INTERNATIONAL FINANCIAL STATISTICS YEARBOOK

WILLIAM F. MAAG LIBRARY
YOUNGSTOWN STATE UNIVERSITY

Other Statistical Publications of the International Monetary Fund

Balance of Payments Statistics Yearbook (BOPSY)
Issued in two parts, this annual publication contains balance of payments data for approximately 140 countries. Part 1 provides aggregated as well as detailed presentations and explanatory notes for countries. Part 2 provides 55 tables of area and world totals of balance of payments components and aggregates. *Price:* US$64.

Direction of Trade Statistics (DOTS)
Quarterly issues of this publication provide, for about 152 countries, tables with current data (or estimates) on the value of imports from and exports to their most important trading partners. In addition, similar summary tables for the world, industrial countries, and developing countries are included. The yearbook provides, for the most recent seven years, detailed trade data by country for approximately 181 countries, the world, and major areas. *Price:* Subscription price is US$104 a year (US$52 to university faculty and students) for the quarterly issues and the yearbook. Price for a quarterly issue only is US$22, the yearbook only is US$34, and a guide only is US$12.50.

Government Finance Statistics Yearbook (GFSY)
This annual publication provides detailed data on revenue, grants, expenditure, lending, financing, and debt of central governments and indicates the amounts represented by social security funds and extrabudgetary operations. Also provided are data for state and local governments, information on the institutional units of government, and lists of sources of information. *Price:* US$58.

A Manual on Government Finance Statistics
Issued in 1986, this manual covers concepts, definitions, and procedures for the compilation of government finance statistics. Emphasis is placed on summarizing and organizing statistics appropriately for analysis, planning, and policy formulation. The text focuses on transactions (taxes, expenditures, borrowing, and lending) and on debt.

Balance of Payments Manual
Revised in 1993, the fifth edition of the manual addresses significant changes that have occurred in international transactions since the fourth edition was published in 1977 and presents salient revisions in the structure and classification of international accounts. The new edition also reflects a major shift in orientation that accords prominence to stocks of external financial assets and liabilities (the international investment position) as well as to balance of payments transactions.

CD-ROM and Tape Subscriptions

International Financial Statistics (IFS) is available on CD-ROM disk and 9-track computer tape. *GFSY, BOPSY,* and *DOTS* are available monthly on 9-track computer tape. *Price of the CD-ROM:* US$1,000 a year for single users (US$350 to university faculty and students); multiple user options are available. *Price of a tape subscription (per publication):* US$1,850 a year to single users (US$950 to university faculty and students) and US$7,500 a year to time sharers.

Subscription Packages

Combined Subscription Package
The combined subscription package includes all issues of *IFS, DOTS, BOPSY, GFSY,* and *Staff Papers,* the Fund's economic journal. *Combined subscription price:* US$360 a year (US$180 to university faculty and students). Airspeed delivery available at additional cost; please inquire.

Combined Statistical Yearbook Subscription
This subscription comprises the *BOPSY,* the *GFSY,* and the yearbooks to *IFS* and *DOTS* at a combined rate of US$150. Because of different publication dates of the four yearbooks, it may take up to one year to service an order. Airspeed delivery available at additional cost; please inquire.

Address orders to
Publication Services, IMF, Washington, DC, USA 20431
Telephone (202) 623-7430   Telefax (202) 623-7201

Note: Prices include the cost of delivery by surface mail. Enhanced delivery is available for an additional charge.

INTERNATIONAL FINANCIAL STATISTICS YEARBOOK

1995

INTERNATIONAL MONETARY FUND

INTERNATIONAL FINANCIAL STATISTICS YEARBOOK
Vol. XLVIII, 1995
Prepared by the IMF Statistics Department
John B. McLenaghan, Director

For information related to this publication, please:
    fax the Public Affairs Division at (202) 623-6278,
    or write Public Affairs Division
        International Monetary Fund
        Washington, D.C. 20431
    or telephone the Statistics Department at (202) 623-6180.
For copyright inquiries, please fax the Editorial Division at (202) 623-6579.
For purchases only, please contact Publication Services (see information below).

Copyright © 1995, International Monetary Fund

International Financial Statistics (IFS) is a standard source of statistics on all aspects of international and domestic finance. *IFS* publishes, for most countries of the world, current data on exchange rates, international liquidity, international banking, money and banking, interest rates, prices, production, international transactions (including balance of payments), government finance, and national accounts. Information is presented in tables for specific countries and in tables for area and world aggregates. *IFS* is published monthly and annually in English, French, and Spanish.

Cutoff Date: July 21, 1995

Price: Subscription price is US$230 a year (US$115 to university faculty and students), which includes the cost of delivery by surface mail, for twelve monthly issues and the yearbook. Single copy price is US$27 for a monthly issue and US$60 for a yearbook issue. Enhanced delivery is available for an additional charge.

Address orders to:
International Monetary Fund
Attention: Publication Services
Washington, D.C. 20431
U.S.A.
Telephone (202) 623-7430
Telefax (202) 623-7201

ISSN 0250-7463
ISBN 1-55775-505-1

POSTMASTER: Send address changes to International Financial Statistics, Publication Services, 700 19th St., N.W., Washington, D.C. 20431. Second class postage paid at Washington, D.C. USPS 049-610

Recycled paper

Table of Contents

Oversize
HG
61
.I57
1995

	Page
IMF: Members and Governors, Board of Executive Directors, Management & Senior Officers	vi
Guides to *IFS* Coverage	viii
Introduction	ix

Charts

International Reserves	2
Interest Rates	3
Exchange Rates	4
Prices	5
Unit Values and Commodity Prices	6
Trade	7
National Accounts	8

World Tables

Article VIII Acceptances	12
Exchange Rates	13
Fund Accounts	19
International Reserves	46
International Banking	74
Measures of Money	88
Interest Rates	108
Real Effective Exchange Rate Indices	114
Prices, Wages, Production, Employment	116
International Trade	124
Balance of Payments	142
Government Finance	156
National Accounts	162
Commodity Prices	178

Country Tables

Islamic State of Afghanistan to Zimbabwe	188–813
Continuation of Notes	814

The term "country," as used in this publication, does not in all cases refer to a territorial entity that is a state as understood by international law and practice; the term also covers some nonsovereign territorial entities, for which statistical data are maintained and provided internationally on a separate and independent basis.

WILLIAM F. MAAG LIBRARY
YOUNGSTOWN STATE UNIVERSITY

IMF Members and Governors

As of August 1, 1995

Member	Governor*	Alternate*
AFGHANISTAN, ISLAMIC STATE OF	Mohamad Hakim	Jan Mohammed Amiry
ALBANIA	Kristaq Luniku	Robert Ceku
ALGERIA	Abdelouahab Keramane	Ali Aissaoui
ANGOLA	Augusto da Silva Tomás	Generoso de Almeida
ANTIGUA AND BARBUDA	Molwyn Joseph	D. Keith L. Hurst
ARGENTINA	Domingo Felipe Cavallo	Roque Benjamin Fernandez
ARMENIA	Hrant A. Bagratian	Levon V. Barkhoudarian
AUSTRALIA	Ralph Willis	E. A. Evans
AUSTRIA	Maria Schaumayer	Thomas Lachs
AZERBAIJAN	Fikret Husseyn Oglu Yusifov	Elman Siradjogly Rustamov
BAHAMAS, THE	William Allen	James H. Smith
BAHRAIN	Ibrahim Abdul Karim	Abdulla Hassan Saif
BANGLADESH	Nasimuddin Ahmed	Khorshed Alam
BARBADOS	Owen S. Arthur	Calvin Springer
BELARUS	Stanislav A. Bogdankevich	Nickolai K. Lisai
BELGIUM	Alfons Verplaetse	Gregoire Brouhns
BELIZE	Manuel Esquivel	Keith A. Arnold
BENIN	Paul Dossou	Paulin L. Cossi
BHUTAN	Dorji Tshering	Sonam Wangchuk
BOLIVIA	Fernando A. Cossio	Juan Fernando Candia Castillo
BOTSWANA	Christopher L. Hermans	Freddy Modise
BRAZIL	Pedro Sampaio Malan	Gustavo J. Laboissière Loyola
BULGARIA	Todor Y. Vulchev	Svetoslav Gavriyski
BURKINA FASO	Zephirin Diabre	Lucien Marie Noel Bembamba
BURUNDI	Mathias Sinamenye	Evariste Nibasumba
CAMBODIA	THOR Peng Leath	TIOULONG Saumura
CAMEROON	Justin Ndioro	Sadou Hayatou
CANADA	Paul Martin	Louise Fréchette
CAPE VERDE	Antonio Gualberto Do Rosario	Oswaldo Miguel Sequeira
CENTRAL AFRICAN REPUBLIC	Emmanuel Dokouna	Auguste Tene-Koyzoa
CHAD	Mahamat Ahmat Alhabo	Tahir Souleyman Haggar
CHILE	Roberto Zahler	Jorge Marshall
CHINA	ZHU Rongji	CHEN Yuan
COLOMBIA	Miguel Urrutia	Guillermo Perry Rubio
COMOROS	Ahmed El-Harif Hamidi	Mohamed Halifa
CONGO	Nguila Moungounga-Nkombo	Ange-Edouard Poungui
COSTA RICA	Rodrígo Bolaños Zamora	Carlos Muñoz Vega
CÔTE D'IVOIRE	Daniel Kablan Duncan	Tiemoko Kone
CROATIA	Pero Jurković	Zdravko Rogić
CYPRUS	A. C. Afxentiou	H. G. Akhniotis
CZECH REPUBLIC	Joseph Tošovský	Vladimír Rudlovčak
DENMARK	Bodil Nyboe Andersen	Michael Dithmer
DJIBOUTI	Luc A. Aden	Ahmed Aden Omar
DOMINICA	Mary Eugenia Charles	Bernard J. Sebastian
DOMINICAN REPUBLIC	Héctor Valdez Albizu	Luis Manuel Piantini
ECUADOR	Ana Lucía Armijos	Augusto P. De la Torre
EGYPT	Mohamed Ahmed El-Razaz	Ismail Hassan Mohamed
EL SALVADOR	Jose Roberto Orellana Milla	Manuel Enrique Hinds
EQUATORIAL GUINEA	Anatolĩo Ndong Mba	Martin-Crisantos Ebe Mba
ERITREA	Andebrhan Weldegiorgis	Ghebriel Fassil
ESTONIA	Siim Kallas	Vahur Kraft
ETHIOPIA	Leikun Berhanu	Nesrudin Mohammed
FIJI	Berenado Vunibobo	Jone Y. Kubuabola
FINLAND	Sirkka Hämäläinen	Matti Vanhala
FRANCE	Alain Madelin	Christian Noyer
GABON	Marcel Doupamby Matoka	Jean-Paul Leyimangoye
GAMBIA, THE	Bala Garba Jahumpa	Momodou Clarke Bajo
GEORGIA	Nadar Javakhishvili	David Iakobidze
GERMANY	Hans Tietmeyer	Theo Waigel
GHANA	Kwesi Botchwey	Godfried Kportufe Agama
GREECE	Lucas D. Papademos	Evangelos Kourakos
GRENADA	Keith Mitchell	Nolan K. Murray
GUATEMALA	Willy Waldemar Zapata Sagastume	Ana Ordóñez de Molina
GUINEA	El Hadj Camara	Kerfalla Yansane
GUINEA-BISSAU	Rui Diã de Sousa	Luis Cândido Lopes Ribeiro
GUYANA	Bharrat Jagdeo	Archibald Livingston Meredith
HAITI	Leslie Delatour	Marie-Michèle Rey
HONDURAS	Hugo Noe Pino	Guillermo Bueso
HUNGARY	Gyorgy Suranyi	Laszlo Akar
ICELAND	Birgir Isl. Gunnarsson	Finnur Sveinbjoernsson
INDIA	Manmohan Singh	Chakravarty Rangarajan
INDONESIA	J. Soedradjad Djiwandono	Jusuf Anwar
IRAN, ISLAMIC REPUBLIC OF	Mohsen Nourbakhsh	Ahmad Azizi
IRAQ	Ahmed Hussein	Abdul Wahid A. Abdullah Al-Makhzoumi
IRELAND	Ruairi Quinn	Maurice O'Connell
ISRAEL	Avraham B. Shochat	David Klein
ITALY	Lamberto Dini	Vacant
JAMAICA	Omar Davies	Jacques Bussieres
JAPAN	Masayoshi Takemura	Yasuo Matsushita
JORDAN	Basil Jardaneh	Mohamed Said Nabulsi
KAZAKHSTAN	Viktor Vasilyevich Sobolev	Daulet Khamitovich Sembayev
KENYA	Musalia Mudavadi	Micah Kiprono Cheserem
KIRIBATI	Beniamina Tinga	Bureti Williams
KOREA	Jae-hyong Hong	Myung-Ho Kim
KUWAIT	Nasser Abdullah Al-Roudan	Salem Abdulaziz Al-Sabah
KYRGYZ REPUBLIC	Marat Sultanov	Askar I. Sarygulov
LAO PEOPLE'S DEM. REP.	Bousbong Souvannavong	Kikham Vongsay
LATVIA	Indra Sãmīte	Einars Repse
LEBANON	Riad Toufic Salameh	Nasser Saidi
LESOTHO	Liphapang T. Tuoane	Anthony Mothae Maruping
LIBERIA	Wilson K. Tarpeh	David K. Vinton
LIBYA	Abdulhafid Mahmoud Zlitni	Mohamed Finaish
LITHUANIA	Kazys Ratkevicius	A. Krizinauskas
LUXEMBOURG	Jean-Claude Juncker	Pierre Jaans
MACEDONIA, FORMER YUGOSLAV REPUBLIC OF	Borko Stanoevski	Tome Nenovski
MADAGASCAR	José Yvon Raserijaona	Raoul J. Ravelomanana
MALAWI	M.A.P. Chikaonda	R. F. Kavinya
MALAYSIA	Anwar Ibrahim	Ahmad Mohd. Don
MALDIVES	Arif Hilmy	Mohamed Jaleel
MALI	Soumaïla Cisse	Mandé Sidibé
MALTA	Francis Vassallo	H. C. de Gabriele
MARSHALL ISLANDS	Ruben R. Zackhras	Vincent Muller
MAURITANIA	Mohamedou Ould Michel	Sidi Mohamed Ould Biya
MAURITIUS	Ramakrishna Sithanen	Indurduth Ramphul
MEXICO	Guillermo Ortiz Martinez	Miguel Mancera Aguayo
MICRONESIA, FEDERATED STATES OF	Aloysius J. Tuuth	Lorin Robert
MOLDOVA	Leonid Talmaci	Valeriu Chiţan
MONGOLIA	Erdeniin Byambajav	Ochirbatyn Chuluunbat
MOROCCO	Mohammed Seqat	Vacant
MOZAMBIQUE	Tomaz Augusto Salomão	Luisa Dias Diogo
MYANMAR	Win Tin	Kyi Aye
NAMIBIA	Helmut K. Angula	Jaafar Ahmad
NEPAL	Hari Shankar Tripathi	Madhab Prasad Ghimire
NETHERLANDS	Wim F. Duisenberg	Henk J. Brouwer
NEW ZEALAND	W.F. Birch	Donald T. Brash
NICARAGUA	José Evenor Taboada Arana	Emilio Pereira
NIGER	Abdallah Boureima	Abdou Maidaji
NIGERIA	Anthony A. Ani	Paul Ogwuma
NORWAY	Torstein Moland	Arne Øien
OMAN	Ahmed Abdul Nabi Macki	Hamood Sangour Hashim
PAKISTAN	Muhammad Yaqub	Javed Talat
PANAMA	Guillermo O. Chapman, Jr.	Jose A. de la Ossa
PAPUA NEW GUINEA	Christopher Haiveta	Koiari Tarata
PARAGUAY	Jacinto Estigarribia Mallada	Luis Enrique Breuer Mojoli
PERU	Germán Suárez Chávez	Jorge Camet Dickmann
PHILIPPINES	Gabriel C. Singson	Roberto F. De Ocampo
POLAND	Grzegorz W. Kolodko	Krzysztof Kalicki
PORTUGAL	Antonio Jose Fernandes de Sousa	Joao António Morais Da Costa Pinto
QATAR	Mohammed bin Khalifa Al-Thani	Abdullah Khalid Al-Attiyah
ROMANIA	Mugur Isarescu	Dan Mogos
RUSSIA	Anatoli Chubais	Vladimir Panskov
RWANDA	Gerard Niyitegeka	Pierre Rwakayigamba
ST. KITTS AND NEVIS	Dwight Venner	Wendell Lawrence
ST. LUCIA	John G. M. Compton	Zenith James
ST. VINCENT AND THE GRENADINES	James F. Mitchell	Maurice Edwards
SAN MARINO	Clelio Galassi	Fiorenzo Stolfi
SÃO TOMÉ AND PRÍNCIPE	Helder D.S. De Barros	Adelino Castelo David
SAUDI ARABIA	Mohammad Abalkhail	Hamad Al-Sayari
SENEGAL	Papa Ousmane Sakho	Mamadou Lamine Loum
SEYCHELLES	James Michel	Aboo Aumeeruddy
SIERRA LEONE	John A. Karimu	Stephen M. Swaray
SINGAPORE	Richard Hu Tsu Tau	Lee Ek Tieng
SLOVAK REPUBLIC	Vladimir Masár	Sergej Kozlík
SLOVENIA	France Arhar	Bogomir Kos
SOLOMON ISLANDS	Rick Nelson Houenipwela	Manasseh Sogavare
SOMALIA	Vacant	Vacant
SOUTH AFRICA	Christian Lodewyk Stals	Estian Calitz
SPAIN	Pedro Solbes	Luis Angel Rojo
SRI LANKA	Chandrika Bandaranaika Kumaratunga	H. B. Disanayaka
SUDAN	Vacant	Vacant
SURINAME	Humphrey S. Hildenberg	Andre Eugene Telting
SWAZILAND	Derek Von Wissell	James Nxumalo
SWEDEN	Urban Bäckström	Svante Öberg
SWITZERLAND	Markus Lusser	Otto Stich
SYRIAN ARAB REP.	Muhammad Imady	Mohamed Al-Sharif
TAJIKISTAN	Anvarsho Muzaffarov	Gulomdzhon Dzhurayevich Babayev

*According to the latest appointments.

IMF MEMBERS AND GOVERNORS (CONT.)

As of August 1, 1995

Member	Governor*	Alternate*	Member	Governor*	Alternate*
TANZANIA	Kighoma A. Malima	Idris M. Rashidi	UNITED STATES	Robert E. Rubin	Alan Greenspan
THAILAND	VIJIT Supinit	RERNGCHAI Marakanond	URUGUAY	Ricardo Pascale	Juan Moreira
TOGO	Elom Emile K. Dadzie	Assiba Amoussou-Guenou	UZBEKISTAN	MULLAJONOV Faizulla Makhsudjonovich	Tatyana N. Guskova
TONGA	James Cecil Cocker	S.T.T. 'Utoikamanu	VANUATU	Willie Jimmy	Sampson Ngwele
TRINIDAD AND TOBAGO	Wendell Mottley	T. Ainsworth Harewood	VENEZUELA	Antonio Casas González	Luis Xavier Grisanti
TUNISIA	Mohamed El Beji Hamda	Tahar Sioud	VIET NAM	Cao Si Kiem	Le Van Chau
TURKEY	Aykon Doğan	Yaman Törüner	WESTERN SAMOA	Tuilaepa S. Malielegaoi	Epa Tuioti
TURKMENISTAN	Valery G. Otchertsov	Khydirkuli M. Achilov	YEMEN, REPUBLIC OF	Alawi Saleh Al-Salami	Mohamed Ahmed Al Junaid
UGANDA	Jehoash Mayanja-Nkangi	Charles N. Kikonyogo	ZAIRE	Vacant	Vacant
UKRAINE	Victor Youshchenko	Boris Sobolev	ZAMBIA	Ronald Damson Siame Penza	Jacob M. Mwanza
UNITED ARAB EMIRATES	Bin Nasser Al-Suwaidi	Mohamed Khalfan Bin Kharbash	ZIMBABWE	A.M. Chambati	Leonard Ladislus Tsumba
UNITED KINGDOM	Kenneth Clarke	Edward A. J. George			

*According to the latest appointments.

179 member countries

BOARD OF EXECUTIVE DIRECTORS

MICHEL CAMDESSUS, CHAIRMAN

Executive Director	From	Alternate	From	Casting Votes of
Karin Lissakers	United States	Barry S. Newman	United States	United States
Stefan Schoenberg	Germany	Bernd Esdar	Germany	Germany
Hachiro Mesaki	Japan	Toshihiko Fukuyama	Japan	Japan
Marc-Antoine Autheman	France	Michel Sirat	France	France
Huw Evans	United Kingdom	Jon Shields	United Kingdom	United Kingdom
Willy Kiekens	Belgium	Johann Prader	Austria	Austria, Belarus, Belgium, Czech Republic, Hungary, Kazakhstan, Luxembourg, Slovak Republic, Slovenia, Turkey
J. de Beaufort Wijnholds	Netherlands	Oleh Havrylyshyn	Canada	Armenia, Bulgaria, Croatia, Cyprus, Georgia, Israel, former Yugoslav Republic of Macedonia, Moldova, Netherlands, Romania, Ukraine
Luis E. Berrizbeitia	Venezuela	Vicente J. Fernandez	Spain	Costa Rica, El Salvador, Guatemala, Honduras, Mexico, Nicaragua, Spain, Venezuela
Giulio Lanciotti	Italy	Nikolaos Coumbis	Greece	Albania, Greece, Italy, Malta, Portugal, San Marino
Ian D. Clark	Canada	Garrett F. Murphy	Ireland	Antigua and Barbuda, The Bahamas, Barbados, Belize, Canada, Dominica, Grenada, Ireland, Jamaica, St. Kitts and Nevis, St. Lucia, St. Vincent and the Grenadines
Jarle Bergo	Norway	Eva Srejber	Sweden	Denmark, Estonia, Finland, Iceland, Latvia, Lithuania, Norway, Sweden
Muhammad Al-Jasser	Saudi Arabia	Abdulrahman A. Al-Tuwaijri	Saudi Arabia	Saudi Arabia
Ewen L. Waterman	Australia	Jung-Ho Kang	Korea	Australia, Kiribati, Korea, Marshall Islands, Federated States of Micronesia, Mongolia, New Zealand, Papua New Guinea, Philippines, Seychelles, Solomon Islands, Vanuatu, Western Samoa
A. Shakour Shaalan	Egypt	Yacoob Yousef Mohammed	Bahrain	Bahrain, Egypt, Iraq, Jordan, Kuwait, Lebanon, Libya, Maldives, Oman, Qatar, Syrian Arab Republic, United Arab Emirates, Republic of Yemen
Dmitri V. Tulin	Russia	Aleksei V. Mozhin	Russia	Russia
J. E. Ismael	Indonesia	Latifah Merican Cheong	Malaysia	Cambodia, Fiji, Indonesia, Lao People's Democratic Republic, Malaysia, Myanmar, Nepal, Singapore, Thailand, Tonga, Viet Nam
Daniel Kaeser	Switzerland	Krzysztof Link	Poland	Azerbaijan, Kyrgyz Republic, Poland, Switzerland, Tajikistan, Turkmenistan, Uzbekistan
Abbas Mirakhor	Islamic Republic of Iran	Mohammed Dairi	Morocco	Islamic State of Afghanistan, Algeria, Ghana, Islamic Republic of Iran, Morocco, Pakistan, Tunisia
Alexandre Kafka	Brazil	Alberto Calderon	Colombia	Brazil, Colombia, Dominican Republic, Ecuador, Guyana, Haiti, Panama, Suriname, Trinidad and Tobago
K. P. Geethakrishnan	India	W. Hettiarachchi	Sri Lanka	Bangladesh, Bhutan, India, Sri Lanka
Barnabas S. Dlamini	Swaziland	Dinah Z. Guti	Zimbabwe	Angola, Botswana, Burundi, Eritrea, Ethiopia, The Gambia, Kenya, Lesotho, Liberia, Malawi, Mozambique, Namibia, Nigeria, Sierra Leone, Swaziland, Tanzania, Uganda, Zambia, Zimbabwe
ZHANG Ming	China	WEI Benhua	China	China
Carlos Saito	Peru	A. Guillermo Zoccali	Argentina	Argentina, Bolivia, Chile, Paraguay, Peru, Uruguay
Yves-Marie T. Koissy	Côte d'Ivoire	Alexandre Barro Chambrier	Gabon	Benin, Burkina Faso, Cameroon, Cape Verde, Central African Republic, Chad, Comoros, Congo, Côte d'Ivoire, Djibouti, Equatorial Guinea, Gabon, Guinea, Guinea-Bissau, Madagascar, Mali, Mauritania, Mauritius, Niger, Rwanda, São Tomé and Príncipe, Senegal, Togo

MANAGEMENT AND SENIOR OFFICERS

Managing Director	Michel Camdessus	Monetary and Exchange Affairs Department	Manuel Guitián, Director
First Deputy Managing Director	Stanley Fischer	Policy Development and Review Department	Jack T. Boorman, Director
Deputy Managing Directors	Alassane D. Ouattara	Research Department	Michael Mussa, Director
	Prabhakar R. Narvekar	Secretary's Department	Leo Van Houtven, Secretary
Economic Counsellor	Michael Mussa[1]	Southeast Asia and Pacific Department	Kunio Saito, Director
Counsellor	Leo Van Houtven[1]	Statistics Department	John B. McLenaghan, Director
Administration Department	K. Burke Dillon, Director	Treasurer's Department	David Williams, Treasurer
African Department	Evangelos A. Calamitsis, Director	Western Hemisphere Department	Claudio M. Loser, Director
Central Asia Department	Hubert Neiss, Director	Special Advisor to the Managing Director	Shigemitsu Sugisaki
European I Department	Massimo Russo, Director	Bureau of Computing Services	Warren N. Minami, Director
European II Department	John Odling-Smee, Director	Bureau of Language Services	Patrick Delannoy, Director
External Relations Department	Shailendra J. Anjaria, Director	Office at the United Nations	J.B. Zulu, Director and Special Representative to the UN
Fiscal Affairs Department	Vito Tanzi, Director		
IMF Institute	Patrick B. de Fontenay, Director	Office in Europe (Paris)	Joaquín Ferrán, Director
Legal Department	François P. Gianviti, General Counsel	Office in Geneva	Alan A. Tait, Director and Special Trade Representative
Middle Eastern Department	Paul Chabrier, Director		
		Office of Budget and Planning	Lindsay A. Wolfe, Director
		Office of Internal Audit and Review	Marcello Caiola, Director

[1] Alphabetical listing

GUIDE TO THE COUNTRY COVERAGE OF *IFS* WORLD TABLES

Country Codes	Country	Reserves	Dep. Bks Fgn A/cs.	Money	Consumer Prices	Exports, Imports	Export Unit Values	Import Unit Values	Balance of Payments	Country Page
001	WORLD									
010	ALL COUNTRIES									
110	*Industrial Countries*									
111	United States	x	x	x	x	x	w	w	x	x
156	Canada	x	x	x	x	x	x	x	x	x
193	Australia	x	x	x	x	x	w	w	x	x
158	Japan	x	x	x	x	x	x	x	x	x
196	New Zealand	x	x	x	x	x	x	x	x	x
122	Austria	x	x	x	x	x	x	x	x	x
124	Belgium	x	x	x	x					x
126	Belgium-Luxembourg					x	x	x	x	
128	Denmark	x	x	x	x	x	x	x	x	x
172	Finland	x	x	x	x	x	x	x	x	x
132	France	x	x	x	x	x	x	x	x	x
134	Germany	x	x	x	x	x	x	x	x	x
174	Greece	x	x	x	x	x	x	x	x	x
176	Iceland	x	x	x	x	x	x	x	x	x
178	Ireland	x	x	x	x	x	x	x	x	x
136	Italy	x	x	x	x	x	x	x	x	x
137	Luxembourg		x		x					x
138	Netherlands	x	x	x	x	x	x	x	x	x
142	Norway	x	x	x	x	x	x	x	x	x
182	Portugal	x	x	x	x	x	w	w	x	x
135	San Marino									
184	Spain	x	x	x	x	x	x	x	x	x
144	Sweden	x	x	x	x	x	x	x	x	x
146	Switzerland	x	x	x	x	x	x	x	x	x
112	United Kingdom	x	x	x	x	x	x	x	x	x
200	*Developing Countries*									
605	*Africa*									
612	Algeria[2]	x	x	x	x	x			x	x
614	Angola					x			x	
638	Benin	x	x	x		x			x	x
616	Botswana[1]	x	x	x	x	x			x	x
748	Burkina Faso	x	x	x	x	x	x	x	x	x
618	Burundi	x	x	x	x	x			x	x
622	Cameroon	x	x	x	x	x			x	x
624	Cape Verde	x	x	x	x	x			x	x
626	C. African Rep.	x	x	x	x	x			x	x
628	Chad	x	x	x	x	x			x	x
632	Comoros	x	x	x	x	x			x	x
634	Congo	x	x	x	x	x			x	x
662	Côte d'Ivoire	x	x	x	x	x	x	x	x	x
611	Djibouti			x		x			x	x
642	Equatorial Guinea	x	x	x	x				x	x
643	Eritrea									
644	Ethiopia	x	x	x	x	x			x	x
646	Gabon	x	x	x	x	x			x	x
648	Gambia, The	x	x	x	x	x			x	x
652	Ghana	x	x	x	x	x			x	x
656	Guinea			x		x			x	x
654	Guinea-Bissau	x		x	x	x			x	x
664	Kenya	x	x	x	x	x	x	x	x	x

Country Codes	Country	Reserves	Dep. Bks Fgn A/cs.	Money	Consumer Prices	Exports, Imports	Export Unit Values	Import Unit Values	Balance of Payments	Country Page
666	Lesotho[1]	x	x		x	x			x	x
668	Liberia	x	x	x	x	x	x	x	x	x
674	Madagascar	x	x	x	x	x			x	x
676	Malawi	x	x	x	x	x	x	x	x	x
678	Mali	x	x	x	x	x			x	x
682	Mauritania	x	x	x	x	x			x	x
684	Mauritius	x	x	x	x	x			x	x
686	Morocco	x	x	x	x	x		x	x	x
688	Mozambique	x			x	x			x	x
728	Namibia	x		x	x	x			x	x
692	Niger	x	x	x	x	x			x	x
694	Nigeria[2]	x	x	x	x	x	x		x	x
696	Réunion		x			x				
714	Rwanda	x	x	x	x	x	w		x	x
856	St. Helena					x				
716	São Tomé & Príncipe					x			x	
722	Senegal	x	x	x	x	x	x	x	x	x
718	Seychelles	x	x	x	x	x			x	x
724	Sierra Leone	x	x	x	x	x			x	x
726	Somalia	x	x	x	x	x			x	x
199	South Africa[1]	x	x	x	x	x	x	x	x	x
732	Sudan	x	x	x	x	x	w		x	x
734	Swaziland[1]	x	x	x	x	x			x	x
738	Tanzania	x	x	x	x	x			x	x
742	Togo	x	x	x	x	x	w	x	x	x
744	Tunisia	x	x	x	x	x	x	w	x	x
746	Uganda	x	x	x	x	x			x	x
636	Zaïre	x	x	x	x	x			x	x
754	Zambia	x	x	x	x	x			x	x
698	Zimbabwe	x	x	x	x	x	x	x	x	x
505	*Asia*									
512	Afghanistan, I.S. of	x	x	x	x	x			x	x
859	American Samoa					x				
513	Bangladesh	x	x	x	x	x			x	x
514	Bhutan	x		x	x	x				x
516	Brunei					x				
522	Cambodia					x				
924	China, People's Rep.	x		x	x	x			x	x
815	Cook Island					x				
819	Fiji	x	x	x	x	x	x		x	x
887	French Polynesia		x			x				
829	Guam					x				
532	Hong Kong		x		x	x				
534	India	x		x	x	x	x	x	x	x
536	Indonesia[2]	x	x	x	x	x	x		x	x
826	Kiribati					x			x	
542	Korea	x	x	x	x	x	x	x	x	x
544	Lao P. D. Rep.	x				x			x	
546	Macao		x			x				
548	Malaysia	x	x	x	x	x	x	x	x	x
556	Maldives	x	x	x	x	x			x	x
867	Marshall Islands									
868	Micronesia, Fed. States of									
948	Mongolia			x	x	x			x	x
518	Myanmar	x	x	x	x	x	x		x	x
836	Nauru					x				
558	Nepal	x	x	x	x	x			x	x
839	New Caledonia		x			x				

Country Codes	Country	Reserves	Dep. Bks Fgn A/cs.	Money	Consumer Prices	Exports, Imports	Export Unit Values	Import Unit Values	Balance of Payments	Country Page
564	Pakistan	x	x	x	x	x	x	x	x	x
853	Papua New Guinea	x	x	x	x	x	x		x	x
566	Philippines	x	x	x	x	x	x	x	x	x
576	Singapore	x	x	x	x	x	w	w	x	x
813	Solomon Islands	x	x	x	x	x	x		x	x
524	Sri Lanka	x	x	x	x	x	x	x	x	x
578	Thailand	x	x	x	x	x	w	x	x	x
866	Tonga			x	x	x			x	x
846	Vanuatu	x	x	x	x	x			x	x
582	Viet Nam	x	x			x				
862	Western Samoa	x		x	x	x			x	x
170	*Europe*									
914	Albania								x	
911	Armenia								x	
912	Azerbaijan									
913	Belarus									
918	Bulgaria								x	
960	Croatia								x	
423	Cyprus	x	x	x	x	x	x	x	x	x
935	Czech Republic	x		x	x	x				x
934	Czechoslovakia	x		x	x	x	x	x	x	
939	Estonia	x		x	x	x			x	x
816	Faeroe Islands					x				
915	Georgia									
823	Gibraltar					x				
944	Hungary	x	x	x	x	x	w	w	x	x
916	Kazakhstan									
917	Kyrgyz Rep.									
941	Latvia									
946	Lithuania									
962	Macedonia, former Yugoslav Rep. of									
181	Malta	x	x	x	x	x	x	x	x	x
921	Moldova	x		x						x
964	Poland	x	x	x	x	x	w	w	x	x
968	Romania	x	x	x	x	x			x	x
922	Russia									
936	Slovak Republic			x	x	x			x	x
961	Slovenia				x	x			x	x
923	Tajikistan									
186	Turkey	x	x	x	x	x	x	x	x	x
925	Turkmenistan									
926	Ukraine									
927	Uzbekistan									
188	Yugoslavia, Socialist Federal Rep. of	x	x	x	x	x			x	
405	*Middle East*									
419	Bahrain	x	x	x	x	x			x	x
469	Egypt	x	x	x	x	x			x	x
429	Iran, I.R. of[2]	x	x	x	x	x	w		x	x
433	Iraq[2]	x	x	x	x	x	w			x
436	Israel	x	x	x	x	x	x	x	x	x
439	Jordan	x	x	x	x	x	x	x	x	x
443	Kuwait[2]	x	x	x	x	x	w		x	x
446	Lebanon	x	x	x		x				x
672	Libya[2]	x	x	x	x	x	w		x	x
449	Oman[2]	x	x	x		x	w		x	x

Country Codes	Country	Reserves	Dep. Bks Fgn A/cs.	Money	Consumer Prices	Exports, Imports	Export Unit Values	Import Unit Values	Balance of Payments	Country Page
453	Qatar[2]	x	x	x	x	x	w			x
456	Saudi Arabia[2]	x	x	x	x	x	w		x	x
463	Syrian Arab Rep.	x	x	x	x	x	x	x	x	x
466	United Arab Emirates[2]	x	x	x		x	w			x
473	Yemen Arab Rep.	x	x	x	x	x			x	
459	Yemen, P. D. Rep.	x	x	x	x	x			x	
474	Yemen, Republic of	x		x					x	x
205	*Western Hemisphere*									
311	Antigua & Barbuda	x	x	x	x	x			x	x
213	Argentina	x	x	x	x	x			x	x
314	Aruba	x		x					x	x
313	Bahamas, The	x	x	x	x	x			x	x
316	Barbados	x	x	x	x	x			x	x
339	Belize	x	x	x		x			x	x
319	Bermuda		x			x				
218	Bolivia	x	x	x	x	x	x		x	x
223	Brazil	x	x	x	x	x	x	x	x	x
377	Cayman Islands		x							
228	Chile	x	x	x	x	x			x	x
233	Colombia	x	x	x	x	x	w	w	x	x
238	Costa Rica	x	x	x	x	x			x	x
928	Cuba	x								
321	Dominica	x	x	x	x	x			x	x
243	Dominican Rep.	x	x	x	x	x	x		x	x
248	Ecuador	x	x	x	x	x	x		x	x
253	El Salvador	x	x	x	x	x			x	x
323	Falkland Islands					x				
326	Greenland					x				
328	Grenada	x	x	x	x	x	x		x	x
329	Guadeloupe		x			x				
258	Guatemala	x	x	x	x	x			x	x
333	Guiana, French		x			x				
336	Guyana	x	x	x	x	x			x	x
263	Haiti	x	x	x	x	x			x	x
268	Honduras	x	x	x	x	x	x		x	x
343	Jamaica	x	x	x	x	x			x	x
349	Martinique		x			x				
273	Mexico	x	x	x	x	x			x	x
351	Montserrat		x			x				
353	Netherlands Ant.	x	x	x	x	x			x	x
278	Nicaragua	x	x	x	x	x			x	x
283	Panama	x	x	x	x	x	x		x	x
288	Paraguay	x	x	x	x	x	x		x	x
293	Peru	x	x	x	x	x	x		x	x
361	St. Kitts & Nevis	x	x	x	x	x			x	x
362	St. Lucia	x	x	x	x	x			x	x
363	St. Pierre & Miquelon			x			x			
364	St. Vincent and the Grenadines	x	x	x	x	x			x	x
366	Suriname	x	x	x	x	x	x		x	x
369	Trinidad & Tobago	x	x	x	x	x	x	x	x	x
298	Uruguay	x	x	x	x	x			x	x
299	Venezuela[2]	x	x	x	x	x	w	w	x	x
999	*Oil Exporting Countries*									
201	*Non-Oil Developing Countries*									

Country pages for 154 countries

[1]South African trade data refer to the South African Common Customs Area and include data for Botswana, Lesotho and Swaziland.
[2]These countries comprise Oil Exporting Countries grouping shown as a memorandum item to the world tables. The memorandum item for Non-Oil Developing Countries shown in the world tables comprises the remaining Developing Countries.
Country indices compiled from specific prices are marked "w."

GUIDE TO THE COMMODITY COVERAGE OF *IFS* COUNTRY PAGES

Commodity Codes (first 2 alphas of lines 66, 70, 72, 74 and 76) **and Country Codes**

dr	Aluminum	156
u	Bananas	248
k	Beef	111 193 213
fl	Butter	196
vr	Coal	193
r	Cocoa beans	223 652
ai	Coconut oil	566
e	Coffee	223 233 386 799
c	Copper	111 112 156 228
ag	Copra	566 813
j	Corn (Maize)	111 578
f	Cotton	111 469 732
al	Fish	176 556 813
z	Fishmeal	176 293
kr	Gold	112 156 199 233
bf	Groundnuts	694
p	Hides, Skins	111
g	Iron ore	223
x	Jute	513
pf	Lamb	196
v	Lead	111 112
vx	Logs	548
w	Manganese	534
ul	Newsprint	111 144 172
pt	Nickel	156
df	Palm kernels	694
dg	Palm oil	548
a	Petroleum	001 111 112 124 142
a	Petroleum (cont.)	156 218 233 248 273 299 369 419 429 433 443 449 453 456 466 536 612 634 672 694 744 968
aw	Phosphates	686
wx	Plywood	566
qr	Potash	156
n	Rice	111 518 578
l	Rubber	111 548 578
rm	Sawnwood	548
bl	Shrimp	111
y	Silver	111
ml	Sisal	639
jf	Soybeans	111
jj	Soybean meal	111
ji	Soybean oil	111
rr	Steel	137
i	Sugar	111 112 193 223 566
as	Superphosphate	111
s	Tea	112 524
q	Tin	112 218 548 578
m	Tobacco	111
ur	Urea	170
d	Wheat	111 193 213
sl	Wood pulp	144
h	Wool	112 193 196
t	Zinc	111 112 156 218

Introduction

The yearbook and the monthly issues of *International Financial Statistics (IFS)* consist of country pages and world tables. The country pages show major economic aggregates used in the analysis of economic developments and normally include data on a country's exchange rates, international liquidity, money and banking, interest rates, production, prices, international transactions, government accounts, and national accounts. Selected series are drawn from the country pages and published in the form of area and world tables in the first part of the yearbook and in monthly issues of *IFS*.

This yearbook reports annual data for the years 1965 through 1994; the historical record of such data from 1948 is maintained in the Fund's Economic Information System (EIS). This earlier data can be consulted in previous issues of the yearbook and are available on CD-ROM and magnetic tape as described in section 15.

The term "country," as used in this publication, does not in all cases refer to a territorial entity that is a state as understood by international law and practice; the term also covers some nonsovereign territorial entities, for which statistical data are maintained and provided internationally on a separate and independent basis.

The following sections describe both the conceptual and technical aspects of various data published in *IFS*. Sections 1 through 10 provide general information regarding the methodologies used in compiling various categories of statistics. Sections 11 through 16 deal with computational and presentational issues such as the calculation of area and world aggregates, the presentation of charts, the standardization of country and line number codes, the use of symbols, conventions, and abbreviations, the production of the *IFS* CD-ROM and subscription tape, and country page notes.

More detailed notes relating to coverage, deviations from the standard methodologies, and discontinuities in the data are published on the individual country pages and world tables of the monthly issues.

1. Exchange Rates and Exchange Rate Arrangements

The country pages carry time series of exchange rates expressed in U.S. dollars per national currency unit or vice versa and a single rate for the SDR (the unit of account for the Fund) in terms of the national currency unit. The exchange rates are classified into three broad categories, reflecting both the role of the authorities in the determination of the exchange rates and/or the multiplicity of exchange rates in a country. The descriptor **market rate** is used to describe exchange rates determined largely by market forces; the **official rate** is an exchange rate determined by the authorities, sometimes in a flexible manner. For countries maintaining multiple exchange arrangements, the rates are labeled **principal rate, secondary rate,** and **tertiary rate**. The SDR values and U.S. dollar exchange rates are classified and coded as follows:

Series **aa** denotes the end-of-period national currency value of the SDR, and series **ac** denotes the end-of-period SDR value of the national currency unit. The SDR rates in terms of U.S. dollars—series **sa, sb, sc,** and **sd**—are also given on the country page for the United States. Series **sa** and **sc** refer to end-of-period values of U.S. dollars per SDR and SDRs per U.S. dollar, respectively; series **sb** and **sd** are the geometric averages of these values during the period.

Series **ae** refers to end of period, and series **rf** refers to period averages of market exchange rates and official exchange rates for countries quoting rates in units of national currency per U.S. dollar. Correspondingly, series **ag** denotes end of period, and series **rh** denotes period averages of market exchange rates and official rates for countries quoting rates in U.S. dollars per unit of national currency. For the period average rates **rf** and **rh**, the data are either the average of market rates or of official rates of the reporting country, or, if those are not available, average rates in New York, or, if those are not available, estimates derived on the basis of a simple average of the end-of-period market rates in the markets of the reporting country.

The end-of-period rates in all forms of expression (**sa** and **sc, aa** and **ac, ae** and **ag**) are reciprocals of each other. Also, the period average SDR rates in terms of the U.S. dollar (**sb** and **sd**) are reciprocals of each other because they are calculated as geometric averages. Other period average rates (**rf** and **rh**) are calculated as arithmetic averages and are not reciprocals.

The country pages carry two U.S. dollar series—**ae** and **rf** (or **ag** and **rh**, depending on the form in which the exchange rate is normally quoted).

All trade figures in *IFS* are converted from national currency values to U.S. dollars and from U.S. dollars to national currency with series **rf**. Conversions are made from the data for the shortest period for which data are available and added to produce longer period data. Conversion is at the longer period rates of only the difference, if any, between the longer period data and the sum of the shorter period data.

The country page notes in the monthly issues of *IFS* identify the exchange rates used.

Apart from the standardized exchange rate lines mentioned above, **w, x,** and **y** lines are presented for members maintaining a dual or multiple exchange rate system. This reflects the wide range of exchange rates in effect. Notes on the relevant country pages in the monthly issues describe the present exchange rate system and identify the exchange rates shown.

European Currency Unit Value

The country pages of the member countries of the European Monetary System (EMS) and the United States carry a time series on the value of the European currency unit (ECU). The **ECU** was issued by the European Monetary Institute (EMI, which has taken over the functions of the European Monetary Cooperation Fund on January 1, 1994) against the gold and U.S. dollar deposits made by the monetary authorities of the member states of the European Union (EU). The ECU is defined as a basket of currencies comprising specific amounts of the currencies of the EU member countries. Each currency's share in the basket is weighted broadly in line with the respective country's gross national product and foreign trade. Representative market exchange rates for the U.S. dollar as reported by the member countries are used to calculate an ECU equivalent, first in U.S. dollars and then in the currencies of the member countries. Series **ea** and **ec** refer to end-of-period values of national currency units per ECU and ECUs per unit of national currency, respectively; series **eb** and **ed** are the arithmetic averages of these values during the period.

Effective Exchange Rates

Measures of effective exchange rates, compiled by the IMF Research Department, are provided in both the country pages and the world tables. (For a description of the latter, see section 11 of this introduction.) A **nominal effective exchange rate** index represents the ratio (expressed on base 1990=100) of an index of the period average exchange rate of the currency in question to a weighted geometric average of exchange rates for the currencies of selected countries. A **real effective exchange rate** index is defined as a nominal effective exchange rate index adjusted for relative movements in national price or cost indicators of the home country and selected countries.

In both cases an increase in the index reflects an appreciation. In view of certain conceptual and data-related limitations, particularly where Fund estimates have been utilized, movements in nominal and real effective exchange rates need to be interpreted with considerable caution. For ease of comparison, the average exchange rate expressed in terms of U.S. dollars per unit of each of the national currencies (*line* **ah**) is also given in an index form on the basis of 1990=100 (*line* **ahx**).

Lines neu and reu

The country pages for 17 industrial countries, for which data are available for normalized unit labor costs in manufacturing, include a nominal effective exchange rate index (*line* **neu**) with weights derived from trade in manufactured goods among all 22 industrial countries. For the 17 countries, a real effective exchange rate index (*line* **reu**)—which is compiled from the nominal effective exchange rate index (*line* **neu**) and from a cost indicator of relative normalized unit labor costs in manufacturing—is also published on the country pages. These indices (*lines* **reu** and **neu**) are discussed more fully in the world tables section of this introduction. A selection of other measures of real effective exchange rates for these countries, using alternative measures of costs and prices, is shown in the world table *Real Effective Exchange Rates Indices*.

Lines nec and rec

The country pages for selected other countries include a nominal effective exchange rate index (*line* **nec**), with weights based on a methodology that takes account of each country's trade in both manufactured goods and primary products with its partner—or competitor—countries. The index is based on 1990=100 in accordance with all indices published in *IFS*. However, the weights are based on disaggregated trade data for manufactured goods and primary products covering the three-year period 1980–82. For manufactured goods, trade by type of good and market is distinguished in the database, so that it is possible to make some allowance at a disaggregated level for competition among various exporters in a foreign market (i.e., third-market competition) as well as that emanating from bilateral trade links. For primary products the weights assigned depend principally on a country's role as a global supplier or purchaser of the product. Trade in crude petroleum, petroleum, and other energy products is excluded.

For these countries a real effective exchange rate index (*line* **rec**) is derived from the nominal effective exchange rate index, adjusted for relative changes in consumer prices. The use of consumer price indices as a measure of domestic costs and prices for these countries typically reflects the use of consumer prices by the reference and partner–or competitor–countries in the compilation of these indices. Consumer price indices are frequently available on a monthly basis.

Line ahx

The notes to the country pages in the monthly issues provide information on exceptions in the choice of the period average exchange rate index (generally *line* **ahx**) and the consumer price index (generally *line 64*). For countries where multiple exchange rates are in effect, Fund staff estimates of a weighted average exchange rate, constructed as an average of the various exchange rates with weights reflecting the share of trade transacted at each rate, are utilized in many cases. For countries where a weighted average exchange rate cannot be calculated, the principal rate, generally *line* **ahx**, is used. For a relatively small number of countries, notes on the country pages in the monthly issues indicate where alternative price indices, such as the wholesale/producer price index or a weighted average of several price indices, are used, where data constraints have made it necessary to use weighting schemes based on aggregate bilateral non-oil trade data, and where trade in services (such as tourism) has been taken into account.

SDR Value

Prior to July 1974, the SDR was valued at the par value of the U.S. dollar, i.e., SDR 1=U.S. dollar 1 through November 1971, SDR 1=U.S. dollar 1.08571 from December 1971 through January 1973, and SDR 1=U.S. dollar 1.20635 from February 1973 through June 1974. Beginning July 1974, the value of the SDR is determined daily by the Fund on the basis of a basket of currencies with each currency assigned a weight in the determination of that value. In the derivation of the SDR value, the currencies of the basket are valued at their market exchange rates for the U.S. dollar, and the U.S. dollar equivalents of each of the currencies are summed to yield the rate of the SDR in terms of the U.S. dollar. The method of calculating the U.S. dollar/SDR exchange rate remains the same, although the number and weights of currencies in the SDR basket have changed over time. The rates for the SDR in terms of other currencies are derived from the market exchange rates of these currencies for the U.S. dollar and the U.S. dollar rate for the SDR.

From July 1974 through June 1978, the currencies included in the basket were those of the countries whose share in world exports of goods and services averaged more than 1 percent in the period 1968–72. This established a basket of 16 currencies with the relative weight for each currency broadly proportionate to the country's exports but modified for the U.S. dollar to reflect its real weight in the world economy. In order to preserve the continuity of valuation, the amount of each of the 16 currencies in the basket used in the calculation was such that on June 28, 1974 the value of SDR 1=U.S. dollar 1.20635.

For the period July 1978 through December 1980, the composition of the basket was changed on the basis of updated data. The revised basket of 16 currencies was based on statistics for the period 1972–76. The weights of some currencies were also changed. The amounts of each of the 16 currencies in the revised basket used in the calculation were such as to ensure that the value of the SDR in terms of any currency on June 30, 1978 was exactly the same in the revised valuation as in the previous valuation.

For the period January 1981 through December 1985, the SDR valuation basket consisted of the currencies of the five members having the largest exports of goods and services during the period 1975–79, i.e., the U.S. dollar, Deutsche mark, French franc, Japanese yen, and pound sterling. The weights for the five currencies (U.S. dollar, 42 percent; Deutsche mark, 19 percent; French franc, Japanese yen, and pound sterling, 13 percent each) broadly reflected the relative importance of these currencies in international trade and finance, based on the value of the exports of goods and services of the members issuing these currencies and the balances of their currencies officially held by members of the Fund over the five-year period 1975–79.

For the period January 1986 through December 1990, the SDR valuation basket consisted of the currencies of the five members having the largest exports of goods and services during the period 1980–84, i.e., the U.S. dollar, Deutsche mark, French franc, Japanese yen, and pound sterling. The weights for the five currencies (U.S. dollar—42 percent, Deutsche mark—19 percent, Japanese yen—15 percent, French franc and pound sterling—12 percent each) broadly reflected the relative importance of these currencies in international trade and finance, based on the value of the exports of goods and services of the members issuing these currencies and the balances of their currencies officially held by members of the Fund over the five-year period 1980–84.

Beginning January 1, 1991, the SDR valuation basket consists of the currencies of the five members having the largest exports of goods and services during the period 1985–89, i.e., the U.S. dollar, Deutsche mark, French franc, Japanese yen, and pound sterling. The weights for the five currencies (U.S. dollar—40 percent, Deutsche mark—21 percent, Japanese yen—17 percent, French franc and pound sterling—11 percent each) broadly reflect the relative importance of these currencies in international trade and finance, based on the value of the exports of goods and services of the members issuing these currencies and the balances of their currencies officially held by members of the Fund over the five-year period 1985–89.

Exchange Rate Tables

The exchange rate table on SDR rates gives the monthly, quarterly, and annual SDR rates in terms of U.S. dollars. The table on market, official, and principal rates provides, in terms of national currency units per SDR, end-of-period rates for the currencies of all Fund members and Netherlands Antilles.

The table on exchange rate arrangements is based mainly on information supplied to the Fund on the exchange rate arrangements that individual member countries apply; such notification is required under Article IV, Section 2(*a*) of the amended Articles of Agreement of the Fund, which entered into force on April 1, 1978. The classification in the table reflects judgments by the Fund staff on the basis of the information obtained from member countries.

Method of Deriving IFS Exchange Rates

For countries that have introduced new currencies, the rates shown in *IFS* for the period prior to the introduction of the most recent currency represent factors that may be used to convert national currency data in *IFS* to U.S. dollar or SDR data. In such cases, the conversion factors are constructed by chain linking the exchange rates of the old and the new currencies, using as a basis the value of the new currency relative to the old currency as established by the issuing agency at the time that the new currency was introduced. Notes on the introduction of new currencies are found on individual country pages.

A detailed description of the method of deriving the *IFS* exchange rates and of the conceptual and technical problems implied in producing these rates is contained in the *IFS Supplement on Exchange Rates*, No. 9 (1985).

2. Fund Accounts

Details of members' positions in the Fund are presented in 12 world tables and in the Fund Position section of the country pages.

The table *Fund Accounts: Arrangements* reports the current status of stand-by, extended, structural adjustment, and enhanced structural adjustment arrangements. The table *Fund Accounts: Position to Date* reports latest monthly data on members' Fund positions, including quota, reserve position in the Fund, total Fund credit and loans outstanding, Fund holdings of currencies, and positions in the SDR Department. The table *Financing Components of Members' Outstanding Obligations to the Fund* reports latest monthly data on the sources of financing of Fund credit and loans outstanding.

The tables *Purchases* and *Repurchases* relate to transactions within the General Resources Account (GRA). The tables *Loan Disbursements* and *Repayments of Loans* relate to the Structural Adjustment Facility (SAF), Enhanced Structural Adjustment Facility (ESAF), and Trust Fund loans. The table *Total Fund Credit and Loans Outstanding* relates to the outstanding use of Fund resources under the GRA and to outstanding loans under the SAF, ESAF, and Trust Fund. The table *Use of Fund Credit: GRA* relates to the outstanding use of Fund resources under the GRA. The table *Fund Accounts: Borrowing Agreements* reports the current status of the Fund's borrowing activities.

The world table *SDRs* shows holdings of SDRs by members and includes a foot table showing SDR holdings by all participants, the IMF, and other holders. The table *Reserve Position in the Fund* relates to members' claims on the Fund.

Monthly issues of *IFS* give a description, in the introduction, of members' positions and the underlying transactions. A more detailed description of the Fund accounts is contained in the IMF's *Financial Organization and Operations of the IMF,* Pamphlet No. 45, 1993.

3. International Liquidity

The international liquidity section on the country pages includes the U.S. dollar value of monetary authorities' holdings of SDRs, reserve position in the Fund, foreign exchange, and the sum of these items, total reserves minus gold. (Monetary authorities comprise central banks and, to the extent that they perform monetary authorities' functions, currency boards, exchange stabilization funds, and treasuries.) The country pages also report data on official holdings of gold expressed in both millions of fine troy ounces and U.S. dollars, the latter valued according to national practice.

Foreign Exchange

Foreign Exchange (line 1d.d) includes monetary authorities' claims on nonresidents in the form of bank deposits, treasury bills, short-term and long-term government securities, European currency units (ECUs, see below), and other claims usable in the event of balance of payments need, without regard as to whether the claim is denominated in the currency of the debtors or the creditors.

Before December 1971, when the U.S. dollar was equivalent to the SDR, foreign exchange data were compiled and expressed in terms of U.S. dollars at official par values. Conversions from national currencies to U.S. dollars from December 1971 through January 1973 were calculated at the cross rates reflecting the parities and central rates agreed to in December 1971. From February 1973 through June 1974, foreign exchange was valued at the cross rates of parities or central rates for countries having effective parities or central rates, and at market rates for the Canadian dollar, the Irish pound, the Italian lira, the Japanese yen, and the pound sterling. Beginning July 1974, foreign exchange is valued at end-of-month market rates or, in the absence of market rate quotations, at other prevailing official rates.

Countries participating in the European Monetary System (Belgium, Denmark, France, Germany, Ireland, Italy, Luxembourg, the Netherlands, the United Kingdom, Greece, Spain, Portugal, Sweden, Austria, and Finland) were issued ECUs against deposits of gold and U.S. dollars with the EMI. For these countries, those reserves that were deposited with the EMI are excluded from gold and foreign exchange holdings, but the equivalent holdings of ECUs are included in foreign exchange.

Other Foreign Assets, Foreign Liabilities

Time series, where significant, are also provided on other foreign assets and foreign liabilities of the monetary authorities. *Other Assets (line 3..d)* usually comprise claims on nonresidents that are of limited usability in the event of balance of payments need, such as balances under bilateral payments agreements and holdings of inconvertible currencies. (These claims are included in *line 11.) Other Liabilities (line 4..d)* comprise foreign liabilities of the monetary authorities other than use of Fund credit (GRA), SAF, ESAF, and Trust Fund loans outstanding; positions with the Fund are reported separately, in terms of SDRs, in the Fund position section of the country pages.

Foreign Accounts of Other Financial Institutions

Where significant, foreign accounts of financial institutions other than the monetary authorities are also reported in the international liquidity section of the country pages. The measures provided are sometimes reported directly in U.S. dollars and may differ slightly in coverage, but they are normally U.S. dollar equivalents of time series reported in the appropriate money and banking sections as follows: *line 7a.d* equals *line 21; line 7b.d* equals *line 26c* plus *line 26cl; line 7e.d* equals *line 41*; and *line 7f.d* equals *line 46c* plus *line 46cl*.

In addition, the international liquidity section for some countries provides summary data on the foreign accounts of special or international license banks that operate locally but are not presently covered in the money and banking section. Their foreign assets are reported as *line 7k.d* and their foreign liabilities as *line 7m.d*, when available (although *7m.d* is not shown separately if it is equal to *line 7k.d*).

Foreign Nonbank Components

Where available and significant, the foreign nonbank components of these time series are also shown separately. These international liquidity lines provide data on the claims of deposit money banks, other banking institutions, and nonbank financial institutions (including international license banks) on foreign nonbanks (*lines 7add, 7edd,* and

7kdd, respectively) and their liabilities to foreign nonbanks (*lines 7bdd, 7fdd,* and *7mdd,* respectively). A country page note indicates if the claims on, or liabilities to, foreign nonbanks are small. In drawing foreign bank/ nonbank distinctions, most countries choose a definition of foreign banks comprising central banks, deposit money banks, and other banking institutions; consequently, the coverage of nonbanks excludes central banks, deposit money banks, and other banking institutions.

World Tables on Reserves

World tables on reserves report all country page time series on reserves, other than gold at national valuation, and present totals for countries, country groups, and the world. There is also a world table on total reserves, with gold valued at SDR 35 per ounce. A foot table to that table reports total reserves of all countries, including gold valued both at SDR 35 per ounce and at market prices. Also included is a world table on the ratio of nongold reserves *(line 1l.d)* to imports *(line 71..d)* expressed in terms of the number of weeks of imports covered by the stock of nongold reserves.

Apart from that table and the world table on gold holdings in physical terms (see next paragraph), world tables on reserves are expressed in SDRs. Foreign exchange holdings are expressed in terms of SDRs by converting the U.S. dollar values shown on the country pages on the basis of the U.S. dollar/SDR rate.

Similarly, a foot table to the world table on gold indicates gold holdings valued at SDR 35 per ounce and at market prices for all countries, the IMF, the EMI, the Bank for International Settlements (BIS), and the world. Gold held by the EMI relates to the amounts deposited against issues of ECUs, as discussed on the preceding page under "Foreign Exchange." A simple addition of the gold held by all of these holders would involve double-counting, because most of the gold deposited with the BIS is also included in countries' official gold reserves. *IFS* therefore reports BIS gold holdings net of gold deposits; negative figures for BIS gold holdings are balanced by forward operations.

This foot table also provides data on (1) the U.S. dollar price of gold on the London market, (2) the U.S. dollar/SDR rate, (3) gold transactions that refer to gold sold by the Fund at auction in connection with the Trust Fund, which derived its resources from the profits of the auctions, from income earned from the investment of those profits, and from voluntary contributions or loans, and (4) the end-period derived market price of gold in terms of SDRs.

4. International Banking

International banking statistics are presented in *IFS* beginning with the January 1984 issue and are more fully discussed in the *IMF Survey,* a topical report of the Fund's activities, published 23 times a year (January 9, 1984, page 1, and June 18, 1984, page 184). With effect from the March 1985 issue of *IFS,* data are based on reports from 33 international banking centers providing detailed geographic analyses of resident deposit banks' external positions.

World Tables

The eight world tables on international banking give geographic analyses of the foreign assets and liabilities of the international banking system. The first two tables, on deposit banks' foreign accounts, summarize available data on foreign accounts of financial institutions other than monetary authorities. The country measures in the table *Deposit Banks' Foreign Liabilities (7y.d)* are normally those shown in *line 7b.d* on the country pages but also include *lines 7f.d* and *7m.d,* where appropriate. The country measures in the table *Deposit Banks' Foreign Assets (7x.d)* are normally those shown in *line 7a.d* on the country pages but also include *lines 7e.d* and *7k.d* where appropriate. Area and world totals include foreign accounts for a number of countries not shown separately. (See page viii for coverage.)

The remaining six tables of international banking statistics recast the available details of deposit banks' external accounts, plus information reported to *IFS* on monetary authorities' accounts with nonresident deposit banks (notably bank deposits classified as foreign exchange reserves, in *line 1d.d),* to form a more comprehensive picture of international banking activity, by residence of debtor or creditor.

To enhance the global symmetry of measures based on debtor and creditor reports, the world totals extend beyond the countries usually reported in *IFS* world tables and seek to identify accounts with deposit banks of international organizations and countries or territories not reporting directly to *IFS.* For this purpose, international organizations have been classified as nonbank transactors. However, the IMF, the EMI, and the BIS are distinguished in measuring international reserves (see foot table to the world table on gold); for consistency they are regarded as international monetary institutions in these tables. In practice, the EMI and the IMF do not have significant accounts with deposit banks.

Two tables on cross-border interbank accounts report on the accounts of monetary authorities and deposit banks with nonresident banks. Identified accounts between monetary authorities have been excluded. Thus, the cross-border interbank market captures positions between monetary authorities and nonresident deposit banks as well as between deposit banks in different countries. Separate analyses are given by country of residence of the borrowing banks and the lending banks.

Series in the table *Cross-Border Interbank Liabilities by Residence of Borrowing Bank (lines 8yad)* are the sum of that portion of *line 7y.d* that is estimated to represent liabilities of deposit banks to nonresident banks and that portion of *line 4..d* that is estimated to represent liabilities of monetary authorities to nonresident banks. Similarly, series in the table *Cross-Border Interbank Claims by Residence of Lending Bank (lines 8xad)* are the sum of that portion of *line 7x.d* estimated to represent claims of deposit banks on nonresident banks and that portion of *line 1d.d* estimated to represent claims of monetary authorities on nonresident banks.

This sum thus includes part of official foreign exchange reserves.

The source for these data is the reports regularly made for *IFS* by the authorities of over 100 countries, supplemented by Fund staff estimates. The line *International Monetary Institutions (BIS)* shows positions of the Bank for International Settlements (BIS) with deposit banks, as derived from the BIS's published balance sheet.

Two tables on international bank credit to nonbanks report on the claims of deposit banks on nonresident nonbanks, and two tables on international bank deposits of nonbanks report on the liabilities of deposit banks to nonresident nonbanks. Each of these two sets of tables gives separate analyses by country of residence of the borrowers and of the lenders or depositors.

The data in the tables *Cross-Border Bank Credit to Nonbanks by Residence of Borrower (lines 7yrd)* and *Cross-Border Bank Deposits of Nonbanks by Residence of Depositor (lines 7xrd)* are derived from detailed reports on the geographic distribution of the foreign assets and liabilities of deposit banks. These reports are made to the Fund by the authorities of 33 international banking centers—Australia, Austria, The Bahamas, Bahrain, Belgium, Canada, the Cayman Islands, Chile, Denmark, Finland, France, Germany, Hong Kong, Ireland, Israel, Italy, Japan, Korea, Lebanon, Luxembourg, the Netherlands, the Netherlands Antilles, Norway, Philippines, Portugal, Saudi Arabia, Singapore, Spain, Sweden, Switzerland, the United Arab Emirates, the United Kingdom, and the United States. Reports provided by the United States for the branches of U.S. banks in The Bahamas, the Cayman Islands, and Panama are also used.

The unallocated items in these two tables arise in large part because the world totals are derived from the "all country" totals in the two tables *Cross-Border Bank Credit to Nonbanks by Residence of Lending Bank (lines 7xdd)* and *Cross-Border Bank Deposits of Nonbanks by Residence of Borrowing Bank (lines 7ydd)*, respectively. The area residuals reflect the extent to which reporting banks identify positions by area but not by individual country as well as all reporting banks' positions with countries not specifically listed; thus, positions with countries specifically listed may be understated.

The line *Nonmonetary International Organizations* shows the positions of nonmonetary international organizations with deposit banks, as derived from the reports of deposit banks in international banking centers. Data in the tables *Cross-Border Bank Credit to Nonbanks by Residence of Lending Bank* and *Cross-Border Bank Deposits of Nonbanks by Residence of Borrowing Bank* are derived from the reports regularly made for *IFS* by the authorities of over 100 countries.

5. Money and Banking

Statistics on the accounts of monetary and other financial institutions are given in sections 10 through 50 on the country pages.

Monetary Authorities

Monetary authorities' data (section 10) measure the creation of reserve money comprising currency in circulation, deposits of the deposit money banks, and deposits of other residents, apart from the central government, with the monetary authorities. The data are categorized by type of financial instrument and by economic sector.

Foreign assets (line 11) reflect the function of the monetary authorities as the holder of international reserves and other foreign claims. Domestic assets are classified as *Claims on Central Government (line 12a)*, *Claims on Deposit Money Banks (line 12e)*, and, if sizable, *Claims on State and Local Governments (line 12b)*; *Claims on Nonfinancial Public Enterprises (line 12c)*; *Claims on the Private Sector (line 12d)*; and *Claims on Nonmonetary Financial Institutions (line 12f)*. In some countries, where insufficient data are available to provide disaggregations of claims on governmental bodies other than the central government, a classification of *Claims on Official Entities (line 12bx)* is used. The principal liabilities of monetary authorities consist of *Reserve Money (line 14)*, *Foreign Liabilities (line 16c)*, and *Central Government Deposits (line 16d)*.

Monetary authorities' data in *IFS* generally consolidate the accounts of the central bank with the accounts arising from monetary functions undertaken by other institutions. These functions include the issuance of currency, the holding of international reserves, and the conducting of Fund account transactions.

Deposit Money Banks

Deposit money banks' data (section 20) measure the creation of deposit money. Major aggregates of the accounts on the assets side are *Reserves (line 20)*, comprising domestic currency holdings and deposits with the monetary authorities, and *Claims on Other Resident Sectors (lines 22*)*, as described in the preceding section on monetary authorities *(lines 12*)*. The principal liabilities consist of *Demand Deposits (line 24)* and *Time, Savings, and Foreign Currency Deposits (line 25)*. Deposit money banks comprise commercial banks and other banks that accept demand deposits.

Monetary Survey

Monetary authorities' and deposit money banks' data, consolidated into a monetary survey (section 30), measure the size and origin of narrow *Money (line 34)*, which includes demand deposits and currency outside banks, and the *Quasi-Money (line 35)* liabilities of these institutions, which include time, savings, and foreign currency deposits. Standard relationships between the monetary survey lines and the component lines in sections 10 and 20 are as follows:

Foreign Assets (Net) (line 31n) equals the sum of foreign asset *lines 11* and *21*, less the sum of foreign liability *lines 16c* and *26c*.

Claims on Central Government (Net) (line 32an) equals claims on central government (the sum of *lines 12a* and *22a*), less central government deposits (the sum of *lines 16d* and *26d)*, plus, where applicable, the counterpart entries of *lines 24..i* and *24..r* (private sector demand deposits with the postal checking system and with the Treasury).

Claims on State and Local Governments (line 32b) equals the sum of *lines 12b* and *22b*. Note that, for some countries, lack of sufficient data to perform the standard classifications of claims has resulted in the use of the alternative classification "claims on official entities" *(line 32bx)*, which is the sum of *lines 12bx* and *22bx*. These series may therefore include state and local governments, public financial institutions, and nonfinancial public enterprises.

Claims on Nonfinancial Public Enterprises (line 32c) equals the sum of *lines 12c* and *22c*.

Claims on Private Sector (line 32d) equals the sum of *lines 12d* and *22d*.

Claims on Other Financial Institutions (line 32f) equals the sum of *lines 12f* and *22f* and therefore includes claims on other banking institutions plus claims on nonbank financial institutions, as applicable.

Domestic Credit (line 32) is the sum of *lines 32an, 32b, 32c, 32d,* and *32f* even when, owing to their small size, data for *lines 32b, 32c,* and *32f* are not published separately. Thus, the data for *line 32* may be larger than the sum of its published components.

Money (line 34) equals the sum of currency outside banks *(line 14a)* and demand deposits other than those of the central government *(lines 14d* and *24)* plus, where applicable, *lines 24..i* and *24..r.*

Quasi-Money (line 35) equals the sum of *lines 15* and *25*, comprising time, savings, and foreign currency deposits of resident sectors other than central government.

The data in *line 34* are frequently referred to as M1, while the sum of *lines 34* and *35* gives a broader measure of money similar to that which is frequently called M2. The yearbook publishes this time series *(line 35l)* immediately following the monetary survey.

Money Market Instruments (line 36aa) equals the sum of *lines 16aa* and *26aa.*

Bonds (line 36ab) equals the sum of *lines 16ab* and *26ab.*

Restricted Deposits (line 36b) equals the sum of *lines 16b* and *26b.*

Long-Term Foreign Liabilities (line 36cl) equals the sum of *lines 16cl* and *26cl.*

Counterpart Funds (line 36e) equals the sum of *lines 16e* and *26e.*

Central Government Lending Funds (line 36f) equals the sum of *lines 16f* and *26f.*

The monetary survey lines listed above give the full range of *IFS* standard lines. Some of these are not applicable to every country, while others may not be published separately in sections 10 and 20 because the data are small. Unpublished lines are included in *Other Items (Net) (lines 17r* and *27r)* but are classified in the appropriate monetary survey aggregates in section 30.

Exceptions to the standard calculations of monetary survey aggregates are indicated in the notes to the country pages in the monthly issues of *IFS.*

Other Banking Institutions

Section 40 contains data on the accounts of other banking institutions. This subsector includes institutions that do not accept transferable deposits but incur liabilities, such as time and savings deposits and securities that mobilize financial resources in a manner similar to the acceptance of deposits. The subsector covers such institutions as savings and mortgage loan institutions, post-office savings institutions, building and loan associations, finance companies that accept deposits or deposit substitutes, development banks, and offshore banking institutions. The major aggregates in section 40 are claims on the various sectors of the economy *(lines 42*)*, as described under "Monetary Authorities" *(lines 12*)*, and quasi-monetary liabilities *(line 45)*, largely in the form of time and savings deposits.

Banking Survey

Where reasonably complete data are available for other banking institutions, a banking survey (section 50) is published, consolidating data for other banking institutions with the monetary institutions data. The banking survey thus provides a broader measure of monetary liabilities. The sectoral classification of assets in the banking survey follows that used in the monetary survey, as outlined in the description of the monetary survey.

Nonbank Financial Institutions

For a few countries, data are shown on the accounts of nonbank financial institutions, such as insurance companies, pension funds, and superannuation funds. Given the nature of their liabilities, these institutions generally exert minimal impact on the liquidity of a given economy; however, they can play a significant role in the distribution of credit from the financial sector to the rest of the economy.

6. Interest Rates

The country pages report up to five groups of interest rates.

The first group refers to the rate at which the monetary authorities lend or discount eligible paper for deposit money banks *(line 60)*. Referred to as the *Discount Rate/Bank Rate*, this series is typically cited on an end-of-month basis, whereas it is preferred in *IFS* to publish the interest rates in the other groups on a period-average basis.

The second group consists of one or more representative short-term money market rates, e.g., the rate at which short-term borrowings are effected between financial institutions *(line 60b)* or the rate at which short-term government paper is issued or traded in the market *(line 60c)*. Typical standardized names for these rates are *Money Market Rate* and *Treasury Bill Rate*, respectively.

The third group comprises bank *Deposit Rates (line 60l)*. These usually refer to rates offered to resident customers for demand, time, or savings deposits. Frequently, rates for time and savings deposits are classified according to maturity and amounts deposited; in addition, deposit money banks and similar deposit-taking institutions may offer short- and medium-term instruments at specified rates for specific amounts and maturities; these are frequently termed "certificates of deposit."

The fourth group relates to bank *Lending Rates (line 60p)*, which usually meet the short- and medium-term financing needs of the private sector. These rates are normally differentiated according to creditworthiness of borrowers and objectives of financing.

The fifth group refers to one or more series representing yields to maturity of government bonds or other bonds that would indicate longer term rates *(line 61*)*. These are usually referred to as *Government Bond Yields*.

The country notes in the monthly issues carry a brief description of the nature and characteristics of the rates reported and of the financial instrument to which they relate. A typical series from each of these groups is included in the world table on national interest rates.

World Table on International Interest Rates

The world table on international interest rates reports data for the years 1980–94 and comprises London interbank offer rates on deposits denominated in SDRs, U.S. dollars, French francs, Deutsche mark, Japanese yen, and Swiss francs and Paris interbank offer rates on deposits denominated in pounds sterling. The table includes the premium or discount on three-month forward rates of currencies of the major industrial countries against the U.S. dollar.

The world table on international interest rates also reports the SDR interest rate and the rate of remuneration. Interest is paid on holdings of SDRs, and charges are levied on participants' cumulative allocations. Interest and charges accrue daily at the same rate and are settled quarterly in SDRs. As a result, participants who have SDR holdings above their net cumulative allocations receive net interest, and those with holdings below their net cumulative allocations pay net charges; other official holders of SDRs—including the Fund's General Resources Account—receive interest on their holdings and pay no charges because they receive no allocations.

The Fund also pays quarterly remuneration to members on their creditor positions arising from the use of their currencies in Fund transactions and operations, which is determined by the positive difference between the remuneration norm and the average daily balances of the member's currency in the General Resources Account.

Effective August 1, 1983, the weekly SDR interest rate has been based on the combined market interest rate, calculated by applying to the specific amounts of the five currencies included in the SDR valuation basket, converted into SDR equivalents, the market rates on specified short-term money market instruments quoted in the five countries.

As of January 1, 1991, the interest rates used in this calculation are market yield for three-month U.S. Treasury bills, three-month interbank deposit rate *(line 60bs)* in Germany, three-month rate for Treasury bills *(line 60cs)* in France, three-month rate on certificates of deposit *(line 60bs)* in Japan, and market yield for three-month U.K. Treasury bills *(line 60cs)*. These series are shown in the table.

The combined market rate is calculated each Friday and enters into effect each Monday. The interest rate on the SDR is 100 percent of the combined market rate, rounded to two nearest decimal places. The rate of remuneration, effective February 2, 1987, is 100 percent of the rate of interest on the SDR.

7. Prices, Wages, Production, and Employment

This section *(lines 62 through 67)* covers domestic prices, production, and labor market indicators. A more detailed discussion of major price indicators is provided in the *IFS Supplement on Price Statistics,* No. 12 (1986).

The index series are compiled from reported versions of national indices and, for some production, employment, and wage series, from absolute data. There is a wide variation between countries and over time in the selection of base years, depending upon the availability of comprehensive benchmark data that permit an adequate review of weighting patterns. The series are linked by using ratio splicing at the first annual overlap, and the linked series are shifted to a common base period 1990=100.

Share Prices

Indices shown for *Share Prices (line 62)* generally relate to common shares of companies traded on national or foreign stock exchanges. All reported indices are adjusted for changes in quoted nominal capital of companies. Indices are in general base-weighted arithmetic averages with market value of outstanding shares as weights.

Producer Price Index (PPI) or Wholesale Price Index (WPI)

Indices shown for *Producer* or *Wholesale Prices* (line 63) are designed to monitor changes in prices of items at the first important commercial transaction. Where a choice is available, preference is given to the PPI because the concept, weighting pattern, and coverage are likely to be more consistent with national accounts and industrial production statistics. In principle, the PPI should include service industries, but in practice it is limited to the domestic agricultural and industrial sectors. The prices should be farm-gate prices for the agricultural sector and ex-factory prices for the industrial sector.

The WPI, when used, covers a mixture of prices of agricultural and industrial goods at various stages of production and distribution, inclusive of imports and import duties. Preference is given to indices that provide broad coverage of the economy, and the indices are computed using the Laspeyres formula, unless otherwise indicated in the country notes in the monthly issues of *IFS*. Subindices are occasionally included for the PPI or the WPI.

Consumer Price Index (CPI)

Indices shown for *Consumer Prices (line 64)* are the most frequently used indicators of inflation and reflect changes in the cost of acquiring a fixed basket of goods and services by the average consumer. Preference is given to series having wider geographical coverage and relating to all income groups, provided they are no less current than more narrowly defined series.

As the weights are usually derived from household expenditure surveys, which may be conducted infrequently, information on the year to which the weights refer is provided in the country page notes in the monthly issues of *IFS*, together with information on any limitations in the coverage of commodities for pricing, income groups, or their expenditures in the chosen index. The Laspeyres formula is used unless otherwise indicated in the country notes in the monthly issues.

Wage Rates or Earnings

Indices shown for *Wages Rates* or *Earnings (line 65)* represent wage rates or earnings per worker employed per specified time period and frequently have the same coverage as the *Industrial Production Index (line 66)* and the *Industrial Employment Index (line 67)*. This is more likely where establishment surveys are the source. Preference is given to data for earnings that include payments in kind and family allowances and that cover salaried employees as well as wage earners. The indices either are computed from absolute wage data or are as reported directly to the Fund.

Industrial Production

Indices shown for *Industrial Production (line 66)* are included as indicators of current economic activity and for some countries are supplemented by indicators relevant to a particular country (such as data on tourism). Generally, the coverage of industrial production indices comprises mining and quarrying, manufacturing and electricity, and gas and water according to the UN *International Standard Industrial Classification (ISIC)*, and the indices are compiled using the Laspeyres formula; for many developing countries the indices refer to the production of a major primary commodity such as crude petroleum (see commodity codes on page viii).

Employment

Indices shown for *Employment (line 67)* are intended to show labor market activity, frequently in the industrial sectors covered by *lines 65* and *66*. The concept of employment conforms (in particular among the industrial countries) to the recommendations adopted by the ILO: Thirteenth International Conference of Labor Statisticians, Geneva, 1982. This covers all persons above a specified age who, during a specified time period, either were in paid employment or were self-employed. In general, national employment statistics are compiled from three main sources: labor force sample surveys, administrative records of social insurance schemes, and establishment surveys and records. The sources used and any divergence in country practice from the recommendations adopted by the ILO are explained in the country notes of the monthly issues of *IFS*.

8. International Transactions

Summary statistics on the international transactions of a country are given in *lines 70* through *79*. There is a section on external trade statistics *(lines 70 through 76)* reporting on the values *(lines 70 and 71)*, volumes *(lines 72 and 73)*, unit values *(lines 74 and 75)*, and prices *(line 76)* for exports and imports. This is followed by a section *(lines 78 through 79)* on balance of payments statistics.

External Trade

Merchandise Exports f.o.b. (line 70) and *Imports c.i.f. (line 71)* are, in general, customs statistics reported under the general trade system according to the recommendations of the UN *International Trade Statistics: Concepts and Definitions*, 1982. For some countries, data relate to the special trade system. The difference between general and special trade lies mainly in the treatment of recording the movement of goods through customs-bonded storage areas (warehouses, free areas, etc.).

Many countries use customs data on exports and imports as the primary source for the recording of goods exports and imports in the balance of payments. However, customs data and the entries for goods in the balance of payments may not be equal, owing to differences in definition. These differences may relate to the coverage of transactions (for example, the goods item in the balance of payments often includes adjustments for certain goods transactions that may not be recorded by customs authorities, e.g., parcel post), the time of recording of transactions (e.g., in the balance of payments, transactions are to be recorded when change of ownership occurs, rather than the moment goods cross the customs border, which generally determines when goods are recorded in customs based trade statistics), and classification differences (e.g., in the balance of payments, repair on goods is part of goods transactions).

The data for *Merchandise Imports f.o.b. (line 71.v)* are either obtained directly from statistical authorities or derived from *line 71* by applying *c.i.f./f.o.b.* factors that are principally taken from balance of payments statistics.

Details of commodity exports are presented for commodities that are traded in the international markets and have an impact on world market prices. Data for petroleum exports are presented only for 12 oil exporting countries. For a number of these countries, data estimated by Fund staff are derived from available data for the volume of production and estimates for prices that are, in part, taken from *Petroleum Intelligence Weekly* and other international sources; details of these estimates are provided in the country notes in the monthly version of the *IFS*.

For a number of countries where data are uncurrent or unavailable, additional lines are included showing data, converted from U.S. dollars to national currency, from *Direction of Trade Statistics (DOTS)*. Exports and imports data published in *DOTS* include reported data, updated where necessary with estimates for the current periods. A description of the nature of the estimates is given in the introduction of the *DOTS* quarterly publication.

Indices for *Volume of Exports (line 72)* and *Volume of Imports (line 73)* are either Laspeyres or Paasche. For 14 countries, as indicated in the country notes in the monthly issues of *IFS*, export volume indices are calculated from reported volume data for individual commodities weighted by reported values.

Indices for *Unit Value of Exports (line 74)* and *Unit Value of Imports (line 75)* are Laspeyres with weights derived from the data for transactions. For about fifteen countries, also as indicated in the country notes, export unit values are calculated from reported value and volume data for individual commodities.

Indices for export and import prices, compiled from survey data for prices at the wholesale level or directly from the exporter or importer (called "direct pricing"), are shown in *line 76*, where available. In the absence of national sources, data for wholesale prices are taken from world commodity markets and are converted into national currency at period average exchange rates. Indices based on direct pricing are generally considered preferable to unit value indices, because problems of unit value bias are reduced.

A more detailed presentation of trade statistics is presented in the *IFS Supplement on Trade Statistics*, No. 15 (1988).

New Presentation of Balance of Payments Data

Beginning with the September 1995 issue of *IFS*, the balance of payments lines are presented on the basis of the methodology and presentation of the fifth edition of the *Balance of Payments Manual (BPM5)*, published by the International Monetary Fund in September 1993. Prior issues of *IFS* presented balance of payments data on the basis of the fourth edition of the manual (*BPM4*). The *BPM5* incorporates several major changes to take account of developments in international trade and finance over the past decade, and to better harmonize the Fund's balance of payments methodology with the methodology of the 1993 *System of National Accounts* (*SNA*). The Fund's balance of payments database, from which the balance of payments lines in *IFS* are published, has been converted for all periods from the *BPM4* basis to the *BPM5* basis; thus the time series conform to the *BPM5* methodology with no methodological breaks.

The major changes in the *BPM5* methodology that significantly affect the meaning and presentation of the balance of payments data presented in *IFS* are:

(1) The *BPM5* coverage of the current account differs from *BPM4*. *BPM5* defines the current account as encompassing transactions in goods, services, income, and the receipts/payments of current transfers; in *BPM4*, the current account was defined to be inclusive of all transfers. Capital transfers now are included in an expanded and redesignated capital and financial account. The distinction between current and capital transfers is based on the guidelines established in the *SNA*, which focus on the special characteristics of capital transfers. First, a transfer in kind is a capital transfer when it consists of the transfer of ownership of a fixed asset, or of the forgiveness of a liability by a creditor when no counterpart is received in return. Second, a transfer of cash is a capital transfer when it is linked to, or conditional on, the acquisition or disposal of a fixed asset (for example, an investment grant) by one or both parties to the transaction.

(2) The coverage of goods in *BPM5* has been expanded to include (a) the value of goods (on a gross basis) received/sent for processing and their subsequent export/import in the form of processed goods; (b) the value of repairs on goods; and (c) the value of goods procured in ports by carriers. In *BPM4*, the value of processing services, repairs of goods, and goods procured in ports by carriers were all included under services.

(3) The *BPM5* reclassifies certain transactions in income and services. In *BPM4*, the distinction between income and services with regard to compensation of employees was not drawn clearly. Labor income included nonresident workers' expenditures in addition to the workers' earnings. In addition, employee compensation of nonresident employees of foreign governments and international organizations was included under government services. Furthermore, *BPM4* classified as property income the payments for the use of patents, copyrights, and similar nonfinancial intangible assets. In *BPM5*, all forms of employee compensation are included in income, whereas nonresident workers' expenditures and payments for the use of patents, etc. are classified as services. Therefore, income now covers investment income plus compensation of employees, whereas it previously included investment income, labor income, and property income, as defined in *BPM4*.

(4) The *BPM4* capital account was expanded and redesignated as the capital and financial account in *BPM5*, and comprises two major categories. The first is the capital account, which covers all transactions that involve (a) the receipt or payment of capital transfers, and (b) the acquisition/disposal of nonproduced, nonfinancial assets. The second is the financial account, roughly equivalent to the former capital account, which covers all transactions associated with changes in ownership of the foreign financial assets and liabilities of an economy. Such changes involve the creation and liquidation of claims on, or by, the rest of the world.

(5) Direct investment, as in *BPM4*, is classified primarily on a directional basis–resident investment abroad and nonresident investment in the reporting economy. However, in *BPM5*, transactions between affiliated banks and between other affiliated financial intermediaries associated with deposits and other claims and liabilities related to usual banking transactions, and similar claims and liabilities of other financial intermediaries, are excluded from the coverage of direct investment. (Such transactions are classified under

portfolio or other investment.) In *BPM4*, only short-term financial flows between banking institutions were excluded from direct investment.

(6) The coverage of portfolio investment was expanded in *BPM5* to reflect the growth of new financial instruments in recent years. In addition to long-term debt and equity securities, money market debt instruments and tradable financial derivatives are included in portfolio investment. (With the exception of long-term debt and equity securities, such instruments were treated as "other capital" in *BPM4*.)

There are also many other changes in the *BPM5* presentation of detailed balance of payments data as compared to the presentation of the *BPM4*. For a detailed description of the new methodology, see the *BPM5*. Nonetheless, all member countries' balance of payments data reported to the Fund will be presented in detailed standard components of the *BPM5* beginning with the 1995 *IMF Balance of Payments Statistics Yearbook*.

Description of Balance of Payments Lines in IFS

All lines are defined in accordance with the *BPM5*.

Goods: Exports f.o.b. and *Goods: Imports f.o.b.* (*lines 78aad* and *78abd*) are both measured on the "free-on-board" (f.o.b.) basis–that is, by the value of the goods at the border of the exporting country; in the case of imports, this excludes the cost of freight and insurance incurred beyond the border of the exporting country. The *Trade Balance* (*line 78acd*) is the difference between exports and imports of goods.

Balance on Goods and Services (*line 78afd*) and *Balance on Goods, Serv., & Inc.* (i.e., Balance on Goods, Services, and Income) (*78aid*) are the relevant credit items minus the debit items.

Current Transfers, n.i.e.: Credit (*line 78ajd*) comprise all current transfers received by the reporting country, except those made to the country to finance its "overall balance" (see below); hence, the label "n.i.e." The latter are included in *Exceptional Financing* (*line 79ded*) (see below). (Note: Some of the capital and financial account lines shown below are also labeled "n.i.e." This is to denote that *Exceptional Financing* items and *Liabilities Constituting Foreign Authorities' Reserves* (LCFARs) (see below) have been excluded from specific capital and financial account components).

Current Account, n.i.e. (*line 78ald*) is the credit lines minus the debit lines of goods, services, income, and current transfers, n.i.e.

Capital Account, n.i.e.: Credit (*line 78bad*) refers mainly to capital transfers linked to the acquisition of a fixed asset other than transactions relating to debt forgiveness (which are classified under *Exceptional Financing*) plus the disposal of nonproduced, nonfinancial assets. *Capital Account: Debit* (*line 78bbd*) refers mainly to capital transfers linked to the disposal of fixed assets by the donor or to the financing of capital formation by the recipient, plus the acquisition of nonproduced, nonfinancial assets. *Capital Account, n.i.e.* (*line 78bcd*) is the credit items minus the debit items of the capital account.

Direct Investment Abroad (*line 78bdd*) and *Direct Investment in Rep. Econ., n.i.e.* (Direct Investment in the Reporting Economy, n.i.e.) (*line 78bed*) represent the flows of direct investment capital out of the reporting economy and those into the reporting economy, respectively. Direct investment capital includes equity capital, reinvested earnings, and other capital associated with various intercompany transactions between affiliated enterprises. Excluded are flows of direct investment capital into the reporting economy for exceptional financing, such as debt-for-equity swaps.

Portfolio Investment Assets (*line 78bfd*) and *Portfolio Investment Liab., n.i.e.* (Portfolio Investment Liabilities) (*line 78bgd*) include transactions with nonresidents in financial securities of any maturity (such as corporate securities, bonds, notes, money market instruments, and financial derivatives) other than those included in direct investment, exceptional financing, LCFARs, and reserve assets.

Other Investment Assets (*line 78bhd*) and *Other Investment Liabilities, n.i.e.* (*line 78bid*) reflect all other transactions with nonresidents in financial assets and liabilities, except exceptional financing, LCFARs, and reserve assets. Major categories are transactions in currency and deposits, loans, and trade credits.

Financial Account, n.i.e. (*line 78bjd*) is the net sum of the balance of direct investment, portfolio investment, and other investment transactions.

Net Errors and Omissions (*line 78cad*) is a residual category needed to ensure that all debit and credit entries in the balance of payments statement sum to zero and reflects statistical inconsistencies in the recording of the credit and debit entries. In the *IFS* presentation, this is equal to the difference between *Reserves and Related Items* (*line 79dad*) (described below) and the sum of the balances of the current account, the capital account, and the financial account.

Overall Balance (*line 78cbd*) is the sum of the balances of the current account, the capital account, the financial account, and net errors and omissions.

Reserves and Related Items (*line 79dad*) is the sum of transactions in reserve assets, LCFARs, exceptional financing, and use of Fund credit and loans.

Reserve Assets (*line 79dbd*) consists of external assets readily available to and controlled by monetary authorities primarily for direct financing of payments imbalances and for indirectly regulating the magnitude of such imbalances through exchange market intervention.

Use of Fund Credit and Loans (*79dcd*) includes purchases and repurchases in the credit tranches of the Fund's General Resource Account, and net borrowings under the Structural Adjustment Facility (SAF), Enhanced Structural Adjustment Facility (ESAF), and the Trust Fund.

Liabs. Constit. For. Auth. Reserves (Liabilities Constituting Foreign Authorities' Reserves) (*line 79ddd*) is a special category of liabilities that have been excluded from the portfolio and other investment liability accounts to represent the liabilities of the reporting country that would generally be classified as reserve assets by the creditor country.

Exceptional Financing (*line 79ded*) includes any other transactions undertaken by the authorities to finance the "overall balance," as an alternative to, or in conjunction with, the use of reserve assets, the use of Fund credit and loans from the Fund, and LCFARs.

9. Government Finance

Summary statistics of government finance are given in section 80. Unless otherwise stated in individual country notes in the monthly issues of IFS, annual data are as reported in the *Government Finance Statistics Yearbook* (*GFSY*) and cover operations of the consolidated central government, i.e., operations of budgetary central government and, where these exist, operations of extrabudgetary units and social security funds as well. The coverage of consolidated central government may not necessarily include all existing extrabudgetary units and/or social security funds. The *GFSY* reproduces, for every country, the institutional tables that identify all the units that belong to budgetary or consolidated central government.

More extensive data for use in cross-country comparisons are published in the *GFSY* and are based on *A Manual on Government Finance Statistics*. The country notes in the monthly issues of IFS identify the principal sources of difference between the data in IFS and *GFSY*.

The data for *lines 80* through *87* are flows and are on a cash basis. The *Deficit or Surplus (line 80)* is calculated as the difference between *Revenue* and, if applicable, *Grants Received* (*lines 81* and *81z*) on the one hand and *Expenditure* and *Lending Minus Repayments* (*lines 82* and *83*) on the other. The deficit/surplus is also equal, with the opposite sign, to the sum of the net borrowing by the government plus the net decrease in government cash, deposits, and securities held for liquidity purposes.

Revenue (line 81) comprises all nonrepayable and nonrepaying government receipts, whether requited or unrequited, other than grants; revenue is shown net of refunds and other adjustment transactions.

Grants Received (line 81z) comprises all unrequited, nonrepayable, noncompulsory receipts from other governments—domestic or foreign—and international institutions. Grants are grouped with revenue because, like revenue, they provide the means whereby expenditure can be made without incurring a debt for future repayment.

Expenditure (line 82) comprises all nonrepayable and nonrepaying payments by government, whether requited or unrequited and whether for current or capital purposes.

Lending Minus Repayments (line 83) comprises government acquisition of claims on others—both loans and equities—for public policy purposes and is net of repayments of lending and sales of equities previously purchased. *Line 83* includes both domestic and foreign lending minus repayments. In determining the deficit or surplus, lending minus repayments is grouped with expenditure, because it is presumed to represent a means of pursuing government policy objectives and not to be an action undertaken to manage government liquidity.

The total of the financing items equals the deficit or surplus with a reverse sign. *Net Borrowing (line 84)* covers the net change in government liabilities to all other sectors, representing either their direct loans or advances to government or their holding of government securities acquired from the government itself or in transactions with others. Where possible, data for *Domestic* and *Foreign Net Borrowing* (*lines 84a* and *85a*) are classified according to the residence of the lender; where this information is not available, the distinction is based on the currency in which the debt instruments are denominated (*lines 84b* and *85b*).

Use of Cash Balances (line 87) is intended to measure changes over a period—resulting from transactions but not revaluations—in government holdings of currency and deposits with the monetary system, corresponding to changes in IFS lines *16d* and *26d*, and where possible, the notes to country pages in the monthly issues give reasons why they may not correspond. All currency issues are regarded as liabilities of the monetary authorities, rather than government debt, and any proceeds reaching the government are regarded as coming from the monetary authorities.

Data for outstanding *Debt (lines 88* and *89)* relate to the direct and assumed debt of the central government and exclude loans guaranteed by the government. The distinction between *Domestic* and *Foreign Debt* (*lines 88a* and *89a*) is based on residence of the lender, where possible, but otherwise on the currency in which the debt instruments are denominated (*lines 88b* and *89b*).

10. National Accounts and Population

The summary data for national accounts are compiled according to the *System of National Accounts*. Country notes in the monthly issues indicate those countries that follow the Material Product System (MPS).

Gross Domestic Product (GDP) (line 99b) is generally presented in IFS as the sum of final expenditures: *Exports of Goods and Services (line 90c), Imports of Goods and Services (line 98c), Private Consumption (line 96f), Government Consumption (line 91f), Gross Fixed Capital Formation (line 93e),* and *Increase/Decrease(-) in Stocks (line 93i). Net Factor Income/Payments(-) Abroad (line 98.n)* is the difference between GDP and *Gross National Product (GNP) (line 99a)*, unless otherwise explained in the country notes.

Statistical discrepancies between aggregate GDP compiled from expenditure flows as against GDP compiled from the production or income accounts (or from a mixture of these accounts) are not shown explicitly. Hence, in some cases, the components of GDP that are shown in IFS may not add up exactly to the total.

Net Material Product (line 99m), compiled in accordance with the MPS, differs from GDP by emphasizing the output of material production sectors (sectors producing goods, and selected services attending to those sectors), rather than total output. In expenditure terms, *line 99m* is the sum of private consumption of goods and material services, consumption of the same items by nonmaterial sectors (such as government, banking, and providers of personal services), net investment and replacement of losses, and net exports of the material production sectors (exports less imports).

Final annual data are generally consistent with the United Nations' *National Accounts Statistics: Main Aggregates and Detailed Tables*. For countries that publish seasonally adjusted data, the data in *IFS* are also on a seasonally adjusted basis (codes ending with *c* or *r*) with the quarterly data shown at annual rates.

Lines 99b.p, 99b.r, 99a.p, and *99a.r* refer to constant price GDP/GNP. The base year prices at which constant price data are expressed are updated by the national compilers. Constant price data for the first overlapping year are used to link different base year series. The linked series are expressed in index form and shifted to a common base period, 1990=100. This index is then applied to current price GDP/GNP data for 1990 to yield an estimated series at 1990 constant prices, which carries a break symbol (χ) preceding the overlapping year used for linking the different base year series.

The *GDP* (or *GNP*) *Deflator (line 99bip, 99bir, 99aip,* or *99air)* series shown in the *IFS Yearbook* is not a direct measurement of prices but is derived implicitly by dividing GDP/GNP at current prices by GDP/GNP at constant prices. The deflator is expressed in index form, with the base 1990=100.

Data on *Population (line 99z)*, which represent midyear estimates, are provided by the UN. These estimates are also published in the UN *Monthly Bulletin of Statistics*.

11. World Tables

World tables presented in the yearbook bring together country data on exchange rates, members' Fund transactions and positions, international reserves, deposit banks' foreign assets and liabilities, reserve money, various measures of money, money plus quasi-money, interest rates, wholesale and consumer prices, wages, production, employment, values and unit values of countries' exports and imports, balance of payments, government finance, GDP (or GNP) at constant prices, GDP (or GNP) deflators, and the shares of consumption and investment in GDP (or GNP). World tables also present series on wholesale prices and unit values (expressed in U.S. dollars) of principal world trade commodities. The *Balance of Payments Statistics Yearbook* and the *Government Finance Statistics Yearbook* should be consulted for world tables dealing with their areas of economic statistics. Tables showing totals or averages of country series may report data for selected countries only. A full listing of countries whose data are included in the calculation of area and world measures is given on page viii.

Country Groups

Countries whose data are included in **world/all countries'** totals and averages are arrayed into two main groups—**industrial countries** and **developing countries.** The developing countries group is further subdivided into area subgroups for **Africa, Asia, Europe,** the **Middle East,** and the **Western Hemisphere.**

In addition, the eight world tables on international banking show aggregated data for **major offshore banking centers,** defined with reference to seven countries (The Bahamas, Bahrain, the Cayman Islands, Hong Kong, the Netherlands Antilles, Panama, and Singapore) where the banking system, acting as financial entrepot, acquires substantial external accounts beyond those associated with economic activity in the country concerned. For major offshore banking centers, the ratio of deposit banks' external assets to exports of goods and services, which serves as an indicator of the relationship between the size of external financial accounts and domestic economic activity, is significantly larger than the world average.

Data for subgroups **oil exporting countries** and **non-oil developing countries** are shown as memorandum items. Oil exporting countries are defined as those countries whose oil exports (net of any imports of crude oil) both represent a minimum of two thirds of their total exports and are at least equivalent to approximately 1 percent of world exports of oil. The calculations presently used to determine which countries meet the above criteria are based on 1976–78 averages.

The country composition of the **world** is all countries for which the topic series are available in the *IFS* files; hence, the country coverage of some areas, mainly Africa and Asia, differs from topic to topic, and area and world totals or averages may be biased to some extent toward the larger reporting countries.

Area and World Indices

Area and world indices are obtained as weighted averages of country indices. Arithmetic means are used for unit values of exports and imports (and terms of trade), where the country indices are expressed in U.S. dollars. Geometric means are used for wholesale and consumer prices, GDP (or GNP) at constant prices, GDP (or GNP) deflator, industrial production, wages, and employment because, unlike arithmetic means, geometric means are not unduly influenced by data for the few countries with extreme growth rates. Geometric means assure that, if all series have constant although different rates of increase, their average will have a constant rate of increase.

The country series included in the calculation of the area averages for wholesale and consumer prices, GDP (or GNP) at constant prices, and GDP (or GNP) deflator are weighted by the 1990 purchasing power parity (PPP) value of GDP[1]. The country series used in the industrial production, wages, and employment tables are weighted by value added in industry, as derived from individual countries' national accounts, expressed in U.S. dollars. The country series used in the export unit values and import unit values tables are

---

[1] See *World Economic Outlook*, May 1993, Annex IV, for a comparison of PPP-based GDP weights and exchange-rate-based GDP weights.

weighted by the 1990 value of exports and imports (both in U.S. dollars), respectively.

Weights are normally updated at about five-year intervals, in accordance with international practice, in order to reflect changes in the importance of each country's data in relation to the data of all other countries. The standard weight base years used are 1953, 1958, 1963, 1970, 1975, 1980, 1984–86, and 1990; the corresponding time spans to which the weights are applied are 1948–55, 1955–60, 1960–68, 1968–73, 1973–78, 1978–83, 1983–88 and 1988 onward. Separate averages are calculated for each time span, and the index series are linked by the splicing at overlap years and shifted to the reference base 1990=100.

The calculation of area totals and averages takes account of the problem that data for some countries do not run through the end of the period for which world and area data should be calculable. Area totals and averages for most topics are estimated for current and for earlier periods if country data are known that contribute at least 60 percent of the area total or index aggregate during recent periods for which data of all countries of an area are available. Area totals or averages are estimated by assuming that the rate of change in the unreported country data is the same as the rate of change in the weighted total or average of the reported country data for that area. These estimates are made for the area totals and averages only; separate country estimates are not calculated.

With the exception of import unit values, the world totals and averages are made from the calculated and estimated data for the two main groups—industrial countries and developing countries. A world total or average is calculated only when totals or averages are available for both of these country groups. For import unit values, world data are calculated directly from country data, because the number of countries for which the series are available and current is insufficient to allow calculation or estimation of the area averages and because the variability of import unit value indices among countries is judged to be less than that for other topics. World estimates are made when data are available for countries whose combined weights represent at least 80 percent of the total country weights.

For the terms of trade index numbers, the world and area data for the export unit values are divided by the corresponding series for the import unit values, where possible. Thus terms of trade averages are available only for areas with both export and import unit values. The country coverage within the areas for the export and import unit values is not identical, leading to a small degree of assymetry in the terms of trade calculation.

Individual World Tables Described

International Reserves: Country series on international reserves begin generally with their appropriate dates and are complete monthly time series; hence, earlier period estimates are not required. When current data of a few countries of an area are not reported, the area total is estimated by carrying forward the last reported country figure.

Deposit Banks' Foreign Assets, Deposit Banks' Foreign Liabilities, Cross-Border Interbank Accounts (two tables), *Cross-Border Bank Credit to Nonbanks* (two tables), and *Cross-Border Bank Deposits of Nonbanks* (two tables): Data in these tables are described in the preceding section on international banking. Six of the eight tables report annual data for the years 1980–94, and two of the tables report annual data for the years 1981–94. For series that are compiled from the regular reports of all contributing national authorities, when data of a few countries of an area are uncurrent, the area total is estimated by carrying forward the last reported figure. For series that are compiled from the reports of major international banking centers, when data of any reporting banking center are uncurrent, reported country totals are estimated by carrying forward the banking center's last reported figures for all reported countries.

Reserve Money, Money, and *Money plus Quasi-Money:* End-of-period stock series are converted to period averages and expressed as index numbers. The percent changes shown in the world tables are calculated from these index numbers.

Ratio of Reserve Money to Money plus Quasi-Money: The measures of money used in calculating this ratio are annual averages of the highest frequency data available.

Income Velocity of Money plus Quasi-Money: The measure of income in this table is *IFS* data on GDP or, if not available, GNP. The data for money plus quasi-money are annual averages of the highest frequency data available. The ratio is then converted into an index number with a base year of 1990.

Real Effective Exchange Rate Indices: This table shows a variety of real effective exchange rate indices for industrial countries. Five of these comprise alternative measures of costs and prices that have been applied to the weighting scheme described next. These alternative measures of costs and prices are derived from *Relative Unit Labor Costs (line 65um), Relative Normalized Unit Labor Costs (line* **reu**), *Relative Value-Added Deflators (line 99by), Relative Wholesale Prices (line 63ey),* and *Relative Export Unit Values (line 74ey).*

The weighting scheme is based on disaggregated data for trade in manufactured goods, averaged over the period 1989–91, with the weights reflecting both the relative importance of a country's trading partners in its direct bilateral trade relations and that resulting from competition in third markets. The measure is expressed as an index 1990=100 in accordance with all indices published in *IFS*.

A discussion of the data sources used to derive the cost and price indicators for the real effective exchange rates shown in the world table is provided in the footnotes to that table. The real effective exchange rate index *Based on Relative Normalized Unit Labor Costs (line* **reu**) is also shown on the country pages (with the exception of Ireland) together with the *Nominal Effective Exchange Rate Index (line* **neu**) from which all five measures are drawn.

Beginning with the October 1992 issue of *IFS*, the data published are from a revised database, based on a comprehensive review and update of the underlying data sources and a change in the method of normalization of output per hour; this uses the Hodrick-Prescott filter, which smoothes a time series by removing short-run fluctuations while retaining changes of a larger amplitude.

In addition, there is a real effective exchange rate index, *Based on Relative Consumer Prices (line* **rec**) as a measure of domestic cost and price developments. It covers trade in manufactured goods and primary products for a range of trading partners—and competitors—by using the same methodology that is used to compile nominal and real effective exchange rates for nonindustrial countries, as discussed in the exchange rate and exchange rate arrangements section of this introduction.

Industrial Production: This table presents seasonally adjusted indices on industrial production for 22 industrial countries together with an aggregate index for the group. The data are those shown on the country pages as either *Industrial Production (lines 66..*)* or *Manufacturing Production (lines 66ey*),* the asterisk representing a wildcard.

Wages: This table presents indices computed either from absolute wage data or from the wage indices reported to the Fund for the industrial sector for 22 industrial countries. The data are those shown in the country pages as *Wage Rates* or *Earnings (line 65).*

Employment: This table presents indices computed from indices of employment or number of persons employed as reported by the countries for the industrial sector for 20 industrial countries. The data are those shown in the country pages as *Employment (line 67).*

Wholesale Prices and *Consumer Prices*: Data are those prices reported in *lines 63** and *64** on the country pages. The percent changes are calculated from the index number series.

Exports and *Imports*: Data are the national currency value series reported on the country pages *(lines 70...* and *71...)* expressed in U.S. dollars at rate **rf**.

Cif/fob Factor: Factors for individual countries use data provided by national authorities or estimated by staff. The factors for the world and areas are derived from the world and area totals of imports, c.i.f., shown in the previous table, and imports, f.o.b.

Export Unit Values and *Import Unit Values*: Data are the index numbers reported on the country pages expressed in U.S. dollars at rate **rf**. The country indices are typically unit value data *(lines 74* and *75);* however, for some countries they are components of wholesale price indices or are derived from specific price quotations *(lines 76, 76.x,* and *76aa).* The exceptions are coded "w" in the tabulation of country coverage on page viii.

Terms of Trade: Data are index numbers computed from the export and import unit value indices and shown in the appropriate world table. The percent changes are calculated from the index number series.

Balance of Payments: For a precise definition of the concepts used in these tables, and for an explanation of changes in definition that are related to the introduction of the fifth edition of the *Balance of Payments Manual,* the reader is referred to section 8, International Transactions.

Trade Balance is the series reported in *line 78acd* of the country pages; Current Account Balance, Excluding Exceptional Financing is the series reported in *line 78ald* of the country pages; Capital and Financial Account, Including New Errors and Omissions but Excluding Reserve Assets, Use of Fund Credit and Loans, Liabilities Constituting Foreign Authorities' Reserves (LCFAR), and Exceptional Financing are the sum of the series reported in *lines 78bcd, 78bjd,* and *78cad* of the country pages.

Overall Balance Excluding Reserve Assets, Use of Fund Credit and Loans, LCFAR, and Exceptional Financing is the series reported in *line 78cbd* (which equals *lines 78ald, 78bcd, 78bjd,* and *78cad*) of the country pages.

Exports/Imports of Goods and Services as Percent of GDP: The data relate to the percent share of exports and imports of goods and services (calculated as the sums of *lines 78aad* and *78add* and *lines 78abd* and *78aed,* respectively) in *Gross Domestic Product (line 99b).* Current Account Balance Excluding Exceptional Financing as Percent of GDP: The data relate to the percent share of the *Current Account n.i.e. (line 78ald)* in *Gross Domestic Product.*

Government Finance: The world tables show, respectively, Deficit/Surplus, Revenue and Grants, and Expenditure and Lending minus Repayments as percent of GDP/GNP. The data, based on the *Government Finance Statistics Yearbook,* are shown for several fiscal years, which may vary from country to country; in calculating the time series as percent of GDP/GNP, the GDP/GNP data have been adjusted to correspond to the same fiscal year. Any changes in the fiscal year basis affecting the time series and the ratios are indicated by a break symbol (⅄).

GDP (or *GNP*) *at Constant Prices*: Data are derived from those series reported in *lines 99b.p* (or *99a.p*) on the country pages. The percent changes are calculated from index numbers.

GDP (or *GNP*) *Deflator*: Data are derived from those series reported in *lines 99bip* (or *99aip*) on the country pages. The percent changes are calculated from index numbers.

Investment as Percent of GDP (or *GNP*): Data are the percent share of investment in GDP (or GNP) at current market prices. Investment comprises *Gross Fixed Capital Formation* and *Increase in Stocks (lines 93e* and *93i,* respectively).

Consumption as Percent of GDP (or *GNP*): Data are the percent share of consumption in GDP (or GNP) at current market prices. Consumption comprises *Government Consumption* and *Private Consumption (91f* and *96f,* respectively).

Commodity Prices: Data are the market prices *(lines 76)* reported on the country pages for important commodities traded internationally, in units of quantity frequently used in the respective commodity markets, expressed in U.S. dollars and as indices. For comparison purposes, unit values *(lines 74)* for corresponding commodities are also shown. The notes to the table in the monthly issues describe the market price series, those unit value series that refer to specific grades of commodities, and the index for all commodities.

12. Charts

The charts following this introduction show the trends over recent years in some key economic time series published in the statistical tables in *IFS*. The underlying data in general relate to the world, area, and regional totals of the time series.

13. Country Codes and *IFS* Line Numbers

Each *IFS* time series carries a unique identification code, which for publication purposes has been truncated to a three-digit country code and to a five-digit topic code referred to as the *IFS* line number.

Country (and area) codes are listed on page viii. They appear also in the upper right-hand corner of the appropriate country pages and as part of the descriptor stub on most of the world tables.

Line numbers apply uniformly across countries, i.e., a given line number measures the same economic variable for each country, subject to data availability. The line numbers take the form of two numerics followed by three alphabetic codes (NN*aaa*), the last of which is referred to as the subset code. Any of these positions may be blank: for publication purposes, blanks in the initial or final positions are omitted whereas imbedded blanks are represented by a period. The line numbers are part of the descriptor stub on the country pages and also appear at the top of most of the world tables.

Production data *(lines 66)*, export data *(lines 70, 72, 74, and 76)*, and import data *(lines 71)* for petroleum carry the commodity codes listed on page viii in the alpha positions of the topic code.

Data expressed in units of money (values or prices) are ordinarily expressed in national currency and in natural form, i.e., without seasonal adjustment. For these data the subset code is blank.

Transformations of these data are denoted by various subset codes. For data that are not seasonally adjusted, subset codes are *d* for U.S. dollar values, *s* for SDR values, and *p* for constant national currency values. For data that are seasonally adjusted for the monthly issues of *IFS*, subset codes are *f* for U.S. dollar values, *u* for SDR values, and *b* for national currency values. For data that are seasonally adjusted by national compilers, subset codes are *c* for national currency values and *r* for constant national currency values.

The subset codes are also used to distinguish separate groups of deposit money banks or other financial institutions when data for separate classes are given.

14. Symbols, Conventions, and Abbreviations

Captions in the middle of the pages identify the units in which data are expressed and whether data are stocks (end of period), flows (transactions during a period), or averages (for a period).

"Billion" means a thousand millions.

(—) Indicates that a figure is zero or less than half of a significant digit or that data do not exist.

(....) Indicates a lack of statistical data that can be reported or calculated from underlying observations.

($\mathbf{I}$) Mark a break in the comparability of data, if explained in the relevant notes. In these instances, data after the symbol do not form a consistent series with those for earlier dates.

However, where no note is shown for many linked series, the use of the symbol marks the fact that a consistent series is not provided by the country, and available series have been spliced by Fund staff by the use of the ratio of the first annual overlap.

(e) In superscript position after the figure marks an observation that is an estimate.

(f) In superscript position after the figure marks an observation that is forecast.

(p) In superscript position after the figure indicates that data are in whole or in part provisional or preliminary.

(n.i.e.) Indicates not included elsewhere.

Because of space limitations in the phototypesetting of descriptor stubs on the country pages and table headings of world tables, abbreviations are sometimes necessary. While most are self-explanatory, the following abbreviation in the table headings of the world tables should be noted:

Use of Fund Credit (GRA) = Use of Fund Credit (General Resources Account).

The following descriptor stub on the country pages should be noted:

Of which: Currency Outside DMBs = Of which: Currency Outside Deposit Money Banks.

Data relating to fiscal years are allocated to calendar years to which most of their months refer. Fiscal years ending June 30 are allocated to that calendar year, e.g., the fiscal year from July 1, 1989 to June 30, 1990 is shown as calendar year 1990.

15. *IFS* Electronic Subscriptions

The *IFS* electronic subscriptions are available in two forms: CD-ROM and magnetic tape. Both forms contain
(1) all time series appearing on *IFS* country pages;
(2) all series published in the *IFS* world tables, except for the daily exchange rates appearing in the *Exchange Rates* tables;
(3) the following exchange rate series as available: **aa, ac, ae, af, ag, ah, b, c, de, dg, ea, eb, ec, ed, g, rb, rd, rf, rh, sa, sb, sc, sd, wa, wc, we, wf, wg, wh, xe, xf, ye, yf, nec, rec, aat, aet, rbt, rft, neu, reu,** and **ahx** (for an explanation of series **af, ah, de, dg, rb,** and **rd**, see *IFS Supplement on Exchange Rates*, No. 9 (1985));
(4) Fund accounts time series, all in SDR terms (*2eb, 2eu, 2ey, 2tl, 1b.s, 1c.s, 2c, 2dus, 2ees, 2egs, 2ehs, 2eqs, 2ers, 2ets, 2f.s, 2h.s, 2krs,* and *2kxs*; and the fol-

lowing series which contain the source code T—*1bf*, *2fz*, *2kk*, *2kl*, *2lk*, *2ll*, and *2tl*);

(5) money index series (*34..x*);
(6) export and import series (*70* and *71*);
(7) export and import unit value index series (*74* and *75*).

The series referred to in item 3 are on tape and CD-ROM for all IMF members, plus Aruba, Hong Kong, and the Netherlands Antilles. The series referred to in items 4 through 8 correspond to all countries for which data are available, though some series are not published in *IFS*. All series on the *IFS* tape and CD-ROM contain control source code F except for the previously mentioned Fund accounts series that contain the source code T.

A partner country code may in some cases be included in the control field. When it exists, it usually is shown in *IFS* either in the midheading (see *Real Effective Exchange Rate Indices* table) or in the notes (see *Commodity Prices* table notes). The series on the U.S. liabilities and claims appearing on the tape and CD-ROM contain partner code 111, but this code is not shown in *IFS*. It should be noted that in some instances the partner country code attached to a commodity price refers to a market (e.g., the London Metals Exchange) rather than the country of origin.

In the book, data expressed in national currency for countries that have undergone periods of high inflation (e.g., Argentina, Brazil, and Peru) are presented in different magnitudes on the same printed line. Users may refer to midheaders on country pages for an indication of the magnitude changes. The practice of expressing different magnitudes on the same line was adopted to prevent early-period data from disappearing from the printed tables.

On the tape the data are stored in a single magnitude per line. Therefore, this data goes to zero as a series moves back in time. On the CD-ROM the data are stored in a scientific notation with eight significant digits for all time periods. Therefore, historical as well as current data may be viewed when using the display options available on the CD-ROM.

16. Country Page Notes

The country page notes in this yearbook explain discontinuities in time series, each of which are identified by a break symbol (Ι). They also explain changes in a country's currency unit over time. Such changes imply discontinuities in time series that express national currencyvalues, but for presentational purposes this problem is eliminated in *IFS* by converting historical data expressed in terms of earlier currency units into their equivalents in terms of the latest currency units.

Other country and world table notes are carried in the monthly issues of *IFS*. Also, all linked series, like the series in section seven of this introduction, show break symbols (Ι) at the point of the splice; the break symbols not otherwise explained on the country pages identify the linkages.

CHARTS

International Reserves

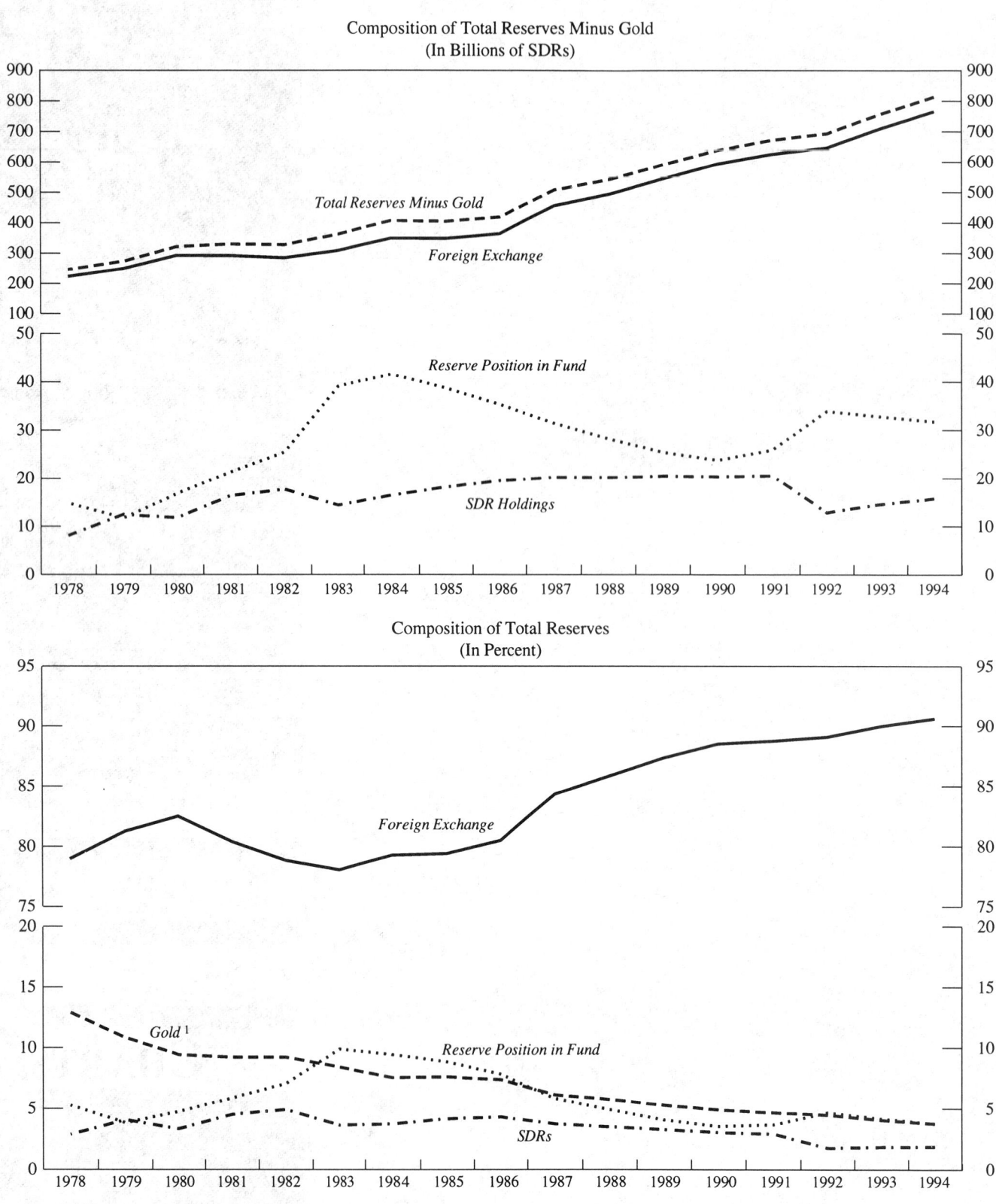

[1] Valued at SDR 35 per ounce.

Interest Rates

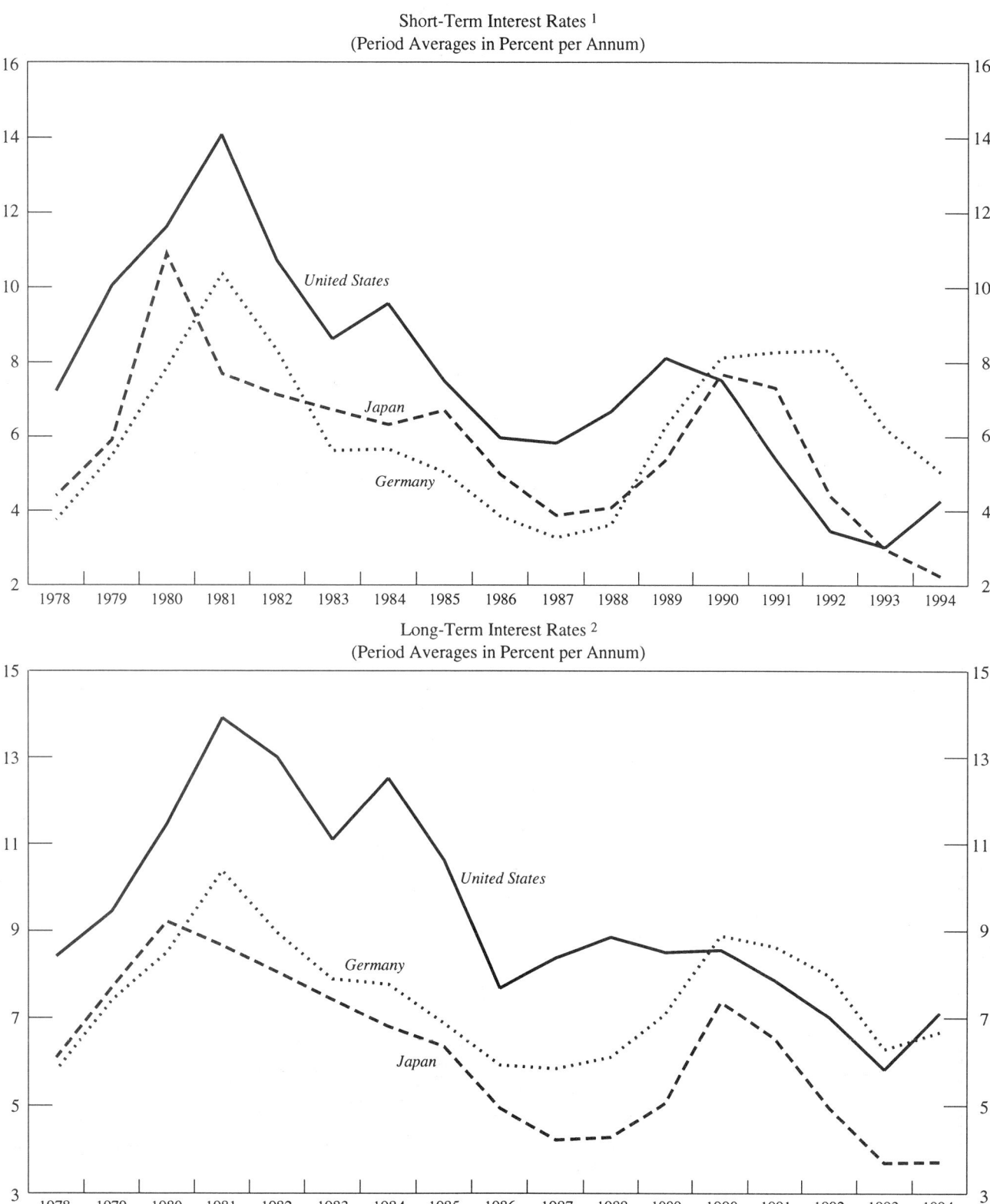

[1] Three-month T-bill rates for U.S. and Germany; private bill rate for Japan.
[2] Long-term government bond yield. (For definitions of the series used, see country notes in the monthly issues of *IFS*.)

Exchange Rates

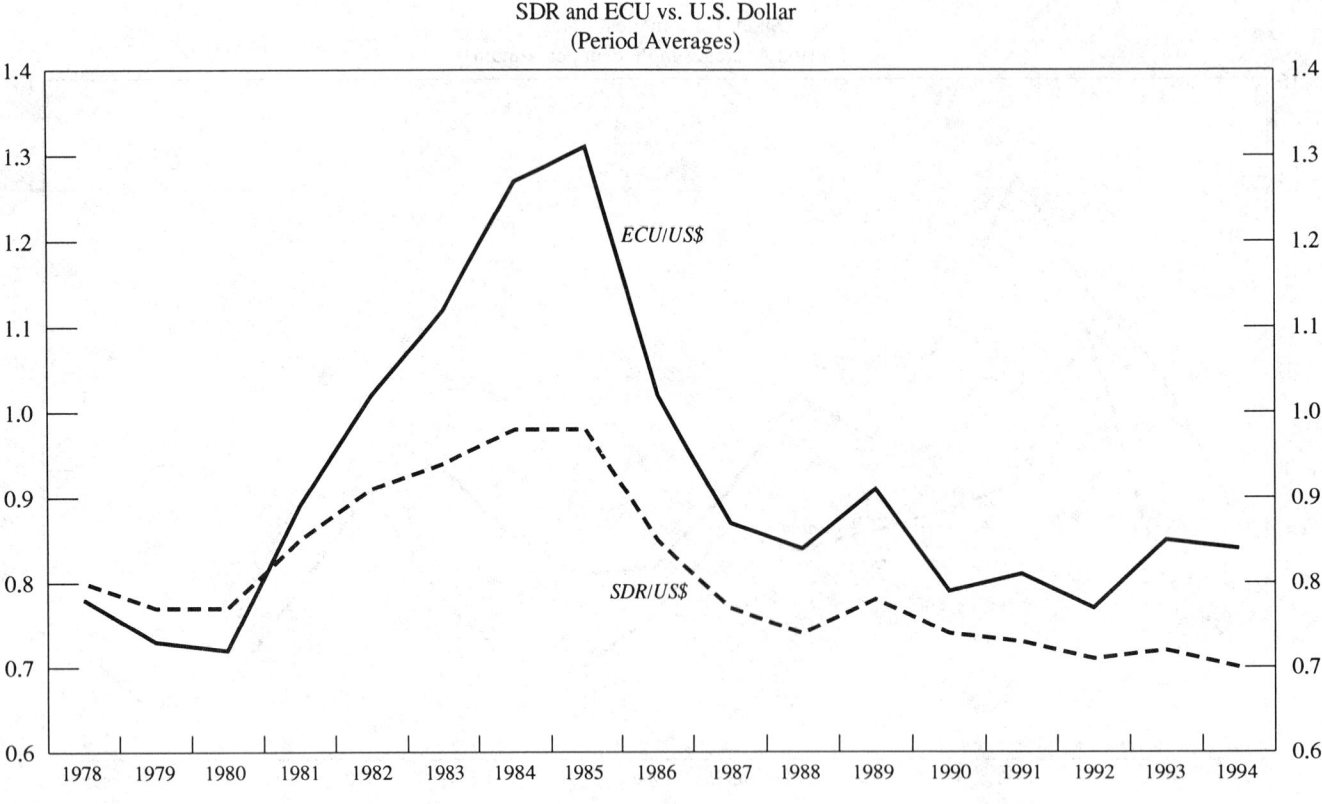

SDR and ECU vs. U.S. Dollar
(Period Averages)

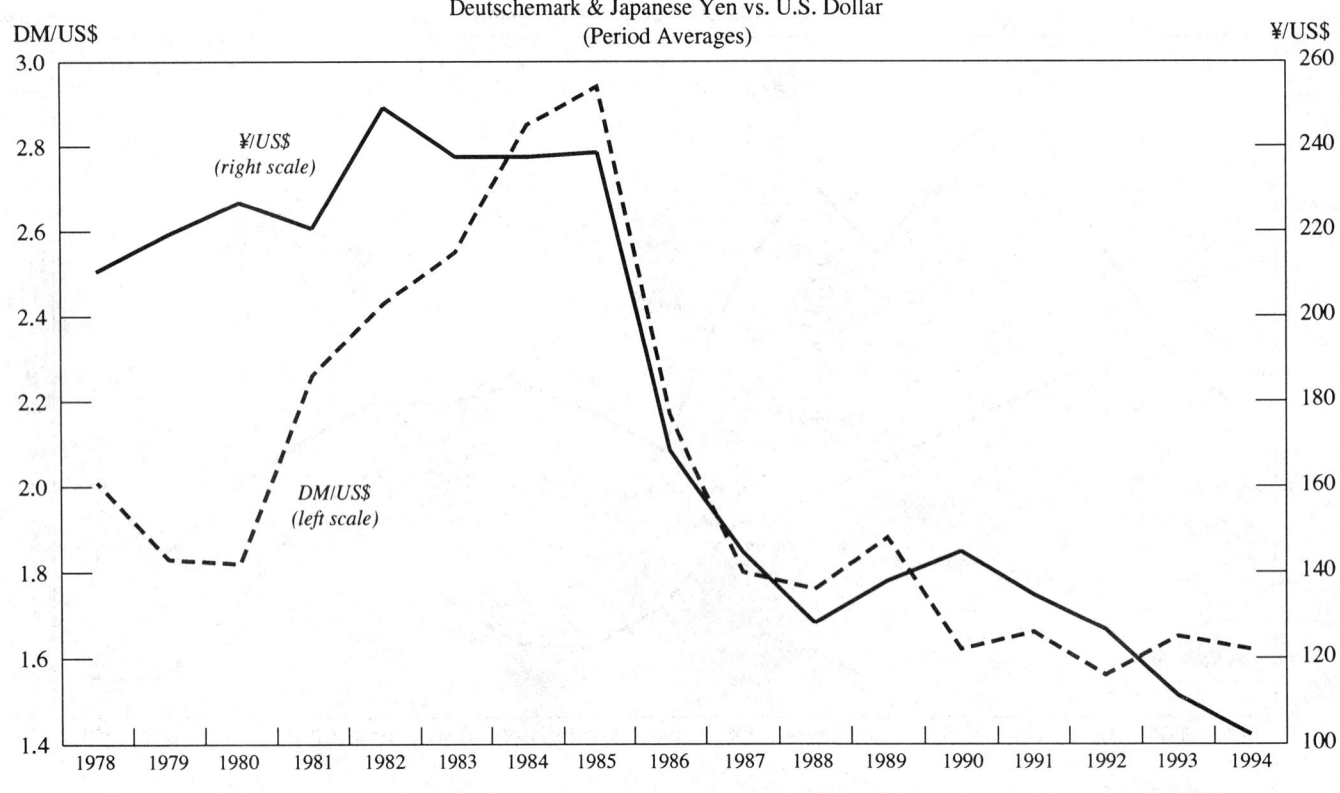

Deutschemark & Japanese Yen vs. U.S. Dollar
(Period Averages)

Prices

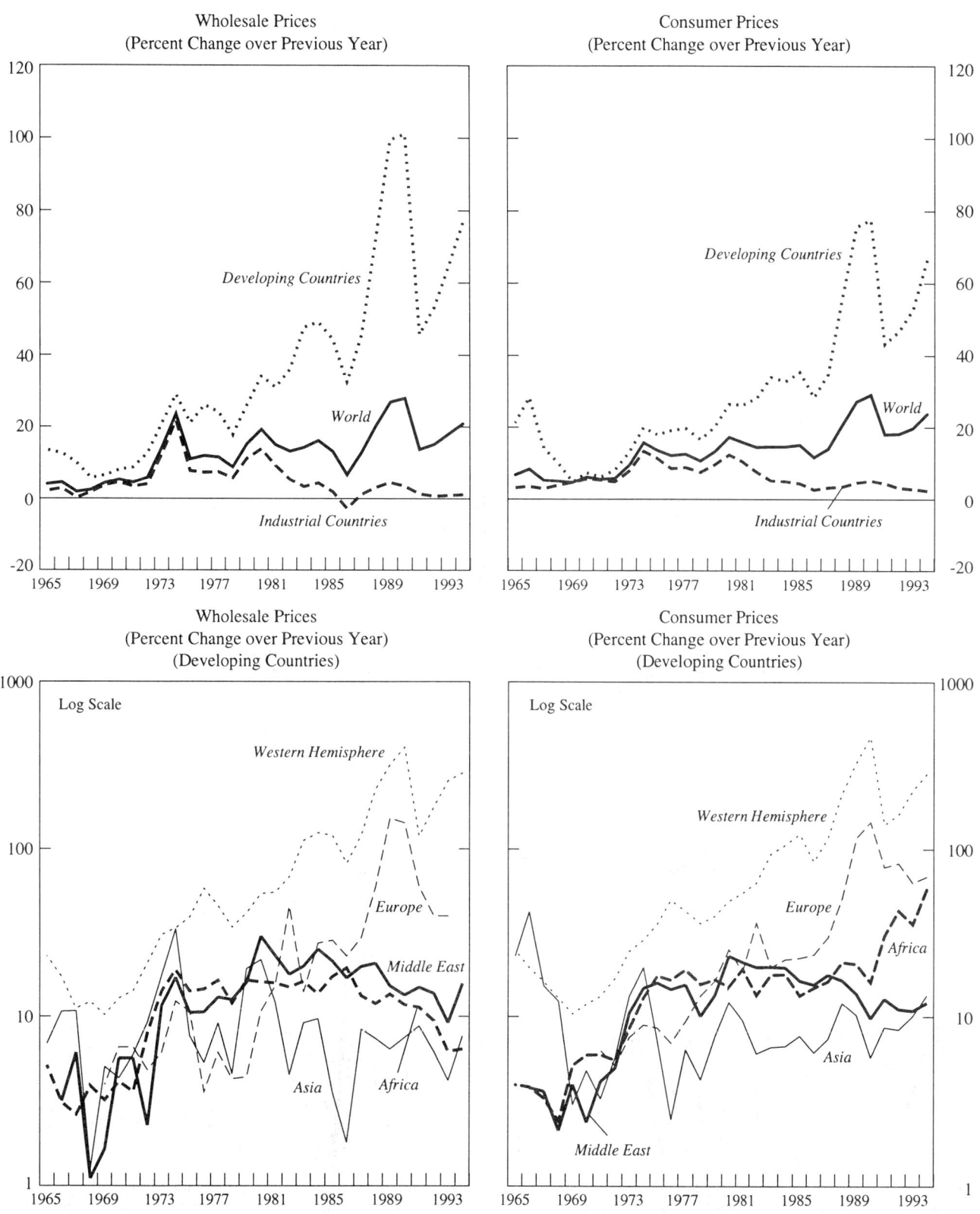

Unit Values and Commodity Prices

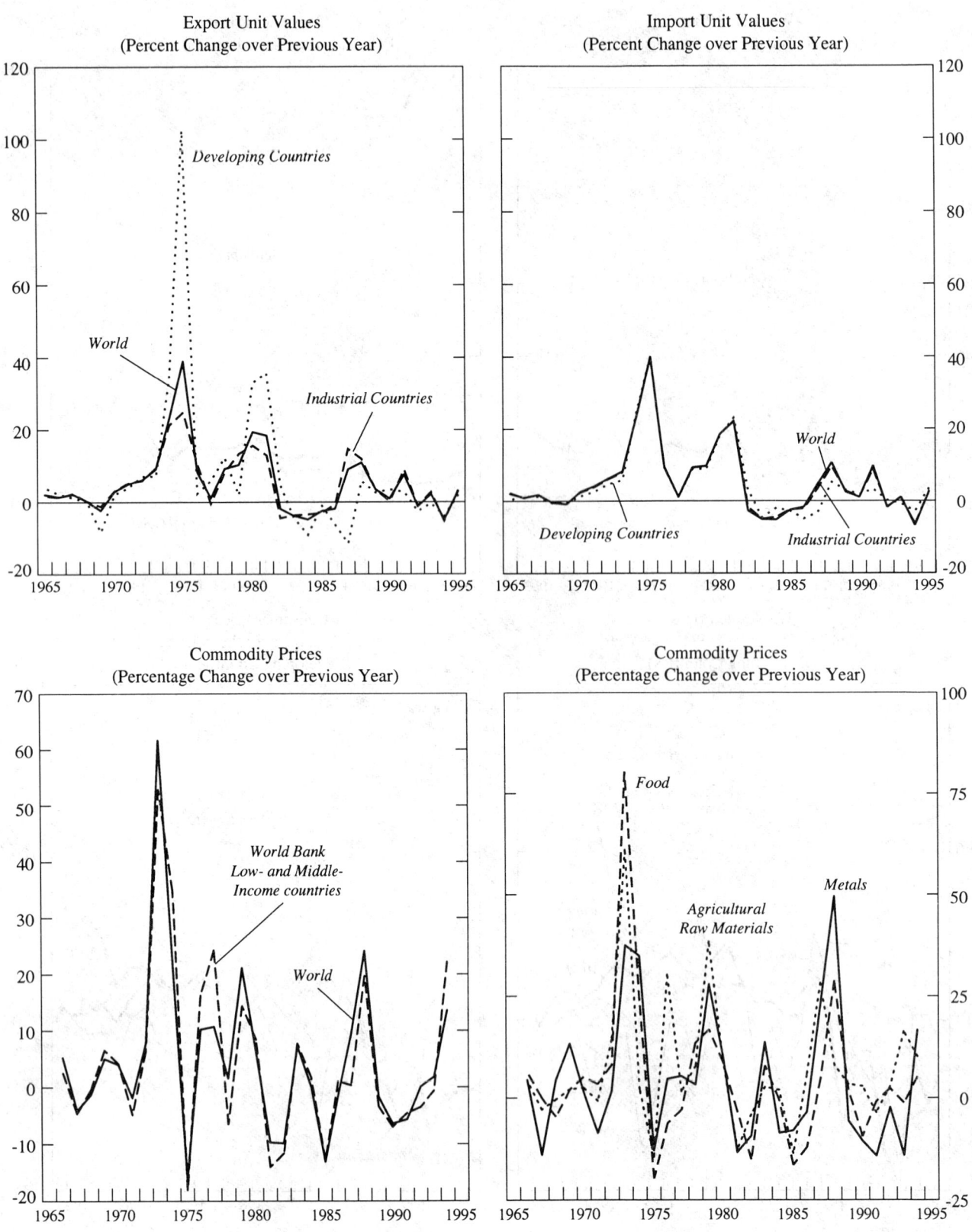

Trade

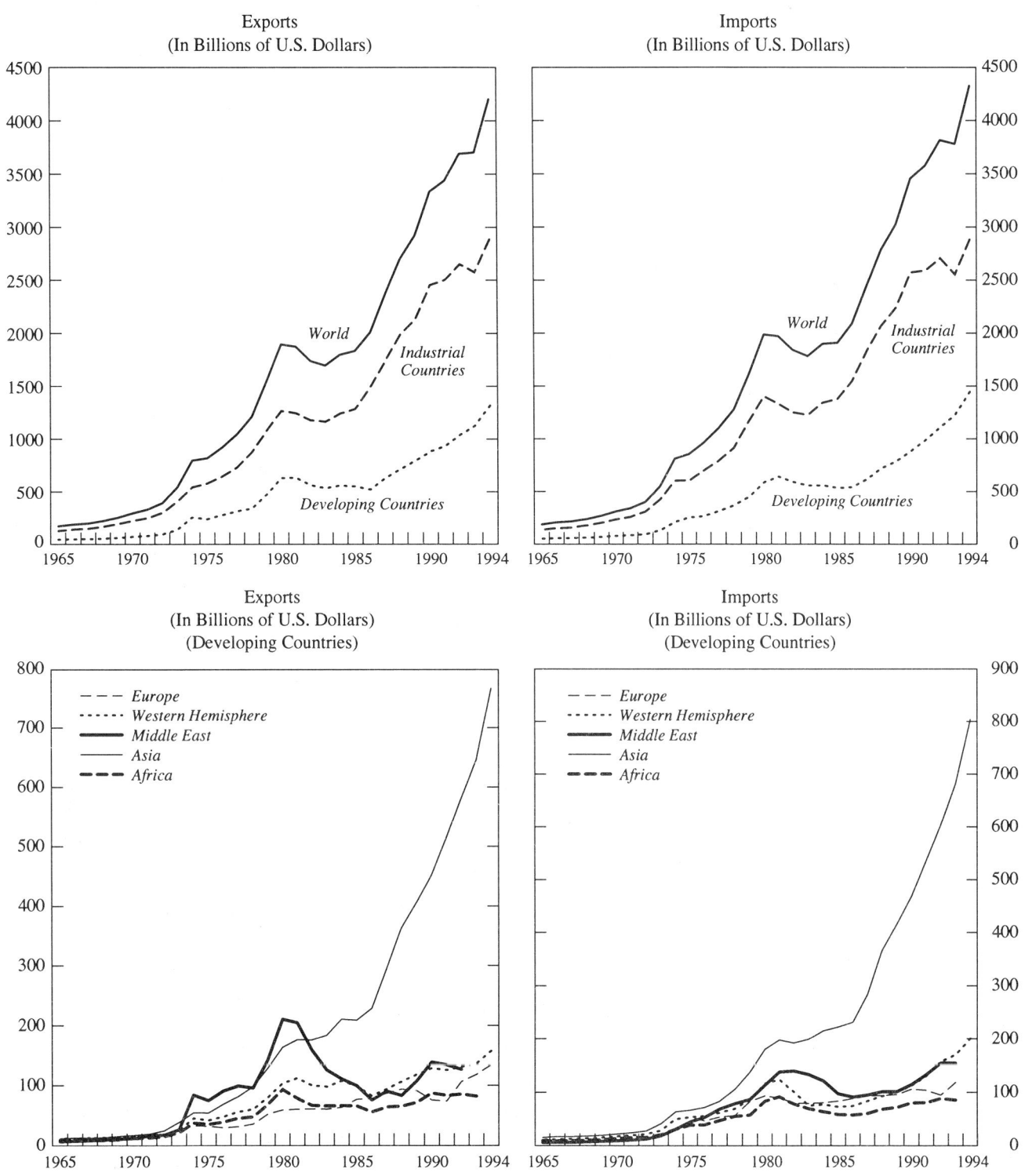

National Accounts

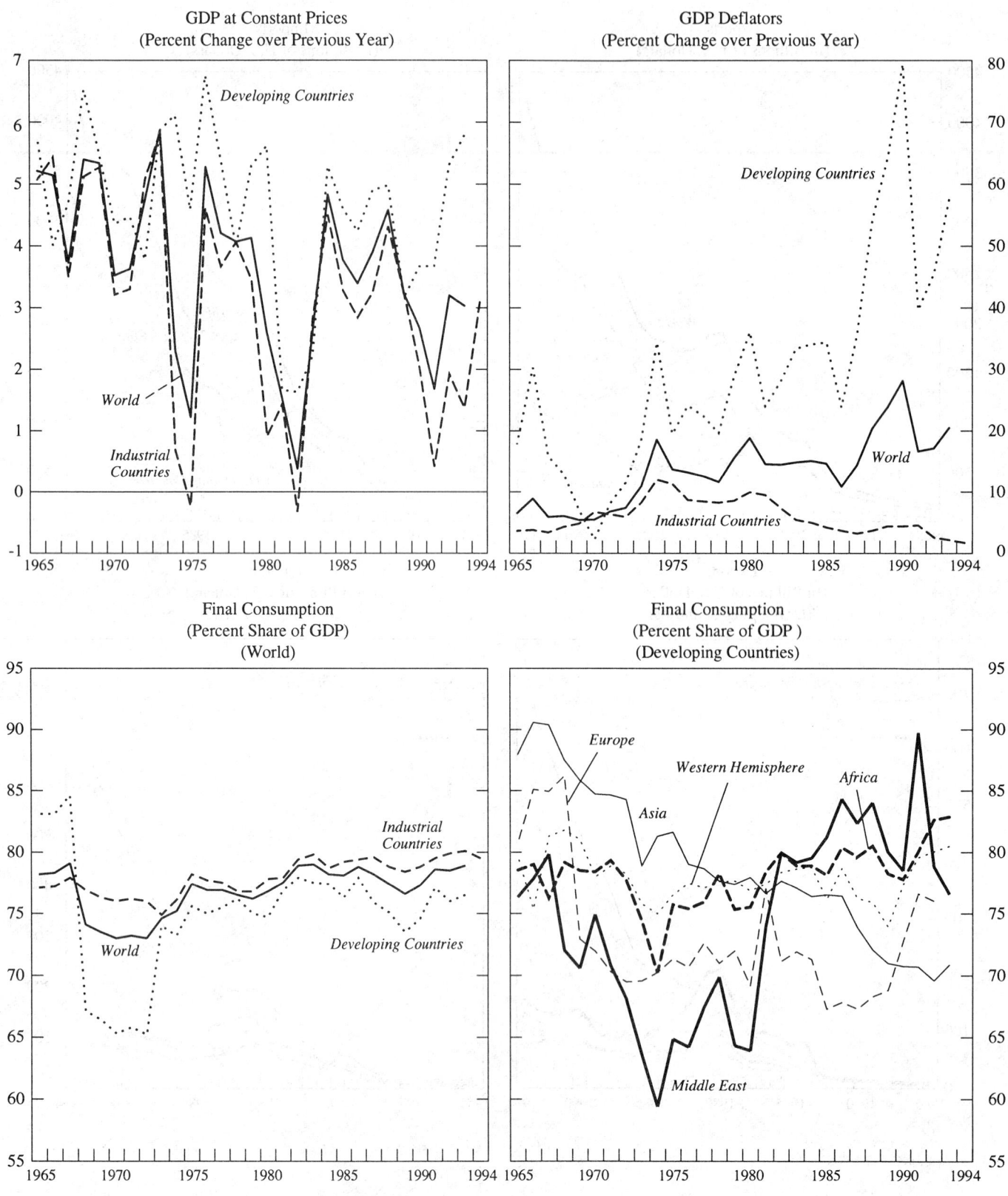

National Accounts

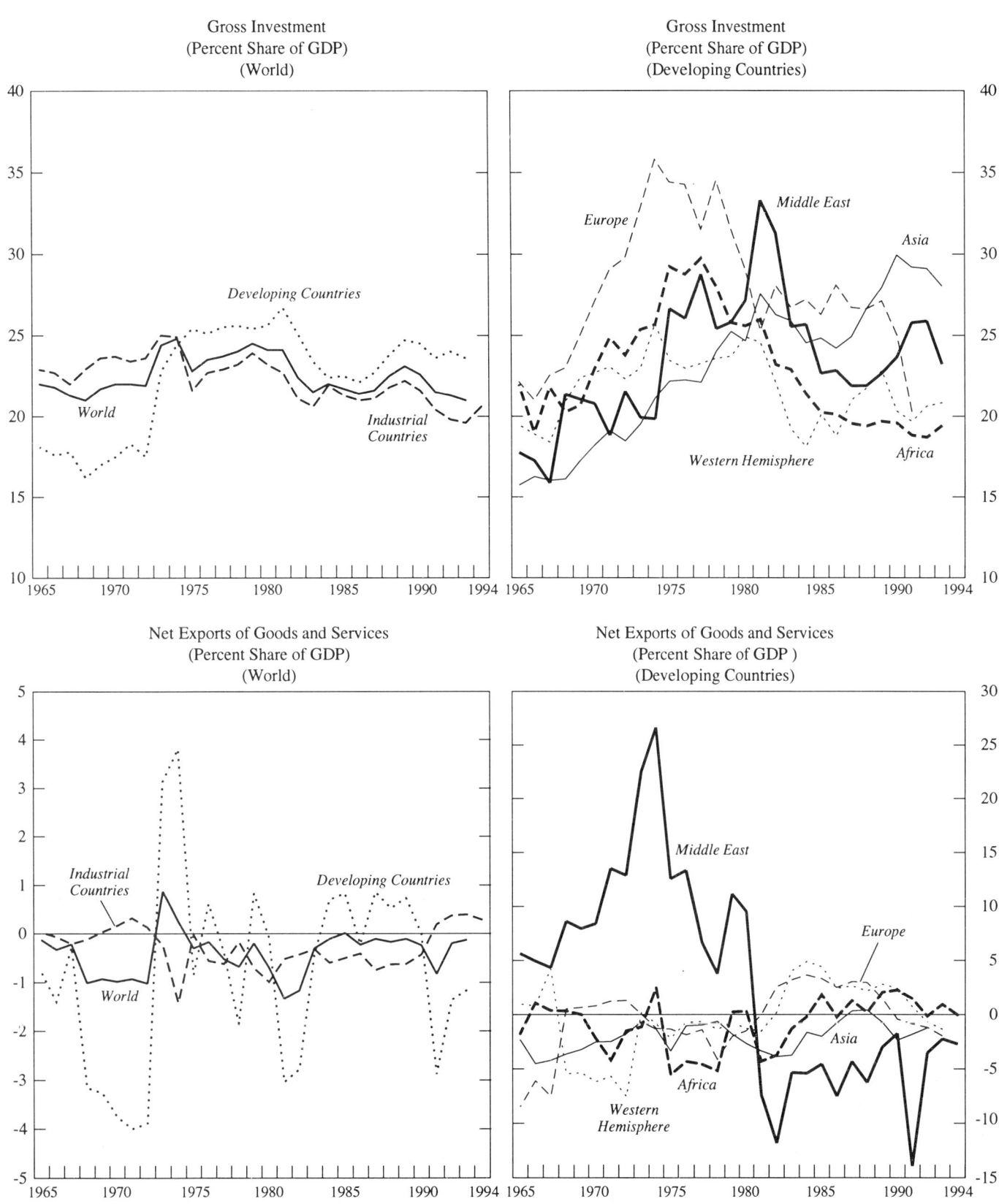

WORLD AND AREA TABLES

Acceptances of Article VIII, Sections 2, 3, and 4

Fund Members That Have Accepted the Obligations of Article VIII, Sections 2, 3, and 4 of the IMF's Articles of Agreement and Effective Date of Acceptance

Article VIII of the Fund's Articles imposes certain obligations on member countries of the Fund. In particular Article VIII, Sections 2 (a) and 3 prohibit members, except with the approval of the Fund, from imposing restrictions on the making of payments and transfers for current international transactions or from engaging in multiple currency practices or discriminatory currency arrangements. Moreover, Article VIII, Section 4 requires Fund members, subject to certain conditions, to purchase balances of their currency from other Fund members, which represent that the balances have been recently acquired as a result of current international transactions or that the conversion is necessary for the purpose of making payments for current transactions.

Article XIV, Section 2 of the Fund's Articles establishes a limited exception to Article VIII, Sections 2, 3, and 4. Thus, member countries that avail themselves of Article XIV, Section 2 may, without seeking Fund approval, maintain and adapt to changing circumstances the restrictions on payments and transfers for current international transactions that were in effect on their date of membership in the Fund; however, if such restrictions are terminated and subsequently reintroduce restrictions are introduced by these members after their date of membership, they are subject to Fund approval under Article VIII. Moreover, members availing themselves of Article XIV are required to consult annually with the Fund with respect to the retention of Article XIV measures.

Members may accept the obligations of Article VIII, Sections 2, 3, and 4 at any time. When a member country accepts these obligations, it may no longer avail itself of the transitional arrangements of Article XIV, Section 2 and may not maintain any exchange measures inconsistent with Article VIII, Sections 2, 3, and 4.

As of September 1, 1995 there were 105 members that had accepted the obligations of Article VIII, Sections 2, 3, and 4.

Member	Effective Date of Acceptance
Antigua and Barbuda	November 22, 1983
Argentina	May 14, 1968
Australia	July 1, 1965
Austria	August 1, 1962
Bahamas, The	December 5, 1973
Bahrain	March 20, 1973
Bangladesh	April 11, 1994
Barbados	November 3, 1993
Belgium	February 15, 1961
Belize	June 14, 1983
Bolivia	June 5, 1967
Canada	March 25, 1952
Chile	July 27, 1977
Costa Rica	February 1, 1965
Croatia	May 29, 1995
Cyprus	January 9, 1991
Denmark	May 1, 1967
Djibouti	September 19, 1980
Dominica	December 13, 1979
Dominican Republic	August 1, 1953
Ecuador	August 31, 1970
El Salvador	November 6, 1946
Estonia	August 15, 1994
Fiji	August 4, 1972
Finland	September 25, 1979
France	February 15, 1961
Gambia, The	January 21, 1993
Germany	February 15, 1961
Ghana	February 21, 1994
Greece	July 7, 1992
Grenada	January 24, 1994
Guatemala	January 27, 1947
Guyana	December 27, 1966
Haiti	December 22, 1953
Honduras	July 1, 1950
Iceland	September 19, 1983
India	August 20, 1994
Indonesia	May 7, 1988
Ireland	February 15, 1961
Israel	September 21, 1993
Italy	February 15, 1961
Jamaica	February 22, 1963
Japan	April 1, 1964
Jordan	February 20, 1995
Kenya	June 30, 1994
Kiribati	August 22, 1986
Korea	November 1, 1988
Kuwait	April 5, 1963
Kyrgyz Republic	March 29, 1995
Latvia	June 10, 1994
Lebanon	July 1, 1993
Lithuania	May 3, 1994
Luxembourg	February 15, 1961
Malaysia	November 11, 1968
Malta	November 30, 1994
Marshall Islands	May 21, 1992
Mauritius	September 29, 1993
Mexico	November 12, 1946
Micronesia, Fed. States of	June 24, 1993
Moldova	June 30, 1995
Morocco	January 21, 1993
Nepal	May 30, 1994
Netherlands	February 15, 1961
New Zealand	August 5, 1982
Nicaragua	July 20, 1964
Norway	May 11, 1967
Oman	June 19, 1974
Pakistan	July 1, 1994
Panama	November 26, 1946
Papua New Guinea	December 4, 1975
Paraguay	August 22, 1994
Peru	February 15, 1961
Poland	June 1, 1995
Portugal	September 12, 1988
Qatar	June 4, 1973
St. Kitts and Nevis	December 3, 1984
St. Lucia	May 30, 1980
St. Vincent and the Grenadines	August 24, 1981
San Marino	September 23, 1992
Saudia Arabia	March 22, 1961
Seychelles	January 3, 1978
Singapore	November 9, 1968
Slovenia	September 1, 1995
Solomon Islands	July 24, 1979
South Africa	September 15, 1973
Spain	July 15, 1986
Sri Lanka	March 15, 1994
Suriname	June 29, 1978
Swaziland	December 11, 1989
Sweden	February 15, 1961
Switzerland	May 29, 1992
Thailand	May 4, 1990
Tonga	March 22, 1991
Trinidad and Tobago	December 13, 1993
Tunisia	January 6, 1993
Turkey	March 22, 1990
Uganda	April 5, 1994
United Arab Emirates	February 13, 1974
United Kingdom	February 15, 1961
United States	December 10, 1946
Uruguay	May 2, 1980
Vanuatu	December 1, 1982
Venezuela	July 1, 1976
Western Samoa	October 6, 1994
Zimbabwe	February 3, 1995

Exchange Rates

SDR Rates: *1975–1995*

sa US Dollars per SDR (*End of Period*)

	Jan.	Feb.	Mar.	April	May	June	July	Aug.	Sept.	Oct.	Nov.	Dec.	I	II	III	IV	Year
1975	1.23890	1.26038	1.24747	1.24144	1.24682	1.23641	1.19098	1.18700	1.16427	1.18578	1.17102	1.17066	1.24747	1.23641	1.16427	1.17066	1.17066
1976	1.16875	1.16873	1.15633	1.15070	1.14231	1.14610	1.14694	1.15077	1.15709	1.15471	1.14982	1.16183	1.15633	1.14610	1.15709	1.16183	1.16183
1977	1.15233	1.15601	1.15916	1.16221	1.16162	1.16587	1.17144	1.16188	1.16354	1.17999	1.18340	1.21471	1.15916	1.16587	1.16354	1.21471	1.21471
1978	1.21512	1.22670	1.23667	1.22609	1.21985	1.23953	1.25986	1.27081	1.28107	1.34879	1.27241	1.30279	1.23667	1.23953	1.28107	1.30279	1.30279
1979	1.28544	1.28917	1.28682	1.27269	1.26893	1.29110	1.30051	1.30030	1.31775	1.28577	1.30805	1.31733	1.28682	1.29110	1.31775	1.31733	1.31733
1980	1.31574	1.30377	1.25118	1.29474	1.31135	1.32438	1.31200	1.31529	1.31244	1.29004	1.27672	1.27541	1.25118	1.32438	1.31244	1.27541	1.27541
1981	1.24418	1.22328	1.22852	1.19858	1.17015	1.15060	1.12723	1.13271	1.14460	1.15118	1.18072	1.16396	1.22852	1.15060	1.14460	1.16396	1.16396
1982	1.14784	1.12689	1.11309	1.12967	1.12410	1.09224	1.09208	1.08309	1.07234	1.06237	1.07953	1.10311	1.11309	1.09224	1.07234	1.10311	1.10311
1983	1.08645	1.08995	1.07867	1.08163	1.07734	1.06835	1.05563	1.04461	1.05684	1.05928	1.05058	1.04695	1.07867	1.06835	1.05684	1.04695	1.04695
1984	1.03409	1.06013	1.06420	1.04712	1.04140	1.03121	1.01333	1.01663	.99901	.99623	.98935	.98021	1.06420	1.03121	.99901	.98021	.98021
1985	.97499	.95942	.99127	.99117	.99295	.99828	1.03737	1.03536	1.05940	1.07165	1.09319	1.09842	.99127	.99828	1.05940	1.09842	1.09842
1986	1.11115	1.15584	1.13827	1.17596	1.14314	1.17757	1.20371	1.20689	1.21342	1.18661	1.21030	1.22319	1.13827	1.17757	1.21342	1.22319	1.22319
1987	1.26759	1.26419	1.28563	1.30626	1.28658	1.27802	1.26723	1.29313	1.27964	1.32109	1.37379	1.41866	1.28563	1.27802	1.27964	1.41866	1.41866
1988	1.36642	1.36101	1.38729	1.38417	1.36483	1.31061	1.29648	1.28818	1.29039	1.34592	1.36637	1.34570	1.38729	1.31061	1.29039	1.34570	1.34570
1989	1.31093	1.32150	1.29271	1.29566	1.24362	1.24639	1.28749	1.24652	1.27981	1.27782	1.28771	1.31416	1.29271	1.24639	1.27981	1.31416	1.31416
1990	1.32559	1.31681	1.30083	1.30247	1.31200	1.32388	1.36564	1.38595	1.39256	1.43078	1.42677	1.42266	1.30083	1.32388	1.39256	1.42266	1.42266
1991	1.43476	1.42053	1.34632	1.34081	1.34084	1.31452	1.33400	1.33698	1.36800	1.36652	1.38072	1.43043	1.34632	1.31452	1.36800	1.43043	1.43043
1992	1.39733	1.38091	1.37174	1.36976	1.39632	1.43117	1.44416	1.48286	1.47284	1.40595	1.37896	1.37500	1.37174	1.43117	1.47284	1.37500	1.37500
1993	1.38188	1.37610	1.39773	1.42339	1.42847	1.40360	1.39072	1.40758	1.41840	1.39293	1.38389	1.37356	1.39773	1.40360	1.41840	1.37356	1.37356
1994	1.38067	1.39930	1.41260	1.42138	1.41733	1.44837	1.44327	1.44770	1.46738	1.48454	1.45674	1.45985	1.41260	1.44837	1.46738	1.45985	1.45985
1995	1.47670	1.49440	1.56050	1.57303	1.57591	1.56876	1.55954						1.56050	1.56876			

sb US Dollars per SDR (*Period Average, geometric*)

	Jan.	Feb.	Mar.	April	May	June	July	Aug.	Sept.	Oct.	Nov.	Dec.	I	II	III	IV	Year
1975	1.23279	1.24495	1.25379	1.24157	1.24626	1.24650	1.21339	1.18871	1.17769	1.17869	1.17919	1.17121	1.24381	1.24477	1.19317	1.17636	1.21415
1976	1.17183	1.16966	1.15767	1.15152	1.14813	1.14380	1.14515	1.14848	1.15366	1.15478	1.15406	1.15588	1.16637	1.14781	1.14909	1.15491	1.15452
1977	1.15717	1.15535	1.15756	1.16047	1.16182	1.16220	1.17292	1.16654	1.16126	1.17239	1.18245	1.20097	1.15669	1.16150	1.16690	1.18521	1.16752
1978	1.21382	1.21823	1.22979	1.23266	1.21687	1.22977	1.24922	1.27049	1.27367	1.32559	1.28498	1.28434	1.22059	1.22641	1.26441	1.29816	1.25200
1979	1.29260	1.28750	1.28693	1.27781	1.27070	1.27705	1.30298	1.30013	1.30451	1.29851	1.29386	1.31215	1.28901	1.27518	1.30254	1.30148	1.29200
1980	1.32035	1.31306	1.27713	1.26728	1.30451	1.32050	1.32753	1.31317	1.31836	1.30825	1.28298	1.26726	1.30338	1.29724	1.31967	1.28605	1.30153
1981	1.26792	1.23225	1.22834	1.21023	1.17871	1.15636	1.13570	1.12234	1.14342	1.15398	1.16596	1.16388	1.24271	1.18156	1.13379	1.16126	1.17916
1982	1.15329	1.13288	1.12347	1.11507	1.13472	1.10209	1.09149	1.08656	1.07979	1.07131	1.06707	1.09407	1.13648	1.11721	1.08594	1.07742	1.10401
1983	1.10004	1.09004	1.08544	1.08220	1.08262	1.06890	1.06292	1.04994	1.05087	1.06228	1.05178	1.04272	1.09182	1.07789	1.05456	1.05223	1.06900
1984	1.03579	1.04674	1.06398	1.05716	1.04100	1.03967	1.02009	1.01633	1.00006	.99278	1.00259	.98749	1.04877	1.04591	1.01212	.99427	1.02501
1985	.97558	.96174	.96366	.99036	.98956	.99703	1.01993	1.03341	1.02830	1.06516	1.08003	1.08972	.96697	.99231	1.02720	1.07826	1.01534
1986	1.09786	1.12904	1.14834	1.15007	1.16859	1.16461	1.18935	1.20849	1.21051	1.21175	1.19840	1.20746	1.12489	1.16106	1.20275	1.20586	1.17317
1987	1.25112	1.26216	1.26933	1.29153	1.30442	1.28656	1.26932	1.26927	1.29137	1.29530	1.34938	1.38310	1.26085	1.29415	1.27661	1.34210	1.29307
1988	1.37723	1.35556	1.37141	1.38197	1.37595	1.34654	1.30514	1.29206	1.29368	1.31949	1.35659	1.35588	1.36804	1.36807	1.29695	1.34387	1.34392
1989	1.32525	1.31652	1.30486	1.29975	1.26560	1.24062	1.27158	1.26166	1.24703	1.27221	1.27724	1.30191	1.31552	1.26843	1.26005	1.28372	1.28176
1990	1.31850	1.32659	1.30170	1.30135	1.31832	1.31442	1.34402	1.37719	1.39049	1.42846	1.44481	1.42654	1.31556	1.31134	1.37042	1.43325	1.35675
1991	1.42291	1.44058	1.38077	1.35123	1.34351	1.31934	1.32155	1.33571	1.35355	1.36201	1.38487	1.40799	1.41453	1.33796	1.33687	1.38483	1.36816
1992	1.40925	1.39042	1.36599	1.37060	1.38810	1.41173	1.44375	1.45645	1.45767	1.43476	1.38701	1.38883	1.38844	1.39004	1.45261	1.40336	1.40838
1993	1.37705	1.37168	1.38045	1.41266	1.41561	1.40969	1.39025	1.40151	1.41756	1.40746	1.38903	1.38404	1.37639	1.41265	1.40306	1.39347	1.39633
1994	1.37343	1.38750	1.40197	1.40425	1.41500	1.42736	1.45706	1.45439	1.46377	1.47720	1.47121	1.45201	1.38759	1.41550	1.45840	1.46676	1.43170
1995	1.46580	1.47826	1.53602	1.57620	1.55819	1.56369	1.55763						1.49305	1.56601			

sc SDRs per US Dollar (*End of Period*)

	Jan.	Feb.	Mar.	April	May	June	July	Aug.	Sept.	Oct.	Nov.	Dec.	I	II	III	IV	Year
1975	.80717	.79341	.80162	.80552	.80204	.80879	.83964	.84246	.85891	.84333	.85396	.85422	.80162	.80879	.85891	.85422	.85422
1976	.85562	.85563	.86481	.86904	.87542	.87253	.87189	.86898	.86424	.86602	.86970	.86071	.86481	.87253	.86424	.86071	.86071
1977	.86781	.86504	.86269	.86043	.86087	.85773	.85365	.86067	.85945	.84746	.84502	.82324	.86269	.85773	.85945	.82324	.82324
1978	.82296	.81519	.80862	.81560	.81977	.80676	.79374	.78690	.78060	.74141	.78591	.76758	.80862	.80676	.78060	.76758	.76758
1979	.77795	.77570	.77711	.78574	.78807	.77454	.76893	.76905	.75887	.77775	.76450	.75911	.77711	.77454	.75887	.75911	.75911
1980	.76003	.76700	.79924	.77235	.76258	.75507	.76220	.76029	.76194	.77517	.78326	.78406	.79924	.75507	.76194	.78406	.78406
1981	.80375	.81747	.81399	.83432	.85459	.86911	.88713	.88284	.87367	.86868	.84694	.85914	.81399	.86911	.87367	.85914	.85914
1982	.87120	.88740	.89840	.88521	.88960	.91555	.91568	.92328	.93254	.94129	.92633	.90653	.89840	.91555	.93254	.90653	.90653
1983	.92043	.91748	.92707	.92453	.92822	.93602	.94730	.95730	.94622	.94404	.95186	.95515	.92707	.93602	.94622	.95515	.95515
1984	.96703	.94328	.93967	.95500	.96025	.96973	.98685	.98364	1.00100	1.00378	1.01077	1.02019	.93967	.96973	1.00100	1.02019	1.02019
1985	1.02565	1.04230	1.00880	1.00891	1.00710	1.00172	.96398	.96584	.94393	.93314	.91476	.91040	1.00880	1.00172	.94393	.91040	.91040
1986	.89997	.86517	.87853	.85037	.87478	.84921	.83077	.82858	.82412	.84273	.82624	.81753	.87853	.84921	.82412	.81753	.81753
1987	.78890	.79102	.77783	.76554	.77725	.78246	.78913	.77332	.78147	.75695	.72791	.70489	.77783	.78246	.78147	.70489	.70489
1988	.73184	.73475	.72083	.72245	.73269	.76300	.77132	.77629	.77496	.74299	.73187	.74311	.72083	.76300	.77496	.74311	.74311
1989	.76282	.75672	.77357	.77181	.80410	.80232	.77670	.80223	.78137	.78258	.77657	.76094	.77357	.80232	.78137	.76094	.76094
1990	.75438	.75941	.76874	.76777	.76219	.75536	.73226	.72153	.71810	.69892	.70089	.70291	.76874	.75536	.71810	.70291	.70291
1991	.69698	.70396	.74277	.74582	.74580	.76074	.74962	.74795	.73100	.73179	.72426	.69909	.74277	.76074	.73100	.69909	.69909
1992	.71565	.72416	.72900	.73006	.71617	.69873	.69244	.67437	.67896	.71127	.72518	.72727	.72900	.69873	.67896	.72727	.72727
1993	.72365	.72669	.71545	.70255	.70005	.71245	.71905	.71044	.70502	.71791	.72260	.72804	.71545	.71245	.70502	.72804	.72804
1994	.72429	.71465	.70792	.70354	.70555	.69043	.69287	.69075	.68149	.67361	.68646	.68500	.70792	.69043	.68149	.68500	.68500
1995	.67719	.66916	.64082	.63572	.63455	.63745	.64121						.64082	.63745			

sd SDRs per US Dollar (*Period Average, geometric*)

	Jan.	Feb.	Mar.	April	May	June	July	Aug.	Sept.	Oct.	Nov.	Dec.	I	II	III	IV	Year
1975	.81117	.80325	.79758	.80543	.80240	.80225	.82414	.84125	.84912	.84840	.84804	.85382	.80398	.80336	.83810	.85008	.82362
1976	.85337	.85495	.86380	.86842	.87098	.87428	.87325	.87071	.86681	.86596	.86651	.86514	.85736	.87122	.87025	.86587	.86616
1977	.86418	.86554	.86388	.86172	.86072	.86044	.85258	.85724	.86114	.85296	.84570	.83266	.86454	.86096	.85697	.84373	.85652
1978	.82385	.82086	.81315	.81125	.82178	.81316	.80050	.78710	.78513	.75438	.77822	.77861	.81928	.81539	.79088	.77032	.79872
1979	.77364	.77670	.77704	.78259	.78697	.78306	.76747	.76915	.76657	.77011	.77288	.76211	.77579	.78420	.76773	.76835	.77399
1980	.75738	.76158	.78300	.78909	.76657	.75729	.75328	.76151	.75852	.76438	.77943	.78910	.76724	.77087	.75776	.77757	.76833
1981	.78869	.81152	.81411	.82629	.84839	.86478	.88051	.89099	.87457	.86656	.85767	.85919	.80469	.84634	.88200	.86113	.84806
1982	.86709	.88270	.89010	.89680	.88128	.90736	.91618	.92034	.92610	.93344	.93714	.91402	.87991	.89509	.92086	.92814	.90579
1983	.90906	.91740	.92128	.92404	.92368	.93554	.94081	.95243	.95160	.94138	.95077	.95903	.91590	.92774	.94826	.95036	.93545
1984	.96545	.95535	.93987	.94593	.96061	.96184	.98031	.98394	.99994	1.00727	.99741	1.01267	.95350	.95611	.98803	1.00577	.97560
1985	1.02503	1.03979	1.03771	1.00974	1.01055	1.00298	.98046	.96767	.97248	.93882	.92590	.91767	1.03416	1.00775	.97352	.92743	.98489
1986	.91086	.88571	.87082	.86951	.85574	.85866	.84080	.82748	.82610	.82526	.83445	.82819	.88898	.86128	.83143	.82929	.85239
1987	.79928	.79229	.78781	.77427	.76662	.77727	.78782	.78785	.77437	.77202	.74108	.72301	.79312	.77271	.78332	.74510	.77335
1988	.72609	.73770	.72918	.72361	.72677	.74264	.76620	.77396	.77299	.75787	.73714	.73753	.73098	.73096	.77104	.74412	.74409
1989	.75458	.75958	.76637	.76938	.79014	.80605	.78642	.79261	.80191	.78603	.78294	.76810	.76016	.78838	.79362	.77899	.78018
1990	.75844	.75381	.76823	.76843	.75854	.76079	.74404	.72612	.71917	.70006	.69213	.70100	.76014	.76258	.72970	.69772	.73706
1991	.70279	.69417	.72423	.74007	.74432	.75795	.75669	.74867	.73880	.73421	.72209	.71023	.70694	.74741	.74802	.72211	.73091
1992	.70960	.71921	.73207	.72961	.72041	.70835	.69264	.68660	.68603	.69698	.72098	.72003	.72024	.71940	.68842	.71258	.71004
1993	.72619	.72903	.72440	.70788	.70641	.70938	.71930	.71352	.70544	.71050	.71993	.72252	.72654	.70789	.71273	.71763	.71616
1994	.72810	.72072	.71328	.71213	.70671	.70059	.68631	.68757	.68317	.67696	.67971	.68870	.72068	.70646	.68568	.68177	.69847
1995	.68222	.67647	.65103	.63444	.64177	.63951	.64200						.66977	.63857			

1995 INTERNATIONAL FINANCIAL STATISTICS YEARBOOK 13

Exchange Rates

Market, Official, or Principal Rate

National Currency Units per SDR: End of Period (aa)

	1965	1966	1967	1968	1969	1970	1971	1972	1973	1974	1975	1976	1977	1978	1979
Industrial Countries															
US dollar	1.0000	1.0000	1.0000	1.0000	1.0000	1.0000	1.0857	1.0857	1.2064	1.2244	1.1707	1.1618	1.2147	1.3028	1.3173
Canadian dollar	1.0750	1.0838	1.0806	1.0728	1.0728	1.0112	1.0881	1.0809	1.2013	1.2136	1.1899	1.1725	1.3294	1.5451	1.5388
Australian dollar	.8941	⅃.8977	.8921	.9009	.8945	.8969	.9116	.8515	.8107	.9226	.9312	1.0694	1.0642	1.1324	1.1916
Japanese yen	360.90	362.47	361.91	357.70	357.80	357.65	341.78	327.88	337.78	368.47	357.23	340.18	291.53	253.52	315.76
New Zealand dollar	.7188	.7220	⅃.8907	.8992	.8930	.8960	.9084	.9084	.8445	.9307	1.1216	1.2230	1.1912	1.2214	1.3358
Austrian schilling	25.890	25.910	25.880	25.880	25.880	25.880	25.742	⅃25.123	23.946	20.973	21.669	19.481	18.385	17.415	16.376
Belgian franc	49.643	50.053	49.628	50.140	49.666	49.675	48.591	47.839	49.846	44.227	46.273	41.806	40.013	37.520	36.948
Danish krone	6.891	6.916	7.462	7.501	7.492	7.489	7.667	7.434	⅃7.588	6.918	7.232	6.724	7.018	6.631	7.067
Finnish markka	3.2200	3.2200	4.2000	4.2000	4.2000	4.1800	4.5057	4.5383	⅃4.6384	4.3477	4.5070	4.3766	4.8807	5.1148	4.8886
French franc	4.9371	4.9371	4.9371	4.9371	5.5542	5.5542	5.5542	5.5542	5.6801	5.4416	5.2510	5.7740	5.7152	5.4457	5.2957
Deutsche mark	4.0056	3.9773	3.9990	3.9995	3.6899	3.6480	3.5486	3.4759	3.2608	2.9501	3.0698	2.7448	2.5570	2.3815	2.2810
Greek drachma	30.00	30.00	30.00	30.00	30.00	30.00	32.57	32.57	35.83	36.73	41.73	43.02	43.13	46.91	50.43
Icelandic krona	.431	.431	.571	.881	.881	.881	.949	1.063	1.013	⅃1.451	1.999	2.204	2.589	4.144	5.202
Irish pound	.35679	.35840	.41558	.41939	.41655	.41776	.42535	.46238	.51926	.52133	.57853	.68247	.63731	.64035	.61414
Italian lira	624.7	624.4	623.9	623.5	625.5	623.0	644.9	632.4	733.4	795.1	800.2	1,016.6	1,058.7	1,081.0	1,059.1
Luxembourg franc	49.643	50.053	49.628	50.140	49.666	49.675	48.591	47.839	49.846	44.227	46.273	41.806	40.013	37.520	36.948
Netherlands guilder	3.6110	3.6140	3.5960	3.6060	3.6240	3.5970	3.5374	3.5030	3.4073	3.0688	3.1473	2.8546	2.7695	2.5652	2.5102
Norwegian krone	7.1500	7.1550	7.1500	7.1500	7.1500	7.1400	7.2851	⅃7.2091	6.9094	6.3727	6.5381	6.0241	6.2430	6.5433	6.4892
Portuguese escudo	28.83	28.98	28.86	28.77	28.65	28.75	29.92	29.31	31.18	30.11	32.16	36.65	48.41	59.94	65.58
Spanish peseta	59.99	60.00	69.70	69.82	70.06	69.72	71.68	69.02	68.70	⅃68.70	69.98	79.34	98.28	91.34	87.14
Swedish krona	5.1800	5.1800	5.1650	5.1800	5.1700	5.1700	5.2820	⅃5.1495	5.5341	4.9960	5.1339	4.7943	5.6721	5.5961	5.4623
Swiss franc	4.3180	4.3270	4.3250	4.3020	4.3180	4.3160	4.2506	4.0975	3.9134	3.1098	3.0671	2.8459	2.4294	2.1105	2.0814
Pound sterling	.35679	.35840	.41558	.41939	.41655	.41776	.42535	⅃.46238	.51926	.52133	.57853	.68247	.63731	.64035	.59232
Developing Countries															
Africa															
Algerian dinar	4.9371	4.9371	4.9371	4.9371	4.9371	4.9371	⅃5.0420	4.9465	5.0486	4.8937	4.8290	5.0644	4.9014	4.9955	4.9472
Benin, CFA franc	245.07	247.59	245.42	247.40	277.91	276.02	283.61	278.00	284.00	272.08	262.55	288.70	285.76	272.28	264.78
Botswana pula	.7144	.7177	.7134	.7196	.7149	.7172	.8308	.8499	.8097	.8444	1.0180	1.0103	1.0060	1.0789	1.0390
Burkina Faso, CFA franc	245.07	247.59	245.42	247.40	277.91	276.02	283.61	278.00	284.00	272.08	262.55	288.70	285.76	272.28	264.78
Burundi franc	87.50	87.50	87.50	87.50	87.50	87.50	95.00	95.00	95.00	96.42	92.19	104.56	109.32	117.25	118.56
Cameroon, CFA franc	245.07	247.59	245.42	247.40	277.91	276.02	283.61	278.00	284.00	272.08	262.55	288.70	285.76	272.28	264.78
Cape Verde escudo	28.83	28.98	28.86	28.77	28.65	28.75	29.92	29.31	31.18	30.11	32.16	36.65	41.18	46.82	50.47
Cent.African Rep.,CFA franc	245.07	247.59	245.42	247.40	277.91	276.02	283.61	278.00	284.00	272.08	262.55	288.70	285.76	272.28	264.78
Chad, CFA franc	245.07	247.59	245.42	247.40	277.91	276.02	283.61	278.00	284.00	272.08	262.55	288.70	285.76	272.28	264.78
Comorian franc	245.07	247.59	245.42	247.40	277.91	276.02	283.61	277.99	284.00	272.08	262.55	288.70	285.76	272.28	264.78
Congo, CFA franc	245.07	247.59	245.42	247.40	277.91	276.02	283.61	278.00	284.00	272.08	262.55	288.70	285.76	272.28	264.78
Côte d'Ivoire, CFA franc	245.07	247.59	245.42	247.40	277.91	276.02	283.61	278.00	284.00	272.08	262.55	288.70	285.76	272.28	264.78
Djibouti franc	214.39	214.39	214.39	214.39	214.39	214.39	214.39	214.39	214.39	217.59	208.05	206.48	215.88	231.53	234.12
Eq. Guinea, CFA franc	245.07	247.59	245.42	247.40	277.91	276.02	283.61	278.00	284.00	272.08	262.55	288.70	285.76	272.28	264.78
Ethiopian birr	2.5000	2.5000	2.5000	2.5000	2.5000	2.5000	2.4971	2.4971	2.4971	2.5344	2.4233	2.4050	2.5144	2.6968	2.7269
Gabon, CFA franc	245.07	247.59	245.42	247.40	277.91	276.02	283.61	278.00	284.00	272.08	262.55	288.70	285.76	272.28	264.78
Gambian dalasi	1.784	1.792	2.078	2.097	2.083	2.089	⅃2.127	2.312	2.077	2.085	2.314	2.730	2.549	2.561	2.369
Ghanaian cedi	.71	.71	1.02	1.02	1.02	1.02	1.97	1.39	1.39	1.41	1.35	1.34	1.40	3.58	3.62
Guinean franc	24.69	24.69	24.69	24.69	24.69	24.69	24.68	24.68	24.91	25.28	24.69	24.69	24.69	24.69	24.69
Guinea-Bissau peso	28.8	29.0	28.9	28.8	28.7	28.8	29.9	29.3	31.2	30.1	32.2	36.7	41.6	44.0	44.0
Kenya shilling	7.143	7.143	7.143	7.143	7.143	7.143	7.755	7.755	8.324	8.745	9.660	9.660	9.660	9.660	9.660
Lesotho loti	.7144	.7177	.7134	.7196	.7149	.7172	.8308	.8500	.8097	.8444	1.0180	1.0103	1.0563	1.1329	1.0892
Liberian dollar	1.0000	1.0000	1.0000	1.0000	1.0000	1.0000	1.0857	1.0857	1.2064	1.2244	1.1707	1.1618	1.2147	1.3028	1.3173
Malagasy franc	245.1	247.6	245.4	247.4	277.9	276.0	283.6	278.0	284.0	272.1	262.5	288.7	285.8	272.3	264.8
Malawi kwacha	.7143	.7143	.8333	.8333	.8333	.8333	.8334	.9280	1.0224	1.0291	1.0541	1.0541	1.0541	1.0541	1.0541
Mali, CFA franc	245.07	247.59	245.42	247.40	277.91	276.02	283.61	278.00	284.00	272.08	262.55	288.70	285.76	272.28	264.78
Mauritanian ouguiya	49.02	49.52	49.09	49.48	55.58	55.21	56.72	55.60	⅃56.80	53.01	52.86	50.70	55.94	60.13	60.39
Mauritian rupee	4.757	4.779	5.541	5.592	5.554	5.570	5.671	6.165	6.923	6.951	7.714	7.714	7.714	7.714	⅃10.000
Moroccan dirham	5.027	5.074	5.035	5.074	5.064	5.029	5.168	5.066	5.175	5.087	4.898	5.210	5.256	5.063	4.925
Mozambique, metical	28.8	29.0	28.9	28.8	28.6	28.7	29.9	29.3	31.2	30.1	32.2	36.7	39.5	42.2	42.5
Namibia dollar	.71441	.71775	.71339	.71955	.71492	.71723	.83085	.85000	.80966	.84435	1.01797	1.01029	1.05627	1.13286	1.08924
Niger, CFA franc	245.07	247.59	245.42	247.40	277.91	276.02	283.61	278.00	284.00	272.08	262.55	288.70	285.76	272.28	264.78
Nigerian naira	.714	.714	.714	.714	.714	.714	.714	.714	.794	.754	.734	.733	.791	.844	.738
Rwanda franc	50.00	100.00	100.00	100.00	100.00	100.00	100.00	100.00	100.00	113.60	108.68	107.86	112.77	120.95	122.30
Sao Tome & Principe dobra	28.83	28.98	28.86	28.77	28.65	28.75	29.92	29.31	31.18	30.11	32.16	36.65	45.25	45.25	45.25
Senegal, CFA franc	245.07	247.59	245.42	247.40	277.91	276.02	283.61	278.00	284.00	272.08	262.55	288.70	285.76	272.28	264.78
Seychelles rupee	4.7571	4.7786	5.5410	5.5919	5.5539	5.5702	5.6713	⅃6.1650	6.9235	6.9511	7.7137	9.0995	8.4974	8.5380	8.3197
Sierra Leonean leone	.71	.72	.83	.84	.83	.84	.85	.92	1.04	1.04	1.16	1.36	1.27	1.37	1.37
Somali shilling	7.14	7.14	7.14	7.14	7.14	7.14	7.56	7.59	7.59	7.71	7.37	7.31	7.65	8.20	8.29
South African rand	.7144	.7177	.7134	.7196	.7149	.7172	.8308	.8500	.8097	.8444	1.0180	1.0103	1.0563	1.1329	1.0892
Sudanese pound	.3482	.3482	.3482	.3482	.3482	.3482	.3781	.3781	.4201	.4264	.4077	.4046	.4230	.5211	.6587
Swaziland lilangeni	.7144	.7177	.7134	.7196	.7149	.7172	.8308	.8500	.8097	.8444	1.0180	1.0103	1.0563	1.1329	1.0892
Tanzanian shilling	7.14	7.14	7.14	7.14	7.14	7.14	7.76	7.76	8.32	8.75	9.66	9.66	9.66	9.66	10.83
Togo, CFA franc	245.07	247.59	245.42	247.40	277.91	276.02	283.61	278.00	284.00	272.08	262.55	288.70	285.76	272.28	264.78
Tunisian dinar	.5200	.5200	.5200	.5200	.5200	.5200	.5211	⅃.5255	.5369	.4978	.4979	.5007	.5005	.5255	.5215
Uganda shilling	.1	.1	.1	.1	.1	.1	.1	.1	.1	.1	.1	.1	.1	.1	.1
Zaire, new zaïre	—	—	—	—	—	—	—	—	—	—	—	—	—	—	—
Zambian kwacha	.714	.714	.714	.714	.714	.714	.776	.776	.776	.788	.753	.922	.922	⅃1.024	1.024
Zimbabwe dollar	.7143	.7143	.7143	.7143	.7143	.7162	.7287	.7079	.7311	.6718	.7314	.7192	.7857	.8796	.8882
Asia															
Afghanistan, afghani	45.000	45.000	45.000	45.000	45.000	45.000	48.857	48.857	54.286	55.096	52.680	52.282	54.662	58.626	55.657
Bangladesh taka	....	....	....	....	....	....	8.068	8.770	9.849	9.888	17.356	17.373	17.486	19.456	20.607
Bhutan, ngultrum	4.775	7.576	7.547	7.628	7.559	7.576	7.903	8.773	9.896	9.978	10.462	10.318	9.971	10.668	10.416
Chinese yuan	2.4618	2.4618	2.4618	2.4618	2.4618	2.4618	2.6728	2.4321	2.4371	2.2524	2.3019	2.1846	2.1014	2.0546	1.9710

⅃ See country notes in the monthly *IFS*

Exchange Rates

Market, Official, or Principal Rate

National Currency Units per SDR: End of Period (aa)

1980	1981	1982	1983	1984	1985	1986	1987	1988	1989	1990	1991	1992	1993	1994	
															Industrial Countries
1.2754	1.1640	1.1031	1.0470	.9802	1.0984	1.2232	1.4187	1.3457	1.3142	1.4227	1.4304	1.3750	1.3736	1.4599	US dollar
1.5237	1.3803	1.3562	1.3028	1.2952	1.5350	1.6886	1.8440	1.6050	1.5215	1.6507	1.6530	1.7478	1.8186	2.0479	Canadian dollar
1.0802	1.0320	1.1249	1.1607	1.1841	1.6132	1.8399	1.9635	1.5730	1.6578	1.8397	1.8826	1.9968	2.0286	1.8793	Australian dollar
258.91	255.95	259.23	243.10	246.13	220.23	194.61	175.20	169.36	188.52	191.21	179.09	171.53	153.63	145.61	Japanese yen
1.3254	1.4119	1.5060	1.5994	2.0524	2.2035	2.3366	2.1577	2.1418	2.2005	2.4203	2.6436	2.6735	2.4581	2.2721	New Zealand dollar
17.612	18.490	18.408	20.249	21.614	18.981	16.770	15.960	16.909	15.527	15.190	15.290	15.612	16.679	16.197	Austrian schilling
40.205	44.766	51.758	58.252	61.832	55.316	49.429	47.032	50.255	46.994	44.078	44.730	45.623	49.599	46.478	Belgian franc
7.672	8.526	9.248	10.339	11.037	9.852	8.981	8.649	9.250	8.683	8.217	8.459	8.601	9.302	8.880	Danish krone
4.8976	5.0714	5.8366	6.0828	6.4008	5.9501	5.8640	5.5980	5.6102	5.3342	5.1699	5.9120	7.2119	7.9454	6.9244	Finnish markka
5.7598	6.6904	7.4184	8.7394	9.4022	8.3052	7.8957	7.5756	8.1536	7.6064	7.2968	7.4096	7.5714	8.0978	7.8044	French franc
2.4985	2.6245	2.6215	2.8517	3.0857	2.7035	2.3740	2.2436	2.3957	2.2312	2.1255	2.1685	2.2193	2.3712	2.2610	Deutsche mark
59.35	67.08	77.85	103.30	125.94	162.30	169.73	178.64	199.30	207.36	224.25	250.73	295.05	342.32	350.51	Greek drachma
7.957	I9.513	18.339	30.016	39.743	46.200	49.221	50.589	62.198	80.387	78.801	79.561	87.890	99.899	99.708	Icelandic krona
.67215	.73668	.78991	.92242	.98861	.88333	.87402	.84671	.89267	.84441	.80127	.81748	.84387	.97360	.94360	Irish pound
1,186.8	1,396.8	1,511.3	1,737.4	1,897.6	1,843.7	1,661.3	1,658.8	1,757.2	1,669.6	1,607.8	1,646.5	2,022.4	2,340.5	2,379.2	Italian lira
40.205	44.766	51.758	58.252	61.832	55.316	49.429	47.032	50.255	46.994	44.078	44.730	45.623	49.599	46.478	Luxembourg franc
2.7160	2.8732	2.8951	3.2084	3.4793	3.0448	2.6812	2.5217	2.6907	2.5173	2.4043	2.4466	2.4944	2.6659	2.5330	Netherlands guilder
6.6066	6.7597	7.7813	8.0847	8.9072	8.3288	9.0516	8.8418	8.8412	8.6932	8.4044	8.5440	9.5212	10.3264	9.8715	Norwegian krone
67.65	75.95	98.25	137.62	165.93	172.99	178.73	184.23	196.97	196.92	190.07	191.94	201.79	242.86	232.25	Portuguese escudo
101.08	113.43	138.55	164.06	169.97	169.32	161.94	154.63	152.67	144.19	137.87	138.31	157.61	195.34	192.32	Spanish peseta
5.5771	6.4844	8.0466	8.3766	8.8116	8.3650	8.3409	8.2963	8.2855	8.1833	8.1063	7.9096	9.6841	11.4054	10.8927	Swedish krona
2.2492	2.0934	2.2002	2.2818	2.5338	2.2809	1.9858	1.8130	2.0239	2.0323	1.8431	1.9389	2.0020	2.0322	1.9146	Swiss franc
.53476	.61004	.68325	.72174	.84757	.76042	.82956	.75803	.74369	.81854	.73789	.76465	.90939	.92733	.93430	Pound sterling
															Developing Countries
															Africa
5.0653	5.0958	5.1135	5.1473	5.0213	5.2425	5.9001	7.0029	9.0576	10.5559	17.3434	30.5996	31.3244	33.1344	62.6166	Algerian dinar
287.99	334.52	370.92	436.97	470.11	415.26	394.78	378.78	407.68	380.32	364.84	370.48	378.57	404.89	I780.44	Benin,CFA franc
.9461	1.0244	1.1704	1.2098	1.5292	2.3076	2.2477	2.2212	2.6049	2.4605	2.6622	2.9646	3.1031	3.5229	3.9670	Botswana pula
287.99	334.52	370.92	436.97	470.11	415.26	394.78	378.78	407.68	380.32	364.84	370.48	378.57	404.89	I780.44	Burkina Faso, CFA franc
114.79	104.76	99.28	122.70	122.70	122.70	151.50	161.00	201.00	232.14	232.14	273.07	322.90	362.99	360.78	Burundi franc
287.99	334.52	370.92	436.97	470.11	415.26	394.78	378.78	407.68	380.32	364.84	370.48	378.57	404.89	I780.44	Cameroon, CFA franc
54.19	59.20	69.54	83.73	91.17	93.78	93.65	93.31	99.13	95.99	94.02	95.08	100.50	118.12	118.45	Cape Verde escudo
287.99	334.52	370.92	436.97	470.11	415.26	394.78	378.78	407.68	380.32	364.84	370.48	378.57	404.89	I780.44	Cent.African Rep.,CFA franc
287.99	334.52	370.92	436.97	470.11	415.26	394.78	378.78	407.68	380.32	364.84	370.48	378.57	404.89	I780.44	Chad, CFA franc
287.98	334.52	370.92	436.97	470.10	415.25	394.78	378.78	407.68	380.31	364.84	370.48	378.57	404.89	I585.33	Comorian franc
287.99	334.52	370.92	436.97	470.11	415.26	394.78	378.78	407.68	380.32	364.84	370.48	378.57	404.89	I780.44	Congo, CFA franc
287.99	334.52	370.92	436.97	470.11	415.26	394.78	378.78	407.68	380.32	364.84	370.48	378.57	404.89	I780.44	Côte d'Ivoire,CFA franc
226.67	206.86	196.05	186.07	174.20	195.21	217.39	252.13	239.16	233.55	252.84	254.22	244.37	244.11	259.45	Djibouti franc
287.99	334.52	370.92	436.97	470.11	415.26	394.78	378.78	407.68	380.32	364.84	370.48	378.57	404.89	I780.44	Eq. Guinea, CFA franc
2.6401	2.4094	2.2834	2.1672	2.0290	2.2737	2.5320	2.9366	2.7856	2.7203	2.9449	2.9610	6.8750	6.8678	8.6861	Ethiopian birr
287.99	334.52	370.92	436.97	470.11	415.26	394.78	378.78	407.68	380.32	364.84	370.48	378.57	404.89	I780.44	Gabon, CFA franc
2.139	2.440	2.733	2.887	4.238	3.802	9.084	9.134	8.961	10.928	10.662	12.813	12.673	13.096	13.983	Gambian dalasi
3.51	3.20	3.03	31.41	49.01	65.89	110.10	249.76	309.36	398.23	490.57	558.76	716.15 p	1,125.87	1,536.68	Ghanaian cedi
24.69	24.69	24.69	24.69	24.69	24.69	288.22	624.21	740.14	814.78	967.41	1,148.56	1,268.31	1,335.67	1,432.15	Guinean franc
44.0	44.0	44.0	88.1	124.7	193.6	291.9	1,207.7	1,833.9	2,611.5	3,568.9	7,093.7	11,901.4	15,746.2	22,436.9	Guinea-Bissau peso
9.660	11.950	14.060	14.417	15.187	17.738	19.135	23.429	25.029	28.387	34.263	40.158	49.797	93.626	65.458	Kenya shilling
.9507	1.1134	1.1873	1.2793	1.9456	2.8093	2.6707	2.7379	3.1997	3.3327	3.6456	3.9237	4.1980	4.6667	5.1730	Lesotho loti
1.2754	1.1640	1.1031	1.0470	.9802	1.0984	1.2232	1.4187	1.3457	1.3142	1.4227	1.4304	1.3750	1.3736	1.4599	Liberian dollar
288.0	334.5	405.6	515.3	645.0	698.4	941.6	1,751.0	2,054.1	2,014.0	2,085.4	2,621.5	2,626.5	2,695.8	5,651.2	Malagasy franc
1.0541	1.0541	1.2122	1.3577	1.5339	1.8445	2.3882	2.9136	3.4120	3.5204	3.7656	3.8104	6.0442	6.1733	22.3337	Malawi kwacha
287.99	334.52	370.92	436.97	470.11	415.26	394.78	378.78	407.68	380.32	364.84	370.48	378.57	404.89	I780.44	Mali, CFA franc
58.71	56.96	58.42	59.71	65.96	84.66	90.61	101.58	101.91	109.80	110.74	111.32	158.26	170.54	187.40	Mauritanian ouguiya
10.000	12.000	12.000	13.321	15.295	15.718	16.069	17.272	18.616	19.707	20.375	21.162	23.372	25.625	26.077	Mauritian rupee
5.528	6.208	6.914	8.439	9.362	10.568	10.656	11.066	11.049	10.673	11.442	11.658	12.442	13.257	13.080	Moroccan dirham
41.8	41.6	42.1	43.1	42.7	45.2	48.1	573.1	842.7	1,077.2	1,476.9	2,639.7	I4,058.2	7,339.2	9,709.5	Mozambique, metical
.95066	1.11341	1.18729	1.27926	1.94563	2.80926	2.67072	2.73793	3.19971	3.33272	3.64557	3.92371	4.19788	4.66667	5.17298	Namibia dollar
287.99	334.52	370.92	436.97	470.11	415.26	394.78	378.78	407.68	380.32	364.84	370.48	378.57	404.89	I780.44	Niger, CFA franc
.694	.741	.739	.784	.792	1.098	4.057	5.874	7.204	10.055	12.805	14.107	27.014	30.056	32.113	Nigerian naira
118.41	108.06	102.41	102.71	102.71	102.71	102.71	102.71	102.71	102.71	171.18	171.18	201.39	201.39	....	Rwanda franc
45.25	45.25	45.25	45.25	45.25	45.25	45.25	103.32	132.12	184.46	200.57	400.55	516.37	709.72	1,730.37	Sao Tome & Principe dobra
287.99	334.52	370.92	436.97	470.11	415.26	394.78	378.78	407.68	380.32	364.84	370.48	378.57	404.89	I780.44	Senegal, CFA franc
8.3197	7.2345	7.2345	7.2345	7.2345	7.2345	7.2345	7.2345	7.2345	7.2345	7.2345	7.2345	7.2345	7.2345	7.2345	Seychelles rupee
1.37	1.37	1.36	2.63	2.46	5.74	43.53	32.69	52.57	85.89	268.43	621.93	723.68	793.41	894.90	Sierra Leonean leone
8.03	7.33	16.50	18.38	25.49	46.68	110.70	141.87	363.34	1,221.51	....	....	....	....	....	Somali shilling
.9507	1.1134	1.1873	1.2793	1.9456	2.8093	2.6707	2.7379	3.1997	3.3327	3.6456	3.9237	4.1979	4.6667	5.1730	South African rand
.6377	1.0486	1.4341	1.3611	1.2743	2.7461	3.0580	6.3846	6.0563	5.9143	6.4026	21.4457	185.8108	298.6000	583.9400	Sudanese pound
.9507	1.1134	1.1873	1.2793	1.9456	2.8093	2.6707	2.7379	3.1997	3.3327	3.6456	3.9237	4.1980	4.6667	5.1730	Swaziland lilangeni
10.44	9.69	10.55	13.04	17.75	18.12	63.26	118.77	168.21	252.71	279.69	334.58	460.63	659.13	764.16	Tanzanian shilling
287.99	334.52	370.92	436.97	470.11	415.26	394.78	378.78	407.68	380.32	364.84	370.48	378.57	404.89	I780.44	Togo, CFA franc
.5340	.6002	.6792	.7612	.8495	.8314	1.0277	1.1035	1.2090	1.1888	1.1904	1.2366	1.3071	1.4376	1.4470	Tunisian dinar
.1	1.0	1.2	2.5	5.1	15.4	17.1	I85.1	222.0	486.2	768.2	1,308.8	1,673.6	1,552.3	1,352.9	Uganda shilling
—	—	—	—	—	—	—	—	—	—	—	.03	.91	48.07	4,744.51	Zaïre, new zaïre
1.024	1.024	1.024	1.280	2.157	6.261	15.546	11.349	13.462	28.451	60.823	127.262	494.604	686.780	1,459.850	Zambian kwacha
.8043	.8347	1.0143	1.1574	1.4727	1.8028	2.0527	2.3593	2.6145	2.9833	3.7508	7.2244	7.5384	9.5256	12.2440	Zimbabwe dollar
															Asia
58.478	58.896	55.817	52.976	49.599	55.580	61.893	71.784	68.092	66.496	71.987	72.380	69.575	69.502	73.868	Afghanistan,afghani
20.726	23.101	26.556	26.174	25.485	34.051	37.674	44.262	43.426	42.408	50.917	55.186	53.625	54.736	58.759	Bangladesh taka
10.114	10.591	10.627	10.986	12.205	13.363	16.051	18.268	20.117	22.387	25.712	36.953	36.025	43.102	45.810	Bhutan,ngultrum
1.9518	2.0317	2.1209	2.0739	2.7404	3.5166	4.5528	5.2804	5.0088	6.2056	7.4293	7.7732	7.9087	7.9666	I12.3302	Chinese yuan

I See country notes in the monthly *IFS*

Exchange Rates

Market, Official, or Principal Rate

National Currency Units per SDR: End of Period (aa)

	1965	1966	1967	1968	1969	1970	1971	1972	1973	1974	1975	1976	1977	1978	1979
Asia (cont.)															
Fiji dollar	.7921	.7956	.8686	.8765	I.8706	.8731	.8890	.9155	.9762	.9795	1.0104	1.0939	1.0575	1.0679	1.1077
Indian rupee	4.775	7.576	7.547	7.628	7.559	7.576	7.903	8.773	9.896	I9.978	10.462	10.318	9.971	10.668	10.416
Indonesian rupiah	....	....	235.0	326.0	326.0	378.0	450.6	450.6	500.6	508.1	485.8	482.2	504.1	814.2	826.0
Kiribati, Aust.dollar	.8941	I.8977	.8921	.9009	.8945	.8969	.9116	.8515	.8107	.9226	.9312	1.0694	1.0642	1.1324	1.1916
Korean won	271.8	271.2	274.6	281.5	304.4	316.6	405.3	433.1	479.5	592.6	566.6	562.3	587.9	630.6	637.6
Lao P.D. Rep.,kip	.12	.12	.12	.12	.12	.12	.13	.33	.36	.37	.44	I2.32	2.43	5.21	I13.17
Malaysian ringgit	3.0592	3.0710	3.0563	3.0650	3.0750	3.0775	3.1334	3.0584	2.9580	2.8317	3.0300	2.9452	2.8734	2.8740	2.8836
Maldivian rufiyaa	4.775	4.775	4.750	4.750	4.750	4.750	4.750	4.750	4.741	4.812	7.170	10.021	10.841	11.237	9.946
Myanmar kyat	4.7820	4.8050	4.8000	4.8100	4.7920	4.8020	5.9377	5.8650	5.8653	5.8891	7.7429	7.7429	8.5085	8.5085	8.5085
Nepalese rupee	7.619	7.616	10.125	10.125	10.125	10.125	10.993	10.993	12.739	12.929	14.633	14.523	15.184	15.633	15.808
Pakistan rupee	4.782	4.805	4.774	4.809	4.791	4.803	5.204	11.976	11.943	12.121	11.590	11.502	12.026	12.898	13.042
Papua New Guinea kina	.8941	I.8977	.8921	.9009	.8945	.8969	.9116	.8515	.8107	.9226	.9312	.9435	.9202	.8966	.9093
Philippine peso	3.910	3.900	3.930	3.930	3.930	I6.435	6.987	7.362	8.119	8.650	8.778	8.630	8.952	9.608	9.768
Singapore dollar	3.0600	3.0800	3.0700	3.0800	3.0900	3.0800	3.1486	3.0617	I2.9991	2.8307	2.9144	2.8529	2.8406	2.8186	2.8441
Solomon Islands dollar	.8941	I.8977	.8921	.9009	.8945	.8969	.9116	.8515	.8107	.9226	.9312	1.0694	1.0642	1.1324	1.1306
Sri Lanka rupee	4.775	4.775	5.928	5.928	5.958	5.958	6.469	7.272	8.140	8.195	9.029	10.257	18.901	20.200	20.346
Thai baht	20.830	20.750	20.800	20.850	20.928	20.928	I22.721	22.721	24.579	24.946	23.881	23.701	24.780	26.564	26.906
Tongan pa'anga	.8941	I.8977	.8921	.9009	.8945	.8969	.9116	.8515	.8107	.9226	.9312	1.0694	1.0642	1.1324	1.1916
Vanuatu, vatu	89.12	90.03	89.25	89.97	89.83	84.44	91.67	89.86	91.80	87.95	84.86	93.32	92.37	88.01	85.59
Vietnamese dong	—	—	—	—	—	—	—	.1	.2	.2	.2	.2	.2	.3	.3
Western Samoa tala	.7192	.7192	.7211	.7211	.7211	.7211	.7336	.7313	.7317	.7427	.8982	.9295	.9093	.9308	1.2002
Europe															
Cyprus pound	.35714	.35714	.41667	.41667	.41667	.41667	.42510	.41622	.43511	.43782	.46044	.47822	.46443	.45760	.45527
Czech Republic koruna	....	....	....	....	....	....	....	....	....	....	....	....	....	....	....
Czechoslovak koruna	....	....	....	....	....	....	....	....	....	26.56	26.31	25.46	24.84	18.03	18.32
Hungarian forint	....	....	....	60.000	60.000	60.000	59.996	59.996	56.400	57.241	50.934	47.984	49.317	46.351	46.868
Maltese lira	.35714	.35714	.41667	.41667	.41667	.41667	.41477	.43067	.46649	.45968	.47257	.49566	.47929	.47383	.45297
Polish zloty	....	....	....	....	....	....	....	....	....	....	....	....	....	....	....
Romanian leu	6.000	6.000	6.000	6.000	6.000	6.000	6.004	6.004	24.127	24.487	23.413	23.237	24.294	23.450	23.712
Turkish lira	9.0	9.0	9.0	9.0	9.0	14.9	15.4	15.4	17.1	17.1	17.7	19.4	23.6	32.9	46.6
Middle East															
Bahrain dinar	....	.47619	.47619	.47619	.47619	.47619	.47619	.47619	.47620	.48330	.46300	.45968	.48060	.50007	.49664
Egyptian pound	.4348	.4348	.4348	.4348	.4348	.4348	.4720	.4720	.4720	.4791	.4581	.4546	.4753	.5098	.9221
Iranian rial	75.75	75.75	75.25	75.09	76.38	76.38	82.93	82.93	81.58	82.80	81.10	82.05	85.61	91.81	92.84
Iraqi dinar	.35714	.35714	.35714	.35714	.35788	.35908	.36621	.36443	.35625	.36157	.34572	.34311	.35872	.38474	.38903
Israeli new sheqel	.0003	.0003	.0003	.0003	.0003	.0003	.0005	.0005	.0005	.0007	.0008	.0010	.0019	.0025	.0047
Jordan dinar	.35714	.35714	.35714	.35714	.35714	.35714	.38775	.38775	.39096	.38567	.38775	.38775	.38775	.38775	.38775
Kuwaiti dinar	.35714	.35714	.35714	.35714	.35714	.35714	.35714	.35584	.35791	.35462	.34435	.33339	.34023	.35410	.35978
Lebanese pound	3.1	3.2	3.1	3.2	3.3	3.3	3.4	3.3	3.0	2.8	2.8	3.4	3.6	3.9	4.3
Libyan dinar	.35714	.35714	.35714	.35714	.35714	.35714	.35714	.35714	.35714	.36247	.34657	.34396	.35962	.38569	.39000
Rial Omani	.35714	.35714	.41667	.41667	.41667	.41667	.41666	.41666	.41667	.42289	.40435	.40130	.41956	.44998	.45501
Qatar riyal	4.7619[p]	4.7619	4.7619	4.7619	4.7619	4.7619	4.7619	4.7619	4.7619	4.8330	4.6679	4.5989	4.8100	5.0008	4.8807
Saudi Arabian riyal	4.5000	4.5000	4.5000	4.5000	4.5000	4.5000	4.5057	4.5057	4.4825	4.3464	4.1324	4.1013	4.2576	4.3187	4.4328
Syrian pound	3.820	3.820	3.820	3.820	3.820	3.820	4.147	4.147	4.584	4.530	4.331	4.560	4.768	5.113	5.171
U.A.Emirates dirham	....	4.7619	4.7619	4.7619	4.7619	4.7619	4.7619	4.7619	4.8344	4.8735	4.6791	4.6206	4.7349	5.0001	4.9611
Yemen,Rep.,Yemeni rial	....	....	....	....	....	....	....	....	....	....	....	....	....	....	....
Western Hemisphere															
Antigua & Barbuda,E.Car.$	1.7126	1.7203	1.9948	2.0131	1.9994	2.0053	2.0417	2.2194	2.4925	2.5024	2.7770	3.1369	3.2797	3.5175	3.5568
Argentine peso	—	—	—	—	—	—	—	—	—	—	—	—	—	—	—
Bahamian dollar	1.0204	I1.0204	1.0204	1.0204	1.0204	1.0000	1.0857	1.0857	—	1.2244	1.1707	1.1618	1.2147	1.3028	1.3173
Barbados dollar	1.7126	1.7203	1.9948	2.0131	1.9994	2.0053	2.0417	2.2194	2.4925	2.5024	2.3458	2.3281	2.4431	2.6203	2.6495
Belize dollar	1.4286	1.4286	1.6623	1.6776	1.6662	1.6711	1.7014	I1.8495	2.0770	2.0853	2.3141	2.7299	2.4294	2.6056	2.6347
Bolivia, boliviano	—	—	—	—	—	—	—	—	—	—	—	—	—	—	—
Brazilian real	—	I—	—	—	—	—	—	—	—	—	I—	—	—	—	—
Chilean peso	—	—	.01	.01	.01	.01	.02	.03	.43	2.29	I9.95	20.24	33.96	44.23	51.38
Colombian peso	13.50	13.50	15.76	16.88	17.85	19.09	22.70	24.74	29.91	35.05	38.58	42.20	46.11	53.41	57.96
Costa Rican colon	6.64	6.64	6.64	6.64	6.64	6.64	7.20	7.20	8.02	10.49	10.03	9.96	10.41	11.16	11.29
Dominica, E.Caribbean dollar	1.7126	1.7203	1.9948	2.0131	1.9994	2.0053	2.0417	2.2194	2.4925	2.5024	2.7770	3.1369	3.2797	3.5175	3.5568
Dominican peso	1.000	1.000	1.000	1.000	1.000	1.000	1.086	1.086	1.206	1.224	1.171	1.162	1.215	1.303	1.317
Ecuadoran sucre	18.0	18.0	18.0	18.0	18.0	25.0	27.1	27.1	30.2	30.6	29.3	29.0	30.4	32.6	32.9
Salvadoran colon	2.5000	2.5000	2.5000	2.5000	2.5000	2.5000	2.7143	2.7143	3.0159	3.0609	2.9267	2.9046	3.0368	3.2570	3.2933
Grenada, E.Caribbean dollar	1.7126	1.7203	1.9948	2.0131	1.9994	2.0053	2.0417	2.2194	2.4925	2.5024	2.7770	3.1369	3.2797	3.5175	3.5568
Guatemalan quetzal	1.0000	1.0000	1.0000	1.0000	1.0000	1.0000	1.0857	1.0857	1.2064	1.2244	1.1707	1.1618	1.2147	1.3028	1.3173
Guyana dollar	1.713	1.720	1.995	2.013	1.999	2.005	2.217	2.410	2.706	2.717	2.985	2.963	3.098	3.322	3.359
Haitian gourde	5.0000	5.0000	5.0000	5.0000	5.0000	5.0000	5.4286	5.4286	6.0318	6.1218	5.8533	5.8092	6.0736	6.5140	6.5867
Honduras lempira	2.0000	2.0000	2.0000	2.0000	2.0000	2.0000	2.1714	2.1714	2.4127	2.4487	2.3413	2.3237	2.4294	2.6056	2.6347
Jamaica dollar	.7136	.7168	.8312	.8388	.8331	.8355	.8507	.9248	I1.0967	1.1130	1.0642	1.0562	1.1043	2.2082	2.3467
Mexican new peso	—	—	—	—	—	—	—	—	—	—	—	—	—	—	—
Netherlands Antilles guilder	1.8812	1.8827	1.8734	1.8786	1.8879	1.8739	1.9543	1.9543	2.1714	2.2038	2.1072	2.0913	2.1865	2.3450	2.3712
Nicaraguan gold córdoba	—	—	—	—	—	—	—	—	—	—	—	—	—	—	I—
Panamanian balboa	1.0000	1.0000	1.0000	1.0000	1.0000	1.0000	1.0857	1.0857	1.2064	1.2244	1.1707	1.1618	1.2147	1.3028	1.3173
Paraguayan guarani	126.0	126.0	126.0	126.0	126.0	126.0	136.8	136.8	152.0	154.3	147.5	146.4	153.1	164.2	166.0
Peruvian new sol	....	....	....	....	....	....	....	....	....	....	....	....	....	....	....
St.Kitts & Nevis, E.C.dollar	1.7126	1.7203	1.9948	2.0131	1.9994	2.0053	2.0417	2.2194	2.4925	2.5024	2.7770	3.1369	3.2797	3.5175	3.5568
St.Lucia, E.Car. dollar	1.7126	1.7203	1.9948	2.0131	1.9994	2.0053	2.0417	2.2194	2.4925	2.5024	2.7770	3.1369	3.2797	3.5175	3.5568
St. Vinc. & Grens.,E.C.$	1.7126	1.7203	1.9948	2.0131	1.9994	2.0053	2.0417	2.2194	2.4925	2.5024	2.7770	3.1369	3.2797	3.5175	3.5568
Suriname guilder	1.886	1.886	1.886	1.886	1.886	1.886	1.835	1.942[p]	....	....	2.185	2.090	2.074	2.168	2.325	2.351
Trinidad & Tobago dollar	1.7126	1.7203	1.9948	2.0131	1.9994	2.0053	2.0417	2.2194	2.4924	2.5024	2.7769	2.7884	2.9153	3.1267	3.1616
Uruguayan peso	—	—	—	—	—	—	—	—	—	—	I—	—	—	—	—
Venezuelan bolivar	4.450	4.450	4.450	4.450	4.450	4.450	4.723	4.723	5.169	5.246	5.016	4.987	5.214	5.592	5.655

I See country notes in the monthly *IFS*

Exchange Rates

Market, Official, or Principal Rate
National Currency Units per SDR: End of Period (aa)

1980	1981	1982	1983	1984	1985	1986	1987	1988	1989	1990	1991	1992	1993	1994	
															Asia (cont.)
1.0089	1.0205	1.0450	1.0954	1.1204	1.2307	1.4010	2.0436	1.8906	1.9632	2.0760	2.1067	2.1511	2.1164	2.0570	Fiji dollar
10.114	10.591	10.627	10.986	12.205	13.363	16.051	18.268	20.117	22.387	25.712	36.953	36.025	43.102	45.810	Indian rupee
799.4	749.6	763.9	1,040.7	1,052.7	1,235.7	2,007.3	2,340.8	2,329.4	2,361.5	2,704.5	2,849.4	2,835.3	2,898.2	3,211.7	Indonesian rupiah
1.0802	1.0320	1.1249	1.1607	1.1841	1.6132	1.8399	1.9635	1.5730	1.6578	1.8397	1.8826	1.9968	2.0286	1.8793	Kiribati,Aust.dollar
841.6	815.4	826.0	832.8	811.0	977.8	1,053.7	1,124.0	920.6	893.1	1,019.2	1,088.3	1,084.1	1,110.0	1,151.4	Korean won
12.75	34.92	38.61	36.64	34.31	104.35	116.20	521.36	608.93	937.65	989.46	1,017.75	985.88	983.47	1,049.63	Lao P.D. Rep.,kip
2.8345	2.6099	2.5606	2.4481	2.3770	2.6653	3.1840	3.5364	3.6540	3.5526	3.8433	3.8965	3.5915	3.7107	3.7372	Malaysian ringgit
9.629	8.788	7.777	7.381	6.910	7.830	8.861	13.328	11.472	12.097	13.686	14.762	14.486	15.253	17.182	Maldivian rufiyaa
8.5085	8.5085	8.5085	8.5085	8.5085	8.5085	8.5085	8.5085	8.5085	8.5085	8.5085	8.5085	8.5085	8.5085	8.5085	Myanmar kyat
15.305	15.364	15.774	15.914	17.644	22.737	26.910	30.643	33.912	37.585	43.249	61.079	59.400	67.634	72.817	Nepalese rupee
12.627	11.523	14.164	14.134	15.056	17.553	21.100	24.756	25.097	28.149	31.156	35.360	35.338	41.372	44.963	Pakistan rupee
.8212	.7921	.8250	.9166	.9227	1.1121	1.1757	1.2462	1.1121	1.1297	1.3558	1.3626	1.3578	1.3479	1.7205	Papua New Guinea kina
9.693	9.544	10.117	14.659	19.369	20.905	25.112	29.508	28.711	29.490	39.834	38.121	34.507	38.046	35.647	Philippine peso
2.6701	2.3836	2.3259	2.2269	2.1349	2.3122	2.6604	2.8352	2.6190	2.4895	2.4818	2.3323	2.2617	2.2087	2.1324	Singapore dollar
1.0172	1.0346	1.1527	1.2788	1.3170	1.7714	2.4299	2.8009	2.8505	3.1500	3.7184	3.9978	4.2622	4.4611	4.8597	Solomon Islands dollar
22.957	23.919	23.518	26.174	25.760	30.105	34.885	43.642	44.453	52.566	57.248	60.908	63.250	68.076	72.963	Sri Lanka rupee
26.312	26.771	25.372	24.080	26.613	29.273	31.962	35.566	33.965	33.761	35.979	36.161	35.090	35.081	36.628	Thai baht
1.0802	1.0320	1.1249	1.1607	1.1841	1.6132	1.8399	1.9635	1.5748	1.6539	1.8435	1.9050	1.9116	1.8946	1.8371	Tongan pa'anga
93.09	106.19	106.06	106.55	100.55	110.12	142.18	142.00	141.37	145.48	155.43	158.48	163.63	165.93	163.62	Vanuatu,vatu
1.3	1.3	1.3	1.3ᵖ	1.3ᵖ	124.7	27.5	399.0	1,513.9	7,063.6	11,559.1	16,449.9	14,526.9	14,892.8	16,131.3	Vietnamese dong
1.1851	1.2794	1.3647	1.6964	2.1397	2.5333	2.6883	2.8527	2.8909	3.0093	3.3193	3.5025	3.5166	3.5816	3.5789	Western Samoa tala
															Europe
.46522	.50355	.53850	.58245	.63138	.59681	.62583	.62263	.62751	.62924	.61828	.62802	.66419	.71398	.69523	Cyprus pound
....	....	....	....	....	....	....	....	....	....	....	....	....	41.14499	40.94733	Czech Republic koruna
18.93	15.32	15.49	15.32	16.79	17.57	17.59	18.44	19.26	18.78	39.83	39.82	39.74	....	....	Czechoslovak koruna
41.084	40.075	43.694	47.315	50.186	52.007	56.177	65.807	70.699	82.192	87.421	108.169	115.459	138.317	161.591	Hungarian forint
.45168	.45075	.45827	.46641	.48208	.46557	.45153	.44221	.44697	.44269	.42788	.43712	.51450	.54272	.53738	Maltese lira
—	—	—	—	—	—	—	—	—	1	1	2	2	3	4	Polish zloty
22.957	17.459	16.547	19.191	17.438	17.278	18.690	19.492	19.338	18.976	49.381	1270.351	632.500	1,752.663	2,579.555	Romanian leu
115.0	155.5	206.0	296.1	435.9	633.6	926.9	1,448.3	2,442.2	3,040.6	4,168.5	7,266.5	11,776.1	19,878.9	56,534.2	Turkish lira
															Middle East
.47955	.43764	.41477	.39365	.36856	.41300	.45992	.53341	.50598	.49412	.53492	.53784	.51700	.51646	.54890	Bahrain dinar
.8928	.8148	.7722	.7329	.6861	.7689	.8562	.9931	.9420	1.4456	2.8453	4.7633	4.5792	4.6294	4.9518	Egyptian pound
92.30	92.30	92.30	92.30	92.30	92.30	92.30	92.30	92.30	92.30	92.30	92.30	92.30	2,415.49	2,534.26	Iranian rial
.37665	.34374	.34291	.32545	.30471	.34145	.38024	.44100	.41832	.40852	.44225	.44466	.42743	.42698	.45381	Iraqi dinar
1.0096	.0182	.0371	.1128	.6261	11.6471	1.8181	2.1828	2.2675	2.5797	2.9136	3.2657	3.8005	4.1015	4.4058	Israeli new sheqel
.38775	.38775	.38775	.38775	.38775	.38775	.38775	.38775	.64191	.85158	.94604	.96553	.95011	.96699	1.02336	Jordan dinar
.34601	.32755	.31847	.30630	.29844	.31745	.35760	.38289	.38031	.38370	....	.40663	.41621	.40990	.43813	Kuwaiti dinar
4.7	5.4	4.2	5.7	8.7	19.9	106.4	645.5	713.2	663.7	1,197.9	1,257.3	2,527.3	2,350.2	2,404.4	Lebanese pound
.37759	.34459	.32658	.30995	.29019	.32519	.38393	.38393	.38393	.38393	.38393	.38393	.41428ᵖ	.44643	.52500	Libyan dinar
.44053	.40203	.38101	.36162	.33856	.37939	.47032	.54547	.51742	.50529	.54701	.55000	.52869	.52813	.56131	Rial Omani
4.6425	4.2368	4.0153	3.8109	3.5680	3.9982	4.4524	5.1639	4.8983	4.7835	5.1785	5.2068	5.0050	4.9998	5.3139	Qatar riyal
4.2407	3.9749	3.7892	3.6591	3.5043	4.0037	4.5808	5.3129	5.0396	4.9215	5.3279	5.3370	5.1494	5.1440	5.4671	Saudi Arabian riyal
5.006	4.569	4.330	4.109	3.847	4.311	4.801	5.568	15.105	14.751	15.969	16.057	15.434	15.418	16.387	Syrian pound
4.6820	4.2729	4.0495	3.8434	3.5984	4.0323	4.4903	5.2079	4.9401	4.8243	5.2226	5.2511	5.0476	5.0423	5.3591	U.A.Emirates dirham
....	....	....	....	....	....	....	....	....	....	17.086	17.179	16.514	16.496	17.533	Yemen,Rep.,Yemeni rial
															Western Hemisphere
3.4436	3.1427	2.9784	2.8268	2.6466	2.9657	3.3026	3.8304	3.6334	3.5482	3.8412	3.8622	3.7125	3.7086	3.9416	Antigua & Barbuda,E. Car.$
—	—	—	—	—	—	—	—	—	.2	.8	1.4	1.4	1.4	1.5	Argentine peso
1.2754	1.1640	1.1031	1.0470	.9802	1.0984	1.2232	1.4187	1.3457	1.3142	1.4227	1.4304	1.3750	1.3736	1.4599	Bahamian dollar
2.5652	2.3411	2.2187	2.1057	1.9715	2.2093	2.4602	2.8534	2.7066	2.6432	2.8614	2.8770	2.7655	2.7626	2.9362	Barbados dollar
2.5508	2.3279	2.2062	2.0939	1.9604	2.1968	2.4464	2.8373	2.6914	2.6283	2.8453	2.8609	2.7500	2.7471	2.9197	Belize dollar
—	—	.0002	.0005	.0086	11.8585	2.3522	13.1352	3.3239	3.9162	4.8370	5.3570	5.6306	6.1467	6.8540	Bolivia, boliviano
—	—	—	—	—	—	—	—	—	—	—	—	1.01	.16	11.24	Brazilian real
49.74	45.39	81.00	91.64	125.70	201.96	250.42	337.84	332.66	390.79	479.56	535.71	525.42	588.53	588.20	Chilean peso
64.94	68.76	77.54	92.94	111.64	189.15	267.88	374.10	451.97	570.24	809.11	1,011.11	1,116.18	1,260.01	1,213.53	Colombian peso
10.93	42.01	44.40	45.44	46.81	58.99	72.02	98.24	106.98	110.85	147.32	193.72	188.97	208.01	240.98	Costa Rican colon
3.4436	3.1427	2.9784	2.8268	2.6466	2.9657	3.3026	3.8304	3.6334	3.5482	3.8412	3.8622	3.7125	3.7086	3.9416	Dominica, E.Caribbean dollar
1.275	1.164	1.103	1.047	.980	3.229	3.763	7.037	8.532	8.332	16.147	18.109	17.291	17.536	19.071	Dominican peso
31.9	29.1	36.6	56.6	65.8	105.2	179.2	314.2	582.0	852.1	1,249.4	1,817.5	2,535.8	2,807.3	3,312.4	Ecuadoran sucre
3.1885	2.9099	2.7578	2.6174	2.4505	2.7461	6.1160	7.0933	6.7285	6.5708	11.4240	11.5579	12.6088	11.9088	12.7737	Salvadoran colon
3.4436	3.1427	2.9784	2.8268	2.6466	2.9657	3.3026	3.8304	3.6334	3.5482	3.8412	3.8622	3.7125	3.7086	3.9416	Grenada, E.Caribbean dollar
1.2754	1.1640	1.1031	1.0470	.9802	1.0984	3.0580	3.5467	3.6401	4.4681	7.1341	7.2142	7.2522	7.9876	8.2460	Guatemalan quetzal
3.252	3.492	3.309	3.141	4.068	4.558	5.382	14.187	13.457	43.367	64.020	174.512	173.250	179.593	208.029	Guyana dollar
6.3771	5.8198	5.5156	5.2348	4.9011	5.4921	6.1160	7.0933	6.7285	6.5708	7.1133	111.7867	15.0604	17.5884	18.9001	Haitian gourde
2.5508	2.3279	2.2062	2.0939	1.9604	2.1968	2.4464	2.8373	2.6914	2.6283	2.8453	7.7243	8.0163	9.9720	13.7227	Honduran lempira
2.2720	2.0735	1.9651	3.4317	4.8324	6.0193	6.7031	7.8026	7.3744	8.5158	11.4348	30.7435	30.5038	44.6057	48.4692	Jamaica dollar
—	—	.1	.2	.2	.4	1.1	3.1	3.1	3.5	4.2	4.4	4.3	4.3	7.8	Mexican new peso
2.2957	2.0951	1.9856	1.8845	1.7644	1.9772	2.2017	2.5536	2.4223	2.3523	2.5466	2.5605	2.4613	2.4587	2.6131	Netherlands Antilles guilder
—	—	—	—	—	—	—	—	—	1	1	7	7	9	10	Nicaraguan gold córdoba
1.2754	1.1640	1.1031	1.0470	.9802	1.0984	1.2232	1.4187	1.3457	1.3142	1.4227	1.4304	1.3750	1.3736	1.4599	Panamanian balboa
160.7	146.7	139.0	131.9	235.3	351.5	672.8	780.3	740.1	1,600.6	1,789.7	1,934.4	2,200.3	2,582.3	2,832.1	Paraguayan guarani
—	—	—	—	—	—	—	—	—	.0007	.0069	.7354	1.1732	2.2413	2.9669	3.1825	Peruvian new sol
3.4436	3.1427	2.9784	2.8268	2.6466	2.9657	3.3026	3.8304	3.6334	3.5482	3.8412	3.8622	3.7125	3.7086	3.9416	St.Kitts & Nevis, E.C. dollar
3.4436	3.1427	2.9784	2.8268	2.6466	2.9657	3.3026	3.8304	3.6334	3.5482	3.8412	3.8622	3.7125	3.7086	3.9416	St.Lucia, E.Car. dollar
3.4436	3.1427	2.9784	2.8268	2.6466	2.9657	3.3026	3.8304	3.6334	3.5482	3.8412	3.8622	3.7125	3.7086	3.9416	St. Vinc. & Grens.,E. Car.$
2.277	2.078	1.969	1.869	1.750	1.961	2.183	2.532	2.402	2.346	2.539	2.553	2.454	2.452	597.809	Suriname guilder
3.0610	2.7935	2.6475	2.5127	2.3525	3.9543	4.4035	5.1072	5.7192	5.5852	6.0463	6.0793	5.8438	7.9860	8.6616	Trinidad & Tobago dollar
—	—	—	—	.1	.1	.2	.4	.6	1.1	2.3	3.6	4.8	16.1	8.2	Uruguayan peso
5.475	4.996	4.735	4.502	7.352	8.238	17.736	20.571	19.513	56.612	71.673	88.048	109.244	145.102	1248.175	Venezuelan bolivar

ɪ See country notes in the monthly *IFS*

Exchange Rate Arrangements

(As of June 30, 1995)[1]

Currency pegged to					Flexibility limited in terms of a single currency or group of currencies		More flexible		
US dollar	French franc	Other currency	SDR	Other composite[2]	Single currency[3]	Cooperative arrangements[4]	Adjusted according to a set of indicators[5]	Other managed floating	Independently floating
Antigua & Barbuda	Benin	Bhutan (Indian rupee)	Libya	Bangladesh	Bahrain	Austria	Chile	Algeria	Afghanistan, Islamic State of
Argentina	Burkina Faso	Estonia (deutsche mark)	Myanmar	Botswana	Qatar	Belgium	Ecuador	Angola	Albania
Bahamas, The	Cameroon	Kiribati (Australian dollar)	Seychelles	Burundi	Saudi Arabia	Denmark	Nicaragua	Belarus	Armenia
Barbados	C. African Rep.	Lesotho (South African rand)		Cape Verde	United Arab Emirates	France		Brazil	Australia
Belize	Chad	Namibia (South African rand)		Cyprus		Germany		Cambodia	Azerbaijan
Djibouti	Comoros	San Marino (Italian lira)		Czech Republic		Ireland		China, P.R.	Bolivia
Dominica	Congo	Swaziland (South African rand)		Fiji		Luxembourg		Colombia	Bulgaria
Grenada	Côte d'Ivoire			Iceland		Netherlands		Croatia	Canada
Iraq	Equatorial Guinea			Jordan		Portugal		Dominican Rep.	Costa Rica
Liberia	Gabon			Kuwait		Spain		Egypt	El Salvador
Lithuania	Mali			Malta				Eritrea	Ethiopia
Marshall Islands	Niger			Mauritania				Georgia	Finland
Micronesia, Fed. States of	Senegal			Morocco				Greece	Gambia, The
Nigeria	Togo			Nepal				Guinea-Bissau	Ghana
Oman				Slovak Republic				Honduras	Guatemala
Panama				Solomon Islands				Hungary	Guinea
St. Kitts & Nevis				Thailand				Indonesia	Guyana
St. Lucia				Tonga				Israel	Haiti
St. Vincent and the Grenadines				Vanuatu				Korea	India
Syrian Arab Rep.				Western Samoa				Lao P.D. Rep	Iran, I. R. of
Turkmenistan								Latvia	Italy
Venezuela								Macedonia, FYR of	Jamaica
Yemen, Republic of								Malaysia	Japan
								Maldives	Kazakhstan
								Mauritius	Kenya
								Pakistan	Kyrgyz Rep.
								Poland	Lebanon
								Russian Federation	Madagascar
								Singapore	Malawi
								Slovenia	Mexico
								Sri Lanka	Moldova
								Sudan	Mongolia
								Tunisia	Mozambique
								Turkey	New Zealand
								Uruguay	Norway
								Viet Nam	Papua New Guinea
									Paraguay
									Peru
									Philippines
									Romania
									Rwanda
									São Tomé and Príncipe
									Sierra Leone
									Somalia
									South Africa
									Suriname
									Sweden
									Switzerland
									Tajikistan, Rep. of
									Tanzania
									Trinidad and Tobago
									Uganda
									Ukraine
									United Kingdom
									United States
									Uzbekistan
									Zaïre
									Zambia
									Zimbabwe

				1992		1993				1994				1995	
Classification status[1]	1989	1990	1991	QIII	QIV	QI	QII	QIII	QIV	QI	QII	QIII	QIV	QI	QII
Currency pegged to															
US dollar	32	25	24	26	24	23	20	20	21	24	23	23	23	23	23
French franc	14	14	14	14	14	14	14	14	14	14	14	14	14	14	14
Russian ruble	—	—	—	5	6	7	7	5	—	—	—	—	—	—	—[6]
Other currency	5	5	4	6	6	6	6	7	8	8	8	8	8	8	7
SDR	7	6	6	5	5	4	4	4	4	4	4	4	4	3	3
Other currency composite	35	35	33	31	29	27	27	26	26	25	25	25	21	20	20
Flexibility limited vis-à-vis a single currency	4	4	4	4	4	4	4	4	4	4	4	4	4	4	4
Cooperative arrangements	9	9	10	11	9	9	9	9	9	9	9	9	10	10	10
Adjusted according to a set of indicators	5	3	5	4	3	4	4	4	4	3	2	2	3	3	3
Managed floating	21	23	27	22	23	21	27	27	29	29	31	31	33	35	36
Independently floating	20	25	29	41	44	48	49	52	56	55	57	57	58	59	59
Total	152	154	156	167	167	167	171	172	175	175	177	177	178	179	179

[1] For members with dual or multiple exchange markets, the arrangement shown is that in the major market.
[2] Comprises currencies which are pegged to various "baskets" of currencies of the members' own choice, as distinct from the SDR basket.
[3] Exchange rates of all currencies have shown limited flexibility in terms of the U.S. dollar.
[4] Refers to the cooperative arrangement maintained under the European Monetary System.
[5] Includes exchange arrangements under which the exchange rate is adjusted at relatively frequent intervals, on the basis of indicators determined by the respective member countries.
[6] Starting May 24, 1994, the Azerbaijan authorities ceased to peg the manat to the Russian ruble and the exchange arrangement was reclassified to "Independently floating".

Fund Accounts: Arrangements

(As of July 31, 1995 and Amounts Expressed in Millions of SDRs)

Member	Date of Arrangement	Date of Expiration	Amount Agreed	Undrawn Balance
Stand-By Arrangements				
Armenia	June 28, 1995	June 27, 1996	43.88	40.50
Cameroon	March 14, 1994	September 13, 1995	81.06	59.15
Croatia	October 14, 1994	April 13, 1996	65.40	52.32
Ecuador	May 11, 1994	March 31, 1996	173.90	75.00
El Salvador	July 21, 1995	September 20, 1996	37.68	37.68
Estonia	April 11, 1995	July 10, 1996	13.95	13.95
Georgia	June 28, 1995	June 27, 1996	72.15	66.60
Haiti	March 8, 1995	March 7, 1996	20.00	3.60
Kazakhstan	June 5, 1995	June 4, 1996	185.60	139.19
Latvia	April 21, 1995	May 20, 1996	27.45	27.45
Lesotho	July 31, 1995	July 30, 1996	7.17	7.17
Macedonia	May 5, 1995	June 4, 1996	22.30	19.80
Mexico	February 1, 1995	August 15, 1996	12,070.20	5,520.30
Moldova	March 22, 1995	March 21, 1996	58.50	39.15
Papua New Guinea	July 14, 1995	January 13, 1997	71.48	47.56
Poland	August 5, 1994	March 4, 1996	693.30	410.00
Romania	May 11, 1994	December 10, 1995	131.97	75.41
Russia	April 11, 1995	April 10, 1996	4,313.10	2,875.40
Slovak Republic	July 22, 1994	March 21, 1996	115.80	83.65
Turkey	July 8, 1994	March 7, 1996	610.50	225.00
Ukraine	April 7, 1995	April 6, 1996	997.30	687.98
Total			19,812.69	10,506.86
Extended Arrangements				
Algeria	May 22, 1995	May 21, 1998	1,169.28	1,012.88
Argentina	March 31, 1992	March 30, 1996	4,020.25	768.55
Egypt	September 20, 1993	September 19, 1996	400.00	400.00
Jamaica	December 11, 1992	December 10, 1995	109.13	22.38
Jordan	May 25, 1994	May 24, 1997	189.30	90.81
Lithuania	October 24, 1994	October 23, 1997	134.55	93.15
Pakistan	February 22, 1994	February 21, 1997	379.10	255.90
Peru	March 18, 1993	March 17, 1996	1,018.10	375.41
Philippines	June 24, 1994	June 23, 1997	474.50	438.00
Zimbabwe	September 11, 1992	September 10, 1995	114.60	27.70
Total			8,008.81	3,484.78
Total (Stand-By and Extended Arrangements)			27,821.49	13,991.63
Structural Adjustment Arrangements				
Ethiopia	October 28, 1992	November 8, 1995	49.42	—
Total			49.42	—
Enhanced Structural Adjustment Arrangements				
Albania	July 14, 1993	July 13, 1996	42.36	11.30
Benin	January 25, 1993	January 24, 1996	51.89	9.06
Bolivia	December 19, 1994	December 18, 1997	100.96	84.14
Burkina Faso	March 31, 1993	March 30, 1996	53.04	17.68
Cambodia	May 6, 1994	May 5, 1997	84.00	56.00
Côte d'Ivoire	March 11, 1994	March 10, 1997	333.48	154.83
Equatorial Guinea	February 3, 1993	February 2, 1996	12.88	8.28
Ghana	June 30, 1995	June 29, 1998	164.40	137.00
Guinea	November 6, 1991	November 5, 1996	57.90	23.16
Guinea-Bissau	January 18, 1995	January 17, 1998	9.45	7.88
Guyana	July 20, 1994	July 19, 1997	53.76	35.84
Honduras	July 24, 1992	July 24, 1997	47.46	23.73
Kyrgyz Republic	July 20, 1994	July 19, 1997	70.95	47.30
Lao, P.D.R.	June 4, 1993	June 3, 1996	35.19	17.60
Mali	August 28, 1992	March 31, 1996	79.24	14.73
Mauritania	January 25, 1995	January 24, 1998	42.75	35.63
Mongolia	June 25, 1993	June 24, 1996	40.81	16.70
Mozambique	June 1, 1990	December 31, 1995	130.05	14.70
Nepal	October 5, 1992	October 4, 1995	33.57	16.79
Nicaragua	June 24, 1994	June 23, 1997	120.12	100.10
Pakistan	February 22, 1994	February 21, 1997	606.60	404.40
Senegal	August 29, 1994	August 28, 1997	130.79	83.23
Sierra Leone	March 28, 1994	March 27, 1997	88.78	20.22
Togo	September 16, 1994	September 15, 1997	65.16	43.44
Uganda	September 6, 1994	September 5, 1997	120.51	87.04
Viet Nam	November 11, 1994	November 10, 1997	362.40	302.00
Zimbabwe	September 11, 1992	September 10, 1995	200.60	48.70
Total			3,139.10	1,821.45
Total (Stand-by, Extended, Structural Adjustment, and Enhanced Structural Adjustment Arrangements)			31,010.01	15,813.08

Fund Accounts: Position to Date

(As of July 31, 1995 and Expressed in Millions of SDRs)

	Quota	Reserve Position in the Fund	Total Fund Credit and Loans Outstanding				Fund Holdings of Currency		SDR Department		
			Total Amount	Percent of Quota	Outstanding Purchases (GRA)	Outstanding Loans	Amount	Percent of Quota	Net Cumulative Allocation	Holdings of SDRs	
										Amount	Percent of Allocation
	(1)	(2)	(3)	(4)	(5)	(6)	(7)	(8)	(9)	(10)	(11)
All Countries	144,954.4	34,756.5	37,729.7	26.0	32,982.3	4,747.4	144,730.3	99.8	21,433.3	19,167.4	89.4
Industrial Countries	88,425.2	30,043.6	—	—	—	—	60,007.0	67.9	14,595.3	14,772.9	101.2
United States	26,526.8	9,465.2	—	—	—	—	17,061.3	64.3	4,899.5	7,365.6	150.3
Canada	4,320.3	793.5	—	—	—	—	3,526.9	81.6	779.3	781.0	100.2
Australia	2,333.2	338.8	—	—	—	—	1,994.4	85.5	470.6	43.2	9.2
Japan	8,241.5	5,277.3	—	—	—	—	4,589.6	55.7	891.7	1,942.4	217.8
New Zealand	650.1	105.0	—	—	—	—	545.1	83.9	141.3	.1	.1
Austria	1,188.3	453.5	—	—	—	—	734.9	61.8	179.1	128.5	71.8
Belgium	3,102.3	646.5	—	—	—	—	2,455.9	79.2	485.3	325.6	67.1
Denmark	1,069.9	353.1	—	—	—	—	716.8	67.0	178.9	101.9	57.0
Finland	861.8	232.6	—	—	—	—	629.2	73.0	142.7	213.8	149.8
France	7,414.6	1,773.0	—	—	—	—	5,641.6	76.1	1,079.9	627.2	58.1
Germany	8,241.5	3,251.0	—	—	—	—	4,990.6	60.6	1,210.8	1,307.3	108.0
Greece	587.6	113.7	—	—	—	—	473.9	80.7	103.5	.9	.8
Iceland	85.3	10.5	—	—	—	—	74.8	87.7	16.4	.2	1.0
Ireland	525.0	163.6	—	—	—	—	361.4	68.8	87.3	104.1	119.3
Italy	4,590.7	1,339.8	—	—	—	—	3,250.9	70.8	702.4	58.8	8.4
Luxembourg	135.5	22.9	—	—	—	—	112.6	83.1	17.0	7.3	43.3
Netherlands	3,444.2	1,025.5	—	—	—	—	2,418.7	70.2	530.3	580.3	109.4
Norway	1,104.6	578.7	—	—	—	—	525.9	47.6	167.8	271.5	161.8
Portugal	557.6	267.6	—	—	—	—	290.0	52.0	53.3	52.3	98.1
San Marino	10.0	2.4	—	—	—	—	7.6	76.5	—	.1	—
Spain	1,935.4	955.9	—	—	—	—	979.5	50.6	298.8	261.5	87.5
Sweden	1,614.0	451.4	—	—	—	—	1,162.6	72.0	246.5	239.0	96.9
Switzerland	2,470.4	863.2	—	—	—	—	1,607.2	65.1	—	33.4	—
United Kingdom	7,414.6	1,558.9	—	—	—	—	5,855.7	79.0	1,913.1	326.9	17.1
Developing Countries	56,529.2	4,713.0	37,729.7	66.7	32,982.3	4,747.4	84,723.3	149.9	6,838.1	4,394.5	64.3
Africa	8,287.6	160.6	6,736.1	81.3	3,948.2	2,788.0	12,075.6	145.7	1,382.5	179.3	13.0
Algeria	914.4	—	965.9	105.6	965.9	—	1,880.3	205.6	128.6	24.8	19.3
Angola	207.3	—	—	—	—	—	207.4	100.1	—	.1	—
Benin	45.3	2.1	57.2	126.3	—	57.2	43.2	95.4	9.4	.1	1.5
Botswana	36.6	19.3	—	—	—	—	17.3	47.4	4.4	26.2	601.6
Burkina Faso	44.2	7.2	41.7	94.3	—	41.7	37.0	83.7	9.4	5.5	58.9
Burundi	57.2	5.9	36.3	63.4	—	36.3	51.3	89.8	13.7	.2	1.3
Cameroon	135.1	.4	27.9	20.7	27.9	—	162.7	120.4	24.5	.3	1.3
Cape Verde	7.0	—	—	—	—	—	7.0	100.0	.6	—	5.1
Central African Rep.	41.2	.1	25.9	62.8	10.7	15.2	51.8	125.8	9.3	.1	1.3
Chad	41.3	.3	26.8	65.0	10.3	16.5	51.3	124.3	9.4	.1	1.3
Comoros	6.5	.5	2.3	34.6	—	2.3	6.0	91.7	.7	.1	12.8
Congo	57.9	.5	13.0	22.5	13.0	—	70.4	121.6	9.7	.1	1.3
Côte d'Ivoire	238.2	.1	247.3	103.8	68.7	178.7	306.8	128.8	37.8	2.3	6.0
Djibouti	11.5	—	—	—	—	—	11.5	100.0	1.2	.1	7.0
Equatorial Guinea	24.3	—	12.7	52.2	—	12.7	24.3	100.0	5.8	.1	1.3
Eritrea	11.5	—	—	—	—	—	11.5	100.0	—	—	—
Ethiopia	98.3	7.0	49.4	50.3	—	49.4	91.3	92.9	11.2	.2	1.9
Gabon	110.3	.1	70.0	63.5	70.0	—	180.3	163.4	14.1	.2	1.3
Gambia, The	22.9	1.5	22.1	96.3	—	22.1	21.4	93.5	5.1	.2	4.2
Ghana	274.0	17.4	473.0	172.6	81.4	391.6	338.0	123.4	63.0	28.9	45.9
Guinea	78.7	.1	54.4	69.2	—	54.4	78.6	99.9	17.6	3.4	19.4
Guinea-Bissau	10.5	—	4.1	39.3	—	4.1	10.5	100.0	1.2	—	1.5
Kenya	199.4	12.3	266.4	133.6	—	266.4	187.1	93.8	37.0	3.4	9.2
Lesotho	23.9	3.5	26.6	111.2	—	26.6	20.4	85.3	3.7	.3	7.3
Liberia	71.3	—	225.8	316.6	201.5	24.3	272.8	382.6	21.0	—	—
Madagascar	90.4	—	54.3	60.1	—	54.3	90.4	100.0	19.3	.2	1.2
Malawi	50.9	2.2	73.2	143.8	12.7	60.5	61.4	120.6	11.0	1.9	16.9
Mali	68.9	8.7	85.3	123.9	—	85.3	60.2	87.3	15.9	.4	2.5
Mauritania	47.5	—	62.6	131.7	—	62.6	47.5	100.0	9.7	—	.1
Mauritius	73.3	7.3	—	—	—	—	66.0	90.0	15.7	21.5	136.6
Morocco	427.7	30.3	57.0	13.3	57.0	—	454.4	106.2	85.7	5.6	6.5
Mozambique	84.0	—	141.0	167.8	—	141.0	84.0	100.0	—	—	—
Namibia	99.6	—	—	—	—	—	99.6	100.0	—	—	—
Niger	48.3	8.6	38.4	79.5	11.1	27.3	50.8	105.3	9.4	.5	5.0
Nigeria	1,281.6	.1	—	—	—	—	1,281.6	100.0	157.2	—	—
Rwanda	59.5	9.8	8.8	14.7	—	8.8	49.7	83.6	13.7	1.5	11.2
São Tomé & Príncipe	5.5	—	.6	11.6	—	.6	5.5	100.1	.6	.1	18.5

Fund Accounts: Position to Date

(As of July 31, 1995 and Expressed in Millions of SDRs)

Quota	Reserve Position in the Fund	Total Fund Credit and Loans Outstanding				Fund Holdings of Currency		SDR Department			
		Total Amount	Percent of Quota	Outstanding Purchases (GRA)	Outstanding Loans	Amount	Percent of Quota	Net Cumulative Allocation	Holdings of SDRs		
									Amount	Percent of Allocation	
(1)	(2)	(3)	(4)	(5)	(6)	(7)	(8)	(9)	(10)	(11)	
											Africa (cont.)
118.9	1.2	224.0	188.4	30.9	193.1	148.6	125.0	24.5	1.7	6.9	Senegal
6.0	.8	—	—	—	—	5.2	86.6	.4	—	4.5	Seychelles
77.2	—	99.0	128.3	—	99.0	77.2	100.0	17.5	4.5	25.8	Sierra Leone
44.2	—	112.0	253.4	96.7	15.3	140.9	318.8	13.7	—	—	Somalia
1,365.4	.1	614.4	45.0	614.4	—	1,979.8	145.0	220.4	14.0	6.4	South Africa
169.7	—	650.5	383.3	586.1	64.4	755.8	445.4	52.2	—	—	Sudan
36.5	3.0	—	—	—	—	33.5	91.8	6.4	5.9	91.7	Swaziland
146.9	10.0	140.2	95.4	—	140.2	136.9	93.2	31.4	.4	1.3	Tanzania
54.3	.3	63.3	116.6	.9	62.4	54.9	101.1	11.0	.4	3.5	Togo
206.0	—	207.3	100.6	207.3	—	413.3	200.6	34.2	20.3	59.2	Tunisia
133.9	—	269.8	201.5	—	269.8	133.9	100.0	29.4	.7	2.5	Uganda
291.0	—	326.7	112.3	181.2	145.5	472.2	162.3	86.3	—	—	Zaïre
270.3	—	548.8	203.1	542.2	6.6	812.5	300.6	68.3	.3	.4	Zambia
261.3	.1	310.0	118.6	158.1	151.9	419.3	160.5	10.2	2.6	25.0	Zimbabwe
13,529.8	**2,548.4**	**5,164.6**	**38.2**	**3,579.2**	**1,585.4**	**14,560.9**	**107.6**	**2,043.7**	**730.5**	**35.7**	**Asia**
120.4	4.9	—	—	—	—	115.5	95.9	26.7	.3	1.2	Afghanistan, I.S. of
392.5	.1	453.2	115.5	—	453.2	392.4	100.0	47.1	63.0	133.6	Bangladesh
4.5	.6	—	—	—	—	3.9	87.3	—	.4	—	Bhutan
65.0	—	34.3	52.7	6.3	28.0	71.3	109.6	15.4	10.6	68.5	Cambodia
3,385.2	646.5	—	—	—	—	2,738.7	80.9	236.8	379.9	160.4	China, People's Rep.
51.1	10.0	—	—	—	—	41.1	80.5	7.0	7.5	108.3	Fiji
3,055.5	212.6	2,304.4	75.4	2,304.4	—	5,147.3	168.5	681.2	12.9	1.9	India
1,497.6	250.6	—	—	—	—	1,247.0	83.3	239.0	.9	.4	Indonesia
4.0	—	—	—	—	—	4.0	100.0	—	—	—	Kiribati
799.6	411.8	—	—	—	—	387.8	48.5	72.9	58.6	80.4	Korea
39.1	—	37.5	96.0	—	37.5	39.1	100.0	9.4	6.7	71.5	Lao P. D. Rep.
832.7	381.5	—	—	—	—	451.2	54.2	139.1	96.4	69.3	Malaysia
5.5	.9	—	—	—	—	4.6	84.0	.3	—	14.7	Maldives
2.5	—	—	—	—	—	2.5	100.0	—	—	—	Marshall Islands
3.5	—	—	—	—	—	3.5	100.0	—	.9	—	Micronesia, Fed.Sts.
37.1	—	33.6	90.7	9.5	24.1	46.6	125.7	—	.5	—	Mongolia
184.9	—	—	—	—	—	184.9	100.0	43.5	.5	1.2	Myanmar
52.0	5.7	35.1	67.4	—	35.1	46.3	89.0	8.1	.1	1.8	Nepal
758.2	.1	1,028.0	135.6	492.6	535.4	1,250.7	165.0	170.0	9.1	5.4	Pakistan
95.3	.1	23.9	25.1	23.9	—	119.2	125.1	9.3	.4	3.9	Papua New Guinea
633.4	87.1	609.6	96.2	609.6	—	1,156.0	182.5	116.6	16.3	14.0	Philippines
357.6	195.8	—	—	—	—	161.8	45.3	16.5	28.5	172.8	Singapore
7.5	.5	—	—	—	—	7.0	92.9	.7	—	2.4	Solomon Islands
303.6	20.2	411.6	135.6	—	411.6	283.4	93.3	70.9	1.4	1.9	Sri Lanka
573.9	315.1	—	—	—	—	258.8	45.1	84.7	26.6	31.4	Thailand
5.0	1.2	—	—	—	—	3.8	76.0	—	—	—	Tonga
12.5	2.5	—	—	—	—	10.0	80.1	—	.3	—	Vanuatu
241.6	—	193.4	80.0	133.0	60.4	374.6	155.0	47.7	6.6	13.9	Viet Nam
8.5	.7	—	—	—	—	7.8	92.2	1.1	2.0	176.7	Western Samoa
11,953.1	**264.6**	**9,312.4**	**77.9**	**9,257.7**	**54.7**	**20,869.1**	**174.6**	**374.2**	**486.3**	**130.0**	**Europe**
35.3	—	44.2	125.2	13.1	31.1	48.4	137.2	—	.3	—	Albania
67.5	—	37.1	55.0	37.1	—	104.6	155.0	—	20.2	—	Armenia
117.0	—	29.3	25.0	29.3	—	146.3	125.0	—	.3	—	Azerbaijan
280.4	—	140.2	50.0	140.2	—	420.6	150.0	—	.5	—	Belarus
464.9	32.6	572.6	123.2	572.6	—	1,004.8	216.1	—	2.0	—	Bulgaria
261.6	—	150.1	57.4	150.1	—	411.7	157.4	44.2	65.5	148.1	Croatia
100.0	25.5	—	—	—	—	74.6	74.6	19.4	.1	.6	Cyprus
589.6	—	—	—	—	—	589.6	100.0	—	.1	—	Czech Republic
46.5	—	62.8	135.0	62.8	—	109.3	235.0	—	.2	—	Estonia
111.0	—	61.1	55.0	61.1	—	172.1	155.0	—	.8	—	Georgia
754.8	56.1	693.9	91.9	693.9	—	1,392.6	184.5	—	12.0	—	Hungary
247.5	—	244.4	98.8	244.4	—	491.9	198.8	—	112.0	—	Kazakhstan
64.5	—	67.5	104.7	43.9	23.7	108.4	168.0	—	14.4	—	Kyrgyz Republic
91.5	—	109.8	120.0	109.8	—	201.3	220.0	—	.8	—	Latvia
103.5	—	155.3	150.0	155.3	—	258.8	250.0	—	9.0	—	Lithuania
49.6	—	28.5	57.4	28.5	—	78.1	157.4	8.4	.9	10.4	Macedonia, former YR
67.5	27.3	—	—	—	—	40.3	59.7	11.3	36.6	324.6	Malta
90.0	—	141.8	157.6	141.8	—	231.8	257.6	—	12.0	—	Moldova
988.5	77.1	—	—	—	—	911.4	92.2	—	4.7	—	Poland
754.1	—	785.0	104.1	785.0	—	1,539.1	204.1	76.0	15.2	20.1	Romania

Fund Accounts: Position to Date

(As of July 31, 1995 and Expressed in Millions of SDRs)

	Quota	Reserve Position in the Fund	Total Fund Credit and Loans Outstanding				Fund Holdings of Currency		SDR Department		
			Total Amount	Percent of Quota	Outstanding Purchases (GRA)	Outstanding Loans	Amount	Percent of Quota	Net Cumulative Allocation	Holdings of SDRs	
										Amount	Percent of Allocation
	(1)	(2)	(3)	(4)	(5)	(6)	(7)	(8)	(9)	(10)	(11)
Europe (cont.)											
Russia	4,313.1	.8	4,313.3	100.0	4,313.3	—	8,625.6	200.0	—	55.8	—
Slovak Republic	257.4	—	351.5	136.6	351.5	—	608.9	236.6	—	.4	—
Slovenia	150.5	12.9	3.6	2.4	3.6	—	141.2	93.8	25.4	.2	.7
Tajikistan	60.0	—	—	—	—	—	60.0	100.0	—	—	—
Turkey	642.0	32.3	385.5	60.0	385.5	—	995.2	155.0	112.3	7.4	6.6
Turkmenistan	48.0	—	—	—	—	—	48.0	100.0	—	—	—
Ukraine	997.3	—	808.0	81.0	808.0	—	1,805.3	181.0	—	114.2	—
Uzbekistan	199.5	—	49.9	25.0	49.9	—	249.4	125.0	—	.8	—
Middle East	**11,309.4**	**1,387.9**	**399.1**	**3.5**	**399.1**	—	**10,320.9**	**91.3**	**986.4**	**1,125.2**	**114.1**
Bahrain	82.8	43.0	—	—	—	—	39.8	48.1	6.2	11.1	179.8
Egypt	678.4	53.8	100.9	14.9	100.9	—	725.5	106.9	135.9	69.3	51.0
Iran, I.R. of	1,078.5	—	—	—	—	—	1,078.5	100.0	244.1	93.3	38.2
Iraq	504.0	—	—	—	—	—	504.0	100.0	68.5	—	—
Israel	666.2	—	156.3	23.5	156.3	—	822.5	123.5	106.4	3.7	3.5
Jordan	121.7	—	142.0	116.7	142.0	—	263.7	216.7	16.9	.7	4.3
Kuwait	995.2	139.8	—	—	—	—	855.4	86.0	26.7	58.3	217.8
Lebanon	146.0	18.8	—	—	—	—	127.2	87.1	4.4	11.9	269.9
Libya	817.6	319.0	—	—	—	—	498.6	61.0	58.8	337.5	574.3
Oman	119.4	34.5	—	—	—	—	85.0	71.2	6.3	6.9	109.5
Qatar	190.5	29.7	—	—	—	—	160.8	84.4	12.8	20.6	160.4
Saudi Arabia	5,130.6	578.3	—	—	—	—	4,552.3	88.7	195.5	432.7	221.3
Syrian Arab Republic	209.9	—	—	—	—	—	209.9	100.0	36.6	—	.1
United Arab Emirates	392.1	171.0	—	—	—	—	221.1	56.4	38.7	55.4	143.1
Yemen, Republic of	176.5	—	—	—	—	—	176.5	100.0	28.7	23.8	—
Western Hemisphere	**11,449.3**	**351.5**	**16,117.3**	**140.8**	**15,798.1**	**319.2**	**26,896.9**	**234.9**	**2,051.3**	**1,873.2**	**91.3**
Antigua and Barbuda	8.5	—	—	—	—	—	8.5	100.0	—	—	—
Argentina	1,537.1	—	3,738.8	243.2	3,738.8	—	5,275.9	343.2	318.4	454.1	142.6
Bahamas, The	94.9	6.2	—	—	—	—	88.7	93.4	10.2	—	.1
Barbados	48.9	—	33.0	67.5	33.0	—	81.9	167.5	8.0	.5	6.8
Belize	13.5	2.9	—	—	—	—	10.6	78.4	—	.4	—
Bolivia	126.2	8.9	171.9	136.2	—	171.9	117.3	93.0	26.7	26.9	100.7
Brazil	2,170.8	—	119.3	5.5	119.3	—	2,290.9	105.5	358.7	1.4	.4
Chile	621.7	—	157.5	25.3	157.5	—	779.1	125.3	121.9	4.6	3.8
Colombia	561.3	120.3	—	—	—	—	441.0	78.6	114.3	117.4	102.7
Costa Rica	119.0	8.7	24.2	20.4	24.2	—	134.5	113.0	23.7	.8	3.4
Dominica	6.0	—	1.4	23.8	—	1.4	6.0	99.9	.6	—	1.3
Dominican Republic	158.8	—	118.7	74.7	118.7	—	277.5	174.7	31.6	3.2	10.0
Ecuador	219.2	17.1	124.6	56.8	124.6	—	326.7	149.0	32.9	5.5	16.8
El Salvador	125.6	—	—	—	—	—	125.6	100.0	25.0	13.6	54.4
Grenada	8.5	—	—	—	—	—	8.5	100.0	.9	—	4.0
Guatemala	153.8	—	—	—	—	—	153.8	100.0	27.7	11.0	39.7
Guyana	67.2	—	119.6	178.0	20.2	99.4	87.4	130.0	14.5	3.6	24.8
Haiti	60.7	—	19.0	31.4	16.4	2.6	77.1	126.9	13.7	.8	5.8
Honduras	95.0	—	70.6	74.3	46.9	23.7	141.9	149.3	19.1	.3	1.7
Jamaica	200.9	—	192.7	95.9	192.7	—	393.7	196.0	40.6	3.3	8.1
Mexico	1,753.3	—	8,765.2	499.9	8,765.2	—	10,518.5	599.9	290.0	807.7	278.5
Nicaragua	96.1	—	30.7	31.9	10.6	20.0	106.8	111.1	19.5	.3	1.3
Panama	149.6	11.9	83.6	55.8	83.6	—	221.3	147.9	26.3	10.4	39.6
Paraguay	72.1	14.5	—	—	—	—	57.6	79.9	13.7	69.1	504.8
Peru	466.1	—	642.7	137.9	642.7	—	1,108.8	237.9	91.3	3.0	3.3
St. Kitts and Nevis	6.5	—	—	—	—	—	6.5	99.8	—	—	—
St. Lucia	11.0	—	—	—	—	—	11.0	100.0	.7	1.4	185.8
St. Vincent & Grens.	6.0	.5	—	—	—	—	5.5	91.7	.4	.1	23.2
Suriname	67.6	—	—	—	—	—	67.6	100.0	7.8	.1	1.2
Trinidad and Tobago	246.8	—	41.6	16.9	41.6	—	288.4	116.9	46.2	1.6	3.4
Uruguay	225.3	15.4	18.2	8.1	18.2	—	228.2	101.3	50.0	1.1	2.2
Venezuela	1,951.3	145.0	1,643.9	84.2	1,643.9	—	3,450.3	176.8	316.9	330.9	104.4
Memorandum Items											
Oil Exporting Ctys	14,872.8	1,667.9	2,609.8	17.5	2,609.8	—	15,815.0	106.3	1,493.0	1,361.2	91.2
Non-Oil Develop.Ctys	41,656.4	3,045.1	35,119.8	84.3	30,372.5	4,747.4	68,908.3	165.4	5,345.1	3,033.2	56.7

Column 6 is comprised of outstanding SAF, ESAF, and Trust Fund loans.

Column 10 does not report separately data on the SDR positions of the Fund's General Resources Account and of Other Holders. Data on the SDR Holdings of the Fund's General Resources Account and of Other Holders are reported in the foot-table to the table on SDRs.

Totals for **All Countries, Developing Countries,** and **Europe** also include positions in the Fund of the two successor states to Yugoslavia not shown separately (the Republic of Bosnia and Herzegovina and the Federal Republic of Yugoslavia [Serbia/Montenegro]).

Financing Components of Members' Outstanding Obligations to the Fund

(As of July 31, 1995 and Expressed in Millions of SDRs)

Total Fund Credit and Loans Outstanding	Outstanding Purchases (GRA)							Outstanding Loans			Trust Fund	
	Total Amount	Ordinary Resources				Borrowed Resources		SAF Arrangements	ESAF Arrangements			
		CCFF	STF	Stand-by/ Credit Tranche	Extended Fund Facility	SFF	EAR	SDA Resources	SDA Resources	ESAF Trust Resources	Administered Accounts	
(1)	(2)	(3)	(4)	(5)	(6)	(7)	(8)	(9)	(10)	(11)	(12)	
37,729.7	32,982.3	2,682.1	3,905.0	15,363.9	8,390.5	188.1	2,452.7	1,190.0	373.2	3,082.4	101.8	**All Countries**
—	—	—	—	—	—	—	—	—	—	—	—	**Industrial Countries**
—	—	—	—	—	—	—	—	—	—	—	—	United States
—	—	—	—	—	—	—	—	—	—	—	—	Canada
—	—	—	—	—	—	—	—	—	—	—	—	Australia
—	—	—	—	—	—	—	—	—	—	—	—	Japan
—	—	—	—	—	—	—	—	—	—	—	—	New Zealand
—	—	—	—	—	—	—	—	—	—	—	—	Austria
—	—	—	—	—	—	—	—	—	—	—	—	Belgium
—	—	—	—	—	—	—	—	—	—	—	—	Denmark
—	—	—	—	—	—	—	—	—	—	—	—	Finland
—	—	—	—	—	—	—	—	—	—	—	—	France
—	—	—	—	—	—	—	—	—	—	—	—	Germany
—	—	—	—	—	—	—	—	—	—	—	—	Greece
—	—	—	—	—	—	—	—	—	—	—	—	Iceland
—	—	—	—	—	—	—	—	—	—	—	—	Ireland
—	—	—	—	—	—	—	—	—	—	—	—	Italy
—	—	—	—	—	—	—	—	—	—	—	—	Luxembourg
—	—	—	—	—	—	—	—	—	—	—	—	Netherlands
—	—	—	—	—	—	—	—	—	—	—	—	Norway
—	—	—	—	—	—	—	—	—	—	—	—	Portugal
—	—	—	—	—	—	—	—	—	—	—	—	Spain
—	—	—	—	—	—	—	—	—	—	—	—	Sweden
—	—	—	—	—	—	—	—	—	—	—	—	Switzerland
—	—	—	—	—	—	—	—	—	—	—	—	United Kingdom
37,729.7	32,982.3	2,682.1	3,905.0	15,363.9	8,390.5	188.1	2,452.7	1,190.0	373.2	3,082.4	101.8	**Developing Countries**
6,736.1	3,948.2	1,281.8	—	1,094.3	742.0	188.1	642.1	569.2	301.1	1,816.0	101.8	**Africa**
965.9	965.9	274.3	—	535.2	156.4	—	—	—	—	—	—	Algeria
—	—	—	—	—	—	—	—	—	—	—	—	Angola
57.2	—	—	—	—	—	—	—	14.4	7.0	35.8	—	Benin
—	—	—	—	—	—	—	—	—	—	—	—	Botswana
41.7	—	—	—	—	—	—	—	6.3	15.8	19.6	—	Burkina Faso
36.3	—	—	—	—	—	—	—	17.1	—	19.2	—	Burundi
27.9	27.9	—	—	27.9	—	—	—	—	—	—	—	Cameroon
—	—	—	—	—	—	—	—	—	—	—	—	Cape Verde
25.9	10.7	—	—	10.7	—	—	—	15.2	—	—	—	Central African Rep.
26.8	10.3	—	—	10.3	—	—	—	16.5	—	—	—	Chad
2.3	—	—	—	—	—	—	—	2.3	—	—	—	Comoros
13.0	13.0	—	—	13.0	—	—	—	—	—	—	—	Congo
247.3	68.7	3.1	—	26.4	—	—	39.2	—	—	178.7	—	Côte d'Ivoire
—	—	—	—	—	—	—	—	—	—	—	—	Djibouti
12.7	—	—	—	—	—	—	—	8.1	3.0	1.7	—	Equatorial Guinea
49.4	—	—	—	—	—	—	—	49.4	—	—	—	Ethiopia
70.0	70.0	21.5	—	41.1	—	—	7.4	—	—	—	—	Gabon
22.1	—	—	—	—	—	—	—	3.6	2.6	15.8	—	Gambia, The
473.0	81.4	47.0	—	—	34.4	—	—	20.5	84.9	286.3	—	Ghana
54.4	—	—	—	—	—	—	—	19.7	—	34.7	—	Guinea
4.1	—	—	—	—	—	—	—	2.6	—	1.6	—	Guinea-Bissau
266.4	—	—	—	—	—	—	—	17.0	64.6	184.7	—	Kenya
26.6	—	—	—	—	—	—	—	8.5	—	18.1	—	Lesotho
225.8	201.5	34.7	—	45.8	—	36.7	84.3	—	—	—	24.3	Liberia
54.3	—	—	—	—	—	—	—	6.6	30.2	17.5	—	Madagascar
73.2	12.7	—	—	12.7	—	—	—	—	23.3	37.2	—	Malawi
85.3	—	—	—	—	—	—	—	20.8	10.2	54.3	—	Mali
62.6	—	—	—	—	—	—	—	7.1	6.1	49.3	—	Mauritania
—	—	—	—	—	—	—	—	—	—	—	—	Mauritius
57.0	57.0	—	—	19.1	—	—	37.9	—	—	—	—	Morocco
141.0	—	—	—	—	—	—	—	25.6	—	115.4	—	Mozambique
—	—	—	—	—	—	—	—	—	—	—	—	Namibia
38.4	11.1	—	—	11.1	—	—	—	7.8	4.9	14.6	—	Niger
—	—	—	—	—	—	—	—	—	—	—	—	Nigeria

Financing Components of Members' Outstanding Obligations to the Fund

(As of July 31, 1995 and Expressed in Millions of SDRs)

	Total Fund Credit and Loans Outstanding	Outstanding Purchases (GRA)							Outstanding Loans			Trust Fund
			Ordinary Resources				Borrowed Resources		SAF Arrangements	ESAF Arrangements		
		Total Amount	CCFF	STF	Stand-by/ Credit Tranche	Extended Fund Facility	SFF	EAR	SDA Resources	SDA Resources	ESAF Trust Resources	Administered Accounts
	(1)	(2)	(3)	(4)	(5)	(6)	(7)	(8)	(9)	(10)	(11)	(12)
Africa (cont.)												
Rwanda	8.8	—	—	—	—	—	—	—	8.8	—	—	—
São Tomé & Príncipe	.6	—	—	—	—	—	—	—	.6	—	—	—
Senegal	224.0	30.9	—	—	30.9	—	—	—	17.9	14.2	161.1	—
Seychelles	—	—	—	—	—	—	—	—	—	—	—	—
Sierra Leone	99.0	—	—	—	—	—	—	—	30.5	—	68.6	—
Somalia	112.0	96.7	28.5	—	12.6	—	—	55.5	8.8	—	—	6.5
South Africa	614.4	614.4	614.4	—	—	—	—	—	—	—	—	—
Sudan	650.5	586.1	82.2	—	89.0	118.8	151.3	144.8	—	—	—	64.4
Swaziland	—	—	—	—	—	—	—	—	—	—	—	—
Tanzania	140.2	—	—	—	—	—	—	—	54.6	—	85.6	—
Togo	63.3	.9	—	—	—	—	—	.9	4.6	17.5	40.3	—
Tunisia	207.3	207.3	—	—	—	207.3	—	—	—	—	—	—
Uganda	269.8	—	—	—	—	—	—	—	28.9	16.9	224.0	—
Zaïre	326.7	181.2	30.3	—	92.3	8.7	—	49.9	145.5	—	—	—
Zambia	548.8	542.2	145.7	—	116.1	58.3	—	222.1	—	—	—	6.6
Zimbabwe	310.0	158.1	—	—	—	158.1	—	—	—	—	151.9	—
Asia	**5,164.6**	**3,579.2**	**751.1**	**30.4**	**2,414.5**	**330.7**	—	**52.5**	**611.3**	—	**974.1**	—
Afghanistan, I.S. of	—	—	—	—	—	—	—	—	—	—	—	—
Bangladesh	453.2	—	—	—	—	—	—	—	108.2	—	345.0	—
Bhutan	—	—	—	—	—	—	—	—	—	—	—	—
Cambodia	34.3	6.3	—	6.3	—	—	—	—	—	—	28.0	—
China, People's Rep.	—	—	—	—	—	—	—	—	—	—	—	—
Fiji	—	—	—	—	—	—	—	—	—	—	—	—
India	2,304.4	2,304.4	555.4	—	1,699.4	—	—	49.6	—	—	—	—
Indonesia	—	—	—	—	—	—	—	—	—	—	—	—
Kiribati	—	—	—	—	—	—	—	—	—	—	—	—
Korea	—	—	—	—	—	—	—	—	—	—	—	—
Lao P. D. Rep.	37.5	—	—	—	—	—	—	—	19.9	—	17.6	—
Malaysia	—	—	—	—	—	—	—	—	—	—	—	—
Maldives	—	—	—	—	—	—	—	—	—	—	—	—
Mongolia	33.6	9.5	—	—	9.5	—	—	—	—	—	24.1	—
Myanmar	—	—	—	—	—	—	—	—	—	—	—	—
Nepal	35.1	—	—	—	—	—	—	—	18.3	—	16.8	—
Pakistan	1,028.0	492.6	91.8	—	277.6	123.2	—	—	333.2	—	202.2	—
Papua New Guinea	23.9	23.9	—	—	23.9	—	—	—	—	—	—	—
Philippines	609.6	609.6	103.9	—	295.3	207.5	—	2.9	—	—	—	—
Singapore	—	—	—	—	—	—	—	—	—	—	—	—
Solomon Islands	—	—	—	—	—	—	—	—	—	—	—	—
Sri Lanka	411.6	—	—	—	—	—	—	—	131.6	—	280.0	—
Thailand	—	—	—	—	—	—	—	—	—	—	—	—
Tonga	—	—	—	—	—	—	—	—	—	—	—	—
Vanuatu	—	—	—	—	—	—	—	—	—	—	—	—
Viet Nam	193.4	133.0	—	24.2	108.8	—	—	—	—	—	60.4	—
Western Samoa	—	—	—	—	—	—	—	—	—	—	—	—
Europe	**9,312.4**	**9,257.7**	**312.5**	**3,874.6**	**4,364.4**	**598.6**	—	**107.7**	—	—	**54.7**	—
Albania	44.2	13.1	—	—	13.1	—	—	—	—	—	31.1	—
Armenia	37.1	37.1	—	33.8	3.4	—	—	—	—	—	—	—
Azerbaijan	29.3	29.3	—	29.3	—	—	—	—	—	—	—	—
Belarus	140.2	140.2	—	140.2	—	—	—	—	—	—	—	—
Bulgaria	572.6	572.6	49.8	116.2	406.5	—	—	—	—	—	—	—
Croatia	150.1	150.1	—	130.8	13.1	—	—	6.2	—	—	—	—
Cyprus	—	—	—	—	—	—	—	—	—	—	—	—
Czech Republic	—	—	—	—	—	—	—	—	—	—	—	—
Estonia	62.8	62.8	—	23.3	39.5	—	—	—	—	—	—	—
Georgia	61.1	61.1	—	55.5	5.6	—	—	—	—	—	—	—
Hungary	693.9	693.9	68.0	—	68.6	557.2	—	—	—	—	—	—
Kazakhstan	244.4	244.4	—	123.8	120.7	—	—	—	—	—	—	—
Kyrgyz Republic	67.5	43.9	—	32.3	11.6	—	—	—	—	—	23.7	—
Latvia	109.8	109.8	—	45.8	64.1	—	—	—	—	—	—	—
Lithuania	155.3	155.3	—	51.8	62.1	41.4	—	—	—	—	—	—
Macedonia, former YR	28.5	28.5	—	24.8	2.5	—	—	1.2	—	—	—	—
Malta	—	—	—	—	—	—	—	—	—	—	—	—
Moldova	141.8	141.8	25.7	45.0	71.1	—	—	—	—	—	—	—

Financing Components of Members' Outstanding Obligations to the Fund

(As of July 31, 1995 and Expressed in Millions of SDRs)

Total Fund Credit and Loans Outstanding	Total Amount	Outstanding Purchases (GRA)						Outstanding Loans			Trust Fund	
		Ordinary Resources				Borrowed Resources		SAF Arrangements	ESAF Arrangements			
		CCFF	STF	Stand-by/ Credit Tranche	Extended Fund Facility	SFF	EAR	SDA Resources	SDA Resources	ESAF Trust Resources	Administered Accounts	
(1)	(2)	(3)	(4)	(5)	(6)	(7)	(8)	(9)	(10)	(11)	(12)	
												Europe (cont.)
—	—	—	—	—	—	—	—	—	—	—	—	Poland
785.0	785.0	112.2	188.5	484.3	—	—	—	—	—	—	—	Romania
4,313.3	4,313.3	—	2,156.6	2,156.7	—	—	—	—	—	—	—	Russia
351.5	351.5	56.8	128.7	101.5	—	—	64.4	—	—	—	—	Slovak Republic
3.6	3.6	—	—	—	—	—	3.6	—	—	—	—	Slovenia
385.5	385.5	—	—	385.5	—	—	—	—	—	—	—	Turkey
808.0	808.0	—	498.7	309.3	—	—	—	—	—	—	—	Ukraine
49.9	49.9	—	49.9	—	—	—	—	—	—	—	—	Uzbekistan
399.1	399.1	156.3	—	144.3	98.5	—	—	—	—	—	—	**Middle East**
—	—	—	—	—	—	—	—	—	—	—	—	Bahrain
100.9	100.9	—	—	100.9	—	—	—	—	—	—	—	Egypt
—	—	—	—	—	—	—	—	—	—	—	—	Iran, I.R. of
—	—	—	—	—	—	—	—	—	—	—	—	Iraq
156.3	156.3	156.3	—	—	—	—	—	—	—	—	—	Israel
142.0	142.0	—	—	43.5	98.5	—	—	—	—	—	—	Jordan
—	—	—	—	—	—	—	—	—	—	—	—	Kuwait
—	—	—	—	—	—	—	—	—	—	—	—	Lebanon
—	—	—	—	—	—	—	—	—	—	—	—	Libya
—	—	—	—	—	—	—	—	—	—	—	—	Oman
—	—	—	—	—	—	—	—	—	—	—	—	Qatar
—	—	—	—	—	—	—	—	—	—	—	—	Saudi Arabia
—	—	—	—	—	—	—	—	—	—	—	—	Syrian Arab Republic
—	—	—	—	—	—	—	—	—	—	—	—	United Arab Emirates
—	—	—	—	—	—	—	—	—	—	—	—	Yemen, Republic of
16,117.3	15,798.1	180.4	—	7,346.5	6,620.7	—	1,650.4	9.5	72.1	237.6	—	**Western Hemisphere**
—	—	—	—	—	—	—	—	—	—	—	—	Antigua and Barbuda
3,738.8	3,738.8	—	—	322.3	3,251.7	—	164.8	—	—	—	—	Argentina
—	—	—	—	—	—	—	—	—	—	—	—	Bahamas, The
33.0	33.0	19.4	—	13.6	—	—	—	—	—	—	—	Barbados
—	—	—	—	—	—	—	—	—	—	—	—	Belize
171.9	—	—	—	—	—	—	—	5.5	37.6	128.8	—	Bolivia
119.3	119.3	—	—	119.3	—	—	—	—	—	—	—	Brazil
157.5	157.5	—	—	—	157.5	—	—	—	—	—	—	Chile
—	—	—	—	—	—	—	—	—	—	—	—	Colombia
24.2	24.2	12.6	—	11.6	—	—	—	—	—	—	—	Costa Rica
1.4	—	—	—	—	—	—	—	1.4	—	—	—	Dominica
118.7	118.7	62.6	—	56.0	—	—	—	—	—	—	—	Dominican Republic
124.6	124.6	—	—	112.8	—	—	11.8	—	—	—	—	Ecuador
—	—	—	—	—	—	—	—	—	—	—	—	El Salvador
—	—	—	—	—	—	—	—	—	—	—	—	Grenada
—	—	—	—	—	—	—	—	—	—	—	—	Guatemala
119.6	20.2	—	—	3.9	—	—	16.2	—	34.4	65.0	—	Guyana
19.0	16.4	—	—	16.4	—	—	—	2.6	—	—	—	Haiti
70.6	46.9	38.6	—	8.3	—	—	—	—	—	23.7	—	Honduras
192.7	192.7	15.1	—	46.4	86.8	—	44.4	—	—	—	—	Jamaica
8,765.2	8,765.2	—	—	6,549.9	883.5	—	1,331.7	—	—	—	—	Mexico
30.7	10.6	—	—	10.6	—	—	—	—	—	20.0	—	Nicaragua
83.6	83.6	32.1	—	51.4	—	—	—	—	—	—	—	Panama
—	—	—	—	—	—	—	—	—	—	—	—	Paraguay
642.7	642.7	—	—	—	642.7	—	—	—	—	—	—	Peru
—	—	—	—	—	—	—	—	—	—	—	—	St. Kitts and Nevis
—	—	—	—	—	—	—	—	—	—	—	—	St. Lucia
—	—	—	—	—	—	—	—	—	—	—	—	St. Vincent & Grens.
—	—	—	—	—	—	—	—	—	—	—	—	Suriname
41.6	41.6	—	—	5.5	—	—	36.1	—	—	—	—	Trinidad and Tobago
18.2	18.2	—	—	18.2	—	—	—	—	—	—	—	Uruguay
1,643.9	1,643.9	—	—	—	1,598.6	—	45.3	—	—	—	—	Venezuela
												Memorandum Items
2,609.8	2,609.8	274.3	—	535.2	1,755.0	—	45.3	—	—	—	—	Oil Exporting Ctys
35,119.8	30,372.5	2,407.8	3,905.0	14,828.7	6,635.5	188.1	2,407.4	1,190.0	373.2	3,082.4	101.8	Non-Oil Develop.Ctys

Purchases*

Expressed in Millions of SDRs

	1965	1966	1967	1968	1969	1970	1971	1972	1973	1974	1975	1976	1977	1978	1979
World	1,939.4	744.6	560.1	1,932.2	1,721.3	948.9	379.9	649.7	342.0	3,087.6	3,935.5	6,019.1	3,344.5	1,208.8	1,695.7
Industrial Countries	1,430.7	142.0	155.5	1,403.8	1,354.6	635.0	—	—	—	1,512.5	1,973.6	2,627.8	2,415.7	98.8	23.8
United States	—	—	—	—	—	—	—	—	—	—	—	—	—	—	—
Canada	—	—	—	—	—	—	—	—	—	—	—	—	—	—	—
Australia	—	—	—	—	—	—	—	—	—	—	—	332.5	—	—	23.8
Japan	—	—	—	—	—	—	—	—	—	—	—	—	—	—	—
New Zealand	30.7	8.0	89.2	—	—	—	—	—	—	85.7	156.6	147.9	—	—	—
Belgium	—	—	—	—	—	—	—	—	—	—	—	—	—	—	—
Denmark	—	—	—	—	—	—	—	—	—	—	—	—	—	—	—
Finland	—	—	62.5	—	—	—	—	—	—	—	71.3	115.1	—	—	—
France	—	—	—	—	500.8	485.0	—	—	—	—	—	—	—	—	—
Germany	—	—	—	—	—	—	—	—	—	—	—	—	—	—	—
Greece	—	—	—	—	—	—	—	—	—	36.2	153.5	58.0	—	—	—
Iceland	—	—	3.8	3.8	3.8	—	—	—	—	15.5	15.9	25.1	—	—	—
Ireland	—	11.5	—	—	—	—	—	—	—	—	—	—	—	—	—
Italy	—	—	—	—	—	—	—	—	—	1,375.1	1,080.2	—	—	90.0	—
Luxembourg	—	—	—	—	—	—	—	—	—	—	—	—	—	—	—
Netherlands	—	—	—	—	—	—	—	—	—	—	—	—	—	—	—
Norway	—	—	—	—	—	—	—	—	—	—	—	—	—	—	—
Portugal	—	—	—	—	—	—	—	—	—	—	—	173.3	75.7	—	—
Spain	—	—	—	—	—	—	—	—	—	—	496.2	75.9	—	98.8	—
United Kingdom	1,400.0	122.5	—	1,400.0	850.0	150.0	—	—	—	—	—	1,700.0	2,250.0	—	—
Developing Countries	508.7	602.6	404.6	528.4	366.7	313.9	379.9	649.7	342.0	1,575.2	1,961.9	3,391.3	928.9	1,110.1	1,671.9
Africa	46.0	87.6	74.4	84.7	33.6	32.1	44.8	83.3	29.5	166.4	326.6	881.4	303.9	285.8	517.3
Algeria	—	—	—	—	—	—	—	—	—	—	—	—	—	—	—
Benin	—	—	—	—	—	—	—	—	—	—	—	—	—	—	—
Burkina Faso	—	—	—	—	—	—	—	—	—	—	—	—	—	—	—
Burundi	1.9	2.9	4.7	4.5	3.5	2.5	1.5	—	—	.1	1.2	—	—	—	9.5
Cameroon	—	—	—	—	—	—	—	—	—	4.6	7.5	21.8	—	—	—
Cape Verde	—	—	—	—	—	—	—	—	—	—	—	—	—	—	—
Central African Rep.	—	—	—	—	—	—	—	—	—	2.7	2.3	6.1	—	—	—
Chad	—	—	—	—	—	2.4	—	—	—	5.0	—	6.5	—	—	—
Comoros	—	—	—	—	—	—	—	—	—	—	—	—	—	—	—
Congo	—	—	—	—	—	—	—	—	—	—	—	—	11.2	3.3	2.0
Côte d'Ivoire	—	—	—	—	—	—	—	—	—	11.2	—	36.4	—	—	—
Djibouti	—	—	—	—	—	—	—	—	—	—	—	—	—	—	—
Equatorial Guinea	—	—	—	—	—	—	—	—	—	—	—	—	—	—	—
Ethiopia	—	—	—	—	—	—	—	—	—	—	—	—	—	—	36.0
Gabon	—	—	—	—	—	—	—	—	—	—	—	—	—	7.5	7.5
Gambia, The	—	—	—	—	—	—	—	—	—	—	—	—	3.5	7.0	—
Ghana	—	46.8	25.0	10.0	5.0	2.0	—	—	—	—	38.6	—	—	—	32.0
Guinea	—	—	—	—	1.0	4.2	—	—	—	9.5	—	—	8.7	—	3.0
Guinea-Bissau	—	—	—	—	—	—	—	—	—	—	—	—	—	—	1.1
Kenya	—	—	—	—	—	—	—	—	—	32.0	48.5	27.1	—	—	86.3
Lesotho	—	—	—	—	—	—	—	—	—	—	—	—	—	—	—
Liberia	3.0	5.2	5.2	3.4	1.4	2.0	1.0	—	1.5	—	3.5	10.9	9.4	—	29.8
Madagascar	—	—	—	—	—	—	—	—	—	—	—	2.4	1.4	5.4	22.1
Malawi	—	—	—	—	—	—	—	—	—	—	—	—	—	—	—
Mali	5.0	1.0	3.0	4.0	2.5	1.5	2.5	2.0	—	4.0	1.0	4.0	—	—	—
Mauritania	—	—	—	—	—	—	—	—	—	—	—	11.8	4.7	—	28.0
Mauritius	—	—	—	—	3.7	—	—	—	—	—	—	—	11.0	—	—
Morocco	—	—	—	36.5	10.0	10.0	8.3	—	—	—	—	115.5	—	56.0	—
Mozambique	—	—	—	—	—	—	—	—	—	—	—	—	—	—	—
Niger	—	—	—	—	—	—	—	—	—	—	—	—	—	—	—
Nigeria	—	—	—	—	—	—	1.5	—	—	—	—	—	—	—	—
Rwanda	—	4.7	2.0	3.0	2.0	—	—	—	—	—	—	—	—	—	—
São Tomé & Príncipe	—	—	—	—	—	—	—	—	—	—	—	—	—	—	—
Senegal	—	—	—	—	—	—	—	—	—	—	25.4	—	—	21.0	10.5
Seychelles	—	—	—	—	—	—	—	—	—	—	—	—	—	—	—
Sierra Leone	—	—	4.6	—	—	—	—	—	—	4.3	.6	17.5	7.0	—	7.5
Somalia	5.6	.9	4.0	3.7	—	—	—	—	—	—	—	—	—	—	—
South Africa	—	—	—	—	—	—	—	—	—	—	—	390.0	162.0	—	—
Sudan	18.8	17.5	19.0	10.0	2.5	—	—	32.5	9.0	45.7	48.3	26.7	—	42.3	83.2
Swaziland	—	—	—	—	—	—	—	—	—	—	—	—	—	—	—
Tanzania	—	—	—	—	—	—	—	—	—	38.9	23.8	21.0	4.7	—	34.0
Togo	—	—	—	—	—	—	—	—	—	—	—	—	7.5	—	—
Tunisia	11.8	8.5	7.0	9.6	2.0	7.5	2.5	—	—	—	—	—	24.0	—	—
Uganda	—	—	—	—	—	—	10.1	—	—	5.0	14.2	20.0	—	—	5.0
Zaïre	—	—	—	—	—	—	—	28.3	—	—	45.0	130.0	33.3	—	20.0
Zambia	—	—	—	—	—	—	19.0	19.0	19.0	—	56.9	38.3	19.0	148.8	100.0
Zimbabwe	—	—	—	—	—	—	—	—	—	—	—	—	—	—	—
Asia	262.2	273.8	127.3	180.6	126.8	91.0	65.7	217.9	144.6	925.2	719.3	752.8	293.8	302.1	355.7
Afghanistan, I.S. of	1.7	9.1	4.0	4.8	13.0	4.0	—	—	7.5	2.5	8.5	—	—	—	—
Bangladesh	—	—	—	—	—	—	—	62.5	—	70.3	58.8	97.2	—	—	57.0
Cambodia	—	—	—	—	—	—	—	6.3	6.3	—	—	—	—	—	—
China, People's Rep.	—	—	—	—	—	—	—	—	—	—	—	—	—	—	—
Fiji	—	—	—	—	—	—	—	—	—	.3	—	—	6.5	—	—
India	200.0	225.0	90.0	—	—	—	—	—	—	497.0	201.3	—	—	—	—
Indonesia	—	—	—	45.0	65.8	38.0	2.9	2.7	—	—	—	—	—	—	—
Kiribati	—	—	—	—	—	—	—	—	—	—	—	—	—	—	—
Korea	—	—	—	—	—	—	—	—	—	110.0	107.3	104.4	—	—	—
Lao P. D. Rep.	—	—	—	—	—	—	—	—	—	—	3.3	3.3	—	4.0	—
Malaysia	—	—	—	—	—	—	7.3	—	—	—	—	93.0	—	—	—
Maldives	—	—	—	—	—	—	—	—	—	—	—	—	—	—	—

*Excludes reserve tranche purchases

Purchases*

Expressed in Millions of SDRs

1980	1981	1982	1983	1984	1985	1986	1987	1988	1989	1990	1991	1992	1993	1994	
3,393.5	6,771.3	7,448.0	12,618.8	7,291.2	4,013.9	3,819.7	3,298.8	2,668.7	3,477.7	4,270.0	7,386.5	4,791.1	5,042.2	4,979.5	**World**
—	—	54.0	354.8	217.2	—	—	—	—	—	—	—	—	—	—	**Industrial Countries**
—	—	—	—	—	—	—	—	—	—	—	—	—	—	—	United States
—	—	—	—	—	—	—	—	—	—	—	—	—	—	—	Canada
—	—	32.5	—	—	—	—	—	—	—	—	—	—	—	—	Australia
—	—	—	—	—	—	—	—	—	—	—	—	—	—	—	Japan
—	—	—	—	—	—	—	—	—	—	—	—	—	—	—	New Zealand
—	—	—	—	—	—	—	—	—	—	—	—	—	—	—	Belgium
—	—	—	—	—	—	—	—	—	—	—	—	—	—	—	Denmark
—	—	—	—	—	—	—	—	—	—	—	—	—	—	—	Finland
—	—	—	—	—	—	—	—	—	—	—	—	—	—	—	France
—	—	—	—	—	—	—	—	—	—	—	—	—	—	—	Germany
—	—	—	—	—	—	—	—	—	—	—	—	—	—	—	Greece
—	—	21.5	—	—	—	—	—	—	—	—	—	—	—	—	Iceland
—	—	—	—	—	—	—	—	—	—	—	—	—	—	—	Ireland
—	—	—	—	—	—	—	—	—	—	—	—	—	—	—	Italy
—	—	—	—	—	—	—	—	—	—	—	—	—	—	—	Luxembourg
—	—	—	—	—	—	—	—	—	—	—	—	—	—	—	Netherlands
—	—	—	—	—	—	—	—	—	—	—	—	—	—	—	Norway
—	—	—	354.8	217.2	—	—	—	—	—	—	—	—	—	—	Portugal
—	—	—	—	—	—	—	—	—	—	—	—	—	—	—	Spain
—	—	—	—	—	—	—	—	—	—	—	—	—	—	—	United Kingdom
3,393.5	6,771.3	7,394.1	12,264.1	7,074.0	4,013.9	3,819.7	3,298.8	2,668.7	3,477.7	4,270.0	7,386.5	4,791.1	5,042.2	4,979.5	**Developing Countries**
821.7	1,859.7	2,118.1	1,702.2	1,188.6	941.8	749.9	479.3	589.7	742.4	176.3	425.6	172.7	678.8	761.5	**Africa**
—	—	—	—	—	—	—	—	—	—	470.9	—	225.0	—	587.5	Algeria
—	—	—	—	—	—	—	—	—	—	—	—	—	—	—	Benin
—	—	—	—	—	—	—	—	—	—	—	—	—	—	—	Burkina Faso
—	—	—	—	—	—	—	—	—	—	—	—	—	—	—	Burundi
—	—	—	—	—	—	—	—	69.5	15.5	—	8.0	—	—	21.9	Cameroon
—	—	—	—	—	—	—	—	—	—	—	—	—	—	—	Cape Verde
4.0	17.0	2.4	4.5	5.0	11.0	6.5	1.0	—	—	—	—	—	—	10.7	Central African Rep.
—	7.1	—	—	—	7.0	—	—	—	—	—	—	—	—	10.3	Chad
—	—	—	—	—	—	—	—	—	—	—	—	—	—	—	Comoros
—	—	—	—	—	—	9.5	—	—	—	4.0	—	—	—	12.5	Congo
—	319.2	115.4	154.9	41.4	60.4	50.5	—	89.8	29.3	112.7	33.1	—	—	—	Côte d'Ivoire
—	—	—	—	—	—	—	—	—	—	—	—	—	—	—	Djibouti
9.4	7.2	—	—	—	5.4	—	—	—	—	—	—	—	—	—	Equatorial Guinea
—	62.0	23.5	—	—	—	35.3	—	—	—	—	—	—	—	—	Ethiopia
—	—	—	—	—	—	27.4	15.1	56.2	4.0	6.5	4.0	—	—	44.7	Gabon
1.6	9.0	16.9	—	2.6	—	5.7	4.1	—	—	—	—	—	—	—	Gambia, The
—	—	—	263.6	213.6	120.0	32.7	71.6	75.0	—	—	—	—	47.0	—	Ghana
—	—	11.5	—	—	—	15.0	6.0	—	—	—	—	—	—	—	Guinea
—	1.9	—	—	1.9	—	—	—	—	—	—	—	—	—	—	Guinea-Bissau
60.0	30.0	150.4	129.8	46.2	123.1	—	—	102.6	—	—	—	—	—	—	Kenya
—	—	—	—	—	—	—	—	—	—	—	—	—	—	—	Lesotho
18.4	46.6	61.7	58.0	35.5	—	—	—	—	—	—	—	—	—	—	Liberia
39.2	39.0	52.4	10.2	41.4	29.0	44.2	20.0	7.8	—	—	—	—	—	—	Madagascar
24.4	30.0	10.9	34.2	37.8	23.0	—	—	9.3	—	—	—	—	—	12.7	Malawi
5.1	—	25.4	15.0	24.0	13.0	9.8	—	2.5	5.1	5.1	—	—	—	—	Mali
19.4	10.3	15.5	—	—	9.6	11.7	8.7	4.0	—	—	—	—	—	—	Mauritania
35.0	68.0	22.5	28.4	24.8	35.5	21.0	—	—	—	—	—	—	—	—	Mauritius
184.5	192.8	433.3	114.4	180.0	215.1	30.0	160.0	110.0	140.0	48.0	—	18.4	—	—	Morocco
—	—	—	—	—	—	—	—	—	—	—	—	—	—	—	Mozambique
—	—	—	30.8	14.4	15.5	12.8	8.1	—	—	—	—	—	—	11.1	Niger
—	—	—	—	—	—	—	—	—	—	—	—	—	—	—	Nigeria
—	—	—	—	—	—	—	—	—	—	—	—	—	—	—	Rwanda
—	—	—	—	—	—	—	—	—	—	—	—	—	—	—	São Tomé & Príncipe
43.3	57.7	53.2	31.5	31.5	55.6	32.5	30.9	12.9	—	—	—	—	—	30.9	Senegal
—	—	—	—	—	—	—	—	—	—	—	—	—	—	—	Seychelles
9.5	33.5	—	20.7	19.0	—	8.0	—	—	—	—	—	—	—	—	Sierra Leone
6.0	25.9	32.3	45.0	—	34.6	18.1	5.5	—	—	—	—	—	—	—	Somalia
—	—	795.0	—	—	—	—	—	—	—	—	—	—	614.4	—	South Africa
142.8	165.6	70.0	183.6	45.5	—	—	—	—	—	—	—	—	—	—	Sudan
—	—	—	10.0	—	—	—	—	—	—	—	—	—	—	—	Swaziland
40.0	15.9	—	—	—	—	33.0	12.5	—	—	—	—	—	—	—	Tanzania
13.3	7.3	—	19.4	18.0	15.0	12.0	—	10.4	2.6	—	—	—	—	—	Togo
—	—	—	—	—	—	149.7	41.0	15.0	—	—	155.5	51.8	—	—	Tunisia
37.5	122.5	85.0	106.5	21.0	—	—	25.0	24.8	—	—	—	—	—	—	Uganda
78.4	194.6	106.9	114.5	158.0	169.0	80.6	69.8	—	—	75.0	—	—	—	—	Zaïre
50.0	359.3	34.0	173.7	147.5	—	103.8	—	—	—	—	—	—	—	—	Zambia
—	37.5	—	153.6	79.6	—	—	—	—	—	—	—	102.5	17.4	19.1	Zimbabwe
1,344.8	3,121.2	2,395.4	3,206.3	1,275.9	896.6	1,156.2	729.1	250.7	430.4	42.8	2,456.3	1,452.0	755.3	220.2	**Asia**
—	—	—	—	—	—	—	—	—	—	—	—	—	—	—	Afghanistan, I.S. of
142.0	106.0	131.2	68.4	—	91.0	96.0	136.9	71.9	—	—	—	—	—	—	Bangladesh
—	—	—	—	—	—	—	—	—	—	—	—	—	6.3	—	Cambodia
—	450.0	—	—	—	—	597.7	—	—	—	—	—	—	—	—	China, People's Rep.
—	—	13.5	—	—	4.8	—	—	—	—	—	—	—	—	—	Fiji
266.0	300.0	1,500.0	1,500.0	600.0	—	—	—	—	—	—	1,988.9	1,109.0	462.0	—	India
—	—	—	425.1	—	—	—	462.9	—	—	—	—	—	—	—	Indonesia
—	—	—	—	—	—	—	—	—	—	—	—	—	—	—	Kiribati
480.0	576.0	106.2	192.0	567.6	135.9	120.0	—	—	—	—	—	—	—	—	Korea
8.0	6.0	—	—	—	—	—	—	—	—	—	—	—	—	—	Lao P. D. Rep.
—	189.8	58.5	113.0	—	—	—	—	—	—	—	—	—	—	—	Malaysia
—	—	—	—	—	—	—	—	—	—	—	—	—	—	—	Maldives

*Excludes reserve tranche purchases

Purchases*

	1965	1966	1967	1968	1969	1970	1971	1972	1973	1974	1975	1976	1977	1978	1979
					Expressed in Millions of SDRs										
Asia (cont.)															
Mongolia	—	—	—	—	—	—	—	—	—	—	—	—	—	—	—
Myanmar	—	—	7.5	—	—	12.0	6.5	—	13.5	29.5	9.5	—	25.0	25.0	15.0
Nepal	—	—	—	—	—	—	—	—	—	—	—	4.5	—	9.5	—
Pakistan	37.5	9.5	—	40.0	35.0	—	—	84.0	60.0	129.9	161.4	107.2	67.0	40.0	21.2
Papua New Guinea	—	—	—	—	—	—	—	—	—	—	—	24.8	—	—	—
Philippines	—	—	—	55.0	—	27.5	35.0	35.0	38.8	38.8	125.9	222.7	108.8	93.1	135.5
Solomon Islands	—	—	—	—	—	—	—	—	—	—	—	—	—	—	1.1
Sri Lanka	23.0	30.3	25.8	35.8	13.0	9.5	14.0	25.3	18.6	46.9	42.1	28.2	55.0	38.0	80.0
Thailand	—	—	—	—	—	—	—	2.2	—	—	—	67.0	—	68.8	45.3
Viet Nam	—	—	—	—	—	—	—	—	—	—	—	—	31.0	22.5	—
Western Samoa	—	—	—	—	—	—	—	—	—	—	1.3	.7	.5	1.3	.7
Europe	50.0	59.0	72.0	27.0	10.0	75.0	91.8	31.8	47.5	145.4	265.5	499.7	72.5	203.6	328.9
Albania	—	—	—	—	—	—	—	—	—	—	—	—	—	—	—
Armenia	—	—	—	—	—	—	—	—	—	—	—	—	—	—	—
Belarus	—	—	—	—	—	—	—	—	—	—	—	—	—	—	—
Bulgaria	—	—	—	—	—	—	—	—	—	—	—	—	—	—	—
Croatia	—	—	—	—	—	—	—	—	—	—	—	—	—	—	—
Cyprus	—	—	—	—	—	—	—	—	—	6.4	1.7	35.0	—	—	9.9
Czech Republic	—	—	—	—	—	—	—	—	—	—	—	—	—	—	—
Czechoslovakia	—	—	—	—	—	—	—	—	—	—	—	—	—	—	—
Estonia	—	—	—	—	—	—	—	—	—	—	—	—	—	—	—
Georgia	—	—	—	—	—	—	—	—	—	—	—	—	—	—	—
Hungary	—	—	—	—	—	—	—	—	—	—	—	—	—	—	—
Kazakhstan	—	—	—	—	—	—	—	—	—	—	—	—	—	—	—
Kyrgyz Republic	—	—	—	—	—	—	—	—	—	—	—	—	—	—	—
Latvia	—	—	—	—	—	—	—	—	—	—	—	—	—	—	—
Lithuania	—	—	—	—	—	—	—	—	—	—	—	—	—	—	—
Macedonia, former YR	—	—	—	—	—	—	—	—	—	—	—	—	—	—	—
Moldova	—	—	—	—	—	—	—	—	—	—	—	—	—	—	—
Poland	—	—	—	—	—	—	—	—	—	—	—	—	—	—	—
Romania	—	—	—	—	—	—	—	—	—	47.5	—	40.0	150.0	72.5	39.1	41.3
Russia	—	—	—	—	—	—	—	—	—	—	—	—	—	—	—
Slovak Republic	—	—	—	—	—	—	—	—	—	—	—	—	—	—	—
Turkey	—	21.5	27.0	27.0	10.0	75.0	15.0	—	—	—	207.6	129.2	—	164.5	70.0
Ukraine	—	—	—	—	—	—	—	—	—	—	—	—	—	—	—
Uzbekistan	—	—	—	—	—	—	—	—	—	—	—	—	—	—	—
Yugoslavia, SFR	50.0	37.5	45.0	—	—	—	76.8	31.8	—	139.0	16.2	185.5	—	—	207.8
Middle East	15.0	10.8	29.5	63.0	22.5	17.5	56.5	25.0	49.9	81.8	190.1	215.9	105.0	147.4	—
Bahrain	—	—	—	—	—	—	—	—	—	—	—	—	—	—	—
Egypt	15.0	7.5	—	63.0	—	17.5	32.0	—	47.0	40.0	—	125.7	105.0	75.0	—
Iran, I.R. of	—	—	—	—	—	—	—	—	—	—	—	—	—	—	—
Iraq	—	—	20.0	—	—	—	—	—	—	—	—	—	—	—	—
Israel	—	—	—	—	22.5	—	20.0	—	—	32.5	175.8	77.0	—	72.4	—
Jordan	—	—	—	—	—	—	4.5	—	2.9	—	—	—	—	—	—
Syrian Arab Republic	—	3.3	9.5	—	—	—	—	25.0	—	—	—	—	—	—	—
Yemen Arab Rep.	—	—	—	—	—	—	—	—	—	—	—	—	—	—	—
Yemen, P.D. Rep.	—	—	—	—	—	—	—	—	—	—	9.3	14.3	13.2	—	—
Yemen, Republic of	—	—	—	—	—	—	—	—	—	—	—	—	—	—	—
Western Hemisphere	135.5	171.5	101.5	173.1	173.9	98.2	121.2	291.8	70.5	256.3	460.4	1,041.5	153.7	171.1	470.1
Antigua and Barbuda	—	—	—	—	—	—	—	—	—	—	—	—	—	—	—
Argentina	—	47.5	—	—	—	—	—	174.0	—	—	186.1	269.5	—	—	—
Barbados	—	—	—	—	—	—	—	—	—	—	—	—	6.5	—	—
Belize	—	—	—	—	—	—	—	—	—	—	—	—	—	—	—
Bolivia	—	—	—	5.1	11.0	—	4.5	4.3	18.2	—	4.7	—	—	15.0	—
Brazil	75.0	—	—	—	—	—	—	—	—	—	—	—	—	—	—
Chile	36.0	30.0	10.0	43.3	29.0	—	39.5	39.5	—	120.5	176.8	124.4	—	—	—
Colombia	—	37.8	71.4	34.8	33.3	29.3	30.0	—	—	—	—	—	—	—	—
Costa Rica	10.0	6.8	2.8	—	—	—	—	—	—	18.8	12.0	6.8	—	—	20.5
Dominica	—	—	—	—	—	—	—	—	—	—	—	—	—	—	1.9
Dominican Republic	5.0	6.6	—	—	14.0	—	7.5	—	—	—	—	21.5	15.0	—	68.3
Ecuador	7.0	6.3	—	—	17.3	10.0	—	8.3	8.3	—	—	—	—	—	—
El Salvador	—	18.8	5.0	3.0	12.3	—	9.0	8.8	—	17.9	—	—	—	—	—
Grenada	—	—	—	—	—	—	—	—	—	—	—	.8	.4	—	.7
Guatemala	—	5.8	10.0	3.0	6.0	—	—	—	—	—	—	—	—	—	—
Guyana	—	—	—	—	—	—	2.2	—	3.9	5.0	—	17.3	—	12.9	12.9
Haiti	2.5	4.6	2.3	—	1.5	—	—	—	—	6.8	4.5	4.9	3.0	—	—
Honduras	—	2.5	—	—	—	—	—	—	—	—	16.8	—	—	—	—
Jamaica	—	—	—	—	—	—	—	—	13.3	13.3	—	55.7	19.2	57.8	145.8
Mexico	—	—	—	—	—	—	—	—	—	—	—	319.1	100.0	—	—
Nicaragua	—	—	—	14.3	13.3	10.0	3.0	4.0	12.0	3.3	12.2	—	—	—	43.1
Panama	—	—	—	2.8	6.4	—	—	—	—	7.4	10.2	25.1	—	—	—
Paraguay	—	—	—	—	—	—	—	—	—	—	—	—	—	—	—
Peru	—	—	—	46.3	30.0	18.0	16.0	30.8	—	—	—	158.8	10.0	85.5	177.0
St. Kitts and Nevis	—	—	—	—	—	—	—	—	—	—	—	—	—	—	—
St. Lucia	—	—	—	—	—	—	—	—	—	—	—	—	—	—	—
St. Vincent & Grens.	—	—	—	—	—	—	—	—	—	—	—	—	—	—	—
Suriname	—	—	—	—	—	—	—	—	—	—	—	—	—	—	—
Trinidad and Tobago	—	—	—	—	—	—	—	—	—	—	—	—	—	—	—
Uruguay	—	5.0	—	20.8	—	31.0	9.5	22.3	15.0	46.6	53.2	38.0	—	—	—
Venezuela	—	—	—	—	—	—	—	—	—	—	—	—	—	—	—
Memorandum Items															
Oil Exporting Ctys	—	—	20.0	45.0	65.8	38.0	2.9	4.2	—	—	—	—	—	—	—
Non-Oil Develop.Ctys	508.7	602.6	384.6	483.4	301.0	275.9	377.1	645.4	342.0	1,575.2	1,961.9	3,391.3	928.9	1,110.1	1,671.9

*Excludes reserve tranche purchases

Purchases*

Expressed in Millions of SDRs

1980	1981	1982	1983	1984	1985	1986	1987	1988	1989	1990	1991	1992	1993	1994	
															Asia (cont.)
—	27.0	25.6	29.2	—	—	—	—	—	—	—	11.2	2.5	—	—	Mongolia
—	—	—	—	—	—	—	—	—	—	—	—	—	—	—	Myanmar
10.5	—	—	—	—	10.3	2.1	6.3	—	—	—	—	—	—	—	Nepal
105.0	482.9	455.2	285.0	—	—	—	—	—	—	194.5	—	122.4	189.6	88.0	123.2	Pakistan
—	45.0	—	—	—	—	—	—	—	—	—	42.8	—	—	—	Papua New Guinea
303.3	200.0	—	288.6	85.0	318.0	229.1	123.0	70.0	235.9	—	—	333.7	151.0	126.6	36.5	Philippines
—	—	.8	1.6	1.0	—	1.3	—	—	—	—	—	—	—	—	Solomon Islands
30.0	175.6	39.2	35.8	20.0	—	—	—	108.8	—	—	—	—	—	—	Sri Lanka
—	531.0	64.4	265.5	—	335.0	110.0	—	—	—	—	—	—	—	—	Thailand
—	28.4	—	—	—	—	—	—	—	—	—	—	—	72.5	60.5	Viet Nam
—	2.8	—	2.8	3.4	1.7	—	—	—	—	—	—	—	—	—	Western Samoa
959.9	1,263.5	1,378.5	1,416.7	1,057.4	255.0	135.0	—	287.8	50.0	550.6	2,715.9	1,674.6	1,700.0	3,177.1	**Europe**
—	—	—	—	—	—	—	—	—	—	—	—	9.7	3.4	—	Albania
—	—	—	—	—	—	—	—	—	—	—	—	—	—	16.9	Armenia
—	—	—	—	—	—	—	—	—	—	—	—	—	70.1	—	Belarus
—	—	—	—	—	—	—	—	—	—	—	289.2	200.3	31.0	232.5	Bulgaria
—	—	—	—	—	—	—	—	—	—	—	—	—	—	78.5	Croatia
8.5	—	—	—	—	—	—	—	—	—	—	—	—	—	—	Cyprus
—	—	—	—	—	—	—	—	—	—	—	—	—	70.0	—	Czech Republic
—	—	—	—	—	—	—	—	—	—	—	917.9	238.6	—	—	Czechoslovakia
—	—	—	—	—	—	—	—	—	—	—	—	7.8	34.1	—	Estonia
—	—	—	—	—	—	—	—	—	—	—	—	—	—	27.8	Georgia
—	—	214.5	332.5	425.0	—	—	—	—	165.4	50.0	127.4	703.8	118.4	56.7	—	Hungary
—	—	—	—	—	—	—	—	—	—	—	—	—	61.9	136.1	Kazakhstan
—	—	—	—	—	—	—	—	—	—	—	—	—	43.9	—	Kyrgyz Republic
—	—	—	—	—	—	—	—	—	—	—	—	25.2	52.6	32.0	Latvia
—	—	—	—	—	—	—	—	—	—	—	—	17.3	70.7	46.6	Lithuania
—	—	—	—	—	—	—	—	—	—	—	—	—	—	12.4	Macedonia, former YR
—	—	—	—	—	—	—	—	—	—	—	—	—	63.0	49.5	Moldova
—	—	—	—	—	—	—	—	—	—	—	357.5	239.1	—	640.3	Poland
121.3	309.5	310.0	183.9	183.6	—	—	—	—	—	—	—	565.8	338.5	245.1	Romania
—	—	—	—	—	—	—	—	—	—	—	—	719.0	1,078.3	1,078.3	Russia
—	—	—	—	—	—	—	—	—	—	—	—	—	64.4	96.5	Slovak Republic
491.6	400.0	300.0	346.3	168.8	—	—	—	—	—	—	—	—	—	235.5	Turkey
—	—	—	—	—	—	—	—	—	—	—	—	—	—	249.3	Ukraine
—	—	—	—	—	—	—	—	—	—	—	—	—	—	—	Uzbekistan
338.5	554.0	554.0	554.0	280.0	255.0	135.0	—	122.4	—	65.7	—	—	—	—	Yugoslavia, SFR
—	—	15.4	9.8	—	57.4	—	116.0	—	66.2	—	60.0	288.0	11.1	65.6	**Middle East**
—	—	—	—	—	—	—	—	—	—	—	—	—	—	—	Bahrain
—	—	—	—	—	—	—	116.0	—	—	—	60.0	87.2	—	—	Egypt
—	—	—	—	—	—	—	—	—	—	—	—	—	—	—	Iran, I.R. of
—	—	—	—	—	—	—	—	—	—	—	—	—	—	—	Iraq
—	—	—	—	—	—	—	—	—	—	—	—	178.6	—	—	Israel
—	—	—	—	—	57.4	—	—	—	66.2	—	—	22.2	11.1	65.6	Jordan
—	—	—	—	—	—	—	—	—	—	—	—	—	—	—	Syrian Arab Republic
—	—	—	9.8	—	—	—	—	—	—	—	—	—	—	—	Yemen Arab Rep.
—	—	15.4	—	—	—	—	—	—	—	—	—	—	—	—	Yemen, P.D. Rep.
—	—	—	—	—	—	—	—	—	—	—	—	—	—	—	Yemen, Republic of
267.2	526.9	1,486.7	5,929.2	3,552.2	1,863.2	1,778.6	1,974.4	1,540.5	2,188.7	3,500.3	1,728.7	1,203.7	1,896.9	755.1	**Western Hemisphere**
—	—	—	—	—	—	—	—	—	—	—	—	—	—	—	Antigua and Barbuda
—	—	—	1,120.6	—	984.5	473.0	969.8	398.7	184.0	322.0	292.5	584.6	1,154.8	612.0	Argentina
—	—	22.2	14.5	7.8	—	—	—	—	—	—	—	36.8	—	—	Barbados
—	—	—	3.6	1.2	4.8	1.2	—	—	—	—	—	—	—	—	Belize
53.4	—	24.5	17.9	—	—	96.8	—	45.3	—	—	—	—	—	—	Bolivia
—	—	498.8	2,027.0	1,744.2	—	—	—	365.3	—	—	—	127.5	—	—	Brazil
—	—	—	579.0	216.0	195.6	250.0	225.0	150.0	139.0	—	—	—	—	—	Chile
—	—	—	—	—	—	—	—	—	—	—	—	—	—	—	Colombia
15.4	52.6	—	110.9	—	34.0	—	—	—	—	—	—	55.3	4.0	—	Costa Rica
—	4.8	2.8	2.4	1.5	—	—	—	—	—	—	—	—	—	—	Dominica
—	—	46.6	179.1	—	76.9	17.1	—	—	—	—	44.8	37.4	53.3	—	Dominican Republic
—	—	—	203.5	39.4	84.4	75.9	37.7	57.8	15.7	23.6	18.6	—	—	98.9	Ecuador
10.8	32.3	59.8	15.5	—	—	—	—	—	—	—	—	—	—	—	El Salvador
—	5.0	—	1.1	—	—	—	—	—	—	—	—	—	—	—	Grenada
—	95.6	—	38.3	19.1	—	—	—	44.8	—	—	—	—	—	—	Guatemala
41.9	16.1	5.9	—	—	—	—	—	—	—	—	39.7	9.8	—	—	Guyana
16.6	17.0	12.0	29.5	14.0	—	—	—	—	—	13.0	2.0	—	—	—	Haiti
16.0	20.7	61.7	45.9	—	—	—	—	—	—	—	21.3	2.3	51.0	—	Honduras
—	203.6	165.2	112.2	100.6	51.0	26.6	95.9	43.7	63.8	41.1	87.0	41.8	36.4	34.4	Jamaica
—	—	200.6	1,003.1	1,203.8	295.8	741.4	600.0	350.0	943.0	1,608.4	932.4	233.1	—	—	Mexico
—	—	—	—	—	—	—	—	—	—	—	17.0	—	—	—	Nicaragua
—	75.3	—	108.9	100.0	35.0	44.0	11.0	—	—	—	—	71.6	9.9	9.9	Panama
—	—	—	—	—	—	—	—	—	—	—	—	—	—	—	Paraguay
111.0	—	299.9	165.0	104.7	—	—	—	—	—	—	—	—	642.7	—	Peru
—	—	—	—	—	—	—	—	—	—	—	—	—	—	—	St. Kitts and Nevis
1.8	2.7	—	—	—	—	—	—	—	—	—	—	—	—	—	St. Lucia
.4	1.3	—	—	—	—	—	—	—	—	—	—	—	—	—	St. Vincent & Grens.
—	—	—	—	—	—	—	—	—	—	—	—	—	—	—	Suriname
—	—	—	—	—	—	—	—	85.1	70.7	75.8	37.5	—	—	—	Trinidad and Tobago
—	—	86.8	151.2	—	101.2	52.7	35.1	—	—	—	—	16.0	—	—	Uruguay
—	—	—	—	—	—	—	—	—	—	759.5	1,357.5	231.5	—	—	Venezuela
															Memorandum Items
—	—	—	425.1	—	—	—	462.9	—	1,230.4	1,357.5	456.5	—	—	587.5	Oil Exporting Ctys
3,393.5	6,771.3	7,394.1	11,839.0	7,074.0	4,013.9	3,819.7	2,835.9	2,668.7	2,247.3	2,912.5	6,930.0	4,791.1	5,042.2	4,392.0	Non-Oil Develop.Ctys

*Excludes reserve tranche purchases

Repurchases

Expressed in Millions of SDRs

	1965	1966	1967	1968	1969	1970	1971	1972	1973	1974	1975	1976	1977	1978	1979
World	372.1	461.9	886.2	788.8	1,448.1	1,197.1	2,206.9	656.3	407.5	374.2	238.9	840.6	2,844.9	4,377.2	3,991.5
Industrial Countries	—	1.3	654.8	346.8	939.1	592.0	1,887.8	250.2	—	—	—	—	1,651.7	2,591.4	2,521.8
United States															
Canada															
Australia	—	—	—	—	—	—	—	—	—	—	—	—	—	85.6	—
Japan															
New Zealand	—	—	—	99.3	20.6	—	—	—	—	—	—	—	—	38.4	92.7
Belgium															
Denmark															
Finland	—	—	—	62.5	—	—	—	—	—	—	—	—	—	34.3	85.7
France	—	—	—	—	—	—	246.3	587.2	—	—	—	—	—	—	—
Greece	—	—	—	—	—	—	—	—	—	—	—	—	71.3	25.8	37.9
Iceland	—	—	—	—	—	7.5	1.8	—	—	—	—	—	—	9.3	12.4
Ireland	—	1.3	—	—	—	—	—	—	—	—	—	—	—	—	—
Italy	—	—	—	—	—	—	—	—	—	—	—	—	966.4	858.9	880.0
Netherlands															
Norway															
Portugal	—	—	—	—	—	—	—	—	—	—	—	—	4.0	29.3	31.9
Spain	—	—	—	—	—	—	—	—	—	—	—	—	—	55.5	410.0
United Kingdom	—	—	654.8	185.0	918.5	338.2	1,298.9	250.2	—	—	—	—	610.0	1,454.3	971.2
Developing Countries	369.6	458.1	228.9	442.0	506.5	605.2	319.1	406.0	407.5	374.2	238.9	840.6	1,193.2	1,785.8	1,469.8
Africa	5.6	11.2	35.7	46.5	40.5	73.9	103.6	44.7	15.0	7.3	64.4	181.1	190.1	217.8	457.0
Algeria															
Burkina Faso															
Burundi	1.9	2.9	4.7	2.0	.2	.2	3.7	5.3	—	—	-.1	—	—	1.2	—
Cameroon	—	—	—	—	—	—	—	—	—	—	—	—	—	2.9	8.0
Central African Rep.	—	—	—	—	—	—	—	—	—	—	—	1.3	—	.9	2.1
Chad	—	—	—	—	—	—	—	—	1.0	2.8	—	—	—	1.9	1.2
Comoros															
Congo	—	—	—	—	—	—	—	—	—	—	—	—	—	3.3	1.1
Côte d'Ivoire	—	—	—	—	—	—	—	—	—	—	—	24.2	10.0	24.1	—
Equatorial Guinea															
Ethiopia															
Gabon															
Gambia, The	—	—	—	—	—	—	—	—	—	—	—	—	—	1.8	3.5
Ghana	3.7	2.0	6.7	—	12.8	24.9	28.1	15.4	1.0	—	—	—	—	4.8	9.7
Guinea	—	—	—	—	.5	—	.5	—	1.9	1.0	2.4	—	—	5.8	4.4
Guinea-Bissau															
Kenya	—	—	—	—	—	—	—	—	—	—	—	12.0	10.6	36.0	2.4	30.6
Lesotho															
Liberia	—	3.6	4.2	3.4	4.4	5.2	3.4	1.4	1.0	—	—	—	—	—	—
Madagascar	—	—	—	—	—	—	—	—	—	—	—	—	8.1	2.6	3.7
Malawi	—	—	—	—	—	—	—	—	—	—	—	—	—	3.8	.8
Mali	—	—	2.0	4.0	4.0	4.0	4.0	1.0	1.0	1.0	1.0	2.5	2.0	1.2	1.8
Mauritania	—	—	—	—	—	—	—	—	—	—	—	—	—	—	.9
Mauritius	—	—	—	—	3.7	—	—	—	—	—	—	—	—	—	—
Morocco	—	—	—	2.4	4.8	14.2	35.8	—	—	—	—	—	—	—	23.2
Niger															
Nigeria	—	—	—	—	—	—	—	—	1.5	—	—	—	—	—	—
Rwanda	—	—	1.0	2.0	3.0	1.0	3.0	—	—	—	—	—	—	—	—
Senegal	—	—	—	—	—	—	—	—	—	—	—	—	—	4.7	6.4
Sierra Leone	—	—	—	—	1.5	5.4	—	—	—	—	—	—	—	1.2	7.3
Somalia	—	—	4.7	11.4	—	—	—	—	—	—	—	—	—	—	—
South Africa	—	—	—	—	—	—	—	—	—	—	—	75.0	85.0	80.0	240.0
Sudan	—	2.5	6.7	8.7	3.1	8.1	15.1	19.0	7.5	2.5	6.0	21.0	19.6	22.6	33.7
Swaziland															
Tanzania	—	—	—	—	—	—	—	—	—	—	—	—	1.6	28.7	13.0
Togo	—	—	—	—	—	—	—	—	—	—	—	—	—	7.5	—
Tunisia	—	.2	5.8	12.6	6.2	7.4	10.0	2.6	—	—	—	—	—	—	—
Uganda	—	—	—	—	—	—	—	—	—	—	5.1	4.9	—	10.0	8.0
Zaïre	—	—	—	—	—	—	—	—	—	—	—	22.6	5.7	9.7	31.5
Zambia	—	—	—	—	—	—	—	—	—	—	—	38.0	19.0	19.0	—	26.3
Zimbabwe															
Asia	131.1	140.6	29.0	155.1	203.3	241.5	73.7	105.0	224.3	117.6	103.1	458.4	555.9	520.8	370.0
Afghanistan, I.S. of	—	4.4	3.2	3.7	8.2	4.6	4.4	4.4	6.0	5.0	4.0	7.5	1.8	—	—
Bangladesh	—	—	—	—	—	—	—	—	—	—	20.5	33.0	41.4	17.7	63.0
Cambodia															
China, People's Rep.															
Fiji															
India	75.0	125.0	7.5	97.5	148.0	175.9	10.0	—	—	—	—	292.0	281.2	201.3	—
Indonesia	39.1	—	12.7	30.0	17.6	3.2	15.0	20.0	87.0	18.2	—	—	—	—	—
Korea	—	—	—	—	—	—	—	—	—	—	—	20.0	10.3	89.5	97.4
Lao P. D. Rep.	—	—	—	—	—	—	—	—	—	—	—	—	—	—	1.6
Malaysia	—	—	—	—	—	—	—	—	7.3	—	—	—	85.7	—	—
Mongolia															
Myanmar	—	—	—	—	—	5.0	10.0	6.5	8.0	5.5	6.0	7.8	16.7	21.9	
Nepal	—	—	—	—	—	—	—	—	—	—	—	—	—	4.1	1.0
Pakistan	—	—	1.9	15.9	14.9	28.4	1.9	15.0	40.0	20.0	25.0	42.0	68.9	84.3	80.7
Papua New Guinea	—	—	—	—	—	—	—	—	—	—	—	—	—	10.0	5.0
Philippines	9.6	—	—	—	—	2.5	14.0	29.5	57.8	47.2	29.1	38.8	38.8	73.7	71.1
Solomon Islands	—	—	—	—	—	—	—	—	—	—	—	—	—	—	1.1
Sri Lanka	7.5	11.3	3.8	8.0	14.6	27.0	23.4	24.0	19.8	19.2	18.7	19.2	19.3	22.8	27.1
Thailand	—	—	—	—	—	—	—	2.1	—	—	—	—	—	—	—
Viet Nam															
Western Samoa	—	—	—	—	—	—	—	—	—	—	—	—	—	.8	.6	.1

Repurchases

	1980	1981	1982	1983	1984	1985	1986	1987	1988	1989	1990	1991	1992	1993	1994	
							Expressed in Millions of SDRs									
	2,428.8	1,880.6	1,505.6	2,030.5	2,284.6	3,625.0	5,664.6	7,881.8	6,671.8	5,912.7	5,853.4	4,744.8	4,201.6	3,804.3	4,572.0	**World**
	850.1	609.0	522.9	116.7	—	—	10.8	209.6	373.1	—	—	—	—	—	—	**Industrial Countries**
	—	—	—	—	—	—	—	—	—	—	—	—	—	—	—	United States
	—	—	—	—	—	—	—	—	—	—	—	—	—	—	—	Canada
	208.9	61.7	—	32.5	—	—	—	—	—	—	—	—	—	—	—	Australia
	—	—	—	—	—	—	—	—	—	—	—	—	—	—	—	Japan
	136.2	98.7	30.8	2.9	—	—	—	—	—	—	—	—	—	—	—	New Zealand
	—	—	—	—	—	—	—	—	—	—	—	—	—	—	—	Belgium
	—	—	—	—	—	—	—	—	—	—	—	—	—	—	—	Denmark
	—	14.3	37.7	14.4	—	—	—	—	—	—	—	—	—	—	—	Finland
	68.8	64.6	13.9	—	—	—	—	—	—	—	—	—	—	—	—	France
	—	—	—	—	—	—	—	—	—	—	—	—	—	—	—	Greece
	19.0	9.8	5.1	.9	—	—	10.8	10.8	—	—	—	—	—	—	—	Iceland
	—	—	—	—	—	—	—	—	—	—	—	—	—	—	—	Ireland
	—	—	—	—	—	—	—	—	—	—	—	—	—	—	—	Italy
	—	—	—	—	—	—	—	—	—	—	—	—	—	—	—	Netherlands
	76.9	46.2	37.7	9.8	—	—	—	198.8	373.1	—	—	—	—	—	—	Norway
	—	63.7	136.9	4.8	—	—	—	—	—	—	—	—	—	—	—	Portugal
	—	250.0	261.0	51.6	—	—	—	—	—	—	—	—	—	—	—	Spain
	340.3	—	—	—	—	—	—	—	—	—	—	—	—	—	—	United Kingdom
	1,578.5	1,271.6	982.7	1,913.8	2,284.6	3,625.0	5,653.8	7,672.2	6,298.8	5,912.7	5,853.4	4,744.8	4,201.6	3,804.3	4,572.0	**Developing Countries**
	413.4	317.3	243.8	424.3	551.5	765.2	1,472.4	1,432.1	952.6	1,122.1	912.0	669.3	601.3	626.5	423.3	**Africa**
	—	—	—	—	—	—	—	—	—	—	—	—	117.7	235.4	136.5	Algeria
	—	—	—	—	—	—	—	—	—	—	—	—	—	—	—	Burkina Faso
	—	—	—	4.8	4.8	—	—	—	—	—	—	—	—	—	—	Burundi
	12.8	8.5	3.0	.5	—	—	—	—	—	—	—	8.7	38.6	33.8	3.9	Cameroon
	4.4	3.1	.6	.3	6.3	9.5	5.3	2.1	6.1	9.0	6.4	2.5	1.1	.6	.4	Central African Rep.
	2.2	5.4	—	—	2.7	3.5	.9	—	.9	—	3.5	2.6	—	—	—	Chad
	.5	.3	—	.3	—	—	—	—	—	—	—	—	—	—	—	Comoros
	5.3	4.6	—	—	—	—	—	—	—	1.2	4.8	3.6	—	.5	2.0	Congo
	—	—	—	—	27.7	97.6	107.2	102.7	127.6	120.1	87.7	76.3	65.2	36.5	53.5	Côte d'Ivoire
	—	.6	—	—	6.1	6.9	1.8	—	.3	3.0	1.8	.4	—	—	—	Equatorial Guinea
	—	—	2.3	18.0	25.2	31.0	26.1	10.1	7.3	14.8	17.6	4.4	—	—	—	Ethiopia
	—	—	2.0	7.5	1.8	—	—	—	—	—	10.7	18.1	25.8	25.7	16.1	Gabon
	—	—	2.2	2.6	1.9	2.8	13.4	5.3	3.2	3.1	3.7	4.4	1.5	—	—	Gambia, The
	9.7	9.7	4.8	15.4	4.0	—	18.7	134.1	196.2	134.4	83.1	56.4	45.3	39.3	27.1	Ghana
	1.1	3.6	.2	—	—	—	5.8	5.8	—	4.1	9.8	6.4	.8	—	—	Guinea
	—	—	.3	.4	.4	.9	.9	.2	.9	.7	—	—	—	—	—	Guinea-Bissau
	7.0	7.2	15.6	41.7	56.7	68.4	89.8	83.9	67.4	98.0	75.2	29.1	58.7	41.5	—	Kenya
	—	—	—	—	—	—	—	—	—	—	1.1	—	—	—	—	Lesotho
	2.4	1.2	—	10.3	19.6	6.9	—	—	1.0	2.2	.7	—	—	—	—	Liberia
	1.5	7.2	.7	3.7	23.5	33.0	40.8	26.5	29.5	38.3	34.7	25.0	11.5	7.4	4.5	Madagascar
	.9	2.6	12.6	10.3	20.4	16.0	20.6	23.6	19.9	19.0	13.8	15.2	13.6	4.2	1.2	Malawi
	2.2	2.3	1.1	1.8	3.2	4.5	13.9	16.5	14.0	15.6	12.9	6.7	4.4	6.3	4.8	Mali
	6.7	6.9	1.5	4.4	9.0	12.4	9.8	5.0	3.4	7.4	11.2	9.6	4.6	1.0	—	Mauritania
	—	11.0	—	14.5	31.5	47.8	37.2	23.4	29.0	28.9	32.1	15.5	—	—	—	Mauritius
	66.4	53.4	32.5	23.3	47.5	143.2	274.2	243.9	169.1	193.3	164.2	125.0	100.8	112.0	106.1	Morocco
	—	—	—	—	—	—	1.5	16.1	21.9	12.9	10.0	8.3	5.4	3.5	2.0	Niger
	—	—	—	—	—	—	—	—	—	—	—	—	—	—	—	Nigeria
	6.4	6.4	13.3	10.5	14.5	40.9	50.4	44.4	41.7	43.4	39.7	34.5	28.1	11.0	2.5	Rwanda
	9.2	8.0	1.3	2.0	8.3	4.4	20.8	—	.7	.9	1.6	5.4	1.4	5.9	42.6	Senegal
	—	—	—	—	2.9	8.8	28.8	16.0	.7	8.8	2.1	—	—	—	—	Sierra Leone
	72.0	—	—	50.0	—	—	347.5	397.5	—	—	—	—	—	—	—	Somalia
	34.7	19.0	30.2	41.6	31.6	4.9	—	—	—	—	1.0	—	—	—	—	South Africa
	—	—	—	—	—	1.0	3.4	3.4	2.3	—	—	—	—	—	—	Sudan
	25.0	26.3	11.1	25.1	24.4	4.8	15.1	4.1	—	2.6	19.6	19.4	3.9	—	—	Swaziland
	—	—	—	—	5.2	8.4	2.9	10.8	17.6	16.8	11.2	5.8	7.1	5.2	2.4	Tanzania
	24.0	—	—	—	—	—	—	—	—	—	82.0	99.1	20.9	3.8	—	Togo
	10.0	10.3	1.5	11.9	37.7	64.2	69.7	51.1	55.4	54.3	30.3	24.4	18.7	3.1	—	Tunisia
	65.5	80.3	20.8	10.4	54.0	103.8	94.0	125.0	78.3	255.6	108.5	35.5	—	—	3.0	Uganda
	44.0	39.8	86.2	113.5	71.3	18.7	122.6	—	—	—	14.7	24.8	26.0	49.8	14.6	Zaïre
	—	—	—	—	—	9.4	—	80.8	58.1	30.0	17.4	4.8	—	—	—	Zambia
	—	—	—	—	—	20.9	49.4	—	—	—	—	—	—	—	—	Zimbabwe
	407.7	381.2	294.3	865.0	899.8	1,608.6	1,589.5	2,422.9	1,824.9	1,427.1	1,695.1	1,350.7	734.3	369.7	1,066.0	**Asia**
	—	—	—	—	—	—	—	—	—	—	—	—	—	—	—	Afghanistan, I.S. of
	69.6	32.6	33.9	21.1	58.0	68.7	104.5	104.1	58.6	81.8	146.4	102.9	56.0	35.9	—	Bangladesh
	—	—	—	—	—	—	—	—	—	—	—	—	6.3	6.3	—	Cambodia
	—	—	—	450.0	—	—	—	—	—	—	298.9	298.9	—	—	—	China, People's Rep.
	6.5	—	—	—	—	5.1	6.8	1.7	1.8	2.4	—	.6	—	—	—	Fiji
	—	—	—	33.3	133.0	174.8	331.3	637.5	787.5	737.5	531.3	362.5	275.0	137.5	821.7	India
	—	—	—	—	3.6	264.9	—	—	42.0	—	115.7	231.4	115.7	—	—	Indonesia
	25.0	40.8	35.2	40.9	261.5	361.8	226.8	896.5	369.8	—	—	—	—	—	—	Korea
	6.5	1.6	—	—	4.7	6.4	1.9	—	—	—	—	—	—	—	—	Lao P. D. Rep.
	—	—	—	46.2	52.2	155.7	107.2	—	—	—	—	—	—	—	—	Malaysia
	—	—	—	—	—	—	—	—	—	—	—	—	—	—	—	Mongolia
	15.1	7.4	2.9	16.2	6.1	13.5	26.7	27.4	10.9	—	—	—	—	—	—	Myanmar
	—	.2	4.8	4.9	5.2	3.9	—	—	—	5.4	8.5	3.9	.8	—	—	Nepal
	107.0	132.6	48.7	24.3	51.6	149.2	269.5	280.3	196.6	143.1	108.1	71.7	116.1	91.4	34.1	Pakistan
	5.0	4.8	—	—	28.3	6.6	10.1	—	—	—	—	—	—	10.7	21.4	Papua New Guinea
	111.6	44.6	67.7	144.6	212.5	147.0	213.1	240.2	119.7	137.9	249.7	215.0	109.9	46.0	188.7	Philippines
	—	—	—	—	.2	—	.4	1.2	1.3	.3	.2	.6	.5	—	—	Solomon Islands
	32.7	39.8	44.6	46.2	22.7	35.9	58.5	69.4	64.1	46.0	31.9	—	63.6	54.4	13.6	Sri Lanka
	16.8	67.4	34.4	35.2	59.3	213.5	230.8	162.5	171.1	271.4	202.9	—	—	—	—	Thailand
	11.5	8.5	21.5	1.3	—	—	—	—	—	—	—	—	—	28.4	—	Viet Nam
	.4	.9	.7	.9	.8	1.4	1.3	2.1	2.6	1.4	.6	.4	.2	—	—	Western Samoa

Repurchases

Expressed in Millions of SDRs

	1965	1966	1967	1968	1969	1970	1971	1972	1973	1974	1975	1976	1977	1978	1979
Europe	30.0	61.5	30.5	17.7	59.2	72.3	37.0	77.1	61.7	21.8	—	21.8	146.0	157.4	169.2
Bulgaria	—	—	—	—	—	—	—	—	—	—	—	—	—	—	—
Croatia	—	—	—	—	—	—	—	—	—	—	—	—	—	—	—
Cyprus	—	—	—	—	—	—	—	—	—	—	—	—	—	10.1	4.8
Czech Republic	—	—	—	—	—	—	—	—	—	—	—	—	—	—	—
Czechoslovakia	—	—	—	—	—	—	—	—	—	—	—	—	—	—	—
Hungary	—	—	—	—	—	—	—	—	—	—	—	—	—	—	—
Macedonia, former YR	—	—	—	—	—	—	—	—	—	—	—	—	—	—	—
Poland	—	—	—	—	—	—	—	—	—	—	—	—	—	—	—
Romania	—	—	—	—	—	—	—	—	—	—	—	—	40.0	47.5	50.0
Slovak Republic	—	—	—	—	—	—	—	—	—	—	—	—	—	—	—
Slovenia	—	—	—	—	—	—	—	—	—	—	—	—	—	24.8	68.5
Turkey	15.0	21.5	19.0	—	21.5	27.0	27.0	62.1	—	—	—	—	—	—	—
Yugoslavia, SFR	15.0	40.0	11.5	17.8	37.8	45.3	10.0	15.0	61.7	21.8	—	21.8	106.0	75.0	45.8
Middle East	35.5	33.6	5.2	96.3	24.0	9.0	16.3	84.6	19.5	23.1	29.9	16.0	28.0	126.4	111.5
Egypt	28.5	28.0	—	69.2	24.0	9.0	11.5	45.0	9.0	9.0	24.5	16.0	28.0	35.0	51.2
Iran, I.R. of	—	—	—	—	—	—	—	—	—	—	—	—	—	—	—
Iraq	—	—	—	20.0	—	—	—	—	—	—	—	—	—	—	—
Israel	—	—	—	—	—	—	—	32.5	—	—	—	—	—	86.4	47.0
Jordan	—	—	—	—	—	—	—	—	5.8	1.6	—	—	—	—	—
Syrian Arab Republic	7.0	5.6	5.2	7.1	—	—	4.8	7.1	4.8	12.5	5.4	—	—	—	—
Yemen Arab Rep.	—	—	—	—	—	—	—	—	—	—	—	—	—	—	—
Yemen, P.D. Rep.	—	—	—	—	—	—	—	—	—	—	—	—	—	5.0	13.3
Yemen, Republic of	—	—	—	—	—	—	—	—	—	—	—	—	—	—	—
Western Hemisphere	167.4	211.2	128.5	126.3	179.5	208.5	88.6	94.5	87.0	204.5	41.5	163.4	273.2	763.5	362.0
Argentina	44.0	76.0	30.0	—	—	—	—	—	—	110.0	—	64.0	103.1	340.8	—
Barbados	—	—	—	—	—	—	—	—	—	—	—	—	—	—	—
Belize	—	—	—	—	—	—	—	—	—	—	—	—	—	—	—
Bolivia	—	—	—	—	8.0	—	4.0	3.0	8.0	3.7	5.1	18.6	—	—	—
Brazil	55.0	39.5	7.5	12.0	—	—	—	—	—	—	—	—	—	—	—
Chile	37.0	44.8	25.2	28.0	51.0	47.3	1.5	—	—	39.5	6.0	53.0	101.6	73.6	130.6
Colombia	24.0	33.5	37.5	13.5	39.7	72.7	31.6	53.3	—	—	—	—	—	—	—
Costa Rica	1.7	5.0	2.8	5.8	9.7	—	—	—	—	—	.9	4.5	3.0	13.0	1.0
Dominica	—	—	—	—	—	—	—	—	—	—	—	—	—	—	—
Dominican Republic	—	—	3.0	7.0	8.0	5.3	3.3	7.0	3.8	—	—	—	—	—	10.8
Ecuador	1.0	—	.8	10.2	5.0	6.5	8.3	5.5	16.5	—	—	—	—	—	—
El Salvador	—	—	5.0	—	15.0	5.0	5.3	10.2	8.8	—	—	—	17.9	—	—
Grenada	—	—	—	—	—	—	—	—	—	—	—	—	—	—	.9
Guatemala	—	.4	—	4.9	8.3	8.4	—	2.1	—	—	3.9	5.6	—	—	2.8
Guyana	—	—	—	—	—	—	—	—	—	—	—	3.7	6.3	1.3	1.9
Haiti	2.3	3.5	1.0	2.0	2.2	2.8	1.4	.8	—	—	—	—	12.5	10.5	—
Honduras	2.5	2.5	2.8	—	—	—	—	—	—	5.5	13.3	—	—	7.7	18.0
Jamaica	—	—	—	—	—	—	—	—	—	—	—	—	—	192.5	126.3
Mexico	—	—	6.5	—	14.3	13.3	—	6.8	8.0	5.5	6.7	6.8	6.7	6.8	—
Nicaragua	—	—	—	.5	1.8	1.7	—	—	—	—	—	—	.5	1.8	8.9
Panama	—	—	—	—	—	—	—	—	—	—	—	—	—	—	—
Paraguay	—	—	—	42.4	5.4	26.9	22.6	3.3	17.1	13.6	—	—	—	—	60.9
Peru	—	—	—	—	—	—	—	—	—	—	—	—	—	—	—
St. Lucia	—	—	—	—	—	—	—	—	—	—	—	—	—	—	—
St. Vincent & Grens.	—	—	—	—	—	—	—	—	—	—	—	—	—	—	—
Trinidad and Tobago	—	—	—	—	—	—	—	—	—	—	—	—	—	—	—
Uruguay	—	6.0	6.5	—	11.2	18.8	10.6	2.7	19.5	15.0	17.3	12.9	21.7	115.5	—
Venezuela	—	—	—	—	—	—	—	—	—	—	—	—	—	—	—
Memorandum Items															
Oil Exporting Ctys	39.1	—	12.7	50.0	17.6	3.2	15.0	20.0	88.5	18.2	—	—	—	—	—
Non-Oil Develop.Ctys	330.6	458.1	216.2	392.0	488.9	602.0	304.1	386.0	319.0	356.0	238.9	840.6	1,193.2	1,785.8	1,469.8

Repurchases

	1980	1981	1982	1983	1984	1985	1986	1987	1988	1989	1990	1991	1992	1993	1994
	Expressed in Millions of SDRs														
Europe	**264.6**	**234.8**	**200.0**	**405.2**	**614.9**	**834.0**	**923.1**	**1,228.8**	**1,289.7**	**918.4**	**539.0**	**168.4**	**444.2**	**234.5**	**1,325.2**
Bulgaria	—	—	—	—	—	—	—	—	—	—	—	—	60.6	—	48.0
Croatia	—	—	—	—	—	—	—	—	—	—	—	—	—	17.2	6.2
Cyprus	11.6	9.0	9.3	6.8	2.3	3.2	—	—	—	—	—	—	—	—	—
Czech Republic	—	—	—	—	—	—	—	—	—	—	—	—	—	70.0	780.7
Czechoslovakia	—	—	—	—	—	—	—	—	—	—	—	—	35.0	—	—
Hungary	—	—	—	—	—	88.3	41.0	272.9	263.9	174.2	242.8	55.3	122.8	36.2	114.7
Macedonia, former YR	—	—	—	—	—	—	—	—	—	—	—	—	—	2.2	1.2
Poland	—	—	—	—	—	—	—	—	—	—	—	—	—	98.9	219.4
Romania	80.0	60.3	35.1	60.9	132.5	172.9	199.3	226.0	250.6	106.9	—	—	153.4	—	89.6
Slovak Republic	—	—	—	—	—	—	—	—	—	—	—	—	—	—	61.9
Slovenia	—	—	—	—	—	—	—	—	—	—	—	—	—	9.9	3.6
Turkey	119.2	91.0	116.4	168.3	210.8	247.5	320.3	344.2	320.9	185.8	36.3	—	—	—	—
Yugoslavia, SFR	53.7	74.6	39.2	169.1	269.3	322.1	362.5	385.8	454.2	451.5	260.0	113.1	72.4	—	—
Middle East	**155.2**	**128.8**	**96.4**	**31.7**	**—**	**13.7**	**23.8**	**23.2**	**36.5**	**28.7**	**36.2**	**58.0**	**36.3**	**33.1**	**48.4**
Egypt	78.9	53.9	33.1	2.7	—	11.8	12.5	12.5	12.5	—	29.0	58.0	29.0	—	22.5
Iran, I.R. of	—	—	—	—	—	—	—	—	—	—	—	—	—	—	—
Iraq	—	—	—	—	—	—	—	—	—	—	—	—	—	—	—
Israel	67.8	68.9	60.4	27.2	—	—	—	—	—	—	—	—	—	—	—
Jordan	—	—	—	—	—	—	—	—	21.5	28.7	7.2	—	7.3	33.1	25.9
Syrian Arab Republic	—	—	—	—	—	—	—	—	—	—	—	—	—	—	—
Yemen Arab Rep.	—	—	—	—	—	—	3.6	4.9	1.2	—	—	—	—	—	—
Yemen, P.D. Rep.	8.4	6.0	2.9	.9	—	1.9	7.7	5.8	—	—	—	—	—	—	—
Yemen, Republic of	—	—	—	.9	—	—	—	—	—	—	—	—	—	—	—
Western Hemisphere	**337.7**	**209.6**	**148.3**	**187.6**	**218.5**	**403.4**	**1,645.0**	**2,565.2**	**2,195.1**	**2,416.5**	**2,671.1**	**2,498.3**	**2,385.6**	**2,540.5**	**1,709.2**
Argentina	—	—	—	—	—	—	337.3	494.4	381.9	558.2	513.6	723.8	637.7	275.1	289.7
Barbados	4.2	1.5	.8	.9	—	—	11.2	16.8	7.8	4.5	2.8	.5	—	—	—
Belize	—	—	—	—	—	—	1.2	1.5	2.3	3.3	2.2	.3	—	—	—
Bolivia	—	1.9	7.5	10.7	20.3	18.2	25.3	19.2	36.3	4.9	31.4	36.9	22.6	17.0	—
Brazil	—	—	—	—	—	64.5	525.5	877.0	691.4	633.5	563.7	414.5	411.3	360.4	93.5
Chile	39.6	54.5	36.1	5.7	—	—	152.4	280.9	199.8	155.1	153.6	143.5	144.4	178.5	147.0
Colombia	—	—	—	—	—	—	—	—	—	—	—	—	—	—	—
Costa Rica	9.4	9.1	4.0	11.7	24.3	21.4	30.7	47.7	40.2	26.1	19.0	5.2	2.8	—	13.8
Dominica	—	—	—	.7	1.8	1.5	1.3	1.6	2.2	1.9	1.0	.7	.4	.1	—
Dominican Republic	49.8	18.2	2.3	8.1	9.5	32.2	38.7	49.0	38.2	68.5	42.8	32.9	10.3	7.2	5.6
Ecuador	—	—	—	—	—	—	5.5	90.2	102.3	69.2	84.8	77.0	54.9	20.8	14.9
El Salvador	—	—	—	—	5.4	26.6	45.8	31.2	3.9	—	—	—	—	—	—
Grenada	.5	.1	.8	—	.9	2.1	1.3	.3	.3	.3	.3	—	—	—	—
Guatemala	—	—	—	—	—	47.8	48.0	15.5	21.0	9.9	8.7	2.1	22.4	22.4	—
Guyana	11.9	9.5	2.2	4.1	1.0	1.0	—	—	—	.8	69.6	1.3	—	2.4	15.3
Haiti	2.2	2.2	1.0	.3	—	11.8	19.7	18.1	14.1	14.3	6.5	1.6	—	—	14.8
Honduras	—	—	—	—	1.6	16.7	41.4	32.4	24.3	.3	22.0	1.3	—	2.1	11.2
Jamaica	14.6	43.6	40.3	41.5	58.3	61.3	103.3	172.1	163.2	130.8	82.1	64.1	55.7	51.9	60.9
Mexico	100.3	—	—	—	—	—	125.4	280.1	419.0	639.6	877.1	807.4	636.1	841.7	841.0
Nicaragua	.6	17.5	3.6	4.3	4.3	9.0	—	—	—	—	—	—	—	—	2.1
Panama	13.4	12.9	4.3	.9	7.5	28.3	38.7	55.7	.1	.6	51.9	40.6	141.7	7.3	.9
Paraguay	—	—	—	—	—	—	—	—	—	—	—	—	—	—	—
Peru	91.2	38.7	43.9	87.5	82.7	49.3	43.5	.1	—	18.4	46.5	37.1	34.7	458.7	—
St. Lucia	—	—	1.5	—	.5	1.7	.3	—	—	—	—	—	—	—	—
St. Vincent & Grens.	—	—	—	—	.5	.7	.3	—	—	—	—	—	—	—	—
Trinidad and Tobago	—	—	—	—	—	—	—	—	—	—	—	—	63.7	92.5	50.4
Uruguay	—	—	—	11.2	—	9.5	48.2	81.5	47.0	76.3	91.6	30.3	18.3	10.2	7.4
Venezuela	—	—	—	—	—	—	—	—	—	—	—	77.2	128.6	192.0	140.6
Memorandum Items															
Oil Exporting Ctys	**—**	**—**	**—**	**—**	**3.6**	**264.9**	**—**	**—**	**42.0**	**—**	**115.7**	**308.6**	**362.0**	**427.5**	**277.1**
Non-Oil Develop.Ctys	**1,578.5**	**1,271.6**	**982.7**	**1,913.8**	**2,280.9**	**3,360.1**	**5,653.8**	**7,672.2**	**6,256.8**	**5,912.7**	**5,737.7**	**4,436.2**	**3,839.6**	**3,376.9**	**4,295.0**

Fund Accounts: Borrowing Agreements

(As of July 31, 1995 and Amounts Expressed in Millions of SDRs)

	Amounts Agreed	Amounts Borrowed	Amounts Repaid	Outstanding Borrowings	Amounts Available for Borrowings
General Department	**36,775.0**	**16,475.0**	**14,849.5**	**1,625.5**	**18,500.0**
GAB and GAB Associated	**18,500.0**	—	—	—	**18,500.0**
Belgium	595.0	—	—	—	595.0
Canada	892.5	—	—	—	892.5
France	1,700.0	—	—	—	1,700.0
Germany	2,380.0	—	—	—	2,380.0
Italy	1,105.0	—	—	—	1,105.0
Japan	2,125.0	—	—	—	2,125.0
Netherlands	850.0	—	—	—	850.0
Saudi Arabia	1,500.0	—	—	—	1,500.0
Sweden	382.5	—	—	—	382.5
Switzerland	1,020.0	—	—	—	1,020.0
United Kingdom	1,700.0	—	—	—	1,700.0
United States	4,250.0	—	—	—	4,250.0
Enlarged Access to Fund Resources	**15,275.0**[1]	**13,475.0**	**13,475.0**	—	—
of which: Saudi Arabia	11,000.0	9,200.0	9,200.0	—	—
Other	**3,000.0**	**3,000.0**	**1,374.5**	**1,625.5**	—
Japan	3,000.0	3,000.0	1,374.5	1,625.5	—
Administered Accounts	**5,046.4**	**3,209.9**	—	**3,209.9**	**1,836.5**
ESAF Trust:					
Loan Account	**4,945.0**[2]	**3,108.5**	—	**3,108.5**	**1,836.5**
Subsidy Account	**101.4**	**101.4**	—	**101.4**	—

[1]In addition to the agreements with the Saudi Arabian Monetary Agency, amounts include agreements with the BIS, Reserve Bank of Australia, National Bank of Belgium, Bank of England, Bank of Finland, Central Bank of Ireland, Bank of Japan, and Swiss National Bank.

[2]Amount includes agreements with Canada, France, Germany, Italy, Japan, Korea, Norway, Saudi Arabia, Spain, Switzerland and others that have not been announced publicly.

Loan Disbursements

	1965	1966	1967	1968	1969	1970	1971	1972	1973	1974	1975	1976	1977	1978	1979
					Expressed in Millions of SDRs										
World	—	—	—	—	—	—	—	—	—	—	—	—	152.9	688.1	526.6
Developing Countries	—	—	—	—	—	—	—	—	—	—	—	—	152.9	688.1	526.6
Africa	—	—	—	—	—	—	—	—	—	—	—	—	49.9	296.7	264.8
Benin	—	—	—	—	—	—	—	—	—	—	—	—	—	5.4	—
Burkina Faso	—	—	—	—	—	—	—	—	—	—	—	—	—	5.4	3.9
Burundi	—	—	—	—	—	—	—	—	—	—	—	—	2.0	5.8	5.8
Cameroon	—	—	—	—	—	—	—	—	—	—	—	—	—	14.5	10.6
Central African Rep.	—	—	—	—	—	—	—	—	—	—	—	—	—	5.4	—
Chad	—	—	—	—	—	—	—	—	—	—	—	—	—	5.4	—
Comoros	—	—	—	—	—	—	—	—	—	—	—	—	—	—	—
Congo	—	—	—	—	—	—	—	—	—	—	—	—	1.4	4.0	3.9
Côte d'Ivoire	—	—	—	—	—	—	—	—	—	—	—	—	—	21.6	—
Djibouti	—	—	—	—	—	—	—	—	—	—	—	—	—	—	—
Equatorial Guinea	—	—	—	—	—	—	—	—	—	—	—	—	—	—	—
Ethiopia	—	—	—	—	—	—	—	—	—	—	—	—	—	11.2	8.2
Gambia, The	—	—	—	—	—	—	—	—	—	—	—	—	.8	2.2	2.1
Ghana	—	—	—	—	—	—	—	—	—	—	—	—	—	—	26.4
Guinea	—	—	—	—	—	—	—	—	—	—	—	—	2.6	7.4	7.3
Guinea-Bissau	—	—	—	—	—	—	—	—	—	—	—	—	—	—	—
Kenya	—	—	—	—	—	—	—	—	—	—	—	—	5.1	14.8	14.5
Lesotho	—	—	—	—	—	—	—	—	—	—	—	—	.5	1.5	1.5
Liberia	—	—	—	—	—	—	—	—	—	—	—	—	3.1	8.9	8.8
Madagascar	—	—	—	—	—	—	—	—	—	—	—	—	—	10.8	—
Malawi	—	—	—	—	—	—	—	—	—	—	—	—	1.6	4.6	4.5
Mali	—	—	—	—	—	—	—	—	—	—	—	—	—	9.1	6.7
Mauritania	—	—	—	—	—	—	—	—	—	—	—	—	1.4	4.0	3.9
Mauritius	—	—	—	—	—	—	—	—	—	—	—	—	—	9.1	—
Morocco	—	—	—	—	—	—	—	—	—	—	—	—	12.1	34.8	34.2
Mozambique	—	—	—	—	—	—	—	—	—	—	—	—	—	—	—
Niger	—	—	—	—	—	—	—	—	—	—	—	—	—	5.4	—
Rwanda	—	—	—	—	—	—	—	—	—	—	—	—	—	—	5.8
São Tomé & Príncipe	—	—	—	—	—	—	—	—	—	—	—	—	—	—	—
Senegal	—	—	—	—	—	—	—	—	—	—	—	—	—	14.1	10.3
Sierra Leone	—	—	—	—	—	—	—	—	—	—	—	—	2.7	7.7	7.6
Somalia	—	—	—	—	—	—	—	—	—	—	—	—	—	29.8	21.8
Sudan	—	—	—	—	—	—	—	—	—	—	—	—	—	—	2.4
Swaziland	—	—	—	—	—	—	—	—	—	—	—	—	—	—	—
Tanzania	—	—	—	—	—	—	—	—	—	—	—	—	4.5	12.9	12.7
Togo	—	—	—	—	—	—	—	—	—	—	—	—	—	6.2	4.5
Uganda	—	—	—	—	—	—	—	—	—	—	—	—	—	—	—
Zaïre	—	—	—	—	—	—	—	—	—	—	—	—	12.1	34.8	34.2
Zambia	—	—	—	—	—	—	—	—	—	—	—	—	—	—	23.0
Zimbabwe	—	—	—	—	—	—	—	—	—	—	—	—	—	—	—
Asia	—	—	—	—	—	—	—	—	—	—	—	—	77.6	302.9	182.1
Afghanistan, I.S. of	—	—	—	—	—	—	—	—	—	—	—	—	—	—	—
Bangladesh	—	—	—	—	—	—	—	—	—	—	—	—	13.4	38.4	37.9
Cambodia	—	—	—	—	—	—	—	—	—	—	—	—	—	—	—
China, People's Rep.	—	—	—	—	—	—	—	—	—	—	—	—	—	—	—
India	—	—	—	—	—	—	—	—	—	—	—	—	—	—	—
Lao P. D. Rep.	—	—	—	—	—	—	—	—	—	—	—	—	—	5.4	3.9
Maldives	—	—	—	—	—	—	—	—	—	—	—	—	—	—	—
Mongolia	—	—	—	—	—	—	—	—	—	—	—	—	—	—	—
Myanmar	—	—	—	—	—	—	—	—	—	—	—	—	6.4	18.5	18.2
Nepal	—	—	—	—	—	—	—	—	—	—	—	—	1.5	4.3	4.2
Pakistan	—	—	—	—	—	—	—	—	—	—	—	—	25.1	72.3	—
Papua New Guinea	—	—	—	—	—	—	—	—	—	—	—	—	—	8.3	—
Philippines	—	—	—	—	—	—	—	—	—	—	—	—	16.6	47.7	47.0
Solomon Islands	—	—	—	—	—	—	—	—	—	—	—	—	—	—	—
Sri Lanka	—	—	—	—	—	—	—	—	—	—	—	—	—	40.6	29.7
Thailand	—	—	—	—	—	—	—	—	—	—	—	—	14.3	41.2	40.6
Viet Nam	—	—	—	—	—	—	—	—	—	—	—	—	—	25.7	—
Western Samoa	—	—	—	—	—	—	—	—	—	—	—	—	.2	.6	.6
Europe	—	—	—	—	—	—	—	—	—	—	—	—	—	—	—
Albania	—	—	—	—	—	—	—	—	—	—	—	—	—	—	—
Kyrgyz Republic	—	—	—	—	—	—	—	—	—	—	—	—	—	—	—
Middle East	—	—	—	—	—	—	—	—	—	—	—	—	23.2	66.7	65.7
Egypt	—	—	—	—	—	—	—	—	—	—	—	—	20.1	57.8	57.0
Yemen Arab Rep.	—	—	—	—	—	—	—	—	—	—	—	—	—	—	—
Yemen, P.D. Rep.	—	—	—	—	—	—	—	—	—	—	—	—	3.1	8.9	8.8
Yemen, Republic of	—	—	—	—	—	—	—	—	—	—	—	—	—	—	—
Western Hemisphere	—	—	—	—	—	—	—	—	—	—	—	—	2.3	21.8	13.9
Bolivia	—	—	—	—	—	—	—	—	—	—	—	—	—	15.3	—
Dominica	—	—	—	—	—	—	—	—	—	—	—	—	—	—	—
El Salvador	—	—	—	—	—	—	—	—	—	—	—	—	.2	.6	.6
Grenada	—	—	—	—	—	—	—	—	—	—	—	—	—	—	—
Guyana	—	—	—	—	—	—	—	—	—	—	—	—	2.0	5.8	5.8
Haiti	—	—	—	—	—	—	—	—	—	—	—	—	—	—	7.6
Honduras	—	—	—	—	—	—	—	—	—	—	—	—	—	—	—
Nicaragua	—	—	—	—	—	—	—	—	—	—	—	—	—	—	—
Memorandum Items															
Non-Oil Develop.Ctys	—	—	—	—	—	—	—	—	—	—	—	—	152.9	688.1	526.6

Loan Disbursements

1980	1981	1982	1983	1984	1985	1986	1987	1988	1989	1990	1991	1992	1993	1994	
							Expressed in Millions of SDRs								
1,256.0	367.7	—	—	—	—	81.8	403.4	410.2	961.1	507.0	781.9	544.3	271.7	910.4	**World**
1,256.0	367.7	—	—	—	—	81.8	403.4	410.2	961.1	507.0	781.9	544.3	271.7	910.4	**Developing Countries**
326.6	4.0	—	—	—	—	54.1	251.0	292.4	543.4	359.3	380.6	273.8	142.1	467.1	**Africa**
7.3	.1	—	—	—	—	—	—	—	6.3	—	9.4	—	15.7	18.1	Benin
3.3	.1	—	—	—	—	—	—	—	—	—	6.3	—	8.8	17.7	Burkina Faso
4.9	.1	—	—	—	—	8.5	—	12.8	8.5	—	4.3	14.9	—	—	Burundi
9.0	.1	—	—	—	—	—	—	—	—	—	—	—	—	—	Cameroon
7.3	.1	—	—	—	—	—	6.1	9.1	—	6.1	—	—	—	—	Central African Rep.
—	—	—	—	—	—	—	6.1	—	9.2	6.1	—	—	—	—	Chad
—	—	—	—	—	—	—	—	—	—	—	—	.9	—	1.4	Comoros
3.3	.1	—	—	—	—	—	—	—	—	—	—	—	—	—	Congo
29.1	.2	—	—	—	—	—	—	—	—	—	—	—	—	119.1	Côte d'Ivoire
—	—	—	—	—	—	—	—	—	—	—	—	—	—	—	Djibouti
4.5	—	—	—	—	—	—	—	3.7	—	—	5.5	—	2.8	1.8	Equatorial Guinea
6.9	.1	—	—	—	—	—	—	—	—	—	—	14.1	21.2	14.1	Ethiopia
1.8	—	—	—	—	—	3.4	5.1	3.4	6.8	6.8	3.4	—	—	—	Gambia, The
22.3	.3	—	—	—	—	—	40.9	86.3	137.8	48.0	116.5	—	—	—	Ghana
6.1	.1	—	—	—	—	—	11.6	—	17.4	—	8.7	8.7	—	8.7	Guinea
—	—	—	—	—	—	—	1.5	—	2.3	—	—	—	—	—	Guinea-Bissau
12.3	.2	—	—	—	—	—	—	28.4	80.5	100.5	35.2	—	22.6	22.6	Kenya
1.3	—	—	—	—	—	—	—	3.0	4.5	3.0	2.3	5.3	6.8	3.8	Lesotho
7.4	.1	—	—	—	—	—	—	—	—	—	—	—	—	—	Liberia
14.5	.1	—	—	—	—	—	13.3	—	25.6	12.8	12.8	—	—	—	Madagascar
3.8	.1	—	—	—	—	—	—	9.3	18.6	18.6	14.9	—	—	5.6	Malawi
5.6	.1	—	—	—	—	—	—	—	10.2	—	15.2	—	10.2	29.5	Mali
3.3	.1	—	—	—	—	6.8	10.2	—	8.5	8.5	—	8.5	8.5	17.0	Mauritania
—	—	—	—	—	—	—	—	—	—	—	—	—	—	—	Mauritius
28.9	.4	—	—	—	—	—	—	—	—	—	—	—	—	—	Morocco
—	—	—	—	—	—	—	12.2	18.3	12.2	9.2	30.5	45.8	15.3	14.7	Mozambique
7.3	.1	—	—	—	—	6.7	10.1	8.4	8.4	6.7	—	—	—	—	Niger
4.9	.1	—	—	—	—	—	—	—	—	—	8.8	—	—	—	Rwanda
—	—	—	—	—	—	—	—	—	.8	—	—	—	—	—	São Tomé & Príncipe
8.7	.1	—	—	—	—	17.0	25.5	29.8	51.1	21.3	42.6	—	—	16.7	Senegal
6.4	.1	—	—	—	—	11.6	—	—	—	—	—	—	—	95.6	Sierra Leone
10.6	.1	—	—	—	—	—	8.8	—	—	—	—	—	—	—	Somalia
18.4	.3	—	—	—	—	—	—	—	—	—	—	—	—	—	Sudan
2.0	—	—	—	—	—	—	—	—	—	—	—	—	—	—	Swaziland
10.8	.2	—	—	—	—	—	21.4	32.1	—	21.4	21.4	64.2	—	—	Tanzania
3.8	.1	—	—	—	—	—	—	7.7	15.4	15.4	—	7.7	—	10.9	Togo
22.4	.2	—	—	—	—	—	19.9	29.9	42.3	59.8	57.3	39.8	—	36.7	Uganda
28.9	.4	—	—	—	—	—	58.2	—	87.3	—	—	—	—	—	Zaïre
19.5	.3	—	—	—	—	—	—	—	—	—	—	—	—	—	Zambia
—	—	—	—	—	—	—	—	—	—	—	—	54.7	30.4	33.4	Zimbabwe
821.8	351.2	—	—	—	—	—	151.2	94.6	372.1	87.8	360.9	209.8	105.5	358.9	**Asia**
—	—	—	—	—	—	—	—	—	—	—	—	—	—	—	Afghanistan, I.S. of
32.0	.5	—	—	—	—	—	143.8	38.8	18.7	43.1	186.9	86.3	28.8	—	Bangladesh
—	—	—	—	—	—	—	—	—	—	—	—	—	—	14.0	Cambodia
—	309.5	—	—	—	—	—	—	—	—	—	—	—	—	—	China, People's Rep.
525.5	3.6	—	—	—	—	—	—	—	—	—	—	—	—	—	India
3.3	.1	—	—	—	—	—	—	—	5.9	—	8.8	5.9	5.9	5.9	Lao P. D. Rep.
—	—	—	—	—	—	—	—	—	—	—	—	—	—	—	Maldives
—	—	—	—	—	—	—	—	—	—	—	—	—	9.3	14.8	Mongolia
15.4	.2	—	—	—	—	—	—	—	—	—	—	—	—	—	Myanmar
3.6	.1	—	—	—	—	—	7.5	11.2	7.5	—	—	5.6	5.6	5.6	Nepal
131.4	.9	—	—	—	—	—	—	—	273.2	—	109.3	—	—	202.2	Pakistan
11.2	.1	—	—	—	—	—	—	—	—	—	—	—	—	—	Papua New Guinea
39.7	.6	—	—	—	—	—	—	—	—	—	—	—	—	—	Philippines
—	—	—	—	—	—	—	—	—	—	—	—	—	—	—	Solomon Islands
25.1	.4	—	—	—	—	—	—	44.6	66.9	44.6	56.0	112.0	56.0	56.0	Sri Lanka
34.3	.5	—	—	—	—	—	—	—	—	—	—	—	—	—	Thailand
—	34.9	—	—	—	—	—	—	—	—	—	—	—	—	60.4	Viet Nam
.5	—	—	—	—	—	—	—	—	—	—	—	—	—	—	Western Samoa
—	—	—	—	—	—	—	—	—	—	—	—	—	8.5	25.0	**Europe**
—	—	—	—	—	—	—	—	—	—	—	—	—	8.5	15.5	Albania
—	—	—	—	—	—	—	—	—	—	—	—	—	—	9.5	Kyrgyz Republic
55.6	.8	—	—	—	—	—	—	—	—	—	—	—	—	—	**Middle East**
48.1	.7	—	—	—	—	—	—	—	—	—	—	—	—	—	Egypt
—	—	—	—	—	—	—	—	—	—	—	—	—	—	—	Yemen Arab Rep.
7.4	.1	—	—	—	—	—	—	—	—	—	—	—	—	—	Yemen, P.D. Rep.
—	—	—	—	—	—	—	—	—	—	—	—	—	—	—	Yemen, Republic of
52.0	11.7	—	—	—	—	27.8	1.2	23.2	45.6	59.9	40.4	60.8	15.6	59.4	**Western Hemisphere**
20.7	.1	—	—	—	—	18.1	—	22.7	45.4	22.7	22.7	36.3	—	30.4	Bolivia
—	—	—	—	—	—	.8	1.2	.5	.3	—	—	—	—	—	Dominica
19.6	.1	—	—	—	—	—	—	—	—	—	—	—	—	—	El Salvador
.5	—	—	—	—	—	—	—	—	—	—	—	—	—	—	Grenada
—	11.3	—	—	—	—	—	—	—	—	37.2	17.7	17.7	8.9	9.0	Guyana
4.9	.1	—	—	—	—	8.8	—	—	—	—	—	—	—	—	Haiti
6.4	.1	—	—	—	—	—	—	—	—	—	—	6.8	6.8	—	Honduras
—	—	—	—	—	—	—	—	—	—	—	—	—	—	20.0	Nicaragua
															Memorandum Items
1,256.0	367.7	—	—	—	—	81.8	403.4	410.2	961.1	507.0	781.9	544.3	271.7	910.4	**Non-Oil Develop.Ctys**

Repayments of Loans

Expressed in Millions of SDRs

	1965	1966	1967	1968	1969	1970	1971	1972	1973	1974	1975	1976	1977	1978	1979
World	—	—	—	—	—	—	—	—	—	—	—	—	—	—	—
Developing Countries	—	—	—	—	—	—	—	—	—	—	—	—	—	—	—
Africa															
Benin	—	—	—	—	—	—	—	—	—	—	—	—	—	—	—
Burkina Faso	—	—	—	—	—	—	—	—	—	—	—	—	—	—	—
Burundi	—	—	—	—	—	—	—	—	—	—	—	—	—	—	—
Cameroon	—	—	—	—	—	—	—	—	—	—	—	—	—	—	—
Central African Rep.	—	—	—	—	—	—	—	—	—	—	—	—	—	—	—
Chad	—	—	—	—	—	—	—	—	—	—	—	—	—	—	—
Comoros	—	—	—	—	—	—	—	—	—	—	—	—	—	—	—
Congo	—	—	—	—	—	—	—	—	—	—	—	—	—	—	—
Côte d'Ivoire	—	—	—	—	—	—	—	—	—	—	—	—	—	—	—
Equatorial Guinea	—	—	—	—	—	—	—	—	—	—	—	—	—	—	—
Ethiopia	—	—	—	—	—	—	—	—	—	—	—	—	—	—	—
Gambia, The	—	—	—	—	—	—	—	—	—	—	—	—	—	—	—
Ghana	—	—	—	—	—	—	—	—	—	—	—	—	—	—	—
Guinea	—	—	—	—	—	—	—	—	—	—	—	—	—	—	—
Guinea-Bissau	—	—	—	—	—	—	—	—	—	—	—	—	—	—	—
Kenya	—	—	—	—	—	—	—	—	—	—	—	—	—	—	—
Lesotho	—	—	—	—	—	—	—	—	—	—	—	—	—	—	—
Liberia	—	—	—	—	—	—	—	—	—	—	—	—	—	—	—
Madagascar	—	—	—	—	—	—	—	—	—	—	—	—	—	—	—
Malawi	—	—	—	—	—	—	—	—	—	—	—	—	—	—	—
Mali	—	—	—	—	—	—	—	—	—	—	—	—	—	—	—
Mauritania	—	—	—	—	—	—	—	—	—	—	—	—	—	—	—
Mauritius	—	—	—	—	—	—	—	—	—	—	—	—	—	—	—
Morocco	—	—	—	—	—	—	—	—	—	—	—	—	—	—	—
Mozambique	—	—	—	—	—	—	—	—	—	—	—	—	—	—	—
Niger	—	—	—	—	—	—	—	—	—	—	—	—	—	—	—
Rwanda	—	—	—	—	—	—	—	—	—	—	—	—	—	—	—
São Tomé & Príncipe	—	—	—	—	—	—	—	—	—	—	—	—	—	—	—
Senegal	—	—	—	—	—	—	—	—	—	—	—	—	—	—	—
Sierra Leone	—	—	—	—	—	—	—	—	—	—	—	—	—	—	—
Somalia	—	—	—	—	—	—	—	—	—	—	—	—	—	—	—
Sudan	—	—	—	—	—	—	—	—	—	—	—	—	—	—	—
Swaziland	—	—	—	—	—	—	—	—	—	—	—	—	—	—	—
Tanzania	—	—	—	—	—	—	—	—	—	—	—	—	—	—	—
Togo	—	—	—	—	—	—	—	—	—	—	—	—	—	—	—
Uganda	—	—	—	—	—	—	—	—	—	—	—	—	—	—	—
Zaïre	—	—	—	—	—	—	—	—	—	—	—	—	—	—	—
Zambia	—	—	—	—	—	—	—	—	—	—	—	—	—	—	—
Asia	—	—	—	—	—	—	—	—	—	—	—	—	—	—	—
Afghanistan, I.S. of	—	—	—	—	—	—	—	—	—	—	—	—	—	—	—
Bangladesh	—	—	—	—	—	—	—	—	—	—	—	—	—	—	—
China, People's Rep.	—	—	—	—	—	—	—	—	—	—	—	—	—	—	—
India	—	—	—	—	—	—	—	—	—	—	—	—	—	—	—
Lao P. D. Rep.	—	—	—	—	—	—	—	—	—	—	—	—	—	—	—
Myanmar	—	—	—	—	—	—	—	—	—	—	—	—	—	—	—
Nepal	—	—	—	—	—	—	—	—	—	—	—	—	—	—	—
Pakistan	—	—	—	—	—	—	—	—	—	—	—	—	—	—	—
Papua New Guinea	—	—	—	—	—	—	—	—	—	—	—	—	—	—	—
Philippines	—	—	—	—	—	—	—	—	—	—	—	—	—	—	—
Solomon Islands	—	—	—	—	—	—	—	—	—	—	—	—	—	—	—
Sri Lanka	—	—	—	—	—	—	—	—	—	—	—	—	—	—	—
Thailand	—	—	—	—	—	—	—	—	—	—	—	—	—	—	—
Viet Nam	—	—	—	—	—	—	—	—	—	—	—	—	—	—	—
Western Samoa	—	—	—	—	—	—	—	—	—	—	—	—	—	—	—
Middle East	—	—	—	—	—	—	—	—	—	—	—	—	—	—	—
Egypt	—	—	—	—	—	—	—	—	—	—	—	—	—	—	—
Yemen Arab Rep.	—	—	—	—	—	—	—	—	—	—	—	—	—	—	—
Yemen, P.D. Rep.	—	—	—	—	—	—	—	—	—	—	—	—	—	—	—
Yemen, Republic of	—	—	—	—	—	—	—	—	—	—	—	—	—	—	—
Western Hemisphere	—	—	—	—	—	—	—	—	—	—	—	—	—	—	—
Bolivia	—	—	—	—	—	—	—	—	—	—	—	—	—	—	—
Dominica	—	—	—	—	—	—	—	—	—	—	—	—	—	—	—
El Salvador	—	—	—	—	—	—	—	—	—	—	—	—	—	—	—
Grenada	—	—	—	—	—	—	—	—	—	—	—	—	—	—	—
Guyana	—	—	—	—	—	—	—	—	—	—	—	—	—	—	—
Haiti	—	—	—	—	—	—	—	—	—	—	—	—	—	—	—
Honduras	—	—	—	—	—	—	—	—	—	—	—	—	—	—	—
Memorandum Items															
Non-Oil Develop.Ctys	—	—	—	—	—	—	—	—	—	—	—	—	—	—	—

Repayments of Loans

Expressed in Millions of SDRs

1980	1981	1982	1983	1984	1985	1986	1987	1988	1989	1990	1991	1992	1993	1994	
—	—	3.15	45.22	173.07	299.63	538.96	550.24	502.52	400.28	270.04	50.65	23.55	133.40	222.33	**World**
—	—	3.15	45.22	173.07	299.63	538.96	550.24	502.52	400.28	269.96	50.65	23.55	133.40	222.33	**Developing Countries**
—	—	2.00	16.58	70.72	121.63	175.45	156.79	137.31	104.48	38.87	3.53	14.02	51.52	144.11	**Africa**
—	—	—	.22	1.08	1.07	2.54	2.53	2.30	1.46	1.45	.05	—	—	.63	Benin
—	—	—	.22	1.08	2.13	2.54	2.53	2.30	1.46	.39	.05	—	—	—	Burkina Faso
—	—	.10	.53	1.58	3.12	3.70	3.60	3.17	2.12	.58	.07	1.71	2.99	4.27	Burundi
—	—	—	.60	2.90	5.75	6.82	6.81	6.21	3.91	1.07	.13	—	—	—	Cameroon
—	—	—	.22	1.08	1.78	2.53	2.53	2.31	1.45	.79	.05	—	.73	2.92	Central African Rep.
—	—	—	.23	1.08	1.07	1.08	1.08	.85	—	—	—	—	1.22	1.22	Chad
.48	.30	—	—	.25	—	—	—	—	—	—	—	—	—	—	Comoros
—	—	.07	.36	1.15	2.13	2.46	2.47	2.16	1.46	.39	.05	—	—	—	Congo
—	—	—	—	4.31	6.97	10.13	10.12	10.12	5.82	3.15	.20	—	—	—	Côte d'Ivoire
—	—	—	—	—	—	.89	.90	.89	.90	.89	.03	—	—	.37	Equatorial Guinea
—	—	—	—	2.24	4.44	5.26	5.25	5.26	3.02	.82	.10	—	—	—	Ethiopia
—	—	—	.20	.58	.50	2.01	1.36	1.17	.78	.21	—	.68	1.71	2.74	Gambia, The
—	—	—	—	1.11	7.08	9.73	9.73	9.72	8.62	2.64	.33	—	8.18	30.52	Ghana
—	—	—	.67	1.99	3.94	4.67	4.67	4.01	2.68	.73	.09	—	2.32	4.05	Guinea
—	—	—	—	—	—	—	—	—	—	—	—	—	.30	.15	Guinea-Bissau
—	—	.26	1.34	4.59	8.21	9.03	9.09	8.00	4.75	1.46	.18	—	2.84	9.70	Kenya
—	—	—	.14	.42	.82	.97	.98	.83	.56	.15	.02	—	—	1.06	Lesotho
—	—	.15	.82	2.40	—	—	—	—	—	—	—	—	—	.69	Liberia
—	—	—	.45	2.16	2.15	5.06	5.07	4.61	2.91	2.90	.10	—	2.66	3.65	Madagascar
—	—	—	.42	1.24	2.47	2.92	2.92	2.50	1.68	.45	.06	—	—	2.79	Malawi
—	—	—	.38	1.83	3.61	4.28	4.29	3.90	2.46	.67	.08	—	—	2.03	Mali
—	—	—	.36	1.24	2.14	2.53	2.53	2.17	1.29	.39	.05	1.36	3.39	4.24	Mauritania
—	—	—	.38	1.83	1.82	1.82	1.83	1.44	—	—	—	—	—	—	Mauritius
—	—	.60	3.16	10.82	18.56	22.00	21.40	18.84	11.19	3.43	.43	—	—	—	Morocco
—	—	—	—	—	—	—	—	—	—	—	—	1.22	4.27	7.32	Mozambique
—	—	—	—	1.07	1.08	2.53	2.53	2.53	1.46	1.45	.05	1.34	3.37	4.38	Niger
—	—	—	—	—	1.54	2.13	2.12	2.13	2.12	.58	.07	—	—	—	Rwanda
—	—	—	—	—	—	—	—	—	—	—	—	—	—	.08	São Tomé & Príncipe
—	—	—	.59	2.82	5.58	6.63	6.62	6.03	3.80	1.03	.13	3.40	8.51	17.45	Senegal
—	—	—	.70	2.07	1.03	7.95	1.31	—	.33	1.83	.09	2.32	—	13.76	Sierra Leone
—	—	—	—	—	—	2.12	2.03	—	.08	—	—	—	—	—	Somalia
—	—	—	—	2.98	—	—	—	—	—	—	—	—	—	—	Sudan
—	—	—	—	—	.65	.90	.90	.89	.90	.26	.03	—	—	—	Swaziland
—	—	.22	1.17	3.49	2.73	12.34	7.96	7.00	4.69	1.28	.16	—	4.28	10.70	Tanzania
—	—	—	.26	1.24	2.47	2.92	2.92	2.66	1.68	.45	.06	—	.77	2.30	Togo
—	—	—	—	—	2.04	4.47	4.48	4.47	4.47	2.43	.15	1.99	3.98	17.09	Uganda
—	—	.60	3.16	9.37	18.56	22.01	21.40	18.84	12.63	3.43	.43	—	—	—	Zaïre
—	—	—	—	.97	6.19	8.48	2.83	—	13.80	3.57	.29	—	—	—	Zambia
—	—	.90	21.98	76.90	131.88	302.72	332.77	311.66	263.75	205.25	44.73	5.75	77.84	61.96	**Asia**
—	—	—	—	—	—	—	—	—	—	—	—	—	—	—	Afghanistan, I.S. of
—	—	—	3.50	10.37	20.53	24.34	24.34	20.83	13.98	3.80	.47	5.75	28.75	38.38	Bangladesh
—	—	—	—	—	—	30.96	61.90	61.91	61.90	61.90	30.95	—	—	—	China, People's Rep.
—	—	—	—	—	—	105.09	105.10	105.09	105.09	105.09	3.55	—	—	—	India
—	—	—	—	1.07	2.14	2.53	2.53	2.53	1.46	.39	.05	—	—	—	Lao P. D. Rep.
—	—	—	1.68	5.75	9.85	11.70	11.69	10.00	5.94	1.83	.23	—	—	—	Myanmar
—	—	.07	.39	1.35	2.29	2.73	2.65	2.34	1.38	.43	.05	—	1.49	3.73	Nepal
—	—	—	6.58	19.48	31.49	45.75	45.75	39.18	26.27	14.26	.89	—	—	10.93	Pakistan
—	—	—	—	1.66	1.66	3.89	3.90	3.89	2.24	2.24	.08	—	—	—	Papua New Guinea
—	—	.82	4.34	14.83	25.47	30.17	29.36	25.84	15.34	4.71	.59	—	—	—	Philippines
—	—	—	—	—	—	—	—	—	—	—	—	—	—	—	Solomon Islands
—	—	—	1.69	9.38	16.10	19.08	19.08	17.39	9.70	2.98	.37	—	4.46	8.92	Sri Lanka
—	—	—	3.75	12.82	22.02	26.09	26.09	22.33	13.27	4.07	.51	—	—	—	Thailand
—	—	—	—	—	—	—	—	—	6.98	3.49	6.98	—	43.14	—	Viet Nam
—	—	.01	.05	.19	.33	.39	.38	.33	.20	.06	.01	—	—	—	Western Samoa
—	—	.15	6.08	20.39	35.66	42.24	42.09	36.18	21.85	6.60	.82	—	—	—	**Middle East**
—	—	—	5.26	17.99	30.89	36.60	36.60	31.34	18.61	5.72	.71	—	—	—	Egypt
—	—	—	—	—	—	—	—	—	—	—	—	—	—	—	Yemen Arab Rep.
—	—	.15	.82	2.40	4.77	5.64	5.49	4.84	3.24	.74	—	—	—	—	Yemen, P. D. Rep.
—	—	—	—	—	—	—	—	—	—	.14	.11	—	—	—	Yemen, Republic of
—	—	.10	.58	5.06	10.46	18.55	18.59	17.37	10.20	19.24	1.57	3.78	4.03	16.26	**Western Hemisphere**
—	—	—	—	3.07	4.96	7.20	7.21	7.20	4.13	2.25	.14	3.62	3.63	10.43	Bolivia
—	—	—	—	—	—	—	—	—	—	—	—	.16	.40	.53	Dominica
—	—	—	—	—	—	3.92	3.91	3.91	3.91	3.92	.13	—	—	—	El Salvador
—	—	—	.05	.17	.33	.39	.38	.28	.28	.06	.01	—	—	—	Grenada
—	—	—	—	—	—	—	.56	.71	—	8.87	1.13	—	—	—	Guyana
—	—	.10	.53	1.82	3.13	3.69	3.60	3.17	1.88	.58	.07	—	—	5.29	Haiti
—	—	—	—	—	2.04	2.79	2.78	2.81	—	3.56	.09	—	—	—	Honduras
															Memorandum Items
—	—	3.15	45.22	173.07	299.63	538.96	550.24	502.52	400.28	269.96	50.65	23.55	133.40	222.33	**Non-Oil Develop.Ctys**

Total Fund Credit & Loans Outstdg.*

Expressed in Millions of SDRs

	1965	1966	1967	1968	1969	1970	1971	1972	1973	1974	1975	1976	1977	1978	1979
World	3,024.42	3,020.78	2,482.33	3,687.85	4,011.06	3,232.34	1,346.99	1,089.16	1,027.39	3,740.09	7,435.03	12,607.69	13,230.58	11,118.36	9,343.59
Industrial Countries	1,937.39	1,897.03	1,199.56	2,303.48	2,751.58	2,440.03	497.39	—	—	1,514.47	3,488.08	6,115.85	6,877.62	4,495.37	1,978.58
United States	—	—	—	—	—	—	—	—	—	—	—	—	—	—	—
Canada	—	—	—	—	—	—	—	—	—	—	—	—	—	—	—
Australia	—	—	—	—	—	—	—	—	—	—	—	332.50	332.50	246.86	270.62
Japan	—	—	—	—	—	—	—	—	—	—	—	—	—	—	—
New Zealand	30.72	30.71	119.91	20.64	—	—	—	—	—	85.68	242.23	390.17	388.06	361.23	270.00
Belgium	—	—	—	—	—	—	—	—	—	—	—	—	—	—	—
Denmark	—	—	—	—	—	—	—	—	—	—	—	—	—	—	—
Finland	—	—	62.46	—	—	—	—	—	—	—	71.25	186.36	186.36	152.07	66.38
France	—	—	—	—	499.21	608.95	—	—	—	—	—	—	—	—	—
Germany	—	—	—	—	—	—	—	—	—	—	—	—	—	—	—
Greece	—	—	—	—	—	—	—	—	—	36.22	189.75	247.75	176.49	185.19	147.27
Iceland	—	—	3.75	7.50	11.26	1.76	—	—	—	15.50	31.35	56.42	56.42	47.27	34.71
Ireland	—	1.46	—	—	—	—	—	—	—	—	—	—	—	—	—
Italy	—	—	—	—	—	—	—	—	—	1,377.07	2,457.30	2,457.30	1,580.89	879.96	—
Luxembourg	—	—	—	—	—	—	—	—	—	—	—	—	—	—	—
Netherlands	—	—	—	—	—	—	—	—	—	—	—	—	—	—	—
Norway	—	—	—	—	—	—	—	—	—	—	—	—	—	—	—
Portugal	—	—	—	—	—	—	—	—	—	—	—	173.26	244.91	202.78	171.74
Spain	—	—	—	—	—	—	—	—	—	—	496.20	572.13	572.12	615.34	205.52
United Kingdom	1,906.67	1,864.86	1,013.44	2,275.34	2,241.11	1,829.32	497.39	—	—	—	—	1,699.96	3,339.87	1,804.67	812.50
Developing Countries	1,079.53	1,118.75	1,280.27	1,381.87	1,259.48	792.31	849.60	1,089.16	1,027.39	2,225.62	3,946.95	6,491.84	6,352.96	6,622.99	7,365.01
Africa	56.14	123.74	163.00	201.87	196.05	147.20	84.62	119.45	133.66	291.94	553.50	1,247.94	1,410.75	1,818.28	2,149.84
Algeria	—	—	—	—	—	—	—	—	—	—	—	—	—	—	—
Angola	—	—	—	—	—	—	—	—	—	—	—	—	—	—	—
Benin	—	—	—	—	—	—	—	—	—	—	—	—	—	5.39	5.39
Burkina Faso	—	—	—	—	—	—	—	—	—	—	—	—	—	5.39	9.33
Burundi	—	—	—	2.47	5.78	7.67	5.34	—	—	—	1.20	1.21	3.25	7.87	23.13
Cameroon	—	—	—	—	—	—	—	—	—	4.62	12.13	33.89	33.89	47.27	49.92
Cape Verde	—	—	—	—	—	—	—	—	—	—	—	—	—	—	—
Central African Rep.	—	—	—	—	—	—	—	—	—	2.66	4.85	9.59	9.59	15.67	13.57
Chad	—	—	—	—	—	2.47	2.32	2.18	1.02	3.11	2.97	9.47	9.47	13.54	12.99
Comoros	—	—	—	—	—	—	—	—	—	—	—	—	—	—	—
Congo	—	—	—	—	—	—	—	—	—	—	—	—	9.34	16.68	21.58
Côte d'Ivoire	—	—	—	—	—	—	—	—	—	11.17	11.17	23.36	13.41	21.55	21.55
Djibouti	—	—	—	—	—	—	—	—	—	—	—	—	—	—	—
Equatorial Guinea	—	—	—	—	—	—	—	—	—	—	—	—	—	11.19	55.77
Ethiopia	—	—	—	—	—	—	—	—	—	—	—	—	—	7.61	15.22
Gabon	—	—	—	—	—	—	—	—	—	—	—	—	—	—	—
Gambia, The	—	—	—	—	—	—	—	—	—	—	—	—	4.26	11.70	10.36
Ghana	—	45.04	63.85	74.71	69.29	46.07	18.31	1.71	—	—	38.60	38.60	38.60	34.43	82.48
Guinea	—	—	—	—	.50	3.45	2.95	2.95	1.02	9.51	7.11	7.11	18.38	19.98	26.16
Guinea-Bissau	—	—	—	—	—	—	—	—	—	—	—	—	—	—	1.10
Kenya	—	—	—	—	—	—	—	—	—	32.05	68.55	85.03	52.79	72.19	142.74
Lesotho	—	—	—	—	—	—	—	—	—	—	—	—	.54	2.08	3.59
Liberia	9.05	9.64	10.60	10.60	7.61	4.35	1.52	—	.06	—	—	—	3.11	12.02	50.98
Madagascar	—	—	—	—	—	—	—	—	—	3.45	14.30	14.30	15.67	24.19	20.65
Malawi	—	—	—	—	—	—	—	—	—	—	2.37	3.73	10.77	11.75	37.70
Mali	9.72	9.89	11.26	11.69	10.68	8.58	7.46	8.30	7.33	10.36	10.62	12.73	11.18	19.21	22.07
Mauritania	—	—	—	—	—	—	—	—	—	—	—	11.82	17.92	22.02	25.08
Mauritius	—	—	—	—	3.70	—	—	—	—	—	—	—	11.00	20.29	48.41
Morocco	—	—	—	34.09	37.49	27.54	—	—	—	—	—	115.46	127.56	220.00	231.88
Mozambique	—	—	—	—	—	—	—	—	—	—	—	—	—	—	—
Namibia	—	—	—	—	—	—	—	—	—	—	—	—	—	—	—
Niger	—	—	—	—	—	—	—	—	—	—	—	—	—	5.39	5.39
Nigeria	—	—	—	—	—	—	—	—	—	—	—	—	—	—	—
Rwanda	—	4.68	5.50	5.93	4.94	2.93	—	—	—	—	—	—	—	—	5.76
São Tomé & Príncipe	—	—	—	—	—	—	—	—	—	—	—	—	—	—	—
Senegal	—	—	—	—	—	—	—	—	—	—	—	25.43	25.43	25.44	57.00	70.51
Seychelles	—	—	—	—	—	—	—	—	—	—	—	—	—	—	—
Sierra Leone	—	—	4.57	4.54	3.04	—	—	—	—	4.32	4.94	22.42	32.10	35.60	43.76
Somalia	8.39	8.37	7.67	—	—	—	—	—	—	—	—	—	—	.14	.14
South Africa	—	—	—	—	—	—	—	—	—	—	—	315.00	391.99	314.38	76.77
Sudan	14.98	26.96	39.22	40.50	39.89	30.87	15.18	28.10	29.03	71.65	113.39	119.08	99.47	150.64	222.44
Swaziland	—	—	—	—	—	—	—	—	—	—	—	—	—	—	2.43
Tanzania	—	—	—	—	—	—	—	—	—	38.85	62.62	83.63	91.23	81.46	115.47
Togo	—	—	—	—	—	—	—	—	—	—	—	—	7.50	7.50	6.22	10.76
Tunisia	14.00	19.16	20.33	17.34	13.13	13.27	2.56	—	—	—	—	—	24.00	24.00	24.00
Uganda	—	—	—	—	—	—	9.99	9.99	9.99	14.97	24.07	32.72	32.72	29.20	26.20
Zaïre	—	—	—	—	—	—	—	28.23	28.23	28.23	73.25	180.64	220.33	247.11	271.57
Zambia	—	—	—	—	—	—	18.99	37.99	56.98	56.99	75.93	95.22	95.24	245.12	342.99
Zimbabwe	—	—	—	—	—	—	—	—	—	—	—	—	—	—	—
Asia	418.83	511.57	622.02	664.90	606.55	372.11	364.61	477.37	396.54	1,202.73	1,817.72	2,112.46	1,909.89	2,088.32	2,258.20
Afghanistan, I.S. of	7.30	10.38	11.22	12.28	17.10	14.53	10.13	5.73	7.23	4.74	9.24	1.75	—	—	—
Bangladesh	—	—	—	—	—	—	—	62.50	62.50	133.31	171.60	235.81	207.76	229.43	262.26
Bhutan	—	—	—	—	—	—	—	—	—	—	—	—	—	—	—
Cambodia	—	—	—	—	—	—	—	6.25	12.50	12.50	12.50	12.50	12.50	12.50	12.50
China, People's Rep.	—	—	—	—	—	—	—	—	—	—	—	—	—	—	—
Fiji	—	—	—	—	—	—	—	—	—	.34	—	—	6.50	6.50	6.50
India	286.96	360.93	456.27	373.57	240.43	10.00	—	—	—	496.99	698.32	406.32	125.10	—	—
Indonesia	63.45	63.45	48.98	63.97	112.10	138.46	125.36	107.12	19.16	—	—	—	—	—	—
Kiribati	—	—	—	—	—	—	—	—	—	—	—	—	—	—	—
Korea	—	—	—	—	—	—	—	—	—	110.00	217.28	301.68	280.37	201.84	104.41
Lao P. D. Rep.	—	—	—	—	—	—	—	—	—	—	3.25	6.50	6.50	15.89	18.30
Malaysia	—	—	—	—	—	—	7.28	7.28	—	—	—	93.00	.36	—	—
Maldives	—	—	—	—	—	—	—	—	—	—	—	—	—	—	—

*Includes outstanding use of Fund's credits within GRA, and SAF, ESAF, and Trust Fund loans.

Total Fund Credit & Loans Outstdg.*

Expressed in Millions of SDRs

1980	1981	1982	1983	1984	1985	1986	1987	1988	1989	1990	1991	1992	1993	1994	
11,109.27	16,358.70	22,297.78	32,841.86	37,675.34	37,650.06	35,348.07	30,618.26	26,523.99	24,649.95	23,303.70	26,681.77	27,791.13	29,159.13	30,262.08	**World**
1,216.11	545.80	138.18	376.25	593.40	593.40	582.65	373.05	—	—	—	—	—	—	—	**Industrial Countries**
—	—	—	—	—	—	—	—	—	—	—	—	—	—	—	United States
—	—	—	—	—	—	—	—	—	—	—	—	—	—	—	Canada
61.71	—	32.46	—	—	—	—	—	—	—	—	—	—	—	—	Australia
—	—	—	—	—	—	—	—	—	—	—	—	—	—	—	Japan
132.33	33.66	2.90	—	—	—	—	—	—	—	—	—	—	—	—	New Zealand
—	—	—	—	—	—	—	—	—	—	—	—	—	—	—	Belgium
—	—	—	—	—	—	—	—	—	—	—	—	—	—	—	Denmark
66.38	52.07	14.39	—	—	—	—	—	—	—	—	—	—	—	—	Finland
—	—	—	—	—	—	—	—	—	—	—	—	—	—	—	France
—	—	—	—	—	—	—	—	—	—	—	—	—	—	—	Germany
78.46	13.91	—	—	—	—	—	—	—	—	—	—	—	—	—	Greece
15.71	5.92	22.35	21.50	21.50	21.50	10.75	—	—	—	—	—	—	—	—	Iceland
—	—	—	—	—	—	—	—	—	—	—	—	—	—	—	Ireland
—	—	—	—	—	—	—	—	—	—	—	—	—	—	—	Italy
—	—	—	—	—	—	—	—	—	—	—	—	—	—	—	Luxembourg
—	—	—	—	—	—	—	—	—	—	—	—	—	—	—	Netherlands
—	—	—	—	—	—	—	—	—	—	—	—	—	—	—	Norway
93.66	47.47	9.78	354.75	571.90	571.90	571.90	373.05	—	—	—	—	—	—	—	Portugal
205.36	141.62	4.75	—	—	—	—	—	—	—	—	—	—	—	—	Spain
562.50	312.50	51.55	—	—	—	—	—	—	—	—	—	—	—	—	United Kingdom
9,893.16	15,751.78	22,159.60	32,465.61	37,081.94	37,056.66	34,765.42	30,245.21	26,523.99	24,649.95	23,303.70	26,681.77	27,791.13	29,159.13	30,262.08	**Developing Countries**
2,728.32	4,274.13	6,146.28	7,407.53	7,973.95	8,028.91	7,185.06	6,326.39	6,118.59	6,177.95	5,762.72	5,896.24	5,727.22	5,871.47	6,532.68	**Africa**
—	—	—	—	—	—	—	—	—	470.90	470.90	695.90	578.18	342.73	793.77	Algeria
—	—	—	—	—	—	—	—	—	—	—	—	—	—	—	Angola
12.65	12.70	12.70	12.48	11.40	10.33	7.79	5.26	2.96	7.76	6.31	15.65	15.65	31.30	48.79	Benin
12.65	12.70	12.70	12.48	11.40	9.27	6.73	4.20	1.90	.44	.05	6.32	6.32	15.16	32.84	Burkina Faso
28.00	28.07	27.97	22.69	16.36	13.24	18.08	14.48	24.12	30.54	29.96	34.16	47.39	44.40	40.13	Burundi
46.04	37.68	34.74	33.60	30.70	24.95	18.13	11.32	74.64	86.18	85.11	84.28	45.66	11.86	29.91	Cameroon
—	—	—	—	—	—	—	—	—	—	—	—	—	—	—	Cape Verde
18.43	32.41	34.19	38.15	35.77	35.49	34.13	36.58	37.33	26.88	25.73	23.28	22.09	20.96	28.34	Central African Rep.
10.81	12.49	12.49	12.26	8.52	10.90	8.93	13.97	12.24	17.92	21.42	21.42	21.42	20.20	29.30	Chad
—	—	—	—	—	—	—	—	—	—	—	.90	.90	.90	2.25	Comoros
17.44	12.70	12.63	12.27	11.12	8.99	16.03	13.56	11.40	8.75	7.61	4.00	4.00	3.50	14.00	Congo
50.62	370.02	485.43	640.31	649.68	605.53	538.67	425.81	377.88	281.25	303.14	259.72	194.46	159.13	224.75	Côte d'Ivoire
—	—	—	—	—	—	—	—	—	—	—	—	—	—	—	Djibouti
12.62	19.24	19.24	19.24	13.19	11.70	9.01	8.11	10.61	6.72	4.10	9.20	9.20	11.96	13.43	Equatorial Guinea
62.29	124.39	145.64	127.64	100.22	64.76	68.76	53.37	40.84	22.98	4.51	—	14.12	35.30	49.42	Ethiopia
11.36	11.34	9.35	1.85	—	—	27.41	42.50	98.68	102.69	98.49	84.34	58.55	32.89	61.42	Gabon
12.67	21.70	36.35	33.52	33.65	30.36	24.13	26.65	25.69	28.67	31.55	30.61	28.39	26.68	23.94	Gambia, The
82.51	73.19	68.35	316.55	525.05	637.97	642.26	610.94	566.36	561.16	523.39	583.12	537.83	537.30	479.70	Ghana
27.45	23.67	34.95	34.28	32.29	28.35	32.93	40.09	36.08	46.65	36.17	38.39	46.32	44.00	48.63	Guinea
1.10	2.95	2.68	2.26	3.73	2.80	1.87	3.14	2.20	3.75	3.75	3.75	3.75	3.45	3.30	Guinea-Bissau
199.06	222.22	356.73	443.47	428.28	474.73	375.90	282.89	338.44	316.12	338.88	344.84	286.08	264.34	277.25	Kenya
4.87	4.89	4.89	4.75	4.33	3.51	2.54	1.56	3.75	7.72	10.59	12.84	18.12	24.92	27.63	Lesotho
69.78	115.27	176.82	223.75	237.25	230.40	230.40	230.40	229.36	227.20	226.52	226.52	226.52	226.52	225.83	Liberia
68.23	100.23	151.95	158.05	173.79	167.63	165.96	167.72	141.39	125.79	100.98	88.67	77.14	67.04	58.86	Madagascar
62.49	89.94	88.24	111.76	127.92	132.47	108.96	82.43	78.55	76.45	80.83	80.45	66.86	62.62	76.90	Malawi
30.33	28.16	52.47	65.32	84.30	89.19	80.77	60.04	54.87	41.93	48.71	41.97	47.53	51.44	74.10	Mali
39.06	42.48	56.42	51.67	41.44	36.51	42.73	54.10	52.54	52.30	49.17	39.50	42.03	46.11	58.82	Mauritania
79.86	136.86	159.35	172.82	164.23	150.11	132.14	106.94	76.51	47.58	15.51	—	—	—	—	Mauritius
358.35	497.37	897.52	985.48	1,107.19	1,160.57	894.39	789.09	711.10	646.57	526.93	401.54	319.10	207.15	101.06	Morocco
—	—	—	—	—	—	—	—	12.20	30.50	42.70	51.85	82.35	126.88	137.86	145.24	Mozambique
—	—	—	—	—	—	—	—	—	—	—	—	—	—	—	Namibia
12.65	12.70	12.70	43.50	56.83	71.25	86.76	86.33	70.32	64.37	59.66	51.30	44.59	37.75	42.46	Niger
—	—	—	—	—	—	—	—	—	—	—	—	—	—	—	Nigeria
10.62	10.69	10.69	10.69	10.69	9.15	7.02	4.90	2.77	.65	.07	8.76	8.76	8.76	8.76	Rwanda
—	—	—	—	—	—	—	—	—	.80	.80	.80	.80	.80	.72	São Tomé & Príncipe
109.88	160.21	200.04	220.45	234.67	243.74	236.25	241.64	236.54	240.42	220.95	228.90	197.36	177.81	205.43	Senegal
—	—	—	—	—	—	—	—	—	—	—	—	—	—	—	Seychelles
46.56	72.16	70.87	88.85	97.47	92.02	82.85	81.54	80.81	79.54	76.16	70.70	66.97	61.01	100.20	Sierra Leone
14.03	39.98	72.22	117.22	114.34	140.13	127.30	123.69	123.01	114.09	112.00	112.00	112.00	112.00	112.00	Somalia
—	—	795.00	745.00	745.00	745.00	397.50	—	—	—	—	—	—	614.43	614.43	South Africa
337.98	484.77	524.61	666.65	677.60	672.68	672.68	672.68	672.68	672.68	671.64	671.64	671.64	671.64	671.61	Sudan
4.47	4.50	4.50	14.48	14.48	12.85	8.57	4.30	1.16	.26	—	—	—	—	—	Swaziland
134.32	125.72	114.38	88.11	60.19	52.62	58.15	80.00	105.10	97.82	98.35	100.20	160.50	156.22	145.52	Tanzania
25.48	32.78	32.78	51.90	63.49	67.60	73.82	60.13	57.89	57.38	61.12	55.29	55.82	49.87	56.04	Togo
—	—	—	—	—	—	—	149.71	190.71	205.71	205.71	123.73	180.10	211.05	207.30	207.30	Tunisia
70.11	182.45	265.92	360.55	343.82	277.59	203.44	192.76	187.59	171.20	198.22	230.91	250.11	243.03	262.59	Uganda
292.75	407.45	492.93	593.87	688.45	735.11	699.67	681.26	584.07	478.19	386.28	330.31	330.31	330.31	327.27	Zaïre
350.80	670.55	618.34	678.51	753.79	728.94	701.63	698.80	698.80	685.00	666.74	641.62	615.62	565.83	551.20	Zambia
—	37.50	37.50	191.10	261.32	240.47	191.06	110.30	52.20	22.24	4.84	—	157.20	205.00	257.50	Zimbabwe
3,827.43	6,909.52	9,009.65	11,329.02	11,628.26	10,669.76	9,933.73	8,058.36	6,267.08	5,378.75	3,608.98	5,030.76	5,952.42	6,365.68	5,816.83	**Asia**
—	—	—	—	—	—	—	—	—	—	—	—	—	—	—	Afghanistan, I.S. of
332.58	398.94	496.22	539.99	471.61	473.29	440.47	592.66	623.88	546.78	439.70	523.24	547.69	511.75	473.37	Bangladesh
—	—	—	—	—	—	—	—	—	—	—	—	—	—	—	Bhutan
12.50	12.50	12.50	12.50	12.50	12.50	12.50	12.50	12.50	12.50	12.50	12.50	6.25	6.25	20.25	Cambodia
—	759.53	759.53	309.53	309.53	309.53	876.30	814.40	752.49	690.59	329.82	.01	.01	.01	.01	China, People's Rep.
—	—	13.50	13.50	13.50	13.19	6.44	4.75	2.97	.59	—	—	—	—	—	Fiji
791.46	1,095.01	2,595.01	4,061.76	4,528.76	4,354.01	3,917.67	3,175.07	2,282.48	1,439.89	803.55	2,426.41	3,260.41	3,584.91	2,763.18	India
—	—	—	—	425.10	421.46	41.96	41.96	504.86	462.90	462.90	347.18	115.73	—	—	Indonesia
—	—	—	—	—	—	—	—	—	—	—	—	—	—	—	Kiribati
535.43	1,070.64	1,141.68	1,292.83	1,598.85	1,373.03	1,266.25	369.78	—	—	—	—	—	—	—	Korea
21.22	25.64	25.64	25.64	19.88	11.36	6.96	4.43	1.90	6.30	5.91	14.65	20.51	26.38	32.24	Lao P. D. Rep.
—	189.75	248.25	315.08	262.86	107.21	—	—	—	—	—	—	—	—	—	Malaysia
—	—	—	—	—	—	—	—	—	—	—	—	—	—	—	Maldives

*Includes outstanding use of Fund's credits within GRA, and SAF, ESAF, and Trust Fund loans.

Total Fund Credit & Loans Outstdg.*

Expressed in Millions of SDRs

	1965	1966	1967	1968	1969	1970	1971	1972	1973	1974	1975	1976	1977	1978	1979
Asia (cont.)															
Mongolia	—	—	—	—	—	—	—	—	—	—	—	—	—	—	—
Myanmar	—	—	7.50	7.50	7.50	16.47	17.97	7.98	14.98	36.48	40.48	34.48	58.10	85.29	97.02
Nepal	—	—	—	—	—	—	—	—	—	—	—	4.49	5.99	15.31	18.56
Pakistan	37.46	37.45	35.80	61.06	81.44	45.38	42.59	110.70	129.82	238.87	374.41	439.55	462.78	492.46	434.76
Papua New Guinea	—	—	—	—	—	—	—	—	—	—	—	24.80	24.80	23.09	18.10
Philippines	—	—	—	55.00	55.00	68.75	89.74	95.25	76.25	67.81	164.68	348.41	435.01	505.53	617.99
Solomon Islands	—	—	—	—	—	—	—	—	—	—	—	—	—	—	—
Sri Lanka	23.66	39.36	62.25	91.52	92.98	78.52	71.54	74.56	74.10	101.69	124.70	134.25	169.94	226.50	304.78
Thailand	—	—	—	—	—	—	—	—	—	—	—	—	67.00	81.34	191.29	278.14
Tonga	—	—	—	—	—	—	—	—	—	—	—	—	—	—	—
Viet Nam	—	—	—	—	—	—	—	—	—	—	—	—	31.00	79.20	80.13
Western Samoa	—	—	—	—	—	—	—	—	—	—	1.26	1.92	1.84	3.49	4.75
Europe	106.10	96.10	132.10	141.34	92.09	74.13	128.88	83.50	69.25	192.88	458.37	936.35	862.85	948.68	1,111.07
Albania	—	—	—	—	—	—	—	—	—	—	—	—	—	—	—
Armenia	—	—	—	—	—	—	—	—	—	—	—	—	—	—	—
Belarus	—	—	—	—	—	—	—	—	—	—	—	—	—	—	—
Bulgaria	—	—	—	—	—	—	—	—	—	—	—	—	—	—	—
Croatia	—	—	—	—	—	—	—	—	—	—	—	—	—	—	—
Cyprus	—	—	—	—	—	—	—	—	—	—	6.38	8.10	43.07	43.07	32.92	37.98
Czech Republic	—	—	—	—	—	—	—	—	—	—	—	—	—	—	—
Czechoslovakia	—	—	—	—	—	—	—	—	—	—	—	—	—	—	—
Estonia	—	—	—	—	—	—	—	—	—	—	—	—	—	—	—
Georgia	—	—	—	—	—	—	—	—	—	—	—	—	—	—	—
Hungary	—	—	—	—	—	—	—	—	—	—	—	—	—	—	—
Kazakhstan	—	—	—	—	—	—	—	—	—	—	—	—	—	—	—
Kyrgyz Republic	—	—	—	—	—	—	—	—	—	—	—	—	—	—	—
Latvia	—	—	—	—	—	—	—	—	—	—	—	—	—	—	—
Lithuania	—	—	—	—	—	—	—	—	—	—	—	—	—	—	—
Macedonia, former YR	—	—	—	—	—	—	—	—	—	—	—	—	—	—	—
Moldova	—	—	—	—	—	—	—	—	—	—	—	—	—	—	—
Poland	—	—	—	—	—	—	—	—	—	—	—	—	—	—	—
Romania	—	—	—	—	—	—	—	—	—	47.50	47.50	87.50	237.50	270.00	255.55	246.80
Russia	—	—	—	—	—	—	—	—	—	—	—	—	—	—	—
Slovak Republic	—	—	—	—	—	—	—	—	—	—	—	—	—	—	—
Slovenia	—	—	—	—	—	—	—	—	—	—	—	—	—	—	—
Turkey	18.89	18.89	21.39	48.38	36.88	74.13	62.13	—	—	—	207.57	336.81	336.81	477.68	480.29
Ukraine	—	—	—	—	—	—	—	—	—	—	—	—	—	—	—
Uzbekistan	—	—	—	—	—	—	—	—	—	—	—	—	—	—	—
Yugoslavia, SFR	87.21	77.21	110.71	92.96	55.21	—	66.75	83.50	21.75	139.00	155.20	318.97	212.97	182.53	346.00
Middle East	113.04	82.55	110.74	81.21	82.64	71.32	111.56	51.51	81.63	140.14	300.13	499.99	600.20	689.39	645.31
Bahrain	—	—	—	—	—	—	—	—	—	—	—	—	—	—	—
Egypt	95.19	70.30	74.24	71.71	50.66	49.34	69.84	24.40	62.17	92.95	68.22	177.90	275.01	374.23	381.37
Iran, I.R. of	—	—	—	—	—	—	—	—	—	—	—	—	—	—	—
Iraq	—	—	19.97	—	—	—	—	—	—	—	—	—	—	—	—
Israel	—	—	—	—	22.48	12.48	32.48	—	—	32.50	208.25	285.25	285.24	271.26	224.21
Jordan	—	—	—	—	—	—	4.49	4.49	1.59	.01	.01	.01	.01	—	—
Syrian Arab Republic	17.85	12.25	16.53	9.50	9.50	9.50	4.75	22.62	17.87	5.37	—	—	—	—	.75
Yemen Arab Rep.	—	—	—	—	—	—	—	—	—	—	—	—	—	—	—
Yemen, P.D. Rep.	—	—	—	—	—	—	—	—	—	—	9.31	23.65	36.83	39.94	43.90	38.98
Yemen, Republic of	—	—	—	—	—	—	—	—	—	—	—	—	—	—	—
Western Hemisphere	385.42	304.79	252.41	292.55	282.15	127.55	159.93	357.33	346.31	397.93	817.23	1,695.10	1,569.27	1,078.32	1,200.59
Antigua and Barbuda	—	—	—	—	—	—	—	—	—	—	—	—	—	—	—
Argentina	76.00	30.00	—	—	—	—	—	174.00	174.00	64.00	250.09	455.59	344.50	—	—
Barbados	—	—	—	—	—	—	—	—	—	—	—	—	6.50	6.50	6.50
Belize	—	—	—	—	—	—	—	—	—	—	—	—	—	—	—
Bolivia	—	—	—	5.09	8.08	6.08	6.60	7.88	18.05	14.32	13.93	—	—	30.33	30.33
Brazil	89.32	44.47	11.97	—	—	—	—	—	—	—	—	—	—	—	—
Chile	99.99	85.19	69.99	78.99	56.99	1.49	39.50	79.00	79.00	159.97	330.79	402.22	300.62	266.49	135.94
Colombia	59.51	57.50	91.40	112.65	106.25	54.85	53.25	—	—	—	—	—	—	—	—
Costa Rica	15.00	15.48	15.48	9.73	—	—	—	—	—	18.84	29.96	32.30	29.31	24.32	43.81
Dominica	—	—	—	—	—	—	—	—	—	—	—	—	—	—	1.90
Dominican Republic	13.75	20.00	16.65	9.30	14.60	6.55	10.75	3.75	—	—	—	21.50	36.50	36.50	94.33
Ecuador	6.00	11.00	10.18	—	12.25	13.75	5.50	8.25	—	—	—	—	—	—	—
El Salvador	—	13.74	13.73	16.72	13.97	6.49	10.19	8.75	—	—	17.89	17.89	12.82	—	—
Grenada	—	—	—	—	—	—	—	—	—	—	—	.81	1.21	1.42	2.03	2.40
Guatemala	—	5.34	15.34	13.39	11.14	—	—	—	—	—	—	—	—	—	—
Guyana	—	—	—	—	—	—	2.06	—	3.87	5.00	—	17.25	17.25	30.27	40.49
Haiti	6.17	6.36	7.67	5.68	5.11	2.19	.80	—	—	6.64	10.97	12.38	10.47	15.51	19.34
Honduras	3.75	2.74	—	—	—	—	—	—	—	—	16.78	16.78	16.78	4.29	—	7.58
Jamaica	—	—	—	—	—	—	—	—	—	13.25	13.25	13.25	68.94	88.14	138.58	266.76
Mexico	—	—	—	—	—	—	—	—	—	—	—	319.12	419.12	229.37	103.11
Nicaragua	8.43	6.49	—	14.25	13.25	8.00	10.99	8.25	12.24	10.06	15.50	8.74	2.00	2.01	43.51
Panama	—	—	—	2.27	2.70	—	—	—	—	—	7.37	17.52	42.62	42.16	40.32	31.45
Paraguay	—	—	—	—	—	—	—	—	—	—	—	—	—	—	—
Peru	—	—	—	3.75	28.31	9.90	3.27	30.75	13.64	—	—	158.75	168.75	256.09	373.14
St. Lucia	—	—	—	—	—	—	—	—	—	—	—	—	—	—	—
St. Vincent & Grens.	—	—	—	—	—	—	—	—	—	—	—	—	—	—	—
Suriname	—	—	—	—	—	—	—	—	—	—	—	—	—	—	—
Trinidad and Tobago	—	—	—	—	—	—	—	—	—	—	—	—	—	—	—
Uruguay	7.50	6.48	—	20.73	9.50	18.25	17.02	36.70	32.26	63.81	99.74	124.88	98.24	—	—
Venezuela	—	—	—	—	—	—	—	—	—	—	—	—	—	—	—
Memorandum Items															
Oil Exporting Ctys	63.45	63.45	68.95	63.97	112.10	138.46	125.36	107.12	19.16	—	—	—	—	—	—
Non-Oil Develop.Ctys	1,016.08	1,055.30	1,211.32	1,317.90	1,147.38	653.85	724.24	982.04	1,008.23	2,225.62	3,946.95	6,491.84	6,352.96	6,622.99	7,365.01

*Includes outstanding use of Fund's credits within GRA, and SAF, ESAF, and Trust Fund loans.

Total Fund Credit & Loans Outstdg.*

Expressed in Millions of SDRs

1980	1981	1982	1983	1984	1985	1986	1987	1988	1989	1990	1991	1992	1993	1994	
															Asia (cont.)
—	—	—	—	—	—	—	—	—	—	—	11.25	13.75	23.03	37.87	Mongolia
87.71	107.55	130.25	141.52	129.71	106.36	67.97	28.90	7.97	2.03	.20	—.03	—.03	—.03	—.03	Myanmar
32.63	32.48	27.66	22.40	15.80	19.83	19.20	30.31	39.16	39.85	30.89	26.90	31.71	35.81	37.67	Nepal
528.49	879.65	1,286.16	1,540.25	1,469.20	1,288.51	973.24	647.20	411.43	709.66	587.26	746.37	819.86	816.50	1,096.83	Pakistan
24.28	64.55	64.55	64.55	34.59	26.33	12.34	8.44	4.55	2.31	42.91	42.83	42.83	32.12	10.70	Papua New Guinea
819.65	974.50	905.92	1,045.55	903.24	1,048.75	1,034.60	888.06	812.55	895.26	640.87	759.02	800.12	880.74	728.56	Philippines
—	.80	2.40	3.36	3.16	2.76	2.83	1.55	1.25	1.09	.47	—	—	—	—	Solomon Islands
306.53	442.63	437.22	425.15	413.04	361.09	283.55	195.11	267.10	278.31	288.10	280.17	337.77	375.71	422.78	Sri Lanka
273.06	737.14	767.16	993.76	921.61	1,021.11	874.18	685.56	492.11	207.45	.51	—	—	—	—	Thailand
															Tonga
57.38	111.80	90.30	88.99	88.99	88.99	88.99	88.99	88.99	88.99	82.01	78.52	71.54	71.54	72.48	Viet Nam
4.51	6.41	5.70	7.56	9.97	9.95	8.28	5.79	2.85	1.23	.59	.16	—	—	193.36	Western Samoa
1,710.74	2,739.41	3,917.91	4,929.39	5,371.81	4,792.79	4,004.67	2,775.86	1,773.89	905.53	917.13	3,464.62	4,695.05	6,159.49	8,036.38	**Europe**
—	—	—	—	—	—	—	—	—	—	—	—	9.69	21.60	37.13	Albania
—	—	—	—	—	—	—	—	—	—	—	—	—	—	16.88	Armenia
—	—	—	—	—	—	—	—	—	—	—	—	—	70.10	70.10	Belarus
—	—	—	—	—	—	—	—	—	—	—	—	289.23	428.90	459.90	644.41	Bulgaria
—	—	—	—	—	—	—	—	—	—	—	—	—	14.82	87.06	Croatia
30.60	21.62	12.30	5.47	3.17	—	—	—	—	—	—	—	—	—	—	Cyprus
—	—	—	—	—	—	—	—	—	—	—	—	—	780.68	—	Czech Republic
—	—	—	—	—	—	—	—	—	—	—	.01	917.94	1,121.50	—	Czechoslovakia
—	—	—	—	—	—	—	—	—	—	—	—	—	7.75	41.85	41.85	Estonia
—	—	—	—	—	—	—	—	—	—	—	—	—	—	27.75	Georgia
—	—	214.50	547.00	972.00	883.71	842.73	569.87	471.30	347.11	231.68	880.21	875.84	896.30	781.58	Hungary
—	—	—	—	—	—	—	—	—	—	—	—	—	61.88	198.00	Kazakhstan
—	—	—	—	—	—	—	—	—	—	—	—	—	43.86	53.32	Kyrgyz Republic
—	—	—	—	—	—	—	—	—	—	—	—	25.16	77.78	109.80	Latvia
—	—	—	—	—	—	—	—	—	—	—	—	17.25	87.98	134.55	Lithuania
—	—	—	—	—	—	—	—	—	—	—	—	—	2.81	14.03	Macedonia, former YR
—	—	—	—	—	—	—	—	—	—	—	—	—	63.00	112.45	Moldova
—	—	—	—	—	—	—	—	—	—	357.50	596.60	596.60	497.69	918.59	Poland
257.42	506.66	781.61	904.65	955.74	782.85	583.53	357.55	106.91	—	—	—	565.80	750.90	906.41	Romania
—	—	—	—	—	—	—	—	—	—	—	—	719.00	1,797.28	2,875.55	Russia
—	—	—	—	—	—	—	—	—	—	—	—	—	405.17	439.81	Slovak Republic
—	—	—	—	—	—	—	—	—	—	—	—	—	8.53	4.94	Slovenia
826.58	1,135.63	1,319.18	1,497.09	1,455.03	1,207.51	887.19	542.97	222.03	36.25	—	—	—	—	235.50	Turkey
—	—	—	—	—	—	—	—	—	—	—	—	—	—	249.33	Ukraine
—	—	—	—	—	—	—	—	—	—	—	—	—	—	—	Uzbekistan
596.14	1,075.50	1,590.32	1,975.18	1,985.87	1,918.72	1,691.22	1,305.47	973.65	522.17	327.94	214.84	142.46	77.36	77.36	Yugoslavia, SFR
516.45	388.52	307.38	280.28	259.88	267.88	201.83	252.57	181.15	196.83	154.06	155.24	407.03	385.02	409.73	**Middle East**
—	—	—	—	—	—	—	—	—	—	—	—	—	—	—	Bahrain
322.06	268.84	235.73	227.77	209.78	167.08	117.98	184.88	141.04	122.43	87.71	89.00	147.20	147.20	132.20	Egypt
—	—	—	.01	—	—	—	—	—	—	—	—	—	—	—	Iran, I.R. of
156.40	87.54	27.15	—	—	—	.01	—	—	—	—	—	178.64	178.64	178.64	Iraq
—	—	—	—	—	57.40	57.40	57.40	35.88	73.41	66.24	66.24	81.19	59.18	98.89	Israel
—	—	—	—	—	—	—	—	—	—	—	—	—	—	—	Jordan
—	—	—	—	—	—	—	—	—	—	—	—	—	—	—	Syrian Arab Republic
—	—	9.75	9.75	9.75	6.11	1.22	—	—	....	....	....	....	....	....	Yemen Arab Rep.
37.99	32.14	44.50	42.75	40.35	33.65	20.33	9.07	4.23	.99	....	....	....	....	....	Yemen, P.D. Rep.
—	—	—	—	—	—	—	—	—	—	.11	—	—	—	—	Yemen, Republic of
1,110.22	1,440.20	2,778.38	8,519.39	11,848.04	13,297.32	13,440.13	12,832.03	12,183.28	11,990.89	12,860.81	12,134.92	11,009.41	10,377.47	9,466.45	**Western Hemisphere**
—	—	—	—	—	—	—	—	—	—	—	—	—	—	—	Antigua and Barbuda
—	—	—	1,120.61	1,120.61	2,105.11	2,240.85	2,716.24	2,733.00	2,358.82	2,167.20	1,735.92	1,682.80	2,562.44	2,884.69	Argentina
2.27	.77	22.18	35.79	43.59	43.59	32.42	15.60	7.75	3.27	.50	—	36.84	36.84	36.84	Barbados
—	—	—	3.60	4.80	9.54	9.54	8.03	5.79	2.52	.30	—	—	—	—	Belize
99.04	97.31	114.25	121.40	98.03	74.85	157.25	130.90	155.32	191.61	180.68	171.13	181.15	160.54	180.54	Bolivia
—	—	498.75	2,525.72	4,269.87	4,205.40	3,679.86	2,802.88	2,476.82	1,843.36	1,279.68	865.14	581.40	221.02	127.50	Brazil
96.31	41.80	5.68	579.00	795.00	990.60	1,088.25	1,032.38	982.58	966.46	812.90	669.38	525.02	346.50	199.48	Chile
—	—	—	—	—	—	—	—	—	—	—	—	—	—	—	Colombia
44.64	88.16	84.18	183.28	158.98	171.64	140.95	93.27	53.03	26.94	7.94	58.03	59.28	59.28	45.46	Costa Rica
1.65	6.47	9.32	11.00	10.66	9.17	8.63	8.23	6.57	4.99	4.00	3.32	2.78	2.26	1.71	Dominica
38.02	19.77	64.06	235.15	225.69	270.43	248.83	199.89	161.76	93.25	50.44	62.37	89.44	135.48	129.88	Dominican Republic
—	—	—	203.53	242.90	327.30	397.68	345.18	300.68	247.23	186.00	127.53	72.61	51.77	135.73	Ecuador
24.95	57.33	117.07	132.57	127.20	100.62	50.86	15.75	7.96	4.05	.13	—	—	—	—	El Salvador
2.21	7.10	6.27	7.32	6.30	3.83	2.13	1.47	.91	.35	.01	—	—	—	—	Grenada
—	95.60	95.60	133.85	152.98	105.18	57.19	41.65	65.40	55.51	46.82	44.76	22.38	—	—	Guatemala
67.40	85.31	89.07	85.01	84.01	83.01	82.45	81.74	81.74	80.91	79.38	104.46	122.17	128.61	122.26	Guyana
35.65	50.56	61.44	90.09	102.27	87.37	72.78	51.05	33.75	30.55	25.45	23.82	23.82	23.82	3.78	Haiti
25.73	46.46	108.16	154.06	152.47	133.72	89.54	54.37	27.29	26.96	22.66	23.55	81.35	86.01	74.81	Honduras
242.49	403.51	528.41	599.08	641.41	631.10	554.42	478.23	358.77	291.75	250.74	273.64	259.69	244.19	217.64	Jamaica
—	—	200.62	1,203.75	2,407.51	2,703.31	3,319.29	3,639.25	3,570.25	3,873.62	4,604.94	4,729.93	4,326.95	3,485.23	2,644.19	Mexico
38.67	21.19	17.54	13.29	9.04	.01	—	—	—	—	—	—	17.03	17.03	34.92	Nicaragua
18.09	80.45	76.12	184.13	276.61	283.36	288.63	243.90	243.79	243.19	191.27	150.69	79.80	82.32	91.27	Panama
—	—	—	—	—	—	—	—	—	—	—	—	—	—	—	Paraguay
371.55	332.86	588.81	666.71	688.28	639.00	595.51	595.44	595.42	576.98	530.46	493.41	458.72	642.69	642.69	Peru
1.35	4.05	2.55	2.55	2.02	.30	—	—	—	—	—	—	—	—	—	St. Lucia
.20	1.50	1.50	1.50	1.01	.33	—	—	—	—	—	—	—	—	—	St. Vincent & Grens.
—	—	—	—	—	—	—	—	—	85.05	155.75	231.55	269.05	205.30	112.80	Suriname
—	—	86.80	226.80	226.80	318.55	323.07	276.58	229.65	153.35	70.78	40.43	38.13	27.90	62.44	Trinidad and Tobago
—	—	—	—	—	—	—	—	—	—	—	—	—	—	20.48	Uruguay
—	—	—	—	—	—	—	—	—	—	759.47	2,116.98	2,271.33	2,142.75	1,950.74	1,810.16	Venezuela
															Memorandum Items
—	—	—	425.11	421.46	41.96	41.96	504.86	462.90	1,693.27	2,935.06	3,082.96	2,720.93	2,293.47	2,603.93	Oil Exporting Ctys
9,893.16	15,751.77	22,159.60	32,040.50	36,660.48	37,014.70	34,723.46	29,740.35	26,061.09	22,956.68	20,368.64	23,598.81	25,070.20	26,865.66	27,658.15	Non-Oil Develop.Ctys

*Includes outstanding use of Fund's credits within GRA, and SAF, ESAF, and Trust Fund loans.

Use of Fund Credit (GRA)

Expressed in Millions of SDRs

	1965	1966	1967	1968	1969	1970	1971	1972	1973	1974	1975	1976	1977	1978	1979
World	3,024.4	3,020.8	2,482.3	3,687.9	4,011.1	3,232.3	1,347.0	1,089.2	1,027.4	3,740.1	7,435.0	12,607.7	13,077.6	10,277.3	7,976.0
Industrial Countries	1,937.4	1,897.0	1,199.6	2,303.5	2,751.6	2,440.0	497.4	—	—	1,514.5	3,488.1	6,115.9	6,877.6	4,495.4	1,978.6
United States	—	—	—	—	—	—	—	—	—	—	—	—	—	—	—
Canada	—	—	—	—	—	—	—	—	—	—	—	—	—	—	—
Australia	—	—	—	—	—	—	—	—	—	—	—	332.50	332.50	246.86	270.62
Japan	—	—	—	—	—	—	—	—	—	—	—	—	—	—	—
New Zealand	30.72	30.71	119.91	20.64	—	—	—	—	—	85.68	242.23	390.17	388.06	361.23	270.00
Belgium	—	—	—	—	—	—	—	—	—	—	—	—	—	—	—
Denmark	—	—	—	—	—	—	—	—	—	—	—	—	—	—	—
Finland	—	—	62.46	—	—	—	—	—	—	—	71.25	186.36	186.36	152.07	66.38
France	—	—	—	—	499.21	608.95	—	—	—	—	—	—	—	—	—
Greece	—	—	—	—	—	—	—	—	—	36.22	189.75	247.75	176.49	185.19	147.27
Iceland	—	—	3.75	7.50	11.26	1.76	—	—	—	15.50	31.35	56.42	56.42	47.27	34.71
Ireland	—	1.46	—	—	—	—	—	—	—	—	—	—	—	—	—
Italy	—	—	—	—	—	—	—	—	—	1,377.07	2,457.30	2,457.30	1,580.89	879.96	—
Netherlands	—	—	—	—	—	—	—	—	—	—	—	—	—	—	—
Norway	—	—	—	—	—	—	—	—	—	—	—	—	—	—	—
Portugal	—	—	—	—	—	—	—	—	—	—	—	173.26	244.91	202.78	171.74
Spain	—	—	—	—	—	—	—	—	—	—	496.20	572.13	572.12	615.34	205.36
United Kingdom	1,906.67	1,864.86	1,013.44	2,275.34	2,241.11	1,829.32	497.39	—	—	—	—	1,699.96	3,339.87	1,804.67	812.50
Developing Countries	1,079.5	1,118.8	1,280.3	1,381.9	1,259.5	792.3	849.6	1,089.2	1,027.4	2,225.6	3,947.0	6,491.8	6,200.0	5,782.0	5,997.4
Africa	56.1	123.7	163.0	201.9	196.1	147.2	84.6	119.5	133.7	291.9	553.5	1,247.9	1,360.9	1,471.7	1,538.5
Algeria	—	—	—	—	—	—	—	—	—	—	—	—	—	—	—
Burkina Faso	—	—	—	—	—	—	—	—	—	—	—	—	—	—	—
Burundi	—	—	—	2.47	5.78	7.67	5.34	—	—	—	1.20	1.21	1.22	—	9.50
Cameroon	—	—	—	—	—	—	—	—	—	4.62	12.13	33.89	33.89	32.76	24.81
Central African Rep.	—	—	—	—	—	—	—	—	—	2.66	4.85	9.59	9.59	10.28	8.18
Chad	—	—	—	—	2.47	2.32	2.18	1.02	—	3.11	2.97	9.47	9.47	8.15	7.60
Comoros	—	—	—	—	—	—	—	—	—	—	—	—	—	—	—
Congo	—	—	—	—	—	—	—	—	—	—	—	—	7.95	11.29	12.25
Côte d'Ivoire	—	—	—	—	—	—	—	—	—	11.17	11.17	23.36	13.41	—	—
Equatorial Guinea	—	—	—	—	—	—	—	—	—	—	—	—	—	—	—
Ethiopia	—	—	—	—	—	—	—	—	—	—	—	—	—	—	36.40
Gabon	—	—	—	—	—	—	—	—	—	—	—	—	—	7.61	15.22
Gambia, The	—	—	—	—	—	—	—	—	—	—	—	—	3.51	8.80	5.34
Ghana	—	45.04	63.85	74.71	69.29	46.07	18.31	1.71	—	—	38.60	38.60	38.60	34.43	56.12
Guinea	—	—	—	—	.50	3.45	2.95	2.95	1.02	9.51	7.11	7.11	15.81	10.03	8.94
Guinea-Bissau	—	—	—	—	—	—	—	—	—	—	—	—	—	—	1.10
Kenya	—	—	—	—	—	—	—	—	—	32.05	68.55	85.03	47.65	52.29	108.30
Lesotho	—	—	—	—	—	—	—	—	—	—	—	—	—	—	—
Liberia	9.05	9.64	10.60	10.60	7.61	4.35	1.52	—	.06	—	—	—	—	—	30.18
Madagascar	—	—	—	—	—	—	—	—	—	3.45	14.30	14.30	15.67	13.41	9.87
Malawi	—	—	—	—	—	—	—	—	—	—	2.37	3.73	9.16	5.53	26.94
Mali	9.72	9.89	11.26	11.69	10.68	8.58	7.46	8.30	7.33	10.36	10.62	12.73	11.18	10.09	6.29
Mauritania	—	—	—	—	—	—	—	—	—	—	—	11.82	16.53	16.63	15.75
Mauritius	—	—	—	—	3.70	—	—	—	—	—	—	—	11.00	11.17	39.29
Morocco	—	—	—	34.09	37.49	27.54	—	—	—	—	—	115.46	115.47	173.16	150.80
Nigeria	—	—	—	—	—	—	—	—	—	—	—	—	—	—	—
Niger	—	—	—	—	—	—	—	—	—	—	—	—	—	—	—
Rwanda	—	4.68	5.50	5.93	4.94	2.93	—	—	—	—	—	—	—	—	—
Senegal	—	—	—	—	—	—	—	—	—	—	25.43	25.43	25.44	42.91	46.11
Sierra Leone	—	—	4.57	4.54	3.04	—	—	—	—	4.32	4.94	22.42	29.42	25.23	25.82
Somalia	8.39	8.37	7.67	—	—	—	—	—	—	—	—	—	—	.14	.14
South Africa	—	—	—	—	—	—	—	—	—	—	—	315.00	391.99	314.38	76.77
Sudan	14.98	26.96	39.22	40.50	39.89	30.87	15.18	28.10	29.03	71.65	113.39	119.08	99.47	120.80	170.79
Swaziland	—	—	—	—	—	—	—	—	—	—	—	—	—	—	—
Tanzania	—	—	—	—	—	—	—	—	—	—	38.85	62.62	83.63	86.74	64.06	85.35
Togo	—	—	—	—	—	—	—	—	—	—	—	—	7.50	7.50	—
Tunisia	14.00	19.16	20.33	17.34	13.13	13.27	2.56	—	—	—	—	—	24.00	24.00	24.00
Uganda	—	—	—	—	—	—	9.99	9.99	9.99	14.97	24.07	32.72	32.72	29.20	26.20
Zaïre	—	—	—	—	—	—	—	28.23	28.23	28.23	73.25	180.64	208.24	200.27	190.49
Zambia	—	—	—	—	—	—	18.99	37.99	56.98	56.99	75.93	95.22	95.24	245.12	319.96
Zimbabwe	—	—	—	—	—	—	—	—	—	—	—	—	—	—	—
Asia	418.8	511.6	622.0	664.9	606.6	372.1	364.6	477.4	396.5	1,202.7	1,817.7	2,112.5	1,832.3	1,707.8	1,695.6
Afghanistan, I.S. of	7.30	10.38	11.22	12.28	17.10	14.53	10.13	5.73	7.23	4.74	9.24	1.75	—	—	—
Bangladesh	—	—	—	—	—	—	—	62.50	62.50	133.31	171.60	235.81	194.38	177.62	172.57
Bhutan	—	—	—	—	—	—	—	—	—	—	—	—	—	—	—
Cambodia	—	—	—	—	—	—	—	6.25	12.50	12.50	12.50	12.50	12.50	12.50	12.50
China, People's Rep.	—	—	—	—	—	—	—	—	—	—	—	—	—	—	—
Fiji	—	—	—	—	—	—	—	—	—	—	.34	—	6.50	6.50	6.50
India	286.96	360.93	456.27	373.57	240.43	10.00	—	—	—	496.99	698.32	406.32	125.10	—	—
Indonesia	63.45	63.45	48.98	63.97	112.10	138.46	125.36	107.12	19.16	—	—	—	—	—	—
Korea	—	—	—	—	—	—	—	—	—	110.00	217.28	301.68	280.37	201.84	104.41
Lao P. D. Rep.	—	—	—	—	—	—	—	—	—	—	3.25	6.50	6.50	10.50	8.97
Malaysia	—	—	—	—	—	—	7.28	7.28	—	—	—	93.00	.36	—	—
Mongolia	—	—	—	—	—	—	—	—	—	—	—	—	—	—	—
Myanmar	—	—	7.50	7.50	7.50	16.47	17.97	7.98	14.98	36.48	40.48	34.48	51.68	60.42	53.97
Nepal	—	—	—	—	—	—	—	—	—	—	—	—	4.49	4.49	9.50	8.51

Use of Fund Credit (GRA)

Expressed in Millions of SDRs

1980	1981	1982	1983	1984	1985	1986	1987	1988	1989	1990	1991	1992	1993	1994	
8,485.7	13,367.6	19,309.6	29,898.9	34,905.5	35,179.8	33,334.9	28,752.0	24,750.1	22,315.1	20,731.9	23,378.6	23,967.2	25,196.8	25,611.7	World
1,216.1	607.2	138.2	376.3	593.4	593.4	582.7	373.1	—	—	—	—	—	—	—	Industrial Countries
—	—	—	—	—	—	—	—	—	—	—	—	—	—	—	United States
—	—	—	—	—	—	—	—	—	—	—	—	—	—	—	Canada
61.71	—	32.46	—	—	—	—	—	—	—	—	—	—	—	—	Australia
—	—	—	—	—	—	—	—	—	—	—	—	—	—	—	Japan
132.33	33.66	2.90	—	—	—	—	—	—	—	—	—	—	—	—	New Zealand
—	—	—	—	—	—	—	—	—	—	—	—	—	—	—	Belgium
—	—	—	—	—	—	—	—	—	—	—	—	—	—	—	Denmark
66.38	52.07	14.39	—	—	—	—	—	—	—	—	—	—	—	—	Finland
—	—	—	—	—	—	—	—	—	—	—	—	—	—	—	France
78.46	13.91	—	—	—	—	—	—	—	—	—	—	—	—	—	Greece
15.71	5.92	22.35	21.50	21.50	21.50	10.75	—	—	—	—	—	—	—	—	Iceland
—	—	—	—	—	—	—	—	—	—	—	—	—	—	—	Ireland
—	—	—	—	—	—	—	—	—	—	—	—	—	—	—	Italy
—	—	—	—	—	—	—	—	—	—	—	—	—	—	—	Netherlands
—	—	—	—	—	—	—	—	—	—	—	—	—	—	—	Norway
93.66	47.47	9.78	354.75	571.90	571.90	571.90	373.05	—	—	—	—	—	—	—	Portugal
205.36	141.62	4.75	—	—	—	—	—	—	—	—	—	—	—	—	Spain
562.50	312.50	51.55	—	—	—	—	—	—	—	—	—	—	—	—	United Kingdom
7,269.6	12,760.5	19,171.4	29,522.7	34,312.1	34,586.4	32,752.3	28,379.0	24,750.1	22,315.1	20,731.9	23,378.6	23,967.2	25,196.8	25,611.7	Developing Countries
1,790.4	3,332.2	5,206.4	6,484.2	7,121.4	7,298.0	6,575.5	5,622.6	5,259.8	4,880.1	4,144.5	3,900.9	3,472.0	3,525.7	3,863.9	Africa
—	—	—	—	—	—	—	—	—	470.90	470.90	695.90	578.18	342.73	793.77	Algeria
—	—	—	—	—	—	—	—	—	—	—	—	—	—	—	Burkina Faso
9.50	9.50	9.50	4.75	—	—	—	—	—	—	—	—	—	—	—	Burundi
11.97	3.48	.54	—	—	—	—	—	69.53	84.98	84.98	84.28	45.66	11.86	29.91	Cameroon
5.78	19.71	21.49	25.67	24.37	25.87	27.04	25.94	19.88	10.84	4.44	2.00	.81	.41	10.71	Central African Rep.
5.42	7.10	7.10	7.10	4.44	7.89	7.00	7.00	6.12	2.62	—	—	—	—	10.33	Chad
—	—	—	—	—	—	—	—	—	—	—	—	—	—	—	Comoros
4.79	—	—	—	—	—	9.50	9.50	9.50	8.31	7.56	4.00	4.00	3.50	14.00	Congo
—	319.20	434.61	589.49	603.17	565.99	509.26	406.52	368.71	277.90	302.94	259.72	194.46	159.13	105.65	Côte d'Ivoire
8.15	14.74	14.74	14.74	8.69	7.20	5.40	5.40	5.11	2.12	.39	—	—	—	—	Equatorial Guinea
36.00	98.00	119.25	101.25	76.07	45.05	54.31	44.17	36.90	22.06	4.41	—	—	—	—	Ethiopia
11.36	11.34	9.35	1.85	—	—	27.41	42.50	98.68	102.69	98.49	84.34	58.55	32.89	61.42	Gabon
5.86	14.86	29.51	26.88	27.59	24.80	17.16	15.91	12.70	9.62	5.90	1.54	—	—	—	Gambia, The
33.88	24.23	19.39	267.59	477.20	597.20	611.22	548.73	427.57	293.19	210.06	153.67	108.38	116.03	88.95	Ghana
4.09	.22	11.50	11.50	11.50	11.50	20.75	21.00	21.00	16.88	7.13	.75	—	—	—	Guinea
1.10	2.95	2.68	2.26	3.73	2.80	1.87	1.64	.70	—	—	—	—	—	—	Guinea-Bissau
152.33	175.31	310.08	398.16	387.56	442.22	352.42	268.50	303.65	205.61	129.37	100.28	41.52	—	—	Kenya
—	—	—	—	—	—	—	—	—	—	—	—	—	—	—	Lesotho
41.55	86.93	148.63	196.38	212.28	205.43	205.43	205.43	204.39	202.23	201.55	201.55	201.55	201.55	201.55	Liberia
42.92	74.82	126.54	133.09	150.99	146.98	150.37	143.92	122.20	83.88	49.15	24.12	12.59	5.15	.63	Madagascar
47.89	75.28	73.58	97.52	114.92	121.94	101.35	77.74	67.06	48.04	34.27	19.07	5.48	1.24	12.73	Malawi
8.91	6.66	30.97	44.20	65.01	73.51	69.37	52.93	41.50	31.02	23.23	16.57	11.97	5.72	.95	Mali
26.41	29.78	43.72	39.33	30.34	27.55	29.52	33.25	33.86	26.43	15.21	5.59	1.00	—	—	Mauritania
70.74	127.74	150.23	164.08	157.32	145.02	128.87	105.50	76.51	47.58	15.51	—	—	—	—	Mauritius
248.35	386.94	787.69	878.81	1,011.34	1,083.28	839.10	755.20	696.05	642.71	526.50	401.54	319.10	207.15	101.06	Morocco
—	—	—	—	—	—	—	—	—	—	—	—	—	—	—	Nigeria
—	—	—	30.80	45.20	60.70	72.00	63.99	42.09	29.17	19.17	10.86	5.49	2.02	11.11	Niger
—	—	—	—	—	—	—	—	—	—	—	—	—	—	—	Rwanda
76.78	126.98	166.81	187.81	204.85	219.50	201.62	188.10	159.25	115.86	76.15	41.68	13.54	2.50	30.91	Senegal
22.22	47.73	46.44	65.12	75.81	71.39	58.59	58.59	57.86	56.92	55.37	50.00	48.59	42.63	—	Sierra Leone
3.41	29.29	61.53	106.53	103.65	129.44	118.73	108.31	107.63	98.79	96.70	96.70	96.70	96.70	96.70	Somalia
—	—	795.00	745.00	745.00	745.00	397.50	—	—	—	—	—	—	614.43	614.43	South Africa
267.89	414.41	454.25	596.29	610.22	605.30	605.30	605.30	605.30	605.30	604.26	604.26	604.26	604.26	604.23	Sudan
—	—	—	9.98	9.98	9.00	5.62	2.25	—	—	—	—	—	—	—	Swaziland
93.44	84.68	73.56	48.46	24.03	19.19	37.06	45.47	45.47	42.88	23.29	3.90	—	—	—	Tanzania
10.88	18.12	18.12	37.50	50.33	56.91	66.05	55.28	48.02	33.83	22.66	16.89	9.74	4.56	2.17	Togo
—	—	—	—	—	—	149.71	190.71	205.71	205.71	123.73	180.10	211.05	207.30	207.30	Tunisia
47.75	159.94	243.41	338.04	321.31	257.12	187.44	161.32	130.74	76.49	46.18	21.75	3.10	—	—	Uganda
182.75	297.02	383.10	487.20	591.15	656.37	642.94	587.73	509.38	328.83	220.35	184.81	184.81	184.81	181.77	Zaïre
308.31	627.78	575.57	635.74	711.99	693.33	674.50	674.50	674.50	674.50	659.81	634.98	608.98	559.19	544.57	Zambia
—	37.50	37.50	191.10	261.32	240.47	191.06	110.30	52.20	22.24	4.84	—	102.50	119.90	139.00	Zimbabwe
2,443.0	5,173.9	7,274.9	9,616.3	9,992.4	9,165.8	8,732.5	7,038.7	5,464.4	4,467.7	2,815.5	3,921.1	4,638.8	5,024.4	4,178.6	Asia
—	—	—	—	—	—	—	—	—	—	—	—	—	—	—	Afghanistan, I.S. of
210.89	276.78	374.06	421.33	363.32	385.53	377.05	409.83	423.07	341.26	194.85	91.99	35.94	—	—	Bangladesh
—	—	—	—	—	—	—	—	—	—	—	—	—	—	—	Bhutan
12.50	12.50	12.50	12.50	12.50	12.50	12.50	12.50	12.50	12.50	12.50	12.50	6.25	6.25	6.25	Cambodia
—	450.00	450.00	—	—	—	597.73	597.73	597.73	597.73	298.86	—	—	—	—	China, People's Rep.
—	—	13.50	13.50	13.50	13.19	6.44	4.75	2.97	.59	—	—	—	—	—	Fiji
266.00	566.00	2,066.00	3,532.75	3,999.75	3,825.00	3,493.75	2,856.25	2,068.75	1,331.25	800.00	2,426.41	3,260.41	3,584.91	2,763.18	India
—	—	—	425.10	421.46	41.96	41.96	504.86	462.90	462.90	347.18	115.73	—	—	—	Indonesia
535.43	1,070.64	1,141.68	1,292.83	1,598.85	1,373.03	1,266.25	369.78	—	—	—	—	—	—	—	Korea
8.57	12.94	12.94	12.94	8.25	1.87	—	—	—	—	—	—	—	—	—	Lao P. D. Rep.
—	189.75	248.25	315.08	262.86	107.21	—	—	—	—	—	—	—	—	—	Malaysia
—	—	—	—	—	—	—	—	—	—	—	—	11.25	13.75	13.75	Mongolia
29.30	48.91	71.61	84.56	78.50	65.00	38.31	10.93	—	—	—	—	—	—	—	Myanmar
19.00	18.80	14.05	9.18	3.93	10.25	12.35	18.65	18.65	13.26	4.73	.79	—	—	—	Nepal

Use of Fund Credit (GRA)

	1965	1966	1967	1968	1969	1970	1971	1972	1973	1974	1975	1976	1977	1978	1979
					Expressed in Millions of SDRs										
Asia (cont.)															
Pakistan	37.46	37.45	35.80	61.06	81.44	45.38	42.59	110.70	129.82	238.87	374.41	439.55	437.64	395.06	337.36
Papua New Guinea	—	—	—	—	—	—	—	—	—	—	—	—	24.80	14.80	9.81
Philippines	—	—	—	55.00	55.00	68.75	89.74	95.25	76.25	67.81	164.68	348.41	418.42	441.28	506.78
Solomon Islands	—	—	—	—	—	—	—	—	—	—	—	—	—	—	—
Sri Lanka	23.66	39.36	62.25	91.52	92.98	78.52	71.54	74.56	74.10	101.69	124.70	134.25	169.94	185.88	234.47
Thailand	—	—	—	—	—	—	—	—	—	—	—	67.00	67.00	135.75	182.00
Viet Nam	—	—	—	—	—	—	—	—	—	—	—	—	31.00	53.50	54.43
Western Samoa	—	—	—	—	—	—	—	—	—	—	1.26	1.92	1.63	2.67	3.32
Europe	106.1	96.1	132.1	141.3	92.1	74.1	128.9	83.5	69.3	192.9	458.4	936.4	862.9	948.7	1,111.1
Albania	—	—	—	—	—	—	—	—	—	—	—	—	—	—	—
Armenia	—	—	—	—	—	—	—	—	—	—	—	—	—	—	—
Belarus	—	—	—	—	—	—	—	—	—	—	—	—	—	—	—
Bulgaria	—	—	—	—	—	—	—	—	—	—	—	—	—	—	—
Croatia	—	—	—	—	—	—	—	—	—	—	—	—	—	—	—
Cyprus	—	—	—	—	—	—	—	—	—	—	6.38	8.10	43.07	43.07	32.92	37.98
Czech Republic	—	—	—	—	—	—	—	—	—	—	—	—	—	—	—
Czechoslovakia	—	—	—	—	—	—	—	—	—	—	—	—	—	—	—
Estonia	—	—	—	—	—	—	—	—	—	—	—	—	—	—	—
Georgia	—	—	—	—	—	—	—	—	—	—	—	—	—	—	—
Hungary	—	—	—	—	—	—	—	—	—	—	—	—	—	—	—
Kazakhstan	—	—	—	—	—	—	—	—	—	—	—	—	—	—	—
Kyrgyz Republic	—	—	—	—	—	—	—	—	—	—	—	—	—	—	—
Latvia	—	—	—	—	—	—	—	—	—	—	—	—	—	—	—
Lithuania	—	—	—	—	—	—	—	—	—	—	—	—	—	—	—
Macedonia, former YR	—	—	—	—	—	—	—	—	—	—	—	—	—	—	—
Moldova	—	—	—	—	—	—	—	—	—	—	—	—	—	—	—
Poland	—	—	—	—	—	—	—	—	—	—	—	—	—	—	—
Romania	—	—	—	—	—	—	—	—	—	47.50	47.50	87.50	237.50	270.00	255.55	246.80
Russia	—	—	—	—	—	—	—	—	—	—	—	—	—	—	—
Slovak Republic	—	—	—	—	—	—	—	—	—	—	—	—	—	—	—
Slovenia	—	—	—	—	—	—	—	—	—	—	—	—	—	—	—
Turkey	18.89	18.89	21.39	48.38	36.88	74.13	62.13	—	—	—	—	207.57	336.81	336.81	477.68	480.29
Ukraine	—	—	—	—	—	—	—	—	—	—	—	—	—	—	—
Uzbekistan	—	—	—	—	—	—	—	—	—	—	—	—	—	—	—
Yugoslavia, SFR	87.21	77.21	110.71	92.96	55.21	—	66.75	83.50	21.75	139.00	155.20	318.97	212.97	182.53	346.00
Middle East	113.0	82.6	110.7	81.2	82.6	71.3	111.6	51.5	81.6	140.1	300.1	500.0	577.0	599.4	489.6
Egypt	95.19	70.30	74.24	71.71	50.66	49.34	69.84	24.40	62.17	92.95	68.22	177.90	254.89	296.30	246.48
Iran, I.R. of	—	—	—	—	—	—	—	—	—	—	—	—	—	—	—
Iraq	—	—	19.97	—	—	—	—	—	—	—	—	—	—	—	—
Israel	—	—	—	—	22.48	12.48	32.48	—	—	32.50	208.25	285.25	285.24	271.26	224.21
Jordan	—	—	—	—	—	—	—	4.49	4.49	1.59	.01	.01	.01	.01	—
Syrian Arab Republic	17.85	12.25	16.53	9.50	9.50	9.50	4.75	22.62	17.87	5.37	—	—	—	—	.75
Yemen Arab Rep.	—	—	—	—	—	—	—	—	—	—	—	—	—	—	—
Yemen, P.D. Rep.	—	—	—	—	—	—	—	—	—	9.31	23.65	36.83	36.83	31.88	18.18
Yemen, Republic of	—	—	—	—	—	—	—	—	—	—	—	—	—	—	—
Western Hemisphere	385.4	304.8	252.4	292.6	282.2	127.6	159.9	357.3	346.3	397.9	817.2	1,695.1	1,567.0	1,054.3	1,162.6
Argentina	76.00	30.00	—	—	—	—	—	174.00	174.00	64.00	250.09	455.59	344.50	—	—
Barbados	—	—	—	—	—	—	—	—	—	—	—	—	6.50	6.50	6.50
Belize	—	—	—	—	—	—	—	—	—	—	—	—	—	—	—
Bolivia	—	—	—	5.09	8.08	6.08	6.60	7.88	18.05	14.32	13.93	—	—	15.00	15.00
Brazil	89.32	44.47	11.97	—	—	—	—	—	—	—	—	—	—	—	—
Chile	99.99	85.19	69.99	78.99	56.99	1.49	39.50	79.00	79.00	159.97	330.79	402.22	300.62	266.49	135.94
Colombia	59.51	57.50	91.40	112.65	106.25	54.85	53.25	—	—	—	—	—	—	—	—
Costa Rica	15.00	15.48	15.48	9.73	—	—	—	—	—	—	18.84	29.96	32.30	29.31	24.32	43.81
Dominica	—	—	—	—	—	—	—	—	—	—	—	—	—	—	1.90
Dominican Republic	13.75	20.00	16.65	9.30	14.60	6.55	10.75	3.75	—	—	—	21.50	36.50	36.50	94.33
Ecuador	6.00	11.00	10.18	—	12.25	13.75	5.50	8.25	—	—	—	—	—	—	—
El Salvador	—	13.74	13.73	16.72	13.97	6.49	10.19	8.75	—	—	17.89	17.89	12.82	—	—
Grenada	—	—	—	—	—	—	—	—	—	—	—	.81	1.21	1.21	1.21	.97
Guatemala	—	5.34	15.34	13.39	11.14	—	—	—	—	—	—	—	—	—	—
Guyana	—	—	—	—	—	—	—	2.06	—	3.87	5.00	—	17.25	17.25	30.27	40.49
Haiti	6.17	6.36	7.67	5.68	5.11	2.19	.80	—	—	—	6.64	10.97	12.38	8.43	7.63	5.71
Honduras	3.75	2.74	—	—	—	—	—	—	—	—	16.78	16.78	16.78	4.29	—
Jamaica	—	—	—	—	—	—	—	—	13.25	13.25	13.25	68.94	88.14	138.58	266.76
Mexico	—	—	—	—	—	—	—	—	—	—	—	319.12	419.12	229.37	103.11
Nicaragua	8.43	6.49	—	14.25	13.25	8.00	10.99	8.25	12.24	10.06	15.50	8.74	2.00	2.01	43.51
Panama	—	—	2.27	2.70	—	—	—	—	—	7.37	17.52	42.62	42.16	40.32	31.45
Paraguay	—	—	—	—	—	—	—	—	—	—	—	—	—	—	—
Peru	—	—	3.75	28.31	9.90	3.27	30.75	13.64	—	—	158.75	168.75	256.09	373.14
St. Lucia	—	—	—	—	—	—	—	—	—	—	—	—	—	—	—
St. Vincent & Grens.	—	—	—	—	—	—	—	—	—	—	—	—	—	—	—
Trinidad and Tobago	—	—	—	—	—	—	—	—	—	—	—	—	—	—	—
Uruguay	7.50	6.48	—	20.73	9.50	18.25	17.02	36.70	32.26	63.81	99.74	124.88	98.24	—	—
Venezuela	—	—	—	—	—	—	—	—	—	—	—	—	—	—	—
Memorandum Items															
Oil Exporting Ctys	63.45	63.45	68.95	63.97	112.10	138.46	125.36	107.12	19.16	—	—	—	—	—	—
Non-Oil Develop.Ctys	1,016.1	1,055.3	1,211.3	1,317.9	1,147.4	653.9	724.2	982.0	1,008.2	2,225.6	3,947.0	6,491.8	6,200.0	5,782.0	5,997.4

Use of Fund Credit (GRA)

Expressed in Millions of SDRs

1980	1981	1982	1983	1984	1985	1986	1987	1988	1989	1990	1991	1992	1993	1994	
															Asia (cont.)
299.73	650.00	1,056.51	1,317.18	1,265.61	1,116.41	846.89	566.60	370.01	421.36	313.22	363.96	437.45	434.09	523.15	Pakistan
4.81	45.00	45.00	45.00	16.70	10.10	—	—	—	—	—	42.84	42.84	32.13	10.71	Papua New Guinea
668.76	823.03	755.27	899.24	771.76	942.74	958.76	841.58	791.91	889.96	640.28	759.02	800.12	880.74	728.56	Philippines
—	.80	2.40	3.36	3.16	2.76	2.83	1.55	1.25	1.09	.47	—	—	—	—	Solomon Islands
211.13	346.86	341.45	331.07	328.34	292.49	234.03	164.67	209.43	163.41	131.56	68.00	13.60	—	—	Sri Lanka
142.62	606.19	636.21	866.56	807.23	928.75	807.91	645.38	474.26	202.87	—	—	—	—	—	Thailand
31.68	51.21	29.71	28.40	28.40	28.40	28.40	28.40	28.40	28.40	28.40	28.40	28.40	72.48	132.96	Viet Nam
2.57	4.46	3.76	5.67	8.27	8.58	7.30	5.19	2.58	1.16	.58	.16	—	—	—	Western Samoa
1,710.7	2,739.4	3,917.9	4,929.4	5,371.8	4,792.8	4,004.7	2,775.9	1,773.9	905.5	917.1	3,464.6	4,695.1	6,151.0	8,002.9	**Europe**
—	—	—	—	—	—	—	—	—	—	—	—	9.69	13.13	13.13	Albania
—	—	—	—	—	—	—	—	—	—	—	—	—	—	16.88	Armenia
—	—	—	—	—	—	—	—	—	—	—	—	—	70.10	70.10	Belarus
—	—	—	—	—	—	—	—	—	—	—	289.23	428.90	459.90	644.41	Bulgaria
—	—	—	—	—	—	—	—	—	—	—	—	—	14.82	87.06	Croatia
30.60	21.62	12.30	5.47	3.17	—	—	—	—	—	—	—	—	—	—	Cyprus
—	—	—	—	—	—	—	—	—	—	—	—	—	780.68	—	Czech Republic
—	—	—	—	—	—	—	—	—	—	—	.01	917.94	1,121.50	....	Czechoslovakia
—	—	—	—	—	—	—	—	—	—	—	—	—	7.75	41.85	Estonia
—	—	—	—	—	—	—	—	—	—	—	—	—	—	27.75	Georgia
—	—	214.50	547.00	972.00	883.71	842.73	569.87	471.30	347.11	231.68	880.21	875.84	896.30	781.58	Hungary
—	—	—	—	—	—	—	—	—	—	—	—	—	61.88	198.00	Kazakhstan
—	—	—	—	—	—	—	—	—	—	—	—	—	43.86	43.86	Kyrgyz Republic
—	—	—	—	—	—	—	—	—	—	—	—	25.16	77.78	109.80	Latvia
—	—	—	—	—	—	—	—	—	—	—	—	17.25	87.98	134.55	Lithuania
—	—	—	—	—	—	—	—	—	—	—	—	—	2.81	14.03	Macedonia, former YR
—	—	—	—	—	—	—	—	—	—	—	—	—	63.00	112.45	Moldova
—	—	—	—	—	—	—	—	—	—	357.50	596.60	596.60	497.69	918.59	Poland
257.42	506.66	781.61	904.65	955.74	782.85	583.53	357.55	106.91	—	—	565.80	750.90	750.90	906.41	Romania
—	—	—	—	—	—	—	—	—	—	—	—	719.00	1,797.28	2,875.55	Russia
—	—	—	—	—	—	—	—	—	—	—	—	—	405.17	439.81	Slovak Republic
—	—	—	—	—	—	—	—	—	—	—	—	—	8.53	4.94	Slovenia
826.58	1,135.63	1,319.18	1,497.09	1,455.03	1,207.51	887.19	542.97	222.03	36.25	—	—	—	—	235.50	Turkey
—	—	—	—	—	—	—	—	—	—	—	—	—	—	249.33	Ukraine
—	—	—	—	—	—	—	—	—	—	—	—	—	—	—	Uzbekistan
596.14	1,075.50	1,590.32	1,975.18	1,985.87	1,918.72	1,691.22	1,305.47	973.65	522.17	327.94	214.84	....	....	....	Yugoslavia, SFR
305.2	176.5	95.5	74.5	74.4	118.1	94.3	187.1	151.9	189.4	153.2	155.2	407.0	385.0	409.7	**Middle East**
139.05	85.12	52.01	49.31	49.31	37.50	25.00	128.50	116.00	116.00	87.00	89.00	147.20	147.20	132.20	Egypt
—	—	—	—	—	—	—	—	—	—	—	—	—	—	—	Iran, I.R. of
—	—	—	.01	—	—	—	—	—	—	—	—	—	—	—	Iraq
156.40	87.54	27.15	—	—	—	.01	—	—	—	—	—	178.64	178.64	178.64	Israel
—	—	—	—	—	57.40	57.40	57.40	35.88	73.41	66.24	66.24	81.19	59.18	98.89	Jordan
—	—	—	—	—	—	—	—	—	—	—	—	—	—	—	Syrian Arab Republic
—	—	—	9.75	9.75	9.75	6.11	1.22	—	—	....	....	....	....	....	Yemen Arab Rep.
9.76	3.80	16.31	15.38	15.38	13.45	5.77	—	—	—	—	—	—	—	—	Yemen, P.D. Rep.
—	—	—	—	—	—	—	—	—	—	—	—	—	—	—	Yemen, Republic of
1,020.2	1,338.5	2,676.8	8,418.4	11,752.1	13,211.8	13,345.4	12,754.7	12,100.1	11,872.3	12,701.6	11,936.8	10,754.3	10,110.8	9,156.6	**Western Hemisphere**
—	—	—	1,120.61	1,120.61	2,105.11	2,240.85	2,716.24	2,733.00	2,358.82	2,167.20	1,735.92	1,682.80	2,562.44	2,884.69	Argentina
2.27	.77	22.18	35.79	43.59	43.59	32.42	15.60	7.75	3.27	.50	—	36.84	36.84	36.84	Barbados
—	—	—	3.60	4.80	9.54	9.54	8.03	5.79	2.52	.30	—	—	—	—	Belize
63.02	61.15	78.09	85.24	64.94	46.72	118.18	99.04	107.98	103.05	71.70	39.62	16.98	—	—	Bolivia
—	—	498.75	2,525.72	4,269.87	4,205.40	3,679.86	2,802.88	2,476.82	1,843.36	1,279.68	865.14	581.40	221.02	127.50	Brazil
96.31	41.80	5.68	579.00	795.00	990.60	1,088.25	1,032.38	982.58	966.45	812.90	669.38	525.02	346.50	199.48	Chile
—	—	—	—	—	—	—	—	—	—	—	—	—	—	—	Colombia
44.64	88.16	84.18	183.28	158.98	171.64	140.95	93.27	53.03	26.94	7.94	58.03	59.28	59.28	45.46	Costa Rica
1.65	6.47	9.32	11.00	10.66	9.17	7.83	6.23	4.03	2.19	1.20	.52	.14	.02	—	Dominica
38.02	19.77	64.06	235.15	225.69	270.43	248.83	199.89	161.76	93.25	50.44	62.37	89.44	135.48	129.88	Dominican Republic
—	—	—	203.53	242.90	327.30	397.68	345.18	300.68	247.23	186.00	127.53	72.61	51.77	135.73	Ecuador
5.38	37.63	97.37	112.87	107.50	80.92	35.08	3.88	—	—	—	—	—	—	—	El Salvador
.27	5.15	4.32	5.42	4.57	2.43	1.12	.84	.56	.28	—	—	—	—	—	Grenada
—	95.60	95.60	133.85	152.98	105.18	57.19	41.65	65.40	55.51	46.82	44.86	22.38	—	—	Guatemala
67.40	74.05	77.81	73.75	72.75	71.75	71.75	71.75	71.75	70.92	41.02	49.50	49.50	47.08	31.77	Guyana
17.15	31.99	42.97	72.15	86.15	74.38	54.66	36.53	22.40	21.08	16.56	15.00	15.00	15.00	.25	Haiti
11.75	32.39	94.09	139.99	138.40	121.69	80.30	47.91	23.64	23.31	22.57	23.55	74.57	72.45	61.25	Honduras
242.49	403.51	528.41	599.08	641.41	631.10	554.42	478.23	358.77	291.75	250.74	273.64	259.69	244.19	217.64	Jamaica
—	—	200.62	1,203.75	2,407.51	2,703.31	3,319.29	3,639.25	3,570.25	3,873.62	4,604.94	4,729.93	4,326.95	3,485.23	2,644.19	Mexico
38.67	21.19	17.54	13.29	9.04	.01	—	—	—	—	—	17.03	17.03	17.03	14.90	Nicaragua
18.09	80.45	76.12	184.13	276.61	283.36	288.63	243.90	243.79	243.19	191.27	150.69	79.80	82.32	91.27	Panama
—	—	—	—	—	—	—	—	—	—	—	—	—	—	—	Paraguay
371.55	332.86	588.81	666.31	688.28	639.00	595.51	595.44	595.42	576.98	530.46	493.41	458.72	642.69	642.69	Peru
1.35	4.05	2.55	2.55	2.02	.30	—	—	—	—	—	—	—	—	—	St. Lucia
.20	1.50	1.50	1.50	1.01	.33	—	—	—	—	—	—	—	—	—	St. Vincent & Grens.
—	—	—	—	—	—	—	—	85.05	155.75	231.55	269.05	205.30	112.80	62.44	Trinidad and Tobago
—	—	86.80	226.80	226.80	318.55	323.07	276.58	229.65	153.35	70.78	40.43	38.13	27.90	20.48	Uruguay
—	—	—	—	—	—	—	—	—	—	759.47	2,116.98	2,271.33	2,142.75	1,950.74	1,810.16	Venezuela
															Memorandum Items
—	—	—	425.11	421.46	41.96	41.96	504.86	462.90	1,693.27	2,935.06	3,082.96	2,720.93	2,293.47	2,603.93	Oil Exporting Ctys
7,269.6	12,760.5	19,171.4	29,097.6	33,890.6	34,544.5	32,710.3	27,874.1	24,287.2	20,621.8	17,796.8	20,295.6	21,246.2	22,903.4	23,007.7	Non-Oil Develop.Ctys

Total Reserves Minus Gold

Millions of SDRs

1l s		1965	1966	1967	1968	1969	1970	1971	1972	1973	1974	1975	1976	1977	1978	1979
All Countries	010	29,394	32,029	35,151	39,068	39,789	56,154	87,056	110,904	116,836	144,001	158,697	186,628	228,473	245,487	272,872
Industrial Countries	110	20,326	21,934	24,390	27,337	26,291	39,647	66,994	81,699	79,948	79,841	84,762	93,575	120,053	144,811	154,907
United States	111	1,385	1,647	2,765	4,818	5,105	3,415	1,942	2,453	2,260	3,456	3,952	6,153	6,250	5,357	5,909
Canada	156	1,886	1,656	1,702	2,183	2,234	3,888	4,457	4,804	4,013	3,990	3,781	4,273	3,023	2,730	2,174
Australia	193	1,317	1,344	1,133	1,185	998	1,454	2,794	5,397	4,465	3,229	2,524	2,470	1,694	1,582	1,081
Japan	158	1,824	1,790	1,692	2,550	3,241	4,308	13,468	16,177	9,412	10,303	10,208	13,553	18,392	24,875	14,819
New Zealand	196	173	179	218	161	209	257	453	766	866	522	365	422	364	346	342
Austria	122	611	632	783	796	822	1,044	1,424	1,775	1,652	2,070	3,060	3,065	2,758	3,874	3,094
Belgium	124	776	825	1,110	663	868	1,377	1,655	2,056	2,751	2,890	3,476	3,004	3,257	3,044	4,132
Denmark	128	490	489	427	335	357	419	601	724	1,034	700	686	724	1,308	2,402	2,456
Finland	172	206	144	139	293	282	425	574	615	476	487	370	398	437	939	1,169
France	132	1,637	1,495	1,760	324	286	1,428	4,078	5,700	3,538	3,697	7,224	4,837	4,834	7,122	13,345
Germany	134	3,020	3,737	3,925	5,409	3,050	9,630	13,108	17,800	23,381	22,346	22,394	25,838	28,573	37,208	39,891
Greece	174	173	153	156	182	187	194	380	828	745	638	823	758	863	1,002	1,019
Iceland	176	53	57	34	27	38	53	63	76	82	39	39	68	81	104	123
Ireland	178	388	471	414	466	652	681	901	1,022	835	1,019	1,292	1,565	1,936	2,048	1,679
Italy	136	2,396	2,497	3,063	2,418	2,089	2,465	3,398	2,721	2,448	2,782	1,116	2,774	6,672	8,527	13,814
Netherlands	138	657	718	908	766	809	1,454	1,588	2,511	3,525	3,782	4,172	4,437	4,727	3,905	5,762
Norway	142	445	509	659	679	685	788	1,030	1,186	1,271	1,541	1,876	1,884	1,808	2,196	3,200
Portugal	182	362	434	535	507	570	602	870	1,189	1,390	948	340	151	301	669	707
Spain	184	612	468	315	364	497	1,319	2,512	4,120	5,114	4,798	4,703	4,049	4,920	7,762	10,039
Sweden	144	770	824	638	590	470	561	822	1,251	1,894	1,215	2,425	1,941	2,811	3,165	2,667
Switzerland	146	402	704	607	1,669	1,783	2,401	3,507	4,052	4,151	4,448	5,996	8,268	8,471	13,634	12,476
United Kingdom	112	739	1,158	1,405	949	1,055	1,479	7,358	4,463	4,633	4,931	3,928	2,905	16,557	12,301	14,986
Developing Countries	200	9,069	10,095	10,761	11,731	13,498	16,506	20,062	29,205	36,889	64,159	73,934	93,053	108,420	100,677	117,967
Africa	605	1,546	1,805	1,664	1,800	2,083	2,565	2,435	3,006	3,776	8,491	8,545	9,059	8,369	6,476	10,133
Algeria	612	179	267	287	286	204	148	275	263	756	1,188	964	1,519	1,386	1,520	2,018
Benin	638	10	10	8	10	7	16	23	26	27	28	13	17	17	12	11
Botswana	616	....	....	....	....	....	....	....	....	....	....	....	64	82	116	203
Burkina Faso	748	14	16	18	23	26	36	40	44	52	68	65	61	46	28	47
Burundi	618	9	7	5	3	7	15	16	17	18	12	26	42	78	62	68
Cameroon	622	27	34	24	41	48	81	68	40	42	64	25	38	35	40	95
Cape Verde	624	....	....	....	....	....	....	....	....	....	....	....	28	35	30	32
Central African Rep.	626	10	6	5	5	1	1	—	2	1	1	3	16	21	19	33
Chad	628	14	7	1	1	1	2	10	9	1	12	3	20	15	9	9
Comoros	632															
Congo	634	6	6	3	7	6	9	10	10	7	20	12	10	11	7	32
Côte d'Ivoire	662	62	62	71	81	74	119	82	80	73	54	88	66	152	344	112
Djibouti	611															
Equatorial Guinea	642															
Ethiopia	644	74	75	60	58	62	63	55	77	138	215	236	254	176	117	131
Gabon	646	18	12	9	5	8	15	23	21	40	84	125	100	8	17	15
Gambia, The	648	8	9	8	7	6	8	10	10	13	23	24	18	20	20	1
Ghana	652	110	106	77	90	66	37	33	86	146	58	107	79	122	213	219
Guinea-Bissau	654															
Kenya	664	20	52	76	100	170	220	157	186	193	158	148	237	430	271	477
Lesotho	666															
Liberia	668	....	....	....	....	....	....	....	....	....	15	16	15	23	14	42
Madagascar	674	50	51	43	31	19	37	43	48	56	40	30	36	57	45	4
Malawi	676	25	21	23	23	21	29	29	33	55	67	52	23	72	57	53
Mali	678	3	—	1	1	1	1	2	3	4	5	4	6	4	6	5
Mauritania	682	10	8	9	7	4	3	7	12	35	85	41	71	41	61	86
Mauritius	684	20	19	13	16	33	46	48	65	55	107	142	77	55	35	22
Morocco	686	78	66	55	64	93	119	139	197	199	319	301	402	416	475	423
Namibia	728															
Niger	692	3	4	1	3	7	19	31	38	42	37	43	71	83	99	100
Nigeria	694	219	195	92	97	112	202	376	327	463	4,576	4,771	4,458	3,484	1,448	4,211
Rwanda	714	4	5	7	6	3	8	5	6	13	11	22	55	68	67	116
Senegal	722	38	46	37	16	6	22	23	35	10	5	27	22	28	14	15
Seychelles	718	....	....	....	....	....	....	....	....	4	4	5	6	9	7	9
Sierra Leone	724	23	20	16	28	35	39	35	43	43	45	24	22	27	27	35
Somalia	726	9	12	10	7	13	21	25	29	29	35	58	73	99	97	33
South Africa	199	175	194	196	228	283	346	245	561	372	308	418	366	342	325	330
Sudan	732	60	57	55	48	36	22	26	33	51	102	31	20	19	22	51
Swaziland	734	....	....	....	....	....	....	....	....	....	11	39	63	78	87	86
Tanzania	738	....	61	62	78	80	65	55	110	120	41	56	97	232	77	52
Togo	742	18	19	22	26	26	35	37	34	31	44	35	57	38	54	50
Tunisia	744	32	24	36	31	33	55	132	201	250	337	325	315	289	340	440
Uganda	746	....	41	35	49	52	57	25	33	24	14	27	38	39	40	17
Zaïre	636	18	17	63	125	144	136	84	113	143	97	41	43	110	97	157
Zambia	754	196	205	175	194	363	508	255	146	154	134	121	80	55	39	61
Zimbabwe	698	....	65	59	4	28	20	6	56	103	58	68	66	60	114	227
Asia *	505	3,022	3,429	3,688	4,058	4,756	5,288	5,649	7,464	8,690	10,435	10,442	15,960	21,459	22,600	26,216
Afghanistan, Islamic State of	512	9	12	5	6	8	13	25	19	18	23	74	113	227	300	335
Bangladesh	513	....	....	....	....	....	....	....	249	119	113	127	249	192	242	293
Bhutan	514															
China, People's Rep. ⅰ	924	....	....	....	....	....	....	....	....	....	....	....	....	1,931	1,195	1,635
Fiji	819	22	18	18	18	27	27	36	64	61	89	127	100	121	103	104
India	534	319	365	419	439	683	763	868	844	704	839	930	2,403	4,011	4,933	5,642
Indonesia	536	17	19	2	183	118	156	171	527	667	1,217	499	1,288	2,065	2,016	3,083
Korea	542	143	242	353	388	550	606	399	482	733	226	667	1,696	2,443	2,122	2,246
Lao, P.D. Rep.	544	7	7	6	6	5	6	8	7	9	12	....	....	....	....	....
Malaysia	548	468	493	426	450	557	616	695	836	1,057	1,264	1,244	2,069	2,292	2,490	2,972
Maldives	556	....	....	....	....	....	....	....	....	....	....	....	....	—	—	1
Myanmar	518	97	100	71	69	46	131	45	37	76	149	113	102	85	74	154
Nepal	558	56	42	43	54	76	89	89	91	97	99	82	110	115	111	121
Pakistan	564	176	154	111	193	278	136	119	203	342	320	291	401	370	313	162
*of which:																
Taiwan Province of China	528	245	275	335	302	361	540	568	877	850	892	917	1,305	1,107	1,079	1,114

ⅰ See country notes in the monthly *IFS*

Total Reserves Minus Gold

1980	1981	1982	1983	1984	1985	1986	1987	1988	1989	1990	1991	1992	1993	1994		ll s
End of Period																
321,284	329,676	327,916	362,314	407,050	404,830	418,613	507,516	542,657	590,920	637,699	671,688	693,064	757,226	812,691	All Countries	010
186,037	186,502	185,560	206,185	226,023	229,440	251,303	324,321	353,065	382,214	414,092	400,659	396,746	413,444	433,835	Industrial Countries	110
12,228	16,258	20,677	21,612	24,319	29,220	30,619	24,474	27,305	48,358	50,791	46,602	43,831	45,395	43,350	United States	111
2,425	3,039	2,730	3,311	2,542	2,278	2,658	5,130	11,437	12,217	12,544	11,362	8,314	9,087	8,416	Canada	156
1,325	1,436	5,776	8,560	7,592	5,251	5,924	6,163	10,105	10,486	11,432	11,559	8,152	8,083	7,730	Australia	193
19,316	24,235	21,153	23,498	26,963	24,325	34,546	57,077	71,879	63,887	55,179	50,376	52,089	71,729	86,214	Japan	158
276	579	576	743	1,823	1,453	3,083	2,298	2,107	2,303	2,902	2,062	2,239	2,430	2,540	New Zealand	196
4,140	4,540	4,805	4,313	4,330	4,340	5,038	5,309	5,475	6,543	6,591	7,223	9,006	10,637	11,523	Austria	122
6,133	4,254	3,560	4,502	4,656	4,414	4,527	6,781	6,935	8,192	8,541	8,515	10,037	8,310	9,505	Belgium	124
2,655	2,189	2,054	3,458	3,070	4,942	4,059	7,096	8,000	4,868	7,445	5,176	8,032	7,499	6,203	Denmark	128
1,466	1,275	1,376	1,182	2,810	3,414	1,461	4,524	4,733	3,889	6,779	5,319	3,792	3,939	7,303	Finland	172
21,436	19,126	14,985	18,961	21,362	24,206	25,715	23,296	18,849	18,728	25,851	21,870	19,657	16,489	17,986	France	132
38,099	37,560	40,578	40,760	40,951	40,403	42,294	55,515	43,492	46,196	47,729	44,043	66,158	56,525	52,994	Germany	134
1,055	878	781	860	973	790	I 1,242	1,890	2,690	2,453	2,398	3,628	3,486	5,672	9,924	Greece	174
136	197	132	143	130	187	253	219	216	257	307	314	362	310	201	Iceland	176
2,243	2,278	2,377	2,521	2,400	2,676	2,646	3,381	3,780	3,087	3,672	4,013	2,502	4,314	4,189	Ireland	178
18,132	17,298	12,774	19,203	21,214	14,198	16,340	21,297	25,797	35,551	44,232	34,031	20,104	20,054	22,102	Italy	136
9,131	8,024	9,185	9,715	9,423	9,816	9,149	11,280	11,945	12,562	12,289	12,442	15,954	22,819	23,655	Netherlands	138
4,742	5,372	6,231	6,332	9,554	12,670	10,239	10,063	9,859	10,489	10,777	9,250	8,684	14,286	13,033	Norway	142
624	459	405	368	527	1,270	1,191	2,345	3,810	7,573	10,182	14,421	13,912	11,532	10,627	Portugal	182
9,302	9,283	6,939	7,070	12,197	10,174	12,062	21,618	27,550	31,554	36,008	46,016	33,094	29,882	28,475	Spain	184
2,680	3,094	3,184	3,853	3,923	5,274	5,355	5,762	6,310	7,274	12,644	12,815	16,454	13,869	15,929	Sweden	144
12,276	12,010	14,015	14,360	15,605	16,402	17,811	19,368	17,985	19,234	20,541	20,277	24,185	23,760	23,790	Switzerland	146
16,192	13,091	11,238	10,831	9,631	11,707	15,061	29,405	32,773	26,457	25,202	29,286	26,648	26,775	28,094	United Kingdom	112
135,247	143,174	142,356	156,129	181,027	175,390	167,310	183,195	189,593	208,706	223,606	271,030	296,318	343,783	378,857	Developing Countries	200
14,956	10,349	7,151	6,842	6,689	8,295	7,022	7,099	7,406	9,028	11,630	14,110	12,293	13,319	15,944	Africa	605
2,958	3,175	2,196	1,796	1,494	2,566	1,357	1,156	669	645	509	1,039	1,060	1,074	1,832	Algeria	612
6	50	4	4	3	4	3	3	3	3	46	134	178	178	177	Benin	638
269	218	266	378	484	713	979	1,450	1,678	2,162	2,380	2,637	2,796	3,024	3,057	Botswana	616
53	61	56	81	108	127	191	227	238	202	211	242	248	278	163	Burkina Faso	748
74	53	27	26	20	27	56	43	52	76	74	99	127	119	140	Burundi	618
148	73	61	152	55	121	48	45	131	61	18	30	15	2	2	Cameroon	622
33	33	39	44	42	50	46	57	60	57	54	46	55	42	. . . .	Cape Verde	624
43	60	42	45	54	45	53	68	81	86	83	72	73	82	144	Central African Rep.	626
4	6	11	27	45	30	13	37	47	85	90	84	59	28	52	Chad	628
5	7	13	14	5	14	19	22	17	23	21	20	20	. . . .	. . . .	Comoros	632
67	106	34	7	4	4	6	2	3	5	4	3	3	1	34	Congo	634
15	15	2	19	5	4	16	6	8	11	3	9	5	2	140	Côte d'Ivoire	662
. . . .	. . . .	. . . .	. . . .	46	46	44	45	48	45	66	70	61	55	51	Djibouti	611
. . . .	. . . .	3	1	1	3	2	—	4	1	—	7	10	—	—	Equatorial Guinea	642
63	229	165	120	45	135	205	86	48	35	14	38	169	332	373	Ethiopia	644
84	171	283	179	203	175	103	8	50	26	192	229	52	1	120	Gabon	646
4	3	8	3	2	2	11	18	14	16	39	47	68	. . . .	67	Gambia, The	648
141	125	126	138	308	436	419	138	164	264	154	385	233	298	400	Ghana	652
. . . .	. . . .	. . . .	. . . .	. . . .	. . . .	25	7	12	16	13	10	13	10	13	Guinea-Bissau	654
386	199	192	359	398	356	338	180	196	217	144	82	39	295	382	Kenya	664
39	37	43	64	50	40	49	48	42	37	51	80	115	184	255	Lesotho	666
4	8	6	19	4	1	2	—	—	6	. . . .	1	1	2	3	Liberia	668
7	23	18	28	60	44	94	131	166	187	65	62	. . . .	. . . .	49	Madagascar	674
54	42	21	15	58	41	20	37	108	76	96	107	29	41	29	Malawi	676
11	15	15	16	27	20	19	11	27	88	134	223	224	242	152	Mali	678
110	139	126	101	79	54	39	51	41	63	38	47	44	32	27	Mauritania	682
71	30	34	17	24	27	111	242	328	394	518	624	596	551	512	Mauritius	684
313	197	197	102	50	105	173	290	407	372	1,453	2,167	2,607	2,661	2,981	Morocco	686
. . . .	. . . .	. . . .	. . . .	. . . .	. . . .	. . . .	. . . .	. . . .	. . . .	. . . .	. . . .	36	97	139	Namibia	728
99	91	27	51	90	124	155	175	172	162	156	142	164	140	76	Niger	692
8,025	3,347	1,462	946	1,492	1,518	884	821	484	1,344	2,716	3,101	703	999	949	Nigeria	694
146	149	116	106	109	103	133	116	88	54	31	77	57	35	. . . .	Rwanda	714
6	7	10	12	4	5	8	6	8	14	8	9	9	2	123	Senegal	722
14	12	12	10	6	8	6	10	6	9	12	19	23	26	21	Seychelles	718
24	14	8	15	8	10	11	4	6	3	4	7	15	24	34	Sierra Leone	724
11	26	6	9	1	2	10	5	11	12	. . . .	. . . .	. . . .	. . . .	. . . .	Somalia	726
569	572	440	786	247	286	303	452	580	730	709	628	721	742	1,154	South Africa	199
38	15	19	16	18	11	48	8	9	12	8	5	20	27	54	Sudan	732
124	83	69	88	82	76	79	90	104	137	152	120	225	192	203	Swaziland	734
16	16	4	19	27	15	50	22	58	41	136	143	238	148	227	Tanzania	738
61	130	152	165	207	270	280	250	172	217	248	255	198	114	65	Togo	742
463	461	550	542	415	212	250	370	668	732	559	552	620	622	1,001	Tunisia	744
2	26	71	102	I 69	25	24	38	37	11	31	41	69	107	220	Uganda	746
160	130	35	97	140	173	220	127	139	148	154	128	114	34	83	Zaïre	636
61	48	53	52	55	182	57	77	100	88	136	129	. . . .	140	. . . .	Zambia	754
167	146	127	72	46	85	87	117	133	72	105	105	162	315	278	Zimbabwe	698
29,702	36,628	43,117	54,593	67,374	66,273	79,811	98,109	110,345	119,884	126,996	155,663	162,578	188,992	227,421	Asia *	505
291	236	234	205	233	269	211	197	194	185	187	164	. . . .	. . . .	. . . .	Afghanistan, Islamic State of	512
235	119	166	501	398	306	334	594	777	382	442	894	1,327	1,755	2,150	Bangladesh	513
. . . .	27	32	38	46	46	50	53	70	75	60	69	57	. . . .	79	Bhutan	514
1,996	4,346	10,288	14,315	I 17,717	11,588	9,363	11,493	13,778	13,666	20,796	30,532	I 14,997	16,298	36,246	China, People's Rep. I	924
131	116	115	111	120	119	140	93	173	161	183	190	230	196	187	Fiji	819
5,444	4,032	3,912	4,716	5,960	5,845	5,229	4,549	3,641	2,936	1,069	2,535	4,187	7,425	13,493	India	534
4,227	4,308	2,851	3,532	4,869	4,529	3,312	3,942	3,751	4,150	5,243	6,472	7,599	8,200	8,311	Indonesia	536
2,293	2,304	2,545	2,241	2,809	2,612	2,714	2,526	9,175	11,577	10,398	9,578	12,451	14,727	17,563	Korea	542
10	11	7	18	11	23	26	15	12	12	43	41	62	112	111	Lao, P.D. Rep.	544
3,440	3,521	3,416	3,614	3,798	4,472	4,928	5,241	4,850	5,922	6,856	7,610	12,529	19,838	17,415	Malaysia	548
1	1	8	4	5	4	6	6	16	19	17	16	21	19	21	Maldives	556
204	197	95	85	63	31	27	19	58	200	220	181	204	221	289	Myanmar	518
143	173	181	127	84	51	71	126	164	161	208	278	340	466	475	Nepal	558
389	620	878	1,884	1,056	735	580	354	293	396	208	368	618	871	2,007	Pakistan	564
															of which:	
1,729	6,216	7,734	11,327	15,980	20,535	37,860	54,099	54,913	55,719	50,919	57,609	59,859	60,844	63,331	Taiwan Province of China	528

I See country notes in the monthly *IFS*

Total Reserves Minus Gold

11 s

		1965	1966	1967	1968	1969	1970	1971	1972	1973	1974	1975	1976	1977	1978	1979
																Millions of SDRs:
Asia (cont.)																
Papua New Guinea	853	….	….	….	….	….	….	….	….	26	27	153	221	351	311	382
Philippines	566	155	150	120	99	76	195	285	442	823	1,192	1,123	1,374	1,218	1,353	1,708
Singapore	576	430	394	496	712	827	1,012	1,338	1,610	1,895	2,297	2,568	2,895	3,176	4,070	4,417
Solomon Islands	813	….	….	….	….	….	….	….	….	….	….	….	….	2	22	28
Sri Lanka	524	73	43	55	52	40	43	46	55	72	63	49	79	241	305	392
Thailand	578	643	832	917	929	893	824	726	887	1,000	1,436	1,434	1,547	1,492	1,542	1,399
Tonga	866	….	….	….	….	….	….	….	….	….	….	….	….	7	8	10
Vanuatu	846	….	….	….	….	….	….	….	….	….	….	….	….	….	….	….
Viet Nam	582	159	281	309	255	204	217	224	226	136	172	….	….	….	….	….
Western Samoa	862	4	3	2	3	5	5	6	4	4	5	5	5	8	4	4
Europe	170	272	311	273	387	619	735	1,144	2,352	3,379	2,878	2,544	3,808	3,270	3,712	3,318
Cyprus	423	84	98	103	141	162	194	247	279	239	204	169	236	258	265	268
Czech Republic	935	….	….	….	….	….	….	….	….	….	….	….	….	….	….	….
Czechoslovakia ɪ	934	….	….	….	….	….	….	….	….	….	….	….	….	….	….	….
Hungary	944	….	….	….	….	….	….	….	….	….	….	….	….	….	….	….
Malta	181	79	90	90	ɪ139	127	148	170	241	257	316	415	523	592	710	769
Poland	964	….	….	….	….	….	….	….	….	….	….	….	….	….	….	429
Romania	968	….	….	….	….	….	….	….	….	….	178	196	461	483	211	289	398
Turkey	186	25	29	22	26	128	304	582	1,162	1,646	1,276	806	853	525	615	500
Yugoslavia, SFR	188	84	94	58	82	202	89	145	622	1,058	886	693	1,713	1,683	1,833	954
Middle East	405	2,081	2,421	2,750	2,596	2,736	3,556	5,948	8,362	10,140	28,344	37,332	44,716	52,886	41,648	46,967
Bahrain	419	23	13	20	42	60	63	79	77	53	107	247	376	415	379	466
Egypt	469	54	63	102	75	51	74	53	47	215	206	166	206	355	377	402
Iran, I.R. of	429	105	138	180	133	152	77	441	754	894	6,716	7,469	7,472	9,966	9,194	11,546
Iraq	433	125	219	254	260	284	319	409	576	1,144	2,530	2,186	3,816	5,614	….	….
Israel	436	587	575	669	617	367	405	635	1,086	1,466	942	971	1,143	1,253	2,015	2,326
Jordan	439	136	164	241	255	233	228	205	222	224	255	392	406	529	680	885
Kuwait	443	72	97	48	51	96	117	178	248	316	1,020	1,274	1,465	2,374	1,919	2,179
Lebanon	446	69	89	88	44	60	98	181	299	392	1,044	1,026	1,121	1,291	1,408	1,163
Libya	672	178	271	317	453	832	1,505	2,370	2,609	1,678	2,868	1,790	2,674	3,940	3,151	4,816
Oman	449	….	….	….	….	….	10	23	34	39	76	138	189	238	195	315
Qatar	453	….	18	23	26	29	30	35	49	56	52	83	111	133	162	219
Saudi Arabia	456	653	679	693	543	488	543	1,223	2,195	3,106	11,559	19,812	23,153	24,617	ɪ14,737	14,631
Syrian Arab Rep.	463	26	34	55	39	31	27	53	97	314	381	600	253	398	293	441
United Arab Emirates	466	….	….	….	….	….	….	….	….	76	370	844	1,641	659	623	1,087
Yemen Arab Rep.	473	….	….	….	….	….	….	….	….	105	162	288	620	1,021	1,120	1,084
Yemen, P.D. Rep.	459	52	61	61	59	55	59	59	61	62	55	46	70	82	144	159
Yemen, Republic of	474	….	….	….	….	….	….	….	….	….	….	….	….	….	….	….
Western Hemisphere	205	2,148	2,129	2,386	2,890	3,304	4,363	4,886	8,021	10,903	14,011	15,071	19,510	22,436	26,241	31,333
Antigua and Barbuda	311	….	….	….	….	….	….	….	….	….	….	6	8	4	5	9
Argentina	213	170	132	643	651	403	533	177	289	952	935	246	1,244	2,596	3,812	7,127
Aruba	314	….	….	….	….	….	….	….	….	….	….	….	….	….	….	….
Bahamas, The	313	….	….	….	44	26	22	27	34	36	41	46	41	ɪ55	45	59
Barbados	316	….	12	9	16	12	17	17	26	27	32	34	24	30	46	50
Belize	339	….	….	….	….	….	….	….	….	….	….	5	7	11	8
Bolivia	218	30	34	29	29	30	33	37	41	46	144	119	130	174	130	135
Brazil	223	421	380	154	212	611	1,142	1,562	3,806	5,272	4,260	3,400	5,584	5,921	9,078	6,806
Chile	228	94	127	81	162	296	342	157	89	101	34	48	349	351	837	1,471
Colombia	233	61	52	52	142	195	189	173	285	428	352	405	947	1,438	1,816	2,918
Costa Rica	238	18	15	16	18	27	14	25	37	40	34	42	82	157	149	90
Dominica	321	….	….	….	….	….	….	….	….	….	….	—	1	2	1	7
Dominican Republic	243	48	41	29	33	37	29	49	51	70	71	96	106	148	118	181
Ecuador	248	35	50	52	31	43	55	34	112	174	260	216	411	513	488	548
El Salvador	253	38	39	37	44	47	45	43	59	34	63	91	160	174	206	108
Grenada	328	….	….	….	….	….	5	5	5	4	4	ɪ4	7	6	7	9
Guatemala	258	46	41	45	45	54	61	69	107	159	148	242	423	551	569	529
Guyana	336	20	17	19	24	21	20	24	34	12	51	86	23	19	45	13
Haiti	263	1	2	2	3	4	4	10	16	14	16	11	24	28	30	42
Honduras	268	23	27	25	31	31	20	20	32	35	36	83	113	148	142	159
Jamaica	343	96	88	85	120	118	139	165	147	106	156	107	28	39	45	48
Mexico	273	380	455	420	492	493	568	693	899	962	1,011	1,182	1,023	1,357	1,414	1,573
Netherlands Antilles	353	….	….	….	20	28	25	34	46	41	50	61	80	83	51	55
Nicaragua	278	57	57	31	48	44	49	54	74	96	85	104	126	122	39	111
Panama	283	6	6	7	11	14	16	19	40	35	32	29	68	58	115	90
Paraguay	288	10	11	12	12	10	18	19	29	47	71	98	136	221	344	462
Peru	293	107	90	106	91	142	ɪ296	351	408	436	756	363	249	294	299	1,154
St. Kitts and Nevis	361	….	….	….	….	….	….	….	….	….	….	….	….	….	….	….
St. Lucia	362	….	….	….	….	….	….	….	….	….	….	3	4	5	5	6
St. Vincent & Grens.	364	….	….	….	….	….	….	….	….	….	….	….	4	4	4	7
Suriname	366	17	17	8	9	24	28	30	35	47	55	78	95	77	102	129
Trinidad and Tobago	369	29	30	30	49	45	43	64	54	39	319	641	872	1,220	1,385	1,625
Uruguay	298	24	30	22	34	19	14	19	64	83	66	50	152	265	271	ɪ245
Venezuela	299	418	376	471	519	530	637	1,010	1,204	1,608	4,928	7,178	6,992	6,368	4,632	5,557
Memorandum Items																
Oil Exporting Countries	999	1,966	2,279	2,365	2,451	2,844	3,744	6,511	8,789	10,803	37,100	47,007	54,779	60,845	44,847	54,913
Non-Oil Developing Countries	201	7,103	7,816	8,395	9,281	10,654	12,763	13,551	20,416	26,085	27,059	26,927	38,274	47,575	55,830	63,054

ɪ See country notes in the monthly *IFS*

Total Reserves Minus Gold

1980	1981	1982	1983	1984	1985	1986	1987	1988	1989	1990	1991	1992	1993	1994		
End of Period															Asia (cont.)	
332	340	411	420	444	403	348	308	292	292	283	226	174	103	66	Papua New Guinea	853
2,232	1,775	805	713	614	560	1,413	683	746	1,078	650	2,269	3,202	3,404	4,122	Philippines	566
5,149	6,486	7,687	8,849	10,626	11,695	10,578	10,733	12,687	15,481	19,505	23,862	29,007	35,208	39,851	Singapore	576
23	19	34	45	46	32	24	26	29	20	12	6	17	15	...	Solomon Islands	813
192	281	319	284	521	411	288	197	165	186	297	479	674	1,186	1,401	Sri Lanka	524
1,223	1,488	1,394	1,535	1,959	1,994	2,293	2,825	4,530	7,241	9,352	12,246	14,806	17,817	20,093	Thailand	578
11	12	14	20	27	25	18	20	23	19	22	23	23	27	24	Tonga	866
....	7	5	6	8	10	18	28	30	27	26	28	31	33	30	Vanuatu	846
....	15	15	12	13	11	10	...	...	...	...	...	...	...	...	Viet Nam	582
2	3	3	7	11	13	19	26	37	42	49	47	44	37	35	Western Samoa	862
4,790	4,865	4,839	6,897	8,469	7,110	7,739	7,524	9,527	14,436	15,218	15,388	14,725	16,729	19,225	Europe	170
289	366	474	496	551	542	615	616	690	855	1,059	972	748	798	1,003	Cyprus	423
...	...	...	...	...	...	...	...	...	...	...	...	...	2,759	4,209	Czech Republic	935
1,442	821	703	767	986	778	912	974	1,176	1,641	775	2,230	I 815	...	...	Czechoslovakia I	934
...	...	...	1,176	1,592	1,960	1,882	1,152	1,090	948	752	2,752	3,220	4,930	4,665	Hungary	944
776	923	982	1,062	1,010	899	936	997	1,014	1,031	1,006	932	922	992	1,267	Malta	181
100	239	586	731	1,128	792	570	1,054	1,527	1,761	3,158	2,540	2,981	2,979	4,002	Poland	964
253	347	408	502	724	181	476	988	580	1,414	368	486	601	725	1,429	Romania	968
844	797	979	1,230	1,296	961	1,154	1,252	1,742	3,638	4,252	3,596	4,480	4,566	4,911	Turkey	186
1,085	1,372	703	933	1,181	997	1,193	492	1,708	3,147	3,848	1,875	...	...	...	Yugoslavia, SFR	188
55,317	58,506	62,777	60,933	58,394	57,307	46,597	44,586	40,341	40,983	36,715	40,549	42,936	46,105	45,125	Middle East	405
748	1,327	1,391	1,362	1,329	1,511	1,218	810	930	799	868	1,059	1,017	948	801	Bahrain	419
820	615	633	737	751	721	678	972	939	1,157	1,886	3,723	7,862	9,395	9,234	Egypt	469
8,015	1,379	5,168	...	...	...	...	...	...	...	...	...	...	...	...	Iran, I.R. of	429
...	...	...	...	...	...	...	...	...	...	...	...	...	...	...	Iraq	433
2,628	3,004	3,480	3,487	3,122	3,350	3,809	4,142	2,984	4,015	4,411	4,390	3,729	4,647	4,653	Israel	436
896	934	801	787	525	385	357	299	81	358	597	577	558	1,192	1,159	Jordan	439
3,080	3,495	5,360	4,959	4,683	4,981	4,497	2,919	1,429	2,360	1,372	2,383	3,743	3,068	2,398	Kuwait	443
1,245	1,303	2,364	1,817	685	978	399	259	727	714	464	892	1,088	1,646	2,661	Lebanon	446
10,264	7,735	6,400	4,985	3,708	5,375	4,867	4,115	3,211	3,297	4,104	3,981	4,496	...	...	Libya	672
456	639	791	728	918	993	791	988	783	1,031	1,176	1,163	1,443	661	671	Oman	449
269	314	350	367	388	406	468	436	353	406	444	467	497	505	451	Qatar	453
18,376	27,695	26,787	26,064	25,248	22,764	14,980	15,990	15,273	12,744	8,201	8,161	4,316	5,408	5,054	Saudi Arabia	456
264	250	180	50	274	76	118	157	143	...	...	...	...	...	...	Syrian Arab Rep.	463
1,580	2,751	I 2,008	1,979	2,333	2,917	2,755	3,331	3,295	3,391	3,222	3,751	4,154	4,444	4,561	United Arab Emirates	466
1,006	826	502	350	325	270	353	380	212	212	...	...	...	...	...	Yemen Arab Rep.	473
183	219	259	269	254	170	113	68	59	58	...	...	...	...	...	Yemen, P.D. Rep.	459
...	...	...	...	...	...	...	...	...	...	297	475	233	106	...	Yemen, Republic of	474
30,482	32,825	24,475	26,868	40,102	36,409	26,155	25,883	21,974	24,376	33,047	45,319	63,785	78,638	71,141	Western Hemisphere	205
6	6	8	9	16	15	23	18	21	21	19	23	37	28	32	Antigua and Barbuda	311
5,268	2,808	2,272	1,120	1,268	I 2,980	2,222	1,140	2,499	1,113	3,228	4,198	7,265	10,040	9,814	Argentina	213
...	...	...	...	...	...	60	55	68	66	69	84	103	132	122	Aruba	314
72	86	103	117	164	166	189	120	128	112	111	127	113	125	121	Bahamas, The	313
62	86	110	118	135	127	124	102	101	83	83	61	102	110	134	Barbados	316
10	9	9	9	6	13	22	26	38	46	49	37	39	28	24	Belize	339
83	86	141	153	257	182	134	69	79	156	117	74	132	163	309	Bolivia	218
4,524	5,673	3,561	4,160	11,740	9,654	I 4,744	4,440	5,181	5,734	5,230	5,616	16,379	22,281	25,393	Brazil	223
2,449	2,761	1,645	1,945	2,350	2,230	1,922	1,765	2,349	2,761	4,266	4,922	6,667	7,018	8,965	Chile	228
3,788	4,073	3,500	1,816	1,392	1,452	2,204	2,175	2,413	2,752	2,960	4,215	5,374	5,498	5,309	Colombia	233
114	113	205	297	413	461	428	345	496	565	366	643	741	746	612	Costa Rica	238
4	3	4	1	5	3	8	13	10	9	10	12	15	14	11	Dominica	321
158	193	117	164	259	310	308	128	189	125	43	309	363	474	173	Dominican Republic	243
794	543	276	616	624	654	527	346	295	411	589	646	631	1,005	1,263	Ecuador	248
61	62	98	153	169	164	139	131	120	202	292	201	307	390	445	El Salvador	253
10	14	8	14	15	19	17	16	13	12	12	12	19	20	21	Grenada	328
349	129	102	201	280	274	296	203	149	233	198	564	557	632	591	Guatemala	258
10	6	10	6	6	6	7	6	3	10	20	87	137	180	169	Guyana	336
13	21	4	9	13	6	13	12	10	10	2	12	...	...	...	Haiti	263
117	87	102	109	131	96	91	75	37	16	28	73	144	71	117	Honduras	268
82	73	99	60	99	147	80	123	109	82	118e	74	236	304	504	Jamaica	343
2,321	3,500	756	3,737	7,419	4,467	4,635	8,786	3,923	4,816	6,933	12,392	13,776	18,281	4,301	Mexico	273
74	116	170	157	120	160	195	153	195	158	151	124	160	170	123	Netherlands Antilles	353
51	96	155	167	...	...	...	12	28	88	75	94	95	40	97	Nicaragua	278
92	103	92	197	220	89	139	55	54	91	241	349	367	435	482	Panama	283
597	692	670	650	680	486	365	350	241	329	465	673	408	460	696	Paraguay	288
1,552	1,031	1,223	1,304	1,663	1,677	1,150	455	380	615	731	1,708	2,072	2,481	4,790	Peru	293
...	3	3	3	6	7	8	7	8	12	11	12	19	21	22	St. Kitts and Nevis	361
6	7	7	8	13	12	21	22	24	29	31	34	40	44	39	St. Lucia	362
6	8	4	5	13	13	21	14	16	17	19	16	24	23	21	St. Vincent & Grens.	364
148	178	159	56	25	21	17	11	9	7	15	—	—	—	—	Suriname	366
2,180	2,876	2,793	2,010	1,384	1,027	388	132	94	188	346	237	125	150	241	Trinidad and Tobago	369
301	369	105	198	137	159	394	374	395	381	368	235	370	552	663	Uruguay	298
5,178	7,014	5,964	7,300	9,081	9,332	5,263	4,203	2,297	3,125	5,849	7,457	6,954	6,709	5,526	Venezuela	299
															Memorandum Items	
67,915	67,872	65,637	65,667	68,065	67,791	50,368	47,621	41,467	42,837	42,421	47,414	44,674	45,062	42,977	Oil Exporting Countries	999
67,332	75,302	76,719	90,462	112,962	107,599	116,942	135,573	148,126	165,870	181,185	223,616	251,644	298,721	335,880	Non-Oil Developing Countries	201

I See country notes in the monthly *IFS*

Nongold Reserves/Imports

1rl s

Weeks of Imports

		1965	1966	1967	1968	1969	1970	1971	1972	1973	1974	1975	1976	1977	1978	1979
World	001	**8.4**	**8.3**	**8.7**	**8.7**	**7.8**	**9.5**	**14.5**	**15.7**	**13.3**	**11.3**	**11.3**	**11.8**	**13.2**	**13.2**	**11.7**
Industrial Countries	110	**7.8**	**7.7**	**8.1**	**8.1**	**6.8**	**8.9**	**14.7**	**15.0**	**11.9**	**8.4**	**8.5**	**8.1**	**9.6**	**10.8**	**9.1**
United States	111	3.1	3.1	5.0	7.1	6.9	4.2	2.3	2.4	1.9	2.0	2.3	2.8	2.5	2.0	1.8
Canada	156	11.4	8.6	8.2	9.3	8.3	14.2	15.3	13.5	10.2	7.4	6.4	6.4	4.5	4.0	2.6
Australia	193	18.2	19.3	15.0	14.1	11.4	14.9	30.2	60.6	37.9	17.2	14.4	12.2	7.9	6.9	4.1
Japan	158	11.6	9.8	7.5	10.2	11.2	11.9	38.6	38.3	15.4	10.6	10.7	12.6	16.3	21.1	9.2
New Zealand	196	8.6	8.5	11.9	9.4	10.8	10.7	19.0	28.4	25.0	9.1	7.0	7.8	6.8	6.7	5.1
Austria	122	15.1	14.1	17.6	16.6	15.1	15.3	19.2	19.2	14.6	14.6	19.8	16.1	12.2	16.4	10.5
Denmark	128	9.0	8.5	7.0	5.4	4.9	4.9	7.4	8.0	8.3	4.5	4.0	3.5	6.2	11.0	9.1
Finland	172	6.5	4.3	4.3	9.6	7.2	8.4	11.5	11.0	6.9	4.5	3.0	3.3	3.6	8.1	7.0
France	132	8.2	6.6	7.4	1.2	.9	3.9	10.8	11.9	5.9	4.4	8.1	4.6	4.3	5.9	8.5
Germany	134	8.9	10.7	11.6	13.9	6.4	16.7	21.6	24.9	26.7	20.4	18.2	17.7	17.8	20.7	17.1
Greece	174	7.9	6.5	6.8	6.8	6.1	5.1	10.2	19.9	13.4	9.2	9.4	7.6	8.0	8.7	7.3
Iceland	176	20.0	18.6	11.0	10.4	15.8	17.4	17.1	18.7	14.3	4.7	4.9	8.8	8.4	10.5	10.3
Ireland	178	19.3	23.4	19.9	19.6	23.0	21.8	27.7	27.4	18.8	17.0	20.8	22.5	22.7	19.5	11.6
Italy	136	16.9	15.1	16.2	12.2	8.7	8.6	12.0	8.0	5.5	4.3	1.8	3.8	8.8	10.2	12.1
Netherlands	138	3.8	3.9	4.8	3.6	3.2	4.9	5.1	7.0	7.9	6.2	6.2	5.8	5.7	4.3	5.1
Norway	142	10.5	11.0	12.5	13.0	12.1	11.1	14.3	15.3	12.7	11.7	11.8	10.2	8.9	12.9	16.0
Portugal	182	21.0	22.3	27.4	25.3	24.0	20.1	27.2	30.5	23.9	13.4	5.4	2.2	4.0	8.6	7.4
Spain	184	10.5	6.8	4.8	5.4	6.1	14.5	28.3	34.1	33.2	19.8	17.6	14.0	17.4	28.1	27.0
Sweden	144	9.1	9.4	7.1	6.0	4.1	4.2	6.6	8.7	10.9	4.6	8.5	6.0	8.8	10.4	6.4
Switzerland	146	5.7	9.4	7.8	19.5	17.8	19.6	27.5	27.0	22.4	19.6	27.4	33.8	29.8	38.8	29.1
United Kingdom	112	2.4	3.6	4.1	2.6	2.7	3.5	17.4	9.1	7.5	5.8	4.5	3.1	16.6	11.0	10.3
Developing Countries	200	**9.8**	**10.0**	**10.3**	**10.5**	**11.0**	**11.1**	**13.6**	**17.6**	**17.6**	**19.5**	**17.9**	**21.4**	**22.1**	**19.0**	**18.5**
Africa	605	**8.7**	**10.4**	**9.0**	**9.3**	**9.7**	**10.1**	**9.1**	**11.0**	**11.6**	**17.8**	**13.7**	**14.2**	**11.5**	**8.2**	**12.4**
Algeria	612	13.8	21.6	23.3	18.3	10.5	6.1	12.7	9.9	21.2	18.7	10.7	18.1	12.3	12.0	16.5
Benin	638	15.2	15.0	8.6	10.6	7.1	12.6	16.6	16.1	15.4	12.2	4.2	4.6	4.0	2.6	2.3
Botswana	616	...	...	...	...	...	...	...	...	...	...	...	18.7	18.3	21.1	25.8
Burkina Faso	748	19.5	22.4	26.2	29.8	27.1	40.3	43.8	40.6	32.9	30.1	26.3	25.8	14.0	8.3	10.6
Burundi	618	25.2	18.9	13.6	6.6	18.0	35.7	30.8	30.4	35.9	17.1	25.9	44.1	66.2	43.0	30.7
Cameroon	622	10.3	13.3	7.1	11.4	12.3	17.3	15.2	7.5	8.0	9.4	2.5	3.7	3.0	2.6	5.1
Cape Verde	624	...	...	...	...	...	...	...	...	...	...	...	56.5	58.0	38.3	41.5
Central African Rep.	626	19.1	9.5	5.6	6.2	1.7	2.1	.3	2.6	1.8	2.0	2.9	17.8	20.8	22.2	32.9
Chad	628	22.5	11.8	.9	1.0	1.2	1.9	9.3	8.5	.9	8.6	1.2	10.5	5.2	2.8	6.9
Comoros	632	...	...	...	...	...	...	...	...	...	...	...	...	...	...	...
Congo	634	3.9	3.9	1.6	4.5	3.7	7.8	6.9	5.8	3.2	9.8	4.1	3.5	3.3	1.9	7.5
Côte d'Ivoire	662	13.5	12.2	14.3	13.4	11.5	15.9	11.6	10.0	6.5	3.5	4.7	3.1	5.5	10.0	3.1
Djibouti	611	...	...	...	...	...	...	...	...	...	...	...	...	...	...	...
Equatorial Guinea	642	...	...	...	...	...	...	...	...	...	...	...	...	...	...	...
Ethiopia	644	25.6	24.0	21.9	17.5	20.9	19.2	16.4	22.8	40.3	49.8	46.0	43.5	31.5	17.5	15.8
Gabon	646	14.6	9.0	7.2	4.4	5.6	9.5	13.6	8.7	13.1	16.2	16.2	12.0	.7	1.9	2.0
Gambia, The	648	25.5	27.0	23.0	16.2	16.0	23.5	26.7	23.9	27.1	31.4	24.9	14.5	16.3	13.5	.7
Ghana	652	12.8	15.6	13.0	15.3	9.9	4.6	4.3	16.8	20.3	4.5	8.1	5.7	6.8	14.6	17.6
Guinea-Bissau	654	...	...	...	...	...	...	...	...	...	...	...	...	...	...	...
Kenya	664	3.7	7.9	11.7	14.6	24.4	25.8	15.9	19.6	19.6	9.8	9.5	14.8	21.1	10.7	19.9
Liberia	668	...	...	...	...	...	...	...	...	...	3.4	3.0	2.2	3.1	1.9	5.6
Lesotho	666	...	...	...	...	...	...	...	...	...	...	...	...	...	...	...
Madagascar	674	18.7	18.8	15.3	9.3	5.5	11.3	11.3	13.2	17.4	9.1	5.1	7.7	10.3	6.9	.4
Malawi	676	20.3	13.0	14.7	14.6	13.2	15.3	15.4	14.6	24.7	22.7	12.6	6.6	19.4	11.5	9.1
Mali	678	4.4	.7	2.0	.8	1.5	1.0	1.9	2.3	2.1	1.7	1.2	2.4	1.7	2.1	.9
Mauritania	682	21.6	17.6	12.3	10.9	4.4	3.0	6.8	10.1	17.2	44.9	15.4	23.9	12.6	22.8	22.9
Mauritius	684	13.5	14.3	9.0	11.2	25.5	32.2	32.0	30.5	20.6	22.0	26.1	13.0	7.8	4.8	2.7
Morocco	686	8.9	7.2	5.5	6.0	8.6	9.0	11.3	14.3	10.9	10.7	7.1	9.3	8.2	10.8	7.9
Namibia	728	...	...	...	...	...	...	...	...	...	...	...	...	...	...	...
Niger	692	4.2	4.3	1.2	3.4	7.2	16.7	32.7	32.7	30.8	24.5	25.9	34.0	26.7	21.9	14.9
Nigeria	694	14.8	14.1	7.7	9.4	8.4	9.9	14.0	12.3	15.6	105.1	48.1	32.8	19.8	7.7	28.2
Rwanda	714	4.6	11.4	17.2	13.3	6.6	13.8	9.1	9.5	22.9	11.6	13.5	32.3	37.2	24.2	41.2
Senegal	722	11.9	14.8	12.2	4.5	1.7	5.9	5.8	7.1	1.7	.7	2.8	2.3	2.2	1.3	1.1
Seychelles	718	...	...	...	...	...	...	...	...	...	8.9	9.3	10.4	8.6	13.1	7.5
Sierra Leone	724	10.9	10.4	9.2	15.8	16.5	17.6	17.7	20.3	17.3	12.8	8.0	8.6	9.6	6.5	7.7
Somalia	726	9.0	15.2	13.0	7.4	13.5	24.4	22.1	21.7	16.8	15.4	23.0	28.4	27.4	27.2	9.3
South Africa	199	3.5	4.2	3.7	4.3	4.6	4.7	3.2	8.0	4.5	2.5	3.1	3.0	3.5	2.9	2.5
Sudan	732	15.0	13.4	13.3	9.6	7.4	3.9	4.4	5.8	7.3	10.1	2.1	1.3	1.1	1.2	3.2
Swaziland	734	...	...	...	...	...	...	...	...	...	5.1	13.2	19.1	27.0	19.0	13.6
Tanzania	738	...	13.4	14.0	15.7	17.4	10.6	8.2	15.3	15.4	3.6	4.4	9.2	20.1	4.5	3.2
Togo	742	20.1	20.4	25.5	28.3	24.4	28.3	29.5	22.3	19.6	23.7	12.3	18.7	8.4	8.1	6.7
Tunisia	744	6.8	5.0	7.2	7.4	6.4	9.4	21.5	24.3	24.8	19.0	13.9	12.4	10.0	10.9	10.6
Uganda	746	...	12.5	11.3	15.7	15.5	17.1	5.6	11.5	9.3	4.1	8.1	13.6	9.9	10.8	6.0
Zaïre	636	9.8	8.5	42.2	63.2	56.9	39.6	23.3	30.7	35.7	17.7	8.3	11.6	34.3	33.3	54.0
Zambia	754	29.5	26.7	17.6	18.6	36.3	47.2	22.2	12.1	14.9	8.8	6.5	5.9	4.4	3.6	4.6
Zimbabwe	698	...	12.4	10.1	.6	4.5	2.8	.7	6.7	10.7	4.3	4.5	5.7	5.3	11.2	16.7
Asia	505	**10.2**	**10.5**	**11.1**	**11.7**	**12.8**	**12.7**	**13.2**	**15.3**	**13.3**	**10.4**	**9.6**	**13.4**	**16.3**	**14.4**	**12.9**
Afghanistan, Islamic State of	512	3.9	4.9	2.2	2.8	3.4	5.7	9.9	6.6	6.5	5.9	12.9	26.1	43.7	51.4	53.9
Bangladesh	513	...	...	...	...	...	...	...	20.6	7.5	6.7	5.8	15.8	10.4	10.8	10.5
China, People's Rep.	924	...	...	...	...	...	...	...	...	...	...	...	...	17.1	7.3	7.2
Fiji	819	15.5	14.7	13.4	12.2	15.7	13.7	15.9	22.6	17.3	20.8	28.8	22.9	24.9	19.7	15.1
India	534	5.8	5.5	7.9	8.9	16.1	18.7	20.2	21.4	13.7	10.4	8.9	25.6	38.1	42.5	39.3
Indonesia	536	1.3	1.9	.2	6.0	7.8	8.1	8.7	19.1	15.3	20.2	6.4	13.7	20.9	20.4	29.3
Korea	542	16.1	17.6	18.4	13.8	15.7	15.9	9.4	10.8	10.9	2.1	5.6	11.7	14.3	9.6	7.6
Lao, P.D. Rep.	544	10.4	8.3	6.0	5.6	3.3	2.8	5.3	6.0	9.6	11.9	...	...	...	...	...
Malaysia	548	22.2	23.2	20.4	20.2	24.6	22.7	27.1	29.8	27.0	19.6	21.2	32.7	31.9	28.4	25.9
Maldives	556	...	...	...	...	...	...	...	...	...	...	...	.1	.4	2.1	1.7
Myanmar	518	20.4	32.9	30.1	31.6	14.4	10.5	15.0	15.8	45.1	53.8	35.1	34.7	22.3	16.3	33.2

Nongold Reserves/Imports

1980	1981	1982	1983	1984	1985	1986	1987	1988	1989	1990	1991	1992	1993	1994		1rl s
Weeks of Imports																
11.0	10.4	10.4	11.4	11.1	12.2	12.8	15.4	13.6	13.5	13.8	14.1	13.3	14.6	12.8	**World**	001
8.8	8.5	8.5	9.2	8.6	9.5	10.3	13.1	11.9	11.7	11.9	11.5	10.5	11.6	11.4	**Industrial Countries**	110
3.2	3.6	4.7	4.4	3.6	4.7	5.1	4.3	4.2	6.7	7.3	6.8	5.7	5.4	4.8	United States	111
2.6	2.6	2.7	2.8	1.7	1.6	2.0	4.1	7.1	7.0	7.5	6.8	4.6	4.7	4.1	Canada	156
3.9	3.3	12.4	21.7	14.9	11.6	14.4	15.5	19.6	15.9	20.1	20.6	13.3	12.7	11.0	Australia	193
9.1	10.3	9.2	10.1	10.1	10.6	17.2	27.9	26.8	20.8	17.3	15.8	16.0	21.2	23.8	Japan	158
3.3	6.1	5.7	7.6	15.0	13.8	32.3	23.3	20.1	17.9	22.6	18.3	17.4	18.0	16.2	New Zealand	196
11.2	13.1	14.1	12.1	11.2	11.8	11.9	12.0	10.6	11.5	9.9	10.6	11.9	15.6	15.8	Austria	122
9.1	7.5	7.1	11.6	9.4	15.5	11.3	20.5	21.6	12.5	17.1	11.9	16.3	17.5	13.5	Denmark	128
6.2	5.4	5.9	5.0	11.5	14.7	6.1	17.0	15.7	10.9	18.6	18.1	12.8	15.6	23.9	Finland	172
10.5	9.6	7.4	9.7	10.4	12.8	12.6	10.8	7.4	6.6	8.2	7.0	5.9	5.8	6.0	France	132
13.4	13.9	15.0	14.5	13.6	14.6	14.1	17.9	12.2	11.7	10.2	8.4	11.8	11.6	10.8	Germany	134
6.6	6.0	4.5	4.9	5.3	4.5	7.0	10.6	15.3	10.4	9.0	12.5	10.7	….	….	Greece	174
9.0	11.7	8.0	9.5	7.9	11.8	14.4	10.2	9.5	12.5	13.5	13.3	15.4	16.4	10.3	Iceland	176
13.3	13.0	14.1	15.0	12.6	15.3	14.5	18.3	17.0	12.1	13.1	14.4	8.0	14.4	….	Ireland	178
11.9	11.1	8.4	13.1	12.7	9.2	10.5	12.5	13.0	15.9	18.0	13.9	7.6	9.7	10.0	Italy	136
6.9	6.4	7.3	7.6	6.9	7.7	7.5	9.1	8.4	8.2	7.2	7.4	8.5	13.1	12.5	Netherlands	138
18.6	20.8	23.1	25.5	35.1	46.5	32.1	32.8	29.7	30.3	29.3	26.9	24.0	42.6	36.2	Norway	142
4.4	2.8	2.4	2.4	3.4	9.5	7.8	12.4	14.9	27.1	29.8	41.1	33.6	33.8	30.3	Portugal	182
18.1	17.5	12.7	13.2	21.6	19.4	21.9	32.5	32.3	30.2	30.4	36.7	23.7	27.1	23.4	Spain	184
5.3	6.5	6.6	8.0	7.6	10.6	10.4	10.4	9.7	10.1	17.2	19.1	23.5	23.2	23.4	Sweden	144
22.4	23.7	28.0	26.8	26.9	30.5	27.6	28.2	22.3	22.6	21.8	22.7	28.0	29.9	28.2	Switzerland	146
9.3	7.7	6.5	5.9	4.7	6.1	7.6	14.0	12.1	9.1	8.4	10.4	8.6	9.3	9.4	United Kingdom	112
15.7	13.9	14.1	15.7	16.9	18.7	19.7	22.0	18.4	18.7	19.3	21.0	19.8	20.9	14.5	**Developing Countries**	200
12.1	7.1	5.4	5.6	5.5	8.4	8.2	9.0	8.0	9.1	11.4	13.9	10.5	12.3	….	**Africa**	605
18.6	17.0	11.7	9.4	7.4	14.9	9.4	12.1	6.4	4.8	3.9	10.3	8.8	9.9	….	Algeria	612
1.3	5.5	.6	.6	.4	.6	.5	.5	.7	.9	12.7	41.3	29.0	36.8	….	Benin	638
25.8	16.5	22.1	28.0	35.4	70.2	87.4	114.1	98.2	98.5	90.5	100.8	107.4	121.6	….	Botswana	616
9.9	10.9	9.3	15.2	26.4	21.9	30.0	38.6	36.8	42.9	29.2	33.8	….	….	….	Burkina Faso	748
29.3	19.8	7.2	7.7	5.5	8.1	17.8	14.9	17.7	27.7	23.7	29.7	40.9	41.5	47.4	Burundi	618
6.1	3.1	2.9	6.8	2.5	6.0	1.8	1.9	7.2	3.3	.8	1.7	.9	….	….	Cameroon	622
32.5	27.8	30.7	27.4	25.7	34.4	27.3	41.8	39.8	34.8	29.5	23.1	21.9	….	….	Cape Verde	624
35.2	38.0	19.5	31.5	31.5	22.9	20.3	24.6	28.1	39.1	39.9	30.0	31.5	….	….	Central African Rep.	626
3.6	3.5	5.9	9.3	12.7	10.5	3.9	12.0	14.4	24.2	23.3	21.0	17.2	10.1	….	Chad	628
11.4	13.5	17.3	16.3	4.2	16.8	24.6	30.8	23.3	37.6	29.9	26.1	20.6	….	….	Comoros	632
7.7	14.4	2.5	.6	.3	.3	.6	.2	.2	.3	.5	.5	.5	.1	….	Congo	634
.3	.4	.1	.6	.2	.1	.5	.2	.3	.4	.1	.3	.1	….	….	Côte d'Ivoire	662
….	….	….	….	10.5	13.2	15.1	16.1	16.6	15.7	22.7	24.3	19.8	….	….	Djibouti	611
….	….	4.7	3.6	4.1	9.0	2.7	.5	4.7	.8	.6	4.2	7.6	.4	….	Equatorial Guinea	642
5.8	18.8	12.0	7.5	2.4	7.7	11.8	6.0	3.0	2.5	1.0	6.0	15.1	30.1	….	Ethiopia	644
8.3	12.3	18.7	14.2	14.3	11.7	7.6	.9	4.4	2.3	18.4	19.3	4.2	—	….	Gabon	646
1.8	1.6	4.2	1.3	1.2	1.0	6.8	10.5	7.2	6.6	14.4	15.9	20.9	….	24.4	Gambia, The	648
8.3	6.8	10.2	3.0	27.1	34.0	34.1	10.3	12.7	14.2	….	….	….	….	15.1	Ghana	652
….	….	….	….	….	….	−.5	….	12.5	15.7	13.9	11.2	11.1	12.0	15.1	Guinea-Bissau	654
12.0	6.2	6.7	14.7	13.8	14.1	13.3	7.6	6.9	6.9	5.0	3.4	1.6	12.3	13.4	Kenya	664
.5	1.1	.8	2.6	.5	.3	.5	.1	.1	….	….	….	….	….	….	Liberia	668
6.1	4.8	5.4	7.1	5.7	6.6	8.8	7.5	5.0	4.3	5.6	7.4	8.4	14.4	….	Lesotho	666
.8	2.5	2.5	3.9	8.4	6.3	16.9	31.9	32.3	34.3	8.4	10.3	….	….	8.6	Madagascar	674
8.1	7.1	3.9	2.6	10.9	8.2	4.9	9.1	18.6	10.4	12.3	11.3	2.9	5.4	….	Malawi	676
1.7	2.5	2.6	2.4	5.0	3.9	1.4	2.2	3.7	17.7	16.4	27.2	….	….	….	Mali	678
25.5	31.8	26.2	24.3	19.4	13.2	11.3	15.9	12.1	19.3	4.4	5.9	….	….	….	Mauritania	682
7.7	3.2	4.2	2.1	2.6	3.0	10.5	18.0	18.2	20.3	23.7	29.5	26.2	22.9	20.2	Mauritius	684
5.0	2.7	2.6	1.5	.6	1.6	2.9	5.1	6.0	4.6	15.8	23.5	25.4	28.1	31.5	Morocco	686
….	….	….	….	….	….	….	….	….	….	….	….	….	2.1	6.0	Namibia	728
11.0	10.7	3.3	8.5	16.0	19.2	26.7	41.6	31.2	30.4	29.7	29.7	….	….	….	Niger	692
31.9	9.7	5.2	4.2	8.1	9.8	13.9	15.5	7.2	21.9	35.7	25.5	6.2	9.5	….	Nigeria	694
39.9	31.8	23.3	20.7	20.0	19.7	24.2	24.3	16.6	11.0	8.0	18.7	14.2	….	….	Rwanda	714
.4	.4	.6	.6	.2	.3	.5	.5	.5	.8	.4	.6	.5	….	….	Senegal	722
9.7	7.7	6.9	5.9	3.2	4.5	3.8	6.3	2.8	3.8	4.6	8.4	8.5	9.8	6.4	Seychelles	718
3.7	2.5	1.5	5.3	2.6	3.7	5.4	2.4	2.5	1.1	1.9	3.1	7.4	11.6	17.2	Sierra Leone	724
2.2	3.1	1.4	1.4	.5	1.2	2.4	2.9	7.2	11.1	….	….	….	….	….	Somalia	726
1.9	1.5	1.4	2.7	.8	1.4	1.5	2.2	2.2	2.7	2.8	2.5	2.6	2.6	3.7	South Africa	199
1.6	.6	.8	.6	.8	.8	3.2	.7	.6	….	….	….	….	….	….	Sudan	732
13.2	8.4	7.5	8.7	9.3	13.4	14.2	15.2	14.1	16.1	17.0	12.5	18.6	….	….	Swaziland	734
.8	.8	.2	1.2	2.1	.4	3.4	1.8	4.9	2.8	9.8	6.9	11.3	6.9	….	Tanzania	738
7.3	18.2	22.2	31.9	39.1	53.5	57.0	43.6	24.8	31.4	31.6	42.7	….	….	….	Togo	742
8.7	7.4	9.2	9.5	6.7	4.4	5.5	9.0	12.7	11.4	7.5	7.9	6.9	7.1	11.5	Tunisia	744
.5	4.5	10.8	14.7	10.3	4.3	4.9	3.3	2.9	2.7	10.8	15.6	11.2	….	19.2	Uganda	746
38.1	35.4	12.6	33.7	866,196.4	749,813.9	803,317.8	331,852.9	204,410.0	93,905.5	53,585.8	2,575.8	90.2	2.6	—	Zaïre	636
3.0	2.3	2.5	3.3	3.9	15.9	5.6	6.9	8.4	6.7	8.2	10.1	….	….	….	Zambia	754
7.7	5.2	4.5	3.3	2.1	4.7	4.9	7.2	7.1	3.0	4.2	3.8	5.2	….	….	Zimbabwe	698
10.9	11.1	12.8	14.8	15.9	16.9	21.8	25.4	21.0	19.6	20.0	21.5	19.2	19.7	21.6	**Asia**	505
23.0	16.1	13.9	10.5	8.6	12.9	9.6	14.6	15.1	15.4	14.8	19.8	….	….	….	Afghanistan, Islamic State of	512
6.0	2.7	4.1	12.6	7.2	6.3	8.6	16.4	17.9	7.1	9.1	19.5	24.4	31.3	34.7	Bangladesh	513
6.6	12.2	31.2	36.5	34.1	15.4	13.7	19.5	17.4	16.0	29.3	36.3	14.0	11.3	24.0	China, People's Rep.	924
15.5	11.1	13.0	12.4	13.6	15.4	20.5	18.1	26.3	18.9	18.3	22.0	26.8	22.1	19.6	Fiji	819
24.3	15.8	15.2	18.3	19.8	21.0	21.6	20.1	13.3	9.8	3.3	9.2	12.7	23.3	38.3	India	534
25.9	19.6	9.7	11.8	17.9	25.2	19.7	22.6	19.8	17.3	17.8	18.6	19.9	20.9	19.7	Indonesia	536
6.8	5.3	6.0	4.7	4.7	4.8	5.5	4.5	12.4	12.9	11.0	8.7	10.9	12.6	13.0	Korea	542
7.5	6.0	3.0	6.5	3.4	6.8	8.9	5.0	4.3	4.5	16.4	14.4	18.2	23.1	15.9	Lao, P.D. Rep.	544
21.1	18.4	15.8	14.9	13.8	20.8	29.0	30.4	20.5	18.0	17.3	15.4	22.4	31.0	22.2	Malaysia	548
1.7	1.9	10.1	4.2	5.0	4.5	8.1	5.3	12.5	11.4	9.2	7.6	7.7	7.3	….	Maldives	556
38.3	31.9	13.3	17.4	13.5	6.2	5.7	5.3	16.5	68.1	60.2	20.8	22.4	19.4	24.8	Myanmar	518

Nongold Reserves/Imports

Weeks of Imports

		1965	1966	1967	1968	1969	1970	1971	1972	1973	1974	1975	1976	1977	1978	1979
Asia (cont.)																
Nepal	558	27.3	28.7	37.3	50.5	46.4	61.1	59.1	60.1	58.9	47.0	29.1	40.7	43.1	34.1	32.5
Pakistan	564	8.7	8.9	5.2	14.9	21.4	9.7	9.9	16.9	22.1	11.8	8.2	11.1	9.5	6.5	2.7
Papua New Guinea	853	....	....	....	....	....	....	....	....	....	4.6	3.3	15.8	26.6	34.5	27.3	29.0
Philippines	566	9.0	8.1	5.3	4.0	3.1	8.2	12.1	17.6	28.7	21.9	18.2	21.1	18.0	17.8	17.7
Singapore	576	18.0	15.4	17.9	22.3	21.1	21.4	26.6	26.8	23.2	17.4	19.2	19.3	19.2	21.1	17.1
Solomon Islands	813	....	....	....	....	....	....	....	....	....	....	....	....	4.5	35.8	27.3
Sri Lanka	524	12.3	5.6	7.8	7.5	5.0	5.8	7.4	8.4	10.5	5.6	3.7	8.2	21.7	21.3	18.3
Thailand	578	45.1	48.6	44.7	41.7	37.2	33.0	31.8	33.7	30.6	29.1	26.6	26.2	20.4	19.5	13.4
Tonga	866	....	....	....	....	....	....	....	....	....	....	....	....	23.9	20.6	22.3
Vanuatu	846	....	....	....	....	....	....	....	....	....	....	....	....	....	....	....
Viet Nam	582	1.4	1.1	1.4	1.6	1.1	3.1	2.7	2.9	3.6	7.0	1.9	—	.2	.3	.5
Western Samoa	862	20.3	17.8	14.3	20.9	26.2	20.0	24.9	12.2	11.2	11.8	9.1	9.2	11.6	4.7	3.4
Europe	170	**2.4**	**2.3**	**1.8**	**2.4**	**3.5**	**2.3**	**4.6**	**8.3**	**10.0**	**5.6**	**3.2**	**5.1**	**4.1**	**5.2**	**3.3**
Cyprus	423	30.3	33.1	32.7	43.2	41.5	43.0	53.1	50.1	33.2	32.0	33.4	33.0	26.2	23.7	18.2
Czech Republic	935	....	....	....	....	....	....	....	....	....	....	....	....	....	....	....
Czechoslovakia	934	....	....	....	....	....	....	....	....	....	....	....	....	....	....	....
Hungary	944	....	....	....	....	....	....	....	....	....	....	....	....	....	....	....
Malta	181	41.7	43.1	41.6	58.5	44.7	47.8	59.8	77.4	67.5	55.7	67.3	74.7	72.6	83.6	69.3
Poland	964	....	....	....	....	....	....	....	....	....	....	....	....	....	....	1.8
Romania	968	....	....	....	....	....	....	....	....	3.0	2.3	4.9	4.4	1.8	2.0	2.3
Turkey	186	2.3	2.1	1.7	1.8	8.3	16.7	28.0	42.2	49.5	21.5	10.4	10.0	5.7	9.1	6.8
Yugoslavia, SFR	188	3.4	3.1	1.8	2.4	4.9	1.6	2.5	10.9	14.7	7.5	5.5	14.0	11.0	12.4	5.1
Middle East	405	**18.9**	**19.6**	**22.8**	**19.0**	**17.1**	**20.6**	**32.4**	**37.9**	**34.2**	**58.4**	**51.1**	**51.7**	**49.0**	**34.7**	**37.2**
Bahrain	419	7.0	3.9	5.0	11.2	14.8	13.2	14.7	11.7	6.4	6.1	12.6	13.6	12.9	12.5	12.9
Egypt	469	3.2	3.1	6.7	5.7	4.2	4.9	3.3	3.1	14.9	5.6	2.7	3.3	4.7	3.8	7.2
Iran, I.R. of	429	6.4	7.7	8.4	5.0	5.2	2.4	13.3	17.7	16.5	78.7	44.0	35.0	44.7	46.0	81.2
Iraq	433	14.2	23.1	31.1	33.4	33.5	32.6	33.0	46.1	80.2	67.9	31.6	66.4	91.0	....	....
Israel	436	36.5	35.9	44.9	24.5	11.5	10.1	15.2	24.8	21.7	11.0	9.9	12.2	13.7	18.4	18.6
Jordan	439	45.2	44.8	81.3	83.6	63.9	64.2	54.0	45.8	42.7	33.3	32.6	24.4	24.2	30.6	30.9
Kuwait	443	9.9	10.9	4.2	4.3	7.7	9.7	15.4	17.5	19.8	41.8	32.4	26.6	31.0	28.3	28.7
Lebanon	446	6.6	7.6	8.3	3.9	5.1	7.5	13.5	18.4	15.9	28.2	30.5	110.6	53.0	49.6	29.5
Libya	672	28.9	34.8	34.6	36.6	64.1	141.1	187.3	138.9	58.3	66.1	30.8	50.3	65.9	46.4	62.1
Oman	449	....	....	....	....	....	29.2	38.3	38.8	21.1	12.3	11.0	15.7	17.2	13.9	17.3
Qatar	453	....	13.4	13.0	31.1	28.1	24.7	18.3	19.8	18.0	12.2	12.2	8.2	6.9	9.2	10.5
Saudi Arabia	456	67.1	59.6	62.7	51.0	34.5	40.7	85.4	109.1	98.8	257.3	286.3	160.9	106.1	49.1	41.0
Syrian Arab Rep.	463	6.3	6.1	10.8	6.5	4.4	3.9	6.9	10.1	32.2	19.8	21.7	6.4	9.3	8.1	9.1
United Arab Emirates	466	....	....	....	....	....	....	....	....	5.8	13.8	19.1	29.7	8.2	7.9	10.7
Yemen Arab Rep.	473	....	....	....	....	....	....	....	....	53.7	54.3	59.7	90.8	62.0	59.1	49.8
Yemen, P.D. Rep.	459	9.0	11.1	15.2	15.0	13.2	15.3	21.2	23.2	22.9	8.3	8.7	10.3	9.5	17.0	11.8
Western Hemisphere	205	**10.0**	**9.0**	**9.7**	**10.8**	**11.2**	**13.0**	**14.0**	**20.4**	**23.3**	**17.5**	**17.2**	**21.1**	**22.9**	**25.6**	**24.9**
Antigua and Barbuda	311	....	....	....	....	....	....	....	....	....	....	5.7	14.3	6.6	6.7	7.8
Argentina	213	7.4	6.1	30.5	28.9	13.3	16.3	5.4	8.6	26.8	16.4	3.8	24.8	39.4	67.4	72.9
Aruba	314	....	....	....	....	....	....	....	....	....	....	....	....	....	....	....
Bahamas, The	313	....	....	....	13.1	4.6	3.3	3.0	4.0	2.9	1.4	1.0	.8	1.0	1.0	1.1
Barbados	316	....	8.3	6.2	9.6	6.7	7.3	7.9	10.3	10.0	10.0	9.5	6.1	7.0	10.0	8.2
Belize	339	....	....	....	....	....	....	....	....	....	....	....	3.9	4.6	6.8	4.1
Bolivia	218	11.6	12.7	9.8	9.7	9.5	10.7	12.2	12.4	12.4	23.5	13.0	14.2	17.8	10.9	10.4
Brazil	223	20.0	13.2	4.8	5.2	14.0	20.8	23.8	44.9	47.3	19.1	15.2	24.6	28.2	40.9	23.5
Chile	228	6.8	7.4	5.2	9.9	15.0	16.7	8.0	4.6	4.9	1.0	1.9	11.3	8.7	16.6	21.0
Colombia	233	7.0	4.0	5.4	11.5	14.8	11.7	10.5	18.7	25.3	14.0	16.5	34.4	48.3	41.4	59.4
Costa Rica	238	5.2	4.4	4.4	4.5	5.7	2.3	4.0	5.7	5.5	3.0	3.7	6.4	9.7	8.6	4.4
Dominica	321	....	....	....	....	....	....	....	....	....	....	....	.9	3.2	5.3	3.5	23.0
Dominican Republic	243	25.6	11.6	7.8	7.6	7.8	5.0	7.7	7.4	9.0	5.6	6.6	7.3	9.6	8.1	10.2
Ecuador	248	10.9	15.0	12.6	6.3	9.2	10.5	5.7	19.8	27.5	24.4	13.3	25.9	27.3	22.0	23.5
El Salvador	253	10.0	9.2	8.6	10.7	11.6	11.0	9.6	12.2	5.7	7.2	9.1	13.1	11.8	13.6	7.1
Grenada	328	....	....	....	....	....	....	12.4	13.0	13.1	12.0	15.4	10.8	16.7	12.3	14.1	14.5
Guatemala	258	10.5	10.2	9.5	9.5	11.2	11.1	13.1	18.7	23.1	13.5	20.1	30.4	33.0	30.0	24.1
Guyana	336	10.0	7.2	7.6	11.2	9.1	7.9	10.1	13.4	4.4	12.8	15.3	3.9	3.8	11.6	2.9
Haiti	263	2.2	3.0	2.7	3.5	4.7	4.1	8.9	13.5	10.6	8.2	4.3	7.0	8.3	8.6	10.5
Honduras	268	9.9	9.5	7.9	8.8	8.7	4.7	5.8	9.4	8.3	6.0	12.6	14.9	16.3	13.8	13.2
Jamaica	343	17.0	13.9	12.7	16.3	13.8	13.9	17.0	12.9	10.0	10.6	5.8	1.8	2.9	3.5	3.3
Mexico	273	12.7	14.7	12.5	13.0	12.3	12.0	16.2	18.7	15.8	10.6	10.9	10.2	15.6	11.8	8.9
Netherlands Antilles	353	....	....	....	1.3	1.8	1.4	2.2	3.0	1.6	.9	1.3	1.3	1.7	1.0	.9
Nicaragua	278	18.5	16.4	8.0	13.4	12.8	12.7	14.4	19.1	18.5	9.7	12.2	14.3	10.1	4.4	21.2
Panama	283	1.4	1.3	1.4	2.2	2.5	2.3	2.8	5.1	4.3	2.5	2.0	4.8	4.3	8.3	5.2
Paraguay	288	9.6	10.1	8.9	8.7	6.5	12.0	13.1	19.8	24.2	22.8	29.1	37.2	45.2	60.9	60.8
Peru	293	7.7	5.7	6.7	7.4	12.1	24.7	26.0	28.9	26.9	31.4	8.7	7.4	9.7	17.3	43.4
St. Kitts and Nevis	361	....	....	....	....	....	....	....	....	....	....	....	....	....	....	....
St. Lucia	362	....	....	....	....	....	....	....	....	....	....	....	3.6	5.6	5.0	4.2	4.2
St. Vincent & Grens.	364	....	....	....	....	....	....	....	....	....	....	....	10.2	8.2	7.6	9.9
Suriname	366	9.7	10.0	4.2	4.7	11.2	12.6	13.6	13.5	18.7	15.3	18.2	19.5	12.3	18.0	21.5
Trinidad and Tobago	369	3.1	3.5	3.9	6.2	4.8	4.1	5.5	4.1	3.1	10.9	26.5	26.8	43.0	47.8	53.4
Uruguay	298	8.2	9.5	6.8	11.1	5.1	3.1	4.6	17.0	18.4	8.6	5.5	15.6	23.0	24.2	13.9
Venezuela	299	15.3	14.9	16.9	16.2	16.0	17.7	27.1	27.6	35.9	75.6	72.8	55.1	36.8	26.7	35.7
Memorandum Items																
Oil Exporting Countries	999	**16.6**	**19.3**	**18.5**	**17.3**	**17.3**	**20.6**	**32.9**	**36.2**	**34.0**	**73.7**	**56.5**	**52.5**	**45.9**	**31.2**	**38.4**
Non-Oil Developing Countries	201	**8.6**	**8.6**	**9.0**	**9.4**	**9.8**	**9.5**	**10.3**	**14.0**	**14.3**	**9.5**	**8.1**	**11.3**	**13.0**	**13.8**	**12.2**

Nongold Reserves/Imports

1980	1981	1982	1983	1984	1985	1986	1987	1988	1989	1990	1991	1992	1993	1994		1rl s
Weeks of Imports															**Asia (cont.)**	
27.8	28.5	26.2	14.9	10.2	6.4	9.8	16.2	16.8	19.0	22.4	27.2	30.7	37.9	....	Nepal	558
4.8	6.7	9.2	19.2	9.2	7.1	6.9	4.5	3.1	3.8	2.1	3.2	4.7	6.6	17.1	Pakistan	564
18.7	16.3	20.1	20.4	20.4	22.8	20.5	19.5	14.7	13.1	17.6	10.4	8.4	5.7	....	Papua New Guinea	853
17.8	12.7	5.6	4.9	4.9	5.9	16.7	7.0	6.0	6.6	3.7	13.2	14.8	13.0	13.9	Philippines	566
14.2	14.2	15.7	17.1	18.9	25.4	26.4	24.3	20.2	21.3	23.7	26.8	28.7	29.5	29.5	Singapore	576
17.3	12.3	27.3	33.4	29.4	22.3	21.4	23.6	21.1	11.9	9.7	4.0	12.5	10.4	....	Solomon Islands	813
6.3	9.2	10.0	8.5	14.2	12.7	9.9	7.1	5.1	5.8	8.2	11.7	14.0	21.2	22.3	Sri Lanka	524
8.8	9.0	9.4	8.1	9.6	12.3	15.9	16.0	15.6	19.2	20.7	24.2	26.0	27.5	....	Thailand	578
19.0	18.1	19.4	29.0	33.3	34.8	28.8	31.3	28.6	23.9	26.4	28.3	26.4	31.4	26.7	Tonga	866
....	7.6	4.9	5.4	6.1	7.9	19.4	30.0	30.0	25.7	20.5	25.1	27.0	31.4	....	Vanuatu	846
—	—	—	—	—	—	—	—	—	—	—	—	—	—	.1	Viet Nam	582
2.3	3.0	3.6	7.8	11.0	14.2	26.2	31.3	33.8	38.0	44.7	37.5	28.9	25.2	32.4	Western Samoa	862
4.1	**4.0**	**4.1**	**5.7**	**6.4**	**4.9**	**5.6**	**6.0**	**7.1**	**12.5**	**13.0**	**13.5**	**13.2**	**12.4**	**14.7**	**Europe**	**170**
15.9	19.0	22.2	22.1	20.6	24.8	30.8	30.6	26.0	25.5	30.5	27.2	16.1	22.0	25.2	Cyprus	423
....	....	....	....	....	....	....	....	....	....	....	....	....	14.8	20.7	Czech Republic	935
7.5	4.2	3.3	3.4	4.2	3.7	4.0	4.4	5.4	7.5	4.2	15.0	4.6	....	....	Czechoslovakia	934
....	....	....	....	7.5	10.0	13.7	12.5	8.6	8.1	7.4	6.5	17.9	20.7	28.0	24.7	Hungary	944
54.9	64.9	71.4	79.0	71.8	67.6	67.1	64.6	52.5	47.6	37.9	32.5	28.3	32.6	39.1	Malta	181
.4	1.1	3.2	3.6	5.2	3.8	3.1	6.9	8.4	11.3	27.8	12.0	13.6	11.3	14.2	Poland	964
1.2	1.6	2.2	2.6	3.3	.9	2.6	8.1	4.9	10.6	2.8	6.2	6.9	7.9	15.3	Romania	968
7.1	5.4	6.4	7.3	6.1	4.8	6.6	6.5	8.5	15.7	14.1	12.7	14.0	11.2	....	Turkey	186
4.8	5.3	3.0	4.2	5.0	4.7	6.5	2.9	9.1	14.5	15.1	9.5	....	....	....	Yugoslavia, SFR	188
32.5	**25.8**	**25.6**	**24.7**	**24.3**	**32.9**	**32.5**	**34.4**	**28.1**	**28.0**	**24.0**	**22.8**	**20.9**	**22.7**	....	**Middle East**	**405**
14.2	19.5	22.1	22.2	19.5	27.8	32.2	22.0	25.1	17.4	17.3	19.1	17.1	17.6	....	Bahrain	419
11.2	4.2	4.0	3.9	3.6	7.5	5.0	9.4	7.6	10.6	15.1	35.2	68.2	82.0	....	Egypt	469
43.4	5.7	24.8	....	....	....	....	....	....	....	....	....	....	....	....	Iran, I.R. of	429
....	....	....	....	....	....	....	....	....	....	....	....	....	....	....	Iraq	433
17.8	17.8	20.7	19.8	16.2	19.4	22.4	21.3	13.9	19.1	19.4	17.5	13.2	14.7	28.3	Israel	436
24.7	17.9	14.2	14.1	9.6	8.0	9.3	8.1	2.1	11.5	17.0	17.1	12.3	24.1	26.0	Jordan	439
31.3	30.3	37.1	36.6	34.6	47.4	50.0	39.2	16.3	25.6	25.6	37.2	36.9	31.1	....	Kuwait	443
22.6	22.5	40.0	27.0	11.8	25.3	11.5	10.2	20.7	....	....	....	....	....	....	Lebanon	446
100.5	55.9	51.2	45.0	30.4	74.9	69.6	64.8	38.3	45.8	56.9	51.5	....	....	....	Libya	672
17.5	16.9	16.9	15.9	17.0	18.0	21.0	40.0	24.9	31.2	32.4	27.1	27.4	11.5	....	Oman	449
12.5	12.5	10.3	13.7	17.0	20.4	27.1	27.7	19.5	20.9	19.4	20.2	17.6	....	....	Qatar	453
40.4	47.5	37.8	36.2	38.2	55.0	49.9	58.7	49.1	41.2	25.2	20.9	9.3	13.7	16.4	Saudi Arabia	456
4.2	2.9	2.6	.6	3.4	1.1	2.7	1.6	4.5	....	....	....	....	....	....	Syrian Arab Rep.	463
12.0	17.3	12.2	13.0	17.1	25.4	27.3	34.0	27.1	23.2	21.3	20.3	17.1	16.3	....	United Arab Emirates	466
36.0	28.4	18.9	11.8	10.6	11.8	19.4	31.8	10.7	....	....	....	....	....	....	Yemen Arab Rep.	473
8.0	9.3	9.3	9.9	8.4	6.7	14.9	....	....	....	....	....	....	....	....	Yemen, P.D. Rep.	459
17.2	**16.1**	**13.9**	**19.4**	**26.6**	**28.6**	**22.5**	**22.8**	**16.5**	**16.4**	**21.7**	**25.9**	**28.8**	**32.9**	**27.2**	**Western Hemisphere**	**205**
3.9	2.8	3.2	4.7	6.1	7.7	7.1	6.0	6.5	6.4	6.8	7.9	....	....	....	Antigua and Barbuda	311
33.1	18.0	24.4	13.5	14.1	44.6	29.9	14.5	32.9	18.1	58.6	37.7	34.9	42.7	34.6	Argentina	213
....	....	....	....	....	....	20.0	17.3	14.1	11.7	....	....	....	....	....	Aruba	314
.6	.7	.9	1.4	2.0	3.1	3.7	2.9	4.0	2.5	2.8	5.2	....	....	13.6	Bahamas, The	313
7.8	9.2	11.5	10.4	10.5	12.0	13.4	14.7	12.1	8.5	8.7	6.5	14.0	13.6	16.8	Barbados	316
4.4	3.3	4.0	4.3	2.4	6.0	11.5	13.2	14.8	14.4	17.2	11.0	10.1	7.2	6.9	Belize	339
8.3	5.7	14.6	14.4	26.8	15.1	12.6	6.6	9.3	17.4	12.6	5.7	8.7	9.6	....	Bolivia	218
12.0	14.3	9.7	13.5	39.3	38.5	19.4	19.8	22.6	19.7	17.2	18.2	50.8	57.4	53.5	Brazil	223
28.0	23.3	23.7	34.3	33.5	41.5	35.6	29.6	31.1	26.4	41.3	45.2	47.1	45.1	57.6	Chile	228
53.0	47.4	36.4	19.9	15.8	20.0	36.3	37.1	33.8	37.6	39.2	63.9	59.0	....	....	Colombia	233
4.9	5.7	13.2	16.4	19.3	24.0	23.7	18.4	24.6	22.5	13.6	25.5	21.7	18.5	15.4	Costa Rica	238
5.5	3.2	4.7	1.7	4.7	3.1	8.9	14.4	8.4	5.7	6.4	8.4	9.6	....	....	Dominica	321
6.4	7.0	4.6	6.1	9.1	11.9	13.7	5.2	7.1	3.8	1.6	11.6	10.4	13.9	5.0	Dominican Republic	243
23.4	14.6	7.3	22.5	19.7	21.1	18.5	11.3	12.1	15.2	23.4	20.0	18.1	28.0	26.3	Ecuador	248
4.2	3.8	6.6	9.3	8.8	9.7	9.4	9.7	8.3	11.9	17.1	10.6	12.9	14.6	15.0	El Salvador	253
13.4	15.4	8.5	12.9	13.2	15.6	12.8	13.3	9.5	8.1	8.7	7.5	12.6	....	....	Grenada	328
14.5	4.6	4.2	9.7	11.2	13.3	19.6	10.3	6.7	9.6	8.9	22.7	15.7	17.4	....	Guatemala	258
1.8	.8	1.9	1.5	1.4	1.5	1.9	1.7	1.0	2.7	4.8	21.1	25.6	....	....	Guyana	336
2.2	2.7	.6	1.1	1.5	.8	2.3	2.2	2.0	2.3	.6	2.1	....	....	....	Haiti	263
7.7	5.5	8.3	7.4	7.5	6.2	6.6	6.7	2.8	1.1	2.2	5.7	9.9	4.5	8.4	Honduras	268
5.0	3.0	4.1	2.2	4.4	7.5	5.3	7.3	5.3	3.0	4.7	3.7	10.1	10.3	....	Jamaica	343
7.9	8.8	2.9	25.4	32.1	18.2	24.6	50.9	14.0	13.5	17.1	24.2	20.5	26.0	5.4	Mexico	273
.9	1.2	1.9	1.9	1.5	6.6	11.2	7.5	9.7	6.7	5.2	4.2	6.1	6.7	....	Netherlands Antilles	353
3.8	5.8	11.5	11.0	....	....	....	1.1	2.5	9.8	8.7	9.3	7.6	3.8	....	Nicaragua	278
4.2	4.0	3.3	7.6	7.9	3.7	7.2	3.1	5.0	6.3	11.6	15.3	13.0	14.2	15.2	Panama	283
64.4	69.9	57.2	64.8	59.1	55.3	40.2	43.4	29.3	29.6	25.4	34.3	20.5	19.4	....	Paraguay	288
41.2	17.9	19.5	27.9	38.3	52.2	25.2	9.4	7.9	15.3	15.6	30.3	30.5	36.2	53.9	Peru	293
....	4.4	4.0	3.2	5.9	7.5	8.2	6.9	5.8	8.3	7.2	7.7	....	....	....	St. Kitts and Nevis	361
3.5	3.1	3.6	3.2	5.4	5.3	8.4	8.9	7.7	7.3	8.6	8.6	9.2	....	....	St. Lucia	362
6.6	8.0	3.8	4.2	8.7	9.1	15.4	10.7	9.3	9.3	10.1	8.4	13.1	12.1	....	St. Vincent & Grens.	364
19.5	19.0	17.8	6.5	3.7	4.1	3.3	2.7	1.9	1.1	2.3	—	....	....	....	Suriname	366
45.8	56.3	45.9	43.7	37.2	37.0	18.3	7.7	5.9	10.5	22.8	10.6	6.2	7.4	....	Trinidad and Tobago	369
11.9	13.6	5.4	13.7	9.0	12.8	28.8	24.1	23.9	21.7	20.3	10.7	13.0	17.0	18.2	Uruguay	298
29.0	32.4	26.4	61.9	59.5	65.8	39.4	32.1	12.6	27.4	59.0	49.8	35.4	39.3	47.2	Venezuela	299
															Memorandum Items	
34.3	26.1	23.4	25.2	27.4	36.4	34.9	38.5	27.9	27.5	26.3	24.3	19.8	20.9	....	Oil Exporting Countries	999
9.7	9.4	10.1	11.8	13.2	14.2	16.4	18.7	16.5	16.4	17.1	19.3	18.8	20.1	13.9	Non-Oil Developing Countries	201

SDRs
1b s

		1965	1966	1967	1968	1969	1970	1971	1972	1973	1974	1975	1976	1977	1978	1979
															Millions	*of SDRs:*
All Countries	010	—	—	—	—	—	3,124.0	5,874.5	8,686.1	8,807.1	8,857.9	8,763.8	8,655.4	8,132.7	8,110.0	12,478.9
Industrial Countries	110	—	—	—	—	—	2,595.0	4,944.9	7,135.0	7,161.3	7,178.3	7,250.3	7,231.4	6,687.0	6,405.1	9,324.7
United States	111	—	—	—	—	—	850.7	1,099.7	1,803.1	1,795.6	1,939.3	1,994.6	2,061.2	2,163.9	1,196.3	2,068.1
Canada	156	—	—	—	—	—	182.1	371.9	465.3	467.3	469.1	474.4	480.1	416.0	401.0	444.8
Australia	193	—	—	—	—	—	90.5	164.0	234.6	234.7	99.9	95.7	36.3	21.8	98.7	31.9
Japan	158	—	—	—	—	—	146.3	282.8	424.5	425.1	431.8	443.9	460.2	494.2	1,053.5	1,281.3
New Zealand	196	—	—	—	—	—	.4	27.7	58.3	58.1	.5	.8	8.4	34.2	46.1	8.9
Austria	122	—	—	—	—	—	38.2	57.0	85.8	85.9	87.0	87.4	95.9	96.6	104.6	155.8
Belgium	124	—	—	—	—	—	204.9	405.4	523.1	626.4	584.2	615.5	397.4	407.1	414.1	475.8
Denmark	128	—	—	—	—	—	17.4	44.8	72.2	119.3	91.5	81.9	81.9	97.1	97.9	137.6
Finland	172	—	—	—	—	—	23.3	47.0	67.5	67.8	68.1	66.2	56.1	41.8	61.8	88.1
France	132	—	—	—	—	—	171.4	347.9	580.6	72.8	202.2	244.4	226.7	233.5	286.3	644.4
Germany	134	—	—	—	—	—	257.8	454.5	822.4	1,387.5	1,439.8	1,450.9	1,747.3	1,176.5	1,378.9	1,576.2
Greece	174	—	—	—	—	—	—	4.5	25.6	25.2	26.7	17.6	16.9	13.4	13.4	.8
Iceland	176	—	—	—	—	—	.5	3.0	6.4	6.3	6.3	4.8	1.8	2.7	1.8	.2
Ireland	178	—	—	—	—	—	13.4	26.4	39.3	39.4	40.6	40.9	45.3	45.6	48.1	70.9
Italy	136	—	—	—	—	—	76.7	227.9	341.5	342.9	180.8	83.0	78.4	118.8	225.7	449.3
Netherlands	138	—	—	—	—	—	144.1	570.0	649.6	475.4	485.8	520.5	531.4	564.1	243.9	393.9
Norway	142	—	—	—	—	—	27.2	54.9	87.9	88.0	88.2	89.0	89.5	92.8	96.3	139.7
Portugal	182	—	—	—	—	—	—	—	—	—	—	—	7.0	8.4	3.8	.6
San Marino	135															
Spain	184	—	—	—	—	—	43.5	86.8	128.7	128.8	133.9	121.4	90.8	48.2	102.7	206.3
Sweden	144	—	—	—	—	—	37.8	72.6	107.1	107.0	107.0	107.0	107.0	107.1	112.0	173.0
Switzerland	146	....	....	....	....	....										
United Kingdom	112	—	—	—	—	—	265.7	590.9	604.4	600.4	688.2	696.3	603.3	500.6	414.5	965.5
Developing Countries	200	—	—	—	—	—	529.0	929.6	1,551.2	1,645.8	1,679.6	1,513.5	1,424.0	1,445.7	1,704.8	3,097.0
Africa	605	—	—	—	—	—	140.8	196.8	320.8	291.0	311.8	322.4	316.5	298.0	312.8	463.1
Algeria	612	—	—	—	—	—	14.1	28.0	41.8	41.9	42.9	43.0	43.1	46.2	46.4	76.3
Angola	614															
Benin	638	—	—	—	—	—	1.7	3.1	4.5	4.5	4.5	4.5	4.5	4.4	4.4	6.1
Botswana	616	....	....	....	....	....	.5	1.0	1.6	1.6	1.6	1.6	1.6	1.6	1.6	2.5
Burkina Faso	748	—	—	—	—	—	1.7	3.1	4.4	4.4	4.4	4.4	4.4	4.4	4.4	6.1
Burundi	618	—	—	—	—	—	2.2	1.8	3.7	3.6	3.6	3.2	3.0	2.8	2.8	5.3
Cameroon	622	—	—	—	—	—	3.1	6.8	10.5	10.5	10.5	10.1	8.8	6.8	3.2	—
Cape Verde	624															
Central African Rep.	626	—	—	—	—	—	—	—	1.2	1.0	.8	2.3	1.6	1.6	1.3	1.4
Chad	628	—	—	—	—	—	—	—	1.1	.4	2.4	2.3	1.9	1.7	1.5	1.6
Comoros	632															.2
Congo	634	—	—	—	—	—	—	1.3	2.6	2.5	2.3	2.2	2.1	1.5	1.3	1.2
Côte d'Ivoire	662	—	—	—	—	—	3.2	9.8	15.3	15.3	15.2	14.5	11.8	8.6	7.4	17.9
Djibouti	611													—	—	.1
Equatorial Guinea	642	—	—	—	—	—	1.0	1.9	1.9	1.9	1.9	1.8	1.8	1.7	1.7	.7
Ethiopia	644	—	—	—	—	—	—	—	—	—	—	—	—	—	—	.4
Gabon	646	—	—	—	—	—	1.6	3.2	4.7	4.7	4.7	4.6	4.6	4.6	4.6	7.2
Gambia, The	648	—	—	—	—	—	.8	1.6	2.2	2.1	2.0	2.0	2.0	.9	1.1	.7
Ghana	652	—	—	—	—	—	—	3.1	10.0	9.7	9.6	7.5	6.7	10.1	9.5	13.7
Guinea	656	—	—	—	—	—	.2	.1	2.9	1.4	3.4	3.1	2.9	2.2	—	—
Guinea-Bissau	654															.1
Kenya	664	—	—	—	—	—	5.8	12.0	17.1	17.1	1.9	3.8	2.8	14.4	11.0	82.1
Lesotho	666	—	—	—	—	—	—	.4	.9	.7	.6	.5	.5	.5	.4	1.1
Liberia	668	—	—	—	—	—	1.0	.1	1.6	3.3	3.2	2.9	3.5	3.3	3.3	6.5
Madagascar	674	—	—	—	—	—	3.2	6.0	8.7	8.7	.2	.9	1.9	6.9	8.7	—
Malawi	676	—	—	—	—	—	1.9	3.5	4.6	4.6	4.6	4.6	4.3	3.9	3.3	3.1
Mali	678	—	—	—	—	—	—	1.3	2.4	2.3	3.0	2.7	2.8	2.7	2.6	1.3
Mauritania	682	—	—	—	—	—	1.7	.9	2.2	2.1	2.0	1.7	1.2	.6	.7	1.3
Mauritius	684	....	....	....	....	....	2.6	5.0	7.3	7.3	2.8	2.6	2.7	2.3	1.6	.6
Morocco	686	—	—	—	—	—	.3	2.4	16.6	16.2	15.8	14.8	10.4	8.5	12.6	15.2
Mozambique	688														....	....
Niger	692	—	—	—	—	—	1.7	3.1	4.4	4.4	4.4	4.4	4.4	4.4	4.4	6.0
Nigeria	694	—	—	—	—	—	16.8	31.2	45.5	45.5	47.5	57.4	61.2	65.8	66.8	107.8
Rwanda	714	—	—	—	—	—	—	1.4	2.4	.4	2.4	2.5	2.4	2.4	2.4	4.6
Senegal	722	—	—	—	—	—	1.2	2.5	5.7	5.3	4.6	3.3	1.2	1.7	9.7	11.5
Seychelles	718														—	.1
Sierra Leone	724	—	—	—	—	—	.5	3.1	5.7	5.7	4.4	3.9	2.9	1.4	.2	—
Somalia	726	—	—	—	—	—	.6	2.6	4.6	4.5	4.4	4.4	4.3	4.2	4.1	6.4
South Africa	199	—	—	—	—	—	39.1	.5	38.2	1.4	39.6	43.4	41.5	39.5	39.3	25.4
Sudan	732	—	—	—	—	—	.1	—	4.9	13.6	21.5	7.3	—	—	6.0	10.0
Swaziland	734	....	....	....	....	....	—	—	.8	.8	.9	1.0	.9	.9	1.0	2.2
Tanzania	738	—	—	—	—	—	1.9	6.3	6.7	6.6	1.7	1.2	5.1	5.6	6.1	2.8
Togo	742	—	—	—	—	—	1.9	3.5	5.1	5.1	5.1	5.1	5.0	4.8	4.4	6.3
Tunisia	744	—	—	—	—	—	—	2.0	7.9	7.6	8.5	8.2	10.0	9.6	8.5	14.6
Uganda	746	—	—	—	—	—	5.4	9.6	13.7	13.4	5.0	3.2	.9	4.5	8.1	8.4
Zaïre	636	—	—	—	—	—	15.6	15.7	7.4	6.9	6.4	20.0	27.1	—	4.4	1.2
Zambia	754	—	—	—	—	—	8.9	18.9	.2	—	11.7	15.7	19.2	11.4	12.1	4.2
Zimbabwe	698														....	....
Asia	505	—	—	—	—	—	98.7	256.8	489.8	507.0	490.0	426.6	388.5	331.7	448.3	785.6
Afghanistan, Islamic State of	512	—	—	—	—	—	1.9	3.2	1.2	4.3	4.5	5.1	5.1	5.7	5.4	13.4
Bangladesh	513	....	....	....	....	....						15.4	16.1	3.9	.1	9.2
Bhutan	514	....	....	....	....	....									....	....
Cambodia	522	—	—	—	—	—	1.6	1.7	4.2	.5	1.1	.6	.3	—	—	1.9
China, People's Rep.	924															
Fiji	819	....	....	....	....	....			1.4	1.4	1.4	1.3	1.3	1.3	1.3	3.1
India	534	—	—	—	—	—	44.2	148.1	246.5	245.3	239.9	212.0	189.1	149.0	225.8	371.0
Indonesia	536	—	—	—	—	—	—	—	35.8	43.3	55.7	6.3	4.1	21.7	57.4	129.2
Korea	542	—	—	—	—	—	10.3	17.6	26.1	26.1	1.4	3.4	6.8	10.0	11.4	18.9
Lao, P.D. Rep.	544	—	—	—	—	—	.5	.9	1.3	1.3	1.3	1.6	1.5	1.5	1.0	.8
Malaysia	548	—	—	—	—	—	23.4	43.3	63.1	60.6	61.6	61.7	65.1	26.6	38.8	87.3
Maldives	556	....	....	....	....	....									—	.1
Myanmar	518	—	—	—	—	—	—	—	5.6	9.7	9.5	8.0	7.6	7.5	2.9	4.7
Nepal	558	—	—	—	—	—	—	1.1	2.2	2.2	2.2	2.2	2.1	1.9	1.2	1.7
Pakistan	564	—	—	—	—	—	10.2	13.3	19.1	26.7	19.9	25.0	32.0	28.7	30.5	34.2
Papua New Guinea	853												—	1.7	.2	.4	.8
Philippines	566	—	—	—	—	—	—	—	21.9	23.9	27.7	23.5	13.6	19.2	13.1	25.6
Singapore	576	....	....	....	....	....			—	—	—	—	—	—	—	12.2
Solomon Islands	813														—	—
Sri Lanka	524	—	—	—	—	—	—	—	12.8	13.4	14.5	10.8	12.4	19.8	26.3	22.2
Thailand	578	—	—	—	—	—	—	14.3	28.5	28.5	29.5	29.6	28.9	30.5	26.6	37.1

SDRs

1980	1981	1982	1983	1984	1985	1986	1987	1988	1989	1990	1991	1992	1993	1994		1b s
End of Period																
11,808.5	16,411.2	17,744.6	14,418.2	16,469.5	18,212.8	19,494.1	20,212.5	20,172.9	20,484.8	20,354.4	20,551.3	12,867.2	14,614.3	15,761.5	All Countries	010
8,888.8	11,940.3	14,093.5	11,521.6	13,374.8	14,902.3	16,135.0	16,476.0	17,559.2	17,663.4	17,615.4	17,455.5	10,468.2	11,454.4	12,485.9	Industrial Countries	110
2,046.0	3,518.5	4,759.1	4,800.0	5,754.6	6,639.4	6,862.9	7,248.3	7,161.0	7,572.0	7,724.3	7,857.6	6,184.2	6,569.4	6,876.4	United States	111
355.4	149.5	64.2	20.1	73.7	198.4	202.2	281.2	1,017.4	1,048.1	1,072.5	1,105.7	755.5	773.5	786.4	Canada	156
—	44.8	77.7	77.0	213.4	282.5	271.0	260.1	248.3	234.0	218.3	202.4	69.6	59.7	49.9	Australia	193
1,362.7	1,661.7	1,895.4	1,848.2	1,966.0	1,926.2	1,813.0	1,736.3	2,182.0	1,862.3	2,138.4	1,803.0	795.5	1,123.4	1,427.0	Japan	158
—	19.6	1.7	2.7	6.8	6.0	9.0	1.0	.7	.4	.4	.3	—	—	.2	New Zealand	196
173.4	185.7	226.5	154.0	224.4	191.2	151.8	205.8	199.5	227.1	195.7	197.5	247.6	160.5	193.8	Austria	122
496.7	627.9	672.0	399.0	454.2	328.4	279.8	493.7	418.0	423.2	398.0	411.0	124.1	124.7	123.4	Belgium	124
137.6	172.6	176.4	118.7	158.1	178.7	207.2	214.5	167.0	213.1	151.6	169.0	66.7	62.4	124.6	Denmark	128
81.3	124.2	104.3	37.0	145.7	156.4	167.3	160.5	199.8	182.0	152.5	157.7	78.4	83.8	222.7	Finland	172
733.4	1,080.1	887.3	421.9	583.7	819.4	1,054.4	1,058.6	1,032.9	1,011.1	901.8	926.8	118.3	240.8	248.3	France	132
1,442.9	1,382.5	1,862.1	1,540.9	1,389.7	1,408.0	1,651.2	1,384.2	1,380.3	1,372.7	1,321.2	1,340.0	611.4	700.1	763.3	Germany	134
—	.1	—	.6	1.1	—	—	.2	.2	.3	.2	.3	—	.1	.2	Greece	174
1.8	3.4	2.0	.2	.4	.4	—	.2	1.9	1.0	—	.3	.1	—	.1	Iceland	176
71.1	90.9	96.4	65.4	89.4	99.0	113.3	126.5	134.3	145.4	158.3	170.0	90.4	96.6	101.3	Ireland	178
521.0	672.8	711.4	564.9	645.3	296.9	480.2	668.2	705.1	759.5	729.2	650.0	173.2	175.4	85.8	Italy	136
439.5	591.7	771.7	501.8	525.0	569.3	597.8	636.8	576.5	590.4	504.4	529.9	402.6	424.4	441.9	Netherlands	138
157.6	195.3	284.3	257.3	262.2	258.0	131.2	318.2	311.2	362.3	345.2	315.5	315.9	139.1	288.4	266.7	Norway	142
—	8.7	2.3	.9	12.5	15.5	54.0	56.1	2.8	1.4	40.3	68.3	33.5	41.9	48.3	Portugal	182
—	—	—	—	—	—	—	—	—	—	—	—	—	—	.1	San Marino	135
230.6	318.6	185.8	65.4	154.5	254.5	353.2	420.4	456.8	523.0	489.4	319.0	134.0	157.4	174.5	Spain	184
174.2	224.5	233.3	123.0	181.4	224.3	261.3	208.5	299.1	259.5	204.0	289.6	32.6	42.2	46.4	Sweden	144
5.1	.1	3.7	12.9	9.3	3.0	—	10.1	15.2	3.6	1.3	1.6	11.7	112.8	162.0	Switzerland	146
447.2	852.0	1,060.7	494.0	506.9	1,029.8	1,269.6	974.3	980.5	870.1	878.0	919.2	393.2	209.9	335.2	United Kingdom	112
2,919.7	4,470.9	3,651.1	2,896.7	3,094.8	3,310.5	3,359.2	3,736.5	2,613.7	2,821.4	2,739.0	3,095.9	2,398.9	3,159.9	3,275.6	Developing Countries	200
328.3	627.5	410.8	268.2	191.3	206.7	263.2	300.4	88.7	100.7	83.6	239.3	148.6	116.3	119.0	Africa	605
75.9	118.9	140.0	102.1	113.2	125.6	136.6	142.7	1.6	3.0	1.9	1.3	.8	4.9	15.7	Algeria	612
—	—	—	—	—	—	—	—	—	—	.1	.1	.1	.1	.1	Angola	614
1.7	2.9	2.0	1.1	.2	—	—	.1	.1	—	.1	.2	—	.1	.1	Benin	638
2.5	5.3	6.2	7.3	8.5	9.7	14.0	15.4	16.8	18.9	21.7	24.1	22.5	24.0	25.4	Botswana	616
5.8	7.5	7.5	7.5	5.6	5.6	5.6	5.7	5.6	5.6	5.7	—	5.6	5.6	5.6	Burkina Faso	748
4.1	5.5	4.2	1.0	.1	.1	.5	—	.1	—	—	2.6	1.1	.5	.1	Burundi	618
—	.2	1.6	.6	6.2	4.2	2.8	.2	—	.2	.5	3.9	.2	.1	—	Cameroon	622
—	.2	—	.1	.1	.1	.1	.1	—	—	—	—	.1	—	—	Cape Verde	624
—	.1	.2	.7	2.6	1.5	.4	4.9	9.2	—	3.4	.5	—	—	—	Central African Rep.	626
—	—	.3	1.5	.4	3.5	1.7	6.4	5.7	1.3	.1	.1	—	—	—	Chad	628
—	—	—	—	.2	.2	.2	.1	.1	.1	.1	—	—	.1	—	Comoros	632
—	.9	1.0	.2	2.1	1.5	3.8	1.9	.8	1.2	1.2	—	—	—	—	Congo	634
2.7	10.6	.1	15.5	.2	.1	7.0	.2	.5	3.9	.8	1.4	.2	.8	.1	Côte d'Ivoire	662
.1	.5	.5	.4	.4	.4	.4	.3	.3	.2	.2	.2	.2	.2	.1	Djibouti	611
—	.1	—	—	—	3.1	.6	.2	—	.1	.1	5.6	5.5	.3	—	Equatorial Guinea	642
—	10.4	3.2	2.3	3.0	.2	—	1.2	—	—	—	.2	.1	.1	.2	.3	Ethiopia	644
5.6	7.0	.7	.4	5.8	2.1	10.1	8.2	6.5	.2	.2	4.4	.1	—	.2	Gabon	646
—	.1	.1	.1	—	—	.6	3.2	1.0	1.0	1.2	.5	.5	.2	.2	Gambia, The	648
—	.6	.2	2.1	.1	17.2	1.6	11.2	.2	22.8	3.1	8.8	3.2	.4	2.9	Ghana	652
—	—	.2	—	—	—	—	.3	.2	.2	—	.2	9.4	7.9	8.5	3.8	Guinea	656
—	.1	—	—	.1	—	—	.1	—	—	—	—	—	—	—	Guinea-Bissau	654
20.2	9.4	14.0	16.6	2.2	.8	9.9	11.4	4.4	8.7	2.8	1.0	.6	.8	.5	Kenya	664
.9	1.4	1.1	1.0	1.0	1.0	.8	.6	1.0	.7	.5	.2	.5	.4	.3	Lesotho	666
—	1.1	—	—	—	—	—	—	—	—	—	—	—	—	—	Liberia	668
—	.3	1.1	.1	1.5	—	—	.1	.1	.1	.1	—	—	.1	—	Madagascar	674
—	5.7	3.6	.8	2.9	—	.4	—	2.4	.3	2.2	.2	.1	.2	4.2	Malawi	676
—	.2	.5	.1	1.7	1.7	—	.2	.2	.1	.3	.3	.1	.1	.1	Mali	678
—	1.1	—	.7	—	3.9	2.6	12.1	.1	.1	.6	.1	.1	.1	—	Mauritania	682
—	5.6	1.7	.1	.1	—	.5	4.1	3.7	5.0	10.3	18.0	17.6	21.0	21.3	Mauritius	684
.5	1.4	.5	.6	.7	.1	15.8	2.9	.3	.4	1.0	102.9	56.3	25.1	18.0	Morocco	686
....	....	....	....	—	—	—	—	—	—	—	—	—	—	—	Mozambique	688
5.8	7.5	7.5	4.6	2.2	—	1.0	.2	.1	.9	—	.3	—	.4	.3	Niger	692
132.5	239.0	40.4	25.7	10.5	1.0	.2	.1	—	.4	.8	—	—	.2	—	Nigeria	694
7.7	9.8	10.8	8.4	8.3	8.2	8.1	8.0	7.9	7.5	7.2	6.7	2.4	2.1	1.7	Rwanda	714
—	3.7	4.9	3.8	.1	.1	2.5	—	—	3.6	.2	.3	—	.3	.7	Senegal	722
—	.2	.2	.1	—	—	—	—	—	—	—	—	—	—	—	Seychelles	718
—	.1	.5	.1	—	—	.3	—	—	—	—	—	1.2	2.8	6.2	Sierra Leone	724
5.5	4.2	.7	.4	.1	—	—	—	—	—	—	—	—	—	—	Somalia	726
37.1	115.5	99.1	27.3	2.3	.5	—	1.2	.8	1.3	1.6	1.2	.1	8.8	.8	South Africa	199
—	.5	—	.1	—	—	—	—	—	—	—	—	—	—	—	Sudan	732
1.8	5.9	5.0	1.5	2.3	.3	2.2	2.8	1.2	.8	8.5	8.7	5.8	5.9	5.9	Swaziland	734
—	.3	—	.1	.1	—	4.6	.1	—	—	—	—	—	—	—	Tanzania	738
5.8	6.5	3.9	1.2	2.1	.1	.5	.1	.1	1.3	.1	.3	.2	.1	—	Togo	742
11.8	17.4	16.0	3.6	1.9	.5	22.6	38.1	21.0	6.4	1.7	23.0	8.8	1.3	1.8	Tunisia	744
—	2.6	10.1	.9	.2	—	—	—	—	—	4.8	7.2	6.6	—	2.1	Uganda	746
—	.6	—	21.0	—	.2	—	.1	—	3.7	—	—	—	—	—	Zaïre	636
—	7.7	14.5	—	—	—	—	—	—	—	—	—	—	—	—	Zambia	754
—	8.8	6.3	6.1	2.3	13.2	5.0	16.3	.5	.5	.2	.1	.3	.6	—	Zimbabwe	698
763.3	1,325.0	1,174.8	713.5	1,026.7	1,101.8	1,063.8	892.7	832.7	761.3	903.6	768.6	523.0	683.4	647.5	Asia	505
12.1	16.3	15.6	10.0	13.5	12.4	11.4	10.5	9.5	8.1	6.3	4.7	3.2	2.0	1.0	Afghanistan, Islamic State of	512
.4	.1	.8	12.9	.3	11.9	8.4	37.6	40.1	2.3	18.1	49.9	30.1	16.6	24.6	Bangladesh	513
....	—	—	—	.1	.1	.1	.1	.2	.2	.3	.3	.3	.4	.4	Bhutan	514
3.8	4.5	3.1	1.6	—	—	—	—	—	—	—	—	—	11.4	10.9	Cambodia	522
72.0	236.3	193.9	320.0	413.8	439.5	465.1	450.9	435.6	411.1	394.8	403.7	305.1	352.0	369.1	China, People's Rep.	924
2.7	4.5	3.7	.3	6.3	5.1	5.8	9.9	15.1	15.9	16.5	9.3	6.0	6.3	7.4	Fiji	819
376.7	468.3	339.4	104.6	337.6	306.2	290.9	112.4	71.1	86.2	222.1	32.3	2.8	72.9	1.4	India	534
137.2	227.2	281.9	3.9	.5	51.2	35.6	4.4	2.0	.7	2.3	2.6	.1	.3	.3	Indonesia	536
9.9	54.1	57.8	60.2	30.9	36.2	14.4	11.6	4.2	1.2	10.1	20.9	30.6	42.3	52.3	Korea	542
—	.6	—	.1	—	—	10.7	—	—	—	—	.3	.6	1.9	7.5	Lao, P.D. Rep.	544
97.8	125.8	118.1	103.1	99.0	105.4	110.2	115.1	119.7	127.1	136.3	145.0	82.3	87.8	92.7	Malaysia	548
.1	.2	.2	—	—	—	—	—	—	—	—	—	—	—	—	Maldives	556
5.4	2.4	1.1	.2	.1	—	—	.1	.1	.4	.6	.1	—	.2	.1	Myanmar	518
.1	—	.8	.2	.1	—	.1	.1	.1	.1	.1	.1	.1	—	.1	Nepal	558
22.6	48.5	45.9	.8	37.4	24.1	10.7	11.1	4.9	1.1	.6	5.2	.1	.5	.2	Pakistan	564
—	33.1	31.0	17.0	5.0	5.9	2.6	3.3	3.0	2.7	—	—	—	—	—	Papua New Guinea	853
.1	1.7	2.5	.9	19.8	35.3	4.7	.1	—	.7	.8	3.1	.4	7.3	16.7	Philippines	566
15.1	27.5	49.4	59.7	58.0	66.0	73.8	81.2	79.0	79.4	81.4	81.3	49.4	56.9	24.1	Singapore	576
1.0	1.2	1.2	1.7	1.3	.8	1.3	.2	—	—	—	.3	.1	—	—	Solomon Islands	813
—	19.9	6.3	.8	.2	.1	—	.1	.1	—	10.3	.3	.2	.1	.3	.2	Sri Lanka	524
6.4	52.3	22.2	15.2	2.4	1.3	27.1	42.5	45.2	12.5	9.0	5.7	8.8	15.9	21.8	Thailand	578

SDRs

1b s

		1965	1966	1967	1968	1969	1970	1971	1972	1973	1974	1975	1976	1977	1978	1979
																Millions of SDRs
Asia (cont.)																
Tonga	866	....	....	....	....	....	....	....	....	....	....	....	....	....	....	....
Vanuatu	846	....	....	....	....	....	....	....	....	....	....	....	....	....	....	....
Viet Nam	582	—	—	—	—	—	6.6	13.2	19.8	19.8	19.8	19.8	.7	4.2	6.2	12.2
Western Samoa	862	....	....	....	....	....	—	—	.2	.2	.2	—	—	—	—	—
Europe	170	—	—	—	—	—	11.8	17.8	60.5	88.1	95.7	79.9	52.4	28.5	22.9	60.7
Albania	914	....	....	....	....	....	....	....	....	....	....	....	....	....	....	....
Belarus	913	—	—	—	—	—	—	—	—	—	—	—	—	—	—	—
Bulgaria	918	—	—	—	—	—	—	—	—	—	—	—	—	—	—	—
Croatia	960	—	—	—	—	—	—	—	—	—	—	—	—	—	—	—
Cyprus	423	—	—	—	—	—	3.9	7.7	10.4	10.5	10.4	10.0	7.9	5.1	1.7	9.9
Czech Republic	935	....	....	....	....	....	....	....	....	....	....	....	....	....	....	....
Czechoslovakia	934	—	—	—	—	—	—	—	—	—	—	—	—	—	—	—
Estonia	939	....	....	....	....	....	....	....	....	....	....	....	....	....	....	....
Hungary	944	....	....	....	....	....	....	....	....	....	....	....	....	....	....	....
Kazakhstan	916	—	—	—	—	—	—	—	—	—	—	—	—	—	—	—
Kyrgyz Republic	917	—	—	—	—	—	—	—	—	—	—	—	—	—	—	—
Latvia	941	—	—	—	—	—	—	—	—	—	—	—	—	—	—	—
Lithuania	946	—	—	—	—	—	—	—	—	—	—	—	—	—	—	—
Macedonia, FYR	962	—	—	—	—	—	—	—	—	—	—	—	—	—	—	—
Malta	181	—	—	—	—	—	1.7	3.4	5.1	5.1	5.1	5.1	5.2	5.5	5.8	9.4
Moldova	921	—	—	—	—	—	—	—	—	—	—	—	—	—	—	—
Poland	964	....	....	....	....	....	....	....	....	....	....	....	....	....	....	....
Romania	968	....	....	....	....	....	—	—	—	—	6.0	5.4	8.1	12.6	6.9	—	.6
Russia	922	—	—	—	—	—	—	—	—	—	—	—	—	—	—	—
Slovak Republic	936	....	....	....	....	....	....	....	....	....	....	....	....	....	....	....
Slovenia	961	—	—	—	—	—	—	—	—	—	—	—	—	—	—	—
Tajikistan	923	—	—	—	—	—	—	—	—	—	—	—	—	—	—	—
Turkey	186	—	—	—	—	—	.1	5.0	38.3	28.5	34.7	27.2	18.5	—	.2	.2
Turkmenistan	925	—	—	—	—	—	—	—	—	—	—	—	—	—	—	—
Ukraine	926	—	—	—	—	—	—	—	—	—	—	—	—	—	—	—
Uzbekistan	927	—	—	—	—	—	—	—	—	—	—	—	—	—	—	—
Yugoslavia, SFR	188	—	—	—	—	—	6.1	1.7	6.7	38.1	40.2	29.5	8.3	11.0	15.2	40.7
Middle East	405	—	—	—	—	—	5.5	44.4	114.1	142.3	123.2	115.9	141.3	169.8	191.3	494.2
Bahrain	419	....	....	....	....	....	....	....	—	—	—	—	—	—	.1	2.2
Egypt	469	—	—	—	—	—	.1	7.5	5.1	31.2	30.9	14.5	20.3	23.7	8.2	.4
Iran, I.R. of	429	—	—	—	—	—	1.0	1.2	34.4	36.9	44.5	55.7	64.3	69.6	96.3	167.3
Iraq	433	—	—	—	—	—	—	11.7	23.2	20.1	23.0	23.0	28.0	34.2	45.5	82.2
Israel	436	—	—	—	—	—	—	13.1	29.2	27.9	2.5	2.0	8.7	22.2	21.0	4.8
Jordan	439	—	—	—	—	—	2.7	5.1	7.6	7.5	7.4	7.4	7.4	7.4	7.4	11.0
Kuwait	443	—	—	—	—	—	—	—	—	—	—	—	—	—	—	—
Lebanon	446	—	—	—	—	—	—	—	—	—	—	—	—	—	—	1.3
Libya	672	—	—	—	—	—	—	—	—	—	—	—	—	—	—	30.7
Oman	449	....	....	....	....	....	—	—	.7	.7	.7	.7	.7	.7	.7	2.8
Qatar	453	....	....	....	....	....	—	—	—	—	—	—	—	—	—	4.2
Saudi Arabia	456	—	—	—	—	—	—	—	—	—	—	—	—	—	—	149.1
Syrian Arab Rep.	463	—	—	—	—	—	—	—	4.0	8.0	8.3	7.3	6.8	6.4	6.0	12.0
United Arab Emirates	466	—	—	—	—	—	—	—	—	—	—	—	—	—	—	15.4
Yemen Arab Rep.	473	—	—	—	—	—	—	1.1	2.1	2.1	2.1	2.1	2.1	2.1	3.2	7.5
Yemen, P.D. Rep.	459	—	—	—	—	—	1.7	4.8	7.8	7.8	3.7	3.2	3.0	3.6	3.0	3.5
Yemen, Republic of	474	—	—	—	—	—	—	—	—	—	—	—	—	—	—	—
Western Hemisphere	205	—	—	—	—	—	272.2	413.9	566.0	617.4	658.8	568.8	525.3	617.7	729.6	1,293.3
Antigua and Barbuda	311	—	—	—	—	—	—	—	—	—	—	—	—	—	—	—
Argentina	213	—	—	—	—	—	59.3	2.8	17.8	66.9	83.8	34.8	78.2	73.9	161.6	247.9
Bahamas, The	313	—	—	—	—	—	—	—	—	—	—	—	—	—	—	3.4
Barbados	316	—	—	—	—	—	—	1.4	2.8	2.8	2.8	2.8	2.8	2.7	2.5	3.9
Belize	339	—	—	—	—	—	—	—	—	—	—	—	—	—	—	—
Bolivia	218	—	—	—	—	—	2.7	2.4	3.0	2.2	2.6	7.0	6.9	5.7	14.1	—
Brazil	223	—	—	—	—	—	62.3	110.5	157.0	157.2	162.8	163.3	171.0	173.2	183.8	290.7
Chile	228	—	—	—	—	—	21.8	38.3	2.0	.3	13.8	20.9	48.3	54.7	20.7	22.0
Colombia	233	—	—	—	—	—	.1	8.3	17.5	23.1	24.5	20.3	24.3	25.6	37.8	71.9
Costa Rica	238	—	—	—	—	—	.2	.1	4.0	3.9	2.0	3.8	1.2	5.5	3.0	4.5
Dominica	321	....	....	....	....	....	....	....	....	....	....	....	....	....	....	....
Dominican Republic	243	—	—	—	—	—	—	—	6.9	6.8	7.2	6.5	6.0	5.2	4.7	7.2
Ecuador	248	—	—	—	—	—	.1	3.4	6.7	5.6	6.5	6.3	6.3	8.2	10.6	19.2
El Salvador	253	—	—	—	—	—	—	—	2.2	3.7	3.8	3.6	3.9	4.0	7.8	7.6	13.2
Grenada	328	—	—	—	—	—	—	—	—	—	—	—	.1	.1	—	—
Guatemala	258	....	—	—	—	—	2.1	7.8	7.6	11.5	11.5	11.5	11.4	11.5	11.6	18.4
Guyana	336	....	—	—	—	—	.1	2.2	4.1	4.0	3.9	3.8	3.5	2.7	2.8	2.8
Haiti	263	—	—	—	—	—	—	1.1	3.1	1.7	2.5	2.0	1.2	1.6	3.8	5.5
Honduras	268	—	—	—	—	—	.2	2.9	5.5	5.4	5.3	4.0	2.7	3.6	3.0	7.7
Jamaica	343	—	—	—	—	—	6.4	12.8	6.9	6.4	5.1	4.3	.8	14.3	4.5	.4
Mexico	273	—	—	—	—	—	47.8	88.3	127.7	127.8	129.0	86.3	.9	46.8	42.6	152.4
Nicaragua	278	—	—	—	—	—	1.0	3.7	6.2	5.7	5.8	4.6	3.5	3.8	4.3	—
Panama	283	—	—	—	—	—	3.2	2.6	2.7	2.6	2.3	6.4	5.2	4.5	4.0	3.9
Paraguay	288	—	—	—	—	—	2.5	4.6	6.6	6.6	6.6	6.6	6.6	6.6	6.6	9.4
Peru	293	—	—	—	—	—	14.3	28.4	41.0	37.3	37.2	37.1	3.3	2.7	4.8	81.3
St. Kitts and Nevis	361	....	....	....	....	....	....	....	....	....	....	....	....	....	....	....
St. Lucia	362	....	....	....	....	....	....	....	....	....	....	....	....	....	....	....
St. Vincent & Grens.	364	....	....	....	....	....	....	....	....	....	....	....	....	....	....	....
Suriname	366	—	—	—	—	—	—	—	—	—	—	—	—	—	—	2.6
Trinidad and Tobago	369	—	—	—	—	—	.5	7.2	7.3	7.1	7.9	7.6	7.6	12.2	16.9	31.2
Uruguay	298	—	—	—	—	—	.1	—	7.8	10.8	12.1	1.6	3.7	8.5	11.4	26.2
Venezuela	299	—	—	—	—	—	47.5	83.1	118.1	118.2	120.3	123.6	126.0	136.5	167.0	267.7
Memorandum Items																
Oil Exporting Countries	999	—	—	—	—	—	79.4	155.2	299.7	306.6	334.6	309.7	327.3	374.5	480.1	1,032.6
Non-Oil Developing Countries	201	—	—	—	—	—	449.6	774.5	1,251.5	1,339.2	1,345.0	1,203.9	1,096.7	1,071.2	1,224.8	2,064.4

SDR Holdings

Millions of SDRs:

		1965	1966	1967	1968	1969	1970	1971	1972	1973	1974	1975	1976	1977	1978	1979
World	001	—	—	—	—	—	3,414.1	6,363.3	9,314.9	9,314.9	9,314.9	9,314.8	9,314.9	9,314.8	9,315.1	13,348.0
All Participants	969	—	—	—	—	—	3,124.0	5,874.5	8,686.1	8,807.1	8,857.9	8,763.8	8,655.4	8,132.7	8,110.0	12,478.9
IMF	992	—	—	—	—	—	290.2	488.9	628.7	507.7	457.0	551.0	659.5	1,182.1	1,205.1	868.9
Other Holders	970	—	—	—	—	—	—	—	—	—	—	—	—	—	—	—

SDRs

SDR Holdings

1980	1981	1982	1983	1984	1985	1986	1987	1988	1989	1990	1991	1992	1993	1994		1b s
End of Period															**Asia (cont.)**	
....	—	—	—	—	—	—	.1	.1	.1	.2	.7	.4	.4	.5	Tonga	866
....	—	—	—	.1	.2	.2	.3	.3	.4	.5	.6	.7	.2	.2	Vanuatu	846
—	.5	—	.4	.2	—	—	—	—	—	—	—	—	4.9	11.0	Viet Nam	582
—	—	—	—	—	—	.8	1.3	2.4	.7	2.9	2.6	1.9	2.0	2.0	Western Samoa	862
28.0	90.5	35.5	77.0	36.2	40.5	43.5	47.2	50.6	129.7	70.2	214.7	103.4	270.1	373.6	**Europe**	170
														.2	Albania	914
													3.2	—	Belarus	913
—	—	—	—	—	—	—	—	—	—	—	—	5.9	.3	.8	Bulgaria	918
													.8	10.4	Bulgaria (?)	
													.8	3.1	Croatia	960
6.5	3.4	.2	.2	.1	.1	—	.3	.1	.1	.1	.1	.1	.1	.1	Cyprus	423
													6.0	—	Czech Republic	935
....	....	....	....	....	....	....	....	....	....	—	—	97.6	30.8	....	Czechoslovakia	934
													7.7	41.6	1.1	Estonia	939
....	—	2.3	44.4	—	.1	—	.2	.2	—	—	.7	.9	2.1	1.1	Hungary	944
													14.0	69.5	Kazakhstan	916
													9.4	.7	Kyrgyz Republic	917
												19.3	71.1	.2	Latvia	941
												.9	54.7	10.4	Lithuania	946
														—	Macedonia, FYR	962
11.3	14.6	21.2	31.0	35.7	39.6	43.1	46.6	50.1	53.6	59.1	64.2	33.1	35.3	35.6	Malta	181
													25.1	14.6	Moldova	921
....	—	—	—	—	—	.1	.1	.1	.1	.6	5.4	.8	.5	1.0	Poland	964
—	.4	11.8	.2	.3	—	.1	—	—	76.0	.1	40.3	7.9	1.4	38.1	Romania	968
												.6	3.7	2.1	Russia	922
													.3	58.9	Slovak Republic	936
....	....	....	....	....	....	....	....	....	....	—	—	—	—	—	Slovenia	961
													—	—	Tajikistan	923
—	.2	.1	1.3	.1	.4	.1	—	—	—	.4	—	—	.1	.8	Turkey	186
													—	—	Turkmenistan	925
													—	123.7	Ukraine	926
													—	—	Uzbekistan	927
10.1	71.9	—	—	.1	.2	—	—	.1	—	9.2	.2	....	....	....	Yugoslavia, SFR	188
644.9	855.3	1,288.8	1,144.9	1,270.5	1,281.2	1,149.2	1,224.2	1,072.9	1,292.2	951.5	913.4	765.4	1,014.4	1,090.4	**Middle East**	405
1.8	5.2	14.0	12.2	13.1	13.6	14.1	14.6	15.1	15.9	16.9	17.8	18.7	10.8	11.0	Bahrain	419
—	.2	.1	.3	.2	.1	—	.2	.3	.1	.4	.9	42.8	50.4	59.2	Egypt	469
240.5	291.2	299.8	309.2	320.3	328.2	335.5	342.3	115.7	304.7	310.4	215.8	7.4	104.8	97.9	Iran, I.R. of	429
87.2	113.7	74.2	8.6	.1	—	—	5.1	—	—	—	—	—	—	—	Iraq	433
8.8	.6	.5	.6	.1	.1	—	.1	.1	.1	.2	.3	.2	.4	.2	Israel	436
11.7	15.5	16.5	17.4	15.8	21.9	19.6	8.5	—	8.4	.7	.8	.4	4.0	.5	Jordan	439
—	35.4	62.3	35.6	76.0	104.3	128.4	148.8	166.8	97.8	113.9	128.3	130.4	49.1	55.0	Kuwait	443
—	1.9	2.0	—	.8	1.8	2.6	3.4	4.2	5.4	6.9	8.3	9.5	10.5	11.4	Lebanon	446
46.6	104.1	129.4	157.7	132.6	156.2	177.6	197.7	218.8	249.6	287.3	322.6	278.3	303.5	324.7	Libya	672
5.1	5.2	7.9	11.1	9.4	10.9	11.4	7.2	8.7	10.9	13.4	15.5	3.4	5.0	6.2	Oman	449
2.7	8.6	14.0	8.7	16.2	18.9	21.1	24.7	26.4	28.7	31.3	33.8	17.1	18.7	19.9	Qatar	453
212.6	212.7	578.7	486.8	586.0	528.7	335.8	370.8	395.5	467.2	69.9	62.0	202.0	402.7	416.0	Saudi Arabia	456
9.8	14.7	11.9	8.8	5.3	2.8	.2	—	—	—	.1	.1	—	—	—	Syrian Arab Rep.	463
8.0	29.5	50.3	61.5	66.0	68.3	76.5	79.8	82.3	85.9	90.8	95.5	52.4	54.1	55.0	United Arab Emirates	466
10.3	12.9	14.1	8.6	8.8	23.2	23.1	19.0	23.9	15.9	....	....	....	....	....	Yemen Arab Rep.	473
—	4.0	13.1	17.0	19.8	2.4	3.4	2.1	14.9	1.8	....	....	....	....	....	Yemen, P.D. Rep.	459
										9.4	11.7	2.9	.5	33.5	Yemen, Republic of	474
1,155.2	1,572.7	741.2	693.1	570.0	680.4	839.5	1,272.0	568.9	537.5	730.2	960.0	858.6	1,075.7	1,045.1	**Western Hemisphere**	205
														—	Antigua and Barbuda	311
256.6	347.1	—	.3	.6	—	—	—	.3	.2	209.0	134.9	272.8	329.5	385.7	Argentina	213
2.7	6.1	5.8	1.1	.7	.4	—	.3	.4	.1	.4	.1	—	—	—	Bahamas, The	313
1.6	1.4	.8	.3	—	—	—	.6	.5	—	—	.5	.1	.1	—	Barbados	316
....	.1	—	—	.1	—	—	.1	—	—	—	.1	.2	.3	.4	Belize	339
—	—	—	—	—	—	2.0	—	—	—	.7	.1	.1	10.2	17.0	Bolivia	218
300.7	388.1	.3	.1	.9	.5	—	.1	.3	—	7.7	8.9	.8	1.7	.3	Brazil	223
3.0	16.4	17.7	5.2	11.7	.3	.2	28.8	32.9	18.5	.7	.5	.5	.9	.5	Chile	228
85.3	119.4	162.4	188.7	.1	—	114.3	114.3	114.3	114.3	114.2	114.2	42.5	114.9	116.4	Colombia	233
—	—	.1	2.9	.1	—	—	—	—	—	1.1	.2	.2	.1	.1	Costa Rica	238
—	.7	.3	.4	—	—	.8	.7	.6	.3	.2	—	.1	—	—	Dominica	321
—	1.6	.5	.2	.4	28.8	—	—	—	—	—	—	.1	10.3	2.5	Dominican Republic	243
19.0	28.9	—	.1	.5	26.2	45.7	.7	1.0	.7	10.3	28.9	.1	3.2	3.0	Ecuador	248
—	.1	1.7	.1	—	—	—	—	—	—	—	—	—	—	.1	El Salvador	253
—	—	—	.1	—	—	—	—	—	—	—	—	—	—	—	Grenada	328
17.7	2.2	—	.6	2.0	—	—	1.2	.1	.6	—	—	11.4	11.4	11.4	Guatemala	258
—	1.0	2.6	—	—	—	—	—	—	—	1.5	1.0	.2	—	.1	Guyana	336
—	—	1.0	1.0	—	—	5.4	—	—	.1	—	—	—	—	—	Haiti	263
—	1.4	1.6	2.1	.2	—	—	.3	1.0	—	—	—	.1	.1	.1	Honduras	268
—	.1	.1	—	—	—	—	—	—	—	.3	—	9.0	9.1	—	Jamaica	343
112.9	152.9	5.3	21.9	3.1	.4	7.2	497.7	292.6	291.5	293.0	409.3	398.8	162.6	121.1	Mexico	273
—	.1	.9	—	—	—	—	—	—	—	—	—	.1	—	—	Nicaragua	278
1.1	2.8	3.8	.4	—	11.7	1.4	—	—	—	19.4	8.1	3.3	.1	—	Panama	283
11.1	15.1	23.7	30.4	35.0	38.8	42.1	44.8	47.4	50.8	54.9	58.8	62.1	65.1	67.6	Paraguay	288
9.7	9.8	29.9	.6	22.9	—	—	—	—	—	—	—	—	.7	.3	Peru	293
....	....	....	....	....	—	—	—	—	—	—	—	—	—	—	St. Kitts and Nevis	361
.1	.2	—	—	—	—	—	—	—	—	1.2	1.3	1.3	1.3	1.4	St. Lucia	362
.1	.2	—	—	—	—	—	—	—	—	—	—	.1	.1	.1	St. Vincent & Grens.	364
2.1	5.4	8.5	1.7	1.3	.8	.3	—	—	—	—	—	—	—	—	Suriname	366
35.8	51.3	73.5	94.4	103.1	107.8	112.0	—	—	6.9	.8	1.5	.2	.2	.1	Trinidad and Tobago	369
26.0	37.2	1.7	3.7	5.1	13.3	9.7	48.1	22.1	17.5	7.9	3.3	—	.3	—	Uruguay	298
269.9	382.1	399.3	336.8	382.1	451.4	498.0	533.6	56.4	36.0	6.7	188.3	54.6	353.6	316.9	Venezuela	299
															Memorandum Items	
1,218.0	1,767.5	2,078.1	1,547.5	1,712.9	1,844.8	1,756.6	1,857.1	1,074.4	1,284.8	928.7	1,065.6	746.3	1,296.7	1,307.6	Oil Exporting Countries	999
1,701.7	2,703.5	1,573.0	1,349.2	1,381.8	1,465.8	1,602.6	1,879.4	1,539.3	1,536.7	1,810.3	2,030.3	1,652.6	1,863.1	1,968.0	Non-Oil Developing Countries	201

End of Period

SDR Holdings

17,385.9	21,433.5	21,437.0	21,446.5	21,450.2	21,451.9	21,448.1	21,466.5	21,484.2	21,480.9	21,479.4	21,474.2	21,480.1	21,480.9	21,476.9	World	001
11,808.5	16,411.2	17,744.6	14,418.2	16,469.5	18,212.8	19,494.1	20,212.5	20,172.9	20,484.8	20,354.4	20,551.3	12,867.2	14,614.3	15,761.5	All Participants	969
5,571.9	5,018.9	3,686.2	6,998.8	4,957.5	3,068.4	1,937.0	1,207.1	769.5	947.1	995.3	819.6	8,561.2	6,687.3	5,510.1	IMF	992
5.6	3.3	6.2	29.4	23.3	170.6	17.1	46.8	541.7	49.0	129.6	103.3	51.7	179.4	205.3	Other Holders	970

Reserve Position in Fund

1c s

Millions of SDRs:

		1965	1966	1967	1968	1969	1970	1971	1972	1973	1974	1975	1976	1977	1978	1979
All Countries	010	5,376.6	6,330.5	5,748.0	6,488.3	6,725.7	7,696.6	6,351.3	6,324.7	6,168.2	8,844.4	12,624.0	17,736.1	18,088.6	14,838.5	11,759.8
Industrial Countries	110	5,024.9	5,799.7	5,186.7	5,828.5	5,950.9	6,646.6	5,347.1	5,288.0	4,963.1	6,225.4	7,712.6	11,846.8	12,245.8	9,612.6	7,763.9
United States	111	604.0	325.7	420.2	1,289.9	2,323.6	1,935.2	584.5	428.0	457.5	1,513.0	1,889.5	3,816.6	4,071.7	803.5	950.9
Canada	156	353.4	448.5	433.4	206.2	478.1	669.6	332.6	315.9	280.4	432.6	553.6	812.9	701.5	427.4	296.5
Australia	193	135.0	170.0	205.4	255.5	260.4	267.0	167.4	167.4	166.8	175.8	166.8	166.6	166.3	161.3	156.4
Japan	158	255.3	321.1	238.6	289.0	626.7	973.2	489.9	570.8	529.4	603.3	686.4	1,143.5	1,329.3	1,641.7	1,120.9
New Zealand	196						50.5	50.5	50.5	50.6					23.0	
Austria	122	72.3	102.1	116.4	159.6	166.2	156.6	142.4	132.5	125.8	130.7	177.2	343.5	324.5	254.3	231.5
Belgium	124	308.7	367.1	328.0	300.8	155.5	391.7	599.4	516.1	492.4	511.1	591.3	814.2	779.3	605.7	524.0
Denmark	128	58.4	66.8	61.9	85.3	1.0	26.4	52.3	65.0	119.1	72.9	61.1	67.0	72.8	68.7	76.8
Finland	172	14.3	31.3		.1	41.3	66.8	63.8	63.8	63.8	63.8				46.1	44.7
France	132	884.4	987.8	885.9	.9			435.9	459.8	377.0	429.0	622.7	843.0	736.4	460.6	478.5
Germany	134	1,076.2	1,257.1	1,051.7	1,515.3	301.9	917.1	1,078.2	1,140.2	1,207.0	1,290.4	1,581.4	2,132.7	2,184.8	3,301.9	2,372.2
Greece	174	15.0	25.0	25.0	25.0	25.0	34.5	34.5	34.5	34.5	—	—	—	—	33.5	32.4
Iceland	176	2.8	3.7	3.7	3.7	—	—	5.7	5.8	5.8	—	—	—	—	—	5.4
Ireland	178	11.0	—	11.0	47.7	58.1	30.3	35.3	40.3	40.3	42.1	39.1	68.7	65.7	59.7	60.7
Italy	136	549.2	884.7	841.7	894.4	862.8	275.5	348.5	330.4	297.2	—	—	—	—	242.5	236.5
Netherlands	138	358.2	412.9	351.7	496.7	439.5	539.3	643.7	553.6	309.4	441.6	746.7	899.8	953.5	631.8	457.7
Norway	142	25.1	42.6	51.3	71.5	87.0	118.8	61.6	69.0	63.4	68.9	111.8	247.4	234.7	205.7	188.1
Portugal	182	15.0	18.8	18.8	18.8	18.8	18.8	29.3	29.3	29.3	29.3	—	—	—	—	—
San Marino	135															
Spain	184	141.0	166.0	—	—	.1	45.0	103.8	103.8	103.8	121.1	—	—	—	136.3	133.4
Sweden	144	142.6	165.3	138.5	164.4	101.0	126.4	83.6	89.3	88.0	89.0	95.1	231.7	225.4	191.0	180.7
Switzerland	146								116.5	116.6	205.9	81.3	250.0	391.2	308.5	207.2
United Kingdom	112											303.7				
Developing Countries	200	351.6	530.8	561.3	659.7	774.8	990.1	1,004.2	1,036.7	1,205.1	2,589.0	4,911.4	5,889.2	5,842.9	5,226.0	3,995.9
Africa	605	107.8	131.9	150.0	148.4	258.3	227.9	252.1	270.6	309.2	258.8	322.1	419.4	414.1	460.8	392.2
Algeria	612	15.0	15.8	16.5	17.3	18.8	32.5	32.5	32.5	32.5	32.5	32.5	33.5	32.5	31.6	30.6
Angola	614															
Benin	638	.8	.9	1.0	1.1	1.4	2.1	2.1	2.1	2.1	2.1	2.1	2.1	2.1	2.0	1.9
Botswana	616				.1	.1	.6	.6	.6	.6	.6	.6	.6	1.2	1.2	2.2
Burkina Faso	748	.8	.9	1.0	1.1	1.4	1.4	2.5	3.1	3.3	3.3	3.3	3.3	4.6	4.6	4.6
Burundi	618	.1	.1	.3	—	—	—	—	.3	.4	—	—	—	—	4.8	4.5
Cameroon	622	1.9	2.1	2.3	2.5	2.7	6.9	6.9	6.9	6.9	—	—	—	—	3.5	6.4
Cape Verde	624															.3
Central African Rep.	626	.7	.8	.9	1.0	1.2	1.3	.1	.3	.4	—	—	—	—	1.7	1.9
Chad	628	.7	.8	.9	1.0	1.3	—	—	—	—	—	—	—	—	1.2	1.8
Comoros	632															
Congo	634	.7	.8	.9	1.0	1.3	1.6	1.7	1.8	1.8	1.9	2.0	2.0	—	—	—
Côte d'Ivoire	662	1.5	1.7	1.9	2.1	2.5	10.8	10.8	10.8	10.8	—	—	—	—	10.4	12.2
Djibouti	611															.8
Equatorial Guinea	642					.5	1.0	1.0	—	—	—	—	1.8	—	—	.2
Ethiopia	644	3.8	4.8	4.8	4.8	4.8	6.8	6.8	6.8	6.8	6.8	6.8	6.8	7.3	—	—
Gabon	646	.7	.8	.9	1.0	1.2	2.4	2.4	2.4	2.5	2.5	2.5	2.5	2.5	—	—
Gambia, The	648			.1	.1	.1	.3	—	.4	.5	.6	1.8	1.7	—	—	—
Ghana	652	1.9	—	—	—	—	—	—	—	—	5.9	10.6	—	—	—	—
Guinea	656	2.8	2.8	2.8	2.8	—	—	—	—	—	—	—	—	—	—	—
Guinea-Bissau	654														.8	
Kenya	664	2.3	4.0	4.0	4.1	4.1	12.0	12.0	12.0	12.3	—	—	—	—	—	—
Lesotho	666				.1	.1	—	.1	.2	.4	.6	1.3	1.3	1.3	1.1	1.1
Liberia	668	—	—	—	—	—	—	—	.3	—	1.4	1.8	—	—	—	—
Madagascar	674	2.3	3.3	3.3	3.3	3.3	5.0	5.0	5.0	5.0	—	—	—	—	—	—
Malawi	676	1.4	1.4	1.4	1.4	1.4	1.4	1.4	1.9	3.8	3.8	—	—	—	—	—
Mali	678															
Mauritania	682	.8	.9	1.0	1.1	1.4	1.5	.6	.8	.9	—	—	—	—	—	—
Mauritius	684				.3	—	1.8	2.5	2.5	2.5	—	—	5.5	5.5	—	—
Morocco	686	10.8	11.7	12.6	—	—	—	—	28.3	28.2	28.2	28.2	—	—	—	—
Mozambique	688															
Niger	692	.8	.9	1.0	1.1	1.4	2.1	2.1	2.1	2.1	2.1	2.1	2.1	3.1	5.0	5.0
Nigeria	694	5.0	8.3	8.3	8.3	11.4	11.4	11.4	12.9	33.0	33.8	212.2	333.8	340.3	365.9	295.2
Rwanda	714	.1	—	—	—	—	—	.1	—	—	—	—	2.1	2.1	2.9	5.5
Senegal	722	2.5	2.5	2.5	2.5	2.5	3.3	3.6	3.9	4.2	—	—	—	—	2.1	—
Seychelles	718														.1	.1	.3
Sierra Leone	724	1.3	.8	—	—	—	4.9	4.9	4.9	4.9	—	—	—	—	—	—
Somalia	726				.1	1.0	3.7	3.8	3.9	3.9	3.9	4.2	4.2	—	—	—
South Africa	199	37.5	50.0	60.0	60.2	153.2	50.4	80.5	80.5	80.5	81.4	—	—	—	—	—
Sudan	732															
Swaziland	734					.2	.1	.2	.3	.2	.4	1.1	2.0	2.0	2.8	2.7
Tanzania	738	2.2	4.0	4.0	4.2	4.4	6.9	6.9	6.9	10.5	—	—	—	—	—	—
Togo	742	1.1	1.1	1.1	1.1	1.1	2.1	2.1	2.1	2.1	2.1	2.1	2.1	2.1	2.0	3.3
Tunisia	744									5.9	12.0	12.0	12.0	12.0	11.7	11.3
Uganda	746	2.3	4.0	4.0	4.0	4.5	6.5	—	—	—	—	—	—	—	5.9	—
Zaïre	636	3.1	3.7	6.1	14.3	22.5	28.3	28.3	28.3	28.3	28.3	—	—	—	—	—
Zambia	754	3.2	3.2	6.3	6.4	8.9	19.0	19.0	—	—	—	—	—	—	—	—
Zimbabwe	698															
Asia	505	57.2	101.2	81.5	76.9	86.4	152.6	194.4	196.6	210.8	143.2	118.5	99.9	174.7	230.1	360.7
Afghanistan, Islamic State of	512	—	—	—	—	—	—	—	—	—	—	—	—	8.3	9.0	9.4
Bangladesh	513								2.0	1.2	—	—	—	—	—	—
Bhutan	514															
Cambodia	522					4.8	6.3	—	—	—	—	—	—	—	—	—
China, People's Rep.	924															
Fiji	819							2.3	2.3	2.3	—	3.3	3.3	3.3	3.2	3.1
India	534	—	—	—	—	—	21.1	76.2	76.2	76.2	—	—	—	—	69.2	161.5
Indonesia	536	—	—	—	—	—	—	—	—	—	28.6	—	—	68.0	69.1	73.7
Korea	542	4.7	6.0	6.0	1.9	—	12.5	12.5	12.5	20.0	—	—	—	—	10.4	18.8
Lao, P.D. Rep.	544	1.9	1.9	1.9	1.9	2.5	2.8	2.8	2.8	2.8	3.3	—	—	—	—	—
Malaysia	548	13.8	20.2	31.7	33.0	35.6	50.9	39.2	39.3	46.5	49.5	53.8	53.8	52.3	53.6	67.5
Maldives	556														.2	.2
Myanmar	518	7.5	7.5	—	—	—	—	—	—	—	—	—	—	—	—	—
Nepal	558	.3	.9	.9	.9	2.4	2.5	2.7	2.9	3.1	3.1	3.1	—	—	2.4	2.3
Pakistan	564															
Papua New Guinea	853															2.4
Philippines	566	4.5	27.5	—	—	—	—	—	—	—	—	—	—	—	—	—
Singapore	576		7.5	7.5	7.5	7.5	7.5	9.3	9.3	9.3	9.3	9.3	9.4	9.4	13.1	21.5
Solomon Islands	813															
Sri Lanka	524	—	—	—	—	—	—	—	—	—	—	—	—	—	—	.4
Thailand	578	19.0	23.8	23.8	23.8	23.8	33.5	33.5	33.5	33.5	33.5	33.5	33.5	33.5	—	—

Reserve Position in Fund

1980	1981	1982	1983	1984	1985	1986	1987	1988	1989	1990	1991	1992	1993	1994		1c s
End of Period																
16,835.5	21,322.8	25,455.2	39,112.6	41,569.6	38,730.8	35,339.3	31,467.1	28,272.9	25,471.0	23,748.9	25,887.8	33,902.9	32,802.3	31,725.7	All Countries	010
10,798.2	13,651.8	17,160.8	25,669.7	27,357.2	25,301.1	23,087.8	20,462.9	19,572.2	19,553.6	19,976.5	22,774.2	29,510.7	28,308.9	27,417.1	Industrial Countries	110
2,236.5	4,342.2	6,660.8	10,805.0	11,774.1	10,876.2	9,589.5	8,000.1	7,241.7	6,884.8	6,379.7	6,632.8	8,552.3	8,589.0	8,240.8	United States	111
454.0	345.7	331.1	671.9	692.1	647.1	561.1	465.7	375.2	401.6	363.7	414.1	734.9	689.9	629.2	Canada	156
255.2	252.5	.1	108.6	186.7	188.7	188.8	188.8	204.6	245.1	245.2	245.3	419.7	400.5	346.9	Australia	193
1,043.9	1,338.8	1,877.5	2,199.3	2,263.8	2,071.1	1,947.3	2,010.8	2,435.8	2,677.0	4,197.3	5,398.2	6,284.3	6,014.5	5,912.3	Japan	158
27.5	27.6	—	28.5	—	.1	.1	.2	8.2	39.8	40.2	54.0	109.1	103.6	100.8	New Zealand	196
228.5	224.0	258.8	447.1	447.2	405.2	361.5	330.0	288.9	274.4	241.8	275.9	389.5	381.6	364.0	Austria	122
489.4	390.2	328.1	496.5	521.3	472.4	462.3	392.4	344.8	341.9	326.3	366.6	586.0	560.2	556.3	Belgium	124
110.9	105.3	99.8	205.0	214.4	207.5	127.2	123.2	234.7	254.9	219.8	248.6	345.7	309.1	294.6	Denmark	128
77.4	77.4	77.5	123.0	133.7	130.3	135.0	141.6	167.6	178.9	151.0	192.3	241.0	220.4	196.1	Finland	172
836.5	883.6	868.3	1,291.6	1,290.9	1,246.8	1,419.3	1,348.9	1,200.5	1,076.2	1,003.6	1,164.9	1,804.9	1,681.8	1,626.7	France	132
1,796.0	2,117.4	2,798.9	3,579.9	3,826.1	3,467.0	3,146.1	2,748.8	2,486.6	2,315.3	2,147.8	2,493.7	3,083.2	2,876.6	2,760.5	Germany	134
55.6	55.6	55.6	86.2	81.4	75.0	70.1	70.1	71.1	89.2	74.7	74.7	116.9	113.7	113.7	Greece	174
9.0	9.0	—	4.0	4.0	4.0	4.0	4.0	4.0	4.0	4.0	4.0	10.5	10.5	10.5	Iceland	176
76.6	75.1	75.2	115.7	124.4	120.8	130.7	130.9	134.3	125.4	104.6	123.9	171.3	155.1	151.9	Ireland	178
645.6	630.6	630.6	945.3	1,095.8	1,056.1	1,036.6	1,019.7	941.1	1,098.5	1,204.6	1,576.2	1,774.1	1,575.4	1,392.8	Italy	136
510.3	497.8	561.3	901.0	963.2	898.2	717.0	652.5	562.6	536.9	518.8	559.0	834.0	795.3	802.2	Netherlands	138
201.4	213.8	246.4	411.0	470.4	463.7	481.8	498.1	451.3	441.4	407.8	399.0	471.4	425.5	440.9	Norway	142
34.8	48.8	48.8	29.7	29.7	29.7	29.7	29.7	29.7	94.9	123.7	188.9	228.3	219.4	230.8	Portugal	182
													2.4	2.4	San Marino	135
205.6	205.6	205.6	321.5	363.0	369.0	423.1	553.6	786.0	929.7	796.8	748.8	831.7	750.6	759.5	Spain	184
193.9	165.6	148.9	240.7	258.3	249.6	253.4	277.4	250.8	253.6	233.9	308.4	451.4	451.4	451.4	Sweden	144
252.4	397.1	467.3	635.8	592.8	500.7	369.5	211.5	102.0	31.6	—	—	580.9	604.5	643.2	Switzerland	146
1,045.2	1,236.1	1,408.1	2,010.2	2,011.8	1,809.7	1,621.0	1,252.6	1,238.6	1,255.7	1,179.0	1,292.7	1,463.6	1,354.4	1,366.1	United Kingdom	112
6,037.3	7,671.0	8,294.5	13,443.0	14,212.4	13,429.7	12,251.5	11,004.2	8,700.7	5,917.4	3,772.4	3,113.6	4,392.1	4,493.4	4,308.6	Developing Countries	200
699.2	800.2	227.0	376.6	347.3	263.1	231.9	188.5	76.3	82.0	76.4	74.7	157.0	157.6	157.6	Africa	605
101.8	116.8	125.6	172.4	165.5	152.9	148.0	107.9	—	—	—	—	—	—	—	Algeria	612
															Angola	614
2.0	2.0	2.0	2.0	2.0	2.0	2.0	2.0	2.0	2.0	2.0	2.0	2.1	2.1	2.1	Benin	638
5.1	9.1	9.2	11.3	12.3	12.9	15.6	15.7	13.6	19.2	16.2	13.5	14.8	16.6	16.3	Botswana	616
5.6	5.6	5.6	5.6	7.5	7.5	7.5	7.5	7.5	7.5	7.2	7.2	7.2	7.2	7.2	Burkina Faso	748
7.3	7.3	7.4	9.4	9.4	9.2	9.2	9.2	9.2	9.2	7.6	7.2	5.9	5.9	5.9	Burundi	618
12.0	12.0	13.9	7.2	.2	.2	.2	.2	.2	.2	.2	.2	.3	.3	.3	Cameroon	622
.6	.6	.6	1.0	1.0	1.0	—	—	—	—	—	—	—	—	—	Cape Verde	624
—	—	1.2	1.6	.1	.1	.1	.1	.1	.1	.1	.1	.1	.1	.1	Central African Rep.	626
3.8	3.8	5.1	3.5	.3	.3	.3	.3	.3	.3	.3	.3	.3	.3	.3	Chad	628
.3	—	—	—	—	—	—	—	—	—	—	—	.5	.5	.5	Comoros	632
—	2.1	3.3	3.0	.5	.5	.5	.5	.5	.5	.5	.5	.5	.5	.5	Congo	634
9.5	—	—	—	—	—	—	—	—	—	—	—	—	.1	.1	Côte d'Ivoire	662
1.2	1.2	1.2	1.2	1.2	1.2	1.2	1.2	1.2	1.2	1.2	1.2	2.1	—	—	Djibouti	611
—	.2	.5	—	—	—	—	—	—	—	—	—	—	—	—	Equatorial Guinea	642
4.1	—	—	4.2	—	—	—	—	—	—	—	—	6.9	7.0	7.0	Ethiopia	644
—	—	—	7.0	—	—	—	—	—	—	—	—	—	—	—	Gabon	646
—	—	—	—	—	—	.1	.1	.1	.1	—	.1	.1	.1	.1	Gambia, The	648
—	—	—	—	—	—	—	—	—	—	—	—	1.5	1.5	1.5	Ghana	652
—	—	—	—	—	—	—	—	—	—	—	—	17.4	17.4	17.4	Guinea	656
—	.6	1.5	—	—	—	—	—	—	—	—	—	—	.1	.1	Guinea-Bissau	654
.5	.2	1.5	9.6	10.9	12.2	12.2	12.2	12.2	12.2	12.2	12.2	12.2	12.2	12.3	Kenya	664
2.0	2.0	.1	1.2	1.3	1.3	1.3	1.3	1.3	1.3	1.3	1.3	3.5	3.5	3.5	Lesotho	666
—	—	—	—	—	—	—	—	—	—	—	—	—	—	—	Liberia	668
—	.3	1.2	—	—	—	—	—	—	—	—	—	—	—	—	Madagascar	674
—	3.8	—	2.2	2.2	2.2	2.2	2.2	2.2	2.2	2.2	2.2	2.2	2.2	2.2	Malawi	676
5.4	7.6	8.7	8.7	8.7	8.7	8.7	8.7	8.7	8.7	8.7	8.7	8.7	8.7	8.7	Mali	678
—	—	—	—	—	—	—	—	—	—	—	—	—	—	—	Mauritania	682
—	—	—	—	—	—	—	—	—	—	—	.1	1.3	6.2	7.3	7.3	Mauritius	684
—	—	—	—	—	—	—	—	—	—	—	—	30.3	30.3	30.3	Morocco	686
															Mozambique	688
6.0	6.0	6.1	8.6	8.6	8.6	8.6	8.6	8.6	8.6	8.6	8.6	8.6	8.6	8.6	Niger	692
370.7	446.1	—	—	—	.1	.1	.1	.1	.1	.1	.1	.1	.1	.1	Nigeria	694
8.4	7.3	7.3	9.6	9.7	9.3	9.3	9.3	7.1	7.1	6.4	6.5	10.4	9.8	9.8	Rwanda	714
—	—	.9	.9	1.0	1.0	1.0	1.0	1.0	1.0	1.0	1.0	1.1	1.1	1.1	Senegal	722
.4	.4	.4	—	—	—	—	—	.1	.1	.1	.1	.8	.8	.8	Seychelles	718
—	1.1	—	—	—	—	—	—	—	—	—	—	—	—	—	Sierra Leone	724
—	—	—	—	—	—	—	—	—	—	—	—	—	—	—	Somalia	726
128.2	107.2	—	70.0	70.0	—	—	—	—	—	—	—	.1	—	.1	South Africa	199
—	—	—	—	—	—	—	—	—	—	—	—	—	—	—	Sudan	732
4.3	4.3	—	1.7	1.7	1.8	—	—	—	—	—	—	3.0	3.0	3.0	Swaziland	734
—	1.7	—	—	—	—	—	—	—	—	—	—	10.0	10.0	10.0	Tanzania	738
—	—	.2	.2	.2	.2	.2	.2	.2	.2	.2	.3	.3	.2	.3	Togo	742
19.2	19.2	19.2	30.1	29.4	26.4	—	—	—	—	—	—	—	—	—	Tunisia	744
—	—	3.5	3.5	3.5	3.5	3.5	—	—	—	—	—	—	—	—	Uganda	746
—	23.5	—	—	—	—	—	—	—	—	—	—	—	—	—	Zaïre	636
—	7.5	—	—	—	—	—	—	—	—	—	—	—	—	—	Zambia	754
—	—	—	—	—	—	—	—	—	—	—	—	.1	.1	.1	Zimbabwe	698
831.6	742.0	880.1	1,196.8	1,236.2	1,210.9	1,220.0	1,213.8	1,231.7	1,409.3	924.3	1,085.5	2,009.0	2,056.7	2,173.8	Asia	505
15.1	15.1	15.1	4.8	4.8	4.8	4.8	4.8	4.9	4.9	4.9	4.9	4.9	4.9	4.9	Afghanistan, Islamic State of	512
—	—	7.5	22.4	22.4	22.4	22.4	22.4	22.4	22.4	—	—	—	.1	.1	Bangladesh	513
....	—	.4	.4	.6	.6	.6	.6	.6	.6	.6	.6	.6	.6	.6	Bhutan	514
															Cambodia	522
150.0	—	—	167.7	260.6	302.6	302.6	302.6	302.6	302.6	302.6	302.6	551.2	512.8	517.3	China, People's Rep.	924
5.3	5.4	5.4	7.8	7.8	7.8	7.9	7.9	7.9	7.9	7.1	6.8	10.4	10.0	10.0	Fiji	819
329.7	329.7	364.3	486.9	487.0	487.1	487.2	487.2	487.2	487.2	—	.2	212.6	212.6	212.6	India	534
160.8	196.3	218.4	72.4	72.4	72.4	72.4	72.4	72.4	72.4	72.4	72.4	194.4	199.7	214.0	Indonesia	536
—	—	—	51.7	—	.7	.7	.7	.7	178.2	224.5	255.4	319.1	339.2	363.6	Korea	542
															Lao, P.D. Rep.	544
116.5	116.5	116.5	159.3	159.4	159.4	159.4	153.0	172.0	169.7	163.9	179.8	240.3	229.1	273.7	Malaysia	548
.3	.3	.3	.5	—	—	—	—	—	—	—	—	.9	.9	.9	Maldives	556
—	9.0	13.0	6.9	6.9	—	—	—	—	—	—	—	—	—	—	Myanmar	518
5.2	5.7	5.7	5.7	5.7	5.7	5.7	5.7	5.7	5.7	5.7	5.7	5.7	5.7	5.7	Nepal	558
—	—	58.8	88.5	88.6	—	.1	.1	.1	.1	.1	.1	.1	.1	.1	Pakistan	564
3.8	—	.1	5.3	5.4	5.4	5.4	6.9	7.0	7.0	—	—	—	.1	.1	Papua New Guinea	853
—	—	—	—	8.8	23.8	38.8	38.8	38.8	38.8	38.8	38.8	87.1	87.1	87.1	Philippines	566
44.3	63.4	67.7	68.5	69.1	80.6	79.9	79.1	77.9	80.1	68.9	60.1	113.4	157.4	172.8	Singapore	576
.7	—	—	.5	.5	.5	.5	.5	.5	.5	.5	.5	.5	.5	.5	Solomon Islands	813
—	.5	5.9	17.1	6.0	6.0	—	—	—	—	—	.1	.1	20.2	20.2	20.2	Sri Lanka	524
—	—	—	28.8	28.8	28.8	28.8	28.8	28.8	28.8	31.8	155.2	243.3	271.5	285.2	Thailand	578

Reserve Position in Fund

Millions of SDRs

		1965	1966	1967	1968	1969	1970	1971	1972	1973	1974	1975	1976	1977	1978	1979
Asia (cont.)																
Tonga	866	...	...	...	...	...	...	...	...	...	...	...	...	...	...	—
Vanuatu	846	...	...	...	...	...	...	...	...	...	...	...	...	...	...	...
Viet Nam	582	5.6	5.9	9.8	9.8	9.8	15.5	15.5	15.5	15.5	15.5	15.5	—	—	—	—
Western Samoa	862	...	...	...	...	...	.4	.4	.4	.4	.4	—	—	—	—	—
Europe	170	—	—	2.2	6.3	6.7	14.8	10.5	86.2	48.3	41.8	7.8	13.8	12.2	81.7	19.4
Albania	914	—	—	—	—	—	—	—	—	—	—	—	—	—	—	—
Belarus	913	—	—	—	—	—	—	—	—	—	—	—	—	—	—	—
Bulgaria	918	—	—	—	—	—	—	—	—	—	—	—	—	—	—	—
Croatia	960	—	—	—	—	—	—	—	—	—	—	—	—	—	—	—
Cyprus	423	—	—	2.2	3.8	4.2	6.5	6.5	6.5	6.5	—	—	—	—	6.5	6.1
Czech Republic	935	...	...	...	...	...	...	...	...	...	...	...	...	...	...	...
Czechoslovakia	934	—	—	—	—	—	—	—	—	—	—	—	—	—	—	—
Estonia	939	...	...	...	...	...	...	...	...	...	...	...	...	...	...	...
Hungary	944	—	—	—	—	—	—	—	—	—	—	—	—	—	—	—
Kazakhstan	916	—	—	—	—	—	—	—	—	—	—	—	—	—	—	—
Kyrgyz Republic	917	—	—	—	—	—	—	—	—	—	—	—	—	—	—	—
Latvia	941	...	...	...	...	...	...	...	...	...	...	...	...	...	...	...
Lithuania	946	...	...	...	...	...	...	...	...	...	...	...	...	...	...	...
Macedonia, FYR	962	...	...	...	...	...	...	...	...	...	...	...	...	...	...	...
Malta	181	...	...	...	2.5	2.5	4.0	4.0	4.0	4.0	4.0	7.8	13.8	12.2	13.2	13.3
Moldova	921	...	...	...	...	...	...	...	...	...	...	...	...	...	...	...
Poland	964	...	...	...	...	...	...	...	...	...	...	...	...	...	...	...
Romania	968	...	...	...	...	...	...	...	...	—	47.5	—	—	—	—	—
Russia	922	...	...	...	...	...	...	...	...	...	...	...	...	...	...	...
Slovak Republic	936	...	...	...	...	...	...	...	...	...	...	...	...	...	...	...
Slovenia	961	...	...	...	...	...	...	...	...	...	...	...	...	...	...	...
Tajikistan	923	—	—	—	—	—	—	—	—	—	—	—	—	—	—	—
Turkey	186	—	—	—	—	—	—	—	—	28.1	37.8	37.8	—	—	—	—
Turkmenistan	925	—	—	—	—	—	—	—	—	—	—	—	—	—	—	—
Ukraine	926	—	—	—	—	—	—	—	—	—	—	—	—	—	—	—
Uzbekistan	927	...	...	...	...	...	...	...	...	...	...	...	...	...	...	...
Yugoslavia, SFR	188	—	—	—	—	—	4.3	—	—	—	—	—	—	—	62.1	—
Middle East	405	70.7	104.2	99.0	88.7	68.1	63.1	75.2	124.0	194.3	1,412.4	3,315.4	4,162.9	4,105.0	3,363.2	2,240.2
Bahrain	419	...	...	...	...	...	...	...	2.5	2.5	5.5	9.6	4.7	4.8	5.8	5.8
Egypt	469	...	...	...	...	...	...	...	...	...	...	...	...	...	...	...
Iran, I.R. of	429	3.5	17.2	31.3	—	—	—	—	19.3	48.0	422.0	958.8	998.0	985.6	725.2	325.1
Iraq	433	16.0	20.0	—	20.0	20.0	—	—	17.3	27.3	27.3	27.3	27.3	27.5	27.7	47.8
Israel	436	12.5	22.5	22.5	22.5	—	—	—	—	32.5	—	—	—	—	—	31.6
Jordan	439	2.7	3.0	3.2	4.0	4.0	5.8	5.8	5.8	5.8	5.8	5.8	5.8	5.8	5.6	10.3
Kuwait	443	12.5	12.5	12.5	12.5	12.5	21.3	20.7	20.7	19.7	255.8	573.6	742.7	722.2	588.4	389.7
Lebanon	446	1.7	1.7	2.3	2.3	2.3	2.3	2.3	2.3	2.3	2.3	2.3	2.3	2.3	2.3	2.1
Libya	672	3.8	4.8	4.8	4.8	4.8	6.0	6.0	6.0	6.0	6.0	6.0	6.0	6.0	5.9	42.4
Oman	449	...	...	...	...	...	...	1.8	1.8	1.8	15.3	24.4	25.0	19.4	13.9	12.8
Qatar	453	...	...	...	...	...	...	...	5.0	5.0	5.0	13.1	16.2	14.5	14.7	13.6
Saudi Arabia	456	18.0	22.5	22.5	22.5	22.5	22.5	33.5	33.5	33.5	595.3	1,570.2	2,205.8	2,215.2	1,895.7	1,289.6
Syrian Arab Rep.	463	—	—	—	.1	—	—	—	—	—	—	—	7.1	12.5	—	—
United Arab Emirates	466	...	...	...	...	...	...	—	3.8	3.8	69.6	114.8	114.1	96.5	71.7	62.1
Yemen Arab Rep.	473	—	—	—	—	—	1.5	1.5	2.5	2.5	2.5	2.5	2.5	5.4	6.3	7.3
Yemen, P.D. Rep.	459	—	—	—	—	2.0	3.8	3.8	3.8	3.8	—	—	—	—	—	—
Yemen, Republic of	474															
Western Hemisphere	205	116.0	193.5	228.7	339.5	355.4	531.7	472.0	359.3	442.4	732.9	1,147.7	1,193.3	1,136.8	1,090.1	983.5
Antigua and Barbuda	311	...	...	...	...	...	...	...	...	...	...	...	...	...	...	...
Argentina	213	—	—	18.0	96.7	117.8	130.2	110.0	—	—	11.3	—	—	—	130.5	154.4
Bahamas, The	313	...	...	...	...	...	...	...	...	...	5.0	5.0	5.0	5.0	4.9	4.7
Barbados	316	...	...	...	...	2.0	2.0	2.0	2.0	2.0	2.0	3.3	3.3	3.3	3.0	2.9
Belize	339	...	...	...	...	...	...	...	...	...	...	...	...	...	...	...
Bolivia	218	1.3	6.9	6.9	—	—	—	—	—	—	—	—	6.4	7.4	9.0	—
Brazil	223	—	12.1	12.5	12.3	12.3	117.4	116.3	116.3	116.3	116.3	116.3	162.2	160.2	138.9	183.2
Chile	228	—	—	—	—	—	—	—	—	—	—	—	—	—	38.3	37.1
Colombia	233	—	—	—	—	—	—	—	—	—	39.3	39.3	39.3	45.3	76.7	70.1	73.6
Costa Rica	238	—	—	—	—	2.0	6.0	.3	.3	.3	—	—	—	—	7.8	7.5
Dominica	321	...	...	...	...	...	...	...	...	...	...	...	...	...	—	—
Dominican Republic	243	—	—	—	—	—	—	—	—	10.8	—	—	—	—	—	—
Ecuador	248	—	—	—	.5	—	—	—	—	—	5.6	9.2	13.2	—	8.0	9.4
El Salvador	253	5.0	—	—	—	—	—	—	—	—	—	—	—	5.1	8.8	8.5
Grenada	328	...	...	...	...	...	...	...	...	...	...	...	...	...	...	...
Guatemala	258	—	—	—	—	—	—	3.0	9.0	9.0	9.0	9.0	9.0	12.0	12.4	12.9	14.1
Guyana	336	...	1.2	1.2	1.2	1.2	1.8	—	.6	—	—	1.8	5.0	—	—	—
Haiti	263	—	—	—	—	—	—	—	2.5	2.9	.2	—	—	—	2.4	4.4
Honduras	268	—	—	2.3	2.3	4.8	—	—	—	—	6.3	—	—	—	6.3	6.1
Jamaica	343	4.8	7.3	7.3	7.3	9.3	9.5	13.3	—	—	—	—	—	—	—	—
Mexico	273	54.5	86.0	95.0	132.9	112.4	135.3	97.8	97.8	97.8	97.8	97.8	97.8	—	—	—
Nicaragua	278	—	—	4.8	—	—	—	—	—	—	—	—	—	—	—	—
Panama	283	.1	.1	.1	—	—	—	1.0	4.4	8.0	8.0	—	—	—	3.7	2.5
Paraguay	288	2.8	3.8	3.8	3.8	3.8	4.8	4.8	4.8	4.8	4.8	4.8	5.8	6.6	6.5	8.2
Peru	293	9.4	11.8	.1	—	—	—	—	—	30.8	30.8	30.8	—	—	—	—
St. Kitts and Nevis	361	...	...	...	...	...	...	...	...	...	...	...	...	...	...	...
St. Lucia	362	...	...	...	...	...	...	...	...	...	...	...	...	...	...	—
St. Vincent & Grens.	364	...	...	...	...	...	...	...	...	...	...	...	...	...	...	...
Suriname	366	...	...	...	...	...	...	...	...	...	...	...	...	...	4.8	4.8
Trinidad and Tobago	369	.5	1.8	1.8	1.8	2.8	6.6	6.6	6.6	—	4.8	18.7	27.8	27.6	29.8	37.8
Uruguay	298	—	—	2.5	—	—	—	—	—	—	—	—	—	—	16.7	16.2
Venezuela	299	37.5	62.5	72.5	80.7	88.9	117.1	111.1	111.1	111.5	401.0	804.6	925.6	832.7	588.0	408.1
Memorandum Items																
Oil Exporting Countries	999	111.3	163.6	168.3	166.0	178.2	210.8	216.9	263.8	322.0	1,892.2	4,337.5	5,428.0	5,360.4	4,397.8	2,990.7
Non-Oil Developing Countries	201	240.4	367.2	393.0	493.7	596.0	779.4	787.3	773.0	883.1	696.8	573.9	461.2	482.5	828.2	1,005.2

Reserve Position in Fund

1980	1981	1982	1983	1984	1985	1986	1987	1988	1989	1990	1991	1992	1993	1994	Country	Code
End of Period																
															Asia (cont.)	
....	....	....	....	....	.7	.7	.7	.7	.7	.7	.7	1.2	1.2	1.2	Tonga	866
....	—	1.0	1.6	1.6	1.6	1.6	1.6	1.6	1.6	1.6	1.6	1.6	2.5	2.5	Vanuatu	846
—	—	—	—	—	—	—	—	—	—	—	—	—	—	—	Viet Nam	582
—	—	—	—	—	—	—	—	—	—	—	.7	.7	.7	.7	Western Samoa	862
15.8	23.7	29.1	157.4	67.8	66.6	69.3	68.2	71.3	73.9	67.0	71.0	255.7	262.8	262.8	**Europe**	170
—	—	—	—	—	—	—	—	—	—	—	—	—	—	—	Albania	914
—	—	—	—	—	—	—	—	—	—	—	—	—	—	—	Belarus	913
—	—	—	—	—	—	—	—	—	—	—	—	38.7	32.6	32.6	Bulgaria	918
—	—	—	—	—	—	—	—	—	—	—	—	—	—	—	Croatia	960
—	—	—	4.7	4.7	4.7	4.7	4.7	11.7	18.1	15.1	17.9	25.5	25.5	25.5	Cyprus	423
....	....	....	....	....	....	....	....	....	....	....	....	—	—	—	Czech Republic	935
....	....	....	....	....	....	....	....	....	....	....	....	—	—	....	Czechoslovakia	934
....	....	....	....	....	....	....	....	....	....	....	....	—	—	—	Estonia	939
....	....	—	38.9	—	—	—	—	—	—	—	—	56.1	56.1	56.1	Hungary	944
—	—	—	—	—	—	—	—	—	—	—	—	—	—	—	Kazakhstan	916
—	—	—	—	—	—	—	—	—	—	—	—	—	—	—	Kyrgyz Republic	917
—	—	—	—	—	—	—	—	—	—	—	—	—	—	—	Latvia	941
—	—	—	—	—	—	—	—	—	—	—	—	—	—	—	Lithuania	946
—	—	—	—	—	—	—	—	—	—	—	—	—	—	—	Macedonia, FYR	962
15.8	23.7	25.8	28.8	30.9	29.7	32.4	31.2	27.3	23.5	19.6	20.8	25.3	25.3	25.4	Malta	181
—	—	—	—	—	—	—	—	—	—	—	—	—	—	—	Moldova	921
....	....	—	—	—	—	—	—	—	—	—	—	77.1	77.1	77.1	Poland	964
—	—	—	—	—	—	—	—	—	—	—	—	—	—	—	Romania	968
—	—	—	—	—	—	—	—	—	—	—	.5	1.0	.8	Russia	922
....	....	....	....	....	....	....	....	....	....	....	....	....	—	—	Slovak Republic	936
....	....	....	....	....	....	....	....	....	....	....	....	....	12.9	12.9	Slovenia	961
—	—	—	—	—	—	—	—	—	—	—	—	—	—	—	Tajikistan	923
—	—	—	32.3	32.3	32.3	32.3	32.3	32.3	32.3	32.3	32.3	32.3	32.3	32.3	Turkey	186
—	—	—	—	—	—	—	—	—	—	—	—	—	—	—	Turkmenistan	925
—	—	—	—	—	—	—	—	—	—	—	—	—	—	—	Ukraine	926
—	—	—	—	—	—	—	—	—	—	—	—	—	—	—	Uzbekistan	927
—	—	3.3	52.7	—	—	—	—	—	—	—	—	....	....	....	Yugoslavia, SFR	188
3,011.7	4,527.2	5,735.9	10,264.1	11,560.0	10,973.4	9,957.2	8,973.5	7,263.0	4,323.8	2,681.7	1,862.3	1,667.2	1,703.3	1,396.5	**Middle East**	405
8.5	8.9	12.5	21.4	23.1	24.6	26.0	27.3	27.7	29.6	28.0	29.6	31.1	40.9	42.2	Bahrain	419
—	—	24.0	30.4	—	—	—	—	—	—	—	—	53.8	53.8	53.8	Egypt	469
234.6	141.4	75.7	70.8	70.8	70.8	70.8	70.8	—	—	—	—	104.6	—	—	Iran, I.R. of	429
111.9	111.9	111.9	—	—	—	—	—	—	—	—	—	—	—	—	Iraq	433
25.6	—	—	34.8	—	—	—	—	—	—	—	—	—	—	—	Israel	436
16.6	16.6	16.6	7.2	—	—	—	—	—	—	—	—	12.0	—	—	Jordan	439
410.5	409.7	461.0	696.7	716.4	639.4	515.8	378.0	247.3	158.2	123.5	111.1	96.7	167.8	142.6	Kuwait	443
6.1	6.1	6.1	18.8	18.8	18.8	18.8	18.8	18.8	18.8	18.8	18.8	18.8	18.8	18.8	Lebanon	446
148.1	189.2	189.2	189.2	243.5	243.5	243.5	243.5	243.5	243.5	243.5	243.5	319.0	319.0	319.0	Libya	672
14.9	16.5	20.8	30.5	33.2	32.1	32.1	32.1	28.7	27.7	25.2	22.7	39.4	37.8	36.0	Oman	449
18.1	18.1	19.4	37.2	38.4	35.8	30.7	27.8	21.1	19.5	17.3	18.7	36.4	33.8	30.7	Qatar	453
1,896.2	3,428.2	4,621.3	8,902.7	10,187.6	9,706.8	8,838.4	8,016.2	6,540.4	3,688.0	2,099.1	1,291.6	797.3	868.6	604.3	Saudi Arabia	456
7.1	7.1	—	—	—	—	—	—	—	—	—	—	—	—	—	Syrian Arab Rep.	463
93.1	147.9	201.4	214.6	222.3	201.7	181.0	159.1	135.3	138.4	126.3	126.1	158.3	162.8	149.1	United Arab Emirates	466
10.8	—	—	6.0	6.0	—	—	—	—	—	—	....	....	....	....	Yemen Arab Rep.	473
9.4	1.6	—	3.9	—	—	—	—	—	—	—	....	....	....	....	Yemen, P.D. Rep.	459
—	—	—	—	—	—	—	—	—	—	—	—	—	—	—	Yemen, Republic of	474
1,479.0	1,577.9	1,422.4	1,448.2	1,001.0	915.6	773.0	560.2	58.4	28.4	23.1	20.2	303.3	313.0	318.0	**Western Hemisphere**	205
—	—	—	—	—	—	—	—	—	—	—	—	—	—	—	Antigua and Barbuda	311
262.8	239.2	91.0	—	—	—	—	—	—	—	—	—	—	—	—	Argentina	213
8.8	6.6	6.7	10.9	10.9	10.9	10.9	10.7	9.0	8.6	7.9	7.2	6.8	6.2	6.2	Bahamas, The	313
5.0	5.0	—	2.2	2.2	2.2	2.2	2.2	2.2	2.2	2.2	—	—	—	—	Barbados	316
....	....	1.3	1.9	1.9	1.9	1.9	1.9	1.9	1.9	1.9	1.9	2.9	2.9	2.9	Belize	339
—	—	—	—	—	—	—	—	—	—	—	—	8.9	8.9	8.9	Bolivia	218
269.5	226.6	259.8	—	—	—	—	—	—	—	—	—	—	—	—	Brazil	223
64.3	64.3	70.5	—	—	—	—	—	—	—	—	—	—	—	—	Chile	228
114.5	151.7	175.2	262.1	—	—	—	—	—	—	—	—	69.0	79.8	86.7	Colombia	233
—	—	—	—	—	—	—	—	—	—	—	—	8.7	8.7	8.7	Costa Rica	238
—	—	—	7.4	—	—	—	—	—	—	—	—	—	—	—	Dominica	321
—	—	—	—	—	—	—	—	—	—	—	—	—	—	—	Dominican Republic	243
21.8	24.8	—	11.4	—	—	—	—	—	—	—	—	17.1	17.1	17.1	Ecuador	248
—	—	—	—	—	—	—	—	—	—	—	—	—	—	—	El Salvador	253
—	—	—	—	—	—	—	—	—	—	—	—	—	—	—	Grenada	328
21.7	8.4	—	7.9	—	—	—	—	—	—	—	—	—	—	—	Guatemala	258
—	—	—	—	—	—	—	—	—	—	—	—	—	—	—	Guyana	336
—	—	.1	.1	.1	.1	.1	.1	.1	.1	.1	.1	.1	—	—	Haiti	263
—	—	—	4.2	—	—	—	—	—	—	—	—	—	—	—	Honduras	268
—	2.4	3.8	—	—	—	—	—	—	—	—	—	—	—	—	Jamaica	343
100.3	161.0	—	90.8	—	—	—	—	—	—	—	—	—	—	—	Mexico	273
—	—	—	—	—	—	—	—	—	—	—	—	—	—	—	Nicaragua	278
8.1	—	—	8.7	—	—	—	—	—	—	—	—	11.9	11.9	11.9	Panama	283
14.9	25.2	27.6	32.3	32.3	31.6	24.9	19.6	15.0	12.5	11.0	11.0	16.9	16.5	14.5	Paraguay	288
—	—	—	—	—	—	—	—	—	—	—	—	—	—	—	Peru	293
....	....	—	—	—	—	—	—	—	—	—	—	—	—	—	St. Kitts and Nevis	361
—	—	—	—	—	—	—	—	—	—	—	—	—	—	—	St. Lucia	362
7.9	7.9	7.9	.4	—	—	—	—	—	—	—	—	.5	.5	.5	St. Vincent & Grens.	364
—	—	—	3.0	—	—	—	—	—	—	—	—	—	—	—	Suriname	366
63.0	78.3	96.7	118.6	126.8	124.4	77.2	53.0	—	—	—	—	—	—	—	Trinidad and Tobago	369
26.7	28.0	—	9.5	—	—	—	—	—	—	—	—	15.4	15.4	15.4	Uruguay	298
489.9	548.6	681.8	877.1	827.0	744.6	655.9	472.8	30.2	3.1	—	—	145.0	145.0	145.0	Venezuela	299
															Memorandum Items	
4,050.6	5,770.7	6,726.4	11,263.5	12,577.0	11,900.0	10,788.8	9,580.5	7,319.1	4,351.0	2,707.3	1,886.3	1,891.0	1,934.5	1,640.7	Oil Exporting Countries	999
1,986.7	1,900.3	1,568.1	2,179.4	1,635.4	1,529.7	1,462.8	1,423.7	1,381.6	1,566.5	1,065.0	1,227.3	2,501.1	2,558.9	2,667.9	Non-Oil Developing Countries	201

Foreign Exchange

1d s

		1965	1966	1967	1968	1969	1970	1971	1972	1973	1974	1975	1976	1977	1978	1979
																Millions of SDRs:
All Countries	010	24,018	25,698	29,403	32,580	33,063	45,333	74,830	95,894	101,861	126,298	137,309	160,236	202,252	222,539	248,633
Industrial Countries	110	15,301	16,134	19,204	21,508	20,340	30,406	56,702	69,276	67,823	66,437	69,800	74,497	101,121	128,793	137,823
United States	111	781	1,321	2,345	3,528	2,781	629	258	222	7	4	68	275	15	3,357	2,890
Canada	156	1,533	1,208	1,269	1,977	1,756	3,037	3,753	4,023	3,266	3,088	2,753	2,980	1,905	1,902	1,433
Australia	193	1,182	1,174	928	930	738	1,096	2,463	4,995	4,063	2,953	2,262	2,267	1,506	1,322	893
Japan	158	1,569	1,469	1,453	2,261	2,614	3,188	12,695	15,182	8,458	9,268	9,078	11,949	16,569	22,180	12,417
New Zealand	196	173	179	218	161	209	206	375	658	758	521	364	414	330	277	333
Austria	122	539	530	667	636	656	849	1,225	1,557	1,440	1,852	2,796	2,625	2,337	3,515	2,706
Belgium	124	467	458	782	362	712	780	650	1,017	1,632	1,794	2,269	1,793	2,070	2,024	3,132
Denmark	128	431	422	365	250	356	375	504	587	796	536	543	575	1,138	2,235	2,242
Finland	172	191	112	139	I293	241	335	463	484	345	355	304	342	395	831	1,036
France	132	753	507	874	323	286	1,257	3,295	4,660	3,088	3,065	6,357	3,767	3,864	6,375	12,222
Germany	134	1,944	2,480	2,873	3,894	2,748	8,455	11,575	15,838	20,787	19,615	19,362	21,958	25,212	32,527	35,942
Greece	174	158	128	131	157	162	159	341	768	685	612	I806	741	850	955	986
Iceland	176	50	53	31	23	38	52	55	64	69	32	34	67	78	102	117
Ireland	178	377	471	403	418	594	637	839	942	755	936	1,212	1,451	1,824	1,940	1,548
Italy	136	1,847	1,612	2,221	1,524	1,226	2,113	2,821	2,049	1,808	2,601	1,033	2,696	6,553	8,059	13,128
Netherlands	138	299	305	556	269	370	771	374	1,308	2,740	2,855	2,905	3,025	3,210	3,030	4,911
Norway	142	420	467	608	607	598	642	914	1,029	1,120	1,384	1,675	1,548	1,480	1,894	2,872
Portugal	182	347	415	516	488	551	583	841	1,160	1,360	919	333	143	297	669	706
Spain	184	471	302	315	364	497	1,231	2,321	3,888	4,882	4,543	4,582	3,958	4,872	7,523	9,699
Sweden	144	627	659	499	426	369	397	666	1,054	1,699	1,018	2,223	1,603	2,479	2,862	2,314
Switzerland	146	402	704	607	1,669	1,783	2,401	3,507	4,052	4,151	4,448	5,915	8,018	8,079	13,326	12,269
United Kingdom	112	739	1,158	1,405	949	1,055	1,213	6,767	3,742	3,916	4,037	2,928	2,302	16,057	11,887	14,021
Developing Countries	200	8,717	9,564	10,199	11,072	12,724	14,927	18,128	26,617	34,038	59,861	67,509	85,739	101,131	93,746	110,817
Africa	605	1,438	1,673	1,514	1,652	1,824	2,196	1,986	2,415	3,176	7,921	7,901	8,323	7,657	5,702	9,278
Algeria	612	164	252	270	269	186	101	215	188	682	1,112	888	1,443	1,307	1,442	1,911
Benin	638	9	9	7	9	6	12	17	20	21	22	6	10	10	5	3
Botswana	616	....	....	....	....	....	....	....	....	....	....	....	62	80	113	198
Burkina Faso	748	13	15	17	22	24	33	34	36	44	61	58	54	37	19	36
Burundi	618	9	7	5	3	7	13	14	13	14	8	23	39	75	55	59
Cameroon	622	25	32	22	38	45	71	54	23	25	54	15	29	28	33	89
Cape Verde	624	....	....	....	....	....	....	....	....	....	1	1	28	35	30	32
Central African Rep.	626	10	6	4	4	—	—	—	—	—	1	1	15	19	16	30
Chad	628	13	7	—	—	—	2	10	8	1	10	—	18	14	6	5
Comoros	632	....	....	....	....	....	....	....	....	....	....	....	....	....	....	....
Congo	634	6	5	2	6	4	7	7	5	2	15	8	6	10	6	31
Côte d'Ivoire	662	60	61	69	79	71	105	62	54	47	38	73	54	144	326	81
Djibouti	611															
Equatorial Guinea	642															
Ethiopia	644	70	70	55	54	58	57	48	70	131	208	230	247	168	117	131
Gabon	646	17	11	9	4	7	11	18	14	33	77	118	93	1	13	8
Gambia, The	648	8	9	8	6	6	7	8	8	11	20	21	14	19	19	1
Ghana	652	108	106	77	90	66	37	30	76	130	38	99	72	112	203	206
Guinea-Bissau	654															
Kenya	664	18	48	72	96	166	202	133	157	164	156	144	234	416	260	394
Lesotho	666															
Liberia	668	....	....	....	....	....	....	....	....	....	11	12	11	19	10	35
Madagascar	674	48	48	40	27	16	29	32	34	43	40	29	34	50	37	4
Malawi	676	24	20	21	21	20	26	25	27	47	58	48	18	68	54	50
Mali	678	3	—	1	1	1	1	1	1	1	2	1	3	2	4	3
Mauritania	682	9	7	8	6	2	—	5	9	32	83	39	69	41	60	85
Mauritius	684	20	19	13	16	33	42	40	55	46	104	134	69	52	34	22
Morocco	686	67	54	42	64	93	119	136	152	155	275	258	392	408	462	408
Namibia	728															
Niger	692	2	3	—	2	5	15	26	32	36	31	36	64	76	89	89
Nigeria	694	214	187	84	89	101	174	333	269	385	4,495	4,502	4,063	3,078	1,016	3,808
Rwanda	714	4	5	7	6	3	7	4	5	10	8	19	51	64	62	106
Senegal	722	36	44	35	14	4	18	17	26	1	1	23	21	26	3	3
Seychelles	718	....	....	....	....	....	....	....	....	4	4	5	6	9	7	9
Sierra Leone	724	21	19	16	28	35	34	27	32	32	40	20	19	26	26	35
Somalia	726	9	12	10	7	12	17	18	20	21	26	50	65	95	93	27
South Africa	199	137	144	136	168	130	256	164	442	290	187	374	324	303	286	304
Sudan	732	60	57	55	48	36	22	26	28	37	80	24	20	19	16	41
Swaziland	734	....	....	....	....	....	....	....	....	....	10	37	60	75	83	81
Tanzania	738	....	57	58	73	76	56	42	97	103	39	55	92	226	71	49
Togo	742	16	18	21	24	25	31	32	26	24	37	28	50	31	47	40
Tunisia	744	32	24	36	31	33	55	130	187	231	317	304	293	268	320	414
Uganda	746	....	37	31	45	48	45	15	19	11	9	23	37	34	26	9
Zaïre	636	15	13	57	111	122	92	40	78	108	62	21	16	110	92	157
Zambia	754	193	202	168	187	354	480	217	146	154	123	106	61	43	27	56
Zimbabwe	698	....	65	59	4	28	20	6	56	103	58	68	66	60	114	227
Asia	505	2,965	3,328	3,607	3,981	4,670	4,976	5,198	6,777	7,973	9,771	9,897	15,471	20,952	21,922	25,013
Afghanistan, Islamic State of	512	9	12	5	6	8	11	22	18	14	18	69	108	213	285	312
Bangladesh	513								247	117	113	111	233	188	242	284
Bhutan	514															
China, People's Rep. I	924													1,931	1,195	1,635
Fiji	819	22	18	18	18	27	27	34	60	58	88	122	96	117	99	97
India	534	319	365	419	439	683	698	644	521	382	600	718	2,214	3,862	4,638	5,110
Indonesia	536	17	19	2	I83	118	156	I171	491	624	1,132	493	1,284	1,976	1,889	2,881
Korea	542	138	236	347	388	550	584	369	443	687	225	664	1,689	2,433	2,100	2,209
Lao, P.D. Rep.	544	5	5	4	4	3	3	4	3	5	8	....	....	....	....	....
Malaysia	548	454	473	394	417	521	542	613	733	950	1,152	1,128	1,950	2,213	2,397	2,817
Maldives	556													—	—	—
Myanmar	518	89	93	71	69	46	I31	45	31	66	139	105	94	78	71	150

I See country notes in the monthly IFS

Foreign Exchange

1d s

1980	1981	1982	1983	1984	1985	1986	1987	1988	1989	1990	1991	1992	1993	1994		
End of Period																
292,640	291,942	284,716	308,783	349,011	347,886	363,780	455,837	494,211	544,965	593,596	625,250	646,323	710,057	765,210	All Countries	010
166,350	160,909	154,306	168,994	185,291	189,236	212,080	287,383	315,933	344,997	376,501	360,429	356,767	373,683	393,934	Industrial Countries	110
7,946	8,397	9,257	6,007	6,790	11,704	14,166	9,226	12,903	33,901	36,687	32,112	29,095	30,237	28,233	United States	111
1,616	2,544	2,334	2,619	1,776	1,433	1,895	4,383	10,044	10,767	11,108	9,842	6,823	7,623	7,000	Canada	156
1,070	1,138	5,698	8,375	7,192	4,780	5,464	5,714	9,652	10,007	10,969	11,112	7,662	7,623	7,334	Australia	193
16,910	21,234	17,380	19,451	22,733	20,327	30,786	53,330	67,262	59,347	48,843	43,174	45,009	64,591	78,875	Japan	158
249	532	575	712	1,816	1,447	3,074	2,297	2,099	2,263	2,862	2,008	2,130	2,326	2,439	New Zealand	196
3,738	4,131	4,320	3,712	3,658	3,744	4,524	4,774	4,987	6,041	6,153	6,750	8,368	10,095	10,966	Austria	122
5,147	3,236	2,560	3,607	3,681	3,613	3,785	5,895	6,172	7,427	7,817	7,738	9,327	7,625	8,826	Belgium	124
2,407	1,911	1,778	3,135	2,697	4,556	3,724	6,758	7,598	4,400	7,073	4,759	7,619	7,128	5,784	Denmark	128
1,308	1,073	1,194	1,022	2,530	3,127	1,159	4,222	4,366	3,528	6,475	4,969	3,472	3,635	6,885	Finland	172
19,867	17,162	13,230	17,247	19,488	22,140	23,241	20,889	16,615	16,640	23,946	19,779	17,734	14,567	16,111	France	132
34,860	34,060	35,917	35,640	35,735	35,528	37,497	51,382	39,625	42,508	44,260	40,210	62,463	52,948	49,470	Germany	134
1,000	822	725	773	891	715	‡1,171	1,820	2,618	2,363	2,323	3,552	3,369	5,558	9,810	Greece	174
125	185	130	138	126	183	249	214	211	253	302	310	352	300	190	Iceland	176
2,095	2,112	2,205	2,340	2,186	2,456	2,402	3,123	3,511	2,817	3,409	3,719	2,240	4,062	3,935	Ireland	178
16,966	15,995	11,432	17,693	19,473	12,845	14,824	19,609	24,151	33,693	42,298	31,805	18,157	18,303	20,623	Italy	136
8,181	6,934	7,852	8,312	7,935	8,348	7,834	9,991	10,806	11,435	11,266	11,353	14,718	21,600	22,411	Netherlands	138
4,383	4,963	5,700	5,664	8,822	11,994	9,439	9,254	9,046	9,702	10,054	8,535	8,073	13,572	12,325	Norway	142
589	401	354	337	485	1,224	1,107	2,259	3,777	7,477	10,018	14,164	13,650	11,271	10,348	Portugal	182
8,865	8,759	6,548	6,683	11,679	9,550	11,286	20,644	26,307	30,101	34,722	44,948	32,128	28,974	27,541	Spain	184
2,312	2,704	2,802	3,489	3,483	4,801	4,841	5,276	5,761	6,761	12,206	12,217	15,970	13,375	15,431	Sweden	144
12,018	11,613	13,544	13,711	15,003	15,898	17,441	19,146	17,868	19,199	20,540	20,275	23,593	23,042	22,985	Switzerland	146
14,700	11,003	8,770	8,327	7,112	8,867	12,171	27,178	30,554	24,341	23,145	27,074	24,791	25,210	26,392	United Kingdom	112
126,290	131,032	130,410	139,790	163,720	158,650	151,699	168,454	178,278	199,968	217,095	264,820	289,556	336,374	371,276	Developing Countries	200
13,929	8,922	6,510	6,194	6,150	7,822	6,513	6,603	7,241	8,845	11,470	13,796	11,988	13,045	15,668	Africa	605
2,780	2,939	1,930	1,522	1,215	2,288	1,073	906	667	641	508	1,037	1,059	1,069	1,816	Algeria	612
3	45	—	—	—	2	1	—	1	1	44	132	176	175	175	Benin	638
262	203	250	359	463	690	950	1,419	1,648	2,124	2,342	2,600	2,759	2,983	3,015	Botswana	616
42	48	43	68	95	114	178	214	225	189	198	229	235	266	150	Burkina Faso	748
63	40	15	15	11	18	47	34	42	67	66	89	120	112	134	Burundi	618
136	61	45	144	49	116	45	45	130	60	17	26	14	1	1	Cameroon	622
33	32	38	43	41	49	46	57	60	57	54	45	55	42		Cape Verde	624
43	59	41	42	51	44	53	63	71	86	80	71	73	81	144	Central African Rep.	626
—	2	6	22	44	27	11	30	41	83	89	83	58	28	52	Chad	628
5	7	10	10	3	10	14	21	17	23	21	20	19	. . . .	. . . .	Comoros	632
67	103	29	4	2	2	1	—	2	3	3	3	2	—	34	Congo	634
3	5	2	3	5	4	9	6	7	7	2	8	5	1	140	Côte d'Ivoire	662
				44	45	42	43	46	44	64	68	58	55	50	Djibouti	611
. . . .	. . . .	2	1	1	—	2	—	4	1	—	1	4	—	—	Equatorial Guinea	642
59	219	162	114	42	135	205	85	48	35	14	38	162	325	366	Ethiopia	644
79	164	282	171	198	173	93	—	44	26	192	224	52	—	120	Gabon	646
4	3	7	3	2	2	10	15	13	15	38	47	66	. . . .	65	Gambia, The	648
141	124	126	136	308	418	418	126	164	242	151	376	212	280	380	Ghana	652
						−1	7	12	16	13	10	13	10	13	Guinea-Bissau	654
365	189	176	333	385	343	316	157	183	196	129	69	26	282	369	Kenya	664
37	34	42	61	47	37	47	46	40	35	49	79	111	180	251	Lesotho	666
4	7	6	19	4	1	2	—	—	6	—	1	1	2	3	Liberia	668
7	22	16	28	59	44	94	130	166	187	65	62	. . . .	. . . .	49	Madagascar	674
54	33	17	12	53	39	18	34	104	74	92	105	27	39	23	Malawi	676
6	7	6	7	17	10	1	2	18	79	125	214	215	233	143	Mali	678
110	138	126	100	79	50	37	38	41	63	37	47	44	32	27	Mauritania	682
71	25	33	17	24	27	111	238	325	389	508	605	573	523	483	Mauritius	684
312	196	197	101	49	105	157	287	406	371	1,452	2,064	2,520	2,605	2,933	Morocco	686
												36	97	139	Namibia	728
87	77	. . . .	13	38	80	116	145	166	164	152	133	155	131	67	Niger	692
7,522	2,662	1,421	920	1,481	1,517	884	821	484	1,343	2,715	3,100	703	999	949	Nigeria	694
130	132	98	88	91	86	115	98	73	39	18	64	44	23	. . . .	Rwanda	714
6	4	4	7	3	4	4	5	7	10	7	8	8	1	121	Senegal	722
14	11	11	9	5	8	6	10	6	9	12	19	22	25	20	Seychelles	718
24	13	7	15	8	10	11	4	5	3	4	7	14	21	28	Sierra Leone	724
6	22	5	8	1	2	10	5	11	12	. . . .	. . . .	. . . .	. . . .	. . . .	Somalia	726
404	350	341	689	174	286	302	450	579	729	707	627	721	734	1,153	South Africa	199
38	14	19	16	18	11	48	8	9	12	8	5	20	27	54	Sudan	732
118	73	64	85	78	74	77	87	103	137	144	112	216	184	195	Swaziland	734
16	14	4	18	27	15	45	22	58	41	136	143	228	138	217	Tanzania	738
55	124	148	164	205	270	279	250	172	216	248	255	198	113	64	Togo	742
432	424	515	508	383	185	227	332	647	725	557	529	611	620	999	Tunisia	744
2	23	57	97	‡66	21	20	38	37	11	26	34	62	107	218	Uganda	746
160	106	35	76	140	173	220	127	139	145	154	128	114	34	83	Zaïre	636
61	33	38	52	55	182	57	77	100	88	136	129	. . . .	140	. . . .	Zambia	754
167	137	121	66	44	72	82	101	132	71	105	104	161	314	277	Zimbabwe	698
28,107	34,562	41,062	52,683	65,111	63,961	77,527	96,003	108,280	117,713	125,168	153,809	160,046	186,253	224,603	Asia	505
264	204	203	190	215	252	195	182	180	172	176	155	. . . .	. . . .	. . . .	Afghanistan, Islamic State of	512
235	119	157	465	375	272	304	534	715	357	424	844	1,297	1,738	2,125	Bangladesh	513
. . . .	27	32	38	45	45	49	52	69	74	60	68	56	. . . .	78	Bhutan	514
1,774	4,109	10,094	13,827	‡17,042	10,846	8,596	10,740	13,040	12,953	20,099	29,826	‡14,140	15,434	35,360	China, People's Rep. ‡	924
123	106	106	103	106	106	126	75	150	137	160	174	214	180	170	Fiji	819
4,738	3,234	3,208	4,124	5,136	5,052	4,451	3,950	3,082	2,363	847	2,503	3,972	7,140	13,279	India	534
3,929	3,884	2,350	3,475	4,796	4,405	3,204	3,865	3,677	4,077	5,168	6,397	7,405	8,000	8,097	Indonesia	536
2,283	2,250	2,487	2,130	2,778	2,575	2,699	2,514	9,170	11,397	10,163	9,302	12,102	14,345	17,147	Korea	542
10	10	7	18	11	23	26	15	12	12	43	40	62	110	103	Lao, P.D. Rep.	544
3,226	3,278	3,181	3,352	3,540	4,207	4,657	4,973	4,558	5,626	6,556	7,285	12,207	19,522	17,048	Malaysia	548
—	1	7	4	5	4	6	6	16	19	17	16	20	18	20	Maldives	556
199	185	80	78	56	31	27	19	57	200	219	181	204	220	289	Myanmar	518

‡ See country notes in the monthly *IFS*

Foreign Exchange

1d *s*

		1965	1966	1967	1968	1969	1970	1971	1972	1973	1974	1975	1976	1977	1978	1979
																Millions of SDRs:
Asia (cont.)																
Nepal	558	56	41	42	53	73	86	85	85	92	94	76	ⲓ108	113	108	117
Pakistan	564	176	154	111	193	278	126	106	184	315	301	266	369	341	282	128
Papua New Guinea	853									26	27	153	220	351	310	379
Philippines	566	151	122	120	99	76	195	285	420	799	1,164	1,099	1,361	1,199	1,340	1,682
Singapore	576	430	387	488	705	819	1,005	1,328	1,601	1,885	2,287	2,559	2,886	3,166	4,057	4,383
Solomon Islands	813													2	22	28
Sri Lanka	524	73	43	55	52	40	43	46	42	58	49	38	67	221	279	370
Thailand	578	624	808	893	905	869	790	678	825	938	1,373	1,371	1,485	1,428	1,515	1,362
Tonga	866													7	8	10
Vanuatu	846															
Viet Nam	582	153	275	299	245	194	195	195	191	101	136					
Western Samoa	862	4	3	2	3	5	5	6	4	4	4	5	5	7	4	4
Europe	170	272	311	271	381	612	708	1,116	2,206	3,242	2,741	2,456	3,742	3,229	3,608	3,238
Cyprus	423	84	98	101	137	158	184	233	262	222	194	159	228	253	257	252
Czech Republic	935															
Czechoslovakia ⲓ	934															
Hungary	944															
Malta	181	79	90	90	ⲓ136	125	143	163	232	248	307	402	504	575	691	746
Poland	964															429
Romania	968									172	191	453	471	204	289	398
Turkey	186	25	29	22	26	128	304	577	1,096	1,580	1,203	779	834	525	615	499
Yugoslavia, SFR	188	84	94	58	82	202	78	143	615	1,019	846	664	1,704	1,672	1,756	913
Middle East	405	2,010	2,317	2,651	2,507	2,668	3,487	5,828	8,124	9,804	26,808	33,901	40,411	48,611	38,093	44,233
Bahrain	419	23	13	20	42	60	63	79	74	51	102	238	371	410	373	458
Egypt	469	54	63	102	75	51	74	45	42	184	175	151	186	331	369	402
Iran, I.R. of	429	102	121	149	133	152	76	440	700	809	6,250	6,454	6,410	8,911	8,372	11,053
Iraq	433	109	199	254	240	264	319	398	536	1,097	2,480	2,136	3,761	5,553		
Israel	436	575	553	646	594	367	405	622	1,057	1,405	940	969	1,135	1,230	1,994	2,289
Jordan	439	134	161	238	251	229	219	194	209	211	242	379	393	516	667	864
Kuwait	443	60	85	35	39	83	96	158	227	296	764	700	722	1,651	1,331	1,789
Lebanon	446	67	87	86	42	58	96	179	297	389	1,042	1,024	1,119	1,289	1,406	1,159
Libya	672	174	267	313	449	828	1,499	2,364	2,603	1,672	2,862	1,784	2,668	3,934	3,145	4,743
Oman	449						10	21	31	37	60	113	163	218	180	300
Qatar	453		18	23	26	29	30	35	44	51	47	70	95	119	147	201
Saudi Arabia	456	635	656	670	520	465	520	1,189	2,162	3,073	10,964	18,242	20,947	22,402	ⲓ12,842	13,192
Syrian Arab Rep.	463	26	34	55	39	31	27	53	93	306	372	585	233	392	287	429
United Arab Emirates	466									72	300	729	1,527	562	551	1,010
Yemen Arab Rep.	473									101	158	284	615	1,013	1,111	1,069
Yemen, P.D. Rep.	459	52	61	61	59	53	53	50	50	51	51	43	67	78	141	156
Yemen, Republic of	474															
Western Hemisphere	205	2,032	1,935	2,157	2,551	2,948	3,559	4,000	7,095	9,843	12,619	13,354	17,792	20,682	24,421	29,056
Antigua and Barbuda	311											6	8	4	5	9
Argentina	213	170	132	625	554	285	343	64	271	885	840	211	1,165	2,522	3,520	6,724
Aruba	314															
Bahamas, The	313				44	26	22	27	34	36	36	41	36	ⲓ50	40	51
Barbados	316		12	9	16	12	15	14	21	22	27	28	18	24	40	43
Belize	339												5	7	11	8
Bolivia	218	29	27	22	29	30	30	34	38	43	141	112	117	161	107	135
Brazil	223	421	368	142	200	599	962	1,336	3,533	4,999	3,981	3,120	5,251	5,587	8,755	6,333
Chile	228	94	127	81	162	296	320	118	87	100	20	27	300	296	778	1,412
Colombia	233	61	52	52	142	195	189	165	267	366	288	346	878	1,336	1,709	2,772
Costa Rica	238	18	15	16	18	25	8	25	33	36	32	38	81	151	138	78
Dominica	321											—	1	2	1	7
Dominican Republic	243	48	41	29	33	37	29	49	44	52	64	90	100	143	114	174
Ecuador	248	35	50	52	31	43	55	31	105	163	245	197	405	505	469	520
El Salvador	253	33	39	37	44	47	45	40	55	30	60	87	156	161	189	87
Grenada	328						5	5	5	4	4	ⲓ4	7	6	7	9
Guatemala	258	46	41	45	45	54	59	58	90	138	128	222	399	527	545	496
Guyana	336	20	16	18	22	19	19	22	29	8	45	77	20	16	42	10
Haiti	263	1	2	2	3	4	4	6	11	12	14	9	23	26	23	32
Honduras	268	23	27	23	29	26	20	17	27	23	31	79	110	144	132	145
Jamaica	343	91	80	78	113	109	123	139	140	99	150	103	27	25	41	48
Mexico	273	325	369	325	359	381	385	507	673	736	784	998	1,022	1,311	1,371	1,420
Netherlands Antilles	353				20	28	25	34	46	41	50	61	80	83	51	55
Nicaragua	278	57	57	27	48	44	48	50	68	91	80	99	122	118	35	111
Panama	283	6	6	7	11	14	11	12	29	24	30	23	63	54	108	84
Paraguay	288	7	8	8	8	6	10	10	18	36	60	87	123	207	331	445
Peru	293	98	78	106	91	142	ⲓ282	322	367	368	688	296	246	291	294	1,073
St. Kitts and Nevis	361															
St. Lucia	362											3	4	5	5	6
St. Vincent & Grens.	364												4	4	4	7
Suriname	366	17	17	8	9	24	28	30	35	47	55	78	95	77	97	121
Trinidad and Tobago	369	28	28	29	48	42	36	50	40	32	306	615	837	1,180	1,339	1,556
Uruguay	298	24	30	20	34	19	14	19	56	73	54	48	148	257	242	ⲓ203
Venezuela	299	380	313	398	438	441	472	816	974	1,379	4,407	6,249	5,941	5,399	3,877	4,881
Memorandum Items																
Oil Exporting Countries	999	1,854	2,116	2,197	2,285	2,665	3,453	6,139	8,225	10,175	34,874	42,360	49,023	55,110	39,969	50,889
Non-Oil Developing Countries	201	6,863	7,448	8,002	8,787	10,058	11,474	11,989	18,392	23,863	24,987	25,149	36,716	46,021	53,777	59,927

ⲓ See country notes in the monthly *IFS*

Foreign Exchange

1980	1981	1982	1983	1984	1985	1986	1987	1988	1989	1990	1991	1992	1993	1994	Country	Code
															Asia (cont.)	
138	168	174	121	78	45	65	120	158	155	202	272	334	460	469	Nepal	558
366	571	773	1,795	930	711	569	343	288	395	207	363	618	871	2,006	Pakistan	564
328	307	379	398	434	392	340	298	282	283	283	226	173	103	66	Papua New Guinea	853
2,231	1,773	802	713	586	501	1,369	644	707	1,039	610	2,227	3,115	3,310	4,018	Philippines	566
5,089	6,395	7,570	8,721	10,499	11,549	10,424	10,573	12,530	15,322	19,354	23,721	28,845	34,994	39,654	Singapore	576
22	17	32	43	44	31	22	25	29	19	12	5	17	14		Solomon Islands	813
192	261	306	266	515	405	288	197	165	176	297	479	654	1,166	1,381	Sri Lanka	524
1,217	1,436	1,372	1,491	1,928	1,964	2,237	2,753	4,456	7,199	9,311	12,085	14,554	17,530	19,786	Thailand	578
11	12	14	20	27	24	18	20	22	18	21	21	22	25	23	Tonga	866
....	7	4	5	7	8	16	26	28	25	24	26	29	31	27	Vanuatu	846
....	14	15	12	13	11	10	....	....	....	....	....	....	....	....	Viet Nam	582
2	3	3	6	11	13	19	25	34	41	46	45	42	34	32	Western Samoa	862
4,746	**4,751**	**4,774**	**6,662**	**8,365**	**7,003**	**7,626**	**7,409**	**9,405**	**14,232**	**15,081**	**15,102**	**14,396**	**16,440**	**18,589**	**Europe**	**170**
282	363	474	491	547	537	611	611	678	837	1,044	954	722	773	978	Cyprus	423
....	....	....	....	....	....	....	....	....	....	....	....	....	2,753	4,209	Czech Republic	935
1,442	821	703	767	986	778	912	974	1,176	1,641	775	2,132	ɪ784	....	....	Czechoslovakia ɪ	934
....	....	....	1,093	1,591	1,960	1,882	1,152	1,090	948	752	2,751	3,162	4,871	4,608	Hungary	944
749	884	935	1,003	944	829	861	919	937	954	928	847	864	931	1,206	Malta	181
100	239	586	731	1,128	792	570	1,054	1,527	1,761	3,157	2,534	2,903	2,901	3,923	Poland	964
253	346	396	501	723	181	476	988	580	1,338	368	445	593	723	1,391	Romania	968
844	797	979	1,197	1,264	929	1,122	1,219	1,710	3,605	4,220	3,564	4,447	4,533	4,878	Turkey	186
1,075	1,300	699	880	1,181	996	1,193	492	1,708	3,147	3,838	1,875	....	....	....	Yugoslavia, SFR	188
51,660	**53,124**	**55,753**	**49,524**	**45,564**	**45,052**	**35,490**	**34,389**	**32,005**	**35,368**	**33,082**	**37,774**	**40,504**	**43,387**	**42,638**	**Middle East**	**405**
737	1,313	1,365	1,329	1,293	1,473	1,177	768	887	754	823	1,011	967	896	748	Bahrain	419
820	591	633	706	751	721	678	971	939	1,157	1,886	3,722	7,765	9,290	9,121	Egypt	469
7,540	947	4,793	....	....	....	....	....	....	....	....	....	....	....	....	Iran, I.R. of	429
....	....	....	....	....	....	....	....	....	....	....	....	....	....	....	Iraq	433
2,593	3,004	3,480	3,451	3,122	3,350	3,809	4,142	2,984	4,015	4,411	4,389	3,729	4,646	4,653	Israel	436
868	902	768	763	510	363	338	291	81	350	596	577	546	1,188	1,159	Jordan	439
2,670	3,049	4,837	4,227	3,890	4,237	3,853	2,393	1,015	2,104	1,134	2,144	3,516	2,851	2,200	Kuwait	443
1,239	1,295	2,356	1,798	665	957	378	237	704	690	438	865	1,060	1,616	2,630	Lebanon	446
10,069	7,441	6,081	4,638	3,331	4,975	4,446	3,674	2,749	2,804	3,574	3,415	3,899	....	....	Libya	672
436	618	762	687	876	950	748	949	746	992	1,137	1,125	1,400	618	629	Oman	449
248	288	317	321	333	352	416	383	305	358	395	414	443	453	400	Qatar	453
16,267	24,054	21,587	16,674	14,474	12,528	5,806	7,603	8,337	8,589	6,032	6,807	3,317	4,137	4,033	Saudi Arabia	456
247	229	168	41	268	73	118	157	143	....	....	....	....	....	....	Syrian Arab Rep.	463
1,479	2,574	ɪ1,757	1,703	2,045	2,647	2,497	3,092	3,077	3,167	3,005	3,529	3,943	4,227	4,357	United Arab Emirates	466
985	813	488	335	310	247	330	361	188	197	....	....	....	....	....	Yemen Arab Rep.	473
174	213	246	248	234	168	109	66	45	57	....	....	....	....	....	Yemen, P.D. Rep.	459
....	....	....	....	....	....	....	....	....	....	287	463	230	105	....	Yemen, Republic of	474
27,847	**29,674**	**22,312**	**24,727**	**38,531**	**34,813**	**24,542**	**24,051**	**21,346**	**23,810**	**32,294**	**44,339**	**62,623**	**77,249**	**69,778**	**Western Hemisphere**	**205**
6	6	8	9	16	15	23	18	21	21	19	23	37	28	32	Antigua and Barbuda	311
4,749	2,222	2,181	1,119	1,267	ɪ2,980	2,222	1,140	2,499	1,113	3,019	4,063	6,992	9,711	9,428	Argentina	213
....	....	....	....	....	....	60	55	68	66	69	84	103	132	122	Aruba	314
61	73	90	104	153	155	178	109	118	103	103	119	106	119	115	Bahamas, The	313
55	80	109	115	133	125	122	100	98	81	80	60	102	109	134	Barbados	316
10	9	8	7	4	12	20	24	36	44	47	35	35	25	20	Belize	339
83	86	141	153	257	182	132	69	79	156	117	74	123	144	283	Bolivia	218
3,953	5,059	3,301	4,160	11,739	9,654	ɪ4,744	4,440	5,181	5,734	5,222	5,607	16,378	22,279	25,392	Brazil	223
2,382	2,680	1,557	1,940	2,338	2,230	1,922	1,736	2,316	2,743	4,265	4,922	6,667	7,018	8,965	Chile	228
3,588	3,802	3,163	1,365	1,392	1,452	2,090	2,061	2,299	2,637	2,846	4,101	5,263	5,303	5,106	Colombia	233
114	113	205	294	413	461	428	345	496	565	365	643	732	737	603	Costa Rica	238
4	2	4	1	5	3	7	12	10	9	10	12	15	14	11	Dominica	321
158	192	116	156	258	281	308	128	189	125	43	309	363	464	170	Dominican Republic	243
753	490	276	604	623	628	481	346	294	411	579	617	614	984	1,243	Ecuador	248
61	62	97	153	169	164	139	131	120	202	292	201	307	390	445	El Salvador	253
10	14	8	13	15	19	17	16	13	12	12	12	19	20	21	Grenada	328
309	118	102	192	278	274	296	202	149	232	198	564	545	620	580	Guatemala	258
10	5	7	6	6	6	7	6	3	10	19	86	137	180	169	Guyana	336
13	21	3	8	13	6	8	12	10	9	2	12	....	....	....	Haiti	263
117	85	100	102	131	96	91	75	37	16	28	73	143	71	117	Honduras	268
82	70	95	60	99	147	80	122	109	82	118ᵉ	74	227	295	504	Jamaica	343
2,108	3,187	751	3,625	7,416	4,466	4,628	8,288	3,630	4,525	6,640	11,982	13,377	18,118	4,179	Mexico	273
74	116	170	157	120	160	195	153	195	158	151	124	160	170	123	Netherlands Antilles	353
51	96	154	167	....	....	....	12	28	88	75	94	95	40	97	Nicaragua	278
83	100	88	188	220	77	138	55	54	91	222	341	352	423	471	Panama	283
571	652	619	587	612	415	298	286	178	266	399	603	329	378	614	Paraguay	288
1,543	1,021	1,194	1,304	1,641	1,677	1,150	455	380	615	731	1,708	2,072	2,480	4,790	Peru	293
....	3	3	3	6	7	8	7	8	12	11	12	19	21	22	St. Kitts and Nevis	361
6	6	7	8	13	12	21	22	24	29	30	33	39	42	38	St. Lucia	362
6	8	4	5	13	13	21	14	16	17	19	16	24	22	20	St. Vincent & Grens.	364
138	165	143	52	24	21	17	11	9	7	15	—	—	—	—	Suriname	366
2,082	2,746	2,622	1,797	1,154	795	198	79	94	181	345	235	125	150	241	Trinidad and Tobago	369
248	304	104	185	132	145	384	326	373	364	360	231	355	536	648	Uruguay	298
4,418	6,084	4,883	6,086	7,872	8,136	4,109	3,197	2,211	3,086	5,842	7,268	6,755	6,211	5,064	Venezuela	299
															Memorandum Items	
62,647	60,334	56,833	52,856	53,776	54,046	37,823	36,184	33,073	37,201	38,785	44,462	42,037	41,831	40,029	Oil Exporting Countries	999
63,643	70,698	73,578	86,934	109,944	104,604	113,877	132,270	145,205	162,767	178,310	220,358	247,520	294,543	331,247	Non-Oil Developing Countries	201

ɪ See country notes in the monthly *IFS*

Gold (Million Ounces)

1ad		1965	1966	1967	1968	1969	1970	1971	1972	1973	1974	1975	1976	1977	1978	1979
														Millions of Ounces:		
All Countries	010	1,193.58	1,165.73	1,126.40	1,107.36	1,112.90	1,059.74	1,030.28	1,021.52	1,024.09	1,022.08	1,019.87	1,015.38	1,030.35	1,037.98	946.89
Industrial Countries	110	1,101.22	1,070.70	1,023.10	972.13	979.68	941.41	919.66	904.66	904.62	905.11	903.74	903.51	908.40	910.07	815.00
United States	111	401.86	378.14	344.71	311.20	338.83	316.34	291.60	275.97	275.97	275.97	274.71	274.68	277.55	276.41	264.60
Canada	156	32.88	29.87	29.00	24.66	24.92	22.59	22.69	21.95	21.95	21.95	21.95	21.62	22.01	22.13	22.18
Australia	193	7.07	6.40	6.60	7.34	7.51	6.83	7.43	7.40	7.37	7.38	7.38	7.36	7.65	7.79	7.93
Japan	158	9.38	9.42	9.68	10.17	11.81	15.22	19.42	21.10	21.11	21.11	21.11	21.11	21.62	23.97	24.23
New Zealand	196	.01	.01	.01	.02	.02	.02	.02	.02	.02	.02	.02	.02	.04	.07	.05
Austria	122	20.01	20.02	20.03	20.41	20.42	20.39	20.82	20.85	20.88	20.88	20.88	20.88	21.00	21.05	21.11
Belgium	124	44.52	43.56	42.26	43.53	43.40	42.01	44.12	43.08	42.17	42.17	42.17	42.17	42.45	42.59	34.21
Denmark	128	2.78	3.09	3.09	3.26	2.54	1.84	1.81	1.81	1.81	1.81	1.81	1.81	1.93	1.98	1.64
Finland	172	2.39	1.29	1.29	1.28	1.29	1.29	.82	1.40	1.40	.82	.82	.82	.90	.95	.99
France	132	134.46	149.66	149.54	110.77	101.34	100.91	100.66	100.69	100.91	100.93	100.93	101.02	101.67	101.99	81.92
Germany	134	126.00	122.62	120.79	129.69	116.56	113.70	116.47	117.36	117.61	117.61	117.61	117.61	118.30	118.64	95.25
Greece	174	2.21	3.42	3.72	3.99	3.71	3.33	2.81	3.50	3.50	3.61	3.63	3.65	3.73	3.77	3.81
Iceland	176	.03	.03	.03	.03	.03	.03	.03	.03	.03	.03	.03	.03	.04	.04	.05
Ireland	178	.60	.66	.71	2.26	1.11	.46	.46	.46	.43	.45	.45	.45	.47	.45	.38
Italy	136	68.68	68.97	68.57	83.52	84.46	82.48	82.40	82.37	82.48	82.48	82.48	82.48	82.91	83.12	66.71
Luxembourg	137	.30	.34	.34	.44	.44	.44	.44	.44	.44	.44	.44	.44	.45	.46	.46
Netherlands	138	50.19	49.45	48.91	48.51	49.16	51.06	54.53	54.17	54.33	54.33	54.33	54.33	54.63	54.78	43.97
Norway	142	.88	.52	.52	.68	.72	.67	.95	.98	.98	.98	.98	.98	1.08	1.13	1.18
Portugal	182	16.46	18.37	19.97	24.46	25.00	25.77	26.31	26.88	27.54	27.84	27.72	27.67	24.11	22.13	22.13
Spain	184	23.15	22.44	22.42	22.42	22.41	14.23	14.23	14.27	14.27	14.27	14.27	14.27	14.44	14.52	14.61
Sweden	144	5.77	5.80	5.80	6.43	6.45	5.72	5.78	5.78	5.79	5.79	5.79	5.79	5.93	6.00	6.07
Switzerland	146	86.91	81.17	88.26	74.97	75.49	78.03	83.11	83.11	83.20	83.20	83.20	83.28	83.28	83.28	83.28
United Kingdom	112	64.70	55.47	36.86	42.09	42.06	38.52	22.18	21.08	21.01	21.03	21.03	21.03	22.23	22.83	18.25
Developing Countries	200	92.36	95.03	103.30	135.23	133.22	118.33	110.62	116.86	119.47	116.97	116.12	111.87	121.94	127.91	131.89
Africa	605	14.15	21.01	24.00	44.40	42.02	28.84	21.32	27.29	28.60	26.64	25.75	20.58	17.87	18.27	18.79
Algeria	612	.16	.16	4.44	5.86	5.86	5.47	5.47	5.47	5.47	5.47	5.47	5.47	5.50	5.53	5.58
Benin	638	....	....	....	....	....	....	....	....	....	....	....	—	.01	.01	.01
Botswana	616	....	....	....	....	....	....	....	....	....	....	....	....	....	....	....
Burkina Faso	748	....	....	....	....	....	....	....	....	....	....	....	....	.01	.01	.01
Burundi	618	....	....	....	—	—	—	....	....	....	....	....	....	.01	.01	.01
Cameroon	622	....	....	....	....	....	....	....	....	....	....	....	....	.02	.02	.03
Cape Verde	624															
Central African Rep.	626	....	....	....	....	....	....	....	....	....	....	....	....	.01	.01	.01
Chad	628	....	....	....	....	....	....	....	....	....	....	....	....	.01	.01	.01
Comoros	632															
Congo	634	....	....	....	....	....	....	....	....	....	....	....	....	.01	.01	.01
Côte d'Ivoire	662	....	....	....	....	....	....	....	....	....	....	....	—	.02	.03	.04
Djibouti	611															
Equatorial Guinea	642															
Ethiopia	644	.09	.11	.13	.23	.27	.23	.24	.25	.26	.28	.28	.28	.29	.29	.29
Gabon	646	....	....	....	....	....	....	....	....	....	....	....	—	.01	.01	.01
Gambia, The	648															
Ghana	652	.16	.16	.16	.16	.16	.16	.16	.16	.16	.16	.16	.16	.20	.22	.22
Guinea-Bissau	654															
Kenya	664	....	....	....	....	....	....	....	....	—	—	—	—	.02	.07	.08
Lesotho	666															
Liberia	668															
Madagascar	674	....	....	....	....	....	....	....	....	....	....	....	....	.01	.01	.01
Malawi	676	....	....	....	....	....	....	....	....	....	....	....	....	.01	.01	.02
Mali	678	....	....	....	....	....	....	....	....	....	....	....	....	.01	.01	.01
Mauritania	682	....	....	....	....	....	....	....	....	....	....	....	....	.01	.03	.04
Mauritius	684															
Morocco	686	.60	.60	.60	.60	.60	.60	.60	.60	.60	.61	.61	.61	.63	.68	.70
Namibia	728															
Niger	692	....	....	....	....	....	....	....	....	....	....	....	....	.01	.01	.01
Nigeria	694	.57	.57	.57	.57	.57	.57	.54	.54	.57	.57	.57	.57	.63	.63	.69
Rwanda	714															
Senegal	722	....	....	....	....	....	....	....	....	....	....	....	—	.01	.02	.03
Seychelles	718															
Sierra Leone	724															
Somalia	726	—	—	—	.02	—	—	—	—	—	—	—	—	.01	.01	.01
South Africa	199	12.14	18.20	16.64	35.51	31.86	19.03	11.72	17.93	18.99	18.25	17.75	12.67	9.72	9.79	10.03
Sudan	732															
Swaziland	734															
Tanzania	738															
Togo	742	....	....	....	....	....	....	....	....	....	....	....	—	.01	.01	.01
Tunisia	744	.11	.11	.12	.12	.12	.13	.13	.13	.13	.13	.13	.13	.15	.16	.17
Uganda	746															
Zaire	636	.09	.10	.12	.36	1.57	1.43	1.44	1.45	1.46	.50	.26	.26	.26	.31	.25
Zambia	754	.22	.36	.36	.18	.18	.18	.20	.20	.20	.17	.17	.17	.17	.20	.22
Zimbabwe	698	....	.63	.86	.80	.80	1.05	.82	.55	.75	.50	.35	.27	.15	.16	.26
Asia	505	19.30	18.62	20.42	21.60	21.02	19.99	19.28	19.00	18.01	18.02	17.33	17.29	31.08	33.07	34.00
Afghanistan, Islamic State of	512	1.04	1.00	.94	.94	.94	.99	.93	.93	.93	.93	.93	.93	.94	.95	.96
Bangladesh	513													.05	.03	.05
Bhutan	514															
China, People's Rep.	924													12.80	12.80	12.80
Fiji	819													.01	.01	.01
India	534	8.03	6.95	6.95	6.95	6.95	6.95	6.95	6.95	6.95	6.95	6.95	6.95	7.36	8.36	8.56
Indonesia	536	.11	.11	.11	.11	.11	.11	.06	.12	.06	.06	.06	.06	.17	.22	.28
Korea	542	.09	.10	.10	.10	.10	.10	.10	.11	.11	.11	.11	.11	.15	.27	.30
Lao, P.D. Rep.	544															
Malaysia	548	.06	.03	.89	1.89	1.80	1.37	1.66	1.66	1.66	1.66	1.66	1.66	1.74	1.89	2.13
Maldives	556															
Myanmar	518	2.39	2.39	2.39	2.39	2.39	1.79	.62	.32	.20	.20	.20	.20	.23	.24	.25
Nepal	558	.09	.09	.09	.27	.23	.15	.14	.14	.13	.13	.13	.13	.13	.15	.15
Pakistan	564	1.55	1.55	1.55	1.56	1.56	1.56	1.58	1.59	1.59	1.59	1.59	1.62	1.62	1.72	1.82
Papua New Guinea	853													.03	.04	.05
Philippines	566	1.09	1.26	1.71	1.77	1.29	1.60	1.91	1.86	1.06	1.06	1.06	1.06	1.06	1.51	1.70
Singapore	576															
Solomon Islands	813															
Sri Lanka	524														.04	.06
Thailand	578	2.76	2.62	2.62	2.62	2.62	2.34	2.34	2.34	2.34	2.34	2.34	2.34	2.40	2.43	2.46
Tonga	866															
Vanuatu	846															
Viet Nam	582	.54	.74	.74	.69	.69	.69	.69	.69	.69	.69	.69	....	....	....	....

Gold (Million Ounces)

1ad

	1980	1981	1982	1983	1984	1985	1986	1987	1988	1989	1990	1991	1992	1993	1994		
End of Period																	
	955.52	**955.15**	**951.23**	**950.11**	**948.98**	**951.45**	**951.44**	**945.94**	**946.65**	**940.93**	**938.90**	**937.80**	**929.29**	**912.60**	**909.79**	**All Countries**	**010**
	813.88	**813.62**	**813.29**	**810.92**	**810.40**	**810.84**	**809.12**	**804.79**	**801.12**	**797.80**	**795.81**	**793.68**	**785.24**	**770.83**	**768.05**	**Industrial Countries**	**110**
	264.32	264.11	264.03	263.39	262.79	262.65	262.04	262.38	261.87	261.93	261.91	261.91	261.84	261.79	261.73	United States	**111**
	20.98	20.46	20.26	20.17	20.14	20.11	19.72	18.52	17.14	16.10	14.76	12.96	9.94	6.05	3.89	Canada	**156**
	7.93	7.93	7.93	7.93	7.93	7.93	7.93	7.93	7.93	7.93	7.93	7.93	7.93	7.90	7.90	Australia	**193**
	24.23	24.23	24.23	24.23	24.23	24.23	24.23	24.23	24.23	24.23	24.23	24.23	24.23	24.23	24.23	Japan	**158**
	.02	.02	.02	.02	.02	.02	.02	.02	.02	—	—	—	—	—	—	New Zealand	**196**
	21.11	21.11	21.12	21.13	21.13	21.14	21.14	21.15	21.15	20.66	20.39	20.03	19.93	18.60	18.34	Austria	**122**
	34.18	34.18	34.18	34.18	34.18	34.18	34.18	33.63	33.67	30.23	30.23	30.23	25.04	25.04	25.04	Belgium	**124**
	1.63	1.63	1.63	1.63	1.63	1.63	1.63	1.63	1.63	1.64	1.65	1.66	1.66	1.64	1.63	Denmark	**128**
	.99	1.27	1.27	1.27	1.27	1.91	1.91	1.96	1.96	2.00	2.00	2.00	2.00	2.00	2.00	Finland	**172**
	81.85	81.85	81.85	81.85	81.85	81.85	81.85	81.85	81.85	81.85	81.85	81.85	81.85	81.85	81.85	France	**132**
	95.18	95.18	95.18	95.18	95.18	95.18	95.18	95.18	95.18	95.18	95.18	95.18	95.18	95.18	95.18	Germany	**134**
	3.84	3.85	3.87	3.88	4.11	4.12	3.31	3.34	3.40	3.40	3.40	3.43	3.43	3.44	3.45	Greece	**174**
	.05	.05	.05	.05	.05	.05	.05	.05	.05	.05	.05	.05	.05	.05	.05	Iceland	**176**
	.36	.36	.36	.36	.36	.36	.36	.36	.36	.36	.36	.36	.36	.36	.36	Ireland	**178**
	66.67	66.67	66.67	66.67	66.67	66.67	66.67	66.67	66.67	66.67	66.67	66.67	66.67	66.67	66.67	Italy	**136**
	.46	.46	.46	.46	.43	.43	.43	.43	.43	.34	.34	.34	.34	.31	.31	Luxembourg	**137**
	43.94	43.94	43.94	43.94	43.94	43.94	43.94	43.94	43.94	43.94	43.94	43.94	43.94	35.05	34.77	Netherlands	**138**
	1.18	1.18	1.18	1.18	1.18	1.18	1.18	1.18	1.18	1.18	1.18	1.18	1.18	1.18	1.18	Norway	**142**
	22.17	22.14	22.09	20.43	20.30	20.23	20.16	20.06	16.07	16.05	15.83	15.87	16.06	16.06	16.07	Portugal	**182**
	14.61	14.61	14.61	14.61	14.63	14.65	14.82	11.92	14.04	15.72	15.61	15.62	15.62	15.62	15.62	Spain	**184**
	6.07	6.07	6.07	6.07	6.07	6.07	6.07	6.07	6.07	6.07	6.07	6.07	6.07	6.07	6.07	Sweden	**144**
	83.28	83.28	83.28	83.28	83.28	83.28	83.28	83.28	83.28	83.28	83.28	83.28	83.28	83.28	83.28	Switzerland	**146**
	18.84	19.03	19.01	19.01	19.03	19.03	19.01	19.01	19.00	18.99	18.94	18.89	18.61	18.45	18.44	United Kingdom	**112**
	141.64	**141.53**	**137.94**	**139.19**	**138.59**	**140.61**	**142.32**	**141.15**	**145.53**	**143.13**	**143.08**	**144.11**	**144.05**	**141.77**	**141.74**	**Developing Countries**	**200**
	21.13	**18.45**	**16.74**	**17.18**	**16.73**	**14.05**	**13.87**	**14.79**	**12.32**	**11.75**	**12.06**	**14.95**	**15.24**	**13.30**	**12.69**	**Africa**	**605**
	5.58	5.58	5.58	5.58	5.58	5.58	5.58	5.58	5.58	5.58	5.14	5.58	5.58	5.58	5.58	Algeria	**612**
	.01	.01	.01	.01	.01	.01	.01	.01	.01	.01	.01	.01	.01	.01	.01	Benin	**638**
	....	....	....	....	....	....	....	....	....	....	....	....	....	....	....	Botswana	**616**
	.01	.01	.01	.01	.01	.01	.01	.01	.01	.01	.01	.01	.01	.01	.01	Burkina Faso	**748**
	.02	.02	.02	.02	.02	.02	.02	.02	.02	.02	.02	.02	.02	.02	.02	Burundi	**618**
	.03	.03	.03	.03	.03	.03	.03	.03	.03	.03	.03	.03	.03	.03	....	Cameroon	**622**
	—	—	—	—	—	—	—	—	—	....	....	....	....	....	....	Cape Verde	**624**
	.01	.01	.01	.01	.01	.01	.01	.01	.01	.01	.01	.01	.01	.01	.01	Central African Rep.	**626**
	.01	.01	.01	.01	.01	.01	.01	.01	.01	.01	.01	.01	.01	.01	....	Chad	**628**
	....	....	....	—	—	—	—	—	—	—	—	—	—	....	....	Comoros	**632**
	.01	.01	.01	.01	.01	.01	.01	.01	.01	.01	.01	.01	.01	.01	.01	Congo	**634**
	.04	.04	.04	.04	.04	.04	.04	.04	.04	.04	.04	.04	.04	.04	.04	Côte d'Ivoire	**662**
	....	....	....	....	....	....	....	....	....	....	....	....	....	....	....	Djibouti	**611**
	....	....	....	....	....	....	....	....	....	....	....	....	....	....	....	Equatorial Guinea	**642**
	.31	.26	.21	.21	.21	.21	.21	.21	.21	.19	.09	.15	.11	.11	.11	Ethiopia	**644**
	.01	.01	.01	.01	.01	.01	.01	.01	.01	.01	.01	.01	.01	.01	....	Gabon	**646**
	....	....	....	....	....	....	....	....	....	....	....	....	....	....	....	Gambia, The	**648**
	.25	.31	.38	.38	.44	.23	.28	.28	.22	.22	.24	.27	.28	.27	.28	Ghana	**652**
	....	....	....	....	....	....	....	....	....	....	....	....	....	....	....	Guinea-Bissau	**654**
	.08	.08	.08	.08	.08	.08	.08	.08	.08	.08	.08	.08	.08	.08	.08	Kenya	**664**
	....	....	....	....	....	....	....	....	....	....	....	....	....	....	....	Lesotho	**666**
	....	....	....	....	....	....	....	....	....	....	....	....	....	....	....	Liberia	**668**
	....	....	....	....	....	....	....	....	....	....	....	....	....	....	....	Madagascar	**674**
	.01	.01	.01	.01	.01	.01	.01	.01	.01	.01	.01	.01	.01	.01	.01	Malawi	**676**
	.02	.02	.02	.02	.02	.02	.02	.02	.02	.02	.02	.02	.02	.02	.02	Mali	**678**
	.01	.01	.01	.01	.01	.01	.01	.01	.01	.01	.01	.01	.01	.01	.01	Mauritania	**682**
	.04	.04	.04	.04	.04	.04	.04	.04	.05	.06	.06	.06	.06	.06	.06	Mauritius	**684**
	.70	.70	.70	.70	.70	.70	.70	.70	.70	.70	.70	.70	.70	.70	.70	Morocco	**686**
	....	....	....	....	....	....	....	....	....	....	—	—	—	—	—	Namibia	**728**
	.01	.01	.01	.01	.01	.01	.01	.01	.01	.01	.01	.01	.01	.01	.01	Niger	**692**
	.69	.69	.69	.69	.69	.69	.69	.69	.69	.69	.69	.69	.69	.69	.69	Nigeria	**694**
	—	—	—	—	—	—	—	—	—	—	—	—	—	—	....	Rwanda	**714**
	.03	.03	.03	.03	.03	.03	.03	.03	.03	.03	.03	.03	.03	.03	.03	Senegal	**722**
	....	....	....	....	....	....	....	....	....	....	....	....	....	....	....	Seychelles	**718**
	....	....	....	....	....	....	....	....	....	....	....	....	....	....	....	Sierra Leone	**724**
	.02	.02	.02	.02	.02	.02	.02	.02	.02	.02	....	....	....	....	....	Somalia	**726**
	12.15	9.29	7.57	7.79	7.36	4.84	4.82	5.83	3.47	3.08	4.09	6.47	6.65	4.76	4.20	South Africa	**199**
	....	....	....	....	....	....	....	....	....	....	....	....	....	....	....	Sudan	**732**
	....	....	....	....	....	....	....	....	....	....	....	....	....	....	....	Swaziland	**734**
	....	....	....	....	....	....	....	....	....	....	....	....	....	....	....	Tanzania	**738**
	.01	.01	.01	.01	.01	.01	.01	.01	.01	.01	.01	.01	.01	.01	.01	Togo	**742**
	.19	.19	.19	.19	.19	.19	.19	.19	.19	.19	.19	.22	.22	.22	.22	Tunisia	**744**
	....	....	....	....	....	....	....	....	....	....	....	....	....	....	....	Uganda	**746**
	.30	.36	.41	.44	.47	.45	.47	.49	.45	.22	.11	.03	.03	.02	.03	Zaïre	**636**
	.22	.22	.22	.22	—	—	—	—	.01	.02	.02	.02	....	....	....	Zambia	**754**
	.35	.47	.39	.59	.70	.77	.54	.42	.40	.45	.38	.41	.55	.50	.47	Zimbabwe	**698**
	37.32	**38.53**	**39.23**	**38.03**	**39.03**	**40.99**	**43.42**	**46.03**	**51.93**	**51.62**	**52.29**	**53.42**	**53.07**	**53.63**	**53.67**	**Asia**	**505**
	.97	.97	.97	.97	.97	.97	.97	.97	.97	.97	.97	.97	....	....	....	Afghanistan, Islamic State of	**512**
	.05	.05	.06	.06	.06	.06	.07	.07	.07	.08	.08	.08	.09	.09	.09	Bangladesh	**513**
	....	....	....	....	....	....	....	....	....	....	....	....	....	....	....	Bhutan	**514**
	12.80	12.70	12.70	12.70	12.70	12.70	12.70	12.70	12.70	12.70	12.70	12.70	12.70	12.70	12.70	China, People's Rep.	**924**
	.01	.01	.01	.01	.01	.01	.01	—	—	—	—	—	—	—	—	Fiji	**819**
	8.59	8.59	8.59	8.59	8.74	9.40	10.45	10.45	10.45	10.45	10.69	11.28	11.35	11.46	11.80	India	**534**
	2.39	3.10	3.10	3.10	3.10	3.10	3.10	3.10	3.10	3.11	3.11	3.11	3.10	3.10	3.10	Indonesia	**536**
	.30	.30	.30	.30	.31	.31	.32	.32	.32	.32	.32	.32	.32	.32	.33	Korea	**542**
	....	....	....	....	....	....	....	....	....	....	....	....	....	....	....	Lao, P.D. Rep.	**544**
	2.32	2.33	2.33	2.33	2.33	2.34	2.34	2.35	2.35	2.37	2.35	2.35	2.39	2.39	2.39	Malaysia	**548**
	....	—	—	—	—	—	—	—	—	—	—	—	—	—	.01	Maldives	**556**
	.25	.25	.25	.25	.25	.25	.25	.25	.25	.25	.25	.25	.25	.25	.25	Myanmar	**518**
	.15	.15	.15	.15	.15	.15	.15	.15	.15	.15	.15	.15	.15	.15	.15	Nepal	**558**
	1.82	1.85	1.85	1.86	1.86	1.90	1.93	1.94	1.95	1.95	1.95	1.96	2.02	2.04	2.05	Pakistan	**564**
	.06	.06	.06	.06	.06	.06	.06	.06	.06	.06	.06	.06	.06	.06	.06	Papua New Guinea	**853**
	1.92	1.66	1.87	.29	.79	1.48	2.26	2.78	2.84	2.45	2.89	3.37	2.80	3.22	2.89	Philippines	**566**
	....	....	....	....	....	....	....	....	....	....	....	....	....	....	....	Singapore	**576**
	....	....	....	....	....	....	....	....	....	....	....	....	....	....	....	Solomon Islands	**813**
	.06	.06	.06	.06	.06	.06	.06	.06	.06	.06	.06	.11	.16	.14	....	Sri Lanka	**524**
	2.49	2.49	2.49	2.49	2.49	2.49	2.49	2.48	2.48	2.48	2.48	2.48	2.47	2.47	2.47	Thailand	**578**
	....	....	....	....	....	....	....	....	....	....	....	....	....	....	....	Tonga	**866**
	....	....	....	....	....	....	....	....	....	....	....	....	....	....	....	Vanuatu	**846**
	....	.69[e]	.69[e]	.69[e]	.69[e]	.69[e]	.69[e]	....	....	....	....	....	....	....	....	Viet Nam	**582**

Gold (Million Ounces)

1ad		1965	1966	1967	1968	1969	1970	1971	1972	1973	1974	1975	1976	1977	1978	1979
																Millions of Ounces:
Europe	170	3.86	3.51	3.40	4.98	5.58	7.64	8.96	9.36	11.75	11.44	11.21	11.73	12.13	13.27	14.76
Cyprus	423	....	....	....	.43	.43	.43	.43	.43	.43	.43	.43	.43	.44	.44	.46
Czech Republic	935	....	....	....	....	....	....	....	....	....	....	....	....	....	....	....
Czechoslovakia	934	....	....	....	....	....	1.85	1.85	1.85	1.85	1.85	1.85	1.85	1.85	1.85	1.85
Hungary	944	....	....	....	....	....	....	1.45	1.67	1.82	1.33	.95	1.32	1.28	1.98	1.78
Malta	181	—	—	—	.35	.35	.28	.35	.35	.35	.35	.35	.35	.36	.36	.37
Poland	964	....	....	....	....	....	....	....	....	....	....	....	....	....	....	1.29
Romania	968	....	....	....	....	....	....	....	....	2.28	2.45	2.60	2.75	3.06	3.35	3.54
Turkey	186	3.31	2.91	2.77	2.77	3.34	3.63	3.43	3.57	3.57	3.57	3.57	3.57	3.63	3.67	3.77
Yugoslavia, SFR	188	.54	.60	.63	1.43	1.46	1.46	1.46	1.49	1.46	1.47	1.47	1.47	1.51	1.63	1.72
Middle East	405	24.23	22.97	25.75	33.64	32.60	30.13	30.78	30.68	31.01	31.66	32.06	34.22	31.43	33.16	33.42
Bahrain	419	....	.24	.24	.24	.24	.24	.24	.24	.24	.24	.15	.15	.15	.15	.15
Egypt	469	3.98	2.67	2.67	2.67	2.67	2.43	2.43	2.43	2.43	2.43	2.43	2.43	2.43	2.47	2.47
Iran, I.R. of	429	4.17	3.71	4.11	4.51	4.51	3.74	3.74	3.74	3.74	3.74	3.74	3.74	3.78	3.82	3.90
Iraq	433	3.14	3.02	3.28	5.50	5.51	4.10	4.10	4.10	4.10	4.10	4.10	4.10	4.14	....	....
Israel	436	1.59	1.31	1.31	1.32	1.31	1.24	1.24	1.14	1.10	1.10	1.10	1.10	1.16	1.17	1.23
Jordan	439	.10	.10	.10	.85	.85	.80	.80	.80	.80	.80	.80	.80	.81	.81	.82
Kuwait	443	1.48	1.92	3.90	3.47	2.46	2.46	2.48	2.48	2.85	3.50	3.99	5.58	2.51	2.53	2.54
Lebanon	446	5.21	5.51	5.51	8.21	8.21	8.21	9.21	9.21	9.22	9.22	9.22	9.22	9.22	9.22	9.22
Libya	672	1.93	1.93	1.93	2.44	2.44	2.44	2.44	2.44	2.44	2.44	2.44	2.44	2.45	2.45	2.46
Oman	449	....	....	....	....	....	.06	.01	.01	.01	.03	.03	.05	.10	.19	.19
Qatar	453	....	—	.14	.18	.18	.18	.19	.19	.19	.19	.19	.19	.18	.25	.27
Saudi Arabia	456	2.09	1.97	1.97	3.40	3.40	3.40	3.09	3.09	3.09	3.08	3.08	3.08	3.08	4.54	4.57
Syrian Arab Rep.	463	.54	.54	.54	.80	.80	.80	.80	.80	.80	.79	.79	.79	.81	.81	.83
United Arab Emirates	466	....	....	....	....	....	....	....	....	—	—	—	.55	.57	.58	.58
Yemen Arab Rep.	473	....	....	....	....	....	....	....	....	—	—	—	—	—	.01	.01
Yemen, P.D. Rep.	459	—	.04	.04	.04	.02	.02	.02	.02	.02	.02	.02	.02	.03	.03	.04
Yemen, Republic of	474	....	....	....	....	....	....	....	....	....	....	....	....	....	....	....
Western Hemisphere	205	30.83	28.92	29.73	30.61	32.00	31.73	30.29	30.54	30.10	29.21	29.77	28.04	29.43	30.13	30.93
Antigua and Barbuda	311	....	....	....	....	....	....	....	....	....	....	....	....	....	....	....
Argentina	213	1.88	2.39	2.39	3.11	3.85	3.99	2.56	3.99	4.00	4.00	4.00	4.00	4.18	4.28	4.37
Aruba	314	....	....	....	....	....	....	....	....	....	....	....	....	....	....	....
Bahamas, The	313	....	....	....	....	....	....	....	....	....	....	....	....	.01	.01	.02
Barbados	316	....	....	....	....	....	....	....	....	....	....	....	....	....	....	....
Belize	339	....	....	....	....	....	....	....	....	....	....	....	....	....	....	....
Bolivia	218	.19	.21	.27	.31	.33	.36	.38	.41	.41	.41	.41	.41	.60	.64	.68
Brazil	223	1.80	1.30	1.30	1.29	1.29	1.29	1.32	1.33	1.33	1.33	1.33	1.33	1.52	1.61	1.70
Chile	228	1.25	1.29	1.29	1.32	1.35	1.33	1.35	1.36	1.38	1.44	1.30	1.34	1.36	1.39	1.52
Colombia	233	1.00	.71	.89	.89	.74	.49	.40	.43	.43	.43	1.13	1.41	1.73	1.96	2.32
Costa Rica	238	.06	.06	.06	.06	.06	.06	.06	.06	.06	.06	.06	.06	.07	.08	.09
Dominica	321	....	....	....	....	....	....	....	....	....	....	....	....	....	....	....
Dominican Republic	243	.09	.09	.09	.09	.09	.09	.09	.09	.09	.09	.09	.09	.10	.10	.11
Ecuador	248	.32	.31	.49	.75	.63	.55	.53	.36	.39	.39	.39	.39	.40	.41	.41
El Salvador	253	.52	.51	.51	.51	.49	.49	.49	.49	.49	.49	.49	.49	.50	.50	.51
Grenada	328	....	....	....	....	....	....	....	....	....	....	....	....	....	....	....
Guatemala	258	.62	.57	.57	.57	.57	.50	.50	.49	.49	.49	.49	.49	.51	.51	.52
Guyana	336	....	....	....	....	....	....	....	....	....	....	....	....	....	....	....
Haiti	263	....	....	....	....	....	....	....	....	—	—	—	—	.01	.01	.02
Honduras	268	....	....	....	....	....	....	....	....	....	....	....	....	.01	.01	.01
Jamaica	343	....	....	....	....	....	....	....	....	....	....	....	....	.01	—	.01
Mexico	273	4.51	3.11	4.74	4.71	4.83	5.03	5.26	4.94	4.63	3.66	3.66	1.60	1.75	1.89	1.98
Netherlands Antilles	353	.56	.56	.56	.56	.56	.56	.55	.55	.55	.55	.55	.55	.55	.55	.55
Nicaragua	278	.01	.03	.02	.02	.01	.02	.02	.01	.02	.02	.02	.02	.03	.03	.02
Panama	283	....	....	....	....	....	....	....	....	....	....	....	....	....	....	....
Paraguay	288	....	....	....	—	—	—	—	—	—	—	—	—	.01	.01	.04
Peru	293	1.92	1.85	.58	.57	.71	1.13	1.13	1.09	1.00	1.00	1.00	1.00	1.00	1.00	1.16
St. Kitts and Nevis	361	....	....	....	....	....	....	....	....	....	....	....	....	....	....	....
St. Lucia	362	....	....	....	....	....	....	....	....	....	....	....	....	....	....	....
St. Vincent & Grens.	364	....	....	....	....	....	....	....	....	....	....	....	....	....	....	....
Suriname	366	.21	.28	.53	.53	.25	.25	.25	.25	.15	.15	.15	.15	.15	.05	.05
Trinidad and Tobago	369	....	....	....	....	....	....	....	....	....	....	....	....	.03	.04	.05
Uruguay	298	4.43	4.19	3.99	3.81	4.71	4.61	4.23	3.54	3.54	3.54	3.54	3.54	3.58	3.64	I 3.31
Venezuela	299	11.46	11.46	11.46	11.51	11.51	10.97	11.17	11.17	11.17	11.18	11.18	11.18	11.32	11.39	11.46
Memorandum Items																
Oil Exporting Countries	999	25.12	24.86	31.92	37.57	36.56	33.51	33.29	33.35	33.68	34.36	34.84	37.00	34.43	36.26	36.66
Non-Oil Developing Countries	201	67.25	70.17	71.38	97.66	96.66	84.81	77.34	83.51	85.79	82.62	81.28	74.88	87.51	91.65	95.23

		1965	1966	1967	1968	1969	1970	1971	1972	1973	1974	1975	1976	1977	1978	1979
Gold Holdings at SDR 35 per oz.																Millions of SDRs:
World	001	43,151	43,080	41,524	40,726	40,833	41,192	41,157	41,365	41,408	41,349	41,269	40,932	41,066	40,811	40,166
All Countries	010	41,775	40,801	39,424	38,758	38,951	37,091	36,060	35,753	35,843	35,773	35,695	35,538	36,062	36,329	33,141
IMF	992	1,869	2,652	2,682	2,288	2,310	4,339	4,732	5,370	5,370	5,369	5,370	5,233	4,605	4,137	3,739
EPU / EF	994	64	51	42	30	52	45	55	41	—	—	—	—	—	—e	—
EMI	977	—	—	—	—	—	—	—	—	—	—	—	—	—	—	2,985
BIS (Net)	993	−558	−424	−624	−349	−480	−282	310	201	195	207	204	160	399	345	301
Gold Holdings at Market Prices																Millions of SDRs:
World	001	43,299	43,313	41,762	48,755	41,066	43,982	47,255	70,648	110,085	179,959	141,262	135,636	159,328	202,277	446,031
All Countries	010	41,919	41,022	39,649	46,399	39,174	39,602	41,402	61,063	95,290	155,689	122,184	117,765	139,914	180,063	368,022
IMF	992	1,875	2,666	2,697	2,739	2,323	4,633	5,433	9,171	14,276	23,367	18,381	17,341	17,867	20,505	41,521
EPU / EF	994	64	51	42	36	52	48	63	70	—	—	—	—	—	—e	....
EMI	977	—	—	—	—	—	—	—	—	—	—	—	—	—	—	33,147
BIS (Net)	993	−560	−426	−627	−418	−483	−301	356	343	518	903	697	531	1,547	1,710	3,342
IMF Gold Transactions																Millions of SDRs:
Distribution(at SDR 35 per ounce)	992	—	—	—	—	—	—	—	—	—	—	—	—	417	213	203
Sale (at SDR 35 per ounce)	992	—	—	—	—	—	—	—	—	—	—	—	137	211	255	195
Sale (at auction price)	992	—	—	—	—	—	—	—	—	—	—	—	414	761	1,111	1,282
Gold Prices and SDR Rates																End of Period
US Dollars per Ounce(London)	112	35.12	35.19	35.20	41.90	35.20	37.37	43.63	64.90	112.25	186.50	140.25	134.75	164.95	226.00	512.00
US Dollars per SDR	111	1.0000	1.0000	1.0000	1.0000	1.0000	1.0000	1.0857	1.0857	1.2064	1.2244	1.1707	1.1618	1.2147	1.3028	1.3173
SDRs per Ounce	112	35.12	35.19	35.20	41.90	35.20	37.37	40.19	59.78	93.05	152.33	119.80	115.98	135.79	173.47	388.66

Gold (Million Ounces)

1980	1981	1982	1983	1984	1985	1986	1987	1988	1989	1990	1991	1992	1993	1994		1ad
End of Period																
16.11	15.43	14.87	16.05	16.76	17.07	16.47	13.76	13.88	14.14	12.09	12.42	12.74	12.78	12.82	Europe	170
.46	.46	.46	.46	.46	.46	.46	.46	.46	.46	.46	.46	.46	.46	.46	Cyprus	423
....	....	....	....	....	....	....	....	....	....	....	....	....	1.95	2.10	Czech Republic	935
3.05	3.14	3.65	3.85	3.91	3.81	3.77	3.66	3.73	3.62	2.49	2.79	3.29	....	....	Czechoslovakia	934
2.07	1.69	.65	1.53	2.06	2.33	2.35	1.64	1.59	1.50	.30	.26	.10	.11	.11	Hungary	944
.43	.46	.46	.47	.47	.47	.47	.47	.47	.23	.16	.12	.12	.10	.11	Malta	181
.76	.47	.47	.47	.47	.47	.47	.47	.47	.47	.47	.47	.47	.47	.47	Poland	964
3.71	3.59	3.55	3.62	3.73	3.82	3.25	1.36	1.45	2.17	2.21	2.25	2.31	2.37	2.63	Romania	968
3.77	3.77	3.77	3.78	3.80	3.86	3.84	3.83	3.82	3.78	4.09	4.16	4.05	4.03	3.82	Turkey	186
1.86	1.86	1.86	1.86	1.86	1.86	1.87	1.87	1.89	1.90	1.91	1.92	....	....	....	Yugoslavia, SFR	188
34.82	35.78	36.04	36.16	36.34	36.16	36.05	35.86	35.65	35.65	35.46	35.07	34.70	34.70	34.65	Middle East	405
.15	.15	.15	.15	.15	.15	.15	.15	.15	.15	.15	.15	.15	.15	.15	Bahrain	419
2.43	2.43	2.43	2.43	2.43	2.43	2.43	2.43	2.43	2.43	2.43	2.43	2.43	2.43	2.43	Egypt	469
4.34	4.34	4.34	4.34	4.34	4.34	4.34	4.34	4.34	4.34	4.34	4.34	4.34	....	....	Iran, I.R. of	429
....	....	....	....	....	....	....	....	....	....	....	....	....	....	....	Iraq	433
1.19	1.19	1.08	1.02	1.02	1.02	1.02	1.02	1.02	1.02	.84	.42	.01	.01	.01	Israel	436
1.02	1.07	1.08	1.09	1.06	1.06	1.06	1.00	.74	.75	.75	.79	.79	.79	.79	Jordan	439
2.54	2.54	2.54	2.54	2.54	2.54	2.54	2.54	2.54	2.54	2.54	2.54	2.54	2.54	2.54	Kuwait	443
9.22	9.22	9.22	9.22	9.22	9.22	9.22	9.22	9.22	9.22	9.22	9.22	9.22	9.22	9.22	Lebanon	446
3.08	3.58	3.58	3.58	3.65	3.60	3.60	3.60	3.60	3.60	3.60	3.60	3.60	....	....	Libya	672
.21	.27	.28	.29	.29	.29	.29	.29	.29	.29	.29	.29	.29	.29	.29	Oman	449
.47	.71	.90	1.07	1.21	1.08	.97	.83	.88	.90	.83	.83	.86	.86	.81	Qatar	453
4.57	4.57	4.60	4.60	4.60	4.60	4.60	4.60	4.60	4.60	4.60	4.60	4.60	4.60	4.60	Saudi Arabia	456
.83	.83	.83	.83	.83	.83	.83	.83	.83	.83	.83	.83	.83	.83	.83	Syrian Arab Rep.	463
.58	.68	.82	.82	.82	.82	.82	.82	.82	.80	.80	.80	.80	.80	.80	United Arab Emirates	466
—	—	—	—	—	—	—	—	—	....	....	....	....	....	....	Yemen Arab Rep.	473
.04	.04	.04	.04	.04	.04	.04	.04	.04	....	....	....	....	....	....	Yemen, P.D. Rep.	459
....	....	....	....	....	....	....	....	....	....	.05	.05	.05	.05	....	Yemen, Republic of	474
32.26	33.35	31.07	31.77	29.73	32.34	32.50	30.71	31.74	29.97	31.19	28.24	28.31	27.36	27.90	Western Hemisphere	205
....	....	....	....	....	....	....	....	....	....	....	....	....	....	....	Antigua and Barbuda	311
4.37	4.37	4.37	4.37	4.37	4.37	4.37	4.37	4.37	4.37	4.23	4.12	4.37	4.37	4.37	Argentina	213
....	....	....	....	....	....	....	....	....	.10	.10	.10	.10	.10	.10	Aruba	314
—	—	—	—	—	—	—	—	—	—	—	—	—	—	—	Bahamas, The	313
....	.01	.01	.01	.01	.01	.01	.01	.01	.01	—	—	—	—	—	Barbados	316
....	....	....	....	....	....	....	....	....	....	....	....	....	....	....	Belize	339
.76	.83	.89	.91	.91	.89	.89	.89	.89	.89	.89	.89	.89	.89	.89	Bolivia	218
1.88	2.20	.15	.54	1.47	3.10	2.43	2.43	2.73	2.98	4.57	2.02	2.23	2.93	3.71	Brazil	223
1.70	1.70	1.71	....	....	....	1.80	1.81	1.82	1.75	1.86	1.86	1.87	1.87	1.86	Chile	228
2.79	3.37	3.82	4.22	1.37	1.84	2.01	.68	1.10	.61	.63	.86	.48	.30	.29	Colombia	233
.09	.03	.05	.09	.02	.06	.07	.06	.02	.01	.01	.03	.04	.03	.03	Costa Rica	238
....	....	....	....	....	....	....	....	....	....	....	....	....	....	....	Dominica	321
.13	.14	.09	.08	.02	.02	.02	.02	.02	.02	.02	.02	.02	.02	.02	Dominican Republic	243
.41	.41	.41	.41	.41	.41	.41	.41	.41	.41	.44	.44	.44	.41	.41	Ecuador	248
.52	.52	.52	.47	.47	.47	.47	.47	.47	.47	.47	.47	.47	.47	.47	El Salvador	253
....	....	....	....	....	....	....	....	....	....	....	....	....	....	....	Grenada	328
.52	.52	.52	.52	.52	.52	.52	.52	.52	.54	.21	.21	.12	.21	.21	Guatemala	258
.02	.02	.02	.02	.02	.02	.02	.02	.02	.02	.02	.02	....	....	....	Guyana	336
.02	.02	.02	.02	.02	.02	.02	.02	.02	.02	.02	.02	.02	.02	.02	Haiti	263
—	—	—	—	—	—	—	—	—	—	—	—	—	—	—	Honduras	268
2.06	2.26	2.07	2.31	2.42	2.36	2.57	2.54	2.55	1.03	.92	.92	.69	.48	.43	Jamaica	343
.55	.55	.55	.55	.55	.55	.55	.55	.55	.55	.55	.55	.55	.55	.55	Mexico	273
.02	.02	.02	.12	....	....	....	.20	.31	.12	.15	.10	.48	.01	.01	Netherlands Antilles	353
....	....	....	....	....	....	....	....	....	....	....	....	....	....	....	Nicaragua	278
.04	.04	.04	.04	.04	.04	.04	.04	.03	.03	.03	.03	.03	.03	.03	Panama	283
....	....	....	....	....	....	....	....	....	....	....	....	....	....	....	Paraguay	288
1.40	1.40	1.40	1.40	1.40	1.95	2.14	1.50	1.71	1.97	2.21	1.83	1.82	1.30	1.12	Peru	293
....	....	....	....	....	....	....	....	....	....	....	....	....	....	....	St. Kitts and Nevis	361
....	....	....	....	....	....	....	....	....	....	....	....	....	....	....	St. Lucia	362
....	....	....	....	....	....	....	....	....	....	....	....	....	....	....	St. Vincent & Grens.	364
.05	.05	.05	.05	.05	.05	.05	.05	.05	.05	.05	.05	.05	.05	.05	Suriname	366
.05	.05	.05	.05	.05	.05	.05	.05	.05	.05	.05	.05	.05	.06	.05	Trinidad and Tobago	369
3.42	3.39	2.86	2.60	2.62	2.62	2.61	2.61	2.61	2.61	2.40	2.26	2.03	1.70	1.70	Uruguay	298
11.46	11.46	11.46	11.46	11.46	11.46	11.46	11.46	11.46	11.46	11.46	11.46	11.46	11.46	11.46	Venezuela	299
															Memorandum Items	
40.05	41.67	42.03	42.20	42.41	42.24	42.13	41.99	42.04	42.05	41.54	41.98	42.00	42.00	41.95	Oil Exporting Countries	999
101.58	99.86	95.91	96.98	96.17	98.37	100.19	99.16	103.49	101.09	101.55	102.14	102.05	99.77	99.79	Non-Oil Developing Countries	201

1980	1981	1982	1983	1984	1985	1986	1987	1988	1989	1990	1991	1992	1993	1994		
End of Period															**Gold Holdings at SDR 35 per oz.**	
40,325	40,317	40,168	40,104	40,065	40,156	40,174	40,073	40,273	40,062	40,028	39,947	39,611	38,998	38,853	World	001
33,443	33,430	33,293	33,254	33,214	33,301	33,300	33,108	33,133	32,933	32,861	32,823	32,525	31,941	31,842	All Countries	010
3,620	3,620	3,620	3,620	3,620	3,620	3,620	3,620	3,620	3,620	3,620	3,620	3,620	3,620	3,620	IMF	992
—	—	—	—	—	—	—	—	—	—	—	—	....	....	....	EPU / EF	994
2,997	2,999	3,000	3,000	3,000	3,000	3,029	3,130	3,289	3,277	3,274	3,273	3,228	3,135	3,146	EMI	977
264	267	255	230	230	234	225	214	231	232	273	230	237	302	244	BIS (Net)	993

End of Period															**Gold Holdings at Market Prices**	
532,519	393,389	475,351	417,528	360,038	341,552	366,818	390,693	350,790	349,271	309,499	282,137	274,290	316,898	291,424	World	001
441,643	326,189	393,993	346,213	298,478	283,247	304,055	322,790	288,594	287,113	254,085	231,822	225,226	259,549	238,843	All Countries	010
47,810	35,325	42,844	37,693	32,534	30,794	33,057	35,298	31,535	31,563	27,993	25,570	25,070	29,419	27,156	IMF	992
....	....	....	....	....	....	....	....	....	....	....	....	....	....	....	EPU / EF	994
39,583	29,265	35,500	31,232	26,959	25,517	27,656	30,520	28,646	28,572	25,314	23,118	22,351	25,478	23,594	EMI	977
3,483	2,610	3,014	2,390	2,066	1,993	2,050	2,087	2,015	2,023	2,107	1,627	1,643	2,453	1,831	BIS (Net)	993

In Period															**IMF Gold Transactions**	
41	—	—	—	—	—	—	—	—	—	—	—	—	—	—	Distribution (at SDR 35 per ounce)	992
78	—	—	—	—	—	—	—	—	—	—	—	—	—	—	Sale (at SDR 35 per ounce)	992
994	—	—	—	—	—	—	—	—	—	—	—	—	—	—	Sale (at auction price)	992

End of Period															**Gold Prices and SDR Rates**	
589.50	397.50	456.90	381.50	308.30	327.00	390.90	484.10	410.25	401.00	385.00	353.60	333.25	390.65	383.25	US Dollars per Ounce (London)	112
1.2754	1.1640	1.1031	1.0470	.9802	1.0984	1.2232	1.4187	1.3457	1.3142	1.4227	1.4304	1.3750	1.3736	1.4599	US Dollars per SDR	111
462.20	341.51	414.19	364.39	314.52	297.70	319.57	341.24	304.86	305.14	270.62	247.20	242.36	284.41	262.53	SDRs per Ounce	112

Total Reserves
1 s
(with Gold at SDR 35 per ounce)

Millions of SDRs:

		1965	1966	1967	1968	1969	1970	1971	1972	1973	1974	1975	1976	1977	1978	1979
All Countries	010	71,170	72,829	74,575	77,826	78,740	93,244	123,115	146,658	152,679	179,773	194,393	222,166	264,535	281,817	306,013
Industrial Countries	110	58,868	59,408	60,199	61,361	60,579	72,597	99,182	113,362	111,609	111,520	116,393	125,198	151,848	176,663	183,431
United States	111	15,450	14,882	14,830	15,710	16,964	14,487	12,148	12,112	11,919	13,115	13,567	15,767	15,965	15,032	15,170
Canada	156	3,037	2,702	2,717	3,046	3,106	4,679	5,251	5,572	4,782	4,758	4,549	5,029	3,793	3,505	2,951
Australia	193	1,317	1,568	1,364	1,442	1,261	1,693	3,054	5,656	4,723	3,487	2,782	2,728	1,962	1,855	1,359
Japan	158	2,152	2,119	2,030	2,906	3,654	4,840	14,148	16,916	10,151	11,042	10,947	14,292	19,149	25,714	15,667
New Zealand	196	173	179	219	162	210	258	454	767	867	522	365	423	366	348	344
Austria	122	1,312	1,333	1,484	1,510	1,537	1,757	2,153	2,505	2,382	2,801	3,791	3,795	3,493	4,610	3,832
Belgium	124	2,334	2,350	2,589	2,186	2,386	2,847	3,199	3,564	4,227	4,366	4,952	4,480	4,743	4,535	5,329
Denmark	128	587	597	535	449	446	484	665	787	1,097	764	749	788	1,375	2,471	2,514
Finland	172	289	189	184	I 338	327	453	623	664	505	515	399	427	469	972	1,204
France	132	6,343	6,733	6,994	4,201	3,833	4,960	7,601	9,224	7,070	7,230	10,757	8,373	8,393	10,691	16,212
Germany	134	7,430	8,029	8,152	9,948	7,129	13,609	17,184	21,908	27,497	26,462	26,510	29,954	32,713	41,360	43,225
Greece	174	250	273	286	322	317	310	478	950	868	765	I 950	886	994	1,134	1,153
Iceland	176	54	58	35	28	39	54	64	77	83	40	40	69	82	106	125
Ireland	178	409	494	439	545	691	697	917	1,038	850	1,034	1,308	1,581	1,952	2,064	1,693
Italy	136	4,800	4,911	5,463	5,342	5,045	5,352	6,281	5,605	5,335	5,669	4,003	5,661	9,574	11,436	16,149
Netherlands	138	2,414	2,449	2,619	2,463	2,530	3,241	3,496	4,407	5,427	5,683	6,074	6,358	6,639	5,823	7,301
Norway	142	476	528	677	702	710	811	1,063	1,220	1,305	1,575	1,911	1,919	1,845	2,235	3,241
Portugal	182	938	1,077	1,234	1,363	1,445	1,504	1,791	2,129	2,354	1,923	1,310	1,120	1,145	1,443	1,481
Spain	184	1,422	1,253	1,100	1,149	1,281	1,818	3,010	4,618	5,614	5,297	5,203	4,549	5,425	8,270	10,550
Sweden	144	972	1,027	841	815	696	761	1,024	1,453	2,097	1,417	2,627	2,144	3,019	3,375	2,880
Switzerland	146	3,444	3,545	3,696	4,293	4,425	5,132	6,416	6,961	7,063	7,360	8,908	11,183	11,385	16,549	15,391
United Kingdom	112	3,004	3,099	2,695	2,422	2,527	2,827	8,135	5,201	5,368	5,667	4,664	3,641	17,335	13,100	15,625
Developing Countries	200	12,302	13,421	14,376	16,464	18,161	20,648	23,934	33,295	41,070	68,253	77,998	96,968	112,688	105,154	122,583
Africa	605	2,041	2,540	2,504	3,354	3,554	3,575	3,181	3,962	4,777	9,424	9,446	9,780	8,995	7,115	10,791
Algeria	612	184	273	442	492	409	339	467	454	948	1,379	1,155	1,711	1,578	1,714	2,214
Benin	638	10	10	8	10	8	16	23	26	27	28	13	17	17	12	11
Botswana	616	....	....	....	....	....	....	....	....	....	....	....	64	82	116	203
Burkina Faso	748	14	16	18	23	26	36	40	44	52	68	65	62	46	28	47
Burundi	618	8	5	3	3	7	15	16	17	18	12	26	42	78	63	69
Cameroon	622	27	34	24	41	48	81	68	40	42	64	25	38	35	41	96
Cape Verde	624	....	....	....	....	....	....	....	....	....	....	....	....	....	....	....
Central African Rep.	626	10	6	5	5	1	1	—	2	1	1	3	16	21	19	34
Chad	628	14	7	1	1	1	2	10	9	1	12	3	20	16	9	9
Comoros	632	....	....	....	....	....	....	....	....	....	....	....	....	....	....	....
Congo	634	6	6	3	7	6	9	10	10	7	20	12	10	11	8	32
Côte d'Ivoire	662	62	62	71	81	74	119	82	80	73	54	88	66	153	345	113
Djibouti	611	....	....	....	....	....	....	....	....	....	....	....	....	....	....	....
Equatorial Guinea	642	....	....	....	....	....	....	....	....	....	....	....	....	....	....	....
Ethiopia	644	77	79	65	66	72	71	63	85	147	225	246	263	186	127	141
Gabon	646	18	12	9	5	8	15	23	21	40	84	125	100	8	18	16
Gambia, The	648	8	9	8	7	6	8	10	10	13	23	24	18	20	20	1
Ghana	652	116	111	83	96	72	42	39	92	152	64	112	85	129	220	227
Guinea-Bissau	654	....	....	....	....	....	....	....	....	....	....	....	....	....	....	....
Kenya	664	20	52	76	100	170	220	157	186	193	158	148	237	431	273	479
Lesotho	666	....	....	....	....	....	....	....	....	....	....	....	....	....	....	....
Liberia	668	....	....	....	....	....	....	....	....	....	15	16	15	23	14	42
Madagascar	674	50	51	43	31	19	37	43	48	56	40	30	36	57	45	4
Malawi	676	25	21	23	23	21	29	29	33	55	67	53	23	72	58	53
Mali	678	3	—	1	1	1	1	2	4	4	5	4	6	5	7	5
Mauritania	682	10	8	9	7	4	3	7	12	35	85	41	71	41	61	87
Mauritius	684	20	19	13	16	33	46	48	65	55	107	142	77	55	36	23
Morocco	686	99	87	76	85	114	140	160	218	220	340	322	423	438	498	447
Niger	692	3	4	1	3	7	19	31	38	42	37	43	71	83	99	100
Nigeria	694	239	215	112	117	132	222	395	346	483	4,596	4,791	4,478	3,506	1,470	4,236
Rwanda	714	4	5	7	6	3	8	5	6	13	11	22	55	68	67	116
Senegal	722	38	46	37	16	6	22	27	36	10	5	27	22	28	15	16
Seychelles	718	....	....	....	....	....	....	....	....	4	4	5	6	9	7	9
Sierra Leone	724	23	20	16	28	35	39	35	43	43	45	24	22	27	27	35
Somalia	726	9	12	10	7	14	21	25	29	29	35	58	73	99	97	34
South Africa	199	599	831	778	1,471	1,398	1,012	655	1,188	1,037	947	1,039	809	683	667	681
Sudan	732	60	57	55	48	36	26	25	26	33	51	102	31	20	19	51
Swaziland	734	....	....	....	....	....	....	....	....	....	....	11	39	63	78	86
Tanzania	738	....	61	62	78	80	65	55	110	120	41	56	97	232	77	52
Togo	742	18	19	22	26	26	35	37	34	31	44	35	35	38	54	50
Tunisia	744	36	28	40	35	37	60	136	205	255	342	329	319	294	346	446
Uganda	746	....	41	35	49	52	57	25	33	24	14	27	38	39	40	17
Zaïre	636	21	21	68	138	199	186	134	164	194	115	50	52	119	107	166
Zambia	754	204	218	187	200	369	514	262	153	161	140	127	86	60	46	68
Zimbabwe	698	....	....	87	89	32	56	57	34	76	130	75	81	75	65	119	236
Asia *	505	3,698	4,081	4,403	4,814	5,492	5,987	6,324	8,129	9,321	11,065	11,049	16,565	22,546	23,758	27,406
Afghanistan, Islamic State of	512	45	47	38	39	41	47	57	52	51	55	107	145	260	333	369
Bangladesh	513	....	....	....	....	....	....	....	249	119	113	127	249	193	243	295
Bhutan	514	....	....	....	....	....	....	....	....	....	....	....	....	....	....	....
China, People's Rep. I	924	....	....	....	....	....	....	....	....	....	....	....	....	2,379	1,643	2,083
Fiji	819	....	....	....	....	27	27	36	64	61	89	127	100	121	104	104
India	534	600	608	662	682	926	1,007	1,111	1,087	947	1,083	1,174	2,646	4,268	5,225	5,942
Indonesia	536	21	23	6	I 87	122	160	I 173	531	669	1,219	501	1,290	2,071	2,024	3,093
Korea	542	146	245	357	391	553	610	403	485	737	230	671	1,700	2,448	2,131	2,257
Lao, P.D. Rep.	544	7	7	6	6	5	6	8	7	9	12	....	....	....	....	....
Malaysia	548	470	494	457	516	620	664	753	894	1,115	1,322	1,302	2,127	2,353	2,556	3,046
Maldives	556	....	....	....	....	....	....	....	....	....	....	....	....	....	....	1
Myanmar	518	181	184	155	153	129	I 94	67	48	83	156	120	109	93	82	163
Nepal	558	60	45	46	63	84	94	93	95	102	104	86	I 114	119	116	126
Pakistan	564	230	208	165	248	333	191	174	259	397	376	346	458	426	373	225
Papua New Guinea	853	....	....	....	....	....	....	....	....	26	27	154	221	352	312	384
Philippines	566	193	194	180	161	121	251	352	507	860	1,229	1,160	1,411	1,255	1,406	1,767
Singapore	576	430	394	496	712	827	1,012	1,338	1,610	1,895	2,297	2,568	2,895	3,176	4,070	4,417
of which:																
Taiwan Province of China	528	300	337	416	383	443	622	649	957	931	972	998	1,383	1,192	1,164	1,198

I See country notes in the monthly IFS

Total Reserves

(with Gold at SDR 35 per ounce)

1980	1981	1982	1983	1984	1985	1986	1987	1988	1989	1990	1991	1992	1993	1994	Country	Code
354,727	363,106	361,209	395,568	440,264	438,130	451,913	540,624	575,790	623,853	670,561	704,511	725,589	789,167	844,534	All Countries	010
214,523	214,978	214,025	234,567	254,387	257,819	279,622	352,489	381,104	410,136	441,946	428,438	424,229	440,423	460,716	Industrial Countries	110
21,479	25,502	29,918	30,831	33,517	38,412	39,790	33,657	36,471	57,525	59,958	55,769	52,995	54,558	52,510	United States	111
3,159	3,755	3,439	4,017	3,246	2,982	3,348	5,778	12,037	12,781	13,060	11,816	8,662	9,299	8,552	Canada	156
1,603	1,713	6,053	8,838	7,869	5,528	6,202	6,441	10,383	10,764	11,710	11,837	8,429	8,359	8,007	Australia	193
20,164	25,083	22,001	24,346	27,811	25,173	35,394	57,925	72,727	64,735	56,027	51,224	52,937	72,577	87,062	Japan	158
277	580	577	744	1,824	1,454	3,084	2,298	2,108	2,303	2,902	2,062	2,239	2,430	2,540	New Zealand	196
4,879	5,279	5,544	5,052	5,070	5,080	5,778	6,049	6,215	7,266	7,305	7,924	9,703	11,288	12,165	Austria	122
7,330	5,451	4,757	5,699	5,853	5,611	5,724	7,958	8,113	9,250	9,599	9,573	10,914	9,187	10,382	Belgium	124
2,712	2,246	2,111	3,515	3,127	4,999	4,116	7,153	8,057	4,925	7,502	5,234	8,090	7,557	6,260	Denmark	128
1,501	1,319	1,420	1,227	2,854	3,481	1,528	4,592	4,801	3,959	6,849	5,389	3,862	4,009	7,374	Finland	172
24,301	21,991	17,850	21,826	24,227	27,071	28,579	26,161	21,713	21,592	28,716	24,735	22,522	19,354	20,851	France	132
41,430	40,892	43,909	44,092	44,282	43,735	45,626	58,846	46,824	49,527	51,060	47,375	69,489	59,856	56,325	Germany	134
1,189	1,013	916	996	1,117	935	1,357	2,007	2,808	2,572	2,517	3,747	3,606	5,792	10,222	Greece	174
138	199	133	144	132	189	255	221	218	258	308	316	364	312	202	Iceland	176
2,255	2,290	2,390	2,534	2,412	2,689	2,658	3,393	3,793	3,100	3,684	4,026	2,514	4,326	4,201	Ireland	178
20,466	19,631	15,108	21,537	23,548	16,531	18,674	23,631	28,131	37,884	46,565	36,365	22,438	22,387	24,435	Italy	136
10,669	9,562	10,723	11,253	10,961	11,354	10,687	12,818	13,483	14,100	13,827	13,980	17,492	24,046	24,872	Netherlands	138
4,783	5,414	6,272	6,373	9,596	12,711	10,281	10,105	9,901	10,531	10,819	9,292	8,725	14,327	13,074	Norway	142
1,399	1,234	1,179	1,083	1,237	1,978	1,896	3,047	4,372	8,135	10,736	14,977	14,474	12,094	11,189	Portugal	182
9,813	9,794	7,450	7,581	12,709	10,686	12,581	22,035	28,041	32,104	36,555	46,562	33,640	30,429	29,021	Spain	184
2,893	3,306	3,397	4,065	4,135	5,487	5,568	5,974	6,523	7,487	12,856	13,028	16,667	14,081	16,141	Sweden	144
15,190	14,925	16,930	17,275	18,520	19,317	20,726	22,283	20,900	22,148	23,456	23,191	27,100	26,674	26,704	Switzerland	146
16,851	13,757	11,904	11,497	10,297	12,373	15,727	30,070	33,439	27,121	25,865	29,948	27,300	27,420	28,739	United Kingdom	112
140,204	148,128	147,184	161,001	185,878	180,312	172,291	188,135	194,686	213,716	228,614	276,074	301,360	348,745	383,818	Developing Countries	200
15,696	10,995	7,737	7,443	7,275	8,787	7,508	7,616	7,838	9,439	12,052	14,633	12,826	13,784	16,388	Africa	605
3,153	3,370	2,391	1,991	1,689	2,762	1,553	1,352	864	840	689	1,234	1,255	1,269	2,027	Algeria	612
7	50	5	4	3	4	4	3	4	3	46	134	179	179	177	Benin	638
269	218	266	378	484	713	979	1,450	1,678	2,162	2,380	2,637	2,796	3,024	3,057	Botswana	616
54	61	56	82	109	127	191	228	239	202	212	242	249	279	163	Burkina Faso	748
75	53	27	26	21	27	57	43	52	76	74	99	127	119	141	Burundi	618
149	74	62	153	56	122	49	46	132	62	19	31	25	12	....	Cameroon	622
33	33	39	44	42	50	46	57	60	....	....	....	....	....	....	Cape Verde	624
44	60	42	45	54	46	54	69	81	86	84	72	73	82	144	Central African Rep.	626
4	7	12	27	45	31	13	37	47	85	90	84	59	29	....	Chad	628
....	....	....	14	5	14	19	22	18	23	21	20	20	....	....	Comoros	632
68	106	34	7	5	4	6	3	4	5	5	4	3	1	35	Congo	634
17	17	4	20	7	6	18	8	9	13	4	11	7	3	141	Côte d'Ivoire	662
....	....	....	....	46	46	44	45	48	45	66	70	61	55	51	Djibouti	611
....	....	3	1	1	3	2	—	4	1	—	7	10	....	—	Equatorial Guinea	642
74	238	172	128	53	142	212	94	55	42	17	43	173	336	377	Ethiopia	644
85	171	283	179	204	176	104	9	51	27	193	229	52	1	....	Gabon	646
4	3	8	3	2	2	11	18	14	16	39	47	68	....	67	Gambia, The	648
150	136	139	152	323	444	429	147	172	272	162	394	242	308	410	Ghana	652
....	....	....	....	....	....	....	25	7	12	16	13	10	13	10	13	Guinea-Bissau	654
388	201	195	362	400	358	341	183	199	219	147	85	41	298	385	Kenya	664
39	37	43	64	50	40	49	48	42	57	51	80	115	184	255	Lesotho	666
4	8	6	19	4	1	2	—	—	6	....	1	1	2	3	Liberia	668
7	23	18	28	60	44	94	131	166	187	65	62	....	....	49	Madagascar	674
54	43	21	15	58	41	21	37	109	77	97	108	30	42	30	Malawi	676
12	16	16	16	28	21	20	12	27	89	135	224	225	243	152	Mali	678
110	139	126	102	79	54	40	51	42	63	38	48	45	33	28	Mauritania	682
72	31	36	18	25	29	113	243	330	396	521	627	599	553	514	Mauritius	684
337	222	222	127	74	129	197	314	431	396	1,477	2,192	2,631	2,686	3,006	Morocco	686
99	91	27	51	91	125	155	176	173	162	157	142	164	140	76	Niger	692
8,049	3,371	1,486	970	1,516	1,542	908	845	508	1,368	2,740	3,125	727	1,023	973	Nigeria	694
146	149	116	106	109	103	133	116	88	54	31	77	57	35	....	Rwanda	714
7	8	11	13	5	6	9	8	9	15	9	10	10	4	124	Senegal	722
14	12	12	10	6	8	6	10	6	9	12	19	23	26	21	Seychelles	718
24	14	8	15	8	10	11	4	6	3	4	7	15	24	34	Sierra Leone	724
12	27	7	9	2	3	11	6	12	12	....	....	....	....	....	Somalia	726
994	898	705	1,059	504	456	471	656	701	838	852	855	954	909	1,301	South Africa	199
38	15	19	16	18	11	48	8	9	12	8	5	20	27	54	Sudan	732
124	83	69	88	82	76	79	90	104	137	152	120	225	192	203	Swaziland	734
16	16	4	19	27	15	50	22	58	41	136	143	238	148	227	Tanzania	738
61	131	152	166	208	270	280	251	173	218	249	256	199	114	65	Togo	742
469	467	556	548	421	218	256	377	675	738	565	560	627	629	1,009	Tunisia	744
2	26	71	102	169	25	24	38	37	11	31	41	69	107	220	Uganda	746
170	143	50	112	156	188	236	145	155	156	158	129	115	34	84	Zaïre	636
69	56	60	60	55	182	58	77	100	89	136	130	....	....	....	Zambia	754
180	162	141	93	71	112	106	142	147	108	147	88	159	181	332	Zimbabwe	698
31,009	37,977	44,490	55,924	68,740	67,708	81,331	99,720	112,162	121,690	128,826	157,533	164,435	190,869	229,300	Asia *	505
325	269	267	238	267	303	245	231	228	219	221	198	....	....	....	Afghanistan, Islamic State of	512
237	121	168	503	400	308	337	597	780	384	445	897	1,330	1,758	2,153	Bangladesh	513
....	....	27	32	38	46	50	53	70	75	60	69	57	....	79	Bhutan	514
2,444	4,790	10,733	14,759	18,161	12,032	9,808	11,938	14,223	14,111	21,241	30,977	15,441	16,743	36,691	China, People's Rep. 1	924
132	116	115	111	120	120	140	93	173	161	183	190	230	196	187	Fiji	819
5,745	4,333	4,213	5,017	6,266	6,174	5,594	4,915	4,006	3,302	1,443	2,930	4,584	7,826	13,907	India	534
4,311	4,416	2,959	3,660	4,978	4,637	3,421	4,051	3,860	4,259	5,352	6,581	7,708	8,308	8,419	Indonesia	536
2,304	2,315	2,556	2,252	2,820	2,623	2,725	2,537	9,186	11,588	10,409	9,590	12,463	14,738	17,574	Korea	542
10	11	7	18	11	23	26	15	12	12	43	41	62	12	111	Lao, P.D. Rep.	544
3,521	3,602	3,497	3,696	3,880	4,554	5,009	5,323	4,932	6,005	6,938	7,692	12,613	19,922	17,498	Malaysia	548
1	1	8	4	5	4	6	6	16	19	17	16	21	19	22	Maldives	556
213	206	103	94	72	40	36	28	66	209	229	189	213	229	298	Myanmar	518
149	179	186	133	89	56	76	131	169	166	213	283	345	471	480	Nepal	558
452	684	943	1,949	1,122	802	647	422	361	464	276	437	689	943	2,078	Pakistan	564
334	343	413	423	446	405	350	310	295	295	286	228	176	105	68	Papua New Guinea	853
2,299	1,833	870	724	642	612	1,492	780	845	1,164	751	2,387	3,300	3,517	4,223	Philippines	566
5,149	6,486	7,687	8,849	10,626	11,695	10,578	10,733	12,687	15,481	19,505	23,862	29,007	35,208	39,851	Singapore	576

of which:

| 1,839 | 6,330 | 7,866 | 11,471 | 16,136 | 20,710 | 38,055 | 54,367 | 55,385 | 56,193 | 51,393 | 58,082 | 60,333 | 61,319 | 63,806 | Taiwan Province of China | 528 |

1 See country notes in the monthly *IFS*

Total Reserves

(with Gold at SDR 35 per ounce)

Millions of SDRs

		1965	1966	1967	1968	1969	1970	1971	1972	1973	1974	1975	1976	1977	1978	1979
Asia (cont.)																
Solomon Islands	813	....	....	....	....	....	....	....	....	....	....	....	....	2	22	28
Sri Lanka	524	73	43	55	52	40	43	46	55	72	64	50	79	240	307	395
Thailand	578	739	923	1,008	1,020	984	905	808	969	1,082	1,518	1,516	1,629	1,576	1,627	1,485
Tonga	866	....	....	....	....	....	....	....	....	....	....	....	....	7	8	10
Vanuatu	846	....	....	....	....	....	....	....	....	....	....	....	....	....	....	....
Viet Nam	582	178	307	335	279	228	241	248	250	160	196	....	....	....	....	....
Western Samoa	862	4	3	2	3	5	5	6	4	4	5	5	5	8	4	4
Europe	170	407	434	392	562	814	1,002	1,458	2,680	3,790	3,279	2,936	4,219	3,694	4,177	3,834
Cyprus	423	84	98	104	156	177	209	262	294	254	219	184	251	273	281	284
Czech Republic	935	....	....	....	....	....	....	....	....	....	....	....	....	....	....	....
Czechoslovakia 1	934	....	....	....	....	....	....	....	....	....	....	....	....	....	....	....
Hungary	944	....	....	....	....	....	....	....	....	....	....	....	....	....	....	....
Malta	181	79	90	90	1 151	139	158	183	253	270	328	427	535	605	723	782
Poland	964	....	....	....	....	....	....	....	....	....	....	....	....	....	....	474
Romania	968	....	....	....	....	....	....	....	....	....	258	282	552	580	318	406	522
Turkey	186	141	131	119	123	245	431	702	1,287	1,771	1,400	931	977	652	743	631
Yugoslavia, SFR	188	103	115	80	132	253	140	196	674	1,109	937	744	1,764	1,736	1,890	1,014
Middle East	405	2,929	3,225	3,651	3,773	3,877	4,610	7,025	9,436	11,226	29,452	38,454	45,913	53,986	42,809	48,137
Bahrain	419	23	22	28	50	68	71	88	85	61	116	253	381	420	384	471
Egypt	469	193	156	195	169	145	159	138	133	300	291	251	291	440	464	488
Iran, I.R. of	429	251	268	324	291	310	208	572	885	1,025	6,847	7,600	7,603	10,098	9,327	11,682
Iraq	433	235	324	369	453	476	462	553	720	1,287	2,673	2,330	3,960	5,759	....	....
Israel	436	643	621	715	663	412	449	679	1,126	1,504	980	1,010	1,182	1,293	2,056	2,369
Jordan	439	140	168	244	284	263	256	233	250	252	283	420	434	558	708	914
Kuwait	443	124	164	184	173	182	203	265	335	415	1,143	1,414	1,660	2,461	2,008	2,268
Lebanon	446	251	282	281	332	347	385	504	622	714	1,367	1,349	1,444	1,614	1,731	1,485
Libya	672	246	339	385	539	918	1,590	2,455	2,694	1,763	2,953	1,875	2,759	4,026	3,236	4,902
Oman	449	....	....	....	....	....	12	23	34	39	77	139	191	242	202	322
Qatar	453	....	18	27	32	35	37	42	56	63	59	89	118	140	171	228
Saudi Arabia	456	726	748	762	662	607	662	1,331	2,303	3,214	11,667	19,920	23,261	24,725	1 14,896	14,790
Syrian Arab Rep.	463	45	53	74	67	59	55	81	125	342	409	627	280	427	321	470
United Arab Emirates	466	....	....	....	....	....	....	....	....	76	370	844	1,660	679	643	1,107
Yemen Arab Rep.	473	....	....	....	....	....	....	....	....	105	162	288	620	1,021	1,120	1,084
Yemen, P.D. Rep.	459	52	62	63	60	56	59	59	62	63	55	47	71	83	145	161
Yemen, Republic of	474	....	....	....	....	....	....	....	....	....	....	....	....	....	....	....
Western Hemisphere	205	3,227	3,141	3,427	3,961	4,424	5,473	5,946	9,089	11,957	15,033	16,113	20,492	23,466	27,296	32,415
Antigua and Barbuda	311	....	....	....	....	....	....	....	....	....	....	6	8	4	5	9
Argentina	213	236	216	727	759	538	672	267	428	1,092	1,074	386	1,383	2,743	3,962	7,280
Aruba	314	....	....	....	....	....	....	....	....	....	....	....	....	....	....	....
Bahamas, The	313	....	....	....	44	26	22	27	34	36	41	46	41	1 56	45	59
Barbados	316	....	12	9	16	12	17	17	26	27	32	34	24	30	46	50
Belize	339	....	....	....	....	....	....	....	....	....	....	....	5	7	11	8
Bolivia	218	37	41	38	40	42	46	50	55	60	158	134	145	195	153	159
Brazil	223	484	426	200	258	657	1,187	1,609	3,853	5,318	4,306	3,447	5,631	5,974	9,134	6,866
Chile	228	137	172	126	208	343	389	204	137	149	84	93	395	399	885	1,525
Colombia	233	96	77	83	173	221	206	187	300	443	367	445	997	1,499	1,885	2,999
Costa Rica	238	20	17	18	21	29	16	27	39	42	36	44	84	159	152	93
Dominica	321	....	....	....	....	....	....	....	....	....	....	—	1	2	1	7
Dominican Republic	243	51	44	32	36	40	32	52	54	73	74	99	109	152	122	185
Ecuador	248	46	61	69	57	65	74	53	124	188	274	230	424	527	502	563
El Salvador	253	56	57	55	62	64	63	60	76	51	80	108	177	191	223	126
Grenada	328	....	....	....	....	....	5	5	5	4	4	1 4	7	6	7	9
Guatemala	258	68	61	65	66	74	78	86	124	176	165	260	440	568	587	547
Guyana	336	20	17	19	24	21	20	24	34	12	51	86	23	19	45	13
Haiti	263	2	2	2	3	4	4	10	17	14	16	11	24	28	30	42
Honduras	268	23	27	25	32	31	20	20	32	35	36	83	113	148	142	159
Jamaica	343	96	88	85	120	118	139	165	147	106	156	107	28	40	45	49
Mexico	273	538	564	586	657	662	744	877	1,072	1,124	1,139	1,310	1,079	1,419	1,480	1,642
Netherlands Antilles	353	....	....	....	40	48	45	53	65	61	69	80	99	102	71	75
Nicaragua	278	57	58	32	48	44	49	54	74	97	86	104	126	123	40	112
Panama	283	6	6	7	11	14	16	19	40	35	32	29	68	58	115	93
Paraguay	288	10	12	12	12	10	18	19	29	47	71	98	136	221	345	464
Peru	293	175	155	126	111	167	1 336	390	446	471	791	399	284	329	334	1,195
St. Kitts and Nevis	361	....	....	....	....	....	....	....	....	....	....	....	....	....	....	....
St. Lucia	362	....	....	....	....	....	....	....	....	....	....	3	4	5	5	6
St. Vincent & Grens.	364	....	....	....	....	....	....	....	....	....	....	....	4	4	4	7
Suriname	366	25	27	27	28	32	36	39	43	52	60	83	100	83	104	131
Trinidad and Tobago	369	29	30	30	49	45	43	64	54	39	319	642	872	1,221	1,387	1,626
Uruguay	298	179	177	162	167	184	175	167	187	207	190	174	276	391	398	1 361
Venezuela	299	819	777	872	922	933	1,021	1,401	1,595	1,999	5,320	7,569	7,384	6,764	5,031	5,958
Memorandum Items																
Oil Exporting Countries	999	2,845	3,149	3,483	3,766	4,124	4,917	7,676	9,956	11,982	38,303	48,227	56,074	62,050	46,116	56,196
Non-Oil Developing Countries	201	9,457	10,271	10,894	12,699	14,037	15,731	16,257	23,339	29,088	29,950	29,772	40,895	50,638	59,037	66,387
(with Gold at SDR 35 per ounce)																*Millions of SDRs*
All Countries	010	71,170	72,829	74,575	77,826	78,740	93,244	123,115	146,658	152,679	179,773	194,393	222,166	264,535	281,817	306,013
(with Gold at market prices)																*Millions of SDRs:*
All Countries	010	71,313	73,051	74,800	85,467	78,963	95,756	128,462	171,967	212,127	299,690	280,844	304,358	368,372	425,540	640,888

1 See country notes in the monthly *IFS*

Total Reserves

(with Gold at SDR 35 per ounce)

1980	1981	1982	1983	1984	1985	1986	1987	1988	1989	1990	1991	1992	1993	1994	Country	Code
															Asia (cont.)	
23	19	34	45	46	32	24	26	29	20	12	6	17	15	....	Solomon Islands	813
195	283	321	286	523	413	290	199	167	188	299	483	679	1,191	....	Sri Lanka	524
1,310	1,575	1,481	1,622	2,046	2,081	2,380	2,911	4,617	7,327	9,439	12,333	14,893	17,904	20,179	Thailand	578
11	12	14	20	27	25	18	20	23	19	22	23	23	27	24	Tonga	866
....	7	5	6	8	10	18	28	30	27	26	28	31	33	30	Vanuatu	846
....	42	43	42	17	15	13	....	....	....	....	....	....	....	....	Viet Nam	582
2	3	3	7	11	13	19	26	37	42	49	47	44	37	35	Western Samoa	862
5,354	5,405	5,359	7,458	9,055	7,707	8,316	8,006	10,013	14,931	15,641	15,823	15,171	17,176	19,674	**Europe**	170
305	382	490	512	568	558	631	632	706	871	1,075	988	764	815	1,019	Cyprus	423
													2,827	4,282	Czech Republic	935
1,549	931	831	902	1,123	911	1,044	1,102	1,307	1,768	862	2,327	ɪ930	....	....	Czechoslovakia ɪ	934
....	....	....	1,230	1,664	2,042	1,964	1,209	1,146	1,001	763	2,761	3,224	4,934	4,669	Hungary	944
791	939	999	1,079	1,027	915	953	1,013	1,030	1,039	1,012	936	927	995	1,271	Malta	181
127	255	603	747	1,145	809	587	1,070	1,544	1,778	3,174	2,556	2,998	2,996	4,018	Poland	964
383	472	532	628	854	315	590	1,036	630	1,491	446	564	681	808	1,521	Romania	968
976	929	1,111	1,362	1,429	1,096	1,288	1,386	1,876	3,770	4,396	3,742	4,621	4,707	5,045	Turkey	186
1,150	1,437	768	998	1,247	1,062	1,259	557	1,774	3,214	3,914	1,942	....	....	....	Yugoslavia, SFR	188
56,536	59,758	64,039	62,198	59,666	58,573	47,859	45,841	41,588	42,231	37,956	41,777	44,151	47,319	46,338	**Middle East**	405
753	1,332	1,397	1,368	1,334	1,516	1,223	815	935	804	873	1,064	1,022	953	806	Bahrain	419
905	700	718	822	836	806	763	1,057	1,024	1,242	1,971	3,808	7,947	9,480	9,319	Egypt	469
8,188	1,591	5,376	....	....	....	....	....	....	....	....	....	....	....	....	Iran, I.R. of	429
....	....	....	....	....	....	....	....	....	....	....	....	....	....	....	Iraq	433
2,670	3,046	3,518	3,523	3,158	3,386	3,845	4,178	3,020	4,050	4,440	4,404	3,729	4,647	4,653	Israel	436
932	971	839	825	562	422	395	334	107	384	623	605	586	1,220	1,187	Jordan	439
3,169	3,583	5,449	5,048	4,772	5,069	4,586	3,008	1,518	2,449	1,461	2,472	3,832	3,157	2,487	Kuwait	443
1,568	1,626	2,687	2,140	1,008	1,300	722	582	1,049	1,037	787	1,214	1,411	1,968	2,983	Lebanon	446
10,372	7,860	6,525	5,110	3,835	5,501	4,993	4,241	3,337	3,423	4,230	4,107	4,622	....	....	Libya	672
463	649	801	738	928	1,003	801	998	793	1,041	1,186	1,173	1,453	671	681	Oman	449
286	339	368	395	414	425	480	440	383	437	473	496	527	535	479	Qatar	453
18,536	27,855	26,948	26,224	25,409	22,924	15,141	16,151	15,434	12,905	8,362	8,322	4,477	5,569	5,214	Saudi Arabia	456
293	280	209	79	303	105	147	186	173	....	....	....	....	....	....	Syrian Arab Rep.	463
1,600	2,775	ɪ2,037	2,008	2,362	2,946	2,784	3,359	3,323	3,419	3,250	3,779	4,182	4,472	4,589	United Arab Emirates	466
1,006	826	502	350	325	270	353	380	212	212	....	....	....	....	....	Yemen Arab Rep.	473
185	220	261	270	255	171	114	70	61	....	....	....	....	....	....	Yemen, P.D. Rep.	459
....	....	....	....	....	....	....	....	....	....	....	299	477	235	108	Yemen, Republic of	474
31,611	33,992	25,563	27,980	41,142	37,541	27,292	26,958	23,085	25,425	34,139	46,308	64,776	79,595	72,118	**Western Hemisphere**	205
6	6	8	9	16	15	23	18	21	21	19	23	37	28	32	Antigua and Barbuda	311
5,421	2,961	2,425	1,273	1,421	ɪ3,133	2,375	1,293	2,652	1,267	3,376	4,342	7,418	10,193	9,967	Argentina	213
....	....	....	....	....	....	64	59	71	70	72	87	107	135	125	Aruba	314
72	86	103	117	164	166	189	120	128	112	111	127	113	125	121	Bahamas, The	313
62	87	110	118	135	127	124	103	101	84	83	61	102	110	134	Barbados	316
10	9	9	9	6	13	22	26	38	46	49	37	39	28	24	Belize	339
110	115	172	185	289	213	165	100	110	187	149	106	163	194	340	Bolivia	218
4,589	5,750	3,566	4,179	11,792	9,763	ɪ4,829	4,525	5,276	5,838	5,390	5,687	16,457	22,383	25,523	Brazil	223
2,508	2,820	1,705	1,999	2,403	2,284	1,985	1,829	2,412	2,822	4,331	4,988	6,733	7,084	9,030	Chile	228
3,885	4,191	3,634	1,963	1,439	1,517	2,274	2,199	2,452	2,773	2,982	4,245	5,391	5,509	5,319	Colombia	233
117	114	207	300	414	463	430	347	497	565	366	644	742	747	613	Costa Rica	238
4	3	4	1	5	3	8	13	10	9	10	12	15	14	11	Dominica	321
163	198	120	166	259	310	308	129	189	125	44	310	364	475	173	Dominican Republic	243
809	558	290	630	638	668	541	361	310	426	605	662	647	1,019	1,278	Ecuador	248
79	80	116	169	186	180	155	148	137	219	308	217	323	407	461	El Salvador	253
10	14	8	14	15	19	17	16	13	12	12	12	19	20	21	Grenada	328
367	147	120	219	298	292	314	221	168	252	205	572	561	639	599	Guatemala	258
10	6	10	6	6	6	7	6	3	10	20	87	137	180	169	Guyana	336
13	21	4	9	14	6	14	13	10	10	3	13	....	....	....	Haiti	263
118	87	102	109	131	97	92	75	38	17	29	74	144	71	118	Honduras	268
82	73	99	60	99	147	80	123	109	82	118ᵉ	74	236	304	504	Jamaica	343
2,393	3,579	828	3,818	7,504	4,549	4,725	8,875	4,012	4,852	6,965	12,424	13,800	18,298	4,316	Mexico	273
93	135	189	176	140	179	215	172	215	177	170	143	179	190	142	Netherlands Antilles	353
51	96	156	171	....	....	....	....	....	....	....	....	....	40	97	Nicaragua	278
95	103	92	197	220	89	139	55	54	91	241	349	367	435	482	Panama	283
599	693	671	651	681	487	366	352	242	330	466	674	410	461	697	Paraguay	288
1,601	1,079	1,272	1,353	1,712	1,745	1,225	508	440	684	808	1,772	2,136	2,527	4,829	Peru	293
....	3	3	3	6	7	8	7	8	12	11	12	19	21	22	St. Kitts and Nevis	361
6	7	7	8	13	12	21	22	24	29	31	34	40	44	39	St. Lucia	362
6	8	4	5	13	13	21	14	16	17	19	16	24	23	21	St. Vincent & Grens.	364
150	180	161	58	27	23	19	13	11	9	17	2	2	2	2	Suriname	366
2,182	2,878	2,794	2,012	1,386	1,029	390	134	96	189	348	239	127	152	243	Trinidad and Tobago	369
421	488	205	289	229	250	485	465	487	473	452	314	441	612	723	Uruguay	298
5,579	7,415	6,365	7,701	9,482	9,733	5,664	4,604	2,698	3,526	6,250	7,858	7,356	7,111	5,927	Venezuela	299
															Memorandum Items	
69,317	69,331	67,108	67,144	69,550	69,270	51,843	49,091	42,938	44,308	43,875	48,883	46,144	46,532	44,445	Oil Exporting Countries	999
70,887	78,797	80,076	93,857	116,328	111,042	120,449	139,044	151,748	169,408	184,739	227,191	255,216	302,213	339,373	Non-Oil Developing Countries	201

End of Period

(with Gold at SDR 35 per ounce)

1980	1981	1982	1983	1984	1985	1986	1987	1988	1989	1990	1991	1992	1993	1994		
354,727	363,106	361,209	395,568	440,264	438,130	451,913	540,624	575,790	623,853	670,561	704,511	725,589	789,167	844,534	All Countries	010

End of Period

(with Gold at market prices)

1980	1981	1982	1983	1984	1985	1986	1987	1988	1989	1990	1991	1992	1993	1994		
763,159	656,411	722,552	709,101	706,500	688,974	723,480	831,014	831,852	878,792	890,382	....	....	....	....	All Countries	010

ɪ See country notes in the monthly *IFS*

Deposit Banks' Foreign Liabilities

7y d

Billions of US Dollars:

		1980	1981	1982	1983	1984	1985	1986	1987	1988	1989	1990	1991	1992	1993	1994
All Countries	010	1,870.5	2,216.7	2,374.6	2,485.4	2,590.5	3,009.5	3,786.2	4,883.3	5,330.0	6,078.4	7,137.1	6,996.8	6,935.0	7,085.6	8,063.8
Industrial Countries	110	1,362.4	1,570.9	1,672.3	1,749.0	1,841.3	2,204.5	2,851.5	3,720.2	4,063.7	4,623.2	5,454.5	5,289.9	5,201.5	5,226.7	5,959.7
United States	111	151.45	189.92	254.55	305.78	338.12	381.26	477.22	572.95	645.26	713.61	733.32	720.46	755.41	823.18	942.65
Canada	156	42.96	61.04	57.74	61.29	61.62	64.64	68.90	71.73	69.48	70.81	77.95	76.71	73.61	67.15	80.51
Australia	193	.66	.73	.73	.65	I 1.28	2.92	I 18.33	21.80	32.08	41.05	45.83	59.62	60.04	....	....
Japan	158	80.21	100.39	100.02	106.65	127.05	179.31	345.99	592.03	772.42	879.72	958.48	845.67	708.62	688.44	723.70
New Zealand	196	.18	.16	.21	.35	.32	.45	.83	1.29	I 3.16	2.84	6.50	6.54	8.96	9.55	....
Austria	122	24.95	25.54	26.12	26.36	28.15	38.03	50.89	62.44	59.37	65.95	74.31	76.57	77.43	74.09	83.36
Belgium	124	72.95	83.10	78.37	80.20	86.38	112.92	144.84	184.79	186.43	205.53	239.79	229.93	226.06	....	....
Denmark	128	4.88	5.27	5.84	7.10	8.29	14.85	16.41	23.42	27.90	35.23	44.80	I 47.38	26.85	27.13	30.14
Finland	172	4.57	4.91	6.29	7.20	9.44	12.81	20.53	32.92	37.76	42.58	59.91	53.45	40.17	31.85	30.36
France	132	146.68	153.79	164.67	167.07	174.37	197.18	228.29	296.36	315.90	384.69	519.67	523.46	526.21	523.08	....
Germany	134	72.09	66.80	64.69	57.92	58.22	75.77	101.29	131.38	131.00	159.90	226.31	231.09	264.43	286.13	378.84
Greece	174	5.15	5.92	6.31	6.60	6.60	7.59	9.12	11.41	12.30	14.37	16.46	17.21	18.13	18.24	....
Ireland	178	10.79	10.42	I 5.72	5.67	5.65	6.98	9.08	11.78	11.77	14.14	19.33	19.00	21.10	21.53	....
Italy	136	51.41	54.28	52.01	55.51	61.81	72.83	90.96	114.42	122.17	161.77	205.38	243.07	249.85	217.13	230.54
Luxembourg	137	98.45	106.70	102.57	94.97	93.35	117.20	151.90	197.77	199.24	241.43	308.09	309.66	320.64	....	....
Netherlands	138	64.35	65.18	62.73	56.22	53.05	65.68	83.46	108.67	109.88	121.33	153.43	157.36	165.53	169.20	186.51
Norway	142	5.96	6.31	6.59	6.66	7.44	11.24	15.57	22.41	21.06	22.19	23.57	17.46	11.81	10.13	9.13
Portugal	182	....	....	7.05	6.85	7.19	8.92	10.20	....	....	....	....	....	....	....	....
Spain	184	....	....	23.51	21.39	22.99	22.45	I 25.41	33.19	37.00	43.63	63.99	73.73	82.35	87.60	101.13
Sweden	144	13.56	15.71	15.49	17.17	16.95	21.54	29.18	42.48	53.33	82.84	I 104.63	99.81	85.28	70.86	73.12
Switzerland	146	108.58	134.80	I 141.20	137.48	I 134.59	163.79	193.72	247.88	243.46	280.48	352.97	345.49	330.22	311.80	384.37
United Kingdom	112	377.71	I 451.40	489.64	519.63	538.22	625.74	758.98	926.53	960.09	1,024.56	1,201.03	I 1113.16	1,114.77	1,133.51	1,278.85
Developing Countries	200	508.14	645.76	702.36	736.37	749.17	804.99	934.69	1,163.10	1,266.31	1,455.22	1,682.65	1,707.92	1,733.52	1,858.89	2,104.08
of which:Major Offshore Bkg.Ctrs.	016	366.97	472.61	508.85	538.35	554.33	603.53	720.34	928.14	1,026.65	1,214.52	1,424.28	1,423.33	1,420.27	1,500.36	1,683.24
Africa	605	8.08	7.87	7.54	7.49	6.98	10.86	14.02	15.78	16.13	16.29	16.49	17.14	15.78	14.18	13.73
Algeria	612	2.95	2.42	2.00	2.09	2.98	5.09	7.20	8.31	8.21	7.73	7.94	7.84	7.01	5.20	4.20
Cameroon	622	.33	.20	.33	.23	.17	.27	.39	.57	.76	.79	.34	.30	.09	.13	.05
Côte d'Ivoire	662	.61	.48	.43	.42	.25	.39	.52	.78	.71	.69	.61	.56	.45	.49	.30
Ethiopia	644	.11	.10	.10	.10	.09	.09	.10	.11	.13	.13	.18	.21	.12	.15	.19
Gabon	646	.08	.11	.08	.04	.02	.09	.12	.06	.03	.14	.14	.15	.12	.09	.04
Kenya	664	.09	.06	.06	.06	.06	.06	.06	.07	.10	.10	.09	.07	.07	.06	....
Morocco	686	.69	.65	.51	.49	.47	.64	.98	1.24	1.27	1.31	1.67	1.85	1.88	1.84	....
Nigeria	694	.17	.22	.35	.39	.12	.27	.25	.23	.11	.19	.05	.12	.13	....	....
Senegal	722	.21	.17	.16	.11	.13	.17	.15	.20	.23	.26	.18	.19	.17	.15	.13
South Africa	199	.80	1.48	1.48	1.62	1.28	1.75	2.14	2.26	2.06	2.37	2.61	....	....	....	....
Sudan	732	.14	.15	.12	.12	.14	.22	.17	.14	.14	.13	.15	.11	.07	.07	.04
Tunisia	744	.68	.66	.65	.69	....	....	....	....	....	....	....	....	....	....	....
Zaïre	636	.04	.04	.05	.02	.01	.02	.04	.05	.05	.07	.05	.04	.03	.03	.03
Zambia	754	.08	.06	.11	.05	.05	.09	.04	.06	.05	.05	.05	.03	.02	.02	.01
Asia	505	111.26	154.17	180.34	197.70	222.75	267.54	357.02	515.93	590.06	686.43	838.41	861.55	871.97	932.05	1,096.74
Hong Kong	532	32.62	45.28	54.12	59.63	65.94	83.33	125.78	229.43	269.58	310.13	402.69	431.63	427.75	438.41	531.77
Indonesia	536	.62	.68	.97	.97	.71	.52	.33	.46	.67	1.79	6.74	6.02	7.89	9.25	10.77
Korea	542	9.97	12.92	16.60	17.87	20.51	24.26	23.14	16.80	14.05	13.15	14.83	21.40	24.43	30.63	42.86
Malaysia	548	1.34	1.62	1.72	3.02	2.53	2.68	2.41	2.01	1.90	....	4.96	7.15	11.66	6.65	....
Pakistan	564	.21	.32	.29	.44	.84	1.10	1.46	1.81	2.00	2.35	2.73	3.57	4.43	2.92	2.78
Philippines	566	8.75	9.66	10.81	8.97	8.55	7.45	5.30	4.89	4.62	4.31	4.40	3.80	4.89	4.88	7.28
Singapore	576	43.46	69.63	82.82	92.64	108.37	129.72	171.15	216.84	252.38	308.37	354.86	329.00	327.95	353.48	381.30
Sri Lanka	524	.16	.26	.50	.75	.62	.64	.63	.66	.60	.65	.75	.82	1.10	1.15	1.28
Thailand	578	1.77	1.93	1.73	2.44	2.68	2.50	2.08	2.34	3.31	4.34	5.90	6.80	11.76	19.41	37.99
Europe	170	....	....	....	....	....	....	....	....	....	....	40.53	40.09	39.12	40.26	35.96
Hungary	944	....	....	1.19	1.20	1.06	1.26	1.78	1.80	....	....	....	....	....	....	....
Romania	968	8.38	9.06	8.03	7.60	6.46	6.05	5.95	5.90	1.97	.51	1.72	.72	.46	.56	.69
Turkey	186	.70	.58	.85	.88	2.19	3.06	I 1.77	2.22	2.09	2.41	4.39	4.69	7.31	10.31	4.04
Yugoslavia	188	8.26	8.99	8.11	7.87	8.29	9.62	11.36	11.76	11.00	10.30	9.64	....	....	....	....
Middle East	405	60.84	75.45	87.88	92.75	90.01	84.49	84.48	96.66	105.09	110.74	100.10	92.82	110.76	102.94	114.94
Bahrain	419	30.98	41.44	48.61	52.26	53.29	48.28	48.12	57.22	62.04	67.48	57.65	51.34	67.46	58.40	63.55
Egypt	469	2.66	3.22	4.44	5.67	5.65	5.75	5.43	5.16	4.72	4.26	4.24	3.85	2.78	2.27	1.92
Iran, I.R. of	429	2.47	2.22	2.16	1.93	.62	....	1.00	1.07	1.08	1.25	1.86	2.27	4.28	3.47	....
Israel	436	7.59	8.66	10.97	10.63	10.31	10.04	10.31	10.26	10.68	9.98	11.02	11.48	12.09	12.16	13.10
Jordan	439	.53	.58	.63	.72	.85	1.00	1.11	1.27	1.23	.84	.77	1.45	2.41	2.28	....
Kuwait	443	6.09	6.99	8.28	8.79	7.85	....	....	6.46	6.92	7.95	....	3.26	....	....	....
Lebanon	446	1.58	1.59	1.78	1.60	1.39	1.02	.75	.90	.94	.89	.90	1.02	.95	1.20	1.58
Libya	672	.11	.26	.24	.20	.15	—	.17	.05	.54	.91	1.02	1.10	.69	....	....
Saudi Arabia	456	2.75	2.66	1.74	1.94	2.23	2.85	3.82	6.54	7.67	9.24	8.06	7.45	7.66	9.96	10.45
Syrian Arab Rep.	463	.38	.64	.72	.99	.93	1.17	1.26	1.31	1.13	1.06	.92	.77	.59	.49	....
United Arab Emirates	466	5.00	6.56	7.57	7.24	6.00	5.73	4.83	5.05	6.45	5.79	6.87	7.16	7.24	7.28	....
Yemen Arab Rep.	473	.05	.06	.08	.06	.10	.25	.19	.18	.20	.22	....	....	....	....	....
Western Hemisphere	205	315.72	392.72	409.68	420.69	411.38	422.70	456.66	506.72	524.53	606.71	687.12	696.32	695.89	769.45	842.71
Argentina	213	....	7.20	7.18	7.84	7.21	6.73	6.56	7.94	9.34	6.09	7.01	7.92	9.67	9.08	10.92
Bahamas, The	313	....	....	....	156.55	148.76	141.45	149.36	160.21	164.81	177.53	181.98	188.11	172.49	160.87	....
Bolivia	218	.23	.26	.24	.36	.33	.21	.21	.12	.10	.06	.07	.11	.19	.32	.47
Brazil	223	16.63	22.10	24.94	24.03	23.89	20.59	20.42	19.44	18.35	18.10	18.05	18.79	23.71	33.58	....
Cayman Islands	377	83.40	107.92	120.07	130.45	138.84	162.17	187.54	233.31	259.38	327.46	401.02	390.53	388.66	445.67	....
Chile	228	3.54	6.24	7.28	6.31	6.73	6.57	6.22	5.07	4.20	3.33	2.97	2.35	3.51	3.79	4.03
Colombia	233	1.53	1.61	1.76	1.68	1.81	....	....	....	....	....	....	2.19	2.80	3.93	5.04
Dominican Republic	243	.19	.37	.34	.12	.11	.06	.10	.15	.14	.04	.10	.11	.10	.10	.15
Jamaica	343	.07	.10	.11	.06	.05	.07	.08	.10	.16	.16	.14	.20	.25	.24	.45
Mexico	273	20.93	31.39	32.21	33.89	34.00	34.79	35.98	36.65	36.59	36.37	34.85	41.71	45.00	54.04	61.08
Netherlands Antilles	353	7.13	10.25	11.42	9.88	7.19	6.08	5.28	6.26	7.81	13.26	15.75	20.06	23.66	28.40	28.58
Nicaragua	278	.27	.11	.10	.13	.10	.10	.02	.03	—	—	—	.02	.02	.02	.03
Panama	283	34.60	41.29	42.87	36.95	31.95	32.52	33.10	....	10.65	....	....	....	....	....	....
Peru	293	.81	.98	.79	.73	.57	.44	.41	.36	.37	.39	.36	.38	.51	.52	.70
Uruguay	298	....	....	1.41	1.20	1.22	1.07	1.13	1.22	1.71	2.26	2.60	2.83	3.34	3.39	3.33
Venezuela	299	2.70	3.23	4.55	4.43	2.98	....	....	....	....	....	....	....	....	....	....
Memorandum Items																
Oil Exporting Countries	999	23.44	25.76	28.44	28.65	24.23	25.42	27.62	31.88	35.65	38.24	41.64	39.23	41.83	43.19	48.93
Non-Oil Developing Countries	201	484.44	619.79	673.67	707.48	724.80	779.43	906.95	1,131.14	1,230.54	1,416.92	1,641.00	1,668.68	1,691.69	1,815.70	2,055.15

Deposit Banks' Foreign Assets

1980	1981	1982	1983	1984	1985	1986	1987	1988	1989	1990	1991	1992	1993	1994		7x d
End of Period																
1,836.0	**2,195.6**	**2,377.4**	**2,461.7**	**2,537.5**	**2,983.4**	**3,742.8**	**4,762.1**	**5,134.8**	**5,839.2**	**6,795.1**	**6,754.6**	**6,773.7**	**7,169.4**	**7,877.1**	**All Countries**	**010**
1,373.5	**1,614.1**	**1,745.8**	**1,797.8**	**1,845.8**	**2,228.8**	**2,847.8**	**3,641.1**	**3,868.8**	**4,377.2**	**5,123.3**	**5,044.5**	**5,054.5**	**5,349.5**	**5,849.3**	**Industrial Countries**	**110**
203.98	292.85	401.53	433.13	443.37	446.78	506.70	549.56	608.04	661.72	652.15	656.28	626.73	600.14	614.17	United States	111
35.19	38.16	38.15	40.97	41.21	44.17	50.74	50.73	46.80	48.82	52.07	46.03	46.85	41.11	57.77	Canada	156
.37	.40	.12	.18	I .91	1.48	I 5.05	5.32	7.85	7.78	10.71	11.31	10.53	....	....	Australia	193
65.67	84.61	90.95	109.06	126.92	194.62	345.33	576.83	733.69	842.06	950.58	942.43	879.19	918.56	1,007.61	Japan	158
.43	.41	.40	.46	.34	.47	.58	.92	I 1.31	.80	1.86	1.28	1.16	2.25	....	New Zealand	196
21.71	22.46	25.04	25.74	26.52	36.75	48.90	58.96	54.60	58.92	65.99	66.19	66.76	68.42	77.00	Austria	122
60.68	69.94	65.75	66.20	71.61	92.63	117.93	149.13	150.37	164.52	192.03	192.02	188.52	....	....	Belgium	124
4.83	5.27	5.87	6.65	7.98	14.16	16.03	24.15	28.78	34.66	45.55	I 49.07	45.63	57.27	50.94	Denmark	128
2.76	3.23	4.15	4.78	6.26	7.67	14.31	18.82	20.54	22.24	27.00	24.27	21.50	21.61	22.23	Finland	172
160.21	158.09	162.96	156.32	158.64	184.38	217.99	290.10	299.72	358.90	458.72	459.92	514.94	583.45	....	France	132
85.17	84.54	81.73	74.76	75.23	112.93	178.48	232.61	230.09	292.86	395.49	402.03	386.84	461.96	484.89	Germany	134
1.19	1.67	1.41	1.39	1.60	1.98	1.79	1.88	2.59	2.97	3.46	4.00	4.71	5.36	....	Greece	174
8.78	8.58	I 2.79	2.59	2.65	3.22	3.84	5.90	6.26	9.86	13.54	14.37	18.61	21.72	....	Ireland	178
34.49	38.92	36.16	36.35	40.14	50.44	60.53	68.51	66.86	87.62	104.05	110.77	114.57	135.53	127.19	Italy	136
104.83	114.20	109.71	103.24	101.71	130.95	171.69	226.52	232.01	280.19	355.12	358.71	376.50	....	....	Luxembourg	137
62.63	66.35	63.92	58.86	57.52	72.88	91.10	115.98	120.57	146.27	185.92	189.05	190.59	195.75	200.37	Netherlands	138
.64	1.90	2.36	2.56	3.02	3.69	6.88	8.68	6.51	6.60	8.08	9.27	11.57	6.71	7.57	Norway	142
1.74	1.55	1.54	1.70	1.84	1.93	1.93	2.74	4.18	4.66	5.49	6.96	9.63	14.89	21.02	Portugal	182
....	....	17.78	16.19	18.10	20.73	24.68	26.94	25.76	29.03	41.40	49.34	72.28	121.39	115.41	Spain	184
8.98	8.73	8.27	9.09	8.68	11.34	14.25	19.54	20.01	38.13	I 40.95	39.76	36.45	30.00	29.39	Sweden	144
139.69	163.45	I 162.40	162.38	I 161.83	205.46	253.44	331.95	319.06	355.60	444.05	428.59	411.93	389.78	459.46	Switzerland	146
356.32	432.71	462.82	485.21	489.71	I 590.07	715.54	875.31	883.08	922.94	1,068.97	I 982.81	1,018.98	1,051.27	1,200.17	United Kingdom	112
462.54	**581.45**	**631.62**	**663.90**	**691.66**	**754.66**	**895.01**	**1,121.00**	**1,266.03**	**1,462.01**	**1,671.83**	**1,710.06**	**1,719.22**	**1,819.89**	**2,027.82**	**Developing Countries**	**200**
373.09	479.42	519.49	546.45	565.85	622.32	758.72	973.34	1,096.62	1,273.63	1,460.55	1,486.13	1,492.65	1,571.14	1,755.62	*of which:Major Offshore Bkg.Ctrs.*	016
4.13	**4.04**	**3.98**	**4.14**	**4.06**	**4.74**	**4.85**	**5.69**	**6.44**	**7.21**	**7.16**	**7.90**	**7.27**	**7.36**	**9.31**	**Africa**	**605**
.68	.66	.65	.44	.42	.38	.38	.25	.57	.68	.74	1.09	.91	.68	1.05	Algeria	612
.03	.15	.07	.13	.28	.43	.13	.28	.40	.48	.14	.17	.10	.09	.14	Cameroon	622
.09	.10	.12	.10	.15	.17	.17	.19	.15	.14	.19	.16	.21	.18	.20	Côte d'Ivoire	662
.05	.06	.09	.07	.07	.06	.07	.06	.07	.07	.05	.15	.19	.24	.54	Ethiopia	644
.02	.03	.03	.02	.02	.03	.04	.04	.04	.08	.09	.09	.06	.05	.08	Gabon	646
.07	.07	.05	.04	.04	.04	.05	.04	.05	.06	.07	.07	.11	.35	....	Kenya	664
.25	.33	.28	.27	.25	.32	.39	.44	.50	.57	.78	.69	.60	.52	.76	Morocco	686
.51	.49	.52	.58	.64	.55	.87	1.07	1.47	1.47	1.16	1.61	1.45	....	....	Nigeria	694
.06	.04	.06	.05	.04	.04	.04	.04	.06	.08	.05	.07	.07	.07	.13	Senegal	722
.54	.46	.48	.61	.47	.73	.83	1.09	.76	.68	.47	....	....	....	....	South Africa	199
.43	.31	.29	.41	.51	.62	.49	.35	.50	.54	.62	.60	.32	.45	.27	Sudan	732
.13	.16	.20	.23	.23	.23	.22	....	....	....	....	....	....	....	....	Tunisia	744
.17	.15	.11	.11	.07	.08	.10	.13	.09	.17	.13	.09	.07	.06	.08	Zaïre	636
.06	.09	.03	.04	.03	.05	.06	.12	.14	.17	.17	.13	.12	.21	....	Zambia	754
102.74	**139.43**	**162.36**	**180.84**	**209.35**	**257.39**	**348.06**	**506.33**	**596.38**	**708.45**	**867.98**	**883.38**	**890.65**	**928.27**	**1,067.91**	**Asia**	**505**
35.77	47.59	58.23	67.56	78.75	101.17	155.23	266.05	309.74	355.64	463.79	502.13	506.93	517.75	614.68	Hong Kong	532
4.36	5.06	3.78	4.55	4.78	5.55	4.99	4.73	4.85	6.03	6.22	5.59	6.34	5.37	5.84	Indonesia	536
3.76	4.39	4.55	4.84	5.25	5.23	4.87	5.73	I 8.87	8.53	10.60	12.49	14.87	21.58	28.84	Korea	542
.87	.89	1.24	2.31	1.08	1.25	1.49	2.01	2.80	2.94	2.80	2.37	2.06	3.93	4.18	Malaysia	548
.31	.32	.33	.46	.55	.56	.69	.80	.83	.93	1.46	1.58	1.38	1.40	1.58	Pakistan	564
3.17	3.36	3.88	2.76	2.85	2.80	2.60	3.15	3.81	4.06	4.42	4.30	5.17	5.29	6.52	Philippines	566
44.63	70.25	81.33	88.23	101.37	120.47	161.97	209.84	248.10	306.06	346.73	322.19	324.00	338.17	365.85	Singapore	576
.24	.32	.55	.75	.66	.67	.67	.68	.72	.79	.95	.87	1.04	.97	1.18	Sri Lanka	524
.92	1.12	1.32	1.07	1.13	1.26	1.61	1.54	1.78	2.73	2.23	2.87	3.05	6.17	6.74	Thailand	578
....	**....**	**....**	**....**	**....**	**....**	**10.90**	**13.02**	**16.08**	**17.93**	**22.48**	**24.62**	**28.78**	**30.19**	**31.15**	**Europe**	**170**
....	....	.07	.13	.12	.35	.64	.66	.78	1.00	1.16	1.41	....	....	....	Hungary	944
.26	.19	.25	.35	.32	1.00	.51	.57	1.02	.80	.68	.26	.13	.22	.13	Romania	968
....	....	....	....	....	....	2.74	3.86	5.04	4.69	5.51	6.11	9.10	11.32	9.13	Turkey	186
1.81	2.17	1.89	1.90	2.28	2.68	2.17	2.04	2.09	2.95	1.69	....	....	....	....	Yugoslavia	188
76.58	**98.97**	**114.35**	**119.76**	**122.80**	**118.18**	**123.06**	**138.85**	**151.77**	**161.46**	**154.36**	**152.10**	**161.63**	**154.29**	**157.60**	**Middle East**	**405**
31.41	42.73	49.84	54.61	55.02	50.71	50.92	59.73	65.22	70.47	59.31	54.03	69.81	60.71	66.10	Bahrain	419
4.64	3.98	6.28	7.64	7.06	7.39	6.84	7.82	7.26	8.52	10.40	12.64	11.37	10.84	11.46	Egypt	469
2.22	1.92	3.19	2.29	1.71	2.05	2.12	1.55	1.46	2.06	3.13	3.02	3.09	1.55	....	Iran, I.R. of	429
5.52	6.27	7.19	6.85	6.64	6.26	6.57	6.45	7.26	7.36	8.32	8.90	10.61	10.14	11.33	Israel	436
.67	.69	.73	.82	.82	1.05	1.17	1.37	1.20	.98	.99	1.92	2.14	2.22	2.40	Jordan	439
9.78	11.46	11.50	12.35	12.77	....	....	12.39	13.76	15.48	....	10.30	....	....	....	Kuwait	443
3.67	4.34	3.70	3.28	2.95	2.56	2.75	3.15	3.20	2.89	2.82	3.48	3.17	4.11	3.81	Lebanon	446
1.13	.98	.93	.72	.70	.55	.48	.37	.38	.18	.29	.28	.46	....	....	Libya	672
9.99	16.00	18.15	18.27	19.21	19.79	23.57	28.40	31.76	32.86	34.16	32.90	28.30	30.95	27.36	Saudi Arabia	456
.11	.07	.29	.24	.14	.15	.22	.24	.30	.50	.99	1.73	2.33	2.67	....	Syrian Arab Rep.	463
5.67	8.25	10.04	10.14	12.56	12.61	13.97	13.64	15.98	16.81	17.52	19.14	18.66	18.12	....	United Arab Emirates	466
.16	.17	.23	.23	.22	.22	.24	.13	.11	.11	....	....	....	....	....	Yemen Arab Rep.	473
273.45	**331.92**	**343.23**	**351.08**	**347.03**	**365.17**	**408.14**	**457.12**	**495.36**	**566.97**	**619.85**	**642.06**	**630.88**	**699.78**	**761.86**	**Western Hemisphere**	**205**
....	1.01	.75	1.22	1.28	1.07	1.07	1.31	1.27	1.56	2.24	2.82	3.65	5.19	5.68	Argentina	213
....	....	....	157.24	147.07	143.06	151.16	163.00	164.37	175.98	174.70	175.80	160.71	159.73	....	Bahamas, The	313
.04	.04	.02	.03	.03	.02	.04	.06	.06	.07	.06	.06	.08	.07	.07	Bolivia	218
1.49	2.11	2.20	2.33	2.41	1.99	3.39	3.55	5.68	8.26	8.73	9.60	11.28	15.29	....	Brazil	223
84.53	109.57	125.96	131.28	143.59	167.20	199.83	242.53	290.73	341.95	389.40	398.98	393.17	448.73	....	Cayman Islands	377
.55	.88	.96	.81	.72	.41	.48	.34	.40	.38	.51	.53	.52	.52	.51	Chile	228
....	1.41	.65	.33	1.15	.84	.78	.73	.87	....	....	....	....	....	....	Colombia	233
.13	.27	.29	.04	.06	.12	.17	.12	.21	.12	.12	.13	.14	.16	.14	Dominican Republic	243
.04	.05	.06	.08	.06	.06	.06	.07	.10	.12	.12	.24	.31	.29	.48	Jamaica	343
1.37	1.02	1.58	2.52	2.30	2.50	2.49	3.20	3.04	2.98	3.87	5.06	6.02	6.91	8.15	Mexico	273
7.39	10.57	11.85	10.25	7.71	6.61	5.97	6.95	8.58	13.93	16.44	21.01	24.98	29.98	29.37	Netherlands Antilles	353
.02	.05	.06	.04	.01	.01	—	.01	—	—	.01	.03	.04	.05	.05	Nicaragua	278
34.21	41.10	43.48	37.29	32.34	33.09	33.64	....	9.87	....	....	....	....	....	....	Panama	283
.41	.59	.45	.38	.36	.27	.34	.41	.45	.65	.59	1.07	1.01	.88	1.15	Peru	293
....	....	.82	.73	.68	.79	.91	1.14	1.45	2.07	2.63	3.33	3.94	3.90	3.65	Uruguay	298
.98	.89	.66	1.42	2.04	....	....	....	....	....	....	....	....	....	....	Venezuela	299
															Memorandum Items	
36.82	**47.72**	**51.58**	**52.99**	**57.80**	**57.95**	**62.18**	**67.52**	**75.66**	**80.41**	**81.16**	**79.18**	**72.39**	**72.54**	**69.42**	**Oil Exporting Countries**	**999**
425.62	**533.60**	**579.93**	**610.83**	**633.74**	**696.66**	**832.83**	**1,053.49**	**1,190.37**	**1,381.60**	**1,590.69**	**1,630.88**	**1,646.82**	**1,747.35**	**1,958.40**	**Non-Oil Developing Countries**	**201**

1995 International Financial Statistics Yearbook 75

Cross-Border Interbank Liabilities by Residence of Borrowing Bank

8ya d

Billions of US Dollars

		1980	1981	1982	1983	1984	1985	1986	1987	1988	1989	1990	1991	1992	1993	1994
World	001	1,546.7	1,794.0	1,843.7	1,918.4	2,011.1	2,351.6	2,997.5	3,956.7	4,341.7	4,911.0	5,632.5	5,487.5	5,433.0	5,540.3	6,262.7
International Monetary Inst. BIS	096	32.85	27.66	29.00	32.50	32.55	41.92	36.23	60.56	58.86	76.84	81.84	68.54	106.62	115.26	130.05
Other Countries n.i.e.	910	....	11.41	8.92	8.18	8.04	10.60	11.90	14.24	15.61	16.99	3.03	2.70	2.40	2.08	2.29
All Countries	010	1,491.8	1,754.9	1,805.8	1,877.7	1,970.5	2,299.1	2,949.4	3,881.9	4,267.2	4,817.2	5,547.5	5,416.3	5,324.0	5,423.0	6,130.3
Industrial Countries	110	1,040.7	1,175.2	1,219.9	1,277.4	1,349.4	1,632.4	2,163.4	2,871.3	3,182.3	3,579.1	4,160.1	3,977.8	3,880.6	3,888.9	4,429.2
United States	111	129.92	162.45	209.01	246.95	270.67	307.42	396.63	491.79	558.42	610.24	640.49	628.32	664.00	726.29	832.85
Canada	156	24.97	37.93	38.75	36.29	34.58	34.30	36.53	40.01	38.37	38.81	42.19	43.20	46.33	42.79	50.69
Australia	193	.35	.33	.32	.36	I.15	.42	I16.80	19.16	27.04	34.66	38.62	51.91			
Japan	158	78.10	97.96	97.53	104.29	123.47	173.10	339.13	584.86	762.51	866.24	945.13	830.51	690.91	669.41	703.91
New Zealand	196	.18	.16	.21	.35	.32	.45	.83	1.29	I3.16	2.84	6.50	6.54	8.96	9.55	....
Austria	122	19.92	18.91	19.82	20.35	20.73	28.34	37.73	46.83	42.45	44.83	50.51	53.02	54.03	51.77	59.29
Belgium-Luxembourg	126	142.60	156.42	148.65	143.47	145.93	185.44	231.12	291.19	280.05	302.63	351.80	329.35	319.02		
Denmark	128	4.46	4.69	5.39	6.75	7.88	13.42	14.47	21.03	24.88	32.42	42.29	I44.15	32.77	22.11	22.32
Finland	172	4.57	4.92	6.80	7.56	9.45	12.82	20.53	32.93	37.78	42.59	59.91	53.46	40.19	31.89	30.39
France	132	121.24	127.02	129.86	128.73	129.22	143.27	168.69	221.29	233.73	286.07	382.24	364.94	349.93	336.05	....
Germany	134	56.98	50.73	49.35	41.97	40.76	53.85	71.82	89.91	94.56	115.61	164.65	167.07	184.03	190.05	259.81
Greece	174	2.68	3.46	4.12	4.65	5.33	7.04	I9.63	....							
Iceland	176	.20	.25	.26	.34	.33	.44	.44	.65	.79	.71	.72	.74	.69	.63	.60
Ireland	178	....		3.05	3.01	3.05	3.41	5.34	7.21	7.34	8.98	12.54	11.65	15.53	14.42	....
Italy	136	49.99	52.92	50.33	53.39	59.50	69.76	86.07	107.95	114.89	146.71	189.17	224.48	232.11	201.21	....
Netherlands	138	52.11	51.11	47.64	42.00	37.69	46.34	57.86	76.32	74.43	75.86	93.86	94.42	105.16	106.31	114.17
Norway	142	2.36	2.77	3.24	3.25	4.03	6.41	7.71	12.65	10.53	10.99	11.77	7.93	4.89	5.10	4.95
Portugal	182	....		7.16	6.90	7.15	8.88	10.13								
Spain	184			13.85	12.02	12.58	10.69	I12.37	17.72	19.70	22.99	38.01	46.02	51.95	58.69	64.34
Sweden	144	12.38	13.88	14.88	15.92	15.70	19.20	27.15	37.35	46.30	71.51	I92.50	85.85	76.06	61.41	65.71
Switzerland	146	34.08	37.34	I31.59	29.57	I28.66	39.49	52.04	69.88	70.34	79.65	100.40	101.14	96.70	95.44	130.26
United Kingdom	112	282.25	I328.00	338.04	369.10	392.12	467.86	560.16	678.73	711.83	758.82	866.28	I798.92	818.77	853.80	984.38
Developing Countries	200	451.12	579.76	585.93	600.33	621.16	666.73	786.00	1,010.59	1,084.96	1,238.09	1,387.56	1,438.47	1,443.42	1,534.11	1,701.15
of which: Major Offshore Bkg.Ctrs.	016	276.48	348.03	372.51	379.80	401.45	429.72	523.96	713.66	788.45	938.33	1,088.29	1,099.76	1,102.94	1,160.81	1,329.13
Africa	605	10.91	18.39	14.14	14.43	14.14	16.67	18.38	19.13	19.42	18.67	18.18	18.23	18.40	17.37	16.90
Algeria	612	1.75	1.37	1.11	1.06	1.45	2.95	4.41	5.13	6.07	5.70	5.04	5.08	4.54	3.15	2.89
Benin	638							.11	.22	.19	.08	.06	.06	.06	.06	.03
Botswana	616	—	.01	—	.01	.01	.01	.01	.02	.01	.01	.02	.01	.01	.03	.01
Burkina Faso	748	.03	.03	.03	.02	.02	.04	.06	.08	.07	.06	.08	.07	.04	.05	.03
Burundi	618	.01	.01	.01	.01	.01	.01	.01	.01	.01	.02	.02	.02	.02	.02	.03
Cameroon	622	.33	.20	.33	.23	.17	.27	.40	.57	.76	.79	.34	.30	.09	.13	....
Cape Verde	624														—	—
Central African Rep.	626	.03	.02	.01	—	—	—	.01	.01	.02	.02	.02	.01	.02	.01	—
Chad	628	.01	.01	.01	—	.01	.01	.01	.01	.02	.02	.03	.03	.03	.03	....
Comoros	632			—		—	—	—	.01	.01	.01	.01	.01			
Congo	634	.06	.10	.08	.10	.11	.14	.17	.09	.07	.06	.06	.06	.10	.06	....
Côte d'Ivoire	662	.97	.97	.76	.89	.51	.36	.50	.96	1.21	1.41	1.65	1.59	1.76	1.68	.19
Djibouti	611					.03	.07	.05	.05	.03	.06	.04	.05	.05	.05	.06
Equatorial Guinea	642															
Ethiopia	644	.10	.07	.07	.06	.05	.06	.07	.08	.11	.13	.18	.18	.26	.27	.28
Gabon	646	.08	.11	.08	.04	.02	.10	.12	.12	.09	.15	.15	.16	.13	.09	.04
Gambia, The	648	.03	.02	.02	.01	.01	.02	.01	.01	.01	.01	.01	.01	.01	.01	.01
Ghana	652	.03	.16	.13	.15	.24	.37	.85	.22	.15	.25	.08	.12	.07	.08	.12
Guinea	656	....	—		.02	.02	.05	.04	.03	.02	.02	.02	.02	.01	.02	.01
Guinea-Bissau	654											.02		—	—	—
Kenya	664	.07	.05	.06	.05	.05	.05	.05	.01	.04	.06	.05	.01	.02	.02	....
Lesotho	666	.01	—	—	.02	—	—	—	—	.01	.01	.01	.01			
Liberia	668	.07	.07	.06	.06	.04	.05	.03	.04	.04	.04	....	.05	.04	.02	.05
Madagascar*	674	.63	.32	.13	.13	.16	.16	.14	.13	.12	.09	.09	.08	.06	.05	.04
Malawi	676	.04	.02	.02	.03	.03	.03	.04	.02	.01	.01	.01	.01	.02	.02	....
Mali	678	....				.02	.04	.09	.11	.06	.07	.08	.05	.03	.03	.03
Mauritania	682	.16	.18	.19	.17	.18	.15	.17	.17	.18	.12	.14	.21	.20	.17	....
Mauritius	684	—	—	—	.01	.01	.01	—	.01	.01	.01	.01	.01	—	.03	.04
Morocco	686	.58	.57	.41	.44	.37										
Mozambique	688	....					—	—	—	—	—	.01	.02	....		
Niger	692	.08	.04	.09	.06	.04	.05	.05	.06	.05	.06	.04	.04	.07	.07	.02
Nigeria	694	.47	.86	.74	.63	.25	.29	.26	.23	.11	.18	.04	.11	.22	....	....
Rwanda	714	.02	.02	.01	.02	.02	.02	.01	.02	.03	.03	.06	.05	.04	.04	....
Senegal	722	.29	.32	.36	.31	.29	.46	.38	.46	.56	.42	.43	.40	.39	.51	.23
Seychelles	718	—	—	—	—	—	—	—	—	—	.01	.01	.01	.01	.01	.01
Sierra Leone	724	.10	.15	.16	.20	.21	.21	.15	.22	.22	.19	.19	.18	.24	.23	.31
Somalia	726	.03	.06	.07	.08	.09	.09	.12	.11	.10	.10	....				
South Africa*	199	....	10.18	6.32	7.32	8.27	8.33	7.39	7.41	6.14	5.58	5.47	5.12	5.44	5.41	6.70
Sudan	732	.75	.96	.89	.68	.56	.48	.33	.23	.20	.17	....			.19	.21
Swaziland	734	.01	.01	.01	.02	.01	—	.01	.01	.02	.02	.02	.01	.02	.02	.02
Tanzania	738	.03	—	.02	....	.05	.40	.75	.34	.56	....			.99	.97	....
Togo	742	.06	.06	.05	.04	.04	.06	.08	.06	.07	.07	....	.05	.06	.05	.04
Tunisia	744	.31	.31	.32	.34											
Uganda	746	.02	.04	.03	.01	.01	.01	.01	.02	.02	.02	.06	.03	.02	.08	....
Zaïre	636	.18	.07	.17	.14	.01	.02	.04	.05	.05	.07	.05	.04	.03	.29	.30
Zambia	754	.69	.64	1.00	.71	.54	.56	.38	.46	.51	.56	.62	.51			
Zimbabwe	698	.04	.18	.25	.35	.11	.07	.07	.07	.06	.06	.21	.44	.47	.71	.61
Asia	505	96.34	134.67	156.38	169.65	194.56	235.29	319.61	469.61	536.94	626.33	764.81	791.40	797.76	855.89	1,013.70
Afghanistan, Islamic State of	512	.01	.02	.01	....											
Bangladesh	513	.29	.27	.28	.20	.18	.19	.16	.17	.22	.28	.34	.67	.70	.79	.89
Bhutan	514	....									.01	.01	.01	.01		
China, People's Rep.	924	5.67	3.87	2.91	3.34	3.65	6.63	8.39	10.16	11.66	10.58	12.87	19.92	19.40	21.93	31.30
Fiji	819	.01	.01	.01	.01	.01	.04	.11	.02	.03	.04	.07	.04	.04	.04	.04
Hong Kong	532	32.62	45.28	54.12	59.63	65.94	83.33	125.78	229.43	269.58	310.13	402.69	431.63	427.75	438.41	531.77
India	534	—	—	—	—	—	—	—	—	—	—			....	....	....
Indonesia	536	.57	.63	.91	.92	.68	.49	.30	.42	.64	1.69	6.58	5.70	7.50	....	....

Cross-Border Interbank Claims by Residence of Lending Bank

1980	1981	1982	1983	1984	1985	1986	1987	1988	1989	1990	1991	1992	1993	1994		8xa d
End of Period																
1,486.0	1,739.2	1,818.3	1,862.8	1,970.3	2,314.9	2,942.5	3,853.5	4,184.4	4,768.4	5,449.4	5,338.3	5,272.9	5,485.0	6,151.9	World	001
29.88	24.89	25.32	28.49	27.17	34.84	32.37	53.42	52.70	65.58	64.94	55.84	83.38	84.75	102.11	International Monetary Inst. BIS	096
....	....	2.22	2.13	4.66	4.65	6.68	7.42	9.00	9.57	9.51	.70	.53	.52	.40	Other Countries n.i.e.	910
1,443.8	1,712.1	1,790.8	1,829.7	1,938.5	2,273.4	2,902.7	3,791.0	4,122.1	4,693.3	5,383.8	5,282.0	5,189.0	5,399.8	6,049.3	All Countries	010
975.9	1,142.9	1,226.7	1,244.4	1,325.5	1,605.3	2,103.9	2,777.7	3,013.1	3,429.2	4,012.6	3,901.3	3,810.2	3,936.3	4,364.9	Industrial Countries	110
146.63	212.64	294.49	312.05	324.36	336.08	396.43	442.02	503.73	558.12	562.19	577.34	540.62	500.58	528.11	United States	111
27.87	28.62	31.02	33.21	33.72	34.38	42.63	40.14	33.90	36.08	39.85	34.07	35.40	28.46	43.44	Canada	156
1.12	.79	.90	1.32	I 2.95	3.23	I 6.17	8.48	12.57	13.02	18.12	18.39				Australia	193
47.62	63.53	67.08	80.94	89.94	136.09	260.01	451.58	593.80	682.34	769.44	751.08	678.64	682.77	764.38	Japan	158
.52	.81	.60	.62	1.65	1.35	3.50	2.31	I 2.22	3.23	2.56	2.23	1.87	3.00	....	New Zealand	196
10.60	10.22	10.64	10.83	11.39	16.91	23.90	31.23	27.87	28.85	32.18	30.71	31.35	35.53	41.40	Austria	122
95.68e	104.58e	98.81e	95.89	99.36	134.16	176.92	239.43	247.61							Belgium-Luxembourg	126
5.37e	5.66e	6.24e	7.23e	8.50	15.06	16.72	27.33	29.16	35.70	42.51	I 42.46	41.29	45.06	38.83	Denmark	128
4.32	4.35	4.78	5.65	8.62	10.93	15.36	24.54	25.75	26.03	34.16	30.41	25.74	25.57	30.99	Finland	172
103.45	97.86	97.10	91.76	94.41	106.06	124.96	179.44	195.79	240.58	310.98	311.08	356.78	403.71	....	France	132
43.89	45.18	43.44	39.26	42.87	67.62	120.49	158.20	159.62	211.70	283.39	277.52	251.91	309.92	318.70	Germany	134
2.39	2.58	2.15	2.09	2.22	2.47	2.73	3.81	5.43	5.26	5.64	7.57	7.62	10.99	....	Greece	174
.07	.07	.06	.04	.05	.10	.15	.16	.16	.17	.26	.22	.22	.21	.20	Iceland	176
....	9.72e	I 4.07	3.80	3.81	4.85	5.60	9.18	9.41	12.19	15.71	15.92	16.79	21.98	....	Ireland	178
33.78	38.05	35.45	35.65	39.41	49.30	58.60	65.49	64.13	....	95.22	94.96	86.60	92.37	....	Italy	136
48.18	50.28	46.13	42.02	42.31	53.81	63.22	83.11	84.98	104.70	139.25	140.03	137.16	139.70	139.36	Netherlands	138
3.95	5.10	5.07	4.00	5.15	5.81	5.32	7.00	7.23	5.16	6.97	7.85	6.57	3.57	3.58	Norway	142
2.49	2.02	1.93	2.06	2.32	3.27	3.28	5.94	9.26	12.71	16.40	23.64	24.93	26.85	33.36	Portugal	182
....	....	19.23	17.41	23.09	23.92	28.90	45.06	42.37	47.03	56.78	64.60	72.86	102.30	99.46	Spain	184
8.16	7.90	7.56	7.14	8.71	12.74	14.88	20.91	20.47	30.30	I 39.56	37.86	40.82	35.97	38.14	Sweden	144
104.75	127.98	I 128.20	113.12	I 133.64	168.08	204.77	265.94	259.86	293.05	370.53	356.58	344.46	313.91	373.37	Switzerland	146
252.83	301.91	320.04	336.56	345.17	I 417.00	526.59	662.64	673.29	703.72	809.04	I 713.58	727.04	728.69	865.96	United Kingdom	112
467.91	569.22	564.09	585.27	613.04	668.05	798.77	1,013.33	1,108.99	1,264.14	1,371.21	1,380.65	1,378.76	1,463.51	1,684.40	Developing Countries	200
245.00	314.66	337.95	361.30	375.02	419.49	548.75	718.55	802.17	920.44	973.56	955.94	931.75	970.11	1,121.73	of which:Major Offshore Bkg.Ctrs.	016
17.93	11.03	9.31	9.29	8.60	11.26	11.31	12.58	13.36	15.26	19.31	22.63	18.71	20.04	25.09	Africa	605
4.12	3.98	2.58	1.90	1.48	2.76	1.53	1.43	1.25	1.29	1.18	1.99	2.01	1.78	3.34	Algeria	612
....	....	....	....	....	....	.02	.02	.02	.01	.08	.24	.31	.34	.38	Benin	638
.33	.24	.24	.32	.39	.44	.50	1.07	1.09	1.18	1.67	1.35	1.28	1.04	1.06	Botswana	616
.06	.06	.05	.08	.10	.13	.23	.34	.33	.29	.34	.37	.37	.42	.27	Burkina Faso	748
.08	.05	.02	.02	.01	.02	.06	.05	.05	.09	.10	....	.17	.16	.21	Burundi	618
.03	.15	.07	.13	.28	.43	.13	.28	.40	.48	.14	.17	.10	.09	....	Cameroon	622
....	....	....	....	....	....	....	....	....	....	....	....	....	.01	.03	Cape Verde	624
.01	.01	.01	.01	.01	.02	.03	.03	.01	.01	.01	.01	.01	.01	....	Central African Rep.	626
.01	.01	.01	.01	.02	.03	.02	.02	.02	.02	.06	.03	.03	.01	....	Chad	628
....	....	—	—	—	—	—	—	.01	—	....	.01	—	....	....	Comoros	632
....	.03	.02	.01	.02	.03	.03	.04	.05	.04	.05	.05	.07	.08	....	Congo	634
.09	.11	.12	.10	.15	.18	.18	.13	.16	.15	.19	.17	.21	.18	.40	Côte d'Ivoire	662
....	....	....	....	.21	.24	.21	.25	.26	.28	.29	.31	.28	.29	.29	Djibouti	611
....	....	....	....	....	.01	....	.01	....	....	.01	.01	.01	—	.01	Equatorial Guinea	642
.09	.27	.23	.15	.07	.18	.29	.17	.10	.08	.04	.18	.37	.70	1.03	Ethiopia	644
.02	.03	.03	.02	.02	.03	.04	.04	.04	.08	.09	.09	.06	.05	....	Gabon	646
.01	.01	.01	—	.01	.01	.02	.02	.03	.03	.05	.07	.10	.11	.10	Gambia, The	648
.13	.09	.11	.16	.26	.44	.81	.16	.14	.32	.32	.61	.38	.50	.55	Ghana	652
....	....	....	.05	.02	.05	.07	.09	.05	.05	.07	.08	.11	.11	.12	Guinea	656
....	....	....	....	....	....	....	....	....	.01	—	....	.01	.01	.01	Guinea-Bissau	654
.40	.18	.12	.35	.35	.36	.39	.23	.26	.29	.26	.17	.20	.60	....	Kenya	664
.09	.07	.09	.12	.09	.08	.09	.08	.08	.07	.12	.17	.24	.26	.37	Lesotho	666
.03	.02	.01	.04	.01	.02	.02	.02	.02	.03	....	.02	.01	.02	.01	Liberia	668
.10	.07	.07	.07	.11	.10	.17	.25	.28	.33	.18	.19	.19	.21	.23	Madagascar	674
.06	.04	.02	.01	.05	.04	.01	.04	.12	.09	.12	.13	.04	.06	.05	Malawi	676
.02	.02	.02	.03	.04	.03	.03	.04	.04	.17	.25	.37	.34	.35	.31	Mali	678
.15	.17	.14	.11	.08	.06	.06	.08	.09	.11	.08	.08	.08	.07	....	Mauritania	682
.10	.03	.05	.03	.03	.05	.15	.21	.33	.37	.59	.84	.78	.70	.60	Mauritius	684
.48	.31	.25	.14	.09	....	....	....	....	....	.01	.01	....	....	....	Morocco	686
....	....	....	....	—	—	—	—	—	—	—	....	....	....	....	Mozambique	688
.13	.11	.02	.05	.09	.13	.19	.25	.24	.22	.23	.21	.24	.20	.14	Niger	692
6.96	1.44	1.65	1.41	1.69	1.77	1.90	2.18	2.07	2.99	4.71	6.07	1.98	....	....	Nigeria	694
....	.16	.13	.10	.11	.11	.16	.17	.13	.08	.06	.13	.10	.06	....	Rwanda	714
.06	.05	.06	.05	.04	.04	.04	.05	.06	.10	.06	.08	.08	.07	.31	Senegal	722
.02	.02	.01	.01	.01	.01	.01	.02	.01	.02	.03	.04	.04	.04	.03	Seychelles	718
.04	.02	.01	.02	.02	.01	.02	.01	.03	.04	.01	.02	.04	.05	.06	Sierra Leone	724
.06	.10	.10	.06	.02	.11	.07	.08	.07	.04	....	....	....	....	....	Somalia	726
1.01	.85	.76	1.33	.62	1.04	1.20	1.70	1.54	1.64	1.47	....	....	....	....	South Africa	199
.46	.31	.30	.41	.52	.62	.50	.36	.50	.54	.42	.60	.23	.45	.27	Sudan	732
.12	.08	.06	.06	.07	.07	.08	.11	.15	.19	.19	.16	.16	.11	.10	Swaziland	734
.19	.14	.17	.23	.11	.07	.10	.05	.10	....	....	....	.34	.23	....	Tanzania	738
.12	.21	.23	.22	.25	.35	.38	.42	.31	.40	.43	.45	.36	.21	.17	Togo	742
.61	.56	.66	.63	.48	.31	.35	....	....	....	....	....	....	....	....	Tunisia	744
.02	.04	.09	.13	.11	.07	.12	.13	.22	.09	.21	.08	.15	.24	....	Uganda	746
.37	.27	.15	.19	.21	.08	.37	.26	.24	.33	.13	.09	.07	.24	.23	Zaïre	636
.12	.11	.05	.07	.07	.22	.10	.18	.28	.35	.54	.43	....	....	....	Zambia	754
.19	.14	.16	.09	.18	.18	.20	.16	.19	.10	.17	.23	.22	.43	.43	Zimbabwe	698
107.04	136.18	151.58	169.29	197.81	248.56	352.93	496.75	565.57	646.93	728.96	702.50	707.00	744.10	886.18	Asia	505
.40	.38	.30	.34	.34	.42	.39	.42	.38	.36	.42	....	....	....	....	Afghanistan, Islamic State of	512
.46	.27	.23	.58	.50	.50	.54	.93	1.18	.74	.92	1.53	2.01	2.64	3.59	Bangladesh	513
....	....	....	.03	.03	.03	.03	.05	.05	.04	.03	.01	.01	....	.01	Bhutan	514
2.26	4.78	11.14	14.48	14.04	8.33	....	....	....	....	....	....	....	....	....	China, People's Rep.	924
.16	.12	.12	.11	.11	.14	.16	.11	.21	.19	.26	.27	.31	.28	.28	Fiji	819
24.55	33.62	42.44	50.20	59.73	81.58	132.64	218.68	252.45	274.20	327.31	313.83	299.10	284.99	357.50	Hong Kong	532
2.56	1.44	1.55	2.24	2.93	2.93	2.98	2.64	1.99	1.31	1.00	3.59	4.70	7.24	16.86	India	534
8.87	8.77	5.54	7.49	8.52	9.18	8.02	9.31	8.97	10.53	12.53	13.85	15.28	....	....	Indonesia	536

Cross-Border Interbank Liabilities by Residence of Borrowing Bank

8ya d

Billions of US Dollars

		1980	1981	1982	1983	1984	1985	1986	1987	1988	1989	1990	1991	1992	1993	1994
Asia (cont.)																
Korea	542	9.87	12.78	16.35	17.43	19.95	23.47	22.57	16.30	13.65	12.85	14.54	21.14	24.17	30.30	42.33
Malaysia	548	1.17	1.48	1.54	1.80	2.29	2.39	2.15	1.84	1.68	....	....	4.55	6.68	10.47	5.69
Maldives	556	—	.01	.01	.02	.03	.03	.02	.02	.02	.03	.03	.02	.02	.02	....
Myanmar	518	—	—	—	—	—	.06	.02	.01	.01	.01	—	....	....	....	....
Nepal	558	—	.01	.01	—	—	.01	.01	.02	.01	.01	.01	....	.01	—	....
Pakistan	564	.12	.23	.19	.34	.70	.93	1.27	1.53	1.82	2.28	2.60	3.38	4.55	2.93	2.54
Papua New Guinea	853	.01	.01	.01	.01	.01	.01	—	.01	.01	.02	.01	.01	—	—	....
Philippines	566	5.07	6.22	7.12	5.67	5.24	7.09	6.12	5.01	4.57	3.65	3.34	3.07	3.12	2.22	2.92
Singapore	576	33.07	54.51	63.51	70.33	85.14	100.22	135.82	173.51	202.95	251.10	284.72	261.92	260.88	286.92	309.92
Solomon Islands	813															
Sri Lanka	524	.14	.22	.51	.72	.51	.49	.45	.51	.44	.58	.72	.78	1.02	1.17	1.28
Thailand	578	1.60	1.71	1.51	2.11	2.35	2.03	1.59	1.70	2.65	3.40	4.97	5.67	8.46	15.63	33.45
Vanuatu	846	....	....	....	....	2.04	1.86	1.75	....	....	....	....	....	....	....	....
Viet Nam	582	—	.37	.23	.20	.21	.31	.35	.41	.42	.44	.52	.48	.40	.40	.44
Western Samoa	862	—	—	—	—	—	—	—	—	—	—	—	—	—	—	—
Europe	170	....	46.94	35.50	30.77	30.11	35.63	41.76	47.53	43.99	43.97	50.75	52.15	47.47	45.83	30.59
Cyprus	423	.04	.04	.05	.04	.04	1.23	.21	.33	.43	.78	1.16	.98	.87	.89	1.06
Czechoslovakia	934						2.85	3.53	3.93	3.78	4.05	....	....	3.33	....	....
Hungary	944	....	....	6.61	6.13	6.29	9.00	12.34	15.22	....	....	....	....	....	....	....
Malta	181	.01	.01	.01	.01	.01	.04	.03	.08	.18	.21	.29	.32	.51	.65	.52
Poland*	964	....	14.21	10.33	8.21	7.97	7.40	8.04	8.83	7.60	7.13	9.16	9.51	8.39	7.48	1.51
Romania*	968	3.65	4.87	3.70	2.89	2.32	2.18	2.00	1.70	.50	.25	1.04	1.13	1.19	1.19	1.33
Turkey*	186	....	3.45	2.97	2.56	2.82	3.93	4.52	5.18	4.02	3.97	6.04	6.34	7.95	10.46	4.47
Yugoslavia, SFR*	188	5.93	9.46	6.71	6.59	6.54	6.99	6.93	6.86	5.95	5.13	4.84	3.73	3.14	2.47	2.49
Middle East	405	51.71	64.21	70.01	72.12	70.87	67.54	67.95	77.26	83.39	87.92	83.08	74.59	94.03	82.47	86.78
Bahrain	419	22.55	29.52	34.93	37.57	38.42	35.21	35.08	42.01	42.66	45.22	40.39	34.51	51.60	39.07	39.01
Egypt	469	7.48	7.68	8.90	7.63	7.63	7.35	7.43	6.54	9.02	10.22	10.93	8.93	12.47	12.18	12.93
Iran, I.R. of*	429	....	2.44	.60	1.06	.66	1.20	1.03	1.11	.94	.82	2.78	4.00	6.31	6.11	8.21
Iraq*	433	....	.32	.21	.72	1.28	2.14	3.11	3.45	4.11	4.36	4.18	4.51	2.29	2.08	1.88
Israel	436	4.21	4.74	5.62	5.03	4.77	4.10	3.88	3.33	2.74	1.85	1.71	1.61	1.51	1.37	.98
Jordan	439	.10	.16	.14	.14	.17	.20	.23	.53	.37	.24	.20	.26	.20	.38	....
Kuwait	443	6.09	6.99	8.28	8.79	7.85	....	....	6.46	6.92	7.95	....	3.26	....	....	....
Lebanon	446	....	1.95	.95	.83	.66	.50	.34	.69	.44	.52	.54	.47	.63	.35	.54
Libya	672	.12	.26	.24	.20	.15	—	.17	.05	.54	.91	1.02	1.10	.69	....	....
Oman	449	.31	.23	.25	.24	.23	.23	.31	.26	.25	.19	.15	.09	.09	.15	.22
Qatar	453	.17	.20	.25	.31	.23	.25	.43	.73	.98	.41	.58	1.19	.06	.05	.04
Saudi Arabia	456	2.75	2.61	1.72	1.92	2.19	2.80	3.78	6.50	7.64	9.21	7.97	7.39	7.25	9.07	8.63
Syrian Arab Rep.*	463	....	.67	.47	.63	.79	.99	1.02	.94	.85	.76	.57	.48	.32	.29	.22
United Arab Emirates	466	4.85	6.35	7.32	6.91	5.66	5.02	4.36	4.42	5.66	4.94	6.18	6.50	6.25	6.27	....
Yemen Arab Rep.	473	.02	.02	.03	.05	.10	.21	.21	.22	.23	.25	....	....	....	....	....
Yemen, P.D. Rep.	459	.03	.05	.09	.07	.07	.07	.04	.03	.04	.07					
Western Hemisphere	205	255.64	315.55	309.90	313.37	311.47	311.60	338.29	397.07	401.22	461.19	470.75	502.10	485.76	532.54	553.17
Antigua and Barbuda	311	.01	.01	.02	.01	.02	.03	.03	.03	.03	.03	.03	.03	.04	.03	.03
Argentina	213	....	6.07	6.06	7.59	7.01	9.45	10.54	12.44	14.57	....	12.52	12.92	7.31	5.41	....
Bahamas, The	313	....	....	....	101.41	92.74	83.31	91.85	101.78	108.79	126.35	124.32	122.26	107.51	109.33	....
Barbados	316	.03	.10	.60	....	....	....	....	....	....	.64	....	....	....	....	....
Belize	339	.02	.02	.02	.02	.03	.02	.01	.01	.01	.01	.01	.01	.02	.04	.04
Bermuda	319	....	....	.59	.90	.11	.15	.12	.08	....	....	....	....	....	....	....
Bolivia	218	.35	.63	.74	1.01	.90	.42	.52	.44	.45	.53	.43	.42	.53	.61	.78
Brazil	223	20.57	25.93	29.64	35.66	38.89	36.10	46.40	64.71	61.86	67.54	57.31	77.31	69.99	80.82	....
Cayman Islands	377	53.38e	69.47	76.17	74.71	91.14	101.06	111.50	149.37	157.34	194.28	222.85	232.54	237.27	265.85	....
Chile	228	3.54	6.24	7.28	6.31	6.73	6.57	6.22	5.07	4.20	3.33	2.97	2.35	3.51	3.79	4.03
Colombia	233	1.58	1.68	1.80	1.75	1.68	....	....	....	....	....	....	....	....	....	....
Costa Rica	238	.97	1.12	1.00	1.91	1.98	2.13	2.25	2.18	2.14	2.02	1.66	1.62	1.59	1.55	1.40
Dominica	321	—	—	—	—	—	—	—	—	—	—	—	—	—	.01	.01
Dominican Republic	243	.71	1.12	1.30	1.19	1.27	1.25	1.38	1.37	1.35	1.34	1.43	1.32	1.09	1.06	1.03
Ecuador	248	.23	.14	.26	.90	1.66	3.03	2.95	2.93	....	....	....	....	....	....	....
El Salvador	253	.01	.02	.02	.04	.05	.04	.02	.02	.03	.05	.02	.02	.03	.05	.14
Grenada	328	—	—	—	—	—	—	—	—	—	.01	—	—	.01	.01	.01
Guatemala	258	.13	.24	.32	.50	.58	.56	.40	.39	.43	.48	.38	.40	.38	.57	.62
Guyana	336	.01	.01	.01	.01	—	....	....	....	....	....	.01	—	.01	....	....
Haiti	263	.10	.11	.13	.14	.15	....	.14	.16	.17	.19	.03	.01	.01	.01	....
Honduras	268	.22	.23	.26	.23	.29	.41	.49	.58	.60	.63	1.78	.55	.50	.49	.55
Jamaica	343	.35	.46	.45	.85	.54	.69	.63	.51	.59	.60	.54	.32	.21	.13	.29
Mexico	273	....	....	30.46	32.23	28.00	27.82	27.87	25.54	24.69	24.18	16.16	18.32	21.70	25.57	26.68
Netherlands Antilles	353	5.52	8.00	8.76	7.59	4.56	3.00	2.48	2.73	2.38	6.47	7.78	10.86	11.08	12.28	17.90
Nicaragua	278	.67	.90	1.20	1.85	2.45	2.82	2.84	3.27	3.64	3.56	3.81	4.14	4.36	3.60	3.53
Panama	283	....	33.03	34.24	28.56	23.51	23.60	21.44	....	4.76	....	....	....	....	....	....
Paraguay	288	....	....	....	....	....	....	....	....	.05	.03	.04	.02	.05	.09	....
Peru	293	.97	1.00	.80	.81	.67	.42	.53	.61	1.10	.92	1.02	1.16	1.16	.59	.76
St. Kitts and Nevis	361	.01	.01	—	.02	.01	.01	.01	.02	.02	.01	.01	.01	.03	.04	.05
St. Lucia	362	.01	.01	.01	.01	.01	.01	.01	.01	.01	.01	.01	.01	.01	.01	.02
St. Vincent & Grens.	364	—	—	—	—	—	—	—	—	—	—	—	—	—	—	—
Suriname	366	.02	.03	.03	.02	.03	.03	.06	.07	.09	.11	.12	.15	.14	....	....
Trinidad and Tobago	369	.05	.04	.05	.05	.07	.04	.11	.11	.08	.10	.14	.13	.13	.16	....
Uruguay	298	....	....	.80	.57	.74	.57	.48	.49	.54	.56	.62	.70	.84	.98	.87
Venezuela*	299	4.68	18.23	6.03	5.89	5.00	5.54	4.55	4.93	5.96	5.17	3.27	2.58	2.82	2.37	1.66
Memorandum Items																
Oil Exporting Countries	999	22.81	40.49	27.66	28.66	25.65	28.17	29.26	33.68	39.81	41.53	43.39	41.53	42.08	42.85	46.89
Non-Oil Developing Countries	201	429.30	537.88	558.29	571.69	595.53	638.57	756.74	976.91	1,045.15	1,196.56	1,344.16	1,396.94	1,401.33	1,491.25	1,654.26

*Data derived from the interbank positions reported by deposit banks in major financial centers.

Cross-Border Interbank Claims by Residence of Lending Bank

1980	1981	1982	1983	1984	1985	1986	1987	1988	1989	1990	1991	1992	1993	1994		
End of Period																
															Asia (cont.)	
6.19	5.84	6.51	6.27	7.33	7.06	5.55	6.57	I 13.98	14.71	16.75	19.21	24.43	29.47	39.80	Korea	542
4.53	3.78	4.26	4.03	3.31	4.63	6.24	7.95	7.75	8.73	....	....	....	....	....	Malaysia	548
—	—	—	—	—	—	—	.01	—	.01	.01	.01	.01	.01	....	Maldives	556
.25	.22	.09	.08	.06	.05	....	....	....	....	....	....	....	....	....	Myanmar	518
.06	.08	.05	.07	.06	.06	.05	.08	.09	.09	.14	.18	.19	.31	....	Nepal	558
.31	.24	.19	.32	.35	.25	.34	.10	.25	.26	.31	.33	.32	.87	.88	Pakistan	564
.45	.38	.31	.42	.43	.44	.46	.50	.47	.39	.40	.35	.29	.28	....	Papua New Guinea	853
5.62	4.96	4.13	2.47	2.29	2.50	2.86	3.15	3.83	4.08	3.92	4.69	6.07	5.90	7.23	Philippines	566
36.97	54.86	56.16	59.27	69.47	90.69	130.68	166.39	193.81	234.38	241.86	215.10	223.33	245.48	272.20	Singapore	576
.01	.01	.03	.04	.03	.02	.02	.03	.04	.03	.02	.01	.02	.02	.02	Solomon Islands	813
.37	.49	.64	.72	.76	.75	.62	.55	.59	.67	.92	1.14	.99	1.16	1.26	Sri Lanka	524
1.75	2.16	2.12	1.88	1.61	2.19	3.10	3.81	6.20	9.71	13.18	15.97	14.45	19.44	23.53	Thailand	578
....	....	....	....	....	2.17	2.29	....	....	....	....	....	....	....	....	Vanuatu	846
....	.08	.06	.06	.05	.05	.06	.10	.09	.15	.30	.47	.42	.32	.39	Viet Nam	582
.01	.01	.01	.01	.02	.02	.03	.04	.05	.06	.07	.07	.06	.05	.05	Western Samoa	862
....	....	....	....	....	18.09	16.79	19.20	23.48	29.70	35.21	32.62	38.47	40.76	45.14	**Europe**	170
....	....	....	....	....	.87	1.06	1.37	1.63	2.47	3.25	3.35	3.30	3.48	4.12	Cyprus	423
....	....	....	....	....	....	....	....	....	....	1.07	3.92	3.31	....	....	Czechoslovakia	934
....	....	1.25	1.73	2.39	3.70	3.88	3.20	2.71	....	....	....	....	....	....	Hungary	944
.98	.99	.98	1.00	.86	.96	1.05	1.06	1.03	1.15	1.21	1.27	1.23	1.44	1.39	Malta	181
....	.78	1.03	1.10	1.40	1.41	1.51	2.72	3.31	3.48	7.15	4.39	6.68	6.12	7.86	Poland*	964
.58	.59	.69	.88	1.03	1.20	1.09	1.97	1.80	2.56	1.21	.90	.95	1.22	1.84	Romania	968
....	....	....	....	....	....	3.99	5.10	6.74	8.29	10.51	10.80	14.47	16.63	15.01	Turkey	186
....	2.52	1.79	1.84	2.31	2.54	1.88	1.63	3.20	6.04	6.42	2.99	2.86	3.51	5.31	Yugoslavia, SFR*	188
134.00	164.33	156.26	149.27	141.93	140.52	134.87	159.33	170.19	180.80	185.10	185.49	190.34	179.90	181.42	**Middle East**	405
23.74	32.95	36.93	39.91	37.81	36.33	38.39	47.64	54.14	59.48	59.98	50.98	45.48	59.54	45.29	Bahrain	419
5.83	5.14	6.85	8.63	7.97	8.13	7.54	8.61	8.77	9.77	14.07	17.87	21.22	23.83	26.29	Egypt	469
....	6.39	8.89	6.69	4.28	5.06	2.39	2.96	2.39	4.03	3.51	2.25	1.93	1.91	2.40	Iran, I.R. of*	429
....	16.38	.90	.32	.36	.55	.45	1.25	1.04	1.97	2.01	1.45	1.15	1.05	1.05	Iraq*	433
7.73	8.57	9.57	8.91	7.82	7.40	7.94	9.47	8.99	9.91	9.99	11.67	10.81	10.22	10.70	Israel	436
1.61	1.57	1.41	1.46	1.17	1.70	2.03	2.27	1.74	1.76	2.04	3.16	3.30	4.25	....	Jordan	439
9.69	11.21	12.65	11.38	10.49	....	....	8.82	8.10	9.84	....	7.00	....	....	....	Kuwait	443
....	7.07	5.49	4.19	2.95	2.85	2.63	2.83	3.17	2.95	2.73	3.96	4.28	6.08	6.88	Lebanon	446
11.91	7.03	4.90	3.82	2.70	5.01	5.18	4.88	3.23	3.18	4.88	4.92	5.70	....	....	Libya	672
.95	1.29	1.62	1.96	2.26	2.06	1.59	2.04	1.89	2.23	2.65	2.78	2.28	1.64	1.75	Oman	449
.97	1.48	1.53	1.35	1.88	1.89	1.99	2.45	2.63	1.96	2.35	2.32	2.36	2.50	2.13	Qatar	453
37.74	53.61	54.17	49.99	48.81	45.69	....	....	....	....	....	....	....	....	....	Saudi Arabia	456
....	1.14	.41	.14	.53	.24	.23	.31	.29	.42	2.01	2.84	3.11	3.64	4.23	Syrian Arab Rep.*	463
6.46	9.58	10.23	9.84	12.31	12.32	13.58	14.47	16.06	16.56	17.76	19.94	19.73	18.90	....	United Arab Emirates	466
.70	.57	.36	.36	.36	.36	.49	.55	.33	.36	....	....	....	....	....	Yemen Arab Rep.	473
.33	.34	.35	.32	.24	.19	.15	.22	.14	.11	....	....	....	....	....	Yemen, P.D. Rep.	459
196.27	242.26	231.67	241.58	248.10	249.62	282.87	325.47	336.38	391.45	402.63	437.41	424.23	478.71	546.57	**Western Hemisphere**	205
.01	.01	.02	.02	.03	.04	.04	.05	.06	.05	.05	.08	.09	.07	.08	Antigua and Barbuda	311
....	3.31	2.87	1.59	1.45	2.35	2.59	1.83	2.49	1.88	4.59	5.23	7.09	4.61	4.17	Argentina	213
....	....	....	111.41	107.93	100.09	111.91	123.58	130.21	140.05	141.64	134.67	121.59	119.10	....	Bahamas, The	313
.09	.15	.14	.14 e	....	....	....	....	....	.67	....	....	....	....	....	Barbados	316
.03	.02	.02	.02	.02	.02	.03	.04	.06	.07	.09	.07	.06	.06	.05	Belize	339
2.44	3.02	3.34	3.50	3.84	3.95	4.60	5.03	....	....	....	....	....	....	....	Bermuda	319
.14	.15	.18	.22	.30	.23	.49	.43	.42	....	....	....	....	....	....	Bolivia	218
5.98	7.23	3.90	4.88	11.55	9.34	6.82	8.00	11.10	14.50	15.53	17.09	32.31	44.79	....	Brazil	223
59.17 e	72.87	80.72	84.60	87.41	97.62	121.48	150.89	164.61	202.86	201.00	232.75	211.46	256.40	....	Cayman Islands	377
.55	.88	.96	.81	.72	.41	.48	.34	.40	.38	.51	.53	.52	.52	.51	Chile	228
....	3.45	2.64	1.03	1.46	1.20	1.80	2.29	2.54	2.68	3.40	4.58	4.86	3.69	4.47	Colombia	233
.18	.20	.30	.37	.44	.55	.60	.58	.75	.84	.62	1.06	1.21	1.16	1.08	Costa Rica	238
.01	.01	.01	.01	.01	.01	.02	.04	.05	.04	.03	.04	.04	.03	.03	Dominica	321
.32	.48	.41	.20	.30	.41	.50	.25	.38	.23	.18	.53	.60	.75	.42	Dominican Republic	243
.94	.55	.29	.71	.57	.64	.53	.43	....	....	....	....	....	....	....	Ecuador	248
.04	.07	.04	.09	.10	.15	.09	.08	.07	.09	.09	.07	.08	.09	.06	El Salvador	253
.02	.03	.01	.02	.02	.03	.03	.03	.04	.02	.03	.03	.05	.05	.07	Grenada	328
.41	.16	.16	.27	.33	.38	.38	.31	.22	.32	.29	.75	.70	.84	.85	Guatemala	258
.03	.02	.02	.01	.01	.01	.02	.02	.02	.04	.08	.14	.22	.27	.26	Guyana	336
.04	.07	.02	.03	.04	.04	.04	.04	.04	.03	.05	.05	....	....	....	Haiti	263
.16	.11	.12	.11	.13	.11	.12	.11	.06	.04	.11	.14	.26	.17	.25	Honduras	268
.13	.12	.13	.13	.15	.22	.16	.24	.24	.22	.27	.34	.49	.45	.83	Jamaica	343
....	....	1.28	4.96	8.42	6.00	6.74	13.33	5.01	4.79	2.92	3.73	4.46	4.67	4.17	Mexico	273
2.75	3.28	5.02	4.40	3.57	3.11	2.59	3.48	4.23	7.04	8.08	10.25	12.61	14.97	17.83	Netherlands Antilles	353
.09	.16	.23	.21	.42	.96	2.21	.03	.04	.12	.11	.17	.17	.10	.19	Nicaragua	278
11.22	10.26	10.75	11.52	9.10	10.07	11.06	....	2.71	....	....	....	....	....	....	Panama	283
.78	.85	.71	.72	.46	.28	.25	.24	.23	....	.72	.82	.68	....	....	Paraguay	288
2.37	1.78	1.76	1.75	1.97	2.10	1.74	1.05	.95	1.45	1.62	3.46	3.85	4.28	8.13	Peru	293
.01	.01	.01	.02	.01	.02	.02	.03	.04	.03	.03	.03	.04	.04	.05	St. Kitts and Nevis	361
.02	.01	.02	.02	.02	.03	.05	.07	.08	.07	.08	.08	.09	.08	.07	St. Lucia	362
.01	.02	.01	.01	.02	.02	.04	.04	.05	.06	.07	.06	.06	.06	.06	St. Vincent & Grens.	364
.23	.24	.21	.09	.04	.03	.03	.03	.02	.03	.04	.02	.02	1.09	....	Suriname	366
1.13	1.36	1.11	.45	.21	.31	.19	.13	.16	.26	.51	.41	.26	.36	....	Trinidad and Tobago	369
....	....	.64	.64	.46	.47	.86	.91	1.02	1.57	2.12	2.46	2.81	2.79	3.00	Uruguay	298
7.93	22.41	7.57	6.47	6.28	8.07	3.98	3.20	2.32	2.19	8.55	7.41	6.49	5.19	5.78	Venezuela*	299
															Memorandum Items	
115.76	143.58	112.23	102.62	101.05	105.10	90.90	103.55	107.24	113.03	129.86	129.45	113.48	111.04	110.58	Oil Exporting Countries	999
350.33	423.58	451.03	482.29	511.82	562.93	707.86	909.77	1,001.74	1,151.10	1,241.34	1,251.18	1,265.28	1,352.47	1,573.82	Non-Oil Developing Countries	201

Cross-Border Bank Credit to Nonbanks by Residence of Borrower

7yr d — *(7yrd 900) Billions of US Dollars:*

		1980	1981	1982	1983	1984	1985	1986	1987	1988	1989	1990	1991	1992	1993	1994
World	001	....	683.4	744.2	785.8	769.3	897.7	1,028.4	1,232.1	1,269.4	1,432.7	1,760.4	1,857.4	1,986.6	2,201.7	2,335.8
Nonmonetary International Orgs.	096	....	.29	4.18	6.01	6.96	11.06	16.14	20.41	17.43	20.50	22.48	25.76	22.19	20.05	22.28
Other Countries n.i.e.	910	....	.42	2.18	1.98	1.82	1.99	2.38	3.06	2.92	2.63	1.36	1.32	1.25	1.13	1.25
All Countries	010	....	682.7	737.8	777.8	760.5	884.6	1,009.9	1,208.6	1,249.1	1,409.6	1,736.5	1,830.4	1,963.2	2,180.5	2,312.3
Industrial Countries	110	....	207.8	285.8	299.8	296.5	365.4	436.1	563.9	622.4	739.0	990.0	1,087.0	1,174.0	1,361.0	1,419.9
United States	111	....	48.50	57.22	58.37	68.75	94.08	120.05	145.60	184.56	218.58	270.25	277.42	307.40	358.76	372.62
Canada	156	....	8.62	10.84	10.60	11.01	13.71	16.67	21.62	20.02	24.24	34.15	37.55	39.82	46.81	48.61
Australia	193	....	1.78	13.22	17.38	19.73	22.26	24.12	26.38	24.98	23.79	25.43	24.86	23.05	21.05	20.15
Japan	158	....	12.73	9.62	11.37	8.63	10.37	16.46	52.13	69.72	101.57	160.70	206.36	229.04	258.64	277.78
New Zealand	196	....	.53	3.68	4.37	5.07	6.80	8.95	10.93	9.82	8.05	8.53	7.11	5.66	7.92	7.17
Austria	122	....	2.61	2.78	3.04	3.35	4.17	5.57	5.93	4.86	4.78	5.76	5.10	6.26	7.88	10.02
Belgium-Luxembourg	126	....	....	11.74	12.01	11.85	12.88	15.24	19.38	18.82	21.82	28.43	31.01	29.05	31.42	33.33
Denmark	128	....	10.98	11.86	12.44	10.33	15.62	18.65	24.89	25.44	27.32	33.46	28.80	22.84	24.01	24.94
Finland	172	....	.34	4.42	4.28	4.66	5.61	6.10	7.24	6.99	9.44	12.48	11.67	11.89	14.53	17.11
France	132	....	10.26	14.35	16.52	17.19	19.71	19.94	21.78	19.29	21.46	29.23	31.58	36.52	46.69	47.12
Germany	134	....	39.77	41.40	40.81	35.24	43.26	49.72	66.47	65.09	69.25	83.89	95.16	121.83	146.16	158.84
Greece	174	....	.99	4.83	5.30	6.05	6.74	6.88	7.32	6.50	7.13	7.34	7.46	7.03	6.97	8.80
Iceland	176	....	.05	.63	.71	.73	.94	.99	1.15	1.32	1.23	1.50	1.54	1.65	1.44	1.21
Ireland	178	....	4.24	5.46	5.50	5.26	7.39	9.51	12.17	10.92	11.76	15.95	20.03	22.54	23.37	24.51
Italy	136	....	20.02	21.64	22.76	19.63	22.73	24.73	29.19	32.39	44.41	73.19	84.58	83.57	82.44	93.53
Netherlands	138	....	5.42	6.37	6.36	7.34	9.39	13.36	20.35	27.03	35.46	55.43	60.88	55.82	60.63	61.74
Norway	142	....	.38	7.90	7.27	6.71	7.45	8.63	9.52	9.70	9.11	10.19	11.96	12.10	12.26	12.01
Portugal	182	....	.52	8.47	9.31	9.15	10.00	8.90	9.54	8.42	8.26	8.06	8.71	9.02	10.34	11.97
Spain	184	....	3.08	15.61	15.94	15.43	13.95	11.29	12.46	13.16	13.76	18.21	19.64	20.32	28.84	28.74
Sweden	144	....	8.46	9.99	10.34	6.96	9.30	10.09	11.98	10.06	12.66	19.18	20.84	34.57	28.39	26.20
Switzerland	146	....	7.57	8.64	7.72	7.32	9.40	12.38	14.70	14.80	18.92	25.77	24.44	24.80	21.25	23.86
United Kingdom	112	....	13.27	13.62	15.89	14.02	16.94	24.69	29.38	33.94	40.94	56.88	65.39	64.32	116.86	104.13
Industrial not specified	189	....	.18	1.52	1.67	1.45	2.12	2.70	3.18	3.78	4.56	5.02	5.91	4.80	4.86	5.40
Developing Countries	200	....	151.35	331.27	346.48	344.55	373.10	383.46	402.12	389.79	390.05	409.41	426.42	473.85	482.83	506.78
of which:Major Offshore Bkg.Ctrs.	016	....	8.28	30.14	30.93	32.77	44.71	52.08	57.63	58.90	67.26	87.34	92.81	105.97	114.41	122.62
Africa	605	....	10.11	48.97	50.11	46.71	52.25	54.67	58.74	53.44	51.64	56.02	52.20	48.33	45.82	48.13
Algeria	612	....	1.31	6.98	6.66	5.90	7.50	8.26	8.80	7.13	6.72	7.75	5.95	4.41	4.11	4.70
Angola	614	....	—	.37	.38	.49	.70	.75	.83	.79	1.09	1.12	1.18	1.34	1.36	1.44
Benin	638	....	.03	.19	.18	.16	.18	.15	.13	.09	.06	.04	.02	.02	.02	.02
Botswana	616	....	.03	.05	.05	.02	.02	.02	.03	.03	.02	.01	.02	.01	.01	.01
Burkina Faso	748	....	—	.03	.04	.03	.03	.03	.03	.02	.02	.01	.02	.02	.03	.01
Burundi	618	....	—	.01	.03	.03	.04	.03	.03	.01	.01	.01	.01	.01	.01	.01
Cameroon	622	....	.02	.73	.81	.79	.86	.97	1.13	1.22	1.15	1.48	1.66	1.40	1.24	1.19
Cape Verde	624	....	—	—	—	—	.01	.01	.01	.01	.01	.01	.01	.01	.01	.01
Central African Rep.	626	....	—	.01	.01	.01	.01	.01	.02	.02	.02	.02	.02	.01	.01	.02
Chad	628	....	—	.01	.01	—	—	—	.01	.02	.01	.01	.02	.01	—	.01
Comoros	632	....	—	—	—	—	—	—	—	—	—	—	—	.01	—	—
Congo	634	....	.02	.78	.81	.73	.93	1.29	1.33	1.12	.93	.87	.93	.84	.91	.74
Côte d'Ivoire	662	....	2.18	2.79	2.38	2.25	2.80	3.01	2.86	2.31	2.02	1.63	1.19	.72	.57	1.88
Djibouti	611	....	—	.01	.01	.04	.06	.03	.01	.03	.04	.04	.03	.02	.02	.01
Equatorial Guinea	642	....	....	....	.01	.01	.01	—	—	.01	—	.02	—	—	—	.01
Ethiopia	644	....	—	.04	.04	.14	.14	.12	.15	.16	.15	.23	.21	.19	.17	.14
Gabon	646	....	.01	.46	.53	.53	.81	1.16	1.34	1.30	1.35	1.30	.96	.82	.72	.77
Gambia, The	648	....	—	.02	.02	.04	.03	.03	.03	.01	.01	.02	.03	.04	.03	.04
Ghana	652	....	.01	.06	.07	.10	.10	.12	.14	.16	.14	.21	.24	.34	.48	.58
Guinea	656	....	—	.14	.12	.09	.11	.10	.13	.13	.11	.15	.13	.12	.11	.09
Guinea-Bissau	654	....	—	.01	.01	.01	.02	.02	.01	.02	.03	.04	.05	.05	.05	.04
Kenya	664	....	.01	1.05	.71	.63	.72	.99	1.23	1.27	1.36	1.66	1.52	1.20	.99	.94
Lesotho	666	....	—	—	—	—	—	—	—	.02	.02	.02	.02	.04	.17	.19	.25
Liberia	668	....	2.80	8.26	8.27	9.76	10.09	10.07	11.37	11.46	11.61	14.03	14.46	14.66	16.15	15.92
Madagascar	674	....	—	.19	.17	.09	.11	.08	.07	.06	.06	.07	.04	.04	.02	.03
Malawi	676	....	—	.10	.10	.09	.07	.07	.07	.08	.07	.06	.05	.05	.05	.24
Mali	678	....	—	.01	.03	.03	.04	.04	.04	.04	.04	.03	.03	.01	.01	.01
Mauritania	682	....	—	.07	.09	.07	.07	.10	.08	.11	.06	.09	.04	.04	.05	.01
Mauritius	684	....	.01	.13	.10	.10	.10	.08	.06	.02	.05	.10	.16	.11	.17	.28
Morocco	686	....	.64	3.72	3.66	3.63	4.06	4.28	4.70	4.53	4.62	4.60	4.33	4.36	3.80	3.92
Mozambique	688	....	—	.24	.28	.35	.38	.34	.38	.31	.34	.61	.60	.61	.59	.55
Niger	692	....	.03	.25	.29	.27	.19	.20	.16	.10	.08	.08	.03	.03	.02	.05
Nigeria	694	....	.54	6.51	7.44	7.02	7.77	8.24	8.33	6.79	5.63	5.41	4.78	4.03	3.43	3.28
Rwanda	714	....	.01	.01	—	.01	.01	.01	.03	.03	.03	.04	.03	.03	.03	.01
Sao Tome & Principe	716	....	—	—	.01	.01	.01	.01	.01	.01	.01	.01	.01	.01	.01	.01
Senegal	722	....	.01	.35	.34	.29	.30	.38	.68	.53	.35	.31	.22	.19	.18	.20
Seychelles	718	....	—	.02	.02	.03	.04	.05	.06	.06	.07	.05	.04	.04	.04	.04
Sierra Leone	724	....	—	.02	.03	.03	.03	.02	.03	.03	.02	.05	.04	.03	.03	.03
Somalia	726	....	—	.06	.07	.06	.07	.05	.05	.03	.02	.02	.02	—	—	—
South Africa	199	....	.64	9.98	11.48	8.45	9.14	8.74	9.50	9.11	8.73	8.94	8.54	7.89	6.41	6.75
Sudan	732	....	.11	.67	.61	.56	.73	.80	.75	.65	.59	.78	.69	.50	.43	.47
Swaziland	734	....	—	.03	.03	.05	.07	.04	.03	.01	.02	.01	.01	.01	.01	—
Tanzania	738	....	.02	.26	.23	.18	.21	.22	.29	.15	.13	.12	.11	.08	.08	.08
Togo	742	....	.01	.24	.17	.11	.11	.10	.12	.10	.08	.08	.07	.05	.04	.05
Tunisia	744	....	.12	1.06	1.13	1.11	1.29	1.43	1.52	1.30	1.16	1.13	.94	.96	.88	.99
Uganda	746	....	—	.06	.05	.06	.04	.06	.06	.06	.07	.08	.04	.03	.03	.03
Zaïre	636	....	.32	.81	.62	.53	.58	.67	.72	.74	.86	.81	.58	.53	.45	.45
Zambia	754	....	—	.37	.35	.31	.30	.38	.27	.28	.18	.27	.26	.19	.16	.21
Zimbabwe	698	....	—	.53	.62	.60	.63	.61	.65	.55	.48	.54	.81	.63	.50	.57
Africa not specified	799	....	1.21	1.28	1.04	.92	.76	.48	.45	.42	1.02	1.04	1.03	1.50	1.21	1.00
Asia	505	....	29.70	59.94	64.60	66.73	72.61	78.99	86.84	87.64	90.65	101.42	114.95	125.16	123.59	132.69
Afghanistan, Islamic State of	512	....	—	.01	.01	—	.01	.01	.01	.01	.01	.05	.04	.05	.03	.04
Bangladesh	513	....	.01	.11	.17	.23	.26	.28	.32	.33	.34	.36	.14	.09	.17	.26
Cambodia	522	....	—	—	—	—	—	—	—	—	—	.02	.02	.02	.02	.02
China, People's Rep.	924	....	.24	.76	.80	1.36	2.06	3.90	6.64	9.64	11.64	13.31	11.77	13.55	13.69	16.74
Fiji	819	....	.02	.05	.06	.06	.06	.07	.04	.03	.01	.01	.01	.03	.05	.05
Hong Kong	532	....	2.16	9.15	8.65	8.00	9.91	11.72	10.57	10.89	12.00	14.75	16.47	17.49	19.77	18.34
India	534	....	.13	1.81	2.62	2.59	4.60	5.23	8.60	9.32	9.99	9.81	9.49	10.50	10.20	10.17
Indonesia	536	....	7.74	10.63	12.88	13.52	14.71	16.57	18.95	19.19	19.46	23.02	28.79	32.97	28.89	31.85
Korea	542	....	5.89	11.01	11.61	12.08	12.24	11.62	11.52	10.41	10.01	10.52	11.49	11.99	12.16	15.53
Lao P. D. Rep.	544	....	—	—	—	.02	.06	—	—	—	—	—	—	—	—	.01

Cross-Border Bank Credit to Nonbanks by Residence of Lending Bank

7xd d

1980	1981	1982	1983	1984	1985	1986	1987	1988	1989	1990	1991	1992	1993	1994		
End of Period																
....	....	....	....	....	....	....	....	....	....	....	....	....	....	....	World	001
....	....	....	....	....	....	....	....	....	....	....	....	....	....	....	Nonmonetary International Orgs.	096
....	....	....	....	....	....	....	....	....	....	....	....	....	....	....	Other Countries n.i.e.	910
572.2	682.8	743.9	785.5	768.9	897.2	1,028.4	1,232.1	1,269.4	1,432.7	1,760.4	1,857.4	1,986.6	2,201.7	2,335.8	All Countries	010
422.4	494.2	538.0	572.1	549.8	657.7	779.3	931.9	926.0	1,024.9	1,209.2	1,251.3	1,336.7	1,496.1	1,582.9	Industrial Countries	110
57.35	80.21	107.04	121.08	119.01	110.69	110.27	107.54	104.30	103.60	89.96	78.94	86.10	99.56	86.06	United States	111
7.33	9.54	7.13	7.76	7.49	9.79	8.12	10.60	12.91	12.74	12.22	11.96	11.45	12.65	14.32	Canada	156
—	—	—	—	—	.97	I.86	.98	.92	.99	.65	.92	....	....	....	Australia	193
18.05	21.07	23.87	28.12	36.99	58.53	85.32	125.25	139.89	159.71	181.14	191.35	200.56	235.79	243.23	Japan	158
....	....	....	....	....	....	....	....	....	....	....	....	....	....	....	New Zealand	196
11.11	12.23	14.39	14.91	15.13	19.85	25.00	27.73	26.73	30.07	33.81	35.48	35.42	32.89	35.61	Austria	122
70.41	80.14	76.90	73.79	74.10	89.65	113.06	138.00	137.81	158.65	196.10	200.15	213.60	....	....	Belgium-Luxembourg	126
.12	.08	.05	.13	.05	.16	.23	.21	.88	.64	6.37	8.55	8.00	15.61	13.88	Denmark	128
....	....	....	....	....	....	....	....	....	....	....	....	....	....	....	Finland	172
56.75	60.23	65.86	64.56	64.23	78.32	93.03	110.66	103.93	118.31	147.75	148.84	158.16	179.73	....	France	132
41.28	39.35	38.29	35.49	32.36	45.31	58.00	74.40	70.47	81.16	112.10	124.51	134.93	152.05	166.19	Germany	134
.02	.02	.03	.02	.09	.09	.10	.07	.06	.07	.07	.11	.23	.24	....	Greece	174
—	—	—	—	—	.01	.01	.01	.01	—	—	—	.01	.01	.01	Iceland	176
....	.79e	I.54	.56	.54	.59	.69	.73	.80	.86	2.06	3.21	4.50	4.52	....	Ireland	178
.72	.87	.72	.71	.73	1.14	1.93	3.02	2.72	....	8.84	15.81	27.97	43.16	....	Italy	136
14.45	16.07	17.79	16.84	15.21	19.06	27.88	32.87	35.59	41.57	46.67	49.01	53.43	56.06	61.02	Netherlands	138
.30	.51	.73	1.32	1.78	2.20	3.57	5.53	3.93	4.66	5.69	5.12	6.20	4.32	4.51	Norway	142
....	....	....	....	....	....	....	....	....	....	....	....	....	....	....	Portugal	182
....	....	5.73	5.74	6.18	7.11	8.36	9.25	8.69	10.41	13.60	17.27	18.00	27.29	27.88	Spain	184
1.79	2.18	1.92	3.14	3.19	3.76	5.28	6.35	7.34	16.71	I18.77	18.86	17.98	14.37	14.21	Sweden	144
34.94	35.47	I34.19	49.26	I28.19	37.38	48.67	66.01	59.20	62.55	73.52	72.01	67.47	75.87	86.09	Switzerland	146
103.50	130.80	142.78	148.65	144.55	I173.08	188.95	212.67	209.79	219.22	259.92	I269.23	291.94	322.58	334.21	United Kingdom	112
....	....	....	....	....	....	....	....	....	....	....	....	....	....	....	Industrial not specified	189
149.72	188.69	205.94	213.42	219.09	239.50	249.09	300.17	343.45	407.80	551.14	606.09	649.86	705.57	752.90	Developing Countries	200
135.77	172.53	187.94	190.22	195.97	214.56	221.38	270.20	310.91	372.63	513.12	562.74	599.70	650.22	691.95	*of which:* Major Offshore Bkg.Ctrs.	016
.46	.52	.59	.61	.56	.58	.72	.79	.84	.97	1.23	1.67	1.45	1.60	2.01	Africa	605
.11	.10	.12	.12	.12	.14	.16	.14	.21	.22	.31	.67	.45	.44	.46	Algeria	612
....	....	....	....	....	....	....	....	....	....	....	....	....	....	....	Angola	614
—	—	—	—	—	—	—	—	—	.01	—	—	—	—	.02	Benin	638
—	—	—	—	—	—	—	—	—	—	—	—	—	—	—	Botswana	616
—	—	—	—	—	—	—	—	—	—	—	—	—	—	.10	Burkina Faso	748
—	—	—	—	—	.01	—	—	—	—	—	—	—	—	—	Burundi	618
....	....	....	....	....	....	....	....	....	....	....	....	....	....	....	Cameroon	622
....	....	....	....	....	....	....	....	....	....	....	....	....	....	....	Cape Verde	624
....	....	....	....	....	....	....	....	....	....	....	....	....	....	....	Central African Rep.	626
....	....	....	....	....	....	....	....	....	....	....	....	....	....	....	Chad	628
....	....	....	....	....	....	....	....	....	....	....	....	....	....	....	Comoros	632
....	....	....	....	....	....	....	.07	....	....	....	....	....	....	....	Congo	634
....	....	....	....	....	....	....	....	....	....	....	....	....	....	....	Côte d'Ivoire	662
—	—	—	—	.01	—	.02	.01	.01	.01	.01	.01	—	—	—	Djibouti	611
....	....	....	....	....	....	....	....	....	....	....	....	....	....	....	Equatorial Guinea	642
.03	.02	.03	.03	.03	.02	.02	.02	.03	.02	.02	.02	.04	.06	.06	Ethiopia	644
....	....	....	....	....	....	....	....	....	....	....	....	....	....	....	Gabon	646
—	—	—	—	—	—	—	—	—	—	—	—	—	—	—	Gambia, The	648
—	—	—	—	—	—	—	—	—	—	.02	.10	.13	.10	.12	Ghana	652
....	....	....	....	....	....	....	....	....	....	....	....	....	....	....	Guinea	656
....	....	....	....	....	....	....	....	....	....	....	....	....	....	....	Guinea-Bissau	654
.03	.02	.02	.02	.02	.02	.02	.02	.02	.04	.04	.03	.04	.19	....	Kenya	664
—	—	—	—	—	—	—	—	—	—	—	.01	—	—	.01	Lesotho	666
—	—	.01	—	—	—	—	—	—	.01	—	....	—	—	.03	Liberia	668
....	....	....	....	....	....	....	....	....	....	....	....	....	....	....	Madagascar	674
....	....	....	....	....	....	....	....	....	....	....	....	....	....	....	Malawi	676
—	—	—	—	—	—	—	—	—	—	—	—	—	—	.02	Mali	678
....	....	....	....	....	....	....	....	....	....	....	....	....	....	....	Mauritania	682
.01	.01	.01	.01	.01	.03	.04	.05	.06	.08	.08	.08	.09	.08	.09	Mauritius	684
.16	.24	.24	.22	.21	—	—	—	—	—	—	—	—	—	—	Morocco	686
—	—	—	—	—	—	—	—	—	—	—	—	—	—	—	Mozambique	688
—	.01	.01	.03	.01	—	.04	—	—	—	—	—	—	—	—	Niger	692
....	.01	—	.01	.01	.01	—	—	—	—	—	—	—	—	—	Nigeria	694
....	....	....	....	....	....	....	....	....	....	....	....	....	....	....	Rwanda	714
....	....	....	....	....	....	....	....	....	....	....	....	....	....	....	Sao Tome & Principe	716
....	....	....	....	....	....	....	....	....	....	....	....	....	....	....	Senegal	722
....	....	....	....	....	....	....	....	....	....	....	....	....	....	....	Seychelles	718
—	—	—	—	—	—	—	—	—	—	—	—	—	—	—	Sierra Leone	724
....	....	....	....	....	....	....	....	....	....	....	....	....	....	....	Somalia	726
....	....	....	....	....	....	....	....	....	....	....	....	....	....	....	South Africa	199
—	—	—	—	—	—	—	—	—	—	—	—	—	—	—	Sudan	732
—	—	—	—	—	—	—	—	—	—	—	—	—	—	—	Swaziland	734
—	—	—	—	—	—	—	—	—	—	—	—	—	—	.04	Tanzania	738
....	....	....	....	....	....	....	....	....	....	....	....	....	....	....	Togo	742
.06	.10	.11	.13	.12	.12	.15	.22	.24	.29	.37	.41	.38	.38	.34	Tunisia	744
....	....	....	....	....	....	....	....	....	....	....	....	....	....	....	Uganda	746
....	....	....	....	....	....	....	....	....	....	....	....	....	....	....	Zaïre	636
—	—	.01	—	—	—	—	—	—	—	—	—	—	—	—	Zambia	754
.03	—	—	—	—	.01	.02	.02	.03	.03	.04	.05	.10	.08	.29	Zimbabwe	698
....	....	....	....	....	....	....	....	....	....	....	....	....	....	....	Africa not specified	799
27.04	37.00	47.60	53.24	57.18	62.04	66.36	108.20	129.99	175.53	271.38	332.71	351.22	378.99	414.71	Asia	505
....	....	....	....	....	....	....	....	....	....	....	....	....	....	....	Afghanistan, Islamic State of	512
.11	.10	.10	.09	.09	.09	.10	.10	.09	.12	.11	.12	.13	.15	.22	Bangladesh	513
....	....	....	....	....	....	....	....	....	....	....	....	....	....	....	Cambodia	522
....	....	....	....	....	....	....	....	....	....	....	....	....	....	....	China, People's Rep.	924
.01	.01	—	—	—	.02	.10	.02	.03	.04	.04	.03	.03	.03	.03	Fiji	819
11.22	13.97	15.78	17.36	19.02	19.60	22.59	47.38	57.29	81.44	136.48	188.30	207.83	232.76	257.17	Hong Kong	532
....	....	....	....	....	....	....	....	....	....	....	....	....	....	....	India	534
....	....	....	....	....	....	....	....	....	....	....	....	....	....	....	Indonesia	536
....	....	....	....	....	....	....	....	....	....	....	....	....	....	....	Korea	542
....	....	....	....	....	....	....	....	....	....	....	....	....	....	....	Lao P. D. Rep.	544

Cross-Border Bank Credit to Nonbanks by Residence of Borrower

7yr d   *(7yrd 900) Billions of US Dollars:*

		1980	1981	1982	1983	1984	1985	1986	1987	1988	1989	1990	1991	1992	1993	1994
Asia (cont.)																
Malaysia	548	....	1.38	7.04	8.43	9.10	8.90	9.59	9.16	7.50	6.56	6.12	6.30	6.20	7.20	7.57
Maldives	556	....	....	....	.01	.01	.01	—	.01	.01	.01	.01	.01	.04	.01	.02
Myanmar	518	....	.01	.17	.20	.17	.21	.21	.23	.18	.14	.13	.07	.04	.03	.03
Nepal	558	....	.01	.01	.01	.03	.02	.03	.04	.07	.06	.05	.05	.04	.05	.04
Pakistan	564	....	.06	.78	.79	.86	1.35	1.46	1.42	1.62	1.60	1.73	1.73	1.84	1.65	1.96
Papua New Guinea	853	....	.19	.50	.64	.60	.61	.62	.65	.64	.71	.61	.52	.44	.43	.18
Philippines	566	....	4.39	6.89	6.07	6.53	6.14	6.30	6.24	5.49	4.71	4.45	4.25	3.83	3.82	3.59
Singapore	576	....	1.54	2.41	2.35	2.27	2.29	1.98	2.11	2.37	2.43	2.62	3.28	3.38	3.69	3.80
Solomon Islands	813	....	—	.01	.01	.02	.02	.08	—	—	—	—	—	—	.01	—
Sri Lanka	524	....	.17	.46	.58	.56	.59	.65	.52	.47	.36	.46	.38	.30	.36	.43
Thailand	578	....	2.30	3.82	3.73	4.51	4.93	5.26	5.95	6.08	6.72	9.47	15.89	18.13	15.48	16.66
Vanuatu	846	....	.12	.07	.08	.09	.06	.17	.20	.29	.29	.39	.56	.15	.14	.07
Viet Nam	582	....	.01	.12	.11	.08	.08	.09	.11	.13	.11	.46	.44	.44	.39	.16
Western Samoa	862	....	—	—	—	—	—	—	—	—	—	—	—	—	.05	—
Asia not specified	598	....	3.33	4.12	4.78	4.02	3.49	3.13	3.55	2.96	3.48	3.07	3.25	3.63	5.32	5.16
Europe	**170**	....	**4.13**	**18.75**	**18.35**	**16.31**	**19.03**	**21.81**	**25.31**	**26.05**	**27.40**	**32.32**	**34.12**	**33.79**	**34.57**	**38.44**
Cyprus	423	....	.09	.53	.61	.62	.81	1.10	1.37	1.69	1.82	2.36	2.68	3.19	3.15	3.45
Czechoslovakia	934	....	.02	.64	.59	.56	.69	.97	1.40	1.57	2.01	2.14	1.84	1.66	1.69	1.91
Hungary	944	....	.62	1.12	1.38	1.41	1.39	1.31	1.02	1.01	1.15	1.22	1.29	1.39	1.53	1.96
Malta	181	....	—	.02	.03	.03	.04	.05	.12	.17	.23	.31	.56	.67	.84	1.26
Poland	964	....	.22	4.07	3.11	2.38	2.95	3.07	3.50	3.04	3.26	3.59	4.00	4.71	4.27	5.61
Romania	968	....	.06	.86	1.03	.87	.86	.89	.85	.24	—	.04	.08	.28	.51	.69
Turkey	186	....	1.11	1.79	2.07	2.35	3.24	4.66	6.31	6.91	7.12	8.97	9.99	10.01	12.40	12.69
Yugoslavia, SFR	188	....	.77	3.56	3.33	3.22	3.51	3.36	3.28	3.10	2.50	2.30	2.02	1.55	1.44	1.33
Europe not specified	884	....	.90	2.17	2.33	1.07	.73	.64	.71	.38	.54	.52	.49	.77	.92	.77
Middle East	**405**	....	**10.74**	**24.69**	**27.62**	**27.26**	**28.20**	**28.59**	**30.13**	**30.19**	**32.65**	**32.75**	**33.37**	**38.82**	**37.26**	**37.62**
Bahrain	419	....	.07	.60	.50	.54	.56	.66	.63	.69	.98	2.32	1.21	1.89	1.90	1.88
Egypt	469	....	.94	2.60	2.82	3.07	3.74	4.27	4.75	4.66	4.36	4.69	3.95	2.77	2.18	1.77
Iran, I.R. of	429	....	.19	1.44	.91	.53	.48	.42	.40	.76	1.48	1.28	2.49	2.94	2.68	2.05
Iraq	433	....	.07	.31	1.33	2.44	3.26	4.26	4.89	4.55	4.19	3.89	2.27	2.97	2.77	3.71
Israel	436	....	1.22	2.49	2.65	2.25	2.68	1.97	2.13	2.41	2.02	2.30	2.32	2.25	2.63	2.99
Jordan	439	....	.12	.66	.75	.81	1.05	1.36	1.86	2.21	2.27	2.33	2.07	1.65	1.21	1.10
Kuwait	443	....	2.41	3.68	3.71	3.16	2.76	2.69	2.57	2.06	2.28	1.84	2.42	6.37	6.39	6.49
Lebanon	446	....	.06	1.00	1.00	.95	.96	1.06	1.22	1.38	1.46	1.59	1.30	1.25	1.30	1.35
Libya	672	....	.08	.34	.41	.24	.30	.16	.08	.35	.27	.16	.13	.12	.14	.13
Oman	449	....	.04	.36	.73	1.12	1.27	1.83	1.66	1.66	1.70	1.34	1.38	1.43	1.43	1.65
Qatar	453	....	.14	.37	.30	.24	.27	.25	.24	.33	.59	.83	.80	.52	.84	1.27
Saudi Arabia	456	....	3.74	6.55	7.75	7.78	7.61	6.29	6.29	5.34	5.65	4.77	7.61	7.77	8.25	8.25
Syrian Arab Rep.	463	....	.10	.24	.18	.16	.20	.21	.26	.19	.24	.39	.36	.41	.34	.39
United Arab Emirates	466	....	.86	2.09	2.37	2.31	2.29	2.24	2.26	2.40	2.95	2.34	1.74	1.62	1.29	1.48
Yemen Arab Rep.	473	....	.04	.12	.18	.15	.17	.16	.14	.13	.14	.19	.17	.12	.10	.07
Yemen, P.D. Rep.	459	....	—	.02	.01	.02	.06	.04	.04	.03	.02	—	—	—	—	—
Middle East not specified	489	....	.63	1.84	2.01	1.49	.56	.73	.71	1.03	2.06	2.51	3.15	4.75	3.82	3.05
Western Hemisphere	**205**	....	**96.66**	**178.92**	**185.80**	**187.54**	**201.02**	**199.41**	**201.09**	**192.46**	**187.71**	**186.92**	**191.77**	**227.74**	**241.58**	**249.91**
Antigua and Barbuda	311	....	....	—	—	.01	.01	.01	.01	.01	—	.01	—	—	.01	.01
Argentina	213	....	8.35	18.28	18.67	18.20	19.86	21.63	23.36	26.30	21.56	20.94	21.39	22.67	22.53	24.05
Bahamas, The	313	....	.24	1.28	1.55	1.56	2.11	6.03	4.99	3.84	4.05	3.92	4.26	4.76	5.13	5.81
Barbados	316	....	—	.06	.08	.14	.12	.13	.17	.20	.29	.32	.40	1.08	1.20	.22
Belize	339	....	....	.02	.01	.01	.01	.01	.01	—	.05	.10	.01	.02	.04	.03
Bermuda	319	....	.47	2.89	3.10	2.94	2.96	3.23	4.79	4.35	6.46	9.90	8.20	13.03	15.03	14.77
Bolivia	218	....	.14	.92	.82	.68	.62	.55	.51	.40	.17	.16	.17	.20	.26	.32
Brazil	223	....	30.97	36.81	36.59	40.32	40.72	32.39	22.95	19.61	13.14	6.42	2.50	20.54	....	....
Cayman Islands	377	....	.58	2.65	2.37	2.38	6.47	5.15	8.34	12.04	16.75	21.96	31.48	39.75	40.57	48.46
Chile	228	....	....	6.39	5.93	5.83	5.61	5.20	4.78	4.38	4.59	5.52	4.74	4.98	....	....
Colombia	233	....	2.51	5.42	5.40	5.33	5.26	5.56	5.41	5.88	5.53	5.81	5.81	6.05	6.45	7.18
Costa Rica	238	....	....	—	.89	.66	.53	.49	.44	.46	.43	.44	.47	.62	.96	1.19
Dominica	321	....	—	—	—	—	—	—	—	—	—	—	—	—	.01	—
Dominican Republic	243	....	....	—	.59	.53	.48	.36	.38	.46	.38	.50	.32	.41	.42	.39
Ecuador	248	....	4.50	4.64	4.17	3.27	2.17	2.36	2.20	2.01	1.64	1.11	.87	.59	.11	.18
El Salvador	253	....	....	....	.23	.26	.28	.30	.31	.11	.14	.16	.18	.22	.26	.34
Grenada	328	....	....	....	....	....	....	....	....	....	....	....	....	....	....	....
Guatemala	258	....	.37	.39	.34	.36	.42	.37	.40	.38	.40	.35	.42	.45	.46	.41
Guyana	336	....	—	.11	.09	.09	.07	.07	.07	.06	.06	.09	.10	.03	.05	.05
Haiti	263	....	.02	.05	.05	.04	.05	.04	.03	.03	.03	.04	.02	.01	.01	.01
Honduras	268	....	.40	.44	.40	.40	.42	.44	.40	.38	.29	.22	.16	.14	.32	.45
Jamaica	343	....	.08	.52	.51	.50	.52	.41	.39	.36	.47	.33	.30	.36	.38	.44
Mexico	273	....	27.85	51.68	56.61	56.77	58.71	57.91	59.02	53.21	52.79	43.37	49.07	47.91	52.15	52.25
Netherlands Antilles	353	....	.84	3.79	5.17	4.87	6.55	7.15	7.69	7.15	10.51	19.10	13.39	16.52	19.77	18.32
Nicaragua	278	....	....	—	.51	.57	.79	.59	.54	.40	.34	.85	.83	.82	.79	.71
Panama	283	....	2.85	10.27	10.34	13.16	16.83	19.39	23.29	21.91	20.54	22.67	22.73	22.18	23.58	26.02
Paraguay	288	....	—	.55	.55	.76	.68	.66	.73	.63	.62	.70	.62	.43	.48	.57
Peru	293	....	1.05	3.07	3.80	4.00	4.02	3.84	3.93	3.39	3.13	2.97	2.85	2.64	2.33	2.35
St. Kitts and Nevis	361	....	....	—	—	—	—	—	—	—	—	—	—	—	—	—
St. Lucia	362	....	—	—	—	—	—	—	—	—	—	—	.01	.01	.01	.01
St. Vincent & Grens.	364	....	—	—	—	—	—	—	—	—	.02	.04	.06	.06	.06	.05
Suriname	366	....	—	.06	.06	.01	.02	.03	.04	.02	.02	.03	.08	.05	.02	.01
Trinidad and Tobago	369	....	.16	.73	.89	.72	.88	.88	.90	.86	.75	.69	.62	.55	.74	.89
Uruguay	298	....	.09	.89	1.42	1.42	1.31	1.38	1.36	1.65	1.25	1.24	1.28	1.37	1.73	1.50
Venezuela	299	....	9.99	23.89	22.66	20.46	20.72	20.73	20.50	19.86	19.19	14.48	15.54	15.76	16.65	13.98
Western Hemisphere not spec.	399	....	.60	.97	1.99	1.29	1.82	2.13	3.15	2.12	2.11	2.36	2.75	3.30	2.98	2.84
Unallocated	**899**	....	**323.56**	**120.70**	**131.54**	**119.46**	**146.10**	**190.31**	**242.61**	**236.91**	**280.60**	**337.14**	**316.95**	**315.29**	**336.65**	**385.61**
Memorandum Items																
Oil Exporting Countries	999	....	28.21	65.57	70.05	66.83	69.91	72.93	76.08	71.78	72.60	69.85	77.22	85.68	80.70	81.77
Non-Oil Developing Countries	201	....	123.30	265.69	276.43	277.72	303.19	310.54	326.05	318.00	317.45	339.56	349.20	388.16	402.13	425.01

Cross-Border Bank Credit to Nonbanks by Residence of Lending Bank

7xd *d*

1980	1981	1982	1983	1984	1985	1986	1987	1988	1989	1990	1991	1992	1993	1994		
End of Period															**Asia (cont.)**	
.42	.36	.33	1.66	.44	.56	.61	.79	.92	1.12	....	....	....	....	....	Malaysia	548
—	—	—	—	—	—	—	—	—	—	—	—	—	—	....	Maldives	556
—	—	—	—	—	—	—	—	—	—	.03	—	—	—	....	Myanmar	518
.02	.02	.01	.01	.02	.02	.02	.02	.02	.02	.03	.03	.04	.04	....	Nepal	558
.17	.24	.26	.33	.39	.42	.50	.70	.69	.78	1.30	1.44	1.25	1.18	1.29	Pakistan	564
.01	.01	.01	—	—	—	—	—	.01	—	—	—	—	.01	....	Papua New Guinea	853
.35	.42	.54	.80	.81	.84	.59	.73	.73	.91	1.17	1.60	1.84	2.21	2.66	Philippines	566
14.15	21.37	29.83	32.33	35.67	39.73	41.02	57.48	69.22	89.86	129.52	137.96	137.67	140.06	150.05	Singapore	576
														—	Solomon Islands	813
.09	.10	.20	.27	.28	.22	.22	.23	.21	.23	.24	.23	.29	.19	.18	Sri Lanka	524
.49	.39	.51	.35	.41	.41	.47	.61	.78	.98	1.06	1.28	1.57	1.78	2.46	Thailand	578
....	....	....	....	.04	.12	.12	.13	.01	.01	—	—	....	....	....	Vanuatu	846
....	....	....	....	....	....	....	....	....	....	....	....	....	....	....	Viet Nam	582
....	....	....	....	....	....	....	....	....	....	....	....	....	....	....	Western Samoa	862
....	....	....	....	....	....	....	....	....	....	....	....	....	....	....	Asia not specified	598
....	3.50	3.01	3.53	4.30	4.91	5.03	4.34	4.84	5.32	6.18	7.14	8.26	7.59	10.25	**Europe**	170
					.14	.21	.26	.33	.45	.76	.75	.73	.86	1.27	Cyprus	423
											.09	.10	.03	....	Czechoslovakia	934
															Hungary	944
.14	.13	.12	.11	.09	.01	.01	—	—	—	—	—	—	—	—		
					.12	.17	.22	.26	.36	.60	.73	.73	.81	1.01	Malta	181
							2.74	2.87	3.01	3.15	4.54	5.38	4.38	6.08	Poland	964
....	....	....	....	....	....	....	....	....	....	....	....	....	....	....	Romania	968
						.32	.41	.65	.76	.92	.37	.74	.89	1.23	Turkey	186
....	....	....	....	....	....	....	....	....	....	....	....	....	....	....	Yugoslavia, SFR	188
....	....	....	....	....	....	....	....	....	....	....	....	....	....	....	Europe not specified	884
15.84	19.50	24.02	27.95	30.66	29.20	29.52	30.43	30.52	31.69	28.65	31.47	38.58	47.96	53.54	**Middle East**	405
8.61	11.31	14.42	16.10	18.48	15.99	13.96	13.17	12.27	11.98	9.50	10.00	11.61	17.30	21.90	Bahrain	419
.12	.11	1.00	.87	.80	.92	1.17	1.31	1.06	.93	.99	1.20	1.29	.93	.85	Egypt	469
....	....	....	....	....	....	....	....	....	....	....	....	....	....	....	Iran, I.R. of	429
															Iraq	433
1.00	1.07	1.03	1.04	.85	1.13	1.21	1.24	.79	.98	1.55	1.40	1.82	2.78	3.63	Israel	436
.01	.01	.03	.05	.04	.04	.05	.05	.05	.05	.03	.04	.03	.08	....	Jordan	439
3.43	3.76	4.17	5.14	5.73	....	....	6.06	6.89	8.01	....	6.23	....	....	....	Kuwait	443
.50	.43	.41	.55	.33	.33	.23	.21	.26	.19	.23	.30	.23	.25	.30	Lebanon	446
—	—	—	—	—	—	—	—	—	—	—	—	—	—	—	Libya	672
.08	.07	.06	.07	.07	.06	.05	.04	.04	.04	.05	.15	.18	.10	.04	Oman	449
.04	.03	.03	.03	.13	.21	.26	.37	.38	.44	.31	.45	.11	.06	.10	Qatar	453
.94	1.05	1.11	2.00	1.99	1.90	3.41	4.42	4.71	4.65	4.83	7.44	13.10	15.56	15.11	Saudi Arabia	456
....	....	....	....	....	....	....	....	....	....	....	....	....	....	....	Syrian Arab Rep.	463
1.09	1.66	1.74	2.08	2.25	3.19	3.45	3.55	4.06	4.41	4.03	4.25	4.35	5.02	....	United Arab Emirates	466
.01	—	—	.01	—	.01	.01	.01	.01	.01	—	—	—	—	—	Yemen Arab Rep.	473
.01	—	.01	.01	—	.01	—	.01	.01	.01	—	—	—	—	—	Yemen, P.D. Rep.	459
															Middle East not specified	489
103.60	128.16	130.73	128.10	126.39	142.77	147.45	156.41	177.26	194.29	243.70	233.11	250.35	269.43	272.39	**Western Hemisphere**	205
										.01	.01	.01	.02	.04	Antigua and Barbuda	311
....	.25	.16	.79	.93	.75	.77	.97	.84	.97	1.58	1.65	1.86	2.06	2.14	Argentina	213
....	....	....	45.83	39.14	42.97	39.25	39.42	34.16	35.93	33.06	41.13	39.12	40.63	....	Bahamas, The	313
—	—	.52	.62[e]	....	....	....	....	....	.32	....	....	....	....	....	Barbados	316
....	....	....	....	....	....	....	....	....	....	....	....	....	....	....	Belize	339
.05	.06	.04	.09	.14	.17	.22	.25	....	....	....	....	....	....	....	Bermuda	319
.22	.39	.49	.39	.53	.40	.35	.30	.64	.53	.58	.51	.72	.80	....	Bolivia	218
25.36[e]	36.70	45.24	46.68	56.19	69.58	78.35	91.64	126.12	139.09	188.40	166.23	181.72	192.33	....	Brazil	223
....	....	....	....	....	....	....	....	....	....	....	....	....	....	....	Cayman Islands	377
.10	.13	.15	.17	.18	.18	.19	.18	.21	....	....	....	....	....	....	Chile	228
															Colombia	233
															Costa Rica	238
—	—	—	—	—	—	.01	—	.01	—	—	—	.01	.01	.01	Dominica	321
															Dominican Republic	243
															Ecuador	248
															El Salvador	253
														.01	.02	Grenada	328
....	....	....	....	....	....	....	....	....	....	....	....	....	....	....	Guatemala	258
.01														.01	Guyana	336
....	....	....	....	....	....	....	....	....	....	....	....	....	....	....	Haiti	263
—	—	—	—	—	—	—	—	—	—	—	—	.01	.01	.01	Honduras	268
.01	.01	.01	.02	—	—	—	—	.01	.01	.01	.01	.05	.07	.13	Jamaica	343
....	....	1.09	1.25	.87	1.00	1.02	1.23	1.79	1.85	2.27	2.65	2.87	3.67	3.97	Mexico	273
4.73	7.42	7.01	6.01	4.26	3.69	3.62	3.69	4.61	7.10	8.57	10.93	12.60	15.25	11.74	Netherlands Antilles	353
															Nicaragua	278
23.08	30.93	32.78	25.92	23.23	23.00	22.59	....	7.24	—	—	—	—	—	—	Panama	283
....	....	....	....	....	....	....	....	....	....	.01	.01	.02	.03	....	Paraguay	288
....	....	....	....	....	....	....	....	....	....	....	....	....	....	....	Peru	293
.02	.01	.01	.01	.01	.01	.01	.02	—	—	—	—	.01	.02	.02	St. Kitts and Nevis	361
—	—	—	—	—	—	—	—	—	—	.01	.01	.01	.01	.01	St. Lucia	362
—	—	—	—	—	.01	.01	—	—	—	.01	.01	.01	.02	.01	St. Vincent & Grens.	364
....	....	....	....	....	....	....	....	....	....	....	....	....	....	....	Suriname	366
.01	.01	.01	.01	.01	—	.01	—	.01	.01	.03	.01	.04	.04	....	Trinidad and Tobago	369
....	....	.30	.27	.34	.43	.46	.65	.88	.91	.95	1.12	1.50	1.55	1.37	Uruguay	298
.03	.03	.02	.02	.03	....	....	....	....	....	....	....	....	....	....	Venezuela	299
....	....	....	....	....	....	....	....	....	....	....	....	....	....	....	Western Hemisphere not spec.	399
....	....	....	....	....	....	....	....	....	....	....	....	....	....	....	**Unallocated**	899
															Memorandum Items	
5.73	6.70	7.27	9.50	10.32	10.95	13.13	14.61	16.32	17.81	16.68	19.22	24.07	27.47	27.63	Oil Exporting Countries	999
143.98	181.99	198.68	203.92	208.77	228.56	235.96	285.57	327.14	389.99	534.46	586.87	625.79	678.10	725.28	Non-Oil Developing Countries	201

Cross-Border Bank Deposits of Nonbanks by Residence of Borrowing Bank

7yd d

Billions of US Dollars:

		1980	1981	1982	1983	1984	1985	1986	1987	1988	1989	1990	1991	1992	1993	1994
World	001	....	....	....	....	....	....	....	....	....	....	....	....	....	....	....
Nonmonetary Internatl. Orgs.	096	....	....	....	....	....	....	....	....	....	....	....	....	....	....	....
Other Countries n.i.e.	910	....	....	....	....	....	....	....	....	....	....	....	....	....	....	....
All Countries	010	447.0	565.5	648.8	693.5	713.0	825.5	973.5	1,135.4	1,193.1	1,389.2	1,712.2	1,722.7	1,739.6	1,789.3	2,003.7
Industrial Countries	110	317.7	393.1	456.2	475.8	496.4	578.2	697.3	858.5	891.7	1,054.9	1,305.8	1,323.3	1,335.3	1,351.4	1,544.6
United States	111	21.53	27.47	45.55	58.83	67.45	73.84	80.59	81.16	86.84	103.37	92.82	92.14	91.42	96.88	109.80
Canada	156	17.99	23.11	18.99	25.00	27.04	30.34	32.38	31.73	31.11	32.00	35.75	33.51	27.29	24.36	29.81
Australia	193	.30	.40	.41	.29	I1.12	2.50	I1.54	2.64	5.04	6.39	7.24	7.74	....	....	....
Japan	158	2.11	2.44	2.49	2.36	3.58	6.20	6.86	7.17	9.91	13.48	13.34	15.16	17.71	19.03	19.78
New Zealand	196	....	....	....	....	....	....	....	....	....	....	....	....	....	....	....
Austria	122	5.13	6.66	6.32	6.04	7.48	9.71	13.19	15.64	16.93	21.15	23.81	23.56	23.41	22.33	24.09
Belgium-Luxembourg	126	28.80	33.38	32.29	31.69	33.80	44.69	65.62	91.38	105.62	144.33	196.07	210.24	227.68	....	....
Denmark	128	.49	.63	.54	.41	.41	1.44	1.93	2.39	3.01	2.81	2.51	3.23	4.08	5.18	7.82
Finland	172	....	....	....	....	....	....	....	....	....	....	....	....	....	....	....
France	132	25.44	26.77	34.81	38.33	45.15	53.91	59.60	75.07	82.17	98.62	137.43	158.51	176.28	187.02	....
Germany	134	15.11	16.07	15.34	15.95	17.47	21.92	29.47	41.47	36.44	44.29	61.73	64.02	80.40	96.08	119.03
Greece	174	4.09	4.61	4.92	5.17	5.40	6.36	7.67	9.57	10.14	11.85	14.21	15.41	16.05	16.52	....
Iceland	176	....	....	....	....	....	....	....	....	....	....	....	....	....	....	....
Ireland	178	....	....	2.67	2.66	2.60	3.57	3.75	4.56	4.43	5.16	6.79	7.35	6.73	7.11	....
Italy	136	1.42	1.37	1.67	2.12	2.31	3.07	4.89	6.47	7.28	15.06	16.21	18.58	17.74	15.92	....
Netherlands	138	12.43	14.18	15.21	14.35	15.44	19.44	25.83	32.45	35.48	45.56	59.66	63.19	60.41	63.04	72.60
Norway	142	3.61	3.55	3.37	3.43	3.42	4.84	7.87	9.76	10.61	11.22	11.82	9.54	7.56	5.66	5.04
Portugal	182	.04	.04	.04	.03	.04	.05	.08	.14	I.17	.23	.40	.38	I1.11	1.04	1.17
Spain	184	....	....	9.67	9.38	10.41	11.78	13.46	15.92	18.12	21.44	26.50	28.19	30.86	29.38	37.31
Sweden	144	1.29	1.91	.68	1.31	1.30	2.40	2.09	5.21	7.02	11.34	I12.13	13.95	9.22	9.45	7.41
Switzerland	146	74.50	97.46	I109.61	107.91	I105.93	124.31	141.68	178.01	173.12	200.83	252.57	244.35	233.52	216.36	254.11
United Kingdom	112	95.46	123.40	151.61	150.53	146.10	157.87	198.82	247.79	248.26	265.74	334.76	I314.24	296.00	279.71	294.47
Industrial not specified	189	....	....	....	....	....	....	....	....	....	....	....	....	....	....	....
Developing Countries	200	129.31	172.35	192.62	217.68	216.61	247.24	276.24	276.86	301.41	334.28	406.43	399.41	404.31	437.90	459.02
of which: Major Offshore Bkg.Ctrs.	016	90.86	124.90	136.69	158.98	153.28	174.36	196.81	214.88	238.66	276.70	336.41	323.00	318.10	340.18	354.73
Africa	605	2.18	2.01	1.87	2.16	2.81	3.72	4.08	5.17	4.18	4.02	4.83	5.11	4.61	4.15	3.64
Algeria	612	1.20	1.06	.90	1.02	1.53	2.14	2.79	3.18	2.14	2.03	2.90	2.75	2.47	2.05	1.31
Angola	614	....	....	....	....	....	....	....	....	....	....	....	....	....	....	....
Benin	638	....	....	....	....	....	....	.02	.02	.02	.02	.03	.02	.01	.01	.01
Botswana	616	—	—	—	—	—	—	—	.01	.01	.01	.01	.01	.01	.03	.02
Burkina Faso	748	.04	.03	.03	.03	.02	.03	.02	.03	.03	.04	.04	.04	.03	.03	.02
Burundi	618	—	—	—	—	—	—	.01	—	—	—	—	—	—	—	—
Cameroon	622	....	....	....	....	....	....	....	....	....	....	....	....	....	....	....
Cape Verde	624	....	....	....	....	....	....	....	....	....	....	....	....	....	....	....
Central African Rep.	626	....	....	....	....	....	....	....	....	....	....	....	....	....	....	....
Chad	628	....	....	....	....	....	....	....	....	....	....	....	....	....	....	....
Comoros	632	....	....	....	....	....	....	....	....	....	....	....	....	....	....	....
Congo	634	....	....	....	....	....	....	....	....	....	....	....	....	....	....	....
Côte d'Ivoire	662	.13	.11	.13	.10	.11	.22	.30	.41	.35	.30	.30	.29	.21	.19	.11
Djibouti	611	....	....	....	....	.07	.04	.03	.03	.03	.04	.03	.03	.03	.04	.04
Equatorial Guinea	642	....	....	....	....	....	....	....	....	....	....	....	....	....	....	....
Ethiopia	644	.02	.03	.04	.05	.04	.04	.04	.04	.05	.05	.06	.05	.03	.04	.05
Gabon	646	....	....	....	....	....	....	....	....	....	....	....	....	....	....	....
Gambia, The	648	—	—	—	—	—	—	—	—	—	—	—	—	—	—	—
Ghana	652	.01	.01	.02	.04	—	—	—	—	.01	.02	.03	.08	.09	.13	.19
Guinea	656	....	....	....	....	....	....	....	....	....	....	....	....	....	....	....
Guinea-Bissau	654	....	....	....	....	....	....	....	....	....	....	—	—	—	—	—
Kenya	664	.02	.02	.01	.01	.02	.02	.01	.06	.06	.06	.05	.06	.05	.04	....
Lesotho	666	—	—	—	—	—	—	—	—	—	—	—	—	—	—	.01
Liberia	668	....	....	....	....	....	....	....	....	....	....	....	....	....	....	....
Madagascar	674	....	....	....	....	....	....	....	....	....	....	....	....	....	....	....
Malawi	676	.01	.01	.01	.01	.01	.01	.01	.01	.01	.01	.01	.01	.01	.01	.02
Mali	678	....	....	....	....	.01	.01	.02	.03	.04	.03	.04	.05	.02	.02	.02
Mauritania	682	....	....	....	....	....	....	....	....	....	....	....	....	....	....	....
Mauritius	684	.02	.01	—	—	.01	....	....	....	....	....	....	....	....	....	....
Morocco	686	.03	.04	.02	.02	.02	....	....	....	....	....	....	....	....	....	....
Mozambique	688	....	....	....	....	....	....	....	....	....	....	....	....	....	....	....
Niger	692	.05	.07	.07	.08	.07	.08	.09	.10	.09	.09	.09	.11	.11	.04	.03
Nigeria	694	—	—	—	—	—	—	—	—	—	—	—	—	.01	.01	....
Rwanda	714	.01	.01	.02	.02	.02	.02	.01	.01	.01	.01	.01	.01	.01	—	....
Sao Tome & Principe	716	....	....	....	....	....	....	....	....	....	....	....	....	....	....	....
Senegal	722	.08	.06	.05	.05	.04	.04	.04	.06	.06	.07	.14	.08	.07	.08	.05	.05
Seychelles	718	....	....	....	....	....	....	....	....	....	....	....	....	....	....	....
Sierra Leone	724	—	—	—	—	—	—	—	—	—	—	—	—	—	—	—
Somalia	726	....	....	....	....	....	....	....	....	....	....	....	....	....	....	....
South Africa	199	....	....	....	....	....	....	....	....	....	....	....	....	....	....	....
Sudan	732	....	....	....	....	....	....	....	....	....	....	....	....	....	.05	.02
Swaziland	734	—	—	—	—	—	—	—	—	—	—	—	—	—	—	—
Tanzania	738	.01	.01	.05	....	.37	.50	.14	.55	.62	....	....	....	.08	.11	....
Togo	742	.03	.02	.02	.01	.01	.01	.03	.04	.03	.03	.04	.04	.04	.03	.01
Tunisia	744	.38	.36	.35	.35	.38	.44	.40	....	.52	.53	.65	1.25	1.23	1.23	1.47
Uganda	746	—	—	—	—	—	—	—	—	—	—	—	—	—	—	—
Zaïre	636	....	....	....	....	....	....	....	....	....	....	....	....	....	....	....
Zambia	754	.04	.04	.04	.03	.02	.01	.01	.01	.01	.02	.01	.01	—	....	....
Zimbabwe	698	.03	.03	.02	.02	.02	.02	.04	.03	.03	.03	.05	.05	.04	.02	.01
Africa not specified	799	....	....	....	....	....	....	....	....	....	....	....	....	....	....	....
Asia	505	16.74	21.64	26.71	29.69	29.77	36.09	40.38	49.26	55.94	62.98	76.70	73.80	77.90	79.23	86.58
Afghanistan, Islamic State of	512	....	....	....	....	....	....	....	....	....	....	....	....	....	....	....
Bangladesh	513	.02	.03	.02	.03	.03	.05	.04	.03	.03	.02	.03	.02	.02	.02	.02
Cambodia	522	....	....	....	....	....	....	....	....	....	....	....	....	....	....	....
China, People's Rep.	924	....	....	....	....	....	....	....	....	....	....	....	....	....	....	....
Fiji	819	.01	.01	.01	.01	.01	.01	.01	.01	.01	.01	.01	.02	.02	.02	.03
Hong Kong	532	....	....	....	....	....	....	....	....	....	....	....	....	....	....	....
India	534	.29	.37	.42	.45	.47	.62	.83	1.27	1.57	1.64	1.93	1.72	....	....	....
Indonesia	536	.05	.05	.05	.05	.04	.03	.03	.03	.03	.10	.16	.32	.40	....	....
Korea	542	.09	.14	.25	.44	.56	.79	.58	.50	.40	.30	.30	.27	.26	.33	.53
Lao P. D. Rep.	544	....	....	....	....	....	....	....	....	....	....	....	....	....	....	....

Cross-Border Bank Deposits of Nonbanks by Residence of Depositor

1980	1981	1982	1983	1984	1985	1986	1987	1988	1989	1990	1991	1992	1993	1994		7xr d
End of Period (7xrd 900)																
....	571.4	648.6	693.2	712.8	825.2	973.8	1,135.4	1,193.1	1,389.1	1,712.2	1,722.7	1,739.6	1,789.3	2,003.7	World	001
....	.33	5.00	5.87	6.20	7.46	7.19	9.77	10.69	11.17	14.57	17.32	16.01	14.90	18.00	Nonmonetary Internatl. Orgs.	096
....	.03	.25	.62	.17	.21	.25	.36	.38	.51	.12	.13	.11	.15	.15	Other Countries n.i.e.	910
....	571.0	643.3	686.7	706.5	817.6	966.4	1,125.2	1,182.0	1,377.5	1,697.5	1,705.3	1,723.5	1,774.2	1,985.5	All Countries	010
....	255.4	287.9	306.5	306.4	348.7	428.0	515.9	549.0	672.1	839.7	833.0	842.7	873.5	975.8	Industrial Countries	110
....	130.65	152.01	167.52	160.87	175.71	203.11	228.79	248.99	255.95	286.28	268.67	256.71	259.18	271.74	United States	111
....	8.97	11.06	11.31	12.64	11.39	13.08	15.41	13.02	13.58	20.39	14.78	12.13	11.45	13.65	Canada	156
....	.29	.92	.91	1.24	2.02	2.13	3.63	3.46	4.82	6.51	6.25	6.11	5.38	6.64	Australia	193
....	1.84	2.08	1.92	2.74	4.22	6.94	9.11	10.57	23.62	22.11	20.12	18.19	16.39	21.35	Japan	158
....	.01	.58	.42	.43	.62	1.03	2.51	2.38	1.17	2.03	1.21	1.02	.90	.99	New Zealand	196
....	1.05	1.33	1.33	1.29	1.70	2.42	2.68	2.82	3.87	4.78	4.43	4.84	4.60	5.26	Austria	122
....	11.77	11.66	10.30	10.97	14.68	20.44	23.27	22.81	31.15	38.46	36.47	38.80	41.17	49.73	Belgium-Luxembourg	126
....	.53	.49	.42	.37	.55	.94	1.78	2.05	2.67	3.73	2.54	2.51	4.35	3.47	Denmark	128
....	.05	.32	.26	.25	.48	.79	.81	1.07	1.40	1.81	2.34	1.88	1.46	1.67	Finland	172
....	13.02	11.86	11.03	9.86	11.49	14.45	19.22	19.10	28.62	44.78	42.36	46.33	40.59	48.53	France	132
....	11.49	10.06	9.93	11.35	15.83	37.45	51.26	52.78	82.11	124.62	137.02	160.27	183.08	200.05	Germany	134
....	1.89	5.12	4.99	4.74	5.87	6.43	7.04	7.29	9.63	11.45	11.34	10.92	10.60	11.88	Greece	174
....	.02	.06	.06	.05	.12	.12	.13	.19	.16	.19	.22	.20	.21	.18	Iceland	176
....	1.32	1.21	1.43	1.24	1.98	2.66	3.27	3.01	4.13	7.50	9.08	11.20	11.55	12.96	Ireland	178
....	11.66	10.30	9.89	8.97	10.90	11.20	14.07	13.68	21.07	31.18	38.08	39.14	36.15	41.25	Italy	136
....	6.68	7.73	10.31	11.69	13.29	17.54	25.02	33.85	46.26	53.22	54.13	57.65	63.56	82.08	Netherlands	138
....	.21	1.30	1.35	.97	1.78	1.70	2.01	2.13	2.16	2.59	2.44	2.75	2.57	2.62	Norway	142
....	1.23	2.48	2.55	2.50	3.12	3.57	3.85	3.75	4.25	4.74	4.59	4.26	6.16	6.94	Portugal	182
....	2.27	4.83	5.10	5.10	5.93	6.44	7.92	8.39	11.17	13.73	14.93	17.94	19.41	21.49	Spain	184
....	.88	.77	.72	.68	1.06	1.63	2.42	2.66	4.02	4.40	4.31	3.29	4.69	5.02	Sweden	144
....	21.03	24.30	24.03	26.86	27.55	29.36	36.15	34.62	48.47	60.94	60.91	58.46	54.27	58.97	Switzerland	146
....	17.97	17.41	20.01	20.15	25.82	31.67	41.09	43.00	51.30	71.79	74.10	64.57	72.28	84.98	United Kingdom	112
....	10.55	10.04	10.73	11.40	12.63	12.93	14.42	17.36	20.53	22.44	22.67	23.52	23.45	24.32	Industrial not specified	189
....	79.93	188.06	212.04	212.89	252.16	274.99	311.98	329.27	388.98	451.92	431.92	412.17	399.91	447.50	Developing Countries	200
....	18.18	47.42	54.68	59.62	70.72	86.35	98.61	101.38	118.93	142.88	137.52	134.65	138.91	165.34	of which:Major Offshore Bkg.Ctrs.	016
....	5.41	14.02	15.02	13.14	17.12	18.72	24.12	25.60	32.42	39.10	36.95	35.19	33.12	35.32	Africa	605
....	.26	.51	.51	.49	.67	.81	.87	.94	1.16	1.59	1.67	1.58	1.43	1.68	Algeria	612
....	.01	.06	.07	.09	.08	.11	.11	.10	.14	.29	.24	.29	.24	.78	Angola	614
....	—	.05	.05	.03	.07	.04	.05	.06	.05	.07	.07	.08	.08	.10	Benin	638
....	.05	.03	.04	.05	.04	.04	.06	.08	.11	.13	.15	.12	.12	.13	Botswana	616
....	—	.03	.02	.01	.03	.03	.06	.05	.05	.06	.06	.07	.08	.10	Burkina Faso	748
....	.03	.06	.07	.07	.07	.12	.09	.09	.09	.14	.13	.13	.13	.15	Burundi	618
....	—	.36	.27	.44	.65	.41	.55	.40	.45	.64	.61	.51	.46	.57	Cameroon	622
....	—	—	—	—	—	—	.05	—	.01	.01	.01	.01	.01	.01	Cape Verde	624
....	—	.02	.02	.02	.03	.03	.05	.06	.06	.07	.07	.08	.09	.09	Central African Rep.	626
....	—	.01	.01	.01	.02	.02	.03	.02	.02	.03	.03	.03	.04	.05	Chad	628
....	—	.01	.01	.01	.01	.01	.01	.01	.02	.03	.03	.02	.03	.03	Comoros	632
....	—	.09	.11	.13	.19	.18	.21	.17	.22	.26	.28	.28	.24	.26	Congo	634
....	.18	.54	.45	.44	.67	.68	.89	.80	1.17	1.48	1.20	1.22	1.16	1.41	Côte d'Ivoire	662
....	—	—	.09	.09	.10	.11	.17	.13	.18	.22	.21	.20	.21	.20	Djibouti	611
....	—	—	.01	—	—	.01	.01	.01	.01	.02	.02	.02	.03	.03	Equatorial Guinea	642
....	—	.11	.11	.11	.10	.10	.12	.16	.19	.23	.22	.23	.24	.22	Ethiopia	644
....	—	.18	.18	.14	.25	.25	.33	.31	.36	.62	.61	.51	.47	.56	Gabon	646
....	—	.01	.02	.02	.08	.04	.08	.07	.07	.11	.09	.10	.09	.11	Gambia, The	648
....	.01	.22	.19	.20	.24	.24	.26	.29	.32	.38	.37	.41	.36	.35	Ghana	652
....	—	—	.03	.03	.04	.05	.11	.06	.06	.09	.09	.10	.11	.10	Guinea	656
....	—	—	—	—	—	—	—	.01	.01	.01	.01	.02	.02	.02	Guinea-Bissau	654
....	.02	1.13	1.07	.99	1.36	1.50	1.84	1.81	2.01	2.64	2.53	2.22	2.08	2.29	Kenya	664
....	—	—	—	—	—	.03	.01	.01	.01	.03	.06	.05	.05	.06	Lesotho	666
....	1.28	3.41	3.73	3.80	4.69	5.47	7.46	9.38	12.60	13.54	12.09	11.97	10.42	10.39	Liberia	668
....	—	—	.11	.11	.13	.17	.22	.21	.28	.32	.33	.35	.28	.35	Madagascar	674
....	—	.05	.04	.04	.06	.06	.08	.08	.08	.10	.12	.11	.10	.10	Malawi	676
....	—	.02	.05	.02	.04	.04	.06	.05	.07	.11	.09	.09	.07	.07	Mali	678
....	—	.05	.07	.04	.03	.05	.04	.08	.05	.10	.10	.09	.09	.12	Mauritania	682
....	—	.05	.05	.05	.07	.08	.13	.11	.14	.19	.19	.17	.19	.22	Mauritius	684
....	.41	.73	.76	.79	.96	1.09	1.31	1.32	1.68	2.10	2.36	2.27	2.12	2.23	Morocco	686
....	—	.05	.05	.04	.04	.06	.08	.06	.09	.11	.11	.11	.13	.12	Mozambique	688
....	—	.08	.04	.03	.06	.07	.06	.05	.09	.13	.07	.07	.08	.08	Niger	692
....	.30	1.38	1.38	1.17	1.50	1.68	2.30	1.96	2.66	3.53	3.47	2.95	3.37	3.46	Nigeria	694
....	.02	.04	.04	.05	.07	.09	.12	.12	.17	.22	.23	.27	.24	.24	Rwanda	714
....	—	—	—	—	—	—	—	—	—	—	—	.01	.01	.01	Sao Tome & Principe	716
....	—	—	.16	.15	.21	.29	.42	.42	.48	.62	.52	.49	.57	.62	Senegal	722
....	—	.04	.03	.03	.04	.04	.06	.09	.10	.09	.09	.09	.09	.10	Seychelles	718
....	—	.08	.06	.06	.19	.11	.12	.10	.34	.43	.14	.12	.12	.13	Sierra Leone	724
....	.01	.05	.07	.07	.09	.09	.11	.10	.12	.16	.14	.09	.08	.06	Somalia	726
....	1.84	2.68	2.85	1.05	1.47	1.68	2.12	2.26	2.57	3.18	3.31	3.02	3.11	3.43	South Africa	199
....	.05	.42	.48	.44	.63	.61	.68	.66	.71	.83	.71	.63	.53	.47	Sudan	732
....	—	.02	.03	.04	.03	.02	.03	.03	.03	.04	.07	.06	.26	.05	Swaziland	734
....	—	.14	.17	.17	.20	.23	.31	.33	.37	.49	.50	.44	.48	.54	Tanzania	738
....	—	.09	.09	.08	.12	.16	.20	.20	.21	.27	.17	.21	.20	.21	Togo	742
....	—	—	.28	.33	.34	.36	.37	.37	.48	.60	.61	.62	.58	.61	Tunisia	744
....	—	.08	.10	.10	.12	.14	.17	.17	.16	.18	.19	.16	.15	.21	Uganda	746
....	.48	.58	.60	.63	.70	.80	1.00	1.04	1.32	1.65	1.48	1.41	1.19	1.25	Zaïre	636
....	—	.23	.24	.21	.36	.28	.36	.40	.42	.42	.44	.42	.34	.39	Zambia	754
....	—	.14	.15	.14	.21	.22	.30	.34	.36	47	.49	.45	.35	.40	Zimbabwe	698
....	.42	.22	.07	.11	.06	.04	.07	.04	.05	.09	.17	.27	.23	.17	Africa not specified	799
....	9.26	25.35	30.52	29.32	37.07	39.75	43.49	48.50	61.12	69.47	69.98	66.17	65.70	72.02	Asia	505
....	—	.11	.11	.08	.09	.08	.11	.12	.12	.13	.12	.14	.11	.11	Afghanistan, Islamic State of	512
....	—	.14	.16	.16	.26	.31	.47	.55	.54	.60	.42	.33	.29	.37	Bangladesh	513
....	—	—	.01	.01	—	—	.01	—	.01	.01	.02	.02	.01	.01	Cambodia	522
....	.04	.49	.39	.29	.55	.65	.63	.67	1.28	1.63	1.57	2.03	1.86	1.85	China, People's Rep.	924
....	—	.01	.01	.01	.01	.01	.02	.02	.02	.02	.03	.03	.03	.03	Fiji	819
....	5.10	14.42	15.44	16.10	19.27	20.75	21.75	24.15	29.71	35.08	35.54	34.28	35.63	37.82	Hong Kong	532
....	—	—	1.75	1.43	2.64	2.32	3.51	3.23	3.79	4.89	4.40	3.77	3.43	4.05	India	534
....	.17	.55	.59	.66	1.09	1.23	1.68	1.75	3.15	3.03	2.97	4.55	2.78	2.76	Indonesia	536
....	.10	.48	.24	.40	.63	.63	.60	.69	.86	.86	.98	1.50	1.38	2.19	Korea	542
....	—	—	.01	.01	.01	.01	.01	.01	.01	.02	.02	.01	.03	.01	.02	Lao P. D. Rep.	544

Cross-Border Bank Deposits of Nonbanks by Residence of Borrowing Bank

7yd d

Billions of US Dollars

		1980	1981	1982	1983	1984	1985	1986	1987	1988	1989	1990	1991	1992	1993	1994
Asia (cont.)																
Malaysia	548	.17	.14	.18	1.22	.24	.30	.26	.19	.22	.33	....	.41	.48	1.20	.96
Maldives	556	—	—	—	—	—	—	—	—	—	—	—	—	—	—	....
Myanmar	518	.39	.52	.51	.61	.60	.74	1.13	1.46	1.60	.05	.04	....	....	....	....
Nepal	558	.01	.01	.01	.01	.02	.02	.02	.03	.03	.03	.03	.04	.06	.07	....
Pakistan	564	.09	.09	.10	.10	.14	.16	.19	.28	.37	.39	.41	.41	.47	.43	.40
Papua New Guinea	853	....	.03	.02	.03	.05	.05	.04	.06	.09	.13	.10	.14	.12	.09	....
Philippines	566	4.88	4.75	5.41	3.90	3.84	2.88	1.06	1.04	1.15	1.37	1.81	1.67	2.32	2.75	4.44
Singapore	576	10.47	15.17	19.35	22.35	23.27	29.66	35.39	43.38	49.47	57.31	70.20	67.15	67.43	66.86	71.67
Solomon Islands	813	—	—	—	—	—	—	—	—	—	—	—	—	—	—	—
Sri Lanka	524	.04	.05	.08	.11	.11	.15	.18	.21	.23	.28	.32	.41	.50	.60	.71
Thailand	578	.17	.23	.23	.32	.33	.47	.49	.64	.67	.95	.93	1.13	3.31	3.79	4.54
Vanuatu	846	....	....	....	.06	.14	.12	.13	.03	.05	.06	.02	....	....	....	....
Viet Nam	582	....	....	....	....	....	....	....	....	....	....	....	....	....	....	....
Western Samoa	862	....	....	....	....	....	....	....	....	....	....	....	....	....	....	....
Asia not specified	598	....	....	....	....	....	....	....	....	....	....	....	....	....	....	....
Europe	170	....	22.18	26.78	28.96	28.49	33.96	39.61	16.92	14.52	13.49	16.22	15.80	19.19	22.80	17.21
Cyprus	423	.14	.17	.20	.24	.27	1.48	.64	.86	1.05	1.44	2.14	2.47	2.87	3.07	3.73
Czechoslovakia	934	.05	.06	.06	.07	.08	.08	.11	.13	.15	.16	....	....	.02	....	....
Hungary	944	.04	.05	.06	.05	.05	.06	.06	.03	....	....	....	....	....	....	....
Malta	181	.01	.02	.02	.03	.02	.03	.04	.06	.08	.11	.20	.26	.12	.11	.10
Poland	964	....	13.81	15.60	16.50	16.07	20.05	23.53	....	....	....	....	—	—	—	.03
Romania	968	....	5.16	5.53	6.01	5.38	5.14	4.92	4.79	1.83	.49	.69	—	—	—	—
Turkey	186	....	....	....	....	....	....	1.62	1.77	1.86	2.04	3.89	4.60	7.19	9.95	3.72
Yugoslavia, SFR	188	....	2.02	4.21	4.87	5.45	6.73	8.69	9.29	9.53	9.22	9.17	....	....	....	....
Europe not specified	884	....	....	....	....	....	....	....	....	....	....	....	....	....	....	....
Middle East	405	13.53	17.77	21.29	23.06	23.10	22.33	22.65	26.08	31.67	34.24	30.05	30.66	32.34	36.26	44.09
Bahrain	419	8.53	11.97	13.70	14.73	14.87	13.10	13.07	15.21	19.46	22.37	17.28	16.85	15.91	19.33	24.54
Egypt	469	.29	.31	.68	1.04	.92	1.07	1.27	1.84	1.98	1.66	1.43	1.16	1.35	1.25	1.36
Iran, I.R. of	429	....	....	....	....	....	....	....	....	....	....	....	....	....	....	....
Iraq	433	....	....	....	....	....	....	....	....	....	....	....	....	....	....	....
Israel	436	3.40	3.94	5.36	5.61	5.56	5.95	6.45	6.97	7.97	8.16	9.34	9.90	10.62	10.83	12.16
Jordan	439	.43	.42	.49	.58	.68	.80	.89	.91	.89	.62	.58	1.20	2.20	1.90	....
Kuwait	443	....	....	....	....	....	....	....	....	....	....	....	....	....	....	....
Lebanon	446	.52	.69	.65	.61	.57	.48	.32	.34	.34	.34	.38	.59	.62	.82	1.01
Libya	672	—	—	—	—	—	—	—	—	—	—	—	—	—	—	—
Oman	449	.02	.02	.03	.04	.04	.03	.04	.02	.06	.08	.05	.02	.01	.02	.02
Qatar	453	—	—	—	—	—	—	—	—	—	—	—	—	—	—	—
Saudi Arabia	456	—	.05	.02	.03	.04	.05	.04	.04	.03	.03	.08	.07	.41	.88	1.83
Syrian Arab Rep.	463	....	....	....	....	....	....	....	....	....	....	....	....	....	....	....
United Arab Emirates	466	.25	.27	.25	.33	.34	.71	.47	.63	.80	.86	.75	.72	1.07	1.10	....
Yemen Arab Rep.	473	.03	.05	.06	.04	.02	.07	.01	.02	.03	.02	....	....	....	....	....
Yemen, P.D. Rep.	459	.06	.05	.04	.05	.06	.08	.08	.09	.11	.12	....	....	....	....	....
Middle East not specified	489	....	....	....	....	....	....	....	....	....	....	....	....	....	....	....
Western Hemisphere	205	80.21	108.75	115.98	133.81	132.44	151.14	169.51	179.43	195.12	219.55	278.63	274.04	270.26	295.45	307.49
Antigua and Barbuda	311	.01	.01	.01	.01	.01	.02	.02	.02	.02	.03	.02	.02	.03	.02	.03
Argentina	213	....	1.41	1.79	1.83	2.35	2.23	2.53	2.41	2.60	1.55	1.89	2.63	2.92	3.82	5.13
Bahamas, The	313	....	....	....	55.14	56.02	58.14	57.51	58.42	56.02	51.18	57.66	65.85	64.98	51.55	....
Barbados	316	.02	.03	.03	.03[e]	....	....	....	....	....	.26	....	....	....	....	....
Belize	339	.01	.01	.01	.01	.02	.01	.02	.02	.02	.02	.02	.02	.02	.01	.01
Bermuda	319	....	....	3.21	3.41	3.77	3.84	4.46	5.03	....	....	....	....	....	....	....
Bolivia	218	.07	.07	.06	.05	.05	.05	.05	.03	.03	.01	.01	.01	....	....	—
Brazil	223	2.20	2.48	2.34	1.93	2.51	3.20	2.48	.01	....	....	....	....	.17	.09	....
Cayman Islands	377	30.02[e]	38.45	43.90	55.74	47.69	61.12	76.04	83.93	102.04	133.18	178.17	157.99	151.38	179.82	....
Chile	228	....	....	....	....	....	....	....	....	....	....	....	....	....	....	....
Colombia	233	.22	.23	.27	.28	.46	....	....	....	....	....	....	....	....	....	....
Costa Rica	238	....	....	....	....	....	....	....	....	....	....	....	....	....	....	....
Dominica	321	—	.01	.01	.01	.01	.01	.01	.01	.01	.02	.02	.02	.02	.03	.03
Dominican Republic	243	....	....	....	....	....	....	....	....	....	....	....	....	....	....	....
Ecuador	248	....	....	....	....	....	....	....	....	....	....	....	....	....	....	....
El Salvador	253	....	....	....	....	....	....	....	....	....	....	....	....	....	....	....
Grenada	328	.01	.01	.01	.01	.01	.01	.01	.02	.02	.02	.02	.02	.02	.03	.03
Guatemala	258	....	....	....	....	....	....	....	....	....	....	....	....	....	....	....
Guyana	336	.01	.01	.02	.02	.01	.01	.02	.01	.01	....	.01	—	....	.01	.02
Haiti	263	....	....	....	....	....	....	....	....	....	....	....	....	....	....	....
Honduras	268	.10	.11	.11	.11	.11	.11	.11	.11	.10	.08	.20	.03	.02	.03	.06
Jamaica	343	.04	.06	.08	.05	.04	.05	.06	.09	.09	.10	.09	.12	.16	.18	.22
Mexico	273	....	....	1.75	1.66	6.00	6.97	8.11	11.11	11.90	12.19	18.69	23.39	23.30	28.47	34.40
Netherlands Antilles	353	1.61	2.25	2.66	2.29	2.63	3.08	2.80	3.53	5.44	6.79	7.97	9.20	12.58	16.13	10.70
Nicaragua	278	....	....	....	....	....	....	....	....	....	....	....	....	....	....	....
Panama	283	....	8.48	8.90	8.73	8.79	9.27	11.99	....	6.23	....	....	....	....	....	....
Paraguay	288	....	....	....	....	....	....	....	....	.08	.05	.05	.08	.09	.10	....
Peru	293	.04	.02	.03	.03	.03	.03	.02	.02	.02	.01	.01	—	.01	.02	.07
St. Kitts and Nevis	361	.01	.01	.01	.01	.01	.01	.01	.01	.01	.01	.02	.02	.01	.02	.02
St. Lucia	362	.01	.01	.01	.01	.01	.01	.01	.01	.01	.02	.02	.02	.03	.03	.03
St. Vincent & Grens.	364	.01	.01	.01	.01	.01	.01	.01	.01	.01	.01	.02	.02	.03	.03	.03
Suriname	366	....	....	....	....	....	....	....	....	....	....	....	....	....	....	....
Trinidad and Tobago	369	.04	.06	.07	.08	.10	.06	.05	.05	.04	.05	.05	.06	.07	.06	....
Uruguay	298	....	....	.87	.74	.58	.57	.73	.82	1.28	1.81	2.17	2.33	2.55	2.46	2.52
Venezuela	299	.56	.93	1.60	1.56	1.13	1.71	1.84	2.68	3.63	.90	.67	.54	.29	.28	.19
Western Hemisphere not spec.	399	....	....	....	....	....	....	....	....	....	....	....	....	....	....	....
Unallocated	899	....	....	....	....	....	....	....	....	....	....	....	....	....	....	....
Memorandum Items																
Oil Exporting Countries	999	2.09	2.38	2.85	3.03	3.11	4.67	5.20	6.59	6.69	3.99	4.63	4.43	4.66	4.89	5.08
Non-Oil Developing Countries	201	127.21	170.01	189.78	214.67	213.50	242.57	271.03	270.27	294.72	330.29	401.80	394.98	399.65	433.01	453.94

Cross-Border Bank Deposits of Nonbanks by Residence of Depositor

1980	1981	1982	1983	1984	1985	1986	1987	1988	1989	1990	1991	1992	1993	1994		7xr d
End of Period (7xrd 900)															**Asia (cont.)**	
....	.14	1.12	1.20	1.38	1.27	.71	.81	1.01	1.54	2.05	1.76	1.32	1.57	1.70	Malaysia................	548
....	—	.02	.01	.01	.01	.01	.01	.01	.02	.03	.02	.02	—	—	.02	Maldives................	556
....	—	.01	.01	.01	.01	.01	.01	.01	.05	.04	.06	.07	.07	.06	.10	Myanmar................	518
....	—	.02	.02	.02	.01	.02	.04	.03	.04	.05	.07	.07	.08	.08	.10	Nepal................	558
....	.04	.76	.85	.88	1.37	1.57	1.72	2.01	2.45	3.19	2.51	2.32	2.07	2.17	Pakistan................	564
....	—	—	.01	.04	.06	.08	.05	.09	.08	.09	.11	.14	.25	.11	Papua New Guinea.........	853
....	.41	.70	.97	1.32	1.35	1.53	1.70	1.33	1.49	1.86	1.73	1.46	1.25	1.50	Philippines................	566
....	1.76	1.71	1.79	1.59	2.26	3.05	3.48	4.82	7.01	5.73	6.66	5.73	6.24	6.75	Singapore................	576
....	—	—	.02	—	—	—	—	.02	.03	.03	.02	.05	.04	.04	Solomon Islands............	813
....	—	.07	.07	.08	.19	.21	.26	.28	.30	.39	.36	.28	.24	.26	Sri Lanka................	524
....	.07	.27	.27	.33	.49	.56	.70	.77	.88	1.00	.91	1.06	.98	1.19	Thailand................	578
....	.01	.03	.02	.03	.04	.05	.05	.10	.08	.11	.08	.06	.06	.05	Vanuatu................	846
....	—	.03	.02	.02	.02	.08	.03	.03	.03	.04	.03	.04	.04	.10	Viet Nam................	582
....	—	—	—	.01	—	—	—	—	—	—	—	.01	.03	.04	Western Samoa............	862
....	1.43	4.40	6.54	4.47	5.38	5.84	5.83	6.70	7.63	8.57	9.57	6.89	7.26	8.66	Asia not specified...........	598
....	2.01	4.94	4.11	3.59	4.42	5.83	6.06	6.75	9.25	12.41	13.58	15.64	18.18	20.58	**Europe**................	170
....	.09	.53	.64	.59	.92	1.16	1.39	1.59	1.64	2.20	2.56	2.38	2.29	2.41	Cyprus................	423
....	—	.03	.05	.03	.04	.05	.07	.08	.14	.18	.28	.49	.57	.65	Czechoslovakia............	934
....	.01	.03	.03	.04	.05	.06	.07	.09	.13	.21	.30	.31	.42	.58	Hungary................	944
....	.02	.25	.29	.28	.41	.49	.66	.74	.87	1.28	1.44	1.33	1.30	1.29	Malta................	181
....	.02	.15	.17	.17	.21	.24	.31	.34	.48	.68	.77	.84	.88	1.08	Poland................	964
....	—	.01	.03	.02	.03	.03	.04	.03	.05	.07	.09	.13	.18	.21	Romania................	968
....	1.65	2.17	2.10	1.80	1.93	2.25	2.50	2.62	3.98	4.86	4.79	5.17	5.45	7.07	Turkey................	186
....	.10	.39	.34	.35	.50	.54	.73	.73	1.04	1.57	2.05	2.42	2.60	2.71	Yugoslavia, SFR............	188
....	.10	1.01	.24	.11	.10	.88	.08	.14	.53	.63	.12	.35	1.40	1.13	Europe not specified.........	884
....	24.28	59.65	61.35	58.79	68.51	67.51	75.84	81.40	98.32	112.24	101.86	95.34	84.91	85.96	**Middle East**............	405
....	.23	1.02	1.33	1.42	1.67	1.57	1.88	2.04	2.47	3.35	3.01	2.94	2.52	2.55	Bahrain................	419
....	.55	2.19	2.12	2.42	3.37	3.10	3.51	3.94	4.60	5.21	5.58	5.22	5.48	5.41	Egypt................	469
....	.47	3.18	2.94	2.57	2.87	2.92	3.38	3.10	3.33	4.12	3.82	3.85	3.59	4.06	Iran, I.R. of................	429
....	.28	1.01	.92	.93	1.09	.99	1.42	1.26	1.43	1.50	1.17	.91	.87	.84	Iraq................	433
....	1.05	2.76	2.82	2.62	2.82	3.07	3.18	3.40	4.20	5.27	5.51	5.70	4.80	5.44	Israel................	436
....	.30	1.01	1.08	1.09	1.20	1.36	1.77	2.35	2.48	2.84	3.20	2.98	2.72	2.73	Jordan................	439
....	1.86	5.05	5.63	5.57	6.43	6.02	8.43	9.00	9.50	12.04	8.96	9.20	7.18	7.37	Kuwait................	443
....	1.95	4.47	4.94	5.39	5.77	6.50	7.35	7.23	7.98	9.46	7.76	7.10	6.36	6.35	Lebanon................	446
....	—	.90	.92	.96	1.34	1.46	1.70	2.27	2.41	2.53	2.02	1.57	1.08	1.14	Libya................	672
....	.41	.98	1.10	1.17	1.89	1.58	1.90	1.87	2.19	2.28	1.14	1.02	.99	.84	Oman................	449
....	.38	1.48	1.23	1.43	1.81	1.55	1.65	1.50	2.10	2.62	2.88	1.89	1.33	1.38	Qatar................	453
....	8.73	22.67	22.54	20.17	22.10	21.50	21.86	24.26	33.20	34.78	30.96	29.13	25.66	24.71	Saudi Arabia................	456
....	.47	1.27	1.48	1.63	1.79	1.86	2.01	1.91	2.24	2.51	2.31	2.20	2.11	2.21	Syrian Arab Rep............	463
....	6.45	10.10	10.35	9.69	12.23	11.93	13.32	14.90	17.65	21.05	20.91	18.84	17.44	18.11	United Arab Emirates........	466
....	.05	.24	.30	.36	.46	.51	.46	.54	.61	.85	.94	.88	.90	.91	Yemen Arab Rep............	473
....	.01	.03	.04	.03	.05	.06	.06	.04	.14	.02	.05	.08	—	—	Yemen, P.D. Rep...........	459
....	1.08	1.28	1.58	1.34	1.62	1.54	1.94	1.78	1.81	1.82	1.65	1.82	1.90	1.92	Middle East not specified.....	489
....	38.97	84.09	101.04	108.05	125.04	143.20	162.47	167.02	187.86	218.69	209.54	199.84	197.99	233.62	**Western Hemisphere**..........	205
....	....	....	—	—	—	.12	—	—	.01	.01	.01	.01	—	—	Antigua and Barbuda........	311
....	3.78	7.21	7.80	7.62	8.51	8.50	9.73	11.12	14.54	17.02	16.95	14.97	12.34	13.51	Argentina................	213
....	.69	3.39	2.68	2.63	3.81	6.99	7.19	7.89	7.26	8.37	8.07	8.45	9.96	10.49	Bahamas, The............	313
....	.11	.11	.10	.13	.14	.34	.53	.63	.66	1.69	.51	.82	.85	1.27	Barbados................	316
....	—	—	—	.01	.03	.03	.12	.03	.05	.09	.10	.03	.08	.07	.12	Belize................	339
....	1.00	7.39	7.79	7.75	8.28	11.15	10.58	11.17	11.95	13.47	13.66	14.00	15.64	15.39	Bermuda................	319
....	.17	.39	.43	.39	.41	.29	.32	.42	.54	.48	.51	.44	.38	.50	Bolivia................	218
....	2.56	4.17	8.03	8.17	9.78	12.01	11.30	12.42	15.61	17.65	18.95	19.91	17.74	19.55	Brazil................	223
....	1.04	3.09	4.26	3.94	5.08	8.03	10.52	14.76	19.30	26.57	28.66	30.94	37.17	51.99	Cayman Islands............	377
....	.98	1.78	2.37	2.11	2.44	2.59	2.65	3.29	4.06	6.94	4.00	3.13	2.84	3.35	Chile................	228
....	....	....	2.84	2.56	2.83	3.11	3.18	4.00	4.61	4.96	4.80	4.01	3.63	4.16	Colombia................	233
....	....	....	.62	.73	.73	.62	.72	.95	.98	1.30	1.30	1.37	1.49	1.63	Costa Rica................	238
....	—	.01	.01	.01	.01	.01	.08	.01	.03	.28	.25	.29	.04	.03	Dominica................	321
....	....	.66	.41	.88	.84	.72	.87	.90	1.08	.99	1.18	1.05	1.17	1.10	Dominican Republic........	243
....	.72	.99	1.12	1.30	1.55	1.45	1.48	1.91	2.00	1.88	2.10	2.17	1.71	1.67	Ecuador................	248
....	....	....	.61	.68	.52	.48	.65	.54	.76	.66	.62	.68	.68	.63	El Salvador................	253
....	....	....	....	....	....	....	....	....	....	....	....	....	....	....	Grenada................	328
....	.69	.99	1.12	1.21	1.32	1.34	1.39	1.57	1.55	1.88	1.77	1.57	1.40	1.56	Guatemala................	258
....	—	.07	.06	.07	.07	.09	.12	.08	.08	.08	.12	.07	.06	.08	Guyana................	336
....	....	.14	.23	.23	.23	.19	.25	.26	.30	.30	.34	.39	.34	.33	Haiti................	263
....	....	....	.38	.38	.39	.47	.45	.45	.48	.51	.51	.66	.50	.66	Honduras................	268
....	.05	.14	.14	.14	.19	.36	.27	.40	.34	.54	.58	.35	.39	.45	Jamaica................	343
....	7.88	10.62	12.85	14.31	16.14	16.29	19.58	20.01	20.48	19.51	18.04	16.01	15.07	17.85	Mexico................	273
....	.89	4.68	7.07	8.68	12.09	14.35	18.59	15.52	13.47	17.78	16.99	17.07	17.37	23.09	Netherlands Antilles........	353
....	....	....	.16	.13	.44	.11	.09	.07	.06	.08	.22	.20	.16	.24	Nicaragua................	278
....	8.47	19.11	22.10	25.25	26.54	31.60	35.20	32.20	39.72	46.00	38.60	35.24	30.02	32.66	Panama................	283
....	—	—	.41	.49	.56	.54	.48	.62	.80	.78	.72	.75	.89	1.10	Paraguay................	288
....	.72	1.21	1.37	1.53	1.72	1.88	2.17	2.58	3.03	2.63	2.46	2.23	2.06	2.37	Peru................	293
....	....	....	....	....	....	....	....	.02	.02	.03	....	....	....	....	St. Kitts and Nevis........	361
....	—	—	—	—	—	—	.01	—	.01	.01	.01	.01	.01	.01	St. Lucia................	362
....	—	—	—	—	—	.01	.01	.02	.06	.06	.18	.19	.21	.29	St. Vincent & Grens........	364
....	—	.11	.08	.09	.13	.12	.14	.16	.18	.21	.26	.23	.22	.24	Suriname................	366
....	.06	.29	.30	.32	.38	.62	.45	.52	.48	.58	.62	.58	.67	.78	Trinidad and Tobago........	369
....	.81	1.43	1.78	1.92	2.20	2.51	2.61	3.03	3.71	4.20	4.07	3.41	2.98	3.27	Uruguay................	298
....	5.13	10.90	11.65	12.49	14.59	13.68	13.85	14.65	15.74	16.20	17.45	15.48	14.84	16.76	Venezuela................	299
....	1.20	1.38	2.26	1.88	3.08	2.51	6.99	4.83	3.81	4.40	4.87	2.68	2.88	4.26	Western Hemisphere not spec.	399
....	235.69	167.33	168.17	187.20	216.68	263.35	297.39	303.80	316.35	405.91	440.38	468.65	500.86	562.25	**Unallocated**................	899
															Memorandum Items	
....	25.71	60.17	61.52	58.78	69.35	67.04	74.39	79.11	96.27	107.04	99.00	92.60	82.31	84.84	Oil Exporting Countries......	999
....	54.21	127.82	150.52	154.11	182.81	207.96	237.59	250.15	292.70	344.89	332.92	319.57	317.59	362.65	Non-Oil Developing Countries..	201

Reserve Money

Percent Change over Previous Year

14 x		1965	1966	1967	1968	1969	1970	1971	1972	1973	1974	1975	1976	1977	1978	1979
Industrial Countries																
United States	111	5.2	5.9	5.4	7.6	5.9	5.1	7.7	6.9	6.9	8.3	4.7	5.9	7.0	9.5	10.3
Canada	156	8.3	7.7	8.4	2.0	9.9	5.7	12.1	14.8	14.8	13.3	16.8	11.2	10.5	12.1	10.7
Australia	193	−.2	−4.3	4.0	5.4	10.1	7.6	7.2	15.4	28.6	2.2	3.7	19.6	17.9	−4.3	7.5
Japan	158	9.5	14.0	15.8	17.5	17.9	19.5	16.4	18.7	34.8	25.0	12.1	4.4	8.0	10.4	10.4
New Zealand	196	−15.6	−9.6	−11.2	−1.8	6.7	7.1	3.7	23.6	77.6	17.2	−9.6	−8.7	6.7	5.6	12.6
Austria	122	10.7	4.8	7.8	1.7	4.1	5.6	6.6	16.3	12.2	.2	13.1	7.0	6.8	9.9	7.0
Belgium	124	7.1	4.2	1.5	3.0	1.9	.1	6.2	10.1	13.8	6.6	5.7	7.7	7.2	7.8	5.5
Denmark	128	7.0	9.5	1.5	13.8	26.6	−7.9	−14.6	11.9	5.4	−6.7	16.7	49.1	−7.6	−4.6	9.2
Finland	172	5.4	7.3	12.4	5.7	−6.9	9.2	9.0	11.0	14.8	13.7	17.4	9.7	7.5	17.5	36.9
France	132	7.7	6.3	6.9	5.8	6.5	−1.6	12.4	13.7	25.1	11.5	−15.1	−1.4	9.1	8.2	12.6
Germany	134	10.5	6.1	−3.0	5.7	10.1	12.1	21.0	16.3	23.6	−1.7	−1.0	8.1	10.1	7.1	10.4
Greece	174	12.9	15.1	13.9	12.0	5.7	5.7	13.4	25.0	26.1	16.7	16.4	21.2	23.5	18.6	14.6
Iceland	176	24.9	14.1	6.7	4.8	21.6	28.2	17.6	20.0	26.8	25.8	33.1	38.6	47.8	42.2	61.0
Ireland	178	5.7	5.1	12.8	18.0	13.8	37.2	13.5	13.6	25.1	18.4	22.7	15.0	12.6	18.1	27.5
Italy	136	10.2	9.8	6.4	7.6	8.2	11.0	17.8	15.5	21.2	29.5	11.5	19.6	16.6	17.3	12.0
Luxembourg	137															
Netherlands	138	9.0	8.2	4.1	2.2	7.1	5.2	6.0	10.3	8.6	1.0	11.9	9.7	9.8	6.8	6.8
Norway	142	5.8	7.1	10.7	2.4	3.6	6.6	10.6	6.5	5.4	12.6	16.4	12.0	12.2	14.8	8.8
Portugal	182	18.7	6.2	6.1	10.0	11.2	7.9	11.5	14.4	22.1	17.9	34.6	20.9	8.1	11.1	18.5
Spain	184	15.0	11.6	12.9	10.4	10.0	10.7	23.5	19.6	21.7	15.6	20.1	17.2	17.1	25.1	35.7
Sweden	144	5.5	5.0	5.4	7.9	7.2	6.1	7.6	11.0	8.7	30.5	15.0	.6	11.9	10.2	20.2
Switzerland	146	5.6	2.3	8.2	5.4	6.7	9.2	27.1	14.8	3.6	—	1.8	2.9	3.2	17.1	5.4
United Kingdom	112	6.4	5.2	4.3	10.4	2.3	6.4	3.7	6.3	30.0	11.3	10.0	13.2	7.9	13.0	5.7
Developing Countries																
Africa																
Algeria	612	6.4	3.6	12.5	13.7	13.5	14.3	15.5	27.1	20.0	21.2	19.1	32.7	26.6	26.8	31.8
Benin	638	3.0	−3.8	−4.1	−2.3	22.0	11.7	15.7	10.6	9.1	9.8	17.5	22.4	13.7	−8.1	15.9
Botswana	616													18.9	7.8	63.7
Burkina Faso	748	8.4	1.4	1.5	.4	10.5	13.1	−.5	−.9	16.1	26.5	26.6	28.9	11.6	1.8	10.6
Burundi	618	10.0	−1.2	7.6	−3.9	5.0	13.1	16.0	7.0	6.0	19.7	2.4	22.2	34.6	46.3	12.5
Cameroon	622	−3.7	8.4	23.2	9.4	10.0	11.6	7.7	3.8	8.0	24.1	12.2	10.2	24.3	21.2	16.8
Cape Verde	624													41.1	14.4	27.3
Central African Rep.	626	30.1	16.1	5.0	21.6	8.7	7.8	4.3	−.3	8.7	15.0	11.8	11.5	29.8	19.3	21.2
Chad	628	−.8	−1.5	−6.7	−6.2	15.9	11.0	9.8	14.7	−1.2	12.9	42.0	13.3	19.8	4.0	43.8
Comoros	632															
Congo	634	−3.3	9.3	20.2	18.4	7.9	9.7	13.4	12.5	16.9	27.5	22.0	9.5	7.0	−1.2	10.2
Côte d'Ivoire	662	5.9	6.6	−1.0	21.9	3.7	4.4	9.3	11.8	10.5	20.0	32.7	16.1	40.1	25.3	9.9
Djibouti	611															
Equatorial Guinea	642															
Ethiopia	644	13.3	6.0	−1.0	4.2	9.2	10.7	−3.9	−.4	25.5	23.3	35.9	29.6	−.8	8.0	8.7
Gabon	646	6.0	−.6	−26.3	6.4	7.5	22.2	16.3	20.5	24.6	64.4	38.5	54.4	22.0	2.4	1.7
Gambia, The	648	14.7	9.4	3.1	16.6	4.5	9.3	13.3	26.5	143.4	45.4	51.1	−8.1	6.7	−38.9	8.7
Ghana	652	14.9	25.6	−25.2	16.1	17.5	18.4	−5.3	51.6	29.5	29.2	43.2	51.4	48.2	77.0	33.1
Guinea	656															
Guinea-Bissau	654															
Kenya	664			71.2	16.0	38.3	34.5	−5.8	.6	33.7	−3.8	2.5	23.4	70.8	4.0	8.0
Lesotho	666										9.2	−7.7	21.9	7.0	7.3	8.8
Liberia	668											7.2	19.1	12.5	57.1	10.4
Madagascar	674	2.3	3.7	3.0	7.0	1.2	12.1	8.6	7.2	5.2	11.0	14.1	20.8	5.0	28.2	16.3
Malawi	676		13.8	8.0	1.0	7.1	11.2	11.0	13.1	57.7	50.5	2.3	−28.8	33.3	1.0	−10.9
Mali	678	5.8	11.7	18.6	−22.4	−7.6	12.6	13.6	9.1	6.4	21.8	36.3	5.8	21.8	12.0	24.3
Mauritania	682	−14.2	−2.0	−2.2	12.8	25.4	14.4	14.0	10.5	39.5	79.2	39.1	−.6	5.7	2.3	61.4
Mauritius	684	−.3	.9	2.9	−1.7	8.6	15.9	12.6	20.2	27.2	43.7	72.0	28.1	21.7	18.8	9.1
Morocco	686	5.4	4.6	4.3	12.4	18.6	10.9	8.1	15.1	14.6	15.3	18.6	20.8	21.7	14.6	15.6
Mozambique	688															
Niger	692	5.0	26.5	8.1	−5.7	3.1	20.1	8.8	23.5	14.2	23.8	29.2	22.8	35.8	16.6	33.8
Nigeria	694	11.2	7.3	9.2	−25.9	35.0	47.7	17.5	6.0	11.0	70.0	124.2	60.2	10.3	7.6	22.0
Rwanda	714	25.8	20.0	16.9	17.5	4.5	31.2	9.5	5.1	23.9	31.1	9.1	7.3	33.9	6.8	13.7
Senegal	722	−1.8	4.2	−5.8	3.7	.1	12.0	4.9	13.9	−2.2	25.7	41.4	31.0	4.8	.7	25.8
Seychelles	718								36.9	12.9	5.0	18.0	33.3	35.6	20.8	41.9
Sierra Leone	724	17.6	3.2	−2.0	14.9	22.0	.9	−6.8	12.9	26.7	14.5	7.9	5.3	24.7	36.9	68.4
Somalia	726	−15.0	11.0	16.1	6.7	26.2	31.8	−23.3	14.7	15.4	20.8	24.3	29.6	22.1	52.1	25.7
South Africa	199	−.2	11.9	6.3	8.3	17.0	8.4	6.1	6.9	12.0	20.7	16.0	11.8	3.6	7.6	13.1
Swaziland	734											205.6	173.8	55.8	36.1	−10.0
Tanzania	738			−10.0	5.9	10.6	23.4	24.6	19.4	13.0	13.6	19.2	19.4	20.6	13.9	32.8
Togo	742	9.6	11.5	3.0	20.3	10.7	12.8	7.8	12.3	4.5	40.9	31.2	25.6	38.8	14.7	19.5
Tunisia	744	.7	13.4	2.8	8.9	14.8	4.1	14.9	23.0	14.2	22.0	21.1	15.4	5.3	14.9	14.8
Zaïre	636	32.1	18.7	21.7	40.4	29.3	5.9	7.7	2.3	14.4	31.2	26.2	52.9	51.2	49.5	56.7
Zambia	754		30.1	26.2	22.2	9.2	21.7	5.6	20.1	15.2	16.5	10.7	29.7	13.1	5.6	4.4
Zimbabwe	698												23.4	11.6	−5.3	16.4
Asia																
Afghanistan, Islamic State of	512	9.0	2.5	−1.5	11.9	14.7	15.4	5.3	12.2	6.5	7.8	16.6	16.4	37.2	22.3	16.2
Bangladesh	513											14.7	−1.3	8.0	19.3	30.3	19.4
Bhutan	514															
China, People' Rep.	924															
Fiji	819	−20.6	−1.7	7.2	−.9	15.4	4.9	18.6	14.2	46.6	30.3	52.0	1.8	−13.1	18.3	8.4
India	534	7.0	8.0	6.5	7.5	10.1	10.5	9.7	9.8	19.3	12.6	2.2	10.7	20.2	18.5	24.8
Indonesia	536															
Korea	542	29.2	65.2	52.9	46.3	39.8	38.1	12.3	7.6	64.3	24.5	35.4	31.8	38.0	47.7	24.7
Maldives	556												−7.3	−30.0	45.3
Myanmar	518	2.4	−1.6	−2.5	3.8	7.9	13.2	6.4	32.7	17.2	40.7	16.5	3.3	−1.9	9.5	15.5
Nepal	558	27.0	14.7	7.0	16.1	15.6	12.4	8.4	10.6	16.7	21.3	5.1	12.2	22.4	14.5	14.7
Pakistan	564	9.2	14.8	6.1	2.0	12.5	7.7	16.2	12.7	14.8	2.4	6.6	17.4	23.7	14.9	27.8
Papua New Guinea	853											27.3	61.1	14.1	63.9	1.2	15.5
Philippines	566	7.7	8.9	16.7	20.2	4.7	10.5	19.3	7.9	25.1	22.2	13.9	10.0	20.8	30.2	16.5
Singapore	576	18.3	12.4	−1.5	2.3	17.3	18.6	13.0	21.2	42.7	11.2	11.5	18.9	15.0	13.5	13.8
Solomon Islands	813															194.7

Reserve Money

14 x

1980	1981	1982	1983	1984	1985	1986	1987	1988	1989	1990	1991	1992	1993	1994		
Percent Change over Previous Year																
															Industrial Countries	
7.1	2.9	5.0	6.1	7.7	7.9	10.4	9.2	7.3	3.9	6.9	4.8	7.6	10.1	9.8	United States	111
7.7	7.2	1.8	2.1	1.4	5.3	6.5	6.1	4.7	5.4	3.8	4.8	4.7	3.1	−2.8	Canada	156
7.9	10.8	9.6	8.1	12.0	15.9	10.6	8.8	10.5	−5.5	−1.2	3.2	4.2	6.5	8.0	Australia	193
11.3	.2	6.4	5.9	6.1	5.2	6.7	11.9	11.0	11.5	9.7	.9	−2.0	3.4	4.5	Japan	158
12.5	−5.7	5.7	23.3	3.8	10.7	−1.4	4.3	12.2	16.7	−4.3	2.9	−1.2	4.0	....	New Zealand	196
6.7	5.1	7.5	7.2	2.2	1.6	5.6	3.2	6.2	5.9	2.8	4.9	7.2	3.7	7.9	Austria	122
.5	2.8	2.0	1.3	1.6	−.4	2.2	4.2	1.2	−.2	−.1	.7	−.2	....	....	Belgium	124
6.9	6.3	5.8	8.3	6.0	58.7	53.1	−37.5	−2.8	−10.6	8.6	9.6	11.7	20.8	21.5	Denmark	128
46.7	10.7	7.7	26.3	37.4	20.8	−3.2	43.5	26.6	15.0	14.1	−23.5	29.5	−4.5	35.3	Finland	172
4.7	14.3	11.7	7.6	9.7	9.0	8.5	6.7	3.0	4.4	.3	−3.5	−11.9	−2.4	−3.2	France	132
1.9	−2.6	6.0	3.3	3.6	3.8	3.9	9.1	9.2	7.4	8.9	12.3	8.0	1.8	−.3	Germany	134
15.2	45.0	37.5	15.1	24.6	20.8	7.9	21.1	12.8	8.5	17.2	11.1	13.0	7.6	15.6	Greece	174
56.1	91.1	52.8	59.4	42.9	19.2	38.1	19.7	18.2	24.3	−4.1	−6.4	6.4	−15.3	−7.8	Iceland	176
4.5	14.2	8.9	4.2	13.0	8.3	4.0	4.7	10.1	3.5	6.8	−1.7	−8.9	4.9	....	Ireland	178
13.1	14.0	15.3	17.1	14.2	17.4	9.7	11.2	8.1	10.4	10.2	5.8	5.4	−7.9	....	Italy	136
....	....	....	....	....	....	135.6	16.8	6.0	2.6	7.6	6.4	−3.0	27.7	28.1	Luxembourg	137
8.8	4.0	3.9	12.3	6.9	5.9	2.6	6.8	10.2	15.7	5.3	1.7	6.4	12.6	13.0	Netherlands	138
4.7	4.9	6.3	2.1	6.5	8.4	7.5	12.1	2.2	5.6	−7.9	.9	10.5	6.9	23.0	Norway	142
25.6	33.6	36.3	22.9	5.7	10.7	1.3	18.3	15.4	85.5	24.7	18.2	17.6	10.0	−5.8	Portugal	182
18.4	13.5	15.0	20.3	8.8	13.4	.1	16.4	7.5	18.4	−26.3	15.0	9.4	−1.4	3.8	Spain	184
10.9	5.2	24.9	−12.6	3.1	4.6	22.5	8.0	14.9	13.5	9.4	21.8	−15.6	18.5	87.5	Sweden	144
−6.3	−3.7	.7	5.3	2.5	2.0	2.7	4.0	−11.3	−4.7	−1.8	1.6	.4	14.1	1.0	Switzerland	146
3.2	5.1	2.7	6.2	−8.0	3.7	5.4	4.5	8.4	6.8	5.9	2.7	1.7	5.3	4.9	United Kingdom	112
															Developing Countries	
															Africa	
24.3	13.3	—	22.6	17.5	11.7	15.9	14.1	8.9	11.6	12.1	14.7	15.0	15.2	−2.5	Algeria	612
31.2	50.3	36.9	−17.3	−5.7	5.5	−2.8	−1.6	−10.2	83.4	67.2	22.6	31.3	3.5	−16.1	Benin	638
19.2	−8.4	60.7	−1.8	3.8	39.0	14.9	40.1	45.2	40.1	6.3	26.9	26.6	20.1	34.3	Botswana	616
22.5	19.4	16.8	19.6	52.8	7.5	15.5	29.4	16.8	−4.8	−11.3	15.2	13.4	12.9	12.3	Burkina Faso	748
5.0	28.7	−4.4	12.5	15.4	18.6	12.5	1.4	.3	2.7	.3	6.8	13.4	7.1	18.0	Burundi	618
19.5	25.9	12.1	16.5	10.3	11.0	20.8	4.1	−5.0	1.7	−1.8	2.0	−12.6	−23.4	19.0	Cameroon	622
8.8	19.5	24.7	20.7	4.1	20.1	18.8	9.5	−.3	2.4	6.8	12.3	16.2	34.7	12.0	Cape Verde	624
34.9	37.1	6.3	5.4	7.8	13.1	4.8	−4.4	9.0	8.2	−1.5	−1.6	1.1	12.9	64.5	Central African Rep.	626
4.2	3.7	1.6	8.9	44.6	27.7	−1.7	.4	17.8	−5.9	−.3	7.2	−9.5	−1.0	22.9	Chad	628
....	....	....	8.0	−5.0	−9.3	45.3	33.1	−2.1	8.4	13.1	−19.9	−5.1	....	....	Comoros	632
35.1	34.0	30.8	13.8	3.6	9.4	2.3	.8	.3	−6.5	14.6	9.0	−10.7	12.1	18.4	Congo	634
5.1	6.7	−.3	−5.3	9.8	39.7	15.7	2.1	−1.5	−14.8	−13.9	−1.8	−2.0	−3.7	42.9	Côte d'Ivoire	662
....	....	....	....	....	−3.1	6.4	13.0	10.0	−5.3	2.5	5.3	11.4	5.9	−.5	Djibouti	611
....	....	....	....	....	....	74.0	14.8	−8.9	−38.3	−41.2	−41.2	34.5	45.8	52.6	Equatorial Guinea	642
13.0	10.2	16.1	.3	17.3	2.7	25.9	11.3	7.3	11.6	17.4	22.6	20.1	12.2	8.2	Ethiopia	644
—	4.9	17.3	11.9	19.5	−6.0	.4	−12.6	2.8	14.0	17.2	20.3	−9.5	−14.4	60.7	Gabon	646
10.3	10.5	36.8	36.7	1.0	15.9	41.4	67.2	19.1	10.4	21.9	13.1	12.3	7.8	5.0	Gambia, The	648
32.0	43.8	25.3	53.1	24.5	40.1	47.2	54.5	46.0	34.0	16.5	−4.0	32.0	44.4	35.4	Ghana	652
....	....	....	....	....	....	....	....	....	....	....	16.7	17.3	−5.5	Guinea	656
....	....	....	....	....	....	....	94.2	83.9	36.2	16.9	88.1	102.3	43.8	30.9	Guinea-Bissau	654
14.4	12.0	6.4	5.2	17.2	9.8	23.5	32.8	7.8	13.9	19.8	13.4	31.3	50.0	....	Kenya	664
−7.2	181.6	−8.9	42.3	39.6	15.2	46.1	20.2	16.5	14.0	−1.5	.4	−5.4	−18.7	9.4	Lesotho	666
28.4	3.6	35.7	14.1	23.6	26.0	36.0	25.5	19.6	20.1	23.8	10.3	−3.4	25.8	27.9	Liberia	668
25.6	12.1	31.2	−20.7	2.2	8.5	59.2	35.2	9.1	19.3	1.8	17.0	45.2	17.9	21.7	Madagascar	674
21.0	42.1	16.4	20.9	34.7	13.2	22.7	81.6	13.5	15.4	−16.5	23.6	1.7	48.8	32.1	Malawi	676
6.4	.7	10.0	11.4	26.8	31.9	8.0	1.1	7.8	10.3	15.2	11.0	11.8	5.3	14.5	Mali	678
−3.3	7.7	11.7	10.4	−2.0	24.5	9.2	13.9	13.6	17.8	−4.6	28.3	35.0	45.8	....	Mauritania	682
2.6	6.2	10.9	6.0	7.6	11.2	18.8	27.0	23.5	21.6	17.9	68.2	59.8	−18.3	−2.6	Mauritius	684
13.2	2.6	14.6	10.6	12.9	8.6	17.3	12.7	11.9	18.4	16.0	27.1	13.4	−8.2	8.5	Morocco	686
....	....	....	....	....	19.5	20.6	36.2	52.9	38.5	29.3	30.1	....	....	....	Mozambique	688
26.6	17.1	3.6	−11.4	24.9	28.4	1.4	8.5	21.0	6.3	−.9	4.0	−2.6	−4.5	.6	Niger	692
20.3	15.6	5.2	10.8	2.2	7.0	3.4	7.3	32.1	46.8	33.1	42.0	....	....	....	Nigeria	694
18.8	2.4	−9.9	7.3	6.5	5.1	10.7	10.5	.5	−9.8	4.6	14.5	16.9	18.9	....	Rwanda	714
−1.8	15.9	33.2	14.6	−5.8	−5.0	16.9	22.4	14.7	10.9	15.6	−12.4	17.2	−16.5	−.4	Senegal	722
42.7	12.4	.6	.8	.5	11.1	−.2	2.4	14.4	10.1	7.9	19.5	18.0	51.8	45.0	Seychelles	718
−5.2	8.6	52.2	49.9	22.7	45.9	88.0	122.4	60.5	48.8	72.2	71.0	36.0	9.2	17.7	Sierra Leone	724
28.8	28.2	13.9	−13.1	34.9	44.2	67.1	59.5	85.2	101.4	....	....	....	....	....	Somalia	726
46.2	36.4	1.6	−.2	14.0	9.1	8.5	12.9	30.2	30.1	20.4	9.5	12.3	.4	12.4	South Africa	199
6.4	3.7	.9	10.3	47.6	51.5	27.6	18.2	−2.3	.7	−2.6	−2.0	21.8	9.6	14.9	Swaziland	734
34.5	24.7	25.6	9.6	22.9	23.3	31.9	37.1	32.5	15.0	3.8	22.2	37.8	111.4	....	Tanzania	738
9.2	58.5	49.1	1.9	19.8	31.7	8.9	−6.3	−5.5	−14.9	10.9	6.5	−3.7	−29.7	−11.5	Togo	742
9.5	23.5	19.4	19.6	19.1	5.4	7.0	−2.1	9.4	14.0	19.8	9.3	13.0	6.7	6.9	Tunisia	744
10.4	67.4	68.9	344.0	−38.1	45.0	32.3	100.2	92.1	111.7	90.6	1,077.8	5,871.7	1,771.1	5,410.8	Zaïre	636
11.3	16.7	14.5	17.1	12.4	19.2	80.6	140.7	21.4	37.9	53.9	221.8	....	....	....	Zambia	754
23.9	36.7	22.5	8.0	10.0	11.5	21.6	10.1	18.4	21.1	25.7	35.6	13.8	44.7	42.0	Zimbabwe	698
															Asia	
23.4	12.0	19.2	15.3	10.6	12.5	12.4	23.6	57.6	38.5	39.7	42.7	....	....	....	Afghanistan, Islamic State of	512
15.4	24.6	3.1	25.3	34.5	19.6	19.3	22.2	29.4	9.7	10.9	−1.0	10.6	26.4	30.0	Bangladesh	513
....	....	....	....	117.3	139.1	27.2	58.7	−1.4	38.7	86.4	47.0	18.2	−22.1	−12.2	Bhutan	514
....	....	....	....	....	....	24.0	15.0	22.7	24.3	30.1	25.7	18.0	27.1	....	China, People' Rep.	924
15.5	−2.4	3.3	7.1	3.6	14.6	6.9	7.1	40.6	−1.2	—	10.0	29.7	−1.0	—	Fiji	819
14.4	15.2	10.7	12.7	20.4	18.4	15.6	21.0	17.8	18.3	18.3	15.1	16.4	12.5	22.9	India	534
....	17.4	12.7	15.0	16.0	15.1	19.6	15.3	6.6	−.9	21.3	9.5	15.2	....	....	Indonesia	536
−4.7	1.8	4.8	16.8	6.5	4.4	8.1	22.8	37.8	36.6	23.4	17.0	12.5	23.5	13.3	Korea	542
48.0	33.1	1.6	4.8	33.4	34.2	30.1	7.0	8.5	19.7	20.6	22.4	24.2	32.5	....	Maldives	556
15.2	13.3	2.5	5.4	15.1	6.4	8.9	3.6	−21.1	220.3	30.4	....	....	....	....	Myanmar	518
16.9	8.8	25.2	15.7	16.5	12.6	25.5	15.9	21.2	19.6	23.1	21.9	18.5	25.0	....	Nepal	558
20.1	13.8	10.6	18.9	11.3	12.6	13.1	20.5	15.4	12.5	16.5	21.5	14.8	15.9	16.3	Pakistan	564
−32.5	−45.4	−2.6	5.7	43.3	−16.3	7.6	1.6	18.6	−1.8	6.3	−1.9	.5	10.0	....	Papua New Guinea	853
14.0	9.9	5.9	−23.7	69.7	14.0	32.0	14.0	13.8	25.6	30.2	25.1	14.9	15.8	4.6	Philippines	566
16.1	11.6	13.8	14.4	8.5	4.7	3.1	9.9	9.0	14.2	11.2	10.5	10.7	9.7	6.2	Singapore	576
−18.3	−43.9	7.0	14.8	87.1	−18.2	−3.5	9.2	6.6	14.3	−5.5	28.6	19.6	2.2	35.8	Solomon Islands	813

Reserve Money

14 x

Percent Change over Previous Year

		1965	1966	1967	1968	1969	1970	1971	1972	1973	1974	1975	1976	1977	1978	1979
Asia (cont.)																
Sri Lanka	524	9.2	–.5	2.9	11.8	4.0	–4.8	3.4	7.3	13.7	17.4	–5.0	16.4	41.8	25.5	16.6
Thailand	578	7.2	16.3	12.1	5.3	7.3	4.9	11.5	15.8	18.5	18.7	9.6	12.2	10.8	14.7	15.1
Tonga	866	....	....	....	....	....	....	....	....	....	....	....	....	....	....	....
Vanuatu	846	....	....	....	....	....	....	....	....	....	....	....	....	18.2	15.8	24.4
Western Samoa	862	....	....	....	28.1	17.8	12.8	18.6	11.3	15.9	19.8	33.5	106.4	27.8	13.9	14.6
Europe																
Cyprus	423	8.5	4.3	6.2	100.8	43.9	–10.4	32.1	21.0	9.8	12.4	6.7	16.4	9.3	18.0	21.4
Czech Republic	935	....	....	....	....	....	....	....	....	....	....	....	....	....	....	....
Czechoslovakia	934	....	....	....	....	....	....	....	....	....	....	....	....	....	....	....
Hungary	944	....	....	....	....	....	....	....	....	....	....	....	....	....	....	....
Malta	181	4.8	8.8	9.1	128.4	46.8	–1.5	17.2	20.5	12.4	12.2	20.5	36.4	18.9	15.9	16.0
Moldova	921	....	....	....	....	....	....	....	....	....	....	....	....	....	....	....
Poland	964	....	....	....	....	....	....	....	....	....	....	....	....	....	....	....
Romania	968	....	....	....	....	....	....	....	....	....	49.9	29.6	4.5	–.7	24.1	25.4
Slovak Republic	936	....	....	....	....	....	....	....	....	....	....	....	....	....	....	....
Slovenia	961	....	....	....	....	....	....	....	....	....	....	....	....	....	....	....
Turkey	186	20.0	13.8	14.5	13.5	14.2	14.6	33.0	33.4	34.1	31.3	25.5	30.6	33.9	40.8	54.5
Yugoslavia, SFR	188	16.2	14.3	5.2	–1.1	17.5	18.2	16.9	38.8	33.6	18.0	8.6	35.6	22.1	59.5	38.5
Middle East																
Bahrain	419	....	39.9	33.4	24.4	23.3	5.2	11.4	9.0	–11.3	–16.2	109.6	37.5	41.4	25.2	–12.0
Egypt	469	16.7	6.5	2.0	–.9	7.2	15.2	.9	6.9	18.5	24.5	19.0	19.9	22.5	20.6	29.5
Iran, I.R. of	429	17.4	4.7	10.1	13.6	18.2	15.1	22.8	29.6	37.6	22.5	42.7	37.0	32.9	30.5	51.6
Israel	436	11.1	3.9	22.3	22.3	2.8	9.4	41.2	108.0	33.7	6.8	43.2	26.8	96.6	164.8	74.6
Jordan	439	29.3	27.3	44.4	33.6	7.9	8.1	11.6	–.8	11.7	18.5	23.0	30.0	14.2	19.1	24.7
Kuwait	443	.1	27.9	27.0	–2.9	–5.8	–3.3	.4	30.1	50.2	12.5	48.8	11.2	49.9	49.3	–31.1
Lebanon	446	8.1	13.6	34.2	9.4	5.5	3.2	11.4	20.3	15.9	28.1	23.7	29.4	18.5	14.8	5.2
Libya	672	49.4	50.3	34.2	26.6	32.7	21.3	46.8	26.0	19.7	36.0	4.1	30.7	31.2	26.6	27.5
Oman	449	....	....	....	....	....	....	....	84.8	63.8	24.4	56.0	80.7	41.8	17.2	8.7
Qatar	453	....	....	52.8	12.4	6.3	–1.4	13.7	30.7	51.6	33.6	64.4	35.1	47.4	35.5	20.2
Saudi Arabia	456	8.7	15.3	11.5	11.1	6.4	3.1	10.5	26.1	58.3	35.9	56.6	85.8	68.5	45.8	3.6
Syrian Arab Rep.	463	10.2	10.6	15.9	20.7	13.4	12.0	13.4	8.1	21.0	31.9	22.4	19.0	27.4	31.6	20.9
United Arab Emirates	466	....	....	....	....	....	....	....	....	....	155.8	54.2	79.0	64.0	9.2	5.6
Yemen, Republic of	474	....	....	....	....	....	....	....	....	....	....	....	....	....	....	....
Western Hemisphere																
Antigua and Barbuda	311	....	....	....	....	....	....	....	....	....	....	....	62.9	–38.4	14.5	63.4
Argentina	213	38.9	26.6	25.0	27.8	7.5	12.2	1,097.0	3.4	420.0	213.4	81.1	369.9	103.3	88.8	86.9
Bahamas, The	313	....	....	....	....	–28.4	–32.6	–1.2	37.0	9.2	5.3	21.1	3.1	6.2	10.8	13.9
Barbados	316	....	....	6.8	65.3	–5.6	2.8	8.6	5.9	10.2	42.0	70.9	5.5	6.5	22.8	22.2
Belize	339	....	....	....	....	....	....	....	....	....	....	....	....	36.1	23.7	13.0
Bolivia	218	25.3	19.5	4.8	5.9	14.9	10.5	12.2	19.6	30.5	41.5	21.7	30.5	33.0	15.7	12.6
Brazil	223	78.8	42.9	29.5	34.9	28.0	24.3	27.6	28.0	32.5	36.9	27.0	49.5	60.3	47.5	58.8
Chile	228	30.3	61.9	19.7	36.6	40.8	79.9	100.6	129.5	318.5	347.2	239.0	264.9	168.3	71.9	41.6
Colombia	233	19.7	10.0	20.3	31.9	27.8	23.1	7.1	20.4	30.7	25.3	13.7	43.2	50.0	43.2	28.1
Costa Rica	238	6.3	3.6	13.6	22.7	16.4	3.5	12.7	23.6	25.5	19.3	18.8	26.8	53.2	19.5	18.7
Dominica	321	....	....	....	....	....	....	....	....	....	....	....	57.0	50.4	–8.5	247.0
Dominican Republic	243	13.4	10.2	–.7	6.5	8.9	23.2	7.3	15.5	18.8	33.3	20.8	–13.8	21.4	13.5	2.8
Ecuador	248	–2.1	12.0	7.6	13.8	13.1	31.6	21.8	18.3	35.3	43.9	15.3	–1.2	42.5	6.5	27.6
El Salvador	253	9.3	24.7	21.3	25.5	6.6	10.1	8.3	20.9	13.2	15.6	30.9	24.2	33.8	–13.1	–18.3
Grenada	328	....	....	....	....	....	....	23.0	14.8	13.5	8.0	10.4	139.6	28.0	13.7	–9.8
Guatemala	258	3.2	11.3	–3.2	4.3	2.3	12.4	1.3	20.6	27.7	15.4	15.5	47.4	21.0	5.8	8.2
Guyana	336	15.4	15.3	4.4	5.7	18.7	2.1	10.3	18.1	14.6	11.9	28.8	27.3	17.2	46.1	7.8
Haiti	263	–7.8	1.0	4.5	10.7	17.3	7.8	17.9	18.5	20.5	12.3	5.4	43.3	23.5	16.1	6.3
Honduras	268	10.9	7.4	–2.3	11.8	14.7	12.2	11.4	–1.4	17.9	11.4	–3.9	26.6	30.5	12.3	14.4
Jamaica	343	.1	9.2	10.9	35.6	8.3	5.0	35.6	4.4	19.8	18.5	30.2	12.7	30.5	8.0	14.9
Mexico	273	7.3	10.3	10.9	13.3	11.1	9.4	16.3	41.4	47.8	39.9	39.5	11.6	24.4	108.9	32.1
Netherlands Antilles	353	....	....	....	....	12.0	9.9	36.8	12.4	26.1	1.2	15.3	32.6	3.7	–.3	7.9
Nicaragua	278	14.1	6.6	.4	–2.0	–.1	30.5	2.9	14.5	32.9	21.6	8.5	25.0	19.6	–3.3	34.9
Panama	283	....	....	....	....	....	14.7	26.9	22.1	37.7	1.1	2.5	30.8	22.0	–3.3	19.6
Paraguay	288	18.1	8.3	9.3	7.1	–3.7	8.1	19.8	16.4	31.7	20.7	16.7	22.1	35.3	29.8	25.1
Peru	293	21.7	.8	8.4	9.9	14.3	40.6	14.4	27.1	15.6	18.4	19.6	12.7	42.6	49.1	87.8
St. Kitts and Nevis	361	....	....	....	....	....	....	....	....	....	....	....	....	....	....	....
St. Lucia	362	....	....	....	....	....	....	....	....	....	....	....	54.8	7.0	26.0	28.8
St. Vincent & Grens.	364	....	....	....	....	....	....	....	....	....	....	....	74.3	9.5	2.2	48.5
Suriname	366	....	....	....	1.6	17.9	4.7	10.7	12.4	605.8	13.9	13.5	37.9	10.9	18.0	11.7
Trinidad and Tobago	369	–8.4	28.4	18.4	11.8	9.9	9.1	20.3	26.2	10.7	25.9	100.1	66.4	–4.9	24.9	19.9
Uruguay	298	81.3	70.7	55.4	82.5	70.2	34.4	29.7	50.8	58.9	81.6	58.0	89.0	39.2	95.8	57.2
Venezuela	299	7.2	3.9	7.1	13.1	1.7	2.0	9.4	17.8	17.6	48.1	46.0	21.2	30.6	11.4	–1.3

Reserve Money

14 x

1980	1981	1982	1983	1984	1985	1986	1987	1988	1989	1990	1991	1992	1993	1994		
Percent Change over Previous Year															**Asia (cont.)**	
21.9	16.2	26.1	20.1	21.3	22.1	13.6	8.6	12.6	17.8	16.9	25.3	15.3	18.0	21.0	Sri Lanka	524
15.9	8.2	9.3	12.8	8.5	6.4	8.3	17.0	16.7	17.4	21.6	10.7	17.8	16.1	16.8	Thailand	578
....	....	....	16.2	30.5	12.6	7.8	31.1	−2.5	14.2	−5.8	8.1	5.2	−44.7	−30.3	Tonga	866
−12.0	−24.4	6.1	10.5	24.5	21.7	12.1	49.9	−16.1	−2.8	6.2	12.2	16.7	13.6	26.2	Vanuatu	846
297.8	83.1	28.1	4.8	11.9	130.5	53.6	39.4	−1.4	29.0	48.4	7.9	−6.3	−20.5	−19.5	Western Samoa	862
															Europe	
21.0	24.9	28.1	15.6	19.7	8.6	4.0	10.2	12.8	−3.6	13.6	16.8	4.6	4.6	8.8	Cyprus	423
....	....	....	....	....	....	....	....	....	....	....	....	....	....	60.4	Czech Republic	935
....	....	....	....	....	....	....	....	−1.3	−4.3	59.4	.7	....	....	....	Czechoslovakia	934
....	....	....	−9.4	−10.7	11.9	7.2	−9.6	−5.1	9.8	32.0	53.7	....	....	....	Hungary	944
6.1	7.9	5.9	8.4	7.9	3.6	−.6	5.6	4.5	−2.0	−5.8	−3.1	7.2	4.6	14.9	Malta	181
....	....	....	....	....	....	....	....	....	....	....	....	539.0	486.6	219.5	Moldova	921
30.4	18.4	13.4	8.7	5.7	6.4	4.8	4.8	94.8	233.4	306.1	59.4	28.8	25.2	18.5	Poland	964
38.2	11.6	11.8	−11.1	−3.3	−6.0	−7.3	44.3	32.9	39.2	−41.7	−27.0	108.3	158.6	109.7	Romania	968
....	....	....	....	....	....	....	....	....	....	....	....	....	....	18.2	Slovak Republic	936
....	....	....	....	....	....	....	....	....	....	....	....	133.1	80.6	39.8	Slovenia	961
53.1	49.5	41.8	37.2	49.4	53.7	27.2	43.0	66.1	72.6	49.6	42.9	71.5	69.9	112.5	Turkey	186
30.5	27.2	36.7	58.6	55.2	60.9	85.2	131.8	229.7	1,036.7	357.8	....	....	....	....	Yugoslavia, SFR	188
															Middle East	
9.8	10.8	17.4	4.2	1.6	13.0	−3.1	5.6	−1.6	3.4	5.5	6.9	−.3	2.5	2.8	Bahrain	419
30.5	25.5	41.9	24.7	18.3	14.3	16.9	9.3	2.3	8.8	18.9	27.8	9.8	14.3	16.5	Egypt	469
28.8	29.1	36.3	22.1	12.3	13.3	14.9	23.9	24.7	20.6	5.9	9.7	13.9	16.0	....	Iran, I.R. of	429
117.5	110.9	127.4	166.6	448.2	288.8	29.5	15.7	2.0	11.9	19.3	8.8	5.3	23.5	4.5	Israel	436
22.2	21.4	10.3	12.8	5.1	.7	7.4	5.8	11.3	17.7	18.1	32.0	5.6	5.1	8.0	Jordan	439
34.1	27.9	46.5	17.1	−19.5	−4.9	−2.4	23.0	−46.0	−9.8	19.5	10.4	−7.4	−1.9	−5.6	Kuwait	443
13.7	13.1	27.5	17.2	16.1	44.7	25.3	87.2	245.8	105.8	53.3	45.4	82.6	32.5	91.5	Lebanon	446
26.9	18.0	−9.0	−16.2	−7.1	9.1	19.4	−1.7	−8.4	8.2	26.2	23.6	3.8	....	....	Libya	672
45.6	23.8	29.7	−11.4	7.6	13.4	6.2	8.9	−10.6	6.6	5.8	3.9	−1.3	2.9	−.1	Oman	449
25.1	.3	14.9	.7	2.3	−.1	21.7	6.8	−4.6	1.7	13.1	4.9	2.2	3.9	−1.7	Qatar	453
−6.3	.6	15.5	3.1	−1.8	−1.3	2.4	7.3	−1.9	−2.0	7.4	11.9	....	....	....	Saudi Arabia	456
23.0	21.4	27.3	37.2	29.8	37.9	17.0	10.4	−.9	5.7	22.3	28.3	23.9	....	....	Syrian Arab Rep.	463
5.6	10.5	17.5	1.5	3.4	18.6	6.1	32.1	10.1	−6.3	−2.4	7.4	16.3	6.5	....	United Arab Emirates	466
....	....	....	....	....	....	....	....	....	....	....	12.0	13.7	23.8	....	Yemen, Republic of	474
															Western Hemisphere	
−15.2	17.2	−38.2	43.5	71.0	17.0	24.3	12.1	−.1	6.7	−8.0	10.1	23.5	−3.3	2.6	Antigua and Barbuda	311
63.3	99.3	491.2	369.7	465.7	414.3	112.9	59.4	255.4	5,698.7	860.2	216.3	62.4	37.4	....	Argentina	213
6.0	4.6	11.3	9.8	21.4	10.6	14.1	13.7	1.0	4.0	6.2	7.2	—	7.7	11.1	Bahamas, The	313
13.7	19.5	3.6	10.8	11.5	11.3	5.0	6.4	16.0	1.9	4.1	−1.3	1.2	−4.0	−.3	Barbados	316
−1.2	16.9	−.5	24.6	3.4	30.6	22.5	12.5	5.5	−3.6	10.0	20.6	1.5	8.8	1.2	Belize	339
35.4	10.6	139.3	238.3	690.1	7,479.5	303.7	39.8	53.2	39.5	42.4	32.5	9.7	21.7	7.5	Bolivia	218
71.4	62.5	85.3	99.2	168.3	210.8	265.8	282.2	325.4	1,057.7	5,413.5	334.0	961.5	1,908.6	3,500.3	Brazil	223
67.6	3.9	18.5	185.7	81.8	108.5	61.9	15.1	−3.7	−1.0	22.1	34.4	22.8	15.1	....	Chile	228
28.7	24.7	21.4	8.8	20.0	23.1	27.2	40.2	19.6	77.8	20.5	10.5	44.4	29.6	30.0	Colombia	233
21.0	81.2	36.9	36.8	19.5	39.2	42.0	14.3	32.2	28.5	25.0	41.9	32.8	8.6	21.3	Costa Rica	238
57.7	−28.6	−36.9	40.3	79.0	10.0	14.3	69.5	1.6	−21.1	10.8	35.8	−4.5	−6.6	−6.1	Dominica	321
8.3	8.4	20.9	14.1	15.2	15.9	55.8	32.0	44.2	46.3	34.3	36.9	31.3	23.6	5.0	Dominican Republic	243
24.1	12.2	9.1	15.4	33.0	20.4	33.9	35.4	51.6	67.7	53.0	63.2	40.2	61.6	41.7	Ecuador	248
3.5	13.0	183.0	4.5	5.1	22.3	23.2	18.7	7.4	5.3	23.6	23.8	19.1	36.2	28.5	El Salvador	253
18.2	13.9	−7.8	4.5	41.3	11.1	12.5	1.0	−5.5	.4	−1.5	16.1	13.5	.5	7.1	Grenada	328
2.6	−1.5	19.4	−.3	1.4	18.9	43.0	14.9	8.6	16.0	29.1	31.0	26.4	18.4	5.7	Guatemala	258
16.0	10.2	55.6	48.3	24.0	13.3	19.2	106.5	34.9	6.7	7.3	77.0	90.2	18.2	−4.8	Guyana	336
16.9	26.0	7.3	4.5	6.1	18.1	13.9	15.6	47.1	−4.5	−2.0	20.9	20.5	29.3	25.8	Haiti	263
11.6	1.8	−3.7	14.6	11.4	3.0	11.2	6.1	14.0	18.8	26.8	31.3	19.7	23.2	15.0	Honduras	268
36.1	1.9	10.1	11.3	100.1	50.7	24.1	22.8	28.2	24.2	28.3	8.8	87.5	50.1	37.8	Jamaica	343
38.2	46.1	82.1	56.0	62.5	26.2	29.4	61.1	73.0	3.9	20.0	36.5	19.1	9.6	20.3	Mexico	273
11.6	−6.5	14.3	7.9	−5.1	.5	87.0	−3.6	−4.4	−11.6	−12.6	−13.7	8.0	22.6	.7	Netherlands Antilles	353
63.4	22.4	29.5	43.0	−53.9	183.4	238.3	593.9	11,540.2	5,411.0	6,382.8	4,126.8	−3.3	6.6	43.4	Nicaragua	278
25.6	22.5	45.3	−.8	−11.8	2.3	4.2	−11.6	−31.2	−17.2	42.5	42.4	−3.7	−2.1	5.7	Panama	283
21.0	21.3	8.2	17.9	26.7	16.7	17.8	52.4	26.0	32.3	25.6	30.7	28.2	26.4	23.3	Paraguay	288
130.0	66.3	61.4	86.1	124.2	202.5	105.7	56.4	283.9	1,619.8	5,370.2	508.8	97.0	101.7	22.9	Peru	293
−26.2	337.9	−4.2	−9.9	45.6	9.4	30.3	19.7	−18.2	14.5	9.7	4.8	33.6	13.9	6.7	St. Kitts and Nevis	361
8.0	−8.0	1.5	11.4	61.1	20.1	28.3	32.6	3.4	2.5	11.2	15.6	2.7	−2.5	−1.1	St. Lucia	362
−5.5	11.3	.3	−7.7	52.0	32.9	42.3	−3.8	−2.0	−17.3	11.7	7.8	21.0	2.0	2.8	St. Vincent & Grens.	364
2.3	21.2	9.6	26.6	30.6	53.7	46.0	22.2	25.6	16.2	4.6	22.1	20.2	32.1	130.6	Suriname	366
39.3	23.6	43.3	14.4	−3.5	−.8	−10.5	−3.5	−19.7	9.5	9.8	13.8	2.1	−2.1	22.4	Trinidad and Tobago	369
34.4	38.2	7.9	102.3	78.3	96.6	69.8	66.2	82.3	87.7	111.4	110.2	45.1	49.5	27.9	Uruguay	298
21.0	7.1	13.1	25.1	35.6	22.6	−10.7	.2	11.0	42.8	61.1	90.1	35.2	8.8	43.5	Venezuela	299

Money

Percent Change over Previous Year

		1965	1966	1967	1968	1969	1970	1971	1972	1973	1974	1975	1976	1977	1978	1979
Industrial Countries																
United States	111	4.3	4.5	4.6	7.2	5.8	3.6	6.9	6.6	6.2	5.4	4.9	5.5	7.6	8.0	8.2
Canada	156	16.5	8.5	15.5	3.7	−2.3	−4.1	9.1	12.5	11.9	5.8	9.7	6.1	7.1	8.9	4.9
Australia	193	.3	2.3	6.8	7.1	8.2	6.0	4.9	11.3	22.9	3.6	13.4	13.9	8.1	8.4	16.2
Japan	158	16.8	16.3	13.4	14.6	18.4	18.3	25.5	22.1	26.1	13.1	10.3	14.2	7.0	10.8	9.9
New Zealand	196	.5	−.8	−3.1	.8	2.9	6.0	7.6	17.2	33.9	10.3	6.2	10.6	3.7	9.3	10.9
Austria	122	8.3	8.5	4.4	6.2	8.0	7.9	9.1	17.4	12.0	6.8	10.9	10.5	6.8	5.9	−6.1
Belgium	124	7.4	6.7	5.0	6.4	3.4	−3.5	10.0	14.7	10.5	6.9	11.6	10.3	7.8	6.9	3.8
Denmark	128	11.1	14.0	11.5	11.5	13.9	4.2	4.1	10.8	12.1	5.0	13.8	17.0	5.9	9.2	12.9
Finland	172	4.8	2.5	1.4	11.5	16.1	15.5	10.5	23.3	19.3	17.7	32.6	14.4	7.8	11.4	16.5
France	132	8.9	8.9	6.2	5.5	6.1	−1.3	13.8	13.1	9.9	12.6	9.9	14.9	7.3	13.0	14.4
Germany	134	9.5	4.5	3.2	8.3	8.6	6.8	12.3	13.7	5.0	6.1	14.1	10.0	8.1	13.5	7.2
Greece	174	12.4	14.3	14.1	11.8	5.8	8.0	13.3	16.4	25.4	19.7	18.5	17.5	19.6	19.4	19.7
Iceland	176	18.1	13.4	−2.7	.2	26.8	34.3	24.1	18.6	33.4	31.3	25.9	33.2	34.0	36.2	46.8
Ireland	178	5.1	3.6	9.8	7.1	6.3	4.6	4.3	13.8	17.7	6.3	15.7	18.4	17.6	24.2	24.0
Italy	136	16.9	14.4	14.0	15.8	17.9	26.4	24.3	18.4	21.9	17.9	5.4	23.7	20.0	24.7	24.0
Luxembourg	137											11.2	7.2	13.3	6.8	6.4
Netherlands	138	10.9	7.2	7.0	8.8	9.4	10.6	16.7	17.7	7.4	3.1	18.8	11.8	14.4	5.3	2.7
Norway	142	4.2	6.8	7.4	9.4	12.4	13.0	15.0	11.2	12.8	12.5	17.2	15.8	19.9	9.2	8.7
Portugal	182	10.9	4.7	7.6	4.9	9.6	9.0	4.9	10.6	30.1	16.8	20.7	14.5	13.6	9.8	17.3
Spain	184	16.3	11.2	6.8	17.2	13.9	8.5	14.8	24.2	26.1	18.8	16.6	21.0	20.7	18.9	13.8
Sweden	144	−18.4	5.4	5.8	7.6	6.0	2.1	7.5	11.3	8.9	13.2	12.7	13.8	9.3	12.0	12.0
Switzerland	146	5.1	3.1	6.2	10.6	9.6	9.7	18.2	13.4	−1.0	−1.7	.7	8.5	4.5	16.2	8.9
United Kingdom	112	3.1	3.1	3.9	3.4	.6	7.1	13.3	16.5	8.7	4.9	15.5	14.0	14.4	19.1	11.4
Developing Countries																
Africa																
Algeria	612	10.2	7.6	26.4	25.5	29.0	7.8	7.9	27.5	24.5	18.2	29.4	23.6	28.8	23.8	14.9
Benin	638	.4	4.1	−1.6	4.3	18.6	16.8	21.6	15.1	2.7	14.5	38.4	22.3	16.0	3.7	14.9
Botswana	616												25.5	18.9	28.9
Burkina Faso	748	5.1	−1.1	3.5	7.5	12.2	16.5	1.4	4.1	23.5	31.3	23.7	30.5	13.4	18.9	6.3
Burundi	618	5.4	−.6	20.0	5.8	−.2	17.3	15.0	8.6	10.6	22.7	2.2	26.0	50.8	13.7	23.8
Cameroon	622	2.1	10.0	17.3	14.2	13.0	14.8	7.9	10.7	10.0	24.9	20.0	15.3	29.9	22.5	20.2
Cape Verde	624													41.1	14.4	27.3
Central African Rep.	626	14.8	6.0	6.4	28.8	2.7	2.8	4.9	9.7	6.4	17.8	7.1	17.9	26.6	14.2	14.3
Chad	628	−.7	.6	−3.3	1.7	17.5	10.4	6.5	6.7	8.3	11.3	30.9	11.4	26.4	10.8	18.2
Comoros	632															
Congo	634	−5.4	6.2	9.9	19.8	8.6	7.1	12.0	7.3	11.2	34.6	20.0	12.5	3.8	1.2	11.9
Côte d'Ivoire	662	7.5	7.5	1.0	23.6	12.2	22.3	13.0	10.2	14.9	22.9	21.8	29.1	48.0	19.5	14.1
Djibouti	611															
Equatorial Guinea	642															
Ethiopia	644	15.1	10.7	—	2.3	8.3	9.5	−4.1	1.2	20.0	31.4	23.8	20.7	2.7	21.1	14.8
Gabon	646	7.1	4.6	−7.3	6.3	14.4	19.7	13.7	21.5	28.0	43.3	56.0	58.8	22.5	−8.9	−6.3
Gambia, The	648	6.3	17.7	−.5	7.6	3.1	14.3	4.0	29.8	12.6	19.7	36.0	22.7	24.2	4.0	19.4
Ghana	652	24.1	−.3	−4.2	5.8	5.4	15.7	−.8	35.5	23.0	24.9	36.6	46.1	50.9	74.2	30.3
Guinea	656															
Guinea-Bissau	654															
Kenya	664			14.6	10.9	8.8	19.7	14.2	9.8	25.9	15.6	3.6	22.5	49.0	8.6	6.6
Lesotho	666															
Liberia	668											−8.1	16.3	16.6	19.9	2.9
Madagascar	674	11.1	4.1	6.6	11.6	4.5	8.8	7.3	7.9	6.6	12.4	12.7	4.9	21.7	21.5	19.1
Malawi	676		19.0	12.8	5.9	9.7	13.9	16.1	8.6	27.4	28.5	16.9	−3.0	17.6	10.1	5.1
Mali	678	7.3	13.5	14.3	7.2	−2.9	5.0	14.0	10.7	13.5	24.3	37.5	13.3	14.5	15.4	17.0
Mauritania	682	−7.9	19.8	22.4	11.0	21.1	13.0	19.1	9.1	19.9	44.3	35.4	13.9	19.4	1.1	33.1
Mauritius	684	−24.1	11.2	5.8	−4.6	6.6	9.0	9.1	28.8	29.5	31.0	58.0	18.7	18.4	13.7	7.4
Morocco	686	3.4	1.5	5.4	10.4	14.0	9.4	8.3	15.6	16.4	22.4	20.5	19.8	20.3	12.7	17.0
Namibia	728															
Niger	692	3.9	10.1	3.5	8.1	5.9	16.3	17.0	21.0	10.7	20.8	27.6	20.6	30.6	26.1	29.7
Nigeria	694	10.9	5.8	6.6	−16.2	33.1	47.5	17.3	8.3	17.8	50.9	95.6	54.1	48.5	13.9	12.6
Rwanda	714	29.2	3.0	15.1	20.2	1.0	23.2	12.9	5.1	31.5	29.0	16.9	18.2	27.0	16.8	22.0
Senegal	722	3.3	−1.7	−2.9	2.4	3.8	6.4	9.5	14.8	2.5	32.7	34.5	27.3	15.2	5.0	17.8
Seychelles	718								48.4	6.9	4.0	14.1	41.4	36.1	16.3	20.6
Sierra Leone	724	10.0	−1.5	2.4	18.1	18.0	2.1	−2.1	13.6	26.5	18.9	8.7	9.1	22.5	29.2	21.9
Somalia	726	−8.0	5.4	12.1	11.2	13.1	6.0	5.5	25.8	20.1	22.7	24.7	29.2	24.3	39.4	29.7
South Africa	199	10.8	8.6	5.1	14.7	14.9	3.2	4.9	12.9	18.3	19.3	13.4	5.2	3.8	6.0	15.3
Sudan	732															
Swaziland	734			−7.0	15.8	17.9	4.9	19.3	14.5	19.2	24.3	23.4	26.0	21.1	13.3	37.4
Tanzania	738															
Togo	742	16.2	15.7	10.6	23.4	14.9	18.8	5.8	9.1	−2.0	69.5	11.7	9.6	41.6	25.8	17.0
Tunisia	744	−.8	10.4	2.0	11.1	9.4	7.3	15.7	21.6	13.0	21.2	20.0	11.1	10.9	15.1	15.0
Uganda	746															
Zaïre	636	20.2	20.1	29.3	32.6	26.8	13.6	13.0	10.2	22.1	35.2	19.5	34.0	52.8	52.8	52.1
Zambia	754		41.4	24.5	25.6	12.7	15.4	9.6	−1.2	17.2	17.8	6.1	24.9	16.9	−5.6	11.6
Zimbabwe	698												8.6	6.4	10.8	11.6
Asia																
Afghanistan, Islamic State of	512	12.4	.4	13.7	9.0	16.7	12.4	5.3	14.0	.3	7.8	17.3	16.3	35.1	21.4	17.6
Bangladesh	513												−2.2	8.9	18.8	25.9	18.4
Bhutan	514															
China, People' Rep.	924														.1	43.1
Fiji	819	−9.1	5.6	1.4	7.5	21.0	11.4	23.1	16.7	17.0	11.4	21.8	14.7	−2.4	9.5	13.8
India	534	9.3	9.8	8.2	8.3	9.8	10.8	12.6	12.8	16.5	14.3	8.1	15.5	18.2	−7.7	14.3
Indonesia	536				147.0	67.4	49.0	32.3	36.7	49.7	40.5	36.9	29.8	29.5	18.9	31.6
Korea	542	23.2	30.5	38.5	42.2	40.4	29.4	20.6	27.9	51.2	26.5	26.3	30.4	39.0	28.2	18.0
Malaysia	548															
Maldives	556													−20.1	−23.6	37.2
Mongolia	948															
Myanmar	518							−6.6	15.6	24.6	25.4	29.6	14.8	4.6	6.9	13.8
Nepal	558	26.7	13.2	6.5	12.5	15.9	13.3	8.6	9.7	17.1	27.9	6.0	9.8	25.8	12.8	15.7
Pakistan	564	10.2	13.8	5.7	3.2	12.6	9.9	16.5	21.1	15.6	2.7	10.1	21.7	24.2	18.5	22.5
Papua New Guinea	853										41.2	18.9	−17.1	28.0	10.2	12.8
Philippines	566	4.7	9.8	10.0	5.1	12.3	15.8	14.2	15.6	27.9	20.9	14.4	15.4	21.1	16.5	11.9
Singapore	576	3.3	14.1	5.0	10.8	17.8	16.4	13.4	24.2	24.7	7.4	18.6	18.1	10.5	11.6	13.1
Solomon Islands	813															41.7

Money

Percent Change over Previous Year

1980	1981	1982	1983	1984	1985	1986	1987	1988	1989	1990	1991	1992	1993	1994	Country	
															Industrial Countries	
8.1	6.9	6.0	10.9	8.0	9.0	15.2	9.4	4.7	.7	9.9	6.7	11.0	10.7	6.0	United States	111
3.9	2.9	2.7	14.5	11.5	31.3	21.4	14.2	3.6	4.3	1.7	5.8	5.4	6.3	8.3	Canada	156
14.6	9.7	1.7	6.6	10.8	10.8	4.7	17.1	24.0	19.8	3.5	8.5	18.1	17.8	15.4	Australia	193
.8	3.7	7.1	3.0	2.9	4.6	7.4	9.0	7.7	4.6	3.2	5.9	6.5	4.2	4.7	Japan	158
8.0	9.6	7.5	10.0	6.0	5.3	16.3	30.6	44.8	39.7	29.0	1.3	2.7	3.7	....	New Zealand	196
7.4	3.7	3.1	12.0	4.0	2.3	4.8	10.0	10.2	6.1	1.7	6.0	5.2	8.6	11.9	Austria	122
-.1	3.5	3.3	4.6	4.0	3.2	6.0	7.0	4.0	3.1	3.1	....	....	....	....	Belgium	124
5.1	12.5	8.1	21.6	15.1	19.2	16.8	7.7	45.6	5.3	5.7	12.6	4.2	.4	9.8	Denmark	128
10.9	10.4	17.5	14.6	7.0	10.2	10.4	9.0	15.9	15.3	14.8	172.1	3.3	6.7	10.8	Finland	172
8.2	11.1	11.2	9.6	11.1	9.0	8.7	4.6	1.9	5.4	5.7	-1.2	-1.8	.3	....	France	132
2.4	.9	3.2	10.3	3.4	4.1	8.7	9.4	10.1	6.5	13.4	15.7	7.1	10.0	9.3	Germany	134
20.3	18.3	24.8	12.5	15.5	21.3	15.9	18.7	14.5	21.5	23.3	15.6	15.5	13.1	....	Greece	174
45.9	70.3	33.8	55.9	52.6	33.7	42.2	40.4	16.6	27.6	35.8	13.8	13.8	.5	10.5	Iceland	176
4.6	13.0	7.2	8.7	10.7	5.5	3.4	5.5	10.6	10.1	4.8	9.5	-2.6	4.5	....	Ireland	178
15.7	12.2	11.9	15.5	12.3	13.2	10.4	10.5	7.8	7.5	8.7	8.3	7.1	5.5	6.5	Italy	136
5.1	5.5	2.5	5.5	3.9	3.3	2.2	7.8	12.2	7.5	8.6	13.4	6.2	....	....	Luxembourg	137
4.2	2.6	5.2	13.1	3.8	6.8	7.9	6.9	7.5	5.5	5.5	3.6	5.5	7.8	6.8	Netherlands	138
8.5	12.4	10.8	10.6	16.4	23.3	12.5	36.4	21.2	24.3	10.8	6.2	7.8	12.1	....	Norway	142
25.4	19.3	14.0	12.3	11.9	21.7	31.7	27.8	12.9	8.9	12.9	21.3	16.3	14.2	8.9	Portugal	182
10.2	11.5	14.7	10.8	6.6	13.7	15.6	13.7	21.1	21.7	17.9	13.0	5.7	-2.2	6.8	Spain	184
8.5	8.9	7.4	8.1	7.6	5.4	8.0	7.4	3.4	6.2	....	....	....	....	....	Sweden	144
-6.8	-2.2	4.6	10.6	4.1	-6.0	2.6	8.0	12.4	-5.5	-4.4	1.1	-.2	10.8	2.9	Switzerland	146
4.9	10.4	13.7	13.4	14.0	16.5	22.4	26.5	13.7	10.8	11.5	9.2	5.7	3.8	....	United Kingdom	112
															Developing Countries	
															Africa	
19.0	17.3	20.6	24.3	29.1	8.0	6.5	6.1	12.1	7.4	.9	15.2	15.0	15.0	13.6	Algeria	612
34.6	35.1	38.1	-1.7	10.5	-3.9	-9.4	-11.4	-10.3	16.7	33.3	8.1	11.9	-4.7	17.5	Benin	638
26.3	17.5	2.8	12.9	13.1	14.4	34.1	28.6	26.9	32.1	20.0	8.0	8.7	4.4	11.1	Botswana	616
8.4	23.9	9.7	7.0	16.7	3.3	15.1	18.1	9.7	5.6	3.3	2.2	.7	4.4	26.7	Burkina Faso	748
8.5	26.2	-3.9	6.5	19.7	15.7	11.5	5.8	5.1	4.1	5.6	....	....	-35.1	....	Burundi	618
21.7	17.1	20.7	18.3	21.6	5.1	3.0	-4.7	-7.2	2.5	3.0	-1.9	-3.7	-35.1	16.9	Cameroon	622
8.8	19.5	24.7	20.7	4.1	20.1	18.8	9.5	-.3	2.4	6.8	12.3	16.2	17.3	7.6	Cape Verde	624
32.1	31.2	3.9	3.3	9.2	13.9	2.8	-5.3	6.4	9.9	-1.3	-6.1	-2.4	7.2	52.7	Central African Rep.	626
-16.1	19.6	13.9	9.1	54.1	31.0	-2.4	-.8	7.8	-10.8	8.4	8.0	-12.3	-9.8	22.9	Chad	628
....	....	....	41.1	.6	-3.0	16.4	7.6	5.6	11.3	12.5	-4.1	3.3	....	....	Comoros	632
36.6	46.8	29.3	9.8	6.2	7.5	-8.8	.1	-5.5	-3.3	12.9	12.0	-4.8	-7.0	14.5	Congo	634
3.0	2.2	3.3	.5	6.4	16.3	6.3	-3.2	-.4	-3.4	-9.3	-3.2	-1.9	-7.0	42.6	Côte d'Ivoire	662
....	....	....	....	....	3.0	8.7	4.1	12.0	-6.3	8.0	10.1	12.9	5.9	3.1	Djibouti	611
....	1.8	9.5	15.5	9.9	13.6	57.5	6.5	-9.1	-34.5	-38.3	-22.8	-5.3	4.5	71.2	Equatorial Guinea	642
9.0	1.8	9.5	15.5	9.9	13.6	19.7	9.8	7.7	10.4	18.8	21.9	14.4	9.9	10.5	Ethiopia	644
3.4	17.4	17.7	12.3	17.3	12.1	-5.4	-16.0	-1.0	4.9	7.9	6.7	-4.8	-22.0	21.5	Gabon	646
-5.7	4.9	21.0	23.2	1.6	24.6	32.4	40.4	12.5	13.3	18.0	16.7	14.6	9.6	-3.3	Gambia, The	648
34.5	35.2	29.3	56.8	37.9	43.2	49.8	52.6	44.0	50.8	29.7	4.3	22.8	48.0	36.6	Ghana	652
....	....	....	....	....	....	....	....	....	....	....	....	....	22.1	21.7	Guinea	656
....	....	....	....	....	....	....	93.4	84.1	30.8	45.5	59.3	50.8	42.7	46.2	Guinea-Bissau	654
12.3	2.8	5.6	12.2	13.2	8.9	22.0	13.6	2.2	11.5	18.7	16.6	29.7	37.4	....	Kenya	664
....	2.8	32.6	17.4	16.7	22.6	20.0	17.9	21.3	24.4	4.4	16.8	7.2	20.1	23.5	Lesotho	666
1.7	-19.0	-.4	21.7	13.1	18.8	39.1	18.4	12.0	11.9	28.3	11.5	-1.1	19.8	29.3	Liberia	668
23.2	21.8	22.3	-7.6	9.6	9.8	17.6	19.7	25.5	26.3	18.1	9.1	21.0	18.4	40.2	Madagascar	674
7.4	8.8	9.8	2.8	11.9	13.6	16.0	42.8	36.7	21.0	3.5	24.7	19.5	27.9	40.4	Malawi	676
10.2	1.7	8.8	13.6	21.9	24.0	-2.5	1.8	1.9	1.6	-7.7	-1.6	5.4	4.8	40.2	Mali	678
.5	25.5	10.9	7.2	10.1	20.5	14.3	11.7	7.4	3.7	-1.6	9.2	10.1	2.2	....	Mauritania	682
5.0	4.0	5.0	10.6	7.0	1.4	13.0	29.3	22.1	20.4	19.6	24.1	11.5	6.2	7.4	Mauritius	684
9.9	9.0	15.6	13.3	9.6	9.4	16.0	12.4	9.5	13.2	13.2	17.1	9.4	4.5	10.2	Morocco	686
....	....	....	....	....	....	....	....	....	....	....	33.8	39.5	26.8	29.9	Namibia	728
26.1	19.3	-1.2	-12.1	9.9	17.1	-2.7	-4.1	4.6	1.2	-2.6	2.7	-8.7	-3.5	37.0	Niger	692
23.0	20.1	3.9	12.8	7.2	10.3	1.5	.6	35.7	37.8	25.9	47.8	....	....	....	Nigeria	694
8.5	11.9	-3.4	3.6	5.9	10.6	11.4	10.2	2.6	-4.1	-2.9	8.9	15.4	14.6	....	Rwanda	714
2.6	3.9	19.4	9.6	-.3	-1.7	7.8	12.7	2.8	-1.6	.7	-3.7	.9	-9.1	29.5	Senegal	722
29.0	11.0	-5.3	-5.0	-7.6	16.5	3.9	3.4	13.6	12.2	5.4	13.8	7.6	14.9	5.2	Seychelles	718
13.9	7.7	25.0	53.8	35.7	68.2	93.9	114.2	38.9	66.6	69.2	70.8	48.3	17.0	12.5	Sierra Leone	724
25.2	33.0	15.9	-5.8	44.5	47.3	41.7	44.8	120.2	130.4	....	....	....	....	....	Somalia	726
29.7	38.7	24.0	24.7	34.1	16.6	-4.5	20.9	31.8	14.2	12.4	....	....	....	....	South Africa	199
....	....	....	....	....	....	....	....	....	....	....	....	....	83.2	63.5	Sudan	732
28.2	12.7	6.5	5.6	10.8	13.5	29.2	21.4	21.1	10.6	13.9	10.4	8.7	15.5	21.0	Swaziland	734
30.8	22.2	18.0	14.7	8.1	9.4	31.3	33.5	34.3	35.7	32.9	32.9	26.2	30.7	....	Tanzania	738
2.2	28.9	30.0	-8.8	-3.6	5.6	2.3	10.8	-17.9	-11.7	5.9	14.4	-13.1	-31.4	57.4	Togo	742
16.0	25.9	18.5	18.5	14.6	9.8	4.6	-2.8	9.7	17.1	6.7	-.2	6.4	-1.4	15.8	Tunisia	744
....	....	....	....	....	....	....	....	....	....	....	....	....	28.9	....	Uganda	746
23.7	52.6	58.1	286.9	-32.1	33.8	38.3	79.7	97.7	105.3	86.7	1,083.4	5,497.6	1,658.0	8,376.8	Zaïre	636
10.7	12.7	9.8	16.0	12.5	26.0	69.9	57.1	42.6	62.2	56.9	99.3	....	....	....	Zambia	754
29.3	16.6	13.7	-.2	7.2	14.1	13.1	8.4	25.6	20.0	26.4	34.5	11.7	40.6	58.0	Zimbabwe	698
															Asia	
23.0	12.2	17.5	14.0	14.2	11.8	11.8	22.1	56.3	40.5	38.3	....	....	....	23.1	Afghanistan, Islamic State of	512
18.4	20.2	4.1	29.9	31.9	18.7	14.6	.7	5.1	7.5	12.5	8.8	14.2	16.9	23.1	Bangladesh	513
....	....	....	....	18.4	24.7	5.8	33.5	20.8	31.7	10.3	21.0	21.9	3.4	10.6	Bhutan	514
24.8	21.8	14.1	14.5	21.4	32.7	18.3	26.4	24.7	7.8	13.4	25.5	31.6	27.9	....	China, People' Rep.	924
8.0	5.5	2.7	9.0	-1.2	8.2	6.2	17.0	30.2	22.5	-5.3	4.4	15.8	12.2	.5	Fiji	819
12.3	15.7	10.8	14.7	17.8	16.0	13.0	14.7	15.1	18.1	18.9	17.5	20.2	10.1	....	India	534
43.2	32.6	25.5	4.1	8.0	14.5	15.9	11.4	10.0	24.0	35.8	12.9	9.6	....	....	Indonesia	536
18.0	11.2	28.6	27.1	9.0	1.5	12.8	18.0	11.5	14.2	22.0	19.7	35.6	18.4	9.8	Korea	542
....	....	....	....	....	....	....	....	....	....	....	....	....	22.6	31.6	Malaysia	548
34.3	32.4	4.9	-13.1	20.2	41.8	32.3	6.5	5.7	11.7	25.5	19.6	19.9	28.9	....	Maldives	556
....	....	....	....	....	....	....	....	....	....	....	....	45.0	77.5	116.4	Mongolia	948
12.2	15.4	9.5	9.0	14.6	8.8	9.1	4.1	-20.8	58.7	39.0	41.6	40.4	....	....	Myanmar	518
15.8	12.6	12.9	15.6	16.2	12.5	23.8	19.5	18.4	17.8	20.5	18.7	22.0	19.3	....	Nepal	558
18.5	14.0	12.9	19.1	6.5	16.0	14.4	18.8	15.2	11.0	16.4	19.0	20.0	8.2	10.9	Pakistan	564
8.0	-7.4	-2.8	1.4	17.6	3.9	1.8	10.3	12.4	6.3	3.6	13.2	14.2	18.6	....	Papua New Guinea	853
14.1	11.0	1.8	10.6	14.7	6.7	17.4	24.6	19.2	18.9	21.4	18.2	15.4	15.5	13.9	Philippines	566
14.2	11.9	12.9	9.3	3.2	2.6	3.8	18.3	6.1	14.3	11.8	4.4	14.0	17.8	11.5	Singapore	576
22.1	9.0	1.5	8.9	54.6	2.4	16.5	10.1	31.7	15.1	18.0	30.5	26.0	24.3	24.9	Solomon Islands	813

Money

Percent Change over Previous Year

		1965	1966	1967	1968	1969	1970	1971	1972	1973	1974	1975	1976	1977	1978	1979
Asia (cont.)																
Sri Lanka	524	6.7	2.1	2.7	6.8	2.3	4.0	6.7	5.0	13.2	18.2	1.8	22.4	32.4	19.8	17.8
Thailand	578	6.2	6.8	10.4	6.1	6.2	4.4	10.1	12.8	20.2	14.7	7.6	13.0	11.9	15.3	16.6
Tonga	866	....	....	....	....	....	....	....	....	....	....	41.5	12.8	51.6	21.4	1.4
Vanuatu	846	....	....	....	....	....	....	....	....	....	....	....	....	8.7	6.7	10.9
Western Samoa	862	−5.7	−3.6	−5.2	2.6	−19.5	41.7	51.6	19.4	29.8	24.2	2.1	30.5	12.8	−2.5	19.2
Europe																
Cyprus	423	9.1	8.7	10.4	9.1	18.8	9.4	9.6	20.9	14.1	6.2	−3.6	13.2	15.3	11.5	27.7
Czech Republic	935	....	....	....	....	....	....	....	....	....	....	....	....	....	....	....
Czechoslovakia	934	....	....	....	....	....	....	....	....	....	....	....	....	....	....	....
Estonia	939	....	....	....	....	....	....	....	....	....	....	....	....	....	....	....
Hungary	944	....	....	....	....	....	....	....	....	....	....	....	....	....	....	....
Malta	181	5.1	12.9	10.5	13.8	13.4	8.1	10.1	13.9	9.2	18.9	17.0	23.0	14.7	16.0	16.2
Moldova	921	....	....	....	....	....	....	....	....	....	....	....	....	....	....	....
Poland	964	....	....	....	....	....	....	....	....	....	....	....	....	....	....	....
Romania	968	....	....	....	....	....	....	....	....	....	....	....	....	....	....	....
Slovak Republic	936	....	....	....	....	....	....	....	....	....	....	....	....	....	....	....
Slovenia	961	....	....	....	....	....	....	....	....	....	....	....	....	....	....	....
Turkey	186	19.3	17.4	14.0	14.7	16.4	13.1	24.2	24.2	28.5	29.7	28.9	29.4	35.9	33.8	54.8
Yugoslavia, SFR	188	22.0	9.4	−1.9	9.7	18.3	16.0	14.7	29.3	44.3	30.8	25.4	49.7	31.3	19.6	17.0
Middle East																
Bahrain	419	....	17.0	17.9	17.9	14.1	2.6	20.8	20.7	6.7	16.4	4.2	58.5	37.6	15.2	2.5
Egypt	469	12.0	6.8	1.2	.1	4.1	6.8	5.9	12.5	20.9	25.9	20.5	26.2	25.6	24.3	23.9
Iran, I.R. of	429	18.0	8.5	12.1	15.3	8.6	10.8	13.7	31.4	36.7	18.1	41.5	37.5	31.2	27.8	50.1
Iraq	433	8.0	10.5	4.2	7.7	14.1	10.5	2.4	10.8	19.7	32.0	40.9	22.9	....	....	....
Israel	436	7.9	7.8	19.3	19.3	7.1	5.0	22.4	30.5	24.4	20.4	30.5	18.0	39.9	37.1	34.2
Jordan	439	13.3	16.1	22.9	25.9	10.9	8.2	8.7	1.5	16.9	20.7	25.5	35.9	16.1	14.1	23.0
Kuwait	443	−5.2	29.9	25.3	−8.3	−4.0	−12.5	1.6	28.1	26.0	18.3	23.8	45.8	20.9	33.0	11.1
Lebanon	446	8.5	6.6	2.0	5.6	3.4	−5.0	12.4	14.5	15.2	10.3	25.1	38.9	3.2	15.9	16.4
Libya	672	44.5	44.5	30.7	27.4	31.7	22.2	43.9	28.2	21.7	46.3	10.0	32.0	29.4	25.2	23.0
Oman	449	....	....	....	....	....	....	....	....	....	31.4	83.5	79.5	23.7	19.6	4.5	7.2
Qatar	453	....	....	30.5	21.2	7.6	−.9	20.4	33.5	34.5	33.0	51.6	76.4	42.7	12.5	7.0
Saudi Arabia	456	7.4	14.7	11.6	10.4	7.1	3.9	8.6	22.7	41.5	39.5	64.1	93.5	60.2	45.7	12.6
Syrian Arab Rep.	463	14.8	11.7	13.5	19.4	14.5	10.0	10.0	15.4	22.6	45.6	27.5	23.6	24.4	27.3	19.8
United Arab Emirates	466	....	....	....	....	....	....	....	....	....	58.4	68.8	82.4	33.2	15.0	4.0
Yemen Arab Rep.	473	....	....	....	....	....	....	....	....	....	30.8	52.0	113.1	76.8	40.4	22.4
Yemen, P.D. Rep.	459	....	9.3	11.3	−9.9	−3.9	.6	9.9	6.2	12.6	18.9	15.7	42.6	40.1	31.0	25.6
Yemen, Republic of	474	....	....	....	....	....	....	....	....	....	....	....	....	....	....	....
Western Hemisphere																
Antigua and Barbuda	311	....	....	....	....	....	....	....	....	....	....	....	27.9	27.4	−5.0	18.5
Argentina	213	2,045.7	37.4	3.6	2.2	2.4	87.7	1.0	9.6	101.5	83.0	92.8	407.0	174.1	144.3	124.9
Bahamas, The	313	....	....	....	....	....	−1.1	−14.5	6.4	4.7	−1.6	−1.2	−.6	6.6	19.5	29.6
Barbados	316	....	....	8.2	18.1	15.1	11.3	1.9	9.3	7.3	8.4	28.4	10.4	11.2	19.8	24.5
Belize	339	....	....	....	....	....	....	....	....	....	....	....	....	....	19.3	27.8
Bolivia	218	22.7	19.9	5.2	7.3	9.6	9.0	10.9	20.8	35.0	42.8	22.6	18.9	31.9	13.5	13.8
Brazil	223	78.5	36.1	36.6	43.9	32.2	28.5	31.7	34.6	37.9	35.7	35.7	42.7	37.0	40.8	51.9
Chile	228	21.1	89.8	24.9	38.0	38.0	52.9	99.3	100.9	265.5	314.1	239.5	275.5	151.0	76.7	61.7
Colombia	233	14.3	16.0	22.2	19.3	21.1	19.8	10.3	19.3	28.3	28.6	9.7	30.2	36.2	29.0	25.2
Costa Rica	238	4.5	2.6	19.6	16.9	12.4	9.6	12.4	19.5	23.0	24.2	18.4	23.7	33.4	21.9	10.4
Dominica	321	....	....	....	....	....	....	....	....	....	....	....	9.6	23.2	51.8	72.0
Dominican Republic	243	−2.5	−1.4	.1	10.6	8.5	14.7	9.5	14.7	17.0	25.6	25.9	−3.0	10.5	15.9	11.6
Ecuador	248	−.9	8.4	15.5	17.5	11.7	22.6	20.5	16.6	31.3	43.4	23.0	9.2	42.8	14.2	20.1
El Salvador	253	2.0	2.9	3.8	.4	5.7	7.6	3.6	13.4	19.0	27.0	14.7	25.4	33.1	−1.2	12.0
Grenada	328	....	....	....	....	....	....	9.8	20.6	9.2	1.0	12.8	22.5	20.4	35.2	23.5
Guatemala	258	3.6	9.3	−3.5	6.9	1.1	6.4	−1.2	12.3	23.8	25.1	7.1	33.9	28.6	12.2	11.0
Guyana	336	8.5	2.6	4.1	8.9	11.7	3.9	8.5	14.9	16.5	24.4	41.4	22.7	23.0	26.0	−8.0
Haiti	263	−3.0	—	3.8	11.3	10.7	10.3	18.0	17.3	22.9	15.1	−.5	37.2	21.3	17.5	7.9
Honduras	268	13.9	6.9	−2.1	14.3	12.8	13.5	3.7	6.4	21.9	11.4	.3	27.5	26.7	11.4	17.2
Jamaica	343	2.7	5.1	7.9	20.3	17.8	13.1	17.7	15.1	19.6	17.2	23.1	6.8	32.6	26.9	7.7
Mexico	273	9.0	8.4	10.1	12.3	12.6	11.3	8.1	13.5	22.8	19.2	21.5	22.3	26.6	34.6	31.5
Netherlands Antilles	353	....	....	....	....	14.3	16.2	15.9	18.8	14.1	9.3	5.1	21.7	15.5	11.0	9.9
Nicaragua	278	17.4	6.8	−.7	−3.6	−1.7	6.6	4.6	17.8	51.4	25.6	−12.4	21.4	15.6	−2.2	20.9
Panama	283	9.6	11.5	8.7	10.1	8.9	12.9	9.9	24.6	24.6	10.0	−7.3	13.1	10.1	13.5	16.1
Paraguay	288	16.0	−.9	5.6	4.1	−7.2	6.3	14.8	14.1	33.0	21.4	16.6	20.6	36.6	34.1	32.2
Peru	293	26.0	15.6	8.9	17.1	12.7	44.8	27.9	17.5	27.3	30.7	27.8	21.2	20.9	34.0	59.9
St. Kitts and Nevis	361	....	....	....	....	....	....	....	....	....	....	....	....	....	....	....
St. Lucia	362	....	....	....	....	....	....	....	....	....	....	....	40.8	13.6	16.3	17.8
St. Vincent & Grens.	364	....	....	....	....	....	....	....	....	....	....	....	20.4	3.3	36.2	22.6
Suriname	366	....	....	....	7.2	14.8	7.0	14.1	10.2	21.6	13.6	11.4	18.8	13.3	12.5	9.2
Trinidad and Tobago	369	−3.9	8.4	4.0	4.7	9.4	5.3	9.7	16.8	14.3	4.3	45.9	48.3	30.9	27.0	24.1
Uruguay	298	83.0	71.9	49.6	87.8	68.2	31.3	31.7	50.1	62.7	79.8	52.7	64.1	46.5	56.5	99.5
Venezuela	299	12.2	5.2	5.5	7.8	9.0	7.2	10.8	16.6	18.9	37.2	49.6	28.5	25.6	21.3	7.7

Money 34 x

1980	1981	1982	1983	1984	1985	1986	1987	1988	1989	1990	1991	1992	1993	1994	Country	Code
\multicolumn{15}{l}{*Percent Change over Previous Year*}	**Asia (cont.)**	
22.2	12.4	18.9	15.7	17.5	13.9	15.2	13.8	23.5	18.1	10.5	14.7	12.0	14.8	18.6	Sri Lanka	524
15.8	5.1	6.5	7.5	8.2	.6	7.9	22.9	18.5	19.7	16.8	2.4	19.7	10.1	20.1	Thailand	578
21.2	1.8	89.1	8.8	19.6	8.5	15.5	19.0	5.9	4.7	8.7	19.6	2.4	10.7	4.3	Tonga	866
–10.1	–22.9	18.8	24.3	24.0	14.2	–2.9	42.6	–12.9	18.0	7.3	3.1	8.9	15.7	6.9	Vanuatu	846
49.1	45.3	22.6	1.8	9.3	11.7	4.7	24.3	10.8	12.3	22.7	2.5	5.5	–6.3	11.0	Western Samoa	862
															Europe	
21.1	18.7	18.1	14.0	9.0	6.3	1.6	7.7	12.0	11.1	10.5	8.7	13.5	5.1	6.3	Cyprus	423
....	....	....	....	....	....	....	....	....	....	....	....	....	....	66.5	Czech Republic	935
....	6.7	7.1	3.9	4.8	1.1	.4	3.6	6.1	4.7	.2	4.4	25.7	....	....	Czechoslovakia	934
....	....	....	....	....	....	....	....	....	....	....	....	291.5	133.2	40.3	Estonia	939
....	....	....	2.7	4.3	18.1	11.8	14.8	–.2	10.9	20.7	17.3	....	....	....	Hungary	944
16.4	12.3	8.5	6.8	2.0	–.4	–2.0	7.7	5.1	3.5	1.5	4.3	5.5	.1	8.6	Malta	181
....	....	....	....	....	....	....	....	....	....	....	....	545.5	520.7	119.6	Moldova	921
12.7	21.1	40.4	9.7	15.5	20.4	21.9	26.8	40.5	137.0	556.1	65.7	31.4	31.8	35.6	Poland	964
....	21.4	20.2	6.3	–2.1	7.3	1.8	5.3	1.1	13.7	7.6	59.8	141.8	90.7	101.1	Romania	968
....	....	....	....	....	....	....	....	....	....	....	....	....	....	9.8	Slovak Republic	936
....	....	....	....	....	....	....	....	....	....	....	....	136.1	72.3	37.2	Slovenia	961
60.5	39.4	26.0	42.8	22.5	41.2	43.6	62.6	44.4	63.7	71.4	45.9	59.2	78.4	72.4	Turkey	186
32.4	24.9	24.5	25.1	31.6	39.3	84.3	96.1	156.1	838.4	689.8	....	....	....	....	Yugoslavia, SFR	188
															Middle East	
5.2	13.9	24.3	3.2	–5.7	–2.1	–2.0	4.1	–1.1	–1.8	6.1	20.5	8.2	10.0	–.4	Bahrain	419
13.2	12.4	19.8	19.7	13.6	16.2	16.1	8.7	15.5	10.7	14.6	12.9	6.3	9.4	11.1	Egypt	469
31.5	30.7	18.5	24.7	12.5	11.1	12.0	17.3	15.2	12.4	15.7	25.4	18.3	22.9	....	Iran, I.R. of	429
....	....	....	....	....	....	....	....	....	....	....	....	....	....	....	Iraq	433
70.0	108.6	99.7	114.9	229.4	344.9	158.4	58.2	31.0	27.6	27.9	26.5	22.8	25.8	19.7	Israel	436
23.2	25.1	15.5	9.5	4.8	–1.5	.7	8.4	13.4	17.2	11.4	11.6	12.2	1.1	4.3	Jordan	439
15.1	30.0	49.2	–13.4	–17.1	–8.6	2.2	2.2	–.8	–4.8	8.4	13.0	–7.6	–.6	2.2	Kuwait	443
10.3	17.0	17.6	16.2	13.8	36.0	32.3	104.9	175.4	79.4	50.7	44.8	79.0	14.0	21.8	Lebanon	446
23.2	32.9	–3.3	–9.1	–4.3	11.6	10.1	–2.9	–6.4	3.8	18.2	19.2	.7	....	....	Libya	672
22.1	26.8	21.5	16.8	5.6	13.4	2.9	1.7	1.7	–2.1	10.4	11.4	7.1	4.7	3.3	Oman	449
8.9	14.5	23.9	–3.4	6.5	–1.0	13.4	11.0	–14.8	–13.0	11.8	–8.6	10.0	3.3	–3.8	Qatar	453
11.8	14.5	19.4	10.1	–3.6	–1.0	.3	5.1	7.3	1.8	4.4	12.5	....	....	–3.1	Saudi Arabia	456
27.0	27.4	14.0	23.6	24.6	16.8	16.4	13.3	14.0	17.5	21.5	27.3	24.5	....	....	Syrian Arab Rep.	463
15.9	13.9	16.4	3.2	–4.7	3.4	–2.5	7.9	6.7	2.4	4.7	7.2	18.7	17.9	....	United Arab Emirates	466
15.1	5.2	22.2	24.9	25.9	20.1	17.7	22.4	4.6	3.0	....	....	....	....	....	Yemen Arab Rep.	473
29.1	13.6	15.7	17.2	7.8	11.0	7.3	3.9	5.0	15.0	....	....	....	....	....	Yemen, P.D. Rep.	459
....	....	....	....	....	....	....	....	....	....	....	15.8	16.1	26.5	....	Yemen, Republic of	474
															Western Hemisphere	
24.4	4.9	7.6	7.9	18.2	10.1	26.6	25.3	19.6	13.0	6.0	20.6	1.3	6.5	15.9	Antigua and Barbuda	311
114.2	12.5	195.7	287.8	521.5	773.6	147.5	98.6	231.9	2,765.5	1,504.9	277.5	79.1	35.4	....	Argentina	213
6.0	5.5	5.7	10.0	10.8	7.4	16.2	14.8	2.9	8.4	6.4	5.8	4.9	5.4	7.5	Bahamas, The	313
22.3	11.7	–2.4	11.6	5.9	8.7	21.1	7.3	14.6	5.5	–5.8	3.5	–7.4	6.4	6.6	Barbados	316
5.8	6.7	–7.7	13.0	9.2	15.0	24.7	14.5	9.2	6.3	13.3	18.3	6.3	8.1	6.4	Belize	339
38.4	15.1	120.6	198.9	790.9	7,574.0	297.0	61.7	27.4	18.6	22.3	49.7	40.1	30.6	27.6	Bolivia	218
76.0	65.1	82.0	95.0	141.1	274.6	503.9	149.2	323.7	852.4	4,406.5	380.6	744.9	1,584.4	....	Brazil	223
57.7	23.8	–5.0	26.2	18.0	13.8	30.6	19.7	39.5	27.0	11.8	43.2	34.7	7.3	....	Chile	228
24.8	24.6	23.1	19.7	21.1	16.6	39.3	30.1	24.5	17.7	13.0	31.7	44.3	31.1	30.7	Colombia	233
9.6	37.5	72.0	45.3	26.2	8.6	26.1	12.7	6.9	24.4	12.9	4.1	33.4	13.4	20.1	Costa Rica	238
36.0	–7.9	–4.5	3.5	28.2	–6.5	7.2	51.1	19.5	–1.2	16.4	9.5	4.9	.7	–2.4	Dominica	321
17.3	1.6	13.7	9.0	30.0	25.6	39.2	41.2	54.5	32.9	53.3	22.1	31.0	19.1	13.5	Dominican Republic	243
25.7	21.7	21.6	22.3	27.2	22.8	21.9	23.8	49.1	48.2	49.1	56.8	42.4	....	....	Ecuador	248
25.2	–2.7	5.6	.2	23.2	23.2	22.3	13.5	4.4	11.0	17.3	16.4	29.4	20.6	13.4	El Salvador	253
14.3	5.8	9.8	2.2	–23.9	20.3	23.3	7.9	9.0	2.7	8.9	2.1	10.7	22.4	10.2	Grenada	328
5.7	1.0	6.6	.1	5.0	24.8	37.8	13.7	10.2	14.4	32.7	19.1	16.6	18.1	34.1	Guatemala	258
4.7	4.6	20.5	24.7	17.1	22.2	28.5	36.1	38.7	47.2	39.0	71.2	43.1	31.4	11.5	Guyana	336
13.4	29.0	4.9	4.0	16.2	10.3	10.7	16.7	52.1	–4.1	–13.2	1.9	18.6	24.8	....	Haiti	263
7.7	8.6	3.1	12.8	13.6	.9	8.6	14.4	13.5	14.6	28.4	20.3	11.9	19.2	23.1	Honduras	268
18.5	7.8	18.7	7.8	23.8	20.5	33.1	24.8	22.5	15.6	11.3	56.7	93.2	44.3	24.5	Jamaica	343
31.1	36.8	43.3	44.1	53.2	53.7	51.3	106.5	110.1	30.6	47.9	91.6	70.3	17.3	10.9	Mexico	273
5.0	7.8	15.3	5.2	.2	–2.2	5.9	11.7	.3	5.9	5.0	4.5	6.5	12.9	8.6	Netherlands Antilles	353
101.3	21.7	19.9	27.5	–34.1	163.3	252.1	637.0	11,353.9	4,219.9	3,997.3	3,726.4	52.8	–1.0	12.8	Nicaragua	278
16.8	8.7	7.0	–.4	4.5	3.3	12.1	6.5	–28.1	–10.9	29.8	21.1	23.9	14.3	12.1	Panama	283
20.4	13.7	–5.5	8.4	37.3	23.2	25.4	46.8	42.6	32.6	27.9	25.1	20.8	20.1	23.8	Paraguay	288
70.8	47.1	36.9	75.6	88.8	199.1	175.4	96.2	261.2	1,585.5	4,930.1	476.4	78.2	76.5	30.7	Peru	293
10.6	189.2	16.3	–5.2	–5.3	10.4	36.0	34.2	–16.9	28.3	–.1	9.4	–.2	23.8	–5.8	St. Kitts and Nevis	361
9.5	14.9	–2.6	1.9	8.6	10.1	23.4	32.1	21.8	13.2	3.5	7.4	18.8	16.9	1.8	St. Lucia	362
1.7	19.5	11.6	9.7	12.8	10.9	18.8	–8.8	18.2	8.8	8.1	–12.3	23.2	16.9	9.2	St. Vincent & Grens.	364
9.5	15.9	12.0	22.0	13.7	42.3	51.9	26.3	28.2	17.0	4.3	18.3	17.9	40.3	....	Suriname	366
20.3	24.7	37.7	15.3	–7.5	–5.8	–2.5	–4.8	–3.0	3.4	13.1	18.6	1.3	6.9	12.1	Trinidad and Tobago	369
34.9	33.9	–.8	27.7	24.0	71.8	102.2	72.6	61.6	60.7	90.1	104.0	93.0	64.5	38.4	Uruguay	298
11.9	11.2	7.8	14.3	27.0	18.1	7.6	21.9	18.4	20.7	25.0	52.6	26.5	–2.5	101.4	Venezuela	299

Money plus Quasi-Money
35l x

Percent Change over Previous Year

		1965	1966	1967	1968	1969	1970	1971	1972	1973	1974	1975	1976	1977	1978	1979
Industrial Countries																
United States	111	8.3	6.9	7.7	8.3	5.8	4.4	12.1	12.1	9.2	6.2	9.9	12.8	12.6	8.4	8.4
Canada	156	16.2	9.0	12.5	12.5	11.7	5.6	10.1	14.0	15.1	24.3	14.4	18.4	15.4	13.6	18.8
Australia	193	9.5	7.4	8.4	8.2	9.1	6.4	7.4	13.5	23.6	15.1	17.8	13.7	9.8	8.3	10.4
Japan	158	16.7	17.4	15.7	15.3	17.3	17.7	21.1	23.1	23.0	12.9	12.7	15.2	11.4	11.9	11.1
New Zealand	196	.4	1.0	-2.0	2.5	6.9	11.3	11.5	24.5	40.3	14.3	7.0	16.5	15.0	17.8	18.7
Austria	122	13.5	11.6	9.5	9.4	11.6	12.8	13.2	15.5	14.1	12.1	15.5	17.0	14.0	11.7	11.1
Belgium	124	8.5	8.4	8.6	9.2	8.0	5.8	10.9	15.0	15.5	12.0	11.4	14.0	9.5	8.2	7.1
Denmark	128	9.3	11.7	11.3	10.2	11.8	6.5	6.0	11.6	14.1	10.0	19.3	21.1	9.9	5.7	8.9
Finland	172	12.3	10.7	10.3	10.1	12.1	14.5	12.2	16.4	15.3	15.9	23.4	14.1	12.1	14.5	15.9
France	132	11.2	12.3	13.5	16.8	11.2	9.2	19.9	21.0	16.1	18.7	15.9	17.5	13.0	12.6	14.4
Germany	134	13.5	11.7	11.5	12.3	13.4	8.3	11.9	13.5	10.8	7.4	9.0	10.6	8.5	10.0	8.2
Greece	174	13.1	13.2	14.1	15.4	14.9	15.5	19.9	23.7	20.4	16.3	23.5	26.1	22.8	21.9	20.6
Iceland	176	20.8	18.1	8.3	6.3	16.9	27.0	22.9	19.0	26.4	27.3	26.8	32.1	34.9	44.7	55.5
Ireland	178	5.7	5.8	11.4	13.3	11.2	8.9	8.2	10.6	18.4	18.7	19.7	17.7	15.9	19.9	23.6
Italy	136	...	...	...	...	...	...	...	...	...	...	18.1	23.3	20.5	22.9	20.5
Luxembourg	137	...	...	...	...	...	...	...	...	...	...	6.6	15.6	12.3	14.3	14.6
Netherlands	138	13.0	7.6	10.6	15.1	12.8	13.1	13.2	14.8	15.4	16.3	13.8	16.5	14.0	11.8	10.4
Norway	142	7.7	8.8	8.9	10.4	12.1	12.9	14.9	11.4	12.6	11.5	13.9	16.3	19.0	12.8	12.5
Portugal	182	14.2	10.8	10.1	11.8	15.3	16.2	14.8	18.7	28.0	18.4	13.7	13.2	19.9	18.5	24.8
Spain	184	19.4	14.5	11.6	20.0	18.8	15.6	20.2	23.6	24.8	20.4	18.8	19.0	19.7	19.8	19.2
Sweden	144	...	...	...	...	...	...	...	...	...	...	...	...	...	...	...
Switzerland	146	7.3	7.5	10.1	11.4	15.9	14.3	14.1	8.2	6.0	7.0	6.9	8.5	8.5	9.2	9.5
United Kingdom	112	6.0	5.9	6.1	8.3	3.6	6.9	12.0	22.0	24.2	18.2	10.5	10.6	9.6	14.5	11.6
Developing Countries																
Africa																
Algeria	612	10.7	8.9	29.0	29.3	31.6	9.0	6.4	24.6	24.3	17.6	27.9	23.8	30.2	24.2	17.9
Benin	638	.2	2.3	-.9	7.4	17.7	16.6	23.9	16.0	8.3	19.6	39.3	23.0	14.9	5.1	21.6
Botswana	616	...	...	...	...	...	...	...	...	...	...	...	...	28.2	12.1	53.5
Burkina Faso	748	4.6	-1.8	2.7	8.3	12.8	16.1	3.1	6.9	24.0	32.2	26.7	33.7	16.8	20.6	15.4
Burundi	618	5.8	.8	15.6	5.0	3.6	18.6	18.3	9.3	15.0	10.8	2.9	25.7	56.3	9.8	24.1
Cameroon	622	...	...	...	...	...	...	...	...	...	...	...	...	...	...	...
Cape Verde	624	...	...	...	...	...	...	...	...	...	...	...	41.0	15.8	30.8	
Central African Rep.	626	...	...	...	...	...	...	...	...	...	...	...	...	...	...	...
Chad	628	1.0	1.3	-3.4	1.5	21.0	9.6	7.7	5.3	10.3	12.2	30.0	10.3	25.5	11.8	18.1
Comoros	632	...	...	...	...	...	...	...	...	...	...	...	...	...	...	...
Congo	634	...	...	...	...	...	...	...	...	...	...	...	...	...	...	...
Côte d'Ivoire	662	14.1	2.4	2.1	27.0	17.0	25.5	12.1	3.3	16.1	34.8	26.2	23.2	53.7	23.3	10.2
Djibouti	611	...	...	...	...	...	...	...	...	...	...	...	...	...	...	...
Equatorial Guinea	642	...	...	...	...	...	...	...	...	...	...	...	...	...	...	...
Ethiopia	644	16.2	10.6	3.2	7.2	11.3	13.6	2.5	7.0	24.4	29.2	6.1	18.6	10.6	15.4	11.9
Gabon	646	7.2	4.8	-7.0	6.6	14.3	19.5	13.4	21.5	28.7	43.8	56.3	59.9	14.4	-86.6	-6.0
Gambia, The	648	6.2	12.8	3.7	10.5	3.7	13.7	3.2	33.0	18.6	24.3	31.8	32.5	25.1	15.6	4.2
Ghana	652	23.5	1.4	.3	9.0	6.9	16.5	3.4	39.8	20.4	24.8	33.7	38.5	44.7	68.9	30.9
Guinea	656	...	...	...	...	...	...	...	...	...	...	...	...	...	...	...
Guinea-Bissau	654	...	...	...	...	...	...	...	...	...	...	...	...	...	...	...
Kenya	664	...	...	19.5	5.7	17.5	22.1	18.4	8.5	24.1	16.4	8.5	24.2	44.7	19.8	8.4
Lesotho	666	...	...	...	...	...	...	...	...	...	...	...	...	...	...	...
Liberia	668	...	...	...	...	...	...	...	...	...	...	-2.5	42.1	12.1	24.7	4.9
Madagascar	674	11.4	5.0	9.1	11.6	6.4	10.6	10.1	9.0	6.5	9.7	13.0	6.4	20.0	21.5	22.1
Malawi	676	...	20.0	11.3	9.6	11.4	13.8	17.5	16.0	26.5	31.6	15.7	-.3	21.4	13.0	15.0
Mali	678	7.8	13.8	13.5	8.7	-2.6	4.6	14.3	10.8	12.9	22.8	37.7	14.4	15.1	19.1	17.9
Mauritania	682	-6.3	20.4	24.9	12.6	24.5	15.1	23.1	5.4	20.7	56.2	44.1	15.5	12.2	-.4	36.7
Mauritius	684	-14.1	8.5	6.2	8.0	8.3	17.0	16.8	30.0	33.2	33.1	59.4	29.4	12.1	18.1	15.9
Morocco	686	3.0	1.6	6.0	11.1	14.5	9.2	8.3	15.8	16.0	22.9	22.2	20.4	20.4	13.8	17.7
Namibia	728	...	...	...	...	...	...	...	...	...	...	...	...	...	...	...
Niger	692	3.0	12.0	9.5	8.6	8.2	15.5	21.1	22.5	9.5	26.0	23.2	22.8	32.9	27.3	28.4
Nigeria	694	14.9	10.6	6.5	-12.4	32.4	43.1	22.6	10.7	20.4	54.1	76.5	56.2	31.6	12.3	18.6
Rwanda	714	29.4	7.7	17.0	20.4	1.6	25.2	13.7	4.8	27.4	29.8	23.2	20.3	27.4	18.3	19.4
Senegal	722	3.8	-2.3	-3.0	2.4	6.1	7.8	10.0	16.7	7.3	36.8	29.7	31.0	17.8	10.0	19.5
Seychelles	718	...	...	...	...	...	...	...	42.9	11.2	3.5	29.9	44.9	37.3	14.1	13.6
Sierra Leone	724	10.9	2.9	3.7	16.5	21.4	4.6	-1.8	14.2	25.9	20.8	9.7	12.9	26.2	32.3	25.6
Somalia	726	-7.3	6.0	13.1	12.4	12.6	9.3	4.6	25.2	20.3	27.3	25.5	26.3	22.3	37.0	32.8
South Africa	199	16.0	8.7	8.5	14.1	12.5	8.0	6.0	12.0	25.7	19.3	21.8	13.0	7.4	13.6	13.8
Sudan	732	...	...	...	...	...	...	...	...	...	...	...	...	...	...	...
Swaziland	734	...	...	...	...	...	...	...	...	...	...	66.2	30.1	25.8	25.7	12.1
Tanzania	738	...	...	-7.3	14.3	18.1	12.4	19.4	17.4	18.6	22.8	23.0	26.3	22.5	15.2	36.0
Togo	742	16.9	16.0	10.6	24.0	24.3	21.8	7.8	5.2	3.4	64.5	21.2	7.9	40.4	25.2	21.8
Tunisia	744	5.5	15.0	5.0	10.5	9.6	9.5	14.4	19.2	17.0	24.8	24.0	18.0	14.3	16.2	16.9
Uganda	746	...	...	...	...	...	...	...	...	...	...	...	...	...	...	...
Zaïre	636	21.1	20.0	31.5	46.5	24.8	9.9	17.6	11.2	28.4	46.8	8.9	30.3	50.9	52.6	51.2
Zambia	754	...	...	...	...	...	...	...	...	...	...	...	...	...	...	...
Zimbabwe	698	...	...	...	...	...	...	...	...	...	...	...	...	...	...	...
Asia																
Afghanistan, Islamic State of	512	23.4	6.6	9.0	4.5	14.3	13.0	7.4	16.1	2.3	9.1	14.8	15.3	32.8	19.4	15.2
Bangladesh	513	...	...	...	...	...	...	...	...	...	...	3.2	14.5	22.0	23.7	23.5
Bhutan	514	...	...	...	...	...	...	...	...	...	...	...	...	...	...	...
China, People' Rep.	924	...	...	...	...	...	...	...	...	...	...	...	...	...	.1	43.1
Fiji	819	-8.3	6.5	5.3	9.8	17.3	12.3	24.6	16.3	17.6	28.5	37.6	16.9	8.9	13.0	16.1
India	534	11.9	11.4	9.2	10.2	12.5	11.5	15.4	15.5	18.7	15.7	12.4	18.1	20.2	20.4	21.2
Indonesia	536	...	...	...	...	95.1	51.7	43.1	48.5	47.0	48.9	37.4	34.0	24.9	17.5	29.5
Korea	542	28.1	63.4	63.2	65.5	70.9	33.6	27.2	24.7	39.4	26.8	27.1	29.5	37.4	37.5	26.7
Malaysia	548	...	...	...	...	...	...	...	...	...	...	...	...	...	...	...
Maldives	556	...	...	...	...	...	...	...	...	...	...	...	...	.2	-15.1	43.0
Mongolia	948	...	...	...	...	...	...	...	...	...	...	...	...	...	...	...
Myanmar	518	-26.2	-33.1	-6.1	-1.2	-3.0	204.7	2.2	13.5	20.1	20.3	25.3	13.3	4.9	9.0	17.4
Nepal	558	24.3	13.2	8.7	18.3	21.3	17.9	14.0	18.0	21.8	25.2	10.4	21.0	26.6	18.3	17.3
Pakistan	564	14.3	17.0	10.8	9.9	10.6	10.0	11.6	17.3	17.6	—	14.5	25.3	22.6	21.3	21.3
Papua New Guinea	853	...	...	...	...	...	...	...	...	...	62.9	7.5	-18.7	48.6	14.5	25.5
Philippines	566	5.2	14.1	19.2	15.0	10.7	11.5	17.8	8.5	22.1	22.6	8.2	18.6	27.5	28.6	16.0
Singapore	576	5.8	14.7	15.6	22.0	21.9	18.1	15.7	20.0	21.1	13.9	17.4	14.8	7.6	9.9	10.9
Solomon Islands	813	...	...	...	...	...	...	...	...	...	...	...	...	...	...	46.6

Money plus Quasi-Money

1980	1981	1982	1983	1984	1985	1986	1987	1988	1989	1990	1991	1992	1993	1994		
Percent Change over Previous Year																
															Industrial Countries	
9.5	10.0	10.8	12.7	9.5	10.4	9.4	6.2	6.5	4.6	7.6	4.7	2.0	.9	1.3	United States	111
14.0	11.4	13.9	.9	2.4	5.6	6.1	9.5	9.8	11.4	9.8	7.2	6.9	11.7	8.6	Canada	156
12.9	12.2	12.0	13.0	12.1	17.9	13.4	12.7	14.3	−26.3	15.8	5.6	4.7	6.9	7.8	Australia	193
7.9	8.8	9.1	6.6	6.8	7.8	9.1	10.2	11.2	10.0	12.1	4.1	1.2	1.4	2.3	Japan	158
15.2	13.8	12.0	10.8	13.7	26.3	21.3	31.6	−15.9	−7.1	64.6	29.8	13.3	5.3	....	New Zealand	196
9.5	11.4	11.0	8.6	3.9	6.8	6.9	8.8	6.7	6.9	7.2	8.4	7.6	6.8	5.8	Austria	122
4.0	6.0	7.1	5.2	8.4	4.5	7.6	10.4	7.3	7.1	7.3	....	....	....	....	Belgium	124
8.7	12.2	10.3	19.3	23.4	15.3	14.7	4.5	−1.9	4.0	6.0	8.8	3.4	6.8	5.8	Denmark	128
15.9	15.3	15.0	13.7	13.4	17.3	13.5	10.7	14.1	18.3	8.6	5.5	1.6	.1	3.1	Finland	172
11.0	11.1	11.2	9.8	10.0	7.8	8.5	6.6	5.6	2.5	3.4	.6	.4	2.2	....	France	132
3.5	4.8	6.1	6.7	4.8	5.3	6.1	7.0	5.8	4.5	12.9	10.4	8.6	8.5	9.3	Germany	134
18.1	27.3	30.7	20.9	23.5	26.7	18.4	21.5	23.6	22.1	18.5	7.4	12.4	4.1	....	Greece	174
55.2	78.5	58.0	76.9	49.3	41.6	43.9	36.0	26.0	26.5	25.5	12.2	9.1	4.4	5.5	Iceland	176
12.1	19.2	12.9	9.8	8.8	7.3	9.0	13.2	13.0	6.5	12.6	10.6	14.2	18.3	....	Ireland	178
13.9	11.4	12.7	16.7	12.1	13.6	7.9	10.0	7.0	8.5	9.0	8.7	8.2	8.3	....	Italy	136
19.1	11.3	.7	.8	9.8	12.0	7.8	12.3	14.4	20.6	16.7	13.4	9.0	....	....	Luxembourg	137
8.5	8.5	8.8	22.8	6.2	6.1	5.7	3.8	3.2	8.8	9.0	5.3	5.3	4.9	3.0	Netherlands	138
11.7	12.7	10.8	10.4	14.3	17.0	9.4	22.8	7.6	8.4	7.7	4.1	4.8	6.5	....	Norway	142
31.5	29.5	23.6	18.9	20.4	25.8	20.5	18.1	14.3	12.5	13.1	20.8	24.9	16.8	8.7	Portugal	182
17.4	15.3	17.1	15.7	4.7	9.0	20.6	7.6	10.4	13.2	13.2	13.9	10.0	7.4	8.3	Spain	184
....	....	....	....	4.0	3.7	13.0	10.2	7.8	9.3	....	....	....	....	....	Sweden	144
6.8	4.3	3.3	8.5	7.4	5.9	2.5	9.2	8.5	5.8	1.7	2.6	2.2	5.5	8.1	Switzerland	146
15.0	21.8	18.4	13.3	10.8	12.8	20.8	24.0	15.2	18.8	15.7	8.0	1.3	5.6	....	United Kingdom	112
															Developing Countries	
															Africa	
20.2	17.3	20.5	22.7	26.6	9.3	8.7	8.0	15.7	8.9	5.5	17.9	19.0	20.6	19.2	Algeria	612
22.7	31.0	33.8	−1.6	14.1	−3.1	8.7	−4.4	−7.6	.3	25.0	15.4	13.4	6.7	15.0	Benin	638
31.2	10.4	−1.5	12.6	28.6	23.9	33.5	38.4	35.5	38.3	12.0	20.0	17.8	6.9	12.2	Botswana	616
9.4	23.1	12.3	8.8	18.3	−.3	18.6	20.8	14.7	7.2	2.4	2.1	4.2	4.5	17.9	Burkina Faso	748
28.1	24.9	8.5	11.3	14.2	12.8	8.2	2.2	6.2	17.0	11.1	....	....	....	....	Burundi	618
....	....	....	....	....	....	....	....	....	5.1	3.2	1.2	−2.8	−26.2	12.0	Cameroon	622
13.9	25.6	28.2	19.5	6.7	23.4	24.2	17.3	10.4	14.5	14.7	16.0	13.9	11.8	17.1	Cape Verde	624
....	....	....	....	....	....	....	....	....	11.0	−1.1	−7.3	−2.4	5.6	51.3	Central African Rep.	626
−15.2	17.6	12.7	8.8	53.3	32.1	−1.5	−.3	8.0	−10.6	7.9	6.7	−10.3	−11.9	22.9	Chad	628
....	....	....	48.3	8.4	−8.0	11.4	15.7	13.3	14.4	9.4	1.7	3.1	....	....	Comoros	632
....	....	....	....	....	....	....	....	....	2.9	12.1	9.1	−1.6	−19.3	11.4	Congo	634
4.2	4.2	6.7	4.1	6.9	22.7	8.1	−2.5	1.9	−1.2	−9.5	−1.8	.9	−5.0	29.7	Côte d'Ivoire	662
....	....	....	....	17.7	8.3	2.7	10.3	.4	.4	4.4	6.6	−3.5	−1.9	3.8	Djibouti	611
....	....	....	....	....	47.8	4.8	−8.4	−32.0	−31.6	−16.9	−3.1	.5	68.6	....	Equatorial Guinea	642
11.5	4.8	10.3	14.9	10.1	13.2	14.4	8.9	8.6	10.7	15.8	19.5	14.8	14.9	14.5	Ethiopia	644
19.3	18.1	17.3	14.7	14.5	19.8	.8	−16.4	−3.9	3.3	5.1	7.2	−3.0	−16.2	23.2	Gabon	646
−.5	9.3	22.6	26.4	10.1	28.5	25.3	38.9	16.9	14.8	15.2	14.1	12.8	15.3	4.4	Gambia, The	648
35.8	36.3	33.1	46.7	33.4	43.7	52.1	56.9	44.2	57.2	27.5	12.1	34.8	39.9	33.7	Ghana	652
....	....	....	....	....	....	....	....	....	....	....	....	....	23.8	1.9	Guinea	656
....	....	....	....	....	....	....	142.3	74.6	36.8	56.0	58.8	69.7	60.9	42.4	Guinea-Bissau	654
11.2	9.1	10.4	9.7	10.4	11.2	24.1	18.3	5.9	15.3	14.0	18.7	29.3	30.6	....	Kenya	664
....	14.5	30.5	21.3	14.7	18.8	17.9	17.0	18.1	17.6	8.7	10.6	5.1	23.2	20.1	Lesotho	666
−10.7	−25.6	21.6	13.9	8.8	11.3	20.1	14.1	7.8	20.7	.4	9.3	13.1	73.8	19.4	Liberia	668
23.4	17.5	22.2	−7.5	8.6	17.2	30.4	17.8	18.3	26.4	21.5	17.0	20.4	27.2	40.2	Madagascar	674
6.2	17.6	18.4	8.2	19.5	13.5	8.3	37.4	22.4	19.4	7.8	22.9	14.0	29.6	34.4	Malawi	676
8.6	3.3	7.7	15.5	25.1	25.7	.6	3.4	6.1	7.8	−5.0	2.1	10.4	4.6	32.1	Mali	678
−4.0	29.7	14.8	5.2	3.9	19.4	16.3	20.3	4.9	−1.0	4.5	10.3	12.2	5.1	....	Mauritania	682
14.0	12.2	16.7	17.4	11.1	23.7	30.7	32.2	29.4	19.1	19.9	21.3	19.7	14.5	16.4	Mauritius	684
11.3	10.5	21.8	15.5	11.6	11.7	17.8	10.7	10.6	14.2	13.6	17.7	12.1	7.8	11.3	Morocco	686
....	....	....	....	....	....	....	....	....	....	....	30.2	27.6	27.3	31.5	Namibia	728
29.0	22.1	−1.1	−12.1	17.5	18.1	5.6	3.3	6.9	6.3	−2.1	−2.2	−8.0	−2.1	18.3	Niger	692
30.8	19.8	8.8	13.3	13.3	10.5	5.9	7.7	32.9	22.5	21.8	42.8	....	....	....	Nigeria	694
12.6	12.0	4.1	6.1	12.1	13.3	13.0	14.1	9.3	1.6	.5	6.4	8.1	9.0	....	Rwanda	714
5.7	5.4	25.9	13.9	3.1	3.5	5.5	10.3	5.3	2.5	3.7	−.8	5.2	−8.8	16.7	Senegal	722
26.6	15.2	−5.1	−.6	5.4	16.3	8.3	13.6	13.5	21.4	12.6	11.8	9.9	18.9	9.0	Seychelles	718
15.3	8.6	28.2	40.7	25.8	56.1	78.6	102.5	45.0	59.7	68.8	76.6	53.5	29.1	13.2	Sierra Leone	724
26.6	33.6	16.1	1.0	45.5	46.4	43.9	50.5	106.5	112.4	....	....	....	....	....	Somalia	726
20.1	25.0	14.8	16.8	16.6	19.3	8.4	10.2	33.3	38.5	18.5	....	....	....	....	South Africa	199
....	....	....	....	....	....	....	....	....	....	....	....	....	82.6	87.2	Sudan	732
10.1	9.9	10.9	16.0	26.4	17.5	12.2	18.2	27.9	31.9	16.5	9.5	13.7	14.0	17.5	Swaziland	734
29.7	22.8	19.3	19.1	11.3	14.0	28.6	29.2	30.4	40.2	39.8	40.6	23.1	29.1	....	Tanzania	738
5.2	27.3	30.0	−.5	6.6	15.4	11.8	9.6	−9.3	−2.6	4.0	7.9	−8.4	−22.0	22.0	Togo	742
16.3	24.5	16.1	16.8	16.7	13.1	8.0	9.9	17.3	17.6	15.3	2.6	9.2	3.6	9.3	Tunisia	744
....	....	....	....	....	....	....	....	....	....	....	....	....	36.9	....	Uganda	746
26.3	47.0	55.7	261.4	−29.9	35.1	36.7	82.6	99.0	105.9	94.1	1,171.1	4,987.5	1,716.5	11,860.6	Zaïre	636
....	....	....	....	....	....	....	....	....	....	69.1	53.4	89.1	....	....	Zambia	754
....	19.0	21.0	7.8	9.4	10.5	10.5	8.7	24.2	23.2	18.4	18.9	1.3	39.0	54.7	Zimbabwe	698
															Asia	
22.1	15.4	18.5	15.6	13.6	9.8	11.4	22.8	52.3	36.4	38.6	....	....	....	....	Afghanistan, Islamic State of	512
19.6	24.0	11.7	31.9	38.6	22.4	18.6	17.0	15.4	17.0	15.2	11.7	14.0	11.9	15.5	Bangladesh	513
....	....	....	....	12.4	26.7	7.7	16.0	20.1	13.5	19.2	21.1	19.1	16.1	25.2	Bhutan	514
24.8	21.8	14.1	14.5	21.4	40.4	89.2	30.7	25.8	16.3	26.2	29.1	28.8	25.7	....	China, People' Rep.	924
18.1	10.8	6.1	11.8	9.0	8.7	8.8	10.7	13.6	11.9	21.6	17.3	16.6	8.5	5.4	Fiji	819
16.0	18.5	13.5	17.0	18.1	17.6	16.9	17.4	17.0	17.8	17.9	16.2	19.8	14.9	....	India	534
46.3	29.3	24.7	21.6	25.6	25.4	22.9	20.1	25.5	29.3	46.8	24.2	20.6	....	....	Indonesia	536
25.9	26.4	28.9	19.7	10.3	11.8	17.5	18.2	18.1	18.3	21.7	19.6	19.2	17.7	15.2	Korea	542
....	....	....	....	....	....	....	....	....	....	....	....	....	21.4	22.4	Malaysia	548
37.4	17.3	.5	−3.1	19.6	31.4	30.5	19.3	11.7	12.6	21.9	21.3	20.9	21.6	....	Maldives	556
....	....	....	....	....	....	....	....	....	....	....	....	56.2	156.1	118.5	Mongolia	948
17.5	19.7	15.0	13.5	17.2	11.2	10.9	7.4	−12.3	35.1	34.0	37.2	35.9	....	....	Myanmar	518
18.2	18.3	19.5	20.3	15.4	17.9	21.9	17.3	22.3	22.8	18.9	20.2	22.6	22.8	....	Nepal	558
18.4	12.9	14.9	23.5	10.1	13.0	14.8	14.9	12.1	5.7	12.4	15.0	24.6	24.5	16.0	Pakistan	564
11.4	−6.1	3.5	6.5	16.4	9.7	13.8	6.0	6.0	2.3	5.4	9.1	18.8	12.4	....	Papua New Guinea	853
17.4	18.9	25.4	17.9	23.6	9.7	1.4	13.0	21.3	27.8	25.7	20.9	12.8	18.7	23.8	Philippines	566
27.9	21.8	14.3	16.3	9.4	3.6	7.8	17.4	12.8	22.8	21.9	14.3	11.7	6.2	11.6	Singapore	576
14.7	−11.6	5.4	18.2	38.3	5.8	12.3	19.9	33.9	13.4	4.8	22.9	19.1	22.6	21.1	Solomon Islands	813

Money plus Quasi-Money

351 x

Percent Change over Previous Year

		1965	1966	1967	1968	1969	1970	1971	1972	1973	1974	1975	1976	1977	1978	1979
Asia (cont.)																
Sri Lanka	524	6.7	4.5	3.3	12.3	7.2	-5.1	10.9	6.5	7.6	17.3	3.2	21.8	35.0	34.3	31.3
Thailand	578	10.3	23.1	18.1	1.8	13.0	11.2	16.1	20.2	24.7	20.9	18.4	18.4	20.4	19.2	15.8
Tonga	866	....	....	....	....	....	....	....	....	....	....	-5.7	16.4	110.7	26.3	8.9
Vanuatu	846	....	....	....	....	....	....	....	....	....	....	....	....	7.9	1.1	3.2
Western Samoa	862	-8.9	3.3	2.4	14.5	14.6	8.3	26.6	11.4	19.5	28.4	8.6	25.7	14.1	11.7	31.7
Europe																
Cyprus	423	12.2	9.8	11.1	11.4	15.9	9.9	15.3	20.9	17.1	14.0	3.7	13.4	17.4	14.5	18.3
Czech Republic	935															
Czechoslovakia	934															
Estonia	939															
Malta	181	4.5	10.4	9.6	12.4	16.4	10.6	15.2	10.3	7.8	9.8	13.1	24.8	15.3	11.8	12.6
Moldova	921															
Poland	964															
Romania	968												24.0	12.4	16.7	14.4	18.4	15.3
Slovak Republic	936															
Slovenia	961															
Turkey	186	20.4	19.5	15.9	15.5	17.0	14.4	28.2	27.3	27.6	27.3	25.3	27.6	32.8	44.7	56.7
Yugoslavia, SFR	188	33.3	27.1	14.8	21.2	23.2	21.2	23.4	20.0	31.1	25.5	25.0	36.8	26.9	25.5	24.6
Middle East																
Bahrain	419	....	22.9	19.3	12.2	19.5	13.3	25.4	25.3	8.2	29.5	39.4	45.4	41.2	18.4	5.8
Egypt	469	6.0	5.8	1.7	1.6	5.4	7.5	3.8	10.2	20.4	28.0	21.4	27.5	26.5	28.7	29.3
Iran, I.R. of	429	17.6	11.9	15.0	19.0	17.5	18.6	17.7	31.1	34.4	28.3	47.4	41.2	31.7	28.9	26.3
Iraq	433	8.2	10.9	4.1	10.6	13.6	10.4	4.4	11.1	20.1	33.2	43.1	24.4	....	....	....
Israel	436	11.2	13.2	29.5	23.8	14.7	13.7	26.5	29.5	21.6	22.1	57.8	33.4	50.8	6.7	55.7
Jordan	439	16.8	18.2	18.6	17.9	11.0	7.6	8.8	4.1	17.4	21.5	25.4	40.5	24.2	28.6	28.0
Kuwait	443	9.6	28.4	21.1	9.8	9.0	-7.4	8.5	21.4	10.3	25.2	19.7	39.7	29.0	25.3	18.7
Lebanon	446	20.5	17.7	-2.4	6.3	.8	8.2	22.6	21.4	19.7	21.9	27.3	6.7	8.7	26.2	22.8
Libya	672	37.0	41.6	22.3	26.5	31.3	21.4	42.3	35.9	30.3	66.8	10.7	18.8	26.8	20.9	20.0
Oman	449						....				.2	60.7	53.7	26.6	33.3	14.0	9.1
Qatar	453	....	....	20.8	8.3	18.2	5.3	27.3	25.4	35.8	23.8	45.4	63.6	45.8	16.1	9.2
Saudi Arabia	456	11.8	15.2	15.4	13.1	7.8	5.9	11.6	25.2	37.6	40.0	62.4	84.0	53.2	44.3	14.8
Syrian Arab Rep.	463	14.0	11.9	12.3	20.5	14.5	10.5	11.1	15.8	22.9	44.6	28.0	24.3	25.5	27.5	20.6
United Arab Emirates	466											171.2	45.5	68.8	35.8	-.1	3.2
Yemen, Republic of	474															
Western Hemisphere																
Antigua and Barbuda	311												8.4	-4.2	10.7	15.4
Argentina	213										146.9	76.2	70.0	321.7	263.6	207.2	167.3
Bahamas, The	313						11.6	-6.5	5.8	4.5	12.2	-2.4	19.3	4.2	7.8	17.7
Barbados	316	....	....	19.4	30.2	12.0	17.8	13.8	13.1	9.2	5.1	20.6	8.1	11.5	20.4	22.4
Belize	339													2.4	11.9	18.2
Bolivia	218	22.3	23.7	10.9	13.3	16.0	13.2	16.4	24.5	32.5	39.8	33.5	38.0	42.6	19.7	11.3
Brazil	223	75.9	51.7	46.4	49.8	34.2	30.3	35.0	34.3	23.5	30.7	34.1	44.4	49.3	62.0	65.4
Chile	228	....	....	....	....	40.1	47.7	85.3	91.9	257.9	305.7	390.9	413.7	136.6	93.8	66.5
Colombia	233	14.8	15.3	22.1	19.2	20.9	19.9	10.5	19.5	28.6	29.0	10.9	29.9	36.5	-82.9	23.4
Costa Rica	238	6.8	2.8	19.1	17.5	11.0	9.5	13.0	31.0	21.2	27.9	37.9	35.5	36.2	26.8	29.4
Dominica	321												12.7	8.7	17.4	41.6
Dominican Republic	243	2.5	3.9	-1.3	8.2	14.3	28.2	14.4	20.7	32.8	34.2	30.5	.1	13.6	10.7	-.5
Ecuador	248	.5	12.3	16.5	21.3	12.7	20.0	21.0	17.2	29.6	40.1	21.5	11.8	36.3	12.3	21.7
El Salvador	253	5.8	6.7	5.9	.3	5.8	10.0	7.2	15.6	19.9	22.3	17.0	23.5	31.5	2.9	11.0
Grenada	328							6.4	18.7	3.0	-1.8	18.6	22.7	14.3	20.8	12.3
Guatemala	258	9.0	13.1	6.0	12.9	8.4	11.7	5.3	18.3	25.0	18.5	16.9	27.8	22.3	14.1	11.6
Guyana	336	15.5	7.6	9.7	11.2	12.2	7.4	11.3	18.9	16.9	15.6	29.7	20.6	16.3	25.0	4.2
Haiti	263	-3.1	.7	3.2	9.3	12.0	12.0	20.8	22.3	27.9	26.3	14.0	40.9	26.6	20.7	11.2
Honduras	268	13.9	11.8	5.4	18.3	15.8	18.0	10.7	10.4	20.4	11.3	3.1	24.2	28.4	16.2	17.8
Jamaica	343	8.3	10.9	12.9	22.2	21.7	16.1	20.2	17.9	12.0	7.8	23.2	11.7	15.7	13.4	16.6
Mexico	273	11.6	8.8	11.3	11.8	13.3	10.2	7.3	13.5	23.0	25.7	16.6	45.7	38.0	33.2	32.8
Netherlands Antilles	353	....	....	....	....	5.3	20.6	17.3	18.2	13.8	16.8	13.6	18.1	10.3	10.3	7.8
Nicaragua	278	27.2	17.5	5.9	2.1	4.6	-4.4	16.5	31.2	39.8	23.6	-3.5	26.4	20.8	-8.4	4.2
Paraguay	288	20.3	4.9	12.1	8.6	2.0	9.9	18.5	17.3	32.2	21.5	21.5	24.6	34.1	30.1	27.5
Peru	293	25.8	17.0	7.7	11.0	8.5	27.8	20.0	15.8	24.5	25.9	25.2	19.1	22.5	43.2	79.4
St. Kitts and Nevis	361															
St. Lucia	362												22.3	5.9	19.7	17.5
St. Vincent & Grens.	364												18.4	9.9	27.5	23.3
Suriname	366	....	....	....	14.1	17.1	10.6	13.6	14.8	20.1	12.7	12.4	31.3	23.1	18.1	12.6
Trinidad and Tobago	369	-1.1	10.6	9.1	10.5	16.9	18.6	19.2	21.0	18.9	16.4	33.1	33.8	27.0	26.5	25.6
Uruguay	298	....	61.2	42.7	89.2	59.8	30.3	33.6	58.2	60.6	77.4	75.6	84.6	77.3	76.8	102.0
Venezuela	299	11.3	7.0	5.8	12.2	9.3	10.9	10.5	20.9	19.1	28.4	46.7	33.4	31.4	15.8	10.0

Money plus Quasi-Money

1980	1981	1982	1983	1984	1985	1986	1987	1988	1989	1990	1991	1992	1993	1994		
Percent Change over Previous Year																351 x
															Asia (cont.)	
27.3	28.8	35.1	16.2	19.5	14.8	6.1	11.6	14.4	14.0	17.7	19.1	20.6	20.2	20.5	Sri Lanka	524
19.3	18.3	20.4	25.2	21.1	15.6	11.3	16.1	18.5	23.3	29.2	20.2	18.2	16.1	13.0	Thailand	578
16.0	6.1	30.9	10.3	16.8	21.4	17.5	24.5	1.7	5.3	8.2	13.9	12.5	-.1	12.4	Tonga	866
-12.9	.4	49.6	20.1	23.2	20.0	14.3	13.3	-10.4	30.4	33.2	-.8	-1.8	7.5	-.1	Vanuatu	846
50.4	41.2	44.7	9.1	-10.0	29.2	15.5	28.8	13.2	12.1	20.5	.7	5.9	-.2	6.1	Western Samoa	862
															Europe	
15.5	18.3	18.4	13.7	13.6	11.1	10.6	11.9	15.6	16.1	17.7	15.3	15.2	13.8	15.4	Cyprus	423
....	....	....	....	....	....	....	....	....	....	....	....	....	....	20.3	Czech Republic	935
....	7.5	8.3	6.4	6.8	4.3	3.7	6.0	6.7	6.3	3.8	10.7	27.6	....	....	Czechoslovakia	934
....	....	....	....	....	....	....	....	....	....	....	....	....	....	52.0	Estonia	939
10.5	9.1	8.8	6.7	8.0	5.9	5.0	9.0	9.0	10.2	10.7	9.7	10.4	9.5	13.5	Malta	181
....	....	....	....	....	....	....	....	....	....	....	....	310.4	433.7	172.4	Moldova	921
13.0	23.0	37.3	14.5	18.5	21.0	26.7	34.6	50.1	238.8	384.3	67.5	49.7	42.6	35.3	Poland	964
-4.8	49.7	13.0	5.8	3.4	8.4	6.0	4.9	1.4	10.8	18.6	35.2	96.3	131.5	137.9	Romania	968
....	....	....	....	....	....	....	....	....	....	....	....	....	....	17.9	Slovak Republic	936
....	....	....	....	....	....	....	....	....	....	....	....	123.2	78.9	48.4	Slovenia	961
65.1	87.3	74.4	37.1	55.6	65.7	41.2	49.4	57.1	74.8	61.3	66.5	88.3	66.8	122.4	Turkey	186
33.4	32.3	31.8	38.2	36.4	57.2	71.6	95.5	192.1	1,015.2	417.1	....	....	....	....	Yugoslavia, SFR	188
															Middle East	
11.6	25.8	27.7	10.3	3.5	1.6	3.3	1.1	4.8	7.8	.8	.2	11.9	7.1	3.2	Bahrain	419
24.1	28.5	32.6	26.7	20.0	18.3	27.7	12.8	25.6	17.8	22.8	28.0	15.2	15.9	11.7	Egypt	469
31.7	21.4	19.5	20.5	10.3	13.4	13.0	19.3	19.6	22.4	18.1	23.4	25.1	27.1	....	Iran, I.R. of	429
....	....	....	....	....	....	....	....	....	....	....	....	....	....	....	Iraq	433
108.6	875.5	140.3	150.3	414.4	319.1	46.9	27.4	20.0	23.7	19.4	19.2	15.7	27.2	24.7	Israel	436
25.9	23.3	19.4	16.2	11.4	7.2	9.4	12.6	14.4	17.6	13.5	6.5	9.9	10.7	4.6	Jordan	439
27.4	26.5	24.3	2.0	2.5	4.5	-1.0	3.2	4.6	9.3	-.4	2.7	-4.8	6.4	6.3	Kuwait	443
29.7	37.3	29.8	22.7	18.7	51.6	88.1	314.2	105.1	36.5	43.2	50.3	108.8	34.2	36.0	Lebanon	446
23.0	30.1	-6.3	-3.0	.2	11.6	9.8	-.9	-1.3	-1.3	12.0	15.2	-.8	....	....	Libya	672
25.9	31.1	32.5	21.5	15.9	21.8	-.1	.2	4.2	8.3	10.6	9.3	5.1	4.4	2.9	Oman	449
24.1	30.6	20.1	2.1	12.7	11.1	13.9	10.4	-.4	-.1	8.2	-8.5	11.1	7.7	10.0	Qatar	453
17.2	23.7	28.9	17.5	5.7	2.4	3.1	6.9	6.2	4.7	3.0	8.5	....	....	-1.5	Saudi Arabia	456
26.4	28.1	15.2	24.9	26.2	17.8	16.2	14.0	16.9	20.1	22.7	33.0	26.2	....	....	Syrian Arab Rep.	463
16.5	25.3	22.4	15.0	18.4	12.2	6.8	4.9	5.7	6.3	2.8	2.1	6.9	1.0	....	United Arab Emirates	466
....	....	....	....	....	....	....	....	....	....	....	....	15.7	15.4	25.0	Yemen, Republic of	474
															Western Hemisphere	
14.4	12.0	14.4	21.1	24.4	12.5	17.3	15.7	13.7	12.7	9.0	12.3	7.4	7.8	12.9	Antigua and Barbuda	311
127.9	63.5	142.3	287.4	567.2	687.2	133.0	133.4	345.5	2,347.3	1,065.8	251.2	78.6	51.1	....	Argentina	213
13.0	12.5	14.3	14.4	10.9	5.7	7.3	13.9	12.2	8.0	16.8	6.1	6.4	9.6	14.4	Bahamas, The	313
17.5	15.8	8.9	8.1	8.5	8.9	9.9	9.8	12.2	9.1	5.7	4.8	1.8	8.0	4.2	Barbados	316
4.3	15.9	1.4	18.2	5.7	6.3	17.0	18.1	13.4	9.2	14.2	14.6	11.2	6.8	6.9	Belize	339
31.8	23.2	146.1	163.1	568.6	8,028.1	532.1	108.8	24.6	19.5	53.1	52.5	38.4	32.4	28.9	Bolivia	218
60.6	64.1	111.6	135.1	268.5	325.8	297.8	171.4	559.5	1,278.5	2,264.6	511.9	1,416.8	2,306.7	....	Brazil	223
60.1	49.1	24.3	27.6	25.1	42.3	33.8	30.2	29.2	26.4	27.7	24.7	27.5	22.9	....	Chile	228
28.6	41.9	30.6	18.2	24.2	21.2	39.0	32.1	22.5	26.0	22.2	20.1	45.1	38.7	35.8	Colombia	233
22.0	51.6	43.6	45.7	19.4	18.6	18.9	17.6	23.5	29.7	28.0	28.0	28.7	17.1	18.5	Costa Rica	238
27.8	4.4	3.0	20.7	12.2	8.0	8.6	27.8	5.2	8.6	18.0	18.7	12.8	2.3	3.6	Dominica	321
15.2	1.1	14.7	15.6	19.0	15.9	55.8	42.8	28.0	46.4	32.7	29.8	39.6	29.8	13.7	Dominican Republic	243
30.3	18.4	23.6	20.3	34.4	32.3	27.0	31.1	57.5	52.1	45.3	52.8	48.9	....	....	Ecuador	248
7.4	5.6	12.1	10.3	13.5	27.4	31.1	15.3	8.5	9.7	25.1	22.6	24.5	24.9	30.9	El Salvador	253
8.7	9.8	1.5	1.8	-4.8	20.8	25.6	13.9	18.6	11.1	8.0	7.7	8.9	18.5	12.3	Grenada	328
8.0	10.5	18.1	4.1	7.0	14.5	31.9	14.0	15.6	15.9	21.3	35.1	47.4	12.1	20.9	Guatemala	258
11.4	15.4	20.7	24.8	19.0	18.3	24.7	31.5	36.0	46.6	52.6	62.0	67.5	42.3	14.0	Guyana	336
14.0	21.2	5.2	6.6	14.0	6.9	8.3	11.9	32.5	2.1	.3	9.1	22.5	29.7	....	Haiti	263
2.6	8.1	9.9	21.4	16.7	2.0	5.0	15.8	20.1	11.9	19.9	21.7	18.4	18.9	19.8	Honduras	268
19.3	23.4	31.6	26.6	21.5	24.4	22.6	22.1	17.1	20.5	14.6	32.8	76.8	45.8	41.9	Jamaica	343
35.7	45.1	63.5	59.6	71.8	46.3	57.5	126.5	77.8	-10.2	104.1	72.4	34.7	21.4	18.2	Mexico	273
10.1	16.6	19.3	8.5	2.4	-4.4	-7.1	12.2	6.3	8.8	6.5	6.2	9.1	11.0	8.0	Netherlands Antilles	353
68.5	53.0	17.9	14.1	-40.4	141.5	235.2	548.7	12,186.2	4,967.1	4,697.4	4,040.7	78.9	18.9	40.2	Nicaragua	278
25.8	23.4	11.5	10.9	20.6	19.1	18.5	41.5	26.6	38.1	52.3	57.0	34.0	34.3	24.9	Paraguay	288
95.4	67.4	70.8	89.0	113.5	164.8	83.1	79.1	271.0	2,081.3	4,825.2	628.3	107.2	98.5	46.0	Peru	293
14.2	17.3	19.6	11.3	14.8	13.9	19.9	-9.3	2.9	23.4	10.8	8.4	12.4	13.1	1.9	St. Kitts and Nevis	361
6.0	21.9	9.0	10.2	14.1	16.7	24.5	20.1	5.1	19.2	11.7	11.4	6.7	1.8	4.2	St. Lucia	362
9.9	14.4	17.1	10.1	12.7	12.3	17.9	7.0	-2.9	20.4	12.1	4.7	3.8	7.4	8.6	St. Vincent & Grens.	364
10.2	13.5	14.5	12.2	14.1	28.4	30.3	24.6	26.4	20.9	4.6	19.4	21.6	36.5	....	Suriname	366
21.6	20.8	33.0	17.6	6.7	2.0	-1.2	1.7	2.1	4.0	4.5	5.9	-4.2	5.3	10.8	Trinidad and Tobago	369
62.0	61.7	31.6	46.1	51.4	81.1	89.1	65.7	75.1	90.9	111.6	92.0	58.8	42.4	35.9	Uruguay	298
13.5	12.8	15.3	14.5	22.8	14.9	15.7	20.6	16.6	35.2	49.7	56.9	25.1	21.8	83.5	Venezuela	299

Ratio of Reserve Money to Money plus Quasi-Money

39ab i

Percent

		1965	1966	1967	1968	1969	1970	1971	1972	1973	1974	1975	1976	1977	1978	1979
Industrial Countries																
United States	111	13.2	13.0	12.7	12.7	12.7	12.8	12.3	11.7	11.5	11.7	11.1	10.4	9.9	10.0	10.2
Canada	156	17.6	17.4	16.7	15.2	14.9	14.9	15.2	15.3	15.3	13.9	14.2	13.4	12.8	12.6	11.8
Australia	193	14.9	13.3	12.8	12.4	12.5	12.7	12.7	12.9	13.4	11.9	10.5	11.0	11.8	10.4	10.2
Japan	158	10.2	9.9	9.9	10.1	10.1	10.3	9.9	9.5	10.5	11.6	11.5	10.4	10.1	10.0	9.9
New Zealand	196	17.9	16.0	14.5	13.9	13.9	13.4	12.4	12.3	15.6	16.0	13.5	10.6	9.8	8.8	8.4
Austria	122	30.4	28.6	28.1	26.1	24.4	22.8	21.5	21.7	21.3	19.0	18.7	17.0	16.0	15.7	15.1
Belgium	124	43.3	41.7	38.9	36.7	34.6	32.8	31.4	30.0	29.6	28.2	26.7	25.2	24.7	24.6	24.3
Denmark	128	24.2	23.7	21.7	22.4	25.3	21.9	17.6	17.7	16.4	13.9	13.6	16.7	14.1	12.7	12.7
Finland	172	10.6	10.3	10.5	10.0	8.3	7.9	7.7	7.4	7.3	7.2	6.8	6.6	6.3	6.5	7.7
France	132	26.6	25.2	23.7	21.5	I20.6	18.6	17.4	16.3	17.6	16.5	12.1	10.2	9.8	9.4	9.3
Germany	134	24.2	23.0	20.0	18.8	18.3	18.9	20.5	21.0	23.4	21.4	19.4	19.0	19.3	18.8	19.1
Greece	174	46.8	47.6	47.5	46.1	42.4	38.8	36.7	37.1	38.8	38.9	36.7	35.3	35.5	34.6	32.8
Iceland	176	31.0	29.9	29.5	29.1	30.2	30.5	29.2	29.5	29.6	29.2	30.7	32.2	35.3	34.7	35.9
Ireland	178	23.4	23.2e	23.5	I22.4	23.0	28.9	30.3	31.2	32.9	32.9	33.7	32.9	32.0	31.5	32.5
Italy	136	....	....	....	....	....	....	....	....	....	....	28.3	26.7	25.9	25.0	23.9	22.2
Luxembourg	137															
Netherlands	138	25.2	25.3	23.8	21.2	20.1	18.7	17.5	16.8	15.8	13.8	13.5	12.7	12.3	11.7	11.3
Norway	142	25.8	25.4	25.8	24.0	22.1	20.9	20.1	19.2	18.0	18.2	18.6	17.9	16.9	17.2	16.6
Portugal	182	I33.3	31.9	30.7	30.2	29.2	27.1	26.3	25.4	24.2	24.1	28.5	30.5	27.5	25.8	24.5
Spain	184	31.7	30.9	31.2	28.8	26.6	25.5	26.2	25.4	24.7	23.8	24.0	23.7	23.1	24.2	27.5
Sweden	144															
Switzerland	146	25.0	23.7	23.3	22.1	20.3	19.4	21.7	23.0	22.4	21.0	20.0	19.0	18.0	19.3	18.6
United Kingdom	112	....	....	....	....	....	....	....	....	....	....	....	16.3	16.0	15.8	15.0
Developing Countries																
Africa																
Algeria	612	56.4	53.8	46.9	41.3	35.5	37.3	40.5	41.3	39.9	41.1	38.3	41.0	39.9	40.7	45.5
Benin	638	57.6	54.2	52.4	47.7	49.4	47.4	44.2	42.2	42.5	39.0	32.9	32.7	32.4	28.3	27.0
Botswana	616	....	....	....	....	....	....	....	....	....	....	....	35.2	32.7	31.4	33.5
Burkina Faso	748	66.7	68.9	68.1	63.2	61.8	60.3	58.1	53.8	50.4	48.3	48.2	46.5	44.5	37.5	36.0
Burundi	618	80.0	78.5	73.1	66.9	67.9	64.7	63.5	62.1	57.2	61.8	61.5	59.8	51.5	68.6	62.2
Cameroon	622															
Cape Verde	624	....	....	....	....	....	....	....	....	....	....	....	98.6	98.7	97.5	94.9
Central African Rep.	626															
Chad	628	73.1	71.1	68.7	63.5	60.8	61.6	62.8	68.4	61.2	61.6	67.3	69.1	66.0	61.4	74.7
Comoros	632															
Congo	634															
Côte d'Ivoire	662	52.9	55.0	53.4	51.2	45.4	44.3	43.2	46.7	44.5	39.6	41.6	39.2	35.8	36.4	36.2
Djibouti	611															
Equatorial Guinea	642															
Ethiopia	644	66.6	63.8	61.2	59.5	58.4	56.9	53.3	49.6	50.0	47.8	61.2	66.8	59.9	56.1	54.5
Gabon	646	4.6	4.4	3.5	3.3	3.3	3.4	3.4	3.4	3.3	3.8	3.3	3.2	3.4	26.3	28.5
Gambia, The	648	28.9	28.1	27.9	29.5	29.7	28.6	31.3	29.8	61.2	71.6	82.0	56.9	48.6	25.7	26.8
Ghana	652	42.7	52.8	39.4	42.0	46.2	47.0	43.0	46.7	50.2	52.0	55.6	60.8	62.3	65.3	66.4
Guinea	656															
Guinea-Bissau	654															
Kenya	664	....	22.1	27.8	30.5	35.9	39.5	31.4	29.2	31.4	26.0	24.5	24.4	28.8	25.0	24.9
Lesotho	666															
Liberia	668	....	....	....	....	....	....	....	....	....	16.9	18.3	15.2	16.2	22.3	20.4
Madagascar	674	56.8	56.1	52.9	50.8	48.3	49.0	48.3	47.5	46.9	47.5	48.0	54.5	47.7	50.3	47.9
Malawi	676	47.6	45.2	43.8	40.4	38.8	37.9	35.9	35.0	43.6	49.9	44.1	31.5	34.6	30.9	24.0
Mali	678	85.2	83.6	87.4	62.4	59.2	63.7	63.3	62.4	58.8	58.3	57.8	53.4	56.5	53.2	56.1
Mauritania	682	54.0	44.0	34.5	34.5	34.8	34.6	32.0	33.6	38.8	44.5	42.9	37.0	34.8	35.8	42.2
Mauritius	684	41.3	38.4	37.2	33.8	33.9	33.6	32.4	29.9	28.6	30.9	33.3	33.0	35.8	36.0	33.9
Morocco	686	37.3	38.4	37.8	38.3	39.7	40.3	40.2	40.0	39.5	37.0	36.0	36.1	36.5	36.7	36.1
Namibia	728															
Niger	692	50.1	56.6	55.9	48.5	46.3	48.1	43.2	43.6	45.5	44.7	46.8	46.8	47.8	43.8	45.6
Nigeria	694	51.3	49.8	51.1	43.2	44.1	45.5	43.6	41.7	38.5	42.4	53.9	55.3	46.4	44.4	45.7
Rwanda	714	69.1	77.0	76.9	75.1	77.2	80.9	77.9	78.1	76.0	76.7	68.0	60.6	63.7	57.5	54.8
Senegal	722	45.5	48.4	47.0	47.6	44.9	46.7	44.5	43.4	39.6	36.4	39.7	39.7	35.3	32.3	34.0
Seychelles	718	....	....	....	....	....	....	26.7	25.6	26.0	26.4	24.0	22.1	21.8	23.1	28.8
Sierra Leone	724	59.7	59.9	56.6	52.9	55.8	56.1	54.1	51.3	50.8	51.1	48.4	47.7	44.4	43.9	45.4	60.9
Somalia	726	60.3	63.2	64.9	61.6	69.1	83.3	61.1	55.9	53.7	50.9	50.5	51.7	51.7	57.4	54.3
South Africa	199	I18.5	19.0	18.6	17.7	18.4	18.4	18.5	17.6	15.7	15.9	15.1	15.0	14.4	13.7	13.6
Sudan	732															
Swaziland	734	....	....	....	....	....	....	....	....	....	9.0	16.6	35.0	43.3	46.9	37.7
Tanzania	738	....	40.2	39.0	36.2	33.9	37.2	38.8	39.5	37.6	34.8	33.7	31.9	31.4	31.0	30.3
Togo	742	56.1	54.0	50.3	48.8	43.4	40.2	40.2	42.9	43.4	37.1	40.2	46.8	46.3	42.4	41.6
Tunisia	744	33.3	32.9	32.2	31.7	33.2	31.6	31.7	32.7	31.9	31.2	30.5	29.8	27.5	27.2	26.7
Uganda	746															
Zaïre	636	80.0	79.2	73.2	70.2	72.7	70.1	64.2	59.1	52.7	47.1	54.5	64.0	64.1	62.8	65.1
Zambia	754															
Zimbabwe	698															
Asia																
Afghanistan, Islamic State of	512	81.7	78.5	71.0	76.0	76.2	77.8	76.3	73.7	76.7	75.7	76.9	77.6	80.2	82.1	82.9
Bangladesh	513	....	....	....	....	....	....	....	....	....	....	35.7	34.1	32.2	31.5	33.1	32.0
Bhutan	514															
China, People's Rep.	924															
Fiji	819	34.9	32.2	32.8	29.6	29.1	27.2	25.9	25.4	31.7	32.2	35.5	30.9	24.7	25.8	24.1
India	534	52.7	51.1	49.8	48.5	47.5	47.1	44.8	42.6	42.8	41.6	37.8	35.5	35.5	34.9	35.9
Indonesia	536	....	....	....	I106.0											
Korea	542	46.5	47.0	44.0	38.9	31.8	32.9	29.1	25.1	29.6	29.0	30.9	31.5	31.6	34.0	33.4
Malaysia	548															
Maldives	556	....	....	....	....	....	....	....	....	....	....	....	....	74.5	68.9	56.9	57.8
Mongolia	948															
Myanmar	518	125.8	184.9	192.0	201.7	224.3	83.2	86.7	101.4	99.0	115.8	107.6	98.1	91.8	92.2	90.7
Nepal	558	77.9	78.9	77.6	76.2	72.6	69.2	65.8	61.8	59.1	57.3	54.5	50.6	48.9	47.3	46.3
Pakistan	564	51.7	50.8	48.6	45.1	45.9	44.9	46.8	45.0	43.9	44.9	41.8	39.2	39.6	37.5	39.5
Papua New Guinea	853	....	....	....	....	....	....	....	....	....	32.5	25.4	38.1	53.4	58.9	52.1	47.9
Philippines	566	38.4	36.6	35.8	37.5	35.4	35.1	35.6	35.4	36.3	36.2	38.1	35.3	33.4	33.8	34.0
Singapore	576	35.9	35.2	30.0	25.1	24.2	24.3	23.7	24.0	28.2	27.6	26.2	27.1	28.9	29.9	30.7
Solomon Islands	813	....	....	....	....	....	....	....	....	....	....	....	....	....	39.8	80.0

Ratio of Reserve Money to Money plus Quasi-Money

1980	1981	1982	1983	1984	1985	1986	1987	1988	1989	1990	1991	1992	1993	1994	Country	Code
															Industrial Countries	
10.0	9.3	8.9	8.3	8.2	8.0	8.1	8.3	8.4	8.3	8.3	8.3	8.7	9.5	10.3	United States	111
11.1	10.7	9.6	9.7	9.6	9.5	9.6	9.3	8.8	8.4	7.9	7.7	7.6	7.0	6.3	Canada	156
9.7	9.6	9.4	9.0	9.0	8.8	8.6	8.3	8.0	10.3	8.8	8.6	8.5	8.5	8.5	Australia	193
10.2	9.4	9.2	9.1	9.1	8.9	8.7	8.8	8.8	8.9	8.7	8.4	8.2	8.3	8.5	Japan	158
8.2	6.8	6.4	7.1	6.5	5.7	4.6	3.7	4.9	6.1	3.6	2.8	2.5	2.4	....	New Zealand	196
14.8	13.9	13.5	13.3	13.1	12.5	12.3	11.7	11.6	11.5	11.0	10.7	10.6	10.3	10.5	Austria	122
23.5	22.8	21.7	20.9	19.6	18.6	17.7	16.7	15.8	14.7	13.7	....	....	....	....	Belgium	124
12.5	11.9	11.4	10.3	8.9	12.2	16.3	9.7	9.6	8.3	8.5	8.6	9.2	10.4	12.0	Denmark	128
9.7	9.3	8.7	9.7	11.7	12.1	10.3	13.3	14.8	14.4	15.1	11.0	14.0	13.3	17.5	Finland	172
8.7	9.0	9.0	8.9	8.8	8.9	8.9	8.9	8.7	8.9	8.6	8.3	7.2	6.9	....	France	132
18.8	17.5	17.5	16.9	16.7	16.5	16.2	16.5	17.0	17.5	16.8	17.1	17.0	16.0	14.6	Germany	134
32.0	36.5	38.4	36.6	36.9	35.2	32.1	32.0	29.2	25.9	25.6	26.5	26.7	27.6	....	Greece	174
36.1	38.7	37.4	33.7	32.3	27.1	26.0	22.9	21.5	21.1	16.1	13.5	13.1	10.7	9.3	Iceland	176
30.3	29.0	28.0	26.6	27.6	27.9	26.6	24.6	24.0	23.3	22.1	19.6	15.7	13.9	....	Ireland	178
22.0	22.6	23.1	23.2	23.6	24.4	24.8	25.1	25.3	25.8	26.1	25.4	24.7	21.0	....	Italy	136
....	....	....	—	—	.5	1.1	1.1	1.1	.9	.8	.8	.7	....	....	Luxembourg	137
11.4	10.9	10.4	9.5	9.6	9.6	9.3	9.5	10.2	10.8	10.5	10.1	10.2	11.0	12.0	Netherlands	138
15.6	14.5	13.9	12.9	12.0	11.1	10.9	10.0	9.5	9.2	7.9	7.6	8.1	8.1	....	Norway	142
23.4	24.1	26.6	27.5	24.1	21.2	17.8	17.9	18.0	29.7	32.8	32.1	30.2	28.5	24.7	Portugal	182
27.8	27.3	26.8	27.9	29.0	30.2	25.1	27.1	26.4	27.6	18.0	18.1	18.1	16.6	15.9	Spain	184
....	....	....	11.6	11.5	11.6	12.6	12.3	13.2	13.7	....	....	....	....	....	Sweden	144
16.3	15.1	14.7	14.3	13.6	13.1	13.1	12.5	10.2	9.2	8.9	8.8	8.7	9.4	8.8	Switzerland	146
13.4	11.6	10.0	9.4	7.8	7.2	6.3	5.3	5.0	4.5	4.1	3.9	3.9	3.9	....	United Kingdom	112
															Developing Countries	
															Africa	
47.0	45.4	37.7	37.7	35.0	35.7	38.1	40.2	37.9	38.8	41.2	40.1	37.3	36.3	34.2	Algeria	612
28.9	33.1	33.9	28.5	23.5	25.6	22.9	23.6	22.9	41.9	56.1	59.6	68.9	66.8	48.8	Benin	638
30.4	25.2	41.2	35.9	29.0	32.6	28.0	28.4	30.4	30.8	29.3	31.0	33.3	37.4	44.7	Botswana	616
40.3	39.1	40.7	44.7	57.8	62.3	60.7	65.0	66.2	58.8	50.9	57.5	62.6	67.6	64.3	Burkina Faso	748
51.0	52.6	46.3	46.8	47.3	49.7	51.7	51.3	48.4	42.5	38.4	....	....	....	....	Burundi	618
....	....	....	....	....	....	....	....	28.6	27.6	26.3	26.5	23.9	24.8	26.3	Cameroon	622
90.6	86.2	83.9	84.7	82.6	80.5	77.0	71.9	64.9	58.0	54.0	52.3	53.3	64.3	61.5	Cape Verde	624
....	....	....	....	....	....	....	....	70.0	68.3	68.0	72.1	74.7	79.9	86.8	Central African Rep.	626
91.9	81.0	73.1	73.2	69.0	66.7	66.5	66.9	73.0	76.8	71.0	71.3	72.0	80.8	80.8	Chad	628
....	....	65.8	47.9	42.0	41.4	54.0	62.2	53.7	50.9	52.6	41.4	38.1	....	....	Comoros	632
....	....	....	....	....	....	....	....	40.7	36.9	37.7	37.7	34.2	47.6	50.6	Congo	634
36.6	37.4	35.0	31.8	32.6	37.1	39.8	41.6	40.3	34.7	33.0	33.0	32.1	32.5	35.8	Côte d'Ivoire	662
....	....	....	....	19.9	16.4	16.1	17.7	17.7	16.7	16.4	16.2	18.7	20.2	19.3	Djibouti	611
....	....	....	....	....	54.9	64.6	70.8	70.4	63.9	54.9	38.9	54.0	78.2	70.8	Equatorial Guinea	642
55.2	58.1	61.1	53.4	56.9	51.6	56.8	58.0	57.3	57.8	58.6	60.0	62.8	61.4	58.0	Ethiopia	644
23.9	21.2	21.2	20.7	21.6	17.0	16.9	17.7	18.9	20.8	23.2	26.1	24.3	24.8	32.4	Gabon	646
29.7	30.0	33.5	36.2	33.3	30.0	33.9	40.7	41.5	39.9	42.2	41.9	41.7	39.0	39.2	Gambia, The	648
64.5	68.1	64.1	66.9	62.5	60.9	59.0	58.1	58.8	50.1	45.8	39.2	38.4	39.7	40.2	Ghana	652
....	....	....	....	....	....	....	....	....	....	....	71.0	66.9	63.1	58.5	Guinea	656
....	....	....	....	....	....	95.6	76.6	80.7	80.3	60.2	71.3	85.1	76.0	69.9	Guinea-Bissau	654
25.6	26.3	25.4	24.3	25.8	25.5	25.4	28.5	29.0	28.6	30.1	28.8	29.2	33.5	....	Kenya	664
14.2	35.0	24.4	28.7	34.9	33.9	41.9	43.1	42.5	41.2	37.3	33.9	30.5	20.1	18.3	Lesotho	666
31.0	40.6	46.8	51.3	57.2	72.1	75.4	83.7	89.0	92.1	....	102.2	86.8	77.9	68.9	Liberia	668
48.8	46.6	50.0	42.9	40.3	37.3	45.6	52.4	48.3	45.6	38.2	38.2	46.0	42.7	37.1	Madagascar	674
27.3	33.0	32.4	36.2	40.8	40.7	46.1	60.9	56.4	54.5	42.2	42.5	37.9	43.5	42.7	Malawi	676
55.0	53.6	54.8	52.9	53.6	56.2	60.4	59.1	60.0	61.4	74.4	80.9	81.9	82.4	71.5	Mali	678
42.5	35.3	34.4	36.1	34.1	35.5	33.3	31.5	34.2	40.7	37.1	43.2	52.0	72.2	....	Mauritania	682
30.5	28.9	27.4	24.8	24.0	21.6	19.6	18.8	18.0	18.3	18.1	25.0	33.4	23.8	19.9	Mauritius	684
36.7	34.1	32.0	30.7	31.1	30.2	30.1	30.6	31.0	32.1	32.8	35.4	35.8	30.5	29.7	Morocco	686
....	....	....	....	....	....	....	....	....	....	5.2	4.3	10.0	8.4	9.0	Namibia	728
44.8	42.9	45.0	45.3	48.2	52.4	50.3	52.8	59.8	59.8	60.6	64.4	68.2	66.5	56.6	Niger	692
42.0	40.5	39.2	38.3	34.6	33.5	32.7	32.6	32.4	38.8	42.4	42.1	....	....	....	Nigeria	694
57.8	52.8	45.7	46.2	43.9	40.7	39.9	38.7	35.5	31.5	32.8	35.3	38.2	41.7	....	Rwanda	714
31.6	34.8	36.8	37.0	33.8	31.1	34.4	38.2	41.6	45.0	50.2	44.3	49.4	45.2	38.6	Senegal	722
32.5	31.7	33.6	34.0	32.4	31.0	28.5	25.7	25.9	23.5	22.5	24.0	25.8	33.0	43.9	Seychelles	718
50.1	50.1	59.5	63.4	61.9	57.9	60.9	66.9	74.0	68.9	70.3	68.1	60.4	51.0	53.1	Sierra Leone	724
55.3	53.0	52.0	44.8	41.5	40.9	47.5	50.3	45.1	42.8	....	....	....	....	....	Somalia	726
16.5	18.0	16.0	13.6	13.3	12.2	12.2	12.5	12.2	11.5	11.7	....	....	....	....	South Africa	199
....	....	....	....	....	....	....	....	....	....	....	....	65.6	61.2	51.7	Sudan	732
36.4	34.3	31.2	29.7	34.6	44.7	50.8	50.8	38.8	29.6	24.8	22.1	23.7	22.8	22.3	Swaziland	734
31.4	31.9	33.6	30.9	34.1	36.9	37.9	40.2	40.8	33.5	24.9	21.6	24.2	39.7	....	Tanzania	738
43.2	53.8	61.7	63.1	71.0	81.0	78.9	67.4	70.3	61.4	61.5	64.6	67.9	61.2	44.4	Togo	742
25.1	24.9	25.6	26.2	26.8	24.9	24.7	22.0	20.6	19.9	20.7	22.0	22.8	23.5	23.0	Tunisia	744
....	....	....	....	....	....	....	....	....	....	....	....	53.6	48.5	....	Uganda	746
56.9	64.8	70.3	86.3	76.2	81.9	79.2	86.9	83.9	86.2	84.7	78.5	92.1	94.9	43.7	Zaïre	636
....	....	....	....	....	....	....	....	....	37.3	30.4	30.5	52.0	....	....	Zambia	754
19.1	22.0	22.2	22.3	22.4	22.6	24.8	25.2	24.0	23.6	25.0	28.5	32.1	33.4	30.7	Zimbabwe	698
															Asia	
83.8	81.2	81.7	81.5	79.4	81.4	82.1	82.6	85.5	86.8	87.5	....	....	....	....	Afghanistan, Islamic State of	512
30.9	31.0	28.6	27.2	26.4	25.8	25.9	27.1	30.4	28.5	27.4	24.3	23.6	26.6	30.0	Bangladesh	513
....	....	....	11.9	23.1	43.6	51.5	70.1	57.5	59.8	93.4	113.4	112.5	75.5	53.0	Bhutan	514
....	....	....	....	....	67.9	44.5	39.1	38.2	40.8	42.0	40.9	37.5	37.9	....	China, People's Rep.	924
23.6	20.8	20.2	19.4	18.4	19.4	19.1	18.5	22.9	20.2	16.6	15.6	17.3	15.8	15.0	Fiji	819
35.5	34.5	33.6	32.4	33.0	33.2	32.9	33.9	34.1	34.2	34.4	34.0	33.1	32.4	....	India	534
45.7	41.5	37.5	35.5	32.7	30.0	29.3	28.1	23.9	18.3	15.1	13.3	12.7	....	....	Indonesia	536
25.3	20.4	16.6	16.2	15.6	14.6	13.4	13.9	16.3	18.8	19.1	18.6	17.6	18.5	18.2	Korea	542
....	....	....	....	....	....	....	....	....	....	....	....	22.7	20.6	22.5	Malaysia	548
62.2	70.6	71.4	77.2	86.1	87.9	87.7	78.6	76.4	81.3	80.3	81.0	83.2	90.6	....	Maldives	556
....	....	....	....	....	....	....	....	....	....	....	18.9	31.2	25.3	33.1	Mongolia	948
88.9	84.1	75.0	69.7	68.5	65.5	64.3	62.0	55.8	132.3	128.8	....	....	....	....	Myanmar	518
45.8	42.1	44.2	42.5	42.9	41.0	42.2	41.6	41.3	40.2	41.6	42.2	40.8	41.5	....	Nepal	558
40.1	40.4	38.9	37.5	37.9	37.7	37.2	39.0	40.1	42.7	44.3	46.8	43.1	40.1	40.2	Pakistan	564
29.0	16.9	15.9	15.8	19.4	14.8	14.0	13.4	15.0	14.4	14.5	13.0	11.0	10.8	....	Papua New Guinea	853
33.0	30.5	25.8	16.7	22.9	23.8	31.0	31.2	29.3	28.8	29.8	30.9	31.4	30.7	25.9	Philippines	566
27.8	25.5	25.4	25.0	24.8	25.0	23.9	22.4	21.7	20.1	18.4	17.8	17.6	18.2	17.3	Singapore	576
57.0	36.1	36.7	35.6	48.2	37.2	32.0	29.1	23.2	23.4	21.1	22.1	22.2	18.5	20.7	Solomon Islands	813

Ratio of Reserve Money to Money plus Quasi-Money

39ab i

Percent

		1965	1966	1967	1968	1969	1970	1971	1972	1973	1974	1975	1976	1977	1978	1979
Asia (cont.)																
Sri Lanka	524	55.3	52.7	52.4	52.1	50.6	50.7	47.3	47.7	50.4	50.4	46.4	44.3	46.5	43.5	38.6
Thailand	578	42.6	40.2	38.2	39.5	37.5	35.4	33.9	32.7	31.1	30.5	28.2	26.7	24.6	23.7	23.5
Tonga	866	....	....	....	....	....	....	....	....	....	....	....	....	....	....	....
Vanuatu	846	....	....	....	....	....	....	....	....	....	....	....	11.6	12.8	14.6	17.6
Western Samoa	862	—	—	3.0	3.3	3.4	3.6	3.3	3.3	3.2	I3.0	3.7	6.1	6.8	6.9	6.0
Europe																
Cyprus	423	19.0	18.1	17.3	31.1	38.6	31.5	36.1	36.1	33.9	33.4	34.3	35.2	32.8	33.8	34.7
Czech Republic	935	....	....	....	....	....	....	....	....	....	....	....	....	....	....	....
Czechoslovakia	934	....	....	....	....	....	....	....	....	....	....	....	....	....	....	....
Estonia	939	....	....	....	....	....	....	....	....	....	....	....	....	....	....	....
Malta	181	36.4	35.8	35.7	I40.8	51.4	45.8	46.6	50.9	53.1	54.3	57.8	63.2	65.2	67.6	69.6
Moldova	921	....	....	....	....	....	....	....	....	....	....	....	....	....	....	....
Poland	964	....	....	....	....	....	....	....	....	....	....	....	....	....	....	95.2
Romania	968	....	....	....	....	....	....	....	....	92.6	111.9	129.1	115.7	100.4	105.2	114.4
Slovak Republic	936	....	....	....	....	....	....	....	....	....	....	....	....	....	....	....
Slovenia	961	....	....	....	....	....	....	....	....	....	....	....	....	....	....	....
Turkey	186	69.1	65.9	65.0	63.9	62.4	62.5	64.9	68.0	71.5	73.7	72.7	74.4	75.0	72.9	71.9
Yugoslavia, SFR	188	46.9	42.2	38.7	31.5	30.1	29.3	27.8	32.1	32.7	30.8	26.8	26.5	25.5	32.4	36.1
Middle East																
Bahrain	419	27.1	30.8	34.5	38.2	39.4	36.6	32.6	28.3	23.2	15.0	22.6	21.4	21.4	22.6	18.8
Egypt	469	60.8	61.2	61.3	59.8	60.8	65.2	63.4	61.5	60.6	58.9	57.7	54.3	52.6	49.3	49.4
Iran, I.R. of	429	48.4	45.3	43.4	41.4	41.7	40.4	42.2	41.7	42.7	40.8	39.5	38.3	38.7	39.2ᵉ	47.0
Iraq	433	71.1	68.5	72.3	71.3	68.6	70.1	69.3	71.6	74.5	72.6	66.2	65.6	....	....	....
Israel	436	49.1	45.0	42.5	42.0	37.7	36.3	40.5	65.0	71.4	62.5	56.7	53.9	70.2	174.4	195.5
Jordan	439	62.9	67.8	82.6	93.6	90.9	91.3	93.7	89.3	84.9	82.8	81.3	75.2	69.1	64.0	62.3
Kuwait	443	17.2	17.2	18.0	15.9	13.7	14.4	13.3	14.2	19.4	17.4	21.7	17.3	20.1	23.9	13.9
Lebanon	446	21.3	20.5	28.2	29.1	30.4	29.0	26.4	26.1	25.3	26.6	25.8	31.3	34.1	31.0	26.6
Libya	672	57.3	60.7	66.7	66.7	67.4	67.4	69.5	64.4	59.2	48.3	45.4	49.9	51.6	54.1	57.4
Oman	449	....	....	....	....	....	....	....	26.5	32.9	32.0	37.6	42.1	37.0	39.7	39.6
Qatar	453	....	14.1	17.8	18.5	16.6	15.5	13.9	14.5	16.1	17.4	19.7	16.3	16.4	19.2	21.1
Saudi Arabia	456	63.7	63.8	61.7	60.6	59.9	58.3	57.7	58.1	66.9	64.9	62.6	63.2	69.5	70.2	63.4
Syrian Arab Rep.	463	80.3	79.3	81.8	82.0	81.2	82.3	84.0	78.4	77.2	70.4	67.4	64.5	65.4	67.5	67.7
United Arab Emirates	466	....	....	....	....	....	....	....	....	....	16.3	15.4	16.3	17.3	20.9	22.9	23.4
Yemen, Republic of	474	....	....	....	....	....	....	....	....	....	....	....	....	....	....	....
Western Hemisphere																
Antigua and Barbuda	311	....	....	....	....	....	....	....	....	....	....	26.7	40.1	25.8	26.7	37.8
Argentina	213	....	....	....	....	....	....	....	....	18.1	63.4	112.8	120.1	133.8	74.8	46.0	32.2
Bahamas, The	313	....	....	....	....	20.3	12.2	12.9	16.8	17.5	16.5	20.4	17.6	18.0	18.5	17.9
Barbados	316	....	16.8	15.0	19.1	I16.1	14.0	13.4	12.6	12.7	17.1	24.3	23.7	22.6	23.1	23.0
Belize	339	....	....	....	....	....	....	....	....	....	....	....	18.4	24.4	27.0	25.8
Bolivia	218	90.7	87.6	82.8	77.4	76.7	74.9	72.2	69.3	68.3	69.1	63.0	59.6	55.6	53.7	54.4
Brazil	223	75.3	71.0	62.8	56.6	54.0	51.5	48.7	46.4	49.8	52.1	49.4	51.1	54.8	49.9	47.9
Chile	228	....	....	....	....	52.4	63.8	69.1	82.6	96.6	106.5	73.5	52.2	59.2	52.5	44.7
Colombia	233	4.8	4.6	4.6	5.0	5.3	5.5	5.3	5.3	5.4	5.3	5.4	6.0	6.5	54.8	56.9
Costa Rica	238	42.6	43.0	41.0	42.8	44.9	42.4	42.3	39.9	41.3	38.5	33.2	31.1	34.9	33.0	30.2
Dominica	321	....	....	....	....	....	....	....	....	....	....	7.0	9.7	13.4	10.4	25.6
Dominican Republic	243	69.6	73.8	74.3	73.1	69.6	67.0	62.8	60.1	53.7	53.4	49.4	42.6	45.5	46.6	48.2
Ecuador	248	59.0	58.8	54.3	51.0	51.2	56.1	56.4	57.0	59.5	61.1	58.0	51.2	53.5	50.8	53.2
El Salvador	253	14.8	17.3	19.8	24.7	24.9	25.0	25.2	26.4	24.9	23.5	26.3	26.5	27.0	22.8	16.8
Grenada	328	....	....	....	....	....	14.3	16.5	15.9	17.6	19.3	18.0	35.1	39.3	37.0	29.8
Guatemala	258	54.8	53.9	49.3	45.5	42.9	43.2	41.6	42.4	43.3	42.2	41.6	48.0	47.5	44.0	42.7
Guyana	336	31.5	33.7	32.1	30.5	32.3	30.7	30.4	30.2	29.6	28.7	28.5	30.0	30.3	35.4	36.7
Haiti	263	70.1	70.3	71.2	72.1	75.5	72.6	70.9	68.8	64.8	57.6	53.3	54.2	52.9	50.8	48.6
Honduras	268	47.5	45.6	42.3	40.0	39.6	37.7	37.9	33.8	33.1	33.2	30.9	31.5	32.0	30.9	30.0
Jamaica	343	21.3	21.0	20.6	22.9	20.4	18.4	20.8	18.4	I19.7	21.6	22.8	23.0	26.0	24.7	24.4
Mexico	273	24.5	24.9	24.8	25.1	24.6	24.5	26.5	33.0	39.7	44.1	52.8	40.5	36.5	57.2	56.9
Netherlands Antilles	353	....	....	....	24.6	26.1	23.8	27.8	26.4	29.3	25.4	25.7	28.9	27.2	24.5	24.6
Nicaragua	278	47.8	43.3	41.1	39.4	37.7	51.4	45.4	39.6	37.6	37.0	35.1	34.7	34.4	36.3	47.0
Paraguay	288	77.9	80.4	78.4	77.3	73.0	71.8	72.6	72.0	71.7	71.3	68.4	67.1	67.7	67.5	66.2
Peru	293	43.7	37.6	37.9	37.5	39.5	43.5	41.4	45.2	42.2	39.7	38.0	35.9	41.8	43.5	45.6
St. Kitts and Nevis	361	....	....	....	....	....	....	....	....	....	....	....	....	....	....	9.2
St. Lucia	362	....	....	....	....	....	....	....	....	....	....	14.0	17.8	18.0	18.9	20.7
St. Vincent & Grens.	364	....	....	....	....	....	....	....	....	....	....	20.5	30.2	30.1	24.1	29.0
Suriname	366	....	....	8.7	7.8	7.8	7.4	7.2	7.1	41.6	42.0	42.4	44.6	40.1	40.1	39.8
Trinidad and Tobago	369	16.7	19.4	21.0	21.3	20.0	18.4	18.6	19.4	18.1	19.5	29.3	36.5	27.3	27.0	25.7
Uruguay	298	I51.7	54.7	59.6	57.5	61.2	63.2	61.4	58.5	57.9	59.3	53.4	54.6	42.9	47.5	36.9
Venezuela	299	38.6	37.5	37.9	38.2	35.6	32.7	32.4	31.6	31.2	36.0	35.8	32.5	32.3	31.1	27.9

Ratio of Reserve Money to Money plus Quasi-Money

39ab i

1980	1981	1982	1983	1984	1985	1986	1987	1988	1989	1990	1991	1992	1993	1994		
Percent																
															Asia (cont.)	
36.9	33.3	31.1	32.1	32.6	34.7	37.1	36.1	35.6	36.8	36.5	38.4	36.8	36.1	36.3	Sri Lanka	524
22.9	20.9	19.0	17.1	15.3	14.1	13.7	13.8	13.6	13.0	12.2	11.2	11.2	11.2	11.6	Thailand	578
....	....	104.8	110.5	123.5	114.6	105.2	110.7	106.1	115.1	100.2	95.2	89.0	49.3	30.5	Tonga	866
17.8	13.4	9.5	8.7	8.8	9.0	8.8	11.6	10.9	8.1	6.5	7.3	8.7	9.2	11.6	Vanuatu	846
16.0	20.7	18.4	17.6	21.9	39.1	52.0	56.3	49.1	56.5	69.6	74.6	66.0	52.7	40.0	Western Samoa	862
															Europe	
36.3	38.4	41.5	42.2	44.5	43.5	40.8	40.2	39.3	32.6	31.4	31.9	28.9	26.6	25.0	Cyprus	423
....	....	....	....	....	....	....	....	....	....	....	....	....	20.2	26.9	Czech Republic	935
....	....	....	....	....	....	....	20.8	19.3	17.3	26.6	24.2	....	....	....	Czechoslovakia	934
....	....	....	....	....	....	....	....	....	....	....	....	....	77.1	57.3	Estonia	939
66.9	66.1	64.4	65.5	65.4	64.0	60.6	58.7	56.2	50.0	42.5	37.6	36.5	34.8	35.3	Malta	181
....	....	....	....	....	....	....	....	....	....	....	35.2	54.8	60.2	70.7	Moldova	921
109.9	105.7	87.3	82.9	74.0	65.1	53.8	41.9	54.4	53.6	44.9	42.7	36.8	32.3	28.3	Poland	964
165.9	123.7	122.4	102.8	96.1	83.3	72.8	100.2	131.3	165.1	81.2	43.8	46.5	52.0	45.8	Romania	968
....	....	....	....	....	....	....	....	....	....	....	....	....	17.3	17.4	Slovak Republic	936
....	....	....	....	....	....	....	....	....	....	....	11.8	12.3	12.4	11.7	Slovenia	961
66.7	53.2	43.3	43.3	41.6	38.6	34.7	33.2	35.1	34.7	32.2	27.6	25.2	25.6	24.5	Turkey	186
35.3	33.9	35.2	40.4	45.9	47.0	50.7	60.2	67.9	69.2	61.3	....	....	....	....	Yugoslavia, SFR	188
															Middle East	
18.5	16.3	15.0	14.2	13.9	15.5	14.5	15.1	14.2	13.6	14.3	15.2	13.6	13.0	12.9	Bahrain	419
51.9	50.7	54.2	53.4	52.6	50.8	46.5	45.0	36.7	33.9	32.8	32.8	31.2	30.8	32.1	Egypt	469
46.0	48.9	55.8	56.5	57.5	57.5	58.5	60.7	63.3	62.4	55.9	49.7	45.3	41.3	....	Iran, I.R. of	429
....	....	....	....	....	....	....	....	....	....	....	....	....	....	....	Iraq	433
203.9	44.1	41.7	44.4	47.4	43.9	38.7	35.2	29.9	27.1	27.0	24.7	22.5	21.8	18.3	Israel	436
60.5	59.6	55.0	53.4	50.4	47.3	46.5	43.7	42.5	42.5	44.2	54.8	52.7	50.0	51.6	Jordan	439
14.6	14.8	17.4	20.0	15.7	14.3	14.1	16.8	8.7	7.2	8.6	9.2	9.0	8.3	7.3	Kuwait	443
23.3	19.2	18.8	18.0	17.6	16.8	11.2	5.1	8.5	12.9	13.8	13.3	11.7	11.5	16.2	Lebanon	446
59.2	53.7	52.2	45.1	41.8	40.9	44.4	44.1	41.0	44.9	50.6	54.3	56.8	....	....	Libya	672
45.8	43.2	42.3	30.9	28.6	26.7	28.3	30.8	26.4	26.0	24.9	23.6	22.2	21.9	21.2	Oman	449
21.3	16.4	15.6	15.4	14.0	12.6	13.5	13.0	12.5	12.7	13.3	15.2	14.0	13.5	12.1	Qatar	453
50.7	41.2	36.9	32.4	30.1	29.0	28.8	28.9	26.7	25.0	26.1	26.9	....	....	....	Saudi Arabia	456
65.9	62.4	69.0	75.8	78.0	91.3	92.0	89.1	75.5	66.4	66.2	63.9	62.8	....	....	Syrian Arab Rep.	463
21.2	18.7	18.0	15.9	13.9	14.6	14.5	18.3	19.1	17.6	16.0	16.8	18.3	19.3	....	United Arab Emirates	466
....	....	....	....	....	....	....	....	....	....	92.6	89.6	88.3	87.4	....	Yemen, Republic of	474
															Western Hemisphere	
28.0	29.3	15.8	18.8	25.8	26.9	28.5	27.6	24.2	22.9	19.4	19.0	21.8	19.6	17.8	Antigua and Barbuda	311
23.0	28.1	68.5	83.0	70.4	46.0	42.0	28.7	22.9	54.3	44.7	40.2	36.6	33.3	....	Argentina	213
16.8	15.6	15.2	14.6	16.0	16.7	17.8	17.7	16.0	15.4	14.0	14.1	13.3	13.1	12.7	Bahamas, The	313
22.3	23.0	21.9	22.4	23.0	23.5	22.5	21.8	22.5	21.1	20.7	19.5	19.4	17.3	16.5	Barbados	316
24.2	24.7	24.2	25.5	25.0	30.6	32.1	30.6	28.5	25.1	24.2	25.4	23.2	23.6	22.4	Belize	339
55.9	50.1	48.7	62.7	74.1	69.1	44.1	29.5	36.3	42.4	39.4	34.2	27.2	25.0	20.8	Bolivia	218
51.1	50.6	44.4	37.6	27.4	20.0	18.4	25.9	16.7	14.0	32.7	23.2	16.2	13.5	....	Brazil	223
46.8	32.6	31.1	69.6	101.2	148.3	179.5	158.7	118.3	92.6	88.5	95.4	91.9	86.1	....	Chile	228
57.0	50.1	46.5	42.8	41.4	42.0	38.4	40.8	39.8	56.2	51.4	51.0	50.7	47.4	45.4	Colombia	233
30.0	35.8	34.1	32.0	32.1	37.6	44.9	43.7	46.8	46.3	45.3	50.2	51.8	48.1	49.2	Costa Rica	238
31.5	21.6	13.2	15.4	24.5	25.0	26.3	34.9	33.7	24.5	23.0	26.3	22.2	20.3	18.4	Dominica	321
45.3	48.5	51.2	50.5	48.9	48.9	48.9	45.2	50.9	50.8	51.4	54.3	51.0	48.6	44.9	Dominican Republic	243
50.7	48.1	42.4	40.7	40.3	36.6	38.6	39.9	38.4	42.3	44.6	47.6	44.8	....	....	Ecuador	248
16.2	17.3	43.6	41.3	38.3	36.8	34.6	35.6	35.2	33.8	33.4	33.8	32.3	35.2	34.6	El Salvador	253
32.4	33.5	30.5	31.2	46.4	42.6	38.2	33.9	27.0	24.4	22.3	24.0	25.0	21.2	20.2	Grenada	328
40.5	36.2	36.5	35.0	33.2	34.4	37.3	37.6	35.3	35.4	37.6	36.5	31.3	33.0	28.9	Guatemala	258
38.2	36.5	47.0	55.9	58.2	55.8	53.3	83.7	83.0	60.4	42.5	46.4	52.7	43.8	36.6	Guyana	336
49.8	51.8	52.8	51.7	48.1	53.2	55.9	57.8	64.2	60.0	58.6	64.9	63.9	63.7	....	Haiti	263
32.7	30.8	27.0	25.5	24.3	24.6	26.0	23.8	22.6	24.0	25.4	27.4	27.7	28.7	27.6	Honduras	268
27.8	22.9	19.2	16.9	27.8	33.7	34.1	34.1	37.4	38.5	43.1	35.3	37.4	38.5	37.4	Jamaica	343
57.9	58.3	65.0	63.5	60.1	51.8	42.6	30.3	29.5	34.1	20.0	15.9	14.0	12.7	12.9	Mexico	273
24.9	20.0	19.1	19.0	17.6	18.5	37.3	32.1	28.8	23.4	19.2	15.6	15.4	17.1	15.9	Netherlands Antilles	353
45.6	36.5	40.1	50.2	38.9	45.6	46.0	49.2	46.6	50.7	68.6	70.0	37.8	33.9	34.7	Nicaragua	278
63.6	62.5	60.7	64.4	67.7	66.4	66.0	71.0	70.7	67.7	55.8	46.4	44.4	41.8	41.3	Paraguay	288
53.7	53.3	50.4	49.6	52.1	59.5	66.8	58.4	60.4	47.6	52.9	44.2	42.0	42.7	35.9	Peru	293
5.9	22.2	17.8	14.4	18.3	17.5	19.1	25.2	20.0	18.6	18.4	17.8	21.1	21.3	22.3	St. Kitts and Nevis	361
21.1	16.0	14.9	15.0	21.2	21.8	22.5	24.8	24.5	21.0	20.9	21.7	20.9	20.0	19.0	St. Lucia	362
24.9	24.3	20.8	17.4	23.5	27.8	33.6	30.2	30.5	23.0	22.9	23.6	27.5	26.1	24.7	St. Vincent & Grens.	364
36.9	39.4	37.7	42.6	48.8	58.4	65.5	64.2	63.9	61.4	61.3	62.8	62.0	60.0	....	Suriname	366
29.5	30.2	32.5	31.6	28.6	27.8	25.2	23.9	18.8	19.8	20.8	22.3	28.0	22.1	24.4	Trinidad and Tobago	369
30.6	26.2	21.5	29.7	35.0	38.0	34.1	34.2	35.6	35.1	35.0	38.3	35.1	36.8	34.7	Uruguay	298
29.7	28.2	27.7	30.2	33.4	35.6	27.5	22.8	21.7	23.0	24.7	30.0	32.4	28.9	22.6	Venezuela	299

Income Velocity of Money plus Quasi-Money

39ad *i*

Index Numbers

		1965	1966	1967	1968	1969	1970	1971	1972	1973	1974	1975	1976	1977	1978	1979
Industrial Countries																
United States	111	106.0	108.7	106.7	107.7	109.8	110.8	107.2	105.2	107.7	109.6	108.5	107.2	106.4	111.0	114.1
Canada	156	130.7	134.2	127.9	124.2	122.4	124.3	123.3	120.8	123.1	118.2	116.5	113.6	108.3	105.7	101.7
Australia	193	66.1	67.1	66.3	67.2	68.4	70.9	74.2	73.1	69.7	72.7	73.5	76.0	76.2	78.0	81.4
Japan	158	161.7	159.9	162.0	166.5	166.7	166.4	151.7	141.0	139.6	147.6	144.7	141.0	141.0	138.7	135.3
New Zealand	196	137.0	141.3	149.3	154.5	ӏ167.3	170.7	180.4	166.6	138.2	132.7	143.3	148.7	136.4	131.1	129.1
Austria	122	170.8	166.8	162.0	159.1	155.7	154.9	152.7	151.1	150.2	152.5	140.1	132.2	127.4	120.7	118.4
Belgium	124	105.6	104.7	103.2	101.1	103.9	109.2	107.8	104.9	103.2	108.0	107.3	107.1	105.8	105.0	104.7
Denmark	128	114.3	113.3	111.9	113.0	114.9	119.2	124.3	128.1	128.8	131.1	122.7	117.7	119.1	125.6	128.6
Finland	172	139.6	135.2	134.5	140.0	142.5	138.9	136.1	136.3	144.0	156.8	145.6	144.3	141.9	137.1	137.7
France	132	123.2	118.7	113.0	105.1	ӏ107.8	111.8	103.9	95.9	94.5	91.7	89.2	87.9	87.7	88.6	88.1
Germany	134	146.8	139.8	127.0	121.9	120.3	125.6	124.7	120.6	121.3	121.2	116.0	114.4	112.5	109.8	109.7
Greece	174	188.2	185.0	175.1	164.8	162.8	158.1	145.7	134.7	143.4	143.6	138.5	134.8	128.3	126.9	129.4
Iceland	176	93.4	94.9	88.5	89.1	94.6	94.4	98.1	102.7	113.2	129.6	144.8	154.5	166.3	179.1	170.9
Ireland	178	75.2	74.8ᵉ	73.5	73.1	76.0	78.7	83.1	90.7	93.4	. . . .	. . . .	. . . .	. . . .	. . . .	. . . .
Italy	136	. . . .	. . . .	. . . .	. . . .	. . . .	. . . .	. . . .	. . . .	. . . .	86.3	91.4	95.3	100.7	99.6	94.4
		. . . .	. . . .	. . . .	. . . .	. . . .	. . . .	. . . .	. . . .	. . . .	77.2	74.2	75.9	77.2	74.3	75.3
Luxembourg	137	. . . .	. . . .	. . . .	. . . .	. . . .	. . . .	. . . .	. . . .	. . . .	182.1	158.3	157.6	144.2	138.0	131.1
Netherlands	138	180.4	182.7	181.1	174.5	175.1	184.4	183.5	180.6	178.6	174.4	168.7	165.9	158.8	153.5	147.9
Norway	142	141.6	140.4	141.1	136.5	132.6	135.1	131.2	130.0	131.2	136.5	137.4	135.6	127.8	126.1	125.5
Portugal	182	86.6	85.6	86.9	84.6	80.5	77.7	75.9	74.4	69.8	70.9	69.3	76.1	84.7	90.0	91.2
Spain	184	121.6	122.9	123.7	115.6	110.6	108.6	102.0	96.9	93.6	95.2	94.1	95.2	100.9	103.1	101.2
Switzerland	146	132.4	132.2	129.3	124.0	115.9	113.0	112.5	117.8	123.8	125.5	116.7	108.9	103.1	98.2	93.7
United Kingdom	112	. . . .	. . . .	. . . .	. . . .	. . . .	. . . .	. . . .	. . . .	. . . .	. . . .	. . . .	177.3	188.5	190.1	200.4
Developing Countries																
Africa																
Algeria	612	229.7	203.4	174.1	155.5	129.5	132.5	127.9	119.7	112.7	165.9	143.7	139.7	126.3	122.2	126.7
Benin	638	183.5	185.9	189.7	186.1	169.9	184.3	157.3	152.9	151.2	152.8	115.0	110.6	107.1	110.9	109.2
Botswana	616	. . . .	. . . .	. . . .	. . . .	. . . .	. . . .	. . . .	. . . .	. . . .	. . . .	. . . .	107.4	97.7	102.4	91.8
Burundi	618	177.1	189.4	176.5	172.8	173.2	166.9	165.3	146.5	143.6	144.8	169.0	159.1	130.5	131.4	131.6
Cameroon	622	. . . .	. . . .	. . . .	. . . .	. . . .	. . . .	. . . .	. . . .	. . . .	. . . .	. . . .	. . . .	. . . .	. . . .	. . . .
Central African Rep.	626	. . . .	. . . .	. . . .	. . . .	. . . .	. . . .	. . . .	. . . .	. . . .	. . . .	. . . .	. . . .	. . . .	. . . .	. . . .
Chad	628	. . . .	. . . .	. . . .	197.1	. . . .	229.9	232.1	209.6	207.6	216.9	207.8	204.6	162.1	187.5	. . . .
Congo	634	. . . .	. . . .	. . . .	. . . .	. . . .	. . . .	. . . .	. . . .	. . . .	. . . .	. . . .	. . . .	. . . .	. . . .	. . . .
Côte d'Ivoire	662	142.3	149.6	156.6	146.1	139.8	126.4	119.5	124.1	128.3	124.2	111.1	121.1	111.8	101.7	100.6
Djibouti	611	. . . .	. . . .	. . . .	. . . .	. . . .	. . . .	. . . .	. . . .	. . . .	. . . .	. . . .	. . . .	. . . .	. . . .	. . . .
Equatorial Guinea	642	. . . .	. . . .	. . . .	. . . .	. . . .	. . . .	. . . .	. . . .	. . . .	. . . .	. . . .	. . . .	. . . .	. . . .	. . . .
Ethiopia	644	285.9	268.4	277.0	275.2	261.4	253.1	260.6	245.4	208.1	178.7	167.5	153.5	157.8	145.6	143.1
Gabon	646	10.1	10.7	12.0	14.5	14.3	13.1	12.5	ӏ11.0	12.7	20.4	16.3	15.8	13.3	77.5	98.6
Gambia, The	648	137.6	135.7	144.1	105.3	126.9	118.1	113.8	114.4	97.3	112.9	119.7	113.7	116.0	101.9	115.2
Ghana	652	61.2	62.5	61.7	64.0	70.5	68.3	73.2	58.9	60.9	64.9	55.0	49.1	58.0	64.6	66.3
Guinea-Bissau	654	. . . .	. . . .	. . . .	. . . .	. . . .	. . . .	. . . .	. . . .	. . . .	. . . .	. . . .	. . . .	. . . .	. . . .	. . . .
Kenya	664	. . . .	132.0	117.6	122.0	112.7	101.9	96.2	99.7	93.2	97.2	105.0	103.1	91.1	84.2	85.7
Lesotho	666	. . . .	. . . .	. . . .	. . . .	. . . .	. . . .	. . . .	. . . .	. . . .	. . . .	. . . .	. . . .	. . . .	. . . .	. . . .
Liberia	668	. . . .	. . . .	. . . .	. . . .	. . . .	. . . .	. . . .	. . . .	. . . .	143.0	176.2	128.5	128.1	112.6	122.1
Madagascar	674	94.7	98.6	96.0	92.9	94.0	94.5	92.4	86.3	88.3	100.8	94.5	94.4	87.7	75.0	75.2
Malawi	676	142.9	135.1	128.0	122.1	118.9	114.1	121.8	112.6	90.2	86.9	86.3	100.0	98.0	95.4	89.5
Mauritania	682	. . . .	. . . .	. . . .	281.0	. . . .	233.4	205.3	206.7	171.7	141.7	121.6	123.3	113.9	114.0	103.3
Mauritius	684	250.7	228.5	228.7	211.0	209.0	180.6	171.3	162.4	157.7	205.8	137.2	127.3	150.6	146.6	154.5
Morocco	686	157.1	150.9	150.8	152.9	156.9	155.2	157.7	144.5	136.9	150.1	133.0	124.6	125.5	122.3	116.8
Namibia	728	. . . .	. . . .	. . . .	. . . .	. . . .	. . . .	. . . .	. . . .	. . . .	. . . .	. . . .	. . . .	. . . .	. . . .	. . . .
Niger	692	285.6	330.4	306.4	276.3	261.6	257.3	226.7	212.4	182.8	180.0	165.7	177.9	162.5	158.7	152.6
Nigeria	694	167.8	163.1	125.1	139.3	140.8	143.6	147.9	144.9	175.1	190.8	125.2	101.4	91.6	89.8	90.6
Rwanda	714	259.4	254.0	250.0	241.1	280.2	260.5	231.2	225.5	189.7	172.4	150.2	146.3	132.9	127.3	128.0
Senegal	722	160.4	169.5	174.8	180.4	169.4	174.2	163.0	154.6	146.6	130.4	120.7	104.1	93.8	86.4	85.0
Seychelles	718	. . . .	. . . .	. . . .	. . . .	. . . .	. . . .	. . . .	87.1	95.4	106.4	99.3	106.6	104.7	110.7	132.1
Sierra Leone	724	120.7	124.0	119.7	107.9	101.7	109.7	ӏ109.5	97.9	85.9	86.4	94.5	89.6	86.1	74.4	71.7
South Africa	199	ӏ113.4	113.6	117.1	111.1	111.1	112.6	117.2	118.1	116.2	120.0	110.8	110.4	114.0	115.4	121.3
Swaziland	734	. . . .	. . . .	. . . .	. . . .	. . . .	. . . .	. . . .	. . . .	. . . .	134.7	95.7	85.1	95.4	85.2	89.9
Tanzania	738	. . . .	145.3	163.5	153.4	136.4	134.7	120.7	117.1	115.7	115.1	111.2	113.1	109.2	105.6	87.5
Tunisia	744	172.8	157.9	156.6	155.9	154.0	155.6	159.6	162.0	150.8	157.2	144.8	135.2	135.4	131.8	133.3
Zaïre	636	. . . .	28.6	. . . .	ӏ29.3	34.4	33.4	31.8	31.5	31.3	26.0	25.4	29.1	26.7	24.2	32.5
Zambia	754	. . . .	. . . .	. . . .	. . . .	. . . .	. . . .	. . . .	. . . .	. . . .	. . . .	. . . .	. . . .	. . . .	. . . .	. . . .
Zimbabwe	698	. . . .	. . . .	. . . .	. . . .	. . . .	. . . .	. . . .	. . . .	. . . .	. . . .	. . . .	. . . .	. . . .	. . . .	. . . .
Asia																
Bangladesh	513	. . . .	. . . .	. . . .	. . . .	. . . .	. . . .	. . . .	. . . .	. . . .	170.1	291.5	217.5	174.8	196.2	187.6
Bhutan	514	. . . .	. . . .	. . . .	. . . .	. . . .	. . . .	. . . .	. . . .	. . . .	. . . .	. . . .	. . . .	406.2	461.8	359.0
China, People' Rep.	924	. . . .	. . . .	. . . .	. . . .	. . . .	. . . .	. . . .	. . . .	. . . .	. . . .	. . . .	. . . .	. . . .	. . . .	. . . .
Fiji	819	181.4	174.9	181.2	161.4	150.4	161.3	143.0	151.6	166.9	172.8	157.0	148.9	144.8	136.3	142.4
India	534	197.8	200.8	215.2	206.8	202.5	194.1	180.3	172.2	176.4	180.4	172.3	157.2	148.0	133.3	120.7
Indonesia	536	. . . .	. . . .	. . . .	821.2	545.7	442.1	339.7	284.3	286.1	304.6	261.8	239.1	235.2	239.5	260.3
Korea	542	353.2	277.3	209.0	163.5	125.0	119.6	116.7	115.5	107.6	118.6	126.0	133.2	125.3	122.7	124.6
Maldives	556	. . . .	. . . .	. . . .	. . . .	. . . .	. . . .	. . . .	. . . .	. . . .	. . . .	. . . .	. . . .	87.3	122.8	113.2
Myanmar	518	135.1	198.9	227.7	278.6	297.2	99.2	100.2	96.2	100.3	109.7	106.2	109.5	112.9	111.2	105.2
Nepal	558	379.3	413.2	352.9	333.5	305.9	285.0	254.9	250.7	197.8	203.0	ӏ237.8	206.3	161.9	156.3	150.0
Pakistan	564	111.1	107.6	103.5	103.6	101.3	92.1	87.3	79.7	83.8	108.9	121.7	113.9	106.8	103.6	94.4
Papua New Guinea	853	. . . .	. . . .	. . . .	. . . .	. . . .	. . . .	. . . .	. . . .	157.9	128.2	115.2	150.8	ӏ133.9	127.3	117.2
Philippines	566	122.9	118.6	111.6	107.4	106.5	115.0	115.3	118.9	125.6	141.0	150.2	149.3	133.5	119.6	126.2
Singapore	576	176.6	173.4	168.7	159.3	152.1	148.9	151.3	150.7	155.7	168.0	152.5	145.6	148.1	149.8	155.5
Solomon Islands	813	. . . .	. . . .	. . . .	. . . .	. . . .	. . . .	. . . .	. . . .	. . . .	. . . .	. . . .	. . . .	. . . .	116.4	104.3

Income Velocity of Money plus Quasi-Money

1990=100   39ad *i*

1980	1981	1982	1983	1984	1985	1986	1987	1988	1989	1990	1991	1992	1993	1994		
															Industrial Countries	
113.4	115.4	108.2	103.8	105.1	101.8	98.4	98.6	99.9	102.3	100.0	99.0	102.1	106.6	111.7	United States	111
100.1	103.3	95.3	102.3	109.5	111.5	111.1	110.7	110.8	106.8	100.0	94.2	89.9	83.2	80.6	Canada	156
81.9	82.9	81.8	79.2	80.7	76.0	73.1	73.1	72.1	109.5	100.0	95.4	94.6	93.1	91.9	Australia	193
136.0	134.3	129.1	126.1	125.9	124.5	119.2	112.6	107.9	104.6	100.0	102.1	103.6	102.9	....	Japan	158
131.4	139.9	140.9	141.2	140.6	128.4	127.3	110.0	140.6	160.8	100.0	76.8	70.8	71.4	....	New Zealand	196
117.1	111.5	107.9	105.2	107.7	106.5	105.1	100.6	99.7	99.6	100.0	98.7	97.4	94.4	94.5	Austria	122
106.4	104.1	105.6	106.5	105.6	108.1	105.8	100.0	99.6	100.0	100.0	....	....	....	....	Belgium	124
127.4	123.9	127.9	118.3	105.7	99.7	94.2	94.7	101.0	101.8	100.0	95.2	94.7	90.9	91.4	Denmark	128
137.3	134.7	131.7	129.1	127.7	118.6	111.8	110.1	108.3	102.6	100.0	88.4	86.3	86.9	89.7	Finland	172
89.8	91.1	93.8	94.5	93.5	93.4	92.9	91.8	93.4	97.8	100.0	103.4	106.6	105.4	....	France	132
112.3	111.9	109.0	107.3	107.5	106.5	105.9	102.2	101.7	103.3	100.0	98.7	96.6	90.3	86.2	Germany	134
131.3	123.6	118.8	117.5	117.7	112.7	113.6	106.4	103.9	98.9	100.0	113.7	116.4	126.4	....	Greece	174
178.3	156.1	159.7	154.4	134.3	129.3	120.6	116.3	113.0	106.1	100.0	97.4	89.9	88.8	88.8	Iceland	176
99.6	101.4	105.8	107.5	109.7	110.9	111.6	105.4	100.3	105.5	100.0	94.1	87.7	79.8	....	Ireland	178
82.8	88.9	92.7	92.3	94.3	92.8	95.4	94.8	98.4	99.1	100.0	100.0	97.6	92.7	....	Italy	136
119.8	114.8	127.7	139.4	140.7	133.2	134.4	121.9	117.2	109.8	100.0	93.5	91.3	....	....	Luxembourg	137
145.3	140.3	I 134.8	113.4	112.2	110.4	107.1	103.5	104.9	101.9	100.0	100.0	....	....	....	Netherlands	138
134.2	136.9	136.7	137.5	135.3	127.8	120.0	106.8	103.1	101.3	100.0	99.8	97.6	95.7	....	Norway	142
87.5	80.7	80.5	84.3	85.7	85.2	88.7	87.9	89.2	94.8	100.0	96.1	87.8	....	....	Portugal	182
99.0	96.5	95.3	94.2	101.9	103.3	98.1	102.0	102.7	101.7	100.0	96.1	94.0	90.3	88.6	Spain	184
94.2	98.0	100.6	96.4	93.9	94.8	98.7	94.6	91.9	94.0	100.0	102.8	102.9	98.8	94.9	Switzerland	146
203.7	I 183.9	170.0	I 163.8	158.2	153.8	137.2	121.7	117.6	108.3	100.0	96.7	99.1	99.1	....	United Kingdom	112
															Developing Countries	
															Africa	
133.7	134.2	120.7	110.8	98.9	100.0	93.6	91.3	80.7	....	....	....	....	....	....	Algeria	612
113.0	105.7	109.3	111.3	109.3	118.5	110.7	106.8	121.4	122.2	100.0	92.1	....	....	....	Benin	638
95.2	97.8	102.1	116.2	109.0	115.6	114.7	96.2	95.9	99.9	100.0	95.1	90.2	....	....	Botswana	616
129.1	107.6	104.8	103.0	105.5	109.7	101.0	100.8	101.1	101.4	100.0	....	....	....	....	Burundi	618
....	....	....	....	....	....	....	....	119.7	107.8	100.0	93.8	87.8	....	....	Cameroon	622
....	....	....	....	....	....	....	....	101.9	95.5	100.0	110.6	111.0	....	....	Central African Rep.	626
179.5	....	127.0	133.4	91.0	91.8	88.2	77.0	90.0	104.5	100.0	104.9	110.0	120.6	....	Chad	628
....	....	....	....	....	....	....	....	98.0	109.6	100.0	88.1	87.1	100.6	....	Congo	634
106.7	109.2	111.0	111.7	119.8	102.4	95.8	94.0	92.9	95.8	100.0	102.5	....	....	....	Côte d'Ivoire	662
....	....	....	....	....	....	101.7	97.8	100.6	100.0	....	....	....	....	Djibouti	611
....	....	....	....	....	63.6	42.0	42.8	42.2	68.5	100.0	126.5	151.0	166.1	....	Equatorial Guinea	642
136.5	133.7	156.7	151.6	130.2	134.7	123.0	120.8	114.8	109.3	100.0	92.8	83.2	92.5	84.9	Ethiopia	644
116.0	113.9	110.0	106.5	102.6	92.7	92.8	72.9	82.9	94.6	100.0	95.7	100.7	....	....	Gabon	646
112.2	112.6	106.2	96.4	109.4	98.9	98.5	97.1	91.4	94.5	100.0	97.4	96.8	....	....	Gambia, The	648
74.2	92.1	82.5	119.7	132.0	116.4	114.1	106.1	103.7	89.0	100.0	113.1	98.0	91.6	....	Ghana	652
....	....	....	....	....	....	83.1	67.5	71.9	109.7	100.0	105.6	111.3	107.0	....	Guinea-Bissau	654
89.3	94.0	99.0	102.2	103.8	105.4	98.9	93.4	101.6	100.0	100.0	95.4	85.2	82.4	....	Kenya	664
89.5	89.4	77.8	67.2	68.3	69.6	67.6	68.9	79.5	85.6	100.0	99.8	113.9	109.5	....	Lesotho	666
I 142.4	213.6	192.3	170.2	146.6	133.2	109.1	101.9	99.0	82.7	....	....	....	....	....	Liberia	668
70.6	68.8	71.1	94.2	120.4	114.8	102.5	108.3	114.7	105.7	100.0	91.2	86.2	78.2	78.4	Madagascar	674
98.0	91.9	87.2	93.0	92.5	92.8	96.8	83.7	89.4	92.0	100.0	101.0	97.1	99.4	....	Malawi	676
110.6	97.1	91.0	95.7	98.7	95.5	96.7	88.7	88.1	100.7	100.0	99.7	....	....	....	Mauritania	682
154.3	161.5	158.8	147.2	149.2	139.5	126.5	114.5	104.4	101.7	100.0	92.9	86.8	86.8	83.6	Mauritius	684
125.4	121.1	116.8	108.0	109.7	113.2	114.8	105.0	110.5	102.9	100.0	95.6	87.0	....	....	Morocco	686
....	....	....	....	....	....	....	....	....	....	100.0	87.2	79.4	70.3	....	Namibia	728
143.1	131.5	146.6	172.7	136.6	117.2	113.1	111.4	105.3	101.2	100.0	101.6	....	....	....	Niger	692
81.6	68.0	63.7	62.1	61.0	62.8	59.9	82.9	83.2	105.1	100.0	87.0	....	....	....	Nigeria	694
126.0	127.7	131.0	133.9	133.7	128.9	111.9	100.4	96.8	100.2	100.0	103.1	97.4	....	....	Rwanda	714
86.9	88.0	89.8	90.9	88.9	96.8	100.1	102.1	104.0	101.0	100.0	103.1	....	....	....	Senegal	722
121.9	109.2	114.6	117.8	120.6	117.0	115.7	110.2	106.3	98.5	100.0	90.0	91.9	....	....	Seychelles	718
69.8	71.9	69.6	57.9	66.9	68.6	69.4	91.6	96.8	96.3	100.0	114.3	111.7	125.7	133.1	Sierra Leone	724
133.1	125.5	123.8	120.4	121.1	I 116.6	125.2	132.4	119.2	103.3	100.0	....	....	....	....	South Africa	199
98.8	106.6	104.9	95.9	86.7	82.8	101.9	101.3	103.3	90.9	100.0	94.2	....	....	....	Swaziland	734
78.3	74.4	73.9	75.1	85.2	101.3	104.3	114.5	128.5	112.6	100.0	98.2	92.3	74.9	....	Tanzania	738
136.8	130.3	129.6	126.9	123.4	120.8	113.6	117.8	109.1	I 101.8	100.0	108.3	113.6	117.1	117.6	Tunisia	744
92.6	86.6	79.3	39.7	113.3	106.0	104.3	101.9	98.6	99.4	100.0	165.9	121.9	....	....	Zaïre	636
....	....	....	....	....	....	....	....	68.7	74.7	100.0	102.4	....	....	....	Zambia	754
92.6	100.3	97.2	109.4	101.5	104.7	108.7	110.7	105.0	102.9	100.0	....	....	....	....	Zimbabwe	698
															Asia	
179.7	170.7	173.7	143.2	125.4	118.6	114.9	113.7	109.1	103.0	100.0	101.3	96.6	90.3	85.4	Bangladesh	513
....	....	....	122.6	128.5	115.2	125.3	138.4	125.7	104.9	100.0	91.2	88.4	85.3	....	Bhutan	514
316.7	277.8	262.9	255.4	251.1	222.2	131.5	119.2	119.4	115.2	100.0	86.0	....	82.5	....	China, People' Rep.	924
139.2	134.9	134.1	123.0	126.1	119.8	122.2	110.7	105.6	110.6	100.0	90.7	85.0	83.7	....	Fiji	819
123.8	122.7	120.6	120.1	113.3	109.2	104.3	101.1	102.7	100.6	100.0	99.0	94.2	91.8	....	India	534
252.5	249.9	215.3	220.0	202.7	174.4	150.3	152.1	138.0	125.5	100.0	93.6	88.7	....	....	Indonesia	536
120.2	118.7	105.6	104.0	108.1	107.1	107.1	106.1	106.7	101.1	100.0	100.5	93.9	88.7	87.9	Korea	542
118.0	117.8	134.8	150.2	144.5	123.0	108.6	111.3	111.8	109.5	100.0	....	....	....	....	Maldives	556
97.8	90.7	86.1	80.8	74.2	69.7	66.2	71.8	90.9	110.0	100.0	89.6	87.5	....	....	Myanmar	518
133.4	131.9	125.3	113.5	114.7	115.0	112.9	110.3	108.6	102.6	100.0	96.8	98.1	90.8	....	Nepal	558
95.8	100.8	102.3	93.1	97.4	96.9	92.0	89.1	93.7	101.1	100.0	103.7	98.8	87.9	88.4	Pakistan	564
110.1	115.4	116.0	123.0	112.4	107.8	101.4	106.1	111.2	104.4	100 0	107.4	103.8	111.1	....	Papua New Guinea	853
120.4	117.0	105.1	103.8	119.3	118.5	124.5	123.5	121.5	119.2	108.0	95.8	92.0	84.6	78.2	Philippines	566
148.6	142.7	139.0	134.4	134.0	125.7	115.8	108.8	113.1	105.8	100.0	96.6	93.6	99.2	....	Singapore	576
96.1	128.4	137.3	103.7	117.5	118.6	112.6	108.8	98.9	94.1	....	....	....	....	....	Solomon Islands	813

Income Velocity of Money plus Quasi-Money

39ad *i*

Index Numbers:

		1965	1966	1967	1968	1969	1970	1971	1972	1973	1974	1975	1976	1977	1978	1979
Asia (cont.)																
Sri Lanka	524	88.8	87.6	91.9	97.0	98.8	121.7	112.8	115.0	128.9	142.0	153.8	143.5	128.1	111.8	104.6
Thailand	578	255.0	249.1	225.3	238.8	232.5	239.7	214.9	198.2	207.5	215.8	197.9	191.0	184.7	187.5	185.3
Tonga	866	....	....	....	....	....	....	....	....	....	....	225.7	191.9	114.0	106.5	107.5
Europe																
Cyprus	423	145.8	144.6	148.7	145.0	143.8	140.6	140.7	132.2	125.4	101.5	82.6	94.7	102.2	106.8	112.3
Czech Republic	935	....	....	....	....	....	....	....	....	....	....	....	....	....	....	....
Czechoslovakia	934	....	....	....	....	....	....	....	....	....	....	....	....	....	....	....
Estonia	939	....	....	....	....	....	....	....	....	....	....	....	....	....	....	....
Malta	181	94.3	95.3	94.2	93.8	92.6	96.9	86.8	82.2	86.3	89.5	99.7	98.1	100.1	103.7	108.1
Poland	964	....	....	....	....	....	....	....	....	....	....	....	....	....	....	44.4
Romania	968	....	....	....	....	....	....	....	....	....	....	....	....	....	....	....
Slovak Republic	936	....	....	....	....	....	....	....	....	....	....	....	....	....	....	....
Slovenia	961	....	....	....	....	....	....	....	....	....	....	....	....	....	....	....
Turkey	186	....	....	....	....	....	....	....	....	....	....	....	....	....	....	....
Middle East																
Bahrain	419	....	....	....	....	....	....	....	....	....	....	184.5	176.8	162.4	161.6	171.5
Egypt	469	163.4	167.6	170.1	171.0	172.6	I176.8	183.6	177.8	158.4	141.7	135.9	136.9	141.6	131.1	129.2
Iran, I.R. of	429	221.9	216.7	208.0	189.1	207.2	167.6	178.9	170.2	184.9	252.4	194.7	184.5	177.3	119.8[e]	109.4
Israel	436	277.6	266.3	208.3	192.8	193.9	200.7	197.4	195.2	207.6	245.3	217.2	206.0	198.8	307.5	370.0
Jordan	439	349.3	245.8	I236.6	239.1	253.1	223.6	219.4	234.7	210.7	196.4	197.7	190.0	186.5	178.3	165.9
Kuwait	443	362.0	320.6	298.1	268.5	256.2	287.0	356.4	311.1	309.0	586.7	448.0	353.1	289.0	242.7	329.0
Libya	672	451.9	408.5	393.8	439.9	381.2	329.6	264.2	214.8	205.8	213.4	187.7	205.1	190.0	155.1	178.2
Oman	449	....	....	....	....	....	....	....	....	84.7	101.6	212.3	175.9	169.7	136.3	119.5	149.3
Qatar	453	....	204.9	194.8	199.9	190.6	194.8	215.6	201.9	178.9	436.2	375.3	302.3	228.2	215.5	273.7
Saudi Arabia	456	278.5	277.6	I264.7	261.2	264.2	271.8	395.4	453.2	806.8	809.8	587.7	398.1	285.5	219.1	295.2
Syrian Arab Rep.	463	182.7	166.2	171.3	155.5	156.3	141.5	149.6	149.2	....	130.0	144.2	145.6	140.5	122.3	115.0	114.7
United Arab Emirates	466	....	....	....	....	....	....	....	....	....	303.4	305.2	266.4	203.8	186.6	178.8	228.1
Western Hemisphere																
Antigua and Barbuda	311	....	....	....	....	....	....	....	....	....	....	83.6	77.2	116.0	119.1	122.3
Argentina	213	....	....	....	....	....	....	....	36.0	24.3	19.3	33.2	41.7	31.7	25.8	26.3
Bahamas, The	313	....	....	....	....	....	....	....	....	....	108.1	103.0	124.4	113.6	130.3	139.0	139.7
Barbados	316	....	94.5	88.0	77.6	I90.7	89.8	87.5	85.8	92.1	129.5	118.8	123.0	112.5	103.3	115.6
Belize	339	....	....	....	....	....	....	....	....	....	....	....	99.5	112.3	114.6	113.2
Bolivia	218	134.9	120.8	123.1	123.3	115.2	113.9	107.1	109.6	125.0	148.6	126.4	105.1	85.2	82.0	88.4
Chile	228	....	....	....	256.6	265.6	258.0	179.6	172.8	236.2	467.1	366.6	259.1	244.9	214.1	203.6
Colombia	233	9.8	10.2	9.5	9.2	8.8	I8.8	9.3	9.5	9.5	9.7	11.0	11.1	11.0	81.5	86.3
Costa Rica	238	197.9	210.2	190.8	179.7	178.5	188.1	182.1	159.9	163.3	166.0	153.0	138.9	129.9	117.5	104.0
Dominica	321	....	....	....	....	....	....	....	....	....	....	107.4	109.8	134.6	143.0	94.5
Dominican Republic	243	113.4	122.9	130.0	123.1	125.9	108.5	106.5	105.2	93.4	87.0	81.9	89.9	91.8	85.6	99.9
Ecuador	248	83.5	81.1	77.8	69.6	68.0	65.8	62.2	62.1	63.6	67.6	64.7	71.3	65.5	67.1	67.4
El Salvador	253	129.7	128.7	127.6	131.6	129.2	126.8	124.3	114.6	110.5	107.0	103.9	107.2	102.4	106.8	107.6
Grenada	328	....	....	....	....	....	....	....	....	80.8	89.2	97.8	96.2	97.4	103.4	108.3
Guatemala	258	119.9	110.8	109.3	107.3	105.4	104.8	103.8	92.8	90.8	94.3	93.0	87.1	89.4	86.7	88.4
Guyana	336	210.4	209.7	209.0	203.2	196.7	195.6	185.1	166.2	153.1	196.1	188.1	149.2	127.0	114.5	115.0
Haiti	263	433.9	450.4	436.3	397.9	378.2	354.2	322.8	270.0	285.6	I204.4	216.1	197.8	174.2	149.1	148.3
Honduras	268	196.6	190.1	196.1	180.1	161.4	146.8	142.2	139.7	130.7	130.5	135.1	130.5	125.9	123.2	121.8
Jamaica	343	146.1	143.2	136.8	123.3	122.7	124.6	113.5	108.1	I115.3	134.3	131.3	122.1	115.6	129.2	126.8
Mexico	273	72.8	75.0	73.0	72.3	70.6	75.9	78.0	79.2	78.8	81.6	85.6	73.2	71.6	67.9	67.1
Nicaragua	278	38.9	35.4	36.2	37.6	38.6	41.9	38.3	30.5	27.3	31.0	33.1	30.1	29.2	30.8	30.1
Paraguay	288	114.7	114.8	108.3	104.7	110.4	107.3	101.2	99.8	97.8	107.8	100.5	90.7	83.3	78.3	82.0
Peru	293	27.7	28.2	30.0	32.0	33.2	29.9	27.4	26.4	25.8	25.6	25.1	29.3	33.1	36.6	I42.5
St. Kitts and Nevis	361	....	....	....	....	....	....	....	....	....	....	....	....	....	....	89.1
St. Lucia	362	....	....	....	....	....	....	....	....	....	....	107.8	109.1	119.0	107.8	110.1
St. Vincent & Grens.	364	....	....	....	....	....	....	....	....	....	....	93.3	93.7	99.1	97.9	92.4
Suriname	366	....	....	549.5	535.4	484.1	463.3	445.1	400.5	366.1	391.8	395.3	333.3	337.3	327.5	309.5
Trinidad and Tobago	369	216.9	192.7	188.5	195.6	171.8	152.7	138.0	134.1	138.9	195.1	185.3	159.2	154.9	139.0	142.9
Uruguay	298	I183.7	216.3	258.4	301.2	254.7	232.2	208.8	227.1	291.6	291.8	298.6	250.3	222.4	195.4	180.2
Venezuela	299	134.7	131.1	130.6	125.3	118.7	120.6	119.8	106.2	106.2	126.7	90.9	78.0	68.4	64.1	71.6

Income Velocity of Money plus Quasi-Money

1980	1981	1982	1983	1984	1985	1986	1987	1988	1989	1990	1991	1992	1993	1994		
1990=100															**Asia (cont.)**	
104.3	103.4	89.4	94.2	99.7	91.7	95.5	93.8	92.5	92.1	100.0	97.1	92.0	90.0	86.5	Sri Lanka	524
184.2	178.6	164.2	143.5	127.2	117.7	113.4	112.0	113.4	109.5	100.0	95.2	90.1	....	....	Thailand	578
122.8	145.2	133.2	130.8	96.7	85.6	91.0	83.9	101.5	99.7	100.0	107.1	97.7	99.2	94.3	Tonga	866
															Europe	
117.3	114.3	112.9	110.1	114.0	113.8	111.1	110.5	107.1	104.3	100.0	90.9	89.0	....	....	Cyprus	423
....	....	....	....	....	....	....	....	....	....	....	....	....	100.0	94.7	Czech Republic	935
129.1	96.1	92.8	89.4	88.8	108.0	106.8	103.2	100.6	97.1	100.0	108.8	....	....	....	Czechoslovakia	934
....	....	....	....	....	....	....	....	....	....	....	....	....	100.0	....	Estonia	939
117.7	120.1	116.8	108.5	101.3	98.7	101.0	99.5	100.7	101.0	100.0	100.2	98.3	96.3	....	Malta	181
I49.4	44.1	64.6	70.5	73.7	74.2	72.6	70.5	82.2	96.9	100.0	83.3	77.5	73.6	....	Poland	964
213.8	144.4	149.0	148.8	152.7	141.2	136.6	131.2	131.2	110.6	100.0	190.1	262.8	357.5	....	Romania	968
....	....	....	....	....	....	....	....	....	....	....	....	....	100.0	99.3	Slovak Republic	936
....	....	....	....	....	....	....	....	....	....	....	....	....	100.0	....	Slovenia	961
....	....	....	....	....	....	....	84.0	90.4	90.5	100.0	97.7	89.4	94.5	....	Turkey	186
															Middle East	
174.7	156.3	128.7	119.6	120.8	112.8	93.9	92.4	93.5	92.6	100.0	....	90.4	98.2	95.8	Bahrain	419
I129.1	111.4	101.7	100.1	101.6	101.4	90.7	97.3	92.7	98.1	100.0	90.4	98.2	95.8	95.4	Egypt	469
92.3	91.8	101.0	106.4	106.8	100.3	91.3	94.1	88.0	89.6	100.0	110.8	117.6	130.6	....	Iran, I.R. of	429
I445.1	108.4	101.5	104.8	100.9	89.7	95.6	95.9	98.6	97.2	100.0	108.2	111.1	99.7	....	Israel	436
165.9	166.8	166.5	I154.0	149.8	142.5	139.5	126.5	113.3	100.9	100.0	100.5	111.9	112.4	118.0	Jordan	439
291.9	209.5	148.8	142.8	147.2	141.4	115.2	133.8	118.5	134.1	100.0	57.4	106.3	122.5	....	Kuwait	443
194.6	132.6	134.0	133.2	118.0	100.6	82.3	....	....	....	....	....	....	....	....	Libya	672
188.2	174.7	138.4	119.4	114.5	106.5	86.4	92.5	86.5	88.2	100.0	88.5	94.9	....	....	Oman	449
290.3	244.8	178.9	149.3	140.3	113.1	81.5	79.6	88.7	95.4	100.0	102.2	99.9	....	....	Qatar	453
339.8	276.8	170.0	129.7	115.8	101.1	84.6	80.4	78.4	81.7	100.0	103.9	....	....	....	Saudi Arabia	456
119.4	119.6	108.6	92.6	75.5	70.8	73.1	82.0	102.1	95.5	100.0	87.3	82.3	....	....	Syrian Arab Rep.	463
269.1	236.9	179.7	143.1	119.6	104.0	77.9	81.6	77.0	84.0	100.0	98.6	95.1	....	....	United Arab Emirates	466
															Western Hemisphere	
117.3	117.8	112.9	104.7	95.4	98.4	98.9	100.3	105.1	102.8	100.0	95.7	91.8	89.1	....	Antigua and Barbuda	311
31.0	37.0	44.6	57.7	62.4	53.2	43.0	43.0	46.0	54.9	100.0	74.7	52.5	39.1	....	Argentina	213
123.8	126.1	111.2	95.4	93.2	102.5	107.2	104.5	103.9	112.1	100.0	93.0	86.5	79.1	....	Bahamas, The	313
126.3	120.1	115.3	113.2	113.7	109.2	109.2	109.5	103.9	105.3	100.0	94.1	86.4	82.8	....	Barbados	316
135.8	128.0	117.3	104.6	110.5	103.1	96.0	98.6	99.1	104.5	100.0	94.5	94.8	96.9	....	Belize	339
91.4	90.6	98.1	129.6	291.5	491.9	242.3	132.3	128.3	128.7	100.0	81.1	....	....	....	Bolivia	218
177.2	140.7	110.2	108.6	105.5	103.8	100.1	102.1	103.0	103.7	100.0	103.9	105.1	101.9	....	Chile	228
89.2	78.9	76.1	78.7	80.0	85.0	83.6	82.3	89.3	91.4	100.0	107.5	94.0	85.8	....	Colombia	233
102.0	92.8	110.3	100.4	106.0	108.5	113.7	111.6	111.0	104.3	100.0	103.1	105.2	106.0	109.6	Costa Rica	238
104.3	112.1	118.6	109.0	109.2	110.9	105.6	102.4	110.7	108.8	100.0	91.4	86.3	86.2	....	Dominica	321
104.6	113.4	108.4	101.5	102.4	119.2	86.4	74.9	84.9	86.7	100.0	118.9	95.6	79.0	78.5	Dominican Republic	243
64.8	65.1	62.8	70.4	76.0	78.4	76.9	76.1	81.4	91.6	100.0	98.1	104.0	....	....	Ecuador	248
103.8	95.4	88.2	90.5	91.6	88.4	93.0	94.4	102.9	110.5	100.0	95.3	89.5	87.0	78.0	El Salvador	253
99.3	97.0	105.5	109.5	124.9	117.1	105.0	106.8	99.4	98.1	100.0	97.3	91.1	....	....	Grenada	328
93.4	92.3	79.2	78.9	77.2	79.6	85.5	83.9	84.2	83.7	100.0	102.0	79.0	83.1	....	Guatemala	258
117.5	107.8	80.9	65.8	64.0	62.5	56.7	65.2	59.0	100.6	100.0	153.6	110.0	93.7	....	Guyana	336
160.7	135.7	134.5	138.7	136.0	140.8	144.7	116.1	86.5	89.7	100.0	104.3	86.4	77.2	....	Haiti	263
137.8	140.0	131.1	114.5	105.9	113.8	113.4	106.7	99.0	98.8	100.0	106.9	104.0	104.4	106.3	Honduras	268
118.2	106.4	89.4	84.2	92.8	89.3	90.4	88.1	88.0	87.7	100.0	108.9	101.2	91.7	....	Jamaica	343
72.1	68.1	66.6	76.1	73.0	80.3	85.2	91.8	104.3	151.0	100.0	73.1	63.9	58.3	....	Mexico	273
25.6	19.7	19.4	19.7	45.2	48.0	54.1	52.9	51.7	48.8	100.0	57.5	39.9	40.3	32.2	Nicaragua	278
84.8	86.9	81.0	81.0	87.9	96.1	106.8	102.6	107.8	108.4	100.0	81.5	71.0	65.5	....	Paraguay	288
37.4	39.2	37.7	35.9	37.1	38.4	40.0	44.9	72.1	81.4	100.0	70.3	54.1	42.5	....	Peru	293
93.9	92.8	83.6	73.4	76.4	74.7	75.2	95.3	108.5	99.4	100.0	95.6	91.1	....	....	St. Kitts and Nevis	361
119.8	111.4	106.7	100.2	95.8	117.4	112.5	100.7	107.9	102.0	100.0	96.6	99.2	....	....	St. Lucia	362
94.1	101.1	100.0	101.9	98.3	96.1	92.0	96.0	111.8	100.5	100.0	103.0	109.4	....	....	St. Vincent & Grens.	364
285.3	281.1	252.7	217.5	186.5	146.8	116.3	102.3	95.2	92.0	100.0	100.9	113.9	172.9	....	Suriname	366
159.2	144.8	126.9	105.4	98.2	93.4	90.4	88.9	87.2	89.1	100.0	98.9	105.7	108.5	....	Trinidad and Tobago	369
178.0	146.2	116.8	108.9	111.2	108.4	106.6	120.1	112.5	104.7	100.0	107.9	118.5	122.2	....	Uruguay	298
77.2	76.8	68.0	59.2	67.4	64.9	61.5	70.4	77.8	97.6	100.0	84.9	92.3	100.0	83.1	Venezuela	299

International Interest Rates

London Interbank Offer Rates on SDR Deposits
(99260lsa, 60lsb, 60lsc)
(Period averages in percent per annum)

	1980	1981	1982	1983	1984	1985	1986	1987	1988	1989	1990	1991	1992	1993	1994
Three-Month	....	....	11.96	9.05	9.29	8.02	6.65	6.22	6.56	8.40	9.07	7.70	6.27	4.74	3.86
Six-Month	....	....	12.13	9.21	9.57	8.17	6.58	6.31	6.70	8.44	9.17	7.71	6.22	4.64	3.97
One-Year	....	....	12.10	9.36	9.94	8.40	6.58	6.48	6.87	8.46	9.28	7.76	6.34	4.59	4.22

London Interbank Offer Rates on US Dollar Deposits
(11160lda, 60ldb, 60ldc, 60ldd, 60lde, 60ldf)
(Period averages in percent per annum)

	1980	1981	1982	1983	1984	1985	1986	1987	1988	1989	1990	1991	1992	1993	1994
Overnight	16.56	19.70	12.61	9.32	10.38	8.04	6.97	6.63	7.56	9.21	8.13	5.78	3.60	3.05	4.24
Seven-Day	13.48	16.84	12.77	9.47	10.53	8.20	6.95	6.82	7.68	9.26	8.20	5.87	3.66	3.08	4.31
One-Month	13.96	16.79	12.95	9.53	10.64	8.23	6.94	6.99	7.81	9.24	8.29	5.90	3.72	3.16	4.46
Three-Month	14.19	16.87	13.29	9.72	10.94	8.40	6.86	7.18	7.98	9.28	8.31	5.99	3.86	3.29	4.74
Six-Month	14.03	16.72	13.60	9.93	11.29	8.64	6.85	7.30	8.13	9.27	8.35	6.08	3.90	3.41	5.07
One-Year	13.44	16.13	13.69	10.18	11.82	9.11	6.95	7.61	8.41	9.31	8.45	6.29	4.20	3.64	5.59

London Interbank Offer Rates on Three-Month Deposits (60ea)
(Pound Sterling Rates Relate to Paris Market)
(Period averages in percent per annum)

	1980	1981	1982	1983	1984	1985	1986	1987	1988	1989	1990	1991	1992	1993	1994
French Franc	12.21	18.16	19.45	16.53	12.77	10.76	9.46	8.64	8.09	9.35	10.29	9.61	10.37	8.57	5.88
Deutsche Mark	8.73	11.89	8.62	5.60	5.83	5.37	4.64	4.06	4.33	7.09	8.51	9.31	9.52	7.30	5.36
Japanese Yen	11.30	7.73	6.99	6.57	6.43	6.68	5.12	4.26	4.51	5.46	7.76	7.38	4.46	3.00	2.31
Swiss Franc	5.64	9.29	5.19	4.19	4.45	5.03	4.33	3.91	3.20	7.07	8.96	8.25	7.88	4.96	4.16
Pound Sterling	16.35	14.32	12.58	10.18	10.02	12.25	10.97	9.80	10.36	13.94	14.79	11.67	9.70	6.05	5.54

London Interbank Offer Rates on Six-Month Deposits (60eb)
(Pound Sterling Rates Relate to Paris Market)
(Period averages in percent per annum)

	1980	1981	1982	1983	1984	1985	1986	1987	1988	1989	1990	1991	1992	1993	1994
French Franc	12.54	18.02	19.64	17.05	13.36	11.11	9.16	8.79	8.32	9.44	10.43	9.64	10.16	7.92	5.95
Deutsche Mark	8.62	11.81	8.67	5.71	6.06	5.50	4.64	4.16	4.47	7.22	8.77	9.40	9.41	6.95	5.35
Japanese Yen	10.86	7.93	7.06	6.55	6.46	6.56	5.02	4.27	4.56	5.50	7.84	7.16	4.32	2.96	2.36
Swiss Franc	5.69	9.35	5.75	4.36	4.61	5.09	4.28	3.96	3.42	7.06	8.94	8.18	7.81	4.76	4.23
Pound Sterling	15.83	14.28	12.60	10.26	10.11	11.99	10.82	9.76	10.50	13.89	14.72	11.40	9.65	5.93	5.80

Discounts (-) or Premiums (60f) on Three-Month Forward Exchange Rates
(End of period in percent per annum based on end-of-period quotation of the currencies against the US dollar)

	1980	1981	1982	1983	1984	1985	1986	1987	1988	1989	1990	1991	1992	1993	1994
Canada	1.04	-1.38	-.65	.23	-1.42	-1.49	-2.12	-1.05	-1.51	-3.90	-3.59	-2.98	-3.37	.24	....
Australia	3.86	-3.69	-1.02	2.67	-3.17	-12.71	-10.05	-5.79	-7.92	-9.51	-5.93	-4.74	-3.93	....	....
Japan	7.00	6.46	1.87	3.70	1.85	.92	-.50	7.97	4.39	1.67	-3.48	-1.50	.03	1.18	3.69
Austria	6.05	12.46	2.80	5.40	1.27	.23	.58	2.84	3.34	-.85	-1.61	-5.65	-5.14	-2.21	3.42
Belgium	5.11	-6.03	-5.29	-1.15	-1.84	-1.75	-1.88	.75	1.77	-1.79	-2.29	-5.50	-4.94	-3.54	1.10
Denmark	-2.56	-.14	-6.56	-.10	-2.49	-.38	-2.86	-2.00	1.30	-3.70	-1.70	-5.80	-11.80	-3.30	.20
Finland	4.90	-.83	-3.10	-7.08	-5.51	-2.73	-6.76	-1.60	-1.97	-7.13	-6.71	-7.79	-6.61	-2.61	.43
France	5.85	—	-3.51	-2.37	-2.00	-1.01	-2.11	-1.27	.59	.01	1.09[p]	-3.32	-6.71	....	....
Germany	8.17	3.16	3.28	3.94	2.92	2.97	1.20	3.67	3.89	-.05	-1.87	-5.54	-5.20	-2.66	1.24
Italy	-3.14[p]	-9.83	-18.25	-8.38	-6.90	-10.25	-4.89	-4.28	-5.06	-4.34	-5.36	-7.97	-10.37	-7.10	-.87
Netherlands	8.17	2.84	4.04	3.85	2.87	2.31	.36	2.81	3.50	-14.93	-1.89	-5.52	-4.77	....	....
Norway	5.71	-.93	-5.50	.58	-4.58	-.58	-11.30	-11.71	-3.07	-3.14	-.51	-7.17	-9.91	-2.47	.09
Spain	1.98	-.92	-8.91	-12.65	.45	-7.95	-12.62	-11.20	-3.46	-16.33	.48	-23.09	-5.51	-.32	-3.67
Sweden	-.61	1.29	-2.74	-1.55	3.74	-4.44	-3.50	-1.64	.45	-3.91	-2.56	-10.63	-54.41	-1.83	-1.66
Switzerland	10.09	5.23	6.12	5.78	2.01	4.91	2.34	4.69	2.93	-1.16	-1.39	-3.10	-2.47	-.95	1.98
United Kingdom	3.34	-1.51	-.99	.72	-1.21	-3.57	-4.56	-1.36	-3.56	-6.30	-5.99	-6.66	-3.53	-1.91	-.12

SDR Interest Rate (99260s) and Rate of Remuneration (99260r)
(Period averages in percent per annum)

	1980	1981	1982	1983	1984	1985	1986	1987	1988	1989	1990	1991	1992	1993	1994
SDR Interest Rate	9.0625	12.6642	11.1725	8.5997	8.9220	7.8064	6.3941	5.8679	6.2544	8.2685	9.0912	7.7229	6.2599	4.6394	4.2858
Rate of Remuneration	8.1563	10.9429	9.5000	7.3088	7.7832	7.1421	6.1074	5.8546	6.2544	8.2685	9.0912	7.7229	6.2599	4.6394	4.2858

National Interest Rates

1978	1979	1980	1981	1982	1983	1984	1985	1986	1987	1988	1989	1990	1991	1992	1993	1994	
						Central Bank Discount Rates (60)											
						except for India (60a)											
						(End of period in percent per annum)											
																	Industrial Countries
9.50	12.00	13.00	12.00	8.50	8.50	8.00	7.50	5.50	6.00	6.50	7.00	6.50	3.50	3.00	3.00	4.75	United States
10.75	14.00	17.26	14.66	10.26	10.04	10.16	9.49	8.49	8.66	11.17	12.47	11.78	7.67	7.36	4.11	7.00	Canada
3.50	6.25	7.25	5.50	5.50	5.00	5.00	5.00	3.00	2.50	2.50	4.25	6.00	4.50	3.25	1.75	1.75	Japan
10.50	13.00	14.00	13.00	13.00	7.50	13.50	19.80	24.60	18.55	15.10	15.00	13.25	8.30	9.15	5.70	....	New Zealand
4.50	3.75	6.75	6.75	4.75	3.75	4.50	4.00	4.00	3.00	4.00	6.50	6.50	8.00	8.00	5.25	4.50	Austria
6.00	10.50	12.00	15.00	11.50	10.00	11.00	9.75	8.00	7.00	7.75	10.25	10.50	8.50	7.75	5.25	4.50	Belgium
8.00	11.00	11.00	11.00	10.00	7.00	7.00	7.00	7.00	7.00	7.00	7.00	8.50	9.50	9.50	6.25	5.00	Denmark
7.25	8.50	9.25	9.25	8.50	9.50	15.07	9.00	7.00	7.00	8.00	8.50	8.50	8.50	9.50	5.50	5.25	Finland
9.50	9.50	9.50	9.50	9.50	9.50	9.50	9.50	9.50	9.50	9.50	9.50	9.50	9.50	9.50	9.50	9.50	France
3.00	6.00	7.50	7.50	5.00	4.00	4.50	4.00	3.50	2.50	3.50	6.00	6.00	8.00	8.25	5.75	4.50	Germany
14.00	19.00	20.50	20.50	20.50	20.50	20.50	20.50	20.50	20.50	19.00	19.00	19.00	19.00	19.00	21.50	20.50	Greece
11.85	ℓ16.50	14.00	16.50	14.00	12.25	14.00	10.25	13.25	9.25	8.00	12.00	11.25	10.75	....	7.00	6.25	Ireland
10.50	15.00	16.50	19.00	18.00	17.00	16.50	15.00	12.00	12.00	12.50	13.50	12.50	12.00	12.00	8.00	7.50	Italy
6.50	9.50	8.00	9.00	5.00	5.00	5.00	5.00	4.50	3.75	4.50	7.00	7.25	8.50	7.75	5.00	....	Netherlands
7.00	9.00	9.00	9.00	ℓ9.20	10.00	10.20	10.70	14.80	13.80	12.00	11.00	10.50	10.00	11.00	7.00	6.75	Norway
16.33	17.33	18.00	18.00	18.75	23.17	25.00	23.50	17.00	14.96	13.71	14.33	14.50	14.50	14.50	13.71	11.63	Portugal
9.02	7.98	10.90	10.51	18.40	21.40	12.50	10.50	11.84	13.50	12.40	14.52	14.71	12.50	13.25	9.00	7.38	Spain
6.50	9.00	10.00	11.00	10.00	8.50	9.50	10.50	7.50	7.50	8.50	10.50	11.50	8.00	ℓ10.00	5.00	7.00	Sweden
1.00	2.00	3.00	6.00	4.50	4.00	4.00	4.00	4.00	2.50	3.50	6.00	6.00	7.00	6.00	4.00	3.50	Switzerland
																	Developing Countries
																	Africa
....	....	....	....	....	....	....	....	9.00	10.00	10.00	13.00	15.00	19.00	19.00	17.00	17.00	Guinea
													42.00	42.00	45.50	41.00	26.00 Guinea-Bissau
5.00	5.00	6.00	6.00	8.00	8.00	10.00	10.00	10.00	12.75	12.75	18.50	18.50	15.50	17.50	26.00	13.50	Nigeria
7.87	4.70	6.54	14.54	14.35	17.75	20.75	13.00	9.50	9.50	14.50	18.00	18.00	17.00	14.00	12.00	13.00	South Africa
12.00	12.00	12.00	12.00	15.00	20.00	20.00	26.00	26.00	29.00	37.00	50.00	45.00	55.00	55.00	95.00	145.00	Zaïre
																	Asia
....	....	....	....	....	18.00	17.50	17.50	15.50	15.50	15.50	15.50	19.00	18.00	14.00	14.00	India	
15.00	15.00	16.00	11.00	5.00	5.00	5.00	5.00	7.00	7.00	8.00	7.00	7.00	7.00	7.00	5.00	5.00	Korea
4.21	3.47	4.46	4.50	5.12	5.20	5.06	4.13	3.89	3.20	3.33	4.44	6.79	7.38	....	....	5.07	Malaysia
															628.80	435.03	Mongolia
10.00	10.00	10.00	10.00	10.00	10.00	10.00	10.00	10.00	10.00	10.00	10.00	10.00	10.00	10.00	....	....	Pakistan
4.00	11.00	4.54	6.69	6.30	8.05	12.11	12.75	10.00	10.00	10.00	12.00	14.00	14.00	14.30	9.40	8.30	Philippines
12.50	12.50	13.50	14.50	12.50	13.00	12.00	11.00	8.00	8.00	8.00	8.00	12.00	11.00	11.00	9.00	9.50	Thailand
																	Europe
....	....	....	....	....	....	....	....	....	....	....	....	....	....	....	8.00	8.50	Czech Republic
....	....	....	....	....	....	....	10.50	9.50	10.00	10.50	14.00	20.00	26.00	20.00	22.00	25.00	Hungary
....	....	....	....	....	3.00	4.00	4.00	4.00	4.00	6.00	140.00	55.00	40.00	38.00	35.00	33.00	Poland
....	....	....	....	....	....	....	....	....	....	....	....	....	....	....	12.00	12.00	Slovak Republic
10.00	10.75	26.00	31.50	31.50	48.50	52.00	52.00	48.00	45.00	54.00	54.00	45.00	45.00	....	....	....	Turkey
6.00	6.00	6.00	6.00	14.00	30.00	47.00	61.00	56.00	131.00	372.00	8,187.00	30.00	40.00	....	....	....	Yugoslavia, SFR
																	Western Hemisphere
9.50	9.00	11.00	9.00	10.00	9.00	9.50	8.50	7.50	7.50	9.00	9.00	9.00	9.00	7.50	7.00	6.50	Bahamas, The
6.00	6.00	7.00	22.00	20.00	16.00	16.00	13.00	8.00	8.00	8.00	13.50	13.50	18.00	12.00	8.00	9.50	Barbados
7.50	10.00	14.00	14.50	13.50	11.50	12.00	20.00	12.00	12.00	10.00	12.00	12.00	12.00	12.00	12.00	12.00	Belize
33	35	ℓ93	121	174	194	272	380	89	401	2,282	38,341	1,083	2,494	1,489	5,757	56	Brazil
22.00	30.00	30.00	30.00	27.00	27.00	27.00	27.00	ℓ33.83	34.82	34.25	36.94	ℓ46.45	44.98	34.42	33.49	44.90	Colombia
15.40	14.80	23.50	23.50	30.00	30.00	28.00	28.00	27.50	31.38	31.50	31.61	37.80	42.50	29.00	35.00	37.75	Costa Rica
8.00	8.00	8.00	15.00	15.00	19.00	23.00	23.00	23.00	23.00	23.00	32.00	35.00	49.00	49.00	33.57	44.88	Ecuador
8.50	10.50	12.50	12.50	14.00	14.00	14.00	14.00	14.00	14.00	14.00	14.00	30.00	30.00	32.50	24.30	17.00	20.25 Guyana
....	....	....	....	....	....	....	....	....	....	....	12,874.63	310.99	10.00	15.00	15.00	11.75	10.50 Nicaragua
....	....	....	....	....	....	....	....	....	....	10.00	21.00	30.00	18.00	18.00	18.00	18.00	Paraguay
28.50	29.50	29.50	44.50	44.50	60.00	60.00	42.58	36.07	29.84	748.04	865.61	289.60	67.65	48.50	28.63	16.08	Peru
6.00	6.00	6.00	6.00	6.00	7.50	7.50	7.50	5.97	7.50	9.50	9.50	9.50	11.50	13.00	13.00	13.00	Trinidad and Tobago
....	....	....	72.10	83.70	112.70	133.20	145.10	138.40	143.40	154.50	219.60	251.60	219.00	162.40	164.30	182.30	Uruguay
7.50	11.00	13.00	14.00	13.00	11.00	11.00	8.00	8.00	8.00	8.00	45.00	43.00	43.00	52.20	71.25	48.00	Venezuela

National Interest Rates

Money Market Rates (60b)
(Period averages in percent per annum)

	1978	1979	1980	1981	1982	1983	1984	1985	1986	1987	1988	1989	1990	1991	1992	1993	1994
Industrial Countries																	
United States	7.93	11.20	13.36	16.38	12.26	9.09	10.23	8.10	6.81	6.66	7.61	9.22	8.10	5.70	3.52	3.02	4.20
Canada	6.61	13.21	18.96	12.82	10.38	9.07	10.05	9.84	8.16	8.50	10.35	12.06	11.62	7.40	6.79	3.79	5.54
Australia	8.72	8.09	9.49	12.07	13.90	9.50	10.84	14.70	15.75	13.06	11.90	16.75	14.81	10.47	6.44	5.11	5.18
Japan	4.36	5.86	10.93	7.43	6.94	6.39	6.10	6.46	4.79	3.51	3.62	4.87	7.24	7.46	4.58	13.06	2.20
Belgium	5.23	7.97	11.22	11.47	11.44	8.18	9.47	8.27	6.64	5.67	5.04	7.00	8.29	19.38	9.38	8.21	5.72
Denmark	15.42	12.63	16.93	14.84	16.92	12.81	11.77	10.33	9.22	10.20	8.52	9.66	10.97	9.78	11.35	10.73	6.21
Finland	11.75	9.26	12.35	11.46	11.66	14.67	16.50	13.46	11.90	10.03	9.97	12.56	14.00	13.08	13.25	7.77	5.35
France	7.98	9.04	11.85	15.30	14.87	12.53	11.74	9.93	7.74	7.98	7.52	9.07	9.85	9.49	10.35	8.75	5.69
Germany	3.36	5.87	9.06	11.26	8.67	5.36	5.55	5.19	4.57	3.72	4.01	6.59	7.92	8.84	9.42	7.49	5.35
Ireland	12.44	16.11	16.39	16.20	17.65	14.45	12.93	11.87	12.28	10.84	7.84	9.55	11.10	10.45	15.12	10.49	5.66
Italy	11.49	11.86	17.17	19.60	20.16	18.44	17.27	15.25	13.41	11.51	11.29	12.69	12.38	12.18	13.97	10.20	....
Netherlands	6.24	9.03	10.13	11.01	8.06	5.28	5.78	6.30	5.83	5.16	4.48	6.99	8.29	9.01	9.27	7.10	5.14
Norway	9.36	8.39	11.16	12.35	13.91	12.27	12.67	12.29	14.15	14.66	13.29	11.31	11.45	10.58	13.71	7.64	5.70
Portugal	18.42	14.87	9.95	9.24	12.42	18.24	21.27	20.17	14.52	13.69	12.34	12.84	13.73	15.81	17.48	13.25	10.62
Spain	20.77	13.13	15.46	16.56	17.21	19.40	12.60	11.60	11.50	16.07	11.30	14.39	14.76	13.20	13.01	....	....
Sweden	7.16	8.19	12.17	14.35	13.29	10.85	11.77	13.85	10.15	9.16	10.08	11.52	13.45	11.81	18.42	9.08	7.36
Switzerland	.66	11.00	2.29	2.93	1.32	1.84	3.34	3.75	3.17	2.51	2.22	6.50	8.33	7.73	7.47	4.94	3.85
United Kingdom	4.29	6.01	15.62	13.12	11.36	9.09	7.62	10.78	10.68	9.66	10.31	13.88	14.68	11.75	9.55	5.46	4.76
Developing Countries																	
Africa																	
South Africa	7.99	5.39	4.40	10.25	16.90	13.98	20.31	18.21	10.92	9.50	13.90	18.77	19.46	17.02	14.11	10.83	10.24
Asia																	
India	8.05	8.47	7.24	8.61	7.27	8.30	9.95	10.00	9.97	9.83	....	....	15.57	19.35	15.23	8.64	7.14
Indonesia	7.29	13.23	12.87	16.26	17.24	13.17	18.63	10.33	13.00p	14.52	15.00	12.57	14.37	15.12	12.14	....	....
Korea	19.32	18.86	22.85	18.14	14.18	13.00	11.39	9.35	9.70	8.93	9.62	13.28	14.03	17.03	14.32	12.12	12.45
Malaysia	2.47	4.37	3.31	3.47	7.90	8.97	8.96	7.57	8.03	2.85	3.22	4.72	6.81	7.83	....	....	....
Pakistan	10.41	8.83	8.63	9.27	9.51	8.15	8.97	8.13	6.59	6.25	6.32	6.30	7.29	7.64	7.51	11.00	8.36
Thailand	10.40	13.28	14.66	17.25	14.95	12.15	13.58	13.48	8.07	5.91	8.66	9.82	12.73	10.58	7.06	....	....
Europe																	
Poland	....	....	....	....	....	....	....	....	....	....	....	....	....	49.93	129.49	24.51	23.32
Yugoslavia, SFR	10	10	11	11	....	....	....	....	64	93	423	4,151	....	....	....	....	....
Middle East																	
Kuwait	....	8.58	10.94	10.13	10.22	6.78	8.90	....	7.53	6.08	6.12	8.70	....	....	....	7.43	6.27
Western Hemisphere																	
Mexico	....	....	....	....	45.86	57.51	49.94	62.44	88.01	95.59	69.01	147.43	37.36	23.58	18.87	17.39	16.47

National Interest Rates

Deposit Rates (60l)
except for United States (60lc)
(Period averages in percent per annum)

1978	1979	1980	1981	1982	1983	1984	1985	1986	1987	1988	1989	1990	1991	1992	1993	1994	
																	Industrial Countries
8.20	11.22	13.07	15.91	12.35	9.09	10.37	8.05	6.52	6.86	7.73	9.09	8.16	5.84	3.68	3.17	4.63	United States
8.83	12.05	12.87	18.16	13.74	7.91	10.06	8.40	8.25	7.67	9.54	12.09	12.81	8.62	6.67	4.92	5.59	Canada
8.52	8.25	8.58	10.38	12.33	10.81	9.75	10.46	13.96	13.77	11.92	15.29	13.70	10.44	....	....	....	Australia
2.69	3.31	5.50	4.44	3.75	3.75	3.50	3.50	2.32	1.76	1.76	1.97	3.56	14.14	3.35	2.14	1.70	Japan
....	....	....	11.00	10.79	9.75	10.46	14.71	16.32	....	13.41	10.92	11.65	8.93	6.58	6.24	....	New Zealand
5.00	5.00	5.00	5.00	5.00	4.21	4.00	3.94	3.63	3.03	2.73	2.98	3.41	3.75	3.69	2.98	2.31	Austria
4.50	5.50	7.69	7.50	7.46	6.67	7.44	6.69	5.33	5.00	4.54	5.13	6.13	6.25	6.25	17.11	4.86	Belgium
....	10.80	10.80	13.02	12.89	9.98	9.00	8.21	6.58	7.07	7.75	8.27	7.93	7.15	7.50	6.52	....	Denmark
....	....	....	9.00	8.56	8.75	9.25	8.75	7.33	7.00	7.75	5.75	7.50	7.50	7.50	4.75	3.27	Finland
6.75	5.81	6.25	7.75	9.31	8.28	7.68	6.80	5.23	5.31	5.01	5.92	6.68	....	....	....	....	France
3.06	5.14	7.95	9.74	7.54	4.56	4.86	4.44	3.71	3.20	3.29	5.50	7.07	7.62	8.01	6.27	4.47	Germany
9.96	11.88	14.50	14.50	14.50	14.50	15.42	15.50	15.50	15.33	17.33	17.14	19.52	20.67	19.92	19.33	18.92	Greece
6.33	10.96	12.00	11.33	12.73	9.27	7.83	6.98	6.50	6.21	3.63	4.54	6.29	5.21	5.42	2.27	.33	Ireland
10.82	10.59	12.70	14.31	15.28	12.91	10.77	8.09	8.89	7.01	6.69	6.93	6.80	6.64	7.11	6.12	4.78	Italy
5.04	5.54	5.96	6.06	5.88	4.03	4.10	4.10	3.93	3.55	3.48	3.49	3.31	3.18	3.20	3.11	2.95	Netherlands
....	5.10	5.00	5.00	5.10	5.30	5.30	10.06	10.97	12.03	11.49	9.63	9.68	9.60	10.69	5.51	5.21	Norway
17.67	19.00	19.00	19.25	21.00	26.08	28.00	25.08	17.13	14.46	13.21	13.00	13.58	14.63	14.59	11.06	8.37	Portugal
....	9.61	13.05	11.41	12.26	12.31	12.30	10.53	9.05	8.97	9.06	9.55	10.65	10.47	10.43	9.33	6.70	Spain
7.00	9.50	11.25	11.75	11.25	9.75	10.75	12.00	9.00	8.75	9.50	19.16	9.93	7.96	17.80	5.10	4.91	Sweden
....	....	....	7.75	4.40	3.31	3.77	4.36	3.51	3.08	4.50	8.08	8.28	7.63	5.50	3.50	3.63	Switzerland
6.08	11.71	14.13	10.67	12.42	11.19	17.14	11.79	9.85	8.57	8.54	11.43	12.22	10.06	7.30	3.76	3.44	United Kingdom
																	Developing Countries
																	Africa
....	6.50	7.50	7.50	7.50	7.50	7.50	7.50	7.35	7.15	7.21	7.50	17.50	7.50	7.50	7.75	8.08	Cameroon
....	....	....	....	....	....	....	4.00	4.00	4.00	4.00	4.00	4.00	4.00	4.00	4.00	4.00	Cape Verde
5.50	4.00	5.50	7.50	7.50	7.50	7.50	7.50	7.35	7.19	7.44	7.50	17.50	7.50	7.50	7.75	8.08	Central African Rep.
4.75	4.50	5.50	5.50	5.50	5.50	5.50	5.50	5.50	5.33	4.31	4.25	17.50	7.50	7.50	7.75	8.08	Chad
5.75	5.50	6.50	6.50	6.50	7.50	7.50	8.25	8.10	7.79	7.81	8.00	17.50	7.50	7.50	7.75	8.08	Congo
....	....	....	....	....	....	....	7.50	8.25	7.88	6.33	6.50	17.50	7.50	7.50	7.75	8.08	Equatorial Guinea
7.50	6.50	7.50	7.50	7.50	7.50	7.50	7.67	8.00	7.94	8.17	8.75	17.50	7.50	7.50	7.75	8.08	Gabon
....	....	....	....	....	....	....	....	....	15.00	....	16.83	19.50	21.00	22.00	23.00	19.75	Guinea
....	....	....	....	....	....	....	....	....	....	....	23.00	28.00	32.67	36.00	39.33	53.92	28.67 Guinea-Bissau
4.15	4.47	5.27	5.72	7.60	7.41	8.25	9.12	9.24	13.09	12.95	14.68	19.78	14.92	18.04	23.24	13.13	Nigeria
7.67	6.00	5.54	8.19	13.00	13.71	18.29	17.02	10.98	8.70	13.54	18.13	18.86	17.30	13.78	11.50	11.11	South Africa
																	Asia
6.00	6.00	6.00	6.00	6.00	6.00	16.00	18.00	15.39	16.78	17.72	18.63	17.30	23.27	20.37	....	....	Indonesia
18.60	18.60	19.50	16.20	8.00	8.00	9.17	10.00	10.00	10.00	10.00	10.00	10.00	10.00	10.00	8.58	8.50	Korea
5.13	5.50	6.23	9.67	9.75	8.02	9.54	8.81	7.17	3.00	....	4.60	5.90	7.18	....	....	....	Malaysia
....	....	....	....	....	....	....	....	300.00	300.00	300.00	300.00	300.00	400.00	500.00	125.20	92.29	Mongolia
8.50	8.67	12.25	13.72	13.74	13.58	21.17	18.91	11.25	8.20	11.32	14.13	19.54	18.80	14.27	9.61	10.54	Philippines
8.00	8.25	12.00	12.50	13.00	13.00	13.00	13.00	9.75	9.50	9.50	9.50	12.25	....	....	....	....	Thailand
																	Europe
....	....	....	....	....	....	....	....	....	....	....	....	....	....	....	7.03	7.07	Czech Republic
3.00	3.00	3.00	3.00	3.50	5.00	5.00	5.00	4.50	4.00	5.25	9.42	19.08	123.83	19.09	13.39	18.18	Hungary
....	....	....	....	....	....	....	....	....	....	....	100.00	41.67	153.50	37.75	34.00	30.58	Poland
....	....	....	....	....	....	....	....	....	....	....	....	....	....	....	8.02	9.32	Slovak Republic
6.00	7.33	8.00	26.50	45.00	45.33	51.42	49.25	40.58	35.00	49.08	53.45	47.60	62.93	68.74	64.58	87.79	Turkey
																	Middle East
5.88	7.00	8.33	10.00	11.00	11.00	11.00	11.00	11.00	11.00	11.00	11.67	12.00	....	....	....	....	Egypt
....	....	....	9.21	9.21	7.13	7.73	7.25	6.80	5.73	5.30	7.40	....	....	7.59	7.07	....	Kuwait
																	Western Hemisphere
....	....	6.00	6.30	7.50	11.00	11.00	9.88	7.71	6.50	6.50	6.50	8.44	8.21	7.44	6.71	6.50	Antigua and Barbuda
131.72	117.29	79.61	157.07	126.24	281.31	396.85	630.03	94.69	175.95	371.85	17,235.81	1,517.88	61.68	16.78	11.34	8.08	Argentina
....	....	6.96	7.48	7.56	7.47	7.44	6.40	5.57	5.50	5.97	6.48	6.57	6.92	6.13	5.19	4.30	Bahamas, The
....	....	5.30	7.39	8.83	6.73	6.07	5.49	4.28	3.61	4.26	4.78	6.28	6.53	6.68	4.39	4.32	Barbados
6.80	6.80	11.18	14.68	14.87	11.30	9.08	11.63	11.83	9.58	8.42	7.86	8.14	8.42	8.15	8.13	8.55	Belize
....	16.00	18.00	28.42	30.33	39.83	108.33	68.75	106.45	33.17	27.74	23.67	23.83	23.78	23.22	22.18	18.43	Bolivia
....	....	115.00	108.00	156.1	154.6	267.6	295.4	109.5	401.0	859.4	15,845.0	9,394.3	913.5	1,560.2	3,293.5	....	Brazil
63.53	45.19	37.72	40.90	48.68	28.01	27.63	31.97	18.99	25.22	15.11	27.72	40.27	22.32	18.26	18.24	15.12	Chile
....	....	....	....	....	....	....	....	31.36	30.79	33.46	33.73	36.44	37.23	26.67	25.84	29.42	Colombia
....	....	....	....	18.29	19.50	14.50	16.50	16.67	14.06	15.18	15.62	21.16	27.32	15.80	16.90	17.72	Costa Rica
4.00	4.00	4.00	....	5.00	5.00	5.00	5.00	4.92	5.04	....	4.54	4.21	4.38	4.08	4.00	4.00	Dominica
....	....	....	....	....	16.00	18.17	21.00	21.39	25.34	34.00	40.24	43.55	41.54	46.81	31.97	33.65	Ecuador
....	....	....	....	....	12.50	12.50	12.50	15.00	15.00	15.00	16.25	18.00	16.11	11.51	15.27	13.57	El Salvador
....	....	4.50	4.50	4.50	5.88	6.98	7.04	6.50	6.08	5.50	5.04	6.50	6.17	5.46	5.00	4.17	Grenada
9.00	9.00	9.00	10.00	12.00	9.00	9.00	9.00	10.17	11.00	12.17	13.00	18.21	24.41	10.44	12.63	9.69	Guatemala
7.00	9.00	11.00	11.00	11.58	12.00	12.00	12.00	12.00	11.08	12.00	15.81	29.18	29.53	22.51	12.26	11.42	Guyana
....	....	....	....	10.60	11.30	10.30	9.93	9.70	9.62	8.63	8.58	8.78	11.45	12.34	11.60	11.56	Honduras
5.68	8.28	9.53	10.55	10.71	13.60	15.86	19.58	18.76	15.64	15.80	15.95	23.88	24.67	33.63	27.59	36.41	Jamaica
11.17	13.23	20.63	29.57	43.62	54.70	48.36	59.48	84.68	97.24	163.65	36.29	31.24	17.10	15.68	15.46	13.26	Mexico
....	....	....	....	....	....	....	....	....	....	—	1,585.90	9.50	11.63	12.01	11.61	11.70	Nicaragua
....	....	....	....	....	....	....	6.50	6.59	7.54	8.49	8.40	7.73	15.67	5.90	6.11	Panama
....	....	....	....	....	....	....	....	....	....	....	22.92	22.53	20.15	22.10	23.12	Paraguay
....	....	....	....	....	....	....	....	....	....	161.78	1,135.59	2,439.56	170.54	59.65	44.14	22.35	Peru
....	....	6.00	6.00	6.00	6.00	6.00	6.33	6.00	5.33	7.00	7.00	7.00	7.00	7.00	5.50	5.50	St. Kitts and Nevis
....	....	5.50	8.00	8.00	8.00	8.58	9.13	7.50	5.04	5.00	5.00	5.58	6.06	5.52	4.96	4.50	St. Lucia
....	....	4.50	4.50	5.50	5.50	5.75	5.92	5.96	5.32	4.82	4.29	4.33	4.44	5.00	4.25	4.04	St. Vincent & Grens.
....	....	....	6.57	6.25	6.40	6.76	5.31	6.04	6.03	....	6.28	5.96	5.79	6.99	7.06	6.91	Trinidad and Tobago
42.60	50.60	50.30	47.40	50.13	71.40	68.39	81.90	61.70	60.83	67.82	84.70	97.83	75.23	54.47	39.38	36.98	Uruguay
....	....	....	....	....	12.29	10.52	8.93	8.94	8.95	29.23	27.78	31.10	35.42	53.75	39.02	Venezuela

National Interest Rates

Lending Rates (60p)
(Period averages in percent per annum)

	1978	1979	1980	1981	1982	1983	1984	1985	1986	1987	1988	1989	1990	1991	1992	1993	1994
Industrial Countries																	
United States	9.06	12.67	15.27	18.87	14.86	10.79	12.04	9.93	8.35	8.21	9.32	10.92	10.01	8.46	6.25	6.00	7.14
Canada	9.69	12.90	14.25	19.29	15.81	11.17	12.06	10.58	10.52	9.52	10.83	13.33	14.06	9.94	7.48	5.94	6.88
Australia	10.46	10.00	10.58	12.92	14.55	14.04	14.46	15.96	19.85	19.83	18.52	21.71	20.48	16.38	12.02	....	....
Japan	6.42	6.37	8.35	7.86	7.31	7.13	6.75	6.60	6.02	5.21	5.03	5.29	6.95	7.53	6.15	‡4.41	4.13
New Zealand	9.65	10.26	12.63	13.50	13.73	13.83	12.53	....	....	‡20.84	17.17	15.78	16.01	14.01	11.39	10.34	....
Belgium	....	....	....	18.00	15.50	13.75	14.00	12.54	10.44	9.33	8.92	11.08	13.00	12.88	12.19	11.81	9.42
Denmark	13.90	15.30	17.20	17.65	18.55	14.49	13.38	14.65	12.98	13.62	12.59	13.44	14.10	11.38	11.60	10.46	....
Finland	8.22	8.03	9.77	9.84	9.32	9.56	10.49	10.41	9.08	8.91	9.72	10.31	11.62	11.80	12.14	9.92	7.91
France	15.12	15.90	18.73	20.77	20.33	18.95	18.85	17.77	16.28	15.82	15.65	16.01	....	....	....	....	....
Germany	7.33	8.63	12.04	14.69	13.50	10.05	9.82	9.53	8.75	8.36	8.33	9.94	11.59	12.46	13.59	12.85	11.48
Greece	13.46	16.71	21.25	21.33	20.50	20.50	20.50	20.50	20.50	21.82	22.89	23.26	27.62	29.45	28.71	28.56	27.44
Ireland	13.00	15.50	15.96	15.50	17.04	14.13	12.92	12.44	12.23	11.15	8.29	9.42	11.29	10.63	....	....	....
Italy	16.05	14.64	19.03	18.36	17.37	22.27	20.38	13.36	15.93	13.58	13.57	14.21	14.08	13.89	15.77	13.86	11.23
Netherlands	13.25	16.50	13.50	14.25	11.17	8.46	8.88	9.25	8.63	8.15	7.77	10.75	11.75	12.40	12.75	10.40	8.29
Norway	....	12.23	12.63	13.90	14.33	14.35	13.69	13.46	14.37	16.31	16.44	14.39	14.15	14.19	14.27	9.17	....
Portugal	17.58	18.75	18.75	20.13	23.00	27.88	29.42	27.29	19.63	‡18.92	‡17.53	19.59	21.71	‡25.02	20.43	16.48	15.01
Spain	14.96	15.77	16.85	15.26	14.98	15.00	16.58	13.52	12.19	16.36	12.43	15.84	16.01	14.38	14.23	12.78	8.95
Sweden	11.16	13.67	15.18	16.73	16.52	14.91	16.00	16.89	‡12.57	12.65	13.29	14.81	16.69	16.05	‡15.20	11.40	10.64
Switzerland	....	....	....	5.56	5.98	5.49	5.49	5.43	5.46	5.24	5.07	5.85	7.42	7.83	7.80	6.40	5.51
United Kingdom	9.25	13.92	16.17	13.25	11.84	9.85	9.75	12.33	10.83	9.64	10.29	13.92	14.75	11.54	9.41	5.92	5.48
Developing Countries																	
Africa																	
Cameroon	....	10.25	13.00	13.00	13.00	14.50	14.50	14.50	13.50	13.00	13.46	15.00	‡18.50	18.15	17.77	17.46	17.42
Cape Verde	6.50	6.50	6.50	6.50	6.50	6.50	6.50	10.00	10.00	10.00	10.00	10.00	10.00	10.00	10.00	10.00	10.67
Central African Rep.	9.50	8.50	10.50	12.00	12.00	12.50	12.50	12.50	12.00	11.42	12.25	13.00	‡18.50	18.15	17.77	17.46	17.42
Chad	10.50	8.50	11.00	11.00	11.00	11.50	11.50	11.50	11.00	10.50	11.79	11.50	‡18.50	18.15	17.77	17.46	17.42
Congo	13.00	9.00	11.00	11.00	11.00	12.00	12.00	12.00	11.50	11.13	11.79	12.50	‡18.50	18.15	17.77	17.46	17.42
Equatorial Guinea	....	....	....	....	....	....	....	15.00	14.50	14.13	14.79	15.50	‡18.50	18.15	17.77	17.46	17.42
Gabon	10.50	8.50	12.50	12.50	12.46	13.00	13.00	12.67	11.50	11.13	11.79	12.50	‡18.50	18.15	17.77	17.46	17.42
Guinea	....	....	....	....	....	....	....	....	....	15.00	15.00	17.25	21.17	24.50	27.00	24.50	22.00
Guinea-Bissau	....	....	....	....	....	....	....	....	18.00	18.00	30.00	38.33	45.75	47.00	50.33	63.58	36.33
Nigeria	6.75	7.79	8.43	8.92	9.54	9.98	10.24	9.43	9.96	13.96	16.62	20.44	25.30	20.04	24.76	31.65	20.48
South Africa	12.13	10.00	9.50	14.00	19.33	16.67	22.33	21.50	14.33	12.50	15.33	19.83	21.00	20.31	18.91	16.16	15.58
Asia																	
Indonesia	....	....	....	....	....	....	....	....	21.49	21.67	22.10	21.70	20.61	....	24.03	20.24	....
Korea	....	....	18.00	17.38	11.79	10.00	10.00	10.00	10.00	10.00	10.13	11.25	10.00	10.00	10.00	8.58	8.50
Malaysia	7.50	7.50	7.75	8.50	8.79	11.08	11.35	11.54	10.80	8.19	7.25	7.00	7.17	8.13	....	....	7.62
Mongolia	....	....	....	....	....	....	....	....	....	....	....	....	....	....	....	300.00	233.56
Thailand	15.00	15.00	18.00	19.00	19.00	17.63	18.75	19.00	17.00	15.00	15.00	15.00	16.54	19.00	....	....	....
Europe																	
Czech Republic	....	....	....	....	....	....	....	....	....	....	....	....	....	....	....	14.07	13.12
Hungary	....	....	....	....	....	....	....	....	....	....	....	....	....	35.15	33.05	25.43	27.40
Poland	....	8.00	8.00	8.00	9.00	9.00	9.00	12.00	12.00	12.00	16.67	64.00	504.17	54.58	39.00	35.25	32.83
Slovak Republic	....	....	....	....	....	....	....	....	....	....	....	....	....	....	....	14.41	14.56
Yugoslavia, SFR	11.50	11.50	11.50	12.00	16.25	34.00	44.50	71.50	82.00	111.25	455.17	4,353.75	....	....	....	....	....
Middle East																	
Kuwait	....	....	....	9.15	9.38	9.17	8.81	9.07	8.96	8.26	7.12	8.30	....	....	7.86	7.94	....
Western Hemisphere																	
Antigua and Barbuda	8.60	8.60	10.00	11.00	13.00	14.00	13.63	13.00	14.25	12.38	11.50	12.17	12.38	15.50	13.00	13.00	12.50
Argentina	....	....	86.88	185.25	201.97	738.97	1,182.30	1,161.16	134.77	252.77	523.69	—	—	71.33	15.11	6.31	7.66
Bahamas, The	9.50	9.13	10.83	11.00	11.00	11.00	11.00	10.33	9.25	9.00	9.00	9.00	9.00	9.00	8.08	7.46	6.88
Barbados	....	....	....	11.46	13.38	11.79	11.50	10.56	9.06	8.75	9.44	9.92	11.42	12.42	13.54	8.92	9.08
Belize	11.30	11.60	16.50	19.28	....	....	....	....	14.69	14.14	13.56	13.77	14.04	14.24	14.32	14.37	14.78
Bolivia	....	27.00	28.00	42.50	45.00	56.83	120.67	172.15	‡297.05	56.87	39.79	37.27	41.81	41.15	45.51	53.88	55.57
Chile	86.13	62.11	47.14	52.02	63.86	42.82	38.33	40.81	26.27	32.80	21.17	35.92	48.83	28.55	23.92	24.33	20.34
Colombia	....	....	....	....	....	....	....	....	....	40.83	41.10	42.69	43.04	45.25	47.13	35.81	40.47
Costa Rica	....	....	....	....	....	25.00	23.25	18.00	20.92	21.80	23.82	28.69	29.17	32.56	38.88	28.46	30.02	33.03
Dominica	8.50	8.50	8.50	9.00	9.50	9.50	10.42	10.04	10.25	10.50	10.50	10.50	10.50	10.29	10.00	10.00	9.58
Ecuador	....	....	9.00	9.00	9.25	12.33	16.17	18.00	18.00	18.42	23.00	30.08	37.50	46.67	60.17	47.83	43.99
El Salvador	....	....	....	....	....	15.00	14.00	14.00	14.00	17.00	17.00	17.00	18.50	21.17	19.67	16.43	19.42	19.03
Grenada	9.00	8.50	9.50	9.50	10.50	10.50	10.50	11.67	11.50	11.42	10.50	10.67	10.50	10.63	10.50	10.50	10.50
Guatemala	11.00	11.00	11.00	12.00	14.50	12.00	12.00	12.00	13.17	14.00	15.17	16.00	23.27	34.08	19.49	24.73	22.93
Guyana	9.50	11.50	13.50	13.50	14.38	15.00	15.00	15.00	15.00	15.00	15.07	18.94	32.75	33.55	28.69	19.36	18.36
Honduras	....	....	....	....	16.50	16.10	16.20	16.30	16.12	15.54	15.38	15.43	17.05	21.88	21.68	22.06	24.68
Jamaica	13.68	13.81	15.63	16.07	16.44	16.97	18.53	24.92	27.34	25.45	25.19	25.22	30.50	31.51	44.81	43.71	49.46
Nicaragua	....	....	....	....	....	....	....	....	....	....	—	—	558.01	22.00	17.92	19.32	18.73	20.14
Panama	....	....	....	....	....	....	....	....	12.36	12.60	12.47	12.92	11.98	11.79	10.61	10.06	10.15
Paraguay	....	....	....	....	....	....	....	....	....	....	....	....	31.00	34.94	27.96	30.78	32.46
Peru	....	....	....	....	....	....	....	....	40.52	35.74	174.28	1,515.86	4,774.53	751.52	173.80	97.37	53.56
St. Kitts and Nevis	....	....	....	9.00	9.00	9.00	10.00	10.21	10.21	12.00	12.00	12.00	12.00	12.00	12.67	13.00	13.00
St. Lucia	7.50	7.50	11.00	13.00	13.00	13.00	13.33	14.00	14.00	11.58	10.58	10.00	10.54	10.50	10.50	10.17	10.13
St. Lucia	7.50	7.50	11.00	13.00	13.00	13.00	13.33	14.00	14.00	11.58	10.58	10.00	10.54	10.50	10.50	10.17	10.13
Trinidad and Tobago	....	....	10.00	11.38	11.50	11.71	12.75	12.69	12.00	11.50	12.58	13.31	12.87	13.17	15.33	15.50	15.98
Uruguay	71.20	68.10	66.62	60.40	58.54	93.64	83.23	94.58	94.73	95.80	101.98	127.58	174.45	152.88	117.77	97.33	95.08
Venezuela	....	....	....	....	....	....	9.57	9.33	8.49	8.48	8.50	22.57	28.23	29.78	33.91	48.88	46.55

National Interest Rates

1978	1979	1980	1981	1982	1983	1984	1985	1986	1987	1988	1989	1990	1991	1992	1993	1994	

Treasury Bill Rates (60c)
(Period averages in percent per annum)

Industrial Countries

1978	1979	1980	1981	1982	1983	1984	1985	1986	1987	1988	1989	1990	1991	1992	1993	1994	Country
7.22	10.04	11.62	14.08	10.72	8.62	9.57	7.49	5.97	5.83	6.67	8.11	7.51	5.41	3.46	3.02	4.27	United States
8.68	11.69	12.79	17.72	13.66	9.31	11.06	9.43	8.97	8.15	9.48	12.05	12.81	8.73	6.59	4.84	5.54	Canada
8.35	8.88	10.67	13.25	14.64	11.06	10.99	15.34	15.39	12.80	12.14	16.80	14.15	9.96	6.27	5.00	5.69	Australia
8.25	10.75	11.25	11.25	11.25	10.13	9.23	....	19.97	20.50	....	13.51	13.78	9.74	6.72	6.21	....	New Zealand
17.10	17.82	18.17	18.87	19.66	14.77	13.03	10.78	9.59	10.99	9.19	....	....	....	....	....	....	Denmark
....	....	....	....	....	....	....	....	....	8.23	7.82	9.38	10.16	9.70	10.48	8.38	5.82	France
3.76	5.48	7.85	10.37	8.31	5.63	5.66	5.04	3.86	3.28	3.62	6.28	8.13	8.27	8.32	6.22	5.05	Germany
11.83	12.96	15.13	15.20	16.33	13.26	13.13	11.78	11.85	10.70	7.81	9.70	10.90	10.12	....	....	....	Ireland
11.99	12.51	15.92	19.70	19.44	17.90	15.37	13.71	11.40	10.73	11.13	12.58	12.38	12.54	14.32	10.58	9.17	Italy
....	....	12.37	13.48	14.37	18.14	21.15	20.90	‖15.56	13.89	12.97	....	13.52	14.19	12.88	....	....	Portugal
14.41	15.70	15.70	15.80	15.70	19.80	13.43	10.90	8.63	8.03	‖10.79	13.57	14.17	12.45	12.44	10.53	8.11	Spain
6.63	6.79	11.58	12.54	13.22	12.34	11.93	14.17	9.83	9.39	10.08	11.50	13.66	11.59	12.85	8.35	7.40	Sweden
....	....	5.15	7.82	3.87	3.04	3.58	4.15	3.54	3.18	3.01	6.60	8.32	7.74	7.76	4.75	3.97	Switzerland
7.84	12.97	15.16	13.03	11.47	9.59	9.30	11.56	10.37	9.25	9.78	13.05	14.08	10.96	8.94	5.18	5.21	United Kingdom

Developing Countries

Africa

7.81	5.26	4.65	9.80	15.59	13.45	19.33	17.56	10.43	8.71	12.03	16.84	17.80	16.68	13.77	11.31	10.93	South Africa

Asia

7.04	7.40	9.16	11.57	11.64	9.35	10.00	11.02	6.76	3.63	5.08	....	....	....	....	....	....	Thailand

Europe

....	....	....	....	....	....	....	....	....	....	....	....	....	....	21.59	16.71	25.25	Hungary
....	....	....	....	....	....	....	....	....	....	....	....	....	....	44.03	33.16	28.81	Poland

Middle East

....	....	6.50	6.50	6.42	5.68	5.68	5.68	5.69	5.48	6.01	8.28	....	....	....	....	....	Kuwait

Western Hemisphere

3.49	3.07	7.37	8.89	8.76	9.11	6.88	5.90	3.47	2.40	4.46	5.21	5.85	6.49	5.32	3.96	1.88	Bahamas, The
4.80	4.88	5.63	9.49	13.25	7.45	6.92	.55	4.42	4.84	4.75	4.90	7.07	9.34	10.88	5.44	7.26	Barbados
6.40	6.40	10.29	11.68	11.06	10.51	9.55	12.76	10.81	8.80	8.32	7.36	7.37	6.71	5.38	4.59	4.27	Belize
31.82	39.85	54.00	71.64	93.06	127.41	190.23	215.06	150.56	195.40	482.65	381.78	....	....	....	....	....	Brazil
7.00	9.08	10.67	11.62	12.28	12.75	12.75	12.75	12.75	11.33	10.25	15.19	30.00	30.94	25.75	16.83	17.66	Guyana
8.26	9.25	9.97	9.83	8.61	12.38	13.29	19.03	20.88	18.16	18.50	19.10	26.21	25.56	34.36	28.85	42.98	Jamaica
10.53	15.02	22.46	30.77	45.75	59.07	49.32	63.20	....	103.07	‖69.15	44.99	34.76	19.28	15.62	15.03	14.10	Mexico
3.60	3.16	3.07	3.06	3.05	3.08	3.39	3.47	3.99	4.63	....	7.13	7.50	7.67	9.26	9.45	....	Trinidad and Tobago

Government Bond Yields (61)
(Average yields to maturity in percent per annum)

Industrial Countries

1978	1979	1980	1981	1982	1983	1984	1985	1986	1987	1988	1989	1990	1991	1992	1993	1994	Country
8.41	9.44	11.46	13.91	13.00	11.11	12.52	10.62	7.68	8.38	8.85	8.50	8.55	7.86	7.01	5.82	7.11	United States
9.27	10.21	12.48	15.22	14.26	11.79	12.75	11.04	9.52	9.95	10.22	9.92	10.85	9.76	8.77	7.85	8.63	Canada
9.06	9.76	11.65	13.96	‖15.35	14.33	13.83	14.10	13.56	13.47	12.31	13.41	13.18	10.69	9.22	7.28	9.04	Australia
6.09	7.69	9.22	8.66	8.06	7.42	6.81	6.34	4.94	4.21	4.27	5.05	7.36	6.53	4.94	3.69	3.71	Japan
9.97	12.04	13.29	12.83	12.91	12.18	12.57	17.71	16.52	‖16.35	13.45	12.78	12.46	10.00	7.87	6.69	....	New Zealand
8.21	7.96	9.24	10.61	9.92	8.17	8.02	7.77	7.33	6.91	6.67	7.14	8.74	8.62	8.27	6.64	6.69	Austria
8.45	9.51	12.04	13.71	13.56	11.86	11.98	10.61	7.93	7.83	7.85	8.64	10.06	9.28	8.64	7.18	7.76	Belgium
14.54	15.82	17.66	18.92	20.39	14.46	‖13.96	11.31	9.91	11.06	9.78	9.75	10.74	9.59	9.47	7.08	7.41	Denmark
8.96	9.48	13.03	15.79	15.69	13.63	12.54	10.94	8.62	9.43	9.06	8.79	9.96	9.05	8.60	6.91	7.35	France
5.80	7.40	8.50	10.38	8.95	7.89	7.78	6.87	5.92	5.84	6.10	7.09	8.88	8.63	7.96	6.28	6.67	Germany
12.83	15.07	15.35	17.26	17.06	13.90	14.62	12.64	11.07	11.27	9.49	8.95	10.08	9.17	9.11	7.72	8.19	Ireland
13.70	14.05	16.11	20.56	20.90	18.02	14.95	13.00	10.52	9.68	10.16	10.72	11.51	‖13.18	13.27	11.31	10.56	Italy
7.74	8.78	10.21	11.55	10.10	8.61	8.33	7.34	6.32	6.40	6.42	7.22	8.92	8.74	8.10	6.51	7.20	Netherlands
8.45	8.59	10.27	12.31	13.20	12.86	12.16	12.58	13.47	13.56	12.97	10.84	10.72	9.87	9.78	6.52	7.13	Norway
16.17	16.68	16.68	16.71	16.79	19.22	21.50	20.75	15.54	15.02	13.87	14.74	15.17	17.77	15.38	12.45	10.83	Portugal
10.09	10.47	11.74	13.49	12.30	12.28	12.28	13.09	10.26	‖11.68	11.35	11.18	13.08	10.69	10.02	8.54	‖9.41	Sweden
3.33	3.45	4.77	5.57	4.83	4.52	4.70	4.78	4.29	4.12	4.15	5.20	‖6.68	6.35	5.48	4.05	5.23	Switzerland
12.47	12.99	13.79	14.74	12.88	10.81	10.69	10.62	9.87	9.48	9.36	9.58	11.08	9.92	9.15	7.87	8.05	United Kingdom

Developing Countries

Africa

10.40	9.26	10.09	12.99	13.51	12.67	15.23	16.79	16.37	15.30	16.37	16.90	16.15	16.34	15.44	13.97	14.83	South Africa

Asia

6.37	6.45	6.71	7.15	7.59	7.99	8.65	8.99	....	....	....	....	....	....	....	....	....	India
9.48	9.75	11.20	9.40	9.36	9.31	9.25	9.19	8.77	8.26	8.32	8.18	8.05	7.88	‖13.15	13.31	13.01	Pakistan
9.25	13.25	13.00	13.06	13.85	11.13	12.41	12.11	9.11	7.48	7.50	8.09	10.60	10.75	10.75	10.75	10.75	Thailand

Western Hemisphere

11.70	12.28	13.61	13.68	13.68	15.16	17.14	22.48	22.62	20.83	20.40	20.17	25.46	26.33	30.50	23.76	26.82	Jamaica
....	....	....	....	....	....	13.15	12.55	12.07	13.49	14.86	17.32	20.06	27.14	31.66	41.03	54.73	Venezuela

Real Effective Exchange Rate Indices

(1990=100)

Industrial Countries

Based on Relative Unit Labor Costs (65um.110)

Country		1980	1981	1982	1983	1984	1985	1986	1987	1988	1989	1990	1991	1992	1993	1994
United States	111	113.4	122.8	133.8	138.4	151.3	156.7	123.1	103.8	98.4	104.2	100.0	98.0	95.2	97.0	....
Canada	156	83.8	86.3	94.6	94.1	86.1	82.4	79.8	85.8	94.1	99.2	100.0	103.9	95.7	88.3	....
Japan	158	85.8	92.1	80.7	87.8	88.8	86.3	114.7	118.2	124.5	114.6	100.0	105.3	112.7	137.1	....
Austria	122	110.2	105.1	103.5	103.6	104.5	105.2	108.3	108.7	101.7	99.6	100.0	97.7	95.9	95.3	....
Belgium	124	135.4	122.9	102.3	92.7	91.9	93.9	97.4	98.1	95.3	93.5	100.0	99.9	99.3	98.9	....
Denmark	128	83.0	78.8	77.7	78.6	79.5	82.7	89.8	98.2	95.5	92.8	100.0	98.5	98.8	....
Finland	172	88.0	91.3	94.1	92.3	95.3	94.7	90.6	88.3	90.5	94.5	100.0	97.7	76.0	61.9	....
France	132	107.5	105.1	101.5	101.5	102.6	105.1	106.9	105.8	100.2	96.6	100.0	98.0	98.0	101.4	....
Germany	134	86.1	79.1	83.1	84.6	83.2	82.0	89.1	98.5	98.8	97.0	100.0	97.7	104.7	114.0	....
Ireland	178	135.1	122.9	128.7	125.3	120.3	115.2	121.2	113.0	105.6	96.0	100.0	97.3	90.2	83.8	....
Italy	136	86.3	86.3	88.1	94.3	92.5	90.6	92.2	91.5	90.4	95.4	100.0	102.1	98.2	81.7	....
Netherlands	138	118.5	107.4	111.1	110.0	99.9	98.0	103.9	108.3	105.2	98.9	100.0	99.0	102.6	105.2	....
Norway	142	93.5	98.0	100.2	101.8	99.9	100.1	99.3	100.6	106.5	102.6	100.0	97.8	97.4	95.1	....
Spain	184	94.2	93.0	91.4	79.8	82.8	81.6	79.4	79.6	85.0	91.9	100.0	100.0	102.5	90.5	....
Sweden	144	104.2	105.7	92.5	81.3	86.0	88.2	88.4	88.4	92.9	98.9	100.0	101.5	98.5	72.5	....
Switzerland	146	105.2	107.4	114.6	115.5	108.0	103.1	106.3	109.7	104.4	96.0	100.0	98.9	93.4	92.6	....
United Kingdom	112	115.0	121.1	114.1	104.4	100.6	103.3	95.0	96.2	103.3	104.0	100.0	103.4	101.4	93.8	....

Based on Relative Normalized Unit Labor Costs (..reu)

Country		1980	1981	1982	1983	1984	1985	1986	1987	1988	1989	1990	1991	1992	1993	1994
United States	111	112.3	123.4	139.4	141.8	149.9	154.3	124.6	108.2	101.5	104.9	100.0	98.5	96.5	100.4	....
Canada	156	83.8	87.8	88.7	91.9	89.6	85.7	81.1	84.6	92.5	98.4	100.0	103.0	97.5	89.9	....
Japan	158	85.8	90.9	79.9	84.8	86.7	85.8	108.1	113.2	119.1	111.9	100.0	105.8	109.1	127.5	....
Austria	122	110.9	105.0	105.4	105.5	104.2	103.6	107.0	108.0	104.2	101.0	100.0	97.0	97.7	97.7	....
Belgium	124	135.7	124.3	103.2	96.9	95.4	94.8	98.1	99.0	96.2	95.7	100.0	100.1	101.9	102.1	....
Denmark	128	84.5	79.7	77.7	80.0	79.5	83.2	86.8	95.2	94.9	93.8	100.0	96.6	96.7	98.8	....
Finland	172	89.7	93.6	95.4	91.6	93.8	93.4	90.4	89.7	92.4	96.6	100.0	92.2	75.8	63.5	....
France	132	105.5	102.8	103.9	101.2	99.9	102.8	104.5	102.4	99.3	97.0	100.0	95.9	96.9	98.9	....
Germany	134	85.1	78.7	80.6	83.7	82.5	82.6	90.0	96.1	96.1	94.6	100.0	99.5	102.3	110.6	....
Ireland	178	133.5	124.8	126.2	123.6	119.9	117.2	120.1	111.7	105.4	98.2	100.0	94.1	92.3	86.2	....
Italy	136	89.6	87.5	87.0	92.0	93.6	90.9	92.3	93.2	92.3	96.3	100.0	101.1	99.2	82.5	....
Netherlands	138	118.4	107.0	109.1	108.2	101.2	98.5	104.2	107.6	104.2	98.8	100.0	98.9	103.0	105.7	....
Norway	142	93.1	95.8	98.6	99.5	100.2	100.1	97.2	101.2	102.8	100.9	100.0	97.5	97.3	94.6	....
Spain	184	97.0	94.6	94.0	81.2	83.9	83.5	81.7	83.2	87.0	94.1	100.0	101.8	102.5	94.0	....
Sweden	144	104.7	103.6	91.8	82.4	87.9	89.0	90.3	90.2	93.4	99.7	100.0	99.1	98.5	74.2	....
Switzerland	146	109.9	108.9	112.1	114.4	108.5	103.2	108.2	109.5	106.4	98.0	100.0	97.6	93.7	92.1	....
United Kingdom	112	114.2	121.7	116.1	107.4	102.8	103.8	95.0	98.6	106.0	106.2	100.0	103.9	103.9	96.7	....

Based on Relative Value-Added Deflators (99by.110)

Country		1980	1981	1982	1983	1984	1985	1986	1987	1988	1989	1990	1991	1992	1993	1994
United States	111	110.3	123.0	133.7	138.3	149.0	150.8	119.7	103.2	97.7	103.9	100.0	100.0	96.4	99.4	....
Canada	156	89.2	89.5	91.7	94.7	90.6	87.3	83.6	89.8	98.1	102.2	100.0	98.9	93.5	90.1	....
Japan	158	89.4	95.3	83.9	87.8	89.8	88.1	112.9	117.3	123.6	113.8	100.0	106.1	110.9	127.1	....
Austria	122	98.1	96.7	99.7	100.8	99.9	99.5	101.0	104.6	100.7	98.8	100.0	99.4	100.8	103.5	....
Belgium	124	121.5	106.2	96.2	89.7	88.3	91.7	94.5	94.9	95.0	94.7	100.0	96.4	98.3	96.9	....
Denmark	128	87.1	83.5	83.4	84.2	85.4	86.5	91.0	96.8	95.3	91.9	100.0	100.2	105.9	109.1	....
Finland	172	93.2	94.1	94.8	92.5	96.9	95.5	89.9	92.9	96.6	102.1	100.0	89.4	77.3	69.4	....
France	132	101.0	97.9	92.8	90.6	90.6	93.6	98.5	99.9	97.9	95.6	100.0	98.1	101.9	104.0	....
Germany	134	94.7	87.2	89.6	91.8	88.2	86.8	94.9	100.9	98.4	96.4	100.0	100.1	104.8	108.5	....
Ireland	178	119.2	111.2	121.6	121.6	118.8	124.4	125.5	117.5	108.4	103.5	100.0	94.5	93.6	91.6	....
Italy	136	94.6	94.5	94.6	96.6	96.4	94.0	95.9	96.7	94.9	98.3	100.0	99.1	94.9	83.1	....
Netherlands	138	103.2	91.6	98.7	98.6	95.7	92.7	98.2	101.0	101.3	98.2	100.0	98.8	99.1	101.0	....
Norway	142	95.6	98.3	97.9	101.1	102.5	100.6	96.5	99.1	106.2	106.4	100.0	100.1	98.2	97.8	....
Spain	184	94.2	93.8	94.4	84.7	90.9	92.0	86.3	86.2	89.4	96.3	100.0	102.6	99.6	88.5	....
Sweden	144	99.9	101.1	91.8	84.0	87.9	88.8	87.7	87.5	91.0	96.2	100.0	105.7	106.4	87.2	....
Switzerland	146	98.2	99.8	103.6	104.4	102.4	99.2	99.9	101.3	100.0	95.5	100.0	97.7	94.5	96.6	....
United Kingdom	112	108.6	115.6	113.5	105.2	98.2	102.7	94.4	94.9	102.1	100.8	100.0	100.1	98.1	92.5	....

The indicators of real effective exchange rates based on *relative unit labor costs (line 65um)* and *relative normalized unit labor costs (line reu)* in manufacturing represent the product of the index of the ratio of the relevant indicator (in national currency) for the country listed to a weighted geometric average of the corresponding indicators for 20 other industrial countries (again in national currency, and including in addition to the other 16 countries listed on this table, Australia, New Zealand, Greece, and Portugal) and the index of the nominal effective exchange rate, which is calculated by weighting the exchange rates for the countries listed in the same manner as the other indicators. This index for the nominal effective exchange rate is presented as line **neu** in the country pages of the 17 countries in the table. Indicators of real effective exchange rates based on *relative value-added deflators (line 99by)*, *relative wholesale prices (line 63ey)*, and *relative export unit values (line 74ey)* in manufacturing are calculated in the same fashion, but using only the 16 other countries listed on this table for weighting the index concerned and the nominal effective exchange rate. The reference base is 1990=100 in accordance with all indices published in *IFS*.

Several of the measures of real effective exchange rates are subject to frequent and sometimes substantial revision. To an important extent, these revisions stem from the procedures used to estimate several of the indicators. Thus, the national data underlying the two labor cost series and the value-added deflator series are calculated by benchmarking the best available monthly or quarterly series on reasonably comprehensive and comparable, but periodically revised, annual data from the national accounts. While such benchmarking makes these series particularly susceptible to revision, it also permits the calculation of up-to-date quarterly series which, on an annual basis, are also reasonably comprehensive and comparable.

The total trade weights used to construct the associated nominal effective exchange rates for the five indices are designed to make them particularly relevant with respect to movements in costs and prices affecting exports and imports of manufactured goods. The weights, which are built up from aggregate trade flows for manufactured goods (SITC 5-8) averaged over the period 1989-91, take into account the relative importance of a country's trading partners in its direct bilateral relations with them, in both the home and foreign markets; of the competitive relations with third countries in particular markets; and of the differences among countries in the importance of foreign trade to the manufacturing sector.

The nature and scope of the various national indicators entering into the indices are briefly described below. While mention is made of specific deficiencies in some of the selected measures of costs and prices, the emphasis is on what they purport to measure. Because these measures of costs and prices contain a considerable amount of staff estimation, they are not published in *IFS*.

Unit labor costs are defined as compensation of employees per unit of real output (or value added) in the manufacturing sector. Account is taken of employer-paid social insurance premia and other employment taxes, as well as wages and salaries. For the most recent quarters, however, indices typically refer more narrowly to wages or wages and salaries per unit of total output of manufactured goods (rather than that of value added in the manufacturing sector).

Normalized unit labor costs in manufacturing are calculated by dividing an index of actual hourly compensation per worker by the normalized index of output per man-hour in local currency. The data printed are the product of this variable after weighting (to obtain the relative measure) and the nominal effective exchange rate (**neu**). The purpose of normalizing output per man-hour is to remove distortions arising from cyclical movements, which occur largely because changes in hours worked do not correspond closely to changes in the effective inputs of labor. The Hodrick-Prescott filter, which smoothes a time series by removing short-run fluctuations while retaining changes of larger amplitude, is the method used to normalize output per man-hour.

Value-added deflators represent the quotient of the current and constant price estimates of value added in the manufacturing sector, adjusted for changes in indirect taxes. Such indicators, which share the

Real Effective Exchange Rate Indices

Industrial Countries

1980	1981	1982	1983	1984	1985	1986	1987	1988	1989	1990	1991	1992	1993	1994	Country	
(1990=100)																

Based on Relative Wholesale Prices (63ey.110)

1980	1981	1982	1983	1984	1985	1986	1987	1988	1989	1990	1991	1992	1993	1994	Country	
107.1	119.4	128.0	130.1	137.3	139.0	113.0	102.5	97.7	103.6	100.0	97.6	95.0	98.3	....	United States	111
93.3	94.1	96.3	99.3	97.1	94.2	91.1	93.6	100.1	102.7	100.0	100.3	95.1	91.7	....	Canada	156
93.5	96.4	86.7	90.8	92.0	90.7	108.9	112.7	119.9	112.5	100.0	106.9	110.0	126.5	....	Japan	158
106.1	104.1	103.4	102.6	101.6	101.3	101.4	102.9	100.2	97.7	100.0	98.2	98.5	99.8	....	Austria	122
116.9	114.3	107.4	106.6	105.5	105.3	101.0	99.5	96.9	97.8	100.0	96.7	97.8	97.0	....	Belgium	124
92.3	92.3	91.5	92.6	92.2	92.0	92.7	95.8	95.0	93.7	100.0	100.9	101.7	103.6	....	Denmark	128
94.0	98.7	99.6	94.8	97.1	92.2	92.9	95.7	100.2	100.0	93.6	82.7	73.8	....		Finland	172
102.0	96.5	92.6	90.8	90.5	93.2	98.8	100.6	99.2	97.6	100.0	96.8	98.3	99.6	....	France	132
99.6	93.6	96.9	97.8	94.0	92.8	99.4	101.6	99.3	97.3	100.0	99.6	103.2	105.8	....	Germany	134
102.9	99.5	102.4	100.5	98.1	98.3	102.7	100.9	100.1	99.4	100.0	96.9	100.2	98.4	....	Ireland	178
90.6	88.2	87.8	89.9	90.2	88.6	90.0	92.0	90.9	93.9	100.0	101.9	99.9	87.7	....	Italy	136
100.5	95.4	98.4	97.4	95.4	93.3	99.1	102.5	99.9	98.3	100.0	99.6	103.6	106.6	....	Netherlands	138
72.8	71.7	71.1	69.7	68.2	78.8	96.8	99.1	102.1	101.3	100.0	99.7	101.9	101.5	....	Norway	142
98.2	94.9	93.7	84.6	89.8	91.0	90.7	90.5	94.0	98.5	100.0	99.3	97.5	87.1	....	Spain	184
100.1	99.3	93.3	88.0	93.1	93.6	93.3	93.9	96.8	101.0	100.0	99.6	98.8	84.0	....	Sweden	144
93.3	92.3	96.2	97.5	94.5	92.2	99.5	103.1	101.7	95.7	100.0	97.8	95.6	98.5	....	Switzerland	146
103.9	107.7	104.9	100.3	97.3	99.8	93.4	94.5	101.2	98.7	100.0	104.7	103.1	97.3	....	United Kingdom	112

Based on Relative Export Unit Values (74ey.110)

1980	1981	1982	1983	1984	1985	1986	1987	1988	1989	1990	1991	1992	1993	1994	Country	
93.6	108.1	119.5	123.8	128.5	129.2	110.6	103.3	101.0	103.6	100.0	100.2	98.0	101.4	....	United States	111
114.2	109.4	104.5	106.0	105.2	101.7	97.8	99.1	101.9	104.0	100.0	97.7	92.4	91.3	....	Canada	156
101.1	105.6	97.5	96.7	98.2	97.2	105.7	105.4	109.2	107.8	100.0	107.2	112.8	126.6	....	Japan	158
102.8	100.1	100.6	98.7	96.9	96.8	99.5	100.7	100.5	97.8	100.0	98.9	100.1	104.0	....	Austria	122
111.0	105.7	101.4	101.6	101.8	100.8	100.3	98.4	96.7	98.4	100.0	97.4	99.2	99.9	....	Belgium	124
91.0	90.9	89.3	89.5	88.6	89.2	97.2	99.9	95.0	93.1	100.0	101.6	103.6	96.0	....	Denmark	128
95.7	97.6	96.9	92.6	95.4	93.8	90.2	91.6	95.3	99.3	100.0	92.3	85.8	78.4	....	Finland	172
104.0	99.8	96.8	95.7	96.5	98.5	101.3	101.8	100.0	98.2	100.0	97.4	97.4	98.9	....	France	132
102.0	93.5	94.7	95.3	91.6	92.0	99.2	102.5	98.8	97.4	100.0	98.2	99.6	97.4	....	Germany	134
....	....	....	....	....	....	....	....	....	....	....	....	....	....	....	Ireland	178
94.9	91.6	90.3	91.9	91.3	89.4	94.7	96.8	94.2	95.9	100.0	100.8	99.8	89.4	....	Italy	136
95.2	95.5	95.9	93.5	93.0	91.6	85.2	82.6	88.5	97.5	100.0	97.0	96.0	96.8	....	Netherlands	138
102.2	101.2	97.2	95.7	100.1	96.4	91.6	92.5	106.8	111.1	100.0	95.1	93.5	87.7	....	Norway	142
81.8	82.7	84.6	80.2	83.0	85.3	90.8	92.3	95.1	95.8	100.0	104.4	105.5	99.8	....	Spain	184
102.5	101.1	94.5	90.0	93.2	93.2	93.5	95.2	96.4	99.2	100.0	100.4	98.7	88.6	....	Sweden	144
79.8	81.6	85.6	89.5	88.0	85.1	94.8	98.7	97.6	93.2	100.0	101.6	100.3	105.1	....	Switzerland	146
112.9	112.4	107.7	103.3	101.2	104.2	99.0	101.0	107.7	101.1	100.0	102.0	103.3	104.0	....	United Kingdom	112

Based on Relative Consumer Prices (..rec)

1980	1981	1982	1983	1984	1985	1986	1987	1988	1989	1990	1991	1992	1993	1994	Country	
102.0	112.1	125.5	131.2	138.8	143.7	120.8	108.8	102.3	105.9	100.0	98.3	96.0	99.1	97.6	United States	111
89.5	94.0	100.3	104.7	102.8	99.1	89.7	89.8	94.7	101.4	100.0	102.8	94.6	89.1	81.1	Canada	156
76.5	81.6	74.0	80.0	83.4	85.5	109.6	115.5	121.9	111.8	100.0	107.4	111.2	130.5	138.5	Japan	158
95.1	91.8	93.0	93.0	93.9	93.6	97.6	100.3	99.7	98.4	100.0	98.6	100.5	102.9	103.1	Austria	122
110.7	102.8	93.8	92.7	92.1	93.3	97.2	100.2	97.5	96.2	100.0	100.8	99.7	99.7	101.2	Belgium	124
94.8	90.2	88.5	89.3	87.7	88.8	94.4	98.8	98.3	96.4	100.0	96.3	97.6	98.9	98.5	Denmark	128
82.2	84.9	87.3	84.8	87.6	88.8	88.8	90.6	92.7	98.0	100.0	95.2	82.7	71.6	76.4	Finland	172
109.0	103.9	99.3	95.5	93.8	96.2	99.6	100.9	98.6	96.5	100.0	97.1	99.0	99.6	99.1	France	132
107.7	98.3	100.1	100.8	96.3	93.7	99.2	102.5	99.9	97.5	100.0	97.9	101.6	105.8	106.7	Germany	134
88.9	88.0	94.4	95.6	95.4	96.6	103.6	102.2	98.7	96.5	100.0	96.9	100.0	94.1	94.4	Ireland	178
82.0	80.0	80.9	85.3	85.9	85.6	91.6	94.4	93.2	95.3	100.0	100.7	99.6	83.7	80.6	Italy	136
109.3	101.4	104.4	103.0	99.6	97.3	102.8	104.7	102.2	98.2	100.0	98.0	100.0	101.7	102.4	Netherlands	138
94.4	97.9	102.0	101.2	99.7	98.5	97.0	99.0	101.4	100.7	100.0	96.5	97.2	93.7	91.6	Norway	142
87.8	82.6	82.5	72.3	74.4	75.8	80.7	84.0	87.5	92.8	100.0	101.3	102.0	89.1	84.5	Spain	184
105.9	105.9	95.4	86.4	90.6	92.5	91.8	91.7	94.0	96.4	100.0	104.7	105.5	87.1	85.7	Sweden	144
90.6	89.7	94.9	96.5	93.4	91.7	97.8	101.6	99.7	93.9	100.0	99.9	98.5	101.3	105.9	Switzerland	146
108.0	111.2	107.2	98.5	94.2	96.0	89.3	89.2	96.4	96.7	100.0	101.9	98.8	88.6	88.7	United Kingdom	112

properties of the corresponding GDP deflator series for the overall economy, are best viewed in this context as composite indicators of the cost (per unit of real value added) of all factors of production. They differ from final product prices in that they abstract from the costs of intermediate inputs obtained by the manufacturing sector from other sectors. Extrapolation beyond the most recent benchmark year is based on wholesale prices for manufacturers adjusted to exclude the influence of changes in raw material prices.

Wholesale prices are intended to measure final product prices (excluding indirect taxes, which are not generally imposed on exported goods). However, the various national indices tend to lack comparability in both concept and commodity composition. Wherever possible, use is made of indices that approximate final product prices (e.g., industry selling prices or finished goods prices).

Export unit values serve as proxies for data on final product prices for traded goods but suffer from some of the same compositional drawbacks as wholesale prices. In addition, because of the less-than-complete homogeneity of the commodity classes upon which the unit values are calculated, the national series are often somewhat erratic. On the other hand, the unit value relatives (each computed as the ratio of one country's index to that of its competitors) tend to be much less variable than relatives derived from other price or cost indicators. This is because of the degree of competition that is characteristic of international trade and the resultant selectivity in the composition of a country's exports. International competition often places severe limits on how far an exporter's prices may diverge from those charged by competitors, so that goods not competitively priced tend to disappear from the trade flows for which unit values are computed. Consequently, export unit values imperfectly reflect underlying cost developments.

An indicator of real effective exchange rates based on relative consumer prices is also shown (*line* **rec**) to afford comparison with a wider group of partner–or competitor–countries. The weighting scheme is based on disaggregated trade data for manufactured goods and primary products covering the three-year period 1980–82 and is derived according to the same methodology as that followed for other countries discussed in the Introduction (section 1). The consumer price index that is used as a cost indicator is that shown on the country pages *(line 64)*. However, it should be borne in mind that, especially for the industrial countries, consumer price indices are in a number of respects conceptually inferior to the other measures of domestic costs and prices discussed above for the purpose of compiling indices of real effective exchange rates, owing to the inclusion of various factors which may differ across countries, for example, indirect taxes.

As indicated in the Introduction, movements in these indices need to be interpreted with considerable caution. While every effort is made to use national data that are as internationally comparable as possible, the degree to which it is practicable to ensure comparability is limited by the character of the available data. For this reason, the table provides a wide array of available indicators.

Production and Labor Indices

66		1965	1966	1967	1968	1969	1970	1971	1972	1973	1974	1975	1976	1977	1978	1979

Industrial Production
Index Numbers: 1990=100

Country		1965	1966	1967	1968	1969	1970	1971	1972	1973	1974	1975	1976	1977	1978	1979
Industrial Countries	110	43.3	46.4	47.8	51.1	55.3	57.1	58.3	62.4	68.2	68.0	62.6	67.7	70.7	73.7	77.5
United States	111	46.6	50.8	51.9	54.7	57.3	55.4	56.1	61.6	66.6	65.6	59.9	65.3	70.5	75.1	78.1
Canada	156	45.8	48.7	50.5	53.9	57.5	58.4	61.5	66.2	72.8	75.3	70.8	74.6	76.3	79.4	84.1
Australia	193	47.5	48.3	51.0	53.9	57.5	60.1	62.5	63.2	69.7	71.9	66.4	69.8	68.7	69.7	73.3
Japan	158	22.0	24.9	29.8	34.4	39.8	45.3	46.5	49.8	57.3	55.2	49.0	54.4	56.7	60.3	64.7
New Zealand	196	....	....	....	....	....	....	....	....	....	....	....	....	88.3	86.1	92.1
Austria	122	37.4	39.2	39.5	42.3	47.1	51.3	54.4	58.7	61.8	64.7	60.6	64.5	67.1	68.8	73.8
Belgium	124	53.2	54.3	55.1	58.2	63.8	66.0	67.8	71.9	76.4	79.2	71.6	77.9	77.8	79.5	83.1
Denmark	128	....	....	....	52.7	59.1	60.7	62.0	66.3	68.8	66.3	62.8	69.1	70.0	71.9	74.6
Finland	172	33.3	34.9	36.2	38.2	43.6	48.1	48.8	54.8	58.7	61.4	59.2	59.7	60.0	63.1	69.8
France	132	50.9	53.5	54.9	56.8	62.8	66.1	70.1	74.0	79.3	81.3	76.0	82.0	83.3	85.3	88.6
Germany	134	55.1	55.7	54.0	59.0	66.6	70.7	71.7	74.3	78.4	76.7	71.5	76.6	78.5	80.0	84.0
Greece	174	32.1	36.8	37.8	40.6	45.1	50.1	55.0	63.6	73.6	72.2	75.4	83.3	84.5	91.0	96.6
Ireland	178	23.7	24.9	26.3	29.7	31.8	33.2	34.4	35.9	39.5	40.6	39.0	42.4	45.8	49.5	53.3
Italy	136	43.0	48.8	52.8	56.2	58.3	62.3	62.0	64.7	71.0	74.1	67.3	75.7	76.5	78.3	83.3
Luxembourg	137	56.9	54.8	55.0	58.3	65.7	66.1	65.2	67.9	76.0	78.6	61.4	62.8	63.1	66.1	68.3
Netherlands	138	47.5	49.2	51.0	55.3	57.9	63.0	67.4	70.0	76.0	79.5	78.6	83.8	83.8	83.8	87.2
Norway	142	29.7	31.0	32.0	33.4	35.5	36.9	38.4	41.3	43.7	45.6	48.0	50.9	50.4	55.7	60.0
Portugal	182	38.5	39.9	39.5	42.0	45.5	48.0	52.1	59.1	66.0	67.6	64.1	67.2	74.9	80.3	111.7
Spain	184	32.0	36.7	37.9	40.8	47.4	50.8	54.2	62.8	69.9	75.1	71.7	76.0	79.9	82.0	82.9
Sweden	144	61.4	63.5	64.8	68.3	73.0	77.8	78.5	80.2	86.0	90.0	88.5	86.2	81.5	80.3	85.9
Switzerland	146	56.9	59.5	60.8	63.3	69.0	75.1	76.2	78.0	82.3	83.4	71.3	72.3	75.5	76.2	77.3
United Kingdom	112	64.2	65.2	65.7	70.7	73.1	73.5	73.1	74.4	81.0	79.4	75.1	77.6	81.6	83.9	87.2

Wages
Index Numbers: 1990=100

Country		1965	1966	1967	1968	1969	1970	1971	1972	1973	1974	1975	1976	1977	1978	1979
Industrial Countries	110	14.1	14.9	15.8	16.9	18.3	19.8	21.7	24.0	26.9	30.9	35.5	39.5	43.8	48.0	52.7
United States	111	24.1	25.1	26.1	27.8	29.4	31.0	33.0	35.3	37.7	40.9	44.6	48.2	52.4	57.0	61.8
Canada	156	14.2	15.1	16.2	17.3	18.8	20.3	22.1	23.8	25.9	29.4	34.0	38.7	42.9	45.9	51.0
Australia	193	9.9	10.4	11.0	11.7	12.7	13.8	15.5	16.8	18.9	23.2	27.4	31.3	34.7	37.7	40.9
Japan	158	12.9	14.2	15.9	17.8	20.2	20.7	23.7	27.4	32.6	40.7	48.0	54.0	59.0	63.2	66.9
New Zealand	196	8.7	9.0	9.5	9.9	10.4	12.1	14.5	15.8	17.7	19.8	22.5	25.5	28.8	32.2	37.2
Austria	122	15.3	17.1	18.5	19.6	20.8	22.7	25.8	28.8	32.5	37.6	42.7	46.5	50.5	53.4	56.5
Belgium	124	13.1	14.5	15.5	16.3	17.6	19.6	22.0	25.1	29.2	35.3	42.4	47.1	51.4	55.0	59.3
Denmark	128	9.1	10.2	11.1	12.4	13.8	15.3	17.5	19.5	22.4	26.8	31.7	35.3	38.8	42.8	47.7
Finland	172	7.2	7.8	8.5	9.4	10.2	11.3	13.0	14.8	17.3	20.7	24.7	28.8	31.6	33.9	37.5
France	132	7.4	7.8	8.4	9.3	10.1	11.3	12.6	14.1	16.0	19.1	23.0	26.8	30.6	35.0	40.3
Germany	134	15.5	17.1	18.1	18.9	20.8	24.5	27.7	30.6	34.6	39.6	44.1	46.7	50.7	54.1	57.9
Greece	174	1.5	1.7	1.9	2.1	2.3	2.4	2.6	2.9	3.3	4.2	5.3	6.8	8.2	10.1	12.2
Iceland	176	....	....	....	.2	.2	.3	.3	.4	.5	.7	.9	1.2	1.7	2.6	3.7
Ireland	178	4.9	5.4	5.8	6.3	7.1	8.1	9.4	10.8	13.0	15.3	20.0	24.0	28.2	32.6	37.2
Italy	136	4.0	4.2	4.4	4.6	4.9	6.0	6.6	7.3	8.9	10.7	13.8	16.6	21.2	24.7	29.5
Netherlands	138	19.6	21.6	23.0	24.7	27.1	30.0	33.6	37.8	42.8	50.1	56.9	62.0	66.3	70.2	73.3
Norway	142	9.5	10.2	11.0	11.9	13.0	14.6	16.4	17.9	19.7	23.1	27.7	32.0	35.6	38.4	39.6
Portugal	182	....	....	....	....	....	....	....	....	....	....	....	....	....	....	15.5
Spain	184	2.5	2.9	3.3	3.6	3.9	4.6	5.2	6.0	7.2	9.1	11.7	15.2	19.8	25.0	30.9
Sweden	144	11.9	13.0	14.2	15.2	16.5	18.3	18.1	20.2	21.8	24.6	28.9	32.8	35.0	38.1	41.0
Switzerland	146	27.6	29.3	30.9	32.1	33.5	35.6	39.0	42.5	46.3	51.1	54.8	55.5	58.2	59.7	61.8
United Kingdom	112	8.4	9.0	9.3	10.0	10.8	12.1	13.5	15.2	17.3	20.3	25.7	29.7	32.7	37.5	43.3

Employment
Index Numbers: 1990=100

Country		1965	1966	1967	1968	1969	1970	1971	1972	1973	1974	1975	1976	1977	1978	1979
Industrial Countries	110	80.7	83.1	83.9	85.6	88.5	89.9	90.3	91.0	93.1	93.9	90.9	91.1	92.0	93.3	94.5
United States	111	55.5	58.4	60.1	62.1	64.3	64.8	65.1	67.3	70.2	71.5	70.3	72.5	75.4	79.2	82.1
Canada	156	98.4	103.7	103.5	102.5	105.2	103.1	102.2	103.9	109.1	112.3	106.1	107.5	106.1	107.2	110.4
Australia	193	....	102.7	105.1	105.3	108.5	110.0	113.7	110.8	115.2	114.5	105.2	106.7	106.4	101.6	101.7
Japan	158	86.0	86.4	89.2	92.9	96.3	100.0	100.6	98.7	99.0	98.6	93.4	91.5	90.7	88.7	88.3
New Zealand	196	....	....	....	....	....	....	....	97.2	96.8	101.1	105.5	103.9	105.5	106.8	102.4	105.7
Austria	122	81.3	81.5	80.6	79.9	80.5	81.6	83.8	85.8	89.1	90.7	90.7	91.7	93.5	94.2	94.7
Denmark	128	....	....	....	....	....	....	....	....	128.6	126.7	123.5	106.7	106.6	106.2	105.1	106.4
Finland	172	90.4	94.5	94.8	93.1	96.1	100.7	103.3	105.1	107.7	113.1	112.3	108.3	107.1	104.2	108.2
France	132	....	....	....	....	....	....	....	....	....	....	....	....	....	....	....
Germany	134	117.9	116.9	109.3	110.1	115.8	119.9	119.1	116.4	116.9	113.8	106.4	103.9	103.0	102.3	102.6
Greece	174	65.3	67.3	66.9	66.4	68.9	72.1	76.5	79.4	84.3	85.3	86.0	91.3	95.5	98.5	101.2
Ireland	178	90.6	91.4	92.4	95.9	101.4	102.8	102.4	102.9	107.8	109.7	102.9	102.5	105.8	107.8	118.2
Italy	136	104.2	102.8	105.6	106.9	110.6	113.1	114.7	113.0	113.2	116.2	116.2	114.5	115.5	114.3	114.5
Luxembourg	137	84.1	83.1	79.1	79.2	81.3	85.8	88.7	91.4	94.0	97.7	98.1	96.1	94.8	93.5	94.3
Netherlands	138	138.2	137.6	133.0	130.6	131.5	131.5	130.0	126.2	122.7	121.2	117.4	113.6	109.8	106.5	104.8
Norway	142	120.2	122.4	122.8	122.1	123.1	125.2	126.9	127.1	131.0	130.1	128.4	128.9	128.2	125.7	123.0
Spain	184	94.9	95.5	96.3	97.0	97.8	98.5	99.2	100.4	99.5	100.9	99.5	99.8	98.8	96.8	94.6
Sweden	144	116.7	114.4	109.2	106.4	108.0	110.8	109.8	109.1	111.1	117.1	119.0	114.2	110.1	106.2	106.7
Switzerland	146	131.7	128.8	127.4	126.6	126.4	125.7	124.0	120.8	119.7	119.4	108.5	101.0	100.6	101.1	101.0
United Kingdom	112	99.6	100.3	98.4	97.7	97.5	96.8	97.3	97.3	99.8	100.3	100.0	99.2	97.3	100.2	101.9

Sector Coverage

Country		Industrial Sector			Other			Country		Industrial Sector			Other		
		Mining	Mfg.	Util.	Constr.	Serv.	Agri.			Mining	Mfg.	Util.	Constr.	Serv.	Agri.
United States	66..c	x	x	x				Belgium	66..b	x	x				
	65ey		x						65	x	x		x	x	
	67..c	x	x	x	x	x		Denmark	66..c	x	x				
Canada	66..c	x	x	x					65		x		x		
	65ey		x						67eyc		x				
	67ey		x					Finland	66..c	x	x		x		
Australia	66..c	x	x	x					65ey		x				
	65	x	x	x	x	x	x		67ez		x				
	67ey		x					France	66..c	x	x		x		
Japan	66..c	x	x						65		x		x		
	65	x	x	x					67..c	x	x		x	x	
	67eyc		x					Germany	66..c	x	x	x	x		
New Zealand	66eyc		x						65..c	x	x				
	65	x	x	x	x	x			67	x	x				
	67ey		x					Greece	66eyb						
Austria	66..b	x	x						65	x	x	x	x		
	65	x	x						67ey	x	x	x	x		
	67	x	x	x	x	x									

Production and Labor Indices

Industrial Production

1980	1981	1982	1983	1984	1985	1986	1987	1988	1989	1990	1991	1992	1993	1994	Country	
(66..i)																
77.6	77.5	75.1	77.2	82.8	85.3	86.3	88.9	94.1	97.9	100.0	99.6	98.2	96.6	100.4	Industrial Countries	110
76.6	78.3	72.7	77.0	85.7	87.4	88.3	91.6	96.5	99.0	100.0	98.1	99.6	101.7	107.9	United States	111
81.3	83.0	74.8	79.7	89.5	94.3	94.2	98.8	103.3	103.4	100.0	95.6	95.9	101.8	108.4	Canada	156
73.7	76.0	75.6	73.3	78.4	84.7	84.5	88.5	93.4	97.6	100.0	96.4	100.3	104.8	113.3	Australia	193
67.8	68.5	68.7	70.7	77.4	80.3	80.1	82.8	90.8	96.1	100.0	101.8	95.6	91.2	91.8	Japan	158
91.1	96.0	100.2	98.3	111.9	110.7	108.9	106.9	103.0	104.0	100.0	95.0	101.0	107.7	112.2	New Zealand	196
75.9	75.0	74.4	74.5	78.9	82.4	83.4	83.8	87.5	93.0	100.0	101.5	100.4	98.7	....	Austria	122
82.1	79.9	80.1	81.6	83.8	85.1	85.9	88.1	93.3	96.5	100.0	98.0	97.9	93.1	....	Belgium	124
75.0	75.0	76.6	79.3	87.9	91.7	98.6	95.7	97.6	100.0	100.0	101.8	103.7	101.3	....	Denmark	128
75.5	77.5	78.2	80.5	84.1	87.4	88.9	93.7	96.9	100.1	100.0	90.3	92.3	97.4	107.6	Finland	172
89.2	88.4	87.7	87.1	87.3	87.6	88.4	90.0	94.3	98.2	100.0	99.9	98.9	95.2	99.2	France	132
84.1	82.1	79.5	79.9	82.1	85.4	87.2	87.4	90.5	94.8	100.0	103.2	101.3	94.5	97.5	Germany	134
97.5	101.0	96.1	94.7	96.0	98.4	97.8	95.8	100.6	102.9	100.0	99.1	97.9	94.4	....	Greece	174
52.6	55.5	55.0	59.5	65.2	67.5	69.0	75.1	85.4	95.7	100.0	102.8	112.9	119.2	134.1	Ireland	178
87.3	85.5	82.9	80.9	83.5	84.7	88.2	90.5	96.8	100.6	100.0	97.8	97.2	94.4	....	Italy	136
66.1	62.3	62.9	66.3	75.1	80.2	82.4	82.8	92.6	99.7	100.0	99.6	98.8	96.1	....	Luxembourg	137
86.4	84.5	80.9	83.9	87.3	90.9	90.9	91.8	94.5	98.2	100.0	102.7	102.7	101.8	105.6	Netherlands	138
63.9	65.4	64.8	71.0	76.7	79.1	81.9	87.3	89.5	98.4	100.0	102.0	108.5	112.7	121.3	Norway	142
118.1	64.3	69.3	71.5	73.6	74.4	79.2	82.8	85.9	91.2	100.0	100.0	97.3	90.7	....	Portugal	182
82.8	82.3	81.4	83.8	84.4	86.1	88.6	92.6	95.6	100.1	100.0	99.3	96.1	....	....	Spain	184
84.9	84.0	82.5	85.9	92.0	94.8	95.2	97.6	98.9	102.5	100.0	94.9	93.4	94.4	104.2	Sweden	144
81.4	80.6	76.6	76.5	79.3	83.2	86.7	87.0	92.8	97.4	100.0	100.4	99.8	....	....	Switzerland	146
81.5	78.9	80.4	83.3	83.4	88.0	90.1	93.7	98.2	100.3	100.0	96.1	95.9	98.1	103.2	United Kingdom	112

Wages

1980	1981	1982	1983	1984	1985	1986	1987	1988	1989	1990	1991	1992	1993	1994	Country	
(65, 65ey, 65..c)																
58.4	64.5	70.2	74.6	78.5	82.4	85.6	88.7	91.3	95.3	100.0	105.1	109.2	112.7	115.6	Industrial Countries	110
67.2	73.8	78.5	81.5	84.8	88.1	89.9	91.5	94.1	96.8	100.0	103.3	105.8	108.5	111.4	United States	111
55.0	61.6	68.9	73.7	78.0	81.0	83.6	85.7	89.7	94.6	100.0	105.5	108.2	110.5	111.5	Canada	156
45.9	51.1	57.1	61.1	66.9	70.3	75.8	79.7	85.2	92.1	100.0	105.1	109.3	111.3	115.0	Australia	193
70.7	74.3	78.1	80.6	83.3	85.9	88.4	90.2	93.4	96.3	100.0	103.4	105.6	107.8	....	Japan	158
44.1	52.6	58.8	59.0	60.4	65.1	75.7	85.7	92.2	95.8	100.0	102.6	103.5	....	....	New Zealand	196
61.0	64.7	68.7	71.8	75.4	79.9	83.5	86.2	89.4	93.3	100.0	105.2	110.3	116.1	120.7	Austria	122
64.8	71.3	75.7	79.0	82.9	85.9	88.3	90.0	90.7	95.8	100.0	105.1	110.1	112.4	114.7	Belgium	124
53.2	57.9	64.1	68.3	71.6	75.1	79.4	87.0	92.6	96.2	100.0	103.9	106.9	....	....	Denmark	128
42.2	47.6	52.8	57.9	63.2	68.0	72.2	77.2	83.5	91.1	100.0	106.4	108.7	....	....	Finland	172
46.7	53.5	64.3	72.5	78.6	83.4	87.1	91.2	94.1	98.5	100.0	104.4	108.4	111.7	115.0	France	132
62.8	67.4	70.9	73.8	76.2	79.3	83.5	87.6	91.0	94.9	100.0	107.2	114.8	121.7	123.6	Germany	134
15.5	19.7	26.3	31.4	39.6	47.5	53.5	58.7	69.5	83.8	100.0	116.7	132.8	146.7	....	Greece	174
5.8	8.8	13.8	21.0	23.4	30.8	38.7	64.6	82.0	92.9	100.0	108.6	112.9	115.0	115.5	Iceland	176
43.9	51.2	57.8	64.6	72.5	78.2	84.1	88.4	92.6	96.3	100.0	104.4	108.6	114.4	....	Ireland	178
35.9	44.5	52.3	60.1	66.8	74.2	77.8	82.9	87.9	93.2	100.0	109.8	115.4	119.8	....	Italy	136
76.5	79.1	84.4	86.6	87.6	91.9	93.4	94.7	95.9	97.2	100.0	103.7	108.2	111.7	113.8	Netherlands	138
43.3	47.8	52.5	57.0	61.8	66.9	73.7	85.6	90.1	94.5	100.0	105.1	108.5	....	....	Norway	142
19.5	23.4	32.7	38.0	45.8	54.2	63.6	72.4	76.0	86.2	100.0	113.5	....	....	....	Portugal	182
36.6	41.2	47.7	54.9	61.3	67.5	74.9	80.5	85.7	92.0	100.0	108.2	116.5	124.4	....	Spain	184
44.4	49.8	53.0	56.4	62.0	66.9	71.0	77.1	83.2	91.5	100.0	104.7	109.5	113.1	117.8	Sweden	144
65.1	69.2	74.2	77.1	79.1	82.1	85.4	87.5	90.7	94.3	100.0	107.5	113.4	116.2	....	Switzerland	146
51.4	58.0	63.4	68.8	73.0	79.0	85.3	92.0	83.5	91.1	100.0	108.0	114.6	118.5	123.3	United Kingdom	112

Employment

1980	1981	1982	1983	1984	1985	1986	1987	1988	1989	1990	1991	1992	1993	1994	Country	
(67, 67ey, 67..c, 67eyc)																
94.8	94.0	92.1	91.1	92.4	93.9	95.0	95.7	97.1	98.8	100.0	99.4	98.5	96.8	96.4	Industrial Countries	110
82.6	83.3	81.8	82.4	86.3	89.0	90.8	93.2	96.2	98.6	100.0	98.9	99.2	100.7	103.7	United States	111
108.3	109.0	98.8	96.0	93.0	94.9	96.9	105.9	107.0	107.5	100.0	87.6	88.5	88.1	90.9	Canada	156
103.9	104.3	101.1	95.3	94.5	94.6	94.9	96.5	99.4	102.7	100.0	93.9	93.0	89.0	92.1	Australia	193
89.2	90.2	91.3	91.8	93.6	95.9	96.9	95.6	96.2	97.9	100.0	102.1	102.8	102.4	....	Japan	158
106.1	104.0	106.2	100.8	104.0	105.1	125.9	119.3	108.9	102.5	100.0	98.8	95.1	100.9	112.0	New Zealand	196
95.2	95.6	94.5	93.4	93.7	94.2	94.9	95.1	96.0	97.7	100.0	102.3	104.3	104.3	104.9	Austria	122
103.1	96.1	95.6	97.1	104.0	108.1	111.2	105.3	102.1	100.9	100.0	96.8	94.7	88.5	....	Denmark	128
112.9	114.5	111.2	109.0	108.0	107.4	106.0	102.5	99.6	101.0	100.0	90.4	81.5	76.2	76.7	Finland	172
116.7	113.1	112.1	109.9	106.9	104.0	102.1	99.7	98.6	99.4	100.0	98.2	95.5	90.8	88.9	France	132
103.3	101.0	97.5	93.5	92.5	93.7	95.3	95.2	95.0	97.3	100.0	101.4	99.0	91.9	85.9	Germany	134
102.3	103.5	103.6	102.4	102.7	101.5	101.6	100.3	101.3	101.6	100.0	93.8	89.2	83.9	....	Greece	174
118.5	115.1	111.5	104.8	101.7	97.4	96.0	95.1	95.3	97.4	100.0	100.5	100.2	100.2	....	Ireland	178
115.1	113.9	111.4	108.3	103.6	101.3	99.7	98.1	98.5	98.5	100.0	100.8	99.0	97.2	95.1	Italy	136
95.1	94.4	93.4	91.3	90.2	91.1	92.9	94.0	97.6	100.2	100.0	99.8	....	....	....	Luxembourg	137
103.7	100.7	86.2	93.5	92.4	93.5	95.3	96.3	96.3	97.9	100.0	100.2	100.7	96.5	....	Netherlands	138
121.6	119.2	115.2	108.2	107.2	113.9	119.0	113.5	108.8	102.5	100.0	95.0	95.3	....	....	Norway	142
90.7	87.6	86.5	85.7	84.8	84.0	88.3	91.0	93.7	97.4	100.0	100.2	98.3	94.1	93.3	Spain	184
106.9	102.7	99.3	98.9	100.0	101.9	102.9	101.3	101.7	102.5	100.0	92.0	84.0	77.2	76.1	Sweden	144
102.7	102.8	99.6	96.1	95.6	96.4	97.7	97.6	97.6	98.5	100.0	98.3	93.2	89.0	85.3	Switzerland	146
101.1	96.3	94.2	92.7	93.4	94.3	94.1	95.0	98.0	99.8	100.0	96.9	94.8	95.2	95.6	United Kingdom	112

Sector Coverage

Country		Industrial Sector			Other			Country		Industrial Sector			Other		
		Mining	Mfg.	Util.	Constr.	Serv.	Agri.			Mining	Mfg.	Util.	Constr.	Serv.	Agri.
Iceland	65		x		x	x		Portugal	66..b	x	x	x			
Ireland	66..c	x	x	x					65ey		x		x	x	
	65ey		x					Spain	66..c	x	x				
	67ey		x						65	x	x	x	x	x	
Italy	66..c	x	x	x					67	x	x	x	x	x	
	65ey		x					Sweden	66..c	x	x				
	67	x	x	x	x				65		x				
Luxembourg	66..b	x	x	x					67	x	x	x			
	67	x	x	x				Switzerland	66..b		x	x			
Netherlands	66..c	x	x	x					65		x				
	65		x						67ey	x	x				
	67	x	x	x				United Kingdom	66..c	x	x	x			
Norway	66..c	x	x	x					65..c	x	x	x	x	x	x
	65		x						67..c	x	x	x	x	x	x
	67ey		x												

(For more information please refer to the country notes in the monthly issues of IFS.)

Wholesale Prices

63 x

Percent Change over Previous Year:

		1965	1966	1967	1968	1969	1970	1971	1972	1973	1974	1975	1976	1977	1978	1979
World	001	4.0	4.5	1.9	2.4	4.3	5.3	4.5	5.9	14.2	23.6	11.1	11.9	11.6	8.8	15.2
Industrial Countries	110	2.2	2.9	.3	1.7	3.8	4.5	3.4	4.0	12.3	21.7	7.7	7.3	7.4	5.8	11.2
United States	111	2.0	3.3	.3	2.5	3.9	3.6	3.3	4.4	13.1	18.8	9.2	4.6	6.1	7.8	12.5
Canada	156	1.3	2.9	1.9	2.1	3.7	2.4	2.0	4.4	11.2	19.0	11.2	5.1	7.9	9.2	14.5
Australia	193	3.4	4.3	2.1	.8	1.4	4.3	4.9	4.8	8.6	15.3	15.1	11.3	10.2	8.2	14.8
Japan	158	.8	2.4	1.8	.8	2.1	3.6	-.7	.8	15.9	31.4	3.0	5.1	1.9	-2.5	7.3
New Zealand	196	2.8	1.6	2.3	7.0	5.1	6.0	7.5	6.9	12.7	8.1	13.3	22.4	16.4	11.5	17.7
Austria	122	3.8	.7	2.4	.9	2.5	4.7	5.2	3.9	1.2	15.2	6.4	5.8	3.0	1.0	4.2
Belgium	124	1.0	2.3	-1.0	.2	5.0	4.8	-.6	4.1	12.3	16.8	1.2	7.1	2.4	-1.9	6.3
Denmark	128	4.0	2.3	1.3	2.8	3.6	7.7	3.3	5.8	14.7	21.7	5.7	8.0	7.4	4.3	9.9
Finland	172	4.2	2.0	3.1	10.9	3.5	4.4	5.0	8.4	17.5	24.3	13.6	8.2	10.1	5.6	9.7
France	132	.7	2.8	-.9	-1.6	10.7	7.5	2.1	4.6	14.7	29.1	-5.7	7.4	5.6	4.3	13.3
Germany	134	2.4	1.8	-.9	-.7	1.9	4.9	4.2	2.6	6.6	13.4	4.6	3.7	2.8	1.1	4.8
Greece	174	1.9	3.1	.6	—	3.9	3.9	3.5	6.3	23.5	30.9	8.3	14.1	13.7	10.3	21.0
Ireland	178	3.7	2.0	2.6	6.0	7.2	5.3	5.4	10.4	17.6	13.5	24.5	19.6	17.2	8.9	12.2
Italy	136	1.4	1.9	-1.6	.3	3.9	7.4	4.0	4.1	17.0	40.7	8.6	22.9	17.4	8.4	15.5
Luxembourg	137															
Netherlands	138	2.8	5.0	1.0	1.8	-2.5	4.7	4.4	4.8	6.2	9.0	6.0	6.9	5.5	1.5	2.6
Norway	142	2.2	1.3	1.8	1.5	3.0	7.1	4.9	3.0	7.9	18.3	9.4	7.8	6.6	4.7	8.6
Portugal	182	3.0	3.8	3.7	4.5	3.4	3.3	2.4	5.5	11.1	28.6	13.2	19.1	29.0	31.4	29.5
Spain	184	10.1	2.6	.5	2.3	2.5	1.6	5.7	6.9	10.2	18.0	9.1	13.3	20.2	16.4	14.5
Sweden	144					4.0	6.7	2.3	4.5	11.3	24.8	6.6	8.9	9.5	8.0	11.9
Switzerland	146	.6	1.9	.3	.1	2.9	4.2	2.2	3.6	10.7	16.1	-2.3	-.6	.3	-3.4	3.8
United Kingdom	112	3.8	2.7	1.0	3.9	3.9	7.1	9.0	5.2	7.5	22.3	23.1	16.5	18.9	9.0	11.8
Developing Countries	200	13.5	12.7	10.0	5.8	6.6	8.1	8.8	12.7	20.9	29.0	21.1	26.1	24.1	17.8	26.1
Africa	605	5.2	3.2	2.7	4.0	3.2	4.2	3.6	8.2	14.6	19.7	14.6	15.1	17.0	12.4	17.0
Central African Rep.	626	7.2	.2	4.7	2.3	1.3	-.2	5.2	6.2	2.4	19.8	18.8	4.8	7.8	7.6	13.8
Congo	634	5.7	4.0	2.6	-.4	-.7	6.6	.7	12.8	5.3	15.3	14.0	13.5	12.3	9.8	8.9
Ghana	652	16.0	.7	3.9	18.7	7.7	8.6	-4.4	18.7	26.1	27.4	24.5	34.7	69.0	47.3	66.1
Morocco	686	4.8	2.1	2.8	-8.5	1.5	7.7	4.2	2.1	17.3	23.2	3.7	4.5	14.2	8.7	8.7
Sierra Leone	724							5.6	11.1	26.2	26.1	16.8	22.5	18.1	17.0	21.1
South Africa	199	3.1	3.7	2.4	1.2	2.7	2.9	5.0	8.3	13.3	17.9	16.8	15.8	13.0	9.9	15.2
Tunisia	744	12.9	3.5	3.7	3.5	1.0	4.0	7.4	1.5	5.4	21.2	9.5	1.2	4.9	3.1	7.3
Zambia	754			-1.2	8.7	9.5	-2.4	-6.2	5.1	22.0	12.8	-6.7	19.3	22.0	16.4	24.3
Asia	505	7.1	11.0	11.1	—	5.1	4.4	6.1	9.5	18.2	34.6	7.9	5.4	9.4	4.7	20.0
China, People's Rep.	924														4.0	22.1
India	534	8.2	11.9	15.1	-.4	2.1	6.2	5.0	8.8	16.4	28.6	3.9	-2.0	7.6	-.2	11.6
Indonesia	536									13.5	38.2	48.0	6.3	14.7	14.0	9.6	49.6
Korea	542	10.0	8.8	6.4	8.1	6.7	9.2	8.6	13.8	6.9	42.1	26.6	12.1	9.0	11.6	18.8
Malaysia	548															
Pakistan	564	6.8	9.6	5.6	-.2	4.7	.9	5.5	10.3	27.2	22.3	22.8	7.4	9.9	6.1	9.7
Philippines	566	2.7	6.9	2.4	1.6	23.7	—	15.7	10.1	23.7	47.7	5.4	13.8	7.5	4.8	19.0
Singapore	576											-1.5	6.7	4.5	1.6	14.4
Sri Lanka	524												3.4	8.2	21.0	15.8	9.5
Thailand	578	3.2	14.2	7.6	-4.6	3.3	-.5	.2	7.8	22.9	28.9	3.7	3.9	7.8	7.5	11.2
Europe	170					4.0	6.7	6.8	4.9	6.3	12.8	11.0	3.6	6.3	4.4	4.5
Cyprus	423					3.0	3.6	2.7	3.5	11.7	27.3	10.6	3.4	7.6	3.9	8.8
Czech Republic	935															
Czechoslovakia	934							—	-.1	.1	-.2	-.1	—	4.7	.5	.7
Hungary	944						6.0	1.7	2.3	1.9	2.9	3.3	10.6	4.6	2.0	3.7
Poland	964														14.9	2.0
Romania	968															
Slovak Republic	936															
Slovenia	961															
Turkey	186															
Yugoslavia, SFR	188	16.9	10.4	3.1	-.2	3.2	9.2	15.2	11.0	13.2	29.9	21.6	6.4	9.6	8.1	12.6
Middle East	405	-.7	3.2	6.2	-2.8	1.7	5.8	5.8	2.3	12.0	17.7	10.9	10.9	13.5	13.0	16.4
Egypt	469	7.8	8.3	7.1	-2.6	-.4	5.1	.2	1.3	6.8	14.3	7.5	7.8	9.3	14.8	9.7
Iran, I.R. of	429	2.9	-1.1	.3	.6	2.8	2.9	6.2	5.7	11.3	17.0	8.0	9.0	17.2	10.1	14.1
Israel	436	3.9	4.7	1.1	2.4	2.1	7.2	9.7	10.5	19.1	51.5	40.8	30.8	38.5	53.2	79.0
Kuwait	443										22.0	10.4	7.6	7.6	7.0	-1.2	6.5
Saudi Arabia	456															
Syrian Arab Rep.	463	-.2	9.2	9.1	-3.6	-2.2	9.8	9.0	-4.6	32.6	13.8	7.6	12.0	9.0	12.9	8.7
Western Hemisphere	205	23.7	17.9	11.5	12.7	10.5	13.3	14.7	21.6	32.0	35.0	40.7	60.8	47.7	35.4	43.2
Argentina	213	30.8	20.6	4.9	9.3	6.4	14.0	39.0	76.7	50.4	19.9	192.5	499.1	149.5	146.0	149.3
Bolivia	218													10.1	15.6	23.9
Brazil	223	51.2	36.8	25.4	24.1	20.1	22.1	20.0	18.6	16.8	29.2	27.2	43.3	42.5	37.6	55.9
Chile	228	24.3	22.9	19.3	30.5	36.4	36.2	18.0	70.0	511.3	1,028.8	481.9	221.1	86.1	43.0	49.8
Colombia	233	8.3	17.4	6.8	6.3	6.7	7.7	11.5	18.3	28.0	36.0	25.4	22.9	26.7	17.6	27.8
Costa Rica	238	-.8	.4	3.4	4.9	4.3	6.5	6.4	5.5	16.3	39.8	21.6	9.3	7.5	7.8	16.1
Ecuador	248												14.0	16.7	8.2	16.7	10.7
El Salvador	253	-1.8	—	1.4	-1.3	-.3	8.7	-5.4	5.9	21.1	25.3	1.8	34.7	47.3	-19.8	7.6
Guatemala	258	-2.2	-.2	.2	4.3	3.3	2.4	2.1	-.7	14.3	22.8	12.3	10.5	13.0	3.6	10.2
Mexico	273	1.8	1.3	2.9	1.9	2.5	6.0	3.4	3.1	15.7	22.3	10.7	22.3	41.2	15.8	18.3
Panama	283			1.1	1.8	1.5	3.1	5.4	8.5	10.5	30.2	14.0	7.8	7.2	5.4	14.0
Paraguay	288	8.9	4.3	-2.2	-2.2	1.8	-4.0	12.9	18.5	33.8	32.5	17.0	1.1	8.0	12.8	26.3
Trinidad and Tobago	369															
Uruguay	298	59.6	92.0	68.9	131.8	15.4	13.7	20.3	90.2	114.9	78.6	72.4	50.6	50.3	48.6	80.4
Venezuela	299	3.2	1.4	1.3	1.7	1.5	1.6	3.5	3.4	6.7	16.7	13.7	7.2	10.3	7.4	9.3
Memorandum Items																
Oil Exporting Countries	999	.9	.7	3.4	-.6	2.3	4.0	5.3	2.6	8.1	24.9	8.7	10.7	12.6	8.3	27.7
Non-Oil Developing Countries	201	14.3	13.4	10.4	6.2	7.2	9.1	10.0	13.9	23.2	24.8	19.6	24.3	22.1	16.5	25.8

Indices

Index Numbers:

		1965	1966	1967	1968	1969	1970	1971	1972	1973	1974	1975	1976	1977	1978	1979
World	001	5.6	5.9	6.0	6.1	6.4	6.7	7.0	7.5	8.5	10.5	11.7	13.1	14.6	15.9	18.3
Industrial Countries	110	26.0	26.8	26.8	27.3	28.3	29.6	30.6	31.8	35.7	43.5	46.9	50.3	54.0	57.2	63.6
Developing Countries	200	.1	.1	.2	.2	.2	.2	.2	.2	.3	.4	.4	.5	.7	.8	1.0
Africa	605	5.6	5.8	5.9	6.2	6.4	6.6	6.9	7.4	8.5	10.2	11.7	13.4	15.7	17.7	20.7
Asia	505	10.4	11.6	12.8	12.8	13.5	14.1	14.9	16.4	19.3	26.0	28.1	29.6	32.4	33.9	40.7
Europe	170				.8	.8	.9	1.0	1.0	1.1	1.2	1.3	1.4	1.5	1.5	1.6
Middle East	405	4.1	4.2	4.5	4.4	4.4	4.7	5.0	5.1	5.7	6.7	7.4	8.2	9.4	10.6	12.3
Western Hemisphere	205	—	—	—	—	—	—	—	—	—	—	—	—	—	—	—

Wholesale Prices

1980	1981	1982	1983	1984	1985	1986	1987	1988	1989	1990	1991	1992	1993	1994		63 x
Calculated from Indices																
19.3	15.0	13.1	14.2	16.1	13.1	6.6	12.9	20.3	26.9	27.9	13.7	15.1	18.0	20.9	World	001
13.8	9.2	5.3	3.3	4.3	1.8	−2.9	1.2	3.1	4.5	3.4	1.2	.7	.9	1.1	Industrial Countries	110
14.1	9.1	2.0	1.3	2.4	−.5	−2.9	2.6	4.0	5.0	3.6	.2	.6	1.5	1.3	United States	111
13.5	10.2	6.0	3.5	4.1	2.7	.8	2.8	4.3	2.0	.3	−1.0	.5	3.3	5.7	Canada	156
14.0	8.4	8.9	8.1	5.4	6.6	5.6	7.3	9.1	5.1	6.0	1.5	1.5	2.1	.8	Australia	193
17.8	1.4	1.8	−2.2	−.3	−1.1	−9.1	−3.8	−1.0	2.6	2.1	.2	−1.5	−3.8	−2.0	Japan	158
22.9	16.9	15.1	5.5	7.1	15.3	5.7	7.9	5.2	7.1	4.6	.9	2.1	2.5	1.4	New Zealand	196
8.6	8.0	3.2	.6	3.7	2.6	−5.3	−2.0	−.2	1.8	2.9	.8	−.2	−.4	1.3	Austria	122
1.3	14.1	13.5	6.7	7.6	2.6	−11.5	−5.0	1.6	6.6	−1.0	−1.0	−1.7	....	....	Belgium	124
17.3	15.7	10.7	5.0	7.5	2.9	−6.8	−.2	4.1	5.8	1.0	1.0	−1.1	−.6	....	Denmark	128
16.4	12.8	7.2	5.6	5.4	4.5	−5.2	.9	4.1	5.0	3.3	.3	1.1	3.0	1.4	Finland	172
8.8	11.0	11.1	11.1	13.3	4.0	....	....	....	....	....	....	....	....	....	France	132
7.6	7.8	5.9	1.5	2.9	2.4	−2.5	−2.5	1.3	3.2	1.7	2.4	1.4	—	.6	Germany	134
28.4	20.5	20.5	20.5	21.4	20.6	16.4	9.8	10.1	13.4	15.9	16.7	11.3	11.9	8.7	Greece	174
10.5	17.3	11.2	6.2	7.7	3.2	−2.2	.6	4.1	5.5	−2.7	1.2	.9	4.7	....	Ireland	178
20.1	17.4	13.8	9.8	10.4	7.3	−.9	2.7	4.7	6.4	7.4	5.2	2.1	....	....	Italy	136
....	10.7	17.9	4.9	6.2	3.0	−2.5	−6.5	2.6	7.6	−2.0	−2.6	−2.7	−1.3	1.5	Luxembourg	137
7.4	8.7	5.7	1.3	4.5	1.6	−2.7	−1.2	.5	3.6	1.0	2.3	2.6	.7	.6	Netherlands	138
14.9	11.2	6.4	6.0	6.3	5.0	2.7	6.0	5.3	5.5	3.7	2.6	—	....	1.4	Norway	142
6.7	21.4	27.6	16.7	27.5	21.2	9.2	....	....	....	....	....	....	....	....	Portugal	182
17.4	15.7	14.4	14.0	12.2	8.0	.9	.8	3.0	4.2	2.1	1.5	1.3	2.5	4.3	Spain	184
14.1	11.2	12.8	11.1	7.7	5.2	−2.8	2.8	5.3	7.7	4.7	1.7	−.7	7.0	4.0	Sweden	144
5.1	5.8	2.6	.5	3.3	2.3	−3.9	−2.0	2.3	4.3	1.5	.4	.1	....	....	Switzerland	146
15.9	10.7	8.6	6.5	6.0	6.2	1.4	3.4	3.7	4.8	6.2	5.4	3.1	3.9	2.5	United Kingdom	112
34.0	31.0	35.9	47.7	49.1	44.4	32.4	45.6	72.1	99.5	101.0	45.7	53.1	64.5	76.6	Developing Countries	200
16.6	16.4	15.5	16.8	14.1	17.9	20.1	13.7	12.3	14.1	12.1	11.7	9.7	6.4	6.6	Africa	605
16.1	14.6	14.4	8.8	5.9	6.7	3.9	.7	−2.1	4.0	1.6	−1.1	....	....	....	Central African Rep.	626
14.0	13.7	15.3	7.0	14.5	6.6	3.8	4.1	2.7	2.2	1.9	−3.5	1.7	3.0	....	Congo	634
43.2	49.5	36.2	128.5	84.3	53.9	63.6	41.4	34.7	26.9	22.7	....	....	....	....	Ghana	652
8.5	17.6	12.1	7.3	13.7	9.6	7.8	1.0	4.3	3.8	4.6	6.4	2.8	4.5	2.3	Morocco	686
22.4	22.0	19.7	44.3	43.8	49.2	....	....	....	....	....	....	....	....	....	Sierra Leone	724
16.2	13.7	14.0	10.5	8.4	16.8	19.6	13.9	13.1	15.2	12.0	11.4	8.2	6.6	8.3	South Africa	199
10.8	12.5	16.9	6.6	8.6	11.3	9.9	9.2	8.8	5.7	2.8	2.6	1.6	2.0	1.7	Tunisia	744
13.4	1.4	6.6	24.1	27.9	47.2	115.9	84.4	11.6	84.2	115.6	91.7	121.3	....	....	Zambia	754
22.6	12.5	4.6	9.4	10.0	3.6	1.8	8.6	7.6	6.6	7.7	9.0	6.3	4.3	7.9	Asia	505
7.2	5.9	2.2	4.4	4.0	8.6	6.4	11.9	23.0	15.0	−2.6	−2.0	....	....	....	China, People's Rep.	924
20.1	12.2	2.4	7.9	6.9	4.6	5.6	7.0	8.7	6.8	9.0	13.5	11.9	7.5	10.5	India	534
26.8	11.1	7.4	17.9	11.0	5.0	2.2	19.2	4.9	8.6	10.0	5.1	5.2	3.7	5.4	Indonesia	536
38.9	20.4	4.7	.2	.7	.9	−1.5	.5	2.7	1.5	4.2	4.7	2.2	1.5	2.7	Korea	542
....	....	....	....	....	−2.1	−6.2	3.7	7.3	3.8	.9	4.0	1.1	1.4	4.9	Malaysia	548
13.4	11.2	6.7	7.4	9.4	2.9	4.9	8.3	9.7	8.4	8.6	12.0	7.2	9.3	18.7	Pakistan	564
18.3	14.6	10.7	16.0	67.3	18.2	−1.6	9.1	13.4	10.6	10.2	13.4	4.5	−1.1	8.2	Philippines	566
19.6	3.9	−4.2	−3.6	−.6	−2.2	−15.1	7.5	−1.8	2.6	1.7	−4.1	−4.4	−4.4	−.4	Singapore	576
33.8	17.0	5.5	25.0	25.6	−15.2	−3.0	13.4	17.8	9.1	22.2	9.2	8.7	7.6	5.0	Sri Lanka	524
20.1	9.5	.9	2.0	−3.1	—	−.4	5.9	8.2	4.6	3.5	6.8	.2	−.4	3.9	Thailand	578
11.0	15.8	47.5	14.4	28.4	29.6	23.8	30.6	62.1	161.7	151.3	62.1	41.5	41.5	....	Europe	170
16.5	11.1	5.2	3.4	5.2	3.2	−4.4	−.3	3.5	3.0	3.5	....	....	....	....	Cyprus	423
....	....	....	....	....	....	....	....	....	....	....	....	....	....	5.3	Czech Republic	935
1.7	4.8	7.7	−.3	8.2	1.8	—	.1	—	−.7	4.4	70.0	....	....	....	Czechoslovakia	934
15.3	6.3	4.7	5.6	4.2	5.3	2.1	3.5	4.6	15.4	22.0	32.6	12.3	12.0	....	Hungary	944
4.2	9.2	122.3	15.3	14.5	16.2	17.8	26.6	59.8	212.8	622.4	48.1	28.0	32.2	30.1	Poland	964
....	....	....	....	....	....	....	....	....	....	....	240.7	203.6	165.0	140.5	Romania	968
....	....	....	....	....	....	....	....	....	....	....	....	....	....	10.0	Slovak Republic	936
....	....	27.0	30.5	50.3	43.2	29.6	32.0	70.5	64.0	52.3	166.0	166.0	21.6	17.7	Slovenia	961
....	....	....	....	....	....	....	....	....	....	....	55.3	62.1	58.0	121.3	Turkey	186
28.7	43.4	24.8	32.7	60.0	84.4	68.5	94.1	203.0	1,306.3	436.5	113.3	....	....	....	Yugoslavia, SFR	188
31.2	23.9	18.4	20.6	26.2	22.1	17.5	20.5	21.5	15.8	13.8	15.5	14.2	9.5	16.3	Middle East	405
21.7	8.0	9.3	16.0	10.0	13.2	17.3	13.7	26.3	27.3	16.8	17.9	12.1	8.6	....	Egypt	469
31.3	23.5	12.7	14.7	7.6	5.3	19.0	32.3	22.2	20.4	20.6	25.8	33.0	25.6	37.6	Iran, I.R. of	429
135.1	122.7	125.7	144.5	396.5	266.1	45.1	18.5	17.5	21.1	11.6	16.1	10.2	8.2	7.8	Israel	436
10.5	6.9	1.1	1.9	−.6	−1.3	.6	3.3	4.6	8.8	....	....	....	....	....	Kuwait	443
....	....	....	....	....	....	3.8	7.2	13.4	1.2	1.7	3.0	1.3	.6	1.8	Saudi Arabia	456
15.0	19.0	10.9	3.0	8.8	10.1	40.5	46.7	46.9	13.9	22.0	14.0	7.9	−4.9	7.7	Syrian Arab Rep.	463
56.6	57.7	71.5	118.3	131.5	127.2	86.2	127.0	241.7	340.5	435.1	125.8	188.0	273.6	303.6	Western Hemisphere	205
75.4	109.6	256.2	360.8	575.1	662.9	63.9	122.9	412.6	3,432.8	1,606.9	110.5	6.0	1.6	.7	Argentina	213
49.3	35.5	227.9	416.0	1,695.4	10,446.9	172.8	10.5	19.0	19.2	20.0	19.2	....	....	....	Bolivia	218
106.4	108.2	93.2	167.4	236.3	229.0	140.2	207.1	697.2	1,268.4	2,703.8	401.4	987.8	2,050.1	2,311.6	Brazil	223
39.6	9.1	7.2	45.5	24.3	43.4	19.8	19.2	5.9	15.1	21.8	21.5	11.7	8.6	7.7	Chile	228
24.2	24.1	25.7	21.7	18.3	24.9	22.0	25.1	28.1	28.2	26.6	27.6	20.1	14.2	17.2	Colombia	233
23.7	65.3	108.2	26.2	7.7	10.4	9.0	10.6	17.9	14.6	14.9	28.1	18.2	6.4	....	Costa Rica	238
7.3	9.6	16.9	14.9	23.1	26.1	28.5	31.6	66.8	80.1	45.5	48.0	54.6	39.1	18.2	Ecuador	248
15.8	10.0	8.5	6.8	5.9	13.8	32.5	.7	5.5	9.7	18.9	6.9	2.2	7.5	7.9	El Salvador	253
16.1	11.7	−6.1	1.2	5.6	23.3	42.9	....	....	....	....	....	....	....	.6	Guatemala	258
24.5	24.5	56.1	107.4	70.3	53.6	88.4	135.6	107.8	16.1	23.3	20.5	13.4	8.9	6.8	Mexico	273
15.3	10.0	8.3	−3.8	1.1	−.4	−16.0	1.5	−6.8	2.4	3.9	.5	1.8	−.2	2.0	Panama	283
7.4	12.6	3.5	22.0	28.3	23.4	45.1	11.9	27.1	21.9	55.1	31.7	....	....	....	Paraguay	288
19.4	16.9	13.8	12.5	5.1	4.7	6.5	4.2	5.9	8.9	1.4	.2	.8	5.4	....	Trinidad and Tobago	369
41.8	23.4	12.9	73.5	77.4	76.6	67.2	63.2	57.4	73.2	107.7	87.6	58.3	33.4	....	Uruguay	298
20.0	13.8	8.6	6.4	17.5	15.2	17.6	44.8	19.3	97.5	27.2	22.3	23.6	35.0	78.2	Venezuela	299
															Memorandum Items	
24.7	13.9	8.2	13.1	10.4	6.3	8.3	22.6	12.1	20.0	12.9	10.9	12.0	11.3	19.1	Oil Exporting Countries	999
35.0	33.5	40.4	52.8	55.3	50.4	36.6	49.5	84.6	116.7	120.1	52.1	61.2	75.6	88.8	Non-Oil Developing Countries	201

Indices

1990=100

1980	1981	1982	1983	1984	1985	1986	1987	1988	1989	1990	1991	1992	1993	1994		
21.8	25.1	28.4	32.4	37.6	42.6	45.4	51.2	61.6	78.2	100.0	113.7	130.9	154.4	186.7	World	001
72.4	79.1	83.3	86.0	89.7	91.4	88.8	89.8	92.6	96.7	100.0	101.2	101.9	102.8	103.9	Industrial Countries	110
1.3	1.7	2.4	3.5	5.2	7.5	10.0	14.5	24.9	49.7	100.0	145.7	223.0	366.9	648.0	Developing Countries	200
24.1	28.1	32.4	37.9	43.2	51.0	61.2	69.6	78.2	89.2	100.0	111.7	122.5	130.3	138.9	Africa	605
49.9	56.1	58.7	64.2	70.7	73.2	74.5	81.0	87.1	92.8	100.0	109.0	115.9	120.9	130.4	Asia	505
1.8	2.1	3.0	3.5	4.5	5.8	7.2	9.4	15.2	39.8	100.0	162.1	229.4	324.6	....	Europe	170
16.2	20.0	23.7	28.6	36.1	44.1	51.8	62.5	75.9	87.8	100.0	115.5	131.9	144.4	167.8	Middle East	405
—	—	—	.1	.1	.3	.5	1.2	4.2	18.7	100.0	225.8	650.3	2,429.3	9,804.1	Western Hemisphere	205

(Notes in the back of the book)

Consumer Prices

64 x

		1965	1966	1967	1968	1969	1970	1971	1972	1973	1974	1975	1976	1977	1978	1979
														Percent Change over Previous Year;		
World	001	6.8	8.4	5.3	5.1	4.7	6.2	5.6	5.8	9.5	15.7	13.7	12.1	12.6	10.7	13.3
Industrial Countries	110	3.1	3.5	2.9	3.9	4.7	5.6	5.3	4.8	7.9	13.4	11.4	8.6	8.8	7.5	9.7
United States	111	1.7	3.0	2.8	4.2	5.4	5.9	4.3	3.3	6.2	11.0	9.1	5.7	6.5	7.6	11.3
Canada	156	2.5	3.7	3.6	4.1	4.5	3.4	2.8	4.8	7.6	10.9	10.8	7.5	8.0	8.9	9.1
Australia	193	4.0	3.0	3.2	2.7	2.9	3.9	6.1	5.9	9.5	15.1	15.1	13.5	12.3	7.9	9.1
Japan	158	6.6	5.1	4.0	5.4	5.2	7.7	6.4	4.9	11.7	23.1	11.8	9.4	8.2	4.1	3.8
New Zealand	196	3.4	2.8	6.1	4.3	4.9	6.5	10.3	6.8	8.2	11.3	14.5	16.8	14.6	11.9	13.7
Austria	122	4.9	2.2	4.0	2.8	3.1	4.4	4.7	6.4	7.5	9.5	8.4	7.3	5.5	3.6	3.7
Belgium	124	4.1	4.2	2.9	2.7	3.7	3.9	4.3	5.4	7.0	12.7	12.8	9.2	7.1	4.5	4.5
Denmark	128	5.5	7.1	8.2	8.0	3.5	6.5	5.9	6.6	9.3	15.3	9.6	9.0	11.1	10.0	9.6
Finland	172	4.8	3.9	5.6	9.2	2.2	2.7	6.5	7.1	11.0	16.7	17.8	14.4	12.7	7.8	7.5
France	132	2.7	2.6	2.8	4.6	6.1	5.9	5.5	6.2	7.3	13.7	11.8	9.6	9.4	9.1	10.8
Germany	134	3.2	3.6	1.6	1.6	1.9	3.4	5.2	5.5	7.0	7.0	5.9	4.3	3.7	2.7	4.1
Greece	174	3.1	5.0	1.7	.3	2.5	2.9	3.0	4.3	15.5	26.9	13.4	13.3	12.2	12.5	19.0
Iceland	176	7.3	10.7	3.3	12.6	22.2	13.1	6.7	9.7	21.0	42.7	49.4	32.8	30.6	44.0	45.4
Ireland	178	5.0	3.1	3.2	4.7	7.4	8.2	9.0	8.6	11.4	17.0	20.9	18.0	13.6	7.6	13.2
Italy	136	4.4	3.2	.5	1.5	2.4	5.0	4.9	5.8	10.8	19.1	16.9	16.8	18.3	12.1	14.8
Luxembourg	137	3.3	3.3	2.2	2.6	2.3	4.6	4.7	5.2	6.1	9.4	10.7	9.8	6.7	3.1	4.5
Netherlands	138	5.8	5.8	3.5	3.7	7.4	3.7	7.5	7.8	8.0	9.6	10.2	9.1	6.5	4.1	4.2
Norway	142	4.3	3.3	4.4	3.5	3.1	10.6	6.3	7.2	7.4	9.4	11.7	9.2	9.0	8.2	4.8
Portugal	182	3.5	5.0	5.5	6.1	7.4	4.5	7.5	8.9	10.4	28.0	20.4	18.2	27.1	22.7	23.6
Spain	184	11.8	7.6	6.4	5.0	2.2	5.7	8.2	8.3	11.4	15.0	17.7	17.6	24.5	19.8	15.7
Sweden	144	5.0	6.4	4.3	1.9	2.7	7.0	7.4	6.0	6.7	9.9	9.8	10.3	11.5	9.9	7.2
Switzerland	146	3.4	4.8	4.0	2.4	2.5	3.6	6.6	6.7	8.8	9.8	6.7	1.7	1.3	1.1	3.6
United Kingdom	112	4.8	3.9	2.4	4.7	5.5	6.4	9.4	7.1	9.2	15.9	24.2	16.5	15.9	8.2	13.5
Developing Countries	200	21.2	28.3	14.3	10.0	4.8	7.4	6.2	8.1	13.2	19.9	18.0	19.1	19.7	16.6	20.2
Africa	605	4.0	3.9	3.4	2.4	5.3	6.1	6.1	5.7	8.7	13.4	18.2	17.2	19.8	16.2	17.3
Algeria	612	...	...	...	...	...	6.6	2.6	3.7	6.2	4.7	9.0	8.9	12.1	17.2	11.5
Botswana	616	...	...	...	...	...	...	...	...	...	...	12.0	11.7	13.2	9.0	11.7
Burkina Faso	748	−.7	2.4	−4.3	−.3	9.7	1.8	2.1	−2.9	7.6	8.7	18.8	−8.4	30.0	8.3	15.0
Burundi	618	...	4.4	−1.1	6.1	4.0	−.2	3.9	3.8	6.0	15.7	15.7	6.9	6.8	23.9	36.5
Cameroon	622	...	...	...	...	−1.1	5.9	4.0	8.1	10.4	17.2	13.6	9.9	14.7	12.5	6.6
Central African Rep.	626	...	...	...	...	...	...	...	...	...	...	...	...	...	...	...
Chad	628	...	...	...	...	...	...	...	...	...	...	...	...	...	...	...
Congo	634	4.1	5.3	3.5	3.8	−.7	1.5	4.1	9.8	3.5	5.4	17.4	7.2	14.0	10.5	8.1
Côte d'Ivoire	662	1.3	5.5	2.3	5.3	4.5	9.4	−1.5	.3	11.1	17.4	11.4	12.1	27.4	13.0	16.6
Equatorial Guinea	642	...	...	...	...	...	...	...	...	...	...	...	...	...	...	...
Ethiopia	644	...	−1.4	.8	.2	1.4	10.1	.5	−6.1	8.9	8.6	6.6	28.5	16.7	14.3	16.0
Gabon	646	2.4	3.6	2.0	2.3	3.0	3.8	3.9	3.5	6.2	12.1	28.5	20.2	13.9	10.8	8.0
Gambia, The	648	1.2	.2	1.4	4.2	5.0	−2.0	3.1	8.7	6.9	9.2	25.9	17.0	12.4	8.9	6.1
Ghana	652	26.4	13.2	−8.4	7.9	7.3	3.0	9.6	10.1	17.7	18.1	29.8	56.1	116.5	73.1	54.4
Guinea-Bissau	654	...	...	...	...	...	...	...	...	...	...	...	...	...	...	...
Kenya	664	3.6	5.0	1.8	.4	−.2	2.2	3.8	5.8	9.3	17.8	19.1	11.4	14.8	16.9	8.0
Liberia	668	...	2.3	5.8	1.5	11.3	1.6	−.8	3.9	19.6	19.0	14.0	5.6	6.2	7.3	11.6
Madagascar	674	4.2	3.2	.8	1.0	3.8	2.9	5.4	5.6	6.1	22.1	8.2	5.0	3.1	6.5	14.1
Malawi	676	...	...	...	...	...	...	...	...	...	...	...	...	...	...	...
Mali	678	...	...	...	...	...	...	...	...	...	...	...	...	...	...	...
Mauritania	682	...	...	...	...	...	...	...	...	...	...	...	...	...	...	...
Mauritius	684	1.7	2.5	1.9	6.9	2.3	1.6	.3	5.4	13.5	29.1	14.8	12.9	9.2	8.5	14.5
Morocco	686	3.5	−1.0	−.7	.4	2.9	1.3	4.2	3.8	4.1	17.6	7.9	8.5	12.6	9.7	8.3
Mozambique	688	...	...	...	...	...	...	...	...	...	...	...	...	...	...	...
Namibia	728	...	...	...	...	...	...	...	...	...	...	...	...	...	...	...
Niger	692	4.4	10.6	.4	−2.9	10.6	1.1	4.2	9.8	11.8	3.4	9.1	23.5	23.3	10.1	7.3
Nigeria	694	4.1	9.7	−3.7	−.5	10.2	13.8	16.0	3.5	5.4	12.7	33.9	24.3	13.8	21.7	11.7
Rwanda	714	...	...	1.5	3.2	.5	.5	.5	3.1	9.4	31.1	30.2	7.2	13.7	13.3	15.7
Senegal	722	...	...	...	.1	4.0	2.8	3.9	6.2	11.3	16.6	31.7	1.1	11.3	3.4	9.7
Seychelles	718	...	...	...	...	...	...	14.9	21.0	18.2	24.5	18.5	14.9	14.9	11.8	12.5
Sierra Leone	724	4.7	4.3	4.9	1.6	3.1	6.4	−1.3	5.5	5.7	14.4	19.9	17.2	8.3	10.9	21.3
Somalia	726	13.0	−3.3	−.3	3.4	6.3	.9	−.6	−3.0	6.5	18.2	19.4	14.2	10.6	10.0	24.3
South Africa	199	3.9	3.6	3.4	2.1	3.2	4.1	5.7	6.5	9.5	11.6	13.5	11.2	11.1	10.2	13.1
Sudan	732	−2.4	1.7	11.0	−10.0	12.6	4.0	1.3	13.6	15.3	26.2	24.0	1.7	17.1	19.2	31.1
Swaziland	734	...	3.2	1.8	3.4	3.2	1.8	2.3	2.4	11.5	19.3	12.0	6.5	20.8	8.5	16.5
Tanzania	738	...	9.8	12.2	15.6	16.4	3.5	4.7	7.6	10.5	19.2	26.5	6.9	11.6	6.6	12.9
Togo	742	...	...	−2.3	.3	6.0	4.5	6.5	7.7	3.6	12.8	18.0	11.6	22.5	.4	7.5
Tunisia	744	...	...	...	...	...	...	...	...	...	...	...	...	...	...	...
Uganda	746	...	...	...	...	...	...	...	...	...	...	...	...	...	...	...
Zaïre	636	−2.7	15.8	36.9	53.3	6.2	8.0	5.8	15.8	15.6	29.5	28.7	80.4	68.9	48.8	101.1
Zambia	754	8.1	10.2	5.0	10.8	2.4	2.7	6.0	5.1	6.5	8.1	10.1	18.8	19.8	16.3	9.7
Zimbabwe	698	2.5	3.1	2.4	1.4	.4	2.1	3.0	2.8	3.1	6.6	10.0	11.0	10.3	5.7	18.2
Asia	505	23.9	44.0	15.8	12.8	3.1	4.9	3.3	5.8	13.7	20.4	7.4	2.5	6.6	4.3	7.9
Afghanistan, Islamic State of	512	...	...	...	...	...	...	...	...	...	...	...	...	...	...	...
Bangladesh	513	7.9	8.0	5.4	2.7	5.0	3.0	−.5	40.7	49.0	54.8	21.9	2.3	4.8	5.3	14.7
Bhutan	514	...	...	...	...	...	...	...	...	...	...	...	...	...	...	...
China, People's Rep.	924	−1.2	−1.2	−.7	.1	1.0	—	−.1	.1	.1	.7	.4	.3	2.5	.9	2.0
Fiji	819	...	...	...	...	...	4.1	9.1	22.0	11.1	14.5	13.1	11.4	7.0	6.1	7.8
Hong Kong	532	.4	2.6	6.3	2.4	3.5	7.1	3.5	6.1	18.2	14.6	2.7	3.8	5.6	5.8	11.7
India	534	9.5	10.8	13.1	3.0	.6	5.1	3.1	6.5	16.9	28.6	5.7	−7.6	8.3	2.5	6.3
Indonesia	536	306.8	1,136.3	106.0	128.8	15.5	12.3	4.4	6.5	31.0	40.6	19.1	19.9	11.0	8.1	16.3
Korea	542	...	...	10.6	10.9	12.5	16.1	13.4	11.7	3.2	24.3	25.3	15.3	10.2	14.5	18.3
Malaysia	548	−.1	1.0	4.6	−.2	−.4	1.8	1.6	3.2	10.6	17.3	4.5	2.6	4.8	4.9	3.7
Maldives	556	...	...	...	...	...	...	...	...	...	...	...	...	...	12.7	27.8
Mongolia	948	...	...	...	...	...	...	...	...	...	...	...	...	...	...	...
Myanmar	518	17.7	25.5	.8	2.4	−4.3	−4.0	2.1	7.6	25.2	25.2	31.7	22.4	−1.2	−6.0	5.7
Nepal	558	8.5	14.4	−2.8	1.2	4.1	15.2	−2.0	8.4	11.4	19.8	7.6	−3.1	9.9	7.3	3.6
Pakistan	564	5.6	7.2	6.8	.2	3.2	5.3	4.7	5.2	23.1	26.7	20.9	7.2	10.1	6.1	8.3
Papua New Guinea	853	...	...	...	...	...	...	...	6.1	8.3	23.2	10.5	7.7	4.5	5.8	5.8
Philippines	566	3.1	4.9	5.7	2.0	1.3	15.3	21.4	8.2	16.6	34.2	6.8	9.2	9.9	7.3	17.5
Singapore	576	.3	2.0	3.3	.6	−.2	.4	1.8	2.1	26.2	22.4	2.6	−1.9	3.2	4.7	4.0
Solomon Islands	813	...	...	...	...	...	...	6.9	3.2	6.9	18.9	10.1	4.3	8.6	6.3	8.1
Sri Lanka	524	.2	−.2	2.2	5.9	7.5	5.9	2.7	6.3	9.6	12.3	6.6	1.3	1.2	12.1	10.7
Thailand	578	.2	4.0	4.3	1.8	2.5	−.1	.5	4.8	15.5	24.3	5.3	4.1	7.6	7.9	9.9
Tonga	866	...	...	...	...	...	...	...	...	...	...	...	...	7.1	17.5	5.5
Vanuatu	846	...	...	...	...	...	...	...	...	...	...	...	...	5.7	6.4	4.2
Western Samoa	862	2.1	2.9	−.5	1.7	4.1	2.7	4.8	7.5	11.8	25.0	8.8	4.9	14.6	2.1	11.1

Consumer Prices

64 x

1980	1981	1982	1983	1984	1985	1986	1987	1988	1989	1990	1991	1992	1993	1994		
Calculated from Indices																
17.3	15.9	14.5	14.7	14.7	15.1	11.7	14.0	20.8	27.2	29.0	18.1	18.2	19.8	23.8	World	001
12.4	**10.4**	**7.7**	**5.2**	**5.0**	**4.4**	**2.6**	**3.2**	**3.5**	**4.6**	**5.2**	**4.4**	**3.1**	**2.8**	**2.3**	**Industrial Countries**	**110**
13.5	10.3	6.2	3.2	4.3	3.6	1.9	3.7	4.0	4.8	5.4	4.2	3.0	3.0	2.6	United States	111
10.2	12.5	10.8	5.8	4.3	4.0	4.2	4.4	4.0	5.0	4.8	5.6	1.5	1.8	.2	Canada	156
10.1	9.7	11.1	10.1	4.0	6.7	9.1	8.5	7.2	7.6	7.3	3.2	1.0	1.8	1.9	Australia	193
7.8	4.9	2.7	1.9	2.2	2.0	.6	.1	.7	2.3	3.1	3.3	1.7	1.3	.7	Japan	158
17.1	15.3	16.2	7.4	6.2	15.4	13.2	15.7	6.4	5.7	6.1	2.6	1.0	1.3	1.7	New Zealand	196
6.3	6.8	5.4	3.3	5.7	3.2	1.7	1.4	1.9	2.6	3.3	3.3	4.0	3.6	3.0	Austria	122
6.7	7.6	8.7	7.7	6.3	4.9	1.3	1.6	1.2	3.1	3.5	3.2	2.4	2.8	2.4	Belgium	124
12.3	11.7	10.1	6.9	6.3	4.7	3.7	4.0	4.6	4.8	2.6	2.4	2.1	1.3	2.0	Denmark	128
11.6	12.0	9.6	8.4	7.1	5.9	2.9	4.1	5.1	6.6	6.1	4.1	2.6	2.1	1.1	Finland	172
13.3	13.4	11.8	9.6	7.4	5.8	2.5	3.3	2.7	3.5	3.4	3.2	2.4	2.1	1.7	France	132
5.4	6.3	5.3	3.3	2.4	2.2	−.1	.2	1.3	2.8	2.7	3.5	4.0	4.1	3.0	Germany	134
24.9	24.5	20.9	20.2	18.4	19.3	23.0	16.4	13.5	13.7	20.4	19.5	15.9	14.4	10.9	Greece	174
58.5	50.8	51.0	84.2	29.2	31.7	21.9	17.7	25.8	20.8	15.5	6.8	4.0	4.1	1.6	Iceland	176
18.2	20.4	17.1	10.5	8.6	5.4	3.8	3.1	2.2	4.1	3.3	3.2	3.1	1.4	2.3	Ireland	178
21.2	19.5	16.5	14.7	10.8	9.2	5.8	4.7	5.1	6.3	6.4	6.3	5.2	4.5	4.0	Italy	136
6.3	8.1	9.4	8.7	5.6	4.1	.3	−.1	1.5	3.4	3.7	3.1	3.2	3.6	2.2	Luxembourg	137
6.5	6.7	5.9	2.8	3.3	2.2	.1	−.7	.7	1.1	2.5	3.1	3.2	2.6	2.8	Netherlands	138
10.9	13.6	11.4	8.4	6.3	5.7	7.2	8.7	6.7	4.6	4.1	3.4	2.3	2.3	1.4	Norway	142
16.6	20.0	22.7	25.1	29.3	19.3	11.7	9.4	9.6	12.6	13.4	11.4	8.9	6.8	4.9	Portugal	182
15.6	14.6	14.4	12.2	11.3	8.8	8.8	5.2	4.8	6.8	6.7	5.9	5.9	4.6	4.7	Spain	184
13.7	12.1	8.6	8.9	8.0	7.4	4.2	4.2	5.8	6.4	10.5	9.3	2.3	4.6	2.2	Sweden	144
4.0	6.5	5.7	3.0	2.9	3.4	.8	1.4	1.9	3.2	5.4	5.8	4.1	3.3	.8	Switzerland	146
18.0	11.9	8.6	4.6	5.0	6.1	3.4	4.1	4.9	7.8	9.5	5.9	3.7	1.6	2.5	United Kingdom	112
26.4	**26.2**	**28.1**	**34.0**	**32.8**	**35.4**	**28.3**	**34.8**	**55.9**	**75.7**	**77.6**	**43.2**	**46.7**	**52.8**	**66.5**	**Developing Countries**	**200**
15.7	**20.0**	**13.9**	**18.4**	**18.6**	**13.8**	**15.4**	**16.8**	**21.9**	**21.4**	**16.6**	**31.5**	**44.9**	**37.2**	**60.6**	**Africa**	**605**
9.5	14.6	6.7	6.0	8.1	10.5	12.4	7.4	5.9	9.3	16.6	25.9	31.7	20.5	29.0	Algeria	612
13.6	16.4	11.1	10.5	8.6	8.1	10.0	9.8	8.4	11.6	11.8	11.8	16.2	14.3	10.5	Botswana	616
12.2	7.6	12.1	8.3	4.8	6.9	−2.6	−2.7	4.1	−.3	−.8	2.5	−2.0	.6	25.2	Burkina Faso	748
2.5	12.2	5.9	8.2	14.3	3.8	1.7	7.1	4.5	11.7	7.0	9.0	4.5	9.7	14.9	Burundi	618
9.6	10.7	12.8	16.7	11.3	11.5	7.7	12.8	−5.5	5.5	1.7	1.9	1.4	....	....	Cameroon	622
....	....	13.3	14.6	2.5	10.4	2.2	−7.0	−4.0	.7	—	−2.8	−1.0	−2.9	....	Central African Rep.	626
....	....	....	....	20.3	5.2	−13.1	−6.0	15.5	−4.9	.6	4.1	−4.1	....	....	Chad	628
7.3	17.0	12.8	7.7	13.2	5.6	2.4	1.6	4.8	3.7	−4.8	9.1	2.2	1.9	....	Congo	634
14.7	8.8	7.3	5.9	4.3	1.8	6.8	6.9	7.0	1.0	−.8	1.7	3.5	2.8	25.9	Côte d'Ivoire	662
....	....	....	....	....	....	−17.8	−12.9	2.3	5.9	1.1	−3.2	−7.2	4.0	....	Equatorial Guinea	642
4.5	1.4	5.9	−.7	8.4	19.1	−9.8	−2.4	7.1	7.8	5.2	35.7	10.5	3.5	....	Ethiopia	644
12.3	8.7	16.7	10.7	5.9	7.4	6.3	−.9	−8.8	6.7	7.7	−8.0	−.9	....	....	Gabon	646
6.8	5.9	10.9	10.6	22.1	18.3	56.6	23.5	11.7	8.3	12.2	8.6	9.5	6.5	1.7	Gambia, The	648
50.1	116.5	22.3	122.9	39.7	10.3	24.6	39.8	31.4	25.2	37.3	18.0	10.1	25.0	24.9	Ghana	652
....	....	....	....	....	....	....	....	60.3	80.8	33.0	57.6	69.6	48.1	15.2	Guinea-Bissau	654
13.9	11.6	20.7	11.4	10.3	13.0	4.8	7.6	11.2	12.9	15.6	19.8	29.5	45.8	29.0	Kenya	664
14.7	7.6	6.0	2.7	1.2	−1.0	4.0	5.0	9.6	9.1	....	....	....	....	....	Liberia	668
18.2	30.5	31.8	19.3	9.9	10.6	14.5	15.0	26.9	9.0	11.8	8.6	14.5	10.0	38.9	Madagascar	674
....	11.8	9.8	13.5	20.0	10.5	14.0	25.2	33.9	12.5	11.8	12.6	22.7	19.7	....	Malawi	676
....	....	....	....	....	....	....	....	....	−.1	....	1.8	−6.2	−.1	....	Mali	678
....	....	....	....	....	....	7.4	8.2	1.3	12.9	6.6	5.6	10.1	9.3	....	Mauritania	682
42.0	14.5	11.4	5.6	7.4	6.7	1.6	.5	9.2	12.7	13.5	7.0	4.6	10.5	7.3	Mauritius	684
9.4	12.5	10.5	6.2	12.4	7.7	8.7	2.7	2.4	3.1	6.9	8.0	5.7	5.2	5.1	Morocco	686
....	....	....	....	....	....	91.0	....	91.0	50.1	40.1	47.0	32.9	45.5	42.2	Mozambique	688
....	14.8	15.5	12.0	9.1	12.0	13.4	12.6	12.9	15.1	12.0	11.9	17.7	8.5	10.8	Namibia	728
10.3	22.9	11.6	−2.5	8.4	−.9	−3.2	−6.7	−1.4	−2.8	−.8	−7.8	−4.5	−1.2	36.0	Niger	692
10.0	20.8	7.7	23.2	39.6	7.4	5.7	11.3	54.5	50.5	7.4	13.0	44.6	57.2	57.0	Nigeria	694
7.2	6.5	12.6	6.6	5.4	1.8	−1.1	4.1	3.0	1.0	4.2	19.6	9.6	12.4	....	Rwanda	714
8.7	5.9	17.4	11.6	11.8	13.0	6.2	−4.1	−1.8	.4	.3	−1.8	−.1	−.6	32.3	Senegal	722
13.6	10.6	−.9	6.1	4.1	.8	.2	2.6	1.8	1.6	3.9	2.0	3.2	1.3	1.8	Seychelles	718
12.9	23.4	26.9	68.5	66.6	76.6	80.9	181.6	31.3	62.8	111.0	102.7	65.5	22.2	24.2	Sierra Leone	724
58.8	44.4	23.6	36.0	91.2	37.8	35.8	28.2	81.9	....	....	....	....	....	....	Somalia	726
13.8	15.2	14.7	12.3	11.5	16.3	18.6	16.1	12.8	14.7	14.4	15.3	13.9	9.7	9.0	South Africa	199
25.4	24.6	25.7	30.6	34.1	45.4	24.5	20.6	64.7	66.7	65.2	123.6	117.6	101.4	....	Sudan	732
18.7	20.1	10.8	11.6	12.9	20.5	13.7	13.4	12.4	8.3	11.0	10.8	8.2	17.0	14.3	Swaziland	734
30.3	25.7	28.9	27.1	36.1	33.3	32.4	30.0	31.2	25.8	19.7	22.3	22.1	23.5	....	Tanzania	738
12.3	19.7	11.1	9.4	−3.5	−1.8	4.1	.1	−.2	−.8	1.0	.4	1.4	−1.0	....	Togo	742
....	....	....	....	8.9	7.3	6.2	8.2	7.2	7.7	6.5	8.2	5.8	4.0	4.7	Tunisia	744
....	108.7	49.3	24.1	42.7	157.7	161.0	200.0	196.1	61.4	33.1	28.1	52.4	6.1	9.7	Uganda	746
46.6	35.4	36.7	76.5	52.2	23.8	46.7	90.4	82.7	104.1	81.3	2,154.4	4,129.2	1,986.9	23,773.1	Zaïre	636
11.6	13.0	13.6	19.6	20.0	37.3	51.8	43.0	55.6	127.9	117.5	92.6	197.4	189.0	....	Zambia	754
5.4	13.2	10.6	23.1	20.2	8.5	14.3	12.5	7.4	12.9	17.4	23.3	42.1	27.6	22.3	Zimbabwe	698
12.6	**9.8**	**6.2**	**6.8**	**6.9**	**7.9**	**6.3**	**7.6**	**12.4**	**10.6**	**5.9**	**8.9**	**8.6**	**10.4**	**13.9**	**Asia**	**505**
.9	4.9	5.8	−3.0	7.7	112.3	−3.2	19.5	19.9	75.1	41.9	56.7	....	....	....	Afghanistan, Islamic State of	512
13.4	16.2	12.5	9.4	10.5	10.7	11.0	9.5	9.3	10.0	8.1	7.2	4.3	—	3.6	Bangladesh	513
....	9.9	9.9	18.0	7.0	1.9	10.0	6.4	10.1	8.8	10.0	12.3	12.7	....	....	Bhutan	514
7.4	2.5	2.0	1.9	2.7	11.9	7.0	8.8	20.7	16.3	1.4	5.1	8.6	17.0	....	China, People's Rep.	924
14.5	11.2	7.0	6.7	5.3	4.4	1.8	5.7	11.8	6.2	8.2	6.5	4.9	5.2	.6	Fiji	819
14.8	13.8	10.6	9.9	8.5	3.4	3.2	5.3	7.4	9.7	9.7	6.9	9.6	8.7	8.6	Hong Kong	532
11.4	13.1	7.9	11.9	8.3	5.6	8.7	8.8	9.4	6.2	9.0	13.9	11.8	6.4	10.2	India	534
18.0	12.2	9.5	11.8	10.5	4.7	5.8	9.3	8.0	6.4	7.8	9.4	7.5	9.2	8.5	Indonesia	536
28.7	21.3	7.2	3.4	2.3	2.5	2.8	3.0	7.1	5.7	8.6	9.3	6.2	4.8	6.3	Korea	542
6.7	9.7	5.8	3.7	3.9	.3	.7	.3	2.6	2.8	2.6	4.4	4.8	3.5	3.7	Malaysia	548
23.8	23.7	22.0	....	....	....	....	....	....	....	7.2	3.6	14.7	16.8	20.2	Maldives	556
....	....	....	....	....	....	....	....	....	....	....	....	....	268.4	87.6	Mongolia	948
.6	.3	5.3	5.7	4.8	6.8	9.3	24.8	16.0	27.2	17.6	32.3	21.9	31.8	24.1	Myanmar	518
14.7	11.1	11.7	12.4	2.8	8.1	19.0	10.8	9.0	8.8	8.2	15.6	17.1	7.5	....	Nepal	558
11.9	11.9	5.9	6.4	6.1	5.6	3.5	4.7	8.8	7.8	9.1	11.8	9.5	9.4	12.5	Pakistan	564
12.1	8.1	5.5	7.9	7.4	3.7	5.5	3.3	5.4	4.5	7.0	7.0	4.3	5.0	2.9	Papua New Guinea	853
18.2	13.1	10.2	10.0	50.3	23.1	.8	3.8	8.8	12.2	14.1	18.7	8.9	7.6	9.1	Philippines	566
8.5	8.2	3.9	1.2	2.6	.5	−1.4	.5	1.5	2.4	3.4	3.4	2.3	2.2	3.1	Singapore	576
13.1	14.6	13.0	6.2	11.0	9.6	13.6	11.0	16.7	14.9	8.7	15.1	2.8	17.3	13.6	Solomon Islands	813
26.1	18.0	10.8	14.0	16.6	1.5	8.0	7.7	14.0	11.6	21.5	12.2	11.4	11.7	8.4	Sri Lanka	524
19.7	12.7	5.3	3.7	.9	2.4	1.8	2.5	3.9	5.4	5.9	5.7	4.1	3.6	5.3	Thailand	578
22.4	14.9	10.8	9.8	.1	16.8	21.7	4.7	9.9	4.1	9.7	10.6	7.9	1.0	1.0	Tonga	866
11.2	26.8	6.7	1.7	5.5	1.1	4.8	16.0	8.8	7.7	4.8	6.5	2.2	5.4	2.3	Vanuatu	846
33.0	20.5	18.3	16.5	11.9	9.1	5.7	4.6	8.5	6.5	15.2	−1.8	9.0	1.7	18.3	Western Samoa	862

1995 INTERNATIONAL FINANCIAL STATISTICS YEARBOOK

Consumer Prices

		1965	1966	1967	1968	1969	1970	1971	1972	1973	1974	1975	1976	1977	1978	1979
														Percent Change over Previous Year;		
Europe	170	....	....	....	....	....	....	6.5	5.3	7.7	9.2	8.8	7.2	9.6	13.8	17.0
Cyprus	423	.2	.5	.7	3.8	2.4	2.4	4.1	4.8	7.8	6.5	14.1	3.9	7.3	7.4	9.5
Czech Republic	935															
Czechoslovakia	934							−.4	−.3	.3	.5	.7	.8	1.3	1.6	3.9
Estonia	939															
Hungary	944									3.4	1.8	3.8	5.2	3.9	4.7	9.0
Malta	181	1.6	.5	.7	2.0	2.3	3.7	2.3	3.4	7.7	7.3	8.8	.6	10.0	4.7	7.1
Poland	964							1.1	−.1	2.5	7.1	2.3	4.4	4.9	8.1	7.0
Romania	968							.6	—	.7	1.1	.2	.5	.6	2.0	1.8
Slovak Republic	936															
Slovenia	961															
Turkey	186	5.9	4.4	6.8	.4	7.9	6.9	15.7	11.7	15.4	15.8	19.2	17.4	27.1	45.3	58.7
Yugoslavia, SFR	188	33.3	25.5	6.6	5.1	9.1	9.5	15.7	15.9	19.5	22.0	23.5	11.2	14.7	14.1	20.7
Middle East	405	.6	3.9	3.7	2.2	4.0	2.4	4.2	5.1	10.8	15.3	16.5	15.1	16.1	10.4	14.0
Bahrain	419		2.1	4.3	3.3	−.2	1.6	5.8	5.1	14.3	24.4	16.2	22.5	17.7	15.8	2.2
Egypt	469	14.8	9.0	.7	−1.7	3.4	3.8	3.1	2.1	5.1	10.0	9.7	10.3	12.7	11.1	9.9
Iran, I.R. of	429	2.2	−.4	1.6	.7	3.6	1.7	4.2	6.4	9.8	14.2	12.9	11.3	27.3	11.7	10.5
Israel	436	7.7	7.9	1.7	2.1	2.4	6.1	12.0	12.9	20.0	39.7	39.3	31.4	34.6	50.6	78.3
Jordan	439						5.9	4.8	7.7	11.1	19.4	12.0	11.5	14.6	6.9	14.2
Kuwait	443									8.3	13.0	8.4	5.2	9.9	8.7	7.1
Libya	672	11.4	12.2	7.3	.4	9.8	−5.3	−3.1	−.3	8.0	7.5	9.1	5.5	6.3	29.4	−6.0
Qatar	453															
Saudi Arabia	456	.4	1.6	2.1	1.6	3.5	.2	4.5	4.3	16.5	21.4	34.6	31.6	11.4	−1.6	1.9
Syrian Arab Rep.	463	−3.9	3.8	6.5	2.8	−2.0	4.6	5.6	2.1	20.4	15.5	11.5	11.4	12.0	4.8	4.6
Yemen Arab Rep.	473									43.0	26.6	24.0	15.4	26.0	12.4	26.2
Yemen, P.D. Rep.	459						5.0	5.3	5.2	19.7	20.3	11.9	3.1	5.5	5.8	7.1
Western Hemisphere	205	25.8	20.3	16.7	13.4	10.7	12.3	13.7	17.5	25.5	29.9	37.2	52.0	44.4	37.5	41.7
Antigua and Barbuda	311													13.8	6.1	16.3
Argentina	213	28.6	31.9	29.2	16.2	7.6	13.6	34.7	58.4	61.2	23.5	182.9	444.0	176.0	175.5	159.5
Bahamas, The	313			5.4	4.5	8.9	6.2	4.6	6.8	5.5	13.1	10.4	4.3	3.2	6.1	9.1
Barbados	316			3.6	7.5	5.8	7.3	7.5	11.9	16.9	38.9	20.3	5.0	8.4	9.5	13.2
Belize	339															
Bolivia	218	2.9	7.0	11.2	5.5	2.2	3.8	3.7	6.5	31.5	62.8	8.0	4.5	8.1	10.4	19.7
Brazil	223	65.7	41.3	30.5	22.0	22.7	22.4	20.1	16.6	12.7	27.6	29.0	42.0	43.7	38.7	52.7
Chile	228	28.8	23.1	18.8	26.3	30.4	32.5	20.0	74.8	361.5	504.7	374.7	211.8	91.9	40.1	33.4
Colombia	233	3.5	19.9	8.2	5.8	10.1	6.8	9.1	13.4	20.8	24.3	22.9	20.2	33.1	17.8	24.7
Costa Rica	238	−.7	.6	1.2	4.1	2.6	4.7	3.1	4.6	15.2	30.1	17.4	3.5	4.2	6.0	9.2
Dominica	321	2.5	2.5	1.0	5.4	4.2	12.4	3.6	3.7	12.1	34.4	19.9	10.9	86.5	−36.7	25.2
Dominican Republic	243	−1.9	.3	1.2	—	1.0	3.8	3.6	8.6	15.1	13.1	14.5	7.8	12.9	3.5	9.2
Ecuador	248	3.1	5.5	3.8	4.3	6.3	5.1	8.4	7.9	13.0	23.3	15.4	10.7	13.0	11.7	10.3
El Salvador	253	.5	−1.2	1.5	2.5	−.2	2.8	.4	1.5	6.4	16.9	19.1	7.0	11.8	13.3	14.6
Grenada	328													18.5	18.1	21.5
Guatemala	258	−.8	.7	.5	1.9	2.1	2.3	−.5	.5	13.8	16.5	13.2	10.7	12.3	8.3	11.3
Guyana	336	2.7	2.1	3.0	3.1	1.3	3.3	1.0	4.9	7.6	17.4	7.9	9.0	8.2	15.2	17.8
Haiti	263	2.3	8.3	−2.9	1.3	1.4	1.4	9.6	3.2	22.7	15.0	16.8	7.0	6.5	−2.7	13.1
Honduras	268	3.2	1.8	2.1	1.9	1.3	2.9	2.2	3.6	5.2	12.8	8.4	4.9	8.4	5.7	12.1
Jamaica	343	2.6	1.9	3.0	5.9	6.3	14.7	5.3	5.4	17.7	27.2	17.4	9.8	11.2	34.9	29.1
Mexico	273	3.6	4.2	3.0	2.3	3.4	5.2	5.3	5.0	12.0	23.8	15.2	15.8	29.0	17.5	18.2
Netherlands Antilles	353	.8	1.1	.8	1.4	1.5	3.5	2.1	4.1	8.1	19.5	15.6	5.4	8.2	11.4	
Nicaragua	278									27.0	13.3	7.5	2.8	11.4	4.6	48.2
Panama	283	.5	.2	1.4	1.6	1.8	3.1	1.9	5.4	6.9	16.3	5.9	4.0	4.6	4.2	8.0
Paraguay	288	3.8	2.9	1.4	.7	2.1	−.7	4.8	9.5	12.5	25.2	6.8	4.6	9.3	10.6	28.3
Peru	293	16.4	8.8	9.8	19.1	6.2	5.0	6.8	7.2	9.5	16.9	23.6	33.5	38.1	57.8	66.7
St. Kitts and Nevis	361															
St. Lucia	362		2.5	3.2	4.0	2.3	13.4	8.4	7.9	13.4	34.2	17.7	9.7	8.9	10.9	9.4
St. Vincent & Grens.	364											6.8	11.3	10.2	8.4	15.6
Suriname	366	1.9	4.7	10.7	.2	11.3	2.6	.2	3.2	12.9	16.9	8.4	10.1	9.7	8.8	14.8
Trinidad and Tobago	369	1.8	4.1	2.1	8.2	2.4	2.5	3.5	9.3	14.8	22.0	17.0	10.7	11.7	10.3	14.7
Uruguay	298	56.6	73.5	89.3	125.3	21.0	16.3	24.0	76.5	97.0	77.2	81.4	50.6	58.2	44.5	66.8
Venezuela	299	1.7	1.8	—	1.3	2.4	2.5	3.2	2.8	4.1	8.3	10.2	7.6	7.8	7.1	12.4
Memorandum Items																
Oil Exporting Countries	999	108.4	273.0	46.4	55.0	7.9	6.2	5.2	4.6	12.0	16.9	17.3	15.3	14.5	10.2	12.3
Non-Oil Developing Countries	201	12.8	11.4	10.5	4.9	7.1	10.0	8.3	10.5	18.0	16.9	14.8	16.2	17.1	14.8	21.6

Indices

Index Numbers:

		1965	1966	1967	1968	1969	1970	1971	1972	1973	1974	1975	1976	1977	1978	1979
World	001	5.0	5.4	5.7	5.9	6.2	6.6	7.0	7.4	8.1	9.3	10.6	11.9	13.4	14.8	16.8
Industrial Countries	110	21.0	21.7	22.4	23.2	24.3	25.7	27.1	28.4	30.6	34.7	38.7	42.0	45.7	49.1	53.9
Developing Countries	200	.4	.5	.5	.6	.6	.7	.7	.8	.9	1.0	1.2	1.4	1.7	2.0	2.4
Africa	605	4.4	4.6	4.8	4.9	5.1	5.4	5.8	6.1	6.6	7.5	8.9	10.4	12.5	14.5	17.0
Asia	505	10.2	14.7	17.0	19.2	19.8	20.8	21.5	22.7	25.8	31.1	33.4	34.2	36.5	38.1	41.1
Europe	170	....	....	....	....	....	.8	.9	.9	1.0	1.1	1.2	1.3	1.4	1.6	1.9
Middle East	405	5.0	5.2	5.4	5.5	5.7	5.8	6.1	6.4	7.1	8.2	9.5	11.0	12.7	14.0	16.0
Western Hemisphere	205	—	—	—	—	—	—	—	—	—	—	—	—	—	—	—

Consumer Prices

64 x

1980	1981	1982	1983	1984	1985	1986	1987	1988	1989	1990	1991	1992	1993	1994		
Calculated from Indices																
26.2	19.3	37.9	20.5	22.8	23.2	24.4	30.9	53.5	123.0	153.8	82.2	86.7	66.2	72.2	Europe	170
13.5	10.7	6.4	5.0	6.0	5.0	1.2	2.8	3.4	3.8	4.5	5.0	6.5	4.9	....	Cyprus	423
....	....	....	....	....	....	....	....	....	....	....	....	....	....	10.1	Czech Republic	935
2.9	.8	5.1	.9	.9	2.3	.5	.1	.1	1.4	10.0	57.7	10.8	....	....	Czechoslovakia	934
....	....	....	....	....	....	....	....	....	....	....	....	1,075.9	89.8	47.7	Estonia	939
9.3	4.5	7.0	6.4	8.7	7.0	5.3	8.7	15.8	16.9	29.0	34.2	22.9	22.5	18.9	Hungary	944
15.7	11.5	5.8	–.9	–.4	–.2	2.0	.4	.9	.8	3.0	2.5	1.6	4.1	4.1	Malta	181
9.7	19.1	103.6	25.5	15.4	11.5	16.5	26.4	58.7	244.6	555.4	76.7	45.3	36.9	33.3	Poland	964
1.5	2.2	16.9	5.2	1.1	–.4	2.2	1.1	2.8	.7	4.2	230.6	211.2	255.2	136.8	Romania	968
....	....	....	....	....	....	....	....	....	....	....	....	....	....	13.4	Slovak Republic	936
....	....	....	....	....	....	....	....	....	....	....	156.6	156.6	31.9	19.8	Slovenia	961
110.2	36.6	30.8	31.4	48.4	45.0	34.6	38.8	73.7	63.3	60.3	66.0	70.1	66.1	106.3	Turkey	186
30.9	39.8	31.5	40.2	54.7	72.3	89.8	120.8	194.1	1,239.9	583.1	117.4	....	....	....	Yugoslavia, SFR	188
23.9	22.0	20.5	20.6	20.3	17.0	16.1	18.4	17.1	14.2	10.1	13.2	11.4	11.2	12.5	Middle East	405
3.9	11.3	8.9	3.0	.3	–2.6	–2.3	–1.7	.3	1.5	.9	.8	–.2	2.5	.8	Bahrain	419
20.7	10.3	14.8	16.1	17.0	12.1	23.9	19.7	17.7	21.3	16.8	19.7	13.6	12.1	8.2	Egypt	469
20.6	24.2	18.7	19.7	12.5	4.4	18.4	28.6	28.7	22.3	7.6	17.1	25.6	21.2	31.5	Iran, I.R. of	429
131.0	116.8	120.4	145.6	373.8	304.6	48.1	19.8	16.3	20.2	17.2	19.0	11.9	10.9	12.3	Israel	436
11.1	7.7	7.4	5.0	3.8	3.0	—	–.2	6.6	25.7	16.2	8.2	4.0	4.7	3.5	Jordan	439
6.9	7.4	7.8	4.7	1.2	1.5	1.0	.7	1.5	3.3	1.9	16.9	....	....	....	Kuwait	443
....	....	....	....	....	....	....	....	....	....	....	....	....	....	....	Libya	672
6.8	8.5	5.7	2.7	1.1	1.9	1.6	2.7	4.6	3.3	3.0	4.4	....	....	....	Qatar	453
3.8	2.8	1.0	.2	–1.6	–3.1	–3.2	–1.5	.9	1.0	2.1	4.9	–.1	1.1	.6	Saudi Arabia	456
19.3	18.4	14.3	6.1	9.2	17.3	36.1	59.5	34.6	11.4	19.4	7.7	9.5	11.8	....	Syrian Arab Rep.	463
5.3	5.0	2.7	5.3	12.8	....	....	....	....	....	....	....	....	....	....	Yemen Arab Rep.	473
13.7	3.8	9.5	11.0	1.1	5.1	....	....	....	....	....	....	....	....	....	Yemen, P.D. Rep.	459
51.5	57.4	66.3	99.0	111.8	130.2	88.7	123.0	229.8	354.4	504.9	148.0	170.9	239.3	301.8	Western Hemisphere	205
19.0	11.5	4.2	2.3	3.9	1.0	....	....	....	....	....	....	....	....	....	Antigua and Barbuda	311
100.8	104.5	164.8	343.8	626.7	672.1	90.1	131.3	343.0	3,079.8	2,314.0	171.7	24.9	10.6	4.2	Argentina	213
12.1	11.1	6.0	4.0	4.0	4.6	5.4	5.8	4.4	5.4	4.7	7.1	5.7	2.7	1.4	Bahamas,The	313
14.4	14.6	10.3	5.2	4.7	3.9	1.3	3.3	4.9	6.2	3.1	6.3	6.1	1.1	.1	Barbados	316
....	11.2	6.8	5.0	3.4	4.2	.8	2.0	5.3	—	3.0	5.6	2.8	1.6	....	Belize	339
47.2	32.1	123.5	275.6	1,281.4	11,749.6	276.3	14.6	16.0	15.2	17.1	21.4	12.1	8.5	....	Bolivia	218
82.8	105.6	97.8	142.1	197.0	226.9	145.2	229.7	682.3	1,287.0	2,937.8	440.9	1,008.7	2,148.4	2,668.5	Brazil	223
35.1	19.7	9.9	27.3	19.9	30.7	19.5	19.9	14.7	17.0	26.0	21.8	15.4	12.7	11.4	Chile	228
26.5	27.5	24.5	19.8	16.1	24.0	18.9	23.3	28.1	25.8	29.1	30.4	27.0	22.6	23.8	Colombia	233
18.1	37.1	90.1	32.6	12.0	15.1	11.8	16.8	20.8	16.5	19.0	28.7	21.8	9.8	13.5	Costa Rica	238
25.2	13.3	4.4	4.1	2.2	3.7	2.8	4.0	2.9	6.2	3.2	5.6	5.5	1.6	1.6	Dominica	321
16.8	7.5	7.6	4.8	27.0	37.5	9.7	15.9	44.4	45.4	59.4	53.9	4.6	5.2	8.3	Dominican Republic	243
13.0	16.4	16.3	48.4	31.2	28.0	23.0	29.5	58.2	75.6	48.5	48.7	54.6	45.0	27.3	Ecuador	248
17.4	14.8	11.7	13.3	11.5	22.3	31.9	24.9	19.8	17.6	24.0	14.4	11.2	18.6	10.6	El Salvador	253
21.2	18.8	7.8	6.1	5.6	2.6	.5	–.9	4.0	5.6	2.7	2.6	3.8	2.8	....	Grenada	328
10.8	11.4	.3	4.5	3.4	18.7	36.9	12.3	10.8	11.4	41.2	33.2	10.0	11.8	....	Guatemala	258
14.1	22.1	21.1	14.9	25.2	15.0	7.9	28.7	39.9	4.0	3.7	2.3	2.6	....	....	Guyana	336
17.8	10.9	7.4	10.2	6.4	10.6	3.3	–11.4	4.1	6.9	21.3	15.4	19.4	22.6	42.6	Haiti	263
18.1	9.4	9.0	8.3	4.7	3.4	4.4	2.5	4.5	9.9	23.3	34.0	8.8	10.7	21.7	Honduras	268
27.3	12.7	6.5	11.6	27.8	25.7	15.1	6.7	8.3	14.3	22.0	51.1	77.3	22.1	35.1	Jamaica	343
26.4	27.9	58.9	101.8	65.5	57.7	86.2	131.8	114.2	20.0	26.7	22.7	15.5	8.7	7.0	Mexico	273
14.6	12.2	6.1	2.8	2.1	.5	1.3	3.8	2.6	3.9	3.7	4.0	1.4	2.1	1.8	Netherlands Antilles	353
35.3	23.9	24.8	31.1	35.4	219.5	681.4	911.9	10,205.0	4,770.4	7,485.2	2,742.2	20.3	....	....	Nicaragua	278
13.8	7.3	4.3	2.1	1.6	1.0	–.1	1.0	.4	.1	.8	1.3	1.8	.5	1.3	Panama	283
22.4	14.0	6.8	13.4	20.3	25.2	31.7	21.8	22.6	26.4	38.2	24.3	15.1	18.3	....	Paraguay	288
59.1	75.4	64.4	111.2	110.2	163.4	77.9	85.8	667.0	3,398.7	7,481.7	409.5	73.5	48.6	23.7	Peru	293
17.7	10.5	5.9	2.3	2.7	2.6	—	.9	.2	5.1	4.2	4.2	2.9	1.8	2.6	St. Kitts and Nevis	361
19.5	15.1	4.6	1.5	1.2	1.4	2.0	7.6	.8	4.1	4.7	5.7	5.1	.8	....	St. Lucia	362
17.2	12.7	7.2	5.5	2.7	2.1	1.0	3.3	.2	2.8	7.6	5.5	3.5	4.3	1.0	St. Vincent & Grens.	364
14.1	8.8	7.3	4.4	3.7	10.9	18.7	53.4	7.3	.8	21.7	26.0	43.7	143.5	....	Suriname	366
17.5	14.3	11.6	15.2	13.3	7.6	7.7	10.8	7.8	11.4	11.1	3.8	6.6	10.7	8.8	Trinidad and Tobago	369
63.5	34.0	19.0	49.2	55.3	72.2	76.4	63.6	62.2	80.4	112.5	102.0	68.5	54.1	44.7	Uruguay	298
21.5	16.0	9.7	6.3	11.6	11.4	11.5	28.1	29.5	84.5	40.7	34.2	31.4	38.1	60.8	Venezuela	299
															Memorandum Items	
15.2	15.5	9.8	12.1	11.7	5.2	8.0	12.4	17.5	19.4	11.0	14.8	17.9	19.5	23.5	Oil Exporting Countries	999
28.2	28.0	31.2	37.6	36.5	40.9	31.8	38.6	62.5	86.0	89.8	47.7	51.2	58.0	73.2	Non-Oil Developing Countries	201

Indices

1990=100

1980	1981	1982	1983	1984	1985	1986	1987	1988	1989	1990	1991	1992	1993	1994		
19.7	22.9	26.2	30.0	34.4	39.6	44.3	50.5	60.9	77.5	100.0	118.1	139.6	167.3	207.1	World	001
60.6	66.9	72.0	75.7	79.5	83.0	85.1	87.8	90.9	95.1	100.0	104.4	107.1	110.7	113.3	Industrial Countries	110
3.1	3.9	4.9	6.6	8.8	11.9	15.3	20.6	32.1	56.3	100.0	143.2	210.1	321.0	534.4	Developing Countries	200
19.7	23.6	26.9	31.9	37.8	43.0	49.6	57.9	70.6	85.8	100.0	131.5	190.6	261.4	419.8	Africa	605
46.3	50.8	53.9	57.6	61.6	66.4	70.6	76.0	85.4	94.4	100.0	108.9	118.3	130.6	148.7	Asia	505
2.4	2.8	3.9	4.7	5.7	7.1	8.8	11.5	17.7	39.4	100.0	182.3	340.2	565.5	973.8	Europe	170
19.8	24.2	29.1	35.1	42.3	49.4	57.4	67.9	79.6	90.9	100.0	113.2	126.2	140.3	157.9	Middle East	405
—	—	—	.1	.1	.3	.5	1.1	3.6	16.5	100.0	248.0	671.7	2,279.4	9,158.2	Western Hemisphere	205

Exports

70 d		1965	1966	1967	1968	1969	1970	1971	1972	1973	1974	1975	1976	1977	1978	1979
																Billions of US Dollars
World	**001**	**172.0**	**188.4**	**198.2**	**220.7**	**252.9**	**293.4**	**328.6**	**391.3**	**542.3**	**796.8**	**816.5**	**919.5**	**1,043.2**	**1,210.1**	**1,545.7**
Industrial Countries	**110**	**126.6**	**139.7**	**147.6**	**166.5**	**191.9**	**222.4**	**248.5**	**296.7**	**405.1**	**542.0**	**578.0**	**643.4**	**729.5**	**873.1**	**1,074.0**
United States	**111**	26.699	29.379	30.934	34.063	37.332	42.659	43.549	49.199	70.823	99.437	108.856	116.794	I 123.182	145.847	186.363
Canada	**156**	8.449	9.971	10.975	13.123	14.293	16.747	18.374	21.185	26.437	34.508	34.074	40.598	43.545	48.431	58.294
Australia	**193**	3.005	3.171	3.478	3.526	4.220	4.770	5.213	6.461	9.559	11.016	11.948	13.193	13.367	14.415	18.663
Japan	**158**	8.451	9.776	10.442	12.971	15.990	19.317	23.995	29.088	37.017	55.469	55.819	67.304	81.083	98.211	102.299
New Zealand	**196**	1.007	1.076	.993	1.010	1.211	1.223	1.361	1.792	2.596	2.435	2.162	2.795	3.196	3.738	4.706
Austria	**122**	1.600	1.684	1.809	1.989	2.412	2.857	3.168	3.883	5.283	7.161	7.519	8.507	9.807	12.180	15.481
Belgium	**126**	6.388	6.824	7.032	8.146	10.006	11.514	12.257	16.034	22.450	28.324	28.801	32.889	37.530	44.944	56.423
Denmark	**128**	2.320	2.453	2.538	2.640	3.019	3.356	3.680	4.432	6.248	7.719	8.712	9.115	10.065	11.883	14.696
Finland	**172**	1.427	1.505	1.513	1.635	1.987	2.306	2.367	2.913	3.837	5.490	5.502	6.342	7.665	8.570	11.172
France	**132**	10.053	10.894	11.383	12.723	14.960	17.879	20.830	26.467	36.675	46.477	53.086	56.874	65.276	79.371	100.692
Germany	**134**	17.912	20.157	21.761	24.888	28.852	34.228	38.845	46.736	67.563	89.368	90.176	102.162	118.072	142.453	171.804
Greece	**174**	.328	.406	.495	.468	.554	.643	.663	.871	1.456	2.031	2.294	2.561	2.758	3.368	3.885
Iceland	**176**	.129	.141	.097	.080	.108	.147	.150	.189	.290	.331	.306	.401	.512	.641	.782
Ireland	**178**	.616	.681	.785	.871	.967	1.120	1.306	1.607	2.129	2.658	3.193	3.313	4.404	5.691	7.143
Italy	**136**	7.198	8.038	8.706	10.186	11.728	13.205	15.105	18.609	22.226	30.465	34.988	37.265	45.305	56.090	72.233
Netherlands	**138**	7.343	7.771	8.361	9.569	11.383	13.355	15.794	19.163	27.348	37.425	39.939	46.157	50.110	57.583	73.567
Norway	**142**	1.443	1.564	1.738	1.938	2.203	2.455	2.553	3.283	4.726	6.282	7.232	7.951	8.880	10.882	13.546
Portugal	**182**	.584	.627	.696	.734	.823	.946	1.049	1.298	1.842	2.277	1.939	1.811	1.970	2.414	3.479
Spain	**184**	.935	1.254	1.362	1.589	1.900	2.388	2.965	3.817	5.200	7.091	7.690	8.730	10.223	13.118	18.208
Sweden	**144**	3.971	4.266	4.528	4.910	5.695	6.795	7.463	8.769	12.201	15.939	17.383	18.435	I 19.082	21.790	27.602
Switzerland	**146**	2.941	3.248	3.468	3.968	4.599	5.065	5.739	6.867	9.538	11.947	12.958	14.889	17.614	23.576	26.538
United Kingdom	**112**	13.810	14.773	14.496	15.458	17.642	19.428	22.098	23.987	29.640	38.197	43.423	45.356	55.862	67.887	86.401
Developing Countries	**200**	**45.352**	**48.737**	**50.615**	**54.177**	**60.994**	**70.985**	**80.078**	**94.613**	**137.221**	**254.782**	**238.499**	**276.025**	**313.731**	**336.983**	**471.705**
Africa	**605**	**8.934**	**9.254**	**9.292**	**10.055**	**11.287**	**12.207**	**13.089**	**15.125**	**21.783**	**37.596**	**35.358**	**38.882**	**45.399**	**47.544**	**68.155**
Algeria	**612**	.637	.621	.723	.830	.934	1.009	.857	1.304	1.887	4.687	4.700	5.259	5.944	6.326	9.551
Angola	**614**	.200	.221	.238	.271	.326	.423	.454	.474	.793	1.202	1.012	....	....	.968	1.091
Benin	**638**	.014	.011	.015	.022	.027	.033	.042	.036	.043	.034	.032	.025	.031	.027	.046
Botswana	**616**	.014	.015	.013	.010	.018	.026	.042	.058	.085	.121	.142	.176	.186	.233	.451
Burkina Faso	**748**	.015	.016	.018	.021	.020	.018	.016	.020	.025	.036	.044	.053	.055	.042	.077
Burundi	**618**	.013	.014	.016	.015	.012	.024	.019	.026	.030	.031	.032	.061	.090	.069	.104
Cameroon	**622**	.146	.132	.122	.189	.225	.227	.208	.221	.353	.478	.447	.511	.704	.802	1.132
Cape Verde	**624**	.001	.001	.001	.001	.002	.002	.002	.002	.002	.002	.002	.002	.002	.002	.002
Central African Rep.	**626**	.027	.031	.029	.036	.035	.031	.035	.039	.037	.048	.047	.061	.082	.072	.080
Chad	**628**	.027	.024	.031	.031	.031	.030	.028	.039	.038	.036	.048	.063	.107	.099	.088
Comoros	**632**	.004	.004	.004	.004	.005	.005	.006	.006	.005	.009	.010	.012	.009	.009	.018
Congo	**634**	.047	.043	.048	.050	.044	.031	.040	.052	.089	.189	.178	.186	.181	.308	.496
Côte d'Ivoire	**662**	.279	.312	.326	.424	.451	.471	.459	.553	.857	1.213	1.181	1.632	2.157	2.322	2.515
Djibouti	**611**	.028	.027	.023	.012	.012	.021	.015	.019	.031	.038	.015	.016	.019	.018	.011
Equatorial Guinea	**642**	.027	.030	.036	.036	.038	.025	.028	.019	.019	.034	.026	.010	.014	.017	.029
Ethiopia	**644**	.116	.111	.101	.106	.119	.122	.126	.167	.238	.269	.240	.280	.333	.306	.418
Gabon	**646**	.105	.100	.121	.124	.142	.122	.188	.214	.298	.906	.983	.932	1.343	1.107	1.848
Gambia, The	**648**	.014	.016	.018	.013	.016	.017	.013	.019	.025	.043	.044	.035	.047	.039	.058
Ghana	**652**	.667	.489	.303	.332	.327	.458	.356	.419	.628	.732	.809	.832	1.014	1.093	.995
Guinea-Bissau	**654**	.004	.003	.004	.004	.004	.004	.002	.003	.004	.004	.007	.006	.013	.012	.013
Kenya	**664**	.228	.260	.242	.252	.271	.305	.314	.359	.477	.603	.606	.790	1.186	1.023	1.090
Liberia	**668**	.135	.150	.159	.169	.196	.214	.222	.244	.324	.400	.394	.460	.447	.504	.537
Madagascar	**674**	.092	.098	.104	.116	.112	.145	.147	.166	.201	.243	.302	.276	.338	.386	.394
Malawi	**676**	.040	.049	.057	.049	.053	.060	.071	.080	.098	.120	.140	.166	.200	.185	.233
Mali	**678**	.009	.009	.008	.011	.017	.033	.029	.034	.058	.065	.053	.084	.125	.102	.148
Mauritania	**682**	.058	.069	.070	.072	.076	.089	.094	.100	.155	.181	.176	.183	.161	.119	.148
Mauritius	**684**	.066	.071	.063	.064	.066	.068	.065	.105	.137	.310	.298	.265	.312	.319	.373
Morocco	**686**	.429	.428	.424	.450	.485	.488	.502	.643	.910	1.708	1.543	1.261	1.302	1.508	1.872
Mozambique	**688**	.108	.112	.122	.154	.142	.156	.163	.176	.225	.298	.198	.150	.149	.162	.255
Niger	**692**	.026	.035	.033	.029	.024	.032	.039	.054	.062	.053	.091	.134	.161	.282	.448
Nigeria	**694**	.749	.796	.677	.591	.891	1.240	1.814	2.180	3.462	9.194	7.845	10.570	11.836	9.960	17.214
Réunion	**696**	.034	.039	.036	.046	.046	.051	.044	.050	.082	.069	.062	.094	.114	.116	.140
Rwanda	**714**	.028	.013	.014	.015	.014	.025	.022	.019	.034	.036	.042	.081	.091	.070	.111
Sao Tome & Principe	**716**	.005	.006	.008	.009	.009	.008	.007	.007	.013	.017	.007	.008	.023	.021	.027
Senegal	**722**	.131	.151	.139	.153	.124	.153	.126	.216	.195	.368	.461	.485	.616	.449	.535
Seychelles	**718**	.002	.002	.002	.003	.003	.002	.002	.003	.004	.007	.006	.009	.011	.015	.022
Sierra Leone	**724**	.088	.083	.070	.096	.106	.101	.098	.115	.131	.144	.118	.099	.136	.170	.200
Somalia	**726**	.033	.033	.028	.030	.032	.031	.035	.043	.054	.062	.089	.095	.063	.107	.112
South Africa	**199**	2.547	2.741	3.011	3.204	3.357	3.344	3.483	4.110	I 6.033	8.695	8.719	7.850	9.904	12.772	18.224
Sudan	**732**	.195	.203	.213	.233	.248	.298	.328	.357	.434	.350	.438	.554	.661	.518	.535
Swaziland	**734**	.043	.054	.056	.055	.062	.071	.078	.082	.107	.179	.199	.183	.165	.196	.231
Tanzania	**738**	.207	.265	.252	.240	.251	.260	.281	.320	.370	.412	.374	.492	.515	.476	.497
Togo	**742**	.027	.036	.032	.039	.044	.055	.050	.050	.061	.189	.126	.105	.159	.340	.219
Tunisia	**744**	.120	.140	.149	.158	.166	.182	.217	.315	.398	.921	.856	.788	.922	1.090	1.791
Uganda	**746**	.021	.022	.022	.022	.022	.028	.026	.028	.029	.032	.026	.036	.059	.341	.436
Zaïre	**636**	.102	.141	.135	.190	.227	.259	.229	.231	.335	.432	.275	.301	.329	.308	.499
Zambia	**754**	.527	.691	.654	.759	1.073	1.001	1.226	.758	1.144	1.407	.810	1.070	.896	.856	1.373
Zimbabwe	**698**	.452	.280	.272	.263	.325	.370	.404	.515	.688	.863	.932	.891	.877	.900	1.053
Asia *	**505**	**11.922**	**12.957**	**12.694**	**13.486**	**15.378**	**16.975**	**19.246**	**24.686**	**38.455**	**54.675**	**54.199**	**68.706**	**81.646**	**97.888**	**128.725**
Afghanistan, Islamic State of	**512**	.074	.067	.066	.072	.082	.086	.100	.122	.143	.230	.217	.291	.306	.321	.474
American Samoa	**859**	.015	.020	.027	.030	.028	.125	.127	.199	.067	.083	.050	.065	.081	.104	.125
Bangladesh	**513**	....	....	....	....	....	....	....	.283	.358	.348	.327	.401	.476	.548	.656
Bhutan	**514**	....	....	....	....	....	....	....	....	....	....	....	....	....	....	....
Brunei	**516**	.065	.074	.081	.092	.088	.095	.106	.176	.347	.980	1.052	1.333	1.640	1.845	2.666
Cambodia	**522**	.105	.067	.083	.089	.064	.039	.011	.007	.015	.019	....	....	....	....	....
China, People's Rep.	**924**	2.563	2.681	2.388	2.340	2.429	2.307	2.783	3.693	5.876	7.108	7.689	6.943	7.520	9.955	13.614
Fiji	**819**	.062	.057	.063	.068	.072	.087	.087	.095	.122	.190	.202	.172	.224	.251	.314
French Polynesia	**887**	.010	.017	.013	.012	.014	.018	.017	.015	.018	.032	.025	.022	.016	.036	.029
Guam	**829**	.008	.007	.008	.009	.001	.006	.010	.016	.020	.020	.028	.025	.031	.034	....
Hong Kong	**532**	1.143	1.324	1.527	1.744	2.177	2.515	2.875	3.436	5.071	5.968	6.026	8.484	9.616	11.453	15.140
India	**534**	1.687	1.954	1.613	1.761	1.835	2.026	2.036	2.448	2.917	3.926	4.355	5.549	6.378	6.671	7.806
Indonesia	**536**	.708	.679	.665	.731	.854	1.108	1.234	1.777	3.211	7.426	7.102	8.547	10.853	11.643	15.591
Korea	**542**	.173	.251	.321	.457	.624	.836	1.067	1.625	3.221	4.462	4.945	7.716	10.048	12.722	15.057
Macao	**546**	.021	.024	.025	.028	.178	.043	.049	.072	.100	.108	.133	.188	.219	.258	.389
**of which:*																
Taiwan Province of China	**528**	.450	.537	.641	.802	1.049	1.428	1.998	2.914	4.384	5.518	5.302	8.155	9.349	12.644	16.083

Exports

70 *d*

Billions of US Dollars

1980	1981	1982	1983	1984	1985	1986	1987	1988	1989	1990	1991	1992	1993	1994		
1,895.6	**1,875.3**	**1,739.1**	**1,696.4**	**1,799.3**	**1,832.8**	**2,009.5**	**2,366.2**	**2,698.5**	**2,921.7**	**3,334.4**	**3,436.3**	**3,690.8**	**3,702.4**	**4,201.3**	**World**	**001**
1,265.1	**1,243.3**	**1,177.2**	**1,162.5**	**1,240.3**	**1,282.0**	**1,488.4**	**1,736.1**	**1,986.1**	**2,127.7**	**2,453.7**	**2,503.3**	**2,651.9**	**2,577.7**	**2,886.0**	**Industrial Countries**	**110**
225.566	238.715	216.442	205.639	223.976	218.815	227.158	254.122	322.427	363.812	393.592	421.730	448.164	464.773	512.521	United States	**111**
67.734	72.726	71.234	76.749	90.272	90.950	90.329	98.168	117.105	121.832	127.629	127.163	134.435	145.178	165.376	Canada	**156**
21.944	21.477	21.360	20.113	23.111	22.604	22.569	26.621	33.233	37.125	39.752	41.854	42.824	42.723	47.572	Australia	**193**
130.441	151.495	138.385	146.965	169.700	177.164	210.757	231.286	264.856	273.932	287.581	314.786	339.885	362.244	397.005	Japan	**158**
5.421	5.622	5.571	5.414	5.518	5.720	5.880	7.195	8.784	8.875	9.488	9.589	9.824	10.537	12.181	New Zealand	**196**
17.489	15.841	15.642	15.427	15.739	17.239	22.508	27.168	31.027	31.905	41.265	41.111	47.270	40.174	45.215	Austria	**122**
64.540	55.688	52.356	51.939	51.893	53.739	68.818	83.098	92.135	100.012	117.703	118.199	123.132	. . . .	. . . .	Belgium	**126**
16.749	16.095	15.397	16.053	15.980	17.090	21.286	25.675	27.653	28.107	35.133	36.001	41.053	37.168	41.417	Denmark	**128**
14.150	14.004	13.088	12.518	13.471	13.617	16.356	20.037	21.748	23.298	26.571	23.080	23.981	23.446	29.658	Finland	**172**
116.030	106.424	96.694	94.943	97.566	101.674	124.948	148.382	167.787	179.397	216.588	217.100	235.871	209.349	235.505	France	**132**
192.860	176.047	176.424	169.417	171.735	183.933	243.326	294.369	323.323	341.231	410.104	402.843	422.271	380.154	419.312	Germany	**134**
5.153	4.246	4.298	4.413	4.816	4.539	5.648	6.533	5.429	7.545	8.105	8.666	9.509	8.434	. . . .	Greece	**174**
.918	.894	.685	.740	.739	.815	1.099	1.375	1.424	1.381	1.592	1.550	1.528	1.399	1.623	Iceland	**176**
8.398	7.678	8.063	8.592	9.642	10.358	12.658	15.999	18.723	20.667	23.743	24.224	28.331	28.611	. . . .	Ireland	**178**
78.104	77.070	73.791	72.877	74.564	76.717	97.204	116.711	127.859	140.556	170.486	169.473	178.155	169.153	189.805	Italy	**136**
85.046	78.597	75.681	73.697	74.860	I 78.008	83.509	93.108	103.213	108.261	131.775	133.631	140.335	139.127	156.580	Netherlands	**138**
18.562	18.218	17.593	17.997	18.886	19.985	18.092	21.490	22.436	27.062	34.047	34.107	35.178	31.853	34.692	Norway	**142**
4.640	4.148	4.164	4.599	5.200	5.685	7.242	9.320	10.989	12.799	16.417	16.280	18.350	15.429	17.534	Portugal	**182**
20.720	20.334	20.498	19.734	23.508	24.247	27.206	34.192	40.341	44.492	55.642	60.177	64.334	59.555	73.295	Spain	**184**
30.906	28.658	26.808	27.446	29.378	30.461	37.263	44.506	49.747	51.547	57.540	55.217	56.118	49.857	61.292	Sweden	**144**
29.632	27.031	26.018	25.592	25.851	27.433	37.455	45.515	50.704	51.525	63.784	61.517	61.377	58.687	66.227	Switzerland	**146**
110.134	102.244	96.984	91.619	93.881	101.252	107.093	131.257	145.165	152.345	185.172	184.964	190.003	180.180	204.491	United Kingdom	**112**
630.445	**632.035**	**561.965**	**533.965**	**559.047**	**550.732**	**521.100**	**630.043**	**712.400**	**793.966**	**880.693**	**933.075**	**1,038.826**	**1,124.669**	**1,315.259**	**Developing Countries**	**200**
93.324	**78.592**	**66.779**	**65.846**	**66.271**	**66.023**	**55.675**	**64.034**	**65.303**	**71.496**	**87.205**	**83.172**	**85.375**	**82.118**	. . . .	**Africa**	**605**
13.871	14.396	. . . .	12.583	12.795	12.841	7.832	8.225	7.810	9.570	12.930	12.570	11.130	10.230	. . . .	Algeria	**612**
1.883	1.856	1.629	1.822	2.033	2.245	1.332	2.168	2.516	3.015	3.944	3.449	3.788	. . . .	. . . .	Angola	**614**
.063	.034	.024	.067	.167	.150	.104	.114	.071	.077	.122	.021	.063	.122	. . . .	Benin	**638**
.502	.397	.454	.635	.660	.728	.862	1.587	1.465	1.857	1.784	1.849	1.742	1.725	. . . .	Botswana	**616**
.090	.074	.056	.058	.079	.071	.083	.155	.142	.095	.152	.106	. . . .	. . . .	. . . .	Burkina Faso	**748**
.065	.075	.088	.080	.103	.112	.154	.091	.133	.078	.075	.090	.072	.068	.106	Burundi	**618**
1.384	1.105	1.064	.976	.886	.722	.782	.806	.927	1.683	2.034	1.932	1.815	. . . .	. . . .	Cameroon	**622**
.004	.003	.004	.003	.002	.006	.004	.008	.003	.007	.006	.006	.005	. . . .	. . . .	Cape Verde	**624**
.116	.079	.107	.080	.086	.092	.066	.130	.130	.134	.120	.126	.124	. . . .	. . . .	Central African Rep.	**626**
.071	.083	.058	.105	.131	.062	.099	.109	.144	.155	.188	.194	.182	.132	. . . .	Chad	**628**
.009	.016	.020	.019	.007	.016	.020	.012	.021	.018	.018	.025	.022	. . . .	. . . .	Comoros	**632**
.911	.811	.993	.640	1.183	1.087	.777	.973	.751	.910	.981	1.066	1.183	1.121	. . . .	Congo	**634**
3.135	2.533	2.350	2.091	2.707	3.198	3.354	3.110	2.770	2.807	3.072	2.686	6.220	. . . .	. . . .	Côte d'Ivoire	**662**
.012	.009	.013	.011	.013	.014	.020	.028	.023	.025	.025	.017	.016	. . . .	. . . .	Djibouti	**611**
.014	.011	.012	.013	.015	.017	.035	.042	.049	.041	.062	.083	.041	.062	. . . .	Equatorial Guinea	**642**
.425	.380	.399	.403	.417	.333	.455	.355	.429	.465	.298	.189	.169	.199	. . . .	Ethiopia	**644**
2.173	2.201	2.161	2.000	2.011	1.951	1.271	1.286	1.196	1.597	2.464	2.273	2.329	. . . .	. . . .	Gabon	**646**
.031	.027	.044	.048	.049	.043	.035	.040	.058	.027	.040	.042	.063	. . . .	.035	Gambia, The	**648**
1.257	1.065	.873	2.624	.528	.617	.863	.977	1.009	1.018	. . . .	. . . .	. . . .	. . . .	. . . .	Ghana	**652**
.011	.014	.012	.009	.017	.012	. . . .	. . . .	.016	.014	.019	.020	.006	.016	.032	Guinea-Bissau	**654**
1.245	1.138	1.021	.876	1.081	.958	1.200	.961	1.071	.970	1.031	1.107	1.339	1.336	1.607	Kenya	**664**
.589	.529	.475	.429	.452	.436	.404	.382	.396	.460	. . . .	. . . .	. . . .	. . . .	. . . .	Liberia	**668**
.401	.316	.308	.263	.334	.274	.315	.331	.274	.321	.319	.305	.277	.261	.277	Madagascar	**674**
.295	.283	.239	.229	.314	.249	.248	.277	.288	.267	.417	.472	.383	.320	. . . .	Malawi	**676**
.205	.155	.146	.165	.133	.124	.212	.179	.215	.247	.359	.354	. . . .	. . . .	. . . .	Mali	**678**
.194	.261	.233	.292	.291	.374	.360	.428	.354	.437	.469	. . . .	. . . .	. . . .	. . . .	Mauritania	**682**
.431	.332	.364	.366	.372	.436	.662	.884	.994	.986	1.194	1.195	1.297	1.299	1.347	Mauritius	**684**
2.493	2.386	2.062	2.006	2.080	2.165	2.454	2.826	3.603	3.307	4.265	4.313	3.984	3.991	4.013	Morocco	**686**
.281	.281	.229	.132	.096	.077	.079	.097	.103	.105	.126	.162	.139	.132	. . . .	Mozambique	**688**
.566	.455	.332	.299	.259	.259	.317	.312	.289	.244	.283	.312	. . . .	. . . .	. . . .	Niger	**692**
25.968	17.845	12.185	10.357	11.856	12.548	5.155	7.365	6.875	7.871	13.670	12.264	11.886	9.914	. . . .	Nigeria	**694**
.130	.133	.110	.115	.096	.117	.137	.168	.159	.161	.187	.146	.212	.168	. . . .	Réunion	**696**
.072	.082	.090	.121	.145	.131	.189	.114	.108	.088	.110	.093	.066	. . . .	. . . .	Rwanda	**714**
.017	.009	. . . .	. . . .	.012	.006	.010	.007	.010	.005	.004	.006	.005	.005	. . . .	Sao Tome & Principe	**716**
.477	.500	.548	.618	.634	.562	.625	.606	.591	.693	.762	.651	.682	. . . .	. . . .	Senegal	**722**
.021	.017	.015	.020	.026	.028	.018	.022	.032	.034	.056	.049	.048	.051	. . . .	Seychelles	**718**
.224	.150	.111	.119	.133	.130	.144	.130	.106	.138	.138	.145	.149	.118	.115	Sierra Leone	**724**
.141	.152	.094	.107	.044	.091	.085	.104	.120	.075	. . . .	. . . .	. . . .	. . . .	. . . .	Somalia	**726**
25.525	20.658	17.673	18.508	17.163	16.293	18.385	21.219	21.871	22.191	23.549	23.306	23.413	24.261	24.987	South Africa	**199**
.543	.657	.498	.624	.629	.374	.333	.504	.509	.672	. . . .	. . . .	. . . .	. . . .	. . . .	Sudan	**732**
.369	.391	.325	.304	.240	.180	.280	.424	.469	.502	.550	.598	.638	.651	. . . .	Swaziland	**734**
.511	.580	.450	.364	.298	.247	.361	.289	.275	.365	.415	.342	.416	.400	. . . .	Tanzania	**738**
.338	.208	.178	.163	.192	.190	.204	.244	.242	.245	.268	.253	. . . .	. . . .	. . . .	Togo	**742**
2.198	2.500	1.986	1.850	1.794	1.738	1.759	2.139	2.395	2.930	3.526	3.699	4.019	3.802	4.657	Tunisia	**744**
.345	.243	.349	.372	.399	.387	.436	.319	.271	.273	.147	.200	.142	.179	.424	Uganda	**746**
.544	.193	.133	.377	I 1.005	.950	1.100	.975	1.120	1.254	.999	.830	.427	.369	.419	Zaïre	**636**
1.298	1.079	1.024	.836	.652	.784	.517	.873	1.179	1.347	1.309	.745	.756	. . . .	. . . .	Zambia	**754**
1.415	1.408	1.276	1.135	1.155	1.113	1.302	1.427	1.643	1.542	1.726	1.532	1.445	. . . .	. . . .	Zimbabwe	**698**
163.673	**176.323**	**175.454**	**183.699**	**210.817**	**209.049**	**228.843**	**295.232**	**363.466**	**405.984**	**451.912**	**515.255**	**581.551**	**646.129**	**766.916**	**Asia ***	**505**
.670	.694	.708	.729	.633	.567	.552	.512	.395	.236	.235	.188	. . . .	. . . .	. . . .	Afghanistan, Islamic State of	**512**
.127	.199	.187	.177	.212	.201	.254	.288	.368	.308	.311	.327	.318	. . . .	. . . .	American Samoa	**859**
.793	.791	.769	.724	.931	.999	.887	1.067	1.291	1.305	1.671	1.689	2.098	2.272	2.650	Bangladesh	**513**
.017	.020	.017	.016	.018	.022	.034	.055	.075	.070	.075	.072	. . . .	. . . .	. . . .	Bhutan	**514**
4.581	4.037	3.794	3.369	3.183	2.934	1.798	1.905	1.720	1.893	2.226	2.480	. . . .	. . . .	. . . .	Brunei	**516**
. . . .	. . . .	. . . .	. . . .	. . . .	. . . .	. . . .	. . . .	. . . .	. . . .	. . . .	. . . .	. . . .	. . . .	. . . .	Cambodia	**522**
18.099	21.560	21.896	22.195	24.982	27.555	31.447	39.542	47.540	51.858	61.269	70.451	80.517	90.970	119.816	China, People's Rep.	**924**
.470	.400	.377	.306	.332	.307	.336	.380	.431	.494	.615	.462	.407	.405	.544	Fiji	**819**
.030	.029	.028	.035	.032	.040	.041	.083	.075	.089	.111	.128	.106	.160	. . . .	French Polynesia	**887**
.035	. . . .	. . . .	. . . .	. . . .	.058	.060	.060	.060	.065	.060	.062	. . . .	. . . .	. . . .	Guam	**829**
19.752	21.827	21.006	21.959	28.323	30.187	35.439	48.476	63.163	73.140	82.160	98.577	119.512	135.248	151.395	Hong Kong	**532**
8.586	8.295	9.358	9.148	9.916	9.140	9.399	11.298	13.325	15.846	17.975	17.664	19.563	21.553	25.051	India	**534**
21.909	22.260	22.293	21.152	21.902	18.590	16.075	17.135	19.465	22.160	25.674	29.543	33.861	36.825	40.054	Indonesia	**536**
17.512	21.268	21.853	24.446	29.245	30.282	34.715	47.281	60.696	62.377	65.016	71.870	76.632	82.236	96.013	Korea	**542**
.538	.691	.726	.760	.911	.905	1.031	1.395	1.491	1.628	1.694	1.660	1.755	1.768	1.844	Macao	**546**
															**of which:*	
19.785	22.518	22.090	25.094	30.424	30.704	39.644	53.483	60.493	66.085	67.142	76.115	81.395	84.678	92.851	Taiwan Province of China	**528**

Exports

70 d		1965	1966	1967	1968	1969	1970	1971	1972	1973	1974	1975	1976	1977	1978	1979
																Billions of US Dollars
Asia (cont.)																
Malaysia	**548**	1.236	1.257	1.217	1.347	1.651	1.686	1.644	1.722	3.050	4.236	3.843	5.296	6.079	7.413	11.077
Maldives	**556**	.002	.002	.003	.002	.003	.004	.004	.003	.004	.004	.003	.003	.003	.004	.005
Mongolia	**948**	....	....	....	....	....	....	....	....	....	....	....	....	....	....	....
Myanmar	**518**	.225	.194	.124	.111	.132	.108	.125	.120	.130	.188	.173	.206	.214	.242	.383
Nepal	**558**	.057	.051	.050	.049	.054	.042	.048	.058	.063	.066	.100	.098	.081	.091	.109
New Caledonia	**839**	.065	.078	.075	.113	.135	.192	.200	.190	.193	.279	.327	.306	.316	.221	.369
Pakistan	**564**	.528	.602	.645	.402	.351	.397	.467	I .692	.955	1.108	1.052	1.167	1.188	1.475	2.056
Papua New Guinea	**853**	.059	.057	.065	.084	.100	.104	.120	.222	.515	.654	.441	.551	.683	.714	.883
Philippines	**566**	.698	.826	.820	.858	.854	1.041	1.098	1.100	1.885	2.725	2.294	2.555	3.127	3.401	4.567
Singapore	**576**	.981	1.102	1.140	1.271	1.549	1.554	1.761	2.190	3.653	5.810	5.375	6.586	8.241	10.134	14.240
Solomon Islands	**813**	.005	.004	.006	.006	.007	.008	.010	.011	.014	.026	.015	.024	.033	.038	.068
Sri Lanka	**524**	.409	.357	.348	.342	.322	.342	.344	.338	.410	.527	.603	.570	.753	.845	.982
Thailand	**578**	.622	.678	.681	.658	.707	.710	.831	1.081	1.564	2.444	2.208	2.980	3.490	4.085	5.298
Tonga	**866**	.003	.004	.004	.004	.004	.003	.002	.003	.005	.007	.006	.004	.007	.005	.007
Vanuatu	**846**	.009	.010	.012	.012	.011	.012	.013	.015	.021	.031	.012	.017	.032	.037	.041
Viet Nam	**582**	.021	.015	.011	.008	.008	.008	.008	.013	.058	.025	I .229	.402	.594	.648	.587
Western Samoa	**862**	.006	.005	.004	.005	.006	.005	.006	.005	.007	.013	.007	.007	.015	.011	.018
Europe	**170**	**5.748**	**6.300**	**6.927**	**7.249**	**8.138**	**14.317**	**15.707**	**19.698**	**26.298**	**32.987**	**32.175**	**29.517**	**31.300**	**35.479**	**52.477**
Cyprus	**423**	.069	.078	.083	.087	.096	.107	.116	.134	.173	.150	.150	.254	.325	.340	.453
Czech Republic	**935**	....	....	....	....	....	....	....	....	....	....	....	....	....	....	....
Czechoslovakia	**934**	....	....	....	....	....	....	....	....	....	....	6.154	....	....	....	10.926
Estonia	**939**	....	....	....	....	....	....	....	....	....	....	....	....	....	....	....
Faeroe Islands	**816**	.026	.022	.026	.021	.024	.034	.038	.046	.079	.080	.081	.105	.144	.141	.144
Hungary	**944**	....	....	....	....	....	1.726	1.847	2.403	3.354	3.942	4.519	4.927	5.825	6.349	7.930
Malta	**181**	.024	.030	.027	.034	.038	.039	.046	.068	.098	.134	.164	.228	.289	.342	.424
Poland	**964**	....	....	....	....	....	3.548	3.872	4.927	6.432	8.321	10.289	11.024	10.666	12.238	14.082
Romania	**968**	1.102	1.186	1.395	1.469	1.633	1.851	2.107	2.601	3.691	4.874	5.341	6.138	7.021	8.086	9.724
Slovak Republic	**936**	....	....	....	....	....	....	....	....	....	....	....	....	....	....	....
Slovenia	**961**	....	....	....	....	....	....	....	....	....	....	....	....	....	....	....
Turkey	**186**	.464	.491	.522	.496	.537	.588	.677	.885	1.317	1.532	1.401	1.960	1.753	2.288	2.261
Yugoslavia, SFR	**188**	1.092	1.220	1.252	1.264	1.475	1.679	1.814	2.237	2.853	3.805	4.072	4.878	5.254	5.671	6.491
Middle East	**405**	**6.572**	**7.470**	**8.462**	**9.719**	**10.880**	**12.014**	**16.517**	**17.733**	**26.485**	**84.024**	**74.851**	**90.674**	**99.334**	**95.817**	**142.465**
Bahrain	**419**	.165	.187	.211	.211	.226	.218	.265	.347	.479	1.272	1.203	1.516	1.845	1.893	2.484
Egypt	**469**	.605	.606	.566	.622	.745	.762	.789	.825	1.121	1.516	1.402	1.522	1.708	1.738	1.840
Iran, I.R. of	**429**	1.305	1.310	1.929	1.881	2.100	2.403	3.824	2.637	3.771	12.408	12.108	12.692	13.094	12.050	13.374
Iraq	**433**	.882	.934	.822	1.039	1.045	1.098	1.556	1.810	3.775	13.010	15.934	18.250	19.011	21.680	42.402
Israel	**436**	.430	.503	.555	.639	.729	.779	.958	1.147	1.449	1.825	1.941	2.415	3.082	3.921	4.546
Jordan	**439**	.028	.029	.032	.040	.041	.034	.032	.048	.073	.155	.153	.207	.249	.298	.403
Kuwait	**443**	1.243	1.304	1.313	1.437	1.540	1.654	2.219	2.531	3.816	10.962	9.184	9.846	9.754	10.427	18.404
Lebanon	**446**	.087	.103	.118	.147	.165	.190	.245	.377	.837	1.487	1.121	.496	.691	.755	.773
Libya	**672**	.789	.986	1.168	1.866	2.164	2.357	2.704	2.939	4.005	8.259	6.834	9.555	11.411	10.200	16.076
Oman	**449**	.002	.002	.026	.105	.141	.143	.154	.167	.239	1.134	1.044	1.134	1.140	1.096	1.570
Qatar	**453**	.163	.180	.202	.211	.223	.240	.315	.397	.628	2.015	1.805	2.211	1.999	2.391	3.789
Saudi Arabia	**456**	1.396	1.651	1.784	1.944	2.053	2.371	3.849	4.772	7.802	35.555	29.682	38.286	43.463	40.664	63.431
Syrian Arab Rep.	**463**	.169	.173	.155	.168	.207	.203	.195	.287	.351	.781	.930	1.075	1.070	1.060	1.644
United Arab Emirates	**466**	....	.241	.262	.335	.407	.523	.871	1.157	1.807	6.414	7.262	9.535	9.636	9.126	13.652
Yemen Arab Rep.	**473**	.005	.003	.004	.004	.004	.003	.004	.004	.008	.013	.011	.008	.011	.007	.014
Yemen, P.D. Rep.	**459**	.187	.190	.137	.110	.134	.135	.096	.096	.100	.228	.172	.177	.181	.192	.466
Western Hemisphere	**205**	**11.695**	**12.278**	**12.864**	**13.213**	**14.792**	**16.379**	**16.456**	**18.697**	**25.688**	**45.234**	**41.915**	**48.245**	**56.053**	**60.256**	**79.884**
Antigua and Barbuda	**311**	.004	.001	.003	.008	.008	.014	.016	.018	.030	.032	.028	.009	.007	.013	.012
Argentina	**213**	1.493	1.593	1.465	1.368	1.612	1.773	1.740	1.941	3.266	3.931	2.961	3.916	5.652	6.400	7.810
Bahamas, The	**313**	.019	.023	.031	.051	.053	.090	.267	.343	.530	1.444	2.508	2.992	3.261	3.058	3.786
Barbados	**316**	.037	.040	.041	.037	.037	.039	.041	.044	.054	.085	.107	.086	.095	.130	.151
Belize	**339**	.012	.013	.014	.015	.017	.019	.019	.026	.032	.045	.067	.042	.062	.080	.087
Bermuda	**319**	.023	.022	.025	.028	.033	.080	.092	.034	.030	.034	.036	.047	.039	.041	.031
Bolivia	**218**	.129	.127	.150	.152	.172	.190	.181	.201	.261	.557	.444	.568	.632	.629	.760
Brazil	**223**	1.596	1.741	1.654	1.881	2.311	2.739	2.904	3.991	6.199	7.951	8.670	10.128	12.120	12.659	15.244
Chile	**228**	.637	.817	.847	.858	1.075	1.249	.997	.855	1.231	2.481	1.552	2.083	2.190	2.478	3.894
Colombia	**233**	.538	.507	.510	.559	.607	.727	.686	.808	1.169	1.509	1.465	1.874	2.403	3.010	3.411
Costa Rica	**238**	.112	.136	.144	.171	.190	.231	.225	.281	.345	.440	.493	.593	.828	.865	.934
Dominica	**321**	.006	.006	.006	.006	.007	.006	.006	.007	.009	.010	.011	.011	.012	.016	.009
Dominican Republic	**243**	.126	.137	.156	.183	.184	.249	.243	.348	.442	.637	.894	.716	.780	.676	.869
Ecuador	**248**	.164	.155	.190	.226	.193	.190	.199	.326	.532	1.124	.974	1.258	1.436	1.558	2.104
El Salvador	**253**	.189	.189	.207	.213	.202	.229	.228	.273	.352	.463	.531	.743	.972	.848	1.223
Greenland	**326**	.013	.015	.013	.012	.014	.014	.019	.022	.031	.092	.087	.086	.092	.102	.165
Grenada	**328**	.006	.006	.005	.005	.008	.006	.005	.005	.007	.009	.012	.013	.014	.017	.021
Guadeloupe	**329**	.038	.035	.032	.038	.035	.038	.042	.040	.065	.058	.084	.090	.079	.112	.113
Guatemala	**258**	.186	.226	.198	.227	.255	.290	.283	.327	.436	.572	.624	.760	1.160	1.089	1.241
Guiana, French	**333**	.003	.003	.004	.003	.005	.004	.003	.005	.005	.001	.002	.004	.007	.007	.017
Guyana	**336**	.103	.109	.113	.108	.120	.135	.128	.139	.136	.268	.357	.275	.251	.291	.287
Haiti	**263**	.037	.036	.034	.036	.037	.040	.047	.044	.053	.072	.080	.124	.149	.155	.185
Honduras	**268**	.127	.143	.155	.181	.168	.179	.189	.205	.259	.289	.295	.400	.513	.608	.734
Jamaica	**343**	.215	.225	.223	.220	.257	.299	.345	.383	.389	.731	.815	.629	.763	.833	.818
Martinique	**349**	.047	.046	.043	.040	.036	.030	.034	.045	.055	.072	.096	.124	.128	.125	.133
Mexico	**273**	1.145	1.199	1.145	1.254	1.430	1.402	1.504	1.694	2.250	2.958	2.904	3.417	4.167	6.005	8.982
Netherlands Antilles	**353**	.603	.592	.607	.599	.625	.675	.725	.757	1.368	3.231	2.395	2.519	2.652	2.976	3.966
Nicaragua	**278**	.149	.142	.152	.162	.159	.179	.187	.249	.278	.381	.375	.542	.637	.646	.567
Panama	**283**	.079	.089	.094	.099	.113	.110	.117	.123	.138	.207	.283	.238	.251	.256	.303
Paraguay	**288**	.056	.049	.047	.046	.050	.063	.064	.085	.124	.167	.176	.181	.279	.257	.305
Peru	**293**	.667	.764	.754	.866	.866	1.048	.893	.944	1.112	1.503	I 1.291	1.360	1.726	1.941	3.491
St. Kitts and Nevis	**361**	.009	.009	.009	.007	.009	.008	.008	.012	.017	.024	.047	.046	.009	.017	.017
St. Lucia	**362**	.007	.007	.007	.006	.008	.009	.006	.008	.010	.016	.017	.021	.025	.029	.036
St. Vincent & Grens.	**364**	.004	.004	.004	.004	.004	.004	.003	.003	.005	.007	.008	.009	.010	.016	.015
Suriname	**366**	.059	.088	.106	.114	.131	.132	.150	.168	.178	.269	.277	.276	.310	.411	I .444
Trinidad and Tobago	**369**	.403	.422	.437	.469	.475	.482	.525	.555	.664	2.014	1.757	2.203	2.175	2.021	2.608
Uruguay	**298**	.191	.186	.159	.179	.200	.233	.206	.214	.322	.382	.384	.546	.608	.686	.788
Venezuela	**299**	2.455	2.373	3.077	2.779	3.083	3.169	3.124	3.166	3.298	11.153	8.800	9.299	9.551	9.187	14.317
Memorandum Items																
Oil Exporting Countries	**999**	**9.447**	**10.143**	**11.827**	**12.709**	**14.390**	**16.216**	**20.964**	**23.027**	**33.925**	**109.207**	**96.366**	**116.933**	**128.681**	**123.071**	**186.969**
Non-Oil Developing Countries	**201**	**36.016**	**38.727**	**38.840**	**41.381**	**46.552**	**54.827**	**59.062**	**71.702**	**104.164**	**145.594**	**146.366**	**163.463**	**189.778**	**219.695**	**292.101**

Billions of US Dollars

	1980	1981	1982	1983	1984	1985	1986	1987	1988	1989	1990	1991	1992	1993	1994	
Asia (cont.)																
Malaysia	12.958	11.765	12.031	14.130	16.590	15.442	13.753	17.939	21.110	25.053	29.416	34.349	40.713	47.122	58.756	548
Maldives	.008	.009	.010	.013	.018	.023	.025	.031	.040	.045	.052	.054	.040	.035	.046	556
Mongolia	....	....	....	....	....	.689	.716	.718	.739	.722	.661	.348	.389	.381	.324	948
Myanmar	.472	.462	.391	.378	.301	.303	.288	.219	.147	.215	.325	.419	.537	.583	.771	518
Nepal	.080	.140	.088	.094	.128	.160	.142	.151	.190	.158	.210	.264	.374	.390	....	558
New Caledonia	.408	.347	.268	.154	.208	.268	.208	.224	.469	.672	.475	.448	.410	.387	....	839
Pakistan	2.618	2.883	2.397	3.077	2.558	2.740	3.384	4.172	4.522	4.709	5.589	6.528	7.317	6.688	7.365	564
Papua New Guinea	1.031	.838	.771	.813	.892	.912	1.033	1.161	1.399	1.404	1.144	1.338	1.810	2.491	2.640	853
Philippines	5.741	5.655	4.968	4.890	5.274	4.607	4.770	5.649	7.032	7.755	8.068	8.767	9.752	11.089	13.342	566
Singapore	19.376	20.967	20.787	21.833	24.070	22.812	22.495	28.687	39.306	44.665	52.752	59.025	63.484	74.012	96.826	576
Solomon Islands	.074	.066	.058	.062	.093	.070	.066	.064	.082	.075	.070	.083	.102	.094	....	813
Sri Lanka	1.067	1.094	1.030	1.066	1.451	1.293	1.215	1.368	1.479	1.545	1.983	2.039	2.455	2.859	3.208	524
Thailand	6.505	7.031	6.945	6.368	7.413	7.121	8.872	11.654	15.953	20.078	23.070	28.428	32.472	37.168	....	578
Tonga	.007	.008	.004	.005	.009	.005	.006	.006	.007	.009	.011	.013	.012	.016	.014	866
Vanuatu	.036	.032	.023	.030	.044	.031	.017	.018	.020	.022	.019	.018	.024	.023	.025	846
Viet Nam	I .339	.401	.527	.617	.650	.699	.789	.854	1.038	1.946	2.404	2.087	2.581	2.971	....	582
Western Samoa	.017	.011	.013	.018	.020	.016	.011	.012	.015	.013	.009	.006	.006	.006	.004	862
Europe	**59.221**	**60.498**	**60.866**	**60.685**	**63.335**	**77.145**	**78.067**	**86.849**	**93.714**	**91.322**	**75.581**	**73.787**	**106.473**	**118.336**	**134.206**	**170**
Cyprus	.532	.562	.544	.503	.573	.476	.451	.568	.705	.791	.957	.980	.987	.867	.967	423
Czech Republic	....	....	....	....	....	....	....	....	....	....	....	....	....	13.205	14.294	935
Czechoslovakia	12.063	11.611	12.059	12.119	11.775	11.900	13.790	15.469	14.887	14.460	11.840	10.939	11.310	....	....	934
Estonia	....	....	....	....	....	....	....	....	....	....	....	....	....	.805	1.299	939
Faeroe Islands	.178	.169	.150	.170	.159	.183	.245	.345	.348	.348	.385	.395	.440	.378	....	816
Hungary	8.638	8.728	8.858	8.767	8.617	8.472	9.170	9.583	9.999	9.672	9.730	10.227	10.680	8.918	10.594	944
Malta	.483	.449	.411	.363	.394	.400	.497	.605	.714	.844	1.133	1.234	1.540	1.355	1.530	181
Poland	14.191	10.675	11.213	11.572	11.750	11.489	12.074	12.205	13.960	13.466	13.627	I 14.903	13.324	14.143	17.042	964
Romania	11.209	12.610	11.559	11.512	12.646	12.167	9.763	10.492	11.392	10.487	5.775	4.266	4.363	4.892	6.151	968
Slovak Republic	....	....	....	....	....	....	....	....	....	....	....	....	....	5.451	6.587	936
Slovenia	....	....	....	....	....	....	....	....	....	....	....	....	....	6.088	6.825	961
Turkey	2.910	4.703	5.746	5.728	7.134	7.958	7.457	10.190	11.662	11.625	12.959	13.594	14.716	15.343	....	186
Yugoslavia, SFR	8.978	10.940	10.284	9.914	10.254	10.700	10.353	11.443	12.663	13.460	14.308	13.953	....	....	....	188
Middle East	**210.623**	**204.554**	**158.818**	**125.791**	**111.100**	**99.671**	**75.652**	**90.199**	**82.984**	**107.048**	**138.594**	**133.859**	**126.282**	....	....	**405**
Bahrain	3.594	4.347	3.789	3.199	3.204	2.897	2.199	2.430	2.411	2.831	3.761	3.513	3.464	3.710	3.454	419
Egypt	3.046	3.233	3.120	3.215	3.140	1.838	2.214	2.037	2.120	2.565	2.585	3.659	3.051	2.244	....	469
Iran, I.R. of	14.705	5.354	13.690	19.378	12.422	13.328	....	....	....	....	....	....	....	....	....	429
Iraq	....	....	....	....	....	....	....	....	....	....	....	....	....	....	....	433
Israel	5.538	5.670	5.255	5.108	5.807	6.260	7.154	8.454	8.198	10.738	11.576	11.921	13.119	14.826	16.884	436
Jordan	.574	.733	.752	.580	.752	.789	.733	.930	1.019	1.107	1.064	1.130	1.215	1.232	1.424	439
Kuwait	19.663	16.044	10.864	11.504	11.623	10.487	7.383	8.264	7.661	11.476	7.042	1.088	6.660	10.248	....	443
Lebanon	.868	.836	.727	.691	.582	.482	.500	.591	.709	....	....	....	....	....	....	446
Libya	21.910	15.571	13.948	11.392	11.136	10.929	8.215	8.694	6.673	8.034	13.225	11.235	....	....	....	672
Oman	2.386	3.203	3.555	4.222	3.926	4.705	2.321	3.198	2.625	4.068	5.508	4.871	....	....	....	449
Qatar	5.672	5.691	4.343	3.345	4.258	4.203	2.720	....	....	....	....	....	....	....	....	453
Saudi Arabia	109.083	119.876	79.077	45.861	37.545	27.481	20.185	23.199	24.377	28.382	44.417	47.797	35.855	30.202	....	456
Syrian Arab Rep.	2.108	2.103	2.026	1.923	1.853	1.637	1.325	3.870	1.345	3.006	4.062	3.143	3.093	3.146	3.547	463
United Arab Emirates	20.676	21.238	16.837	14.672	14.192	14.043	12.387	14.165	13.934	17.596	23.544	24.436	24.756	....	....	466
Yemen Arab Rep.	.023	.047	.039	.027	.016	.013	.008	.048	....	....	....	....	....	....	....	473
Yemen, P.D. Rep.	.777	.607	.795	.674	.645	.579	.290	....	....	....	....	....	....	....	....	459
Western Hemisphere	**103.603**	**112.067**	**100.048**	**97.944**	**107.524**	**98.845**	**82.864**	**93.683**	**106.193**	**117.928**	**128.295**	**125.542**	**130.716**	**136.205**	**157.389**	**205**
Antigua and Barbuda	.030	.040	.021	.020	.018	.013	.020	.017	.022	.032	.033	.032	....	....	....	311
Argentina	8.021	9.143	7.625	7.836	8.107	8.396	6.852	6.360	9.135	9.579	12.353	11.978	12.235	13.118	15.659	213
Bahamas, The	5.009	6.189	4.534	3.970	3.540	2.707	2.657	2.728	2.147	2.786	2.593	1.517	....	....	....	313
Barbados	.226	.195	.257	.321	.390	.352	.275	.154	.173	.186	.209	.205	.191	.179	....	316
Belize	.111	.119	.091	.078	.093	.090	.093	.087	.095	.094	.105	.102	.116	.115	.119	339
Bermuda	.037	.029	.017	.023	.041	.023	.065	.029	.031	.050	.060	.055	.085	....	....	319
Bolivia	.942	.912	.828	.755	.725	.623	.638	.570	.600	.822	.926	.849	.710	.728	1.032	218
Brazil	20.132	23.293	20.175	21.899	27.005	25.639	22.349	26.224	33.494	34.383	31.414	31.620	35.793	38.597	43.558	223
Chile	4.705	3.837	3.706	3.831	3.651	3.804	4.191	5.224	7.052	8.080	8.373	8.942	10.007	9.199	11.539	228
Colombia	3.924	2.916	3.024	3.001	3.462	3.552	5.102	4.642	5.037	5.717	6.766	7.232	6.917	7.116	8.399	233
Costa Rica	1.002	1.008	.870	.873	1.006	.976	1.121	1.158	1.246	1.415	1.448	1.598	1.829	2.049	2.215	238
Dominica	.010	.019	.024	.027	.026	.028	.043	.048	.054	.045	.055	.054	.056	....	....	321
Dominican Republic	.962	1.188	.768	.785	.868	.735	.718	.711	.890	.924	.735	.658	.562	.511	.633	243
Ecuador	2.481	2.451	2.327	2.348	2.620	2.905	2.172	1.928	2.192	2.354	2.714	2.852	3.007	2.904	3.717	248
El Salvador	.967	.797	.699	.735	.717	.679	.755	.591	.609	.498	.582	.588	.598	.732	.844	253
Greenland	.211	.204	.169	.173	.172	.174	.257	.346	.391	.418	.452	.341	.333	....	....	326
Grenada	.017	.019	.019	.019	.018	.023	.031	.032	.033	.028	.027	.023	.020	....	....	328
Guadeloupe	.107	.092	.096	.083	.086	.075	.112	.093	.289	.107	.122	.147	.130	.128	....	329
Guatemala	1.520	1.226	1.120	1.159	1.129	1.057	1.044	.987	1.022	1.108	1.163	1.202	1.295	1.340	....	258
Guiana, French	.025	.035	.032	.039	.037	.037	.037	.054	.053	.057	.093	.070	.096	.120	....	333
Guyana	.396	.352	.256	.189	.210	.206	.214	.242	.230	.227	.251	.248	.302	.423	.439	336
Haiti	.226	.152	.178	.166	.179	.168	.184	.214	.179	.144	.158	.181	.084	.089	.062	263
Honduras	.829	.761	.660	.672	.725	.780	.854	.791	.842	.859	.831	.792	.802	.814	.843	268
Jamaica	.963	.974	.767	.718	.747	.566	.589	.706	.831	.967	1.135	1.053	1.102	1.069	....	343
Martinique	.142	.133	.095	.115	.105	.145	.210	.195	.197	.190	.272	.194	.242	.191	....	349
Mexico	15.570	19.646	21.214	21.819	24.407	22.112	16.347	20.887	20.765	23.048	27.131	27.318	27.722	30.241	34.530	273
Netherlands Antilles	5.162	5.417	4.891	4.409	3.732	1.031	I .924	1.308	1.133	1.454	1.789	1.599	1.559	1.284	....	353
Nicaragua	.451	.508	.406	.429	.386	.302	.247	.273	.233	.311	.331	.275	.218	.267	....	278
Panama	.358	.328	.371	.321	.274	.334	.349	.358	.307	.318	.340	.358	.502	.553	.584	283
Paraguay	.310	.296	.330	.269	.335	.304	.233	.353	.510	1.009	.959	.737	.657	.725	....	288
Peru	3.898	3.255	3.259	3.015	3.147	2.979	2.531	2.661	2.701	3.488	3.231	3.329	3.484	3.463	4.507	293
St. Kitts and Nevis	.024	.024	.019	.018	.021	.020	.026	.028	.029	.033	.025	.021	....	....	....	361
St. Lucia	.058	.046	.045	.055	.049	.057	.087	.080	.116	.109	.127	.110	.123	....	....	362
St. Vincent & Grens.	.015	.024	.032	.041	.054	.063	.064	.052	.085	.075	.083	.067	.078	.058	.043	364
Suriname	.514	.480	.429	.367	.356	.329	.335	.306	.409	.541	.472	.420	....	....	....	366
Trinidad and Tobago	3.955	3.761	3.079	2.384	2.156	2.196	1.376	1.460	1.391	1.558	1.718	1.985	1.869	1.612	....	369
Uruguay	1.059	1.215	1.023	1.045	.934	.909	1.088	1.189	1.405	1.599	1.693	1.605	1.703	1.645	1.913	298
Venezuela	19.221	20.980	16.590	13.937	15.997	14.438	8.660	10.577	10.244	13.286	17.497	15.155	14.185	14.066	15.480	299
Memorandum Items																
Oil Exporting Countries	**275.064**	**262.457**	**206.840**	**168.404**	**157.651**	**143.593**	**98.950**	**114.981**	**110.810**	**137.504**	**184.042**	**178.923**	**173.263**	**170.070**	....	**999**
Non-Oil Developing Countries	**365.173**	**377.971**	**363.587**	**374.573**	**411.413**	**404.025**	**420.837**	**514.923**	**600.045**	**660.354**	**716.759**	**774.571**	**883.346**	**962.112**	**1,129.132**	**201**

Imports

71 *d*

		1965	1966	1967	1968	1969	1970	1971	1972	1973	1974	1975	1976	1977	1978	1979
															Billions of US Dollars	
World	**001**	**185.9**	**204.5**	**213.4**	**236.6**	**269.4**	**309.7**	**340.2**	**399.6**	**551.4**	**811.0**	**855.7**	**959.4**	**1,099.2**	**1,276.2**	**1,614.5**
Industrial Countries	**110**	**134.7**	**149.0**	**156.3**	**175.6**	**201.9**	**232.4**	**257.3**	**307.4**	**422.0**	**603.3**	**603.9**	**696.2**	**788.2**	**911.2**	**1,168.0**
United States	**111**	23.233	27.791	28.819	35.438	38.498	42.389	48.342	58.862	73.199	110.875	105.880	132.498	I 160.411	186.045	222.228
Canada	**156**	8.597	10.028	10.796	12.236	13.963	14.251	16.472	20.038	24.713	34.248	36.106	40.243	42.083	46.278	56.642
Australia	**193**	3.762	3.612	3.924	4.366	4.538	5.056	5.228	5.028	7.393	11.982	10.697	12.232	13.511	15.567	18.191
Japan	**158**	8.169	9.522	11.663	12.987	15.023	18.881	19.712	23.863	38.389	61.948	57.860	64.894	71.340	79.922	109.831
New Zealand	**196**	1.052	1.095	.955	.895	1.003	1.245	1.348	1.523	2.176	3.648	3.155	3.254	3.361	3.491	4.553
Austria	**122**	2.101	2.328	2.310	2.496	2.825	3.549	4.190	5.216	7.119	9.022	9.394	11.516	14.245	16.019	20.253
Belgium	**126**	6.458	7.150	7.154	8.198	9.966	11.340	12.221	15.392	22.082	29.878	30.784	35.503	40.417	48.596	60.921
Denmark	**128**	2.823	3.003	3.153	3.236	3.813	4.407	4.608	5.087	7.802	9.927	10.368	12.427	13.265	14.808	18.401
Finland	**172**	1.646	1.726	1.676	1.592	2.025	2.638	2.807	3.165	4.341	6.813	7.628	7.392	7.608	7.866	11.398
France	**132**	10.342	11.848	12.406	14.009	17.267	19.119	21.313	26.950	37.483	52.915	54.222	64.082	70.637	81.788	107.009
Germany	**134**	17.612	18.167	17.545	20.295	24.876	29.947	34.293	40.378	54.891	69.661	74.930	88.421	101.458	121.754	159.646
Greece	**174**	1.134	1.223	1.186	1.393	1.594	1.958	2.098	2.346	3.477	4.406	5.357	6.061	6.853	7.829	9.614
Iceland	**176**	.138	.159	.162	.134	.123	.157	.210	.231	.359	.518	.484	.467	.605	.675	.815
Ireland	**178**	1.043	1.045	1.081	1.236	1.472	1.622	1.834	2.105	2.793	3.814	3.778	4.193	5.396	7.121	9.884
Italy	**136**	7.378	8.590	9.829	10.285	12.470	14.974	15.969	19.319	27.798	41.089	38.526	43.905	48.092	56.496	77.895
Netherlands	**138**	8.925	9.540	9.875	11.009	12.965	15.562	17.599	20.270	27.940	38.844	40.854	46.114	52.230	61.314	77.310
Norway	**142**	2.211	2.404	2.747	2.706	2.942	3.702	4.073	4.372	6.289	8.420	9.705	11.121	12.883	11.497	13.707
Portugal	**182**	.897	1.013	1.015	1.043	1.232	1.556	1.803	2.204	3.015	4.496	3.839	4.220	4.744	5.237	6.534
Spain	**184**	3.040	3.591	3.441	3.505	4.233	4.747	5.009	6.829	9.667	15.428	16.265	17.474	17.835	18.711	25.438
Sweden	**144**	4.377	4.582	4.701	5.126	5.909	7.007	7.067	8.110	10.907	16.683	17.450	19.628	I 20.137	20.589	28.735
Switzerland	**146**	3.642	3.889	4.068	4.443	5.209	6.376	7.193	8.480	11.628	14.445	13.305	14.770	17.940	23.812	29.357
United Kingdom	**112**	16.128	16.666	17.803	18.960	19.961	21.866	23.863	27.658	38.528	54.193	53.343	55.744	63.191	75.813	99.602
Developing Countries	**200**	**51.214**	**55.495**	**57.072**	**60.997**	**67.526**	**77.351**	**82.912**	**92.168**	**129.374**	**207.752**	**251.817**	**263.267**	**311.002**	**364.956**	**446.502**
Africa	**605**	**9.256**	**9.145**	**9.694**	**10.167**	**11.222**	**13.392**	**15.305**	**15.645**	**20.513**	**30.691**	**38.334**	**39.000**	**46.734**	**54.683**	**57.123**
Algeria	**612**	.671	.643	.639	.815	1.009	1.257	1.227	1.494	2.236	4.035	5.498	5.081	7.125	8.548	8.403
Angola	**614**	.195	.209	.275	.308	.323	.368	.430	.392	.545	.614	.429	....	....	.885	1.112
Benin	**638**	.035	.034	.049	.049	.055	.064	.077	.092	.112	.147	.188	.219	.268	.311	.320
Botswana	**616**	.023	.026	.031	.033	.046	.057	.083	.110	.166	.185	.218	.209	.285	.371	.538
Burkina Faso	**748**	.037	.038	.036	.041	.050	.047	.051	.061	.099	.144	.151	.144	.209	.227	.301
Burundi	**618**	.019	.019	.019	.023	.021	.022	.030	.032	.031	.043	.062	.058	.074	.098	.152
Cameroon	**622**	.135	.131	.178	.187	.204	.243	.252	.303	.334	.437	.599	.613	.735	1.056	1.275
Cape Verde	**624**	.006	.006	.007	.007	.011	.016	.020	.024	.034	.034	.040	.030	.038	.053	.053
Central African Rep.	**626**	.028	.035	.044	.040	.038	.034	.035	.034	.052	.046	.069	.055	.063	.057	.070
Chad	**628**	.031	.032	.059	.054	.053	.062	.063	.061	.082	.092	.133	.116	.189	.217	.085
Comoros	**632**	.007	.007	.008	.007	.008	.009	.010	.012	.015	.026	.023	.013	.016	.019	.029
Congo	**634**	.083	.083	.085	.086	.080	.059	.082	.092	.128	.127	.174	.180	.210	.262	.291
Côte d'Ivoire	**662**	.238	.267	.258	.314	.333	.390	.402	.454	.710	.969	1.127	1.296	1.756	2.326	2.492
Djibouti	**611**	.061	.059	.057	.050	.049	.049	.053	.066	.072	.082	.140	.120	.107	.164	.188
Equatorial Guinea	**642**	.026	.028	.032	.032	.033	.024	.028	.027	.027	.015	.020	.004	.010	.009	.019
Ethiopia	**644**	.150	.162	.143	.173	.155	.172	.188	.189	.214	.275	.313	.352	.352	.455	.567
Gabon	**646**	.063	.067	.068	.064	.077	.080	.097	.139	.190	.332	.469	.503	.716	.617	.532
Gambia, The	**648**	.016	.018	.019	.021	.020	.018	.021	.025	.031	.047	.060	.074	.078	.100	.141
Ghana	**652**	.448	.352	.307	.308	.347	.411	.439	.290	.452	.822	.802	.844	1.143	.989	.852
Guinea-Bissau	**654**	.015	.015	.016	.018	.023	.027	.031	.032	.044	.043	.038	.037	.037	.049	.061
Kenya	**664**	.282	.346	.337	.356	.361	.442	.560	.535	.619	1.026	.945	.969	1.289	1.711	1.636
Liberia	**668**	.105	.114	.125	.108	.115	.150	.157	.179	.193	.288	.332	.399	.464	.481	.506
Madagascar	**674**	.138	.142	.145	.170	.182	.170	.214	.205	.203	.281	.366	.285	.347	.443	.641
Malawi	**676**	.065	.086	.080	.080	.083	.099	.108	.129	.140	.188	.253	.206	.235	.338	.399
Mali	**678**	.033	.029	.026	.037	.039	.047	.056	.084	.107	.183	.176	.150	.160	.203	.361
Mauritania	**682**	.024	.023	.037	.035	.042	.056	.057	.069	.128	.120	.161	.179	.206	.181	.259
Mauritius	**684**	.077	.070	.077	.076	.067	.075	.084	.119	.168	.310	.330	.357	.444	.496	.565
Morocco	**686**	.454	.477	.518	.552	.562	.686	.693	.779	1.144	1.896	2.567	2.617	3.199	2.969	3.662
Mozambique	**688**	.174	.208	.206	.238	.261	.326	.341	.330	.460	.467	.411	.300	.328	.521	.571
Niger	**692**	.038	.045	.046	.041	.048	.058	.053	.066	.086	.097	.101	.126	.197	.305	.461
Nigeria	**694**	.770	.718	.626	.540	.696	1.059	1.514	1.505	1.862	2.772	6.041	8.213	11.095	12.821	10.218
Réunion	**696**	.098	.105	.116	.123	.146	.161	.190	.198	.306	.336	.410	.445	.492	.597	.759
Rwanda	**714**	.042	.023	.020	.023	.024	.029	.033	.035	.035	.058	.099	.103	.116	.188	.192
Sao Tome & Principe	**716**	.005	.006	.005	.006	.008	.009	.008	.008	.010	.010	.011	.009	.014	.018	.020
Senegal	**722**	.166	.162	.159	.185	.194	.194	.220	.280	.361	.457	.583	.575	.789	.755	.931
Seychelles	**718**	.002	.004	.005	.006	.007	.010	.015	.021	.025	.028	.032	.039	.046	.058	.084
Sierra Leone	**724**	.108	.100	.090	.090	.112	.116	.113	.119	.155	.222	.185	.153	.181	.279	.316
Somalia	**726**	.050	.042	.040	.048	.052	.045	.063	.075	.108	.143	.155	.156	.228	.241	.246
South Africa	**199**	2.563	2.395	2.780	2.789	3.189	3.843	4.363	3.943	I 5.136	7.865	8.226	7.285	6.270	7.615	8.980
Sudan	**732**	.208	.222	.214	.258	.257	.288	.331	.320	.436	.642	.887	.980	1.081	1.194	1.109
Swaziland	**734**	.037	.034	.049	.048	.050	.060	.067	.069	.096	.138	.180	.200	.182	.311	.434
Tanzania	**738**	.197	.237	.229	.257	.241	.319	.381	.406	.488	.730	.780	.638	.728	1.144	1.104
Togo	**742**	.045	.047	.045	.047	.056	.065	.071	.085	.101	.119	.174	.185	.284	.450	.510
Tunisia	**744**	.246	.250	.261	.218	.266	.306	.345	.466	.634	1.128	1.424	1.529	1.825	2.119	2.849
Uganda	**746**	.161	.170	.160	.162	.175	.172	.249	.162	.163	.210	.200	.171	.248	.254	.197
Zaïre	**636**	.097	.104	.078	.103	.132	.179	.203	.208	.251	.349	.300	.224	.203	.196	.199
Zambia	**754**	.345	.398	.516	.540	.520	.559	.648	.679	.647	.968	1.138	.812	.787	.741	.905
Zimbabwe	**698**	.386	.273	.301	.333	.321	.378	.456	.478	.606	.865	.932	.703	.710	.685	.929
Asia *	**505**	**15.345**	**16.872**	**17.241**	**17.937**	**19.414**	**21.802**	**24.167**	**27.617**	**41.365**	**63.584**	**66.358**	**71.366**	**82.658**	**105.679**	**137.867**
Afghanistan, Islamic State of	**512**	.121	.128	.126	.114	.126	.114	.141	.164	.172	.243	.350	.261	.328	.395	.425
American Samoa	**859**	.010	.006	.004	.012	.012	.018	.020	.024	.036	.047	.053	.051	.055	.073	.040
Bangladesh	**513**	....	....	....	....	....	....	....	.683	.986	1.078	1.321	.952	1.163	1.513	1.908
Bhutan	**514**	....	....	....	....	....	....	....	....	....	....	....	....	....	....	....
Brunei	**516**	.036	.051	.045	.069	.073	.084	.150	.106	.132	.185	.274	.260	.279	.281	.396
Cambodia	**522**	.103	.111	.096	.116	.102	.054	.057	.080	.227	.273	....	....	....	....	....
China, People's Rep.	**924**	2.246	2.482	2.169	2.068	1.917	2.279	2.129	2.851	5.208	7.791	7.926	6.660	7.148	11.131	15.621
Fiji	**819**	.073	.064	.071	.079	.089	.104	.129	.159	.222	.273	.268	.264	.307	.355	.470
French Polynesia	**887**	.107	.167	.114	.174	.109	.135	.140	.156	.211	.287	.286	.296	.327	.403	.476
Guam	**829**	.040	.039	.064	.063	.056	.096	.115	.162	.211	.259	.266	.268	.269	.272	....
Hong Kong	**532**	1.569	1.767	1.818	2.058	2.458	2.905	3.391	3.856	5.655	6.778	6.766	8.838	10.446	13.394	17.127
India	**534**	2.838	3.440	2.773	2.570	2.212	2.124	2.424	2.223	3.211	5.136	6.381	5.665	6.647	7.865	9.827
Indonesia	**536**	.695	.527	.649	.716	.781	1.002	1.103	1.562	2.729	3.842	4.770	5.673	6.230	6.690	7.202
Korea	**542**	.463	.716	.996	1.463	1.824	1.984	2.394	2.522	4.240	6.852	7.274	8.774	10.811	14.972	20.339
Macao	**546**	.047	.051	.043	.050	.060	.065	.075	.104	.158	.638	.161	.161	.199	.249	.351
**of which:*																
Taiwan Province of China	**528**	.557	.622	.808	.906	1.216	1.528	1.849	2.518	3.801	6.983	5.959	7.609	8.522	11.051	14.793

Imports

71 *d*

Billions of US Dollars

1980	1981	1982	1983	1984	1985	1986	1987	1988	1989	1990	1991	1992	1993	1994		
1,986.3	**1,970.0**	**1,840.5**	**1,781.6**	**1,898.2**	**1,907.7**	**2,089.3**	**2,443.9**	**2,788.1**	**3,023.3**	**3,455.4**	**3,578.3**	**3,815.5**	**3,780.9**	**4,324.9**	**World**	**001**
1,400.3	**1,328.9**	**1,248.0**	**1,225.3**	**1,339.8**	**1,374.2**	**1,548.1**	**1,829.5**	**2,067.7**	**2,238.8**	**2,573.1**	**2,591.2**	**2,706.1**	**2,554.3**	**2,881.3**	**Industrial Countries**	**110**
256.984	273.352	254.884	269.878	346.364	352.463	382.295	424.442	459.542	492.922	516.987	508.363	553.923	603.438	689.215	United States	111
62.544	70.010	58.128	64.789	77.789	80.640	85.494	92.593	112.711	119.792	123.244	124.782	129.262	139.035	155.072	Canada	156
22.399	26.215	26.667	21.458	25.919	25.889	26.104	29.318	36.095	44.933	42.032	41.697	43.807	45.577	53.425	Australia	193
141.296	142.866	131.499	126.437	136.176	130.488	127.553	151.033	187.378	209.715	235.368	236.999	233.246	241.624	275.235	Japan	158
5.472	5.734	5.782	5.333	6.203	5.992	6.063	7.276	7.342	8.784	9.501	8.381	9.202	9.636	11.913	New Zealand	196
24.444	21.043	19.502	19.423	19.629	20.986	26.863	32.724	36.223	38.980	49.146	50.815	54.112	48.578	55.343	Austria	122
71.860	62.426	58.227	55.313	55.459	56.182	68.603	83.233	92.436	98.473	119.702	120.182	125.047	....	....	Belgium	126
19.340	17.580	16.692	16.266	16.613	18.245	22.878	25.499	25.941	26.690	32.228	32.402	35.174	30.542	34.878	Denmark	128
15.635	14.192	13.401	12.826	12.433	13.232	15.339	19.634	21.130	24.436	27.001	21.809	21.208	18.032	23.214	Finland	172
134.866	120.953	115.714	105.907	104.362	108.251	129.401	158.476	178.857	192.986	234.436	231.784	239.638	201.838	229.344	France	132
188.002	163.941	155.323	152.877	153.022	158.488	190.872	228.441	250.467	269.702	346.153	389.908	402.441	348.631	373.172	Germany	134
10.548	8.810	10.026	9.500	9.435	10.134	11.350	13.168	12.323	16.151	19.777	21.580	23.220	20.818	....	Greece	174
.999	1.024	.944	.818	.841	.905	1.119	1.590	1.597	1.401	1.680	1.760	1.684	1.349	1.472	Iceland	176
11.153	10.608	9.702	9.159	9.675	10.020	11.621	13.642	15.567	17.420	20.669	20.771	22.477	21.386	....	Ireland	178
100.741	94.261	87.332	79.808	85.162	87.692	99.376	125.661	138.553	153.011	181.968	182.679	188.451	148.273	167.685	Italy	136
88.392	76.030	71.796	69.230	69.395	I 73.268	78.058	91.307	99.474	104.330	126.098	125.873	134.650	124.428	143.598	Netherlands	138
16.926	15.650	15.477	13.497	13.885	15.556	20.301	22.639	23.220	23.666	27.231	25.572	25.905	23.956	27.308	Norway	142
9.309	9.800	9.572	8.240	7.961	7.652	9.649	13.967	17.866	19.072	25.263	26.113	29.581	24.337	26.624	Portugal	182
34.078	32.150	31.465	29.193	28.831	29.963	35.057	49.113	59.643	71.469	87.715	93.306	99.758	78.626	92.510	Spain	184
33.438	28.840	27.585	26.098	26.426	28.547	32.693	40.706	45.627	48.975	54.264	49.990	50.017	42.681	51.725	Sweden	144
36.341	30.697	28.678	29.192	29.522	30.696	41.051	50.652	56.363	58.194	69.681	66.485	61.737	56.716	64.074	Switzerland	146
115.545	102.708	99.646	100.080	104.725	108.957	126.330	154.407	189.340	197.731	222.977	209.947	221.551	205.390	226.793	United Kingdom	112
586.021	**641.146**	**592.411**	**556.306**	**558.386**	**533.500**	**541.245**	**614.395**	**720.427**	**784.438**	**882.301**	**987.099**	**1,109.370**	**1,226.614**	**1,443.572**	**Developing Countries**	**200**
83.337	**91.158**	**77.904**	**69.184**	**63.547**	**58.435**	**57.100**	**60.115**	**68.003**	**71.312**	**79.910**	**80.363**	**88.150**	**84.972**	....	**Africa**	**605**
10.559	11.303	10.754	10.399	10.288	9.841	9.228	7.042	7.342	9.210	9.715	7.538	8.573	7.770	....	Algeria	612
1.328	1.662	.886	.686	.774	.678	.625	.447	.998	1.150	1.577	....	....	....	....	Angola	614
.331	.543	.464	.318	.288	.331	.387	.349	.327	.207	.265	.241	.440	.344	....	Benin	638
.692	.797	.689	.735	.697	.580	.713	.937	1.196	1.500	1.946	1.947	1.861	1.776	....	Botswana	616
.359	.338	.347	.291	.209	.332	.405	.434	.454	.322	.536	.533	....	....	....	Burkina Faso	748
.168	.161	.213	.182	.186	.189	.202	.212	.204	.187	.231	.248	.221	.204	.224	Burundi	618
1.602	1.427	1.210	1.224	1.112	1.151	1.704	1.723	1.273	1.261	1.564	1.351	1.175	....	....	Cameroon	622
.068	.071	.072	.087	.083	.084	.107	.100	.106	.112	.136	.147	.180	....	....	Cape Verde	624
.081	.095	.123	.077	.087	.113	.167	.204	.201	.150	.154	.179	.165	....	....	Central African Rep.	626
.074	.108	.109	.157	.181	.166	.212	.226	.228	.240	.286	.297	.243	.201	....	Chad	628
.029	.032	.033	.034	.043	.036	.037	.052	.053	.043	.052	.058	.069	....	....	Comoros	632
.580	.446	.767	.648	.618	.598	.597	.979	1.113	1.030	.621	.472	.451	.518	....	Congo	634
2.967	2.383	2.180	1.839	1.497	1.749	2.055	2.370	2.080	2.111	2.098	2.103	5.347	....	....	Côte d'Ivoire	662
.213	.224	.226	.221	.222	.201	.184	.205	.201	.196	.215	.214	.219	....	....	Djibouti	611
.026	.027	.031	.019	.018	.020	.052	.058	.061	.055	.061	.117	.092	.060	....	Equatorial Guinea	642
.716	.739	.786	.875	.942	.993	1.102	1.066	1.129	.943	1.081	.472	.799	.787	....	Ethiopia	644
.674	.841	.867	.685	.724	.855	.866	.732	.791	.767	.772	.884	.886	.835	....	Gabon	646
.165	.126	.103	.115	.100	.093	.104	.127	.138	.161	.199	.222	.234	....	.209	Gambia, The	648
1.129	1.106	.705	2.513	.580	.731	.783	.988	.905	1.273	....	....	....	....	....	Ghana	652
.055	.050	.050	.055	....	....	....	....	.066	.069	.068	.067	.084	.062	.063	Guinea-Bissau	654
2.125	1.939	1.644	1.334	1.469	1.436	1.613	1.755	1.975	2.148	2.124	1.797	1.713	1.711	2.166	Kenya	664
.535	.449	.410	.412	.363	.284	.267	.308	.272	....	....	....	....	....	....	Liberia	668
.600	.545	.417	.387	.366	.402	.353	.302	.360	.371	.571	.450	.448	.468	.434	Madagascar	674
.439	.359	.304	.311	.271	.285	.260	.295	.406	.503	.581	.703	.718	.546	....	Malawi	676
.439	.365	.332	.353	.278	.299	.444	.374	.504	.340	.602	....	....	....	....	Mali	678
.286	.265	.276	.227	.208	.234	.221	.235	.240	.222	.639	....	....	....	....	Mauritania	682
.609	.563	.464	.441	.470	.523	.676	.993	1.261	1.325	1.618	1.576	1.630	1.715	1.926	Mauritius	684
4.164	4.411	4.315	3.592	3.911	3.849	3.803	4.230	4.773	5.492	6.800	6.873	7.348	6.760	7.188	Morocco	686
.800	.801	.836	.636	.540	.424	.543	.642	.736	.808	.878	.899	.855	.955	....	Mozambique	688
.594	.510	.466	.324	.288	.369	.368	.311	.387	.363	.389	.355	....	....	....	Niger	692
16.660	20.877	16.061	12.254	9.364	8.877	4.034	3.912	4.717	4.187	5.627	9.031	8.119	7.508	....	Nigeria	694
.887	.788	.807	.841	.789	.830	1.135	1.456	1.688	1.734	2.156	2.128	2.316	2.057	....	Réunion	696
.243	.283	.286	.279	.278	.298	.349	.352	.370	.333	.288	.306	.288	....	....	Rwanda	714
.019	.017	....	....	....	.010	.017	.014	.014	.018	.021	.025	.025	.022	....	Sao Tome & Principe	716
1.052	1.076	.992	1.025	.981	.826	.961	1.024	1.080	1.221	1.314	1.097	1.170	....	....	Senegal	722
.099	.093	.098	.088	.088	.099	.106	.113	.159	.165	.186	.172	.192	.189	.244	Seychelles	718
.427	.328	.298	.160	.157	.151	.132	.137	.156	.183	.149	.163	.146	.147	.150	Sierra Leone	724
.348	.512	.250	.346	.103	.112	.279	.132	.110	.072	....	....	....	....	....	Somalia	726
I 19.598	22.925	18.407	15.813	15.955	11.319	12.992	15.277	18.723	18.498	18.399	18.834	19.761	20.017	23.387	South Africa	199
1.576	1.553	1.282	1.354	1.147	.771	.961	.871	1.060	....	....	....	....	....	....	Sudan	732
.623	.594	.526	.551	.447	.324	.352	.435	.516	.583	.663	.718	.866	....	....	Swaziland	734
1.252	1.213	1.166	.832	.665	1.324	.937	.929	.823	.990	1.027	1.533	1.510	1.523	....	Tanzania	738
.551	.434	.393	.282	.271	.288	.312	.424	.487	.472	.581	.444	....	....	....	Togo	742
3.540	3.791	3.420	3.107	3.174	2.757	2.890	3.039	3.689	4.374	5.542	5.189	6.431	6.214	6.581	Tunisia	744
.293	.345	.377	.377	.344	.327	.307	.848	.887	.271	.213	.196	.439	....	.870	Uganda	746
.278	.223	.160	.157	I .685	.792	.875	.756	.763	.850	.888	.711	.420	.372	.382	Zaïre	636
1.339	1.261	1.201	.851	.730	.654	.648	.816	.835	.906	1.220	.948	....	....	....	Zambia	754
1.448	1.696	1.639	1.205	1.098	1.031	1.132	1.205	1.301	1.623	1.847	2.055	2.220	....	....	Zimbabwe	698
180.069	**197.921**	**192.052**	**199.102**	**215.372**	**222.520**	**231.133**	**283.522**	**365.630**	**415.156**	**467.809**	**534.795**	**603.056**	**681.839**	**803.473**	**Asia** *	**505**
.841	.886	.962	1.064	1.390	1.194	1.404	.996	.900	.822	.936	.616	....	....	....	Afghanistan, Islamic State of	512
.095	.234	.198	.227	.284	.296	.313	.346	.339	.378	.360	.372	.418	....	....	American Samoa	859
2.599	2.699	2.307	2.165	2.825	2.772	2.486	2.680	3.046	3.648	3.598	3.401	3.888	4.001	4.701	Bangladesh	513
.050	.068	.068	.072	.073	.084	.102	.092	.135	.099	.108	.102	....	....	....	Bhutan	514
.572	.594	.731	.724	.622	.606	.656	.642	.721	.883	1.019	1.084	....	....	....	Brunei	516
....	....	....	....	....	....	....	....	....	....	....	....	....	....	....	Cambodia	522
19.941	21.572	18.906	21.345	26.482	42.896	43.411	43.392	55.278	58.437	52.523	62.567	76.354	103.088	114.563	China, People's Rep.	924
.562	.631	.509	.484	.450	.442	.435	.379	.462	.581	.743	.642	.614	.634	.724	Fiji	819
.547	.556	.520	.534	.534	.549	.738	.829	.808	.790	.928	.914	.894	.918	....	French Polynesia	887
.400	....	....	....	....	.350	.380	.300	.350	.390	.410	.420	....	....	....	Guam	829
22.447	24.797	23.575	24.017	28.568	29.703	35.367	48.465	63.896	72.155	82.474	100.255	123.430	138.658	161.777	Hong Kong	532
14.864	15.418	14.786	14.061	15.322	15.928	15.421	16.675	19.149	20.535	23.642	20.418	23.580	22.761	26.762	India	534
10.834	13.272	16.859	16.352	13.882	10.262	10.718	12.891	13.249	16.360	21.837	25.869	27.280	28.086	31.985	Indonesia	536
22.292	26.131	24.251	26.192	30.631	31.136	31.585	41.020	51.811	61.465	69.844	81.525	81.775	83.800	102.348	Korea	542
.544	.711	.719	.727	.795	.778	.879	1.120	1.289	1.481	1.532	1.842	1.949	1.992	2.098	Macao	546
															*of which:	
19.764	21.153	18.827	20.308	22.002	20.124	24.230	34.802	49.763	52.507	54.830	63.078	72.181	77.099	85.519	Taiwan Province of China	528

1995 INTERNATIONAL FINANCIAL STATISTICS YEARBOOK 129

Imports

71 d		1965	1966	1967	1968	1969	1970	1971	1972	1973	1974	1975	1976	1977	1978	1979
																Billions of US Dollars
Asia (cont.)																
Malaysia	548	1.097	1.104	1.087	1.160	1.178	1.412	1.446	1.581	2.453	4.114	3.566	3.828	4.542	5.928	7.849
Maldives	556	.002	.002	.003	.002	.003	.002	.004	.005	.007	.007	.007	.006	.010	.014	.021
Mongolia	948	....	....	....	....	....	....	....	....	....	....	....	....	....	....	....
Myanmar	518	.247	.158	.124	.114	.165	.155	.169	.133	.106	.176	.197	.177	.241	.307	.319
Nepal	558	.108	.075	.060	.056	.085	.075	.085	.085	.104	.134	.171	.163	.168	.221	.254
New Caledonia	839	.077	.067	.079	.093	.127	.230	.234	.211	.219	.281	.347	.277	.292	.292	.361
Pakistan	564	1.047	.900	1.101	.673	.676	.731	.678	1.680	.971	1.729	2.158	2.181	2.446	3.285	4.056
Papua New Guinea	853	.123	.149	.178	.178	.220	.300	.356	.332	.356	.518	.592	.502	.642	.770	.903
Philippines	566	.894	.959	1.180	1.290	1.265	1.236	1.325	1.418	1.800	3.471	3.756	3.942	4.270	5.144	6.612
Singapore	576	1.243	1.328	1.439	1.660	2.039	2.461	2.838	3.395	5.127	8.380	8.133	9.071	10.471	13.061	17.643
Solomon Islands	813	.008	.011	.011	.012	.011	.013	.015	.017	.018	.027	.033	.030	.033	.042	.070
Sri Lanka	524	.310	.400	.365	.359	.420	.386	.354	.368	.430	.720	.816	.585	.700	.969	1.466
Thailand	578	.742	.890	1.067	1.159	1.248	1.299	1.288	1.484	2.049	3.143	3.280	3.572	4.617	5.356	7.158
Tonga	866	.004	.005	.006	.006	.006	.006	.007	.009	.011	.017	.017	.014	.020	.026	.029
Vanuatu	846	.007	.008	.010	.010	.011	.013	.018	.029	.035	.050	.040	.034	.040	.051	.062
Viet Nam	582	.208	.286	.365	.316	.453	.373	.594	.692	.616	.321	1.102	1.171	1.372	1.485	1.599
Western Samoa	862	.009	.008	.008	.008	.010	.014	.013	.019	.023	.026	.037	.030	1.041	.052	.074
Europe	170	....	....	....	....	....	....	....	....	....	....	53.655	46.486	53.447	56.541	82.622
Cyprus	423	.144	.154	.165	.170	.203	.235	.263	.315	.452	.407	.308	.432	.623	.758	1.010
Czech Republic	935															
Czechoslovakia	934	....	....	....	....	....	....	....	....	....	....	7.050	....	....	....	11.940
Estonia	939															
Faeroe Islands	816	.026	.028	.027	.028	.033	.030	.041	.047	.068	.100	.113	.131	.152	.184	.205
Hungary	944	....	....	....	....	....	1.877	2.248	2.356	3.018	4.453	5.400	5.534	6.526	7.938	8.682
Malta	181	.098	.109	.112	.123	.148	.161	.161	.176	.239	.361	.375	.423	.516	.575	.759
Poland	964	....	....	....	....	....	3.608	....	....	....	....	11.155	12.898	13.420	14.744	16.142
Romania	968	1.163	1.310	1.670	1.738	1.880	2.117	2.278	2.827	3.738	5.555	5.769	6.583	7.579	9.638	11.789
Slovak Republic	936															
Slovenia	961															
Turkey	186	.572	.718	.685	.764	.801	.948	1.171	1.563	2.086	3.778	4.739	5.129	5.796	4.599	5.070
Yugoslavia, SFR	188	1.288	1.575	1.707	1.797	2.134	2.874	3.252	3.233	4.511	7.542	7.697	7.367	9.634	9.989	12.863
Middle East	405	5.716	6.443	6.271	7.117	8.318	8.960	10.374	12.460	18.689	30.934	44.594	52.452	68.226	78.742	86.830
Bahrain	419	.168e	.176	.206	.193	.209	.247	.303	.371	.521	1.124	1.198	1.669	2.029	2.045	2.477
Egypt	469	.879	1.071	.792	.680	.636	.786	.904	.877	.906	2.349	3.751	3.808	4.808	6.727	3.837
Iran, I.R. of	429	.859	.931	1.119	1.383	1.527	1.662	1.873	2.409	3.393	5.433	10.343	12.894	14.070	13.549	9.738
Iraq	433	.456	.494	.424	.404	.440	.508	.701	.705	.894	2.371	4.214	3.470	3.899	4.213	7.179
Israel	436	.838	.833	.774	1.307	1.653	2.079	2.363	2.473	4.240	5.437	5.997	5.669	5.787	7.415	8.576
Jordan	439	.157	.191	.154	.159	.190	.184	.215	.274	.330	.488	.732	1.006	1.381	1.504	1.963
Kuwait	443	.377	.463	.593	.611	.646	.625	.652	.797	1.047	1.552	2.390	3.324	4.840	4.595	5.200
Lebanon	446	.543	.608	.549	.594	.610	.677	.758	.917	1.541	2.355	2.048	.612	1.539	1.922	2.700
Libya	672	.320	.405	.477	.645	.676	.555	.714	1.060	1.806	2.762	3.542	3.212	3.777	4.603	5.311
Oman	449	.009	.010	.010	.010	.013	.018	.033	.049	.116	.393	.765	.725	.875	.947	1.246
Qatar	453	.070	.070	.090	.043	.053	.064	.109	.141	.195	.271	.413	.817	1.225	1.185	1.424
Saudi Arabia	456	.506	.592	.574	.553	.735	.693	.808	1.136	1.972	2.860	4.213	8.695	14.656	20.349	24.465
Syrian Arab Rep.	463	.213	.289	.265	.313	.370	.360	.439	.540	.612	1.225	1.685	2.389	2.702	2.459	3.329
United Arab Emirates	466	....	....	....	....	.307	.267	.309	.482	.821	1.705	2.685	3.337	5.055	5.371	6.966
Yemen Arab Rep.	473	.019	.027	.035	.020	.036	.033	.034	.080	.123	.190	.294	.413	1.040	1.284	1.492
Yemen, P.D. Rep.	459	.301	.285	.210	.203	.218	.200	.156	.149	.171	.419	.323	.412	.544	.575	.925
Western Hemisphere	205	11.158	12.213	12.697	13.829	15.209	17.436	19.489	21.613	28.417	49.827	53.257	55.539	61.340	69.027	85.916
Antigua and Barbuda	311	.019	.026	.023	.025	.029	.036	.044	.047	.048	.070	.067	.035	.041	.046	.075
Argentina	213	1.199	1.124	1.096	1.169	1.576	1.694	1.868	1.905	2.230	3.635	3.947	3.033	4.162	3.834	6.700
Aruba	314															
Bahamas, The	313	.105	.139	.163	.176	.296	.337	.511	.485	.764	1.908	2.697	3.125	3.568	3.150	3.514
Barbados	316	.067	.076	.077	.084	.097	.118	.124	.141	.168	.204	.216	.237	.274	.313	.421
Belize	339	.024	.027	.026	.027	.030	.033	.036	.043	.044	.064	.088	.073	.090	.106	.132
Bermuda	319	.064	.073	.075	.080	.094	.116	.119	.120	.135	.165	.178	.182	.204	.233	.257
Bolivia	218	.134	.138	.151	.153	.165	.159	.170	.185	.230	.390	.558	.555	.618	.808	.894
Brazil	223	1.096	1.496	1.667	2.132	2.265	2.849	3.701	4.783	6.999	14.168	13.592	13.726	13.257	15.054	19.804
Chile	228	.718	.892	.819	.852	1.028	1.063	1.109	1.086	1.290	2.148	1.525	1.864	2.539	3.408	4.808
Colombia	233	.454	.675	.497	.643	.685	.843	.929	.859	1.062	1.597	1.495	1.662	1.880	2.971	3.364
Costa Rica	238	.178	.179	.191	.214	.245	.317	.350	.373	.455	.720	.694	.770	1.021	1.166	1.397
Dominica	321	.010	.010	.010	.010	.012	.016	.017	.017	.016	.019	.021	.019	.022	.028	.022
Dominican Republic	243	.097	.181	.197	.222	.246	.304	.358	.388	.489	.808	.889	.878	.975	.987	1.213
Ecuador	248	.165	.174	.214	.255	.242	.274	.340	.319	.397	.678	.987	.958	1.189	1.505	1.600
El Salvador	253	.201	.221	.224	.214	.208	.214	.249	.272	.377	.562	.614	.735	.929	1.028	1.037
Greenland	326	.034	.038	.046	.048	.050	.053	.061	.072	.095	.106	.128	.129	.160	.179	.275
Grenada	328	.011	.013	.014	.013	.017	.022	.023	.022	.022	.018	.024	.025	.032	.036	.044
Guadeloupe	329	.085	.093	.100	.102	.106	.128	.125	.148	.202	.230	.307	.318	.375	.424	.598
Guatemala	258	.229	.207	.247	.249	.250	.284	.297	.324	.431	.700	.733	.839	1.053	1.286	1.504
Guiana, French	333	.020	.028	.042	.052	.050	.045	.040	.045	.056	.056	.072	.086	.144	.191	.251
Guyana	336	.104	.123	.129	.110	.118	.134	.135	.143	.166	.253	.342	.363	.314	.260	.318
Haiti	263	.034	.038	.036	.038	.039	.055	.060	.069	.083	.125	.149	.207	.213	.233	.272
Honduras	268	.122	.149	.165	.186	.184	.221	.194	.193	.262	.382	.400	.456	.575	.693	.826
Jamaica	343	.293	.327	.348	.384	.443	.522	.548	.643	.662	.936	1.122	.914	.860	.885	.994
Martinique	349	.091	.093	.106	.109	.126	.146	.155	.173	.244	.293	.326	.420	.428	.493	.676
Mexico	273	1.560	1.605	1.748	1.960	2.080	2.461	2.407	2.718	3.814	6.057	6.580	6.028	5.489	8.109	12.086
Netherlands Antilles	353	.721	.721	.776	.781	.807	.926	.877	.869	1.591	3.602	2.956	3.661	3.129	3.491	4.394
Nicaragua	278	.160	.182	.204	.185	.177	.199	.210	.218	.327	.562	.517	.532	.762	.596	.360
Panama	283	.208	.235	.251	.266	.294	.357	.396	.440	.502	.822	.892	.848	.861	.942	1.184
Paraguay	288	.055	.059	.071	.073	.082	.076	.083	.083	.122	.198	.206	.220	.308	.383	.521
Peru	293	.730	.829	.825	.646	.613	.623	.763	.796	1.019	1.531	2.550	2.037	1.911	1.175	1.820
St. Kitts and Nevis	361	.009	.009	.009	.009	.010	.012	.015	.016	.018	.019	.024	.017	.011	.024	.032
St. Lucia	362	.013	.017	.017	.015	.021	.027	.035	.036	.038	.044	.046	.048	.059	.083	.101
St. Vincent & Grens.	364	.009	.009	.009	.010	.012	.015	.018	.018	.019	.025	.025	.024	.030	.036	.047
Suriname	366	.093	.090	.103	.100	.111	.115	.127	.144	.157	.229	.262	.294	.398	.382	1.411
Trinidad and Tobago	369	.471	.447	.406	.413	.483	.539	.662	.741	.782	1.865	1.471	1.967	1.791	1.963	2.084
Uruguay	298	.151	.164	.171	.157	.197	.231	.229	.212	.285	.487	.556	.587	.730	.757	1.206
Venezuela	299	1.421	1.307	1.445	1.665	1.720	1.869	2.103	2.463	2.812	4.148	6.000	7.663	10.938	11.767	10.670
Memorandum Items																
Oil Exporting Countries	999	6.155	6.158	6.646	7.385	8.603	9.579	11.147	13.802	19.884	32.144	50.875	63.105	83.785	94.639	98.024
Non-Oil Developing Countries	201	46.118	50.618	51.572	54.885	60.407	69.848	74.067	81.043	113.324	180.124	203.886	203.621	230.449	273.666	353.294

Imports

Billions of US Dollars

1980	1981	1982	1983	1984	1985	1986	1987	1988	1989	1990	1991	1992	1993	1994		71 *d*
															Asia (cont.)	
10.820	11.581	12.395	13.198	14.069	12.301	10.823	12.701	16.551	22.496	29.258	36.648	39.926	45.657	59.581	Malaysia	548
.029	.031	.043	.057	.053	.053	.045	.081	.090	.113	.138	.161	.189	.185	.222	Maldives	556
....	....	....	....	....	1.096	1.140	1.105	1.114	.963	.924	.361	.418	.362	.223	Mongolia	948
.353	.373	.409	.268	.239	.283	.304	.268	.244	.201	.270	.646	.651	.814	.886	Myanmar	518
.342	.369	.395	.464	.416	.453	.459	.570	.681	.580	.686	.758	.792	.880	....	Nepal	558
.456	.408	.367	.303	.311	.342	.500	.627	.604	.764	.883	.865	.915	.924	....	New Caledonia	839
5.350	5.631	5.465	5.329	5.853	5.890	5.374	5.822	6.590	7.143	7.376	8.439	9.379	9.500	8.889	Pakistan	564
1.176	1.261	1.170	1.120	1.110	1.008	1.080	1.165	1.393	1.530	1.193	1.614	1.485	1.299	1.521	Papua New Guinea	853
8.295	8.479	8.263	7.976	6.432	5.459	5.394	7.144	8.721	11.171	13.041	12.786	15.449	18.754	22.531	Philippines	566
24.007	27.572	28.167	28.158	28.667	26.285	25.511	32.559	43.864	49.667	60.899	66.293	72.179	85.234	102.670	Singapore	576
.089	.091	.071	.074	.079	.083	.072	.081	.098	.114	.094	.110	.098	.101	....	Solomon Islands	813
2.037	1.849	1.831	1.820	1.867	1.843	1.857	2.058	2.262	2.188	2.685	3.054	3.445	3.991	4.776	Sri Lanka	524
9.214	9.955	8.549	10.287	10.398	9.242	9.173	13.023	20.285	25.771	33.379	37.591	40.686	46.208	....	Thailand	578
.038	.040	.042	.038	.041	.041	.041	.048	.055	.054	.062	.059	.063	.061	.069	Tonga	866
.073	.058	.060	.064	.069	.070	.058	.070	.070	.071	.096	.083	.082	.075	....	Vanuatu	846
I 1.314	1.382	1.472	1.527	1.745	1.857	2.155	2.455	2.757	2.566	2.752	2.338	2.541	3.415	....	Viet Nam	582
.062	.056	.050	.048	.050	.051	.047	.062	.076	.075	.080	.094	.110	.105	.082	Western Samoa	862
93.373	**88.956**	**80.100**	**78.768**	**80.553**	**83.065**	**88.007**	**92.718**	**93.716**	**95.460**	**105.619**	**103.567**	**94.841**	**118.118**	....	**Europe**	**170**
1.202	1.166	1.223	1.219	1.364	1.247	1.272	1.484	1.859	2.288	2.568	2.659	3.313	2.590	3.018	Cyprus	423
....	....	....	....	....	....	....	....	....	....	....	....	....	13.341	15.465	Czech Republic	935
12.774	11.894	12.271	12.250	11.852	12.149	14.666	16.340	15.298	14.988	13.712	11.072	12.594	....	....	Czechoslovakia	934
....	....	....	....	....	....	....	....	....	....	....	....	....	.896	1.660	Estonia	939
.223	.214	.192	.238	.261	.254	.328	.514	.478	.323	.296	.265	.333	.253	....	Faeroe Islands	816
9.219	9.159	8.867	8.553	8.128	8.183	9.594	9.859	9.372	8.781	8.621	11.449	11.123	12.597	14.318	Hungary	944
.938	.860	.789	.733	.717	.759	.887	1.139	1.353	1.479	1.964	2.130	2.331	2.174	2.461	Malta	181
16.690	12.792	10.648	10.927	10.985	11.855	11.535	11.215	12.712	10.659	8.413	I 15.757	15.701	18.834	21.383	Poland	964
13.843	13.454	10.525	10.414	11.161	11.267	11.437	8.978	8.254	9.122	9.843	5.793	6.260	6.522	7.109	Romania	968
....	....	....	....	....	....	....	....	....	....	....	....	....	6.655	6.823	Slovak Republic	936
....	....	....	....	....	....	....	....	....	....	....	....	....	6.498	7.334	Slovenia	961
7.910	8.933	8.843	9.235	10.757	11.343	11.105	14.158	14.335	15.792	22.302	21.047	22.872	29.174	....	Turkey	186
15.076	15.727	13.453	12.154	11.996	12.207	11.751	12.632	13.171	14.829	18.871	14.737	....	....	....	Yugoslavia, SFR	188
113.244	**137.720**	**139.786**	**132.859**	**121.120**	**96.900**	**90.804**	**94.724**	**100.581**	**100.642**	**113.925**	**132.620**	**154.146**	**154.221**	....	**Middle East**	**405**
3.483	4.124	3.614	3.342	3.480	3.107	2.405	2.714	2.593	3.134	3.712	4.115	4.263	3.858	3.737	Bahrain	419
4.860	8.839	9.078	10.275	10.766	5.495	8.680	7.596	8.657	7.434	9.216	7.862	8.245	8.184	....	Egypt	469
12.246	14.693	11.955	18.320	15.370	11.635	10.521	9.570	9.454	12.807	15.716	21.688	....	....	....	Iran, I.R. of	429
13.942	20.735	21.534	12.166	11.078	10.556	10.190	7.415	10.268	....	....	....	....	....	....	Iraq	433
9.784	10.235	9.655	9.574	9.819	9.875	10.806	14.348	15.018	14.347	16.791	18.658	20.253	22.624	....	Israel	436
2.402	3.165	3.240	3.036	2.784	2.733	2.432	2.710	2.732	2.125	2.600	2.508	3.255	3.539	3.382	Jordan	439
6.529	6.978	8.282	7.373	6.896	6.005	5.717	5.493	6.143	6.295	3.972	4.761	7.261	7.036	....	Kuwait	443
3.650	3.499	3.391	3.661	2.948	2.203	2.203	1.880	2.457	....	....	....	....	....	....	Lebanon	446
6.777	8.382	7.175	6.029	6.222	4.101	4.445	4.684	5.869	4.923	5.336	5.361	....	....	....	Libya	672
1.732	2.288	2.682	2.492	2.748	3.153	2.402	1.822	2.202	2.257	2.681	3.194	3.769	4.114	....	Oman	449
1.423	1.518	1.947	1.456	1.162	1.139	1.099	1.161	1.267	1.326	1.695	1.720	2.015	....	....	Qatar	453
30.166	35.269	40.644	39.197	33.696	23.622	19.112	20.110	21.784	21.154	24.069	29.079	33.244	28.224	23.344	Saudi Arabia	456
4.124	5.172	4.028	4.542	4.116	3.967	2.728	7.112	2.231	2.097	2.526	3.151	3.490	4.140	5.369	Syrian Arab Rep.	463
8.746	9.646	9.440	8.294	6.936	6.549	6.422	7.226	8.522	10.010	11.199	13.746	17.410	19.520	....	United Arab Emirates	466
1.853	1.758	1.521	1.618	1.556	1.313	1.159	.883	1.384	....	....	....	....	....	....	Yemen Arab Rep.	473
1.527	1.419	1.599	1.483	1.543	1.448	.483	....	....	....	....	....	....	....	....	Yemen, P.D. Rep.	459
116.349	**123.603**	**100.573**	**75.103**	**76.745**	**72.579**	**74.202**	**83.317**	**92.461**	**99.464**	**112.100**	**129.886**	**157.097**	**169.889**	**200.423**	**Western Hemisphere**	**205**
.106	.138	.139	.109	.132	.112	.207	.222	.225	.228	.210	.215	....	....	....	Antigua and Barbuda	311
10.541	9.430	5.337	4.504	4.585	3.814	4.724	5.818	5.322	4.203	4.076	8.275	14.872	16.784	21.527	Argentina	213
....	....	....	....	....	....	.192	.236	.336	.387	....	....	....	....	....	Aruba	314
7.546	7.284	6.349	4.616	4.098	3.078	3.289	3.041	2.263	3.001	2.920	1.801	....	....	....	Bahamas, The	313
.524	.571	.551	.616	.657	.607	.587	.515	.582	.673	.700	.694	.521	.574	.608	Barbados	316
.150	.162	.128	.112	.130	.128	.122	.143	.181	.216	.211	.251	.273	.281	.258	Belize	339
.343	.355	.386	.416	.455	.402	.492	.420	.488	.535	.595	.510	.562	.535	....	Bermuda	319
.665	.917	.554	.577	.489	.691	.674	.766	.591	.611	.687	.970	1.090	1.206	1.209	Bolivia	218
24.961	24.079	21.069	16.801	15.210	14.332	15.557	16.581	16.055	19.875	22.524	22.950	23.068	27.740	35.997	Brazil	223
5.797	7.181	3.989	3.085	3.574	3.072	3.436	4.396	5.292	7.144	7.678	8.094	10.129	11.125	11.825	Chile	228
4.739	5.201	5.480	4.963	4.498	4.141	3.862	4.322	5.002	5.004	5.590	4.906	6.516	9.832	11.883	Colombia	233
1.540	1.209	.889	.988	1.094	1.098	1.148	1.383	1.410	1.717	1.990	1.877	2.440	2.885	3.025	Costa Rica	238
.048	.050	.047	.045	.058	.055	.056	.066	.088	.107	.118	.110	.111	....	....	Dominica	321
1.640	1.668	1.444	1.471	1.446	1.487	1.433	1.830	1.849	2.258	2.062	1.988	2.501	2.436	2.626	Dominican Republic	243
2.253	I 2.246	2.169	1.487	1.616	1.767	1.810	2.252	1.714	1.855	1.862	2.399	2.501	2.562	3.642	Ecuador	248
.966	.986	.857	.891	.977	.961	.935	.994	1.007	1.161	1.263	1.406	1.699	1.912	2.249	El Salvador	253
.328	.294	.273	.261	.279	.296	.360	.507	.519	.399	.445	.408	.456	....	....	Greenland	326
.050	.054	.056	.057	.056	.069	.084	.089	.092	.099	.105	.121	.107	....	....	Grenada	328
.679	.588	.624	.665	.598	.646	.792	1.039	1.203	1.205	1.677	1.644	1.518	1.394	....	Guadeloupe	329
1.598	1.688	1.388	1.126	1.279	1.175	.959	1.447	1.557	1.654	1.649	1.851	2.532	2.599	....	Guatemala	258
.255	.249	.250	.280	.247	.255	.297	.395	.518	.567	.786	.769	.671	.501	....	Guiana, French	333
.365	.438	.283	.231	.213	.226	.241	.265	.216	.258	.311	.307	.382	....	....	Guyana	336
.375	.461	.387	.441	.450	.442	.360	.399	.344	.291	.279	.420	.327	.228	.287	Haiti	263
1.009	.949	.701	.803	.893	.888	.875	.827	.940	.969	.935	.955	1.037	1.130	1.056	Honduras	268
1.095	1.473	1.381	1.494	1.146	1.111	.972	1.238	1.440	1.852	1.859	1.491	1.668	2.097	....	Jamaica	343
.787	.742	.722	.736	.636	.687	.885	1.116	1.291	1.246	1.655	1.602	1.747	1.557	....	Martinique	349
19.460	24.068	15.128	8.023	11.788	13.993	11.997	12.731	19.591	24.438	29.969	38.124	48.160	50.147	60.979	Mexico	273
5.676	5.862	5.087	4.526	4.033	1.388	I 1.112	1.502	1.404	1.610	2.146	2.173	1.869	1.807	....	Netherlands Antilles	353
.887	.999	.776	.826	.848	.964	.857	.827	.805	.615	.638	.751	.892	.746	....	Nicaragua	278
1.449	1.540	1.570	1.412	1.423	1.392	1.229	1.306	.751	.986	1.539	1.695	2.024	2.188	2.404	Panama	283
.615	.600	.672	.546	.586	.502	.578	.595	.574	.760	1.352	1.460	1.422	1.689	....	Paraguay	288
2.499	3.482	3.601	2.548	2.212	1.835	2.909	3.562	3.348	2.749	3.470	4.195	4.860	4.901	6.752	Peru	293
.045	.048	.044	.052	.050	.051	.065	.080	.093	.103	.117	.112	....	....	....	St. Kitts and Nevis	361
.124	.129	.118	.144	.119	.125	.155	.179	.220	.274	.271	.295	.313	....	....	St. Lucia	362
.057	.058	.065	.070	.077	.079	.087	.099	.122	.127	.136	.140	.132	.134	.135	St. Vincent & Grens.	364
.504	.568	.514	.472	.346	.299	.327	.294	.351	.443	.472	.470	....	....	....	Suriname	366
3.161	3.089	3.492	2.505	1.898	1.586	1.345	1.261	1.123	1.217	1.121	1.667	1.434	1.448	....	Trinidad and Tobago	369
1.680	1.641	1.110	.788	.777	.708	.870	1.142	1.157	1.203	1.343	1.637	2.045	2.324	2.773	Uruguay	298
11.827	13.106	12.944	6.419	7.774	8.106	8.504	I 9.659	12.726	7.803	7.335	11.147	14.066	12.200	8.879	Venezuela	299
															Memorandum Items	
131.441	**158.067**	**160.277**	**140.751**	**125.417**	**103.845**	**92.391**	**90.986**	**103.542**	**106.936**	**121.200**	**147.787**	**169.596**	**162.140**	....	**Oil Exporting Countries**	**999**
459.435	**485.276**	**436.566**	**419.055**	**436.071**	**433.784**	**454.584**	**534.375**	**630.426**	**694.071**	**785.289**	**864.729**	**968.393**	**1,081.079**	**1,273.639**	**Non-Oil Developing Countries**	**201**

CIF/FOB Factor

		1965	1966	1967	1968	1969	1970	1971	1972	1973	1974	1975	1976	1977	1978	1979
World	001	**1.092**	**1.093**	**1.091**	**1.089**	**1.087**	**1.086**	**1.090**	**1.083**	**1.081**	**1.083**	**1.081**	**1.076**	**1.074**	**1.074**	**1.072**
Industrial Countries	110	**1.083**	**1.083**	**1.081**	**1.079**	**1.077**	**1.076**	**1.076**	**1.071**	**1.069**	**1.069**	**1.065**	**1.060**	**1.056**	**1.056**	**1.055**
United States	111	1.087	1.088	1.075	1.067	1.068	1.061	1.061	1.059	1.054	1.073	1.066	1.063	1.059	1.057	1.057
Canada	156	1.032	1.032	1.032	1.032	1.032	1.033	1.031	1.031	1.029	1.025	1.027	1.027	1.026	1.024	1.024
Australia	193	1.114	1.114	1.114	1.119	1.117	1.117	1.113	1.115	1.088	1.070	1.076	1.070	1.095	1.104	1.102	1.100
Japan	158	1.214	1.222	1.221	1.217	1.203	1.200	1.187	1.177	1.159	1.136	1.132	1.119	1.106	1.108	1.105
New Zealand	196	1.079	1.088	1.080	1.075	1.067	1.071	1.076	1.071	1.075	1.091	1.095	1.080	1.086	1.080	1.102
Austria	122	1.026	1.026	1.026	1.030	1.028	1.028	1.028	1.027	1.028	1.032	1.035	1.035	1.031	1.030	1.029
Belgium-Luxembourg	126	1.052	1.052	1.037	1.038	1.037	1.036	1.038	1.036	1.037	1.061	1.063	1.052	1.031	1.031	1.031
Denmark	128	1.058	1.058	1.058	1.058	1.058	1.067	1.058	1.056	1.055	1.047	1.043	.998	1.042	1.030	1.048
Finland	172	1.070	1.070	1.070	1.070	1.070	1.070	1.070	1.069	1.070	1.070	1.049	1.049	1.049	1.049	1.049
France	132	1.077	1.074	1.075	1.075	1.075	1.067	1.066	1.066	1.073	1.076	1.063	1.044	1.049	1.046	1.038	1.038
Germany	134	1.068	1.068	1.070	1.066	1.055	1.066	1.066	1.058	1.056	1.046	1.041	1.035	1.033	1.034	1.033
Greece	174	1.130	1.130	1.130	1.130	1.130	1.130	1.130	1.130	1.130	1.130	1.130	1.130	1.130	1.130	1.130
Iceland	176	1.104	1.112	1.120	1.155	1.150	1.150	1.147	1.150	1.114	1.080	1.100	1.100	1.100	1.100	1.100
Ireland	178	1.050	1.050	1.050	1.050	1.050	1.050	1.049	1.050	1.050	1.050	1.050	1.050	1.050	1.050	1.050
Italy	136	1.099	1.099	1.099	1.099	1.099	1.067	1.099	1.099	1.081	1.067	1.068	1.071	1.070	1.071	1.075
Netherlands	138	1.060	1.060	1.060	1.060	1.060	1.065	1.063	1.058	1.065	1.064	1.059	1.055	1.055	1.057	1.057
Norway	142	1.028	1.028	1.028	1.030	1.029	1.027	1.024	1.028	1.030	1.022	1.031	1.025	1.025	1.025	1.024
Portugal	182	1.120	1.120	1.120	1.120	1.120	1.120	1.120	1.120	1.113	1.104	1.103	1.111	1.104	1.103	1.103
Spain	184	1.110	1.110	1.110	1.110	1.105	1.105	1.099	1.105	1.105	1.094	1.082	1.081	1.074	1.074	1.068
Sweden	144	1.071	1.071	1.071	1.072	1.074	1.075	1.075	1.075	1.075	1.075	1.075	1.075	1.075	1.076	1.018
Switzerland	146	1.014	1.014	1.014	1.014	1.014	1.013	1.014	1.015	1.020	1.022	1.026	1.023	1.025	1.029	1.029
United Kingdom	112	1.113	1.105	1.103	1.106	1.112	1.119	1.111	1.091	1.088	1.076	1.072	1.070	1.065	1.081	1.071
Developing Countries	200	**1.119**	**1.120**	**1.119**	**1.120**	**1.120**	**1.116**	**1.137**	**1.125**	**1.125**	**1.124**	**1.123**	**1.122**	**1.121**	**1.122**	**1.119**
Africa	605	**1.099**	**1.098**	**1.095**	**1.104**	**1.107**	**1.107**	**1.110**	**1.111**	**1.112**	**1.120**	**1.120**	**1.118**	**1.114**	**1.116**	**1.119**
Algeria	612	1.080	1.080	1.080	1.080	1.080	1.080	1.080	1.080	1.080	1.105	1.087	1.100	1.098	1.105	1.100
Benin	638	1.130	1.130	1.129	1.120	1.138	1.130	1.129	1.126	1.130	1.168	1.176	1.192	1.185	1.194	1.205
Botswana	616	1.180	1.180	1.180	1.180	1.180	1.180	1.180	1.180	1.180	1.176	1.177	1.176	1.177	1.177	1.177
Burkina Faso	748	1.260	1.260	1.260	1.260	1.263	1.259	1.256	1.264	1.249	1.220	1.228	1.247	1.235	1.209	1.236
Burundi	618	1.150	1.150	1.150	1.150	1.150	1.150	1.150	1.150	1.150	1.150	1.150	1.150	1.150	1.150	1.150
Cameroon	622	1.042	1.042	1.042	1.042	1.042	1.042	1.067	1.097	1.056	1.084	1.076	1.072	1.105	1.100	1.100
Cape Verde	624	1.150	1.150	1.150	1.150	1.150	1.150	1.150	1.150	1.150	1.150	1.150	1.150	1.150	1.150	1.150
Central African Rep.	626	1.430	1.430	1.430	1.427	1.428	1.429	1.132	1.218	1.360	1.327	1.324	1.312	1.312	1.312	1.194
Chad	628	1.246	1.246	1.246	1.250	1.330	1.330	1.330	1.330	1.330	1.330	1.330	1.330	1.330	1.330	1.330
Congo	634	1.140	1.140	1.140	1.140	1.140	1.140	1.136	1.120	1.238	1.186	1.185	1.160	1.168	1.223	1.215
Côte d'Ivoire	662	1.110	1.110	1.110	1.108	1.110	1.111	1.110	1.112	1.109	1.137	1.146	1.182	1.174	1.172	1.192
Djibouti	611	1.130	1.130	1.130	1.130	1.130	1.130	1.130	1.130	1.130	1.130	1.130	1.130	1.130	1.130	1.130
Ethiopia	644	1.180	1.180	1.180	1.178	1.190	1.190	1.190	1.190	1.190	1.191	1.201	1.212	1.233	1.254	1.197	1.196
Gabon	646	1.110	1.110	1.110	1.114	1.156	1.000	1.098	1.089	1.083	1.152	1.159	1.192	1.178	1.173	1.200
Gambia, The	648	1.060	1.060	1.060	1.060	1.060	1.060	1.060	1.085	1.110	1.197	1.168	1.167	1.167	1.167	1.167
Ghana	652	1.110	1.110	1.111	1.106	1.135	1.149	1.137	1.120	1.132	1.134	1.131	1.131	1.065	1.085	1.069
Kenya	664	1.140	1.140	1.140	1.141	1.140	1.143	1.146	1.145	1.152	1.150	1.147	1.142	1.149	1.166	1.168
Liberia	668	1.140	1.140	1.140	1.140	1.140	1.140	1.140	1.140	1.140	1.140	1.140	1.140	1.136	1.136	1.158	1.157
Madagascar	674	1.190	1.190	1.190	1.190	1.191	1.211	1.209	1.219	1.250	1.244	1.265	1.273	1.267	1.251	1.229
Malawi	676	1.156	1.156	1.127	1.127	1.127	1.156	1.156	1.138	1.138	1.138	1.138	1.140	1.138	1.136	1.126
Mali	678	1.240	1.240	1.240	1.240	1.240	1.240	1.240	1.241	1.188	1.386	1.386	1.386	1.429	1.429	1.330
Mauritania	682	1.100	1.130	1.130	1.130	1.130	1.130	1.130	1.130	1.130	1.130	1.130	1.130	1.130	1.130	1.130
Mauritius	684	1.150	1.140	1.156	1.162	1.164	1.167	1.177	1.187	1.163	1.148	1.182	1.177	1.200	1.196	1.210
Morocco	686	1.135	1.078	1.079	1.080	1.090	1.097	1.100	1.099	1.099	1.136	1.137	1.136	1.136	1.136	1.136
Mozambique	688	1.120	1.120	1.120	1.120	1.120	1.120	1.120	1.120	1.120	1.120	1.120	1.120	1.120	1.120	1.120
Niger	692	1.270	1.270	1.270	1.270	1.267	1.265	1.281	1.264	1.270	1.384	1.397	1.366	1.247	1.208	1.181
Nigeria	694	1.091	1.091	1.091	1.091	1.091	1.094	1.098	1.097	1.098	1.096	1.108	1.109	1.107	1.107	1.107
Rwanda	714	1.250	1.250	1.250	1.250	1.250	1.250	1.250	1.250	1.251	1.271	1.278	1.231	1.238	1.471	1.494
Senegal	722	1.130	1.130	1.130	1.134	1.127	1.133	1.127	1.127	1.131	1.159	1.132	1.128	1.122	1.128	1.113
Seychelles	718	1.120	1.120	1.120	1.120	1.120	1.120	1.120	1.150	1.150	1.150	1.150	1.150	1.150	1.150	1.150
Sierra Leone	724	1.100	1.100	1.099	1.098	1.099	1.099	1.098	1.099	1.099	1.099	1.099	1.099	1.099	1.099	1.099
Somalia	726	1.120	1.120	1.120	1.123	1.135	1.129	1.128	1.149	1.149	1.149	1.150	1.149	1.149	1.149	1.149
South Africa	199	1.042	1.040	1.035	1.060	1.067	1.078	1.081	1.078	1.088	1.089	1.097	1.081	1.065	1.057	1.076
Sudan	732	1.120	1.120	1.120	1.120	1.120	1.120	1.120	1.120	1.098	1.097	1.098	1.099	1.099	1.099	1.110
Swaziland	734	1.019	1.019	1.019	1.019	1.019	1.019	1.019	1.019	1.019	1.019	1.020	1.024	1.017	1.023	1.011
Tanzania	738	1.160	1.160	1.162	1.154	1.158	1.154	1.156	1.154	1.152	1.151	1.150	1.149	1.149	1.149	1.149
Togo	742	1.140	1.140	1.140	1.140	1.136	1.131	1.135	1.150	1.129	1.187	1.272	1.208	1.205	1.210	1.202
Tunisia	744	1.071	1.071	1.071	1.071	1.071	1.044	1.045	1.056	1.065	1.073	1.066	1.060	1.058	1.068	1.063
Uganda	746	1.110	1.110	1.110	1.110	1.110	1.110	1.110	1.110	1.110	1.110	1.110	1.110	1.110	1.110	1.110
Zaïre	636	1.200	1.211	1.193	1.186	1.180	1.180	1.180	1.180	1.151	1.153	1.154	1.160	1.160	1.160	1.160
Zambia	754	1.156	1.156	1.173	1.182	1.191	1.172	1.167	1.201	1.214	1.229	1.225	1.205	1.173	1.199	1.208
Zimbabwe	698	1.150	1.150	1.150	1.150	1.150	1.150	1.150	1.150	1.150	1.150	1.150	1.150	1.150	1.150	1.150
Asia	505	**1.108**	**1.112**	**1.108**	**1.107**	**1.106**	**1.106**	**1.105**	**1.100**	**1.102**	**1.098**	**1.096**	**1.092**	**1.093**	**1.092**	**1.091**
Afghanistan, Islamic State of	512	1.150	1.150	1.150	1.150	1.150	1.150	1.150	1.150	1.150	1.150	1.150	1.150	1.150	1.150	1.150
Bangladesh	513	....	....	....	....	....	....	1.122	1.107	1.122	1.124	1.146	1.104	1.108	1.111
China, People's Rep.	924	1.090	1.090	1.090	1.090	1.090	1.090	1.090	1.090	1.090	1.090	1.090	1.090	1.090	1.090	1.090
Fiji	819	1.110	1.110	1.110	1.110	1.111	1.110	1.136	1.135	1.134	1.157	1.158	1.159	1.159	1.169	1.137
Hong Kong	532	1.100	1.100	1.100	1.100	1.100	1.100	1.100	1.100	1.100	1.100	1.100	1.100	1.100	1.100	1.100
India	534	1.180	1.180	1.180	1.180	1.184	1.179	1.164	1.142	1.134	1.143	1.132	1.128	1.130	1.123	1.121
Indonesia	536	1.100	1.126	1.107	1.111	1.128	1.127	1.121	1.115	1.115	1.129	1.133	1.130	1.136	1.132	1.121

CIF/FOB Factor

1980	1981	1982	1983	1984	1985	1986	1987	1988	1989	1990	1991	1992	1993	1994		v
1.070	1.073	1.072	1.071	1.069	1.066	1.064	1.057	1.061	1.061	1.061	1.062	1.065	1.066	1.066	World	001
1.052	**1.052**	**1.051**	**1.050**	**1.049**	**1.048**	**1.047**	**1.040**	**1.046**	**1.046**	**1.047**	**1.046**	**1.046**	**1.044**	**1.044**	**Industrial Countries**	**110**
1.048	1.047	1.045	1.046	1.047	1.047	1.046	1.045	1.042	1.042	1.044	1.041	1.040	1.039	1.038	United States	111
1.025	1.025	1.026	1.026	1.024	1.025	1.025	1.025	1.025	1.025	1.025	1.025	1.025	1.025	1.025	Canada	156
1.101	1.108	1.130	1.123	1.142	1.118	1.093	1.087	1.083	1.098	1.080	1.075	1.076	1.073	1.070	Australia	193
1.088	1.080	1.078	1.074	1.079	1.082	1.090	1.025	1.090	1.090	1.090	1.090	1.090	1.090	1.090	Japan	158
1.086	1.079	1.081	1.082	1.082	1.082	1.082	1.082	1.082	1.082	1.082	1.082	1.084	1.086	1.081	New Zealand	196
1.033	1.041	1.038	1.046	1.047	1.047	1.047	1.047	1.047	1.047	1.047	1.047	1.047	1.047	1.047	Austria	122
1.031	1.031	1.031	1.031	1.031	1.031	1.031	1.031	1.031	1.031	1.031	1.031	1.031	1.031	1.031	Belgium-Luxembourg	126
1.048	1.045	1.046	1.046	1.046	1.046	1.046	1.047	1.046	1.047	1.030	1.046	1.093	1.046	1.046	Denmark	128
1.049	1.049	1.050	1.048	1.047	1.045	1.045	1.045	1.045	1.045	1.045	1.045	1.045	1.045	1.045	Finland	172
1.035	1.030	1.083	1.065	1.045	1.040	1.038	1.032	1.032	1.036	1.038	1.041	1.043	1.044	1.044	France	132
1.030	1.033	1.031	1.031	1.030	1.028	1.027	1.025	1.026	1.026	1.024	1.026	1.026	1.028	1.028	Germany	134
1.130	1.130	1.130	1.130	1.130	1.130	1.130	1.130	1.130	1.130	1.130	1.130	1.130	1.130	....	Greece	174
1.100	1.100	1.100	1.100	1.100	1.100	1.100	1.100	1.100	1.100	1.100	1.100	1.100	1.100	1.100	Iceland	176
1.050	1.050	1.050	1.050	1.050	1.050	1.050	1.050	1.050	1.050	1.050	1.050	1.050	1.050	1.050	Ireland	178
1.072	1.068	1.069	1.069	1.069	1.069	1.069	1.069	1.069	1.069	1.069	1.069	1.069	1.069	1.069	Italy	136
1.057	1.060	1.057	1.051	1.057	1.056	1.056	1.056	1.056	1.056	1.056	1.056	1.056	1.056	1.056	Netherlands	138
1.021	1.022	1.020	1.027	1.026	1.026	1.026	1.026	1.029	1.029	1.044	1.049	1.026	1.026	1.026	Norway	142
1.103	1.103	1.103	1.100	1.103	1.103	1.103	1.103	1.103	1.103	1.103	1.103	1.103	1.103	1.103	Portugal	182
1.059	1.058	1.053	1.059	1.060	1.060	1.060	1.060	1.060	1.060	1.060	1.060	1.060	1.060	1.060	Spain	184
1.015	1.017	1.028	1.024	1.023	1.023	1.023	1.023	1.023	1.023	1.023	1.023	1.023	1.023	1.023	Sweden	144
1.035	1.031	1.015	1.011	1.010	1.010	1.010	1.010	1.010	1.010	1.010	1.010	1.010	1.010	1.010	Switzerland	146
1.087	1.079	1.067	1.062	1.045	1.045	1.049	1.036	1.047	1.042	1.046	1.045	1.045	1.019	1.017	United Kingdom	112
1.117	**1.119**	**1.120**	**1.120**	**1.118**	**1.113**	**1.115**	**1.111**	**1.107**	**1.107**	**1.106**	**1.107**	**1.112**	**1.113**	**1.112**	**Developing Countries**	**200**
1.112	**1.117**	**1.114**	**1.114**	**1.116**	**1.129**	**1.127**	**1.122**	**1.116**	**1.117**	**1.115**	**1.125**	**1.118**	**1.133**	....	**Africa**	**605**
1.100	1.100	1.087	1.092	1.114	1.114	1.100	1.100	1.100	1.100	1.100	1.100	1.100	1.100	....	Algeria	612
1.205	1.205	1.205	1.205	1.205	1.205	1.205	1.205	1.205	1.205	1.205	1.205	1.205	1.205	1.205	Benin	638
1.176	1.176	1.177	1.176	1.176	1.176	1.176	1.176	1.176	1.176	1.176	1.176	1.176	1.176	1.176	Botswana	616
1.279	1.282	1.282	1.282	1.282	1.282	1.282	1.282	1.282	1.282	1.282	1.282	1.282	1.282	....	Burkina Faso	748
1.150	1.150	1.150	1.150	1.150	1.150	1.150	1.150	1.150	1.150	1.150	1.150	1.150	1.150	1.150	Burundi	618
1.100	1.100	1.100	1.100	1.100	1.100	1.100	1.100	1.100	1.100	1.100	1.100	1.100	1.100	1.100	Cameroon	622
1.150	1.150	1.150	1.150	1.150	1.150	1.150	1.150	1.150	1.150	1.150	1.150	1.150	1.150	1.150	Cape Verde	624
1.194	1.181	1.107	1.089	1.089	1.089	1.089	1.089	1.089	1.089	1.089	1.089	1.089	1.089	1.089	Central African Rep.	626
1.330	1.330	1.330	1.330	1.330	1.340	1.350	1.350	1.350	1.350	1.350	1.350	1.350	1.350	1.350	Chad	628
1.222	1.228	1.224	1.229	1.229	1.229	1.229	1.229	1.229	1.229	1.229	1.229	1.229	1.229	....	Congo	634
1.223	1.251	1.214	1.244	1.244	1.244	1.244	1.244	1.244	1.244	1.244	1.244	1.244	1.244	1.244	Côte d'Ivoire	662
1.130	1.130	1.130	1.130	1.130	1.130	1.130	1.130	1.130	1.130	1.130	1.130	1.130	1.130	....	Djibouti	611
1.176	1.172	1.165	1.182	1.178	1.186	1.186	1.186	1.186	1.186	1.186	1.186	1.186	1.186	....	Ethiopia	644
1.201	1.203	1.203	1.210	1.211	1.211	1.211	1.211	1.211	1.211	1.211	1.211	1.211	1.211	....	Gabon	646
1.167	1.167	1.167	1.167	1.167	1.167	1.167	1.167	1.167	1.167	1.167	1.167	1.167	1.167	1.167	Gambia, The	648
1.069	1.069	1.069	1.069	1.069	1.069	1.069	1.069	1.069	1.069	1.069	1.069	1.069	1.069	....	Ghana	652
1.149	1.163	1.159	1.164	1.152	1.163	1.163	1.163	1.163	1.163	1.163	1.163	1.163	1.163	....	Kenya	664
1.158	1.169	1.158	1.163	1.155	1.155	1.155	1.155	1.155	1.155	1.155	1.155	1.155	1.155	....	Liberia	668
1.244	1.198	1.171	1.205	1.205	1.205	1.205	1.205	1.205	1.205	1.205	1.205	1.205	1.205	....	Madagascar	674
1.138	1.135	1.138	1.142	1.124	1.667	1.667	1.667	1.667	1.667	1.667	1.667	1.667	1.670	....	Malawi	676
1.428	1.429	1.428	1.429	1.429	1.429	1.429	1.429	1.429	1.429	1.429	1.429	1.429	1.429	1.429	Mali	678
1.130	1.130	1.130	1.130	1.130	1.130	1.130	1.130	1.130	1.130	1.130	1.130	1.130	....	....	Mauritania	682
1.210	1.168	1.169	1.157	1.147	1.162	1.109	1.114	1.103	1.105	1.096	1.098	1.101	1.148	1.148	Mauritius	684
1.136	1.148	1.136	1.135	1.099	1.099	1.099	1.099	1.099	1.099	1.099	1.174	1.099	1.099	1.099	Morocco	686
1.120	1.120	1.120	1.120	1.120	1.120	1.120	1.120	1.120	1.120	1.120	1.120	1.120	1.120	1.120	Mozambique	688
1.246	1.140	1.100	1.100	1.100	1.173	1.173	1.173	1.173	1.173	1.173	1.173	1.173	1.173	1.173	Niger	692
1.107	1.107	1.107	1.107	1.107	1.107	1.107	1.107	1.107	1.107	1.107	1.107	1.107	1.107	....	Nigeria	694
1.514	1.380	1.429	1.418	1.436	1.436	1.436	1.436	1.436	1.436	1.436	1.436	1.436	1.436	....	Rwanda	714
1.144	1.144	1.144	1.144	1.144	1.144	1.144	1.144	1.144	1.144	1.144	1.144	1.144	1.144	1.144	Senegal	722
1.150	1.150	1.150	1.150	1.150	1.150	1.150	1.150	1.150	1.150	1.150	1.150	1.150	1.150	....	Seychelles	718
1.099	1.118	1.136	1.136	1.136	1.136	1.136	1.136	1.136	1.136	1.136	1.136	1.136	1.136	1.136	Sierra Leone	724
1.149	1.149	1.149	1.149	1.149	1.149	1.149	1.149	1.149	1.149	1.149	1.149	1.149	1.149	1.149	Somalia	726
1.051	1.076	1.093	1.081	1.087	1.101	1.105	1.087	1.081	1.088	1.068	1.074	1.172	1.113	1.087	South Africa	199
1.099	1.099	1.099	1.099	1.090	1.066	1.066	1.066	1.066	1.066	1.066	1.066	1.066	1.066	1.066	Sudan	732
1.006	1.016	1.016	1.015	1.014	1.014	1.014	1.014	1.014	1.014	1.014	1.014	1.014	1.014	1.014	Swaziland	734
1.177	1.176	1.176	1.176	1.176	1.176	1.176	1.176	1.176	1.176	1.176	1.176	1.176	1.176	1.176	Tanzania	738
1.217	1.217	1.218	1.211	1.164	1.164	1.164	1.164	1.164	1.164	1.164	1.164	1.164	1.164	1.164	Togo	742
1.058	1.057	1.057	1.072	1.072	1.072	1.072	1.072	1.072	1.072	1.072	1.072	1.072	1.072	1.072	Tunisia	744
1.111	1.113	1.110	1.110	1.110	1.110	1.110	1.110	1.110	1.110	1.110	1.110	1.110	1.110	1.110	Uganda	746
1.160	1.160	1.160	1.160	1.160	1.160	1.160	1.160	1.160	1.160	1.160	1.160	1.160	1.160	1.160	Zaïre	636
1.230	1.185	1.200	1.546	1.224	.906	1.086	1.009	.987	1.017	1.029	1.159	1.200	1.200	1.200	Zambia	754
1.150	1.150	1.150	1.150	1.150	1.150	1.150	1.150	1.150	1.150	1.150	1.150	1.150	1.150	1.150	Zimbabwe	698
1.093	**1.089**	**1.091**	**1.089**	**1.089**	**1.088**	**1.087**	**1.086**	**1.086**	**1.086**	**1.086**	**1.086**	**1.086**	**1.087**	**1.086**	**Asia**	**505**
1.150	1.150	1.150	1.150	1.150	1.150	1.150	1.150	1.150	1.150	1.150	1.150	1.150	1.150	1.150	Afghanistan, Islamic State of	512
1.111	1.111	1.190	1.111	1.111	1.111	1.111	1.111	1.111	1.111	1.101	1.131	1.061	1.113	1.137	Bangladesh	513
1.090	1.090	1.090	1.090	1.090	1.090	1.090	1.090	1.090	1.090	1.090	1.090	1.090	1.090	1.090	China, People's Rep.	924
1.136	1.136	1.136	1.136	1.136	1.136	1.136	1.136	1.136	1.136	1.136	1.136	1.136	1.136	1.136	Fiji	819
1.100	1.100	1.100	1.100	1.100	1.100	1.100	1.100	1.100	1.100	1.100	1.100	1.100	1.100	1.100	Hong Kong	532
1.117	1.117	1.115	1.117	1.117	1.117	1.117	1.117	1.117	1.117	1.117	1.117	1.117	1.122	1.117	India	534
1.120	1.120	1.120	1.120	1.120	1.120	1.120	1.120	1.120	1.120	1.120	1.120	1.120	1.120	1.120	Indonesia	536

CIF/FOB Factor

		1965	1966	1967	1968	1969	1970	1971	1972	1973	1974	1975	1976	1977	1978	1979
Asia (cont.)																
Korea	542	1.092	1.092	1.092	1.092	1.092	1.098	1.099	1.104	1.105	1.094	1.077	1.065	1.067	1.070	1.078
Malaysia	548	1.056	1.056	1.056	1.056	1.075	1.077	1.082	1.080	1.085	1.091	1.092	1.105	1.108	1.113	1.111
Maldives	556	1.100	1.100	1.100	1.100	1.100	1.100	1.100	1.100	1.100	1.100	1.100	1.100	1.100	1.100	1.100
Myanmar	518	1.100	1.100	1.100	1.100	1.100	1.100	1.100	1.100	1.100	1.100	1.100	1.100	1.100	1.100	1.100
Nepal	558	1.050	1.050	1.050	1.050	1.050	1.050	1.050	1.050	1.050	1.050	1.050	1.050	1.050	1.050	1.050
New Caledonia	839	1.140	1.140	1.140	1.140	1.140	1.140	1.140	1.140	1.140	1.140	1.140	1.140	1.140	1.140	1.140
Pakistan	564	1.100	1.100	1.098	1.100	1.097	1.097	1.096	1.085	1.103	1.099	1.095	1.093	1.095	1.102	1.094
Papua New Guinea	853	1.132	1.126	1.120	1.126	1.132	1.132	1.143	1.148	1.167	1.170	1.151	1.132	1.132	1.140	1.145
Philippines	566	1.110	1.120	1.110	1.110	1.108	1.111	1.122	1.114	1.121	1.104	1.092	1.088	1.091	1.087	1.077
Singapore	576	1.064	1.064	1.064	1.064	1.064	1.066	1.067	1.071	1.069	1.069	1.070	1.065	1.064	1.059	1.059
Solomon Islands	813	1.150	1.150	1.150	1.150	1.150	1.150	1.150	1.150	1.150	1.150	1.150	1.150	1.150	1.200	1.200
Sri Lanka	524	1.110	1.110	1.110	1.110	1.110	1.111	1.111	1.111	1.111	1.111	1.111	1.111	1.111	1.111	1.111
Thailand	578	1.110	1.110	1.110	1.108	1.108	1.108	1.110	1.110	1.111	1.111	1.107	1.109	1.114	1.113	1.118
Tonga	866	1.100	1.100	1.100	1.100	1.100	1.100	1.100	1.100	1.100	1.100	1.100	1.100	1.100	1.100	1.100
Vanuatu	846	1.140	1.140	1.140	1.140	1.140	1.140	1.140	1.140	1.140	1.140	1.140	1.140	1.140	1.140	1.140
Western Samoa	862	1.110	1.110	1.110	1.111	1.100	1.100	1.100	1.100	1.100	1.116	1.100	1.100	1.099	1.099	1.099
Europe	170	....	....	....	....	....	....	....	....	....	....	1.195	1.193	1.195	1.195	1.197
Cyprus	423	1.100	1.100	1.103	1.105	1.104	1.105	1.107	1.108	1.107	1.109	1.108	1.111	1.111	1.106	1.110
Czech Republic	935	....	....	....	....	....	1.050	1.050	1.050	1.050	1.050	1.050	1.050	1.050	1.050	1.050
Czechoslovakia	934	....	....	....	....	....	1.050	1.050	1.050	1.050	1.050	1.050	1.050	1.050	1.050	1.050
Hungary	944	1.108e	1.108e	1.108e	1.108e	1.108e	1.108e	1.108e	1.108e	1.108e	1.108e	1.018	1.020	1.017	1.017	1.016
Malta	181	1.118	1.118	1.118	1.118	1.117	1.118	1.118	1.118	1.112	1.111	1.111	1.110	1.111	1.111	1.111
Poland	964	1.039	1.039	1.039	1.039	1.039	1.039	1.039	1.039	1.039	1.039	1.039	1.039	1.034	1.037	1.041
Romania	968	1.080	1.080	1.080	1.080	1.080	1.080	1.080	1.080	1.080	1.080	1.080	1.080	1.080	1.080	1.080
Turkey	186	1.120	1.120	1.123	1.124	1.123	1.123	1.123	1.123	1.124	1.053	1.053	1.053	1.053	1.053	1.053
Yugoslavia, SFR	188	1.091	1.091	1.090	1.084	1.090	1.090	1.090	1.090	1.090	1.090	1.090	1.090	1.091	1.090	1.090
Middle East	405	1.103	1.104	1.109	1.110	1.109	1.108	1.111	1.112	1.110	1.127	1.136	1.139	1.131	1.133	1.128
Bahrain	419	1.120	1.120	1.120	1.120	1.120	1.120	1.120	1.120	1.120	1.120	1.145	1.145	1.145	1.110	1.110
Egypt	469	1.099	1.099	1.099	1.098	1.099	1.099	1.099	1.099	1.099	1.099	1.099	1.099	1.111	1.111	1.111
Iran, I.R. of	429	1.130	1.130	1.130	1.131	1.138	1.137	1.154	1.150	1.160	1.191	1.213	1.188	1.161	1.160	1.160
Iraq	433	1.120	1.120	1.120	1.116	1.106	1.107	1.107	1.108	1.104	1.126	1.113	1.110	1.110	1.110	1.110
Israel	436	1.082	1.079	1.082	1.079	1.085	1.079	1.077	1.070	1.068	1.077	1.082	1.076	1.071	1.070	1.069
Jordan	439	1.120	1.120	1.120	1.120	1.120	1.120	1.120	1.123	1.124	1.123	1.123	1.124	1.123	1.123	1.124
Kuwait	443	1.140	1.140	1.140	1.140	1.140	1.139	1.139	1.139	1.139	1.139	1.139	1.135	1.149	1.159	1.154
Libya	672	1.130	1.130	1.130	1.130	1.127	1.152	1.169	1.158	1.141	1.178	1.160	1.111	1.111	1.111	1.111
Oman	449	1.190	1.190	1.190	1.190	1.190	1.190	1.190	1.190	1.190	1.185	1.177	1.181	1.149	1.155	1.129
Qatar	453	1.100	1.100	1.100	1.100	1.120	1.120	1.120	1.120	1.120	1.120	1.120	1.120	1.120	1.120	1.120
Saudi Arabia	456	1.100	1.100	1.115	1.158	1.122	1.129	1.116	1.126	1.118	1.167	1.152	1.199	1.160	1.170	1.170
Syrian Arab Rep.	463	1.079	1.079	1.079	1.079	1.079	1.081	1.079	1.080	1.080	1.080	1.080	1.080	1.113	1.117	1.090
United Arab Emirates	466	1.100	1.100	1.100	1.100	1.100	1.100	1.100	1.100	1.100	1.100	1.100	1.100	1.100	1.100	1.100
Yemen Arab Rep.	473	1.180	1.180	1.180	1.180	1.180	1.180	1.180	1.180	1.180	1.180	1.177	1.150	1.153	1.150	1.167	1.140
Yemen, P.D. Rep.	459	1.050	1.050	1.050	1.050	1.050	1.050	1.050	1.050	1.050	1.050	1.063	1.075	1.076	1.076	1.049
Western Hemisphere	205	1.124	1.126	1.124	1.123	1.121	1.107	1.166	1.121	1.120	1.110	1.111	1.104	1.103	1.104	1.104
Argentina	213	1.131	1.132	1.130	1.130	1.130	1.130	1.791	1.130	1.123	1.121	1.124	1.106	1.094	1.098	1.109
Bahamas, The	313	1.081	1.081	1.081	1.081	1.081	1.081	1.064	1.064	1.064	1.064	1.064	1.064	1.064	1.064	1.064
Barbados	316	1.100	1.100	1.100	1.101	1.101	1.100	1.101	1.100	1.100	1.100	1.100	1.100	1.087	1.087	1.089
Belize	339	1.100	1.100	1.100	1.100	1.100	1.100	1.100	1.100	1.100	1.100	1.100	1.100	1.100	1.100	1.100
Bolivia	218	1.177	1.173	1.172	1.173	1.173	1.177	1.176	1.298	1.187	1.071	1.050	.986	.959	1.171	1.328
Brazil	223	1.138	1.124	1.131	1.125	1.114	1.114	1.141	1.130	1.131	1.121	1.117	1.116	1.103	1.102	1.087
Chile	228	1.190	1.188	1.133	1.147	1.133	1.130	1.132	1.154	1.175	1.124	1.140	1.135	1.124	1.135	1.140
Colombia	233	1.121	1.133	1.153	1.124	1.140	1.130	1.142	1.135	1.156	1.116	1.111	1.106	1.111	1.110	1.110
Costa Rica	238	1.112	1.111	1.111	1.111	1.112	1.112	1.112	1.112	1.111	1.111	1.111	1.111	1.111	1.111	1.111
Dominican Republic	243	1.120	1.129	1.129	1.130	1.134	1.140	1.150	1.150	1.160	1.200	1.150	1.150	1.150	1.148	1.150
Ecuador	248	1.148	1.147	1.150	1.151	1.157	1.149	1.143	1.159	1.153	1.150	1.143	1.127	1.141	1.136	1.129
El Salvador	253	1.095	1.095	1.093	1.092	1.098	1.100	1.100	1.100	1.115	1.100	1.080	1.087	1.082	1.079	1.082	1.094
Grenada	328	1.100	1.100	1.100	1.100	1.100	1.100	1.100	1.100	1.100	1.100	1.100	1.100	1.100	1.100	1.109
Guatemala	258	1.089	1.100	1.092	1.093	1.091	1.089	1.066	1.119	1.108	1.122	1.094	1.094	1.136	1.091	1.078
Guyana	336	1.106	1.105	1.101	1.100	1.110	1.110	1.108	1.107	1.108	1.100	1.107	1.100	1.100	1.100	1.100
Haiti	263	1.122	1.112	1.140	1.140	1.140	1.140	1.160	1.160	1.160	1.160	1.165	1.185	1.162	1.166	1.152
Honduras	268	1.100	1.102	1.105	1.111	1.110	1.108	1.123	1.128	1.115	1.098	1.098	1.100	1.104	1.102	1.103
Jamaica	343	1.134	1.148	1.158	1.161	1.163	1.163	1.162	1.163	1.163	1.154	1.159	1.153	1.290	1.153	1.136
Mexico	273	1.050	1.050	1.050	1.050	1.050	1.050	1.050	1.050	1.050	1.050	1.050	1.052	1.053	1.052	1.050
Netherlands Antilles	353	1.143	1.143	1.142	1.140	1.139	1.134	1.177	1.170	1.170	1.170	1.170	1.120	1.120	1.120	1.120
Nicaragua	278	1.092	1.095	1.095	1.092	1.096	1.112	1.105	1.108	1.092	1.113	1.109	1.104	1.156	1.103	1.074
Panama	283	1.099	1.094	1.093	1.094	1.054	1.094	1.103	1.098	1.106	1.088	1.094	1.088	1.107	1.115	1.114
Paraguay	288	1.169	1.171	1.168	1.184	1.168	1.194	1.185	1.183	1.167	1.157	1.153	1.222	1.207	1.206	1.190
Peru	293	1.250	1.250	1.250	1.250	1.248	1.248	1.248	1.248	1.249	1.200	1.200	1.200	1.200	1.200	1.200
St. Kitts and Nevis	361	1.100	1.100	1.100	1.100	1.100	1.100	1.100	1.100	1.100	1.100	1.100	1.100	1.100	1.100	1.100
St. Lucia	362	1.100	1.100	1.100	1.100	1.100	1.100	1.100	1.100	1.100	1.100	1.100	1.100	1.100	1.100	1.100
St. Vincent & Grens.	364	1.100	1.100	1.100	1.100	1.100	1.100	1.100	1.100	1.100	1.100	1.100	1.100	1.100	1.100	1.100
Suriname	366	1.090	1.090	1.090	1.090	1.090	1.090	1.090	1.090	1.090	1.090	1.090	1.091	1.111	1.111	1.111
Trinidad and Tobago	369	1.079	1.076	1.090	1.176	1.168	1.160	1.153	1.041	1.047	1.026	1.064	1.054	1.069	1.078	1.094
Uruguay	298	1.180	1.180	1.180	1.176	1.186	1.173	1.185	1.201	1.165	1.159	1.132	1.099	1.086	1.092	1.093
Venezuela	299	1.109	1.109	1.111	1.106	1.114	1.110	1.120	1.116	1.110	1.104	1.127	1.129	1.120	1.110	1.110
Memorandum Items																
Oil Exporting Countries	999	1.108	1.112	1.114	1.116	1.116	1.116	1.121	1.120	1.119	1.136	1.140	1.142	1.131	1.133	1.131
Non-Oil Developing Countries	201	1.099	1.100	1.098	1.099	1.099	1.095	1.117	1.103	1.104	1.099	1.095	1.091	1.091	1.092	1.091

CIF/FOB Factor

1980	1981	1982	1983	1984	1985	1986	1987	1988	1989	1990	1991	1992	1993	1994		
															Asia (cont.)	
1.093	1.071	1.070	1.063	1.063	1.056	1.056	1.056	1.056	1.056	1.056	1.056	1.056	1.056	1.056	Korea	542
1.109	1.108	1.104	1.107	1.106	1.103	1.105	1.105	1.105	1.105	1.105	1.105	1.105	1.105	1.105	Malaysia	548
1.100	1.100	1.100	1.100	1.100	1.100	1.100	1.100	1.100	1.100	1.100	1.100	1.100	1.100	1.100	Maldives	556
1.100	1.100	1.100	1.100	1.100	1.100	1.100	1.100	1.100	1.100	1.100	1.100	1.100	1.100	1.100	Myanmar	518
1.050	1.050	1.050	1.050	1.050	1.050	1.050	1.050	1.050	1.050	1.050	1.050	1.050	1.050	1.050	Nepal	558
1.140	1.140	1.140	1.140	1.140	1.140	1.140	1.140	1.140	1.140	1.140	1.140	1.140	1.140	....	New Caledonia	839
1.095	1.095	1.095	1.095	1.095	1.095	1.095	1.095	1.095	1.095	1.095	1.095	1.095	1.095	....	Pakistan	564
1.150	1.150	1.150	1.150	1.150	1.150	1.150	1.150	1.150	1.150	1.150	1.150	1.150	1.150	1.150	Papua New Guinea	853
1.080	1.067	1.080	1.065	1.085	1.087	1.043	1.067	1.070	1.072	1.068	1.067	1.065	1.067	....	Philippines	566
1.059	1.057	1.064	1.060	1.060	1.060	1.060	1.060	1.060	1.060	1.060	1.060	1.060	1.060	1.060	Singapore	576
1.200	1.200	1.200	1.200	1.200	1.200	1.200	1.200	1.200	1.200	1.200	1.200	1.200	1.200	1.200	Solomon Islands	813
1.111	1.111	1.111	1.111	1.111	1.111	1.111	1.111	1.111	1.111	1.111	1.111	1.111	1.111	1.111	Sri Lanka	524
1.112	1.111	1.109	1.110	1.110	1.108	1.108	1.108	1.108	1.108	1.108	1.108	1.108	1.108	....	Thailand	578
1.100	1.100	1.100	1.097	1.090	1.090	1.090	1.090	1.090	1.090	1.090	1.090	1.090	1.090	....	Tonga	866
1.140	1.140	1.140	1.140	1.140	1.140	1.140	1.140	1.140	1.140	1.140	1.140	1.140	1.140	....	Vanuatu	846
1.099	1.099	1.099	1.099	1.099	1.099	1.099	1.099	1.099	1.099	1.099	1.099	1.099	1.099	1.099	Western Samoa	862
1.201	**1.202**	**1.199**	**1.197**	**1.199**	**1.210**	**1.216**	**1.209**	**1.212**	**1.212**	**1.212**	**1.205**	**1.290**	**1.287**	....	**Europe**	170
1.110	1.111	1.111	1.111	1.101	1.102	1.102	1.102	1.102	1.102	1.102	1.102	1.102	1.102	1.102	Cyprus	423
1.050	1.050	1.050	1.050	1.050	1.050	1.050	1.050	1.050	1.050	1.050	1.050	1.050	1.050	1.050	Czech Republic	935
1.050	1.050	1.050	1.050	1.050	1.050	1.050	1.050	1.050	1.050	1.050	1.050	1.050	1.050	1.050	Czechoslovakia	934
1.018	1.021	1.018	1.016	1.017	1.020	1.018	1.018	1.019	1.007	.995	1.018	1.018	1.018	1.018	Hungary	944
1.111	1.111	1.111	1.099	1.111	1.111	1.111	1.111	1.111	1.111	1.111	1.111	1.111	1.111	1.111	Malta	181
1.047	1.050	1.039	1.034	1.033	1.032	1.029	1.034	1.038	1.037	1.199	1.000	1.150	1.150	1.150	Poland	964
1.080	1.080	1.080	1.080	1.080	1.080	1.080	1.080	1.080	1.081	1.070	1.078	1.082	1.083	1.083	Romania	968
1.053	1.043	1.052	1.054	1.061	1.057	1.057	1.057	1.057	1.057	1.057	1.057	1.057	1.057	1.057	Turkey	186
1.090	1.091	1.091	1.090	1.091	1.091	1.091	1.091	1.091	1.091	1.091	1.091	1.091	1.091	....	Yugoslavia, SFR	188
1.124	**1.126**	**1.129**	**1.132**	**1.128**	**1.105**	**1.104**	**1.101**	**1.102**	**1.104**	**1.103**	**1.104**	**1.105**	**1.106**	....	**Middle East**	405
1.110	1.110	1.110	1.110	1.110	1.110	1.110	1.110	1.110	1.110	1.110	1.110	1.110	1.110	1.110	Bahrain	419
1.111	1.111	1.111	1.111	1.111	1.111	1.111	1.111	1.111	1.111	1.111	1.111	1.111	1.111	....	Egypt	469
1.160	1.160	1.160	1.160	1.160	1.160	1.160	1.160	1.160	1.160	1.160	1.160	1.160	1.160	1.160	Iran, I.R. of	429
1.110	1.110	1.110	1.110	1.110	1.110	1.110	1.110	1.110	1.110	1.110	1.110	1.110	1.110	1.110	Iraq	433
1.063	1.078	1.080	1.082	1.080	1.080	1.080	1.080	1.080	1.080	1.080	1.080	1.080	1.080	1.080	Israel	436
1.124	1.123	1.124	1.123	1.124	1.124	1.124	1.124	1.124	1.124	1.124	1.124	1.124	1.124	1.124	Jordan	439
1.153	1.155	1.155	1.155	1.153	1.153	1.153	1.153	1.153	1.153	1.153	1.153	1.153	1.153	1.153	Kuwait	443
1.111	1.111	1.111	1.111	1.111	1.111	1.111	1.111	1.111	1.111	1.111	1.111	1.111	1.111	1.111	Libya	672
1.124	1.126	1.120	1.118	1.119	1.120	1.120	1.120	1.120	1.120	1.120	1.120	1.120	1.120	1.120	Oman	449
1.120	1.120	1.120	1.120	1.120	1.120	1.120	1.120	1.120	1.120	1.120	1.120	1.120	1.120	1.120	Qatar	453
1.170	1.170	1.170	1.170	1.162	1.078	1.070	1.070	1.070	1.070	1.070	1.070	1.070	1.070	1.070	Saudi Arabia	456
1.029	1.041	1.085	1.093	1.090	1.090	1.090	1.090	1.090	1.090	1.090	1.090	1.090	1.090	1.090	Syrian Arab Rep.	463
1.100	1.100	1.100	1.100	1.100	1.100	1.100	1.100	1.100	1.100	1.100	1.100	1.100	1.100	1.100	United Arab Emirates	466
1.128	1.138	1.110	1.111	1.102	1.113	1.113	1.113	1.113	1.113	1.113	1.113	1.113	1.113	1.113	Yemen Arab Rep.	473
1.049	1.059	1.056	1.060	1.062	1.062	1.062	1.062	1.062	1.062	1.062	1.062	1.062	1.062	1.062	Yemen, P.D. Rep.	459
1.094	**1.095**	**1.095**	**1.099**	**1.097**	**1.091**	**1.100**	**1.101**	**1.097**	**1.091**	**1.091**	**1.089**	**1.093**	**1.089**	**1.083**	**Western Hemisphere**	205
1.124	1.119	1.099	1.092	1.091	1.085	1.093	1.089	1.088	1.088	1.094	1.100	1.092	1.142	1.095	Argentina	213
1.064	1.064	1.064	1.064	1.064	1.064	1.064	1.064	1.064	1.064	1.064	1.064	1.064	1.064	1.064	Bahamas, The	313
1.087	1.087	1.087	1.087	1.087	1.100	1.100	1.100	1.100	1.100	1.100	1.100	1.100	1.100	1.100	Barbados	316
1.100	1.100	1.100	1.100	1.100	1.100	1.100	1.100	1.100	1.100	1.100	1.100	1.100	1.100	1.100	Belize	339
1.158	1.108	1.117	1.163	1.185	1.223	1.195	1.186	1.193	1.085	1.085	1.085	1.085	1.085	....	Bolivia	218
1.089	1.090	1.086	1.092	1.093	1.090	1.114	1.084	1.099	1.088	1.090	1.091	1.122	1.089	1.085	Brazil	223
1.060	1.103	1.095	1.084	1.087	1.052	1.109	1.101	1.095	1.099	1.091	1.101	1.097	1.093	1.087	Chile	228
1.110	1.110	1.110	1.111	1.110	1.110	1.083	1.106	1.104	1.094	1.086	1.087	1.090	1.088	....	Colombia	233
1.111	1.111	1.111	1.107	1.107	1.107	1.107	1.107	1.107	1.107	1.107	1.107	1.107	1.107	1.107	Costa Rica	238
1.150	1.150	1.150	1.150	1.150	1.150	1.150	1.150	1.150	1.150	1.150	1.150	1.150	1.150	1.150	Dominican Republic	243
1.132	1.185	1.143	1.140	1.158	1.144	1.149	1.136	1.129	1.135	1.132	1.134	1.266	1.152	1.131	Ecuador	248
1.100	1.110	1.110	1.110	1.110	1.110	1.110	1.110	1.110	1.110	1.110	1.110	1.110	1.110	1.110	El Salvador	253
1.109	1.113	1.102	1.117	1.117	1.117	1.117	1.117	1.117	1.117	1.117	1.117	1.117	1.117	1.117	Grenada	328
1.085	1.096	1.081	1.068	1.083	1.091	1.095	1.086	1.102	1.105	1.155	1.107	1.086	1.090	....	Guatemala	258
1.100	1.100	1.100	1.100	1.100	1.100	1.100	1.100	1.100	1.100	1.100	1.100	1.100	1.100	1.100	Guyana	336
1.150	1.150	1.150	1.150	1.150	1.150	1.150	1.150	1.150	1.150	1.150	1.150	1.150	1.150	1.150	Haiti	263
1.106	1.103	1.100	1.111	1.102	1.105	1.105	1.105	1.173	1.227	1.173	1.200	1.105	1.105	1.105	Honduras	268
1.134	1.156	1.142	1.139	1.141	1.139	1.139	1.139	1.139	1.139	1.139	1.139	1.139	1.139	1.139	Jamaica	343
1.050	1.047	1.043	1.053	1.049	1.041	1.047	1.047	1.047	1.047	1.047	1.047	1.047	1.047	1.047	Mexico	273
1.120	1.120	1.120	1.120	1.120	1.120	1.120	1.120	1.120	1.120	1.120	1.120	1.120	1.120	1.120	Netherlands Antilles	353
1.079	1.072	1.072	1.061	1.061	1.098	1.096	1.126	1.124	1.124	1.124	1.083	1.124	1.099	....	Nicaragua	278
1.124	1.106	1.116	1.114	1.115	1.123	1.114	1.121	1.115	1.137	1.149	1.113	1.105	....	....	Panama	283
1.189	1.185	1.156	1.141	1.142	1.134	1.135	1.150	1.160	1.150	1.133	1.145	1.149	1.143	....	Paraguay	288
1.200	1.200	1.200	1.200	1.200	1.200	1.200	1.200	1.200	1.200	1.200	1.200	1.200	1.200	1.200	Peru	293
1.100	1.100	1.100	1.100	1.100	1.100	1.100	1.100	1.100	1.100	1.100	1.100	1.100	1.100	1.100	St. Kitts and Nevis	361
1.100	1.100	1.100	1.100	1.100	1.100	1.100	1.100	1.100	1.100	1.100	1.100	1.100	1.100	1.100	St. Lucia	362
1.100	1.100	1.100	1.100	1.100	1.100	1.100	1.100	1.100	1.100	1.100	1.100	1.100	1.100	1.100	St. Vincent & Grens.	364
1.111	1.121	1.121	1.121	1.121	1.123	1.123	1.123	1.123	1.123	1.123	1.123	1.123	1.123	1.123	Suriname	366
1.081	1.083	1.100	1.113	1.113	1.111	1.111	1.111	1.111	1.111	1.111	1.111	1.111	1.111	1.111	Trinidad and Tobago	369
1.090	1.094	1.069	1.065	1.059	1.048	1.048	1.048	1.048	1.048	1.048	1.048	1.048	1.048	1.048	Uruguay	298
1.110	1.110	1.110	1.110	1.110	1.110	1.110	1.110	1.110	1.110	1.110	1.110	1.110	1.110	1.110	Venezuela	299
															Memorandum Items	
1.129	**1.129**	**1.129**	**1.134**	**1.133**	**1.111**	**1.109**	**1.108**	**1.108**	**1.110**	**1.110**	**1.111**	**1.111**	**1.113**	....	Oil Exporting Countries	999
1.089	**1.090**	**1.090**	**1.089**	**1.089**	**1.090**	**1.089**	**1.088**	**1.087**	**1.087**	**1.087**	**1.086**	**1.091**	**1.093**	**1.091**	Non-Oil Developing Countries	201

Export Unit Values

Indices of Unit Values (Prices) In Terms of US Dollars:

		1965	1966	1967	1968	1969	1970	1971	1972	1973	1974	1975	1976	1977	1978	1979
World	001	21.4	21.9	21.9	21.4	22.0	23.1	24.6	26.8	33.0	45.9	49.8	50.3	55.0	60.7	72.4
Industrial Countries	110	23.6	24.2	24.2	23.9	24.7	26.0	27.5	30.1	36.6	45.7	50.5	50.3	54.4	61.6	71.3
United States	111	25.8	26.5	27.1	27.4	28.3	29.9	30.8	31.8	37.1	47.3	52.9	54.7	56.7	60.6	68.9
Canada	156	28.1	29.3	29.9	30.6	31.3	33.3	34.8	36.8	41.6	56.6	60.1	62.9	62.5	63.4	74.7
Australia	193	28.6	30.1	28.2	27.9	28.5	27.7	28.3	34.0	52.2	61.9	59.1	60.2	61.3	65.6	77.4
Japan	158	24.6	24.7	25.8	25.7	26.8	28.1	29.4	33.5	39.7	49.6	50.0	49.7	55.1	66.3	69.6
New Zealand	196	30.8	30.4	26.9	24.1	25.7	25.7	28.3	35.9	52.3	52.6	44.8	48.9	54.8	62.3	74.5
Austria	122	25.2	24.6	24.6	23.6	24.3	26.6	28.7	31.5	39.2	47.9	53.4	51.8	58.0	66.0	74.6
Belgium	126	23.7	24.2	24.1	23.9	25.1	26.5	26.9	30.1	36.8	45.8	50.3	50.7	55.6	63.1	74.3
Denmark	128	23.0	24.0	23.3	22.1	23.1	24.4	25.3	28.4	36.6	43.1	50.2	51.2	55.1	62.3	71.0
Finland	172	17.1	16.9	16.1	15.6	16.2	17.5	18.7	20.0	24.6	35.2	42.5	41.7	46.2	48.2	57.4
France	132	23.8	24.5	24.3	24.1	24.6	25.4	27.0	30.1	37.5	43.7	51.7	50.3	54.1	61.8	71.8
Germany	134	20.3	20.7	20.9	20.7	21.7	22.5	24.4	27.7	34.7	41.7	47.5	45.3	50.4	58.8	67.9
Greece	174	33.1	34.0	33.3	32.6	32.9	33.7	33.6	35.1	44.9	59.7	62.0	59.7	64.9	68.0	72.8
Iceland	176	20.3	20.7	18.3	15.2	17.4	20.7	25.0	26.1	36.5	44.1	40.3	45.6	53.4	58.2	64.6
Ireland	178	23.1	23.3	23.3	21.7	22.8	24.5	26.6	31.2	39.0	43.5	48.9	49.1	54.9	63.2	73.8
Italy	136	20.1	19.9	20.1	20.0	20.9	21.7	22.9	25.1	29.8	37.8	41.9	40.1	45.1	50.2	60.1
Netherlands	138	22.9	22.9	22.6	22.4	22.9	23.8	25.0	27.6	33.9	45.1	50.4	51.1	56.6	63.0	73.8
Norway	142	23.1	23.2	22.9	22.2	22.7	24.8	26.1	27.7	34.7	47.3	54.5	53.5	58.5	62.8	76.1
Portugal	182	....	....	....	....	....	....	....	....	....	....	....	....	....	....	....
Spain	184	28.4	29.6	30.5	29.3	28.7	I29.1	28.9	32.2	40.4	50.2	52.9	48.0	49.7	55.3	69.1
Sweden	144	21.3	21.5	21.7	21.7	22.5	24.4	25.8	28.9	34.7	43.6	54.1	54.7	56.2	58.7	69.7
Switzerland	146	30.4	31.7	32.6	32.9	33.2	34.6	38.1	43.2	53.6	64.6	76.3	78.2	83.2	107.6	119.3
United Kingdom	112	22.6	23.4	23.4	22.0	22.7	24.2	25.9	28.0	30.9	37.5	43.6	42.5	48.8	58.7	71.9
Developing Countries	200	16.9	17.1	17.1	15.7	16.0	16.6	17.8	19.1	25.7	52.0	53.3	56.4	63.4	64.6	85.8
Africa	605	20.3	21.2	21.0	20.3	21.0	21.3	21.5	22.5	30.6	49.7	51.5	53.0	59.8	60.6	76.4
Burkina Faso (1985=100)	748	....	46.5	46.6	45.8	47.4	37.4	39.3	40.7	50.7	69.0	78.1	90.2	98.4	102.0	110.8
Côte d'Ivoire (1985=100)	662	....	....	....	....	....	....	33.7	34.8	50.6	60.2	61.1	73.0	112.4	105.9	120.6
Ethiopia	644	39.3	39.4	35.2	36.5	36.6	45.6	40.7	46.3	58.6	63.2	56.6	100.4	101.8	101.2	110.0
Kenya	664	38.5	38.5	38.5	38.9	39.4	43.3	41.5	43.3	50.6	65.8	73.6	87.3	125.4	113.5	125.1
Liberia (1985=100)	668	44.7	40.2	40.3	38.6	42.2	38.5	42.8	42.8	47.5	62.5	81.8	84.2	98.1	88.3	103.9
Malawi (1985=100)	676	56.9	55.1	51.4	49.7	52.1	55.4	60.3	59.7	65.2	80.6	92.0	97.3	129.7	124.9	116.2
Mauritius	684	17.5	18.2	18.7	15.9	16.2	17.3	19.0	23.1	26.6	63.0	78.5	58.0	57.6	60.5	66.8
Morocco	686	33.5	33.9	33.7	32.5	31.8	32.0	33.1	36.3	43.9	85.2	98.9	71.0	65.6	75.3	95.0
Rwanda	714	35.3	62.9	54.8	54.1	51.2	65.4	55.4	61.3	75.9	79.4	70.4	119.5	188.5	130.5	119.4
Senegal (1985=100)	722	....	32.5	37.2	36.7	30.1	31.6	35.1	37.6	50.3	88.6	84.2	73.7	86.1	101.2	114.9
South Africa	199	33.2	33.5	32.6	32.6	33.8	34.2	33.2	33.2	44.1	56.7	59.0	58.4	63.1	68.1	80.0
Tunisia	744	14.0	14.1	14.6	14.4	14.8	14.9	16.3	18.4	26.6	53.7	58.8	48.8	50.5	56.1	79.0
Asia	505	23.7	23.3	23.0	26.1	27.2	28.6	28.9	30.6	41.5	61.9	59.3	61.3	69.1	72.9	88.3
Bangladesh	513	....	....	....	....	....	....	....	....	....	....	....	....	....	95.8	112.8
Fiji (1985=100)	819	34.2	36.6	30.6	29.6	34.0	36.5	36.3	47.3	59.0	96.0	127.4	101.4	107.7	126.0	126.4
India	534	33.4	32.9	32.2	30.9	32.8	32.8	33.8	36.2	39.4	45.7	55.6	56.0	60.8	72.9	73.5
Indonesia	536	11.1	10.6	10.1	10.1	I11.7	I17.2	17.1	20.6	29.9	65.4	69.1	72.6	81.1	82.2	115.5
Korea	542	28.1	30.6	32.0	33.0	31.3	32.7	32.3	32.7	41.4	52.3	48.6	54.3	59.4	65.7	78.6
Malaysia	548	37.0	34.4	32.9	28.8	31.0	34.8	34.2	32.8	50.4	85.5	77.1	79.3	95.5	99.8	135.4
Myanmar	518	33.9	35.5	39.5	47.1	39.2	30.0	28.7	28.8	59.9	121.0	98.0	92.7	100.4	105.2	108.3
Pakistan	564	....	....	....	....	....	31.9	30.4	31.4	47.6	62.1	54.8	59.7	71.5	81.6	94.5
Papua New Guinea	853	....	....	....	....	....	....	....	....	52.7	81.5	55.0	65.0	86.4	85.3	115.1
Philippines	566	47.9	48.3	49.2	52.3	52.4	53.2	50.6	47.9	69.9	116.1	92.3	80.8	82.0	92.0	113.1
Singapore	576	....	....	....	....	....	....	....	....	....	....	....	....	....	....	85.4
Solomon Islands	813	....	....	....	....	....	51.8	56.9	49.2	71.1	133.6	79.4	116.0	153.9	150.5	217.7
Sri Lanka	524	41.6	39.0	35.6	35.3	35.3	35.3	35.4	35.2	38.6	57.6	51.2	50.0	76.7	79.2	86.6
Thailand	578	31.9	32.9	32.6	32.5	33.6	31.9	30.7	32.0	50.6	75.7	66.8	65.0	66.4	71.9	85.6
Europe	170	....	....	....	....	....	52.6	54.2	58.8	71.3	85.9	92.7	96.5	110.4	118.7	132.0
Cyprus (1985=100)	423	52.6	58.2	55.5	50.9	54.6	58.4	57.8	64.7	81.4	89.5	104.5	99.8	101.0	110.5	124.8
Czechoslovakia	934	....	....	....	....	....	....	....	....	....	40.5	46.4	50.9	50.7	79.1	88.0
Hungary	944	....	....	....	....	....	50.1	50.4	55.6	67.2	77.5	84.8	85.6	89.9	96.5	107.1
Malta (1985=100)	181	45.6	44.5	42.2	39.4	41.0	46.1	46.3	55.0	62.8	76.3	81.3	82.0	85.6	102.0	118.5
Poland	964	....	....	....	....	....	....	....	....	....	....	107.2	116.2	118.7	128.6	138.7
Middle East	405	6.6	6.6	6.7	6.7	6.7	6.7	8.2	8.9	12.2	41.1	42.8	45.6	49.8	50.6	84.9
Iran, I.R. of (1985=100)	429	5.4	5.4	5.4	5.4	5.4	5.4	6.7	7.4	9.9	36.3	38.9	41.4	45.6	45.6	68.9
Iraq (1985=100)	433	5.2	5.2	5.2	5.2	5.2	5.2	6.5	7.3	9.8	35.6	38.1	40.7	44.7	44.6	65.9
Israel	436	I21.3	22.6	22.2	21.9	22.9	22.6	23.4	I25.5	31.8	37.2	38.8	I39.5	46.7	I61.8	I70.9
Jordan	439	....	....	....	....	....	37.7	31.8	29.5	35.6	39.0	80.9	92.4	82.8	83.5	86.6	88.8
Kuwait (1985=100)	443	5.1	5.1	5.1	5.1	5.1	5.1	6.6	7.0	9.7	38.4	38.8	41.2	45.3	44.8	67.7
Libya (1985=100)	672	7.8	7.8	7.8	7.8	7.8	7.8	9.6	10.2	14.5	43.3	38.8	41.0	46.0	45.5	70.0
Oman (1985=100)	449	....	....	6.0	6.0	6.0	6.0	7.3	8.2	11.3	39.6	41.6	43.1	47.6	48.2	74.0
Qatar (1985=100)	453	6.0	6.0	6.0	6.0	6.0	6.0	6.7	7.4	10.1	36.4	38.4	40.3	44.9	44.9	67.2
Saudi Arabia	456	....	....	....	....	....	....	....	....	9.8	34.9	37.5	40.2	43.0	44.1	85.3
Syrian Arab Rep.	463	43.5	35.2	42.7	45.3	45.3	44.0	52.8	61.6	76.9	148.1	127.1	155.7	164.8	176.8	230.7
United Arab Emirates (1985=100)	466	5.8	5.8	5.8	5.8	5.8	5.8	6.9	7.8	10.9	38.7	39.4	42.2	45.6	46.9	70.1
Western Hemisphere	205	24.1	24.3	24.6	I24.4	24.5	26.4	27.9	30.2	I41.4	77.4	70.2	77.2	92.4	I86.4	104.4
Bolivia	218	16.7	15.8	15.0	15.0	16.3	21.1	17.1	17.8	40.8	70.6	66.8	76.0	97.8	114.2	136.8
Brazil	223	34.6	33.2	33.1	32.7	33.6	38.0	36.6	41.4	57.0	71.8	71.8	82.8	101.0	92.9	102.0
Colombia	233	33.3	26.8	32.5	33.1	33.5	I41.6	39.5	44.3	55.7	74.8	73.9	108.2	158.9	132.8	131.0
Costa Rica	238	....	....	....	....	....	....	47.3	49.3	55.6	66.7	75.8	85.7	109.6	102.3	107.1
Dominican Republic	243	39.7	43.2	43.1	36.0	33.6	34.0	21.8	36.4	43.7	66.8	101.8	70.1	78.5	71.3	77.0
Ecuador	248	24.2	21.6	24.4	20.8	16.1	21.9	22.7	19.0	24.1	61.5	60.9	66.0	74.6	70.6	115.5
Guatemala	258	....	....	....	....	....	....	....	....	....	....	....	....	....	80.1	88.1
Guyana	336	240.8	247.1	243.7	245.1	259.1	294.5	314.6	355.4	35.2	64.5	85.6	75.2	89.0	80.1	88.1
Honduras	268	....	....	....	....	....	....	....	....	....	....	53.3	74.4	121.1	104.1	93.9
Panama	283	69.8	70.7	71.7	73.4	69.3	68.0	66.6	71.2	75.2	88.4	101.8	99.7	89.6	89.3	99.3
Paraguay (1985=100)	288	118.6	121.4	110.3	118.8	121.6	130.6	132.7	146.8	184.0	92.4	83.3	104.2	142.5	127.9	133.0
Peru	293	24.8	31.4	29.6	31.9	35.2	35.7	30.3	30.5	49.7	89.7	55.4	62.1	67.7	67.6	105.9
Suriname (1985=100)	366	39.1	39.1	39.1	40.0	41.4	44.3	45.4	45.9	46.0	62.2	83.4	91.4	101.3	109.9	120.3
Trinidad and Tobago	369	....	12.0	12.4	11.7	11.7	11.9	13.5	14.1	18.1	46.2	50.5	52.0	57.5	57.5	76.0
Venezuela	299	9.6	9.4	9.4	9.5	9.2	9.5	12.1	12.8	19.1	49.7	53.1	54.4	61.6	58.7	86.2
Memorandum Items																	
Oil Exporting Countries	999	9.1	9.1	9.1	7.2	7.1	7.3	9.1	9.9	13.9	46.1	48.3	51.3	56.2	56.4	92.6
Non-Oil Developing Countries	201	32.0	32.5	32.6	31.4	32.5	34.1	33.7	35.8	46.3	63.2	63.0	66.3	76.7	78.8	90.8

Export Unit Values

74 *d*

1980	1981	1982	1983	1984	1985	1986	1987	1988	1989	1990	1991	1992	1993	1994		
1990=100																
85.8	**84.1**	**80.8**	**76.9**	**75.0**	**73.5**	**80.2**	**89.0**	**92.1**	**92.9**	**100.0**	**98.7**	**100.9**	**95.8**	**98.5**	**World**	**001**
80.5	**76.9**	**74.1**	**71.5**	**69.3**	**68.9**	**79.0**	**88.5**	**91.6**	**91.7**	**100.0**	**98.9**	**101.6**	**96.3**	**99.4**	**Industrial Countries**	**110**
78.3	85.4	86.4	87.3	88.5	87.8	88.7	90.2	96.6	99.1	100.0	100.9	101.0	101.4	103.6	United States	**111**
87.0	90.2	88.3	88.2	87.8	83.9	80.8	86.1	93.3	99.3	100.0	98.2	95.3	94.4	94.6	Canada	**156**
90.3	92.7	85.5	81.7	79.9	71.4	69.2	75.3	94.0	100.4	100.0	91.2	87.7	82.3	86.0	Australia	**193**
74.9	79.3	73.9	72.3	72.2	71.3	85.4	93.5	101.6	100.9	100.0	107.2	114.0	124.5	134.1	Japan	**158**
82.0	82.6	78.8	74.1	71.4	67.6	69.8	83.4	98.3	102.0	100.0	92.6	93.2	96.2	101.2	New Zealand	**196**
80.9	69.8	68.0	64.5	59.9	58.9	78.1	92.0	94.7	86.2	100.0	94.2	98.0	88.6	....	Austria	**122**
82.1	70.4	65.3	62.7	59.9	59.8	73.5	83.3	86.9	87.5	100.0	96.0	100.5	....	....	Belgium	**126**
75.3	67.9	64.7	61.2	58.2	58.8	74.8	86.8	87.8	86.0	100.0	96.9	101.6	91.4	....	Denmark	**128**
66.6	63.9	60.9	56.5	55.4	55.2	66.1	77.9	86.1	90.1	100.0	94.5	90.9	75.3	....	Finland	**172**
80.3	70.7	66.0	62.4	59.2	59.8	73.3	83.8	87.8	86.8	100.0	96.2	99.6	90.1	98.3	France	**132**
74.9	64.1	62.3	60.0	55.7	55.9	73.3	86.3	89.0	86.9	100.0	96.8	102.1	92.0	92.9	Germany	**134**
91.0	86.2	85.8	78.2	70.5	65.8	69.8	77.2	89.2	89.7	100.0	95.3	97.2	83.0	....	Greece	**174**
69.8	69.8	64.8	61.0	57.4	58.3	72.4	87.8	89.8	83.4	100.0	109.4	109.1	96.2	....	Iceland	**176**
82.3	74.0	72.7	69.0	65.6	66.7	78.6	86.8	95.4	94.6	100.0	96.6	99.3	92.7	....	Ireland	**178**
70.4	65.3	63.3	60.6	57.4	57.1	69.7	81.0	84.8	85.5	100.0	99.4	100.8	87.9	....	Italy	**136**
84.6	78.1	75.4	70.6	67.6	66.7	76.8	84.2	86.2	86.6	100.0	95.8	98.6	90.9	....	Netherlands	**138**
101.7	101.5	96.5	88.3	86.8	85.6	74.7	79.2	82.1	86.8	100.0	92.4	88.7	78.1	....	Norway	**142**
....	....	....	63.2	62.5	62.0	73.0	84.0	90.7	87.9	100.0	98.9	103.6	....	....	Portugal	**182**
77.0	69.3	64.2	57.0	57.6	57.8	67.1	77.9	86.4	89.1	100.0	97.5	99.4	83.7	83.6	Spain	**184**
80.2	73.2	66.1	60.3	59.9	59.7	71.6	82.6	88.3	90.1	100.0	98.7	98.9	81.2	78.1	Sweden	**144**
131.0	114.9	114.9	113.3	106.3	100.0	133.9	167.6	....	....	....	....	....	....	....	Switzerland	**146**
89.9	84.7	78.7	73.8	69.9	71.0	73.1	84.8	92.7	89.0	100.0	100.4	101.7	97.5	101.6	United Kingdom	**112**
116.5	**121.8**	**116.3**	**105.6**	**104.5**	**97.9**	**86.6**	**91.7**	**94.1**	**97.3**	**100.0**	**97.4**	**97.0**	**93.1**	**91.8**	**Developing Countries**	**200**
102.6	**100.2**	**91.5**	**81.4**	**80.0**	**72.3**	**80.4**	**89.4**	**92.9**	**89.2**	**100.0**	**98.2**	**99.4**	**91.8**	....	**Africa**	**605**
121.6	104.3	99.3	97.5	87.5	100.0	91.3	109.0	106.9	....	....	....	....	....	....	Burkina Faso (1985=100)	**748**
134.3	94.3	82.5	81.1	92.8	100.0	108.9	103.2	....	....	....	....	....	....	....	Côte d'Ivoire (1985=100)	**662**
101.2	....	....	107.3	110.4	110.1	146.0	106.9	111.5	107.9	100.0	105.4	....	....	....	Ethiopia	**644**
151.7	136.4	124.1	122.2	135.5	117.2	127.0	103.8	110.8	102.8	100.0	106.5	102.7	102.4	108.9	Kenya	**664**
121.1	100.6	109.1	101.9	100.5	100.0	98.2	93.6	....	....	....	....	....	....	....	Liberia (1985=100)	**668**
120.9	153.5	142.8	131.0	134.7	100.0	103.3	114.1	118.2	128.5	....	....	....	....	....	Malawi (1985=100)	**676**
75.5	70.2	64.0	63.6	60.0	61.2	74.3	86.9	88.5	92.9	100.0	101.0	108.7	104.0	107.0	Mauritius	**684**
117.4	107.2	96.0	86.5	86.6	85.1	92.5	96.1	118.7	93.6	100.0	94.2	92.1	84.6	....	Morocco	**686**
105.2	133.7	I 141.3	164.3	157.2	159.5	197.0	115.6	....	118.8	100.0	86.4	65.3	....	....	Rwanda	**714**
113.2	120.7	96.6	92.8	103.1	100.0	90.9	99.6	....	....	....	....	....	....	....	Senegal (1985=100)	**722**
99.3	97.5	85.5	93.3	79.9	66.8	75.2	87.6	90.3	94.0	100.0	98.9	101.2	96.6	....	South Africa	**199**
105.1	108.0	98.9	89.2	85.1	79.6	75.0	81.9	84.6	87.0	100.0	92.6	94.7	84.2	....	Tunisia	**744**
104.5	**103.4**	**98.0**	**93.6**	**96.5**	**89.7**	**81.8**	**87.2**	**94.3**	**97.9**	**100.0**	**99.7**	**99.6**	**97.7**	**98.6**	**Asia**	**505**
131.4	99.2	88.2	89.9	117.3	130.6	93.8	92.7	105.5	101.9	100.0	98.9	....	....	....	Bangladesh	**513**
173.7	146.3	131.3	127.3	118.3	100.0	136.7	170.2	141.5	....	....	....	....	....	....	Fiji (1985=100)	**819**
79.8	75.2	78.3	78.1	79.4	81.6	81.0	82.5	99.6	102.0	100.0	97.2	97.3	92.9	....	India	**534**
168.8	169.0	165.0	146.4	144.6	124.5	82.9	81.4	77.4	82.2	100.0	87.9	84.3	77.3	47.8	Indonesia	**536**
82.1	84.7	81.8	I 78.7	81.4	78.4	80.0	88.1	I 100.1	101.9	100.0	100.6	99.0	99.4	101.1	Korea	**542**
158.0	148.4	136.6	130.1	140.7	119.0	79.1	96.7	102.0	101.1	100.0	100.8	....	....	....	Malaysia	**548**
130.8	131.4	102.8	96.9	98.1	99.4	96.9	89.9	91.3	105.4	100.0	102.3	91.3	83.0	89.7	Myanmar	**518**
100.8	104.6	95.9	93.0	96.7	85.0	98.8	103.8	101.8	96.5	100.0	94.5	92.1	89.5	96.4	Pakistan	**564**
126.9	98.8	89.0	91.6	94.3	87.2	88.6	103.5	125.8	106.4	100.0	99.5	99.9	110.2	....	Papua New Guinea	**853**
117.8	115.2	95.7	I 100.5	110.9	97.4	86.5	95.1	104.9	102.9	100.0	101.9	....	....	....	Philippines	**566**
107.0	112.5	107.6	103.8	98.8	94.0	81.6	87.2	90.0	I 92.5	100.0	99.3	98.4	96.9	98.4	Singapore	**576**
244.6	187.1	171.2	147.9	199.7	162.6	97.3	100.3	116.9	134.8	100.0	50.6	....	....	....	Solomon Islands	**813**
91.0	85.0	76.7	87.1	102.6	85.3	73.7	81.3	88.0	91.5	100.0	98.6	105.5	105.7	103.7	Sri Lanka	**524**
100.9	97.5	86.0	87.3	84.1	75.2	79.8	87.4	96.3	97.5	100.0	103.6	105.3	106.6	....	Thailand	**578**
146.5	**149.2**	**147.1**	**143.7**	**129.2**	**122.1**	**133.4**	**138.7**	**131.0**	**127.0**	**100.0**	**103.5**	....	....	....	**Europe**	**170**
136.1	134.1	116.6	110.3	105.9	100.0	110.1	121.4	....	....	....	....	....	....	....	Cyprus (1985=100)	**423**
97.0	112.1	109.8	107.7	91.6	90.3	103.5	113.4	110.9	111.9	100.0	57.9	....	....	....	Czechoslovakia	**934**
115.6	113.7	107.6	97.3	90.4	89.2	98.7	99.3	98.6	97.2	100.0	110.7	....	....	....	Hungary	**944**
128.3	122.9	118.8	106.3	101.4	100.0	122.3	145.8	168.5	167.4	....	....	....	....	....	Malta (1985=100)	**181**
146.0	135.5	131.8	122.5	113.7	109.8	109.9	106.0	111.1	107.0	100.0	106.7	....	100.7	103.4	Poland	**964**
138.9	**156.3**	**151.7**	**132.7**	**129.6**	**128.1**	**80.7**	**85.0**	**72.2**	**81.7**	**100.0**	**86.4**	**87.2**	**79.1**	**80.2**	**Middle East**	**405**
121.9	130.0	109.2	101.2	99.3	100.0	48.9	64.4	55.1	58.4	....	....	....	....	....	Iran, I.R. of (1985=100)	**429**
107.2	125.5	118.4	104.4	100.7	100.0	54.0	59.8	49.2	....	....	....	....	....	....	Iraq (1985=100)	**433**
I 79.9	I 77.1	73.0	I 71.1	I 69.9	69.1	71.4	76.1	86.8	92.3	I 100.0	100.4	101.2	101.7	100.2	Israel	**436**
106.4	110.0	112.7	100.0	102.9	97.2	94.4	90.6	95.4	97.0	100.0	108.5	104.7	103.8	....	Jordan	**439**
109.2	128.4	118.2	101.8	99.9	100.0	73.5	60.8	46.7	....	....	....	....	....	....	Kuwait (1985=100)	**443**
119.5	132.8	117.8	102.5	100.0	100.0	....	....	....	....	....	....	....	....	....	Libya (1985=100)	**672**
119.3	135.5	127.8	112.3	105.9	100.0	49.8	63.9	50.1	....	....	....	....	....	....	Oman (1985=100)	**449**
108.6	127.1	118.7	102.6	100.9	100.0	....	....	....	....	....	....	....	....	....	Qatar (1985=100)	**453**
142.2	160.4	163.9	142.2	138.7	135.9	97.0	85.2	68.8	79.0	100.0	81.1	84.9	73.8	74.1	Saudi Arabia	**456**
299.6	332.6	290.7	272.7	278.7	272.7	200.8	185.9	62.0	77.0	100.0	98.0	68.0	67.0	....	Syrian Arab Rep.	**463**
111.7	128.9	123.1	107.6	104.6	100.0	49.3	62.7	48.7	....	....	....	....	....	....	United Arab Emirates (1985=100)	**466**
130.1	**135.9**	**124.4**	**I 115.9**	**106.4**	**95.5**	**85.9**	**85.8**	**I 93.0**	**95.9**	**100.0**	**89.9**	....	....	....	**Western Hemisphere**	**205**
176.1	176.5	171.2	174.2	171.0	166.0	115.0	108.8	102.4	115.0	100.0	96.2	76.2	64.2	....	Bolivia	**218**
108.1	101.7	95.6	90.4	92.2	87.0	92.9	92.9	102.0	101.0	100.0	96.0	....	....	....	Brazil	**223**
146.0	130.6	129.6	130.0	138.8	129.8	146.9	112.8	117.9	96.2	100.0	92.9	78.1	....	....	Colombia	**233**
120.9	110.6	108.2	107.1	109.1	108.8	122.5	103.5	106.5	104.0	100.0	104.1	104.4	106.6	....	Costa Rica	**238**
91.7	117.6	76.2	71.6	83.1	71.1	75.6	63.3	89.7	104.1	100.0	94.8	82.3	75.1	87.1	Dominican Republic	**243**
161.8	157.0	149.3	129.0	125.5	127.8	76.3	86.1	72.4	85.2	100.0	87.5	96.6	75.0	83.7	Ecuador	**248**
....	....	....	....	....	....	....	168.6	165.0	154.2	100.0	70.6	67.0	67.6	....	Guatemala	**258**
117.8	1,113.1	1,043.5	955.3	94.6	81.9	83.7	94.2	97.6	90.3	100.0	121.5	102.4	78.3	76.3	Guyana	**336**
112.1	94.5	92.8	86.5	95.5	98.3	127.3	100.2	107.5	105.0	100.0	98.3	77.0	78.4	89.4	Honduras	**268**
109.9	109.7	99.2	110.2	110.8	106.1	93.2	103.1	93.5	95.3	100.0	100.7	....	....	....	Panama	**283**
138.5	146.8	136.5	149.1	172.3	100.0	74.0	109.4	153.2	156.5	....	....	....	....	....	Paraguay (1985=100)	**288**
139.2	116.8	100.3	104.5	95.4	84.8	69.2	85.4	95.1	104.2	100.0	87.6	87.2	74.1	84.4	Peru	**293**
148.4	160.6	155.0	138.2	130.4	100.0	97.1	102.9	134.3	....	....	....	....	....	....	Suriname (1985=100)	**366**
121.4	133.9	128.2	127.3	126.5	118.3	78.4	82.2	73.1	83.6	100.0	....	....	....	....	Trinidad and Tobago	**369**
128.6	142.3	132.3	122.0	105.3	98.8	57.2	60.8	64.8	81.1	100.0	77.3	74.4	65.6	....	Venezuela	**299**
															Memorandum Items	
150.8	**168.3**	**162.3**	**141.6**	**136.6**	**131.0**	**79.2**	**80.9**	**71.4**	**80.8**	**100.0**	**83.5**	**83.3**	**75.1**	**63.5**	**Oil Exporting Countries**	**999**
104.5	**101.2**	**95.5**	**92.0**	**91.9**	**85.3**	**85.0**	**90.8**	**96.3**	**98.3**	**100.0**	**100.1**	**99.7**	**96.6**	....	**Non-Oil Developing Countries**	**201**

Import Unit Values
75 d

Indices of Unit Values (Prices) In Terms of US Dollars:

		1965	1966	1967	1968	1969	1970	1971	1972	1973	1974	1975	1976	1977	1978	1979
World	001	22.7	23.1	22.9	22.8	23.3	24.2	25.7	27.7	34.2	47.9	52.3	52.9	57.8	63.4	75.1
Industrial Countries	110	22.2	22.6	22.5	22.3	22.8	23.8	25.3	27.3	33.7	47.2	51.7	52.2	57.1	62.7	74.3
United States	111	19.5	20.1	20.2	20.4	21.1	22.5	23.7	25.4	30.1	44.6	48.6	50.2	54.3	58.6	69.9
Canada	156	25.9	26.3	26.4	27.0	27.7	29.1	30.8	32.1	34.2	43.2	47.7	50.5	53.6	56.6	64.7
Australia	193	19.0	19.3	19.4	19.1	19.7	20.4	21.9	24.0	28.6	40.3	46.3	47.5	52.0	57.2	67.6
Japan	158	22.2	22.3	22.2	22.0	21.8	23.2	24.2	25.7	31.7	51.5	54.8	56.2	60.1	63.0	78.7
New Zealand	196	25.5	25.5	25.4	24.6	25.5	27.1	29.1	31.9	38.0	49.5	56.5	57.6	61.8	68.5	76.1
Austria	122	24.4	24.6	24.1	23.1	23.9	25.4	27.6	29.9	36.6	45.7	50.9	50.5	56.9	64.7	74.1
Belgium	126	23.4	23.7	23.5	23.5	24.1	25.2	26.0	28.7	34.7	44.3	49.5	50.3	55.0	62.5	73.2
Denmark	128	21.3	21.5	21.4	21.0	21.4	22.6	24.2	25.8	32.9	44.8	49.1	50.5	55.5	60.4	72.1
Finland	172	18.0	18.0	17.6	17.4	17.8	19.2	20.8	22.2	27.0	39.3	43.9	44.7	49.7	53.7	65.9
France	132	24.7	25.2	25.3	24.5	24.8	25.7	26.7	29.6	36.0	48.9	53.9	53.2	58.1	63.8	74.6
Germany	134	21.4	21.3	20.7	20.7	21.7	22.1	23.4	25.9	33.1	43.9	47.5	47.5	53.3	59.8	73.0
Greece	174	25.8	26.1	25.9	26.1	26.1	27.2	28.2	30.6	37.0	53.7	59.3	58.1	60.3	64.9	79.0
Iceland	176	22.6	23.0	22.3	19.6	21.0	22.0	23.5	24.8	29.9	40.2	43.7	44.1	47.6	51.8	63.2
Ireland	178	22.6	22.6	22.2	20.9	21.7	23.2	24.9	26.7	29.6	41.3	47.2	45.6	51.8	58.6	71.5
Italy	136	18.1	18.3	18.5	18.6	18.7	19.4	20.5	22.4	29.3	44.9	47.3	46.8	51.1	55.8	68.0
Netherlands	138	21.0	21.2	21.0	20.4	21.0	22.4	24.0	26.1	32.2	45.3	50.4	51.1	56.6	63.1	75.9
Norway	142	25.2	25.3	25.1	24.5	25.0	26.9	28.6	30.9	37.6	49.2	55.5	56.7	62.8	67.0	76.6
Portugal	182	31.3	32.5	33.4	34.3	34.3	34.0	35.0	37.7	47.6	60.2	66.7	67.2	73.6	76.8	83.8
Spain	184	25.9	25.4	24.6	I23.5	24.0	I25.3	26.9	28.9	36.5	52.5	56.5	53.6	56.0	60.8	71.3
Sweden	144	22.1	22.8	22.8	23.0	23.4	25.2	26.9	29.4	36.1	48.5	54.4	55.0	59.5	64.5	78.0
Switzerland (1985=100)	146	33.0	33.8	34.2	34.2	34.9	37.1	39.7	43.8	56.5	72.0	79.3	78.0	85.8	102.7	117.2
United Kingdom	112	22.2	22.5	22.4	21.8	22.4	23.5	24.9	26.7	33.2	45.9	49.3	49.0	54.9	62.0	72.9
Developing Countries	200	26.6	27.0	26.8	26.7	27.0	27.7	29.0	30.7	38.2	53.5	58.4	59.0	64.3	70.0	82.7
Africa	605	23.6	23.7	23.6	23.4	23.4	23.9	25.3	27.7	33.8	45.4	52.0	51.7	54.7	62.8	77.2
Burkina Faso (1985=100)	748	....	37.6	38.9	37.6	38.8	35.3	38.6	46.2	55.8	64.9	84.3	85.9	91.8	97.7	111.8
Côte d'Ivoire (1985=100)	662	....	....	....	....	....	....	33.5	40.3	47.8	59.6	75.2	77.3	80.1	91.8	110.5
Kenya	664	15.8	15.8	15.8	16.0	16.2	16.6	18.0	20.3	24.5	36.0	43.3	45.2	49.4	55.8	66.8
Liberia (1985=100)	668	....	....	....	....	....	....	32.8	36.7	42.0	61.6	66.9	64.2	78.9	80.9	93.6
Malawi (1985=100)	676	....	....	33.9	31.5	32.0	31.6	33.7	36.4	41.5	54.6	64.6	69.9	78.6	84.5	99.4
Mauritius	684	22.6	23.1	23.2	23.7	22.9	22.7	25.3	27.4	35.0	54.5	58.3	59.0	65.0	73.9	86.6
Morocco	686	31.8	28.2	26.5	25.9	26.9	27.5	29.0	34.4	43.0	58.9	63.9	57.9	44.5	53.9	75.9
Senegal (1985=100)	722	....	44.2	46.3	35.5	33.1	31.7	37.2	42.1	54.3	71.9	85.5	80.7	85.4	91.8	109.4
South Africa	199	21.1	22.1	21.7	20.9	21.5	22.1	22.8	24.4	29.5	38.9	44.7	46.4	52.4	60.2	76.7
Tunisia (1985=100)	744	45.7	47.4	47.4	48.1	48.8	50.7	52.9	58.8	70.6	91.1	109.1	100.4	102.8	108.3	119.1
Asia	505	26.4	26.7	26.4	26.3	26.3	26.7	27.5	28.6	37.8	56.9	60.8	60.1	62.6	67.5	80.9
Bangladesh	513	....	....	....	....	....	....	....	....	....	....	....	....	92.0	92.0	....
India	534	30.9	29.5	29.4	27.9	29.0	28.7	28.2	28.4	28.7	39.5	66.3	72.2	71.7	70.2	80.4
Korea	542	28.7	28.0	28.3	28.0	27.6	28.6	28.5	29.0	38.6	60.0	61.7	60.5	61.8	65.3	79.8
Malaysia (1985=100)	548	27.8	28.1	27.5	28.6	28.9	30.1	31.0	35.2	47.1	67.7	72.0	69.0	73.0	79.6	90.3
Pakistan	564	....	....	....	....	....	23.5	25.7	24.1	29.5	50.7	57.5	55.0	56.9	60.0	67.9
Philippines	566	22.8	23.2	23.7	25.9	26.4	27.3	27.9	29.2	37.7	61.9	64.2	63.5	70.5	71.9	84.6
Sri Lanka	524	17.0	17.0	16.7	17.3	18.6	19.8	21.1	22.2	27.6	46.5	51.5	38.6	44.9	47.2	71.9
Thailand	578	19.5	19.0	18.9	18.0	17.6	19.0	20.0	21.1	24.9	40.7	45.4	47.9	51.5	55.7	64.1
Europe	170	36.5	36.1	36.2	35.4	36.9	39.6	41.1	44.0	55.6	73.6	78.6	80.3	94.4	101.8	116.2
Cyprus (1985=100)	423	49.2	49.8	49.1	44.3	47.0	49.9	53.1	57.9	69.2	89.1	97.2	88.9	94.1	103.3	121.5
Czechoslovakia	934	....	....	....	....	....	....	....	....	34.0	38.8	44.5	45.8	69.7	75.0	84.9
Hungary	944	....	....	....	....	....	37.9	38.8	42.9	52.5	67.1	77.3	76.3	83.0	89.6	101.3
Malta (1985=100)	181	33.4	32.6	34.1	31.0	31.6	33.5	35.3	41.0	52.9	68.9	73.8	72.5	79.4	92.4	112.1
Poland	964	....	....	....	....	....	....	....	....	....	....	111.2	116.6	122.6	132.7	147.1
Middle East	405	22.1	23.0	23.1	22.6	23.1	23.7	24.9	27.1	34.3	47.0	50.9	51.9	54.0	63.8	77.6
Israel	436	I21.1	21.5	21.5	21.1	21.9	22.3	22.8	I24.3	31.4	42.6	44.5	I43.5	47.4	I58.2	I72.3
Jordan	439	....	....	....	....	29.3	31.8	37.0	40.4	45.9	59.5	82.3	77.2	79.4	83.1	90.6
Syrian Arab Rep.	463	32.2	35.2	35.6	34.2	33.2	34.2	39.7	47.6	58.5	84.2	94.4	114.3	103.3	110.4	137.1
Western Hemisphere	205	29.1	29.6	29.6	I30.2	30.4	31.1	33.1	34.0	I41.1	58.2	63.2	65.9	69.8	I74.0	85.0
Brazil	223	23.8	24.4	24.9	25.6	25.1	25.6	26.2	26.2	35.5	52.0	56.5	58.1	60.4	64.6	77.3
Chile	228	28.6	25.5	23.7	24.3	25.3	25.4	30.1	30.0	35.8	69.2	63.9	72.5	87.9	80.6	97.1
Colombia	233	....	....	....	....	....	38.8	39.4	42.0	49.7	63.8	68.2	71.2	75.3	84.4	93.1
Costa Rica	238	38.2	38.5	40.3	40.4	40.7	41.9	I41.7	44.3	49.1	67.3	73.6	70.0	73.7	78.0	89.5
Guatemala	258	....	....	....	....	....	....	....	....	....	....	....	....	....	....	....
Trinidad and Tobago	369	....	9.6	9.5	9.7	10.1	10.5	11.7	13.1	15.0	32.6	35.4	37.2	38.9	40.6	46.0
Venezuela	299	43.8	45.7	47.0	47.9	48.9	50.3	52.9	55.9	60.2	70.3	79.1	84.8	91.1	97.5	104.5
Memorandum Items																
Oil Exporting Countries	999	43.8	45.7	46.9	47.8	48.8	50.3	52.9	56.5	60.3	70.3	79.1	84.8	91.0	97.4	104.4
Non-Oil Developing Countries	201	26.2	26.5	26.3	26.2	26.5	27.1	28.3	30.0	37.7	53.3	58.1	58.4	63.6	69.2	82.0

Import Unit Values

75 d

1980	1981	1982	1983	1984	1985	1986	1987	1988	1989	1990	1991	1992	1993	1994		
1990=100																
91.8	90.2	85.7	81.9	79.9	78.2	80.9	88.6	91.0	92.0	100.0	98.4	99.1	92.8	....	World	001
90.7	88.2	83.6	79.3	77.3	76.0	79.5	88.0	90.2	91.1	100.0	98.2	99.2	92.4	94.7	Industrial Countries	110
87.6	92.4	90.9	87.2	88.8	86.5	83.6	89.7	94.0	96.9	100.0	100.0	100.8	100.1	101.8	United States	111
78.2	87.0	88.1	87.8	88.4	86.5	84.7	87.6	92.8	96.7	100.0	100.4	99.2	98.6	99.1	Canada	156
87.2	89.6	84.4	81.4	81.3	76.8	80.3	89.2	97.2	97.4	100.0	100.8	99.3	99.4	105.1	Australia	193
105.7	109.2	100.9	96.0	93.4	89.7	80.4	86.4	91.4	95.0	100.0	97.4	96.3	97.0	97.2	Japan	158
94.0	95.2	91.9	88.7	85.5	82.5	85.1	91.7	101.1	99.6	100.0	97.7	97.1	97.1	103.1	New Zealand	196
84.7	76.0	71.2	66.8	62.3	62.5	77.8	89.8	92.0	88.2	100.0	97.6	102.2	93.4	....	Austria	122
84.5	76.0	70.6	67.7	64.8	64.0	73.1	82.6	86.3	86.4	100.0	96.5	99.2	....	....	Belgium	126
82.1	76.0	71.6	67.3	64.3	64.2	76.5	86.0	88.7	87.6	100.0	97.3	99.7	89.2	....	Denmark	128
80.1	77.5	72.7	67.3	65.1	65.2	71.3	80.9	87.1	87.9	100.0	96.8	96.7	86.0	....	Finland	172
89.0	82.0	76.7	71.5	68.5	67.4	73.6	83.5	86.6	87.0	100.0	95.5	97.9	87.0	92.1	France	132
86.1	78.8	73.8	69.9	66.4	65.8	75.1	85.1	87.8	88.2	100.0	99.0	102.0	91.1	94.6	Germany	134
93.7	83.1	85.9	75.4	73.3	69.2	77.0	77.8	91.3	89.2	100.0	95.6	97.3	81.9	....	Greece	174
70.6	69.3	64.0	62.9	61.1	61.4	70.2	80.6	86.1	85.1	100.0	101.9	106.3	98.7	....	Iceland	176
85.1	79.5	75.8	69.3	66.9	66.9	75.6	83.4	91.1	90.2	100.0	99.5	103.1	94.1	....	Ireland	178
85.0	82.9	78.4	73.1	70.3	69.6	73.3	83.2	86.2	88.0	100.0	95.8	95.9	....	....	Italy	136
88.0	80.7	77.1	72.9	68.3	66.7	74.6	84.7	86.5	88.6	100.0	97.0	100.7	90.8	....	Netherlands	138
88.2	81.3	75.6	70.0	63.8	64.5	74.9	84.4	90.0	90.0	100.0	95.0	97.2	85.8	....	Norway	142
96.0	90.1	82.0	76.8	78.5	72.2	75.2	84.8	88.8	87.5	100.0	98.9	100.6	....	....	Portugal	182
90.9	91.1	86.2	80.2	80.3	76.9	77.4	84.7	88.5	89.0	100.0	95.2	92.2	79.6	80.6	Spain	184
89.8	82.1	75.1	69.4	66.6	66.2	72.6	84.5	90.5	90.1	100.0	97.3	98.4	80.9	75.8	Sweden	144
140.6	116.6	111.2	108.3	100.9	100.0	122.8	142.6	....	....	....	....	....	....	....	Switzerland (1985=100)	146
87.6	81.9	76.8	72.7	69.2	69.9	76.1	87.0	94.0	89.9	100.0	100.3	100.7	94.2	99.3	United Kingdom	112
101.8	105.0	100.2	98.2	95.4	90.7	87.8	92.4	95.2	96.9	100.0	100.2	99.4	96.5	....	Developing Countries	200
95.6	93.3	87.6	86.9	81.8	75.5	81.5	87.6	91.0	89.5	100.0	98.1	98.8	94.4	....	Africa	605
118.9	111.0	111.7	105.5	95.6	100.0	124.5	127.8	127.7	....	....	....	....	....	....	Burkina Faso (1985=100)	748
126.5	122.8	120.9	114.2	108.2	100.0	113.0	129.5	....	....	....	....	....	....	76.0	Côte d'Ivoire (1985=100)	662
88.2	92.6	88.2	92.6	87.5	90.8	87.2	87.2	89.0	92.7	100.0	92.8	91.7	82.3	76.4	Kenya	664
109.0	98.3	103.6	98.6	107.9	100.0	105.0	111.5	....	....	....	....	....	....	....	Liberia (1985=100)	668
121.9	126.7	116.5	116.7	115.0	100.0	118.7	135.7	145.3	154.8	....	....	....	....	....	Malawi (1985=100)	676
103.9	95.5	97.1	88.5	84.2	82.8	76.9	83.3	87.1	91.3	100.0	99.4	102.1	99.4	104.7	Mauritius	684
93.3	90.6	80.9	78.7	77.1	75.0	74.1	79.0	82.3	88.4	100.0	91.2	88.4	89.1	....	Morocco	686
143.3	124.9	116.7	110.1	105.3	100.0	93.9	102.9	....	....	....	....	....	....	....	Senegal (1985=100)	722
99.7	99.5	96.9	101.4	85.0	72.0	81.7	95.8	94.1	92.1	100.0	102.9	106.0	100.5	....	South Africa	199
134.9	130.4	118.1	107.2	100.2	100.0	109.3	109.6	....	....	....	....	....	....	....	Tunisia (1985=100)	744
100.8	102.7	95.0	91.9	92.6	87.6	79.9	84.6	92.3	95.9	100.0	99.3	98.3	96.1	99.7	Asia	505
101.9	97.9	91.2	98.3	99.2	97.9	98.8	106.7	97.0	97.0	100.0	114.5	....	....	....	Bangladesh	513
94.7	98.1	91.9	88.0	72.4	85.5	82.9	70.0	87.3	91.8	100.0	88.7	83.9	70.0	....	India	534
96.0	101.2	93.7	I 89.3	90.4	86.6	81.3	87.3	I 96.5	98.5	100.0	100.0	98.4	94.7	95.2	Korea	542
108.9	117.1	115.6	111.4	107.1	100.0	84.8	87.9	....	....	....	....	....	....	....	Malaysia (1985=100)	548
84.7	97.3	91.9	83.3	85.4	78.6	71.6	83.0	89.3	92.0	100.0	97.9	95.2	90.8	97.8	Pakistan	564
104.9	116.5	99.6	I 100.1	113.1	106.4	87.6	88.0	87.3	92.8	100.0	95.7	....	....	....	Philippines	566
86.0	85.7	82.5	76.2	73.8	74.9	67.2	72.1	82.7	87.5	100.0	100.6	103.5	101.7	104.7	Sri Lanka	524
79.4	88.0	85.6	80.8	79.3	75.6	72.4	80.1	89.8	94.7	100.0	104.7	105.7	106.3	....	Thailand	578
133.8	138.6	136.9	137.1	127.7	120.5	131.4	134.0	112.9	103.8	100.0	123.1	....	....	....	Europe	170
140.5	131.4	117.7	107.9	103.3	100.0	100.9	103.6	....	....	....	....	....	....	....	Cyprus (1985=100)	423
93.4	111.9	111.5	113.8	105.1	100.0	102.5	118.2	126.3	120.0	115.1	100.0	82.8	....	....	Czechoslovakia	934
108.9	108.0	104.7	97.1	92.2	91.8	105.4	105.0	101.8	97.7	100.0	123.7	....	....	....	Hungary	944
125.7	124.0	117.6	112.1	103.2	100.0	114.8	131.4	138.8	136.0	....	....	....	....	....	Malta (1985=100)	181
155.0	142.9	138.0	134.7	124.5	117.5	115.5	107.4	111.5	92.1	100.0	120.3	....	96.0	96.5	Poland	964
97.0	104.0	96.4	97.0	96.0	90.2	91.3	98.3	89.2	92.6	100.0	96.2	95.2	92.0	94.2	Middle East	405
I 88.8	I 85.9	78.6	I 75.0	I 75.0	73.4	73.0	80.3	87.0	92.9	I 100.0	95.1	95.2	92.0	93.8	Israel	436
113.3	124.1	118.4	105.0	109.8	104.1	88.4	95.0	90.8	85.8	100.0	97.7	92.4	92.2	....	Jordan	439
178.0	231.4	217.2	251.0	235.0	197.6	235.0	237.4	102.0	99.0	100.0	101.0	98.0	93.0	....	Syrian Arab Rep.	463
105.3	116.0	115.5	I 114.4	103.9	101.5	91.0	95.3	I 103.6	102.8	100.0	94.8	....	....	....	Western Hemisphere	205
99.0	110.0	106.4	100.8	95.7	90.2	70.0	81.8	89.1	96.0	100.0	92.6	....	....	....	Brazil	223
127.7	133.3	113.2	118.9	122.0	115.7	103.5	100.7	98.2	99.1	100.0	98.2	....	....	....	Chile	228
102.1	108.3	110.7	108.3	111.7	105.5	98.1	97.6	101.5	104.3	100.0	95.7	85.7	....	....	Colombia	233
101.5	108.5	105.4	101.2	99.7	96.1	86.1	88.6	91.3	95.7	100.0	97.6	101.9	102.2	....	Costa Rica	238
....	....	....	....	....	....	....	178.8	183.1	177.6	100.0	85.8	106.7	94.4	....	Guatemala	258
69.0	78.0	88.3	88.9	89.0	86.4	79.8	91.4	94.7	98.6	100.0	....	....	....	....	Trinidad and Tobago	369
119.6	135.6	145.5	154.1	111.2	119.4	131.2	121.6	142.1	112.5	100.0	98.2	96.2	97.4	107.6	Venezuela	299
															Memorandum Items	
119.5	135.5	145.4	154.0	114.0	119.9	133.6	121.5	142.0	121.1	100.0	98.1	96.3	97.2	107.2	Oil Exporting Countries	999
100.8	102.7	97.6	94.8	93.1	88.7	86.6	90.5	93.6	95.3	100.0	99.9	99.4	95.3	....	Non-Oil Developing Countries	201

Terms of Trade

74tx d

		1965	1966	1967	1968	1969	1970	1971	1972	1973	1974	1975	1976	1977	1978	1979
														Percent Change over Previous Year:		
Industrial Countries	110	.4	.6	.6	-.3	.6	1.2	-.3	1.1	-1.6	-10.8	1.1	-1.5	-1.0	3.3	-2.5
United States	111	2.2	.2	1.1	.3	.2	-1.2	-2.0	-3.5	-2.1	-13.8	2.6	.2	-4.2	-.9	-4.6
Canada	156	1.3	2.7	1.4	.2	-.2	1.2	-1.0	1.2	6.4	7.6	-4.0	-1.0	-6.4	-4.0	3.1
Australia	193	-9.7	3.5	-6.6	.3	-1.0	-6.3	-4.8	10.0	28.6	-15.9	-17.0	-.5	-7.2	-2.7	-.1
Japan	158	-4.9	-.2	5.4	.2	5.2	-1.4	.3	7.5	-3.9	-23.2	-5.3	-2.9	3.4	15.0	-16.1
New Zealand	196	-2.6	-1.4	-11.4	-7.2	2.5	-5.8	2.5	15.7	22.0	-22.8	-25.3	7.1	4.5	2.6	7.6
Austria	122	2.1	-3.1	2.1	—	-.3	3.1	-1.0	1.2	1.9	-2.1	—	-2.1	-.7	-.1	-1.3
Belgium	126	1.7	.7	.7	-.8	1.9	1.0	-1.6	1.7	1.0	-2.7	-1.6	-.8	.3	-.1	.5
Denmark	128	-.1	3.0	-1.9	-3.8	2.9	—	-3.3	5.0	1.2	-13.4	6.1	-.8	-2.1	3.8	-4.6
Finland	172	3.6	-.9	-2.9	-1.4	1.4	—	-1.5	.4	.8	-1.4	8.2	-3.7	-.3	-3.4	-3.2
France	132	-.4	.9	-1.2	2.1	1.0	-.5	2.7	.5	2.4	-14.1	7.2	-1.3	-1.7	4.1	-.7
Germany	134	-.8	2.4	3.8	-.6	-.6	2.3	2.6	2.4	-2.1	-9.2	5.2	-4.5	-1.0	4.0	-5.4
Greece	174	-3.4	1.2	-1.0	-2.8	.7	-1.6	-3.8	-3.9	6.2	-8.6	-5.9	-1.7	4.7	-2.6	-12.1
Iceland	176	10.6	.1	-9.3	-5.1	6.9	13.7	12.9	-1.0	16.1	-10.0	-16.0	11.9	8.8	.1	-9.1
Ireland	178	-1.1	1.3	1.6	-.8	1.0	.3	1.3	9.2	12.9	-20.0	-1.7	3.9	-1.7	1.9	-4.3
Italy	136	-2.8	-2.2	-.1	-1.0	3.6	.5	-.2	.3	-9.2	-17.3	5.3	-3.3	2.9	2.1	-1.8
Netherlands	138	1.0	-1.0	—	2.0	-1.0	-2.8	-1.9	2.0	-.9	-5.1	.3	—	—	—	-2.6
Norway	142	3.7	.5	-.7	-.7	-.1	1.6	-1.0	1.9	2.9	4.2	2.3	-3.9	-1.3	.5	6.2
Portugal	182	....	....	....	....	....	....	....	....	....	....	....	....	....	....	....
Spain	184	1.7	6.6	6.4	.5	-4.1	-4.1	-6.4	3.6	-.7	-13.6	-2.1	-4.4	-.8	2.4	6.6
Sweden	144	2.8	-1.8	.9	-.9	1.8	.7	-.8	2.2	-2.3	-6.5	10.7	—	-5.1	-3.6	-1.8
Switzerland	146	1.3	2.0	1.6	1.1	-1.1	-2.1	3.0	2.8	-3.8	-5.5	7.2	4.2	-3.3	8.1	-2.9
United Kingdom	112	2.7	2.4	.5	-3.6	.3	1.8	.9	.9	-11.3	-12.1	8.2	-2.0	2.7	6.4	4.1
Developing Countries	200	.8	—	.7	-8.0	.8	1.3	2.4	1.2	8.0	44.6	-6.3	4.8	3.1	-6.4	12.6
Africa	605	-3.8	3.9	-.5	-2.3	3.4	-1.0	-4.3	-4.8	11.5	21.2	-9.6	3.4	6.8	-11.7	2.4
Benin	638	....	....	....	....	-7.5	9.8	-1.3	-19.4	19.5	-3.1	-18.5	22.3	16.7	12.0	-7.3
Burkina Faso	748	....	....	-3.3	1.9	.4	-13.3	-4.0	-13.3	2.9	17.2	-12.8	13.2	2.1	-2.6	-5.1
Côte d'Ivoire	662	....	....	....	....	....	....	-14.2	22.7	-4.5	-19.6	16.3	48.6	-17.8	-5.4	
Ethiopia	644	-.1	-3.5	-12.5	1.1	-.3	23.2	-15.2	2.0	9.7	-3.1	-15.0	68.1	-5.9	-10.5	.2
Kenya	664	-2.9	—	—	-.2	-.2	7.2	-11.6	-7.3	-3.4	-11.6	-8.9	16.2	31.5	-19.9	-7.9
Liberia	668	....	....	....	....	....	....	-10.7	-2.9	-10.4	20.6	7.3	-5.2	-12.2	1.6	
Malawi	676	....	....	....	3.9	3.2	7.7	2.1	-8.5	-4.0	-6.1	-3.6	-2.4	18.6	-10.4	-20.9
Mauritius	684	-19.0	2.0	1.8	-16.3	5.3	7.4	-1.4	12.3	-10.0	52.5	16.3	-26.9	-9.9	-7.6	-5.9
Morocco	686	-2.7	14.5	5.4	-1.2	-5.9	-1.5	-2.1	-7.1	-3.6	41.9	7.0	-20.7	20.0	-5.2	-10.4
Niger	692	....	....	1.4	15.3	-24.5	11.8	-12.5	20.6	-9.3	15.3	21.1	4.9	-2.9	27.2	-10.8
Senegal	722	....	....	9.1	28.8	-12.1	9.6	-5.2	-5.6	4.0	32.9	-20.2	-7.2	10.4	9.4	-4.8
Seychelles	718	....	....	....	....	....	....	-1.9	-7.6	23.8	7.4	-29.0	15.0	25.6	11.2	-7.5
South Africa	199	-1.9	-3.6	-1.0	3.8	1.0	-1.8	-6.2	-6.3	10.1	-2.7	-8.5	-4.7	-4.4	-6.0	-7.7
Tanzania	738	-14.6	-1.0	-6.5	5.6	-1.9	-3.4	4.8	-16.7	5.3	10.2	-16.3	21.9	21.8	-17.2	-10.7
Togo	742	....	....	-.5	7.9	2.5	-5.7	-9.9	-10.5	4.5	95.0	-9.7	-35.0	23.2	-9.2	.5
Tunisia	744	5.2	-2.4	3.1	-2.5	1.2	-3.2	5.1	1.6	20.4	56.5	-8.5	-9.9	1.1	5.4	28.1
Zambia	754	....	27.1	-24.4	4.3	28.6	-10.1	-31.0	-7.4	31.4	-3.0	-49.1	8.0	-6.8	-14.2	12.8
Asia	505	4.8	-2.8	-.1	13.6	4.4	3.9	-2.1	2.1	2.5	-.9	-10.5	4.7	8.3	-2.0	1.0
Bangladesh	513	....	....	....	....	....	....	....	....	....	....	....	....	....	....	17.7
India	534	2.6	3.0	-1.7	1.2	2.0	1.0	5.0	6.3	7.6	-15.6	-27.5	-7.5	9.3	22.6	-12.0
Korea	542	2.0	11.8	3.4	4.3	-3.6	.9	-.9	-.4	-5.1	-18.6	-9.7	14.1	7.0	4.8	-2.1
Malaysia	548	10.1	-7.9	-2.3	-16.1	6.5	12.3	-8.3	-15.5	14.6	18.2	-15.3	7.5	13.6	-4.1	19.5
Pakistan	564	....	....	....	....	....	....	-13.1	10.3	23.6	-24.1	-22.1	14.0	15.7	8.1	2.4
Philippines	566	—	-.8	-.5	-2.6	-1.4	-2.1	-6.9	-9.6	13.3	1.1	-23.3	-11.5	-8.6	10.0	4.4
Singapore	576	....	....	....	....	....	....	....	....	....	....	....	....	....	....	....
Sri Lanka	524	9.1	-6.3	-6.7	-4.6	-6.7	-6.3	-5.9	-5.6	-11.8	-11.4	-19.8	30.6	31.5	-1.8	-28.3
Thailand	578	.7	5.3	-.2	4.9	5.7	-12.4	-8.4	-1.5	34.5	-8.6	-20.9	-7.8	-5.0	.2	3.3
Europe	170	....	....	....	....	....	....	-1.0	1.5	-4.0	-9.1	1.2	1.7	-2.6	-.3	-2.7
Cyprus	423	1.0	9.2	-3.2	1.8	1.2	.5	-7.0	2.8	5.1	-14.5	6.9	4.4	-4.3	-.4	-4.0
Czechoslovakia	934	....	....	....	....	....	....	....	....	....	.2	-4.2	-3.2	-3.7	-1.1	-1.8
Hungary	944	....	....	....	....	....	....	-1.7	-.2	-1.3	-9.6	-5.1	2.3	-3.4	-.6	-1.8
Malta	181	....	.1	-9.5	2.8	2.0	6.2	-4.6	2.2	-11.4	-6.8	-.6	2.8	-4.7	2.4	-4.3
Poland	964	....	....	....	....	....	....	....	....	....	....	....	3.4	-2.9	.1	-2.7
Turkey	186	....	....	....	....	-.9	-2.4	.9	6.4	2.5	-8.0	-15.5	2.7	-.5	-7.0	-.2
Yugoslavia, SFR	188	-.1	3.6	.9	-1.7	-1.9	2.1	.6	.4	-.5	-10.3	3.8	1.5	-1.1	4.1	-2.6
Middle East	405	.2	-4.4	.3	2.6	-2.1	-2.3	16.6	.2	7.4	146.3	-3.9	4.6	4.8	-13.9	38.0
Israel	436	2.1	4.1	-1.9	1.0	.2	-3.3	1.5	2.3	-3.3	-13.9	-.1	4.1	8.4	7.7	-7.5
Jordan	439	....	....	....	....	....	....	-22.4	-20.2	10.5	-3.7	60.1	-17.4	-4.4	-2.1	-.9	-5.9
Syrian Arab Rep.	463	4.2	-26.3	20.1	10.4	3.1	-5.8	3.4	-2.6	1.6	33.7	-23.4	1.2	17.1	.4	5.1
Western Hemisphere	205	-28.3	-.9	1.2	-2.9	-.2	5.5	-.7	5.3	13.4	32.4	-16.6	5.6	12.9	-11.8	5.2
Brazil	223	-.4	-6.2	-2.3	-4.2	4.9	10.9	-7.2	14.6	1.4	-13.7	-8.1	12.3	17.4	-13.9	-8.3
Chile	228	....	....	....	....	....	....	....	....	....	....	....	....	....	....	....
Colombia	233	....	....	....	....	....	....	-6.5	....	5.1	6.5	4.4	-7.5	40.3	38.7	-25.4	-10.6
Costa Rica	238	....	....	....	....	....	....	....	-1.9	1.8	-12.5	3.9	18.9	21.4	-11.9	-8.6
El Salvador	253	3.2	-21.0	8.8	4.6	-3.2	18.3	-4.7	1.1	6.4	-12.5	-6.8	50.3	31.1	-24.7	1.9
Guatemala	258	....	....	....	....	....	....	....	....	....	....	....	....	....	....	....
Nicaragua	278	1.3	-8.0	1.0	-6.8	4.3	-8.7	-3.5	3.6	-1.2	-2.9	-23.1	33.5	17.7	-10.9	-3.9
Trinidad and Tobago	369	....	....	3.0	-7.2	-3.8	-2.1	1.9	-6.7	12.2	17.3	.7	-1.9	5.8	-4.3	16.7
Venezuela	299	-80.4	-5.8	-2.9	-.2	-5.5	-.2	21.7	—	38.5	123.3	-5.2	-4.4	5.4	-10.9	37.0
Memorandum Items																
Oil Exporting Countries	999	-5.5	-4.0	-2.8	-22.1	-2.9	-.7	18.4	1.5	32.3	183.9	-6.9	-1.0	2.0	-6.3	53.4
Non-Oil Developing Countries	201	1.9	.5	.8	-3.1	2.5	2.2	-5.5	.3	3.1	-3.4	-8.6	4.7	6.1	-5.5	-2.7

Indices

Index Numbers:

		1965	1966	1967	1968	1969	1970	1971	1972	1973	1974	1975	1976	1977	1978	1979
Industrial Countries	110	106.4	107.0	107.7	107.4	108.0	109.3	108.9	110.2	108.4	96.7	97.8	96.2	95.3	98.4	96.0
Developing Countries	200	63.6	63.5	64.0	58.9	59.4	60.2	61.6	62.4	67.4	97.4	91.3	95.7	98.7	92.3	103.9
Africa	605	86.0	89.4	88.9	86.9	89.8	88.9	85.1	81.1	90.4	109.6	99.1	102.4	109.4	96.5	98.9
Asia	505	89.7	87.2	87.1	99.0	103.3	107.3	105.1	107.3	109.9	108.9	97.4	101.9	110.4	108.1	109.2
Europe	170	....	....	....	....	....	133.0	131.6	133.7	128.3	116.6	118.0	120.1	117.0	116.7	113.5
Middle East	205	82.8	82.1	83.1	80.6	80.4	84.8	84.2	80.6	88.7	100.6	133.2	111.0	117.2	132.3	116.7	122.8
Western Hemisphere	405	30.1	28.8	28.9	29.7	29.0	28.4	33.1	33.1	35.6	87.7	84.3	88.1	92.4	79.5	109.7

Terms of Trade

74tx d

1980	1981	1982	1983	1984	1985	1986	1987	1988	1989	1990	1991	1992	1993	1994	Country	Code
Calculated from Indices																
-7.4	-1.8	1.5	1.9	-.6	1.1	9.6	1.1	1.0	-.8	-.7	.8	1.7	1.7	.7	Industrial Countries	110
-9.4	3.5	2.8	5.4	-.4	1.8	4.5	-5.1	2.1	-.4	-2.2	.9	-.7	1.2	.4	United States	111
-3.5	-6.9	-3.3	.3	-1.2	-2.3	-1.7	3.1	2.3	2.1	-2.6	-2.2	-1.8	-.3	-.4	Canada	156
-9.5	-.1	-2.1	-1.0	-2.1	-5.3	-7.4	-1.9	14.5	6.5	-2.9	-9.6	-2.3	-6.3	-1.1	Australia	193
-19.8	2.5	.8	2.8	2.7	2.9	33.7	1.8	2.7	-4.4	-5.8	10.0	7.6	8.3	7.6	Japan	158
-10.9	-.6	-1.1	-2.5	-.2	-1.8	—	11.0	6.8	5.4	-2.3	-5.2	1.4	3.2	-1.0	New Zealand	196
-5.1	-4.0	4.1	1.0	-.3	-2.0	6.4	2.0	.6	-5.1	2.3	-3.5	-.6	-1.0	...	Austria	122
-4.3	-4.6	-.3	.3	-.4	1.1	7.6	.4	-.2	.7	-1.3	-.6	1.9	...	...	Belgium	126
-6.8	-2.6	1.0	.8	-.6	1.4	6.6	3.3	-1.9	-.8	1.9	-.4	2.3	.6	...	Denmark	128
-4.4	-.9	1.8	.1	1.3	-.4	9.5	3.9	2.5	3.8	-2.5	-2.3	-3.8	-6.9	...	Finland	172
-6.3	-4.4	-.3	1.2	-.8	2.8	12.2	.6	1.2	-1.7	.3	.8	1.0	1.8	3.0	France	132
-6.4	-6.6	3.7	1.7	-2.3	1.3	15.1	3.7	—	-2.7	1.5	-2.3	2.4	.9	-2.8	Germany	134
5.3	6.9	-3.7	3.8	-7.3	-1.0	-4.7	9.4	-1.5	2.9	-.5	-.3	.2	1.5	...	Greece	174
-3.4	2.0	.6	-4.3	-3.0	1.1	8.5	5.6	-4.2	-6.0	2.0	7.4	-4.4	-5.1	...	Iceland	176
-6.3	-3.8	3.0	3.9	-1.5	1.6	4.4	—	.6	.2	-4.6	-3.0	-.7	2.3	...	Ireland	178
-6.2	-4.9	2.5	2.5	-1.6	.6	15.8	2.5	1.0	-1.2	2.9	3.7	1.3	...	...	Italy	136
-1.1	.5	1.2	-1.1	2.3	1.0	3.0	-3.5	.4	-1.9	2.2	-1.2	-.9	2.2	...	Netherlands	138
15.9	8.4	2.1	-1.2	7.9	-2.4	-24.8	-6.0	-2.8	5.7	3.7	-2.7	-6.3	-.2	...	Norway	142
...	...	...	18.2	-3.3	7.9	13.0	2.1	3.1	-1.6	-.5	—	3.0	...	...	Portugal	182
-12.6	-10.2	-2.1	-4.5	.9	4.7	15.4	6.1	6.1	2.6	-.1	2.4	5.3	-2.5	-1.4	Spain	184
—	-.2	-1.4	-1.1	3.5	.2	9.4	-.9	-.2	2.5	—	1.5	-1.0	-.1	2.7	Sweden	144
-8.4	5.7	4.8	1.2	.8	-5.1	9.0	7.8	...	...	...	...	...	...	...	Switzerland	146
4.1	.8	-.9	-.9	-.7	.6	-5.4	1.4	1.1	.2	1.4	.1	.8	2.6	-1.5	United Kingdom	112
10.3	1.4	.1	-7.3	1.8	-1.4	-8.7	.6	-.4	1.6	-.4	-2.8	.4	-1.1	...	Developing Countries	200
8.5	—	-2.8	-10.2	4.4	-2.2	3.2	3.4	—	-2.4	.4	.1	.5	-3.4	...	Africa	605
-17.4	-1.0	11.8	-10.8	...	...	...	...	...	...	...	...	...	...	...	Benin	638
3.2	-8.2	-5.3	3.9	-.9	9.2	-26.7	16.3	-1.8	...	...	...	...	...	...	Burkina Faso	748
-2.8	-27.7	-11.1	4.1	20.7	16.7	-3.6	-17.3	...	...	...	...	...	...	...	Côte d'Ivoire	662
-18.1	...	...	...	...	...	...	...	...	...	...	...	...	...	...	Ethiopia	644
-8.2	-14.3	-4.4	-6.3	17.3	-16.7	12.9	-18.2	4.6	-10.9	-9.9	14.8	-2.5	11.1	...	Kenya	664
.1	-7.8	2.8	-1.8	-9.8	7.3	-6.5	-10.3	...	...	...	...	...	...	...	Liberia	668
-15.1	22.2	1.1	-8.3	4.3	-14.6	-12.9	-3.4	-3.2	2.1	...	...	...	...	...	Malawi	676
-5.7	1.1	-10.5	9.2	-.9	3.8	30.6	8.1	-2.7	.2	-1.7	1.6	4.8	-1.7	-2.4	Mauritius	684
.5	-6.0	.3	-7.3	2.1	1.1	10.0	-2.5	18.5	-26.6	-5.6	3.3	.8	-8.9	...	Morocco	686
-11.2	-13.5	2.3	-6.6	...	...	...	...	...	...	...	...	...	...	...	Niger	692
-24.7	22.2	-14.3	1.8	16.1	2.1	-3.2	—	...	...	...	...	...	...	...	Senegal	722
-20.2	-.6	-6.7	...	...	...	...	...	...	...	...	...	...	...	...	Seychelles	718
-4.6	-1.6	-9.8	4.1	2.2	-1.3	-.9	-.5	5.0	6.2	-1.9	-3.9	-.6	.7	...	South Africa	199
1.5	...	...	...	...	...	...	...	...	...	...	...	...	...	...	Tanzania	738
-12.4	-7.3	1.4	-5.9	37.9	18.8	...	...	...	...	...	...	...	...	...	Togo	742
17.5	6.3	1.1	-.6	2.0	-6.2	-13.8	9.0	...	...	...	...	...	...	...	Tunisia	744
-30.9	...	...	...	...	...	...	...	...	...	...	...	...	...	...	Zambia	754
-5.0	-2.9	2.4	-1.2	2.2	-1.8	.1	.6	-.9	—	-2.1	.3	.9	.5	-2.7	Asia	505
5.2	-21.4	-4.6	-5.4	29.3	12.9	-28.8	-8.5	25.2	-3.5	-4.8	-13.6	...	...	...	Bangladesh	513
-7.9	-9.0	11.2	4.1	23.5	-13.0	2.4	20.5	-3.1	-2.6	-10.0	9.5	5.8	14.4	...	India	534
-13.3	-2.1	4.3	.9	2.2	.5	8.8	2.4	2.8	-.3	-3.3	.6	—	4.3	1.2	Korea	542
-3.1	-13.2	-6.2	-1.2	12.5	-9.4	-21.6	17.9	...	...	...	...	...	...	...	Malaysia	548
-14.5	-9.6	-2.9	6.9	1.5	-4.4	27.5	-9.4	-8.9	-7.9	-4.7	-3.4	.2	2.0	—	Pakistan	564
-15.9	-12.0	-2.7	4.4	-2.3	-6.7	7.9	9.5	11.0	-7.6	-9.9	6.5	...	...	...	Philippines	566
5.6	2.1	1.4	-2.2	-3.2	.7	-2.7	-4.5	-1.8	-.4	1.4	-2.3	-3.3	-.2	-3.1	Singapore	576
-12.1	-6.3	-6.2	23.0	21.7	-18.1	-3.6	2.8	-5.8	-1.6	-4.4	-1.9	4.0	1.9	-4.7	Sri Lanka	524
-4.8	-12.9	-9.3	7.5	-1.7	-6.3	10.8	-1.1	-1.8	-3.9	-2.9	-1.0	.7	.7	...	Thailand	578
-3.6	-1.6	-.2	-2.5	-3.4	.1	.2	1.9	12.1	5.5	-18.3	-15.9	...	...	...	Europe	170
-5.7	5.4	-2.9	3.1	.3	-2.4	9.2	7.3	...	...	...	...	...	...	...	Cyprus	423
.3	-3.6	-1.7	-3.9	-7.9	1.1	-.8	2.6	2.9	5.2	2.8	-30.0	...	...	...	Czechoslovakia	934
.3	-.8	-2.3	-2.5	-2.1	-.9	-3.6	.9	2.4	2.8	.4	-10.6	...	...	...	Hungary	944
-3.4	-3.0	1.9	-6.1	3.7	1.7	6.5	4.1	9.5	1.4	...	...	...	...	...	Malta	181
-.1	.7	.8	-4.8	.5	2.3	1.9	3.6	1.0	16.6	-13.9	-11.3	...	...	2.1	Poland	964
-22.8	-8.5	-4.7	-1.7	12.0	...	...	...	...	...	...	...	...	...	...	Turkey	186
-.9	-1.5	4.4	-1.9	...	...	...	...	...	...	...	...	...	...	...	Yugoslavia, SFR	188
30.9	5.0	4.7	-13.1	-1.3	5.2	-38.0	-1.8	-6.5	8.8	13.4	-10.2	2.0	-6.1	-1.0	Middle East	405
-8.3	-.2	3.4	2.2	-1.8	1.1	3.9	-3.2	5.3	-.3	.6	5.6	.7	3.9	-3.4	Israel	436
-4.3	-5.7	7.5	—	-1.5	-.4	14.3	-10.6	10.2	7.6	-11.5	11.0	2.0	-.6	...	Jordan	439
—	-14.6	-6.9	-18.8	9.2	16.4	-38.1	-8.3	-22.4	28.0	28.6	-3.0	-28.5	3.8	...	Syrian Arab Rep.	463
.6	-5.3	-8.1	-5.9	1.1	-8.1	.3	-4.6	-.4	3.9	7.2	-5.1	...	...	...	Western Hemisphere	205
-17.3	-15.3	-2.9	-.1	7.4	.1	37.6	-14.3	.7	-8.0	-5.0	3.6	...	...	...	Brazil	223
...	-17.1	-24.6	-39.6	-25.8	-39.5	-4.4	3.6	18.2	-5.3	...	...	...	...	...	Chile	228
1.7	-5.3	-2.9	2.5	3.5	-1.0	21.8	-22.9	.6	-20.6	8.4	-2.9	-6.1	...	...	Colombia	233
-.5	-14.4	.6	3.1	3.4	3.5	25.6	-17.8	-.2	-6.8	-8.0	6.7	-4.0	1.8	...	Costa Rica	238
-18.8	-16.2	-11.4	-13.2	-14.1	...	...	...	...	...	...	...	...	...	...	El Salvador	253
...	...	...	...	...	...	...	...	-4.4	-3.6	15.2	-17.8	-23.6	14.0	...	Guatemala	258
-10.6	4.3	-2.6	-3.4	6.0	-12.3	14.1	9.3	-3.4	...	...	...	...	...	...	Nicaragua	278
6.4	-2.4	-15.4	-1.5	-.7	-3.5	-28.3	-8.4	-14.2	9.8	18.0	...	...	...	...	Trinidad and Tobago	369
30.4	-2.5	-13.3	-13.0	19.6	-12.6	-47.3	14.8	-8.7	57.9	38.8	-21.3	-1.8	-12.9	...	Venezuela	299

Memorandum Items

1980	1981	1982	1983	1984	1985	1986	1987	1988	1989	1990	1991	1992	1993	1994		
42.2	-1.6	-10.1	-17.7	30.4	-8.8	-45.8	12.5	-24.6	32.7	49.9	-14.9	1.7	-10.8	-23.3	Oil Exporting Countries	999
-6.4	-5.0	-.7	-.8	1.7	-2.5	2.0	2.3	2.6	.2	-3.0	.2	.1	1.0	...	Non-Oil Developing Countries	201

Indices

1990=100

1980	1981	1982	1983	1984	1985	1986	1987	1988	1989	1990	1991	1992	1993	1994		
88.8	87.2	88.6	90.2	89.7	90.7	99.4	100.5	101.5	100.7	100.0	100.8	102.5	104.2	105.0	Industrial Countries	110
114.6	116.2	116.2	107.8	109.7	108.1	98.6	99.2	98.8	100.4	100.0	97.2	97.5	96.5	...	Developing Countries	200
107.3	107.3	104.4	93.7	97.8	95.7	98.7	102.0	102.1	99.6	100.0	100.1	100.6	97.3	...	Africa	605
103.8	100.7	103.2	101.9	104.2	102.3	102.4	103.0	102.1	102.1	100.0	100.3	101.2	101.7	99.0	Asia	505
109.4	107.6	107.4	104.8	101.2	101.3	101.5	103.5	116.1	122.4	100.0	84.1	...	...	...	Europe	170
123.6	117.1	107.7	101.3	102.4	94.1	94.4	90.1	89.7	93.2	100.0	94.9	...	...	...	Middle East	205
143.6	150.8	157.9	137.2	135.4	142.5	88.3	86.7	81.0	88.2	100.0	89.8	91.6	86.0	85.2	Western Hemisphere	405

Balance of Payments

Trade Balance
Expressed in Millions of US Dollars

	1978	1979	1980	1981	1982	1983	1984	1985	1986	1987	1988	1989	1990	1991	1992	1993	1994
All Countries	10,399	28,402	38,220	23,686	104	3,836	11,272	11,965	6,662	27,729	36,244	24,440	35,161	34,872	37,866	55,259	47,207
Industrial Countries	1,347	-46,442	-74,519	-30,311	-23,290	-25,611	-47,611	-41,525	-9,189	-28,665	-8,267	-33,734	-36,072	9,001	45,425	100,247	91,899
United States	-33,950	-27,540	-25,510	-28,019	-36,480	-67,090	-112,480	-122,180	-145,060	-159,560	-126,960	-115,250	-109,022	-74,060	-96,100	-132,570	-166,360
Canada	4,188	4,183	8,005	6,584	14,996	14,989	15,984	12,587	7,677	8,961	8,157	5,985	8,334	3,871	5,699	7,927	12,202
Australia	90	2,518	1,367	-2,207	-2,147	45	-776	-969	-1,841	275	-716	-3,418	368	3,514	1,555	-127	-3,199
Japan	24,300	1,740	2,130	19,960	18,080	31,460	44,260	55,990	92,820	96,420	95,000	76,890	63,580	103,090	132,400	141,570	145,930
New Zealand	602	290	303	257	-280	337	-472	-59	95	582	2,164	973	897	2,072	1,674	1,714	....
Austria	-3,301	-4,279	-6,489	-4,944	-3,046	-3,172	-3,242	-3,137	-4,016	-4,809	-4,765	-5,552	-6,969	-8,560	-8,443	-7,281	-8,869
Belgium-Luxembourg	-1,212	-3,016	-3,859	-3,474	-2,300	-666	-191	492	2,305	1,294	2,705	2,575	2,602	2,079	3,510	6,126	....
Denmark	-2,356	....	-2,008	-927	-794	252	-195	-764	-1,050	795	1,883	2,425	4,875	4,748	7,204	7,812	....
Finland	1,077	345	-683	354	201	147	1,480	870	1,634	1,375	1,132	-228	718	2,309	3,944	6,384	7,651
France	-33	-3,626	-14,076	-10,139	-15,449	-8,412	-4,494	-4,814	-1,347	-7,775	-7,649	-10,240	-13,230	-9,594	2,344	7,749	9,132
Germany	23,253	15,140	7,917	15,432	24,194	19,478	21,431	28,528	54,771	68,110	76,328	75,043	68,617	18,510	26,936	39,679	51,102
Greece	-3,494	-5,006	-5,542	-5,337	-4,699	-4,270	-4,222	-5,013	-4,375	-5,435	-6,027	-7,327	-10,106	-10,022	-11,561	-10,499	....
Iceland	22	6	20	-29	-152	20	-13	—	97	-52	-14	134	80	-47	1	181	....
Ireland	-1,065	-2,320	-2,222	-2,255	-1,162	-252	237	631	1,145	2,614	3,822	4,003	3,969	4,167	6,813	8,172	....
Italy	3,455	-155	-15,911	-11,314	-7,980	-1,710	-5,132	-5,367	5,047	83	-924	-1,664	1,373	-445	3,085	32,825	35,497
Netherlands	-984	-669	-94	5,035	5,630	5,541	6,531	6,273	7,815	6,434	9,741	9,148	11,654	12,417	13,083	14,411	14,416
Norway	-512	146	1,896	3,035	2,386	4,351	5,158	4,728	-2,115	-759	-209	3,770	7,761	8,696	9,303	7,995	8,321
Portugal	-2,001	-2,575	-3,943	-6,948	-4,759	-2,985	-2,051	-1,430	-1,611	-3,513	-5,377	-4,742	-6,684	-7,688	-9,387	-6,636	....
Spain	-4,064	-5,684	-11,725	-10,113	-9,254	-7,806	-4,643	-4,759	-7,197	-13,742	-18,703	-25,406	-29,158	-30,335	-30,420	-14,946	-14,581
Sweden	2,574	-695	-2,198	163	-222	1,901	3,422	2,385	5,035	4,485	4,880	4,015	3,402	6,359	6,723	7,669	9,583
Switzerland	-2,178	-4,900	-5,250	-2,384	-3,219	-5,391	-1,089	-1,561	-4,960	-5,427	-4,576	-4,323	-6,391	-3,806	490	2,237	....
United Kingdom	-3,064	-6,973	3,353	6,960	3,167	-2,377	-7,114	-3,955	-14,058	-19,019	-38,160	-40,544	-32,742	-18,274	-23,428	-20,146	-16,009
Developing Countries	9,052	74,844	112,739	53,997	23,394	29,446	58,883	53,489	15,851	56,395	44,511	58,174	71,233	25,870	-7,558	-44,988	-44,691
Africa	-1,811	9,855	17,944	-3,292	-3,864	3,253	8,167	15,711	8,052	11,486	6,732	8,894	16,717	13,177	7,460	6,054	27
Algeria	-976	1,664	4,037	4,012	3,594	3,199	3,547	4,214	169	2,398	935	1,144	4,179	5,468	....	....	....
Angola	....	....	....	....	....	....	....	900	260	1,019	1,120	1,676	2,306	2,102	1,845	1,438	....
Benin	-159	-156	-148	-139	-379	-154	-67	-24	-109	-120	-132	-138	-141	-154	-198	-239	....
Botswana	-72	—	-58	-286	-119	25	94	234	244	783	482	635	147	....	....	....	....
Burkina Faso	-148	-179	-208	-189	-233	-196	-129	-217	-288	-245	-238	-272	-321	-318	-355	-367	....
Burundi	....	....	....	....	....	....	....	-36	-36	-61	-42	-58	-116	-105	-102	-98	....
Cameroon	144	83	37	42	140	141	524	490	442	254	620	717	778	784	951	502	....
Cape Verde	-56	-67	-71	-80	-93	-101	-76	-81	-82	-85	-99	-100	-114	-128	-169	....	....
Central African Rep.	-7	-11	-38	-27	-25	-14	-26	-37	-72	-69	-45	-38	-91	-53	-42	....	....
Chad	-64	24	16	2	-24	-21	-19	-104	-113	-116	-83	-85	-29	-56	-61	-66	....
Comoros	....	....	-11	-8	-6	-9	-26	-13	-8	-33	-23	-18	-27	-29	....	....	....
Congo	26	133	365	269	445	417	651	515	160	457	320	629	876	613	740	617	....
Côte d'Ivoire	573	489	399	367	558	431	1,137	1,351	1,547	1,086	922	920	1,327	979	994	1,072	....
Djibouti	....	....	....	....	....	....	....	....	....	....	....	....	....	....	-191	-191	....
Equatorial Guinea	....	....	....	....	....	....	....	....	....	-9	-12	-11	-15	-24	....	....	....
Ethiopia	-130	-93	-230	-256	-272	-337	-382	-508	-455	-577	-556	-374	-620	-303	-823	-507	....
Gabon	751	1,260	1,398	1,359	1,438	1,275	1,285	1,097	95	555	404	874	1,684	1,367	1,373	1,305	....
Gambia, The	-41	-41	-89	-84	-36	-35	-9	-12	-20	-20	-23	-25	-30	-42	-31	....	....
Ghana	112	263	195	-244	18	-61	33	-36	61	-125	-112	-195	-308	-321	-470	....	....
Guinea	....	....	....	....	....	....	....	....	84	164	1	64	85	-8	-91	-22	....
Guinea-Bissau	....	....	....	....	-50	-50	-43	-48	-42	-29	-43	-55	-49	-47	-77	-38	....
Kenya	-575	-474	-914	-641	-422	-214	-266	-279	-235	-660	-729	-962	-915	-512	-495	-239	....
Lesotho	-210	-278	-366	-403	-410	-451	-405	-302	-316	-405	-496	-526	-613	-736	-823	-778	....
Liberia	....	79	122	105	87	46	121	167	149	63	....	....	....	....	....	....	....
Madagascar	1	-249	-328	-179	-124	-68	-23	-44	-8	11	-34	1	-248	-102	-138	....	....
Malawi	-79	-95	-27	28	26	30	150	69	94	100	40	-35	67	53	-32	—	....
Mali	-105	-125	-103	-115	-87	-74	-66	-152	-133	-80	-108	-70	-95	-93	-145	-120	....
Mauritania	-149	-139	-125	-116	-187	-63	-8	38	18	43	89	99	61	37	-55	3	....
Mauritius	-98	-97	-82	-147	-30	-17	-41	-26	58	-16	-166	-210	-270	-204	-171	-254	....
Morocco	-1,112	-1,289	-1,321	-1,520	-1,746	-1,227	-1,401	-1,353	-1,053	-1,066	-760	-1,697	-2,108	-1,981	-1,799	-1,466	....
Mozambique	....	....	-439	-440	-523	-441	-390	-305	-409	-481	-559	-622	-663	-647	-659	....	....
Namibia	....	....	....	....	....	....	....	....	....	....	....	....	-28	102	79	122	118
Niger	-123	-42	-101	-107	-134	4	33	-86	22	2	-24	-58	-34	11	-1	-6	....
Nigeria	-1,169	4,924	11,176	-831	-2,731	-1,089	2,992	5,616	2,313	3,448	2,626	4,178	8,653	4,441	4,611	....	....
Rwanda	-33	43	-62	-94	-106	-74	-55	-93	-75	-146	-161	-149	-125	-133	-172	....	....
São Tomé & Príncipe	6	11	1	-15	-18	-9	-11	-13	-13	-7	-5	-8	-9	....	....	....	....
Senegal	-309	-296	-405	-417	-251	-275	-186	-248	-189	-248	-243	-240	-264	-290	-368	-383	....
Seychelles	-45	-65	-78	-75	-79	-70	-69	-80	-85	-88	-118	-125	-130	-127	-143	....	....
Sierra Leone	-59	-125	-159	-116	-138	-18	-11	-5	20	27	-30	-18	8	17	....	....	....
Somalia	-130	-237	-268	-195	-301	-264	-411	-240	-247	-265	-158	-279	....	....	....	....	....
South Africa	3,819	6,107	7,430	10	645	4,039	2,174	5,842	7,200	7,163	5,222	5,589	6,783	6,134	5,429	5,781	....
Sudan	-61	-222	-438	-841	-349	-189	-81	-135	-307	-430	-522	-507	-322	-836	-597	....	....
Swaziland	-49	-122	-170	-116	-115	-161	-141	-96	-19	54	25	-22	-31	-36	-128	-125	....
Tanzania	-516	-415	-506	-448	-539	-325	-362	-541	-577	-713	-646	-655	-779	-923	-913	-838	....
Togo	-149	-174	-48	-36	-63	-18	28	-22	-56	-40	-69	-58	-118	-59	-96	-34	....
Tunisia	-846	-930	-970	-967	-1,163	-1,084	-1,166	-886	-947	-731	-1,102	-1,212	-1,685	-1,199	-2,063	-2,073	....
Uganda	....	....	2	-56	10	25	121	110	46	-142	-257	-311	-313	-204	-271	-278	....
Zaïre	....	....	....	....	304	473	742	606	561	356	533	518	599	....	....	....	....
Zambia	213	652	343	-69	-61	212	280	226	175	267	502	566	-257	420	....	....	....
Zimbabwe	270	205	106	-83	-160	84	184	201	311	381	501	375	243	48	-255	122	....
Asia	-7,565	-10,007	-15,599	-19,627	-18,127	-15,451	-927	-8,853	2,848	20,539	11,719	6,652	3,521	783	-81	-13,918	-20,087
Afghanistan, I.S. of	....	-136	-69	-207	-121	-162	-417	-293	-642	-366	-278	-371	....	....	....	....	....
Bangladesh	-790	-1,070	-1,560	-1,644	-1,453	-1,207	-1,408	-1,287	-1,421	-1,369	-1,443	-1,995	-1,587	-1,386	-1,256	-1,283	....
China, People's Rep.	....	....	....	....	4,249	1,990	14	-13,123	-9,140	-1,661	-5,315	-5,620	9,165	8,743	5,183	-10,654	....
Fiji	-95	-142	-117	-233	-155	-181	-135	-146	-105	-22	-16	-48	-150	-103	-101	-210	....
India	-884	-2,222	-5,644	-5,711	-4,820	-4,098	-4,025	-5,616	-5,438	-5,777	-6,581	-6,110	-5,151	....	....	....	....
Indonesia	....	....	....	6,806	1,893	963	5,707	5,822	2,458	4,674	5,678	6,664	5,352	4,801	7,022	8,231	....
Kiribati	....	8	-17	-21	-20	-14	-7	-11	-13	-13	-17	-17	-22	-23	....	....	....
Korea	-1,780	-4,395	-4,384	-3,628	-2,594	-1,763	-1,036	-19	4,206	7,659	11,445	4,597	-2,004	-6,980	-2,146	1,860	-3,146

Balance of Payments

Trade Balance

1978	1979	1980	1981	1982	1983	1984	1985	1986	1987	1988	1989	1990	1991	1992	1993	1994	
Expressed in Millions of US Dollars																	
																	Asia (cont.)
....	....	....	....	....	....	-118	-140	-131	-152	-92	-131	-107	-101	-100	-148	....	Lao P. D. Rep.
1,620	3,160	2,393	-115	-731	438	2,931	3,573	3,214	5,783	5,427	4,277	2,525	391	3,150	3,011	....	Malaysia
-8	-11	-31	-26	-29	-38	-38	-33	-36	-32	-43	-60	-63	-83	-117	-139	....	Maldives
....	....	....	-803	-834	-806	-713	-799	-1,098	-1,011	-1,021	-1,118	-583	....	....	....	....	Mongolia
-223	-369	-360	-330	-490	-353	-200	-202	-290	-233	-205	-82	-302	....	....	....	....	Myanmar
-131	-141	-226	-218	-319	-367	-273	-283	-294	-350	-471	-407	-449	-482	-376	-462	....	Nepal
-1,824	-2,341	-2,876	-2,926	-3,403	-2,715	-3,753	-3,230	-2,780	-2,316	-2,693	-2,571	-2,714	-2,262	-2,790	-2,552	....	Pakistan
25	227	-35	-256	-249	-154	-47	51	102	114	91	-23	67	79	629	1,370	....	Papua New Guinea
-1,307	-1,541	-1,939	-2,224	-2,646	-2,482	-679	-482	-202	-1,017	-1,085	-2,598	-4,020	-3,211	-4,695	-6,222	....	Philippines
-1,967	-2,202	-2,971	-4,695	-5,181	-4,358	-2,643	-1,508	-1,019	-1,253	-1,216	-858	-3,099	-1,952	-4,323	-6,417	....	Singapore
—	10	-1	-10	-1	1	26	-1	-4	-6	-23	-20	-7	-9	14	....	....	Solomon Islands
-53	-323	-784	-632	-780	-664	-237	-523	-556	-472	-540	-550	-473	-805	-715	-742	-871	Sri Lanka
-858	-1,550	-1,902	-2,029	-731	-2,861	-1,898	-1,332	388	-424	-2,074	-2,916	-6,751	-5,989	-4,161	-4,146	....	Thailand
-11	-17	-20	-30	-31	-34	-26	-24	-26	-28	-38	-38	-40	-41	-36	-38	....	Tonga
....	....	....	....	-33	-28	-19	-34	-38	-43	-43	-44	-66	-59	-49	-47	....	Vanuatu
-38	-49	-40	-41	-32	-26	-27	-30	-32	-44	-51	-54	-61	-71	-84	-81	....	Western Samoa
-822	-1,647	-3,425	-2,185	446	3,542	8,094	10,815	15,744	18,898	12,323	16,745	14,440	13,897	8,672	7,405	4,339	Asia not specified
-9,447	**-12,591**	**-13,470**	**-10,271**	**-3,555**	**-2,776**	**-921**	**-2,397**	**-4,090**	**-2,050**	**2,385**	**-3,622**	**-15,164**	**-10,592**	**-13,208**	**-30,594**	**-16,059**	**Europe**
....	....	13	35	-78	-42	-34	-41	-5	-4	-38	-62	-134	-208	-471	-490	-460	Albania
....	....	....	....	....	....	....	....	....	....	....	....	....	....	....	-98	-181	Armenia
....	....	646	-308	-290	-406	-178	-505	-1,183	-1,011	-606	-692	-1,314	-32	-212	-885	152	Bulgaria
....	....	....	....	....	....	....	....	....	....	....	....	....	....	....	-763	-969	Croatia
-345	-455	-551	-491	-536	-598	-652	-647	-639	-707	-957	-1,275	-1,356	-1,419	-1,989	....	....	Cyprus
....	....	11	257	346	348	352	277	-386	-270	385	143	-1,422	-121	-1,834	....	....	Czechoslovakia
....	....	....	....	....	....	....	....	....	....	....	....	....	....	-90	-145	-361	Estonia
....	....	....	....	410	434	780	448	-465	80	583	1,043	534	358	-11	-4,021	-3,716	Hungary
-145	-212	-347	-278	-264	-253	-213	-237	-252	-372	-442	-436	-561	-573	-500	-555	....	Malta
-2,292	-2,384	-1,776	-2,181	-84	303	659	347	467	790	1,089	47	3,589	-711	-131	-3,505	....	Poland
-606	-1,216	-1,661	103	1,814	1,869	2,312	1,772	1,680	2,178	3,750	2,050	-3,344	-1,106	-1,194	-1,128	-330	Romania
....	....	....	....	....	....	....	....	....	....	....	....	....	....	....	-912	....	Slovak Republic
....	....	....	....	....	....	....	....	....	....	....	....	....	....	791	-154	-146	Slovenia
-2,081	-2,554	-4,603	-3,864	-2,628	-2,990	-2,942	-2,975	-3,081	-3,229	-1,777	-4,219	-9,555	-7,326	-8,190	-14,162	....	Turkey
-3,768	-6,058	-4,899	-3,163	-2,022	-1,231	-789	-588	-702	82	779	58	-2,676	512	....	....	....	Yugoslavia, SFR
31,880	**86,490**	**125,138**	**89,170**	**41,128**	**14,081**	**13,748**	**16,096**	**-7,409**	**6,386**	**247**	**18,514**	**37,730**	**12,442**	**6,339**	**6,899**	**11,416**	**Middle East**
19	404	446	618	527	184	72	101	35	-13	77	11	421	-190	-313	....	....	Bahrain
-2,804	-3,578	-2,960	-3,919	-3,715	-4,558	-6,216	-5,215	-4,538	-4,980	-6,608	-5,722	-6,379	-5,667	-5,231	-6,378	....	Egypt
5,872	15,650	1,450	-1,307	7,900	3,480	2,358	2,169	-3,414	-89	101	-367	975	-6,529	-3,406	....	....	Iran, I.R. of
-2,710	-3,247	-3,255	-3,599	-3,253	-3,253	-2,584	-2,382	-1,838	-3,702	-2,897	-1,926	-3,091	-5,025	-5,030	-5,661	-6,141	Israel
-1,042	-1,341	-1,561	-2,082	-2,127	-2,120	-1,721	-1,638	-1,426	-1,467	-1,411	-773	-1,237	-1,173	-1,780	-1,899	....	Jordan
5,908	13,243	13,877	9,287	3,008	4,584	5,607	4,655	1,955	3,280	1,709	4,987	3,179	-4,204	-689	3,499	5,221	Kuwait
4,136	7,334	11,551	168	2,725	3,370	2,564	4,599	1,468	472	-109	765	3,777	....	....	....	....	Libya
441	994	1,968	2,400	1,840	1,895	1,781	1,943	552	2,036	1,235	1,842	2,885	1,759	1,928	1,336	....	Oman
17,514	37,860	76,011	82,533	39,759	12,646	8,987	7,115	3,119	4,916	4,571	9,154	22,924	21,776	16,932	19,150	....	Saudi Arabia
-1,142	-1,407	-1,898	-2,193	-1,633	-2,106	-1,853	-2,090	-1,326	-869	-639	1,192	2,094	1,084	159	-322	....	Syrian Arab Republic
-942	-1,407	-1,855	-1,714	-1,921	-1,756	-1,393	-1,071	-780	-1,141	-862	-677	....	....	....	....	....	Yemen Arab Rep.
-328	-348	-539	-592	-653	-643	-704	-581	-417	-386	-514	-440	....	....	....	....	....	Yemen, P.D. Rep.
....	....	....	....	....	....	....	....	....	....	....	....	-103	-723	-841	-971	-52	Yemen, Republic of
6,958	22,334	31,902	9,571	-1,329	2,358	6,848	8,490	-798	8,327	5,593	10,469	12,285	9,323	3,639	-569	-2,238	Middle East not spec
-4,005	**1,097**	**-1,274**	**-1,983**	**7,811**	**30,339**	**38,816**	**32,933**	**16,449**	**20,033**	**23,428**	**27,736**	**28,429**	**10,060**	**-8,068**	**-13,429**	**-19,988**	**Western Hemisphere**
-29	-56	-55	-74	-77	-63	-115	-147	-193	-202	-184	-227	-212	-217	-221	-229	....	Antigua and Barbuda
2,913	1,782	-1,373	712	2,764	3,716	3,982	4,878	2,446	1,017	4,242	5,709	8,628	4,419	-1,450	-2,428	....	Argentina
....	....	....	....	....	....	....	....	-181	-205	-267	-290	-425	-524	-377	-392	-311	Aruba
-241	-350	-437	-477	-444	-510	-522	-542	-583	-652	-642	-811	-791	-653	-688	-760	....	Bahamas, The
-157	-224	-253	-335	-250	-251	-215	-207	-244	-297	-343	-415	-411	-413	-274	-330	....	Barbados
....	....	....	....	....	....	-23	-24	-16	-24	-42	-64	-59	-98	-104	-119	....	Belize
-97	21	368	85	332	259	312	161	-51	-128	-48	-6	55	-44	-432	....	....	Bolivia
-1,158	-2,717	-2,823	1,185	778	6,469	13,086	12,466	8,304	11,158	19,168	16,112	10,747	10,578	15,239	13,072	....	Brazil
-426	-355	-764	-2,677	63	986	362	884	1,092	1,309	2,209	1,578	1,335	1,588	772	-982	659	Chile
603	463	-297	-1,572	-2,244	-1,494	246	-23	1,922	1,868	827	1,474	1,971	2,959	1,233	....	....	Colombia
-186	-315	-374	-88	64	-42	5	-62	40	-139	-98	-255	-443	-200	-472	-666	....	Costa Rica
-10	-26	-38	-25	-18	-15	-25	-24	-5	-10	-20	-48	-48	-41	-43	-51	....	Dominica
-187	-269	-558	-264	-490	-494	-389	-547	-630	-880	-718	-1,039	-1,058	-1,071	-1,612	-1,607	....	Dominican Republic
-175	54	278	174	140	927	1,054	1,294	543	-33	619	661	1,003	644	925	588	445	Ecuador
-149	178	178	-100	-100	-74	-189	-216	-124	-349	-356	-592	-600	-706	-961	-1,035	....	El Salvador
-16	-21	-31	-37	-41	-39	-33	-43	-52	-57	-59	-71	-80	-90	-83	-91	....	Grenada
-191	-180	47	-249	-114	36	-50	-17	168	-355	-340	-358	-217	-443	-1,044	-1,021	....	Guatemala
42	4	2	-53	-13	-32	15	5	....	....	....	....	....	....	....	....	....	Guyana
-58	-82	-103	-209	-125	-139	-123	-122	-112	-101	-103	-111	-177	-247	-139	-185	....	Haiti
-23	-20	-94	-106	4	-49	-139	-86	23	-41	-34	-45	-12	-72	-151	-91	....	Honduras
81	-64	-76	-323	-442	-439	-335	-436	-248	-352	-357	-590	-502	-392	-425	-822	....	Jamaica
....	-2,142	-3,056	-3,877	7,047	14,105	13,186	8,399	5,019	8,786	2,611	405	-881	-7,279	-15,934	-13,481	-18,465	Mexico
-165	143	-123	-187	-216	-171	-300	-322	-521	-614	-654	-704	-810	-817	-836	-828	....	Netherlands Antilles
93	227	-353	-414	-318	-290	-323	-489	-420	-439	-483	-229	-237	-420	-548	-392	434	Nicaragua
-476	-633	-525	-609	-537	-585	-741	700	-502	-427	-42	-356	-426	-760	-788	-766	-902	Panama
-76	-193	-275	-374	-315	-225	-288	-194	-288	-321	-159	164	-254	-747	-869	-1,019	....	Paraguay
340	1,540	826	-553	-428	293	1,007	1,172	-65	-521	-99	1,197	339	-165	-565	-580	....	Peru
....	....	-17	-19	-21	-28	-27	-26	-30	-42	-55	-62	-70	-69	-52	-57	....	St. Kitts and Nevis
-48	-60	-67	-76	-66	-50	-60	-62	-53	-77	-75	-129	-111	-151	-147	-144	....	St. Lucia
-15	-23	-31	-23	-26	-22	-15	-8	-13	-34	-22	-37	-37	-52	-37	-60	....	St. Vincent & Grens.
68	74	60	-33	-32	-35	-17	27	33	64	119	218	91	-1	68	84	99	Suriname
243	425	939	962	-169	-131	469	787	169	357	405	506	1,013	564	696	547	....	Trinidad and Tobago
-24	-378	-610	-362	218	417	192	178	273	102	292	463	426	61	-122	-387	....	Uruguay
-2,060	4,356	8,398	8,058	2,932	8,350	8,829	6,977	798	1,694	-1,863	5,694	10,706	4,900	1,322	2,958	....	Venezuela
																	Memorandum Items
40,287	**115,989**	**172,299**	**123,499**	**62,185**	**42,860**	**51,601**	**53,011**	**9,820**	**32,357**	**21,578**	**45,528**	**76,760**	**46,599**	**38,509**	**42,287**	**46,726**	**Oil Exporting Ctys**
-31,234	**-41,145**	**-59,561**	**-69,502**	**-38,790**	**-13,414**	**7,282**	**478**	**6,031**	**24,038**	**22,934**	**12,646**	**-5,527**	**-20,729**	**-46,068**	**-87,275**	**-91,418**	**Non-Oil Develop.Ctys**

Balance of Payments

Current Account Balance
Excluding Exceptional Financing

Expressed in Millions of US Dollars

	1978	1979	1980	1981	1982	1983	1984	1985	1986	1987	1988	1989	1990	1991	1992	1993	1994
All Countries	-25,593	-15,193	-35,056	-78,894	-114,675	-88,613	-87,411	-91,855	-80,996	-68,032	-77,131	-96,817	-118,555	-126,298	-124,853	-96,721	-104,091
Industrial Countries	10,249	-27,119	-65,117	-29,024	-32,444	-30,443	-57,221	-66,815	-38,087	-68,696	-65,855	-89,825	-116,937	-38,824	-52,230	16,517	-9,220
United States	-15,770	-129	2,150	4,841	-11,600	-44,667	-99,837	-125,580	-151,357	-167,307	-128,469	-102,969	-91,979	-7,209	-68,297	-104,359	-156,157
Canada	-4,604	-4,608	-1,691	-6,022	1,185	-1,635	-927	-4,769	-10,351	-12,420	-18,023	-23,790	-22,577	-24,571	-22,592	-23,391	-17,388
Australia	-4,577	-2,767	-4,461	-8,645	-8,418	-6,406	-9,049	-9,314	-9,995	-8,459	-11,714	-19,227	-16,585	-11,658	-11,776	-10,707	-15,224
Japan	16,530	-8,740	-10,750	4,770	6,850	20,800	35,000	49,170	85,831	87,020	79,610	56,990	35,860	72,905	117,650	131,540	129,240
New Zealand	-438	-802	-973	-1,045	-1,694	-960	-1,842	-1,642	-1,713	-1,761	-367	-1,501	-1,301	-1,140	-1,343	-1,251	....
Austria	-1,490	-1,954	-3,865	-3,042	703	276	-178	-158	204	-263	-242	248	1,166	61	-631	-762	-2,452
Belgium-Luxembourg	-823	-3,080	-4,931	-4,168	-2,594	-495	-55	669	3,055	2,794	3,594	3,197	4,950	4,731	6,468	12,588	....
Denmark	-1,502	....	-2,453	-1,875	-2,259	-1,382	-1,718	-2,767	-4,490	-3,002	-1,340	-1,118	1,372	1,983	4,268	4,711	....
Finland	680	-163	-1,403	-478	-923	-1,124	-21	-806	-682	-1,717	-2,681	-5,781	-6,939	-6,741	-4,922	-959	1,068
France	7,064	5,142	-4,208	-4,811	-12,082	-5,166	-876	-35	2,430	-4,446	-4,795	-4,726	-9,942	-6,469	3,934	10,301	8,832
Germany	9,391	-5,351	-13,311	-3,408	5,019	4,739	9,573	17,782	41,115	46,660	49,840	57,332	48,456	-18,620	-21,590	-15,443	-20,926
Greece	-955	-1,886	-2,209	-2,408	-1,892	-1,878	-2,132	-3,276	-1,676	-1,223	-958	-2,561	-3,537	-1,574	-2,140	-747	....
Iceland	20	-19	-76	-148	-261	-56	-133	-115	16	-188	-231	-102	-147	-312	-206	-6	....
Ireland	-849	-2,100	-2,132	-2,601	-1,935	-1,219	-950	-628	-728	100	224	-381	146	1,541	2,555	3,735	....
Italy	6,054	5,913	-10,589	-10,466	-7,379	699	-3,190	-4,084	2,306	-2,723	-7,271	-12,841	-17,676	-24,746	-28,844	9,170	14,301
Netherlands	-1,199	119	-979	3,623	4,769	4,937	6,360	4,195	4,066	4,208	6,990	9,889	9,158	7,764	6,885	10,201	11,249
Norway	-2,118	-1,047	1,079	2,131	640	1,962	2,886	3,038	-4,551	-4,102	-3,896	212	3,992	5,032	2,982	2,152	3,645
Portugal	-463	-54	-1,064	-4,686	-3,258	-1,632	-623	380	1,166	435	-1,066	153	-181	-716	-184	947	....
Spain	1,251	757	-5,580	-5,363	-4,548	-3,013	1,778	2,785	3,914	-263	-3,795	-10,924	-18,653	-20,137	-21,996	-6,048	-6,832
Sweden	-191	-2,349	-4,331	-2,778	-3,285	-725	736	-1,010	32	-21	-534	-3,104	-6,338	-4,632	-8,790	-4,078	826
Switzerland	2,075	-245	-201	3,427	2,534	1,211	6,143	6,040	4,654	6,286	8,843	8,042	6,942	10,325	14,190	16,696	....
United Kingdom	2,163	-783	6,862	14,127	7,985	5,292	1,835	3,309	-1,334	-8,304	-29,574	-36,862	-33,037	-14,643	-17,850	-17,776	-12
Developing Countries	-35,842	11,926	30,061	-49,870	-82,230	-58,170	-30,190	-25,039	-42,908	664	-11,276	-6,992	-1,618	-87,474	-72,624	-113,239	-94,871
Africa	-12,705	-3,498	-898	-21,769	-21,566	-12,091	-5,910	1,092	-5,630	-2,916	-7,963	-4,985	64	-3,346	-4,799	-8,425	-13,128
Algeria	-3,540	-1,632	249	90	-183	-85	74	1,015	-2,230	141	-2,040	-1,081	1,420	2,367	....	....	....
Angola	....	....	....	....	....	....	....	195	-303	447	-469	-132	-236	-580	-735	-669	....
Benin	-96	-52	-36	-93	-377	-135	-57	5	-66	-74	-83	-13	-1	-11	-45	-52	....
Botswana	-116	-61	-151	-304	-145	-79	-59	82	109	628	194	492	131	....	....	....	....
Burkina Faso	-60	-64	-49	-42	-92	-60	-3	-60	-21	-51	-49	33	-102	-104	-97	-118	....
Burundi	....	....	....	....	....	....	....	41	-36	-95	-70	-11	-66	-31	-54	-25	....
Cameroon	-187	-126	-446	-482	-386	-412	-169	-562	-452	-893	-431	-298	-478	-405	-339	-565	....
Cape Verde	-9	-1	4	-22	-15	-13	-6	-9	2	14	—	-5	-12	-8	-4	....	....
Central African Rep.	-23	-16	-43	-4	-43	-29	-33	-49	-87	-73	-35	-33	-89	-62	-57	....	....
Chad	-46	-8	9	20	19	38	9	-87	-59	-26	26	-56	-46	-66	-86	-84	....
Comoros	....	....	-9	-8	-11	-11	-33	-14	-16	-21	-7	5	-9	-9	....	....	....
Congo	-181	-99	-167	-461	-332	-401	210	-161	-601	-223	-445	-85	-251	-462	-317	-507	....
Côte d'Ivoire	-839	-1,383	-1,826	-1,411	-1,017	-931	-77	64	-300	-970	-1,241	-967	-1,210	-1,490	-1,428	-1,229	....
Djibouti	....	....	....	....	....	....	....	....	....	....	....	....	....	....	-89	-88	....
Equatorial Guinea	....	....	....	....	....	....	....	....	....	-25	-21	-21	-19	-25	....	....	....
Ethiopia	-112	-91	-226	-250	-195	-170	-130	106	-327	-217	-228	-144	-294	103	-120	-54	....
Gabon	74	248	384	403	309	98	113	-162	-1,057	-449	-616	-192	168	75	-168	-269	....
Gambia, The	-45	-35	-87	-50	-23	-34	8	7	4	6	26	15	34	13	37	....	....
Ghana	-46	123	30	-419	-107	-172	-39	-134	-43	-96	-65	-98	-228	-252	-377	....	....
Guinea	....	....	....	....	....	....	....	....	-124	-38	-222	-180	-203	-289	-263	65	....
Guinea-Bissau	....	....	....	....	-80	-72	-66	-76	-63	-57	-68	-93	-60	-79	-104	-65	....
Kenya	-661	-495	-878	-563	-308	-50	-130	-118	-47	-503	-472	-591	-527	-213	-180	124	....
Lesotho	9	—	56	4	22	41	6	-12	-3	24	-25	10	65	83	38	22	....
Liberia	....	16	46	75	3	-104	-2	55	-18	-145	....	....	....	....	....	....	....
Madagascar	-79	-426	-556	-363	-299	-247	-193	-184	-143	-141	-150	-74	-255	-192	-139	....	....
Malawi	-175	-266	-260	-147	-113	-132	-43	-127	-85	-61	-72	-137	-134	-225	-293	-96	....
Mali	-146	-114	-130	-143	-115	-113	-121	-210	-254	-219	-234	-191	-250	-179	-250	-244	....
Mauritania	-79	-115	-134	-147	-277	-214	-111	-116	-195	-147	-96	-19	-10	-30	-118	-139	....
Mauritius	-116	-141	-116	-151	-42	-23	-55	-29	95	66	-60	-103	-119	-17	—	-92	....
Morocco	-1,311	-1,502	-1,408	-1,833	-1,864	-888	-986	-893	-209	182	473	-787	-196	-392	213	36	....
Mozambique	....	....	-367	-407	-497	-415	-308	-301	-409	-389	-359	-460	-415	-344	-381	....	....
Namibia	....	....	....	....	....	....	....	....	....	....	....	....	10	114	58	144	150
Niger	-219	-144	-277	-193	-233	-64	-7	-69	25	-90	-83	-111	-109	-25	-45	-29	....
Nigeria	-3,757	1,669	5,127	-6,164	-7,285	-4,354	115	2,566	366	-69	-194	1,090	4,988	1,203	2,268	....	....
Rwanda	-46	46	-48	-74	-90	-49	-41	-64	-69	-135	-145	-123	-108	-34	-85	....	....
São Tomé & Príncipe	6	9	1	-18	-26	-11	-11	-18	-19	-13	-11	-11	-14	....	....	....	....
Senegal	-236	-264	-387	-462	-267	-306	-274	-273	-268	-307	-261	-198	-216	-205	-268	-305	....
Seychelles	-4	-12	-16	-19	-41	-26	-13	-19	-33	-21	-28	-23	—	4	-2	....	....
Sierra Leone	-112	-179	-165	-132	-170	-18	-23	3	141	-30	-3	-60	-69	11	....	....	....
Somalia	-65	-206	-136	-83	-177	-142	-139	-103	-126	-114	-98	-157	....	....	....	....	....
South Africa	1,582	3,445	3,508	-4,489	-3,178	9	-1,589	2,622	3,163	2,934	1,204	1,564	2,065	2,243	1,376	1,804	....
Sudan	-110	-258	-317	-648	-249	-219	36	149	-26	-232	-358	-150	-372	-955	-506	....	....
Swaziland	-71	-119	-130	-81	-114	-107	-77	-38	12	63	65	4	47	25	5	-37	....
Tanzania	-467	-346	-522	-408	-524	-305	-360	-375	-322	-446	-376	-367	-425	-451	-422	-408	....
Togo	-217	-213	-95	-44	-87	-48	16	-33	-66	-61	-87	-51	-101	-55	-107	-98	....
Tunisia	-459	-300	-353	-381	-662	-570	-765	-581	-615	-54	219	-116	-469	-464	-961	-905	....
Uganda	....	....	-83	1	-70	-72	104	5	-43	-112	-195	-260	-263	-170	-100	-107	....
Zaïre	....	....	....	....	-752	-350	-325	-290	-415	-645	-580	-610	-643	....	....	....	....
Zambia	-281	78	-516	-729	-562	-263	-147	-395	-348	-245	-293	-219	-594	-306	....	-116	....
Zimbabwe	54	-56	-149	-546	-632	-398	-43	-64	17	58	125	17	-140	-457	-604	....	....
Asia	-4,579	-10,161	-15,087	-19,743	-17,201	-15,093	-4,948	-13,876	3,789	23,261	13,215	5,740	3,979	1,890	1,412	-13,673	-10,296
Afghanistan, I.S. of	....	-100	54	-206	-67	-139	-451	-243	-537	-167	26	-143	....	....	....	....	....
Bangladesh	-386	-419	-704	-1,019	-505	-49	-481	-458	-627	-238	-273	-1,100	-398	65	181	197	....
China, People's Rep.	....	....	....	....	5,682	4,248	2,040	-11,411	-7,084	214	-4,093	-4,482	11,894	13,017	5,810	-12,399	....
Fiji	....	-58	-15	-165	-86	-57	-20	19	14	1	71	75	-10	52	59	13	....
India	683	48	-1,785	-2,698	-2,524	-1,953	-2,343	-4,177	-4,598	-5,192	-7,148	-6,826	-7,037	....	....	....	....
Indonesia	....	....	....	-566	-5,324	-6,338	-1,856	-1,923	-3,911	-2,098	-1,397	-1,108	-2,988	-4,260	-2,780	-2,016	....
Kiribati	....	19	—	-6	-6	1	10	6	7	8	5	6	6	12	....	....	....
Korea	-1,085	-4,151	-5,325	-4,649	-2,651	-1,608	-1,377	-893	4,611	9,849	14,155	5,047	-2,179	-8,398	-4,122	859	-4,095

Balance of Payments

Current Account Balance
Excluding Exceptional Financing
Expressed in Millions of US Dollars

1978	1979	1980	1981	1982	1983	1984	1985	1986	1987	1988	1989	1990	1991	1992	1993	1994	
																	Asia (cont.)
....	....	....	....	....	....	-100	-114	-110	-137	-81	-88	-59	-63	-57	-53	....	Lao P. D. Rep.
127	941	-266	-2,469	-3,585	-3,482	-1,657	-600	-101	2,575	1,867	315	-870	-4,183	-1,788	-2,411	....	Malaysia
2	-5	-22	-20	-19	-24	-16	-6	—	8	9	11	9	-9	-20	-48	....	Maldives
....	....	....	-808	-847	-825	-740	-813	-1,061	-991	-1,033	-1,231	-644	....	....	....	....	Mongolia
-215	-359	-347	-314	-499	-350	-218	-205	-294	-180	-176	-68	-431	....	....	....	....	Myanmar
-26	-11	-39	-19	-85	-146	-95	-122	-119	-123	-271	-243	-289	-304	-181	-223	....	Nepal
-718	-1,113	-920	-913	-801	27	-1,195	-1,078	-645	-560	-1,423	-1,334	-1,654	-1,396	-1,868	-2,935	....	Pakistan
-32	107	-289	-484	-445	-337	-290	-122	-73	-185	-296	-313	-78	-151	97	554	....	Papua New Guinea
-1,095	-1,496	-1,917	-2,096	-3,212	-2,771	-1,294	-36	952	-444	-390	-1,456	-2,695	-1,034	-1,000	-3,289	....	Philippines
-453	-736	-1,563	-1,470	-1,296	-610	-385	-4	319	-157	889	2,785	2,094	3,992	3,748	2,039	....	Singapore
3	10	-12	-27	-25	-15	—	-28	-12	-17	-38	-33	-28	-36	-1	....	....	Solomon Islands
-68	-228	-657	-446	-549	-466	1	-418	-417	-326	-394	-414	-298	-595	-451	-382	-547	Sri Lanka
-1,153	-2,087	-2,076	-2,571	-1,003	-2,873	-2,109	-1,537	247	-366	-1,654	-2,498	-7,281	-7,571	-6,355	-6,928	....	Thailand
-1	-2	-3	-7	3	1	—	-2	1	5	-11	-12	13	-2	-2	3	....	Tonga
....	....	....	....	-8	-8	3	-10	-12	-24	-15	-12	-6	-14	-14	-21	....	Vanuatu
-18	-22	-13	-15	-7	4	1	2	7	7	8	13	7	-29	-52	-39	....	Western Samoa
1,112	-475	-1,957	-1,031	707	2,750	7,622	10,298	17,232	21,798	14,880	18,840	17,177	17,953	14,397	15,401	13,641	Asia not specified
-6,560	-10,518	-11,842	-8,941	-2,808	-2,338	167	-603	-2,352	925	6,909	2,755	-7,034	-3,569	-3,562	-19,398	-2,534	**Europe**
....	....	16	45	-67	-38	-28	-36	-3	5	-27	-39	-118	-168	-51	15	-157	Albania
....	....	....	....	....	....	....	....	....	....	....	....	....	....	....	-67	-106	Armenia
....	....	954	122	177	36	535	-136	-951	-720	-402	-769	-1,710	-77	-360	-1,098	139	Bulgaria
....	....	....	....	....	....	....	....	....	....	....	....	....	....	....	105	102	Croatia
-185	-240	-258	-172	-178	-205	-222	-180	-32	69	-13	-152	47	-215	-260	....	....	Cyprus
....	....	....	28	422	677	708	691	169	371	1,093	936	-1,227	908	-31	....	....	Czechoslovakia
....	....	....	....	....	....	....	....	....	....	....	....	....	....	36	23	-170	Estonia
....	....	....	....	-531	-181	39	-455	-1,365	-676	-572	-588	379	403	352	-4,262	-4,054	Hungary
73	47	39	86	12	-5	8	-26	7	23	61	-9	-61	-14	26	-70	....	Malta
-2,545	-3,365	-3,417	-3,986	-1,941	-1,581	-1,083	-982	-1,106	-379	-107	-1,409	3,067	-2,146	-3,104	-5,788	....	Poland
-759	-1,653	-2,420	-833	1,040	1,160	1,719	1,381	1,395	2,043	3,922	2,514	-3,254	-1,012	-1,506	-1,162	-259	Romania
....	....	....	....	....	....	....	....	....	....	....	....	....	....	....	-580	....	Slovak Republic
....	....	....	....	....	....	....	....	....	....	....	....	....	....	926	188	492	Slovenia
-1,265	-1,413	-3,408	-1,936	-952	-1,923	-1,407	-1,013	-1,465	-806	1,596	938	-2,625	272	-942	-6,380	....	Turkey
-1,273	-3,659	-2,317	-959	-473	275	478	833	1,100	1,248	2,487	2,427	-2,364	-1,161	....	....	....	Yugoslavia, SFR
7,522	55,452	87,812	43,050	468	-20,914	-18,529	-9,180	-22,024	-10,908	-13,678	-2,810	3,275	-64,926	-31,367	-27,231	-21,362	**Middle East**
-388	-223	184	430	426	103	218	39	-69	-200	190	-130	245	-796	-993	....	....	Bahrain
-1,220	-1,542	-438	-2,136	-1,851	-330	-1,988	-2,166	-1,811	-246	-1,048	-1,309	185	1,903	2,812	2,299	....	Egypt
104	11,968	-2,438	-3,446	5,733	358	-414	-476	-5,155	-2,090	-1,869	-191	327	-9,448	-6,504	....	....	Iran, I.R. of
-1,009	-920	-871	-1,361	-2,125	-2,099	-1,423	1,023	1,339	-1,183	-474	558	-66	-1,104	-706	-2,322	-4,008	Israel
-288	-6	374	-39	-333	-391	-265	-260	-40	-352	-294	385	-227	-394	-835	-629	....	Jordan
6,130	14,032	15,302	13,699	4,963	5,311	6,428	4,798	5,620	4,557	4,602	9,136	3,886	-26,690	-467	2,412	3,763	Kuwait
738	3,771	8,214	-3,963	-1,560	-1,643	-1,456	1,906	-166	-1,128	-1,826	-1,026	2,201	....	....	....	....	Libya
-50	549	942	1,237	489	494	303	-10	-1,040	784	-309	305	1,106	-244	-496	-1,069	....	Oman
-2,212	10,206	41,503	39,627	7,575	-16,852	-18,401	-12,932	-11,795	-9,773	-7,340	-9,538	-4,117	-27,589	-20,967	-14,218	....	Saudi Arabia
-15	946	251	-308	-250	-844	-794	-958	-504	-298	-151	1,222	1,762	699	55	-607	....	Syrian Arab Republic
16	-242	-685	-655	-607	-559	-301	-287	-125	-452	-694	-579	....	....	....	....	....	Yemen Arab Rep.
-30	-16	-125	-79	-100	-184	-253	-231	-176	-130	-404	-417	....	....	....	....	....	Yemen, P.D. Rep.
....	....	....	....	....	....	....	....	....	....	....	....	460	-895	-1,163	-1,316	-74	Yemen, Republic of
5,746	16,930	25,599	46	-11,891	-4,279	-183	373	-8,102	-398	-4,060	-1,227	-2,487	-792	-1,458	-5,783	-6,919	Middle East not spec
-19,519	-19,349	-29,924	-42,466	-41,124	-7,735	-971	-2,471	-16,691	-9,697	-9,759	-7,692	-1,902	-17,522	-34,307	-44,511	-47,552	**Western Hemisphere**
-2	-20	-19	-33	-42	-9	1	-23	-117	-111	-43	-79	-26	-29	-28	-19	....	Antigua and Barbuda
1,856	-513	-4,774	-4,712	-2,353	-2,436	-2,495	-952	-2,859	-4,235	-1,572	-1,305	4,552	-647	-6,546	-7,452	....	Argentina
....	....	....	....	....	....	....	....	-19	-23	-44	-47	-158	-209	44	42	81	Aruba
44	18	-14	-80	-61	-32	-43	29	47	-31	-43	-58	-71	-83	-30	-68	....	Bahamas, The
-31	-34	-26	-119	-35	-37	20	54	9	-23	42	24	-16	-25	144	64	....	Barbados
....	....	....	....	....	....	-5	9	12	9	-3	-19	15	-26	-29	-49	....	Belize
-332	-397	-6	-469	-174	-142	-179	-286	-389	-432	-304	-270	-199	-263	-534	....	....	Bolivia
-6,996	-10,516	-12,880	-11,817	-16,342	-6,850	6	-302	-5,329	-1,476	4,137	1,001	-3,919	-1,693	6,089	-637	....	Brazil
-1,088	-1,189	-1,971	-4,733	-2,304	-1,117	-2,111	-1,413	-1,192	-735	-234	-705	-536	112	-708	-2,096	-757	Chile
258	438	-206	-1,961	-3,054	-3,003	-1,401	-1,809	383	336	-216	-201	542	2,349	912	....	....	Colombia
-363	-558	-664	-409	-272	-313	-251	-291	-161	-376	-304	-447	-494	-99	-380	-470	....	Costa Rica
-1	6	-14	-13	-8	-2	-7	-6	5	-3	-6	-33	-31	-21	-23	....	....	Dominica
-312	-331	-720	-389	-443	-418	-163	-108	-183	-364	-19	-216	-106	-36	-445	-161	....	Dominican Republic
-703	-630	-642	-998	-1,182	-115	-273	76	-596	-1,172	-611	-594	-210	-542	-73	-530	-697	Ecuador
-279	32	34	-251	-120	-148	-189	-189	-17	-68	-129	-330	-235	-213	-195	-118	....	El Salvador
1	-1	—	-14	-18	-15	2	2	-3	-20	-17	-30	-28	-35	-24	-28	....	Grenada
-271	-206	-163	-573	-399	-224	-377	-246	-18	443	-414	-367	-233	-184	-706	-702	....	Guatemala
-30	-83	-129	-185	-142	-157	-99	-97	....	....	....	....	....	....	....	....	....	Guyana
-45	-53	-101	-149	-99	-111	-103	-95	-45	-31	-40	-63	-88	-123	-41	-78	....	Haiti
-157	-192	-317	-303	-228	-232	-374	-309	-225	-263	-181	-206	-228	-258	-351	-309	....	Honduras
-22	-107	-136	-307	-383	-339	-315	-273	-18	-126	47	-28	-312	-240	29	-214	....	Jamaica
....	-5,409	-10,422	-16,240	-5,889	5,866	4,183	800	-1,377	4,247	-2,374	-5,825	-7,451	-14,888	-24,442	-23,400	-28,784	Mexico
-25	24	1	53	178	88	175	403	51	-49	75	38	-44	-6	12	-15	....	Netherlands Antilles
-25	180	-411	-592	-514	507	597	-726	-688	-679	-715	-362	-305	-5	-834	-644	-729	Nicaragua
-208	-311	-311	56	-51	416	218	286	355	318	611	155	47	-158	-84	2	-331	Panama
-113	-206	-277	-374	-375	-248	-317	-252	-365	-490	-210	256	-172	-324	-600	-603	....	Paraguay
-193	730	-101	-1,733	-1,612	-875	-235	90	-1,173	-1,640	-1,246	75	-901	-1,331	-1,710	-1,800	....	Peru
....	....	-3	-5	-9	-15	-4	-7	-5	-10	-21	-34	-44	-32	-12	-21	....	St. Kitts and Nevis
-23	-28	-33	-40	-31	-5	-13	-13	2	-4	-12	-56	-57	-69	-51	-42	....	St. Lucia
3	-4	-9	-1	-11	-3	-1	4	-2	-14	-8	-18	-5	-24	-13	-42	....	St. Vincent & Grens.
29	44	18	-27	-55	-158	-77	-10	-21	76	64	164	37	-75	14	44	59	Suriname
54	-19	357	415	-599	-947	-467	-48	-412	-225	-89	-39	459	-5	139	113	....	Trinidad and Tobago
-127	-357	-709	-461	-235	-63	-129	-98	42	-141	22	134	186	42	-9	-227	....	Uruguay
-5,735	350	4,728	4,000	-4,246	4,427	4,651	3,327	-2,245	-1,390	-5,809	2,161	8,279	1,736	-3,753	-2,223	....	Venezuela
																	Memorandum Items
-4,064	59,091	102,271	45,305	-12,720	-21,784	-9,581	-864	-28,448	-11,263	-20,043	-1,379	13,966	-60,359	-30,449	-25,391	-14,551	Oil Exporting Ctys
-31,778	-47,166	-72,210	-95,175	-69,511	-36,387	-20,610	-24,175	-14,461	11,927	8,767	-5,613	-15,584	-27,115	-42,175	-87,848	-80,320	Non-Oil Develop.Ctys

Balance of Payments

Capital and Financial Account

Incl. Net Errors & Omissions, but Excl. Res.Assets, Use of Fund Credit,
Exceptional Financing, & Liabs. Constituting Fgn. Authorities' Reserves

	1978	1979	1980	1981	1982	1983	1984	1985	1986	1987	1988	1989	1990	1991	1992	1993	1994
							Expressed in Millions of US Dollars										
All Countries	24,437	18,471	52,298	37,560	38,156	49,677	64,209	70,081	45,528	110,278	38,255	94,888	133,550	136,033	82,851	59,689	65,361
Industrial Countries	−15,447	−415	57,110	14,652	27,988	29,489	53,505	58,693	27,759	96,307	60,225	96,094	140,231	18,478	−13,417	−65,185	−19,805
United States	−16,109	13,763	−10,040	−6,083	13,629	40,613	100,553	131,375	117,575	110,449	92,199	119,897	62,172	−14,572	26,102	35,706	114,420
Canada	−515	4,682	416	6,756	−2,850	1,587	−895	1,489	9,775	15,198	25,582	24,083	23,202	22,086	16,785	22,899	12,244
Australia	4,490	2,066	5,059	8,502	13,321	9,437	7,742	7,032	10,700	8,829	16,965	19,855	18,312	11,342	7,039	10,652	14,268
Japan	−6,571	−4,398	15,776	−1,134	−11,555	−19,250	−32,880	−49,754	−70,991	−49,081	−63,093	−69,751	−42,447	−79,522	−117,018	−103,880	−103,957
New Zealand	−446	−164	−451	−1,057	−519	−154	296	−491	−898	−487	−2,554	276	1,565	−372	−135	−522	....
Austria	2,837	925	5,206	3,420	−496	−804	245	173	439	595	733	742	−1,181	775	3,224	2,964	3,273
Belgium-Luxembourg	808	103	5,481	1,978	1,820	129	666	−441	−2,663	−521	−3,698	−5,291	−4,493	−4,227	−5,803	−14,669	....
Denmark	2,998	....	2,546	1,162	1,962	2,757	1,351	4,289	2,511	7,445	2,656	−2,704	2,003	−5,286	−4,494	−859	....
Finland	30	554	1,683	254	1,123	896	1,838	1,393	−1,598	5,739	2,936	4,723	10,874	4,852	2,758	1,235	3,653
France	−4,064	−3,390	10,268	45	8,477	9,332	3,662	2,415	−1,012	−3,883	4,728	2,377	21,765	653	−17,028	−8,101	−3,802
Germany	3,525	1,913	3,668	925	−2,174	−6,691	−9,920	−15,553	−35,690	−25,165	−65,264	−54,535	−41,144	12,642	58,128	−20	18,810
Greece	1,149	1,894	2,073	2,215	1,330	2,078	1,930	2,880	2,326	2,197	1,895	2,213	3,817	3,778	1,766	4,186	....
Iceland	31	56	111	219	165	67	117	179	83	170	232	157	221	322	276	−54	....
Ireland	992	1,514	2,844	2,594	2,056	1,407	908	676	634	787	368	−556	602	−1,077	−6,096	181	....
Italy	−2,874	−5,428	11,382	9,505	2,672	5,184	5,768	−3,506	23	8,216	15,687	24,111	29,299	18,028	4,852	−12,305	−12,726
Netherlands	282	−707	2,159	−4,450	−2,988	−5,164	−6,322	−3,444	−4,452	−1,347	−5,364	−9,439	−8,881	−7,687	−459	−3,659	−10,839
Norway	2,755	2,332	803	−1,701	69	−2,061	181	414	1,340	3,882	3,758	753	−3,578	−7,782	−3,837	1,986	−2,194
Portugal	766	330	1,421	4,544	3,376	370	629	528	−1,276	1,341	1,933	4,501	3,723	6,430	28	−3,794	....
Spain	2,508	2,693	4,785	4,636	1,444	2,748	3,039	−5,061	−1,571	12,969	12,212	15,640	25,832	34,437	4,186	1,206	6,868
Sweden	−502	−519	−1,067	−13	−1,006	−4,756	−6,570	−3,641	145	783	1,472	4,328	13,833	4,765	15,743	6,608	1,505
Switzerland	−2,982	−3,689	538	−3,947	965	−828	−4,662	−4,815	−3,561	−3,080	−11,269	−6,623	−5,770	−9,355	−9,770	−16,292	....
United Kingdom	−4,555	−17,846	−7,551	−13,720	−2,832	−7,409	−14,171	−7,443	5,920	1,270	28,110	21,336	30,505	28,251	10,336	11,350	−18,678
Developing Countries	39,884	18,885	−4,811	22,909	10,168	20,187	10,705	11,389	17,769	13,971	−21,970	−1,206	−6,681	117,554	96,268	124,873	85,166
Africa	9,956	6,928	4,090	10,870	10,805	5,664	1,266	−4,471	594	−4,524	−3,894	−3,353	−2,344	−2,691	−10,037	−5,614	−360
Algeria	3,633	2,116	1,092	30	−886	−336	−408	6	732	−493	1,081	307	−1,431	−1,319	....	....	....
Angola	....	....	....	....	....	....	....	−201	44	−779	−456	−798	−973	−920	−403	−651	....
Benin	77	48	13	125	329	97	34	−34	−6	3	−16	−53	11	72	−33	12	....
Botswana	155	177	242	230	200	203	183	172	198	−67	188	85	177	....	....	....	....
Burkina Faso	28	72	55	56	92	97	39	66	63	68	74	−181	84	152	115	135	....
Burundi	....	....	....	....	....	....	....	57	65	93	77	49	62	64	79	35	....
Cameroon	174	186	524	422	375	529	83	620	371	423	267	164	−392	−327	−970	−315	....
Cape Verde	6	4	−4	17	20	17	2	23	−2	9	−2	−2	10	−5	12	....	....
Central African Rep.	11	33	42	−3	8	15	34	24	83	62	21	22	71	23	34	....	....
Chad	21	−22	−32	−6	−14	−29	7	64	42	25	−60	86	23	47	49	33	....
Comoros	....	....	5	12	15	13	27	20	19	30	3	—	4	2	....	....	....
Congo	165	122	214	502	248	369	−272	81	203	−266	−21	−317	−113	3	−113	55	....
Côte d'Ivoire	976	1,054	1,162	808	710	232	−402	−240	−79	37	−162	−343	−356	226	38	39	....
Djibouti	....	....	....	....	....	....	....	....	....	....	....	....	....	....	72	80	....
Equatorial Guinea	....	....	....	....	....	....	....	....	....	—	3	5	9	1	....	....	....
Ethiopia	23	72	124	358	119	117	73	56	441	109	205	190	95	−459	−146	146	....
Gabon	−66	−264	−288	−285	−163	−187	−100	102	862	314	615	96	−404	−295	−276	−152	....
Gambia, The	28	15	51	44	−7	11	−28	−13	−36	5	−2	−11	−30	4	−18	....	....
Ghana	−16	−54	−31	131	89	−9	74	148	−18	236	246	253	333	361	320	....	....
Guinea	....	....	....	....	....	....	....	....	27	2	70	71	120	159	133	−98	....
Guinea-Bissau	....	....	....	59	54	53	84	30	26	27	23	29	8	53	7	....	....
Kenya	441	566	506	258	148	148	191	66	184	478	428	713	435	169	−77	287	....
Lesotho	−11	−3	−15	−4	−14	−15	2	18	15	−23	18	−18	−48	−41	12	81	....
Liberia	....	−89	−93	−124	−126	−24	−151	−259	−276	−155	....	....	....	....	....	....	....
Madagascar	69	295	308	198	90	−22	−10	16	27	−22	32	−100	−23	−42	−136	....	....
Malawi	162	183	238	120	75	34	46	101	85	106	132	85	163	241	246	120	....
Mali	129	94	97	130	89	81	122	183	205	205	279	203	185	219	124	158	....
Mauritania	89	120	91	122	220	171	78	85	177	−10	23	13	−63	46	135	−162	....
Mauritius	46	48	88	19	−18	−8	16	27	28	155	246	247	351	207	43	99	....
Morocco	1,239	1,391	1,119	1,514	1,473	662	877	859	539	116	−209	808	1,893	1,559	333	195	....
Mozambique	....	....	335	340	356	115	−87	−65	−49	−52	−41	2	−17	−191	−90	....	....
Namibia	....	....	....	....	....	....	....	....	....	....	....	....	27	−126	−64	−53	−75
Niger	208	134	272	184	170	50	−25	18	−73	56	70	32	−2	−63	28	−34	....
Nigeria	1,648	1,535	−755	1,442	1,672	1,365	−1,082	−3,799	−1,352	−4,426	−4,759	−3,753	−3,947	−2,725	−7,906	....	....
Rwanda	47	16	71	67	54	30	49	65	99	124	95	56	85	99	81	....	....
São Tomé & Príncipe	1	−8	−13	11	12	4	4	4	7	8	9	6	6	5	....	....	....
Senegal	176	237	328	330	32	196	176	182	233	209	147	35	−13	25	162	157	....
Seychelles	3	16	24	13	40	24	12	19	32	25	24	26	4	7	6	....	....
Sierra Leone	103	124	89	25	90	−75	−73	−77	−237	−23	−69	11	48	9	....	....	....
Somalia	92	98	105	88	213	64	112	91	29	16	−83	−33	....	....	....	....	....
South Africa	−1,003	−2,971	−2,713	2,290	2,933	278	1,008	−3,129	−2,670	−1,573	−2,590	−1,677	−661	−736	−1,245	−4,599	....
Sudan	8	150	−209	252	47	−4	−154	−570	−175	−111	71	−42	128	682	347	....	....
Swaziland	87	111	164	33	105	119	69	34	−4	−41	−51	48	−35	−12	87	−10	....
Tanzania	217	174	172	321	252	217	138	−112	−31	155	−8	41	343	88	133	56	....
Togo	237	197	62	−2	9	10	−37	30	22	−70	39	23	73	13	−52	−89	....
Tunisia	541	407	430	444	825	605	664	356	531	180	222	181	346	409	1,059	911	....
Uganda	....	....	−132	−128	−10	−9	−37	29	16	58	158	175	221	138	124	165	....
Zaïre	....	....	....	....	56	−182	−224	−93	−104	84	−144	51	−118	....	....	....	....
Zambia	−62	−10	292	265	171	241	58	215	214	3	61	112	816	126	....	....	....
Zimbabwe	21	176	63	538	610	224	−3	146	39	66	−24	−64	226	502	409	342	....
Asia	10,589	15,385	21,196	23,631	20,481	19,661	12,901	20,818	19,642	20,475	8,239	13,360	19,855	36,096	26,859	61,376	78,778
Afghanistan, I.S. of	....	95	−125	168	59	79	521	269	518	178	−52	123	....	....	....	....	....
Bangladesh	428	95	381	802	405	402	475	378	751	434	405	790	622	369	454	500	....
China, People's Rep.	....	....	....	....	623	−106	−1,902	8,971	5,036	4,569	6,467	4,003	153	1,520	−7,870	14,168	....
Fiji	....	64	56	141	64	50	27	−24	13	−64	41	−89	46	−43	−6	−55	....
India	1,237	785	122	520	825	1,201	3,412	3,780	4,189	5,325	7,131	7,064	5,099	....	....	....	....
Indonesia	....	....	....	192	3,471	6,521	2,837	2,433	2,908	2,728	1,284	1,603	5,239	5,788	4,850	2,603	....
Kiribati	....	−13	−2	−2	2	−5	−15	−6	−5	−5	−2	1	1	−2	....	....	....
Korea	1,816	5,025	5,636	4,320	2,656	1,372	1,937	1,085	−4,534	−7,745	−4,839	−1,927	971	7,250	7,846	2,150	8,709

Balance of Payments

Capital and Financial Account
Incl. Net Errors & Omissions, but Excl. Res.Assets, Use of Fund Credit,
Exceptional Financing, & Liabs. Constituting Fgn. Authorities' Reserves

1978	1979	1980	1981	1982	1983	1984	1985	1986	1987	1988	1989	1990	1991	1992	1993	1994	
																	Expressed in Millions of US Dollars
																	Asia (cont.)
....	....	....	....	....	....	97	137	121	128	86	83	60	78	61	69	....	Lao P. D. Rep.
152	−140	734	2,017	3,323	3,467	2,143	1,752	1,557	−1,456	−2,298	916	2,823	5,421	8,444	13,754	....	Malaysia
−1	5	22	19	25	20	11	7	−4	−7	5	−8	−10	8	25	48	....	Maldives
....	....	....	807	848	820	754	838	1,075	1,067	1,034	1,360	542	....	....	....	....	Mongolia
151	416	378	285	370	325	209	190	343	218	256	219	440	....	....	....	....	Myanmar
4	39	26	70	87	138	74	28	87	187	265	201	309	468	337	288	....	Nepal
625	639	709	656	561	515	236	661	488	384	1,570	896	1,068	812	2,676	2,857	....	Pakistan
28	2	205	433	409	435	338	120	77	187	243	254	101	65	−169	−636	....	Papua New Guinea
1,855	1,812	2,808	1,531	2,483	−725	846	874	182	386	1,064	1,756	2,650	2,789	2,689	3,578	....	Philippines
1,117	1,252	2,225	2,379	2,473	1,670	1,909	1,341	219	1,252	770	−47	3,337	205	2,352	5,539	....	Singapore
12	−3	3	20	30	18	−11	13	−6	10	33	20	14	23	16	....	....	Solomon Islands
69	235	341	406	501	461	319	320	327	272	293	462	363	915	675	1,124	845	Sri Lanka
1,128	1,998	1,871	2,614	772	2,553	2,638	1,642	467	1,311	4,250	7,527	10,516	12,190	9,280	14,097	....	Thailand
4	3	7	8	−2	−1	6	6	—	−4	12	—	−12	1	5	4	....	Tonga
....	....	....	....	11	9	−9	10	16	23	11	20	11	11	14	25	....	Vanuatu
11	21	10	9	3	4	7	3	—	1	2	−2	4	27	40	29	....	Western Samoa
−815	493	2,423	5,023	479	437	−3,960	−4,013	5,816	11,096	−9,793	−11,864	−14,568	−2,415	−6,505	−5,368	−973	Asia not specified
6,075	7,789	9,064	−1,498	−5,858	−3,163	−4,377	−1,948	−1,393	−3,261	−14,104	−28	−2,927	−6,230	1,613	18,190	279	**Europe**
....	....	−13	−19	53	−3	16	19	2	6	161	364	−120	−56	15	34	164	Albania
....	....	....	....	....	....	....	....	....	....	....	....	....	....	....	74	78	Armenia
....	....	−719	−483	−51	176	−118	434	66	223	1,059	335	−2,744	94	631	776	−142	Bulgaria
....	....	....	....	....	....	....	....	....	....	....	....	....	....	....	5	327	Croatia
203	228	295	260	318	247	318	151	191	−5	83	381	251	111	41	....	....	Cyprus
....	....	....	−909	−582	−640	−542	−802	91	−111	−886	−373	100	−119	−391	....	....	Czechoslovakia
....	....	....	....	....	....	....	....	....	....	....	....	....	....	22	141	188	Estonia
....	....	....	....	−9	56	27	991	1,497	395	730	760	−791	1,392	418	6,807	3,579	Hungary
53	9	13	61	40	109	24	−41	−11	−27	−26	24	−14	−71	19	73	....	Malta
2,674	3,640	2,780	−1,692	−5,223	−3,337	−3,187	−1,358	−4,095	−3,227	−10,928	−1,906	−8,569	−4,928	−1,226	2,237	....	Poland
909	1,791	2,174	−548	−233	−1,150	−1,591	−1,698	−783	−1,002	−4,207	−1,262	1,760	335	1,368	1,108	658	Romania
....	....	....	....	....	....	....	....	....	....	....	....	....	....	....	591	....	Slovak Republic
....	....	....	....	....	....	....	....	....	....	....	....	....	....	−294	−64	155	Slovenia
−72	255	2,080	1,549	204	1,291	510	229	2,005	1,386	−443	1,772	3,568	−1,471	2,426	6,688	....	Turkey
1,464	2,110	1,932	−150	−958	−552	−375	−674	−264	−1,010	−534	−496	3,732	−1,636	....	....	....	Yugoslavia, SFR
−11,943	−39,008	−68,292	−47,817	−16,117	17,271	12,431	12,425	11,275	14,520	7,574	9,789	−14,576	67,259	28,697	11,447	9,969	**Middle East**
369	344	159	160	−430	−211	−228	319	−107	−142	−97	−59	−63	1,078	911	....	....	Bahrain
156	1,527	1,048	2,189	1,606	417	1,741	1,966	1,780	560	946	775	−10,409	−3,976	548	−2,281	....	Egypt
−819	−8,899	−7,409	3,076	−846	−1,607	−3,722	1,031	3,941	1,866	859	2,491	−651	7,354	6,339	....	....	Iran, I.R. of
1,954	1,131	1,412	1,912	3,039	1,599	876	−624	−346	1,845	−696	840	581	931	−751	3,804	4,077	Israel
540	327	71	200	233	444	76	219	82	493	498	80	648	2,419	698	−232	....	Jordan
−6,572	−13,666	−14,256	−13,416	−2,989	−4,309	−6,311	−4,253	−5,703	−6,404	−6,530	−7,861	−4,784	27,965	2,319	−3,897	−3,709	Kuwait
−1,359	−1,551	−1,807	−182	−453	−143	−265	456	389	46	434	1,318	−1,043	....	....	....	....	Libya
1	−393	−146	11	256	−143	16	132	427	−676	−158	18	−971	774	775	10	....	Oman
−4,488	−9,972	−37,566	−30,059	−9,883	15,344	16,921	12,222	4,176	12,413	5,821	6,030	−1,259	27,638	15,303	15,714	....	Saudi Arabia
−87	−751	−505	257	158	699	1,010	772	565	377	119	−1,288	−1,726	−627	21	671	....	Syrian Arab Republic
185	215	470	318	163	343	198	237	194	510	408	569	....	....	....	....	....	Yemen Arab Rep.
95	33	155	90	108	187	236	141	118	82	378	401	....	....	....	....	....	Yemen, P.D. Rep.
....	....	....	....	....	....	....	....	....	....	....	....	−485	899	1,150	1,313	121	Yemen, Republic of
−1,919	−7,353	−9,918	−12,372	−7,079	4,652	1,883	−193	5,758	3,552	5,591	6,475	5,586	3,005	984	4,042	5,446	Middle East not spec
25,208	27,792	29,131	37,722	857	−19,245	−11,516	−15,434	−12,349	−13,238	−19,785	−20,974	−6,690	23,120	49,135	39,475	−3,501	**Western Hemisphere**
3	24	15	31	38	3	−1	20	121	91	25	40	−21	−4	9	−10	....	Antigua and Barbuda
−62	4,486	1,890	1,072	−2,335	−2,687	8	325	720	−138	266	−8,257	−5,135	−181	8,975	−9,539	....	Argentina
....	....	....	....	....	....	....	....	70	35	44	68	170	232	−21	−8	−84	Aruba
−52	−3	25	85	75	42	82	−10	−78	−29	42	31	80	96	1	87	....	Bahamas, The
52	39	43	140	37	45	−37	−32	12	30	−3	−67	−23	−15	−116	−43	....	Barbados
....	....	....	....	....	....	—	−7	—	2	24	35	—	9	29	34	....	Belize
278	206	−422	−18	−187	−255	52	−39	94	38	23	−130	82	168	409	....	....	Bolivia
11,624	7,729	9,174	12,370	7,167	−3,096	−5,562	−8,792	−8,494	−11,058	−10,015	−13,320	−5,732	−2,992	5,177	7,527	....	Brazil
1,818	2,141	3,216	4,800	946	−3,168	36	−1,337	−1,614	−1,189	−890	1,092	2,907	1,125	3,208	2,681	3,961	Chile
311	1,058	1,124	1,901	2,204	1,158	1,016	1,964	913	55	410	564	96	−516	297	....	....	Colombia
318	432	174	41	−75	−46	−175	−90	−206	−310	−47	20	−63	255	401	361	....	Costa Rica
1	−1	10	4	6	−3	13	6	1	11	5	33	36	25	26	24	....	Dominica
193	194	596	351	15	−61	254	231	303	292	20	−25	−311	289	382	195	....	Dominican Republic
694	656	888	630	−190	−1,767	−1,283	−883	−1,573	−453	−563	−392	−581	−319	−732	100	265	Ecuador
304	−166	−296	93	113	42	−33	20	−96	−52	−55	232	260	65	61	177	....	El Salvador
—	3	1	10	16	15	−4	4	2	21	9	23	23	35	32	28	....	Grenada
319	161	−162	115	−7	109	−94	−85	−266	114	78	280	−10	816	692	874	....	Guatemala
56	21	23	−29	−18	−73	−39	−42	....	....	....	....	....	....	....	....	....	Guyana
52	53	45	111	97	74	93	96	50	40	38	46	55	134	35	55	....	Haiti
149	190	198	208	144	119	250	156	46	97	−17	−178	−71	100	104	125	....	Honduras
−135	−45	50	18	260	−23	467	213	−48	429	27	93	418	235	277	363	....	Jamaica
....	5,724	11,239	17,514	−5,748	−5,174	−2,034	−3,529	896	−113	−7,688	5,614	9,669	22,861	26,187	30,632	11,118	Mexico
−19	−17	14	—	−127	−114	−214	−331	47	20	−42	−82	14	−36	47	59	....	Netherlands Antilles
−104	−183	−32	323	296	−74	202	167	−311	47	355	−158	−342	−459	−478	−375	−55	Nicaragua
294	284	322	−129	36	−473	−334	−415	−361	−820	−1,615	−987	−408	−264	−230	−409	....	Panama
290	366	428	413	318	198	302	106	139	430	−1	−264	287	687	650	792	....	Paraguay
−129	−121	365	959	1,416	−186	−1,336	−1,461	−1,094	−1,182	−1,070	−1,329	−570	652	1,284	1,253	....	Peru
....	....	1	5	5	16	6	9	8	11	21	41	44	32	22	24	....	St. Kitts and Nevis
24	30	31	35	33	4	14	14	9	13	14	62	63	77	58	46	....	St. Lucia
−3	7	7	1	7	3	6	3	14	9	9	20	10	20	24	40	....	St. Vincent & Grens.
13	−17	8	40	12	49	25	2	−19	−85	−69	−165	−27	31	−26	−31	−24	Suriname
283	363	291	154	393	74	−226	−253	−310	−31	−141	−138	−637	−272	−243	45	....	Trinidad and Tobago
265	431	827	495	−181	−3	45	164	240	185	−61	−69	−50	40	147	415	....	Uruguay
4,670	3,748	−965	−4,021	−3,914	−3,981	−3,015	−1,628	−1,637	184	1,074	−3,829	−6,765	225	2,405	1,720	....	Venezuela
																	Memorandum Items
−3,927	−32,234	−69,678	−54,960	−21,394	17,228	6,880	6,253	10,059	9,189	4,898	2,898	−11,108	65,863	21,388	9,009	−4,572	Oil Exporting Ctys
43,812	51,119	64,867	77,868	31,562	2,959	3,825	5,136	7,710	4,783	−26,868	−4,105	4,427	51,691	74,880	115,865	89,738	Non-Oil Develop.Ctys

Balance of Payments

Overall Balance

Excluding Reserves Assets, Use of Fund Credit, Exceptional Financing, and Liabilities Constituting Foreign Authorities' Reserves

Expressed in Millions of US Dollars

	1978	1979	1980	1981	1982	1983	1984	1985	1986	1987	1988	1989	1990	1991	1992	1993	1994
All Countries	−1,155	3,278	17,242	−41,333	−76,519	−38,937	−23,202	−21,773	−35,467	42,247	−38,877	−1,929	14,995	9,735	−42,002	−37,032	−38,730
Industrial Countries	−5,198	−27,533	−8,008	−14,372	−4,457	−954	−3,716	−8,123	−10,328	27,611	−5,631	6,269	23,294	−20,346	−65,646	−48,667	−29,025
United States	−31,879	13,635	−7,890	−1,242	2,029	−4,054	716	5,795	−33,782	−56,858	−36,270	16,928	−29,807	−21,781	−42,195	−68,653	−41,737
Canada	−5,119	74	−1,275	734	−1,665	−49	−1,822	−3,280	−576	2,778	7,558	293	625	−2,486	−5,807	−492	−5,144
Australia	−88	−701	598	−143	4,902	3,031	−1,307	−2,282	705	371	5,251	628	1,727	−316	−4,737	−55	−955
Japan	9,959	−13,138	5,026	3,636	−4,705	1,550	2,120	−584	14,840	37,939	16,517	−12,761	−6,587	−6,617	632	27,660	25,283
New Zealand	−883	−966	−1,424	−2,102	−2,214	−1,114	−1,546	−2,134	−2,612	−2,248	−2,921	−1,226	178	−1,511	−1,477	−1,773	....
Austria	1,347	−1,029	1,341	379	207	−528	67	15	643	333	491	990	−15	836	2,593	2,202	821
Belgium-Luxembourg	−15	−2,977	550	−2,190	−774	−366	611	228	392	2,273	−104	−2,094	457	504	665	−2,081	....
Denmark	1,496	....	93	−713	−297	1,375	367	1,522	−1,979	4,443	1,316	−3,821	3,374	−3,303	−226	3,851	....
Finland	710	391	280	−224	200	−228	1,817	586	−2,280	4,022	255	−1,058	3,935	−1,889	−2,163	276	4,721
France	3,000	1,752	6,060	−4,766	−3,606	4,166	2,786	2,380	1,418	−8,329	−67	−2,350	11,823	−5,816	−13,094	2,201	5,029
Germany	12,916	−3,438	−9,643	−2,483	2,845	−1,952	−348	2,229	5,426	21,495	−15,423	2,797	7,313	−5,978	36,538	−15,462	−2,116
Greece	194	8	−136	−193	−562	200	−202	−396	650	974	937	−348	280	2,204	−374	3,439	....
Iceland	51	37	34	72	−96	11	−15	64	99	−18	1	55	74	10	70	−60	....
Ireland	142	−586	712	−8	121	188	−43	48	−94	886	592	−937	748	464	−3,542	3,915	....
Italy	3,180	485	793	−961	−4,707	5,883	2,578	−7,590	2,329	5,493	8,416	11,270	11,623	−6,718	−23,992	−3,135	1,575
Netherlands	−917	−588	1,180	−827	1,781	−228	38	751	−386	2,861	1,626	450	277	77	6,427	6,542	410
Norway	637	1,285	1,882	431	708	−98	3,068	3,452	−3,211	−220	−138	965	414	−2,751	−855	4,138	1,451
Portugal	304	276	357	−142	118	−1,262	6	908	−111	1,777	867	4,654	3,542	5,713	−156	−2,847	....
Spain	3,759	3,450	−795	−727	−3,104	−265	4,817	−2,275	2,344	12,706	8,416	4,716	7,179	14,300	−17,810	−4,842	36
Sweden	−693	−2,868	−5,398	−2,790	−4,291	−5,481	−5,834	−4,651	177	762	938	1,223	7,495	133	6,952	2,530	2,331
Switzerland	−906	−3,934	337	−520	3,499	384	1,480	1,224	1,093	3,206	−2,426	1,419	1,172	970	4,420	404	....
United Kingdom	−2,392	−18,628	−689	407	5,153	−2,117	−12,336	−4,134	4,586	−7,035	−1,464	−15,525	−2,533	13,608	−7,513	−6,426	−18,691
Developing Countries	4,043	30,811	25,250	−26,961	−72,062	−37,983	−19,486	−13,650	−25,140	14,636	−33,246	−8,198	−8,299	30,080	23,644	11,635	−9,706
Africa	−2,750	3,430	3,192	−10,899	−10,761	−6,426	−4,644	−3,379	−5,036	−7,441	−11,857	−8,338	−2,279	−6,037	−14,836	−14,039	−13,488
Algeria	93	484	1,341	120	−1,070	−421	−333	1,020	−1,498	−352	−959	−774	−10	1,047	....	....	....
Angola	....	....	....	....	....	....	−6	−259	−332	−925	−930	−1,209	−1,500	−1,138	−1,320	....	....
Benin	−19	−4	−23	31	−48	−37	−23	−29	−71	−71	−98	−66	10	62	−78	−40	....
Botswana	39	116	90	−74	55	124	124	254	307	562	382	576	307	....	....	....	....
Burkina Faso	−31	8	7	14	—	37	36	6	42	17	24	−148	−18	48	18	17	....
Burundi	....	....	....	....	....	....	....	16	29	−3	7	38	−3	33	26	10	....
Cameroon	−13	59	78	−60	−11	117	−86	59	−81	−470	−164	−134	−870	−732	−1,309	−880	....
Cape Verde	−3	3	—	−5	5	3	−5	14	−1	23	−2	−7	−2	−13	8	....	....
Central African Rep.	−13	16	−1	−7	−34	−14	1	−25	−3	−12	−13	−12	−18	−39	−24	....	....
Chad	−26	−30	−24	15	5	9	16	−23	−17	—	−34	30	−23	−19	−36	−51	....
Comoros	....	....	−4	4	4	2	−6	6	3	9	−4	5	−5	−7	....	....	....
Congo	−15	23	47	42	−84	−32	−61	−81	−398	−489	−467	−402	−364	−458	−430	−452	....
Côte d'Ivoire	137	−329	−664	−603	−307	−699	−479	−176	−379	−933	−1,403	−1,311	−1,566	−1,264	−1,390	−1,190	....
Djibouti	....	....	....	....	....	....	....	....	....	....	....	....	....	....	−17	−8	....
Equatorial Guinea	....	....	....	....	....	....	....	....	....	−26	−17	−16	−10	−23	....	....	....
Ethiopia	−88	−19	−102	108	−75	−53	−57	162	114	−107	−22	45	−198	−356	−266	92	....
Gabon	8	−16	96	118	147	−89	13	−61	−195	−135	−1	−96	−237	−220	−444	−421	....
Gambia, The	−17	−20	−36	−5	−29	−22	−20	−6	−32	11	25	4	4	17	19	....	....
Ghana	−62	70	−1	−288	−18	−181	36	14	−61	140	181	156	105	109	−57	....	....
Guinea	....	....	....	....	....	....	....	....	−97	−36	−152	−109	−83	−130	−130	−33	....
Guinea-Bissau	....	....	....	....	−20	−18	−12	8	−33	−31	−41	−70	−32	−71	−52	−58	....
Kenya	−220	72	−371	−306	−160	98	61	−52	137	−25	−44	122	−93	−44	−257	412	....
Lesotho	−2	−3	41	1	8	26	9	6	13	1	−6	−8	17	42	50	102	....
Liberia	....	−73	−47	−49	−124	−128	−153	−203	−294	−300	....	....	....	....	....	....	....
Madagascar	−11	−131	−248	−165	−209	−269	−203	−167	−116	−163	−118	−174	−278	−235	−276	....	....
Malawi	−13	−83	−22	−27	−38	−98	4	−26	−1	45	60	−52	29	16	−47	24	....
Mali	−18	−20	−33	−13	−26	−32	—	−27	−50	−14	46	13	−66	41	−126	−85	....
Mauritania	10	6	−43	−25	−57	−43	−34	−32	−18	−157	−73	−5	−72	16	17	−300	....
Mauritius	−70	−93	−28	−131	−60	−31	−39	−2	123	221	185	145	232	191	43	7	....
Morocco	−72	−111	−289	−319	−391	−226	−109	−34	331	298	264	21	1,697	1,167	546	231	....
Mozambique	....	....	−32	−67	−141	−301	−396	−366	−459	−441	−400	−458	−433	−536	−472	....	....
Namibia	....	....	....	....	....	....	....	....	....	....	....	....	37	−12	−7	91	75
Niger	−11	−9	−5	−8	−64	−14	−31	−50	−48	−34	−14	−79	−111	−88	−16	−63	....
Nigeria	−2,109	3,204	4,372	−4,722	−5,613	−2,988	−968	−1,233	−986	−4,495	−4,953	−2,663	1,041	−1,523	−5,638	....	....
Rwanda	1	62	23	−7	−37	−18	8	2	30	−11	−50	−67	−23	65	−4	....	....
São Tomé & Príncipe	7	1	−13	−7	−14	−7	−7	−11	−11	−4	−4	−6	−9	....	....	....	....
Senegal	−59	−27	−58	−133	−234	−110	−98	−91	−35	−97	−115	−163	−228	−180	−107	−148	....
Seychelles	−1	4	8	−5	—	−2	−2	—	−1	4	−4	4	4	10	4	....	....
Sierra Leone	−9	−55	−76	−107	−80	−93	−96	−74	−97	−53	−72	−48	−21	19	....	....	....
Somalia	28	−107	−31	4	36	−78	−27	−12	−97	−98	−182	−190	....	....	....	....	....
South Africa	580	474	795	−2,200	−245	287	−581	−507	493	1,361	−1,386	−113	1,405	1,506	131	−2,795	....
Sudan	−102	−107	−526	−396	−202	−223	−118	−421	−201	−343	−287	−193	−244	−273	−159	....	....
Swaziland	16	−9	34	−49	−9	12	−9	−4	7	22	15	51	11	13	92	−48	....
Tanzania	−251	−172	−350	−86	−273	−88	−221	−487	−353	−292	−384	−327	−82	−363	−288	−352	....
Togo	20	−16	−33	−46	−78	−38	−21	−3	−43	−130	−48	−28	−28	−42	−158	−187	....
Tunisia	82	107	76	63	163	35	−100	−225	−84	126	441	65	−123	−55	97	7	....
Uganda	....	....	−214	−127	−80	−81	67	33	−27	−54	−37	−85	−42	−32	24	58	....
Zaïre	....	....	....	....	−696	−532	−549	−383	−519	−561	−724	−559	−761	....	....	....	....
Zambia	−342	68	−225	−464	−390	−21	−89	−181	−134	−242	−232	−106	222	−179	....	....	....
Zimbabwe	75	120	−86	−18	−22	−174	−46	82	55	124	102	−47	86	45	−195	226	....
Asia	6,010	5,224	6,109	3,888	3,280	4,568	7,953	6,942	23,431	43,736	21,454	19,100	23,834	37,985	28,271	47,702	68,482
Afghanistan, I.S. of	....	−5	−72	−38	−8	−59	70	26	−19	11	−26	−20	....	....	....	....	....
Bangladesh	42	−324	−324	−217	−100	352	−6	−80	124	196	132	−309	224	434	635	698	....
China, People's Rep.	....	....	....	....	6,305	4,142	138	−2,440	−2,048	4,783	2,374	−479	12,047	14,537	−2,060	1,769	....
Fiji	....	5	40	−24	−22	−6	7	−5	28	−63	112	−14	36	10	53	−42	....
India	1,920	832	−1,663	−2,178	−1,698	−752	1,070	−397	−409	133	−16	239	−1,937	....	....	....	....
Indonesia	....	....	....	−374	−1,853	183	981	510	−1,003	630	−113	495	2,251	1,528	2,070	587	....
Kiribati	....	6	−2	−9	−4	−5	−4	—	2	3	3	7	7	10	....	....	....
Korea	731	874	311	−329	5	−236	560	192	77	2,104	9,316	3,120	−1,208	−1,148	3,724	3,009	4,614

Balance of Payments

Overall Balance
Excluding Reserves Assets, Use of Fund Credit, Exceptional Financing, and Liabilities Constituting Foreign Authorities' Reserves

Expressed in Millions of US Dollars

1978	1979	1980	1981	1982	1983	1984	1985	1986	1987	1988	1989	1990	1991	1992	1993	1994	
																	Asia (cont.)
....	....	....	....	....	....	−3	23	12	−8	4	−4	1	15	4	16	....	Lao P. D. Rep.
279	802	468	−452	−262	−15	486	1,151	1,455	1,119	−430	1,230	1,953	1,238	6,655	11,343	....	Malaysia
—	—	—	−1	6	−4	−5	2	−4	1	14	2	−1	−1	5	—	....	Maldives
....	....	....	−1	2	−4	14	25	15	76	1	130	−102	....	....	....	....	Mongolia
−64	57	31	−29	−128	−24	−9	−15	49	38	80	151	9	....	....	....	....	Myanmar
−22	27	−13	51	2	−8	−21	−93	−33	64	−6	−42	20	163	155	66	....	Nepal
−93	−474	−211	−257	−240	542	−958	−417	−157	−177	147	−439	−585	−584	808	−78	....	Pakistan
−4	109	−84	−51	−36	97	49	−1	3	2	−53	−59	23	−86	−72	−82	....	Papua New Guinea
760	316	891	−565	−729	−3,496	−448	838	1,134	−58	674	300	−45	1,755	1,689	289	....	Philippines
665	516	663	909	1,177	1,059	1,524	1,337	538	1,095	1,659	2,738	5,431	4,198	6,100	7,578	....	Singapore
15	8	−9	−7	5	4	−11	−15	−18	−7	−5	−13	−14	−13	14	....	....	Solomon Islands
1	6	−316	−39	−48	−5	320	−98	−90	−54	−101	48	65	320	224	742	298	Sri Lanka
−25	−88	−206	43	−231	−320	529	105	714	945	2,596	5,029	3,235	4,618	2,925	7,169	....	Thailand
3	1	3	—	2	—	6	4	—	1	1	−2	1	−1	4	8	....	Tonga
....	....	....	....	3	1	−6	—	5	−1	−5	8	5	−3	1	3	....	Vanuatu
−7	−1	−2	−6	−3	7	7	5	7	7	9	10	11	−2	−13	−9	....	Western Samoa
297	18	466	3,992	1,186	3,187	3,662	6,285	23,048	32,894	5,087	6,975	2,609	15,538	7,892	10,033	12,668	Asia not specified
−485	**−2,729**	**−2,778**	**−10,439**	**−8,666**	**−5,502**	**−4,209**	**−2,552**	**−3,745**	**−2,336**	**−7,195**	**2,727**	**−9,960**	**−9,799**	**−1,949**	**−1,208**	**−2,255**	**Europe**
....	....	3	26	−14	−41	−12	−18	−1	12	134	325	−238	−224	−36	49	7	Albania
....	....	....	....	....	....	....	....	....	....	....	....	....	....	....	7	−28	Armenia
....	....	235	−361	126	212	417	298	−885	−497	657	−434	−4,454	17	271	−322	−3	Bulgaria
....	....	....	....	....	....	....	....	....	....	....	....	....	....	....	110	429	Croatia
18	−12	37	88	140	42	96	−30	159	64	71	229	297	−104	−219	....	....	Cyprus
....	....	....	−881	−160	36	166	−112	260	260	207	563	−1,127	789	−422	....	....	Czechoslovakia
....	....	....	....	....	....	....	....	....	....	....	....	....	....	58	165	17	Estonia
....	....	....	....	−540	−125	66	536	132	−281	158	172	−413	1,795	770	2,545	−475	Hungary
125	55	51	148	52	104	32	−67	−5	−5	35	14	−75	−85	45	3	....	Malta
129	275	−637	−5,678	−7,164	−4,918	−4,270	−2,340	−5,201	−3,606	−11,035	−3,315	−5,502	−7,074	−4,330	−3,551	....	Poland
150	138	−246	−1,381	807	10	128	−317	612	1,041	−285	1,252	−1,494	−677	−138	−54	399	Romania
....	....	....	....	....	....	....	....	....	....	....	....	....	....	....	11	....	Slovak Republic
....	....	....	....	....	....	....	....	....	....	....	....	....	....	633	125	647	Slovenia
−1,337	−1,158	−1,328	−387	−748	−632	−897	−784	540	580	1,153	2,710	943	−1,199	1,484	308	....	Turkey
191	−1,549	−385	−1,109	−1,431	−277	103	159	836	238	1,953	1,931	1,368	−2,797	....	....	....	Yugoslavia, SFR
−4,421	**16,444**	**19,520**	**−4,767**	**−15,648**	**−3,644**	**−6,098**	**3,244**	**−10,749**	**3,612**	**−6,105**	**6,979**	**−11,301**	**2,334**	**−2,670**	**−15,784**	**−11,392**	**Middle East**
−18	122	343	589	−4	−109	−10	357	−176	−343	93	−188	182	282	−82	....	....	Bahrain
−1,064	−16	610	53	−245	87	−247	−200	34	315	−102	−533	−10,224	−2,073	3,360	18	....	Egypt
−715	3,069	−9,847	−370	4,887	−1,249	−4,136	555	−1,214	−224	−1,010	2,300	−324	−2,094	−165	....	....	Iran, I.R. of
945	211	541	550	914	−500	−547	399	993	661	−1,170	1,398	515	−173	−1,457	1,481	69	Israel
252	321	445	161	−100	53	−189	−42	43	141	204	465	421	2,025	−137	−861	....	Jordan
−443	366	1,045	283	1,975	1,002	117	545	−83	−1,847	−1,928	1,275	−897	1,276	1,851	−1,485	53	Kuwait
−621	2,220	6,407	−4,145	−2,013	−1,786	−1,721	2,362	224	−1,082	−1,392	292	1,158	....	....	....	....	Libya
−49	155	796	1,247	744	351	319	122	−613	108	−467	324	135	530	280	−1,058	....	Oman
−6,700	234	3,937	9,568	−2,308	−1,508	−1,480	−709	−7,619	2,640	−1,519	−3,508	−5,376	49	−5,664	1,496	....	Saudi Arabia
−103	195	−254	−51	−92	−145	216	−186	61	79	−32	−66	36	72	76	64	....	Syrian Arab Republic
201	−27	−215	−338	−444	−216	−102	−50	69	58	−286	−10	....	....	....	....	....	Yemen Arab Rep.
65	17	30	11	8	3	−17	−90	−58	−48	−26	−16	....	....	....	....	....	Yemen, P.D. Rep.
....	....	....	....	....	....	....	....	....	....	....	....	....	−25	4	−13	−3	47	Yemen, Republic of
3,827	9,577	15,681	−12,326	−18,970	374	1,700	180	−2,344	3,153	1,532	5,248	3,099	2,213	−474	−1,741	−1,473	Middle East not spec
5,689	**8,443**	**−794**	**−4,744**	**−40,267**	**−26,980**	**−12,487**	**−17,905**	**−29,041**	**−22,936**	**−29,544**	**−28,667**	**−8,592**	**5,598**	**14,828**	**−5,037**	**−51,052**	**Western Hemisphere**
1	5	−4	−2	−3	−6	—	−3	4	−20	−18	−39	−47	−34	−19	−30	....	Antigua and Barbuda
1,794	3,973	−2,884	−3,640	−4,688	−5,123	−2,487	−627	−2,139	−4,373	−1,306	−9,562	−583	−828	2,429	−16,991	....	Argentina
....	....	....	....	....	....	....	....	51	13	—	22	12	23	23	33	−3	Aruba
−9	15	11	5	14	11	39	19	−31	−60	−1	−27	9	13	−29	19	....	Bahamas, The
21	5	18	21	2	8	−17	22	20	7	40	−43	−39	−40	28	21	....	Barbados
....	....	....	....	....	....	−5	2	12	12	22	16	15	−16	—	−14	....	Belize
−54	−191	−429	−487	−361	−397	−126	−324	−294	−394	−281	−400	−116	−94	−125	....	....	Bolivia
4,628	−2,787	−3,706	553	−9,175	−9,946	−5,556	−9,094	−13,823	−12,534	−5,878	−12,319	−9,651	−4,685	11,266	6,890	....	Brazil
730	952	1,245	67	−1,358	−4,285	−2,075	−2,750	−2,806	−1,924	−1,124	387	2,371	1,237	2,500	585	3,204	Chile
569	1,496	919	−60	−850	−1,845	−385	155	1,296	391	194	363	638	1,834	1,209	....	....	Colombia
−45	−127	−490	−368	−346	−358	−426	−381	−366	−686	−351	−427	−557	156	21	−109	....	Costa Rica
—	6	−4	−9	−2	−4	6	−1	7	8	−1	—	5	4	3	1	....	Dominica
−118	−138	−123	−39	−428	−479	90	124	120	−72	1	−241	−418	253	−63	34	....	Dominican Republic
−10	25	246	−368	−1,372	−1,882	−1,556	−807	−2,169	−1,625	−1,174	−986	−791	−861	−805	−430	−432	Ecuador
25	−134	−262	−158	−7	−106	−222	−169	−113	−120	−184	−98	25	−148	−134	59	....	El Salvador
1	2	1	−4	−2	—	−2	6	—	1	−8	−7	−5	—	9	−1	....	Grenada
48	−45	−325	−458	−406	−115	−471	−331	−283	−329	−336	−87	−243	632	−14	173	....	Guatemala
27	−62	−106	−213	−161	−231	−138	−139	....	....	....	....	....	....	....	....	....	Guyana
7	—	−56	−38	−1	−37	−10	1	5	9	−2	−16	−34	10	−6	−23	....	Haiti
−8	−3	−118	−95	−84	−113	−124	−153	−179	−166	−198	−384	−299	−158	−247	−183	....	Honduras
−157	−151	−87	−289	−124	−362	152	−60	−66	303	73	−189	106	−5	306	149	....	Jamaica
....	315	817	1,274	−11,637	692	2,149	−2,729	481	4,134	−10,062	−211	2,218	7,973	1,745	7,232	−17,666	Mexico
−44	7	15	53	51	−26	−39	72	98	−30	33	−44	−30	−42	59	44	....	Netherlands Antilles
−129	−3	−443	−269	−218	−582	−395	−559	−999	−632	−360	−520	−647	−464	−1,312	−1,019	−784	Nicaragua
86	−27	11	−73	−15	−57	−115	−129	−6	−501	−1,004	−832	−361	−422	−314	−407	....	Panama
177	160	151	39	−56	−50	−16	−146	−226	−59	−211	−8	114	363	50	189	....	Paraguay
−322	609	264	−774	−196	−1,061	−1,571	−1,371	−2,267	−2,822	−2,316	−1,254	−1,471	−679	−426	−547	....	Peru
....	....	−2	—	−4	1	2	2	3	1	—	6	—	1	10	3	....	St. Kitts and Nevis
1	2	−2	−5	2	—	—	1	11	9	2	6	6	8	7	4	....	St. Lucia
....	4	−2	—	−4	—	5	6	11	−5	2	1	4	−4	11	−1	....	St. Vincent & Grens.
42	27	26	13	−43	−109	−53	−8	−40	−9	−5	—	10	−44	−12	13	34	Suriname
337	344	648	569	−207	−873	−693	−301	−722	−256	−229	−177	−178	−277	−104	159	....	Trinidad and Tobago
138	74	118	34	−416	−66	−84	66	282	44	−38	65	136	82	138	189	....	Uruguay
−1,065	4,098	3,763	−21	−8,160	446	1,636	1,699	−3,882	−1,206	−4,735	−1,668	1,514	1,961	−1,348	−503	....	Venezuela
																	Memorandum Items
−7,991	26,857	32,593	−9,655	−34,113	−4,555	−2,701	5,388	−18,388	−2,074	−15,145	1,520	2,858	5,504	−9,062	−16,382	−19,124	Oil Exporting Ctys
12,034	3,954	−7,343	−17,307	−37,949	−33,428	−16,785	−19,039	−6,751	16,710	−18,102	−9,717	−11,157	24,576	32,705	28,017	9,418	Non-Oil Develop.Ctys

Balance of Payments

Exports of Goods and Services

As percent of GDP

	1978	1979	1980	1981	1982	1983	1984	1985	1986	1987	1988	1989	1990	1991	1992	1993	1994
All Countries																	
Industrial Countries																	
United States	8.0	9.0	10.0	9.7	8.7	7.8	7.7	7.1	7.2	7.7	8.8	9.3	9.7	10.1	10.2	10.1	10.4
Canada	25.3	27.2	28.2	27.2	25.8	25.5	28.3	28.2	27.3	26.4	26.3	25.2	25.0	24.4	26.2	29.4	33.2
Australia	14.7	16.9	17.1	15.0	15.4	14.6	15.2	16.9	16.4	16.9	16.9	16.4	17.0	18.1	18.6	19.3	19.0
Japan	11.2	11.6	13.9	14.8	14.7	14.1	15.1	14.7	11.6	10.6	10.2	10.8	11.0	10.6	10.5	9.7	9.7
New Zealand	27.9	29.9	28.5	28.2	27.8	28.7	30.6	31.2	26.3	25.6	25.8	26.3	26.8	28.7	30.2	30.2	....
Austria	32.5	34.4	34.7	36.1	37.8	37.2	38.7	40.8	36.8	35.6	37.6	39.8	40.2	39.9	39.4	37.9	37.6
Belgium-Luxembourg	50.5	56.1	59.7	65.4	69.6	72.4	76.2	75.1	69.4	69.4	71.7	75.3	73.2	71.3	69.1	68.2	....
Denmark	29.4	....	34.5	38.4	37.8	38.1	38.7	39.0	33.6	32.8	34.2	36.5	37.9	39.4	39.1	37.0	....
Finland	30.0	31.4	32.7	33.0	30.8	30.2	30.6	29.5	26.8	25.7	24.9	23.8	22.9	22.6	26.8	33.1	35.5
France	21.8	22.6	23.1	24.7	23.4	23.9	25.6	25.4	22.4	21.8	22.4	24.0	23.9	24.1	24.7	23.5	23.6
Germany	25.9	26.1	27.6	30.2	31.5	30.2	32.2	34.3	31.5	30.3	30.8	32.6	31.4	29.1	27.6	25.9	26.9
Greece	18.2	19.3	20.2	23.9	19.8	20.1	21.2	20.8	19.8	21.7	20.8	20.1	19.6	20.0	19.0	18.2	....
Iceland	37.8	39.3	36.9	35.3	32.0	39.5	38.8	41.5	39.6	35.5	32.8	35.5	35.1	32.0	31.1	33.4	....
Ireland	50.2	50.1	50.0	48.7	48.2	51.9	59.0	60.2	52.7	56.3	60.3	63.6	59.6	59.9	62.4	67.7	....
Italy	23.2	24.0	21.5	22.9	22.5	21.7	22.4	22.7	20.0	19.3	18.9	19.9	20.1	19.1	19.7	23.0	24.5
Netherlands	44.6	49.0	52.9	58.8	58.7	57.9	63.0	63.6	53.1	51.5	53.9	57.7	56.2	56.0	54.1	52.7	53.5
Norway	40.9	44.1	47.2	47.7	45.6	45.7	47.3	47.3	37.8	35.7	36.7	42.2	44.9	44.9	43.1	43.2	43.8
Portugal	21.5	25.6	26.6	25.1	24.6	29.5	35.9	37.1	32.8	34.0	34.6	36.5	35.9	31.4	28.4	....	....
Spain	14.7	14.6	15.2	17.5	18.3	20.5	22.7	22.7	19.8	19.3	18.9	18.3	17.0	16.9	17.3	19.4	22.4
Sweden	28.8	31.5	30.5	31.0	32.8	36.2	36.9	36.0	32.7	32.8	32.9	32.7	30.7	28.9	28.9	33.4	37.5
Switzerland	40.4	41.7	47.8	49.9	44.6	42.6	48.4	48.5	43.8	40.4	42.0	44.7	41.7	39.6	40.7	40.4	....
United Kingdom	28.2	27.8	27.1	26.6	26.2	26.2	28.1	28.8	25.4	25.2	22.8	23.5	24.3	23.3	23.6	25.1	26.0
Developing Countries																	
Africa																	
Algeria	25.2	29.9	33.4	32.9	31.1	27.5	25.3	23.4	13.7	14.9	15.0	19.5	22.6	29.8	....	....	....
Angola								35.4	22.7	32.6	32.7	33.9	38.8				
Benin	22.9	19.4	19.5	41.1	14.5	16.7	26.4	35.1	27.2	30.3	29.9	17.4	21.9	24.0	....	....	....
Botswana	55.0	72.4	65.0	47.6	64.4	71.7	73.3	83.6	73.9	102.3	76.1	71.1	57.3				
Burkina Faso	13.3	14.7	16.3	16.8	16.0	15.1	18.8	16.0	....								
Burundi	....	....	....	....	....	....	....	10.8	11.4	9.5	12.5	9.6	7.8	9.5	8.1	8.6	....
Cameroon	30.4	32.0	32.1	27.2	27.0	26.3	27.4	24.5	21.3	17.1	18.5	21.3	20.4	21.0	21.4	....	....
Cape Verde	6.8	10.1	13.0	16.3	21.7	26.0	22.5	21.7	18.7	18.9	15.1	....					
Central African Rep.	26.7	24.7	25.2	21.1	22.0	24.1	23.4	25.3	19.4	18.7	17.8	20.0	16.9	13.7	13.2	....	....
Chad	12.9	....	7.5	....	10.5	18.2	28.6	14.2	17.5	22.0	21.5	19.5	22.2	17.0	15.8	13.8	....
Comoros																	
Congo	42.9	47.3	59.9	58.0	54.8	55.0	61.5	56.4	42.0	42.4	42.3	52.8	52.2	45.6	45.4	48.6	....
Côte d'Ivoire	38.3	35.4	35.2	34.0	37.0	36.4	43.8	45.3	40.0	34.5	31.7	32.6	33.2	30.7	....	....	....
Djibouti																	
Equatorial Guinea	....	....	....	....	....	....	....	....	....	....	33.8	41.9	31.1	29.2	28.5		
Ethiopia	11.0	13.4	13.3	12.0	9.9	8.9	10.5	9.3	10.3	8.7	8.7	9.0	6.9	4.6	6.0	9.2	....
Gabon	61.9	66.8	56.3	65.0	64.4	63.5	64.7	59.6	26.1	40.3	36.8	45.4	49.7	47.0	44.1	....	....
Gambia, The	30.9	33.9	27.7	28.8	36.3	36.0	56.7	39.1	59.8	59.0	59.6	64.8	60.1	74.8	68.7	....	....
Ghana	8.4	11.3	7.8	3.1	2.3	2.3	8.1	10.6	14.2	18.5	18.3	16.8	15.6	15.6	15.9	....	....
Guinea																	
Guinea-Bissau	....	....	....	....	....	....	....	....	4.2	9.3	10.3	7.2	8.3	8.7	2.9	6.8	....
Kenya	28.1	25.8	28.3	26.4	25.0	25.0	26.2	25.6	25.8	21.3	22.0	23.1	26.1	27.3	27.1	41.8	....
Lesotho	18.7	19.9	24.5	21.3	18.5	18.6	17.1	16.5	16.5	20.0	21.2	20.0	15.7	16.4	19.7	21.6	....
Liberia	....	62.9	66.9	52.9	45.6	40.7	45.7	43.5	44.2	38.1	....						
Madagascar	20.4	17.4	15.8	13.6	13.2	12.5	13.3	12.2	12.2	16.5	16.5	18.6	16.6	18.1	16.7	....	....
Malawi	22.1	24.3	25.3	25.5	22.7	22.5	28.0	24.0	22.7	25.9	24.9	19.7	25.1	23.6	23.1	17.7	....
Mali	13.6	15.7	18.5	14.3	15.5	19.3	21.9	18.8	16.0	17.1	16.9	16.8	17.1	18.1	....	....	....
Mauritania	28.3	28.7	36.6	42.6	38.3	44.0	44.6	57.7	52.5	46.7	49.4	49.1	44.8	41.1	....	....	....
Mauritius	43.7	39.9	50.3	41.7	46.7	45.5	47.3	54.8	60.9	66.9	66.6	65.5	67.3	65.1	62.1	61.1	....
Morocco	16.2	16.8	17.2	19.9	18.9	20.9	23.5	24.4	21.0	22.3	24.3	21.8	24.0	21.9	24.8	....	....
Mozambique	....	....	16.6	17.0	16.1	11.9	8.1	5.6	4.7	13.0	15.6	15.0	15.9	21.6	24.5	....	....
Namibia														56.6	59.8	58.4	59.1
Niger	20.1	25.0	24.3	23.7	21.0	20.8	22.9	20.7	17.4	20.8	18.3	16.7	15.1	14.4	....	....	....
Nigeria	19.9	25.0	29.1	23.2	16.5	13.6	14.8	16.6	15.0	28.7	22.7	27.6	44.9	40.2	40.4	....	....
Rwanda	14.4	21.6	14.2	11.4	10.1	10.1	11.0	9.4	11.7	7.7	6.9	6.1	6.2	8.2	6.1	....	....
São Tomé & Príncipe	....	....	31.7	20.5	36.8	27.4	29.5	....	21.1	14.8	22.6	20.4	14.6				
Senegal	30.8	29.9	27.2	39.9	33.8	36.4	39.4	33.7	30.0	24.2	23.2	26.6	26.5	25.2	....	....	....
Seychelles	82.3	70.6	65.7	60.6	55.2	55.9	66.1	69.1	61.1	61.4	64.0	65.9	69.8	67.8	61.5	....	....
Sierra Leone	26.0	24.9	25.0	18.2	11.4	14.3	16.0	18.7	31.1	29.5	15.7	20.7	35.3	35.5	....	....	....
Somalia	11.7	9.2	7.2	7.1	9.4	7.9	3.4	5.7	5.7	5.8	....						
South Africa	33.9	36.6	37.0	29.2	27.1	25.5	26.7	33.0	32.5	28.7	28.4	27.4	25.4	23.8	22.8	23.6	....
Sudan	8.4	7.7	9.9	10.6	12.4	11.1	8.9	13.6	6.8	3.7	5.7	4.5	2.0	1.4	....	....	....
Swaziland	64.5	65.9	74.6	75.2	70.9	66.3	61.1	61.2	68.7	80.1	76.2	83.7	73.5	79.3	....	....	....
Tanzania	14.5	15.5	14.6	13.5	8.4	7.7	8.7	6.3	8.9	11.2	15.1	18.8	21.0	15.8	20.2	35.1	....
Togo	35.6	33.6	48.7	50.0	52.8	44.0	51.2	49.0	44.2	41.7	....						
Tunisia	27.7	35.3	37.6	41.9	36.9	35.4	33.6	32.3	30.7	34.6	42.0	44.5	42.2	39.3	38.4	39.7	....
Uganda	....	....	1.8	5.1	8.3	9.5	14.3	9.0	9.0	6.4	4.5	5.3	4.8	6.4	5.7	8.1	....
Zaïre	....	....	....	....	12.1	16.2	25.9	27.5	24.7	25.4	26.3	25.9	24.5				
Zambia	33.6	45.4	41.4	28.7	27.5	30.8	35.6	38.4	43.9	43.3	34.4	35.7	36.4	37.0	....	....	....
Zimbabwe	28.6	28.1	30.1	24.7	21.8	20.9	25.8	31.3	29.7	29.0	30.7	31.1	32.5				
Asia																	
Afghanistan, I.S. of	....	13.2	17.6	15.6	14.1	11.7	9.5	7.1	5.1	....							
Bangladesh	6.7	7.1	7.8	7.7	8.2	8.0	8.3	8.5	7.2	7.6	8.3	8.0	9.7	9.3	11.1	11.7	....
China, People's Rep.	....	....	....	....	10.5	9.7	11.0	11.8	13.0	15.6	14.5	13.7	19.0	21.9	18.1	20.1	....
Fiji	43.4	45.3	48.0	42.9	43.6	43.7	42.9	44.6	41.5	45.0	55.7	61.8	63.3	57.6	54.8	56.8	....
India	6.4	6.9	6.5	6.1	6.5	6.4	6.6	6.1	5.8	5.9	6.1	7.2	7.5	....	....	....	....
Indonesia	....	....	....	25.9	21.4	22.5	24.3	22.2	19.0	24.1	24.8	26.3	27.6	27.8	29.0	25.7	....
Kiribati	....	64.8	27.7	36.8	27.2	29.1	43.8	33.8	22.2	31.9	30.5	23.3	22.5	17.7	....	....	....
Korea	33.4	29.5	35.0	37.9	37.0	35.9	35.9	34.0	37.6	40.4	38.1	32.3	29.3	27.8	28.6	29.0	29.9

Balance of Payments

Exports of Goods and Services

As percent of GDP

1978	1979	1980	1981	1982	1983	1984	1985	1986	1987	1988	1989	1990	1991	1992	1993	1994	
																	Asia (cont.)
....	....	....	....	....	....	....	....	....	....	....	....	....	....	....	....	....	Lao P. D. Rep.
49.0	55.9	57.6	52.3	50.9	52.0	54.4	55.0	56.4	63.8	67.3	73.0	76.3	80.8	77.7	81.5	....	Malaysia
67.6	139.8	153.5	149.8	127.3	115.9	111.0	107.7	100.0	121.4	118.5	129.8	145.9	....	....	....	....	Maldives
....	....	....	....	....	....	....	....	....	....	....	....	....	....	....	....	....	Mongolia
6.5	7.6	8.2	10.3	8.4	7.1	6.7	5.7	4.9	2.8	1.8	1.5	1.3	....	....	....	....	Myanmar
11.6	12.0	13.2	13.5	10.6	11.7	12.1	12.5	12.2	13.0	12.6	11.1	12.0	15.9	18.6	20.9	....	Nepal
10.1	12.7	13.6	12.0	11.5	13.1	10.9	11.8	13.0	14.9	14.0	16.0	17.3	18.4	17.5	17.3	....	Pakistan
34.6	42.2	37.2	34.1	33.6	34.9	38.6	41.2	41.7	42.7	43.7	41.9	42.8	47.1	53.6	55.4	....	Papua New Guinea
18.4	19.3	22.3	21.1	18.4	20.5	22.4	22.3	25.8	24.3	25.0	25.9	25.8	27.5	27.5	29.5	....	Philippines
169.0	189.1	207.2	203.6	190.9	171.0	161.1	157.8	155.2	172.4	190.6	187.8	182.2	175.0	166.6	168.5	....	Singapore
41.0	57.1	59.2	49.0	44.1	62.7	59.0	50.2	55.5	57.6	60.7	60.4	56.4	....	....	....	....	Solomon Islands
34.8	33.7	32.1	30.4	27.4	26.3	28.8	26.1	23.6	25.8	26.0	26.5	28.5	28.3	30.1	33.1	33.8	Sri Lanka
20.3	22.9	24.5	24.4	23.4	20.4	22.3	23.4	25.8	29.0	33.1	35.0	34.1	36.2	36.8	....	....	Thailand
32.2	27.0	23.9	20.9	23.2	17.4	29.3	41.0	30.9	31.1	22.4	27.3	31.3	21.7	21.6	19.4	....	Tonga
....	....	....	....	48.6	54.9	73.3	54.9	38.9	50.8	53.3	38.3	48.3	47.1	48.2	43.4	....	Vanuatu
....	....	....	....	20.1	26.9	27.6	31.1	26.5	28.3	35.4	40.0	....	....	....	....	....	Western Samoa
																	Europe
....	....	....	....	....	....	....	....	....	....	....	....	....	....	....	....	....	Albania
....	....	....	....	....	....	....	....	....	....	....	....	....	....	....	....	....	Armenia
....	....	....	....	....	....	....	35.2	27.8	27.1	23.0	20.3	33.5	53.2	....	....	....	Bulgaria
....	....	....	....	....	....	....	....	....	....	....	....	....	....	....	....	....	Croatia
44.1	46.3	46.9	51.9	52.5	52.0	56.1	50.1	46.4	48.6	49.4	52.7	53.1	48.1	52.7	....	....	Cyprus
....	....	....	38.6	39.3	39.6	43.3	35.3	34.9	34.7	34.8	33.9	31.6	40.8	....	....	....	Czechoslovakia
....	....	....	....	....	....	....	....	....	....	....	....	....	....	....	66.3	....	Estonia
....	....	....	....	41.8	45.5	47.6	44.6	41.8	41.9	38.8	40.7	36.6	39.5	38.0	30.3	....	Hungary
87.0	88.8	89.8	80.8	67.1	65.1	67.7	69.9	69.4	76.1	78.2	79.9	84.4	85.9	90.9	93.6	....	Malta
....	30.5	28.3	23.1	20.5	18.0	18.1	18.4	18.9	22.3	23.7	19.5	30.6	23.2	22.2	20.7	....	Poland
....	....	35.3	32.4	25.5	27.3	35.2	22.9	20.1	19.4	20.4	21.1	16.7	17.1	25.9	23.0	....	Romania
....	....	....	....	....	....	....	....	....	....	....	....	....	....	....	66.8	....	Slovak Republic
....	....	....	....	....	....	....	....	....	....	....	....	....	....	....	59.9	....	Slovenia
....	....	....	....	....	....	....	....	....	15.9	19.3	17.0	13.5	13.9	14.6	14.2	....	Turkey
15.5	14.7	19.5	22.3	25.2	29.5	31.2	32.3	25.5	23.1	28.7	19.4	....	....	....	....	....	Yugoslavia, SFR
																	Middle East
96.3	105.4	122.6	130.9	116.9	93.3	102.9	102.8	93.0	103.9	98.6	103.4	118.7	....	....	....	....	Bahrain
14.3	23.6	28.3	26.7	23.0	18.5	15.2	12.9	9.9	9.2	8.2	8.1	16.0	30.2	27.2	24.4	....	Egypt
28.3	30.4	13.9	12.1	16.6	14.2	10.7	8.4	3.6	4.4	3.4	3.5	3.7	2.6	2.0	....	....	Iran, I.R. of
44.5	40.9	39.8	38.0	33.8	30.7	35.2	40.7	36.3	36.4	32.7	34.3	32.0	28.2	29.3	32.2	....	Israel
34.6	37.2	40.8	43.8	38.6	33.8	36.5	38.2	29.0	34.1	40.1	56.9	62.5	59.2	51.9	50.3	....	Jordan
70.5	77.7	76.2	69.0	54.5	59.1	60.1	53.7	46.2	41.4	42.9	52.4	44.9	16.9	42.7	52.3	....	Kuwait
52.3	60.8	62.1	47.2	46.4	43.4	43.8	42.8	28.7	25.9	25.1	31.1	38.2	....	....	....	....	Libya
58.6	61.2	63.4	65.2	58.6	53.8	50.3	49.9	39.2	48.9	44.1	49.1	52.9	48.4	48.5	....	....	Oman
53.3	54.8	68.2	77.0	65.0	46.4	41.8	35.8	31.1	35.0	35.0	37.2	45.3	42.9	41.6	....	....	Saudi Arabia
16.0	20.4	19.0	15.8	14.2	13.3	12.2	11.8	6.3	6.0	12.2	21.0	21.0	16.2	13.3	13.1	....	Syrian Arab Republic
3.8	5.0	6.3	6.3	4.8	5.1	4.7	3.9	3.6	4.2	....	....	....	....	....	....	....	Yemen Arab Rep.
....	....	....	....	....	....	....	....	....	....	....	....	....	....	....	....	....	Yemen, Republic of
....	....	....	....	....	....	....	....	....	....	....	....	....	....	....	....	....	Yemen, P.D. Rep.
																	Western Hemisphere
57.5	57.9	109.3	96.9	86.0	75.3	111.9	103.0	95.1	89.6	88.5	91.8	100.6	99.7	106.0	110.1	....	Antigua and Barbuda
11.4	8.5	4.7	6.4	10.9	8.9	8.2	11.4	8.0	7.5	8.8	15.4	10.5	7.6	6.5	6.2	....	Argentina
....	....	....	....	....	....	....	....	....	....	....	....	....	....	....	....	....	Aruba
256.5	330.7	447.2	303.1	226.7	246.2	214.5	143.3	101.9	89.9	76.4	85.7	86.7	67.6	67.9	68.6	....	Bahamas, The
63.8	62.5	63.5	55.3	59.9	62.5	66.9	62.9	53.8	44.0	47.8	49.3	46.3	46.6	48.9	50.8	....	Barbados
....	....	....	....	....	....	61.0	61.3	59.4	57.4	57.6	61.6	57.9	57.9	59.0	53.9	....	Belize
18.7	19.6	20.6	16.4	14.6	14.3	12.3	11.1	14.4	13.1	12.8	15.8	17.7	15.1	....	....	....	Bolivia
6.9	7.6	9.3	9.7	7.9	12.0	14.5	12.4	9.0	9.5	10.9	9.7	8.0	9.0	10.6	9.8	....	Brazil
19.1	22.3	21.6	15.3	19.1	23.4	22.5	27.3	29.5	30.7	33.7	34.0	33.8	32.3	29.1	25.9	27.6	Chile
16.9	16.3	16.0	11.8	11.4	9.8	13.6	12.9	18.4	18.8	17.2	18.5	21.5	22.1	21.2	....	....	Colombia
28.5	27.2	24.7	44.7	42.6	35.8	34.7	30.9	31.5	31.9	34.9	34.9	34.4	38.8	38.3	39.6	....	Costa Rica
42.5	46.2	26.6	35.4	44.0	45.0	41.6	39.2	52.8	52.5	53.9	45.8	52.3	51.5	50.4	48.1	....	Dominica
17.5	20.6	19.2	20.8	14.3	14.4	13.2	29.5	26.0	30.8	41.0	31.1	26.4	25.1	23.8	....	....	Dominican Republic
22.3	25.8	24.6	21.0	19.6	21.0	22.4	20.7	23.3	23.2	26.4	29.2	30.4	29.0	28.7	26.0	27.0	Ecuador
30.0	36.8	34.0	22.0	26.7	22.8	22.0	19.1	15.8	25.0	19.6	17.1	12.6	16.5	16.9	16.3	16.4	El Salvador
52.2	54.0	50.8	47.0	41.5	40.5	39.1	45.9	58.5	53.0	51.9	45.7	45.8	46.0	45.6	....	....	Grenada
21.0	21.0	22.0	16.8	14.7	13.0	13.0	10.4	13.8	16.0	16.2	16.9	20.5	18.0	18.2	17.9	....	Guatemala
63.1	59.9	69.1	65.1	54.8	46.0	55.5	56.7	....	....	....	....	....	....	....	....	....	Guyana
20.9	19.0	22.1	17.1	18.6	17.9	17.6	16.8	13.1	16.0	13.9	11.3	13.5	11.7	8.2	9.6	....	Haiti
36.2	37.9	36.7	31.3	26.4	26.0	25.5	25.0	26.6	22.9	22.2	20.5	33.9	33.1	30.5	30.8	....	Honduras
42.1	48.1	50.9	47.2	38.3	33.9	53.4	58.5	52.9	51.6	47.5	46.9	52.2	60.1	70.3	61.0	....	Jamaica
....	12.4	11.6	11.3	16.2	20.2	19.3	17.1	20.4	23.6	21.4	20.5	20.0	18.0	16.8	17.0	....	Mexico
....	....	....	....	....	....	....	....	....	....	....	....	....	....	....	....	....	Netherlands Antilles
52.1	64.7	35.1	33.4	23.3	22.3	15.1	11.6	6.4	1.2	22.2	33.6	17.7	....	....	18.7	24.6	Nicaragua
33.8	36.2	92.1	92.6	81.1	64.9	62.3	65.1	69.2	70.1	76.9	79.9	88.7	97.8	104.9	100.8	....	Panama
17.0	15.0	12.7	9.9	8.8	7.1	10.7	13.6	14.0	17.0	19.3	36.1	35.7	32.4	29.6	38.9	....	Paraguay
22.4	26.3	22.3	16.1	16.4	19.5	19.2	22.1	13.1	8.4	11.0	11.0	12.0	9.9	10.2	10.6	....	Peru
....	....	67.1	61.5	53.4	53.6	57.8	55.4	61.4	63.9	59.3	55.3	51.6	58.7	63.3	....	....	St. Kitts and Nevis
77.0	77.4	88.4	72.2	74.6	84.9	85.5	65.0	74.7	75.2	88.7	83.1	84.6	81.4	83.2	....	....	St. Lucia
64.3	62.1	65.6	67.1	56.9	62.4	70.8	73.1	73.0	64.1	77.5	66.5	67.2	53.9	54.8	....	....	St. Vincent & Grens.
57.5	58.6	68.8	56.8	49.7	43.9	44.3	38.9	35.9	37.9	29.3	37.7	28.2	17.7	12.7	5.8	....	Suriname
43.9	44.9	50.3	45.9	34.9	30.1	31.5	32.6	34.4	33.8	38.7	42.4	45.2	41.1	39.4	39.7	....	Trinidad and Tobago
17.9	16.3	15.1	15.0	16.6	28.3	26.7	26.6	25.8	21.7	23.1	25.4	25.8	21.9	22.2	19.7	....	Uruguay
24.9	30.9	33.7	31.5	25.9	23.4	29.0	25.5	15.6	24.4	18.3	32.7	38.7	30.7	25.7	26.0	....	Venezuela

Balance of Payments

Imports of Goods and Services

As percent of GDP

	1978	1979	1980	1981	1982	1983	1984	1985	1986	1987	1988	1989	1990	1991	1992	1993	1994
All Countries																	
Industrial Countries																	
United States	9.3	10.0	10.7	10.2	9.5	9.5	10.6	10.2	10.5	11.0	11.1	11.0	11.1	10.6	10.9	11.3	11.9
Canada	24.8	26.5	26.4	26.1	22.1	22.1	24.9	25.8	26.4	25.5	25.8	25.5	25.4	25.5	27.1	29.8	32.5
Australia	16.6	16.8	17.9	18.1	18.5	16.2	17.6	19.6	19.2	18.1	18.1	19.2	18.2	17.8	19.1	19.9	20.1
Japan	9.5	12.5	14.8	14.2	14.1	12.5	12.6	11.4	7.6	7.5	8.1	9.5	10.4	8.8	8.1	7.4	7.6
New Zealand	27.2	31.7	30.8	30.3	32.2	29.3	34.3	33.0	27.6	25.3	22.3	25.9	26.6	25.9	28.6	28.0	....
Austria	34.2	36.6	38.9	39.9	36.0	36.2	38.4	40.5	35.8	35.0	37.0	38.8	38.9	38.9	38.6	37.4	38.0
Belgium-Luxembourg	51.4	58.5	62.9	68.5	71.0	71.5	75.2	73.4	66.0	66.8	68.5	72.6	70.0	68.7	65.5	62.3	....
Denmark	31.5	....	35.4	38.0	37.7	36.5	37.7	39.1	34.5	31.5	31.3	33.3	32.1	32.8	31.4	29.6	....
Finland	26.2	30.0	33.7	31.7	30.0	29.8	28.2	28.8	25.3	25.4	25.3	25.9	24.6	23.5	25.6	27.7	29.7
France	19.9	21.4	23.5	25.1	24.8	23.9	24.7	24.4	21.2	21.5	22.1	23.7	23.7	23.5	23.0	21.5	21.5
Germany	23.1	25.4	27.8	28.9	28.7	28.0	29.4	30.1	25.9	24.9	25.4	27.1	27.7	29.0	27.6	25.4	26.2
Greece	23.8	26.7	27.8	32.3	27.3	28.2	29.5	32.2	26.7	27.8	26.6	29.2	29.4	28.5	27.4	26.2	....
Iceland	33.9	36.9	35.8	35.6	35.8	36.5	38.0	40.4	35.1	35.9	33.1	32.6	33.1	32.7	30.7	29.9	....
Ireland	59.4	65.7	62.6	62.3	55.1	54.3	58.8	57.7	50.1	50.4	52.3	56.3	53.5	53.3	52.2	54.0	....
Italy	21.2	22.9	24.4	25.2	23.9	21.3	22.9	23.2	18.6	18.8	18.9	20.1	20.1	19.1	19.8	19.7	20.9
Netherlands	44.8	49.7	53.6	55.4	54.4	54.2	58.1	59.3	49.6	49.2	50.5	53.7	51.7	52.1	50.4	48.2	49.0
Norway	41.8	41.5	41.2	39.8	39.9	37.8	38.3	39.3	41.6	37.9	37.5	37.8	36.9	36.1	35.9	36.6	37.4
Portugal	31.4	35.9	40.4	52.4	44.7	42.8	44.4	40.8	35.4	40.8	45.7	44.8	45.2	41.4	38.6	....	....
Spain	14.1	14.4	18.0	19.9	20.3	21.5	20.7	20.6	17.7	19.4	20.3	21.6	20.5	20.4	20.4	20.2	22.5
Sweden	27.0	32.0	31.9	30.7	33.4	34.1	33.4	34.2	30.3	31.1	31.4	32.1	30.7	27.4	27.1	29.7	33.1
Switzerland	40.7	45.1	51.0	50.2	45.6	45.3	46.8	47.0	44.3	40.3	41.7	44.3	41.9	38.3	37.5	36.0	....
United Kingdom	26.9	27.5	24.9	23.7	24.4	25.5	28.5	27.9	26.3	26.5	26.5	27.7	27.0	24.5	25.1	26.4	26.9
Developing Countries																	
Africa																	
Algeria	35.0	30.6	29.1	28.9	27.8	24.5	22.3	19.6	15.7	12.5	14.8	18.7	17.0	18.8	....	....	....
Angola	....	....	....	....	....	....	....	....	29.7	26.0	23.3	31.3	27.0	32.9	....	....	....
Benin	51.7	42.2	36.2	60.4	51.1	34.6	36.0	40.6	37.7	41.7	41.5	28.0	30.7	33.0	....	....	....
Botswana	79.8	85.9	82.4	85.9	87.1	78.4	72.2	65.0	59.3	60.2	59.0	52.0	57.4	....	....	....	....
Burkina Faso	39.6	41.3	44.8	44.7	48.8	45.6	44.1	47.5	....	....	....	....	....	....	....	....	....
Burundi	....	....	....	....	....	....	....	20.4	21.7	25.1	25.8	21.6	27.4	27.2	26.5	27.6	....
Cameroon	33.0	32.5	36.4	31.6	29.8	28.3	24.9	23.9	21.6	20.2	17.1	19.8	19.5	20.4	17.3	....	....
Cape Verde	55.7	62.9	59.3	71.2	75.5	82.6	68.3	66.8	52.9	45.9	42.4	....	....	....	....	....	....
Central African Rep.	38.4	38.7	41.1	29.5	33.9	36.5	35.5	39.2	35.9	33.5	30.0	30.9	31.6	24.6	23.1	....	....
Chad	28.9	....	8.4	....	18.2	31.4	42.6	48.2	46.2	51.8	42.8	44.5	39.8	34.6	35.2	32.9	....
Comoros	....	....	....	....	....	....	....	....	....	....	....	....	....	....	....	....	....
Congo	61.6	48.7	60.1	76.1	62.9	65.6	46.0	53.5	63.3	41.4	48.9	43.2	45.0	48.4	42.9	52.2	....
Côte d'Ivoire	39.7	39.3	40.7	39.1	39.0	38.4	33.8	31.1	32.2	31.9	30.3	30.8	31.1	31.2	....	....	....
Djibouti	....	....	....	....	....	....	....	....	....	....	....	....	....	....	....	....	....
Equatorial Guinea	....	....	....	....	....	....	....	....	....	67.0	87.3	59.1	60.9	69.7	....	....	....
Ethiopia	16.7	18.1	20.9	19.9	16.3	15.9	18.4	16.6	17.2	16.6	16.6	14.0	14.7	7.9	18.7	19.3	....
Gabon	47.5	42.8	34.5	44.3	45.6	50.7	52.6	54.5	40.6	42.7	41.8	39.2	33.0	32.1	30.6	....	....
Gambia, The	62.0	58.7	74.9	75.1	57.3	52.7	60.0	42.2	67.8	66.3	63.2	68.7	64.1	86.1	73.8	....	....
Ghana	9.0	10.4	7.6	4.7	2.6	3.0	9.3	13.3	16.4	24.5	24.0	24.3	24.0	23.4	26.6	....	....
Guinea	....	....	....	....	....	....	....	....	....	....	....	....	....	....	....	....	....
Guinea-Bissau	....	....	....	....	....	....	....	....	28.4	36.3	49.0	45.3	34.8	35.0	45.1	27.8	....
Kenya	38.7	32.4	40.1	35.0	29.0	25.7	27.9	26.6	25.8	26.7	27.4	30.1	31.7	29.0	27.4	37.3	....
Lesotho	102.4	121.3	128.9	134.6	143.7	152.0	154.9	145.4	140.4	138.5	139.2	133.9	118.3	134.6	132.6	124.3	....
Liberia	....	59.8	60.1	47.2	43.1	42.8	39.5	32.2	32.3	34.4	....	....	....	....	....	....	....
Madagascar	26.6	33.2	32.9	25.3	22.9	19.4	17.5	17.6	16.5	21.1	23.3	22.0	27.3	25.4	24.4	....	....
Malawi	40.4	42.6	39.3	31.6	28.6	28.1	25.1	28.3	24.1	27.1	33.8	35.2	34.2	35.8	41.5	29.1	....
Mali	36.3	35.6	36.6	31.3	32.2	37.8	40.6	47.7	37.8	33.5	35.6	32.6	33.8	34.0	....	....	....
Mauritania	63.4	54.9	65.0	68.8	77.9	70.8	66.5	77.6	72.6	61.3	59.1	55.6	49.5	48.4	....	....	....
Mauritius	55.9	51.3	60.5	52.5	49.5	46.1	50.9	56.5	54.1	64.8	72.0	73.1	74.9	68.9	65.5	67.5	....
Morocco	29.7	29.6	27.7	34.5	33.4	30.0	34.1	33.8	27.3	26.7	24.7	27.3	30.0	27.6	29.2	....	....
Mozambique	....	....	35.0	37.0	42.7	37.2	30.2	18.7	21.3	55.7	70.9	69.3	69.0	73.0	84.1	....	....
Namibia	....	....	....	....	....	....	....	....	....	....	....	....	....	69.7	70.7	69.9	65.1
Niger	36.1	36.9	37.7	35.5	36.1	26.9	27.0	32.8	20.7	25.2	23.6	23.4	22.1	18.2	....	....	....
Nigeria	25.6	21.5	21.6	29.2	23.9	17.5	12.8	11.3	11.8	18.3	16.0	16.6	21.3	31.4	28.3	....	....
Rwanda	29.9	29.3	27.4	24.9	23.8	20.6	19.6	19.4	21.0	18.9	17.2	15.4	15.3	20.0	21.8	....	....
São Tomé & Príncipe	....	....	34.7	64.7	126.1	67.4	70.1	....	53.2	39.9	46.1	47.4	40.8	....	....	....	....
Senegal	43.6	40.3	40.9	61.5	46.9	50.3	51.9	46.4	38.5	31.7	29.8	32.4	31.4	30.7	....	....	....
Seychelles	93.1	84.3	84.0	77.8	84.5	78.4	79.5	84.9	78.5	72.7	76.3	77.2	71.9	68.8	63.6	....	....
Sierra Leone	38.1	42.0	42.8	30.6	25.7	17.6	18.1	21.5	29.7	25.3	17.4	23.9	36.1	32.9	....	....	....
Somalia	25.7	28.6	19.4	14.4	22.2	21.6	18.9	19.3	28.5	30.2	....	....	....	....	....	....	....
South Africa	26.2	26.3	28.5	30.6	27.5	21.5	24.7	23.3	22.4	21.1	23.5	22.3	19.7	19.1	19.3	20.0	....
Sudan	9.9	10.9	15.0	18.3	15.3	14.8	10.2	15.3	10.2	7.6	11.5	7.8	3.6	4.8	....	....	....
Swaziland	91.7	107.8	114.0	105.8	108.5	107.2	102.2	100.2	79.8	77.1	81.1	88.3	80.9	89.9	....	....	....
Tanzania	29.7	27.1	26.9	22.2	18.3	13.7	16.1	15.6	23.2	34.8	38.9	47.3	56.7	50.0	60.8	82.1	....
Togo	65.1	60.9	61.2	59.0	66.3	52.4	52.3	57.9	56.0	51.2	....	....	....	....	....	....	....
Tunisia	36.0	40.5	43.4	47.6	46.5	44.0	44.3	38.7	37.5	35.6	41.5	48.0	48.7	43.6	44.9	46.4	....
Uganda	....	....	2.4	7.2	11.8	12.7	12.5	9.0	10.5	13.3	12.7	15.7	18.4	20.4	20.5	21.0	....
Zaïre	....	....	....	....	14.0	17.3	23.8	25.6	24.0	27.4	28.7	28.9	26.2	....	....	....	....
Zambia	36.5	36.1	45.4	41.2	36.5	31.5	33.2	36.7	42.6	38.9	26.9	30.5	50.7	32.9	....	....	....
Zimbabwe	25.5	27.7	32.3	32.2	27.9	24.1	26.4	30.5	26.4	25.5	26.0	28.5	32.3	....	....	....	....
Asia																	
Afghanistan, I.S. of	....	17.9	21.8	23.0	18.1	15.6	16.2	11.4	12.9	....	....	....	....	....	....	....	....
Bangladesh	16.3	18.9	22.1	22.3	22.2	19.9	20.4	19.1	18.3	16.9	17.8	19.7	18.6	16.5	17.8	18.7	....
China, People's Rep.	....	....	....	....	8.4	8.6	11.0	17.0	16.3	15.5	15.8	15.1	15.5	18.0	16.9	22.8	....
Fiji	46.9	50.9	51.4	57.6	49.8	49.1	44.1	45.0	41.5	44.2	51.6	56.9	65.4	56.9	53.0	57.8	....
India	7.0	8.5	9.8	9.4	9.3	8.5	8.8	9.0	8.5	8.7	8.9	10.0	9.7	....	....	....	....
Indonesia	....	....	....	23.4	24.0	25.8	22.0	20.4	20.2	22.4	21.9	23.0	25.9	26.9	27.2	23.6	....
Kiribati	....	55.3	106.8	128.8	113.3	90.6	77.2	97.6	95.0	124.0	120.7	117.1	135.2	123.6	....	....	....
Korea	35.2	34.9	41.0	41.2	37.2	35.2	34.6	32.4	31.6	32.3	30.3	29.8	30.1	30.6	29.9	28.8	30.9

Balance of Payments

Imports of Goods and Services

As percent of GDP

1978	1979	1980	1981	1982	1983	1984	1985	1986	1987	1988	1989	1990	1991	1992	1993	1994	
																	Asia (cont.)
....	....	....	....	....	....	....	....	....	....	....	....	....	....	....	....	....	Lao P. D. Rep.
43.5	47.2	55.2	59.0	60.0	57.5	52.6	50.0	50.5	49.6	56.9	66.8	74.2	84.7	75.6	80.5	....	Malaysia
85.6	156.2	205.1	188.2	155.7	145.9	125.1	100.5	89.2	103.6	107.2	121.2	130.6	....	....	....	....	Maldives
....	....	....	....	....	....	....	....	....	....	....	....	....	....	....	....	....	Mongolia
11.3	14.9	14.7	16.2	17.0	13.0	9.9	9.0	8.4	4.8	3.4	1.9	2.5	....	....	....	....	Myanmar
17.0	17.6	21.4	20.6	21.0	24.0	21.0	21.9	21.0	22.0	24.7	21.8	23.7	29.1	27.9	31.7	....	Nepal
21.5	25.8	26.7	23.4	24.5	23.7	24.5	23.8	23.2	22.9	22.9	24.2	25.8	25.5	25.6	25.0	....	Pakistan
41.8	41.0	47.8	53.0	53.1	51.0	51.9	48.4	46.5	47.9	49.8	49.3	46.9	51.4	46.8	38.0	....	Papua New Guinea
23.8	24.8	28.2	26.9	25.6	27.8	23.1	19.5	19.7	23.8	25.0	28.1	31.5	30.5	31.8	38.0	....	Philippines
173.9	196.0	216.0	209.1	195.3	172.8	163.8	160.2	155.2	172.5	187.4	179.9	178.3	167.5	160.8	166.4	....	Singapore
53.8	60.9	71.1	70.3	58.9	77.7	61.0	71.9	80.9	81.6	99.8	101.1	92.2	....	....	....	....	Solomon Islands
39.5	45.7	54.6	46.5	45.8	41.3	34.5	38.4	35.3	35.9	36.7	37.5	36.9	39.7	39.6	42.6	43.8	Sri Lanka
24.6	29.7	30.9	30.8	25.2	27.7	26.7	26.2	23.8	28.5	34.7	37.7	41.9	43.0	41.8	....	....	Thailand
56.2	59.6	53.2	55.4	54.4	60.4	67.7	83.0	72.7	64.2	61.3	61.1	57.7	50.4	50.0	47.2	....	Tonga
....	....	....	....	58.7	61.3	70.0	70.3	61.8	74.0	72.8	54.6	67.5	58.7	51.7	50.7	....	Vanuatu
....	....	....	....	53.6	56.7	59.3	67.7	61.4	71.1	71.6	78.4	....	....	....	....	....	Western Samoa
																	Europe
....	....	....	....	....	....	....	....	....	....	....	....	....	....	....	....	....	Albania
....	....	....	....	....	....	....	....	....	....	....	....	....	....	....	....	....	Armenia
....	....	....	....	....	....	....	35.6	30.2	28.3	23.2	20.8	38.7	54.7	....	....	....	Bulgaria
....	....	....	....	....	....	....	....	....	....	....	....	....	....	....	....	....	Croatia
62.9	63.8	62.5	63.3	64.2	64.0	67.1	58.8	48.4	47.5	50.6	57.1	53.4	52.8	57.1	....	....	Cyprus
....	....	....	36.8	36.7	37.0	40.4	33.1	34.2	33.8	32.4	32.1	34.3	38.3	....	....	....	Czechoslovakia
....	....	....	....	....	....	....	....	....	....	....	....	....	....	....	70.3	....	Estonia
....	....	....	39.5	43.0	43.5	42.9	43.7	41.0	37.3	38.4	33.5	36.7	35.9	40.9	....	....	Hungary
89.9	94.4	99.4	90.5	85.3	81.9	84.9	87.8	81.9	87.0	89.2	91.6	98.8	97.8	98.8	104.8	....	Malta
....	35.2	31.4	26.8	20.0	17.3	17.0	17.5	18.2	20.8	22.0	19.3	24.2	23.2	21.5	24.1	....	Poland
....	....	40.1	31.9	21.6	23.2	29.0	18.7	16.4	15.2	13.5	16.6	25.9	21.5	33.5	28.0	....	Romania
....	....	....	....	....	....	....	....	....	....	....	....	....	....	....	72.6	....	Slovak Republic
....	....	....	....	....	....	....	....	....	....	....	....	....	....	....	58.3	....	Slovenia
....	....	....	....	....	....	....	....	....	17.6	17.7	17.8	17.1	15.8	16.7	19.1	....	Turkey
23.2	24.6	27.4	27.4	30.3	33.6	34.1	34.2	27.3	25.0	29.7	22.2	....	....	....	....	....	Yugoslavia, SFR
																	Middle East
94.6	92.4	112.7	120.2	106.9	92.0	94.4	88.7	78.2	93.6	85.2	94.2	102.3	....	....	....	....	Bahrain
25.2	43.6	41.4	42.5	35.3	29.8	29.2	23.0	16.7	14.7	14.2	13.4	22.7	36.4	32.9	32.6	....	Egypt
28.5	16.8	17.2	16.1	12.4	14.4	11.2	8.8	6.2	5.2	4.0	4.3	4.1	4.2	2.9	....	....	Iran, I.R. of
63.6	58.4	52.8	53.3	48.7	44.5	46.8	49.5	43.2	47.7	40.3	40.1	40.1	38.8	37.9	42.8	....	Israel
79.2	90.1	83.6	97.3	88.2	76.6	73.8	72.5	53.5	56.7	62.1	71.4	88.8	81.7	84.1	80.2	....	Jordan
39.9	28.7	34.2	38.2	52.4	50.4	47.3	45.7	51.0	40.3	49.3	43.3	39.0	92.3	62.8	51.3	....	Kuwait
37.5	40.0	35.6	54.9	44.3	39.2	41.7	30.9	26.7	29.7	32.1	33.7	29.9	....	....	....	....	Libya
49.3	40.7	38.8	40.4	43.4	38.4	37.5	37.4	40.9	28.8	34.6	33.3	31.7	40.0	39.7	....	....	Oman
46.9	42.0	35.7	45.2	57.2	65.4	61.6	53.3	51.1	50.5	45.6	47.1	41.9	54.9	51.0	....	....	Saudi Arabia
33.7	36.7	34.7	31.1	25.1	26.1	23.9	23.2	12.0	9.0	15.8	14.0	12.4	12.1	12.2	13.2	....	Syrian Arab Republic
53.8	67.0	80.7	60.2	52.2	43.7	36.1	31.1	24.3	34.7	....	....	....	....	....	....	....	Yemen Arab Rep.
....	....	....	....	....	....	....	....	....	....	....	....	....	....	....	....	....	Yemen, P.D. Rep.
....	....	....	....	....	....	....	....	....	....	....	....	....	....	....	....	....	Yemen, Republic of
																	Western Hemisphere
67.1	89.9	138.4	135.3	126.3	89.5	121.0	122.9	140.8	124.1	97.4	107.0	98.7	102.0	107.4	111.8	....	Antigua and Barbuda
7.7	8.2	6.3	7.0	8.2	6.1	5.5	6.5	6.5	7.3	6.0	8.7	4.8	6.1	8.1	8.1	....	Argentina
....	....	....	....	....	....	....	....	....	....	....	....	....	....	....	....	....	Aruba
239.7	318.9	438.0	298.2	222.4	239.6	207.1	132.2	90.9	83.2	71.2	82.0	84.0	64.0	63.7	65.9	....	Bahamas, The
74.7	71.1	69.8	69.9	65.5	66.9	65.5	57.8	52.6	44.7	44.8	47.4	47.8	48.1	41.3	46.3	....	Barbados
....	....	....	....	....	....	69.1	67.6	65.1	62.5	68.1	69.1	62.6	67.9	68.0	65.5	....	Belize
25.2	25.6	16.6	18.8	11.5	12.3	10.0	10.9	18.1	18.5	16.2	18.8	19.6	18.4	....	....	....	Bolivia
8.3	9.8	11.8	10.4	9.0	9.9	8.8	7.6	6.8	6.6	6.0	6.2	6.4	7.3	7.4	8.0	....	Brazil
23.6	25.3	25.6	25.4	20.8	20.7	23.4	24.3	26.0	26.6	27.4	30.3	30.3	27.7	27.4	28.0	26.3	Chile
14.7	14.0	16.3	16.6	17.2	14.9	13.9	14.6	14.6	15.1	15.8	15.5	17.0	15.4	18.5	....	....	Colombia
36.3	37.8	34.4	49.8	40.1	36.5	34.3	32.7	30.6	36.1	36.9	38.9	41.1	39.6	43.4	45.5	....	Costa Rica
65.6	96.5	92.8	78.8	69.5	62.2	67.0	64.7	61.6	64.5	69.7	79.2	81.1	71.3	67.9	66.4	....	Dominica
24.4	27.0	28.9	25.0	19.3	18.3	15.0	34.8	30.1	38.4	43.2	36.3	29.4	28.0	31.3	....	....	Dominican Republic
28.5	28.5	25.1	22.9	21.0	15.1	16.2	14.1	20.1	25.8	22.0	23.7	22.2	24.9	22.4	22.9	25.3	Ecuador
39.3	36.5	32.8	33.6	29.4	26.6	24.8	20.7	29.1	26.3	23.9	22.3	27.5	30.4	32.3	30.9	....	El Salvador
62.6	73.4	80.0	86.5	86.2	78.7	68.3	75.2	82.2	78.1	73.0	71.6	70.1	72.2	66.3	....	....	Grenada
27.1	25.9	24.9	23.5	18.7	14.5	15.1	11.2	12.4	22.5	22.1	22.1	23.7	21.6	27.3	26.3	....	Guatemala
63.1	69.3	83.5	87.8	72.3	66.2	67.8	67.8	....	....	....	....	....	....	....	....	....	Guyana
30.5	29.3	34.8	36.5	31.9	30.6	29.0	27.7	21.2	25.0	24.3	21.3	24.7	27.1	21.6	29.2	....	Haiti
40.9	42.1	44.0	37.7	28.4	29.7	32.2	29.9	28.3	25.9	24.7	23.0	37.0	37.1	36.1	34.6	....	Honduras
39.6	50.2	52.6	57.2	49.8	42.2	61.3	70.4	49.2	50.6	51.5	57.5	56.3	62.0	71.4	71.3	....	Jamaica
....	13.8	14.2	14.3	13.3	11.0	12.0	12.9	17.0	17.2	20.0	20.7	21.3	21.3	22.5	21.4	....	Mexico
....	....	....	....	....	....	....	....	....	....	....	....	....	....	....	....	....	Netherlands Antilles
47.7	49.3	64.3	62.2	43.0	39.0	29.0	31.2	18.7	3.3	69.6	65.7	30.8	....	....	41.5	51.9	Nicaragua
44.9	49.0	101.4	102.7	85.9	61.1	63.2	64.0	65.3	64.8	61.3	73.2	83.4	97.9	105.5	101.1	....	Panama
20.6	21.4	18.9	17.4	16.4	10.9	16.2	18.5	20.1	25.9	22.1	30.2	39.8	38.6	38.7	47.7	....	Paraguay
19.3	16.2	19.1	19.6	19.4	19.3	15.3	16.3	14.6	10.6	12.4	9.0	12.2	11.4	13.1	13.6	....	Peru
....	....	97.2	90.9	87.5	98.2	80.5	73.1	78.1	85.4	85.4	84.3	84.3	81.5	72.0	....	....	St. Kitts and Nevis
124.5	124.2	137.7	127.0	116.7	106.1	111.7	81.1	82.9	86.9	96.6	104.4	98.4	98.1	94.5	....	....	St. Lucia
84.8	98.3	107.0	91.2	87.4	83.3	84.0	79.1	82.3	81.9	86.0	85.4	79.3	74.7	67.6	....	....	St. Vincent & Grens.
56.8	58.5	73.9	70.6	65.1	58.4	52.1	39.7	37.7	30.9	24.3	27.7	27.2	21.4	13.0	5.3	....	Suriname
39.7	39.3	39.0	36.2	42.2	40.1	32.9	28.2	38.0	32.3	33.8	34.4	28.2	32.9	28.6	30.4	....	Trinidad and Tobago
19.0	20.5	21.2	18.5	17.1	23.9	22.1	21.5	20.5	19.6	18.8	19.5	19.9	19.6	20.9	20.5	....	Uruguay
38.5	29.3	25.5	25.7	28.9	13.4	17.1	15.9	16.4	23.7	24.7	21.7	19.4	25.6	28.4	26.4	....	Venezuela

Balance of Payments

Current Account Balance
Excluding Exceptional Financing

As percent of GDP

	1978	1979	1980	1981	1982	1983	1984	1985	1986	1987	1988	1989	1990	1991	1992	1993	1994
All Countries																	
Industrial Countries																	
United States	-.7	—	.1	.2	-.4	-1.3	-2.6	-3.1	-3.5	-3.7	-2.6	-2.0	-1.7	-.1	-1.1	-1.6	-2.3
Canada	-2.2	-2.0	-.6	-2.0	.4	-.5	-.3	-1.4	-2.8	-3.0	-3.7	-4.3	-3.9	-4.2	-4.0	-4.2	-3.2
Australia	-4.0	-2.1	-3.0	-5.0	-5.0	-3.9	-5.0	-5.8	-6.0	-4.3	-4.7	-6.8	-5.6	-3.9	-4.1	-3.8	-4.7
Japan	1.7	-.9	-1.0	.4	.6	1.8	2.8	3.7	4.3	3.6	2.7	2.0	1.2	2.2	3.2	3.1	2.8
New Zealand	-2.5	-4.0	-4.3	-4.3	-7.2	-4.1	-8.2	-7.3	-6.0	-4.8	-.8	-3.5	-3.2	-2.7	-3.3	-2.9	….
Austria	-2.6	-2.8	-5.0	-4.6	1.1	.4	-.3	-.2	.2	-.2	-.2	.2	.7	—	-.3	-.4	-1.2
Belgium-Luxembourg	-.8	-2.8	-4.2	-4.3	-3.0	-.6	-.1	.8	2.7	2.0	2.4	2.1	2.6	2.4	2.9	6.0	….
Denmark	-2.7	….	-3.7	-3.3	-4.1	-2.5	-3.1	-4.8	-5.5	-2.9	-1.2	-1.1	1.1	1.5	3.0	3.5	….
Finland	2.0	-.4	-2.7	-1.0	-1.8	-2.3	—	-1.5	-1.0	-2.0	-2.6	-5.1	-5.1	-5.7	-4.6	-1.1	1.1
France	1.5	.9	-.6	-.8	-2.2	-1.0	-.2	—	.3	-.5	-.5	-.5	-.8	-.5	.3	.8	.7
Germany	1.5	-.7	-1.6	-.5	.8	.7	1.5	2.9	4.6	4.2	4.2	4.8	3.2	-1.2	-1.2	-.9	-1.2
Greece	-3.0	-4.9	-5.5	-6.5	-4.9	-5.4	-6.3	-9.8	-4.3	-2.6	-1.8	-4.7	-5.3	-2.2	-2.8	-1.0	….
Iceland	.8	-.7	-2.3	-4.3	-8.1	-2.0	-4.7	-3.9	.4	-3.5	-3.9	-1.9	-2.3	-4.6	-3.0	-.1	….
Ireland	-6.6	-13.0	-11.1	-14.2	-10.2	-6.6	-5.3	-3.3	-2.7	.3	.6	-1.1	.3	3.4	5.0	7.8	….
Italy	2.0	1.6	-2.3	-2.6	-1.8	.2	-.8	-1.0	.4	-.4	-.9	-1.5	-1.6	-2.2	-2.4	.9	1.4
Netherlands	-.9	.1	-.6	2.6	3.5	3.7	5.1	3.3	2.3	1.9	3.0	4.3	3.2	2.7	2.2	3.3	3.4
Norway	-5.2	-2.2	1.9	3.7	1.1	3.6	5.2	5.2	-6.6	-4.9	-4.4	.2	3.8	4.8	2.6	2.1	3.3
Portugal	-2.6	-.3	-4.2	-19.2	-14.0	-7.9	-3.2	1.8	3.9	1.2	-2.6	.3	-.3	-1.0	-.2	….	….
Spain	.8	.4	-2.6	-2.9	-2.5	-1.9	1.1	1.7	1.7	-.1	-1.1	-2.9	-3.8	-3.8	-3.8	-1.3	-1.4
Sweden	-.2	-2.2	-3.5	-2.4	-3.3	-.8	.8	-1.0	—	—	-.3	-1.6	-2.8	-1.9	-3.6	-2.2	.4
Switzerland	2.4	-.3	-.2	3.6	2.6	1.2	6.8	6.5	3.4	3.7	4.8	4.5	3.1	4.5	5.9	7.2	….
United Kingdom	.7	-.2	1.3	2.8	1.6	1.1	.4	.7	-.2	-1.2	-3.5	-4.4	-3.4	-1.4	-1.7	-1.9	—
Developing Countries																	
Africa																	
Algeria	-13.4	-4.9	.6	.2	-.4	-.2	.1	1.7	-3.5	.2	-3.8	-2.1	2.4	5.5	….	….	….
Angola	….	….	….	….	….	….	….	….	2.8	-4.7	6.0	-5.9	-1.4	-2.3	….	….	….
Benin	-13.5	-5.7	-3.1	-8.4	-29.7	-12.3	-5.3	.4	-4.5	-4.8	-5.1	-.9	-.1	-.6	….	….	….
Botswana	-23.2	-8.7	-15.2	-29.0	-16.5	-7.5	-5.5	8.5	8.4	37.6	9.3	18.1	4.0	….	….	….	….
Burkina Faso	-6.0	-5.4	-3.8	-3.5	-8.4	-6.0	-.4	-5.9	….	….	….	….	….	….	….	….	….
Burundi	….	….	….	….	….	….	….	-3.5	-2.9	-8.2	-6.4	-1.0	-5.7	-2.6	-4.5	-2.4	….
Cameroon	-4.4	-2.4	-6.9	-7.3	-5.8	-6.0	-2.3	-6.5	-3.8	-7.3	-3.5	-2.7	-3.9	-3.6	-3.1	….	….
Cape Verde	-7.5	-.8	2.9	-14.9	-10.3	-9.4	-4.7	-6.3	.9	5.5	.2	….	….	….	….	….	….
Central African Rep.	-4.3	-2.5	-5.4	-.5	-5.7	-4.4	-5.2	-6.9	-9.1	-7.0	-3.1	-3.1	-6.9	-4.8	-4.3	….	….
Chad	-5.0	….	.9	….	3.2	6.8	1.8	-13.1	-7.3	-3.1	2.4	-5.5	-3.7	-5.0	-6.5	-7.0	….
Comoros	….	….	….	….	….	….	….	….	….	….	….	….	….	….	….	….	….
Congo	-20.6	-8.3	-9.8	-23.1	-15.3	-19.1	9.6	-7.5	-32.5	-9.7	-20.1	-3.6	-8.8	-17.5	-11.6	-21.3	….
Côte d'Ivoire	-10.6	-15.1	-17.9	-16.7	-13.4	-13.6	-1.1	.9	-3.3	-9.6	-12.1	-9.9	-11.2	-14.2	….	….	….
Djibouti	….	….	….	….	….	….	….	….	….	….	….	….	….	….	….	….	….
Equatorial Guinea	….	….	….	….	….	….	….	….	….	-19.3	-17.1	-16.9	-13.1	-16.8	….	….	….
Ethiopia	-3.2	-2.4	-5.5	-5.9	-3.6	-2.8	-2.3	1.6	-4.7	-2.9	-2.9	-1.8	-3.4	1.1	-1.6	-1.0	….
Gabon	3.1	8.2	9.0	10.4	8.6	2.8	3.4	-4.6	-23.0	-12.9	-16.1	-4.6	3.1	1.4	-2.8	….	….
Gambia, The	-25.9	-15.6	-36.3	-21.8	-9.9	-14.8	3.9	3.3	2.7	2.9	10.9	5.9	11.3	4.4	11.2	….	….
Ghana	-.4	1.2	.2	-1.6	-.3	-.8	-.5	-2.1	-.7	-2.0	-1.3	-1.9	-3.7	-3.6	-5.5	….	….
Guinea	….	….	….	….	….	….	….	….	….	….	….	….	….	….	….	….	….
Guinea-Bissau	….	….	….	….	….	….	….	….	-27.1	-34.2	-44.1	-46.8	-25.9	-33.8	-47.2	-27.9	….
Kenya	-12.4	-8.1	-12.4	-8.4	-4.8	-.8	-2.1	-1.9	-.6	-6.3	-5.5	-7.1	-6.2	-2.7	-2.3	2.2	….
Lesotho	3.2	….	15.3	1.1	6.4	11.6	2.1	-4.9	-1.0	6.4	-5.5	2.1	10.2	12.6	4.9	2.7	….
Liberia	….	1.8	5.0	7.3	.2	-9.2	-.2	5.2	-1.7	-12.9	….	….	….	….	….	….	….
Madagascar	-3.7	-15.2	-17.0	-12.5	-10.5	-8.7	-6.6	-6.4	-4.4	-5.5	-6.1	-2.9	-8.3	-7.2	-4.6	….	….
Malawi	-18.4	-25.1	-21.0	-11.9	-9.6	-10.8	-3.5	-11.2	-7.2	-5.1	-5.4	-9.0	-7.5	-10.4	-15.8	-4.8	….
Mali	-15.2	-9.3	-9.1	-10.2	-9.4	-10.5	-11.5	-16.9	-14.9	-11.1	-11.8	-9.5	-10.2	-7.4	….	….	….
Mauritania	-14.6	-17.1	-19.3	-19.7	-36.9	-27.2	-15.4	-16.9	-23.1	-15.7	-10.0	-1.9	-.9	-2.6	….	….	….
Mauritius	-11.4	-11.7	-10.3	-13.2	-3.9	-2.1	-5.2	-2.7	6.5	3.6	-2.9	-4.9	-4.7	-.6	—	-3.0	….
Morocco	-9.9	-9.4	-7.5	-12.0	-12.1	-6.4	-7.7	-6.9	-1.2	1.0	2.1	-3.4	-.8	-1.4	.7	….	….
Mozambique	….	….	-15.2	-17.5	-23.7	-22.3	-16.0	-11.7	-13.6	-28.8	-29.8	-34.6	-28.8	-24.0	-30.7	….	….
Namibia	….	….	….	….	….	….	….	….	….	….	….	….	.5	5.0	2.3	5.8	….
Niger	-13.7	-6.9	-10.9	-8.7	-11.6	-3.5	-.5	-4.8	1.3	-4.0	-3.7	-5.1	-4.4	-1.1	….	….	….
Nigeria	-6.6	2.3	5.5	-7.5	-9.5	-5.5	.1	3.2	.9	-.3	-.6	3.6	15.4	3.7	7.1	….	….
Rwanda	-5.3	4.4	-4.2	-5.6	-6.4	-2.3	-2.6	-3.7	-3.6	-6.2	-6.0	-5.1	-4.6	-2.0	-5.2	….	….
São Tomé & Príncipe	….	….	1.1	-39.7	-88.7	-29.7	-22.9	….	-29.4	-23.4	-22.0	-24.7	-26.5	….	….	….	….
Senegal	-10.8	-9.7	-13.0	-18.8	-10.2	-11.8	-12.0	-10.9	-7.6	-6.7	-5.2	-4.3	-3.9	-3.7	….	….	….
Seychelles	-4.7	-9.6	-10.6	-12.2	-27.5	-17.8	-8.8	-11.4	-15.9	-8.5	-10.0	-7.5	-.1	1.0	-.4	….	….
Sierra Leone	-13.8	-18.4	-15.0	-11.8	-13.1	-1.8	-2.1	.3	28.7	-4.9	-.3	-7.0	-11.7	1.7	….	….	….
Somalia	-5.2	-13.2	-4.9	-2.4	-6.6	-6.4	-4.5	-4.6	-7.6	-7.1	….	….	….	….	….	….	….
South Africa	3.6	6.3	4.5	-5.5	-4.3	—	-2.2	4.7	5.0	3.6	1.4	1.7	1.9	2.0	1.2	1.5	….
Sudan	-1.3	-2.8	-3.2	-5.7	-3.5	-3.1	.4	2.5	-.3	-1.9	-3.4	-.8	-1.5	-3.4	….	….	….
Swaziland	-20.8	-28.8	-23.9	-14.2	-22.6	-20.6	-17.3	-11.5	2.6	10.6	9.4	.5	5.1	2.9	….	….	….
Tanzania	-11.2	-7.8	-10.2	-6.9	-8.4	-4.8	-6.2	-5.4	-6.6	-12.7	-11.3	-12.9	-16.4	-14.2	-15.6	-19.6	….
Togo	-26.0	-21.3	-8.4	-4.7	-10.6	-6.1	2.3	-4.4	-6.2	-4.9	….	….	….	….	….	….	….
Tunisia	-7.7	-4.1	-4.1	-4.5	-8.1	-7.0	-9.5	-7.0	-7.0	-.6	2.2	-1.2	-3.8	-3.6	-6.2	-6.2	….
Uganda	….	….	-.5	—	-1.7	-1.9	3.5	.1	-.9	-2.1	-3.3	-4.9	-7.1	-5.6	-3.0	-3.0	….
Zaïre	….	….	….	….	….	-5.5	-3.2	-4.1	-4.0	-5.1	-8.4	-6.5	-6.8	-6.9	….	….	….
Zambia	-10.0	2.3	-13.3	-18.2	-14.5	-7.9	-5.4	-17.5	-20.6	-11.8	-8.1	-5.5	-15.9	-9.0	….	….	….
Zimbabwe	1.6	-1.4	-2.8	-8.5	-9.2	-6.4	-.8	-1.4	.3	1.0	2.1	.3	-2.3	….	….	….	….
Asia																	
Afghanistan, I.S. of	….	-2.3	1.3	-4.5	-1.3	-2.1	-5.2	-2.6	-5.2	….	….	….	….	….	….	….	….
Bangladesh	-4.0	-3.8	-5.5	-7.9	-4.2	-.4	-3.5	-3.2	-4.1	-1.4	-1.5	-5.4	-1.9	.3	.8	.8	….
China, People's Rep.	….	….	….	….	2.5	1.8	.8	-4.8	-3.1	.1	-1.3	-1.3	3.9	4.3	1.3	-2.9	….
Fiji	….	-5.7	-1.3	-13.3	-7.2	-5.0	-1.7	1.7	1.1	.1	6.4	6.0	-.7	3.6	3.8	.8	….
India	.5	—	-1.0	-1.5	-1.3	-1.0	-1.2	-2.0	-2.0	-2.0	-2.5	-2.4	-2.3	….	….	….	….
Indonesia	….	….	….	-.6	-5.6	-7.4	-2.1	-2.2	-4.9	-2.8	-1.7	-1.2	-2.8	-3.7	-2.2	-1.3	….
Kiribati	….	45.2	.5	-22.0	-20.9	2.7	30.2	25.2	30.3	33.5	15.9	17.2	19.6	35.6	….	….	….
Korea	-2.2	-6.4	-8.5	-6.7	-3.6	-1.9	-1.5	-.9	4.2	7.2	7.8	2.3	-.9	-2.9	-1.3	.3	-1.1

Balance of Payments

Current Account Balance
Excluding Exceptional Financing
As percent of GDP

1978	1979	1980	1981	1982	1983	1984	1985	1986	1987	1988	1989	1990	1991	1992	1993	1994	Country
																	Asia (cont.)
....	.8	4.4	-1.1	-9.9	-13.4	-11.6	-4.9	-1.9	-.4	8.1	5.4	.8	-2.0	-8.9	-3.1	-3.8	Lao P. D. Rep.
....	8.5	-16.1	-52.3	-40.6	-31.7	-36.6	-21.4	-6.5	-.3	8.7	8.2	9.2	7.1	....	....	....	Malaysia
....	....	....	....	....	....	....	....	....	....	....	....	....	....	....	....	....	Maldives
....	-4.7	-6.8	-5.9	-5.3	-8.3	-5.6	-3.4	-3.1	-3.7	-1.7	-1.5	-.4	-1.8	....	....	....	Mongolia
....	-1.6	-.6	-2.0	-.9	-3.7	-6.3	-4.0	-4.8	-4.5	-4.2	-8.2	-7.4	-8.2	-9.4	-5.2	-6.4	Myanmar
....	-4.0	-5.7	-3.9	-3.2	-2.9	.1	-4.0	-3.6	-2.1	-1.7	-3.8	-3.6	-4.2	-3.3	-3.9	-6.1	Nepal
....	-1.5	4.3	-10.4	-17.8	-17.3	-13.1	-11.4	-5.1	-2.8	-5.9	-8.1	-8.8	-2.4	-4.0	2.3	10.9	Pakistan
....	-4.5	-5.1	-5.9	-5.9	-8.6	-8.3	-4.1	-.1	3.2	-1.3	-1.0	-3.4	-6.1	-2.3	-1.9	-6.0	Papua New Guinea
....	-5.8	-7.8	-13.3	-10.6	-8.5	-3.5	-2.1	—	1.8	-.8	3.6	9.5	5.7	9.4	7.7	3.7	Philippines
....	3.4	7.9	-8.5	-16.4	-15.3	-11.9	.1	-17.4	-8.2	-11.5	-22.0	-19.8	-16.4	....	....	....	Singapore
....	-2.5	-6.8	-16.3	-10.1	-11.5	-9.0	—	-7.0	-6.5	-4.9	-5.7	-5.9	-3.7	-6.6	-4.6	-3.7	Solomon Islands
....	-4.8	-7.6	-6.4	-7.4	-2.7	-7.2	-5.0	-4.0	.6	-.7	-2.7	-3.5	-8.5	-7.7	-5.8	....	-4.7 Sri Lanka
....	-1.7	-5.4	-5.3	-9.8	4.2	1.0	-.4	-3.7	.8	6.1	-10.1	-1.6	10.3	-1.3	-1.2	2.3	Thailand
....	....	....	....	....	-7.8	-8.1	3.0	-10.0	-11.6	-24.8	-14.6	-8.7	-4.0	-8.0	-7.5	-11.7	Tonga
....	....	....	....	....	-6.1	3.5	.7	2.1	8.0	7.3	6.7	11.7	....	....	....	....	Vanuatu
																	Western Samoa
																	Europe
....	....	....	....	....	....	....	....	....	....	....	....	....	....	....	....	....	Albania
....	....	....	....	....	....	....	....	....	....	....	....	....	....	....	....	....	Armenia
....	....	....	....	....	....	....	-.4	-2.7	-1.7	-.9	-1.6	-8.3	-1.0	....	....	....	Bulgaria
....	....	....	....	....	....	....	....	....	....	....	....	....	....	....	....	....	Croatia
-13.6	-13.5	-12.0	-8.3	-8.3	-9.5	-9.8	-7.4	-1.0	1.9	-.3	-3.3	.8	-3.7	-3.9	....	....	Cyprus
....	....	....	.1	1.2	1.9	2.2	1.7	.4	.7	2.1	1.9	-2.7	2.7	....	....	....	Czechoslovakia
....	....	....	....	....	....	....	....	....	....	....	....	....	....	....	1.3	....	Estonia
....	....	....	....	-2.3	-.9	.2	-2.2	-5.7	-2.6	-2.0	-2.0	1.2	1.3	1.0	-11.8	....	Hungary
10.1	5.1	3.4	7.7	1.1	-.5	.8	-2.5	.5	1.4	3.3	-.5	-2.7	-.5	.9	-2.9	....	Malta
....	-6.8	-6.0	-7.4	-3.0	-2.1	-1.4	-1.4	-1.5	-.6	-.2	-1.7	4.9	-2.8	-3.7	-6.7	....	Poland
....	....	....	-7.1	-2.0	2.1	2.6	4.5	2.9	2.7	3.5	6.5	4.7	-8.5	-3.5	-7.8	-4.7	Romania
....	....	....	....	....	....	....	....	....	....	....	....	....	....	....	-5.2	....	Slovak Republic
....	....	....	....	....	....	....	....	....	....	....	....	....	....	....	1.5	....	Slovenia
....	....	....	....	....	....	....	....	....	-.9	1.8	.9	-1.7	.2	-.6	-3.6	....	Turkey
-2.3	-5.4	-3.3	-1.4	-.8	.6	1.1	1.9	1.8	1.8	4.1	2.5	....	....	....	....	....	Yugoslavia, SFR
																	Middle East
-16.5	-8.3	6.0	12.4	11.7	2.7	5.6	1.0	-2.2	-6.3	5.7	-3.6	6.3	....	....	....	....	Bahrain
-4.9	-8.7	-2.0	-8.7	-6.2	-.9	-4.4	-4.1	-3.0	-.3	-1.2	-1.5	.3	5.2	6.7	4.9	....	Egypt
.1	14.1	-2.6	-3.4	4.5	.2	-.3	-.3	-2.5	-.7	-.6	—	.1	-1.3	-.6	....	....	Iran, I.R. of
-7.4	-5.3	-4.0	-5.9	-8.6	-7.7	-5.5	4.2	4.5	-3.3	-1.1	1.2	-.1	-1.9	-1.1	-3.6	....	Israel
-11.5	-.2	9.7	-.9	-6.9	-7.8	-5.1	-5.1	-.6	-5.4	-4.9	9.3	-5.6	-9.4	-16.3	-11.2	....	Jordan
39.5	56.5	53.3	54.3	23.0	25.4	29.6	22.4	31.4	20.4	22.2	37.6	21.1	-242.4	-2.5	10.8	....	Kuwait
3.8	14.2	23.1	-12.6	-5.2	-5.7	-5.7	7.8	-.8	-4.5	-7.9	-4.3	7.3	....	....	....	....	Libya
-1.8	14.7	15.9	17.1	6.5	6.2	3.4	-.1	-14.2	10.0	-4.1	3.6	10.5	-2.4	-4.3	....	....	Oman
-3.0	8.9	26.5	25.5	6.3	-15.6	-18.5	-14.9	-16.1	-13.3	-9.6	-11.5	-3.9	-23.4	-17.3	....	....	Saudi Arabia
-.2	9.5	1.9	-1.8	-1.4	-4.5	-4.1	-4.5	-2.0	-.9	-.9	6.6	7.4	2.5	.2	-1.7	....	Syrian Arab Republic
.7	-9.4	-24.7	-18.7	-13.9	-11.7	-6.5	-6.8	-3.1	-10.7	....	....	....	....	....	....	....	Yemen Arab Rep.
....	....	....	....	....	....	....	....	....	....	....	....	....	....	....	....	....	Yemen, P.D. Rep.
....	....	....	....	....	....	....	....	....	....	....	....	....	....	....	....	....	Yemen, Republic of
																	Western Hemisphere
-3.0	-22.5	-19.7	-30.5	-35.4	-6.9	.4	-13.3	-57.1	-46.3	-15.1	-25.1	-7.9	-8.2	-7.5	-5.0	....	Antigua and Barbuda
2.8	-.5	-2.3	-2.8	-2.8	-2.3	-2.1	-1.1	-2.7	-3.9	-1.2	-1.7	3.2	-.3	-2.9	-2.9	....	Argentina
....	....	....	....	....	....	....	....	....	....	....	....	....	....	....	....	....	Aruba
4.0	1.4	-1.1	-5.3	-4.1	-2.2	-2.7	1.5	2.3	-1.3	-1.6	-1.9	-2.3	-2.7	-1.0	-2.2	....	Bahamas, The
-6.4	-5.1	-3.0	-12.5	-3.6	-3.5	1.7	4.5	.7	-1.6	2.8	1.4	-1.0	-1.5	9.1	3.9	....	Barbados
....	....	....	....	....	....	-2.5	4.3	5.2	3.4	-.8	-5.2	3.9	-6.0	-6.0	-9.3	....	Belize
-8.8	-9.0	-.1	-7.7	-2.8	-2.4	-2.7	-4.4	-8.4	-8.7	-5.8	-4.9	-3.6	-4.3	....	....	....	Bolivia
-3.5	-4.8	-5.5	-4.5	-5.9	-3.5	—	-.1	-2.0	-.5	1.3	.3	-.9	-.4	1.6	-.1	....	Brazil
-7.1	-5.7	-7.1	-14.5	-9.5	-5.7	-11.0	-8.6	-6.7	-3.6	-1.0	-2.5	-1.8	.3	-1.7	-4.6	-1.5	Chile
1.1	1.6	-.6	-5.4	-7.8	-7.8	-3.7	-5.2	1.1	.9	-.6	-.5	1.3	5.7	2.1	-4.6	....	Colombia
-10.3	-13.8	-13.7	-15.6	-10.4	-9.9	-6.9	-7.4	-3.6	-8.3	-6.6	-8.6	-8.7	-1.8	-5.6	-6.3	....	Costa Rica
-2.9	15.1	-24.3	-19.4	-11.4	-2.3	-8.0	-6.5	4.9	-2.5	-4.1	-21.2	-18.6	-11.8	-11.9	-11.7	....	Dominica
-6.6	-6.0	-10.9	-5.4	-5.6	-4.8	-1.6	-2.4	-3.4	-7.2	-.4	-3.2	-1.4	-.5	-5.1	....	....	Dominican Republic
-9.2	-6.7	-5.5	-7.2	-8.5	-.9	-2.1	.5	-5.3	-11.1	-6.1	-6.0	-2.0	-4.6	-.6	-3.7	-4.2	Ecuador
-9.1	.9	1.0	-7.2	-3.3	-3.6	-4.0	-3.3	-.4	-1.5	-2.4	-5.1	-4.4	-4.0	-3.3	-1.7	....	El Salvador
1.6	-1.5	.3	-17.4	-20.0	-16.1	1.8	1.9	-2.0	-13.3	-9.9	-16.7	-14.0	-16.6	-11.1	....	....	Grenada
-4.5	-3.2	-2.1	-6.7	-4.6	-2.5	-4.0	-2.2	-.2	-6.2	-5.3	-4.4	-3.0	-2.0	-6.8	-6.2	....	Guatemala
-5.9	-15.9	-21.7	-32.5	-29.5	-32.2	-22.3	-20.9	....	....	....	....	....	....	....	....	....	Guyana
-4.4	-4.7	-7.3	-10.5	-6.7	-6.8	-5.7	-4.7	-2.0	-1.6	-2.0	-3.0	-3.8	-5.6	-3.0	-6.4	....	Haiti
-8.3	-8.7	-12.3	-10.7	-7.9	-7.5	-11.3	-8.5	-5.9	-6.3	-3.9	-4.0	-7.5	-8.4	-10.3	-8.9	....	Honduras
-.8	-4.4	-5.1	-10.3	-11.6	-9.4	-13.3	-13.6	-.7	-4.1	1.3	-7.0	-7.3	-6.6	.9	-5.6	....	Jamaica
....	-4.0	-5.4	-6.5	-3.4	3.9	2.4	.4	-1.1	3.0	-1.4	-2.8	-3.1	-5.2	-7.4	-6.5	....	Mexico
....	....	....	....	....	....	....	....	....	....	....	....	....	....	....	....	....	Netherlands Antilles
-1.8	17.3	-29.2	-35.7	-26.8	-22.7	-19.6	-24.5	-15.4	-2.5	-58.2	-35.7	-13.8	....	....	-32.7	-39.5	Nicaragua
-8.5	-11.1	-8.7	1.4	-1.2	9.4	4.7	5.8	6.8	5.9	13.3	3.3	.9	-2.9	-1.4	....	....	Panama
-4.4	-6.0	-6.2	-6.6	-6.4	-3.8	-6.0	-5.5	-6.7	-10.8	-3.5	5.9	-3.3	-5.2	-9.3	-8.8	....	Paraguay
-1.8	4.7	-.5	6.9	-6.5	-4.6	-1.2	.5	-4.5	-3.8	-3.7	.2	-2.7	-3.1	-4.0	-4.4	....	Peru
....	....	-5.5	-8.4	-14.5	-25.1	-6.2	-8.6	-5.1	-9.6	-16.9	-24.0	-27.8	-19.2	-7.0	....	....	St. Kitts and Nevis
-32.5	-33.1	-34.0	-35.9	-26.6	-4.1	-10.2	-6.7	1.0	-1.8	-4.6	-18.6	-17.1	-19.3	-12.9	....	....	St. Lucia
5.9	-6.8	-15.7	-1.1	-12.8	-2.8	-1.0	3.3	-1.9	-10.0	-4.7	-10.6	-2.8	-11.4	-5.4	....	....	St. Vincent & Grens.
3.5	5.0	2.0	-2.7	-5.3	-16.0	-8.0	-1.0	-2.0	6.9	4.9	10.8	2.2	-3.6	.5	.7	....	Suriname
1.5	-.4	5.7	6.1	-7.5	-12.1	-6.0	-.6	-8.6	-4.7	-2.0	-.9	9.1	-.1	2.6	2.4	....	Trinidad and Tobago
-2.5	-4.9	-7.0	-4.1	-2.5	-1.2	-2.7	-2.1	.7	-1.9	.3	1.7	2.2	.4	-.1	-1.7	....	Uruguay
-14.6	.7	8.0	6.0	-6.3	6.5	8.0	5.6	-3.7	-3.0	-9.6	5.0	17.0	3.2	-6.2	-3.7	....	Venezuela

Government Finance

Central Government Deficit/Surplus

As Percent of GDP

	1978	1979	1980	1981	1982	1983	1984	1985	1986	1987	1988	1989	1990	1991	1992	1993	1994
Industrial Countries																	
United States	-2.73	-1.48	-2.88	-2.66	-4.02	-6.11	-4.82	-5.34	-5.04	-3.31	-3.23	-2.78	-3.99	-4.84	-4.93	-4.05	-3.32 f
Canada	-4.80	-3.70	-3.34	-2.32	-5.49	-6.04	-6.37	-5.90	-3.91	-2.47	-2.19	-2.52	-3.11	-3.62	....	....	....
Australia	-3.45	-2.88	-1.69	-.77	-.37	-2.68	-4.10	-3.14	-2.39	-1.03	.82	1.85	2.24	.62	-2.32 P	....	....
Japan	-7.30	-7.25	-6.88	-6.45	-6.43	-6.60	-5.67	-4.82	-4.72	-3.45	-2.56	-2.90	-1.57	....	....	....	....
New Zealand	-8.91	-5.72	-6.67	-7.54	-7.57	-9.16	-8.15	-4.55	-3.62	1.03	2.01	....	I4.03	1.94	-2.27	....	....
Austria	-4.15	-3.84	-3.37	-3.08	-4.81	-5.98	-4.56	-4.70	-5.92	-5.50	-5.00	-3.76	-4.49	-4.77	-3.91	....	....
Belgium	-6.84	-7.59	-8.17	-12.49	-11.10	-12.51	-13.45	-11.34	-9.96	-7.76	-6.54	-6.59	-5.68	-6.82	-7.06	....	....
Denmark	-.34	I-.74	-2.68	-6.05	-8.08	-6.86	-3.93	-.61	4.51	3.92	2.20	1.06	-.69	-1.05	-1.55 P	-2.34 P	....
Finland	-1.86	-2.48	-2.17	-.91	-2.08	-2.93	-1.02	-.81	.11	-1.73	.40	1.81	.18	-6.95	-14.76	....	....
France	-1.36	-1.49	-.07	-2.31	-3.36	-3.51	-2.67	-2.72	-3.36	-1.21	-2.34	-1.93	-2.10	-1.25	-3.76	....	....
Germany	-2.06	-1.99	-1.83	-2.37	-2.02	-1.98	-1.85	-1.10	-.91	-1.08	-1.70	-.16	I-1.63	-2.36	....	....	....
Greece	-4.29	-3.87	-5.00	-10.91	-18.55	-5.23	-14.03	-14.45	10.98	-1340	-15.21	-26.38	-28.91	I-18.92	-11.98	-15.66 P	....
Iceland	-2.41	-2.01	-1.24	-.70	-2.42	-2.93	-1.81	-3.90	-4.74	-2.05	-3.78	-2.58	-2.46	-4.37	3.14	....	....
Ireland	-11.37	-11.92	-13.08	-14.63	I-14.83	-12.51	-10.70	-11.68	-10.86	-9.22	-4.20	-1.34	-2.00	-.69	-2.02	....	....
Italy	-8.34	-8.86	-10.70	-11.21	-9.92	-11.29	-13.13	-13.35	-14.23	-14.90	I-10.56	I-10.50	-10.25	-9.90	-10.91	....	....
Luxembourg	3.39	-.24	1.50	-1.83	.75	-2.03	5.31	10.48	7.34	3.55	3.04	3.26	5.63	-11.67	....	....	....
Netherlands	-3.10	-4.60	-4.62	-6.51	-7.60	-7.76	-7.48	-5.49	-1.88	-3.13	-4.21	-4.33	-4.78	-2.76	-3.40	-.95	....
Norway	-6.79	-6.28	-1.89	2.08	1.07	2.35	1.98	3.65	3.37	.06	-.16	-1.23	.70	....	....	....	....
Portugal	-11.79	-10.10	-9.67	-11.96	-10.54	-9.55	-9.67	-14.81	-12.29	-10.41	-8.71	-4.00	-5.25	....	....	....	....
Spain	-2.34	-3.53	I-4.19	-5.13	-5.54	-6.25	-8.28	-6.96	-4.53	-3.89	-3.59	-2.25	I-3.23	-3.67	....	....	....
Sweden	-5.23	-7.60	-8.83	-9.25	-8.66	-10.31	-8.32	-7.40	-6.31	.41	.76	.57	.63	-1.06	-2.30	-11.85	....
Switzerland	-.09	-.69	-.20	.11	-.06	-.38	-.09	....	....	....	....	....	....	....	....	....	....
United Kingdom	-5.23	-5.63	-4.63	-4.76	-3.41	-4.39	-3.16	-2.87	-2.37	-.68	1.55	1.54	.73	-.99	-5.02	....	....
Developing Countries																	
Africa																	
Benin	3.13	-.52	....	....	....	....	....	....	....	....	....	....	....	....	....	....	....
Botswana	-1.31	2.97	-.15	-2.05	-1.84	7.75	10.95	18.21	19.90	14.16	15.63	9.58	11.70	10.00	....	....	....
Burkina Faso	.67	-2.23	.32	-1.44	-1.72	.15	-.86	I1.39	....	....	....	....	....	....	....	....	....
Burundi	-2.94	-5.52	-3.78	-5.54	....	....	....	....	....	....	....	....	....	....	....	....	....
Cameroon	.42	2.79	.53	-3.26	-2.54	1.29	....	....	....	....	....	....	-3.15	I-5.93	-5.50	I-2.81	....
Central African Rep.	....	....	....	-3.06	....	....	....	....	....	....	....	....	....	....	....	....	....
Chad	....	....	....	....	....	....	....	....	....	I-3.19	-3.40	-3.83	-7.83	-6.76	-7.29 P	....	....
Congo	....	....	I-5.21	.07	-13.12	-3.33	....	....	....	....	....	....	....	....	....	....	....
Côte d'Ivoire	....	-8.65	-10.85	....	....	....	....	....	....	....	....	....	....	....	....	....	....
Djibouti	....	4.10	6.73	I7.84	3.98	6.40	....	....	....	....	I-1.04	....	....	....	....	....	....
Ethiopia	-5.81	-3.19	-4.48	-3.83	I-5.46	-13.84	-6.32	-8.68	-7.38	-6.05	-6.62	....	-8.28	-13.99	I-12.32	-10.51 P	-11.19 P
Gabon	....	-.54	6.09	.78	2.95	-1.23	.21	.07	....	....	....	I-4.77	3.41	-1.64	....	....	....
Gambia, The	-9.94	-9.04	-4.45	-11.10	-6.49	....	....	....	....	....	....	....	I-.82	....	....	....	....
Ghana	-11.80	-7.32	-5.09	-8.16	-6.10	I-2.68	-1.79	-2.21	.06	.54	.37	.73	.17	1.51	-4.80	....	....
Guinea-Bissau	....	....	....	....	....	....	....	....	-16.03	-19.37	-18.35	-14.92	....	....	....	....	....
Kenya	-4.15	-6.96	-4.91	-7.08	-8.36	-5.12	I-5.07	-6.57	-4.71	-6.70	-4.42	-6.94	-4.04	-2.76	-.44	-3.99	....
Lesotho	....	....	....	....	....	....	....	....	....	....	-21.31	-17.66	-7.96	-1.11	-.57	....	....
Liberia	-7.60	-17.07	-9.83	-11.38	-10.89	-9.15	-5.58	-8.19	-8.57	-7.73	I-7.83	....	....	....	....	....	....
Madagascar	....	....	....	....	....	....	....	....	....	....	I-3.48	-4.08	-.76	-5.54	....	....	....
Malawi	-9.10	-8.40	-15.55	-12.06	-7.35	-6.77	-5.00	-8.10	-9.46	-8.03	-5.67	-2.71	-1.56	....	....	....	....
Mauritius	-12.43	-12.70	-10.98	-13.68	-12.66	I-7.98	-4.78	-3.75	-1.91	.25	I.34	I-1.56	-.45	—	I-.79	I.04	....
Morocco	-10.47	-9.73	-9.70	-13.36	-11.44	-7.75	-6.02	-7.28	-7.67	-4.48	-3.20	-5.13	-2.22	-2.11	-1.37	....	....
Namibia	....	....	....	....	....	....	....	....	....	5.93	-3.78	.04	6.12	I-1.26	-2.90	-5.80 P	....
Niger	-3.69	-2.87	-4.92	....	....	....	....	....	....	....	....	....	....	....	....	....	....
Nigeria	-1.77	....	....	....	....	....	-4.41 P	-2.76 P	-3.38 P	-8.22 P	....	....	....	....	....	....	....
Rwanda	-1.59	-1.66	-1.74	....	....	....	....	....	....	....	....	....	-3.27 P	-5.82 P	-3.55 P	-6.92 P	....
Senegal	.30	-.79	I.90	-3.49	I-6.83	-5.99	-8.28	....	....	....	....	....	....	....	....	....	....
Seychelles	....	....	....	....	....	....	....	-10.59	-14.97	-1.67	-3.68	-6.96	....	....	....	....	....
Sierra Leone	-9.32	-11.56	-12.83	-9.34	-10.43	-14.46	-7.53	-7.85	-2.45	-16.94	-7.42	-6.52	-2.91	-5.91	-6.34	-4.85	....
South Africa	-5.23	-3.94	I-2.29	-3.84	-3.70	-5.01	-4.56	I-3.92	-5.26	-6.88	-5.18	-.23	-4.15	-4.16 P	....	....	....
Sudan	-4.66	-3.42	-2.62	....	-4.86	....	....	....	....	....	....	....	....	....	....	....	....
Swaziland	-12.95	1.05	6.24	-9.54	-5.74	-3.26	-.53	-3.39	-4.56	1.66	3.62	4.89	....	....	....	....	....
Tanzania	-7.75	-15.71	-9.02 P	-7.17 P	....	....	....	-5.21	....	....	....	....	....	....	....	....	....
Togo	-31.13	-8.43	-1.97	-5.74	-1.78	-1.88	-2.51	-1.80	-4.56	-2.52	....	....	....	....	....	....	....
Tunisia	-4.07	-4.75	-2.82	-2.53	-5.77	-8.35	-4.92	I-5.13	-7.28	-4.65	-3.76	I-4.32	-5.42	-4.14 P	-2.54 f	....	....
Uganda	-.28	-4.22	-3.33	-5.00	-4.41	-2.69	-2.90	-3.76	-3.21	....	....	-7.99	....	-6.52	-14.37	I-12.06	....
Zaïre	-10.86	-4.94	-.83	-3.92	-4.44	....	....	....	....	....	....	....	....	....	....	....	....
Zambia	-14.42	-9.06	-18.52	-12.90	-18.59	-7.83	-8.39	-15.17	I-21.38	-12.89	-11.55	-5.00 P	....	....	....	....	....
Zimbabwe	-10.75	-10.40	-10.93	-5.90	-10.49	-6.24	-10.11	I-7.48	-8.14	-11.08	-9.95	-9.21	-8.02 P	....	....	....	....
Asia																	
Bangladesh	2.92	.51	2.51	-3.17	1.18 P	3.12 P	.82 P	-1.46 P	....	....	....	....	....	....	....	....	....
Bhutan	....	....	....	....	.65	-1.25	1.46	-8.31	-3.27	....	I.68	I-10.38	-8.33	-2.58 P	....	....	....
China, People's Rep.	....	....	....	....	....	....	....	....	....	....	....	....	-2.04	-2.44	....	....	....
Fiji	-4.35	-2.91	-3.00	-4.29	-6.32	-3.79	-3.04	-2.69	-4.83	-5.05	-.75	-2.95	-2.22	-2.30	....	....	....
India	-4.87	-5.51	-6.52	-5.47	-6.03	-6.42	-7.60	-8.49	-9.28	-8.37	-8.10	-7.92	-8.17	-5.82	-5.19 P	....	....
Indonesia	-3.01	-2.16	-2.27	-1.98	-1.80	-2.31	1.33	-.96	-3.35	-.80	-2.96	-1.93	.39	.42	-.41	.64	....
Korea	-1.23	-1.74	-2.23	-3.34	-3.04	-1.04	-1.16	-1.15	-.09	.43	1.51	.19	-.67	-1.62	-.49	.64	....
Malaysia	-6.22	-3.02	-5.97	-14.88	-16.14	-9.70	-6.48	I-2.55	-9.19	-6.63	-.25	-.45	-1.30	-.24	.70	1.62 P	....
Maldives	....	-12.46	-23.83	-7.03	-4.54	-15.61	-4.68	-5.10	-12.11	2.26	2.70	-4.08	-14.15	....	....	....	....
Myanmar	.62	2.41	1.23	1.65	.72	.62	-.17	-.79	-2.51	-2.21	-3.02	-4.16	-5.13	-4.81	-2.85	....	....
Nepal	-2.95	I-2.65	-3.02	-2.67	-5.13	-8.75	-7.58	-7.61	-7.21	-6.59	-6.21	-10.31	-7.71 P	-6.18 f	....	....	....
Pakistan	-7.51	-9.23	-5.70	-5.80	-4.74	-6.80	-6.18	-7.16	-9.12	-8.52	-6.28	-7.40	-5.40	-7.55	-7.88	-7.40	....
Papua New Guinea	I-1.40	-3.54	-1.78	-5.90	-5.12	-4.41	-.93	I-2.31	-3.11	-1.36	I-1.03	-1.15	-3.47	-1.89	-5.32	....	....
Philippines	-1.22	-.16	-1.39	-4.32	-4.54	-2.02	-1.90	-1.95	-5.03	-2.45	-2.91	-2.11	-3.45	-2.11	-1.18	-1.48	....
Singapore	.79	2.16	2.06	.71	3.26	1.76	4.13	2.10	1.41	-2.62	6.72	9.87	10.59	8.66	12.47	....	....

Government Finance

Central Government Deficit/Surplus

As Percent of GDP

1978	1979	1980	1981	1982	1983	1984	1985	1986	1987	1988	1989	1990	1991	1992	1993	1994	
																	Asia (cont.)
.84	−2.61	−3.02	−6.55	−8.23	−9.46	−2.95	−8.16ᴾ	−5.96ᴾ	−11.63ᴾ	−9.25ᴾ	....	....	....	....	....	....	Solomon Islands
−12.40	−12.03	−18.27	−12.37	−14.03	−10.56	−6.82	−9.66	−10.14	−8.68	−12.70	−8.65	−7.82	−9.45	−5.39	−6.46ᴾ	....	Sri Lanka
−3.79	−3.77	−5.05	−3.47	−6.52	−4.04	−3.47	−5.33	−4.30	−2.30	.71	3.07	4.71	4.88	2.94ᴾ	....	....	Thailand
....	....	−1.50	−2.25	−1.91	1.23	.44	−2.63	−4.78	−5.83	.44	−.04	−1.20ᴾ	−5.20 ᶠ	....	....	....	Tonga
....	....	....	....	−3.58	−.56	3.51	−.50	−7.02	3.82	−4.19	....	....	....	....	....	....	Vanuatu
																	Europe
−5.69	−6.61	−9.21	−5.34	−4.73	−7.16	−5.47	−4.41	−3.63	−4.21	−3.19	−1.38	−2.32	−4.42	....	....	....	Cyprus
....	....	....	....	....	....	....	....	....	....	....	....	....	....	....	2.64ᴾ	....	Czech Republic
....	....	....	−2.83	−1.90	−.71	1.60	−.98	−2.84	−3.29	−.22	−1.91	.80	....	....	....	....	Hungary
4.06	....	ɪ1.09	1.27	−1.65	1.60	.45	−4.04	−3.81	−6.68	−.03	−4.65	−5.18	−5.05	−3.12	....	....	Malta
....	....	....	....	....	....	−.47	−1.73	−.32	−1.43	−2.27	....	....	....	....	....	....	Poland
....	....	.49	1.66	3.00	3.22	6.48	2.55	4.29	7.11	5.83	8.22	.94	1.94	−4.72	....	....	Romania
−3.85	−5.45	−3.45	−1.73	....	ɪ−4.19	−9.97	−7.44	−3.21	−4.02	−3.83	−4.47	−4.17	....	....	....	....	Turkey
																	Middle East
−3.37	2.17	5.87	8.50	2.34	−6.85	−1.57	.98	−4.33	−10.25	....	−8.59	−7.03	....	....	....	....	Bahrain
−12.74	−15.74	....	ɪ−6.39	−17.13	−9.13	−10.33	−9.23	−10.94	−5.07	−7.66	−5.37	−5.72	−.96	−3.47	....	....	Egypt
−8.67	−3.88	−13.79	−10.50	−5.72	−6.30	−4.03	−3.77	−8.34	−7.11	ɪ−9.15	−3.92	−1.82	−2.25	−1.43	ɪ−.26	....	Iran, I.R. of
−11.92	−12.12	ɪ−12.89	−18.09	−13.37	−19.61	−12.94	−2.79	.70	−3.30	−8.03	−3.90	−4.33	ɪ−8.01	ɪ−3.86	−1.81ᴾ	....	Israel
−20.88	−8.18	−9.55	−8.12	−7.83	ɪ−6.14	−7.39	−7.77	−6.15	−11.46	−9.39	−5.90	−3.61	−2.79	5.59	....	....	Jordan
27.27	31.51	62.19	40.89	8.54	8.00	12.47	7.78	29.01	....	....	....	....	....	....	....	....	Kuwait
−7.95	6.59	.44	1.95	−8.52	−8.84	−11.38	−10.54	−25.00	−4.87	−11.85	−8.96	−.81	−7.26	−13.23	....	....	Oman
−9.06	.78	−9.71	−6.32	....	....	....	....	−8.27	−2.63	1.25	−.61	.34	1.32	1.69	....	....	Syrian Arab Republic
−.83	.25	2.10	1.94	....	....	....	−.49	−.68	−.71	−.36	−.77	.37	−.50	.82	....	....	United Arab Emirates
																	Western Hemisphere
—	—	−2.60	−6.69	−5.03	−7.95	−3.38	−5.51	−1.97	−2.86	−1.88	−.38	....	....	....	....	....	Argentina
−1.24	.52	1.45	−2.27	−3.00	−3.54	.90	.24	−.84ᴾ	....	....	....	....	....	....	....	....	Bahamas, The
−.40	−1.45	−3.43	−6.69	ɪ−3.77	−1.19	−3.91	−2.89	−2.94	−7.22	−2.79	−.96	....	....	....	....	....	Barbados
−1.08	ɪ−1.78	ɪ−1.64	....	....	−1.24	−3.32	....	....	....	6.87	−.77	.70	−3.13	−3.34	....	....	Belize
....	....	....	....	....	....	....	....	−.06	.66	−.64	−1.24	−1.49	−.06	....	....	....	Bolivia
−2.76	—	−2.41	−2.46	−2.82	−4.21	−5.09	−11.12	−13.30	−12.04	−15.17	−16.07	−5.66	−.43	−3.63	....	....	Brazil
−.11	4.82	5.41	2.59	−.98	−2.63	ɪ−2.97	−2.29	−.92	.44	−.21	ɪ1.80	.84	1.55	2.29	1.99	....	Chile
.68	−.77	−1.76	−3.05	−4.73	−4.19	−4.32	−2.71	−.86	−.69	ɪ−1.33	−1.90	....	....	....	....	....	Colombia
−5.00	−6.77	−7.39	−2.87	−.88	−2.01	−.74	−1.25	−4.48	ɪ−2.91	—	−2.13	−3.14	−1.33	.94	−.20	....	Costa Rica
−2.50	−6.95	....	....	....	....	....	....	....	....	....	....	....	....	....	....	....	Dominica
−1.49	−5.73	−2.61	−2.50	−3.10	−2.51	−1.10	−1.88	.49	−.70	−1.99	.04	.54	....	....	....	....	Dominican Republic
−1.20	−.65	−1.40	−4.83	−4.45	−2.51	−.83	1.98	−2.24	−2.28	−.05	1.88	1.89ᴾ	....	....	....	....	Ecuador
−1.39	−1.00	−5.75	−7.50	−7.59	−5.35	−4.47	−.74	.94	.61	−.28	−1.86	−.78	−2.05	−.79	....	....	El Salvador
−1.17	−2.16	−3.44	−5.52	−4.35	−3.05	ɪ−3.81	−1.80	−.58	−.76	−1.06	−1.72	....	....	....	....	....	Guatemala
−10.15	−17.53	−29.19	−28.37	....	....	....	....	....	....	....	....	....	....	....	....	....	Guyana
....	−4.03	−4.94	....	−3.20	....	....	....	....	....	....	....	....	....	....	....	....	Haiti
−13.23	−12.29	−15.07	−13.23	−14.53	−18.33	−5.57	−8.11	....	....	....	....	....	....	....	....	....	Honduras
−2.70	−3.33	−3.00	−6.40	−14.84	−7.62	−7.11	−8.40	−13.14	−13.57	−10.33	−5.22	.74ᴾ	....	....	....	....	Jamaica
−5.88	−6.47	−6.85	−10.74	−20.29	−31.34	−23.59	−21.97	−14.75	....	−23.65	−1.91	−17.84	5.54	−2.10	....	....	Mexico
−6.51	−13.28	−5.50	−8.53	−11.16	−6.15	−7.38	−3.13	−4.25	−4.25	−2.35	−2.88	3.20	5.74	4.29	....	....	Nicaragua
.95	1.01	.32	−1.49	.40	−.94	−1.90	−.50	.03	−.04	.65	ɪ2.44	2.93	−.16	.80	....	....	Panama
−5.07	ɪ−.54	−2.36	−3.98	−3.22	−7.52	ɪ−4.45	−2.42	−4.10	−6.23	−5.62	−3.65	−1.43	−1.77	ɪ−.80	....	....	Paraguay
....	....	....	....	....	....	....	....	−6.52	1.12	−16.47	ɪ−7.08	−.99	−.01	....	....	....	Peru
....	....	....	....	....	....	....	....	....	....	....	....	....	....	....	....	....	St. Kitts and Nevis
−.74	1.99	−4.71	−2.59	−5.02	4.32	....	−2.10	−1.86	1.21	2.54	1.30	−.12	....	....	....	....	St. Lucia
....	....	−.20	.90	−3.35	−.17	....	2.10	1.36	1.43	−1.39	....	....	....	....	....	....	St. Vincent & Grens.
....	....	....	....	....	....	−15.23	−19.99	−24.72	....	....	....	....	....	....	....	....	Suriname
3.07	−.87	7.22	2.91	−12.24	−11.84	−8.89	−5.15	−5.87	−5.86	−5.69	−3.86	....	....	....	....	....	Trinidad and Tobago
−.91	—	.03	−1.50	−9.06	−4.15	−5.65	−2.43	−.70	−.85	−1.67	−3.02	.37	.91	.63	....	....	Uruguay
−4.08	1.91	.04	−1.37	−4.35	ɪ−1.51	3.34	5.26	−2.02	ɪ−5.85	−7.73	−1.61	1.11	4.41	−3.17	−2.99ᴾ	....	Venezuela

Government Finance

Central Government Revenue and Grants

As Percent of GDP

	1978	1979	1980	1981	1982	1983	1984	1985	1986	1987	1988	1989	1990	1991	1992	1993	1994
Industrial Countries																	
United States	19.33	20.10	20.65	21.58	21.12	19.70	19.44	19.94	19.51	20.43	20.01	20.22	19.86	20.60	19.71	19.73	....
Canada	16.71	16.91	17.90	19.92	19.31	18.57	18.83	18.74	19.31	19.73	19.31	20.14	20.76	20.99	....	....	....
Australia	25.48	24.30	24.86	25.84	26.49	26.75	25.89	27.40	27.78	28.49	28.18	26.89	27.05	27.09	25.38 P	....	....
Japan	9.94	10.78	11.46	12.13	12.08	11.87	12.07	12.46	12.35	13.38	13.86	13.91	14.41	....	....	....	....
New Zealand	33.53	34.68	34.12	34.84	35.51	33.45	34.54	36.99	37.88	42.64	40.40	....	I42.97	38.94	36.04	....	....
Austria	34.48	34.64	34.93	36.26	35.12	34.81	35.83	35.35	35.03	34.90	35.62	34.95	34.94	35.40	36.85	....	....
Belgium	42.54	42.82	43.78	44.68	45.89	45.10	46.09	46.49	45.56	45.56	44.25	43.23	43.98	44.15	....	....	....
Denmark	34.50	I35.37	37.16	36.38	35.84	37.57	39.57	40.89	42.86	42.24	42.00	41.29	39.85	40.24	40.60 P	41.60 P	....
Finland	28.86	27.68	27.67	28.87	28.77	28.92	29.23	30.30	31.94	30.27	31.60	31.94	31.84	32.25	33.99	....	....
France	36.38	38.01	40.06	40.73	41.34	41.78	42.13	42.15	41.49	41.85	41.47	41.05	41.07	41.65	41.35	....	....
Germany	27.55	27.39	28.97	29.46	30.27	29.61	30.11	30.41	29.90	29.72	29.00	29.60	I28.93	30.81	....	....	....
Greece	30.12	30.01	30.76	29.42	33.99	38.74	36.06	35.95	38.20	39.25	37.32	34.04	37.09	I26.27	21.61	27.46 P	....
Iceland	26.55	27.35	26.24	27.01	27.21	25.66	26.51	25.85	26.04	26.58	28.61	30.85	29.64	29.61	30.88	....	....
Ireland	33.39	34.46	37.92	38.97	I41.90	44.09	43.81	43.13	41.59	41.63	41.38	37.16	38.03	39.54	39.70	....	....
Italy	30.12	30.53	31.90	31.31	34.14	36.43	34.88	34.36	37.16	36.76	I36.77	I38.08	38.82	39.80	41.60	....	....
Luxembourg	50.04	47.69	49.92	50.98	50.13	51.74	50.12	51.24	49.27	50.18	48.41	48.49	50.20	52.11	53.08	....	....
Netherlands	48.44	48.97	50.36	50.94	51.55	52.80	51.76	51.26	51.25	51.28	50.50	47.68	47.11	50.03	49.59	50.76	....
Norway	38.81	38.92	41.34	43.12	42.73	44.15	43.13	44.88	47.87	45.81	46.72	45.76	47.35	....	....	....	....
Portugal	27.69	27.43	30.26	32.14	32.68	35.27	33.93	33.70	36.43	36.00	35.59	39.95	39.36	....	....	....	....
Spain	23.58	24.13	I24.23	24.26	25.39	26.11	26.37	27.50	29.21	30.51	30.53	32.24	I31.05	31.59	....	....	....
Sweden	39.53	38.08	38.32	38.39	39.75	40.90	40.97	42.32	41.67	44.74	44.58	45.31	46.19	44.37	43.54	39.31	....
Switzerland	20.78	20.26	I20.32	20.03	20.49	20.64	21.42	....	....	....	....	....	....	....	....	....	....
United Kingdom	32.73	32.56	35.40	36.40	38.62	37.36	37.35	37.64	36.53	35.97	36.08	35.61	36.97	37.51	36.20	....	....
Developing Countries																	
Africa																	
Benin	25.19	23.72	....	....	....	....	....	....	....	....	....	....	....	....	....	....	....
Botswana	30.45	33.75	35.51	35.25	35.57	41.77	46.02	49.31	55.74	50.80	50.38	45.86	54.79	53.10	....	....	....
Burkina Faso	14.49	13.89	15.86	15.03	15.17	14.31	16.15	I15.70	....	....	....	....	....	....	....	....	....
Burundi	20.02	18.33	17.19	18.09	....	....	....	....	....	....	....	....	....	....	....	....	....
Cameroon	18.47	19.59	17.01	17.51	17.97	25.66	24.90	....	22.34	20.10	17.13	17.21	I15.46	17.23	I17.25	....	....
Central African Rep.	....	....	....	16.07	....	....	....	....	....	....	....	....	....	....	....	....	....
Chad	....	....	....	....	....	....	....	....	I21.74	29.82	23.65	26.40	24.32	23.99 P	....	....	....
Congo	....	....	I44.40	39.70	36.95	35.53	....	....	....	....	....	....	....	....	....	....	....
Côte d'Ivoire	....	24.02	24.07	....	....	....	....	....	....	....	I30.57	....	....	....	....	....	....
Djibouti	....	48.91	52.03	I34.46	39.55	39.92	....	....	....	....	....	....	....	....	....	....	....
Ethiopia	17.29	17.99	18.87	20.58	20.88	22.42	23.43	23.64	25.51	25.68	29.35	32.79	25.51	I19.95	16.17 P	19.09 P	....
Gabon	....	42.66	39.12	40.35	41.08	38.59	41.69	41.14	....	20.10	....	I21.46	25.32	29.20	....	....	....
Gambia, The	28.49	20.91	26.49	21.58	25.87	....	....	11.75	14.40	14.89	14.63	15.14	I27.13	15.17	12.17	....	....
Ghana	8.67	10.57	8.30	5.68	6.11	I5.57	8.37	11.75	14.40	14.89	14.63	15.14	13.16	15.17	12.17	....	....
Guinea-Bissau	....	....	....	....	....	....	....	....	24.49	37.45	34.34	41.29	....	....	....	....	....
Kenya	23.90	23.33	24.89	24.71	23.38	22.18	I21.59	21.41	22.11	23.43	24.20	25.72	25.89	28.62	26.51	26.47	....
Lesotho	....	....	....	....	....	....	....	52.57	....	45.52	48.15	45.38	52.11	54.05	55.74	....	....
Liberia	26.72	27.12	25.07	25.01	25.99	23.37	23.75	21.56	19.40	18.29	I18.12	....	....	....	....	....	....
Madagascar	26.70	28.29	19.28	....	....	....	....	....	....	....	I13.78	12.90	13.34	9.51	....	....	....
Malawi	20.73	23.52	22.90	22.55	21.02	20.66	21.55	22.97	23.09	22.25	22.29	23.68	23.44	....	....	....	....
Mauritius	21.10	20.41	22.19	21.93	20.87	I24.38	24.30	24.26	24.02	24.91	I26.01	I25.63	25.61	25.23	I25.26	I24.27	....
Morocco	24.20	25.47	23.62	25.84	26.25	24.73	23.75	23.33	21.25	23.67	24.93	25.39	26.47	25.93	28.47	....	....
Namibia	....	....	....	....	....	....	....	....	....	47.50	40.68	38.45	43.19	I35.24	40.00	38.76 P	....
Niger	14.75	14.82	15.10	....	....	....	....	....	....	....	....	....	....	....	....	....	....
Nigeria	16.44	....	....	....	....	....	11.16 P	....	12.41 P	15.30 P	14.73 P	....	16.18 P	14.96 P	18.67 P	18.19 P	....
Rwanda	11.32	12.81	12.78	....	....	....	....	....	....	....	....	....	....	....	....	....	....
Senegal	20.00	20.05	I25.49	23.44	I23.59	21.20	21.81	....	....	....	....	....	....	....	....	....	....
Seychelles	....	....	....	....	....	....	....	46.77	46.25	52.75	52.90	57.50	....	....	....	....	....
Sierra Leone	19.95	18.72	17.06	18.33	11.94	9.09	9.74	6.83	7.96	10.67	9.07	9.61	7.03	11.52	15.57	17.47	....
South Africa	22.47	21.88	I22.99	21.97	23.11	22.90	23.92	I26.15	25.30	24.79	25.77	29.32	27.12	26.91 P	....	....	....
Sudan	12.40	13.78	13.45	....	15.38	....	....	....	....	....	....	....	....	....	....	....	....
Swaziland	34.12	36.52	35.41	26.57	33.16	30.91	32.45	29.79	23.87	25.99	26.17	29.90	....	....	....	....	....
Tanzania	22.25	21.57	21.78 P	22.61 P	....	....	....	....	19.23	....	....	....	....	....	....	....	....
Togo	29.97	32.90	30.58	27.48	30.27	28.83	32.73	34.48	32.98	29.01	....	....	....	....	....	....	....
Tunisia	31.66	32.38	32.23	32.05	34.50	33.73	36.63	I33.74	34.24	31.52	31.76	I32.22	31.45	29.38 P	29.34 f	....	....
Uganda	10.26	3.21	3.41	1.54	8.36	10.81	12.28	9.81	7.71	....	....	....	....	....	....	....	....
Zaïre	16.68	22.11	11.63	10.74	9.15	....	....	....	....	....	12.11	13.61	12.24	6.10	I3.25	....	....
Zambia	25.56	23.30	25.81	23.85	24.17	25.52	22.58	22.27	24.37	22.04	18.78	14.29 P	....	....	....	....	....
Zimbabwe	24.29	21.67	24.11	25.52	29.47	29.96	32.95	I33.65	33.28	34.38	36.08	36.13	37.42 P	....	....	....	....
Asia																	
Bangladesh	14.81	13.94	14.18	12.89	15.55 P	15.34 P	12.68 P	11.87 P	....	....	....	....	....	....	....	....	....
Bhutan	....	....	....	....	31.36	36.17	36.30	38.89	37.38	....	I37.92	I36.10	31.89	38.96 P	....	....	....
China, People's Rep.	....	....	....	....	....	....	....	....	....	....	....	....	....	9.36	8.06	....	....
Fiji	22.37	22.77	22.81	24.89	23.78	25.71	25.81	25.80	23.26	22.94	24.55	24.70	25.79	23.20	....	....	....
India	12.69	12.93	12.17	12.50	12.86	12.45	13.01	13.96	14.51	14.58	14.23	14.95	13.71	14.64	15.16 P	....	....
Indonesia	17.47	19.93	21.40	23.24	19.34	19.22	20.43	20.67	19.70	19.19	16.23	16.69	19.44	17.99	18.75	....	....
Korea	16.89	17.39	17.96	18.12	18.34	18.08	17.35	16.97	16.55	16.64	17.19	17.40	17.87	17.07	18.22	19.11	....
Malaysia	23.25	22.54	26.36	27.50	26.57	26.57	25.86	I30.15	30.02	25.43	25.73	25.72	27.14	28.73	28.81	27.54 P	....
Maldives	....	10.90	18.03	22.05	27.74	26.14	30.51	27.59	35.62	42.99	43.89	54.76	47.35	....	....	....	....
Myanmar	15.73	17.03	17.07	17.66	17.31	16.15	15.20	14.66	13.36	11.31	8.93	10.65	9.82	8.34	....	....	....
Nepal	10.08	I10.46	11.22	11.84	11.70	11.45	10.63	10.74	11.26	11.92	13.36	11.86	11.64 P	11.89 f	....	....	....
Pakistan	14.89	15.57	17.05	17.24	16.33	16.45	17.39	16.75	18.31	17.87	18.54	19.64	19.98	17.75	18.50	18.69	....
Papua New Guinea	I 28.10	25.88	30.56	30.46	29.29	28.76	31.91	I29.43	29.37	28.79	I28.42	32.81	32.50	33.65	27.00	....	....
Philippines	13.51	13.48	14.10	12.69	11.98	12.36	10.83	12.06	13.01	15.12	14.12	16.47	16.79	17.69	17.96	17.65	....
Singapore	22.95	23.91	25.31	28.82	29.94	31.19	29.41	37.99	37.75	31.04	27.88	28.95	31.87	31.17	32.63	....	....

Government Finance

Central Government Revenue and Grants

As Percent of GDP

1978	1979	1980	1981	1982	1983	1984	1985	1986	1987	1988	1989	1990	1991	1992	1993	1994	Country
																	Asia (cont.)
32.80	28.69	30.94	26.49	24.45	28.57	23.64	23.32ᴾ	32.67ᴾ	34.05ᴾ	33.67ᴾ	....	....	....	....	....	....	Solomon Islands
27.91	25.86	24.15	20.58	19.74	22.03	24.30	24.36	22.84	23.80	21.78	23.97	23.20	22.65	22.12	21.45ᴾ	....	Sri Lanka
13.56	14.19	15.22	15.97	14.72	16.22	16.21	16.05	15.96	16.20	17.21	18.15	19.51	19.99	18.74ᴾ	....	....	Thailand
....	....	33.53	36.33	32.86	29.53	36.79	51.08	34.64	39.01	35.41	38.71	43.68ᴾ	53.42 f	....	....	....	Tonga
....	....	....	....	29.78	28.62	31.44	29.48	27.27	42.91	37.69	....	....	....	....	....	....	Vanuatu
																	Europe
22.41	21.72	22.85	23.21	24.62	25.46	25.75	26.32	26.68	25.92	26.85	28.02	27.89	27.13	....	....	....	Cyprus
....	....	....	....	....	....	....	....	....	....	....	....	....	....	....	41.71ᴾ	....	Czech Republic
43.34	....	I36.57	41.96	41.88	43.63	42.03	52.14	55.73	53.85	55.04	54.16	53.18	....	....	....	....	Hungary
....	....	....	....	....	....	43.74	41.40	37.09	34.39	38.59	35.66	39.23	39.56	35.47	....	....	Malta
....	....	....	....	....	....	....	43.45	41.82	38.96	37.17	....	....	....	....	....	....	Poland
....	....	45.28	41.75	35.12	30.80	35.39	44.15	46.78	47.78	42.48	48.29	34.73	37.33	36.78	....	....	Romania
20.56	19.82	20.51	21.36	....	I20.02	14.94	17.55	17.95	17.92	17.44	18.70	20.00	....	....	....	....	Turkey
																	Middle East
30.18	29.89	38.48	41.15	40.43	34.93	35.61	38.87	38.37	34.74	....	32.73	33.74	....	....	....	....	Bahrain
39.05	37.56	....	I47.12	46.82	42.78	39.14	37.33	37.31	34.66	33.22	30.76	25.87	34.40	38.11	....	....	Egypt
33.53	29.83	21.56	24.00	25.60	22.38	20.19	18.79	12.43	12.59	I11.91	13.78	18.06	16.75	18.68	I26.85	....	Iran, I.R. of
55.38	55.17	I49.63	49.10	50.73	52.70	52.07	61.43	61.48	54.50	47.12	44.78	45.36	I44.07	I45.31	45.12ᴾ	....	Israel
30.07	42.26	36.25	34.97	33.18	I32.50	26.37	30.46	29.05	27.28	28.40	32.91	33.00	35.68	39.02	....	....	Jordan
73.35	65.56	94.73	85.86	64.59	67.58	69.83	59.12	81.54	....	....	....	....	....	....	....	....	Kuwait
47.27	50.59	40.50	45.19	38.29	41.02	39.85	40.47	31.96	39.95	35.21	35.70	39.17	32.79	30.31	....	....	Oman
32.14	39.99	38.47	32.23	....	....	....	....	26.21	25.13	23.83	24.80	22.14	25.60	24.81	....	....	Syrian Arab Republic
11.51	11.09	16.04	18.55	....	....	....	15.64	16.14	14.47	14.78	12.56	12.05	11.75	12.94	....	....	United Arab Emirates
																	Western Hemisphere
19.11	21.05	15.63	12.04	10.53	9.68	9.90	15.62	15.20	13.98	9.26	9.85	....	....	....	....	....	Argentina
16.86	17.44	20.80	21.07	20.73	22.93	23.58	23.21	21.67ᴾ	....	....	....	....	....	....	....	....	Bahamas, The
30.69	26.14	26.83	26.63	I28.33	29.48	28.59	30.32	28.57	28.53	32.59	32.69	....	....	....	....	....	Barbados
25.85	I25.38	I23.60	23.51	26.95	24.65	23.37	22.98	....	....	24.98	26.35	27.62	25.88	25.98	....	....	Belize
....	....	....	....	....	....	....	8.11	11.35	11.56	11.72	11.83	12.97	14.47	....	....	....	Bolivia
22.12	23.49	22.49	24.99	25.76	27.46	24.87	26.51	22.56	34.55	20.18	22.34	30.63	26.07	25.86	....	....	Brazil
32.29	34.12	34.14	32.94	30.21	27.74	I28.91	28.36	26.93	26.55	26.20	I21.46	20.83	22.77	23.37	23.65	....	Chile
12.18	11.70	12.01	11.57	11.35	11.39	11.12	12.02	12.91	13.04	I12.85	12.86	....	....	....	....	....	Colombia
19.04	18.27	17.82	17.84	17.47	21.74	22.32	20.72	22.13	I24.63	25.09	24.55	23.09	23.55	24.90	25.80	....	Costa Rica
39.87	44.67	....	....	....	....	....	....	....	....	....	....	....	....	....	....	....	Dominica
14.67	13.45	14.41	13.68	10.37	11.60	12.38	12.38	15.57	15.79	16.98	14.58	11.38	....	....	....	....	Dominican Republic
9.96	9.86	12.80	11.27	11.06	10.74	12.29	17.07	13.51	13.19	15.26	16.09	16.58ᴾ	....	....	....	....	Ecuador
13.13	13.81	11.40	12.55	12.11	11.95	14.59	17.02	14.77	13.30	10.82	8.62	9.63	10.01	10.22	....	....	El Salvador
10.90	9.65	9.44	8.59	8.34	8.16	I7.02	7.71	9.23	10.46	11.15	10.25	8.13	9.10	10.63	9.05	....	Guatemala
31.90	36.26	35.79	41.73	45.02	45.84	....	49.01	....	....	....	....	....	....	....	....	....	Guyana
....	14.71	13.39	....	15.08	....	....	....	....	....	....	....	....	....	....	....	....	Haiti
13.67	14.27	14.58	13.14	....	....	....	....	....	....	....	....	....	....	....	....	....	Honduras
29.08	26.06	28.16	30.69	27.96	24.27	29.35	31.50	....	....	....	....	....	....	....	....	....	Jamaica
13.78	14.31	15.10	14.61	15.51	18.02	16.20	16.50	15.97	17.42	17.28	18.29	14.05ᴾ	....	....	....	....	Mexico
13.29	14.80	23.95	28.70	29.17	36.41	40.40	37.68	37.66	....	23.11	28.79	18.31	33.72	28.15	....	....	Nicaragua
24.37	24.88	26.89	26.26	27.84	29.91	28.35	29.65	29.70	27.19	24.39	28.06	32.36	32.30	....	....	....	Panama
12.67	11.90	11.10	10.28	11.66	10.27	9.58	9.72	9.75	10.16	9.75	I11.42	12.32	11.85	14.42	....	....	Paraguay
15.68	I15.79	16.96	14.45	14.41	12.01	14.02	14.99	12.61	9.20	9.36	7.07	9.31	9.21	11.14	I13.58	....	Peru
....	....	....	....	....	....	....	31.79	30.20	31.31	I31.17	31.16	29.55	....	....	....	....	St. Kitts and Nevis
32.78	40.47	36.90	39.65	43.55	46.58	....	30.63	30.35	33.24	32.81	33.30	29.35	30.59ᴾ	....	....	....	St. Lucia
28.11	29.57	31.10	33.05	32.21	33.01	31.31	33.31	32.65	31.19	29.43	....	....	....	....	....	....	St. Vincent & Grens.
....	....	....	....	....	....	30.03	28.16	27.60	....	....	....	....	....	....	....	....	Suriname
35.89	36.42	42.67	42.76	36.85	35.00	35.52	37.44	31.61	30.69	28.62	27.09	....	....	....	....	....	Trinidad and Tobago
22.38	21.15	22.26	23.75	21.33	22.88	20.48	22.84	24.74	23.79	24.50	23.90	26.55	28.45	29.48	....	....	Uruguay
25.38	24.60	26.28	34.30	28.85	I26.67	25.79	28.19	22.08	I19.90	19.18	20.41	23.48	24.17	18.91	17.73ᴾ	....	Venezuela

Government Finance

Central Government Expenditure and Lending Minus Repayments

As Percent of GDP

	1978	1979	1980	1981	1982	1983	1984	1985	1986	1987	1988	1989	1990	1991	1992	1993	1994
Industrial Countries																	
United States	22.06	21.58	23.53	24.24	25.14	25.81	24.26	25.28	24.55	23.75	23.25	23.00	23.85	25.45	24.64	23.78	23.70 f
Canada	21.51	20.61	21.24	22.25	24.80	24.61	25.20	24.64	23.22	22.21	21.50	22.65	23.87	24.62	....	....	....
Australia	28.92	27.17	26.56	26.61	26.86	29.43	29.98	30.54	30.17	29.52	27.37	25.04	24.82	26.47	27.71 P	....	....
Japan	17.25	18.02	18.33	18.59	18.51	18.47	17.74	17.28	17.07	16.82	16.43	16.81	15.98	....	....	....	....
New Zealand	42.44	40.40	40.79	42.39	43.08	42.61	42.69	41.54	41.50	41.62	38.39	....	I38.94	37.00	38.32	....	....
Austria	38.62	38.48	38.30	39.34	39.93	40.39	40.39	40.05	40.95	40.41	40.63	38.71	39.43	40.17	40.76	....	....
Belgium	49.38	50.41	51.95	57.17	56.99	57.61	59.54	57.83	55.53	53.32	50.79	49.82	49.67	50.47	51.21	....	....
Denmark	34.84	I36.12	39.84	42.43	43.92	44.43	43.51	41.50	38.35	38.32	39.80	40.23	40.54	41.28	42.16 P	43.93 P	....
Finland	30.72	30.16	29.84	29.77	30.85	31.85	30.25	31.11	31.83	32.00	31.20	30.13	31.66	39.20	48.75	....	....
France	38.28	39.10	39.95	42.75	45.20	45.06	45.20	45.16	44.75	43.36	43.25	42.42	42.42	44.34	45.07	....	....
Germany	29.53	29.20	30.76	31.76	32.21	31.59	31.82	31.37	30.61	30.80	30.60	29.74	I29.93	33.12	....	....	....
Greece	34.41	33.88	35.76	40.33	52.54	43.97	50.09	50.40	49.18	52.65	52.52	60.42	66.00	I45.19	33.58	43.12 P	....
Iceland	28.96	29.36	27.48	27.71	29.63	28.59	28.32	29.76	30.78	28.63	32.39	33.43	32.10	33.98	34.01	....	....
Ireland	44.75	46.38	51.00	53.61	I56.73	56.60	54.51	54.81	52.45	50.85	45.58	48.49	40.03	40.23	41.72	....	....
Italy	38.47	39.39	42.60	42.52	44.06	47.72	48.01	47.71	51.39	51.67	I47.34	I48.57	49.06	49.70	52.51	....	....
Luxembourg	46.65	47.93	48.77	51.07	51.64	53.32	47.60	46.88	45.42	47.27	46.42	43.40	47.32	50.79	52.15	....	....
Netherlands	51.34	53.04	54.85	57.21	59.24	60.00	59.10	55.90	52.98	54.77	54.48	52.53	51.57	52.48	53.09	51.97	....
Norway	45.60	45.20	43.24	41.04	41.65	41.80	41.15	41.22	44.50	45.76	46.87	46.99	46.65	....	....	....	....
Portugal	39.48	37.53	39.93	44.10	43.22	44.81	43.60	48.51	48.72	46.41	44.30	43.95	44.61	....	....	....	....
Spain	25.92	27.65	I28.42	29.39	30.93	32.36	34.65	34.46	33.73	34.40	34.12	34.49	I34.28	35.26	....	....	....
Sweden	44.76	45.68	47.15	47.65	48.41	51.21	49.29	49.72	47.98	44.32	43.82	44.74	45.56	45.43	45.84	51.16	....
Switzerland	20.86	20.94	20.52	19.92	20.55	21.02	21.51	....	....	....	....	....	....	....	....	....	....
United Kingdom	37.95	38.20	40.03	41.16	42.03	41.75	40.50	40.51	38.90	36.65	34.53	34.06	36.25	38.50	41.22	....	....
Developing Countries																	
Africa																	
Benin	22.06	24.24	....	....	....	....	....	....	....	....	....	....	....	....	....	....	....
Botswana	31.76	30.79	35.66	37.30	37.41	34.02	35.07	31.10	35.84	36.64	34.75	36.28	43.09	43.10	....	....	....
Burkina Faso	13.95	16.31	15.54	16.47	16.89	14.17	17.01	I14.31	....	....	....	....	....	....	....	....	....
Burundi	22.96	23.85	20.97	23.63	....	....	....	23.72	....	....	....	....	....	....	....	....	....
Cameroon	18.05	16.80	16.48	20.77	20.51	24.37	....	21.95	....	....	....	....	20.36	I21.39	22.74	I20.06	....
Central African Rep.	....	....	....	19.33	....	....	....	....	....	....	....	....	....	....	....	....	....
Chad	....	....	....	....	....	....	....	....	....	I24.93	33.22	27.47	34.23	31.08	31.28 P	....	....
Congo	....	32.67	I49.60	39.63	50.07	38.86	....	....	....	....	....	....	....	....	....	....	....
Côte d'Ivoire	....	....	34.92	....	....	....	....	....	....	....	I31.61	....	....	....	....	....	....
Djibouti	....	44.81	45.30	I26.62	35.56	33.52	....	....	....	....	....	....	....	....	....	....	....
Ethiopia	23.10	21.17	23.35	24.41	I26.34	36.27	29.74	32.32	32.89	31.73	35.97	41.07	39.50	I32.28	26.68 P	30.28 P	....
Gabon	....	....	43.21	33.02	39.56	38.13	39.83	41.47	41.07	....	....	....	I26.24	21.90	30.84	....	....
Gambia, The	38.44	29.95	30.94	32.68	32.36	....	....	....	....	....	....	....	I27.94	....	....	....	....
Ghana	20.47	17.88	13.39	13.84	12.21	I8.25	10.16	13.96	14.34	14.34	14.26	14.41	12.99	13.66	16.97	....	....
Guinea-Bissau	....	....	....	....	....	....	....	....	....	40.52	56.82	56.21	....	....	....	....	....
Kenya	28.06	30.29	29.80	31.78	31.73	27.30	I26.66	27.98	26.82	30.13	28.62	32.65	29.92	31.39	26.95	30.46	....
Lesotho	....	....	....	....	....	....	....	....	....	69.46	63.04	60.07	55.16	56.31	....	....	....
Liberia	34.31	44.19	34.90	36.39	36.88	32.52	29.33	29.75	27.98	26.01	....	....	....	....	....	....	....
Madagascar	....	....	....	....	....	....	....	....	....	....	I17.26	16.98	14.10	15.06	....	....	....
Malawi	29.84	31.91	38.45	34.61	28.36	27.43	26.55	31.07	32.54	30.28	27.95	26.39	25.00	....	....	....	....
Mauritius	33.53	33.10	33.17	35.61	33.53	I32.36	29.08	28.01	25.93	24.66	I25.67	I27.19	26.06	25.22	I26.06	I24.23	....
Morocco	34.67	35.21	33.32	39.19	37.69	32.48	29.77	30.61	28.93	28.15	28.14	30.52	28.69	28.04	29.84	....	....
Namibia	....	....	....	....	....	....	....	....	....	41.57	44.45	38.40	37.07	I36.50	42.90	44.56 P	....
Niger	18.45	17.68	20.02	....	....	....	....	....	....	....	....	....	....	....	....	....	....
Nigeria	18.21	....	....	....	....	....	15.57 P	15.17 P	18.68 P	22.95 P	....	....	19.45 P	20.78 P	22.22 P	25.10 P	....
Rwanda	12.91	14.47	14.52	....	....	....	....	....	....	....	....	....	....	....	....	....	....
Senegal	19.70	20.85	I24.59	26.93	I30.42	27.18	30.09	....	....	....	....	....	....	....	....	....	....
Seychelles	....	....	....	....	....	....	....	57.36	61.22	54.42	56.57	64.46	....	....	....	....	....
Sierra Leone	29.27	30.29	29.88	27.67	22.37	23.55	17.27	14.68	10.40	27.61	16.49	16.13	9.94	17.43	21.91	22.32	....
South Africa	27.70	25.82	I25.28	25.81	26.81	27.91	28.47	I30.06	30.56	31.68	30.95	29.55	31.27	31.07 P	....	....	....
Sudan	17.06	17.20	16.07	....	20.24	....	....	....	....	....	....	....	....	....	....	....	....
Swaziland	47.07	35.47	29.18	36.11	36.20	34.17	32.98	33.18	28.43	24.33	22.55	25.02	....	....	....	....	....
Tanzania	30.00	37.27	30.81 P	29.78 P	....	....	....	24.45	....	....	....	....	....	....	....	....	....
Togo	61.10	41.33	32.54	33.22	32.05	30.71	35.23	36.28	37.54	31.53	....	....	....	....	....	....	....
Tunisia	35.73	37.13	35.05	34.59	40.28	42.08	41.55	I38.87	41.52	36.17	35.53	I36.54	36.88	33.53 P	31.88 f	....	....
Uganda	10.55	7.43	6.74	6.54	12.77	13.50	15.18	13.57	10.93	....	....	....	....	....	....	....	....
Zaïre	27.46	27.06	12.46	14.66	13.59	....	....	....	....	....	....	20.09	13.60	18.76	20.47	I15.27	....
Zambia	39.97	32.37	44.33	36.74	42.76	33.35	30.97	37.44	I45.75	34.92	30.32	19.28 P	....	45.45 P	....	....	....
Zimbabwe	35.04	32.06	35.04	31.42	39.96	36.21	43.06	I41.13	41.42	45.46	46.03	45.35	45.45 P	....	....	....	....
Asia																	
Bangladesh	11.89	13.44	11.66	16.07	14.37 P	12.22 P	11.85 P	13.33 P	....	....	I37.23	I46.48	40.22	41.54 P	....	....	....
Bhutan	....	....	....	....	30.71	37.43	34.84	47.20	40.65	....	....	....	11.39	10.50	....	....	....
China, People's Rep.	26.72	25.68	25.81	29.17	30.10	29.50	28.85	28.49	28.09	27.99	25.30	27.65	28.02	25.50	....	....	....
Fiji	17.57	18.43	18.68	17.97	18.88	18.87	20.60	22.44	23.79	22.95	22.34	22.87	21.88	20.46	20.36 P	....	....
India	20.47	22.09	23.67	25.22	21.14	21.53	19.10	21.64	23.05	19.99	19.19	18.62	19.04	17.57	19.16	....	....
Indonesia	18.12	19.13	20.20	21.46	21.38	19.11	18.51	18.12	16.64	16.21	15.68	17.21	18.55	18.69	18.72	18.47	....
Korea	29.47	25.56	32.34	42.38	42.71	36.27	32.34	I32.70	39.20	32.07	25.98	26.17	28.45	28.97	28.11	25.92 P	....
Malaysia	....	23.36	41.86	29.08	32.28	41.75	35.19	32.68	47.73	40.72	41.19	58.85	61.50	....	....	....	....
Maldives	15.12	14.62	15.85	16.01	16.59	15.53	15.37	15.45	15.87	13.51	11.95	13.78	15.78	14.63	11.18	....	....
Myanmar	13.03	I13.10	14.24	14.51	16.84	20.20	18.21	18.35	18.48	18.51	19.57	22.11	19.35 P	18.07 f	....	....	....
Nepal	22.40	24.80	22.75	23.04	21.06	23.25	23.57	23.90	27.43	26.40	24.82	27.05	25.38	25.31	26.38	26.09	....
Pakistan	29.50	29.42	32.34	36.36	34.41	33.17	32.84	I31.74	32.48	30.15	I29.45	33.96	35.97	35.53	32.32	....	....
Papua New Guinea	14.73	13.64	15.49	17.01	16.52	14.38	12.73	14.01	18.05	17.57	17.03	18.58	20.25	19.80	19.14	19.14	....
Philippines	22.16	21.75	23.26	28.12	26.68	29.43	25.28	35.89	36.34	33.66	21.16	19.08	21.28	22.51	20.16	....	....
Singapore																	

Government Finance

Central Government Expenditure and Lending Minus Repayments

As Percent of GDP

	1978	1979	1980	1981	1982	1983	1984	1985	1986	1987	1988	1989	1990	1991	1992	1993	1994	
																		Asia (cont.)
	31.96	31.29	33.97	33.04	32.68	38.03	26.59	31.48ᴾ	38.63ᴾ	45.68ᴾ	42.92ᴾ	38.35ᴾ	....	....	27.50	27.92ᴾ	....	Solomon Islands
	40.30	37.89	42.42	32.96	33.77	32.60	31.11	34.02	32.98	32.48	34.48	32.62	31.02	32.10	27.50	27.92ᴾ	....	Sri Lanka
	17.34	17.96	20.27	19.44	21.24	20.26	19.68	21.38	20.26	18.51	16.50	15.08	14.79	15.11	15.80ᴾ	....	....	Thailand
	....	....	35.03	38.58	34.77	28.30	36.36	53.71	39.42	44.83	34.97	38.75	44.88ᴾ	58.63ᶠ	....	....	....	Tonga
	....	....	....	....	33.37	29.18	27.94	29.97	34.30	39.10	41.89	....	....	....	....	....	....	Vanuatu
																		Europe
	28.10	28.33	32.06	28.55	29.35	32.62	31.21	30.73	30.31	30.14	30.05	29.40	30.21	31.56	....	....	....	Cyprus
	....	....	....	....	....	....	....	....	....	....	....	....	....	....	....	39.08ᴾ	....	Czech Republic
	....	....	....	56.44	53.64	54.88	53.09	53.12	58.57	57.13	55.26	56.07	52.38	....	....	....	....	Hungary
	39.29	....	ɪ35.48	40.69	43.53	42.03	41.58	45.43	40.90	41.07	38.62	40.30	44.41	44.61	38.58	....	....	Malta
	....	....	....	....	....	....	44.20	45.17	42.14	40.38	39.44	....	....	....	....	....	....	Poland
	....	....	44.79	40.09	32.12	27.58	28.90	41.60	42.49	40.68	36.65	40.07	33.79	35.39	41.50	....	....	Romania
	24.41	25.27	23.95	23.09	....	ɪ24.21	24.91	24.99	21.16	21.94	21.27	23.17	24.17	....	....	....	....	Turkey
																		Middle East
	33.55	27.72	32.61	32.66	38.09	41.78	37.18	37.88	42.71	44.99	....	41.32	40.77	....	....	....	....	Bahrain
	51.78	53.31	....	ɪ53.51	63.95	51.91	49.46	46.56	48.25	39.74	40.88	36.13	31.59	35.36	41.59	....	....	Egypt
	42.21	33.70	35.35	34.50	31.32	28.68	24.22	22.55	20.77	19.70	ɪ21.06	17.70	19.87	19.00	20.10	ɪ27.11	....	Iran, I.R. of
	67.31	67.28	ɪ62.52	67.19	64.10	72.31	65.01	64.22	60.77	57.80	55.15	48.68	49.69	ɪ52.08	ɪ49.18	46.93ᴾ	....	Israel
	50.95	50.45	45.80	43.10	41.01	ɪ38.64	33.75	38.23	35.20	38.74	37.80	38.81	36.61	38.47	33.43	....	....	Jordan
	46.08	34.05	32.54	44.96	56.05	59.58	57.36	51.34	52.54	....	....	....	....	....	....	....	....	Kuwait
	55.22	44.00	40.05	43.24	46.81	49.86	51.23	51.01	56.96	44.81	47.06	44.66	39.98	40.04	43.54	....	....	Oman
	41.21	39.21	48.18	38.55	....	....	....	....	34.48	27.75	22.58	25.40	21.79	24.28	23.12	....	....	Syrian Arab Republic
	12.33	10.84	13.94	16.60	....	....	....	16.13	16.82	15.19	15.14	13.33	11.68	12.25	12.13	....	....	United Arab Emirates
																		Western Hemisphere
	19.11	21.05	18.23	18.73	15.56	17.63	13.28	21.13	17.17	16.84	11.14	10.23	....	....	....	....	....	Argentina
	18.10	16.92	19.35	23.35	23.73	26.47	22.68	22.97	22.51ᴾ	....	....	....	....	....	....	....	....	Bahamas, The
	31.09	27.59	30.26	33.32	ɪ32.10	30.67	32.50	33.21	31.51	35.75	35.38	33.65	....	....	....	....	....	Barbados
	26.94	ɪ27.16	ɪ25.24	....	....	....	24.61	26.30	....	....	18.11	27.13	26.93	29.01	29.33	....	....	Belize
	....	....	....	....	....	....	....	....	11.42	10.91	12.36	13.08	14.46	14.53	....	....	....	Bolivia
	24.88	23.49	24.90	27.45	28.58	31.67	29.96	37.64	35.86	46.59	35.35	38.40	36.29	26.50	29.50	....	....	Brazil
	32.39	29.30	28.73	30.34	31.20	30.37	ɪ31.88	30.65	27.85	26.11	26.40	ɪ19.66	19.99	21.22	21.08	21.66	....	Chile
	11.51	12.47	13.76	14.62	16.08	15.58	15.43	14.73	13.77	13.73	ɪ14.18	14.76	....	....	....	....	....	Colombia
	24.04	25.04	25.21	20.72	18.35	23.75	23.05	21.97	26.60	ɪ27.55	25.09	26.67	26.22	24.88	23.96	26.00	....	Costa Rica
	42.38	51.62	....	....	....	....	....	....	....	....	....	....	....	....	....	....	....	Dominica
	16.16	19.18	17.02	16.18	13.47	14.11	13.48	14.25	15.08	16.49	18.97	14.53	10.85	....	....	....	....	Dominican Republic
	11.16	10.51	14.20	16.10	15.51	13.25	13.12	15.09	15.76	15.48	13.66	14.22	14.69ᴾ	....	....	....	....	Ecuador
	14.52	14.81	17.14	20.05	19.69	17.30	19.06	17.77	13.84	12.69	11.10	10.48	10.41	12.06	11.01	....	....	El Salvador
	12.07	11.81	12.88	14.11	12.69	11.21	ɪ10.83	9.52	9.81	11.21	12.21	11.97	....	....	....	....	....	Guatemala
	42.06	53.79	64.98	70.09	....	....	....	....	....	....	....	....	....	....	....	....	....	Guyana
	18.21	18.74	18.33	20.62	18.27	....	....	....	....	....	....	....	....	....	....	....	....	Haiti
	42.31	38.35	43.23	43.92	42.49	42.60	34.92	39.61	....	....	....	....	....	....	....	....	....	Honduras
	....	....	....	....	....	....	....	....	....	....	....	....	....	....	....	....	....	Jamaica
	16.51	17.64	18.10	21.00	30.35	25.64	23.30	24.90	29.11	30.99	27.61	23.51	13.30ᴾ	....	....	....	....	Mexico
	19.16	21.27	30.79	39.44	49.45	67.76	63.99	59.66	52.41	....	46.77	30.70	36.14	28.18	30.25	....	....	Nicaragua
	30.87	38.15	32.39	34.79	39.00	36.06	37.18	31.48	33.90	33.95	29.53	27.27	24.87	26.62	28.01	....	....	Panama
	11.72	10.90	10.77	11.77	11.25	11.22	11.30	9.53	8.37	9.32	9.10	ɪ8.97	9.39	12.01	13.62	....	....	Paraguay
	20.75	ɪ16.33	19.32	18.43	17.63	19.53	ɪ18.47	17.41	16.71	15.43	12.96	12.69	12.95	10.64	12.91	ɪ14.38	....	Peru
	....	....	....	....	....	....	....	38.31	29.08	47.78	ɪ38.25	32.15	29.57	....	....	....	....	St. Kitts and Nevis
	33.52	38.48	41.61	42.24	48.57	42.26	....	32.73	32.21	32.02	30.27	32.01	29.47	....	....	....	....	St. Lucia
	....	....	31.30	32.15	35.56	33.18	34.43	31.21	31.29	29.76	30.83	30.96	34.10	....	....	....	....	St. Vincent & Grens.
	....	....	....	....	....	....	45.26	48.15	52.33	....	....	....	....	....	....	....	....	Suriname
	32.82	37.28	35.45	39.85	49.09	46.84	44.42	42.59	37.48	36.54	34.32	30.95	....	....	....	....	....	Trinidad and Tobago
	23.29	21.15	22.23	25.24	30.39	27.03	26.13	25.28	25.44	24.64	26.17	26.93	26.19	27.55	28.86	....	....	Uruguay
	29.46	22.69	26.24	35.67	33.20	ɪ28.18	22.45	22.93	24.10	ɪ25.75	26.91	22.02	22.38	19.75	22.08	20.72ᴾ	....	Venezuela

GDP at Constant Prices

99bp x

Percent Change over Previous Year

		1965	1966	1967	1968	1969	1970	1971	1972	1973	1974	1975	1976	1977	1978	1979
World	001	5.2	5.1	3.7	5.4	5.3	3.5	3.6	4.8	5.9	2.3	1.2	5.3	4.2	4.1	4.1
Industrial Countries	110	5.1	5.4	3.5	5.1	5.3	3.2	3.3	5.1	5.8	.7	-.2	4.6	3.7	4.1	3.4
United States	111	5.6	6.0	2.6	4.1	2.7	—	3.1	4.8	5.2	-.6	-.8	4.9	4.5	4.8	2.5
Canada	156	6.6	6.8	2.9	5.4	5.4	2.6	5.8	5.7	7.7	4.4	2.6	6.2	3.6	4.6	3.9
Australia	193	5.6	6.3	3.3	5.9	5.9	6.3	5.2	3.5	5.0	2.2	2.9	3.7	.9	3.2	4.7
Japan*	158	5.8	10.4	11.0	12.2	12.1	10.2	4.3	8.4	7.6	-.8	2.9	4.2	4.8	5.0	5.6
New Zealand	196	6.0	3.8	-.9	2.2	5.0	3.7	2.5	4.4	7.2	4.0	1.7	.1	-2.7	-.3	2.6
Austria	122	3.0	5.1	2.8	4.1	5.5	6.4	5.1	6.2	4.9	3.9	-.4	4.6	4.5	.1	4.7
Belgium	124	3.7	2.8	4.0	4.3	6.6	6.3	3.7	5.4	5.9	4.3	-1.5	5.7	.6	2.9	2.2
Denmark	128	4.8	2.2	3.7	3.8	6.5	2.3	2.4	5.4	3.8	-.9	-.7	6.5	1.6	1.5	3.5
Finland	172	5.3	2.4	2.2	2.3	9.6	7.5	2.1	7.6	6.7	3.0	1.1	-.4	.2	2.1	7.0
France	132	4.8	5.2	4.7	4.3	7.0	5.7	4.8	4.4	5.4	3.1	-.3	4.2	3.2	3.3	3.2
Germany*	134	5.3	2.9	-.2	5.6	7.6	5.0	3.0	4.3	4.8	.1	-1.3	5.5	2.6	3.4	4.0
Greece	174	9.3	6.1	5.5	6.6	9.9	7.9	7.1	8.9	7.3	-3.6	6.1	6.4	3.4	6.7	3.7
Iceland*	176	7.1	8.5	-1.9	-6.1	3.2	8.3	12.8	5.7	7.7	3.5	-2.2	2.8	11.6	5.9	5.0
Ireland	178	2.0	1.0	5.2	8.1	6.1	3.5	3.4	6.5	6.2	4.1	2.4	1.4	8.2	7.2	3.1
Italy	136	3.3	6.0	7.2	6.5	6.1	5.3	—	4.3	7.1	5.4	-2.7	6.3	3.7	3.7	6.1
Luxembourg	137	2.2	1.1	.6	4.6	11.0	3.7	2.7	6.6	8.3	4.2	-6.6	2.5	1.6	4.1	2.2
Netherlands	138	5.5	2.9	5.4	6.5	12.4	5.7	4.2	3.3	4.7	4.0	-.1	5.1	2.3	2.5	2.4
Norway	142	5.3	3.8	6.3	2.3	4.5	2.0	4.6	5.2	4.1	5.2	4.2	6.8	3.6	4.7	5.1
Portugal	182	....	....	7.9	8.8	1.9	9.3	6.6	8.0	11.2	1.2	-4.3	6.9	5.6	3.4	6.1
Spain	184	6.3	7.1	4.3	6.8	8.9	4.1	4.6	8.1	7.8	5.6	.5	3.3	2.8	1.5	—
Sweden	144	3.8	2.2	3.4	3.6	5.0	6.6	.9	2.3	4.0	3.2	2.6	1.1	-1.6	1.8	3.8
Switzerland	146	3.1	2.4	3.0	3.7	5.6	6.4	4.3	3.5	3.2	1.2	-6.7	-.8	2.4	.6	2.4
United Kingdom	112	2.5	1.9	2.3	4.1	2.1	2.3	2.0	3.5	7.4	-1.7	-.7	2.8	2.4	3.5	2.8
Developing Countries	200	5.8	4.0	4.7	6.5	5.5	4.4	4.5	3.8	5.9	6.1	4.6	6.7	5.4	4.0	5.3
Africa	605	4.8	-.2	5.2	5.5	4.6	5.9	3.4	3.5	5.3	6.4	1.3	4.7	3.7	1.5	4.2
Algeria	612	3.5	-8.4	5.3	8.2	5.4	7.3	-1.9	10.2	7.6	1.2	10.3	9.0	7.6	8.5	8.9
Benin	638	....	....	....	....	....	....	2.0	8.9	2.3	-7.5	4.4	4.3	5.7	2.8	5.0
Botswana	616	-5.4	6.5	7.0	1.9	15.1	14.9	17.2	29.8	24.8	24.2	-1.3	19.0	3.5	19.5	9.9
Burkina Faso	748	....	....	....	....	....	....	....	....	....	....	....	....	....	....	....
Burundi	618	....	....	....	....	....	....	7.9	-10.8	7.2	-.8	1.0	7.9	12.4	-1.1	2.0
Cameroon	622	....	....	....	....	....	3.6	3.0	4.3	1.5	4.5	5.1	1.9	5.7	10.4	11.2
Chad	628	....	....	....	....	....	....	1.8	-6.8	-4.9	13.6	17.3	-1.5	-7.4	-.3	-.3
Congo	634	3.7	1.0	1.5	4.0	6.2	3.8	5.6	5.1	6.2	15.1	-3.3	-.1	-5.5	-1.6	9.8
Côte d'Ivoire	662	....	....	....	....	....	....	....	....	....	....	....	....	4.7	9.9	1.9
Ethiopia	644	5.9	3.9	4.5	3.0	6.0	4.5	4.5	4.8	2.7	1.4	.1	2.3	.6	-1.1	5.3
Gambia, The	648	....	....	....	....	....	....	15.6	7.3	4.5	53.9	-4.1	6.6	-7.2	5.8	-9.1
Ghana	652	1.4	.1	-3.0	6.4	5.9	6.8	5.6	-2.5	15.3	3.4	-12.9	-3.5	2.3	8.5	-3.2
Kenya	664	....	....	....	8.6	5.5	7.4	6.9	9.5	6.8	1.5	3.4	7.0	9.4	10.8	3.7
Liberia	668	1.7	19.0	-.7	4.8	7.3	6.5	5.0	3.8	-2.5	7.4	-15.1	4.0	-.8	4.0	4.4
Madagascar	674	-.5	2.0	5.5	6.8	3.7	4.0	2.4	-3.2	-2.0	3.3	3.0	-4.0	-2.6	9.8	9.8
Malawi	676	18.2	9.9	11.7	-5.6	6.4	1.5	14.4	7.5	12.4	7.4	5.5	6.2	4.3	8.3	3.3
Mali	678	-2.0	-.5	4.4	18.3	-.2	13.2	-4.6	-7.2	15.1	-1.8	-.9	.9	.9	.7	-.7
Mauritius	684	3.9	-3.4	4.0	-6.6	5.1	-.9	4.5	8.0	11.8	8.0	1.3	16.7	6.6	3.8	3.5
Morocco	686	1.9	-1.4	6.5	12.4	.9	5.0	5.8	2.1	3.8	14.3	4.1	7.0	6.5	3.4	4.5
Mozambique	688	....	....	....	....	....	....	....	....	....	....	....	....	....	....	....
Niger	692	6.6	23.4	-3.4	-7.8	-1.6	9.3	-3.4	-7.6	-10.9	6.2	18.8	15.3	4.3	9.8	2.3
Nigeria	694	....	....	....	....	....	....	....	....	....	12.1	-3.0	10.9	8.1	-7.3	9.4
Rwanda	714	9.0	.4	9.5	9.3	11.0	11.0	1.2	.2	3.4	.7	2.0	1.8	5.2	9.8	9.4
Senegal	722	....	....	....	....	....	....	....	....	....	....	....	....	-2.7	-3.9	10.1
Seychelles	718	....	....	....	....	....	....	....	....	....	....	....	....	7.9	6.7	15.0
Sierra Leone	724	....	....	....	....	....	....	....	-1.1	3.1	4.0	3.0	-3.0	1.4	.3	7.4
Somalia	726	....	....	....	....	....	....	....	....	....	....	....	....	....	....	....
South Africa	199	6.1	4.4	7.2	4.2	4.7	5.2	4.3	1.7	4.6	6.1	1.7	2.2	-.1	3.0	3.8
Swaziland	734	....	....	....	....	....	....	....	....	....	....	....	....	....	9.9	14.5
Tanzania	738	....	12.8	4.0	5.2	1.8	5.8	4.2	6.7	3.1	2.5	5.7	6.6	-.4	2.1	2.4
Togo	742	....	....	....	....	....	....	....	6.0	3.8	-4.2	4.3	-.6	-.5	5.6	10.1	5.4
Tunisia	744	....	....	....	....	4.6	7.5	11.6	17.2	.5	10.0	8.1	8.2	4.9	6.2	7.2
Uganda	746	....	....	....	....	....	....	2.9	.7	-.6	.2	-2.0	.7	1.6	-5.5	-11.0
Zaïre	636	....	....	....	....	....	....	6.0	.2	8.1	3.1	-5.0	-5.2	.8	-5.3	.3
Zambia	754	29.4	-4.1	5.0	2.6	3.2	3.2	-.1	9.2	-.9	6.7	-2.4	4.3	-4.8	.6	-3.0
Zimbabwe	698	....	....	....	....	....	....	....	....	....	1.7	17.3	-3.6	-1.1	-5.1	-2.2	3.8
Asia	505	-.1	3.8	5.2	5.5	7.0	6.0	4.0	3.0	7.1	4.2	6.4	6.0	7.5	7.2	4.3
Bangladesh	513	....	....	....	....	....	....	....	....	....	12.1	3.4	12.3	1.3	6.5	4.6
Bhutan	514	....	....	....	....	....	....	....	....	....	....	....	....	....	....	....
China, People's Rep.	924	....	....	....	....	....	....	....	....	....	....	....	....	....	....	7.6
Fiji	819	....	....	....	....	....	....	....	....	....	....	....	....	....	....	....
India	534	-4.3	1.1	8.2	2.8	6.4	5.8	2.3	-.7	3.6	.2	9.7	1.5	8.2	6.6	-4.8
Indonesia	536	—	2.3	2.3	11.1	6.0	7.5	7.0	9.4	11.3	7.6	5.0	6.9	8.8	7.8	6.3
Korea	542	5.7	12.2	5.9	11.3	13.8	8.8	9.2	5.9	14.4	7.9	7.1	12.9	10.1	9.7	7.6
Malaysia	548	....	....	....	....	....	....	7.1	9.4	11.7	8.3	.8	11.6	7.8	6.7	9.3
Maldives	556	....	....	....	....	....	....	....	....	....	....	-2.1	26.0	16.1	14.9	10.4
Mongolia	948	....	....	....	....	....	....	....	....	....	....	....	....	....	....	....
Myanmar	518	....	....	....	10.1	8.0	1.3	2.4	-1.0	2.6	2.7	4.1	6.1	6.0	6.5	5.2
Nepal	558	2.5	7.0	-1.6	.7	4.5	2.6	-1.2	3.1	-.5	6.3	1.5	4.4	3.0	4.4	2.4
Pakistan	564	3.5	7.7	-4.5	5.0	5.3	-2.4	.7	.4	6.9	5.5	4.6	4.6	3.8	8.0	4.8
Papua New Guinea	853	....	....	....	....	....	....	....	....	....	3.8	.9	-1.6	-4.3	8.6	1.8
Philippines	566	5.2	4.4	6.1	5.6	4.8	4.5	4.9	4.8	9.2	5.0	6.4	8.0	6.1	5.5	6.2
Singapore	576	7.5	11.1	11.8	13.9	13.7	13.7	12.5	13.4	11.5	6.3	4.1	7.5	7.8	8.6	9.3
Solomon Islands	813	....	....	....	....	....	....	....	....	....	....	....	....	....	....	....
Sri Lanka	524	2.4	5.1	6.1	4.4	8.2	15.8	-.1	3.0	3.5	4.0	4.7	4.4	3.8	7.4	6.1
Thailand	578	7.9	12.2	7.8	8.5	7.9	10.5	5.0	4.1	9.9	4.4	4.8	9.4	9.9	10.4	5.3
Tonga	866	....	....	....	....	....	....	....	....	....	....	....	....	.8	4.8	1.9	1.9
Vanuatu	846	....	....	....	....	....	....	....	....	....	....	....	....	....	....	....
Western Samoa	862	-5.6	-.6	—	7.8	4.4	6.8	13.2	1.7	7.3	-10.6	-4.0	9.5	-1.0	6.3	13.3

GDP at Constant Prices

1980	1981	1982	1983	1984	1985	1986	1987	1988	1989	1990	1991	1992	1993	1994		99bp x
Calculated from Indices																
2.6	1.5	.4	2.6	4.8	3.8	3.4	3.9	4.6	3.2	2.7	1.7	3.2	3.0	....	World	001
.9	1.4	−.3	2.8	4.5	3.3	2.8	3.3	4.3	3.2	2.0	.4	1.9	1.4	3.1	Industrial Countries	110
−.5	1.8	−2.2	3.9	6.2	3.2	2.9	3.1	3.9	2.5	.8	−1.2	3.3	3.1	4.1	United States	111
1.5	3.7	−3.2	3.2	6.3	4.8	3.3	4.3	4.9	2.4	−.2	−1.8	.8	2.2	4.6	Canada	156
2.3	3.6	−.6	1.0	7.5	4.5	2.0	4.8	4.2	4.2	1.3	−1.6	2.5	4.0	4.9	Australia	193
3.5	3.4	3.4	2.8	4.3	5.2	2.6	4.3	6.2	4.8	4.8	4.3	1.4	.1	.6	Japan*	158
1.1	4.9	2.3	5.8	5.2	−.2	3.3	.6	1.5	−1.3	−.9	−2.5	1.9	5.2	....	New Zealand	196
2.9	−.3	1.1	2.0	1.4	2.5	1.2	1.7	4.1	3.8	4.2	2.9	1.8	−.1	2.7	Austria	122
4.1	−1.0	1.5	.4	2.3	.8	1.4	2.0	4.9	3.5	3.2	2.3	1.9	−1.7	2.3	Belgium	124
−.4	−.9	3.0	2.5	4.4	4.3	3.6	.3	1.2	.6	1.4	1.3	.8	1.5	4.4	Denmark	128
5.3	1.9	3.2	2.7	3.0	3.4	2.4	4.1	4.9	5.7	—	−7.1	−3.6	−1.6	3.9	Finland	172
1.6	1.2	2.5	.7	1.3	1.9	2.5	2.3	4.5	4.3	2.5	.8	1.3	−1.5	2.7	France	132
1.0	.1	−1.1	1.9	3.1	1.8	2.2	1.5	3.7	4.0	4.9	3.6	1.2	−2.3	1.6	Germany*	134
1.7	.1	.4	.4	2.7	3.1	1.6	−.5	4.5	3.5	−.9	3.2	.8	−.5	....	Greece	174
6.2	4.7	1.6	−3.0	3.6	3.6	6.8	9.0	−1.0	−.1	.6	1.2	−3.4	1.1	3.2	Iceland*	176
3.1	3.3	2.3	.8	4.3	3.1	3.7	4.7	4.3	7.4	8.6	2.9	5.0	4.0	....	Ireland	178
4.1	.6	.2	1.0	2.7	2.6	2.9	3.1	4.1	2.9	2.1	1.3	.9	....	....	Italy	136
1.0	−.6	1.1	3.0	6.2	2.9	4.8	2.9	5.7	6.7	3.2	3.1	1.8	....	....	Luxembourg	137
.9	−.7	−1.5	1.4	3.1	2.6	2.0	3.3	2.6	4.7	3.9	2.3	1.8	.4	2.5	Netherlands	138
4.2	.9	.3	4.6	5.7	5.3	4.2	2.0	−.5	.6	1.7	1.6	3.4	2.4	5.1	Norway	142
4.8	1.3	2.1	−.2	−1.8	3.0	4.1	5.1	4.0	4.9	4.1	2.1	1.1	....	....	Portugal	182
1.3	−.2	1.6	2.2	1.5	2.6	3.2	5.6	5.2	4.7	3.7	2.2	.7	−1.1	2.0	Spain	184
1.7	—	1.1	1.8	4.0	2.2	2.2	2.8	2.7	2.4	1.4	−1.7	−1.4	−2.6	2.2	Sweden	144
4.4	1.4	−.9	1.0	1.8	3.7	2.9	2.0	2.9	3.9	2.3	—	−.3	−.9	2.1	Switzerland	146
−2.2	−1.3	1.7	3.7	2.3	3.8	4.3	4.8	5.0	2.2	.4	−2.0	−.5	2.3	3.8	United Kingdom	112
5.6	1.7	1.6	2.2	5.3	4.6	4.2	4.9	5.0	3.2	3.7	3.7	5.3	5.8	....	Developing Countries	200
5.1	1.4	—	−1.0	2.2	3.3	2.7	1.9	5.1	3.1	3.1	1.0	−.4	1.9	....	Africa	605
16.4	1.8	−5.3													Algeria	612
11.0	5.8	10.8	−4.3	7.9	7.5	2.1	−1.5	3.0	−.7	....	....	....	....	....	Benin	638
14.3	9.5	7.5	16.0	11.5	7.2	7.5	8.9	15.3	13.1	5.7	8.8	....	....	....	Botswana	616
1.7	4.4	2.2	−1.2	1.6	13.1	....	....	....	....	....	....	....	....	....	Burkina Faso	748
7.9	10.9	−.4	3.1	−.1	11.7	3.8	4.1	3.7	1.5	3.5	5.0	2.3	....	....	Burundi	618
4.2	17.1	7.6	7.0	7.8	8.9	7.2	−5.0	−7.2	−6.0	2.1	....	....	....	....	Cameroon	622
−.3	11.6	11.6	11.6	−5.0	26.0	−2.7	−5.6	....	....	....	....	....	....	....	Chad	628
15.8	21.2	23.6	5.6	7.2	−1.2	−6.9	.2	1.8	1.8	....	....	....	....	....	Congo	634
7.7	3.5	....	....	....	....	....	....	....	....	....	....	....	....	....	Côte d'Ivoire	662
5.5	6.1	1.0	7.7	−4.9	−5.9	6.9	9.6	1.9	1.6	−.4	−6.0	....	....	....	Ethiopia	644
−3.4	−4.5	7.7	−7.2	−.2	5.7	5.4	19.8	6.7	5.7	3.2	4.0	−9.5	....	....	Gambia, The	648
—	−1.8	−7.2	.7	2.6	5.1	5.2	4.8	5.6	5.1	3.3	5.3	3.9	5.0	....	Ghana	652
5.6	4.3	1.5	1.3	1.8	4.3	7.1	5.9	6.2	4.7	4.2	1.4	.4	−.2	....	Kenya	664
−4.7	2.2	−2.9	−.7	−.9	−1.4	2.9	2.7	—	....	....	....	....	....	....	Liberia	668
.8	−8.6	−1.8	.8	2.2	1.2	2.0	1.2	3.4	4.1	3.1	−6.3	1.2	2.1	.2	Madagascar	674
−.4	−5.2	2.8	3.5	4.4	4.5	1.1	2.1	3.4	4.1	4.8	7.8	−7.9	10.8	....	Malawi	676
.7	4.3	6.2	−5.2	.7	8.5	16.1	−2.4	.2	7.5	2.4	−.2	....	....	....	Mali	678
−10.1	5.9	5.5	.4	4.8	6.9	9.7	10.2	6.8	4.6	7.2	4.1	6.2	5.4	....	Mauritius	684
3.4	−2.8	9.6	−.6	4.3	6.3	8.4	−2.6	10.4	2.5	3.7	5.2	−2.9	−.2	....	Morocco	686
....	....	....	....	....	1.2	−2.4	14.8	8.6	5.9	.9	5.6	−.9	8.8	....	Mozambique	688
2.1	−6.3	....	....	....	....	....	....	....	....	....	....	....	....	....	Niger	692
5.3	−8.4	−.3	−5.4	−5.1	9.4	3.1	−.5	9.9	7.4	8.2	4.7	3.0	2.3	1.3	Nigeria	694
−3.6	2.5	4.1	6.0	−4.2	4.4	5.5	−.6	5.0	.5	2.0	.8	.5	....	....	Rwanda	714
−6.0	−1.2	15.3	2.2	−4.0	3.8	4.6	4.0	5.1	−1.5	....	....	....	....	....	Senegal	722
−3.1	−6.6	−1.5	−1.7	8.0	10.3	1.2	4.4	5.3	10.3	7.5	2.2	....	....	....	Seychelles	718
3.0	6.2	1.6	−1.4	1.4	−2.7	−2.4	5.4	2.7	2.2	4.5	2.3	−1.8	−2.4	....	Sierra Leone	724
....	6.3	2.8	−11.6	3.3	9.5	−2.1	10.1	....	....	....	....	....	....	....	Somalia	726
6.6	5.4	−.4	−1.8	5.1	−1.2	—	2.1	4.2	2.4	−.3	−1.0	−2.2	1.1	2.3	South Africa	199
−4.4	6.9	1.2	1.2	6.2	3.8	9.4	18.4	29.8	14.9	16.5	....	....	....	....	Swaziland	734
3.0	−.5	.6	−2.4	3.4	2.6	3.3	5.1	4.2	4.0	4.8	3.9	3.6	....	....	Tanzania	738
1.9	−3.5	−3.8	.7	1.3	3.1	3.4	1.5	....	....	....	....	....	....	....	Togo	742
9.4	6.5	−.5	4.7	5.7	5.7	−1.4	6.7	.1	1.7	7.8	3.9	8.0	2.1	4.4	Tunisia	744
−3.4	3.9	6.0	7.8	4.0	−.1	.5	7.0	7.3	7.2	5.3	4.8	4.4	7.9	....	Uganda	746
−22.4	.9	−.4	1.3	4.9	1.1	4.7	2.6	.6	−1.4	−2.5	−12.3	−10.5	....	....	Zaïre	636
3.0	6.2	−2.8	−2.0	−.4	1.6	.7	2.7	6.3	−1.0	−.5	−1.8	....	....	....	Zambia	754
10.6	12.5	2.6	1.6	−1.9	6.9	2.6	−1.0	9.3	5.5	8.9	1.7	....	....	....	Zimbabwe	698
6.8	5.9	5.0	7.4	8.2	6.8	6.5	7.7	9.2	5.7	5.7	5.7	8.4	8.2	9.2	Asia	505
1.3	6.8	.8	3.6	4.2	3.7	4.7	4.0	2.9	2.5	6.6	3.4	4.2	4.5	4.6	Bangladesh	513
....	10.0	5.3	8.0	7.0	3.7	10.2	17.8	1.2	4.9	4.6	....	....	....	....	Bhutan	514
7.8	4.5	8.3	10.4	14.6	12.9	8.5	11.1	11.2	4.3	3.9	8.0	13.2	13.8	11.9	China, People's Rep.	924
....	6.7	−1.1	−7.2	7.2	2.8	−.7	2.3	5.4	6.9	6.7	....	....	....	....	Fiji	819
6.5	6.5	3.8	7.4	3.7	5.5	4.9	4.8	9.9	6.6	5.7	.5	4.6	3.5	....	India	534
9.9	7.9	2.2	4.2	7.0	2.5	5.9	4.9	5.8	7.5	7.2	7.0	6.5	6.5	7.3	Indonesia	536
−2.2	6.7	7.3	11.8	9.4	6.9	11.6	11.5	11.3	6.4	9.5	9.1	5.1	5.8	8.4	Korea	542
7.4	6.9	5.9	6.3	7.8	−1.0	1.0	5.4	8.9	9.2	9.7	8.7	7.8	8.3	8.7	Malaysia	548
8.6	28.7	−2.9	16.1	27.2	13.7	8.6	8.9	8.7	9.3	16.2	7.6	6.3	6.2	....	Maldives	556
....	8.3	8.3	5.8	6.0	5.7	8.3	4.5	5.1	4.2	−2.5	−9.2	−11.6	....	....	Mongolia	948
22.4	4.4	5.4	4.4	4.9	2.9	−1.1	−4.0	−11.4	3.7	2.8	−2.4	11.3	6.0	....	Myanmar	518
−2.3	8.3	3.8	−3.0	9.7	6.1	4.6	1.7	7.7	4.3	4.6	6.4	4.1	3.1	7.6	Nepal	558
8.7	6.9	6.5	6.8	5.1	7.6	5.5	6.5	7.6	5.0	4.5	5.5	7.8	1.9	4.0	Pakistan	564
−2.3	1.1	.8	3.4	−1.0	3.6	5.7	2.8	2.9	−1.4	−3.0	9.5	11.8	14.4	....	Papua New Guinea	853
5.2	2.9	3.6	1.9	−7.3	−7.3	3.4	4.3	6.8	6.2	3.0	−.6	.3	2.1	4.3	Philippines	566
9.7	9.6	6.9	8.2	8.3	−1.6	1.8	9.4	11.1	9.2	8.8	6.7	6.0	9.9	....	Singapore	576
....	6.7	−1.1	3.9	8.3	2.6	−2.2	−5.1	....	....	....	....	....	....	....	Solomon Islands	813
5.7	5.5	−15.7	5.0	5.1	5.0	4.3	1.5	2.7	2.3	6.2	4.8	....	....	....	Sri Lanka	524
4.8	5.9	5.4	5.6	5.8	4.6	5.5	9.5	13.3	12.2	11.6	8.1	7.6	....	....	Thailand	578
15.8	14.0	14.8	5.8	44.1	5.6	8.8	1.7	−3.5	1.1	4.7	5.9	−3.8	−.1	4.8	Tonga	866
....	....	....	....	6.9	1.1	−2.0	.4	.6	4.5	4.7	5.2	4.1	.8	3.8	Vanuatu	846
−6.1	−9.1	−1.0	.5	....	....	....	....	....	....	....	....	....	....	....	Western Samoa	862

GDP at Constant Prices

99bp x

Percent Change over Previous Year:

		1965	1966	1967	1968	1969	1970	1971	1972	1973	1974	1975	1976	1977	1978	1979
Europe	170	....	....	....	....	....	....	....	....	....	....	....	....	....	....	....
Cyprus	423	21.3	7.1	13.1	5.3	9.8	3.0	13.0	6.8	2.6	−16.9	−19.0	18.0	15.8	7.6	9.9
Czechoslovakia	934															
Hungary	944							6.2	6.1	6.9	5.9	6.2	3.6	7.6	4.4	2.7
Malta	181	6.9	10.8	6.9	10.1	6.4	12.6	2.5	5.8	9.8	10.0	19.6	17.0	12.2	11.2	10.5
Romania	968															
Turkey*	186															
Yugoslavia, SFR	188					9.6	5.6	8.1	4.3	4.9	8.6	3.6	3.9	8.0	6.9	7.0
Middle East	405	10.9	3.5	.7	17.6	9.1	9.1	10.5	10.1	10.5	6.5	7.1	14.1	5.6	−1.8	6.5
Bahrain	419												23.7	14.7	8.1	−1.1
Egypt	469															
Iran, I.R. of	429	12.3	10.0	11.3	15.0	13.0	10.6	12.4	16.3	8.6	8.9	2.8	18.3	7.6	−21.1	−9.3
Iraq	433	13.6	4.3	−7.2	18.0	2.7	1.7	4.4	−2.5	18.7	7.2	15.0	12.1	17.3	12.2	11.7
Israel	436						33.3	—	—	50.0	—	16.7	3.7	−21.4	13.6	24.0
Jordan	439						−10.2	1.5	3.8	−5.4	−5.2	12.6	21.2	6.4	14.8	4.5
Kuwait	443							7.9	5.6	−2.9	−6.5	−12.3	6.6	−2.4	7.2	13.7
Libya	672	27.9	18.4	11.3	33.5	13.0	3.9	−5.3	9.1	1.9	22.2	4.0	22.6	8.9	2.6	8.3
Oman	449	.6	4.8	66.2	82.0	25.6	3.3	1.0	9.2	−14.0	28.2	28.6	16.0	17.6	17.7	4.6
Saudi Arabia	456					6.8	15.3	32.0	19.7	15.1	.3	8.6	15.1	5.9	6.7	10.1
Syrian Arab Rep.	463	2.3	−2.9	5.3	4.4	20.0	−5.9	9.5	21.6	−3.0	19.3	21.1	8.9	−1.4	7.9	3.6
United Arab Emirates	466											14.5	6.2	15.0	17.4	−2.3	24.9
Western Hemisphere	205	11.7	5.9	4.3	6.9	6.6	4.8	6.6	6.8	8.0	7.2	3.8	5.9	4.1	4.6	6.7
Antigua and Barbuda	311														9.5	7.7
Argentina	213	11.6	10.1	.8	3.3	4.9	2.6	3.4	1.9	3.2	6.3	−.7	−.2	6.2	−3.3	7.3
Bahamas, The	313															
Barbados	316	2.5	6.4	9.0	11.7	8.6	9.1	1.6	1.0	2.0	13.4	−2.0	4.5	3.7	4.9	7.9
Belize	339															
Bolivia	218	4.9	7.2	6.3	8.5	4.6	7.8	4.9	5.8	6.7	5.1	6.6	6.1	4.2	3.4	1.8
Brazil	223	23.1	3.5	5.4	10.8	9.8	2.6	12.2	10.9	13.5	9.7	5.6	9.7	2.9	5.0	6.8
Chile	228	.8	11.2	3.2	3.6	3.7	2.1	9.0	−1.2	−5.6	1.0	−12.9	3.5	9.9	8.2	8.3
Colombia	233					6.3	6.6	6.0	7.7	6.7	5.7	2.3	4.7	4.2	8.5	5.4
Costa Rica	238	9.8	7.9	5.7	8.5	5.5	7.5	6.8	8.2	7.7	5.5	2.1	5.5	8.9	6.3	4.9
Dominica	321													3.5	12.0	−17.2
Dominican Republic	243	−10.9	13.1	3.4	.5	12.2	9.0	10.9	10.4	12.9	6.0	5.2	6.7	5.0	2.1	4.5
Ecuador	248		2.4	6.9	4.0	2.3	6.5	6.3	14.4	25.3	6.4	5.6	9.2	6.5	6.6	5.3
El Salvador	253	5.4	7.2	5.4	3.2	3.5	3.0	4.8	5.5	5.1	6.4	5.6	4.0	6.1	6.4	−1.7
Grenada	328												9.0	5.7	8.1	2.4
Guatemala	258	4.4	5.5	4.1	8.8	4.7	5.7	5.6	7.3	6.8	6.4	1.9	7.4	7.8	5.0	4.7
Guyana	336	11.1	—	8.7	.2	4.7	3.4	2.8	−2.0	1.7	7.0	10.4	2.9	−4.8	−1.7	−11.7
Haiti	263			−2.1	3.2	3.8	.7	6.5	.9	4.0	5.8	1.1	8.4	.5	4.9	7.6
Honduras	268	10.3	5.9	4.6	7.3	.3	4.7	5.4	4.0	5.6	−.1	−3.0	10.5	10.4	8.3	6.3
Jamaica	343	7.8	3.9	2.6	6.1	6.5	7.7	4.4	7.8	2.8	−5.4	−1.2	−6.3	−2.4	.7	−1.8
Mexico	273	6.5	6.9	6.3	8.1	6.3	6.9	4.2	8.5	8.4	6.1	5.6	4.2	3.4	8.3	9.2
Nicaragua	278	9.5	3.3	7.0	1.4	6.2	1.3	4.9	3.2	7.5	14.2	−.2	5.2	8.4	−7.8	−26.4
Panama	283	9.2	7.6	8.6	7.0	8.4	7.0	9.6	4.6	5.4	2.4	1.7	1.7	1.1	9.8	4.5
Paraguay	288	5.7	1.1	6.3	3.6	3.9	6.2	4.4	5.1	7.2	8.2	6.3	7.0	10.9	11.4	11.4
Peru	293	4.9	8.4	3.8	.4	3.8	5.9	4.2	2.9	5.4	9.3	3.4	2.0	.4	.3	5.8
St. Kitts and Nevis	361															
St. Lucia	362															3.7
St. Vincent & Grens.	364												10.3	2.8	−3.1	4.7
Suriname	366											−7.2	10.1	16.5	11.3	−1.9	241.0
Trinidad and Tobago	369			2.0	5.2	2.7	3.5	1.0	5.8	1.7	3.8	1.5	6.4	9.1	10.0	3.6
Uruguay	298	1.2	3.4	−3.9	1.1	6.3	4.8	−1.0	−1.6	.4	3.1	5.9	4.0	1.2	5.3	6.2
Venezuela	299	6.0	2.5	3.8	4.9	4.5	8.8	3.0	2.7	6.3	6.1	6.1	8.8	6.7	2.1	1.3
Memorandum Items																
Oil Exporting Countries	999	4.4	—	2.9	10.8	7.1	8.2	7.4	9.1	8.9	6.7	4.6	11.7	8.3	−.4	5.2
Non-Oil Developing Countries	201	6.1	4.9	5.1	5.6	8.4	7.1	7.1	6.7	9.2	4.4	3.5	4.0	3.4	4.2	5.3

Indices

Index Numbers:

		1965	1966	1967	1968	1969	1970	1971	1972	1973	1974	1975	1976	1977	1978	1979
World	001	40.6	42.7	44.2	46.6	49.1	50.9	52.7	55.2	58.5	59.8	60.5	63.7	66.4	69.1	71.9
Industrial Countries	110	45.1	47.6	49.2	51.7	54.5	56.2	58.1	61.0	64.6	65.0	64.9	67.8	70.3	73.2	75.7
Developing Countries	200	33.1	34.4	36.0	38.4	40.5	42.2	44.1	45.8	48.5	51.5	53.8	57.4	60.5	63.0	66.3
Africa	605	44.8	44.8	47.1	49.7	52.0	55.0	56.9	58.9	62.1	66.0	66.9	70.1	72.7	73.7	76.8
Asia	505	22.9	23.8	25.0	26.4	28.2	29.9	31.1	32.0	34.3	35.8	38.1	40.3	43.4	46.5	48.5
Europe	170	....	....	....	....	....	....	....	....	....	....	....	....	....	....	....
Middle East	405	30.6	31.7	32.0	37.6	41.0	44.8	49.5	54.5	60.2	64.1	68.7	78.4	82.8	81.3	86.6
Western Hemisphere	205	37.1	39.3	41.0	43.8	46.7	48.9	52.2	55.7	60.2	64.5	67.0	71.0	73.9	77.3	82.4

*GNP used in calculation

GDP at Constant Prices

99bp x

Calculated from Indices

1980	1981	1982	1983	1984	1985	1986	1987	1988	1989	1990	1991	1992	1993	1994		
....	−2.7	−.5	3.0	4.1	2.2	3.3	1.4	1.8	−.7	−1.8	−8.5	....	....	....	Europe	170
5.9	3.1	6.3	5.3	8.8	4.7	3.7	7.1	8.6	8.0	7.3	1.2	8.5	....	....	Cyprus	423
....	−.1	.2	2.3	3.5	3.0	2.6	2.1	2.3	.7	−1.5	−19.2	....	....	....	Czechoslovakia	934
.2	2.9	2.8	.7	2.6	−.3	2.4	3.8	5.5	.7	−3.5	−11.9	....	....	....	Hungary	944
7.0	3.3	2.3	−.6	.9	2.6	3.9	4.1	8.4	8.2	6.3	6.3	4.3	....	....	Malta	181
....	.1	4.0	6.1	5.9	−.1	2.3	.8	....	−.5	−5.8	−7.3	−12.9	−13.5	....	Romania	968
....	....	....	....	....	....	....	....	....	2.3	.3	.8	9.2	5.0	5.8	Turkey*	186
2.3	1.4	.5	−1.0	2.0	.5	3.6	−1.0	−2.0	....	....	....	....	....	....	Yugoslavia, SFR	188
.6	−6.0	1.1	2.4	1.5	1.9	−1.1	3.8	1.6	.4	9.1	7.0	5.0	2.7	....	**Middle East**	405
6.6	−6.6	−7.5	8.5	4.9	−2.0	1.6	−1.2	7.3	2.5	1.2	....	....	....	....	Bahrain	419
....	....	....	6.4	6.0	12.1	9.1	6.4	5.4	5.0	5.7	1.1	4.4	2.9	4.0	Egypt	469
−13.9	−2.5	13.1	13.2	.9	.2	−15.1	1.2	−8.7	3.3	11.7	11.4	5.7	1.8	....	Iran, I.R. of	429
11.7	−18.0	−1.1	−8.3	.2	—	8.1	19.4	3.1	−7.2	....	....	....	....	....	Iraq	433
3.2	4.5	1.3	2.5	2.1	4.0	4.1	6.1	3.1	1.3	5.8	6.2	6.6	3.0	6.5	Israel	436
17.6	9.8	5.6	2.5	1.4	4.1	7.0	3.9	−2.8	−13.4	1.0	1.8	16.1	5.8	5.7	Jordan	439
−20.4	−18.9	−11.8	7.9	5.2	−4.3	8.5	−4.0	3.5	....	....	....	....	....	....	Kuwait	443
.6	....	....	....	....	....	....	....	....	....	....	....	....	....	....	Libya	672
5.7	17.0	11.5	16.0	16.7	13.8	3.3	−3.7	6.0	3.1	7.5	9.2	6.8	....	....	Oman	449
7.9	1.7	−10.7	−.1	−2.2	−4.1	5.6	−1.4	7.6	.2	10.7	9.7	1.0	....	....	Saudi Arabia	456
12.0	9.5	2.1	1.4	−4.1	6.1	−4.9	1.9	13.3	−9.0	7.6	7.1	10.5	3.9	....	Syrian Arab Rep.	463
26.4	2.9	−8.3	−2.6	4.5	−2.5	−21.2	3.6	−.2	15.3	17.5	.8	2.7	....	....	United Arab Emirates	466
6.4	.4	−.8	−2.8	3.7	3.5	3.7	3.3	.8	1.3	.3	3.0	2.4	3.1	4.5	**Western Hemisphere**	205
1.4	4.9	.4	6.9	7.5	8.8	9.7	9.0	7.7	6.3	3.5	4.3	1.7	3.4	....	Antigua and Barbuda	311
1.5	−5.7	−3.1	3.7	1.8	−6.6	7.3	2.6	−1.9	−6.2	.1	8.9	8.7	6.0	7.1	Argentina	213
....	18.9	.8	−7.5	3.0	13.5	3.6	4.9	....	....	....	....	....	....	....	Bahamas, The	313
4.5	−1.9	−4.9	.4	3.7	1.1	5.1	2.6	3.5	3.6	−3.3	−4.0	....	....	....	Barbados	316
5.7	.9	−.3	−2.2	2.0	1.0	4.6	11.6	9.0	13.0	9.3	4.6	9.0	4.2	....	Belize	339
.6	.9	−4.4	−4.5	−.6	−1.0	−2.5	2.6	3.0	2.8	4.1	4.6	3.4	....	....	Bolivia	218
9.1	−4.4	.6	−2.9	5.4	7.9	7.5	3.5	−.1	3.1	−4.4	.2	−.8	4.1	5.7	Brazil	223
7.8	5.5	−14.1	−.7	6.4	2.5	5.6	6.6	7.3	9.9	3.3	7.3	11.0	6.3	4.2	Chile	228
4.1	2.3	.9	1.6	3.4	3.1	5.8	5.4	4.1	3.4	4.3	2.0	3.8	5.3	....	Colombia	233
.8	−2.3	−7.3	2.9	8.0	.7	5.5	4.8	3.4	5.7	3.6	2.3	7.7	6.3	4.5	Costa Rica	238
17.0	8.0	3.3	2.1	5.4	1.7	6.8	6.8	7.4	−1.1	6.4	2.3	2.8	1.8	....	Dominica	321
6.1	4.1	1.6	6.9	1.3	−2.1	3.5	10.1	2.2	4.8	−5.9	.8	7.8	3.0	4.3	Dominican Republic	243
4.9	3.9	1.2	−2.8	4.2	4.3	3.1	−6.0	10.5	.3	3.0	5.0	3.6	2.0	4.0	Ecuador	248
−8.7	−8.3	−5.6	.8	2.3	2.0	.6	2.7	1.6	1.1	3.4	3.6	7.5	7.4	6.0	El Salvador	253
.2	2.1	5.3	1.2	5.6	4.9	5.5	6.0	5.3	5.7	5.2	2.9	.6	....	....	Grenada	328
3.7	.7	−3.5	−2.6	.5	−.6	.1	3.5	3.9	3.9	3.1	3.6	4.8	3.9	4.4	Guatemala	258
1.6	−.3	−10.4	−9.3	2.1	1.0	.2	.8	−2.6	−3.3	−4.7	6.0	7.8	8.2	....	Guyana	336
7.3	−2.9	−3.4	.8	.3	.2	1.0	.1	.9	.4	−1.2	−.6	−14.8	−5.2	−13.2	Haiti	263
.7	2.5	−1.4	−.9	4.3	4.2	.7	6.0	4.6	4.3	.1	3.3	5.6	6.1	−1.4	Honduras	268
−5.7	2.6	1.2	2.3	−.9	−4.6	1.7	7.7	2.9	6.8	5.5	.5	1.9	.7	....	Jamaica	343
8.3	7.9	−.6	−4.2	3.6	2.6	−3.8	1.9	1.2	3.3	4.4	3.6	2.8	.6	....	Mexico	273
4.5	5.4	−.8	4.6	−1.6	−4.1	−1.0	−.7	−12.4	−1.7	—	−.2	.4	−.4	3.2	Nicaragua	278
14.5	4.0	5.6	.6	−.4	4.7	3.3	2.4	−15.6	−.4	4.6	9.6	8.5	5.4	4.7	Panama	283
11.4	8.7	−1.0	−3.0	3.1	4.0	—	4.3	6.4	5.8	3.1	2.5	1.8	4.1	....	Paraguay	288
4.9	5.1	−.2	−12.6	5.8	2.1	9.3	8.3	−8.2	−11.0	−4.3	2.8	−2.3	6.4	....	Peru	293
....	5.1	6.3	−1.1	9.0	5.6	6.2	7.4	9.8	6.7	3.0	3.9	3.5	4.0	....	St. Kitts and Nevis	361
−.8	1.2	3.0	4.1	5.0	6.0	11.9	1.5	12.1	4.6	4.0	1.6	6.6	....	....	St. Lucia	362
3.8	6.6	5.8	5.2	5.3	5.4	7.3	6.3	8.6	7.2	7.0	3.1	6.5	1.4	....	St. Vincent & Grens.	364
−8.6	7.1	−4.2	−3.9	−1.9	2.0	.8	−6.2	8.2	3.8	—	3.5	5.8	−4.5	....	Suriname	366
10.4	4.6	4.0	−9.2	−6.2	−4.1	−3.3	−4.6	−3.9	−.8	1.5	2.7	−1.7	−1.7	....	Trinidad and Tobago	369
6.0	1.9	−9.4	−5.9	−1.1	1.5	8.9	7.9	—	1.3	.9	3.2	7.9	2.5	5.1	Uruguay	298
−2.0	−.3	.7	−5.6	−1.4	1.4	6.3	4.5	6.2	−7.8	6.9	9.7	6.1	−.4	−3.3	Venezuela	299
															Memorandum Items	
4.0	−2.7	.3	.6	1.8	1.4	.9	3.4	3.3	2.7	8.8	7.9	4.9	3.8	4.1	Oil Exporting Countries	999
5.9	2.5	1.9	2.5	5.8	5.1	4.8	5.1	5.3	3.3	2.9	3.0	5.3	6.0	....	Non-Oil Developing Countries	201

Indices

1990 = 100

1980	1981	1982	1983	1984	1985	1986	1987	1988	1989	1990	1991	1992	1993	1994		
73.8	74.9	75.2	77.2	80.9	84.0	86.8	90.2	94.4	97.4	100.0	101.7	104.9	108.1	....	World	001
76.4	77.5	77.2	79.4	83.0	85.7	88.2	91.0	95.0	98.0	100.0	100.4	102.3	103.7	106.9	Industrial Countries	110
70.0	71.2	72.4	74.0	77.9	81.5	84.9	89.1	93.5	96.5	100.0	103.7	109.2	115.5	....	Developing Countries	200
80.7	81.8	81.8	81.0	82.8	85.6	87.9	89.6	94.1	97.0	100.0	101.0	100.5	102.4	....	Africa	605
51.8	54.8	57.6	61.8	66.9	71.5	76.1	82.0	89.5	94.6	100.0	105.7	114.6	124.0	135.4	Asia	505
90.7	88.2	87.7	90.3	94.1	96.2	99.3	100.7	102.6	101.8	100.0	91.5	....	....	....	Europe	170
87.1	81.8	82.7	84.7	86.0	87.6	86.6	89.9	91.4	91.7	100.0	107.0	112.4	115.5	....	Middle East	405
87.7	88.1	87.4	85.0	88.1	91.2	94.5	97.6	98.4	99.7	100.0	103.0	105.4	108.7	113.6	Western Hemisphere	205

GDP Deflators

99bi x

Percent Change over Previous Year;

		1965	1966	1967	1968	1969	1970	1971	1972	1973	1974	1975	1976	1977	1978	1979
World	001	6.5	8.9	5.9	6.0	5.4	5.5	6.8	7.4	10.9	18.5	13.7	13.2	12.5	11.6	15.6
Industrial Countries	110	3.7	3.8	3.4	4.3	4.8	6.7	6.3	5.9	8.2	12.0	11.3	8.7	8.4	8.3	8.5
United States	111	2.7	3.3	3.1	4.9	5.0	5.3	5.3	5.0	6.3	8.8	9.6	6.3	6.9	7.9	8.7
Canada	156	3.4	4.8	4.2	3.7	4.5	4.6	3.2	5.6	8.9	14.4	9.9	8.7	6.2	6.0	10.0
Australia	193	2.5	2.5	3.8	3.5	4.9	3.9	6.9	7.9	12.3	17.4	15.9	13.3	9.1	7.4	10.1
Japan	158	5.2	5.2	5.6	5.5	4.8	7.0	5.5	5.8	13.1	20.1	7.4	7.8	6.4	5.0	2.7
New Zealand	196	1.9	.4	4.5	3.8	10.2	9.5	14.9	10.1	8.6	5.5	13.7	20.7	8.5	13.6	13.9
Austria	122	5.5	3.6	3.4	3.2	3.5	5.4	6.2	7.6	8.0	9.5	6.5	5.6	5.1	5.7	4.1
Belgium	124	5.0	4.5	3.1	2.6	4.1	4.6	5.6	6.2	7.3	12.5	12.3	7.7	7.5	4.4	4.5
Denmark	128	7.1	8.3	6.0	7.2	6.8	8.1	7.9	9.0	10.5	13.1	12.4	9.1	9.4	9.9	7.6
Finland	172	5.0	4.7	7.4	12.1	4.2	3.9	7.6	8.4	14.1	22.5	13.3	13.5	9.9	8.4	8.8
France	132	2.7	2.9	3.2	4.2	6.6	7.1	6.3	7.0	8.5	11.9	13.0	11.1	9.3	10.1	10.1
Germany*	134	3.8	3.4	1.5	2.4	4.1	7.7	7.8	5.3	6.3	7.0	5.8	3.6	3.7	4.2	3.9
Greece	174	4.1	4.8	2.4	1.8	3.3	3.9	3.2	5.0	19.4	20.9	12.3	15.4	12.9	13.0	18.6
Iceland*	176	12.7	10.6	2.9	13.9	20.4	16.9	13.2	17.8	29.4	40.8	44.8	37.0	30.1	47.1	41.3
Ireland	178	4.4	4.3	3.9	4.3	8.9	8.9	10.5	13.4	14.8	5.3	23.9	21.0	13.3	10.5	13.7
Italy	136	4.2	2.2	2.8	1.7	4.1	14.2	8.6	4.8	13.2	19.8	16.6	18.7	18.2	14.1	15.1
Luxembourg	137	2.5	3.8	.3	4.9	5.3	10.9	−.8	5.8	12.2	17.0	−.9	12.2	1.2	5.1	6.5
Netherlands	138	5.8	5.8	4.1	4.1	.7	12.8	8.1	9.4	9.0	9.2	10.2	8.9	6.7	5.4	3.9
Norway	142	4.8	4.0	3.0	4.4	4.2	12.8	6.7	5.0	9.2	10.3	10.0	7.5	8.3	6.3	6.6
Portugal	182	....	....	3.6	—	7.5	2.7	5.1	7.7	8.0	18.9	16.2	16.3	26.4	21.7	19.1
Spain	184	9.4	8.1	7.7	5.0	4.4	9.1	7.8	8.5	11.8	16.0	16.8	16.5	23.4	20.6	16.9
Sweden	144	6.0	6.6	5.0	2.4	3.4	6.2	7.1	7.0	7.0	9.5	14.5	11.9	10.5	9.5	7.9
Switzerland	146	3.9	4.9	4.5	3.0	2.6	4.7	8.9	9.5	8.0	7.2	6.5	2.1	.3	3.5	2.0
United Kingdom	112	5.1	4.5	2.9	4.2	5.5	7.3	9.4	8.2	7.0	14.9	27.1	15.1	13.9	11.6	14.4
Developing Countries	200	17.8	30.3	15.9	12.8	7.0	2.2	8.1	11.5	18.5	34.4	19.5	24.1	22.4	19.6	28.9
Africa	605	4.7	4.6	4.1	5.0	7.6	−27.3	5.0	8.1	12.3	30.5	10.9	13.9	14.9	15.8	17.7
Algeria	612	4.5	5.2	4.9	6.7	3.9	4.0	4.7	5.8	8.7	71.0	.5	10.3	9.5	10.8	12.3
Benin	638	....	....	....	....	....	....	3.7	3.2	4.9	30.7	.5	13.5	5.1	6.0	14.1
Botswana	616	.7	5.3	7.2	2.1	1.4	4.3	9.2	.7	5.5	12.3	19.0	14.2	12.7	−1.6	25.1
Burkina Faso	748	....	....	....	....	....	....	....	....	....	....	....	....	....	....	....
Burundi	618	....	....	....	....	....	....	8.6	8.7	5.2	12.6	19.0	9.7	14.1	11.8	21.8
Cameroon	622	....	....	....	....	....	17.2	3.9	6.2	10.9	17.7	12.0	11.1	13.7	11.0	5.5
Central African Rep.	626	−14.2	4.3	−.8	7.3	−.4	3.8	4.2	4.1	.7	18.8	15.9	7.0	7.5	....	....
Côte d'Ivoire	662	....	....	....	....	....	....	....	....	....	....	....	....	35.6	2.0	7.0
Ethiopia	644	5.1	−.1	1.9	3.4	−.3	6.2	1.0	−3.9	2.7	9.3	−.6	6.3	13.0	7.7	4.4
Gambia, The	648	....	....	....	....	....	....	−14.0	24.5	−3.5	−6.2	45.7	18.1	37.5	−4.0	29.7
Ghana	652	16.9	3.4	2.1	6.2	11.1	5.9	4.9	15.4	7.9	28.7	30.1	28.0	67.3	73.3	38.9
Kenya	664	−1.3	13.3	−30.5	1.0	2.9	2.8	4.5	2.7	8.6	19.6	13.4	13.9	16.9	−.1	6.4
Liberia	668	2.0	−1.0	6.6	.1	−2.3	−2.6	.9	5.0	4.8	13.9	41.6	−.3	12.7	5.4	9.0
Madagascar	674	4.4	7.1	.7	1.0	3.9	7.0	5.2	5.1	11.2	21.3	2.9	10.7	7.9	6.8	11.4
Malawi	676	−.6	3.3	−5.6	10.8	1.9	7.7	9.6	−.3	−9.8	18.0	8.8	8.8	.4	1.5	4.5
Mali	678	4.5	5.1	4.8	6.6	3.7	−.6	15.0	14.1	−9.6	8.1	33.6	36.7	13.6	5.6	20.3
Mauritania	682	....	....	....	....	....	....	....	....	....	11.6	33.4	6.1	7.6	2.1	....
Mauritius	684	1.1	2.4	2.2	6.7	2.1	2.0	6.0	14.2	15.6	60.8	4.9	3.0	24.5	10.8	17.9
Morocco	686	3.4	−1.1	−.5	.1	16.5	2.9	4.0	3.9	5.8	18.0	4.0	5.3	13.9	7.2	7.6
Mozambique	688	....	....	....	....	....	....	....	....	....	....	....	....	....	....	....
Niger	692	4.7	5.0	5.2	6.2	4.1	3.9	10.4	24.2	5.8	16.8	−4.5	14.4	16.4	13.3	20.6
Nigeria	694	....	....	....	....	....	....	....	....	....	49.8	19.4	14.2	9.8	18.9	16.6
Rwanda	714	4.5	5.1	5.1	6.3	6.4	4.8	−.3	2.0	3.6	17.2	5.2	15.1	10.0	3.2	9.8
Senegal	722	....	....	....	....	....	....	....	....	....	....	....	....	9.1	5.5	6.8
Seychelles	718	....	....	....	....	....	....	....	....	21.7	15.5	21.1	73.6	25.0	13.1	17.9
Sierra Leone	724	....	....	....	....	....	....	....	....	3.2	7.3	16.8	16.4	10.5	19.6	13.9	12.7
Somalia	726	....	....	....	....	....	....	....	....	....	....	....	....	....	....	....
South Africa	199	2.9	4.3	4.3	3.9	7.5	4.0	5.8	11.0	18.3	16.2	10.6	10.2	10.9	11.6	15.3
Swaziland	734	....	....	....	....	....	....	....	....	....	....	....	....	....	2.1	3.2
Tanzania	738	....	1.6	.2	2.0	3.1	4.8	2.7	6.7	13.8	19.1	12.5	20.5	17.7	9.1	10.1
Togo	742	....	....	....	....	....	....	4.6	3.1	7.7	38.6	−1.2	6.7	17.3	1.7	6.8
Tunisia	744	....	....	....	....	3.5	2.8	5.2	3.3	8.4	18.2	5.7	1.9	9.1	6.5	10.3
Uganda	746	....	....	....	....	....	....	6.6	9.1	14.4	23.6	43.3	16.7	80.8	40.1	74.1
Zaïre	636	34.2	—	53.9	37.9	17.0	−98.2	5.6	10.1	17.9	18.2	12.3	57.4	37.3	46.3	102.1
Zambia	754	9.5	24.3	7.4	8.1	19.9	−10.1	−3.1	4.6	19.2	11.2	−14.0	14.8	10.1	12.7	21.9
Zimbabwe	698	....	....	....	....	....	....	....	....	5.9	1.5	13.0	9.8	7.0	9.7	15.2
Asia	505	29.2	64.0	25.7	17.9	7.8	6.8	5.4	10.1	19.6	25.8	8.8	7.8	7.6	8.4	16.5
Bangladesh	513	....	....	....	....	....	....	....	....	....	40.6	71.1	−23.9	−3.2	30.4	12.9
Bhutan	514	....	....	....	....	....	....	....	....	....	....	....	....	....	....	....
China, People's Rep.	924	....	....	....	....	....	....	....	....	....	....	....	....	....	....	....
Fiji	819	....	....	−3.6	−3.5	6.5	6.8	3.4	14.7	16.0	29.7	25.0	8.9	9.7	4.5	8.3
Hong Kong	532	−.4	−4.5	6.4	3.5	5.1	8.7	7.4	8.6	13.9	11.8	4.8	8.8	3.0	7.0	17.2
India	534	10.3	11.8	8.2	3.0	3.5	1.0	4.8	11.1	17.3	17.9	−2.0	6.2	4.6	1.7	15.3
Indonesia	536	232.4	1,204.4	162.4	122.6	22.3	14.3	2.7	13.6	32.9	47.3	12.5	14.5	13.0	10.9	32.5
Korea	542	6.1	14.3	16.2	16.2	14.8	17.6	13.6	16.5	13.5	29.5	26.1	21.3	17.3	22.7	19.7
Malaysia	548	....	....	....	....	....	....	−.5	.3	17.9	12.7	−3.1	12.7	6.9	9.8	12.1
Maldives	556	....	....	....	....	....	....	....	....	....	....	....	....	....	3.9	19.4
Mongolia	948	....	....	....	....	....	....	....	....	....	....	....	....	....	....	....
Myanmar	518	....	....	....	9.8	−4.2	.5	.7	10.0	22.1	28.2	16.5	10.1	1.9	.8	5.6
Nepal	558	8.8	15.2	−5.6	11.1	6.6	7.0	3.2	12.5	−3.4	20.8	27.5	.5	−3.6	9.4	10.0
Pakistan	564	6.1	5.2	11.5	4.8	2.7	2.5	5.0	6.6	15.7	23.0	22.4	12.1	10.7	9.0	5.5
Papua New Guinea	853	....	....	....	....	....	....	....	....	....	27.4	−4.3	8.2	37.9	.3	13.5
Philippines	566	4.0	5.5	5.7	4.9	4.8	15.0	12.5	6.8	18.1	31.0	8.3	9.2	7.4	9.2	15.2
Singapore	576	1.3	1.4	.6	1.1	2.3	1.7	4.5	5.4	12.2	15.6	2.4	1.9	1.6	2.4	5.3
Solomon Islands	813	....	....	....	....	....	....	....	....	....	....	....	....	....	....	....
Sri Lanka	524	1.3	−1.9	2.2	13.6	.9	.9	2.9	5.3	16.6	24.3	6.8	8.8	16.1	9.1	15.8
Thailand	578	4.6	7.2	−.9	−.6	2.0	3.8	−.8	6.5	18.9	20.5	3.6	4.5	6.0	9.6	8.7
Vanuatu	846	....	....	....	....	....	....	....	....	....	....	....	....	....	....	....
Western Samoa	862	1.9	3.3	−.6	1.8	3.5	3.0	4.6	7.7	12.1	24.8	8.8	5.0	14.5	2.2	11.8

GDP Deflators

1980	1981	1982	1983	1984	1985	1986	1987	1988	1989	1990	1991	1992	1993	1994	Country	Code
Calculated from Indices																99bi x
18.8	14.5	14.5	14.8	15.1	14.6	10.8	14.3	20.3	23.8	28.1	16.6	17.2	20.5	....	World	001
9.9	9.5	7.4	5.4	5.0	4.2	3.7	3.2	3.7	4.4	4.4	4.6	2.6	2.2	1.7	Industrial Countries	110
9.4	10.0	6.2	4.1	4.5	3.6	2.7	3.2	3.9	4.5	4.3	4.8	1.9	2.2	2.1	United States	111
10.6	10.8	8.7	5.0	3.1	2.6	2.4	4.6	4.7	4.8	3.1	2.9	1.2	1.1	.6	Canada	156
11.0	9.5	11.3	8.4	6.2	6.1	6.9	7.5	8.3	7.4	4.4	2.3	1.3	1.2	1.5	Australia	193
4.6	3.7	1.7	1.4	2.3	1.6	1.8	—	.4	1.9	2.2	2.0	1.5	.5	—	Japan	158
16.0	15.6	10.2	4.9	7.6	15.6	16.4	13.0	5.9	7.6	3.3	2.3	2.4	1.0	....	New Zealand	196
5.2	6.5	6.2	3.9	4.9	3.1	4.3	2.4	1.6	2.9	3.3	4.0	4.2	3.6	3.2	Austria	122
1.5	4.7	7.1	5.6	5.1	6.1	3.9	2.3	1.9	4.8	3.1	2.7	3.4	4.4	2.3	Belgium	124
8.2	10.1	10.6	7.6	5.7	4.3	4.6	4.7	3.4	4.2	2.7	2.2	2.0	1.1	1.9	Denmark	128
9.7	11.1	8.9	8.6	8.9	5.3	4.6	4.7	7.0	6.1	5.8	.4	2.8	2.4	2.5	Finland	172
11.4	11.4	11.7	9.7	7.5	5.8	5.2	3.0	2.8	3.0	3.1	3.3	2.1	2.5	1.5	France	132
4.9	4.1	4.4	3.4	2.1	2.2	3.3	1.9	1.5	2.6	3.8	5.2	4.4	3.2	2.0	Germany*	134
17.7	19.7	25.1	19.1	20.3	17.7	17.5	14.3	15.6	12.3	21.0	18.3	14.1	13.6	....	Greece	174
52.5	49.2	59.0	76.3	25.3	31.6	25.7	20.3	23.7	18.9	17.6	8.0	4.3	2.0	2.2	Iceland*	176
14.7	17.4	15.2	10.6	6.4	5.3	5.8	2.2	3.1	4.3	-1.7	1.1	1.3	3.6	....	Ireland	178
20.2	19.0	17.2	15.1	11.6	8.9	7.9	6.0	6.6	6.2	7.6	7.4	4.7	....	....	Italy	136
7.8	7.2	10.8	6.8	4.4	3.0	3.8	-1.0	4.0	6.0	2.9	3.0	4.5	....	....	Luxembourg	137
5.6	5.5	6.1	1.9	1.9	3.6	.9	-2.5	1.2	1.2	2.6	2.6	2.1	1.6	2.0	Netherlands	138
14.6	14.0	10.2	6.1	6.4	5.0	-1.4	7.2	4.4	5.9	4.6	2.3	-1.0	2.0	.3	Norway	142
20.4	18.0	20.8	24.6	24.6	21.5	20.5	11.3	11.5	14.0	14.5	13.6	12.9	....	....	Portugal	182
13.4	12.6	13.9	11.8	11.6	7.7	11.1	5.8	5.7	7.1	7.3	7.1	6.7	4.4	4.1	Spain	184
12.4	9.6	8.3	10.0	7.6	6.7	6.9	5.1	6.0	8.0	8.8	8.2	1.0	2.7	3.0	Sweden	144
2.9	6.9	7.1	3.0	2.8	3.1	3.8	2.6	2.4	4.2	5.7	5.5	2.6	2.1	1.7	Switzerland	146
19.5	11.4	7.6	5.2	4.7	5.8	3.5	5.0	6.0	7.1	6.4	6.5	4.4	3.3	2.1	United Kingdom	112
36.1	23.9	28.0	33.4	34.1	34.4	23.8	35.6	54.2	64.3	79.4	39.6	45.4	57.6	....	Developing Countries	200
24.2	14.8	13.6	20.4	17.7	14.5	12.4	24.5	20.2	24.3	16.4	39.8	54.0	18.4	....	Africa	605
8.9	15.7	14.5	....	....	....	....	....	....	....	....	....	....	....	....	Algeria	612
14.4	15.8	25.0	4.8	3.8	-2.2	-.6	-6.3	1.9	1.7	....	....	....	....	....	Benin	638
19.1	3.6	-4.3	10.4	8.2	22.7	23.1	6.6	17.2	27.4	6.0	4.8	....	....	....	Botswana	616
6.0	14.2	8.5	7.2	.9	3.2	....	....	....	....	....	....	....	....	....	Burkina Faso	748
16.5	-6.2	6.1	6.1	17.2	5.1	-4.0	-2.1	2.7	15.7	5.8	7.7	9.2	....	....	Burundi	618
14.6	13.1	12.5	12.6	13.2	11.9	-1.0	-5.9	7.8	.6	-6.2	....	....	....	....	Cameroon	622
....	....	....	....	....	....	....	....	....	....	....	....	....	....	....	Central African Rep.	626
2.6	3.0	....	....	....	....	....	....	....	....	....	....	....	....	....	Côte d'Ivoire	662
.8	-3.3	28.1	3.2	-.6	24.4	-2.3	-2.4	1.3	3.8	6.4	18.0	3.8	14.8	....	Ethiopia	644
.2	14.9	7.4	23.7	25.2	10.0	18.4	14.3	3.1	12.4	18.1	6.9	23.9	....	....	Gambia, The	648
51.8	72.3	28.4	111.4	43.2	20.6	41.7	39.2	33.4	28.3	38.8	20.3	12.5	24.5	....	Ghana	652
9.8	10.1	14.5	11.8	10.2	8.3	8.7	5.4	8.5	8.4	9.4	11.5	15.1	26.6	....	Kenya	664
9.3	9.1	12.8	1.6	-5.4	2.5	-4.5	3.8	4.8	....	....	....	....	....	....	Liberia	668
15.0	25.2	28.6	21.6	35.8	10.4	14.2	23.0	21.2	12.0	11.5	13.9	12.5	13.0	40.3	Madagascar	674
16.7	16.3	9.3	11.5	13.8	9.0	11.8	16.5	26.4	18.1	11.8	15.1	19.1	19.7	....	Malawi	676
14.9	21.3	-.1	7.5	12.0	10.9	-8.6	2.8	-1.2	1.4	1.3	3.1	....	....	....	Mali	678
....	....	....	....	....	....	....	....	....	....	....	....	....	....	....	Mauritania	682
26.6	10.9	8.9	8.4	7.4	8.3	8.0	8.6	10.4	11.0	10.0	8.2	5.3	8.7	....	Mauritius	684
15.4	9.7	7.2	7.3	8.6	8.4	10.2	4.0	5.4	3.8	6.4	7.0	5.1	....	....	Morocco	686
....	....	....	....	....	33.7	12.6	180.6	47.8	48.2	34.1	45.2	53.4	60.5	....	Mozambique	688
18.4	19.8	....	....	....	....	....	....	....	....	....	....	....	....	....	Niger	692
11.9	8.9	2.2	16.8	17.3	4.0	-2.1	49.7	21.4	44.1	7.2	18.7	64.8	24.0	27.0	Nigeria	694
15.0	10.7	2.6	2.4	16.9	4.6	-7.1	3.0	.4	4.6	-1.6	8.9	1.6	....	....	Rwanda	714
14.9	8.0	11.4	12.8	5.1	8.5	4.4	8.1	2.1	1.1	....	....	....	....	....	Senegal	722
20.6	10.5	1.1	4.0	-.1	2.3	5.8	3.7	3.9	2.1	6.4	-1.5	....	....	....	Seychelles	718
9.0	5.3	22.2	18.6	43.5	64.4	85.2	153.7	49.2	55.3	67.8	97.2	52.9	49.0	....	Sierra Leone	724
....	19.7	28.4	36.5	71.6	28.0	39.1	29.7	....	....	....	....	....	....	....	Somalia	726
23.6	11.8	13.7	15.7	11.5	16.2	16.3	14.2	15.1	17.2	15.1	13.5	12.4	11.1	10.4	South Africa	199
26.6	11.0	7.9	4.8	7.6	8.2	26.2	-.7	.5	10.0	10.1	....	....	....	....	Swaziland	734
12.7	17.2	17.9	24.0	21.9	32.2	28.2	34.9	40.3	18.2	18.5	32.9	11.7	....	....	Tanzania	738
10.0	12.1	8.7	9.7	3.9	4.6	4.4	.3	....	....	....	....	....	....	....	Togo	742
9.1	11.3	16.0	9.3	7.4	4.8	3.1	6.7	8.5	7.9	5.1	7.0	6.2	4.6	5.2	Tunisia	744
40.5	89.8	40.0	40.3	71.1	160.1	135.4	219.7	163.6	73.4	29.4	32.8	59.4	7.6	....	Uganda	746
364.3	36.2	43.3	78.2	90.8	25.0	28.4	73.8	91.4	110.5	100.2	2,303.3	4,077.0	....	....	Zaïre	636
11.8	7.2	6.1	18.6	18.4	41.1	84.1	46.9	42.8	85.7	106.4	97.0	....	....	....	Zambia	754
10.3	14.5	14.2	19.4	3.5	6.5	11.8	11.9	7.8	14.4	5.6	....	....	....	....	Zimbabwe	698
14.7	8.9	5.3	6.9	7.9	7.1	4.0	7.4	9.4	8.8	8.1	9.0	6.7	11.3	16.1	Asia	505
13.1	10.3	12.7	5.0	16.4	11.7	9.7	11.4	7.6	7.7	4.9	9.4	4.2	.1	4.4	Bangladesh	513
....	6.3	11.0	8.9	10.0	9.5	6.9	9.3	7.8	6.2	8.7	....	....	....	....	Bhutan	514
....	2.3	.1	1.2	4.5	9.0	4.7	5.0	11.8	9.0	6.4	5.7	5.1	14.8	24.8	China, People's Rep.	924
27.4	.6	6.6	10.5	4.2	.4	11.9	-2.1	2.8	9.7	3.0	5.3	....	....	....	Fiji	819
15.0	10.1	9.8	3.9	9.9	5.7	3.6	8.9	9.6	12.3	7.5	9.2	9.7	8.8	7.6	Hong Kong	532
11.7	10.3	7.4	8.5	7.5	7.5	6.5	8.6	8.1	8.3	10.9	14.5	9.1	8.1	....	India	534
29.1	18.5	5.1	19.2	8.2	5.3	—	15.8	7.6	9.5	9.1	8.7	7.3	19.1	6.6	Indonesia	536
24.1	17.0	6.9	5.5	4.8	4.3	4.6	5.0	6.7	5.3	9.9	10.1	6.1	5.1	5.3	Korea	542
6.9	1.1	2.5	5.2	5.5	-1.5	-8.6	5.5	4.7	3.4	2.9	2.9	5.8	1.8	4.5	Malaysia	548
31.9	-9.0	18.4	-7.0	-9.6	-1.6	6.0	12.3	3.3	.9	-4.2	....	....	....	....	Maldives	556
....	1.5	2.0	1.0	-3.2	-1.5	-8.2	-.2	.9	—	—	99.1	183.1	....	....	Mongolia	948
-10.7	6.4	3.6	2.0	2.5	1.6	6.6	21.2	25.2	57.7	18.5	26.0	19.2	29.1	....	Myanmar	518
7.6	7.9	9.3	12.3	6.4	11.4	14.4	12.7	11.8	11.3	10.7	9.4	19.3	10.3	7.7	Nepal	558
10.5	11.1	9.4	5.3	9.7	4.5	3.3	4.5	9.6	8.6	6.5	13.1	10.1	8.7	12.1	Pakistan	564
7.1	-2.7	3.2	9.2	7.4	1.6	1.3	8.0	7.9	-2.5	4.1	7.0	2.7	5.1	....	Papua New Guinea	853
6.5	12.3	8.7	14.2	53.3	17.6	3.0	7.5	9.6	9.0	13.0	16.5	7.9	6.9	9.7	Philippines	566
11.5	6.7	4.2	3.9	.7	-1.2	-2.5	.8	5.5	5.2	5.9	3.5	2.1	2.4	....	Singapore	576
....	10.7	14.0	-14.1	44.8	4.2	9.0	22.2	....	....	....	....	....	....	....	Solomon Islands	813
20.2	21.1	38.6	16.7	20.3	.6	6.0	8.0	9.9	10.9	20.3	10.4	....	....	....	Sri Lanka	524
13.1	8.4	5.1	3.6	1.4	2.2	1.7	4.7	5.9	6.1	5.7	5.8	4.1	....	....	Thailand	578
....	....	....	....	-6.4	6.9	—	—	—	44.3	3.9	3.1	6.0	3.0	....	Vanuatu	846
22.0	16.2	20.7	18.1	....	....	....	....	....	....	....	....	....	....	....	Western Samoa	862

1995 INTERNATIONAL FINANCIAL STATISTICS YEARBOOK

GDP Deflators

99bi x

Percent Change over Previous Year;

		1965	1966	1967	1968	1969	1970	1971	1972	1973	1974	1975	1976	1977	1978	1979
Europe	170	....	....	....	....	....	....	....	....	....	....	....	....	....	....	....
Cyprus	423	3.8	1.7	1.0	3.0	4.7	4.3	2.2	6.3	8.3	11.1	4.2	10.1	9.5	11.2	13.2
Czech Republic	935															
Czechoslovakia	934															
Estonia	939															
Hungary	944							2.1	2.1	2.7	-1.2	1.2	5.8	2.2	3.6	5.5
Malta	181	.2	.7	1.3	1.6	8.1	2.7	.8	-1.4	3.1	3.4	5.4	5.0	4.9	4.1	6.2
Romania	968															
Slovak Republic	936															
Turkey*	186	4.2	6.3	6.7	3.9	5.3	11.4	17.9	16.4	21.9	27.8	16.4	17.9	24.7	43.5	70.3
Yugoslavia	188					7.8	14.1	17.0	14.7	19.2	19.2	25.6	30.2	13.7	13.4	19.4
Middle East	405	-1.7	4.2	7.3	.1	6.6	-4.6	14.4	7.6	24.6	66.3	8.2	9.7	14.7	7.8	28.8
Bahrain	419												12.6	13.1	9.0	13.5
Egypt	469															
Iran, I.R. of	429	-2.3	-.7	-.7	-6.0	14.0	-13.2	11.8	7.3	34.4	60.9	10.6	13.0	17.7	10.3	27.1
Iraq	433	-3.7	3.9	8.8	-3.8	1.8	6.9	7.1	3.0	-4.9	93.8	3.5	3.3	10.5	6.6	33.1
Israel	436					15.4	-11.8	24.5	28.1	-13.8	44.3	19.8	22.0	85.2	45.2	51.1
Jordan	439						5.8	5.3	7.2	11.4	19.5	12.0	11.4	14.6	7.1	14.0
Kuwait	443							24.8	.3	12.8	154.2	4.2	3.3	8.3	-1.9	41.5
Lebanon	446	—	2.8	3.7	-.7	4.6	—	1.6	5.1	6.6						
Libya	672	5.3	8.1	5.9	5.8	.6	1.1	20.5	1.3	22.5	41.5	-6.4	5.8	7.9	-3.8	27.4
Oman	449	1.3	2.1	-3.5	11.4	1.1	3.4	16.0	3.0	39.9	161.7	-.9	5.3	-9.0	-15.0	30.2
Saudi Arabia	456					2.1	-5.5	23.1	19.9	112.8	40.2	8.5	8.3	3.8	3.8	40.4
Syrian Arab Rep.	463	-1.9	4.8	9.9	4.8	-4.1	6.3	7.3	-5.0	10.4	34.5	6.6	10.2	10.8	11.2	16.1
United Arab Emirates	466										138.3	19.6	12.2	5.9	-2.0	5.4
Western Hemisphere	205	16.2	17.6	13.2	13.6	10.7	14.6	14.0	19.8	33.4	36.2	39.3	53.2	45.3	36.2	44.4
Antigua and Barbuda	311														3.8	10.0
Argentina	213	19.5	13.6	19.0	12.9	8.9	9.7	39.7	58.5	61.5	31.8	194.0	432.1	159.7	158.5	153.8
Bahamas, The	313															
Barbados	316	2.8	1.1	2.0	2.8	20.5	6.8	9.2	9.8	14.9	30.3	12.9	7.1	-1.7	5.4	27.0
Belize	339										27.8	21.6	-2.3	10.9	5.9	-21.6
Bolivia	218	5.9	3.3	6.2	4.6	3.6	3.9	4.4	20.4	41.6	58.1	6.5	8.1	10.9	11.6	17.8
Brazil	223	32.2	42.2	25.1	25.6	19.7	25.1	18.4	21.0	30.1	32.7	33.5	41.9	48.2	38.2	54.4
Chile	228	39.0	28.5	25.8	33.8	39.9	40.6	18.4	86.9	417.9	694.4	342.5	250.7	103.6	56.5	46.3
Colombia	233					8.2	12.3	10.8	13.0	20.2	25.4	22.8	25.5	29.2	17.1	24.0
Costa Rica	238	-.9	1.2	2.3	2.0	4.6	7.3	2.4	6.4	14.8	23.2	24.5	16.6	16.9	7.9	9.1
Dominica	321													28.8	11.5	13.0
Dominican Republic	243	-4.7	-.5	1.0	2.0	4.2	1.4	1.2	8.0	4.5	17.9	16.7	2.9	10.6	1.0	11.1
Ecuador	248		6.6	4.5	4.4	7.5	9.1	7.6	2.3	6.0	40.0	10.0	12.9	17.5	7.9	16.1
El Salvador	253	1.1	-1.1	—	—	—	5.4	—	1.0	10.2	11.1	7.5	22.5	1.1	13.8
Grenada	328										8.3	50.7	10.7	9.4	18.7	14.8
Guatemala	258	-1.4	-1.0	.4	1.9	1.7	5.0	-1.3	-1.3	14.5	15.7	13.1	11.5	16.4	5.5	8.6
Guyana	336	-2.5	7.3	.6	7.8	3.7	3.3	2.4	9.0	5.8	38.4	12.7	-7.1	4.0	14.7	18.4
Haiti	263			2.1	-3.4	2.6	4.2	3.4	1.3	29.1	-14.6	19.2	18.9	10.9	-1.5	2.9
Honduras	268	.9	2.2	3.9	1.2	3.4	2.5	1.8	4.3	6.6	11.7	9.6	8.5	12.2	5.1	9.6
Jamaica	343	.2	4.6	5.1	3.8	13.7	9.5	5.0	4.1	16.3	32.7	21.9	10.8	12.2	25.7	16.6
Mexico	273	6.9	5.0	1.9	2.4	4.0	10.8	5.9	6.2	12.9	22.7	15.8	19.6	30.4	16.8	20.2
Nicaragua	278	.9	3.7	1.3	4.5	1.2	2.4	1.4	1.5	16.3	23.0	3.1	9.3	8.0	5.0	38.3
Panama	283	.6	1.3	2.6	.6	1.2	1.0	2.9	5.0	8.5	11.6	9.4	4.5	4.7	7.9	9.2
Paraguay	288	2.8	3.9	-.6	1.4	3.4	.7	7.1	10.1	20.8	23.7	6.6	5.0	11.0	9.9	19.9
Peru	293	13.2	9.8	10.5	18.0	8.4	8.8	5.4	8.4	15.7	14.0	18.9	36.3	37.8	58.1	96.6
St. Kitts and Nevis	361															
St. Lucia	362															15.7
St. Vincent & Grens.	364												7.8	13.1	30.0	11.0
Suriname	366										29.9	3.1	-5.0	12.0	17.0	-68.8
Trinidad and Tobago	369			4.6	8.9	-.1	1.9	6.6	11.1	21.2	57.5	24.6	8.0	13.3	3.2	24.7
Uruguay	298	59.2	83.4	77.3	118.0	27.2	13.3	21.4	74.7	105.4	72.1	69.7	48.8	55.8	47.5	75.5
Venezuela	299	.4	1.7	1.5	2.6	-.9	3.6	6.5	4.3	12.1	44.5	-.8	5.2	8.0	6.3	21.3
Memorandum Items																
Oil Exporting Countries	999	56.9	163.1	46.4	37.0	8.7	1.9	9.7	7.8	25.6	61.2	8.2	10.2	10.6	8.7	25.6
Non-Oil Developing Countries	201	11.1	13.0	10.4	8.4	10.5	3.0	12.2	15.9	29.0	20.4	17.6	21.6	19.9	17.7	29.5

Indices

Index Numbers:

		1965	1966	1967	1968	1969	1970	1971	1972	1973	1974	1975	1976	1977	1978	1979
World	001	4.6	5.0	5.3	5.6	5.9	6.2	6.6	7.1	7.9	9.4	10.7	12.1	13.6	15.2	17.5
Industrial Countries	110	21.1	21.9	22.6	23.6	24.7	26.4	28.0	29.7	32.1	36.0	40.0	43.5	47.2	51.1	55.5
Developing Countries	200	.3	.3	.4	.4	.5	.5	.5	.6	.7	.9	1.1	1.3	1.6	2.0	2.5
Africa	605	5.3	5.6	5.8	6.1	6.5	4.7	5.0	5.4	6.1	7.9	8.8	10.0	11.5	13.3	15.6
Asia	505	5.5	9.0	11.3	13.4	14.4	15.4	16.2	17.9	21.3	26.8	29.2	31.5	33.9	36.8	42.8
Europe	170	....	....	....	....	....	....	....	....	....	....	....	....	....	....	....
Middle East	405	4.1	4.3	4.6	4.6	4.9	4.7	5.3	5.7	7.1	11.9	12.8	14.1	16.1	17.4	22.4
Western Hemisphere	205	—	—	—	—	—	—	—	—	—	—	—	—	—	—	—

*GNP used in calculation

GDP Deflators

99bi x

1980	1981	1982	1983	1984	1985	1986	1987	1988	1989	1990	1991	1992	1993	1994		
Calculated from Indices																
....	....	....	....	....	....	....	....	....	....	93.9	69.6	....	....	....	Europe	170
14.0	11.8	10.1	5.3	8.1	5.8	4.2	3.9	3.2	4.7	5.2	3.6	3.9	....	....	Cyprus	423
....	....	....	....	....	....	....	....	....	....	....	....	....	....	11.6	Czech Republic	935
....	−2.6	4.6	.1	2.9	−.2	−.1	.2	1.6	1.2	10.0	53.0	....	....	....	Czechoslovakia	934
....	....	....	....	....	....	....	....	....	....	....	....	785.0	73.8	....	Estonia	939
5.4	5.1	5.7	4.9	6.4	5.9	2.8	8.5	10.9	18.3	26.0	26.0	....	....	....	Hungary	944
12.4	7.8	3.4	−.3	−.2	.6	3.5	3.1	1.9	2.1	3.2	3.4	3.9	....	....	Malta	181
....	1.0	12.2	−.4	.3	.3	.3	—	1.9	−.9	15.7	195.0	214.0	....	....	Romania	968
....	....	....	....	....	....	....	....	....	....	....	....	....	....	11.7	Slovak Republic	936
102.3	42.0	28.3	28.8	49.4	43.9	31.6	−100.0	65.2	74.5	63.2	61.4	63.9	66.6	....	Turkey*	186
30.2	37.8	24.3	37.9	54.6	77.8	88.4	125.0	211.8	....	....	....	....	....	....	Yugoslavia	188
34.3	12.9	16.2	13.3	17.1	11.0	3.3	12.8	10.5	15.1	16.1	11.9	13.1	18.6	....	Middle East	405
6.7	20.6	13.7	−5.6	−.3	−3.2	−15.3	.7	−1.3	4.1	7.6	....	....	....	....	Bahrain	419
....	....	....	17.2	14.9	5.3	4.8	13.7	13.4	18.8	18.4	14.5	19.8	9.9	7.0	Egypt	469
29.1	23.8	16.4	12.1	9.7	6.3	21.2	21.5	22.4	20.6	18.0	22.7	25.5	38.6	....	Iran, I.R. of	429
33.1	−14.8	15.9	13.1	12.4	3.8	−10.1	−.5	8.6	7.6	....	....	....	....	....	Iraq	433
143.0	127.3	122.0	152.2	384.8	258.3	50.4	20.3	19.7	20.4	16.2	21.3	11.6	10.8	....	Israel	436
7.0	12.8	12.9	4.9	6.8	−2.0	.1	−1.7	5.5	21.0	11.4	5.1	5.4	5.1	4.0	Jordan	439
41.9	12.0	—	−9.3	.4	4.9	−25.7	24.8	−10.5	....	....	....	....	....	....	Kuwait	443
....	....	....	....	....	....	....	....	....	....	....	....	....	....	....	Lebanon	446
33.5	....	....	....	....	....	....	....	....	....	....	....	....	....	....	Libya	672
50.1	4.0	−5.9	−9.6	−4.7	−.4	−21.5	11.3	−8.0	7.1	16.6	−11.4	5.6	....	....	Oman	449
25.0	−.8	−11.3	−10.3	−3.4	−6.9	−18.2	3.0	−3.8	8.8	14.0	2.8	1.9	....	....	Saudi Arabia	456
17.5	17.2	2.4	5.0	7.2	4.1	26.3	25.4	28.6	23.3	19.3	8.4	7.6	3.5	....	Syrian Arab Rep.	463
8.7	7.2	1.2	−6.0	−5.3	.1	1.5	6.0	—	.6	4.2	4.1	−.1	.4	....	United Arab Emirates	466
60.6	55.5	69.9	99.0	118.0	129.1	82.0	120.6	231.6	286.2	559.3	135.0	175.9	250.3	....	Western Hemisphere	205
8.3	7.2	9.1	5.1	5.4	6.7	7.5	7.6	10.6	3.8	2.5	3.1	1.4	1.2	....	Antigua and Barbuda	311
165.4	106.5	201.9	383.1	609.3	618.2	75.4	127.8	385.1	3,014.6	2,023.2	141.0	15.4	6.1	2.2	Argentina	213
....	−3.5	−.1	6.2	5.3	2.3	8.3	5.9	....	....	....	....	....	....	....	Bahamas, The	313
22.9	12.2	9.9	5.8	5.1	3.5	4.5	7.4	2.8	6.7	3.8	2.8	....	....	....	Barbados	316
18.2	8.3	−6.8	7.8	9.4	−1.8	4.1	8.7	4.5	2.0	—	3.7	2.4	4.8	....	Belize	339
35.5	20.9	178.8	263.7	1,412.7	13,750.0	219.3	11.2	17.4	16.6	14.3	18.3	....	....	....	Bolivia	218
91.5	105.1	102.4	136.4	207.2	248.4	146.4	204.4	648.7	765.8	3,955.2	422.6	991.9	2,081.2	....	Brazil	223
29.2	12.2	13.3	26.6	14.3	36.7	22.1	24.6	21.5	15.8	19.2	20.9	16.2	12.0	13.9	Chile	228
27.6	22.8	24.8	20.4	22.2	24.9	29.2	23.4	27.7	24.7	28.2	26.5	22.3	20.2	....	Colombia	233
18.8	41.1	84.2	28.9	16.7	20.5	18.1	10.1	18.8	15.2	18.5	29.1	21.9	10.9	17.3	Costa Rica	238
20.6	3.8	5.5	8.7	6.7	7.9	6.4	5.5	6.0	7.9	2.0	6.1	3.6	.4	....	Dominica	321
13.7	5.3	7.9	1.3	18.6	37.9	9.1	12.5	42.1	42.7	62.7	53.0	4.2	4.1	8.3	Dominican Republic	243
19.5	14.4	17.8	38.7	39.2	30.9	20.9	38.0	52.3	70.7	54.0	42.7	52.4	38.6	27.4	Ecuador	248
13.5	5.7	9.7	12.4	12.6	20.4	37.1	13.9	16.5	16.5	9.5	12.7	8.8	13.1	10.7	El Salvador	253
−.5	5.1	4.9	4.4	3.0	7.9	6.7	9.4	5.0	3.7	4.7	1.8	1.3	....	....	Grenada	328
10.0	8.5	5.0	6.5	4.2	18.8	41.5	8.0	11.7	10.9	40.5	33.0	8.8	13.7	8.8	Guatemala	258
11.9	6.2	1.1	11.9	13.4	14.4	12.8	49.9	26.5	158.2	59.1	134.6	11.3	12.0	....	Guyana	336
15.1	5.3	8.0	9.1	11.5	10.4	10.2	−10.3	−2.2	5.6	13.2	14.5	19.2	22.3	54.0	Haiti	263
15.2	7.2	4.4	7.0	3.4	5.2	3.9	2.8	6.5	7.1	21.2	26.0	9.1	12.5	23.6	Honduras	268
17.9	8.4	9.2	16.5	35.0	25.5	22.0	11.1	13.6	12.5	23.9	43.9	61.3	31.2	....	Jamaica	343
34.5	27.0	60.8	90.5	59.1	56.7	73.6	139.7	99.5	25.8	29.5	21.6	14.6	10.0	....	Mexico	273
37.1	11.7	16.7	11.0	39.0	167.2	281.5	539.5	13,611.6	4,772.6	9,719.9	2,285.3	23.7	20.4	8.5	Nicaragua	278
12.0	4.9	4.5	1.8	4.6	2.5	1.5	.9	1.7	1.2	3.2	.2	.9	3.5	....	Panama	283
16.8	16.3	5.0	14.4	26.9	25.2	31.5	30.3	25.1	31.2	36.3	24.8	14.7	19.1	....	Paraguay	288
64.2	66.8	64.6	106.0	108.7	168.2	74.7	85.4	549.8	2,667.1	6,221.6	398.0	63.3	46.4	....	Peru	293
....	10.4	1.3	−1.1	9.6	5.4	13.7	6.9	6.7	5.9	8.2	−.2	3.4	....	....	St. Kitts and Nevis	361
16.2	12.0	1.3	−.5	3.9	35.0	6.5	5.9	.5	7.7	5.4	5.9	2.8	....	....	St. Lucia	362
8.0	15.1	9.7	6.6	3.3	4.2	5.1	5.0	4.1	1.0	4.2	4.6	3.5	....	....	St. Vincent & Grens.	364
11.1	4.4	7.4	.5	−.3	−.2	4.2	16.7	8.7	12.6	13.7	16.4	29.8	117.0	....	Suriname	366
22.7	5.0	12.1	7.5	6.1	1.3	−1.3	4.9	4.2	7.2	15.5	2.0	4.2	9.9	....	Trinidad and Tobago	369
51.0	30.3	16.0	44.8	56.2	74.0	70.9	72.9	64.1	75.3	100.4	100.7	61.8	44.7	....	Uruguay	298
24.8	12.5	1.4	5.7	41.6	9.1	3.1	32.1	21.4	84.1	43.6	21.4	28.2	32.4	57.7	Venezuela	299
															Memorandum Items	
24.5	10.7	7.2	11.3	10.7	3.9	−1.3	18.8	10.4	21.5	14.5	12.2	18.3	25.1	18.7	Oil Exporting Countries	999
38.7	26.6	32.5	37.4	38.2	40.0	28.5	38.2	62.3	71.7	90.1	43.8	49.5	62.2	....	Non-Oil Developing Countries	201

Indices

1990=100

1980	1981	1982	1983	1984	1985	1986	1987	1988	1989	1990	1991	1992	1993	1994		
20.8	23.8	27.3	31.3	36.1	41.3	45.8	52.4	63.0	78.0	100.0	116.6	136.7	164.7	....	World	001
61.0	66.8	71.7	75.6	79.3	82.7	85.7	88.5	91.7	95.8	100.0	104.6	107.3	109.6	111.5	Industrial Countries	110
3.4	4.3	5.5	7.3	9.8	13.1	16.2	22.0	33.9	55.7	100.0	139.6	203.1	319.9	....	Developing Countries	200
19.4	22.3	25.3	30.5	35.9	41.1	46.2	57.5	69.1	85.9	100.0	139.8	215.2	254.8	....	Africa	605
49.1	53.5	56.4	60.3	65.0	69.6	72.4	77.8	85.0	92.5	100.0	109.0	116.3	129.5	150.3	Asia	505
....	....	....	....	....	....	....	....	....	51.6	100.0	169.6	....	....	....	Europe	170
30.1	34.0	39.5	44.8	52.4	58.2	60.1	67.7	74.8	86.1	100.0	111.9	126.6	150.1	....	Middle East	405
—	—	—	.1	.1	.3	.5	1.2	3.9	15.2	100.0	235.0	648.4	2,271.4	....	Western Hemisphere	205

Investment as Percent of GDP

93e r		1965	1966	1967	1968	1969	1970	1971	1972	1973	1974	1975	1976	1977	1978	1979
																Percentages
World	001	22.0	21.8	21.3	21.0	21.7	22.0	22.0	21.9	24.4	24.8	22.8	23.5	23.7	24.0	24.5
Industrial Countries	110	22.9	22.7	22.0	22.9	23.6	23.7	23.4	23.6	25.0	24.9	21.6	22.7	22.9	23.2	23.9
United States	111	19.7	19.8	18.7	18.9	19.2	17.7	18.7	19.8	20.7	19.8	17.2	18.9	20.6	21.9	21.8
Canada	156	26.0	26.7	23.8	22.8	23.6	21.6	22.6	22.7	24.1	25.9	25.2	24.8	23.9	23.0	24.8
Australia	193	29.2	28.3	27.2	27.8	27.0	27.4	27.2	24.4	24.8	27.4	23.4	24.5	24.5	24.2	25.3
Japan	158	31.9	32.4	35.4	36.8	37.6	39.0	35.8	35.5	38.1	37.3	32.8	31.8	30.8	30.9	32.5
New Zealand	196	27.4	27.2	24.1	23.6	22.3	24.3	25.1	24.5	37.0	37.0	31.8	30.8	24.7	21.6	23.0
Austria	122	28.0	29.8	27.6	27.4	27.1	29.7	29.7	30.6	30.9	31.1	26.0	27.3	27.9	26.0	26.6
Belgium	124	22.5	23.6	23.1	22.1	22.9	24.0	23.2	21.5	22.4	24.6	21.6	21.8	21.6	21.4	21.1
Denmark	128	23.8	24.8	23.7	23.6	25.8	25.7	24.8	24.8	26.1	25.2	20.9	21.9	22.9	21.5	21.3
Finland	172	25.9	25.7	24.9	24.9	26.8	30.2	30.8	28.1	30.6	35.4	33.2	27.6	23.3	21.2	25.5
France	132	24.9	25.7	25.6	25.1	26.1	26.9	26.2	26.4	27.2	28.1	23.5	25.4	24.4	23.2	23.7
Germany	134	28.5	26.5	23.0	24.4	26.1	27.6	26.7	25.9	25.2	22.0	19.8	21.5	20.9	21.1	24.7
Greece	174	26.3	22.3	22.4	23.1	25.9	28.1	27.9	29.5	35.8	29.3	27.0	26.3	26.4	27.7	30.2
Iceland*	176	27.7	27.5	30.9	30.1	25.1	23.1	31.6	26.4	29.7	33.9	33.1	26.6	27.9	23.3	23.9
Ireland	178	23.7	20.6	19.7	22.0	25.7	24.5	24.0	25.1	27.6	29.1	23.3	25.4	27.9	29.0	33.0
Italy	136	20.0	19.6	20.5	20.3	21.7	27.4	24.9	24.0	27.2	30.1	23.9	26.9	24.9	24.1	24.7
Luxembourg	137	29.7	27.9	20.4	19.6	20.6	25.8	29.7	28.5	27.5	21.1	22.9	22.8	20.4	24.9	22.1
Netherlands	138	27.0	27.4	27.1	27.4	28.3	27.9	26.5	24.1	24.5	24.3	20.6	20.6	21.6	21.9	21.5
Norway	142	29.9	30.5	30.6	26.2	24.5	30.5	31.6	27.7	30.1	33.6	35.2	37.1	36.3	28.5	27.5
Portugal	182	25.0	23.5	24.8	24.1	24.2	26.4	27.7	29.3	29.4	28.5	20.3	24.7	29.0	30.9	31.7
Spain	184	24.7	24.9	23.6	23.6	25.7	26.8	24.7	25.8	27.1	30.1	28.5	26.9	24.9	22.9	22.3
Sweden	144	27.0	25.6	24.8	24.0	24.3	25.2	22.4	21.7	20.7	23.9	23.3	22.1	20.1	17.2	19.6
Switzerland	146	30.4	29.3	29.1	28.1	28.3	32.3	32.5	31.8	31.3	31.2	23.0	20.7	20.7	21.7	23.9
United Kingdom	112	19.7	19.2	19.8	20.4	19.9	19.5	19.1	18.5	21.9	22.1	18.6	20.3	19.8	19.5	19.7
Developing Countries	200	18.1	17.6	17.8	16.2	17.0	17.5	18.3	17.5	22.8	24.4	25.1	25.5	25.6	25.4	
Africa	605	22.0	19.0	21.8	20.3	20.7	22.9	24.9	23.8	25.3	25.7	29.2	28.7	29.7	28.0	25.8
Algeria	612	18.8	14.8	19.9	25.3	29.8	36.0	36.3	40.2	44.5	39.7	45.2	43.1	46.8	52.1	42.5
Benin	638	13.5	13.8	18.6	18.1	17.5	17.0	16.3	20.5	18.3	20.7	25.5	18.9	18.6	17.8	23.9
Botswana	616	6.1	18.2	22.3	27.3	33.6	39.1	45.5	53.0	52.4	51.7	46.0	38.3	28.1	34.6	34.9
Burkina Faso	748	15.2	14.6	11.8	9.5	9.7	9.9	14.7	17.4	21.2	26.6	25.5	26.4	22.2	20.7	31.6
Burundi	618	5.8	7.2	7.2	7.2	7.2	7.2	5.0	3.2	5.3	4.1	11.1	9.1	11.1	14.1	15.4
Cameroon	622	14.9	15.7	16.3	15.8	14.7	17.0	17.6	19.4	21.0	18.0	20.8	18.5	23.0	24.7	24.0
Chad	628	....	....	....	11.5	11.0	10.6	11.0	12.4	11.4	15.3	18.6	17.8	18.2	....	....
Congo	634														27.4	31.3
Côte d'Ivoire	662	18.7	19.4	17.6	17.5	19.6	22.0	21.8	20.6	22.9	22.0	24.3	22.9	26.5	29.8	28.0
Ethiopia	644	12.2	13.2	14.2	14.0	13.4	11.5	11.8	12.7	11.4	9.9	10.5	9.6	8.9	7.5	8.8
Gabon	646	25.0	29.6	30.6	29.2	29.8	29.6	39.6	48.1	37.5	51.8	62.7	73.5	58.1	35.0	32.7
Gambia, The	648	13.6	14.3	16.4	21.8	17.3	9.4	17.5	....	....	....	....	....	....	....	....
Ghana	652	17.9	12.9	10.3	11.1	11.8	14.2	14.1	7.1	9.0	13.0	12.7	8.9	11.1	6.8	6.5
Kenya	664	14.6	18.8	20.3	19.2	19.6	21.9	25.3	22.1	19.9	28.5	18.2	20.2	23.7	29.7	22.7
Liberia	668	21.2	25.0	25.4	20.0	15.8	24.5	23.7	25.6	17.3	24.0	40.5	38.0	40.5	36.3	36.5
Madagascar	674	10.2	13.4	14.6	16.2	16.9	15.6	18.0	13.9	14.3	13.6	12.8	12.8	12.9	14.5	25.3
Malawi	676	13.9	17.3	13.6	16.3	18.6	26.1	19.4	24.7	22.4	27.8	34.1	23.9	24.7	38.4	37.9
Mali	678															
Mauritania	682	....	....	....	....	....	22.8	23.7	34.0	27.7	44.9	44.4	50.8	43.7	27.0	26.2
Mauritius	684	16.8	14.6	15.0	14.6	13.9	13.8	15.8	16.0	25.9	23.3	33.3	40.5	30.0	30.7	31.2
Morocco	686	10.8	10.7	14.1	17.6	11.7	15.9	15.6	12.6	14.4	20.6	25.2	28.1	34.2	25.7	24.5
Mozambique	688															
Niger	692	11.1	8.9	9.0	10.1	6.4	9.5	7.4	9.0	14.7	13.9	28.5	26.4	28.9	31.6	31.8
Nigeria	694	18.3	16.7	16.4	15.2	14.3	15.7	18.1	18.2	23.4	16.8	25.3	31.1	30.3	27.4	22.2
Rwanda	714	....	....	....	42.4	46.1	45.8	46.5	47.2	47.2	47.8	13.8	13.9	15.1	16.5	11.9
Senegal	722	....	....	....	11.5	13.4	15.7	16.3	17.0	18.9	22.2	17.8	16.5	17.4	14.7	18.8
Seychelles	718												38.9	40.0	43.3	32.9
Sierra Leone	724	11.7	15.3	12.9	11.9	12.9	15.7	15.3	11.7	11.7	15.8	15.7	11.3	13.1	11.3	13.4
Somalia	726	....	....	....	....	....	....	14.4	12.4	15.3	1.4	3.8	26.3	30.9	34.4	27.1
South Africa	199	26.9	24.0	26.9	24.8	25.6	28.0	30.4	25.7	26.0	29.6	32.0	28.5	26.9	25.2	26.8
Sudan	732	14.9	12.7	15.3	13.6	13.9	9.2	9.1	8.5	8.4	15.2	14.3	20.8	17.5	16.1	5.5
Swaziland	734	....	....	23.9	19.3	19.6	16.2	22.8	23.3	21.1	20.3	24.6	28.2	27.0	48.0	42.5
Tanzania	738	14.6	15.5	17.9	17.7	15.5	22.5	26.4	21.8	21.1	22.0	21.1	22.9	26.1	25.2	26.1
Togo	742	23.6	16.4	12.7	11.0	13.2	14.4	18.2	20.1	23.6	17.0	28.5	27.0	38.9	49.3	50.7
Tunisia	744	27.6	25.0	24.8	23.0	22.7	19.7	20.0	21.6	20.7	23.0	31.3	30.1	30.0	30.5	29.5
Uganda	746	....	....	....	14.9	16.8	13.8	16.4	10.5	8.5	10.6	7.6	5.7	4.7	3.9	....
Zaïre	636	....	....	....	23.3	24.6	26.1	32.9	33.4	30.0	30.6	31.9	25.9	38.5	18.4	19.6
Zambia	754	24.3	28.9	30.8	32.4	18.1	29.6	37.3	35.3	29.2	36.4	40.5	23.8	24.7	23.9	14.1
Zimbabwe	698	13.7	16.6	22.9	22.3	20.2	20.4	21.9	20.7	24.8	27.9	27.1	18.9	19.1	11.9	12.7
Asia	505	15.8	16.3	16.1	16.1	17.3	18.2	19.1	18.5	19.5	21.1	22.2	22.3	22.1	24.0	25.2
Bhutan	514															
Fiji	819	22.3	22.3	22.6	25.9	24.9	22.2	24.8	24.0	22.2	18.9	20.6	21.5	23.2	25.3	30.1
India	534	16.9	18.0	16.5	15.1	16.0	17.1	18.5	17.1	18.3	19.8	20.8	20.9	19.8	22.1	22.9
Indonesia	536	6.7	4.5	8.0	8.8	11.7	13.6	15.8	18.8	17.9	16.8	20.3	20.7	20.1	20.5	20.9
Korea	542	15.1	21.9	22.3	26.2	29.2	25.4	25.1	22.1	25.5	31.4	29.6	25.7	25.3	28.5	36.0
Malaysia	548	15.7	15.7	16.1	15.8	14.6	20.3	20.9	21.3	23.6	29.6	25.5	22.8	23.8	26.7	28.9
Maldives	556															
Myanmar	518	18.4	4.3	12.2	12.8	14.2	11.8	12.2	10.8	10.2	10.3	10.0	10.3	13.0	18.2	22.3
Nepal	558	....	....	....	....	....	....	....	....	....	....	14.5	15.1	16.0	17.8	15.8
Pakistan	564	15.5	17.4	16.1	16.1	15.8	15.8	15.6	14.2	12.9	13.4	16.4	18.5	19.3	17.9	17.9
Papua New Guinea	853	20.2	22.8	22.0	21.8	21.7	35.4	46.9	38.8	18.6	12.9	22.1	18.1	20.0	19.4	21.7
Philippines	566	20.8	19.7	20.9	21.1	20.4	21.2	20.9	20.6	20.2	25.2	29.5	31.0	28.8	28.9	31.1
Singapore	576	21.9	21.9	22.2	24.9	28.6	38.7	40.2	41.1	39.2	44.6	37.6	40.8	36.2	39.0	43.4
Solomon Islands	813															
Sri Lanka	524	12.5	14.3	15.2	15.9	19.3	18.9	17.1	17.3	13.7	15.7	15.6	16.2	14.4	20.0	25.8
Thailand	578	20.2	23.6	23.7	25.2	26.4	25.6	24.2	21.7	27.0	26.6	26.7	24.0	26.9	28.2	27.2
Vanuatu	846															

Investment as Percent of GDP

1980	1981	1982	1983	1984	1985	1986	1987	1988	1989	1990	1991	1992	1993	1994		
Percentages																
24.1	**24.1**	**22.4**	**21.5**	**22.0**	**21.7**	**21.4**	**21.6**	**22.5**	**23.1**	**22.6**	**21.5**	**21.3**	**21.0**	....	World	001
23.2	**22.7**	**21.1**	**20.6**	**21.9**	**21.3**	**21.0**	**21.1**	**21.8**	**22.2**	**21.6**	**20.4**	**19.8**	**19.6**	**20.6**	Industrial Countries	110
20.0	20.9	18.4	18.4	21.2	20.1	19.4	18.9	18.4	18.2	16.9	15.3	15.6	16.6	18.5	United States	111
23.4	24.5	19.1	19.3	20.1	20.2	20.6	21.7	22.5	23.0	20.7	19.0	18.1	18.2	18.9	Canada	156
24.7	26.7	25.0	22.0	24.0	24.8	23.8	24.3	25.3	26.7	22.7	19.6	19.5	20.3	21.2	Australia	193
32.2	31.1	29.9	28.1	28.0	28.2	27.8	28.7	30.6	31.8	32.8	32.5	31.1	29.9	28.9	Japan	158
20.8	24.6	25.9	26.2	28.8	26.9	24.1	22.2	20.3	22.9	19.9	16.5	18.8	21.1	....	New Zealand	196
28.4	26.3	23.0	22.0	23.8	23.4	23.5	24.0	24.8	25.1	25.5	25.8	25.2	24.6	25.7	Austria	122
21.8	17.8	17.5	15.7	16.6	14.9	15.2	16.2	18.1	19.5	20.3	19.4	19.1	17.6	....	Belgium	124
18.5	15.5	16.3	16.0	18.4	19.6	21.5	19.0	17.9	18.4	17.3	16.4	15.2	14.2	14.7	Denmark	128
28.7	25.9	25.2	25.1	23.8	24.2	23.2	24.0	26.6	29.7	28.1	18.8	16.7	14.6	16.4	Finland	172
24.2	21.7	21.9	19.9	19.0	18.9	19.6	20.2	21.4	22.3	22.5	21.5	19.8	17.1	17.9	France	132
25.0	23.2	22.0	22.4	22.2	21.7	21.8	21.7	22.6	23.4	24.4	25.7	25.1	24.0	24.8	Germany	134
28.6	25.4	21.1	21.9	20.1	21.3	19.7	17.6	19.3	20.9	19.4	20.3	19.6	18.5	....	Greece	174
25.7	25.2	26.9	20.2	21.0	18.5	16.8	18.6	18.5	16.4	18.0	18.9	17.4	15.8	15.1	Iceland*	176
27.8	28.4	27.8	23.6	22.6	19.8	18.1	16.5	15.9	17.9	20.7	18.7	15.3	14.3	....	Ireland	178
27.0	24.7	23.5	21.8	22.9	22.5	20.9	21.0	21.5	21.3	21.0	20.5	19.4	....	....	Italy	136
25.2	24.5	24.8	24.3	24.7	20.3	23.5	24.8	27.1	27.6	28.3	31.4	30.2	....	....	Luxembourg	137
21.5	18.3	17.9	18.4	19.1	20.0	21.3	20.7	21.4	22.6	22.2	21.4	20.5	19.4	19.9	Netherlands	138
27.7	25.6	26.5	24.6	25.7	24.2	29.5	28.2	27.1	24.3	20.5	18.8	18.4	19.5	19.8	Norway	142
34.4	38.6	37.1	29.1	22.2	20.6	22.4	27.4	29.8	29.6	29.5	28.5	28.1	....	....	Portugal	182
23.2	21.9	22.2	21.5	19.7	19.2	20.0	21.5	23.7	25.1	25.4	24.6	22.7	19.9	19.7	Spain	184
21.3	18.2	17.6	17.2	17.8	19.2	17.9	18.9	19.9	21.9	21.3	17.9	16.5	13.5	14.4	Sweden	144
27.2	25.4	24.0	24.0	24.1	24.4	26.0	27.2	27.9	29.7	29.3	27.0	23.4	21.5	22.9	Switzerland	146
16.8	15.1	15.6	16.4	17.3	17.2	17.1	18.0	20.3	21.0	19.2	16.1	15.4	15.1	15.5	United Kingdom	112
25.6	**26.7**	**25.1**	**23.4**	**22.4**	**22.5**	**22.1**	**22.7**	**23.8**	**24.7**	**24.5**	**23.6**	**24.0**	**23.6**	....	Developing Countries	200
25.6	**26.0**	**23.2**	**22.9**	**21.4**	**20.2**	**20.1**	**19.6**	**19.4**	**19.7**	**19.6**	**18.8**	**18.7**	**19.4**	....	Africa	605
39.1	37.0	37.3	37.6	35.1	33.2	33.5	30.0	30.7	29.7	28.7	29.1	28.8	27.5	....	Algeria	612
23.6	21.7	27.6	17.3	14.1	15.4	19.3	14.5	15.6	11.6	14.3	14.6	....	....	....	Benin	638
37.7	40.6	43.6	30.1	26.3	30.4	16.2	24.5	7.3	41.8	....	....	....	....	....	Botswana	616
26.6	23.8	25.5	24.4	24.1	28.3	....	....	....	....	....	....	....	....	....	Burkina Faso	748
13.9	16.1	17.5	17.9	18.1	14.3	15.7	17.3	14.2	16.4	15.8	16.5	15.9	12.7	11.5	Burundi	618
21.8	27.2	24.8	26.0	25.9	24.5	23.1	29.0	27.3	27.3	28.8	....	....	....	....	Cameroon	622
....	....	....	....	....	....	....	....	....	....	....	....	....	....	....	Chad	628
35.8	48.1	60.3	35.6	30.4	30.3	29.5	13.9	18.6	16.2	....	....	....	....	....	Congo	634
26.5	25.9	23.2	18.1	11.6	13.0	12.1	12.3	7.8	8.9	6.7	7.5	....	....	....	Côte d'Ivoire	662
10.0	10.6	13.4	11.9	16.3	10.5	16.0	15.1	19.9	14.0	12.2	10.5	9.4	12.6	16.8	Ethiopia	644
....	....	....	....	32.7	37.9	34.6	31.9	....	....	....	....	....	....	....	Gabon	646
....	....	....	....	....	....	....	....	....	....	....	....	....	....	....	Gambia, The	648
5.6	4.6	3.4	3.7	6.9	9.6	9.4	10.4	10.9	13.5	12.3	12.7	12.9	22.0	....	Ghana	652
30.0	28.4	21.8	20.8	20.7	25.5	21.8	24.3	25.0	24.7	24.3	21.3	17.5	16.0	....	Kenya	664
33.3	19.4	21.1	20.4	18.4	12.6	11.7	11.4	10.1	8.5	....	....	....	....	....	Liberia	668
23.5	18.1	13.4	13.2	10.8	11.5	....	....	....	....	....	....	....	....	....	Madagascar	674
31.9	23.3	23.6	27.2	12.9	18.6	12.3	15.4	18.7	21.2	19.7	20.1	18.8	12.3	....	Malawi	676
....	24.5	17.6	14.6	15.2	12.2	19.7	22.2	21.5	25.1	23.2	14.9	....	....	....	Mali	678
32.1	44.1	48.2	45.8	35.3	....	....	....	....	....	....	....	....	....	....	Mauritania	682
20.7	25.3	18.2	17.6	22.0	23.5	21.9	25.3	30.6	30.7	30.4	28.0	28.6	30.6	31.9	Mauritius	684
24.2	26.1	28.2	24.0	25.3	27.1	22.7	21.1	21.0	23.7	25.0	22.9	23.8	....	....	Morocco	686
19.2	19.5	22.8	20.0	22.0	17.1	18.9	45.5	57.4	56.2	59.0	60.8	64.5	68.8	....	Mozambique	688
31.5	28.0	27.3	15.6	5.2	15.3	13.3	10.6	19.9	12.3	12.5	....	....	....	....	Niger	692
22.5	22.8	18.8	13.1	6.7	7.1	10.6	8.8	6.5	8.2	11.9	11.0	10.7	11.7	9.4	Nigeria	694
16.1	13.3	17.7	13.5	15.8	17.3	15.9	15.4	14.4	13.3	12.7	12.3	14.8	....	....	Rwanda	714
15.5	16.4	16.5	21.1	17.3	18.4	15.3	12.5	12.7	11.8	13.1	15.4	....	....	....	Senegal	722
38.3	32.6	32.3	21.3	21.7	22.7	24.4	19.8	25.5	27.5	24.6	22.3	21.2	....	....	Seychelles	718
16.2	19.1	13.4	14.3	12.7	10.9	10.6	9.8	7.1	11.5	12.1	11.5	14.7	7.8	....	Sierra Leone	724
9.1	6.5	6.8	11.5	10.4	11.8	17.8	21.5	....	....	....	....	....	....	....	Somalia	726
30.8	32.4	25.2	25.8	24.9	20.3	19.1	18.5	21.0	21.1	17.6	16.9	15.9	16.0	18.1	South Africa	199
-3.6	-2.3	....	....	....	....	8.5	5.3	7.8	2.5	7.0	10.1	....	....	....	Sudan	732
40.7	31.0	32.2	35.0	31.6	32.0	20.0	14.7	23.6	24.2	20.7	19.2	....	....	....	Swaziland	734
23.0	24.7	21.0	13.6	15.3	15.7	19.5	30.4	30.6	34.4	46.6	38.5	42.4	63.5	....	Tanzania	738
34.8	30.7	26.3	21.8	15.0	25.5	29.1	25.3	....	....	....	....	....	....	....	Togo	742
29.0	32.3	31.6	29.3	32.0	26.6	23.5	20.6	19.4	23.7	26.6	26.2	30.0	29.5	29.5	Tunisia	744
....	....	....	....	8.5	7.2	8.7	11.2	10.4	10.2	13.8	15.7	14.3	14.3	....	Uganda	746
10.7	10.8	8.3	9.3	10.5	12.5	13.2	14.2	14.4	14.3	9.1	5.6	6.9	....	....	Zaïre	636
23.3	19.3	16.8	13.8	14.7	14.9	23.5	14.4	11.4	10.8	17.3	14.7	14.1	10.7	....	Zambia	754
18.8	23.1	21.2	15.9	18.1	19.8	18.4	18.5	17.0	19.8	....	....	....	....	....	Zimbabwe	698
24.6	**27.5**	**26.3**	**25.9**	**24.5**	**24.8**	**24.2**	**24.9**	**26.6**	**27.9**	**29.9**	**29.2**	**29.1**	**28.0**	....	Asia	505
31.0	38.5	40.5	39.8	36.3	45.4	40.5	30.2	38.6	33.1	33.2	31.1	47.4	....	....	Bhutan	514
31.8	34.3	25.6	21.1	19.8	19.1	18.2	16.0	12.9	13.8	17.4	13.5	13.1	15.1	....	Fiji	819
20.9	25.0	22.9	21.1	21.2	24.2	23.2	22.5	24.5	24.3	25.7	22.9	23.3	21.3	....	India	534
20.9	29.8	27.9	28.7	26.2	28.0	28.3	31.4	31.5	35.2	36.1	35.5	35.9	33.2	34.0	Indonesia	536
31.7	29.5	28.6	29.0	30.1	29.6	28.7	29.8	31.1	33.6	36.9	38.9	36.6	35.1	35.9	Korea	542
30.4	35.0	37.3	37.8	33.6	27.6	26.0	23.2	26.0	28.6	31.3	35.9	33.5	35.0	38.5	Malaysia	548
23.7	26.2	24.4	24.7	30.8	38.9	36.5	60.5	57.4	65.5	64.8	....	....	....	....	Maldives	556
21.5	22.9	22.2	18.0	15.1	15.5	12.7	11.6	12.8	9.2	13.4	15.3	13.6	12.1	....	Myanmar	518
18.3	17.6	17.1	19.6	18.7	21.9	19.0	20.2	19.8	21.7	18.4	20.8	21.2	21.4	....	Nepal	558
18.5	18.8	19.3	18.8	18.3	18.3	18.8	19.1	18.0	18.9	18.9	19.0	20.1	20.7	19.9	Pakistan	564
23.4	25.3	29.8	29.4	27.2	18.8	18.7	20.0	27.2	23.2	24.4	27.4	23.8	18.8	....	Papua New Guinea	853
29.1	27.5	27.9	29.6	20.3	14.3	15.2	17.5	18.7	21.6	24.2	20.2	21.3	24.5	25.3	Philippines	566
46.3	46.3	47.9	47.9	48.5	42.5	38.5	39.0	36.9	35.5	39.5	38.0	40.4	43.8	....	Singapore	576
....	....	....	....	23.0	26.2	26.2	23.1	37.1	....	....	....	....	....	....	Solomon Islands	813
33.8	27.8	30.8	28.9	25.8	23.8	23.7	23.3	22.8	21.7	22.2	22.9	24.3	25.6	27.0	Sri Lanka	524
29.1	29.7	26.5	30.0	29.5	28.2	25.9	27.9	32.6	35.1	41.1	42.0	40.1	....	....	Thailand	578
....	....	....	25.7	25.7	29.7	34.8	33.3	29.5	37.1	43.2	30.0	30.0	30.1	....	Vanuatu	846

Investment as Percent of GDP

93e r		1965	1966	1967	1968	1969	1970	1971	1972	1973	1974	1975	1976	1977	1978	1979
																Percentages
Europe	170	22.1	21.0	22.5	23.0	....	27.1	29.1	29.8	32.8	35.8	34.4	34.3	31.5	34.5	31.5
Cyprus	423	21.1	19.5	20.6	20.3	23.5	24.4	23.5	23.6	30.2	26.3	22.5	26.6	34.9	37.2	38.7
Czech Republic	935	....	....	....	....	....	....	....	....	....	....	....	....	....	....	....
Czechoslovakia	934	....	....	....	....	....	26.0	24.5	24.8	26.3	28.4	28.9	29.0	25.2	24.9	24.6
Hungary	944	....	....	....	....	....	37.4	38.7	33.4	33.4	40.6	37.8	35.9	37.2	41.3	34.0
Malta	181	25.6	26.0	29.2	32.3	32.7	32.7	29.0	25.0	22.1	27.1	23.5	27.5	26.0	23.5	25.5
Poland	964	....	....	25.2	26.3	25.0	24.6	28.9	31.7	36.3	38.7	36.7	36.9	33.3	31.8	29.0
Romania	968	....	....	....	....	....	....	....	....	....	....	....	....	....	....	....
Turkey	186	....	....	....	....	....	....	....	....	....	....	....	....	....	....	....
Yugoslavia, SFR	188	40.9	39.4	34.7	34.8	36.6	41.6	42.4	36.1	38.3	43.0	41.4	40.1	44.5	42.8	45.5
Middle East	405	17.7	17.3	15.9	21.4	21.1	20.8	18.8	21.5	19.9	19.8	26.6	26.0	28.8	25.4	25.8
Egypt	469	17.2	18.6	15.6	13.5	11.8	14.4	13.0	13.7	13.7	17.4	27.2	25.2	29.1	31.0	30.4
Iran, I.R. of	429	17.9	17.2	20.7	33.4	31.2	34.6	28.7	33.6	27.9	18.3	28.5	28.5	27.3	22.2	21.7
Iraq	433	15.8	16.1	15.9	13.7	14.0	15.8	14.6	19.0	22.1	28.1	30.3	22.2	24.5	20.1	28.8
Israel	436	26.1	21.1	16.9	23.3	26.6	28.4	32.0	31.3	25.8	35.7	31.3	27.3	24.4	27.0	27.1
Jordan	439	16.6	18.9	14.1	14.5	17.8	10.4	15.6	16.8	14.8	21.8	23.4	29.3	33.1	29.0	30.6
Kuwait	443	14.6	17.7	19.3	18.0	19.1	12.1	9.4	9.3	9.5	6.8	12.7	16.5	23.3	20.2	13.6
Lebanon	446	....	....	20.2	18.1	19.3	18.6	19.6	20.2	20.6	....	....	....	20.9	18.6	18.0
Libya	672	27.1	27.2	25.8	24.8	23.8	17.3	18.5	25.1	29.6	26.5	30.6	24.0	25.0	27.3	25.0
Oman	449	....	....	31.2	12.6	9.3	13.8	28.5	29.8	26.2	30.6	35.6	35.9	30.6	28.9	26.0
Qatar	453	....	....	....	....	....	....	....	....	....	....	....	....	....	....	....
Saudi Arabia	456	14.4	19.5	17.9	21.3	21.0	16.1	12.4	13.8	9.3	13.2	20.9	25.4	33.1	27.8	20.7
Syrian Arab Rep.	463	10.5	12.4	11.5	13.0	14.9	13.7	14.8	20.1	12.4	24.8	28.7	31.4	35.5	27.4	26.2
United Arab Emirates	466	....	....	....	....	....	....	....	27.3	25.4	15.4	30.6	33.3	39.1	38.7	34.5
Yemen Arab Rep.	473	....	....	....	....	.4	16.4	17.6	16.8	20.2	18.5	20.3	21.4	43.4	39.2	40.7
Western Hemisphere	205	19.5	18.9	18.4	20.9	22.4	22.7	23.1	22.3	23.0	25.7	23.4	23.0	23.3	23.6	23.7
Antigua and Barbuda	311	....	....	....	....	....	....	....	....	....	....	....	....	....	....	37.8
Argentina	213	25.0	20.0	16.7	14.3	25.0	22.2	23.1	19.0	17.1	18.4	26.6	27.1	27.2	23.9	22.6
Bahamas, The	313	....	....	....	....	....	....	....	....	18.3	15.9	10.3	8.5	9.3	8.6	9.3
Barbados	316	....	....	....	....	....	....	....	23.3	24.5	21.6	20.0	27.0	21.8	25.8	23.5
Belize	339	....	....	....	....	....	....	....	....	29.6	27.8	32.3	37.8	32.5	30.0	33.9
Bolivia	218	17.0	16.2	14.3	16.1	17.2	17.1	17.2	19.8	20.7	16.4	24.4	21.2	20.8	24.7	20.8
Brazil	223	....	....	....	25.2	26.4	25.7	27.9	27.7	28.5	33.7	23.3	22.4	21.3	22.3	22.8
Chile	228	15.0	16.3	16.1	16.3	15.1	16.4	14.5	12.2	7.9	21.2	13.1	12.8	14.4	17.8	17.8
Colombia	233	17.7	20.4	18.5	21.2	20.5	20.3	19.9	18.4	18.1	21.5	17.0	17.6	18.8	18.3	18.2
Costa Rica	238	19.5	19.1	19.4	18.0	20.0	20.5	24.3	22.0	24.0	26.7	21.6	23.7	24.3	23.5	25.3
Dominica	321	....	....	....	....	....	....	....	....	....	....	18.8	22.3	26.5	20.6	24.0	38.3
Dominican Republic	243	8.9	15.9	15.0	14.0	18.7	19.1	17.9	19.7	22.1	23.5	24.5	22.3	21.8	23.9	25.4
Ecuador	248	14.0	15.3	17.4	18.0	17.5	18.2	23.2	20.0	19.5	22.5	26.7	23.8	26.5	28.4	25.3
El Salvador	253	15.4	17.1	14.7	11.1	12.7	13.2	15.6	14.2	18.3	22.6	22.1	19.6	23.4	23.8	18.1
Grenada	328	....	....	....	....	....	....	....	....	....	....	....	6.5	13.2	15.6	8.4	15.8
Guatemala	258	13.3	10.8	12.9	15.1	11.4	12.8	14.4	12.1	13.7	18.6	16.1	21.4	20.0	21.6	18.7
Guyana	336	22.3	23.9	25.8	22.3	20.8	22.9	18.7	19.8	27.2	26.4	33.0	37.4	29.1	20.5	31.0
Haiti	263	6.9	5.7	5.8	5.6	6.9	8.4	8.8	9.5	8.8	15.2	16.3	16.0	15.8	16.9	16.8
Honduras	268	14.6	16.0	19.6	18.4	19.1	20.9	16.1	15.2	18.4	25.6	19.0	19.2	23.1	27.2	26.5
Jamaica	343	20.3	21.9	23.8	28.1	35.2	31.5	32.1	27.3	31.5	24.3	25.8	18.2	12.2	15.0	19.2
Mexico	273	17.5	18.8	19.5	20.8	21.1	22.7	20.2	20.3	21.4	23.2	23.7	22.3	22.8	23.6	26.0
Netherlands Antilles	353	12.8	15.5	16.9	18.2	....	....	....	....	....	....	....	....	....	....	....
Nicaragua	278	....	....	....	....	....	....	....	....	....	....	....	....	....	....	....
Panama	283	17.5	21.9	21.0	22.3	23.6	27.8	30.4	31.8	33.6	33.6	30.8	31.6	23.7	26.6	28.1
Paraguay	288	15.1	15.8	16.5	15.9	16.0	14.7	14.6	15.1	19.0	21.0	24.1	24.6	24.7	27.2	28.6
Peru	293	18.6	20.1	19.8	13.9	13.3	12.9	15.0	14.2	15.6	18.9	19.8	17.9	15.0	14.2	21.6
St. Kitts and Nevis	361	....	....	....	....	....	....	....	....	29.0	24.6	20.8	39.9	76.3	54.3	69.2
St. Lucia	362	....	....	....	....	....	....	....	....	....	....	46.1	43.0	49.8	65.3	68.0
St. Vincent & Grens.	364	....	....	....	....	....	....	....	....	....	....	26.2	20.4	27.2	22.7	34.2
Suriname	366	42.3	32.8	21.5	20.5	18.0	18.3	17.6	21.7	23.0	29.9	38.0	29.5	37.3	32.4	22.8
Trinidad and Tobago	369	25.9	23.1	17.6	19.8	17.2	25.9	34.0	31.3	26.0	21.8	27.3	24.6	26.7	30.2	29.1
Uruguay	298	10.9	12.0	13.8	10.1	10.9	11.6	12.6	11.8	12.6	11.5	13.5	14.8	15.2	16.0	17.3
Venezuela	299	20.8	20.0	20.3	28.4	26.0	29.6	29.7	31.2	29.3	24.0	30.9	34.4	41.5	42.8	31.6
Memorandum Items																
Oil Exporting Countries	999	14.6	12.6	15.2	20.5	20.9	22.3	21.7	24.4	24.1	20.8	27.4	28.2	30.3	28.6	26.0
Non-Oil Developing Countries	201	19.1	18.9	18.5	24.6	25.6	26.6	27.4	27.1	17.9	20.2	19.5	19.1	19.0	24.8	25.3

*GNP used in calculation

Investment as Percent of GDP

1980	1981	1982	1983	1984	1985	1986	1987	1988	1989	1990	1991	1992	1993	1994		
Percentages																
29.1	**25.3**	**28.1**	**26.7**	**27.2**	**26.3**	**28.1**	**26.7**	**26.6**	**27.1**	**25.0**	**20.3**	....	....	....	Europe	170
37.8	33.8	31.7	30.1	33.6	30.3	25.9	25.5	27.4	30.9	27.1	26.1	27.8	....	....	Cyprus	423
....	....	....	....	....	....	....	....	....	....	....	....	....	18.4	20.4	Czech Republic	935
21.2	19.6	19.7	18.8	19.0	15.1	16.2	14.9	13.5	12.9	15.7	13.3	....	....	....	Czechoslovakia	934
30.7	29.7	28.5	26.5	25.7	25.0	26.9	26.7	26.1	26.1	24.0	20.8	19.5	22.6	....	Hungary	944
24.6	27.1	31.5	30.0	28.9	28.1	25.5	27.5	28.8	29.6	33.4	31.6	27.5	30.0	....	Malta	181
26.4	18.5	28.0	25.0	26.3	27.7	28.9	28.8	32.6	38.5	27.5	21.5	....	....	....	Poland	964
39.8	36.3	33.7	34.0	34.2	33.0	34.4	31.8	28.4	26.8	30.2	28.0	31.0	27.4	....	Romania	968
....	....	....	....	....	....	....	25.8	25.8	24.2	26.8	22.4	23.2	26.1	....	Turkey	186
42.8	44.5	43.0	40.9	42.5	41.7	40.8	39.7	39.5	47.7	....	....	....	....	....	Yugoslavia, SFR	188
27.1	**33.3**	**31.3**	**25.5**	**25.7**	**22.7**	**22.8**	**21.9**	**21.9**	**22.7**	**23.7**	**25.8**	**25.9**	**23.2**	....	Middle East	405
28.0	30.4	30.1	32.2	29.2	28.7	30.7	26.1	33.2	31.3	29.4	24.0	19.8	16.2	16.6	Egypt	469
29.6	22.8	15.9	23.1	24.3	21.1	22.1	25.5	19.1	23.8	28.6	33.2	35.4	29.2	....	Iran, I.R. of	429
30.5	63.0	57.7	14.9	18.1	23.7	19.0	19.7	21.4	8.1	....	....	....	....	....	Iraq	433
22.4	21.1	23.5	23.3	21.7	18.5	19.4	19.1	17.3	15.9	18.7	24.3	24.3	24.0	....	Israel	436
40.3	49.1	38.3	32.3	28.8	20.5	20.5	23.3	23.5	23.7	31.9	25.9	34.6	31.8	27.6	Jordan	439
13.9	16.5	22.9	24.8	21.0	18.9	22.1	17.5	15.7	12.3	17.6	39.6	19.1	22.9	....	Kuwait	443
....	....	....	....	....	....	....	....	....	....	....	....	....	....	....	Lebanon	446
23.9	31.4	26.1	....	....	....	....	....	....	....	....	....	....	....	....	Libya	672
22.7	23.4	27.0	26.9	30.0	27.6	32.1	18.8	17.5	13.7	13.1	16.9	17.0	....	....	Oman	449
17.0	17.7	27.5	21.9	16.6	17.8	18.5	14.4	....	....	....	....	....	....	....	Qatar	453
21.7	19.5	27.2	30.3	33.0	20.9	19.9	19.0	20.9	21.6	19.5	21.2	23.7	....	....	Saudi Arabia	456
27.5	23.2	23.7	23.9	24.0	24.1	22.5	18.2	14.0	16.2	16.5	18.0	23.2	25.8	....	Syrian Arab Rep.	463
28.3	26.3	28.6	31.3	28.9	25.2	30.1	23.9	24.9	23.4	20.6	21.8	24.5	....	....	United Arab Emirates	466
39.5	38.3	29.8	19.4	17.4	14.4	13.0	14.6	....	....	....	....	....	....	....	Yemen Arab Rep.	473
24.9	**24.5**	**22.1**	**19.2**	**18.1**	**20.1**	**18.8**	**21.0**	**21.8**	**22.8**	**20.3**	**19.7**	**20.6**	**20.8**	....	Western Hemisphere	205
45.0	58.5	55.4	23.8	28.9	....	17.6	18.5	19.6	18.6	15.5	14.0	14.6	16.7	18.4	Antigua and Barbuda	311
25.3	22.7	21.8	20.9	20.0	17.6	17.5	19.6	20.9	15.5	14.0	14.6	16.7	18.4	20.0	Argentina	213
13.9	20.5	21.0	17.7	19.1	21.1	20.9	22.5	20.9	24.1	22.2	20.5	20.9	21.0	....	Bahamas, The	313
24.5	27.6	22.7	19.9	16.2	15.4	16.0	16.0	17.3	18.8	18.9	16.2	11.0	13.4	....	Barbados	316
26.7	26.0	20.8	20.2	23.5	21.6	20.4	21.9	25.4	30.3	28.5	29.8	29.9	31.8	....	Belize	339
14.6	13.3	12.5	12.2	10.6	16.9	13.4	14.9	11.3	9.8	9.2	13.2	....	....	....	Bolivia	218
23.2	23.2	21.5	17.2	15.3	21.3	19.1	22.2	22.7	28.6	22.9	19.6	19.6	20.4	....	Brazil	223
21.0	22.7	11.3	9.8	13.6	17.2	18.9	22.2	22.8	25.5	26.3	24.5	26.8	28.8	26.8	Chile	228
19.1	20.6	20.5	19.9	19.0	19.0	18.0	20.0	22.0	20.0	18.5	16.0	17.2	20.5	....	Colombia	233
26.6	29.0	24.7	24.2	22.7	25.9	25.2	27.1	24.5	26.5	27.3	25.0	29.1	29.9	27.8	Costa Rica	238
50.1	31.9	30.9	28.1	36.9	28.5	23.3	23.2	31.1	41.2	40.8	31.6	31.0	31.2	....	Dominica	321
25.1	23.6	20.0	21.1	21.3	20.0	22.7	27.8	28.6	27.4	23.4	20.9	22.4	23.2	22.7	Dominican Republic	243
26.1	23.2	25.2	17.6	17.2	18.2	20.9	22.7	21.5	20.7	17.5	22.2	21.2	21.1	22.0	Ecuador	248
13.3	14.2	13.2	12.1	12.0	10.8	13.3	12.4	12.8	15.3	13.9	15.4	14.5	18.6	18.8	El Salvador	253
27.7	44.3	44.7	40.2	29.7	29.5	33.2	36.9	37.4	40.0	42.0	43.7	34.5	....	....	Grenada	328
15.9	17.0	14.1	11.1	11.6	11.5	10.3	13.9	13.7	13.5	13.6	14.3	18.3	17.4	....	Guatemala	258
29.8	33.2	26.3	26.9	22.9	20.9	26.4	37.2	21.5	34.2	42.3	35.3	53.7	....	....	Guyana	336
17.9	17.7	16.7	16.4	15.9	16.7	14.4	15.4	15.2	16.1	9.9	....	....	....	....	Haiti	263
24.8	21.1	14.1	13.8	17.4	17.3	13.9	17.4	21.0	19.1	23.0	24.7	26.0	28.9	26.0	Honduras	268
15.9	20.3	20.9	22.3	23.1	25.3	18.5	22.3	25.7	28.8	28.0	27.4	28.5	34.7	....	Jamaica	343
29.6	28.4	22.9	24.0	21.8	21.2	18.5	19.3	20.4	21.4	21.9	22.4	23.3	22.0	....	Mexico	273
....	....	....	....	22.1	23.1	16.8	15.8	26.8	27.2	19.3	20.2	19.3	18.9	22.5	Netherlands Antilles	353
27.5	29.8	27.4	21.1	16.5	15.2	16.6	17.3	6.8	3.4	17.1	18.1	22.8	25.0	....	Nicaragua	278
28.8	28.8	25.6	21.4	22.9	22.0	25.0	25.1	24.4	23.8	22.9	24.8	22.9	22.9	....	Panama	283
28.9	34.3	33.6	24.3	20.6	18.4	21.4	22.0	24.2	17.9	15.7	16.7	16.4	18.6	21.5	Paraguay	288
38.2	30.6	33.9	37.9	30.2	30.3	27.3	33.6	55.9	58.2	55.3	42.7	40.1	....	....	Peru	293
68.6	66.4	46.3	36.0	35.7	....	....	....	....	....	....	....	....	....	....	St. Kitts and Nevis	361
39.3	33.4	30.7	31.2	27.2	25.0	29.3	....	....	....	....	....	....	....	....	St. Lucia	362
26.5	31.2	27.7	15.6	11.8	14.4	21.7	25.8	16.7	20.8	21.4	22.3	22.8	23.0	....	St. Vincent & Grens.	364
30.6	27.6	28.3	26.5	22.1	18.8	21.6	19.3	13.0	16.6	12.6	13.4	12.3	13.1	....	Suriname	366
17.3	15.4	14.4	14.3	12.1	11.4	11.2	14.3	13.2	11.3	11.0	13.5	13.3	14.0	13.9	Trinidad and Tobago	369
24.7	22.9	25.9	11.8	18.1	19.1	20.8	25.2	27.9	12.9	10.2	18.7	23.7	18.7	10.2	Uruguay	298
															Venezuela	299
															Memorandum Items	
25.8	31.2	29.6	24.7	24.2	23.1	23.7	24.3	24.3	24.7	25.5	27.6	28.3	25.8	....	Oil Exporting Countries	999
25.6	25.6	23.9	22.9	21.8	22.2	21.4	22.1	23.5	24.6	24.2	23.0	23.2	23.3	....	Non-Oil Developing Countries	201

Consumption as Percent of GDP

96f r

		1965	1966	1967	1968	1969	1970	1971	1972	1973	1974	1975	1976	1977	1978	1979
																Percentages
World	001	78.2	78.3	79.1	74.1	73.5	73.0	73.2	73.0	74.6	75.2	77.4	76.9	76.9	76.5	76.2
Industrial Countries	110	77.1	77.2	77.9	76.9	76.3	76.0	76.2	76.0	74.9	76.1	78.2	77.7	77.5	76.8	76.8
United States	111	79.8	80.0	81.1	81.3	80.9	82.2	81.6	80.8	79.2	80.4	81.9	81.2	80.6	79.3	79.1
Canada	156	74.7	73.9	75.5	76.3	76.2	76.6	76.6	76.6	74.5	73.4	76.3	75.7	76.3	76.5	74.5
Australia	193	73.5	72.9	74.5	74.3	73.2	73.3	73.0	72.4	71.7	72.9	75.6	75.9	76.9	77.9	75.6
Japan*	158	66.7	66.0	64.4	62.1	60.8	59.7	61.5	62.2	61.9	63.4	67.2	67.4	67.5	67.4	68.4
New Zealand	196	75.3	74.6	76.1	73.2	77.7	77.4	74.1	73.2	72.4	75.8	75.7	71.6	75.0	78.5	78.3
Austria	122	72.5	71.6	73.2	72.9	71.7	69.3	69.6	68.8	68.8	69.2	73.4	74.2	74.8	74.0	73.8
Belgium	124	77.3	77.4	76.8	77.8	76.3	73.7	74.9	75.2	75.6	75.1	78.2	78.0	79.3	79.6	81.0
Denmark	128	77.9	76.7	77.8	77.4	76.3	77.3	77.1	74.6	75.8	77.7	80.1	80.7	80.8	80.7	81.5
Finland	172	75.7	75.9	76.0	73.5	72.2	71.1	71.1	71.7	70.0	68.3	72.8	74.4	75.0	74.8	72.9
France	132	74.1	74.0	74.1	74.7	74.6	72.6	72.7	72.6	71.9	72.9	75.3	75.3	75.4	75.5	75.7
Germany	134	71.3	71.8	73.4	71.9	71.0	70.4	71.5	72.0	71.8	73.6	77.3	76.2	76.7	76.3	76.0
Greece	174	84.5	84.1	85.4	84.7	81.9	81.8	80.5	77.8	74.9	81.5	82.7	80.8	81.8	81.1	79.7
Iceland*	176	70.7	73.3	77.2	77.8	72.4	74.4	74.5	75.0	71.9	75.8	75.0	72.4	72.3	73.0	74.2
Ireland	178	85.3	85.3	83.4	84.4	83.3	83.5	83.3	80.3	79.1	85.5	82.7	82.6	81.2	80.9	83.4
Italy	136	79.2	80.1	79.7	78.7	77.9	73.3	75.3	76.3	75.8	75.0	77.2	75.4	75.3	75.3	76.0
Luxembourg	137	69.3	69.9	71.0	69.7	63.6	61.0	66.5	65.3	60.2	57.6	72.7	71.3	75.4	73.6	73.8
Netherlands	138	73.7	74.1	73.8	72.7	78.1	73.8	73.8	73.2	72.3	73.0	76.0	76.0	77.2	78.0	79.0
Norway	142	71.0	71.0	71.2	71.8	73.3	70.8	71.7	71.6	70.3	69.3	71.5	72.4	74.4	72.4	69.8
Portugal	182	80.3	80.9	78.5	80.3	80.8	80.1	78.9	76.7	77.6	86.8	92.1	88.7	86.6	82.8	81.3
Spain	184	83.1	82.8	82.7	82.1	76.4	74.1	74.5	74.0	73.7	74.7	75.4	77.6	77.1	76.4	77.4
Sweden	144	74.0	75.0	75.3	76.2	75.9	74.6	75.3	75.7	75.4	76.5	75.4	77.5	80.8	81.5	81.1
Switzerland	146	70.4	70.6	70.3	70.3	70.5	69.4	69.1	69.1	69.8	70.7	74.2	76.0	76.7	75.9	76.6
United Kingdom	112	80.9	80.9	81.7	80.9	79.5	79.5	80.2	81.2	80.8	84.0	84.3	83.0	80.4	79.9	80.1
Developing Countries	200	83.1	83.1	84.6	67.1	66.4	65.3	65.8	65.2	74.0	73.2	75.6	75.0	75.5	76.2	75.0
Africa	605	78.5	79.0	76.3	79.2	78.5	78.4	79.3	77.7	74.4	70.2	75.7	75.4	75.9	78.3	75.3
Algeria	612	82.1	82.9	76.7	74.0	73.1	70.8	72.9	68.0	69.3	57.0	64.0	61.0	64.4	62.5	59.2
Benin	638	97.7	97.6	95.5	93.8	92.1	90.5	89.1	90.7	91.6	83.4	97.0	99.1	103.6	105.7	100.3
Botswana	616	112.8	103.5	108.0	112.8	106.1	93.3	82.1	72.2	72.6	73.0	78.3	79.1	86.3	87.1	77.8
Burkina Faso	748	94.1	94.3	96.2	98.1	99.7	101.3	101.5	99.4	98.3	91.8	99.2	93.8	101.9	101.9	95.6
Burundi	618	96.4	92.9	92.9	92.9	92.9	92.9	100.7	100.2	97.0	101.7	96.9	93.9	88.2	94.0	95.5
Cameroon	622	84.5	85.8	84.5	85.9	84.3	80.9	85.6	86.7	85.1	76.6	82.1	84.6	79.4	76.0	81.4
Central African Rep.	626	89.2	93.0	98.8	95.5	97.9	96.4	93.5	94.4	92.1	91.5	92.7	88.0	87.8	....	....
Chad	628	....	....	....	96.8	96.6	96.5	96.2	95.5	89.5	91.7	97.9	91.3	93.0	....	....
Congo	634	75.7	76.4	98.6	101.3	99.0	98.1	97.4	103.4	90.5	83.3	102.6	105.0	101.5	82.4	69.5
Côte d'Ivoire	662	68.1	67.5	69.1	65.8	63.0	75.0	77.5	77.4	77.0	72.6	77.4	71.1	64.2	71.1	75.1
Ethiopia	644	89.7	89.7	88.0	87.9	88.7	88.8	90.1	89.1	86.6	87.0	93.4	91.3	94.2	98.1	96.5
Gabon	646	66.5	67.8	63.5	59.4	59.0	59.1	55.0	51.2	61.3	34.0	35.7	27.0	41.6	50.1	45.1
Gambia, The	648	86.6	90.1	88.1	105.7	90.9	93.7	104.1	....	....	....	....	101.2	91.7	99.1	95.8
Ghana	652	91.7	92.2	92.4	87.2	87.2	86.5	89.6	87.1	85.7	89.2	86.4	91.5	90.0	94.6	93.4
Kenya	664	84.5	81.3	80.6	81.5	79.7	79.8	81.3	80.1	81.4	79.1	86.5	79.1	72.9	80.0	83.3
Liberia	668	67.7	62.6	63.1	59.1	56.5	56.2	59.0	57.1	61.3	61.2	54.3	58.7	68.4	70.0	67.3
Madagascar	674	96.3	93.0	91.8	91.2	91.3	88.1	88.5	89.4	86.6	90.3	91.5	88.5	88.8	90.9	92.0
Malawi	676	98.2	96.7	95.5	97.2	94.6	86.7	90.7	87.8	87.6	83.6	83.0	82.2	79.9	79.5	79.8
Mali	678	....	....	....	....	....	....	....	....	....	....	....	79.5	77.4	83.7	86.6
Mauritania	682	....	....	....	....	....	69.0	68.3	68.5	74.9	74.3	81.1	86.9	92.0	107.5	102.6
Mauritius	684	83.7	88.4	87.8	89.5	80.8	85.9	83.1	80.2	73.3	63.6	67.9	67.4	80.7	81.6	80.5
Morocco	686	86.2	88.3	86.9	82.5	88.8	87.3	86.6	87.5	85.8	78.8	84.4	89.9	84.5	86.6	87.1
Mozambique	688	....	....	....	....	....	....	....	....	....	....	....	....	....	....	....
Niger	692	89.6	93.6	94.1	95.3	100.3	97.6	94.4	95.5	93.0	103.8	89.9	83.6	82.3	83.1	79.4
Nigeria	694	83.7	84.5	87.0	88.1	86.2	84.0	80.6	78.7	70.4	65.2	73.1	68.5	69.9	81.3	71.4
Rwanda	714	....	....	....	61.6	58.2	56.4	57.0	57.4	54.2	57.5	94.7	91.0	88.4	92.4	89.8
Senegal	722	92.2	91.2	92.0	95.6	94.7	88.7	90.8	87.3	91.3	84.1	87.7	91.6	90.6	103.3	98.3
Seychelles	718	....	....	....	....	....	....	....	....	....	....	....	77.1	64.0	57.9	73.0
Sierra Leone	724	90.8	88.7	91.2	91.2	84.5	82.5	85.8	89.7	86.8	85.6	94.3	96.7	94.3	93.6	94.8
Somalia	726	....	....	....	....	....	90.9	94.6	89.8	114.9	118.7	88.1	83.2	76.9	86.6	92.3
South Africa	199	71.2	71.6	69.3	70.7	70.7	73.2	75.3	73.6	69.5	67.2	70.8	71.9	72.0	69.6	67.2
Sudan	732	89.5	89.6	87.8	89.0	89.4	82.4	82.3	76.3	62.3	67.9	74.6	90.0	94.0	92.6	100.2
Swaziland	734	....	....	67.0	68.9	76.8	73.2	67.7	74.6	78.1	90.4	86.5	87.7	76.4	75.8	92.9
Tanzania	738	83.1	85.4	82.1	83.3	82.5	82.9	82.4	83.4	85.8	91.6	91.7	79.3	77.2	90.0	86.7
Togo	742	82.6	85.3	86.7	86.9	85.1	87.9	85.4	87.8	86.5	64.0	89.5	82.9	79.8	80.6	76.7
Tunisia	744	85.5	84.6	84.7	79.9	81.7	84.8	82.0	79.6	81.7	76.6	73.5	76.2	77.9	79.1	75.5
Uganda	746	....	....	....	....	....	....	....	....	....	....	....	....	....	....	....
Zaïre	636	85.2	84.8	78.9	73.4	70.5	72.4	76.0	79.0	75.7	76.2	87.2	92.5	91.5	95.9	76.9
Zambia	754	60.1	56.9	63.0	60.7	48.6	56.8	64.8	63.1	55.0	54.1	79.0	71.1	77.9	79.5	76.9
Zimbabwe	698	68.7	81.1	77.5	81.6	77.3	77.4	78.6	76.5	75.9	75.7	75.7	77.2	78.5	84.7	87.5
Asia	505	88.0	90.6	90.4	87.5	85.9	84.7	84.6	84.3	78.9	81.3	81.6	79.0	78.7	77.7	77.4
Bhutan	514	....	....	....	....	....	....	....	....	....	....	....	....	....	....	....
Fiji	819	83.8	81.0	78.2	80.9	82.9	78.9	84.0	83.6	89.8	86.3	80.0	83.2	78.4	81.7	77.9
India	534	86.8	88.9	89.9	85.8	84.7	84.3	85.5	85.1	78.4	85.7	82.7	80.5	81.1	81.5	81.2
Indonesia	536	93.6	104.8	100.1	95.9	94.1	89.4	86.4	83.6	81.5	75.0	79.1	77.9	76.5	72.6	72.6
Korea	542	93.5	89.3	90.2	86.1	82.1	84.6	85.3	83.1	76.7	79.4	81.9	76.8	73.0	71.2	71.8
Malaysia	548	79.9	80.4	81.3	81.0	75.5	78.0	77.8	79.8	70.7	71.3	76.2	67.7	68.6	67.8	62.2
Maldives	556	....	....	....	....	....	....	....	....	....	....	....	....	....	....	....
Nepal	558	....	....	....	....	....	....	....	....	....	....	90.0	88.3	86.5	87.1	88.4
Pakistan	564	87.7	87.5	86.6	87.0	86.9	86.9	87.1	87.3	86.5	90.4	92.6	89.2	89.2	91.2	92.9
Papua New Guinea	853	96.3	100.0	101.7	99.3	100.2	96.1	91.7	95.2	83.4	68.8	84.6	89.7	80.0	81.5	78.0
Philippines	566	85.4	85.1	83.9	83.1	82.2	77.9	79.5	80.6	75.3	76.5	76.1	74.1	75.8	76.0	75.8
Singapore	576	89.6	87.3	86.4	84.1	79.7	79.5	79.0	74.3	73.1	71.4	71.4	69.3	68.5	67.9	64.7
Solomon Islands	813	....	....	....	....	....	101.1	96.8	92.0	....	....	....	....	....	....	....
Sri Lanka	524	87.1	89.1	87.6	87.1	87.0	84.2	84.9	84.3	87.5	91.8	91.9	86.1	81.9	84.7	86.2
Thailand	578	79.4	74.9	79.0	80.2	78.2	81.3	79.8	80.1	76.8	77.4	80.0	79.6	78.0	75.7	77.1
Tonga	866	....	....	....	....	....	....	....	....	....	....	....	101.9	109.9	103.0	108.3	112.7
Vanuatu	846	....	....	....	....	....	....	....	....	....	....	....	....	....	....	....

Consumption as Percent of GDP

1980	1981	1982	1983	1984	1985	1986	1987	1988	1989	1990	1991	1992	1993	1994		
Percentages																
76.8	**77.5**	**78.9**	**79.0**	**78.2**	**78.1**	**78.8**	**78.2**	**77.4**	**76.6**	**77.3**	**78.6**	**78.5**	**78.9**	....	**World**	001
77.8	**77.9**	**79.4**	**79.8**	**78.7**	**79.2**	**79.4**	**79.6**	**78.8**	**78.4**	**78.8**	**79.5**	**79.9**	**80.1**	79.5	**Industrial Countries**	110
80.6	79.6	82.3	83.1	81.5	82.8	83.7	84.2	83.8	83.3	84.3	85.0	84.9	84.7	83.7	United States	111
74.8	74.4	77.2	77.9	76.6	77.4	78.6	77.7	76.6	77.3	79.1	82.3	83.0	82.6	80.5	Canada	156
76.4	76.9	78.8	80.0	77.1	78.0	78.7	76.4	75.0	74.6	76.9	80.1	81.1	80.1	79.1	Australia	193
68.7	68.1	69.3	70.2	69.2	68.5	68.2	68.2	67.1	66.8	66.5	65.7	66.5	67.7	69.0	Japan*	158
79.3	77.3	77.9	75.8	75.4	76.9	76.1	76.1	76.7	77.3	79.5	79.9	77.9	75.4	....	New Zealand	196
73.5	75.0	75.4	76.7	76.0	76.4	75.6	75.5	74.6	74.0	73.2	73.3	73.5	74.3	74.0	Austria	122
80.7	83.8	83.6	82.7	81.9	82.6	81.0	80.8	78.3	77.3	77.0	77.8	77.3	77.2	....	Belgium	124
82.5	83.8	83.3	82.0	80.3	80.1	78.9	79.2	78.9	78.3	77.3	77.5	77.8	78.8	78.9	Denmark	128
72.1	72.7	73.9	74.4	73.5	74.7	75.2	75.4	73.6	72.2	73.4	81.8	81.9	80.0	77.4	Finland	172
77.0	79.1	80.0	80.3	80.4	80.5	79.3	79.7	78.5	77.6	77.6	78.1	78.9	80.7	79.9	France	132
77.2	78.3	78.3	77.7	77.3	76.8	75.2	75.6	74.8	73.7	72.6	72.3	72.5	73.5	72.7	Germany	134
80.9	85.4	85.7	85.5	84.2	85.9	86.8	89.0	88.2	90.6	92.4	90.5	91.7	91.6	....	Greece	174
73.7	75.7	77.8	77.8	79.2	81.4	79.4	82.5	82.5	81.3	80.7	82.5	82.8	81.2	79.6	Iceland*	176
85.7	85.8	79.6	79.2	77.7	78.3	79.6	77.9	76.6	75.1	73.4	74.8	74.8	71.9	....	Ireland	178
77.2	78.5	79.1	79.1	78.9	79.4	78.7	79.3	79.1	79.3	79.4	79.9	80.8	....	....	Italy	136
75.4	78.3	76.7	75.4	73.5	74.5	72.2	76.0	73.5	70.1	71.9	74.3	73.4	....	....	Luxembourg	137
79.0	78.2	77.8	77.8	75.7	75.2	74.9	76.7	74.7	73.5	73.2	73.8	75.0	75.5	74.8	Netherlands	138
66.2	66.5	67.8	67.4	65.2	67.6	74.1	73.8	73.7	71.3	71.9	72.4	74.3	73.8	73.9	Norway	142
82.5	82.8	83.2	85.6	88.4	86.6	83.3	83.2	84.3	82.4	82.5	84.0	84.4	....	....	Portugal	182
79.1	80.2	79.7	79.4	78.2	78.8	77.9	78.3	77.5	78.1	78.0	78.6	80.1	80.7	80.2	Spain	184
80.8	82.2	83.0	80.7	78.7	78.8	78.6	78.9	78.2	77.5	78.3	80.5	81.7	82.8	81.4	Sweden	144
76.3	75.5	75.5	76.1	76.2	75.2	72.8	71.9	71.7	70.5	70.2	71.6	73.0	73.5	72.3	Switzerland	146
81.4	82.7	82.8	83.0	82.9	81.9	83.8	83.2	83.4	83.2	83.6	85.0	86.0	86.2	85.5	United Kingdom	112
74.7	**76.9**	**77.9**	**77.5**	**77.4**	**76.3**	**77.9**	**75.9**	**75.1**	**73.5**	**74.6**	**77.1**	**76.0**	**76.5**	....	**Developing Countries**	200
75.5	**78.4**	**79.9**	**78.9**	**78.9**	**78.1**	**80.4**	**79.6**	**80.5**	**78.2**	**77.8**	**80.1**	**82.6**	**82.9**	....	**Africa**	605
56.9	59.3	60.8	60.3	62.6	63.6	70.6	68.1	68.4	70.6	72.8	65.2	70.0	72.9	....	Algeria	612
98.4	100.1	93.0	99.3	91.6	89.1	95.2	96.6	95.5	94.5	93.6	94.5	....	....	....	Benin	638
72.3	75.8	84.0	75.0	70.3	67.1	59.2	60.9	57.1	44.7	....	....	....	....	....	Botswana	616
102.5	104.8	107.8	106.7	98.6	103.3	....	....	....	....	....	....	....	....	....	Burkina Faso	748
98.0	95.9	97.9	95.2	94.3	93.6	91.3	94.4	95.3	95.8	102.5	101.1	102.4	106.6	103.2	Burundi	618
82.7	76.9	79.6	75.1	72.4	72.2	76.3	82.6	77.7	77.6	83.0	....	....	....	....	Cameroon	622
....	....	....	111.9	132.2	148.0	116.3	115.6	....	....	....	....	....	....	....	Central African Rep.	626
															Chad	628
58.6	54.2	53.0	54.7	53.6	58.0	84.4	77.1	81.2	72.9	....	....	....	....	....	Congo	634
79.6	81.2	79.7	80.7	74.8	72.7	78.6	83.9	84.7	88.1	88.7	89.5	....	....	....	Côte d'Ivoire	662
95.2	95.1	96.1	94.8	92.6	97.5	91.9	93.0	88.1	91.6	92.4	96.6	96.9	96.4	98.2	Ethiopia	644
....	....	....	....	49.1	51.2	51.5	70.0	....	....	....	....	....	....	....	Gabon	646
102.6	96.6	....	....	....	....	....	....	....	....	....	....	....	....	....	Gambia, The	648
95.1	96.1	96.3	96.7	93.4	92.4	92.3	91.8	89.3	94.0	96.4	95.3	97.9	94.1	....	Ghana	652
81.4	80.6	81.9	79.6	80.6	75.4	78.2	80.8	80.3	82.7	80.9	80.0	82.4	79.0	....	Kenya	664
66.8	85.8	78.7	81.5	81.5	80.1	75.5	78.2	74.6	69.1	....	....	....	....	....	Liberia	668
93.3	93.0	95.2	93.3	94.2	98.7	93.1	94.1	91.6	90.0	94.0	100.8	97.2	97.7	97.6	Madagascar	674
82.1	82.5	82.7	80.4	85.2	87.1	89.9	87.0	90.8	95.3	93.4	92.1	98.1	98.2	....	Malawi	676
86.2	92.6	99.1	104.9	102.2	107.7	102.2	93.0	96.2	92.4	94.6	98.3	....	....	....	Mali	678
100.2	115.2	104.6	98.4	94.1	....	....	....	....	....	....	....	....	....	....	Mauritania	682
89.5	85.2	84.9	82.7	81.3	78.4	71.5	72.6	74.5	76.8	77.0	75.9	74.8	75.8	77.1	Mauritius	684
87.1	89.1	86.7	86.7	87.8	85.2	86.8	87.1	79.0	81.3	80.2	82.0	81.2	....	....	Morocco	686
100.0	100.0	102.5	105.3	100.0	95.5	95.9	93.1	94.6	94.6	90.8	87.5	87.3	87.0	....	Mozambique	688
81.3	80.0	85.1	88.8	96.2	93.9	92.1	92.0	91.3	90.9	94.1	96.3	....	....	....	Niger	692
72.3	81.1	83.4	85.7	86.3	84.9	87.2	78.7	84.2	66.2	60.6	72.5	77.2	85.7	89.0	Nigeria	694
95.8	98.7	94.8	95.6	91.2	91.7	90.9	92.4	94.7	95.1	95.6	101.8	101.9	....	....	Rwanda	714
102.7	104.9	97.2	93.2	93.8	94.3	93.9	93.2	93.2	93.6	91.4	89.4	....	....	....	Senegal	722
72.9	84.8	96.7	101.0	91.8	92.8	92.9	91.5	86.8	83.9	77.6	78.9	81.0	....	....	Seychelles	718
99.1	97.6	98.6	96.7	89.1	99.6	85.4	82.8	82.6	80.7	84.8	86.3	77.6	81.5	....	Sierra Leone	724
103.0	102.2	105.2	103.9	100.7	101.1	98.8	99.9	....	....	....	....	....	....	....	Somalia	726
64.6	67.5	70.7	71.8	72.4	70.8	72.5	74.1	74.3	74.2	76.9	78.7	81.5	80.8	80.3	South Africa	199
104.1	104.2	....	....	....	....	95.8	89.2	88.7	89.9	91.9	90.4	....	....	....	Sudan	732
92.6	98.6	98.0	101.1	104.6	103.5	83.1	73.3	71.0	74.0	69.6	79.7	....	....	....	Swaziland	734
90.2	83.8	86.4	91.6	92.8	92.9	94.5	88.5	104.8	97.3	88.5	95.6	95.4	20.4	....	Tanzania	738
78.4	85.0	87.8	86.2	85.7	82.8	83.1	84.9	....	....	....	....	....	....	....	Togo	742
76.4	76.1	78.9	79.3	79.7	79.6	83.8	80.4	80.2	80.6	80.0	78.6	76.5	77.3	77.4	Tunisia	744
....	....	....	....	96.0	99.3	101.1	101.5	105.5	104.2	80.6	100.8	101.9	98.3	....	Uganda	746
89.4	90.9	90.6	89.1	87.7	83.6	85.6	88.7	87.9	85.0	83.0	93.1	90.5	....	....	Zaïre	636
80.7	93.2	92.1	87.4	81.5	84.6	76.5	82.0	81.3	96.2	82.2	68.4	88.9	90.5	....	Zambia	754
84.2	84.2	84.8	87.2	80.5	79.0	77.3	77.5	77.6	77.1	....	....	....	....	....	Zimbabwe	698
77.9	**76.6**	**77.7**	**77.1**	**76.4**	**76.5**	**76.4**	**73.9**	**72.1**	**71.0**	**70.7**	**70.7**	**69.6**	**70.9**	....	**Asia**	505
92.1	93.0	90.7	91.6	92.6	86.4	86.2	81.9	81.3	79.0	77.8	78.3	78.3	....	....	Bhutan	514
74.4	78.9	79.8	85.8	81.5	82.8	77.0	82.9	85.5	81.0	83.4	86.6	85.4	86.7	....	Fiji	819
82.6	80.8	80.5	80.5	80.3	78.6	79.6	79.0	77.0	74.9	73.2	73.2	70.9	72.6	....	India	534
70.8	66.7	72.3	71.0	70.3	70.2	72.7	67.1	66.0	62.5	63.3	64.1	61.8	64.7	64.7	Indonesia	536
76.2	76.1	75.0	71.4	69.0	68.6	65.2	62.3	60.6	63.5	63.8	63.6	64.8	64.6	64.5	Korea	542
67.1	71.2	71.4	67.9	64.5	67.3	67.9	62.7	63.7	65.2	66.6	67.9	64.5	64.1	63.1	Malaysia	548
95.4	104.8	98.9	98.8	81.1	101.4	98.8	89.7	82.9	91.9	89.5	....	....	....	....	Maldives	556
88.9	89.1	90.1	91.4	90.1	86.6	89.4	88.5	90.1	88.6	92.7	90.5	89.2	88.3	....	Nepal	558
92.2	90.7	91.7	91.5	92.3	93.7	89.1	86.1	87.6	87.4	86.5	82.6	83.0	85.2	84.4	Pakistan	564
86.4	93.6	91.5	87.8	88.1	90.4	84.4	84.8	81.5	88.9	83.9	82.5	80.3	72.2	....	Papua New Guinea	853
73.4	73.2	74.7	72.6	76.1	81.2	81.0	79.0	78.9	79.7	81.3	83.4	85.1	86.2	84.6	Philippines	566
61.2	58.3	57.7	55.0	54.7	59.4	60.7	60.0	57.5	55.6	54.0	53.3	52.4	52.1	....	Singapore	576
....	....	....	....	78.5	92.3	96.4	99.5	105.9	112.7	....	....	....	....	....	Solomon Islands	813
88.8	88.3	88.1	86.2	80.1	88.1	88.0	87.2	88.0	87.8	85.7	87.2	85.0	84.0	84.8	Sri Lanka	524
77.7	78.0	76.7	78.0	76.8	75.7	74.1	71.4	66.8	65.0	65.3	64.8	65.2	....	....	Thailand	578
95.2	112.2	111.1	118.0	....	....	....	....	....	....	....	....	....	....	....	Tonga	866
....	....	....	89.8	89.8	94.1	95.3	91.4	93.5	94.3	91.2	89.4	86.0	80.7	....	Vanuatu	846

Consumption as Percent of GDP

96f r

Percentages

		1965	1966	1967	1968	1969	1970	1971	1972	1973	1974	1975	1976	1977	1978	1979
Europe	170	80.7	85.1	84.9	86.2	72.9	71.9	70.3	69.5	69.5	70.2	71.3	70.7	72.6	71.0	72.0
Cyprus	423	77.5	84.3	83.6	84.6	83.4	85.2	84.1	83.7	83.3	93.6	98.7	92.0	89.7	87.4	81.0
Czech Republic	935	....	....	....	....	....	....	....	....	....	....	....	....	....	....	....
Czechoslovakia	934	....	....	....	....	72.8	70.7	71.8	72.1	73.1	72.5	72.1	73.6	76.5	76.2	75.2
Hungary	944	....	....	....	....	....	68.7	68.6	67.0	65.8	68.7	69.7	68.2	67.3	67.9	69.3
Malta	181	91.7	87.8	89.6	91.7	94.8	97.3	96.6	98.0	97.6	101.7	90.0	84.2	88.4	83.8	79.7
Poland	964	....	....	73.4	71.9	73.6	73.2	69.5	68.2	68.3	68.8	70.9	69.4	71.7	71.5	73.7
Romania	968	....	....	....	....	....	....	....	....	....	....	....	....	....	....	....
Turkey	186	....	....	....	....	....	....	....	....	....	....	....	....	....	....	....
Yugoslavia, SFR	188	58.2	59.2	64.5	65.7	64.5	64.2	62.6	64.5	63.8	62.9	64.6	65.2	64.1	63.6	62.9
Middle East	405	76.3	77.8	79.8	72.0	70.6	74.9	70.8	68.1	63.5	59.4	64.8	64.2	67.4	69.9	64.3
Egypt	469	85.8	85.9	85.5	91.8	90.9	93.1	91.8	92.0	91.7	94.6	92.0	86.6	80.6	83.0	85.6
Iran, I.R. of	429	80.8	82.3	79.7	77.0	69.6	82.1	81.1	76.2	66.1	58.9	64.0	61.2	64.4	72.4	71.2
Iraq	433	69.7	69.6	70.2	68.0	68.4	68.5	65.2	....	....	....	75.1	74.7	81.0	58.3	40.5
Israel	436	85.3	88.7	96.9	94.8	95.1	96.0	90.7	86.5	98.6	97.8	102.6	103.3	96.6	99.4	97.0
Jordan	439	104.3	135.4	92.8	96.7	99.1	99.9	98.2	97.6	99.2	99.0	98.1	94.0	91.2	92.1	106.3
Kuwait	443	38.9	41.0	43.1	46.4	46.3	52.1	42.9	42.8	40.8	22.1	32.8	38.0	48.1	49.1	36.4
Lebanon	446	98.4	98.1	97.3	96.1	96.6	96.8	96.3	96.1	97.5	99.2	100.9	102.7	112.6	109.5	109.6
Libya	672	50.2	50.2	51.2	44.2	47.1	50.8	48.4	50.2	52.0	46.1	59.2	51.4	50.0	59.0	49.7
Oman	449	....	....	57.5	32.0	28.0	32.2	37.9	54.5	61.2	43.4	47.5	47.8	54.4	61.5	53.7
Qatar	453	....	....	....	....	....	....	....	....	....	....	....	....	....	....	....
Saudi Arabia	456	43.9	41.4	50.8	50.0	52.5	53.3	39.6	32.6	19.8	24.3	32.1	36.8	45.1	56.3	46.6
Syrian Arab Rep.	463	90.0	93.3	92.6	90.1	89.6	89.9	90.1	85.4	91.3	84.8	87.5	83.4	87.0	88.9	90.7
United Arab Emirates	466	....	....	....	....	....	....	....	....	27.3	24.6	15.8	24.1	30.0	34.1	31.0
Yemen Arab Rep.	473	....	....	....	....	125.9	107.3	107.3	110.6	107.9	110.3	113.1	128.3	108.2	122.7	124.7
Western Hemisphere	205	79.7	75.3	81.3	81.8	81.0	78.0	78.9	78.2	75.8	75.0	76.5	77.5	77.1	77.6	77.7
Antigua and Barbuda	311	....	....	....	....	....	....	....	....	....	....	....	....	....	....	94.3
Argentina	213	75.0	60.0	83.3	85.7	87.5	77.8	76.9	76.2	80.0	79.6	74.1	68.5	69.7	72.2	77.2
Bahamas, The	313	....	....	....	....	....	....	....	....	72.6	78.1	73.3	73.8	66.0	63.2	58.9
Barbados	316	....	....	....	....	....	....	....	....	95.6	96.4	90.6	85.9	91.3	102.7	98.8	87.1
Belize	339	....	....	....	....	....	....	....	....	83.0	75.0	73.8	86.8	86.7	82.6	84.5
Bolivia	218	88.1	89.0	89.2	87.9	85.6	83.1	85.6	82.9	80.2	77.1	81.2	81.1	82.0	82.7	82.4
Brazil	223	79.7	79.6	83.4	84.2	80.6	75.7	76.7	75.0	69.8	71.7	73.8	79.0	78.5	78.4	80.6
Chile	228	84.2	82.5	82.5	82.9	82.5	82.9	86.5	91.3	93.9	78.2	88.9	82.9	87.4	85.5	85.0
Colombia	233	81.3	82.5	81.0	80.1	80.7	81.0	84.6	81.4	79.5	79.6	81.2	79.3	77.6	78.9	80.1
Costa Rica	238	91.0	86.8	87.0	86.6	85.3	86.2	86.0	84.3	82.1	88.2	84.8	82.3	81.2	84.4	85.0
Dominica	321	....	....	....	....	....	....	....	....	....	....	102.7	97.4	91.9	99.5	100.8	129.4
Dominican Republic	243	93.4	90.6	89.7	91.6	86.5	88.2	89.2	81.9	80.1	82.9	75.5	81.9	82.4	83.0	81.0
Ecuador	248	89.4	87.1	86.5	87.6	88.5	86.4	86.3	83.6	77.3	72.4	79.7	77.6	76.5	77.2	74.1
El Salvador	253	87.0	88.1	88.4	90.6	89.9	86.5	86.4	84.9	84.7	85.6	84.5	81.7	75.9	85.4	82.1
Grenada	328	....	....	....	....	....	....	....	....	....	86.7	89.2	94.1	91.1	94.0	103.4	102.1
Guatemala	258	89.5	89.4	90.4	86.6	88.2	86.4	87.0	87.5	85.6	84.7	85.7	84.6	81.8	84.2	85.8
Guyana	336	80.1	80.9	77.0	76.8	76.7	77.5	78.0	80.1	89.7	70.7	67.0	87.5	86.5	79.4	79.3
Haiti	263	84.2	84.7	....	105.3	104.9	104.7	104.3	102.8	96.3	92.1	92.4	93.3	93.8	92.7	93.7
Honduras	268	84.2	84.7	81.7	82.0	83.2	85.7	84.9	84.1	82.7	86.2	90.4	85.8	81.8	77.8	78.3
Jamaica	343	84.7	83.5	83.4	82.3	71.6	72.6	75.0	81.0	78.1	85.9	84.6	90.6	89.3	83.7	82.4
Mexico	273	82.9	81.2	81.2	80.7	79.7	79.2	80.8	80.4	79.7	79.0	79.0	79.1	77.1	77.0	75.3
Netherlands Antilles	353	88.6	85.7	86.8	84.6	....	....	....	....	79.9	77.7	....	....	....	....	....
Nicaragua	278	82.4	84.2	87.8	86.2	84.1	84.1	84.8	81.3	85.8	82.3	88.0	80.3	79.1	83.6	92.1
Panama	283	84.5	80.6	79.8	76.8	77.5	75.5	73.4	73.1	70.4	75.8	76.5	75.4	79.9	78.1	80.7
Paraguay	288	85.7	87.1	86.9	88.6	88.6	86.5	88.0	85.0	80.3	80.7	80.4	78.7	78.3	76.5	76.9
Peru	293	82.8	81.5	83.0	82.9	85.9	82.7	84.3	84.3	85.0	86.0	90.1	87.8	88.6	82.2	66.8
St. Kitts and Nevis	361	....	....	....	....	....	....	....	....	....	119.0	105.4	93.4	85.5	78.3	84.2	89.5
St. Lucia	362	....	....	....	....	....	....	....	....	....	....	....	97.2	88.8	83.8	99.4	104.4
St. Vincent & Grens.	364	....	....	....	....	....	....	....	....	....	....	....	103.7	100.4	109.3	96.4	110.7
Suriname	366	79.2	67.7	77.4	74.2	75.1	76.7	74.6	72.8	73.8	69.1	68.8	70.7	69.5	69.9	77.5
Trinidad and Tobago	369	78.9	71.3	73.9	70.8	78.6	73.0	71.2	75.3	68.3	53.7	54.9	59.7	60.7	65.4	65.2
Uruguay	298	82.5	82.6	85.0	87.1	88.0	89.9	88.7	87.8	86.2	91.1	90.1	86.0	87.7	86.5	87.2
Venezuela	299	69.5	70.5	70.2	64.3	66.8	65.9	64.1	65.5	61.1	51.3	61.2	64.2	66.2	70.3	66.5
Memorandum Items																
Oil Exporting Countries	999	81.4	85.9	82.6	74.0	72.7	73.6	70.4	67.8	63.1	56.1	63.0	62.2	65.1	67.0	61.2
Non-Oil Developing Countries	201	83.6	82.5	85.1	99.7	98.5	97.4	97.2	95.9	60.9	61.8	62.7	62.3	62.1	78.6	78.6

*GNP used in calculation

Consumption as Percent of GDP

1980	1981	1982	1983	1984	1985	1986	1987	1988	1989	1990	1991	1992	1993	1994		96f r
Percentages																
69.2	**77.0**	**71.1**	**71.9**	**71.3**	**67.3**	**67.8**	**67.3**	**68.3**	**68.8**	**72.7**	**76.6**	**76.0**	....	....	**Europe**	170
80.5	80.1	80.9	82.5	77.8	77.9	75.3	73.3	74.4	72.7	72.6	79.0	80.0	....	....	Cyprus	423
....	....	....	....	....	....	....	....	....	....	....	....	....	79.8	79.9	Czech Republic	935
60.3	77.6	76.9	77.7	77.0	62.8	63.6	64.6	64.9	65.7	67.4	65.9	....	....	....	Czechoslovakia	934
71.5	71.4	70.7	71.6	71.1	72.9	74.5	73.8	72.3	70.6	72.3	82.1	81.7	85.3	....	Hungary	944
80.8	81.3	84.6	85.0	86.3	87.7	84.6	81.8	81.3	81.3	80.3	79.5	79.5	80.8	....	Malta	181
76.1	83.6	70.9	73.6	72.6	70.8	70.2	68.9	65.3	57.3	64.0	78.1	76.8	....	....	Poland	964
63.0	66.0	64.4	60.3	60.5	60.2	59.3	61.2	62.1	70.5	79.2	75.9	76.6	....	....	Romania	968
....	....	....	....	....	....	....	76.4	73.0	77.4	79.7	80.3	79.7	79.7	....	Turkey	186
61.9	60.7	60.5	59.9	59.0	58.8	59.5	58.8	58.9	53.8	....	....	....	....	....	Yugoslavia, SFR	188
63.9	**74.0**	**79.9**	**79.2**	**79.5**	**81.2**	**84.3**	**82.3**	**84.0**	**80.0**	**78.5**	**89.7**	**78.9**	**76.6**		**Middle East**	405
87.7	81.6	81.3	78.7	83.4	82.2	79.9	84.0	84.7	83.1	83.0	83.9	83.0	83.3	84.9	Egypt	469
74.0	79.0	74.5	74.2	75.1	76.5	78.9	74.9	81.2	78.2	76.8	73.9	72.4	69.6	....	Iran, I.R. of	429
38.0	68.2	82.2	93.0	85.8	80.9	90.6	83.1	81.7	89.0	....	....	....	....	....	Iraq	433
92.8	96.3	95.8	94.3	92.7	94.9	93.5	98.4	95.0	92.4	92.2	90.2	89.1	92.0	....	Israel	436
104.3	107.2	113.8	112.2	110.2	115.2	105.6	102.2	98.5	95.0	99.0	97.4	98.5	98.8	97.1	Jordan	439
41.1	51.5	73.0	65.4	63.5	70.2	79.7	67.0	78.5	76.7	95.5	294.1	95.4	69.6	....	Kuwait	443
114.1	117.3	164.2	....	....	....	....	....	....	....	....	....	....	....	....	Lebanon	446
44.4	62.6	71.8	....	....	....	....	....	....	....	....	....	....	....	....	Libya	672
52.6	50.1	57.7	57.7	57.3	59.8	69.6	61.4	73.0	69.3	64.8	73.5	72.7	....	....	Oman	449
35.3	43.0	47.5	59.2	59.8	60.3	75.1	76.4	....	....	....	....	....	....	....	Qatar	453
37.8	48.6	67.0	74.9	79.8	87.0	90.9	88.3	83.1	77.7	70.4	75.5	73.1	....	....	Saudi Arabia	456
89.7	94.1	87.4	89.5	87.6	89.4	88.5	95.1	95.3	83.8	83.1	89.7	88.2	88.3	....	Syrian Arab Rep.	463
28.2	38.3	43.4	45.2	44.4	48.1	61.8	59.1	65.7	61.4	54.0	58.3	63.2	....	....	United Arab Emirates	466
125.5	115.8	117.6	119.2	114.0	112.9	108.9	109.9	....	....	....	....	....	....	....	Yemen Arab Rep.	473
76.9	**77.4**	**78.4**	**78.6**	**78.8**	**76.1**	**78.7**	**76.2**	**75.9**	**73.9**	**77.4**	**79.6**	**80.1**	**80.5**	....	**Western Hemisphere**	205
99.1	97.4	96.8	92.5	93.6	....	....	....	....	....	....	....	....	....	....	Antigua and Barbuda	311
76.2	77.8	75.7	75.8	77.2	76.9	80.7	80.1	78.0	78.0	80.3	83.6	84.8	83.4	82.4	Argentina	213
57.8	56.7	62.1	68.8	69.2	64.2	63.5	63.6	58.0	90.2	87.9	91.4	88.8	....	....	Bahamas, The	313
77.4	81.7	80.0	78.9	79.0	76.7	81.7	83.5	82.0	80.9	83.8	85.6	82.8	83.9	....	Barbados	316
87.8	95.9	101.8	95.7	84.2	91.2	82.2	80.2	80.5	79.1	69.2	79.6	78.3	77.8	....	Belize	339
79.9	80.0	77.5	77.7	84.4	70.9	77.5	82.4	82.3	81.4	82.0	82.9	....	....	....	Bolivia	218
78.5	77.7	81.0	83.2	82.3	75.3	78.2	74.2	72.0	66.5	75.6	78.3	76.9	77.4	....	Brazil	223
83.2	87.6	90.6	87.5	87.4	80.4	78.1	74.9	70.3	70.0	70.3	71.5	71.8	73.5	71.8	Chile	228
80.3	82.9	83.8	82.9	81.6	79.7	75.2	76.0	75.6	75.8	75.7	76.6	80.9	83.5	....	Colombia	233
83.8	75.9	72.4	76.6	76.9	75.9	73.9	77.0	77.3	77.3	79.6	75.8	76.0	77.4	77.1	Costa Rica	238
120.7	112.3	97.4	91.4	95.9	94.9	82.9	87.4	85.7	92.2	88.0	89.1	88.1	92.0	....	Dominica	321
84.6	80.6	84.9	85.5	84.8	85.5	81.8	80.6	73.6	78.0	82.7	83.6	86.8	81.7	80.2	Dominican Republic	243
74.1	75.8	77.1	78.4	76.3	75.9	79.0	83.6	80.6	81.1	77.1	76.2	75.0	78.3	81.0	Ecuador	248
85.8	92.7	92.5	93.4	94.8	96.7	91.1	94.7	93.7	95.1	98.8	97.9	97.8	95.9	96.2	El Salvador	253
100.4	92.1	101.2	94.8	99.1	99.0	97.7	91.7	89.8	87.1	86.1	88.0	86.3	....	....	Grenada	328
86.9	89.5	89.8	90.5	90.6	90.1	88.2	92.5	92.1	91.7	90.4	89.7	91.5	91.6	....	Guatemala	258
81.7	87.2	90.7	93.1	87.0	89.4	84.5	79.4	83.2	74.4	74.5	67.0	63.9	64.5	....	Guyana	336
98.8	106.4	97.5	96.9	95.6	94.3	93.7	93.6	95.2	94.0	93.1	86.8	96.2	95.7	90.3	Haiti	263
83.0	85.0	87.3	89.2	88.9	87.4	87.9	85.5	81.6	84.2	79.8	78.4	78.1	76.9	77.2	Honduras	268
86.2	90.0	90.7	89.8	83.6	84.9	79.4	77.4	78.1	81.8	76.1	81.0	69.2	73.7	....	Jamaica	343
75.1	75.1	72.1	69.7	72.3	73.7	77.6	74.6	78.0	78.8	79.3	80.8	82.3	82.3	....	Mexico	273
....	....	....	....	....	....	....	....	....	....	....	....	....	....	....	Netherlands Antilles	353
102.5	96.1	91.5	88.3	90.9	84.0	91.3	86.2	113.5	105.0	99.2	109.7	113.8	107.1	104.9	Nicaragua	278
73.9	73.3	74.5	76.0	82.9	82.1	77.8	78.2	78.6	86.1	78.7	78.9	76.7	76.1	....	Panama	283
77.5	78.0	82.0	85.6	83.3	83.0	84.9	82.6	75.0	72.5	83.7	84.9	85.2	82.7	....	Paraguay	288
68.2	69.5	69.5	75.5	75.4	75.1	80.0	79.7	78.6	80.5	83.0	84.8	86.4	84.4	81.8	Peru	293
92.1	98.9	96.7	107.3	97.8	92.2	89.4	87.9	70.1	70.8	77.5	77.0	72.6	....	....	St. Kitts and Nevis	361
91.0	97.8	107.7	101.7	104.6	....	....	....	....	....	....	....	....	....	....	St. Lucia	362
111.7	99.3	101.8	99.5	86.0	77.5	77.2	85.2	76.8	94.0	85.0	97.3	87.8	....	....	St. Vincent & Grens.	364
78.9	82.8	87.7	99.1	93.6	88.7	78.4	68.8	78.4	69.3	77.8	81.4	77.6	77.6	....	Suriname	366
57.9	62.7	78.9	82.8	77.4	77.1	85.5	79.3	82.1	75.5	70.5	78.3	76.8	77.4	....	Trinidad and Tobago	369
88.3	88.6	88.7	83.7	82.7	83.0	82.9	83.3	82.2	82.4	83.0	83.3	85.8	86.5	87.0	Uruguay	298
67.1	71.2	77.2	77.4	73.8	74.8	79.6	76.7	78.8	75.5	70.5	76.2	78.8	81.9	80.0	Venezuela	299
															Memorandum Items	
60.5	67.4	73.2	73.3	73.1	74.1	78.7	73.7	74.3	69.6	68.1	75.3	70.2	72.1	....	**Oil Exporting Countries**	999
78.4	79.5	79.3	79.0	78.8	77.3	77.9	76.8	75.6	74.7	76.4	77.8	77.6	77.8	....	**Non-Oil Developing Countries**	201

Commodity Prices

z

		1965	1966	1967	1968	1969	1970	1971	1972	1973	1974	1975	1976	1977	1978	1979
														Wholesale Prices (lines 76) and Unit Values (lines 74)		
Aluminum (US cents/pound)																
All Origins (London) *	156	24.50	24.50	24.50	25.08	26.69	27.86	28.48	26.77	27.18	34.69	39.39	40.37	51.88	60.10	72.70
Bananas (US cents/pound)																
Latin America (US Ports) *	248	7.25	6.99	7.15	6.93	7.24	7.53	6.37	7.34	7.47	8.34	11.15	11.73	12.38	13.00	14.78
Beef (US cents/pound)																
Australia-NZ (US Ports) *	193	39.99	46.37	47.22	49.22	55.47	59.16	61.05	67.14	91.19	71.77	60.20	71.71	68.33	96.99	130.82
United States (New York)	111	29.60	35.42	35.68	36.02	38.91	41.30	42.49	49.74	63.64	53.17	44.99	52.35	50.88	71.26	91.66
Argentina (frozen)	213	28.37	25.76	21.46	28.02	25.51	33.14	40.16	51.84	71.16	76.26	38.87	41.09	52.61	52.54	83.65
Argentina (corned)	213	37.68	38.90	40.15	41.42	39.72	39.29	61.70	65.67	82.33	113.12	78.95	74.13	74.99	75.93	119.19
Butter (US cents/pound)																
New Zealand (London)	196	41.51	37.65	36.98	32.14	32.14	33.47	47.16	54.19	44.24	53.06	72.10	76.51	84.22	109.48	130.61
New Zealand	196	38.24	34.62	33.10	28.22	28.30	28.58	38.24	50.62	44.15	44.09	50.46	49.32	57.42	68.08	69.34
Coal (US $/metric ton)																
Australia	193	....	....	9.13	9.26	9.94	10.96	12.03	13.56	16.19	24.06	38.43	45.33	42.94	45.37	43.84
Cocoa Beans (US cents/pound)																
Brazil	223	13.66	20.45	23.47	27.58	40.02	29.42	23.50	26.24	48.51	73.35	56.59	77.02	183.53	153.53	140.73
New York and London *	652	16.57	23.48	27.13	32.70	40.97	30.57	24.43	29.15	51.29	70.77	56.51	92.79	171.96	154.43	149.36
Coconut Oil (US cents/pound)																
Philippines (New York)	566	15.84	14.15	14.45	17.52	15.74	17.19	15.99	11.23	23.27	45.26	17.85	18.95	26.23	30.99	44.66
Philippines	566	13.10	10.91	11.67	13.71	11.33	12.80	11.81	8.21	15.94	39.91	17.00	15.71	24.19	27.01	41.95
Coffee (US cents/pound)																
Other Milds (New York) *	386	45.38	42.13	39.21	39.33	39.78	52.01	44.99	50.33	62.31	65.84	65.41	142.75	234.67	162.82	173.53
Brazil (New York)	223	43.75	40.56	37.72	37.36	40.90	55.80	44.71	52.57	69.19	73.34	82.58	149.48	267.14	165.29	178.47
Brazil	223	39.62	34.32	31.83	31.72	32.89	44.26	33.88	42.73	52.68	56.83	49.57	122.37	203.51	142.11	154.72
Colombia (New York)	233	48.49	47.43	41.94	42.60	44.94	56.66	49.01	55.71	72.66	77.86	81.60	156.72	241.59	185.20	183.40
Colombia	233	46.01	46.08	40.00	40.34	40.13	54.22	46.00	49.84	66.81	68.40	62.38	117.49	216.69	166.86	137.47
Uganda (New York) *	799	30.77	33.53	33.53	33.85	33.10	41.44	42.26	45.18	49.89	58.68	61.05	127.62	223.75	147.48	165.47
Copper (US cents/pound)																
United Kingdom (London) *	112	58.11	69.32	50.95	56.15	66.44	64.04	49.02	48.58	80.58	93.23	56.10	63.64	59.41	61.92	89.49
Copra (US $/metric ton)																
Philippines (Europ. Ports)	566	226.17	185.42	201.75	232.17	201.75	223.08	189.58	142.33	343.92	668.67	256.00	275.08	402.33	470.58	672.67
Cotton (US cents/pound)																
United States (10 markets)	111	30.40	26.40	23.00	27.20	25.40	25.08	27.68	34.25	56.06	57.87	45.07	67.97	61.56	57.63	62.10
Liverpool Index *	111	28.84	28.24	30.69	30.76	27.83	28.93	33.88	36.26	62.09	65.13	53.09	77.24	71.33	71.95	77.14
Egypt (Liverpool) *	469	51.18	49.95	53.24	58.67	63.20	62.60	61.72	65.09	98.36	153.80	129.41	136.30	149.20	138.60	153.21
Egypt (Long Staple)	469	49.71	47.68	47.76	53.45	59.71	61.06	61.54	64.93	85.11	150.42	138.39	118.46	155.53	119.42	123.40
Egypt (Long Medium)	469	41.08	43.01	36.68	44.98	60.35	49.83	49.22	48.10	68.20	127.61	109.72	84.92	125.75	101.98	109.27
Fish Meal (US $/metric ton)																
All Origins (Hamburg) *	293	201.83	181.92	147.92	128.83	172.25	196.83	168.08	238.67	542.00	372.00	245.33	376.17	453.92	409.92	394.92
Iceland	176	....	....	....	....	....	185.86	192.75	166.41	415.35	403.38	222.96	277.64	420.08	415.93	375.80
Gold (US $/fine ounce)																
United Kingdom (London)	112	35.00	35.00	35.00	38.63	41.08	35.94	40.80	58.16	97.33	159.25	161.03	124.82	147.72	193.24	306.67
Groundnuts (US $/metric ton)																
Nigeria (London)	694	206.54	186.64	179.28	166.06	206.77	228.18	250.91	253.95	391.31	739.06	432.96	422.99	546.86	630.93	562.74
Groundnut Meal (US $/metric ton)																
All Origins (Europe)	694	114.68	106.99	107.27	101.17	108.11	115.34	110.56	137.21	299.29	196.33	157.76	198.02	245.23	230.78	237.72
Groundnut Oil (US $/metric ton)																
West Africa (Europe) *	694	324.92	296.33	283.00	270.75	331.67	378.25	445.50	425.67	544.00	1,058.25	778.17	690.58	845.75	1,079.17	888.67
Hides (US cents/pound)																
United States (Chicago) *	111	14.30	17.69	11.98	11.24	14.59	12.90	14.47	29.60	34.30	23.60	23.28	33.57	36.95	47.54	73.13
Australia	193	35.62	38.03	29.33	25.24	30.36	24.79	19.48	28.62	78.35	66.72	43.92	56.63	67.36	73.87	90.58
Iron Ore (US $/metric ton)																
Brazil (North Sea Ports) *	223	15.69	15.25	13.50	12.62	11.68	15.22	13.40	12.79	17.13	19.00	22.81	22.72	21.59	19.39	23.44
Jute (US $/metric ton)																
Bangladesh (Chitta.-Chalna)	513	250.50	302.07	287.23	266.56	280.83	269.51	281.40	293.70	284.03	347.67	370.75	295.42	319.00	397.83	384.92
Lamb (US cents/pound)																
New Zealand (London) *	196	34.06	32.95	31.17	29.88	34.47	33.80	36.58	48.51	63.43	64.98	67.79	71.86	78.08	100.65	109.02
New Zealand	196	25.79	23.29	21.46	21.38	24.30	24.33	24.21	27.30	43.51	46.28	39.80	40.90	48.16	55.62	63.94
Lead (US cents/pound)																
United Kingdom (London) *	112	14.41	11.90	10.30	10.90	13.13	13.80	11.50	13.70	19.38	26.80	18.92	20.24	28.02	29.95	54.56
United States (New York)	111	16.01	15.01	14.01	13.21	14.91	15.71	13.90	15.38	16.39	22.29	21.56	22.98	30.72	33.75	52.98
Linseed Oil (US $/metric ton)																
Any Origin	001	213.67	191.75	202.83	235.00	222.58	216.33	187.08	197.00	544.50	1,094.58	700.75	545.58	461.50	434.17	644.00
Maize (US $/bushel)																
United States (Chicago)	111	1.30	1.37	1.30	1.19	1.24	1.37	1.40	1.31	2.30	3.23	2.90	2.69	2.22	2.32	2.63
United States (U.S. Gulf Ports) *	111	1.40	1.47	1.38	1.21	1.32	1.48	1.48	1.42	2.48	3.36	3.04	2.85	2.42	2.56	2.94
Thailand	578	1.47	1.53	1.52	1.29	1.40	1.66	1.49	1.38	2.64	3.39	3.38	2.92	2.70	2.52	3.49
Manganese (US $/long ton)																
India (US Ports)	534	76.38	77.17	73.78	63.34	53.00	55.33	63.83	64.50	76.17	114.17	140.00	147.33	150.33	144.38	140.00
Newsprint (US $/short ton)																
United States (New York)	111	132.44	136.24	140.04	141.44	146.14	150.54	157.04	163.25	170.48	210.78	256.78	276.08	297.73	315.55	345.32
Finland	172	112.66	113.76	114.52	110.93	110.98	114.89	120.10	125.47	146.55	235.47	315.57	295.04	322.14	332.27	368.04
Sweden	144	119.22	119.61	119.01	114.85	111.60	117.98	123.07	134.25	163.71	243.88	327.47	318.17	343.77	355.64	394.51
Nickel (US cents/pound)																
United Kingdom(N.Europ.ports)*	156	78.60	78.73	86.53	92.87	103.88	127.63	133.00	139.67	153.00	173.92	207.33	225.25	236.00	209.17	271.00
Palm Kernels (US $/metric ton)																
Malaysia (Rotterdam)	548	318.58	271.33	....	354.92	305.75	367.33	335.50	219.08	489.75	1,045.83	408.58	433.25	620.42	763.92	1,049.25
Palm Oil (US $/metric ton)																
Malaysia (N.W.Europe) *	548	273.42	233.75	223.00	168.25	184.83	259.50	262.08	217.42	375.92	691.33	420.25	397.33	530.08	600.33	653.83
Malaysia	548	244.54	212.35	200.60	142.20	140.12	214.82	217.35	187.08	239.32	500.45	474.94	359.85	525.18	533.35	594.21
Pepper,Black (US cents/pound)																
Malaysia (New York)	548	47.90	43.30	38.40	37.80	46.41	57.30	50.06	46.24	57.97	84.86	90.95	89.08	113.62	106.43	96.12

Commodity Prices

1980	1981	1982	1983	1984	1985	1986	1987	1988	1989	1990	1991	1992	1993	1994	Country of Origin and, for Wholesale Prices, Pricing Point in Parentheses	z
															Aluminum (US cents/pound)	
80.51	57.28	44.98	65.25	56.77	47.21	52.15	70.99	115.51	88.48	74.37	59.15	56.98	51.71	66.93	All Origins (London) *	156
															Bananas (US cents/pound)	
17.01	18.21	17.00	19.47	16.76	17.15	17.32	17.11	21.73	24.80	24.60	25.46	21.69	20.10	19.91	Latin America (US Ports) *	248
															Beef (US cents/pound)	
125.19	112.12	108.39	110.67	103.11	97.67	94.98	108.18	114.17	116.46	116.27	120.83	111.34	118.74	105.82	Australia-NZ (US Ports) *	193
86.71	88.25	98.56	95.57	97.14	89.70	76.63	81.38	81.55	87.13	94.27	90.43	90.11	93.44	86.73	United States (New York)	111
97.41	84.12	64.07	66.59	90.89	86.61	111.04	162.19	154.87	148.59	130.90	194.67	253.91	303.09	230.30	Argentina (frozen)	213
143.68	136.27	99.99	91.28	87.24	82.23	90.67	111.79	82.38	95.27	102.80	120.14	93.41	111.75	124.98	Argentina (corned)	213
															Butter (US cents/pound)	
151.39	140.88	129.18	111.41	93.93	101.45	115.14	113.49	140.56	148.26	147.94	140.87	150.53	140.98	140.51	New Zealand (London)	196
73.80	96.88	97.16	91.25	76.27	60.22	56.89	63.64	69.52	90.97	87.34	78.39	91.60	81.66	84.46	New Zealand	196
															Coal (US $/metric ton)	
45.31	52.16	56.69	49.12	45.19	39.92	39.27	34.98	36.29	41.61	42.72	43.66	41.42	39.40	37.36	Australia	193
															Cocoa Beans (US cents/pound)	
107.06	87.50	68.29	83.10	105.32	94.97	92.04	83.96	72.68	56.85	49.07	47.54	44.99	44.47	55.91	Brazil	223
118.09	94.19	79.01	96.10	108.67	102.27	93.82	90.62	71.84	56.34	57.52	54.10	49.87	50.41	63.31	New York and London *	652
															Coconut Oil (US cents/pound)	
30.51	25.86	21.19	33.10	52.39	26.77	13.45	20.06	25.62	23.44	15.32	19.64	26.22	20.47	27.51	Philippines (New York)	566
28.06	23.27	19.75	24.15	44.83	24.18	12.10	16.74	23.34	22.39	13.99	16.13	24.71	19.42	....	Philippines	566
															Coffee (US cents/pound)	
154.20	128.09	139.72	131.69	144.17	145.56	192.74	112.29	135.10	106.96	89.15	85.03	63.66	69.94	148.53	Other Milds (New York) *	386
208.79	186.38	143.68	142.75	149.65	148.93	231.19	106.37	121.84	98.76	83.80	72.88	56.26	66.58	143.32	Brazil (New York)	223
143.75	83.34	94.88	101.16	112.72	103.97	190.39	89.98	100.76	74.58	58.80	57.28	43.25	50.08	115.54	Brazil	223
178.83	128.09	139.71	131.69	144.25	145.56	194.54	112.29	135.10	106.96	89.15	84.97	63.64	....	....	Colombia (New York)	233
161.70	121.77	134.62	126.13	133.35	134.87	202.33	113.13	127.15	110.58	79.86	83.93	60.29	....	....	Colombia	233
147.15	102.91	111.04	124.12	138.18	121.24	148.32	102.34	95.11	75.69	54.99	49.83	43.63	53.50	119.82	Uganda (New York) *	799
															Copper (US cents/pound)	
99.12	79.05	67.21	72.23	62.46	64.29	62.13	80.79	117.93	129.15	120.72	106.07	103.64	86.86	104.58	United Kingdom (London) *	112
															Copra (US $/metric ton)	
453.00	378.92	314.00	496.00	710.08	386.42	197.58	310.33	395.92	348.02	229.92	295.85	381.85	295.42	416.84	Philippines (Europ. Ports) *	566
															Cotton (US cents/pound)	
81.28	72.02	60.04	68.43	68.15	58.68	52.72	63.45	57.35	64.21	71.82	70.65	54.72	55.85	73.73	United States (10 markets)	111
93.73	83.97	72.51	84.10	80.94	59.92	47.74	74.77	63.52	75.95	82.56	76.91	57.94	58.02	79.72	Liverpool Index *	111
153.49	151.99	124.87	139.96	163.82	163.97	157.23	162.95	218.45	289.31	300.12	278.66	212.79	201.19	171.54	Egypt (Liverpool) *	469
123.22	121.73	109.69	110.62	142.85	138.35	142.53	173.66	275.29	617.57	516.94	256.14	164.99	130.01	....	Egypt (Long Staple)	469
109.17	108.07	80.66	86.85	112.31	133.21	136.23	132.11	254.53	555.71	436.98	215.20	110.82	99.20	....	Egypt (Long Medium)	469
															Fish Meal (US $/metric ton)	
504.42	467.50	353.75	452.50	373.17	280.08	320.58	383.42	544.42	409.08	412.17	477.85	481.52	364.69	376.66	All Origins (Hamburg) *	293
467.76	470.40	313.51	536.62	330.30	304.59	344.64	386.27	476.67	535.48	480.63	499.53	522.16	405.15	452.21	Iceland	176
															Gold (US $/fine ounce)	
607.86	459.75	375.80	422.47	360.36	317.18	367.68	446.52	437.15	381.28	383.51	362.18	343.42	359.73	384.22	United Kingdom (London)	112
															Groundnuts (US $/metric ton)	
1,236.58	1,257.42	827.50	965.33	836.58	675.75	993.58	758.50	935.75	817.50	1,325.50	1,237.83	799.13	1,092.15	954.80	Nigeria (London)	694
															Groundnut Meal (US $/metric ton)	
271.41	269.26	208.33	229.00	187.50	146.25	166.00	161.92	209.42	200.42	184.75	150.08	152.58	168.08	168.33	All Origins (Europe)	694
															Groundnut Oil (US $/metric ton)	
858.75	1,042.75	585.17	710.92	1,016.67	905.25	569.42	499.75	590.50	774.75	963.67	894.83	609.58	737.88	1,022.64	West Africa (Europe) *	694
															Hides (US cents/pound)	
45.92	41.72	38.56	45.13	58.87	51.18	63.96	79.84	87.65	90.02	92.23	79.45	75.86	80.03	86.82	United States (Chicago) *	111
84.64	60.76	57.72	48.72	51.94	47.08	58.09	86.35	105.67	80.10	59.75	45.23	51.59	33.07	53.06	Australia	193
															Iron Ore (US $/metric ton)	
28.09	28.09	32.50	29.00	26.15	26.56	26.26	24.50	23.50	26.50	30.80	33.25	31.60	28.11	25.47	Brazil (North Sea Ports) *	223
															Jute (US $/metric ton)	
313.50	278.25	283.08	298.25	530.75	582.92	271.75	320.58	370.00	373.33	408.33	365.42	279.17	271.25	295.67	Bangladesh (Chitta.-Chalna) *	513
															Lamb (US cents/pound)	
131.17	124.98	108.65	87.88	87.70	83.56	92.57	98.45	109.46	105.31	121.14	104.88	115.42	124.12	125.67	New Zealand (London) *	196
72.28	78.46	72.04	62.54	57.29	49.50	49.61	56.93	164.07	69.05	88.53	79.08	82.82	100.78	97.97	New Zealand	196
															Lead (US cents/pound)	
41.07	32.93	24.76	19.29	20.05	17.72	18.40	27.05	29.73	30.51	36.72	25.30	24.65	18.48	24.89	United Kingdom (London) *	112
43.52	37.48	26.70	22.54	27.01	19.63	20.31	35.93	36.58	38.38	45.21	33.08	35.21	31.59	37.19	United States (New York)	111
															Linseed Oil (US $/metric ton)	
697.08	659.92	519.08	484.50	571.50	627.08	419.17	317.50	521.50	756.67	709.25	438.88	396.34	448.50	516.74	Any Origin	001
															Maize (US $/bushel)	
3.00	3.17	2.52	3.23	3.27	2.66	2.11	1.71	2.51	2.65	2.61	2.51	2.49	2.45	2.59	United States (Chicago)	111
3.19	3.32	2.75	3.45	3.45	2.85	2.23	1.92	2.72	2.83	2.78	2.73	2.65	2.59	2.74	United States (U.S. Gulf Ports) *	111
4.11	3.78	3.25	3.52	3.47	2.59	2.23	2.35	3.17	3.42	3.33	3.17	3.68	3.41	....	Thailand	578
															Manganese (US $/long ton)	
155.25	167.80	164.12	151.82	143.21	141.01	140.83	134.00	149.21	204.75	341.67	391.58	373.75	298.09	212.93	India (US Ports)	534
															Newsprint (US $/short ton)	
388.64	428.60	440.83	422.53	450.84	463.54	453.95	493.36	522.58	507.90	495.63	501.02	455.17	464.39	482.88	United States (New York)	111
410.92	405.48	390.37	329.32	317.02	328.07	407.71	465.84	550.46	526.07	575.21	556.29	469.86	377.58	401.99	Finland	172
437.43	415.44	396.49	353.88	326.73	342.60	432.82	509.13	581.45	549.43	597.91	591.00	489.22	....	....	Sweden	144
															Nickel (US cents/pound)	
295.68	270.03	219.43	211.96	215.56	222.22	176.39	221.00	624.97	603.87	402.07	370.28	318.22	240.78	287.21	United Kingdom(N.Europ.ports)*	156
															Palm Kernels (US $/metric ton)	
725.50	588.25	458.17	709.00	1,037.17	551.17	288.17	426.08	538.75	472.00	333.58	416.33	581.83	437.84	627.75	Malaysia (Rotterdam)	548
															Palm Oil (US $/metric ton)	
583.08	570.67	445.08	501.42	728.83	500.92	257.00	342.50	437.17	350.42	289.83	339.00	393.69	377.73	529.15	Malaysia (N.W.Europe) *	548
529.53	490.91	416.81	437.54	650.55	493.83	269.80	318.62	416.12	348.83	287.10	329.78	382.41	382.97	381.06	Malaysia	548
															Pepper, Black (US cents/pound)	
90.43	71.84	70.43	81.40	136.52	183.10	267.57	263.23	208.74	129.33	81.30	64.34	66.70	104.90	....	Malaysia (New York)	548

Commodity Prices

z		1965	1966	1967	1968	1969	1970	1971	1972	1973	1974	1975	1976	1977	1978	1979
													Wholesale Prices (lines 76) and Unit Values (lines 74)			
Petroleum, spot (US $/barrel)																
Average Crude Price	001	2.11	2.11	2.11	2.11	2.11	2.11	2.57	2.80	3.14	11.22	10.60	11.83	12.84	12.95	29.22
Dubai Fateh	466	1.80	1.80	1.80	1.80	1.80	1.80	2.21	2.48	2.86	10.98	10.43	11.63	12.57	12.92	29.82
U.K. Brent	112	2.23	2.23	2.23	2.23	2.23	2.23	3.21	3.61	4.25	12.93	11.50	13.14	14.31	14.26	32.11
Alaskan North Slope	111	2.30	2.30	2.30	2.30	2.30	2.30	2.30	2.30	2.30	9.76	9.85	10.71	11.64	11.67	25.74
West Texas Intermediate	111	....	....	....	....	....	....	....	....	....	....	....	....	....	....	....
Phosphate Rock (US $/metric ton)																
Morocco (Casablanca) *	686	14.00	13.00	12.00	11.50	11.25	11.00	11.25	11.50	13.75	52.77	68.00	35.83	30.67	29.00	33.00
Potash (US $/metric ton)																
Canada (Vancouver)	156	21.75	27.50	25.50	24.00	22.00	31.50	32.50	33.50	42.50	60.50	81.33	55.50	51.17	56.38	76.48
Plywood (US cents/sheet)																
Philippines (Tokyo)	566	61.00	73.61	80.09	79.51	84.40	103.06	81.68	96.89	189.78	152.74	121.83	147.71	161.53	189.58	262.49
Pulp (US $/metric ton)																
Sweden (Swedish Ports)	144	113.86	109.80	107.86	103.03	105.93	130.29	141.24	135.98	164.60	256.96	374.25	341.26	280.32	246.54	357.41
Sweden	144	142.13	134.73	133.34	127.31	136.45	162.04	174.86	173.05	207.96	295.17	410.31	388.84	345.16	302.72	393.27
Rice (US $/metric ton)																
United States (New Orleans)	111	182.93	182.93	187.33	191.74	187.33	188.25	190.82	215.80	395.79	555.21	418.56	307.82	333.90	399.10	381.10
Thailand (Bangkok) *	578	136.25	165.67	221.00	204.67	185.08	143.00	130.33	149.92	296.58	541.50	363.17	254.08	272.42	368.50	334.33
Thailand	578	110.20	127.59	150.92	169.92	138.39	113.77	88.74	101.00	205.32	466.24	301.86	213.70	222.65	319.06	273.02
Myanmar	518	102.49	106.49	123.12	144.30	121.72	83.33	75.09	75.28	117.32	370.31	257.50	168.04	172.11	201.54	223.85
Rubber (US cents/pound)																
All Origins (New York)	111	25.66	23.60	19.89	19.85	26.15	21.07	18.02	18.11	35.11	39.74	29.87	39.50	41.53	49.89	64.16
Malaysia (Singapore) *	548	22.90	21.39	17.70	17.33	22.78	18.47	15.08	15.05	30.75	34.09	25.44	35.10	36.95	44.71	57.25
Malaysia	548	22.42	21.60	18.10	17.11	22.21	18.98	15.61	15.30	28.40	34.65	26.30	34.33	37.68	43.69	56.34
Thailand	578	20.67	20.04	16.26	15.70	21.02	17.66	13.49	12.78	25.76	30.92	23.28	31.54	34.10	40.50	52.67
Shrimp (US $/pound)																
United States (U.S. Gulf Ports)	111	.84	1.05	1.04	1.17	1.30	1.24	1.50	1.88	2.27	2.11	2.67	3.79	3.59	3.64	5.43
Silver (US cents/troy ounce)																
United States (New York)	111	129.3	129.3	155.0	214.5	179.1	177.1	154.6	168.4	255.8	470.8	441.9	435.3	462.3	540.1	1,109.0
Sisal (US $/metric ton)																
East African (Europe)	639	222.00	209.00	178.00	161.00	172.00	152.00	170.00	240.00	526.75	1,055.50	580.33	467.50	511.25	474.83	712.92
Sorghum (US $/metric ton)																
United States (US Gulf Ports)	111	47.21	51.71	50.40	46.51	50.05	51.80	55.70	56.20	93.39	120.94	111.87	105.22	89.24	93.84	108.11
Soybeans (US $/metric ton)																
United States (Rotterdam) *	111	116.92	126.25	112.58	105.92	103.00	116.92	125.58	140.00	290.33	276.92	221.67	231.17	280.17	268.33	297.75
Soybean Meal (US $/metric ton)																
United States (Rotterdam) *	111	73.00	86.50	85.33	98.00	95.08	102.58	101.83	129.17	302.58	184.33	155.00	198.33	229.83	213.33	243.00
Soybean Oil (US $/metric ton)																
All Origins (Dutch Ports)	111	270.00	261.50	216.83	178.08	197.17	286.33	303.75	240.58	436.00	832.17	563.33	438.33	580.25	607.00	662.17
Sugar (US cents/pound)																
EU Import Price *	112	5.82	5.94	5.87	5.09	5.09	5.09	5.16	6.81	6.67	10.65	15.44	13.39	14.01	15.91	19.29
Caribbean (New York) *	001	2.12	1.87	2.00	1.99	3.39	3.76	4.53	7.48	9.62	29.94	20.56	11.56	8.11	7.82	9.66
U.S. Import Price *	111	6.18	6.39	6.68	6.93	7.14	7.50	7.93	8.53	10.29	29.48	22.47	13.31	11.00	13.97	15.53
Brazil	223	3.39	3.64	3.64	4.49	4.75	5.10	5.50	7.22	8.96	25.38	29.18	11.52	8.24	7.70	8.79
Australia	193	3.91	3.37	2.98	2.85	3.95	4.97	4.88	6.52	7.63	18.38	19.95	14.35	11.74	12.07	13.30
Philippines	566	5.40	6.15	6.60	6.78	6.89	6.62	7.25	7.78	9.24	21.03	27.03	13.25	8.71	8.18	7.61
Superphosphate (US $/metric ton)																
United States (US Gulf Ports)	111	47.25	47.25	47.00	37.50	39.00	42.50	43.00	67.50	100.00	308.00	202.50	91.50	97.92	98.04	143.33
Tea (US cents/pound)																
Average Auction (London) *	112	57.64	56.67	57.03	47.24	44.28	49.55	47.80	47.81	47.97	63.29	62.68	69.70	122.02	99.29	97.87
Sri Lanka	524	50.77	48.14	45.21	42.40	40.12	40.91	42.13	46.42	43.41	52.86	58.78	56.62	96.39	96.52	88.88
Timber (US $/cubic meter)																
Hardwood Logs																
Malaysia, Sarawak	548	34.87	36.86	39.25	40.31	38.92	43.17	43.26	40.57	68.05	81.53	67.51	92.00	92.57	97.36	170.04
Hardwood Sawnwood																
Malaysia	548	81.37	73.14	76.72	84.12	90.19	93.23	92.59	109.45	156.09	143.08	166.44	168.13	154.09	205.68	339.08
Softwood Logs																
United States	111	....	....	....	....	....	....	....	....	....	....	....	....	....	....	....
Softwood Sawnwood																
United States	111	....	....	....	....	....	....	....	....	....	....	....	....	....	....	....
Tin (US cents/pound)																
All Origins (London) *	112	176.48	162.09	150.05	141.83	155.47	166.63	159.30	169.64	217.83	371.23	311.92	344.08	490.08	584.01	700.68
Malaysia (Penang) *	548	172.02	158.09	147.02	138.56	153.39	162.86	155.14	166.73	211.88	354.16	301.95	338.33	484.34	564.38	672.01
Malaysia	548	171.61	159.79	148.08	139.44	151.34	160.86	153.59	165.89	201.76	335.35	293.23	334.15	471.98	564.11	665.56
Bolivia	218	174.21	161.25	150.39	142.73	155.15	174.41	158.53	169.63	207.74	361.28	312.55	343.90	475.13	566.91	672.37
Thailand	578	124.05	151.86	146.58	137.08	151.80	158.65	156.53	166.18	197.46	332.00	300.19	329.69	471.06	557.12	656.45
Tobacco (US $/metric ton)																
United States (All Markets) *	111	59.40	64.50	164.38	1,204.47	1,112.38	1,055.44	1,100.62	1,073.64	1,128.02	1,482.07	1,841.99	2,186.72	2,253.93	2,268.02	2,344.43
Urea (US $/metric ton)																
Any Origin (Europe)	170	94.75	89.25	79.25	65.50	56.00	48.25	46.00	59.25	94.75	315.75	197.67	111.67	127.42	144.83	172.88
Wheat (US $/bushel)																
Australia (Sydney)	193	1.53	1.68	1.66	1.59	1.54	1.48	1.58	1.84	3.97	5.32	4.03	3.50	2.91	3.70	4.28
Australia	193	1.55	1.64	1.67	1.57	1.65	1.42	1.53	1.61	2.03	4.73	4.57	3.92	2.90	3.10	3.94
United States (US Gulf Pts) *	111	1.62	1.71	1.79	1.71	1.59	1.49	1.68	1.90	3.81	4.89	4.06	3.62	2.81	3.48	4.36
Argentina	213	1.52	1.52	1.70	1.56	1.59	1.48	1.62	1.81	2.65	5.26	4.68	3.65	2.63	3.20	3.98
Wool (US cents/kilogram)																
Australia-NZ(UK) 48s *	112	186.71	188.43	153.69	126.41	131.17	120.28	121.70	208.48	364.06	285.13	234.39	320.48	338.57	347.34	422.30
Australia-NZ(UK) 64s *	112	246.20	273.08	249.77	242.03	225.98	196.45	178.38	297.59	698.62	492.00	386.50	398.64	429.53	442.92	524.88
Australia (greasy wool)	193	125.98	136.37	121.96	116.60	131.86	98.20	79.68	117.80	305.06	251.91	182.41	197.99	227.00	234.83	259.60
New Zealand	196	114.56	114.67	93.21	69.15	78.32	73.81	72.64	106.86	237.50	214.65	147.59	202.92	256.35	249.63	300.35
Zinc (US cents/pound)																
United Kingdom (London) *	112	14.17	12.76	12.34	11.93	12.99	13.42	14.06	17.14	38.16	56.13	33.83	32.32	26.74	26.92	33.61
United States (New York)	111	15.00	15.00	14.40	14.00	15.20	15.83	16.11	17.71	21.05	35.78	38.86	37.46	34.48	31.46	37.78
Bolivia	218	14.07	13.51	12.06	11.46	13.37	13.95	15.25	17.64	23.76	34.85	36.93	36.08	33.08	27.48	35.90

Commodity Prices

Country of Origin and, for Wholesale Prices, Pricing Point in Parentheses

1980	1981	1982	1983	1984	1985	1986	1987	1988	1989	1990	1991	1992	1993	1994	Commodity	z
															Petroleum, spot (US $/barrel)	
35.48	34.12	31.38	28.37	28.25	26.98	13.82	17.79	14.15	17.19	22.05	18.30	18.22	16.13	15.47	Average Crude Price	001
35.85	34.29	31.76	28.73	27.49	26.46	13.08	16.94	13.22	15.70	20.46	16.54	17.19	14.96	14.76	Dubai Fateh	466
37.89	36.68	33.42	29.83	28.80	27.33	14.50	18.34	14.97	18.22	23.99	19.99	19.34	17.04	15.82	U.K. Brent	112
32.69	31.38	28.98	26.55	28.54	27.14	13.89	18.08	14.26	17.65	22.03	18.35	18.15	16.40	15.76	Alaskan North Slope	111
....	....	....	30.42	29.38	28.14	15.10	19.16	15.96	19.60	24.45	21.46	20.56	18.46	17.10	West Texas Intermediate	111
															Phosphate Rock (US $/metric ton)	
46.71	49.50	42.38	36.92	38.25	33.92	34.26	31.00	36.00	40.83	40.50	42.50	41.75	33.00	33.00	Morocco (Casablanca) *	686
															Potash (US $/metric ton)	
115.71	112.46	80.75	75.46	83.71	83.96	68.79	69.04	87.54	98.88	98.13	108.85	112.08	107.42	105.72	Canada (Vancouver)	156
															Plywood (US cents/sheet)	
273.84	245.46	234.35	229.87	227.03	210.91	274.15	398.72	358.84	350.32	354.87	372.38	380.77	661.42	599.50	Philippines (Tokyo)	566
															Pulp (US $/metric ton)	
447.37	412.98	336.90	289.57	364.23	327.47	342.24	467.05	569.32	609.42	649.79	548.23	461.91	354.02	399.39	Sweden (Swedish Ports)	144
486.43	479.95	426.49	373.91	440.91	386.36	431.20	558.95	668.11	747.36	767.29	570.21	535.43	402.30	477.69	Sweden	144
															Rice (US $/metric ton)	
494.97	565.31	366.59	378.34	379.63	382.38	342.73	323.43	429.77	409.20	389.50	418.02	401.14	389.15	466.68	United States (New Orleans)	111
433.67	482.83	293.38	276.83	252.25	217.42	210.17	229.75	301.50	320.33	287.17	312.58	287.44	267.94	358.03	Thailand (Bangkok) *	578
340.29	398.55	258.63	252.25	237.60	204.16	170.76	198.64	269.37	288.07	270.20	287.14	291.03	257.18	....	Thailand	578
274.95	311.36	211.00	185.41	186.11	164.87	139.78	119.92	170.19	211.34	205.49	232.27	211.99	173.25	171.53	Myanmar	518
															Rubber (US cents/pound)	
73.43	56.97	45.26	56.14	49.56	41.77	41.18	44.08	48.81	48.70	50.17	47.63	46.67	47.34	48.93	All Origins (New York)	111
64.62	50.93	38.90	48.27	43.44	34.42	36.58	44.66	53.75	43.99	39.22	37.46	39.08	37.71	51.07	Malaysia (Singapore) *	548
63.07	49.21	37.42	45.80	44.67	35.05	36.89	43.50	56.52	44.47	38.42	39.20	40.55	40.03	49.73	Malaysia	548
60.13	47.73	34.37	41.88	42.16	32.84	34.27	40.88	52.00	41.92	35.89	35.20	35.28	35.07	....	Thailand	578
															Shrimp (US $/pound)	
4.60	4.41	6.21	6.00	5.24	4.76	5.85	5.18	5.64	5.09	4.90	5.24	4.97	5.16	5.93	United States (U.S. Gulf Ports)	111
															Silver (US cents/troy ounce)	
2,057.7	1,051.8	794.9	1,144.1	814.1	614.2	546.9	700.9	653.5	549.9	482.0	404.0	393.6	429.8	528.4	United States (New York)	111
															Sisal (US $/metric ton)	
764.83	645.25	593.17	570.83	583.75	525.67	514.17	512.08	550.58	653.08	715.00	669.17	505.58	615.42	604.58	East African (Europe)	639
															Sorghum (US $/metric ton)	
128.86	126.36	108.35	128.73	118.19	103.01	82.41	72.76	98.46	105.94	103.94	105.11	102.76	99.03	103.87	United States (US Gulf Ports)	111
															Soybeans (US $/metric ton)	
296.25	288.42	244.50	281.67	282.08	224.42	208.42	215.75	303.50	275.00	246.75	239.56	235.52	255.25	252.82	United States (Rotterdam) *	111
															Soybean Meal (US $/metric ton)	
258.58	252.67	218.00	237.83	197.17	157.17	184.75	203.25	267.50	247.33	200.08	197.08	204.33	208.08	192.52	United States (Rotterdam) *	111
															Soybean Oil (US $/metric ton)	
598.25	506.92	447.33	526.92	725.17	576.00	342.42	334.25	463.42	431.50	447.50	453.90	428.65	479.98	616.20	All Origins (Dutch Ports)	111
															Sugar (US cents/pound)	
22.09	18.93	18.12	17.57	16.03	16.12	18.60	21.44	23.82	22.75	26.45	27.77	28.48	28.10	28.20	EU Import Price *	112
28.67	16.89	8.41	8.47	5.20	4.05	6.05	6.76	10.19	12.81	12.51	8.98	9.07	10.02	12.11	Caribbean (New York) *	001
30.03	19.73	19.92	22.04	21.74	20.35	20.95	21.83	22.12	22.81	23.25	21.55	21.30	21.61	22.03	U.S. Import Price *	111
21.79	16.92	9.42	9.46	9.17	6.66	7.03	6.80	8.42	12.14	15.94	11.87	11.12	11.62	13.15	Brazil	223
21.07	19.16	9.99	10.32	7.82	5.84	7.97	7.49	9.57	12.34	12.65	10.76	10.44	10.68	12.14	Australia	193
16.22	20.65	15.09	13.44	12.70	14.94	17.59	16.63	19.01	19.02	19.46	19.09	19.02	14.13	....	Philippines	566
															Superphosphate (US $/metric ton)	
180.33	161.00	138.38	134.67	131.25	121.38	121.17	138.00	158.38	144.00	131.82	133.12	120.74	111.95	132.11	United States (US Gulf Ports)	111
															Tea (US cents/pound)	
101.06	91.59	87.62	105.44	156.79	89.98	87.48	77.45	81.18	91.25	92.17	83.57	90.60	84.20	83.15	Average Auction (London) *	112
91.64	82.83	76.35	101.26	137.66	101.24	72.08	81.60	79.79	84.20	103.91	92.23	84.84	85.58	83.81	Sri Lanka	524
															Timber (US $/cubic meter)	
															Hardwood Logs	
141.51	101.60	101.94	91.24	113.34	82.24	97.29	167.46	167.21	167.34	160.28	179.63	196.69	388.98	316.32	Malaysia, Sarawak	548
															Hardwood Sawnwood	
369.65	314.14	226.31	202.56	251.63	182.58	215.98	371.80	371.23	467.71	517.12	524.76	607.21	758.24	821.44	Malaysia	548
															Softwood Logs	
....	....	89.43	78.22	73.43	72.30	75.22	88.60	103.41	106.21	123.56	125.67	152.47	217.94	201.23	United States	111
															Softwood Sawnwood	
....	....	151.63	141.44	137.10	136.07	149.33	160.30	162.65	184.18	206.26	216.17	234.64	277.44	299.55	United States	111
															Tin (US cents/pound)	
761.03	642.69	581.95	589.11	554.76	523.40	279.48	303.45	319.86	387.12	276.03	253.83	276.88	234.40	247.66	All Origins (London) *	112
744.24	636.74	584.43	589.95	564.38	542.19	270.43	302.98	320.27	392.89	287.08	265.98	284.23	242.32	248.06	Malaysia (Penang)	548
751.14	633.57	593.23	587.60	568.07	524.49	282.68	304.37	322.62	392.91	287.07	266.00	287.78	242.33	248.06	Malaysia	548
760.36	633.80	574.63	586.48	554.40	539.32	252.64	308.97	320.22	400.71	286.88	253.36	273.91	249.26	....	Bolivia	218
740.29	628.38	615.91	585.82	548.99	524.89	283.11	301.24	305.53	381.08	280.53	249.24	261.43	232.36	....	Thailand	578
															Tobacco (US $/metric ton)	
2,275.86	2,321.69	2,563.96	2,656.55	2,786.32	2,611.82	2,659.18	2,745.55	2,467.90	3,167.57	3,392.19	3,500.07	3,439.54	2,695.34	2,974.85	United States (All Markets) *	111
															Urea (US $/metric ton)	
222.08	215.88	157.50	134.96	171.29	136.33	107.00	116.58	155.00	132.17	157.00	172.00	140.33	106.75	147.92	Any Origin (Europe)	170
															Wheat (US $/bushel)	
4.77	4.73	4.35	4.34	3.76	3.84	3.26	3.11	4.08	4.81	5.29	3.59	5.41	4.20	4.41	Australia (Sydney)	193
4.91	5.07	4.41	4.67	3.89	3.50	3.14	2.43	3.71	4.59	4.25	2.91	4.20	3.73	3.51	Australia	193
4.70	4.76	4.36	4.28	4.15	3.70	3.13	3.07	3.95	4.61	3.69	3.50	4.11	3.82	4.08	United States (US Gulf Pts) *	111
5.01	5.27	4.54	3.91	3.60	3.13	2.66	2.44	3.18	4.05	3.93	2.44	3.27	3.57	3.58	Argentina	213
															Wool (US cents/kilogram)	
429.78	391.43	342.76	320.24	315.54	301.48	325.99	407.89	467.57	421.67	343.33	262.69	272.34	255.21	318.95	Australia-NZ(UK) 48s *	112
597.25	612.58	572.64	539.86	558.93	495.33	465.48	713.30	1,164.83	926.58	807.83	556.01	498.33	384.74	619.00	Australia-NZ(UK) 64s *	112
302.48	328.54	306.49	269.29	282.04	258.53	259.54	343.18	567.10	520.86	446.65	307.49	302.60	240.38	323.51	Australia (greasy wool)	193
316.68	274.56	239.68	221.93	230.74	234.94	248.52	333.01	403.17	386.27	341.47	249.33	242.87	234.22	287.92	New Zealand	196
															Zinc (US cents/pound)	
34.52	38.37	33.78	34.68	41.82	35.53	34.20	36.20	56.26	75.12	68.85	50.86	56.33	43.73	45.28	United Kingdom (London) *	112
38.07	45.67	40.01	42.82	49.95	43.22	40.50	44.08	57.76	77.48	71.32	52.79	56.96	45.32	46.66	United States (New York)	111
35.98	41.04	39.10	36.61	45.86	39.41	35.72	37.43	50.55	74.47	67.09	49.63	55.15	43.78	....	Bolivia	218

*See the Commodity Prices note in the monthly IFS.

Commodity Price Index

Indices of Wholesale Prices (lines 76) and of Unit Values (lines 74)
1990=100

d		1965	1966	1967	1968	1969	1970	1971	1972	1973	1974	1975	1976	1977	1978	1979
World (non-fuel comm. with *)	001	37.7	39.9	38.4	37.8	39.4	40.4	39.7	42.8	69.2	83.9	70.2	77.3	85.6	86.9	105.3
Food	001	44.0	46.8	46.8	44.6	45.5	47.8	49.4	53.3	96.2	119.0	95.5	89.5	86.8	98.4	114.8
Beverages	001	48.6	51.0	51.4	51.9	54.6	59.5	54.0	59.2	75.1	91.0	85.7	158.5	275.3	205.8	214.4
Agricultural Raw Materials	001	23.8	24.7	24.0	23.9	24.4	25.0	24.8	28.3	45.6	46.5	39.8	51.8	52.6	56.6	78.3
Metals	001	34.9	36.5	31.3	32.7	37.0	37.5	34.2	34.8	47.8	64.5	56.1	58.7	61.8	63.7	81.5
Fertilizers	001	34.6	32.2	29.7	28.4	27.8	27.2	27.8	28.4	34.0	130.5	168.2	88.6	75.8	71.7	81.6
World Bank LMICs	200	40.7	41.8	39.9	39.7	42.3	44.1	42.0	44.6	68.2	92.0	75.4	87.7	109.0	101.8	116.5
Aluminum (US cents/pound)																
All Origins (London) *	156	32.9	32.9	32.9	33.7	35.9	37.5	38.3	36.0	36.5	46.6	53.0	54.3	69.8	80.8	97.8
Bananas (US cents/pound)																
Latin America (US Ports) *	248	29.5	28.4	29.1	28.2	29.4	30.6	25.9	29.8	30.4	33.9	45.3	47.7	50.3	52.9	60.1
Beef (US cents/pound)																
Australia-NZ (US Ports) *	193	34.4	39.9	40.6	42.3	47.7	50.9	52.5	57.8	78.4	61.7	51.8	61.7	58.8	83.4	112.5
United States (New York)	111	31.4	37.6	37.8	38.2	41.3	43.8	45.1	52.8	67.5	56.4	47.7	55.5	54.0	75.6	97.2
Argentina (frozen)	213	21.7	19.7	16.4	21.4	19.5	25.3	30.7	39.6	54.4	58.3	29.7	31.4	40.2	40.1	63.9
Argentina (corned)	213	36.6	37.8	39.1	40.3	38.6	38.2	60.0	63.9	80.1	110.0	76.8	72.1	72.9	73.9	115.9
Butter (US cents/pound)																
New Zealand (London)	196	28.1	25.4	25.0	21.7	21.7	22.6	31.9	36.6	29.9	35.9	48.7	51.7	56.9	74.0	88.3
New Zealand	196	43.8	39.6	37.9	32.3	32.4	32.7	43.8	58.0	50.6	50.5	57.8	56.5	65.7	78.0	79.4
Coal (US $/metric ton)																
Australia	193	....	....	21.4	21.7	23.3	25.7	28.2	31.7	37.9	56.3	90.0	106.1	100.5	106.2	102.6
Cocoa Beans (US cents/pound)																
Brazil	223	27.8	41.7	47.8	56.2	81.5	60.0	47.9	53.5	98.9	149.5	115.3	157.0	374.0	312.9	286.8
New York and London *	652	28.8	40.8	47.2	56.9	71.2	53.1	42.5	50.7	89.2	123.0	98.3	161.3	299.0	268.5	259.7
Coconut Oil (US cents/pound)																
Philippines (New York)	566	103.4	92.4	94.4	114.4	102.8	112.2	104.4	73.3	151.9	295.5	116.5	123.7	171.3	202.3	291.6
Philippines	566	93.7	78.0	83.4	98.0	81.0	91.5	84.4	58.7	113.9	285.3	121.5	112.3	172.9	193.0	299.9
Coffee (US cents/pound)																
Other Milds (New York) *	386	50.9	47.3	44.0	44.1	44.6	58.3	50.5	56.5	69.9	73.9	73.4	160.1	263.2	182.6	194.7
Brazil (New York)	223	52.2	48.4	45.0	44.4	48.8	66.6	53.4	62.7	82.6	87.5	98.5	178.4	318.8	197.2	213.0
Brazil	223	67.4	58.4	54.1	53.9	55.9	75.3	57.6	72.7	89.6	96.7	84.3	208.1	346.1	241.7	263.1
Colombia (New York)	233	54.4	53.2	47.0	47.8	50.4	63.6	55.0	62.5	81.5	87.3	91.5	175.8	271.0	207.7	205.7
Colombia	233	57.6	57.7	50.1	50.5	50.3	67.9	57.6	62.4	83.7	85.7	78.1	147.1	271.3	208.9	172.2
Uganda (New York) *	799	56.0	61.0	61.0	61.6	60.2	75.4	76.8	82.2	90.7	106.7	111.0	232.1	406.9	268.2	300.9
Copper (US cents/pound)																
United Kingdom (London) *	112	48.1	57.4	42.2	46.5	55.0	53.1	40.6	40.2	66.8	77.2	46.5	52.7	49.2	51.3	74.1
Copra (US $/metric ton)																
Philippines (Europ. Ports)	566	98.4	80.6	87.7	101.0	87.7	97.0	82.5	61.9	149.6	290.8	111.3	119.6	175.0	204.7	292.6
Cotton (US cents/pound)																
United States (10 markets)	111	42.3	36.8	32.0	37.9	35.4	34.9	38.5	47.7	78.1	80.6	62.8	94.6	85.7	80.2	86.5
Liverpool Index *	111	34.9	34.2	37.2	37.3	33.7	35.0	41.0	43.9	75.2	78.9	64.3	93.6	86.4	87.1	93.4
Egypt (Liverpool) *	469	17.1	16.6	17.7	19.5	21.1	20.9	20.6	21.7	32.8	51.2	43.1	45.4	49.7	46.2	51.1
Egypt (Long Staple)	469	9.6	9.2	9.2	10.3	11.6	11.8	11.9	12.6	16.5	29.1	26.8	22.9	30.1	23.1	23.9
Egypt (Long Medium)	469	9.4	9.8	8.4	10.3	13.8	11.4	11.3	11.0	15.6	29.2	25.1	19.4	28.8	23.3	25.0
Fish Meal (US $/metric ton)																
All Origins (Hamburg) *	293	49.0	44.1	35.9	31.3	41.8	47.8	40.8	57.9	131.5	90.3	59.5	91.3	110.1	99.5	95.8
Iceland	176	....	....	....	....	....	38.7	40.1	34.6	86.4	83.9	46.4	57.8	87.4	86.5	78.2
Gold (US $/fine ounce)																
United Kingdom (London)	112	9.1	9.1	9.1	10.1	10.7	9.4	10.6	15.2	25.4	41.5	42.0	32.5	38.5	50.4	80.0
Groundnuts (US $/metric ton)																
Nigeria (London)	694	15.6	14.1	13.5	12.5	15.6	17.2	18.9	19.2	29.5	55.8	32.7	31.9	41.3	47.6	42.5
Groundnut Meal (US $/metric ton)																
All Origins (Europe)	694	62.1	57.9	58.1	54.8	58.5	62.4	59.8	74.3	162.0	106.3	85.4	107.2	132.7	124.9	128.7
Groundnut Oil (US $/metric ton)																
West Africa (Europe) *	694	33.7	30.8	29.4	28.1	34.4	39.3	46.2	44.2	56.5	109.8	80.8	71.7	87.8	112.0	92.2
Hides (US cents/pound)																
United States (Chicago) *	111	15.5	19.2	13.0	12.2	15.8	14.0	15.7	32.1	37.2	25.6	25.2	36.4	40.1	51.5	79.3
Australia	193	59.6	63.6	49.1	42.2	50.8	41.5	32.6	47.9	131.1	111.7	73.5	94.8	112.7	123.6	151.6
Iron Ore (US $/metric ton)																
Brazil (North Sea Ports) *	223	50.9	49.5	43.8	41.0	37.9	49.4	43.5	41.5	55.6	61.7	74.0	73.8	70.1	62.9	76.1
Jute (US $/metric ton)																
Bangladesh (Chitta.-Chalna)	513	61.3	74.0	70.3	65.3	68.8	66.0	68.9	71.9	69.6	85.1	90.8	72.3	78.1	97.4	94.3
Lamb (US cents/pound)																
New Zealand (London) *	196	28.1	27.2	25.7	24.7	28.5	27.9	30.2	40.0	52.4	53.6	56.0	59.3	64.4	83.1	90.0
New Zealand	196	29.1	26.3	24.2	24.1	27.5	27.5	27.3	30.8	49.1	52.3	45.0	46.2	54.4	62.8	72.2
Lead (US cents/pound)																
United Kingdom (London) *	112	39.2	32.4	28.1	29.7	35.8	37.6	31.3	37.3	52.8	73.0	51.5	55.1	76.3	81.6	148.6
United States (New York)	111	35.4	33.2	31.0	29.2	33.0	34.7	30.7	34.0	36.3	49.3	47.7	50.8	68.0	74.7	117.2
Linseed Oil (US $/metric ton)																
Any Origin	001	30.1	27.0	28.6	33.1	31.4	30.5	26.4	27.8	76.8	154.3	98.8	76.9	65.1	61.2	90.8
Maize (US $/bushel)																
United States (Chicago)	111	50.0	52.5	49.9	45.5	47.5	52.6	53.8	50.3	88.3	123.7	111.1	103.1	85.0	88.8	100.9
United States (US Gulf Pts) *	111	50.6	53.1	49.6	43.5	47.6	53.3	53.3	51.0	89.2	121.1	109.4	102.7	87.3	92.2	105.8
Thailand	578	44.3	45.8	45.8	38.8	41.9	49.9	44.7	41.5	79.2	101.9	101.5	87.7	81.1	75.6	104.7
Manganese (US $/long ton)																
India (US Ports)	534	22.4	22.6	21.6	18.5	15.5	16.2	18.7	18.9	22.3	33.4	41.0	43.1	44.0	42.3	41.0
Newsprint (US $/short ton)																
United States (New York)	111	26.7	27.5	28.3	28.5	29.5	30.4	31.7	32.9	34.4	42.5	51.8	55.7	60.1	63.7	69.7
Finland	172	19.6	19.8	19.9	19.3	19.3	20.0	20.9	21.8	25.5	40.9	54.9	51.3	56.0	57.8	64.0
Sweden	144	19.9	20.0	19.9	19.2	18.7	19.7	20.6	22.5	27.4	40.8	54.8	53.2	57.5	59.5	66.0
Nickel (US cents/pound)																
United Kingdom (N.Europ.ports)*	156	19.5	19.6	21.5	23.1	25.8	31.7	33.1	34.7	38.1	43.3	51.6	56.0	58.7	52.0	67.4
Palm Kernels (US $/metric ton)																
Malaysia (Rotterdam)	548	95.5	81.3	....	106.4	91.7	110.1	100.6	65.7	146.8	313.5	122.5	129.9	186.0	229.0	314.5
Palm Oil (US $/metric ton)																
Malaysia (N.W. Europe) *	548	94.3	80.6	76.9	58.1	63.8	89.5	90.4	75.0	129.7	238.5	145.0	137.1	182.9	207.1	225.6
Malaysia	548	85.2	74.0	69.9	49.5	48.8	74.8	75.7	65.2	83.4	174.3	165.4	125.3	182.9	185.8	207.0
Pepper, Black (US cents/pound)																
Malaysia (New York)	548	58.9	53.3	47.2	46.5	57.1	70.5	61.6	56.9	71.3	104.4	111.9	109.6	139.7	130.9	118.2

Commodity Price Index

d

1980	1981	1982	1983	1984	1985	1986	1987	1988	1989	1990	1991	1992	1993	1994		
Country of Origin and,for Wholesale Prices,Pricing Point in Parentheses																
1990=100																
111.7	**100.8**	**90.8**	**96.3**	**97.9**	**85.1**	**82.0**	**88.8**	**109.0**	**108.4**	**100.0**	**95.6**	**95.4**	**91.8**	**103.2**	**World (non-fuel comm. with *)**	**001**
124.7	**120.8**	**102.5**	**110.5**	**109.8**	**91.6**	**80.5**	**84.3**	**108.6**	**110.6**	**100.0**	**99.1**	**101.3**	**100.0**	**105.1**	**Food**	**001**
187.3	**148.4**	**149.1**	**158.2**	**183.0**	**163.8**	**192.5**	**134.6**	**138.3**	**114.6**	**100.0**	**93.5**	**80.5**	**85.6**	**149.7**	**Beverages**	**001**
85.6	**74.7**	**71.6**	**73.4**	**74.8**	**64.6**	**68.1**	**87.3**	**94.2**	**97.3**	**100.0**	**96.4**	**99.0**	**115.0**	**126.6**	**Agricultural Raw Materials**	**001**
89.7	**77.7**	**70.3**	**79.9**	**72.9**	**67.0**	**64.7**	**79.4**	**118.8**	**112.0**	**100.0**	**85.7**	**83.7**	**71.9**	**83.8**	**Metals**	**001**
115.5	**122.4**	**104.8**	**96.0**	**96.8**	**87.4**	**87.8**	**88.9**	**102.5**	**104.7**	**100.0**	**103.2**	**98.0**	**83.0**	**89.6**	**Fertilizers**	**001**
126.3	**108.6**	**95.9**	**103.3**	**105.1**	**91.7**	**92.6**	**92.9**	**111.3**	**107.5**	**100.0**	**95.5**	**92.1**	**91.6**	**111.9**	**World Bank LMICs**	**200**
															Aluminum (US cents/pound)	
108.3	77.0	60.5	87.7	76.3	63.5	70.1	95.5	155.3	119.0	100.0	79.5	76.6	69.5	90.0	All Origins (London) *	**156**
															Bananas (US cents/pound)	
69.2	74.0	69.1	79.1	68.1	69.7	70.4	69.6	88.3	100.8	100.0	103.5	88.2	81.7	81.0	Latin America (US Ports) *	**248**
															Beef (US cents/pound)	
107.7	96.4	93.2	95.2	88.7	84.0	81.7	93.0	98.2	100.2	100.0	103.9	95.8	102.1	91.0	Australia-NZ (US Ports) *	**193**
92.0	91.6	104.5	101.4	103.0	95.2	81.3	86.3	86.5	I 92.4	100.0	95.9	95.6	99.1	92.0	United States (New York)	**111**
74.4	64.3	48.9	50.9	69.4	66.2	84.8	123.9	118.3	113.5	100.0	148.7	194.0	231.5	175.9	Argentina (frozen)	**213**
139.8	132.5	97.3	88.8	84.9	80.0	88.2	108.7	80.1	92.7	100.0	116.9	90.9	108.7	121.6	Argentina (corned)	**213**
															Butter (US cents/pound)	
102.3	95.2	87.3	75.3	63.5	68.6	77.8	76.7	95.0	100.2	100.0	95.2	101.7	95.3	95.0	New Zealand (London)	**196**
84.5	110.9	111.2	104.5	87.3	68.9	65.1	72.9	79.6	104.2	100.0	89.8	104.9	93.5	96.7	New Zealand	**196**
															Coal (US $/metric ton)	
106.1	122.1	132.7	115.0	105.8	93.4	91.9	81.9	85.0	97.4	100.0	102.2	97.0	92.2	87.5	Australia	**193**
															Cocoa Beans (US cents/pound)	
218.2	178.3	139.2	169.3	214.6	193.5	187.6	171.1	148.1	115.9	100.0	96.9	91.7	90.6	113.9	Brazil	**223**
205.3	163.8	137.4	167.1	188.9	177.8	163.1	157.5	124.9	98.0	100.0	94.1	86.7	87.6	110.1	New York and London *	**652**
															Coconut Oil (US cents/pound)	
199.2	168.8	138.4	216.1	342.0	174.8	87.8	131.0	167.3	153.1	100.0	128.2	171.2	133.6	179.6	Philippines (New York)	**566**
200.6	166.3	141.1	172.6	320.5	172.8	86.5	119.7	166.9	160.0	100.0	115.3	176.6	138.8	....	Philippines	**566**
															Coffee (US cents/pound)	
173.0	143.7	156.7	147.7	161.7	163.3	216.2	126.0	151.5	120.0	100.0	95.4	71.4	78.5	166.6	Other Milds (New York) *	**386**
249.1	222.4	171.5	170.3	178.6	177.7	275.9	126.9	145.4	117.8	100.0	87.0	67.1	79.4	171.0	Brazil (New York)	**223**
244.4	141.7	161.4	172.0	191.7	176.8	323.8	153.0	171.3	126.8	100.0	97.4	73.5	85.2	196.5	Brazil	**223**
200.6	143.7	156.7	147.7	161.8	163.3	218.2	126.0	151.5	120.0	100.0	95.3	71.4	....	....	Colombia (New York)	**233**
202.5	152.5	168.6	157.9	167.0	168.9	253.4	141.7	159.2	138.5	100.0	105.1	75.5	....	....	Colombia	**233**
267.6	187.2	201.9	225.7	251.3	220.5	269.7	186.1	173.0	137.7	100.0	90.6	79.3	97.3	217.9	Uganda (New York) *	**799**
															Copper (US cents/pound)	
82.1	65.5	55.7	59.8	51.7	53.3	51.5	66.9	97.7	107.0	100.0	87.9	85.9	72.0	86.6	United Kingdom (London) *	**112**
															Copra (US $/metric ton)	
197.0	164.8	136.6	215.7	308.8	168.1	85.9	135.0	172.2	151.4	100.0	128.7	166.1	128.5	181.3	Philippines (Europ. Ports)	**566**
															Cotton (US cents/pound)	
113.2	100.3	83.6	95.3	94.9	81.7	73.4	88.4	79.9	I 89.4	100.0	98.4	76.2	77.8	102.7	United States (10 markets)	**111**
113.5	101.7	87.8	101.9	98.0	72.6	58.1	90.6	76.9	92.0	100.0	93.2	70.2	70.3	96.6	Liverpool Index *	**111**
51.1	50.6	41.6	46.6	54.6	54.6	52.4	54.3	72.8	96.4	100.0	92.9	70.9	67.0	57.2	Egypt (Liverpool) *	**469**
23.8	23.5	21.2	21.4	27.6	26.8	27.6	33.6	53.3	119.5	100.0	49.5	31.9	25.2	....	Egypt (Long Staple)	**469**
25.0	24.7	18.5	19.9	25.7	30.5	31.2	30.2	58.2	127.2	100.0	49.2	25.4	22.7	....	Egypt (Long Medium)	**469**
															Fish Meal (US $/metric ton)	
122.4	113.4	85.8	109.8	90.5	68.0	77.8	93.0	132.1	99.3	100.0	115.9	116.8	88.5	91.4	All Origins (Hamburg) *	**293**
97.3	97.9	65.2	111.6	68.7	63.4	71.7	80.4	99.2	111.4	100.0	103.9	108.6	84.3	94.1	Iceland	**176**
															Gold (US $/fine ounce)	
158.5	119.9	98.0	110.2	94.0	82.7	95.9	116.4	114.0	99.4	100.0	94.4	89.5	93.8	100.2	United Kingdom (London)	**112**
															Groundnuts (US $/metric ton)	
93.3	94.9	62.4	72.8	63.1	51.0	75.0	57.2	70.6	61.7	100.0	93.4	60.3	82.4	72.0	Nigeria (London)	**694**
															Groundnut Meal (US $/metric ton)	
146.9	145.7	112.8	124.0	101.5	79.2	89.9	87.6	113.4	108.5	100.0	81.2	82.6	91.0	91.1	All Origins (Europe)	**694**
															Groundnut Oil (US $/metric ton)	
89.1	108.2	60.7	73.8	105.5	93.9	59.1	51.9	61.3	80.4	100.0	92.9	63.3	76.6	106.1	West Africa (Europe) *	**694**
															Hides (US cents/pound)	
49.8	45.2	41.8	48.9	63.8	55.5	69.3	86.6	95.0	97.6	100.0	86.1	82.3	86.8	94.1	United States (Chicago) *	**111**
141.6	101.7	96.6	81.5	86.9	78.8	97.2	144.5	176.8	134.1	100.0	75.7	86.3	55.3	88.8	Australia	**193**
															Iron Ore (US $/metric ton)	
91.2	91.2	105.5	94.2	84.9	86.2	85.3	79.5	76.3	86.0	100.0	108.0	102.6	91.3	82.7	Brazil (North Sea Ports) *	**223**
															Jute (US $/metric ton)	
76.8	68.1	69.3	73.0	130.0	142.8	66.6	78.5	90.6	91.4	100.0	89.5	68.4	66.4	72.4	Bangladesh (Chitta.-Chalna)	**513**
															Lamb (US cents/pound)	
108.3	103.2	89.7	72.5	72.4	69.0	76.4	81.3	90.4	86.9	100.0	86.6	95.3	102.5	103.7	New Zealand (London) *	**196**
81.6	88.6	81.4	70.6	64.7	55.9	56.0	64.3	72.4	78.0	100.0	89.3	93.6	113.8	110.7	New Zealand	**196**
															Lead (US cents/pound)	
111.8	89.7	67.4	52.5	54.6	48.3	50.1	73.7	81.0	83.1	100.0	68.9	67.1	50.3	67.8	United Kingdom (London) *	**112**
96.3	82.9	59.1	49.9	59.8	43.4	44.9	79.5	80.9	I 84.9	100.0	73.2	77.9	69.9	82.3	United States (New York)	**111**
															Linseed Oil (US $/metric ton)	
98.3	93.0	73.2	68.3	80.6	88.4	59.1	44.8	73.5	106.7	100.0	61.9	55.9	63.2	72.9	Any Origin	**001**
															Maize (US $/bushel)	
115.0	121.5	96.6	123.9	125.1	102.0	80.8	65.4	96.0	I 101.5	100.0	96.2	95.2	93.8	99.2	United States (Chicago)	**111**
115.0	119.5	98.9	124.4	124.3	102.8	80.3	69.1	97.9	101.9	100.0	98.3	95.4	93.4	98.6	United States (US Gulf Pts) *	**111**
123.5	113.4	97.6	105.8	104.1	77.7	66.9	70.6	95.0	102.8	100.0	95.1	110.5	102.4	....	Thailand	**578**
															Manganese (US $/long ton)	
45.4	49.1	48.0	44.4	41.9	41.3	41.2	39.2	43.7	59.9	100.0	114.6	109.4	87.2	62.3	India (US Ports)	**534**
															Newsprint (US $/short ton)	
78.4	86.5	88.9	85.3	91.0	93.5	91.6	99.5	105.4	I 102.5	100.0	101.1	91.8	93.7	97.4	United States (New York)	**111**
71.4	70.5	67.9	57.3	55.1	57.0	70.9	81.0	95.7	91.5	100.0	96.7	81.7	65.6	69.9	Finland	**172**
73.2	69.5	66.3	59.2	54.6	57.3	72.4	85.2	97.2	91.9	100.0	98.8	81.8	....	....	Sweden	**144**
															Nickel (US cents/pound)	
73.5	67.2	54.6	52.7	53.6	55.3	43.9	55.0	155.4	150.2	100.0	92.1	79.1	59.9	71.4	United Kingdom (N.Europ.ports)*	**156**
															Palm Kernels (US $/metric ton)	
217.5	176.3	137.3	212.5	310.9	165.2	86.4	127.7	161.5	141.5	100.0	124.8	174.4	131.3	188.2	Malaysia (Rotterdam)	**548**
															Palm Oil (US $/metric ton)	
201.2	196.9	153.6	173.0	251.5	172.8	88.7	118.2	150.8	120.9	100.0	117.0	135.8	130.3	182.6	Malaysia (N.W. Europe) *	**548**
184.4	171.0	145.2	152.4	226.6	172.0	94.0	111.0	144.9	121.5	100.0	114.9	133.2	133.4	132.7	Malaysia	**548**
															Pepper,Black (US cents/pound)	
111.2	88.4	86.6	100.1	167.9	225.2	329.1	323.8	256.7	159.1	100.0	79.1	82.0	129.0	....	Malaysia (New York)	**548**

Commodity Price Index

Indices of Wholesale Prices (lines 76) and of Unit Values (lines 74)
1990=100

d		1965	1966	1967	1968	1969	1970	1971	1972	1973	1974	1975	1976	1977	1978	1979
Petroleum, spot (US $/barrel)																
Average Crude Price	001	9.6	9.6	9.6	9.6	9.6	9.6	11.7	12.7	14.2	50.9	48.1	53.6	58.2	58.7	132.6
Dubai Fateh	466	8.8	8.8	8.8	8.8	8.8	8.8	10.8	12.1	14.0	53.6	51.0	56.8	61.4	63.1	145.7
U.K. Brent	112	9.3	9.3	9.3	9.3	9.3	9.3	13.4	15.1	17.7	53.9	47.9	54.8	59.6	59.4	133.9
Alaskan North Slope	111	10.4	10.4	10.4	10.4	10.4	10.4	10.4	10.4	10.4	44.3	44.7	48.6	52.9	53.0	116.9
West Texas Intermediate	111	....	....	....	....	....	....	....	....	....	....	....	....	....	....	....
Phosphate Rock (US $/metric ton)																
Morocco (Casablanca)	686	34.6	32.1	29.6	28.4	27.8	27.2	27.8	28.4	34.0	130.3	167.9	88.5	75.7	71.6	81.5
Potash (US $/metric ton)																
Canada (Vancouver)	156	22.2	28.0	26.0	24.5	22.4	32.1	33.1	34.1	43.3	61.7	82.9	56.6	52.1	57.5	77.9
Plywood (US cents/sheet)																
Philippines (Tokyo)	566	17.2	20.7	22.6	22.4	23.8	29.0	23.0	27.3	53.5	43.0	34.3	41.6	45.5	53.4	74.0
Pulp (US $/metric ton)																
Sweden (Swedish Ports)	144	17.5	16.9	16.6	15.9	16.3	20.1	21.7	20.9	25.3	39.5	57.6	52.5	43.1	37.9	55.0
Sweden	144	18.5	17.6	17.4	16.6	17.8	21.1	22.8	22.6	27.1	38.5	53.5	50.7	45.0	39.5	51.3
Rice (US $/metric ton)																
United States (New Orleans)	111	47.0	47.0	48.1	49.2	48.1	48.3	49.0	55.4	101.6	142.5	107.5	79.0	85.7	102.5	97.8
Thailand (Bangkok) *	578	47.4	57.7	77.0	71.3	64.5	49.8	45.4	52.2	103.7	188.6	126.5	88.5	94.9	128.3	116.4
Thailand	578	40.8	47.2	55.9	62.9	51.2	42.1	32.8	37.4	76.0	172.6	111.7	79.1	82.4	118.1	101.0
Myanmar	518	49.9	51.8	59.9	70.2	59.2	40.6	36.5	36.6	57.1	180.2	125.3	81.8	83.8	98.1	108.9
Rubber (US cents/pound)																
All Origins (New York)	111	51.1	47.0	39.6	39.6	52.1	42.0	35.9	36.1	70.0	79.2	59.5	78.7	82.8	99.4	127.9
Malaysia (Singapore) *	548	58.4	54.5	45.1	44.2	58.1	47.1	38.5	38.4	78.4	86.9	64.9	89.5	94.2	114.0	146.0
Malaysia	548	58.4	56.2	47.1	45.7	57.8	49.4	40.6	39.8	73.9	90.2	68.5	89.4	98.1	113.7	146.7
Thailand	578	57.6	55.8	45.3	43.8	58.6	49.2	37.6	35.6	71.8	86.2	64.9	87.9	95.0	112.9	146.8
Shrimp (US $/pound)																
United States (U.S. Gulf Ports)	111	17.1	21.5	21.2	24.0	26.6	25.2	30.7	38.3	46.4	43.1	54.6	77.3	73.4	74.3	110.9
Silver (US cents/troy ounce)																
United States (New York)	111	26.8	26.8	32.2	44.5	37.2	36.7	32.1	34.9	53.1	97.7	91.7	90.3	95.9	112.1	230.1
Sisal (US $/metric ton)																
East Africa (Europe)	639	31.0	29.2	24.9	22.5	24.1	21.3	23.8	33.6	73.7	147.6	81.2	65.4	71.5	66.4	99.7
Sorghum (US $/metric ton)																
United States (US Gulf Ports)	111	45.4	49.8	48.5	44.7	48.2	49.8	53.6	54.1	89.9	116.4	107.6	101.2	85.9	90.3	104.0
Soybeans (US $/metric ton)																
United States (Rotterdam) *	111	47.4	51.2	45.6	42.9	41.7	47.4	50.9	56.7	117.7	112.2	89.8	93.7	113.5	108.7	120.7
Soybean Meal (US $/metric ton)																
United States (Rotterdam) *	111	36.5	43.2	42.6	49.0	47.5	51.3	50.9	64.6	151.2	92.1	77.5	99.1	114.9	106.6	121.4
Soybean Oil (US $/metric ton)																
All Origins (Dutch Ports) *	111	60.3	58.4	48.5	39.8	44.1	64.0	67.9	53.8	97.4	186.0	125.9	98.0	129.7	135.6	148.0
Sugar (US cents/pound)																
EU Import Price *	112	22.0	22.5	22.2	19.2	19.2	19.2	19.5	25.7	25.2	40.2	58.4	50.6	53.0	60.2	72.9
Caribbean (New York) *	001	16.9	14.9	16.0	15.9	27.1	30.0	36.2	59.8	76.9	239.3	164.3	92.4	64.8	62.5	77.2
U.S. Import Price *	111	26.6	27.5	28.7	29.8	30.7	32.3	34.1	36.7	44.3	126.8	96.6	57.2	47.3	60.1	66.8
Brazil	223	21.2	22.8	22.9	28.2	29.8	32.0	34.5	45.3	56.2	159.2	183.0	72.3	51.7	48.3	55.1
Australia	193	30.9	26.6	23.6	22.5	31.2	39.3	38.6	51.5	60.3	145.3	157.7	113.4	92.8	95.4	105.2
Philippines	566	27.8	31.6	33.9	34.8	35.4	34.0	37.3	40.0	47.5	108.1	138.9	68.1	44.8	42.0	39.1
Superphosphate (US $/metric ton)																
United States (US Gulf Ports)	111	35.8	35.8	35.7	28.4	29.6	32.2	32.6	51.2	75.9	233.7	153.6	69.4	74.3	74.4	108.7
Tea (US cents/pound)																
Average Auction (London) *	112	62.5	61.5	61.9	51.3	48.0	53.8	51.9	51.9	52.0	68.7	68.0	75.6	132.4	107.7	106.2
Sri Lanka	524	48.9	46.3	43.5	40.8	38.6	39.4	40.5	44.7	41.8	50.9	56.6	54.5	92.8	92.9	85.5
Timber (US $/cubic meter)																
Hardwood Logs																
Malaysia, Sarawak	548	21.8	23.0	24.5	25.1	24.3	26.9	27.0	25.3	42.5	50.9	42.1	57.4	57.8	60.7	106.1
Hardwood Sawnwood																
Malaysia	548	15.7	14.1	14.8	16.3	17.4	18.0	17.9	21.2	30.2	27.7	32.2	32.5	29.8	39.8	65.6
Softwood Logs																
United States	111	....	....	....	....	....	....	....	....	....	....	....	....	....	....	....
Softwood Sawnwood																
United States	111	....	....	....	....	....	....	....	....	....	....	....	....	....	....	....
Tin (US cents/pound)																
All Origins (London) *	112	63.9	58.7	54.4	51.4	56.3	60.4	57.7	61.5	78.9	134.5	113.0	124.7	177.5	211.6	253.8
Malaysia (Penang)	548	59.9	55.1	51.2	48.3	53.4	56.7	54.0	58.1	73.4	123.4	105.2	117.9	168.7	196.6	234.1
Malaysia	548	59.8	55.7	51.6	48.6	52.7	56.0	53.5	57.8	70.3	116.8	102.1	116.4	164.4	196.5	231.8
Bolivia	218	60.7	56.2	52.4	49.8	54.1	60.8	55.3	59.1	72.4	125.9	108.9	119.9	165.6	197.6	234.4
Thailand	578	44.2	54.1	52.3	48.9	54.1	56.6	55.8	59.2	70.4	118.3	107.0	117.5	167.9	198.6	234.0
Tobacco (US $/metric ton)																
United States (All Markets) *	111	1.8	1.9	4.8	35.5	32.8	31.1	32.4	31.7	33.3	43.7	54.3	64.5	66.4	66.9	69.1
Urea (US $/metric ton)																
Any Origin (Europe)	170	60.4	56.8	50.5	41.7	35.7	30.7	29.3	37.7	60.4	201.1	125.9	71.1	81.2	92.3	110.1
Wheat (US $/bushel)																
Australia (Sydney)	193	28.9	31.8	31.5	30.0	29.0	28.1	29.8	34.8	75.1	100.7	76.2	66.2	55.1	69.9	80.9
Australia	193	36.4	38.5	39.4	37.1	38.8	33.4	36.1	37.8	47.8	111.5	107.7	92.4	68.2	72.9	92.7
United States (US Gulf Pts) *	111	43.9	46.5	48.5	46.3	43.1	40.5	45.5	51.5	103.2	132.6	110.0	98.1	76.2	94.3	118.3
Argentina	213	38.8	38.7	43.2	39.6	40.6	37.7	41.2	46.1	67.4	134.0	119.1	92.8	67.0	81.5	101.3
Wool (US cents/kilogram)																
Australia-NZ(UK) 48s *	112	54.4	54.9	44.8	36.8	38.2	35.0	35.4	60.7	106.0	83.0	68.3	93.3	98.6	101.2	123.0
Australia-NZ(UK) 64s *	112	30.5	33.8	30.9	30.0	28.0	24.3	22.1	36.8	86.5	60.9	47.8	49.3	53.2	54.8	65.0
Australia (greasy wool)	193	28.2	30.5	27.3	26.1	29.5	22.0	17.8	26.4	68.3	56.4	40.8	44.3	50.8	52.6	58.1
New Zealand	196	33.5	33.6	27.3	20.2	22.9	21.6	21.3	31.3	69.6	62.9	43.2	59.4	75.1	73.1	88.0
Zinc (US cents/pound)																
United Kingdom (London) *	112	20.6	18.5	17.9	17.3	18.9	19.5	20.4	24.9	55.4	81.5	49.1	46.9	38.8	39.1	48.8
United States (New York)	111	21.0	21.0	20.2	19.6	21.3	22.2	22.6	24.8	29.5	50.2	54.5	52.5	48.4	44.1	53.0
Bolivia	218	21.0	20.1	18.0	17.1	19.9	20.8	22.7	26.3	35.4	51.9	55.0	53.8	49.3	41.0	53.5

*See the Commodity Prices note in the monthly IFS.
₤ Prior to 1982, the World index and all components (food, beverages, agricultural raw materials, and metals), except fertilizer, were calculated by backward recursion of percent changes based on the previously published indices. (00176axd)

Commodity Price Index

Country of Origin and, for Wholesale Prices, Pricing Point in Parentheses
1990=100

1980	1981	1982	1983	1984	1985	1986	1987	1988	1989	1990	1991	1992	1993	1994		
															Petroleum, spot (US $/barrel)	
160.9	154.7	142.3	128.7	128.1	122.4	62.7	80.7	64.2	78.0	100.0	83.0	82.6	73.2	70.2	Average Crude Price	001
175.2	167.6	155.2	140.4	134.4	129.3	63.9	82.8	64.6	76.7	100.0	80.9	84.0	73.1	72.1	Dubai Fateh	466
158.0	152.9	139.3	124.4	120.1	113.9	60.4	76.5	62.4	76.0	100.0	83.3	80.6	71.0	65.9	U.K. Brent	112
148.4	142.5	131.6	120.5	129.6	123.2	63.1	82.1	64.7	80.2	100.0	83.3	82.4	74.5	71.6	Alaskan North Slope	111
....	....	....	124.4	120.2	115.1	61.8	78.4	65.3	80.1	100.0	87.8	84.1	75.5	70.0	West Texas Intermediate	111
															Phosphate Rock (US $/metric ton)	
115.3	122.2	104.6	91.2	94.4	83.7	84.6	76.5	88.9	100.8	100.0	104.9	103.1	81.5	81.5	Morocco (Casablanca)	686
															Potash (US $/metric ton)	
117.9	114.6	82.3	76.9	85.3	85.6	70.1	70.4	89.2	100.8	100.0	110.9	114.2	109.5	107.7	Canada (Vancouver)	156
															Plywood (US cents/sheet)	
77.2	69.2	66.0	64.8	64.0	59.4	77.3	112.4	101.1	98.7	100.0	104.9	107.3	186.4	168.9	Philippines (Tokyo)	566
															Pulp (US $/metric ton)	
68.8	63.6	51.8	44.6	56.1	50.4	52.7	71.9	87.6	93.8	100.0	84.4	71.1	54.5	61.5	Sweden (Swedish Ports)	144
63.4	62.6	55.6	48.7	57.5	50.4	56.2	72.8	87.1	97.4	100.0	74.3	69.8	52.4	62.3	Sweden	144
															Rice (US $/metric ton)	
127.1	145.1	94.1	97.1	97.5	98.2	88.0	83.0	110.3	105.1	100.0	107.3	103.0	99.9	119.8	United States (New Orleans)	111
151.0	168.1	102.2	96.4	87.8	75.7	73.2	80.0	105.0	111.5	100.0	108.8	100.1	93.3	124.7	Thailand (Bangkok) *	578
125.9	147.5	95.7	93.4	88.0	75.6	63.2	73.5	99.7	106.6	100.0	106.3	107.7	95.2	....	Thailand	578
133.8	151.5	102.7	90.2	90.6	80.2	68.0	58.4	82.8	102.8	100.0	113.0	103.2	84.3	83.5	Myanmar	518
															Rubber (US cents/pound)	
146.4	113.6	90.2	111.9	98.8	83.3	82.1	87.9	97.3	97.1	100.0	94.9	93.0	94.4	97.5	All Origins (New York)	111
164.7	129.9	99.2	123.1	110.8	87.7	93.3	113.9	137.0	112.2	100.0	95.5	99.6	96.1	130.2	Malaysia (Singapore) *	548
164.2	128.1	97.4	119.2	116.3	91.2	96.0	113.2	147.1	115.7	100.0	102.0	105.6	104.2	129.5	Malaysia	548
167.6	133.0	95.8	116.7	117.5	91.5	95.5	113.9	144.9	116.8	100.0	98.1	98.3	97.7	....	Thailand	578
															Shrimp (US $/pound)	
93.9	90.0	126.7	122.6	106.9	97.1	119.6	105.8	115.2	104.0	100.0	106.9	101.4	105.4	121.2	United States (U.S. Gulf Ports)	111
															Silver (US cents/troy ounce)	
426.9	218.2	164.9	237.4	168.9	127.4	113.5	145.4	135.6	114.1	100.0	83.8	81.7	89.2	109.6	United States (New York)	111
															Sisal (US $/metric ton)	
107.0	90.2	83.0	79.8	81.6	73.5	71.9	71.6	77.0	91.3	100.0	93.6	70.7	86.1	84.6	East Africa (Europe)	639
															Sorghum (US $/metric ton)	
124.0	121.6	104.2	123.9	113.7	99.1	79.3	70.0	94.7	101.9	100.0	101.1	98.9	95.3	99.9	United States (US Gulf Ports)	111
															Soybeans (US $/metric ton)	
120.1	116.9	99.1	114.2	114.3	90.9	84.5	87.4	123.0	111.4	100.0	97.1	95.4	103.4	102.5	United States (Rotterdam) *	111
															Soybean Meal (US $/metric ton)	
129.2	126.3	109.0	118.9	98.5	78.6	92.3	101.6	133.7	123.6	100.0	98.5	102.1	104.0	96.2	United States (Rotterdam) *	111
															Soybean Oil (US $/metric ton)	
133.7	113.3	100.0	117.7	162.0	128.7	76.5	74.7	103.6	96.4	100.0	101.4	95.8	107.3	137.7	All Origins (Dutch Ports) *	111
															Sugar (US cents/pound)	
83.5	71.6	68.5	66.4	60.6	60.9	70.3	81.0	90.0	86.0	100.0	105.0	107.6	106.2	106.6	EU Import Price *	112
229.2	135.0	67.2	67.7	41.6	32.4	48.4	54.0	81.5	102.4	100.0	71.8	72.5	80.1	96.8	Caribbean (New York) *	001
129.2	84.9	85.7	94.8	93.5	87.5	90.1	93.9	95.1	98.1	100.0	92.7	91.6	92.9	94.7	U.S. Import Price *	111
136.7	106.1	59.1	59.4	57.5	41.8	44.1	42.7	52.8	76.2	100.0	74.4	69.8	72.9	82.5	Brazil	223
166.6	151.5	78.9	81.6	61.8	46.2	63.0	59.2	75.6	97.5	100.0	85.1	82.5	84.4	95.9	Australia	193
83.4	106.1	77.5	69.1	65.3	76.8	90.4	85.4	97.7	97.7	100.0	98.1	97.8	72.6	....	Philippines	566
															Superphosphate (US $/metric ton)	
136.8	122.1	105.0	102.2	99.6	92.1	91.9	104.7	120.1	109.2	100.0	101.0	91.6	84.9	100.2	United States (US Gulf Ports)	111
															Tea (US cents/pound)	
109.6	99.4	95.1	114.4	170.1	97.6	94.9	84.0	88.1	99.0	100.0	90.7	98.3	91.4	90.2	Average Auction (London) *	112
88.2	79.7	73.5	97.4	132.5	97.4	69.4	78.5	76.8	81.0	100.0	88.8	81.6	82.4	80.7	Sri Lanka	524
															Timber (US $/cubic meter)	
															Hardwood Logs	
88.3	63.4	63.6	56.9	70.7	51.3	60.7	104.5	104.3	104.4	100.0	112.1	122.7	242.7	197.4	Malaysia, Sarawak	548
															Hardwood Sawnwood	
71.5	60.7	43.8	39.2	48.7	35.3	41.8	71.9	71.8	90.4	100.0	101.5	117.4	146.6	158.9	Malaysia	548
															Softwood Logs	
....	....	72.4	63.3	59.4	58.5	60.9	71.7	83.7	86.0	100.0	101.7	123.4	176.4	162.9	United States	111
															Softwood Sawnwood	
....	....	73.5	68.6	66.5	66.0	72.4	77.7	78.9	89.3	100.0	104.8	113.8	134.5	145.2	United States	111
															Tin (US cents/pound)	
275.7	232.8	210.8	213.4	201.0	189.6	101.2	109.9	115.9	140.2	100.0	92.0	100.3	84.9	89.7	All Origins (London) *	112
259.2	221.8	203.6	205.5	196.6	188.9	94.2	105.5	111.6	136.9	100.0	92.7	99.0	84.4	86.4	Malaysia (Penang)	548
261.7	220.7	206.6	204.7	197.9	182.7	98.5	106.0	112.4	136.9	100.0	92.7	100.2	84.4	86.4	Malaysia	548
265.0	220.9	200.3	204.4	193.3	188.0	88.1	107.7	111.6	139.7	100.0	88.3	95.5	86.9	....	Bolivia	218
263.9	224.0	219.6	208.8	195.7	187.1	100.9	107.4	108.9	135.8	100.0	88.8	93.2	82.8	....	Thailand	578
															Tobacco (US $/metric ton)	
67.1	68.4	75.6	78.3	82.1	77.0	78.4	80.9	72.8	93.4	100.0	103.2	101.4	79.5	87.7	United States (All Markets) *	111
															Urea (US $/metric ton)	
141.5	137.5	100.3	86.0	109.1	86.8	68.2	74.3	98.7	84.2	100.0	109.6	89.4	68.0	94.2	Any Origin (Europe)	170
															Wheat (US $/bushel)	
90.3	89.4	82.2	82.1	71.1	72.7	61.6	58.9	77.3	90.9	100.0	67.9	102.3	79.5	83.4	Australia (Sydney)	193
115.7	119.4	103.9	110.0	91.6	82.5	74.0	57.3	87.4	108.0	100.0	68.5	98.9	87.8	82.6	Australia	193
127.5	129.1	118.3	116.2	112.4	100.2	84.8	83.3	107.1	124.9	100.0	94.9	111.5	103.5	110.5	United States (US Gulf Pts) *	111
127.6	134.2	115.6	99.4	91.6	79.8	67.8	62.2	81.0	103.1	100.0	62.2	83.4	90.9	91.2	Argentina	213
															Wool (US cents/kilogram)	
125.2	114.0	99.8	93.3	91.9	87.8	94.9	118.8	136.2	122.8	100.0	76.5	79.3	74.3	92.9	Australia-NZ(UK) 48s *	112
73.9	75.8	70.9	66.8	69.2	61.3	57.6	88.3	144.2	114.7	100.0	68.8	61.7	47.6	76.6	Australia-NZ(UK) 64s *	112
67.7	73.6	68.8	60.3	63.1	57.9	58.1	76.8	127.0	116.6	100.0	68.8	67.7	53.8	72.4	Australia (greasy wool)	193
92.7	80.4	70.2	65.0	67.6	68.8	72.8	97.5	118.1	113.1	100.0	73.0	71.1	68.6	84.3	New Zealand	196
															Zinc (US cents/pound)	
50.1	55.7	49.1	50.4	60.7	51.6	49.7	52.6	81.7	109.1	100.0	73.9	81.8	63.5	65.8	United Kingdom (London) *	112
53.4	64.0	56.1	60.0	70.0	60.6	56.8	61.8	81.0	108.6	100.0	74.0	79.9	63.6	65.4	United States (New York)	111
53.6	61.2	58.3	54.6	68.4	58.7	53.2	55.8	75.3	111.0	100.0	74.0	82.2	65.2	....	Bolivia	218

COUNTRY
TABLES

Afghanistan, I.S. of

512

		1965	1966	1967	1968	1969	1970	1971	1972	1973	1974	1975	1976	1977	1978	1979
Exchange Rates														*Afghanis per SDR:*		
Principal Rate	aa	45.000	45.000	45.000	45.000	45.000	45.000	48.857	48.857	54.286	55.096	52.680	52.282	54.662	58.626	55.657
														Afghanis per US Dollar:		
Principal Rate	ae	45.000	45.000	45.000	45.000	45.000	45.000	45.000	45.000	45.000	45.000	45.000	45.000	45.000	45.000	42.250
Principal Rate	rf	45.000	45.000	45.000	45.000	45.000	45.000	45.000	45.000	45.000	45.000	45.000	45.000	45.000	45.000	43.733[e]
Fund Position														*Millions of SDRs:*		
Quota	2f.s	22.50	29.00	29.00	29.00	29.00	37.00	37.00	37.00	37.00	37.00	37.00	37.00	37.00	45.00	45.00
SDRs	1b.s	—	—	—	—	—	1.91	3.16	1.20	4.28	4.45	5.32	5.12	5.68	5.38	13.42
Reserve Position in the Fund	1c.s	—	—	—	—	—	—	—	—	—	—	—	—	8.25	8.97	9.43
Total Fund Cred.&Loans Outstg.	2tl	7.30	10.38	11.22	12.28	17.10	14.53	10.13	5.73	7.23	4.74	9.24	1.75	—	—	—
International Liquidity											*Millions of US Dollars Unless Otherwise Indicated:*					
Total Reserves minus Gold	1l.d	8.98	12.10	5.30	6.12	8.18	12.53	26.95	20.80	21.61	27.64	86.55	130.92	275.82	390.56	441.21
SDRs	1b.d	—	—	—	—	—	1.91	3.43	1.30	5.16	5.45	6.23	5.95	6.90	7.01	17.68
Reserve Position in the Fund	1c.d	—	—	—	—	—	—	—	—	—	—	—	—	10.02	11.69	12.42
Foreign Exchange	1d.d	8.98	12.10	5.30	6.12	8.18	10.62	23.52	19.50	16.45	22.19	80.32	124.97	258.90	371.86	411.11
Gold (Million Fine Troy Ounces)	1ad	1.038	.995	.944	.942	.943	.989	.932	.932	.932	.932	.932	.932	.941	.949	.964
Gold (National Valuation)	1and	....	....	....	....	31.01	31.01	29.01	35.40	39.35	39.35	39.35	39.35	39.69	40.02	42.97
Monetary Authorities: Other Liab.	4..d	2.74	6.09	1.47	4.98	3.08	2.16	6.16	4.91	.93	1.19	2.34	3.16	2.70	27.47	42.29
Deposit Money Banks: Assets	7a.d	2.07	2.80	3.00	3.66	4.92	1.33	7.52	5.13	6.26	8.44	10.92	10.37	20.55	40.81	54.51
Monetary Authorities														*Millions of Afghanis:*		
Foreign Assets	11	2,240	2,256	1,934	1,689	ℐ1,830	2,148	2,722	2,821	3,185	3,550	6,848	9,350	15,864	19,506	21,399
Claims on Central Government	12a	5,476	5,736	6,082	7,486	ℐ7,614	8,363	9,859	11,657	11,355	12,270	13,204	15,466	16,486	21,716	23,900
Claims on Local Government	12b	119	88	142	260	ℐ177	287	129	9	11	770	1,313	400	11	11	188
Claims on Nonfin.Pub.Enterprises	12c	....	....	....	....	....	....	....	....	....	....	....	....	....	....	....
Claims on Private Sector	12d	485	628	517	662	ℐ1,097	1,020	833	1,186	1,261	1,706	2,273	3,678	2,773	3,139	5,474
Claims on Deposit Money Banks	12e	70	130	174	109	ℐ130	658	266	367	408	1,153	825	415	255	426	816
Claims on Other Financial Insts.	12f	....	....	....	....	....	....	....	....	....	....	....	....	....	....	....
Reserve Money	14	5,996	6,032	6,035	7,180	ℐ7,803	8,759	9,512	10,335	10,886	12,409	14,545	17,765	23,725	27,528	ℐ33,476
of which: Currency Outside DMBs	14a	4,797	4,722	4,614	5,111	ℐ5,769	6,540	6,435	7,518	8,979	9,693	11,427	14,225	17,784	21,667	ℐ26,641
Private Sector Deposits	14d	992	1,158	1,128	1,792	ℐ1,630	1,419	2,297	2,134	1,616	2,019	2,494	3,002	4,544	5,551	5,758
Time, Savings,& Fgn.Currency Dep.	15	297	253	295	263	ℐ589	680	681	811	1,254	1,748	1,445	2,306	2,647	2,500	2,941
Restricted Deposits	16b	....	....	....	....	291	522	611	552	585	1,043	2,179	4,020	2,728	4,961	4,215
Foreign Liabilities	16c	452	741	571	777	ℐ908	751	772	501	434	315	592	234	121	1,236	1,787
Central Government Deposits	16d	774	1,309	1,070	1,121	ℐ1,105	1,436	1,397	1,987	1,589	2,469	3,863	3,623	3,582	5,523	4,661
Capital Accounts	17a	813	841	689	692	ℐ787	985	1,325	1,510	1,579	1,512	1,627	1,702	2,151	2,438	2,983
Other Items (Net)	17r	58	−338	190	174	ℐ−635	−657	−491	1,084	−107	−44	214	−342	434	612	1,714
Deposit Money Banks														*Millions of Afghanis:*		
Reserves	20	150	117	212	229	ℐ321	509	519	604	308	539	462	520	1,319	430	887
Foreign Assets	21	93	126	135	165	ℐ222	40	339	231	282	380	492	467	925	1,837	2,303
Claims on Nonfin.Pub.Enterprises	22c	....	....	....	....	....	....	....	....	....	....	....	....	....	....	....
Claims on Private Sector	22d	1,767	1,767	1,932	1,826	ℐ1,992	2,563	2,326	2,795	3,020	3,509	2,743	2,565	2,720	3,632	4,315
Claims on Other Financial Insts.	22f	....	....	....	....	....	....	....	....	....	....	....	....	....	....	....
Demand Deposits	24	315	263	359	381	ℐ772	719	936	911	723	810	1,054	1,095	1,424	1,407	1,788
Time, Savings,& Fgn.Currency Dep.	25	654	665	639	667	ℐ825	973	1,211	1,541	1,612	1,825	1,679	1,851	2,372	2,326	2,533
Restricted Deposits	26b	....	....	....	....	....	....	....	....	....	....	....	....	....	....	....
Foreign Liabilities	26c	....	....	....	....	....	....	....	....	....	....	....	....	....	....	....
Long-Term Foreign Liabilities	26cl	....	....	....	....	....	....	....	....	....	....	....	....	....	....	....
Central Government Deposits	26d	116	85	135	164	ℐ76	85	79	104	116	105	120	6	19	16	41
Credit from Monetary Authorities	26g	....	....	....	....	....	....	....	....	....	....	....	....	....	....	....
Capital Accounts	27a	1,064	1,119	1,229	1,257	1,278	1,199	1,210	1,226	1,317	1,275	1,237	1,274	1,375	1,587	1,862
Other Items (Net)	27r	−139	−122	−82	−249	ℐ−416	136	−253	−152	−159	413	−393	−674	−226	563	1,281
Monetary Survey														*Millions of Afghanis:*		
Foreign Assets (Net)	31n	1,881	1,641	1,498	1,077	ℐ1,143	1,437	2,288	2,550	3,032	3,615	6,748	9,583	16,667	20,107	21,915
Domestic Credit	32	6,957	6,825	7,468	8,949	ℐ9,699	10,712	11,670	13,556	13,942	15,681	15,552	18,481	18,389	22,958	29,176
Claims on Central Govt. (Net)	32an	4,586	4,342	4,877	6,201	ℐ6,433	6,842	8,383	9,565	9,651	9,697	9,222	11,837	12,885	16,177	19,198
Claims on Local Government	32b	119	88	142	260	ℐ177	287	129	9	11	770	1,313	400	11	11	188
Claims on Nonfin.Pub.Enterprises	32c	....	....	....	....	....	....	....	....	....	....	....	....	....	....	....
Claims on Private Sector	32d	2,252	2,395	2,449	2,488	ℐ3,089	3,583	3,159	3,982	4,280	5,215	5,016	6,243	5,494	6,770	9,790
Claims on Other Financial Insts.	32f	....	....	....	....	....	....	....	....	....	....	....	....	....	....	....
Money	34	6,104	6,143	6,101	7,284	8,171	8,678	9,668	10,563	11,318	12,522	14,975	18,322	23,752	28,625	34,187
Quasi-Money	35	951	918	934	930	ℐ1,414	1,653	1,892	2,352	2,866	3,573	3,124	4,157	5,020	4,826	5,474
Restricted Deposits	36b	....	....	....	....	291	522	611	552	585	1,043	2,179	4,020	2,728	4,961	4,215
Long-Term Foreign Liabilities	36cl	....	....	....	....	....	....	....	....	....	....	....	....	....	....	....
Other Items (Net)	37r	1,783	1,405	1,931	1,813	ℐ965	1,295	1,787	3,530	2,205	2,158	2,022	1,566	3,557	4,653	7,216
Money plus Quasi-Money	35l	7,055	7,061	7,035	8,214	ℐ9,692	10,391	11,566	13,178	14,163	16,075	18,100	22,479	28,772	33,451	39,661
Prices														*Index Numbers (1990=100):*		
Consumer Prices	64	....	....	....	....	....	....	....	....	....	....	....	....	....	....	11.7

Afghanistan, I.S. of

512

1980	1981	1982	1983	1984	1985	1986	1987	1988	1989	1990	1991	1992	1993	1994		
End of Period															**Exchange Rates**	
58.478	58.896	55.817	52.976	49.599	55.580	61.893	71.784	68.092	66.496	71.987	72.380	69.575	69.502	73.868	Principal Rate	aa
End of Period (ae) Period Average (rf)																
45.850	50.600	50.600	50.600	50.600	50.600	50.600	50.600	50.600	50.600	50.600	50.600	50.600	50.600	50.600	Principal Rate	ae
44.129	49.481	50.600	50.600	50.600	50.600	50.600	50.600	50.600	50.600	50.600	50.600	50.600	50.600	50.600	Principal Rate	rf
End of Period															**Fund Position**	
67.50	67.50	67.50	86.70	86.70	86.70	86.70	86.70	86.70	86.70	86.70	86.70	86.70	120.40	120.40	Quota	2f. s
12.12	16.29	15.58	9.97	13.50	12.42	11.44	10.51	9.51	8.09	6.34	4.66	3.18	2.01	.96	SDRs	1b. s
15.07	15.08	15.09	4.80	4.81	4.82	4.84	4.84	4.85	4.88	4.90	4.90	4.93	4.93	4.93	Reserve Position in the Fund	1c. s
—	—	—	—	—	—	—	—	—	—	—	—	—	—	—	Total Fund Cred.&Loans Outstg.	2tl
End of Period															**International Liquidity**	
371.17	274.29	257.75	214.16	228.71	295.21	258.52	279.68	261.12	243.69	266.40	234.89	....	....	....	Total Reserves minus Gold	1l. d
15.46	18.96	17.19	10.44	13.23	13.64	13.99	14.91	12.80	10.63	9.02	6.67	4.37	2.76	1.40	SDRs	1b. d
19.22	17.55	16.65	5.03	4.71	5.29	5.92	6.87	6.53	6.41	6.97	7.01	6.78	6.77	7.19	Reserve Position in the Fund	1c. d
336.49	237.78	223.92	198.70	210.76	276.27	238.61	257.90	241.80	226.65	250.41	221.22	....	....	....	Foreign Exchange	1d. d
.965	.965	.965	.965	.965	.965	.965	.965	.965	.965	.965	.965	....	....	....	Gold (Million Fine Troy Ounces)	1ad
270.32	245.04	245.04	245.04	245.05	245.06	245.06	245.06	245.06	245.06	245.06	245.06	....	....	....	Gold (National Valuation)	1and
3.08	7.92	3.69	3.23	72.17	223.00	291.80	163.74	120.25	216.43	592.30	1,066.78	....	....	....	Monetary Authorities: Other Liab.	4..d
61.34	146.32	75.26	136.84	131.63	138.96	148.53	159.79	133.40	136.17	164.83	....	....	....	....	Deposit Money Banks: Assets	7a. d
Data as of the 20th of December															**Monetary Authorities**	
36,682	39,802	I 36,879	32,834	24,031	27,419	25,656	26,839	25,781	24,833	25,941	24,330	....	....	....	Foreign Assets	11
17,065	22,779	I 21,400	35,131	48,080	63,813	77,255	141,662	202,463	287,513	440,191	651,358	....	....	....	Claims on Central Government	12a
—	1,839	I 225	651	406	482	1,023	374	358	503	446	443	....	....	....	Claims on Local Government	12b
....	....	7,844	10,304	15,580	18,275	22,589	13,443	2,358	4,269	3,412	4,331	....	....	....	Claims on Nonfin.Pub.Enterprises	12c
5,014	5,859	I 189	473	138	176	517	616	134	424	575	322	....	....	....	Claims on Private Sector	12d
1,258	249	I 249	349	746	746	906	873	1,046	942	892	841	....	....	....	Claims on Deposit Money Banks	12e
....	....	811	885	1,140	1,121	1,213	1,597	1,407	1,164	1,306	1,494	....	....	....	Claims on Other Financial Insts.	12f
39,356	45,071	I 52,245	60,613	66,109	73,124	83,168	130,644	176,525	246,696	347,968	524,013	....	....	....	Reserve Money	14
32,316	38,750	I 46,674	53,782	58,716	64,390	71,402	112,488	152,330	222,720	311,929	454,750	....	....	....	*of which: Currency Outside DMBs*	14a
5,676	4,786	I 3,628	4,534	5,561	7,212	8,006	9,564	12,695	12,838	13,928	19,368	....	....	....	*Private Sector Deposits*	14d
3,405	4,709	I 6,221	6,794	6,138	7,126	7,460	9,643	11,128	14,472	21,031	16,665	....	....	....	Time, Savings,& Fgn.Currency Dep.	15
4,540	7,974	I 3,779	4,811	4,868	6,047	6,381	9,258	10,433	11,393	10,978	14,954	....	....	....	Restricted Deposits	16b
141	401	I 187	164	3,652	11,284	14,765	8,285	6,085	10,951	29,970	53,979	....	....	....	Foreign Liabilities	16c
5,943	6,496	I 2,169	4,639	4,433	8,101	7,788	15,344	14,981	12,814	25,169	31,227	....	....	....	Central Government Deposits	16d
4,154	5,990	I 8,077	9,288	10,565	10,709	13,091	12,532	12,094	13,563	14,271	13,516	....	....	....	Capital Accounts	17a
2,479	–113	–5,081	–5,680	–5,643	–4,356	–3,495	–303	2,302	9,759	23,376	28,765	....	....	....	Other Items (Net)	17r
Data as of the 20th of December															**Deposit Money Banks**	
1,455	1,396	I 2,292	....	872	1,084	2,250	5,670	5,817	6,462	15,924	....	....	....	....	Reserves	20
2,813	7,404	I 3,808	....	6,661	7,031	7,516	8,086	6,750	6,890	8,340	....	....	....	....	Foreign Assets	21
....	....	725	....	1,150	682	830	695	658	680	701	....	....	....	....	Claims on Nonfin.Pub.Enterprises	22c
4,589	4,194	I 3,996	....	4,650	6,552	8,256	12,083	17,446	19,548	25,972	....	....	....	....	Claims on Private Sector	22d
....	....	89	....	76	106	92	239	230	245	223	....	....	....	....	Claims on Other Financial Insts.	22f
1,786	2,128	I 1,850	....	2,946	3,705	4,127	5,642	9,531	11,699	18,217	....	....	....	....	Demand Deposits	24
3,161	4,059	I 5,217	....	7,339	7,156	9,218	12,223	15,604	17,132	25,269	....	....	....	....	Time, Savings,& Fgn.Currency Dep.	25
....	....	1,166	....	1,150	2,091	3,020	3,836	3,573	3,420	4,847	....	....	....	....	Restricted Deposits	26b
....	1,845	I 173	....	776	444	488	1,379	320	198	147	....	....	....	....	Foreign Liabilities	26c
....	624	I 559	....	463	439	—	—	298	239	182	....	....	....	....	Long-Term Foreign Liabilities	26cl
55	92	I 146	....	55	26	31	85	—	462	248	....	....	....	....	Central Government Deposits	26d
....	....	51	....	466	1,061	498	16	107	25	25	....	....	....	....	Credit from Monetary Authorities	26g
2,079	2,250	I 2,472	....	3,435	3,255	3,555	3,997	4,405	5,224	10,718	....	....	....	....	Capital Accounts	27a
1,775	1,997	–723	....	–3,222	–2,721	–1,994	–405	–2,937	–4,573	–8,492	....	....	....	....	Other Items (Net)	27r
Data as of the 20th of December															**Monetary Survey**	
39,353	44,960	40,328	....	26,264	22,723	17,918	25,260	26,126	20,574	4,163	....	....	....	....	Foreign Assets (Net)	31n
20,670	28,083	32,964	....	66,732	83,082	103,956	155,278	210,073	301,072	447,411	....	....	....	....	Domestic Credit	32
11,067	16,191	19,085	....	43,592	55,687	69,437	126,233	187,482	274,237	414,774	....	....	....	....	Claims on Central Govt. (Net)	32an
—	1,839	225	....	406	482	1,023	374	358	503	446	....	....	....	....	Claims on Local Government	32b
....	....	8,569	....	16,730	18,957	23,419	14,136	3,016	4,951	4,114	....	....	....	....	Claims on Nonfin.Pub.Enterprises	32c
9,603	10,053	4,185	....	4,788	6,728	8,773	12,699	17,580	19,973	26,547	....	....	....	....	Claims on Private Sector	32d
....	....	900	....	1,216	1,227	1,305	1,836	1,637	1,409	1,529	....	....	....	....	Claims on Other Financial Insts.	32f
39,779	45,664	52,973	....	68,638	76,359	85,113	131,419	179,414	251,062	351,025	....	....	....	....	Money	34
6,565	8,768	11,439	....	13,476	14,282	16,678	21,866	26,732	31,604	46,305	....	....	....	....	Quasi-Money	35
4,540	7,974	I 4,944	....	6,018	8,138	9,401	13,094	14,006	14,813	15,825	....	....	....	....	Restricted Deposits	36b
....	624	I 559	....	463	439	—	—	298	239	182	....	....	....	....	Long-Term Foreign Liabilities	36cl
9,139	10,014	3,377	....	4,402	6,588	10,681	14,158	15,750	23,928	38,237	....	....	....	....	Other Items (Net)	37r
46,345	54,433	64,412	....	82,114	90,641	101,791	153,285	206,146	282,666	397,330	....	....	....	....	Money plus Quasi-Money	35l
Period Averages															**Prices**	
11.8	12.4	13.1	12.7	13.7	29.0	28.1	33.6	40.2	70.5	100.0	156.7	....	....	....	Consumer Prices	64

Afghanistan, I.S. of

512

		1965	1966	1967	1968	1969	1970	1971	1972	1973	1974	1975	1976	1977	1978	1979
International Transactions														*Millions of US Dollars: Year Ending March 20*		
Exports	70..d	73.9	67.4	66.4	71.8	81.9	85.6	99.7	122.5	143.2	230.0	217.4	291.3	306.1	320.7	474.0
Imports, cif	71..d	121.0	128.0	126.0	114.0	126.0	114.0	141.0	164.0	172.0	243.0	350.0	260.9	328.0	394.8	425.5
Imports, fob	71.vd	105.2	111.3	109.6	99.1	109.6	99.1	122.6	142.6	149.6	211.3	304.3	226.9	285.2	343.3	370.0
Balance of Payments															*Millions of US Dollars:*	
Goods: Exports f.o.b.	78aa d	....	....	....	....	....	....	....	....	....	....	....	....	....	....	493.7
Goods: Imports f.o.b.	78ab d	....	....	....	....	....	....	....	....	....	....	....	....	....	....	−629.3
Trade Balance	78ac d	....	....	....	....	....	....	....	....	....	....	....	....	....	....	−135.6
Services: Credit	78ad d	....	....	....	....	....	....	....	....	....	....	....	....	....	....	75.1
Services: Debit	78ae d	....	....	....	....	....	....	....	....	....	....	....	....	....	....	−144.6
Balance on Goods and Services	78af d	....	....	....	....	....	....	....	....	....	....	....	....	....	....	−205.1
Income: Credit	78ag d	....	....	....	....	....	....	....	....	....	....	....	....	....	....	46.7
Income: Debit	78ah d	....	....	....	....	....	....	....	....	....	....	....	....	....	....	−23.5
Balance on Goods, Serv., & Inc.	78ai d	....	....	....	....	....	....	....	....	....	....	....	....	....	....	−181.9
Current Transfers, n.i.e.: Credit	78aj d	....	....	....	....	....	....	....	....	....	....	....	....	....	....	82.3
Current Transfers: Debit	78ak d	....	....	....	....	....	....	....	....	....	....	....	....	....	....	—
Current Account, n.i.e.	78al d	....	....	....	....	....	....	....	....	....	....	....	....	....	....	−99.6
Capital Account, n.i.e.: Credit	78ba d	....	....	....	....	....	....	....	....	....	....	....	....	....	....	—
Capital Account: Debit	78bb d	....	....	....	....	....	....	....	....	....	....	....	....	....	....	—
Capital Account, n.i.e.	78bc d	....	....	....	....	....	....	....	....	....	....	....	....	....	....	—
Direct Investment Abroad	78bd d	....	....	....	....	....	....	....	....	....	....	....	....	....	....	—
Dir. Invest. in Rep. Econ., n.i.e.	78be d	....	....	....	....	....	....	....	....	....	....	....	....	....	....	—
Portfolio Investment Assets	78bf d	....	....	....	....	....	....	....	....	....	....	....	....	....	....	—
Portfolio Investment Liab., n.i.e.	78bg d	....	....	....	....	....	....	....	....	....	....	....	....	....	....	—
Other Investment Assets	78bh d	....	....	....	....	....	....	....	....	....	....	....	....	....	....	−21.0
Other Investment Liab., n.i.e.	78bi d	....	....	....	....	....	....	....	....	....	....	....	....	....	....	136.3
Financial Account, n.i.e.	78bj d	....	....	....	....	....	....	....	....	....	....	....	....	....	....	115.3
Net Errors and Omissions	78ca d	....	....	....	....	....	....	....	....	....	....	....	....	....	....	−20.5
Overall Balance	78cb d	....	....	....	....	....	....	....	....	....	....	....	....	....	....	−4.8
Reserves and Related Items	79da d	....	....	....	....	....	....	....	....	....	....	....	....	....	....	4.8
Reserve Assets	79db d	....	....	....	....	....	....	....	....	....	....	....	....	....	....	4.8
Use of Fund Credit and Loans	79dc d	....	....	....	....	....	....	....	....	....	....	....	....	....	....	—
Liabs.Constit.For.Auth.Reserves	79dd d	....	....	....	....	....	....	....	....	....	....	....	....	....	....	—
Exceptional Financing	79de d	....	....	....	....	....	....	....	....	....	....	....	....	....	....	....
																Millions:
Population	99z	13.53	13.77	14.05	14.25	14.54	14.87	15.22	15.57	15.92	16.29	16.67	17.05	ℓ14.74	15.11	15.55

Monetary Authorities: ℓ Monetary statistics from 1969 have been revised to accommodate wider coverages in both Da Afghanistan Bank and commercial bank data. Da Afghanistan Bank data now include all departments of the central bank, and the commercial bank data include branch offices. ℓ Beginning in 1982, data are based on improved classification.
Deposit Money Banks: ℓ See note to section 10.
Monetary Survey: ℓ See note to section 10.

Afghanistan, I.S. of

512

	1980	1981	1982	1983	1984	1985	1986	1987	1988	1989	1990	1991	1992	1993	1994		
of Following Year																**International Transactions**	
	670.2	694.3	707.6	728.6	632.9	566.8	551.9	511.9	394.7	235.9	235.1	188.2	....	....	....	Exports	70..*d*
	840.9	886.3	961.8	1,064.3	1,389.5	1,194.2	1,403.5	995.9	900.3	821.7	936.4	616.4	....	....	....	Imports, cif	71..*d*
	731.2	770.7	836.3	925.5	1,208.3	1,038.4	1,220.4	866.0	782.9	714.5	814.3	536.0	....	....	....	Imports, fob	71.v*d*
Minus Sign Indicates Debit																**Balance of Payments**	
	705.2	690.8	707.8	728.8	787.7	628.2	497.0	538.7	453.8	252.3	....	....	....	....	....	Goods: Exports f.o.b.	78aa*d*
	−773.8	−897.3	−829.1	−890.9	−1,204.7	−921.6	−1,138.8	−904.5	−731.8	−623.5	....	....	....	....	....	Goods: Imports f.o.b.	78ab*d*
	−68.6	−206.5	−121.3	−162.1	−417.0	−293.4	−641.8	−365.8	−278.0	−371.2	....	....	....	....	....	Trade Balance	78ac*d*
	35.6	31.9	49.0	49.7	33.4	40.0	29.3	35.6	69.6	8.2	....	....	....	....	....	Services: Credit	78ad*d*
	−143.8	−163.1	−140.4	−150.6	−196.2	−154.1	−181.3	−156.3	−120.0	−103.4	....	....	....	....	....	Services: Debit	78ae*d*
	−176.8	−337.7	−212.7	−263.0	−579.8	−407.5	−793.8	−486.5	−328.4	−466.4	....	....	....	....	....	Balance on Goods and Services	78af*d*
	51.9	43.6	41.2	27.7	20.4	29.2	23.8	19.2	23.3	20.1	....	....	....	....	....	Income: Credit	78ag*d*
	−6.9	−20.1	−20.1	−21.4	−18.5	−8.6	−34.6	−11.3	−11.5	−7.9	....	....	....	....	....	Income: Debit	78ah*d*
	−131.8	−314.2	−191.6	−256.7	−577.9	−386.9	−804.6	−478.6	−316.6	−454.2	....	....	....	....	....	Balance on Goods, Serv., & Inc.	78ai*d*
	192.2	136.9	133.4	120.2	127.3	143.7	267.4	311.7	342.8	312.1	....	....	....	....	....	Current Transfers, n.i.e.: Credit	78aj*d*
	−6.8	−28.5	−9.1	−2.3	—	—	—	—	—	−1.2	....	....	....	....	....	Current Transfers: Debit	78ak*d*
	53.6	−205.8	−67.3	−138.8	−450.6	−243.2	−537.2	−166.9	26.2	−143.3	....	....	....	....	....	Current Account, n.i.e.	78al*d*
	—	—	—	—	—	—	—	—	—	—	....	....	....	....	....	Capital Account, n.i.e.: Credit	78ba*d*
	—	—	—	—	—	—	—	—	—	—	....	....	....	....	....	Capital Account: Debit	78bb*d*
	—	—	—	—	—	—	—	—	—	—	....	....	....	....	....	Capital Account, n.i.e.	78bc*d*
	—	—	—	—	—	—	—	—	—	—	....	....	....	....	....	Direct Investment Abroad	78bd*d*
	—	—	—	—	—	—	—	—	—	—	....	....	....	....	....	Dir. Invest. in Rep. Econ., n.i.e.	78be*d*
	—	—	—	—	—	—	—	—	—	—	....	....	....	....	....	Portfolio Investment Assets	78bf*d*
	—	—	—	—	—	—	—	—	—	—	....	....	....	....	....	Portfolio Investment Liab., n.i.e.	78bg*d*
	−259.1	−27.2	67.2	124.7	119.5	—	—	—	—	—	....	....	....	....	....	Other Investment Assets	78bh*d*
	153.7	94.2	69.3	59.3	193.7	100.8	302.1	−33.9	−4.1	−59.6	....	....	....	....	....	Other Investment Liab., n.i.e.	78bi*d*
	−105.4	67.0	136.5	184.0	313.2	100.8	302.1	−33.9	−4.1	−59.6	....	....	....	....	....	Financial Account, n.i.e.	78bj*d*
	−19.9	100.9	−77.2	−104.5	207.6	168.4	216.4	211.6	−47.7	182.8	....	....	....	....	....	Net Errors and Omissions	78ca*d*
	−71.7	−37.9	−8.0	−59.3	70.2	26.0	−18.7	10.8	−25.6	−20.1	....	....	....	....	....	Overall Balance	78cb*d*
	71.7	37.9	8.0	59.3	−70.2	−26.0	18.7	−10.8	25.6	20.1	....	....	....	....	....	Reserves and Related Items	79da*d*
	71.7	37.9	8.0	59.3	−70.2	−26.0	18.7	−10.8	25.6	20.1	....	....	....	....	....	Reserve Assets	79db*d*
	—	—	—	—	—	—	—	—	—	—	....	....	....	....	....	Use of Fund Credit and Loans	79dc*d*
	—	—	—	—	—	—	—	—	—	—	....	....	....	....	....	Liabs.Constit.For.Auth.Reserves	79dd*d*
	....	....	....	....	....	....	....	....	....	....	....	....	....	....	....	Exceptional Financing	79de*d*
Midyear Estimates																	
	15.95	16.36	16.79	17.22	17.67	18.14	18.61	15.22	15.51	15.81	16.12	16.43	16.62	17.69	....	Population	99z

Algeria
612

		1965	1966	1967	1968	1969	1970	1971	1972	1973	1974	1975	1976	1977	1978	1979
Exchange Rates																*Dinars per SDR:*
Official Rate	aa	4.937	4.937	4.937	4.937	4.937	4.937	I 5.042	4.946	5.049	4.894	4.829	5.064	4.901	4.996	4.947
																Dinars per US Dollar:
Official Rate	ae	4.937	4.937	4.937	4.937	4.937	4.937	I 4.644	4.556	4.185	3.997	4.125	4.359	4.035	3.835	3.756
Official Rate	rf	4.937	4.937	4.937	4.937	4.937	4.937	I 4.913	4.481	3.962	4.181	3.949	4.164	4.147	3.966	3.853
Fund Position																*Millions of SDRs:*
Quota	2f.s	60	63	66	69	75	130	130	130	130	130	130	130	130	285	285
SDRs	1b.s	—	—	—	—	—	14	28	42	42	43	43	43	46	46	76
Reserve Position in the Fund	1c.s	15	16	17	17	19	33	33	33	33	33	33	34	33	32	31
Total Fund Cred.&Loans Outstg.	2tl	—	—	—	—	—	—	—	—	—	—	—	—	—	—	—
International Liquidity										*Millions of US Dollars Unless Otherwise Indicated:*						
Total Reserves minus Gold	1l.d	178	267	287	286	204	148	299	285	912	1,454	1,128	1,765	1,684	1,981	2,659
SDRs	1b.d	—	—	—	—	—	14	30	45	50	52	50	50	56	60	100
Reserve Position in the Fund	1c.d	15	16	16	17	19	32	35	35	39	40	38	39	40	41	40
Foreign Exchange	1d.d	164	252	270	269	186	101	233	204	823	1,362	1,040	1,676	1,588	1,879	2,518
Gold (Million Fine Troy Ounces)	1ad	.16	.16	4.44	5.86	5.86	5.47	5.47	5.47	5.47	5.47	5.47	5.47	5.50	5.53	5.58
Gold (National Valuation)	1and	6	6	155	205	205	191	208	208	231	234	224	222	234	252	257
Monetary Authorities: Other Assets	3..d	13	9	6	2	17	3	16	22	16	33	132	64	49	44	5
Other Liab.	4..d	57	50	72	55	63	71	222	114	99	152	55	60	52	60	76
Deposit Money Banks: Assets	7a.d	39	54	76	106	311	58	64	120	172	507	351	497	633	800	656
of which: Claims on Nonbanks	7ad d	...	15	10	26	14	—	—	—	—	85	106	137	160	196	107
Deposit Money Banks: Liabilities	7b.d	34	38	42	59	199	23	24	168	800	996	1,353	1,433	1,756	2,609	2,972
of which: Liab. to Nonbanks	7bd d	...	—	—	—	—	—	—	25	91	153	326	286	467	1,099	1,302
Monetary Authorities																*Billions of Dinars:*
Foreign Assets	11	.98	1.40	2.22	2.44	2.11	1.70	2.39	2.35	4.76	7.03	6.25	8.95	8.03	8.85	11.05
Claims on Central Government	12a	1.59	1.51	1.12	1.51	2.05	3.63	4.39	2.97	.95	.45	.57	2.69	6.43	15.23	14.35
Claims on Deposit Money Banks	12e	.28	.13	.18	.17	.56	.17	.91	3.09	4.75	6.29	7.65	8.78	8.52	7.33	11.54
Reserve Money	14	2.89	3.00	3.37	3.81	4.27	4.83	5.96	7.18	9.33	10.61	13.63	18.68	21.96	28.77	35.88
of which: Currency Outside DMBs	14a	2.77	2.84	3.23	3.70	4.16	4.74	5.70	7.05	8.82	10.45	12.74	17.24	20.57	27.37	35.40
Foreign Liabilities	16c	.28	.25	.35	.27	.31	.35	1.03	.52	.41	.61	.23	.26	.21	.23	.29
Central Government Deposits	16d	.27	.34	.15	.26	.42	.31	.59	.49	.33	1.84	.56	.18	.12	.08	.09
Other Items (Net)	17r	−.59	−.54	−.35	−.22	−.29	.02	.11	.22	.40	.71	.05	1.30	.69	2.34	.68
Deposit Money Banks																*Billions of Dinars:*
Reserves	20	.11	.15	.12	.14	.14	.15	.16	.14	.51	.14	.89	.85	.98	1.34	.87
Foreign Assets	21	.19	.27	.38	.52	1.54	.28	.30	.55	.70	2.03	1.45	2.17	2.55	3.07	2.46
Claims on Central Government	22a	.38	.38	1.01	1.54	1.55	1.57	1.07	1.59	3.17	1.97	3.45	3.19	4.11	4.02	5.39
Claims on Nonfin.Pub.Enterprises	22c	...	...	...	...	...	...	...	...	...	...	...	...	...	...	...
Claims on Private Sector	22d	1.52	1.30	2.08	3.73	5.99	6.12	7.73	13.26	15.56	21.52	28.67	36.92	39.77	51.33	59.66
Demand Deposits	24	1.86	2.13	3.29	4.99	5.64	5.78	6.10	8.43	8.68	10.57	15.11	20.56	23.85	28.84	29.49
Time Deposits	25	.13	.23	.49	.84	1.11	1.45	.97	1.39	1.44	1.52	1.77	2.53	3.40	5.25	7.48
Foreign Liabilities	26c	.17	.19	.21	.29	.98	.12	.11	.17	.46	1.28	.98	1.03	1.29	.65	.86
Long-Term Foreign Liabilities	26cl								.60	2.81	2.70	4.60	5.22	5.79	9.35	10.30
Central Government Deposits	26d	—	.02	—	.07	.05	.04	.06	.11	.12	.19	.28	.11	.17	.31	.35
Central Govt. Lending Funds	26f	—	.16	.20	.28	1.07	.61	.92	1.54	1.64	2.78	3.13	3.01	2.94	2.55	3.57
Credit from Monetary Authorities	26g	.28	.13	.18	.17	.56	.17	.91	3.09	4.75	6.29	7.65	8.78	8.52	7.33	11.54
Other Items (Net)	27r	−.23	−.75	−.78	−.70	−.19	−.04	.18	.20	.04	.33	.94	1.89	1.45	5.47	4.79
Post Office: Checking Deposits	24..i	.34	.33	.35	.40	.51	.66	.92	1.11	1.33	1.96	2.56	2.87	3.46	5.28	6.60
Treasury: Checking Deposits	24..r	.20	.25	.16	.23	.21	.44	.23	.16	.09	1.26	1.56	.40	.67	.72	.73
Monetary Survey																*Billions of Dinars:*
Foreign Assets (Net)	31n	.72	1.23	2.04	2.46	2.35	1.52	1.54	2.20	4.59	7.17	6.49	9.82	9.08	11.03	12.36
Domestic Credit	32	5.00	4.41	5.27	7.68	10.37	12.42	14.04	18.85	21.00	25.47	36.32	46.12	54.48	76.53	86.61
Claims on Central Govt. (Net)	32an	2.24	2.12	2.49	3.35	3.85	5.97	5.97	5.24	5.10	3.62	7.31	8.86	14.38	24.86	26.62
Claims on Nonfin.Pub.Enterprises	32c															
Claims on Private Sector	32d	2.76	2.29	2.78	4.32	6.52	6.45	8.07	13.61	15.90	21.85	29.01	37.25	40.11	51.66	59.99
Money	34	5.16	5.55	7.02	9.32	10.51	11.62	12.95	16.75	18.93	24.25	31.98	41.08	48.55	62.21	72.21
Quasi-Money	35	.13	.23	.49	.84	1.11	1.45	.97	1.39	1.44	1.52	1.77	2.53	3.40	5.25	7.48
Long-Term Foreign Liabilities	36cl								.60	2.81	2.70	4.60	5.22	5.79	9.35	10.30
Central Govt. Lending Funds	36f	—	.16	.20	.28	1.07	.61	.92	1.54	1.64	2.78	3.13	3.01	2.94	2.55	3.57
Other Items (Net)	37r	.43	−.29	−.40	−.30	.03	.25	.74	.78	.77	1.39	1.33	4.11	2.89	8.19	5.41
Money plus Quasi-Money	35l	5.29	5.78	7.51	10.16	11.62	13.08	13.93	18.14	20.36	25.77	33.75	43.60	51.95	67.46	79.69
Other Banking Institutions																*Billions of Dinars:*
Deposits	45	...	.04	.09	.15	.25	.38	.66	.86	1.06	1.35	1.69	2.28	3.29	4.61	6.60
Liquid Liabilities	55l	...	5.82	7.60	10.31	11.87	13.45	14.59	19.00	21.42	27.12	35.44	45.88	55.24	72.07	86.29
Prices and Production																*Index Numbers (1990=100):*
Consumer Prices	64	...	...	...	...	16.5	17.6	18.1	18.7	19.9	20.8	22.7	24.7	27.7	32.5	36.2
Crude Petroleum Production	66aa	72.6	92.9	107.2	117.7	122.9	132.2	99.7	137.3	140.4	133.5	123.6	140.7	143.7	155.3	146.0
International Transactions																*Millions of Dinars*
Exports	70	3,146	3,067	3,571	4,098	4,611	4,980	4,208	5,854	7,479	19,594	18,563	21,897	24,650	25,088	36,802
Petroleum	70a	2,432	2,509	2,628	2,878	2,990	3,360	3,016	4,614	6,030	17,838	16,963	19,950	23,064	23,224	33,700
Crude Petroleum	70aa	2,294	2,367	2,479	2,781	2,929	3,287	2,972	4,565	5,648	16,953	15,885	18,992	22,457	21,518	30,794
Refined Petroleum	70ab	138	142	149	97	61	73	44	49	382	885	1,078	958	607	1,706	2,906
Imports, cif	71	3,314	3,153	3,154	4,023	4,981	6,205	6,028	6,694	8,859	16,821	23,755	22,226	29,534	34,439	32,378
Imports, fob	71.v	3,069	2,919	2,920	3,725	4,612	5,745	5,581	6,198	8,203	15,223	21,854	20,205	26,898	31,167	29,435
Imports, cif, from DOTS	71y	...	...	...	...	...	...	...	...	...	...	...	...	...	...	...
Volume of Exports																*1990=100*
Petroleum	72a	126	164	186	201	215	232	178	238	234	219	214	234	247	257	256
Crude Petroleum	72aa	175	228	260	281	301	325	250	333	321	301	292	322	343	351	350
Refined Petroleum	72ab	3	4	4	4	3	4	2	4	17	16	19	16	10	26	23
Export Prices																*1990=100*
Crude Petroleum	76aa d	...	7.9	7.3	7.3	7.7	7.7	9.1	11.5	17.3	49.6	49.2	54.0	59.2	58.2	86.5

Algeria

612

	1980	1981	1982	1983	1984	1985	1986	1987	1988	1989	1990	1991	1992	1993	1994		
Exchange Rates																	
End of Period	5.065	5.096	5.113	5.147	5.021	5.243	5.900	7.003	9.058	10.556	17.343	30.600	31.324	33.134	62.617	Official Rate	aa
End of Period (ae) Period Average (rf)	3.972	4.378	4.636	4.917	5.123	4.773	4.824	4.936	6.731	8.032	12.191	21.392	22.781	24.123	42.893	Official Rate	ae
	3.837	4.316	4.592	4.789	4.983	5.028	4.702	4.850	5.915	7.609	8.958	18.473	21.836	23.345	35.059	Official Rate	rf
Fund Position																	
End of Period	428	428	428	623	623	623	623	623	623	623	623	623	623	914	914	914 Quota	2f.s
	76	119	140	102	113	126	137	143	2	3	2	1	1	5	16	SDRs	1b.s
	102	117	126	172	165	153	148	108	—	—	—	—	—	—	—	Reserve Position in the Fund	1c.s
	—	—	—	—	—	—	—	—	—	—	471	471	696	578	343	794 Total Fund Cred.&Loans Outstg.	2tl
International Liquidity																	
End of Period	3,773	3,695	2,422	1,880	1,464	2,819	1,660	1,640	900	847	725	1,486	1,457	1,475	2,674	Total Reserves minus Gold	1l.d
	97	138	154	107	111	138	167	202	2	4	3	2	1	7	23	SDRs	1b.d
	130	136	139	180	162	168	181	153	—	—	—	—	—	—	—	Reserve Position in the Fund	1c.d
	3,546	3,421	2,129	1,593	1,191	2,513	1,312	1,285	898	843	722	1,484	1,456	1,468	2,651	Foreign Exchange	1d.d
	5.58	5.58	5.58	5.58	5.58	5.58	5.58	5.58	5.58	5.58	5.14	5.58	5.58	5.58	5.58	Gold (Million Fine Troy Ounces)	1ad
	249	227	216	205	192	215	239	277	263	257	256	280	269	268	285	Gold (National Valuation)	1an d
	4	5	4	3	3	3	3	3	2	2	1	1	13	12	1	Monetary Authorities: Other Assets	3..d
	108	54	51	49	47	51	53	52	38	32	85	152	120	464	466	Other Liab.	4..d
	682	663	649	441	416	382	376	253	569	679	741	1,085	914	683	1,046	Deposit Money Banks: Assets	7a.d
	113	102	120	122	122	139	164	138	208	219	307	666	447	438	461	of which: Claims on Nonbanks	7ad d
	2,953	2,423	2,001	2,089	2,983	5,092	7,203	8,305	8,208	7,728	7,941	7,837	7,010	5,201	4,200	Deposit Money Banks: Liabilities	7b.d
	1,199	1,058	896	1,024	1,528	2,143	2,791	3,179	2,142	2,025	2,901	2,753	2,467	2,046	1,310	of which: Liab. to Nonbanks	7bd d
Monetary Authorities																	
End of Period	16.06	17.24	12.03	10.24	8.51	14.54	9.19	9.45	7.17	7.89	10.43	35.52	I 36.69	38.66	120.39	Foreign Assets	11
	19.74	9.85	16.23	29.24	39.23	42.16	65.86	82.41	104.35	110.40	98.85	100.57	I 162.76	273.80	255.57	Claims on Central Government	12a
	11.78	22.63	27.04	22.20	26.88	22.05	23.24	18.17	16.90	30.74	65.70	108.40	I 78.31	29.39	50.45	Claims on Deposit Money Banks	12e
	43.26	48.58	50.58	60.99	69.97	78.72	91.06	102.36	111.49	124.97	137.92	160.28	I 196.28	250.41	237.22	Reserve Money	14
	42.34	48.06	49.16	60.02	67.46	76.64	89.36	96.87	109.76	119.87	135.26	157.20	I 184.61	211.31	222.99	of which: Currency Outside DMBs	14a
	.43	.24	.24	.24	.24	.25	.25	.26	.26	5.23	9.21	24.54	I 20.84	22.55	69.68	Foreign Liabilities	16c
	.31	.10	.32	.54	.44	.44	.15	.44	3.89	1.72	5.36	5.97	I 2.31	2.94	9.25	Central Government Deposits	16d
	3.59	.79	4.18	-.08	3.97	-.65	6.82	6.96	12.78	17.11	22.49	53.71	I 58.32	65.96	110.26	Other Items (Net)	17r
Deposit Money Banks																	
End of Period	.70	.52	1.22	1.09	2.25	2.32	1.61	5.66	3.54	4.57	4.04	4.97	5.86	37.89	7.32	Reserves	20
	2.71	2.90	3.01	2.17	2.13	1.83	1.81	1.25	3.83	5.45	9.03	23.22	20.82	16.47	44.88	Foreign Assets	21
	5.22	6.48	7.13	9.17	13.23	16.82	19.71	20.27	21.12	21.57	44.83	32.14	14.76	293.13	190.62	Claims on Central Government	22a
	....	....	....	....	....	....	....	....	....	....	....	295.63	127.42	203.61	Claims on Nonfin.Pub.Enterprises	22c
	68.20	88.21	112.48	132.63	155.70	174.53	176.84	180.53	191.91	209.30	246.98	....	325.85	I 126.02	99.12	115.15 Claims on Private Sector	22d
	33.50	40.08	61.99	76.88	95.28	104.62	95.94	103.80	115.53	101.89	105.55	133.11	140.84	188.93	196.45	Demand Deposits	24
	9.11	11.23	12.59	13.17	14.28	21.63	22.20	33.99	40.76	58.13	72.92	90.28	146.18	180.52	247.68	Time Deposits	25
	1.83	1.08	.84	.82	1.08	1.23	1.43	1.30	1.46	1.59	3.71	9.89	14.00	12.94	35.14	Foreign Liabilities	26c
	9.90	9.53	8.44	9.45	14.21	23.07	33.32	39.70	53.79	60.48	93.09	157.77	145.70	112.52	145.02	Long-Term Foreign Liabilities	26cl
	.24	.86	1.05	1.04	1.98	2.87	3.85	2.29	1.26	1.29	.87	2.46	5.88	90.19	38.82	Central Government Deposits	26d
	3.15	3.66	3.92	6.09	6.62	8.35	9.60	10.31	11.25	12.82	13.56	11.64	14.00	13.19	13.61	Central Govt. Lending Funds	26f
	11.78	22.75	27.16	21.95	27.29	23.32	22.43	13.50	10.49	30.74	66.33	108.56	I 78.66	29.39	50.69	Credit from Monetary Authorities	26g
	7.32	8.91	7.86	15.67	12.57	10.39	11.21	2.82	-14.14	-26.05	-51.16	-127.53	I -82.17	-53.65	-165.82	Other Items (Net)	27r
	7.83	8.57	12.28	14.07	15.95	18.32	18.31	22.25	25.88	26.96	27.16	31.95	39.83	40.98	68.50	Post Office: Checking Deposits	24..i
	.77	1.22	1.87	1.80	1.74	2.65	1.21	.99	1.04	1.30	2.43	2.21	4.20	5.68	7.97	Treasury: Checking Deposits	24..r
Monetary Survey																	
End of Period	16.51	18.83	13.97	11.35	9.32	14.89	9.32	9.15	9.28	6.52	6.54	24.31	I 22.67	19.65	60.45	Foreign Assets (Net)	31n
	101.54	113.69	148.97	185.66	223.77	251.25	278.01	303.80	339.24	366.59	414.02	484.29	I 639.24	748.09	794.45	Domestic Credit	32
	33.01	25.15	36.15	52.69	67.74	76.63	101.09	123.19	147.25	157.21	167.04	158.44	I 213.36	520.45	474.59	Claims on Central Govt. (Net)	32an
	....	....	....	....	....	....	....	....	....	....	....	....	295.63	127.42	203.61	Claims on Nonfin.Pub.Enterprises	32c
	68.53	88.54	112.82	132.97	156.03	174.61	176.92	180.61	191.99	209.39	246.98	325.85	I 126.02	99.17	115.19	Claims on Private Sector	32d
	84.43	97.92	125.30	152.76	180.43	202.23	204.82	223.91	252.21	250.01	270.40	324.47	I 377.00	450.32	505.72	Money	34
	9.11	11.23	12.59	13.17	14.28	21.63	22.20	33.99	40.76	58.13	72.92	90.28	146.18	180.52	247.68	Quasi-Money	35
	9.90	9.53	8.44	9.45	14.21	23.07	33.32	39.70	53.79	60.48	93.09	157.77	145.70	112.52	145.02	Long-Term Foreign Liabilities	36cl
	3.15	3.66	3.92	6.09	6.62	8.35	9.60	10.31	11.25	12.82	13.56	11.64	14.00	13.19	13.61	Central Govt. Lending Funds	36f
	11.47	10.17	12.69	15.54	17.55	10.86	17.40	5.04	-9.49	-8.33	-29.42	-75.55	I -20.96	11.19	-57.13	Other Items (Net)	37r
	93.54	109.15	137.89	165.93	194.72	223.86	227.02	257.90	292.97	308.15	343.32	414.75	I 523.18	630.84	753.40	Money plus Quasi-Money	35l
Other Banking Institutions																	
End of Period	10.30	12.08	16.23	19.09	21.92	25.60	30.67	37.99	46.18	58.11	65.07	....	....	....	....	Deposits	45
	103.84	121.24	154.12	185.02	216.63	249.46	257.68	295.89	339.15	366.26	408.39	....	....	....	....	Liquid Liabilities	55l
Prices and Production																	
Period Averages	39.6	45.4	I 48.5	51.4	55.5	61.4	68.9	74.1	78.4	85.7	I 100.0	125.9	165.8	199.8	257.8	Consumer Prices	64
	123.4	105.6	90.6	88.3	83.6	82.5	78.5	83.0	83.7	90.8	100.0	104.9	103.1	99.3	96.7	Crude Petroleum Production	66aa
International Transactions																	
Millions of Dinars	52,648	62,837	60,478	60,722	63,758	64,564	36,828	41,736	45,421	71,937	114,392	233,589	243,087	....	....	Exports	70
	48,532	56,041	....	45,334	45,793	....	....	....	....	....	....	....	....	....	....	Petroleum	70a
	40,980	44,302	26,562	32,281	31,780	....	....	....	....	....	....	....	....	....	....	Crude Petroleum	70aa
	7,552	11,739	22,896	13,053	14,013	....	....	....	....	....	....	....	....	....	....	Refined Petroleum	70ab
	40,519	48,780	49,384	49,782	51,257	49,491	43,393	34,153	43,427	70,072	87,018	139,241	188,406	....	....	Imports, cif	71
	36,835	44,345	45,431	45,588	46,012	44,426	39,448	31,048	39,479	63,702	79,107	126,583	171,278	....	....	Imports, fob	71.v
	....	48,636	49,311	49,782	52,235	49,491	43,393	34,153	43,767	69,905	86,708	141,943	188,836	186,063	323,879	Imports, cif, from DOTS	71y
1990=100																Volume of Exports	
	208	185	148	....	....	....	....	....	87	93	100	98	95	103	....	Petroleum	72a
	271	233	154	88	84	83	78	83	79	93	100	100	93	107	....	Crude Petroleum	72aa
	51	69	133	....	....	....	....	....	107	93	100	93	100	93	....	Refined Petroleum	72ab
Index of Prices in US Dollars																Export Prices	
	152.9	162.9	147.4	129.8	125.5	125.5	....	....	66.6	76.1	100.0	84.1	84.4	71.2	....	Crude Petroleum	76aa d

Algeria

612

		1965	1966	1967	1968	1969	1970	1971	1972	1973	1974	1975	1976	1977	1978	1979
															Millions of US Dollars:	
Balance of Payments																
Goods: Exports f.o.b.	78aa d	...	...	...	...	...	...	...	...	...	...	...	...	6,009	6,340	9,484
Goods: Imports f.o.b.	78ab d	...	...	...	...	...	...	...	...	...	...	...	...	−6,213	−7,316	−7,820
Trade Balance	78ac d	...	...	...	...	...	...	...	...	...	...	...	...	−204	−976	1,664
Services: Credit	78ad d	...	...	...	...	...	...	...	...	...	...	...	...	288	326	468
Services: Debit	78ae d	...	...	...	...	...	...	...	...	...	...	...	...	−1,520	−1,939	−2,379
Balance on Goods and Services	78af d	...	...	...	...	...	...	...	...	...	...	...	...	−1,436	−2,589	−247
Income: Credit	78ag d	...	...	...	...	...	...	...	...	...	...	...	...	87	69	156
Income: Debit	78ah d	...	...	...	...	...	...	...	...	...	...	...	...	−1,258	−1,335	−1,863
Balance on Goods, Serv., & Inc.	78ai d	...	...	...	...	...	...	...	...	...	...	...	...	−2,607	−3,855	−1,953
Current Transfers, n.i.e.: Credit	78aj d	...	...	...	...	...	...	...	...	...	...	...	...	391	451	474
Current Transfers: Debit	78ak d	...	...	...	...	...	...	...	...	...	...	...	...	−110	−136	−153
Current Account, n.i.e.	78al d	...	...	...	...	...	...	...	...	...	...	...	...	−2,325	−3,540	−1,632
Capital Account, n.i.e.: Credit	78ba d	...	...	...	...	...	...	...	...	...	...	...	...	—	—	—
Capital Account: Debit	78bb d	...	...	...	...	...	...	...	...	...	...	...	...	—	—	—
Capital Account, n.i.e.	78bc d	...	...	...	...	...	...	...	...	...	...	...	...	—	—	—
Direct Investment Abroad	78bd d	...	...	...	...	...	...	...	...	...	...	...	...	−6	—	−16
Dir. Invest. in Rep. Econ., n.i.e.	78be d	...	...	...	...	...	...	...	...	...	...	...	...	178	135	26
Portfolio Investment Assets	78bf d	...	...	...	...	...	...	...	...	...	...	...	...			
Portfolio Investment Liab., n.i.e.	78bg d	...	...	...	...	...	...	...	...	...	...	...	...	—	—	1
Other Investment Assets	78bh d	...	...	...	...	...	...	...	...	...	...	...	...	−114	−299	−193
Other Investment Liab., n.i.e.	78bi d	...	...	...	...	...	...	...	...	...	...	...	...	1,959	3,653	2,705
Financial Account, n.i.e.	78bj d	...	...	...	...	...	...	...	...	...	...	...	...	2,019	3,489	2,523
Net Errors and Omissions	78ca d	...	...	...	...	...	...	...	...	...	...	...	...	−41	143	−407
Overall Balance	78cb d	...	...	...	...	...	...	...	...	...	...	...	...	−347	93	484
Reserves and Related Items	79da d	...	...	...	...	...	...	...	...	...	...	...	...	347	−93	−484
Reserve Assets	79db d	...	...	...	...	...	...	...	...	...	...	...	...	328	−73	−484
Use of Fund Credit and Loans	79dc d	...	...	...	...	...	...	...	...	...	...	...	...			
Liabs.Constit.For.Auth.Reserves	79dd d	...	...	...	...	...	...	...	...	...	...	...	...	20	−20	—
Exceptional Financing	79de d	...	...	...	...	...	...	...	...	...	...	...	...	—	—	—
															Millions of Dinars:	
Government Finance																
Deficit (−) or Surplus	80	−1,041	−601	−958	−1,437	I−996	−1,989	−1,753	−917	−3,133	2,034	...	...	...	...	...
Revenue	81	2,790	3,503	3,873	4,553	I6,009	6,704	7,086	9,358	10,925	23,752	...	...	...	...	...
Expenditure	82	3,831	4,105	4,831	5,990	I5,665	6,014	6,796	7,729	9,913	12,495	...	...	...	...	...
Lending Minus Repayments	83	...	...	...	...	1,340	2,680	2,043	2,545	4,144	9,223	...	...	...	...	...
Financing																
Net Borrowing: Domestic	84a	1,191	452	871	1,483	I1,030	2,420	2,097	1,001	3,181	−1,597	...	...	...	...	...
Foreign	85a	−150	149	87	−46	I−48	−431	−348	−49	14	30	...	...	...	...	...
Use of Cash Balances	87	...	...	...	...	15	—	5	−35	−63	−466	...	...	...	...	...
															Billions of Dinars	
National Accounts																
Exports of Goods & Services	90c	3.4	3.7	3.8	4.2	4.5	5.4	4.7	6.9	8.1	21.4	20.7	24.4	26.6	26.7	39.9
Government Consumption	91f	2.9	3.0	3.4	3.5	3.7	4.0	4.3	4.6	5.0	5.9	8.0	9.2	11.6	14.6	17.5
Gross Fixed Capital Formation	93e	2.4	2.2	2.7	4.1	5.7	7.6	8.6	10.3	13.3	17.0	24.0	31.4	38.4	50.8	50.4
Increase/Decrease(−) in Stocks	93i	.5	—	.5	.6	.4	.7	−.1	.8	1.0	5.1	3.9	.6	2.4	3.8	4.1
Private Consumption	96f	9.6	9.1	9.1	10.3	11.3	12.2	12.8	14.1	17.3	25.7	31.5	35.9	44.6	50.9	58.5
Imports of Goods & Serv.	98c	−3.5	−3.3	−3.2	−4.1	−5.1	−7.0	−6.9	−9.2	−12.6	−19.6	−26.4	−27.4	−36.3	−42.0	−42.1
Gross Domestic Product	99b	15.2	14.7	16.2	18.7	20.5	22.9	23.5	27.4	32.1	55.6	61.6	74.1	87.2	104.8	128.2
Gross Dom. Prod. 1980 Prices	99b.p	65.7	60.2	63.4	68.6	72.3	77.6	76.1	83.9	90.3	91.4	100.8	109.9	118.2	128.2	139.6
GDP Deflator (1980=100)	99bi p	23.2	24.4	25.6	27.3	28.4	29.5	30.9	32.7	35.5	60.8	61.1	67.4	73.8	81.8	91.8
															Millions:	
Population	99z	11.92	12.66	13.08	13.50	13.91	14.33	14.77	15.27	15.77	16.28	16.78	17.30	17.91	I17.58	18.19

Monetary Authorities: I Beginning in January 1992, data reflect the introduction of a new reporting system.
Deposit Money Banks: I Beginning in September 1992, data reflect improved classification including the separate identification of claims on nonfinancial public enterprises, which were previously included with claims on private sector.
Monetary Survey: I See notes to sections 10 and 20.

Government Finance: I Beginning in 1969, lending minus repayments and use of cash balances are shown separately; they were previously included in revenue and expenditure and in net domestic borrowing respectively.

Algeria

612

	1980	1981	1982	1983	1984	1985	1986	1987	1988	1989	1990	1991	1992	1993	1994		
Minus Sign Indicates Debit																**Balance of Payments**	
	13,652	14,117	13,509	12,742	12,792	13,034	8,065	9,029	7,620	9,534	12,965	12,330	....	....	....	Goods: Exports f.o.b.	78aa *d*
	−9,614	−10,105	−9,916	−9,543	−9,245	−8,820	−7,896	−6,630	−6,685	−8,390	−8,786	−6,862	....	....	....	Goods: Imports f.o.b.	78ab *d*
	4,037	4,012	3,594	3,199	3,547	4,214	169	2,398	935	1,144	4,179	5,468	....	....	....	Trade Balance	78ac *d*
	476	474	528	679	599	531	549	565	470	496	497	393	....	....	....	Services: Credit	78ad *d*
	−2,697	−2,705	−2,644	−2,410	−2,573	−2,565	−2,019	−1,441	−1,337	−1,214	−1,321	−1,163	....	....	....	Services: Debit	78ae *d*
	1,817	1,781	1,477	1,469	1,573	2,180	−1,301	1,523	68	425	3,355	4,698	....	....	....	Balance on Goods and Services	78af *d*
	372	481	328	186	179	191	172	110	71	111	73	70	....	....	....	Income: Credit	78ag *d*
	−2,241	−2,482	−2,318	−1,978	−1,858	−1,735	−1,865	−2,009	−2,570	−2,157	−2,341	−2,618	....	....	....	Income: Debit	78ah *d*
	−52	−219	−512	−323	−106	636	−2,994	−376	−2,430	−1,622	1,087	2,151	....	....	....	Balance on Goods, Serv., & Inc.	78ai *d*
	512	513	529	414	350	529	917	628	477	603	400	269	....	....	....	Current Transfers, n.i.e.: Credit	78aj *d*
	−211	−204	−200	−176	−169	−151	−153	−111	−86	−62	−67	−53	....	....	....	Current Transfers: Debit	78ak *d*
	249	90	−183	−85	74	1,015	−2,230	141	−2,040	−1,081	1,420	2,367	....	....	....	Current Account, n.i.e.	78al *d*
	—	—	—	—	—	—	—	—	—	—	—	—	....	....	....	Capital Account, n.i.e.: Credit	78ba *d*
	—	—	—	—	—	—	—	—	—	—	—	—	....	....	....	Capital Account: Debit	78bb *d*
	—	—	—	—	—	—	—	—	—	—	—	—	....	....	....	Capital Account, n.i.e.	78bc *d*
	−34	−15	−11	−15	−15	−2	5	−15	−5	−8	−5	−50	....	....	....	Direct Investment Abroad	78bd *d*
	349	13	−54	—	1	—	5	4	13	12	—	12	....	....	....	Dir. Invest. in Rep. Econ., n.i.e.	78be *d*
	—	—	—	2	—	—	—	—	2	—	—	—	....	....	....	Portfolio Investment Assets	78bf *d*
	—	—	−3	—	—	—	—	—	—	—	—	—	....	....	....	Portfolio Investment Liab., n.i.e.	78bg *d*
	−122	−158	−196	2	49	−285	−23	73	−131	−97	−229	−145	....	....	....	Other Investment Assets	78bh *d*
	762	176	−535	−519	−246	166	602	248	865	848	−860	−837	....	....	....	Other Investment Liab., n.i.e.	78bi *d*
	955	16	−799	−529	−211	−121	590	309	744	755	−1,094	−1,020	....	....	....	Financial Account, n.i.e.	78bj *d*
	137	14	−88	193	−197	127	142	−802	337	−448	−336	−299	....	....	....	Net Errors and Omissions	78ca *d*
	1,341	120	−1,070	−421	−333	1,020	−1,498	−352	−959	−774	−10	1,047	....	....	....	Overall Balance	78cb *d*
	−1,341	−120	1,070	421	333	−1,020	1,498	352	959	774	10	−1,047	....	....	....	Reserves and Related Items	79da *d*
	−1,341	−120	1,070	421	333	−1,020	1,498	352	757	121	−138	−1,356	....	....	....	Reserve Assets	79db *d*
	—	—	—	—	—	—	—	—	—	584	—	308	....	....	....	Use of Fund Credit and Loans	79dc *d*
	—	—	—	—	—	—	—	—	—	—	—	—	....	....	....	Liabs.Constit.For.Auth.Reserves	79dd *d*
	—	—	—	—	—	—	—	—	201	69	148	—	....	....	....	Exceptional Financing	79de *d*
Year Ending December 31																**Government Finance**	
	....	....	....	....	....	....	....	....	....	....	....	....	....	....	....	Deficit (−) or Surplus	80
	....	....	....	....	....	....	....	....	....	....	....	....	....	....	....	Revenue	81
	....	....	....	....	....	....	....	....	....	....	....	....	....	....	....	Expenditure	82
	....	....	....	....	....	....	....	....	....	....	....	....	....	....	....	Lending Minus Repayments	83
																Financing	
	....	....	....	....	....	....	....	....	....	....	....	....	....	....	....	Net Borrowing: Domestic	84a
	....	....	....	....	....	....	....	....	....	....	....	....	....	....	....	Foreign	85a
	....	....	....	....	....	....	....	....	....	....	....	....	....	....	....	Use of Cash Balances	87
Billions of Dinars																**National Accounts**	
	55.8	66.2	64.2	65.3	67.7	68.6	38.7	45.8	I 48.9	76.2	130.3	244.3	263.6	251.9	....	Exports of Goods & Services	90c
	22.4	26.4	30.7	34.7	39.5	45.8	52.9	58.0	I 60.0	63.2	89.2	124.3	165.2	202.1	....	Government Consumption	91f
	54.9	63.0	71.5	80.3	87.5	92.8	101.3	92.9	I 97.3	121.8	153.0	230.1	279.3	300.3	....	Gross Fixed Capital Formation	93e
	8.6	7.8	5.9	7.5	5.0	4.0	−2.0	1.0	I 1.0	5.2	—	—	—	—	....	Increase/Decrease(−) in Stocks	93i
	70.2	87.2	95.6	106.2	125.8	139.7	156.4	154.9	I 158.8	195.5	298.6	390.1	512.8	594.7	....	Private Consumption	96f
	−49.3	−59.1	−60.2	−60.3	−61.6	−59.5	−50.8	−40.0	I −46.0	−70.1	−138.6	−199.3	−251.9	−255.9	....	Imports of Goods & Services	98c
	162.5	191.5	207.6	233.8	263.9	291.6	296.6	312.7	I 320.0	391.8	532.5	789.5	969.0	1,093.1	....	Gross Domestic Product	99b
	162.5	165.5	156.7	....	....	....	....	....	....	....	....	....	....	....	....	Gross Dom. Prod. 1980 Prices	99b.*p*
	100.0	115.7	132.4	....	....	....	....	....	....	....	....	....	....	....	....	GDP Deflator (1980=100)	99bi *p*
Midyear Estimates																	
	18.67	19.25	19.86	20.52	21.25	21.85	22.52	23.02	23.73	24.33	25.01	25.53	26.13	26.72	....	Population	99z

Antigua and Barbuda

311

		1965	1966	1967	1968	1969	1970	1971	1972	1973	1974	1975	1976	1977	1978	1979
Exchange Rates												E. Caribbean Dollars per SDR: End of Period (aa)				
Official Rate	aa	1.7126	1.7203	1.9948	2.0131	1.9994	2.0053	2.0417	2.2194	2.4925	2.5024	2.7770	3.1369	3.2797	3.5175	3.5568
Official Rate	ae	1.7126	1.7203	1.9948	2.0131	1.9994	2.0053	1.8805	2.0442	2.0661	2.0439	2.3721	2.7000	2.7000	2.7000	2.7000
														Index Numbers (1990=100):		
Official Rate	ah x	157.3	157.1	154.5	134.6	134.5	134.8	137.3	140.7	137.9	131.6	125.0	103.5	100.0	100.0	100.0
Nominal Effective Exchange Rate	ne c	....	....	....	....	....	....	....	....	....	....	....	....	....	....	93.6
Real Effective Exchange Rate	re c	....	....	....	....	....	....	....	....	....	....	....	....	....	....	100.0
Fund Position												Millions of SDRs:				
Quota	2f. s	....	....	....	....	....	....	....	....	....	....	....	....	....	....	....
SDRs	1b. s	....	....	....	....	....	....	....	....	....	....	....	....	....	....	....
Reserve Position in the Fund	1c. s	....	....	....	....	....	....	....	....	....	....	....	....	....	....	....
International Liquidity												Millions of US Dollars:				
Total Reserves minus Gold	1l. d	....	....	....	....	....	....	....	....	....	....	7.32	9.67	5.10	5.97	11.23
SDRs	1b. d															
Reserve Position in the Fund	1c. d															
Foreign Exchange	1d. d	....	....	....	....	....	....	....	....	....	....	7.32	9.67	5.10	5.97	11.23
Deposit Money Banks: Assets	7a. d	....	....	....	....	....	....	....	....	....	....	14.16	3.68	2.31	4.55	5.58
of which: Claims on Nonbanks	7ad d											—	—	.37	.37	.50
Deposit Money Banks: Liabilities	7b. d	....	....	....	....	....	....	....	....	....	....	15.91	18.28	10.50	14.87	17.20
of which: Liab. to Nonbanks	7bd d	....	....	....	....	....	....	....	....	....	....	4.51	4.74	4.33	5.85	7.57
Monetary Authorities												Millions of E. Caribbean Dollars:				
Foreign Assets	11	....	....	....	....	....	....	....	....	....	....	17.35	26.10	13.78	16.13	30.33
Claims on Central Government	12a	....	....	....	....	....	....	....	....	....	....	2.12	5.62	5.77	6.26	6.26
Claims on Deposit Money Banks	12e															
Reserve Money	14	....	....	....	....	....	....	....	....	....	....	19.47	31.72	19.55	22.39	36.59
of which: Currency Outside DMBs	14a	....	....	....	....	....	....	....	....	....	....	10.77	11.92	13.15	15.13	17.09
Foreign Liabilities	16c											—	—	—	—	—
Central Government Deposits	16d											....	....	....	....	....
Other Items (Net)	17r											—	—	—	—	—
Deposit Money Banks												Millions of E. Caribbean Dollars:				
Reserves	20	....	....	....	....	....	....	....	....	....	....	8.70	19.80	6.40	7.26	19.50
Foreign Assets	21	....	....	....	....	....	....	....	....	....	....	33.60	9.93	6.24	12.29	15.07
Claims on Central Government	22a	....	....	....	....	....	....	....	....	....	....	13.29	32.18	20.04	20.02	31.74
Claims on Local Government	22b															
Claims on Nonfin.Pub.Enterprises	22c	....	....	....	....	....	....	....	....	....	....	1.26	2.65	2.33	2.75	6.01
Claims on Private Sector	22d	....	....	....	....	....	....	....	....	....	....	65.35	74.32	83.74	90.54	85.88
Claims on Nonbank Financial Insts	22f											—	—	—	—	1.44
Demand Deposits	24	....	....	....	....	....	....	....	....	....	....	8.20	12.35	17.76	14.24	17.72
Time, Savings,& Fgn.Currency Dep.	25	....	....	....	....	....	....	....	....	....	....	79.05	82.23	71.61	83.84	95.93
Foreign Liabilities	26c	....	....	....	....	....	....	....	....	....	....	37.75	49.36	28.36	40.16	46.45
Central Government Deposits	26d															.63
Credit from Monetary Authorities	26g															
Capital Accounts	27a	....	....	....	....	....	....	....	....	....	....	3.00	3.00	3.00	3.00	3.26
Other Items (Net)	27r	....	....	....	....	....	....	....	....	....	....	-5.79	-8.05	-2.00	-8.39	-4.36
Monetary Survey												Millions of E. Caribbean Dollars:				
Foreign Assets (Net)	31n	....	....	....	....	....	....	....	....	....	....	13.20	-13.33	-8.34	-11.74	-1.05
Domestic Credit	32	....	....	....	....	....	....	....	....	....	....	82.02	114.77	111.87	119.57	130.69
Claims on Central Govt. (Net)	32an	....	....	....	....	....	....	....	....	....	....	15.41	37.80	25.81	26.28	37.37
Claims on Local Government	32b															
Claims on Nonfin.Pub.Enterprises	32c	....	....	....	....	....	....	....	....	....	....	1.26	2.65	2.33	2.75	6.01
Claims on Private Sector	32d	....	....	....	....	....	....	....	....	....	....	65.35	74.32	83.74	90.54	85.88
Claims on Nonbank Financial Inst	32f											—	—	—	—	1.44
Money	34	....	....	....	....	....	....	....	....	....	....	18.97	24.26	30.91	29.37	34.81
Quasi-Money	35	....	....	....	....	....	....	....	....	....	....	79.05	82.23	71.61	83.84	95.93
Other Items (Net)	37r	....	....	....	....	....	....	....	....	....	....	-2.79	-5.05	1.01	-5.39	-1.10
Money plus Quasi-Money	35l	....	....	....	....	....	....	....	....	....	....	98.02	106.49	102.53	113.21	130.74
Interest Rates												Percent Per Annum				
Treasury Bill Rate	60c	....	....	....	....	....	....	....	....	....	....	....	....	....	....	....
Deposit Rate	60l	....	....	....	....	....	....	....	....	....	....	....	....	....	....	....
Lending Rate	60p	....	....	....	....	....	....	....	....	....	....	....	....	....	8.6	8.6
Prices												Index Numbers (1985=100):				
Consumer Prices	64	....	....	....	....	....	....	....	....	....	....	....	48.0	54.6	57.9	67.4

Antigua and Barbuda

1980	1981	1982	1983	1984	1985	1986	1987	1988	1989	1990	1991	1992	1993	1994		
\multicolumn{15}{l}{E. Caribbean Dollars per US Dollar: End of Period (ae)}	**Exchange Rates**	
3.4436	3.1427	2.9784	2.8268	2.6466	2.9657	3.3026	3.8304	3.6334	3.5482	3.8412	3.8622	3.7125	3.7086	3.9416	Official Rate	aa
2.7000	2.7000	2.7000	2.7000	2.7000	2.7000	2.7000	2.7000	2.7000	2.7000	2.7000	2.7000	2.7000	2.7000	2.7000	Official Rate	ae
\multicolumn{15}{l}{Period Averages}		
100.0	100.0	100.0	100.0	100.0	100.0	100.0	100.0	100.0	100.0	100.0	100.0	100.0	100.0	100.0	Official Rate	ahx
92.1	95.7	100.0	103.2	108.2	110.5	105.7	101.6	98.7	101.6	100.0	100.6	101.9	106.5	107.4	Nominal Effective Exchange Rate	nec
102.7	107.6	109.1	110.1	113.9	112.4	104.9	100.6	100.1	101.2	100.0	100.9^e	100.7^e	105.1^e	105.9	Real Effective Exchange Rate	rec
\multicolumn{15}{l}{End of Period}	**Fund Position**	
....	....	3.60	5.00	5.00	5.00	5.00	5.00	5.00	5.00	5.00	5.00	5.00	8.50	8.50	Quota	2f. s
....	....	—	—	—	—	—	—	—	—	—	—	—	—	—	SDRs	1b. s
		—	—	—	—	—	—	—	—	—	—	—	—	—	Reserve Position in the Fund	1c. s
\multicolumn{15}{l}{End of Period}	**International Liquidity**	
7.82	7.34	8.52	9.93	15.44	16.58	28.26	25.60	28.03	28.07	27.50	32.54	50.52	38.31	46.31	Total Reserves minus Gold	1l. d
....	....	—	—	—	—	—	—	—	—	—	—	—	.01	.01	SDRs	1b. d
		—	—	—	—	—	—	—	—	—	—	—	—	—	Reserve Position in the Fund	1c. d
7.82	7.34	8.52	9.93	15.44	16.58	28.26	25.60	28.03	28.07	27.50	32.54	50.52	38.30	46.30	Foreign Exchange	1d. d
4.45	8.49	11.02	8.39	19.27	27.64	19.09	30.99	37.31	29.32	30.28	49.41	53.62	56.99	77.30	Deposit Money Banks: Assets	7a. d
1.27	1.42	4.08	1.49	1.79	1.08	2.68	3.86	4.36	4.41	6.52	6.08	14.39	20.97	39.57	of which: Claims on Nonbanks	7ad d
14.78	18.16	26.10	20.64	30.98	49.21	49.06	51.50	56.23	57.00	55.81	50.14	66.79	52.73	60.72	Deposit Money Banks: Liabilities	7b. d
8.81	10.50	11.02	10.95	12.98	15.57	18.96	18.88	24.09	25.38	22.13	21.67	26.30	24.48	28.13	of which: Liab. to Nonbanks	7bd d
\multicolumn{15}{l}{End of Period}	**Monetary Authorities**	
21.52	20.28	23.67	30.00	37.85	52.07	78.64	70.50	75.83	76.30	75.07	86.26	134.95	101.88	123.68	Foreign Assets	11
9.40	9.60	11.56	11.56	32.49	33.95	37.10	36.38	40.55	38.46	45.78	44.71	36.10	39.48	39.11	Claims on Central Government	12a
—	—	—	—	4.04	.26	1.92	4.58	7.35	4.15	2.47	1.88	1.60	1.46	1.33	Claims on Deposit Money Banks	12e
30.51	29.41	34.69	39.79	71.60	83.15	115.33	109.33	121.49	116.44	120.61	132.75	172.53	142.83	164.12	Reserve Money	14
15.26	16.27	16.32	17.47	23.97	26.50	32.46	42.24	51.31	61.47	57.52	57.91	64.31	61.21	65.87	of which: Currency Outside DMBs	14a
—	—	—	—	—	—	—	—	—	—	—	—	—	—	—	Foreign Liabilities	16c
.41	.48	.54	1.78	2.78	3.14	2.33	2.13	2.25	2.48	2.71	.11	.11	—	—	Central Government Deposits	16d
															Other Items (Net)	17r
\multicolumn{15}{l}{End of Period}	**Deposit Money Banks**	
15.24	13.14	18.38	22.31	55.24	61.25	85.53	59.17	65.82	56.66	63.31	77.17	98.34	87.99	96.82	Reserves	20
12.02	22.92	29.75	22.67	52.03	74.62	51.54	83.67	100.75	79.18	81.75	133.42	144.76	153.87	208.72	Foreign Assets	21
34.91	32.99	39.64	38.33	46.59	48.25	57.57	69.18	85.96	79.98	64.88	80.60	95.19	117.80	124.62	Claims on Central Government	22a
—	—	—	—	—	—	—	—	.12	13.53	19.94	—	—	.81	.23	Claims on Local Government	22b
6.24	3.79	8.54	4.56	1.56	5.07	8.17	12.04	9.58	9.78	7.27	5.70	9.30	9.69	9.53	Claims on Nonfin.Pub.Enterprises	22c
102.72	131.35	137.75	180.13	211.80	258.34	295.34	352.05	412.52	468.64	503.09	547.45	586.67	598.33	616.83	Claims on Private Sector	22d
1.82	1.59	1.65	.36	.11	1.11	.66	2.29	6.30	13.84	22.35	25.23	6.00	5.92	21.50	Claims on Nonbank Financial Insts	22f
23.31	26.89	25.38	33.62	34.44	41.95	54.91	68.39	76.88	79.63	99.22	109.73	118.20	123.26	154.13	Demand Deposits	24
106.79	125.38	149.55	185.71	227.68	251.47	290.76	338.82	371.65	425.03	436.34	515.42	539.27	599.16	649.27	Time, Savings, & Fgn.Currency Dep.	25
39.90	49.04	70.47	55.73	83.65	132.87	132.46	139.04	151.82	153.90	150.68	135.38	180.35	142.36	163.95	Foreign Liabilities	26c
1.56	1.09	.79	2.73	2.39	1.95	4.76	9.43	28.51	27.93	28.18	35.77	49.61	39.82	53.83	Central Government Deposits	26d
—	—	.09	1.42	1.20	.51	2.20	4.76	8.69	4.83	2.49	1.76	2.12	1.94	1.29	Credit from Monetary Authorities	26g
4.55	5.72	6.92	5.67	15.18	17.32	21.84	27.90	27.51	30.75	35.85	96.00	81.18	91.18	110.08	Capital Accounts	27a
-3.17	-2.34	-17.49	-16.51	2.79	2.57	-8.12	-9.94	15.99	-.46	9.85	-24.51	-29.75	-23.33	-54.32	Other Items (Net)	27r
\multicolumn{15}{l}{End of Period}	**Monetary Survey**	
-6.36	-5.84	-17.05	-3.06	6.23	-6.18	-2.28	15.13	24.76	1.57	6.13	84.30	99.36	113.39	168.45	Foreign Assets (Net)	31n
153.11	177.75	197.82	230.44	287.37	341.64	391.76	460.37	524.26	593.82	632.43	667.81	684.25	732.20	757.98	Domestic Credit	32
42.34	41.02	49.88	45.39	73.91	77.12	87.59	93.99	95.75	88.03	79.78	89.43	81.56	117.47	109.90	Claims on Central Govt. (Net)	32an
—	—	—	—	—	—	—	—	.12	13.53	19.94	—	.72	.81	.23	Claims on Local Government	32b
6.24	3.79	8.54	4.56	1.56	5.07	8.17	12.04	9.58	9.78	7.27	5.70	9.30	9.69	9.53	Claims on Nonfin.Pub.Enterprises	32c
102.72	131.35	137.75	180.13	211.80	258.34	295.34	352.05	412.52	468.64	503.09	547.45	586.67	598.33	616.83	Claims on Private Sector	32d
1.82	1.59	1.65	.36	.11	1.11	.66	2.29	6.30	13.84	22.35	25.23	6.00	5.92	21.50	Claims on Nonbank Financial Inst	32f
38.57	43.16	41.70	51.10	58.40	68.45	87.37	110.62	128.19	141.09	156.74	167.64	182.62	184.61	220.18	Money	34
106.79	125.38	149.55	185.71	227.68	251.47	290.76	338.82	371.65	425.03	436.34	515.42	539.27	599.16	649.27	Quasi-Money	35
1.38	3.38	-10.49	-9.43	7.52	15.54	11.36	26.06	49.19	29.27	45.49	69.05	61.72	61.82	56.98	Other Items (Net)	37r
145.37	168.54	191.25	236.80	286.08	319.92	378.13	449.44	499.84	566.12	593.08	683.06	721.89	783.77	869.45	Money plus Quasi-Money	35l
\multicolumn{15}{l}{Percent Per Annum}	**Interest Rates**	
7.0	7.0	7.0	7.0	7.0	7.0	7.0	7.0	7.0	7.0	7.0	7.0	7.0	7.0	7.0	Treasury Bill Rate	60c
6.0	6.3	7.5	11.0	11.0	9.9	7.7	6.5	6.5	6.5	6.5	8.4	8.2	7.4	6.7	6.5 Deposit Rate	60l
10.0	11.0	13.0	14.0	13.6	13.0	14.3	12.4	11.5	12.2	12.4	15.5	13.0	13.0	12.5	Lending Rate	60p
\multicolumn{15}{l}{Period Averages}	**Prices**	
80.2	89.4	93.1	95.3	99.0	100.0	....	....	....	....	....	....	....	....	....	Consumer Prices	64

Antigua and Barbuda
311

		1965	1966	1967	1968	1969	1970	1971	1972	1973	1974	1975	1976	1977	1978	1979
International Transactions																*Millions of E. Caribbean Dollars*
Exports	70	6.34	2.37	4.97	16.04	16.87	27.26	32.23	34.64	59.45	66.47	59.92	23.61	17.82	34.02	32.40
Imports, cif	71	32.42	43.91	39.99	49.74	57.58	72.65	86.77	90.98	94.50	143.75	145.14	91.84	109.35	125.01	201.15
Imports, fob	71.v	29.47	39.92	36.35	45.22	52.35	66.35	79.24	83.08	86.31	131.28	132.55	83.87	99.90	113.64	182.84
Balance of Payments																*Millions of US Dollars:*
Goods: Exports f.o.b.	78aa d	....	....	....	....	....	....	....	....	....	....	....	....	6.60	12.60	12.00
Goods: Imports f.o.b.	78ab d	....	....	....	....	....	....	....	....	....	....	....	....	−37.00	−42.09	−67.72
Trade Balance	78ac d	....	....	....	....	....	....	....	....	....	....	....	....	−30.40	−29.49	−55.72
Services: Credit	78ad d	....	....	....	....	....	....	....	....	....	....	....	....	24.70	29.50	38.20
Services: Debit	78ae d	....	....	....	....	....	....	....	....	....	....	....	....	−6.50	−7.01	−10.28
Balance on Goods and Services	78af d	....	....	....	....	....	....	....	....	....	....	....	....	−12.20	−7.00	−27.80
Income: Credit	78ag d	....	....	....	....	....	....	....	....	....	....	....	....	.30	.10	.80
Income: Debit	78ah d	....	....	....	....	....	....	....	....	....	....	....	....	−.50	−.50	−2.60
Balance on Goods, Serv., & Inc.	78ai d	....	....	....	....	....	....	....	....	....	....	....	....	−12.40	−7.40	−29.60
Current Transfers, n.i.e.: Credit	78aj d	....	....	....	....	....	....	....	....	....	....	....	....	2.90	5.40	11.20
Current Transfers: Debit	78ak d	....	....	....	....	....	....	....	....	....	....	....	....	−.10	−.20	−1.10
Current Account, n.i.e.	78al d	....	....	....	....	....	....	....	....	....	....	....	....	−9.60	−2.20	−19.50
Capital Account, n.i.e.: Credit	78ba d	....	....	....	....	....	....	....	....	....	....	....	....	—	—	—
Capital Account: Debit	78bb d	....	....	....	....	....	....	....	....	....	....	....	....			
Capital Account, n.i.e.	78bc d	....	....	....	....	....	....	....	....	....	....	....	....	—	—	—
Direct Investment Abroad	78bd d	....	....	....	....	....	....	....	....	....	....	....	....			
Dir. Invest. in Rep. Econ., n.i.e.	78be d	....	....	....	....	....	....	....	....	....	....	....	....	2.20	−6.90	8.50
Portfolio Investment Assets	78bf d	....	....	....	....	....	....	....	....	....	....	....	....	—	—	—
Portfolio Investment Liab., n.i.e.	78bg d	....	....	....	....	....	....	....	....	....	....	....	....			
Other Investment Assets	78bh d	....	....	....	....	....	....	....	....	....	....	....	....	1.74	−2.24	−.90
Other Investment Liab., n.i.e.	78bi d	....	....	....	....	....	....	....	....	....	....	....	....	−1.13	14.77	11.26
Financial Account, n.i.e.	78bj d	....	....	....	....	....	....	....	....	....	....	....	....	2.81	5.63	18.86
Net Errors and Omissions	78ca d	....	....	....	....	....	....	....	....	....	....	....	....	2.33	−2.66	5.60
Overall Balance	78cb d	....	....	....	....	....	....	....	....	....	....	....	....	−4.46	.77	4.96
Reserves and Related Items	79da d	....	....	....	....	....	....	....	....	....	....	....	....	4.46	−.77	−4.96
Reserve Assets	79db d	....	....	....	....	....	....	....	....	....	....	....	....	4.46	−.77	−5.36
Use of Fund Credit and Loans	79dc d	....	....	....	....	....	....	....	....	....	....	....	....	—	—	—
Liabs.Constit.For.Auth.Reserves	79dd d	....	....	....	....	....	....	....	....	....	....	....	....			
Exceptional Financing	79de d	....	....	....	....	....	....	....	....	....	....	....	....	—	—	.40
National Accounts																*Millions of E. Caribbean Dollars*
Exports of Goods & Services	90c	....	....	....	....	....	....	....	....	....	....	....	....	....	....	135.5
Government Consumption	91f	....	....	....	....	....	....	....	....	....	....	....	....	....	....	47.8
Gross Capital Formation	93	....	....	....	....	....	....	....	....	....	....	....	....	....	....	88.5
Private Consumption	96f	....	....	....	....	....	....	....	....	....	....	....	....	....	....	173.0
Imports of Goods & Services	98c	....	....	....	....	....	....	....	....	....	....	....	....	....	....	−210.6
Gross Domestic Product	99b	....	....	....	....	....	....	....	....	99.9	111.6	120.6	120.8	173.8	197.6	234.2
Gross Dom. Prod. 1990 Prices	99b.p	....	....	....	....	....	....	....	....	....	....	....	....	404.6	442.9	477.1
GDP Deflator (1990=100)	99bi p	....	....	....	....	....	....	....	....	....	....	....	....	43.0	44.6	49.1
																Millions:
Population	99z	....	....	....	....	....	.07	.07	.07	.07	.07	.07	.07	.07	.07	.07

Antigua and Barbuda

	1980	1981	1982	1983	1984	1985	1986	1987	1988	1989	1990	1991	1992	1993	1994		
Millions of E. Caribbean Dollars																**International Transactions**	
	82.08	107.56	57.38	53.29	47.49	35.64	52.88	46.48	60.04	....	....	....	....	....	....	Exports	70
	284.85	371.96	375.02	294.06	356.11	301.80	560.23	600.09	608.79	....	....	....	....	....	....	Imports, cif	71
	258.93	338.11	340.89	267.30	323.71	274.37	509.30	545.54	553.45	....	....	....	....	....	....	Imports, fob	71.v
Minus Sign Indicates Debit																Balance of Payments	
	59.50	51.40	49.30	36.50	35.20	28.30	19.59	16.84	17.00	15.70	18.98	35.43	54.67	66.91	....	Goods: Exports f.o.b.	78aa d
	−114.71	−125.26	−126.71	−99.72	−150.17	−174.80	−212.36	−218.86	−201.07	−242.25	−230.74	−252.57	−275.74	−296.26	....	Goods: Imports f.o.b.	78ab d
	−55.21	−73.86	−77.41	−63.22	−114.97	−146.50	−192.78	−202.02	−184.07	−226.55	−211.76	−217.15	−221.07	−229.34	....	Trade Balance	78ac d
	44.60	52.50	51.70	62.80	132.10	150.30	174.79	198.02	235.76	273.33	317.17	322.47	337.82	359.44	....	Services: Credit	78ad d
	−17.09	−19.74	−21.59	−18.28	−30.63	−38.40	−75.49	−78.71	−77.23	−94.57	−98.83	−113.64	−121.70	−136.90	....	Services: Debit	78ae d
	−27.70	−41.10	−47.30	−18.70	−13.50	−34.60	−93.47	−82.70	−25.53	−47.80	6.58	−8.32	−4.96	−6.79	....	Balance on Goods and Services	78af d
	2.80	3.20	6.60	5.00	5.10	2.40	1.44	1.41	1.43	1.20	2.49	2.66	3.37	2.76	....	Income: Credit	78ag d
	−4.00	−5.20	−10.30	−6.00	−5.50	−5.10	−37.47	−41.37	−31.21	−44.83	−45.96	−33.13	−33.36	−24.19	....	Income: Debit	78ah d
	−28.90	−43.10	−51.00	−19.70	−13.90	−37.30	−129.50	−122.66	−55.30	−91.43	−36.89	−38.79	−34.95	−28.23	....	Balance on Goods, Serv., & Inc.	78ai d
	12.40	12.60	11.10	12.60	16.60	16.80	14.94	14.60	15.29	17.74	15.74	15.62	14.26	15.89	....	Current Transfers, n.i.e.: Credit	78aj d
	−2.30	−2.20	−1.70	−2.00	−2.10	−2.60	−2.12	−2.95	−3.17	−5.47	−5.31	−6.30	−7.07	−6.84	....	Current Transfers: Debit	78ak d
	−18.80	−32.70	−41.60	−9.10	.60	−23.10	−116.69	−111.01	−43.18	−79.16	−26.46	−29.47	−27.75	−19.19	....	Current Account, n.i.e.	78al d
	—	—	—	—	—	—	—	—	—	—	—	—	—	—	....	Capital Account, n.i.e.: Credit	78ba d
	—	—	—	—	—	—	—	—	—	—	—	—	—	—	....	Capital Account: Debit	78bb d
	—	—	—	—	—	—	—	—	—	—	—	—	—	—	....	Capital Account, n.i.e.	78bc d
	—	—	—	—	—	—	—	—	—	—	—	—	—	—	....	Direct Investment Abroad	78bd d
	19.60	22.40	23.00	5.00	4.40	15.60	22.60	38.60	31.10	41.26	58.76	52.43	19.60	9.35	....	Dir. Invest. in Rep. Econ., n.i.e.	78be d
	—	—	—	—	—	—	—	—	—	—	—	—	—	—	....	Portfolio Investment Assets	78bf d
	1.15	−19.65	7.61	2.70	10.40	17.80	—	—	—	8.69	—	−23.97	8.47	—	....	Portfolio Investment Liab., n.i.e.	78bg d
	1.54	34.20	4.80	−11.50	−15.70	−13.20	95.11	37.95	−6.05	−14.03	−44.46	−23.14	−23.81	−30.45	....	Other Investment Assets	78bh d
	22.29	36.95	35.41	−3.80	−.90	20.20	117.71	76.54	25.05	35.91	14.30	5.32	4.26	−21.10	....	Other Investment Liab., n.i.e.	78bi d
	−7.30	−6.13	3.00	6.80	−.10	—	3.30	14.58	.28	4.24	−35.30	−9.37	4.62	10.78	....	Financial Account, n.i.e.	78bj d
	−3.81	−1.88	−3.20	−6.10	−.40	−2.90	4.32	−19.89	−17.85	−39.00	−47.46	−33.52	−18.87	−29.51	....	Net Errors and Omissions	78ca d
	3.81	1.88	3.20	6.10	.40	2.90	−4.32	19.89	17.85	39.00	47.46	33.52	18.87	29.51	....	Overall Balance	78cb d
	3.21	.38	−1.20	−1.40	−7.10	−3.30	−10.14	2.48	−2.59	−.04	.57	−5.26	−17.98	11.84	....	Reserves and Related Items	79da d
	—	—	—	—	—	—	—	—	—	—	—	—	—	—	....	Reserve Assets	79db d
	—	—	—	—	—	—	—	—	—	—	—	—	—	—	....	Use of Fund Credit and Loans	79dc d
	—	—	—	—	—	—	—	—	—	—	—	—	—	—	....	Liabs.Constit.For.Auth.Reserves	79dd d
	.60	1.50	4.40	7.50	7.50	6.20	5.81	17.41	20.44	39.04	46.89	38.78	36.85	17.66	....	Exceptional Financing	79de d
Millions of E. Caribbean Dollars																**National Accounts**	
	203.9	248.4	248.1	292.4	393.9	....	....	....	....	....	....	....	....	....	....	Exports of Goods & Services	90c
	57.1	68.2	78.7	68.0	84.2	....	....	....	....	....	....	....	....	....	....	Government Consumption	91f
	115.8	169.4	175.8	84.6	116.7	....	....	....	....	....	....	....	....	....	....	Gross Capital Formation	93
	197.8	213.8	228.3	261.3	293.4	....	....	....	....	....	....	....	....	....	....	Private Consumption	96f
	−293.8	−381.0	−385.0	−317.2	−453.6	....	....	....	....	....	....	....	....	....	....	Imports of Goods & Services	98c
	257.2	289.4	317.1	356.1	403.5	468.3	552.1	647.5	771.1	850.2	901.8	969.2	999.4	1,045.7	....	Gross Domestic Product	99b
	483.5	507.4	509.4	544.6	585.2	636.5	698.3	761.3	820.1	871.4	901.8	940.2	955.9	988.2	....	Gross Dom. Prod. 1990 Prices	99b.p
	53.2	57.0	62.2	65.4	69.0	73.6	79.1	85.1	94.0	97.6	100.0	103.1	104.6	105.8	....	GDP Deflator (1990=100)	99bi p
Midyear Estimates																	
	.08	.08	.08	.07	.08	.08	.08	.06	.06	.06	.06	.06	.06	.06	....	**Population**	99z

Argentina

213

		1965	1966	1967	1968	1969	1970	1971	1972	1973	1974	1975	1976	1977	1978	1979
Exchange Rates													*Pesos per Bill. SDRs through 1977, per Mill. SDRs from 1978 to 1983,*			
Official Rate	aa	.01885	.02473	.03500	.03500	.03500	.04000	.05429	.05429	.06032	.06122	.71276	3.18922	7.25789	ɪ.01307	.02132
													Pesos per Billion US$ through 1977, per Million US$ from 1978 to 1983,			
Official Rate	ae	.01885	.02473	.03500	.03500	.03500	.04000	.05000	.05000	.05000	.05000	.60885	2.74500	5.97500	ɪ.01004	.01619
Official Rate	rf	.01696	.02092	.03334	.03500	.03500	.03792	.04522	.05000	.05000	.05000	.36575	1.39983	4.07633	ɪ.00796	.01317
Fund Position															*Millions of SDRs:*	
Quota	2f. s	280.0	350.0	350.0	350.0	350.0	440.0	440.0	440.0	440.0	440.0	440.0	440.0	440.0	535.0	535.0
SDRs	1b. s	—	—	—	—	—	59.3	2.8	—	17.8	66.9	83.8	34.8	78.2	73.9	161.6	247.9
Reserve Position in the Fund	1c. s	—	—	18.0	96.7	117.8	130.2	110.0	—	—	—	11.3	—	—	—	130.5	154.4
Total Fund Cred.&Loans Outstg.	2tl	76.0	30.0	—	—	—	—	—	174.0	174.0	64.0	250.1	455.6	344.5	—	—
International Liquidity													*Millions of US Dollars Unless Otherwise Indicated:*			
Total Reserves minus Gold	1l. d	170	132	643	651	403	533	192	313	1,149	1,144	288	1,445	3,154	4,966	9,388
SDRs	1b. d	—	—	—	—	—	59	3	19	81	103	41	91	90	211	327
Reserve Position in the Fund	1c. d	—	—	18	97	118	130	119	—	—	—	14	—	—	170	203
Foreign Exchange	1d. d	170	132	625	554	285	343	70	294	1,068	1,028	247	1,354	3,064	4,586	8,858
Gold (Million Fine Troy Ounces)	1ad	1.882	2.392	2.392	3.107	3.850	3.993	2.564	3.993	3.996	3.996	3.996	3.996	4.184	4.278	4.372
Gold (National Valuation)	1and	66	84	84	109	135	140	97	152	169	169	169	169	177	181	184
Monetary Authorities: Other Assets	3..d	46	48	40	50	41	67	66	121	151	166	389	592	877	1,059	1,069
Other Liab.	4..d	152	79	266	217	120	36	111	176	353	383	457	1,182	871	21	86
Deposit Money Banks: Assets	7a. d	....	....	....	....	137	158	127	183	265	254	329	441	420	478	454
of which: Claims on Nonbanks	7ad d	....	....	....	....	....	....	....	....	....	....	....	....	....	....	....
Deposit Money Banks: Liabilities	7b. d	....	....	....	....	....	....	....	....	....	....	....	....	....	....	....
of which: Liab. to Nonbanks	7bd d	....	....	....	....	....	....	....	....	....	....	....	....	....	....	....
Other Banking Insts.: Assets	7e. d	....	....	....	....	....	....	....	....	....	....	....	....	....	....	....
of which: Claims on Nonbanks	7ed d	....	....	....	....	....	....	....	....	....	....	....	....	....	....	....
Other Banking Insts.: Liabilities	7f. d	....	....	....	....	....	....	....	....	....	....	....	....	....	....	....
of which: Liab. to Nonbanks	7fd d	....	....	....	....	....	....	....	....	....	....	....	....	....	....	....
Monetary Authorities												*Thousandths (.000) of Pesos through 1978; Pesos from 1979 to 1984;*				
Foreign Assets	11	4	5	23	25	20	29	17	29	73	74	515	6,052	25,132	62,161	ɪ172
Claims on Central Government	12a	30	41	48	53	54	62	90	140	310	540	1,790	4,760	13,570	30,160	ɪ43
Claims on Deposit Money Banks	12e	9	8	2	11	12	14	19	30	800	1,200	3,600	14,700	4,900	5,700	ɪ8
Claims on Other Banking Insts.	12f	4	4	5	5	5	—	—	—	—	100	200	200	1,200	1,300	600	ɪ2
Reserve Money	14	41	52	66	84	90	101	109	150	1,300	1,990	5,490	25,140	36,000	71,100	ɪ132
of which: Currency Outside DMBs	14a	30	40	51	59	66	76	100	130	300	400	1,200	4,100	10,700	33,300	ɪ79
Foreign Liabilities	16c	3	2	9	7	4	1	6	18	28	23	457	4,699	7,706	215	ɪ1
Central Government Deposits	16d	—	—	—	—	—	—	—	—	10	10	—	120	210	400	ɪ1
Capital Accounts	17a	—	—	—	—	—	2	6	8	9	9	209	686	1,507	2,894	ɪ6
Other Items (Net)	17r	2	4	3	4	-3	1	6	23	-64	-19	-51	-3,933	-521	24,012	ɪ85
Deposit Money Banks																
Reserves	20	11	12	23	25	18	24	40	60	1,000	1,590	4,090	19,840	24,000	36,000	ɪ55
Foreign Assets	21	—	—	—	—	—	—	—	—	—	—	—	—	—	—	ɪ—
Claims on Central Government	22a	10	12	15	16	17	20	20	20	210	200	700	2,500	9,600	33,500	ɪ99
Claims on Official Entities	22bx	—	—	—	—	—	—	—	—	—	—	—	—	—	—	ɪ—
Claims on Private Sector	22d	43	59	77	112	143	171	290	460	740	1,170	2,980	12,110	43,350	121,870	ɪ400
Demand Deposits	24	20	28	58	77	100	100	100	200	400	700	2,100	8,300	19,400	42,900	ɪ105
Time, Savings,& Fgn.Currency Dep.	25	23	29	38	53	62	100	100	300	400	600	800	5,900	31,900	95,300	ɪ315
Foreign Liabilities	26c	—	—	—	—	—	—	—	—	—	—	—	—	—	—	ɪ—
Central Government Deposits	26d	11	13	2	2	3	—	—	—	—	—	100	200	500	1,200	ɪ3
Credit from Monetary Authorities	26g	9	8	10	11	34	57	80	100	900	1,300	3,600	14,500	5,100	5,200	ɪ10
Capital Accounts	27a	6	8	11	17	21	24	62	100	100	100	300	2,200	10,200	27,200	ɪ81
Other Items (Net)	27r	-5	-2	-4	-7	-42	-67	8	-160	150	260	870	3,350	9,850	19,570	ɪ41
Monetary Survey												*Thousandths (.000) of Pesos through 1978; Pesos from 1979 to 1984;*				
Foreign Assets (Net)	31n	1	3	15	18	16	28	11	11	45	51	58	1,353	17,426	61,946	ɪ171
Domestic Credit	32	76	102	143	185	216	253	400	620	1,350	2,100	5,570	20,250	67,110	184,530	ɪ540
Claims on Central Govt. (Net)	32an	29	40	62	67	68	82	110	160	510	730	2,390	6,940	22,460	62,060	ɪ138
Claims on Official Entities	32bx	—	—	—	—	—	—	—	—	—	—	—	—	—	—	ɪ—
Claims on Private Sector	32d	43	59	77	112	143	171	290	460	740	1,170	2,980	12,110	43,350	121,870	ɪ400
Claims on Other Banking Insts.	32f	4	4	5	5	5	—	—	—	100	200	200	1,200	1,300	600	ɪ2
Money	34	50	67	109	136	166	176	200	330	700	1,100	3,500	13,600	31,900	78,600	ɪ185
Quasi-Money	35	23	29	38	53	62	100	100	300	400	600	800	5,900	31,900	95,300	ɪ315
Capital Accounts	37a	6	8	11	17	21	26	68	108	109	109	509	2,886	11,707	30,094	ɪ87
Other Items (Net)	37r	-2	1	—	-2	-17	-21	43	-107	186	341	819	-783	9,029	42,482	ɪ125
Money plus Quasi-Money	35l	73	96	148	189	228	276	300	630	1,100	1,700	4,300	19,500	63,800	173,900	ɪ500
Other Banking Institutions												*Thousandths (.000) of Pesos through 1978; Pesos from 1979 to 1984;*				
Cash	40	—	—	—	—	—	—	—	—	—	100	200	1,300	200	500	ɪ1
Foreign Assets	41	—	—	—	—	—	—	—	—	—	—	—	—	—	—	ɪ—
Claims on Central Government	42a	—	—	—	—	10	—	—	—	—	—	—	—	240	400	ɪ1
Claims on Official Entities	42bx	—	—	—	—	—	—	—	—	—	—	—	—	—	100	ɪ—
Claims on Private Sector	42d	6	8	11	16	32	40	10	20	50	80	210	1,770	8,840	23,800	ɪ64
Claims on Deposit Money Banks	42e	—	—	—	—	—	—	—	—	—	—	—	200	3,200	5,900	ɪ9
Time, Savings,& Fgn.Currency Dep.	45	2	4	7	11	16	20	—	10	20	70	110	1,210	7,910	22,700	ɪ59
Foreign Liabilities	46c	—	—	—	—	—	—	—	—	—	—	—	—	—	—	ɪ—
Credit from Monetary Authorities	46g	4	4	4	5	5	7	10	10	30	110	200	1,200	1,500	1,800	ɪ2
Capital Accounts	47a	—	—	—	—	—	—	—	—	—	—	—	200	800	2,200	ɪ5
Other Items (Net)	47r	—	—	-1	—	11	23	—	—	—	—	100	660	2,370	3,900	ɪ9
Banking Survey												*Thousandths (.000) of Pesos through 1978; Pesos from 1979 to 1984;*				
Foreign Assets (Net)	51n	1	3	15	18	16	28	11	11	45	51	58	1,353	17,426	61,946	ɪ171
Domestic Credit	52	78	106	149	196	243	303	410	640	1,300	1,980	5,580	20,820	74,990	208,130	ɪ604
Claims on Central Govt. (Net)	52an	29	40	62	67	68	92	110	160	510	730	2,390	6,940	22,700	62,460	ɪ139
Claims on Official Entities	52bx	—	—	—	—	—	—	—	—	—	—	—	—	100	—	ɪ—
Claims on Private Sector	52d	49	67	88	128	175	211	300	480	790	1,250	3,190	13,880	52,190	145,670	ɪ465
Liquid Liabilities	55l	75	100	155	200	245	296	300	640	1,120	1,670	4,210	19,410	71,510	196,100	ɪ558
Capital Accounts	57a	6	8	11	17	21	26	68	108	109	109	509	3,086	12,507	32,294	ɪ92
Other Items (Net)	57r	-2	2	-2	-3	-6	9	53	-97	116	251	919	-323	8,399	41,682	ɪ126

Argentina

1980	1981	1982	1983	1984	1985	1986	1987	1988	1989	1990	1991	1992	1993	1994		
per Thous. SDRs from 1984 to 1988, per SDR thereafter: End of Period															**Exchange Rates**	
.02541	.08436	.53550	2.43531	ɪ.01752	.08793	.15375	.53200	1.79920	ɪ.23589	.79456	1.42828	1.36194	1.37150	1.45912	Official Rate	aa
per Thous.US$ from 1984 to 1988, per US$ after:End Per.(ae) Per.Avg.(rf)																
.01993	.07248	.48545	2.32610	ɪ.01787	.08005	.12570	.37500	1.33700	ɪ.17950	.55850	.99850	.99050	.99850	.99950	Official Rate	ae
.01837	.04403	.25923	1.05300	ɪ.00676	.06018	.09430	.21443	.87526	ɪ.04233	.48759	.95355	.99064	.99895	.99901	Official Rate	rf
End of Period															**Fund Position**	
802.5	802.5	802.5	1,113.0	1,113.0	1,113.0	1,113.0	1,113.0	1,113.0	1,113.0	1,113.0	1,113.0	1,537.1	1,537.1	1,537.1	Quota	2f. s
256.6	347.1	—	.3	.6	—	—	—	—	.3	.2	209.0	134.9	272.8	329.5	385.7 SDRs	1b. s
262.8	239.2	91.0	—	—	—	—	—	—	—	—	—	—	—	—	Reserve Position in the Fund	1c. s
—	—	—	1,120.6	1,120.6	2,105.1	2,240.9	2,716.2	2,733.0	2,358.8	2,167.2	1,735.9	1,682.8	2,562.4	2,884.7	Total Fund Cred.&Loans Outstg.	2tl
End of Period															**International Liquidity**	
6,719	3,268	2,506	1,172	1,243	ɪ3,273	2,718	1,617	3,363	1,463	4,592	6,005	9,990	13,791	14,327	Total Reserves minus Gold	1l. d
327	404	—	—	1	—	—	—	—	—	—	297	193	375	453	563 SDRs	1b. d
335	278	100	—	—	—	—	—	—	—	—	—	—	—	—	Reserve Position in the Fund	1c. d
6,057	2,586	2,406	1,172	1,242	ɪ3,273	2,718	1,617	3,363	1,463	4,295	5,812	9,615	13,339	13,764	Foreign Exchange	1d. d
4.372	4.372	4.372	4.372	4.372	4.372	4.373	4.373	4.373	4.373	4.373	4.233	4.123	4.373	4.373	4.374 Gold (Million Fine Troy Ounces)	1ad
185	185	185	1,421	1,421	1,421	1,421	1,421	1,421	1,421	1,421	1,421	1,430	1,446	1,672	1,651 Gold (National Valuation)	1an d
1,070	1,173	1,247	1,369	1,815	2,100	....	....	....	....	1,154	772	—	—	—	57 Monetary Authorities: Other Assets	3..d
194	271	679	1,572	2,155	4,952	6,506	6,906	7,826	....	7,394	7,629	—	558	161	Other Liab.	4..d
2,155	1,008	751	1,217	1,275	1,068	1,063	1,312	1,270	1,557	2,234	2,812	3,642	5,153	5,650	Deposit Money Banks: Assets	7a. d
....	254	164	785	923	746	766	972	842	966	1,580	1,651	1,860	2,050	2,130	*of which: Claims on Nonbanks*	7ad d
....	7,196	7,172	7,839	7,206	6,732	6,555	7,937	9,338	6,092	7,011	7,869	9,558	9,051	10,882	Deposit Money Banks: Liabilities	7b. d
....	1,407	1,790	1,825	2,352	2,231	2,526	2,405	2,597	1,552	1,886	2,581	2,814	3,807	5,100	*of which: Liab. to Nonbanks*	7bd d
....	2	2	2	2	4	3	1	1	3	5	10	12	32	25	Other Banking Insts.: Assets	7e. d
....	1	—	—	—	4	2	1	1	—	3	4	4	9	6	*of which: Claims on Nonbanks*	7ed d
....	8	5	4	3	1	1	2	—	—	2	49	117	26	40	Other Banking Insts.: Liabilities	7f. d
....	2	1	3	1	—	—	—	—	—	2	48	106	18	32	*of which: Liab. to Nonbanks*	7fd d
Thousands from 1985 to 1988;Millions Beginning 1989: End of Period															**Monetary Authorities**	
159	335	1,929	9,270	90,586	ɪ533	888	2,002	10,635	....	ɪ4,114	9,009	11,236	15,448	....	Foreign Assets	11
127	485	1,438	16,667	84,202	ɪ715	1,247	4,814	17,641	ɪ475	ɪ5,334	10,879	9,272	11,432	....	Claims on Central Government	12a
101	367	4,167	12,308	85,568	....	....	....	....	....	ɪ14,510	17,922	23,408	22,527	....	Claims on Deposit Money Banks	12e
17	52	617	1,631	9,462	....	....	....	....	....	ɪ6	6	5	5	....	Claims on Other Banking Insts.	12f
236	513	4,332	19,765	105,849	ɪ515	694	1,352	7,000	ɪ528	ɪ3,617	7,823	11,010	14,989	....	Reserve Money	14
164	302	874	4,634	31,340	ɪ202	399	926	4,319	ɪ182	ɪ2,259	5,222	7,686	10,067	....	*of which: Currency Outside DMBs*	14a
4	20	329	6,386	58,153	ɪ581	1,162	4,035	15,381	....	ɪ5,857	10,102	2,843	3,677	....	Foreign Liabilities	16c
—	3	290	903	653	ɪ26	10	204	100	ɪ79	ɪ156	1,097	1,378	1,338	....	Central Government Deposits	16d
9	66	299	1,509	23,878	ɪ149	250	1,102	4,074	ɪ446	ɪ5,557	3,786	6,394	7,217	....	Capital Accounts	17a
155	637	2,900	11,313	81,286	ɪ455	834	4,583	24,604	....	ɪ8,777	15,008	22,296	22,191	....	Other Items (Net)	17r
Thousands from 1985 to 1988;Millions Beginning 1989: End of Period															**Deposit Money Banks**	
75	206	3,190	14,248	71,978	ɪ309	305	428	2,550	ɪ189	ɪ1,342	2,900	3,481	5,488	5,329	Reserves	20
—	107	365	2,832	23,408	ɪ86	134	493	1,698	ɪ280	ɪ1,249	2,809	3,606	5,148	5,650	Foreign Assets	21
168	644	2,314	7,636	55,179	ɪ247	464	1,552	7,247	ɪ948	ɪ6,197	9,830	9,871	11,657	9,638	Claims on Central Government	22a
—	—	—	—	4,502	ɪ37	107	310	1,381	ɪ36	ɪ713	795	1,103	1,509	1,931	Claims on Official Entities	22bx
835	2,220	6,844	29,079	190,221	ɪ898	1,650	4,882	22,248	ɪ1,279	ɪ10,702	22,550	34,564	42,600	51,113	Claims on Private Sector	22d
196	330	613	2,361	18,191	ɪ146	264	491	2,078	ɪ91	ɪ809	2,404	3,678	5,052	6,068	Demand Deposits	24
597	1,283	2,970	15,521	122,633	ɪ568	1,291	3,727	21,528	ɪ379	ɪ4,845	11,471	19,666	30,334	35,843	Time, Savings,& Fgn.Currency Dep.	25
—	763	3,484	18,243	128,780	ɪ539	825	2,984	12,485	ɪ1,096	ɪ13,919	7,861	9,462	9,042	10,882	Foreign Liabilities	26c
5	23	849	3,666	11,078	ɪ167	216	345	1,387	ɪ76	ɪ524	1,976	2,958	5,054	3,443	Central Government Deposits	26d
80	266	3,627	7,439	34,349	ɪ240	446	1,363	5,083	ɪ237	ɪ10,082	18,292	22,967	22,336	22,228	Credit from Monetary Authorities	26g
158	482	2,053	9,952	75,135	ɪ344	620	1,728	6,073	ɪ533	ɪ5,966	9,608	10,802	12,503	13,383	Capital Accounts	27a
41	29	-884	-3,388	-45,147	ɪ-429	-1,002	-2,972	-13,511	ɪ319	ɪ-5,942	-12,728	-16,908	-17,919	-18,186	Other Items (Net)	27r
Thousands from 1985 to 1988;Millions Beginning 1989: End of Period															**Monetary Survey**	
155	-341	-1,520	-12,527	-73,207	ɪ-502	-966	-4,524	-15,532	....	ɪ-4,413	-6,145	2,537	7,877	....	Foreign Assets (Net)	31n
1,141	3,376	10,073	50,444	331,835	....	....	....	....	....	....	ɪ22,272	40,987	50,479	60,811	Domestic Credit	32
289	1,104	2,612	19,733	127,650	ɪ769	1,485	5,818	23,400	ɪ1,267	ɪ10,851	17,636	14,807	16,697	....	Claims on Central Govt. (Net)	32an
—	—	—	—	4,502	ɪ37	107	310	1,381	ɪ36	ɪ713	795	1,103	1,509	....	Claims on Official Entities	32bx
835	2,220	6,844	29,079	190,221	ɪ898	1,650	4,882	22,248	ɪ1,279	ɪ10,702	22,550	34,564	42,600	....	Claims on Private Sector	32d
17	52	617	1,631	9,462	....	....	....	....	....	ɪ6	6	5	5	....	Claims on Other Banking Insts.	32f
362	639	1,623	7,500	51,170	ɪ350	664	1,418	6,402	ɪ273	ɪ3,068	7,626	11,364	15,119	....	Money	34
597	1,283	2,970	15,521	122,633	ɪ568	1,291	3,727	21,528	ɪ379	ɪ4,845	11,471	19,666	30,334	....	Quasi-Money	35
167	549	2,352	11,462	99,013	ɪ494	869	2,829	10,147	ɪ979	ɪ11,523	13,394	17,196	19,720	....	Capital Accounts	37a
171	566	1,608	3,434	-14,188	....	....	....	....	....	ɪ-1,577	2,351	4,790	3,515	....	Other Items (Net)	37r
958	1,921	4,593	23,021	173,803	ɪ918	1,955	5,145	27,929	ɪ652	ɪ7,913	19,097	31,030	45,453	....	Money plus Quasi-Money	35l
Thousands from 1985 to 1988;Millions Beginning 1989: End of Period															**Other Banking Institutions**	
2	13	138	589	1,952	ɪ2	2	4	21	ɪ1	ɪ7	12	17	20	21	Cash	40
—	—	—	1	4	44	ɪ—	—	—	2	ɪ3	10	12	32	25	Foreign Assets	41
1	10	30	75	311	ɪ1	1	5	18	ɪ5	ɪ26	37	24	26	36	Claims on Central Government	42a
—	—	—	—	—	ɪ—	—	1	11	ɪ—	ɪ2	5	6	—	—	Claims on Official Entities	42bx
141	288	566	1,707	7,517	ɪ23	39	87	337	ɪ9	ɪ51	220	441	644	850	Claims on Private Sector	42d
8	30	29	104	385	ɪ2	3	3	22	ɪ—	ɪ2	5	5	5	10	Claims on Deposit Money Banks	42e
120	297	264	1,218	4,513	ɪ16	38	98	567	ɪ5	ɪ43	121	272	412	502	Time, Savings,& Fgn.Currency Dep.	45
—	1	2	8	59	ɪ—	—	—	1	—	ɪ1	49	116	26	40	Foreign Liabilities	46c
10	32	490	620	2,139	ɪ10	18	16	35	ɪ1	ɪ6	6	5	5	7	Credit from Monetary Authorities	46g
11	37	129	510	2,926	ɪ7	8	19	178	ɪ8	ɪ76	133	167	202	237	Capital Accounts	47a
11	-26	-122	123	573	ɪ-5	-18	-33	-368	ɪ1	ɪ-35	20	-55	82	156	Other Items (Net)	47r
Thousands from 1985 to 1988;Millions Beginning 1989: End of Period															**Banking Survey**	
155	-341	-1,521	-12,532	-73,222	ɪ-502	-966	-4,524	-15,530	....	ɪ-4,411	-6,184	2,433	7,883	....	Foreign Assets (Net)	51n
1,266	3,621	10,052	50,595	330,201	ɪ1,728	3,282	11,103	47,395	ɪ2,597	ɪ22,345	41,243	50,945	61,476	....	Domestic Credit	52
290	1,113	2,642	19,808	127,961	ɪ769	1,486	5,823	23,418	ɪ1,272	ɪ10,877	17,673	14,831	16,723	....	Claims on Central Govt. (Net)	52an
—	—	—	—	4,502	ɪ37	107	311	1,392	ɪ36	ɪ715	800	1,109	1,509	....	Claims on Official Entities	52bx
975	2,508	7,409	30,787	197,738	ɪ921	1,688	4,969	22,585	ɪ1,288	ɪ10,753	22,770	35,005	43,244	....	Claims on Private Sector	52d
1,077	2,206	4,720	23,651	176,364	ɪ932	1,991	5,239	28,476	ɪ657	ɪ7,949	19,206	31,285	45,845	....	Liquid Liabilities	55l
178	585	2,481	11,971	101,938	ɪ501	877	2,848	10,324	ɪ987	ɪ11,599	13,527	17,363	19,922	....	Capital Accounts	57a
167	489	1,329	2,441	-21,324	ɪ-207	-552	-1,509	-6,935	....	ɪ-1,614	2,326	4,730	3,592	....	Other Items (Net)	57r

Argentina
213

		1965	1966	1967	1968	1969	1970	1971	1972	1973	1974	1975	1976	1977	1978	1979
Interest Rates																*Percent Per Annum*
Deposit Rate	60l	....	....	....	....	....	....	....	....	....	....	....	....	115	132	117
Lending Rate	60p	....	....	....	....	....	....	....	....	....	....	....	....			
Prices and Production																*Index Numbers (1990=100):*
W'sale Prices(1990=100,000)	63.b	—	—	—	—	—	—	—	—	—	—	—	—	—	—	—
Wholesale Prices	63.c	—	—	—	—	—	—	—	—	—	—	—	—	—	—	—
Cons.Prices (1990=100,000)	64.b	—	—	—	—	—	—	—	—	—	—	—	—	—	—	—
Consumer Prices	64.c	....	....	....	....	....	....	....	....	....	....	....	....	....	....	....
Manufacturing Prod. (1985=100)	66ey	80	76	77	82	88	97	103	107	111	118	115	111	120	108	119
Crude Petroleum Production	66aa	55.9	59.6	65.3	71.4	74.0	81.6	87.9	90.2	87.5	86.0	82.5	82.7	89.5	94.0	98.4
International Transactions																*Millions of US Dollars*
Exports	70..d	1,493.4	1,593.2	1,464.5	1,367.9	1,612.1	1,773.2	1,740.4	1,941.2	3,266.0	3,930.7	2,961.3	3,916.1	5,651.8	6,399.5	7,809.9
Meat	70k.d	328.8	397.1	382.4	335.1	432.8	438.0	412.3	686.3	778.8	437.1	281.5	510.5	622.4	781.0	1,202.5
Wheat	70d.d	372.7	279.6	122.1	139.1	138.5	125.9	48.8	109.6	273.8	305.0	300.7	431.5	541.4	174.3	606.0
Imports, cif	71..d	1,198.6	1,124.3	1,095.5	1,169.2	1,576.1	1,694.0	1,868.1	1,904.7	2,229.5	3,634.9	3,946.5	3,033.0	4,161.5	3,833.7	6,700.1
Imports, fob	71.v d	1,059.8	993.2	969.5	1,034.7	1,394.8	1,499.1	1,042.8	1,685.6	1,985.0	3,242.0	3,512.0	2,743.0	3,803.3	3,491.6	6,040.9
Volume of Exports																*1990=100*
Meat	72k	168.8	205.5	211.3	170.5	225.9	209.4	133.4	190.2	154.0	70.0	60.0	122.3	135.5	158.0	153.3
Wheat	72d	116.4	88.3	36.0	42.3	41.0	40.2	14.0	28.7	52.2	30.3	30.7	55.2	98.5	28.1	74.8
Unit Value of Exports																*1990=100:*
Frozen Beef	74ka.d	21.7	19.7	16.4	21.4	19.5	25.3	30.7	39.6	54.4	58.3	29.7	31.4	40.2	40.1	63.9
Corned Beef	74kd.d	36.6	37.8	39.1	40.3	38.6	38.2	60.0	63.9	80.1	110.0	76.8	72.1	72.9	73.9	115.9
Wheat	74d.d	38.8	38.7	43.2	39.6	40.6	37.7	41.2	46.1	67.4	134.0	119.1	92.8	67.0	81.5	101.3
Balance of Payments																*Millions of US Dollars:*
Goods: Exports f.o.b.	78aa d	....	....	....	....	....	....	....	....	....	....	....	3,918	5,651	6,401	7,810
Goods: Imports f.o.b.	78ab d	....	....	....	....	....	....	....	....	....	....	....	−2,765	−3,799	−3,488	−6,028
Trade Balance	78ac d	....	....	....	....	....	....	....	....	....	....	....	1,153	1,852	2,913	1,782
Services: Credit	78ad d	....	....	....	....	....	....	....	....	....	....	....	714	951	1,087	1,369
Services: Debit	78ae d	....	....	....	....	....	....	....	....	....	....	....	−742	−967	−1,544	−2,814
Balance on Goods and Services	78af d	....	....	....	....	....	....	....	....	....	....	....	1,125	1,836	2,456	337
Income: Credit	78ag d	....	....	....	....	....	....	....	....	....	....	....	59	136	348	737
Income: Debit	78ah d	....	....	....	....	....	....	....	....	....	....	....	−551	−877	−1,016	−1,644
Balance on Goods, Serv., & Inc.	78ai d	....	....	....	....	....	....	....	....	....	....	....	633	1,095	1,788	−570
Current Transfers, n.i.e.: Credit	78aj d	....	....	....	....	....	....	....	....	....	....	....	30	43	85	88
Current Transfers: Debit	78ak d	....	....	....	....	....	....	....	....	....	....	....	−12	−12	−17	−31
Current Account, n.i.e.	78al d	....	....	....	....	....	....	....	....	....	....	....	651	1,126	1,856	−513
Capital Account, n.i.e.: Credit	78ba d	....	....	....	....	....	....	....	....	....	....	....	—	—	—	—
Capital Account: Debit	78bb d	....	....	....	....	....	....	....	....	....	....	....	—	—	—	—
Capital Account, n.i.e.	78bc d	....	....	....	....	....	....	....	....	....	....	....	—	—	—	—
Direct Investment Abroad	78bd d	....	....	....	....	....	....	....	....	....	....	....	—	1	23	59
Dir. Invest. in Rep. Econ., n.i.e.	78be d	....	....	....	....	....	....	....	....	....	....	....	—	144	250	206
Portfolio Investment Assets	78bf d	....	....	....	....	....	....	....	....	....	....	....				
Portfolio Investment Liab., n.i.e.	78bg d	....	....	....	....	....	....	....	....	....	....	....	−66	−1	101	222
Other Investment Assets	78bh d	....	....	....	....	....	....	....	....	....	....	....	328	−382	−83	496
Other Investment Liab., n.i.e.	78bi d	....	....	....	....	....	....	....	....	....	....	....	−816	843	−365	3,260
Financial Account, n.i.e.	78bj d	....	....	....	....	....	....	....	....	....	....	....	−554	605	−74	4,243
Net Errors and Omissions	78ca d	....	....	....	....	....	....	....	....	....	....	....	−218	134	12	243
Overall Balance	78cb d	....	....	....	....	....	....	....	....	....	....	....	−121	1,865	1,794	3,973
Reserves and Related Items	79da d	....	....	....	....	....	....	....	....	....	....	....	121	−1,865	−1,794	−3,973
Reserve Assets	79db d	....	....	....	....	....	....	....	....	....	....	....	−1,156	−1,714	−1,716	−4,225
Use of Fund Credit and Loans	79dc d	....	....	....	....	....	....	....	....	....	....	....	237	−132	−423	—
Liabs.Constit.For.Auth.Reserves	79dd d	....	....	....	....	....	....	....	....	....	....	....	—	—	4	65
Exceptional Financing	79de d	....	....	....	....	....	....	....	....	....	....	....	1,040	−20	341	187
Government Finance																*Thousandths (.000) of Pesos through 1978; Pesos from 1979 to 1984;*
Deficit (-) or Surplus	80	....	....	....	....	....	....	....	−100.0	−200.0	−300.0	−1,500.0	−5,400.0	−5,800.0	−16,800.0	I−37.1
Revenue	81	....	....	....	....	....	....	....	300.0	400.0	800.0	1,600.0	9,300.0	29,500.0	83,500.0	I 234.4
Exp. & Lending Minus Repay.	82z	....	....	....	....	....	....	....	400.0	600.0	1,100.0	3,100.0	14,700.0	35,300.0	100,300.0	I 271.5
Expenditure	82	....	....	....	....	....	....	....	400.0	600.0	1,000.0	2,800.0	13,400.0	32,500.0	92,600.0	I 248.3
Lending Minus Repayments	83	....	....	....	....	....	....	....	—	—	100.0	300.0	1,300.0	2,800.0	7,700.0	I 23.2
Financing																
Domestic	84a	....	....	....	....	....	....	....	100.0	200.0	300.0	1,500.0	5,100.0	5,300.0	11,600.0	I 33.6
Foreign	85a	....	....	....	....	....	....	....	I —	—	—	—	300.0	500.0	5,200.0	I 3.5
Debt: Domestic	88a	....	....	....	....	....	....	....	....	....	....	2,300.0	9,800.0	20,500.0	36,500.0	I 81.6
Foreign	89a	....	....	....	....	....	....	....	....	....	....	300.0	4,700.0	12,500.0		I 25.1
National Accounts																*Thousandths (.000) of Pesos through 1978; Pesos from 1979 to 1984;*
Exports of Goods & Services	90c	—	—	100	100	100	100	100	200	400	500	1,100	9,400	27,300	61,000	I 126
Government Consumption	91f	—	—	100	100	100	100	100	200	400	700	1,900	7,400	19,700	60,900	I 164
Gross Fixed Capital Formation	93e	100	100	100	100	200	200	300	400	600	900	3,700	20,400	56,900	127,600	I 324
Increase/Decrease(-) in Stocks	93i	—	—	—	—	—	—	—	—	—	—	100	200	—	−2,700	I −2
Private Consumption	96f	300	300	400	500	600	600	900	1,400	2,400	3,200	8,700	44,600	126,200	317,100	I 936
Imports of Goods & Services	98c	—	—	—	−100	−100	−100	−100	−200	−300	−400	−1,200	−6,100	−20,800	−40,500	I −122
Gross Domestic Product	99b	400	500	600	700	800	900	1,300	2,100	3,500	4,900	14,300	75,900	209,300	523,400	I 1,425
Net Factor Inc/Pmts(-) Abroad	98.n	−1	−6	−8	−9	−10	−11	−20	−29	−40	−30	−200	−1,200	−2,400	−6,200	I −14
Gross Nat'l Expenditure = GNP	99a	300	400	500	600	700	800	1,100	2,000	3,200	4,786	14,100	74,700	206,900	517,200	I 1,412
GDP 1990 Prices (Millions)	99b.p	47,795	52,603	53,028	54,795	57,482	I 58,967	60,971	62,140	64,145	68,154	67,653	67,486	71,662	69,323	74,369
GDP Deflator (1990=100)	99bi p	—	—	—	—	—	—	—	—	—	—	—	—	—	—	—
																Millions:
Population	99z	22.18	22.49	22.80	23.11	23.43	23.75	24.07	24.39	24.82	25.22	I 26.05	26.48	26.91	27.35	27.79

Exchange Rates: On June 1, 1983, the peso argentino, equal to 10,000 pesos, was introduced. On June 14, 1985, the austral, equal to 1,000 pesos argentino, was introduced. On January 1, 1992, the peso argentino, equal to 10,000 australes, was introduced.

Monetary Authorities: I Beginning in January 1990, data may not be comparable with data for earlier periods because of a change in the valuation system and adjustments to the accounts of the Central Bank of the Republic of Argentina. Accounts classified as central government include also positions with nonfinancial public enterprises.

Deposit Money Banks: I Beginning in January 1990, data are based on an improved reporting system. Accounts classified as central government include also positions with nonfinancial public enterprises.

Monetary Survey: I See notes to sections 10 and 20.
Other Banking Institutions: I See note to section 20.
Banking Survey: I See notes to sections 10 and 20.

Government Finance: I Beginning in 1970, annual data are as reported in the *Government Finance Statistics Yearbook* and cover consolidated central government (including all extrabudgetary and social security funds). However, data on outstanding debt cover budgetary central government only.

Argentina

213

	1980	1981	1982	1983	1984	1985	1986	1987	1988	1989	1990	1991	1992	1993	1994		
Percent Per Annum																**Interest Rates**	
	80	157	126	281	397	630	95	176	372	17,236	1,518	62	17	11	8	Deposit Rate	60l
	87	185	202	739	1,182	1,161	135	253	524	1,387,179	9,695,422	71	15	6	8	Lending Rate	60p
Period Averages																**Prices and Production**	
	—	—	—	—	1	9	15	32	‡166	5,858	100,000	....	....	....	....	W'sale Prices(1990=100,000)	63.b
	....	....	....	....	....	....	....	....	....	....	100	210	223	227	228	Wholesale Prices	63.c
	—	—	—	—	1	7	13	29	‡130	4,143	100,000	....	....	....	....	Cons.Prices (1990=100,000)	64.b
	....	....	....	....	....	....	....	....	....	....	100	272	339	375	391	Consumer Prices	64.c
	114	96	91	101	105	100	113	....	....	....	....	....	....	....	....	Manufacturing Prod. (1985=100)	66ey
	102.3	103.2	101.8	101.9	99.6	95.5	90.1	88.7	93.5	95.3	100.0	101.0	115.6	96.0	138.3	Crude Petroleum Production	66aa
Millions of US Dollars																**International Transactions**	
	8,021.4	9,143.0	7,624.9	7,836.1	8,107.4	8,396.1	6,852.2	6,360.2	9,134.8	9,579.3	12,352.5	11,977.8	12,235.0	13,117.8	15,659.3	Exports	70..d
	935.8	907.7	804.9	602.6	404.3	385.7	464.7	599.3	607.2	716.3	873.2	....	....	....	....	Meat	70k.d
	816.1	763.6	676.2	1,474.0	965.8	1,133.2	395.1	351.0	355.2	657.5	870.9	496.3	715.8	734.8	657.0	Wheat	70d.d
	10,540.6	9,430.2	5,336.9	4,504.2	4,584.7	3,814.2	4,724.1	5,817.8	5,321.6	4,203.2	4,076.0	8,275.3	14,871.8	16,783.5	21,527.3	Imports, cif	71..d
	9,381.1	8,429.9	4,857.3	4,125.7	4,200.7	3,515.1	4,322.7	5,341.0	4,890.4	3,864.0	3,724.7	7,525.2	13,622.6	14,693.7	19,660.9	Imports, fob	71.v d
1990=100																Volume of Exports	
	98.5	104.3	111.8	88.2	58.0	58.8	64.2	60.1	73.8	86.3	100.0	....	....	....	....	Meat	72k
	78.6	65.8	66.4	178.0	126.7	167.5	70.2	73.3	47.8	73.7	100.0	95.7	180.7	99.6	88.6	Wheat	72d
Indexes of Unit Values in US Dollars																Unit Value of Exports	
	74.4	64.3	48.9	50.9	69.4	66.2	84.8	123.9	118.3	113.5	100.0	148.7	194.0	231.5	175.9	Frozen Beef	74ka d
	139.8	132.5	97.3	88.8	84.9	80.0	88.2	108.7	80.1	92.7	100.0	116.9	90.9	108.7	121.6	Corned Beef	74kd d
	127.6	134.2	115.6	99.4	91.6	79.8	67.8	62.2	81.0	103.1	100.0	62.2	83.4	90.9	91.2	Wheat	74d. d
Minus Sign Indicates Debit																Balance of Payments	
	8,021	9,143	7,623	7,835	8,100	8,396	6,852	6,360	9,134	9,573	12,354	11,978	12,235	13,117	....	Goods: Exports f.o.b.	78aa d
	-9,394	-8,431	-4,859	-4,119	-4,118	-3,518	-4,406	-5,343	-4,892	-3,864	-3,726	-7,559	-13,685	-15,545	....	Goods: Imports f.o.b.	78ab d
	-1,373	712	2,764	3,716	3,982	4,878	2,446	1,017	4,242	5,709	8,628	4,419	-1,450	-2,428	....	Trade Balance	78ac d
	1,876	1,716	1,574	1,455	1,511	1,651	1,597	1,794	2,015	2,193	2,446	2,408	2,560	2,656	....	Services: Credit	78ad d
	-3,788	-3,434	-2,018	-2,224	-2,289	-2,187	-2,500	-2,566	-2,702	-2,793	-3,120	-4,007	-4,749	-5,137	....	Services: Debit	78ae d
	-3,285	-1,006	2,320	2,947	3,204	4,342	1,543	245	3,555	5,109	7,954	2,820	-3,639	-4,909	....	Balance on Goods and Services	78af d
	1,305	946	558	474	298	282	392	252	211	276	1,854	1,746	1,369	1,502	....	Income: Credit	78ag d
	-2,817	-4,630	-5,265	-5,873	-5,999	-5,576	-4,796	-4,724	-5,338	-6,698	-6,254	-6,006	-5,025	-4,491	....	Income: Debit	78ah d
	-4,797	-4,690	-2,387	-2,452	-2,497	-952	-2,861	-4,227	-1,572	-1,313	3,554	-1,440	-7,295	-7,898	....	Balance on Goods, Serv., & Inc.	78ai d
	85	70	51	35	21	18	21	11	2	18	1,015	821	798	597	....	Current Transfers, n.i.e.: Credit	78aj d
	-62	-92	-17	-19	-19	-18	-19	-19	-2	-10	-17	-28	-49	-151	....	Current Transfers: Debit	78ak d
	-4,774	-4,712	-2,353	-2,436	-2,495	-952	-2,859	-4,235	-1,572	-1,305	4,552	-647	-6,546	-7,452	....	Current Account, n.i.e.	78al d
	—	—	—	—	—	—	—	—	—	—	—	—	—	—	....	Capital Account, n.i.e.: Credit	78ba d
	—	—	—	—	—	—	—	—	—	—	—	—	—	—	....	Capital Account: Debit	78bb d
	—	—	—	—	—	—	—	—	—	—	—	—	—	—	....	Capital Account, n.i.e.	78bc d
	110	107	30	-2	—	—	—	—	—	—	—	—	—	—	....	Direct Investment Abroad	78bd d
	678	837	227	185	268	919	574	-19	1,147	1,028	1,836	2,439	4,179	6,305	....	Dir. Invest. in Rep. Econ., n.i.e.	78be d
	—	—	—	—	—	—	—	—	—	—	—	-241	-8,261	-7,537	-5,655	Portfolio Investment Assets	78bf d
	154	1,125	299	649	372	-617	-542	-572	-718	-1,098	-1,105	8,227	6,857	-3,380	....	Portfolio Investment Liab., n.i.e.	78bg d
	-440	-1,605	-552	-374	-241	26	-286	104	879	-399	661	426	-1,633	-4,980	....	Other Investment Assets	78bh d
	1,696	813	-1,938	-2,698	-336	529	672	461	-877	-7,539	-7,001	-2,671	6,972	-1,916	....	Other Investment Liab., n.i.e.	78bi d
	2,198	1,277	-1,934	-2,240	63	857	418	-26	431	-8,008	-5,850	160	8,838	-9,626	....	Financial Account, n.i.e.	78bj d
	-308	-205	-401	-447	-55	-532	302	-112	-165	-249	715	-341	137	87	....	Net Errors and Omissions	78ca d
	-2,884	-3,640	-4,688	-5,123	-2,487	-627	-2,139	-4,373	-1,306	-9,562	-583	-828	2,429	-16,991	....	Overall Balance	78cb d
	2,884	3,640	4,688	5,123	2,487	627	2,139	4,373	1,306	9,562	583	828	-2,429	16,991	....	Reserves and Related Items	79da d
	2,598	3,193	669	1,230	-166	-2,016	745	1,302	-1,888	1,826	-3,121	-2,040	-4,477	-3,758	....	Reserve Assets	79db d
	—	—	—	1,227	—	987	146	615	30	-478	-257	-590	-73	1,211	....	Use of Fund Credit and Loans	79dc d
	107	78	-38	-151	194	-219	-8	126	-62	-75	-34	22	-21	-7	....	Liabs.Constit.For.Auth.Reserves	79dd d
	179	369	4,057	2,817	2,459	1,875	1,256	2,330	3,226	8,289	3,996	3,436	2,142	19,545	....	Exceptional Financing	79de d
Thousands from 1985 to 1988; Millions Beginning 1989: Yr. Ending Dec. 31																**Government Finance**	
	-101.2	-446.3	-1,055.8	-8,699.5	-26,700.0	‡-292.4	-196.4	-667.5	-2,087.1	‡-12.4	....	....	....	....	....	Deficit (-) or Surplus	80
	486.9	918.6	2,322.1	10,632.1	78,300.0	‡828.6	1,517.9	3,262.7	10,285.4	‡319.4	....	....	....	....	....	Revenue	81
	588.1	1,364.9	3,377.9	19,331.6	105,000.0	‡1,121.0	1,714.3	3,930.2	12,372.5	‡331.8	....	....	....	....	....	Exp. & Lending Minus Repay.	82z
	537.7	1,226.7	3,048.8	14,879.2	88,500.0	‡938.1	1,599.5	3,552.8	12,011.0	‡305.6	....	....	....	....	....	Expenditure	82
	50.4	138.2	329.1	4,452.4	16,500.0	‡182.9	114.8	377.4	361.5	‡26.2	....	....	....	....	....	Lending Minus Repayments	83
																Financing	
	99.0	370.3	985.0	8,085.5	26,400.0	‡282.4	35.7	219.7	1,089.8	‡-20.9	....	....	....	....	....	Domestic	84a
	2.2	76.0	70.8	614.0	300.0	‡10.0	160.7	447.8	997.3	‡33.3	....	....	....	....	....	Foreign	85a
	134.6	596.5	2,300.0	14,700.0	50,600.0	....	270.5	1,046.0	2,572.4	‡357.0	....	....	....	....	....	Debt: Domestic	88a
	35.5	300.0	2,004.2	13,300.0	145,400.0	....	2,248.8	8,487.5	13,869.8	‡339.1	....	....	....	....	....	Foreign	89a
Thousands from 1985 to 1988; Millions Beginning 1989																**National Accounts**	
	194	517	1,986	10,020	60,030	‡623	815	1,837	10,586	‡424	7,140	13,883	15,271	16,237	19,167	Exports of Goods & Services	90c
	—	—	—	—	—	‡—	—	—	—	‡—	—	—	—	—	—	Government Consumption	91f
	970	1,696	4,754	22,870	157,900	‡933	1,743	4,563	20,702	‡503	9,647	26,478	37,854	47,070	55,809	Gross Fixed Capital Formation	93e
	—	—	—	—	—	‡—	—	—	—	‡—	—	—	—	—	—	Increase/Decrease(-) in Stocks	93i
	2,925	5,812	16,537	82,990	610,610	‡4,082	8,057	18,700	86,673	‡2,531	55,326	151,252	192,348	212,889	230,126	Private Consumption	96f
	-249	-551	-1,425	-6,390	-37,620	‡-333	-631	-1,768	-6,899	‡-213	-3,192	-10,715	-18,526	-20,870	-25,702	Imports of Goods & Services	98c
	3,840	7,474	21,852	109,500	790,920	‡5,305	9,984	23,332	111,062	‡3,244	68,922	180,897	226,847	255,326	279,400	Gross Domestic Product	99b
	-32	-229	-1,266	-6,222	-41,830	‡-346	-417	-982	-4,768	‡-270	-1,948	-2,194	-2,102	-1,819	-2,145	Net Factor Inc/Pmts(-) Abroad	98.n
	2,801	5,247	13,495	62,044	486,270	‡3,613	7,014	16,737	73,711	‡2,975	67,974	178,703	224,745	252,507	277,255	Gross Nat'l Expenditure = GNP	99a
	‡75,506	71,169	68,928	71,501	72,809	67,993	72,969	74,852	73,444	68,878	68,922	75,059	81,554	86,474	92,607	GDP 1990 Prices (Millions)	99b.p
	—	—	—	—	—	—	—	—	—	5	100	241	278	295	302	GDP Deflator (1990=100)	99bi p
Midyear Estimates																	
	28.24	28.66	29.09	29.51	29.88	30.32	30.77	31.22	31.67	32.11	32.55	32.97	33.37	33.67	34.18	Population	99z

Aruba

314

	1965	1966	1967	1968	1969	1970	1971	1972	1973	1974	1975	1976	1977	1978	1979

Exchange Rates

Aruban Florins per SDR:

Official Rate .... **aa** ....

Aruban Florins per US Dollar

Official Rate .... **ae** ....
Official Rate .... **rf** ....

International Liquidity

Millions of US Dollars:

Total Reserves minus Gold .... **1l.**d ....
  Foreign Exchange .... **1d.**d ....
Gold (Million Fine Troy Ounces) ..... **1ad** ....
Gold (National Valuation) .... **1an**d ....
Deposit Money Banks: Assets .... **7a.**d ....
  of which: Claims on Nonbanks ..... **7ad**d ....
Deposit Money Banks: Liabilities .... **7b.**d ....
  of which: Liab. to Nonbanks .... **7bd**d ....

Monetary Authorities

Millions of Aruban Florins

Foreign Assets .... **11** ....
Reserve Money .... **14** ....
  of which: Currency Outside DMBs ..... **14a** ....
Central Government Deposits .... **16d** ....
Capital Accounts .... **17a** ....
Other Items (Net) .... **17r** ....

Deposit Money Banks

Millions of Aruban Florins

Reserves .... **20** ....
Foreign Assets .... **21** ....
Claims on Central Government .... **22a** ....
Claims on Private Sector .... **22d** ....
Demand Deposits .... **24** ....
Time and Savings Deposits .... **25** ....
Foreign Liabilities .... **26c** ....
Central Government Deposits .... **26d** ....
Capital Accounts .... **27a** ....
Other Items (Net) .... **27r** ....

Monetary Survey

Millions of Aruban Florins

Foreign Assets (Net) .... **31n** ....
Domestic Credit .... **32** ....
  Claims on Central Govt. (Net) .... **32an** ....
  Claims on Private Sector .... **32d** ....
Money .... **34** ....
Quasi-Money .... **35** ....
Other Items (Net) .... **37r** ....
Money plus Quasi-Money .... **35l** ....

Interest Rates

Percent Per Annum:

Discount Rate .... **60** ....
Deposit Rate .... **60l** ....
Lending Rate .... **60p** ....

Prices and Tourism

Index Numbers (1990=100):

Consumer Prices .... **64** ....
Number of Tourists .... **66ta** ....
Number of Tourist Nights .... **66tb** ....

International Transactions

Millions of Aruban Florins

Exports .... **70** ....
Imports, cif .... **71** ....

Balance of Payments

Millions of US Dollars:

Goods: Exports f.o.b. .... **78aa**d ....
Goods: Imports f.o.b. .... **78ab**d ....
  Trade Balance .... **78ac**d ....
Services: Credit .... **78ad**d ....
Services: Debit .... **78ae**d ....
  Balance on Goods and Services .. **78af**d ....
Income: Credit .... **78ag**d ....
Income: Debit .... **78ah**d ....
  Balance on Goods, Serv., & Inc. .. **78ai**d ....
Current Transfers, n.i.e.: Credit ...... **78aj**d ....
Current Transfers: Debit .... **78ak**d ....
  Current Account, n.i.e. .... **78al**d ....
Capital Account, n.i.e.: Credit .... **78ba**d ....
Capital Account: Debit .... **78bb**d ....
  Capital Account, n.i.e. .... **78bc**d ....
Direct Investment Abroad .... **78bd**d ....
Dir. Invest. in Rep. Econ., n.i.e. ..... **78be**d ....
Portfolio Investment Assets .... **78bf**d ....
Portfolio Investment Liab., n.i.e. .... **78bg**d ....
Other Investment Assets .... **78bh**d ....
Other Investment Liab., n.i.e. .... **78bi**d ....
  Financial Account, n.i.e. .... **78bj**d ....
Net Errors and Omissions .... **78ca**d ....
  Overall Balance .... **78cb**d ....
Reserves and Related Items .... **79da**d ....
  Reserve Assets .... **79db**d ....
  Use of Fund Credit and Loans .... **79dc**d ....
  Liabs.Constit.For.Auth.Reserves .. **79dd**d ....
  Exceptional Financing .... **79de**d ....

Millions:

Population .... **99z** ....

Aruba
314

	1980	1981	1982	1983	1984	1985	1986	1987	1988	1989	1990	1991	1992	1993	1994		
End of Period																**Exchange Rates**	
	....	....	....	....	....	....	2.1895	2.5394	2.4088	2.3523	2.5466	2.5605	2.4613	2.4587	2.6131	Official Rate	**aa**
End of Period (ae) Period Average (rf)																	
	....	....	....	....	....	....	1.7900	1.7900	1.7900	1.7900	1.7900	1.7900	1.7900	1.7900	1.7900	Official Rate	**ae**
	....	....	....	....	....	....	1.7900	1.7900	1.7900	1.7900	1.7900	1.7900	1.7900	1.7900	1.7900	Official Rate	**rf**
End of Period																**International Liquidity**	
	....	....	....	....	....	....	73.63	78.73	90.92	87.07	97.93	119.59	142.11	181.24	177.59	Total Reserves minus Gold	**1l.d**
	....	....	....	....	....	....	73.63	78.73	90.92	87.07	97.93	119.59	142.11	181.24	177.59	Foreign Exchange	**1d.d**
	....	....	....	....	....	....	—	—	—	.100	.100	.100	.100	.100	.100	Gold (Million Fine Troy Ounces)	**1ad**
	....	....	....	....	....	....	5.587	5.587	5.587	26.465	26.465	26.465	25.630	25.630	25.630	Gold (National Valuation)	**1and**
	....	....	....	....	....	....	37.15	64.90	109.14	129.41	160.73	194.37	197.89	213.42	222.37	Deposit Money Banks: Assets	**7a.d**
	....	....	....	....	....	....	7.22	14.66	53.92	44.78	39.60	38.74	47.64	53.30	64.09	*of which:* Claims on Nonbanks	**7ad d**
	....	....	....	....	....	....	43.52	64.48	121.87	112.54	132.85	153.29	143.36	163.04	150.87	Deposit Money Banks: Liabilities	**7b.d**
	....	....	....	....	....	....	23.97	47.22	103.36	90.00	109.79	130.13	121.45	131.28	132.09	*of which:* Liab. to Nonbanks	**7bd d**
End of Period																**Monetary Authorities**	
	....	....	....	....	....	....	142.11	150.94	173.25	203.37	222.78	261.44	300.25	370.30	363.77	Foreign Assets	**11**
	....	....	....	....	....	....	97.45	116.28	133.47	128.67	152.55	190.64	225.48	249.57	233.57	Reserve Money	**14**
	....	....	....	....	....	....	32.04	34.56	41.07	48.32	59.22	66.16	76.23	81.66	87.56	*of which:* Currency Outside DMBs	**14a**
	....	....	....	....	....	....	30.70	11.57	16.41	13.76	12.54	15.88	23.72	58.57	72.18	Central Government Deposits	**16d**
	....	....	....	....	....	....	10.00	13.87	19.86	57.84	59.37	59.50	59.80	58.60	57.80	Capital Accounts	**17a**
	....	....	....	....	....	....	3.96	9.22	3.51	3.10	−1.67	−4.58	−8.74	3.57	.22	Other Items (Net)	**17r**
End of Period																**Deposit Money Banks**	
	....	....	....	....	....	....	62.88	71.03	85.52	70.08	82.94	112.89	147.13	168.16	147.54	Reserves	**20**
	....	....	....	....	....	....	66.50	116.16	195.36	231.64	287.71	347.93	354.22	382.02	386.94	Foreign Assets	**21**
	....	....	....	....	....	....	9.27	29.91	15.66	21.65	23.01	34.34	36.23	43.16	67.94	Claims on Central Government	**22a**
	....	....	....	....	....	....	286.51	344.33	467.52	539.79	609.05	690.37	742.74	793.09	927.54	Claims on Private Sector	**22d**
	....	....	....	....	....	....	66.27	120.59	145.66	192.43	200.69	242.76	252.72	293.14	326.99	Demand Deposits	**24**
	....	....	....	....	....	....	215.55	274.97	331.13	391.71	478.82	560.40	663.16	673.52	747.96	Time and Savings Deposits	**25**
	....	....	....	....	....	....	77.90	115.41	218.15	201.44	237.80	274.40	256.62	291.84	272.87	Foreign Liabilities	**26c**
	....	....	....	....	....	....	30.14	14.91	1.97	1.15	4.06	25.96	10.57	20.90	36.75	Central Government Deposits	**26d**
	....	....	....	....	....	....	40.00	48.71	49.95	55.37	64.53	72.93	62.81	56.56	69.53	Capital Accounts	**27a**
	....	....	....	....	....	....	−4.68	−13.16	17.29	21.06	16.81	9.08	34.45	50.48	75.86	Other Items (Net)	**27r**
End of Period																**Monetary Survey**	
	....	....	....	....	....	....	130.39	151.15	149.57	231.13	270.16	334.85	396.84	448.02	464.19	Foreign Assets (Net)	**31n**
	....	....	....	....	....	....	234.95	347.76	464.81	546.53	615.47	682.86	744.69	756.79	886.55	Domestic Credit	**32**
	....	....	....	....	....	....	−51.57	3.43	−2.72	6.74	6.42	−7.50	1.95	−36.30	−40.99	Claims on Central Govt. (Net)	**32an**
	....	....	....	....	....	....	286.51	344.33	467.52	539.79	609.05	690.37	742.74	793.09	927.54	Claims on Private Sector	**32d**
	....	....	....	....	....	....	100.18	157.56	189.82	243.35	264.13	313.97	331.28	377.89	418.36	Money	**34**
	....	....	....	....	....	....	215.55	285.50	336.28	392.51	481.08	570.04	663.66	674.03	748.49	Quasi-Money	**35**
	....	....	....	....	....	....	49.61	55.85	88.35	141.79	140.42	133.71	146.59	152.88	183.89	Other Items (Net)	**37r**
	....	....	....	....	....	....	315.73	443.06	526.10	635.87	745.21	884.01	994.94	1,051.93	1,166.85	Money plus Quasi-Money	**35l**
End of Period																**Interest Rates**	
	....	....	....	....	....	....	9.5	9.5	9.5	9.5	9.5	9.5	9.5	9.5	9.5	Discount Rate	**60**
	....	....	....	....	....	....	6.4	6.7	6.7	6.7	6.7	6.3	5.7	4.2	4.4	Deposit Rate	**60l**
	....	....	....	....	....	....	11.0	10.3	10.3	10.6	10.6	10.6	10.6	10.6	10.6	Lending Rate	**60p**
Period Averages																**Prices and Tourism**	
	....	....	....	....	....	84.1	85.0	88.1	90.9	94.5	100.0	105.6	109.6	115.4	122.6	Consumer Prices	**64**
	44	....	....	....	49	48	42	54	64	80	100	116	125	130	135	Number of Tourists	**66ta**
	34	....	....	....	41	41	38	48	62	79	100	111	115	119	125	Number of Tourist Nights	**66tb**
Millions of Aruban Florins																**International Transactions**	
	....	....	....	....	....	....	42.5	46.7	54.6	41.0	....	....	....	....	....	Exports	**70**
	....	....	....	....	....	....	343.5	422.6	602.1	693.0	....	....	....	....	....	Imports, cif	**71**
Minus Sign Indicates Debit																**Balance of Payments**	
	....	....	....	....	....	....	29.6	45.1	87.4	107.5	155.5	878.8	1,069.2	1,154.4	1,296.8	Goods: Exports f.o.b.	**78aa d**
	....	....	....	....	....	....	−210.4	−249.8	−354.6	−397.4	−580.8	−1,402.8	−1,446.7	−1,546.5	−1,607.3	Goods: Imports f.o.b.	**78ab d**
	....	....	....	....	....	....	−180.9	−204.7	−267.3	−289.9	−425.4	−524.1	−377.5	−392.1	−310.6	Trade Balance	**78ac d**
	....	....	....	....	....	....	216.9	260.1	326.2	351.3	411.0	472.7	571.2	604.1	624.2	Services: Credit	**78ad d**
	....	....	....	....	....	....	−50.6	−62.8	−85.3	−100.2	−134.9	−147.8	−159.8	−169.1	−228.7	Services: Debit	**78ae d**
	....	....	....	....	....	....	−14.6	−7.4	−26.3	−38.8	−149.3	−199.2	33.9	42.8	85.0	Balance on Goods and Services	**78af d**
	....	....	....	....	....	....	7.3	8.9	10.9	13.4	14.5	17.9	14.5	13.4	9.6	Income: Credit	**78ag d**
	....	....	....	....	....	....	−13.6	−21.2	−27.9	−24.7	−22.6	−25.7	−21.8	−24.6	−22.3	Income: Debit	**78ah d**
	....	....	....	....	....	....	−20.9	−19.7	−43.4	−50.1	−157.0	−207.0	26.5	31.6	72.3	Balance on Goods, Serv., & Inc.	**78ai d**
	....	....	....	....	....	....	18.4	15.4	14.9	18.0	33.8	38.1	45.9	43.4	47.5	Current Transfers, n.i.e.: Credit	**78aj d**
	....	....	....	....	....	....	−16.1	−18.3	−15.8	−14.6	−34.9	−40.6	−28.7	−33.3	−38.7	Current Transfers: Debit	**78ak d**
	....	....	....	....	....	....	−18.7	−22.6	−44.3	−46.7	−158.2	−209.5	43.8	41.7	81.1	Current Account, n.i.e.	**78al d**
	....	....	....	....	....	....	—	—	—	—	—	.8	.9	.9	.3	Capital Account, n.i.e.: Credit	**78ba d**
	....	....	....	....	....	....	—	—	—	—	—	−3.8	−2.4	−2.8	−4.4	Capital Account: Debit	**78bb d**
	....	....	....	....	....	....	—	—	—	—	—	−3.0	−1.5	−1.8	−4.1	Capital Account, n.i.e.	**78bc d**
	....	....	....	....	....	....	—	—	—	—	—	—	—	—	—	Direct Investment Abroad	**78bd d**
	....	....	....	....	....	....	—	—	—	—	130.5	184.7	−37.0	−17.9	−73.2	Dir. Invest. in Rep. Econ., n.i.e.	**78be d**
	....	....	....	....	....	....	—	—	—	—	8.7	13.1	11.3	10.8	16.5	Portfolio Investment Assets	**78bf d**
	....	....	....	....	....	....	—	—	—	—	−15.1	−25.4	−18.2	−14.6	−25.8	Portfolio Investment Liab., n.i.e.	**78bg d**
	....	....	....	....	....	....	1.1	−27.7	−48.9	−19.4	−10.2	−17.1	13.6	−25.8	5.8	Other Investment Assets	**78bh d**
	....	....	....	....	....	....	61.7	52.3	105.7	67.3	58.3	73.4	6.0	39.2	1.3	Other Investment Liab., n.i.e.	**78bi d**
	....	....	....	....	....	....	62.8	24.6	56.8	47.8	172.2	228.8	−24.1	−8.4	−75.4	Financial Account, n.i.e.	**78bj d**
	....	....	....	....	....	....	7.1	10.9	−12.8	20.4	−2.4	6.5	4.4	2.0	−4.7	Net Errors and Omissions	**78ca d**
	....	....	....	....	....	....	51.3	12.9	−.4	21.5	11.7	22.8	22.6	33.4	−3.2	Overall Balance	**78cb d**
	....	....	....	....	....	....	−51.3	−12.9	.4	−21.5	−11.7	−22.8	−22.6	−33.4	3.2	Reserves and Related Items	**79da d**
	....	....	....	....	....	....	−51.3	−12.9	.4	−21.5	−11.7	−22.8	−22.6	−33.4	3.2	Reserve Assets	**79db d**
	....	....	....	....	....	....	—	—	—	—	—	—	—	—	—	Use of Fund Credit and Loans	**79dc d**
	....	....	....	....	....	....	—	—	—	—	—	—	—	—	—	Liabs.Constit.For.Auth.Reserves	**79dd d**
	....	....	....	....	....	....	....	....	....	....	....	....	....	....	....	Exceptional Financing	**79de d**
Midyear Estimates																	
	.06	.07	.06	.06	.06	.06	.06	.06	.06	.06	.06	.07	.07	.08	....	Population	**99z**

Australia

		1965	1966	1967	1968	1969	1970	1971	1972	1973	1974	1975	1976	1977	1978	1979
Exchange Rates														SDRs per Australian Dollar:		
Market Rate	ac	1.1185	‡1.1140	1.1210	1.1100	1.1180	1.1150	1.0970	1.1743	1.2335	1.0838	1.0738	.9351	.9396	.8831	.8392
														US Dollars per Australian Dollar:		
Market Rate	ag	1.1185	‡1.1140	1.1210	1.1100	1.1180	1.1150	1.1910	1.2750	1.4880	1.3270	1.2571	1.0864	1.1414	1.1505	1.1055
Market Rate	rh	1.1200	1.1200	1.1200	1.1200	1.1200	1.1200	1.1342	1.1923	1.4215	1.4394	1.3102	1.2252	1.1090	1.1447	1.1179
														Index Numbers (1990=100):		
Market Rate	ahx	142.6	142.4	142.4	142.4	142.2	142.5	145.4	152.6	202.8	184.0	167.7	156.8	141.9	146.5	143.1
Nominal Effective Exchange Rate	nec	....	....	....	....	....	....	....	....	....	....	....	....	....	....	106.8
Real Effective Exchange Rate	rec	....	....	....	....	....	....	....	....	....	....	....	....	....	....	107.0
Fund Position														Millions of SDRs:		
Quota	2f.s	400	500	500	500	500	665	665	665	665	665	665	665	665	790	790
SDRs	1b.s	—	—	—	—	—	90	164	235	235	100	96	36	22	99	32
Reserve Position in the Fund	1c.s	135	170	205	255	260	267	167	167	167	176	167	167	166	161	156
Total Fund Cred.&Loans Outstg.	2tl	—	—	—	—	—	—	—	—	—	—	—	333	333	247	271
International Liquidity												Millions of US Dollars Unless Otherwise Indicated:				
Total Reserves minus Gold	1l.d	1,317	1,344	1,133	1,185	998	1,454	3,034	5,860	5,386	3,953	2,955	2,870	2,058	2,062	1,424
SDRs	1b.d	—	—	—	—	—	90	178	255	283	122	112	42	27	129	42
Reserve Position in the Fund	1c.d	135	170	205	255	260	267	182	182	201	215	195	194	202	210	206
Foreign Exchange	1d.d	1,182	1,174	928	930	738	1,096	2,674	5,423	4,902	3,616	2,647	2,634	1,829	1,723	1,176
Gold (Million Fine Troy Ounces)	1ad	7.07	6.40	6.60	7.34	7.51	6.83	7.43	7.40	7.37	7.38	7.38	7.36	7.65	7.79	7.93
Gold (National Valuation)	1and	248	224	231	258	263	239	....	280	311	316	299	300	1,228	1,619	3,676
Deposit Money Banks: Assets	7a.d	59	81	68	96	185	99	157	209	199	202	275	251	183	272	216
Deposit Money Banks: Liabilities	7b.d	....	....	....	....	....	....	143	242	315	390	277	304	310	375	429
of which: Liab. to Nonbanks	7bdd	....	....	....	....	....	....	....	85	100	119	134	118	148	150	
Monetary Authorities												Millions of Australian Dollars: Average of Weekly				
Foreign Assets	11	1,288	1,336	1,224	1,279	1,165	1,542	2,785	4,794	3,953	3,260	2,907	2,772	3,053	3,334	4,148
Claims on Central Government	12a	1,011	893	970	1,183	1,349	1,138	629	289	584	1,058	2,796	4,741	5,005	5,039	6,562
Reserve Money	14	2,147	2,122	2,279	2,489	2,728	2,713	3,211	3,871	4,875	4,296	5,504	6,160	6,516	6,456	7,026
of which: Currency Outside DMBs	14a	828	909	992	1,069	1,194	1,330	1,477	1,665	1,965	2,355	2,761	3,127	3,550	3,955	4,375
Foreign Liabilities	16c	—	—	—	—	—	—	—	—	—	—	—	356	354	280	322
Central Government Deposits	16d															
Other Items (Net)	17r	152	107	–84	–27	–214	–33	203	1,211	–338	22	200	998	1,188	1,637	3,362
Deposit Money Banks												Millions of Australian Dollars: Average of Weekly				
Reserves	20	1,293	1,207	1,256	1,394	1,497	1,341	1,706	2,200	2,771	1,794	2,589	3,059	2,848	2,350	2,518
Foreign Assets	21	53	72	61	86	165	88	‡129	164	134	152	219	231	160	236	195
Claims on Central Government	22a	3,295	3,583	3,776	3,657	3,898	4,141	4,339	5,602	5,799	5,724	7,324	7,386	6,718	7,439	7,957
Claims on Official Entities	22bx	1,170	1,294	1,459	1,605	1,776	1,916	2,122	2,380	2,770	3,118	3,731	4,313	4,764	5,255	5,677
Claims on Private Sector	22d	4,778	5,363	6,067	6,870	7,721	8,217	9,286	10,790	14,011	16,683	19,321	23,091	25,860	29,222	33,822
Demand Deposits	24	3,075	3,291	3,500	3,678	4,006	4,111	4,266	5,227	6,076	5,620	6,998	7,550	7,826	8,740	10,266
Time and Savings Deposits	25	6,938	7,483	8,244	8,883	9,729	10,252	11,317	13,525	16,726	19,055	22,798	25,911	27,369	30,116	33,136
Foreign Liabilities	26c	....	....	....	....	....	....	118	190	212	294	220	280	272	326	388
Central Government Deposits	26d	245	238	286	307	341	396	499	536	756	604	897	1,562	1,626	1,624	1,748
Other Items (Net)	27r	331	507	589	744	981	945	1,383	1,658	‡1,715	1,898	2,269	2,775	3,258	3,696	4,632
Monetary Survey												Millions of Australian Dollars: Average of Weekly				
Foreign Assets (Net)	31n	1,368	1,399	1,279	1,375	1,291	1,599	2,796	4,768	3,875	3,118	2,906	2,587	2,965	3,633	
Domestic Credit	32	9,974	10,781	11,954	12,832	14,402	14,909	15,522	18,009	21,775	25,215	31,416	36,944	39,986	44,214	50,722
Claims on Central Govt. (Net)	32an	4,061	4,237	4,460	4,533	4,906	4,883	4,469	5,355	5,627	6,178	9,222	10,565	10,097	10,853	12,771
Claims on Official Entities	32bx	1,170	1,294	1,459	1,605	1,776	1,916	2,122	2,380	2,770	3,118	3,731	4,313	4,764	5,255	5,677
Claims on Private Sector	32d	4,900	5,457	6,278	7,009	8,130	8,591	9,534	10,990	14,132	16,815	19,480	23,214	26,343	29,466	34,024
Money	34	3,907	4,203	4,495	4,752	5,205	5,446	5,749	6,899	8,050	7,990	9,807	10,681	11,390	12,709	14,661
Quasi-Money	35	6,938	7,483	8,244	8,883	9,729	10,252	11,317	13,525	16,726	19,055	22,798	25,911	27,369	30,116	33,136
Other Items (Net)	37r	497	494	494	572	759	810	1,253	2,353	874	1,287	1,717	2,719	3,814	4,354	6,558
Money plus Quasi-Money	35l	10,845	11,686	12,739	13,635	14,934	15,698	17,066	20,424	24,776	27,045	32,605	36,592	38,759	42,825	47,797
Interest Rates														Percent Per Annum		
Discount Rate	60	....	....	....	....	....	6.03	6.08	4.89	6.13	10.22	8.71	8.67	9.91	9.35	9.53
Money Market Rate	60b	....	....	....	....	....	5.19	5.46	4.65	4.98	7.52	9.49	7.09	8.49	8.72	8.09
Treasury Bill Rate	60c	....	....	....	....	4.79	5.38	5.41	4.32	5.21	9.07	7.51	7.51	8.52	8.35	8.88
Deposit Rate	60l	....	....	....	....	....	5.00	5.25	5.00	5.50	8.00	9.00	8.63	9.00	8.52	8.25
Lending Rate	60p	....	....	....	....	....	....	....	....	....	....	11.50	10.50	10.50	10.46	10.00
Govt. Bond Yield: Short-Term	61a	4.85	4.92	4.55	4.81	5.25	6.26	6.14	4.91	6.30	9.33	8.46	8.69	9.74	8.80	9.62
Long-Term	61	5.21	5.25	5.25	5.21	5.71	6.72	6.87	5.99	7.11	9.07	9.75	10.18	10.28	9.06	9.76
Prices, Production, Employment														Index Numbers (1990=100):		
Share Prices	62	14.6	14.5	17.0	24.4	‡26.8	‡25.7	21.5	25.8	24.2	17.9	16.9	20.9	20.0	22.7	27.9
Prices: Manufacturing Output	63	16.2	16.9	17.3	‡17.4	17.6	18.4	19.3	20.2	22.0	25.3	29.2	32.5	35.8	38.7	44.4
Consumer Prices	64	14.6	15.0	15.5	15.9	16.4	17.0	18.1	19.1	20.9	24.1	27.7	31.5	35.4	38.2	‡41.6
Wages, Weekly Earnings	65	9.9	10.4	11.0	11.7	12.7	13.8	15.5	16.8	18.9	23.2	27.4	31.3	34.7	37.7	40.9
Industrial Production	66..c	47.5	48.3	51.0	53.9	57.5	60.1	62.5	63.2	69.7	71.9	66.4	69.8	‡68.7	69.7	73.3
Manufacturing Employment	67ey	....	102.7	105.1	105.3	108.5	110.0	113.7	110.8	115.2	114.5	105.2	106.7	106.4	101.6	101.7
International Transactions														Millions of Australian Dollars		
Exports	70	2,683	2,831	3,105	3,148	3,768	4,259	4,599	5,419	6,719	7,685	9,123	10,774	12,050	12,591	16,711
Wheat	70d	337	235	448	255	324	363	432	361	201	868	1,062	919	926	765	1,515
Coal	70vr	....	....	76	102	142	179	210	267	325	489	890	1,185	1,394	1,479	1,608
Greasy Wool	70ha	693	719	678	671	819	585	467	699	1,212	834	736	1,103	1,068	1,112	1,325
Sugar	70i	88	93	102	120	115	143	161	257	253	477	566	649	600	483	455
Imports, cif	71	3,359	3,225	3,504	3,898	4,052	4,515	4,613	4,217	5,177	8,358	8,173	9,999	12,186	13,591	16,279
Imports, fob	71.v	3,015	2,895	3,130	3,489	3,626	4,056	4,139	3,876	4,840	7,769	7,636	9,134	11,036	12,329	14,801
															1990=100	
Volume of Exports	72	24.6	25.1	28.8	29.9	34.2	39.0	42.9	46.3	46.3	43.4	47.3	51.9	52.7	51.9	58.1
Wheat	72d	60.0	39.5	73.6	44.6	54.1	70.5	78.4	65.9	34.6	64.6	74.7	70.2	87.1	69.5	105.6
Coal	72vr	....	....	8.3	11.0	14.2	16.2	17.5	20.9	25.3	26.0	27.0	28.5	32.0	33.1	36.4
Greasy Wool	72ha	154.5	148.1	156.0	161.6	174.3	167.2	166.6	177.3	141.5	119.4	132.6	171.1	130.8	135.8	143.0
Sugar	72i	39.5	48.2	60.0	74.1	50.8	50.5	58.4	73.6	73.6	58.3	58.1	86.5	88.6	71.6	59.8
Volume of Imports	73	....	....	31.6	36.1	36.8	40.0	39.2	35.8	45.2	57.7	45.7	51.4	51.8	53.9	55.7
Export Prices	76	20.0	21.0	‡19.7	19.5	19.9	19.3	19.5	22.3	28.7	33.7	‡35.2	38.5	43.2	44.7	54.0
Wheat	76d	20.1	22.2	21.9	20.9	20.2	19.6	20.5	22.8	41.2	54.7	45.5	42.3	38.8	47.7	56.5
Coal (Unit Value)	74vr	....	....	14.9	15.1	16.2	17.9	19.4	20.8	20.8	30.6	53.6	67.7	70.8	72.5	71.7
Import Prices	76.x	13.3	‡13.5	13.5	13.3	13.7	14.2	15.1	15.7	15.7	21.9	27.6	30.3	36.6	39.0	‡47.2

1980	1981	1982	1983	1984	1985	1986	1987	1988	1989	1990	1991	1992	1993	1994		
End of Period															**Exchange Rates**	
.9257	.9690	.8889	.8616	.8445	.6199	.5435	.5093	.6357	.6032	.5436	.5312	.5008	.4930	.5321	Market Rate	ac
End of Period (ag) Period Average (rh)																
1.1807	1.1279	.9806	.9020	.8278	.6809	.6648	.7225	.8555	.7927	.7733	.7598	.6886	.6771	.7768	Market Rate	ag
1.1395	1.1493	1.0174	.9024	.8796	.7008	.6709	.7009	.7842	.7925	.7813	.7791	.7353	.6801	.7317	Market Rate	rh
Period Averages																
145.9	147.1	130.2	115.5	112.6	89.7	85.9	89.7	100.4	101.4	100.0	99.7	94.1	87.1	93.6	Market Rate	ahx
110.8	122.1	119.3	112.7	118.8	100.0	83.7	81.0	89.2	97.7	100.0	102.9	99.7	99.2	111.7	Nominal Effective Exchange Rate	nec
107.8	116.9	117.2	114.8	118.1	99.5	87.0	86.9	95.5	102.6	100.0	98.6	89.7	83.4	87.2	Real Effective Exchange Rate	rec
End of Period															**Fund Position**	
1,185	1,185	1,185	1,619	1,619	1,619	1,619	1,619	1,619	1,619	1,619	1,619	2,333	2,333	2,333	Quota	2f.s
—	45	78	77	213	283	271	260	248	234	218	202	70	60	50	SDRs	1b.s
255	252	—	109	187	189	189	189	205	245	245	245	420	400	347	Reserve Position in the Fund	1c.s
62	—	32	—	—	—	—	—	—	—	—	—	—	—	—	Total Fund Cred.&Loans Outstg.	2tl
End of Period															**International Liquidity**	
1,690	1,671	6,371	8,962	7,441	5,768	7,246	8,744	13,598	13,780	16,265	16,535	11,208	11,102	11,285	Total Reserves minus Gold	1l.d
—	52	86	81	209	310	332	369	334	307	311	290	96	82	73	SDRs	1b.d
325	294	—	114	183	207	231	268	275	322	349	351	577	550	506	Reserve Position in the Fund	1c.d
1,365	1,325	6,285	8,768	7,049	5,250	6,684	8,107	12,989	13,150	15,605	15,894	10,536	10,470	10,706	Foreign Exchange	1d.d
7.93	7.93	7.93	7.93	7.93	7.93	7.93	7.93	7.93	7.93	7.93	7.93	7.93	7.90	7.90	Gold (Million Fine Troy Ounces)	1ad
4,722	3,247	3,527	3,080	2,539	2,551	3,100	3,855	3,319	3,248	3,064	2,804	2,639	3,086	3,023	Gold (National Valuation)	1and
367	396	120	179	I 913	1,483	3,631	5,399	6,409	7,184	10,602	10,456	10,803	11,702	10,601	Deposit Money Banks: Assets	7a.d
655	730	727	647	I 1,276	2,922	8,967	12,070	13,667	22,075	33,523	38,895	37,768	41,587	39,272	Deposit Money Banks: Liabilities	7b.d
305	403	410	289	I 1,123	2,502	....	....	....	....	....	....	....	....	....	*of which:* Liab. to Nonbanks	7bdd
Figures for Last Month of Period															**Monetary Authorities**	
5,878	4,263	9,745	13,390	12,003	12,412	15,477	17,439	19,561	I 21,234	24,205	24,506	20,212	21,415	18,344	Foreign Assets	11
6,710	7,764	4,102	3,880	5,803	8,640	9,189	8,031	5,257	I 4,194	4,280	5,499	14,312	14,337	13,613	Claims on Central Government	12a
7,717	8,536	9,286	10,472	11,639	13,221	14,320	15,917	17,478	I 17,549	18,917	19,478	20,648	21,987	23,779	Reserve Money	14
4,975	5,533	6,023	6,882	7,855	8,632	9,538	10,841	12,267	I 13,018	14,342	15,328	16,326	17,279	18,332	*of which: Currency Outside DMBs*	14a
67	—	37	—	—	—	—	—	—	I 8	37	47	63	109	214	Foreign Liabilities	16c
....	....	....	....	....	....	....	....	2,710	1,576	1,350	1,937	2,719	2,634	999	Central Government Deposits	16d
4,804	3,490	4,525	6,798	6,167	7,831	10,346	9,554	I 4,630	6,295	8,181	8,543	11,094	11,022	6,965	Other Items (Net)	17r
Figures for Last Month of Period															**Deposit Money Banks**	
2,619	2,910	3,264	3,451	3,648	4,280	4,472	4,813	5,111	I 4,447	4,281	4,083	4,265	4,674	5,376	Reserves	20
311	351	122	198	I 1,103	2,178	5,462	7,473	7,491	I 9,456	14,827	15,458	17,863	20,203	17,199	Foreign Assets	21
9,201	9,146	10,599	13,137	12,929	14,100	17,930	20,156	21,525	I 26,618	21,445	24,902	28,627	30,929	28,457	Claims on Central Government	22a
6,116	6,557	6,752	7,761	8,114	7,817	7,016	6,513	7,064	I 5,477	6,197	5,397	6,195	4,664	3,233	Claims on Official Entities	22bx
38,015	43,991	48,833	55,334	64,627	86,991	105,049	122,489	151,623	I 225,978	255,585	261,094	274,929	290,052	320,144	Claims on Private Sector	22d
12,191	12,488	11,960	13,862	14,615	14,650	16,391	20,352	I 28,178	30,478	32,336	34,606	43,927	53,720	60,743	Demand Deposits	24
37,275	41,819	48,194	54,196	61,300	75,505	82,305	94,385	111,923	I 151,346	172,678	170,963	177,370	180,926	197,449	Time and Savings Deposits	25
555	647	741	717	I 1,541	4,291	13,488	16,706	15,975	I 27,848	43,350	51,191	54,848	61,419	50,556	Foreign Liabilities	26c
1,033	1,129	1,393	1,261	1,733	1,131	917	595	438	I 1,758	1,923	2,694	3,587	3,637	2,989	Central Government Deposits	26d
5,209	6,873	7,282	9,846	11,231	19,788	26,828	29,406	36,300	I 60,546	52,048	51,480	52,147	50,820	62,672	Other Items (Net)	27r
Figures for Last Month of Period															**Monetary Survey**	
5,567	3,967	9,089	12,871	I 11,565	10,299	7,451	8,206	11,077	I 2,834	–4,355	–11,274	–16,836	–19,910	–15,227	Foreign Assets (Net)	31n
57,371	64,500	66,874	76,620	86,837	112,132	133,981	157,040	185,404	I 260,509	285,584	294,198	320,476	336,345	362,458	Domestic Credit	32
14,878	15,781	13,308	15,755	16,999	21,609	26,203	27,592	I 26,344	I 27,478	22,452	25,770	36,633	38,995	38,082	Claims on Central Govt. (Net)	32an
6,116	6,557	6,752	7,761	8,114	7,817	7,016	6,513	7,064	I 5,477	6,197	5,397	6,195	4,664	3,233	Claims on Official Entities	32bx
38,278	44,347	49,128	55,697	64,778	87,191	105,108	122,490	151,623	I 225,978	255,585	261,094	274,929	290,052	320,144	Claims on Private Sector	32d
17,220	18,063	18,032	20,796	22,492	23,298	25,947	31,218	I 40,470	43,514	46,699	49,983	60,292	71,027	79,134	Money	34
37,275	41,819	48,194	54,196	61,300	75,505	82,305	94,385	111,923	I 151,346	172,678	170,963	177,370	180,926	197,449	Quasi-Money	35
8,443	8,585	9,737	14,499	I 14,610	23,627	33,180	39,644	44,089	I 68,483	61,852	61,978	65,978	64,482	70,648	Other Items (Net)	37r
54,495	59,882	66,226	74,992	83,792	98,803	108,252	125,603	152,392	I 194,860	219,377	220,946	237,662	251,953	276,583	Money plus Quasi-Money	35l
Percent Per Annum															**Interest Rates**	
11.11	13.53	15.76	12.14	12.03	15.98	16.93	14.95	13.20	17.23	15.24	10.99	6.96	5.83	5.75	Discount Rate	60
9.49	12.07	13.90	9.50	10.84	14.70	15.75	13.06	11.90	16.75	14.81	10.47	6.44	5.11	5.18	Money Market Rate	60b
10.67	13.25	14.64	11.06	10.99	15.34	15.39	12.80	12.14	16.80	14.15	9.96	6.27	5.00	5.69	Treasury Bill Rate	60c
8.58	10.38	12.33	10.81	9.75	10.46	13.96	13.77	11.92	15.29	13.70	10.44	....	....	....	Deposit Rate	60l
10.58	12.92	14.55	14.04	14.46	15.96	19.85	19.83	18.52	21.71	20.48	16.38	12.02	....	....	Lending Rate	60p
11.50	13.76	I 15.18	12.84	12.25	14.03	13.97	13.17	12.18	15.14	13.46	9.94	7.25	5.63	7.65	Govt. Bond Yield: Short-Term	61a
11.65	13.96	I 15.35	14.33	13.83	14.10	13.56	13.47	12.31	13.41	13.18	10.69	9.22	7.28	9.04	Long-Term	61
Period Averages															**Prices, Production, Employment**	
41.7	43.5	33.2	41.9	48.8	59.9	80.7	115.8	98.6	105.7	100.0	100.8	105.0	120.9	138.1	Share Prices	62
50.6	54.9	59.8	64.7	68.2	72.7	76.7	82.3	89.8	94.4	100.0	101.5	103.0	105.2	105.9	Prices: Manufacturing Output	63
45.8	50.3	55.9	61.6	64.0	68.3	74.5	80.8	86.7	93.2	I 100.0	103.2	104.2	106.1	108.1	Consumer Prices	64
45.9	51.1	I 57.1	61.1	66.9	70.3	75.8	79.7	85.2	92.1	100.0	105.1	109.3	111.3	115.0	Wages, Weekly Earnings	65
73.7	76.0	75.6	73.3	78.4	84.7	84.5	88.5	93.4	97.6	100.0	I 96.4	100.3	104.8	113.3	Industrial Production	66..c
103.9	104.3	101.1	95.3	95.4	94.6	94.9	96.5	99.4	102.7	100.0	93.9	93.0	89.0	92.1	Manufacturing Employment	67ey
Millions of Australian Dollars															**International Transactions**	
19,269	18,686	21,032	22,306	26,366	32,408	33,716	37,947	42,369	47,005	50,892	53,728	58,383	62,840	64,962	Exports	70
1,967	1,471	1,974	1,156	2,454	2,570	2,877	2,006	1,409	2,562	2,215	1,582	1,530	2,224	2,283	Wheat	70d
1,683	2,290	2,533	3,343	3,937	5,061	5,318	5,043	4,612	5,080	6,157	6,757	7,245	7,712	6,701	Coal	70vr
1,300	1,392	1,513	1,525	1,549	2,326	2,374	3,457	4,657	4,101	2,281	2,447	2,461	1,951	2,392	Greasy Wool	70ha
982	1,022	548	610	597	532	645	650	796	1,024	1,036	736	797	1,120	1,536	Sugar	70i
19,632	22,824	26,210	23,839	29,560	37,054	39,033	41,816	45,925	56,801	53,785	53,427	59,732	66,910	72,881	Imports, cif	71
17,826	20,592	23,194	21,220	25,877	33,130	35,716	38,469	42,416	51,726	49,807	49,678	55,513	62,385	68,086	Imports, fob	71.v
1990=100																
59.3	56.7	62.2	58.9	69.8	77.5	80.8	89.1	88.9	92.6	100.0	115.3	120.7	127.8	....	Volume of Exports	72
112.0	81.8	111.4	54.7	136.0	125.8	150.3	141.7	72.8	108.5	100.0	104.1	65.7	99.6	116.8	Wheat	72d
37.6	44.8	40.4	54.5	68.0	78.9	80.7	89.7	88.5	85.9	100.0	107.1	114.2	118.2	116.5	Coal	72vr
122.7	122.1	125.9	128.1	121.1	158.0	153.8	176.9	161.4	156.4	100.0	155.4	149.9	138.3	135.6	Greasy Wool	72ha
83.0	95.8	87.0	83.2	104.8	99.5	84.6	95.1	101.7	102.7	100.0	83.4	87.7	111.6	144.7	Sugar	72i
58.3	64.5	67.7	59.4	72.7	77.8	74.1	75.0	87.5	105.0	100.0	98.6	107.2	114.2	....	Volume of Imports	73
61.9	63.0	65.8	70.8	71.0	79.8	80.8	84.0	93.9	I 99.1	100.0	91.4	93.2	94.4	91.8	Export Prices	76
61.9	60.8	63.2	71.1	63.3	81.3	71.9	65.6	77.2	89.7	100.0	68.1	108.7	91.2	89.0	Wheat	76d
72.7	83.0	101.9	99.6	94.0	104.2	107.1	91.3	84.6	96.0	100.0	102.5	103.0	106.0	93.4	Coal (Unit Value)	74vr
59.8	I 60.8	65.0	70.6	72.3	85.9	93.8	99.4	97.2	96.2	I 100.0	101.1	105.6	114.1	112.2	Import Prices	76.x

Australia

		1965	1966	1967	1968	1969	1970	1971	1972	1973	1974	1975	1976	1977	1978	1979
Balance of Payments															*Millions of US Dollars:*	
Goods: Exports f.o.b.	78aa d	2,941	3,088	3,394	3,431	4,015	4,623	5,065	6,279	9,271	10,763	11,692	12,972	13,198	14,114	18,578
Goods: Imports f.o.b.	78ab d	−3,279	−2,987	−3,344	−3,697	−3,754	−4,109	−4,476	−4,295	−6,461	−10,625	−9,481	−10,943	−12,174	−14,025	−16,060
Trade Balance	78ac d	−338	101	49	−267	261	514	589	1,984	2,810	138	2,211	2,029	1,024	90	2,518
Services: Credit	78ad d	528	536	635	697	775	917	985	1,139	1,458	2,013	2,166	2,269	2,293	2,926	3,494
Services: Debit	78ae d	−932	−965	−1,100	−1,220	−1,340	−1,504	−1,660	−1,868	−2,703	−3,794	−3,842	−4,262	−4,422	−5,168	−5,786
Balance on Goods and Services	78af d	−743	−328	−416	−790	−304	−73	−86	1,254	1,565	−1,643	536	36	−1,105	−2,152	227
Income: Credit	78ag d	112	118	112	124	153	166	231	358	643	751	570	487	496	582	711
Income: Debit	78ah d	−464	−461	−570	−689	−752	−864	−941	−1,051	−1,639	−1,707	−1,846	−2,154	−2,158	−2,543	−3,197
Balance on Goods, Serv., & Inc.	78ai d	−1,094	−672	−874	−1,354	−902	−771	−796	561	568	−2,599	−740	−1,631	−2,767	−4,114	−2,259
Current Transfers, n.i.e.: Credit	78aj d	93	90	104	122	139	171	197	235	296	403	490	304	323	380	410
Current Transfers: Debit	78ak d	−196	−216	−254	−239	−269	−302	−318	−420	−530	−693	−810	−679	−719	−843	−918
Current Account, n.i.e.	78al d	−1,197	−799	−1,024	−1,471	−1,032	−902	−916	376	334	−2,888	−1,060	−2,006	−3,163	−4,577	−2,767
Capital Account, n.i.e.: Credit	78ba d	92	108	119	143	146	166	156	203	242	252	216	228	246	319	387
Capital Account: Debit	78bb d	−21	−25	−29	−31	−40	−49	−64	−99	−156	−166	−167	−157	−148	−177	−185
Capital Account, n.i.e.	78bc d	71	83	90	112	105	116	92	104	86	85	49	72	98	142	203
Direct Investment Abroad	78bd d	−46	−34	−54	−59	−108	−112	−104	−129	−259	−245	−160	−266	−266	−236	−343
Dir. Invest. in Rep. Econ., n.i.e.	78be d	617	488	514	659	628	898	1,149	1,054	147	1,332	455	1,043	1,139	1,678	1,487
Portfolio Investment Assets	78bf d	4	−2	−2	−2	4	−10	11	−6	−26	−13	5	−10	−7	−10	−3
Portfolio Investment Liab., n.i.e.	78bg d	125	188	310	474	335	264	635	559	−751	−826	412	−132	124	302	600
Other Investment Assets	78bh d	20	−40	−26	−34	−168	−2	−10	−156	138	−563	−133	−1	−434	−341	−1,017
Other Investment Liab., n.i.e.	78bi d	15	−92	184	196	−54	−131	33	209	−70	821	134	1,208	1,489	2,199	1,347
Financial Account, n.i.e.	78bj d	736	508	926	1,233	638	907	1,714	1,531	−820	507	714	1,842	2,046	3,590	2,071
Net Errors and Omissions	78ca d	66	221	7	202	102	220	476	710	81	663	−575	−292	−135	757	−208
Overall Balance	78cb d	−325	14	−1	77	−186	342	1,366	2,720	−319	−1,633	−872	−384	−1,154	−88	−701
Reserves and Related Items	79da d	325	−14	1	−77	186	−342	−1,366	−2,720	319	1,633	872	384	1,154	88	701
Reserve Assets	79db d	322	−19	−2	−79	182	−349	−1,371	−2,725	301	1,618	919	8	947	194	715
Use of Fund Credit and Loans	79dc d	—	—	—	—	—	—	—	—	—	—	—	381	—	−105	31
Liabs.Constit.For.Auth.Reserves	79dd d	2	6	2	2	3	7	6	5	18	15	−46	−5	207	−1	−45
Exceptional Financing	79de d	—	—	—	—	—	—	—	—	—	—	—	—	—	—	—
Government Finance															*Millions of Australian Dollars:*	
Deficit (-) or Surplus	80	−268	−424	−661	−653	−307	I−260	−78	130	−409	−241	−2,479	−3,609	−2,702	−3,290	−3,133
Revenue	81	4,832	5,178	5,299	5,730	6,442	I 7,323	8,241	9,131	9,740	12,296	15,749	18,853	22,076	24,219	26,336
Expenditure	82	5,100	5,602	5,960	6,383	6,749	I 6,423	7,473	8,284	9,441	11,240	15,679	20,370	23,260	26,173	28,424
Lending Minus Repayments	83	....	....	....	....	....	I 1,160	846	717	708	1,297	2,549	2,092	1,518	1,336	1,045
Financing (by Residence of Lender)																
Domestic	84a	....	....	....	....	....	I 391	161	−83	475	371	2,479	3,483	2,345	1,678	1,755
Foreign	85a	....	....	....	....	....	I−131	−83	−47	−66	−130	1	126	357	1,612	1,377
Debt: Domestic	88a	....	....	....	....	....	....	....	....	....	....	....	....	....	....	....
Foreign	89a	....	....	....	....	....	....	....	....	....	....	....	....	....	....	....
Financing (by Currency)																
Net Borrowing: Australian Dollars	84b	213	574	440	449	354	....	....	....	....	....	....	....	....	....	....
Foreign Currency	85b	42	−136	155	151	−37	....	....	....	....	....	....	....	....	....	....
Other Financing	86c	−18	1	14	5	49	....	....	....	....	....	....	....	....	....	....
Use of Cash Balances	87	31	−15	52	42	−61	....	....	....	....	....	....	....	....	....	....
Commonwealth and States																
Debt: Australian Dollars	88b	7,162	7,462	8,012	8,510	8,692	9,008	9,245	9,964	13,479	14,275	16,587	19,013	21,420	23,287	25,752
Held By: Reserve Bank	88ba	805	692	815	1,041	846	1,190	910	501	611	1,443	1,276	2,739	4,239	4,392	5,197
Deposit Money Banks	88bb	3,011	3,236	3,379	3,452	3,652	3,508	3,749	4,168	5,085	5,164	6,571	6,641	6,395	6,382	7,256
Life Insur. Companies	88bc	745	834	978	1,093	1,150	1,195	1,325	1,483	1,632	1,786	1,862	2,055	2,226	2,447	2,602
Others	88be	2,601	2,700	2,840	2,924	3,044	3,115	3,261	3,812	6,151	5,882	6,878	7,578	8,560	10,066	10,697
Intragovernmental Debt	88bg	1,532	1,673	1,666	1,847	2,123	2,617	2,700	2,628	2,610	2,575	3,052	2,490	2,572	3,114	3,180
Debt: Foreign Currency	89b	1,529	1,505	1,532	1,558	1,698	1,580	1,545	1,442	1,265	1,032	1,182	1,325	1,870	....	....
Local and Other Governments																
Total Debt	88.. i	3,344	3,597	3,892	4,205	4,574	4,903	5,268	6,060	6,609	....	....	....	....	....	....
National Accounts															*Billions of Australian Dollars*	
Exports of Goods & Services	90c. c	3.09	3.26	3.59	3.68	4.30	4.95	5.35	6.22	7.55	8.93	10.57	12.46	13.95	14.86	19.75
Government Consumption	91f. c	2.70	2.96	3.44	3.82	4.11	4.57	5.25	5.88	7.13	9.22	12.11	14.52	16.25	18.29	20.01
Gross Fixed Capital Formation	93e. c	5.72	6.03	6.38	7.10	7.85	8.63	9.84	10.36	11.96	13.87	16.70	19.88	21.74	24.24	27.32
Increase/Decrease(-) in Stocks	93i. c	.48	.60	.35	.45	.29	.51	.33	−.16	.29	2.32	−.16	.42	.62	.29	2.15
Private Consumption	96f. c	12.89	13.88	15.00	16.34	17.98	19.83	22.05	24.41	28.23	33.90	41.22	48.35	53.98	60.52	68.12
Imports of Goods & Services	98c. c	−3.68	−3.45	−3.89	−4.30	−4.45	−4.91	−5.33	−5.07	−6.31	−9.94	−10.02	−12.27	−14.79	−16.53	−19.25
Gross Domestic Product	99b. c	21.21	23.10	24.77	27.13	30.15	33.29	37.42	41.82	49.32	59.17	70.54	82.88	91.29	101.19	116.63
Net Factor Inc/Pmts(-) Abroad	98.n c	−.29	−.28	−.33	−.37	−.41	−.52	−.52	−.47	−.53	−.45	−.64	−.98	−1.11	−1.31	−1.79
Gross Nat'l Expenditure = GNP	99a. c	20.93	22.82	24.44	26.77	29.75	32.77	36.90	41.35	48.79	58.72	69.89	81.90	90.18	99.88	114.84
Nat'l Income, Market Prices	99e. c	18.28	19.99	21.27	23.27	25.87	28.47	32.04	35.88	42.49	50.79	59.88	70.12	76.69	84.71	97.65
Gross Dom. Prod. 1990 Prices	99b. r	151.05	160.55	165.90	175.62	186.05	197.70	207.90	215.26	226.03	230.96	237.64	246.45	248.72	256.76	268.88
GDP Deflator (1990=100)	99bi r	14.0	14.4	14.9	15.5	16.2	16.8	18.0	19.4	21.8	25.6	29.7	33.6	36.7	39.4	43.4
																Millions:
Population	99z	11.39	11.60	11.80	12.01	12.26	12.51	12.94	13.18	13.38	13.70	13.89	14.03	14.19	14.36	14.52

Exchange Rates: On February 14, 1966 the Australian dollar, equal to one half the Australian pound, was introduced.

Monetary Authorities: I Beginning in 1989, the Reserve Bank introduced an improved sectoral classification of accounts.

Deposit Money Banks: I Before 1971, data relate to net foreign assets. I Beginning in December 1984, foreign assets and liabilities are compiled under a new, more comprehensive statistical collection. I Beginning in 1989, the coverage of accounts has been expanded to include domestic assets and liabilities denominated in foreign currencies as well as foreign assets and foreign liabilities denominated in Australian dollars.

Monetary Survey: I See notes to sections 10 and 20.

Interest Rates: *Deposit Rate:* I Beginning in 1991, deposit rate refers to average rate on certificates of deposit.

Government Bond Yield: I Beginning in 1982, the government bond yield short- and long-term series (lines 61a and 61) comprise assessed secondary market yields on non-rebate bonds with maturity of 2 and 10 years, respectively.

Government Finance: I Beginning in 1970, annual data are as reported in the *Government Finance Statistics Yearbook* and cover consolidated central government. Also beginning in 1970, data relate to a fiscal year different from calendar year.

Australia

1980	1981	1982	1983	1984	1985	1986	1987	1988	1989	1990	1991	1992	1993	1994		
Minus Sign Indicates Debit															**Balance of Payments**	
21,560	21,330	21,303	19,497	22,856	22,629	22,423	27,014	33,182	36,893	39,332	42,005	42,375	42,236	47,073	Goods: Exports f.o.b.	78aa *d*
−20,192	−23,537	−23,450	−19,452	−23,632	−23,598	−24,265	−26,739	−33,898	−40,311	−38,964	−38,491	−40,820	−42,363	−50,272	Goods: Imports f.o.b.	78ab *d*
1,367	−2,207	−2,147	45	−776	−969	−1,841	275	−716	−3,418	368	3,514	1,555	−127	−3,199	Trade Balance	78ac *d*
4,192	4,627	4,673	4,444	4,824	4,518	5,095	6,510	8,921	9,417	10,737	11,534	11,682	12,331	14,451	Services: Credit	78ad *d*
−6,842	−7,650	−7,752	−7,151	−8,365	−7,942	−8,008	−9,157	−11,379	−13,845	−14,735	−14,391	−14,636	−13,913	−14,782	Services: Debit	78ae *d*
−1,282	−5,230	−5,226	−2,662	−4,318	−4,393	−4,755	−2,372	−3,174	−7,847	−3,630	657	−1,399	−1,709	−3,530	Balance on Goods and Services	78af *d*
916	942	984	1,235	1,582	1,394	1,521	2,455	2,916	3,484	3,148	3,048	3,443	3,935	4,190	Income: Credit	78ag *d*
−3,649	−3,857	−3,599	−4,521	−5,846	−6,056	−6,583	−8,467	−11,391	−14,894	−16,411	−15,346	−13,672	−12,685	−15,451	Income: Debit	78ah *d*
−4,015	−8,145	−7,841	−5,949	−8,583	−9,055	−9,817	−8,385	−11,650	−19,258	−16,892	−11,641	−11,628	−10,459	−14,791	Balance on Goods, Serv., & Inc.	78ai *d*
554	619	649	730	774	741	861	979	1,204	1,366	1,758	1,414	1,232	1,118	1,186	Current Transfers, n.i.e.: Credit	78aj *d*
−1,000	−1,119	−1,226	−1,187	−1,241	−999	−1,040	−1,053	−1,268	−1,335	−1,450	−1,432	−1,380	−1,366	−1,619	Current Transfers: Debit	78ak *d*
−4,461	−8,645	−8,418	−6,406	−9,049	−9,314	−9,995	−8,459	−11,714	−19,227	−16,585	−11,658	−11,776	−10,707	−15,224	Current Account, n.i.e.	78al *d*
504	595	615	757	781	880	979	1,311	1,790	2,213	2,077	2,212	1,657	842	976	Capital Account, n.i.e.: Credit	78ba *d*
−184	−232	−233	−253	−262	−205	−207	−219	−252	−300	−342	−365	−353	−311	−363	Capital Account: Debit	78bb *d*
320	363	381	504	518	674	771	1,092	1,538	1,913	1,735	1,847	1,303	531	612	Capital Account, n.i.e.	78bc *d*
−461	−733	−697	−521	−1,407	−1,879	−3,327	−5,114	−4,984	−3,319	−186	−3,126	−113	−1,087	−5,908	Direct Investment Abroad	78bd *d*
1,870	2,347	2,363	2,985	375	2,063	3,484	3,921	8,056	7,936	7,077	4,903	4,912	3,381	3,789	Dir. Invest. in Rep. Econ., n.i.e.	78be *d*
−16	−31	−338	−342	−355	−937	−1,848	−950	−1,665	−2,350	1,450	−2,532	591	−2,361	280	Portfolio Investment Assets	78bf *d*
1,913	704	2,736	1,525	1,092	3,081	3,034	5,273	7,497	2,820	1,024	7,030	−1,110	6,395	15,229	Portfolio Investment Liab., n.i.e.	78bg *d*
−494	395	−666	−347	−1,824	−1,846	−593	−2,702	396	−2,487	−831	−817	−1,811	−2,521	1,282	Other Investment Assets	78bh *d*
1,394	4,728	9,152	4,421	8,147	6,331	8,734	7,885	10,022	13,997	5,287	7,145	7,206	7,793	−3,681	Other Investment Liab., n.i.e.	78bi *d*
4,204	7,410	12,550	7,720	6,028	6,812	9,484	8,313	19,323	16,598	13,822	12,602	9,675	11,600	10,992	Financial Account, n.i.e.	78bj *d*
535	730	390	1,214	1,196	454	444	−576	−3,896	1,344	2,754	−3,107	−3,940	−1,479	2,664	Net Errors and Omissions	78ca *d*
598	−143	4,902	3,031	−1,307	−2,282	705	371	5,251	628	1,727	−316	−4,737	−55	−955	Overall Balance	78cb *d*
−598	143	−4,902	−3,031	1,307	2,282	−705	−371	−5,251	−628	−1,727	316	4,737	55	955	Reserves and Related Items	79da *d*
−175	8	−4,766	−2,996	1,294	2,301	−703	−374	−5,279	−601	−1,740	324	4,726	42	960	Reserve Assets	79db *d*
−272	−71	35	−34	—	—	—	—	—	—	—	—	—	—	—	Use of Fund Credit and Loans	79dc *d*
−150	207	−171	−1	12	−19	−2	4	28	−28	13	−8	11	13	−4	Liabs.Constit.For.Auth.Reserves	79dd *d*
—	—	—	—	—	—	—	—	—	—	—	—	—	—	—	Exceptional Financing	79de *d*
Year Ending June 30															**Government Finance**	
−2,085	−1,078	−590	−4,601	−7,983	−6,800	−5,744	−2,719	2,440	6,304	8,307	2,355	−9,047 [p]	….	….	Deficit (−) or Surplus	80
30,584	36,244	41,814	45,936	50,450	59,298	66,793	75,486	84,235	91,574	100,426	103,135	98,835 [p]	….	….	Revenue	81
31,847	36,358	41,379	49,186	57,315	65,179	71,714	77,673	82,337	85,507	93,401	102,332	109,929 [p]	….	….	Expenditure	82
822	964	1,025	1,351	1,118	919	823	532	−542	−237	−1,282	−1,552	−2,047 [p]	….	….	Lending Minus Repayments	83
															Financing (by Residence of Lender)	
1,837	1,283	222	585	234	908	1,271	724	−1,373	−3,150	−2,671	−300	9,611 [p]	….	….	Domestic	84a
248	−205	368	4,016	7,749	5,892	4,473	1,995	−1,067	−3,154	−5,636	−2,055	−564 [p]	….	….	Foreign	85a
….	….	25,707	30,152	38,353	44,627	49,258	52,710	50,710	48,060	42,526	….	….	….	….	Debt: Domestic	88a
….	….	5,352	6,919	7,084	9,857	13,832	15,064	12,670	9,328	6,953	….	….	….	….	Foreign	89a
															Financing (by Currency)	
….	….	….	….	….	….	….	….	….	….	….	….	….	….	….	Net Borrowing: Australian Dollars	84b
….	….	….	….	….	….	….	….	….	….	….	….	….	….	….	Foreign Currency	85b
….	….	….	….	….	….	….	….	….	….	….	….	….	….	….	Other Financing	86c
….	….	….	….	….	….	….	….	….	….	….	….	….	….	….	Use of Cash Balances	87
															Commonwealth and States	
27,250	27,820	….	….	….	….	….	….	….	….	….	….	….	….	….	Debt: Australian Dollars	88b
5,217	4,779	….	….	….	….	….	….	….	….	….	….	….	….	….	Held By: Reserve Bank	88ba
7,548	9,027	….	….	….	….	….	….	….	….	….	….	….	….	….	Deposit Money Banks	88bb
2,798	3,012	….	….	….	….	….	….	….	….	….	….	….	….	….	Life Insur. Companies	88bc
11,687	11,002	….	….	….	….	….	….	….	….	….	….	….	….	….	Others	88be
….	….	….	….	….	….	….	….	….	….	….	….	….	….	….	Intragovernmental Debt	88bg
….	….	….	….	….	….	….	….	….	….	….	….	….	….	….	Debt: Foreign Currency	89b
															Local and Other Governments	
….	….	….	….	….	….	….	….	….	….	….	….	….	….	….	Total Debt	88.. *i*
Billions of Australian Dollars															**National Accounts**	
22.55	22.55	25.51	26.47	31.44	38.75	40.92	47.53	53.46	58.30	63.85	68.44	73.36	79.81	82.93	Exports of Goods & Services	90c. *c*
23.26	26.79	30.48	34.08	38.08	42.54	47.37	50.35	54.70	59.08	65.06	69.63	72.76	75.41	78.43	Government Consumption	91f. *c*
31.97	38.67	42.06	41.41	47.30	56.54	61.06	68.05	77.71	90.39	85.57	77.56	78.40	82.32	91.98	Gross Fixed Capital Formation	93e. *c*
.79	1.50	−.51	−1.42	2.62	.57	−1.33	.64	2.95	5.05	.20	−2.84	−1.20	2.13	1.92	Increase/Decrease(−) in Stocks	93i. *c*
77.86	88.70	100.54	111.39	121.97	137.02	150.18	165.97	184.72	207.49	225.32	235.11	247.69	257.62	271.65	Private Consumption	96f. *c*
−23.36	−26.73	−30.19	−28.97	−35.68	−44.34	−47.21	−50.08	−56.40	−67.13	−67.25	−66.44	−74.05	−80.96	−88.18	Imports of Goods & Services	98c. *c*
132.40	150.26	166.22	181.92	207.69	230.33	251.15	282.96	319.32	357.40	377.83	380.46	395.03	415.74	442.57	Gross Domestic Product	99b. *c*
−1.98	−2.48	−3.23	−4.31	−5.28	−7.16	−8.22	−9.31	−11.66	−15.71	−17.77	−16.54	−14.82	−13.56	−14.55	Net Factor Inc/Pmts(−) Abroad	98.n *c*
130.42	147.78	162.98	177.61	202.41	223.18	242.93	273.65	307.66	341.69	360.06	363.92	380.20	402.18	428.02	Gross Nat'l Expenditure = GNP	99a. *c*
110.65	125.08	136.87	148.68	171.35	188.32	202.86	228.98	258.70	287.96	302.79	304.96	319.03	338.29	361.57	Nat'l Income, Market Prices	99e. *c*
275.06	285.10	283.43	286.29	307.74	321.63	327.99	343.65	358.19	373.15	377.83	371.79	381.01	396.18	415.70	Gross Dom. Prod. 1990 Prices	99b. *r*
48.1	52.7	58.6	63.5	67.5	71.6	76.6	82.3	89.1	95.8	100.0	102.3	103.7	104.9	106.5	GDP Deflator (1990=100)	99bi *r*
Midyear Estimates																
14.70	14.92	15.18	15.39	15.56	15.79	16.02	16.26	16.52	16.81	17.06	17.28	17.48	17.66	17.84	**Population**	99z

Austria
122

		1965	1966	1967	1968	1969	1970	1971	1972	1973	1974	1975	1976	1977	1978	1979
Exchange Rates																*Schillings per SDR:*
Official Rate	aa	25.890	25.910	25.880	25.880	25.880	25.880	25.742	I25.123	23.946	20.973	21.669	19.481	18.385	17.415	16.376
																Schillings per US Dollar:
Official Rate	ae	25.890	25.910	25.880	25.880	25.880	25.880	23.710	I23.140	19.850	17.130	18.510	16.768	15.135	13.368	12.431
Official Rate	rf	26.000	26.000	26.000	26.000	26.000	26.000	24.986	23.115	19.580	18.693	17.417	17.940	16.527	14.522	13.368
																Index Numbers (1990=100):
Official Rate	ahx	43.9	43.9	43.9	43.9	43.8	43.8	82.3	49.1	58.3	60.8	65.3	63.3	68.7	78.2	85.0
Nominal Effective Exchange Rate	neu	70.3	70.3	70.4	71.3	71.0	68.7	69.1	69.0	71.9	75.3	77.4	79.8	83.4	84.0	86.1
Real Effective Exchange Rate	reu	....	....	....	....	....	....	....	....	....	reu	109.3	110.0	110.3	110.5	107.2
Fund Position																*Millions of SDRs:*
Quota	2f.s	75	175	175	175	175	175	270	270	270	270	270	270	270	330	330
SDRs	1b.s	—	—	—	—	—	38	57	86	86	87	87	96	97	105	156
Reserve Position in the Fund	1c.s	72	102	116	160	166	157	142	132	126	131	177	344	325	254	232
of which: Outstg.Fund Borrowing	2c	—	—	—	—	—	—	—	—	—	—	24	100	98	79	66
International Liquidity												*Millions of US Dollars Unless Otherwise Indicated:*				
Total Reserves minus Gold	1l.d	611	632	783	796	822	1,044	1,547	1,927	1,992	2,535	3,583	3,560	3,351	5,047	4,075
SDRs	1b.d	—	—	—	—	—	38	62	93	104	107	102	111	117	136	205
Reserve Position in the Fund	1c.d	72	102	116	160	166	157	155	144	152	160	207	399	394	331	305
Foreign Exchange	1d.d	539	530	667	636	656	849	1,330	1,690	1,737	2,268	3,273	3,050	2,839	4,579	3,565
Gold (Million Fine Troy Ounces)	1ad	20.01	20.02	20.03	20.41	20.42	20.39	20.82	20.85	20.88	20.88	20.88	20.88	21.00	21.05	21.11
Gold (National Valuation)	1and	698	698	699	713	713	712	756	775	905	1,049	971	1,072	1,195	2,213	3,182
Monetary Authorities: Other Liab.	4..d	16	12	11	10	7	8	21	26	20	19	24	37	59	202	397
Deposit Money Banks: Assets	7a.d	289	263	391	460	684	1,043	1,479	2,077	3,341	4,518	5,404	7,669	10,290	13,704	19,329
Liabilities	7b.d	280	363	451	388	515	962	1,611	2,272	3,358	4,591	5,353	7,974	10,983	14,699	20,272
Monetary Authorities																*Billions of Schillings:*
Foreign Assets	11	33.9	34.5	38.4	39.1	39.8	45.5	53.9	62.8	57.7	61.2	84.1	77.5	68.6	96.8	90.0
Claims on Central Government	12a	5.0	6.2	6.1	6.5	6.5	6.4	4.6	5.0	5.6	5.7	6.1	6.2	6.2	6.2	5.9
Claims on Deposit Money Banks	12e	6.9	7.3	7.3	6.7	8.6	7.6	6.7	8.7	10.4	15.7	7.5	15.9	29.9	28.5	48.6
Reserve Money	14	37.8	40.6	44.1	44.7	46.6	49.4	55.4	63.6	64.9	71.4	83.4	87.2	91.0	105.1	107.1
of which: Currency Outside DMBs	14a	26.8	28.9	30.3	31.2	32.7	34.0	37.3	42.9	46.1	48.7	52.3	55.2	58.7	63.2	67.0
Central Government Deposits	16d	2.9	2.5	2.3	1.9	2.0	2.0	3.0	4.5	2.3	2.8	3.2	2.9	3.9	4.0	3.4
Capital Accounts	17a	3.5	3.8	4.3	4.8	5.3	6.7	8.2	9.3	9.9	10.2	11.3	12.6	13.9	17.6	27.1
Other Items (Net)	17r	1.7	1.2	1.1	.9	1.0	1.4	-1.4	-.9	-3.4	-1.8	-.3	-3.1	-4.2	4.9	7.0
Deposit Money Banks																*Billions of Schillings:*
Reserves	20	11.4	11.7	14.0	13.7	13.7	15.3	17.9	20.6	18.9	22.8	31.3	32.1	32.2	41.8	40.2
Foreign Assets	21	7.5	6.9	10.2	12.0	17.8	27.1	34.5	48.4	70.1	I77.4	100.0	128.6	155.7	183.2	240.3
Claims on Central Government	22a	18.8	19.5	22.6	25.4	29.1	32.6	38.3	44.0	56.3	59.9	86.9	116.4	137.2	158.7	183.2
Claims on State and Local Govts.	22b	....	....	....	....	....	....	....	....	....	....	....	....	....	....	....
Claims on Private Sector	22d	100.7	115.1	124.6	135.5	156.4	178.7	211.1	254.8	282.6	326.7	360.8	440.5	510.1	577.3	679.3
Demand Deposits	24	20.5	20.8	22.6	25.0	28.1	30.8	36.4	46.4	49.8	52.7	65.3	70.4	68.5	74.7	58.4
Time and Savings Deposits	25	80.4	91.3	101.8	113.7	129.8	150.4	173.3	196.6	227.8	262.3	314.6	377.6	421.6	489.5	552.8
Bonds	26ab	6.5	7.2	8.7	10.1	12.9	15.8	19.9	26.5	29.9	34.8	43.0	55.2	69.7	87.6	127.9
Foreign Liabilities	26c	7.3	9.4	11.7	10.1	13.4	25.0	37.5	52.9	70.4	I78.7	99.1	133.7	166.2	196.5	252.0
Central Government Deposits	26d	5.0	5.4	5.5	6.0	6.4	6.6	8.6	11.3	12.9	11.8	17.6	19.3	23.2	25.7	28.0
Credit from Monetary Authorities	26g	6.9	7.3	7.3	6.7	8.6	7.6	6.7	8.7	10.4	15.7	7.5	15.9	29.9	28.5	48.6
Capital Accounts	27a	8.6	11.7	12.8	13.9	15.3	16.5	18.7	20.8	22.7	25.1	28.3	33.3	38.3	44.0	47.1
Other Items (Net)	27r	3.1	.1	1.0	1.1	2.4	1.0	.6	4.6	4.6	5.8	5.3	12.1	17.7	14.5	28.1
Banking Survey																*Billions of Schillings:*
Foreign Assets (Net)	31n	33.8	31.6	36.6	40.7	44.0	47.4	50.3	57.6	56.9	59.6	84.6	71.8	57.2	80.8	73.3
Domestic Credit	32	116.6	133.5	145.8	159.8	183.5	209.2	242.4	288.0	329.2	377.6	432.9	540.9	626.4	712.5	837.1
Claims on Central Govt. (Net)	32an	15.9	17.9	20.8	23.9	27.2	30.5	31.3	33.2	46.6	51.0	72.1	100.4	116.3	135.2	157.8
Claims on State and Local Govts.	32b	....	....	....	....	....	....	....	....	....	....	....	....	....	....	....
Claims on Private Sector	32d	100.7	115.7	125.0	135.9	156.4	178.7	211.1	254.8	282.6	326.7	360.8	440.5	510.1	577.3	679.3
Money	34	47.3	49.6	52.9	56.2	60.8	64.8	73.7	89.2	95.9	101.4	115.9	125.5	127.3	137.9	125.4
Quasi-Money	35	80.4	91.3	101.8	113.7	129.8	150.4	173.3	196.6	227.8	262.3	314.6	377.6	421.6	489.5	552.8
Other Items (Net)	37r	22.7	24.2	27.7	30.7	36.9	41.5	45.7	59.8	62.9	73.7	87.0	109.4	134.8	166.0	232.1
Money plus Quasi-Money	35l	127.7	140.9	154.7	169.9	190.6	215.1	247.0	285.8	323.2	363.6	430.5	503.2	548.9	627.4	678.3
Money (National Definitions)																*Billions of Schillings:*
Central Bank Money	14na	....	....	....	47.59	49.67	53.00	60.24	70.32	69.83	78.85	92.26	98.63	104.05	119.11	I110.42
Extended Monetary Base	14nb	....	....	....	....	....	....	....	....	....	....	....	....	....	....	....
Money, M1	34n	51.80	54.17	57.78	61.73	66.52	70.98	82.88	102.06	108.29	114.05	134.30	146.98	153.66	165.63	I142.93
Interest Rates																*Percent Per Annum*
Discount Rate (End of Period)	60	4.50	4.50	3.75	3.75	4.75	5.00	5.00	5.50	5.50	6.50	6.00	4.00	5.50	4.50	3.75
Money Market Rate	60b	....	....	4.75	4.14	4.49	5.67	4.39	5.17	6.94	7.26	5.48	4.67	7.49	6.45	5.59
Deposit Rate	60l	....	....	....	....	....	....	....	....	....	....	....	....	....	5.00	5.00
Government Bond Yield	61	6.52	6.93	7.24	7.74	7.52	7.82	7.71	7.37	8.25	9.74	9.61	8.75	8.74	8.21	7.96
Prices, Production, Employment																*Index Numbers (1990=100):*
Share Prices	62	15.8	15.1	14.1	I13.9	16.4	18.1	18.3	20.1	23.7	22.4	22.3	22.6	21.1	19.8	20.1
Wholesale Prices	63	45.8	46.1	47.2	47.7	48.9	51.1	53.8	55.9	56.7	65.2	69.3	I73.4	75.6	76.3	79.5
Consumer Prices	64	32.8	I33.5	34.8	35.8	36.9	38.5	40.3	42.9	46.1	50.5	54.8	I58.8	62.0	64.2	66.6
Wages: Monthly Earnings	65	15.3	17.1	18.5	19.6	20.8	22.7	25.8	28.8	32.5	37.6	42.7	46.5	50.5	53.4	56.5
Industrial Production	66	37.4	39.2	39.5	42.3	47.1	51.3	I54.4	58.7	61.8	64.7	60.6	I64.5	67.1	68.8	73.8
Employment	67	81.3	81.5	80.6	79.9	80.5	81.6	83.8	85.8	89.1	90.7	90.7	91.7	93.5	94.2	94.7

Austria

122

	1980	1981	1982	1983	1984	1985	1986	1987	1988	1989	1990	1991	1992	1993	1994		
End of Period																**Exchange Rates**	
	17.612	18.490	18.408	20.249	21.614	18.981	16.770	15.960	16.909	15.527	15.190	15.290	15.612	16.679	16.197	Official Rate	aa
End of Period (ae) Period Average (rf)																	
	13.809	15.885	16.687	19.341	22.050	17.280	13.710	11.250	12.565	11.815	10.677	10.689	11.354	12.143	11.095	Official Rate	ae
	12.938	15.927	17.059	17.963	20.009	20.690	15.267	12.643	12.348	13.231	11.370	11.676	10.989	11.632	11.422	Official Rate	rf
Period Averages																	
	87.8	71.5	66.6	63.3	56.9	55.3	74.6	89.8	92.0	85.8	100.0	97.5	103.4	97.5	99.5	Official Rate	ah x
	87.8	87.0	89.8	91.9	91.8	92.3	95.9	98.5	98.2	97.9	100.0	99.6	101.3	104.0	103.9	Nominal Effective Exchange Rate	ne u
	110.9	105.0	105.4	105.5	104.2	103.6	107.0	108.0	104.2	101.0	100.0	97.0	97.7	97.7	....	Real Effective Exchange Rate	re u
End of Period																**Fund Position**	
	495	495	495	776	776	776	776	776	776	776	776	776	1,188	1,188	1,188	Quota	2f. s
	173	186	226	154	224	191	152	206	199	227	196	197	248	161	194	SDRs	1b. s
	228	224	259	447	447	405	361	330	289	274	242	276	390	382	364	Reserve Position in the Fund	1c. s
	56	43	42	50	47	41	32	19	10	4	—	—	—	—	—	*of which:* Outstg.Fund Borrowing	2c
End of Period																**International Liquidity**	
	5,280	5,285	5,300	4,515	4,244	4,767	6,162	7,532	7,368	8,598	9,376	10,332	12,383	14,611	16,822	Total Reserves minus Gold	1l. d
	221	216	250	161	220	210	186	292	268	298	278	282	341	220	283	SDRs	1b. d
	291	261	285	468	438	445	442	468	389	361	344	395	536	524	531	Reserve Position in the Fund	1c. d
	4,768	4,808	4,765	3,886	3,586	4,112	5,534	6,772	6,711	7,939	8,754	9,655	11,506	13,866	16,008	Foreign Exchange	1d. d
	21.11	21.11	21.12	21.13	21.13	21.14	21.14	21.15	21.15	20.66	20.39	20.03	19.93	18.60	18.34	Gold (Million Fine Troy Ounces)	1ad
	2,863	2,488	2,369	2,044	1,793	2,283	2,888	3,523	3,153	3,277	3,581	3,510	3,291	2,871	3,099	Gold (National Valuation)	1an d
	92	31	29	33	52	25	37	30	15	20	19	10	15	9	17	Monetary Authorities: Other Liab.	4.. d
	21,711	22,458	25,039	25,743	26,515	36,754	48,900	58,955	54,604	58,919	65,991	66,189	66,763	68,418	77,001	Deposit Money Banks: Assets	7a. d
	24,955	25,538	26,118	26,355	28,153	38,026	50,891	62,440	59,370	65,954	74,306	76,570	77,427	74,089	83,363	Liabilities	7b. d
End of Period																**Monetary Authorities**	
	112.4	123.7	128.3	127.1	133.9	122.4	124.0	123.7	131.9	140.9	137.1	147.5	177.5	211.6	217.5	Foreign Assets	11
	5.9	5.8	6.2	6.7	7.3	7.0	6.4	6.0	6.2	6.7	7.6	8.3	8.8	9.2	9.6	Claims on Central Government	12a
	37.2	42.3	44.2	62.6	66.1	72.1	76.9	71.8	70.2	75.4	79.3	77.4	70.8	64.0	62.0	Claims on Deposit Money Banks	12e
	114.7	122.1	126.8	135.0	138.0	139.9	150.0	145.9	147.7	168.4	168.6	171.9	189.7	205.0	214.2	Reserve Money	14
	71.6	73.2	75.7	84.1	83.9	84.5	87.9	93.0	98.7	102.6	106.6	113.3	120.9	127.4	133.6	*of which:* Currency Outside DMBs	14a
	2.8	3.8	2.8	3.5	3.4	.8	.6	.2	.2	.3	.2	.2	.2	.3	.3	Central Government Deposits	16d
	33.2	40.7	46.8	59.2	67.6	63.7	61.0	60.7	68.0	60.6	62.3	68.1	76.7	90.4	88.2	Capital Accounts	17a
	4.8	5.2	2.3	−1.4	−1.7	−2.9	−4.3	−5.3	−7.5	−6.2	−7.1	−6.9	−9.5	−10.9	−13.5	Other Items (Net)	17r
End of Period																**Deposit Money Banks**	
	43.4	48.9	50.6	50.6	54.0	55.4	62.0	52.7	48.8	65.3	61.8	59.4	69.8	77.4	80.5	Reserves	20
	299.8	356.7	417.8	497.9	584.7	635.1	670.4	663.2	686.1	696.1	704.6	707.5	758.0	830.8	854.3	Foreign Assets	21
	204.5	220.8	255.5	297.4	I 288.8	321.8	381.8	463.0	467.3	484.6	499.5	526.5	531.7	561.8	624.4	Claims on Central Government	22a
	....	....	....	....	299.6	231.4	362.3	404.7	427.1	438.3	452.9	466.5	478.8	479.7	551.4	Claims on State and Local Govts.	22b
	754.2	840.7	896.0	959.8	I 789.0	928.8	882.7	920.3	1,023.7	1,165.2	1,329.6	1,460.2	1,565.5	1,653.9	1,716.1	Claims on Private Sector	22d
	73.5	68.5	77.5	86.3	92.5	97.4	105.7	120.5	133.5	132.4	140.6	152.5	162.0	181.2	201.1	Demand Deposits	24
	620.0	702.0	782.8	814.3	870.9	928.3	1,012.4	1,083.0	1,139.7	1,234.3	1,363.9	1,465.1	1,567.3	1,643.1	1,721.0	Time and Savings Deposits	25
	141.6	147.4	161.2	189.0	203.8	236.5	264.4	300.7	332.5	357.6	386.6	401.0	419.7	491.9	538.7	Bonds	26ab
	344.6	405.7	435.8	509.7	620.8	657.1	697.7	702.5	746.0	779.2	793.4	818.5	879.1	899.7	924.9	Foreign Liabilities	26c
	22.8	26.1	32.3	44.2	49.8	53.6	71.6	73.6	59.1	63.8	58.4	77.9	59.6	55.2	74.0	Central Government Deposits	26d
	37.2	42.3	44.2	62.6	66.1	72.1	76.9	71.8	70.2	75.4	79.3	77.4	70.8	64.0	62.0	Credit from Monetary Authorities	26g
	51.4	54.7	58.9	65.4	72.0	77.8	90.2	110.6	128.5	147.4	165.7	180.1	194.7	211.4	226.6	Capital Accounts	27a
	11.0	20.3	27.2	33.9	39.5	49.7	40.6	41.2	43.3	59.4	60.6	48.1	50.7	57.0	78.3	Other Items (Net)	27r
End of Period																**Banking Survey**	
	66.4	74.3	109.8	114.6	96.7	100.0	96.2	84.2	71.9	57.5	48.2	36.4	56.3	142.6	146.7	Foreign Assets (Net)	31n
	939.1	1,037.3	1,122.6	1,216.1	I 1,331.4	1,434.6	1,561.0	1,720.3	1,865.0	2,030.8	2,231.1	2,383.4	2,525.1	2,649.0	2,827.2	Domestic Credit	32
	184.9	196.6	226.6	256.3	I 242.8	274.4	316.0	395.2	414.2	427.3	448.5	456.7	480.8	515.5	559.7	Claims on Central Govt. (Net)	32an
	....	....	....	....	299.6	231.4	362.3	404.7	427.1	438.3	452.9	466.5	478.8	479.7	551.4	Claims on State and Local Govts.	32b
	754.2	840.7	896.0	959.8	I 789.0	928.8	882.7	920.3	1,023.7	1,165.2	1,329.6	1,460.2	1,565.5	1,653.9	1,716.1	Claims on Private Sector	32d
	145.1	141.6	153.3	170.4	176.4	181.9	193.5	213.5	232.1	235.0	247.3	265.8	283.0	308.7	334.7	Money	34
	620.0	702.0	782.8	814.3	870.9	928.3	1,012.4	1,083.0	1,139.7	1,234.3	1,363.9	1,465.1	1,567.3	1,643.1	1,721.0	Quasi-Money	35
	240.4	268.0	296.3	345.9	380.2	424.4	451.4	508.0	565.0	619.1	668.1	689.5	731.1	839.9	918.2	Other Items (Net)	37r
	765.0	843.6	936.1	984.7	1,047.3	1,110.2	1,205.9	1,296.5	1,371.9	1,469.3	1,611.2	1,730.9	1,850.3	1,951.8	2,055.7	Money plus Quasi-Money	35l
End of Period																**Money (National Definitions)**	
	117.51	125.90	129.53	138.57	141.42	140.71	150.64	146.12	147.82	168.69	168.80	172.09	189.88	205.24	214.47	*Central Bank Money*	14na
	....	....	....	142.48	140.85	143.04	152.79	161.11	166.89	182.88	195.58	205.76	216.26	224.39	235.17	*Extended Monetary Base*	14nb
	157.14	152.86	165.66	185.02	189.71	192.32	201.58	222.15	240.93	249.20	262.72	284.19	301.81	334.64	355.58	*Money, M1*	34n
Percent Per Annum																**Interest Rates**	
	6.75	6.75	4.75	3.75	4.50	4.00	4.00	3.00	4.00	6.50	6.50	8.00	8.00	5.25	4.50	Discount Rate *(End of Period)*	60
	10.38	10.82	8.00	5.36	6.57	6.11	5.19	4.35	4.59	7.46	8.53	9.10	9.35	7.22	5.03	Money Market Rate	60b
	5.00	5.00	5.00	4.21	4.00	3.94	3.63	3.03	2.73	2.98	3.41	3.75	3.69	2.98	2.31	Deposit Rate	60l
	9.24	10.61	9.92	8.17	8.02	7.77	7.33	6.91	6.67	7.14	8.74	8.62	8.27	6.64	6.69	Government Bond Yield	61
Period Averages																**Prices, Production, Employment**	
	20.8	18.5	16.5	17.9	18.5	35.2	44.1	37.5	35.6	61.6	100.0	85.2	66.9	65.5	74.9	Share Prices	62
	86.4	93.3	96.3	96.9	100.5	103.1	I 97.7	95.7	95.5	97.2	100.0	100.8	100.6	100.2	101.5	Wholesale Prices	63
	70.8	75.6	79.7	82.4	87.0	89.8	I 91.4	92.6	94.4	96.8	100.0	103.3	107.5	111.4	114.7	Consumer Prices	64
	61.0	64.7	68.7	71.8	75.4	79.9	83.5	86.2	89.4	93.3	100.0	105.2	110.3	116.1	120.7	Wages: Monthly Earnings	65
	75.9	I 75.0	74.4	74.5	78.9	82.4	I 83.4	83.8	87.5	93.0	100.0	I 101.5	100.4	98.4	102.4	Industrial Production	66
	95.2	95.6	94.5	93.4	93.7	94.2	94.9	95.1	96.0	97.7	100.0	102.3	104.3	104.3	104.9	Employment	67

Austria 122

		1965	1966	1967	1968	1969	1970	1971	1972	1973	1974	1975	1976	1977	1978	1979
International Transactions																*Billions of Schillings*
Exports	70	41.60	43.77	47.03	51.71	62.72	74.27	78.99	89.75	101.98	133.36	130.88	152.11	161.78	176.11	206.25
Imports, cif	71	54.61	60.52	60.05	64.90	73.46	92.27	104.48	120.58	137.87	168.27	163.38	206.08	234.84	231.89	269.86
Imports, fob	71.v	53.23	58.99	58.55	63.02	71.47	89.77	101.60	117.35	134.18	163.10	157.90	199.12	227.87	225.24	262.26
																1990=100
Volume of Exports	72	15.2	16.3	17.6	I20.2	24.0	25.9	26.8	29.9	32.5	36.3	33.7	39.1	40.3	44.3	I50.1
Volume of Imports	73	18.1	19.8	20.0	I22.6	24.7	29.3	31.8	36.4	40.2	41.3	38.5	47.4	52.0	51.2	I56.6
Export Prices	74	57.5	56.3	56.3	I54.0	55.5	60.9	63.0	64.0	67.6	78.8	81.7	81.7	84.2	84.2	I87.7
Import Prices	75	55.8	56.3	55.2	I52.9	54.6	58.0	60.6	60.9	63.1	75.2	78.0	79.7	82.7	82.6	I87.2
Balance of Payments																*Millions of US Dollars:*
Goods: Exports f.o.b.	78aa d	....	....	1,796	1,969	2,417	2,862	3,160	3,890	5,291	7,570	7,620	8,472	9,737	12,203	15,474
Goods: Imports f.o.b.	78ab d	....	....	-2,309	-2,461	-2,809	-3,550	-4,086	-5,018	-6,865	-8,879	-9,587	-11,073	-13,602	-15,504	-19,753
Trade Balance	78ac d	....	....	-513	-492	-392	-688	-926	-1,128	-1,574	-1,309	-1,967	-2,602	-3,865	-3,301	-4,279
Services: Credit	78ad d	....	....	833	932	1,073	1,335	1,706	2,207	3,017	3,150	3,729	4,359	5,211	6,632	8,166
Services: Debit	78ae d	....	....	-478	-542	-619	-690	-806	-1,026	-1,455	-1,789	-2,223	-2,850	-3,670	-4,330	-5,386
Balance on Goods and Services	78af d	....	....	-158	-103	62	-42	-26	53	-13	52	-461	-1,094	-2,323	-999	-1,500
Income: Credit	78ag d	....	....	54	68	96	129	161	169	256	530	598	614	724	974	1,551
Income: Debit	78ah d	....	....	-88	-124	-140	-175	-212	-253	-390	-637	-735	-829	-1,062	-1,460	-2,035
Balance on Goods, Serv., & Inc.	78ai d	....	....	-192	-159	18	-88	-77	-30	-147	-56	-598	-1,309	-2,661	-1,485	-1,984
Current Transfers, n.i.e.: Credit	78aj d	....	....	97	93	102	103	120	140	197	254	305	356	416	547	726
Current Transfers: Debit	78ak d	....	....	-52	-56	-62	-92	-116	-172	-288	-428	-450	-475	-557	-552	-696
Current Account, n.i.e.	78al d	....	....	-147	-122	57	-78	-73	-63	-238	-230	-744	-1,429	-2,801	-1,490	-1,954
Capital Account, n.i.e.: Credit	78ba d	....	....	3	3	4	4	6	9	13	15	14	16	16	18	21
Capital Account: Debit	78bb d	....	....	-2	-3	-4	-5	-4	-11	-9	-7	-8	-10	-15	-22	-22
Capital Account, n.i.e.	78bc d	....	....	1	—	—	-1	2	-2	4	7	6	6	1	-4	-1
Direct Investment Abroad	78bd d	....	....	-2	-17	-12	-9	-36	-38	-39	-20	-26	-56	-86	-90	-85
Dir. Invest. in Rep. Econ., n.i.e.	78be d	....	....	31	50	66	113	143	145	161	177	79	91	97	142	187
Portfolio Investment Assets	78bf d	....	....	-21	-42	-78	-56	-47	-84	-282	-26	-77	-133	-70	-63	-236
Portfolio Investment Liab., n.i.e.	78bg d	....	....	59	64	27	-1	8	191	133	309	963	647	1,249	1,267	414
Other Investment Assets	78bh d	....	....	-143	-70	-218	-394	-290	-550	-1,021	-516	-1,250	-1,599	-1,660	-2,302	-4,658
Other Investment Liab., n.i.e.	78bi d	....	....	305	94	95	440	507	666	900	738	1,511	1,821	2,183	2,828	4,361
Financial Account, n.i.e.	78bj d	....	....	230	79	-120	93	284	330	-148	661	1,199	771	1,712	1,782	-17
Net Errors and Omissions	78ca d	....	....	71	63	97	168	182	99	210	-50	711	535	737	1,059	943
Overall Balance	78cb d	....	....	155	19	34	182	395	365	-172	388	1,172	-116	-350	1,347	-1,029
Reserves and Related Items	79da d	....	....	-155	-19	-34	-182	-395	-365	172	-388	-1,172	116	350	-1,347	1,029
Reserve Assets	79db d	....	....	-155	-19	-34	-182	-395	-365	172	-388	-1,172	116	350	-1,347	1,029
Use of Fund Credit and Loans	79dc d	....	....	—	—	—	—	—	—	—	—	—	—	—	—	—
Liabs.Constit.For.Auth.Reserves	79dd d	....	....	—	—	—	—	—	—	—	—	—	—	—	—	—
Exceptional Financing	79de d	....	....	—	—	—	—	—	—	—	—	—	—	—	—	—
Government Finance																*Billions of Schillings:*
Federal Government																
Deficit (-) or Surplus	80	-3.30	-3.62	-7.83	-8.44	-7.18	I-1.80	.24	-.85	-8.96	-9.76	-26.34	-34.06	-30.21	-34.92	-35.31
Revenue	81	47.49	52.43	54.43	59.72	66.54	I109.24	123.56	141.63	163.39	189.04	204.75	225.96	253.31	288.56	315.84
Grants Received	81z	....	....	....	....	....	I1.09	1.21	1.47	.58	.68	1.01	1.11	1.25	1.85	2.32
Expenditure	82	50.79	56.05	62.26	68.16	73.72	I109.34	122.64	141.00	168.77	192.98	228.37	255.06	280.05	317.46	343.96
Lending Minus Repayments	83	....	....	....	....	....	I2.79	1.89	2.95	4.16	6.50	3.73	6.07	4.72	7.87	9.51
Financing																
Net Borrowing	84	3.60	3.33	7.81	8.25	8.44	I2.93	1.57	3.89	6.67	7.17	37.90	35.77	34.78	35.94	37.17
Domestic	84a	....	....	....	....	....	I2.17	2.61	5.49	7.32	2.31	19.80	32.03	21.50	24.13	31.25
Foreign	85a	....	....	....	....	....	I.76	-1.04	-1.60	-.65	4.86	18.10	3.74	13.28	11.81	5.92
Use of Cash Balances	87	-.28	.29	.03	.20	-1.28	I-1.13	-1.81	-3.04	2.29	2.59	-11.56	-1.71	-4.57	-1.02	-1.86
Debt: Domestic	88a	....	....	....	....	....	33.58	35.00	40.17	47.44	48.13	68.51	98.85	117.95	139.15	167.73
Foreign	89a	....	....	....	....	....	13.50	12.14	10.31	9.03	13.55	32.07	34.96	47.42	60.02	63.65
National Accounts																*Billions of Schillings*
Exports of Goods & Services	90c	61.9	67.3	71.5	78.8	95.0	116.8	128.7	146.4	165.9	204.2	209.0	236.3	256.9	280.8	327.7
Government Consumption	91f	32.9	36.7	41.6	45.3	50.5	55.2	62.0	70.1	81.9	97.4	113.1	127.8	138.7	154.1	166.0
Gross Fixed Capital Formation	93e	67.4	74.8	76.0	78.9	84.0	97.2	116.9	144.9	155.0	175.7	174.9	188.7	212.9	215.6	231.9
Increase/Decrease(-) in Stocks	93i	1.7	5.3	2.9	5.1	6.9	14.5	7.7	2.0	12.8	16.9	-4.3	9.1	9.1	3.4	12.8
Private Consumption	96f	145.9	155.7	167.4	178.4	189.7	205.3	230.0	259.8	291.8	330.6	368.3	410.2	456.9	468.9	511.7
Imports of Goods & Services	98c	-63.3	-71.1	-73.8	-79.6	-91.0	-113.1	-125.7	-143.7	-163.9	-206.3	-204.4	-247.3	-278.4	-280.4	-331.6
Gross Domestic Product	99b	246.5	268.5	285.6	306.8	335.0	375.9	419.6	479.6	543.5	618.6	656.1	724.8	796.2	842.3	918.5
Net Factor Inc/Pmts(-) Abroad	98.n	-.9	-.9	-1.3	-1.9	-1.7	-2.0	-1.9	-2.7	-3.4	-3.0	-3.6	-5.1	-6.9	-8.4	-7.8
Gross Nat'l Expenditure = GNP	99a	245.6	267.6	284.3	305.0	333.3	373.9	417.7	476.9	540.1	615.6	652.5	719.7	789.3	834.0	910.7
Nat'l Income, Market Prices	99e	215.8	235.3	249.3	267.9	293.9	330.1	368.2	420.6	477.7	544.1	575.1	637.2	698.7	736.3	806.5
Gross Dom. Prod. 1990 Prices	99b.p	806.1	847.5	871.5	907.4	957.0	1,018.5	1,070.6	1,137.1	1,192.6	1,239.6	1,235.2	I1,291.7	1,350.4	1,351.2	1,415.2
GDP Deflator (1990=100)	99bi p	30.6	31.7	32.8	33.8	35.0	36.9	39.2	42.2	45.6	49.9	53.1	56.1	59.0	62.3	64.9
																Millions:
Population	99z	7.25	7.29	7.32	7.36	7.39	7.43	7.46	7.49	7.53	7.53	I7.58	7.57	7.57	7.56	7.55

Deposit Money Banks: I From 1974, banks' external accounts are based on the foreign exchange record which provides an improved resident/nonresident distinction. **I** Beginning in 1984, data are based on improved classification.
Banking Survey: I See note to section 20.

Government Finance: I Beginning in 1970, annual data are as reported in the *Government Finance Statistics Yearbook* and cover consolidated central government.

Austria

	1980	1981	1982	1983	1984	1985	1986	1987	1988	1989	1990	1991	1992	1993	1994		
Billions of Schillings																**International Transactions**	
	226.17	251.77	266.86	277.14	314.50	353.97	342.48	342.43	383.22	429.31	466.07	479.03	487.56	467.66	511.89	Exports	70
	315.85	334.51	332.55	348.34	392.09	430.97	407.96	411.85	451.44	514.69	556.23	591.90	593.92	565.56	629.42	Imports, cif	71
	305.74	321.29	320.32	333.08	374.45	411.53	389.64	393.36	431.17	491.59	531.26	565.33	567.26	540.17	601.17	Imports, fob	71.v
1990=100																	
	51.5	54.1	54.7	57.1	62.5	68.8	69.3	71.1	I79.6	90.3	100.0	105.7	110.8	108.0	....	Volume of Exports	72
	59.5	57.0	55.8	59.7	64.9	68.0	71.6	75.3	I81.5	90.1	100.0	101.3	106.6	105.8	....	Volume of Imports	73
	92.1	97.7	102.1	101.8	105.4	107.3	104.8	102.2	I102.9	100.3	100.0	96.7	94.8	90.6	....	Export Prices	74
	96.4	106.5	106.9	105.6	109.6	113.8	104.5	99.9	I99.9	102.6	100.0	100.2	98.8	95.5	....	Import Prices	75
Minus Sign Indicates Debit																**Balance of Payments**	
	17,227	15,769	15,552	15,292	15,475	16,876	21,725	26,626	30,158	31,960	40,414	40,353	43,932	39,785	44,561	Goods: Exports f.o.b.	78aa d
	−23,716	−20,713	−18,598	−18,464	−18,717	−20,012	−25,741	−31,434	−34,922	−37,512	−47,383	−48,913	−52,375	−47,066	−53,430	Goods: Imports f.o.b.	78ab d
	−6,489	−4,944	−3,046	−3,172	−3,242	−3,137	−4,016	−4,809	−4,765	−5,552	−6,969	−8,560	−8,443	−7,281	−8,869	Trade Balance	78ac d
	9,423	8,198	9,557	9,613	9,240	9,697	12,561	15,116	17,550	18,377	23,279	25,560	29,400	29,162	29,257	Services: Credit	78ad d
	−6,204	−5,752	−5,343	−5,715	−5,768	−6,389	−7,627	−9,635	−12,077	−11,527	−14,197	−15,333	−19,551	−20,990	−21,355	Services: Debit	78ae d
	−3,271	−2,499	1,169	726	229	171	918	672	708	1,298	2,114	1,667	1,406	892	−967	Balance on Goods and Services	78af d
	2,502	3,168	3,147	2,598	2,876	3,194	3,783	4,484	5,324	6,789	9,145	9,544	8,716	8,773	8,418	Income: Credit	78ag d
	−3,030	−3,631	−3,559	−2,966	−3,226	−3,448	−4,459	−5,346	−6,243	−7,723	−10,087	−11,020	−9,884	−9,620	−9,048	Income: Debit	78ah d
	−3,799	−2,962	757	359	−120	−83	242	−190	−210	364	1,172	192	238	45	−1,597	Balance on Goods, Serv., & Inc.	78ai d
	778	695	673	619	605	630	866	1,115	1,258	1,227	1,657	1,699	1,364	1,324	1,433	Current Transfers, n.i.e.: Credit	78aj d
	−844	−775	−726	−702	−663	−705	−903	−1,188	−1,289	−1,343	−1,663	−1,830	−2,233	−2,131	−2,288	Current Transfers: Debit	78ak d
	−3,865	−3,042	703	276	−178	−158	204	−263	−242	248	1,166	61	−631	−762	−2,452	Current Account, n.i.e.	78al d
	30	26	20	27	23	18	35	36	40	50	63	152	217	177	564	Capital Account, n.i.e.: Credit	78ba d
	−52	−33	−40	−25	−25	−35	−38	−43	−44	−62	−55	−97	−288	−290	−252	Capital Account: Debit	78bb d
	−22	−7	−20	2	−2	−17	−3	−7	−5	−12	8	55	−71	−114	311	Capital Account, n.i.e.	78bc d
	−101	−211	−139	−189	−70	−73	−317	−313	−310	−867	−1,701	−1,293	−1,947	−1,396	−1,247	Direct Investment Abroad	78bd d
	239	328	208	216	115	173	187	410	436	587	653	360	891	770	1,309	Dir. Invest. in Rep. Econ., n.i.e.	78be d
	−126	−35	−46	−497	−757	−999	−489	−1,012	−1,451	−1,791	−1,695	−1,739	−2,744	−1,739	−4,223	Portfolio Investment Assets	78bf d
	1,701	1,837	1,557	954	1,266	1,660	2,061	1,357	3,376	3,338	3,062	2,920	4,714	10,477	4,237	Portfolio Investment Liab., n.i.e.	78bg d
	−5,091	−3,572	−3,939	−4,776	−4,680	−2,285	−1,697	−287	−2,668	−1,374	−1,347	−2,740	−6,794	−12,083	−3,579	Other Investment Assets	78bh d
	6,268	3,176	1,498	3,802	4,314	1,856	1,925	881	1,033	1,473	1,008	2,481	6,923	7,829	6,308	Other Investment Liab., n.i.e.	78bi d
	2,890	1,522	−862	−490	188	332	1,670	1,035	415	1,367	−19	−12	1,043	3,859	2,805	Financial Account, n.i.e.	78bj d
	2,338	1,905	385	−315	60	−143	−1,228	−433	322	−613	−1,170	731	2,253	−782	157	Net Errors and Omissions	78ca d
	1,341	379	207	−528	67	15	643	333	491	990	−15	836	2,593	2,202	821	Overall Balance	78cb d
	−1,341	−379	−207	528	−67	−15	−643	−333	−491	−990	15	−836	−2,593	−2,202	−821	Reserves and Related Items	79ad
	−1,341	−379	−207	528	−67	−15	−643	−333	−491	−990	15	−836	−2,593	−2,202	−821	Reserve Assets	79db d
	—	—	—	—	—	—	—	—	—	—	—	—	—	—	—	Use of Fund Credit and Loans	79dc d
	—	—	—	—	—	—	—	—	—	—	—	—	—	—	—	Liabs.Constit.For.Auth.Reserves	79dd d
	—	—	—	—	—	—	—	—	—	—	—	—	—	—	—	Exceptional Financing	79de d
Year Ending December 31																**Government Finance**	
																Federal Government	
	−33.57	−32.52	−54.53	−71.84	−58.22	−63.33	−84.22	−81.55	−78.40	−62.84	−80.89	−91.69	−79.62	....	....	Deficit (−) or Surplus	80
	344.44	379.50	395.04	414.91	454.23	473.11	494.54	513.84	554.26	580.73	626.21	676.25	746.63	....	....	Revenue	81
	2.97	3.43	3.04	3.26	3.20	3.59	3.75	3.23	3.78	3.99	3.19	4.36	3.44	....	....	Grants Received	81z
	371.62	408.40	443.57	477.54	504.95	530.04	569.22	595.22	629.00	648.44	691.73	751.76	808.53	....	....	Expenditure	82
	9.36	7.05	9.04	12.47	10.70	9.99	13.29	3.40	7.44	−.88	18.56	20.54	21.16	....	....	Lending Minus Repayments	83
																Financing	
	30.66	30.62	51.19	74.96	59.67	66.52	101.57	87.33	63.26	70.08	74.60	86.81	68.09	....	....	Net Borrowing	84
	22.11	13.99	34.91	63.21	64.32	64.63	95.37	89.86	57.61	66.25	65.68	73.36	46.73	....	....	Domestic	84a
	8.55	16.63	16.28	11.75	−4.65	1.89	6.20	−2.53	5.65	3.83	8.92	13.45	21.36	....	....	Foreign	85a
	2.91	1.90	3.34	−3.12	−1.45	−3.19	−17.35	−5.78	15.14	−7.24	6.29	4.88	11.53	....	....	Use of Cash Balances	87
	188.62	201.29	233.24	291.21	351.54	407.94	494.25	573.81	617.25	677.00	731.80	797.15	828.70	....	....	Debt: Domestic	88a
	72.64	94.56	108.43	125.59	118.96	118.72	124.61	124.74	130.80	125.83	135.36	148.46	172.14	....	....	Foreign	89a
Billions of Schillings																**National Accounts**	
	366.2	404.5	431.2	449.7	497.7	549.1	523.0	527.1	587.5	664.3	724.3	770.4	803.4	803.4	852.5	Exports of Goods & Services	90c
	178.7	195.2	214.3	226.9	237.8	255.0	270.7	280.4	288.4	302.9	319.9	349.6	377.1	405.6	427.5	Government Consumption	91f
	255.5	268.0	262.9	269.6	282.9	304.4	324.0	342.1	371.2	405.8	442.4	488.2	511.1	511.3	550.1	Gross Fixed Capital Formation	93e
	27.4	10.2	−2.6	−5.8	21.0	11.2	10.3	13.8	17.6	14.1	17.5	8.8	4.2	8.7	25.9	Increase/Decrease(−) in Stocks	93i
	552.5	596.5	640.2	694.8	733.2	775.5	804.4	837.8	880.5	935.3	999.2	1,064.0	1,127.1	1,168.3	1,234.8	Private Consumption	96f
	−385.7	−418.5	−412.4	−433.9	−495.7	−546.8	−509.8	−519.8	−578.7	−649.4	−702.0	−753.0	−776.8	−779.4	−846.0	Imports of Goods & Services	98c
	994.7	1,056.0	1,133.5	1,201.2	1,276.8	1,348.4	1,422.5	1,481.4	1,566.4	1,672.9	1,801.3	1,928.3	2,046.1	2,117.8	2,244.9	Gross Domestic Product	99b
	−8.4	−8.8	−8.4	−8.8	−8.6	−7.1	−12.0	−12.9	−13.7	−14.4	−13.2	−19.5	−9.7	−9.1	....	Net Factor Inc/Pmts(−) Abroad	98.n
	986.4	1,047.2	1,125.1	1,192.4	1,268.2	1,341.4	1,410.5	1,468.5	1,552.9	1,658.5	1,788.1	1,908.8	2,036.4	2,108.7	....	Gross Nat'l Expenditure = GNP	99a
	870.3	918.7	984.4	1,043.2	1,110.0	1,173.8	1,234.3	1,284.6	1,358.8	1,451.5	1,566.7	1,658.9	1,761.5	1,830.4	....	Nat'l Income, Market Prices	99e
	1,456.5	1,452.3	1,467.8	1,497.1	1,517.5	1,554.8	1,573.2	1,599.3	1,664.2	1,727.9	1,801.3	1,854.3	1,888.6	1,887.5	1,939.2	Gross Dom. Prod. 1990 Prices	99b.p
	68.3	72.7	77.2	80.2	84.1	86.7	90.4	92.6	94.1	96.8	100.0	104.0	108.3	112.2	115.8	GDP Deflator (1990=100)	99bi p
Midyear Estimates																	
	7.55	7.56	7.57	7.55	7.55	7.56	7.56	7.57	7.60	7.62	7.79	7.84	7.88	7.99	....	Population	99z

Bahamas, The
313

		1965	1966	1967	1968	1969	1970	1971	1972	1973	1974	1975	1976	1977	1978	1979
Exchange Rates																*Bahamian Dollars per SDR:*
Principal Rate........aa=	wa	1.0204	1.0204	1.0204	1.0204	1.0204	1.0000	1.0857	1.0857	....	1.2244	1.1707	1.1618	1.2147	1.3028	1.3173
														Bahamian Dollars per US Dollar:		
Principal Rate........ae=	we	1.0204	1.0204	1.0204	1.0204	1.0204	1.0000	1.0000	1.0000	....	1.0000	1.0000	1.0000	1.0000	1.0000	1.0000
Secondary Rate.........................	xe	....	....	....	....	....	....	....	....	....	....	....	....	....	1.1850	1.1750
Secondary Rate.........................	xf	....	....	....	....	....	....	....	....	....	....	....	....	....	1.1867	1.1637
													Index Numbers (1990=100):			
Principal Rate...........................	ahx	98.0	98.0	98.0	98.0	98.0	99.7	100.0	100.0	100.0	100.0	100.0	100.0	100.0	100.0	100.0
Nominal Effective Exchange Rate.........	nec	....	....	....	....	....	....	....	....	....	....	....	....	....	....	74.6
Real Effective Exchange Rate..................	rec	....	....	....	....	....	....	....	....	....	....	....	....	....	....	94.0
Fund Position																*Millions of SDRs:*
Quota..	2f. s	....	....	....	....	....	....	....	....	20.0	20.0	20.0	20.0	20.0	33.0	33.0
SDRs..	1b. s	....	....	....	....	....	....	....	....	—	—	—	—	—	—	3.4
Reserve Position in the Fund............	1c. s	....	....	....	....	....	....	....	....	—	5.0	5.0	5.0	5.0	4.9	4.7
International Liquidity												*Millions of US Dollars Unless Otherwise Indicated:*				
Total Reserves minus Gold........	1l. d	....	....	....	44.4	26.1	21.7	29.5	37.1	43.2	49.8	53.3	47.4	↑67.1	58.1	77.5
SDRs..	1b. d	....	....	....	....	....	....	....	....	—	—	—	—	—	—	4.5
Reserve Position in the Fund.........	1c. d	....	....	....	....	....	....	....	....	—	6.1	5.9	5.8	6.1	6.3	6.2
Foreign Exchange....................	1d. d	....	....	....	44.4	26.1	21.7	29.5	37.1	43.2	43.7	47.4	41.6	↑61.0	51.8	66.8
Deposit Money Banks: Assets.........	7a. d	....	....	....	2,053	2,635	4,107	5,840	5,565	12,223	16,788	23,877	26,870	31,900	30,097	
of which: Claims on Nonbanks.........	7ad d	....	....	....	....	....	....	....	....	3,272	4,044	5,751	8,129	5,696	5,977	6,653
Deposit Money Banks: Liabilities.......	7b. d	....	....	....	....	2,056	2,836	4,270	5,806	5,734	12,347	16,869	23,931	27,023	32,036	30,203
of which: Liab. to Nonbanks..........	7bd d	....	....	....	....	....	....	....	....	1,208	2,708	3,669	3,299	3,767	4,590	4,858
Branches of US Banks: Assets........	7k. d	....	....	....	....	2,966	4,515	8,146	12,472	20,235	26,624	37,505	53,778	61,580	71,407	79,712
of which: Claims on Nonbanks.........	7kd d	....	....	....	....	1,332	1,759	3,922	5,300	8,798	12,407	17,058	24,340	27,321	28,705	29,136
Branches of US Banks: Liab..........	7m. d	....	....	....	....	2,961	4,508	8,053	12,479	20,268	26,673	37,333	53,931	61,530	71,898	80,238
of which: Liab. to Nonbanks........	7md d	....	....	....	....	890	1,277	1,734	2,246	2,609	3,608	4,734	8,211	12,259	15,137	18,768
Monetary Authorities																*Millions of Bahamian Dollars:*
Foreign Assets..........................	11	....	....	....	47.8	29.1	23.7	30.7	36.1	43.5	49.8	53.4	47.5	67.2	58.6	78.2
Claims on Central Government.........	12a	....	....	....	8.0	9.5	9.5	10.7	9.0	.5	9.7	9.9	18.6	12.3	14.9	22.5
Claims on Deposit Money Banks........	12e	....	....	....	.1	2.1	1.5	.1	—	.7	1.6	—	—	—	—	2.0
Claims on Other Financial Insts.........	12f	....	....	....	....	....	....	....	....	....	....	....	....	....	....	....
Reserve Money.........................	14	....	....	....	39.5	28.3	25.9	27.1	37.4	35.6	41.7	44.7	44.3	46.4	54.7	64.3
of which: Currency Outside DMBs.......	14a	....	....	....	....	17.4	17.8	15.3	21.3	20.2	19.3	20.1	20.5	23.3	26.5	29.8
Central Government Deposits..........	16d	....	....	....	16.1	10.8	6.7	9.8	4.1	3.2	8.2	9.0	9.5	21.1	3.9	15.2
Capital Accounts.......................	17a	....	....	....	.4	1.5	2.5	3.9	3.1	5.6	4.7	10.6	10.5	11.8	13.3	17.8
Other Items (Net)......................	17r	....	....	....	−.1	.1	−.4	.7	.5	.3	6.5	−1.0	1.8	.2	1.6	5.4
Deposit Money Banks																*Millions of Bahamian Dollars:*
Reserves................................	20	....	....	....	....	10.9	8.1	11.8	16.0	15.4	20.7	22.3	21.3	20.4	25.0	30.9
Foreign Assets (Net)..................	21n	....	....	....	....	−3.4	−201.1	−163.2	34.1	−169.3	−124.6	−80.4	−53.9	−135.2	−135.0	−105.9
Claims on Central Government........	22a	....	....	....	....	4.0	19.6	156.1	18.9	26.4	59.6	68.5	80.2	94.5	90.6	88.8
Claims on Official Entities.............	22bx	....	....	....	....	....	....	....	....	—	2.1	.4	10.6	24.6	21.7	20.0
Claims on Private Sector............	22d	....	....	....	....	323.0	349.1	220.8	241.7	369.7	264.8	294.1	264.9	286.6	309.3	348.4
Claims on Other Financial Insts......	22f	....	....	....	....	....	....	....	....	1.7	1.0	3.4	.7	1.9	2.2	9.4
Demand Deposits....................	24	....	....	....	....	70.6	62.7	53.5	63.6	60.2	58.5	53.6	57.0	66.2	80.6	108.5
Time, Savings,& Fgn.Currency Dep....	25	....	....	....	....	112.8	103.1	120.4	119.6	136.3	137.0	159.8	231.4	193.8	213.4	237.2
Central Government Deposits..........	26d	....	....	....	....	1.8	4.6	6.5	.2	2.1	2.4	7.4	6.4	2.7	4.5	12.4
Credit from Monetary Authorities.......	26g	....	....	....	....	....	....	....	....	3.0	13.0	4.0	—	—	—	2.0
Capital Accounts.....................	27a	....	....	....	....	30.3	37.4	41.1	43.4	43.2	14.9	23.4	26.2	23.8	33.5	34.4
Other Items (Net)......................	27r	....	....	....	....	119.1	−32.2	4.0	83.9	−.9	−2.2	60.4	2.8	−11.7	−18.4	−2.9
Monetary Survey																*Millions of Bahamian Dollars:*
Foreign Assets (Net).................	31n	....	....	....	....	25.7	−177.4	−132.5	70.2	−125.8	−74.8	−27.0	−6.4	−86.0	−76.6	−27.7
Domestic Credit.......................	32	....	....	....	....	323.9	366.9	371.3	265.3	393.0	326.6	360.2	359.1	396.1	430.3	461.5
Claims on Central Govt. (Net)........	32an	....	....	....	....	.9	17.8	150.5	23.6	21.6	58.7	62.3	82.9	83.0	97.1	83.7
Claims on Official Entities............	32bx	....	....	....	....	....	....	....	....	—	2.1	.4	10.6	24.6	21.7	20.0
Claims on Private Sector.............	32d	....	....	....	....	323.0	349.1	220.8	241.7	369.7	264.8	294.1	264.9	286.6	309.3	348.4
Claims on Other Financial Insts.......	32f	....	....	....	....	....	....	....	....	1.7	1.0	3.4	.7	1.9	2.2	9.4
Money..................................	34	....	....	....	....	88.0	80.5	68.8	84.9	80.4	77.8	73.7	77.5	89.5	107.1	138.3
Quasi-Money..........................	35	....	....	....	....	112.8	103.1	120.4	119.6	136.3	137.0	159.8	231.4	193.8	213.4	237.2
Other Items (Net).....................	37r	....	....	....	....	148.8	5.9	49.6	131.0	50.5	37.0	99.7	43.8	26.8	33.2	58.3
Money plus Quasi-Money..............	35l	....	....	....	....	200.8	183.6	189.2	204.5	216.7	214.8	233.5	308.9	283.3	320.5	375.5
Other Banking Institutions																*Millions of Bahamian Dollars*
Cash...................................	40	....	....	....	....	....	....	....	....	—	2.1	2.3	2.5	2.9	3.3	4.2
Foreign Assets (Net).................	41n	....	....	....	....	....	....	....	....	12.6	−4.7	−2.0	4.1	10.5	5.2	4.9
Claims on Central Government.......	42a	....	....	....	....	....	....	....	....	2.6	4.0	7.2	6.0	8.6	11.6	9.6
Claims on Private Sector............	42d	....	....	....	....	....	....	....	....	51.3	59.9	65.1	65.1	66.6	75.2	93.2
Claims on Deposit Money Banks.....	42e	....	....	....	....	....	....	....	....	9.3	6.3	4.9	41.6	6.6	4.7	10.0
Demand Deposits....................	44	....	....	....	....	....	....	....	....	—	—	—	—	—	—	—
Time, Savings,& Fgn.Currency Dep....	45	....	....	....	....	....	....	....	....	36.2	41.5	45.7	50.4	57.9	71.0	85.6
Central Government Deposits.........	46d	....	....	....	....	....	....	....	....	—	—	—	—	—	—	—
Credit from Monetary Authorities.....	46g	....	....	....	....	....	....	....	....	—	—	—	—	—	—	—
Credit from Deposit Money Banks.....	46h	....	....	....	....	....	....	....	....	1.7	1.0	3.4	.7	1.9	2.2	9.4
Capital Accounts.....................	47a	....	....	....	....	....	....	....	....	22.7	25.3	25.2	31.6	38.0	26.4	27.2
Other Items (Net)....................	47r	....	....	....	....	....	....	....	....	15.2	−.2	3.2	36.6	−2.6	.4	−.3

Bahamas, The

1980	1981	1982	1983	1984	1985	1986	1987	1988	1989	1990	1991	1992	1993	1994		
End of Period															**Exchange Rates**	
1.2754	1.1640	1.1031	1.0470	.9802	1.0984	1.2232	1.4187	1.3457	1.3142	1.4227	1.4304	1.3750	1.3736	1.4599	Principal Rate..............aa=	wa
End of Period (we and xe) Period Average (xf)																
1.0000	1.0000	1.0000	1.0000	1.0000	1.0000	1.0000	1.0000	1.0000	1.0000	1.0000	1.0000	1.0000	1.0000	1.0000	Principal Rate..............ae=	we
1.2250	1.2350	1.2350	1.2350	1.1750	1.1750	1.1750	1.2250	1.2250	1.2250	1.2250	1.2250	1.2250	1.2250	1.2250	Secondary Rate.................	xe
1.2135	1.2265	1.2350	1.2350	1.1950	1.1800	1.1750	1.1989	1.2250	1.2250	1.2250	1.2250	1.2250	1.2250	1.2250	Secondary Rate.................	xf
Period Averages																
100.0	100.0	100.0	100.0	100.0	100.0	100.0	100.0	100.0	100.0	100.0	100.0	100.0	100.0	100.0	Principal Rate.................	ahx
75.3	79.4	83.3	87.0	91.7	95.1	90.8	88.8	90.3	96.0	100.0	103.9	108.1	117.1	124.5	Nominal Effective Exchange Rate........	nec
93.6	98.2	100.9	103.8	106.6	108.9	105.3	103.2	101.7	103.7	100.0	103.1	105.4	107.6	106.0	Real Effective Exchange Rate.............	rec
End of Period															**Fund Position**	
49.5	49.5	49.5	66.4	66.4	66.4	66.4	66.4	66.4	66.4	66.4	66.4	66.4	94.9	94.9	Quota.................	2f.s
2.7	6.1	5.8	1.1	.7	.4	—	.3	.4	.1	.4	.1	—	—	—	SDRs.................	1b.s
8.8	6.6	6.7	10.9	10.9	10.9	10.9	10.7	9.0	8.6	7.9	7.2	6.8	6.2	6.2	Reserve Position in the Fund.................	1c.s
End of Period															**International Liquidity**	
92.3	100.2	113.5	122.0	161.1	182.5	231.5	170.1	172.0	146.8	158.2	181.3	155.3	172.3	176.6	Total Reserves minus Gold.................	1l.d
3.5	7.1	6.3	1.2	.7	.4	—	.4	.5	.2	.5	.2	—	—	—	SDRs.................	1b.d
11.3	7.7	7.3	11.4	10.7	12.0	13.4	15.2	12.2	11.4	11.2	10.2	9.4	8.6	9.1	Reserve Position in the Fund.................	1c.d
77.5	85.4	99.8	109.4	149.8	170.1	218.1	154.5	159.4	135.3	146.4	170.9	145.9	163.7	167.5	Foreign Exchange.................	1d.d
33,513	43,317	34,716	31,959	32,107	29,423	29,189	39,794	44,487	36,116	33,945	26,719	32,327	35,701	42,829	Deposit Money Banks: Assets.................	7a.d
7,886	6,409	3,601	4,140	5,947	5,805	5,887	6,198	5,647	5,185	5,390	5,903	6,411	6,591	7,002	*of which:* Claims on Nonbanks.................	7add
33,580	43,396	34,811	32,036	32,135	29,494	29,287	39,909	44,646	36,317	34,181	26,978	32,537	35,924	43,080	Deposit Money Banks: Liabilities.................	7b.d
5,707	6,739	5,657	5,898	5,021	4,487	4,868	5,098	4,719	5,608	6,184	5,794	6,447	9,430	10,266	*of which:* Liab. to Nonbanks.................	7bdd
88,917	103,698	94,778	99,867	94,148	91,390	90,656	104,854	109,722	115,359	113,088	105,310	87,983	87,620	....	Branches of US Banks: Assets.................	7k.d
27,819	26,560	18,573	19,498	18,822	15,330	14,173	14,520	11,794	14,450	14,381	15,721	16,105	15,137	....	*of which:* Claims on Nonbanks.................	7kdd
89,847	104,531	96,094	101,082	94,979	91,657	92,441	106,805	112,386	117,579	105,864	108,549	90,049	89,058	....	Branches of US Banks: Liab.................	7m.d
25,206	34,952	34,412	39,484	37,937	39,094	38,664	40,788	40,033	33,979	28,806	31,644	25,295	28,365	....	*of which:* Liab. to Nonbanks.................	7mdd
End of Period															**Monetary Authorities**	
92.3	100.2	113.4	123.2	162.0	182.6	231.5	171.8	172.5	147.3	159.6	172.3	144.0	162.7	170.4	Foreign Assets.................	11
42.1	34.2	28.4	35.8	43.8	30.3	31.5	53.1	47.0	89.9	111.5	123.1	136.7	114.7	143.6	Claims on Central Government.................	12a
10.0	19.0	19.5	—	—	—	—	12.0	21.0	13.0	7.0	—	.5	—	—	Claims on Deposit Money Banks.................	12e
—	.4	—	—	—	1.0	2.1	2.5	2.5	2.5	2.4	2.3	2.1	3.2	3.1	Claims on Other Financial Insts.................	12f
75.1	74.2	85.7	95.9	105.3	121.5	141.5	149.6	168.5	170.8	182.8	207.0	201.0	199.6	223.5	Reserve Money.................	14
33.4	37.4	41.1	45.5	51.0	57.8	65.0	74.8	78.8	79.5	80.2	78.7	84.4	83.7	89.4	*of which:* Currency Outside DMBs.................	14a
24.9	31.4	22.7	9.9	45.9	34.4	60.3	19.6	4.0	12.8	20.9	14.1	11.7	8.9	20.4	Central Government Deposits.................	16d
26.6	46.7	50.6	50.2	53.4	54.4	63.2	64.8	69.6	72.1	73.3	80.0	82.3	87.6	88.4	Capital Accounts.................	17a
17.8	1.5	2.3	3.0	1.2	3.6	.1	5.4	.9	-3.0	3.4	-3.4	-11.7	-15.5	-15.2	Other Items (Net).................	17r
End of Period															**Deposit Money Banks**	
36.4	31.7	38.6	41.8	44.5	53.7	62.4	58.5	72.4	72.9	86.3	112.5	101.4	105.0	123.0	Reserves.................	20
-67.2	-79.7	-95.2	-77.2	-27.8	-70.5	-98.5	-115.4	-158.6	-201.1	-236.4	-259.1	-210.0	-222.7	-251.3	Foreign Assets (Net).................	21n
69.1	91.2	100.8	126.1	127.2	122.6	124.3	119.9	164.2	159.8	186.8	220.6	225.1	329.6	295.7	Claims on Central Government.................	22a
36.9	22.3	47.3	33.2	24.9	9.6	15.6	27.9	39.9	81.9	106.0	113.0	105.5	88.8	72.9	Claims on Official Entities.................	22bx
402.8	443.4	483.1	509.7	534.9	592.3	677.1	788.5	851.9	927.2	1,122.4	1,163.4	1,215.4	1,400.0	1,591.6	Claims on Private Sector.................	22d
4.2	5.3	1.7	5.4	6.6	5.3	12.8	13.6	13.0	6.9	7.3	4.9	5.5	10.6	20.4	Claims on Other Financial Insts.................	22f
102.9	106.1	118.6	131.4	136.7	150.3	184.2	202.9	218.5	218.8	247.3	276.0	280.2	288.3	321.9	Demand Deposits.................	24
289.2	328.9	393.4	455.6	483.4	496.0	537.0	627.8	680.9	764.6	890.5	958.7	1,023.0	1,237.5	1,339.1	Time, Savings,& Fgn.Currency Dep.................	25
15.9	6.0	5.8	8.2	9.5	13.0	22.7	21.8	18.4	15.6	19.8	34.6	29.4	29.5	35.7	Central Government Deposits.................	26d
24.0	22.0	12.0	.7	26.0	24.0	20.0	33.1	33.0	23.0	19.0	—	.5	—	—	Credit from Monetary Authorities........	26g
60.5	55.5	40.7	46.6	56.6	20.6	14.4	27.1	50.6	50.0	98.1	91.1	93.8	128.7	135.2	Capital Accounts.................	27a
-10.3	-4.3	5.8	-3.5	-1.9	9.1	15.4	-19.7	-18.4	-24.4	-2.3	-5.1	16.0	27.3	20.4	Other Items (Net).................	27r
End of Period															**Monetary Survey**	
25.1	20.5	18.2	46.0	134.2	112.1	132.9	56.4	13.9	-53.8	-76.8	-86.8	-66.0	-60.0	-80.9	Foreign Assets (Net).................	31n
514.3	559.4	632.8	692.1	682.0	713.7	780.4	964.1	1,096.1	1,239.8	1,495.8	1,578.6	1,649.2	1,908.5	2,071.2	Domestic Credit.................	32
70.4	88.0	100.7	143.8	115.6	105.5	72.8	131.6	188.8	221.3	257.6	295.0	320.7	405.9	383.2	Claims on Central (Net).................	32an
36.9	22.3	47.3	33.2	24.9	9.6	15.6	27.9	39.9	81.9	106.0	113.0	105.5	88.8	72.9	Claims on Official Entities.................	32bx
402.8	443.4	483.1	509.7	534.9	592.3	677.1	788.5	851.9	927.2	1,122.4	1,163.4	1,215.4	1,400.0	1,591.6	Claims on Private Sector.................	32d
4.2	5.7	1.7	5.4	6.6	6.3	14.9	16.1	15.5	9.4	9.7	7.2	7.6	13.8	23.5	Claims on Other Financial Insts...........	32f
136.3	143.5	159.7	176.9	187.7	208.1	249.2	277.7	297.1	298.3	327.5	354.7	364.6	372.0	411.3	Money.................	34
289.2	328.9	393.4	455.6	483.4	496.0	537.0	627.8	680.9	764.6	890.5	958.7	1,023.0	1,237.5	1,339.1	Quasi-Money.................	35
113.9	107.5	97.9	105.6	145.1	121.7	127.5	115.0	132.0	123.1	200.8	178.4	195.6	239.0	239.9	Other Items (Net).................	37r
425.5	472.4	553.1	632.5	671.1	704.1	786.2	905.5	978.0	1,062.9	1,218.0	1,313.4	1,387.6	1,609.5	1,750.4	Money plus Quasi-Money.................	35l
End of Period															**Other Banking Institutions**	
5.0	5.7	6.8	8.3	9.8	11.8	14.6	17.4	18.7	19.2	16.4	16.5	16.9	12.9	12.8	Cash.................	40
42.7	59.5	92.4	93.7	159.1	191.5	224.3	199.8	130.7	107.0	166.5	240.6	279.0	370.1	429.6	Foreign Assets (Net).................	41n
8.2	7.0	6.1	8.4	10.2	12.9	13.5	18.3	21.4	21.8	19.1	20.4	33.6	23.7	22.1	Claims on Central Government.................	42a
113.2	125.8	142.6	167.1	201.9	248.0	303.6	371.6	388.8	404.5	343.8	351.9	364.4	268.1	266.9	Claims on Private Sector.................	42d
6.2	7.6	14.7	24.9	15.9	10.7	14.4	8.8	5.8	18.4	11.6	25.6	28.4	24.5	26.1	Claims on Deposit Money Banks.............	42e
—	—	—	—	—	.1	.1	1.0	3.3	7.1	7.3	9.4	8.3	7.8	Demand Deposits.................	44	
99.8	116.7	138.4	168.4	196.6	245.6	293.9	353.1	363.3	370.2	312.7	317.1	325.8	245.2	242.9	Time, Savings,& Fgn.Currency Dep........	45
—	1.1	1.1	1.9	1.1	1.2	2.3	2.5	3.8	3.5	5.2	1.9	3.1	.3	—	Central Government Deposits.................	46d
—	.4	—	—	3.0	3.0	3.0	3.0	—	—	—	—	—	—	—	Credit from Monetary Authorities........	46g
4.2	5.3	1.7	5.4	6.6	5.3	9.4	10.2	9.6	3.5	3.4	3.0	1.1	1.1	3.7	Credit from Deposit Money Banks........	46h
89.9	94.7	123.7	159.1	207.9	251.4	292.7	337.6	269.6	249.4	231.9	272.5	302.2	315.7	323.4	Capital Accounts.................	47a
-18.6	-12.6	-2.3	-32.4	-18.3	-31.6	-31.0	-90.6	-81.9	-58.9	-2.7	55.2	80.7	126.1	171.6	Other Items (Net).................	47r

Bahamas, The
313

		1965	1966	1967	1968	1969	1970	1971	1972	1973	1974	1975	1976	1977	1978	1979
Banking Survey													*Millions of Bahamian Dollars:*			
Foreign Assets (Net)	51n	....	....	....	....	25.7	−177.4	−132.6	70.5	−113.2	−79.5	−29.1	−2.3	−75.7	−71.5	−22.8
Domestic Credit	52	....	....	....	....	....	....	....	....	445.2	389.5	429.1	429.5	469.4	514.9	554.9
Claims on Central Govt. (Net)	52an	....	....	....	....	.9	17.8	150.5	23.6	24.2	62.7	69.5	88.9	91.6	108.7	93.3
Claims on Official Entities	52bx	....	....	....	....	....	....	....	....	—	2.1	.4	10.6	24.6	21.7	20.0
Claims on Private Sector	52d	....	....	....	....	323.0	349.1	220.8	241.7	421.0	324.7	359.2	330.0	353.2	384.5	441.6
Liquid Liabilities	55l	....	....	....	....	....	....	....	....	252.9	254.2	276.9	356.8	338.3	388.2	456.9
Capital Accounts	57a	....	....	....	....	31.8	39.9	45.0	46.5	71.5	44.9	59.2	68.3	73.6	73.2	79.4
Other Items (Net)	57r	....	....	....	....	....	....	....	....	7.6	10.9	63.9	2.1	−18.2	−18.0	−4.2
Interest Rates													*Percent Per Annum*			
Bank Rate *(End of Period)*	60	....	....	....	....	....	9.50	9.50	9.50	9.50	9.50	9.50	9.50	9.50	9.50	9.00
Treasury Bill Rate	60c	....	....	....	....	....	....	....	7.18	7.02	7.44	6.64	5.32	4.92	3.49	3.07
Deposit Rate	60l	....	....	....	....	....	....	....	....	....	....	....	....	....	....	....
Lending Rate	60p	....	....	....	....	....	....	....	....	....	....	....	9.50	9.50	9.50	9.13
Prices													*Index Numbers (1990=100):*			
Consumer Prices	64	....	22.3	23.5	24.6	26.8	28.5	29.8	31.8	33.6	37.9	41.9	43.7	45.0	47.8	52.1
International Transactions													*Millions of Bahamian Dollars*			
Exports	70	19	23	32	52	54	90	267	343	530	1,444	2,508	2,992	3,261	3,058	3,786
Imports, cif	71	107	142	166	180	302	338	511	485	764	1,908	2,697	3,125	3,568	3,150	3,514
Imports, fob	71.v	99	131	154	167	279	313	480	456	718	1,793	2,535	2,937	3,353	2,961	3,303
Balance of Payments													*Millions of US Dollars:*			
Goods: Exports f.o.b.	78aa *d*	....	....	....	....	....	....	....	....	....	....	....	2,716.2	2,661.9	2,214.4	3,601.8
Goods: Imports f.o.b.	78ab *d*	....	....	....	....	....	....	....	....	....	....	....	−2,865.5	−2,841.2	−2,455.0	−3,951.5
Trade Balance	78ac *d*	....	....	....	....	....	....	....	....	....	....	....	−149.3	−179.3	−240.6	−349.7
Services: Credit	78ad *d*	....	....	....	....	....	....	....	....	....	....	....	449.3	497.3	602.2	694.0
Services: Debit	78ae *d*	....	....	....	....	....	....	....	....	....	....	....	−128.0	−155.1	−177.8	−190.9
Balance on Goods and Services	78af *d*	....	....	....	....	....	....	....	....	....	....	....	172.0	162.9	183.8	153.4
Income: Credit	78ag *d*	....	....	....	....	....	....	....	....	....	....	....	4.5	4.0	6.9	10.9
Income: Debit	78ah *d*	....	....	....	....	....	....	....	....	....	....	....	−80.1	−87.6	−134.7	−144.5
Balance on Goods, Serv., & Inc.	78ai *d*	....	....	....	....	....	....	....	....	....	....	....	96.4	79.3	56.0	19.8
Current Transfers, n.i.e.: Credit	78aj *d*	....	....	....	....	....	....	....	....	....	....	....	7.2	7.2	9.0	13.8
Current Transfers: Debit	78ak *d*	....	....	....	....	....	....	....	....	....	....	....	−4.2	−17.6	−21.5	−15.6
Current Account, n.i.e.	78al *d*	....	....	....	....	....	....	....	....	....	....	....	99.4	68.9	43.5	18.0
Capital Account, n.i.e.: Credit	78ba *d*	....	....	....	....	....	....	....	....	....	....	....	....	....	....	....
Capital Account: Debit	78bb *d*	....	....	....	....	....	....	....	....	....	....	....	−14.6	−2.8	−2.2	−2.2
Capital Account, n.i.e.	78bc *d*	....	....	....	....	....	....	....	....	....	....	....	−14.6	−2.8	−2.2	−2.2
Direct Investment Abroad	78bd *d*	....	....	....	....	....	....	....	....	....	....	....	....	....	....	....
Dir. Invest. in Rep. Econ., n.i.e.	78be *d*	....	....	....	....	....	....	....	....	....	....	....	14.6	31.4	−1.1	9.6
Portfolio Investment Assets	78bf *d*	....	....	....	....	....	....	....	....	....	....	....	....	....	....	....
Portfolio Investment Liab., n.i.e.	78bg *d*	....	....	....	....	....	....	....	....	....	....	....	−1.5	6.9	−2.3	−3.2
Other Investment Assets	78bh *d*	....	....	....	....	....	....	....	....	....	....	....	−12.0	9.7	.5	−33.1
Other Investment Liab., n.i.e.	78bi *d*	....	....	....	....	....	....	....	....	....	....	....	−3.5	2.4	−21.9	2.4
Financial Account, n.i.e.	78bj *d*	....	....	....	....	....	....	....	....	....	....	....	−2.4	50.4	−24.8	−24.3
Net Errors and Omissions	78ca *d*	....	....	....	....	....	....	....	....	....	....	....	−88.3	−97.4	−25.5	23.3
Overall Balance	78cb *d*	....	....	....	....	....	....	....	....	....	....	....	−5.9	19.1	−9.0	14.8
Reserves and Related Items	79da *d*	....	....	....	....	....	....	....	....	....	....	....	5.9	−19.1	9.0	−14.8
Reserve Assets	79db *d*	....	....	....	....	....	....	....	....	....	....	....	5.9	−19.1	9.0	−14.8
Use of Fund Credit and Loans	79dc *d*	....	....	....	....	....	....	....	....	....	....	....	—	—	—	—
Liabs.Constit.For.Auth.Reserves	79dd *d*	....	....	....	....	....	....	....	....	....	....	....	....	....	....	....
Exceptional Financing	79de *d*	....	....	....	....	....	....	....	....	....	....	....	—	—	—	—
Government Finance													*Millions of Bahamian Dollars:*			
Deficit (−) or Surplus	80	....	....	....	....	−8.3	−17.5	−9.8	1.5	2.9	−32.8	−14.1	−23.3	−27.7	−33.0	−8.2
Revenue	81	....	....	....	....	74.6	81.3	77.5	97.8	108.8	114.5	118.3	129.3	136.9	164.0	202.1
Expenditure	82	....	....	....	....	78.4	97.2	92.1	97.8	107.8	121.5	127.8	151.5	159.7	185.9	205.1
Lending Minus Repayments	83	....	....	....	....	4.5	1.6	−4.7	−1.6	−2.0	25.9	4.6	1.2	4.9	11.1	5.2
Financing																
Net Borrowing: Domestic	84a	....	....	....	....	11.8	18.2	10.8	−2.9	−17.1	27.1	23.3	25.5	32.0	24.8	34.7
Foreign	85a	....	....	....	....	−.2	−1.8	−2.2	−1.8	10.7	2.9	−5.1	−5.0	3.6	−5.8	−7.7
Use of Cash Balances	87	....	....	....	....	−3.2	1.0	1.2	3.1	3.4	2.9	−4.1	2.8	−7.9	14.0	−18.7
Debt: Domestic	88a	7.6	9.6	11.3	20.2	28.2	39.1	50.0	46.7	38.5	71.8	95.8	123.4	149.2	173.5	213.5
Monetary Authorities	88ab	....	....	....	....	....	....	....	....	.5	9.9	9.8	18.7	12.3	14.9	22.6
Deposit Money Banks	88ac	....	....	....	....	....	....	....	....	34.0	55.5	66.7	76.6	84.5	85.0	88.0
Other Domestic	88ad	....	....	....	....	....	....	....	....	4.0	6.4	19.3	28.1	52.4	73.6	102.9
Debt: Foreign	89a	7.7	25.5	20.8	24.3	24.1	22.3	20.1	18.6	33.5	36.4	31.4	26.4	34.8	29.1	21.3
National Accounts													*Millions of Bahamian Dollars*			
Exports of Goods & Services	90c	....	....	....	....	....	....	....	....	465.8	601.4	617.3	676.8	643.4	779.0	947.4
Government Consumption	91f	....	....	....	....	....	....	....	....	76.8	85.8	86.9	107.0	109.3	128.4	147.2
Gross Fixed Capital Formation	93e	....	....	....	....	....	....	....	....	106.7	99.0	75.4	68.1	89.2	94.4	120.3
Private Consumption	96f	....	....	....	....	....	....	....	....	345.9	400.2	451.1	482.9	521.0	565.9	617.8
Imports of Goods & Services	98c	....	....	....	....	....	....	....	....	−413.0	−564.3	−497.1	−535.9	−407.5	−469.4	−533.8
Gross Domestic Product	99b	....	....	....	....	....	....	....	....	582.2	622.1	733.6	798.9	955.4	1,098.3	1,298.9
													Millions:			
Population	99z	.14	.14	.15	.16	.16	.17	.18	.18	.18	.19	.19	.19	.20	.20	.21

Exchange Rates: On May 25, 1966 the Bahamian dollar, equal to .35 Bahamian pound, was introduced.
International Liquidity: **l** Prior to January 1977, data for *line 1d.d* included small foreign exchange holdings by the government, which were transferred to the Central Bank of The Bahamas at this date.

Bahamas, The

	1980	1981	1982	1983	1984	1985	1986	1987	1988	1989	1990	1991	1992	1993	1994		
End of Period																**Banking Survey**	
	67.8	80.0	110.6	139.7	293.3	303.6	357.2	256.2	144.6	53.2	89.9	153.8	213.0	310.1	348.7	Foreign Assets (Net)	51n
	631.5	685.4	778.7	860.3	886.4	967.1	1,080.3	1,335.4	1,487.0	1,653.2	1,843.7	1,941.8	2,036.5	2,186.2	2,336.7	Domestic Credit	52
	78.6	93.9	105.7	150.3	124.7	117.2	84.0	147.4	206.4	239.6	271.5	313.5	351.2	429.3	405.3	Claims on Central Govt. (Net)	52an
	36.9	22.3	47.3	33.2	24.9	9.6	15.6	27.9	39.9	81.9	106.0	113.0	105.5	88.8	72.9	Claims on Official Entities	52bx
	516.0	569.2	625.7	676.8	736.8	840.3	980.7	1,160.1	1,240.7	1,331.7	1,466.2	1,515.3	1,579.8	1,668.1	1,858.5	Claims on Private Sector	52d
	520.3	583.4	684.7	792.6	857.9	937.9	1,065.6	1,241.3	1,323.6	1,417.2	1,521.4	1,621.3	1,705.9	1,850.1	1,988.3	Liquid Liabilities	55l
	177.0	196.9	215.0	255.9	317.9	326.4	370.3	429.5	389.8	371.5	403.3	443.6	478.3	532.0	547.0	Capital Accounts	57a
	2.0	-14.9	-10.4	-48.5	3.9	6.4	1.7	-79.2	-81.8	-82.2	8.8	30.7	65.3	114.2	150.1	Other Items (Net)	57r
Percent Per Annum																**Interest Rates**	
	11.00	9.00	10.00	9.00	9.50	8.50	7.50	7.50	9.00	9.00	9.00	9.00	7.50	7.00	6.50	Bank Rate *(End of Period)*	60
	7.37	8.89	8.76	9.11	6.88	5.90	3.47	2.40	4.46	5.21	5.85	6.49	5.32	3.96	1.88	Treasury Bill Rate	60c
	6.96	7.48	7.56	7.47	7.44	6.40	5.57	5.50	5.97	6.48	6.57	6.92	6.13	5.19	4.30	Deposit Rate	60l
	10.83	11.00	11.00	11.00	11.00	10.33	9.25	9.00	9.00	9.00	9.00	9.00	8.08	7.46	6.88	Lending Rate	60p
Period Averages																**Prices**	
	58.5	64.9	68.9	71.6	74.4	77.9	82.1	86.8	90.7	95.5	100.0	107.1	113.3	116.3	118.0	Consumer Prices	64
Millions of Bahamian Dollars																**International Transactions**	
	5,009	6,189	4,534	3,970	3,393	2,728	2,701	2,728	2,164	2,786	2,678	1,517	....	....	....	Exports	70
	7,546	7,284	6,349	4,616	4,098	3,078	3,289	3,041	2,263	3,001	2,920	1,801	....	....	....	Imports, cif	71
	7,092	6,846	5,967	4,339	3,851	2,893	3,091	2,858	2,127	2,820	2,744	1,693	....	....	....	Imports, fob	71.v
Minus Sign Indicates Debit																**Balance of Payments**	
	5,030.2	3,694.6	2,579.6	2,693.0	2,461.6	1,527.3	890.4	808.6	702.0	1,129.6	1,250.3	780.0	738.4	697.6	....	Goods: Exports f.o.b.	78aa d
	-5,467.4	-4,171.5	-3,023.4	-3,203.0	-2,983.5	-2,068.8	-1,473.8	-1,461.0	-1,344.4	-1,940.2	-2,041.2	-1,433.1	-1,426.2	-1,457.1	....	Goods: Imports f.o.b.	78ab d
	-437.2	-476.9	-443.8	-510.0	-521.9	-541.5	-583.4	-652.4	-642.4	-810.6	-790.9	-653.1	-687.8	-759.5	....	Trade Balance	78ac d
	783.5	823.8	824.3	935.9	964.7	1,131.3	1,230.5	1,268.7	1,269.5	1,448.3	1,463.6	1,307.6	1,337.9	1,405.2	....	Services: Credit	78ad d
	-226.2	-274.3	-315.9	-329.0	-324.0	-383.2	-417.7	-461.9	-491.2	-525.8	-589.3	-546.2	-521.2	-564.0	....	Services: Debit	78ae d
	120.1	72.6	64.6	96.9	118.8	206.6	229.4	154.4	135.9	111.9	83.4	108.3	128.9	81.7	....	Balance on Goods and Services	78af d
	13.0	17.0	23.8	15.3	18.8	20.4	19.5	18.1	15.3	16.1	15.0	15.1	11.6	9.5	....	Income: Credit	78ag d
	-147.5	-168.9	-155.4	-153.8	-183.9	-201.0	-203.1	-201.4	-182.2	-189.3	-184.3	-229.1	-187.6	-176.4	....	Income: Debit	78ah d
	-14.4	-79.3	-67.0	-41.6	-46.3	26.0	45.8	-28.9	-31.0	-61.3	-85.9	-105.7	-47.1	-85.2	....	Balance on Goods, Serv., & Inc.	78ai d
	19.5	13.3	23.6	19.6	17.5	16.8	16.3	16.7	17.4	21.6	24.7	30.9	31.1	31.5	....	Current Transfers, n.i.e.: Credit	78aj d
	-18.9	-13.6	-17.8	-9.8	-14.0	-14.3	-15.1	-18.6	-28.9	-17.9	-9.9	-8.4	-13.5	-14.4	....	Current Transfers: Debit	78ak d
	-13.8	-79.6	-61.2	-31.8	-42.8	28.5	47.0	-30.8	-42.5	-57.6	-71.1	-83.2	-29.5	-68.1	....	Current Account, n.i.e.	78al d
	—	—	—	—	—	—	—	—	—	—	—	—	—	—	....	Capital Account, n.i.e.: Credit	78ba d
	-2.5	-2.5	-2.0	-2.7	-2.7	-2.5	-1.5	-1.7	-3.0	-2.7	-4.2	-2.9	-4.2	-4.4	....	Capital Account: Debit	78bb d
	-2.5	-2.5	-2.0	-2.7	-2.7	-2.5	-1.5	-1.7	-3.0	-2.7	-4.2	-2.9	-4.2	-4.4	....	Capital Account, n.i.e.	78bc d
	—	—	—	—	—	—	—	—	—	—	—	—	—	—	....	Direct Investment Abroad	78bd d
	4.1	34.4	2.8	-6.0	-4.9	-30.2	-13.2	10.8	36.7	25.0	-17.2	—	7.4	-24.1	....	Dir. Invest. in Rep. Econ., n.i.e.	78be d
	—	—	—	—	—	—	—	—	—	—	—	—	—	—	....	Portfolio Investment Assets	78bf d
	-2.3	-3.0	-3.2	—	—	—	—	—	—	—	—	—	—	—	....	Portfolio Investment Liab., n.i.e.	78bg d
	7.3	17.1	8.5	-19.3	-26.8	24.3	27.0	11.9	39.3	44.6	32.9	11.9	-37.9	1.1	....	Other Investment Assets	78bh d
	7.7	114.2	75.2	25.3	-1.9	-5.6	12.4	-37.6	-2.8	25.2	41.4	165.0	43.4	20.3	....	Other Investment Liab., n.i.e.	78bi d
	16.8	162.7	83.3	—	-33.6	-11.5	26.2	-14.9	73.2	94.8	57.1	176.9	12.9	-2.7	....	Financial Account, n.i.e.	78bj d
	10.2	-75.3	-6.1	45.1	118.2	4.2	-102.5	-12.5	-28.4	-61.1	27.5	-77.8	-7.9	94.2	....	Net Errors and Omissions	78ca d
	10.7	5.3	14.0	10.6	39.1	18.7	-30.8	-59.9	-.7	-26.6	9.3	13.0	-28.7	19.0	....	Overall Balance	78cb d
	-10.7	-5.3	-14.0	-10.6	-39.1	-18.7	30.8	59.9	.7	26.6	-9.3	-13.0	28.7	-19.0	....	Reserves and Related Items	79da d
	-10.7	-5.3	-14.0	-10.6	-39.1	-18.7	30.8	59.9	.7	26.6	-9.3	-13.0	28.7	-19.0	....	Reserve Assets	79db d
	—	—	—	—	—	—	—	—	—	—	—	—	—	—	....	Use of Fund Credit and Loans	79dc d
	—	—	—	—	—	—	—	—	—	—	—	—	—	—	....	Liabs.Constit.For.Auth.Reserves	79dd d
	—	—	—	—	—	—	—	—	—	—	—	—	—	—	....	Exceptional Financing	79de d
Year Ending December 31																**Government Finance**	
	-7.8	-62.2	-78.2	-68.5	-16.4	-28.4	-12.3	-21.4	-76.0	-123.5	-75.8	-132.5	-88.1	-86.6	-23.6	Deficit (-) or Surplus	80
	244.1	282.2	273.5	298.2	333.5	376.8	398.8	436.1	432.6	456.7	497.8	490.4	534.6	536.8	615.7	Revenue	81
	246.9	289.3	302.3	314.3	343.2	406.0	420.1	462.0	513.8	580.8	554.2	584.6	597.8	583.6	602.1	Expenditure	82
	5.1	55.1	49.5	52.4	6.7	-.9	-9.0	-4.5	-5.2	-.6	19.4	38.3	24.9	39.8	37.2	Lending Minus Repayments	83
																Financing	
	15.6	18.0	17.5	52.0	37.2	48.5	-15.5	26.4	82.7	134.0	83.9	157.1	85.0	95.3	51.6	Net Borrowing: Domestic	84a
	-7.5	31.3	65.9	20.0	1.7	-3.6	55.7	-18.5	-18.1	3.2	7.9	4.1	-4.7	-14.6	-10.3	Foreign	85a
	-.3	12.9	-5.1	-3.5	-22.5	-16.6	-27.9	13.5	11.4	-13.7	-16.0	-28.7	7.8	5.9	-17.7	Use of Cash Balances	87
	228.4	235.0	258.1	313.6	328.9	365.7	400.2	419.4	474.0	545.8	643.7	738.1	777.1	954.1	1,032.9	Debt: Domestic	88a
	42.3	35.0	28.4	35.8	43.9	30.4	31.5	53.2	47.1	90.9	112.1	124.3	137.5	115.0	144.8	Monetary Authorities	88ab
	68.2	85.4	97.0	105.2	101.6	100.6	115.4	109.8	130.9	116.5	148.2	175.6	134.3	288.3	271.9	Deposit Money Banks	88ac
	117.9	114.6	132.7	172.6	183.4	234.7	253.3	256.4	296.0	338.4	383.4	438.2	505.3	550.8	616.2	Other Domestic	88ad
	14.7	46.0	93.5	112.9	114.5	112.5	122.5	108.5	100.4	126.0	129.4	133.5	125.2	110.6	100.4	Debt: Foreign	89a
Millions of Bahamian Dollars																**National Accounts**	
	1,156.6	1,200.4	1,189.8	1,238.2	1,293.2	1,511.9	1,605.1	1,773.0	2,100.8	1,423.5	1,516.0	1,416.4	1,404.8	1,358.4	....	Exports of Goods & Services	90c
	173.3	207.3	218.8	250.6	267.6	294.4	306.3	333.8	370.1	409.0	427.9	442.9	447.5	452.3	....	Government Consumption	91f
	172.1	266.2	301.1	311.3	300.8	381.3	419.1	512.7	510.7	712.4	671.2	643.9	634.5	638.9	....	Gross Fixed Capital Formation	93e
	577.7	637.4	713.6	763.1	838.3	897.6	1,015.9	1,137.5	1,126.9	2,301.6	2,323.4	2,380.7	2,268.7	....	....	Private Consumption	96f
	-788.7	-860.4	-935.7	-1,039.7	-1,106.3	-1,239.4	-1,281.2	-1,451.6	-1,557.0	-1,789.4	-1,839.8	-1,761.3	-1,688.6	-1,718.1	....	Imports of Goods & Services	98c
	1,299.9	1,490.9	1,501.8	1,473.9	1,597.4	1,855.4	2,081.7	2,311.7	2,578.9	3,006.4	3,131.2	3,090.3	3,059.1	3,065.1	....	Gross Domestic Product	99b
Midyear Estimates																	
	.21	.21	.22	.22	.23	.23	.23	.24	.25	.25	.26	.26	.26	.27	....	**Population**	99z

Bahrain

419

		1965	1966	1967	1968	1969	1970	1971	1972	1973	1974	1975	1976	1977	1978	1979
Exchange Rates																*SDRs per Dinar:*
Official Rate	ac	....	2.1000	2.1000	2.1000	2.1000	2.1000	2.1000	2.1000	2.1000	2.0691	2.1598	2.1754	2.0807	1.9997	2.0135
																US Dollars per Dinar:
Official Rate	ag	....	2.1000	2.1000	2.1000	2.1000	2.1000	2.2800	2.2800	2.5333	2.5333	2.5284	2.5275	2.5275	2.6052	2.6525
Official Rate	rh	....	2.1000	2.1000	2.1000	2.1000	2.1000	2.1064	2.2800	2.5046	2.5333	2.5284	2.5278	2.5275	2.5809	2.6206
																Index Numbers (1990=100):
Official Rate	ahx	....	79.0	79.0	79.0	79.0	79.0	79.2	85.7	94.2	95.3	95.1	95.0	95.0	97.0	98.5
Nominal Effective Exchange Rate	nec	....	....	....	....	....	....	....	....	....	....	....	....	....	....	100.6
Real Effective Exchange Rate	rec	....	....	....	....	....	....	....	....	....	....	....	....	....	....	179.6
Fund Position																*Millions of SDRs:*
Quota	2f.s	....	....	....	....	....	....	....	10.0	10.0	10.0	10.0	10.0	10.0	20.0	20.0
SDRs	1b.s	....	....	....	....	....	....	....	—	—	—	—	—	—	.1	2.2
Reserve Position in the Fund	1c.s	....	....	....	....	....	....	....	2.5	2.5	5.5	9.6	4.7	4.8	5.8	5.8
International Liquidity													*Millions of US Dollars Unless Otherwise Indicated:*				
Total Reserves minus Gold	11.d	22.7	13.1	20.0	41.7	59.6	62.8	86.0	83.5	64.0	131.3	289.5	436.4	503.9	493.4	613.9
SDRs	1b.d	....	....	....	....	....	....	....	....	....	....	....	—	.1	2.9
Reserve Position in the Fund	1c.d	....	....	....	....	....	....	....	2.7	3.0	6.7	11.2	5.5	5.8	7.5	7.6
Foreign Exchange	1d.d	22.7	13.1	20.0	41.7	59.6	62.8	86.0	80.8	61.0	124.6	278.3	430.9	498.1	485.8	603.4
Monetary Agency	1da d	22.7	13.1	20.0	28.8	35.6	40.1	50.0	54.8	30.0	43.3	148.8	336.4	443.0	434.5	429.3
Government	1db d	—	—	—	12.9	24.0	22.7	36.0	26.0	31.0	81.3	129.5	94.5	55.1	51.3	174.1
Gold (Million Fine Troy Ounces)	1ad	....	.240	.237	.237	.237	.237	.237	.237	.237	.238	.150	.150	.150	.150	.150
Gold (National Valuation)	1and	....	8.4	8.3	8.3	8.3	8.3	9.0	8.2	....	10.1	6.3	6.3	6.3	6.5	6.6
Monetary Authorities: Other Liab.	4..d	....	....	....	....	....	....	....	....	....	—	16.4	122.1	154.4	97.4	8.5
Deposit Money Banks: Assets	7a.d	....	35.4	43.9	52.0	48.4	57.2	87.1	106.6	114.4	250.5	406.0	479.8	566.3	635.1	627.8
of which: Claims on Nonbanks	7ad d	....	....	....	.3	.1	1.0	.6	3.6	35.6	42.3	39.6	56.7	70.4	71.4	134.6
Deposit Money Banks: Liabilities	7b.d	....	1.2	1.9	5.1	12.4	9.4	22.8	39.4	58.4	154.2	328.0	389.9	499.8	499.7	625.4
OBU: Foreign Assets	7k.d	....	....	....	....	....	....	....	....	....	....	1,687	5,568	13,527	20,445	23,074
of which: Claims on Nonbanks	7kd d	....	....	....	....	....	....	....	....	....	....	....	1,734	3,706	6,166	6,688
OBU: Foreign Liabilities	7m.d	....	....	....	....	....	....	....	....	....	....	1,687	5,617	13,561	20,440	23,076
of which: Liab. to Nonbanks	7md d	....	....	....	....	....	....	....	....	....	....	—	598	3,513	4,786	7,009
Monetary Authorities																*Millions of Dinars:*
Foreign Assets	11	10.81	10.23	13.52	23.08	30.92	32.52	39.71	33.04	23.56	55.96	116.72	174.68	201.46	195.03	235.96
Reserve Money	14	7.08	9.91	13.44	16.96	18.59	20.06	22.87	25.32	16.15	19.30	49.20	72.80	69.70	76.00	93.60
of which: Currency Outside DMBs	14a	6.43	9.06	12.70	15.40	17.22	18.86	21.23	23.81	14.91	16.88	24.02	34.22	43.78	44.14	49.90
Foreign Liabilities	16c	—	—	—	—	—	—	—	—	—	—	6.50	48.30	61.10	37.40	3.20
Central Government Deposits	16d	—	—	—	5.38	10.01	9.48	13.80	16.57	13.00	34.86	57.22	44.68	51.16	52.53	111.83
Capital Accounts	17a	—	—	—	—	—	—	—	—	—	3.60	9.70	15.00	28.00	41.60	49.93
Other Items (Net)	17r	3.73	.33	.08	.75	2.32	2.98	3.04	−8.85	−5.59	−1.80	−5.90	−6.10	−8.50	−12.50	−22.60
Deposit Money Banks																*Millions of Dinars:*
Reserves	20	.65	.85	.73	1.55	1.37	1.20	1.64	1.51	1.24	2.42	25.25	38.46	25.36	33.94	36.89
Foreign Assets	21	11.94	16.84	20.92	24.75	23.05	27.23	38.18	46.76	45.15	98.88	160.59	189.85	224.05	243.79	236.67
Claims on Central Government	22a	—	—	—	—	.30	—	1.90	9.10	2.90	1.13	1.34	3.58	9.17	23.76	26.77
Claims on Private Sector	22d	14.78	10.03	12.11	18.14	23.55	24.73	37.57	53.13	76.36	120.87	160.76	267.90	310.76	325.44	375.84
Demand Deposits	24	13.95	14.78	15.66	19.40	17.21	19.09	27.35	31.40	44.46	44.43	53.75	93.72	108.71	127.20	136.21
Time and Savings Deposits	25	5.86	8.45	8.72	9.14	14.00	18.49	24.56	32.67	40.27	84.52	106.45	175.89	203.01	231.00	225.76
Foreign Liabilities	26c	.43	.57	.89	2.43	5.89	4.50	10.01	17.26	23.05	60.85	129.74	154.24	197.75	191.80	235.79
Central Government Deposits	26d	6.10	2.04	7.90	11.69	8.96	8.23	11.78	13.67	11.30	32.05	50.51	68.67	49.02	66.87	50.77
Capital Accounts	27a	.76	.85	.98	.95	1.46	1.20	1.96	3.45	6.21	7.61	9.39	14.17	21.50	24.32	34.66
Other Items (Net)	27r	.28	1.04	−.39	.84	.75	1.66	3.64	12.05	.37	−6.16	−1.89	−6.92	−10.66	−14.27	−7.02
Monetary Survey																*Millions of Dinars:*
Foreign Assets (Net)	31n	22.32	26.51	33.55	45.41	48.08	55.26	67.88	62.55	45.66	93.99	141.07	161.98	166.65	209.63	233.64
Domestic Credit	32	8.68	7.99	4.20	1.07	4.88	7.02	13.89	31.99	54.96	55.10	54.37	158.12	219.76	229.79	240.01
Claims on Central Govt. (Net)	32an	−6.10	−2.04	−7.90	−17.07	−18.67	−17.71	−23.68	−21.14	−21.40	−65.77	−106.39	−109.77	−91.01	−95.65	−135.83
Claims on Private Sector	32d	14.78	10.03	12.11	18.14	23.55	24.73	37.57	53.13	76.36	120.87	160.76	267.90	310.76	325.44	375.84
Money	34	20.38	23.83	28.36	34.80	34.43	37.95	48.57	55.22	59.37	61.31	77.77	127.94	152.49	171.34	186.11
Quasi-Money	35	5.86	8.45	8.72	9.14	14.00	18.49	24.56	32.67	40.27	84.52	106.45	175.89	203.01	231.00	225.76
Other Items (Net)	37r	4.77	2.21	.67	2.53	4.53	5.84	8.64	6.65	.99	3.25	11.22	16.27	30.91	37.08	61.78
Money plus Quasi-Money	35l	26.24	32.28	37.08	43.94	48.43	56.44	73.13	87.88	99.64	145.83	184.22	303.83	355.50	402.35	411.87
Interest Rates																*Percent Per Annum*
Money Market Rate	60b	....	....	....	....	....	....	....	....	....	....	....	....	....	....	....
Treasury Bill Rate	60c	....	....	....	....	....	....	....	....	....	....	....	....	....	....	....
Deposit Rate	60l	....	....	....	....	....	....	....	....	....	....	....	6.5	6.5	6.5	6.8
Lending Rate	60p	....	....	....	....	....	....	....	....	....	....	....	....	....	....	....
Prices and Production																*Index Numbers (1990=100):*
Consumer Prices	64	22.9	23.4	24.4	25.2	25.1	25.5	27.0	28.4	32.5	40.4	46.9	57.5	67.6	78.3	80.0
Crude Petr. Prod.(1985=100)	66aa	72.3	68.8	79.8	94.8	97.2	101.3	105.0	103.7	108.7	116.4	80.2	99.3	109.0	111.2	105.7
Refined Petroleum Production	66ab	74.3	76.5	92.7	87.9	91.6	101.8	98.7	91.5	94.1	96.1	83.9	85.6	102.2	97.1	98.0

Bahrain

	1980	1981	1982	1983	1984	1985	1986	1987	1988	1989	1990	1991	1992	1993	1994		
End of Period																**Exchange Rates**	
	2.0853	2.2850	2.4110	2.5403	2.7133	2.4213	2.1743	1.8747	1.9764	2.0238	1.8695	1.8593	1.9343	1.9363	1.8218	Official Rate	ac
End of Period (ag) Period Average (rh)																	
	2.6596	2.6596	2.6596	2.6596	2.6596	2.6596	2.6596	2.6596	2.6596	2.6596	2.6596	2.6596	2.6596	2.6596	2.6596	Official Rate	ag
	2.6525	2.6596	2.6596	2.6596	2.6596	2.6596	2.6596	2.6596	2.6596	2.6596	2.6596	2.6596	2.6596	2.6596	2.6596	Official Rate	rh
Period Averages																	
	99.7	100.0	100.0	100.0	100.0	100.0	100.0	100.0	100.0	100.0	100.0	100.0	100.0	100.0	100.0	Official Rate	ah x
	101.1	110.1	120.8	126.8	134.3	138.8	118.0	106.3	100.3	104.5	100.0	99.3	97.1	100.4	97.5	Nominal Effective Exchange Rate	ne c
	130.3	144.1	161.4	167.4	171.3	166.4	135.6	117.2	107.7	108.9	100.0	95.9	90.8	94.1	90.1	Real Effective Exchange Rate	re c
End of Period																**Fund Position**	
	30.0	30.0	30.0	48.9	48.9	48.9	48.9	48.9	48.9	48.9	48.9	48.9	48.9	82.8	82.8	Quota	2f. s
	1.8	5.2	14.0	12.2	13.1	13.6	14.1	14.6	15.1	15.9	16.9	17.8	18.7	10.8	11.0	SDRs	1b. s
	8.5	8.9	12.5	21.4	23.1	24.6	26.00	27.3	27.7	29.6	28.0	29.6	31.1	40.9	42.2	Reserve Position in the Fund	1c. s
End of Period																**International Liquidity**	
	953.4	1,544.1	1,534.8	1,426.4	1,302.4	1,659.7	1,489.4	1,148.5	1,251.7	1,050.0	1,234.9	1,514.6	1,398.5	1,302.2	1,169.7	Total Reserves minus Gold	1l. d
	2.2	6.1	15.4	12.8	12.8	15.0	17.3	20.7	20.4	20.9	24.0	25.5	25.7	14.8	16.1	SDRs	1b. d
	10.9	10.4	13.8	22.4	22.6	27.0	31.8	38.7	37.3	38.9	39.8	42.4	42.7	56.2	61.6	Reserve Position in the Fund	1c. d
	940.3	1,527.7	1,505.6	1,391.2	1,267.0	1,617.7	1,440.3	1,089.1	1,194.0	990.3	1,171.1	1,446.7	1,330.0	1,231.2	1,092.0	Foreign Exchange	1d. d
	544.0	812.4	768.2	762.3	619.4	774.0	740.3	923.5	692.2	693.7	922.2	1,196.3	1,079.6	980.4	841.5	Monetary Agency	1da d
	396.3	715.3	737.4	628.9	647.6	843.7	700.0	165.6	501.8	296.6	248.9	250.4	250.4	250.8	250.4	Government	1db d
	.150	.150	.150	.150	.150	.150	.150	.150	.150	.150	.150	.150	.150	.150	.150	Gold (Million Fine Troy Ounces)	1ad
	6.6	6.6	6.6	6.6	6.6	6.6	6.6	6.6	6.6	6.6	6.6	6.6	6.6	6.6	6.6	Gold (National Valuation)	1an d
	101.1	48.4	21.8	43.1	3.2	27.5	25.4	—	74.7	116.3	16.4	16.9	48.8	—	—	Monetary Authorities: Other Liab.	4..d
	851.0	912.6	952.3	1,250.2	1,159.1	1,560.6	1,847.4	1,846.7	2,276.3	3,113.0	2,505.1	2,844.5	2,672.6	3,034.3	3,732.9	Deposit Money Banks: Assets	7a. d
	116.2	69.2	100.9	120.3	83.9	121.0	102.4	73.1	62.7	115.9	94.0	201.8	303.5	446.1	529.7	of which: Claims on Nonbanks	7ad d
	627.7	326.7	333.0	398.7	279.2	339.5	403.2	390.2	425.9	867.5	762.8	759.9	888.2	1,219.4	1,674.3	Deposit Money Banks: Liabilities	7b. d
	30,555	41,819	48,890	53,361	53,861	49,148	49,069	57,879	62,942	67,355	56,806	51,187	67,142	57,673	62,363	OBU: Foreign Assets	7k. d
	8,493	11,242	14,316	15,977	18,392	15,873	13,862	13,097	12,206	11,866	9,405	9,796	11,304	16,853	21,369	of which: Claims on Nonbanks	7kd d
	30,349	41,116	48,275	51,864	53,010	47,939	47,720	56,828	61,613	66,614	56,888	50,585	66,569	57,180	61,875	OBU: Foreign Liabilities	7m. d
	8,530	11,968	13,698	14,734	14,872	13,097	13,072	15,207	19,455	22,373	17,276	16,853	15,907	19,330	24,540	of which: Liab. to Nonbanks	7md d
End of Period																**Monetary Authorities**	
	399.33	601.04	589.37	556.05	536.85	649.79	600.18	470.47	529.62	547.80	473.81	579.84	548.02	493.35	499.48	Foreign Assets	11
	91.20	105.00	125.80	124.38	116.76	136.00	128.53	142.26	133.50	144.56	158.19	151.18	154.58	162.96	163.99	Reserve Money	14
	58.32	63.35	70.46	73.53	78.17	78.97	79.98	84.06	84.37	84.77	105.25	99.01	99.86	103.81	105.51	of which: Currency Outside DMBs	14a
	38.00	18.20	8.20	16.20	1.19	10.33	9.54	—	28.09	43.73	6.15	6.37	18.36	—	—	Foreign Liabilities	16c
	220.74	419.43	356.80	317.88	350.50	386.82	335.65	174.40	249.55	246.57	141.23	185.41	263.29	160.08	173.06	Central Government Deposits	16d
	61.99	66.51	86.17	92.46	100.60	134.40	151.12	167.77	166.55	170.41	183.85	200.26	205.84	220.85	218.75	Capital Accounts	17a
	-12.60	-8.10	12.40	5.13	-32.20	-17.75	-24.66	-13.96	-48.29	-57.48	-15.61	36.62	-94.06	-50.54	-56.32	Other Items (Net)	17r
End of Period																**Deposit Money Banks**	
	37.76	40.81	53.93	36.26	39.99	56.47	47.39	54.07	48.65	53.46	196.71	141.51	116.55	73.22	66.32	Reserves	20
	319.96	343.12	358.07	470.05	435.82	586.79	694.62	694.34	855.88	1,170.47	941.90	1,069.52	1,004.90	1,140.91	1,403.57	Foreign Assets	21
	27.16	13.77	26.22	33.68	97.91	89.17	126.55	253.00	114.92	127.76	161.21	137.93	139.64	133.08	137.52	Claims on Central Government	22a
	434.89	487.48	544.64	606.88	640.20	598.43	566.09	498.02	491.64	482.37	474.61	457.30	514.81	656.40	745.46	Claims on Private Sector	22d
	133.92	185.42	196.48	176.47	161.13	164.17	155.69	162.61	154.51	149.91	153.30	205.85	252.01	261.14	239.21	Demand Deposits	24
	331.83	481.78	513.28	593.12	588.47	660.17	649.50	721.78	768.72	817.76	672.18	816.89	815.62	866.49	962.66	Time and Savings Deposits	25
	236.01	122.84	125.21	149.80	104.99	127.65	151.62	146.73	160.13	326.19	286.82	285.73	333.98	458.49	629.52	Foreign Liabilities	26c
	84.96	59.88	58.91	114.10	240.48	242.62	270.82	318.62	334.55	448.13	511.12	461.01	362.32	372.74	455.59	Central Government Deposits	26d
	42.57	62.73	122.28	137.59	130.89	167.79	252.73	201.92	172.34	169.48	132.81	111.88	155.69	169.10	194.58	Capital Accounts	27a
	-9.52	-27.47	-33.30	-24.29	-12.04	-31.53	-45.70	-52.22	-79.17	-77.40	18.19	-75.10	-143.71	-124.35	-128.67	Other Items (Net)	27r
End of Period																**Monetary Survey**	
	445.28	803.13	814.04	860.01	866.49	1,098.61	1,133.64	1,018.09	1,197.28	1,348.35	1,122.74	1,357.27	1,200.58	1,175.77	1,273.53	Foreign Assets (Net)	31n
	156.35	21.93	155.14	208.57	147.13	58.16	86.17	258.00	22.46	-84.57	-16.53	-51.20	28.84	256.66	254.34	Domestic Credit	32
	-278.54	-465.54	-389.50	-398.30	-493.07	-540.27	-479.92	-240.02	-469.18	-566.94	-491.15	-508.50	-485.97	-399.74	-491.13	Claims on Central Govt. (Net)	32an
	434.89	487.48	544.64	606.88	640.20	598.43	566.09	498.02	491.64	482.37	474.61	457.30	514.81	656.40	745.46	Claims on Private Sector	32d
	192.24	248.76	266.93	250.00	239.29	243.14	235.67	246.67	238.88	234.67	258.56	304.86	351.87	364.95	344.72	Money	34
	331.83	481.78	513.28	593.12	588.47	660.17	649.50	721.78	768.72	817.76	672.18	816.89	815.62	866.49	962.66	Quasi-Money	35
	77.57	94.52	188.97	225.47	185.86	253.46	334.65	307.64	212.13	211.35	175.47	184.32	61.93	200.98	220.49	Other Items (Net)	37r
	524.06	730.54	780.21	843.11	827.76	903.31	885.17	968.45	1,007.60	1,052.43	930.74	1,121.74	1,167.49	1,231.45	1,307.38	Money plus Quasi-Money	35l
Percent Per Annum																**Interest Rates**	
	....	....	....	....	....	....	7.2	7.1	8.0	9.2	8.5	6.3	4.0	3.5	5.2	Money Market Rate	60b
	....	....	....	....	....	....	....	6.4	7.4	9.1	....	5.9	3.8	3.3	4.8	Treasury Bill Rate	60c
	7.9	9.0	8.6	7.0	7.0	6.7	5.6	5.0	5.5	7.3	....	....	....	....	....	Deposit Rate	60l
	....	....	....	....	....	....	9.0	7.5	7.8	....	....	....	....	....	....	Lending Rate	60p
Period Averages																**Prices and Production**	
	83.1	92.6	100.8	103.8	I 104.1	101.4	99.1	97.3	97.6	99.1	100.0	100.8	100.6	103.1	104.0	Consumer Prices	64
	93.4	88.5	81.2	83.9	88.5	100.0	89.0	88.4	89.5	....	....	....	....	....	....	Crude Petr. Prod.(1985=100)	66aa
	96.4	103.0	77.9	70.1	80.7	74.5	98.4	97.6	97.1	97.6	100.0	102.8	103.3	98.7	99.3	Refined Petroleum Production	66ab

Bahrain

419

		1965	1966	1967	1968	1969	1970	1971	1972	1973	1974	1975	1976	1977	1978	1979
International Transactions																*Millions of Dinars*
Exports	70	....	89.2	100.4	100.5	107.6	103.7	125.8	152.4	191.5	502.0	475.8	599.8	730.1	733.5	948.0
Imports, cif	71	....	83.8	98.1	91.9	99.4	117.7	144.0	162.9	208.1	443.8	473.8	660.4	802.7	792.3	945.3
Imports, fob	71.v	....	74.8	87.6	82.1	88.8	105.1	128.6	145.4	185.8	396.2	413.8	576.7	701.0	713.7	851.6
Balance of Payments																*Millions of US Dollars:*
Goods: Exports f.o.b.	78aa d	....	....	....	....	....	....	....	....	....	....	1,203.0	1,518.0	1,848.9	1,891.8	2,499.1
Goods: Imports f.o.b.	78ab d	....	....	....	....	....	....	....	....	....	....	−1,090.0	−1,510.1	−1,837.0	−1,873.3	−2,094.8
Trade Balance	78ac d	....	....	....	....	....	....	....	....	....	....	113.0	7.8	11.9	18.6	404.3
Services: Credit	78ad d	....	....	....	....	....	....	....	....	....	....	156.3	201.5	255.8	364.2	313.7
Services: Debit	78ae d	....	....	....	....	....	....	....	....	....	....	−179.3	−243.2	−296.2	−342.8	−369.7
Balance on Goods and Services	78af d	....	....	....	....	....	....	....	....	....	....	90.0	−33.9	−28.6	40.0	348.3
Income: Credit	78ag d	....	....	....	....	....	....	....	....	....	....	45.5	66.7	76.3	106.9	112.2
Income: Debit	78ah d	....	....	....	....	....	....	....	....	....	....	−262.2	−309.4	−369.5	−494.0	−687.6
Balance on Goods, Serv., & Inc.	78ai d	....	....	....	....	....	....	....	....	....	....	−126.7	−276.5	−321.7	−347.1	−227.2
Current Transfers, n.i.e.: Credit	78aj d	....	....	....	....	....	....	....	....	....	....	—	1.3	100.8	94.7	98.0
Current Transfers: Debit	78ak d	....	....	....	....	....	....	....	....	....	....	−76.4	−84.9	−103.1	−135.2	−93.5
Current Account, n.i.e.	78al d	....	....	....	....	....	....	....	....	....	....	−203.0	−360.2	−324.0	−387.7	−222.7
Capital Account, n.i.e.: Credit	78ha d	....	....	....	....	....	....	....	....	....	....	—	—	—	—	—
Capital Account: Debit	78bb d	....	....	....	....	....	....	....	....	....	....	—	—	—	—	—
Capital Account, n.i.e.	78bc d	....	....	....	....	....	....	....	....	....	....	—	—	—	—	—
Direct Investment Abroad	78bd d	....	....	....	....	....	....	....	....	....	....	—	—	—	—	—
Dir. Invest. in Rep. Econ., n.i.e.	78be d	....	....	....	....	....	....	....	....	....	....	—	—	—	23.0	145.2
Portfolio Investment Assets	78bf d	....	....	....	....	....	....	....	....	....	....	—	—	—	−145.3	−83.6
Portfolio Investment Liab., n.i.e.	78bg d	....	....	....	....	....	....	....	....	....	....	96.1	139.0	195.1	112.0	42.2
Other Investment Assets	78bh d	....	....	....	....	....	....	....	....	....	....	−164.1	−98.6	−120.8	−76.7	−6.8
Other Investment Liab., n.i.e.	78bi d	....	....	....	....	....	....	....	....	....	....	217.7	313.2	387.0	83.6	−61.3
Financial Account, n.i.e.	78bj d	....	....	....	....	....	....	....	....	....	....	149.7	353.6	461.3	−3.4	35.6
Net Errors and Omissions	78ca d	....	....	....	....	....	....	....	....	....	....	222.3	153.2	−70.0	372.8	308.7
Overall Balance	78cb d	....	....	....	....	....	....	....	....	....	....	168.9	146.6	67.3	−18.2	121.6
Reserves and Related Items	79da d	....	....	....	....	....	....	....	....	....	....	−168.9	−146.6	−67.3	18.2	−121.6
Reserve Assets	79db d	....	....	....	....	....	....	....	....	....	....	−168.9	−146.6	−67.3	18.0	−123.2
Use of Fund Credit and Loans	79dc d	....	....	....	....	....	....	....	....	....	....	—	—	—	—	—
Liabs.Constit.For.Auth.Reserves	79dd d	....	....	....	....	....	....	....	....	....	....	—	—	—	.3	1.6
Exceptional Financing	79de d	....	....	....	....	....	....	....	....	....	....	....	....	....	....	....
Government Finance																*Millions of Dinars:*
Deficit (−) or Surplus	80	....	....	....	....	....	....	....	....	....	39.6	5.5	−36.2	−12.9	−30.6	22.1
Revenue	81	....	....	....	....	....	....	....	....	....	115.3	129.0	186.4	227.4	247.5	277.9
Grants Received	81z	....	....	....	....	....	....	....	....	....	2.2	—	.3	27.7	26.4	26.4
Expenditure	82	....	....	....	....	....	....	....	....	....	67.0	112.3	190.9	242.5	285.3	254.5
Lending Minus Repayments	83	....	....	....	....	....	....	....	....	....	10.9	11.2	32.0	25.5	19.2	27.7
Financing																
Total Financing	80h	....	....	....	....	....	....	....	....	....	−39.6	−5.5	36.2	12.9	30.6	−22.1
Domestic	84a	....	....	....	....	....	....	....	....	....	−45.2	−7.9	26.2	10.4	−.7	14.2
Foreign	85a	....	....	....	....	....	....	....	....	....	5.6	2.4	10.0	2.5	31.3	−36.3
Debt: Domestic	88a	....	....	....	....	....	....	....	....	....	—	—	—	—	20.0	20.0
Foreign	89a	....	....	....	....	....	....	....	....	4.2	9.7	12.1	22.1	24.6	54.5	64.6
National Accounts																*Millions of Dinars*
Exports of Goods & Services	90c	....	....	....	....	....	....	....	....	....	....	531.5	674.0	817.0	826.7	1,050.7
Government Consumption	91f	....	....	....	....	....	....	....	....	....	....	64.6	85.2	111.1	132.3	152.1
Gross Fixed Capital Formation	93e	....	....	....	....	....	....	....	....	....	....	129.1	249.3	349.6	359.5	329.8
Increase/Decrease(−) in Stocks	93i	....	....	....	....	....	....	....	....	....	....	26	18	9	60	92
Private Consumption	96f	....	....	....	....	....	....	....	....	....	....	170.8	262.7	336.7	390.6	404.0
Imports of Goods & Services	98c	....	....	....	....	....	....	....	....	....	....	−495.7	−695.4	−853.7	−861.0	−1,010.6
Gross Domestic Product	99b	....	....	....	....	....	....	....	....	....	....	425.9	593.5	770.0	907.6	1,018.2
Net Factor Inc/Pmts(−) Abroad	98.n	....	....	....	....	....	....	....	....	....	....	....	....	....	....	....
Gross Nat'l Expenditure = GNP	99a	....	....	....	....	....	....	....	....	....	....	....	....	....	....	....
Nat'l Income, Market Prices	99e	....	....	....	....	....	....	....	....	....	....	....	....	....	....	....
Gross Dom. Prod. 1990 Prices	99b.p	....	....	....	....	....	....	....	....	....	....	843.5	1,043.7	1,197.2	1,294.4	1,280.0
GDP Deflator (1990=100)	99bi p	....	....	....	....	....	....	....	....	....	....	50.5	56.9	64.3	70.1	79.5
																Millions:
Population	99z	.18	.19	.19	.20	.21	.22	.22	.23	.24	.26	.26	.26	.30	.32	.33

Bahrain

	1980	1981	1982	1983	1984	1985	1986	1987	1988	1989	1990	1991	1992	1993	1994		
Millions of Dinars																**International Transactions**	
	1,355.0	1,634.6	1,424.8	1,202.8	1,204.7	1,089.2	827.0	913.5	906.7	1,064.5	1,414.0	1,320.9	1,302.6	1,395.0	1,298.8	Exports	70
	1,313.1	1,550.6	1,358.9	1,256.6	1,308.3	1,168.1	904.3	1,020.3	975.1	1,178.2	1,395.6	1,547.3	1,602.8	1,450.6	1,405.0	Imports, cif	71
	1,183.0	1,397.0	1,224.3	1,132.1	1,178.6	1,052.3	814.7	919.2	878.5	1,061.4	1,257.3	1,394.0	1,444.0	1,306.9	1,265.8	Imports, fob	71.v
Minus Sign Indicates Debit																**Balance of Payments**	
	3,433.2	4,177.1	3,695.0	3,119.4	3,204.0	2,896.8	2,199.5	2,429.5	2,411.4	2,831.1	3,760.6	3,513.0	3,417.3	....	....	Goods: Exports f.o.b.	78aa d
	−2,987.5	−3,559.3	−3,167.8	−2,935.6	−3,131.6	−2,796.0	−2,164.6	−2,442.3	−2,334.0	−2,820.2	−3,339.9	−3,703.5	−3,730.3	....	....	Goods: Imports f.o.b.	78ab d
	445.6	617.8	527.2	183.8	72.3	100.8	34.8	−12.8	77.4	10.9	420.7	−190.4	−313.0	....	....	Trade Balance	78ac d
	332.9	360.9	567.6	366.8	813.8	911.4	764.4	864.1	899.5	872.9	873.7	933.8	1,018.9	....	....	Services: Credit	78ad d
	−473.7	−610.1	−729.8	−499.5	−555.1	−488.6	−327.1	−525.0	−529.3	−556.4	−651.1	−708.2	−1,010.1	....	....	Services: Debit	78ae d
	304.8	368.6	364.9	51.1	331.1	523.7	472.1	326.3	447.6	327.4	643.4	35.1	−304.3	....	....	Balance on Goods and Services	78af d
	314.1	517.8	489.9	415.7	335.6	322.6	277.9	282.2	263.0	377.7	322.3	282.7	245.2	....	....	Income: Credit	78ag d
	−522.3	−544.7	−501.3	−404.5	−447.3	−692.8	−675.0	−678.5	−694.1	−738.0	−906.6	−912.2	−763.6	....	....	Income: Debit	78ah d
	96.6	341.8	353.5	62.2	219.4	153.5	75.0	−69.9	16.5	−33.0	59.0	−594.4	−822.6	....	....	Balance on Goods, Serv., & Inc.	78ai d
	183.6	194.4	189.6	142.6	124.5	120.2	120.7	113.3	368.1	102.1	458.8	101.9	100.0	....	....	Current Transfers, n.i.e.: Credit	78aj d
	−95.8	−106.6	−117.6	−102.1	−125.5	−234.8	−264.6	−243.6	−194.7	−198.9	−272.3	−303.5	−270.7	....	....	Current Transfers: Debit	78ak d
	184.4	429.5	425.6	102.7	218.4	38.8	−68.9	−200.3	189.9	−129.8	245.5	−796.0	−993.4	....	....	Current Account, n.i.e.	78al d
	—	—	—	—	—	—	—	—	—	—	—	—	—	....	....	Capital Account: Credit	78ba d
	—	—	—	—	—	—	—	—	—	—	—	—	—	....	....	Capital Account: Debit	78bb d
	—	—	—	—	—	—	—	—	—	—	—	—	—	....	....	Capital Account, n.i.e.	78bc d
	−418.0	—	28.5	64.1	140.7	101.3	−31.9	−35.9	222.1	180.9	−3.5	−6.9	−8.5	....	....	Direct Investment Abroad	78bd d
	−8.8	−16.8	−16.0	−47.9	—	—	—	—	—	—	−80.6	−34.6	—	....	....	Dir. Invest. in Rep. Econ., n.i.e.	78be d
	121.5	69.9	—	—	—	—	—	—	—	—	—	—	—	....	....	Portfolio Investment Assets	78bf d
	—	—	—	—	—	—	—	—	—	—	—	—	—	....	....	Portfolio Investment Liab., n.i.e.	78bg d
	−250.4	−88.6	−127.1	−314.6	−17.6	−410.6	−298.9	−7.2	−437.0	−916.8	601.6	−345.2	165.4	....	....	Other Investment Assets	78bh d
	318.0	−467.6	43.6	132.4	−158.8	−138.3	257.2	−10.6	.5	470.2	−61.2	39.6	209.3	....	....	Other Investment Liab., n.i.e.	78bi d
	−237.7	−502.9	−71.0	−166.0	−35.6	−447.6	−73.7	−53.7	−214.4	−265.7	456.4	−347.1	366.2	....	....	Financial Account, n.i.e.	78bj d
	396.3	662.7	−358.9	−45.2	−192.8	766.2	−33.2	−88.7	117.0	207.0	−519.6	1,424.7	545.3	....	....	Net Errors and Omissions	78ca d
	343.0	589.3	−4.4	−108.5	−10.1	357.4	−175.7	−342.7	92.5	−188.5	182.2	281.6	−81.9	....	....	Overall Balance	78cb d
	−343.0	−589.3	4.4	108.5	10.1	−357.4	175.7	342.7	−92.5	188.5	−182.2	−281.6	81.9	....	....	Reserves and Related Items	79da d
	−342.0	−589.3	4.4	108.5	10.1	−357.4	175.7	342.7	−92.5	188.5	−182.2	−281.6	81.9	....	....	Reserve Assets	79db d
	−1.1	—	—	—	—	—	—	—	—	—	—	—	—	....	....	Use of Fund Credit and Loans	79dc d
	....	....	....	....	....	....	....	....	....	....	....	....	....	....	....	Liabs.Constit.For.Auth.Reserves	79dd d
	....	....	....	....	....	....	....	....	....	....	....	....	....	....	....	Exceptional Financing	79de d
Year Ending December 31																**Government Finance**	
	68.0	110.8	32.1	−96.2	−23.0	13.7	−51.9	−122.2	49.1	−115.8	−103.1	−67.6	−115.1	−1.9	....	Deficit (−) or Surplus	80
	388.9	478.3	497.8	443.5	485.4	503.8	422.2	376.4	360.6	403.4	468.9	471.2	465.4	545.7	....	Revenue	81
	56.8	58.3	56.4	47.0	37.6	37.6	37.6	37.6	37.6	37.6	37.6	26.3	37.6	37.6	18.8	Grants Received	81z
	317.2	380.2	473.7	535.1	538.6	508.5	495.1	418.0	445.5	467.5	505.1	503.6	548.7	595.1	....	Expenditure	82
	60.5	45.6	48.4	51.6	7.4	19.2	16.6	118.2	−96.4	89.3	93.2	72.8	69.4	−28.7	....	Lending Minus Repayments	83
																Financing	
	−68.0	−110.8	−32.1	96.2	23.0	−13.7	51.9	122.2	−49.1	115.8	103.1	67.6	115.1	1.9	....	Total Financing	80h
	3.5	5.6	21.4	52.0	9.5	37.5	−3.6	−73.4	80.3	40.3	−35.9	71.7	114.1	2.3	....	Domestic	84a
	−71.5	−116.4	−53.5	44.2	13.5	−51.2	55.5	195.6	−129.4	75.5	139.0	−4.1	1.0	−.4	....	Foreign	85a
	20.0	20.0	20.0	30.0	30.0	30.0	....	102.5	193.8	215.4	84.9	233.5	328.5	323.6	....	Debt: Domestic	88a
	77.1	81.3	91.0	87.3	93.8	71.1	....	59.9	60.7	58.1	53.9	50.8	52.0	54.7	....	Foreign	89a
Millions of Dinars																**National Accounts**	
	1,421.1	1,714.0	1,621.0	1,344.2	1,455.0	1,397.0	1,133.8	1,216.5	1,228.6	1,341.7	1,742.4	....	....	....	....	Exports of Goods & Services	90c
	150.9	188.6	233.3	254.5	302.2	312.8	312.4	310.9	339.8	356.7	378.7	....	....	....	....	Government Consumption	91f
	356.9	380.5	451.9	576.1	647.0	487.8	390.8	359.2	344.8	386.0	400.8	....	....	....	....	Gross Fixed Capital Formation	93e
	164	160	57	42	−43	−10	−65	9	−15	29	59	....	....	....	....	Increase/Decrease(−) in Stocks	93i
	370.3	427.7	472.9	481.6	499.2	438.3	399.8	389.5	440.7	505.0	526.2	....	....	....	....	Private Consumption	96f
	−1,304.8	−1,567.3	−1,465.5	−1,294.4	−1,381.3	−1,233.6	−973.4	−1,093.1	−1,076.7	−1,270.9	−1,500.9	....	....	....	....	Imports of Goods & Services	98c
	1,158.1	1,303.9	1,370.8	1,404.4	1,468.5	1,392.9	1,198.2	1,191.8	1,262.9	1,347.5	1,467.5	....	....	....	....	Gross Domestic Product	99b
	−46.6	−15.0	−38.0	−60.8	−57.5	−109.7	−113.1	−107.7	−168.0	−98.7	−128.7	....	....	....	....	Net Factor Inc/Pmts(−) Abroad	98.n
	1,111.5	1,288.9	1,332.8	1,343.6	1,411.0	1,283.2	1,085.1	1,084.1	1,095.3	1,248.8	1,338.8	....	....	....	....	Gross Nat'l Expenditure = GNP	99a
	991.0	1,153.4	1,183.8	1,176.8	1,212.0	1,079.3	875.1	875.3	869.0	1,024.2	1,109.5	....	....	....	....	Nat'l Income, Market Prices	99e
	1,364.0	1,273.1	1,177.8	1,277.6	1,340.2	1,312.8	1,333.9	1,317.5	1,414.3	1,449.7	1,467.5	....	....	....	....	Gross Dom. Prod. 1990 Prices	99b.p
	84.9	102.4	116.4	109.9	109.6	106.1	89.8	90.5	89.3	93.0	100.0	....	....	....	....	GDP Deflator (1990=100)	99bi p
Midyear Estimates																	
	.34	.35	.37	.39	.39	.41	.42	.44	.45	.47	.49	.50	.52	.54	....	**Population**	99z

Bangladesh
513

		1965	1966	1967	1968	1969	1970	1971	1972	1973	1974	1975	1976	1977	1978	1979
Exchange Rates																
															Taka per SDR:	
Official Rate......aa= ......wa		....	....	....	....	....	....	8.068	8.770	9.849	9.888	17.356	17.373	17.486	19.456	20.607
															Taka per US Dollar:	
Official Rate......ae= ......we		....	....	....	....	....	....	7.431	8.078	8.164	8.077	14.826	14.953	14.396	14.934	15.643
Official Rate......rf= ......wf		....	....	....	....	....	....	7.761	7.594	7.742	8.113	12.019	15.347	15.375	15.016	15.552
Fund Position															Millions of SDRs:	
Quota .... 2f. s		....	....	....	....	....	....	....	125.0	125.0	125.0	125.0	125.0	125.0	152.0	152.0
SDRs .... 1b. s		....	....	....	....	....	....	....	—	—	—	15.4	16.1	3.9	.1	9.2
Reserve Position in the Fund ...... 1c. s		....	....	....	....	....	....	....	2.0	1.2	—	—	—	—	—	—
Total Fund Cred.&Loans Outstg. .. 2tl		....	....	....	....	....	....	....	62.5	62.5	133.3	171.6	235.8	207.8	229.4	262.3
International Liquidity											Millions of US Dollars Unless Otherwise Indicated:					
Total Reserves minus Gold .... 1l. d		....	....	....	....	....	....	....	270.5	143.2	138.2	148.3	288.9	232.7	315.2	386.3
SDRs .... 1b. d		....	....	....	....	....	....	....	—	—	—	18.1	18.7	4.8	.1	12.1
Reserve Position in the Fund ...... 1c. d		....	....	....	....	....	....	....	2.2	1.5	—	—	—	—	—	—
Foreign Exchange .... 1d. d		....	....	....	....	....	....	....	268.3	141.7	138.2	130.2	270.2	227.9	315.1	374.2
Gold (Million Fine Troy Ounces) 1ad		....	....	....	....	....	....	....	....	....	....	....	....	.054	.027	.054
Gold (National Valuation) 1and		....	....	....	....	....	....	....	—	—	—	—	—	2.3	1.2	15.7
Monetary Authorities: Other Liab. .. 4..d		....	....	....	....	....	....	....	.1	—	—	—	21.2	42.2	35.5	80.6
Deposit Money Banks: Assets ...... 7a. d		....	....	....	....	....	....	....	....	....	118.2	121.4	104.2	111.0	127.7	176.1
of which: Claims on Nonbanks .. 7ad d		....	....	....	....	....	....	....	....	....	91.2	106.4	92.5	65.5	65.8	87.8
Deposit Money Banks: Liabilities .... 7b. d		....	....	....	....	....	....	....	....	....	25.2	21.8	26.4	61.2	67.7	77.9
of which: Liab. to Nonbanks ...... 7bd d		....	....	....	....	....	....	....	....	....	17.5	8.5	5.5	11.3	12.8	19.8
Monetary Authorities															Millions of Taka:	
Foreign Assets 11		....	....	....	....	....	....	....	....	1,174	1,115	2,084	4,318	3,385	4,728	6,332
Claims on Central Government 12a		....	....	....	....	....	....	....	....	3,326	4,212	5,170	6,983	7,331	7,715	7,259
Claims on Nonfin.Pub.Enterprises .. 12c		....	....	....	....	....	....	....	....	—	160	160	160	160	160	511
Claims on Deposit Money Banks .. 12e		....	....	....	....	....	....	....	....	635	1,799	2,220	832	2,625	3,752	5,705
Claims on Other Financial Insts. .. 12f		....	....	....	....	....	....	....	....	270	223	156	169	172	305	924
Reserve Money 14		....	....	....	....	....	....	....	....	4,095	5,157	5,033	5,158	6,679	8,541	9,914
of which: Currency Outside DMBs .. 14a		....	....	....	....	....	....	....	....	3,212	4,103	3,618	3,817	4,902	6,329	7,114
Foreign Liabilities 16c		....	....	....	....	....	....	....	....	617	1,318	2,979	4,414	4,240	4,994	6,665
Central Government Deposits 16d		....	....	....	....	....	....	....	....	—	—	—	—	—	—	—
Central Govt. Lending Funds 16f		....	....	....	....	....	....	....	....	....	....	....	....	....	....	....
Capital Accounts 17a		....	....	....	....	....	....	....	....	103	133	183	223	263	303	682
Other Items (Net) 17r		....	....	....	....	....	....	....	....	590	900	1,595	2,666	2,491	2,822	3,470
Deposit Money Banks															Millions of Taka:	
Reserves 20		....	....	....	....	....	....	....	....	....	1,145	1,276	1,378	1,736	2,051	2,645
Foreign Assets 21		....	....	....	....	....	....	....	....	....	955	1,799	1,558	1,077	1,363	1,919
Claims on Central Government 22a		....	....	....	....	....	....	....	....	....	2,401	1,942	2,462	3,185	2,961	4,153
Claims on Nonfin.Pub.Enterprises .. 22c		....	....	....	....	....	....	....	....	....	5,194	6,502	6,623	7,622	10,013	12,015
Claims on Private Sector 22d		....	....	....	....	....	....	....	....	....	2,603	3,309	4,455	7,450	9,105	12,650
Claims on Other Financial Insts. .. 22f		....	....	....	....	....	....	....	....	....	690	137	270	318	645	794
Demand Deposits 24		....	....	....	....	....	....	....	....	....	4,284	4,662	5,399	6,764	8,306	11,240
Time Deposits 25		....	....	....	....	....	....	....	....	....	5,603	6,458	8,255	9,943	12,667	15,049
Foreign Liabilities 26c		....	....	....	....	....	....	....	....	....	155	128	181	564	540	612
Central Government Deposits 26d		....	....	....	....	....	....	....	....	....	....	....	....	....	....	....
Central Govt. Lending Funds 26f		....	....	....	....	....	....	....	....	....	480	622	411	432	571	701
Credit from Monetary Authorities .. 26g		....	....	....	....	....	....	....	....	....	1,769	1,962	845	2,446	3,385	5,707
Capital Accounts 27a		....	....	....	....	....	....	....	....	....	431	423	793	920	959	1,039
Other Items (Net) 27r		....	....	....	....	....	....	....	....	....	266	712	862	319	−290	−172
Monetary Survey															Millions of Taka:	
Foreign Assets (Net) 31n		....	....	....	....	....	....	....	....	....	597	776	1,281	−343	557	975
Domestic Credit 32		....	....	....	....	....	....	....	....	....	15,483	17,376	21,122	26,238	30,905	38,305
Claims on Central Govt. (Net) 32an		....	....	....	....	....	....	....	....	....	6,613	7,112	9,445	10,516	10,676	11,412
Claims on Nonfin.Pub.Enterprise .. 32c		....	....	....	....	....	....	....	....	....	....	....	....	....	....	....
Claims on Private Sector 32d		....	....	....	....	....	....	....	....	....	2,603	3,309	4,455	7,450	9,105	12,650
Claims on Other Financial Insts. .. 32f		....	....	....	....	....	....	....	....	....	913	293	439	490	950	1,718
Money 34		....	....	....	....	....	....	....	....	....	8,391	8,283	9,216	11,667	14,636	18,356
Quasi-Money 35		....	....	....	....	....	....	....	....	....	5,603	6,458	8,255	9,943	12,667	15,049
Central Govt. Lending Funds 36f		....	....	....	....	....	....	....	....	....	480	622	411	432	571	701
Other Items (Net) 37r		....	....	....	....	....	....	....	....	....	1,606	2,789	4,521	3,853	3,589	5,174
Money plus Quasi-Money 35l		....	....	....	....	....	....	....	....	....	13,994	14,741	17,471	21,610	27,302	33,405
Interest Rates															Percent Per Annum	
Discount Rate (End of Period) 60		....	....	....	....	....	....	5.00	5.00	5.00	8.00	8.00	8.00	8.00	8.00	8.00
Deposit Rate 60k		....	....	....	....	....	....	....	....	....	....	....	....	....	....	....
Lending Rate 60p		....	....	....	....	....	....	....	....	....	....	....	11.00	11.00	11.00	11.00
Prices and Production															Index Numbers (1990=100):	
Consumer Prices 64		4.9	5.3	5.6	5.8	6.1	6.3	6.2	8.8	13.1	20.2	24.6	25.2	26.4	27.8	31.9
Industrial Production 66		....	....	....	....	....	....	....	....	....	80.7	85.8	82.9	82.9	78.4	176.8

Bangladesh

	1980	1981	1982	1983	1984	1985	1986	1987	1988	1989	1990	1991	1992	1993	1994		
End of Period																**Exchange Rates**	
	20.726	23.101	26.556	26.174	25.485	34.051	37.674	44.262	43.426	42.408	50.917	55.186	53.625	54.736	58.759	Official Rate......aa=	wa
End of Period (we)	*Period Average (wf)*																
	16.251	19.847	24.074	25.000	26.000	31.000	30.800	31.200	32.270	32.270	35.790	38.580	39.000	39.850	40.250	Official Rate......ae=	we
	15.454	17.987	22.118	24.615	25.354	I 27.995	30.407	30.950	31.733	32.270	34.569	36.596	38.951	39.567	40.212	Official Rate......rf=	wf
End of Period																**Fund Position**	
	228.0	228.0	228.0	287.5	287.5	287.5	287.5	287.5	287.5	287.5	287.5	287.5	392.5	392.5	392.5	Quota	2f. s
	.4	.1	.8	12.9	.3	11.9	8.4	37.6	40.1	2.3	18.1	49.9	30.1	16.6	24.6	SDRs	1b. s
	—	—	7.5	22.4	22.4	22.4	22.4	22.4	22.4	22.4	—	—	—	.1	.1	Reserve Position in the Fund	1c. s
	332.6	398.9	496.2	540.0	471.6	473.3	440.5	592.7	623.9	546.8	439.7	523.2	547.7	511.8	473.4	Total Fund Cred.&Loans Outstg.	2tl
End of Period																**International Liquidity**	
	299.6	138.4	182.6	524.1	389.9	336.5	409.1	843.1	1,046.1	501.5	628.7	1,278.2	1,824.6	2,410.8	3,138.7	Total Reserves minus Gold	1l. d
	.4	.1	.8	13.5	.3	13.1	10.3	53.3	54.0	3.0	25.8	71.3	41.4	22.8	36.0	SDRs	1b. d
	—	—	8.3	23.5	22.0	24.6	27.4	31.8	30.1	29.4	—	—	—	.1	.1	Reserve Position in the Fund	1c. d
	299.2	138.3	173.5	487.1	367.7	298.8	371.4	758.1	961.9	469.0	602.9	1,206.9	1,783.2	2,387.9	3,102.6	Foreign Exchange	1d. d
	.054	.054	.057	.057	.059	.060	.066	.068	.074	.076	.080	.084	.087	.092	.094	Gold (Million Fine Troy Ounces)	1ad
	21.5	16.9	24.5	17.5	15.8	12.9	16.8	22.8	24.0	21.4	20.8	21.5	22.7	25.9	27.2	Gold (National Valuation)	1an d
	143.1	179.0	197.6	213.6	130.0	95.3	74.6	120.8	127.8	83.9	129.8	421.6	475.4	574.1	627.7	Monetary Authorities: Other Liab.	4.. d
	272.2	228.3	153.0	188.0	221.0	289.0	273.0	275.9	306.6	391.3	431.7	436.7	356.5	402.5	703.4	Deposit Money Banks: Assets	7a. d
	110.2	98.6	96.4	92.6	93.4	89.4	101.1	99.8	92.3	122.7	114.8	116.6	128.1	150.3	220.9	of which: Claims on Nonbanks	7ad d
	171.0	115.4	94.7	54.0	96.0	127.0	119.0	160.7	211.3	212.7	237.6	269.0	242.0	241.7	283.7	Deposit Money Banks: Liabilities	7b. d
	23.8	25.5	24.3	26.7	32.4	50.1	35.4	29.9	29.4	20.3	25.4	22.7	18.5	21.5	20.2	of which: Liab. to Nonbanks	7bd d
End of Period																**Monetary Authorities**	
	5,252	3,052	I 5,708	16,157	13,404	13,349	14,381	29,153	37,745	19,721	27,491	54,133	76,832	101,805	130,199	Foreign Assets	11
	10,350	15,406	13,268	13,180	12,763	14,183	11,266	13,769	9,999	15,384	16,162	12,469	10,426	5,366	5,697	Claims on Central Government	12a
	460	500	800	750	580	I 580	580	1,046	1,079	874	821	825	649	597	594	Claims on Nonfin.Pub.Enterprises	12c
	8,554	9,841	15,074	10,596	18,808	22,681	23,117	23,130	25,389	36,600	37,122	34,292	27,399	24,409	26,275	Claims on Deposit Money Banks	12e
	1,675	2,138	2,695	3,605	5,644	7,261	8,810	7,918	8,228	8,427	8,475	8,440	8,231	11,721	13,153	Claims on Other Financial Insts.	12f
	11,767	12,912	I 14,272	19,139	25,867	29,435	31,535	45,994	51,021	56,878	59,502	59,431	71,850	89,417	118,017	Reserve Money	14
	8,267	9,143	9,744	13,444	17,250	17,672	19,027	22,490	25,282	27,286	29,950	31,330	37,990	44,987	57,248	of which: Currency Outside DMBs	14a
	9,218	12,769	19,075	20,910	17,819	21,138	20,977	I 30,000	31,215	25,896	24,836	32,450	30,952	32,005	32,807	Foreign Liabilities	16c
	10	5	I 13	5	411	10	10	557	980	977	2,180	2,179	3,670	9,717	4,868	Central Government Deposits	16d
	....	....	12	907	1,806	2,418	3,081	3,403	4,865	5,328	9,055	16,099	16,661	13,272	18,977	Central Govt. Lending Funds	16f
	1,245	1,862	2,172	2,487	2,867	3,247	3,627	4,007	4,387	4,650	5,035	5,424	5,966	6,346	6,726	Capital Accounts	17a
	4,052	3,389	I 2,001	840	2,429	1,806	−1,077	−8,945	−10,029	−12,723	−10,537	−5,424	−5,562	−6,859	−5,477	Other Items (Net)	17r
End of Period																**Deposit Money Banks**	
	3,378	3,798	4,227	5,642	7,867	9,312	10,387	24,298	27,181	31,140	31,430	30,470	36,687	48,324	60,215	Reserves	20
	3,498	4,106	5,703	5,939	6,179	8,955	8,415	I 8,607	9,894	12,628	15,450	16,848	13,903	16,039	28,313	Foreign Assets	21
	5,423	4,616	5,054	10,362	13,004	11,927	17,876	I 17,486	21,156	19,599	19,271	27,904	47,353	54,135	64,899	Claims on Central Government	22a
	14,774	17,179	22,978	22,567	23,160	26,021	30,385	I 27,829	29,840	36,273	37,442	40,592	43,412	45,951	33,731	Claims on Nonfin.Pub.Enterprises	22c
	16,205	22,423	26,566	37,799	59,386	75,530	83,242	99,537	119,538	147,546	167,104	175,944	173,881	191,744	220,332	Claims on Private Sector	22d
	1,225	1,243	I 1,335	1,761	1,823	1,844	2,031	I 5,606	6,012	5,839	5,891	5,865	11,543	11,614	14,644	Claims on Other Financial Insts.	22f
	11,903	13,570	I 13,589	18,191	25,016	28,279	30,968	I 28,510	27,883	32,718	35,785	39,474	42,452	48,294	62,802	Demand Deposits	24
	20,213	24,443	I 29,442	42,262	58,314	68,322	82,794	I 106,643	125,955	152,535	168,474	194,874	217,606	236,020	272,844	Time Deposits	25
	1,582	2,291	2,279	1,345	2,306	3,949	3,768	I 4,724	6,255	6,219	7,893	9,779	8,873	9,122	11,064	Foreign Liabilities	26c
	....	....	1,682	2,634	3,055	3,800	5,296	I 12,419	15,686	12,565	13,355	18,279	23,726	26,845	32,200	Central Government Deposits	26d
	1,292	1,741	2,284	3,393	4,383	5,615	5,939	5,619	4,208	4,040	4,352	4,458	4,952	5,341	5,423	Central Govt. Lending Funds	26f
	8,995	9,971	15,012	9,985	16,432	20,358	21,551	21,852	25,630	38,210	39,408	35,708	30,019	27,192	28,781	Credit from Monetary Authorities	26g
	1,132	1,255	1,523	2,641	3,223	3,534	3,964	4,962	5,973	6,489	7,023	7,491	13,101	18,515	21,068	Capital Accounts	27a
	−614	93	I 48	3,619	−1,313	−277	−1,939	I −1,366	2,033	248	294	−12,440	−13,946	−3,522	−12,050	Other Items (Net)	27r
End of Period																**Monetary Survey**	
	−2,050	−7,902	I −8,804	−159	−542	−2,783	−1,949	3,036	10,169	234	10,212	28,752	50,910	76,717	114,641	Foreign Assets (Net)	31n
	50,101	63,499	I 71,000	87,385	112,894	133,536	148,884	160,102	179,186	220,400	239,631	251,581	268,099	284,566	315,982	Domestic Credit	32
	15,763	20,017	I 16,627	20,903	22,301	22,300	23,836	18,269	14,489	21,441	19,898	19,915	30,383	22,939	33,528	Claims on Central Govt. (Net)	32an
	....	....	....	23,317	23,740	26,601	30,965	28,875	30,919	37,147	38,263	41,417	44,061	46,548	34,325	Claims on Nonfin.Pub.Enterprise	32c
	16,205	22,423	26,566	37,799	59,386	75,530	83,242	99,537	119,538	147,546	167,104	175,944	173,881	191,744	220,332	Claims on Private Sector	32d
	2,899	3,380	I 4,030	5,366	7,467	9,105	10,841	13,421	14,240	14,266	14,366	14,305	19,774	23,335	27,797	Claims on Other Financial Insts.	32f
	20,171	22,716	I 23,336	31,636	42,269	45,955	49,996	50,950	53,165	60,004	65,735	70,804	80,442	93,281	120,050	Money	34
	20,213	24,443	I 29,442	42,262	58,314	68,322	82,794	106,643	125,955	152,535	168,474	194,874	217,606	236,020	272,844	Quasi-Money	35
	1,292	1,741	I 2,296	4,300	6,189	8,033	9,020	9,022	9,073	9,368	13,407	20,557	21,613	18,613	24,400	Central Govt. Lending Funds	36f
	6,375	6,697	I 7,121	9,029	5,583	8,447	5,128	−3,477	1,164	−1,273	2,223	−5,902	−648	13,369	13,327	Other Items (Net)	37r
	40,384	47,159	52,778	73,898	100,583	114,277	132,790	157,593	179,120	212,539	234,209	265,678	298,048	329,301	392,894	Money plus Quasi-Money	35l
Percent Per Annum																**Interest Rates**	
	10.50	10.50	10.50	10.50	10.50	11.25	10.75	10.75	10.75	10.75	9.75	9.25	8.50	6.00	5.50	Discount Rate (End of Period)	60
	8.50	8.50	8.50	8.50	8.50	....	....	11.50	11.50	11.50	11.50	11.75	10.75	9.04	7.67	Deposit Rate	60k
	11.33	12.00	12.00	12.00	12.00	12.00	14.00	16.00	16.00	16.00	16.00	15.92	15.00	15.00	14.42	Lending Rate	60p
Period Averages																**Prices and Production**	
	36.2	42.0	47.3	51.7	57.1	63.3	70.2	76.9	84.1	92.5	100.0	107.2	111.8	111.8	115.8	Consumer Prices	64
	80.5	87.1	81.9	83.3	87.5	88.5	86.9	95.1	I 95.5	99.8	100.0	107.5	118.9	130.3	....	Industrial Production	66

Bangladesh
513

		1965	1966	1967	1968	1969	1970	1971	1972	1973	1974	1975	1976	1977	1978	1979
International Transactions															*Millions of Taka:*	
Exports	70	....	....	....	....	....	....	....	1,992	2,764	2,819	3,689	6,150	7,314	8,251	10,242
Imports, c. & f.	71	....	....	....	....	....	....	....	5,207	7,624	8,729	16,251	14,584	17,831	22,832	29,762
Imports, fob	71.v	....	....	....	....	....	....	....	4,640	6,886	7,783	14,452	12,725	16,157	20,603	26,783
															1990=100	
Unit Value of Exports	74	....	....	....	....	....	....	....	....	....	....	....	....	....	41.6	50.7
Unit Value of Imports	75	....	....	....	....	....	....	....	....	....	....	....	....	....	40.0	41.4
Balance of Payments															*Millions of US Dollars:*	
Goods: Exports f.o.b.	78aa d	....	....	....	....	....	....	....	....	....	....	....	400.5	476.4	549.3	655.6
Goods: Imports f.o.b.	78ab d	....	....	....	....	....	....	....	....	....	....	....	−820.1	−1,019.1	−1,339.6	−1,725.8
Trade Balance	78ac d	....	....	....	....	....	....	....	....	....	....	....	−419.5	−542.6	−790.3	−1,070.2
Services: Credit	78ad d	....	....	....	....	....	....	....	....	....	....	....	68.3	64.1	101.0	132.6
Services: Debit	78ae d	....	....	....	....	....	....	....	....	....	....	....	−131.9	−184.9	−253.1	−372.2
Balance on Goods and Services	78af d	....	....	....	....	....	....	....	....	....	....	....	−483.2	−663.4	−942.5	−1,309.8
Income: Credit	78ag d	....	....	....	....	....	....	....	....	....	....	....	16.4	26.5	34.5	64.4
Income: Debit	78ah d	....	....	....	....	....	....	....	....	....	....	....	−40.2	−58.7	−61.5	−65.9
Balance on Goods, Serv., & Inc.	78ai d	....	....	....	....	....	....	....	....	....	....	....	−507.1	−695.5	−969.5	−1,311.3
Current Transfers, n.i.e.: Credit	78aj d	....	....	....	....	....	....	....	....	....	....	....	229.1	412.8	583.3	893.0
Current Transfers: Debit	78ak d	....	....	....	....	....	....	....	....	....	....	....	−.7	−.5	−.3	−.2
Current Account, n.i.e.	78al d	....	....	....	....	....	....	....	....	....	....	....	−278.7	−283.3	−386.4	−418.5
Capital Account, n.i.e.: Credit	78ba d	....	....	....	....	....	....	....	....	....	....	....	—	—	—	—
Capital Account: Debit	78bb d	....	....	....	....	....	....	....	....	....	....	....	—	—	—	—
Capital Account, n.i.e.	78bc d	....	....	....	....	....	....	....	....	....	....	....	—	—	—	—
Direct Investment Abroad	78bd d	....	....	....	....	....	....	....	....	....	....	....	—	—	—	—
Dir. Invest. in Rep. Econ., n.i.e.	78be d	....	....	....	....	....	....	....	....	....	....	....	—	—	—	—
Portfolio Investment Assets	78bf d	....	....	....	....	....	....	....	....	....	....	....	—	—	—	—
Portfolio Investment Liab., n.i.e.	78bg d	....	....	....	....	....	....	....	....	....	....	....	—	—	—	—
Other Investment Assets	78bh d	....	....	....	....	....	....	....	....	....	....	....	−15.4	−73.5	−60.8	−99.0
Other Investment Liab., n.i.e.	78bi d	....	....	....	....	....	....	....	....	....	....	....	331.4	333.5	467.2	197.9
Financial Account, n.i.e.	78bj d	....	....	....	....	....	....	....	....	....	....	....	315.9	260.0	406.5	98.9
Net Errors and Omissions	78ca d	....	....	....	....	....	....	....	....	....	....	....	13.8	−14.7	21.6	−4.3
Overall Balance	78cb d	....	....	....	....	....	....	....	....	....	....	....	51.1	−38.0	41.6	−324.0
Reserves and Related Items	79da d	....	....	....	....	....	....	....	....	....	....	....	−51.1	38.0	−41.6	324.0
Reserve Assets	79db d	....	....	....	....	....	....	....	....	....	....	....	−146.4	63.5	−70.6	−96.0
Use of Fund Credit and Loans	79dc d	....	....	....	....	....	....	....	....	....	....	....	74.5	−32.7	26.5	43.5
Liabs.Constit.For.Auth.Reserves	79dd d	....	....	....	....	....	....	....	....	....	....	....	20.1	4.8	—	21.4
Exceptional Financing	79de d	....	....	....	....	....	....	....	....	....	....	....	.7	2.3	2.5	355.1
Government Finance															*Millions of Taka:*	
Deficit (−) or Surplus	80	....	....	....	....	....	....	....	....	−864	−330	1,444	−3,728	209	4,274	874
Revenue	81	....	....	....	....	....	....	....	....	3,885	5,295	9,087	9,243	12,371	16,361	18,695
Grants Received	81z	....	....	....	....	....	....	....	....	138	675	2,776	1,520	3,541	5,311	5,403
Expenditure	82	....	....	....	....	....	....	....	....	4,251	5,299	8,153	11,995	13,167	15,085	21,215
Lending Minus Repayments	83	....	....	....	....	....	....	....	....	635	1,001	2,266	2,496	2,536	2,313	2,009
Financing																
Total Financing	84	....	....	....	....	....	....	....	....	864	330	−1,444	3,728	−209	−4,274	−874
Net Borrowing: Domestic	84a	....	....	....	....	....	....	....	....	913	1,151	855	3,292	−3,586	−6,685	−4,632
Foreign	85a	....	....	....	....	....	....	....	....	—	−211	−368	2,812	875	2,411	3,758
Use of Cash Balances	87	....	....	....	....	....	....	....	....	−49	−610	−1,931	−2,376	2,502	....	....
National Accounts															*Billions of Taka:*	
Gross Domestic Product	99b	....	....	....	....	....	....	....	....	45.11	71.09	125.74	107.46	105.36	146.37	172.82
Gross Dom. Prod. 1990 Prices	99b.p	....	....	....	....	....	....	....	....	335.85	376.50	389.23	436.96	442.76	471.58	493.09
GDP Deflator (1990=100)	99bi p	....	....	....	....	....	....	....	....	13.4	18.9	32.3	24.6	23.8	31.0	35.0
															Millions:	
Population	99z	....	....	....	....	....	....	....	72.39	74.37	77.03	78.96	80.82	82.72	84.66	86.64

Monetary Authorities: I The sectorization and classification of accounts have been revised from June 1982 and again from June 1987.
Deposit Money Banks: I See note to section 10.
Monetary Survey: I See note to section 10.

Bangladesh

	1980	1981	1982	1983	1984	1985	1986	1987	1988	1989	1990	1991	1992	1993	1994		
Millions of Taka																**International Transactions**	
	11,728	14,169	17,049	17,837	23,640	27,997	26,761	33,030	40,967	42,108	57,885	61,866	81,724	90,183	106,581	Exports	70
	40,121	48,736	54,240	53,305	71,673	70,867	77,471	84,087	96,558	117,797	124,880	124,857	145,328	158,123	189,057	Imports, c. & f.	71
	36,108	43,861	45,577	47,975	64,522	63,780	69,724	75,678	86,902	106,018	113,435	110,430	137,000	142,055	166,246	Imports, fob	71.v
1990=100																	
	58.7	51.6	56.4	64.0	86.0	105.7	82.5	83.0	96.9	95.1	100.0	104.7	....	....	....	Unit Value of Exports	74
	45.6	51.0	58.4	70.0	72.8	79.3	86.9	95.5	89.0	90.6	100.0	121.2	....	....	....	Unit Value of Imports	75
Minus Sign Indicates Debit																**Balance of Payments**	
	793.2	790.5	768.4	723.9	931.7	999.5	880.0	1,076.9	1,291.0	1,304.8	1,672.4	1,688.7	2,097.9	2,277.9	....	Goods: Exports f.o.b.	78aa d
	−2,352.8	−2,434.8	−2,221.1	−1,930.7	−2,340.0	−2,286.4	−2,300.7	−2,445.6	−2,734.4	−3,300.1	−3,259.4	−3,074.5	−3,353.8	−3,560.9	....	Goods: Imports f.o.b.	78ab d
	−1,559.6	−1,644.3	−1,452.6	−1,206.8	−1,408.3	−1,287.0	−1,420.7	−1,368.8	−1,443.4	−1,995.3	−1,587.0	−1,385.8	−1,255.9	−1,282.9	....	Trade Balance	78ac d
	211.5	211.1	218.2	215.9	207.5	237.9	215.0	247.9	277.6	334.4	391.6	431.0	483.4	530.5	....	Services: Credit	78ad d
	−481.2	−463.5	−439.7	−405.1	−478.0	−477.9	−503.0	−494.2	−613.1	−726.4	−700.5	−695.3	−788.8	−922.3	....	Services: Debit	78ae d
	−1,829.3	−1,896.7	−1,674.2	−1,395.9	−1,678.8	−1,527.0	−1,708.7	−1,615.0	−1,778.9	−2,387.3	−1,895.8	−1,650.0	−1,561.4	−1,674.7	....	Balance on Goods and Services	78af d
	76.3	41.8	28.9	35.9	41.6	31.7	47.4	54.8	88.7	64.2	70.0	100.1	100.1	....		Income: Credit	78ag d
	−69.7	−97.3	−154.2	−117.8	−135.8	−153.7	−167.2	−172.5	−180.7	−196.9	−179.8	−166.9	−166.0	−173.5	....	Income: Debit	78ah d
	−1,822.7	−1,952.2	−1,799.4	−1,477.8	−1,746.4	−1,639.1	−1,844.2	−1,740.1	−1,904.8	−2,495.5	−2,011.4	−1,747.0	−1,627.3	−1,748.0	....	Balance on Goods, Serv., & Inc.	78ai d
	1,118.8	932.9	1,294.6	1,428.6	1,265.6	1,181.6	1,217.5	1,502.6	1,633.0	1,396.6	1,614.2	1,811.9	1,808.8	1,946.8	....	Current Transfers, n.i.e.: Credit	78aj d
	−.4	−.2	−.1	−.3	−.2	−.4	−.3	−.4	−1.5	−.7	−.7	−.3	−.7	−1.5	....	Current Transfers: Debit	78ak d
	−704.3	−1,019.5	−505.0	−49.5	−481.0	−457.9	−627.0	−237.9	−273.2	−1,099.6	−397.9	64.6	180.8	197.3	....	Current Account, n.i.e.	78al d
	—	—	—	—	—	—	—	—	—	—	—	—	—	—	....	Capital Account, n.i.e.: Credit	78ba d
	—	—	—	—	—	—	—	—	—	—	—	—	—	—	....	Capital Account: Debit	78bb d
	—	—	—	—	—	—	—	—	—	—	—	—	—	—	....	Capital Account, n.i.e.	78bc d
	—	—	—	—	—	—	—	—	—	—	—	—	—	—	....	Direct Investment Abroad	78bd d
	—	—	—	.4	−.6	—	2.4	3.2	1.8	.2	3.2	1.4	3.7	14.0	....	Dir. Invest. in Rep. Econ., n.i.e.	78be d
	—	—	—	—	—	—	—	—	—	—	—	—	—	—	....	Portfolio Investment Assets	78bf d
	—	—	—	1.3	1.6	−7.2	—	−.1	—	1.7	.3	2.2	8.7	8.4	....	Portfolio Investment Liab., n.i.e.	78bg d
	−76.8	−115.9	−134.3	−91.5	−60.9	−13.7	−18.0	−21.0	−229.1	−152.0	−207.8	−267.1	−196.0	−26.1	....	Other Investment Assets	78bh d
	531.4	824.5	623.1	518.2	630.3	467.0	757.9	576.0	625.9	983.2	902.0	731.1	722.0	492.0	....	Other Investment Liab., n.i.e.	78bi d
	454.6	708.6	488.8	428.3	570.5	446.2	742.4	558.1	398.6	833.2	697.8	467.6	538.4	488.2	....	Financial Account, n.i.e.	78bj d
	−74.1	93.7	−83.4	−26.4	−95.2	−67.8	8.7	−123.8	6.6	−43.1	−75.7	−98.4	−84.0	12.0	....	Net Errors and Omissions	78ca d
	−323.8	−217.1	−99.6	352.5	−5.7	−79.6	124.1	196.5	132.0	−309.5	224.2	433.8	635.2	697.6	....	Overall Balance	78cb d
	323.8	217.1	99.6	−352.5	5.7	79.6	−124.1	−196.5	−132.0	309.5	−224.2	−433.8	−635.2	−697.6	....	Reserves and Related Items	79aa d
	117.7	140.7	−56.1	−357.6	98.3	79.4	−47.9	−352.3	−176.1	447.8	−78.9	−544.5	−670.1	−647.0	....	Reserve Assets	79db d
	89.2	79.1	108.2	46.2	−69.9	1.8	−38.0	196.5	43.6	−99.6	−145.3	110.7	34.9	−50.6	....	Use of Fund Credit and Loans	79dc d
	114.7	−5.5	43.2	−44.7	−26.1	−4.3	−40.0	−41.5	—	−38.8	—	—	—	—	....	Liabs.Constit.For.Auth.Reserves	79dd d
	2.2	2.9	4.3	3.7	3.4	2.8	1.8	.8	.4	—	—	—	—	—	....	Exceptional Financing	79de d
Year Ending June 30																**Government Finance**	
	4,976	−7,396	3,135ᴾ	9,003ᴾ	2,873ᴾ	−5,924ᴾ	....	....	....	....	....	....	....	....	....	Deficit (−) or Surplus	80
	22,628	27,604	32,194ᴾ	31,945ᴾ	32,446ᴾ	39,436ᴾ	....	....	....	....	....	....	....	....	....	Revenue	81
	5,440	2,474	9,038ᴾ	12,312ᴾ	11,909ᴾ	8,688ᴾ	....	....	....	....	....	....	....	....	....	Grants Received	81z
	20,026	32,445	34,007ᴾ	32,680ᴾ	38,314ᴾ	50,482ᴾ	....	....	....	....	....	....	....	....	....	Expenditure	82
	3,066	5,029	4,090ᴾ	2,574ᴾ	3,168ᴾ	3,566ᴾ	....	....	....	....	....	....	....	....	....	Lending Minus Repayments	83
																Financing	
	−4,976	7,396	−3,135ᴾ	−9,003ᴾ	−2,873ᴾ	5,924ᴾ	....	....	....	....	....	....	....	....	....	Total Financing	84
	....	1,623	....	....	....	−8,430ᴾ	....	....	....	....	....	....	....	....	....	Net Borrowing: Domestic	84a
	....	5,773	....	....	....	14,354ᴾ	....	....	....	....	....	....	....	....	....	Foreign	85a
	....	....	....	....	....	....	....	....	....	....	....	....	....	....	....	Use of Cash Balances	87
Year Ending June 30																**National Accounts**	
	197.99	233.26	265.14	288.42	349.92	405.41	465.61	539.20	597.14	659.60	737.57	834.39	906.50	947.90	1,035.46	Gross Domestic Product	99b
	499.57	533.37	537.76	557.19	580.72	602.31	630.68	655.77	674.73	691.73	737.57	762.65	794.89	830.51	868.80	Gross Dom. Prod. 1990 Prices	99b.p
	39.6	43.7	49.3	51.8	60.3	67.3	73.8	82.2	88.5	95.4	100.0	109.4	114.0	114.1	119.2	GDP Deflator (1990=100)	99bi p
Midyear Estimates																	
	88.68	90.46	92.59	94.65	97.27	99.43	101.67	102.56	104.53	106.51	108.12	110.34	112.71	115.20	....	Population	99z

Barbados

316

		1965	1966	1967	1968	1969	1970	1971	1972	1973	1974	1975	1976	1977	1978	1979
Exchange Rates														*Barbados Dollars per SDR: End of Period (aa)*		
Official Rate	aa	1.7126	1.7203	1.9948	2.0131	1.9994	2.0053	2.0417	2.2194	2.4925	2.5024	2.3458	2.3281	2.4431	2.6203	2.6495
Official Rate	ae	1.7126	1.7203	1.9948	2.0131	1.9994	2.0053	1.8805	2.0442	2.0661	2.0439	2.0038	2.0038	2.0113	2.0113	2.0113
Fund Position														*Millions of SDRs:*		
Quota	2f.s	....	....	....	....	....	13.00	13.00	13.00	13.00	13.00	13.00	13.00	13.00	17.00	17.00
SDRs	1b.s	....	....	....	....	....	—	1.39	2.77	2.77	2.77	2.77	2.77	2.72	2.49	3.94
Reserve Position in the Fund	1c.s	....	....	....	....	....	2.00	2.00	2.00	2.00	2.01	3.26	3.27	3.27	2.98	2.89
Total Fund Cred.&Loans Outstg.	2tl						—	—	—	—	—	—	—	6.50	6.50	6.50
International Liquidity														*Millions of US Dollars Unless Otherwise Indicated:*		
Total Reserves minus Gold	1l.d	....	12.11	9.25	15.52	12.47	16.58	18.86	27.99	32.37	39.15	39.58	27.98	37.01	59.84	66.12
SDRs	1b.d	....	....	....	....	....	—	1.51	3.01	3.34	3.39	3.24	3.22	3.30	3.24	5.19
Reserve Position in the Fund	1c.d	....	....	....	....	....	2.00	2.17	2.17	2.41	2.46	3.82	3.80	3.97	3.88	3.81
Foreign Exchange	1d.d	....	12.11	9.25	15.52	12.47	14.58	15.18	22.81	26.62	33.30	32.52	20.96	29.73	52.71	57.12
Monetary Authorities	1da.d	....	6.98	5.94	11.58	7.83	8.60	11.01	10.50	16.43	19.06	26.12	12.71	22.03	42.51	45.11
Government	1db.d	....	5.13	3.31	3.94	4.64	5.98	4.17	I12.31	10.19	14.24	6.40	8.25	7.70	10.20	12.01
Gold (Million Fine Troy Ounces)	1ad	....	....	....	....	....	....	....	....	....	....	....	....	....	....	....
Gold (National Valuation)	1an.d						—	—	—	—	—	—	—	.12	.25	
Monetary Authorities: Other Liab.	4..d													9.94	9.94	7.96
Deposit Money Banks: Assets	7a.d	....	8.22	11.15	13.25	8.65	18.70	21.77	19.65	19.39	15.79	16.31	14.48	17.61	15.70	24.26
of which: Claims on Nonbanks	7ad.d	....	....	....	....	....	....	....	....	2.19	2.81	4.02	4.72	5.01	3.16	3.51
Deposit Money Banks: Liabilities	7b.d	....	5.07	3.80	3.05	17.90	27.10	36.43	40.99	51.00	43.36	37.44	41.87	44.66	39.36	42.19
of which: Liab. to Nonbanks	7bd.d	....	....	....	....	....	....	....	....	14.97	13.82	16.14	16.25	14.61	13.67	16.85
Monetary Authorities														*Millions of Barbados Dollars:*		
Foreign Assets	11	....	20.8	18.5	31.1	24.9	33.2	34.7	54.1	69.7	64.4	85.2	58.2	74.7	120.3	135.6
Claims on Central Government	12a	....	1.4	2.0	1.9	2.8	3.8	5.8	5.8	5.7	20.5	20.2	30.3	72.3	46.7	83.6
Claims on Deposit Money Banks	12e	....	3.2	3.8	3.9	4.3	6.4	4.3	8.8	2.6	2.6	.3	3.0	4.5	—	1.2
Claims on Other Banking Insts.	12f	....	....	....	....	....	....	....	....	—	6.8	12.9	20.1	14.1	24.0	14.4
Reserve Money	14	....	16.2	17.3	28.6	22.5	27.0	29.2	33.5	44.4	59.1	80.2	76.5	93.1	109.9	146.5
of which: Currency Outside DMBs	14a	....	11.8	12.7	14.3	15.7	21.2	21.4	23.7	26.9	34.1	41.8	47.0	55.7	65.9	80.2
Foreign Liabilities	16c													35.9	37.0	33.2
Central Government Deposits	16d	....	9.2	6.9	8.2	9.6	16.3	12.9	29.6	25.9	24.5	29.8	27.5	19.5	26.7	32.3
Capital Accounts	17a									9.1	12.3	15.2	15.6	17.0	18.6	24.0
Other Items (Net)	17r	....	—	.1	.1	—	—	2.8	5.5	-1.3	-1.7	-6.6	-8.1	.1	-1.2	-1.2
Deposit Money Banks														*Millions of Barbados Dollars:*		
Reserves	20	....	4.3	4.6	14.3	6.8	5.9	7.8	9.8	18.8	14.3	25.8	17.7	33.3	43.6	60.4
Foreign Assets	21	....	14.1	22.3	26.5	17.3	37.4	40.1	36.2	40.1	32.3	32.7	29.0	35.4	31.6	48.8
Claims on Central Government	22a	....	.5	.9	7.2	6.7	8.0	17.4	19.1	9.0	42.5	60.6	82.1	80.0	141.0	138.2
Claims on Private Sector	22d	....	66.7	72.2	83.4	132.3	165.8	189.1	214.9	249.9	250.1	271.8	302.9	326.8	362.6	443.9
Claims on Other Banking Insts.	22f	....	....	....	....	....	....	....	....	3.2	5.1	3.5	5.1	7.8	10.7	14.4
Demand Deposits	24	....	27.1	29.4	37.6	I41.1	34.5	41.1	44.1	47.2	51.5	62.9	65.6	77.0	93.2	140.4
Time, Savings,& Fgn.Currency Dep.	25	....	51.0	65.4	90.4	I96.1	120.8	146.4	168.5	149.4	190.5	212.3	243.0	256.3	320.2	392.5
Foreign Liabilities	26c	....	8.7	7.6	6.1	I35.8	54.2	67.1	75.5	105.4	88.6	75.0	83.9	89.8	79.2	84.9
Central Government Deposits	26d	....	1.2	2.3	6.1	10.7	12.2	17.9	19.7	35.5	33.3	57.6	50.9	66.2	86.0	91.5
Credit from Monetary Authorities	26g	....	31.7	37.9	38.6	43.0	64.2	42.9	87.5	2.6	2.6	.3	3.0	4.5	—	1.2
Capital Accounts	27a									1.6	3.7	3.9	2.4	5.3	13.2	16.6
Other Items (Net)	27r	....	-2.4	-4.7	-8.8	-20.6	-4.6	-18.1	-27.8	-20.6	-26.0	-17.7	-11.9	-15.9	-2.2	-21.2
Monetary Survey														*Millions of Barbados Dollars:*		
Foreign Assets (Net)	31n	....	26.2	33.2	51.5	I6.4	16.4	7.7	14.8	4.4	8.0	42.9	3.3	-15.6	35.7	66.3
Domestic Credit	32	....	58.2	67.1	78.2	125.7	161.1	199.2	210.0	206.4	267.0	281.5	362.0	415.1	472.3	570.8
Claims on Central Govt. (Net)	32an	....	-8.5	-6.3	-5.2	-10.8	-16.7	-7.6	-24.4	-46.6	5.1	-6.7	33.9	66.5	75.1	98.1
Claims on Private Sector	32d	....	66.7	72.2	83.4	132.3	165.8	189.1	214.9	249.9	250.1	271.8	302.9	326.8	362.6	443.9
Claims on Other Banking Insts.	32f	....	....	....	....	....	....	....	....	3.2	11.9	16.4	25.2	21.9	34.6	28.8
Money	34	....	38.9	42.1	51.9	I56.8	55.7	62.5	67.8	74.1	88.6	106.5	113.7	135.7	160.7	222.2
Quasi-Money	35	....	51.0	65.4	90.4	96.1	120.8	146.4	168.5	149.4	190.5	212.3	243.0	256.3	320.2	392.5
Other Items (Net)	37r	....	-5.5	-7.2	-12.6	-20.8	1.0	-2.0	-11.5	-12.6	-4.0	5.5	8.6	7.6	27.1	22.4
Money plus Quasi-Money	35l	....	89.9	107.5	142.3	152.9	176.5	208.9	236.3	223.5	279.1	318.8	356.7	391.9	480.9	614.7
Other Banking Institutions														*Millions of Barbados Dollars:*		
Claims on Central Government	42a	....	....	....	10.2	10.3	12.3	12.6	.5	.5	.5	.5	.9	.4	.6	.5
Claims on Private Sector	42d	....	....	....	9.9	10.5	12.4	12.7	2.8	4.9	8.2	13.3	20.2	25.9	34.9	51.4
Claims on Deposit Money Banks	42e	....	....	....	.4	.9	2.3	3.5	2.0	4.8	3.3	7.1	4.7	2.3	5.8	7.3
Time Deposits	45	....	16.7	17.4	16.8	16.6	17.8	19.7	3.9	8.5	10.5	19.8	23.6	26.0	36.3	39.3
Central Government Deposits	46d				—	—	—	—	—	—	—	—	—	4.2	22.3	
Credit from Deposit Money Banks	46h								.1	.1	.1	.1	.6	.8	1.7	.9
Capital Accounts	47a	....	2.9	2.5	3.2	4.1	6.1	6.5	1.5	1.5	1.5	1.5	1.5	1.8	2.0	2.5
Other Items (Net)	47r	....	....	....	.5	1.0	3.1	2.6	-.1	.1	—	-.6	.3	—	-3.1	-5.8
Banking Survey														*Millions of Barbados Dollars:*		
Foreign Assets (Net)	51n	....	35.9	42.9	60.8	15.7	25.1	17.6	14.8	4.4	8.1	42.9	3.3	-15.6	35.7	66.3
Domestic Credit	52	....	....	....	98.3	142.4	173.8	206.8	193.8	208.6	263.9	278.9	357.9	419.5	468.9	571.6
Claims on Central Govt. (Net)	52an	....	....	....	5.0	-.4	-4.4	5.0	-23.9	-46.1	5.6	-6.2	34.8	66.9	71.4	76.4
Claims on Private Sector	52d	....	76.1	81.7	93.3	142.8	178.2	201.8	217.7	254.8	258.3	285.1	323.1	352.7	397.5	495.2
Liquid Liabilities	55l	....	106.6	124.8	158.8	169.5	193.9	228.6	240.2	203.8	249.3	275.7	309.4	342.1	427.2	546.0
Capital Accounts	57a											12.2	17.4	20.5	19.5	24.1	33.8	43.1
Other Items (Net)	57r	....	....	....	.3	-7.3	17.0	-4.2	-31.6	-2.9	5.3	25.6	32.3	37.8	43.6	48.7

Barbados

316

	1980	1981	1982	1983	1984	1985	1986	1987	1988	1989	1990	1991	1992	1993	1994		
	Barbados Dollars per US Dollar: End of Period (ae)															**Exchange Rates**	
	2.5652	2.3411	2.2187	2.1057	1.9715	2.2093	2.4602	2.8534	2.7066	2.6432	2.8614	2.8770	2.7655	2.7626	2.9362	Official Rate	**aa**
	2.0113	2.0113	2.0113	2.0113	2.0113	2.0113	2.0113	2.0113	2.0113	2.0113	2.0113	2.0113	2.0113	2.0113	2.0113	Official Rate	**ae**
	End of Period															**Fund Position**	
	25.50	25.50	25.50	34.10	34.10	34.10	34.10	34.10	34.10	34.10	34.10	34.10	48.90	48.90	48.90	Quota	**2f. s**
	1.56	1.44	.79	.29	.02	.01	—	.63	.46	—	.01	.50	.11	.05	.03	SDRs	**1b. s**
	5.02	5.01	—	2.15	2.16	2.16	2.16	2.17	2.18	2.18	2.18	—	.03	.03	.03	Reserve Position in the Fund	**1c. s**
	2.27	.77	22.18	35.79	43.59	43.59	32.42	15.60	7.75	3.27	.50	—	36.84	36.84	36.84	Total Fund Cred.&Loans Outstg.	**2tl**
	End of Period															**International Liquidity**	
	78.92	100.56	121.60	123.27	132.52	139.77	151.71	145.21	135.46	109.46	117.54	87.25	139.96	150.45	195.77	Total Reserves minus Gold	**1l. d**
	1.99	1.68	.87	.30	.02	.01	—	.89	.62	—	.01	.72	.15	.07	.04	SDRs	**1b. d**
	6.40	5.83	—	2.25	2.12	2.37	2.64	3.08	2.93	2.86	3.10	—	.04	.03	.04	Reserve Position in the Fund	**1c. d**
	70.53	93.05	120.73	120.72	130.38	137.39	149.07	141.24	131.91	106.60	114.42	86.53	139.77	150.35	195.69	Foreign Exchange	**1d. d**
	56.33	76.62	101.23	101.07	107.91	117.24	131.34	125.83	109.10	92.73	104.81	80.06	133.14	143.21	188.28	Monetary Authorities	**1da d**
	14.20	16.43	19.50	19.65	22.47	20.15	17.73	15.41	22.81	13.87	9.61	6.47	6.63	7.14	7.41	Government	**1db d**
	.0028	.0061	.0061	.0061	.0061	.0061	.0061	.0061	.0061	.0061	.0061	—	—	—	—	Gold (Million Fine Troy Ounces)	**1ad**
	1.75	3.36	3.36	3.36	3.36	3.89	3.89	3.89	3.89	3.11	—	—	—	—	—	Gold (National Valuation)	**1an d**
	5.97	55.80	60.14	40.85	37.71	27.92	39.73	33.32	35.97	59.80	76.40	78.44	64.35	48.58	33.94	Monetary Authorities: Other Liab.	**4.. d**
	26.23	25.08	26.28	26.64	46.05	50.12	58.78	119.95	74.42	69.05	76.98	87.98	90.43	95.11	125.82	Deposit Money Banks: Assets	**7a. d**
	3.29	4.77	4.99	5.61	11.21	8.89	9.98	34.83	12.62	14.72	10.10	15.15	11.39	13.73	11.49	*of which:* Claims on Nonbanks	**7ad d**
	48.36	65.93	65.24	80.84	86.12	88.29	106.49	168.45	107.06	106.52	125.47	139.81	142.62	151.70	172.14	Deposit Money Banks: Liabilities	**7b. d**
	23.44	26.51	28.47	31.14	33.38	34.80	34.57	68.16	66.93	67.37	89.90	88.03	106.82	107.02	147.11	*of which:* Liab. to Nonbanks	**7bd d**
	End of Period															**Monetary Authorities**	
	163.9	207.9	251.5	259.9	253.3	287.3	327.4	306.2	290.0	250.6	260.0	207.1	315.2	335.8	442.2	Foreign Assets	**11**
	75.9	118.4	126.0	122.8	110.2	134.6	131.7	119.2	110.1	160.4	199.8	259.9	235.1	220.9	219.8	Claims on Central Government	**12a**
	1.2	7.5	17.9	22.1	14.9	1.9	.7	2.4	3.7	29.8	27.8	33.6	31.2	5.0	—	Claims on Deposit Money Banks	**12e**
	23.8	50.7	47.8	43.3	70.4	55.7	56.8	58.0	52.4	61.4	69.3	61.3	62.3	25.3	10.1	Claims on Other Banking Insts.	**12f**
	164.0	180.8	189.6	226.1	233.9	256.1	260.4	313.6	327.9	317.4	379.0	324.6	367.6	324.6	318.4	Reserve Money	**14**
	101.6	111.2	110.6	114.1	118.1	123.5	137.4	156.6	171.3	182.7	192.9	178.7	176.8	177.0	189.6	*of which:* Currency Outside DMBs	**14a**
	17.8	114.0	170.2	157.5	161.8	152.5	159.7	111.5	93.3	128.9	155.1	172.2	245.5	213.6	184.6	Foreign Liabilities	**16c**
	35.7	49.5	48.8	45.9	55.0	113.3	141.2	121.1	87.7	121.5	75.4	86.2	107.4	105.2	212.0	Central Government Deposits	**16d**
	28.2	30.8	29.8	28.9	27.9	29.8	31.8	34.9	33.8	28.7	35.5	35.1	34.2	34.2	35.6	Capital Accounts	**17a**
	19.1	9.4	4.9	−10.4	−29.6	−72.1	−76.5	−95.3	−86.3	−94.4	−88.1	−56.2	−110.9	−90.6	−78.4	Other Items (Net)	**17r**
	End of Period															**Deposit Money Banks**	
	58.1	66.1	71.0	78.6	86.9	83.0	103.3	122.3	140.4	118.4	181.1	127.2	167.4	129.3	114.1	Reserves	**20**
	52.8	50.5	52.9	53.6	92.6	100.8	118.2	241.3	149.7	138.9	154.8	177.0	181.9	191.3	253.1	Foreign Assets	**21**
	154.8	170.8	201.0	202.9	247.3	263.1	315.7	359.6	394.7	354.3	428.6	441.0	555.1	594.9	603.4	Claims on Central Government	**22a**
	521.5	618.0	645.0	729.8	741.9	769.4	811.0	898.6	965.1	1,102.8	1,104.3	1,144.5	1,121.0	1,128.9	1,268.1	Claims on Private Sector	**22d**
	12.5	19.0	22.8	29.6	41.7	55.5	44.6	34.4	73.2	79.2	106.9	84.3	66.7	83.7	159.3	Claims on Other Banking Insts.	**22f**
	140.5	135.6	137.4	166.7	159.1	198.9	231.0	278.5	329.8	260.3	320.6	293.4	305.1	280.8	309.6	Demand Deposits	**24**
	449.7	540.6	589.0	618.3	696.2	739.9	799.6	899.1	992.2	1,075.3	1,219.3	1,232.0	1,311.0	1,389.0	1,514.5	Time, Savings,& Fgn.Currency Dep.	**25**
	97.3	132.6	131.2	162.6	173.2	177.6	214.2	338.8	215.3	214.3	252.6	281.2	286.9	305.1	346.2	Foreign Liabilities	**26c**
	116.8	103.4	110.3	117.8	137.6	136.0	112.2	104.6	114.0	125.9	157.2	106.0	125.5	101.3	173.5	Central Government Deposits	**26d**
	1.2	5.4	16.2	26.1	24.3	15.1	13.5	20.3	22.4	40.4	42.9	54.1	38.3	19.7	10.1	Credit from Monetary Authorities	**26g**
	19.9	20.7	18.3	13.1	27.2	26.9	37.9	37.6	36.9	33.6	34.1	32.6	43.5	46.5	92.2	Capital Accounts	**27a**
	−25.8	−14.0	−9.8	−10.2	−7.3	−22.6	−15.6	−22.7	12.5	43.8	−50.6	−25.3	−18.2	−14.4	−48.2	Other Items (Net)	**27r**
	End of Period															**Monetary Survey**	
	101.6	11.7	3.0	−6.7	10.9	58.1	71.8	97.2	131.0	46.3	7.4	−69.3	−35.3	8.3	164.4	Foreign Assets (Net)	**31n**
	635.9	824.1	883.5	964.7	1,018.9	1,029.0	1,106.4	1,244.1	1,393.9	1,510.7	1,676.3	1,798.8	1,807.3	1,847.1	1,875.2	Domestic Credit	**32**
	78.1	136.4	168.0	161.9	164.9	148.4	193.9	253.0	303.2	267.3	395.9	508.7	557.3	609.3	437.6	Claims on Central Govt. (Net)	**32an**
	521.5	618.0	645.0	729.8	741.9	769.4	811.0	898.6	965.1	1,102.8	1,104.3	1,144.5	1,121.0	1,128.9	1,268.1	Claims on Private Sector	**32d**
	36.3	69.7	70.6	72.9	112.1	111.2	101.4	92.5	125.6	140.6	176.1	145.6	129.0	109.0	169.4	Claims on Other Banking Insts.	**32f**
	244.8	249.6	251.5	312.9	305.7	353.5	395.4	466.9	524.8	459.0	526.2	495.0	502.3	476.6	516.3	Money	**34**
	449.7	540.6	589.0	618.3	696.2	739.9	799.6	899.1	992.2	1,075.3	1,219.3	1,232.0	1,311.0	1,389.0	1,514.5	Quasi-Money	**35**
	42.9	45.7	46.0	26.8	27.9	−6.3	−16.8	−24.7	8.0	22.7	−61.9	2.4	−41.3	−10.2	8.8	Other Items (Net)	**37r**
	694.5	790.1	840.5	931.2	1,002.0	1,093.4	1,194.9	1,366.0	1,517.0	1,534.3	1,745.5	1,727.0	1,813.3	1,865.6	2,030.8	Money plus Quasi-Money	**35l**
	End of Period															**Other Banking Institutions**	
	.5	.8	.5	.1	1.0	1.5	3.7	2.0	1.6	1.4	1.8	1.0	.4	7.1	.5	Claims on Central Government	**42a**
	71.5	105.1	127.6	131.1	141.7	149.3	180.1	231.7	283.3	340.1	360.9	384.4	387.1	403.5	417.5	Claims on Private Sector	**42d**
	1.9	1.4	6.6	11.0	16.7	15.0	9.9	6.0	19.1	1.6	14.4	13.3	15.9	8.6	2.1	Claims on Deposit Money Banks	**42e**
	50.3	68.3	88.5	98.7	109.0	114.9	120.6	201.6	216.2	241.0	269.3	295.4	306.9	339.4	301.8	Time Deposits	**45**
	19.6	24.6	30.7	27.0	27.5	33.3	54.0	17.1	45.6	55.4	51.1	50.8	49.8	26.2	34.5	Central Government Deposits	**46d**
	1.6	5.0	6.6	5.6	8.4	1.1	2.5	3.7	10.9	8.6	18.4	17.5	4.6	6.3	46.8	Credit from Deposit Money Banks	**46h**
	2.5	3.0	3.6	3.6	3.6	3.6	4.8	4.8	4.8	4.8	4.8	4.8	4.8	5.0	5.1	Capital Accounts	**47a**
	−.1	6.3	5.4	7.3	10.9	12.9	11.7	12.5	26.5	33.3	33.4	30.2	37.2	42.4	32.0	Other Items (Net)	**47r**
	End of Period															**Banking Survey**	
	101.6	11.7	3.0	−6.7	10.9	58.1	71.8	97.2	131.0	46.3	7.4	−69.3	−35.3	8.3	164.4	Foreign Assets (Net)	**51n**
	652.0	835.7	910.4	996.0	1,022.0	1,035.2	1,134.7	1,368.2	1,507.6	1,656.3	1,811.7	1,987.8	2,015.9	2,122.6	2,089.3	Domestic Credit	**52**
	59.0	112.6	137.8	135.0	138.4	116.6	143.5	237.9	259.2	213.4	346.6	458.9	507.9	590.2	403.7	Claims on Central Govt. (Net)	**52an**
	593.0	723.1	772.6	860.9	883.6	918.7	991.1	1,130.3	1,248.4	1,442.9	1,465.1	1,528.9	1,508.0	1,532.3	1,685.7	Claims on Private Sector	**52d**
	627.2	732.1	790.1	860.1	918.2	1,033.2	1,168.4	1,408.4	1,571.1	1,637.2	1,823.0	1,872.1	1,878.0	2,021.5	2,093.5	Liquid Liabilities	**55l**
	50.6	54.5	51.7	45.6	58.6	60.3	74.5	77.4	75.5	67.2	74.3	72.6	82.5	85.6	132.9	Capital Accounts	**57a**
	75.8	60.8	71.6	83.6	56.1	−.1	−36.4	−20.4	−8.0	−1.8	−78.3	−26.2	20.1	23.7	27.3	Other Items (Net)	**57r**

Barbados
316

		1965	1966	1967	1968	1969	1970	1971	1972	1973	1974	1975	1976	1977	1978	1979
Interest Rates															*Percent Per Annum*	
Bank Rate (End of Period)	60	...	...	...	...	...	...	...	...	...	...	...	...	6.00	6.00	6.00
Treasury Bill Rate	60c	...	...	5.35	5.83	6.12	7.01	7.17	5.95	6.57	8.96	5.67	4.43	4.63	4.80	4.88
Deposit Rate	60l	...	...	...	...	...	...	...	...	...	...	...	...	...	...	...
Lending Rate	60p	...	...	...	...	...	...	...	...	...	...	...	...	...	...	...
Prices and Production															*Index Numbers (1990=100):*	
Consumer Prices	64	...	12.0	12.4	13.4	14.2	15.2	16.3	18.3	21.3	29.6	35.7	37.4	40.6	44.4	ɪ50.3
Industrial Production	66	...	...	...	...	...	57.4	62.7	70.0	74.1	70.3	75.9	88.1	90.5	94.6	95.2
International Transactions															*Millions of Barbados Dollars*	
Exports	70	64.4	69.0	71.5	80.5	74.3	79.0	81.2	84.5	103.7	175.0	217.9	172.5	193.0	261.2	303.9
Imports, cif	71	114.7	130.8	134.3	168.1	194.6	235.1	243.6	270.4	328.6	418.3	437.2	474.1	545.1	628.7	850.8
Imports, fob	71.v	104.2	118.9	122.1	152.7	176.8	213.6	221.2	245.8	298.7	380.3	397.5	436.1	501.5	578.4	781.2
Balance of Payments															*Millions of US Dollars:*	
Goods: Exports f.o.b.	78aa d	...	...	...	...	...	40.4	41.3	44.2	53.4	85.7	108.8	87.8	104.1	130.9	155.1
Goods: Imports f.o.b.	78ab d	...	...	...	...	...	-106.9	-112.2	-128.0	-152.6	-185.5	-197.0	-219.1	-250.2	-288.0	-379.1
Trade Balance	78ac d	...	...	...	...	...	-66.5	-70.9	-83.9	-99.1	-99.8	-88.2	-131.3	-146.1	-157.1	-224.0
Services: Credit	78ad d	...	...	...	...	...	53.3	61.8	73.2	85.2	91.8	97.0	108.9	143.3	181.1	263.7
Services: Debit	78ae d	...	...	...	...	...	-34.5	-31.0	-37.1	-44.0	-46.8	-56.1	-59.7	-65.2	-77.4	-97.6
Balance on Goods and Services	78af d	...	...	...	...	...	-47.7	-40.1	-47.8	-57.9	-54.8	-47.3	-82.0	-68.0	-53.4	-58.0
Income: Credit	78ag d	...	...	...	...	...	8.0	7.6	7.9	10.7	12.3	14.9	13.5	12.7	17.6	22.8
Income: Debit	78ah d	...	...	...	...	...	-7.3	-8.1	-9.8	-12.4	-12.3	-16.3	-8.2	-12.0	-12.0	-20.9
Balance on Goods, Serv., & Inc.	78ai d	...	...	...	...	...	-47.0	-40.5	-49.8	-59.6	-54.8	-48.6	-76.8	-67.3	-47.9	-56.1
Current Transfers, n.i.e.: Credit	78aj d	...	...	...	...	...	7.7	8.2	9.4	11.2	11.0	11.9	18.4	21.4	22.0	30.7
Current Transfers: Debit	78ak d	...	...	...	...	...	-2.5	-2.8	-2.9	-3.9	-3.9	-4.7	-5.7	-5.4	-5.3	-8.8
Current Account, n.i.e.	78al d	...	...	...	...	...	-41.8	-35.1	-43.3	-52.3	-47.8	-41.3	-64.2	-51.4	-31.3	-34.2
Capital Account, n.i.e.: Credit	78ba d	...	...	...	...	...	—	—	—	—	—	—	—	—	—	—
Capital Account: Debit	78bb d	...	...	...	...	...	—	—	—	—	—	—	—	—	—	—
Capital Account, n.i.e.	78bc d	...	...	...	...	...	—	—	—	—	—	—	—	—	—	—
Direct Investment Abroad	78bd d	...	...	...	...	...	-.2	-1.3	.1	-.8	-.1	-.8	-.9	-.4	—	-.2
Dir. Invest. in Rep. Econ., n.i.e.	78be d	...	...	...	...	...	8.7	16.1	17.3	5.6	2.4	22.9	6.9	4.9	8.9	5.3
Portfolio Investment Assets	78bf d	...	...	...	...	...	-.6	-.2	—	-.3	.7	-.1	.1	5.0	—	-3.1
Portfolio Investment Liab., n.i.e.	78bg d	...	...	...	...	...	—	.8	.5	.4	-.9	.3	—	.5	2.0	.3
Other Investment Assets	78bh d	...	...	...	...	...	-10.6	-3.4	-4.6	-6.2	1.9	1.6	-6.1	-8.2	-22.6	-41.0
Other Investment Liab., n.i.e.	78bi d	...	...	...	...	...	14.1	12.7	7.6	35.8	-11.1	-2.4	25.2	26.3	27.8	48.0
Financial Account, n.i.e.	78bj d	...	...	...	...	...	11.3	24.6	20.8	34.5	-7.1	21.4	25.2	28.2	16.2	9.2
Net Errors and Omissions	78ca d	...	...	...	...	...	24.6	22.2	25.5	17.4	48.3	28.6	27.0	14.9	36.1	29.7
Overall Balance	78cb d	...	...	...	...	...	-5.9	11.7	3.1	-.4	-6.7	8.7	-12.0	-8.3	21.1	4.8
Reserves and Related Items	79da d	...	...	...	...	...	5.9	-11.7	-3.1	.4	6.7	-8.7	12.0	8.3	-21.1	-4.8
Reserve Assets	79db d	...	...	...	...	...	5.9	-11.7	-3.1	.4	6.7	-8.7	12.0	-9.2	-21.1	-4.8
Use of Fund Credit and Loans	79dc d	...	...	...	...	...	—	—	—	—	—	—	—	7.6	—	—
Liabs.Constit.For.Auth.Reserves	79dd d	...	...	...	...	...	—	—	—	—	—	—	—	—	—	—
Exceptional Financing	79de d	...	...	...	...	...	—	—	—	—	—	—	—	10.0	—	—
Government Finance															*Millions of Barbados Dollars:*	
Deficit (-) or Surplus	80	...	...	...	...	...	9.53	-2.74	-5.45	ɪ-8.00	-33.80	-22.00	ɪ-20.00	-58.50	-62.80	-4.30	-20.90
Revenue	81	...	...	...	...	...	82.20	98.49	113.01	ɪ119.50	138.60	177.50	ɪ214.20	230.30	266.20	328.20	376.70
Grants Received	81z	...	...	...	...	...	.70	...	...	ɪ—	—	—	ɪ—	—	.80	1.80	.80
Expenditure	82	...	...	...	...	...	79.77	100.49	116.54	ɪ123.70	167.80	197.80	ɪ233.60	287.60	328.30	324.90	395.90
Lending Minus Repayments	83	...	...	...	...	...	-6.40	.74	1.92	ɪ3.80	4.60	1.70	ɪ.60	1.20	1.50	9.40	2.50
Financing																	
Domestic	84a	...	...	...	...	...	-4.33	4.44	5.61	ɪ4.30	13.70	18.40	...	...	...	...	...
Foreign	85a	...	...	...	...	...	-5.20	-1.70	-.16	ɪ3.70	20.10	3.60	...	...	...	...	...
Unclassified Financing	87c	...	...	...	...	...	...	...	...	...	...	...	...	...	...	...
Debt: Domestic	88a	...	...	...	...	...	40.8	51.2	ɪ71.9	98.1	143.8	ɪ165.8	219.1	274.8	267.9	301.2
Foreign	89a	...	...	...	...	...	30.2	30.2	ɪ32.1	52.4	42.3	ɪ47.9	52.1	65.2	105.2	114.7
National Accounts															*Millions of Barbados Dollars*	
Exports of Goods & Services	90c	...	...	...	...	...	...	...	252	298	386	469	406	493	646	882
Government Consumption	91f	...	...	...	...	...	...	...	81	111	100	102	151	172	190	210
Gross Fixed Capital Formation	93e	...	...	...	...	...	...	...	95	117	152	156	236	194	254	317
Private Consumption	96f	...	...	...	...	...	...	...	308	349	539	568	646	742	782	965
Imports of Goods & Services	98c	...	...	...	...	...	...	...	-329	-398	-472	-515	-566	-607	-760	-1,027
Gross Domestic Product = GDP	99b	158	170	189	217	284	331	367	407	477	705	780	873	890	984	1,348
Gross Dom. Prod. 1990 Prices	99b.p	1,373	1,461	1,593	1,780	1,933	2,109	2,142	2,164	2,208	ɪ2,505	2,454	2,563	2,657	2,786	3,005
GDP Deflator (1990=100)	99bi p	11.5	11.6	11.9	12.2	14.7	15.7	17.1	18.8	21.6	28.1	31.8	34.1	33.5	35.3	44.9
																Millions:
Population	99z	.24	.24	.24	.24	.24	.24	.24	.24	.24	.24	.25	.25	.25	.26	.25

Exchange Rates: On October 6, 1965 the East Caribbean dollar, equal to the West Indian dollar, was introduced. On December 3, 1973 the Barbados dollar, equal to the East Caribbean dollar, was introduced.
International Liquidity: ɪ Beginning in January 1972, line 1dbd includes sinking funds held against domestic government debt.
Deposit Money Banks: ɪ Prior to June 1969, deposits by nonresidents are included in *lines 24* and *25* rather than in *line 26c*.
Monetary Survey: ɪ See note to section 20.

Government Finance: ɪ Beginning in 1972, data are as reported in the *Government Finance Statistics Yearbook* and cover consolidated central government. ɪ Beginning in 1975, data exclude all transactions of several special funds previously included. ɪ Beginning in 1982, data include transactions of two extrabudgetary accounts.

Barbados

316

	1980	1981	1982	1983	1984	1985	1986	1987	1988	1989	1990	1991	1992	1993	1994		
	Percent Per Annum															**Interest Rates**	
	7.00	22.00	20.00	16.00	16.00	13.00	8.00	8.00	8.00	13.50	13.50	18.00	12.00	8.00	9.50	Bank Rate *(End of Period)*	60
	5.63	9.49	13.25	7.45	6.92	.55	4.42	4.84	4.75	4.90	7.07	9.34	10.88	5.44	7.26	Treasury Bill Rate	60c
	5.30	7.39	8.83	6.73	6.07	5.49	4.28	3.61	4.26	4.78	6.28	6.53	6.68	4.39	4.32	Deposit Rate	60l
	....	11.46	13.38	11.79	11.50	10.56	9.06	8.75	9.44	9.92	11.42	12.42	13.54	8.92	9.08	Lending Rate	60p
	Period Averages															**Prices and Production**	
	57.5	65.9	72.7	76.5	80.1	83.2	84.3	87.1	91.4	97.0	100.0	106.3	112.7	114.0	114.1	Consumer Prices	64
	97.9	94.9	90.7	91.6	‡87.7	91.9	82.9	85.2	98.6	97.1	100.0	97.7	91.6	88.3	94.1	Industrial Production	66
	Millions of Barbados Dollars															**International Transactions**	
	455.4	391.0	517.5	646.0	787.4	698.5	552.3	313.5	354.2	375.5	421.1	411.6	383.8	359.7	....	Exports	70
	1,049.1	1,151.1	1,107.5	1,249.0	1,324.7	1,210.7	1,181.1	1,035.9	1,163.9	1,354.3	1,407.9	1,394.0	1,048.4	1,153.9	1,222.2	Imports, cif	71
	965.1	1,059.0	1,018.9	1,149.0	1,218.7	1,100.6	1,073.7	941.7	1,058.1	1,231.2	1,279.9	1,267.3	953.1	1,049.0	1,111.1	Imports, fob	71.v
	Minus Sign Indicates Debit															Balance of Payments	
	227.6	192.0	256.7	320.9	391.3	352.0	279.6	161.7	175.8	185.7	213.1	203.9	190.5	181.5	....	Goods: Exports f.o.b.	78aa *d*
	−480.8	−527.2	−507.0	−571.5	−606.1	−559.2	−523.3	−459.0	−518.7	−600.3	−624.1	−617.4	−464.7	−511.3	....	Goods: Imports f.o.b.	78ab *d*
	−253.2	−335.2	−250.3	−250.6	−214.8	−207.2	−243.7	−297.2	−342.9	−414.7	−410.9	−413.5	−274.2	−329.8	....	Trade Balance	78ac *d*
	318.4	331.6	335.7	336.0	374.9	401.2	428.2	475.1	560.2	654.3	579.1	581.3	581.1	646.8	....	Services: Credit	78ad *d*
	−119.6	−134.5	−141.1	−131.6	−144.3	−133.2	−170.0	−188.1	−172.2	−206.9	−194.3	−194.6	−186.5	−244.2	....	Services: Debit	78ae *d*
	−54.4	−138.1	−55.7	−46.2	15.8	60.9	14.5	−10.2	45.1	32.7	−26.2	−26.7	120.5	72.8	....	Balance on Goods and Services	78af *d*
	26.7	31.9	29.8	26.1	35.9	34.8	46.1	48.5	46.9	47.9	44.2	46.8	50.7	53.8	....	Income: Credit	78ag *d*
	−19.3	−30.3	−32.1	−36.9	−45.4	−46.6	−63.1	−66.8	−66.0	−61.7	−76.9	−78.2	−67.7	−83.1	....	Income: Debit	78ah *d*
	−47.1	−136.6	−58.0	−57.1	6.3	49.0	−2.5	−28.5	26.0	18.9	−58.9	−58.1	103.5	43.5	....	Balance on Goods, Serv., & Inc.	78ai *d*
	33.9	37.5	30.7	34.0	33.2	32.3	38.4	37.8	47.4	51.0	54.4	48.8	54.8	43.1	....	Current Transfers, n.i.e.: Credit	78aj *d*
	−12.4	−19.5	−7.9	−13.9	−19.5	−27.2	−27.2	−32.0	−31.0	−46.2	−11.9	−15.8	−14.5	−22.3	....	Current Transfers: Debit	78ak *d*
	−25.7	−118.6	−35.2	−37.0	20.0	54.1	8.6	−22.7	42.5	23.7	−16.4	−25.1	143.8	64.3	....	Current Account, n.i.e.	78al *d*
	—	—	—	—	—	—	—	—	—	—	—	—	—	—	....	Capital Account: Credit	78ba *d*
	—	—	—	—	—	—	—	—	—	—	—	—	—	—	....	Capital Account: Debit	78bb *d*
	—	—	—	—	—	—	—	—	—	—	—	—	—	—	....	Capital Account, n.i.e.	78bc *d*
	−.6	−1.2	−.5	−1.4	−1.5	−2.2	−2.7	−2.4	−.9	−2.9	−1.4	−1.3	−.8	−2.6	....	Direct Investment Abroad	78bd *d*
	2.8	8.4	4.6	3.6	—	4.8	7.7	7.1	11.5	8.3	11.1	7.3	14.4	9.3	....	Dir. Invest. in Rep. Econ., n.i.e.	78be *d*
	.3	−.2	−2.4	−.6	−.4	−2.9	−5.5	−1.8	−.5	−5.1	−6.0	−8.2	−4.1	−9.8	....	Portfolio Investment Assets	78bf *d*
	.5	1.0	−3.3	−.3	−.2	.1	.1	.2	.3	.4	—	−.6	—	.9	....	Portfolio Investment Liab., n.i.e.	78bg *d*
	−43.0	−55.3	−42.9	−39.2	−78.3	−16.7	4.2	31.9	3.1	−23.3	−18.6	−2.2	−4.2	−6.2	....	Other Investment Assets	78bh *d*
	90.5	153.3	87.7	109.7	74.2	18.3	71.9	50.9	34.1	.2	62.9	22.9	−99.2	9.6	....	Other Investment Liab., n.i.e.	78bi *d*
	50.5	106.0	43.2	71.8	−6.2	1.4	75.7	85.9	47.5	−22.4	48.0	17.8	−94.0	1.2	....	Financial Account, n.i.e.	78bj *d*
	−7.2	33.9	−5.8	−27.2	−30.4	−33.3	−64.2	−56.0	−50.4	−44.1	−70.6	−32.6	−21.5	−44.7	....	Net Errors and Omissions	78ca *d*
	17.6	21.2	2.2	7.6	−16.6	22.3	20.1	7.2	39.5	−42.8	−38.9	−39.9	28.3	20.9	....	Overall Balance	78cb *d*
	−17.6	−21.2	−2.2	−7.6	16.6	−22.3	−20.1	−7.2	−39.5	42.8	38.9	39.9	−28.3	−20.9	....	Reserves and Related Items	79aj *d*
	−12.1	−19.5	−23.7	−22.1	8.5	−22.3	−7.1	15.3	−27.4	48.6	42.0	40.6	−79.8	−20.9	....	Reserve Assets	79db *d*
	−5.5	−1.7	22.9	14.5	8.1	—	−13.0	−21.6	−10.6	−5.8	−3.7	−.7	51.5	—	....	Use of Fund Credit and Loans	79dc *d*
	—	—	—	—	—	—	—	−.9	−1.5	—	.6	—	—	—	....	Liabs.Constit.For.Auth.Reserves	79dd *d*
	—	—	−1.5	—	—	—	—	—	—	—	—	—	—	—	....	Exceptional Financing	79de *d*
	Year Beginning April 1															**Government Finance**	
	−60.90	−128.80	‡−76.10	−25.70	−91.00	−71.40	−79.70	−213.80	−88.70	−32.80	....	....	....	....	....	Deficit (−) or Surplus	80
	473.80	512.00	‡570.70	634.00	662.10	747.20	773.10	842.20	1,034.00	1,120.40	....	....	....	....	....	Revenue	81
	2.20	.90	‡1.80	2.90	4.00	1.30	2.00	2.20	2.70	1.10	....	....	....	....	....	Grants Received	81z
	531.90	625.30	‡608.00	636.40	706.60	797.20	824.00	1,007.70	1,071.20	1,136.80	....	....	....	....	....	Expenditure	82
	5.00	16.40	‡40.60	26.20	50.50	22.70	30.80	50.50	54.20	17.50	....	....	....	....	....	Lending Minus Repayments	83
																Financing	
	....	43.70	‡30.60	5.70	38.40	−3.60	27.80	75.20	12.00	....	....	....	....	....	....	Domestic	84a
	....	85.10	‡45.50	20.00	60.60	75.00	51.90	132.60	75.50	....	....	....	....	....	....	Foreign	85a
	....	—	‡—	—	−8.00	—	—	6.00	1.20	....	....	....	....	....	....	Unclassified Financing	87c
	330.0	325.1	‡349.9	362.6	362.0	423.2	499.8	522.5	549.3	611.2	....	....	....	....	....	Debt: Domestic	88a
	177.8	274.2	‡316.7	344.4	401.3	441.3	595.7	714.6	789.9	823.9	....	....	....	....	....	Foreign	89a
	Millions of Barbados Dollars															**National Accounts**	
	1,214	1,138	1,270	1,490	1,656	1,633	1,496	1,340	1,510	1,724	1,689	1,610	1,587	1,577	....	Exports of Goods & Services	90c
	258	321	329	346	388	456	469	498	537	614	694	642	640	732	....	Government Consumption	91f
	424	525	451	421	374	372	424	467	535	645	651	551	350	440	....	Gross Fixed Capital Formation	93e
	1,081	1,235	1,263	1,321	1,432	1,392	1,692	1,934	2,004	2,158	2,189	2,262	1,988	2,019	....	Private Consumption	96f
	−1,247	−1,315	−1,323	−1,466	−1,547	−1,448	−1,435	−1,325	−1,495	−1,725	−1,780	−1,701	−1,344	−1,500	....	Imports of Goods & Services	98c
	1,731	1,905	1,990	2,113	2,303	2,410	2,646	2,914	3,099	3,427	3,440	3,393	3,171	3,281	....	Gross Domestic Product = GDP	99b
	3,140	3,080	2,928	2,939	3,047	3,079	3,236	3,319	3,434	3,558	3,440	3,301	....	....	....	Gross Dom. Prod. 1990 Prices	99b.*p*
	55.1	61.8	68.0	71.9	75.6	78.3	81.8	87.8	90.2	96.3	100.0	102.8	....	....	....	GDP Deflator (1990=100)	99bi *p*
	Midyear Estimates																
	.25	.25	.25	.25	.25	.25	.25	.25	.25	.26	.26	.26	.26	.26	....	**Population**	99z

Belgium 124

		1965	1966	1967	1968	1969	1970	1971	1972	1973	1974	1975	1976	1977	1978	1979
Exchange Rates																*Francs per SDR:*
Market Rate......aa=	wa	49.642	50.052	49.627	50.140	49.666	49.675	48.591	47.839	49.846	44.227	46.273	41.806	40.013	37.520	36.948
																Francs per US Dollar:
Market Rate......ae=	we	49.643	50.053	49.628	50.140	49.666	49.675	44.755	44.063	41.320	36.123	39.528	35.983	32.940	28.800	28.048
Market Rate......rf=	wf	49.637	49.830	49.684	49.930	50.135	49.650	48.781	44.015	38.977	38.952	36.779	38.605	35.843	31.492	29.319
Secondary Rate	xe	49.96	50.46	49.85	52.10	50.19	49.70	44.75	44.38	41.24	36.10	40.32	35.70	32.99	29.39	28.99
Secondary Rate	xf	49.89	50.75	50.09	50.74	52.51	50.17	48.56	43.96	39.01	39.76	37.80	40.24	35.89	31.95	30.14
																Francs per ECU:
ECU Rate	ea	....	....	....	....	....	....	....	....	....	....	....	....	....	....	40.318
ECU Rate	eb	....	....	....	....	....	....	....	....	....	....	....	42.921	40.884	40.059	40.166
																Index Numbers (1990=100):
Market Rate	ahx	67.1	66.9	67.1	66.7	66.5	67.1	120.9	75.7	85.8	85.7	90.9	86.5	93.0	106.0	113.7
Nominal Effective Exchange Rate	neu	85.7	85.7	86.0	87.9	88.3	87.5	87.3	90.2	91.8	93.4	94.9	98.1	103.7	106.7	108.5
Real Effective Exchange Rate	reu	....	....	....	....	....	....	....	....	....	....	148.5	149.6	153.1	148.6	141.3
Fund Position																*Millions of SDRs:*
Quota	2f.s	338	422	422	422	422	650	650	650	650	650	650	650	650	890	890
SDRs	1b.s	—	—	—	—	—	205	405	523	626	584	615	397	407	414	476
Reserve Position in the Fund	1c.s	309	367	328	301	156	392	599	516	492	511	591	814	779	606	524
of which: Outstg. Fund Borrowing	2c	68	68	38	100	—	—	—	—	—	—	50	200	230	207	151
International Liquidity												*Millions of US Dollars Unless Otherwise Indicated:*				
Total Reserves minus Gold	1l.d	776	825	1,110	663	867	1,377	1,797	2,232	3,319	3,538	4,069	3,491	3,956	3,966	5,443
SDRs	1b.d	—	—	—	—	—	205	440	568	756	715	720	462	495	540	627
Reserve Position in the Fund	1c.d	309	367	328	301	155	392	651	560	594	626	692	946	947	789	690
Foreign Exchange	1d.d	467	458	782	362	712	780	706	1,104	1,969	2,197	2,656	2,083	2,515	2,637	4,126
Gold (Million Fine Troy Ounces)	1ad	44.52	43.56	42.26	43.53	43.40	42.01	44.12	43.08	42.17	42.17	42.17	42.17	42.45	42.59	34.21
Gold (National Valuation)	1and	1,558	1,524	1,480	1,524	1,518	1,470	1,723	1,682	1,780	1,780	1,780	1,780	1,793	1,797	1,445
Monetary Authorities: Other Assets	3..d	136	153	164	287	198	40	130	375	409	332	300	386	621	908	789
Other Liab.	4..d	14	14	14	20	14	20	78	38	79	91	91	92	823	1,132	1,191
Deposit Money Banks: Assets	7a.d	1,004	1,368	1,602	2,326	3,362	4,922	6,611	8,207	12,049	16,577	17,777	21,505	28,543	39,438	49,162
of which: Claims on Nonbanks	7ad.d	390	428	500	814	1,090	1,784	2,550	2,687	3,623	5,351	5,705	6,945	8,579	10,896	13,609
Deposit Money Banks: Liabilities	7b.d	1,518	2,052	2,382	3,052	4,086	5,734	7,386	9,222	13,708	19,254	20,148	23,914	31,852	44,514	58,635
of which: Liab. to Nonbanks	7bd.d	292	346	368	618	840	918	1,053	1,118	1,788	2,220	2,525	3,585	4,317	5,712	6,999
Monetary Authorities																*Billions of Francs:*
Foreign Assets	11	123.5	125.2	137.6	123.8	129.1	144.4	166.9	194.9	222.5	227.3	253.2	226.9	247.9	243.1	253.9
Claims on Central Government	12a	45.5	46.3	39.4	51.9	52.0	49.5	40.8	37.1	42.9	46.1	45.5	61.9	78.7	78.7	79.4
Reserve Money	14	172.1	177.1	180.2	184.1	184.4	189.8	203.4	232.0	260.9	272.0	290.0	309.1	336.4	361.3	372.8
of which: Currency Outside DMBs	14a	166.8	171.8	173.6	178.8	178.1	183.2	196.4	216.8	231.5	248.9	281.2	299.5	327.4	349.7	359.0
Other Items (Net)	17r	−3.1	−5.6	−3.2	−8.3	−3.2	4.1	4.3	....	4.5	1.4	8.7	−20.3	−9.8	−39.5	−39.5
Deposit Money Banks																
Commercial Banks																*Billions of Francs:*
Reserves	20	10.6	10.5	11.7	10.5	15.9	13.3	14.8	20.7	30.1	26.7	14.3	14.5	14.8	15.4	19.3
Foreign Assets	21	50.2	68.4	80.1	116.3	168.1	246.1	296.3	367.8	486.0	598.8	702.7	773.8	940.2	1,135.8	1,378.9
Claims on Central Government	22a	93.0	102.6	113.0	116.0	132.6	135.5	153.6	181.9	214.9	235.3	266.3	300.6	313.6	359.4	423.9
Claims on Official Entities	22bx	14.0	17.6	21.6	27.1	36.1	51.3	58.4	63.7	79.7	96.1	107.2	120.7	155.4	165.7	186.3
Claims on Private Sector	22d	109.6	129.9	156.1	178.2	195.1	226.3	258.4	311.2	366.2	410.6	491.2	567.1	667.3	740.1	876.2
Demand Deposits	24	95.1	103.6	113.1	122.8	109.4	124.5	144.0	173.3	185.9	195.1	236.3	248.1	278.6	291.7	296.8
Time & Foreign Currency Deposits	25	81.8	94.7	116.2	134.5	185.3	204.4	240.1	283.9	355.3	399.1	457.5	550.5	596.9	654.0	722.9
Bonds	26ab	11.4	12.0	13.5	16.5	21.0	25.5	30.4	35.8	41.8	48.7	58.2	74.3	104.4	125.6	153.0
Foreign Liabilities	26c	75.9	102.6	119.1	152.6	204.3	286.7	331.0	413.3	552.9	695.5	796.4	860.5	1,049.2	1,282.0	1,644.6
Other Items (Net)	27r	13.2	16.1	20.6	21.7	27.8	31.5	36.0	39.0	40.9	29.0	33.3	43.3	62.2	63.1	67.3
Other Monetary Institutions																*Billions of Francs:*
Claims on Central Government	22a.j	53.4	55.0	55.4	63.7	58.5	62.3	63.0	72.0	72.1	73.3	78.8	87.5	90.6	94.7	92.4
Claims on Nonfin.Pub.Enterprise	22bx.j	6.8	9.7	8.1	10.1	10.2	10.9	12.8	17.4	17.2	21.9	25.9	28.4	35.9	38.5	44.8
Claims on Private Sector	22d.j	1.5	1.2	2.5	1.4	2.4	1.6	.3	.8	3.2	3.0	7.0	3.5	3.4	3.9	.6
Monetary Liabilities	24..j	62.1	69.5	69.0	79.5	75.7	77.2	87.8	99.7	103.7	112.4	127.5	141.7	140.9	148.0	155.2
of which: To Private Sector	24x.j	44.5	48.8	46.0	53.4	51.5	57.7	59.6	71.7	74.8	77.0	85.1	92.4	97.3	103.5	104.0
To Govt. & Off. Ent.	24y.j	11.8	14.9	17.4	20.8	14.1	12.4	19.7	21.8	27.6	31.5	35.9	43.1	36.8	39.6	43.6
Other Items (Net)	27r..j	−.4	−3.6	−3.0	−4.3	−4.6	−2.3	−11.6	−9.7	−11.6	−14.2	−15.8	−22.3	−11.0	−10.9	−17.4
Monetary Survey																*Billions of Francs:*
Foreign Assets (Net)	31n	94.9	89.2	97.1	86.0	93.7	105.0	131.4	147.7	152.2	127.5	156.9	137.2	112.7	64.7	−45.2
Domestic Credit	32	329.8	370.6	402.4	461.0	496.7	543.6	598.7	703.1	821.5	908.8	1,034.5	1,203.6	1,386.8	1,536.1	1,764.0
Claims on Central Govt. (Net)	32an	191.9	203.9	207.8	231.6	243.1	247.3	257.4	291.0	329.9	354.7	390.6	450.0	482.5	532.8	595.7
Claims on Official Entities	32bx	21.2	27.7	30.2	37.8	47.0	63.0	72.5	82.5	98.3	119.4	134.5	150.5	192.7	205.5	232.4
Claims on Private Sector	32d	116.7	139.0	164.4	191.6	206.6	233.3	268.8	329.6	393.3	434.7	509.4	603.1	711.2	797.8	935.9
Money	34	318.6	339.6	350.5	375.9	353.5	378.1	420.3	484.2	520.3	552.6	639.4	684.1	741.0	784.4	804.1
Quasi-Money	35	81.8	94.7	116.2	134.5	185.3	204.4	240.1	283.9	355.3	399.1	457.5	550.5	596.9	654.0	722.9
Other Items (Net)	37r	24.3	25.5	32.8	36.7	51.7	66.3	69.8	82.5	97.6	84.7	94.3	106.2	161.6	162.4	191.8
Money plus Quasi-Money	35l	400.4	434.3	466.7	510.4	538.8	582.5	660.4	768.1	875.6	951.7	1,096.9	1,234.6	1,337.9	1,438.4	1,527.0
Interest Rates																*Percent Per Annum*
Discount Rate (End of Period)	60	4.75	5.25	4.00	4.50	7.50	6.50	5.50	5.00	7.75	8.75	6.00	9.00	9.00	6.00	10.50
Money Market Rate	60b	3.14	3.89	3.22	2.85	5.28	6.26	3.72	2.51	4.80	9.24	4.68	8.31	5.49	5.23	7.97
Treasury Bill Rate	60c	5.34	5.74	5.72	6.41	6.89	7.05	6.83	6.68	7.17	9.87	6.49	9.53	6.64	6.89	10.51
Deposit Rate	60l	3.50	3.65	3.67	3.10	4.56	5.92	4.65	2.90	4.27	6.75	5.41	5.62	5.46	4.50	5.50
Lending Rate	60p															
Government Bond Yield	61	6.44	6.62	6.70	6.54	7.20	7.81	7.35	7.04	7.44	8.68	8.54	9.05	8.80	8.45	9.51

Belgium

124

1980	1981	1982	1983	1984	1985	1986	1987	1988	1989	1990	1991	1992	1993	1994	
End of Period															**Exchange Rates**
40.205	44.766	51.758	58.252	61.832	55.316	49.429	47.032	50.255	46.994	44.078	44.730	45.623	49.599	46.478	Market Rate....................aa= .... **wa**
End of Period (we) Period Average (wf)															
31.523	38.460	46.920	55.640	63.080	50.360	40.410	33.153	37.345	35.760	30.983	31.270	33.180	36.110	31.838	Market Rate....................ae= .... **we**
29.242	37.129	45.691	51.132	57.784	59.378	44.672	37.334	36.768	39.404	33.418	34.148	32.150	34.597	33.456	Market Rate....................rf= .... **wf**
31.65	42.55	48.10	56.55	63.30	50.68	40.82	33.22	37.28	35.59	....	....	....	....	....	Secondary Rate.. **xe**
29.66	39.31	49.05	52.02	58.65	59.74	45.08	37.57	37.01	39.51	....	....	....	....	....	Secondary Rate.. **xf**
End of Period (ea) Period Average (eb)															
41.335	41.747	45.321	46.097	44.717	44.645	43.233	43.154	43.576	42.592	42.184	41.931	40.178	40.287	39.161	ECU Rate .... **ea**
40.601	41.301	44.680	45.430	45.438	44.913	43.803	43.039	43.427	43.378	42.423	42.222	41.604	40.466	39.662	ECU Rate .... **eb**
Period Averages															
114.1	90.2	73.3	65.4	57.8	56.5	74.9	89.4	90.8	84.7	100.0	98.0	103.9	96.5	99.9	Market Rate .... **ah*x***
106.9	102.2	93.1	90.9	89.6	90.4	94.5	97.7	96.5	95.8	100.0	100.0	101.9	103.2	105.1	Nominal Effective Exchange Rate .... **ne*u***
135.7	124.3	103.2	96.9	95.4	94.8	98.1	99.0	96.2	95.7	100.0	100.1	101.9	102.1	....	Real Effective Exchange Rate .... **re*u***
End of Period															**Fund Position**
1,335	1,335	1,335	2,080	2,080	2,080	2,080	2,080	2,080	2,080	2,080	2,080	3,102	3,102	3,102	Quota .... **2f. *s***
497	628	672	399	454	328	280	494	418	423	398	411	124	125	123	SDRs .... **1b. *s***
489	390	328	496	521	472	462	392	345	342	326	367	586	560	556	Reserve Position in the Fund .... **1c. *s***
117	75	28	10	7	4	1	—	—	—	—	—	—	—	—	*of which:* Outstg.Fund Borrowing **2c**
End of Period															**International Liquidity**
7,823	4,952	3,927	4,714	4,564	4,849	5,538	9,620	9,333	10,766	12,151	12,180	13,801	11,415	13,876	Total Reserves minus Gold...................... **1l. *d***
633	731	741	418	445	361	342	700	563	556	566	588	171	171	180	SDRs .... **1b. *d***
624	454	362	520	511	519	565	557	464	449	464	524	806	769	812	Reserve Position in the Fund .... **1c. *d***
6,565	3,767	2,824	3,776	3,608	3,969	4,630	8,363	8,306	9,760	11,121	11,068	12,825	10,474	12,884	Foreign Exchange .... **1d. *d***
34.18	34.18	34.18	34.18	34.18	34.18	34.18	33.63	33.67	30.23	30.23	30.23	25.04	25.04	25.04	Gold (Million Fine Troy Ounces)............ **1ad**
1,443	1,443	1,443	1,443	1,443	1,443	1,443	1,421	1,421	1,277	1,277	10,774	8,321	....	....	Gold (National Valuation)...................... **1an *d***
247	838	701	560	194	335	109	82	86	512	609	254	165	140	115	Monetary Authorities: Other Assets .... **3.. *d***
222	315	524	985	98	133	144	151	273	131	274	339	241	....	....	Other Liab. .... **4.. *d***
60,680	69,943	65,748	66,202	71,607	92,631	117,926	149,126	150,374	164,516	192,031	192,024	188,522	....	....	Deposit Money Banks: Assets .... **7a. *d***
16,766	19,932	19,256	19,330	20,961	25,550	33,143	38,923	39,175	43,451	52,856	52,076	54,688	....	....	*of which:* Claims on Nonbanks............ **7ad *d***
72,953	83,102	78,374	80,196	86,376	112,925	144,838	184,795	186,432	205,526	239,787	229,933	226,055	....	....	Deposit Money Banks: Liabilities .... **7b. *d***
7,836	8,947	8,668	9,143	9,957	13,036	18,243	24,420	27,672	34,723	44,361	49,937	56,127	....	....	*of which:* Liab. to Nonbanks .... **7bd *d***
End of Period															**Monetary Authorities**
331.0	281.5	265.1	328.0	336.2	306.7	272.9	365.6	393.5	446.5	447.4	752.1	731.7	....	....	Foreign Assets **11**
80.1	80.8	82.5	84.2	85.3	86.9	88.8	91.9	95.6	98.8	103.3	48.9	51.9	....	....	Claims on Central Government **12a**
376.9	383.5	383.6	397.2	399.8	396.1	415.6	426.9	431.2	443.6	429.0	432.0	430.4	....	....	Reserve Money **14**
364.2	370.1	369.5	383.3	381.9	379.9	400.5	410.7	415.0	422.6	408.6	412.2	410.2	....	....	*of which: Currency Outside DMBs* **14a**
34.2	-21.2	-36.0	15.0	21.7	-2.5	-53.9	30.6	57.8	101.5	122.0	369.1	353.3	....	....	Other Items (Net) **17r**
															Deposit Money Banks
End of Period															Commercial Banks
19.5	17.1	17.0	16.9	21.7	20.0	22.9	21.6	20.9	23.2	23.2	....	....	....	....	Reserves **20**
1,912.8	2,690.0	3,084.9	3,683.5	4,517.0	4,664.9	4,765.4	4,943.9	5,615.7	5,883.1	5,949.6	....	....	....	....	Foreign Assets **21**
542.8	660.8	843.7	1,119.3	1,230.5	1,435.0	1,558.2	1,655.8	1,711.7	1,811.5	1,942.7	....	....	....	....	Claims on Central Government **22a**
188.9	258.7	283.7	304.4	344.7	372.1	433.7	528.9	426.9	420.9	401.5	....	....	....	....	Claims on Official Entities **22bx**
968.2	1,021.3	1,049.3	1,101.3	1,181.0	1,222.3	1,342.4	1,493.8	1,769.5	2,220.8	2,327.6	....	....	....	....	Claims on Private Sector......................... **22d**
293.7	306.9	334.6	393.7	393.3	427.6	468.4	502.6	545.6	574.9	584.8	....	....	....	....	Demand Deposits **24**
771.4	853.8	941.6	1,016.9	1,102.2	1,179.8	1,328.8	1,495.0	1,573.0	1,787.4	1,900.2	....	....	....	....	Time & Foreign Currency Deposits **25**
201.0	245.0	300.2	356.8	393.5	444.5	451.1	461.4	468.7	530.0	676.1	....	....	....	....	Bonds **26ab**
2,299.7	3,196.1	3,677.3	4,462.1	5,448.6	5,686.9	5,852.9	6,126.4	6,962.3	7,349.6	7,429.2	....	....	....	....	Foreign Liabilities..................................... **26c**
66.4	46.1	24.9	-4.1	-42.7	-24.5	21.7	58.4	-5.0	117.2	54.1	....	....	....	....	Other Items (Net)....................................... **27r**
End of Period															Other Monetary Institutions
98.5	102.3	101.3	99.3	85.5	98.6	109.6	105.8	108.0	121.3	115.6	....	....	....	....	Claims on Central Government.............**22a. *j***
44.6	35.5	39.6	42.4	62.7	47.3	45.7	52.6	64.6	72.8	91.4	....	....	....	....	Claims on Nonfin.Pub.Enterprise.........**22bx *j***
2.0	3.2	1.4	.9	.8	3.3	.3	—	—	—	—	....	....	....	....	Claims on Private Sector ....**22d. *j***
156.5	151.8	156.4	157.4	163.0	160.7	178.4	180.3	192.4	215.0	228.6	....	....	....	....	Monetary Liabilities ....**24.. *j***
106.5	110.9	112.7	111.7	102.4	115.2	131.2	128.6	132.9	157.3	160.2	....	....	....	....	*of which: To Private Sector*..................**24x. *j***
41.3	34.7	37.9	40.1	53.8	38.8	36.5	43.1	51.9	52.1	63.0	....	....	....	....	*To Govt. & Off. Ent.* ....**24y. *j***
-11.4	-10.8	-14.1	-14.8	-14.0	-11.5	-22.8	-21.8	-19.9	-20.9	-21.5	....	....	....	....	Other Items (Net)...................................**27r. *j***
End of Period															**Monetary Survey**
-60.2	-235.7	-351.8	-500.8	-599.6	-719.8	-819.2	-821.9	-963.3	-1,024.7	-1,040.7	....	....	....	....	Foreign Assets (Net) **31n**
1,967.4	2,219.0	2,456.1	2,806.8	2,991.8	3,276.0	3,579.8	3,929.8	4,177.1	4,764.0	4,997.6	....	....	....	....	Domestic Credit **32**
721.4	843.9	1,027.5	1,302.8	1,401.3	1,620.5	1,756.6	1,853.5	1,915.3	2,031.6	2,161.6	....	....	....	....	Claims on Central Govt. (Net) **32an**
234.8	295.7	324.5	347.7	408.4	420.4	480.5	582.5	492.3	494.5	493.5	....	....	....	....	Claims on Official Entities **32bx**
1,011.2	1,079.4	1,104.1	1,156.3	1,182.1	1,235.1	1,342.7	1,493.8	1,769.5	2,237.9	2,342.5	....	....	....	....	Claims on Private Sector **32d**
806.1	823.5	855.8	929.8	932.5	962.4	1,037.3	1,086.0	1,145.9	1,207.4	1,217.0	....	....	....	....	Money **34**
771.4	853.8	941.6	1,016.9	1,102.2	1,179.8	1,328.8	1,495.0	1,573.0	1,787.4	1,900.2	....	....	....	....	Quasi-Money.. **35**
329.7	306.0	306.9	359.3	357.5	414.0	394.8	526.8	494.6	743.9	839.9	....	....	....	....	Other Items (Net) **37r**
1,577.5	1,677.3	1,797.4	1,946.7	2,034.7	2,142.2	2,366.1	2,581.0	2,718.9	2,994.8	3,117.2	....	....	....	....	Money plus Quasi-Money **35l**
Percent Per Annum															**Interest Rates**
12.00	15.00	11.50	10.00	11.00	9.75	8.00	7.00	7.75	10.25	10.50	8.50	7.75	5.25	4.50	Discount Rate *(End of Period)*.................... **60**
11.22	11.47	11.44	8.18	9.47	8.27	6.64	5.67	5.04	7.00	8.29	9.38	9.38	8.21	5.72	Money Market Rate **60b**
13.90	14.88	13.96	10.38	11.60	9.44	8.09	7.00	6.61	8.45	9.62	9.23	9.36	8.52	5.57	Treasury Bill Rate **60c**
7.69	7.50	7.46	6.67	7.44	6.69	5.33	5.00	4.54	5.13	6.13	6.25	6.25	7.11	4.86	Deposit Rate... **60l**
....	18.00	15.50	13.75	14.00	12.54	10.44	9.33	8.92	11.08	13.00	12.88	13.00	11.81	9.42	Lending Rate **60p**
12.04	13.71	13.56	11.86	11.98	10.61	7.93	7.83	7.85	8.64	10.06	9.28	8.64	7.18	7.76	Government Bond Yield **61**

Belgium

124

		1965	1966	1967	1968	1969	1970	1971	1972	1973	1974	1975	1976	1977	1978	1979
Prices and Production																*Index Numbers (1990=100):*
Industrial Share Prices	62	34	28	28	30	33	31	34	38	46	37	35	33	30	30	33
Producer Prices																
Home and Import Goods	63	40.9	41.9	41.4	41.5	43.6	45.7	45.4	47.3	53.1	62.0	62.8	67.2	68.8	67.5	71.8
Industrial Production Prices	63b	40.1	40.5	40.5	41.0	42.4	45.0	45.8	47.7	51.2	61.5	64.1	67.2	69.0	69.4	72.1
Consumer Prices	64	26.5	27.7	28.5	29.2	30.3	31.5	32.9	34.7	37.1	41.8	I47.1	51.4	55.1	57.5	60.1
Wages: Hourly Earnings	65	13.1	14.5	15.5	16.3	17.6	19.6	22.0	25.1	29.2	35.3	42.4	47.1	51.4	55.0	I59.3
Industrial Production	66..b	53.2	54.3	55.1	58.2	63.8	66.0	67.8	71.9	76.4	79.2	71.6	77.9	77.8	79.5	83.1
International Transactions																*Billions of Francs*
(BLEU: Country Code 126)																
Exports	70	319.7	341.6	354.1	408.6	504.5	580.0	620.2	711.0	870.1	1,099.8	1,056.9	1,266.5	1,344.7	1,410.3	1,661.2
Imports, cif	71	325.1	359.1	364.3	419.8	501.1	570.6	629.1	681.8	856.1	1,160.7	1,130.9	1,369.0	1,448.0	1,526.0	1,784.4
Imports, fob	71.v	309.0	341.3	351.3	404.4	483.2	550.8	606.1	658.1	825.7	1,094.0	1,063.9	1,301.3	1,404.5	1,480.1	1,730.7
																1990=100
Volume of Exports	72	24	25	25	30	35	39	41	47	53	54	50	56	I58	60	65
Volume of Imports	73	24	26	26	30	35	39	43	47	54	58	53	61	I62	65	70
Unit Value of Exports	74	35	36	36	36	38	40	39	40	43	53	55	59	I60	59	65
Unit Value of Imports	75	35	36	35	35	36	38	38	38	40	52	55	58	I59	59	64
Import Price(Belgium: Code 124)	76.x	38.5	39.9	37.8	37.3	39.3	41.3	40.4	41.0	48.5	60.7	56.8	60.2	59.5	58.0	65.5
Balance of Payments																*Millions of US Dollars:*
(BLEU: Country Code 126)																
Goods: Exports f.o.b.	78aa d	....	....	....	....	....	....	9,760	13,241	19,024	24,878	23,797	26,886	32,699	40,055	51,410
Goods: Imports f.o.b.	78ab d	....	....	....	....	....	....	−9,552	−12,136	−17,798	−24,516	−24,191	−27,574	−34,537	−41,267	−54,426
Trade Balance	78ac d	....	....	....	....	....	....	208	1,105	1,226	363	−394	−687	−1,838	−1,212	−3,016
Services: Credit	78ad d	....	....	....	....	....	....	476	2,520	3,404	4,676	5,555	6,018	8,277	9,006	11,016
Services: Debit	78ae d	....	....	....	....	....	....	−394	−2,397	−3,327	−4,360	−4,957	−5,136	−7,071	−8,659	−10,703
Balance on Goods and Services	78af d	....	....	....	....	....	....	204	1,027	1,052	278	204	195	−632	−865	−2,703
Income: Credit	78ag d	....	....	....	....	....	....	1,003	1,412	2,313	4,178	4,479	4,430	5,263	7,380	11,527
Income: Debit	78ah d	....	....	....	....	....	....	−916	−1,130	−2,003	−3,739	−3,889	−3,670	−4,563	−6,585	−11,007
Balance on Goods, Serv., & Inc.	78ai d	....	....	....	....	....	....	291	1,308	1,362	717	795	955	68	−71	−2,184
Current Transfers, n.i.e.: Credit	78aj d	....	....	....	....	....	....	371	471	676	637	755	918	1,232	1,588	1,928
Current Transfers: Debit	78ak d	....	....	....	....	....	....	−533	−672	−984	−1,016	−1,368	−1,438	−1,854	−2,341	−2,825
Current Account, n.i.e.	78al d	....	....	....	....	....	....	129	1,108	1,054	338	181	435	−554	−823	−3,080
Capital Account, n.i.e.: Credit	78ba d	....	....	....	....	....	....	—	—	—	—	—	—	—	—	—
Capital Account: Debit	78bb d	....	....	....	....	....	....	—	—	—	—	—	—	—	—	—
Capital Account, n.i.e.	78bc d	....	....	....	....	....	....	—	—	—	—	—	—	—	—	—
Direct Investment Abroad	78bd d	....	....	....	....	....	....	−93	−62	−151	−344	−238	−352	−465	−560	−1,341
Dir. Invest. in Rep. Econ., n.i.e.	78be d	....	....	....	....	....	....	257	257	448	524	955	872	1,275	1,436	1,130
Portfolio Investment Assets	78bf d	....	....	....	....	....	....	—	—	—	−26	−1,039	−763	−1,373	−864	−216
Portfolio Investment Liab., n.i.e.	78bg d	....	....	....	....	....	....	—	—	—	−76	−35	213	230	−94	829
Other Investment Assets	78bh d	....	....	....	....	....	....	—	−353	−707	−820	−8,376	−9,946	−14,827	−18,165	−32,136
Other Investment Liab., n.i.e.	78bi d	....	....	....	....	....	....	—	—	—	—	8,112	8,152	15,140	18,836	31,975
Financial Account, n.i.e.	78bj d	....	....	....	....	....	....	163	−158	−410	−651	−622	−1,824	−20	589	242
Net Errors and Omissions	78ca d	....	....	....	....	....	....	−207	−706	−503	−529	419	113	129	219	−138
Overall Balance	78cb d	....	....	....	....	....	....	85	243	141	−843	−21	−1,276	−445	−15	−2,977
Reserves and Related Items	79da d	....	....	....	....	....	....	−85	−243	−141	843	21	1,276	445	15	2,977
Reserve Assets	79db d	....	....	....	....	....	....	−85	−243	−141	38	−546	635	−422	275	906
Use of Fund Credit and Loans	79dc d	....	....	....	....	....	....	—	—	—	—	—	—	—	—	—
Liabs.Constit.For.Auth.Reserves	79dd d	....	....	....	....	....	....	—	—	—	805	567	640	868	−259	2,071
Exceptional Financing	79de d	....	....	....	....	....	....	—	—	—	—	—	—	—	—	—
Government Finance																*Billions of Francs:*
Deficit (-) or Surplus	80	4.6	1.5	6.0	7.8	.1	I−21.2	−39.6	−67.9	−61.8	−46.6	−109.0	−147.5	−168.3	−209.2	−247.7
Revenue	81	173.2	201.2	219.8	239.4	266.6	I448.1	493.7	553.6	646.9	779.0	924.8	1,056.1	1,180.1	1,296.8	1,393.4
Grants Received	81z	....	....	....	....	....	I1.3	2.0	2.4	3.2	2.6	3.1	3.9	3.4	3.9	4.7
Expenditure	82	168.6	199.7	213.8	231.6	266.5	I468.3	530.6	619.9	706.8	820.2	1,025.9	1,194.0	1,340.2	1,482.3	1,625.6
Lending Minus Repayments	83	....	....	....	....	....	I2.3	4.7	4.0	5.1	8.0	11.0	13.5	11.6	27.6	20.2
Financing																
Net Borrowing: Domestic	84a	26.4	11.1	25.4	37.3	22.1	I33.1	69.1	82.3	68.4	40.6	109.1	150.7	167.4	172.7	207.1
Foreign	85a	−4.3	6.0	−2.4	−3.2	6.0	I−11.3	−28.5	−15.0	−3.5	−1.4	.2	−.4	−.3	13.4	43.0
Use of Cash Balances	87	....	....	....	....	....	I−.6	−1.0	.6	−3.1	7.4	−.3	−2.8	1.2	23.1	−2.4
Debt: Domestic	88a	434.8	449.8	466.5	509.4	532.1	I554.2	615.7	693.7	749.1	807.9	917.0	1,050.4	1,218.2	1,387.5	1,556.3
Foreign	89a	49.8	53.7	58.9	57.9	63.7	I55.0	26.8	11.8	8.3	6.9	7.1	6.7	6.4	19.9	62.9
National Accounts																*Billions of Francs*
Exports of Goods & Services	90c	306	328	352	402	483	562	609	683	846	1,116	1,065	1,266	1,474	1,540	1,798
Government Consumption	91f	110	121	133	144	160	175	202	232	264	314	388	441	489	544	588
Gross Fixed Capital Formation	93e	185	206	218	221	244	288	306	328	374	467	512	565	606	646	668
Increase/Decrease(-) in Stocks	93i	4	8	5	9	20	20	18	10	25	46	−13	10	8	8	20
Private Consumption	96i	541	580	612	663	719	769	848	948	1,084	1,256	1,421	1,613	1,769	1,890	2,057
Imports of Goods & Services	98c	−305	−337	−351	−400	−474	−533	−581	−633	−811	−1,109	−1,061	−1,261	−1,499	−1,570	−1,866
Gross Domestic Product	99b	842	905	970	1,038	1,151	1,281	1,402	1,569	1,782	2,091	2,313	2,633	2,847	3,058	3,265
Net Factor Inc/Pmts(-) Abroad	98.n	7	7	8	8	8	11	10	12	9	12	13	17	12	10	−4
Gross Nat'l Expenditure = GNP	99a	849	912	977	1,046	1,160	1,292	1,412	1,581	1,792	2,103	2,326	2,650	2,859	3,068	3,261
Nat'l Income, Market Prices	99e	769	826	885	947	1,051	1,167	1,278	1,432	1,630	1,910	2,113	2,419	2,597	2,786	2,959
Gross Dom. Prod. 1990 Prices	99b.p	3,050	3,137	3,261	3,400	3,623	I3,853	3,996	4,210	4,458	4,648	4,578	4,838	4,866	5,005	5,113
GDP Deflator (1990=100)	99bi p	27.6	28.9	29.7	30.5	31.8	33.2	35.1	37.3	40.0	45.0	50.5	54.4	58.5	61.1	63.9
																Millions:
Population	99z	9.46	9.53	9.58	9.62	9.65	9.66	9.67	9.71	9.74	9.77	9.79	9.81	9.82	9.83	9.84

Interest Rates: *Money Market Rate:* I Beginning in January 1991, the averages of borrowing and lending rates for three-month interbank transactions. Prior to that date, the call money rate was used.
Deposit Rate: I Beginning in January 1993, the average rate on time deposits with maturities between one month and one year. Prior to that date, the rate on three-month time deposits at commercial banks.

Government Finance: I Beginning in 1970, annual data are as reported in the *Government Finance Statistics Yearbook* and cover consolidated central government.

Belgium 124

	1980	1981	1982	1983	1984	1985	1986	1987	1988	1989	1990	1991	1992	1993	1994		
Period Averages																**Prices and Production**	
	33	26	31	39	50	56	80	95	94	108	100	97	95	99	114	Industrial Share Prices	62
																Producer Prices	
	72.7	82.9	94.1	100.4	108.0	110.8	98.1	93.3	94.8	101.0	100.0	99.0	97.2	....	....	Home and Import Goods	63
	73.8	82.9	92.2	98.0	103.9	106.8	97.1	92.9	94.0	99.4	100.0	98.9	99.1	98.1	99.5	Industrial Production Prices	63b
	64.1	69.0	75.0	80.8	‡85.9	90.1	91.3	92.7	‡93.8	96.7	100.0	103.2	105.7	108.6	111.2	Consumer Prices	64
	64.8	71.3	75.7	79.0	82.9	85.9	88.3	‡90.0	90.7	95.8	100.0	105.1	110.1	112.4	114.7	Wages: Hourly Earnings	65
	82.1	79.9	80.1	81.6	83.8	85.1	85.9	88.1	93.3	96.5	100.0	98.0	97.9	93.1	....	Industrial Production	66..b
Billions of Francs																**International Transactions**	
																(BLEU: Country Code 126)	
	1,890.4	2,062.3	2,393.2	2,651.3	2,992.1	3,167.7	3,070.3	3,100.1	3,382.3	3,943.1	3,944.5	4,023.4	3,969.8	....	....	Exports	70
	2,100.8	2,309.8	2,653.4	2,820.9	3,195.8	3,317.8	3,065.2	3,110.1	3,393.6	3,883.9	4,011.6	4,116.3	4,023.3	....	....	Imports, cif	71
	2,037.6	2,240.3	2,573.6	2,736.1	3,099.7	3,218.0	2,973.0	3,016.6	3,291.6	3,767.1	3,891.0	3,992.5	3,902.3	....	....	Imports, fob	71.v
1990=100																	
	‡67	67	68	70	73	76	79	84	90	97	100	104	104	....	....	Volume of Exports	72
	‡71	68	69	68	71	73	78	84	89	95	100	104	105	....	....	Volume of Imports	73
	‡72	78	89	96	104	106	98	93	96	103	100	98	97	....	....	Unit Value of Exports	74
	‡74	84	97	104	112	114	98	92	95	102	100	99	95	....	....	Unit Value of Imports	75
	‡71.4	82.7	95.2	102.0	111.0	114.1	98.8	93.3	95.3	101.8	100.0	98.9	96.0	....	....	Import Price(Belgium: Code 124)	76.x
																Balance of Payments	
																(BLEU: Country Code 126)	
Minus Sign Indicates Debit																	
	57,573	50,719	48,243	47,598	48,001	49,178	62,914	77,948	87,436	92,112	110,230	108,566	116,277	106,550	....	Goods: Exports f.o.b.	78aa d
	−61,432	−54,193	−50,543	−48,264	−48,192	−48,686	−60,608	−76,654	−84,731	−89,538	−107,628	−106,487	−112,767	−100,424	....	Goods: Imports f.o.b.	78ab d
	−3,859	−3,474	−2,300	−666	−191	492	2,305	1,294	2,705	2,575	2,602	2,079	3,510	6,126	....	Trade Balance	78ac d
	12,925	12,341	10,971	10,770	10,423	10,796	14,618	18,908	21,045	23,178	30,512	32,177	36,401	36,959	....	Services: Credit	78ad d
	−12,827	−11,804	−9,908	−9,392	−9,464	−9,942	−13,167	−16,466	−18,897	−21,677	−26,913	−29,177	−31,912	−30,846	....	Services: Debit	78ae d
	−3,761	−2,937	−1,237	712	768	1,346	3,756	3,735	4,854	4,076	6,201	5,078	7,998	12,240	....	Balance on Goods and Services	78af d
	18,427	24,197	22,883	18,333	18,943	20,830	23,665	27,496	33,127	46,547	63,883	73,527	86,105	80,854	....	Income: Credit	78ag d
	−18,366	−24,189	−23,063	−18,441	−18,934	−20,851	−23,420	−27,011	−32,631	−45,708	−63,169	−72,124	−85,148	−77,918	....	Income: Debit	78ah d
	−3,700	−2,928	−1,417	604	776	1,325	4,001	4,220	5,350	4,915	6,915	6,482	8,955	15,176	....	Balance on Goods, Serv., & Inc.	78ai d
	1,743	1,403	1,249	1,259	1,300	1,524	1,968	2,500	2,602	2,435	3,945	4,388	4,323	4,184	....	Current Transfers, n.i.e.: Credit	78aj d
	−2,973	−2,643	−2,426	−2,358	−2,131	−2,180	−2,913	−3,927	−4,357	−4,153	−5,911	−6,138	−6,810	−6,772	....	Current Transfers: Debit	78ak d
	−4,931	−4,168	−2,594	−495	−55	669	3,055	2,794	3,594	3,197	4,950	4,731	6,468	12,588	....	Current Account, n.i.e.	78al d
	—	—	—	—	—	—	—	—	—	—	—	—	—	—	....	Capital Account, n.i.e.: Credit	78ba d
	—	—	—	—	—	—	—	—	—	—	—	—	—	—	....	Capital Account: Debit	78bb d
	—	—	—	—	—	—	—	—	—	—	—	—	—	—	....	Capital Account, n.i.e.	78bc d
	−196	−104	69	−355	−293	−296	−1,723	−2,782	−3,784	−6,812	−6,262	−6,165	−11,259	−4,023	....	Direct Investment Abroad	78bd d
	1,545	1,386	1,472	1,290	389	1,051	730	2,355	5,212	7,057	8,056	9,377	11,286	10,650	....	Dir. Invest. in Rep. Econ., n.i.e.	78be d
	−789	−1,583	−2,237	−3,788	−4,141	−6,269	−7,039	−4,435	−12,302	−14,137	−14,799	−33,993	−62,887	−58,433	....	Portfolio Investment Assets	78bf d
	1,485	812	246	113	161	267	447	2,006	7,729	11,237	7,267	26,872	59,016	50,238	....	Portfolio Investment Liab., n.i.e.	78bg d
	−45,092	−17,604	−27,519	−4,785	−31,332	−51,671	−61,223	−122,240	6,361	−1,634	−52,146	−10,358	−16,117	−33,858	....	Other Investment Assets	78bh d
	47,547	20,412	30,083	8,082	35,730	56,739	65,923	124,586	−6,975	−915	56,231	11,031	12,312	21,696	....	Other Investment Liab., n.i.e.	78bi d
	4,500	3,319	2,114	557	514	−179	−2,885	−510	−3,758	−5,204	−1,654	−3,235	−7,650	−13,731	....	Financial Account, n.i.e.	78bj d
	981	−1,341	−294	−428	152	−262	222	−55	34	−78	−2,839	−992	1,847	−938	....	Net Errors and Omissions	78ca d
	550	−2,190	−774	−366	611	228	392	2,273	−104	−2,094	457	504	665	−2,081	....	Overall Balance	78cb d
	−550	2,190	774	366	−611	−228	−392	−2,273	104	2,094	−457	−504	−665	2,081	....	Reserves and Related Items	79da d
	−133	2,394	588	−265	−305	197	−29	−2,434	−861	−226	−457	−504	−665	2,081	....	Reserve Assets	79db d
	−417	−204	186	631	−306	−426	−362	161	965	2,320	—	—	—	—	....	Use of Fund Credit and Loans	79dc d
	—	—	—	—	—	—	—	—	—	—	—	—	—	—	....	Liabs.Constit.For.Auth.Reserves	79dd d
	—	—	—	—	—	—	—	—	—	—	—	—	—	—	....	Exceptional Financing	79de d
Year Ending December 31																**Government Finance**	
	−282.0	−446.9	−431.6	−515.9	−596.1	−537.6	−497.3	−404.0	−364.0	−397.0	−364.6	−457.2	−496.6	....	....	Deficit (−) or Surplus	80
	1,508.6	1,595.5	1,781.9	1,857.3	2,040.0	2,201.6	2,271.4	2,369.9	2,459.7	2,603.4	2,818.9	2,924.5	3,101.0	....	....	Revenue	81
	2.4	3.0	2.9	2.8	3.1	2.5	2.6	2.7	2.2	2.8	2.0	2.4	3.6	....	....	Grants Received	81z
	1,758.3	2,016.1	2,185.0	2,346.9	2,493.6	2,624.5	2,727.4	2,735.4	2,798.4	2,973.0	3,154.7	3,370.0	3,590.6	....	....	Expenditure	82
	34.7	29.3	31.4	29.1	145.6	117.2	43.9	41.2	27.5	30.2	30.8	14.1	10.6	....	....	Lending Minus Repayments	83
																Financing	
	211.5	234.6	220.4	394.0	405.8	504.4	417.7	356.3	330.1	332.2	355.2	476.3	622.2	....	....	Net Borrowing: Domestic	84a
	83.5	214.1	189.4	127.0	181.1	26.8	74.1	31.8	22.9	68.8	−19.4	−8.0	−107.6	....	....	Foreign	85a
	−13.0	−1.8	21.8	−5.1	9.2	6.4	5.5	15.9	11.0	−4.0	28.8	−11.1	−18.0	....	....	Use of Cash Balances	87
	1,761.0	2,000.3	2,299.2	2,706.0	3,077.3	3,694.2	4,295.6	4,693.2	5,256.1	5,624.8	6,083.3	6,656.8	7,297.6	....	....	Debt: Domestic	88a
	154.9	374.4	591.0	724.8	882.0	919.8	968.5	999.9	1,087.4	1,131.0	1,111.8	1,107.0	1,010.5	....	....	Foreign	89a
Billions of Francs																**National Accounts**	
	2,170	2,439	2,794	3,079	3,505	3,645	3,523	3,609	4,029	4,630	4,739	4,847	4,979	5,071	....	Exports of Goods & Services	90c
	614	664	701	722	755	809	839	845	845	891	933	1,006	1,045	1,112	....	Government Consumption	91f
	724	642	672	669	709	741	783	834	983	1,160	1,303	1,306	1,345	1,285	....	Gross Fixed Capital Formation	93e
	29	−4	8	−22	26	−35	−27	11	24	18	—	−1	13	—	....	Increase/Decrease(-) in Stocks	93i
	2,172	2,334	2,550	2,688	2,876	3,106	3,202	3,361	3,513	3,770	4,012	4,243	4,445	4,514	....	Private Consumption	96f
	−2,258	−2,497	−2,834	−3,004	−3,429	−3,526	−3,327	−3,452	−3,826	−4,436	−4,565	−4,657	−4,724	−4,638	....	Imports of Goods & Services	98c
	3,451	3,578	3,889	4,124	4,433	4,741	4,991	5,208	5,564	6,032	6,422	6,743	7,102	7,285	7,621	Gross Domestic Product	99b
	−26	−30	−58	−63	−60	−76	−60	−50	−53	−34	−66	−26	−41	33	....	Net Factor Inc/Pmts(-) Abroad	98.n
	3,425	3,548	3,831	4,061	4,373	4,664	4,931	5,158	5,510	5,998	6,356	6,717	7,061	7,318	7,661	Gross Nat'l Expenditure = GNP	99a
	3,135	3,246	3,492	3,710	4,004	4,273	4,527	4,691	5,019	5,427	5,758	6,106	6,389	6,610	....	Nat'l Income, Market Prices	99e
	‡5,325	5,272	5,352	5,376	5,497	5,543	5,618	5,730	6,011	6,220	6,422	6,567	6,689	6,575	6,726	Gross Dom. Prod. 1990 Prices	99b.p
	64.8	67.9	72.7	76.7	80.6	85.5	88.8	90.9	92.6	97.0	100.0	102.7	106.2	110.8	113.3	GDP Deflator (1990=100)	99bi p
Midyear Estimates																	
	9.85	9.85	9.86	9.86	9.86	9.86	9.86	9.87	9.89	9.94	9.97	9.98	10.05	10.05	....	Population	99z

Belize
339

		1965	1966	1967	1968	1969	1970	1971	1972	1973	1974	1975	1976	1977	1978	1979
Exchange Rates													*Belize Dollars per SDR: End of Period (aa)*			
Official Rate	aa	1.4286	1.4286	1.6623	1.6776	1.6662	1.6711	1.7014	1.8495	2.0770	2.0853	2.3141	2.7299	2.4294	2.6056	2.6347
Official Rate	ae	1.4286	1.4286	1.6623	1.6776	1.6662	1.6711	1.5671	1.7035	1.7218	1.7032	1.9768	2.3496	2.0000	2.0000	2.0000
													Index Numbers (1990=100):			
Official Rate	ah x	140.0	140.0	137.7	119.7	119.5	119.8	122.2	125.1	122.6	117.0	111.1	90.3	100.0	100.0	100.0
Nominal Effective Exchange Rate	ne c	....	....	....	....	....	....	....	....	....	....	....	....	....	....	61.5
Real Effective Exchange Rate	re c	....	....	....	....	....	....	....	....	....	....	....	....	....	....	....
Fund Position													*Millions of SDRs:*			
Quota	2f. s	....	....	....	....	....	....	....	....	....	....	....	....	....	....	....
SDRs	1b. s	....	....	....	....	....	....	....	....	....	....	....	....	....	....	....
Reserve Position in the Fund	1c. s	....	....	....	....	....	....	....	....	....	....	....	....	....	....	....
Total Fund Cred.&Loans Outstg.	2tl	....	....	....	....	....	....	....	....	....	....	....	....	....	....	....
International Liquidity													*Millions of US Dollars Unless Otherwise Indicated:*			
Total Reserves minus Gold	1l. d	....	....	....	....	....	....	....	....	....	....	....	5.49	8.02	13.98	10.46
SDRs	1b. d	....	....	....	....	....	....	....	....	....	....	....	....	....	....	....
Reserve Position in the Fund	1c. d	....	....	....	....	....	....	....	....	....	....	....	....	....	....	....
Foreign Exchange	1d. d	....	....	....	....	....	....	....	....	....	....	....	5.49	8.02	13.98	10.46
Monetary Authorities: Other Liab.	4.. d	....	....	....	....	....	....	....	....	....	....	....	—	.26	1.08	.45
Deposit Money Banks: Assets	7a. d	....	....	....	....	....	....	....	....	....	....	....	1.31	4.79	7.68	12.71
Liabilities	7b. d	....	....	....	....	....	....	....	....	....	....	....	4.59	6.31	6.41	14.81
Other Banking Insts.: Assets	7e. d	....	....	....	....	....	....	....	....	....	....	....	....	....	....	.01
Other Banking Insts.: Liabilities	7f. d	....	....	....	....	....	....	....	....	....	....	....	....	....	6.04	6.61
of which: Liab. to Nonbanks	7fd d	....	....	....	....	....	....	....	....	....	....	....	....	....	6.04	6.61
Monetary Authorities													*Millions of Belize Dollars:*			
Foreign Assets	11	....	....	....	....	....	....	....	....	....	....	....	12.90	16.04	27.96	20.93
Claims on Central Government	12a	....	....	....	....	....	....	....	....	....	....	....	1.90	4.67	4.73	10.77
Reserve Money	14	....	....	....	....	....	....	....	....	....	....	....	13.64	18.58	25.45	22.92
of which: Currency Outside DMBs	14a	....	....	....	....	....	....	....	....	....	....	....	11.27	12.55	16.72	16.68
Foreign Liabilities	16c	....	....	....	....	....	....	....	....	....	....	....	—	.52	2.16	.91
Central Government Deposits	16d	....	....	....	....	....	....	....	....	....	....	....	—	—	.49	—
Capital Accounts	17a	....	....	....	....	....	....	....	....	....	....	....	.64	2.00	4.74	7.99
Other Items (Net)	17r	....	....	....	....	....	....	....	....	....	....	....	.52	−.39	−.15	−.11
Deposit Money Banks													*Millions of Belize Dollars:*			
Reserves	20	....	....	....	....	....	....	....	....	....	....	....	2.37	5.79	8.38	6.22
Foreign Assets	21	....	....	....	....	....	....	....	....	....	....	....	3.09	9.59	15.36	25.41
Claims on Central Government	22a	....	....	....	....	....	....	....	....	....	....	....	1.57	3.50	7.01	2.59
Claims on Official Entities	22bx	....	....	....	....	....	....	....	....	....	....	....	4.04	4.38	6.25	8.13
Claims on Private Sector	22d	....	....	....	....	....	....	....	....	....	....	....	57.66	52.68	55.32	70.73
Demand Deposits	24	....	....	....	....	....	....	....	....	....	....	....	10.03	12.14	19.26	20.19
Time, Savings,& Fgn.Currency Dep.	25	....	....	....	....	....	....	....	....	....	....	....	50.28	48.74	56.92	59.04
Foreign Liabilities	26c	....	....	....	....	....	....	....	....	....	....	....	10.79	12.62	12.82	29.62
Central Government Deposits	26d	....	....	....	....	....	....	....	....	....	....	....	.76	.75	1.09	1.41
Credit from Monetary Authorities	26g	....	....	....	....	....	....	....	....	....	....	....	....	....	....	....
Capital Accounts	27a	....	....	....	....	....	....	....	....	....	....	....	.70	5.40	5.21	7.25
Other Items (Net)	27r	....	....	....	....	....	....	....	....	....	....	....	−3.82	−3.71	−2.97	−4.43
Monetary Survey													*Millions of Belize Dollars:*			
Foreign Assets (Net)	31n	....	....	....	....	....	....	....	....	....	....	....	5.19	12.49	28.34	15.82
Domestic Credit	32	....	....	....	....	....	....	....	....	....	....	....	64.42	64.48	71.73	90.81
Claims on Central Govt. (Net)	32an	....	....	....	....	....	....	....	....	....	....	....	2.71	7.42	10.16	11.95
Claims on Official Entities	32bx	....	....	....	....	....	....	....	....	....	....	....	4.04	4.38	6.25	8.13
Claims on Private Sector	32d	....	....	....	....	....	....	....	....	....	....	....	57.66	52.68	55.32	70.73
Money	34	....	....	....	....	....	....	....	....	....	....	....	21.30	24.69	36.01	36.89
Quasi-Money	35	....	....	....	....	....	....	....	....	....	....	....	50.28	48.74	56.92	59.04
Capital Accounts	37a	....	....	....	....	....	....	....	....	....	....	....	1.34	7.40	9.94	15.23
Other Items (Net)	37r	....	....	....	....	....	....	....	....	....	....	....	−3.31	−3.85	−2.80	−4.55
Money plus Quasi-Money	35l	....	....	....	....	....	....	....	....	....	....	....	71.58	73.43	92.93	95.94
Other Banking Institutions													*Millions of Belize Dollars:*			
Reserves	40	....	....	....	....	....	....	....	....	....	....	....	....	....	1.01	.83
Foreign Assets	41	....	....	....	....	....	....	....	....	....	....	....	....	....	.01	.03
Claims on Central Government	42a	....	....	....	....	....	....	....	....	....	....	....	....	....	1.66	1.41
Claims on Official Entities	42bx	....	....	....	....	....	....	....	....	....	....	....	....	....	1.67	1.67
Claims on Private Sector	42d	....	....	....	....	....	....	....	....	....	....	....	....	....	12.00	12.74
Foreign Liabilities	46c	....	....	....	....	....	....	....	....	....	....	....	....	....	12.07	13.23
Other Items (Net)	47r	....	....	....	....	....	....	....	....	....	....	....	....	....	4.27	3.45
Interest Rates													*Percent Per Annum*			
Discount Rate (End of Period)	60	....	....	....	....	....	....	....	....	....	....	....	....	7.00	7.50	10.00
Treasury Bill Rate	60c	....	....	....	....	....	....	....	....	....	....	....	....	5.91	6.40	6.40
Deposit Rate	60l	....	....	....	....	....	....	....	....	....	....	....	7.1	6.7	6.8	6.8
Lending Rate	60p	....	....	....	....	....	....	....	....	....	....	....	11.5	11.3	11.3	11.6
Prices													*Index Numbers (1990=100):*			
Consumer Prices	64	....	....	....	....	....	....	....	....	....	....	....	....	....	....	....

Belize

	1980	1981	1982	1983	1984	1985	1986	1987	1988	1989	1990	1991	1992	1993	1994		
																Exchange Rates	
Belize Dollars per US Dollar: End of Period (ae)																	
	2.5508	2.3279	2.2062	2.0939	1.9604	2.1968	2.4464	2.8373	2.6914	2.6283	2.8453	2.8609	2.7500	2.7471	2.9197	Official Rate	aa
	2.0000	2.0000	2.0000	2.0000	2.0000	2.0000	2.0000	2.0000	2.0000	2.0000	2.0000	2.0000	2.0000	2.0000	2.0000	Official Rate	ae
Period Averages																	
	100.0	100.0	100.0	100.0	100.0	100.0	100.0	100.0	100.0	100.0	100.0	100.0	100.0	100.0	100.0	Official Rate	ah x
	61.5	66.5	71.4	76.3	82.0	89.6	85.7	82.9	84.5	92.2	100.0	105.7	110.0	122.2	129.5	Nominal Effective Exchange Rate	ne c
	96.9	105.5	111.7	117.7	122.3	129.8	116.1	107.7	106.4	104.9	100.0	100.1	98.8	101.7	98.6	Real Effective Exchange Rate	re c
																Fund Position	
End of Period																	
	....	....	7.20	9.50	9.50	9.50	9.50	9.50	9.50	9.50	9.50	9.50	13.50	13.50	13.50	Quota	2f. s
	....	....	—	.02	.01	—	—	.06	.02	—	.01	.08	.15	.29	.37	SDRs	1b. s
	....	....	1.32	1.90	1.90	1.90	1.90	1.91	1.91	1.91	1.91	1.91	2.91	2.91	2.91	Reserve Position in the Fund	1c. s
	....	....	—	3.60	4.80	9.54	9.54	8.03	5.79	2.52	.30	—	—	—	—	Total Fund Cred.&Loans Outstg.	2tl
																International Liquidity	
End of Period																	
	12.68	10.33	9.84	9.31	6.07	14.81	26.90	36.41	51.66	59.88	69.78	53.02	52.94	38.75	34.52	Total Reserves minus Gold	1l. d
	....	....	—	.02	.01	—	—	.09	.03	—	.01	.11	.21	.39	.54	SDRs	1b. d
	....	....	1.46	1.99	1.86	2.09	2.32	2.71	2.57	2.51	2.72	2.73	4.00	4.00	4.25	Reserve Position in the Fund	1c. d
	12.68	10.33	8.38	7.30	4.20	12.73	24.57	33.62	49.06	57.37	67.05	50.17	48.74	34.35	29.72	Foreign Exchange	1d. d
	.45	.19	.19	.45	1.77	.68	.58	.86	.56	1.65	4.14	7.51	8.79	6.81	6.21	Monetary Authorities: Other Liab.	4..d
	13.51	14.05	7.79	9.36	9.77	10.17	8.48	8.04	6.95	12.38	19.39	16.31	12.31	23.64	24.27	Deposit Money Banks: Assets	7a. d
	17.29	19.04	23.68	23.04	26.11	21.74	13.17	11.14	10.51	8.53	4.58	7.48	15.81	34.51	38.64	Liabilities	7b. d
	.01	.01	.01	.01	1.59	1.35	.59	.36	.12	—	—	—	.01	—	—	Other Banking Insts.: Assets	7e. d
	8.51	10.77	12.00	12.98	16.06	11.81	17.93	19.37	19.42	17.67	16.79	16.05	15.53	14.11	14.20	Other Banking Insts.: Liabilities	7f. d
	8.51	10.77	12.00	12.98	16.06	11.81	17.93	19.37	19.42	17.67	16.79	16.05	15.53	14.11	14.20	*of which:* Liab. to Nonbanks	7fd d
																Monetary Authorities	
End of Period																	
	25.35	20.67	19.67	18.63	12.34	29.63	53.55	73.15	103.51	120.22	139.84	105.88	105.86	77.27	68.94	Foreign Assets	11
	11.91	28.08	33.70	39.52	56.70	65.57	61.47	50.45	33.64	27.00	5.19	21.95	31.40	61.47	67.54	Claims on Central Government	12a
	26.11	31.58	37.15	34.99	47.14	54.09	63.94	71.45	68.31	85.16	83.72	86.79	105.38	104.63	102.50	Reserve Money	14
	17.51	19.01	20.61	21.53	22.77	22.64	25.90	29.56	34.11	40.44	43.46	47.91	50.98	54.19	56.74	*of which:* Currency Outside DMBs	14a
	.90	.39	.38	8.45	12.94	22.31	24.50	24.50	16.70	9.93	9.13	15.01	17.58	13.62	12.41	Foreign Liabilities	16c
	1.52	5.34	—	—	3.77	6.41	7.63	39.41	33.28	35.28	10.08	13.30	15.06	17.88	Central Government Deposits	16d
	9.55	10.46	10.46	11.14	11.73	15.24	15.36	14.84	15.49	15.99	16.91	17.36	19.85	17.18	17.78	Capital Accounts	17a
	−.82	.99	5.38	3.57	−2.78	−.22	4.81	5.18	−2.76	2.86	−.01	−1.41	−18.85	−11.75	−14.08	Other Items (Net)	17r
																Deposit Money Banks	
End of Period																	
	8.49	12.54	16.52	13.70	19.81	21.07	22.74	25.43	29.43	42.32	37.91	37.30	53.40	49.95	45.13	Reserves	20
	27.02	28.11	15.58	18.71	19.55	20.34	16.95	16.08	13.90	24.76	38.78	32.62	24.62	47.28	48.53	Foreign Assets	21
	9.82	6.68	16.17	32.07	30.10	33.58	47.98	48.32	39.87	37.24	51.20	45.44	60.75	48.93	52.99	Claims on Central Government	22a
	7.00	8.66	9.58	7.00	13.05	3.16	2.74	9.04	7.96	5.45	7.25	4.88	1.16	.31	.27	Claims on Official Entities	22bx
	77.32	90.79	107.66	117.16	116.14	120.47	119.77	146.60	197.95	231.08	268.35	331.10	372.01	385.99	405.27	Claims on Private Sector	22d
	24.03	20.52	18.76	20.84	22.67	24.44	29.60	36.80	42.92	56.58	59.45	68.97	74.45	81.65	86.81	Demand Deposits	24
	66.55	78.25	85.67	105.75	104.62	109.13	128.06	157.35	170.33	187.40	224.80	245.60	285.11	288.57	316.35	Time, Savings,& Fgn.Currency Dep.	25
	34.59	38.08	47.35	46.09	52.22	43.48	26.34	22.28	21.03	17.07	9.17	14.96	31.62	69.02	77.28	Foreign Liabilities	26c
	.57	2.38	6.18	8.37	10.96	12.20	15.43	16.44	31.64	58.30	75.19	86.80	74.24	49.30	43.86	Central Government Deposits	26d
	.40	—	—	—	6.80	.61	1.35	5.84	4.76	3.60	2.86	2.20	7.98	5.32	1.66	Credit from Monetary Authorities	26g
	7.63	8.23	8.35	10.30	10.61	11.29	12.13	13.36	17.08	19.00	21.25	25.06	28.41	31.00	31.04	Capital Accounts	27a
	−4.12	−.69	−.82	−2.71	−9.23	−2.51	−2.73	−6.59	1.34	−1.10	10.78	7.75	10.12	7.60	−4.81	Other Items (Net)	27r
																Monetary Survey	
End of Period																	
	16.88	10.31	−12.48	−17.19	−33.28	−15.82	19.67	42.45	79.68	117.98	160.33	108.53	81.29	41.92	27.78	Foreign Assets (Net)	31n
	103.95	126.63	161.15	187.53	205.23	207.05	210.41	230.69	208.37	209.19	221.53	306.49	377.78	432.35	464.44	Domestic Credit	32
	19.64	27.04	43.69	63.22	75.84	83.18	87.61	74.70	2.46	−27.34	−54.08	−29.49	4.60	46.03	58.80	Claims on Central Govt. (Net)	32an
	7.00	8.66	9.58	7.00	13.05	3.16	2.74	9.04	7.96	5.45	7.25	4.88	1.16	.31	.27	Claims on Official Entities	32bx
	77.32	90.79	107.66	117.16	116.14	120.47	119.77	146.60	197.95	231.08	268.35	331.10	372.01	385.99	405.27	Claims on Private Sector	32d
	41.65	39.56	39.40	42.41	50.01	58.61	71.03	84.30	81.78	99.87	105.99	118.30	126.33	136.35	144.18	Money	34
	66.55	78.25	85.67	105.75	104.62	109.13	128.06	157.35	170.33	187.40	224.80	245.60	285.11	288.57	316.35	Quasi-Money	35
	17.18	18.69	18.81	21.44	22.34	26.53	27.49	28.20	32.57	34.99	38.16	42.42	48.26	48.18	48.82	Capital Accounts	37a
	−4.54	.44	4.78	.73	−5.02	−3.04	3.49	3.28	3.36	4.91	12.90	8.70	−.64	1.17	−17.13	Other Items (Net)	37r
	108.20	117.81	125.07	148.16	154.63	167.73	199.10	241.65	252.11	287.27	330.80	363.90	411.45	424.92	460.53	Money plus Quasi-Money	35l
																Other Banking Institutions	
End of Period																	
	.91	.53	.89	2.31	.95	.11	1.34	1.09	2.49	.83	3.44	4.91	2.38	1.28	1.41	Reserves	40
	.02	.02	.02	.02	3.19	2.70	1.17	.71	.23	−.50	—	—	.02	—	—	Foreign Assets	41
	1.09	.64	.24	.77	.64	—	1.09	1.11	—	—	—	—	—	—	—	Claims on Central Government	42a
	1.60	1.38	1.39	1.49	1.29	—	1.03	.94	.55	.50	.52	.17	.17	.17	—	Claims on Official Entities	42bx
	17.12	22.04	24.20	27.35	30.01	32.26	36.84	34.65	34.64	35.55	33.71	32.87	36.59	40.66	45.70	Claims on Private Sector	42d
	17.02	21.55	23.99	25.96	32.13	23.62	35.86	38.74	38.84	35.34	33.57	32.10	31.05	28.22	28.41	Foreign Liabilities	46c
	3.72	3.07	2.74	5.98	3.95	11.44	5.62	−.24	−.93	1.04	4.10	5.85	8.10	13.90	18.69	Other Items (Net)	47r
																Interest Rates	
Percent Per Annum																	
	14.00	14.50	13.50	11.50	12.00	20.00	12.00	12.00	10.00	12.00	12.00	12.00	12.00	12.00	12.00	Discount Rate *(End of Period)*	60
	10.29	11.68	11.06	10.51	9.55	12.76	10.81	8.80	8.32	7.36	7.37	6.71	5.38	4.59	4.27	Treasury Bill Rate	60c
	11.2	14.7	14.9	11.3	9.1	11.6	11.8	9.6	8.4	7.9	8.1	8.4	8.2	8.1	8.6	Deposit Rate	60l
	16.5	19.3	....	....	....	....	14.7	14.1	13.6	13.8	14.0	14.2	14.3	14.4	14.8	Lending Rate	60p
																Prices	
Period Averages																	
	66.7	74.2	79.3	83.2	86.0	89.6	90.3	92.2	97.1	97.1	100.0	105.6	108.6	110.2	....	Consumer Prices	64

Belize
339

	1965	1966	1967	1968	1969	1970	1971	1972	1973	1974	1975	1976	1977	1978	1979
International Transactions													*Millions of Belize Dollars*		
Exports 70	17.46	19.24	20.47	25.19	28.08	31.33	31.69	40.89	52.69	76.86	120.40	94.04	124.16	159.57	173.46
Imports, cif 71	34.99	38.76	36.95	44.20	49.35	55.61	58.59	69.26	72.32	109.18	159.23	161.51	180.15	212.99	263.68
Imports, fob 71.v	31.81	35.24	33.59	40.18	44.86	50.55	53.26	62.96	65.75	99.25	144.75	146.83	163.77	193.63	239.71
Balance of Payments													*Millions of US Dollars:*		
Goods: Exports f.o.b. .... 78aa d	....	....	....	....	....	....	....	....	....	....	....	....	....	....	....
Goods: Imports f.o.b. .... 78ab d	....	....	....	....	....	....	....	....	....	....	....	....	....	....	....
Trade Balance .... 78ac d	....	....	....	....	....	....	....	....	....	....	....	....	....	....	....
Services: Credit .... 78ad d	....	....	....	....	....	....	....	....	....	....	....	....	....	....	....
Services: Debit .... 78ae d	....	....	....	....	....	....	....	....	....	....	....	....	....	....	....
Balance on Goods and Services ...... 78af d	....	....	....	....	....	....	....	....	....	....	....	....	....	....	....
Income: Credit .... 78ag d	....	....	....	....	....	....	....	....	....	....	....	....	....	....	....
Income: Debit .... 78ah d	....	....	....	....	....	....	....	....	....	....	....	....	....	....	....
Balance on Goods, Serv., & Inc. ...... 78ai d	....	....	....	....	....	....	....	....	....	....	....	....	....	....	....
Current Transfers, n.i.e.: Credit .... 78aj d	....	....	....	....	....	....	....	....	....	....	....	....	....	....	....
Current Transfers: Debit .... 78ak d	....	....	....	....	....	....	....	....	....	....	....	....	....	....	....
Current Account, n.i.e. .... 78al d	....	....	....	....	....	....	....	....	....	....	....	....	....	....	....
Capital Account, n.i.e.: Credit .... 78ba d	....	....	....	....	....	....	....	....	....	....	....	....	....	....	....
Capital Account: Debit .... 78bb d	....	....	....	....	....	....	....	....	....	....	....	....	....	....	....
Capital Account, n.i.e. .... 78bc d	....	....	....	....	....	....	....	....	....	....	....	....	....	....	....
Direct Investment Abroad .... 78bd d	....	....	....	....	....	....	....	....	....	....	....	....	....	....	....
Dir. Invest. in Rep. Econ., n.i.e. .... 78be d	....	....	....	....	....	....	....	....	....	....	....	....	....	....	....
Portfolio Investment Assets .... 78bf d	....	....	....	....	....	....	....	....	....	....	....	....	....	....	....
Portfolio Investment Liab., n.i.e. .... 78bg d	....	....	....	....	....	....	....	....	....	....	....	....	....	....	....
Other Investment Assets .... 78bh d	....	....	....	....	....	....	....	....	....	....	....	....	....	....	....
Other Investment Liab., n.i.e. .... 78bi d	....	....	....	....	....	....	....	....	....	....	....	....	....	....	....
Financial Account, n.i.e. .... 78bj d	....	....	....	....	....	....	....	....	....	....	....	....	....	....	....
Net Errors and Omissions .... 78ca d	....	....	....	....	....	....	....	....	....	....	....	....	....	....	....
Overall Balance .... 78cb d	....	....	....	....	....	....	....	....	....	....	....	....	....	....	....
Reserves and Related Items .... 79da d	....	....	....	....	....	....	....	....	....	....	....	....	....	....	....
Reserve Assets .... 79db d	....	....	....	....	....	....	....	....	....	....	....	....	....	....	....
Use of Fund Credit and Loans .... 79dc d	....	....	....	....	....	....	....	....	....	....	....	....	....	....	....
Liabs.Constit.For.Auth.Reserves ...... 79dd d	....	....	....	....	....	....	....	....	....	....	....	....	....	....	....
Exceptional Financing .... 79de d	....	....	....	....	....	....	....	....	....	....	....	....	....	....	....
Government Finance													*Thousands of Belize Dollars:*		
Deficit (-) or Surplus 80	....	....	....	....	....	....	....	....	....	....	....	....	-12,112	-2,613	ʃ-5,018
Revenue 81	....	....	....	....	....	....	....	....	....	....	....	....	41,913	54,914	ʃ63,326
Grants Received 81z	....	....	....	....	....	....	....	....	....	....	....	....	8,167	7,577	ʃ8,359
Expenditure 82	....	....	....	....	....	....	....	....	....	....	....	....	61,296	62,568	ʃ73,914
Lending Minus Repayments 83	....	....	....	....	....	....	....	....	....	....	....	....	896	2,536	ʃ2,789
Financing															
Domestic 84a	....	....	....	....	....	....	....	....	....	....	....	....	8,237	2,513	ʃ6,223
Foreign 85a	....	....	....	....	....	....	....	....	....	....	....	....	3,875	100	ʃ-1,205
Debt: Domestic 88a	....	....	....	....	....	....	....	....	....	....	....	....	....	....	....
Foreign 89a	....	....	....	....	....	....	....	....	....	....	....	....	....	....	....
National Accounts													*Millions of Belize Dollars*		
Exports of Goods & Services 90c	....	....	....	....	....	....	....	....	63.1	111.4	150.1	113.9	155.7	205.9	173.8
Government Consumption 91f	....	....	....	....	....	....	....	....	16.5	22.0	22.8	27.1	29.5	33.9	53.0
Gross Fixed Capital Formation 93e	....	....	....	....	....	....	....	....	27.0	38.6	53.0	58.0	62.9	69.1	81.0
Increase/Decrease(-) in Stocks 93i	....	....	....	....	....	....	....	....	5.7	4.2	8.0	11.2	5.8	3.3	14.7
Private Consumption 96f	....	....	....	....	....	....	....	....	75.0	93.6	116.6	131.9	154.0	165.7	185.5
Imports of Goods & Services 98c	....	....	....	....	....	....	....	....	-77.1	-115.6	-161.7	-159.0	-196.3	-236.5	-225.6
Gross Domestic Product = GDP 99b	....	....	....	....	....	....	....	....	110.3	154.2	188.8	183.2	211.6	241.7	282.4
Gross Dom. Prod. 1990 Prices 99b.p	....	....	....	....	....	....	....	....	....	....	....	....	....	....	470.8
GDP Deflator (1990=100) .... 99bi p	....	....	....	....	....	....	....	....	42.9	54.9	66.7	65.2	72.3	76.5	60.0
													Millions:		
Population 99z	.10	.11	.11	.11	.12	.12	.12	.13	.13	.13	.13	.14	.14	.14	.14

Government Finance: ʃ Beginning in 1985, annual data cover budgetary and social security funds. Prior to 1985, data cover budgetary funds only. ʃ Beginning in 1979, data relate to a fiscal year different from calendar year. Data for 1979 cover 15 months.

Belize

1980	1981	1982	1983	1984	1985	1986	1987	1988	1989	1990	1991	1992	1993	1994		
Millions of Belize Dollars															**International Transactions**	
221.30	238.01	182.03	155.46	186.40	179.39	185.21	205.66	232.51	249.07	258.10	252.00	282.24	263.16	288.11	Exports	70
299.51	323.93	256.00	223.58	260.27	256.26	243.93	285.89	361.95	431.39	422.50	501.50	545.89	561.82	516.95	Imports, cif	71
272.28	294.48	232.73	203.25	236.61	232.96	221.75	259.90	329.05	392.17	384.09	455.91	496.26	510.75	469.95	Imports, fob	71.v
Minus Sign Indicates Debit															Balance of Payments	
....	....	....	....	93.2	90.2	92.6	102.9	119.4	124.4	129.2	126.1	140.6	132.0	....	Goods: Exports f.o.b.	78aa d
....	....	....	....	−116.3	−113.8	−108.3	−127.0	−161.3	−188.5	−188.4	−223.6	−244.5	−250.5	....	Goods: Imports f.o.b.	78ab d
....	....	....	....	−23.1	−23.7	−15.7	−24.1	−41.9	−64.1	−59.2	−97.5	−103.9	−118.5	....	Trade Balance	78ac d
....	....	....	....	35.4	38.1	42.8	56.0	74.5	85.9	115.4	122.7	142.6	150.5	....	Services: Credit	78ad d
....	....	....	....	−29.4	−27.6	−40.2	−46.0	−53.4	−62.5	−60.0	−68.2	−81.6	−92.5	....	Services: Debit	78ae d
....	....	....	....	−17.1	−13.1	−13.1	−14.1	−20.8	−40.8	−3.9	−43.0	−42.9	−60.5	....	Balance on Goods and Services	78af d
....	....	....	....	1.3	2.9	9.2	5.9	8.0	9.7	10.6	8.3	6.7	5.9	....	Income: Credit	78ag d
....	....	....	....	−14.8	−13.2	−11.6	−13.4	−15.7	−19.1	−20.8	−19.1	−22.8	−23.4	....	Income: Debit	78ah d
....	....	....	....	−30.6	−23.4	−15.5	−21.6	−28.5	−50.2	−14.1	−53.8	−59.0	−78.0	....	Balance on Goods, Serv., & Inc.	78ai d
....	....	....	....	27.9	34.5	31.3	35.1	29.4	34.5	33.6	32.3	35.4	33.8	....	Current Transfers, n.i.e.: Credit	78aj d
....	....	....	....	−2.6	−2.1	−3.9	−4.1	−3.6	−3.4	−4.2	−4.3	−5.0	−4.3	....	Current Transfers: Debit	78ak d
....	....	....	....	−5.3	9.1	12.0	9.4	−2.6	−19.1	15.4	−25.8	−28.6	−48.5	....	Current Account, n.i.e.	78al d
....	....	....	....	—	—	—	—	—	—	—	—	—	—	....	Capital Account, n.i.e.: Credit	78ba d
....	....	....	....	—	—	—	—	—	—	—	—	—	—	....	Capital Account: Debit	78bb d
....	....	....	....	—	—	—	—	—	—	—	−1.5	−2.2	−2.1	....	Capital Account, n.i.e.	78bc d
....	....	....	....	−3.7	3.7	4.6	6.9	14.0	18.7	17.2	15.1	17.8	11.3	....	Dir. Invest. in Rep. Econ., n.i.e.	78be d
....	....	....	....	—	—	—	—	—	—	—	—	—	—	....	Portfolio Investment Assets	78bf d
....	....	....	....	.7	.7	—	—	—	—	—	—	.2	7.0	....	Portfolio Investment Liab., n.i.e.	78bg d
....	....	....	....	—	—	—	—	1.8	—	—	3.0	3.7	−11.6	....	Other Investment Assets	78bh d
....	....	....	....	−.6	5.0	−3.9	−4.2	11.6	6.9	7.9	5.6	3.0	28.2	....	Other Investment Liab., n.i.e.	78bi d
....	....	....	....	−3.6	9.4	.7	2.7	27.3	25.5	25.1	22.2	22.4	32.8	....	Financial Account, n.i.e.	78bj d
....	....	....	....	3.6	−16.1	−.9	−.2	−2.9	9.1	−25.0	−12.8	6.3	1.5	....	Net Errors and Omissions	78ca d
....	....	....	....	−5.3	2.3	11.8	11.9	21.8	15.5	15.4	−16.4	.1	−14.2	....	Overall Balance	78cb d
....	....	....	....	5.3	−2.3	−11.8	−11.9	−21.8	−15.5	−15.4	16.4	−.1	14.2	....	Reserves and Related Items	79da d
....	....	....	....	2.9	−7.2	−11.8	−9.9	−18.7	−11.3	−12.5	16.8	−.1	14.2	....	Reserve Assets	79db d
....	....	....	....	1.2	4.9	—	−2.0	−3.0	−4.2	−3.0	−.4	—	—	....	Use of Fund Credit and Loans	79dc d
....	....	....	....	—	—	—	—	—	—	—	—	—	—	....	Liabs.Constit.For.Auth.Reserves	79dd d
....	....	....	....	1.2	—	—	—	—	—	—	—	—	—	....	Exceptional Financing	79de d
Year Beginning April 1															**Government Finance**	
−5,916	....	....	....	−5,214 ⟦−14,208	....	....	44,922	−5,733	5,633	−27,701	−32,819	−93,487	−115,597	Deficit (−) or Surplus	80	
80,565	83,621	79,514	78,908	92,795 ⟦96,896	....	....	161,443	190,169	210,747	216,191	245,214	247,864	265,920 f	Revenue	81	
4,688	5,461	18,426	16,954	5,600 ⟦1,400	....	....	1,868	5,600	13,000	12,836	9,848	28,070	33,354 f	Grants Received	81z	
89,072	102,989	107,655	105,856	105,026 ⟦111,895	....	....	152,670	202,550	228,824	278,901	320,779	375,174	419,365 f	Expenditure	82	
2,097	....	....	....	−1,417 ⟦609	....	....	−34,281	−1,048	−10,710	−22,173	−32,898	−5,753	−4,494	Lending Minus Repayments	83	
															Financing	
4,857	....	....	....	....	....	....	....	−54,966	−1,651	−25,951	8,318	13,893	....	....	Domestic	84a
1,059	....	....	....	....	....	....	....	10,044	7,384	20,318	19,383	18,926	....	....	Foreign	85a
....	....	....	....	....	....	....	....	77,270	75,272	73,808	77,626	....	....	....	Debt: Domestic	88a
....	....	....	....	....	....	....	....	123,962	140,002	145,516	177,141	....	....	....	Foreign	89a
Millions of Belize Dollars															**National Accounts**	
215.7	206.0	172.0	185.5	263.4	202.8	253.0	334.4	390.6	433.9	514.0	507.2	575.5	600.4	....	Exports of Goods & Services	90c
66.8	73.4	84.2	89.7	93.0	95.4	102.8	127.1	132.0	146.5	155.1	166.6	175.5	205.7	....	Government Consumption	91f
88.7	95.6	80.8	71.5	85.7	72.7	79.5	118.8	161.6	198.8	207.9	245.9	279.5	328.0	....	Gross Fixed Capital Formation	93e
5.7	4.9	−6.4	4.9	13.6	17.7	13.3	2.5	−1.8	21.2	18.3	10.3	7.1	4.9	....	Increase/Decrease(−) in Stocks	93i
243.3	296.6	280.9	272.1	262.0	286.1	272.0	316.5	374.7	428.0	394.2	517.7	576.1	609.7	....	Private Consumption	96f
−267.1	−290.7	−253.0	−245.7	−295.9	−256.4	−264.9	−346.2	−427.3	−502.1	−496.2	−587.8	−654.1	−700.9	....	Imports of Goods & Services	98c
353.1	385.8	358.5	378.0	421.8	418.4	455.8	553.0	629.8	726.0	793.4	859.9	959.6	1,047.8	....	Gross Domestic Product = GDP	99b
497.8	⟦502.3	500.9	490.1	499.9	505.0	528.2	589.6	642.5	726.1	793.4	829.5	904.1	942.4	....	Gross Dom. Prod. 1990 Prices	99b.p
70.9	76.8	71.6	77.1	84.4	82.9	86.3	93.8	98.0	100.0	100.0	103.7	106.1	111.2	....	GDP Deflator (1990=100)	99bi p
Midyear Estimates																
.14	.15	.15	.16	.16	.17	.17	.17	.18	.18	.19	.19	.20	.21	.21	Population	99z

Benin

638

		1965	1966	1967	1968	1969	1970	1971	1972	1973	1974	1975	1976	1977	1978	1979
Exchange Rates																*Francs per SDR:*
Official Rate	aa	245.07	247.59	245.42	247.40	277.91	276.02	283.61	278.00	284.00	272.08	262.55	288.70	285.76	272.28	264.78
																Francs per US Dollar:
Official Rate	ae	245.08	247.59	245.43	247.41	277.92	276.03	261.23	256.05	235.43	222.22	224.27	248.49	235.25	209.00	201.00
Official Rate	rf	245.06	245.68	246.00	247.56	259.96	276.40	275.59	252.03	222.89	240.70	214.31	238.95	245.68	225.66	212.72
Fund Position																*Millions of SDRs:*
Quota	2f. s	7.5	8.0	8.5	9.0	10.0	13.0	13.0	13.0	13.0	13.0	13.0	13.0	13.0	16.0	16.0
SDRs	1b. s	—	—	—	—	—	1.7	3.1	4.5	4.5	4.5	4.5	4.5	4.4	4.4	6.1
Reserve Position in the Fund	1c. s	.8	.9	1.0	1.1	1.4	2.1	2.1	2.1	2.1	2.1	2.1	2.1	2.1	2.0	1.9
Total Fund Cred.&Loans Outstg.	2tl	—	—	—	—	—	—	—	—	—	—	—	—	—	5.4	5.4
International Liquidity												*Millions of US Dollars Unless Otherwise Indicated:*				
Total Reserves minus Gold	1l. d	10.2	9.7	8.0	10.0	7.5	15.5	24.6	28.4	33.1	34.6	15.0	19.2	20.4	15.5	14.2
SDRs	1b. d	—	—	—	—	—	1.7	3.3	4.8	5.4	5.4	5.2	5.2	5.4	5.8	8.0
Reserve Position in the Fund	1c. d	.8	.9	1.0	1.1	1.4	2.1	2.3	2.3	2.6	2.6	2.5	2.5	2.6	2.6	2.6
Foreign Exchange	1d. d	9.4	8.8	7.0	8.9	6.1	11.7	19.0	21.3	25.2	26.6	7.3	11.6	12.4	7.1	3.6
Gold (Million Fine Troy Ounces)	1ad	....	....	....	....	....	....	....	....	....	....	....	—	.006	.008	.011
Gold (National Valuation)	1and	....	....	....	....	....	....	....	....	....	....	....	—	.2	.4	.5
Monetary Authorities: Other Liab.	4.. d	—	.5	—	.5	.1	.1	—	.3	.2	.1	.9	1.0	1.8	10.6	22.8
Deposit Money Banks: Assets	7a. d	1.38	2.47	1.66	3.27	2.55	5.19	7.78	3.59	5.09	13.62	60.42	7.20	8.15	6.59	5.52
Deposit Money Banks: Liabilities	7b. d	6.24	4.90	5.23	5.51	5.98	7.67	11.02	10.77	21.54	19.81	52.00	65.60	70.60	75.60	80.60
of which: Liab. to Nonbanks	7bdd d	....	....	....	....	....	....	....	....	....	....	....	....	....	....	....
Monetary Authorities																*Billions of Francs:*
Foreign Assets	11	2.51	2.40	1.98	2.47	2.09	4.30	6.29	7.27	7.62	7.69	3.37	4.78	4.79	3.24	2.86
Claims on Central Government	12a	.21	.68	.73	.88	1.16	.53	—	.89	1.33	1.27	.84	.43	—	2.30	5.61
Claims on Deposit Money Banks	12e	.90	.74	1.06	.77	1.40	1.52	.98	1.38	1.06	2.33	7.87	7.69	9.33	11.34	15.00
Claims on Other Financial Insts.	12f	—	—	—	—	—	—	—	—	—	—	—	—	—	—	—
Reserve Money	14	3.45	3.50	3.33	3.48	4.17	4.79	5.39	6.35	6.53	6.69	8.73	10.27	10.46	10.00	14.37
of which: Currency Outside DMBs	14a	3.31	3.28	3.15	3.33	3.97	4.51	4.97	5.80	6.02	6.07	8.45	9.36	9.92	7.96	13.26
Foreign Liabilities	16c	—	.13	—	.12	.02	.02	.01	.08	.04	.02	.21	.24	.42	5.22	7.54
Central Government Deposits	16d	.17	.20	.43	.52	.46	1.05	1.02	1.87	2.20	3.30	1.94	1.05	1.97	1.93	1.38
Other Items (Net)	17r	—	−.01	.01	—	—	.49	.85	1.24	1.24	1.29	1.20	1.34	1.27	−.27	.18
Deposit Money Banks																*Billions of Francs:*
Reserves	20	.10	.15	.14	I.14	.16	.21	.42	.56	.30	.60	.40	.50	.60	3.60	1.36
Foreign Assets	21	.34	.61	.41	I.81	.71	1.44	1.99	.92	1.17	3.03	13.55	....	....	....	1.11
Claims on Central Government	22a	....	....	....	.02	.31	.19	.16	.41	.03	.05	.03	.05	.05	.25	I.84
Claims on Private Sector	22d	4.52	4.26	4.57	4.89	6.28	7.40	8.54	10.42	12.74	16.45	32.44	32.10	37.60	45.10	I63.51
Claims on Other Financial Insts.	22f	....	....	....	....	....	....	....	....	....	....	....	....	....	....	....
Demand Deposits	24	2.26	2.66	2.44	3.13	3.69	4.52	5.91	6.11	5.38	8.68	17.26	14.70	17.60	20.60	I18.07
Time Deposits	25	.11	.08	.27	.36	.36	.40	.74	1.19	2.46	2.72	4.99	5.00	5.60	8.00	I7.00
Foreign Liabilities	26c	.53	.30	.53	.79	1.15	1.71	2.12	2.04	4.29	3.61	11.21	....	....	....	....
Long-Term Foreign Liabilities	26cl	1.01	.91	.76	.59	.51	.42	.70	.71	.67	.79	.68	.69	.92	1.58	2.11
Central Government Deposits	26d	.15	.14	.12	.13	.13	.41	.60	.73	1.25	1.43	3.05	3.30	6.00	8.00	I24.09
Credit from Monetary Authorities	26g	.90	.74	1.06	.77	1.40	1.52	.98	1.38	1.06	2.33	7.87	7.69	9.33	11.34	I15.00
Other Items (Net)	27r	—	.19	−.05	.12	.21	.26	.05	.14	−.88	.57	1.38	3.05	.73	.81	I.55
Treasury Claims: Private Sector	22d. i	—	—	—	.25	.28	—	—	—	—	—	—	—	—	—	—
Post Office: Checking Deposits	24.. i	.47	.44	.46	.48	.53	.60	.64	.80	.93	.98	1.17	1.57	1.79	2.46	2.42
Monetary Survey																*Billions of Francs:*
Foreign Assets (Net)	31n	2.32	2.58	1.86	2.38	1.63	4.01	6.15	6.06	4.46	7.04	5.48	6.33	6.29	.87	I−2.14
Domestic Credit	32	4.88	5.04	5.21	5.62	7.68	7.25	7.72	9.91	11.57	14.03	29.49	29.80	31.48	40.18	I46.92
Claims on Central Govt. (Net)	32an	.36	.78	.64	.48	1.12	−.15	−.82	−.51	−1.17	−2.42	−2.95	−2.30	−6.12	−4.92	I−16.60
Claims on Private Sector	32d	4.52	4.26	4.57	5.14	6.56	7.40	8.54	10.42	12.74	16.45	32.44	32.10	37.60	45.10	I63.51
Claims on Other Financial Insts.	32f	....	....	....	....	....	....	....	....	....	....	....	....	....	....	....
Money	34	6.04	6.38	6.05	6.94	8.19	9.63	11.52	12.71	12.33	15.73	26.87	25.63	29.32	31.02	I33.74
Quasi-Money	35	.11	.08	.27	.36	.36	.40	.74	1.19	2.46	2.72	4.99	5.00	5.60	8.00	I7.00
Long-Term Foreign Liabilities	36cl	1.01	.91	.76	.59	.51	.42	.70	.71	.67	.79	.68	.69	.92	1.58	2.11
Other Items (Net)	37r	.04	.26	−.01	.11	.27	.82	.91	1.36	.57	1.83	2.43	4.80	1.93	.45	I.49
Money plus Quasi-Money	35l	6.15	6.46	6.32	7.30	8.55	10.03	12.26	13.90	14.79	18.45	31.86	30.63	34.92	39.02	I40.74
Other Banking Institutions																*Billions of Francs:*
Savings Deposits	45	.32	.33	.34	.37	.40	.46	.53	.60	.64	.67	.83	.87	.91	.95	1.00
Liquid Liabilities	55l	6.47	6.79	6.66	7.67	8.96	10.49	12.79	14.50	15.43	19.12	32.69	31.50	35.83	39.97	I41.74
Interest Rates																*Percent Per Annum*
Discount Rate (End of Period)	60	3.50	3.50	3.50	3.50	3.50	3.50	3.50	3.50	5.50	5.50	8.00	8.00	8.00	8.00	8.00
Money Market Rate	60b	....	....	....	....	....	....	....	....	....	....	....	7.28	7.38	7.40	7.72
Deposit Rate	60l	....	....	....	....	3.00	3.00	3.00	3.00	5.75	5.75	5.88	6.00	6.00	6.00	6.00
Lending Rate	60p	....	....	....	....	....	....	....	....	....	....	....	....	12.00	12.00	12.00
International Transactions																*Billions of Francs*
Exports	70	3.36	2.58	3.77	5.52	7.07	9.06	11.65	9.19	9.79	8.31	6.79	5.96	7.64	6.14	9.77
Exports, from DOTS	70y	....	....	....	....	....	....	....	....	....	....	....	....	....	....	....
Imports, cif	71	8.50	8.26	11.95	12.22	14.13	17.66	21.20	23.09	24.86	35.30	40.28	52.30	65.79	70.20	68.10
Imports, fob	71.v	7.52	7.31	10.58	10.91	12.41	15.63	18.79	20.50	21.99	30.24	34.25	43.87	55.51	58.78	56.54
Imports, cif, from DOTS	71y	....	....	....	....	....	....	....	....	....	....	....	....	....	....	....

Benin

1980	1981	1982	1983	1984	1985	1986	1987	1988	1989	1990	1991	1992	1993	1994		
End of Period															**Exchange Rates**	
287.99	334.52	370.92	436.97	470.11	415.26	394.78	378.78	407.68	380.32	364.84	370.48	378.57	404.89	ℐ780.44	Official Rate	aa
End of Period (ae) Period Average (rf)																
225.80	287.40	336.25	417.37	479.60	378.05	322.75	267.00	302.95	289.40	256.45	259.00	275.33	294.78	ℐ534.60	Official Rate	ae
211.28	271.73	328.61	381.06	436.96	449.26	346.30	300.54	297.85	319.01	272.26	282.11	264.69	283.16	ℐ555.20	Official Rate	rf
															Fund Position	
24.0	24.0	24.0	31.3	31.3	31.3	31.3	31.3	31.3	31.3	31.3	31.3	45.3	45.3	45.3	Quota	2f. s
1.7	2.9	2.0	1.1	.2	—	—	.1	.1	—	.1	.2	—	.1	—	SDRs	1b. s
2.0	2.0	2.0	2.0	2.0	2.0	2.0	2.0	2.0	2.0	2.0	2.0	2.1	2.1	2.1	Reserve Position in the Fund	1c. s
12.7	12.7	12.7	12.5	11.4	10.3	7.8	5.3	3.0	7.8	6.3	15.7	15.7	31.3	48.8	Total Fund Cred.&Loans Outstg.	2tl
End of Period															**International Liquidity**	
8.1	57.6	4.9	3.7	2.5	4.1	3.9	3.6	4.2	3.4	64.9	191.6	245.2	244.0	258.2	Total Reserves minus Gold	1l. d
2.2	3.4	2.2	1.2	.1	—	—	.1	.1	—	.1	.2	—	.1	—	SDRs	1b. d
2.6	2.4	2.2	2.1	2.0	2.2	2.5	2.9	2.7	2.7	2.9	2.9	2.8	2.9	3.1	Reserve Position in the Fund	1c. d
3.4	51.9	.5	.4	.3	1.9	1.4	.6	1.4	.7	61.9	188.5	242.4	241.0	255.1	Foreign Exchange	1d. d
.011	.011	.011	.011	.011	.011	.011	.011	.011	.011	.011	.011	.011	.011	.011	Gold (Million Fine Troy Ounces)	1ad
.5	4.7	4.7	4.3	3.7	3.6	4.5	5.2	4.6	4.3	4.2	3.9	3.8	4.1	4.1	Gold (National Valuation)	1and
8.7	4.1	12.2	47.9	41.6	63.7	74.9	128.7	143.9	26.4	5.7	8.1	4.7	13.6	3.8	Monetary Authorities: Other Liab.	4.. d
3.59	6.05	2.91	16.77	14.54	13.31	23.23	20.60	18.45	8.87	25.89	52.95	72.69	96.18	143.87	Deposit Money Banks: Assets	7a. d
85.60	90.60	95.60	100.60	37.16	48.49	56.43	111.67	67.36	72.28	81.13	71.16	56.21	50.72	30.38	Deposit Money Banks: Liabilities	7b. d
....	....	....	....	....	21.89	24.89	20.34	23.18	25.93	19.15	5.89	7.10	5.95		*of which:* Liab. to Nonbanks	7bd d
End of Period															**Monetary Authorities**	
1.84	16.57	1.66	1.53	1.18	1.55	1.26	.96	1.28	.98	16.65	49.63	67.52	71.91	138.06	Foreign Assets	11
6.45	7.97	9.98	13.82	15.22	13.73	16.13	15.49	16.88	20.99	30.63	29.50	28.74	23.18	28.33	Claims on Central Government	12a
22.76	19.94	34.91	39.30	39.98	42.43	44.55	48.93	63.35	51.83	50.77	50.33	50.33	50.33	—	Claims on Deposit Money Banks	12e
													—	—	Claims on Other Financial Insts.	12f
17.94	29.03	29.81	23.80	29.29	23.96	28.42	23.45	28.16	50.57	80.77	100.60	123.34	107.41	109.70	Reserve Money	14
16.32	28.10	28.84	22.51	28.06	20.26	26.17	19.61	23.69	36.39	41.07	46.48	51.73	25.52	78.14	*of which:* Currency Outside DMBs	14a
9.11	8.96	12.34	28.91	28.48	31.20	30.45	38.39	45.95	11.20	3.79	7.90	7.23	16.69	40.12	Foreign Liabilities	16c
5.47	7.58	5.76	3.70	.90	4.58	3.68	2.13	4.38	9.02	9.53	16.68	11.61	17.43	17.92	Central Government Deposits	16d
-1.47	-1.09	-1.37	-1.75	-2.28	-2.04	-.61	1.41	3.03	3.01	3.95	4.28	4.40	3.91	-1.36	Other Items (Net)	17r
End of Period															**Deposit Money Banks**	
1.44	1.72	1.77	1.29	1.22	3.38	2.09	3.63	1.46	7.73	36.14	52.61	71.03	93.16	30.91	Reserves	20
.81	1.74	.98	7.00	6.98	5.03	7.50	5.50	5.59	2.57	6.64	13.71	20.01	28.35	76.91	Foreign Assets	21
.64	2.70	3.00	3.40	3.72	3.77	3.68	7.01	12.54	13.63	14.62	7.17	6.44	7.15	44.39	Claims on Central Government	22a
85.00	87.00	125.90	132.90	116.86	145.43	132.61	124.80	137.84	103.43	102.07	86.21	69.40	67.72	75.00	Claims on Private Sector	22d
														1.02	Claims on Other Financial Insts.	22f
26.00	30.00	52.00	56.60	59.56	63.63	49.86	38.90	42.30	39.90	58.53	67.35	72.89	84.59	106.32	Demand Deposits	24
16.00	15.00	15.00	15.00	21.12	24.53	30.22	34.97	25.91	19.82	29.47	31.66	47.87	59.28	66.13	Time Deposits	25
....	....	....	....	ℐ17.82	18.33	14.19	24.70	16.51	16.11	15.90	14.77	14.91	14.03	14.92	Foreign Liabilities	26c
2.61	3.84	5.18	—	—	—	4.02	5.12	3.90	4.81	4.91	3.66	.56	.92	1.33	Long-Term Foreign Liabilities	26cl
19.17	24.00	20.00	17.00	6.40	10.32	10.94	11.44	22.25	31.59	26.95	29.54	19.70	25.60	35.02	Central Government Deposits	26d
22.76	19.94	34.91	39.30	39.98	40.68	44.97	48.93	64.17	51.78	56.99	50.77	50.33	50.33	—	Credit from Monetary Authorities	26g
1.35	-.42	4.56	16.69	-16.10	.12	-8.32	-23.12	-17.61	-36.66	-33.27	-38.05	-39.39	-38.37	4.51	Other Items (Net)	27r
—	—	—	—	—	—	—	—	—	—	—	—	—	—	—	Treasury Claims: Private Sector	22d. i
2.36	2.33	2.59	2.89	2.98	2.90	2.74	3.00	3.41	3.47	1.59	1.48	1.94	.64	—	Post Office: Checking Deposits	24.. i
End of Period															**Monetary Survey**	
-2.83	13.49	-4.99	-14.92	-38.15	-42.95	-35.89	-56.63	-55.59	-23.76	3.60	40.67	65.39	69.55	159.93	Foreign Assets (Net)	31n
69.82	68.42	115.72	132.32	131.49	150.93	140.54	136.73	144.05	100.91	112.43	78.16	75.20	55.66	95.79	Domestic Credit	32
-15.18	-18.58	-10.19	-.58	14.63	5.50	7.93	11.93	6.21	-2.52	10.36	-8.05	5.80	-12.06	19.77	Claims on Central Govt. (Net)	32an
85.00	87.00	125.90	132.90	116.86	145.43	132.61	124.80	137.84	103.43	102.07	86.21	69.40	67.72	75.00	Claims on Private Sector	32d
														1.02	Claims on Other Financial Insts.	32f
44.68	60.44	83.44	82.00	90.60	87.09	78.93	61.84	71.95	84.37	104.55	116.66	128.21	111.34	184.98	Money	34
16.00	15.00	15.00	15.00	21.12	24.53	30.22	34.97	25.91	19.82	29.47	31.66	47.87	59.28	66.13	Quasi-Money	35
2.61	3.84	5.18	—	—	—	4.02	5.12	3.90	4.81	4.91	3.66	.56	.92	1.33	Long-Term Foreign Liabilities	36cl
.06	-2.31	2.40	14.95	-18.38	-3.64	-8.51	-21.83	-13.30	-31.84	-22.90	-33.16	-36.00	-46.33	3.28	Other Items (Net)	37r
60.68	75.44	98.44	97.00	111.72	111.62	109.14	96.81	97.86	104.19	134.02	148.32	176.08	170.62	251.11	Money plus Quasi-Money	35l
End of Period															**Other Banking Institutions**	
1.14	1.46	1.57	1.66	1.72	2.12	2.36	3.29	3.10	3.09	....	....	....	....	....	Savings Deposits	45
61.82	76.90	100.01	98.66	113.44	113.74	111.50	100.10	100.96	107.28	....	....	....	....	....	Liquid Liabilities	55l
Percent Per Annum															**Interest Rates**	
10.50	10.50	12.50	10.50	10.50	10.50	8.50	8.50	9.50	11.00	11.00	11.00	12.50	10.50	10.00	Discount Rate (End of Period)	60
10.13	13.68	14.66	12.23	11.84	10.66	8.58	8.37	8.72	10.07	10.98	10.94	11.44	....	....	Money Market Rate	60b
6.19	6.25	7.75	7.50	7.25	7.25	6.08	5.25	5.25	6.42	7.00	7.00	7.75	....	....	Deposit Rate	60l
14.50	14.50	16.00	14.50	14.50	14.50	13.50	13.50	13.58	15.08	16.00	16.00	16.75	....	....	Lending Rate	60p
Billions of Francs															**International Transactions**	
13.27	9.14	7.84	25.35	72.82	67.35	36.01	34.27	21.00	24.58	33.25	5.98	16.77	34.50	....	Exports	70
....	8.50	7.90	26.85	72.97	67.82	36.01	34.41	20.99	24.58	33.25	12.94	16.77	38.50	....	Exports, from DOTS	70y
69.97	147.50	152.55	121.02	125.88	148.78	133.85	104.98	97.26	66.13	72.19	68.05	72.19	97.48	....	Imports, cif	71
58.07	122.41	126.60	100.43	104.46	123.47	111.08	87.12	80.71	54.88	59.91	56.48	96.71	80.90	....	Imports, fob	71.v
....	147.50	156.29	121.11	131.47	152.76	133.85	105.04	97.26	66.13	72.19	68.05	116.96	97.74	....	Imports, cif, from DOTS	71y

Benin
638

		1965	1966	1967	1968	1969	1970	1971	1972	1973	1974	1975	1976	1977	1978	1979
Balance of Payments																*Millions of US Dollars:*
Goods: Exports f.o.b.	78aa d	...	...	...	...	...	...	...	...	...	93.0	116.1	85.9	129.1	125.6	132.9
Goods: Imports f.o.b.	78ab d	...	...	...	...	...	...	...	...	...	−148.3	−205.6	−208.6	−255.5	−284.8	−289.0
Trade Balance	78ac d	...	...	...	...	...	...	...	...	...	−55.3	−89.5	−122.7	−126.4	−159.2	−156.1
Services: Credit	78ad d	...	...	...	...	...	...	...	...	...	22.0	28.1	30.8	32.5	38.7	43.4
Services: Debit	78ae d	...	...	...	...	...	...	...	...	...	−40.6	−57.9	−61.0	−71.3	−85.5	−94.9
Balance on Goods and Services	78af d	...	...	...	...	...	...	...	...	...	−73.9	−119.3	−152.9	−165.2	−206.0	−207.6
Income: Credit	78ag d	...	...	...	...	...	...	...	...	...	4.1	3.5	3.2	3.4	3.9	6.0
Income: Debit	78ah d	...	...	...	...	...	...	...	...	...	−1.8	−4.8	−3.2	−3.6	−3.7	−4.8
Balance on Goods, Serv., & Inc.	78ai d	...	...	...	...	...	...	...	...	...	−71.6	−120.6	−152.8	−165.4	−205.8	−206.3
Current Transfers, n.i.e.: Credit	78aj d	...	...	...	...	...	...	...	...	...	46.9	72.3	83.2	108.6	114.4	160.7
Current Transfers: Debit	78ak d	...	...	...	...	...	...	...	...	...	−4.6	−5.1	−3.2	−3.9	−5.0	−6.2
Current Account, n.i.e.	78al d	...	...	...	...	...	...	...	...	...	−29.3	−53.4	−72.8	−60.7	−96.4	−51.9
Capital Account, n.i.e.: Credit	78ba d										—	—	—	—	—	—
Capital Account: Debit	78bb d										—	—	—	—	—	—
Capital Account, n.i.e.	78bc d										—	—	—	—	—	—
Direct Investment Abroad	78bd d															−.2
Dir. Invest. in Rep. Econ., n.i.e.	78be d										−2.3	1.9	2.5	3.1	.8	3.6
Portfolio Investment Assets	78bf d															
Portfolio Investment Liab., n.i.e.	78bg d															
Other Investment Assets	78bh d										−15.0	−71.6	−26.0	−38.0	−30.5	−41.8
Other Investment Liab., n.i.e.	78bi d										36.4	80.3	68.6	71.5	93.3	74.6
Financial Account, n.i.e.	78bj d										19.1	10.6	45.1	36.7	63.6	36.1
Net Errors and Omissions	78ca d										10.7	23.0	24.9	20.1	13.6	12.1
Overall Balance	78cb d										.5	−19.9	−2.8	−3.9	−19.2	−3.6
Reserves and Related Items	79da d										−.5	19.9	2.8	3.9	19.2	3.6
Reserve Assets	79db d										−.5	19.9	−5.2	−.1	6.5	3.6
Use of Fund Credit and Loans	79dc d														6.7	
Liabs.Constit.For.Auth.Reserves	79dd d															
Exceptional Financing	79de d										—	—	8.0	4.0	6.1	—
Government Finance																*Millions of Francs:*
Deficit (−) or Surplus	80										...	...	...	1,434	5,052	−1,010
Revenue	81										...	...	24,781	27,518	31,611	34,200
Grants Received	81z													14,477	9,096	11,705
Expenditure	82													37,006	34,304	42,065
Lending Minus Repayments	83													3,555	1,351	4,850
Financing																
Net Borrowing: Domestic	84a													−430	2,071	147
Foreign	85a													887	1,802	2,457
Use of Cash Balances	87													−1,891	−8,925	−1,594
National Accounts																*Billions of Francs:*
Exports of Goods & Services	90c	6.1	6.9	8.8	...	...	19.3	23.6	21.6	25.4	27.8	30.6	31.6	43.3	50.0	50.3
Government Consumption	91f	7.7	7.5	8.5			9.0	9.3	10.5	11.2	11.8	13.4	12.8	14.7	14.4	17.4
Gross Fixed Capital Formation	93e	5.9	6.3	8.6			10.2	10.3	14.9	14.1	20.2	22.8	22.0	22.9	23.2	38.8
Increase/Decrease(−) in Stocks	93i	.4	.4	.4			1.6	1.7	2.2	2.2	2.1	6.0	3.3	4.8	5.5	7.5
Private Consumption	96f	37.7	39.5	38.0			54.1	56.4	64.8	70.4	77.9	96.0	119.5	139.1	156.3	176.7
Imports of Goods & Services	98c	−11.3	−12.3	−15.7			−24.5	−27.5	−30.9	−33.2	−35.4	−55.7	−54.8	−73.7	−80.9	−97.2
Gross Domestic Product	99b	46.5	48.2	48.7	51.3	55.1	69.7	73.7	83.1	89.0	107.6	112.8	133.5	148.5	161.6	193.5
Net Factor Inc/Pmts(−) Abroad	98.n	−.1	.1	—			.7	−.7	...	...	−.3	−.1	.2	.1	.2	.2
Gross Nat'l Expenditure = GNP	99a	46.4	48.2	48.6									134.5	151.3	168.8	193.7
Nat'l Income, Market Prices	99e	44.0	45.5	45.4			57.1				103.5	107.7	126.0	142.4	157.9	181.3
Gross Dom. Prod. 1985 Prices	99b.p						261.3	266.4	290.2	296.8	274.5	286.5	298.7	315.7	324.4	340.5
GDP Deflator (1985=100)	99bi p						26.7	27.7	28.6	30.0	39.2	39.4	44.7	47.0	49.8	56.8
																Millions:
Population	99z	2.37	2.44	2.51	2.58	2.65	2.72	2.79	2.87	2.95	3.03	3.11	3.20	3.29	3.38	ⅼ 3.38

Deposit Money Banks: ⅼ Beginning in October 1979, *Central Government Deposits* include the deposits of public establishments of an administrative or social nature (EPAS) and exclude those of the savings bank; *Demand* and *Time Deposits* include deposits of the savings bank and exclude deposits of EPAS; and *Claims on Private Sector* exclude claims on other financial institutions.

Monetary Survey: ⅼ Beginning in October 1979, *line 32f* includes claims of deposit money banks on other financial institutions; see deposit money bank notes for explanation of other break symbols.

Benin

	1980	1981	1982	1983	1984	1985	1986	1987	1988	1989	1990	1991	1992	1993	1994		
Minus Sign Indicates Debit																**Balance of Payments**	
	164.0	388.0	135.4	132.3	223.8	314.1	303.2	363.4	379.1	178.4	287.2	328.6	362.3	332.7	....	Goods: Exports f.o.b.	78aa *d*
	−312.2	−526.8	−514.5	−286.3	−290.9	−337.7	−412.4	−483.8	−511.0	−316.6	−427.9	−482.4	−560.7	−571.4	....	Goods: Imports f.o.b.	78ab *d*
	−148.3	−138.8	−379.1	−154.0	−67.1	−23.6	−109.2	−120.5	−131.9	−138.2	−140.7	−153.8	−198.3	−238.7	....	Trade Balance	78ac *d*
	62.3	66.8	48.0	50.2	58.3	70.1	88.4	100.5	106.8	87.8	114.6	122.6	141.7	134.6	....	Services: Credit	78ad *d*
	−108.6	−142.7	−133.7	−92.4	−93.8	−106.2	−131.1	−155.4	−163.2	−111.6	−135.2	−138.6	−157.5	−155.4	....	Services: Debit	78ae *d*
	−194.6	−214.6	−464.8	−196.3	−102.6	−59.7	−151.9	−175.4	−188.4	−162.1	−161.2	−169.8	−214.2	−259.6	....	Balance on Goods and Services	78af *d*
	15.1	10.6	10.7	4.9	7.4	7.1	11.0	11.3	12.1	—	—	—	—	—	....	Income: Credit	78ag *d*
	−6.9	−10.0	−29.6	−51.8	−55.4	−46.5	−65.0	−73.6	−75.5	−38.2	−38.9	−30.5	−61.6	−39.9	....	Income: Debit	78ah *d*
	−186.5	−214.1	−483.7	−243.2	−150.7	−99.1	−205.9	−237.6	−251.8	−200.3	−200.2	−200.3	−275.8	−299.5	....	Balance on Goods, Serv., & Inc.	78ai *d*
	157.5	127.2	111.1	113.2	100.2	110.8	149.6	174.7	180.3	196.2	211.2	203.1	247.8	263.8	....	Current Transfers, n.i.e.: Credit	78aj *d*
	−6.8	−6.5	−4.5	−4.8	−6.6	−7.1	−9.2	−11.0	−11.4	−9.1	−12.5	−13.5	−16.6	−16.6	....	Current Transfers: Debit	78ak *d*
	−35.7	−93.4	−377.2	−134.8	−57.1	4.7	−65.5	−73.9	−82.9	−13.2	−1.5	−10.6	−44.6	−52.3	....	Current Account, n.i.e.	78al *d*
	—	—	—	—	—	—	—	—	—	—	—	—	—	—	....	Capital Account, n.i.e.: Credit	78ba *d*
	—	—	—	—	—	—	—	—	—	—	—	—	—	—	....	Capital Account: Debit	78bb *d*
	—	—	—	—	—	—	—	—	—	—	—	—	—	—	....	Capital Account, n.i.e.	78bc *d*
	—	—	−.5	−.5	−.5	—	—	—	—	—	—	—	—	—	....	Direct Investment Abroad	78bd *d*
	4.3	2.1	—	—	—	—	—	—	—	—	—	—	—	—	....	Dir. Invest. in Rep. Econ., n.i.e.	78be *d*
	—	—	—	—	—	—	—	—	—	—	—	—	—	—	....	Portfolio Investment Assets	78bf *d*
	—	—	—	—	—	—	—	—	—	—	—	—	—	—	....	Portfolio Investment Liab., n.i.e.	78bg *d*
	16.8	−98.4	106.5	−29.6	−9.1	19.8	5.2	45.3	−15.8	9.5	−14.9	−25.1	−23.8	−7.0	....	Other Investment Assets	78bh *d*
	16.8	223.9	212.2	117.5	7.7	−10.7	−21.7	−1.0	8.1	9.1	65.3	77.2	−16.8	52.0	....	Other Investment Liab., n.i.e.	78bi *d*
	37.9	127.5	318.2	87.4	−1.9	9.1	−16.5	44.3	−7.7	18.6	50.4	52.1	−40.7	45.0	....	Financial Account, n.i.e.	78bj *d*
	−24.7	−8.0	10.9	10.0	35.6	−43.3	10.8	−41.6	−7.8	−71.3	−39.0	20.4	7.7	−32.8	....	Net Errors and Omissions	78ca *d*
	−22.6	31.2	−48.1	−37.4	−23.3	−29.5	−71.2	−71.3	−98.4	−65.9	10.0	61.9	−77.5	−40.1	....	Overall Balance	78cb *d*
	22.6	−31.2	48.1	37.4	23.3	29.5	71.2	71.3	98.4	65.9	−10.0	−61.9	77.5	40.1	....	Reserves and Related Items	79da *d*
	7.5	−51.6	45.9	1.4	1.3	−1.1	.7	.9	−.9	.7	−57.6	−116.5	−67.5	−15.3	....	Reserve Assets	79db *d*
	9.6	.1	—	−.2	−1.1	−1.1	−2.9	−3.2	−3.1	5.9	−1.9	12.5	—	21.9	....	Use of Fund Credit and Loans	79dc *d*
	—	—	—	—	—	—	—	—	—	—	—	—	—	—	....	Liabs.Constit.For.Auth.Reserves	79dd *d*
	5.4	20.3	2.2	36.2	23.1	31.6	73.3	73.6	102.4	59.2	49.6	42.2	145.1	33.5	....	Exceptional Financing	79de *d*
Year Ending December 31																**Government Finance**	
	....	....	....	....	....	....	....	....	....	....	....	....	....	....	....	Deficit (-) or Surplus	80
	....	....	....	....	....	....	....	....	....	....	....	....	....	....	....	Revenue	81
	....	....	....	....	....	....	....	....	....	....	....	....	....	....	....	Grants Received	81z
	....	....	....	....	....	....	....	....	....	....	....	....	....	....	....	Expenditure	82
	....	....	....	....	....	....	....	....	....	....	....	....	....	....	....	Lending Minus Repayments	83
																Financing	
	....	....	....	....	....	....	....	....	....	....	....	....	....	....	....	Net Borrowing: Domestic	84a
	....	....	....	....	....	....	....	....	....	....	....	....	....	....	....	Foreign	85a
	....	....	....	....	....	....	....	....	....	....	....	....	....	....	....	Use of Cash Balances	87
Billions of Francs																**National Accounts**	
	59.5	65.1	107.6	83.5	91.9	106.7	78.0	128.7	93.4	87.6	102.3	118.0	....	....	....	Exports of Goods & Services	90c
	21.7	25.2	43.7	60.2	41.8	42.2	43.6	68.7	63.7	62.3	66.1	64.3	....	....	....	Government Consumption	91f
	48.2	52.3	112.7	69.4	60.5	77.5	82.8	66.7	72.8	59.7	67.4	72.6	....	....	....	Gross Fixed Capital Formation	93e
	9.7	13.1	2.3	2.9	5.2	−1.6	13.6	−.1	2.6	−3.1	4.0	5.0	....	....	....	Increase/Decrease(-) in Stocks	93i
	220.0	276.1	343.8	354.1	386.5	395.9	431.8	376.4	398.0	399.3	401.3	437.6	....	....	....	Private Consumption	96f
	−113.5	−130.7	−193.6	−152.8	−118.3	−129.2	−150.6	−179.0	−146.8	−117.4	−141.6	−166.6	....	....	....	Imports of Goods & Services	98c
	245.6	301.0	416.6	417.4	467.6	491.5	499.2	460.6	483.7	488.4	499.5	530.9	....	....	....	Gross Domestic Product	99b
	.2	−.2	....	....	....	....	....	....	−12.8	−17.2	−15.6	−16.1	....	....	....	Net Factor Inc/Pmts(-) Abroad	98.n
	245.8	300.8	....	....	....	....	....	....	471.7	462.0	486.7	519.5	....	....	....	Gross Nat'l Expenditure = GNP	99a
	226.0	277.8	....	....	....	....	....	....	....	....	....	....	....	....	....	Nat'l Income, Market Prices	99e
	ⅠI377.8	399.7	ⅠI442.7	423.5	457.1	491.5	502.1	494.5	509.5	505.9	....	....	....	....	....	Gross Dom. Prod. 1985 Prices	99b.*p*
	65.0	75.3	94.1	98.6	102.3	100.0	99.4	93.1	94.9	96.5	....	....	....	....	....	GDP Deflator (1985=100)	99bi *p*
Midyear Estimates																	
	3.46	3.58	3.69	3.81	3.93	4.06	4.19	4.32	4.46	4.61	4.74	4.89	5.05	5.22	5.34	**Population**	99z

Bhutan
514

		1965	1966	1967	1968	1969	1970	1971	1972	1973	1974	1975	1976	1977	1978	1979
Exchange Rates														*Ngultrum per SDR:*		
Official Rate	aa	4.775	7.576	7.547	7.628	7.559	7.576	7.903	8.773	9.896	9.978	10.462	10.318	9.971	10.668	10.416
														Ngultrum per US Dollar:		
Official Rate	ae	4.775	7.576	7.547	7.628	7.559	7.576	7.279	8.080	8.203	8.150	8.937	8.881	8.209	8.188	7.907
Official Rate	rf	4.762	6.359	7.500	7.500	7.500	7.500	7.492	7.594	7.742	8.102	8.376	8.960	8.739	8.193	8.126
Fund Position														*Millions of SDRs:*		
Quota	2f.s	...	...	...	...	...	...	...	...	...	...	...	...	...	...	...
SDRs	1b.s	...	...	...	...	...	...	...	...	...	...	...	...	...	...	...
Reserve Position in the Fund	1c.s	...	...	...	...	...	...	...	...	...	...	...	...	...	...	...
International Liquidity													*Millions of US Dollars Unless Otherwise Indicated:*			
Total Reserves minus Gold	1l.d	...	...	...	...	...	...	...	...	...	...	...	...	...	...	...
SDRs	1b.d	...	...	...	...	...	...	...	...	...	...	...	...	...	...	...
Reserve Position in the Fund	1c.d	...	...	...	...	...	...	...	...	...	...	...	...	...	...	...
Foreign Exchange	1d.d	...	...	...	...	...	...	...	...	...	...	...	...	...	...	...
of which: Convertible Currency	1dx.d	...	...	...	...	...	...	...	...	...	...	...	...	...	...	...
Deposit Money Banks: Assets	7a.d	...	...	...	...	...	...	...	...	...	...	...	...	...	...	...
Liabilities	7b.d	...	...	...	...	...	...	...	...	...	...	...	...	...	...	...
Monetary Authorities														*Millions of Ngultrum*		
Foreign Assets	11	...	...	...	...	...	...	...	...	...	...	...	...	...	...	...
Claims on Other Financial Insts.	12f	...	...	...	...	...	...	...	...	...	...	...	...	...	...	...
Reserve Money	14	...	...	...	...	...	...	...	...	...	...	...	...	...	...	...
of which: Currency Outside DMBs	14a	...	...	...	...	...	...	...	...	...	...	...	...	...	...	...
Central Government Deposits	16d	...	...	...	...	...	...	...	...	...	...	...	...	...	...	...
Other Items (Net)	17r	...	...	...	...	...	...	...	...	...	...	...	...	...	...	...
Deposit Money Banks														*Millions of Ngultrum*		
Reserves	20	...	...	...	...	...	...	...	...	...	...	...	...	...	...	...
Foreign Assets	21	...	...	...	...	...	...	...	...	...	...	...	...	...	...	...
Claims on Central Government	22a	...	...	...	...	...	...	...	...	...	...	...	...	...	...	...
Claims on Nonfin.Pub.Enterprises	22c	...	...	...	...	...	...	...	...	...	...	...	...	...	...	...
Claims on Private Sector	22d	...	...	...	...	...	...	...	...	...	...	...	...	...	...	...
Demand Deposits	24	...	...	...	...	...	...	...	...	...	...	...	...	...	...	...
Time and Fgn. Currency Deposits	25	...	...	...	...	...	...	...	...	...	...	...	...	...	...	...
Foreign Liabilities	26c	...	...	...	...	...	...	...	...	...	...	...	...	...	...	...
Central Government Deposits	26d	...	...	...	...	...	...	...	...	...	...	...	...	...	...	...
Capital Accounts	27a	...	...	...	...	...	...	...	...	...	...	...	...	...	...	...
Other Items (Net)	27r	...	...	...	...	...	...	...	...	...	...	...	...	...	...	...
Monetary Survey														*Millions of Ngultrum:*		
Foreign Assets (Net)	31n	...	...	...	...	...	...	...	...	...	...	...	...	...	...	...
Domestic Credit	32	...	...	...	...	...	...	...	...	...	...	...	...	...	...	...
Claims on Central Govt. (Net)	32an	...	...	...	...	...	...	...	...	...	...	...	...	...	...	...
Claims on Nonfin.Pub.Enterprises	32c	...	...	...	...	...	...	...	...	...	...	...	...	...	...	...
Claims on Private Sector	32d	...	...	...	...	...	...	...	...	...	...	...	...	...	...	...
Money	34	...	...	...	...	...	...	...	...	...	...	...	...	...	...	...
Quasi-Money	35	...	...	...	...	...	...	...	...	...	...	...	...	...	...	...
Other Items (Net)	37r	...	...	...	...	...	...	...	...	...	...	...	...	...	...	...
Money plus Quasi-Money	35l	...	...	...	...	...	...	...	...	...	...	...	...	...	...	...
Interest Rates														*Percent Per Annum*		
Deposit Rate	60l	...	...	...	...	...	...	...	...	...	...	...	...	...	...	...
Lending Rate	60p	...	...	...	...	...	...	...	...	...	...	...	...	...	...	...
Prices, Production, and Tourism														*Index Numbers (1990=100):*		
Consumer Prices	64	...	...	...	...	...	...	...	...	...	...	...	...	...	...	...
Electricity Production	66ae	...	...	...	...	...	...	...	...	...	...	...	...	...	...	...
Tourist Arrivals	66ta	...	...	...	...	...	...	...	...	...	...	...	...	...	...	...
International Transactions														*Millions of Ngultrum:*		
Exports	70	...	...	...	...	...	...	...	...	...	...	...	...	...	...	...
Imports, cif	71	...	...	...	...	...	...	...	...	...	...	...	...	...	...	...
Government Finance														*Millions of Ngultrum:*		
Deficit (-) or Surplus	80	...	...	...	...	...	...	...	...	...	...	...	...	...	...	...
Revenue	81	...	...	...	...	...	...	...	...	...	...	...	...	...	...	...
Grants Received	81z	...	...	...	...	...	...	...	...	...	...	...	...	...	...	...
Expenditure	82	...	...	...	...	...	...	...	...	...	...	...	...	...	...	...
Lending Minus Repayments	83	...	...	...	...	...	...	...	...	...	...	...	...	...	...	...
Financing																
Total Financing	84	...	...	...	...	...	...	...	...	...	...	...	...	...	...	...
Domestic	84a	...	...	...	...	...	...	...	...	...	...	...	...	...	...	...
Foreign	85a	...	...	...	...	...	...	...	...	...	...	...	...	...	...	...
Debt: Domestic	88a	...	...	...	...	...	...	...	...	...	...	...	...	...	...	...
Foreign	89a	...	...	...	...	...	...	...	...	...	...	...	...	...	...	...
National Accounts														*Millions of Ngultrum:*		
Exports of Goods & Services	90c	...	...	...	...	...	...	...	...	...	...	...	...	...	...	...
Government Consumption	91f	...	...	...	...	...	...	...	...	...	...	...	...	...	...	...
Gross Fixed Capital Formation	93e	...	...	...	...	...	...	...	...	...	...	...	...	...	...	...
Increase/Decrease(-) in Stocks	93i	...	...	...	...	...	...	...	...	...	...	...	...	...	...	...
Private Consumption	96f	...	...	...	...	...	...	...	...	...	...	...	...	...	...	...
Imports of Goods & Services	98c	...	...	...	...	...	...	...	...	...	...	...	...	...	...	...
Gross Domestic Product	99b	...	...	...	...	...	...	...	...	...	...	...	...	...	...	...
Net Factor Inc/Pmts(-) Abroad	98.n	...	...	...	...	...	...	...	...	...	...	...	...	...	...	...
Gross Nat'l Product = GNP	99a	...	...	...	...	...	...	...	...	...	...	...	...	...	...	...
Gross Dom. Prod. 1990 Prices	99b.p	...	...	...	...	...	...	...	...	...	...	...	...	...	...	...
GDP Deflator (1990=100)	99bi.p	...	...	...	...	...	...	...	...	...	...	...	...	...	...	...
														Millions:		
Population	99z	...	...	...	...	...	...	...	...	...	...	...	...	...	...	...

Government Finance: I Data relate to a fiscal year different from calendar year (fiscal year ends March 31 through 1986 and ends June 30 beginning in 1988). Data for 1988 cover 15 months.

Bhutan

	1980	1981	1982	1983	1984	1985	1986	1987	1988	1989	1990	1991	1992	1993	1994		
End of Period																**Exchange Rates**	
	10.114	10.591	10.627	10.986	12.205	13.363	16.051	18.268	20.117	22.387	25.712	36.953	36.025	43.102	45.810	Official Rate	aa
End of Period (ae) Period Average (rf)																	
	7.930	9.099	9.634	10.493	12.451	12.166	13.122	12.877	14.949	17.035	18.073	25.834	26.200	31.380	31.380	Official Rate	ae
	7.863	8.659	9.455	10.099	11.363	12.369	12.611	12.962	13.917	16.226	17.505	22.742	25.918	30.493	31.374	Official Rate	rf
																Fund Position	
	....	1.700	1.700	1.700	2.500	2.500	2.500	2.500	2.500	2.500	2.500	2.500	2.500	4.500	4.500	Quota	2f. s
	....	—	—	.020	.050	.080	.110	.140	.160	.200	.250	.300	.340	.376	.405	SDRs	1b. s
	....	—	.370	.370	.570	.570	.570	.570	.570	.570	.570	.570	.570	.570	.570	Reserve Position in the Fund	1c. s
End of Period																**International Liquidity**	
	....	31.11	35.51	40.22	44.81	50.30	61.00	74.94	94.12	98.51	86.01	98.92	77.87	....	115.20	Total Reserves minus Gold	1l. d
	....	—	—	.02	.05	.09	.13	.20	.22	.26	.36	.43	.47	.52	.59	SDRs	1b. d
	....	—	.41	.39	.56	.63	.70	.81	.77	.75	.81	.82	.78	.78	.83	Reserve Position in the Fund	1c. d
	....	31.11	35.10	39.81	44.21	49.59	60.17	73.93	93.14	97.50	84.85	97.68	76.62	....	113.78	Foreign Exchange	1d. d
	....	....	....	4.22	7.12	17.42	21.59	35.26	44.57	46.39	61.29	85.44	75.29	....	110.39	of which: Convertible Currency	1dx d
	....	....	....	30.58	34.78	34.60	33.06	49.46	49.09	40.67	25.50	13.50	8.11	....	8.88	Deposit Money Banks: Assets	7a. d
	....	....	....	2.53	3.68	4.38	2.84	3.32	3.08	5.13	6.53	5.30	13.63	....	—	Liabilities	7b. d
End of Period																**Monetary Authorities**	
	....	....	....	51	103	228	304	483	697	841	1,145	2,268	2,027	....	3,533	Foreign Assets	11
	....	....	....	—	14	16	17	24	24	30	39	48	44	....	....	Claims on Other Financial Insts.	12f
	....	....	....	39	85	204	259	433	384	691	1,260	1,593	1,257	....	1,589	Reserve Money	14
	....	....	....	22	46	70	91	104	149	188	194	246	345	....	348	of which: Currency Outside DMBs	14a
	....	....	....	13	24	22	19	9	180	78	65	116	20	....	30	Central Government Deposits	16d
	....	....	....	−1	8	18	42	65	156	102	−141	607	794	....	....	Other Items (Net)	17r
End of Period																**Deposit Money Banks**	
	....	....	....	9	13	119	143	310	244	502	1,009	1,253	828	....	1,416	Reserves	20
	....	....	....	321	433	421	434	637	734	693	461	349	213	....	279	Foreign Assets	21
	....	....	....	23	59	120	104	12	3	3	3	3	3	....	5	Claims on Central Government	22a
	....	....	....	57	41	27	20	14	32	28	53	65	770	....	....	Claims on Nonfin.Pub.Enterprises	22c
	....	....	....	43	58	55	67	82	116	192	216	306	426	....	2,485	Claims on Private Sector	22d
	....	....	....	155	164	191	186	213	263	358	345	504	496	....	697	Demand Deposits	24
	....	....	....	147	157	202	222	236	312	430	539	648	746	....	1,351	Time and Fgn. Currency Deposits	25
	....	....	....	27	46	53	37	43	46	87	118	137	357	....	....	Foreign Liabilities	26c
	....	....	....	—	89	78	118	307	221	202	299	315	200	....	140	Central Government Deposits	26d
	....	....	....	121	111	133	150	176	177	229	240	236	534	....	324	Capital Accounts	27a
	....	....	....	4	38	85	55	80	110	110	200	136	−95	....	....	Other Items (Net)	27r
End of Period																**Monetary Survey**	
	....	....	....	346	490	595	700	1,077	1,384	1,446	1,488	2,480	1,883	....	3,812	Foreign Assets (Net)	31n
	....	....	....	110	59	118	71	−185	−227	−27	−54	−10	1,022	....	....	Domestic Credit	32
	....	....	....	10	−54	20	−33	−305	−399	−277	−361	−428	−218	....	−165	Claims on Central Govt. (Net)	32an
	....	....	....	57	41	27	20	14	32	28	53	65	770	....	....	Claims on Nonfin.Pub.Enterprises	32c
	....	....	....	43	58	55	67	82	116	192	216	306	426	....	2,485	Claims on Private Sector	32d
	....	....	....	177	210	262	277	317	412	546	540	750	841	....	1,044	Money	34
	....	....	....	147	157	202	222	236	312	430	539	648	746	....	1,351	Quasi-Money	35
	....	....	....	132	182	249	272	339	434	442	355	1,072	1,317	....	....	Other Items (Net)	37r
	....	....	....	325	367	464	499	553	724	977	1,079	1,398	1,587	....	2,395	Money plus Quasi-Money	35l
Percent Per Annum																**Interest Rates**	
	....	....	....	5.5	5.5	6.1	6.5	6.5	6.5	6.5	6.5	6.5	8.0	8.0	8.0	Deposit Rate	60l
	....	....	....	15.0	15.0	15.0	15.0	15.0	15.0	15.0	15.0	15.0	17.0	17.0	16.6	Lending Rate	60p
Period Averages																**Prices, Production, and Tourism**	
	41.7	45.9	50.4	59.5	63.7	64.9	71.4	75.9	83.6	90.9	100.0	112.3	126.6	....	....	Consumer Prices	64
	....	....	....	....	....	1.5	1.3	23.7	95.9	80.9	99.7	100.0	100.2	....	....	Electricity Production	66ae
	91.3	79.9	104.4	123.8	123.4	123.1	156.2	163.9	142.7	96.1	100.0	133.4	185.3	194.6	....	Tourist Arrivals	66ta
Year Ending June 30																**International Transactions**	
	131.5	171.7	159.4	160.7	206.4	272.0	427.1	711.9	1,041.3	1,132.3	1,306.4	1,632.0	....	....	....	Exports	70
	394.6	585.9	646.5	730.0	825.2	1,041.6	1,285.4	1,194.6	1,874.5	1,613.9	1,889.8	2,319.9	....	....	....	Imports, cif	71
Fiscal Year (see note)																**Government Finance**	
	....	....	10.3	−23.4	31.8	−207.2	−98.3	....	I 31.9	I−431.6	−390.0	−135.0ᵖ	....	....	....	Deficit (−) or Surplus	80
	....	....	137.8	197.3	278.1	268.3	345.0	....	I 841.7	I 815.3	970.2	1,001.8ᵖ	....	....	....	Revenue	81
	....	....	360.3	478.4	512.1	701.7	777.4	....	I 929.9	I 685.6	523.0	1,040.6ᵖ	....	....	....	Grants Received	81z
	....	....	487.8	697.5	753.4	1,098.1	1,064.3	....	I 1,621.3	I 1,551.5	1,893.3	2,220.7ᵖ	....	....	....	Expenditure	82
	....	....	—	1.6	5.0	79.1	156.4	....	I 118.4	I 381.0	−10.1	−43.3ᵖ	....	....	....	Lending Minus Repayments	83
																Financing	
	....	....	−10.3	23.4	−31.8	207.2	98.3	....	I−31.9	I 431.6	390.0	135.0ᵖ	....	....	....	Total Financing	84
	....	....	−18.9	14.4	−49.8	115.9	−73.6	....	I−242.2	I−53.4	332.7	139.8ᵖ	....	....	....	Domestic	84a
	....	....	8.6	9.0	18.0	91.3	171.9	....	I 210.3	I 485.0	57.3	−4.8ᵖ	....	....	....	Foreign	85a
	....	....	12.6	37.2	14.1	126.3	77.8	....	I 8.9	I 3.9	89.0	116.3ᵖ	....	....	....	Debt: Domestic	88a
	....	....	12.2	22.4	45.8	135.5	316.2	....	I 560.8	I 1,141.1	2,473.9	3,266.2ᵖ	....	....	....	Foreign	89a
Calendar Year																**National Accounts**	
	145.4	207.4	213.2	227.8	290.2	367.5	550.5	767.5	1,200.8	1,348.7	1,484.9	1,743.4	....	....	....	Exports of Goods & Services	90c
	275.9	287.3	326.7	442.9	513.0	560.9	576.3	633.6	641.1	879.0	948.7	1,015.1	1,215.2	....	....	Government Consumption	91f
	330.4	425.8	555.7	690.7	754.9	1,002.9	1,103.1	1,249.7	1,508.0	1,573.5	1,685.9	1,781.6	2,663.1	....	....	Gross Fixed Capital Formation	93e
	14.7	74.7	59.8	21.3	10.4	81.6	32.0	−161.5	10.4	−121.1	−33.9	−71.3	351.0	....	....	Increase/Decrease(−) in Stocks	93i
	748.6	922.2	1,053.8	1,195.1	1,435.8	1,506.3	1,837.5	2,320.8	2,558.2	2,581.8	2,926.3	3,292.7	3,758.1	....	....	Private Consumption	96f
	−402.1	−616.2	−687.6	−789.0	−898.9	−1,127.8	−1,297.8	−1,202.6	−1,983.7	−1,879.5	−2,100.0	−2,431.3	....	....	....	Imports of Goods & Services	98c
	1,112.9	1,301.2	1,521.6	1,788.8	2,105.6	2,391.4	2,801.6	3,607.5	3,933.7	4,381.6	4,982.6	5,501.5	6,353.6	7,120.9	....	Gross Domestic Product	99b
	−200.0	−269.6	−321.5	−456.6	−387.9	−449.7	−467.0	−349.5	−344.3	−171.6	−296.3	−439.8	−645.1	−645.1	....	Net Factor Inc/Pmts(−) Abroad	98.n
	912.9	1,031.6	1,200.1	1,332.2	1,717.7	1,941.7	2,334.6	3,258.0	3,589.4	4,210.0	4,686.1	5,061.7	5,708.5	6,475.8	....	Gross Nat'l Product = GNP	99a
	2,492.0	2,741.9	2,888.4	3,118.3	3,335.6	3,458.8	3,810.8	4,490.4	4,543.4	4,764.4	4,982.4	....	....	....	....	Gross Dom. Prod. 1990 Prices	99b. p
	44.7	47.5	52.7	57.4	63.1	69.1	73.5	80.3	86.6	92.0	100.0	....	....	....	....	GDP Deflator (1990=100)	99bi p
Midyear Estimates																	
	1.24	1.27	1.29	1.32	1.35	1.38	1.41	1.45	1.48	1.52	1.54	1.57	1.58	1.60	....	Population	99z

Bolivia
218

		1965	1966	1967	1968	1969	1970	1971	1972	1973	1974	1975	1976	1977	1978	1979
Exchange Rates																
										Bolivianos per Million sdrs through 1983; per Thousand SDRs in 1984						
Market Rate	aa	11.880	11.880	11.880	11.880	11.880	11.880	12.898	21.714	24.127	24.487	23.413	23.237	24.294	26.056	32.288
										Bolivianos per Million US$ through 1983; per Thousand US$ in 1984						
Market Rate	ae	11.880	11.880	11.880	11.880	11.880	11.880	11.880	20.000	20.000	20.000	20.000	20.000	20.000	20.000	24.510
Market Rate	rf	11.880	11.880	11.880	11.880	11.880	11.880	11.880	13.295	20.010	20.010	20.010	20.010	20.010	20.010	20.403
															Index Numbers (1990=100):		
Market Rate	ah x	....	....	....	....	....	....	....	....	....	....	....	....	....	....	....
Nominal Effective Exchange Rate	ne c	....	....	....	....	....	....	....	....	....	....	....	....	....	....	....
Real Effective Exchange Rate	re c	....	....	....	....	....	....	....	....	....	....	....	....	....	....	150.11
Fund Position															Millions of SDRs:		
Quota	2f. s	22.5	29.0	29.0	29.0	29.0	37.0	37.0	37.0	37.0	37.0	37.0	37.0	37.0	45.0	45.0
SDRs	1b. s	—	—	—	—	—	2.7	2.4	3.0	2.2	2.6	7.0	6.9	5.7	14.1	—
Reserve Position in the Fund	1c. s	1.3	6.9	6.9	—	—	—	—	—	—	—	—	6.4	7.4	9.0	—
Total Fund Cred.&Loans Outstg.	2tl	—	—	—	5.1	8.1	6.1	6.6	7.9	18.1	14.3	13.9	—	—	—	30.3
International Liquidity											Millions of US Dollars Unless Otherwise Indicated:						
Total Reserves minus Gold	1l. d	29.9	33.9	28.6	28.6	30.3	32.8	39.6	44.3	54.9	176.2	139.5	151.1	211.1	169.8	178.2
SDRs	1b. d	—	—	—	—	—	2.7	2.6	3.3	2.6	3.2	8.2	8.0	6.9	18.4	—
Reserve Position in the Fund	1c. d	1.3	6.9	6.9	—	—	—	—	—	—	—	—	7.5	9.0	11.7	—
Foreign Exchange	1d. d	28.6	27.0	21.7	28.6	30.3	30.1	37.0	41.0	52.3	173.0	131.3	135.6	195.2	139.7	178.2
Gold (Million Fine Troy Ounces)	1ad	.191	.209	.266	.311	.334	.362	.384	.407	.407	.408	.410	.414	.602	.645	.683
Gold (National Valuation)	1an d	6.7	7.3	9.3	10.9	11.8	12.8	13.6	15.4	15.5	17.2	17.3	17.6	25.4	27.2	28.8
Monetary Authorities: Other Liab.	4. d	13.3	13.2	17.9	14.4	13.2	14.7	18.8	13.6	28.7	30.4	33.0	29.0	33.1	28.6	218.5
Deposit Money Banks: Assets	7a. d	2.1	1.8	1.9	1.8	1.3	2.9	4.1	6.4	5.1	7.2	14.9	21.0	22.9	23.9	32.8
Liabilities	7b. d	1.9	2.8	3.3	3.4	2.0	3.1	7.2	8.1	15.0	36.0	41.0	41.0	90.0	173.0	203.0
Other Banking Insts.: Liabilities	7f. d	2.9	3.8	5.0	7.8	9.8	14.1	16.8	12.3	16.8	24.1	37.7	51.9	56.9	65.0	62.5
of which: Liab. to Nonbanks	7fd d	2.9	3.8	5.0	7.8	9.8	14.1	16.8	12.3	16.8	24.1	37.7	51.9	56.9	65.0	62.5
Monetary Authorities											Bolivianos through 1982; Thousands from 1983 to 1984;						
Foreign Assets	11	406	489	450	469	499	541	573	1,196	1,384	3,868	3,142	3,853	4,726	4,004	5,534
Claims on Central Government	12a	999	1,168	1,349	1,381	1,496	1,711	2,039	2,805	3,330	3,666	5,681	8,941	12,173	13,842	21,593
Claims on State & Local Govts.	12b	....	....	....	....	....	....	....	....	....	....	....	....	....	....	....
Claims on Nonfin.Pub.Enterprises	12c	....	....	....	....	....	....	....	....	....	....	....	....	....	....	....
Claims on Deposit Money Banks	12e	13	30	69	86	115	132	102	262	601	621	935	765	791	1,212	1,775
Claims on Other Banking Insts.	12f	52	49	45	51	57	84	179	218	459	648	661	973	1,454	1,461	1,151
Claims on Nonbank Financial Insts	12g	....	....	....	....	....	....	....	....	....	....	....	....	....	....	....
Reserve Money	14	850	1,032	1,080	1,145	1,267	1,414	1,679	1,974	2,768	3,668	4,348	6,315	7,884	8,836	9,832
of which: Currency Outside DMBs	14a	740	883	905	949	1,041	1,153	1,281	1,598	2,073	2,746	3,054	3,968	4,864	5,810	7,211
Time,Savings,& Fgn.Currency Dep.	15	....	....	....	....	....	....	....	....	....	....	....	....	....	....	....
Foreign Liabilities	16c	158	157	213	232	253	109	173	222	613	546	569	330	439	587	5,476
Long-Term Foreign Liabilities	16cl	—	—	—	—	—	137	135	222	396	413	417	250	224	776	860
Central Government Deposits	16d	198	274	300	323	429	474	564	1,004	1,452	3,258	4,410	6,875	9,861	9,972	13,711
Central Govt. Lending Funds	16f	....	....	....	....	....	....	....	....	....	....	....	....	....	....	....
Capital Accounts	17a	....	....	....	....	....	....	....	....	....	....	....	....	....	....	....
Other Items (Net)	17r	265	273	320	287	218	334	344	1,060	545	918	676	762	737	348	174
Deposit Money Banks											Bolivianos through 1982; Thousands from 1983 to 1984;						
Reserves	20	97	136	144	173	204	261	346	357	677	929	1,269	2,314	2,918	2,947	2,800
Foreign Assets	21	25	22	23	21	15	35	48	129	101	145	298	419	459	479	803
Claims on Private Sector	22d	253	341	389	520	582	692	798	1,143	1,830	3,005	3,713	5,136	7,365	9,746	12,241
Demand Deposits	24	180	229	237	280	307	365	429	576	849	1,461	1,607	2,430	2,882	2,856	2,924
Time and Savings Deposits	25a	39	81	125	201	272	342	457	581	660	945	1,498	2,571	3,502	3,671	3,586
Foreign Currency Deposits	25b	11	16	24	22	32	37	35	50	143	244	454	830	1,455	1,972	2,731
Foreign Liabilities	26c	22	33	39	41	24	37	86	162	252	552	794	807	1,610	2,666	2,561
Long-Term Foreign Liabilities	26cl	2	2	2	2	1	—	—	—	56	169	32	5	184	802	2,422
Central Govt. Lending Funds	26f	....	....	....	....	....	....	....	....	....	....	....	....	....	....	....
Credit from Monetary Authorities	26g	44	57	51	76	93	118	100	166	491	531	654	719	792	966	1,592
Capital Accounts	27a	102	121	118	127	133	136	163	238	290	377	573	793	1,243	1,347	1,458
Other Items (Net)	27r	−25	−42	−40	−35	−61	−47	−77	−145	−133	−200	−332	−286	−927	−1,108	−1,429
Monetary Survey											Bolivianos through 1982; Thousands from 1983 to 1984;						
Foreign Assets (Net)	31n	251	320	221	218	238	430	363	940	620	2,914	2,078	3,135	3,136	1,229	−1,699
Domestic Credit	32	1,161	1,340	1,538	1,685	1,765	2,071	2,510	3,219	4,223	4,118	5,702	8,232	11,188	15,135	21,274
Claims on Central Govt. (Net)	32an	857	950	1,104	1,115	1,126	1,295	1,533	1,858	1,935	465	1,328	2,123	2,369	3,927	7,882
Claims on State & Local Govt.	32b	....	....	....	....	....	....	....	....	....	....	....	....	....	....	....
Claims on Nonfin.Pub.Enterprises	32c	....	....	....	....	....	....	....	....	....	....	....	....	....	....	....
Claims on Private Sector	32d	253	341	389	520	582	692	798	1,143	1,830	3,005	3,713	5,136	7,365	9,746	12,241
Claims on Other Banking Insts.	32f	52	49	45	51	57	84	179	218	459	648	661	973	1,454	1,461	1,151
Claims on Nonbank Fin. Insts.	32g	....	....	....	....	....	....	....	....	....	....	....	....	....	....	....
Money	34	943	1,153	1,192	1,287	1,361	1,532	1,766	2,210	2,969	4,257	4,759	6,497	7,855	8,831	10,304
Quasi-Money	35	52	100	151	226	306	381	493	634	807	1,192	1,956	3,405	4,960	5,650	6,328
Long-Term Foreign Liabilities	36cl	2	2	2	2	1	137	135	222	453	582	449	255	408	1,578	3,282
Central Govt. Lending Funds	36f	....	....	....	....	....	....	....	....	....	....	....	....	....	....	....
Capital Accounts	37a	....	....	....	....	....	....	....	....	....	....	....	....	....	....	....
Other Items (Net)	37r	416	405	415	389	334	450	479	1,093	615	1,002	617	1,209	1,102	306	−338
Money plus Quasi-Money	35l	995	1,253	1,343	1,513	1,667	1,913	2,259	2,844	3,776	5,449	6,715	9,903	12,815	14,481	16,631
Other Banking Institutions											Bolivianos through 1982; Thousands from 1983 to 1984;						
Cash	40	16	26	19	25	24	22	48	33	39	59	94	102	124	172	178
Foreign Assets	41	3	1	2	2	3	5	4	5	17	−17	11	5	8	32	−31
Claims on Private Sector	42d	204	205	210	248	289	369	388	551	949	1,421	1,905	2,335	2,887	3,275	3,889
Quasi-Monetary Liabilities	45	21	31	26	21	22	30	36	28	157	47	187	217	270	330	236
Foreign Liabilities	46c	....	....	....	....	....	....	....	....	....	....	....	....	....	....	....
Long-Term Foreign Liabilities	46cl	34	46	59	93	117	167	200	245	336	483	754	1,038	1,137	1,301	1,532
Central Government Deposits	46d	7	30	14	11	16	27	22	22	64	83	116	115	45	72	80
Central Govt. Lending Funds	46f	....	....	....	....	....	....	....	....	....	....	....	....	....	....	....
Credit from Monetary Authorities	46g	5	22	43	51	53	61	156	207	340	614	823	916	1,289	1,477	1,127
Capital Accounts	47a	114	112	108	119	122	120	114	105	118	89	292	455	700	952	1,811
Other Items (Net)	47r	40	−7	−18	−20	−14	−9	−89	−18	−9	147	−162	−300	−423	−653	−750

Bolivia

1980	1981	1982	1983	1984	1985	1986	1987	1988	1989	1990	1991	1992	1993	1994		
															Exchange Rates	
\multicolumn{15}{l}{*and per SDR thereafter: End of Period*}		
31.260	28.529	218.305	528.605	‡8.609	‡1.859	2.352	3.135	3.324	3.916	4.837	5.357	5.631	6.147	6.854	Market Rate	aa
\multicolumn{15}{l}{*and per US$ thereafter: End of Period (ae) Period Average (rf)*}		
24.510	24.510	197.900	504.900	‡8.783	‡1.692	1.923	2.210	2.470	2.980	3.400	3.745	4.095	4.475	4.695	Market Rate	ae
24.520	24.520	64.072	231.630	‡3.136	‡.440	1.922	2.055	2.350	2.692	3.173	3.581	3.901	4.265	4.621	Market Rate	rf
\multicolumn{15}{l}{*Period Averages*}		
....	....	....	46,329.72	10,211.88	6,523.17	164.98	154.42	134.96	118.15	100.00	88.51	81.30	74.34	68.60	Market Rate	ah x
....	....	....	....	....	466.55	14.11	16.00	22.90	45.25	100.00	144.00	200.42	314.13	508.22	Nominal Effective Exchange Rate	nec
163.89	206.37	223.77	205.84	267.09	457.79	134.93	130.08	123.32	118.61	100.00	103.87	101.24	97.63	89.91	Real Effective Exchange Rate	rec
															Fund Position	
\multicolumn{15}{l}{*End of Period*}		
67.5	67.5	67.5	90.7	90.7	90.7	90.7	90.7	90.7	90.7	90.7	90.7	126.2	126.2	126.2	Quota	2f. s
—	.1	—	.1	—	—	2.0	—	—	—	—	.7	.1	10.2	17.0	SDRs	1b. s
—	—	—	—	—	—	—	—	—	—	—	—	.1	8.9	8.9	Reserve Position in the Fund	1c. s
99.0	97.3	114.3	121.4	98.0	74.9	157.3	130.9	155.3	191.6	180.7	171.1	181.2	160.5	180.5	Total Fund Cred.&Loans Outstg.	2tl
															International Liquidity	
\multicolumn{15}{l}{*End of Period*}		
106.1	99.8	155.9	160.1	251.6	200.0	163.7	97.3	105.8	204.9	166.8	106.4	181.8	223.4	451.0	Total Reserves minus Gold	1l. d
—	.1	—	.1	—	—	2.5	—	—	—	1.0	.1	.1	14.0	24.8	SDRs	1b. d
—	—	—	—	—	—	—	—	—	—	—	—	12.2	12.2	13.0	Reserve Position in the Fund	1c. d
106.1	99.7	155.9	160.0	251.6	200.0	161.2	97.3	105.8	204.9	165.8	106.3	169.5	197.2	413.2	Foreign Exchange	1d. d
.759	.829	.890	.914	.913	.894	.894	.894	.894	.894	.894	.894	.894	.894	.893	Gold (Million Fine Troy Ounces)	1ad
31.2	34.2	36.1	37.0	37.9	37.8	37.8	37.8	37.8	37.8	37.8	37.8	37.8	37.8	39.6	Gold (National Valuation)	1and
190.7	443.4	557.7	693.2	618.6	260.0	362.3	352.0	386.5	475.6	370.7	316.7	343.5	288.8	311.1	Monetary Authorities: Other Liab.	4..d
43.2	36.8	18.0	34.0	25.0	15.0	41.6	50.1	52.1	66.0	61.3	62.4	79.3	72.2	74.9	Deposit Money Banks: Assets	7a. d
161.0	191.0	182.0	314.0	282.0	156.6	157.0	89.5	67.0	50.1	60.0	101.0	189.0	318.1	469.1	Liabilities	7b. d
67.5	68.1	60.1	48.7	47.6	54.0	50.4	30.5	31.7	6.2	7.1	5.6	4.1	4.1	4.2	Other Banking Insts.: Liabilities	7f. d
67.5	68.1	60.1	48.7	47.6	54.0	50.4	30.5	31.7	6.2	7.1	5.6	4.1	4.1	4.2	of which: Liab. to Nonbanks	7fd d
															Monetary Authorities	
\multicolumn{15}{l}{*Millions of Bolivianos Beginning 1985: End of Period*}		
3,482	3,989	41,972	‡120	2,814	‡463	963	‡1,137	1,288	1,475	1,714	1,969	2,343	2,917	3,702	Foreign Assets	11
32,163	43,298	241,541	‡726	13,115	‡2,444	2,673	‡2,375	2,797	3,208	4,189	5,108	5,906	4,700	5,009	Claims on Central Government	12a
....	....	....	....	....	....	....	76	89	111	125	129	150	20	18	Claims on State & Local Govts.	12b
....	....	....	....	....	....	....	570	621	846	1,086	1,241	1,461	814	891	Claims on Nonfin.Pub.Enterprises	12c
2,618	3,230	13,334	‡27	542	‡80	227	‡361	631	942	1,039	1,538	1,789	1,392	2,513	Claims on Deposit Money Banks	12e
1,363	1,540	7,704	‡27	428	‡50	133	‡179	223	327	404	—	—	—	—	Claims on Other Banking Insts.	12f
....	....	....	....	....	....	....	1	18	27	54	73	84	91	108	Claims on Nonbank Financial Insts	12g
13,741	16,195	63,726	‡195	3,345	‡201	380	‡533	873	1,110	1,413	1,827	1,925	2,557	2,705	Reserve Money	14
9,461	10,852	39,093	‡125	2,888	‡174	294	‡398	529	502	642	754	886	1,034	1,416	of which: Currency Outside DMBs	14a
....	....	....	....	....	....	....	417	351	226	438	526	570	568	1,754	Time,Savings,& Fgn.Currency Dep.	15
5,851	9,970	105,586	‡144	1,974	‡304	367	‡496	548	877	662	340	199	−35	−105	Foreign Liabilities	16c
1,918	3,673	29,729	‡270	4,303	‡391	700	‡692	893	1,166	1,253	1,398	1,641	1,674	1,898	Long-Term Foreign Liabilities	16cl
19,005	26,586	154,752	‡450	10,189	‡2,649	3,211	‡2,998	3,340	3,621	4,415	5,390	6,220	2,524	2,582	Central Government Deposits	16d
....	....	....	....	....	....	....	81	263	637	1,033	1,369	1,741	2,238	2,690	Central Govt. Lending Funds	16f
....	....	....	....	....	....	....	436	412	392	599	341	205	1,075	1,673	Capital Accounts	17a
−888	−4,368	−49,243	‡−159	−2,911	‡−509	−662	‡−953	−1,014	−1,092	−1,202	−1,135	−767	−666	−956	Other Items (Net)	17r
															Deposit Money Banks	
\multicolumn{15}{l}{*Millions of Bolivianos Beginning 1985: End of Period*}		
4,010	5,332	25,717	‡73	674	‡111	183	‡111	251	563	664	974	1,030	1,539	1,205	Reserves	20
1,058	902	3,553	‡17	226	‡25	80	‡111	129	197	209	234	325	323	352	Foreign Assets	21
14,350	18,546	69,281	‡141	1,526	‡291	732	‡1,086	1,543	2,311	3,320	5,093	7,599	10,740	12,217	Claims on Private Sector	22d
4,820	6,299	17,699	‡50	432	‡24	69	‡110	159	206	350	693	1,037	1,466	1,800	Demand Deposits	24
5,707	8,626	38,357	‡87	675	‡53	166	‡133	138	119	146	159	128	138	225	Time and Savings Deposits	25a
2,712	3,195	849	‡1	9	‡36	282	‡510	841	1,418	2,203	3,564	5,039	7,036	7,366	Foreign Currency Deposits	25b
1,970	2,197	17,889	‡112	1,859	‡117	150	‡144	129	39	84	164	402	1,028	1,533	Foreign Liabilities	26c
1,974	2,484	17,676	‡45	678	‡148	152	‡54	36	111	120	215	372	396	670	Long-Term Foreign Liabilities	26cl
....	....	....	....	....	....	....	59	92	122	140	133	160	—	—	Central Govt. Lending Funds	26f
2,405	3,229	9,818	‡14	297	‡53	144	‡235	472	830	929	1,014	1,297	1,334	1,107	Credit from Monetary Authorities	26g
1,936	1,993	11,347	‡26	698	‡165	206	‡421	500	642	743	972	1,278	1,576	1,875	Capital Accounts	27a
−2,105	−3,243	−15,083	‡−104	−2,220	‡−170	−174	‡−358	−444	−415	−520	−612	−759	−373	−802	Other Items (Net)	27r
															Monetary Survey	
\multicolumn{15}{l}{*Millions of Bolivianos Beginning 1985: End of Period*}		
−3,280	−7,276	−77,950	‡−119	−792	‡67	526	‡607	739	756	1,178	1,699	2,067	2,248	2,626	Foreign Assets (Net)	31n
28,871	36,796	163,773	‡445	4,881	‡136	327	‡1,280	1,937	3,202	4,749	6,242	9,056	13,821	15,690	Domestic Credit	32
13,159	16,711	86,789	‡276	2,927	‡−205	−538	‡−632	−556	−420	−240	−294	−237	2,156	2,457	Claims on Central Govt. (Net)	32an
....	....	....	....	....	....	....	76	89	111	125	129	150	20	18	Claims on State & Local Govt.	32b
....	....	....	....	....	....	....	570	621	846	1,086	1,241	1,461	814	891	Claims on Nonfin.Pub.Enterprises	32c
14,350	18,546	69,281	‡141	1,526	‡291	732	‡1,086	1,543	2,311	3,320	5,093	7,599	10,740	12,217	Claims on Private Sector	32d
1,363	1,540	7,704	‡27	428	‡50	133	‡179	223	327	404	—	—	—	—	Claims on Other Banking Insts.	32f
....	....	....	....	....	....	....	1	18	27	54	73	84	91	108	Claims on Nonbank Fin. Insts	32g
14,694	17,587	57,827	‡178	3,370	‡198	369	‡516	698	715	997	1,447	1,923	2,499	3,216	Money	34
8,430	11,831	39,375	‡88	684	‡89	448	‡1,060	1,329	1,762	2,787	4,249	5,737	7,743	9,344	Quasi-Money	35
3,893	6,157	47,404	‡315	4,981	‡539	852	‡746	929	1,277	1,373	1,613	2,013	2,069	2,568	Long-Term Foreign Liabilities	36cl
....	....	....	....	....	....	....	140	356	760	1,172	1,502	1,901	2,238	2,690	Central Govt. Lending Funds	36f
....	....	....	....	....	....	....	857	912	1,034	1,342	1,313	1,483	2,651	3,548	Capital Accounts	37a
−1,425	−6,055	−58,783	‡−255	−4,946	‡−623	−816	‡−1,431	−1,548	−1,589	−1,745	−2,183	−1,933	−1,131	−3,050	Other Items (Net)	37r
23,124	29,418	97,201	‡265	4,053	‡287	817	‡1,576	2,027	2,477	3,784	5,696	7,660	10,242	12,560	Money plus Quasi-Money	35l
															Other Banking Institutions	
\multicolumn{15}{l}{*Millions of Bolivianos Beginning 1985: End of Period*}		
283	283	1,100	‡5	70	‡2	6	‡4	15	8	7	3	—	—	1	Cash	40
−13	−32	−300	‡—	43	‡13	14	‡14	10	3	6	1	—	—	—	Foreign Assets	41
4,664	5,529	27,800	‡74	1,240	‡160	244	‡290	309	318	390	390	393	389	349	Claims on Private Sector	42d
376	629	2,100	‡6	102	‡18	12	‡24	20	2	1	2	1	1	1	Quasi-Monetary Liabilities	45
....	....	....	....	....	....	....	....	10	12	—	5	—	—	—	Foreign Liabilities	46c
1,655	1,670	11,900	‡25	418	‡91	97	‡58	66	19	19	21	17	18	19	Long-Term Foreign Liabilities	46cl
129	119	800	‡3	80	‡10	3	‡6	7	6	2	1	1	1	1	Central Government Deposits	46d
....	....	....	....	....	....	....	9	1	11	15	10	122	—	—	Central Govt. Lending Funds	46f
1,541	1,876	4,000	‡19	409	‡56	120	‡26	33	61	92	112	307	292	272	Credit from Monetary Authorities	46g
1,973	1,792	2,900	‡8	684	‡100	135	‡328	366	325	434	257	73	34	21	Capital Accounts	47a
−741	−306	6,900	‡17	−340	‡−100	−103	‡−153	−170	−94	−165	−8	−128	43	36	Other Items (Net)	47r

Bolivia

		1965	1966	1967	1968	1969	1970	1971	1972	1973	1974	1975	1976	1977	1978	1979
Banking Survey														Bolivianos through 1982; Thousands from 1983 to 1984;		
Foreign Assets (Net)	51n	254	322	224	221	240	435	366	946	637	2,897	2,089	3,140	3,144	1,261	−1,730
Domestic Credit	52	1,307	1,466	1,689	1,871	1,980	2,329	2,697	3,530	4,650	4,808	6,830	9,478	12,576	16,876	23,933
Claims on Central Govt.(Net)	52an	850	920	1,090	1,104	1,109	1,268	1,511	1,836	1,871	382	1,212	2,008	2,324	3,855	7,803
Claims on State & Local Govts.	52b	....	....	....	....	....	....	....	....	....	....	....	....	....	....	....
Claims on Nonfin.Pub.Enterprises	52c	....	....	....	....	....	....	....	....	....	....	....	....	....	....	....
Claims on Private Sector	52d	457	546	599	768	871	1,061	1,186	1,694	2,779	4,426	5,618	7,471	10,252	13,021	16,131
Claims on Nonbank Fin. Insts	52g	....	....	....	....	....	....	....	....	....	....	....	....	....	....	....
Liquid Liabilities	55l	1,001	1,258	1,350	1,509	1,665	1,921	2,247	2,840	3,894	5,437	6,807	10,018	12,961	14,639	16,689
Long-Term Foreign Liabilities	56cl	36	48	61	94	118	305	335	467	789	1,064	1,203	1,293	1,545	2,878	4,814
Central Govt. Lending Funds	56f	....	....	....	....	....	....	....	....	....	....	....	....	....	....	....
Capital Accounts	57a	114	112	108	119	122	120	114	105	118	89	292	455	700	952	1,811
Other Items (Net)	57r	409	370	394	370	315	418	367	1,065	487	1,115	617	852	514	−332	−1,112
Interest Rates															Percent Per Annum	
Discount Rate (End of Period)	60	16.0	16.0	16.0	16.0	16.0	12.0	13.0	11.0	11.0	13.0	13.0	13.0	13.0	13.0	18.0
Deposit Rate	60l	....	....	....	....	....	....	....	....	....	....	....	....	....	....	16.0
Lending Rate	60p	....	....	....	....	....	....	....	....	....	....	....	....	....	....	27.0
Prices and Production														Index Numbers (1990=100):		
Consumer Prices	64	—	—	—	—	—	—	—	—	—	—	—	—	—	—	—
Crude Petroleum Production	66aa	45.3	79.7	190.2	196.3	193.5	115.5	172.9	209.1	226.1	217.3	192.3	194.5	166.0	155.1	133.4
International Transactions														Millions of US Dollars		
Exports	70..d	129.0	127.4	149.9	152.1	172.3	190.2	181.1	201.2	260.5	556.5	444.1	568.2	631.7	628.8	759.8
Tin	70q.d	93.0	93.3	90.9	92.5	102.5	108.1	105.9	113.5	131.0	230.1	171.4	216.3	328.8	374.2	395.6
Zinc	70t.d	4.2	5.0	4.4	3.0	7.8	14.3	15.3	15.4	26.0	37.7	40.3	39.1	44.7	31.5	42.7
Imports, cif	71..d	133.9	138.4	151.0	152.9	165.0	159.2	169.6	185.4	230.2	390.0	557.9	554.6	617.9	807.8	894.3
Imports, fob	71.v d	113.7	118.0	128.8	130.3	140.7	135.2	144.2	142.8	194.0	364.0	531.5	562.3	644.0	689.8	673.6
																1990=100
Volume of Exports	72	90.9	111.4	140.4	147.4	156.6	142.7	156.0	161.3	98.6	98.6	92.7	100.6	106.2	100.9	100.7
Tin	72q	142.8	154.8	161.7	173.5	176.7	164.2	178.6	178.9	167.6	170.8	147.0	168.7	183.4	175.5	157.0
Zinc	72t	13.9	16.9	16.9	11.9	26.9	47.2	46.0	40.2	50.2	49.7	50.2	49.9	62.2	52.7	54.6
																1990=100:
Unit Value of Exports	74..d	16.7	15.8	15.0	15.0	16.3	21.1	17.1	17.8	40.8	70.6	66.8	76.0	97.8	114.2	136.8
Tin	74q.d	60.7	56.2	52.4	49.8	54.1	60.8	55.3	59.1	72.4	125.9	108.9	119.9	165.6	197.6	234.4
Zinc	74t.d	21.0	20.1	18.0	17.1	19.9	20.8	22.7	26.3	35.4	51.9	55.0	53.8	49.3	41.0	53.5
Balance of Payments														Millions of US Dollars:		
Goods: Exports f.o.b.	78aa d	....	....	....	....	....	....	....	....	....	....	....	563.0	634.3	627.3	759.8
Goods: Imports f.o.b.	78ab d	....	....	....	....	....	....	....	....	....	....	....	−512.3	−579.0	−723.9	−738.4
Trade Balance	78ac d	....	....	....	....	....	....	....	....	....	....	....	50.7	55.3	−96.6	21.4
Services: Credit	78ad d	....	....	....	....	....	....	....	....	....	....	....	60.4	60.8	76.2	105.2
Services: Debit	78ae d	....	....	....	....	....	....	....	....	....	....	....	−147.1	−181.9	−224.2	−392.5
Balance on Goods and Services	78af d	....	....	....	....	....	....	....	....	....	....	....	−36.0	−65.8	−244.6	−265.9
Income: Credit	78ag d	....	....	....	....	....	....	....	....	....	....	....	12.8	5.6	2.5	8.4
Income: Debit	78ah d	....	....	....	....	....	....	....	....	....	....	....	−44.3	−72.7	−116.4	−190.7
Balance on Goods, Serv., & Inc.	78ai d	....	....	....	....	....	....	....	....	....	....	....	−67.5	−132.9	−358.5	−448.2
Current Transfers, n.i.e.: Credit	78aj d	....	....	....	....	....	....	....	....	....	....	....	16.0	18.0	30.0	53.0
Current Transfers: Debit	78ak d	....	....	....	....	....	....	....	....	....	....	....	−2.0	−3.0	−3.0	−1.8
Current Account, n.i.e.	78al d	....	....	....	....	....	....	....	....	....	....	....	−53.5	−117.9	−331.5	−397.0
Capital Account, n.i.e.: Credit	78ba d	....	....	....	....	....	....	....	....	....	....	....	—	—	—	—
Capital Account: Debit	78bb d	....	....	....	....	....	....	....	....	....	....	....	—	—	—	—
Capital Account, n.i.e.	78bc d	....	....	....	....	....	....	....	....	....	....	....	—	—	—	—
Direct Investment Abroad	78bd d	....	....	....	....	....	....	....	....	....	....	....	—	—	—	—
Dir. Invest. in Rep. Econ., n.i.e.	78be d	....	....	....	....	....	....	....	....	....	....	....	−8.1	−1.2	11.5	35.0
Portfolio Investment Assets	78bf d	....	....	....	....	....	....	....	....	....	....	....	—	—	—	2.5
Portfolio Investment Liab., n.i.e.	78bg d	....	....	....	....	....	....	....	....	....	....	....	—	—	—	−1.1
Other Investment Assets	78bh d	....	....	....	....	....	....	....	....	....	....	....	−20.1	−135.1	−63.7	−8.8
Other Investment Liab., n.i.e.	78bi d	....	....	....	....	....	....	....	....	....	....	....	200.9	358.1	414.8	182.3
Financial Account, n.i.e.	78bj d	....	....	....	....	....	....	....	....	....	....	....	172.7	221.8	362.6	209.9
Net Errors and Omissions	78ca d	....	....	....	....	....	....	....	....	....	....	....	−63.4	−79.0	−84.9	−4.1
Overall Balance	78cb d	....	....	....	....	....	....	....	....	....	....	....	55.8	24.9	−53.8	−191.2
Reserves and Related Items	79da d	....	....	....	....	....	....	....	....	....	....	....	−55.8	−24.9	53.8	191.2
Reserve Assets	79db d	....	....	....	....	....	....	....	....	....	....	....	−35.1	−67.4	64.8	−18.5
Use of Fund Credit and Loans	79dc d	....	....	....	....	....	....	....	....	....	....	....	−16.1	—	38.2	—
Liabs.Constit.For.Auth.Reserves	79dd d	....	....	....	....	....	....	....	....	....	....	....	−4.6	5.5	−12.2	60.0
Exceptional Financing	79de d	....	....	....	....	....	....	....	....	....	....	....	....	37.0	−37.0	149.7
Government Finance													Bolivianos through 1982; Thousands from 1983 to 1984;			
Deficit (−) or Surplus	80	−198	−248	−358	−568	−457	−238	−522	−595	−873	....	....	....	−3,313	−3,002	−6,651
Revenue	81	632	741	792	862	901	1,131	1,151	1,389	2,479	....	....	....	7,641	8,540	8,384
Grants Received	81z	98	34	27	10	1	29	35	34	18	....	....	....	....	....	....
Expenditure	82	928	1,023	1,177	1,440	1,360	1,399	1,708	2,019	3,370	....	....	....	10,954	11,542	15,035
Lending Minus Repayments	83	....	....	....	....	....	....	....	....	....	....	....	....	....	....	....
Financing																
Domestic	84a	113	128	110	136	107	19	352	434	357	....	....	....	....	....	....
Foreign	85a	84	120	248	432	351	219	171	161	516	....	....	....	....	....	....
National Accounts													Bolivianos through 1982; Thousands from 1983 to 1984;			
Exports of Goods & Services	90c	1,541	1,690	2,020	2,016	2,255	2,494	2,336	2,963	5,878	12,448	10,474	12,698	14,512	17,000	21,800
Government Consumption	91f	827	924	977	1,078	1,154	1,324	1,520	1,920	2,814	4,461	5,699	6,700	8,559	9,500	13,600
Gross Fixed Capital Formation	93e	1,051	949	1,155	1,574	1,741	1,792	1,951	2,623	4,519	6,550	9,055	10,685	12,414	16,400	17,400
Increase/Decrease(−) in Stocks	93i	167	342	129	65	162	319	375	797	878	558	2,971	1,264	1,149	2,200	....
Private Consumption	96f	5,497	6,150	7,034	7,881	8,300	8,955	10,074	12,376	18,081	28,928	34,244	39,056	44,940	52,700	60,700
Imports of Goods & Services	98c	−1,903	−2,105	−2,336	−2,422	−2,568	−2,514	−2,713	−3,430	−6,114	−9,620	−13,242	−13,956	−16,354	−22,600	−24,700
Gross Domestic Product = GDP	99b	7,180	7,950	8,979	10,192	11,044	12,370	13,543	17,249	26,056	43,325	49,201	56,447	65,220	75,200	90,200
Net Factor Inc/Pmts(−) Abroad	98.n	−46	−29	−226	−262	−346	−284	−179	−309	−488	−822	−792	−896	−1,684	−2,334	−3,572
Gross National Product = GNP	99a	7,134	7,921	8,753	9,930	10,698	12,086	13,364	16,940	25,568	42,503	48,409	55,551	63,536	72,900	86,600
Nat'l Income, Market Prices	99e	6,730	7,506	8,299	9,408	10,259	11,330	12,489	15,791	23,957	40,207	45,516	52,138	59,172	69,194	82,543
GDP 1990 Prices (Millions)	99b.p	8,100	8,680	9,229	10,016	10,474	11,290	11,843	12,530	13,367	14,055	14,984	15,897	16,566	17,122	17,436
GDP Deflator (1990=100)	99bi p	—	—	—	—	—	—	—	—	—	—	—	—	—	—	—
																Millions:
Population	99z	4.33	4.45	4.48	4.51	4.55	4.58	4.62	4.64	4.67	4.75	4.89	5.03	5.16	5.30	5.45

1980	1981	1982	1983	1984	1985	1986	1987	1988	1989	1990	1991	1992	1993	1994		
Millions of Bolivianos Beginning 1985: End of Period															**Banking Survey**	
-3,294	-7,308	-78,250	I-119	-749	I80	540	I611	737	759	1,178	1,700	2,068	2,248	2,626	Foreign Assets (Net)	**51n**
32,043	40,667	183,070	I488	5,612	I235	435	I1,384	2,017	3,188	4,734	6,631	9,450	14,211	16,042	Domestic Credit	**52**
13,030	16,592	85,989	I272	2,847	I-215	-541	I-638	-563	-426	-241	-295	-237	2,158	2,460	Claims on Central Govt.(Net)	**52an**
....	....	....	....	....	....	....	76	89	111	125	129	150	20	18	Claims on State & Local Govts.	**52b**
....	....	....	....	....	....	....	570	621	846	1,086	1,241	1,461	814	891	Claims on Nonfin.Pub.Enterprises	**52c**
19,014	24,075	97,081	I215	2,766	I451	976	I1,376	1,852	2,629	3,710	5,484	7,992	11,129	12,566	Claims on Private Sector	**52d**
....	....	....	....	....	....	....	1	18	27	54	73	84	91	108	Claims on Nonbank Fin. Insts	**52g**
23,217	29,764	98,201	I266	4,086	I303	823	I1,596	2,032	2,471	3,778	5,694	7,661	10,243	12,560	Liquid Liabilities	**55l**
5,548	7,827	59,304	I340	5,399	I630	949	I803	996	1,295	1,392	1,634	2,029	2,087	2,587	Long-Term Foreign Liabilities	**56cl**
....	....	....	....	....	....	....	149	356	771	1,187	1,512	2,023	2,238	2,690	Central Govt. Lending Funds	**56f**
1,973	1,792	2,900	I8	684	I100	135	I1,184	1,278	1,358	1,776	1,570	1,556	2,685	3,569	Capital Accounts	**57a**
-1,988	-6,024	-55,585	I-246	-5,305	I-717	-932	I-1,737	-1,908	-1,948	-2,221	-2,079	-1,752	-793	-2,739	Other Items (Net)	**57r**
Percent Per Annum															**Interest Rates**	
19.9	26.0	37.0	61.0	149.0	....	....	....	....	....	....	....	....	....	....	Discount Rate *(End of Period)*	**60**
18.0	28.4	30.3	39.8	108.3	68.8	I106.5	33.2	27.7	23.7	23.8	23.8	23.2	22.2	18.4	Deposit Rate	**60l**
28.0	42.5	45.0	56.8	120.7	172.2	I297.1	56.9	39.8	37.3	41.8	41.1	45.5	53.9	55.6	Lending Rate	**60p**
Period Averages															**Prices and Production**	
—	—	—	I—	.1	14.8	55.8	63.9	74.1	85.4	100.0	121.4	I136.1	147.7	....	Consumer Prices	**64**
114.0	106.0	116.9	105.8	99.8	94.9	84.0	90.2	91.9	95.3	100.0	106.0	101.5	....	....	Crude Petroleum Production	**66aa**
Millions of US Dollars															**International Transactions**	
942.2	912.4	827.7	755.2	724.5	623.4	637.8	569.5	600.2	821.8	926.1	848.6	710.1	727.5	1,032.4	Exports	**70..d**
378.2	343.1	278.4	207.9	247.8	186.7	103.3	68.9	76.9	126.5	106.5	99.7	107.3	83.3	....	Tin	**70q.d**
36.7	40.4	38.4	33.4	37.3	29.5	28.0	32.7	60.2	132.2	146.0	139.7	173.0	119.5	....	Zinc	**70t.d**
665.4	917.1	554.1	576.7	488.5	690.9	674.0	766.3	590.5	610.9	687.2	969.5	1,090.3	1,205.9	1,209.0	Imports, cif	**71..d**
574.4	827.7	496.0	496.0	412.3	565.1	564.0	646.3	495.1	563.1	633.5	893.7	1,005.0	1,111.6	....	Imports, fob	**71.vd**
1990=100																
100.9	109.5	104.7	93.6	96.8	87.6	91.9	79.7	84.6	95.3	100.0	101.5	99.3	92.8	....	Volume of Exports	**72**
132.9	143.0	129.1	94.6	119.6	95.2	99.2	59.6	63.7	85.9	100.0	105.3	104.1	94.4	....	Tin	**72q**
46.8	45.3	45.1	41.9	37.4	34.4	36.0	40.2	54.7	81.6	100.0	129.4	144.2	125.4	....	Zinc	**72t**
Indices of Unit Values in US Dollars																
176.1	176.5	171.2	174.2	171.0	166.0	115.0	108.8	102.4	115.0	100.0	96.2	76.2	64.2	....	Unit Value of Exports	**74..d**
265.0	220.9	200.3	204.4	193.3	188.0	88.1	107.7	111.6	139.7	100.0	88.3	95.5	86.9	....	Tin	**74q.d**
53.6	61.2	58.3	54.6	68.4	58.7	53.2	55.8	75.3	111.0	100.0	74.0	82.2	65.2	....	Zinc	**74t.d**
Minus Sign Indicates Debit															Balance of Payments	
942.2	912.4	827.7	755.1	724.5	623.4	545.5	518.7	542.5	723.5	830.8	760.3	608.4	....	....	Goods: Exports f.o.b.	**78aad**
-574.4	-827.7	-496.0	-496.0	-412.3	-462.8	-596.5	-646.3	-590.9	-729.5	-775.6	-804.2	-1,040.8	....	....	Goods: Imports f.o.b.	**78abd**
367.8	84.7	331.7	259.1	312.2	160.6	-51.0	-127.6	-48.4	-6.0	55.2	-43.9	-432.4	....	....	Trade Balance	**78acd**
87.9	93.0	82.3	103.0	93.5	96.5	121.1	131.5	128.3	143.3	145.9	157.0	164.6	....	....	Services: Credit	**78add**
-258.5	-319.8	-221.7	-244.6	-253.5	-246.1	-245.8	-270.2	-254.8	-298.2	-310.6	-311.2	-311.0	....	....	Services: Debit	**78aed**
197.2	-142.1	192.3	117.5	152.2	11.0	-175.7	-266.3	-174.9	-160.9	-109.5	-198.1	-578.8	....	....	Balance on Goods and Services	**78afd**
15.6	16.2	8.4	40.9	30.0	17.5	17.6	16.2	18.2	23.9	18.8	24.6	17.7	....	....	Income: Credit	**78agd**
-278.7	-378.4	-419.1	-402.7	-444.9	-390.4	-326.1	-293.9	-283.0	-283.0	-267.4	-271.6	-215.4	....	....	Income: Debit	**78ahd**
-65.9	-504.3	-218.4	-244.3	-262.7	-361.9	-484.2	-544.0	-439.7	-420.0	-358.1	-445.1	-776.5	....	....	Balance on Goods, Serv., & Inc.	**78aid**
62.0	38.0	46.2	106.8	87.0	80.3	97.0	113.9	140.0	152.5	161.2	185.8	246.3	....	....	Current Transfers, n.i.e.: Credit	**78ajd**
-2.5	-2.2	-2.2	-4.1	-2.8	-4.2	-1.7	-2.2	-4.7	-2.6	-2.0	-3.3	-3.7	....	....	Current Transfers: Debit	**78akd**
-6.4	-468.5	-174.4	-141.6	-178.5	-285.8	-388.9	-432.3	-304.4	-270.1	-198.9	-262.6	-533.9	....	....	Current Account, n.i.e.	**78ald**
—	3.0	1.0	3.0	3.8	4.2	5.0	5.5	1.3	5.9	.8	.5	.6	....	....	Capital Account, n.i.e.: Credit	**78bad**
—	-.2	-.3	-.3	-.2	-.8	-.3	—	—	—	—	—	—	....	....	Capital Account: Debit	**78bbd**
—	2.8	.7	2.7	3.6	3.4	4.7	5.5	1.3	5.9	.8	.5	.6	....	....	Capital Account, n.i.e.	**78bcd**
-.5	-.1	-.1	-.1	—	—	—	-1.7	-1.9	-1.0	-1.1	-2.0	-2.0	....	....	Direct Investment Abroad	**78bdd**
47.0	75.7	31.1	7.0	7.0	10.0	10.0	38.1	-10.1	-24.4	27.2	52.0	93.1	....	....	Dir. Invest. in Rep. Econ., n.i.e.	**78bed**
-2.6	—	—	—	—	—	—	—	-7.2	-7.3	-6.6	—	—	....	....	Portfolio Investment Assets	**78bfd**
-.9	-.9	-15.0	-1.8	-.9	-.9	—	—	7.2	7.3	6.6	—	—	....	....	Portfolio Investment Liab., n.i.e.	**78bgd**
-15.3	-4.0	-156.4	-101.5	178.6	15.2	112.2	-98.7	-85.5	-161.8	-32.1	-16.3	-13.0	....	....	Other Investment Assets	**78bhd**
-38.1	95.2	-81.4	-233.2	-124.0	-256.3	-168.7	-79.4	72.8	83.8	99.0	80.9	295.8	....	....	Other Investment Liab., n.i.e.	**78bid**
-10.4	165.9	-221.8	-329.6	60.7	-232.0	-46.5	-141.7	-24.7	-103.4	93.0	114.6	373.9	....	....	Financial Account, n.i.e.	**78bjd**
-412.0	-187.1	34.2	71.5	-12.1	190.0	136.3	174.6	46.6	-32.1	-11.4	53.3	34.3	....	....	Net Errors and Omissions	**78cad**
-428.8	-486.9	-361.3	-397.0	-126.3	-324.4	-294.4	-393.9	-281.2	-399.7	-116.5	-94.2	-125.1	....	....	Overall Balance	**78cbd**
428.8	486.9	361.3	397.0	126.3	324.4	294.4	393.9	281.2	399.7	116.5	94.2	125.1	....	....	Reserves and Related Items	**79dad**
96.1	—	-46.5	-49.3	-95.0	58.0	-214.5	82.0	12.8	57.3	-5.0	-8.4	-41.2	....	....	Reserve Assets	**79dbd**
89.5	-2.0	18.6	8.3	-24.0	-23.5	99.8	-33.6	30.6	47.5	-13.2	-13.9	14.7	....	....	Use of Fund Credit and Loans	**79dcd**
-6.4	199.4	142.3	-230.4	-37.7	-62.7	-59.2	-43.5	-12.4	95.7	-44.9	-52.9	-6.5	....	....	Liabs.Constit.For.Auth.Reserves	**79ddd**
249.7	289.6	246.9	668.4	282.9	352.6	468.3	389.0	250.2	199.2	179.5	169.5	158.1	....	....	Exceptional Financing	**79ded**
Millions of Bolivianos Beginning 1985: Year Ending December 31															**Government Finance**	
-9,729	-10,217	-110,959	I-310	-7,659	I-1,182	I-6	67	-79	-184	-262	-13	-450	-457	....	Deficit (-) or Surplus	**80**
11,793	14,069	19,316	I46	562	I202	I1,001	1,164	1,354	1,619	2,112	2,842	3,378	3,480	....	Revenue	**81**
....	....	....	....	....	....	13	13	88	127	163	297	732	1,769	....	Grants Received	**81z**
21,522	24,286	130,275	I356	8,221	I1,384	I1,010	1,110	1,515	1,929	2,530	3,221	4,461	5,877	....	Expenditure	**82**
....	....	....	....	....	....	9	—	6	—	7	-69	100	-170	....	Lending Minus Repayments	**83**
															Financing	
....	....	....	....	....	....	69	-18	30	94	155	-35	-56	-325	....	Domestic	**84a**
....	....	....	....	....	....	-63	-49	50	89	107	48	506	782	....	Foreign	**85a**
Millions of Bolivianos Beginning 1985															**National Accounts**	
31,500	40,000	140,000	I430	2,910	I830	2,587	2,493	2,993	3,951	5,116	5,875	....	....	....	Exports of Goods & Services	**90c**
15,900	20,000	40,000	I110	4,700	I238	705	942	1,326	1,620	2,012	2,491	....	....	....	Government Consumption	**91f**
17,500	20,000	50,000	I160	2,260	I336	959	1,146	1,414	1,694	1,927	2,594	....	....	....	Gross Fixed Capital Formation	**93e**
500	—	—	I10	-50	I148	234	368	-26	-243	-317	274	....	....	....	Increase/Decrease(-) in Stocks	**93i**
82,300	100,000	270,000	I970	12,930	I1,793	6,214	7,440	8,803	10,392	12,366	15,500	....	....	....	Private Consumption	**96f**
-24,800	-30,000	-100,000	I-300	-1,860	I-479	-1,775	-2,211	-2,209	-2,665	-3,562	-5,042	....	....	....	Imports of Goods & Services	**98c**
122,900	150,000	400,000	I1,390	20,900	I2,867	8,924	10,179	12,301	14,749	17,542	21,690	....	....	....	Gross Domestic Product = GDP	**99b**
....	....	....	....	....	....	....	....	....	....	....	....	....	....	....	Net Factor Inc/Pmts(-) Abroad	**98.n**
....	....	....	....	....	....	....	....	....	....	....	....	....	....	....	Gross National Product = GNP	**99a**
113,832	....	....	....	....	....	....	....	....	....	....	....	....	....	....	Nat'l Income, Market Prices	**99e**
I17,535	17,697	16,925	16,170	16,073	15,918	15,521	15,925	I16,396	16,857	17,542	18,342	18,973	....	....	GDP 1990 Prices *(Millions)*	**99b.p**
—	—	—	—	—	18	57	64	75	87	100	118	....	....	....	GDP Deflator (1990=100)	**99bip**
Midyear Estimates																
5.60	5.76	5.92	6.08	6.25	6.43	6.61	6.80	6.99	7.19	7.40	7.61	7.83	8.06	....	**Population**	**99z**

(Notes in the back of the book)

Botswana
616

		1965	1966	1967	1968	1969	1970	1971	1972	1973	1974	1975	1976	1977	1978	1979
Exchange Rates																*SDRs per Pula:*
Official Rate	ac	1.3998	1.3933	1.4018	1.3898	1.3988	1.3943	1.2036	1.1766	1.2351	1.1843	.9824	.9898	.9941	.9269	.9625
																US Dollars per Pula:
Official Rate	ag	1.3998	1.3933	1.4018	1.3898	1.3988	1.3943	1.3068	1.2774	1.4900	1.4501	1.1500	1.1500	1.2075	1.2075	1.2679
Official Rate	rh	1.4000	1.4000	1.4000	1.4000	1.4000	1.4000	1.3982	1.3018	1.4441	1.4722	1.3663	1.1500	1.1883	1.2075	1.2276
Fund Position																*Millions of SDRs:*
Quota	2f. s	....	....	....	3.00	3.00	5.00	5.00	5.00	5.00	5.00	5.00	5.00	5.00	9.00	9.00
SDRs	1b. s	....	....	....	—	—	.50	1.04	1.57	1.57	1.57	1.57	1.57	1.57	1.57	2.50
Reserve Position in the Fund	1c. s	....	....	....	.10	.10	.61	.61	.61	.62	.62	.62	.61	1.24	1.22	2.18
International Liquidity													*Millions of US Dollars Unless Otherwise Indicated:*			
Total Reserves minus Gold	1l. d	....	....	....	....	....	....	....	....	....	....	....	74.86	100.11	150.57	267.28
SDRs	1b. d	....	....	....	....	....	....	.50	1.13	1.70	1.89	1.92	1.84	1.82	1.91	2.05	3.29
Reserve Position in the Fund	1c. d	....	....	....	.10	.10	.61	.66	.66	.75	.76	.73	.71	1.51	1.59	2.87
Foreign Exchange	1d. d	....	....	....	....	....	....	....	....	....	....	....	72.32	96.70	146.94	261.12
Deposit Money Banks: Assets	7a. d	....	....	....	....	....	....	....	26.31	37.64	50.13	69.11	.68	3.37	3.23	4.97
Liabilities	7b. d	....	....	....	....	....	....	....	7.58	5.17	19.82	33.99	1.13	3.08	3.31	2.84
Monetary Authorities																*Millions of Pula:*
Foreign Assets	11	....	....	....	....	....	....	....	....	....	....	....	65.1	82.9	124.7	210.8
Reserve Money	14	....	....	....	....	....	....	....	....	....	....	....	32.8	36.4	35.6	57.1
of which: Currency Outside DMBs	14a	....	....	....	....	....	....	....	....	....	....	....	10.4	12.4	15.8	17.9
Time Deposits	15	....	....	....	....	....	....	....	....	....	....	....	.1	.5	7.9	50.2
Central Government Deposits	16d	....	....	....	....	....	....	....	....	....	....	....	29.4	39.2	62.6	84.4
Capital Accounts	17a	....	....	....	....	....	....	....	....	....	....	....	4.6	8.0	17.3	14.8
Other Items (Net)	17r	....	....	....	....	....	....	....	....	....	....	....	-2.0	-1.3	1.3	4.3
Deposit Money Banks																*Millions of Pula:*
Reserves	20	....	....	....	....	....	....	....	.9	1.6	1.7	2.7	22.3	24.0	19.5	38.5
Foreign Assets	21	....	....	....	....	....	....	....	20.6	26.5	34.6	60.1	.6	2.8	2.7	3.9
Claims on Central Government	22a	....	....	....	....	....	....	....	1.8	1.4	1.4	2.8	11.6	12.6	9.3	7.4
Claims on Nonfin.Pub.Enterprises	22c	....	....	....	....	....	....	....	.6	.1	.5	1.8	1.3	3.7	3.7	.3
Claims on Private Sector	22d	....	....	....	....	....	....	....	11.6	20.9	35.6	50.8	66.3	67.9	69.5	84.5
Claims on Other Financial Insts.	22f	....	....	....	....	....	....	....	—	—	—	—	.1	.6	1.1	1.6
Demand Deposits	24	....	....	....	....	....	....	....	13.1	16.6	20.3	21.2	33.1	45.8	45.2	64.2
Time and Savings Deposits	25	....	....	....	....	....	....	....	11.9	16.8	21.5	25.8	42.6	49.9	52.1	66.7
Foreign Liabilities	26c	....	....	....	....	....	....	....	5.9	3.6	13.7	29.6	1.0	2.5	2.7	2.2
Capital Accounts	27a	....	....	....	....	....	....	....	—	—	—	—	3.6	5.7	7.5	9.4
Other Items (Net)	27r	....	....	....	....	....	....	....	4.5	13.6	18.4	41.5	21.9	7.7	-1.7	-6.4
Monetary Survey																*Millions of Pula:*
Foreign Assets (Net)	31n	....	....	....	....	....	....	....	....	....	....	....	64.7	83.1	124.6	212.5
Domestic Credit	32	....	....	....	....	....	....	....	....	....	....	....	27.6	32.5	17.5	8.4
Claims on Central Govt. (Net)	32an	....	....	....	....	....	....	....	....	....	....	....	-40.1	-39.8	-57.0	-78.4
Claims on Nonfin.Pub.Enterprises	32c	....	....	....	....	....	....	....	.6	.1	.5	1.8	1.3	3.7	3.7	.3
Claims on Private Sector	32d	....	....	....	....	....	....	....	11.6	20.9	35.6	50.8	66.3	67.9	69.5	84.5
Claims on Other Financial Insts.	32f	....	....	....	....	....	....	....	—	—	—	—	.1	.6	1.1	1.6
Money	34	....	....	....	....	....	....	....	....	....	....	....	43.5	58.2	60.9	82.1
Quasi-Money	35	....	....	....	....	....	....	....	11.9	16.8	21.5	25.8	42.7	50.4	60.0	116.9
Other Items (Net)	37r	....	....	....	....	....	....	....	....	....	....	....	5.9	7.0	21.2	21.9
Money plus Quasi-Money	35l	....	....	....	....	....	....	....	....	....	....	....	86.2	108.6	120.9	199.0
Interest Rates																*Percent Per Annum*
Bank Rate (End of Period)	60	....	....	....	....	....	....	....	....	....	....	....	8.25	7.75	6.75	5.75
Deposit Rate	60l	....	....	....	....	....	....	....	....	....	....	....	....	....	....	....
Lending Rate	60p	....	....	....	....	....	....	....	....	....	....	....	....	....	....	....
Prices and Production																*Index Numbers (1990=100):*
Consumer Prices	64	....	....	....	....	....	....	....	....	....	18.7	20.9	23.4	26.5	28.9	32.2
Mining Production	66zx	....	....	....	....	....	....	1.9	7.6	7.8	11.1	13.6	19.4	20.2	24.1	28.6
International Transactions																*Millions of Pula*
Exports	70	10.2	10.8	9.2	7.5	13.1	18.3	30.3	44.8	59.2	82.0	105.0	153.2	156.7	192.7	367.3
Imports, cif	71	16.6	18.8	22.4	23.2	32.7	40.9	59.1	84.2	115.0	125.4	159.3	181.4	239.6	307.1	438.3
Imports, fob	71.v	14.1	16.0	19.0	19.7	27.7	34.7	50.1	71.3	97.4	106.6	135.4	154.2	203.6	261.0	372.5

Botswana

616

	1980	1981	1982	1983	1984	1985	1986	1987	1988	1989	1990	1991	1992	1993	1994		
Exchange Rates																	
End of Period																	
Official Rate	1.0569	.9762	.8544	.8266	.6539	.4333	.4449	.4502	.3839	.4064	.3756	.3373	.3223	.2839	.2521		ac
End of Period (ag) Period Average (rh)																	
Official Rate	1.3480	1.1362	.9425	.8654	.6410	.4760	.5442	.6387	.5166	.5341	.5344	.4825	.4431	.3899	.3680		ag
Official Rate	1.2871	1.2004	.9788	.9122	.7789	.5296	.5354	.5960	.5507	.4969	.5376	.4957	.4689	.4134	.3727		rh
Fund Position																	
End of Period																	
Quota	13.50	13.50	13.50	22.10	22.10	22.10	22.10	22.10	22.10	22.10	22.10	22.10	36.60	36.60	36.60		2f. s
SDRs	2.45	5.25	6.19	7.26	8.53	9.70	14.01	15.38	16.79	18.91	21.70	24.10	22.46	24.03	25.39		1b. s
Reserve Position in the Fund	5.12	9.13	9.15	11.31	12.34	12.93	15.58	15.73	13.64	19.22	16.17	13.45	14.79	16.60	16.34		1c. s
International Liquidity																	
End of Period																	
Total Reserves minus Gold	343.69	253.43	292.97	395.67	474.29	783.21	1,197.67	2,057.08	2,258.09	2,841.11	3,385.34	3,772.37	3,844.64	4,153.14	4,462.40		1l. d
SDRs	3.12	6.11	6.83	7.60	8.36	10.65	17.14	21.82	22.59	24.85	30.87	34.47	30.88	33.00	37.07		1b. d
Reserve Position in the Fund	6.53	10.63	10.09	11.84	12.10	14.20	19.06	22.32	18.36	25.26	23.00	19.24	20.34	22.79	23.86		1c. d
Foreign Exchange	334.04	236.69	276.05	376.23	453.83	758.35	1,161.48	2,012.95	2,217.14	2,791.00	3,331.46	3,718.66	3,793.42	4,097.34	4,401.47		1d. d
Deposit Money Banks: Assets	3.29	1.64	4.65	6.34	20.01	17.49	22.77	31.27	33.78	24.06	80.39	74.31	64.91	61.17	63.42		7a. d
Liabilities	3.97	7.67	3.06	10.78	11.01	10.33	19.30	25.91	23.86	19.72	34.14	23.80	19.40	54.32	24.22		7b. d
Monetary Authorities																	
End of Period																	
Foreign Assets	255.0	223.1	310.8	457.2	711.4	1,645.4	2,201.0	3,152.1	4,371.1	5,225.4	6,257.4	7,708.2	8,561.2	10,506.3	10,566.9		11
Reserve Money	62.5	52.9	96.3	106.5	127.7	161.5	165.8	278.2	399.2	502.9	447.7	718.9	767.2	1,181.8	1,320.0		14
of which: Currency Outside DMBs	24.4	29.6	29.0	30.2	35.2	43.4	58.5	68.6	95.8	117.6	143.7	158.1	163.0	180.0	194.9		14a
Time Deposits	91.3	30.3	15.2	65.0	12.3	183.2	187.9	480.3	482.3	832.6	359.0	491.1	604.5	452.2	568.3		15
Central Government Deposits	91.1	75.8	105.5	184.6	368.4	642.4	1,269.8	1,817.1	2,347.9	3,059.3	4,000.7	4,287.1	5,099.6	5,630.3	6,733.9		16d
Capital Accounts	17.9	38.2	61.2	64.8	64.9	464.6	384.9	373.9	829.1	846.7	865.6	1,464.0	1,364.6	2,167.2	2,934.6		17a
Other Items (Net)	-7.8	25.9	32.6	36.2	138.1	193.7	192.6	202.6	312.7	-.5	556.7	743.4	725.2	1,074.9	-989.9		17r
Deposit Money Banks																	
End of Period																	
Reserves	35.8	22.4	67.9	79.6	88.1	117.9	102.9	197.6	313.5	377.5	291.5	427.5	467.6	554.7	653.4		20
Foreign Assets	2.4	1.4	4.9	7.3	31.2	36.7	41.9	49.0	65.4	45.1	150.4	154.0	146.5	156.9	172.3		21
Claims on Central Government	5.2	9.2	—	—	—	—	—	—	—	—	—	—	—	—	2.2		22a
Claims on Nonfin.Pub.Enterprises	1.7	5.1	7.8	14.7	18.3	25.3	34.2	22.5	25.8	55.3	56.8	60.2	75.9	93.7	147.9		22c
Claims on Private Sector	93.1	135.8	134.6	154.6	204.1	181.5	217.1	261.4	321.1	435.2	661.8	945.3	1,284.8	1,434.2	1,624.8		22d
Claims on Other Financial Insts.	2.6	3.5	6.0	7.8	16.0	17.0	21.5	1.2	21.0	38.8	37.0	33.4	35.1	32.1	70.0		22f
Demand Deposits	66.2	85.2	98.4	107.2	115.4	144.9	184.9	243.6	310.7	388.9	442.4	455.5	444.0	516.4	578.8		24
Time and Savings Deposits	55.0	81.5	103.1	113.9	206.0	185.9	174.8	220.9	339.5	458.4	600.9	1,083.8	1,267.0	1,386.2	1,572.8		25
Foreign Liabilities	2.9	6.7	3.3	12.5	17.2	21.7	35.5	40.6	46.2	36.9	63.9	49.3	43.8	139.3	65.8		26c
Capital Accounts	9.5	13.8	20.9	24.8	29.5	40.3	41.3	55.8	62.7	99.4	118.6	160.1	220.7	244.4	308.0		27a
Other Items (Net)	7.3	-9.7	-4.5	5.7	-10.4	-14.4	-18.9	-29.3	-12.2	-31.8	-28.3	-128.3	34.5	-14.5	83.0		27r
Monetary Survey																	
End of Period																	
Foreign Assets (Net)	254.5	217.7	312.5	452.1	725.4	1,660.5	2,207.4	3,160.5	4,390.3	5,233.6	6,344.0	7,812.9	8,663.9	10,523.9	10,673.4		31n
Domestic Credit	6.1	77.3	42.8	-7.7	-129.7	-418.9	-996.8	-1,531.9	-1,981.1	-2,532.7	-3,250.1	-3,260.3	-3,710.8	-4,098.7	-4,903.5		32
Claims on Central Govt. (Net)	-91.9	-67.3	-105.8	-184.9	-368.4	-642.7	-1,270.0	-1,817.3	-2,349.6	-3,062.1	-4,006.2	-4,301.5	-5,108.5	-5,661.6	-6,747.9		32an
Claims on Nonfin.Pub.Enterprises	1.7	5.1	7.8	14.7	18.3	25.3	34.2	22.5	25.8	55.3	56.8	60.2	75.9	93.7	147.9		32c
Claims on Private Sector	93.1	135.8	134.6	154.6	204.1	181.5	217.1	261.4	321.1	435.2	661.8	945.3	1,284.8	1,434.2	1,624.8		32d
Claims on Other Financial Insts.	2.6	3.5	6.0	7.8	16.0	17.0	21.5	1.2	21.0	38.8	37.0	33.4	35.1	32.1	70.0		32f
Money	90.6	114.8	127.4	137.3	150.6	188.2	243.5	312.1	406.5	506.5	586.1	613.6	607.0	696.3	773.7		34
Quasi-Money	146.3	111.7	118.2	178.9	218.3	369.2	362.7	701.2	821.9	1,290.8	959.8	1,574.9	1,871.5	1,838.4	2,141.1		35
Other Items (Net)	23.7	68.5	109.5	128.1	226.8	684.2	604.4	615.2	1,181.1	919.1	1,520.2	2,360.4	2,474.6	3,890.6	2,792.9		37r
Money plus Quasi-Money	236.9	226.5	245.6	316.3	368.9	557.4	606.2	1,013.4	1,228.3	1,797.3	1,545.9	2,188.5	2,478.5	2,534.7	2,914.8		35l
Interest Rates																	
Percent Per Annum																	
Bank Rate (End of Period)	5.75	8.50	12.00	10.50	9.00	9.00	9.00	8.50	6.50	6.50	8.50	12.00	14.25	14.25	13.50		60
Deposit Rate	5.0	8.7	10.8	11.9	10.0	9.0	8.7	7.5	5.0	5.6	6.1	11.4	12.5	13.5	10.4		60l
Lending Rate	8.5	9.6	24.2	13.4	12.0	11.5	11.0	10.0	7.8	7.7	7.9	11.8	14.0	14.9	13.9		60p
Prices and Production																	
Period Averages																	
Consumer Prices	36.6	‡42.7	47.4	52.4	56.9	61.5	67.6	74.3	80.5	89.8	100.0	‡111.8	129.8	148.4	164.1		64
Mining Production	31.3	‡32.9	46.7	65.0	76.5	75.0	77.2	77.6	90.2	88.7	100.0	95.7	....	....	....		66zx
International Transactions																	
Millions of Pula																	
Exports	390.4	332.3	467.5	696.7	857.1	1,384.3	1,619.3	2,664.7	2,678.3	3,742.6	3,319.1	3,738.0	3,675.0	4,179.4	....		70
Imports, cif	537.8	663.9	703.9	805.9	895.3	1,095.2	1,331.4	1,572.5	2,172.2	3,019.6	3,619.5	3,927.7	3,970.1	4,297.0	....		71
Imports, fob	457.1	564.3	598.2	685.1	761.3	931.3	1,132.2	1,337.1	1,847.1	2,567.7	3,077.8	3,339.9	3,375.9	3,653.9	....		71.v

Botswana

	1965	1966	1967	1968	1969	1970	1971	1972	1973	1974	1975	1976	1977	1978	1979
Balance of Payments															*Millions of US Dollars:*
Goods: Exports f.o.b. .... 78aa d	....	....	....	....	....	....	....	....	....	....	142.0	169.7	191.6	223.4	442.2
Goods: Imports f.o.b. .... 78ab d	....	....	....	....	....	....	....	....	....	....	−181.2	−180.2	−226.4	−295.0	−442.1
Trade Balance .... 78ac d	....	....	....	....	....	....	....	....	....	....	−39.2	−10.5	−34.8	−71.6	.1
Services: Credit .... 78ad d	....	....	....	....	....	....	....	....	....	....	30.8	46.8	51.4	50.5	61.1
Services: Debit .... 78ae d	....	....	....	....	....	....	....	....	....	....	−76.0	−78.4	−89.9	−101.9	−155.1
Balance on Goods and Services ... 78af d	....	....	....	....	....	....	....	....	....	....	−84.4	−42.1	−73.3	−123.0	−93.9
Income: Credit .... 78ag d	....	....	....	....	....	....	....	....	....	....	47.1	59.3	68.3	58.9	72.3
Income: Debit .... 78ah d	....	....	....	....	....	....	....	....	....	....	6.9	−51.9	−54.4	−68.5	−69.4
Balance on Goods, Serv., & Inc. ... 78ai d	....	....	....	....	....	....	....	....	....	....	−30.4	−34.6	−59.4	−132.6	−91.0
Current Transfers, n.i.e.: Credit ... 78aj d	....	....	....	....	....	....	....	....	....	....	30.6	57.7	95.0	80.7	109.1
Current Transfers: Debit ...... 78ak d	....	....	....	....	....	....	....	....	....	....	−35.7	−43.5	−62.6	−63.6	−78.6
Current Account, n.i.e. .... 78al d	....	....	....	....	....	....	....	....	....	....	−35.6	−20.4	−27.0	−115.6	−60.6
Capital Account, n.i.e.: Credit ... 78ba d	....	....	....	....	....	....	....	....	....	....	—	5.6	6.1	6.4	7.4
Capital Account: Debit .... 78bb d	....	....	....	....	....	....	....	....	....	....				−2.3	−.7
Capital Account, n.i.e. .... 78bc d	....	....	....	....	....	....	....	....	....	....	—	5.6	6.1	4.1	6.6
Direct Investment Abroad ... 78bd d	....	....	....	....	....	....	....	....	....	....		−.1	−.2	—	
Dir. Invest. in Rep. Econ., n.i.e. ... 78be d	....	....	....	....	....	....	....	....	....	....	−38.3	11.3	12.2	40.8	127.9
Portfolio Investment Assets ... 78bf d	....	....	....	....	....	....	....	....	....	....					
Portfolio Investment Liab., n.i.e. ... 78bg d	....	....	....	....	....	....	....	....	....	....		—	—	4.2	—
Other Investment Assets ..... 78bh d	....	....	....	....	....	....	....	....	....	....	−50.4	72.6	10.2	5.6	−28.0
Other Investment Liab., n.i.e. ... 78bi d	....	....	....	....	....	....	....	....	....	....	132.3	−10.1	−6.7	40.1	−12.4
Financial Account, n.i.e. .... 78bj d	....	....	....	....	....	....	....	....	....	....	43.5	73.6	15.6	90.7	87.5
Net Errors and Omissions ... 78ca d	....	....	....	....	....	....	....	....	....	....	−8.0	13.0	23.1	60.1	82.5
Overall Balance .... 78cb d	....	....	....	....	....	....	....	....	....	....		71.9	17.7	39.3	116.0
Reserves and Related Items ... 79da d	....	....	....	....	....	....	....	....	....	....	—	−71.9	−17.7	−39.3	−116.0
Reserve Assets .... 79db d	....	....	....	....	....	....	....	....	....	....		−71.9	−18.1	−39.1	−116.0
Use of Fund Credit and Loans ... 79dc d	....	....	....	....	....	....	....	....	....	....					
Liabs.Constit.For.Auth.Reserves ... 79dd d	....	....	....	....	....	....	....	....	....	....	—	—	.4	−.2	—
Exceptional Financing .... 79de d	....	....	....	....	....	....	....	....	....	....	—	—	—	—	—
Government Finance															*Millions of Pula:*
Deficit (-) or Surplus 80	....	....	....	....	....	....	−11.22	−21.00	−14.05	−5.67	1.24	−20.75	−4.58	−6.91	21.38
Revenue 81	....	....	....	....	....	....	16.44	27.12	39.36	60.60	77.92	68.39	97.39	132.24	206.09
Grants Received 81z	....	....	....	....	....	....	2.74	1.73	6.27	5.29	11.36	16.48	18.09	28.58	37.08
Exp. & Lending Minus Repayments ... 82z	....	....	....	....	....	....									
Expenditure 82	....	....	....	....	....	....	23.14	29.74	42.38	62.11	77.61	98.24	112.71	156.34	200.43
Lending Minus Repayments ... 83	....	....	....	....	....	....	7.26	20.11	17.30	9.45	10.43	7.38	7.35	11.39	21.36
Financing															
Net Borrowing: Domestic ... 84a	....	....	....	....	....	....	.42	2.43	.26	1.04	2.51	5.41	2.92	−3.48	.53
Foreign ... 85a	....	....	....	....	....	....	11.80	24.57	21.69	18.03	13.65	10.74	6.15	14.54	12.02
Use of Cash Balances 87	....	....	....	....	....	....	−1.00	−6.00	−7.90	−13.40	−17.40	4.60	−4.49	−4.15	−33.93
Debt: Domestic 88a	....	....	....	....	....	....	....	....	....	....	....	....	15.35	14.49	14.28
Foreign 89a	....	....	....	....	....	....	....	....	....	....	....	....	101.66	109.50	87.61
National Accounts															*Millions of Pula:*
Exports of Goods and Services ... 90c	10.4	10.8	....	10.2	11.7	....	....	39.8	....	....	76.4	93.8	135.2	190.8	196.3	312.8
Government Consumption ... 91f	7.9	9.3	....	11.6	11.3	....	....	16.0	....	....	31.7	41.5	58.2	80.2	95.9	110.7
Gross Fixed Capital Formation ... 93e	7.2	8.1	....	9.9	9.9	....	....	53.1	....	....	79.6	57.3	79.1	77.8	110.1	162.9
Increase/Decrease(-) in Stocks ... 93i	−5.2	−1.4	....	2.1	7.3	....	....	1.3	....	....	17.8	44.4	35.9	20.9	32.4	34.7
Private Consumption 96f	29.1	28.8	....	37.9	43.0	....	....	58.1	....	....	105.7	131.8	179.6	222.6	262.9	330.4
Imports of Goods and Services ... 98c	−16.6	−18.8	....	−27.8	−32.0	....	....	−65.7	....	....	−121.8	−147.6	−187.5	−241.6	−285.5	−384.6
Gross Domestic Product = GDP ... 99b	32.8	36.8	42.2	43.9	51.2	61.3	78.5	102.6	135.0	188.3	221.2	300.5	350.7	412.1	566.9
Net Factor Inc/Pmts(-) Abroad ... 98.n	−1.1	−1.2	....	....	....	....	....	—	....	9.3	15.1	18.5	−24.4	−31.9	−44.7
Gross National Product = GNP ... 99a	36.7	31.6	....	....	....	....	....	....	....	....	....	....	....	....	....
Nat'l Income, Market Price ... 99e	34.8	37.2	....	....	....	....	....	97.2	159.3	163.6	217.0	256.1	283.1	419.8	583.7
Gross Dom. Prod. 1990 Prices ... 99b. p	352.2	375.2	401.4	409.1	470.7	540.7	633.9	822.6	1,026.4	1,275.2	1,258.5	1,497.6	1,550.7	1,852.7	2,036.8
GDP Deflator (1990=100) ... 99bi p	9.3	9.8	10.5	10.7	10.9	11.3	12.4	12.5	13.2	14.8	17.6	20.1	22.6	22.2	27.8
															Millions:
Population 99z	.52	.54	.55	.56	.57	.58	.59	.63	.65	.66	.69	.69	.71	.73	.79

Exchange Rates: On August 23, 1976 the pula, equal to the South African rand, was introduced.

Botswana

Balance of Payments

	1980	1981	1982	1983	1984	1985	1986	1987	1988	1989	1990	1991	1992	1993	1994		
Minus Sign Indicates Debit																	
Goods: Exports f.o.b.	544.5	401.3	460.6	640.3	677.7	727.6	852.5	1,586.6	1,468.9	1,819.7	1,753.2	....	....	....	....	78aa	*d*
Goods: Imports f.o.b.	−602.5	−687.1	−579.8	−615.3	−583.4	−493.8	−608.4	−803.9	−986.9	−1,185.1	−1,606.2	....	....	....	....	78ab	*d*
Trade Balance	−58.0	−285.8	−119.2	25.1	94.3	233.8	244.0	782.7	482.0	634.6	147.0	....	....	....	....	78ac	*d*
Services: Credit	100.9	97.0	102.5	113.0	107.2	76.3	100.0	125.1	110.3	110.5	134.1	....	....	....	....	78ad	*d*
Services: Debit	−215.9	−211.8	−181.6	−209.4	−190.2	−130.5	−155.0	−203.4	−238.8	−228.0	−285.1	....	....	....	....	78ae	*d*
Balance on Goods and Services	−173.1	−400.5	−198.3	−71.4	11.2	179.7	189.1	704.4	353.6	517.1	−4.0	....	....	....	....	78af	*d*
Income: Credit	102.2	106.0	82.4	82.7	92.7	84.9	116.5	171.8	220.1	244.8	363.2	....	....	....	....	78ag	*d*
Income: Debit	−135.1	−49.7	−45.1	−129.9	−190.6	−216.3	−245.7	−415.3	−546.8	−483.6	−497.0	....	....	....	....	78ah	*d*
Balance on Goods, Serv., & Inc.	−206.0	−344.2	−161.0	−118.6	−86.7	48.2	60.0	460.9	26.9	278.3	−137.8	....	....	....	....	78ai	*d*
Current Transfers, n.i.e.: Credit	144.4	141.6	115.0	145.7	124.8	102.7	133.5	280.8	301.8	266.8	335.0	....	....	....	....	78aj	*d*
Current Transfers: Debit	−89.4	−101.1	−98.6	−106.0	−96.9	−68.9	−84.8	−113.2	−134.7	−53.2	−66.7	....	....	....	....	78ak	*d*
Current Account, n.i.e.	−151.1	−303.7	−144.6	−78.9	−58.8	81.9	108.7	628.5	193.9	491.9	130.5	....	....	....	....	78al	*d*
Capital Account, n.i.e.: Credit	9.1	9.6	7.8	8.4	7.9	5.6	3.2	7.0	—	7.0	7.8	....	....	....	....	78ba	*d*
Capital Account: Debit	−.9	−.8	−1.1	−1.1	−.5	−.4	−.7	−1.1	—	−.7	−.8	....	....	....	....	78bb	*d*
Capital Account, n.i.e.	8.2	8.7	6.7	7.3	7.3	5.2	2.5	5.8	—	6.3	7.0	....	....	....	....	78bc	*d*
Direct Investment Abroad	−2.3	.1		1.3	.2	−1.5			—			....	....	....	....	78bd	*d*
Dir. Invest. in Rep. Econ., n.i.e.	111.6	88.4	21.1	23.8	62.2	53.6	70.4	113.6	39.9	42.2	38.2	....	....	....	....	78be	*d*
Portfolio Investment Assets	—	—	—	—	—	—	—	—	—	—	—	....	....	....	....	78bf	*d*
Portfolio Investment Liab., n.i.e.	—	—	—	—	—	—	—	—	—	—	—	....	....	....	....	78bg	*d*
Other Investment Assets	−12.7	−25.3	−17.5	6.6	−16.7	−16.7	−28.7	−251.6	−68.3	−34.6	−110.7	....	....	....	....	78bh	*d*
Other Investment Liab., n.i.e.	47.5	47.7	87.2	63.1	66.9	87.7	63.9	48.3	3.1	105.4	264.0	....	....	....	....	78bi	*d*
Financial Account, n.i.e.	144.0	110.9	90.8	94.7	112.5	123.1	105.6	−89.8	−25.3	113.0	191.5	....	....	....	....	78bj	*d*
Net Errors and Omissions	89.3	110.3	102.0	100.6	63.2	44.0	90.2	16.9	213.7	−34.7	−21.7	....	....	....	....	78ca	*d*
Overall Balance	90.4	−73.8	54.9	123.6	124.3	254.3	306.9	561.5	382.3	576.5	307.2	....	....	....	....	78cb	*d*
Reserves and Related Items	−90.4	73.8	−54.9	−123.6	−124.3	−254.3	−306.9	−561.5	−382.3	−576.5	−307.2	....	....	....	....	79da	*d*
Reserve Assets	−90.4	73.8	−54.9	−123.6	−124.3	−254.3	−306.9	−561.5	−382.3	−576.5	−307.2	....	....	....	....	79db	*d*
Use of Fund Credit and Loans	—	—	—	—	—	—	—	—	—	—	—	....	....	....	....	79dc	*d*
Liabs.Constit.For.Auth.Reserves	—	—	—	—	—	—	—	—	—	—	—	....	....	....	....	79dd	*d*
Exceptional Financing	—	—	—	—	—	—	—	—	—	—	—	....	....	....	....	79de	*d*

Government Finance

	1980	1981	1982	1983	1984	1985	1986	1987	1988	1989	1990	1991	1992	1993	1994	
Year Beginning April 1																
Deficit (−) or Surplus	−1.27	−18.34	−20.09	103.22	188.32	413.83	539.77	502.42	789.71	571.48	793.37	760.50	897.40	....		80
Revenue	263.88	275.27	340.39	507.97	750.82	1,079.45	1,444.37	1,705.64	2,427.73	2,694.50	3,596.48	3,969.00	4,503.60	....		81
Grants Received	37.81	39.79	47.21	48.20	40.33	41.23	67.62	97.29	117.71	41.48	117.77	70.00	90.10	....		81z
Exp. & Lending Minus Repayments	....	....	407.70	453.00	602.80	706.90	972.20	1,300.50	1,755.70	2,164.50	2,920.90	3,278.50		....		82z
Expenditure	261.91	300.13	372.61	401.16	526.23	642.83	909.17	1,169.39	1,469.79	1,848.24	2,368.33	2,691.30	3,209.30	....		82
Lending Minus Repayments	41.05	33.27	35.08	51.79	76.60	64.02	63.05	131.12	285.94	316.26	552.55	587.20	487.00	....		83
Financing																
Net Borrowing: Domestic	−3.31	−11.65	1.47	−2.16	1.82	.49	−1.37	22.01	3.39	19.91	−53.41	140.40	−136.70	....		84a
Foreign	10.86	11.85	58.86	20.13	33.67	13.22	73.09	75.40	92.35	56.52	2.49	36.00	79.50	....		85a
Use of Cash Balances	−6.28	18.14	−40.24	−121.19	−223.81	−427.54	−611.49	−599.83	−885.45	−647.91	−742.45	−936.90	−840.20	....		87
Debt: Domestic	14.67	1.35	.57	.58	.50	.50	.50	.34	—	—	—	—	—	....		88a
Foreign	98.73	132.45	199.23	232.37	380.62	410.96	474.12	557.51	713.95	744.22	801.92	965.80	1,096.30	....		89a

National Accounts

	1980	1981	1982	1983	1984	1985	1986	1987	1988	1989	1990	1991	1992	1993	1994	
Year Ending June 30																
Exports of Goods and Services	410.5	464.5	428.7	711.7	884.9	1,074.5	1,737.5	1,838.8	3,119.0	3,706.0	....	....	....	....		90c
Government Consumption	148.7	203.2	242.6	301.9	362.8	443.1	531.8	722.6	1,052.3	1,208.2	....	....	....	....		91f
Gross Fixed Capital Formation	248.8	306.6	304.6	320.3	337.6	484.0	457.9	669.9	1,081.8	2,232.0	....	....	....	....		93e
Increase/Decrease(−) in Stocks	42.1	49.2	87.9	26.8	28.7	71.6	−64.6	18.6	−804.3	56.1	....	....	....	....		93i
Private Consumption	408.9	460.3	513.2	563.2	615.1	784.8	901.8	987.4	1,116.0	1,236.5	....	....	....	....		96f
Imports of Goods and Services	−487.4	−608.3	−677.1	−770.8	−838.2	−1,029.4	−1,143.8	−1,427.5	−1,769.2	−2,966.8	....	....	....	....		98c
Gross Domestic Product = GDP	771.6	875.5	899.9	1,153.1	1,390.9	1,828.6	2,420.6	2,809.8	3,795.6	5,472.0	6,130.1	6,995.0	7,810.1	....		99b
Net Factor Inc/Pmts(−) Abroad	....	....	64.9	125.1	104.9	195.2	322.8	251.7	465.1	....	....	....	....	....		98.n
Gross National Product = GNP	725.1	764.4	835.0	1,028.0	1,286.0	1,633.4	2,097.8	2,558.2	3,316.1	....	....	....	....	....		99a
Nat'l Income, Market Price	615.6															99e
Gross Dom. Prod. 1990 Prices	2,328.0	2,549.3	2,739.4	3,178.6	3,544.8	3,799.1	4,083.7	4,447.3	5,126.5	5,798.9	6,130.1	6,671.5	....	....		99b.*p*
GDP Deflator (1990=100)	33.1	34.3	32.8	36.3	39.2	48.1	59.3	63.2	74.0	94.4	100.0	104.8	....	....		99bi *p*
Midyear Estimates																
Population	.89	.94	.97	1.01	1.05	1.09	1.13	1.17	1.21	1.24	1.30	1.35	1.39	1.44	....	99z

Brazil
223

		1965	1966	1967	1968	1969	1970	1971	1972	1973	1974	1975	1976	1977	1978	1979
Exchange Rates												*Reais per Trillion SDRs through 1983, per Bill. 1984-88, per Mill.*				
Principal Rate	aa	.81	.81	.99	1.40	1.59	1.80	2.23	2.46	2.73	3.32	3.86	5.22	7.09	9.91	20.37
											Reais per Trillion US$ through 1983, per Bill.US$ 1984-88, per Mill.US$					
Principal Rate	ae	.81	.81	.99	1.40	1.59	1.80	2.05	2.27	2.27	2.71	3.30	4.49	5.84	7.61	15.47
Principal Rate	rf	.69	.81	.97	1.23	1.48	1.67	1.92	2.16	2.23	2.47	2.95	3.88	5.14	6.57	9.79
Fund Position															*Millions of SDRs:*	
Quota	2f. s	280	350	350	350	350	440	440	440	440	440	440	440	440	665	665
SDRs	1b. s	—	—	—	—	—	62	110	157	157	163	163	171	173	184	291
Reserve Position in the Fund	1c. s	—	12	12	12	12	117	116	116	116	116	116	162	160	139	183
Total Fund Cred.&Loans Outstg.	2tl	89	44	12	—	—	—	—	—	—	—	—	—	—	—	—
International Liquidity												*Millions of US Dollars Unless Otherwise Indicated:*				
Total Reserves minus Gold	1l. d	421	380	154	212	611	1,142	1,696	4,133	6,360	5,216	3,980	6,488	7,192	11,826	8,966
SDRs	1b. d	—	—	—	—	—	62	120	170	190	199	191	199	210	239	383
Reserve Position in the Fund	1c. d	—	12	12	12	12	117	126	126	140	142	136	188	195	181	241
Foreign Exchange	1d. d	421	368	142	200	599	962	1,450	3,836	6,030	4,874	3,653	6,101	6,787	11,406	8,342
Other Liquid Foreign Assets	1e. d	....	....	....	....	....	....	....	....	....	....	....	....	....	....	....
Gold (Million Fine Troy Ounces)	1ad	1.80	1.30	1.30	1.29	1.29	1.29	1.32	1.33	1.33	1.33	1.33	1.33	1.52	1.61	1.70
Gold (National Valuation)	1an d	33	45	45	45	45	45	50	50	56	56	56	56	64	68	75
Monetary Authorities: Other Assets	3..d	215	235	202	183	333	299	316	476	665	896	1,195	1,473	1,599	1,513	1,613
Other Liab.	4..d	1,260	9	842	796	553	440	405	618	574	940	1,162	1,765	1,956	3,286	4,504
Deposit Money Banks: Assets	7a. d	79	103	123	154	162	192	335	436	895	1,161	929	1,175	1,214	2,043	1,817
of which: Claims on Nonbanks	7ad d	....	....	....	....	....	....	....	....	....	....	....	....	....	....	....
Deposit Money Banks: Liabilities	7b. d	79	103	123	789	930	1,633	893	1,452	2,258	2,973	2,778	4,797	5,849	8,365	8,109
of which: Liab. to Nonbanks	7bd d	....	....	....	....	....	....	....	....	....	....	....	....	....	....	....
Other Banking Insts.: Assets	7e. d	....	....	....	....	....	....	....	....	....	....	....	....	....	—	—
of which: Claims on Nonbanks	7ed d	....	....	....	....	....	....	....	....	....	....	....	....	....	....	....
Other Banking Insts.: Liabilities	7f. d	....	....	....	....	233	204	357	1,290	1,613	1,757	2,111	2,276	2,704	4,183	4,823
Monetary Authorities											*Millionths of Reais through 1974; Thousandths 1975-85; Reais 1986-89;*					
Foreign Assets	11	559	528	394	609	1,555	2,659	ℐ4,000	10,182	15,636	16,000	ℐ16	34	48	ℐ102	165
Claims on Central Government	12a	831	865	1,162	1,588	1,425	930	ℐ−2,545	−727	−2,545	−9,455	ℐ−17	−20	−18	ℐ35	43
Claims on State and Local Govt.	12b	127	93	120	157	138	323	ℐ—	—	—	—	ℐ—	—	1	ℐ6	8
Claims on Private Sector	12d	575	903	1,292	2,150	3,279	4,428	ℐ9,455	12,727	18,182	32,000	ℐ54	86	125	ℐ154	253
Claims on Deposit Money Banks	12e	86	129	160	347	529	560	ℐ1,455	2,182	3,273	6,545	ℐ12	17	24	ℐ26	35
Claims on Other Banking Insts.	12f	—	—	—	—	—	—	ℐ364	1,091	1,455	5,091	ℐ9	16	28	ℐ25	27
Claims on Nonbank Financial Insts	12g															
Reserve Money	14	1,871	2,365	2,969	4,323	5,586	6,649	ℐ8,000	9,091	13,455	18,545	ℐ26	40	60	ℐ86	160
of which: Currency Outside DMBs	14a	629	852	1,071	1,484	1,960	2,443	ℐ3,273	4,364	5,818	8,000	ℐ11	17	24	ℐ34	61
Liabs. of Central Bank: Securities	16ac	....	....	....	....	....	....	....	....	....	....	....	....	....	....	....
Restricted Deposits	16b	228	137	81	221	208	218	ℐ—	—	—	—	ℐ3	15	16	ℐ23	30
Foreign Liabilities	16c	7	7	35	123	38	4	ℐ727	1,091	1,091	1,091	ℐ1	4	6	ℐ3	4
Long-Term Foreign Liabilities	16cl	1,213	1,117	1,248	1,670	1,847	1,801	ℐ364	364	364	1,455	ℐ3	4	5	ℐ22	65
Central Government Deposits	16d														88	79
Capital Accounts	17a	364	364	364	727	1,455	2,545	ℐ3,636	6,182	8,727	15,636	ℐ24	36	55	ℐ64	88
Other Items (Net)	17r	−1,505	−1,472	−1,568	−2,213	−2,207	−2,317	ℐ—	8,727	12,364	13,455	ℐ18	35	67	ℐ62	107
Deposit Money Banks											*Millionths of Reais through 1974; Thousandths 1975-85; Reais 1986-89;*					
Reserves	20	743	804	1,040	1,408	1,478	1,513	ℐ2,182	2,545	3,636	4,000	ℐ4	7	19	ℐ29	51
Other Claims on Monetary Author.	20c	....	....	....	....	....	....	....	....	....	....	....	....	....	....	....
Blocked Financial Assets	20d	....	....	....	....	....	....	....	....	....	....	....	....	....	....	....
Foreign Assets	21	63	83	121	213	255	344	ℐ727	1,091	2,182	3,273	ℐ3	5	7	ℐ15	28
Claims on Central Government	22a	32	112	358	441	760	1,152	ℐ1,818	2,909	4,364	5,818	ℐ9	15	19	ℐ26	37
Claims on State and Local Govt.	22b	49	111	227	298	484	679	ℐ1,091	1,455	1,818	1,818	ℐ3	6	10	ℐ19	38
Claims on Nonfin.Pub.Enterprises	22c														23	49
Claims on Private Sector	22d	1,455	1,814	2,985	4,823	6,707	9,036	ℐ13,091	19,273	27,636	41,455	ℐ63	95	143	ℐ205	337
Claims on Other Banking Insts.	22f	—	—	—	—	—	—	ℐ—	—	364	364	ℐ—	—	1	ℐ1	4
Demand Deposits	24	2,109	2,252	3,499	4,902	6,113	7,808	ℐ10,182	14,182	21,091	28,364	ℐ41	55	77	ℐ103	176
Time and Savings Deposits	25	80	310	545	877	1,378	1,858	ℐ1,091	2,182	2,545	2,909	ℐ4	7	16	ℐ34	56
Money Market Instruments	26aa	....	....	....	....	....	....	....	....	....	....	....	....	....	....	....
Restricted Deposits	26b	....	....	....	....	....	....	....	....	....	....	....	....	....	....	....
Foreign Liabilities	26c	43	41	109	782	1,370	2,104	ℐ727	1,091	2,545	3,636	ℐ3	10	15	ℐ30	51
Long-Term Foreign Liabilities	26cl	—	—	—	364	364	727	ℐ1,091	2,182	2,545	4,364	ℐ6	11	19	ℐ33	73
Central Government Deposits	26d	—	—	—	—	—	—	ℐ364	364	364	364	ℐ1	1	1	ℐ47	57
Credit from Monetary Authorities	26g	84	149	223	412	568	609	ℐ1,455	2,182	3,273	6,182	ℐ12	17	25	ℐ21	33
Liabilities to Other Banking Insts	26i	....	....	....	....	....	....	....	....	....	....	....	....	....	....	....
Capital Accounts	27a	362	511	753	1,061	1,529	2,043	ℐ2,909	4,000	5,455	7,273	ℐ10	16	26	ℐ47	64
Other Items (Net)	27r	−336	−339	−397	−1,214	−1,639	−2,426	ℐ1,091	1,091	2,182	3,636	ℐ6	14	19	ℐ3	34
Monetary Survey											*Millionths of Reais through 1974; Thousandths 1975-85; Reais 1986-89;*					
Foreign Assets (Net)	31n	572	563	371	−83	402	894	ℐ3,273	9,091	14,182	14,545	ℐ15	25	34	ℐ85	138
Domestic Credit	32	3,068	3,897	6,145	9,457	12,792	16,549	ℐ22,909	36,364	50,909	76,727	ℐ121	197	309	ℐ368	683
Claims on Central Govt. (Net)	32an	862	977	1,520	2,029	2,185	2,083	ℐ−1,091	1,818	1,455	−4,000	ℐ−9	−7	−1	ℐ−74	−55
Claims on State and Local Govt.	32b	176	204	348	455	622	1,002	ℐ1,091	1,455	1,818	1,818	ℐ3	6	11	ℐ25	46
Claims on Nonfin.Pub.Enterprises	32c	—	—	—	—	—	—	ℐ—	—	—	—	ℐ—	—	1	ℐ32	70
Claims on Private Sector	32d	2,030	2,716	4,277	6,973	9,985	13,465	ℐ22,545	32,000	45,818	73,455	ℐ117	181	269	ℐ359	590
Claims on Other Banking Insts.	32f	—	—	—	—	—	—	ℐ364	1,091	1,818	5,455	ℐ9	16	29	ℐ26	32
Claims on Nonbank Financ. Insts	32g	....	....	....	....	....	....	....	....	....	....	....	....	....	....	....
Money	34	2,966	3,379	5,029	7,109	9,068	11,523	ℐ15,636	21,455	31,273	42,909	ℐ61	84	116	ℐ158	276
Quasi-Money	35	108	343	618	996	1,585	2,191	ℐ3,273	2,182	2,545	2,909	ℐ4	7	16	ℐ34	56
Money Market Instruments	36aa	....	....	....	....	....	....	....	....	....	....	....	....	....	....	....
Liabs. of Central Bank: Securities	36ac	....	....	....	....	....	....	....	....	....	....	....	....	....	....	....
Restricted Deposits	36b	228	137	81	221	208	218	ℐ—	—	—	—	ℐ3	15	16	ℐ23	30
Long-Term Foreign Liabilities	36cl	1,213	1,117	1,248	2,034	2,210	2,529	ℐ1,455	2,545	2,909	5,818	ℐ8	15	24	ℐ56	139
Liabilities to Other Banking Insts	36i	....	....	....	....	....	....	....	....	....	....	....	....	....	....	....
Capital Accounts	37a	725	874	1,117	1,788	2,984	4,589	ℐ6,545	10,182	14,182	22,909	ℐ33	52	81	ℐ111	152
Other Items (Net)	37r	−1,601	−1,390	−1,576	−2,773	−2,861	−3,606	ℐ−727	9,091	14,182	16,727	ℐ25	49	91	ℐ73	168
Money plus Quasi-Money	35l	3,074	3,722	5,647	8,105	10,653	13,714	ℐ18,909	23,636	33,818	45,818	ℐ65	91	132	ℐ192	332

Brazil

1980	1981	1982	1983	1984	1985	1986	1987	1988	1989	1990	1991	1992	1993	1994		
1989-92, per Thous.SDRs thereafter: End of Period															**Exchange Rates**	
30.38	54.09	101.35	374.62	ⱡ1.13	4.19	6.63	37.27	374.50	ⱡ5.43	91.60	555.94	6,193.75	ⱡ162.88	1,235.03	Principal Rate	aa
1989-92, per Thous.US$ thereafter: End of Per. (ae) Per. Average(rf)																
23.82	46.47	91.88	357.82	ⱡ1.16	3.81	5.42	26.27	278.29	ⱡ4.13	64.39	388.65	4,504.55	ⱡ118.58	846.00	Principal Rate	ae
19.16	33.85	65.25	209.73	ⱡ.67	2.25	4.96	14.26	95.27	ⱡ1.03	24.84	147.86	1,641.09	ⱡ32.16	....	Principal Rate	rf
End of Period															**Fund Position**	
998	998	998	1,461	1,461	1,461	1,461	1,461	1,461	1,461	1,461	1,461	2,171	2,171	2,171	Quota	2f. s
301	388	—	—	1	1	—	—	—	—	8	9	1	2	....	SDRs	1b. s
270	227	260	—	—	—	—	—	—	—	—	—	—	—	—	Reserve Position in the Fund	1c. s
—	—	499	2,526	4,270	4,205	3,680	2,803	2,477	1,843	1,280	865	581	221	128	Total Fund Cred.&Loans Outstg.	2tl
End of Period															**International Liquidity**	
5,769	6,604	3,928	4,355	11,508	10,605	ⱡ5,803	6,299	6,972	7,535	7,441	8,033	22,521	30,604	37,070	Total Reserves minus Gold	1l. d
384	452	—	—	1	1	—	—	—	—	11	13	1	2	....	SDRs	1b. d
344	264	287	—	—	—	—	—	—	—	—	—	—	—	—	Reserve Position in the Fund	1c. d
5,042	5,888	3,641	4,355	11,507	10,604	ⱡ5,803	6,299	6,971	7,535	7,430	8,020	22,520	30,602	37,069	Foreign Exchange	1d. d
....	....	....	....	....	....	....	....	1,024	950	798	643	486	501	319	Other Liquid Foreign Assets	1e. d
1.88	2.20	.15	.54	1.47	3.10	2.43	2.43	2.73	2.98	4.57	2.02	2.23	2.93	3.71	Gold (Million Fine Troy Ounces)	1ad
1,143	905	65	207	488	1,004	958	1,159	1,144	1,194	1,735	731	747	1,107	1,418	Gold (National Valuation)	1an d
4,333	3,050	2,804	3,818	4,463	4,965	2,445	3,315	2,446	2,751	2,425	2,095	2,331	2,056	1,851	Monetary Authorities: Other Assets	3..d
6,810	6,846	8,557	14,928	18,888	19,198	29,939	46,405	44,539	50,770	40,814	59,819	47,574	48,514	8,874	Other Liab.	4..d
1,489	2,088	2,099	1,924	2,274	1,983	3,379	3,544	5,551	8,186	8,628	9,573	11,143	14,589	....	Deposit Money Banks: Assets	7a. d
216	389	492	393	531	404	349	300	622	519	568	507	720	794	....	*of which:* Claims on Nonbanks	7ad d
11,292	15,764	18,150	16,997	17,325	14,053	14,128	13,138	14,167	15,252	15,696	16,776	21,472	31,054	....	Deposit Money Banks: Liabilities	7b. d
2,172	2,442	2,305	1,851	2,494	3,201	2,456	10	3	3	5	3	166	91	....	*of which:* Liab. to Nonbanks	7bd d
—	24	99	401	136	8	7	9	126	77	100	27	141	702	....	Other Banking Insts.: Assets	7e. d
....	....	....	....	....	....	....	....	16	7	16	2	2	5	....	*of which:* Claims on Nonbanks	7ed d
5,337	6,336	6,794	7,032	6,564	6,539	6,287	6,307	4,183	2,849	2,352	2,013	2,242	2,527	....	Other Banking Insts.: Liabilities	7f. d
Thousands 1990-92; Millions Beginning 1993: End of Period															**Monetary Authorities**	
267	488	621	2,984	18,960	62,094	ⱡ47	269	ⱡ3,520	55,952	ⱡ835	4,957	123,520	ⱡ4,217	35,415	Foreign Assets	11
157	330	618	1,235	3,144	12,698	ⱡ224	901	ⱡ18,140	300,863	ⱡ5,747	29,354	363,345	ⱡ7,934	26,506	Claims on Central Government	12a
9	19	30	67	92	257	ⱡ—	—	ⱡ—	—	ⱡ194	862	172	ⱡ9	—	Claims on State and Local Govt.	12b
435	720	1,253	2,504	5,876	23,337	ⱡ—	—	ⱡ8	49	ⱡ—	—	—	ⱡ—	3	Claims on Private Sector	12d
57	129	244	486	1,769	4,977	ⱡ114	445	ⱡ64	3,733	ⱡ151	651	17,214	ⱡ120	20,556	Claims on Deposit Money Banks	12e
37	66	89	132	191	756	ⱡ2	9	ⱡ2	474	ⱡ6	6	163	ⱡ1	5	Claims on Other Banking Insts.	12f
....	....	....	....	....	....	ⱡ—	1	ⱡ20	8	ⱡ—	1	5	ⱡ—	—	Claims on Nonbank Financial Insts	12g
252	429	801	1,649	5,409	18,981	ⱡ75	413	ⱡ1,686	42,411	ⱡ821	4,897	61,120	ⱡ1,533	34,666	Reserve Money	14
105	190	367	684	2,272	8,671	ⱡ31	92	ⱡ760	14,677	ⱡ356	1,314	14,564	ⱡ340	....	*of which:* Currency Outside DMBs	14a
....	....	....	....	....	....	ⱡ74	594	ⱡ—	—	ⱡ11	987	94,933	ⱡ867	39,288	Liabs. of Central Bank: Securities	16ac
12	5	3	1	35	134	ⱡ33	152	ⱡ1,148	16,137	ⱡ1,498	4,449	5,014	ⱡ75	306	Restricted Deposits	16b
41	84	629	2,535	8,086	21,143	ⱡ30	270	ⱡ1,083	32,590	ⱡ947	7,401	29,516	ⱡ807	896	Foreign Liabilities	16c
120	233	204	3,720	18,495	69,276	ⱡ156	1,047	ⱡ12,173	186,023	ⱡ1,667	16,327	188,383	ⱡ4,982	6,750	Long-Term Foreign Liabilities	16cl
171	478	636	808	7,861	31,981	ⱡ36	134	ⱡ780	35,195	ⱡ874	3,036	42,889	ⱡ1,023	12,094	Central Government Deposits	16d
76	–17	–424	–3,272	–12,809	–38,888	ⱡ35	48	ⱡ4,468	42,509	ⱡ128	727	70,673	ⱡ1,838	998	Capital Accounts	17a
289	541	1,006	1,965	2,957	1,491	ⱡ–52	–1,034	ⱡ415	6,214	ⱡ988	–1,992	11,894	ⱡ1,156	–12,513	Other Items (Net)	17r
Thousands 1990-92; Millions Beginning 1993: End of Period															**Deposit Money Banks**	
84	132	276	552	1,906	5,900	ⱡ41	351	ⱡ1,597	21,710	ⱡ387	2,325	30,779	ⱡ901	....	Reserves	20
....	....	....	....	....	....	....	....	97	299	ⱡ9	119	46,131	ⱡ320	....	Other Claims on Monetary Author.	20c
....	....	....	....	....	....	....	....	....	....	ⱡ1,251	3,612	1	ⱡ—	....	Blocked Financial Assets	20d
35	97	192	685	2,620	7,528	ⱡ18	93	ⱡ1,537	33,645	ⱡ529	3,720	50,194	ⱡ1,730	....	Foreign Assets	21
90	269	524	1,091	4,616	17,369	ⱡ28	88	ⱡ1,596	122,967	ⱡ336	1,055	27,547	ⱡ1,027	....	Claims on Central Government	22a
73	219	498	1,521	4,874	17,612	ⱡ36	220	ⱡ2,960	44,977	ⱡ669	3,770	57,656	ⱡ1,522	....	Claims on State and Local Govt.	22b
98	251	583	2,037	6,415	21,781	ⱡ105	673	ⱡ2,931	53,009	ⱡ636	3,040	42,715	ⱡ1,158	....	Claims on Nonfin.Pub.Enterprises	22c
572	1,170	2,377	5,731	19,269	67,785	ⱡ286	949	ⱡ20,041	305,429	ⱡ3,595	19,971	348,163	ⱡ11,589	....	Claims on Private Sector	22d
11	26	98	241	537	3,646	ⱡ5	59	ⱡ10	2,903	ⱡ18	135	3,046	ⱡ79	....	Claims on Other Banking Insts.	22f
304	561	900	1,866	5,418	25,740	ⱡ125	265	ⱡ1,748	22,619	ⱡ550	2,581	24,073	ⱡ497	....	Demand Deposits	24
67	152	412	1,448	7,287	29,729	ⱡ100	311	ⱡ10,823	172,322	ⱡ2,000	16,548	313,207	ⱡ9,996	....	Time and Savings Deposits	25
....	....	....	....	....	....	....	....	5	4,909	ⱡ53	328	9,140	ⱡ283	....	Money Market Instruments	26aa
....	....	....	....	....	....	....	....	....	....	ⱡ1,645	4,543	3,507	ⱡ—	....	Restricted Deposits	26b
120	309	586	1,966	7,914	22,805	ⱡ40	210	ⱡ809	19,268	ⱡ275	1,736	70,000	ⱡ2,568	....	Foreign Liabilities	26c
153	449	1,075	4,085	11,751	30,547	ⱡ36	134	ⱡ3,114	43,416	ⱡ688	4,783	26,719	ⱡ1,115	....	Long-Term Foreign Liabilities	26cl
104	247	489	745	2,692	6,707	ⱡ15	35	ⱡ6,017	111,428	ⱡ654	3,194	44,179	ⱡ1,394	....	Central Government Deposits	26d
60	132	246	555	1,809	1,950	ⱡ115	784	ⱡ133	5,335	ⱡ181	500	13,019	ⱡ146	....	Credit from Monetary Authorities	26g
....	....	....	....	....	....	....	....	1,095	17,081	ⱡ165	1,241	31,747	ⱡ1,083	....	Liabilities to Other Banking Insts	26i
111	289	656	2,007	6,881	24,946	ⱡ77	370	ⱡ5,855	121,551	ⱡ1,471	10,726	143,861	ⱡ4,069	....	Capital Accounts	27a
45	26	184	–813	–3,516	–802	ⱡ10	325	ⱡ1,170	67,008	ⱡ–250	–8,435	–73,220	ⱡ–2,824	....	Other Items (Net)	27r
Thousands 1990-92; Millions Beginning 1993: End of Period															**Monetary Survey**	
141	192	–401	–832	5,579	25,675	ⱡ–5	–118	ⱡ3,165	37,738	ⱡ143	–459	74,198	ⱡ2,572	....	Foreign Assets (Net)	31n
1,234	2,408	5,024	14,036	39,106	157,157	ⱡ609	2,654	ⱡ38,912	684,056	ⱡ9,674	51,964	755,745	ⱡ20,901	....	Domestic Credit	32
–28	–126	17	773	–2,792	–8,621	ⱡ175	742	ⱡ12,939	277,207	ⱡ4,555	24,180	303,823	ⱡ6,544	....	Claims on Central Govt. (Net)	32an
83	239	528	1,588	4,966	17,869	ⱡ36	220	ⱡ2,960	44,977	ⱡ863	4,632	57,828	ⱡ1,531	....	Claims on State and Local Govt.	32b
125	313	662	3,067	11,059	52,386	ⱡ105	674	ⱡ2,931	53,009	ⱡ636	3,040	42,715	ⱡ1,158	....	Claims on Nonfin.Pub.Enterprises	32c
1,006	1,890	3,629	8,235	25,145	91,122	ⱡ286	949	ⱡ20,049	305,478	ⱡ3,595	19,971	348,165	ⱡ11,589	....	Claims on Private Sector	32d
48	92	187	372	728	4,402	ⱡ7	68	ⱡ12	3,377	ⱡ24	140	3,209	ⱡ79	....	Claims on Other Banking Insts.	32f
....	....	....	....	....	....	....	....	1	20	8	ⱡ—	1	5	ⱡ—	Claims on Nonbank Financ. Insts	32g
468	855	1,441	2,922	8,887	38,600	ⱡ166	524	ⱡ2,623	37,697	ⱡ917	4,856	52,539	ⱡ1,113	....	Money	34
67	152	412	1,448	7,287	29,729	ⱡ100	311	ⱡ10,823	172,322	ⱡ2,000	16,548	313,207	ⱡ9,996	....	Quasi-Money	35
....	....	....	....	....	....	....	....	5	4,909	ⱡ53	328	9,140	ⱡ283	....	Money Market Instruments	36aa
....	....	....	....	....	....	ⱡ74	594	ⱡ–97	–299	ⱡ—	868	48,802	ⱡ547	....	Liabs. of Central Bank: Securities	36ac
12	5	3	1	35	134	ⱡ33	152	ⱡ1,148	16,137	ⱡ3,143	8,991	8,521	ⱡ75	....	Restricted Deposits	36b
273	682	1,279	7,806	30,246	99,823	ⱡ193	1,181	ⱡ15,287	229,439	ⱡ2,355	21,110	215,102	ⱡ6,097	....	Long-Term Foreign Liabilities	36cl
....	....	....	....	....	....	....	....	1,095	17,081	ⱡ165	1,241	31,747	ⱡ1,083	....	Liabilities to Other Banking Insts	36i
188	271	233	–1,265	–5,928	–13,942	ⱡ112	418	ⱡ10,323	164,060	ⱡ1,599	11,453	214,534	ⱡ5,908	....	Capital Accounts	37a
367	635	1,256	2,292	4,159	28,488	ⱡ–73	–643	ⱡ869	80,447	ⱡ–417	–13,893	–63,648	ⱡ–1,627	....	Other Items (Net)	37r
535	1,007	1,853	4,370	16,174	68,329	ⱡ266	834	ⱡ13,447	210,019	ⱡ2,918	21,404	365,746	ⱡ11,109	....	Money plus Quasi-Money	35l

Brazil
223

		1965	1966	1967	1968	1969	1970	1971	1972	1973	1974	1975	1976	1977	1978	1979
Other Banking Institutions											*Millionths of Reais through 1974; Thousandths 1975-85; Reais 1986-89;*					
Reserves	40	...	...	...	...	364	364	I364	727	727	1,091	I1	2	2	I2	4
Other Claims on Monetary Author.	40c															
Blocked Financial Assets	40d															
Foreign Assets	41	...	...	...	...	—	—	I—	—	—	—	I—	—	—	I—	—
Claims on Central Government	42a	...	...	...	...	364	727	I1,091	2,545	3,636	5,818	I11	18	28	I43	81
Claims on State and Local Govt.	42b	...	...	...	...	364	364	I—	364	364	364	I—	1	2	I7	16
Claims on Nonfin.Pub.Enterprises	42c														33	59
Claims on Private Sector	42d	...	...	...	...	4,727	8,364	I12,727	20,727	32,000	51,636	I84	143	224	I304	516
Claims on Deposit Money Banks	42e	...	...	...	...	364	364	I727	1,091	1,818	4,000	I7	13	22	I23	50
Demand Deposits	44	...	...	...	...	727	727	I727	727	1,091	1,455	I2	4	5	I5	9
Time and Savings Deposits	45	...	...	...	...	727	1,818	I3,636	6,545	11,636	18,909	I34	59	97	I153	272
Money Market Instruments	46aa	...	...	...	...	364	727	I1,091	1,818	2,182	2,909	I3	4	4	I4	5
Restricted Deposits	46b															
Foreign Liabilities	46c															
Long-Term Foreign Liabilities	46cl	...	...	...	...	364	364	I727	2,909	3,636	4,727	I7	10	16	I32	75
Central Government Deposits	46d														130	230
Credit from Monetary Authorities	46g	...	...	...	...	—	—	I364	727	1,455	3,273	I6	10	17	I25	32
Credit from Deposit Money Banks	46h															
Capital Accounts	47a	...	...	...	...	1,818	2,909	I4,727	6,545	9,818	15,636	I24	37	51	I71	109
Other Items (Net)	47r	...	...	...	...	2,182	3,636	I3,636	6,182	8,727	16,000	I27	52	88	I-8	-5
Banking Survey											*Millionths of Reais through 1974; Thousandths 1975-85; Reais 1986-89;*					
Foreign Assets (Net)	51n	...	...	...	...	402	894	I3,273	9,091	14,182	14,545	I15	25	34	I85	138
Domestic Credit	52	...	...	...	...	18,247	26,004	I36,364	58,909	85,091	129,091	I207	343	535	I600	1,094
Claims on Central Govt. (Net)	52an	...	...	...	...	2,549	2,810	I—	4,364	5,091	1,818	I2	11	28	I-161	-203
Claims on State and Local Govt.	52b	...	...	...	...	985	1,365	I1,091	1,818	2,182	2,182	I4	7	13	I32	61
Claims on Nonfin.Pub.Enterprises	52c	...	...	...	...	—	—	I—	—	—	—	I—	—	1	I66	129
Claims on Private Sector	52d	...	...	...	...	14,712	21,828	I35,273	52,727	77,818	125,091	I201	324	493	I663	1,106
Claims on Nonbank Fin. Insts	52g															
Liquid Liabilities	55l	...	...	...	...	11,744	15,896	I22,909	30,182	45,818	65,091	I100	152	232	I348	609
Money Market Instruments	56aa	...	...	...	...	364	727	I1,091	1,818	2,182	2,909	I3	4	4	I4	5
Liabs. of Central Bank: Securities	56ac															
Restricted Deposits	46b															
Long-Term Foreign Liabilities	56cl	...	...	...	...	2,574	2,892	I2,182	5,455	6,545	10,545	I15	25	40	I88	213
Capital Accounts	57a	...	...	...	...	4,802	7,498	I11,273	16,727	24,000	38,545	I57	89	132	I182	262
Other Items (Net)	57r	...	...	...	...	-1,043	-333	I2,182	13,818	20,727	26,545	I43	83	145	I41	113
Nonbank Financial Institutions											*Reais through 1989; Thousands of Reais from 1990 through 1992;*					
Reserves	40..n															
Other Claims on Monetary Author.	40c.n															
Blocked Financial Assets	40d.n															
Foreign Assets	41..n															
Claims on Central Government	42a.n															
Claims on State and Local Govt.	42b.n															
Claims on Nonfin.Pub.Enterprises	42c.n															
Claims on Private Sector	42d.n															
Claims on Deposit Money Banks	42e.n															
Claims on Other Banking Insts.	42f.n															
Money Market Instruments	46aan															
Restricted Deposits	46b.n															
Long-Term Foreign Liabilities	46cln															
Central Government Deposits	46d.n															
Liabilities to Other Banking Insts	46i.n															
Capital Accounts	47a.n															
Other Items (Net)	47r.n															
Interest Rates															*Percent Per Annum*		
Bank Rate (End of Period)	60	12	12	22	22	20	20	20	20	18	18	18	28	30	33	35
Treasury Bill Rate	60c	...	39	34	23	22	19	20	20	14	21	30	30	36	32	40
Savings Rate	60k															
Deposit Rate	60l															
Prices															*Index Numbers (1990=100):*		
W'sale Prices(1990=100 million)	63.a	—	1	1	1	1	2	2	2	3	3	4	6	8	12	18
W'sale Prices(1990=1 million)	63.b															
Wholesale Prices (1990=1)	63.c															
Cons. Prices (1990=100 million)	64.a	1	1	1	1	2	2	2	3	3	4	5	7	10	14	21
Cons. Prices (1990=1 million)	64.b															
Consumer Prices (1990=1)	64.c															
International Transactions															*Millions of US Dollars*		
Exports	70..d	1,596	1,741	1,654	1,881	2,311	2,739	2,904	3,991	6,199	7,951	8,670	10,128	12,120	12,659	15,244
Coffee	70e.d	707	764	705	775	813	939	773	989	1,244	864	855	2,173	2,299	1,947	1,918
Imports, cif	71..d	1,096	1,496	1,667	2,132	2,265	2,849	3,701	4,783	6,999	14,168	13,592	13,726	13,257	15,054	19,804
Imports, fob	71.v d	941	1,303	1,441	1,855	1,993	2,507	3,247	4,232	6,192	12,642	12,210	12,383	12,023	13,683	18,084
Volume of Exports																*1990=100*	
Including Coffee	72	15	17	16	19	21	22	23	29	34	35	38	39	39	44	48
Coffee	72e	95	118	118	130	131	113	121	123	126	81	92	94	60	73	66
Volume of Imports	73	20	27	29	36	37	45	55	73	78	112	92	103	95	106	113
Export Prices																*1990=100:*	
Exports (Unit Value)	74..d	35	33	33	33	34	38	37	41	57	72	72	83	101	93	102
Coffee (Unit Value)	74e.d	67	58	54	54	56	75	58	73	90	97	84	208	346	242	263
Coffee (Wholesale Price)	76eb d	52	48	45	45	49	67	53	63	83	88	99	178	319	197	213
Unit Value of Imports	75..d	24	24	25	26	25	26	27	26	36	52	57	58	60	65	77

Brazil

1980	1981	1982	1983	1984	1985	1986	1987	1988	1989	1990	1991	1992	1993	1994		
Thousands 1990-92; Millions Beginning 1993: End of Period																**Other Banking Institutions**
4	12	25	49	156	3,488	....	....	‡443	3,260	‡15	113	2,064	‡53	....	Reserves	40
....	....	....	....	....	....	....	....	1	—	‡—	—	829	‡15	....	Other Claims on Monetary Author.	40c
....	....	....	....	....	....	....	....	—	—	‡74	265	—	‡—	....	Blocked Financial Assets	40d
—	1	9	143	157	31	‡—	—	‡35	315	‡6	11	634	‡83	....	Foreign Assets	41
129	374	909	2,641	7,771	20,817	....	....	‡229	1,671	‡3	17	2,965	‡95	....	Claims on Central Government	42a
32	60	180	574	1,999	7,328	‡13	86	‡701	7,763	‡113	434	5,852	‡156	....	Claims on State and Local Govt.	42b
102	291	686	1,735	4,532	26,232	‡40	188	‡1,845	22,984	‡311	1,703	15,257	‡355	....	Claims on Nonfin.Pub.Enterprises	42c
907	2,013	4,452	11,843	38,604	119,282	....	....	‡6,629	72,398	‡898	5,766	82,942	‡1,981	....	Claims on Private Sector	42d
106	252	530	1,351	4,153	17,997	....	....	‡663	8,845	‡397	2,144	31,115	‡1,025	....	Claims on Deposit Money Banks	42e
18	34	60	128	361	1,487	‡7	17	‡—	—	‡—	—	—	‡—	....	Demand Deposits	44
499	1,214	2,807	8,482	29,133	98,264	....	....	‡2,953	20,834	‡146	856	25,462	‡684	....	Time and Savings Deposits	45
6	10	11	29	49	46	....	....	‡131	603	‡7	26	427	‡9	....	Money Market Instruments	46aa
....	....	....	....	....	....	....	....	—	—	‡98	242	4	‡—	....	Restricted Deposits	46b
....	....	....	....	....	....	....	....	10	120	‡2	3	1,068	‡39	....	Foreign Liabilities	46c
126	294	621	2,504	7,562	24,823	‡34	165	‡1,148	11,589	‡142	780	9,032	‡261	....	Long-Term Foreign Liabilities	46cl
419	957	2,159	6,056	20,002	70,455	‡81	429	‡4,237	62,980	‡599	3,170	40,373	‡1,086	....	Central Government Deposits	46d
34	62	104	173	404	1,257	‡2	16	‡281	3,993	‡45	188	2,537	‡57	....	Credit from Monetary Authorities	46g
....	....	....	....	....	....	....	....	1,107	18,033	‡177	672	7,865	‡145	....	Credit from Deposit Money Banks	46h
186	422	1,061	2,974	10,040	32,843	....	....	‡2,624	39,943	‡467	3,824	54,101	‡1,382	....	Capital Accounts	47a
−6	9	−33	−2,010	−10,179	−33,999	....	....	‡−1,945	−40,859	‡135	693	788	‡100	....	Other Items (Net)	47r
Thousands 1990-92; Millions Beginning 1993: End of Period																**Banking Survey**
141	193	−392	−689	5,736	25,706	‡−5	−118	‡3,190	37,933	‡147	−451	73,764	‡2,617	....	Foreign Assets (Net)	51n
1,938	4,096	8,904	24,400	71,282	255,960	....	....	‡44,067	722,515	‡10,376	56,574	819,179	‡22,323	....	Domestic Credit	52
−317	−709	−1,234	−2,643	−15,023	−58,259	....	....	‡8,932	215,898	‡3,960	21,027	266,415	‡5,554	....	Claims on Central Govt. (Net)	52an
115	299	708	2,163	6,965	25,196	‡49	306	‡3,661	52,740	‡976	5,066	63,679	‡1,687	....	Claims on State and Local Govt.	52b
227	604	1,348	4,802	15,591	78,618	‡145	862	‡4,776	75,992	‡947	4,743	57,972	‡1,513	....	Claims on Nonfin.Pub.Enterprises	52c
1,913	3,903	8,081	20,078	63,749	210,404	....	....	‡26,678	377,876	‡4,493	25,737	431,107	‡13,570	....	Claims on Private Sector	52d
....	....	....	....	....	....	‡—	1	‡20	8	‡—	1	5	‡—	....	Claims on Nonbank Fin. Insts	52g
1,047	2,243	4,695	12,931	45,511	164,591	....	....	‡15,957	227,593	‡3,049	22,147	389,144	‡11,740	....	Liquid Liabilities	55l
6	10	11	29	49	46	....	....	‡136	5,512	‡59	355	9,567	‡292	....	Money Market Instruments	56aa
....	....	....	....	....	....	‡74	594	‡−97	−299	‡2	868	47,972	‡532	....	Liabs. of Central Bank: Securities	56ac
....	....	....	....	....	....	....	....	—	—	‡98	242	4	‡—	....	Restricted Deposits	46b
399	976	1,900	10,309	37,808	124,646	‡227	1,346	‡16,435	241,029	‡2,497	21,890	224,134	‡6,358	....	Long-Term Foreign Liabilities	56cl
374	693	1,293	1,709	4,112	18,901	....	....	‡12,947	204,003	‡2,066	15,277	268,634	‡7,289	....	Capital Accounts	57a
241	362	610	−1,268	−10,496	−26,653	....	....	‡730	66,473	‡−390	−13,648	−55,035	‡−1,346	....	Other Items (Net)	57r
Millions of Reais Beginning 1993: End of Period																**Nonbank Financial Institutions**
....	....	....	....	....	....	....	....	33	456	‡7	38	353	‡—	....	Reserves	40..n
....	....	....	....	....	....	....	....	56	5	‡1	4	2,804	‡8	....	Other Claims on Monetary Author.	40c.n
....	....	....	....	....	....	....	....	—	—	‡26	91	1	‡—	....	Blocked Financial Assets	40d.n
....	....	....	....	....	....	....	....	—	25	‡—	1	22	‡1	....	Foreign Assets	41..n
....	....	....	....	....	....	....	....	163	20,154	‡48	57	1,528	‡65	....	Claims on Central Government	42a.n
....	....	....	....	....	....	....	....	449	11,326	‡55	56	547	‡26	....	Claims on State and Local Govt.	42b.n
....	....	....	....	....	....	....	....	109	2,605	‡34	171	1,775	‡4	....	Claims on Nonfin.Pub.Enterprises	42c.n
....	....	....	....	....	....	....	....	2,196	2,430	‡12	309	1,515	‡91	....	Claims on Private Sector	42d.n
....	....	....	....	....	....	....	....	223	5,147	‡51	135	6,165	‡178	....	Claims on Deposit Money Banks	42e.n
....	....	....	....	....	....	....	....	9	67	‡—	1	13	‡1	....	Claims on Other Banking Insts.	42f.n
....	....	....	....	....	....	....	....	47	486	‡7	208	3,919	‡131	....	Money Market Instruments	46aa.n
....	....	....	....	....	....	....	....	—	—	‡6	15	8	‡—	....	Restricted Deposits	46b.n
....	....	....	....	....	....	....	....	130	2,397	‡34	315	4,757	‡170	....	Long-Term Foreign Liabilities	46cl.n
....	....	....	....	....	....	....	....	—	—	‡—	—	5	‡—	....	Central Government Deposits	46d.n
....	....	....	....	....	....	....	....	272	2,248	‡19	6	4,608	‡204	....	Liabilities to Other Banking Insts	46i.n
....	....	....	....	....	....	....	....	552	12,104	‡131	1,025	15,086	‡444	....	Capital Accounts	47a.n
....	....	....	....	....	....	....	....	2,237	24,980	‡36	−703	−13,658	‡−575	....	Other Items (Net)	47r.n
Percent Per Annum																**Interest Rates**
‡93	121	174	194	272	380	89	401	2,282	38,341	1,083	2,494	1,489	5,757	56	Bank Rate (End of Period)	60
54	72	93	127	190	215	151	195	483	382	....	....	....	....	....	Treasury Bill Rate	60c
....	....	....	....	....	255	114	511	1,101	3,478	21,938	690	1,255	2,743	4,206	Savings Rate	60k
115	108	156	155	268	295	109	401	859	‡5,845	9,394	913	1,560	3,294	5,175	Deposit Rate	60l
Period Averages																**Prices**
37	78	150	401	....	....	....	....	....	....	....	....	....	....	....	W'sale Prices(1990=100 million)	63.a
....	1	1	4	13	44	106	327	2,606	35,665	1,000,000	....	....	....	....	W'sale Prices(1990=1 million)	63.b
....	....	....	....	....	....	....	....	....	....	1	5	55	1,173	28,280	Wholesale Prices (1990=1)	63.c
....	39	81	160	387	....	....	....	....	....	....	....	....	....	....	Cons. Prices (1990=100 million)	64.a
....	....	....	4	11	38	92	303	2,373	32,918	1,000,000	....	....	....	....	Cons. Prices (1990=1 million)	64.b
....	....	....	....	....	....	....	....	....	....	1	5	60	1,348	37,331	Consumer Prices (1990=1)	64.c
Millions of US Dollars																**International Transactions**
20,132	23,293	20,175	21,899	27,005	25,639	22,349	26,224	33,494	34,383	31,414	31,620	35,793	38,597	43,558	Exports	70..d
2,486	1,517	1,858	2,096	2,564	2,369	2,006	1,959	2,009	1,560	1,106	1,382	970	1,065	2,219	Coffee	70e.d
24,961	24,079	21,069	16,801	15,210	14,332	15,557	16,581	16,055	19,875	22,524	22,950	23,068	27,740	35,997	Imports, cif	71..d
22,955	22,091	19,395	15,429	13,916	13,153	14,044	15,052	14,605	18,263	20,661	21,041	20,554	25,480	33,167	Imports, fob	71.vd
1990=100																Volume of Exports
59	71	65	74	91	96	79	92	109	109	100	104	....	....	....	Including Coffee	72
92	97	104	110	121	121	56	116	106	111	100	128	119	113	102	Coffee	72e
102	93	86	72	70	69	92	90	80	92	100	110	....	....	....	Volume of Imports	73
Indices of Unit Values in US Dollars																Export Prices
108	102	96	90	92	87	93	93	102	101	100	96	....	....	....	Exports (Unit Value)	74..d
244	142	161	172	192	177	324	153	171	127	100	97	74	85	196	Coffee (Unit Value)	74e.d
249	222	171	170	179	178	276	127	145	118	100	87	67	79	171	Coffee (Wholesale Price)	76eb.d
99	110	106	101	96	90	70	82	89	96	100	93	....	....	....	Unit Value of Imports	75..d

Brazil
223

		1965	1966	1967	1968	1969	1970	1971	1972	1973	1974	1975	1976	1977	1978	1979
Balance of Payments																*Millions of US Dollars:*
Goods: Exports f.o.b.	78aa d	...	...	...	...	...	...	...	...	...	...	8,492	9,961	11,923	12,473	15,244
Goods: Imports f.o.b.	78ab d	...	...	...	...	...	...	...	...	...	...	−12,042	−12,347	−12,023	−13,631	−17,961
Trade Balance	78ac d	...	...	...	...	...	...	...	...	...	...	−3,550	−2,386	−100	−1,158	−2,717
Services: Credit	78ad d	...	...	...	...	...	...	...	...	...	...	1,060	1,018	1,207	1,350	1,475
Services: Debit	78ae d	...	...	...	...	...	...	...	...	...	...	−2,504	−2,603	−2,793	−3,074	−3,799
Balance on Goods and Services	78af d	...	...	...	...	...	...	...	...	...	...	−4,994	−3,971	−1,686	−2,882	−5,041
Income: Credit	78ag d	...	...	...	...	...	...	...	...	...	...	387	304	380	666	1,279
Income: Debit	78ah d	...	...	...	...	...	...	...	...	...	...	−2,404	−2,891	−3,806	−4,892	−6,733
Balance on Goods, Serv., & Inc.	78ai d	...	...	...	...	...	...	...	...	...	...	−7,011	−6,558	−5,112	−7,108	−10,495
Current Transfers, n.i.e.: Credit	78aj d	...	...	...	...	...	...	...	...	...	...	71	49	85	157	180
Current Transfers: Debit	78ak d	...	...	...	...	...	...	...	...	...	...	−28	−11	−22	−45	−201
Current Account, n.i.e.	78al d	...	...	...	...	...	...	...	...	...	...	−6,968	−6,520	−5,049	−6,996	−10,516
Capital Account, n.i.e.: Credit	78ba d	...	...	...	...	...	...	...	...	...	...	62	62	42	96	50
Capital Account: Debit	78bb d	...	...	...	...	...	...	...	...	...	...	−102	−96	−105	−136	−12
Capital Account, n.i.e.	78bc d	...	...	...	...	...	...	...	...	...	...	−40	−34	−63	−40	38
Direct Investment Abroad	78bd d	...	...	...	...	...	...	...	...	...	...	−112	−183	−146	−124	−196
Dir. Invest. in Rep. Econ., n.i.e.	78be d	...	...	...	...	...	...	...	...	...	...	1,302	1,555	1,833	2,006	2,419
Portfolio Investment Assets	78bf d	...	...	...	...	...	...	...	...	...	...	—	—	—	—	3
Portfolio Investment Liab., n.i.e.	78bg d	...	...	...	...	...	...	...	...	...	...	—	—	—	—	657
Other Investment Assets	78bh d	...	...	...	...	...	...	...	...	...	...	165	−516	−260	−653	16
Other Investment Liab., n.i.e.	78bi d	...	...	...	...	...	...	...	...	...	...	5,026	7,879	4,834	10,134	3,558
Financial Account, n.i.e.	78bj d	...	...	...	...	...	...	...	...	...	...	6,381	8,735	6,261	11,363	6,457
Net Errors and Omissions	78ca d	...	...	...	...	...	...	...	...	...	...	−438	491	−628	301	1,234
Overall Balance	78cb d	...	...	...	...	...	...	...	...	...	...	−1,065	2,672	521	4,628	−2,787
Reserves and Related Items	79da d	...	...	...	...	...	...	...	...	...	...	1,065	−2,672	−521	−4,628	2,787
Reserve Assets	79db d	...	...	...	...	...	...	...	...	...	...	1,065	−2,672	−521	−4,628	2,900
Use of Fund Credit and Loans	79dc d	...	...	...	...	...	...	...	...	...	...	—	—	—	—	−113
Liabs.Constit.For.Auth.Reserves	79dd d	...	...	...	...	...	...	...	...	...	...	—	—	—	—	—
Exceptional Financing	79de d	...	...	...	...	...	...	...	...	...	...	—	—	—	—	—
Government Finance												*Millionths of Reais through 1974; Thousandths 1975-85; Reais 1986-89:*				
Deficit (−) or Surplus	80	−364	−364	−364	−727	−364	I −364	−727	−364	727	3,273	I−2	−1	−8	−23	−13
Revenue	81	1,455	2,182	2,545	3,636	5,091	I 12,727	17,455	24,000	34,182	50,182	I 71	116	203	301	493
Grants Received	81z	...	...	...	...	...	—	—	—	364	364	I —	1	2	1	4
Expenditure	82	1,818	2,545	2,909	4,364	5,455	I 12,364	16,727	21,818	29,091	42,545	I 67	106	169	260	398
Lending Minus Repayments	83	...	...	...	...	...	727	1,455	2,545	4,727	4,727	I 7	12	44	65	111
Financing																
Domestic	84a	...	...	...	...	...	...	...	...	...	...	...	...	...	...	...
Other	84b	...	...	...	...	...	...	...	...	...	...	...	...	...	...	...
Foreign	85a	...	...	...	...	...	...	...	...	...	...	...	...	...	...	...
Debt: Domestic	88a	...	...	...	...	...	...	...	...	...	...	...	...	...	...	...
Foreign	89a	...	...	...	...	...	...	...	...	...	...	...	...	...	...	...
National Accounts												*Millionths of Reais through 1974; Thousandths 1975-85; Reais 1986-89:*				
Exports of Goods & Services	90c	1,091	1,455	1,818	2,545	3,636	5,091	6,182	9,091	14,545	20,727	I 27	42	66	88	157
Government Consumption	91f	1,818	2,545	3,273	4,727	6,182	8,000	10,545	13,455	18,545	25,455	I 39	62	85	127	215
Gross Fixed Capital Formation	93e	2,909	4,728	6,182	9,455	13,092	17,092	23,638	31,638	45,457	72,004	I 89	133	193	293	507
Increase/Decrease (−) in Stocks	93i	...	...	...	1,091	1,455	1,091	2,545	3,273	7,636	19,273	I —	—	—	—	−13
Private Consumption	96f	10,545	15,636	21,818	30,546	38,182	45,455	61,455	81,091	111,273	168,728	I 243	407	626	904	1,532
Imports of Goods and Services	98c	−727	−1,455	−1,818	−2,909	−3,636	−5,455	−7,636	−11,273	−16,727	−36,000	I −42	−56	−72	−104	−202
Gross Domestic Product = GDP	99b	15,513	22,833	30,102	41,891	55,055	70,655	93,927	126,036	186,109	270,945	I 382	594	907	1,315	2,168
Net Factor Inc/Pmts (−) Abroad	98.n	—	363	363	363	363	726	1,089	1,089	1,815	2,178	I 5	9	15	30	59
Gross National Product = GNP	99a	15,990	22,895	30,891	44,337	58,510	70,503	94,125	124,289	174,077	255,120	I 362	581	889	1,337	2,235
Nat'l Income, Market Prices	99e	15,273	21,818	29,455	41,818	55,636	66,909	89,091	117,818	165,091	241,818	I 343	552	845	1,272	2,125
GDP 1990 Prices (Millions)	99b.p	3,046	3,152	3,321	3,681	4,040	4,146	4,654	5,162	5,860	6,431	I 6,790	7,448	7,665	8,046	8,590
GDP Deflator (1990=100)	99bi p	—	—	—	—	—	—	—	—	—	—	—	—	—	—	—
																Millions:
Population	99z	81.01	82.93	85.24	87.62	90.07	92.52	95.17	97.85	99.92	102.40	104.94	107.54	110.21	112.94	115.74

Exchange Rates: On February 28, 1986 the cruzado, equal to 1,000 cruzeiros, was introduced. On January 15, 1989 the new cruzado, equal to 1,000 old cruzados, was introduced. On March 16, 1990 the cruzeiro replaced the new cruzado at an exchange rate of one new cruzado for one cruzeiro. On August 1, 1993 the cruzeiro real, equal to 1,000 cruzeiros, was introduced. On July 1, 1994 the real, equal to 2,750 cruzeiros reais, was introduced.

Monetary Authorities: ɪ Beginning in December 1971, in 1978, and again in June 1988, data are based on improved sectorization of the accounts. ɪ Beginning in January 1986, comprises only the Central Bank of Brazil.

Deposit Money Banks: ɪ See note to section 10. ɪ Comprises only commercial banks through December 1985. Beginning in January 1986, consolidates the accounts of the commercial banks and the Bank of Brazil. ɪ Beginning in June 1988, data reflect the introduction of a new accounting system, which provides an improved sectorization of the accounts.

Monetary Survey: ɪ See notes to sections 10 and 20.

Other Banking Institutions: ɪ Beginning in December 1978, the accounts of the National Bank of Cooperative Credit are also consolidated in this category. ɪ See note to section 20.

Banking Survey: ɪ See notes to sections 10, 20, and 40.

Interest Rates: *Bank Rate (End of Period):* ɪ Beginning in January 1980, overnight rate on repurchase agreements based on federal securities capitalized daily.

Deposit Rate: ɪ Beginning in January 1989, annualized interest rate paid on 30-day certificates of deposit.

Government Finance: ɪ Beginning in 1970, data are as reported in the *Government Finance Statistics Yearbook* and cover consolidated central government.

Brazil

	1980	1981	1982	1983	1984	1985	1986	1987	1988	1989	1990	1991	1992	1993	1994		Balance of Payments	
	\.\.\.\.	\.\.\.\.	\.\.\.\.	\.\.\.\.	\.\.\.\.	\.\.\.\.	\.\.\.\.	\.\.\.\.	\.\.\.\.	\.\.\.\.	\.\.\.\.	\.\.\.\.	\.\.\.\.	\.\.\.\.	\.\.\.\.			
Minus Sign Indicates Debit																		
	20,132	23,276	20,173	21,898	27,002	25,634	22,348	26,210	33,773	34,375	31,408	31,619	35,793	38,783		\.\.\.\.	Goods: Exports f.o.b.	78aa *d*
	−22,955	−22,091	−19,395	−15,429	−13,916	−13,168	−14,044	−15,052	−14,605	−18,263	−20,661	−21,041	−20,554	−25,711		\.\.\.\.	Goods: Imports f.o.b.	78ab *d*
	−2,823	1,185	778	6,469	13,086	12,466	8,304	11,158	19,168	16,112	10,747	10,578	15,239	13,072		\.\.\.\.	Trade Balance	78ac *d*
	1,737	2,265	1,809	1,724	1,947	2,086	1,816	1,952	2,279	3,132	3,762	3,319	4,088	4,113		\.\.\.\.	Services: Credit	78ad *d*
	−4,871	−5,138	−5,397	−4,131	−3,696	−3,790	−4,389	−4,316	−5,302	−5,917	−7,523	−7,210	−7,430	−9,117		\.\.\.\.	Services: Debit	78ae *d*
	−5,957	−1,688	−2,810	4,062	11,337	10,762	5,731	8,794	16,145	13,327	6,986	6,687	11,897	8,068		\.\.\.\.	Balance on Goods and Services	78af *d*
	1,406	1,382	1,487	719	1,256	1,589	967	568	771	1,310	1,157	904	1,118	1,050		\.\.\.\.	Income: Credit	78ag *d*
	−8,424	−11,644	−14,981	−11,726	−12,722	−12,779	−12,089	−10,882	−12,851	−13,856	−12,765	−10,555	−9,115	−11,408		\.\.\.\.	Income: Debit	78ah *d*
	−12,975	−11,950	−16,304	−6,945	−129	−428	−5,391	−1,520	4,065	781	−4,622	−2,964	3,900	−2,290		\.\.\.\.	Balance on Goods, Serv., & Inc.	78ai *d*
	257	282	158	129	155	148	116	134	108	237	738	1,302	2,260	1,759		\.\.\.\.	Current Transfers, n.i.e.: Credit	78aj *d*
	−162	−149	−196	−34	−20	−22	−54	−90	−36	−17	−35	−31	−71	−106		\.\.\.\.	Current Transfers: Debit	78ak *d*
	−12,880	−11,817	−16,342	−6,850	6	−302	−5,329	−1,476	4,137	1,001	−3,919	−1,693	6,089	−637		\.\.\.\.	Current Account, n.i.e.	78al *d*
	80	88	37	20	37	31	32	31	23	28	138	297	54	—		\.\.\.\.	Capital Account, n.i.e.: Credit	78ba *d*
	−6	−22	−7	−7	−1	−2	−7	−5	−1	−4	−7	−12	—	—		\.\.\.\.	Capital Account: Debit	78bb *d*
	74	66	30	13	36	29	25	26	22	24	131	285	54	—		\.\.\.\.	Capital Account, n.i.e.	78bc *d*
	−367	−207	−376	−187	−42	−81	−143	−138	−175	−523	−665	−1,014	−137	−1,094		\.\.\.\.	Direct Investment Abroad	78bd *d*
	1,911	2,520	2,910	1,560	1,598	1,348	320	1,225	2,969	1,267	901	972	1,580	802		\.\.\.\.	Dir. Invest. in Rep. Econ., n.i.e.	78be *d*
	—	−3	−3	−8	−4	−3	1	—	—	—	−30	414	—	—		\.\.\.\.	Portfolio Investment Assets	78bf *d*
	354	1	2	−278	−268	−234	−451	−428	−498	−391	98	3,808	7,366	12,872		\.\.\.\.	Portfolio Investment Liab., n.i.e.	78bg *d*
	−405	−1,397	−553	348	−3,325	190	1,385	−401	−1,994	−894	−2,864	−3,140	−99	—		\.\.\.\.	Other Investment Assets	78bh *d*
	7,947	11,808	5,532	−3,958	−3,956	−9,511	−9,697	−10,540	−9,512	−11,954	−3,451	−4,755	−2,194	−4,200		\.\.\.\.	Other Investment Liab., n.i.e.	78bi *d*
	9,440	12,722	7,512	−2,523	−5,997	−8,291	−8,585	−10,282	−9,210	−12,525	−5,567	−4,129	6,516	8,380		\.\.\.\.	Financial Account, n.i.e.	78bj *d*
	−340	−418	−375	−586	399	−530	66	−802	−827	−819	−296	852	−1,393	−853		\.\.\.\.	Net Errors and Omissions	78ca *d*
	−3,706	553	−9,175	−9,946	−5,556	−9,094	−13,823	−12,534	−5,878	−12,319	−9,651	−4,685	11,266	6,890		\.\.\.\.	Overall Balance	78cb *d*
	3,706	−553	9,175	9,946	5,556	9,094	13,823	12,534	5,878	12,319	9,651	4,685	−11,266	−6,890		\.\.\.\.	Reserves and Related Items	79da *d*
	3,469	−622	4,655	−269	−7,169	573	3,856	−1,014	−1,250	−893	−474	369	−14,670	−8,709		\.\.\.\.	Reserve Assets	79db *d*
	—	—	546	2,160	1,801	−62	−625	−1,151	−462	−808	−771	−566	−399	−504		\.\.\.\.	Use of Fund Credit and Loans	79dc *d*
	237	69	1,634	−1,305	491	−385	396	525	73	1,099	126	−739	−627	—		\.\.\.\.	Liabs.Constit.For.Auth.Reserves	79dd *d*
	—	—	2,340	9,360	10,434	8,968	10,195	14,174	7,516	12,921	10,771	5,621	4,430	2,323		\.\.\.\.	Exceptional Financing	79de *d*
Thousands Beginning 1990: Year Ending December 31																	**Government Finance**	
	−111	−218	−463	−1,762	−6,829	−56,093	Ɪ−178	−507	−4,777	−74,291	Ɪ−672	−549	−24,389	\.\.\.\.		\.\.\.\.	Deficit (-) or Surplus	80
	1,009	2,183	4,604	11,267	33,010	132,883	Ɪ297	1,441	6,318	102,291	Ɪ3,628	15,553	173,586	\.\.\.\.		\.\.\.\.	Revenue	81
	7	26	46	116	371	836	Ɪ4	13	38	982	Ɪ8	40	115	\.\.\.\.		\.\.\.\.	Grants Received	81z
	912	1,814	3,840	9,069	28,990	127,735	Ɪ371	1,044	9,852	160,545	Ɪ4,027	14,975	187,242	\.\.\.\.		\.\.\.\.	Expenditure	82
	215	613	1,272	4,076	11,219	62,079	Ɪ108	917	1,280	17,018	Ɪ281	1,167	10,848	\.\.\.\.		\.\.\.\.	Lending Minus Repayments	83
																	Financing	
	\.\.\.\.	Ɪ221	529	1,545	5,996	57,222	Ɪ177	\.\.\.\.	\.\.\.\.	\.\.\.\.	\.\.\.\.	\.\.\.\.	\.\.\.\.	\.\.\.\.		\.\.\.\.	Domestic	84a
	\.\.\.\.	−3	−69	218	833	−1,127	Ɪ1	\.\.\.\.	\.\.\.\.	\.\.\.\.	\.\.\.\.	\.\.\.\.	\.\.\.\.	\.\.\.\.		\.\.\.\.	Other	84b
	365	909	1,558	3,480	10,139	74,070	Ɪ227	\.\.\.\.	\.\.\.\.	\.\.\.\.	\.\.\.\.	\.\.\.\.	\.\.\.\.	\.\.\.\.		\.\.\.\.	Foreign	85a
	153	248	248	455	1,287	169	Ɪ1	\.\.\.\.	\.\.\.\.	\.\.\.\.	\.\.\.\.	\.\.\.\.	\.\.\.\.	\.\.\.\.		\.\.\.\.	Debt: Domestic	88a
																\.\.\.\.	Foreign	89a
Thousands 1990-92; Millions Beginning 1993																	**National Accounts**	
	408	840	1,399	4,870	19,020	61,455	Ɪ117	397	3,427	38,004	Ɪ853	5,107	64,600	Ɪ1,378		\.\.\.\.	Exports of Goods & Services	90c
	414	831	1,839	4,119	11,632	49,455	Ɪ142	510	3,951	65,948	Ɪ1,839	8,600	101,936	Ɪ2,317		\.\.\.\.	Government Consumption	91f
	1,031	2,046	3,940	7,731	22,182	96,364	Ɪ255	936	7,151	114,496	Ɪ2,500	11,200	121,300	Ɪ2,863		\.\.\.\.	Gross Fixed Capital Formation	93e
	20	13	−63	−617	−1,600	11,273	Ɪ—	—	—	—	Ɪ—	—	—	Ɪ—		\.\.\.\.	Increase/Decrease (-) in Stocks	93i
	3,139	6,064	12,785	30,378	98,771	330,572	Ɪ902	2,612	18,727	200,000	Ɪ6,400	36,100	373,700	Ɪ8,555		\.\.\.\.	Private Consumption	96f
	−509	−874	−1,521	−3,841	−11,125	−35,636	Ɪ−85	−260	−1,792	−23,243	Ɪ−660	−3,945	−42,900	Ɪ−1,064		\.\.\.\.	Imports of Goods and Services	98c
	4,527	8,876	18,065	41,455	134,218	504,364	Ɪ1,336	4,209	31,491	400,000	Ɪ10,900	57,100	618,600	Ɪ14,049		\.\.\.\.	Gross Domestic Product = GDP	99b
	−147	−368	−940	−2,483	−7,964	−26,909	Ɪ−59	−159	−1,200	−13,954	Ɪ−300	−1,603	−15,200	Ɪ−389		\.\.\.\.	Net Factor Inc/Pmts(-) Abroad	98.n
	4,353	8,501	17,112	38,948	126,182	477,455	Ɪ1,276	4,050	30,230	448,503	Ɪ10,600	55,500	603,400	Ɪ13,654		\.\.\.\.	Gross National Product = GNP	99a
	4,409	8,489	15,745	\.\.\.\.	\.\.\.\.	\.\.\.\.	\.\.\.\.	\.\.\.\.	\.\.\.\.	\.\.\.\.	\.\.\.\.	\.\.\.\.	\.\.\.\.	\.\.\.\.		\.\.\.\.	Nat'l Income, Market Prices	99e
	9,369	8,957	Ɪ9,009	8,745	9,217	9,941	10,685	11,063	11,056	11,404	10,900	10,926	10,841	11,288	11,928	GDP 1990 Prices *(Millions)*		99b.*p*
	—	—	—	—	—	—	—	—	2	100	523	5,706	124,461	\.\.\.\.		GDP Deflator (1990=100)		99bi *p*
Midyear Estimates																		
	121.29	124.07	126.90	129.77	132.66	135.56	138.49	141.45	144.43	147.40	150.37	153.32	156.28	159.22	\.\.\.\.	**Population**		99z

Burkina Faso
748

		1965	1966	1967	1968	1969	1970	1971	1972	1973	1974	1975	1976	1977	1978	1979
Exchange Rates																*Francs per SDR:*
Official Rate	aa	245.07	247.59	245.42	247.40	277.91	276.02	283.61	278.00	284.00	272.08	262.55	288.70	285.76	272.28	264.78
																Francs per US Dollar:
Official Rate	ae	245.08	247.59	245.43	247.41	277.92	276.03	261.23	256.05	235.43	222.22	224.27	248.49	235.25	209.00	201.00
Official Rate	rf	245.06	245.68	246.00	247.56	259.96	276.40	275.59	252.03	222.89	240.70	214.31	238.95	245.68	225.66	212.72
Fund Position																*Millions of SDRs:*
Quota	2f. s	7.5	8.0	8.5	9.0	10.0	13.0	13.0	13.0	13.0	13.0	13.0	13.0	13.0	16.0	16.0
SDRs	1b. s	—	—	—	—	—	1.7	3.1	4.4	4.4	4.4	4.4	4.4	4.4	4.4	6.1
Reserve Position in the Fund	1c. s	.8	.9	1.0	1.1	1.4	1.4	2.5	3.1	3.3	3.3	3.3	3.3	4.6	4.6	4.6
Total Fund Cred.&Loans Outstg.	2tl														5.4	9.3
International Liquidity												*Millions of US Dollars Unless Otherwise Indicated:*				
Total Reserves minus Gold	1l. d	14.1	16.3	18.4	23.4	25.8	36.4	42.9	47.5	62.6	83.6	76.5	71.4	56.2	36.3	61.6
SDRs	1b. d	—	—	—	—	—	1.7	3.3	4.8	5.3	5.4	5.2	5.1	5.4	5.8	8.0
Reserve Position in the Fund	1c. d	.8	.9	1.0	1.1	1.4	1.4	2.7	3.4	3.9	4.0	3.8	3.8	5.6	6.0	6.0
Foreign Exchange	1d. d	13.3	15.4	17.4	22.3	24.4	33.3	36.9	39.3	53.4	74.2	67.5	62.5	45.2	24.6	47.5
Gold (Million Fine Troy Ounces)	1ad	....	....	....	....	....	....	....	....	....	....	....	—	.006	.008	.011
Gold (National Valuation)	1an d	....	....	....	....	....	....	....	....	....	....	....	—	.2	.4	.5
Monetary Authorities: Other Liab.	4.. d	—	—	.2	.8	.2	.1	.2	.3	—	2.3	5.1	11.1	2.4	5.2	6.4
Deposit Money Banks: Assets	7a. d	1.0	.7	.8	2.5	1.2	1.2	4.9	.5	6.4	2.7	3.1	1.2	3.8	4.2	1.4
Deposit Money Banks: Liabilities	7b. d	4.4	3.2	3.6	4.9	5.4	6.0	9.6	8.3	12.5	23.3	22.2	28.6	53.9	58.3	61.9
of which: Liab. to Nonbanks	7bd d											18.9	19.3	36.2	40.8	43.7
Monetary Authorities																*Billions of Francs:*
Foreign Assets	11	3.45	4.02	4.55	5.78	7.17	10.11	10.99	12.14	14.42	18.58	17.17	17.75	13.23	7.59	12.38
Claims on Central Government	12a	.20	.37	.15	—	—	—	—	—	—	—	—	—	1.97	3.50	4.43
Claims on Deposit Money Banks	12e	1.05	.55	.66	.34	.88	.12	.20	.28	.44	1.51	2.48	6.12	7.51	13.29	11.51
Claims on Other Financial Insts.	12f	....	....	....	....	....	....	....	....	....	....	....	.17	.44	.40	.34
Reserve Money	14	4.48	4.72	4.68	4.88	5.73	5.87	5.79	6.22	7.56	8.95	11.74	13.32	15.68	15.19	19.87
of which: Currency Outside DMBs	14a	4.43	4.69	4.60	4.77	5.54	5.74	5.65	5.77	7.13	8.51	10.65	12.85	14.75	13.50	17.36
Foreign Liabilities	16c	.01	.01	.05	.20	.07	.03	.06	.07	.01	.51	1.14	2.77	.56	4.08	6.35
Central Government Deposits	16d	.20	.21	.63	1.04	2.26	3.86	4.36	4.79	5.94	9.37	5.73	6.57	5.61	5.37	3.30
Other Items (Net)	17r	.01	—	—	—	—	.47	.98	1.34	1.35	1.26	1.04	1.38	1.30	.15	-.86
Deposit Money Banks																*Billions of Francs:*
Reserves	20	.04	.04	.08	.20	.17	.13	.10	.40	.40	.39	1.09	.57	.89	1.50	2.10
Foreign Assets	21	.25	.17	.19	.61	.33	.33	1.25	.13	1.46	.61	.69	.30	.90	.87	.27
Claims on Central Government	22a	....	....	....	.03	.02	.01	.02	.05	.06	.28	5.29	4.84	1.94	5.91	‡6.69
Claims on Private Sector	22d	3.85	3.36	3.53	3.92	5.58	5.51	5.97	7.14	9.01	15.16	21.37	31.95	45.28	54.83	‡56.66
Claims on Other Financial Insts.	22f	....	....	....	....	....	....	....	....	....	....	....	....	....	....	.53
Demand Deposits	24	1.46	1.44	1.65	2.33	2.58	2.97	3.37	3.62	5.82	7.26	10.71	13.64	14.67	18.76	‡15.81
Time Deposits	25	.14	.09	.06	.14	.20	.23	.46	.71	.99	1.16	1.82	4.00	4.79	8.12	‡11.48
Foreign Liabilities	26c	.73	.37	.50	.74	.81	.78	1.41	.58	.59	1.34	.82	2.64	7.69	6.95	7.23
Long-Term Foreign Liabilities	26cl	.35	.41	.40	.48	.69	.89	1.05	1.55	2.29	3.83	4.16	4.47	4.99	5.24	5.20
Central Government Deposits	26d	....	....	....	.12	.27	.30	.31	.63	.67	.50	5.32	5.83	6.59	8.33	‡10.72
Credit from Monetary Authorities	26g	1.05	.55	.65	.34	.88	.12	.20	.28	.44	1.51	2.48	6.12	7.51	13.29	11.51
Other Items (Net)	27r	.41	.72	.55	.61	.66	.71	.55	.36	.13	.84	3.12	.96	2.77	2.42	4.29
Treasury Claims: Private Sector	22d. i	.23	.26	.21	.14	.11	.12	.14	.17	.15	.23	.30	.46	.81	1.13	1.02
Post Office: Checking Deposits	24.. i	.38	.40	.34	.36	.38	.43	.44	.50	.55	.60	1.14	1.07	1.36	2.14	1.60
Monetary Survey																*Billions of Francs:*
Foreign Assets (Net)	31n	2.96	3.81	4.19	5.45	6.63	9.63	10.77	11.63	15.29	17.35	15.90	12.64	5.87	-2.57	-.93
Domestic Credit	32	4.21	3.92	3.39	3.14	3.45	1.79	1.65	2.17	2.89	6.11	16.74	25.62	38.79	53.08	‡56.23
Claims on Central Govt. (Net)	32an	.13	.30	-.35	-.92	-2.24	-3.84	-4.45	-5.15	-6.27	-9.28	-4.92	-6.96	-7.74	-3.28	‡-2.32
Claims on Private Sector	32d	4.08	3.62	3.74	4.06	5.69	5.63	6.11	7.32	9.16	15.39	21.66	32.41	46.09	55.96	‡57.68
Claims on Other Financial Insts.	32f	....	....	....	....	....	....	....	....	....	....	....	.17	.44	.40	1.87
Money	34	6.27	6.53	6.59	7.45	8.51	9.14	9.47	9.89	13.50	16.38	22.50	27.55	30.78	34.40	‡34.76
Quasi-Money	35	.14	.09	.06	.14	.20	.23	.46	.71	.99	1.16	1.82	4.00	4.79	8.12	‡11.48
Long-Term Foreign Liabilities	36cl	.35	.41	.40	.48	.69	.89	1.05	1.55	2.29	3.83	4.16	4.47	4.99	5.24	5.20
Other Items (Net)	37r	.42	.71	.54	.51	.68	1.18	1.45	1.65	1.39	2.09	4.16	2.24	4.09	4.04	3.85
Money plus Quasi-Money	35l	6.41	6.62	6.65	7.60	8.71	9.36	9.93	10.59	14.49	17.53	24.32	31.55	35.57	42.52	‡46.24
Other Banking Institutions																*Billions of Francs:*
Savings Deposits	45	.48	.54	.70	.78	.87	1.00	1.05	1.12	1.37	1.65	2.04	2.50	2.82	2.94	3.37
Liquid Liabilities	55l	6.89	7.16	7.35	8.37	9.58	10.37	10.98	11.71	15.86	19.18	26.36	34.05	38.39	45.46	‡49.62
Interest Rates																*Percent Per Annum*
Discount Rate (End of Period)	60	3.50	3.50	3.50	3.50	3.50	3.50	3.50	3.50	5.50	5.50	8.00	8.00	8.00	8.00	8.00
Money Market Rate	60b	....	....	....	....	....	....	....	....	....	....	....	7.28	7.42	7.72
Deposit Rate	60l	....	....	....	....	....	3.00	3.00	3.00	5.75	5.75	5.88	6.00	6.00	6.00	6.00
Lending Rate	60p	....	....	....	....	....	....	....	....	....	....	....	....	12.00	12.00	12.00
Prices																*Index Numbers (1990=100):*
Consumer Prices	64	28.1	28.7	27.5	27.4	30.1	30.6	31.2	30.3	32.6	35.5	42.1	38.6	50.2	54.3	62.4

Burkina Faso

748

	1980	1981	1982	1983	1984	1985	1986	1987	1988	1989	1990	1991	1992	1993	1994		
	End of Period															**Exchange Rates**	
	287.99	334.52	370.92	436.97	470.11	415.26	394.78	378.78	407.68	380.32	364.84	370.48	378.57	404.89	I780.44	Official Rate	aa
	End of Period (ae) Period Average (rf)																
	225.80	287.40	336.25	417.37	479.60	378.05	322.75	267.00	302.95	289.40	256.45	259.00	275.33	294.78	I534.60	Official Rate	ae
	211.28	271.73	328.61	381.06	436.96	449.26	346.30	300.54	297.85	319.01	272.26	282.11	264.69	283.16	I555.20	Official Rate	rf
	End of Period															**Fund Position**	
	24.0	24.0	24.0	24.0	31.6	31.6	31.6	31.6	31.6	31.6	31.6	31.6	44.2	44.2	44.2	Quota	2f. s
	5.8	7.5	7.5	7.5	5.6	5.6	5.6	5.7	5.6	5.6	5.7	5.6	5.6	5.6	5.6	SDRs	1b. s
	5.6	5.6	5.6	5.6	7.5	7.5	7.5	7.5	7.5	7.5	7.5	7.2	7.2	7.2	7.2	Reserve Position in the Fund	1c. s
	12.7	12.7	12.7	12.5	11.4	9.3	6.7	4.2	1.9	.4	.1	6.3	6.3	15.2	32.8	Total Fund Cred.&Loans Outstg.	2tl
	End of Period															**International Liquidity**	
	68.2	70.8	61.8	85.0	106.3	139.5	233.5	322.6	320.9	265.5	300.5	346.1	341.3	382.3	237.2	Total Reserves minus Gold	1l. d
	7.4	8.7	8.3	7.9	5.5	6.2	6.9	8.0	7.6	7.4	8.0	8.0	7.7	7.7	8.1	SDRs	1b. d
	7.2	6.6	6.2	5.9	7.4	8.3	9.2	10.7	10.1	9.9	10.2	10.3	9.9	9.9	10.5	Reserve Position in the Fund	1c. d
	53.6	55.6	47.3	71.2	93.4	125.1	217.4	303.9	303.1	248.2	282.2	327.7	323.7	364.7	218.6	Foreign Exchange	1d. d
	.011	.011	.011	.011	.011	.011	.011	.011	.011	.011	.011	.011	.011	.011	.011	Gold (Million Fine Troy Ounces)	1ad
	.5	4.7	4.8	4.3	3.7	3.6	4.5	5.2	4.6	4.3	4.2	3.9	3.8	4.1	4.1	Gold (National Valuation)	1and
	7.2	5.1	8.6	6.0	12.6	21.4	46.3	59.6	53.7	42.6	41.8	40.4	32.5	29.8	14.9	Monetary Authorities: Other Liab.	4..d
	7.0	3.5	2.8	4.7	5.8	9.0	10.3	34.8	30.9	43.5	54.9	38.7	48.6	53.1	155.5	Deposit Money Banks: Assets	7a. d
	56.5	55.2	53.0	51.6	32.4	45.4	41.4	50.6	45.7	57.8	75.7	66.6	43.1	42.5	39.7	Deposit Money Banks: Liabilities	7b. d
	38.1	33.1	32.9	34.4	22.6	28.7	24.6	33.4	32.0	37.4	38.9	39.4	32.5	27.0	23.9	of which: Liab. to Nonbanks	7bd d
	End of Period															**Monetary Authorities**	
	15.40	20.36	20.77	35.48	50.99	52.75	75.36	86.12	97.20	76.83	77.06	89.63	93.97	112.68	126.83	Foreign Assets	11
	5.08	6.14	10.13	12.38	13.84	11.92	12.21	16.57	17.21	18.23	19.35	21.60	22.60	26.29	44.84	Claims on Central Government	12a
	11.80	8.94	10.53	11.20	9.61	7.01	7.50	8.09	4.45	4.30	3.89	9.00	9.00	9.00	—	Claims on Deposit Money Banks	12e
	.41	.49	.62	.76	.80	.77	1.13	1.18	1.33	1.60	1.61	1.27	.96	.90	.36	Claims on Other Financial Insts.	12f
	21.63	26.34	28.63	42.03	57.34	51.76	73.29	86.60	94.92	80.98	82.06	99.17	105.65	121.40	120.40	Reserve Money	14
	19.90	24.83	27.03	31.74	31.24	30.97	43.43	43.71	49.31	53.28	58.69	60.94	66.24	78.48	94.91	of which: Currency Outside DMBs	14a
	8.77	9.23	11.10	11.41	14.62	14.50	20.37	19.15	17.80	12.67	10.76	12.81	11.35	14.94	33.60	Foreign Liabilities	16c
	3.52	1.27	2.69	7.23	4.77	5.24	2.61	4.03	4.02	4.10	5.33	5.53	5.59	8.43	19.45	Central Government Deposits	16d
	-1.23	-.92	-.37	-.83	-1.49	.95	-.08	2.20	3.45	3.20	3.77	3.99	3.95	4.11	-1.43	Other Items (Net)	17r
	End of Period															**Deposit Money Banks**	
	1.62	1.40	1.96	10.23	25.85	20.19	29.27	41.92	42.37	26.17	22.32	36.35	37.68	41.04	20.95	Reserves	20
	1.58	1.01	.93	1.94	2.80	3.40	3.32	9.30	9.35	12.60	14.09	10.03	13.38	15.66	83.13	Foreign Assets	21
	8.65	14.14	13.40	12.47	12.66	6.67	6.82	5.59	6.87	14.69	19.70	15.21	13.99	13.52	35.32	Claims on Central Government	22a
	58.56	64.96	73.38	76.11	74.42	91.15	96.17	102.05	114.51	135.96	141.43	108.40	94.87	87.65	72.27	Claims on Private Sector	22d
	.45	.59	1.16	1.53	1.67	1.69	2.01	1.49	1.51	1.61	—	1.57	1.21	.35	.25	Claims on Other Financial Insts.	22f
	20.33	22.55	25.96	27.29	33.41	36.36	39.75	44.09	47.25	48.47	42.07	45.80	41.39	42.00	69.84	Demand Deposits	24
	11.55	14.89	17.02	19.73	26.26	23.78	28.77	36.33	47.83	48.89	49.87	51.01	56.80	57.37	62.55	Time Deposits	25
	8.40	11.48	13.54	17.09	12.84	14.52	9.82	9.50	9.16	10.25	14.47	11.16	6.42	6.95	12.19	Foreign Liabilities	26c
	4.36	4.39	4.28	4.43	2.71	2.66	3.53	4.00	4.68	6.47	4.95	6.10	5.45	5.57	9.03	Long-Term Foreign Liabilities	26cl
	13.43	17.14	19.15	23.95	28.02	31.13	39.46	53.18	57.92	68.59	75.82	51.37	50.90	47.82	59.00	Central Government Deposits	26d
	11.80	8.94	10.54	11.20	9.61	7.01	7.50	8.09	4.45	4.30	3.89	9.00	9.00	9.00	—	Credit from Monetary Authorities	26g
	1.07	2.71	.34	-1.41	4.54	7.65	8.76	5.15	3.33	4.07	6.48	-2.88	-8.82	-10.51	-.68	Other Items (Net)	27r
	1.58	1.76	2.49	1.92	1.81	2.60	2.43	2.61	2.61	2.08	2.13	2.06	2.20	.90	1.56	Treasury Claims: Private Sector	22d. i
	1.43	1.45	1.37	1.31	1.84	1.98	2.14	2.79	1.75	2.21	2.26	1.90	1.90	1.61	2.37	Post Office: Checking Deposits	24.. i
	End of Period															**Monetary Survey**	
	-.19	.66	-2.94	8.92	26.32	27.14	48.49	66.77	79.59	66.51	65.92	75.69	89.58	106.45	164.17	Foreign Assets (Net)	31n
	57.72	69.35	78.22	73.38	72.44	77.80	78.40	72.46	81.25	101.61	103.21	93.05	79.03	74.07	76.96	Domestic Credit	32
	-3.38	1.55	.57	-6.94	-6.25	-18.41	-23.33	-34.87	-38.71	-39.64	-41.96	-20.25	-20.21	-15.73	2.52	Claims on Central Govt. (Net)	32an
	60.24	66.72	75.87	78.03	76.22	93.75	98.59	104.66	117.12	138.04	143.56	110.46	97.07	88.55	73.83	Claims on Private Sector	32d
	.86	1.08	1.78	2.29	2.47	2.46	3.13	2.67	2.84	3.20	1.61	2.84	2.18	1.24	.61	Claims on Other Financial Insts.	32f
	41.67	48.83	54.36	60.33	66.51	69.54	85.43	91.18	100.87	105.28	103.63	109.34	110.57	122.61	170.32	Money	34
	11.55	14.89	17.02	19.73	26.26	23.78	28.77	36.33	47.83	48.89	49.87	51.01	56.80	57.37	62.55	Quasi-Money	35
	4.36	4.39	4.28	4.43	2.71	2.66	3.53	4.00	4.68	6.47	4.95	6.10	5.45	5.57	9.03	Long-Term Foreign Liabilities	36cl
	-.05	1.90	-.39	-2.19	3.29	8.96	9.15	7.72	7.47	7.48	10.69	2.29	-4.19	-5.03	-.77	Other Items (Net)	37r
	53.22	63.72	71.38	80.06	92.77	93.33	114.19	127.51	148.69	154.17	153.49	160.35	167.36	179.98	232.88	Money plus Quasi-Money	35l
	End of Period															**Other Banking Institutions**	
	3.81	4.27	4.36	4.25	4.08	5.47	6.58	6.69	6.68	6.80	6.56	6.63	10.17	....	....	Savings Deposits	45
	57.02	67.99	75.74	84.31	96.85	98.79	120.77	134.20	155.37	160.97	160.05	166.98	177.54	....	....	Liquid Liabilities	55l
	Percent Per Annum															**Interest Rates**	
	10.50	10.50	12.50	10.50	10.50	10.50	8.50	8.50	9.50	11.00	11.00	11.00	12.50	10.50	10.00	Discount Rate (End of Period)	60
	10.55	13.68	14.66	12.23	11.84	10.67	8.58	8.37	8.72	10.07	10.98	10.94	11.44	....	....	Money Market Rate	60b
	6.19	6.25	7.75	7.50	7.25	7.25	6.08	5.25	5.25	6.42	7.00	7.00	7.75	....	....	Deposit Rate	60l
	14.50	14.50	16.00	14.50	14.50	14.50	13.50	13.50	13.58	15.13	16.00	16.00	16.75	....	....	Lending Rate	60p
	Period Averages															**Prices**	
	70.1	75.4	84.4	I91.5	95.9	102.5	99.9	97.2	101.1	100.8	100.0	102.5	100.5	101.0	126.5	Consumer Prices	64

Burkina Faso

748

		1965	1966	1967	1968	1969	1970	1971	1972	1973	1974	1975	1976	1977	1978	1979
International Transactions																*Billions of Francs*
Exports	70	3.68	3.99	4.43	5.29	5.33	5.06	4.41	5.14	5.60	8.70	9.37	12.69	13.61	9.60	16.24
Imports, cif	71	9.17	9.29	8.97	10.80	13.99	13.70	15.61	17.27	21.69	34.66	32.39	34.42	51.36	51.08	63.92
Imports, fob	71.v	7.28	7.38	7.12	8.57	11.08	10.88	12.43	13.66	17.37	28.42	26.37	27.61	41.60	42.26	51.73
																1985=100
Unit Value of Exports	74	....	25.4	25.5	25.3	27.4	23.0	24.1	22.8	25.1	37.0	Ɪ37.3	48.0	53.8	51.2	52.5
Unit Value of Imports	75	....	20.5	21.3	20.7	22.4	21.7	23.7	25.9	27.7	34.7	Ɪ40.2	45.7	50.2	49.1	52.9
Balance of Payments																*Millions of US Dollars*
Goods: Exports f.o.b.	78aa d	....	....	....	....	....	....	....	....	....	66.0	73.5	83.1	94.8	107.8	132.7
Goods: Imports f.o.b.	78ab d	....	....	....	....	....	....	....	....	....	-147.8	-187.8	-167.4	-220.7	-255.4	-312.1
Trade Balance	78ac d	....	....	....	....	....	....	....	....	....	-81.8	-114.3	-84.4	-125.9	-147.6	-179.4
Services: Credit	78ad d	....	....	....	....	....	....	....	....	....	9.4	14.3	17.0	17.5	23.7	41.6
Services: Debit	78ae d	....	....	....	....	....	....	....	....	....	-51.5	-74.2	-77.2	-95.1	-135.2	-178.6
Balance on Goods and Services	78af d	....	....	....	....	....	....	....	....	....	-123.9	-174.2	-144.5	-203.5	-259.1	-316.5
Income: Credit	78ag d	....	....	....	....	....	....	....	....	....	9.0	7.4	6.4	6.2	4.9	7.1
Income: Debit	78ah d	....	....	....	....	....	....	....	....	....	-11.3	-19.3	-15.8	-26.2	-15.5	-16.0
Balance on Goods, Serv., & Inc.	78ai d	....	....	....	....	....	....	....	....	....	-126.1	-186.1	-153.9	-223.4	-269.7	-325.5
Current Transfers, n.i.e.: Credit	78aj d	....	....	....	....	....	....	....	....	....	134.9	157.3	147.9	171.9	255.6	315.3
Current Transfers: Debit	78ak d	....	....	....	....	....	....	....	....	....	-14.0	-25.4	-27.5	-32.8	-45.4	-53.6
Current Account, n.i.e.	78al d	....	....	....	....	....	....	....	....	....	-5.3	-54.3	-33.5	-84.3	-59.5	-63.8
Capital Account, n.i.e.: Credit	78ba d	....	....	....	....	....	....	....	....	....	—	—	—	—	—	—
Capital Account: Debit	78bb d	....	....	....	....	....	....	....	....	....	—	—	—	—	—	—
Capital Account, n.i.e.	78bc d	....	....	....	....	....	....	....	....	....	—	—	—	—	—	—
Direct Investment Abroad	78bd d	....	....	....	....	....	....	....	....	....	-.4	-.7	-.3	-.4	-.8	-.4
Dir. Invest. in Rep. Econ., n.i.e.	78be d	....	....	....	....	....	....	....	....	....	2.7	.3	2.1	5.0	1.2	1.5
Portfolio Investment Assets	78bf d	....	....	....	....	....	....	....	....	....	-.6	-.8	-.9	-1.4	.4	—
Portfolio Investment Liab., n.i.e.	78bg d	....	....	....	....	....	....	....	....	....	.2	.2	1.2	.1	.4	—
Other Investment Assets	78bh d	....	....	....	....	....	....	....	....	....	-4.6	7.1	-7.5	-2.1	-2.0	-3.6
Other Investment Liab., n.i.e.	78bi d	....	....	....	....	....	....	....	....	....	22.5	26.5	38.1	54.1	28.5	69.9
Financial Account, n.i.e.	78bj d	....	....	....	....	....	....	....	....	....	19.9	32.6	32.7	55.3	27.7	67.5
Net Errors and Omissions	78ca d	....	....	....	....	....	....	....	....	....	1.7	15.5	1.3	9.2	.6	4.6
Overall Balance	78cb d	....	....	....	....	....	....	....	....	....	16.3	-6.3	.5	-19.8	-31.2	8.3
Reserves and Related Items	79da d	....	....	....	....	....	....	....	....	....	-16.3	6.3	-.5	19.8	31.2	-8.3
Reserve Assets	79db d	....	....	....	....	....	....	....	....	....	-16.3	6.3	-1.5	18.4	24.6	-20.6
Use of Fund Credit and Loans	79dc d	....	....	....	....	....	....	....	....	....	—	—	—	—	6.7	5.1
Liabs.Constit.For.Auth.Reserves	79dd d	....	....	....	....	....	....	....	....	....	—	—	—	—	—	—
Exceptional Financing	79de d	....	....	....	....	....	....	....	....	....	—	—	1.0	1.3	—	7.2
Government Finance																*Millions of Francs:*
Deficit (-) or Surplus	80	....	....	....	....	....	....	....	....	354	2,212	-1,664	-1,272	Ɪ4,313	1,495	-5,622
Revenue	81	....	....	....	....	....	....	....	....	12,111	14,998	15,235	20,630	Ɪ27,965	32,235	34,071
Grants Received	81z	....	....	....	....	....	....	....	....	751	975	550	800	Ɪ800	—	1,000
Adj. Unalloc. Revenue & Grants	81c	....	....	....	....	....	....	....	....	—	—	877	335	Ɪ2,649	307	480
Expenditure	82	....	....	....	....	....	....	....	....	11,804	13,181	16,246	20,963	Ɪ26,954	30,734	40,319
Lending Minus Repayments	83	....	....	....	....	....	....	....	....	704	580	2,080	2,074	Ɪ147	313	854
Financing																
Domestic	84a	....	....	....	....	....	....	....	....	....	....	....	....	....	....	....
Foreign	85a	....	....	....	....	....	....	....	....	....	....	....	....	....	....	....
Unclassified Financing	87c	....	....	....	....	....	....	....	....	....	....	....	....	....	....	....
National Accounts																*Billions of Francs*
Exports of Goods and Services	90c	6.0	6.7	....	7.0	....	8.6	9.1	11.6	11.8	18.7	18.4	23.9	27.4	29.0	36.2
Government Consumption	91f	6.3	6.0	....	10.5	....	7.9	8.5	9.5	10.9	13.4	23.2	21.2	26.5	30.0	49.2
Gross Fixed Capital Formation	93e	7.0	7.0	....	6.7	....	7.5	12.2	15.5	20.0	28.8	29.5	33.2	35.9	39.2	74.8
Increase/Decrease (-) in Stocks	93i	1.6	1.5	....	.8	—	2.3	2.7	3.5	3.3	6.0	5.6	6.2	5.1	6.8	5.0
Private Consumption	96f	46.8	48.9	....	67.0	....	92.1	94.6	99.2	96.9	106.9	113.4	118.9	161.9	196.7	192.1
Imports of Goods and Services	98c	-11.3	-11.9	....	-13.1	....	-19.6	-25.5	-29.9	-33.2	-42.8	-52.4	-54.0	-71.9	-79.2	-104.8
Gross Domestic Product	99b	56.4	58.2	....	79.0	83.9	98.7	101.6	109.4	109.7	131.0	137.7	149.4	184.9	222.5	252.5
Net Factor Inc/Pmts(-) Abroad	98.n	1.7	2.2	.1	-2.1	-2.1	-10.1	-13.0	-2.2	-.2	-.2	.3	.5	-.8	-1.5	-1.3
Gross Nat'l Expenditure = GNP	99a	58.1	60.4	....	76.9	81.8	88.6	88.6	107.2	109.5	130.8	138.0	149.4	184.1	221.1	252.2
Gross Dom. Prod. 1985 Prices	99b.p	....	....	....	....	....	....	....	....	....	....	....	....	....	....	380.9
GDP Deflator (1985=100)	99bi p	....	....	....	....	....	....	....	....	....	....	....	....	....	....	68.2
																Millions:
Population	99z	4.86	4.96	5.05	5.18	5.28	5.38	5.49	5.61	Ɪ5.45	5.54	5.64	5.74	5.84	5.94	6.04

Deposit Money Banks: Ɪ Beginning in October 1979, *Central Government Deposits* include the deposits of public establishments of an administrative or social nature (EPAS) and exclude those of the savings bank; *Demand* and *Time Deposits* include deposits of the savings bank and exclude deposits of EPAS; and *Claims on Private Sector* exclude claims on other financial institutions.
   Monetary Survey: Ɪ Beginning in October 1979, *line 32f* includes claims of deposit money banks on other financial institutions; see deposit money bank notes for explanation of other break symbols.

Government Finance: Ɪ Beginning in 1977, annual data cover social security funds in addition to budgetary accounts. Ɪ Beginning in 1985, data also cover extrabudgetary accounts.

Burkina Faso

	1980	1981	1982	1983	1984	1985	1986	1987	1988	1989	1990	1991	1992	1993	1994		
Billions of Francs																**International Transactions**	
	19.07	19.92	18.11	21.71	34.87	31.16	28.67	46.59	41.95	30.28	41.28	29.89	....	....	....	Exports	70
	75.61	91.44	114.01	109.57	111.26	146.24	139.64	130.53	134.94	125.35	145.83	150.26	....	....	....	Imports, cif	71
	59.13	71.33	88.93	85.47	86.79	114.07	108.92	101.82	105.26	97.78	113.75	117.20	....	....	....	Imports, fob	71.v
1985=100																	
	57.2	63.1	72.7	82.7	85.1	100.0	70.4	72.9	70.9	....	....	....	....	....	....	Unit Value of Exports	74
	55.9	67.2	81.7	89.5	93.0	100.0	96.0	85.5	84.6	....	....	....	....	....	....	Unit Value of Imports	75
Minus Sign Indicates Debit																**Balance of Payments**	
	160.6	159.4	126.4	112.9	140.9	135.6	149.0	229.9	249.1	229.8	272.2	283.2	287.5	276.5	....	Goods: Exports f.o.b.	78aa *d*
	−368.3	−348.4	−359.9	−308.9	−270.1	−352.8	−437.5	−475.2	−486.8	−501.6	−593.2	−601.5	−642.3	−643.4	....	Goods: Imports f.o.b.	78ab *d*
	−207.7	−189.1	−233.4	−196.0	−129.2	−217.2	−288.5	−245.2	−237.7	−271.8	−321.0	−318.3	−354.8	−366.9	....	Trade Balance	78ac *d*
	49.1	40.9	48.3	37.7	27.1	27.1	39.7	34.9	34.9	39.5	49.6	48.6	56.3	50.7	....	Services: Credit	78ad *d*
	−209.0	−185.1	−174.0	−146.9	−124.3	−129.3	−147.8	−185.0	−208.2	−208.8	−249.4	−246.7	−263.7	−259.8	....	Services: Debit	78ae *d*
	−367.6	−333.6	−359.2	−305.2	−226.4	−319.5	−396.6	−395.3	−410.9	−441.1	−520.8	−516.5	−562.2	−576.0	....	Balance on Goods and Services	78af *d*
	15.6	8.9	9.0	5.9	7.0	9.8	12.1	14.0	14.1	13.2	15.4	14.9	16.6	15.5	....	Income: Credit	78ag *d*
	−19.1	−18.4	−19.2	−16.0	−14.4	−16.5	−33.6	−28.3	−27.2	−28.5	−23.5	−30.8	−28.0	−29.7	....	Income: Debit	78ah *d*
	−371.1	−343.1	−369.4	−315.2	−233.8	−326.2	−418.1	−409.6	−424.0	−456.4	−528.9	−532.4	−573.5	−590.2	....	Balance on Goods, Serv., & Inc.	78ai *d*
	387.2	354.3	319.9	301.2	270.9	310.2	453.2	442.9	460.4	576.5	511.6	510.8	568.6	555.5	....	Current Transfers, n.i.e.: Credit	78aj *d*
	−64.8	−53.2	−42.6	−46.1	−40.5	−44.2	−55.8	−84.2	−85.6	−87.5	−84.8	−82.6	−92.2	−83.3	....	Current Transfers: Debit	78ak *d*
	−48.7	−42.1	−92.1	−60.1	−3.5	−60.1	−20.7	−50.9	−49.3	32.6	−102.1	−104.2	−97.1	−118.0	....	Current Account, n.i.e.	78al *d*
	—	—	—	—	—	—	—	—	—	—	—	—	—	—	....	Capital Account, n.i.e.: Credit	78ba *d*
	—	—	—	—	—	—	—	—	—	—	—	—	—	—	....	Capital Account: Debit	78bb *d*
	—	—	—	—	—	—	—	—	—	—	—	—	—	—	....	Capital Account, n.i.e.	78bc *d*
	—	—	−.2	—	—	—	—	—	—	—	—	—	—	—	....	Direct Investment Abroad	78bd *d*
	—	2.4	1.9	2.0	1.7	−1.4	3.1	—	—	—	—	—	—	—	....	Dir. Invest. in Rep. Econ., n.i.e.	78be *d*
	−1.1	−.2	.9	.4	—	1.2	1.3	—	—	—	—	—	—	—	....	Portfolio Investment Assets	78bf *d*
	.5	—	—	—	—	—	—	—	—	—	—	—	—	—	....	Portfolio Investment Liab., n.i.e.	78bg *d*
	−13.1	−4.4	−7.0	−10.7	−7.5	−1.9	−26.0	−19.9	−.2	−10.2	−5.5	14.4	−12.7	−8.1	....	Other Investment Assets	78bh *d*
	77.0	66.6	80.9	95.5	38.9	68.3	81.3	93.6	76.1	−189.7	95.0	119.1	137.0	121.6	....	Other Investment Liab., n.i.e.	78bi *d*
	63.3	64.4	76.5	87.2	33.1	66.2	59.6	73.7	76.0	−199.9	89.5	133.5	124.3	113.5	....	Financial Account, n.i.e.	78bj *d*
	−7.9	−8.1	15.4	9.5	6.2	−.4	3.0	−5.3	−2.4	19.2	−5.2	18.8	−9.0	21.9	....	Net Errors and Omissions	78ca *d*
	6.6	14.2	−.2	36.6	35.9	5.7	41.9	17.5	24.3	−148.0	−17.7	48.1	18.3	17.4	....	Overall Balance	78cb *d*
	−6.6	−14.2	.2	−36.6	−35.9	−5.7	−41.9	−17.5	−24.3	148.0	17.7	−48.1	−18.3	−17.4	....	Reserves and Related Items	79da *d*
	−10.9	−14.3	.2	−36.3	−34.8	−5.5	−66.1	−36.5	−35.9	62.7	−1.6	−44.3	−16.0	−64.9	....	Reserve Assets	79db *d*
	4.3	.1	—	−.2	−1.1	−2.2	−3.0	−3.3	−3.1	−1.9	−.5	8.7	—	12.5	....	Use of Fund Credit and Loans	79dc *d*
	—	—	—	—	—	—	—	—	—	—	—	—	—	—	....	Liabs.Constit.For.Auth.Reserves	79dd *d*
	—	—	—	—	2.0	27.1	22.3	14.8	87.1	19.8	−12.4	−2.3	35.0	—	....	Exceptional Financing	79de *d*
Year Ending December 31																**Government Finance**	
	879	−4,674	−6,185	562	−3,350	I6,339	−747	1,976	....	....	....	....	....	....	....	Deficit (−) or Surplus	80
	42,461	45,809	54,170	53,529	62,278	I70,798	78,967	89,852	....	....	....	....	....	....	....	Revenue	81
	678	2,911	390	1,011	810	I790	273	112	....	....	....	....	....	....	....	Grants Received	81z
						I										Adj. Unalloc. Revenue & Grants	81c
	44,047	50,063	63,037	52,614	64,691	I62,883	77,659	85,377	....	....	....	....	....	....	....	Expenditure	82
	−1,787	3,331	−2,292	1,364	1,747	I2,366	2,328	2,611	....	....	....	....	....	....	....	Lending Minus Repayments	83
Financing																	
	−132	4,548	4,289	760	4,314	....	....	....	....	....	....	....	....	....	....	Domestic	84a
	1,305	2,900	4,031	2,053	3,346	....	....	....	....	....	....	....	....	....	....	Foreign	85a
	−2,052	−2,774	−2,135	−3,375	−4,310	....	....	....	....	....	....	....	....	....	....	Unclassified Financing	87c
Billion of Francs																**National Accounts**	
	43.6	53.6	56.2	55.9	88.1	79.1	....	....	....	....	....	....	....	....	....	Exports of Goods and Services	90c
	47.4	60.9	72.5	78.8	76.9	72.6	....	....	....	....	....	....	....	....	....	Government Consumption	91f
	66.0	69.9	84.0	90.3	90.8	113.5	....	....	....	....	....	....	....	....	....	Gross Fixed Capital Formation	93e
	6.4	7.2	7.8	2.6	3.3	15.5	....	....	....	....	....	....	....	....	....	Increase/Decrease (−) in Stocks	93i
	231.3	278.7	315.1	327.6	308.3	398.5	....	....	....	....	....	....	....	....	....	Private Consumption	96f
	−122.7	−146.1	−176.0	−174.2	−176.8	−223.3	....	....	....	....	....	....	....	....	....	Imports of Goods and Services	98c
	272.0	324.2	359.6	381.0	390.6	455.9	....	....	....	....	....	....	....	....	....	Gross Domestic Product	99b
	1.1	−.5	−1.0	−.7	−.8	−15.2	....	....	....	....	....	....	....	....	....	Net Factor Inc/Pmts(−) Abroad	98.n
	273.1	323.7	358.6	380.3	389.8	440.7	....	....	....	....	....	....	....	....	....	Gross Nat'l Expenditure = GNP	99a
	387.2	404.3	413.3	408.4	415.0	469.3	....	....	....	....	....	....	....	....	....	Gross Dom. Prod. 1985 Prices	99b.*p*
	72.3	82.5	89.6	96.0	96.9	100.0	....	....	....	....	....	....	....	....	....	GDP Deflator (1985=100)	99bi *p*
Midyear Estimates																	
	6.91	7.09	7.28	7.48	7.68	7.89	8.10	8.31	8.54	8.77	9.00	9.19	9.43	9.68	9.89	Population	99z

Burundi

618

		1965	1966	1967	1968	1969	1970	1971	1972	1973	1974	1975	1976	1977	1978	1979
Exchange Rates															*Francs per SDR:*	
Official Rate	aa	87.50	87.50	87.50	87.50	87.50	87.50	95.00	95.00	95.00	96.42	92.19	104.56	109.32	117.25	118.56
															Francs per US Dollar:	
Official Rate	ae	87.50	87.50	87.50	87.50	87.50	87.50	87.50	87.50	78.75	78.75	78.75	90.00	90.00	90.00	90.00
Official Rate	rf	84.38	87.50	87.50	87.50	87.50	87.50	87.50	87.50	80.03	78.75	78.75	86.25	90.00	90.00	90.00
													Index Numbers (1990=100):			
Official Rate	ah x	205.3	195.5	195.5	195.5	195.5	195.5	137.8	195.5	214.0	217.2	217.2	199.1	190.0	190.0	190.0
Nominal Effective Exchange Rate	ne c	....	....	....	....	....	....	....	....	....	....	....	....	....	....	146.3
Real Effective Exchange Rate	re c	....	....	....	....	....	....	....	....	....	....	....	....	....	....	140.8
Fund Position															*Millions of SDRs:*	
Quota	2f. s	11.25	15.00	15.00	15.00	15.00	19.00	19.00	19.00	19.00	19.00	19.00	19.00	19.00	23.00	23.00
SDRs	1b. s	—	—	—	—	—	2.18	1.81	3.65	3.60	3.56	3.24	3.03	2.82	2.76	5.32
Reserve Position in the Fund	1c. s	.13	.14	.33	—	—	—	—	.28	.39	—	—	—	—	4.75	4.47
Total Fund Cred.&Loans Outstg.	2tl	—	—	—	2.47	5.78	7.67	5.34	—	—	—	—	1.20	1.21	3.25	7.87	23.13
International Liquidity												*Millions of US Dollars Unless Otherwise Indicated:*				
Total Reserves minus Gold	1l. d	9.22	7.04	5.05	2.91	7.42	15.36	17.69	18.49	21.48	14.19	30.71	49.03	94.41	81.30	89.99
SDRs	1b. d	—	—	—	—	—	2.18	1.97	3.96	4.34	4.36	3.79	3.52	3.43	3.60	7.01
Reserve Position in the Fund	1c. d	.13	.14	.33	—	—	—	—	.30	.47	—	—	—	—	6.19	5.89
Foreign Exchange	1d. d	9.09	6.90	4.72	2.91	7.42	13.18	15.72	14.22	16.67	9.83	26.92	45.51	90.98	71.52	77.09
Gold (Million Fine Troy Ounces)	1ad	....	....	—	.001	.001	.001	.001	.001	.001	.001	.001	.001	.009	.009	.013
Gold (National Valuation)	1an d	....	....	—	.03	.03	.03	.03ᵉ	....	....	.16	.13	.13	1.50	2.05	8.87
Monetary Authorities: Other Liab.	4..d	1.02	1.82	2.74	3.87	7.44	9.09	7.15	2.29	.97	1.91	4.41	5.98	7.04	5.24	22.60
Deposit Money Banks: Assets	7a. d	1.61	1.10	1.12	1.67	1.42	2.13	2.38	2.12	1.96	3.00	1.75	2.99	3.57	5.57	8.07
Deposit Money Banks: Liabilities	7b. d	.65	.25	.21	.48	.66	.70	.66	2.03	1.31	2.27	2.71	4.35	3.85	4.49	3.57
of which: Liab. to Nonbanks	7bd d	....	....	—	—	—	—	—	—	—	—	—	—	—	—	—
Other Banking Insts.: Assets	7e. d	....	....	....	....	....	....	....	....	....	....	....	.65	2.38	4.23	4.65	6.70
Liabilities	7f. d	....	....	....	....	....	....	....	....	....	....	....	....	....	....	—
Monetary Authorities															*Millions of Francs:*	
Foreign Assets	11	806	616	I442	257	652	1,347	1,550	1,621	1,695	1,130	2,429	4,424	8,632	7,502	8,897
Claims on Central Government	12a	329	506	I563	772	781	855	705	833	1,031	1,192	860	1,509	1,880	2,909	5,170
Claims on Nonfin.Pub.Enterprises	12c	—	—	I—	—	—	—	—	—	—	—	—	5	5	5	14
Claims on Private Sector	12d	—	—	I76	105	120	127	126	127	135	27	26	32	65	93	116
Claims on Deposit Money Banks	12e	—	—	I—	105	—	4	113	83	46	959	—	16	—	—	1,166
Claims on Other Financial Insts.	12f	—	5	I10	10	28	10	10	10	10	10	70	26	108	306	155
Reserve Money	14	1,214	1,106	I1,099	1,122	1,158	1,332	1,547	1,631	1,753	2,103	2,052	3,452	4,788	5,617	5,346
of which: Currency Outside DMBs	14a	854	900	I1,013	1,037	1,032	1,192	1,333	1,370	1,548	1,873	1,710	2,411	3,225	4,542	4,876
Nonfin.Pub.Ent. Deps.	14e	—	—	33	29	72	111	164	112	91	207	117	612	478	514	407
Bonds	16ab	....	....	—	39	38	134	127	147	166	243	233	349	259	364	889
Restricted Deposits	16b	90	85	I67	65	48	101	93	186	212	238	183	345	546	683	530
Stabilization Fund	16bb	....	....	—	—	2	15	48	55	20	128	2	413	1,727	470	1,065
Foreign Liabilities	16c	89	159	I240	339	651	796	625	200	76	151	347	539	846	1,341	3,603
Long-Term Foreign Liabilities	16cl	....	....	....	100	113	113	113	129	140	—	—	—	—	2	4
Central Government Deposits	16d	106	78	I74	99	83	161	227	251	410	399	332	1,076	2,197	1,718	1,773
Capital Accounts	17a	....	....	713	676	673	724	773	1,036	996	934	1,241	992	1,741	2,529	3,989
Other Items (Net)	17r	-363	-301	I-1,170	-1,164	-1,136	-942	-1,050	-960	-855	-876	-1,003	-1,153	-1,413	-1,239	-1,639
Deposit Money Banks																
Commercial Banks															*Millions of Francs:*	
Reserves	20	357	207	I61	55	55	29	48	150	109	22	237	448	1,379	457	108
Foreign Assets	21	141	96	I98	147	125	186	208	186	154	237	138	269	321	501	727
Claims on Central Government	22a	5	7	124	162	249	163	263	233	311	162	713	680	462	103	203
Claims on Nonfin.Pub.Enterprises	22c	....	....	....	....	....	....	....	....	....	....	....	....	....	....	....
Claims on Private Sector	22d	348	363	I451	483	366	698	932	945	1,149	2,459	932	1,454	1,507	3,309	5,106
Claims on Other Financial Insts.	22f	....	....	24	23	28	19	19	19	15	15	15	15	15	15	15
Demand Deposits	24	465	364	I559	569	577	759	891	1,035	1,274	1,485	1,507	2,201	2,779	3,274	3,834
Savings Deposits	25	79	86	I52	53	78	138	124	131	295	199	274	256	529	725	639
Foreign Liabilities	26c	57	22	I19	42	58	61	57	177	103	179	214	391	346	404	289
Central Government Deposits	26d	—	—	I—	21	19	34	41	30	38	48	8	10	8	3	4
Credit from Monetary Authorities	26g	—	—	I—	88	—	4	13	83	—	966	3	—	—	—	1,197
Capital Accounts	27a	116	136	I140	144	152	159	164	168	233	252	265	307	313	301	402
Other Items (Net)	27r	134	64	I-58	-2	-20	14	254	80	26	-28	68	109	62	120	197
Other Monetary Institutions															*Millions of Francs:*	
Reserves	20..h	....	....	....	....	....	....	....	....	....	....	23	49	63	198	889
Claims on Central Government	22a.h	....	....	....	....	....	....	....	....	....	....	....	....	....	....	111
Claims on Nonfin.Pub.Enterprise	22c.h	....	....	....	....	....	....	....	....	....	....	....	....	....	....	....
Claims on Private Sector	22d.h	4	5	12	15	28	26	34	29	37	37	43	68	112	296	I391
Claims on Other Financial Insts.	22f.h	....	....	....	....	....	....	....	....	....	....	....	....	....	....	101
Demand Deposits	24..h	....	....	7	5	4	8	6	8	10	10	13	14	43	45	456
Time and Savings Deposits	25..h	60	76	98	110	139	135	157	117	98	100	153	283	536	1,021	1,508
Foreign Liabilities	26c.h	....	....	....	....	....	....	....	....	....	....	....	....	....	....	33
Central Government Deposits	26d.h	....	....	8	6	9	10	9	11	21	26	50	86	96	154	472
Cred.from Monetary Authorities	26g.h	....	....	....	....	....	....	....	....	....	....	....	....	....	....	....
Other Items (Net)	27r.h	....	....	....	....	....	....	....	....	....	....	....	....	....	....	20
Monetary Survey															*Millions of Francs:*	
Foreign Assets (Net)	31n	801	531	I351	23	68	676	1,076	1,429	1,670	1,037	2,007	3,763	7,760	6,258	5,700
Domestic Credit	32	589	810	I1,179	1,439	1,474	1,684	1,793	1,895	2,213	3,429	2,293	2,664	2,166	6,159	10,960
Claims on Central Govt. (Net)	32an	241	442	I620	819	932	831	706	794	905	918	1,246	1,116	180	1,336	3,718
Claims on Nonfin.Pub.Enterprises	32c	—	—	I—	—	—	—	—	—	—	—	—	55	21	291	1,101	1,358
Claims on Private Sector	32d	348	363	I526	587	486	824	1,057	1,072	1,283	2,486	958	1,487	1,572	3,401	5,613
Claims on Other Financial Insts.	32f	....	5	34	33	56	29	29	29	25	25	35	41	123	321	270
Money	34	1,332	1,271	I1,608	1,610	1,653	2,001	2,321	2,310	2,825	3,307	3,209	4,548	6,155	8,406	9,058
Quasi-Money	35	79	86	I52	53	78	138	124	131	163	144	141	165	396	496	419
Long-Term Foreign Liabilities	36cl	....	....	....	100	113	113	113	129	140	—	—	—	—	2	4
Other Items (Net)	37r	-20	-17	I-249	-279	-262	114	157	772	757	946	807	1,589	3,194	3,287	6,392
Money plus Quasi-Money	35l	1,411	1,357	I1,659	1,662	1,731	2,138	2,444	2,440	2,988	3,451	3,350	4,713	6,550	8,902	9,477

Burundi

	1980	1981	1982	1983	1984	1985	1986	1987	1988	1989	1990	1991	1992	1993	1994		
Exchange Rates																	
End of Period																	
	114.79	104.76	99.28	122.70	122.70	122.70	151.50	161.00	201.00	232.14	232.14	273.07	322.90	362.99	360.78	Official Rate	aa
End of Period (ae) Period Average (rf)																	
	90.00	90.00	90.00	117.41	124.95	111.97	124.17	114.47	149.94	175.43	165.35	191.10	236.55	264.38	246.94	Official Rate	ae
	90.00	90.00	90.00	92.95	119.71	120.69	114.17	123.56	140.40	158.67	171.26	181.51	208.30	242.78	252.66	Official Rate	rf
Period Averages																	
	190.0	190.0	190.0	185.0	142.9	141.9	150.3	138.5	122.9	107.9	100.0	94.8	82.3	70.5	67.7	Official Rate	ahx
	146.5	174.0	198.5	212.2	182.8	190.7	167.0	138.6	121.8	116.3	100.0	97.8	83.0	77.5	73.9	Nominal Effective Exchange Rate	nec
	129.8	156.5	172.3	185.9	172.3	175.9	151.1	129.4	113.8	115.2	100.0	100.5	84.6	81.9	85.1	Real Effective Exchange Rate	rec
Fund Position																	
End of Period																	
	34.50	34.50	34.50	42.70	42.70	42.70	42.70	42.70	42.70	42.70	42.70	42.70	57.20	57.20	57.20	Quota	2f.s
	4.14	5.53	4.16	.99	.11	.11	.53	.04	.08	.01	.04	2.62	1.08	.51	.14	SDRs	1b.s
	7.34	7.34	7.37	9.42	9.42	9.16	9.16	9.16	9.16	9.16	7.55	7.24	5.86	5.86	5.86	Reserve Position in the Fund	1c.s
	28.00	28.07	27.97	22.69	16.36	13.24	18.08	14.48	24.12	30.54	29.96	34.16	47.39	44.40	40.13	Total Fund Cred.&Loans Outstg.	2tl
International Liquidity																	
End of Period																	
	94.50	61.30	29.49	26.94	19.73	29.47	69.07	60.73	69.38	99.62	105.04	141.38	174.17	162.98	204.70	Total Reserves minus Gold	1l.d
	5.28	6.44	4.59	1.04	.11	.12	.65	.06	.11	.01	.06	3.75	1.49	.70	.21	SDRs	1b.d
	9.36	8.54	8.13	9.86	9.23	10.06	11.20	12.99	12.33	12.04	10.74	10.36	8.06	8.05	8.56	Reserve Position in the Fund	1c.d
	79.86	46.32	16.77	16.04	10.39	19.29	57.22	47.68	56.95	87.57	94.24	127.28	164.63	154.23	195.94	Foreign Exchange	1d.d
	.017	.017	.017	.017	.017	.017	.017	.017	.017	.017	.017	.017	.017	.017	.017	Gold (Million Fine Troy Ounces)	1ad
	10.15	6.85	7.87	6.60	5.33	5.62	6.93	8.53	7.14	7.03	6.55	6.44	5.79	6.66	6.59	Gold (National Valuation)	1and
	21.29	18.12	19.85	10.56	7.10	4.06	22.65	17.50	29.59	41.18	46.92	52.69	54.84	48.45	42.95	Monetary Authorities: Other Liab.	4..d
	3.47	3.74	1.63	5.64	6.41	5.24	9.70	6.11	5.32	4.46	5.32	6.64	6.51	9.66	19.33	Deposit Money Banks: Assets	7a.d
	6.22	4.24	5.57	9.25	4.46	6.67	9.42	6.32	4.93	3.65	5.50	8.77	8.08	7.70	12.95	Deposit Money Banks: Liabilities	7b.d
	.07	.02	.05	3.96	3.78	3.98	6.52	3.81	2.98	1.66	1.76	—	—	—	—	of which: Liab. to Nonbanks	7bd.d
	—	.24	.65	2.73	.81	1.72	1.49	1.31	.79	.84	1.00	....	—	—	—	Other Banking Insts.: Assets	7e.d
	5.87	6.15	5.58	6.28	6.77	7.50	6.92	10.69	11.65	13.23	11.54	12.68	12.24	14.00	18.21	Liabilities	7f.d
Monetary Authorities																	
	9,419	6,134	3,363	3,934	3,134	3,962	9,508	7,881	10,621	18,792	18,270	28,244	43,387	46,912	54,230	Foreign Assets	11
	5,808	7,959	9,299	12,355	14,588	17,119	16,414	17,161	15,837	15,237	15,040	13,450	11,885	9,170	8,698	Claims on Central Government	12a
	1,381	598	482	412	362	324	303	306	312	315	316	25	25	25	25	Claims on Nonfin.Pub.Enterprises	12c
	110	110	111	124	134	148	126	140	213	244	265	276	325	421	420	Claims on Private Sector	12d
	506	3,075	2,095	640	498	51	215	61	2,683	2,153	4,872	2,827	550	3,355	2,538	Claims on Deposit Money Banks	12e
	144	161	510	693	335	112	105	105	117	446	272	915	1,616	1,487	634	Claims on Other Financial Insts.	12f
	5,916	8,145	6,999	8,916	9,607	11,962	12,160	12,176	11,763	12,478	13,068	15,121	16,797	17,617	22,292	Reserve Money	14
	4,972	7,059	6,419	7,262	7,498	7,254	8,008	8,734	9,605	9,868	10,766	....	....	....	....	of which: Currency Outside DMBs	14a
	521	646	372	532	1,222	1,966	2,210	1,416	1,315	1,525	1,302	990	990	1,118	649	Nonfin.Pub.Ent. Deps.	14e
	971	992	568	768	1,032	765	660	886	2,961	1,422	1,481	2,091	2,743	2,174	1,285	Bonds	16ab
	549	750	382	804	766	910	1,109	580	954	1,294	979	1,429	1,123	1,019	842	Restricted Deposits	16b
	547	21	94	338	510	300	1,190	527	1,143	590	1	68	452	4	4	Stabilization Fund	16bb
	4,039	3,576	3,624	3,441	2,895	2,079	4,222	2,962	4,995	7,375	7,775	10,069	12,971	12,809	10,606	Foreign Liabilities	16c
	4	1	—	—	—	—	133	—	—	—	—	—	—	—	—	Long-Term Foreign Liabilities	16cl
	2,113	1,592	1,658	1,548	1,550	2,477	3,022	3,983	3,338	6,533	8,967	6,307	6,966	8,299	7,710	Central Government Deposits	16d
	4,241	3,663	4,052	3,598	3,838	3,644	4,492	4,981	5,717	8,020	6,918	9,730	11,654	12,490	12,242	Capital Accounts	17a
	−1,015	−707	−1,504	−1,237	−1,147	−420	−834	−793	−1,089	−524	−154	922	5,081	6,958	11,563	Other Items (Net)	17r
Deposit Money Banks																	
Commercial Banks																	
End of Period																	
	79	65	71	1,095	595	2,075	463	1,678	353	812	737	2,525	2,469	1,761	2,171	Reserves	20
	312	337	147	662	801	587	1,204	699	798	782	879	1,269	1,539	2,553	4,773	Foreign Assets	21
	4	5	13	49	317	778	776	1,179	1,597	1,157	1,017	901	460	2,441	5,311	Claims on Central Government	22a
	....	....	....	....	2,525	3,576	3,782	3,926	5,398	6,128	7,123	6,338	5,793	1,591	2,749	Claims on Nonfin.Pub.Enterprises	22c
	5,592	8,415	7,422	6,949	14,559	4,812	5,986	5,930	8,839	12,137	16,437	22,500	23,832	31,557	34,022	Claims on Private Sector	22d
	32	32	382	1,070	889	607	231	346	887	827	1,124	346	127	114	142	Claims on Other Financial Insts.	22f
	3,840	3,871	3,927	5,183	5,325	8,185	8,729	8,637	8,768	9,025	10,399	12,462	13,841	14,721	19,095	Demand Deposits	24
	499	1,254	1,453	2,818	2,227	2,432	881	1,382	3,671	7,334	8,067	11,147	10,695	10,185	14,951	Savings Deposits	25
	492	334	453	1,048	531	717	1,140	689	672	593	863	1,636	1,872	1,969	3,155	Foreign Liabilities	26c
	8	4	4	—	—	—	—	—	—	—	—	—	—	—	526	Central Government Deposits	26d
	906	2,884	1,561	48	415	—	250	59	2,821	2,147	4,269	2,845	1,134	4,044	2,602	Credit from Monetary Authorities	26g
	512	583	733	845	919	1,068	1,148	1,180	2,131	2,423	3,211	3,924	5,111	7,085	8,281	Capital Accounts	27a
	518	76	115	−86	−76	−191	116	1,810	−184	322	509	1,866	1,328	1,536	1,008	Other Items (Net)	27r
Other Monetary Institutions																	
End of Period																	
	1,828	373	146	147	294	654	679	304	309	219	303	....	....	....	....	Reserves	20..h
	1,615	1,900	2,199	2,178	2,102	2,269	2,417	2,659	3,067	2,941	2,540	....	....	....	....	Claims on Central Government	22a.h
	305	675	1,178	1,438	1,493	1,458	1,436	1,589	2,021	2,184	2,092	1,776	1,241	1,286	1,071	Claims on Nonfin.Pub.Enterprise	22c.h
	711	739	855	1,107	1,110	1,111	1,737	1,936	1,672	1,699	2,533	....	....	....	....	Claims on Private Sector	22d.h
	200	270	20	20	40	680	70	—	356	116	6	6	6	6	6	Claims on Other Financial Insts.	22f.h
	1,683	887	108	869	718	1,049	962	999	819	694	767	....	....	....	....	Demand Deposits	24..h
	2,345	2,157	3,025	2,775	3,217	3,298	3,557	3,685	4,064	3,498	4,081	....	....	....	....	Time and Savings Deposits	25..h
	69	48	48	38	27	29	29	34	67	47	47	41	41	66	43	Foreign Liabilities	26c.h
	1,676	958	890	933	1,360	1,862	1,982	1,643	2,085	2,442	1,843	....	....	....	....	Central Government Deposits	26d.h
	—	—	472	535	—	—	—	11	—	—	476	189	469	749	303	Cred.from Monetary Authorities	26g.h
	1−130	−93	−145	−260	−286	−234	−279	−140	−612	−986	−1,003	....	....	....	....	Other Items (Net)	27r.h
Monetary Survey																	
End of Period																	
	5,132	2,513	−616	69	482	1,723	5,321	4,895	5,685	11,559	10,464	17,768	30,042	34,621	45,198	Foreign Assets (Net)	31n
	13,106	18,308	19,907	23,915	25,544	28,655	28,377	29,649	34,891	34,458	37,954	....	....	....	....	Domestic Credit	32
	4,630	7,309	8,959	12,101	14,097	15,828	14,602	15,373	15,078	10,360	7,787	....	....	....	....	Claims on Central Govt. (Net)	32an
	1,687	1,273	1,660	1,850	4,379	5,357	5,521	5,820	7,730	8,627	9,531	8,139	7,059	2,902	3,844	Claims on Nonfin.Pub.Enterprises	32c
	6,414	9,264	8,388	8,180	5,803	6,071	7,849	8,005	10,723	14,080	19,234	....	....	....	....	Claims on Private Sector	32d
	376	462	911	1,783	1,265	1,399	406	450	1,360	1,390	1,403	1,267	1,749	1,607	782	Claims on Other Financial Insts.	32f
	10,016	12,463	10,827	13,845	14,762	18,453	19,909	19,786	20,507	21,112	23,233	....	....	....	....	Money	34
	2,844	3,411	4,478	5,593	5,444	5,730	4,438	5,067	7,735	10,832	12,148	....	....	....	....	Quasi-Money	35
	4	1	—	—	—	—	133	—	—	—	—	—	—	—	—	Long-Term Foreign Liabilities	36cl
	6,236	5,175	3,986	4,744	5,820	6,194	9,218	9,690	12,335	14,072	13,037	....	....	....	....	Other Items (Net)	37r
	12,860	15,874	15,305	19,439	20,206	24,183	24,347	24,854	28,241	31,944	35,381	....	....	....	....	Money plus Quasi-Money	35l

Burundi
618

		1965	1966	1967	1968	1969	1970	1971	1972	1973	1974	1975	1976	1977	1978	1979
Other Banking Institutions																*Millions of Francs:*
Cash	40..f	....	....	—	1	1	1	3	1	—	—	1	—	—	—	—
Foreign Assets	41..f	....	....	—	—	—	—	—	—	—	—	—	—	—	—	—
Claims on Central Government	42a.f	....	....	40	15	—	—	—	—	—	—	—	—	—	—	—
Claims on Private Sector	42d.f	....	....	16	56	107	127	160	131	141	164	294	506	715	1,009	1,209
Bonds	46ab f															
Long-Term Foreign Liabilities	46cl f	....	....	—	—	—	—	—	—	—	—	51	214	381	418	603
Central Govt. Lending Funds	46f.f	....	....	—	—	—	—	—	—	—	—	87	87	87	124	110
Credit from Monetary Authorities	46g.f	....	....	—	—	18	—	—	2	—	—	—	6	86	286	166
Credit from Depos. Money Banks	46h.f	....	....	—	—	—	—	—	—	—	—	—	14	—	—	—
Capital Accounts	47a.f	....	....	60	122	124	126	130	133	136	135	182	187	192	217	259
Other Items (Net)	47r.f															
Banking Survey																*Millions of Francs:*
Foreign Assets (Net)	51n															
Domestic Credit	52	....	....	1,202	1,478	1,525	1,782	1,923	1,997	2,329	3,568	2,551	3,130	2,758	6,847	11,899
Claims on Central Govt. (Net)	52an	....	....	660	834	932	831	706	794	905	918	1,246	1,116	180	1,336	3,718
Claims on Nonfin.Pub.Enterprises	52c	—	—	Ⅰ	—	—	—	—	—	—	—	55	21	291	1,101	1,358
Claims on Private Sector	52d	....	....	542	643	593	951	1,217	1,203	1,424	2,650	1,251	1,993	2,287	4,410	6,822
Liquid Liabilities	55l	1,447	1,447	Ⅰ1,659	1,661	1,730	2,137	2,441	2,439	2,988	3,451	3,349	4,713	6,550	8,902	9,477
Other Items (Net)	57r															
Interest Rates																*Percent Per Annum*
Discount Rate (End of Period)	60	....	....	....	....	....	....	....	....	....	....	5.50	5.50	5.50	5.50	7.00
Deposit Rate	60l											2.50	2.50	2.50	2.50	2.50
Lending Rate	60p														12.00	12.00
Prices																*Index Numbers (1990=100):*
Consumer Prices	64	14.0	14.6	14.5	15.3	16.0	15.9	16.5	17.2	18.2	21.1	24.4	26.1	27.8	34.5	47.1
International Transactions																*Millions of Francs*
Exports	70	1,101	1,213	1,443	1,298	1,039	2,132	1,701	2,302	2,444	2,440	2,515	5,420	8,011	6,243	9,361
Imports, cif	71	1,580	1,698	1,694	1,994	1,880	1,956	2,619	2,736	2,495	3,396	4,856	5,027	6,678	8,843	13,721
Imports, fob	71.v	1,374	1,477	1,473	1,734	1,635	1,701	2,277	2,379	2,170	2,953	4,223	4,371	5,807	7,690	11,931
Balance of Payments																*Millions of US Dollars:*
Goods: Exports f.o.b.	78aa d															
Goods: Imports f.o.b.	78ab d															
Trade Balance	78ac d															
Services: Credit	78ad d															
Services: Debit	78ae d															
Balance on Goods and Services	78af d															
Income: Credit	78ag d															
Income: Debit	78ah d															
Balance on Goods, Serv., & Inc.	78ai d															
Current Transfers, n.i.e.: Credit	78aj d															
Current Transfers: Debit	78ak d															
Current Account, n.i.e.	78al d															
Capital Account, n.i.e.: Credit	78ba d															
Capital Account: Debit	78bb d															
Capital Account, n.i.e.	78bc d															
Direct Investment Abroad	78bd d															
Dir. Invest. in Rep. Econ., n.i.e.	78be d															
Portfolio Investment Assets	78bf d															
Portfolio Investment Liab., n.i.e.	78bg d															
Other Investment Assets	78bh d															
Other Investment Liab., n.i.e.	78bi d															
Financial Account, n.i.e.	78bj d															
Net Errors and Omissions	78ca d															
Overall Balance	78cb d															
Reserves and Related Items	79da d															
Reserve Assets	79db d															
Use of Fund Credit and Loans	79dc d															
Liabs.Constit.For.Auth.Reserves	79dd d															
Exceptional Financing	79de d															
Government Finance																*Millions of Francs:*
Deficit (-) or Surplus	80	....	....	−12.3	−70.1	−46.1	119.8	329.7	202.3	155.1	300.4	−80.7	238.9	468.7	6.2	67.1
Revenue	81	....	....	1,633.1	1,850.3	1,782.1	2,175.5	2,390.3	2,607.5	2,847.7	3,302.2	3,224.6	5,106.6	7,216.3	9,265.5	11,052.3
Expenditure	82	....	....	1,635.5	1,881.8	1,822.4	2,046.6	2,045.9	2,377.0	2,663.4	2,937.9	3,267.8	4,839.9	6,714.3	9,264.1	10,986.9
Lending Minus Repayments	83	....	....	9.9	38.6	5.8	9.1	14.7	28.2	29.2	63.9	37.5	27.8	33.3	−4.8	−1.7
Financing																
Net Borrowing: Domestic	84a	....	....	91.5	39.0	26.8	−73.8	−232.5	−210.2	112.0	−303.2	143.4	485.0	−3.5	478.7	1,667.0
Foreign	85a	....	....	−21.2	9.2	10.3	16.6	−18.3	−46.5	−53.5	−48.0	38.1	−213.2	−238.0	−198.6	−229.2
Use of Cash Balances	87	....	....	−58.0	21.9	9.0	−62.6	−78.9	54.4	−213.5	50.8	−100.8	−510.7	−227.2	−286.3	−1,504.9
Debt: National Currency	88b	506	723	926	1,114	1,167	1,154	1,145	1,194	1,475	1,474	1,726	2,573	2,872	3,989	6,361
Central Bank	88ba	329	506	563	760	801	855	705	833	1,031	1,192	857	1,509	1,855	2,881	5,150
Commercial Banks	88bb	5	7	123	162	248	163	263	233	311	162	713	680	462	103	203
Other Financial Institutions	88bc	38	68	92	60	45	29	29	33	6	6	16	78	233	487	826
Others (Incl. P.O. Dep.)	88bd	134	142	148	132	73	107	148	95	126	113	140	306	322	517	182
Debt: Foreign Currency	89b	334	343	389	526	555	639	651	589	562	629	1,726	2,026	3,449	5,353	8,437
National Accounts																*Millions of Francs*
Exports of Goods & Services	90c	1,388	2,082	2,244	2,306	2,394	2,735	1,866	2,534	2,683	2,652	2,899	5,309	8,671	6,661	9,985
Government Consumption	91f	932	1,991	2,146	2,205	2,289	2,615	2,342	2,791	2,821	3,421	4,642	3,368	5,495	9,574	11,436
Gross Fixed Capital Formation	93e	743	763	1,037	1,066	1,107	1,265	1,121	1,137	1,392	1,768	4,181	3,515	5,517	7,709	10,505
Increase/Decrease(-) in Stocks	93i	30	86	92	95	99	113	—	−450	−98	−666	−556	—	—	—	—
Private Consumption	96f	12,024	11,460	12,350	12,690	13,175	15,052	20,084	18,839	20,805	24,238	27,029	32,938	38,227	41,932	53,586
Imports of Goods & Services	98c	−1,682	−2,106	−2,270	−2,332	−2,421	−2,766	−3,135	−3,256	−3,247	−4,224	−5,523	−6,454	−8,332	−11,055	−17,426
Gross Domestic Product	99b	13,436	14,476	15,601	16,030	16,643	19,014	22,278	21,595	24,355	27,190	32,672	38,676	49,578	54,821	68,086
Net Factor Inc/Pmts(-) Abroad	98.n	....	....	....	....	....	....	....	−997	−708	−681	−971	−1,231	−1,301	—	−914
Gross National Product	99a	....	....	....	....	....	....	24,818	20,598	23,686	26,482	32,472	37,705	48,347	53,520	67,172
Gross Dom. Prod. 1990 Prices	99b.p	....	....	....	....	....	96,439	104,059	92,832	99,496	98,668	99,665	107,512	120,819	119,490	Ⅰ121,847
GDP Deflator (1990=100)	99bi p	....	....	....	....	....	19.7	21.4	23.3	24.5	27.6	32.8	36.0	41.0	45.9	55.9
																Millions:
Population	99z	Ⅰ3.21	3.24	3.27	3.30	3.55	3.62	3.69	3.74	3.80	3.86	Ⅰ3.74	3.82	3.90	3.98	4.03

Monetary Authorities: Ⅰ Beginning in 1967, data are based on improved classification.
Deposit Money Banks: Ⅰ See note to section 10. Ⅰ Beginning in 1980, data are based on an improved sectorization of accounts.
Monetary Survey: Ⅰ See notes to sections 10 and 20.

Burundi

618

	1980	1981	1982	1983	1984	1985	1986	1987	1988	1989	1990	1991	1992	1993	1994		
End of Period																**Other Banking Institutions**	
	118	55	84	73	44	250	1,017	2,423	26	155	....	....	....	....	....	Cash	**40.. f**
	—	22	59	321	101	193	185	151	119	147	....	....	....	....	....	Foreign Assets	**41.. f**
	—	—	—	187	100	99	98	1,144	1,544	1,284	....	....	....	....	....	Claims on Central Government	**42a. f**
	1,684	2,223	2,929	4,539	4,619	4,950	5,624	7,627	8,500	9,536	....	....	....	....	....	Claims on Private Sector	**42d. f**
	49	53	94	169	505	558	846	3,415	3,958	4,179	....	....	....	....	....	Bonds	**46ab f**
	528	553	503	737	846	839	860	1,223	1,747	2,322	1,908	2,423	2,896	....	4,496	Long-Term Foreign Liabilities	**46cl f**
	62	82	182	221	240	266	2,213	3,942	974	891	897	1,040	1,213	....	1,151	Central Govt. Lending Funds	**46f. f**
	105	120	430	617	224	10	—	—	98	293	110	777	1,347	....	....	Credit from Monetary Authorities	**46g. f**
	—	—	350	1,039	789	945	26	200	739	766	1,013	—	—	....	....	Credit from Depos. Money Banks	**46h. f**
	748	998	1,652	2,341	2,060	2,501	2,828	2,958	3,299	3,385	....	....	....	....	....	Capital Accounts	**47a. f**
	309	490	-141	-9	92	120	-199	-672	-844	-931	....	....	....	....	....	Other Items (Net)	**47r. f**
End of Period																**Banking Survey**	
	5,131	2,534	-559	388	580	1,916	5,506	5,046	5,804	11,706	....	....	....	....	....	Foreign Assets (Net)	**51n**
	14,414	20,069	21,924	26,858	I 28,998	32,304	33,694	37,970	43,575	43,888	....	....	....	....	....	Domestic Credit	**52**
	4,630	7,309	8,959	12,288	14,197	15,926	14,700	16,517	16,622	11,644	....	....	....	....	....	Claims on Central Govt. (Net)	**52an**
	1,687	1,273	1,660	1,850	4,379	5,357	5,521	5,820	7,730	8,627	9,531	8,139	7,059	2,902	3,844	Claims on Nonfin.Pub.Enterprises	**52c**
	8,097	11,486	11,316	12,719	I 10,422	11,020	13,473	15,633	19,223	23,617	....	....	....	....	....	Claims on Private Sector	**52d**
	12,741	15,820	15,220	19,365	20,162	23,933	23,330	22,431	28,215	31,789	....	....	....	....	....	Liquid Liabilities	**55l**
	7,176	7,012	6,145	8,078	9,415	10,287	15,870	20,585	21,165	23,805	....	....	....	....	....	Other Items (Net)	**57r**
Percent Per Annum																**Interest Rates**	
	7.00	7.00	7.00	7.00	7.00	7.00	5.00	7.00	7.00	....	....	....	....	....	....	Discount Rate *(End of Period)*	**60**
	2.50	4.50	5.00	4.50	4.50	4.50	5.96	5.33	4.00	....	....	....	....	....	....	Deposit Rate	**60l**
	12.00	12.00	12.00	12.00	12.00	12.00	12.00	12.00	12.00	....	....	....	....	....	....	Lending Rate	**60p**
Period Averages																**Prices**	
	I 48.3	54.1	57.3	62.0	70.9	73.5	74.8	80.1	83.7	93.5	100.0	109.0	I 113.9	124.9	143.5	Consumer Prices	**64**
Millions of Francs																**International Transactions**	
	5,884	6,744	7,901	7,522	12,367	13,533	17,674	11,117	18,589	12,304	12,784	16,698	15,355	16,802	26,500	Exports	**70**
	15,114	14,509	19,280	17,075	22,383	22,754	23,195	25,465	28,885	29,910	40,179	46,154	46,106	49,702	56,468	Imports, cif	**71**
	13,143	12,617	16,765	14,848	19,463	19,786	20,170	22,143	25,117	26,009	34,938	40,134	40,092	43,219	49,103	Imports, fob	**71.v**
Minus Sign Indicates Debit																Balance of Payments	
	....	....	....	....	....	113.6	129.1	98.3	124.4	93.2	72.9	90.7	79.3	75.0	....	Goods: Exports f.o.b.	**78aa d**
	....	....	....	....	....	-149.7	-165.3	-159.2	-166.1	-151.4	-189.0	-195.9	-181.8	-172.8	....	Goods: Imports f.o.b.	**78ab d**
	....	....	....	....	....	-36.1	-36.2	-60.8	-41.7	-58.2	-116.1	-105.2	-102.5	-97.9	....	Trade Balance	**78ac d**
	....	....	....	....	....	13.2	11.7	11.9	11.9	15.3	16.6	25.5	17.3	14.2	....	Services: Credit	**78ad d**
	....	....	....	....	....	-89.4	-102.9	-132.1	-114.9	-92.6	-125.5	-137.0	-133.8	-112.5	....	Services: Debit	**78ae d**
	....	....	....	....	....	-112.3	-127.3	-181.0	-144.7	-135.5	-225.0	-216.8	-218.9	-196.2	....	Balance on Goods and Services	**78af d**
	....	....	....	....	....	1.6	2.1	2.9	2.9	8.9	8.2	9.7	14.0	11.2	....	Income: Credit	**78ag d**
	....	....	....	....	....	-19.9	-22.7	-31.3	-25.8	-26.5	-23.0	-20.7	-27.6	-22.2	....	Income: Debit	**78ah d**
	....	....	....	....	....	-130.6	-147.9	-209.4	-167.6	-153.1	-239.8	-227.8	-232.5	-207.2	....	Balance on Goods, Serv., & Inc.	**78ai d**
	....	....	....	....	....	93.6	115.8	118.3	103.4	142.7	175.5	198.1	180.6	183.8	....	Current Transfers, n.i.e.: Credit	**78aj d**
	....	....	....	....	....	-4.3	-4.0	-4.1	-5.9	-1.1	-1.3	-1.7	-1.9	-1.8	....	Current Transfers: Debit	**78ak d**
	....	....	....	....	....	-41.4	-36.2	-95.2	-70.1	-11.5	-65.6	-31.4	-53.8	-25.1	....	Current Account, n.i.e.	**78al d**
	....	....	....	....	....	—	—	—	—	—	—	—	—	—	....	Capital Account, n.i.e.: Credit	**78ba d**
	....	....	....	....	....	-.8	-1.4	-1.2	-.5	-.6	-.5	-.7	-.8	-1.2	....	Capital Account: Debit	**78bb d**
	....	....	....	....	....	-.8	-1.4	-1.2	-.5	-.6	-.5	-.7	-.8	-1.2	....	Capital Account, n.i.e.	**78bc d**
	....	....	....	....	....	—	—	—	—	-.1	—	—	—	-.1	....	Direct Investment Abroad	**78bd d**
	....	....	....	....	....	.5	1.5	1.4	1.2	.6	1.3	.9	.6	.5	....	Dir. Invest. in Rep. Econ., n.i.e.	**78be d**
	....	....	....	....	....	—	—	—	—	—	—	—	—	—	....	Portfolio Investment Assets	**78bf d**
	....	....	....	....	....	—	—	—	—	—	—	—	—	—	....	Portfolio Investment Liab., n.i.e.	**78bg d**
	....	....	....	....	....	.3	8.0	1.4	-11.5	-7.6	4.1	-3.5	-1.0	-1.5	....	Other Investment Assets	**78bh d**
	....	....	....	....	....	—	—	—	—	—	—	—	—	—	....	Other Investment Liab., n.i.e.	**78bi d**
	....	....	....	....	....	66.1	85.0	131.1	84.3	64.4	78.0	70.5	98.9	52.9	....	Financial Account, n.i.e.	**78bj d**
	....	....	....	....	....	-8.0	-18.9	-37.3	-6.6	-14.3	-15.1	-5.8	-18.7	-16.3	....	Net Errors and Omissions	**78ca d**
	....	....	....	....	....	15.9	28.5	-2.6	7.1	38.0	-3.2	32.6	25.5	10.2	....	Overall Balance	**78cb d**
	....	....	....	....	....	-15.9	-28.5	2.6	-7.1	-38.0	3.2	-32.6	-25.5	-10.2	....	Reserves and Related Items	**79da d**
	....	....	....	....	....	.3	-.5	.6	-.4	.1	2.2	-3.1	4.2	.8	....	Reserve Assets	**79db d**
	....	....	....	....	....	-3.2	6.0	-4.6	13.3	8.1	-.8	5.8	18.5	-4.1	....	Use of Fund Credit and Loans	**79dc d**
	....	....	....	....	....	—	—	—	—	—	—	—	—	—	....	Liabs.Constit.For.Auth.Reserves	**79dd d**
	....	....	....	....	....	—	—	—	—	—	—	—	—	—	....	Exceptional Financing	**79de d**
Year Ending December 31																**Government Finance**	
	-1,708.0	-1,873.0	-1,362.1	-917.8	231.4	-148.5	3,475.0	-1,433.2	1,116.1	4,649.1	1,273.7	4,219.3	1,796.8	3,442.6	....	Deficit (-) or Surplus	**80**
	11,441.0	12,321.1	14,046.8	12,855.9	16,350.6	19,254.1	23,133.4	20,060.8	25,084.9	38,583.8	37,079.4	42,820.3	45,618.7	49,933.2	....	Revenue	**81**
	13,149.8	14,194.2	15,409.0	13,773.7	16,119.2	19,402.6	19,658.4	21,494.0	23,968.8	33,934.7	35,805.7	38,601.0	43,821.9	46,490.6	....	Expenditure	**82**
	-.8	-.1	-.1	—	—	—	—	—	—	—	—	—	—	—	....	Lending Minus Repayments	**83**
																Financing	
	1,680.2	1,829.5	1,338.3	1,043.8	683.2	1,451.5	-1,000.2	2,194.6	-916.1	-3,358.8	-821.0	-5,619.4	-4,710.5	-3,023.7	....	Net Borrowing: Domestic	**84a**
	7.3	-358.1	-318.6	-570.1	-810.8	-1,402.8	-323.7	1,215.3	-108.2	301.0	147.0	263.7	2,291.7	-654.9	....	Foreign	**85a**
	20.5	401.6	342.4	444.1	-103.8	99.8	-2,151.1	-1,976.7	-91.8	-1,591.3	-599.7	1,136.4	622.0	236.0	....	Use of Cash Balances	**87**
	8,186	10,638	12,519	15,624	18,633	21,986	22,169	24,455	25,937	22,935	22,662	18,080	15,591	13,784	12,742	Debt: National Currency	**88b**
	5,796	7,953	9,296	12,355	14,588	17,119	16,414	17,161	16,040	15,237	15,040	13,450	11,671	9,258	8,689	Central Bank	**88ba**
	4	5	2	49	317	778	776	1,179	1,597	1,157	1,017	901	444	2,417	2,540	Commercial Banks	**88bb**
	1,529	1,791	2,114	2,039	1,946	2,137	2,292	3,493	4,725	3,969	3,402	2,635	1,811	451	204	Other Financial Institutions	**88bc**
	856	888	1,106	1,181	1,782	1,951	2,689	2,622	3,575	2,572	3,203	1,094	1,665	1,658	1,309	Others (Incl. P.O. Dep.)	**88bd**
	11,030	13,025	16,276	32,368	41,099	47,080	65,415	83,311	116,475	147,270	139,289	170,242	219,716	258,973	265,129	Debt: Foreign Currency	**89b**
Millions of Francs																**National Accounts**	
	7,328	6,999	8,697	9,683	11,782	13,937	15,625	13,015	17,298	15,697	15,333	21,246	20,310	21,426	31,276	Exports of Goods & Services	**90c**
	13,746	15,583	18,183	20,414	21,132	22,793	24,252	28,570	31,491	36,547	38,334	39,556	40,653	48,318	42,041	Government Consumption	**91f**
	10,955	11,948	17,170	19,541	20,364	20,113	18,860	21,114	25,701	26,115	32,234	38,307	41,066	34,492	27,004	Gross Fixed Capital Formation	**93e**
	921	2,429	-741	-1,083	1,410	73	3,247	3,762	-4,029	3,247	-1,177	-1,616	-1,678	-2,663	3,929	Increase/Decrease(-) in Stocks	**93i**
	70,133	69,823	73,894	77,516	92,484	109,478	104,340	107,015	114,298	135,449	163,216	185,294	213,769	218,822	236,175	Private Consumption	**96f**
	-17,476	-17,696	-23,109	-23,179	-26,721	-25,047	-25,482	-29,886	-31,852	-37,507	-51,602	-60,402	-65,724	-69,710	-70,841	Imports of Goods & Services	**98c**
	85,607	89,086	94,094	102,892	120,451	141,347	140,842	143,590	152,907	179,548	196,656	222,385	248,395	250,686	269,584	Gross Domestic Product	**99b**
	822	455	68	-382	-980	-1,436	-1,697	-2,092	-2,457	-2,008	-2,551	-2,041	-2,845	-2,674	-4,275	Net Factor Inc/Pmts(-) Abroad	**98.n**
	86,429	89,541	94,162	102,510	119,471	139,911	139,145	141,498	150,450	177,540	194,105	220,344	245,550	248,012	265,309	Gross National Product	**99a**
	131,503	145,853	145,225	149,740	149,591	167,072	173,453	180,585	187,229	189,952	196,656	206,483	211,166	....	....	Gross Dom. Prod. 1990 Prices	**99b.p**
	65.1	61.1	64.8	68.7	80.5	84.6	81.2	79.5	81.7	94.5	100.0	107.7	117.6	....	....	GDP Deflator (1990=100)	**99bi p**
Midyear Estimates																	
	4.12	4.23	4.34	4.46	4.58	4.72	4.86	5.00	5.15	5.30	5.46	5.62	5.78	5.96	6.13	**Population**	**99z**

Cameroon
622

		1965	1966	1967	1968	1969	1970	1971	1972	1973	1974	1975	1976	1977	1978	1979
Exchange Rates																*Francs per SDR:*
Official Rate	aa	245.07	247.59	245.42	247.40	277.91	276.02	283.61	278.00	284.00	272.08	262.55	288.70	285.76	272.28	264.78
																Francs per US Dollar:
Official Rate	ae	245.08	247.59	245.43	247.41	277.92	276.03	261.23	256.05	235.43	222.22	224.27	248.49	235.25	209.00	201.00
Official Rate	rf	245.06	245.68	246.00	247.56	259.96	276.40	275.59	252.03	222.89	240.70	214.31	238.95	245.68	225.66	212.72
															Index Numbers (1990=100):	
Official Rate	ahx	110.8	110.5	110.4	109.7	104.8	98.2	98.6	107.8	122.3	112.8	126.9	113.8	110.5	120.6	127.7
Nominal Effective Exchange Rate	nec	....	....	....	....	....	....	....	....	....	....	....	....	....	....	75.5
Real Effective Exchange Rate	rec	....	....	....	....	....	....	....	....	....	....	....	....	....	....	90.4
Fund Position																*Millions of SDRs:*
Quota	2f.s	15.00	15.80	16.60	17.40	18.20	35.00	35.00	35.00	35.00	35.00	35.00	35.00	35.00	45.00	45.00
SDRs	1b.s	—	—	—	—	—	3.06	6.80	10.51	10.51	10.47	10.11	8.79	6.75	3.23	.01
Reserve Position in the Fund	1c.s	1.90	2.10	2.30	2.50	2.70	6.90	6.90	6.90	6.90	—	—	—	—	3.47	6.39
Total Fund Cred.&Loans Outstg.	2tl	—	—	—	—	—	—	—	—	—	4.62	12.13	33.89	33.89	47.27	49.92
International Liquidity														*Millions of US Dollars Unless Otherwise Indicated:*		
Total Reserves minus Gold	1l.d	26.70	33.70	24.35	40.85	48.09	80.81	73.60	43.64	51.15	78.53	28.83	43.80	42.39	52.28	125.70
SDRs	1b.d	—	—	—	—	—	3.06	7.38	11.41	12.68	12.82	11.84	10.21	8.20	4.21	.01
Reserve Position in the Fund	1c.d	1.90	2.10	2.30	2.50	2.70	6.90	7.49	7.49	8.32	—	—	—	—	4.52	8.42
Foreign Exchange	1d.d	24.80	31.60	22.05	38.35	45.39	70.85	58.73	24.74	30.15	65.71	16.99	33.59	34.19	43.56	117.27
Gold (Million Fine Troy Ounces)	1ad	....	....	....	....	....	....	....	....	....	....	....	....	.015	.015	.030
Gold (National Valuation)	1and	....	....	....	....	....	....	....	....	....	....	....	....	2.46	2.95	15.59
Monetary Authorities: Other Liab.	4..b	.65	.08	.57	.11	.18	.14	.06	.06	.05	8.59	2.80	4.38	2.89	3.78	2.85
Deposit Money Banks: Assets	7a.d	10.45	5.55	2.84	6.66	13.58	9.81	11.29	8.51	16.76	6.73	5.85	14.68	28.57	34.00	32.24
Liabilities	7b.d	15.76	13.57	15.60	22.19	24.09	29.14	24.75	30.95	24.08	26.92	32.41	20.29	51.35	109.22	126.81
Monetary Authorities																*Billions of Francs:*
Foreign Assets	11	6.59	8.32	6.01	10.08	13.35	22.44	18.83	11.16	11.78	17.45	6.47	10.88	10.55	11.55	28.42
Claims on Central Government	12a	....	....	....	....	....	....	....	....	2.00	7.65	15.77	25.35	26.01	30.49	29.69
Claims on Deposit Money Banks	12e	11.26	11.62	13.18	12.44	13.40	13.64	14.59	17.17	20.28	18.77	25.07	24.97	44.32	61.20	61.11
Claims on Other Banking Insts.	12f	....	....	....	....	....	....	....	....	....	....	....	....	....	....	....
Reserve Money	14	11.76	15.58	15.78	18.32	21.30	22.73	23.78	24.38	28.66	34.98	36.39	43.09	56.13	65.33	77.58
of which: Currency Outside DMBs	14a	10.77	14.46	14.64	17.09	19.18	20.63	22.18	22.78	26.65	32.20	33.71	38.85	50.72	60.05	70.27
Foreign Liabilities	16c	.16	.02	.14	.03	.05	.04	.02	.02	.01	3.17	3.81	10.87	10.36	13.66	13.79
Central Government Deposits	16d	5.81	4.01	3.30	4.26	5.36	12.49	7.34	.90	2.21	4.24	3.91	3.45	9.87	19.26	18.11
Capital Accounts	17a	....	....	....	....	....	....	....	....	....	.06	.06	.06	.06	.05	.05
Other Items (Net)	17r	.11	.35	−.03	−.09	.04	.82	2.29	3.04	3.11	1.42	3.14	3.74	4.46	4.92	9.71
Deposit Money Banks																*Billions of Francs:*
Reserves	20	.59	.75	.81	1.23	2.12	2.11	1.61	1.60	2.02	2.79	2.67	4.24	5.41	5.29	7.30
Foreign Assets	21	2.58	1.37	.70	1.64	3.77	2.72	2.89	2.18	3.86	1.50	1.31	3.65	I6.72	7.11	6.48
Claims on Central Government	22a	1.34	1.41	1.54	3.01	3.70	3.58	4.18	5.25	5.73	7.31	8.59	10.96	15.85	21.06	21.47
Claims on Nonfin.Pub.Enterprises	22c	....	....	....	....	....	....	....	....	....	....	....	....	....	....	....
Claims on Private Sector	22d	27.33	29.93	34.18	34.82	39.55	45.20	48.16	57.67	64.90	89.30	114.79	144.09	I204.59	266.82	323.75
Claims on Other Banking Insts.	22f	....	....	....	....	....	....	....	....	....	....	....	....	....	....	....
Claims on Nonbank Financial Insts.	22g	....	....	....	....	....	....	....	....	....	....	....	....	....	....	....
Demand Deposits	24	10.06	10.32	11.82	14.58	17.29	18.85	21.97	24.57	28.93	41.46	43.49	57.34	I77.70	88.48	116.01
Time and Savings Deposits	25	2.29	2.35	2.89	3.47	5.26	7.07	8.39	10.35	15.06	21.60	30.05	37.96	56.87	65.37	75.84
Bonds	26ab	....	....	....	....	....	....	....	....	....	....	....	....	....	....	....
Foreign Liabilities	26c	3.89	2.07	2.50	3.88	5.13	6.53	4.99	6.49	3.98	4.12	6.04	3.76	11.04	20.77	11.14
Long-Term Foreign Liabilities	26cl	—	1.28	1.35	1.60	1.56	1.56	1.34	1.43	1.56	1.86	1.23	1.29	1.04	2.06	14.35
Central Government Deposits	26d	3.48	4.67	4.48	3.34	4.16	4.39	4.01	4.82	5.59	6.84	9.38	29.26	34.19	43.99	66.70
Credit from Monetary Authorities	26g	11.26	11.62	13.18	12.44	13.40	13.64	14.59	17.17	20.28	23.99	27.56	28.75	47.82	65.77	64.38
Capital Accounts	27a	2.38	3.09	2.84	3.34	3.52	3.94	5.34	5.97	7.20	8.31	11.36	12.67	13.53	17.46	24.33
Other Items (Net)	27r	−1.52	−1.94	−1.83	−1.94	−1.18	−2.37	−3.80	−4.10	−6.09	−7.30	−1.74	−8.09	I−9.63	−3.62	−13.94
Monetary Survey																*Billions of Francs:*
Foreign Assets (Net)	31n	5.12	7.60	4.07	7.83	11.95	18.59	16.71	6.84	11.64	11.66	−2.08	−.09	I−4.13	−15.78	9.97
Domestic Credit	32	19.75	23.78	28.54	30.23	33.72	31.91	40.99	57.21	64.83	93.17	125.86	147.69	I202.38	255.12	289.90
Claims on Central Govt. (Net)	32an	I−7.58	−6.15	−5.64	−4.59	−5.82	−13.30	−7.17	−.47	−.07	3.87	11.07	3.60	−2.21	−11.70	−33.85
Claims on Nonfin.Pub.Enterprises	32c	....	....	....	....	....	....	....	....	....	....	....	....	....	....	....
Claims on Private Sector	32d	I27.33	29.93	34.18	34.82	39.55	45.20	48.16	57.67	64.90	89.30	114.79	144.09	I204.59	266.82	323.75
Claims on Other Banking Insts.	32f	....	....	....	....	....	....	....	....	....	....	....	....	....	....	....
Claims on Nonbk. Financial Insts.	32g	....	....	....	....	....	....	....	....	....	....	....	....	....	....	....
Money	34	20.83	24.78	26.46	31.67	36.47	39.48	44.14	47.35	55.57	73.66	77.20	96.19	I128.42	148.53	186.28
Quasi-Money	35	2.29	2.35	2.89	3.47	5.26	7.07	8.39	10.35	15.06	21.60	30.05	37.96	56.87	65.37	75.84
Bonds	36ab	....	....	....	....	....	....	....	....	....	....	....	....	....	....	....
Other Items (Net)	37r	....	....	....	2.92	3.94	3.95	5.17	6.35	5.84	9.56	16.53	13.44	I12.95	25.45	37.75
Money plus Quasi-Money	35l	23.12	27.13	29.35	35.14	41.73	46.54	52.53	57.70	70.63	95.26	107.24	134.15	I185.29	213.89	262.12
Interest Rates																*Percent Per Annum*
Discount Rate (End of Period)	60	....	....	....	4.50	4.50	4.50	4.50	4.50	4.50	4.50	5.50	5.50	6.50	6.50	8.50
Deposit Rate	60l	....	....	....	....	....	....	....	....	....	....	....	....	....	....	6.50
Lending Rate	60p	....	....	....	....	....	....	....	....	....	....	....	....	....	....	10.25
Prices																*Index Numbers (1990=100):*
Consumer Prices	64	....	....	....	15.7	15.5	16.4	17.0	18.4	20.3	23.8	27.1	29.8	34.1	38.4	40.9

Cameroon

1980	1981	1982	1983	1984	1985	1986	1987	1988	1989	1990	1991	1992	1993	1994		
End of Period															**Exchange Rates**	
287.99	334.52	370.92	436.97	470.11	415.26	394.78	378.78	407.68	380.32	364.84	370.48	378.57	404.89	ⅼ780.44	Official Rate	**aa**
End of Period (ae)		*Period Average (rf)*														
225.80	287.40	336.25	417.37	479.60	378.05	322.75	267.00	302.95	289.40	256.45	259.00	275.33	294.78	ⅼ534.60	Official Rate	**ae**
211.28	271.73	328.61	381.06	436.96	449.26	346.30	300.54	297.85	319.01	272.26	282.11	264.69	283.16	ⅼ555.20	Official Rate	**rf**
Period Averages																
128.7	100.5	83.1	71.6	62.3	60.9	78.6	90.5	91.4	85.2	100.0	96.6	102.8	96.0	49.0	Official Rate	**ah** x
77.2	72.3	69.2	67.3	66.8	69.5	75.1	78.8	81.5	85.6	100.0	103.6	113.1	121.0	68.5	Nominal Effective Exchange Rate	**ne** c
88.9	81.6	79.8	82.8	84.0	87.9	97.2	108.9	105.4	97.3	100.0	96.5	94.7	88.0	59.1	Real Effective Exchange Rate	**re** c
End of Period															**Fund Position**	
67.50	67.50	67.50	92.70	92.70	92.70	92.70	92.70	92.70	92.70	92.70	92.70	135.10	135.10	135.10	Quota	**2f.** s
—	.23	1.64	.62	6.23	4.21	2.82	.18	.02	.22	.45	3.89	.20	.06	.03	SDRs	**1b.** s
12.04	12.04	13.90	7.20	.20	.20	.20	.20	.22	.22	.22	.23	.29	.34	.34	Reserve Position in the Fund	**1c.** s
46.04	37.68	34.74	33.60	30.70	24.95	18.13	11.32	74.64	86.18	85.11	84.28	45.66	11.86	29.91	Total Fund Cred.&Loans Outstg.	**2tl**
End of Period															**International Liquidity**	
188.86	85.19	67.23	159.09	53.85	132.46	59.02	63.76	175.85	79.86	25.54	43.04	20.37	2.45	2.26	Total Reserves minus Gold	**1l.** d
—	.27	1.81	.65	6.11	4.62	3.45	.26	.03	.29	.64	5.56	.28	.09	.05	SDRs	**1b.** d
15.36	14.01	15.33	7.54	.20	.22	.24	.28	.30	.29	.31	.33	.40	.47	.49	Reserve Position in the Fund	**1c.** d
173.50	70.90	50.08	150.90	47.55	127.62	55.32	63.22	175.52	79.28	24.59	37.15	19.70	1.90	1.72	Foreign Exchange	**1d.** d
.030	.030	.030	.030	.030	.030	.030	.030	.030	.030	.030	.030	.030	.030	....	Gold (Million Fine Troy Ounces)	**1ad**
17.65	11.99	13.45	11.33	9.27	9.70	11.74	14.45	12.17	12.01	11.48	10.58	9.95	11.91	ⅼ22.66	Gold (National Valuation)	**1an** d
2.12	.98	1.20	.92	2.89	.97	1.46	1.63	406.28	340.18	441.53	477.54	594.53	719.56	605.19	Monetary Authorities: Other Liab.	**4..** d
34.31	151.65	71.16	129.92	279.74	431.08	127.71	279.70	396.82	481.78	142.84	173.78	98.99	88.27	135.55	Deposit Money Banks: Assets	**7a.** d
326.04	195.46	333.63	228.43	167.14	268.42	394.45	567.80	759.14	791.18	338.28	301.01	90.26	125.49	50.01	Liabilities	**7b.** d
End of Period															**Monetary Authorities**	
46.65	27.93	27.12	71.17	30.27	53.78	22.83	20.91	ⅼ56.99	26.59	9.51	13.89	8.34	4.18	7.37	Foreign Assets	**11**
28.79	30.94	32.14	46.11	62.79	63.88	106.70	91.00	ⅼ117.18	133.24	131.32	ⅼ320.40	331.57	319.09	340.51	Claims on Central Government	**12a**
68.99	107.19	132.02	162.67	162.33	129.98	192.56	341.55	ⅼ327.91	294.33	273.36	ⅼ77.58	51.63	52.06	27.07	Claims on Deposit Money Banks	**12e**
....	....	....	....	....	....	....	....	....	....	....	....	....	....	—	Claims on Other Banking Insts.	**12f**
89.78	119.76	126.50	162.95	159.97	183.44	216.13	200.71	ⅼ206.40	219.98	200.59	199.14	168.61	129.79	180.77	Reserve Money	**14**
80.84	105.26	111.02	131.24	141.08	155.94	171.52	175.28	ⅼ166.12	162.85	155.98	170.25	149.02	116.13	136.33	of which: Currency Outside DMBs	**14a**
13.74	12.89	13.29	15.07	15.82	10.73	7.63	4.72	ⅼ153.51	131.23	144.28	154.91	180.97	216.91	346.88	Foreign Liabilities	**16c**
29.85	19.24	36.71	85.15	61.27	37.64	86.94	223.70	ⅼ123.32	82.72	52.00	43.38	23.62	14.85	44.83	Central Government Deposits	**16d**
3.78	3.23	4.41	4.67	4.35	3.61	3.97	4.17	ⅼ4.33	3.90	3.27	3.52	2.90	3.69	3.08	Capital Accounts	**17a**
7.29	10.94	10.92	12.11	13.97	12.22	7.42	20.16	ⅼ14.51	16.34	14.05	10.90	ⅼ15.45	10.09	-200.61	Other Items (Net)	**17r**
End of Period															**Deposit Money Banks**	
8.94	14.51	15.48	31.71	18.89	27.50	44.57	25.41	ⅼ30.91	48.78	41.25	27.69	17.22	12.39	42.57	Reserves	**20**
7.75	43.58	23.93	54.23	134.16	162.97	41.22	74.68	ⅼ120.22	139.43	36.63	45.01	27.25	26.02	72.46	Foreign Assets	**21**
29.32	35.35	49.81	61.87	69.38	82.40	115.69	140.92	ⅼ125.18	119.49	86.05	108.85	ⅼ126.05	154.08	185.76	Claims on Central Government	**22a**
....	....	....	....	....	....	....	....	132.76	191.13	182.57	171.91	77.03	52.68	39.45	Claims on Nonfin.Pub.Enterprises	**22c**
416.61	559.68	678.74	808.76	806.13	878.29	986.21	1,014.56	ⅼ897.65	887.42	894.45	892.95	400.06	368.81	369.54	Claims on Private Sector	**22d**
....	....	....	....	....	....	....	....	.01	.31	—	.01	—	.01	.03	Claims on Other Banking Insts.	**22f**
....	....	....	....	....	....	....	....	2.49	2.60	2.10	2.96	3.06	3.05	4.43	Claims on Nonbank Financial Insts.	**22g**
130.15	157.12	190.89	249.43	276.35	278.38	280.31	215.90	ⅼ246.49	281.20	259.29	258.45	159.94	150.06	223.09	Demand Deposits	**24**
107.18	146.69	184.92	235.35	325.47	437.84	383.07	290.71	ⅼ303.19	316.98	337.98	340.37	290.32	278.67	329.79	Time and Savings Deposits	**25**
....	....	....	....	....	....	....	....	16.88	16.50	15.00	15.93	6.22	5.01	3.85	Bonds	**26ab**
45.17	15.50	47.42	50.74	19.22	50.14	83.61	98.90	ⅼ132.47	151.48	54.22	ⅼ47.17	22.92	32.58	17.44	Foreign Liabilities	**26c**
28.45	40.67	64.77	44.60	60.94	51.33	43.70	52.71	ⅼ97.51	77.49	32.53	ⅼ30.80	1.93	4.41	9.30	Long-Term Foreign Liabilities	**26cl**
76.16	173.82	158.06	127.47	138.50	143.65	120.76	221.57	ⅼ177.08	189.77	199.60	189.05	ⅼ82.24	77.65	97.04	Central Government Deposits	**26d**
71.14	110.72	132.02	162.67	162.33	129.98	192.56	341.55	ⅼ327.91	294.33	273.37	ⅼ77.58	51.63	52.06	27.07	Credit from Monetary Authorities	**26g**
26.84	42.16	49.24	62.36	46.64	64.22	82.43	101.34	ⅼ95.05	119.51	131.29	ⅼ370.23	77.27	75.87	84.39	Capital Accounts	**27a**
-22.47	-33.56	-59.36	23.94	-.88	-4.38	1.25	-67.11	ⅼ-87.37	-58.11	-60.24	-80.20	ⅼ-41.80	-59.27	-77.72	Other Items (Net)	**27r**
End of Period															**Monetary Survey**	
-4.51	43.12	-9.66	59.59	129.39	155.87	-27.19	-8.03	ⅼ-206.28	-194.18	-184.89	ⅼ-173.97	-170.23	-223.70	-293.78	Foreign Assets (Net)	**31n**
368.71	432.91	566.47	704.12	738.53	843.28	1,000.90	801.21	ⅼ974.85	1,061.70	1,044.89	1,264.64	ⅼ831.91	805.22	797.85	Domestic Credit	**32**
-47.90	-126.77	-112.27	-104.64	-67.60	-35.00	14.68	-213.35	ⅼ-58.05	-19.76	-34.24	196.81	ⅼ351.76	380.67	384.40	Claims on Central Govt. (Net)	**32an**
....	....	....	....	....	....	....	....	132.76	191.13	182.57	171.91	77.03	52.68	39.45	Claims on Nonfin.Pub.Enterprises	**32c**
416.61	559.68	678.74	808.76	806.13	878.29	986.21	1,014.56	ⅼ897.65	887.42	894.45	892.95	400.06	368.81	369.54	Claims on Private Sector	**32d**
....	....	....	....	....	....	....	....	.01	.31	—	.01	—	.01	.03	Claims on Other Banking Insts.	**32f**
....	....	....	....	....	....	....	....	2.49	2.60	2.10	2.96	3.06	3.05	4.43	Claims on Nonbk. Financial Insts.	**32g**
210.99	262.37	301.91	380.67	417.43	434.32	451.87	391.21	ⅼ421.98	452.40	418.63	429.90	311.33	267.46	361.29	Money	**34**
107.18	146.69	184.92	235.35	325.47	437.84	383.07	290.71	ⅼ303.19	316.98	337.98	340.37	290.32	278.67	329.79	Quasi-Money	**35**
....	....	....	....	....	....	....	....	16.88	16.50	15.00	15.93	6.22	5.01	3.85	Bonds	**36ab**
46.03	66.97	69.97	147.68	125.02	127.00	138.77	111.27	ⅼ26.52	81.64	88.38	ⅼ304.46	ⅼ53.82	30.38	-190.86	Other Items (Net)	**37r**
318.17	409.06	486.83	616.02	742.90	872.16	834.94	681.91	ⅼ725.18	769.38	756.61	770.28	601.65	546.13	691.08	Money plus Quasi-Money	**35l**
Percent Per Annum															**Interest Rates**	
8.50	8.50	8.50	8.50	8.50	9.00	8.00	8.00	9.50	10.00	11.00	10.75	12.00	11.50	....	Discount Rate (End of Period)	**60**
7.50	7.50	7.50	7.50	7.50	7.50	7.35	7.15	7.21	7.50	ⅼ7.50	7.50	7.50	7.75	8.08	Deposit Rate	**60l**
13.00	13.00	13.00	14.50	14.50	14.50	13.50	13.00	13.46	15.00	ⅼ18.50	18.15	17.77	17.46	17.42	Lending Rate	**60p**
Period Averages															**Prices**	
44.8	ⅼ49.6	56.0	65.4	72.8	81.2	87.4	98.7	93.2	98.3	100.0	101.9	103.3	....	....	Consumer Prices	**64**

Cameroon

622

		1965	1966	1967	1968	1969	1970	1971	1972	1973	1974	1975	1976	1977	1978	1979
International Transactions															*Billions of Francs*	
Exports	70	35.66	32.41	29.96	46.72	58.57	62.78	57.28	55.70	78.32	114.90	96.13	122.03	172.88	181.70	240.62
Imports, cif	71	33.01	32.27	43.78	46.31	53.00	67.24	69.37	76.47	74.23	104.84	128.10	146.98	180.68	237.25	271.14
Imports, fob	71.v	31.68	30.97	42.02	44.44	50.86	64.50	65.04	69.69	70.29	96.72	119.01	137.08	163.58	215.71	246.49
Balance of Payments															*Millions of US Dollars:*	
Goods: Exports f.o.b.	78aa d													809.1	1,095.8	1,354.1
Goods: Imports f.o.b.	78ab d													-719.2	-951.5	-1,270.8
Trade Balance	78ac d													89.9	144.3	83.3
Services: Credit	78ad d													161.8	206.5	351.5
Services: Debit	78ae d													-335.1	-464.1	-464.7
Balance on Goods and Services	78af d													-83.4	-113.3	-29.9
Income: Credit	78ag d													8.1	16.3	12.4
Income: Debit	78ah d													-49.3	-90.4	-108.3
Balance on Goods, Serv., & Inc.	78ai d													-124.6	-187.5	-125.8
Current Transfers, n.i.e.: Credit	78aj d													64.2	53.1	71.0
Current Transfers: Debit	78ak d													-32.7	-52.7	-71.7
Current Account, n.i.e.	78al d													-93.1	-187.1	-126.5
Capital Account, n.i.e.: Credit	78ba d													—	—	—
Capital Account: Debit	78bb d													—	—	—
Capital Account, n.i.e.	78bc d													—	—	—
Direct Investment Abroad	78bd d													-4.4	-6.9	2.2
Dir. Invest. in Rep. Econ., n.i.e.	78be d													8.7	40.5	62.1
Portfolio Investment Assets	78bf d													—	—	—
Portfolio Investment Liab., n.i.e.	78bg d													—	—	—
Other Investment Assets	78bh d													-42.7	8.3	-90.5
Other Investment Liab., n.i.e.	78bi d													130.8	131.5	211.3
Financial Account, n.i.e.	78bj d													92.5	173.5	185.1
Net Errors and Omissions	78ca d													-2.1	.6	.9
Overall Balance	78cb d													-2.7	-13.1	59.5
Reserves and Related Items	79da d													2.7	13.1	-59.5
Reserve Assets	79db d													3.6	-4.7	-62.2
Use of Fund Credit and Loans	79dc d														16.6	3.5
Liabs.Constit.For.Auth.Reserves	79dd d													-1.5	.4	-1.5
Exceptional Financing	79de d													.7	.7	.8
Government Finance															*Billions of Francs:*	
Deficit (-) or Surplus	80											-12.98	-15.85	-3.02	4.07	31.72
Revenue	81											86.82	104.32	128.16	178.78	222.43
Grants Received	81z											4.14	5.29	4.59		
Expenditure	82											103.12	125.27	133.53	168.45	188.98
Lending Minus Repayments	83											.82	.19	2.24	6.26	1.73
Financing																
Domestic	84a											5.20	6.61	-16.50	-4.33	-26.47
Foreign	85a											7.78	9.24	19.52	.26	-5.25
Adj. to Total Financing	84x											—	—	—	—	—
Debt: Domestic	88a															
Foreign	89a												130.70	209.23		
National Accounts															*Billions of Francs:*	
Exports of Goods & Services	90c	38.4	34.9	36.5	44.5	52.0	85.1	82.0	73.7	89.7	137.9	145.6	150.4	202.6	249.9	259.4
Government Consumption	91f	28.4	31.0	31.9	34.3	38.8	39.1	41.5	46.0	49.0	57.3	68.4	74.8	81.9	102.8	116.3
Gross Fixed Capital Formation	93e	25.0	27.9	31.7	34.6	30.6	44.7	50.5	60.3	74.0	74.7	99.2	118.7	163.5	204.7	251.7
Increase/Decrease(-) in Stocks	93i	—	—	—	—	5.8	6.3	6.2	8.6	10.3	14.0	21.3	3.0	18.3	34.1	20.9
Private Consumption	96f	113.3	121.0	132.4	154.2	169.6	203.7	233.6	262.6	291.9	320.0	408.1	481.4	545.3	632.9	807.8
Imports of Goods & Services	98c	-37.4	-37.5	-38.0	-48.2	-49.5	-78.5	-92.5	-95.2	-114.4	-111.3	-162.5	-171.1	-221.7	-256.3	-310.1
Gross Domestic Product	99b	167.7	177.2	194.5	219.4	247.3	300.3	321.3	355.9	400.5	492.6	580.2	657.2	789.9	968.1	1,135.4
Net Factor Inc/Pmts(-) Abroad	98.n					6.2	11.0	.3	-52.2	-63.9	-108.8	-109.2	-119.6	-162.0		
Gross Nat'l Expenditure = GNP	99a					253.5	311.4	321.6	303.7	336.6	383.8	471.0	537.6	627.9		
Nat'l Income, Market Prices	99e				243.7	243.7	272.7	307.6	338.8	373.6	415.1	515.3	583.1	709.5	872.0	1,047.8
Gross Dom. Prod. 1990 Prices	99b.p					1,363.1	I 1,412.3	1,454.6	1,517.6	1,539.7	1,608.3	1,691.1	1,723.5	1,821.3	2,010.8	2,236.0
GDP Deflator (1990=100)	99bi p					18.1	21.3	22.1	23.5	26.0	30.6	34.3	38.1	43.4	48.1	50.8
															Millions:	
Population	99z	I 5.31	5.42	5.52	6.10	6.65	6.78	6.92	7.06	7.21	7.37	7.53	7.70	7.91	I 8.18	8.40

Monetary Authorities: I Beginning in March 1988, the sectorization and classification of accounts have been revised. I Beginning in September 1991, *Claims on Central Government* include government assumption of certain nonperforming bank loans. I Beginning in December 1992, the coverage of the banking system has been revised. Claims and deposits of nonactive banks or banks in the process of liquidation have been excluded from the monetary accounts.
Deposit Money Banks: I Beginning in September 1991, the counterpart of government assumption of certain nonperforming bank loans was reclassified from *Credit from Monetary Authorities* to *Capital Accounts*. I See note to section 10.
Monetary Survey: I See notes to sections 10 and 20.

Interest Rates: *Deposit Rate:* I Beginning in October 1990, minimum rate offered by deposit money banks on savings accounts.
Lending Rate: I Beginning in October 1990, maximum rate charged by deposit money banks on all loans, excluding charges and fees.
Government Finance: I Data prior to 1990 cover budgetary, extrabudgetary, and social security accounts. I Data for 1990 and 1991 cover the general budget units, *Caisse nationale de prevoyance sociale* (National Social Security Fund), and *Caisse autonome d'amortissement* (Autonomous Amortization Fund). I Beginning in 1992, data cover the general budget units and *Caisse autonome d'amortissement* only. Data relate to a fiscal year different from calendar year.

Cameroon

	1980	1981	1982	1983	1984	1985	1986	1987	1988	1989	1990	1991	1992	1993	1994		
Billions of Francs																**International Transactions**	
	290.62	299.72	348.63	372.22	381.33	321.76	271.63	241.92	464.36	536.84	553.84	545.11	480.39	….	….	Exports	70
	337.58	386.09	394.57	467.02	484.43	508.74	590.45	517.28	432.63	402.24	425.81	381.15	311.09	….	….	Imports, cif	71
	306.89	350.99	358.70	424.56	440.39	462.49	536.77	470.25	393.30	365.68	387.10	346.50	282.81	….	….	Imports, fob	71.v
Minus Sign Indicates Debit																**Balance of Payments**	
	1,657.5	1,410.6	1,357.9	1,366.7	1,589.0	1,626.3	2,077.0	1,688.7	1,841.2	1,853.8	2,125.4	1,957.5	1,934.1	1,507.7	….	Goods: Exports f.o.b.	78aa *d*
	–1,620.3	–1,368.8	–1,217.6	–1,225.2	–1,064.7	–1,135.9	–1,634.5	–1,434.8	–1,220.8	–1,136.8	–1,347.2	–1,173.1	–983.3	–1,005.3	….	Goods: Imports f.o.b.	78ab *d*
	37.2	41.8	140.3	141.5	524.2	490.4	442.5	253.9	620.5	717.0	778.1	784.3	950.8	502.4	….	Trade Balance	78ac *d*
	401.0	389.5	427.3	440.8	414.7	498.7	467.2	411.4	456.2	475.7	382.2	406.0	407.5	390.9	….	Services: Credit	78ad *d*
	–716.8	–723.3	–752.1	–717.3	–755.8	–936.2	–944.1	–1,052.5	–901.4	–1,032.4	–1,045.1	–1,122.3	–907.3	–741.1	….	Services: Debit	78ae *d*
	–278.6	–292.0	–184.4	–135.0	183.1	53.0	–34.4	–387.2	175.3	160.3	115.2	68.0	450.9	152.2	….	Balance on Goods and Services	78af *d*
	38.3	29.8	14.9	28.2	35.7	38.1	36.9	12.4	16.9	16.8	8.3	18.3	41.8	17.0	….	Income: Credit	78ag *d*
	–214.6	–213.2	–209.1	–307.4	–363.1	–634.0	–354.4	–419.0	–510.9	–430.8	–566.1	–442.7	–823.9	–669.5	….	Income: Debit	78ah *d*
	–454.8	–475.4	–378.6	–414.3	–144.4	–542.9	–351.9	–793.7	–318.7	–253.7	–442.6	–356.4	–331.2	–500.3	….	Balance on Goods, Serv., & Inc.	78ai *d*
	140.2	132.7	118.3	145.9	107.0	147.6	71.8	61.2	63.8	88.0	82.3	57.0	141.0	65.2	….	Current Transfers, n.i.e.: Credit	78aj *d*
	–131.4	–139.4	–125.6	–143.5	–131.6	–166.2	–171.8	–160.2	–176.0	–132.3	–117.5	–105.4	–148.3	–130.2	….	Current Transfers: Debit	78ak *d*
	–446.0	–482.1	–386.0	–411.9	–168.9	–561.5	–451.8	–892.7	–431.0	–298.0	–477.8	–404.8	–338.5	–565.4	….	Current Account, n.i.e.	78al *d*
	—	—	—	—	—	—	7.7	—	6.4	5.0	2.9	8.0	17.1	6.4	….	Capital Account, n.i.e.: Credit	78ba *d*
	—	—	—	—	—	—	–.4	—	–.1	–.1	–.1	–.1	–.1	–.1	….	Capital Account: Debit	78bb *d*
	—	—	—	—	—	—	7.3	—	6.4	5.0	2.8	7.9	17.0	6.3	….	Capital Account, n.i.e.	78bc *d*
	8.2	.4	–4.3	–5.2	–10.1	–10.6	–15.7	–11.5	–28.6	–26.1	–15.1	–21.5	–33.1	–22.1	….	Direct Investment Abroad	78bd *d*
	129.8	135.4	111.4	213.8	17.7	316.2	–90.7	12.0	92.4	–85.7	–112.5	–14.5	29.2	5.1	….	Dir. Invest. in Rep. Econ., n.i.e.	78be *d*
	—	—	—	—	—	—	11.0	—	–10.9	–1.0	55.6	–2.2	–46.5	–106.3	….	Portfolio Investment Assets	78bf *d*
	—	—	—	—	—	—	—	—	—	—	—	—	—	—	….	Portfolio Investment Liab., n.i.e.	78bg *d*
	–213.6	–185.8	–64.9	–271.6	–418.0	–141.3	490.5	299.7	–93.9	–8.9	481.5	–112.3	16.8	105.5	….	Other Investment Assets	78bh *d*
	606.3	467.7	329.0	586.6	614.6	347.0	–2.6	33.7	79.8	441.1	636.1	–211.7	–312.9	–286.7	….	Other Investment Liab., n.i.e.	78bi *d*
	530.8	417.7	371.2	523.5	204.1	511.3	392.5	333.8	38.7	319.4	–226.9	–362.2	–346.4	–304.6	….	Financial Account, n.i.e.	78bj *d*
	–6.4	4.3	3.9	5.2	–121.6	108.9	–29.0	89.3	221.8	–160.7	–168.2	26.9	–640.7	–16.2	….	Net Errors and Omissions	78ca *d*
	78.3	–60.2	–10.9	116.8	–86.4	58.7	–81.1	–469.7	–164.1	–134.3	–870.2	–732.3	–1,308.7	–879.9	….	Overall Balance	78cb *d*
	–78.3	60.2	10.9	–116.8	86.4	–58.7	81.1	469.7	164.1	134.3	870.2	732.3	1,308.7	879.9	….	Reserves and Related Items	79da *d*
	–72.9	69.4	13.5	–115.6	88.9	–53.5	88.6	7.3	–94.6	96.8	64.6	–31.6	20.9	14.9	….	Reserve Assets	79db *d*
	–5.3	–10.2	–3.2	–1.2	–3.0	–5.8	–8.0	–8.7	81.6	14.5	–1.4	–1.2	–54.6	–47.4	….	Use of Fund Credit and Loans	79dc *d*
	–.8	.5	.4	–.1	.5	.5	.4	–1.1	.7	6.2	–.4	1.1	3.5	–5.4	….	Liabs.Constit.For.Auth.Reserves	79dd *d*
	.6	.5	.1	.1	—	—	—	472.1	176.4	16.7	807.4	763.9	1,338.9	917.8	….	Exceptional Financing	79de *d*
Year Ending June 30																**Government Finance**	
	7.24	–58.50	–55.22	33.87	….	….	….	….	….	–110.24	ⱡ–198.44	–174.88	ⱡ–81.16	–54.74	….	Deficit (-) or Surplus	80
	230.64	314.54	390.44	612.27	790.52	….	919.06	742.78	633.08	601.65	ⱡ517.51	547.90	ⱡ498.47	448.41	….	Revenue	81
	.10	—	—	59.56	4.89	.12	4.80	—	.12	—	ⱡ—	—	ⱡ—	—	….	Grants Received	81z
	221.92	371.63	445.56	546.71	….	813.81	….	….	….	707.47	ⱡ709.71	719.76	ⱡ578.43	501.15	….	Expenditure	82
	1.58	1.41	.10	91.25	….	41.36	….	….	….	4.42	ⱡ6.24	3.02	ⱡ1.20	2.00	….	Lending Minus Repayments	83
Financing																	
	–17.17	….	….	–56.47	….	….	….	….	….	14.53	ⱡ39.68	37.27	ⱡ14.27	12.45	….	Domestic	84a
	9.93	….	….	22.60	….	….	….	….	….	95.71	ⱡ176.01	141.09	ⱡ106.73	61.16	….	Foreign	85a
	—	—	—	—	—	—	—	—	—	—	ⱡ–17.25	–3.48	ⱡ–39.84	–18.87	….	Adj. to Total Financing	84x
	….	291.89	359.54	431.53	112.56	125.88	172.74	228.30	153.87	….	ⱡ141.50	356.43	ⱡ377.90	374.16	….	Debt: Domestic	88a
	….	….	….	….	….	….	….	….	….	….	ⱡ1054.40	1,275.81	ⱡ1496.02	1,852.61	….	Foreign	89a
Year Ending June 30																**National Accounts**	
	378.6	388.5	434.8	547.5	646.5	799.9	881.9	615.4	579.3	547.1	553.4	….	….	….	….	Exports of Goods & Services	90c
	136.8	159.1	192.0	248.7	306.4	345.3	465.5	409.6	385.6	364.1	376.9	….	….	….	….	Government Consumption	91f
	282.4	441.4	507.2	654.5	809.5	939.0	927.6	1,052.3	990.6	935.4	943.4	….	….	….	….	Gross Fixed Capital Formation	93e
	13.5	47.0	31.5	25.6	19.4	16.3	29.4	21.3	20.1	18.9	22.0	….	….	….	….	Increase/Decrease(-) in Stocks	93i
	985.3	1,222.5	1,538.5	1,716.5	2,008.0	2,466.3	2,689.7	2,641.7	2,486.7	2,348.3	2,402.4	….	….	….	….	Private Consumption	96f
	–386.5	–462.1	–531.2	–574.7	–594.7	–727.9	–859.0	–735.5	–692.4	–653.8	–659.7	….	….	….	….	Imports of Goods & Services	98c
	1,356.2	1,796.4	2,172.8	2,618.1	3,195.0	3,896.0	4,135.0	3,696.0	3,697.0	3,496.0	3,347.0	3,179.0	2,890.0	….	….	Gross Domestic Product	99b
	….	….	….	….	….	….	….	….	….	….	….	….	….	….	….	Net Factor Inc/Pmts(-) Abroad	98.n
	….	….	….	….	….	….	….	….	….	….	….	….	….	….	….	Gross Nat'l Expenditure = GNP	99a
	1,283.2	1,619.6	1,965.6	2,400.3	2,967.7	….	….	….	….	….	….	….	….	….	….	Nat'l Income, Market Prices	99e
	ⱡ2,330.0	2,727.7	2,933.9	3,140.4	3,386.3	3,688.9	3,955.4	3,758.8	3,487.3	3,278.1	3,347.0	….	….	….	….	Gross Dom. Prod. 1990 Prices	99b.*p*
	58.2	65.9	74.1	83.4	94.3	105.6	104.5	98.3	106.0	106.6	100.0	….	….	….	….	GDP Deflator (1990=100)	99bi *p*
Midyear Estimates																	
	8.50	8.97	9.28	9.57	9.87	10.17	10.46	10.82	10.88	11.54	11.53	11.85	12.18	12.52	….	Population	99z

Canada
156

		1965	1966	1967	1968	1969	1970	1971	1972	1973	1974	1975	1976	1977	1978	1979
Exchange Rates															*Canadian Dollars per SDR:*	
Market Rate	aa	1.0750	1.0838	1.0806	1.0728	1.0728	1.0112	1.0881	1.0809	1.2013	1.2136	1.1899	1.1725	1.3294	1.5451	1.5388
															Canadian Dollars per US Dollar:	
Market Rate	ae	1.0750	1.0838	1.0806	1.0728	1.0728	1.0112	1.0022	.9956	.9958	.9912	1.0164	1.0092	1.0944	1.1860	1.1681
Market Rate	rf	1.0811	1.0811	1.0811	1.0811	1.0811	1.0477	1.0098	.9899	1.0001	.9780	1.0172	.9860	1.0635	1.1407	1.1714
															Index Numbers (1990=100):	
Market Rate	ah x	108.2	108.3	108.1	108.3	108.3	111.8	115.5	117.9	116.7	119.3	114.7	118.3	109.8	102.3	99.6
Nominal Effective Exchange Rate	ne u	115.3	115.3	115.4	115.9	116.0	119.6	123.5	123.9	120.5	124.1	119.0	124.3	114.6	104.1	100.9
Real Effective Exchange Rate	re u	....	....	....	....	....	....	....	....	....	....	95.2	104.2	96.9	87.3	84.8
Fund Position															*Millions of SDRs:*	
Quota	2f. s	550	740	740	740	740	1,100	1,100	1,100	1,100	1,100	1,100	1,100	1,100	1,357	1,357
SDRs	1b. s	—	—	—	—	—	182	372	465	467	469	474	480	416	401	445
Reserve Position in the Fund	1c. s	353	448	433	206	478	670	333	316	280	433	554	813	701	427	297
of which: Outstg.Fund Borrowing	2c	50	50	35	—	96	120	—	—	—	141	247	247	205	129	26
International Liquidity												*Millions of US Dollars Unless Otherwise Indicated:*				
Total Reserves minus Gold	1l. d	1,886	1,656	1,702	2,183	2,234	3,888	4,839	5,216	4,841	4,885	4,426	4,964	3,672	3,557	2,864
SDRs	1b. d	—	—	—	—	—	182	404	505	564	574	555	558	505	522	586
Reserve Position in the Fund	1c. d	353	448	433	206	478	670	361	343	338	530	648	944	852	557	391
Foreign Exchange	1d. d	1,533	1,208	1,269	1,977	1,756	3,037	4,074	4,368	3,940	3,781	3,223	3,462	2,315	2,478	1,888
of which: US Dollars	1dx d	1,520	1,195	1,255	1,965	1,744	3,022	4,061	4,355	3,927	3,768	3,207	3,446	2,299	2,463	1,864
Gold (Million Fine Troy Ounces)	1a d	32.88	29.87	29.00	24.66	24.92	22.59	22.69	21.95	21.95	21.95	21.95	21.62	22.01	22.13	22.18
Gold (National Valuation)	1an d	1,151	1,046	1,015	863	872	791	792	834	927	941	899	879	936	1,009	1,023
Deposit Money Banks: Assets	7a. d	2,740	2,954	3,505	4,207	6,246	7,600	6,993	8,203	12,343	13,942	13,852	17,237	18,150	21,657	25,406
of which: Claims on Nonbanks	7ad d	....	....	....	....	....	....	....	....	1,467	2,090	2,715	3,528	4,014	4,304	5,254
Deposit Money Banks: Liabilities	7b. d	2,378	2,159	2,369	2,724	4,298	5,501	6,282	8,134	12,632	13,333	14,095	16,475	18,874	24,645	32,042
of which: Liab. to Nonbanks	7bd d	....	....	....	....	....	....	....	....	3,702	4,932	5,630	6,455	6,563	11,010	14,803
Monetary Authorities															*Billions of Canadian Dollars:*	
Foreign Assets	11	3.26	2.93	2.94	3.27	3.33	4.73	5.71	6.02	5.74	5.77	5.41	5.90	5.04	5.42	4.54
Claims on Central Government	12a	.45	1.00	1.23	1.10	1.30	.27	.09	.74	2.04	2.86	4.61	5.09	7.73	9.20	11.77
Reserve Money	14	3.85	4.15	4.39	4.75	5.00	5.28	6.08	7.03	8.16	9.31	10.75	11.75	13.18	14.74	16.01
of which: Currency Outside DMBs	14a	2.41	2.58	2.82	3.05	3.33	3.56	3.99	4.56	5.20	5.86	6.78	7.32	8.08	8.95	9.45
Other Items (Net)	17r	-2.29	-2.76	-3.05	-3.56	-3.99	-4.50	-4.90	-5.54	-6.86	-9.36	-10.00	-8.49	-6.59	-4.76	-2.79
Deposit Money Banks															*Billions of Canadian Dollars:*	
Reserves	20	1.42	1.55	1.55	1.68	1.65	1.70	2.07	2.45	2.94	3.44	4.02	4.48	5.13	5.83	6.63
Foreign Assets	21	2.96	3.19	3.79	4.55	6.75	7.69	7.01	8.17	11.90	13.41	13.61	16.93	19.39	25.24	29.19
Claims on Central Government	22a	3.73	3.89	4.63	5.56	5.07	6.60	7.33	7.13	7.24	8.06	7.73	8.58	9.51	9.75	9.93
Claims on Local Government	22b	1.27	1.34	1.46	1.53	1.62	1.69	1.79	1.86	2.19	2.45	3.04	3.05	2.65	2.64	2.73
Claims on Private Sector	22d	13.22	14.04	15.67	17.83	20.10	21.17	25.86	31.45	38.90	47.92	56.05	67.34	80.03	100.24	120.00
Demand Deposits	24	7.00	7.54	Ɪ13.21	12.88	11.92	11.82	13.59	15.18	16.23	15.90	19.12	18.94	20.92	22.02	21.91
Savings & Fgn Currency Deposits	25	10.94	11.87	Ɪ9.64	12.91	15.78	18.63	19.53	22.93	29.99	39.53	44.82	58.02	67.09	81.36	100.80
Foreign Liabilities	26c	2.57	2.33	2.56	2.95	4.65	5.56	6.30	8.10	11.49	11.62	12.27	14.65	18.27	26.73	34.69
Central Government Deposits	26d	.80	.92	.62	.67	1.31	1.26	2.24	2.41	2.36	4.68	3.66	3.10	4.73	6.47	2.42
Other Items (Net)	27r	1.29	1.34	1.07	1.74	1.53	1.58	2.40	2.44	3.09	3.54	4.52	5.62	5.64	7.06	8.57
Monetary Survey															*Billions of Canadian Dollars:*	
Foreign Assets (Net)	31n	3.64	3.77	4.14	4.85	5.41	6.83	6.40	6.05	6.12	7.48	6.71	8.08	6.05	3.87	-1.05
Domestic Credit	32	20.13	22.09	25.44	28.82	30.70	32.92	37.87	44.54	55.19	66.24	78.03	89.45	101.93	120.38	145.28
Claims on Central Govt. (Net)	32an	3.24	3.89	5.17	5.92	4.96	5.36	5.08	5.37	6.89	6.22	8.65	10.48	12.38	12.34	19.12
Claims on Local Government	32b	1.27	1.34	1.46	1.53	1.62	1.69	1.79	1.86	2.19	2.45	3.04	3.05	2.65	2.64	2.73
Claims on Private Sector	32d	15.62	16.86	18.82	21.37	24.13	25.87	31.00	37.31	46.11	57.57	66.35	75.92	86.90	105.40	123.44
Money	34	9.43	10.13	Ɪ16.19	15.97	15.30	15.57	17.61	19.77	21.50	21.83	25.97	26.36	29.10	31.12	31.56
Quasi-Money	35	10.94	11.87	Ɪ9.64	12.91	15.78	18.48	19.53	22.93	29.99	39.53	44.82	58.02	67.09	81.36	100.80
Other Items (Net)	37r	1.14	1.07	Ɪ-.73	-.77	1.45	1.49	2.51	2.63	3.37	3.72	4.67	5.45	5.64	7.17	8.87
Money plus Quasi-Money	35l	20.37	22.00	Ɪ25.83	28.88	31.08	34.05	37.15	42.71	51.49	61.36	70.79	84.38	96.19	112.48	132.37
Other Banking Institutions															*Billions of Canadian Dollars:*	
Cash	40	....	.21	.80	.92	.81	1.10	1.41	2.12	Ɪ1.54	1.91	2.66	2.85	3.36	3.83	4.01
Claims on Central Government	42a	....	....	....	....	....	....	....	....	.56	.49	.49	.55	.75	.98	1.20
Claims on State and Local Govt	42b	.47	.50	.90	.93	.93	1.03	1.33	1.31	Ɪ1.17	1.11	1.10	1.10	1.20	1.19	1.16
Claims on Private Sector	42d	....	5.37	8.04	9.03	10.31	11.66	13.31	15.95	Ɪ32.98	39.00	44.46	51.13	59.51	69.22	80.14
Demand Deposits	44	.71	.72	.72	.73	.60	.55	.61	.71	Ɪ.74	.66	.79	.81	.94	1.04	1.02
Time and Savings Deposits	45	....	5.09	Ɪ11.57	13.15	14.27	16.27	18.95	21.87	Ɪ18.51	22.16	26.60	32.39	39.05	46.94	55.41
Money Market Instruments	46aa	....	....	....	....	....	....	....	....	2.67	3.25	3.23	3.43	3.66	4.26	4.35
Bonds	46ab	....	....	....	....	....	....	....	....	2.61	2.76	3.22	3.95	4.31	4.63	4.82
Capital Accounts	47a	.61	.64	2.19	2.35	2.45	2.58	2.73	3.08	Ɪ4.76	5.16	5.95	6.74	7.71	8.69	9.17
Other Items (Net)	47r	....	.99	2.27	2.40	2.19	2.31	2.43	3.44	Ɪ-.49	.09	-.38	-1.34	-1.15	-1.31	.08
Banking Survey															*Billions of Canadian Dollars:*	
Foreign Assets (Net)	51n	3.64	3.77	4.14	4.85	5.41	6.83	6.40	6.05	6.12	7.48	6.71	8.08	6.05	3.87	-1.05
Domestic Credit	52	....	....	....	....	....	....	....	....	90.67	107.86	125.28	143.59	164.82	193.31	229.66
Claims on Central Govt. (Net)	52an	....	....	....	....	....	....	....	....	7.45	6.71	9.14	11.03	13.13	13.32	20.31
Claims on State and Local Govt.	52b	....	....	....	....	....	....	....	....	3.36	3.56	4.13	4.14	3.84	3.84	3.88
Claims on Private Sector	52d	....	....	....	....	....	....	....	....	79.86	97.59	112.01	128.42	147.84	176.15	205.46
Liquid Liabilities	55l	....	27.61	Ɪ33.22	37.17	40.72	44.98	49.97	57.23	Ɪ70.32	83.72	97.62	116.83	135.48	159.57	188.43
Money Market Instruments	56aa	....	....	....	....	....	....	....	....	2.67	3.25	3.23	3.43	3.66	4.26	4.35
Bonds	56ab	....	....	....	....	....	....	....	....	2.61	2.76	3.22	3.95	4.31	4.63	4.82
Other Items (Net)	57r	....	....	....	....	....	....	....	....	7.76	9.17	10.44	10.96	12.32	14.75	18.55

Canada

1980	1981	1982	1983	1984	1985	1986	1987	1988	1989	1990	1991	1992	1993	1994		
End of Period															**Exchange Rates**	
1.5237	1.3803	1.3562	1.3028	1.2952	1.5350	1.6886	1.8440	1.6050	1.5215	1.6507	1.6530	1.7478	1.8186	2.0479	Market Rate	**aa**
End of Period (ae) Period Average (rf)																
1.1947	1.1859	1.2294	1.2444	1.3214	1.3975	1.3805	1.2998	1.1927	1.1578	1.1603	1.1556	1.2711	1.3240	1.4028	Market Rate	**ae**
1.1692	1.1989	1.2337	1.2324	1.2951	1.3655	1.3895	1.3260	1.2307	1.1840	1.1668	1.1457	1.2087	1.2901	1.3656	Market Rate	**rf**
Period Averages																
99.8	97.3	94.6	94.7	90.1	85.5	84.0	88.0	94.8	98.5	100.0	101.8	96.6	90.5	85.4	Market Rate	**ah** x
100.8	100.6	100.0	101.1	97.6	93.1	87.2	89.0	94.8	99.8	100.0	101.7	95.8	90.3	84.7	Nominal Effective Exchange Rate	**ne** u
83.8	87.8	88.7	91.9	89.6	85.7	81.1	84.6	92.5	98.4	100.0	103.0	97.5	89.9	....	Real Effective Exchange Rate	**re** u
End of Period															**Fund Position**	
2,036	2,036	2,036	2,941	2,941	2,941	2,941	2,941	2,941	2,941	2,941	2,941	2,941	4,320	4,320	4,320	Quota	**2f.** s
355	150	64	20	74	198	202	281	1,017	1,048	1,072	1,106	756	773	786	SDRs	**1b.** s
454	346	331	672	692	647	561	466	375	402	364	414	735	690	629	Reserve Position in the Fund	**1c.** s
13	13	13	124	164	161	155	120	30	—	—	—	—	—	—	*of which:* Outstg.Fund Borrowing	**2c**
End of Period															**International Liquidity**	
3,093	3,537	3,011	3,466	2,491	2,503	3,251	7,277	15,391	16,055	17,845	16,252	11,431	12,481	12,286	Total Reserves minus Gold	**1l.** d
453	174	71	21	72	218	247	399	1,369	1,377	1,526	1,582	1,039	1,062	1,148	SDRs	**1b.** d
579	402	365	703	678	711	686	661	505	528	517	592	1,011	948	919	Reserve Position in the Fund	**1c.** d
2,061	2,961	2,575	2,742	1,741	1,574	2,318	6,218	13,517	14,150	15,802	14,079	9,382	10,471	10,219	Foreign Exchange	**1d.** d
2,038	2,865	2,455	2,373	1,692	1,524	2,274	6,163	12,608	11,489	11,476	9,440	7,864	9,950	9,693	*of which:* US Dollars	**1dx** d
20.98	20.46	20.26	20.17	20.14	20.11	19.72	18.52	17.14	16.10	14.76	12.96	9.94	6.05	3.89	Gold (Million Fine Troy Ounces)	**1a** d
937	834	782	739	691	773	845	920	807	741	735	649	478	292	198	Gold (National Valuation)	**1an** d
35,194	38,160	38,150	40,965	41,212	44,169	50,745	50,734	46,804	48,819	52,068	46,031	46,851	41,108	54,608	Deposit Money Banks: Assets	**7a.** d
7,328	9,540	7,126	7,756	7,492	9,786	8,117	10,596	12,907	12,740	12,216	11,962	11,454	12,649	11,166	*of which:* Claims on Nonbanks	**7ad** d
42,959	61,040	57,738	61,289	61,619	64,637	68,905	71,734	69,480	70,807	77,946	76,711	73,613	67,151	80,507	Deposit Money Banks: Liabilities	**7b.** d
17,985	23,110	18,991	24,996	27,040	30,336	32,379	31,726	31,107	31,999	35,755	33,513	27,288	24,361	29,812	*of which:* Liab. to Nonbanks	**7bd** d
End of Period															**Monetary Authorities**	
4.81	5.18	4.66	5.23	4.20	4.58	5.65	10.65	19.32	19.45	21.56	19.53	15.14	16.91	17.51	Foreign Assets	**11**
13.48	14.04	14.39	14.57	15.86	14.15	16.58	13.94	6.89	7.59	6.00	9.20	15.13	12.92	13.24	Claims on Central Government	**12a**
17.62	18.02	18.73	18.98	19.34	20.44	22.04	23.94	25.19	26.11	26.73	28.48	29.14	28.46	29.09	Reserve Money	**14**
10.40	10.71	11.62	12.80	13.50	14.61	15.59	16.92	18.24	19.64	20.05	21.22	23.17	22.52	23.97	*of which:* Currency Outside DMBs	**14a**
−.87	1.21	.33	.82	.73	−1.70	.19	.65	1.02	.93	.83	.25	1.12	1.36	1.66	Other Items (Net)	**17r**
End of Period															**Deposit Money Banks**	
7.28	7.36	7.15	6.08	5.85	5.68	6.24	6.77	6.71	6.29	6.58	7.15	5.88	5.92	5.04	Reserves	**20**
41.60	44.19	45.29	49.23	52.17	59.91	68.41	63.92	52.88	53.09	57.13	50.81	57.44	51.74	78.36	Foreign Assets	**21**
9.75	9.85	11.55	16.10	14.72	14.84	17.40	15.18	20.94	20.58	24.47	38.35	50.68	69.59	78.33	Claims on Central Government	**22a**
2.88	3.6	3.21	3.18	2.73	3.06	2.52	3.67	3.86	4.32	4.74	7.67	8.57	9.67	13.15	Claims on Local Government	**22b**
136.54	**I** 189.45	191.61	184.94	199.78	216.85	223.58	244.52	272.27	306.67	334.55	348.75	372.22	415.63	450.46	Claims on Private Sector	**22d**
24.32	**I** 26.00	28.16	31.11	38.86	54.05	64.31	67.91	71.54	75.47	75.92	78.98	84.63	91.73	97.65	Demand Deposits	**24**
110.18	**I** 140.62	146.34	140.45	143.14	137.07	142.03	156.35	177.06	207.78	230.30	241.92	266.91	301.33	327.17	Savings & Fgn Currency Deposits	**25**
48.48	68.85	67.37	73.11	78.04	86.57	90.46	87.33	76.73	74.38	82.41	81.13	87.68	82.23	105.94	Foreign Liabilities	**26c**
4.09	7.14	6.91	6.06	2.80	4.35	2.05	1.82	1.84	2.08	3.23	2.08	1.41	2.44	2.78	Central Government Deposits	**26d**
10.88	**I** 11.53	10.03	8.81	12.42	18.30	19.32	20.65	29.49	31.24	35.60	48.63	54.16	74.82	91.80	Other Items (Net)	**27r**
End of Period															**Monetary Survey**	
−2.13	−19.63	−17.55	−18.75	−21.85	−22.20	−16.48	−13.11	−4.75	−2.14	−4.02	−11.22	−15.49	−13.94	−10.57	Foreign Assets (Net)	**31n**
160.02	**I** 209.27	213.69	212.56	230.22	243.87	257.91	275.34	301.63	336.85	366.31	401.78	445.14	505.20	552.00	Domestic Credit	**32**
18.89	16.32	18.87	24.44	27.71	23.96	31.80	27.15	25.50	25.86	27.02	45.36	64.36	79.90	88.39	Claims on Central Govt. (Net)	**32an**
2.88	3.50	3.21	3.18	2.73	3.06	2.52	3.67	3.86	4.32	4.74	7.67	8.57	9.67	13.15	Claims on Local Government	**32b**
138.25	**I** 189.45	191.61	184.94	199.78	216.85	223.58	244.52	272.27	306.67	334.55	348.75	372.22	415.63	450.46	Claims on Private Sector	**32d**
34.75	**I** 36.75	39.82	44.09	52.44	68.91	80.22	85.20	90.12	95.45	96.22	100.45	108.02	114.40	121.79	Money	**34**
110.18	**I** 140.62	146.34	140.45	143.14	137.07	142.03	156.35	177.06	207.78	230.30	241.92	266.91	301.33	327.17	Quasi-Money	**35**
11.34	**I** 12.05	9.99	9.27	12.80	15.69	19.18	20.68	29.70	31.48	35.77	48.18	54.72	75.53	92.46	Other Items (Net)	**37r**
144.93	**I** 177.37	186.16	184.54	195.57	205.98	222.25	241.55	267.18	303.22	326.52	342.37	374.93	415.72	448.96	Money plus Quasi-Money	**35l**
End of Period															**Other Banking Institutions**	
4.04	5.28	6.31	4.86	5.54	5.42	6.79	7.50	13.24	15.17	14.99	15.86	17.21	15.12	....	Cash	**40**
1.93	1.61	2.19	3.39	3.28	3.50	5.23	3.87	4.80	6.91	8.53	9.23	8.92	7.56	....	Claims on Central Government	**42a**
1.54	1.43	1.61	1.66	2.06	1.73	1.63	1.52	1.83	1.36	1.64	2.54	3.01	2.13	....	Claims on State and Local Govt.	**42b**
87.89	92.30	90.54	98.70	98.62	110.83	123.81	142.37	162.70	184.34	196.45	197.92	196.92	166.14	....	Claims on Private Sector	**42d**
1.56	1.86	2.47	3.66	5.29	7.77	8.43	8.92	9.21	11.46	11.41	11.62	11.38	9.47	8.97	Demand Deposits	**44**
63.45	69.46	74.75	81.48	88.31	95.27	108.63	121.48	139.60	158.26	172.10	176.79	179.50	150.01	....	Time and Savings Deposits	**45**
4.26	4.31	3.89	5.84	7.41	7.81	8.78	9.59	9.84	11.09	10.28	8.44	7.73	7.09	9.46	Money Market Instruments	**46aa**
4.61	4.61	3.68	3.15	3.34	4.13	5.35	6.89	8.02	8.27	9.25	9.83	9.02	8.92	9.19	Bonds	**46ab**
9.66	**I** 6.01	5.67	6.09	5.99	6.07	6.34	7.71	9.13	10.38	11.05	11.45	11.30	10.58	....	Capital Accounts	**47a**
.47	**I** −.79	−.93	−2.75	−.73	−.08	−1.06	.07	2.09	6.27	6.47	7.12	7.01	4.89	....	Other Items (Net)	**47r**
End of Period															**Banking Survey**	
−2.13	−19.63	−17.55	−18.75	−21.85	−22.20	−16.48	−13.11	−4.75	−2.14	−4.02	−11.22	−15.49	−13.94	....	Foreign Assets (Net)	**51n**
253.38	304.60	308.03	316.30	334.18	359.92	388.58	423.09	470.96	529.45	572.93	611.46	654.00	681.03	....	Domestic Credit	**52**
20.82	17.93	21.06	27.83	30.99	27.46	37.03	31.01	30.30	32.77	35.55	54.59	73.28	87.46	....	Claims on Central Govt. (Net)	**52an**
4.41	4.92	4.82	4.84	4.79	4.79	4.15	5.19	5.69	5.67	6.38	10.21	11.58	11.80	....	Claims on State and Local Govt.	**52b**
228.14	281.75	282.15	283.63	298.40	327.67	347.39	386.89	434.97	491.01	530.99	546.67	569.14	581.77	....	Claims on Private Sector	**52d**
211.37	243.41	257.06	264.82	283.64	303.60	332.52	364.44	402.75	457.77	495.04	514.92	548.60	560.08	....	Liquid Liabilities	**55l**
4.26	4.31	3.89	5.84	7.41	7.81	8.78	9.59	9.84	11.09	10.28	8.44	7.73	7.09	....	Money Market Instruments	**56aa**
4.61	4.61	3.68	3.15	3.34	4.13	5.35	6.89	8.02	8.27	9.25	9.83	9.02	8.92	....	Bonds	**56ab**
21.78	17.28	14.73	12.60	18.06	21.68	24.45	28.46	40.92	48.13	53.28	66.75	73.04	91.00	....	Other Items (Net)	**57r**

Canada
156

		1965	1966	1967	1968	1969	1970	1971	1972	1973	1974	1975	1976	1977	1978	1979
Nonbank Financial Institutions																*Millions of Canadian Dollars:*
Cash	40..s	66	56	60	76	89	132	133	211	187	168	273	319	444	438	568
Claims on Central Government	42a.s	525	433	410	437	442	503	487	546	484	512	554	746	989	1,650	2,595
Claims on Local Government	42b.s	1,770	1,779	1,862	1,824	1,772	1,780	1,860	2,010	2,105	2,142	2,252	2,612	2,897	3,185	3,289
Claims on Private Sector	42d.s	8,190	8,897	9,524	10,252	10,767	11,286	12,065	13,900	15,364	16,700	18,685	20,460	22,827	25,303	27,985
Incr.in Total Assets(Within Per.)	49z.s	786	703	785	755	667	626	2,066	1,385	1,636	1,609	2,441	2,662	3,205	3,962	4,503
Interest Rates																*Percent Per Annum*
Bank Rate *(End of Period)*	60	4.75	5.25	6.00	6.50	8.00	6.00	4.75	4.75	7.25	8.75	9.00	8.50	7.50	10.75	14.00
Money Market Rate	60b	....	....	....	....	....	....	....	....	....	....	9.23	8.45	5.88	6.61	13.21
Corporate Paper Rate	60bc	5.02	6.27	5.85	6.82	7.85	7.34	4.51	5.10	7.45	10.51	7.94	9.17	7.48	8.83	12.07
Treasury Bill Rate	60c	3.98	5.00	4.64	6.27	7.19	5.99	3.56	3.56	5.47	7.82	7.40	8.87	7.33	8.68	11.69
Deposit Rate	60l	....	....	....	....	....	....	4.75	5.36	6.87	....	7.78	9.31	7.53	8.83	12.05
Lending Rate	60p	5.77	6.00	5.92	6.92	7.96	8.17	6.48	6.00	7.65	10.75	9.42	10.04	8.50	9.69	12.90
Govt. Bond Yield: Med.-Term	61a	4.90	5.55	5.64	6.68	7.66	7.11	5.56	6.26	6.98	8.12	7.72	8.35	7.90	9.00	10.42
Long-Term	61	5.21	5.69	5.94	6.75	7.58	7.91	6.95	7.23	7.56	8.90	9.04	9.18	8.70	9.27	10.21
Prices, Production, Employment																*Index Numbers (1990=100):*
Industrial Share Prices	62	25.7	24.4	25.9	27.2	30.3	26.6	28.3	33.3	35.6	29.7	29.2	30.3	29.5	33.9	46.1
Prices: Industry Selling	63	24.4	25.1	25.6	26.1	27.1	27.8	28.3	29.6	32.9	39.1	43.5	45.7	49.4	53.9	61.7
Consumer Prices	64	21.5	22.3	23.1	24.0	25.1	25.9	26.7	28.0	30.1	33.4	37.0	39.7	42.9	46.7	51.0
Wages: Hourly Earnings (Mfg)	65ey	14.2	15.1	16.2	17.3	18.8	20.3	22.1	23.8	25.9	29.4	34.0	38.7	42.9	45.9	50.0
Industrial Production	66..c	45.8	48.7	50.5	53.9	57.5	58.4	I61.5	66.2	72.8	75.3	70.8	74.6	76.3	79.4	I84.1
Crude Petroleum Production	66aa	....	....	....	....	....	....	....	....	....	....	....	86.2	86.8	85.6	96.5
Gold Production	66kr	67.9	62.0	56.1	51.9	48.2	45.6	42.8	39.3	37.0	32.1	30.7	32.0	32.8	32.8	31.1
Manufacturing Employment	67ey	98.4	103.7	103.5	102.5	105.2	103.1	102.2	103.9	109.1	112.3	106.1	107.5	106.1	107.2	110.4
International Transactions																*Millions of Canadian Dollars*
Exports	70	9,134	10,779	11,865	14,187	15,452	17,527	18,552	20,955	26,438	33,743	34,662	40,015	46,337	55,311	68,269
Wheat	70d	840	1,061	742	684	473	687	833	927	1,034	1,644	1,260	1,262	1,412	1,447	1,685
Wood Pulp	70sl	493	520	543	628	754	785	798	830	1,082	1,889	1,835	2,186	2,158	2,181	3,083
Newsprint	70ul	870	968	955	990	1,126	1,111	1,085	1,158	1,288	1,726	1,746	2,003	2,382	2,886	3,222
Imports, cif	71	9,295	10,841	11,671	13,229	15,095	14,928	16,631	19,823	24,715	33,492	36,726	39,666	44,758	52,853	66,334
Imports, fob	71.v	9,006	10,505	11,309	12,818	14,628	14,454	16,135	19,231	24,027	32,674	35,761	38,619	43,634	51,613	64,756
																1990=100
Volume of Exports	72	22.4	25.4	I27.5	I32.2	34.1	37.5	39.5	43.2	47.8	46.0	42.6	47.7	52.0	57.2	58.2
Wheat	72d	78	101	66	63	45	73	82	87	79	62	51	58	83	80	66
Wood Pulp	72sl	55	58	60	70	82	79	80	86	95	102	78	96	95	104	111
Newsprint	72ul	79	86	82	82	91	89	86	89	93	96	77	85	88	96	94
Volume of Imports	73	20.7	23.3	I26.1	I29.0	32.5	31.5	34.6	40.5	47.0	51.7	48.9	52.7	53.0	54.7	60.8
Unit Value of Exports	74	26.1	27.2	I27.7	I28.3	29.0	29.9	30.1	31.2	35.7	47.4	52.4	53.2	56.9	61.9	75.0
Wheat	74d	32	31	33	32	31	28	30	31	38	78	73	64	50	53	75
Wood Pulp	74sl	27	26	27	26	27	29	29	28	34	55	69	67	67	62	82
Newsprint	74ul	19	20	20	21	22	22	22	23	24	32	40	41	47	53	60
Unit Value of Imports	75	24.0	24.4	I24.5	I25.0	25.6	26.1	26.6	27.2	29.3	36.2	I41.6	42.7	48.8	55.3	65.0
Balance of Payments																*Millions of US Dollars:*
Goods: Exports f.o.b.	78aad	8,426	9,931	10,856	13,112	14,397	16,716	18,321	21,214	26,565	34,488	34,024	40,026	43,198	48,175	57,664
Goods: Imports f.o.b.	78abd	−8,262	−9,659	−10,271	−11,660	−13,421	−13,665	−15,635	−19,033	−23,381	−32,394	−34,293	−38,138	−40,059	−43,987	−53,481
Trade Balance	78acd	164	272	585	1,452	976	3,050	2,685	2,181	3,185	2,094	−269	1,888	3,139	4,188	4,183
Services: Credit	78add	1,489	1,687	2,239	1,834	2,108	2,470	2,639	2,778	3,181	4,148	4,242	4,860	4,880	5,376	6,432
Services: Debit	78aed	−1,756	−1,978	−2,175	−2,384	−2,954	−3,352	−3,702	−3,983	−4,633	−5,797	−6,361	−7,779	−8,144	−8,609	−9,072
Balance on Goods and Services	78afd	−103	−19	649	903	130	2,168	1,622	975	1,733	445	−2,388	−1,032	−124	955	1,543
Income: Credit	78agd	456	476	457	575	826	1,004	982	1,036	1,234	1,478	1,703	1,703	1,695	2,062	2,261
Income: Debit	78ahd	−1,374	−1,509	−1,600	−1,705	−1,943	−2,291	−2,476	−2,508	−2,967	−3,762	−4,201	−5,288	−5,981	−7,244	−8,369
Balance on Goods, Serv., & Inc.	78aid	−1,020	−1,051	−494	−227	−986	881	129	−497	....	−1,839	−4,885	−4,617	−4,410	−4,227	−4,565
Current Transfers, n.i.e.: Credit	78ajd	246	280	305	299	318	380	451	479	553	697	725	803	827	862	1,039
Current Transfers: Debit	78akd	−247	−319	−367	−300	−368	−432	−463	−542	−596	−727	−902	−885	−956	−1,239	−1,082
Current Account, n.i.e.	78ald	−1,021	−1,090	−556	−228	−1,036	829	117	−560	−43	−1,869	−5,062	−4,698	−4,538	−4,604	−4,608
Capital Account, n.i.e.: Credit	78bad	200	249	304	343	339	374	428	448	522	717	653	738	650	540	683
Capital Account: Debit	78bbd	−195	−183	−197	−193	−189	−191	−183	−164	−171	−166	−167	−184	−221	−220	−218
Capital Account, n.i.e.	78bcd	5	66	107	150	150	183	244	284	351	551	486	554	428	320	465
Direct Investment Abroad	78bdd	−116	−5	−116	−208	−342	−287	−232	−347	−694	−746	−854	−505	−628	−1,885	−1,916
Dir. Invest. in Rep. Econ., n.i.e.	78bed	495	731	639	546	666	794	956	681	554	821	711	−549	149	459	1,182
Portfolio Investment Assets	78bfd	−79	−371	−400	−432	94	59	195	245	70	49	−19	78	205	25	−495
Portfolio Investment Liab., n.i.e.	78bgd	454	660	794	1,338	1,796	691	183	1,209	706	1,919	4,799	9,983	5,490	2,594	3,402
Other Investment Assets	78bhd	−157	−68	156	77	−902	−1,632	−630	−2,028	−4,836	−1,333	−847	−4,594	−3,136	−5,894	−6,175
Other Investment Liab., n.i.e.	78bid	815	−38	−133	−181	−202	1,242	1,326	2,429	4,272	1,689	1,680	4,071	2,726	6,675	10,526
Financial Account, n.i.e.	78bjd	1,412	910	941	1,139	1,111	866	1,797	2,189	72	2,400	5,469	8,485	4,805	1,974	6,524
Net Errors and Omissions	78cad	−250	−219	−477	−738	−165	−435	−1,387	−1,693	−847	−1,057	−1,291	−3,815	−2,043	−2,809	−2,307
Overall Balance	78cbd	146	−333	15	323	60	1,442	772	221	−466	25	−398	525	−1,348	−5,119	74
Reserves and Related Items	79dad	−146	333	−15	−323	−60	−1,442	−772	−221	466	−25	398	−525	1,348	5,119	−74
Reserve Assets	79dbd	−146	333	−15	−323	−60	−1,442	−772	−221	466	−25	398	−525	1,348	191	941
Use of Fund Credit and Loans	79dcd	—	—	—	—	—	—	—	—	—	—	—	—	—	—	—
Liabs.Constit.For.Auth.Reserves	79ddd	—	—	—	—	—	—	—	—	—	—	—	—	—	—	—
Exceptional Financing	79ded	—	—	—	—	—	—	—	—	—	—	—	—	—	4,928	−1,015

Canada

1980	1981	1982	1983	1984	1985	1986	1987	1988	1989	1990	1991	1992	1993	1994		
End of Period															**Nonbank Financial Institutions**	
689	1,138	1,383	950	1,150	1,357	1,448	....	....	....	....	....	....	....	....	Cash	40..s
3,087	3,483	4,458	5,379	7,740	10,327	10,176	....	....	....	....	....	....	....	....	Claims on Central Government	42a.s
3,503	4,168	4,628	5,204	6,530	7,426	7,989	....	....	....	....	....	....	....	....	Claims on Local Government	42b.s
31,950	34,943	37,135	40,711	42,385	47,339	53,453	....	....	....	....	....	....	....	....	Claims on Private Sector	42d.s
5,487	4,971	5,213	6,075	6,678	9,061	7,655	....	....	....	....	....	....	....	....	Incr.in Total Assets(Within Per.)	49z.s
Percent Per Annum															**Interest Rates**	
17.26	14.66	10.26	10.04	10.16	9.49	8.49	8.66	11.17	12.47	11.78	7.67	7.36	4.11	7.00	Bank Rate *(End of Period)*	60
18.96	12.82	10.38	9.07	10.05	9.84	8.16	8.50	10.35	12.06	11.62	7.40	6.79	3.79	5.54	Money Market Rate	60b
13.15	18.33	14.15	9.45	11.19	9.56	9.16	8.38	9.67	12.21	13.03	8.91	6.74	4.97	5.66	Corporate Paper Rate	60bc
12.79	17.72	13.66	9.31	11.06	9.43	8.97	8.15	9.48	12.05	12.81	8.73	6.59	4.84	5.54	Treasury Bill Rate	60c
12.87	18.16	13.74	7.91	10.06	8.40	8.25	7.67	9.54	12.09	12.81	8.62	6.67	4.92	5.59	Deposit Rate	60l
14.25	19.29	15.81	11.17	12.06	10.58	10.52	9.52	10.83	13.33	14.06	9.94	7.48	5.94	6.88	Lending Rate	60p
12.37	15.68	14.00	10.61	11.91	10.39	9.21	9.42	9.77	10.20	11.19	9.16	7.43	6.46	7.79	Govt. Bond Yield: Med.-Term	61a
12.48	15.22	14.26	11.79	12.75	11.04	9.52	9.95	10.22	9.92	10.85	9.76	8.77	7.85	8.63	Long-Term	61
Period Averages															**Prices, Production, Employment**	
62.1	63.1	47.9	69.2	68.4	79.3	88.0	104.3	96.5	111.1	100.0	101.4	99.5	114.1	125.2	Industrial Share Prices	62
70.0	77.1	81.8	84.6	88.0	‡90.4	‡91.1	93.7	97.7	99.7	100.0	99.0	99.5	102.7	108.6	Prices: Industry Selling	63
56.2	‡63.2	70.0	74.1	77.3	80.4	83.7	87.4	90.9	95.5	100.0	105.6	107.2	109.2	109.4	Consumer Prices	64
55.0	61.6	68.9	‡73.7	78.0	81.0	83.6	85.7	89.7	94.6	100.0	105.5	108.2	110.5	111.5	Wages: Hourly Earnings (Mfg)	65ey
81.3	83.0	74.8	79.7	89.3	94.3	‡94.2	98.8	103.3	103.4	100.0	95.6	95.9	101.8	108.4	Industrial Production	66..c
92.3	82.9	81.8	86.6	91.9	94.1	94.0	98.3	103.3	100.4	100.0	....	....	....	....	Crude Petroleum Production	66aa
29.8	28.6	39.4	44.7	50.8	53.3	62.6	70.5	82.0	95.8	100.0	104.2	95.3	90.9	88.1	Gold Production	66kr
108.3	109.0	98.8	‡96.0	93.0	94.9	96.9	105.9	107.0	107.5	100.0	87.6	88.5	88.1	90.9	Manufacturing Employment	67ey
Millions of Canadian Dollars															**International Transactions**	
79,208	87,164	87,911	94,603	116,965	124,249	125,497	130,089	144,038	144,248	148,912	145,658	162,596	187,346	225,908	Exports	70
2,745	2,743	3,509	3,358	4,710	3,416	1,878	....	....	....	....	....	....	....	....	Wheat	70d
3,873	3,819	3,221	3,058	3,912	3,388	3,995	5,464	6,323	6,810	....	....	....	....	....	Wood Pulp	70sl
3,684	4,325	4,086	4,005	3,703	5,692	7,093	6,380	6,190	5,741	....	....	....	....	....	Newsprint	70ul
73,150	83,925	71,706	79,857	100,746	110,130	118,785	122,718	138,802	141,866	143,837	142,913	156,246	179,425	211,792	Imports, cif	71
71,353	81,867	69,892	77,855	98,339	107,477	115,887	119,725	135,416	138,406	140,329	139,427	152,435	175,049	206,626	Imports, fob	71.v
1990=100																
57.5	‡59.1	58.8	63.1	74.8	79.6	‡83.2	86.2	94.2	95.5	100.0	101.0	110.0	120.9	140.4	Volume of Exports	72
90	83	114	112	128	100	73	51	57	30	....	....	....	....	....	Wheat	72d
113	105	96	106	110	100	109	117	116	115	....	....	....	....	....	Wood Pulp	72sl
91	89	78	82	90	91	84	97	96	95	100	96	....	....	....	Newsprint	72ul
57.3	‡59.0	49.3	54.7	65.5	72.3	‡78.1	83.0	94.7	99.9	100.0	102.4	109.5	120.0	138.5	Volume of Imports	73
87.2	‡92.7	93.4	93.2	97.4	98.2	‡96.2	97.9	98.4	100.8	100.0	96.5	98.7	104.4	110.7	Unit Value of Exports	74
89	96	90	88	108	100	75	129	194	202	....	....	....	....	....	Wheat	74d
101	107	100	85	105	100	108	138	161	175	....	....	....	....	....	Wood Pulp	74sl
71	86	92	85	73	110	148	116	114	106	....	....	....	....	....	Newsprint	74ul
78.3	89.4	93.2	92.7	98.1	101.2	‡100.9	99.6	97.9	98.2	100.0	98.6	102.8	109.0	116.0	Unit Value of Imports	75
Minus Sign Indicates Debit															**Balance of Payments**	
67,491	72,533	70,506	75,699	88,643	89,665	89,027	98,052	115,431	122,969	128,440	126,153	132,115	143,953	163,492	Goods: Exports f.o.b.	78aad
−59,486	−65,949	−55,510	−60,710	−72,659	−77,077	−81,350	−89,091	−107,273	−116,984	−120,106	−122,282	−126,415	−136,026	−151,290	Goods: Imports f.o.b.	78abd
8,005	6,584	14,996	14,989	15,984	12,587	7,677	8,961	8,157	5,985	8,334	3,871	5,699	7,927	12,202	Trade Balance	78acd
7,377	8,266	7,786	8,210	8,605	9,105	10,382	11,635	14,087	15,448	15,249	17,743	17,729	18,298	18,999	Services: Credit	78add
−10,558	−11,608	−11,451	−12,166	−12,788	−13,269	−14,644	−16,901	−19,798	−23,271	−25,521	−28,567	−28,541	−28,716	−27,145	Services: Debit	78aed
4,825	3,242	11,330	11,033	11,801	8,423	3,415	3,695	2,447	−1,838	−1,938	−6,953	−5,113	−2,491	4,056	Balance on Goods and Services	78afd
3,112	3,329	4,440	4,299	6,151	6,236	5,057	7,337	8,372	9,078	9,542	8,938	8,451	7,763	8,649	Income: Credit	78agd
−9,801	−12,786	−14,708	−16,859	−18,495	−18,999	−18,775	−22,792	−28,182	−30,230	−29,113	−25,679	−25,038	−27,962	−29,792	Income: Debit	78ahd
−1,865	−6,215	1,062	−1,527	−543	−4,340	−10,303	−11,760	−17,363	−22,990	−21,510	−23,694	−21,700	−22,690	−17,087	Balance on Goods, Serv., & Inc.	78aid
1,308	1,392	1,454	1,351	1,349	1,296	1,779	1,549	2,066	2,035	2,290	2,292	2,233	2,281	2,284	Current Transfers, n.i.e.: Credit	78ajd
−1,135	−1,200	−1,331	−1,459	−1,732	−1,725	−1,827	−2,208	−2,727	−2,835	−3,358	−3,169	−3,125	−2,982	−2,586	Current Transfers: Debit	78akd
−1,691	−6,022	1,185	−1,635	−927	−4,769	−10,351	−12,420	−18,023	−23,790	−22,577	−24,571	−22,592	−23,391	−17,388	Current Account, n.i.e.	78ald
284	413	537	346	366	377	409	790	1,100	1,257	1,251	1,260	1,297	1,293	1,281	Capital Account, n.i.e.: Credit	78bad
−128	−130	−144	−156	−149	−149	−161	−172	−179	−202	−218	−273	−264	−264	−264	Capital Account: Debit	78bbd
156	283	393	191	218	228	248	617	921	1,055	1,033	986	1,033	1,029	1,017	Capital Account, n.i.e.	78bcd
−2,754	−4,895	−1,082	−2,641	−3,636	−3,866	−3,502	−8,540	−3,854	−4,587	−4,725	−5,655	−3,635	−5,825	−4,781	Direct Investment Abroad	78bdd
−420	−3,829	−1,209	1,999	4,754	1,283	2,777	8,040	6,425	5,029	7,855	2,740	4,517	4,997	6,043	Dir. Invest. in Rep. Econ., n.i.e.	78bed
−154	−24	−438	−1,036	−1,601	−961	−1,621	−1,470	−2,443	−3,393	−2,239	−6,695	−6,933	−10,687	−6,414	Portfolio Investment Assets	78bfd
5,304	10,230	8,512	5,754	7,160	7,311	17,790	12,058	18,489	19,220	15,925	27,012	20,679	39,817	12,881	Portfolio Investment Liab., n.i.e.	78bgd
−12,886	−11,052	−4,499	−2,722	−4,652	−742	−7,740	2,504	4,445	−3,166	−5,371	6,136	679	7,527	−12,945	Other Investment Assets	78bhd
12,263	23,149	−3,230	4,029	1,587	2,827	3,776	4,389	2,158	9,425	12,127	209	−859	−6,705	13,546	Other Investment Liab., n.i.e.	78bid
1,353	13,579	−1,946	5,385	3,612	5,852	11,480	16,981	25,219	22,527	23,571	23,748	14,448	29,124	8,331	Financial Account, n.i.e.	78bjd
−1,092	−7,106	−1,297	−3,989	−4,724	−4,591	−1,952	−2,400	−558	501	−1,402	−2,649	1,304	−7,255	2,896	Net Errors and Omissions	78cad
−1,275	734	−1,665	−49	−1,822	−3,280	−576	2,778	7,558	293	625	−2,486	−5,807	−492	−5,144	Overall Balance	78cbd
1,275	−734	1,665	49	1,822	3,280	576	−2,778	−7,558	−293	−625	2,486	5,807	492	5,144	Reserves and Related Items	79dad
655	−149	579	−449	866	73	−479	−3,342	−7,558	−293	−625	2,486	5,807	492	1,227	Reserve Assets	79dbd
—	—	—	—	—	—	—	—	—	—	—	—	—	—	—	Use of Fund Credit and Loans	79dcd
—	—	—	—	—	—	—	—	—	—	—	—	—	—	—	Liabs.Constit.For.Auth.Reserves	79ddd
620	−586	1,086	497	956	3,207	1,055	564	—	—	—	—	—	—	3,917	Exceptional Financing	79ded

Canada

156

		1965	1966	1967	1968	1969	1970	1971	1972	1973	1974	1975	1976	1977	1978	1979
Government Finance															*Billions of Canadian Dollars:*	
Deficit (-) or Surplus	80	-.02	-.71	-1.31	-.82	I.22	-.99	-1.91	-1.74	-1.70	I-1.97	-5.70	-6.30	-9.41	-11.95	-10.56
Revenue	81	8.86	9.64	10.57	11.82	I16.41	17.23	19.11	22.04	25.85	I31.62	34.89	37.72	38.24	41.64	48.22
Grants Received	81z	....	....	....	....	....	....	....	....	....	—	—	—	—	—	—
Expenditure	82	8.11	9.11	10.46	11.67	I14.27	15.99	18.42	21.32	24.68	I30.08	36.00	39.69	45.06	50.51	55.54
Lending Minus Repayments	83	.77	1.24	1.42	.97	I1.92	2.23	2.60	2.45	2.88	I3.51	4.59	4.33	2.59	3.08	3.23
Financing																
Net Borrowing	84	-.07	.96	1.56	.44	I.01	1.41	2.16	2.25	1.37	I3.67	4.79	5.40	9.80	15.64	5.42
Domestic	84a	....	....	....	....	....	....	....	....	....	I3.73	4.82	5.40	9.80	9.59	6.50
Foreign	85a	....	....	....	....	....	....	....	....	....	I-.06	-.04	—	.01	6.05	-1.08
Use of Cash Balances	87	.09	-.25	-.25	.38	I-.23	-.42	-.25	-.51	.33	I-1.70	.91	.89	-.39	-3.68	5.14
Debt: Domestic	88a	....	....	....	....	....	....	....	....	....	I34.53	39.28	43.94	51.30	60.79	67.12
Foreign	89a	....	....	....	....	....	....	....	....	....	I.20	.16	.16	2.25	8.29	7.22
															Millions of Canadian Dollars:	
Total Debt (by Holder)	88	20,124	20,263	21,196	22,572	22,869	24,740	27,709	29,262	29,130	....	....	....	....	....	....
Held By: Bank of Canada	88aa	3,472	3,473	3,807	3,942	4,112	4,295	4,866	5,453	6,025	....	....	....	....	....	....
Chartered Banks	88ab	3,724	3,890	4,630	5,573	5,091	6,603	7,324	7,132	7,291	....	....	....	....	....	....
Other Finan.Institutions	88ac	1,793	1,914	1,978	2,010	2,177	2,251	2,118	2,220	1,971	....	....	....	....	....	....
Other Dom. Investors	88ae	10,052	10,176	10,087	10,088	10,527	10,865	12,720	13,613	13,102	....	....	....	....	....	....
Foreigners	88c	1,085	810	695	958	959	726	681	844	741	....	....	....	....	....	....
Intragovernmental Debt	88s	557	848	814	985	1,033	1,005	569	611	607	....	....	....	....	....	....
National Accounts															*Billions of Canadian Dollars:*	
Exports of Goods & Services	90c. c	10.72	12.56	14.16	16.17	17.84	20.08	21.17	23.74	29.77	37.81	38.95	44.25	51.18	61.15	75.07
Government Consumption	91f. c	8.27	9.64	11.09	12.69	14.19	16.45	18.23	20.14	22.85	27.48	33.27	38.27	43.41	47.39	52.29
Gross Fixed Capital Formation	93e. c	13.67	15.92	16.25	16.49	18.14	19.01	21.57	23.88	28.86	35.78	41.85	46.71	50.23	54.58	63.44
Increase/Decrease(-) in Stocks	93i. c	1.30	1.28	.21	.74	1.48	.24	.37	.78	1.86	3.59	1.37	2.33	1.86	1.05	4.99
Private Consumption	96f. c	34.71	37.95	41.07	44.84	49.09	51.85	56.27	63.02	72.07	84.23	97.57	111.50	123.56	137.43	153.39
Imports of Goods & Services	98c. c	-10.83	-12.58	-13.46	-15.19	-17.71	-17.83	-19.53	-22.78	-28.02	-37.37	-41.36	-45.28	-51.25	-60.05	-73.28
Gross Domestic Product	99b. c	57.52	64.39	69.06	75.42	83.03	89.12	97.29	108.63	127.37	152.11	171.54	197.92	217.88	241.60	276.10
Net Factor Inc/Pmts(-) Abroad	98.n c	-.99	-1.12	-1.24	-1.22	-1.21	-1.35	-1.51	-1.46	-1.73	-2.24	-2.54	-3.54	-4.57	-5.95	-7.16
Gross Nat'l Expenditure = GNP	99a. c	56.53	63.27	67.82	74.20	81.82	87.77	95.78	107.17	125.64	149.87	169.00	194.39	213.31	235.65	268.94
Nat'l Income, Market Prices	99e. c	49.85	55.90	59.94	65.79	72.67	77.82	85.02	95.43	112.01	133.43	150.24	172.93	189.51	209.04	238.20
Gross Dom. Prod. 1990 Prices	99b. r	256.84	274.27	282.31	297.42	313.35	321.48	339.99	359.48	387.20	404.25	414.76	440.32	456.24	477.10	495.57
GDP Deflator (1990=100)	99bi r	22.4	23.5	24.5	25.4	26.5	27.7	28.6	30.2	32.9	37.6	41.4	44.9	47.8	50.6	55.7
															Millions:	
Population	99z	19.68	20.05	20.41	20.73	21.03	21.32	21.59	21.83	22.07	22.40	22.73	23.03	23.28	23.49	23.70

Deposit Money Banks: I Beginning in 1967, data for *lines 24* and *25* refer to averages of Wednesdays, because an adequate classification at month ends is not available. I Beginning in November 1981, all wholly- and majority-owned subsidiaries of the chartered banks (including mortgage loan subsidiaries and foreign banking subsidiaries) are consolidated in accordance with Canadian banking law. Unconsolidated data are not available on a monthly basis. In addition, data for *lines 24* and *25,* which were previously calculated from monthly averages of Wednesday figures, in the absence of an adequate classification of month ends, are now calculated mostly from month-end figures.

Monetary Survey: I See note to section 20.

Other Banking Institutions: I Prior to 1973, data relate to savings institutions. After this date, other banklike institutions are included in the consolidation of the banking survey. I From November 1981, mortgage loan companies affiliated with chartered banks have been excluded from this group, as they have been consolidated with the accounts of chartered banks in their reporting to the Bank of Canada. Prior to November 1981, this group comprised all trust and mortgage loan companies, local credit unions, *caisses populaires,* Quebec savings banks, and sales finance and consumer loan companies.

Banking Survey: I Prior to 1973, data relate to savings institutions. After this date, other banklike institutions are included in the consolidation of the banking survey.

Government Finance: I Beginning in 1969, data include nonbudgetary transactions. I Beginning in 1974, annual data are as reported in the *Government Finance Statistics Yearbook* and cover consolidated central government. Non-debt data relate to a fiscal year different from calendar year.

Canada 156

	1980	1981	1982	1983	1984	1985	1986	1987	1988	1989	1990	1991	1992	1993	1994		
Year Beginning April 1																**Government Finance**	
	−10.73	−8.43	−20.81	−25.16	−28.87	−28.68	−20.11	−14.00	−13.51	−16.57	−20.81	−24.59	....	....	....	Deficit (-) or Surplus	80
	57.49	72.28	73.24	77.33	85.30	91.10	99.21	111.55	119.31	132.54	138.79	142.40	....	....	....	Revenue	81
	—	—	—	—	—	—	.02	.11	.05	.09	.08	.09	....	....	....	Grants Received	81z
	65.52	76.15	89.36	98.81	111.38	117.20	119.33	127.08	133.26	148.96	159.45	166.67	....	....	....	Expenditure	82
	2.70	4.56	4.68	3.67	2.79	2.58	.01	−1.41	−.39	.24	.23	.41	....	....	....	Lending Minus Repayments	83
																Financing	
	12.25	9.35	21.84	25.67	28.48	28.15	25.88	22.14	22.03	14.47						Net Borrowing	84
	10.50	8.02	20.59	24.50	20.38	22.89	15.62	14.29	9.07	9.39						Domestic	84a
	1.75	1.33	1.26	1.17	8.10	5.26	10.26	7.85	12.96	5.08						Foreign	85a
	−1.51	−.92	−1.03	−.51	.40	.53	−5.78	−8.13	−8.53	2.10						Use of Cash Balances	87
	77.17	84.99	105.63	133.26	156.36	179.53	194.94	209.76	220.12	233.72	....					Debt: Domestic	88a
	8.97	10.30	11.55	12.72	20.81	26.08	36.34	43.60	56.57	62.08	....					Foreign	89a
Year Ending December 31																	
	....	....	....	....	....	....	....	....	....	....	....	....	....	....	....	Total Debt (by Holder)	88
	....	....	....	....	....	....	....	....	....	....	....	....	....	....	....	Held By: Bank of Canada	88aa
	....	....	....	....	....	....	....	....	....	....	....	....	....	....	....	Chartered Banks	88ab
	....	....	....	....	....	....	....	....	....	....	....	....	....	....	....	Other Finan. Institutions	88ac
	....	....	....	....	....	....	....	....	....	....	....	....	....	....	....	Other Dom. Investors	88ae
	....	....	....	....	....	....	....	....	....	....	....	....	....	....	....	Foreigners	88c
	....	....	....	....	....	....	....	....	....	....	....	....	....	....	....	Intragovernmental Debt	88s
Billions of Canadian Dollars																**National Accounts**	
	87.58	96.88	96.65	103.44	126.04	134.92	138.12	145.42	159.31	163.90	168.92	164.85	181.19	209.37	249.37	Exports of Goods & Services	90c. c
	59.25	68.79	78.66	84.57	89.09	95.52	100.13	105.79	114.47	124.11	135.15	144.89	150.39	152.16	150.76	Government Consumption	91f. c
	72.29	86.12	81.33	81.23	84.70	94.20	101.56	116.72	132.79	146.08	141.38	132.01	128.92	128.88	139.19	Gross Fixed Capital Formation	93e. c
	.34	1.19	−9.75	−2.85	4.76	2.28	2.56	3.07	3.80	3.62	−2.84	−3.24	−3.70	1.10	2.82	Increase/Decrease(-) in Stocks	93i. c
	172.42	196.19	210.51	231.45	251.65	274.50	297.48	322.77	349.94	378.94	394.32	411.96	422.52	436.54	452.86	Private Consumption	96f. c
	−81.93	−93.00	−82.60	−89.83	−110.63	−123.39	−133.37	−140.50	−156.38	−166.09	−171.13	−172.81	−187.25	−212.53	−243.76	Imports of Goods & Services	98c. c
	309.89	355.99	374.44	405.72	444.74	477.99	505.67	551.60	605.91	650.75	669.51	676.48	690.12	712.86	750.05	Gross Domestic Product	99b. c
	−7.83	−11.34	−12.67	−11.60	−13.49	−14.33	−16.40	−16.45	−18.71	−21.50	−23.86	−21.87	−24.24	−23.99	−26.27	Net Factor Inc/Pmts(-) Abroad	98.n c
	302.06	344.66	361.77	394.11	431.25	463.66	489.26	535.15	587.19	629.25	645.61	654.61	665.88	688.86	723.78	Gross Nat'l Expenditure = GNP	99a. c
	266.54	303.98	317.42	347.05	380.37	407.73	428.67	471.04	519.07	556.90	567.02	572.28	580.58	600.96	630.81	Nat'l Income, Market Prices	99e. c
	502.93	521.40	504.63	520.59	553.43	579.81	599.04	624.59	655.06	671.09	669.51	657.55	662.58	677.29	708.35	Gross Dom. Prod. 1990 Prices	99b. r
	61.6	68.3	74.2	77.9	80.4	82.4	84.4	88.3	92.5	97.0	100.0	102.9	104.2	105.3	105.9	GDP Deflator (1990=100)	99bi r
Midyear Estimates																	
	24.04	24.34	24.58	24.79	24.98	25.16	25.35	25.62	25.91	26.24	26.58	I 28.12	28.43	28.94	29.25	Population	99z

Cape Verde
624

		1965	1966	1967	1968	1969	1970	1971	1972	1973	1974	1975	1976	1977	1978	1979
Exchange Rates																*Escudos per SDR:*
Official Rate	aa	28.830	28.980	28.860	28.770	28.650	28.750	29.922	29.314	31.178	30.114	32.160	36.655	41.179	46.822	50.467
																Escudos per US Dollar:
Official Rate	ae	28.830	28.980	28.860	28.770	28.650	28.750	27.560	27.000	25.845	24.596	27.472	31.549	33.900	35.940	38.310
Official Rate	rf	28.750	28.750	28.750	28.750	28.750	28.750	28.360	27.053	24.515	25.408	25.543	30.229	34.046	35.501	37.433
Fund Position																*Millions of SDRs:*
Quota	2f.s	....	....	....	....	....	....	....	....	....	....	....	....	....	2.00	2.00
SDRs	1b.s	....	....	....	....	....	....	....	....	....	....	....	....	....	—	.01
Reserve Position in the Fund	1c.s	....	....	....	....	....	....	....	....	....	....	....	....	....	—	.32
International Liquidity													*Millions of US Dollars Unless Otherwise Indicated:*			
Total Reserves minus Gold	1l.d	....	....	....	....	....	....	....	....	....	....	....	32.70	42.02	39.37	42.32
SDRs	1b.d	....	....	....	....	....	....	....	....	....	....	....	....	....	—	.01
Reserve Position in the Fund	1c.d	....	....	....	....	....	....	....	....	....	....	....	....	....	—	.42
Foreign Exchange	1d.d	....	....	....	....	....	....	....	....	....	....	....	32.70	42.02	39.37	41.89
Monetary Authorities: Other Liab.	4..d	....	....	....	....	....	....	....	....	....	....	....	.47	.11	2.27	1.75
Deposit Money Banks: Assets	7a.d	....	....	....	....	....	....	....	....	....	....	....	....	....	....	....
Liabilities	7b.d	....	....	....	....	....	....	....	....	....	....	....	....	....	....	....
Monetary Authorities																*Millions of Escudos:*
Foreign Assets	11	....	....	....	....	....	....	....	....	....	....	....	1,031.5	1,424.6	1,414.9	1,621.4
Claims on Central Government	12a	....	....	....	....	....	....	....	....	....	....	....	87.9	91.8	91.8	121.8
Claims on Local Government	12b	....	....	....	....	....	....	....	....	....	....	....	—	—	.9	.6
Claims on Nonfin.Pub.Enterprises	12c	....	....	....	....	....	....	....	....	....	....	....	—	—	125.3	142.8
Claims on Private Sector	12d	....	....	....	....	....	....	....	....	....	....	....	316.4	308.3	435.0	591.1
Claims on Deposit Money Banks	12e	....	....	....	....	....	....	....	....	....	....	....	....	....	....	....
Claims on Other Banking Insts.	12f	....	....	....	....	....	....	....	....	....	....	....	1.5	1.5	1.5	1.5
Reserve Money	14	....	....	....	....	....	....	....	....	....	....	....	1,000.4	1,411.3	1,614.8	1,822.6
of which: Currency Outside DMBs	14a	....	....	....	....	....	....	....	....	....	....	....	464.8	537.2	638.3	736.4
Time and Foreign Currency Deposits	15	....	....	....	....	....	....	....	....	....	....	....	17.1	23.8	52.3	135.2
Foreign Liabilities	16c	....	....	....	....	....	....	....	....	....	....	....	14.9	3.8	81.5	67.1
Central Government Deposits	16d	....	....	....	....	....	....	....	....	....	....	....	252.8	214.6	88.2	50.8
Capital Accounts	17a	....	....	....	....	....	....	....	....	....	....	....	186.6	357.1	515.0	723.0
Other Items (Net)	17r	....	....	....	....	....	....	....	....	....	....	....	−34.5	−184.4	−282.4	−319.5
Deposit Money Banks																*Millions of Escudos:*
Reserves	20	....	....	....	....	....	....	....	....	....	....	....	....	....	....	....
Foreign Assets	21	....	....	....	....	....	....	....	....	....	....	....	....	....	....	....
Claims on Central Government	22a	....	....	....	....	....	....	....	....	....	....	....	....	....	....	....
Claims on Local Government	22b	....	....	....	....	....	....	....	....	....	....	....	....	....	....	....
Claims on Nonfin.Pub.Enterprises	22c	....	....	....	....	....	....	....	....	....	....	....	....	....	....	....
Claims on Private Sector	22d	....	....	....	....	....	....	....	....	....	....	....	....	....	....	....
Demand Deposits	24	....	....	....	....	....	....	....	....	....	....	....	....	....	....	....
Time, Savings,& Fgn.Currency Dep.	25	....	....	....	....	....	....	....	....	....	....	....	....	....	....	....
Restricted Deposits	26b	....	....	....	....	....	....	....	....	....	....	....	....	....	....	....
Foreign Liabilities	26c	....	....	....	....	....	....	....	....	....	....	....	....	....	....	....
Central Government Deposits	26d	....	....	....	....	....	....	....	....	....	....	....	....	....	....	....
Credit from Monetary Authorities	26g	....	....	....	....	....	....	....	....	....	....	....	....	....	....	....
Liab. to Nonbank Financial Insts.	26j	....	....	....	....	....	....	....	....	....	....	....	....	....	....	....
Capital Accounts	27a	....	....	....	....	....	....	....	....	....	....	....	....	....	....	....
Other Items (Net)	27r	....	....	....	....	....	....	....	....	....	....	....	....	....	....	....
Monetary Survey																*Millions of Escudos:*
Foreign Assets (Net)	31n	....	....	....	....	....	....	....	....	....	....	....	1,016.6	1,420.8	1,333.4	1,554.3
Domestic Credit	32	....	....	....	....	....	....	....	....	....	....	....	153.0	187.0	566.3	807.0
Claims on Central Govt.(Net)	32an	....	....	....	....	....	....	....	....	....	....	....	−164.9	−122.8	3.6	71.0
Claims on Local Government	32b	....	....	....	....	....	....	....	....	....	....	....	—	—	.9	.6
Claims on Nonfin.Pub.Enterprises	32c	....	....	....	....	....	....	....	....	....	....	....	—	—	125.3	142.8
Claims on Private Sector	32d	....	....	....	....	....	....	....	....	....	....	....	316.4	308.3	435.0	591.1
Claims on Other Banking Insts	32f	....	....	....	....	....	....	....	....	....	....	....	1.5	1.5	1.5	1.5
Money	34	....	....	....	....	....	....	....	....	....	....	....	1,000.4	1,411.3	1,614.8	1,822.6
Quasi-Money	35	....	....	....	....	....	....	....	....	....	....	....	17.1	23.8	52.3	135.2
Restricted Deposits	36b	....	....	....	....	....	....	....	....	....	....	....	4.1	6.2	6.9	7.9
Liab. to Nonbank Financial Insts.	36j	....	....	....	....	....	....	....	....	....	....	....	....	....	....	....
Capital Accounts	37a	....	....	....	....	....	....	....	....	....	....	....	186.6	357.1	515.0	723.0
Other Items (Net)	37r	....	....	....	....	....	....	....	....	....	....	....	−38.6	−190.6	−289.3	−327.4
Money plus Quasi-Money	35l	....	....	....	....	....	....	....	....	....	....	....	1,017.5	1,435.1	1,667.1	1,957.8
Other Banking Institutions																*Millions of Escudos:*
Cash	40	....	....	....	....	....	....	....	....	....	....	....	31.5	38.8	46.2	50.7
Foreign Assets	41	....	....	....	....	....	....	....	....	....	....	....	.1	.1	.1	.1
Claims on Private Sector	42d	....	....	....	....	....	....	....	....	....	....	....	84.1	86.6	96.6	121.2
Time, Savings,& Fgn.Currency Dep.	45	....	....	....	....	....	....	....	....	....	....	....	57.0	64.6	81.8	99.0
Credit from Monetary Authorities	46g	....	....	....	....	....	....	....	....	....	....	....	1.5	1.5	1.5	1.5
Capital Accounts	47a	....	....	....	....	....	....	....	....	....	....	....	—	—	—	—
Other Items (Net)	47r	....	....	....	....	....	....	....	....	....	....	....	57.2	59.4	59.6	71.5
Banking Survey																*Millions of Escudos:*
Foreign Assets (Net)	51n	....	....	....	....	....	....	....	....	....	....	....	1,016.7	1,420.9	1,333.5	1,554.4
Domestic Credit	52	....	....	....	....	....	....	....	....	....	....	....	250.4	286.0	674.0	936.9
Claims on Central Govt. (Net)	52an	....	....	....	....	....	....	....	....	....	....	....	−164.7	−122.6	3.8	71.2
Claims on Local Government	52b	....	....	....	....	....	....	....	....	....	....	....	7.4	7.1	7.5	5.7
Claims on Nonfin.Pub.Enterprises	52c	....	....	....	....	....	....	....	....	....	....	....	7.2	6.6	131.1	147.7
Claims on Private Sector	52d	....	....	....	....	....	....	....	....	....	....	....	400.5	394.9	531.6	712.3
Liquid Liabilities	55l	....	....	....	....	....	....	....	....	....	....	....	1,043.0	1,460.9	1,702.7	2,006.1
Restricted Deposits	56b	....	....	....	....	....	....	....	....	....	....	....	4.1	6.2	6.9	7.9
Capital Accounts	57a	....	....	....	....	....	....	....	....	....	....	....	186.6	357.1	515.0	723.0
Other Items (Net)	57r	....	....	....	....	....	....	....	....	....	....	....	33.4	−117.3	−217.1	−245.7

Cape Verde

624

1980	1981	1982	1983	1984	1985	1986	1987	1988	1989	1990	1991	1992	1993	1994		
End of Period															**Exchange Rates**	
54.192	59.199	69.540	83.730	91.174	93.778	93.654	93.312	99.131	95.993	94.016	95.081	100.497	118.115	118.452	Official Rate	**aa**
End of Period (ae) Period Average (rf)																
42.490	50.860	63.040	79.975	93.015	85.375	76.565	65.775	73.665	73.045	66.085	66.470	73.089	85.992	81.140	Official Rate	**ae**
40.175	48.695	58.293	71.686	84.878	91.632	80.145	72.466	72.068	77.978	70.031	71.408	68.018	80.427	81.891	Official Rate	**rf**
End of Period															**Fund Position**	
3.00	3.00	3.00	4.50	4.50	4.50	4.50	4.50	4.50	4.50	4.50	4.50	7.00	7.00	7.00	Quota	**2f.*s***
—	.18	.15	.11	.10	.10	.10	.07	.03	.04	.03	.04	.05	.02	.05	SDRs	**1b.*s***
.58	.58	.58	.95	.95	.95	—	—	—	—	—	—	—	—	—	Reserve Position in the Fund	**1c.*s***
End of Period															**International Liquidity**	
42.40	37.83	42.74	45.90	40.99	55.36	56.36	80.73	81.33	74.74	76.97	65.10	75.76	57.69	....	Total Reserves minus Gold	**1l.*d***
—	.21	.17	.12	.10	.11	.12	.10	.04	.05	.04	.06	.07	.03	.07	SDRs	**1b.*d***
.74	.68	.64	.99	.93	1.04	—	—	—	—	—	—	—	—	—	Reserve Position in the Fund	**1c.*d***
41.66	36.94	41.93	44.79	39.96	54.20	56.24	80.63	81.29	74.69	76.93	65.04	75.69	57.66	....	Foreign Exchange	**1d.*d***
.42	2.14	3.36	7.32	2.87	8.02	.93	1.73	1.65	1.23	1.13	2.49	2.90	.81	.74	Monetary Authorities: Other Liab.	**4..*d***
....	....	....	....	....	....	....	....	....	....	....	....	....	14.47	32.32	Deposit Money Banks: Assets	**7a.*d***
....	....	....	....	....	....	....	....	....	....	....	....	....	2.47	3.38	Liabilities	**7b.*d***
End of Period															**Monetary Authorities**	
1,801.6	1,924.0	2,694.3	3,671.1	3,812.7	4,726.2	4,315.2	5,310.0	5,991.4	5,459.2	5,086.5	4,327.2	5,536.9	5,591.2	4,088.5	Foreign Assets	**11**
157.0	548.1	547.7	669.0	727.1	938.0	1,248.8	1,441.8	1,653.9	1,902.8	2,217.0	3,101.0	4,118.6	5,068.2	4,467.6	Claims on Central Government	**12a**
3.5	19.6	31.8	32.9	34.9	32.2	34.5	28.3	48.3	60.0	79.7	70.3	68.8	27.6	—	Claims on Local Government	**12b**
587.1	770.6	1,046.1	1,030.0	1,346.1	1,483.4	1,517.3	1,422.1	2,724.6	2,986.1	3,151.2	3,602.4	3,694.1	2,136.9	119.7	Claims on Nonfin.Pub.Enterprises	**12c**
506.3	720.3	802.6	1,222.8	1,437.6	2,110.2	2,565.1	3,179.0	2,223.3	2,877.3	3,444.5	3,948.0	4,731.8	2,005.7	1,091.2	Claims on Private Sector	**12d**
....	....	....	....	....	....	....	....	....	....	....	....	....	612.8	592.1	Claims on Deposit Money Banks	**12e**
1.5	1.5	1.5	1.5	1.5	—	—	32.7	137.2	214.2	258.4	308.0	301.4	—	—	Claims on Other Banking Insts.	**12f**
2,302.0	2,552.7	3,227.8	3,956.2	4,201.6	4,843.2	5,620.6	5,710.4	6,037.9	6,410.5	6,926.4	7,538.1	9,906.6	12,763.8	8,101.2	Reserve Money	**14**
872.2	1,040.5	1,251.9	1,332.9	1,433.6	1,628.1	1,826.4	1,955.9	2,219.2	2,490.3	2,842.4	2,971.9	3,191.3	2,072.3	3,298.2	*of which: Currency Outside DMBs*	**14a**
254.1	486.1	616.1	628.3	914.7	1,297.1	1,966.0	2,527.1	3,591.6	4,659.4	5,754.3	7,195.0	6,730.7	—	173.9	Time and Foreign Currency Deposits	**15**
17.9	109.0	211.7	585.4	267.2	685.0	71.1	114.0	121.8	89.5	74.6	165.3	211.8	69.4	59.8	Foreign Liabilities	**16c**
130.9	119.4	235.3	188.2	364.9	689.6	640.0	722.6	929.6	928.9	968.9	649.0	803.9	—	21.2	Central Government Deposits	**16d**
880.9	982.3	1,358.7	1,844.4	1,936.9	2,300.0	2,277.7	2,434.1	2,213.3	2,459.5	2,970.3	2,725.2	3,002.9	2,781.5	2,671.5	Capital Accounts	**17a**
–528.8	–265.4	–525.6	–575.2	–325.4	–524.9	–894.5	–94.3	–115.5	–1,048.2	–2,457.2	–2,915.7	–2,204.3	–172.3	–668.5	Other Items (Net)	**17r**
End of Period															**Deposit Money Banks**	
....	....	....	....	....	....	....	....	....	....	....	....	....	10,604.3	4,861.0	Reserves	**20**
....	....	....	....	....	....	....	....	....	....	....	....	....	1,244.4	2,622.3	Foreign Assets	**21**
....	....	....	....	....	....	....	....	....	....	....	....	....	—	5,966.7	Claims on Central Government	**22a**
....	....	....	....	....	....	....	....	....	....	....	....	....	48.7	190.2	Claims on Local Government	**22b**
....	....	....	....	....	....	....	....	....	....	....	....	....	433.9	422.3	Claims on Nonfin.Pub.Enterprises	**22c**
....	....	....	....	....	....	....	....	....	....	....	....	....	5,499.4	6,229.4	Claims on Private Sector	**22d**
....	....	....	....	....	....	....	....	....	....	....	....	....	7,049.3	7,471.0	Demand Deposits	**24**
....	....	....	....	....	....	....	....	....	....	....	....	....	9,039.4	10,323.0	Time, Savings,& Fgn.Currency Dep.	**25**
....	....	....	....	....	....	....	....	....	....	....	....	....	300.9	203.8	Restricted Deposits	**26b**
....	....	....	....	....	....	....	....	....	....	....	....	....	212.8	274.3	Foreign Liabilities	**26c**
....	....	....	....	....	....	....	....	....	....	....	....	....	847.8	1,013.1	Central Government Deposits	**26d**
....	....	....	....	....	....	....	....	....	....	....	....	....	612.8	574.6	Credit from Monetary Authorities	**26g**
....	....	....	....	....	....	....	....	....	....	....	....	....	3.4	20.3	Liab. to Nonbank Financial Insts.	**26j**
....	....	....	....	....	....	....	....	....	....	....	....	....	1,091.5	1,427.2	Capital Accounts	**27a**
....	....	....	....	....	....	....	....	....	....	....	....	....	–1,327.2	–1,015.4	Other Items (Net)	**27r**
End of Period															**Monetary Survey**	
1,783.7	1,815.0	2,482.6	3,085.7	3,545.5	4,041.2	4,244.1	5,196.0	5,869.6	5,369.7	5,011.9	4,161.9	5,325.1	6,553.4	6,376.7	Foreign Assets (Net)	**31n**
1,124.5	1,940.7	2,194.4	2,768.0	3,182.3	3,874.2	4,725.7	5,381.3	5,857.7	7,111.5	8,181.9	10,380.7	12,110.8	14,372.6	17,452.8	Domestic Credit	**32**
26.1	428.7	312.4	480.8	362.2	248.4	608.8	719.2	724.3	973.9	1,248.1	2,452.0	3,314.7	4,220.4	9,400.0	Claims on Central Govt.(Net)	**32an**
3.5	19.6	31.8	32.9	34.9	32.2	34.5	28.3	48.3	60.0	79.7	70.3	68.8	76.3	190.2	Claims on Local Government	**32b**
587.1	770.6	1,046.1	1,030.0	1,346.1	1,483.4	1,517.3	1,422.1	2,724.6	2,986.1	3,151.2	3,602.4	3,694.1	2,570.8	542.0	Claims on Nonfin.Pub.Enterprises	**32c**
506.3	720.3	802.6	1,222.8	1,437.6	2,110.2	2,565.1	3,179.0	2,223.3	2,877.3	3,444.5	3,948.0	4,731.8	7,505.1	7,320.6	Claims on Private Sector	**32d**
1.5	1.5	1.5	1.5	1.5	—	—	32.7	137.2	214.2	258.4	308.0	301.4	—	—	Claims on Other Banking Insts	**32f**
2,302.0	2,552.7	3,227.8	3,956.2	4,201.6	4,843.2	5,620.6	5,710.4	6,037.9	6,410.5	6,926.4	7,538.1	9,906.6	9,157.1	10,811.2	Money	**34**
254.1	486.1	616.1	628.3	914.7	1,297.1	1,966.0	2,527.1	3,591.6	4,659.4	5,754.3	7,195.0	6,730.7	9,039.4	10,496.9	Quasi-Money	**35**
7.1	8.0	10.0	13.5	296.7	379.2	272.0	228.1	321.8	185.2	289.2	141.6	142.5	300.9	203.8	Restricted Deposits	**36b**
....	....	....	....	....	....	....	....	....	....	....	....	....	3.4	20.3	Liab. to Nonbank Financial Insts.	**36j**
880.9	982.3	1,358.7	1,844.4	1,936.9	2,300.0	2,277.7	2,434.1	2,213.3	2,459.5	2,970.3	2,725.2	3,002.9	3,873.0	4,098.7	Capital Accounts	**37a**
–535.9	–273.4	–535.6	–588.7	–622.1	–904.1	–1,166.5	–322.4	–437.3	–1,233.4	–2,746.4	–3,057.3	–2,346.8	–1,447.8	–1,801.4	Other Items (Net)	**37r**
2,556.1	3,038.8	3,843.9	4,584.5	5,116.3	6,140.3	7,586.6	8,237.5	9,629.5	11,069.9	12,680.7	14,733.1	16,637.3	18,196.5	21,308.1	Money plus Quasi-Money	**35l**
End of Period															**Other Banking Institutions**	
21.4	16.6	21.8	75.0	6.7	9.5	54.3	33.4	42.6	43.8	47.6	57.0	74.6	....	....	Cash	**40**
.1	.2	.3	.3	.3	.3	.2	.2	.2	.2	.2	.2	.2	....	....	Foreign Assets	**41**
178.2	217.3	230.2	265.6	232.2	274.2	254.2	378.5	548.5	717.5	1,013.3	1,016.1	1,126.4	....	....	Claims on Private Sector	**42d**
116.7	150.5	167.3	235.4	230.2	257.1	256.5	308.5	368.4	432.0	506.7	569.7	623.8	....	....	Time, Savings,& Fgn.Currency Dep.	**45**
1.5	1.5	1.5	1.5	—	—	—	33.8	137.5	214.2	245.4	327.6	301.4	....	....	Credit from Monetary Authorities	**46g**
—	—	—	—	—	—	—	—	—	—	—	—	—	....	....	Capital Accounts	**47a**
81.5	82.1	83.5	104.0	9.0	26.9	52.2	69.8	85.4	115.3	309.0	176.0	276.0	....	....	Other Items (Net)	**47r**
End of Period															**Banking Survey**	
1,783.8	1,815.2	2,482.9	3,086.0	3,545.8	4,041.5	4,244.3	5,196.2	5,869.8	5,369.9	5,012.1	4,162.1	5,325.3	....	....	Foreign Assets (Net)	**51n**
1,309.9	2,163.8	2,429.0	3,036.6	3,416.1	4,150.9	4,979.9	5,727.1	6,269.1	7,614.8	8,936.8	11,088.8	12,935.8	....	....	Domestic Credit	**52**
26.3	428.9	312.6	481.0	362.4	248.6	608.8	719.2	724.3	973.9	1,248.1	2,452.0	3,314.7	....	....	Claims on Central Govt. (Net)	**52an**
8.0	23.5	35.1	35.6	37.0	33.7	34.5	28.3	48.4	60.0	79.7	70.3	68.8	....	....	Claims on Local Government	**52b**
591.1	773.8	1,048.5	1,031.6	1,346.9	1,484.2	1,517.3	1,422.1	2,724.6	2,986.1	3,151.2	3,602.4	3,694.1	....	....	Claims on Nonfin.Pub.Enterprises	**52c**
684.5	937.6	1,032.8	1,488.4	1,669.8	2,384.4	2,819.3	3,557.5	2,771.8	3,594.8	4,457.8	4,964.1	5,858.2	....	....	Claims on Private Sector	**52d**
2,651.4	3,172.7	3,989.4	4,744.9	5,339.8	6,387.9	7,788.8	8,512.6	9,955.3	11,458.1	13,139.8	15,245.8	17,186.5	....	....	Liquid Liabilities	**55l**
7.1	8.0	10.0	13.5	296.7	379.2	272.0	228.1	321.8	185.2	289.2	141.6	142.5	....	....	Restricted Deposits	**56b**
880.9	982.3	1,358.7	1,844.4	1,936.9	2,300.0	2,277.7	2,434.1	2,213.3	2,459.5	2,970.3	2,725.2	3,002.9	....	....	Capital Accounts	**57a**
–445.7	–184.0	–446.2	–480.2	–611.5	–874.7	–1,114.3	–251.5	–351.5	–1,118.1	–2,450.4	–2,861.7	–2,070.8	....	....	Other Items (Net)	**57r**

Cape Verde
624

		1965	1966	1967	1968	1969	1970	1971	1972	1973	1974	1975	1976	1977	1978	1979
Interest Rates																*Percent Per Annum*
Deposit Rate	60l	....	....	....	....	....	....	....	....	....	....	....	....	....	....	....
Lending Rate	60p	....	....	....	....	....	....	....	....	....	6.5	6.5	6.5	6.5	6.5	6.5
Prices															*Index Numbers (1990=100):*	
Consumer Prices	64	....	....	....	....	....	....	....	....	....	....	....	....	....	....	....
International Transactions															*Millions of Escudos*	
Exports	70	28.0	33.0	31.0	41.0	45.0	47.7	45.6	48.0	47.8	52.7	61.3	48.0	74.5	75.1	92.1
Imports, cif	71	164.6	162.0	203.0	212.6	324.6	469.4	573.5	656.9	833.1	869.3	1,010.9	911.5	1,284.7	1,908.2	1,986.9
Imports, fob	71.v	143.1	140.9	176.5	184.9	282.3	408.2	498.7	571.2	724.4	755.9	879.0	792.6	1,117.1	1,659.3	1,727.7
Balance of Payments															*Millions of US Dollars:*	
Goods: Exports f.o.b.	78aa d	....	....	....	....	....	....	....	....	....	....	....	....	1.24	3.07	4.12
Goods: Imports f.o.b.	78ab d	....	....	....	....	....	....	....	....	....	....	....	....	−45.08	−58.75	−71.25
Trade Balance	78ac d	....	....	....	....	....	....	....	....	....	....	....	....	−43.84	−55.67	−67.12
Services: Credit	78ad d	....	....	....	....	....	....	....	....	....	....	....	....	.96	4.68	8.19
Services: Debit	78ae d	....	....	....	....	....	....	....	....	....	....	....	....	−3.66	−4.62	−5.48
Balance on Goods and Services	78af d	....	....	....	....	....	....	....	....	....	....	....	....	−46.54	−55.61	−64.41
Income: Credit	78ag d	....	....	....	....	....	....	....	....	....	....	....	....	1.13	.90	2.12
Income: Debit	78ah d	....	....	....	....	....	....	....	....	....	....	....	....	−.14	−.26	−.83
Balance on Goods, Serv., & Inc.	78ai d	....	....	....	....	....	....	....	....	....	....	....	....	−45.55	−54.98	−63.12
Current Transfers, n.i.e.: Credit	78aj d	....	....	....	....	....	....	....	....	....	....	....	....	52.95	48.69	65.59
Current Transfers: Debit	78ak d	....	....	....	....	....	....	....	....	....	....	....	....	−1.57	−2.29	−3.49
Current Account, n.i.e.	78al d	....	....	....	....	....	....	....	....	....	....	....	....	5.84	−8.57	−1.02
Capital Account, n.i.e.: Credit	78ba d	....	....	....	....	....	....	....	....	....	....	....	....	—	—	—
Capital Account: Debit	78bb d	....	....	....	....	....	....	....	....	....	....	....	....			
Capital Account, n.i.e.	78bc d	....	....	....	....	....	....	....	....	....	....	....	....	—	—	—
Direct Investment Abroad	78bd d	....	....	....	....	....	....	....	....	....	....	....	....			
Dir. Invest. in Rep. Econ., n.i.e.	78be d	....	....	....	....	....	....	....	....	....	....	....	....	—	—	—
Portfolio Investment Assets	78bf d	....	....	....	....	....	....	....	....	....	....	....	....			
Portfolio Investment Liab., n.i.e.	78bg d	....	....	....	....	....	....	....	....	....	....	....	....	—	—	—
Other Investment Assets	78bh d	....	....	....	....	....	....	....	....	....	....	....	....			
Other Investment Liab., n.i.e.	78bi d	....	....	....	....	....	....	....	....	....	....	....	....	2.02	3.75	.42
Financial Account, n.i.e.	78bj d	....	....	....	....	....	....	....	....	....	....	....	....	2.02	3.75	.42
Net Errors and Omissions	78ca d	....	....	....	....	....	....	....	....	....	....	....	....	1.47	2.17	3.27
Overall Balance	78cb d	....	....	....	....	....	....	....	....	....	....	....	....	9.33	−2.66	2.67
Reserves and Related Items	79da d	....	....	....	....	....	....	....	....	....	....	....	....	−9.33	2.66	−2.67
Reserve Assets	79db d	....	....	....	....	....	....	....	....	....	....	....	....	−9.33	2.66	−2.67
Use of Fund Credit and Loans	79dc d	....	....	....	....	....	....	....	....	....	....	....	....	—	—	—
Liabs.Constit.For.Auth.Reserves	79dd d	....	....	....	....	....	....	....	....	....	....	....	....			
Exceptional Financing	79de d	....	....	....	....	....	....	....	....	....	....	....	....	—	—	—
National Accounts															*Millions of Escudos*	
Exports of Goods & Services	90c	....	....	....	....	....	....	....	....	321	....	....	185	325	437	610
Government Consumption	91f	....	....	....	....	....	....	....	....	124	....	....	368	498	628	649
Gross Fixed Capital Formation	93e	....	....	....	....	....	....	....	....	279	....	....	553	847	1,537	1,655
Net Increase/Decrease(−) in Stocks	93i	....	....	....	....	....	....	....	....	56	....	....	−34	121	11	24
Private Consumption	96f	....	....	....	....	....	....	....	....	1,312	....	....	2,574	2,955	3,605	4,282
Imports of Goods & Services	98c	....	....	....	....	....	....	....	....	−1,016	....	....	−1,199	−1,684	−2,187	−2,711
Gross Domestic Product = GDP	99b	....	....	....	....	....	....	....	....	1,075	....	....	2,424	3,172	4,038	4,569
Gross Dom. Prod. 1985 Prices	99b.p	.....	.....	.....	.....	.....	.....	.....	.....	.....	.....	.....	.....	.....	.....	.....
GDP Deflator (1985=100)	99bi p	.....	.....	.....	.....	.....	.....	.....	.....	.....	.....	.....	.....	.....	.....	.....
																Millions:
Population	99z	.22	.23	.24	.25	.25	.27	.27	.29	.29	.29	.29	.30	.29	.29	.30

Cape Verde

624

	1980	1981	1982	1983	1984	1985	1986	1987	1988	1989	1990	1991	1992	1993	1994		
Percent Per Annum																**Interest Rates**	
	....	....	....	....	....	4.0	4.0	4.0	4.0	4.0	4.0	4.0	4.0	4.0	4.0	Deposit Rate	60l
	6.5	6.5	6.5	6.5	6.5	10.0	10.0	10.0	10.0	10.0	10.0	10.0	10.0	10.0	10.7	Lending Rate	60p
Period Averages																**Prices**	
	....	....	....	62	68	72	80	83	86	90	100	110	113	120	....	Consumer Prices	64
Millions of Escudos																**International Transactions**	
	170.5	147.0	191.0	246.0	212.0	524.0	355.0	567.0	237.0	527.0	398.0	438.0	327.0	....	....	Exports	70
	2,742.3	3,451.7	5,102.0	6,237.0	7,036.0	7,663.0	8,601.0	7,281.0	7,652.0	8,706.0	9,495.0	10,469.0	12,234.0	....	....	Imports, cif	71
	2,384.6	3,001.4	4,436.5	5,423.5	6,118.3	6,663.5	7,479.1	6,331.3	6,653.9	7,570.4	8,256.5	9,103.5	10,638.3	....	....	Imports, fob	71.v
Minus Sign Indicates Debit																**Balance of Payments**	
	9.12	6.26	3.97	3.30	6.93	6.12	4.00	7.78	3.28	6.74	5.64	4.14	4.43	....	....	Goods: Exports f.o.b.	78aa d
	−79.97	−85.90	−96.71	−104.59	−82.47	−86.74	−85.93	−92.83	−101.78	−106.86	−119.46	−132.15	−173.29	....	....	Goods: Imports f.o.b.	78ab d
	−70.85	−79.64	−92.74	−101.29	−75.54	−80.61	−81.93	−85.05	−98.50	−100.12	−113.82	−128.00	−168.86	....	....	Trade Balance	78ac d
	10.08	17.39	27.45	33.48	23.73	24.81	32.25	39.09	39.84	50.44	55.20	48.93	53.62	....	....	Services: Credit	78ad d
	−7.47	−17.17	−12.62	−12.20	−10.45	−8.60	−16.78	−21.11	−19.68	−28.55	−32.78	−19.11	−26.79	....	....	Services: Debit	78ae d
	−68.24	−79.42	−77.90	−80.01	−62.26	−64.40	−66.45	−67.07	−78.34	−78.23	−91.40	−98.18	−142.03	....	....	Balance on Goods and Services	78af d
	3.48	2.88	1.66	1.32	1.62	1.90	2.64	4.17	5.14	6.84	6.06	5.35	5.51	....	....	Income: Credit	78ag d
	−.09	−2.36	−6.13	−8.19	−6.12	−5.98	−5.33	−4.37	−4.54	−3.99	−4.15	−4.13	−4.30	....	....	Income: Debit	78ah d
	−64.85	−78.90	−82.37	−86.88	−66.75	−68.47	−69.14	−67.28	−77.74	−75.38	−89.50	−96.97	−140.82	....	....	Balance on Goods, Serv., & Inc.	78ai d
	73.48	61.39	71.29	77.58	63.99	63.37	72.29	82.82	80.17	72.88	79.48	94.74	142.98	....	....	Current Transfers, n.i.e.: Credit	78aj d
	−4.30	−4.11	−3.76	−4.05	−3.65	−3.84	−1.41	−1.85	−1.98	−2.08	−1.92	−5.70	−5.70	....	....	Current Transfers: Debit	78ak d
	4.32	−21.61	−14.84	−13.35	−6.42	−8.94	1.73	13.69	.45	−4.58	−11.94	−7.93	−3.55	....	....	Current Account, n.i.e.	78al d
	—	—	—	—	—	—	—	—	—	—	—	—	—	....	....	Capital Account, n.i.e.: Credit	78ba d
	—	—	—	—	—	—	—	—	—	—	—	—	—	....	....	Capital Account: Debit	78bb d
	—	—	—	—	—	—	—	—	—	—	—	—	—	....	....	Capital Account, n.i.e.	78bc d
	—	—	—	—	—	—	—	—	—	—	—	—	—	....	....	Direct Investment Abroad	78bd d
	—	—	—	—	—	−.01	2.78	.41	−.59	−.06	1.20	−.75		....	....	Dir. Invest. in Rep. Econ., n.i.e.	78be d
	—	—	—	—	—	—	—	—	—	—	—	—	—	....	....	Portfolio Investment Assets	78bf d
	—	—	—	—	—	—	—	—	—	—	—	—	—	....	....	Portfolio Investment Liab., n.i.e.	78bg d
	1.14	20.56	21.66	20.24	6.41	18.24	9.24	5.39	−2.16	−.48	5.12	1.47	6.82	....	....	Other Investment Assets	78bh d
														....	....	Other Investment Liab., n.i.e.	78bi d
	1.14	20.56	21.66	20.24	6.41	18.24	9.23	8.17	−1.74	−1.07	5.05	2.67	6.07	....	....	Financial Account, n.i.e.	78bj d
	−5.63	−3.69	−1.86	−3.69	−4.84	4.94	−11.57	.90	−.65	−1.22	5.15	−7.28	5.49	....	....	Net Errors and Omissions	78ca d
	−.18	−4.74	4.96	3.20	−4.84	14.24	−.61	22.76	−1.94	−6.86	−1.73	−12.55	8.01	....	....	Overall Balance	78cb d
	.18	4.74	−4.96	−3.20	4.84	−14.24	.61	−22.76	1.94	6.86	1.73	12.55	−8.01	....	....	Reserves and Related Items	79da d
	.18	4.74	−4.96	−3.20	4.84	−14.24	−.89	−24.35	−.61	6.60	−2.23	11.87	−13.30	....	....	Reserve Assets	79db d
	—	—	—	—	—	—	—	—	—	—	—	—	—	....	....	Use of Fund Credit and Loans	79dc d
	—	—	—	—	—	—	—	—	—	—	—	—	—	....	....	Liabs.Constit.For.Auth.Reserves	79dd d
	—	—	—	—	—	1.50	1.59	2.55	.27	3.96	.68	5.29		....	....	Exceptional Financing	79de d
Millions of Escudos																**National Accounts**	
	1,089	1,588	1,880	2,451	2,562	2,887	2,733	2,984	3,190	....	....	....	....	....	....	Exports of Goods & Services	90c
	807	980	1,495	1,954	2,438	2,748	3,380	3,673	3,968	....	....	....	....	....	....	Government Consumption	91f
	2,214	3,271	4,222	4,840	4,966	5,957	6,440	7,053	7,721	....	....	....	....	....	....	Gross Fixed Capital Formation	93e
	214	−175	149	21	−37	−246	439	328	−434	....	....	....	....	....	....	Net Increase/Decrease(-) in Stocks	93i
	5,386	6,141	7,113	8,498	10,193	11,471	13,407	15,134	17,848	....	....	....	....	....	....	Private Consumption	96f
	−3,793	−4,753	−6,420	−7,622	−8,575	−9,736	−10,841	−11,189	−11,653	....	....	....	....	....	....	Imports of Goods & Services	98c
	5,919	7,053	8,438	10,140	11,548	13,081	15,558	17,984	20,640	....	....	....	....	....	....	Gross Domestic Product = GDP	99b
	9,665	10,281	10,646	11,628	12,052	13,081	13,437	14,455	15,558	....	....	....	....	....	....	Gross Dom. Prod. 1985 Prices	99b.p
	61.2	68.6	79.3	87.2	95.8	100.0	115.8	124.4	132.7	....	....	....	....	....	....	GDP Deflator (1985=100)	99bi p
Midyear Estimates																	
	.30	.29	.30	.32	.33	.33	.34	.35	.33	.33	.34	.35	.36	.37	....	**Population**	99z

Central African Rep.
626

		1965	1966	1967	1968	1969	1970	1971	1972	1973	1974	1975	1976	1977	1978	1979
Exchange Rates															*Francs per SDR:*	
Official Rate	aa	245.07	247.59	245.42	247.40	277.91	276.02	283.61	278.00	284.00	272.08	262.55	288.70	285.76	272.28	264.78
															Francs per US Dollar:	
Official Rate	ae	245.08	247.59	245.43	247.41	277.92	276.03	261.23	256.05	235.43	222.22	224.27	248.49	235.25	209.00	201.00
Official Rate	rf	245.06	245.68	246.00	247.56	259.96	276.40	275.59	252.03	222.89	240.70	214.31	238.95	245.68	225.66	212.72
														Index Numbers (1990=100):		
Official Rate	ah x	110.8	110.5	110.4	109.7	104.8	98.2	98.6	107.8	122.3	112.8	126.9	113.8	110.5	120.6	127.7
Nominal Effective Exchange Rate	ne c	....	....	....	....	....	....	....	....	....	....	....	....	....	....	64.2
Real Effective Exchange Rate	re c	....	....	....	....	....	....	....	....	....	....	....	....	....	....	101.5
Fund Position															*Millions of SDRs:*	
Quota	2f. s	7.50	8.00	8.50	9.00	9.50	13.00	13.00	13.00	13.00	13.00	13.00	13.00	13.00	16.00	16.00
SDRs	1b. s	—	—	—	—	—	.01	—	1.21	1.02	.81	2.25	1.62	1.56	1.30	1.36
Reserve Position in the Fund	1c. s	.65	.77	.90	1.02	1.15	1.33	.14	.29	.44	—	—	—	—	1.66	1.85
Total Fund Cred.&Loans Outstg.	2tl	—	—	—	—	—	—	—	—	—	2.66	4.85	9.59	9.59	15.67	13.57
International Liquidity											*Millions of US Dollars Unless Otherwise Indicated:*					
Total Reserves minus Gold	1l. d	10.16	6.42	4.75	4.70	1.20	1.39	.21	1.72	1.78	1.74	3.83	18.83	25.35	24.13	44.11
SDRs	1b. d	—	—	—	—	—	.01	—	1.31	1.23	.99	2.63	1.88	1.89	1.69	1.79
Reserve Position in the Fund	1c. d	.65	.77	.90	1.02	1.15	1.33	.15	.31	.53	—	—	—	—	2.16	2.44
Foreign Exchange	1d. d	9.51	5.65	3.85	3.67	.04	.05	.06	.09	.02	.75	1.19	16.95	23.46	20.28	39.88
Gold (Million Fine Troy Ounces)	1ad	....	....	....	....	....	....	....	....	....	....	....	—	.006	.009	.011
Gold (National Valuation)	1an d	....	....	....	....	....	....	....	....	....	....	....	....	.92	1.94	5.79
Monetary Authorities: Other Liab.	4. d	—	.04	.04	.28	.16	.16	.31	.32	.27	2.40	2.37	1.08	1.85	1.21	2.23
Deposit Money Banks: Assets	7a. d	.53	.57	.77	2.42	1.16	6.55	6.69	6.96	12.91	.83	.77	8.56	4.10	8.36	12.23
Liabilities	7b. d	2.84	2.39	4.09	4.84	7.26	9.36	10.33	9.46	16.71	23.29	24.14	20.20	24.17	26.57	25.16
Monetary Authorities															*Billions of Francs:*	
Foreign Assets	11	2.51	1.59	1.17	1.16	.33	.39	.05	.44	.41	.39	.86	4.68	6.18	5.45	10.04
Claims on Central Government	12a	—	—	.08	.73	1.51	2.15	1.73	2.27	2.63	3.09	3.88	5.38	5.84	7.66	7.06
Claims on Deposit Money Banks	12e	1.71	2.38	2.87	2.99	4.42	5.32	4.78	5.29	6.66	7.23	6.80	3.37	3.42	7.67	8.47
Claims on Other Banking Insts.	12f	....	....	....	....	....	....	....	....	....	....	....	....	....	....	....
Reserve Money	14	3.40	3.56	3.76	4.57	4.87	5.24	5.14	5.78	5.99	7.58	7.87	9.28	11.49	13.73	18.16
of which: Currency Outside DMBs	14a	3.33	3.48	3.69	4.44	4.80	5.19	5.05	5.71	5.85	7.44	7.52	8.99	11.19	13.45	17.98
Foreign Liabilities	16c	—	.01	.01	.07	.04	.04	.08	.08	.06	1.26	1.80	3.04	3.18	4.52	4.04
Central Government Deposits	16d	.80	.38	.30	.13	1.16	1.94	.75	.19	2.54	.20	1.39	.35	.19	.88	.59
Capital Accounts	17a	—	—	—	—	—	—	—	—	.01	.01	.01	.02	.01	.01	.01
Other Items (Net)	17r	—	.02	.04	.11	.18	.62	.59	1.94	1.10	1.67	.46	.74	.57	1.63	2.76
Deposit Money Banks															*Billions of Francs:*	
Reserves	20	.03	.08	.05	.13	.08	.05	.10	.07	.14	.14	.36	.29	.30	.28	.18
Foreign Assets	21	.13	.14	.19	.60	.32	1.82	1.71	1.78	2.97	.18	.17	2.13	1.97	1.75	2.46
Claims on Central Government	22a	—	—	.01	.14	.19	.59	1.40	1.22	2.63	4.31	5.29	5.06	5.25	5.36	5.22
Claims on Nonfin.Pub.Enterprises	22c	....	....	....	....	....	....	....	....	....	....	....	....	....	....	....
Claims on Private Sector	22d	5.32	6.26	7.37	8.34	9.91	10.27	8.13	8.98	9.83	14.62	13.33	12.04	14.73	18.24	15.62
Claims on Other Banking Insts.	22f	....	....	....	....	....	....	....	....	....	....	....	....	....	....	....
Claims on Nonbank Financial Insts.	22g	....	....	....	....	....	....	....	....	....	....	....	....	....	....	....
Demand Deposits	24	2.00	1.80	2.08	2.98	2.04	2.48	2.72	3.42	3.38	4.88	4.62	7.94	7.04	7.16	8.19
Time and Savings Deposits	25	.23	.43	.47	.58	.86	.81	.79	.81	1.13	1.09	1.35	2.22	2.29	1.99	.97
Foreign Liabilities	26c	.70	.36	.68	.54	1.14	1.72	1.90	1.68	3.24	4.67	4.96	4.57	4.78	4.65	5.06
Long-Term Foreign Liabilities	26cl	—	.23	.33	.65	.88	.88	.74	.74	.60	.50	.45	.45	.91	.91	—
Central Government Deposits	26d	.20	.22	.14	.19	.11	.20	.16	.19	.25	.22	.20	.26	.28	.31	.04
Credit from Monetary Authorities	26g	1.71	2.38	2.87	2.99	4.42	5.32	4.78	5.29	6.66	7.23	6.80	3.37	3.42	7.67	8.47
Capital Accounts	27a	.85	1.09	1.14	1.22	1.30	1.24	.58	.52	.73	.92	1.09	1.27	3.27	3.60	3.70
Other Items (Net)	27r	−.21	−.03	−.09	.06	−.23	.08	−.33	−.58	−.42	−.26	−.33	−.55	−.74	−.66	−2.95
Post Office: Checking Deposits	24.. i	.11	.09	.10	.12	.12	.16	.15	.16	.16	.27	.39	.45	.33	.30	.23
Postal Debt	26c. i	....	.21	.02	.02	.07	.41	1.21	1.03	2.39	3.88	4.74	4.47	4.87	5.03	4.95
Monetary Survey															*Billions of Francs:*	
Foreign Assets (Net)	31n	1.94	1.36	.67	1.14	−.52	.44	−.22	.46	.08	−5.36	−5.73	−.80	−.81	−1.97	3.40
Domestic Credit	32	4.32	5.66	7.02	8.88	10.35	10.87	10.35	12.09	12.31	21.60	20.91	21.87	25.34	30.06	27.28
Claims on Central Govt. (Net)	32an	−1.00	−.60	−.35	.55	.44	.60	2.22	3.11	2.48	6.98	7.58	9.83	10.61	11.83	11.66
Claims on Nonfin.Pub.Enterprises	32c	....	....	....	....	....	....	....	....	....	....	....	....	....	....	....
Claims on Private Sector	32d	5.32	6.26	7.37	8.34	9.91	10.27	8.13	8.98	9.83	14.62	13.33	12.04	14.73	18.24	15.62
Claims on Other Banking Insts.	32f	....	....	....	....	....	....	....	....	....	....	....	....	....	....	....
Claims on Nonbk.Financial Insts.	32g	....	....	....	....	....	....	....	....	....	....	....	....	....	....	....
Money	34	5.33	5.28	5.77	7.42	6.83	7.67	7.77	9.13	9.23	12.32	12.13	16.93	18.23	20.61	26.17
Quasi-Money	35	.23	.43	.47	.58	.86	.81	.79	.81	1.13	1.09	1.35	2.22	2.29	1.99	.97
Other Items (Net)	37r	....	....	....	2.03	2.13	2.83	1.57	2.61	2.03	2.83	1.69	1.93	4.02	5.50	3.53
Money plus Quasi-Money	35l	5.56	5.71	6.24	8.00	7.69	8.49	8.56	9.94	10.36	13.41	13.49	19.15	20.51	22.60	27.15
Interest Rates															*Percent Per Annum*	
Discount Rate (End of Period)	60	....	....	....	4.50	4.50	4.50	4.50	4.50	4.50	4.50	5.50	5.50	6.50	6.50	8.50
Deposit Rate	60l	....	....	....	....	....	....	....	....	....	....	....	....	....	5.50	4.00
Lending Rate	60p	....	....	....	....	....	....	....	....	....	....	....	....	....	9.50	8.50
Prices															*Index Numbers (1990=100):*	
Wholesale Prices	63	20.2	20.2	21.2	21.7	22.0	21.9	23.1	24.5	25.1	30.0	35.7	37.4	40.3	43.4	49.4
Consumer Prices	64	....	....	....	....	....	....	....	....	....	....	....	....	....	....	....

Central African Rep.

626

1980	1981	1982	1983	1984	1985	1986	1987	1988	1989	1990	1991	1992	1993	1994		
End of Period															**Exchange Rates**	
287.99	334.52	370.92	436.97	470.11	415.26	394.78	378.78	407.68	380.32	364.84	370.48	378.57	404.89	ⅼ780.44	Official Rate	aa
End of Period (ae) Period Average (rf)																
225.80	287.40	336.25	417.37	479.60	378.05	322.75	267.00	302.95	289.40	256.45	259.00	275.33	294.78	ⅼ534.60	Official Rate	ae
211.28	271.73	328.61	381.06	436.96	449.26	346.30	300.54	297.85	319.01	272.26	282.11	264.69	283.16	ⅼ555.20	Official Rate	rf
Period Averages																
128.7	100.5	83.1	71.6	62.3	60.9	78.6	90.5	91.4	85.2	100.0	96.6	102.8	96.0	49.0	Official Rate	ahx
66.3	63.5	62.1	61.8	63.7	68.6	74.6	78.8	81.8	86.5	100.0	103.8	112.6	119.9	67.5	Nominal Effective Exchange Rate	nec
106.0	101.8	101.3	98.5	95.5	98.5	105.0	105.1	102.5	97.3	100.0	94.2	94.1	89.1	55.4	Real Effective Exchange Rate	rec
End of Period															**Fund Position**	
24.00	24.00	24.00	30.40	30.40	30.40	30.40	30.40	30.40	30.40	30.40	30.40	41.20	41.20	41.20	Quota	2f.s
—	.07	.17	.71	2.59	1.54	.43	4.93	9.15	—	3.42	.49	.04	.03	.01	SDRs	1b.s
—	—	1.21	1.61	.11	.11	.11	.11	.11	.11	.09	.09	.09	.09	.09	Reserve Position in the Fund	1c.s
18.43	32.41	34.19	38.15	35.77	35.49	34.13	36.58	37.33	26.88	25.73	23.28	22.09	20.96	28.34	Total Fund Cred.&Loans Outstg.	2tl
End of Period															**International Liquidity**	
54.98	69.27	46.37	46.79	52.68	49.62	65.35	96.73	108.47	113.06	118.63	102.98	100.12	111.98	210.01	Total Reserves minus Gold	1l.d
—	.08	.19	.74	2.54	1.69	.53	6.99	12.31	—	4.87	.70	.06	.04	.01	SDRs	1b.d
—	—	1.33	1.69	.11	.11	.13	.16	.15	.14	.13	.13	.12	.13	.14	Reserve Position in the Fund	1c.d
54.98	69.19	44.85	44.36	50.03	47.81	64.69	89.58	96.01	112.92	113.63	102.15	99.94	111.81	209.86	Foreign Exchange	1d.d
.011	.011	.011	.011	.011	.011	.011	.011	.011	.011	.011	.011	.011	.011	.011	Gold (Million Fine Troy Ounces)	1ad
6.56	4.45	5.00	4.21	3.44	3.60	4.36	5.37	4.52	3.52	3.98	3.94	3.70	4.42	....	Gold (National Valuation)	1and
1.59	.70	1.74	2.60	1.47	1.12	.52	1.14	13.12	10.53	9.16	8.50	9.54	.81	.19	Monetary Authorities: Other Liab.	4..d
14.61	11.70	5.65	9.11	9.68	21.94	28.04	29.74	13.02	10.57	12.65	9.43	9.12	6.85	11.45	Deposit Money Banks: Assets	7a.d
23.83	17.87	4.16	1.31	2.46	3.26	12.24	12.67	16.24	14.24	16.18	13.22	14.34	12.04	12.10	Liabilities	7b.d
End of Period															**Monetary Authorities**	
13.90	21.19	17.27	21.30	26.91	20.12	22.50	27.27	ⅼ34.25	34.01	31.52	27.69	28.59	34.29	114.56	Foreign Assets	11
8.67	15.19	15.77	21.82	21.37	20.23	21.55	20.92	ⅼ22.68	17.94	17.41	ⅼ27.66	28.23	28.34	41.99	Claims on Central Government	12a
11.69	11.12	16.40	15.74	12.13	18.13	18.85	13.11	ⅼ9.15	7.60	11.67	ⅼ2.51	2.18	3.66	—	Claims on Deposit Money Banks	12e
....	....	....	....	....	....	....	....	....	....	....	....	....	....	—	Claims on Other Banking Insts.	12f
24.81	32.43	31.77	35.41	37.91	38.27	43.03	42.89	ⅼ39.00	42.82	43.13	43.14	43.80	52.46	96.65	Reserve Money	14
24.38	31.99	31.39	34.93	37.33	38.03	40.95	42.28	ⅼ38.71	42.24	41.84	42.26	43.36	52.16	88.53	*of which:* Currency Outside DMBs	14a
5.67	11.04	13.27	17.76	17.52	15.16	13.64	14.16	ⅼ19.37	13.44	11.68	10.83	10.99	8.72	22.22	Foreign Liabilities	16c
.54	.85	.68	.89	.77	.90	1.19	1.72	ⅼ5.14	1.09	2.05	.59	.63	1.69	1.89	Central Government Deposits	16d
1.53	1.30	1.69	1.78	1.65	1.36	1.41	1.44	ⅼ1.46	1.34	1.11	1.23	.99	1.27	1.02	Capital Accounts	17a
1.72	1.87	2.04	3.02	2.55	2.79	3.63	1.09	ⅼ1.10	.87	2.63	2.07	ⅼ2.59	2.16	34.77	Other Items (Net)	17r
End of Period															**Deposit Money Banks**	
.43	.43	.38	.48	.58	.24	2.07	.61	ⅼ.29	.58	1.29	.88	.44	.30	8.11	Reserves	20
3.30	3.36	1.90	3.80	4.64	8.29	9.05	7.94	ⅼ4.01	3.06	3.24	2.44	2.51	2.02	6.12	Foreign Assets	21
5.17	5.31	1.44	.51	1.01	.40	3.15	1.72	ⅼ1.96	2.20	2.28	3.76	ⅼ4.22	5.21	5.07	Claims on Central Government	22a
....	....	....	....	....	....	....	....	4.45	6.32	11.03	9.35	4.25	4.54	5.84	Claims on Nonfin.Pub.Enterprises	22c
23.47	24.43	30.35	30.84	30.62	35.03	31.97	29.46	ⅼ27.96	30.21	29.15	26.60	16.85	15.93	18.70	Claims on Private Sector	22d
....	....	....	....	....	....	....	....	—	—	—	—	—	—	—	Claims on Other Banking Insts.	22f
....	....	....	....	....	....	....	....	....	....	....	....	....	....	....	Claims on Nonbank Financial Insts.	22g
10.25	10.37	9.34	10.47	11.01	14.39	11.58	12.09	ⅼ11.03	14.42	12.71	10.77	7.68	7.26	14.86	Demand Deposits	24
2.01	3.01	2.73	3.15	3.87	5.01	6.17	6.48	ⅼ7.32	7.75	7.47	6.49	6.20	5.16	11.89	Time and Savings Deposits	25
5.38	5.14	1.40	.55	1.18	1.23	3.95	3.38	ⅼ2.77	2.43	2.66	ⅼ1.83	3.53	3.18	5.80	Foreign Liabilities	26c
....	....	....	....	....	....	....	....	ⅼ2.15	1.69	1.49	ⅼ1.60	.42	.37	.66	Long-Term Foreign Liabilities	26cl
.41	1.53	1.45	3.14	4.94	2.16	1.64	1.59	ⅼ3.01	3.75	5.59	5.30	ⅼ2.41	1.98	3.55	Central Government Deposits	26d
11.69	11.12	16.40	15.74	12.13	18.15	18.85	13.11	ⅼ9.15	7.60	11.67	ⅼ2.51	2.18	3.66	—	Credit from Monetary Authorities	26g
3.67	4.78	5.76	6.33	8.60	8.87	10.70	10.75	ⅼ7.19	7.49	7.74	ⅼ19.97	8.01	8.10	8.70	Capital Accounts	27a
-1.03	-2.41	-3.02	-3.75	-4.87	-5.84	-6.65	-7.66	ⅼ-3.95	-2.75	-2.34	-5.43	ⅼ-2.15	-1.71	-1.62	Other Items (Net)	27r
.30	.38	.33	.37	.32	.32	.31	.31	.31	....	....	....	....	....	....	Post Office: Checking Deposits	24..i
4.84	4.81	.95	—	—	—	2.35	1.17	....	....	....	....	....	....	....	Postal Debt	26c.i
End of Period															**Monetary Survey**	
6.15	8.37	4.50	6.80	12.86	12.02	13.96	17.67	ⅼ13.97	19.52	18.94	ⅼ15.88	16.16	24.04	92.00	Foreign Assets (Net)	31n
36.36	42.54	45.43	49.14	47.29	52.61	53.84	48.79	ⅼ48.90	51.83	52.23	ⅼ61.47	ⅼ50.52	50.35	66.15	Domestic Credit	32
12.89	18.11	15.09	18.30	16.67	17.57	21.87	19.33	ⅼ16.49	15.30	12.05	ⅼ25.53	ⅼ29.41	29.88	41.61	Claims on Central Govt. (Net)	32an
....	....	....	....	....	....	....	....	4.45	6.32	11.03	9.35	4.25	4.54	5.84	Claims on Nonfin.Pub.Enterprises	32c
23.47	24.43	30.35	30.84	30.62	35.03	31.97	29.46	ⅼ27.96	30.21	29.15	26.60	16.85	15.93	18.70	Claims on Private Sector	32d
....	....	....	....	....	....	....	....	—	—	—	—	—	—	—	Claims on Other Banking Insts.	32f
....	....	....	....	....	....	....	....	....	....	....	....	....	....	....	Claims on Nonbk.Financial Insts.	32g
34.63	42.36	40.73	45.40	48.33	52.42	52.54	54.37	ⅼ49.74	56.66	54.56	53.03	51.05	59.42	103.40	Money	34
2.01	3.01	2.73	3.15	3.87	5.01	6.17	6.48	ⅼ7.32	7.75	7.47	6.49	6.20	5.16	11.89	Quasi-Money	35
5.88	5.55	6.47	7.39	7.94	7.19	9.09	5.61	ⅼ5.81	6.94	9.14	ⅼ17.84	ⅼ9.44	9.82	42.87	Other Items (Net)	37r
36.63	45.37	43.46	48.55	52.20	57.43	58.71	60.85	ⅼ57.06	64.41	62.03	59.52	57.24	64.58	115.29	Money plus Quasi-Money	35l
Percent Per Annum															**Interest Rates**	
8.50	8.50	8.50	8.50	8.50	9.00	8.00	8.00	9.50	10.00	11.00	10.75	12.00	11.50	....	Discount Rate (End of Period)	60
5.50	7.50	7.50	7.50	7.50	7.50	7.35	7.19	7.44	7.50	ⅼ7.50	7.50	7.50	7.75	8.08	Deposit Rate	60l
10.50	12.00	12.00	12.50	12.50	12.50	12.00	11.42	12.25	13.00	ⅼ18.50	18.15	17.77	17.46	17.42	Lending Rate	60p
Period Averages															**Prices**	
57.3	ⅼ65.7	75.1	81.7	86.6	92.4	96.0	96.7	94.7	98.4	100.0	98.9	....	....	....	Wholesale Prices	63
....	74.0	83.8	96.0	98.5	108.8	111.2	103.4	99.3	100.0	100.0	97.2	96.2	93.4	....	Consumer Prices	64

Central African Rep.

		1965	1966	1967	1968	1969	1970	1971	1972	1973	1974	1975	1976	1977	1978	1979
International Transactions																*Millions of Francs*
Exports	70	6,507	7,591	7,166	8,816	9,196	8,434	8,939	9,930	8,328	11,622	10,120	14,623	20,033	16,182	16,937
Imports, cif	71	6,776	8,623	10,908	9,820	9,766	9,492	9,053	8,547	11,496	11,090	14,615	13,155	15,540	12,775	14,816
Imports, fob	71.v	4,738	6,030	7,628	6,883	6,838	6,641	7,997	7,015	8,453	8,357	11,042	10,026	11,845	9,737	12,410
Balance of Payments																*Millions of US Dollars:*
Goods: Exports f.o.b.	78aa d	...	...	...	...	...	...	...	...	...	...	...	...	104.5	110.3	122.2
Goods: Imports f.o.b.	78ab d	...	...	...	...	...	...	...	...	...	...	...	...	−103.9	−117.7	−132.9
Trade Balance	78ac d	...	...	...	...	...	...	...	...	...	...	...	...	.6	−7.4	−10.7
Services: Credit	78ad d	...	...	...	...	...	...	...	...	...	...	...	...	23.4	32.7	35.0
Services: Debit	78ae d	...	...	...	...	...	...	...	...	...	...	...	...	−70.2	−87.9	−113.3
Balance on Goods and Services	78af d	...	...	...	...	...	...	...	...	...	...	...	...	−46.3	−62.6	−89.0
Income: Credit	78ag d	...	...	...	...	...	...	...	...	...	...	...	...	2.8	3.7	2.6
Income: Debit	78ah d	...	...	...	...	...	...	...	...	...	...	...	...	−3.4	−2.5	−8.0
Balance on Goods, Serv., & Inc.	78ai d	...	...	...	...	...	...	...	...	...	...	...	...	−46.9	−61.5	−94.4
Current Transfers, n.i.e.: Credit	78aj d	...	...	...	...	...	...	...	...	...	...	...	...	43.0	56.7	89.9
Current Transfers: Debit	78ak d	...	...	...	...	...	...	...	...	...	...	...	...	−15.1	−18.3	−11.5
Current Account, n.i.e.	78al d	...	...	...	...	...	...	...	...	...	...	...	...	−19.0	−23.1	−16.1
Capital Account, n.i.e.: Credit	78ba d	...	...	...	...	...	...	...	...	...	...	...	...	—	—	—
Capital Account: Debit	78bb d	...	...	...	...	...	...	...	...	...	...	...	...	—	—	—
Capital Account, n.i.e.	78bc d	...	...	...	...	...	...	...	...	...	...	...	...	—	—	—
Direct Investment Abroad	78bd d	...	...	...	...	...	...	...	...	...	...	...	...	−.1	1.3	−.3
Dir. Invest. in Rep. Econ., n.i.e.	78be d	...	...	...	...	...	...	...	...	...	...	...	...	−2.8	6.1	22.8
Portfolio Investment Assets	78bf d	...	...	...	...	...	...	...	...	...	...	...	...	—	—	—
Portfolio Investment Liab., n.i.e.	78bg d	...	...	...	...	...	...	...	...	...	...	...	...	—	—	−6.0
Other Investment Assets	78bh d	...	...	...	...	...	...	...	...	...	...	...	...	.5	−12.7	−6.0
Other Investment Liab., n.i.e.	78bi d	...	...	...	...	...	...	...	...	...	...	...	...	17.0	7.6	26.2
Financial Account, n.i.e.	78bj d	...	...	...	...	...	...	...	...	...	...	...	...	14.6	2.3	42.6
Net Errors and Omissions	78ca d	...	...	...	...	...	...	...	...	...	...	...	...	9.3	8.2	−10.0
Overall Balance	78cb d	...	...	...	...	...	...	...	...	...	...	...	...	4.9	−12.6	16.5
Reserves and Related Items	79da d	...	...	...	...	...	...	...	...	...	...	...	...	−4.9	12.6	−16.5
Reserve Assets	79db d	...	...	...	...	...	...	...	...	...	...	...	...	−6.1	3.1	−16.9
Use of Fund Credit and Loans	79dc d	...	...	...	...	...	...	...	...	...	...	...	...	—	7.5	−2.7
Liabs.Constit.For.Auth.Reserves	79dd d	...	...	...	...	...	...	...	...	...	...	...	...	1.1	1.5	1.3
Exceptional Financing	79de d	...	...	...	...	...	...	...	...	...	...	...	...	.1	.4	1.9
Government Finance																*Millions of Francs:*
Deficit (−) or Surplus	80	...	...	...	...	...	...	...	...	...	...	...	...	...	...	...
Revenue	81	...	...	...	...	...	...	...	...	...	...	...	...	...	...	...
Grants Received	81z	...	...	...	...	...	...	...	...	...	...	...	...	...	...	...
Expenditure	82	...	...	...	...	...	...	...	...	...	...	...	...	...	...	...
Lending Minus Repayments	83	...	...	...	...	...	...	...	...	...	...	...	...	...	...	...
Overall Cash Adjustment	80x	...	...	...	...	...	...	...	...	...	...	...	...	...	...	...
Financing																
Net Borrowing: Domestic	84a	...	...	...	...	...	...	...	...	...	...	...	...	...	...	...
Foreign	85a	...	...	...	...	...	...	...	...	...	...	...	...	...	...	...
Use of Cash Balances	87	...	...	...	...	...	...	...	...	...	...	...	...	...	...	...
National Accounts																*Billions of Francs*
Gross Domestic Product	99b	36.9	38.8	40.3	44.3	46.9	49.7	52.7	55.6	57.1	72.0	83.8	94.1	106.9	120.8	135.3
																Millions:
Population	99z	1.43	1.47	1.50	1.54	1.58	1.82	1.87	1.91	1.96	2.01	2.05	2.10	2.17	2.22	2.28

Monetary Authorities: Beginning in March 1988, the sectorization and classification of accounts have been revised. Beginning in September 1991, *Claims on Central Government* include government assumption of certain nonperforming bank loans. Beginning in December 1992, the coverage of the banking system has been revised. Claims and deposits of nonactive banks or banks in the process of liquidation have been excluded from the monetary accounts.

Deposit Money Banks: Beginning in September 1991, the counterpart of government assumption of certain nonperforming bank loans was reclassified from *Credit from Monetary Authorities* to *Capital Accounts*. See note to section 10.

Monetary Survey: Beginning in 1965, data for *line 32d* include Treasury claims on the private sector with the contra-entry reported in *line 32an*. See notes to sections 10 and 20.

Interest Rates: *Deposit Rate:* Beginning in October 1990, minimum rate offered by deposit money banks on savings accounts.

Lending Rate: Beginning in October 1990, maximum rate charged by deposit money banks on all loans, excluding charges and fees.

Central African Rep.

626

	1980	1981	1982	1983	1984	1985	1986	1987	1988	1989	1990	1991	1992	1993	1994		
International Transactions																	
Millions of Francs																	
Exports	24,384	21,323	35,461	28,405	37,022	41,217	22,975	39,180	38,750	42,866	32,770	35,440	32,700	....	....		70
Imports, cif	17,009	25,646	41,306	25,951	38,193	50,686	57,841	61,370	59,760	47,994	42,050	50,400	43,700	....	....		71
Imports, fob	14,245	21,712	37,327	23,835	35,072	46,544	53,114	56,354	54,876	44,072	38,613	46,281	40,129	....	....		71.v
Balance of Payments																	
Minus Sign Indicates Debit																	
Goods: Exports f.o.b.	147.2	117.7	124.4	123.4	114.4	131.0	129.5	128.9	133.7	148.1	150.5	125.6	123.5	....	....		78aa *d*
Goods: Imports f.o.b.	−185.1	−144.6	−149.7	−137.5	−140.1	−167.7	−201.0	−197.7	−179.1	−186.0	−241.6	−178.7	−165.1	....	....		78ab *d*
Trade Balance	−37.9	−26.9	−25.3	−14.1	−25.6	−36.7	−71.5	−68.8	−45.4	−37.9	−91.1	−53.0	−41.6	....	....		78ac *d*
Services: Credit	53.8	51.7	41.6	35.7	34.8	46.8	56.0	67.8	62.3	65.6	69.1	50.5	53.6	....	....		78ad *d*
Services: Debit	−142.3	−92.1	−106.4	−103.7	−86.4	−108.0	−141.6	−154.4	−151.0	−144.4	−168.5	−136.7	−143.9	....	....		78ae *d*
Balance on Goods and Services	−126.4	−67.2	−90.1	−82.1	−77.2	−98.0	−157.2	−155.4	−134.1	−116.8	−190.5	−139.2	−131.9	....	....		78af *d*
Income: Credit	4.4	8.0	5.0	3.1	2.7	6.7	2.8	2.8	—	.7	.8	5.5	6.4	....	....		78ag *d*
Income: Debit	−1.8	−4.7	−12.2	−13.8	−12.4	−14.0	−15.2	−21.9	−21.2	−21.4	−22.4	−19.0	−25.3	....	....		78ah *d*
Balance on Goods, Serv., & Inc.	−123.8	−63.9	−97.4	−92.8	−86.9	−105.3	−169.5	−174.5	−155.3	−137.5	−212.1	−152.7	−150.7	....	....		78ai *d*
Current Transfers, n.i.e.: Credit	107.6	81.6	76.8	86.2	75.7	78.9	111.5	136.3	156.7	138.3	164.2	129.7	134.9	....	....		78aj *d*
Current Transfers: Debit	−26.8	−22.0	−22.1	−22.7	−22.3	−22.2	−28.5	−35.2	−36.0	−34.2	−41.2	−38.8	−41.6	....	....		78ak *d*
Current Account, n.i.e.	−43.1	−4.3	−42.6	−29.3	−33.4	−48.6	−86.5	−73.4	−34.6	−33.4	−89.1	−61.8	−57.4	....	....		78al *d*
Capital Account, n.i.e.: Credit	—	—	—	—	—	—	—	—	—	—	—	—	—	....	....		78ba *d*
Capital Account: Debit	—	—	—	—	—	—	—	—	—	—	—	—	—	....	....		78bb *d*
Capital Account, n.i.e.	—	—	—	—	—	—	—	—	—	—	—	—	—	....	....		78bc *d*
Direct Investment Abroad	—	—	−.3	−.4	−.3	−.6	−1.3	−2.6	−4.8	−3.8	−3.8	−3.5	−5.7	....	....		78bd *d*
Dir. Invest. in Rep. Econ., n.i.e.	5.3	5.8	9.2	4.5	5.1	3.0	8.2	11.9	−3.8	1.3	.7	−4.9	−3.0	....	....		78be *d*
Portfolio Investment Assets	—	—	—	—	—	—	—	—	—	—	—	—	—	....	....		78bf *d*
Portfolio Investment Liab., n.i.e.	—	—	—	—	—	—	—	—	—	—	—	—	—	....	....		78bg *d*
Other Investment Assets	−4.0	−28.0	.4	−17.7	−8.7	−22.3	−16.8	−12.7	−9.0	−13.3	−16.3	−11.2	−20.4	....	....		78bh *d*
Other Investment Liab., n.i.e.	53.0	30.6	−3.1	21.3	31.0	51.4	86.1	66.8	27.1	36.0	88.6	44.1	62.0	....	....		78bi *d*
Financial Account, n.i.e.	54.3	8.4	6.1	7.6	27.3	31.6	76.2	63.4	9.5	20.2	69.3	24.5	32.9	....	....		78bj *d*
Net Errors and Omissions	−12.1	−11.4	2.1	7.6	6.7	−7.8	7.0	−1.6	11.7	1.4	1.4	−1.9	.7	....	....		78ca *d*
Overall Balance	−.8	−7.3	−34.4	−14.1	.6	−24.8	−3.3	−11.6	−13.4	−11.9	−18.5	−39.1	−23.9	....	....		78cb *d*
Reserves and Related Items	.8	7.3	34.4	14.1	−.6	24.8	3.3	11.6	13.4	11.9	18.5	39.1	23.9	....	....		79da *d*
Reserve Assets	−14.5	−25.5	21.4	−3.2	−5.0	18.6	−4.9	−14.2	−32.4	.8	9.4	13.8	1.4	....	....		79db *d*
Use of Fund Credit and Loans	6.3	17.0	2.0	4.3	−2.5	−.5	−1.3	3.1	1.1	−13.4	−1.6	−3.3	−1.7	....	....		79dc *d*
Liabs.Constit.For.Auth.Reserves	7.1	5.2	−7.8	.7	−1.0	—	−.3	—	.1	−4.8	−2.6	−.5	—	....	....		79dd *d*
Exceptional Financing	1.9	10.6	18.9	12.3	7.9	6.7	9.7	22.7	44.6	29.3	13.3	29.2	24.2	....	....		79de *d*
Government Finance																	
Year Ending December 31																	
Deficit (−) or Surplus	....	−6,671	....	....	....	....	....	....	....	....	....	....	....	....	....		80
Revenue	....	30,365	....	....	....	....	....	....	....	....	....	....	....	....	....		81
Grants Received	....	4,686	....	....	....	....	....	....	....	....	....	....	....	....	....		81z
Expenditure	....	41,538	....	....	....	....	....	....	....	....	....	....	....	....	....		82
Lending Minus Repayments	....	618	....	....	....	....	....	....	....	....	....	....	....	....	....		83
Overall Cash Adjustment	....	434	....	....	....	....	....	....	....	....	....	....	....	....	....		80x
Financing																	
Net Borrowing: Domestic	....	4,489	....	....	....	....	....	....	....	....	....	....	....	....	....		84a
Foreign	....	3,925	....	....	....	....	....	....	....	....	....	....	....	....	....		85a
Use of Cash Balances	....	−1,743	....	....	....	....	....	....	....	....	....	....	....	....	....		87
National Accounts																	
Billions of Francs																	
Gross Domestic Product	168.4	218.1	248.0	251.5	278.7	316.2	330.9	315.7	327.5	340.6	353.0	362.1	354.5	....	....		99b
Midyear Estimates																	
Population	2.31	2.38	2.44	2.50	2.56	2.61	2.74	2.72	2.88	2.99	2.93	3.00	3.08	3.16	....		99z

Chad

		1965	1966	1967	1968	1969	1970	1971	1972	1973	1974	1975	1976	1977	1978	1979
Exchange Rates															*Francs per SDR:*	
Official Rate	aa	245.07	247.59	245.42	247.40	277.91	276.02	283.61	278.00	284.00	272.08	262.55	288.70	285.76	272.28	264.78
															Francs per US Dollar:	
Official Rate	ae	245.08	247.59	245.43	247.41	277.92	276.03	261.23	256.05	235.43	222.22	224.27	248.49	235.25	209.00	201.00
Official Rate	rf	245.06	245.68	246.00	247.56	259.96	276.40	275.59	252.03	222.89	240.70	214.31	238.95	245.68	225.66	212.72
Fund Position															*Millions of SDRs:*	
Quota	2f. s	7.50	8.00	8.50	9.00	10.00	13.00	13.00	13.00	13.00	13.00	13.00	13.00	13.00	16.00	16.00
SDRs	1b. s	—	—	—	—	—	.04	—	1.12	.38	2.41	2.27	1.91	1.70	1.46	1.55
Reserve Position in the Fund	1c. s	.65	.77	.90	1.02	1.28	—	—	—	—	—	—	—	—	1.24	1.84
Total Fund Cred.&Loans Outstg.	2tl	—	—	—	—	—	2.47	2.32	2.18	1.02	3.11	2.97	9.47	9.47	13.54	12.99
International Liquidity												*Millions of US Dollars Unless Otherwise Indicated:*				
Total Reserves minus Gold	1l. d	13.62	7.37	.98	1.02	1.28	2.31	11.22	10.07	1.47	15.27	3.06	23.27	18.78	11.79	11.27
SDRs	1b. d	—	—	—	—	—	.04	—	1.22	.46	2.95	2.66	2.22	2.07	1.90	2.04
Reserve Position in the Fund	1c. d	.65	.77	.90	1.02	1.28	—	—	—	—	—	—	—	—	1.62	2.42
Foreign Exchange	1d. d	12.97	6.60	.08	—	—	2.27	11.22	8.86	1.01	12.32	.40	21.06	16.72	8.27	6.80
Gold (Million Fine Troy Ounces)	1ad	....	....	....	....	....	....	....	....	....	....	....	—	.006	.009	.011
Gold (National Valuation)	1an d	....	....	....	....	....	....	....	....	....	....	....	—	.92	1.94	5.79
Monetary Authorities: Other Liab.	4.. d	.20	.04	2.35	.01	.01										7.14
Deposit Money Banks: Assets	7a. d	.65	.12	.20	.81	.22	2.82	2.86	3.24	6.74	2.69	5.73	8.84	6.32	14.83	16.05
Liabilities	7b. d	3.61	5.35	5.35	6.68	5.73	5.22	4.45	6.19	6.94	9.43	10.52	7.95	10.11	11.00	7.65
Monetary Authorities															*Billions of Francs:*	
Foreign Assets	11	3.36	1.82	.24	−.55	−1.34	.64	2.87	2.58	.34	3.39	.69	5.78	4.63	2.87	3.44
Claims on Central Government	12a	.33	.48	.90	.35	.62	1.54	1.52	1.91	2.61	3.22	3.30	4.79	5.81	6.79	9.72
Claims on Deposit Money Banks	12e	2.49	2.88	4.54	4.83	5.75	3.45	3.16	3.46	4.07	5.10	11.16	7.27	8.55	14.80	23.95
Claims on Other Banking Insts.	12f	....	....	....	....	....	....	....	....	....	....	....	....	....	....	....
Reserve Money	14	4.98	4.91	4.28	4.65	5.09	5.61	6.32	7.06	6.97	9.21	11.81	14.04	15.38	17.64	23.97
of which: Currency Outside DMBs	14a	4.94	4.64	4.15	4.54	4.91	5.31	6.20	6.90	6.49	8.53	10.88	13.00	14.37	16.49	22.54
Foreign Liabilities	16c	.05	.01	.58	.83	1.71	.65	.64	.57	.25	.63	.57	2.55	2.51	3.47	4.87
Central Government Deposits	16d	1.13	.44	.53	.44	.50	.59	.74	.33	.31	.17	.61	.67	.55	1.08	.84
Capital Accounts	17a	....	....	....	....	....	....	....	....	....	....	....	....	....	....	....
Other Items (Net)	17r	.07	−.17	.87	−.47	−.56	−.57	.49	.55	−.25	2.33	2.73	3.13	3.07	5.74	12.30
Deposit Money Banks															*Billions of Francs:*	
Reserves	20	.05	.07	.25	.11	.18	.29	.12	.16	.48	.68	.92	1.04	1.01	1.15	1.43
Foreign Assets	21	.16	.03	.05	.20	.06	.78	.73	.83	1.55	.60	1.28	2.20	1.49	3.10	3.23
Claims on Central Government	22a	.15	.14	.16	.14	.13	.18	.16	.16	.15	.16	.14	.14	.14	.12	.17
Claims on Nonfin.Pub.Enterprises	22c	....	....	....	....	....	....	....	....	....	....	....	....	....	....	....
Claims on Private Sector	22d	5.65	6.65	8.99	10.07	11.50	9.97	8.94	9.09	10.89	14.59	22.25	19.28	23.45	31.09	38.17
Claims on Other Banking Insts.	22f	....	....	....	....	....	....	....	....	....	....	....	....	....	....	....
Claims on Nonbank Financial Insts.	22g	....	....	....	....	....	....	....	....	....	....	....	....	....	....	....
Demand Deposits	24	1.52	1.59	2.20	2.52	2.63	3.17	2.94	2.57	3.16	5.42	4.44	6.33	7.92	10.87	8.83
Time and Savings Deposits	25	.22	.18	.19	.12	.37	.59	.51	.49	.86	.99	1.17	1.34	1.20	1.85	1.66
Foreign Liabilities	26c	.89	.40	.26	.47	.47	.48	.20	.65	.77	1.23	1.49	1.64	2.15	1.89	1.16
Long-Term Foreign Liabilities	26cl	—	.92	1.06	1.19	1.12	.97	.94	.94	.82	.87	.87	.34	.23	.41	.38
Central Government Deposits	26d	.17	.13	.16	.15	.22	.25	.23	.09	.10	.11	.69	1.17	1.06	.73	.69
Credit from Monetary Authorities	26g	2.49	2.88	4.54	4.83	5.75	4.19	3.73	4.16	5.29	5.10	12.37	8.58	10.19	16.79	23.95
Capital Accounts	27a	.90	.97	.97	1.15	1.31	1.61	1.81	1.90	2.83	4.16	5.00	4.78	5.09	5.04	5.04
Other Items (Net)	27r	−.18	−.18	.07	.09	—	−.04	−.40	−.57	−.77	−1.85	−1.44	−1.52	−1.74	−2.12	1.29
Post Office: Checking Deposits	24.. i	.13	.14	.16	.24	.14	.12	.13	.16	.15	.19	.19	.17	.22	.20	.20
Postal Debt	26c. i	....	....	....	.09	.26	.30	.39	1.08	1.78	2.09	2.76	3.73	3.28	2.82	2.81
Monetary Survey															*Billions of Francs:*	
Foreign Assets (Net)	31n	2.58	1.44	−.55	−1.74	−3.72	—	2.37	1.11	−.91	.04	−2.84	.06	−1.83	−2.21	−2.18
Domestic Credit	32	4.96	6.84	9.52	10.29	11.93	11.26	10.19	11.98	15.18	19.95	27.34	26.25	31.31	39.22	49.55
Claims on Central Govt. (Net)	32an	−1.54	−.73	−.23	−.51	−.54	.29	.78	2.56	3.89	5.11	4.93	6.90	7.71	8.01	11.37
Claims on Nonfin.Pub.Enterprises	32c	....	....	....	....	....	....	....	....	....	....	....	....	....	....	....
Claims on Private Sector	32d	6.50	7.57	9.75	10.80	12.47	10.97	9.41	9.42	11.29	14.84	22.41	19.35	23.60	31.20	38.17
Claims on Other Banking Insts.	32f	....	....	....	....	....	....	....	....	....	....	....	....	....	....	....
Claims on Nonbk.Financial Insts.	32g	....	....	....	....	....	....	....	....	....	....	....	....	....	....	....
Money	34	6.59	6.37	6.51	7.30	7.68	8.60	9.27	9.64	9.80	14.13	15.51	19.49	22.51	27.57	31.57
Quasi-Money	35	.22	.18	.19	.12	.37	.59	.51	.49	.86	.99	1.17	1.34	1.20	1.85	1.66
Other Items (Net)	37r	.72	1.73	2.27	1.97	1.88	2.70	2.77	3.02	4.35	4.88	7.81	5.48	5.77	7.59	14.13
Money plus Quasi-Money	35l	6.81	6.55	6.70	7.41	8.04	9.20	9.78	10.13	10.66	15.12	16.69	20.83	23.71	29.42	33.24
Interest Rates															*Percent Per Annum*	
Discount Rate *(End of Period)*	60	....	....	....	4.50	4.50	4.50	4.50	4.50	4.50	5.50	5.50	6.50	6.50	6.50	8.50
Deposit Rate	60l	....	....	....	....	....	....	....	....	....	....	....	....	....	4.75	4.50
Lending Rate	60p	....	....	....	....	....	....	....	....	....	....	....	....	....	10.50	8.50
Prices															*Index Numbers (1990=100):*	
Consumer Prices	64	....	....	....	....	....	....	....	....	....	....	....	....	....	....	....

Chad

	1980	1981	1982	1983	1984	1985	1986	1987	1988	1989	1990	1991	1992	1993	1994		
	End of Period															**Exchange Rates**	
	287.99	334.52	370.92	436.97	470.11	415.26	394.78	378.78	407.68	380.32	364.84	370.48	378.57	404.89	I780.44	Official Rate	aa
	End of Period (ae) Period Average (rf)																
	225.80	287.40	336.25	417.37	479.60	378.05	322.75	267.00	302.95	289.40	256.45	259.00	275.33	294.78	I534.60	Official Rate	ae
	211.28	271.73	328.61	381.06	436.96	449.26	346.30	300.54	297.85	319.01	272.26	282.11	264.69	283.16	I555.20	Official Rate	rf
	End of Period															**Fund Position**	
	24.00	24.00	24.00	30.60	30.60	30.60	30.60	30.60	30.60	30.60	30.60	30.60	41.30	41.30	41.30	Quota	2f. s
	—	.02	.26	1.47	.37	3.52	1.69	6.35	5.72	1.34	.10	.11	.02	.01	—	SDRs	1b. s
	3.84	3.84	5.06	3.46	.26	.26	.26	.26	.26	.26	.26	.27	.27	.28	.28	Reserve Position in the Fund	1c. s
	10.81	12.49	12.49	12.26	8.52	10.90	8.93	13.97	12.24	17.92	21.42	21.42	21.42	20.20	29.30	Total Fund Cred.&Loans Outstg.	2tl
	End of Period															**International Liquidity**	
	5.05	7.31	12.41	28.00	44.16	33.46	15.91	52.11	63.08	111.73	127.78	119.79	80.48	38.94	76.01	Total Reserves minus Gold	1l. d
	—	.02	.29	1.54	.36	3.87	2.07	9.01	7.70	1.76	.14	.16	.03	.01	—	SDRs	1b. d
	4.90	4.47	5.58	3.62	.25	.29	.32	.37	.35	.34	.37	.39	.37	.38	.41	Reserve Position in the Fund	1c. d
	.16	2.82	6.54	22.84	43.54	29.31	13.52	42.73	55.04	109.63	127.27	119.25	80.08	38.54	75.60	Foreign Exchange	1d. d
	.011	.011	.011	.011	.011	.011	.011	.011	.011	.011	.011	.011	.011	.011	....	Gold (Million Fine Troy Ounces)	1ad
	6.56	4.45	5.00	4.21	3.44	3.60	4.36	5.37	4.52	3.52	3.98	3.94	3.70	4.42	....	Gold (National Valuation)	1and
	6.30	5.64	5.27	1.61	2.07	4.05	3.60	4.76	9.97	10.85	11.64	12.95	6.10	....	.75	Monetary Authorities: Other Liab.	4..d
	14.29	10.85	9.25	7.27	17.42	26.99	16.86	18.58	15.63	18.66	57.22	31.08	31.02	8.55	11.09	Deposit Money Banks: Assets	7a.d
	6.81	6.48	3.54	2.85	3.50	3.20	4.17	13.61	13.12	22.32	22.99	25.12	28.40	26.43	22.36	Liabilities	7b. d
	End of Period															**Monetary Authorities**	
	2.63	3.38	5.85	13.46	22.83	14.02	6.54	15.36	I20.50	33.56	33.87	I32.05	23.18	12.75	42.93	Foreign Assets	11
	9.58	10.63	9.95	9.72	10.35	8.69	9.92	11.55	I10.93	11.60	15.39	I14.62	31.52	33.79	48.48	Claims on Central Government	12a
	23.23	17.97	17.81	17.81	22.36	36.68	42.93	38.64	I28.12	20.46	15.12	I16.45	9.83	5.88	.50	Claims on Deposit Money Banks	12e
	....	....	....	....	....	....	....	....	4.62	4.56	4.44	4.32	—	—	—	Claims on Other Banking Insts.	12f
	20.87	22.83	24.64	30.18	46.36	47.79	47.35	52.20	I46.75	52.68	49.07	I50.47	47.94	38.25	47.24	Reserve Money	14
	17.45	22.14	23.61	29.20	44.93	47.35	46.67	46.70	I40.27	43.06	46.81	I49.45	46.95	35.84	39.69	of which: Currency Outside DMBs	14a
	4.54	5.80	6.41	6.03	5.00	6.06	4.69	6.56	I8.01	9.96	10.80	11.29	9.79	8.12	23.27	Foreign Liabilities	16c
	.66	.39	.42	1.08	2.97	3.65	2.21	4.15	I5.10	1.67	2.42	I.28	.44	.56	3.61	Central Government Deposits	16d
												1.28	1.02	1.25	1.04	Capital Accounts	17a
	13.91	8.77	8.55	9.73	6.21	7.95	9.84	9.20	12.32	15.84	17.33	15.39	15.13	12.36	40.02	Other Items (Net)	17r
	End of Period															**Deposit Money Banks**	
	3.42	.69	1.03	.99	1.43	.44	.67	5.49	I6.19	9.57	2.18	.93	.86	1.98	6.17	Reserves	20
	3.23	3.12	3.11	3.03	8.35	10.20	5.44	4.96	I4.78	5.40	14.68	I8.05	8.54	2.52	5.93	Foreign Assets	21
	.17	.17	.18	.18	.18	.18	.18	.63	I3.97	4.40	1.14	I4.45	5.71	6.37	7.98	Claims on Central Government	22a
	....	....	....	....	....	....	....	....	34.08	24.05	16.06	23.38	12.95	6.71	7.13	Claims on Nonfin.Pub.Enterprises	22c
	37.48	31.26	29.99	32.46	45.93	64.95	75.00	74.17	I31.31	29.56	29.03	I31.54	30.29	20.86	23.75	Claims on Private Sector	22d
	....	....	....	....	....	....	....	....						—	—	Claims on Other Banking Insts.	22f
	....	....	....	....	....	....	....	....						—	—	Claims on Nonbank Financial Insts.	22g
	8.83	9.34	9.35	11.36	20.00	20.79	22.34	23.68	I21.25	23.35	19.45	19.32	15.79	9.19	18.73	Demand Deposits	24
	1.66	1.48	1.49	1.64	2.63	3.55	3.58	4.79	I3.91	4.31	3.73	I4.12	3.62	2.20	2.86	Time and Savings Deposits	25
	1.16	1.49	.81	.81	1.30	.83	.97	1.75	I2.29	2.04	1.49	I2.31	3.14	7.58	11.22	Foreign Liabilities	26c
	.38	.38	.38	.38	.38	.38	.38	1.89	I4.40	4.42	4.40	I4.20	4.67	.21	.73	Long-Term Foreign Liabilities	26cl
	.69	.89	.89	.90	2.35	6.52	4.16	7.35	I11.11	10.78	14.77	I13.06	8.14	6.53	4.91	Central Government Deposits	26d
	23.23	18.01	17.81	17.81	22.36	36.68	42.93	38.64	I28.12	20.46	15.12	I16.45	9.83	5.88	.50	Credit from Monetary Authorities	26g
	5.04	5.16	5.16	5.16	5.52	7.58	8.74	8.59	I7.04	7.63	8.58	I9.45	27.43	10.64	11.95	Capital Accounts	27a
	3.30	-1.51	-1.58	-1.40	1.35	-.56	-1.80	-1.43	2.23	—	-4.47	-.54	-14.28	-3.79	.06	Other Items (Net)	27r
	.20	.20	.20	.20	.20	.20	.13	.22	....	....	....	....	....	....	....	Post Office: Checking Deposits	24.. i
	2.81	2.81	2.81	2.81	2.80	2.80	2.80	2.80	....	....	....	....	....	....	....	Postal Debt	26c. i
	End of Period															**Monetary Survey**	
	-2.65	-3.60	-1.07	6.84	22.08	14.54	3.52	9.21	I10.58	22.46	31.85	22.30	14.11	-.64	13.64	Foreign Assets (Net)	31n
	48.88	43.79	41.82	43.39	54.14	66.66	81.67	77.88	I68.72	61.24	47.98	64.97	71.91	61.15	79.22	Domestic Credit	32
	11.41	12.53	11.83	10.94	8.21	1.71	6.67	3.70	I-1.30	3.56	-.67	5.74	28.64	33.07	47.94	Claims on Central Govt. (Net)	32an
	....	....	....	....	....	....	....	....	34.08	24.05	16.06	23.38	12.95	6.71	7.13	Claims on Nonfin.Pub.Enterprises	32c
	37.48	31.26	29.99	32.46	45.93	64.95	75.00	74.17	I31.31	29.06	28.15	31.54	30.29	20.86	23.75	Claims on Private Sector	32d
	....	....	....	....	....	....	....	....	4.62	4.56	4.44	4.32	—	—	—	Claims on Other Banking Insts.	32f
	....	....	....	....	....	....	....	....				.01	.03	.51	.40	Claims on Nonbk.Financial Insts.	32g
	26.48	31.68	33.16	40.75	65.13	68.34	69.14	70.60	I61.57	66.46	66.34	68.86	62.86	45.47	59.79	Money	34
	1.66	1.48	1.49	1.64	2.63	3.55	3.58	4.79	I3.91	4.31	2.75	4.12	3.62	2.20	2.86	Quasi-Money	35
	18.09	7.03	6.10	7.84	8.46	9.29	12.48	11.70	13.82	12.93	10.75	14.29	19.55	12.85	30.20	Other Items (Net)	37r
	28.14	33.16	34.65	42.39	67.76	71.90	72.71	75.38	I65.48	70.77	69.09	72.98	66.48	47.67	62.66	Money plus Quasi-Money	35l
	Percent Per Annum															**Interest Rates**	
	8.50	8.50	8.50	9.00	9.00	9.00	8.00	8.00	9.50	10.00	11.00	10.75	12.00	11.50	....	Discount Rate (End of Period)	60
	5.50	5.50	5.50	5.50	5.50	5.50	5.50	5.33	4.31	4.25	I7.50	7.50	7.50	7.75	8.08	Deposit Rate	60l
	11.00	11.00	11.00	11.50	11.50	11.50	11.00	10.50	10.79	11.50	I18.50	18.15	17.77	17.46	17.42	Lending Rate	60p
	Period Averages															**Prices**	
	....	....	....	87.5	105.3	110.7	I96.2	90.5	104.5	99.4	100.0	104.1	99.8	....	....	Consumer Prices	64

Chad

628

		1965	1966	1967	1968	1969	1970	1971	1972	1973	1974	1975	1976	1977	1978	1979
International Transactions																*Millions of Francs*
Exports	70	6,722	5,848	7,534	7,580	8,026	8,206	7,787	9,028	8,483	9,056	10,103	14,861	26,177	22,329	18,776
Imports, cif	71	7,705	7,962	14,494	13,361	13,900	17,216	17,219	15,675	18,213	20,859	28,325	27,593	46,465	49,034	18,132
Imports, fob	71.v	6,185	6,391	11,634	10,689	10,451	12,944	12,947	11,786	13,694	15,683	21,297	20,747	⌶34,936	36,868	13,633
Volume of Exports																*1990=100*
Cotton	72f	50	43	54	56	63	52	46	54	48	50	72	79			
Balance of Payments															*Millions of US Dollars:*	
Goods: Exports f.o.b.	78aa d	...	...	...	...	...	...	...	...	...	...	...	...	106.5	99.0	88.3
Goods: Imports f.o.b.	78ab d	...	...	...	...	...	...	...	...	...	...	...	...	−142.2	−163.4	−64.1
Trade Balance	78ac d	...	...	...	...	...	...	...	...	...	...	...	...	−35.7	−64.4	24.2
Services: Credit	78ad d	...	...	...	...	...	...	...	...	...	...	...	...	24.2	20.6	4.6
Services: Debit	78ae d	...	...	...	...	...	...	...	...	...	...	...	...	−103.4	−104.1	−54.4
Balance on Goods and Services	78af d	...	...	...	...	...	...	...	...	...	...	...	...	−114.9	−148.0	−25.6
Income: Credit	78ag d	...	...	...	...	...	...	...	...	...	...	...	...	1.6	—	—
Income: Debit	78ah d	...	...	...	...	...	...	...	...	...	...	...	...	−3.9	−3.7	−8.6
Balance on Goods, Serv., & Inc.	78ai d	...	...	...	...	...	...	...	...	...	...	...	...	−117.2	−151.6	−34.2
Current Transfers, n.i.e.: Credit	78aj d	...	...	...	...	...	...	...	...	...	...	...	...	106.2	118.8	35.9
Current Transfers: Debit	78ak d	...	...	...	...	...	...	...	...	...	...	...	...	−17.6	−13.6	−10.0
Current Account, n.i.e.	78al d	...	...	...	...	...	...	...	...	...	...	...	...	−28.5	−46.4	−8.3
Capital Account, n.i.e.: Credit	78ba d	...	...	...	...	...	...	...	...	...	...	...	...	—	—	—
Capital Account: Debit	78bb d	...	...	...	...	...	...	...	...	...	...	...	...	—	—	—
Capital Account, n.i.e.	78bc d	...	...	...	...	...	...	...	...	...	...	...	...	—	—	—
Direct Investment Abroad	78bd d	...	...	...	...	...	...	...	...	...	...	...	...	—	1.0	−1.3
Dir. Invest. in Rep. Econ., n.i.e.	78be d	...	...	...	...	...	...	...	...	...	...	...	...	21.2	34.1	—
Portfolio Investment Assets	78bf d	...	...	...	...	...	...	...	...	...	...	...	...	—	—	—
Portfolio Investment Liab., n.i.e.	78bg d	...	...	...	...	...	...	...	...	...	...	...	...	—	—	—
Other Investment Assets	78bh d	...	...	...	...	...	...	...	...	...	...	...	...	−3.4	−2.1	−.3
Other Investment Liab., n.i.e.	78bi d	...	...	...	...	...	...	...	...	...	...	...	...	13.7	−7.1	−17.6
Financial Account, n.i.e.	78bj d	...	...	...	...	...	...	...	...	...	...	...	...	31.5	26.0	−19.1
Net Errors and Omissions	78ca d	...	...	...	...	...	...	...	...	...	...	...	...	−7.0	−5.4	−2.4
Overall Balance	78cb d	...	...	...	...	...	...	...	...	...	...	...	...	−4.0	−25.8	−29.9
Reserves and Related Items	79da d	...	...	...	...	...	...	...	...	...	...	...	...	4.0	25.8	29.9
Reserve Assets	79db d	...	...	...	...	...	...	...	...	...	...	...	...	4.7	7.6	3.0
Use of Fund Credit and Loans	79dc d	...	...	...	...	...	...	...	...	...	...	...	...	—	5.0	−.7
Liabs.Constit.For.Auth.Reserves	79dd d	...	...	...	...	...	...	...	...	...	...	...	...	−.6	.1	.1
Exceptional Financing	79de d	...	...	...	...	...	...	...	...	...	...	...	...	—	13.0	27.5
Government Finance																*Millions of Francs:*
Deficit (−) or Surplus	80	...	...	...	...	...	...	...	−2,783	−3,910	−2,543	−2,130	−2,848	...	...	...
Revenue	81	...	...	...	...	...	...	...	11,295	11,478	13,836	14,290	15,122	...	...	...
Grants Received	81z	...	...	...	...	...	...	...	1,557	1,972	2,871	3,901	5,170	...	...	...
Expenditure	82	...	...	...	...	...	...	...	15,637	17,373	19,245	20,341	23,169	...	...	...
Lending Minus Repayments	83	...	...	...	...	...	...	...	−2	−13	5	−20	−29	...	...	...
Financing																
Domestic	84a	...	...	...	...	...	...	...	2,128	2,793	1,733	584	1,399	...	...	...
Foreign	85a	...	...	...	...	...	...	...	655	1,117	810	1,546	1,449	...	...	...
Debt: Domestic	88a	...	...	...	...	...	...	...	...	...	...	...	...	...	...	...
Foreign	89a	...	...	...	...	...	...	...	...	...	...	...	...	...	...	...
National Accounts																*Billions of Francs*
Gross Domestic Product	99b	...	...	...	59	...	91	98	94	102	120	149	162	161	209	...
Gross Dom. Prod. 1985 Prices	99b.p	...	...	...	...	...	165	168	157	149	169	199	196	181	...	...
GDP Deflator (1985=100)	99bi p	...	...	...	...	...	55	58	60	69	71	75	83	89	...	...
																Millions:
Population	99z	3.31	3.37	3.43	3.50	3.57	3.64	3.72	3.79	3.86	3.95	4.03	4.12	4.21	4.31	4.38

Monetary Authorities: ⌶ Beginning in March 1988, the sectorization and classification of accounts have been revised. ⌶ Beginning in September 1991, *Claims on Central Government* include government assumption of certain nonperforming bank loans. ⌶ Beginning in December 1992, the coverage of the banking system has been revised. Claims and deposits of nonactive banks or banks in the process of liquidation have been excluded from the monetary accounts.
Deposit Money Banks: ⌶ Beginning in September 1991, the counterpart of government assumption of certain nonperforming bank loans was reclassified from *Credit from Monetary Authorities* to *Capital Accounts*. ⌶ See note to section 10.
Monetary Survey: ⌶ See notes to sections 10 and 20.

Interest Rates: *Deposit Rate:* ⌶ Beginning in October 1990, minimum rate offered by deposit money banks on savings accounts.
Lending Rate: ⌶ Beginning in October 1990, maximum rate charged by deposit money banks on all loans, excluding charges and fees.
Government Finance: ⌶ Prior to 1986, data cover budgetary central government only. Beginning in 1986, data cover budgetary central government and the Autonomous Amortization Fund.

Chad

	1980	1981	1982	1983	1984	1985	1986	1987	1988	1989	1990	1991	1992	1993	1994		
Millions of Francs																**International Transactions**	
	14,999	22,665	18,968	39,824	57,384	27,781	34,145	32,892	42,900	49,561	51,202	54,710	48,250	37,330	....	Exports	70
	15,533	29,349	35,701	59,707	79,272	74,708	73,437	67,894	68,000	76,657	77,742	83,670	64,320	56,910	....	Imports, cif	71
	11,679	22,067	26,843	44,892	59,603	55,752	54,398	50,292	50,370	56,783	57,587	61,978	47,644	42,156	....	Imports, fob	71.v
1990=100																Volume of Exports	
	....	....	33	50	67	28	48	43	56	64	100	....	....	....	....	Cotton	72f
Minus Sign Indicates Debit																**Balance of Payments**	
	71.0	83.4	57.7	78.2	109.7	61.8	98.6	109.4	145.9	155.4	230.3	193.5	182.3	135.8	....	Goods: Exports f.o.b.	78aa d
	-55.3	-81.2	-81.7	-99.1	-128.3	-166.3	-212.1	-225.9	-228.4	-240.3	-259.5	-249.9	-243.0	-201.3	....	Goods: Imports f.o.b.	78ab d
	15.7	2.2	-24.0	-20.9	-18.7	-104.5	-113.5	-116.5	-82.5	-84.9	-29.2	-56.3	-60.7	-65.5	....	Trade Balance	78ac d
	.4	4.1	2.4	24.2	36.8	32.6	44.5	70.4	78.7	42.3	40.9	30.9	26.7	28.8	....	Services: Credit	78ad d
	-24.2	-25.3	-22.1	-77.6	-90.1	-153.9	-165.7	-198.0	-217.9	-210.0	-228.2	-208.0	-224.1	-191.9	....	Services: Debit	78ae d
	-8.1	-19.0	-43.7	-74.3	-71.9	-225.7	-234.7	-244.0	-221.7	-252.6	-216.5	-233.4	-258.1	-228.6	....	Balance on Goods and Services	78af d
	—	—	1.9	4.4	1.3	5.0	3.5	2.9	2.1	1.3	3.0	8.9	17.6	8.8	....	Income: Credit	78ag d
	-3.7	-1.1	-1.0	-3.3	-6.3	-7.3	-12.4	-13.1	-15.5	-10.8	-23.8	-11.2	-14.9	-22.7	....	Income: Debit	78ah d
	-11.8	-20.1	-42.7	-73.3	-76.8	-228.0	-243.5	-254.2	-235.0	-262.0	-237.2	-235.7	-255.5	-242.5	....	Balance on Goods, Serv., & Inc.	78ai d
	24.5	41.1	61.9	118.1	94.0	153.5	204.7	257.0	301.4	241.4	239.3	215.5	222.3	198.7	....	Current Transfers, n.i.e.: Credit	78aj d
	-4.1	-.6	-.7	-6.9	-8.1	-12.8	-20.6	-28.3	-40.8	-35.2	-47.7	-45.3	-52.5	-39.9	....	Current Transfers: Debit	78ak d
	8.6	20.4	18.5	38.0	9.0	-87.2	-59.4	-25.5	25.5	-55.9	-45.6	-65.6	-85.7	-83.7	....	Current Account, n.i.e.	78al d
	—	—	—	—	—	—	—	—	—	—	—	—	—	—	....	Capital Account, n.i.e.: Credit	78ba d
	—	—	—	—	—	—	—	—	—	—	—	—	—	—	....	Capital Account: Debit	78bb d
	—	—	—	—	—	—	—	—	—	—	—	—	—	—	....	Capital Account, n.i.e.	78bc d
	-.4	-.1	-.1	-.1	—	-.3	-.4	-8.0	-13.8	-12.5	—	-10.5	-13.8	—	....	Direct Investment Abroad	78bd d
	—	—	—	—	9.2	53.7	28.2	8.2	1.3	18.7	—	4.2	2.0	—	....	Dir. Invest. in Rep. Econ., n.i.e.	78be d
	—	—	—	—	—	—	—	—	—	—	—	—	—	—	....	Portfolio Investment Assets	78bf d
	—	—	—	—	—	—	—	—	—	—	—	—	—	—	....	Portfolio Investment Liab., n.i.e.	78bg d
	—	—	—	—	-12.0	-4.1	13.1	12.1	10.3	3.5	—	24.2	3.9	—	....	Other Investment Assets	78bh d
	-10.9	-3.5	-6.0	-21.8	-3.4	20.3	-8.6	-3.6	26.4	64.7	56.1	42.0	47.9	67.3	....	Other Investment Liab., n.i.e.	78bi d
	-11.3	-3.6	-6.2	-21.9	-6.3	69.6	32.2	8.6	24.2	74.4	56.1	59.9	40.0	67.3	....	Financial Account, n.i.e.	78bj d
	-21.0	-1.9	-7.8	-7.5	13.6	-5.5	9.7	16.5	-83.7	11.1	-33.3	-13.0	9.2	-34.8	....	Net Errors and Omissions	78ca d
	-23.7	14.9	4.6	8.6	16.4	-23.2	-17.4	-.3	-34.0	29.6	-22.9	-18.6	-36.5	-51.2	....	Overall Balance	78cb d
	23.7	-14.9	-4.6	-8.6	-16.4	23.2	17.4	.3	34.0	-29.6	22.9	18.6	36.5	51.2	....	Reserves and Related Items	79da d
	8.0	-.9	-2.4	-17.7	-21.6	18.6	17.5	-25.0	14.8	-41.3	3.6	8.2	32.9	52.9	....	Reserve Assets	79db d
	-2.9	2.5	—	-.2	-3.7	2.5	-2.2	6.6	-2.3	6.9	4.6	—	—	-1.7	....	Use of Fund Credit and Loans	79dc d
	-.1	-.2	-.1	.3	.3	-.4	-1.5	.5	—	—	—	-.9	-6.3	—	....	Liabs.Constit.For.Auth.Reserves	79dd d
	18.7	-16.4	-2.0	9.0	8.6	2.4	3.6	18.3	21.5	4.8 e	14.7	11.4	9.9	—	....	Exceptional Financing	79de d
Year Ending December 31																**Government Finance**	
	....	....	....	....	....	....	I -9,029	-8,365	-11,893	-25,458	-22,451	-26,502 P	....	....	....	Deficit (-) or Surplus	80
	....	....	....	....	....	....	I 17,577	19,471	24,775	28,022	31,567	32,241 P	....	....	....	Revenue	81
	....	....	....	....	....	....	I 43,953	53,909	48,715	57,767	49,234	55,028 P	....	....	....	Grants Received	81z
	....	....	....	....	....	....	I 70,559	81,745	85,341	110,945	103,252	113,771 P	....	....	....	Expenditure	82
	....	....	....	....	....	....	I —	—	42	302	—	— P	....	....	....	Lending Minus Repayments	83
																Financing	
	....	....	....	....	....	....	I 1,845	660	-1,506	-4,629	-1,185	-1,725 P	....	....	....	Domestic	84a
	....	....	....	....	....	....	I 7,184	7,705	13,399	30,087	23,636	28,227 P	....	....	....	Foreign	85a
	....	....	....	....	....	....	....	....	....	....	29,975	26,321 P	....	....	....	Debt: Domestic	88a
	....	....	....	....	....	....	....	....	96,923	114,997	123,918	150,597 P	....	....	....	Foreign	89a
Billions of Francs																**National Accounts**	
	200	....	188	214	224	299	283	246	311	323	333	373	351	339	....	Gross Domestic Product	99b
	180	....	....	250	237	299	291	275	....	....	....	....	....	....	....	Gross Dom. Prod. 1985 Prices	99b. p
	111	....	....	86	95	100	97	90	....	....	....	....	....	....	....	GDP Deflator (1985=100)	99bi p
Midyear Estimates																	
	4.48	4.58	4.68	4.80	4.91	5.02	5.12	5.22	5.32	5.56	5.69	5.82	5.96	6.09	6.21	Population	99z

Chile

228		1965	1966	1967	1968	1969	1970	1971	1972	1973	1974	1975	1976	1977	1978	1979
Exchange Rates																*Pesos per Thousand SDRs through 1973*
Principal Rate.................aa=	wa	3.47	4.37	5.79	7.67	9.98	12.23	17.15	27.14	434.29	I 2.29	9.95	20.24	33.96	44.23	51.38
																Pesos per Thousand US Dollars through 1973
Principal Rate.................ae=	we	3.47	4.37	5.79	7.67	9.98	12.23	15.80	25.00	360.00	I 1.87	8.50	17.42	27.96	33.95	39.00
Principal Rate.................rf=	wf	3.12	3.96	5.02	6.80	8.97	12.02	12.40	19.48	110.80	I .83	4.91	13.05	21.53	31.66	37.25
Secondary Rate	xe	....	....	10.00	10.00	10.00	10.00	30.00	50.00	750.00	I 2.00	8.50	17.42	....	....	....
																Index Numbers (1990=100):
Principal Rate	ahx	....	....	....	....	....	....	....	....	665,400.8	44,680.0	7,614.6e	2,409.6e	1,441.9e	965.0e	819.7e
Nominal Effective Exchange Rate	nec	....	....	....	....	....	....	....	....	....	....	....	....	....	....	91.9
Real Effective Exchange Rate	rec	....	....	....	....	....	....	....	....	....	....	....	....	....	....	171.3
Fund Position																*Millions of SDRs:*
Quota	2f.s	100.0	100.0	100.0	125.0	125.0	158.0	158.0	158.0	158.0	158.0	158.0	158.0	158.0	217.0	217.0
SDRs	1b.s	—	—	—	—	—	21.8	38.3	2.0	.3	13.8	20.9	48.3	54.7	20.7	22.0
Reserve Position in the Fund	1c.s	—	—	—	—	—	—	—	—	—	—	—	—	—	38.3	37.1
Total Fund Cred.&Loans Outstg.	2tl	100.0	85.2	70.0	79.0	57.0	1.5	39.5	79.0	79.0	160.0	330.8	402.2	300.6	266.5	135.9
International Liquidity																*Millions of US Dollars Unless Otherwise Indicated:*
Total Reserves minus Gold	1l.d	93.6	126.9	81.3	162.0	296.0	341.8	170.1	96.8	121.6	41.1	55.9	405.1	426.5	1,090.1	1,938.3
SDRs	1b.d	—	—	—	—	—	21.8	41.6	2.2	.4	16.9	24.5	56.1	66.4	27.0	28.9
Reserve Position in the Fund	1c.d	—	—	—	—	—	—	—	—	—	—	—	—	—	49.9	48.9
Foreign Exchange	1d.d	93.6	126.9	81.3	162.0	296.0	320.0	128.5	94.6	121.2	24.2	31.4	349.0	360.1	1,013.2	1,860.5
Gold (Million Fine Troy Ounces)	1ad	1.251	1.291	1.286	1.323	1.354	1.334	1.346	1.355	1.376	1.438	1.297	1.336	1.364	1.390	1.524
Gold (National Valuation)	1and	43.9	45.4	45.1	46.4	47.5	46.7	47.1	51.5	58.1	60.7	54.8	56.4	57.6	58.7	439.5
Monetary Authorities: Other Liab.	4..d	188.2	143.6	102.7	89.4	80.7	61.2	85.5	274.2	490.8	490.8	603.3	157.2	687.4	595.3	1,260.2
Deposit Money Banks: Assets	7a.d	....	....	....	....	100.0	82.0	63.3	40.0	66.7	98.4	96.1	124.2	104.7	143.8	298.8
Liabilities	7b.d	....	....	....	....	100.0	82.0	126.6	240.0	336.1	368.4	323.6	296.5	410.9	831.0	1,579.4
Monetary Authorities																*Thousands of Pesos through 1971; Millions from 1972 to 1976;*
Foreign Assets	11	476.0	752.0	735.0	1,600.0	3,456.0	4,833.7	3,436.8	I 3.9	87.9	445.2	1,635.7	I 10476.0	I 18.9	48.6	109.7
Claims on Central Government	12a	2,148.0	3,022.0	4,059.0	5,144.0	6,683.0	9,575.0	29,917.0	I 88.1	759.8	3,737.1	18,708.2	I 39597.0	I 87.8	92.1	116.8
Claims on Nonfin.Pub.Enterprises	12c	....	....	....	....	....	....	....	....	....	....	....	1,616.0	I 1.9	2.1	.7
Claims on Private Sector	12d	113.0	244.0	352.0	403.0	506.0	745.0	416.0	I .5	6.8	41.5	120.1	I 7,874.0	I 2.1	34.0	52.5
Claims on Deposit Money Banks	12e	56.0	71.0	228.0	439.0	665.0	686.0	1,871.0	I 6.9	8.5	216.2	875.7	I 3,176.0	I 6.1	18.0	20.8
Claims on Other Banking Insts.	12f	....	....	....	....	....	....	....	....	....	....	....	253.0	I .6	.9	1.0
Reserve Money	14	1,272.0	2,060.0	2,466.0	3,369.0	4,899.0	7,740.0	21,442.0	I 60.0	310.9	1,003.5	3,568.2	I 15110.0	I 29.2	50.2	71.1
of which: Currency Outside DMBs	14a	230.0	1,227.0	1,318.0	1,697.0	2,360.0	4,380.0	8,973.0	I 28.2	95.7	349.3	1,358.2	I 4,480.0	I 9.3	16.4	24.9
Time, Savings,& Fgn.Currency Dep.	15	....	....	....	....	....	....	....	....	....	....	....	5,435.0	I 6.3	8.0	8.1
Foreign Liabilities	16c	906.0	960.0	1,166.0	1,291.9	1,373.8	767.2	2,028.7	I 8.7	211.2	1,283.8	8,424.0	I —	I —	—	—
Long-Term Foreign Liabilities	16cl	....	....	....	....	....	....	....	....	....	....	....	10,879.0	I 25.3	26.7	43.5
Central Government Deposits	16d	38.0	72.0	122.0	165.0	544.0	330.0	808.0	I 3.2	49.4	177.8	505.2	I 5,701.0	I 12.9	25.5	50.6
Capital Accounts	17a	50.0	78.0	168.0	297.0	531.0	1,775.0	3,432.0	I 6.4	70.9	475.1	2,384.4	I 8,821.0	I 22.3	51.4	109.4
Other Items (Net)	17r	527.0	919.0	1,452.0	2,463.1	3,962.2	5,227.5	7,930.1	I 21.1	220.6	1,499.8	6,457.9	I 17046.0	I 21.4	33.9	18.9
Deposit Money Banks																*Thousands of Pesos through 1971; Millions from 1972 to 1976;*
Reserves	20	572.0	1,100.0	1,203.0	1,803.0	2,692.0	3,598.0	12,209.0	I 33.5	241.1	764.5	3,281.0	I 9,742.0	I 20.5	31.1	41.8
Foreign Assets	21	79.0	207.0	297.0	405.0	597.0	826.0	713.0	I 1.3	24.4	183.7	817.3	I 2,159.0	I 3.4	5.7	12.4
Claims on Central Government	22a	301.0	325.0	505.0	670.0	1,113.0	1,822.0	3,439.0	I 10.9	85.2	343.0	1,359.4	I 1,090.0	I 2.2	3.4	8.5
Claims on Local Government	22b	....	....	....	....	....	....	....	....	....	....	....	1.0	I —	—	—
Claims on Nonfin.Pub.Enterprises	22c	....	....	....	....	....	....	....	....	....	....	....	3,179.0	I 3.2	3.4	3.3
Claims on Private Sector	22d	1,885.0	2,440.0	3,131.0	4,345.0	5,594.0	7,446.0	11,474.0	I 22.3	69.9	541.0	2,952.7	I 12844.0	I 55.5	107.1	211.4
Claims on Other Banking Insts.	22f	....	....	....	....	....	....	....	....	....	....	....	—	I —	.1	.7
Demand Deposits	24	1,137.0	1,367.0	1,922.0	2,774.0	3,698.0	5,647.0	12,300.0	I 25.9	132.9	487.4	1,620.5	I 5,242.0	I 8.9	17.6	30.2
Time, Savings,& Fgn.Currency Dep.	25	764.0	1,164.0	1,583.0	2,402.0	3,441.0	4,976.0	9,027.0	I 20.0	93.0	441.0	2,218.0	I 10737.0	I 27.3	60.4	107.5
Bonds	26ab	....	....	....	....	....	....	....	....	....	....	....	—	I —	1.3	8.3
Foreign Liabilities	26c	277.0	281.0	387.0	428.0	503.0	685.0	1,562.0	I 6.0	121.0	689.0	2,751.2	I 5,165.0	I 15.1	17.0	27.3
Long-Term Foreign Liabilities	26cl	....	....	....	....	....	....	....	....	....	....	....	—	I —	11.3	39.7
Central Government Deposits	26d	412.0	630.0	602.0	1,170.0	1,912.0	2,332.0	4,892.0	I 17.7	142.7	476.6	2,069.8	I 4,655.0	I 15.1	17.5	27.3
Credit from Monetary Authorities	26g	127.0	289.0	420.0	594.0	904.0	993.0	2,184.0	I 8.9	25.0	237.8	701.2	I 2,113.0	I 8.9	15.8	21.6
Liabilities to Other Financ. Insts.	26i	....	....	....	....	....	....	....	....	....	....	....	—	I —	—	.7
Capital Accounts	27a	533.0	663.0	900.0	1,072.0	1,466.0	2,012.0	2,372.0	I 4.0	45.0	617.0	3,642.9	I 10688.0	I 20.1	25.7	41.9
Other Items (Net)	27r	–413.0	–322.0	–678.0	–1,217.0	–1,928.0	–2,953.0	–4,502.0	I –14.5	–139.0	–1,116.6	–4,593.2	I –9585.0	I –10.6	–15.8	–26.5
Monetary Survey																*Thousands of Pesos through 1971; Millions from 1972 to 1976;*
Foreign Assets (Net)	31n	–628.0	–282.0	–521.0	285.1	2,176.2	4,207.5	559.2	I –9.5	–219.9	–1,343.9	–8,722.2	I –3409.0	I –18.1	–.7	11.7
Domestic Credit	32	3,997.0	5,329.0	7,323.0	9,227.0	11,440.0	16,926.0	39,546.0	I 100.9	729.6	4,008.2	20,565.4	I 56098.0	I 125.3	200.0	316.9
Claims on Central Govt. (Net)	32an	1,999.0	2,645.0	3,840.0	4,479.0	5,340.0	8,735.0	27,656.0	I 78.1	652.9	3,425.7	17,492.6	I 30331.0	I 62.0	52.5	47.3
Claims on Local Government	32b	....	....	....	....	....	....	....	....	....	....	....	1.0	I —	—	—
Claims on Nonfin.Pub.Enterpr.	32c	....	....	....	....	....	....	....	....	....	....	....	4,795.0	I 5.1	5.5	4.0
Claims on Private Sector	32d	1,998.0	2,684.0	3,483.0	4,748.0	6,100.0	8,191.0	11,890.0	I 22.8	76.7	582.5	3,072.8	I 20718.0	I 57.6	141.1	263.9
Claims on Other Banking Insts.	32f	....	....	....	....	....	....	....	....	....	....	....	253.0	I .6	1.0	1.7
Money	34	1,367.0	2,594.0	3,240.0	4,471.0	6,058.0	10,027.0	21,273.0	I 54.1	228.6	836.7	2,978.7	I 10603.0	I 19.8	35.0	56.6
Quasi-Money	35	764.0	1,164.0	1,583.0	2,402.0	3,441.0	4,976.0	9,027.0	I 20.0	93.0	441.0	2,218.0	I 16172.0	I 33.6	68.4	115.6
Bonds	36ab	....	....	....	....	....	....	....	....	....	....	....	—	I —	1.3	8.3
Liabilities to Other Financ. Insts.	36i	....	....	....	....	....	....	....	....	....	....	....	—	I —	—	.7
Capital Accounts	37a	....	....	....	....	....	....	....	....	....	....	....	19,509.0	I 42.4	77.0	151.3
Other Items (Net)	37r	1,238.0	1,289.0	1,979.0	2,639.1	4,117.2	6,130.5	9,805.2	I 17.3	188.1	1,386.6	6,646.5	I 6,405.0	I 11.4	17.6	–3.9
Money plus Quasi-Money	35l	2,131.0	3,758.0	4,823.0	6,873.0	9,499.0	15,003.0	30,300.0	I 74.1	321.6	1,277.7	5,196.7	I 26775.0	I 53.4	103.4	172.2
Other Banking Institutions																*Billions of Pesos:*
Reserves	40	....	....	....	....	....	....	....	....	....	....	....	....	....	....	.9
Foreign Assets	41	....	....	....	....	....	....	....	....	....	....	....	....	....	....	—
Claims on Central Government	42a	....	....	....	....	....	....	....	....	....	....	....	....	....	....	4.5
Claims on Local Government	42b	....	....	....	....	....	....	....	....	....	....	....	....	....	....	—
Claims on Nonfin.Pub.Enterprises	42c	....	....	....	....	....	....	....	....	....	....	....	....	....	....	.1
Claims on Private Sector	42d	....	....	....	....	....	....	....	....	....	....	....	....	....	....	15.9
Claims on Deposit Money Banks	42e	....	....	....	....	....	....	....	....	....	....	....	....	....	....	.9
Time, Savings,& Fgn.Currency Dep.	45	....	....	....	....	....	....	....	....	....	....	....	....	....	....	16.8
Bonds	46ab	....	....	....	....	....	....	....	....	....	....	....	....	....	....	—
Foreign Liabilities	46c	....	....	....	....	....	....	....	....	....	....	....	....	....	....	—
Long-Term Foreign Liabilities	46cl	....	....	....	....	....	....	....	....	....	....	....	....	....	....	.8
Central Government Deposits	46d	....	....	....	....	....	....	....	....	....	....	....	....	....	....	—
Credit from Monetary Authorities	46g	....	....	....	....	....	....	....	....	....	....	....	....	....	....	.1
Credit from Deposit Money Banks	46h	....	....	....	....	....	....	....	....	....	....	....	....	....	....	1.7
Capital Accounts	47a	....	....	....	....	....	....	....	....	....	....	....	....	....	....	3.1
Other Items (Net)	47r	....	....	....	....	....	....	....	....	....	....	....	....	....	....	—

Chile

228

1980	1981	1982	1983	1984	1985	1986	1987	1988	1989	1990	1991	1992	1993	1994		
															Exchange Rates	
and per SDR Thereafter: End of Period																
49.74	45.39	81.00	91.64	125.70	201.96	250.42	337.84	332.66	390.79	479.56	535.71	525.42	588.53	588.20	Principal Rate..................aa=	wa
and per US Dollar thereafter: End of Period (we and xe) Period Avg. (wf)																
39.00	39.00	73.43	87.53	128.24	183.86	204.73	238.14	247.20	297.37	337.09	374.51	382.12	428.47	402.92	Principal Rate..................ae=	we
39.00	39.00	50.91	78.84	98.66	161.08	193.02	219.54	245.05	267.16	305.06	349.37	362.59	404.35	420.08	Principal Rate..................rf=	wf
....	....	58.47	72.81	89.02	183.66	205.00	238.11	247.49	296.58	336.86	374.87	382.33	431.04	404.09	Secondary Rate	xe
Period Averages																
780.8e	780.8e	634.8e	387.4e	314.1	191.8	157.9	139.0	124.3	114.4	100.0	87.2	84.0	75.4	72.5	Principal Rate	ahx
94.9	112.1	108.4	82.6	83.7	64.5	53.0	48.3	52.9	72.7	100.0	114.7	139.5	173.8	225.5	Nominal Effective Exchange Rate	nec
199.1	234.9	212.3	172.9	169.9	136.9	115.7	107.4	100.4	102.8	100.0	103.2	109.0	109.9	112.1	Real Effective Exchange Rate	rec
End of Period															**Fund Position**	
325.5	325.5	325.5	440.5	440.5	440.5	440.5	440.5	440.5	440.5	440.5	440.5	621.7	621.7	621.7	Quota	2f.s
3.0	16.4	17.7	5.2	11.7	.3	.2	28.8	32.9	18.5	.7	.5	.5	.9	.5	SDRs	1b.s
64.3	64.3	70.5	—	—	—	—	—	—	—	—	—	—	—	—	Reserve Position in the Fund	1c.s
96.3	41.8	5.7	579.0	795.0	990.6	1,088.3	1,032.4	982.6	966.5	812.9	669.4	525.0	346.5	199.5	Total Fund Cred.&Loans Outstg.	2tl
End of Period															**International Liquidity**	
3,123.2	3,213.3	1,815.0	2,036.3	2,303.2	2,449.9	2,351.3	2,504.2	3,160.5	3,628.6	6,068.5	7,041.3	9,167.7	9,640.3	13,087.6	Total Reserves minus Gold	1l.d
3.8	19.1	19.5	5.4	11.5	.3	.2	40.8	44.3	24.4	1.0	.8	.6	1.3	.7	SDRs	1b.d
82.0	74.8	77.8	—	—	—	—	—	—	—	—	—	—	—	—	Reserve Position in the Fund	1c.d
3,037.5	3,119.4	1,717.7	2,030.9	2,291.7	2,449.6	2,351.1	2,463.4	3,116.2	3,604.2	6,067.5	7,040.5	9,167.0	9,639.0	13,086.9	Foreign Exchange	1d.d
1.704	1.702	1.712	....	....	....	1.795	1.811	1.824	1.752	1.858	1.863	1.867	1.865	1.864	Gold (Million Fine Troy Ounces)	1ad
963.4	660.4	655.9	566.7e	540.1	518.6	668.1	757.4	679.4	592.0	641.5	596.9	574.0	612.0	652.0	Gold (National Valuation)	1and
1,184.3	836.0	766.9	2,218.8	3,717.9	4,420.8	4,423.5	4,912.1	3,921.8	2,605.2	2,380.4	2,103.0	1,995.2	1,917.0	2,388.1	Monetary Authorities: Other Liab.	4..d
548.2	881.4	959.2	814.0	722.0	413.0	480.0	342.0	395.0	378.0	507.0	526.6	520.0	524.0	547.0	Deposit Money Banks: Assets	7a.d
3,535.3	6,238.2	7,282.2	6,311.0	6,733.0	6,572.0	6,221.0	5,071.0	4,197.0	3,331.0	2,972.0	2,354.2	3,505.0	3,793.0	4,258.0	Liabilities	7b.d
Billions of Pesos Beginning 1977: End of Period															**Monetary Authorities**	
165.6	147.1	185.5	231.3	364.1	534.7	630.0	783.3	971.9	1,209.2	2,313.6	2,923.2	4,115.5	4,749.6	....	Foreign Assets	11
108.6	58.0	53.5	163.2	425.8	1,129.9	1,519.4	1,879.5	2,177.3	2,197.4	2,795.4	3,143.0	3,432.4	3,814.8	....	Claims on Central Government	12a
1.3	.5	.9	.6	.8	.8	.9	—	.6	—	—	—	—	—	....	Claims on Nonfin.Pub.Enterprises	12c
54.6	59.7	176.4	228.6	278.6	357.5	412.8	465.7	511.7	86.6	106.9	127.1	146.7	167.5	....	Claims on Private Sector	12d
25.4	39.2	152.3	601.8	876.1	1,695.6	1,886.9	2,039.0	1,826.0	1,879.9	2,168.9	2,378.0	2,393.0	2,484.2	....	Claims on Deposit Money Banks	12e
3.0	2.5	12.9	26.3	47.9	53.8	43.1	45.7	42.3	53.6	56.7	58.1	56.1	51.1	....	Claims on Other Banking Insts.	12f
116.5	104.3	225.2	517.4	912.8	1,912.3	2,317.4	2,492.5	2,400.4	2,321.7	3,675.4	4,507.4	5,238.3	6,001.8	....	Reserve Money	14
35.6	44.5	43.0	51.9	64.2	79.5	108.5	135.7	181.6	221.8	285.5	368.4	480.5	582.1	....	*of which: Currency Outside DMBs*	14a
11.0	11.3	72.1	158.4	165.5	285.9	328.9	404.7	441.1	545.1	570.4	365.7	303.7	285.7	....	Time, Savings,& Fgn.Currency Dep.	15
—	—	15.2	79.3	161.1	254.2	267.5	392.5	330.1	358.7	407.1	362.3	305.3	222.0	....	Foreign Liabilities	16c
36.9	20.6	46.8	181.9	412.9	735.3	891.8	1,096.8	979.3	735.6	770.9	804.3	843.8	888.6	....	Long-Term Foreign Liabilities	16cl
43.5	33.0	22.9	22.6	29.2	87.7	118.4	188.4	219.7	245.1	473.2	806.3	1,200.6	1,371.0	....	Central Government Deposits	16d
132.4	139.4	195.5	229.5	172.8	223.4	263.4	327.0	378.3	453.8	613.2	730.0	837.3	898.2	....	Capital Accounts	17a
18.2	-1.4	3.9	62.8	138.9	273.5	305.8	311.4	780.9	766.8	931.3	1,053.5	1,414.6	1,600.0	....	Other Items (Net)	17r
Billions of Pesos Beginning 1977: End of Period															**Deposit Money Banks**	
55.5	40.0	24.4	39.4	43.0	96.0	102.2	127.5	160.3	153.1	178.1	337.0	528.6	575.8	....	Reserves	20
21.6	35.5	70.6	71.3	96.7	63.8	96.6	81.0	98.7	107.0	179.4	197.3	207.9	225.7	....	Foreign Assets	21
1.5	1.9	56.5	75.2	109.7	191.9	187.5	163.6	23.4	22.2	23.0	26.3	27.8	51.3	....	Claims on Central Government	22a
.1	—	—	.2	.1	.1	.2	.2	.4	.3	.4	—	.4	.4	....	Claims on Local Government	22b
5.7	7.8	13.9	15.7	24.9	52.3	74.2	98.1	50.9	81.2	301.6	247.1	174.7	165.8	....	Claims on Nonfin.Pub.Enterprises	22c
412.1	590.8	845.5	925.8	1,256.5	1,448.4	1,696.3	2,122.2	2,606.7	3,531.5	4,152.1	5,155.6	6,892.8	8,933.2	....	Claims on Private Sector	22d
9.0	21.1	1.3	.9	1.4	1.8	1.5	2.0	1.9	2.5	.9	2.5	.4	9.9	....	Claims on Other Banking Insts.	22f
49.7	37.4	49.2	60.3	66.1	68.7	106.3	93.3	203.7	219.7	231.9	415.4	456.7	603.4	....	Demand Deposits	24
180.6	265.3	319.9	317.1	424.3	626.6	785.3	1,159.8	1,453.6	2,003.8	2,607.7	3,582.9	4,596.7	5,729.9	....	Time, Savings,& Fgn.Currency Dep.	25
28.3	48.5	82.1	110.5	155.0	199.3	241.9	284.2	336.1	440.9	610.8	843.3	1,086.3	1,449.9	....	Bonds	26ab
52.2	76.0	147.4	124.4	85.2	92.0	164.1	218.9	309.7	452.6	608.6	564.8	1,173.1	1,316.6	....	Foreign Liabilities	26c
96.7	193.9	388.2	428.0	775.3	926.4	1,089.1	978.2	734.5	489.3	443.2	317.3	316.4	318.4	....	Long-Term Foreign Liabilities	26cl
72.5	59.5	49.0	52.8	59.5	86.0	105.0	134.4	192.5	156.4	255.9	301.6	357.7	425.4	....	Central Government Deposits	26d
26.3	34.6	48.1	463.5	663.1	1,150.9	1,183.2	1,167.3	912.1	901.0	841.4	836.7	692.0	538.2	....	Credit from Monetary Authorities	26g
1.9	4.9	10.8	3.5	16.0	40.6	86.1	158.9	218.8	230.1	322.0	345.3	270.6	287.2	....	Liabilities to Other Financ. Insts.	26i
66.8	78.3	99.2	93.7	93.4	699.9	859.0	998.4	823.7	1,080.7	1,385.4	1,161.1	1,278.7	1,619.8	....	Capital Accounts	27a
-69.6	-101.3	-181.6	-525.2	-805.5	-2,036.0	-2,461.4	-2,598.9	-2,242.2	-2,076.8	-2,471.3	-2,402.4	-2,395.7	-2,326.7	....	Other Items (Net)	27r
Billions of Pesos Beginning 1977: End of Period															**Monetary Survey**	
1.4	-107.9	-341.5	-510.9	-973.8	-1,409.4	-1,685.9	-1,822.1	-1,283.0	-720.0	263.2	1,071.9	1,684.7	2,229.8	....	Foreign Assets (Net)	31n
479.8	649.8	1,089.2	1,361.2	2,057.1	3,062.9	3,712.5	4,454.2	5,003.0	5,573.7	6,707.9	7,652.0	9,172.8	11,397.4	....	Domestic Credit	32
-5.9	-32.7	38.2	163.1	446.8	1,148.1	1,483.5	1,720.2	1,788.5	1,818.1	2,089.3	2,061.4	1,901.8	2,069.6	....	Claims on Central Govt. (Net)	32an
.1	—	—	.2	.1	.1	.2	.2	.4	.3	.4	—	.4	.4	....	Claims on Local Government	32b
7.0	8.3	14.8	16.3	25.7	53.1	75.1	98.1	51.5	81.2	301.7	247.1	174.7	165.8	....	Claims on Nonfin.Pub.Enterpr.	32c
466.7	650.5	1,021.9	1,154.4	1,535.2	1,805.9	2,109.1	2,587.9	3,118.4	3,618.1	4,258.9	5,282.8	7,039.5	9,100.7	....	Claims on Private Sector	32d
12.0	23.6	14.3	27.3	49.3	55.6	44.6	47.7	44.2	56.0	57.6	60.6	56.4	60.9	....	Claims on Other Banking Insts.	32f
87.0	82.5	92.4	113.0	130.4	148.4	214.9	229.2	385.5	441.6	517.6	784.2	937.5	1,186.0	....	Money	34
191.7	276.6	392.0	475.5	589.9	912.5	1,114.2	1,564.5	1,894.6	2,548.9	3,178.1	3,948.6	4,900.4	6,015.5	....	Quasi-Money	35
28.3	48.5	82.1	110.5	155.0	199.3	241.9	284.2	336.1	440.9	610.8	843.3	1,086.3	1,449.9	....	Bonds	36ab
1.9	4.9	10.8	3.5	16.0	40.6	86.1	158.9	218.8	230.1	322.0	345.3	270.6	287.2	....	Liabilities to Other Financ. Insts.	36i
199.2	217.6	294.8	323.2	266.2	923.2	1,122.4	1,325.4	1,202.0	1,534.4	1,998.6	1,891.1	2,116.0	2,518.0	....	Capital Accounts	37a
-26.8	-88.1	-124.3	-175.4	-74.2	-570.5	-752.8	-930.1	-317.0	-342.3	344.1	911.4	1,546.7	2,170.6	....	Other Items (Net)	37r
278.7	359.0	484.4	588.5	720.3	1,060.9	1,329.1	1,793.7	2,280.2	2,990.5	3,695.7	4,732.7	5,838.0	7,201.5	....	Money plus Quasi-Money	35l
End of Period															**Other Banking Institutions**	
4.9	1.7	1.4	4.7	8.0	8.0	4.4	4.4	5.0	5.2	8.4	19.3	22.2	12.9	....	Reserves	40
—	—	—	.1	.1	—	—	—	—	—	—	—	—	—	....	Foreign Assets	41
—	—	.1	.6	.5	1.5	2.3	2.3	.7	.4	.4	—	—	—	....	Claims on Central Government	42a
—	—	—	—	—	—	—	—	—	—	—	—	—	—	....	Claims on Local Government	42b
.1	.1	.4	.4	.1	.1	.5	.7	.2	.3	2.3	.1	—	4.7	....	Claims on Nonfin.Pub.Enterprises	42c
37.0	25.8	19.8	18.4	25.5	32.5	34.7	44.9	58.9	84.6	100.6	141.4	249.1	390.9	....	Claims on Private Sector	42d
2.3	1.6	2.8	1.9	2.7	4.1	1.9	3.8	4.6	6.1	6.4	14.6	16.6	29.7	....	Claims on Deposit Money Banks	42e
28.3	19.6	15.0	15.9	23.0	27.0	27.6	37.8	46.9	62.0	75.4	119.9	211.9	313.3	....	Time, Savings,& Fgn.Currency Dep.	45
.1	2.1	1.9	2.3	3.6	4.8	5.4	5.3	5.2	5.8	6.7	7.9	10.4	15.0	....	Bonds	46ab
—	—	—	—	—	.2	—	—	—	—	—	—	—	—	....	Foreign Liabilities	46c
.9	1.2	.8	.9	.8	.5	.2	—	—	—	—	—	—	—	....	Long-Term Foreign Liabilities	46cl
.1	—	.1	.5	.2	.3	.7	.9	1.9	.5	.3	.3	.8	.6	....	Central Government Deposits	46d
1.5	—	4.1	4.8	4.9	6.5	4.6	4.8	3.1	3.3	2.4	2.6	2.8	3.9	....	Credit from Monetary Authorities	46g
8.8	3.3	1.3	.2	1.0	3.1	3.2	2.8	3.1	9.3	4.1	6.4	17.0	35.2	....	Credit from Deposit Money Banks	46h
4.7	3.5	3.2	3.0	3.7	4.7	3.3	4.5	5.5	7.5	13.3	16.4	24.1	32.9	....	Capital Accounts	47a
—	-.2	-1.6	-1.4	-.4	-.8	-1.2	—	3.8	8.1	15.9	21.8	21.0	37.2	....	Other Items (Net)	47r

Chile
228

		1965	1966	1967	1968	1969	1970	1971	1972	1973	1974	1975	1976	1977	1978	1979
Nonbank Financial Institutions																*Billions of Pesos*
Claims on Monetary Authorities	40x.p	...	...	...	...	...	...	...	...	...	...	...	...	...	...	...
Foreign Assets	41..p	...	...	...	...	...	...	...	...	...	...	...	...	...	...	...
Claims on Central Government	42a.p	...	...	...	...	...	...	...	...	...	...	...	...	...	...	...
Claims on Private Sector	42d.p	...	...	...	...	...	...	...	...	...	...	...	...	...	...	...
Claims on Deposit Money Banks	42e.p	...	...	...	...	...	...	...	...	...	...	...	...	...	...	...
Reserve Funds and Capital	47a.p	...	...	...	...	...	...	...	...	...	...	...	...	...	...	...
Other Items (Net)	47r.p	...	...	...	...	...	...	...	...	...	...	...	...	...	...	...
Interest Rates															*Percent Per Annum*	
Deposit Rate	60l														94.92	63.53	45.19
Lending Rate	60p														163.15	86.13	62.11
Prices and Production															*Index Numbers (1990=100):*		
Industrial Share Prices	62	...	...	...	...	...	...	...	...	...	I—	I—	.2	.6	1.7	2.7
Prices: Home & Import Goods	63	—	—	—	I—	—	—	—	—	—	—	I—	1	3	5	7	11
Home Goods	63a	—	—	—	I—	—	—	—	—	—	—	I—	1	3	5	7	11
Consumer Prices	64	I—	—	—	—	—	—	I—	—	—	—	—	I1	3	6	9	12
Wages and Salaries	65	...	...	...	...	...	...	...	...	...	...	...	—	2	I4	7	10
Wages, Hourly (Apr.93=100)	65a	...	...	...	...	...	...	...	...	...	...	...	...	...	...	...	...
Manufacturing Production	66ey	63	68	67	I67	70	70	80	82	79	76	55	57	63	68	73
Mining Production	66zx	45	48	I46	I47	49	49	50	48	49	59	55	63	64	62	66
Copper Production	66c	37	42	41	I42	44	45	45	46	47	57	52	64	66	65	67
International Transactions															*Millions of US Dollars*		
Exports	70..d	637	817	847	858	1,075	1,249	997	855	1,231	2,481	1,552	2,083	2,190	2,478	3,894
Imports, cif	71..d	718	892	819	852	1,028	1,063	1,109	1,086	1,290	2,148	1,525	1,864	2,539	3,408	4,808
Imports, fob	71.vd	604	751	722	743	907	941	980	941	1,098	1,911	1,338	I1,643	2,259	3,002	4,218
															1990=100		
Import Prices	76.x	—	—	—	—	—	—	—	—	—	I.2	1.0	3.1	6.2	8.4	11.9
Balance of Payments															*Millions of US Dollars:*		
Goods: Exports f.o.b.	78aa d	...	...	...	...	...	...	...	...	...	...	1,590	2,116	2,186	2,460	3,835
Goods: Imports f.o.b.	78ab d	...	...	...	...	...	...	...	...	...	...	-1,520	-1,473	-2,151	-2,886	-4,190
Trade Balance	78ac d											70	643	35	-426	-355
Services: Credit	78ad d											248	297	417	481	785
Services: Debit	78ae d											-535	-515	-734	-751	-1,048
Balance on Goods and Services	78af d											-217	425	-282	-696	-618
Income: Credit	78ag d											4	12	18	43	126
Income: Debit	78ah d											-289	-337	-383	-532	-802
Balance on Goods, Serv., & Inc.	78ai d											-502	100	-647	-1,185	-1,294
Current Transfers, n.i.e.: Credit	78aj d											16	52	101	127	143
Current Transfers: Debit	78ak d											-4	-4	-5	-30	-38
Current Account, n.i.e.	78al d											-490	148	-551	-1,088	-1,189
Capital Account, n.i.e.: Credit	78ba d											—	—	—	—	—
Capital Account: Debit	78bb d											—	—	—	—	—
Capital Account, n.i.e.	78bc d											—	—	—	—	—
Direct Investment Abroad	78bd d											—	—	-5	-4	-11
Dir. Invest. in Rep. Econ., n.i.e.	78be d											50	-1	21	181	244
Portfolio Investment Assets	78bf d											—	—	—	—	—
Portfolio Investment Liab., n.i.e.	78bg d											-6	-6	-7	—	50
Other Investment Assets	78bh d											185	67	50	108	5
Other Investment Liab., n.i.e.	78bi d											-235	134	504	1,661	1,864
Financial Account, n.i.e.	78bj d											-6	194	563	1,946	2,152
Net Errors and Omissions	78ca d											-109	69	114	-128	-12
Overall Balance	78cb d											-605	411	126	730	952
Reserves and Related Items	79da d											605	-411	-126	-730	-952
Reserve Assets	79db d											80	-413	-51	-700	-887
Use of Fund Credit and Loans	79dc d											207	82	-118	-44	-170
Liabs.Constit.For.Auth.Reserves	79dd d											-61	53	38	14	9
Exceptional Financing	79de d											380	-133	5	—	96
Government Finance											*Thousands of Pesos through 1971; Millions from 1972 to 1976;*					
Deficit (-) or Surplus	80	-700.0	-500.0	-200.0	-400.0	300.0	-2,800.0	-10,000.0	I-30.0	-84.0	-495.0	45.0	1,756.0	I-3.2	-.5	37.2
Revenue	81	3,100.0	4,900.0	6,300.0	8,700.0	13,100.0	16,000.0	23,100.0	I71.0	326.0	2,548.0	11,450.0	39,192.0	I87.9	150.7	251.8
Grants Received	81z								I—	—	59.0	1,009.0	1,855.0	I3.6	6.7	11.7
Expenditure	82	3,800.0	5,400.0	6,500.0	9,100.0	12,800.0	18,800.0	33,100.0	I98.0	399.0	3,042.0	12,164.0	38,757.0	I92.1	155.0	221.6
Lending Minus Repayments	83	...	...	...	...	...	...	...	I3.0	11.0	60.0	250.0	534.0	I2.6	2.9	4.7
Financing																	
Net Borrowing	84	600.0	500.0	400.0	300.0	100.0	3,100.0	10,000.0	I32.0	146.0	684.0	970.0	1,547.0	I13.4	4.3	-10.7
Net Borrowing: Domestic	84a	...	...	...	-44,640	-62,610	-98,180	-152,000	I32.0	149.0	592.0	1,916.0	4,176.0	I16.8	6.6	-3.3
Foreign	85a	...	...	...	...	...	...	...	I—	-3.0	92.0	-946.0	-2,629.0	I-3.4	-2.3	-7.5
Use of Cash Balances	87	—	—	-100.0	—	-300.0	-300.0	—	I-2.0	-62.0	-189.0	-1,016.0	-3,303.0	I-10.2	-3.8	-26.5
Debt: Domestic	88a	...	...	...	...	...	...	...	...	...	...	...	...	...	...	...
Foreign	89a	...	...	...	...	...	...	...	...	...	...	...	...	...	...	...
Intragovernmental Debt	88s	...	...	...	...	...	...	...	...	...	...	...	...	...	...	...
National Accounts									*Thousands of Pesos through 1971; Millions from 1972 to 1976;*							
Exports of Goods & Services	90c	2,500	3,000	4,931	6,649	11,430	14,591	13,900	I23	138	1,880	9,040	32,320	I59	100	180
Government Consumption	91f	1,972	2,951	3,815	5,244	7,629	12,588	19,381	I38	151	1,448	5,560	17,990	I42	70	110
Gross Fixed Capital Formation	93e	2,711	3,738	4,860	6,972	9,807	14,771	18,500	I31	147	1,559	6,271	17,068	I38	72	115
Increase/Decrease(-) in Stocks	93i	42	557	632	742	560	1,405	-96	I-2	-56	386	-1,626	-621	I3	15	22
Private Consumption	96f	13,530	18,734	24,350	33,942	48,993	69,001	90,493	I176	927	5,742	25,941	88,669	I210	347	546
Imports of Goods & Services	98c	-2,400	...	-44,640	-62,610	-98,180	-143,540	-152,000	I-392	-166	-1,815	-9,726	-26,752	I-65	-117	-202
Gross Domestic Product = GDP	99b	18,401	26,280	34,124	47,288	68,601	98,417	126,979	I234	1,147	9,199	35,447	128,676	I288	488	772
Net Factor Inc/Pmts(-) Abroad	98.n	-409	-731	-1,067	-1,401	-2,094	-2,324	-1,461	I-1	-12	-144	-1,388	-4,204	I-8	-13	-25
Gross National Product = GNP	99a	17,992	25,549	33,057	45,887	66,507	96,093	125,518	I233	1,134	9,055	34,058	124,472	I280	474	747
Nat'l Income, Market Prices	99e	16,335	23,455	30,330	42,166	61,293	88,930	115,168	I214	1,016	8,055	29,106	108,303	I249	423	676
GDP 1990 Prices (Billions)	99b.p	4,269	4,745	4,899	5,074	5,263	5,371	5,852	5,781	5,460	5,513	4,801	4,970	5,460	5,909	6,398
GDP Deflator (1990=100)	99bi p										.2	.7	2.6	5.3	8.3	12.1
																Millions
Population	99z	8.51	8.68	8.85	9.03	9.20	9.37	9.53	9.70	9.86	10.03	10.20	10.37	10.55	I10.82	10.98

Exchange Rates: On September 29, 1975 the Chilean peso, equal to 1,000 escudos, was introduced.
Monetary Authorities: I Beginning in January 1976, data are based on improved sectorization.
Deposit Money Banks: I See note to section 10.
Monetary Survey: I See note to section 10.

International Transactions: I Trade data, which are derived from customs returns, have been updated with central bank payments data for current periods.

Chile

	1980	1981	1982	1983	1984	1985	1986	1987	1988	1989	1990	1991	1992	1993	1994		
End of Period																**Nonbank Financial Institutions**	
	....	....	....	....	26.8	57.4	112.9	192.1	267.4	508.7	956.3	1,412.4	1,904.5	2,656.8	3,462.9	Claims on Monetary Authorities	40x.p
	....	....	....	....	....	....	....	....	....	....	....	....	....	38.7	80.5	Foreign Assets	41..p
	....	....	....	41.6	62.7	89.7	75.3	48.4	46.4	35.9	34.7	35.5	32.8	108.3	Claims on Central Government	42a.p
	....	....	....	2.9	3.1	19.9	57.0	129.2	256.2	505.0	1,320.1	1,601.7	2,693.5	3,536.8	Claims on Private Sector	42d.p
	....	....	....	90.5	158.4	211.4	319.6	446.4	523.4	751.5	1,006.9	1,195.8	1,415.5	1,807.2	Claims on Deposit Money Banks	42e.p
	....	....	....	161.6	281.8	433.4	644.7	885.9	1,329.3	2,244.5	3,769.2	4,736.5	6,831.4	8,983.6	Reserve Funds and Capital	47a.p
	....	....	....	.2	–.2	.5	–.7	5.5	5.3	4.2	5.0	.9	5.9	12.2	Other Items (Net)	47r.p
Percent Per Annum																**Interest Rates**	
37.72	40.90	48.68	28.01	27.63	31.97	18.99	25.22	15.11	27.72	40.27	22.32	18.26	18.24	15.12	Deposit Rate	60l
47.14	52.02	63.86	42.82	38.33	40.81	26.27	32.80	21.17	35.92	48.83	28.55	23.92	24.33	20.34	Lending Rate	60p
Period Averages																**Prices and Production**	
7.3	6.1	4.8	4.1	5.5	6.8	14.8	27.1	40.2	64.7	100.0	180.8	249.3	281.7	392.0	Industrial Share Prices	62
16	17	18	26	33	47	56	67	ⅼ71	82	100	122	136	147	159	Prices: Home & Import Goods	63
15	17	18	26	32	44	55	66	ⅼ70	81	100	123	140	151	163	Home Goods	63a
16	19	21	26	32	41	49	59	ⅼ68	79	100	122	141	158	177	Consumer Prices	64
15	20	21	24	29	37	45	53	65	78	100	128	154	....	....	Wages and Salaries	65
....	....	....	....	....	....	....	....	....	....	....	....	....	....	120.9	Wages, Hourly (Apr.93=100)	65a
77	77	66	69	76	76	82	86	92	99	100	ⅼ105	118	121	124	Manufacturing Production	66ey
68	71	81	80	84	87	88	87	90	ⅼ99	100	112	119	123	131	Mining Production	66zx
67	68	79	79	82	85	88	88	91	ⅼ102	100	115	122	131	138	Copper Production	66c
Millions of US Dollars																**International Transactions**	
4,705	3,837	3,706	3,831	3,651	3,804	4,191	5,224	7,052	8,080	8,373	8,942	10,007	9,199	11,539	Exports	70..d
5,797	7,181	3,989	3,085	3,574	3,072	3,436	4,396	5,292	7,144	7,678	8,094	10,129	11,125	11,825	Imports, cif	71..d
5,469	6,513	3,643	2,845	3,288	2,920	3,099	3,994	4,833	6,502	7,037	7,354	9,237	10,181	10,879	Imports, fob	71.vd
1990=100																	
16.3	17.0	18.9	30.7	39.5	61.1	65.5	72.4	78.9	86.7	100.0	112.5	....	....	....	Import Prices	76.x
Minus Sign Indicates Debit																Balance of Payments	
4,705	3,836	3,706	3,831	3,650	3,804	4,191	5,303	7,053	8,080	8,372	8,942	10,008	9,199	11,537	Goods: Exports f.o.b.	78aa d
–5,469	–6,513	–3,643	–2,845	–3,288	–2,920	–3,099	–3,994	–4,844	–6,502	–7,037	–7,354	–9,236	–10,181	–10,878	Goods: Imports f.o.b.	78ab d
–764	–2,677	63	986	362	884	1,092	1,309	2,209	1,578	1,335	1,588	772	–982	659	Trade Balance	78ac d
1,263	1,172	936	797	664	692	1,042	1,045	1,089	1,495	1,913	2,170	2,426	2,601	2,847	Services: Credit	78ad d
–1,583	–1,780	–1,410	–1,236	–1,207	–1,080	–1,506	–1,501	–1,781	–2,051	–2,167	–2,177	–2,477	–2,596	–2,828	Services: Debit	78ae d
–1,084	–3,285	–411	547	–181	496	628	853	1,517	1,022	1,081	1,581	721	–977	678	Balance on Goods and Services	78af d
308	606	512	203	322	201	228	176	185	241	356	473	441	497	497	Income: Credit	78ag d
–1,308	–2,162	–2,514	–1,964	–2,359	–2,257	–2,132	–1,902	–2,118	–2,183	–2,173	–2,283	–2,301	–2,002	–2,272	Income: Debit	78ah d
–2,084	–4,841	–2,413	–1,214	–2,218	–1,560	–1,276	–873	–416	–920	–736	–229	–1,139	–2,482	–1,097	Balance on Goods, Serv., & Inc.	78ai d
194	193	186	161	165	203	106	172	219	241	228	359	450	405	360	Current Transfers, n.i.e.: Credit	78aj d
–81	–85	–77	–64	–58	–56	–22	–34	–37	–26	–28	–18	–19	–19	–20	Current Transfers: Debit	78ak d
–1,971	–4,733	–2,304	–1,117	–2,111	–1,413	–1,192	–735	–234	–705	–536	112	–708	–2,096	–757	Current Account, n.i.e.	78al d
—	—	—	—	—	—	—	—	—	—	—	—	—	—	—	Capital Account, n.i.e.: Credit	78ba d
—	—	—	—	—	—	—	—	—	—	—	—	—	—	—	Capital Account: Debit	78bb d
—	—	—	—	—	—	—	—	—	—	—	—	—	—	—	Capital Account	78bc d
213	383	401	135	—	–11	–2	–3	–6	–16	–10	–8	–123	–378	–431	–925	Direct Investment Abroad	78bd d
–43	–21	–17	–3	78	144	316	891	968	1,289	590	523	699	841	1,795	Dir. Invest. in Rep. Econ., n.i.e.	78be d
—	—	—	—	—	—	—	—	—	—	—	—	—	—	–90	–351	Portfolio Investment Assets	78bf d
—	—	—	—	—	—	—	—	—	87	359	225	452	837	1,373	Portfolio Investment Liab., n.i.e.	78bg d
128	–484	–720	242	153	435	576	258	370	297	553	1,298	–273	457	–143	Other Investment Assets	78bh d
2,867	4,820	1,351	–3,610	–374	–1,845	–2,727	–2,189	–2,095	–452	1,557	–1,100	2,384	1,163	2,779	Other Investment Liab., n.i.e.	78bi d
3,165	4,698	1,015	–3,236	–154	–1,268	–1,838	–1,046	–773	1,211	3,051	823	2,884	2,777	4,528	Financial Account, n.i.e.	78bj d
51	102	–69	68	190	–69	224	–143	–117	–119	–144	302	324	–96	–567	Net Errors and Omissions	78ca d
1,245	67	–1,358	–4,285	–2,075	–2,750	–2,806	–1,924	–1,124	387	2,371	1,237	2,500	585	3,204	Overall Balance	78cb d
–1,245	–67	1,358	4,285	2,075	2,750	2,806	1,924	1,124	–387	–2,371	–1,237	–2,500	–585	–3,204	Reserves and Related Items	79da d
–1,269	–73	1,379	4,750	–94	–312	–103	137	–66	–756	–549	–2,122	–1,052	–2,344	–171	–2,922	Reserve Assets	79db d
–52	–64	–40	623	220	205	115	–70	–70	–21	–209	–197	–203	–249	–210	Use of Fund Credit and Loans	79dc d
76	70	–181	12	74	–4	–25	77	93	130	–37	9	47	–156	–64	Liabs.Constit.For.Auth.Reserves	79dd d
—	—	200	3,744	2,094	2,652	2,579	1,982	1,857	53	–3	2	—	–9	–8	Exceptional Financing	79de d
Billions of Pesos Beginning 1977; Year Ending December 31																**Government Finance**	
58.2	33.0	–12.2	–40.9	ⅼ–56.2	–60.7	–31.4	20.0	–12.2	ⅼ135.3	77.6	184.2	341.9	351.2	....	Deficit (–) or Surplus	80
352.4	401.1	365.7	432.2	ⅼ547.4	752.1	921.0	1,205.6	1,550.3	ⅼ1,610.3	1,917.3	2,702.8	3,495.1	4,177.5	....	Revenue	81
14.7	18.2	8.7	—	ⅼ—	—	—	—	—	—	—	—	—	—	....	Grants Received	81z
301.2	374.9	422.8	497.2	ⅼ617.1	806.1	969.3	1,217.8	1,620.4	ⅼ1,571.1	1,884.5	2,542.0	3,152.0	3,842.7	....	Expenditure	82
7.7	11.4	–36.2	–24.2	ⅼ–13.6	6.7	–16.9	–32.2	–57.9	ⅼ–96.1	–44.8	–23.4	1.2	–16.4	....	Lending Minus Repayments	83
															Financing	
–50.8	–45.0	–7.1	40.9	ⅼ56.2	60.7	31.4	–20.0	12.2	....	....	....	....	....	....	Net Borrowing	84
–42.7	–38.3	–3.4	41.2	ⅼ42.0	–5.5	–72.4	–92.6	–106.9	....	....	....	....	....	....	Net Borrowing: Domestic	84a
–8.1	–6.7	–3.7	–.3	ⅼ14.2	66.2	103.8	72.6	119.1	....	....	....	....	....	....	Foreign	85a
–7.4	12.0	19.3	....	....	....	....	....	....	....	....	....	....	....	....	Use of Cash Balances	87
....	....	122.0	....	....	....	....	....	....	....	....	....	....	....	....	Debt: Domestic	88a
....	....	1,338.0	....	....	....	....	....	....	....	....	....	....	....	....	Foreign	89a
....	....	26.8	....	....	....	....	....	....	....	....	....	....	....	....	Intragovernmental Debt	88s
Billions of Pesos Beginning 1977																**National Accounts**	
245	209	240	374	459	746	995	1,374	2,046	2,639	3,194	3,943	4,615	4,916	6,180	Exports of Goods & Services	90c
134	167	190	221	274	356	430	494	613	742	906	1,147	1,457	1,788	2,041	Government Consumption	91f
179	237	181	187	234	447	586	882	1,202	1,733	2,159	2,510	3,517	4,715	5,322	Gross Fixed Capital Formation	93e
47	52	–42	–34	24	9	60	128	146	187	276	435	636	591	549	Increase/Decrease(–) in Stocks	93i
760	948	933	1,142	1,382	1,776	2,239	2,906	3,545	4,527	5,609	7,450	9,664	11,778	13,693	Private Consumption	96f
–290	–341	–263	–332	–480	682	–890	–1,244	–1,634	–2,298	–2,875	–3,468	–4,390	–5,335	–5,867	Imports of Goods & Services	98c
1,075	1,273	1,239	1,558	1,893	2,652	3,419	4,541	5,918	7,529	9,270	12,017	15,500	18,454	21,918	Gross Domestic Product = GDP	99b
–36	–57	–96	–134	–193	–335	–374	–384	–485	–532	–568	–647	–692	–629	–769	Net Factor Inc/Pmts(–) Abroad	98.n
1,039	1,216	1,107	1,398	1,705	2,317	3,045	4,154	5,433	6,971	8,839	10,961	13,139	15,658	....	Gross National Product = GNP	99a
940	1,100	1,016	1,217	1,479	2,108	....	....	....	....	....	....	....	....	....	Nat'l Income, Market Prices	99e
6,896	7,277	6,252	6,206	6,601	ⅼ6,764	7,143	7,614	8,170	8,977	9,270	9,942	11,040	11,733	12,231	GDP 1990 Prices (Billions)	99b.p
15.6	17.5	19.8	25.1	28.7	39.2	47.9	59.6	72.4	83.9	100.0	120.9	140.4	157.3	179.2	GDP Deflator (1990=100)	99bi p
Midyear Estimates																	
11.14	11.33	11.52	11.72	11.92	12.12	12.33	12.54	12.75	12.96	13.17	13.39	13.60	13.81	13.99	Population	99z

Government Finance: ⅼ Beginning in 1972, annual data are as reported in the *Government Finance Statistics Yearbook* and cover consolidated central government (including all extrabudgetary and social security funds). ⅼ Data for 1984-88 also cover accounts of some nonfinancial public enterprises and one public financial institution included in national sources. ⅼ Beginning in 1989, data exclude the operations of nonfinancial public enterprises.

China, People's Rep.
924

		1965	1966	1967	1968	1969	1970	1971	1972	1973	1974	1975	1976	1977	1978	1979
Exchange Rates																*Yuan per SDR:*
Market Rate......aa=	wa	2.4618	2.4618	2.4618	2.4618	2.4618	2.4618	2.6728	2.4321	2.4371	2.2524	2.3019	2.1846	2.1014	2.0546	1.9710
																Yuan per US Dollar:
Market Rate......ae=	we	2.4618	2.4618	2.4618	2.4618	2.4618	2.4618	2.4618	2.2401	2.0202	1.8397	1.9663	1.8803	1.7300	1.5771	1.4962
Market Rate......rf=	wf	2.4618	2.4618	2.4618	2.4618	2.4618	2.4618	2.4618	2.2451	1.9894	1.9612	1.8598	1.9414	1.8578	1.6836	1.5550
Fund Position																*Millions of SDRs:*
Quota	2f.s	....	....	....	....	....	....	....	....	....	....	....	....	....	....	....
SDRs	1b.s	....	....	....	....	....	....	....	....	....	....	....	....	....	....	....
Reserve Position in the Fund	1c.s	....	....	....	....	....	....	....	....	....	....	....	....	....	....	....
Total Fund Cred.&Loans Outstg.	2tl	....	....	....	....	....	....	....	....	....	....	....	....	....	....	....
International Liquidity													*Millions of US Dollars Unless Otherwise Indicated:*			
Total Reserves Minus Gold	11.d	....	....	....	....	....	....	....	....	....	....	....	....	2,345	1,557	2,154
SDRs	1b.d	....	....	....	....	....	....	....	....	....	....	....	....	....	....	....
Reserve Position in the Fund	1c.d	....	....	....	....	....	....	....	....	....	....	....	....	....	....	....
Foreign Exchange	1d.d	....	....	....	....	....	....	....	....	....	....	....	....	2,345	1,557	2,154
Gold (Million Fine Troy Ounces)	1ad	....	....	....	....	....	....	....	....	....	....	....	....	12.8	12.8	12.8
Gold (National Valuation)	1and	....	....	....	....	....	....	....	....	....	....	....	....	544	584	590
Monetary Authorities: Other Assets	3..d	....	....	....	....	....	....	....	....	....	....	....	....	322	701	828
Deposit Money Banks: Liabilities	7b.d	....	....	....	....	....	....	....	....	....	....	....	....	1,916	2,542	4,373
Monetary Authorities																*Billions of Yuan:*
Foreign Assets	11	....	....	....	....	....	....	....	....	....	....	....	....	....	....	....
Claims on Central Government	12a	....	....	....	....	....	....	....	....	....	....	....	....	....	....	....
Claims on Other Dom.Transactors	12d	....	....	....	....	....	....	....	....	....	....	....	....	....	....	....
Claims on Deposit Money Banks	12e	....	....	....	....	....	....	....	....	....	....	....	....	....	....	....
Reserve Money	14	....	....	....	....	....	....	....	....	....	....	....	....	....	....	....
Currency Outside DMBs	14a	....	....	....	....	....	....	....	....	....	....	....	....	....	....	....
Banks' Reserves	14c	....	....	....	....	....	....	....	....	....	....	....	....	....	....	....
Deposits of Other Dom.Trans.	14d	....	....	....	....	....	....	....	....	....	....	....	....	....	....	....
Foreign Liabilities	16c	—	—	—	—	—	—	—	—	—	—	—	—	—	—	—
Central Government Deposits	16d	....	....	....	....	....	....	....	....	....	....	....	....	....	....	....
Capital Accounts	17a	....	....	....	....	....	....	....	....	....	....	....	....	....	....	....
Other Items (Net)	17r	....	....	....	....	....	....	....	....	....	....	....	....	....	....	....
Deposit Money Banks																*Billions of Yuan:*
Specialized Banks																
Reserves	20	....	....	....	....	....	....	....	....	....	....	....	....	....	....	....
Foreign Assets	21	....	....	....	....	....	....	....	....	....	....	....	....	....	....	....
Claims on Other Dom.Transactors	22d	....	....	....	....	....	....	....	....	....	....	....	....	....	....	....
Demand Deposits	24	....	....	....	....	....	....	....	....	....	....	....	....	....	....	....
Savings Deposits	25a	....	....	....	....	....	....	....	....	....	....	....	....	....	....	....
Time Deposits	25b	....	....	....	....	....	....	....	....	....	....	....	....	3.31	4.01	6.54
Foreign Liabilities	26c	....	....	....	....	....	....	....	....	....	....	....	....	....	....	....
Credit from Monetary Authorities	26g	....	....	....	....	....	....	....	....	....	....	....	....	....	....	....
Capital Accounts	27a	....	....	....	....	....	....	....	....	....	....	....	....	....	....	....
Other Items (Net)	27r	....	....	....	....	....	....	....	....	....	....	....	....	....	....	....
Rural Credit Co-operatives																*Billions of Yuan:*
Reserves at Specialized Banks	20..g	....	....	....	....	....	....	....	....	....	....	....	....	....	....	....
Claims on Oth. Dom.Transactors	22d.g	....	....	....	....	....	....	....	....	....	....	....	....	....	....	....
Demand Deposits	24..g	....	....	....	....	....	....	....	....	....	....	....	....	....	....	....
Savings Deposits	25a.g	....	....	....	....	....	....	....	....	....	....	....	....	....	....	....
Time Deposits	25b.g	....	....	....	....	....	....	....	....	....	....	....	....	....	....	....
Credit from Specialized Banks	26g.g	....	....	....	....	....	....	....	....	....	....	....	....	....	....	....
Other Items (Net)	27r.g	....	....	....	....	....	....	....	....	....	....	....	....	....	....	....
Monetary Survey																*Billions of Yuan:*
Foreign Assets (Net)	31n	....	....	....	....	....	....	....	....	....	....	....	....	2.41	.54	−1.64
Domestic Credit	32	....	....	....	....	....	....	....	....	....	....	....	....	126.24	139.31	198.11
Claims on Central Govt. (Net)	32an	....	....	....	....	....	....	....	....	....	....	....	....	−40.09	−45.69	−5.85
Claims on Oth. Dom.Transactors	32d	....	....	....	....	....	....	....	....	....	....	....	....	166.33	185.00	203.96
Money	34	....	....	....	....	....	....	....	....	....	....	....	....	58.01	58.04	92.15
Quasi-Money	35	....	....	....	....	....	....	....	....	....	....	....	....	27.83	30.93	40.63
Other Items (Net)	37r	....	....	....	....	....	....	....	....	....	....	....	....	42.81	50.88	50.56
Money plus Quasi-Money	35l	....	....	....	....	....	....	....	....	....	....	....	....	85.84	88.97	132.78
Interest Rates																*Percent per Annum*
Deposit Rate	60l	....	....	....	....	....	....	....	....	....	....	....	....	....	....	....
Lending Rate	60p	....	....	....	....	....	....	....	....	....	....	....	....	....	....	....
Prices, Production, Employment																*Index Numbers (1990=100):*
Prices: Ind. Goods (1985=100)	63a	....	....	....	....	....	....	....	....	....	....	....	....	35.1	36.5	44.5
Prices: Agricultural Goods	63b	....	....	....	....	....	....	....	....	....	....	....	....	....	....	....
Consumer Prices	64	43.2	42.7	42.4	42.4	42.8	42.8	42.8	42.9	42.9	43.2	143.3	43.5	44.6	45.0	45.9
Wages: Average Annual Earnings	65	27.6	27.2	27.4	27.0	26.9	26.2	26.2	27.5	27.4	27.3	27.1	26.9	26.9	28.7	31.2
Industrial Production	66	7.0	8.5	7.3	6.9	9.3	12.3	14.2	15.1	16.6	16.7	19.3	19.7	22.6	25.7	27.9
Agricultural Production	66bx	33.9	36.8	37.4	36.5	36.8	39.0	40.2	39.8	43.1	44.6	46.0	45.8	45.6	49.3	53.1
Industrial Employment	67	27.3	....	....	....	....	....	....	....	....	....	....	....	....	68.3	71.1

China, People's Rep.

1980	1981	1982	1983	1984	1985	1986	1987	1988	1989	1990	1991	1992	1993	1994		
End of Period															**Exchange Rates**	
1.9518	2.0317	2.1209	2.0739	2.7404	3.5166	4.5528	5.2804	5.0088	6.2056	7.4293	7.7732	7.9087	7.9666	12.3302	Market Rate............aa=	**wa**
End of Period (we) Period Average (wf)																
1.5303	1.7455	1.9227	1.9809	2.7957	3.2015	3.7221	3.7221	3.7221	4.7221	5.2221	5.4342	5.7518	5.8000	8.4462	Market Rate............ae=	**we**
1.4984	1.7045	1.8925	1.9757	2.3200	2.9367	3.4528	3.7221	3.7221	3.7651	4.7832	5.3234	5.5146	5.7620	8.6187	Market Rate............rf=	**wf**
															Fund Position	
1,800	1,800	1,800	2,391	2,391	2,391	2,391	2,391	2,391	2,391	2,391	2,391	2,391	3,385	3,385	Quota	2f. s
72	236	194	320	414	440	465	451	436	411	395	404	305	352	369	SDRs	1b. s
150	—	—	168	261	303	303	303	303	303	303	303	551	513	517	Reserve Position in the Fund	1c. s
—	760	760	310	310	310	876	814	752	691	330	—	—	—	—	Total Fund Cred.&Loans Outstg.	2tl
															International Liquidity	
2,545	5,058	11,349	14,987 ‡17,366		12,728	11,453	16,305	18,541	17,960	29,586	43,674	‡20,620	22,387	52,914	Total Reserves Minus Gold	1l. d
92	275	214	335	406	483	569	640	586	540	562	577	419	484	539	SDRs	1b. d
191	—	—	176	255	332	370	429	407	398	430	433	758	704	755	Reserve Position in the Fund	1c. d
2,262	4,783	11,135	14,476 ‡16,705		11,913	10,514	15,236	17,548	17,022	28,594	42,664	‡19,443	21,199	51,620	Foreign Exchange	1d. d
12.8	12.7	12.7	12.7	12.7	12.7	12.7	12.7	12.7	12.7	12.7	12.7	12.7	12.7	12.7	Gold (Million Fine Troy Ounces)......	1ad
571	516	491	464	435	486	541	629	594	587	623	634	610	612	646	Gold (National Valuation)	1and
908	798	742	829	897	943	1,108	1,450	1,399	1,127	2,006	1,575	1,786	1,498	....	Monetary Authorities: Other Assets ..	3..d
5,667	3,874	2,907	3,337	3,646	6,634	8,389	10,155	11,660	10,582	12,868	19,918	19,398	21,925	31,298	Deposit Money Banks: Liabilities	7b. d
End of Period															**Monetary Authorities**	
....	....	....	....	....	14.57	14.40	25.47	28.22	40.50	82.05	139.96	133.04	145.99	....	Foreign Assets	11
....	....	....	....	....	27.51	37.01	51.50	57.65	68.46	80.11	106.78	124.11	158.21	....	Claims on Central Government	12a
....	....	....	....	....	7.84	14.05	24.42	32.92	38.18	46.37	52.28	73.50	95.51	....	Claims on Other Dom.Transactors ..	12d
....	....	....	....	....	224.86	268.16	275.64	336.44	420.95	509.07	591.81	678.02	962.57	....	Claims on Deposit Money Banks	12e
....	....	....	....	....	228.41	281.86	318.17	398.36	491.12	638.73	793.14	922.80	1,254.02	....	Reserve Money	14
....	....	....	....	....	98.78	121.84	145.45	213.26	234.21	264.12	317.40	432.94	585.55	....	Currency Outside DMBs	14a
....	....	....	....	....	96.37	120.08	127.41	145.38	208.15	312.66	399.98	420.51	596.41	....	Banks' Reserves	14c
....	....	....	....	....	33.26	39.94	45.31	39.72	48.76	61.95	75.76	69.35	72.06	....	Deposits of Other Dom.Trans.	14d
—	1.54	1.61	.64	.85	1.09	3.99	4.30	3.77	4.29	2.45	—	—	—	—	Foreign Liabilities	16c
....	....	....	....	....	36.84	31.15	30.70	27.11	43.80	38.04	48.58	23.06	48.73	....	Central Government Deposits	16d
....	....	....	....	....	23.36	23.23	26.38	26.40	30.62	36.29	52.70	68.27	96.75	....	Capital Accounts	17a
....	....	....	....	....	-16.47	-3.58	-2.52	-.40	-1.74	2.09	-3.59	-5.47	-37.20	....	Other Items (Net)	17r
															Deposit Money Banks	
															Specialized Banks	
....	....	....	....	....	96.07	111.56	113.99	128.86	178.15	263.81	359.32	367.80	526.69	....	Reserves	20
....	....	....	....	....	29.67	31.40	45.83	52.76	54.17	91.39	113.86	147.05	149.70	....	Foreign Assets	21
....	....	....	....	....	554.44	718.68	850.26	1,001.68	1,181.11	1,445.09	1,718.70	2,050.08	2,494.01	....	Claims on Other Dom.Transactors ..	22d
....	....	....	....	....	153.68	204.50	244.69	270.01	274.71	344.53	466.35	608.11	694.72	....	Demand Deposits	24
....	....	....	....	....	21.61	27.96	41.01	59.72	61.37	76.43	101.70	154.83	218.88	....	Savings Deposits	25a
....	....	....	....	....	107.51	143.54	192.68	230.36	342.72	488.18	595.68	771.46	944.42	....	Time Deposits	25b
8.67	6.76	5.59	6.61	10.19	21.24	31.22	37.80	43.40	49.97	67.20	108.24	111.57	127.17	264.35	Foreign Liabilities	26c
....	....	....	....	....	224.86	268.39	274.99	336.10	420.15	508.29	590.56	670.99	961.26	....	Credit from Monetary Authorities	26g
....	....	....	....	....	65.34	74.13	81.46	91.42	99.32	111.49	131.30	131.30	171.92	....	Capital Accounts	27a
....	....	....	....	....	85.90	111.90	137.45	152.29	165.19	204.17	198.05	116.67	52.04	....	Other Items (Net)	27r
End of Period															*Rural Credit Co-operatives*	
....	....	....	....	32.72	40.14	49.33	59.13	57.97	65.82	77.36	91.59	108.05	137.60	....	Reserves at Specialized Banks........	20..g
....	....	....	....	35.45	40.00	56.82	77.13	90.86	109.49	141.09	180.86	245.40	314.39	....	Claims on Oth. Dom.Transactors	22d.g
....	....	....	....	18.69	16.01	19.62	21.95	25.75	25.74	30.35	39.27	61.03	72.09	....	Demand Deposits	24..g
....	....	....	....	15.26	18.08	22.62	29.74	35.08	33.25	38.72	43.37	59.23	73.10	....	Savings Deposits	25a.g
....	....	....	....	28.55	38.40	53.99	70.83	79.15	107.96	145.39	188.29	227.50	284.52	....	Time Deposits	25b.g
....	....	....	....	3.12	3.29	4.15	3.77	3.60	3.77	4.19	5.08	6.06	6.03	....	Credit from Specialized Banks	26g.g
....	....	....	....	2.55	4.36	5.80	9.97	5.25	4.59	-.19	-3.56	-.37	16.25	....	Other Items (Net)	27r.g
End of Period															**Monetary Survey**	
-2.78	2.67	16.14	23.95	27.03	‡21.91	10.59	29.20	33.81	40.42	103.79	145.58	168.52	168.53	....	Foreign Assets (Net)	31n
242.25	273.99	304.67	343.70	451.45	‡592.95	795.41	972.61	1,156.00	1,353.44	1,674.62	2,010.04	2,470.03	3,013.39	....	Domestic Credit	32
.82	-2.48	-.56	.59	9.49	‡-9.33	5.86	20.80	30.54	24.66	42.07	58.20	101.05	109.48	....	Claims on Central Govt. (Net)	32an
241.43	276.47	305.23	343.11	441.96	‡602.28	789.55	951.81	1,125.46	1,328.78	1,632.55	1,951.84	2,368.98	2,903.91	....	Claims on Oth. Dom.Transactors	32d
114.88	134.52	148.84	174.89	244.94	‡301.73	385.90	457.40	548.74	583.42	700.95	898.78	1,171.43	1,424.42	....	Money	34
52.23	63.25	77.73	96.39	114.91	‡185.76	248.96	338.34	411.47	555.89	767.24	961.11	1,261.30	1,583.15	....	Quasi-Money	35
55.19	55.97	65.76	66.39	85.29	‡125.78	174.21	206.08	229.61	254.54	310.23	295.73	205.81	174.36	....	Other Items (Net)	37r
167.11	197.77	226.57	271.28	359.85	‡487.49	634.86	795.74	960.21	1,139.31	1,468.19	1,859.89	2,432.73	3,007.57	....	Money plus Quasi-Money	35l
Percent per Annum															**Interest Rates**	
5.40	5.40	5.76	5.76	5.76	7.20	7.20	7.20	8.64	....	....	....	....	....	....	Deposit Rate	60l
5.04	5.04	7.20	7.20	7.20	7.74	7.92	7.92	8.28	11.15	....	....	....	....	....	Lending Rate	60p
Period Averages															**Prices, Production, Employment**	
91.0	91.9	93.4	94.3	97.1	100.0	108.4	116.9	134.5	....	....	....	....	....	....	Prices: Ind. Goods(1985=100)	63a
47.7	50.5	51.6	53.9	56.1	60.9	64.8	72.6	89.3	102.7	100.0	98.0	....	....	....	Prices: Agricultural Goods	63b
49.3	50.5	51.5	52.5	53.9	60.3	64.6	70.2	84.8	98.6	100.0	105.1	114.1	‡133.5	....	Consumer Prices	64
35.6	36.1	37.3	38.6	45.5	53.6	62.1	68.2	81.6	90.4	100.0	109.3	....	....	....	Wages: Average Annual Earnings......	65
30.5	31.8	34.3	38.2	44.4	53.9	60.1	70.8	85.5	92.8	100.0	114.5	....	....	....	Industrial Production	66
53.8	56.9	63.3	68.3	76.7	79.3	81.9	86.7	90.1	92.9	100.0	103.7	....	....	....	Agricultural Production	66bx
74.7	78.1	80.2	81.6	83.8	87.1	90.6	93.6	96.6	97.6	100.0	102.7	....	....	....	Industrial Employment	67

China, People's Rep.
924

		1965	1966	1967	1968	1969	1970	1971	1972	1973	1974	1975	1976	1977	1978	1979
International Transactions																*Billions of Yuan*
Exports	70	6.31	6.60	5.88	5.76	5.98	5.68	6.85	8.29	11.69	13.94	14.30	13.48	13.97	16.76	21.17
Imports, cif	71	5.53	6.11	5.34	5.09	4.72	5.61	5.24	6.40	10.36	15.28	14.74	12.93	13.28	18.74	24.29
Imports, fob	71.v	5.07	5.61	4.90	4.67	4.33	5.15	4.81	5.87	9.50	14.02	13.52	11.86	12.18	17.19	22.28
Balance of Payments																*Millions of US Dollars:*
Goods: Exports f.o.b.	78aa d	....	....	....	....	....	....	....	....	....	....	....	....	....	....	....
Goods: Imports f.o.b.	78ab d	....	....	....	....	....	....	....	....	....	....	....	....	....	....	....
Trade Balance	78ac d	....	....	....	....	....	....	....	....	....	....	....	....	....	....	....
Services: Credit	78ad d	....	....	....	....	....	....	....	....	....	....	....	....	....	....	....
Services: Debit	78ae d	....	....	....	....	....	....	....	....	....	....	....	....	....	....	....
Balance on Goods and Services	78af d	....	....	....	....	....	....	....	....	....	....	....	....	....	....	....
Income: Credit	78ag d	....	....	....	....	....	....	....	....	....	....	....	....	....	....	....
Income: Debit	78ah d	....	....	....	....	....	....	....	....	....	....	....	....	....	....	....
Balance on Goods, Serv., & Inc.	78ai d	....	....	....	....	....	....	....	....	....	....	....	....	....	....	....
Current Transfers, n.i.e.: Credit	78aj d	....	....	....	....	....	....	....	....	....	....	....	....	....	....	....
Current Transfers: Debit	78ak d	....	....	....	....	....	....	....	....	....	....	....	....	....	....	....
Current Account, n.i.e.	78al d	....	....	....	....	....	....	....	....	....	....	....	....	....	....	....
Capital Account, n.i.e.: Credit	78ba d	....	....	....	....	....	....	....	....	....	....	....	....	....	....	....
Capital Account: Debit	78bb d	....	....	....	....	....	....	....	....	....	....	....	....	....	....	....
Capital Account, n.i.e.	78bc d	....	....	....	....	....	....	....	....	....	....	....	....	....	....	....
Direct Investment Abroad	78bd d	....	....	....	....	....	....	....	....	....	....	....	....	....	....	....
Dir. Invest. in Rep. Econ., n.i.e.	78be d	....	....	....	....	....	....	....	....	....	....	....	....	....	....	....
Portfolio Investment Assets	78bf d	....	....	....	....	....	....	....	....	....	....	....	....	....	....	....
Portfolio Investment Liab., n.i.e.	78bg d	....	....	....	....	....	....	....	....	....	....	....	....	....	....	....
Other Investment Assets	78bh d	....	....	....	....	....	....	....	....	....	....	....	....	....	....	....
Other Investment Liab., n.i.e.	78bi d	....	....	....	....	....	....	....	....	....	....	....	....	....	....	....
Financial Account, n.i.e.	78bj d	....	....	....	....	....	....	....	....	....	....	....	....	....	....	....
Net Errors and Omissions	78ca d	....	....	....	....	....	....	....	....	....	....	....	....	....	....	....
Overall Balance	78cb d	....	....	....	....	....	....	....	....	....	....	....	....	....	....	....
Reserves and Related Items	79da d	....	....	....	....	....	....	....	....	....	....	....	....	....	....	....
Reserve Assets	79db d	....	....	....	....	....	....	....	....	....	....	....	....	....	....	....
Use of Fund Credit and Loans	79dc d	....	....	....	....	....	....	....	....	....	....	....	....	....	....	....
Liabs.Constit.For.Auth.Reserves	79dd d	....	....	....	....	....	....	....	....	....	....	....	....	....	....	....
Exceptional Financing	79de d	....	....	....	....	....	....	....	....	....	....	....	....	....	....	....
Government Finance																*Billions of Yuan:*
Deficit(-) or Surplus	80													3.10	1.01	−17.06
Revenue	81													87.45	112.11	110.33
Expenditure	82													84.35	111.10	127.39
National Accounts																*Billions of Yuan*
Gross Domestic Product	99b	....	....	....	....	....	....	....	....	....	....	....	....	....	....	....
Net Factor Inc/Pmts(-) Abroad	98.n	....	....	....	....	....	....	....	....	....	....	....	....	....	....	....
Gross National Product	99a											283.9			358.8	398.8
Gross Dom. Prod. 1990 Prices	99b.p														649.0	698.4
Gross Nat. Prod. 1990 Prices	99a.p														648.9	698.2
GDP Deflator (1990=100)	99bi p															
GNP Deflator (1990=100)	99ai p														55.3	57.1
																Millions:
Population	99z	725.4	745.4	763.7	785.3	806.7	829.9	852.3	871.8	892.1	908.6	924.2	937.2	949.7	962.6	975.4

International Liquidity: ⅼ Beginning in December 1984, *Foreign Exchange* (line 1d.d) includes foreign government securities. ⅼ Starting July 1992, *Foreign Exchange* includes foreign exchange holdings of the People's Bank of China only. Prior to that date, it included foreign exchange holdings of the Bank of China.
Monetary Survey: ⅼ Beginning in 1979, data are based on improved classification. ⅼ Data prior to the fourth quarter of 1985 exclude the rural credit cooperatives and the People's Construction Bank of China.
International Transactions: ⅼ Prior to 1980, the data are provided by the Ministry of Foreign Trade and exclude exports of complete plants in the form of foreign aid. Beginning in 1980, data are provided by the Customs Office and are more comprehensive.

China, People's Rep.

924

	1980	1981	1982	1983	1984	1985	1986	1987	1988	1989	1990	1991	1992	1993	1994	International Transactions	
Billions of Yuan																	
	27.12	36.75	41.44	43.85	57.96	80.92	108.58	147.18	176.95	195.25	293.06	375.04	444.02	524.16	1,032.66	Exports	70
	29.88	36.77	35.78	42.17	61.44	125.97	149.89	161.51	205.75	220.02	251.23	333.07	421.06	593.99	987.39	Imports, cif	71
	27.41	33.73	32.83	38.69	56.37	115.57	137.51	148.17	188.76	201.85	230.49	305.57	386.29	544.94	905.86	Imports, fob	71.v
Minus Sign Indicates Debit																Balance of Payments	
	....	....	21,125	20,707	23,905	25,108	25,756	34,734	41,054	43,220	51,519	58,919	69,568	75,659	....	Goods: Exports f.o.b.	78aa d
	....	....	−16,876	−18,717	−23,891	−38,231	−34,896	−36,395	−46,369	−48,840	−42,354	−50,176	−64,385	−86,313	....	Goods: Imports f.o.b.	78ab d
	....	....	4,249	1,990	14	−13,123	−9,140	−1,661	−5,315	−5,620	9,165	8,743	5,183	−10,654	....	Trade Balance	78ac d
	....	....	2,512	2,479	2,811	3,055	3,827	4,386	4,823	4,550	5,803	6,905	9,189	11,146	....	Services: Credit	78ad d
	....	....	−2,024	−1,994	−2,857	−2,524	−2,276	−2,485	−3,603	−3,910	−4,352	−4,121	−9,414	−12,014	....	Services: Debit	78ae d
	....	....	4,737	2,475	−32	−12,592	−7,589	240	−4,095	−4,980	10,616	11,527	4,958	−11,522	....	Balance on Goods and Services	78af d
	....	....	1,092	1,549	2,008	1,478	1,100	1,027	1,504	1,947	3,069	3,793	5,655	4,437	....	Income: Credit	78ag d
	....	....	−641	−295	−388	−546	−924	−1,191	−1,630	−1,665	−1,962	−2,879	−5,367	−5,696	....	Income: Debit	78ah d
	....	....	5,188	3,729	1,588	−11,660	−7,413	76	−4,221	−4,698	11,723	12,441	5,246	−12,781	....	Balance on Goods, Serv., & Inc.	78ai d
	....	....	670	620	596	439	458	295	269	306	267	613	613	497	....	Current Transfers, n.i.e.: Credit	78aj d
	....	....	−176	−101	−144	−190	−129	−157	−141	−90	−96	−37	−49	−115	....	Current Transfers: Debit	78ak d
	....	....	5,682	4,248	2,040	−11,411	−7,084	214	−4,093	−4,482	11,894	13,017	5,810	−12,399	....	Current Account, n.i.e.	78al d
	....	....	2	—	—	—	58	94	299	171	109	277	593	793	....	Capital Account, n.i.e.: Credit	78ba d
	....	....	−10	−8	−10	−6	−8	−8	−8	−6	−6	−22	−2	−3	....	Capital Account: Debit	78bb d
	....	....	−8	−8	−10	−6	50	86	291	165	103	255	591	790	....	Capital Account, n.i.e.	78bc d
	....	....	−44	−93	−134	−629	−450	−645	−850	−780	−830	−913	−4,000	−4,400	....	Direct Investment Abroad	78bd d
	....	....	430	636	1,258	1,659	1,875	2,314	3,194	3,393	3,487	4,366	11,156	27,515	....	Dir. Invest. in Rep. Econ., n.i.e.	78be d
	....	....	−20	−641	−1,721	2,263	−40	−140	−340	−320	−241	−330	−450	−597	....	Portfolio Investment Assets	78bf d
	....	....	41	20	83	764	1,608	1,191	1,216	140	—	565	393	3,646	....	Portfolio Investment Liab., n.i.e.	78bg d
	....	....	−790	−638	−625	−1,101	−328	82	−781	−229	−231	−156	−3,267	−2,114	....	Other Investment Assets	78bh d
	....	....	721	490	136	6,015	3,279	3,199	4,694	1,519	1,070	4,500	−4,082	−576	....	Other Investment Liab., n.i.e.	78bi d
	....	....	338	−226	−1,003	8,971	5,944	6,001	7,133	3,723	3,255	8,032	−250	23,474	....	Financial Account, n.i.e.	78bj d
	....	....	293	128	−889	6	−958	−1,518	−957	115	−3,205	−6,767	−8,211	−10,096	....	Net Errors and Omissions	78ca d
	....	....	6,305	4,142	138	−2,440	−2,048	4,783	2,374	−479	12,047	14,537	−2,060	1,769	....	Overall Balance	78cb d
	....	....	−6,305	−4,142	−138	2,440	2,048	−4,783	−2,374	479	−12,047	−14,537	2,060	−1,769	....	Reserves and Related Items	79da d
	....	....	−6,305	−3,658	−138	2,440	1,369	−4,704	−2,291	558	−11,555	−14,083	2,060	−1,769	....	Reserve Assets	79db d
	....	....	—	−483	—	—	679	−79	−82	−79	−492	−454	—	—	....	Use of Fund Credit and Loans	79dc d
	....	....	—	—	—	—	—	—	—	—	—	—	—	—	....	Liabs.Constit.For.Auth.Reserves	79dd d
	....	....	—	—	—	—	—	—	—	—	—	—	—	—	....	Exceptional Financing	79de d
Year Ending December 31																Government Finance	
	−12.75	−2.55	−2.93	−4.35	−4.45	2.16	−7.05	−7.96	−7.86	−9.23	−13.96	−20.27	−23.66	−19.93	−63.80	Deficit(−) or Surplus	80
	108.52	108.95	112.40	124.90	150.19	186.64	226.03	236.89	262.80	294.79	331.26	361.09	415.31	508.81	518.18	Revenue	81
	121.27	111.50	115.33	129.25	154.64	184.48	233.08	244.85	270.66	304.02	345.22	381.36	438.97	528.74	581.98	Expenditure	82
Billions of Yuan																National Accounts	
	447.0	478.0	518.0	579.0	693.0	853.0	969.0	1,131.0	1,407.0	1,600.0	1,768.0	2,019.0	2,402.0	3,138.0	4,380.0	Gross Domestic Product	99b
	—	−.7	1.3	1.9	3.2	2.8	.6	−.9	−.2	−.7	1.5	4.6	1.6	13.4	11.8	Net Factor Inc/Pmts(−) Abroad	98.n
	447.0	477.3	519.3	580.9	696.2	855.8	969.6	1,130.1	1,406.8	1,599.3	1,769.5	2,023.6	2,403.6	3,151.4	4,391.8	Gross National Product	99a
	752.9	786.6	851.5	940.5	1,077.4	1,216.3	1,319.5	1,466.2	1,631.1	1,701.8	1,768.0	1,909.5	2,161.3	2,459.9	2,752.0	Gross Dom. Prod. 1990 Prices	99b.p
	752.7	786.5	855.2	944.1	1,083.0	1,221.2	1,320.5	1,464.6	1,630.0	1,700.7	1,769.5	1,914.2	2,163.4	....	....	Gross Nat. Prod. 1990 Prices	99a.p
	59.4	60.8	60.8	61.6	64.3	70.1	73.4	77.1	86.3	94.0	100.0	105.7	111.1	127.6	159.2	GDP Deflator (1990=100)	99bi p
	59.4	60.7	60.7	61.5	64.3	70.1	73.4	77.2	86.3	94.0	100.0	105.7	111.1	....	....	GNP Deflator (1990=100)	99ai p
Midyear																	
	996.1	1,008.4	1,020.6	1,039.6	1,054.9	1,070.2	1,086.7	1,104.2	1,121.9	1,139.2	1,153.3	1,170.1	1,183.6	1,196.4	....	Population	99z

Colombia

233

		1965	1966	1967	1968	1969	1970	1971	1972	1973	1974	1975	1976	1977	1978	1979
Exchange Rates																*Pesos per SDR:*
Principal Rate	aa	13.50	13.50	15.76	16.88	17.85	19.09	22.70	24.74	29.91	35.05	38.58	42.20	46.11	53.41	57.96
																Pesos per US Dollar:
Principal Rate	ae	13.50	13.50	15.76	16.88	17.85	19.09	20.91	22.79	24.79	28.63	32.96	36.32	37.96	41.00	44.00
Principal Rate	rf	10.48	13.50	14.51	16.29	17.32	18.44	19.93	21.87	23.64	26.06	30.93	34.69	36.77	39.09	42.55
																Index Numbers (1990=100):
Principal Rate	ahx	4,951.7	3,715.0	3,471.4	3,078.7	2,894.9	2,719.4	2,516.8	2,294.1	2,122.0	1,926.0	1,623.5	1,446.0	1,363.7	1,283.0	1,178.6
Nominal Effective Exchange Rate	nec	....	....	....	....	....	....	....	....	....	....	....	....	....	....	300.5
Real Effective Exchange Rate	rec	....	....	....	....	....	....	....	....	....	....	....	....	....	....	196.1
Fund Position																*Millions of SDRs:*
Quota	2f.s	100	125	125	125	125	157	157	157	157	157	157	157	157	193	193
SDRs	1b.s	—	—	—	—	—	—	8	18	23	25	20	24	26	38	72
Reserve Position in the Fund	1c.s	—	—	—	—	—	—	—	—	39	39	39	45	77	70	74
Total Fund Cred.&Loans Outstg.	2tl	60	58	91	113	106	55	53	—	—						
International Liquidity												*Millions of US Dollars Unless Otherwise Indicated:*				
Total Reserves minus Gold	1l.d	61	52	52	142	195	189	188	309	516	431	475	1,101	1,747	2,366	3,844
SDRs	1b.d	—	—	—	—	—	—	9	19	28	30	24	28	31	49	95
Reserve Position in the Fund	1c.d	—	—	—	—	—	—	—	—	47	48	46	53	93	91	97
Foreign Exchange	1d.d	61	52	52	142	195	189	179	290	441	353	405	1,020	1,623	2,226	3,652
Gold (Million Fine Troy Ounces)	1ad	1.000	.714	.886	.886	.743	.486	.400	.429	.429	.429	1.126	1.413	1.731	1.961	2.317
Gold (National Valuation)	1and	35	25	31	31	26	17	14	16	16	18	48	60	73	137	215
Monetary Authorities: Other Assets	3..d	24	36	36	14	5	12	24	24	—	—	28	8	18	—	7
Other Liab.	4..d	62	75	48	33	64	64	73	112	132	137	135	142	175	229	259
Deposit Money Banks: Assets	7a.d	11	9	5	9	6	6	4	4	5	21	35	57	62	64	89	145
of which: Claims on Nonbanks	7add	....	....	....	....	....	....	....	....	....	....	....	....	....	44	63
Deposit Money Banks: Liabilities	7b.d	41	62	71	129	181	239	331	325	310	578	533	637	476	486	869
Other Banking Insts.: Liabilities	7f.d	....	....	....	....	....	....	....	....	....	102	152	139	175	229	292
Monetary Authorities												*Millions of Pesos through 1973;*				
Foreign Assets	11	1,170.0	1,020.0	1,600.0	2,520.0	3,980.0	4,040.0	4,560.0	7,780.0	12,675.1	‡11.6	16.4	40.7	69.4	98.6	175.9
Claims on Central Government	12a	4,517.0	4,899.0	5,782.0	5,718.0	5,894.0	5,611.0	6,832.0	6,990.0	6,200.0	‡8.0	10.9	9.0	8.8	‡9.5	9.7
Claims on Nonfin.Pub.Enterprises	12c	....	....	....	....	....	....	....	....	334.0	‡.3	.3	.2	.2	.2	.1
Claims on Deposit Money Banks	12e	1,212.0	1,143.0	1,105.0	1,784.0	2,414.0	3,249.0	3,618.0	3,394.0	5,790.0	‡7.6	8.1	7.4	13.9	‡32.1	36.0
Claims on Other Banking Insts.	12f	1,202.0	1,393.0	1,959.0	2,718.0	3,241.0	3,689.0	4,772.0	5,875.0	8,055.0	‡11.3	19.2	20.6	35.3	‡27.8	25.2
Claims on Nonbank Financial Insts.	12g	....	....	....	....	....	....	....	....	....	....	....	....	....	....	....
Reserve Money	14	5,288.0	5,791.0	7,055.0	9,264.0	11,840.0	13,700.0	15,363.0	18,919.0	24,808.0	‡30.1	37.7	53.4	74.9	‡115.0	148.1
of which: Currency Outside DMBs	14a	3,538.0	4,037.0	4,689.0	5,470.0	6,506.0	7,809.0	8,534.0	10,729.0	12,424.0	‡15.9	20.8	28.8	40.5	‡53.7	67.3
Time, Savings,& Fgn.Currency Dep.	15	....	....	....	....	....	....	....	....	....	....	....	....	....	....	....
Money Market Instruments	16aa	....	....	....	....	....	....	....	....	504.0	‡1.0	1.6	5.1	16.3	‡27.3	39.9
Restricted Deposits	16b	1,709.0	1,737.0	1,561.0	1,879.0	2,159.0	2,401.0	2,144.0	2,496.0	3,661.0	‡3.8	2.0	.9	5.1	‡5.9	10.1
Foreign Liabilities	16c	1,636.0	1,771.0	2,009.0	1,948.0	2,277.0	1,226.0	1,121.0	297.0	812.0	‡1.0	.2	.2	.2	‡1.4	.3
Long-Term Foreign Liabilities	16cl	5.0	15.0	186.0	515.0	762.0	1,046.0	1,621.0	2,264.0	2,464.0	‡3.0	4.3	5.0	6.4	‡9.0	11.1
Central Government Deposits	16d	321.0	1,007.0	968.0	1,099.0	1,488.0	1,632.0	1,304.0	1,536.0	1,594.0	‡1.9	1.8	2.8	4.1	‡5.8	28.7
Capital Accounts	17a	....	....	....	....	....	....	....	....	2,530.0	‡2.4	2.5	2.7	2.9	‡3.6	5.1
Other Items (Net)	17r	−858.0	−1,866.0	−1,333.0	−1,965.0	−2,997.0	−3,416.0	−1,771.0	−1,473.0	−3,318.9	‡−4.4	4.8	7.8	17.6	‡1.1	2.9
Deposit Money Banks												*Millions of Pesos through 1973;*				
Reserves	20	1,343.0	1,399.0	2,115.0	3,176.0	4,446.0	5,209.0	5,410.0	6,758.0	10,690.0	‡12.6	17.0	24.8	34.3	‡60.5	79.3
Foreign Assets	21	145.0	115.0	74.0	157.0	104.0	113.0	85.0	109.0	510.0	‡1.0	1.9	2.2	2.4	‡3.6	6.0
Claims on Central Government	22a	760.0	810.0	940.0	1,174.0	1,560.0	1,990.0	2,352.0	2,968.0	4,822.0	‡6.9	6.9	9.3	14.6	‡15.1	15.6
Claims on Local Government	22b	....	....	....	....	....	....	....	....	....	....	....	....	....	....	....
Claims on Nonfin.Pub.Enterprises	22c	....	....	....	....	....	....	....	....	....	....	....	....	....	1.6	1.0
Claims on Private Sector	22d	6,819.0	8,253.0	9,921.0	12,101.0	14,173.0	17,582.0	21,515.0	25,095.0	29,976.0	‡45.1	55.6	73.5	88.6	‡108.0	138.1
Claims on Other Banking Insts.	22f	659.0	992.0	1,197.0	1,247.0	1,632.0	1,840.0	2,240.0	3,081.0	4,465.0	‡7.0	10.5	12.1	14.7	‡9.1	12.0
Demand Deposits	24	5,937.0	6,994.0	8,726.0	9,964.0	12,080.0	14,005.0	15,647.0	20,055.0	28,151.0	‡31.7	40.9	54.8	69.4	‡76.5	93.6
Time, Savings,& Fgn.Currency Dep.	25	1,521.0	1,575.0	1,790.0	2,039.0	2,416.0	2,972.0	3,545.0	5,127.0	7,408.0	‡13.1	17.0	24.0	34.3	‡44.0	51.7
Money Market Instruments	26aa	....	....	....	....	....	....	....	....	....	....	....	....	....	....	....
Bonds	26ab	....	....	....	....	....	....	....	....	....	....	....	....	....	—	—
Restricted Deposits	26b	....	....	....	....	....	....	....	....	....	....	....	....	....	....	....
Foreign Liabilities	26c	514.0	751.0	974.0	2,003.0	3,004.0	4,285.0	6,576.0	7,068.0	7,363.0	‡16.2	17.3	22.9	17.8	‡19.3	37.7
Long-Term Foreign Liabilities	26cl	34.0	80.0	151.0	167.0	218.0	287.0	338.0	331.0	334.0	‡.3	.3	.2	.2	‡1.3	.3
Central Government Deposits	26d	....	....	....	....	....	....	....	....	....	....	....	....	....	.7	.9
Credit from Monetary Authorities	26g	1,211.0	1,141.0	1,436.0	2,107.0	2,372.0	3,018.0	2,751.0	2,394.0	4,320.0	‡6.2	6.4	5.2	16.0	‡31.5	35.5
Liabilities to Other Banking Insts	26i	....	....	....	....	....	....	....	....	....	....	....	....	....	....	....
Capital Accounts	27a	1,558.0	1,821.0	2,230.0	2,486.0	2,810.0	3,752.0	4,456.0	5,183.0	6,102.0	‡5.6	6.8	9.1	11.6	‡22.9	28.8
Other Items (Net)	27r	−1,049.0	−793.0	−1,060.0	−911.0	−985.0	−1,585.0	−1,711.0	−2,147.0	−3,215.0	‡−.4	3.1	5.8	5.5	‡2.8	3.6
Monetary Survey												*Millions of Pesos through 1973;*				
Foreign Assets (Net)	31n	−835.0	−1,387.0	−1,309.0	−1,274.0	−1,197.0	−1,358.0	−3,052.0	524.0	5,010.1	‡−4.5	.8	19.8	53.7	‡82.4	143.9
Domestic Credit	32	14,556.0	17,174.0	20,510.0	23,881.0	28,217.0	33,060.0	39,145.0	45,937.0	55,469.0	‡78.7	104.5	124.4	161.6	‡169.3	178.4
Claims on Central Govt. (Net)	32an	4,564.0	4,279.0	5,224.0	5,139.0	5,024.0	4,696.0	6,333.0	6,413.0	5,800.0	‡8.8	10.8	14.9	19.2	‡18.1	−4.3
Claims on Local Government	32b	....	....	....	....	....	....	....	....	....	....	....	....	....	....	....
Claims on Nonfin.Pub.Enterprises	32c	....	....	....	....	....	....	....	....	334.0	‡.3	.3	.2	.2	1.8	1.1
Claims on Private Sector	32d	7,755.0	10,091.0	11,620.0	14,130.0	17,385.0	21,569.0	24,260.0	28,559.0	33,521.0	‡47.4	58.9	76.5	92.3	‡112.4	144.4
Claims on Other Banking Insts.	32f	1,861.0	2,385.0	3,156.0	3,965.0	4,873.0	5,529.0	7,012.0	8,956.0	12,520.0	‡18.4	29.7	32.7	50.1	‡36.9	37.2
Claims on Nonbank Fin. Insts.	32g	....	....	....	....	....	....	....	....	....	....	....	....	....	....	....
Money	34	9,638.0	11,237.0	13,682.0	15,858.0	19,396.0	22,397.0	25,063.0	31,854.0	41,647.0	‡49.1	58.9	79.4	103.5	‡132.9	165.9
Quasi-Money	35	2,189.0	1,809.0	2,103.0	2,216.0	2,696.0	3,381.0	4,127.0	5,856.0	9,250.0	‡14.6	19.6	25.8	37.2	‡47.1	55.1
Money Market Instruments	36aa	....	....	....	....	....	....	....	....	504.0	‡1.1	1.6	5.1	16.3	27.3	39.9
Bonds	36ab	....	....	....	....	....	....	....	....	....	....	....	....	....	....	....
Restricted Deposits	36b	1,709.0	1,737.0	1,561.0	1,879.0	2,159.0	2,402.0	2,144.0	2,496.0	3,661.0	‡3.8	2.0	.9	5.1	‡5.9	10.1
Long-Term Foreign Liabilities	36cl	39.0	95.0	337.0	682.0	980.0	1,333.0	1,959.0	2,595.0	2,798.0	‡3.3	4.5	5.2	6.7	‡9.3	11.4
Liabilities to Other Banking Insts	36i	....	....	....	....	....	....	....	....	....	....	....	....	....	....	....
Capital Accounts	37a	....	....	....	....	....	....	....	....	8,632.0	‡8.0	9.4	11.8	14.6	‡26.5	34.0
Other Items (Net)	37r	146.0	909.0	1,518.0	1,972.0	1,789.0	2,189.0	2,800.0	3,660.0	−6,012.9	‡−5.7	9.4	16.1	32.0	‡2.7	5.9
Money plus Quasi-Money	35l	11,827.0	13,046.0	15,785.0	18,074.0	22,092.0	25,778.0	29,190.0	37,710.0	50,897.0	‡63.7	78.5	105.1	140.7	‡180.0	221.0

Colombia

1980	1981	1982	1983	1984	1985	1986	1987	1988	1989	1990	1991	1992	1993	1994		
End of Period															**Exchange Rates**	
64.94	68.76	77.54	92.94	111.64	189.15	267.88	374.10	451.97	570.24	809.11	1,011.11	1,116.18	1,260.01	1,213.53	Principal Rate	aa
End of Period (ae) Period Average (rf)																
50.92	59.07	70.29	88.77	113.89	172.20	219.00	263.70	335.86	433.92	568.73	706.86	811.77	917.33	831.27	Principal Rate	ae
47.28	54.49	64.08	78.85	100.82	ɪ142.31	194.26	242.61	299.17	382.57	502.26	633.05	759.28	863.06	844.84	Principal Rate	rf
Period Averages																
1,061.6	921.7	784.2	639.2	499.1	356.3	258.3	206.4	167.7	131.2	100.0	79.2	65.6	57.9	59.2	Principal Rate	ah x
286.0	280.5	272.4	258.1	236.3	192.4	135.1	112.0	104.0	103.5	100.0	95.4	102.3	114.7	142.9	Nominal Effective Exchange Rate	ne c
200.9	216.1	230.4	229.4	210.1	183.3	136.6	121.8	117.4	113.2	100.0	103.5	112.9	118.5	132.6	Real Effective Exchange Rate	re c
End of Period															**Fund Position**	
290	290	290	394	394	394	394	394	394	394	394	394	561	561	561	Quota	2f. s
85	119	162	189	—	—	114	114	114	114	114	114	42	115	116	SDRs	1b. s
115	152	175	262	—	—	—	—	—	—	—	—	69	80	87	Reserve Position in the Fund	1c. s
—	—	—	—	—	—	—	—	—	—	—	—	—	—	—	Total Fund Cred.&Loans Outstg.	2tl
End of Period															**International Liquidity**	
4,831	4,741	3,861	1,901	1,364	1,595	2,696	3,086	3,248	3,616	4,212	6,029	7,389	7,552	7,750	Total Reserves minus Gold	1l. d
109	139	179	198	—	—	140	162	154	150	163	163	58	158	170	SDRs	1b. d
146	177	193	274	—	—	—	—	—	—	—	—	95	110	127	Reserve Position in the Fund	1c. d
4,576	4,425	3,489	1,429	1,364	1,595	2,556	2,924	3,094	3,466	4,049	5,866	7,236	7,285	7,453	Foreign Exchange	1d. d
2.787	3.366	3.817	4.223	1.367	1.842	2.009	.682	1.102	.614	.626	.863	.484	.302	.293	Gold (Million Fine Troy Ounces)	1ad
525	764	933	1,025ᵉ	426	597	698	290	468	249	248	323	172	....	....	Gold (National Valuation)	1an d
77	57	7	23	6	10	1	—	—	104	202	224	238	238	250	Monetary Authorities: Other Assets	3..d
302	321	334	348	345	607	776	694	580	829	860	870	800	602	383	Other Liab.	4..d
170	179	177	385	528	272	312	321	492	....	269	420	425	544	506	Deposit Money Banks: Assets	7a. d
80	100	121	136	143	145	155	147	172	....	4	19	10	12	20	of which: Claims on Nonbanks	7ad d
1,093	1,147	1,222	1,151	1,202	1,096	961	944	1,176	....	984	782	1,019	1,655	1,854	Deposit Money Banks: Liabilities	7b. d
435	466	539	530	608	....	....	....	....	....	1,201	1,338	1,785	2,271	3,182	Other Banking Insts.: Liabilities	7f. d
Billions of Pesos Beginning 1974: End of Period															**Monetary Authorities**	
259.3	308.0	314.8	242.6	145.4	360.5	987.9	1,182.9	1,212.8	ɪ1,735.1	2,664.8	4,286.3	5,941.7	6,597.2	6,928.5	Foreign Assets	11
13.1	13.7	46.7	106.8	252.3	310.9	410.6	466.7	526.2	ɪ538.5	574.5	798.0	827.3	757.3	867.9	Claims on Central Government	12a
.1	.1	-1.0	2.2	—	.3	47.9	97.7	130.2	ɪ221.3	263.6	9.2	9.7	9.3	—	Claims on Nonfin.Pub.Enterprises	12c
38.0	48.6	67.8	104.3	121.1	140.3	132.3	135.3	158.1	ɪ396.8	445.0	148.8	117.5	75.6	66.3	Claims on Deposit Money Banks	12e
27.3	30.0	34.3	53.3	84.4	94.9	126.1	130.3	171.3	ɪ244.9	182.4	260.3	267.9	312.3	335.2	Claims on Other Banking Insts.	12f
....	....	....	....	....	....	....	....	....	52.9	64.4	25.1	22.2	10.3	3.8	Claims on Nonbank Financial Insts	12g
192.4	239.1	281.2	333.4	411.9	483.6	581.5	848.9	1,017.6	ɪ1,694.4	2,077.3	2,647.5	3,619.3	4,530.3	5,721.7	Reserve Money	14
84.1	101.6	130.3	167.7	211.7	186.7	....	418.8	530.7	....	ɪ837.0	1,054.9	1,438.6	1,804.4	2,376.1	of which: Currency Outside DMBs	14a
....	....	....	....	....	....	....	....	....	279.9	303.9	22.9	28.9	32.1	50.0	Time, Savings,& Fgn.Currency Dep.	15
62.0	65.8	106.7	69.6	69.1	178.7	474.9	504.3	547.1	ɪ174.7	328.6	1,299.4	1,673.8	1,307.2	573.0	Money Market Instruments	16aa
12.8	12.0	10.0	25.6	35.9	54.1	62.0	84.5	125.3	ɪ128.5	157.7	.4	.4	.4	.4	Restricted Deposits	16b
.2	.1	.1	7.4	8.3	43.2	11.7	11.7	14.5	ɪ116.5	138.7	159.1	135.9	158.8	235.1	Foreign Liabilities	16c
15.2	18.8	23.4	23.5	31.0	61.4	158.2	171.4	180.2	ɪ231.7	334.9	391.2	454.2	324.7	82.7	Long-Term Foreign Liabilities	16cl
30.4	32.5	19.3	42.1	39.3	78.7	270.5	247.4	79.3	ɪ282.1	375.2	528.9	589.0	413.9	475.2	Central Government Deposits	16d
7.4	10.0	11.8	15.5	48.5	61.8	74.9	144.7	223.0	ɪ255.4	383.5	408.2	498.2	1,104.3	1,388.1	Capital Accounts	17a
17.5	21.9	10.0	-8.0	-40.7	-54.4	71.0	-.3	11.5	ɪ26.3	94.9	69.9	186.2	-109.7	-324.5	Other Items (Net)	17r
Billions of Pesos Beginning 1974: End of Period															**Deposit Money Banks**	
106.0	134.5	149.7	169.5	202.2	268.8	....	483.9	560.8	....	ɪ1,000.6	1,323.1	1,791.6	2,461.1	2,881.9	Reserves	20
8.4	10.3	12.2	28.1	50.9	44.7	....	83.7	166.7	....	ɪ148.0	265.6	313.6	437.3	419.7	Foreign Assets	21
15.5	22.6	30.2	40.6	62.0	52.5	....	79.5	101.0	....	ɪ138.2	98.3	158.1	337.8	484.0	Claims on Central Government	22a
....	....	....	....	....	....	....	....	....	....	146.5	240.7	233.0	347.3	878.5	Claims on Local Government	22b
1.1	2.8	3.4	10.9	13.5	16.8	....	38.3	40.3	....	ɪ69.8	59.2	50.0	8.1	49.2	Claims on Nonfin.Pub.Enterprises	22c
220.7	298.1	374.2	479.2	584.8	747.8	....	1,229.3	1,680.3	....	ɪ3,142.1	3,481.4	4,902.7	7,701.0	10,854.2	Claims on Private Sector	22d
15.0	18.6	22.3	26.3	28.7	34.5	....	61.4	68.5	....	ɪ155.9	351.4	581.2	560.7	158.1	Claims on Other Banking Insts.	22f
121.4	147.2	180.8	220.9	267.3	341.2	....	577.4	723.0	....	ɪ1,140.8	1,502.7	2,164.1	2,883.8	3,776.7	Demand Deposits	24
103.2	171.4	196.8	250.6	309.1	417.8	....	739.6	817.7	....	ɪ1,476.8	1,898.3	2,777.6	4,217.7	6,203.3	Time, Savings,& Fgn.Currency Dep.	25
....	....	....	....	....	....	....	....	....	....	193.8	246.0	191.5	221.5	290.0	Money Market Instruments	26aa
—	—	—	—	—	2.1	....	26.1	28.8	....	ɪ—	—	40.5	69.7	220.3	Bonds	26ab
....	....	....	....	....	....	....	....	....	....	147.1	34.6	8.2	5.8	5.5	Restricted Deposits	26b
55.2	67.4	85.7	102.0	136.8	188.7	....	249.0	394.9	....	ɪ463.4	444.9	745.3	1,283.3	1,448.5	Foreign Liabilities	26c
.2	.2	.1	.1	—	—	....	—	—	....	ɪ79.0	49.6	6.5	46.6	88.7	Long-Term Foreign Liabilities	26cl
1.3	1.5	2.5	2.8	3.2	3.8	....	6.8	8.7	....	ɪ230.4	374.4	589.8	816.7	738.4	Central Government Deposits	26d
36.7	47.0	68.4	101.2	119.1	148.2	....	173.3	273.2	....	ɪ416.4	207.5	138.5	119.6	115.8	Credit from Monetary Authorities	26g
....	....	....	....	....	....	....	....	....	....	374.5	730.1	999.2	1,463.1	1,862.3	Liabilities to Other Banking Insts	26i
40.3	52.4	66.3	71.9	75.9	21.9	....	75.4	155.3	....	ɪ508.9	696.1	1,076.4	1,719.5	2,580.1	Capital Accounts	27a
8.3	-.1	-8.7	30.7	41.4	....	....	128.6	216.1	....	ɪ-230.0	-364.7	-707.4	-994.0	-1,604.0	Other Items (Net)	27r
Billions of Pesos Beginning 1974: End of Period															**Monetary Survey**	
212.3	250.7	241.2	161.5	51.3	173.3	....	1,006.0	970.1	....	ɪ2,210.7	3,947.8	5,374.1	5,592.4	5,664.5	Foreign Assets (Net)	31n
266.5	364.6	498.5	686.3	996.5	1,218.3	....	1,890.7	2,695.4	....	ɪ4,137.7	4,424.0	5,877.4	8,819.7	13,339.3	Domestic Credit	32
-3.1	2.3	55.1	102.5	271.8	280.8	....	291.8	539.2	....	ɪ107.1	-7.0	-193.4	-135.5	138.3	Claims on Central Govt. (Net)	32an
....	....	....	....	....	....	....	....	....	....	146.5	240.7	233.0	347.3	878.5	Claims on Local Government	32b
1.2	2.9	2.4	13.1	13.5	17.1	....	136.0	170.5	....	ɪ333.4	68.4	59.7	17.4	49.2	Claims on Nonfin.Pub.Enterprises	32c
226.0	306.1	384.4	493.3	598.0	791.0	....	1,271.1	1,745.9	....	ɪ3,146.9	3,484.9	4,907.2	7,707.2	10,906.4	Claims on Private Sector	32d
42.3	48.6	56.6	79.7	113.1	129.4	....	191.7	239.8	....	ɪ338.3	611.7	849.1	873.0	493.3	Claims on Other Banking Insts.	32f
....	....	....	....	....	....	....	....	....	....	65.5	25.3	22.2	10.3	873.6	Claims on Nonbank Fin. Insts	32g
212.4	256.4	321.4	396.7	492.4	545.3	....	1,019.6	1,282.0	....	ɪ2,116.2	2,786.2	4,020.4	5,135.8	6,695.0	Money	34
108.1	178.4	204.2	262.5	324.4	436.8	....	795.7	916.4	....	ɪ1,780.7	1,921.2	2,806.5	4,249.8	6,253.3	Quasi-Money	35
62.0	70.0	106.7	69.6	69.1	180.8	....	530.4	575.9	....	ɪ522.4	1,545.4	1,865.3	1,528.7	863.0	Money Market Instruments	36aa
—	—	—	—	—	2.1	....	26.1	28.8	....	ɪ—	—	40.5	69.7	220.3	Bonds	36ab
12.8	12.0	10.0	25.6	35.9	54.1	....	84.5	125.3	....	ɪ304.8	35.0	8.6	6.2	5.9	Restricted Deposits	36b
15.4	19.0	23.5	23.6	31.0	61.4	....	171.4	180.2	....	ɪ413.9	440.8	460.7	371.3	171.4	Long-Term Foreign Liabilities	36cl
....	....	....	....	....	....	....	....	....	....	374.5	730.1	999.2	1,463.1	1,862.3	Liabilities to Other Banking Insts	36i
47.7	62.4	78.1	87.5	124.5	83.8	....	220.1	378.3	....	ɪ892.4	1,104.3	1,574.6	2,823.8	3,968.2	Capital Accounts	37a
20.4	17.1	-4.3	-17.6	-29.6	27.3	....	48.7	178.7	....	ɪ-56.5	-191.1	-523.9	-1,236.3	-1,035.5	Other Items (Net)	37r
320.5	434.7	525.6	659.2	816.8	982.1	....	1,815.3	2,198.4	....	ɪ3,896.9	4,707.4	6,826.9	9,385.6	12,948.3	Money plus Quasi-Money	35l

Colombia
233

		1965	1966	1967	1968	1969	1970	1971	1972	1973	1974	1975	1976	1977	1978	1979
Other Banking Institutions														*Millions of Pesos through 1973;*		
Reserves	40	276.0	284.0	528.0	884.0	1,379.0	....	....	....	....	I 13.1	4.5	6.0	8.8	11.6	13.9
Foreign Assets	41										I .3	.4	.5	.7	.6	.4
Claims on Central Government	42a										I .5	1.2	2.9	2.1	3.6	4.1
Claims on Local Government	42b															
Claims on Nonfin.Pub.Enterprises	42c										I .3	.4	.5	.5	.5	.5
Claims on Private Sector	42d	4,731.0	5,515.0	6,606.0	8,716.0	11,233.0					I 48.1	61.8	75.7	103.6	140.5	178.9
Claims on Deposit Money Banks	42e										I 2.8	3.5	5.2	6.8	8.9	12.4
Demand Deposits	44	487.0	537.0	638.0	817.0	1,094.0	733.0	798.0	1,030.0	1,450.0	I 1.8	2.4	3.1	4.2	4.7	6.8
Time, Savings,& Fgn.Currency Dep.	45	1,100.0	1,282.0	1,455.0	1,818.0	2,365.0					I 13.3	21.0	32.9	45.7	66.9	87.7
Money Market Instruments	46aa															
Bonds	46ab										I 11.5	12.0	12.8	8.4	16.6	25.0
Restricted Deposits	46b															
Foreign Liabilities	46c										I 1.6	1.8	1.7	2.6	4.3	5.9
Long-Term Foreign Liabilities	46cl										I 1.3	3.2	3.3	4.0	5.0	7.0
Central Government Deposits	46d										I .3	.4	.4	.3	.5	.5
Credit from Monetary Authorities	46g	947.0	1,056.0	1,371.0	1,657.0	2,113.0					I 11.8	13.6	13.6	21.1	28.5	25.2
Credit from Deposit Money Banks	46h	1,406.0	1,653.0	2,211.0	2,186.0	2,580.0					I 5.7	6.5	7.8	9.6	12.6	10.1
Capital Accounts	47a										I 6.2	6.7	11.0	14.4	19.9	26.1
Other Items (Net)	47r	1,067.0	1,271.0	1,459.0	3,122.0	4,460.0					I 11.9	4.2	4.2	12.2	6.6	16.1
Banking Survey														*Millions of Pesos through 1973;*		
Foreign Assets (Net)	51n	-830.0	-1,390.0	-1,310.0	-1,270.0	-1,200.0					I -5.6	-.2	19.0	52.3	78.7	138.5
Domestic Credit	52										I 104.6	134.1	164.7	217.7	276.4	324.3
Claims on Central Govt. (Net)	52an										I 9.0	11.6	10.9	21.1	21.2	-.7
Claims on Local Government	52b															
Claims on Nonfin.Pub.Enterprises	52c	6,820.0	8,254.0	9,922.0	12,104.0	14,175.0	17,582.0	21,516.0	25,095.0	334.0	I .6	.7	.7	.7	2.3	1.7
Claims on Private Sector	52d	12,481.0	15,605.0	18,226.0	22,846.0	28,613.0					I 95.5	120.7	152.2	195.9	252.9	323.3
Claims on Nonbank Fin. Inst.	52g															
Liquid Liabilities	55l	13,138.0	14,581.0	17,350.0	19,825.0	24,172.0					I 52.8	68.8	103.1	181.8	240.0	301.5
Money Market Instruments	56aa										I 12.5	13.6	17.9	24.7	43.9	64.9
Bonds	56ab														16.6	25.0
Restricted Deposits	56b	1,710.0	1,740.0	1,560.0	1,880.0	2,160.0	2,400.0	2,140.0	2,500.0	3,661.0	I 3.8	2.0	.1	5.1	5.9	10.1
Long-Term Foreign Liabilities	56cl										I 4.6	7.7	8.5	10.7	14.3	18.3
Capital Accounts	57a										I 14.2	16.0	15.4	29.0	46.3	60.1
Other Items (Net)	57r										I 11.0	25.7	38.7	18.7	-12.1	-17.2
Interest Rates														*Percent Per Annum*		
Discount Rate (End of Period)	60	8.0	8.0	8.0	8.0	8.0	14.0	14.0	14.0	14.0	16.0	16.0	20.0	20.0	22.0	30.0
Deposit Rate	60l															
Lending Rate	60p															
Prices, Production, Employment														*Index Numbers (1990=100):*		
Share Prices	62	6.9	6.3	6.7	7.7	8.9	9.9	8.5	7.1	7.7	7.6	6.7	8.3	11.7	17.3	22.5
Producer Prices	63	.9	1.0	1.1	1.2	1.2	I 1.3	1.5	1.8	2.3	3.1	3.9	4.7	6.0	7.1	9.0
Consumer Prices	64	1.1	1.3	1.4	1.5	1.6	1.8	I 1.9	2.2	2.6	3.3	4.0	4.8	6.4	7.6	9.5
Manufacturing Production	66ey															
Volume of Gold Produced	66kr	33.6	29.6	27.2	25.2	23.1	21.3	20.0	19.8	22.7	27.9	32.5	32.0	27.1	25.7	28.8
Crude Petroleum Production	66aa	45.4	44.8	43.2	39.6	48.2	49.9	49.0	44.7	41.8	38.3	35.7	33.3	31.3	29.8	28.2
Manufacturing Employment	67ey															
International Transactions														*Millions of US Dollars*		
Exports	70..d	537.8	506.5	509.9	558.5	607.4	726.7	686.0	807.5	1,168.6	1,508.6	1,465.0	1,873.8	2,403.4	3,009.8	3,410.6
Coffee	70e..d	343.9	339.2	322.4	351.5	343.9	466.9	399.7	430.4	597.9	624.8	674.5	977.4	1,525.7	1,993.9	2,024.3
Imports, cif	71..d	453.8	674.5	497.1	643.4	684.7	843.0	929.4	858.9	1,061.5	1,597.2	1,494.8	1,661.9	1,880.0	2,971.0	3,364.1
Imports, fob	71.vd	404.5	595.1	431.0	572.3	601.1	746.0	813.8	756.7	918.3	1,431.2	1,345.5	1,544.4	1,825.7	2,555.2	2,912.8
Volume of Exports															*1990=100*	
Coffee	72e	41	40	44	47	46	47	47	47	49	50	59	45	38	65	80
Export Prices in Pesos	76	1	1	1	1	1	2	2	2	3	4	5	7	12	10	11
Import Prices in Pesos	76.x						1	2	2	2	3	4	5	6	7	8
Export Prices															*1990=100:*	
Coffee	76e..d	54.4	53.2	47.0	47.8	50.4	63.6	55.0	62.5	81.5	87.3	91.5	175.8	271.0	207.7	205.7
Balance of Payments														*Millions of US Dollars:*		
Goods: Exports f.o.b.	78aad				605	672	788	754	979	1,263	1,495	1,683	2,202	2,660	3,155	3,441
Goods: Imports f.o.b.	78abd				-615	-648	-802	-903	-850	-983	-1,511	-1,415	-1,654	-1,970	-2,552	-2,978
Trade Balance	78acd				-10	24	-14	-148	129	280	-17	268	548	690	603	463
Services: Credit	78add				158	178	192	218	226	281	366	431	568	730	780	1,105
Services: Debit	78aed				-243	-283	-334	-382	-383	-440	-566	-597	-647	-773	-857	-941
Balance on Goods and Services	78afd				-95	-81	-156	-313	-28	121	-217	102	468	647	526	627
Income: Credit	78agd				24	30	39	25	21	44	88	66	80	112	164	305
Income: Debit	78ahd				-124	-162	-212	-200	-222	-255	-273	-388	-437	-430	-505	-596
Balance on Goods, Serv., & Inc.	78aid				-195	-213	-329	-488	-226	-89	-403	-220	112	329	185	336
Current Transfers, n.i.e.: Credit	78ajd				38	57	50	46	46	45	61	80	83	84	109	114
Current Transfers: Debit	78akd				-7	-19	-14	-12	-11	-11	-10	-32	-32	-38	-36	-12
Current Account, n.i.e.	78ald				-164	-175	-293	-454	-191	-55	-352	-172	163	375	258	438
Capital Account, n.i.e.: Credit	78bad				—	—	—	—	—	—	—	—	—	—	—	—
Capital Account: Debit	78bbd				—	—	—	—	—	—	—	—	—	—	—	—
Capital Account, n.i.e.	78bcd				—	—	—	—	—	—	—	—	—	—	—	—
Direct Investment Abroad	78bdd				-2	-4	-4	-3	-1	-1	-6	-4	-11	-22	-41	-24
Dir. Invest. in Rep. Econ., n.i.e.	78bed				50	54	43	43	18	24	41	37	25	65	107	127
Portfolio Investment Assets	78bfd															
Portfolio Investment Liab., n.i.e.	78bgd				-4	-3	-2	-6	-1	42	-4	-2	-2	-3	-2	-11
Other Investment Assets	78bhd				-22	-1	-32	-19	-52	-57	-238	-7	—	-9	-244	80
Other Investment Liab., n.i.e.	78bid				195	229	322	331	282	139	479	92	185	-56	255	788
Financial Account, n.i.e.	78bjd				217	275	327	346	246	146	272	116	196	-25	75	960
Net Errors and Omissions	78cad				12	-45	-18	90	106	70	-14	118	255	298	236	98
Overall Balance	78cbd				65	55	16	-18	160	161	-94	62	614	648	569	1,496
Reserves and Related Items	79dad				-65	-55	-16	18	-160	-161	94	-62	-614	-648	-569	-1,496
Reserve Assets	79dbd				-86	-49	33	20	-107	-166	88	-59	-621	-649	-596	-1,513
Use of Fund Credit and Loans	79dcd				21	-6	-51	-2	-58	—	—	—	—	—	—	—
Liabs.Constit.For.Auth.Reserves	79ddd				—	—	2	—	4	5	6	-4	7	1	27	17
Exceptional Financing	79ded															

Colombia
233

1980	1981	1982	1983	1984	1985	1986	1987	1988	1989	1990	1991	1992	1993	1994		
Billions of Pesos Beginning 1974: End of Period															**Other Banking Institutions**	
19.3	28.1	33.3	29.1	43.0	....	....	....	....	....	I237.2	240.7	513.4	548.5	762.1	Reserves	40
1.0	.8	2.4	3.3	4.3	....	....	....	....	....	I8.7	68.3	53.7	120.0	140.6	Foreign Assets	41
7.0	9.0	11.3	28.1	34.2	....	....	....	....	....	I114.4	105.0	172.7	202.0	401.4	Claims on Central Government	42a
....	....	....	....	....	....	....	....	....	....	1.6	11.2	13.1	30.8	782.1	Claims on Local Government	42b
1.1	1.4	1.9	2.5	3.3	4.9	....	....	....	....	I452.6	945.1	1,191.3	1,329.9	666.0	Claims on Nonfin.Pub.Enterprises	42c
255.0	344.8	469.0	628.5	841.3	....	....	....	....	....	I3,079.5	3,803.4	5,122.1	7,623.3	11,668.9	Claims on Private Sector	42d
15.4	21.1	25.2	30.3	37.5	....	....	89.4	124.0	....	I80.7	799.4	1,234.2	1,560.4	2,319.0	Claims on Deposit Money Banks	42e
8.7	10.6	14.6	20.2	24.4	33.1	41.5	53.2	64.8	....	I4.7	4.3	6.8	—	1.7	Demand Deposits	44
137.2	198.2	267.0	360.0	445.5	....	....	....	....	....	I2,357.8	3,266.9	4,360.4	6,064.6	10,063.1	Time, Savings,& Fgn.Currency Dep.	45
....	....	....	....	....	....	....	....	....	....	9.9	20.3	16.3	15.2	94.1	Money Market Instruments	46aa
32.6	44.9	49.9	58.5	74.0	....	....	135.0	78.0	....	I272.6	652.1	625.3	869.0	1,035.8	Bonds	46ab
....	....	....	....	....	....	....	....	....	....	17.5	3.8	28.4	7.6	7.8	Restricted Deposits	46b
11.1	14.3	19.3	22.7	18.2	....	....	....	....	....	I175.2	125.9	387.6	741.6	1,467.9	Foreign Liabilities	46c
11.0	13.3	18.6	24.3	51.0	....	....	—	....	....	I486.5	720.1	929.4	1,083.3	1,171.0	Long-Term Foreign Liabilities	46cl
.1	—	—	—	—	....	....	....	....	....	I96.1	215.0	215.5	261.5	426.7	Central Government Deposits	46d
23.9	31.5	40.8	63.3	102.4	....	....	....	....	....	I140.6	203.7	215.5	250.2	287.6	Credit from Monetary Authorities	46g
11.3	13.4	23.9	29.1	33.4	....	....	....	....	....	I39.6	340.4	437.4	628.0	1,103.6	Credit from Deposit Money Banks	46h
36.6	47.4	72.4	88.8	112.0	....	....	....	....	....	I489.6	1,073.6	1,544.8	1,985.7	2,932.3	Capital Accounts	47a
26.0	31.7	36.7	55.0	102.7	....	....	....	....	....	I–115.4	–653.0	–466.9	–491.8	–1,851.5	Other Items (Net)	47r
Billions of Pesos Beginning 1974: End of Period															**Banking Survey**	
202.1	237.2	224.3	142.0	37.3	....	....	....	....	....	I2,044.2	3,890.3	5,040.2	4,970.8	4,337.3	Foreign Assets (Net)	51n
487.1	666.3	924.1	1,285.4	1,762.3	....	....	....	....	....	I7,351.6	8,462.0	11,312.4	16,871.2	26,046.3	Domestic Credit	52
3.7	11.3	66.3	130.6	306.1	....	....	....	....	....	I125.4	–117.0	–236.2	–195.0	113.0	Claims on Central Govt. (Net)	52an
....	....	....	....	....	....	....	....	....	....	148.1	251.9	246.1	378.1	1,660.6	Claims on Local Government	52b
2.3	4.2	4.3	15.6	16.8	22.0	....	....	....	....	I786.0	1,013.5	1,251.0	1,347.3	715.2	Claims on Nonfin.Pub.Enterprises	52c
481.1	650.9	853.4	1,121.9	1,439.4	....	....	....	....	....	I6,226.4	7,288.3	10,029.3	15,330.5	22,575.3	Claims on Private Sector	52d
....	....	....	....	....	....	....	....	....	....	65.7	25.3	22.2	10.3	982.2	Claims on Nonbank Fin. Inst.	52g
447.2	615.3	773.9	1,010.3	1,243.7	....	....	....	....	....	I6,022.2	7,737.9	10,680.7	14,901.7	22,251.0	Liquid Liabilities	55l
94.6	114.9	156.6	128.1	143.0	....	....	....	....	....	I532.3	1,565.7	1,881.6	1,543.9	957.1	Money Market Instruments	56aa
32.6	44.9	49.9	58.5	74.0	....	....	161.1	106.7	....	I272.6	652.1	665.8	938.7	1,256.1	Bonds	56ab
12.8	12.0	10.0	25.6	35.9	54.1	62.0	84.5	125.3	....	I322.3	38.8	37.0	13.8	13.7	Restricted Deposits	56b
26.5	32.3	42.1	47.9	82.0	....	....	....	....	....	I900.4	1,160.9	1,390.1	1,454.6	1,342.4	Long-Term Foreign Liabilities	56cl
84.3	109.8	150.5	176.3	236.5	....	....	....	....	....	I1,382.0	2,177.9	3,119.4	4,809.5	6,900.5	Capital Accounts	57a
–8.7	–25.7	–34.5	–19.2	–15.6	....	....	....	....	....	I–36.0	–981.0	–1,422.0	–1,820.2	–2,337.2	Other Items (Net)	57r
Percent Per Annum															**Interest Rates**	
30.0	30.0	27.0	27.0	27.0	27.0	I33.8	34.8	34.3	36.9	I46.5	45.0	34.4	33.5	44.9	Discount Rate *(End of Period)*	60
....	....	....	....	....	....	31.4	30.8	33.5	33.7	36.4	37.2	26.7	25.8	29.4	Deposit Rate	60l
....	....	....	....	....	....	40.8	41.1	42.7	43.0	45.2	47.1	37.3	35.8	40.5	Lending Rate	60p
Period Averages															**Prices, Production, Employment**	
19.4	22.8	33.9	25.3	20.6	19.0	28.9	54.7	73.7	81.0	100.0	13.6	41.6	46.7	85.2	Share Prices	62
11.2	13.9	17.5	21.3	25.2	31.5	I38.4	48.1	61.6	79.0	100.0	I127.6	153.3	....	....	Producer Prices	63
12.0	15.3	19.0	22.7	26.4	32.8	39.0	48.0	I61.5	77.4	100.0	130.4	165.6	203.1	251.5	Consumer Prices	64
74.4	67.5	70.0	69.7	76.6	78.7	84.2	90.2	93.5	95.1	100.0	....	....	....	....	Manufacturing Production	66ey
52.4	54.4	48.4	45.4	77.0	120.4	134.8	89.9	98.3	100.0	100.0	117.6	108.8	92.8	....	Volume of Gold Produced	66kr
28.6	30.5	32.3	33.8	37.9	40.1	69.0	87.6	85.5	92.0	100.0	96.8	100.0	103.0	....	Crude Petroleum Production	66aa
112.5	107.4	101.9	95.0	94.0	92.6	92.6	95.4	98.4	99.1	I100.0	....	....	....	....	Manufacturing Employment	67ey
Millions of US Dollars															**International Transactions**	
3,924.3	2,916.3	3,023.6	3,000.6	3,461.6	3,551.6	5,101.6	4,642.2	5,037.0	5,716.5	6,765.8	7,232.1	6,916.5	7,115.7	8,398.6	Exports	70..*d*
2,375.2	1,458.8	1,577.4	1,536.6	1,798.8	1,784.0	3,046.0	1,688.5	1,646.1	1,583.5	1,472.9	1,398.4	1,321.3	....	....	Coffee	70e.*d*
4,738.6	5,200.8	5,479.8	4,963.4	4,497.5	4,140.9	3,861.5	4,321.9	5,001.8	5,004.1	5,589.5	4,906.1	6,516.4	9,831.5	11,882.9	Imports, cif	71..*d*
4,200.5	4,685.4	4,936.8	4,471.6	4,052.1	3,731.5	3,564.0	3,907.2	4,531.6	4,573.3	5,144.9	4,568.6	5,980.4	....	....	Imports, fob	71.v*d*
1990=100															Volume of Exports	
80	65	64	66	73	72	82	81	70	78	100	90	119	....	....	Coffee	72e
14	14	17	20	28	37	I57	54	70	73	100	117	118	....	....	Export Prices in Pesos	76
10	12	14	17	22	30	I38	47	60	79	100	121	130	....	....	Import Prices in Pesos	76.x
Indices of Prices in US Dollars															Export Prices	
200.6	143.7	156.7	147.7	161.8	163.3	218.2	126.0	151.5	120.0	100.0	95.3	71.4	....	....	Coffee	76e.*d*
Minus Sign Indicates Debit															Balance of Payments	
3,986	3,158	3,114	2,970	4,273	3,650	5,331	5,661	5,343	6,031	7,079	7,507	7,263	....	....	Goods: Exports f.o.b.	78aa*d*
–4,283	–4,730	–5,358	–4,464	–4,027	–3,673	–3,409	–3,793	–4,516	–4,557	–5,108	–4,548	–6,030	....	....	Goods: Imports f.o.b.	78ab*d*
–297	–1,572	–2,244	–1,494	246	–23	1,922	1,868	827	1,474	1,971	2,959	1,233	....	....	Trade Balance	78ac*d*
1,342	1,148	1,335	844	927	855	1,108	1,166	1,408	1,291	1,600	1,594	1,978	....	....	Services: Credit	78ad*d*
–1,170	–1,295	–1,346	–1,302	–1,298	–1,427	–1,684	–1,709	–1,670	–1,565	–1,750	–1,812	–2,037	....	....	Services: Debit	78ae*d*
–126	–1,719	–2,255	–1,952	–125	–595	1,346	1,325	565	1,200	1,821	2,741	1,174	....	....	Balance on Goods and Services	78af*d*
532	708	525	289	128	111	175	202	257	287	347	390	454	....	....	Income: Credit	78ag*d*
–777	–1,192	–1,494	–1,504	–1,703	–1,786	–1,923	–2,192	–2,002	–2,586	–2,652	–2,480	–2,450	....	....	Income: Debit	78ah*d*
–371	–2,203	–3,223	–3,167	–1,700	–2,270	–402	–665	–1,180	–1,099	–484	651	–822	....	....	Balance on Goods, Serv., & Inc.	78ai*d*
178	257	187	186	316	479	801	1,022	994	928	1,043	1,743	1,871	....	....	Current Transfers, n.i.e.: Credit	78aj*d*
–13	–15	–17	–22	–17	–18	–16	–21	–30	–30	–17	–45	–137	....	....	Current Transfers: Debit	78ak*d*
–206	–1,961	–3,054	–3,003	–1,401	–1,809	383	336	–216	–201	542	2,349	912	....	....	Current Account, n.i.e.	78al*d*
—	—	—	—	—	—	—	—	—	—	—	—	—	....	....	Capital Account, n.i.e.: Credit	78ba*d*
—	—	—	—	—	—	—	—	—	—	—	—	—	....	....	Capital Account: Debit	78bb*d*
—	—	—	—	—	—	—	—	—	—	—	—	—	....	....	Capital Account, n.i.e.	78bc*d*
–106	–37	–29	–104	–23	–7	–32	–26	–44	–29	–16	–24	–50	....	....	Direct Investment Abroad	78bd*d*
157	265	366	618	584	1,023	674	319	203	576	500	457	790	....	....	Dir. Invest. in Rep. Econ., n.i.e.	78be*d*
—	—	—	—	—	—	—	—	—	—	—	—	—	....	....	Portfolio Investment Assets	78bf*d*
–3	–2	–7	–2	–3	–1	30	48		179	–4	81	60	....	....	Portfolio Investment Liab., n.i.e.	78bg*d*
–303	–33	–42	–360	–562	–111	–217	–295	–315	–95	–102	–522	–647	....	....	Other Investment Assets	78bh*d*
1,210	1,807	1,969	1,277	944	1,333	709	–58	1,096	–224	–352	–777	130	....	....	Other Investment Liab., n.i.e.	78bi*d*
956	2,000	2,256	1,429	940	2,237	1,164	–12	940	407	26	–785	283	....	....	Financial Account, n.i.e.	78bj*d*
168	–99	–52	–270	76	–273	–251	67	–530	157	70	269	14	....	....	Net Errors and Omissions	78ca*d*
919	–60	–850	–1,845	–385	155	1,296	391	194	363	638	1,834	1,209	....	....	Overall Balance	78cb*d*
–919	60	850	1,845	385	–155	–1,296	–391	–194	–363	–638	–1,834	–1,209	....	....	Reserves and Related Items	79da*d*
–908	21	874	1,839	381	–154	–1,292	–402	–193	–434	–610	–1,836	–1,092	....	....	Reserve Assets	79db*d*
—	—	—	—	—	—	—	—	—	—	—	—	—	....	....	Use of Fund Credit and Loans	79dc*d*
–11	39	–24	5	4	–1	–4	11	–1	71	–28	2	–117	....	....	Liabs.Constit.For.Auth.Reserves	79dd*d*
—	—	—	—	—	—	—	—	—	—	—	—	—	....	....	Exceptional Financing	79de*d*

Colombia
233

		1965	1966	1967	1968	1969	1970	1971	1972	1973	1974	1975	1976	1977	1978	1979
Government Finance														*Millions of Pesos through 1973;*		
Deficit (-) or Surplus	80	−392.0	55.0	−231.0	−574.0	−824.0	−1,140.0	ⅼ−2526.0	−4,701.0	−5,578.0	ⅼ−4.1	−.9	5.3	4.5	6.2	−9.2
Revenue and Grants	81	3,948.0	6,028.0	6,688.0	8,194.0	9,581.0	11,950.0	ⅼ17262.0	20,069.0	25,209.0	ⅼ34.2	51.3	63.6	84.1	110.9	139.0
Revenue	81y	....	....	....	....	....	....	ⅼ17171.0	19,649.0	25,070.0	ⅼ32.5	48.2	61.7	82.3	106.4	138.8
Grants	81z	....	....	....	....	....	....	ⅼ91.0	420.0	139.0	ⅼ1.8	3.1	1.8	1.8	4.5	.2
Exp. & Lending Minus Repay.	82z	4,340.0	5,973.0	6,919.0	8,768.0	10,405.0	13,090.0	ⅼ19788.0	24,770.0	30,787.0	ⅼ38.3	52.2	58.2	79.6	104.8	148.2
Expenditure	82							ⅼ19187.0	24,169.0	29,991.0	ⅼ38.0	50.7	57.3	81.1	106.9	143.8
Lending Minus Repayments	83	....	....	....	....	....	....	ⅼ601.0	601.0	796.0	ⅼ.3	1.5	.9	−1.5	−2.2	4.4
Financing																
Net Borrowing: Domestic	84a	548.0	34.0	−205.0	−456.0	−368.0	16.0	ⅼ667.0	547.0	1,210.0	ⅼ3.5	1.5	−4.3	−3.2	−4.1	....
Foreign	85a	−95.0	79.0	367.0	1,063.0	1,273.0	1,458.0	ⅼ1,859.0	4,154.0	4,368.0	ⅼ.6	−.5	−1.0	−1.3	−2.1	....
Use of Cash Balances	87	−59.0	−166.0	69.0	−31.0	−83.0	−333.0									
Debt: Pesos	88b	5,141.0	6,524.0	6,929.0	7,551.0	8,890.0	9,776.0	10,012.0	12,086.0	13,435.0	ⅼ14.6	17.8	20.2	19.5	18.6	23.1
Foreign Currency	89b	3,073.0	3,503.0	5,029.0	6,249.0	9,282.0	12,282.0	16,478.0	21,119.0	26,180.0	ⅼ27.8	34.9	40.2	45.9	49.5	76.6
National Accounts														*Millions of Pesos through 1973;*		
Exports of Goods & Services	90c	6,943	8,916	9,950	12,519	14,675	ⅼ17,620	18,650	25,130	36,290	ⅼ47	64	91	121	151	181
Government Consumption	91f	3,954	4,910	5,717	6,580	7,833	ⅼ12,280	17,100	18,140	23,010	ⅼ28	36	44	55	78	111
Gross Fixed Capital Formation	93e	9,504	12,304	14,729	18,815	21,230	ⅼ24,000	28,000	31,000	38,000	ⅼ53	62	85	104	140	183
Increase/Decrease(-) in Stocks	93i	1,238	2,737	612	1,591	1,485	ⅼ2,940	2,960	3,890	6,010	ⅼ16	7	9	30	26	32
Private Consumption	96f	45,482	55,843	61,596	70,696	81,677	ⅼ95,330	114,840	136,230	170,230	ⅼ229	293	378	500	640	841
Imports of Goods & Services	98c	−6,324	−11,098	−9,521	−13,779	−15,947	ⅼ−19,320	−24,970	−24,270	−30,790	ⅼ−50	−57	−74	−95	−126	−160
Gross Domestic Product	99b	60,797	73,612	83,083	96,421	110,953	ⅼ132,770	155,890	189,610	243,160	ⅼ322	405	532	716	909	1,189
Net Factor Inc/Pmts(-) Abroad	98.n	−898	−1,243	−1,471	−2,002	−2,676	−2,830	−2,820	−3,600	−4,480	ⅼ−4	−7	−9	−8	−8	−7
Gross Nat'l Expenditure = GNP	99a	59,899	72,369	81,612	94,419	108,277	ⅼ129,940	153,070	186,010	238,680	ⅼ319	399	523	708	902	1,182
GDP 1990 Prices *(Billions)*	99b,p	....	....	....	7,463	7,937	ⅼ8,460	8,964	9,651	10,300	10,892	11,145	11,672	12,158	13,187	13,897
GDP Deflator (1990=100)	99bi p	....	....	....	1.3	1.4	1.6	1.7	2.0	2.4	3.0	3.6	4.6	5.9	6.9	8.6
																Millions:
Population	99z	18.04	18.47	18.96	19.46	19.98	20.53	21.09	21.67	22.34	22.98	23.64	24.33	ⅼ24.23	24.91	25.38

Monetary Authorities: ⅼ Beginning in 1978, the financial funds (for the financing of agriculture, industry, housing, etc.) are considered as part of the Bank of the Republic in the treatment of the accounts of these funds with commercial and specialized banks. ⅼ Beginning in 1989, data reflect the introduction of a new system of accounts, which provides an improved sectorization of the balance sheet.

Deposit Money Banks: ⅼ See note to section 10. Beginning in 1978, data exclude the accounts of the Agricultural Bank (Caja de Crédito Agrario, Industrial y Minero). ⅼ Beginning in December 1990, includes the Agricultural Bank and Social Savings Bank. Data reflect the introduction of a new system of accounts, which provides an improved sectorization of the balance sheet.

Monetary Survey: ⅼ See note to section 10.

Other Banking Institutions: ⅼ Beginning in 1974, data cover a wider range of institutions. ⅼ Beginning in December 1990, includes commercial financing companies and financial cooperative institutions and excludes the Agricultural Bank and Social Savings Bank. Data reflect the introduction of a new system of accounts, which provides an improved sectorization of the balance sheet. Beginning in December 1991, includes the Banco de Comercio Exterior (BANCOLDEX), Fondo para el Financiamiento del Sector Agropecuario (FINAGRO), and Financiera de Desarrollo Territorial (FINDETER).

Banking Survey: ⅼ See note to section 10.

Interest Rates: *Discount Rate (End of Period):* ⅼ Beginning in September 1986, corresponds to DTF (see note for deposit rate in monthly issue of *IFS*) plus two points. ⅼ Beginning in October 1990, corresponds to DTF plus eight points.

Government Finance: ⅼ Beginning in 1971, annual data are as reported in the *Government Finance Statistics Yearbook* and cover consolidated central government (including all social security funds and most extrabudgetary funds). ⅼ Beginning in 1988, extrabudgetary accounts include six funds and agencies only.

Colombia

1980	1981	1982	1983	1984	1985	1986	1987	1988	1989	1990	1991	1992	1993	1994		
Billions of Pesos Beginning 1974: Year Ending December 31															**Government Finance**	
−27.7	−60.4	−118.0	−127.9	−166.5	−134.7	−58.6	−61.0	ⅼ−156.3	−286.7	....	....	....	....	....	Deficit (-) or Surplus	80
189.6	229.4	283.5	348.0	428.7	597.0	876.2	1,150.9	ⅼ1,507.7	1,945.8	....	....	....	....	....	Revenue and Grants	81
189.2	229.1	283.3	347.6	428.2	597.0	852.8	1,148.7	ⅼ1,494.3	1,919.0	....	....	....	....	....	Revenue	81y
.3	.3	.2	.4	.5	—	23.4	2.2	ⅼ13.4	26.8	....	....	....	....	....	Grants	81z
217.3	289.8	401.5	475.9	595.2	731.7	934.8	1,211.9	ⅼ1,664.0	2,232.5	....	....	....	....	....	Exp. & Lending Minus Repay.	82z
211.2	277.2	399.7	465.3	584.5	698.0	923.5	1,209.4	ⅼ1,607.6	2,158.4	....	....	....	....	....	Expenditure	82
6.1	12.6	1.8	10.6	10.7	33.7	11.3	2.5	ⅼ56.4	74.1	....	....	....	....	....	Lending Minus Repayments	83
															Financing	
....	....	....	....	....	....	....	....	ⅼ48.0	160.4	....	....	....	....	....	Net Borrowing: Domestic	84a
....	....	....	....	....	....	....	....	ⅼ108.3	126.3	....	....	....	....	....	Foreign	85a
....	....	....	....	....	....	....	....	ⅼ—	—	....	....	....	....	....	Use of Cash Balances	87
27.7	28.0	37.7	104.2	287.7	455.0	595.1	700.3	....	....	....	....	....	....	....	Debt: Pesos	88b
106.4	129.7	162.9	....	....	....	....	....	....	....	....	....	....	....	....	Foreign Currency	89b
Billions of Pesos Beginning 1974															**National Accounts**	
256	235	273	319	458	686	1,279	1,496	1,911	2,723	4,160	5,572	5,883	7,255	....	Exports of Goods & Services	90c
159	207	273	335	426	531	666	868	1,183	1,597	2,076	2,685	3,656	5,039	....	Government Consumption	91f
265	350	436	525	654	870	1,204	1,537	2,288	2,733	3,365	3,810	5,214	8,027	....	Gross Fixed Capital Formation	93e
36	59	76	83	77	75	18	227	292	288	387	354	493	557	....	Increase/Decrease(-) in Stocks	93i
1,109	1,438	1,820	2,197	2,722	3,425	4,436	5,835	7,684	9,876	13,239	17,317	23,171	29,958	....	Private Consumption	96f
−246	−306	−379	−404	−481	−622	−814	−1,140	−1,626	−2,090	−2,998	−3,631	−5,274	−8,904	....	Imports of Goods & Services	98c
1,579	1,983	2,497	3,054	3,857	4,966	6,788	8,824	11,731	15,127	20,228	26,107	33,144	41,932	....	Gross Domestic Product	99b
−6	−11	−51	−76	−128	−206	−302	−430	−484	−766	−1,075	−1,229	−1,282	—	....	Net Factor Inc/Pmts(-) Abroad	98.n
1,573	1,972	2,447	2,978	3,728	4,760	6,486	8,395	11,248	14,360	19,153	24,878	31,861	41,932	....	Gross Nat'l Expenditure = GNP	99a
14,465	14,794	14,934	15,169	15,678	16,165	17,106	18,024	18,757	19,398	20,228	20,634	21,423	22,554	....	GDP 1990 Prices *(Billions)*	99b.*p*
10.9	13.4	16.7	20.1	24.6	30.7	39.7	49.0	62.5	78.0	100.0	126.5	154.7	185.9	....	GDP Deflator (1990=100)	99bi*p*
Midyear Estimates																
25.89	26.43	26.97	27.50	28.06	28.62	29.19	29.73	30.24	31.74	32.30	32.84	33.39	33.95	34.52	**Population**	99z

Comoros
632

		1965	1966	1967	1968	1969	1970	1971	1972	1973	1974	1975	1976	1977	1978	1979
Exchange Rates																*Francs per SDR:*
Official Rate	aa	245.07	247.59	245.42	247.40	277.91	276.02	283.61	277.99	284.00	272.08	262.55	288.70	285.76	272.28	264.78
																Francs per US Dollar:
Official Rate	ae	245.07	247.59	245.42	247.40	277.91	276.02	261.22	256.05	235.42	222.22	224.27	248.48	235.25	209.00	201.00
Official Rate	rf	245.06	245.68	246.00	247.57	259.96	276.40	275.59	252.03	222.89	240.71	214.31	238.95	245.68	225.66	212.72
Fund Position																*Millions of SDRs:*
Quota	2f. s	....	....	....	....	....	....	....	....	....	....	....	1.90	1.90	2.30	2.30
SDRs	1b. s	....	....	....	....	....	....	....	....	....	....	....	—	—	—	.24
Reserve Position in the Fund	1c. s	....	....	....	....	....	....	....	....	....	....	....	—	—	—	—
Total Fund Cred.&Loans Outstg.	2tl	....	....	....	....	....	....	....	....	....	....	....	—	—	—	—
International Liquidity												*Millions of US Dollars Unless Otherwise Indicated:*				
Total Reserves minus Gold	1l. d	....	....	....	....	....	....	....	....	....	....	....	....	....	....	....
SDRs	1b. d	....	....	....	....	....	....	....	....	....	....	....	—	—	—	.32
Reserve Position in the Fund	1c. d	....	....	....	....	....	....	....	....	....	....	....	—	—	—	—
Foreign Exchange	1d. d	....	....	....	....	....	....	....	....	....	....	....	....	....	....	....
Gold (Million Fine Troy Ounces)	1ad	....	....	....	....	....	....	....	....	....	....	....	....	....	....	....
Gold (National Valuation)	1an d	....	....	....	....	....	....	....	....	....	....	....	....	....	....	....
Deposit Money Banks: Assets	7a. d	....	....	....	....	....	....	....	....	....	....	....	....	....	....	....
Liabilities	7b. d	....	....	....	....	....	....	....	....	....	....	....	....	....	....	....
Monetary Authorities																*Millions of Francs:*
Foreign Assets	11	....	....	....	....	....	....	....	....	....	....	....	....	....	....	....
Claims on Central Government	12a	....	....	....	....	....	....	....	....	....	....	....	....	....	....	....
Reserve Money	14	....	....	....	....	....	....	....	....	....	....	....	....	....	....	....
of which: Currency Outside DMBs	14a	....	....	....	....	....	....	....	....	....	....	....	....	....	....	....
Foreign Liabilities	16c	....	....	....	....	....	....	....	....	....	....	....	....	....	....	....
Central Government Deposits	16d	....	....	....	....	....	....	....	....	....	....	....	....	....	....	....
Capital Accounts	17a	....	....	....	....	....	....	....	....	....	....	....	....	....	....	....
Other Items (Net)	17r	....	....	....	....	....	....	....	....	....	....	....	....	....	....	....
Deposit Money Banks																*Millions of Francs:*
Reserves	20	....	....	....	....	....	....	....	....	....	....	....	....	....	....	....
Foreign Assets	21	....	....	....	....	....	....	....	....	....	....	....	....	....	....	....
Claims on Central Government	22a	....	....	....	....	....	....	....	....	....	....	....	....	....	....	....
Claims on Private Sector	22d	....	....	....	....	....	....	....	....	....	....	....	....	....	....	....
Demand Deposits	24	....	....	....	....	....	....	....	....	....	....	....	....	....	....	....
Time and Savings Deposits	25	....	....	....	....	....	....	....	....	....	....	....	....	....	....	....
Foreign Liabilities	26c	....	....	....	....	....	....	....	....	....	....	....	....	....	....	....
Central Government Deposits	26d	....	....	....	....	....	....	....	....	....	....	....	....	....	....	....
Credit From Monetary Authorities	26g	....	....	....	....	....	....	....	....	....	....	....	....	....	....	....
Capital Accounts	27a	....	....	....	....	....	....	....	....	....	....	....	....	....	....	....
Other Items (Net)	27r	....	....	....	....	....	....	....	....	....	....	....	....	....	....	....
Monetary Survey																*Millions of Francs:*
Foreign Assets (Net)	31n	....	....	....	....	....	....	....	....	....	....	....	....	....	....	....
Domestic Credit	32	....	....	....	....	....	....	....	....	....	....	....	....	....	....	....
Claims on Central Govt. (Net)	32an	....	....	....	....	....	....	....	....	....	....	....	....	....	....	....
Claims on Private Sector	32d	....	....	....	....	....	....	....	....	....	....	....	....	....	....	....
Money	34	....	....	....	....	....	....	....	....	....	....	....	....	....	....	....
Quasi-Money	35	....	....	....	....	....	....	....	....	....	....	....	....	....	....	....
Other Items (Net)	37r	....	....	....	....	....	....	....	....	....	....	....	....	....	....	....
Money plus Quasi-Money	35l	....	....	....	....	....	....	....	....	....	....	....	....	....	....	....
Other Banking Institutions																*Millions of Francs:*
Reserves	40	....	....	....	....	....	....	....	....	....	....	....	....	....	....	....
Claims on Central Government	42a	....	....	....	....	....	....	....	....	....	....	....	....	....	....	....
Claims on Private Sector	42d	....	....	....	....	....	....	....	....	....	....	....	....	....	....	....
Time Deposits	45	....	....	....	....	....	....	....	....	....	....	....	....	....	....	....
Central Government Deposits	46d	....	....	....	....	....	....	....	....	....	....	....	....	....	....	....
Long-Term Foreign Liabilities	46cl	....	....	....	....	....	....	....	....	....	....	....	....	....	....	....
Central Govt. Lending Funds	46f	....	....	....	....	....	....	....	....	....	....	....	....	....	....	....
Other Items (Net)	47r	....	....	....	....	....	....	....	....	....	....	....	....	....	....	....
Banking Survey																*Millions of Francs:*
Foreign Assets (Net)	51n	....	....	....	....	....	....	....	....	....	....	....	....	....	....	....
Domestic Credit	52	....	....	....	....	....	....	....	....	....	....	....	....	....	....	....
Claims on Central Govt. (Net)	52an	....	....	....	....	....	....	....	....	....	....	....	....	....	....	....
Claims on Private Sector	52d	....	....	....	....	....	....	....	....	....	....	....	....	....	....	....
Liquid Liabilities	55l	....	....	....	....	....	....	....	....	....	....	....	....	....	....	....
Money	54	....	....	....	....	....	....	....	....	....	....	....	....	....	....	....
Quasi-Money	55	....	....	....	....	....	....	....	....	....	....	....	....	....	....	....
Central Govt. Lending Funds	56f	....	....	....	....	....	....	....	....	....	....	....	....	....	....	....
Other Items (Net)	57r	....	....	....	....	....	....	....	....	....	....	....	....	....	....	....

Comoros

632

	1980	1981	1982	1983	1984	1985	1986	1987	1988	1989	1990	1991	1992	1993	1994		
End of Period (aa)																**Exchange Rates**	
	287.98	334.52	370.92	436.97	470.10	415.25	394.78	378.78	407.68	380.31	364.84	370.48	378.57	404.89	ℐ585.33	Official Rate	aa
End of Period (ae) Period Average (rf)																	
	225.80	287.40	336.25	417.37	479.59	378.05	322.75	267.00	302.95	289.40	256.45	259.00	275.32	294.77	ℐ400.95	Official Rate	ae
	211.28	271.73	328.61	381.07	436.96	449.27	346.31	300.54	297.85	319.01	272.27	282.11	264.69	283.16	ℐ416.40	Official Rate	rf
End of Period																**Fund Position**	
	3.50	3.50	3.50	3.50	4.50	4.50	4.50	4.50	4.50	4.50	4.50	4.50	6.50	6.50	6.50	Quota	2f. s
	—	.01	—	—	.23	.21	.18	.14	.11	.06	.08	.02	.02	.07	.03	SDRs	1b. s
	.30	—	—	—	—	—	—	—	—	—	—	—	.50	.50	.52	Reserve Position in the Fund	1c. s
	—	—	—	—	—	—	—	—	—	—	—	.90	.90	.90	2.25	Total Fund Cred.&Loans Outstg.	2tl
End of Period																**International Liquidity**	
	6.37	8.39	10.83	10.79	3.51	11.75	17.55	30.67	23.54	30.77	29.69	29.18	27.09	....	....	Total Reserves minus Gold	1l. d
	—	.01	—	—	.23	.23	.22	.20	.15	.08	.11	.03	.03	.09	.05	SDRs	1b. d
	.38	—	—	—	—	—	—	—	—	—	—	—	.69	.69	.76	Reserve Position in the Fund	1c. d
	5.99	8.38	10.83	10.79	3.28	11.52	17.33	30.48	23.39	30.69	29.58	29.15	26.38	....	....	Foreign Exchange	1d. d
	....	....	....	.001	.001	.001	.001	.001	.001	.001	.001	.001	.001			Gold (Million Fine Troy Ounces)	1ad
	....	....	—	.22	.19	.20	.24	.30	.24	.24	.22	.21	.19			Gold (National Valuation)	1an d
	....	....	2.36	1.61	.15	3.76	2.11	.40	5.50	3.90	3.89	5.84	4.35	....	....	Deposit Money Banks: Assets	7a. d
	....	....	.12	.33	.10	1.21	3.81	6.26	6.30	5.46	6.28	6.93	4.76	....	....	Liabilities	7b. d
End of Period																**Monetary Authorities**	
	....	....	3,642	4,597	1,775	4,515	5,740	8,275	7,205	8,977	7,654	7,595	7,512	....	....	Foreign Assets	11
	....	....	670	786	978	1,202	1,251	1,312	1,624	1,830	1,819	2,475	2,510	....	....	Claims on Central Government	12a
	....	....	3,554	3,864	3,461	3,745	5,181	7,239	5,541	7,755	6,480	5,764	5,873			Reserve Money	14
	....	....	2,434	3,427	3,142	3,448	3,118	3,151	3,688	3,618	4,274	4,046	4,082			of which: Currency Outside DMBs	14a
	....	....	171	335	177	172	193	88	115	182	196	575	505			Foreign Liabilities	16c
	....	....	92	337	80	189	161	959	1,638	230	752	756	657			Central Government Deposits	16d
	....	....	1,289	1,469	1,674	1,540	1,724	1,706	1,809	2,585	2,728	2,802	2,976			Capital Accounts	17a
	....	....	−798	−622	−2,639	71	−268	−405	−274	56	−683	−115	−222			Other Items (Net)	17r
End of Period																**Deposit Money Banks**	
	....	....	481	266	419	66	1,804	3,774	1,722	3,728	1,637	1,261	1,599	....	....	Reserves	20
	....	....	795	671	73	1,420	681	106	1,667	1,130	997	1,512	1,198	....	....	Foreign Assets	21
	....	....	457	457	457	458	385	328	273	178	51	—	—	....	....	Claims on Central Government	22a
	....	....	3,485	4,436	6,313	3,428	3,982	4,734	6,826	6,277	9,023	9,627	9,998	....	....	Claims on Private Sector	22d
	....	....	1,688	2,783	2,016	2,636	2,904	3,024	3,831	4,065	4,244	3,465	3,866	....	....	Demand Deposits	24
	....	....	1,168	1,229	959	1,015	1,432	3,035	3,559	4,608	4,574	5,829	5,720	....	....	Time and Savings Deposits	25
	....	....	42	139	50	457	1,231	1,671	1,908	1,580	1,611	1,795	1,311	....	....	Foreign Liabilities	26c
	....	....	129	70	206	—	348	277	83	127	—	—	—	....	....	Central Government Deposits	26d
	....	....	—	—	2,516	17	—	—	—	—	84	—	—	....	....	Credit From Monetary Authorities	26g
	....	....	350	514	581	617	566	592	632	835	951	1,174	1,405	....	....	Capital Accounts	27a
	....	....	1,843	1,094	934	630	373	343	475	98	244	370	493	....	....	Other Items (Net)	27r
End of Period																**Monetary Survey**	
	....	....	4,224	4,794	1,621	5,306	4,997	6,622	6,849	8,345	6,844	6,737	6,894	....	....	Foreign Assets (Net)	31n
	....	....	4,993	6,120	8,399	5,820	5,984	6,516	8,163	10,067	11,918	13,277	14,403	....	....	Domestic Credit	32
	....	....	1,447	1,621	2,046	2,392	1,982	1,763	1,304	3,727	2,829	3,523	4,316	....	....	Claims on Central Govt. (Net)	32an
	....	....	3,546	4,499	6,353	3,428	4,002	4,753	6,859	6,340	9,089	9,754	10,087	....	....	Claims on Private Sector	32d
	....	....	5,202	7,292	6,254	7,177	7,232	7,812	8,879	10,256	10,888	9,932	10,857	....	....	Money	34
	....	....	1,168	1,229	959	1,015	1,432	3,035	3,559	4,608	4,574	5,829	5,720	....	....	Quasi-Money	35
	....	....	2,845	2,392	2,807	2,934	2,319	2,291	2,574	3,549	3,300	3,838	4,127	....	....	Other Items (Net)	37r
	....	....	6,370	8,521	7,213	8,192	8,664	10,847	12,438	14,864	15,462	15,761	16,577	....	....	Money plus Quasi-Money	35l
End of Period																**Other Banking Institutions**	
	....	....	245	137	60	143	134	148	129	337	267	443	511	....	....	Reserves	40
	....	....	2	5	16	12	70	163	116	162	166	246	—	....	....	Claims on Central Government	42a
	....	....	576	925	1,226	1,498	1,749	2,052	2,114	1,995	1,922	2,000	1,991	....	....	Claims on Private Sector	42d
	....	....	97	182	277	318	375	397	345	308	376	456	472	....	....	Time Deposits	45
	....	....	—	—	38	32	66	75	3	4	4	4	4	....	....	Central Government Deposits	46d
	....	....	—	—	—	—	—	221	448	713	635	1,042	1,284	....	....	Long-Term Foreign Liabilities	46cl
	....	....	413	514	643	896	1,089	1,156	1,008	866	595	445	235	....	....	Central Govt. Lending Funds	46f
	....	....	313	371	344	406	423	514	555	603	745	742	511	....	....	Other Items (Net)	47r
End of Period																**Banking Survey**	
	....	....	4,224	4,794	1,621	5,307	4,998	6,402	6,403	7,633	6,211	5,695	5,612	....	....	Foreign Assets (Net)	51n
	....	....	5,571	7,050	9,603	7,298	7,737	8,656	10,390	12,220	14,002	15,519	16,394	....	....	Domestic Credit	52
	....	....	1,449	1,626	2,024	2,372	1,986	1,851	1,417	3,885	2,991	3,765	4,316	....	....	Claims on Central Govt. (Net)	52an
	....	....	4,122	5,424	7,579	4,926	5,751	6,805	8,973	8,335	11,011	11,754	12,078	....	....	Claims on Private Sector	52d
	....	....	6,466	8,702	7,489	8,368	8,909	11,094	12,658	14,841	15,589	15,791	16,569	....	....	Liquid Liabilities	55l
	....	....	5,201	7,291	6,253	7,035	7,102	7,662	8,754	9,925	10,639	9,506	10,377	....	....	Money	54
	....	....	1,265	1,411	1,236	1,333	1,807	3,432	3,904	4,916	4,950	6,285	6,192	....	....	Quasi-Money	55
	....	....	763	864	993	1,246	1,439	1,506	1,358	1,216	945	795	585	....	....	Central Govt. Lending Funds	56f
	....	....	2,564	2,277	2,742	2,990	2,389	2,458	2,777	3,797	3,679	4,213	4,259	....	....	Other Items (Net)	57r

Comoros

632

		1965	1966	1967	1968	1969	1970	1971	1972	1973	1974	1975	1976	1977	1978	1979
Interest Rates															*Percent Per Annum*	
Discount Rate *(End of Period)*	60	....	....	....	....	....	....	....	....	....	....	....	....	....	....	....
Deposit Rate	60l	....	....	....	....	....	....	....	....	....	....	....	....	....	....	....
Lending Rate	60p	....	....	....	....	....	....	....	....	....	....	....	....	....	....	....
International Transactions															*Millions of Francs*	
Exports	70	915	953	938	1,008	1,289	1,278	1,572	1,511	1,106	2,138	2,036	2,824	2,203	2,099	3,729
Imports, cif	71	1,623	1,783	1,850	1,763	2,092	2,373	2,835	2,932	3,369	6,203	4,974	3,119	4,053	4,329	6,135
Balance of Payments															*Millions of US Dollars:*	
Goods: Exports f.o.b.	78aa*d*	....	....	....	....	....	....	....	....	....	....	....	....	....	....	....
Goods: Imports f.o.b.	78ab*d*	....	....	....	....	....	....	....	....	....	....	....	....	....	....	....
Trade Balance	78ac*d*	....	....	....	....	....	....	....	....	....	....	....	....	....	....	....
Services: Credit	78ad*d*	....	....	....	....	....	....	....	....	....	....	....	....	....	....	....
Services: Debit	78ae*d*	....	....	....	....	....	....	....	....	....	....	....	....	....	....	....
Balance on Goods and Services	78af*d*	....	....	....	....	....	....	....	....	....	....	....	....	....	....	....
Income: Credit	78ag*d*	....	....	....	....	....	....	....	....	....	....	....	....	....	....	....
Income: Debit	78ah*d*	....	....	....	....	....	....	....	....	....	....	....	....	....	....	....
Balance on Goods, Serv., & Inc.	78ai*d*	....	....	....	....	....	....	....	....	....	....	....	....	....	....	....
Current Transfers, n.i.e.: Credit	78aj*d*	....	....	....	....	....	....	....	....	....	....	....	....	....	....	....
Current Transfers: Debit	78ak*d*	....	....	....	....	....	....	....	....	....	....	....	....	....	....	....
Current Account, n.i.e.	78al*d*	....	....	....	....	....	....	....	....	....	....	....	....	....	....	....
Capital Account, n.i.e.: Credit	78ba*d*	....	....	....	....	....	....	....	....	....	....	....	....	....	....	....
Capital Account: Debit	78bb*d*	....	....	....	....	....	....	....	....	....	....	....	....	....	....	....
Capital Account, n.i.e.	78bc*d*	....	....	....	....	....	....	....	....	....	....	....	....	....	....	....
Direct Investment Abroad	78bd*d*	....	....	....	....	....	....	....	....	....	....	....	....	....	....	....
Dir. Invest. in Rep. Econ., n.i.e.	78be*d*	....	....	....	....	....	....	....	....	....	....	....	....	....	....	....
Portfolio Investment Assets	78bf*d*	....	....	....	....	....	....	....	....	....	....	....	....	....	....	....
Portfolio Investment Liab., n.i.e.	78bg*d*	....	....	....	....	....	....	....	....	....	....	....	....	....	....	....
Other Investment Assets	78bh*d*	....	....	....	....	....	....	....	....	....	....	....	....	....	....	....
Other Investment Liab., n.i.e.	78bi*d*	....	....	....	....	....	....	....	....	....	....	....	....	....	....	....
Financial Account, n.i.e.	78bj*d*	....	....	....	....	....	....	....	....	....	....	....	....	....	....	....
Net Errors and Omissions	78ca*d*	....	....	....	....	....	....	....	....	....	....	....	....	....	....	....
Overall Balance	78cb*d*	....	....	....	....	....	....	....	....	....	....	....	....	....	....	....
Reserves and Related Items	79da*d*	....	....	....	....	....	....	....	....	....	....	....	....	....	....	....
Reserve Assets	79db*d*	....	....	....	....	....	....	....	....	....	....	....	....	....	....	....
Use of Fund Credit and Loans	79dc*d*	....	....	....	....	....	....	....	....	....	....	....	....	....	....	....
Liabs.Constit.For.Auth.Reserves	79dd*d*	....	....	....	....	....	....	....	....	....	....	....	....	....	....	....
Exceptional Financing	79de*d*	....	....	....	....	....	....	....	....	....	....	....	....	....	....	....
Government Finance															*Millions of Francs:*	
Deficit (-) or Surplus	80	....	....	....	....	....	....	....	....	....	....	....	....	....	....	....
Revenue	81	....	....	....	....	....	....	....	....	....	....	....	....	....	....	....
Grants Received	81z	....	....	....	....	....	....	....	....	....	....	....	....	....	....	....
Cash Adj.& Unall.Rev. & Grants	81x	....	....	....	....	....	....	....	....	....	....	....	....	....	....	....
Expenditure	82	....	....	....	....	....	....	....	....	....	....	....	....	....	....	....
Lending Minus Repayments	83	....	....	....	....	....	....	....	....	....	....	....	....	....	....	....
Financing																
Domestic	84a	....	....	....	....	....	....	....	....	....	....	....	....	....	....	....
Foreign	85a	....	....	....	....	....	....	....	....	....	....	....	....	....	....	....
Debt: Domestic	88a	....	....	....	....	....	....	....	....	....	....	....	....	....	....	....
Foreign	89a	....	....	....	....	....	....	....	....	....	....	....	....	....	....	....
National Accounts															*Billions of Francs*	
Gross Domestic Product	99b	5.5	6.2	6.5	6.5	7.5	8.0	8.9	10.0	11.0	16.8	15.0	14.4	....	....	....
															Millions:	
Population	99z	.24	.24	.25	.25	.26	.27	.28	.28	.29	.31	.32	.34	.35	.36	.38

Comoros

632

	1980	1981	1982	1983	1984	1985	1986	1987	1988	1989	1990	1991	1992	1993	1994		
Percent Per Annum																**Interest Rates**	
	....	....	....	10.00	10.00	10.00	10.00	8.50	8.50	....	....	....	....	....	....	Discount Rate (End of Period)	60
	....	....	....	7.50	7.50	7.50	7.50	6.50	6.50	....	....	....	....	....	....	Deposit Rate	60l
	....	....	....	15.00	15.00	15.00	15.00	13.00	13.00	....	....	....	....	....	....	Lending Rate	60p
Millions of Francs																**International Transactions**	
	1,961	4,461	6,435	7,419	3,079	7,048	7,053	3,485	6,398	5,758	4,883	7,028	5,847	....	....	Exports	70
	6,147	8,791	10,725	13,099	18,778	16,495	12,849	15,560	15,647	13,575	14,040	16,399	18,139	....	....	Imports, cif	71
Minus Sign Indicates Debit																Balance of Payments	
	11.19	16.42	19.58	19.47	7.05	15.69	20.37	11.60	21.48	18.05	17.93	24.36	....	....	....	Goods: Exports f.o.b.	78aa d
	−22.37	−24.88	−25.10	−28.80	−32.65	−28.22	−28.54	−44.15	−44.29	−35.65	−45.23	−53.60	....	....	....	Goods: Imports f.o.b.	78ab d
	−11.18	−8.47	−5.52	−9.33	−25.60	−12.53	−8.17	−32.55	−22.81	−17.60	−27.29	−29.24	....	....	....	Trade Balance	78ac d
	2.24	1.10	2.56	2.64	2.65	4.22	6.76	14.44	16.85	17.54	16.86	24.70	....	....	....	Services: Credit	78ad d
	−11.92	−25.31	−25.41	−21.85	−37.66	−35.89	−42.27	−41.80	−42.29	−39.61	−42.73	−44.38	....	....	....	Services: Debit	78ae d
	−20.86	−32.67	−28.38	−28.54	−60.61	−44.21	−43.68	−59.91	−48.26	−39.66	−53.16	−48.92	....	....	....	Balance on Goods and Services	78af d
	.63	.81	1.27	1.27	1.04	.57	1.50	1.80	1.76	4.30	3.35	2.81	....	....	....	Income: Credit	78ag d
	−.04	−.56	−.71	−1.73	−1.61	−1.97	−3.13	−2.92	−3.94	−2.94	−4.21	−3.74	....	....	....	Income: Debit	78ah d
	−20.27	−32.43	−27.82	−29.00	−61.18	−45.60	−45.32	−61.03	−50.44	−38.31	−54.02	−49.85	....	....	....	Balance on Goods, Serv., & Inc.	78ai d
	12.88	28.09	21.85	22.09	33.89	36.61	36.97	45.86	48.40	49.16	49.41	47.44	....	....	....	Current Transfers, n.i.e.: Credit	78aj d
	−1.52	−3.82	−4.98	−4.14	−5.43	−5.27	−7.34	−6.19	−4.48	−5.45	−4.67	−6.50	....	....	....	Current Transfers: Debit	78ak d
	−8.91	−8.16	−10.96	−11.05	−32.72	−14.26	−15.69	−21.37	−6.52	5.41	−9.29	−8.91	....	....	....	Current Account, n.i.e.	78al d
	—	—	—	—	—	—	—	—	—	—	—	—	....	....	....	Capital Account, n.i.e.: Credit	78ba d
	—	—	—	—	—	—	—	—	—	—	—	—	....	....	....	Capital Account: Debit	78bb d
	—	—	—	—	—	—	—	—	—	—	—	—	....	....	....	Capital Account, n.i.e.	78bc d
	—	—	—	—	—	—	—	—	—	—	−1.10	—	....	....	....	Direct Investment Abroad	78bd d
	—	—	—	—	—	—	—	7.55	3.77	3.27	.39	2.51	....	....	....	Dir. Invest. in Rep. Econ., n.i.e.	78be d
	−.41	−.31	.40	—	—	.02	—	—	—	—	—	—	....	....	....	Portfolio Investment Assets	78bf d
	—	—	—	—	—	—	−.24	—	—	—	—	—	....	....	....	Portfolio Investment Liab., n.i.e.	78bg d
	—	—	—	−.53	—	—	−3.00	−1.49	8.83	−13.70	−6.73	3.05	−17.43	....	....	Other Investment Assets	78bh d
	21.00	15.17	18.01	15.74	27.35	21.82	22.68	13.14	14.13	11.01	11.32	15.51	....	....	....	Other Investment Liab., n.i.e.	78bi d
	20.59	14.86	18.42	15.21	27.35	18.60	21.18	29.51	4.19	7.54	13.67	.58	....	....	....	Financial Account, n.i.e.	78bj d
	−15.19	−3.19	−3.75	−2.08	−.49	1.77	−2.02	.65	−1.39	−7.60	−9.23	1.70	....	....	....	Net Errors and Omissions	78ca d
	−3.51	3.51	3.71	2.08	−5.85	6.12	3.48	8.79	−3.72	5.35	−4.85	−6.62	....	....	....	Overall Balance	78cb d
	3.51	−3.51	−3.71	−2.08	5.85	−6.12	−3.48	−8.79	3.72	−5.35	4.85	6.62	....	....	....	Reserves and Related Items	79da d
	3.51	−3.51	−3.71	−2.08	5.85	−6.12	−3.48	−8.79	3.72	−5.35	4.85	1.87	....	....	....	Reserve Assets	79db d
	—	—	—	—	—	—	—	—	—	—	—	1.19	....	....	....	Use of Fund Credit and Loans	79dc d
	—	—	—	—	—	—	—	—	—	—	—	—	....	....	....	Liabs.Constit.For.Auth.Reserves	79dd d
	—	—	—	—	—	—	—	—	—	—	—	3.57	....	....	....	Exceptional Financing	79de d
Year Ending December 31																**Government Finance**	
	....	....	−4,084	−6,353	−8,587	−8,126	−4,816	....	....	....	....	....	....	....	....	Deficit (−) or Surplus	80
	....	....	5,036	6,844	6,977	6,482	8,979	6,820^p	....	....	....	....	....	....	....	Revenue	81
	....	....	4,750	6,868	9,279	9,532	9,496	....	....	....	....	....	....	....	....	Grants Received	81z
	....	....	—	−235	−211	−145	3	35	....	....	....	....	....	....	....	Cash Adj.& Unall.Rev. & Grants	81x
	....	....	13,706	19,825	24,636	24,142	23,326	21,037^p	....	....	....	....	....	....	....	Expenditure	82
	....	....	−70	28	61	1	—	67^p	....	....	....	....	....	....	....	Lending Minus Repayments	83
																Financing	
	....	....	154	238	−391	563	2,357	....	....	....	....	....	....	....	....	Domestic	84a
	....	....	3,930	6,115	8,977	7,563	2,460	....	....	....	....	....	....	....	....	Foreign	85a
	....	....	....	....	797	....	....	....	....	....	....	....	....	....	....	Debt: Domestic	88a
	....	....	....	....	81,626	....	....	....	....	....	....	....	....	....	....	Foreign	89a
Billions of Francs																**National Accounts**	
	....	....	....	....	....	....	....	....	....	....	....	....	....	....	....	Gross Domestic Product	99b
Midyear Estimates																	
	.38	.41	.42	.42	.44	.45	.48	.49	.51	.52	.54	.56	.58	.61	....	Population	99z

Congo

634

		1965	1966	1967	1968	1969	1970	1971	1972	1973	1974	1975	1976	1977	1978	1979
Exchange Rates																*Francs per SDR:*
Official Rate	aa	245.07	247.59	245.42	247.40	277.91	276.02	283.61	278.00	284.00	272.08	262.55	288.70	285.76	272.28	264.78
																Francs per US Dollar:
Official Rate	ae	245.08	247.59	245.43	247.41	277.92	276.03	261.23	256.05	235.43	222.22	224.27	248.49	235.25	209.00	201.00
Official Rate	rf	245.06	245.68	246.00	247.56	259.96	276.40	275.59	252.03	222.89	240.70	214.31	238.95	245.68	225.66	212.72
Fund Position																*Millions of SDRs:*
Quota	2f. s	7.50	8.00	8.50	9.00	10.00	13.00	13.00	13.00	13.00	13.00	13.00	13.00	13.00	17.00	17.00
SDRs	1b. s	—	—	—	—	—	.03	1.32	2.58	2.46	2.33	2.15	2.06	1.48	1.31	1.20
Reserve Position in the Fund	1c. s	.65	.77	.90	1.02	1.27	1.56	1.65	1.75	1.84	1.93	2.03	2.03			
Total Fund Cred.&Loans Outstg.	2tl	—	—	—	—	—	—	—	—	—	—	—	—	9.34	16.68	21.58
International Liquidity														*Millions of US Dollars Unless Otherwise Indicated:*		
Total Reserves minus Gold	1l. d	6.19	6.18	2.62	7.41	5.74	8.88	10.82	10.34	7.86	24.10	13.81	12.17	13.53	9.43	42.23
SDRs	1b. d	—	—	—	—	—	.03	1.43	2.80	2.97	2.85	2.52	2.39	1.80	1.71	1.58
Reserve Position in the Fund	1c. d	.65	.77	.90	1.02	1.27	1.56	1.79	1.90	2.22	2.37	2.38	2.36			
Foreign Exchange	1d. d	5.54	5.41	1.72	6.38	4.47	7.29	7.59	5.63	2.67	18.88	8.92	7.41	11.73	7.72	40.65
Gold (Million Fine Troy Ounces)	1ad	....	....	....	....	....	....	....	....	....	....	—	.006	.009	.011	
Gold (National Valuation)	1an d	....	....	....	....	....	....	....	....	....	....	....	....	.92	1.94	5.79
Monetary Authorities: Other Liab.	4.. d	.20	.28	.08	.03	.40	.03	.09	.09	.04	.08	.06	3.62	3.96	2.76	2.14
Deposit Money Banks: Assets	7a. d	.85	.81	1.62	4.46	2.43	2.65	4.82	2.59	3.35	4.99	3.21	5.80	6.84	14.11	15.93
Liabilities	7b. d	4.98	8.77	8.87	11.85	10.23	7.63	7.37	11.78	9.10	12.06	21.07	24.97	57.31	63.37	64.79
Monetary Authorities																*Billions of Francs:*
Foreign Assets	11	1.53	1.53	.65	1.83	1.59	2.47	2.77	2.64	1.81	5.36	3.10	3.02	3.40	2.38	9.66
Claims on Central Government	12a	1.08	.96	1.54	1.19	1.41	2.03	1.59	2.65	3.98	4.20	7.86	9.06	11.08	13.71	13.94
Claims on Deposit Money Banks	12e	2.17	3.18	3.12	2.75	3.18	2.78	3.81	4.74	5.41	4.55	5.91	7.58	8.77	11.24	10.27
Claims on Other Banking Insts.	12f	....	....	....	....	....	....	....	....	....	....	....	....	....	....	....
Reserve Money	14	3.15	3.74	4.36	5.11	5.60	6.48	7.13	8.36	9.43	12.35	15.31	16.43	17.30	17.55	21.26
of which: Currency Outside DMBs	14a	2.91	3.50	4.15	4.90	5.37	6.02	6.71	7.99	9.15	11.86	14.34	15.29	16.13	16.53	19.17
Foreign Liabilities	16c	.05	.07	.02	.01	.11	.01	.02	.02	.01	.02	.01	.90	3.60	5.12	6.14
Central Government Deposits	16d	1.56	1.82	.86	.56	.37	.25	.09	.36	.34	.44	.29	.72	.41	1.31	1.62
Capital Accounts	17a	....	....	....	—	—	—	—	—	.02	.02	.02	.04	.04	.04	.04
Other Items (Net)	17r	.02	.04	.07	.10	.10	.54	.91	1.29	1.40	1.28	1.23	1.56	1.89	3.32	4.82
Deposit Money Banks																*Billions of Francs:*
Reserves	20	.21	.22	.19	.21	.23	.46	.43	.37	.29	.48	.97	1.14	1.17	1.02	2.09
Foreign Assets	21	.21	.20	.40	1.10	.68	.74	1.23	.66	.77	1.11	.72	1.44	I1.61	2.95	3.20
Claims on Central Government	22a	.07	.47	.47	1.87	2.19	1.84	1.90	2.73	2.60	3.92	5.45	6.36	9.14	10.54	9.02
Claims on Nonfin.Pub.Enterprises	22c	....	....	....	....	....	....	....	....	....	....	....	....	....	....	....
Claims on Private Sector	22d	9.78	10.55	11.26	11.23	11.66	12.38	14.25	16.06	18.50	21.26	28.23	35.83	I38.93	39.42	45.59
Claims on Other Banking Insts.	22f	....	....	....	....	....	....	....	....	....	....	....	....	....	....	....
Claims on Nonbank Financial Insts	22g	....	....	....	....	....	....	....	....	....	....	....	....	....	....	....
Demand Deposits	24	4.26	4.25	5.03	5.50	5.79	7.06	7.40	6.93	8.03	12.13	12.83	16.06	I14.76	16.65	20.65
Time and Savings Deposits	25	.44	.61	.62	.99	.78	.92	1.12	1.27	1.41	1.86	2.14	2.61	3.87	3.92	5.30
Foreign Liabilities	26c	1.23	1.56	1.64	2.49	2.46	1.89	1.67	2.89	1.23	1.20	2.01	2.25	8.50	7.75	7.52
Long-Term Foreign Liabilities	26cl	—	.61	.55	.43	.38	.23	.21	.12	.87	1.48	2.71	3.95	4.98	5.49	5.50
Central Government Deposits	26d	1.04	.41	.50	.56	.49	.73	1.49	1.34	1.38	1.54	1.67	1.32	2.28	1.50	.97
Credit from Monetary Authorities	26g	2.17	3.18	3.12	2.13	2.65	2.35	3.25	4.21	4.54	4.27	5.55	6.66	8.77	11.24	10.27
Capital Accounts	27a	1.23	1.49	1.61	1.70	1.94	2.20	2.52	2.86	3.19	3.70	4.33	6.61	6.46	7.04	9.03
Other Items (Net)	27r	–.10	–.67	–.75	.61	.27	.03	.14	.20	1.52	.61	4.13	5.32	I1.22	.33	.65
Post Office: Checking Deposits	24.. i	.24	.19	.30	.32	.31	.32	.26	.31	.28	.43	.55	.60	.53	.53	.53
Postal Debt	26c. i	....	....	....	.96	1.22	.89	.89	1.61	1.45	2.36	3.03	3.99	6.06	6.78	6.05
Monetary Survey																*Billions of Francs:*
Foreign Assets (Net)	31n	.46	.10	–.61	.43	–.30	1.31	2.30	.39	1.35	5.25	1.79	1.31	I–7.09	–7.54	–.80
Domestic Credit	32	8.33	9.75	11.91	13.17	14.40	15.27	16.15	19.74	23.37	27.41	39.59	49.20	I56.46	60.86	65.96
Claims on Central Govt. (Net)	32an	I–1.45	–.80	.65	1.94	2.74	2.89	1.90	3.68	4.87	6.14	11.35	13.37	17.53	21.44	20.38
Claims on Nonfin.Pub.Enterprises	32c	....	....	....	....	....	....	....	....	....	....	....	....	....	....	....
Claims on Private Sector	32d	I9.78	10.55	11.26	11.23	11.66	12.38	14.25	16.06	18.50	21.26	28.23	35.83	I38.93	39.42	45.59
Claims on Other Banking Insts.	32f	....	....	....	....	....	....	....	....	....	....	....	....	....	....	....
Claims on Nonbk.Financial Insts	32g	....	....	....	....	....	....	....	....	....	....	....	....	....	....	....
Money	34	7.17	7.75	9.18	10.40	11.16	13.08	14.11	14.92	17.18	24.00	27.17	31.34	I30.89	33.18	39.82
Quasi-Money	35	.44	.61	.62	.99	.78	.92	1.12	1.27	1.41	1.86	2.14	2.61	3.87	3.92	5.30
Other Items (Net)	37r	1.18	1.49	1.50	2.22	2.16	2.58	3.23	3.94	6.14	6.80	12.07	16.56	I14.60	16.21	20.04
Money plus Quasi-Money	35l	7.61	8.36	9.80	11.39	11.94	14.00	15.23	16.19	18.58	25.85	29.31	33.95	I34.76	37.10	45.12
Interest Rates																*Percent Per Annum*
Discount Rate (End of Period)	60	....	....	....	4.50	4.50	4.50	4.50	4.50	4.50	5.50	5.50	6.50	6.50	6.50	8.50
Deposit Rate	60l	....	....	....	....	....	....	....	....	....	....	....	....	....	5.75	5.50
Lending Rate	60p	....	....	....	....	....	....	....	....	....	....	....	....	....	13.00	9.00
Prices and Production																*Index Numbers (1990=100):*
Wholesale Prices	63	16.4	17.1	17.5	17.5	17.3	18.5	18.6	21.0	22.1	25.5	29.0	32.9	I37.0	40.6	44.3
Consumer Prices	64	20.9	22.0	22.8	23.7	23.5	23.9	24.8	27.3	28.2	29.7	34.9	37.4	42.7	47.2	51.0
Crude Petroleum Production	66aa	.9	.8	.6	.5	.3	.2	.2	4.2	26.0	28.6	22.3	26.2	22.9	30.5	34.1

Congo 634

1980	1981	1982	1983	1984	1985	1986	1987	1988	1989	1990	1991	1992	1993	1994		
															Exchange Rates	
End of Period																
287.99	334.52	370.92	436.97	470.11	415.26	394.78	378.78	407.68	380.32	364.84	370.48	378.57	404.89	I780.44	Official Rate	aa
End of Period (ae) Period Average (rf)																
225.80	287.40	336.25	417.37	479.60	378.05	322.75	267.00	302.95	289.40	256.45	259.00	275.33	294.78	I534.60	Official Rate	ae
211.28	271.73	328.61	381.06	436.96	449.26	346.30	300.54	297.85	319.01	272.26	282.11	264.69	283.16	I555.20	Official Rate	rf
															Fund Position	
End of Period																
25.50	25.50	25.50	37.30	37.30	37.30	37.30	37.30	37.30	37.30	37.30	37.30	37.30	57.90	57.90	57.90 Quota	2f. s
—	.90	.96	.21	2.13	1.51	3.80	1.91	.84	1.21	1.17	.04	.04	.01	.03	SDRs	1b. s
—	—	2.06	3.30	2.98	.48	.48	.48	.48	.48	.47	.47	.47	.47	.47	Reserve Position in the Fund	1c. s
17.44	12.70	12.63	12.27	11.12	8.99	16.03	13.56	11.40	8.75	7.61	4.00	4.00	3.50	14.00	Total Fund Cred.&Loans Outstg.	2tl
															International Liquidity	
End of Period																
85.90	123.37	37.01	7.36	4.11	3.96	6.82	3.40	4.70	6.10	5.91	4.76	4.01	1.34	50.36	Total Reserves minus Gold	1l. d
—	1.05	1.06	.22	2.09	1.66	4.65	2.71	1.13	1.59	1.66	.06	.06	.02	.05	SDRs	1b. d
—	2.40	3.64	3.12	.47	.53	.59	.68	.65	.63	.67	.67	.65	.64	.68	Reserve Position in the Fund	1c. d
85.90	119.92	32.32	4.02	1.56	1.78	1.58	.01	2.93	3.88	3.58	4.03	3.31	.68	49.63	Foreign Exchange	1d. d
.011	.011	.011	.011	.011	.011	.011	.011	.011	.011	.011	.011	.011	.011	.011	Gold (Million Fine Troy Ounces)	1ad
6.56	4.45	5.00	4.21	3.44	3.60	4.36	5.37	4.52	3.52	3.98	3.94	3.70	4.42	....	Gold (National Valuation)	1an d
1.65	1.53	.72	.47	1.40	.85	.69	1.50	107.06	124.90	21.37	57.98	28.30	23.55	1.08	Monetary Authorities: Other Liab.	4.. d
13.89	26.31	19.88	13.84	20.93	32.19	30.89	38.61	47.75	39.22	48.90	50.71	68.00	82.84	41.43	Deposit Money Banks: Assets	7a. d
56.79	93.93	81.13	95.05	106.82	138.92	169.43	85.21	71.80	60.61	59.31	63.58	96.22	58.86	50.04	Liabilities	7b. d
															Monetary Authorities	
End of Period																
20.89	37.02	14.12	4.84	3.62	2.87	3.60	2.35	I5.81	5.87	6.74	2.25	2.12	1.67	29.21	Foreign Assets	11
14.01	12.05	31.70	35.60	46.23	41.39	58.23	58.41	I53.37	53.37	55.19	I51.63	73.25	72.61	77.25	Claims on Central Government	12a
4.08	8.82	21.94	30.68	38.27	40.65	46.11	41.55	I28.66	31.44	28.14	I14.85	6.84	1.51	1.54	Claims on Deposit Money Banks	12e
....	....	....	....	....	....	....	....	12.39	11.94	13.03	12.26	—	—	—	Claims on Other Banking Insts.	12f
27.73	33.03	46.00	47.90	47.39	52.94	53.91	59.53	I53.72	52.70	71.02	57.29	66.33	63.50	85.97	Reserve Money	14
23.06	31.21	44.21	44.33	45.03	50.19	51.09	56.87	I51.20	49.91	66.20	53.28	59.32	53.71	69.49	of which: Currency Outside DMBs	14a
5.40	4.69	4.93	5.56	5.90	4.06	6.55	5.54	I37.08	39.47	8.26	16.50	9.31	8.36	11.50	Foreign Liabilities	16c
2.03	16.61	12.48	12.17	29.11	22.33	36.83	28.86	I2.48	4.51	17.40	4.22	4.01	4.95	22.34	Central Government Deposits	16d
1.42	1.21	1.61	1.70	1.57	1.35	1.47	1.51	I1.46	1.39	1.19	1.29	1.76	2.16	1.77	Capital Accounts	17a
2.40	2.35	2.76	3.79	4.14	4.23	9.18	6.87	I5.48	4.55	5.24	1.69	I.80	-3.18	-13.58	Other Items (Net)	17r
															Deposit Money Banks	
End of Period																
4.67	1.83	1.78	3.58	2.36	2.75	2.78	2.63	I2.35	2.46	4.09	3.84	4.42	9.68	12.05	Reserves	20
3.14	7.56	6.69	5.78	10.04	12.17	9.97	10.31	I14.03	11.35	12.54	13.13	18.72	24.42	22.15	Foreign Assets	21
10.15	12.73	17.54	28.15	40.24	38.42	44.01	30.95	I45.16	41.45	39.81	36.96	I36.78	17.84	30.76	Claims on Central Government	22a
....	....	....	....	....	....	....	....	38.92	32.17	27.23	27.62	26.78	11.28	10.17	Claims on Nonfin.Pub.Enterprises	22c
56.00	94.20	131.15	151.95	180.56	201.24	202.88	186.91	I107.02	112.32	119.58	122.97	122.33	66.02	75.62	Claims on Private Sector	22d
....	....	....	....	....	....	....	....	.53	.95	1.09	1.26	.41	.06	.01	Claims on Other Banking Insts.	22f
....	....	....	....	....	....	....	....	.78	.29	.69	.62	.26	.40	.60	Claims on Nonbank Financial Insts	22g
31.50	44.47	54.41	47.58	57.66	63.73	48.12	47.08	I46.17	46.35	54.10	58.73	57.40	41.94	60.57	Demand Deposits	24
7.06	17.01	18.35	23.33	20.92	35.62	32.99	36.13	I39.07	45.13	46.84	48.61	49.86	28.48	24.78	Time and Savings Deposits	25
6.98	13.79	9.46	25.29	19.36	14.89	13.39	12.70	I13.41	14.60	12.87	I12.81	24.81	17.18	26.75	Foreign Liabilities	26c
5.84	13.21	17.82	14.39	31.88	37.63	41.30	10.06	I3.03	2.94	2.34	I3.66	1.68	.17	—	Long-Term Foreign Liabilities	26cl
1.37	4.86	17.38	33.02	41.95	42.15	53.15	49.93	I52.16	16.95	17.15	19.48	I18.08	2.61	6.10	Central Government Deposits	26d
5.08	9.11	21.94	30.74	38.27	40.65	46.11	41.55	I28.66	31.44	28.14	I14.85	6.84	1.51	1.54	Credit from Monetary Authorities	26g
12.81	13.17	20.99	23.74	28.70	33.95	39.53	40.75	I36.59	54.45	57.07	I56.84	57.41	36.24	41.05	Capital Accounts	27a
3.32	.72	-3.19	-8.63	-5.53	-14.04	-14.93	-7.38	I-10.30	-10.86	-13.50	-8.58	I-6.38	1.57	-9.42	Other Items (Net)	27r
.53	.53	2.59	3.65	5.07	5.43	5.46	5.26	2.56	....	....	....	....	....	....	Post Office: Checking Deposits	24.. i
6.19	5.56	1.18	3.20	2.57	.35	.83	1.17	....	....	....	....	....	....	....	Postal Debt	26c. i
															Monetary Survey	
End of Period																
11.65	26.10	6.42	-20.23	-11.60	-3.90	-6.36	-5.57	I-33.68	-39.79	-4.18	I-17.59	-14.95	.38	13.11	Foreign Assets (Net)	31n
76.75	97.51	150.54	170.51	195.96	216.57	215.15	197.48	I203.52	231.04	222.06	I229.61	I237.72	160.65	165.98	Domestic Credit	32
20.76	3.31	19.39	18.56	15.41	15.33	12.27	10.57	I43.88	73.37	60.45	I64.89	I87.94	82.89	79.58	Claims on Central Govt. (Net)	32an
....	....	....	....	....	....	....	....	38.92	32.17	27.23	27.62	26.78	11.28	10.17	Claims on Nonfin.Pub.Enterprises	32c
56.00	94.20	131.15	151.95	180.56	201.24	202.88	186.91	I107.02	112.32	119.58	122.97	122.33	66.02	75.62	Claims on Private Sector	32d
....	....	....	....	....	....	....	....	12.92	12.89	14.12	13.52	.41	.06	.01	Claims on Other Banking Insts.	32f
....	....	....	....	....	....	....	....	.78	.29	.69	.62	.26	.40	.60	Claims on Nonbk.Financial Insts	32g
54.56	75.67	98.62	91.91	102.69	113.92	99.24	103.98	I97.54	96.59	121.03	112.17	119.32	95.76	134.49	Money	34
7.06	17.01	18.35	23.33	20.92	35.62	32.99	36.13	I39.07	45.13	46.84	48.61	49.86	28.48	24.78	Quasi-Money	35
26.78	30.93	39.99	35.05	60.75	63.13	76.56	51.81	I33.23	49.53	50.01	I51.24	I53.59	36.79	19.82	Other Items (Net)	37r
61.62	92.68	116.97	115.24	123.61	149.54	132.22	140.10	I136.61	141.72	167.87	160.79	169.17	124.24	159.27	Money plus Quasi-Money	35l
															Interest Rates	
Percent Per Annum																
8.50	8.50	8.50	8.50	8.50	9.00	8.00	8.00	9.50	10.00	11.00	10.75	12.00	11.50	....	Discount Rate (End of Period)	60
6.50	6.50	6.50	7.50	7.50	8.25	8.10	7.79	7.81	8.00	I7.50	7.50	7.50	7.75	8.08	Deposit Rate	60l
11.00	11.00	11.00	12.00	12.00	12.00	11.50	11.13	11.79	12.50	I18.50	18.15	17.77	17.46	17.42	Lending Rate	60p
															Prices and Production	
Period Averages																
50.5	57.4	66.2	70.8	81.1	86.4	89.7	93.4	96.0	98.1	100.0	96.5	98.1	101.1	....	Wholesale Prices	63
54.7	I64.0	72.1	77.7	88.0	92.9	95.1	96.6	101.3	105.0	100.0	109.1	111.5	113.6	....	Consumer Prices	64
40.9	51.1	56.7	66.8	75.0	73.9	74.1	78.7	87.7	99.2	100.0	100.3	....	....	....	Crude Petroleum Production	66aa

Congo

634

International Transactions

		1965	1966	1967	1968	1969	1970	1971	1972	1973	1974	1975	1976	1977	1978	1979
															Billions of Francs	
Exports	70	11.55	10.66	11.73	12.19	11.38	8.56	10.96	15.00	19.62	54.86	38.25	52.95	65.51	69.56	105.43
Imports, cif	71	16.45	17.70	20.85	21.23	20.90	16.39	22.57	26.27	28.56	30.54	36.33	41.16	50.82	58.26	61.95
Imports, fob	71.v	14.43	15.53	18.29	18.62	18.33	14.37	19.86	23.45	23.08	25.75	30.66	35.48	43.51	47.62	51.00

Balance of Payments

Millions of US Dollars:

		1978	1979
Goods: Exports f.o.b.	78aa d	308.2	495.7
Goods: Imports f.o.b.	78ab d	−282.1	−363.0
Trade Balance	78ac d	26.1	132.7
Services: Credit	78ad d	68.8	69.7
Services: Debit	78ae d	−259.2	−219.8
Balance on Goods and Services	78af d	−164.3	−17.4
Income: Credit	78ag d	3.4	3.3
Income: Debit	78ah d	−58.0	−96.3
Balance on Goods, Serv., & Inc.	78ai d	−218.9	−110.4
Current Transfers, n.i.e.: Credit	78aj d	67.1	50.5
Current Transfers: Debit	78ak d	−28.7	−39.4
Current Account, n.i.e.	78al d	−180.6	−99.4
Capital Account, n.i.e.: Credit	78ba d	—	—
Capital Account: Debit	78bb d	—	—
Capital Account, n.i.e.	78bc d	—	—
Direct Investment Abroad	78bd d	—	—
Dir. Invest. in Rep. Econ., n.i.e.	78be d	4.1	16.5
Portfolio Investment Assets	78bf d	—	—
Portfolio Investment Liab., n.i.e.	78bg d	—	—
Other Investment Assets	78bh d	−17.7	−14.0
Other Investment Liab., n.i.e.	78bi d	180.5	90.1
Financial Account, n.i.e.	78bj d	166.9	92.6
Net Errors and Omissions	78ca d	−1.4	29.9
Overall Balance	78cb d	−15.1	23.1
Reserves and Related Items	79da d	15.1	−23.1
Reserve Assets	79db d	4.6	−28.5
Use of Fund Credit and Loans	79dc d	9.0	6.4
Liabs.Constit.For.Auth.Reserves	79dd d	1.5	−.8
Exceptional Financing	79de d	—	−.1

Government Finance

Millions of Francs:

		1965	1966	1967	1968	1969	1970	1971	1972	1973	1974	1975	1976	1977	1978	1979
Deficit (−) or Surplus	80	....	....	....	....	....	−1,090	−2,400	....	....	....	....	....	....	....	....
Revenue	81	....	....	....	....	....	16,680	17,610	18,780	20,080	44,120	47,800	48,290	....	....	....
Grants Received	81z	....	....	....	....	....	30	—	20	20	—	30	10	....	....	....
Expenditure	82	....	....	....	....	....	17,800	20,010	....	....	....	....	....	....	....	....
Lending Minus Repayments	83	....	....	....	....	....	—	—	....	....	....	....	....	....	....	....
Financing																
Domestic	84a	....	....	....	....	....	....	....	....	....	....	....	....	....	....	....
Foreign	85a	....	....	....	....	....	....	....	....	....	....	....	....	....	....	....

National Accounts

Billions of Francs

		1965	1966	1967	1968	1969	1970	1971	1972	1973	1974	1975	1976	1977	1978	1979
Exports of Goods & Services	90c	24.9	23.3	17.8	18.9	22.1	26.4	28.9	29.3	38.2	75.0	59.4	71.2	....	78.6	....
Government Consumption	91f	7.5	9.2	14.1	15.7	17.1	18.1	22.9	27.6	28.2	37.8	54.3	61.2	61.2	45.5	....
Gross Fixed Capital Formation	93e	9.2	13.9	15.6	15.9	17.8	18.9	19.9	21.2	23.9	31.7	41.2	36.1	32.8	46.4	....
Increase/Decrease(−) in Stocks	93i														7.9	
Private Consumption	96f	29.3	32.2	43.5	47.3	51.1	55.0	57.3	66.5	64.7	76.3	109.5	120.9	123.2	117.9	....
Imports of Goods & Services	98c	−22.3	−24.4	−32.6	−35.6	−39.2	−43.9	−46.7	−53.6	−52.4	−83.3	−104.8	−116.0	....	−97.9	....
Gross Domestic Product	99b	48.6	54.2	58.4	62.2	68.9	74.5	82.3	91.0	102.6	137.0	159.6	173.4	181.7	198.3	254.5

Millions:

		1965	1966	1967	1968	1969	1970	1971	1972	1973	1974	1975	1976	1977	1978	1979
Population	99z	1.07	1.09	1.12	1.14	1.17	1.20	1.23	1.26	1.29	1.32	1.35	1.39	1.44	1.45	1.49

Monetary Authorities: ℐ Beginning in March 1988, the sectorization and classification of accounts have been revised. ℐ Beginning in September 1991, *Claims on Central Government* include government assumption of certain nonperforming bank loans. ℐ Beginning in December 1992, the coverage of the banking system has been revised. Claims and deposits of nonactive banks or banks in the process of liquidation have been excluded from the monetary accounts.

Deposit Money Banks: ℐ See note to section 10. ℐ Beginning in September 1991, the counterpart of government assumption of certain nonperforming bank loans was reclassified from *Credit from Monetary Authorities* to *Capital Accounts*.

Monetary Survey: ℐ Beginning with 1965, data for *line 32d* include Treasury claims on the private sector with the contra-entry reported in *line 32an*. ℐ See notes to sections 10 and 20.

Interest Rates: *Deposit Rate:* ℐ Beginning in October 1990, minimum rate offered by deposit money banks on savings accounts.

Lending Rate ℐ Beginning in October 1990, maximum rate charged by deposit money banks on all loans, excluding charges and fees.

Government Finance: ℐ Prior to 1980, data cover budgetary central government only. Beginning in 1980, data cover consolidated central government, including all extrabudgetary and social security funds.

Congo

634

	1980	1981	1982	1983	1984	1985	1986	1987	1988	1989	1990	1991	1992	1993	1994		
Billions of Francs																**International Transactions**	
	192.40	220.43	326.15	243.82	516.76	488.52	268.99	292.44	223.70	290.30	267.10	300.60	313.20	317.30	....	Exports	70
	122.54	121.31	251.90	246.97	269.95	268.70	206.65	294.37	331.45	328.49	169.02	133.18	119.48	146.78	....	Imports, cif	71
	100.30	98.76	205.75	200.96	219.60	218.63	168.14	239.52	269.69	267.28	137.53	108.36	97.22	119.43	....	Imports, fob	71.v
Minus Sign Indicates Debit																**Balance of Payments**	
	910.6	1,072.7	1,108.5	1,066.2	1,268.4	1,144.8	672.6	876.7	843.2	1,160.5	1,388.7	1,107.7	1,178.7	1,107.5	....	Goods: Exports f.o.b.	78aa d
	−545.2	−803.6	−663.8	−649.5	−617.6	−630.1	−512.4	−419.9	−522.7	−532.0	−512.7	−494.5	−438.2	−490.9	....	Goods: Imports f.o.b.	78ab d
	365.4	269.1	444.7	416.7	650.8	514.7	160.2	456.8	320.5	628.5	876.0	613.2	740.5	616.6	....	Trade Balance	78ac d
	110.6	84.0	77.6	87.8	80.3	74.7	103.1	97.2	92.3	95.3	99.2	99.3	66.1	53.3	....	Services: Credit	78ad d
	−480.1	−713.3	−697.3	−727.4	−391.3	−525.6	−656.8	−532.1	−560.1	−494.0	−769.1	−786.6	−737.5	−755.4	....	Services: Debit	78ae d
	−4.0	−360.2	−175.1	−222.9	339.8	63.8	−393.5	21.9	−147.4	229.8	206.1	−74.1	69.1	−85.5	....	Balance on Goods and Services	78af d
	8.0	16.6	19.6	5.4	6.5	9.1	8.1	30.5	7.5	2.2	14.7	18.8	12.5	11.7	....	Income: Credit	78ag d
	−169.6	−128.8	−158.0	−179.3	−133.5	−237.2	−234.2	−286.2	−313.3	−363.3	−474.9	−401.6	−380.4	−375.1	....	Income: Debit	78ah d
	−165.6	−472.3	−313.4	−396.8	212.9	−164.2	−619.6	−233.8	−453.2	−131.3	−254.2	−456.9	−298.8	−448.9	....	Balance on Goods, Serv., & Inc.	78ai d
	85.3	71.6	37.2	51.3	55.1	51.0	69.1	88.8	79.8	119.7	86.3	74.1	54.8	40.3	....	Current Transfers, n.i.e.: Credit	78aj d
	−86.4	−59.9	−55.3	−55.4	−57.8	−48.0	−50.3	−77.7	−72.0	−73.4	−83.4	−78.7	−73.3	−98.9	....	Current Transfers: Debit	78ak d
	−166.7	−460.7	−331.5	−400.9	210.2	−161.3	−600.7	−222.7	−445.5	−85.0	−251.2	−461.5	−317.4	−507.5	....	Current Account, n.i.e.	78al d
	—	—	—	—	—	—	—	—	—	—	—	—	—	—	....	Capital Account, n.i.e.: Credit	78ba d
	—	—	—	—	—	—	—	—	—	—	—	—	—	—	....	Capital Account: Debit	78bb d
	—	—	—	—	—	—	—	—	—	—	—	—	—	—	....	Capital Account, n.i.e.	78bc d
	—	—	—	—	—	—	—	—	—	—	—	—	—	—	....	Direct Investment Abroad	78bd d
	40.0	30.8	35.3	56.1	34.9	12.7	22.4	43.4	9.1	—	—	—	—	—	....	Dir. Invest. in Rep. Econ., n.i.e.	78be d
	—	—	—	—	—	—	—	—	—	—	—	—	—	—	....	Portfolio Investment Assets	78bf d
	—	—	—	—	—	—	—	—	—	—	—	—	—	—	....	Portfolio Investment Liab., n.i.e.	78bg d
	−93.8	−183.8	−44.4	33.9	−255.5	8.6	157.8	−150.8	−59.0	−7.8	−67.9	35.1	−24.9	−25.4	....	Other Investment Assets	78bh d
	229.0	480.5	211.7	208.1	−71.5	17.6	−25.9	−186.1	−12.1	−317.5	−4.0	−25.5	−128.8	115.8	....	Other Investment Liab., n.i.e.	78bi d
	175.2	327.6	202.7	298.0	−292.1	38.9	154.4	−293.4	−62.0	−325.4	−72.0	9.6	−153.8	90.4	....	Financial Account, n.i.e.	78bj d
	38.5	174.6	45.0	70.9	20.5	41.7	48.1	27.6	40.6	8.5	−40.6	−6.3	41.2	−35.4	....	Net Errors and Omissions	78ca d
	47.0	41.5	−83.9	−31.9	−61.4	−80.7	−398.2	−488.5	−466.8	−401.8	−363.9	−458.2	−429.9	−452.4	....	Overall Balance	78cb d
	−47.0	−41.5	83.9	31.9	61.4	80.7	398.2	488.5	466.8	401.8	363.9	458.2	429.9	452.4	....	Reserves and Related Items	79da d
	−49.3	−57.1	82.2	32.4	7.8	1.8	−2.0	4.7	−1.7	—	−112.9	32.1	−26.8	−1.7	....	Reserve Assets	79db d
	−5.3	−5.7	−.1	−.4	−1.2	−2.2	8.7	−3.1	−2.9	−3.4	−1.5	−4.9	—	−.7	....	Use of Fund Credit and Loans	79dc d
	−.3	.3	−.6	−.1	.6	−.3	−.1	.3	−.4	−1.4	—	—	—	—	....	Liabs.Constit.For.Auth.Reserves	79dd d
	7.8	21.0	2.4	—	54.2	81.4	391.6	486.6	471.8	406.6	478.2	431.0	456.8	454.9	....	Exceptional Financing	79de d
Year Ending December 31																**Government Finance**	
	₤−18,760	400	−93,380	−26,650	....	....	....	....	....	....	....	....	....	....	....	Deficit (-) or Surplus	80
	₤157,420	214,250	261,700	280,510	....	....	....	....	....	....	....	....	....	....	....	Revenue	81
	₤2,580	800	1,190	3,500	....	....	....	....	....	....	....	....	....	....	....	Grants Received	81z
	₤177,900	214,250	355,600	310,450	....	....	....	....	....	....	....	....	....	....	....	Expenditure	82
	₤860	400	670	210	....	....	....	....	....	....	....	....	....	....	....	Lending Minus Repayments	83
																Financing	
	₤4,890	−340	24,170	−14,970	....	....	....	....	....	....	....	....	....	....	....	Domestic	84a
	₤13,870	−60	69,210	41,620	....	....	....	....	....	....	....	....	....	....	....	Foreign	85a
Billions of Francs																**National Accounts**	
	203.0	314.3	383.5	454.2	590.7	551.9	255.2	288.3	267.7	368.1	....	....	....	....	....	Exports of Goods & Services	90c
	63.4	72.8	95.8	120.0	141.7	159.7	159.8	142.1	138.7	144.6	....	....	....	....	....	Government Consumption	91f
	118.7	239.7	404.7	280.2	277.3	276.9	182.9	104.0	129.2	126.7	....	....	....	....	....	Gross Fixed Capital Formation	93e
	10.2	21.1	24.0	4.3	14.0	17.1	5.7	−7.8	−6.5	−3.8	....	....	....	....	....	Increase/Decrease(-) in Stocks	93i
	147.9	220.6	281.6	317.0	372.2	403.6	380.5	390.7	396.3	408.5	....	....	....	....	....	Private Consumption	96f
	−182.8	−326.9	−478.1	−376.3	−437.3	−438.3	−343.7	−266.7	−266.4	−270.6	....	....	....	....	....	Imports of Goods & Services	98c
	360.4	541.7	711.5	799.4	958.5	970.8	640.1	690.6	659.0	758.2	776.1	746.0	725.3	675.7	....	Gross Domestic Product	99b
Midyear Estimates																	
	1.53	1.72	1.77	1.81	1.87	1.92	1.98	2.04	2.10	2.16	2.23	2.30	2.37	2.44	....	Population	99z

Costa Rica
238

		1965	1966	1967	1968	1969	1970	1971	1972	1973	1974	1975	1976	1977	1978	1979
Exchange Rates																
Market Rate	aa	6.63	6.63	6.63	6.63	6.63	6.63	7.20	7.20	8.02	10.49	10.03	9.96	10.41	11.16	11.29
															Colones per US Dollar:	
Market Rate	ae	6.64	6.64	6.64	6.64	6.64	6.64	6.64	6.64	6.65	8.57	8.57	8.57	8.57	8.57	8.57
Market Rate	rf	6.63	6.63	6.63	6.63	6.63	6.63	6.63	6.64	6.65	7.93	8.57	8.57	8.57	8.57	8.57
													Index Numbers (1990=100):			
Market Rate	ah x	1,375.7	1,375.7	1,375.7	1,375.7	1,375.7	1,375.7	1,375.7	1,375.7	1,373.2	1,161.9	1,065.1	1,065.1	1,065.1	1,065.1	1,065.1
Nominal Effective Exchange Rate	nec	....	....	....	....	....	....	....	....	....	....	....	....	....	....	380.8
Real Effective Exchange Rate	rec	....	....	....	....	....	....	....	....	....	....	....	....	....	....	147.8
Fund Position															*Millions of SDRs:*	
Quota	2f. s	20.00	25.00	25.00	25.00	25.00	32.00	32.00	32.00	32.00	32.00	32.00	32.00	32.00	41.00	41.00
SDRs	1b. s	—	—	—	—	—	.20	.06	3.99	3.88	1.96	3.81	1.24	5.53	3.00	4.46
Reserve Position in the Fund	1c. s	—	—	—	—	2.02	6.03	.29	.28	.28	—	—	—	—	7.78	7.54
Total Fund Cred.&Loans Outstg.	2tl	15.00	15.48	15.48	9.73	—	—	—	—	—	18.84	29.96	32.30	29.31	24.32	43.81
International Liquidity											*Millions of US Dollars Unless Otherwise Indicated:*					
Total Reserves minus Gold	1l. d	17.73	15.00	16.07	18.45	27.06	14.16	27.19	40.62	48.49	42.13	48.82	95.41	190.49	193.89	118.63
SDRs	1b. d	—	—	—	—	—	.20	.07	4.33	4.68	2.40	4.46	1.44	6.72	3.91	5.88
Reserve Position in the Fund	1c. d	—	—	—	—	2.02	6.03	.31	.30	.34	—	—	—	—	10.14	9.93
Foreign Exchange	1d. d	17.73	15.00	16.07	18.45	25.04	7.93	26.81	35.98	43.47	39.73	44.36	93.97	183.77	179.85	102.82
Gold (Million Fine Troy Ounces)	1ad	.060	.060	.060	.060	.060	.060	.060	.060	.060	.060	.060	.060	.073	.080	.087
Gold (National Valuation)	1an d	2.08	2.08	2.08	2.10	2.10	2.10	2.10	2.28	2.54	2.53	2.53	2.53	11.69	15.46	36.00
Deposit Money Banks: Assets	7a. d	4.48	4.53	9.03	10.75	9.62	10.88	11.88	18.20	27.55	22.89	11.74	28.67	40.28	55.15	47.06
Liabilities	7b. d	11.00	12.32	10.45	15.38	21.69	21.01	20.47	24.15	36.80	31.20	45.12	65.99	94.92	87.63	120.04
Other Banking Insts.: Liabilities	7f. d	9.89	10.70	11.53	14.23	16.08	17.37	17.10	16.95	11.98	8.73	7.93	7.41	9.85	8.59	7.27
Monetary Authorities															*Millions of Colones:*	
Foreign Assets	11	132	113	128	141	195	118	235	321	395	383	444	837	1,728	1,786	1,315
Claims on Central Government	12a	113	181	250	316	298	333	345	424	376	538	762	1,132	1,641	2,314	3,161
Claims on Official Entities	12bx	....	....	....	....	....	....	....	....	....	....	....	....	....	1,381	2,151
Claims on Deposit Money Banks	12e	247	232	128	114	102	226	253	292	279	815	855	795	1,061	1,267	3,941
Claims on Other Banking Insts.	12f	59	55	60	60	60	64	76	83	105	125	142	174	205	307	407
Reserve Money	14	356	364	455	503	598	596	766	926	1,082	1,238	1,648	2,210	3,236	3,224	4,977
of which: Currency Outside DMBs	14a	237	253	282	306	350	380	434	521	643	734	853	1,117	1,409	1,704	1,955
Time, Savings,& Fgn.Currency Dep.	15	7	—	10	—	—	—	—	—	—	56	6	205	342	649	1,734
Bonds	16ab	—	—	—	16	38	5	4	—	—	—	—	—	297	417	371
Foreign Liabilities	16c	102	200	110	66	1	9	5	70	34	400	304	365	393	789	1,023
Long-Term Foreign Liabilities	16cl	157	94	77	76	55	41	69	102	96	226	581	818	1,190	1,527	2,773
Central Government Deposits	16d	23	25	16	35	45	137	96	117	127	236	199	359	270	302	228
Capital Accounts	17a	30	29	30	27	31	53	78	101	109	154	154	147	132	151	201
Other Items (Net)	17r	−124	−131	−132	−91	−112	−100	−111	−197	−293	−450	−690	−1,166	−1,224	−4	−332
of which: Valuation Adjustment	17rv	....	....	....	....	....	....	....	....	....	....	....	....	....	−839	−784
Deposit Money Banks															*Millions of Colones:*	
Reserves	20	113	101	158	193	245	213	324	398	436	484	771	1,072	1,570	1,433	2,966
Foreign Assets	21	30	30	60	71	64	72	79	121	183	196	101	246	345	473	403
Claims on Central Government	22a	44	44	15	20	15	31	65	120	167	322	481	578	862	1,154	3,206
Claims on Official Entities	22bx	....	....	....	....	....	....	....	....	....	....	....	....	....	178	182
Claims on Private Sector	22d	820	835	881	921	1,002	1,197	1,570	1,785	2,029	3,050	4,184	5,115	6,024	7,474	8,941
Claims on Other Banking Insts.	22f	44	50	43	42	42	52	96	92	87	184	182	128	135	179	317
Demand Deposits	24	360	367	547	539	606	623	875	973	1,225	1,395	1,889	2,273	3,065	3,857	4,231
Time, Savings,& Fgn.Currency Dep.	25	178	186	237	219	236	270	494	665	767	1,244	2,127	2,977	3,818	4,793	6,908
Bonds	26ab	—	—	—	6	4	2	1	1	—	—	—	—	—	—	—
Foreign Liabilities	26c	1	—	—	7	7	9	28	42	55	49	41	28	73	95	178
Long-Term Foreign Liabilities	26cl	72	82	69	95	137	130	108	119	189	219	346	538	741	656	851
Central Government Deposits	26d	1	1	1	63	87	120	144	168	199	338	296	578	482	548	606
Credit from Monetary Authorities	26g	247	232	128	114	97	223	240	277	270	805	851	799	1,056	1,270	3,892
Capital Accounts	27a	223	222	225	234	237	241	244	255	259	278	296	298	325	331	362
Other Items (Net)	27r	−31	−30	−51	−30	−42	−53	−1	21	−63	−90	−128	−351	−624	−659	−1,013
Monetary Survey															*Millions of Colones:*	
Foreign Assets (Net)	31n	59	−57	78	139	251	172	280	330	489	130	200	691	1,607	1,375	517
Domestic Credit	32	1,056	1,139	1,232	1,260	1,284	1,420	1,910	2,223	2,439	3,645	5,291	6,244	8,175	12,200	17,603
Claims on Central Govt. (Net)	32an	133	200	248	237	180	107	169	259	217	286	748	773	1,751	2,618	5,533
Claims on Official Entities	32bx	....	....	....	....	....	....	....	....	....	....	....	....	....	1,559	2,333
Claims on Private Sector	32d	820	835	881	921	1,002	1,197	1,570	1,785	2,029	3,050	4,219	5,170	6,084	7,537	9,013
Claims on Other Banking Insts.	32f	103	105	103	102	102	116	171	178	193	309	324	301	340	486	724
Money	34	598	622	832	849	959	1,006	1,317	1,501	1,874	2,146	2,771	3,408	4,504	5,625	6,226
Quasi-Money	35	185	186	248	219	236	270	494	665	767	1,300	2,133	3,182	4,160	5,442	8,642
Bonds	36ab	—	—	—	22	42	7	5	1	—	—	—	—	297	417	371
Long-Term Foreign Liabilities	36cl	228	176	146	171	191	171	177	221	285	445	928	1,356	1,931	2,183	3,624
Capital Accounts	37a	253	251	255	261	268	294	322	356	368	432	451	445	457	481	563
Other Items (Net)	37r	−149	−153	−171	−121	−161	−156	−125	−190	−366	−547	−792	−1,455	−1,567	−573	−1,306
Money plus Quasi-Money	35l	783	808	1,080	1,069	1,195	1,277	1,811	2,166	2,640	3,446	4,904	6,590	8,664	11,067	14,869
Other Banking Institutions															*Millions of Colones:*	
Cash	40	—	—	—	—	—	—	—	—	5	—	—	1	20	2	2
Claims on Central Government	42a	3	1	4	1	1	4	7	8	13	9	6	10	5	5	4
Claims on Official Entities	42bx	....	....	....	....	....	....	....	....	....	....	....	....	....	1	1
Claims on Private Sector	42d	353	353	388	408	425	460	542	581	568	650	731	797	921	1,139	1,251
Demand Deposits	44	—	—	—	1	1	1	1	1	1	—	1	1	—	—	—
Time, Savings,& Fgn.Currency Dep.	45	—	—	—	—	—	—	—	—	—	—	—	—	—	16	83
Bonds	46ab	110	107	126	119	123	130	133	135	142	84	124	182	207	284	181
Long-Term Foreign Liabilities	46cl	66	71	76	94	107	115	113	112	79	75	68	64	84	74	62
Central Government Deposits	46d															
Credit from Monetary Authorities	46g	59	55	60	60	60	64	87	97	113	133	144	175	207	273	307
Credit from Deposit Money Banks	46h	44	41	38	42	42	52	96	96	79	176	174	122	129	173	311
Capital Accounts	47a	81	87	89	91	94	99	105	115	106	112	121	126	131	137	141
Other Items (Net)	47r	−3	−7	3	3	—	3	15	33	66	79	106	138	187	190	173

Costa Rica

238

1980	1981	1982	1983	1984	1985	1986	1987	1988	1989	1990	1991	1992	1993	1994		
															Exchange Rates	
End of Period																
10.93	42.01	44.40	45.44	46.81	58.99	72.02	98.24	106.98	110.85	147.32	193.72	188.97	208.01	240.98	Market Rate	**aa**
End of Period (ae) Period Average (rf)																
8.57	36.09	40.25	43.40	47.75	53.70	58.88	69.25	79.50	84.35	103.55	135.43	137.43	151.44	165.07	Market Rate	**ae**
8.57	21.76	37.41[e]	41.09	44.53	50.45	55.99	62.78	75.80	81.50	91.58	122.43	134.51	142.17	157.07	Market Rate	**rf**
Period Averages																
1,065.1	463.2	244.7[e]	222.9	205.2	180.6	163.2	145.7	120.5	112.0	100.0	75.0	67.9	64.3	58.1	Market Rate	**ahx**
391.7	182.6	106.8	108.4	110.5	111.3	103.8	96.0	87.0	92.7	100.0	83.2	82.3	89.4	91.8	Nominal Effective Exchange Rate	**nec**
162.6	103.2	117.9	135.6	133.3	131.5	118.2	107.3	98.2	101.9	100.0	91.2	93.0	91.5	89.4	Real Effective Exchange Rate	**rec**
															Fund Position	
End of Period																
61.50	61.50	61.50	84.10	84.10	84.10	84.10	84.10	84.10	84.10	84.10	84.10	119.00	119.00	119.00	Quota	**2f.s**
—	—	.07	2.85	.11	.02	.01	.01	.01	.04	1.14	.21	.17	.12	.12	SDRs	**1b.s**
—	—	—	—	—	—	—	—	—	—	—	—	8.73	8.73	8.73	Reserve Position in the Fund	**1c.s**
44.64	88.16	84.18	183.28	158.98	171.64	140.95	93.27	53.03	26.94	7.94	58.03	59.28	59.28	45.46	Total Fund Cred.&Loans Outstg.	**2tl**
															International Liquidity	
End of Period																
145.57	131.42	226.12	311.27	405.00	506.37	523.37	488.86	667.98	742.57	520.63	919.80	1,018.65	1,024.03	893.20	Total Reserves minus Gold	**1l.d**
—	—	.08	2.98	.11	.02	.01	.01	.01	.05	1.62	.30	.23	.16	.18	SDRs	**1b.d**
—	—	—	—	—	—	—	—	—	—	—	—	12.00	11.98	12.74	Reserve Position in the Fund	**1c.d**
145.57	131.42	226.04	308.29	404.89	506.35	523.36	488.85	667.97	742.52	519.01	919.50	1,006.41	1,011.89	880.28	Foreign Exchange	**1d.d**
.087	.029	.052	.088	.023	.058	.069	.063	.021	.008	.011	.032	.040	.035	.034	Gold (Million Fine Troy Ounces)	**1ad**
53.86	7.19	22.60	....	....	19.05	26.10	....	....	....	....	....	95.97	....	....	Gold (National Valuation)	**1and**
30.05	65.47	69.44	60.30	38.91	48.51	74.07	86.89	85.96	100.57	96.51	136.31	200.90	151.99	199.11	Deposit Money Banks: Assets	**7a.d**
126.72	131.10	139.95	68.41	88.65	79.44	61.32	55.45	50.67	54.80	58.64	51.06	49.73	90.29	102.24	Liabilities	**7b.d**
5.93	71.21	71.73	68.80	59.48	54.69	32.70	4.62	1.85	5.12	4.70	4.27	4.21	3.81	3.58	Other Banking Insts.: Liabilities	**7f.d**
															Monetary Authorities	
End of Period																
3,379	5,288	9,777	18,430	20,577	28,272	32,430	35,484	53,444	62,417	58,124	130,934	148,627	162,319	155,900	Foreign Assets	**11**
4,088	9,650	6,070	9,326	9,793	10,807	17,265	18,065	21,856	25,333	31,800	37,940	42,756	51,965	71,534	Claims on Central Government	**12a**
3,100	3,860	7,152	20,086	23,355	24,288	30,868	30,615	34,768	32,800	37,450	40,521	34,277	28,759	23,536	Claims on Official Entities	**12bx**
6,189	1,779	1,727	6,348	5,451	8,786	13,454	18,401	19,584	20,390	24,289	27,996	28,784	30,906	62,739	Claims on Deposit Money Banks	**12e**
465	614	769	1,127	1,408	1,683	1,434	1,303	3,278	2,967	2,874	4,145	3,522	3,485	3,303	Claims on Other Banking Insts.	**12f**
5,911	13,097	14,277	19,010	23,020	32,924	42,585	48,806	70,608	82,242	99,495	161,467	190,262	208,398	269,980	Reserve Money	**14**
2,255	3,501	5,436	6,941	8,588	9,938	13,241	14,777	24,734	21,922	27,506	34,667	47,864	54,672	74,862	*of which: Currency Outside DMBs*	**14a**
1,906	6,720	3,232	3,352	2,789	866	680	433	709	5,886	10,287	7,616	9,203	8,856	4,787	Time, Savings,& Fgn.Currency Dep.	**15**
301	1,542	5,264	5,081	4,895	5,592	6,228	11,443	23,376	30,221	27,970	33,266	37,026	43,979	71,200	Bonds	**16ab**
3,759	17,896	12,342	15,174	12,330	13,631	14,037	14,192	11,496	8,710	16,821	20,941	17,700	14,337	11,642	Foreign Liabilities	**16c**
3,867	19,074	23,275	70,123	82,539	103,706	122,820	141,512	159,860	159,583	149,314	201,998	204,200	217,995	213,013	Long-Term Foreign Liabilities	**16cl**
678	1,035	2,360	3,681	3,446	5,861	7,798	2,573	9,276	12,541	16,514	16,870	11,688	14,088	9,329	Central Government Deposits	**16d**
251	1,293	1,400	1,797	1,979	3,333	4,639	5,176	5,953	8,641	9,923	15,789	24,472	25,064	26,804	Capital Accounts	**17a**
549	-39,466	-36,655	-62,901	-70,414	-92,077	-103,336	-120,267	-148,348	-163,917	-175,787	-216,411	-236,585	-255,283	-289,743	Other Items (Net)	**17r**
-835	-34,098	-47,646	-58,982	-84,057	-110,462	-125,162	-161,563	-188,262	-213,398	-257,567	-248,812	-274,583	-293,341	-335,010	*of which:* Valuation Adjustment	**17rv**
															Deposit Money Banks	
End of Period																
3,305	8,184	8,628	11,471	14,619	23,685	28,733	34,937	52,497	61,618	79,582	129,962	144,687	157,237	203,946	Reserves	**20**
258	2,363	2,795	2,617	1,858	2,605	4,361	6,017	6,834	8,483	9,994	18,460	27,609	23,018	32,867	Foreign Assets	**21**
5,306	1,416	3,069	3,980	4,234	5,236	5,308	5,675	10,279	12,945	21,331	14,136	7,765	6,562	34,584	Claims on Central Government	**22a**
277	279	431	750	1,056	989	777	831	1,252	2,346	3,257	3,104	2,597	2,646	2,762	Claims on Official Entities	**22bx**
10,205	11,191	16,068	24,820	29,239	34,144	40,188	51,336	59,270	66,164	78,944	93,117	138,699	190,338	222,923	Claims on Private Sector	**22d**
252	379	404	647	934	934	911	1,056	1,090	1,767	1,745	1,605	2,750	2,929	2,584	Claims on Other Banking Insts.	**22f**
4,862	7,185	12,888	18,401	21,399	22,367	29,016	27,624	40,186	41,903	38,781	45,039	61,103	62,437	86,600	Demand Deposits	**24**
8,059	14,719	19,313	27,172	32,843	42,697	48,991	64,102	84,250	104,973	146,177	210,709	252,338	301,349	355,059	Time, Savings,& Fgn.Currency Dep.	**25**
—	—	5	5	56	52	44	38	30	29	28	29	—	—	19	Bonds	**26ab**
414	1,931	2,101	998	1,587	523	777	1,441	1,456	1,114	2,334	2,570	3,097	8,578	7,281	Foreign Liabilities	**26c**
672	2,800	3,532	1,971	2,646	3,743	2,833	2,399	2,572	3,508	3,738	4,345	3,737	5,095	9,596	Long-Term Foreign Liabilities	**26cl**
710	1,402	423	634	629	1,243	1,065	1,588	1,578	1,697	3,879	3,701	4,992	5,610	41,400	Central Government Deposits	**26d**
6,151	1,753	1,675	6,179	5,183	9,214	9,956	14,529	17,420	18,004	20,626	19,212	18,677	17,400	45,834	Credit from Monetary Authorities	**26g**
373	4,199	575	1,104	1,895	3,809	4,548	6,492	11,346	14,423	20,383	31,406	35,518	43,040	31,832	Capital Accounts	**27a**
-1,639	-10,177	-9,117	-12,179	-14,298	-16,055	-16,952	-18,361	-27,616	-32,328	-41,093	-56,627	-55,355	-60,779	-77,955	Other Items (Net)	**27r**
															Monetary Survey	
End of Period																
-536	-12,177	-1,871	4,875	8,518	16,723	21,977	25,868	47,326	61,076	48,963	125,883	155,439	162,422	169,844	Foreign Assets (Net)	**31n**
22,364	24,999	31,180	56,421	65,944	70,977	87,888	104,720	120,939	130,084	157,008	173,997	215,686	266,986	310,497	Domestic Credit	**32**
8,005	8,629	6,356	8,991	9,952	8,939	13,710	19,579	21,281	24,040	32,738	31,505	33,841	38,829	55,389	Claims on Central Govt. (Net)	**32an**
3,377	4,139	7,583	20,836	24,411	25,277	31,645	31,446	36,020	35,146	40,707	43,625	36,874	31,405	26,298	Claims on Official Entities	**32bx**
10,265	11,238	16,068	24,820	29,239	34,144	40,188	51,336	59,270	66,164	78,944	93,117	138,699	190,338	222,923	Claims on Private Sector	**32d**
717	993	1,173	1,774	2,342	2,617	2,345	2,359	4,368	4,734	4,619	5,750	6,272	6,414	5,887	Claims on Other Banking Insts.	**32f**
7,271	10,832	18,448	25,619	30,132	32,439	42,487	42,611	65,267	63,975	66,484	79,794	109,517	117,193	161,568	Money	**34**
9,965	21,439	22,545	30,524	35,632	43,563	49,671	64,535	84,959	110,859	156,464	218,325	261,541	310,205	359,846	Quasi-Money	**35**
301	1,542	5,269	5,086	4,951	5,644	6,272	11,481	23,406	30,250	27,998	33,295	37,026	43,979	71,219	Bonds	**36ab**
4,538	21,874	26,807	72,094	85,185	107,449	125,653	143,911	162,432	163,091	153,052	206,343	207,937	223,090	222,609	Long-Term Foreign Liabilities	**36cl**
625	5,492	1,975	2,901	3,874	7,142	9,187	11,668	17,299	23,064	30,306	47,195	59,990	68,104	58,636	Capital Accounts	**37a**
-872	-48,357	-45,735	-74,928	-85,312	-108,537	-123,405	-143,618	-185,098	-200,079	-228,333	-285,072	-304,886	-333,163	-393,537	Other Items (Net)	**37r**
17,235	32,270	40,993	56,143	65,764	76,002	92,158	107,146	150,226	174,834	222,948	298,119	371,058	427,398	521,414	Money plus Quasi-Money	**35l**
															Other Banking Institutions	
End of Period																
2	72	269	226	578	434	238	—	54	950	713	851	22	60	43	Cash	**40**
12	4	69	42	23	27	288	77	25	162	79	409	609	769	449	Claims on Central Government	**42a**
3	24	24	24	23	110	21	—	—	—	—	—	—	—	—	Claims on Official Entities	**42bx**
1,284	2,059	2,200	2,828	3,215	3,508	3,929	2,606	2,833	3,409	3,859	3,847	4,768	4,985	7,284	Claims on Private Sector	**42d**
—	25	27	36	44	68	5	211	1	5	—	—	—	—	—	Demand Deposits	**44**
132	224	389	778	1,214	561	285	408	458	899	947	1,168	546	434	466	Time, Savings,& Fgn.Currency Dep.	**45**
230	354	283	293	331	506	1,121	476	710	718	606	922	1,403	2,006	2,086	Bonds	**46ab**
51	2,570	2,887	2,986	2,840	2,937	1,925	320	147	432	487	578	579	577	591	Long-Term Foreign Liabilities	**46cl**
—	7	6	6	6	6	5	—	—	—	1	—	—	—	—	Central Government Deposits	**46d**
312	613	769	1,125	1,419	1,880	2,938	478	443	804	839	1,024	653	650	2,447	Credit from Monetary Authorities	**46g**
246	122	184	442	697	931	1,062	804	1,008	283	1,816	1,676	2,148	2,305	2,150	Credit from Deposit Money Banks	**46h**
143	245	279	334	344	355	423	234	235	231	194	196	158	144	177	Capital Accounts	**47a**
188	-2,001	-2,262	-2,880	-3,056	-3,165	-3,288	-248	-90	1,149	-239	-457	-88	-302	-141	Other Items (Net)	**47r**

Costa Rica
238

		1965	1966	1967	1968	1969	1970	1971	1972	1973	1974	1975	1976	1977	1978	1979
Banking Survey															*Millions of Colones:*	
Foreign Assets (net)	51n	59	−57	78	139	251	172	280	330	489	130	200	691	1,607	1,375	517
Domestic Credit	52	....	....	....	1,567	1,608	1,768	2,288	2,633	2,827	3,995	5,704	6,751	8,761	12,858	18,136
Claims on Central Govt. (Net)	52an	136	201	252	238	181	111	176	267	230	295	754	783	1,756		5,537
Claims on Official Entities	52bx														1,560	2,334
Claims on Private Sector	52d	1,173	1,188	1,269	1,329	1,427	1,657	2,112	2,366	2,597	3,700	4,950	5,968	7,005	8,675	10,264
Liquid Liabilities	55l	783	808	1,080	1,069	1,195	1,277	1,812	2,166	2,636	3,446	4,905	6,590	8,645	11,081	14,949
Bonds	56ab	110	107	126	141	165	137	137	136	142	84	124	182	504	701	552
Long-Term Foreign Liabilities	56cl	294	247	223	265	298	286	290	333	364	520	996	1,419	2,016	2,257	3,687
Capital Accounts	57a	334	338	344	351	362	393	427	471	474	544	571	571	588	618	704
Other Items (Net)	57r	....	....	....	−119	−161	−154	−99	−143	−301	−469	−692	−1,321	−1,384	−423	−1,239
Interest Rates															*Percent Per Annum*	
Discount Rate (End of Period)	60	4.00	5.00	5.00	5.00	5.00	5.00	5.00	5.00	5.00	7.00	7.00	8.00	8.00	15.40	14.80
Deposit Rate	60l	....	....	....	....	....	....	....	....	....	....	....	....	....	....	....
Lending Rate	60p	....	....	....	....	....	....	....	....	....	....	....	....	....	....	....
Prices															*Index Numbers (1990=100):*	
Prices: Home & Import Goods	63	2.1	I2.1	2.2	2.3	2.4	2.6	2.7	2.9	3.3	4.7	5.7	6.2	6.7	I7.2	8.4
Producer Prices (1991=100)	63p															
Consumer Prices	64	3.2	3.2	3.3	3.4	3.5	3.7	3.8	4.0	4.6	5.9	I7.0	7.2	7.5	8.0	8.7
International Transactions															*Millions of US Dollars*	
Exports	70..d	111.8	135.5	143.8	170.8	189.7	231.2	225.4	280.9	344.5	440.3	493.3	592.9	828.2	864.9	934.4
Imports, cif	71..d	178.2	178.5	190.7	213.9	245.1	316.7	349.7	372.8	455.3	719.7	694.0	770.4	1,021.4	1,165.7	1,396.8
Imports, fob	71.vd	160.3	160.6	171.6	192.5	220.5	284.8	314.6	335.3	409.8	647.8	624.7	693.3	919.3	1,049.1	1,257.1
Balance of Payments															*Millions of US Dollars:*	
Goods: Exports f.o.b.	78aa d													827.8	863.9	942.1
Goods: Imports f.o.b.	78ab d													−925.1	−1,049.4	−1,257.2
Trade Balance	78ac d													−97.3	−185.5	−315.1
Services: Credit	78ad d													129.9	141.9	154.8
Services: Debit	78ae d													−199.0	−228.7	−266.8
Balance on Goods and Services	78af d													−166.4	−272.3	−427.1
Income: Credit	78ag d													11.4	19.2	14.4
Income: Debit	78ah d													−86.4	−126.7	−157.7
Balance on Goods, Serv., & Inc.	78ai d													−241.4	−379.8	−570.4
Current Transfers, n.i.e.: Credit	78aj d													26.4	28.0	30.1
Current Transfers: Debit	78ak d													−10.6	−11.4	−17.9
Current Account, n.i.e.	78al d													−225.6	−363.2	−558.2
Capital Account, n.i.e.: Credit	78ba d													—	—	—
Capital Account: Debit	78bb d													—	—	—
Capital Account, n.i.e.	78bc d													—	—	—
Direct Investment Abroad	78bd d														−1.6	−1.1
Dir. Invest. in Rep. Econ., n.i.e.	78be d													62.5	48.6	43.5
Portfolio Investment Assets	78bf d															—
Portfolio Investment Liab., n.i.e.	78bg d													3.5	20.9	—
Other Investment Assets	78bh d													−22.6	−49.2	−113.7
Other Investment Liab., n.i.e.	78bi d													308.0	349.8	423.8
Financial Account, n.i.e.	78bj d													351.4	368.5	352.5
Net Errors and Omissions	78ca d													−27.4	−50.5	79.2
Overall Balance	78cb d													98.4	−45.2	−126.5
Reserves and Related Items	79da d													−98.4	45.2	126.5
Reserve Assets	79db d													−107.3	−20.8	93.2
Use of Fund Credit and Loans	79dc d													−3.5	−6.6	25.3
Liabs.Constit.For.Auth.Reserves	79dd d													4.4	54.5	−35.5
Exceptional Financing	79de d													8.0	18.1	43.5
Government Finance															*Millions of Colones*	
Deficit (-) or Surplus	80						−66	−285	I−356	−380	−89	−371	−704	−818	−1,507	−2,341
Revenue and Grants	81						975	1,008	I1,260	1,620	2,449	3,027	3,648	4,393	5,755	6,317
Expenditure	82						1,041	1,293	I1,506	1,846	2,415	3,217	4,148	5,085	7,000	8,601
Lending Minus Repayments	83								I110	155	122	180	203	127	261	58
Financing																
Net Borrowing: Domestic	84a						157	148								
Foreign	85a						6	104								
Use of Cash Balances	87	20	5	11	23	56	−97	33								
Debt (by Residence of Lender)																
Debt: Domestic	88a								I1,391	1,594	1,697	1,777	2,237	2,787	3,850	5,671
Foreign	89a								I657	820	1,149	1,348	1,551	1,967	2,929	3,614
Debt (by Currency)																
Debt: Colones	88b	662	760	911	1,105	1,150	1,528	1,698								
Foreign Currency	89b	284	302	325	315	302	349	484								
National Accounts															*Millions of Colones*	
Exports of Goods & Services	90c	896	1,072	1,168	1,445	1,523	1,816	1,912	2,483	3,130	4,380	5,052	5,977	8,128	8,509	9,311
Government Consumption	91f	495	537	586	636	706	820	990	1,182	1,417	1,889	2,558	3,306	4,208	5,069	6,243
Gross Fixed Capital Formation	93e	730	736	834	882	1,024	1,270	1,579	1,800	2,252	3,175	3,695	4,846	5,889	6,952	9,050
Increase/Decrease(-) in Stocks	93i	37	81	63	42	109	70	158	10	187	359	−58	46	502	132	−295
Private Consumption	96f	3,080	3,186	3,444	3,804	4,116	4,805	5,146	5,748	6,924	9,772	12,036	13,718	17,171	20,412	23,139
Imports of Goods & Services	98c	−1,309	−1,324	−1,461	−1,683	−1,821	−2,256	−2,648	−3,007	−3,747	−6,360	−6,478	−7,218	−9,567	−10,879	−12,863
Gross Domestic Product = GDP	99b	3,929	4,288	4,634	5,127	5,655	6,525	7,137	8,216	10,162	13,216	16,805	20,676	26,331	30,194	34,584
Net Factor Inc/Pmts(-) Abroad	98.n	−83	−93	−109	−125	−106	−88	−98	−253	−285	−312	−543	−627	−655	−903	−1,279
Gross National Product = GNP	99a	3,845	4,195	4,525	5,002	5,549	6,436	7,033	7,958	9,875	12,910	16,283	20,077	25,705	29,315	33,307
Nat'l Income, Market Prices	99e	3,607	3,939	4,240	4,678	5,195	6,020	6,583	7,454	9,308	12,212	15,391	18,953	24,352	27,730	31,461
Gross Dom. Prod. 1990 Prices	99b.p	169,759	183,120	193,467	209,860	221,385	237,996	254,128	274,911	296,104	312,522	319,086	336,691	366,672	389,654	408,908
GDP Deflator (1990=100)	99bi p	2.3	2.3	2.4	2.4	2.6	2.7	2.8	3.0	3.4	4.2	5.3	6.1	7.2	7.7	8.5
																Millions:
Population	99z	1.49	1.54	1.59	1.63	1.69	1.73	1.80	1.84	1.87	1.92	1.96	2.01	2.07	2.12	2.17

Government Finance: I Beginning in 1972, annual data are as reported in the *Government Finance Statistics Yearbook* and cover consolidated central government (including some social security funds but excluding all extrabudgetary accounts). I Beginning in 1987, social security coverage has been expanded and, in addition, data cover operations of extrabudgetary accounts.

Costa Rica

238

Series	Code	1980	1981	1982	1983	1984	1985	1986	1987	1988	1989	1990	1991	1992	1993	1994
Banking Survey (*End of Period*)																
Foreign Assets (net)	51n	-536	-12,177	-1,871	4,875	8,518	16,723	21,977	25,868	47,326	61,076	48,963	125,883	155,439	162,422	169,844
Domestic Credit	52	22,946	26,086	32,294	57,535	66,857	71,999	89,776	105,044	119,429	128,921	156,326	172,503	214,791	266,326	312,343
Claims on Central Govt. (Net)	52an	8,016	8,626	6,419	9,027	9,969	8,960	13,993	19,656	21,306	24,202	32,816	31,914	34,450	39,598	55,838
Claims on Official Entities	52bx	3,380	4,163	7,607	20,860	24,434	25,387	31,666	31,446	36,020	35,146	40,707	43,625	36,874	31,405	26,298
Claims on Private Sector	52d	11,549	13,297	18,268	27,648	32,454	37,652	44,117	53,942	62,103	69,573	82,803	96,964	143,467	195,323	230,207
Liquid Liabilities	55l	17,365	32,447	41,140	56,731	66,444	76,197	92,210	107,765	150,631	174,788	223,182	298,436	371,582	427,772	521,837
Bonds	56ab	531	1,896	5,552	5,379	5,282	6,150	7,393	11,957	24,116	30,968	28,604	34,217	38,429	45,985	73,305
Long-Term Foreign Liabilities	56cl	4,589	24,444	29,694	75,080	88,025	110,386	127,578	144,231	162,579	163,523	153,539	206,921	208,516	223,667	223,200
Capital Accounts	57a	768	5,737	2,254	3,235	4,218	7,497	9,610	11,902	17,534	23,295	30,500	47,391	60,148	68,248	58,813
Other Items (Net)	57r	-844	-50,616	-48,217	-78,015	-88,594	-111,508	-125,038	-144,943	-188,105	-202,577	-230,536	-288,579	-308,445	-336,924	-394,968
Interest Rates (*Percent Per Annum*)																
Discount Rate (*End of Period*)	60	23.50	23.50	30.00	30.00	28.00	28.00	27.50	31.38	31.50	31.61	37.80	42.50	29.00	35.00	37.75
Deposit Rate	60l	....	....	18.29	19.50	14.50	16.50	16.67	14.06	15.18	15.62	21.16	27.32	15.80	16.90	17.72
Lending Rate	60p	....	....	25.00	23.25	18.00	20.92	21.80	23.82	28.69	29.17	32.56	38.88	28.46	30.02	33.03
Prices (*Period Averages*)																
Prices: Home & Import Goods	63	10.4	17.1	35.6	45.0	48.4	53.4	58.3	64.4	75.9	87.0	100.0	128.1	151.4	161.1	....
Producer Prices (1991=100)	63p	....	....	....	....	....	....	....	....	....	....	....	100.0	118.4	124.5	140.8
Consumer Prices	64	10.3	14.1	26.7	35.5	39.7	45.7	51.1	59.7	72.1	84.0	100.0	128.7	156.8	172.1	I195.4
International Transactions (*Millions of US Dollars*)																
Exports	70..*d*	1,001.7	1,008.1	870.4	872.6	1,006.4	976.0	1,120.5	1,158.3	1,245.7	1,414.6	1,448.2	1,597.7	1,828.9	2,049.4	2,215.3
Imports, cif	71..*d*	1,540.4	1,208.5	889.0	987.8	1,093.7	1,098.2	1,147.5	1,382.5	1,409.8	1,717.4	1,989.7	1,876.6	2,440.0	2,884.7	3,025.1
Imports, fob	71.v*d*	1,386.4	1,087.5	800.2	892.4	988.1	992.1	1,036.6	1,248.9	1,273.5	1,551.4	1,797.4	1,695.2	2,204.1	2,605.8	2,732.7
Balance of Payments (*Minus Sign Indicates Debit*)																
Goods: Exports f.o.b.	78aa*d*	1,000.9	1,002.6	869.0	852.5	997.5	939.1	1,084.8	1,106.7	1,180.7	1,322.7	1,354.2	1,498.1	1,739.1	1,944.6	....
Goods: Imports f.o.b.	78ab*d*	-1,375.2	-1,090.6	-804.9	-894.3	-992.9	-1,001.0	-1,045.2	-1,245.2	-1,278.6	-1,577.2	-1,796.7	-1,697.6	-2,210.9	-2,610.4	....
Trade Balance	78ac*d*	-374.3	-88.0	64.1	-41.8	4.6	-61.9	39.6	-138.5	-97.9	-254.5	-442.5	-199.5	-471.8	-665.8	....
Services: Credit	78ad*d*	194.2	170.8	242.2	275.2	272.5	274.7	303.0	337.1	430.3	499.3	609.0	691.4	841.3	1,035.2	....
Services: Debit	78ae*d*	-286.2	-217.0	-240.3	-253.4	-261.3	-281.7	-303.6	-391.1	-423.7	-455.7	-549.7	-534.8	-710.6	-806.4	....
Balance on Goods and Services	78af*d*	-466.3	-134.2	66.0	-20.0	15.8	-68.9	39.0	-192.5	-91.3	-210.9	-383.2	-42.9	-341.1	-437.0	....
Income: Credit	78ag*d*	23.5	25.9	32.2	44.9	43.7	56.4	52.4	48.5	47.8	69.6	130.3	111.4	112.8	101.9	....
Income: Debit	78ah*d*	-235.6	-327.9	-400.8	-373.8	-351.5	-332.2	-323.3	-338.4	-390.4	-401.4	-363.0	-285.3	-315.4	-287.8	....
Balance on Goods, Serv., & Inc.	78ai*d*	-678.4	-436.2	-302.6	-348.9	-292.0	-344.7	-231.9	-482.4	-433.9	-542.7	-615.9	-216.8	-543.7	-622.9	....
Current Transfers, n.i.e.: Credit	78aj*d*	33.5	36.9	38.9	45.6	51.3	64.2	82.1	117.2	141.9	99.6	126.0	121.1	168.9	160.1	....
Current Transfers: Debit	78ak*d*	-19.0	-9.8	-8.0	-9.3	-10.4	-10.6	-10.8	-11.2	-11.5	-3.8	-4.1	-3.5	-5.6	-7.2	....
Current Account, n.i.e.	78al*d*	-663.9	-409.1	-271.7	-312.6	-251.1	-291.1	-160.6	-376.4	-303.5	-446.9	-494.0	-99.2	-380.4	-470.0	....
Capital Account, n.i.e.: Credit	78ba*d*	—	—	—	—	—	—	—	—	—	—	—	—	—	—	....
Capital Account: Debit	78bb*d*	—	—	—	—	—	—	—	—	—	—	—	—	—	—	....
Capital Account, n.i.e.	78bc*d*	—	—	—	—	—	—	—	—	—	—	—	—	—	—	....
Direct Investment Abroad	78bd*d*	-4.5	-3.4	-2.4	-5.4	-3.9	-4.7	-3.6	-4.5	-.9	-1.5	-2.1	-5.6	-4.4	—	....
Dir. Invest. in Rep. Econ., n.i.e.	78be*d*	52.6	69.6	28.9	60.7	55.9	69.9	61.0	80.3	122.3	116.4	162.5	178.4	226.0	275.0	....
Portfolio Investment Assets	78bf*d*	—	-.5	-.3	—	—	.7	—	—	—	—	—	—	—	—	....
Portfolio Investment Liab., n.i.e.	78bg*d*	122.0	-1.9	-1.6	-2.6	-.2	-14.2	-2.5	—	-6.0	-13.2	-28.2	-13.0	-16.9	-5.1	....
Other Investment Assets	78bh*d*	-163.2	-131.2	-145.7	-25.8	-161.8	-95.8	-42.4	-72.3	-77.3	-37.8	-160.6	75.6	84.8	90.0	....
Other Investment Liab., n.i.e.	78bi*d*	236.8	39.1	-117.1	-150.9	-169.2	-188.4	-315.7	-444.6	-310.0	-266.0	-88.9	-80.4	-90.1	-24.7	....
Financial Account, n.i.e.	78bj*d*	243.7	-28.3	-238.2	-124.0	-279.2	-232.5	-303.2	-441.1	-271.9	-202.1	-119.8	155.0	199.4	335.2	....
Net Errors and Omissions	78ca*d*	-69.5	69.6	163.7	78.4	104.4	142.9	97.5	131.1	224.6	221.9	56.4	99.9	201.9	19.8	....
Overall Balance	78cb*d*	-489.7	-367.8	-346.2	-358.3	-426.0	-380.7	-366.3	-686.4	-350.8	-427.1	-557.4	155.7	20.9	-109.2	....
Reserves and Related Items	79da*d*	489.7	367.8	346.2	358.3	426.0	380.7	366.3	686.4	350.8	427.1	557.4	-155.7	-20.9	109.2	....
Reserve Assets	79db*d*	-92.9	-1.5	-120.9	-152.7	79.7	-72.1	-58.0	25.0	-188.0	-112.1	222.6	-416.1	-176.8	59.6	....
Use of Fund Credit and Loans	79dc*d*	.8	50.1	-4.4	105.6	-24.5	12.2	-36.4	-62.3	-54.1	-33.4	-25.6	67.7	1.7	—	....
Liabs.Constit.For.Auth.Reserves	79dd*d*	130.2	-3.9	11.9	-25.3	-51.2	-54.4	1.6	-5.5	8.0	-4.2	-6.9	7.1	-6.6	-29.0	....
Exceptional Financing	79de*d*	451.7	323.0	459.6	430.6	422.0	495.0	459.2	729.2	585.0	576.7	369.8	185.6	160.8	84.5	....
Government Finance (*Year Ending December 31*)																
Deficit (-) or Surplus	80	-3,062	-1,640	-864	-2,591	-1,195	-2,467	-11,034	I-8,290	10	-9,060	-16,410	-9,200	8,540	-2,170	....
Revenue and Grants	81	7,373	10,199	17,027	28,115	36,382	41,011	54,564	I70,090	87,750	104,540	120,720	162,520	225,230	277,910	....
Expenditure	82	10,369	11,994	17,944	30,490	37,198	43,136	65,127	I77,410	85,740	111,090	133,920	171,100	216,390	279,960	....
Lending Minus Repayments	83	67	-156	-54	216	378	342	471	I970	2,000	2,510	3,210	620	300	120	....
Financing																
Net Borrowing: Domestic	84a	I2,157	265	-233	627	....	....	....	I6,560	3,800	5,990	14,870	-1,630	-11,010	....	....
Foreign	85a	I463	1,136	1,097	1,964	....	....	....	I1,730	760	3,070	1,540	10,830	2,470	-9,340	....
Use of Cash Balances	87	I442	239	....	....	....	....	....	....	-4,570	....	....	....	....	....	....
Debt (by Residence of Lender)																
Debt: Domestic	88a	8,605	10,231	12,316	21,010	....	....	....	....	....	....	....	....	....	....	....
Foreign	89a	4,431	11,620	13,492	15,300	....	....	....	....	....	....	....	....	....	....	....
Debt (by Currency)																
Debt: Colones	88b	....	....	....	....	23,830	26,434	44,072	54,390	80,560	100,963	137,089	....	....	....	....
Foreign Currency	89b	....	....	....	....	17,482	19,018	20,584	22,304	22,408	23,640	21,738	....	....	....	....
National Accounts (*Millions of Colones*)																
Exports of Goods & Services	90c	10,963	24,708	43,959	46,601	56,046	60,807	77,280	90,004	118,998	148,435	179,509	265,470	344,296	411,466	514,664
Government Consumption	91f	7,544	8,987	14,192	19,527	25,503	31,175	37,951	42,652	54,630	72,283	94,948	111,876	144,448	178,685	226,930
Gross Fixed Capital Formation	93e	9,895	13,737	19,808	23,269	32,679	38,240	46,023	56,313	66,211	87,224	117,071	136,098	188,318	248,535	273,049
Increase/Decrease(-) in Stocks	93i	1,109	2,837	4,262	8,001	4,324	13,000	16,139	20,857	19,358	25,519	25,672	36,544	75,805	70,987	90,980
Private Consumption	96f	27,140	34,344	56,397	79,481	99,837	118,974	144,381	176,475	215,794	256,923	321,143	411,105	544,608	648,463	781,887
Imports of Goods & Services	98c	-15,245	-27,510	-41,113	-47,565	-55,378	-64,277	-75,195	-101,768	-125,247	-164,473	-215,508	-270,903	-391,166	-489,595	-578,603
Gross Domestic Product = GDP	99b	41,405	57,103	97,505	129,314	163,011	197,920	246,579	284,533	349,743	425,911	522,835	690,190	906,309	1,068,542	1,308,906
Net Factor Inc/Pmts(-) Abroad	98.n	-1,987	-6,434	-16,087	-13,673	-13,804	-14,115	-15,099	-18,616	-25,661	-30,740	-21,480	-21,819	-27,268	-31,921	-32,786
Gross National Product = GNP	99a	39,417	50,669	81,418	115,641	149,207	183,805	231,480	265,917	324,082	395,171	501,355	668,371	879,041	1,036,621	1,276,120
Nat'l Income, Market Prices	99e	37,237	47,958	77,531	111,432	144,346	178,317	225,350	258,803	315,163	384,550	488,138	650,011	856,820	1,010,886	1,244,697
Gross Dom. Prod. 1990 Prices	99b.*p*	411,982	402,673	373,338	384,013	414,843	417,832	440,934	461,943	477,828	504,900	522,835	534,663	575,998	612,508	639,879
GDP Deflator (1990=100)	99bi*p*	10.1	14.2	26.1	33.7	39.3	47.4	55.9	61.6	73.2	84.4	100.0	129.1	157.3	174.5	204.6
Midyear Estimates																
Population	99z	2.25	2.27	2.42	2.50	2.57	2.64	2.72	2.78	2.85	2.92	I2.80	2.87	2.94	3.00	3.07

Côte d'Ivoire

662

		1965	1966	1967	1968	1969	1970	1971	1972	1973	1974	1975	1976	1977	1978	1979
Exchange Rates																*Francs per SDR:*
Official Rate	aa	245.07	247.59	245.42	247.40	277.91	276.02	283.61	278.00	284.00	272.08	262.55	288.70	285.76	272.28	264.78
																Francs per US Dollar:
Official Rate	ae	245.08	247.59	245.43	247.41	277.92	276.03	261.23	256.05	235.43	222.22	224.27	248.49	235.25	209.00	201.00
Official Rate	rf	245.06	245.68	246.00	247.56	259.96	276.40	275.59	252.03	222.89	240.70	214.31	238.95	245.68	225.66	212.72
																Index Numbers (1990=100):
Official Rate	ah$x$	110.8	110.5	110.4	109.7	104.8	98.2	98.6	107.8	122.3	112.8	126.9	113.8	110.5	120.6	127.7
Nominal Effective Exchange Rate	ne c	....	....	....	....	....	....	....	....	....	....	....	....	....	....	43.5
Real Effective Exchange Rate	re c	....	....	....	....	....	....	....	....	....	....	....	....	....	....	103.3
Fund Position																*Millions of SDRs:*
Quota	2f. s	15.0	15.8	16.6	17.4	19.0	52.0	52.0	52.0	52.0	52.0	52.0	52.0	52.0	76.0	76.0
SDRs	1b. s	—	—	—	—	—	3.2	9.8	15.3	15.3	15.2	14.5	11.8	8.6	7.4	17.9
Reserve Position in the Fund	1c. s	1.5	1.7	1.9	2.1	2.5	10.8	10.8	10.8	10.8	—	—	—	—	10.4	12.2
Total Fund Cred.&Loans Outstg.	2tl	—	—	—	—	—	—	—	—	—	11.2	11.2	23.4	13.4	21.6	21.6
International Liquidity													*Millions of US Dollars Unless Otherwise Indicated:*			
Total Reserves minus Gold	1l. d	61.8	62.4	71.1	80.7	73.9	118.8	89.4	87.2	88.4	65.7	102.8	76.4	184.8	448.0	147.0
SDRs	1b. d	—	—	—	—	—	3.2	10.6	16.6	18.5	18.6	16.9	13.7	10.4	9.6	23.6
Reserve Position in the Fund	1c. d	1.5	1.7	1.9	2.1	2.5	10.7	11.7	11.7	13.0	—	—	—	—	13.5	16.1
Foreign Exchange	1d. d	60.3	60.7	69.2	78.6	71.4	104.9	67.2	58.9	56.9	47.1	85.8	62.7	174.4	424.9	107.3
Gold (Million Fine Troy Ounces)	1ad	....	....	....	....	....	....	....	....	....	....	.022	.034	.045		
Gold (National Valuation)	1an d											—	1.0	1.5	2.1	
Monetary Authorities: Other Liab.	4.. d	1.1	.3	.4	4.4	.8	3.2	.5	1.0	7.3	4.1	11.5	2.8	10.7	31.7	31.5
Deposit Money Banks: Assets	7a. d	34.6	46.1	23.8	59.1	77.6	91.1	101.2	31.6	47.9	165.7	36.9	111.0	147.0	118.6	94.9
Deposit Money Banks: Liabilities	7b. d	30.4	29.3	34.0	42.3	46.8	50.6	54.5	63.5	85.3	116.1	149.9	215.3	212.3	371.7	495.1
of which: Liab. to Nonbanks	7bd d	....	....	....	....	....	....	....	....	....	....	47.0	50.3	63.4	83.7	145.0
Monetary Authorities																*Billions of Francs:*
Foreign Assets	11	14.9	15.0	17.1	19.3	19.8	29.1	22.9	22.3	20.3	14.6	23.0	19.0	43.5	93.6	29.6
Claims on Central Government	12a	—	1.2	1.8	.4	—	—	1.5	4.8	.1	—	—	9.3	—	6.0	36.0
Claims on Deposit Money Banks	12e	12.0	13.3	12.7	15.6	19.6	22.9	29.2	35.0	51.5	91.1	90.4	103.0	165.2	173.6	197.7
Claims on Other Financial Insts.	12f	—	—	—	—	—	—	—	—	—	—	—	2.9	4.4	5.7	6.4
Reserve Money	14	25.4	28.8	30.9	33.3	37.4	45.0	50.2	56.7	62.5	87.5	99.3	120.6	167.4	221.0	230.1
of which: Currency Outside DMBs	14a	22.9	26.4	27.6	30.6	34.0	39.8	47.0	51.5	57.0	77.5	89.6	106.7	137.3	164.5	193.7
Foreign Liabilities	16c	.3	.1	.1	1.1	.2	.9	.1	.3	1.7	3.9	5.5	7.4	6.3	18.5	18.0
Central Government Deposits	16d	1.2	.6	.6	.9	1.8	5.2	.8	1.1	3.8	13.4	6.7	2.4	33.2	40.7	21.0
Other Items (Net)	17r	—	—	—	—	—	.9	2.5	4.0	4.0	.8	2.1	3.8	6.2	−1.4	.6
Deposit Money Banks																*Billions of Francs:*
Reserves	20	2.4	2.2	2.8	2.6	3.2	4.7	3.1	5.0	5.1	9.1	8.2	12.0	30.0	55.5	32.6
Foreign Assets	21	8.5	11.4	5.9	14.6	21.5	25.3	25.9	8.1	11.0	36.8	8.3	27.6	34.6	24.8	19.1
Claims on Central Government	22a	5.2	4.7	5.5	1.6	1.7	.1	.2	.2	.2	.3	.3	5.1	2.8	6.4	1 24.8
Claims on Private Sector	22d	41.6	45.8	52.2	62.4	76.1	89.3	107.5	128.8	167.4	238.5	286.4	377.3	581.7	673.3	1 773.7
Claims on Other Financial Insts.	22f	....	....	....	....	....	....	....	....	....	....	....	....	....	....	11.2
Demand Deposits	24	18.1	19.0	19.6	27.2	34.2	42.0	43.2	50.0	59.5	82.8	87.9	151.7	243.4	248.3	1 240.0
Time Deposits	25	6.6	7.5	9.7	13.4	22.2	23.2	25.5	19.7	30.0	60.4	64.7	89.7	141.4	166.1	1 132.4
Foreign Liabilities	26c	4.7	4.0	4.8	6.7	8.1	8.4	8.1	10.0	12.6	18.0	23.5	41.7	35.7	61.0	73.5
Long-Term Foreign Liabilities	26cl	2.8	3.2	3.6	3.7	4.9	5.7	5.9	6.2	7.1	7.8	10.1	11.8	14.3	16.7	26.0
Central Government Deposits	26d	8.4	11.3	9.0	9.6	7.4	9.5	15.3	11.5	15.1	25.2	16.8	23.6	28.6	64.4	1 141.5
Credit from Monetary Authorities	26g	12.0	13.3	12.7	15.6	19.7	22.9	29.2	35.0	51.5	91.1	90.4	103.4	165.2	173.5	196.6
Other Items (Net)	27r	5.1	5.7	7.0	4.9	6.2	7.8	9.6	9.7	8.0	−.6	9.6	.2	20.6	30.1	51.3
Treasury Claims: Private Sector	22d. i	3.1	2.4	2.5	3.2	2.9	3.4	3.9	4.2	7.9	5.2	6.2	11.7	19.4	17.3	12.2
Post Office: Checking Deposits	24.. i	1.3	1.1	1.3	1.3	1.6	1.7	1.9	1.6	1.4	2.5	2.3	1.6	2.4	2.6	
Monetary Survey																*Billions of Francs:*
Foreign Assets (Net)	31n	18.4	22.3	18.1	26.1	33.1	45.2	40.5	20.1	17.1	29.5	2.3	−2.6	36.1	38.9	−42.9
Domestic Credit	32	38.5	40.9	51.2	55.2	70.2	76.4	95.1	122.7	150.2	205.6	267.2	370.4	529.5	588.8	1 689.6
Claims on Central Govt. (Net)	32an	−6.2	−7.3	−3.6	−10.3	−8.8	−16.2	−16.2	−10.2	−25.2	−38.1	−25.3	−21.6	−76.0	−107.5	1 −114.0
Claims on Private Sector	32d	44.7	48.2	54.8	65.5	79.1	92.7	111.4	132.9	175.4	243.7	292.5	389.0	601.2	690.7	1 785.9
Claims on Other Financial Insts.	32f	—	—	—	—	—	—	—	—	—	—	—	2.9	4.4	5.7	1 17.7
Money	34	42.2	46.4	48.5	59.1	69.8	83.5	92.1	103.2	117.9	162.8	179.8	260.1	383.1	415.6	1 433.8
Quasi-Money	35	6.6	7.5	9.7	13.4	22.2	23.2	25.5	19.7	30.0	60.4	64.7	89.7	141.4	166.1	1 132.4
Long-Term Foreign Liabilities	36cl	2.8	3.2	3.6	3.7	4.9	5.7	5.9	6.2	7.1	7.8	10.1	11.8	14.3	16.7	26.0
Other Items (Net)	37r	5.3	6.0	7.4	5.0	6.5	9.2	12.2	13.7	12.3	4.1	14.9	6.2	26.6	35.4	54.5
Money plus Quasi-Money	35l	48.9	54.0	58.2	72.5	91.9	106.8	117.6	122.8	147.9	223.2	244.6	349.8	524.5	581.6	1 566.2
Other Banking Institutions																*Billions of Francs:*
Savings Deposits	45	.48	.52	.64	.74	.81	.95	1.09	1.16	1.25	1.47	1.54	1.79	2.06	2.06	....
Liquid Liabilities	55l	49.34	54.47	58.87	73.28	92.73	107.73	118.69	123.99	149.16	224.68	246.10	351.54	526.55	583.67	566.16
Interest Rates																*Percent Per Annum*
Discount Rate *(End of Period)*	60	3.50	3.50	3.50	3.50	3.50	3.50	3.50	3.50	5.50	5.50	8.00	8.00	8.00	8.00	8.00
Money Market Rate	60b	....	....	....	....	....	....	....	....	....	....	....	7.28	7.38	7.40	7.72
Deposit Rate	60l	....	....	....	....	....	3.00	3.00	3.00	5.75	5.75	5.88	6.00	6.00	6.00	6.00
Lending Rate	60p	....	....	....	....	....	....	....	....	....	....	....	....	12.00	12.00	12.00

Côte d'Ivoire
662

	1980	1981	1982	1983	1984	1985	1986	1987	1988	1989	1990	1991	1992	1993	1994		
																Exchange Rates	
End of Period																	
	287.99	334.52	370.92	436.97	470.11	415.26	394.78	378.78	407.68	380.32	364.84	370.48	378.57	404.89	ℐ780.44	Official Rate	**aa**
End of Period (ae) Period Average (rf)																	
	225.80	287.40	336.25	417.37	479.60	378.05	322.75	267.00	302.95	289.40	256.45	259.00	275.33	294.78	ℐ534.60	Official Rate	**ae**
	211.28	271.73	328.61	381.06	436.96	449.26	346.30	300.54	297.85	319.01	272.26	282.11	264.69	283.16	ℐ555.20	Official Rate	**rf**
Period Averages																	
	128.7	100.5	83.1	71.6	62.3	60.9	78.6	90.5	91.4	85.2	100.0	96.6	102.8	96.0	49.0	Official Rate	**ah***x*
	45.0	41.5	39.6	41.3	43.0	47.0	55.8	63.7	69.5	77.7	100.0	108.4	127.1	146.1	88.3	Nominal Effective Exchange Rate	**ne** *c*
	105.4	90.3	82.3	79.2	75.8	74.9	91.8	102.1	103.6	98.1	100.0	97.2	102.1	99.7	61.2	Real Effective Exchange Rate	**re** *c*
End of Period																**Fund Position**	
	114.0	114.0	114.0	165.5	165.5	165.5	165.5	165.5	165.5	165.5	165.5	165.5	165.5	238.2	238.2	Quota	**2f.** *s*
	2.7	10.6	.1	15.5	.2	.1	7.0	.2	.5	3.9	.8	1.4	.2	.8	.1	SDRs	**1b.** *s*
	9.5	—	—	—	—	—	—	—	—	—	—	—	—	.1	.1	Reserve Position in the Fund	**1c.** *s*
	50.6	370.0	485.4	640.3	649.7	605.5	538.7	425.8	377.9	281.3	303.1	259.7	194.5	159.1	224.8	Total Fund Cred.&Loans Outstg.	**2tl**
End of Period																**International Liquidity**	
	19.7	17.8	2.2	19.7	5.4	4.7	19.6	8.9	10.4	15.0	4.0	13.4	6.9	2.3	204.3	Total Reserves minus Gold	**1l.** *d*
	3.5	12.3	.1	16.2	.2	.1	8.5	.2	.7	5.1	1.2	2.0	.3	1.1	.2	SDRs	**1b.** *d*
	12.1	—	—	—	—	—	—	—	—	—	—	—	—	—	.1	Reserve Position in the Fund	**1c.** *d*
	4.1	5.6	2.1	3.5	5.2	4.7	11.0	8.7	9.7	9.8	2.8	11.4	6.7	1.1	204.0	Foreign Exchange	**1d.** *d*
	.045	.045	.045	.045	.045	.045	.045	.045	.045	.045	.045	.045	.045	.045	.045	Gold (Million Fine Troy Ounces)	**1a***d*
	2.0	18.7	19.0	17.2	14.8	14.4	18.0	21.0	18.5	17.4	16.9	15.8	15.4	16.6	16.6	Gold (National Valuation)	**1an***d*
	483.0	590.8	453.7	571.8	380.8	190.7	274.1	597.8	845.5	1,019.8	1,330.7	1,316.0	1,519.8	1,382.4	1.7	Monetary Authorities: Other Liab.	**4.**.*d*
	95.0	100.9	122.8	99.6	146.5	174.8	167.4	191.8	154.6	141.3	189.6	163.6	206.9	176.5	202.1	Deposit Money Banks: Assets	**7a.** *d*
	612.0	483.3	433.2	422.8	247.6	388.3	520.7	775.3	713.5	687.1	614.6	558.6	449.6	486.4	299.8	Deposit Money Banks: Liabilities	**7b.** *d*
	129.2	107.8	128.8	103.8	115.0	219.8	295.9	409.7	351.1	301.1	298.1	288.8	211.9	192.7	111.0	*of which*: Liab. to Nonbanks	**7bd** *d*
End of Period																**Monetary Authorities**	
	4.4	5.1	.7	8.2	2.6	1.8	6.3	2.4	3.2	4.3	1.0	3.5	1.9	.7	109.2	Foreign Assets	**11**
	91.9	166.0	245.3	316.4	333.5	327.4	327.6	289.6	279.1	245.6	250.3	245.0	239.1	273.2	433.2	Claims on Central Government	**12a**
	266.2	366.8	405.7	466.9	433.3	392.2	412.9	498.8	497.5	452.0	523.9	521.5	533.6	506.6	130.0	Claims on Deposit Money Banks	**12e**
	5.7	5.5	6.4	7.8	8.6	9.9	11.1	11.7	11.9	10.7	10.1	9.4	9.3	10.6	5.1	Claims on Other Financial Insts.	**12f**
	232.6	255.2	239.6	257.6	309.2	389.1	405.4	413.0	356.4	278.8	296.4	305.1	271.1	295.8	462.4	Reserve Money	**14**
	210.9	229.8	219.1	232.0	278.7	307.1	317.7	304.7	298.5	254.1	270.7	258.5	252.1	272.5	392.6	*of which:* Currency Outside DMBs	**14a**
	137.5	307.5	346.5	532.4	500.8	334.4	313.2	328.4	413.8	403.5	451.9	437.1	492.1	471.9	176.3	Foreign Liabilities	**16c**
	3.5	2.9	87.0	37.7	19.7	25.0	28.0	33.2	1.9	3.1	16.7	18.5	8.2	13.1	45.8	Central Government Deposits	**16d**
	-5.4	-22.1	-14.9	-28.4	-51.7	-17.2	11.3	27.9	19.6	27.3	20.3	18.7	12.5	10.3	-6.9	Other Items (Net)	**17r**
End of Period																**Deposit Money Banks**	
	31.5	25.0	20.9	26.6	39.2	78.1	90.3	107.7	61.7	26.9	24.8	38.9	22.1	20.6	66.6	Reserves	**20**
	21.4	29.0	41.3	41.6	70.3	66.1	54.0	51.2	46.8	40.9	48.6	42.4	57.0	52.0	108.0	Foreign Assets	**21**
	12.6	13.9	17.0	17.4	19.4	52.7	74.5	98.4	107.0	81.3	76.6	83.1	226.8	224.7	314.9	Claims on Central Government	**22a**
	861.2	947.2	1,010.3	1,091.1	1,076.8	1,053.8	1,061.8	1,142.8	1,143.8	1,091.8	1,062.7	1,053.7	928.9	878.5	828.2	Claims on Private Sector	**22d**
	17.5	16.6	13.9	15.9	18.9	21.4	30.7	37.6	29.9	27.3	20.5	11.7	11.2	6.2	5.8	Claims on Other Financial Insts.	**22f**
	227.7	234.5	238.2	253.1	290.6	311.2	317.1	292.3	278.3	255.6	254.4	250.1	234.5	219.2	403.3	Demand Deposits	**24**
	143.1	175.3	200.0	203.9	251.5	319.3	327.5	331.4	366.0	356.5	319.0	336.3	346.9	331.0	412.1	Time Deposits	**25**
	111.7	110.5	108.7	137.5	70.8	78.7	89.6	109.3	124.5	128.6	93.0	82.3	78.1	95.8	112.5	Foreign Liabilities	**26c**
	26.6	28.4	36.9	39.0	48.0	68.1	78.2	97.7	91.7	70.3	64.6	62.4	45.7	47.6	47.8	Long-Term Foreign Liabilities	**26cl**
	140.6	106.4	89.3	78.0	90.8	121.5	118.6	164.2	114.4	80.7	97.7	82.5	74.9	92.5	171.1	Central Government Deposits	**26d**
	270.0	365.2	407.0	457.0	449.3	393.5	414.5	480.7	458.4	444.9	514.7	516.4	524.7	497.3	134.4	Credit from Monetary Authorities	**26g**
	24.7	12.0	23.2	24.2	23.6	-20.2	-34.5	-37.9	-44.1	-68.3	-110.1	-100.3	-58.9	-101.3	42.3	Other Items (Net)	**27r**
	15.1	9.3	12.0	10.2	11.8	13.7	12.2	14.6	6.4	14.7	10.0	12.3	17.5	17.8	26.7	Treasury Claims: Private Sector	**22d.** *i*
	—	—	2.9	2.8	5.0	1.8	1.4	1.5	1.1	1.5	1.3	1.4	2.5	1.7	2.1	Post Office: Checking Deposits	**24..** *i*
End of Period																**Monetary Survey**	
	-223.3	-383.9	-413.2	-620.0	-498.7	-345.2	-342.7	-384.2	-488.3	-486.8	-495.3	-473.6	-511.3	-515.0	-71.5	Foreign Assets (Net)	**31n**
	844.9	1,040.5	1,119.6	1,335.7	1,351.6	1,320.5	1,360.5	1,384.1	1,456.5	1,374.3	1,307.1	1,303.3	1,334.6	1,289.3	1,372.4	Domestic Credit	**32**
	-54.7	61.5	77.0	210.7	235.6	221.8	244.7	177.5	264.5	229.9	203.8	216.2	367.7	376.1	506.5	Claims on Central Govt. (Net)	**32an**
	876.3	957.0	1,022.3	1,101.3	1,088.6	1,067.4	1,074.0	1,157.4	1,150.3	1,106.5	1,072.7	1,065.9	946.4	896.3	854.9	Claims on Private Sector	**32d**
	23.2	22.0	20.3	23.7	27.4	31.2	41.7	49.3	41.8	38.0	30.6	21.0	20.5	16.9	10.9	Claims on Other Financial Insts.	**32f**
	438.7	464.4	460.3	488.0	574.6	620.2	636.4	598.6	578.0	511.2	526.4	510.1	489.4	494.0	798.8	Money	**34**
	143.1	175.3	200.0	203.9	251.5	319.3	327.5	331.4	366.0	356.5	319.0	336.3	346.9	331.0	412.1	Quasi-Money	**35**
	26.6	28.4	36.9	39.0	48.0	68.1	78.2	97.7	91.7	70.3	64.6	62.4	45.7	47.6	47.8	Long-Term Foreign Liabilities	**36cl**
	13.2	-11.5	9.1	-15.2	-21.1	-32.3	-24.3	-27.7	-67.4	-50.5	-98.2	-79.1	-58.7	-98.3	42.1	Other Items (Net)	**37r**
	581.8	639.7	660.3	692.0	826.1	939.4	963.9	930.0	944.0	867.7	845.4	846.4	836.4	825.0	1,210.9	Money plus Quasi-Money	**35l**
End of Period																**Other Banking Institutions**	
	....	....	....	....	....	....	....	....	....	....	....	....	....	....	88.1	Savings Deposits	**45**
	ℐ581.82	....	....	....	....	....	....	....	....	....	....	....	....	....	61.2	Liquid Liabilities	**55l**
Percent Per Annum																**Interest Rates**	
	10.50	10.50	12.50	10.50	10.50	10.50	8.50	8.50	9.50	11.00	11.00	11.00	12.50	10.50	10.00	Discount Rate (End of Period)	**60**
	10.13	13.68	14.66	12.23	11.84	10.66	8.58	8.37	8.72	10.07	10.98	10.94	11.44	....	....	Money Market Rate	**60b**
	6.19	6.25	7.75	7.50	7.25	7.25	6.08	5.25	5.25	6.42	7.00	7.00	7.75	....	....	Deposit Rate	**60l**
	14.50	14.50	16.00	14.50	14.50	14.50	13.50	13.50	13.58	15.08	16.00	16.00	16.75	....	....	Lending Rate	**60p**

Côte d'Ivoire

662

		1965	1966	1967	1968	1969	1970	1971	1972	1973	1974	1975	1976	1977	1978	1979
Prices and Production															*Index Numbers (1990=100):*	
Consumer Prices	64	15.4	16.3	16.7	17.6	18.3	20.1	19.8	19.8	22.0	25.9	28.8	32.3	41.1	46.5	54.2
Industrial Production	66	....	....	....	19.9	22.7	26.8	31.7	35.9	41.3	43.8	53.4	66.7	77.6	89.4	⅃97.0
International Transactions															*Billions of Francs*	
Exports	70	68.42	76.66	80.26	104.89	118.22	130.19	126.56	139.54	190.86	291.77	254.57	392.50	529.21	524.38	534.85
Imports, cif	71	58.34	62.79	65.05	75.83	86.28	107.70	110.84	114.32	157.52	232.29	241.39	311.61	429.57	522.50	528.85
Imports, fob	71.v	52.56	56.57	58.60	68.43	77.71	96.90	99.89	102.82	142.09	204.29	210.59	263.71	365.89	445.90	443.66
															1985=100	
Export Prices	74	....	....	....	....	....	....	20.7	19.5	25.1	32.3	⅃29.1	38.8	61.5	53.2	57.1
Unit Value of Imports	75	....	....	....	....	....	....	20.6	22.6	23.7	31.9	⅃35.9	41.1	43.8	46.1	52.3
Balance of Payments															*Millions of US Dollars:*	
Goods: Exports f.o.b.	78aa d											1,238.8	1,735.1	2,412.1	2,615.9	2,722.8
Goods: Imports f.o.b.	78ab d											−1,012.1	−1,161.3	−1,597.2	−2,042.9	−2,233.4
Trade Balance	78ac d											226.8	573.8	814.9	573.0	489.4
Services: Credit	78ad d											225.8	235.2	324.8	410.4	510.5
Services: Debit	78ae d											−550.1	−642.1	−823.9	−1,097.0	−1,363.8
Balance on Goods and Services	78af d											−97.5	166.8	315.8	−113.6	−363.9
Income: Credit	78ag d											38.7	28.0	42.3	60.3	59.2
Income: Debit	78ah d											−178.2	−185.0	−235.3	−367.4	−506.8
Balance on Goods, Serv., & Inc.	78ai d											−237.0	9.9	122.8	−420.7	−811.4
Current Transfers, n.i.e.: Credit	78aj d											130.2	128.7	160.3	186.0	199.1
Current Transfers: Debit	78ak d											−272.0	−387.9	−460.4	−604.5	−771.0
Current Account, n.i.e.	78al d											−378.9	−249.3	−177.3	−839.2	−1,383.3
Capital Account, n.i.e.: Credit	78ba d											—	—	—	—	—
Capital Account: Debit	78bb d											—	—	—	—	—
Capital Account, n.i.e.	78bc d											—	—	—	—	—
Direct Investment Abroad	78bd d											—	—	—	—	—
Dir. Invest. in Rep. Econ., n.i.e.	78be d											69.1	44.8	14.7	83.3	74.7
Portfolio Investment Assets	78bf d											−.9	−5.0	−9.4	−6.6	1.4
Portfolio Investment Liab., n.i.e.	78bg d											−.5	.8	−2.4	.4	
Other Investment Assets	78bh d											−14.9	−190.4	−371.2	−24.4	205.0
Other Investment Liab., n.i.e.	78bi d											228.2	411.8	711.9	955.9	851.8
Financial Account, n.i.e.	78bj d											280.9	262.0	343.5	1,008.6	1,132.9
Net Errors and Omissions	78ca d											5.6	−3.7	−48.2	−32.2	−78.8
Overall Balance	78cb d											−92.4	9.0	118.1	137.3	−329.2
Reserves and Related Items	79da d											92.4	−9.0	−118.1	−137.3	329.2
Reserve Assets	79db d											84.5	−37.1	−115.2	−164.1	329.9
Use of Fund Credit and Loans	79dc d											—	14.6	−11.6	9.9	—
Liabs.Constit.For.Auth.Reserves	79dd d											7.9	−7.5	8.1	15.1	−.9
Exceptional Financing	79de d											—	21.1	.5	1.9	.2
Government Finance															*Millions of Francs:*	
Deficit (-) or Surplus	80														....	−168,301
Revenue	81															467,070
Grants Received	81z															43
Expenditure	82															611,831
Lending Minus Repayments	83															23,583
Financing																
Total Financing	84															168,301
Net Borrowing: Domestic	84a															33,590
Foreign	85a															134,711
Use of Cash Balances	87															....
Debt: Domestic	88a															....
Foreign	89a															....
National Accounts															*Billions of Francs*	
Exports of Goods & Services	90c	73.5	81.6	87.2	117.7	136.7	150.6	153.1	170.2	215.8	337.6	315.2	465.0	656.1	651.0	673.1
Government Consumption	91f	9.6	10.6	11.5	14.1	19.9	64.9	73.9	77.2	95.6	118.7	141.8	180.3	209.7	290.4	353.8
Gross Fixed Capital Formation	93e	43.6	44.6	45.9	54.0	61.8	83.9	92.4	94.3	122.0	143.6	199.4	247.2	397.7	529.0	526.7
Increase/Decrease(-) in Stocks	93i	1.3	5.5	2.7	3.0	10.0	7.4	3.6	3.1	7.8	19.1	3.4	8.9	23.1	1.8	16.9
Private Consumption	96f	153.6	163.6	178.9	200.6	210.6	246.1	267.1	287.8	340.1	418.1	504.1	616.4	811.9	978.1	1,106.7
Imports of Goods & Services	98c	−67.7	−73.1	−77.6	−91.9	−106.3	−129.6	−141.6	−149.6	−203.4	−286.6	−326.0	−403.8	−559.2	−667.3	−732.5
Gross Domestic Product	99b	239.6	258.0	275.7	326.5	365.6	414.9	439.9	471.8	566.2	739.0	834.5	1,120.4	1,590.4	1,783.0	1,944.7
Net Factor Inc/Pmts(-) Abroad	98.n	−8.7	−9.8	−8.1	−8.9	−4.7	−11.5	−15.2	−12.7	−12.6	−20.5	−27.2	−41.1	−50.5	−69.4	....
Gross Nat'l Expenditure = GNP	99a	230.9	248.2	266.3	316.2	358.7	403.4	424.6	459.1	553.6	718.5	807.3	1,072.9	1,488.8	1,713.6	....
Nat'l Income, Market Prices	99e	222.4	239.2	258.1	306.7	348.0	388.4	405.6	437.1	528.6	688.5	767.3	1,017.9	1,406.8	1,591.2	1,702.0
Gross Dom. Prod. 1980 Prices	99b.p	....	....	....	....	....	....	....	....	....	....	....	1,702.6	1,782.5	1,959.0	1,996.2
GDP Deflator (1980=100)	99bi p	....	....	....	....	....	....	....	....	....	....	....	65.8	89.2	91.0	97.4
															Millions:	
Population	99z	3.84	3.93	4.02	⅃4.50	5.06	5.55	5.58	5.86	6.15	6.43	6.77	7.05	7.34	7.61	7.92

Deposit Money Banks: ⅃ Beginning in October 1979, *Central Government Deposits* include the deposits of public establishments of an administrative or social nature (*EPAS*) and exclude those of the savings bank; *Demand* and *Time Deposits* include deposits of the savings bank and exclude deposits of EPAS; and *Claims on Private Sector* exclude claims on other financial institutions.

Monetary Survey: ⅃ Beginning in October 1979, *line 32f* includes claims of deposit money banks on other financial institutions; see deposit money bank notes for explanation of other break symbols.

Côte d'Ivoire

	1980	1981	1982	1983	1984	1985	1986	1987	1988	1989	1990	1991	1992	1993	1994		
Period Averages																**Prices and Production**	
	62.2	67.6	72.6	76.9	80.2	‡81.7	87.2	93.3	99.8	100.8	100.0	101.7	105.3	‡108.3	136.3	Consumer Prices	64
	111.7	112.8	108.4	92.3	‡100.0	103.1	111.5	111.5	108.3	106.5	100.0	97.4	99.0	….	….	Industrial Production	66
Billions of Francs																**International Transactions**	
	663.92	689.30	747.45	796.77	1,184.34	1,318.06	1,160.44	929.14	826.47	895.60	836.43	757.76	751.70	….	….	Exports	70
	636.96	653.32	718.59	704.25	658.57	772.98	709.04	673.90	619.92	673.45	571.10	593.37	613.17	….	….	Imports, cif	71
	520.74	522.22	591.69	566.34	529.40	621.37	569.97	541.72	498.33	541.36	459.08	476.99	492.90	….	….	Imports, fob	71.v
1985=100																	
	63.2	57.0	60.4	68.8	90.2	100.0	83.9	69.0	….	….	….	….	….	….	….	Export Prices	74
	59.5	74.3	88.4	96.8	105.3	100.0	87.1	86.6	….	….	….	….	….	….	….	Unit Value of Imports	75
Minus Sign Indicates Debit																Balance of Payments	
	3,012.6	2,435.1	2,347.2	2,066.3	2,624.8	2,761.0	3,187.4	2,949.7	2,691.3	2,696.8	3,027.9	2,686.2	2,880.0	2,734.1	….	Goods: Exports f.o.b.	78aa d
	-2,613.6	-2,067.9	-1,789.7	-1,635.2	-1,487.3	-1,409.9	-1,639.9	-1,863.3	-1,769.4	-1,777.1	-1,700.6	-1,706.8	-1,885.6	-1,662.3	….	Goods: Imports f.o.b.	78ab d
	399.0	367.3	557.5	431.2	1,137.4	1,351.1	1,547.5	1,086.4	921.9	919.7	1,327.4	979.4	994.4	1,071.8	….	Trade Balance	78ac d
	564.2	434.3	450.7	425.1	370.5	399.1	471.6	535.4	555.7	485.9	557.9	529.9	569.3	546.3	….	Services: Credit	78ad d
	-1,531.2	-1,225.5	-1,163.4	-990.1	-824.3	-763.5	-1,313.6	-1,352.6	-1,342.3	-1,230.4	-1,662.0	-1,568.6	-1,567.9	-1,392.5	….	Services: Debit	78ae d
	-568.0	-423.9	-155.2	-133.8	683.6	986.7	705.4	269.2	135.3	175.2	223.3	-59.2	-4.2	225.7	….	Balance on Goods and Services	78af d
	63.0	46.0	46.0	46.7	37.5	39.4	67.3	77.9	71.8	55.8	23.9	23.0	18.9	17.7	….	Income: Credit	78ag d
	-615.8	-554.2	-545.3	-548.5	-530.9	-705.4	-714.1	-957.3	-992.8	-995.9	-1,130.5	-1,219.4	-1,196.1	-1,251.6	….	Income: Debit	78ah d
	-1,120.8	-932.2	-654.6	-635.6	190.2	320.7	58.6	-610.2	-785.6	-764.9	-883.3	-1,255.6	-1,181.4	-1,008.3	….	Balance on Goods, Serv., & Inc.	78ai d
	242.3	205.2	189.4	174.2	149.9	130.5	184.2	276.1	208.8	316.0	365.0	357.7	381.2	293.5	….	Current Transfers, n.i.e.: Credit	78aj d
	-948.0	-684.5	-552.0	-469.7	-417.0	-387.5	-543.2	-635.9	-664.4	-518.5	-691.2	-592.0	-628.3	-514.2	….	Current Transfers: Debit	78ak d
	-1,826.5	-1,411.4	-1,017.3	-931.1	-76.8	63.7	-300.3	-970.0	-1,241.3	-967.3	-1,209.6	-1,489.9	-1,428.5	-1,229.0	….	Current Account, n.i.e.	78al d
	—	—	—	—	—	—	—	—	—	—	—	—	—	—	….	Capital Account, n.i.e.: Credit	78ba d
	—	—	—	—	—	—	—	—	—	—	—	—	—	—	….	Capital Account: Debit	78bb d
	—	—	—	—	—	—	—	—	—	—	—	—	—	—	….	Capital Account, n.i.e.	78bc d
	—	—	—	—	—	—	—	—	—	—	—	—	—	—	….	Direct Investment Abroad	78bd d
	94.7	32.8	47.5	37.5	21.7	29.2	70.7	87.5	51.7	18.5	31.6	80.8	77.1	30.4	….	Dir. Invest. in Rep. Econ., n.i.e.	78be d
	2.8	.7	—	1.3	-.9	-1.1	-.3	-5.3	-13.4	1.9	—	—	—	—	….	Portfolio Investment Assets	78bf d
	—	—	-1.2	-1.0	-.7	-.2	—	-2.7	-.7	-.6	—	—	—	—	….	Portfolio Investment Liab., n.i.e.	78bg d
	-30.3	-27.6	-10.7	-64.0	-94.5	-30.3	96.2	-3.0	50.4	21.6	8.1	91.1	140.5	27.2	….	Other Investment Assets	78bh d
	1,171.9	900.9	710.0	412.3	-208.3	-321.6	-190.3	-52.2	-225.9	-345.8	-298.6	1.1	-214.6	-80.9	….	Other Investment Liab., n.i.e.	78bi d
	1,239.1	906.8	745.6	386.0	-282.6	-324.1	-23.7	24.3	-137.2	-304.4	-258.9	173.0	3.0	-23.3	….	Financial Account, n.i.e.	78bj d
	-76.9	-98.1	-35.2	-154.1	-119.1	84.2	-55.3	12.6	-24.4	-38.8	-97.1	53.0	35.0	61.9	….	Net Errors and Omissions	78ca d
	-664.3	-603.5	-306.8	-699.2	-478.6	-176.1	-379.3	-933.2	-1,403.3	-1,310.6	-1,565.6	-1,263.8	-1,390.4	-1,190.4	….	Overall Balance	78cb d
	664.3	603.5	306.8	699.2	478.6	176.1	379.3	933.2	1,403.3	1,310.6	1,565.6	1,263.8	1,390.4	1,190.4	….	Reserves and Related Items	79da d
	135.5	6.2	20.3	-19.1	10.0	4.8	-10.7	-17.2	-.3	11.3	16.3	-.5	-84.4	24.2	….	Reserve Assets	79db d
	37.0	372.0	125.6	165.3	9.9	-45.4	-78.4	-145.8	-63.0	-123.9	33.4	-58.5	-91.9	-49.0	….	Use of Fund Credit and Loans	79dc d
	-23.7	-.7	4.0	-1.6	1.8	6.9	-12.7	9.0	-21.5	-.9	55.1	-10.3	-33.2	-3.5	….	Liabs.Constit.For.Auth.Reserves	79dd d
	515.4	226.1	157.0	554.6	456.8	209.8	481.1	1,087.2	1,488.0	1,424.1	1,460.8	1,333.2	1,600.0	1,218.7	….	Exceptional Financing	79de d
Year Ending December 31																**Government Finance**	
	-233,189	….	….	….	….	….	….	….	….	….	….	….	….	….	….	Deficit (-) or Surplus	80
	516,696	….	….	….	….	….	….	….	….	….	….	….	….	….	….	Revenue	81
	860	….	….	….	….	….	….	….	….	….	….	….	….	….	….	Grants Received	81z
	681,163	….	….	….	….	….	….	….	….	….	….	….	….	….	….	Expenditure	82
	69,582	….	….	….	….	….	….	….	….	….	….	….	….	….	….	Lending Minus Repayments	83
																Financing	
	233,189	….	….	….	….	….	….	….	….	….	….	….	….	….	….	Total Financing	84
	107,339	….	….	….	….	….	….	….	….	….	….	….	….	….	….	Net Borrowing: Domestic	84a
	139,553	….	….	….	….	….	….	….	….	….	….	….	….	….	….	Foreign	85a
	-13,703	….	….	….	….	….	….	….	….	….	….	….	….	….	….	Use of Cash Balances	87
	68,079	….	….	….	….	….	….	….	….	….	….	….	….	….	….	Debt: Domestic	88a
	611,435	….	….	….	….	….	….	….	….	….	….	….	….	….	….	Foreign	89a
Billions of Francs																**National Accounts**	
	752.5	806.0	905.7	963.1	1,250.4	1,353.3	1,252.7	1,013.5	931.3	997.1	931.5	887.9	….	….	….	Exports of Goods & Services	90c
	362.4	403.6	432.5	439.3	453.3	441.6	485.9	501.8	530.1	575.8	499.2	488.4	….	….	….	Government Consumption	91f
	523.6	558.4	538.7	461.8	387.5	369.1	374.8	356.8	350.8	321.2	249.9	253.8	….	….	….	Gross Fixed Capital Formation	93e
	46.9	36.0	37.8	8.9	-39.3	36.9	7.7	16.6	35.6	-43.7	-53.1	-32.6	….	….	….	Increase/Decrease(-) in Stocks	93i
	1,349.8	1,456.3	1,549.7	1,663.5	1,783.5	1,836.4	2,007.8	2,041.0	2,058.0	2,167.0	2,108.8	2,161.8	….	….	….	Private Consumption	96f
	-885.3	-968.9	-977.9	-930.7	-742.7	-815.7	-957.2	-898.0	-852.0	-904.9	-797.0	-799.3	….	….	….	Imports of Goods & Services	98c
	2,149.9	2,291.4	2,486.5	2,605.9	2,989.4	3,134.8	3,171.7	3,031.7	3,054.5	3,112.8	2,939.3	2,960.0	….	….	….	Gross Domestic Product	99b
	….	….	….	….	….	….	-237.0	-285.8	-300.2	-359.4	-374.3	-411.3	….	….	….	Net Factor Inc/Pmts(-) Abroad	98.n
	….	….	….	….	….	….	2,934.7	2,745.9	2,754.3	2,753.4	2,565.0	2,548.7	….	….	….	Gross Nat'l Expenditure = GNP	99a
	….	….	….	….	….	….	….	….	….	….	….	….	….	….	….	Nat'l Income, Market Prices	99e
	2,149.9	2,225.1	….	….	….	….	….	….	….	….	….	….	….	….	….	Gross Dom. Prod. 1980 Prices	99b.p
	100.0	103.0	….	….	….	….	….	….	….	….	….	….	….	….	….	GDP Deflator (1980=100)	99bi p
Midyear Estimates																	
	8.33	8.52	8.85	9.30	9.56	9.93	10.32	10.72	10.82	11.26	11.72	12.19	12.67	13.18	13.70	Population	99z

Cyprus

		1965	1966	1967	1968	1969	1970	1971	1972	1973	1974	1975	1976	1977	1978	1979
Exchange Rates															*SDRs per Pound:*	
Official Rate	ac	2.8000	2.8000	2.4000	2.4000	2.4000	2.4000	2.3524	2.4026	2.2983	2.2841	2.1719	2.0911	2.1532	2.1853	2.1965
															US Dollars per Pound:	
Official Rate	ag	2.8000	2.8000	2.4000	2.4000	2.4000	2.4000	2.5540	2.6085	2.7725	2.7965	2.5425	2.4295	2.6155	2.8470	2.8935
Official Rate	rh	2.8000	2.8000	2.7667	2.4000	2.4000	2.4000	2.4355	2.6071	2.8612	2.7426	2.7162	2.4371	2.4510	2.6796	2.8220
														Index Numbers (1990=100):		
Official Rate	ahx	128.0	128.0	125.8	109.7	109.7	109.7	111.7	119.2	130.8	125.4	124.2	111.4	112.1	122.5	129.0
Nominal Effective Exchange Rate	nec	....	....	....	....	....	....	....	....	....	....	....	....	....	....	81.8
Real Effective Exchange Rate	rec	....	....	....	....	....	....	....	....	....	....	....	....	....	....	151.3
Fund Position															*Millions of SDRs:*	
Quota	2f.s	11.3	15.0	15.0	20.0	20.0	26.0	26.0	26.0	26.0	26.0	26.0	26.0	26.0	34.0	34.0
SDRs	1b.s	—	—	—	—	—	3.9	7.7	10.4	10.5	10.4	10.0	7.9	5.1	1.7	9.9
Reserve Position in the Fund	1c.s	—	—	2.2	3.8	4.2	6.5	6.5	6.5	6.5	—	—	—	—	6.5	6.1
Total Fund Cred.&Loans Outstg.	2tl	—	—	—	—	—	—	—	—	—	6.4	8.1	43.1	43.1	32.9	38.0
International Liquidity											*Millions of US Dollars Unless Otherwise Indicated:*					
Total Reserves minus Gold	1l.d	83.7	98.2	103.5	140.9	161.9	194.0	268.7	303.3	288.7	250.1	197.7	274.5	313.5	345.7	353.1
SDRs	1b.d	—	—	—	—	—	3.9	8.3	11.3	12.6	12.8	11.8	9.2	6.2	2.2	13.0
Reserve Position in the Fund	1c.d	—	—	2.2	3.8	4.2	6.5	7.1	7.1	7.9	—	—	—	—	8.5	8.0
Foreign Exchange	1d.d	83.7	98.2	101.3	137.1	157.7	183.6	253.3	284.9	268.2	237.3	185.9	265.3	307.3	335.0	332.0
Gold (Million Fine Troy Ounces)	1ad	....	....	....	.428	.428	.428	.428	.428	.428	.428	.428	.428	.440	.443	.459
Gold (National Valuation)	1and	....	....	....	15.0	15.0	15.0				18.1	17.5	15.9	15.2	16.8	19.1	20.8
Monetary Authorities: Other Liab.	4..d	1.0	1.0	.3	.6	.7	1.4	4.6	4.9	2.5	4.4	7.7	8.4	7.6	10.2	6.7
Deposit Money Banks: Assets	7a.d	48.2	50.0	50.0	16.7	16.7	15.9	16.5	13.7	16.0	19.4	11.7	20.8	21.1	33.4	43.9
of which: Claims on Nonbanks	7add	12.8	11.7	11.1	8.2	9.4	7.6	7.9	7.7	9.4	5.9	7.6	9.6	11.5	16.8	21.2
Deposit Money Banks: Liabilities	7b.d	20.4	25.3	23.4	29.1	32.3	32.0	42.9	47.5	58.2	50.5	37.1	48.3	64.9	83.5	118.1
of which: Liab. to Nonbanks	7bdd	11.6	14.6	16.2	20.7	23.6	24.4	33.4	37.0	44.6	41.1	33.5	41.6	56.0	73.3	101.7
Other Banking Insts.: Liabilities	7f.d	1.2	1.8	3.2	14.5	4.7	8.9	9.8	12.2	13.5	15.5	11.9	11.2	14.4	19.8	28.0
of which: Liab. to Nonbanks	7fdd	1.2	1.8	3.2	4.5	4.3	7.4	9.0	10.9	11.9	11.9	8.4	7.8	8.5	10.2	11.2
Monetary Authorities															*Millions of Pounds:*	
Foreign Assets	11	30.4	35.7	43.7	65.5	74.5	88.2	110.9	118.0	110.8	102.0	85.9	122.2	127.7	128.6	129.9
Claims on Central Government	12a	1.9	1.7	-.3	-.9	.8	-.6	-2.0	-.3	—	12.9	12.8	28.3	25.1	31.5	59.9
Claims on Deposit Money Banks	12e	—	—	—	—	—	—	—	.8	.1	—	.9	2.3	5.1	5.5	9.8
Reserve Money	14	13.5	14.0	15.7	36.0	40.7	41.4	54.2	64.7	67.8	78.0	79.2	97.6	110.1	127.8	153.1
of which: Currency Outside DMBs	14a	11.7	12.2	13.6	15.5	17.2	18.4	21.8	26.3	29.7	35.8	33.7	39.3	43.7	51.2	64.0
Foreign Liabilities	16c	.4	.4	.1	.2	.3	.6	1.8	1.9	.9	4.4	6.7	24.1	22.9	18.7	19.6
Central Government Deposits	16d	17.4	22.0	24.5	24.8	29.6	37.0	43.1	43.4	32.9	22.9	6.9	23.6	17.7	10.5	12.6
Other Items (Net)	17r	1.0	1.0	3.1	3.7	4.7	8.7	9.9	8.6	9.3	9.6	6.8	7.6	7.2	8.6	14.3
Deposit Money Banks															*Millions of Pounds:*	
Reserves	20	1.6	1.6	2.5	20.2	23.2	23.1	32.1	38.0	37.4	42.3	35.0	47.5	54.9	58.7	66.6
Foreign Assets	21	17.2	17.9	20.8	7.0	7.0	6.6	6.3	5.3	5.5	7.0	4.6	8.6	8.1	11.7	15.2
Claims on Central Government	22a	1.3	1.6	2.8	2.6	5.1	9.0	15.9	18.8	13.9	13.6	5.3	34.1	21.0	20.7	18.1
Claims on Private Sector	22d	49.1	57.5	61.9	70.7	81.2	88.2	98.3	119.2	147.3	172.1	178.4	195.6	247.7	292.2	354.6
Demand Deposits	24	12.5	13.7	15.5	17.2	20.8	24.2	25.0	31.2	31.1	31.3	28.4	40.7	42.8	49.6	65.5
Time and Savings Deposits	25	44.3	49.4	55.1	62.3	71.1	76.1	95.8	114.8	132.4	157.6	164.4	191.5	226.0	257.5	296.9
Foreign Liabilities	26c	7.3	9.0	9.8	12.1	13.5	13.3	16.5	18.2	20.1	18.1	14.6	19.9	24.8	29.3	40.8
Central Government Deposits	26d	2.4	2.7	2.2	2.7	3.1	3.4	3.5	3.8	4.6	4.4	5.0	6.8	7.6	10.7	15.7
Credit from Monetary Authorities	26g	—	—	—	—	—	—	—	.8	.1	—	.9	2.3	5.1	5.5	9.8
Other Items (Net)	27r	2.7	3.6	5.5	6.3	8.2	9.9	12.0	12.5	15.9	23.7	20.1	24.6	25.4	30.8	25.7
Monetary Survey															*Millions of Pounds:*	
Foreign Assets (Net)	31n	39.9	44.1	54.7	60.2	67.7	81.0	99.0	103.1	95.4	86.5	69.2	86.8	88.1	92.3	84.7
Domestic Credit	32	32.6	36.0	37.8	45.0	54.7	56.4	65.7	90.7	123.9	171.8	195.3	228.2	269.1	323.9	406.3
Claims on Central Govt. (Net)	32an	-16.5	-21.4	-24.2	-25.7	-26.7	-31.9	-32.6	-28.5	-23.6	-.8	16.2	32.1	20.7	31.0	49.6
Claims on Local Government	32b	....	....	....	....	....	....	....	....	....	....	....	....	....	....	....
Claims on Nonfin.Pub.Enterprises	32c	....	....	....	....	....	....	....	....	....	....	....	....	....	....	....
Claims on Private Sector	32d	49.1	57.5	61.9	70.7	81.4	88.4	98.3	119.3	147.5	172.6	179.1	196.1	248.4	292.9	356.7
Money	34	24.3	25.9	29.1	32.7	38.0	42.6	46.7	57.4	60.9	67.0	62.1	80.0	85.9	100.8	129.5
Quasi-Money	35	44.3	49.4	55.1	62.6	71.3	77.8	98.3	117.7	136.1	161.4	167.6	195.1	230.1	262.5	304.0
Other Items (Net)	37r	3.9	4.9	8.2	9.9	13.1	17.0	19.7	18.6	22.3	29.9	34.8	39.9	41.2	52.9	57.4
Money plus Quasi-Money	35l	68.6	75.3	84.2	95.3	109.3	120.4	145.0	175.2	197.0	228.5	229.7	275.1	316.0	363.3	433.5
Other Banking Institutions															*Millions of Pounds:*	
Reserves	40	1.1	1.5	2.5	2.1	3.2	6.4	6.0	6.5	8.5	5.5	4.6	7.2	7.2	8.6	12.0
Foreign Assets	41	1.1	1.4	1.4	.7	—	—	—	—	—	—	—	—	—	—	—
Claims on Private Sector	42d	5.0	6.1	7.6	10.3	13.0	14.2	16.2	21.2	26.7	29.9	30.9	33.5	43.2	50.9	56.4
Liquid Liabilities	45l	5.6	7.0	8.4	9.2	11.5	13.0	13.4	17.2	23.3	22.0	22.6	26.2	33.7	39.8	42.2
Foreign Liabilities	46c	.4	.6	1.3	1.9	1.9	3.7	3.8	4.7	4.7	5.5	4.7	4.6	5.5	7.0	9.7
Capital Accounts	47a	1.3	1.6	1.8	2.0	2.2	2.6	2.8	3.1	3.4	4.0	4.8	5.5	6.7	7.9	9.8
Other Items (Net)	47r	-.1	-.2	—	—	.6	1.3	2.2	2.8	3.8	3.9	3.6	4.4	4.5	4.9	6.8
Banking Survey															*Millions of Pounds:*	
Foreign Assets (Net)	51n	40.6	44.9	54.8	59.0	65.8	77.3	95.3	98.5	90.7	81.0	64.5	82.2	82.6	85.4	75.0
Domestic Credit	52	37.5	42.2	45.3	55.3	67.7	70.4	81.9	111.8	150.3	201.1	225.4	261.4	312.3	375.0	461.5
Claims on Central Govt. (Net)	52an	-16.5	-21.4	-24.2	-25.7	-26.6	-32.0	-32.6	-28.5	-23.7	-.9	16.1	32.3	21.4	31.9	50.5
Claims on Local Government	52b	....	....	....	....	....	....	....	....	....	....	....	....	....	....	....
Claims on Nonfin.Pub.Enterprises	52c	....	....	....	....	....	....	....	....	....	....	....	....	....	....	....
Claims on Private Sector	52d	54.1	63.6	69.5	80.9	94.2	102.4	114.5	140.4	174.0	202.0	209.3	229.1	291.0	343.1	411.0
Monetary Liabilities	54	23.4	25.0	27.3	31.5	35.9	37.1	42.2	53.6	56.0	64.7	63.4	78.8	90.1	103.4	130.1
Quasi-Monetary Liabilities	55	49.5	55.8	62.8	71.1	81.7	90.0	110.2	132.3	155.8	180.2	187.4	218.9	256.6	296.0	340.5
Other Items (Net)	57r	5.2	6.3	10.0	11.6	15.8	20.7	24.5	24.5	29.2	37.1	39.1	46.0	48.2	60.9	65.7
Liquid Liabilities	55l	73.0	80.8	90.1	102.3	117.6	127.0	152.5	185.8	211.9	245.0	247.6	294.1	342.5	394.5	463.7

Cyprus

1980	1981	1982	1983	1984	1985	1986	1987	1988	1989	1990	1991	1992	1993	1994		
End of Period															**Exchange Rates**	
2.1495	1.9859	1.8570	1.7169	1.5838	1.6756	1.5979	1.6061	1.5936	1.5892	1.6174	1.5923	1.5056	1.4006	1.4384	Official Rate	ac
End of Period (ag)	*Period Average (rh)*															
2.7415	2.3115	2.0485	1.7975	1.5525	1.8405	1.9545	2.2785	2.1445	2.0885	2.3010	2.2777	2.0702	1.9238	2.0998	Official Rate	ag
2.8338	2.3829	2.1071	1.9015	1.7039	1.6407	1.9353	2.0802	2.1447	2.0272	2.1874	2.1670	2.2212	2.0120	2.0347	Official Rate	rh
Period Averages																
129.6	108.9	96.3	86.9	77.9	75.0	88.5	95.1	98.1	92.7	100.0	99.1	101.5	92.0	93.0	Official Rate	ahx
83.9	83.0	84.4	85.7	87.8	91.5	91.8	89.1	90.6	94.1	100.0	103.7	108.1	111.6	117.8	Nominal Effective Exchange Rate	nec
127.3	122.5	119.7	117.1	115.8	116.0	111.6	105.8	103.7	101.8	100.0	100.2	102.6	102.3	103.4	Real Effective Exchange Rate	rec
End of Period															**Fund Position**	
51.0	51.0	51.0	69.7	69.7	69.7	69.7	69.7	69.7	69.7	69.7	69.7	100.0	100.0	100.0	Quota	2f.s
6.5	3.4	.2	.2	.1	.1	.1	—	.3	.1	.1	.1	.1	.1	.1	SDRs	1b.s
—	—	—	4.7	4.7	4.7	4.7	4.7	11.7	18.1	15.1	17.9	25.5	25.5	25.5	Reserve Position in the Fund	1c.s
30.6	21.6	12.3	5.5	3.2	—	—	—	—	—	—	—	—	—	—	Total Fund Cred.&Loans Outstg.	2tl
End of Period															**International Liquidity**	
368.3	426.4	523.2	519.1	540.5	595.3	752.7	873.5	927.9	1,124.0	1,506.9	1,390.2	1,027.9	1,096.7	1,464.5	Total Reserves minus Gold	1l.d
8.3	4.0	.2	.2	.1	.1	—	.4	.1	.1	.1	.1	.1	.1	.2	SDRs	1b.d
—	—	—	4.9	4.6	5.1	5.7	6.6	15.7	23.7	21.5	25.5	35.0	35.0	37.2	Reserve Position in the Fund	1c.d
360.0	422.4	523.0	514.0	535.9	590.0	747.0	866.5	912.1	1,100.2	1,485.3	1,364.5	992.8	1,061.6	1,427.2	Foreign Exchange	1d.d
.459	.459	.459	.459	.459	.459	.459	.459	.459	.459	.459	.459	.459	.460	.459	Gold (Million Fine Troy Ounces)	1ad
19.7	16.7	14.8	13.0	11.2	13.3	14.1	16.4	15.5	15.1	16.6	16.4	15.0	14.2	....	Gold (National Valuation)	1and
1.2	1.3	1.0	1.0	.8	2.7	2.8	11.0	23.7	29.4	69.1	76.8	77.2	53.9	55.7	Monetary Authorities: Other Liab.	4..d
45.8	55.5	60.7	66.8	84.6	124.3	178.4	232.0	318.7	553.2	701.9	1,093.0	1,396.6	1,554.3	1,915.4	Deposit Money Banks: Assets	7a.d
23.9	31.9	22.6	21.5	21.0	34.5	27.8	31.9	55.5	54.2	62.0	71.6	83.3	98.7	383.4	of which: Claims on Nonbanks	7add
147.7	174.2	212.3	249.1	286.2	364.5	462.7	600.2	714.8	924.8	1,400.8	1,728.8	2,010.5	2,187.8	2,676.5	Deposit Money Banks: Liabilities	7b.d
128.3	159.8	196.6	237.4	269.2	347.1	425.6	549.3	657.9	859.7	1,316.5	1,610.0	1,884.2	2,036.7	2,493.7	of which: Liab. to Nonbanks	7bdd
31.7	36.1	35.5	29.8	24.5	335.6	389.6	578.6	735.1	1,271.1	1,837.0	1,639.4	1,647.7	1,722.9	2,052.7	Other Banking Insts.: Liabilities	7f.d
11.2	8.6	6.7	5.4	4.5	I 128.5	216.6	313.1	389.9	582.2	828.1	855.4	985.3	1,036.9	1,232.6	of which: Liab. to Nonbanks	7fdd
															Monetary Authorities	
142.0	191.9	262.9	298.4	356.1	331.5	393.3	408.0	440.9	546.0	662.3	618.0	504.3	578.1	705.6	Foreign Assets	11
87.5	92.9	75.3	84.2	89.1	122.1	86.7	119.1	166.5	92.5	186.1	240.8	415.2	407.3	398.5	Claims on Central Government	12a
14.2	14.9	20.7	24.5	31.4	42.6	58.7	69.0	83.7	10.4	24.1	24.6	34.2	13.4	12.4	Claims on Deposit Money Banks	12e
195.4	240.0	297.5	344.5	404.9	419.2	453.0	501.8	I 569.2	506.9	696.7	714.0	763.6	775.6	872.4	Reserve Money	14
76.0	89.5	101.6	115.9	122.2	127.9	130.7	142.6	157.6	169.1	183.5	195.5	215.2	229.4	246.6	of which: Currency Outside DMBs	14a
14.7	11.5	7.1	3.7	2.5	1.5	1.4	4.8	11.0	14.1	30.1	33.7	37.3	28.0	26.6	Foreign Liabilities	16c
14.5	20.5	20.6	18.3	21.3	21.0	17.4	18.2	23.9	94.6	111.0	115.8	131.7	154.8	175.2	Central Government Deposits	16d
19.1	27.7	33.6	40.5	47.8	54.5	67.0	71.2	I 87.0	33.3	34.8	19.9	21.1	40.4	42.4	Other Items (Net)	17r
End of Period															**Deposit Money Banks**	
94.0	118.9	154.8	181.0	228.0	230.4	253.7	278.0	327.3	334.8	485.6	504.4	542.0	538.0	612.4	Reserves	20
16.7	24.0	29.6	37.2	54.5	67.6	91.3	101.8	148.6	264.9	305.0	479.9	674.6	807.9	912.2	Foreign Assets	21
31.6	47.0	54.7	69.4	90.5	98.0	121.5	181.2	222.8	234.6	285.4	310.2	342.5	519.9	566.5	Claims on Central Government	22a
402.4	460.0	539.7	605.6	683.9	788.6	874.7	981.0	I 1,147.7	1,345.6	1,611.6	1,839.3	2,158.9	2,436.7	2,754.2	Claims on Private Sector	22d
77.2	98.4	116.6	132.5	137.1	157.2	151.4	171.1	201.2	214.6	245.3	265.7	289.3	317.2	326.8	Demand Deposits	24
341.2	406.6	483.8	534.6	631.0	696.4	801.0	911.0	1,084.2	1,289.0	1,529.1	1,793.7	2,064.1	2,440.9	2,794.8	Time and Savings Deposits	25
53.9	75.4	103.6	138.6	184.3	198.1	236.7	263.4	333.3	442.8	608.4	759.0	971.2	1,137.3	1,274.7	Foreign Liabilities	26c
28.3	18.9	15.0	20.6	21.3	33.6	31.4	35.0	35.3	36.1	34.3	36.4	36.4	38.1	38.2	Central Government Deposits	26d
14.2	14.9	20.7	24.5	31.4	42.6	58.7	69.0	83.7	10.4	24.1	24.6	34.2	13.4	12.4	Credit from Monetary Authorities	26g
29.7	35.7	39.1	42.4	51.7	56.7	61.9	72.4	92.4	108.7	187.2	246.6	254.3	322.8	355.5	Other Items (Net)	27r
End of Period															**Monetary Survey**	
90.1	129.1	181.8	193.2	223.7	199.5	246.4	241.6	245.2	353.9	328.9	305.2	170.4	220.8	316.6	Foreign Assets (Net)	31n
481.0	562.9	637.0	724.2	825.6	958.4	1,039.2	1,234.0	I 1,496.8	1,558.9	1,969.3	2,279.6	2,797.6	3,225.9	3,579.3	Domestic Credit	32
76.2	100.6	94.3	114.7	137.0	165.5	159.4	247.0	330.1	196.4	326.2	398.5	589.6	734.2	751.6	Claims on Central Govt. (Net)	32an
....	....	....	....	....	....	....	....	6.3	9.8	19.3	28.7	34.5	37.5	42.9	Claims on Local Government	32b
....	....	....	....	....	....	....	....	7.0	6.0	7.3	10.3	12.0	14.9	28.1	Claims on Nonfin.Pub.Enterprises	32c
404.7	462.4	542.7	609.5	688.7	792.9	879.8	987.0	I 1,153.4	1,346.7	1,616.3	1,841.8	2,161.5	2,439.2	2,756.8	Claims on Private Sector	32d
153.3	188.3	218.5	248.5	259.4	285.3	282.5	314.0	358.9	385.0	429.1	462.4	506.3	549.1	576.9	Money	34
347.9	413.2	491.0	542.7	640.1	707.0	813.0	924.4	I 1,102.7	1,300.8	1,539.7	1,800.2	2,070.2	2,448.0	2,803.7	Quasi-Money	35
69.9	90.6	109.3	126.3	149.8	165.6	190.2	237.1	I 280.3	227.0	329.4	322.1	391.5	449.5	515.3	Other Items (Net)	37r
501.2	601.4	709.5	791.1	899.4	992.3	1,095.5	1,238.4	I 1,461.7	1,685.8	1,968.8	2,262.6	2,576.5	2,997.1	3,380.6	Money plus Quasi-Money	35l
End of Period															**Other Banking Institutions**	
14.5	15.9	19.3	21.1	23.1	27.1	29.3	27.0	27.6	18.6	24.1	9.7	10.1	18.3	27.0	Reserves	40
—	—	—	—	—	.1	.1	I 340.1	606.0	795.7	718.6	795.1	894.9	977.1	Foreign Assets	41
65.1	69.1	73.8	74.8	83.5	93.0	106.2	115.2	I 635.4	768.3	909.0	1,059.4	1,235.1	1,405.8	1,599.8	Claims on Private Sector	42d
46.6	49.4	55.7	61.2	70.4	81.9	88.5	99.6	I 712.3	835.1	977.8	1,111.1	1,276.6	1,475.7	1,685.0	Liquid Liabilities	45l
11.6	15.6	17.3	16.6	15.8	25.3	22.9	20.8	I 342.8	608.6	798.3	719.8	795.9	895.6	977.6	Foreign Liabilities	46c
11.4	14.7	15.1	10.9	13.6	16.0	18.2	20.2	23.5	26.6	30.5	33.3	34.9	38.3	41.9	Capital Accounts	47a
10.0	5.3	4.9	7.1	6.8	-3.1	6.0	1.7	I –75.5	–77.5	–77.9	–76.5	–67.0	–90.6	–100.6	Other Items (Net)	47r
End of Period															**Banking Survey**	
78.6	113.4	164.4	176.7	207.9	174.2	223.6	220.9	I 242.5	351.3	326.2	304.0	169.6	220.1	316.1	Foreign Assets (Net)	51n
544.7	630.7	711.1	797.9	909.2	1,060.6	1,147.5	1,347.3	I 2,132.1	2,342.0	2,886.5	3,343.2	4,035.8	4,635.8	5,182.3	Domestic Credit	52
77.2	101.7	97.7	117.5	141.8	179.1	166.6	251.2	335.6	212.4	339.4	405.5	595.3	740.9	757.4	Claims on Central Govt. (Net)	52an
....	....	....	....	....	....	....	....	6.3	9.8	19.3	28.7	34.5	37.5	42.9	Claims on Local Government	52b
....	....	....	....	....	....	....	....	7.0	6.0	7.3	10.3	12.0	14.9	28.1	Claims on Nonfin.Pub.Enterprises	52c
467.5	529.0	613.4	680.4	767.4	881.6	980.9	1,096.1	I 1,783.1	2,113.8	2,520.6	2,898.7	3,394.0	3,842.5	4,354.0	Claims on Private Sector	52d
148.9	182.7	210.5	239.0	249.1	273.0	267.0	302.3	346.5	381.0	427.8	460.2	503.8	539.8	560.8	Monetary Liabilities	54
391.1	458.8	542.7	600.3	706.7	784.7	899.8	1,022.1	I 1,794.3	2,121.6	2,504.3	2,903.7	3,339.3	3,915.3	4,478.1	Quasi-Monetary Liabilities	55
83.2	102.7	122.4	135.2	161.3	177.1	204.4	243.8	I 233.8	190.7	280.6	283.3	362.3	400.8	459.4	Other Items (Net)	57r
533.3	634.9	745.9	831.2	946.7	1,047.1	1,154.8	1,311.0	I 2,146.3	2,502.3	2,922.5	3,364.0	3,843.0	4,454.6	5,038.5	Liquid Liabilities	55l

Cyprus
423

		1965	1966	1967	1968	1969	1970	1971	1972	1973	1974	1975	1976	1977	1978	1979
Interest Rates															*Percent Per Annum*	
Discount Rate (End of Period)	60	....	....	....	....	6.00	6.00	6.00	6.00	6.00	6.00	6.00	6.00	6.00	6.00	6.00
Deposit Rate	60l	....	....	....	....	....	....	5.00	5.00	5.00	5.00	5.06	5.75	5.75	5.75	5.75
Lending Rate	60p	....	....	....	....	....	6.00	6.00	6.00	6.00	6.00	....	9.00	9.00	9.00	9.00
Prices and Production															*Index Numbers (1990=100):*	
Wholesale Prices	63	....	....	....	27.8	28.6	29.6	30.4	31.5	35.2	44.8	49.5	51.2	55.1	57.2	62.3
Wholesale Prices: Home Goods	63a	....	....	....	27.5	28.6	29.3	29.6	I30.8	34.2	42.9	47.8	I49.9	53.3	54.3	62.2
Consumer Prices	64	26.5	26.7	26.8	27.8	28.5	29.2	30.4	31.9	I34.4	36.6	I41.8	43.6	46.6	50.0	54.8
Industrial Production	66	26.9	29.5	32.8	34.8	37.7	41.3	45.6	51.8	54.8	42.0	35.7	I43.3	50.0	I55.3	59.9
Mining Production	66zx	213.7	216.0	216.0	206.7	216.0	227.6	248.5	232.3	239.2	162.6	I132.4	132.4	145.6	I177.4	169.2
International Transactions															*Millions of Pounds*	
Exports	70	25.29	29.24	29.70	36.96	40.90	45.19	47.28	51.31	60.47	55.29	56.01	106.33	129.75	128.37	161.87
Imports, cif	71	51.41	55.37	59.71	70.94	86.46	98.23	106.87	121.48	157.44	148.03	113.71	177.76	254.01	282.69	357.60
Imports, fob	71.v	46.73	50.33	54.13	64.23	78.30	88.90	96.55	109.65	142.26	133.46	102.59	160.07	228.71	255.59	322.30
															1985=100	
Volume of Exports	72	35	I36	40	47	47	48	53	52	I55	43	38	63	80	76	88
Volume of Imports	73	I24	I26	29	33	38	40	42	47	I55	39	27	41	56	62	70
Unit Value of Exports	74	31	34	33	35	37	40	39	41	I46	53	63	67	67	67	72
Unit Value of Imports	75	I29	29	I29	30	32	34	36	36	I40	53	59	60	63	63	70
Balance of Payments															*Millions of US Dollars:*	
Goods: Exports f.o.b.	78aa d	....	....	....	....	....	....	....	....	....	....	....	....	....	339.2	451.1
Goods: Imports f.o.b.	78ab d	....	....	....	....	....	....	....	....	....	....	....	....	....	−683.8	−906.2
Trade Balance	78ac d	....	....	....	....	....	....	....	....	....	....	....	....	....	−344.6	−455.1
Services: Credit	78ad d	....	....	....	....	....	....	....	....	....	....	....	....	....	258.6	371.3
Services: Debit	78ae d	....	....	....	....	....	....	....	....	....	....	....	....	....	−169.5	−226.8
Balance on Goods and Services	78af d	....	....	....	....	....	....	....	....	....	....	....	....	....	−255.4	−310.6
Income: Credit	78ag d	....	....	....	....	....	....	....	....	....	....	....	....	....	60.8	74.2
Income: Debit	78ah d	....	....	....	....	....	....	....	....	....	....	....	....	....	−35.1	−50.2
Balance on Goods, Serv., & Inc.	78ai d	....	....	....	....	....	....	....	....	....	....	....	....	....	−229.7	−286.6
Current Transfers, n.i.e.: Credit	78aj d	....	....	....	....	....	....	....	....	....	....	....	....	....	46.6	49.1
Current Transfers: Debit	78ak d	....	....	....	....	....	....	....	....	....	....	....	....	....	−1.9	−2.3
Current Account, n.i.e.	78al d	....	....	....	....	....	....	....	....	....	....	....	....	....	−185.0	−239.8
Capital Account, n.i.e.: Credit	78ba d	....	....	....	....	....	....	....	....	....	....	....	....	....	24.1	26.5
Capital Account: Debit	78bb d	....	....	....	....	....	....	....	....	....	....	....	....	....	−1.3	−1.7
Capital Account, n.i.e.	78bc d	....	....	....	....	....	....	....	....	....	....	....	....	....	22.8	24.8
Direct Investment Abroad	78bd d	....	....	....	....	....	....	....	....	....	....	....	....	....	—	—
Dir. Invest. in Rep. Econ., n.i.e.	78be d	....	....	....	....	....	....	....	....	....	....	....	....	....	57.0	70.5
Portfolio Investment Assets	78bf d	....	....	....	....	....	....	....	....	....	....	....	....	....	—	—
Portfolio Investment Liab., n.i.e.	78bg d	....	....	....	....	....	....	....	....	....	....	....	....	....	—	—
Other Investment Assets	78bh d	....	....	....	....	....	....	....	....	....	....	....	....	....	−7.5	−9.6
Other Investment Liab., n.i.e.	78bi d	....	....	....	....	....	....	....	....	....	....	....	....	....	110.6	110.9
Financial Account, n.i.e.	78bj d	....	....	....	....	....	....	....	....	....	....	....	....	....	160.1	171.8
Net Errors and Omissions	78ca d	....	....	....	....	....	....	....	....	....	....	....	....	....	20.3	31.1
Overall Balance	78cb d	....	....	....	....	....	....	....	....	....	....	....	....	....	18.2	−12.0
Reserves and Related Items	79da d	....	....	....	....	....	....	....	....	....	....	....	....	....	−18.2	12.0
Reserve Assets	79db d	....	....	....	....	....	....	....	....	....	....	....	....	....	−5.9	5.4
Use of Fund Credit and Loans	79dc d	....	....	....	....	....	....	....	....	....	....	....	....	....	−12.8	6.6
Liabs.Constit.For.Auth.Reserves	79dd d	....	....	....	....	....	....	....	....	....	....	....	....	....	—	—
Exceptional Financing	79de d	....	....	....	....	....	....	....	....	....	....	....	....	....	.5	—
Government Finance															*Millions of Pounds:*	
Deficit (−) or Surplus	80	....	5.67	4.26	.09	−.21	1.42	.32	−4.81	−12.14	−20.90	−20.38	−24.90	−12.71	−28.84	−41.64
Revenue	81	....	29.05	30.41	31.55	35.47	41.37	46.91	52.28	60.42	54.82	59.48	64.29	83.20	100.00	123.52
Grants Received	81z	....	....	....	—	—	—	.12	.10	—	6.33	7.41	14.48	23.61	13.50	13.25
Expenditure	82	....	23.30	25.71	29.77	34.87	38.35	45.36	54.14	70.26	79.20	84.58	100.39	116.52	136.63	174.11
Lending Minus Repayments	83	....	.07	.45	1.69	.81	1.60	1.35	3.05	2.30	2.85	2.69	3.28	3.00	5.71	4.30
Financing																
Net Borrowing: Domestic	84a	....	−.05	−.14	.04	5.57	3.98	4.63	6.58	−4.49	2.98	5.42	14.43	−6.29	17.82	28.93
Foreign	85a	....	.11	.03	−.20	−.23	.74	−.99	.15	1.66	.84	1.98	10.92	16.20	18.42	11.68
Use of Cash Balances	87	....	−5.74	−4.14	.08	−5.12	−6.14	−3.96	−1.92	14.97	17.08	12.98	−.45	2.80	−7.40	1.03
Debt: Domestic	88a	....	....	....	....	....	13.93	18.56	25.15	27.58	32.73	35.36	49.99	43.98	57.29	87.74
Foreign	89a	....	....	....	....	....	5.17	4.23	4.27	6.66	8.82	10.69	23.22	39.79	59.26	70.14
National Accounts															*Millions of Pounds*	
Exports of Goods & Services	90c	46.7	54.2	57.8	69.0	79.4	85.9	99.0	115.3	131.6	115.8	91.2	166.1	202.3	214.4	281.4
Government Consumption	91f	5.0	14.5	15.3	17.1	19.7	21.6	25.5	29.6	35.8	43.1	44.9	54.5	59.2	66.3	80.5
Gross Fixed Capital Formation	93e	24.9	28.8	31.3	37.4	46.0	53.3	58.5	67.2	94.3	80.0	50.5	70.3	124.6	170.4	219.5
Increase/Decrease(−) in Stocks	93i	3.8	.1	3.5	−.2	3.5	1.9	3.0	2.8	5.4	.1	7.4	18.4	23.0	18.1	24.4
Private Consumption	96f	100.2	110.2	125.9	138.1	156.2	171.5	194.3	218.9	238.9	242.1	208.7	252.7	320.4	376.6	429.7
Imports of Goods & Services	98c	−54.8	−59.9	−64.8	−78.0	−93.9	−107.6	−118.8	−136.7	−176.1	−176.5	−145.7	−209.1	−286.7	−318.7	−401.6
Gross Domestic Product	99b	135.8	147.9	169.0	183.4	210.9	226.6	261.5	296.9	329.9	304.6	257.0	333.9	423.1	506.5	629.8
Net Factor Inc/Pmts(−) Abroad	98.n	5.1	3.0	4.3	4.3	6.6	7.4	8.1	8.9	11.1	11.9	14.2	13.9	18.8	20.2	22.1
Gross Nat'l Expenditure = GNP	99a	140.9	150.9	173.3	187.7	217.5	234.0	269.6	306.0	341.0	316.5	271.2	347.8	441.9	526.7	651.9
Nat'l Income, Market Prices	99e	134.6	144.1	165.5	179.6	207.7	223.5	257.5	292.0	307.0	284.8	244.1	319.6	408.2	484.2	597.6
Gross Dom. Prod. 1990 Prices	99b.p	674.2	722.0	816.8	860.2	944.8	972.9	1,099.0	1,173.4	I1,203.4	999.8	809.8	I955.3	1,106.0	1,190.6	1,308.1
GDP Deflator (1990=100)	99bi p	20.1	20.5	20.7	21.3	22.3	23.3	23.8	25.3	27.4	30.5	31.7	35.0	38.3	42.5	48.1
															Millions:	
Population	99z	.59	.60	.60	.61	.61	.61	.61	.61	.62	.63	.62	.61	.61	.62	.62

Monetary Authorities: I Beginning in 1988, the data reflect improved classification in the report forms.
Deposit Money Banks: I See note to section 10.
Monetary Survey: I See note to section 10.
Other Banking Institutions: I Beginning in 1988, comprises specialized credit institutions, co-operative credit institutions, and offshore banks. Prior to 1988, only specialized credit institutions were included.

Government Finance: I Beginning in 1992, annual data on domestic and foreign net borrowing include the use of cash balances.

Cyprus

1980	1981	1982	1983	1984	1985	1986	1987	1988	1989	1990	1991	1992	1993	1994		
Percent Per Annum															**Interest Rates**	
6.00	6.00	6.00	6.00	6.00	6.00	6.00	6.00	6.00	6.50	6.50	6.50	6.50	6.50	6.50	Discount Rate *(End of Period)*	60
5.75	5.75	5.75	5.75	5.75	5.75	5.75	5.75	5.75	5.75	5.75	5.75	5.75	5.75	5.75	Deposit Rate	60l
9.00	9.00	9.00	9.00	9.00	9.00	9.00	9.00	9.00	9.00	9.00	9.00	9.00	9.00	8.83	Lending Rate	60p
Period Averages															**Prices and Production**	
I72.5	80.6	84.7	87.6	92.2	95.1	90.9	90.7	93.8	96.6	100.0	....	....	....	....	Wholesale Prices	63
79.7	90.9	96.5	98.1	102.2	105.5	95.0	92.3	94.7	95.5	100.0	....	....	....	....	Wholesale Prices: Home Goods	63a
62.2	I68.8	73.3	77.0	81.6	85.7	I86.7	89.2	92.2	95.7	100.0	105.0	I111.9	117.3	....	Consumer Prices	64
64.2	68.0	69.8	72.0	75.8	74.9	I77.3	84.8	91.2	94.5	I100.0	100.7	104.5	97.8	101.2	Industrial Production	66
170.5	147.5	137.1	128.1	109.5	128.3	116.6	123.8	121.1	99.8	I100.0	98.1	100.1	122.4	132.3	Mining Production	66zx
Millions of Pounds															**International Transactions**	
188.04	234.77	263.81	260.53	336.83	290.61	260.16	297.99	330.86	393.05	435.60	441.79	443.72	431.40	475.47	Exports	70
424.29	489.54	577.55	641.96	796.52	762.31	659.07	711.42	866.77	1,130.30	1,174.54	1,215.83	1,490.76	1,260.05	1,481.66	Imports, cif	71
382.19	440.73	519.96	577.96	723.14	691.75	598.07	645.57	786.54	1,025.68	1,065.82	1,103.29	1,352.77	1,143.42	1,344.52	Imports, fob	71.v
1985=100																
94	105	104	97	113	100	95	115	....	....	....	....	....	....	....	Volume of Exports	72
73	75	88	96	104	100	108	117	....	....	....	....	....	....	....	Volume of Imports	73
78	92	90	95	102	100	93	95	....	....	....	....	....	....	....	Unit Value of Exports	74
81	90	91	93	99	100	85	81	....	....	....	....	....	....	....	Unit Value of Imports	75
Minus Sign Indicates Debit															**Balance of Payments**	
527.7	551.5	554.1	495.4	573.1	474.9	502.8	619.8	709.6	797.1	952.2	965.6	1,009.3	....	....	Goods: Exports f.o.b.	78aa *d*
−1,079.2	−1,042.6	−1,090.3	−1,093.5	−1,224.9	−1,121.9	−1,141.6	−1,326.8	−1,666.8	−2,072.1	−2,308.3	−2,385.1	−2,998.6	....	....	Goods: Imports f.o.b.	78ab *d*
−551.5	−491.2	−536.2	−598.1	−651.8	−647.0	−638.8	−706.9	−957.3	−1,274.9	−1,356.1	−1,419.4	−1,989.2	....	....	Trade Balance	78ac *d*
481.8	526.5	577.2	627.4	701.6	738.4	932.0	1,181.0	1,404.3	1,612.5	2,000.2	1,839.0	2,521.4	....	....	Services: Credit	78ad *d*
−267.7	−273.6	−294.5	−287.7	−300.5	−301.7	−354.7	−431.1	−498.0	−539.2	−660.1	−694.1	−828.7	....	....	Services: Debit	78ae *d*
−337.3	−238.2	−253.5	−258.4	−250.7	−210.3	−61.6	43.0	−51.0	−201.6	−16.0	−274.5	−296.6	....	....	Balance on Goods and Services	78af *d*
97.7	102.3	115.3	102.9	110.0	115.6	129.5	141.3	159.9	186.2	238.5	245.9	238.1	....	....	Income: Credit	78ag *d*
−63.4	−74.5	−89.4	−103.3	−105.5	−107.3	−123.9	−136.4	−152.6	−157.4	−199.0	−205.3	−214.0	....	....	Income: Debit	78ah *d*
−303.1	−210.5	−227.6	−258.8	−246.3	−201.9	−56.0	48.0	−43.7	−172.8	23.5	−233.9	−272.5	....	....	Balance on Goods, Serv., & Inc.	78ai *d*
46.2	39.9	50.5	54.9	25.8	22.7	25.5	21.6	32.4	22.1	24.8	20.8	13.9	....	....	Current Transfers, n.i.e.: Credit	78aj *d*
−1.4	−1.2	−1.1	−1.1	−1.2	−1.0	−1.1	−1.0	−1.3	−1.6	−1.7	−1.7	−1.3	....	....	Current Transfers: Debit	78ak *d*
−258.3	−171.8	−178.2	−205.1	−221.6	−180.2	−31.7	68.6	−12.6	−152.4	46.5	−214.9	−259.9	....	....	Current Account, n.i.e.	78al *d*
31.2	26.1	24.2	22.4	20.7	20.6	22.8	24.9	22.9	21.3	22.3	21.9	22.5	....	....	Capital Account, n.i.e.: Credit	78ba *d*
−2.5	−2.1	−2.1	−1.9	−1.9	−1.5	−1.7	−1.7	−1.9	−1.8	−2.7	−3.7	−4.0	....	....	Capital Account: Debit	78bb *d*
28.6	24.0	22.1	20.5	18.9	19.1	21.0	23.3	21.0	19.5	19.7	18.2	18.5	....	....	Capital Account, n.i.e.	78bc *d*
—	—	—	—	—	—	—	—	—	—	—	−3.2	−15.6	−14.4	....	Direct Investment Abroad	78bd *d*
85.0	78.3	71.5	68.4	52.7	58.0	46.3	52.0	62.1	69.9	129.9	82.3	121.5	....	....	Dir. Invest. in Rep. Econ., n.i.e.	78be *d*
—	—	—	—	—	—	—	—	—	—	—	—	—	....	....	Portfolio Investment Assets	78bf *d*
—	—	—	—	—	—	—	—	—	—	92.8	−37.4	123.3	53.9	....	Portfolio Investment Liab., n.i.e.	78bg *d*
−9.1	−16.6	−16.8	−21.1	−32.8	−60.7	−55.8	−59.4	−85.1	−213.0	−486.9	−91.5	−368.9	−377.9	....	Other Investment Assets	78bh *d*
174.8	176.8	221.1	168.2	249.7	110.4	206.7	88.3	171.9	460.6	463.3	422.9	540.6	....	....	Other Investment Liab., n.i.e.	78bi *d*
250.7	238.5	275.8	215.5	269.5	107.6	197.2	80.9	148.9	410.3	461.1	244.1	323.7	....	....	Financial Account, n.i.e.	78bj *d*
16.1	−2.7	20.5	10.8	29.1	23.9	−27.1	−109.0	−86.6	−48.9	−229.9	−151.3	−300.9	....	....	Net Errors and Omissions	78ca *d*
37.1	88.0	140.2	41.7	95.9	−29.6	159.5	63.7	70.7	228.5	297.4	−103.9	−218.6	....	....	Overall Balance	78cb *d*
−37.1	−88.0	−140.2	−41.7	−95.9	29.6	−159.5	−63.7	−70.7	−228.5	−297.4	103.9	218.6	....	....	Reserves and Related Items	79da *d*
−27.8	−77.3	−129.9	−34.3	−93.5	32.8	−159.5	−63.7	−70.7	−228.5	−297.4	103.9	218.6	....	....	Reserve Assets	79db *d*
−9.3	−10.6	−10.3	−7.4	−2.3	−3.2	—	—	—	—	—	—	—	....	....	Use of Fund Credit and Loans	79dc *d*
—	—	—	—	—	—	—	—	—	—	—	—	—	....	....	Liabs.Constit.For.Auth.Reserves	79dd *d*
—	—	—	—	—	—	—	—	—	—	—	—	—	....	....	Exceptional Financing	79de *d*
Year Ending December 31															**Government Finance**	
−70.01	−46.75	−48.48	−81.34	−73.11	−65.40	−58.07	−75.06	−63.78	−31.16	−59.01	−118.13	−110.30	−77.80	....	Deficit (−) or Surplus	80
161.22	191.25	232.83	275.62	333.39	380.39	418.10	454.73	529.10	627.24	706.42	720.83	874.00	987.90	....	Revenue	81
12.55	12.09	19.52	13.79	10.96	9.71	8.99	6.98	6.96	5.37	4.04	3.78	1.10	3.80	....	Grants Received	81z
221.52	255.58	297.03	357.34	409.52	437.44	477.31	520.79	588.70	656.42	759.27	824.65	970.10	1,053.80	....	Expenditure	82
22.26	−5.49	3.80	13.41	7.94	18.06	7.85	15.98	11.14	7.35	10.20	18.09	15.30	15.70	....	Lending Minus Repayments	83
															Financing	
40.62	26.72	8.54	38.93	44.73	69.35	−8.88	81.44	99.45	−3.79	168.55	125.75	I160.50	168.90	....	Net Borrowing: Domestic	84a
29.61	25.45	51.96	32.14	39.47	18.61	84.51	7.13	−1.74	69.96	−31.66	75.07	I−50.20	−91.10	....	Foreign	85a
−.22	−5.42	−12.02	10.27	−11.09	−22.56	−17.56	−13.51	−33.93	−35.01	−77.88	−82.69	....	....	....	Use of Cash Balances	87
131.95	156.17	164.48	203.22	247.39	316.83	305.71	388.12	488.12	487.45	500.12	699.66	825.40	....	....	Debt: Domestic	88a
95.44	133.95	199.05	254.52	321.39	326.28	448.47	459.15	456.22	521.62	489.50	566.69	....	....	....	Foreign	89a
Millions of Pounds															**National Accounts**	
344.1	440.2	521.9	573.0	731.0	722.4	721.0	841.8	959.6	1,161.5	1,312.6	1,262.8	1,538.8	....	....	Exports of Goods & Services	90c
103.4	127.5	151.5	171.9	188.7	208.5	225.9	246.5	275.0	298.1	339.1	388.4	429.2	....	....	Government Consumption	91f
260.0	275.9	304.7	316.0	412.5	403.0	384.0	417.9	490.8	621.4	628.9	647.8	780.9	....	....	Gross Fixed Capital Formation	93e
27.5	20.3	20.4	26.3	36.8	46.7	31.0	36.6	57.2	75.8	62.3	49.7	55.0	....	....	Increase/Decrease(−) in Stocks	93i
508.4	573.8	678.0	765.8	851.5	945.8	979.2	1,059.8	1,210.2	1,343.3	1,510.9	1,722.3	1,980.4	....	....	Private Consumption	96f
−479.5	−554.7	−658.4	−727.2	−897.4	−872.0	−775.4	−845.7	−1,010.3	−1,288.7	−1,355.1	−1,413.9	−1,722.7	....	....	Imports of Goods & Services	98c
760.4	876.0	1,024.9	1,136.7	1,337.4	1,482.2	1,600.9	1,781.2	1,996.4	2,257.5	2,547.4	2,670.5	3,011.8	....	....	Gross Domestic Product	99b
26.6	27.0	30.5	21.8	24.2	25.8	25.8	27.0	30.0	42.6	50.4	52.9	63.2	....	....	Net Factor Inc/Pmts(−) Abroad	98.n
787.0	903.0	1,055.4	1,158.5	1,361.6	1,508.0	1,626.7	1,808.2	2,026.4	2,300.1	2,598.3	2,723.4	3,075.0	....	....	Gross Nat'l Expenditure = GNP	99a
716.6	814.2	951.3	1,039.5	1,221.6	1,349.7	1,455.9	1,613.3	1,813.6	2,058.6	2,325.5	2,437.4	2,749.7	....	....	Nat'l Income, Market Prices	99e
1,385.5	1,427.8	1,517.5	1,598.0	1,739.2	I1,821.7	1,889.2	2,023.2	2,197.4	2,374.2	2,547.4	2,576.9	2,796.7	....	....	Gross Dom. Prod. 1990 Prices	99b.p
54.9	61.4	67.5	71.1	76.9	81.4	84.7	88.0	90.9	95.1	100.0	103.6	107.7	....	....	GDP Deflator (1990=100)	99bi p
Midyear Estimates																
.63	.63	.64	.65	.66	.67	.67	.68	.69	.69	.70	.71	.72	.73	....	Population	99z

Czech Republic

935

		1965	1966	1967	1968	1969	1970	1971	1972	1973	1974	1975	1976	1977	1978	1979

Exchange Rates — *Koruny per SDR:*

Official Rate	aa	...	...	...	...	...	...	...	...	...	...	...	...	...	...	...

Koruny per US Dollar:

Official Rate	ae	...	...	...	...	...	...	...	...	...	...	...	...	...	...	...
Official Rate	rf	...	...	...	...	...	...	...	...	...	...	...	...	...	...	...

Fund Position — *Millions of SDRs:*

Quota	2f. s	...	...	...	...	...	...	...	...	...	...	...	...	...	...	...
SDRs	1b. s	...	...	...	...	...	...	...	...	...	...	...	...	...	...	...
Reserve Position in the Fund	1c. s	...	...	...	...	...	...	...	...	...	...	...	...	...	...	...
Total Fund Cred.&Loans Outstg.	2tl	...	...	...	...	...	...	...	...	...	...	...	...	...	...	...

International Liquidity — *Millions of US Dollars Unless Otherwise Indicated:*

Total Reserves minus Gold	1l. d	...	...	...	...	...	...	...	...	...	...	...	...	...	...	...
SDRs	1b. d	...	...	...	...	...	...	...	...	...	...	...	...	...	...	...
Reserve Position in the Fund	1c. d	...	...	...	...	...	...	...	...	...	...	...	...	...	...	...
Foreign Exchange	1d. d	...	...	...	...	...	...	...	...	...	...	...	...	...	...	...
Gold (Million Fine Troy Ounces)	1ad	...	...	...	...	...	...	...	...	...	...	...	...	...	...	...
Gold (National Valuation)	1and	...	...	...	...	...	...	...	...	...	...	...	...	...	...	...
Other Fgn. Assets: Convertible	3a. d	...	...	...	...	...	...	...	...	...	...	...	...	...	...	...
Nonconvertible	3b. d	...	...	...	...	...	...	...	...	...	...	...	...	...	...	...
Monetary Authorities: Other Liab.	4.. d	...	...	...	...	...	...	...	...	...	...	...	...	...	...	...
Dep.Money Banks: Assets Conv.	7ax d	...	...	...	...	...	...	...	...	...	...	...	...	...	...	...
Assets Nonconv.	7ay d	...	...	...	...	...	...	...	...	...	...	...	...	...	...	...
Dep.Money Banks: Liab. Conv.	7bx d	...	...	...	...	...	...	...	...	...	...	...	...	...	...	...
Liab. Nonconv.	7by d	...	...	...	...	...	...	...	...	...	...	...	...	...	...	...

Monetary Authorities — *Millions of Koruny:*

Foreign Assets	11	...	...	...	...	...	...	...	...	...	...	...	...	...	...	...
of which: Nonconv. Fgn. Assets	11..y	...	...	...	...	...	...	...	...	...	...	...	...	...	...	...
Claims on Central Government	12a	...	...	...	...	...	...	...	...	...	...	...	...	...	...	...
Claims on Nonfin.Pub.Enterprises	12c	...	...	...	...	...	...	...	...	...	...	...	...	...	...	...
Claims on Deposit Money Banks	12e	...	...	...	...	...	...	...	...	...	...	...	...	...	...	...
Reserve Money	14	...	...	...	...	...	...	...	...	...	...	...	...	...	...	...
of which: Currency Outside DMBs	14a	...	...	...	...	...	...	...	...	...	...	...	...	...	...	...
Time Deposits	15	...	...	...	...	...	...	...	...	...	...	...	...	...	...	...
Foreign Liabilities	16c	...	...	...	...	...	...	...	...	...	...	...	...	...	...	...
of which: Nonconv. Fgn. Liab.	16c.y	...	...	...	...	...	...	...	...	...	...	...	...	...	...	...
Long-Term Foreign Liabilities	16cl	...	...	...	...	...	...	...	...	...	...	...	...	...	...	...
o/w: L-T Nonconv. Fgn. Liab.	16cly	...	...	...	...	...	...	...	...	...	...	...	...	...	...	...
Central Government Deposits	16d	...	...	...	...	...	...	...	...	...	...	...	...	...	...	...
Capital Accounts	17a	...	...	...	...	...	...	...	...	...	...	...	...	...	...	...
Other Items (Net)	17r	...	...	...	...	...	...	...	...	...	...	...	...	...	...	...

Deposit Money Banks — *Millions of Koruny:*

Reserves	20	...	...	...	...	...	...	...	...	...	...	...	...	...	...	...
Foreign Assets	21	...	...	...	...	...	...	...	...	...	...	...	...	...	...	...
of which: Nonconv. Fgn. Assets	21..y	...	...	...	...	...	...	...	...	...	...	...	...	...	...	...
Claims on Central Government	22a	...	...	...	...	...	...	...	...	...	...	...	...	...	...	...
Claims on National Property Fund	22ae	...	...	...	...	...	...	...	...	...	...	...	...	...	...	...
Claims on Local Government	22b	...	...	...	...	...	...	...	...	...	...	...	...	...	...	...
Claims on Nonfin.Pub.Enterprises	22c	...	...	...	...	...	...	...	...	...	...	...	...	...	...	...
Claims on Private Sector	22d	...	...	...	...	...	...	...	...	...	...	...	...	...	...	...
Demand Deposits	24	...	...	...	...	...	...	...	...	...	...	...	...	...	...	...
Time & Fgn. Currency Deposits	25	...	...	...	...	...	...	...	...	...	...	...	...	...	...	...
of which: Fgn. Currency Deposits	25b	...	...	...	...	...	...	...	...	...	...	...	...	...	...	...
Bonds	26ab	...	...	...	...	...	...	...	...	...	...	...	...	...	...	...
Foreign Liabilities	26c	...	...	...	...	...	...	...	...	...	...	...	...	...	...	...
of which: Nonconv. Fgn. Liab.	26c.y	...	...	...	...	...	...	...	...	...	...	...	...	...	...	...
Long-Term Foreign Liabilities	26cl	...	...	...	...	...	...	...	...	...	...	...	...	...	...	...
o/w: L-T Nonconv. Fgn. Liab.	26cly	...	...	...	...	...	...	...	...	...	...	...	...	...	...	...
Central Government Deposits	26d	...	...	...	...	...	...	...	...	...	...	...	...	...	...	...
National Property Fund Deposits	26de	...	...	...	...	...	...	...	...	...	...	...	...	...	...	...
Local Government Deposits	26db	...	...	...	...	...	...	...	...	...	...	...	...	...	...	...
Credit from Monetary Authorities	26g	...	...	...	...	...	...	...	...	...	...	...	...	...	...	...
Capital Accounts	27a	...	...	...	...	...	...	...	...	...	...	...	...	...	...	...
Other Items (Net)	27r	...	...	...	...	...	...	...	...	...	...	...	...	...	...	...

Monetary Survey — *Millions of Koruny:*

Foreign Assets (Net)	31n	...	...	...	...	...	...	...	...	...	...	...	...	...	...	...
Domestic Credit	32	...	...	...	...	...	...	...	...	...	...	...	...	...	...	...
Claims on General Govt. (Net)	32an	...	...	...	...	...	...	...	...	...	...	...	...	...	...	...
Claims on Nonfin.Pub.Enterprises	32c	...	...	...	...	...	...	...	...	...	...	...	...	...	...	...
Claims on Private Sector	32d	...	...	...	...	...	...	...	...	...	...	...	...	...	...	...
Money	34	...	...	...	...	...	...	...	...	...	...	...	...	...	...	...
Quasi-Money	35	...	...	...	...	...	...	...	...	...	...	...	...	...	...	...
Bonds	36ab	...	...	...	...	...	...	...	...	...	...	...	...	...	...	...
Long-Term Foreign Liabilities	36cl	...	...	...	...	...	...	...	...	...	...	...	...	...	...	...
Capital Accounts	37a	...	...	...	...	...	...	...	...	...	...	...	...	...	...	...
Other Items (Net)	37r	...	...	...	...	...	...	...	...	...	...	...	...	...	...	...
Money plus Quasi-Money	35l	...	...	...	...	...	...	...	...	...	...	...	...	...	...	...

Czech Republic

1980	1981	1982	1983	1984	1985	1986	1987	1988	1989	1990	1991	1992	1993	1994		
End of Period															**Exchange Rates**	
....	....	....	....	....	....	....	....	....	....	....	....	....	41.145	40.947	Official Rate	aa
End of Period (ae) Period Averages (rf)																
....	....	....	....	....	....	....	....	....	....	....	....	....	29.955	28.049	Official Rate	ae
....	....	....	....	....	....	....	....	....	....	....	....	....	29.153	28.785	Official Rate	rf
End of Period															**Fund Position**	
....	....	....	....	....	....	....	....	....	....	....	....	....	589.6	589.6	Quota	2f. s
....	....	....	....	....	....	....	....	....	....	....	....	....	6.0	—	SDRs	1b. s
....	....	....	....	....	....	....	....	....	....	—	—	—	—	—	Reserve Position in the Fund	1c. s
....	....	....	....	....	....	....	....	....	....	....	....	....	780.7	—	Total Fund Cred.&Loans Outstg.	2tl
End of Period															**International Liquidity**	
....	....	....	....	....	....	....	....	....	....	....	....	....	3,789	6,145	Total Reserves minus Gold	1l. d
....	....	....	....	....	....	....	....	....	....	....	....	....	8	—	SDRs	1b. d
....	....	....	....	....	....	....	....	....	....	—	—	—	—	—	Reserve Position in the Fund	1c. d
....	....	....	....	....	....	....	....	....	....	....	....	....	3,781	6,145	Foreign Exchange	1d. d
....	....	....	....	....	....	....	....	....	....	....	....	....	1.950	2.098	Gold (Million Fine Troy Ounces)	1ad
....	....	....	....	....	....	....	....	....	....	....	....	....	129	140	Gold (National Valuation)	1an d
....	....	....	....	....	....	....	....	....	....	....	....	....	1,766	1,773	Other Fgn. Assets: Convertible	3a. d
....	....	....	....	....	....	....	....	....	....	....	....	....	2,012	1,857	Nonconvertible	3b. d
....	....	....	....	....	....	....	....	....	....	....	....	....	2,905	1,791	Monetary Authorities: Other Liab.	4.. d
....	....	....	....	....	....	....	....	....	....	....	....	....	2,517	2,716	Dep.Money Banks: Assets Conv.	7ax d
....	....	....	....	....	....	....	....	....	....	....	....	....	285	487	Assets Nonconv.	7ay d
....	....	....	....	....	....	....	....	....	....	....	....	....	1,342	2,279	Dep.Money Banks: Liab. Conv.	7bx d
....	....	....	....	....	....	....	....	....	....	....	....	....	117	185	Liab. Nonconv.	7by d
End of Period															**Monetary Authorities**	
....	....	....	....	....	....	....	....	....	....	....	....	....	185,197	205,202	Foreign Assets	11
....	....	....	....	....	....	....	....	....	....	....	....	....	61,633	24,578	of which: Nonconv. Fgn. Assets	11..y
....	....	....	....	....	....	....	....	....	....	....	....	....	44,339	35,716	Claims on Central Government	12a
....	....	....	....	....	....	....	....	....	....	....	....	....	2,153	4,956	Claims on Nonfin.Pub.Enterprises	12c
....	....	....	....	....	....	....	....	....	....	....	....	....	76,906	75,088	Claims on Deposit Money Banks	12e
....	....	....	....	....	....	....	....	....	....	....	....	....	164,477	223,899	Reserve Money	14
....	....	....	....	....	....	....	....	....	....	....	....	....	59,039	83,581	of which: Currency Outside DMBs	14a
....	....	....	....	....	....	....	....	....	....	....	....	....	136	9,219	Time Deposits	15
....	....	....	....	....	....	....	....	....	....	....	....	....	37,395	1,102	Foreign Liabilities	16c
....	....	....	....	....	....	....	....	....	....	....	....	....	644	644	of which: Nonconv. Fgn. Liab.	16c.y
....	....	....	....	....	....	....	....	....	....	....	....	....	81,754	49,146	Long-Term Foreign Liabilities	16cl
....	....	....	....	....	....	....	....	....	....	....	....	....	55,214	24,611	o/w: L-T Nonconv. Fgn. Liab.	16cl y
....	....	....	....	....	....	....	....	....	....	....	....	....	33,405	51,858	Central Government Deposits	16d
....	....	....	....	....	....	....	....	....	....	....	....	....	9,124	16,857	Capital Accounts	17a
....	....	....	....	....	....	....	....	....	....	....	....	....	-17,696	-31,119	Other Items (Net)	17r
End of Period															**Deposit Money Banks**	
....	....	....	....	....	....	....	....	....	....	....	....	....	71,445	80,778	Reserves	20
....	....	....	....	....	....	....	....	....	....	....	....	....	83,948	89,843	Foreign Assets	21
....	....	....	....	....	....	....	....	....	....	....	....	....	8,540	13,654	of which: Nonconv. Fgn. Assets	21..y
....	....	....	....	....	....	....	....	....	....	....	....	....	65,456	83,780	Claims on Central Government	22a
....	....	....	....	....	....	....	....	....	....	....	....	....	10,800	12,200	Claims on National Property Fund	22ae
....	....	....	....	....	....	....	....	....	....	....	....	....	1,980	—	Claims on Local Government	22b
....	....	....	....	....	....	....	....	....	....	....	....	....	222,994	221,076	Claims on Nonfin.Pub.Enterprises	22c
....	....	....	....	....	....	....	....	....	....	....	....	....	508,672	683,189	Claims on Private Sector	22d
....	....	....	....	....	....	....	....	....	....	....	....	....	201,961	307,642	Demand Deposits	24
....	....	....	....	....	....	....	....	....	....	....	....	....	428,214	426,431	Time & Fgn. Currency Deposits	25
....	....	....	....	....	....	....	....	....	....	....	....	....	56,731	59,059	of which: Fgn. Currency Deposits	25b
....	....	....	....	....	....	....	....	....	....	....	....	....	3,784	21,213	Bonds	26ab
....	....	....	....	....	....	....	....	....	....	....	....	....	37,506	61,172	Foreign Liabilities	26c
....	....	....	....	....	....	....	....	....	....	....	....	....	2,100	2,534	of which: Nonconv. Fgn. Liab.	26c.y
....	....	....	....	....	....	....	....	....	....	....	....	....	6,198	7,949	Long-Term Foreign Liabilities	26cl
....	....	....	....	....	....	....	....	....	....	....	....	....	1,395	2,662	o/w: L-T Nonconv. Fgn. Liab.	26cl y
....	....	....	....	....	....	....	....	....	....	....	....	....	18,307	51,016	Central Government Deposits	26d
....	....	....	....	....	....	....	....	....	....	....	....	....	43,477	29,938	National Property Fund Deposits	26de
....	....	....	....	....	....	....	....	....	....	....	....	....	16,941	30,147	Local Government Deposits	26db
....	....	....	....	....	....	....	....	....	....	....	....	....	76,347	77,711	Credit from Monetary Authorities	26g
....	....	....	....	....	....	....	....	....	....	....	....	....	160,746	185,367	Capital Accounts	27a
....	....	....	....	....	....	....	....	....	....	....	....	....	-28,186	-27,720	Other Items (Net)	27r
End of Period															**Monetary Survey**	
....	....	....	....	....	....	....	....	....	....	....	....	....	194,244	232,771	Foreign Assets (Net)	31n
....	....	....	....	....	....	....	....	....	....	....	....	....	744,271	877,969	Domestic Credit	32
....	....	....	....	....	....	....	....	....	....	....	....	....	10,445	-31,263	Claims on General Govt. (Net)	32an
....	....	....	....	....	....	....	....	....	....	....	....	....	225,147	226,032	Claims on Nonfin.Pub.Enterprises	32c
....	....	....	....	....	....	....	....	....	....	....	....	....	508,679	683,200	Claims on Private Sector	32d
....	....	....	....	....	....	....	....	....	....	....	....	....	268,969	403,973	Money	34
....	....	....	....	....	....	....	....	....	....	....	....	....	428,350	435,650	Quasi-Money	35
....	....	....	....	....	....	....	....	....	....	....	....	....	3,784	21,213	Bonds	36ab
....	....	....	....	....	....	....	....	....	....	....	....	....	87,952	57,095	Long-Term Foreign Liabilities	36cl
....	....	....	....	....	....	....	....	....	....	....	....	....	169,870	202,224	Capital Accounts	37a
....	....	....	....	....	....	....	....	....	....	....	....	....	-20,410	-9,415	Other Items (Net)	37r
....	....	....	....	....	....	....	....	....	....	....	....	....	697,319	839,623	Money plus Quasi-Money	35l

Czech Republic

935

	1965	1966	1967	1968	1969	1970	1971	1972	1973	1974	1975	1976	1977	1978	1979
Interest Rates															*Percent Per Annum*
Discount Rate *(End of Period)* ... 60	....	....	....	....	....	....	....	....	....	....	....	....	....	....	....
Refinancing Rate ... 60a	....	....	....	....	....	....	....	....	....	....	....	....	....	....	....
Deposit Rate ... 60l	....	....	....	....	....	....	....	....	....	....	....	....	....	....	....
Lending Rate ... 60p	....	....	....	....	....	....	....	....	....	....	....	....	....	....	....
Prices, Production, Employment															*Index Numbers (1990=100):*
Producer Prices ... 63	....	....	....	....	....	....	....	....	....	....	....	....	....	....	....
Consumer Prices ... 64	....	....	....	....	....	....	....	....	....	....	....	....	....	....	....
Wages ... 65	....	....	....	....	....	....	....	....	....	....	....	....	....	....	....
Industrial Production ... 66	....	....	....	....	....	....	....	....	....	....	....	....	....	....	....
Employment ... 67	....	....	....	....	....	....	....	....	....	....	....	....	....	....	....
International Transactions															*Millions of Koruny*
Exports ... 70	....	....	....	....	....	....	....	....	....	....	....	....	....	....	....
Imports, fob ... 71.v	....	....	....	....	....	....	....	....	....	....	....	....	....	....	....
Balance of Payments															*Millions of US Dollars:*
Goods: Exports f.o.b. ... 78aa *d*	....	....	....	....	....	....	....	....	....	....	....	....	....	....	....
Goods: Imports f.o.b. ... 78ab *d*	....	....	....	....	....	....	....	....	....	....	....	....	....	....	....
Trade Balance ... 78ac *d*	....	....	....	....	....	....	....	....	....	....	....	....	....	....	....
Services: Credit ... 78ad *d*	....	....	....	....	....	....	....	....	....	....	....	....	....	....	....
Services: Debit ... 78ae *d*	....	....	....	....	....	....	....	....	....	....	....	....	....	....	....
Balance on Goods and Services ... 78af *d*	....	....	....	....	....	....	....	....	....	....	....	....	....	....	....
Income: Credit ... 78ag *d*	....	....	....	....	....	....	....	....	....	....	....	....	....	....	....
Income: Debit ... 78ah *d*	....	....	....	....	....	....	....	....	....	....	....	....	....	....	....
Balance on Goods, Serv., & Inc. ... 78ai *d*	....	....	....	....	....	....	....	....	....	....	....	....	....	....	....
Current Transfers, n.i.e.: Credit ... 78aj *d*	....	....	....	....	....	....	....	....	....	....	....	....	....	....	....
Current Transfers: Debit ... 78ak *d*	....	....	....	....	....	....	....	....	....	....	....	....	....	....	....
Current Account, n.i.e. ... 78al *d*	....	....	....	....	....	....	....	....	....	....	....	....	....	....	....
Capital Account, n.i.e.: Credit ... 78ba *d*	....	....	....	....	....	....	....	....	....	....	....	....	....	....	....
Capital Account: Debit ... 78bb *d*	....	....	....	....	....	....	....	....	....	....	....	....	....	....	....
Capital Account, n.i.e. ... 78bc *d*	....	....	....	....	....	....	....	....	....	....	....	....	....	....	....
Direct Investment Abroad ... 78bd *d*	....	....	....	....	....	....	....	....	....	....	....	....	....	....	....
Dir. Invest. in Rep. Econ., n.i.e. ... 78be *d*	....	....	....	....	....	....	....	....	....	....	....	....	....	....	....
Portfolio Investment Assets ... 78bf *d*	....	....	....	....	....	....	....	....	....	....	....	....	....	....	....
Portfolio Investment Liab., n.i.e. ... 78bg *d*	....	....	....	....	....	....	....	....	....	....	....	....	....	....	....
Other Investment Assets ... 78bh *d*	....	....	....	....	....	....	....	....	....	....	....	....	....	....	....
Other Investment Liab., n.i.e. ... 78bi *d*	....	....	....	....	....	....	....	....	....	....	....	....	....	....	....
Financial Account, n.i.e. ... 78bj *d*	....	....	....	....	....	....	....	....	....	....	....	....	....	....	....
Net Errors and Omissions ... 78ca *d*	....	....	....	....	....	....	....	....	....	....	....	....	....	....	....
Overall Balance ... 78cb *d*	....	....	....	....	....	....	....	....	....	....	....	....	....	....	....
Reserves and Related Items ... 79da *d*	....	....	....	....	....	....	....	....	....	....	....	....	....	....	....
Reserve Assets ... 79db *d*	....	....	....	....	....	....	....	....	....	....	....	....	....	....	....
Use of Fund Credit and Loans ... 79dc *d*	....	....	....	....	....	....	....	....	....	....	....	....	....	....	....
Liabs.Constit.For.Auth.Reserves ... 79dd *d*	....	....	....	....	....	....	....	....	....	....	....	....	....	....	....
Exceptional Financing ... 79de *d*	....	....	....	....	....	....	....	....	....	....	....	....	....	....	....
Government Finance															*Billions of Koruny:*
Deficit (-) or Surplus ... 80	....	....	....	....	....	....	....	....	....	....	....	....	....	....	....
Revenue ... 81	....	....	....	....	....	....	....	....	....	....	....	....	....	....	....
Expenditure ... 82	....	....	....	....	....	....	....	....	....	....	....	....	....	....	....
Lending Minus Repayments ... 83	....	....	....	....	....	....	....	....	....	....	....	....	....	....	....
Financing															
Domestic ... 84a	....	....	....	....	....	....	....	....	....	....	....	....	....	....	....
Foreign ... 85a	....	....	....	....	....	....	....	....	....	....	....	....	....	....	....
Debt: Domestic ... 88a	....	....	....	....	....	....	....	....	....	....	....	....	....	....	....
Foreign ... 89a	....	....	....	....	....	....	....	....	....	....	....	....	....	....	....
National Accounts															*Billions of Koruny*
Exports of Goods & Services ... 90c	....	....	....	....	....	....	....	....	....	....	....	....	....	....	....
Government Consumption ... 91f	....	....	....	....	....	....	....	....	....	....	....	....	....	....	....
Gross Fixed Capital Formation ... 93e	....	....	....	....	....	....	....	....	....	....	....	....	....	....	....
Increase/Decrease(-) in Stocks ... 93i	....	....	....	....	....	....	....	....	....	....	....	....	....	....	....
Private Consumption ... 96f	....	....	....	....	....	....	....	....	....	....	....	....	....	....	....
Imports of Goods & Services ... 98c	....	....	....	....	....	....	....	....	....	....	....	....	....	....	....
Gross Domestic Product ... 99b	....	....	....	....	....	....	....	....	....	....	....	....	....	....	....
Gross Dom. Prod. 1990 Prices ... 99b.*p*	....	....	....	....	....	....	....	....	....	....	....	....	....	....	....
GDP Deflator (1990=100) ... 99bi *p*	....	....	....	....	....	....	....	....	....	....	....	....	....	....	....
															Millions:
Population ... 99z	....	....	....	....	....	....	....	....	....	....	....	....	....	....	....

Czech Republic

1980	1981	1982	1983	1984	1985	1986	1987	1988	1989	1990	1991	1992	1993	1994		
Percent Per Annum															**Interest Rates**	
....	....	....	....	....	....	....	....	....	....	....	....	....	8.00	8.50	Discount Rate *(End of Period)*	60
....	....	....	....	....	....	....	....	....	....	....	....	....	11.50	11.00	Refinancing Rate	60a
....	....	....	....	....	....	....	....	....	....	....	....	....	7.03	7.07	Deposit Rate	60l
....	....	....	....	....	....	....	....	....	....	....	....	....	14.07	13.12	Lending Rate	60p
Period Averages															**Prices, Production, Employment**	
....	....	....	....	....	....	....	....	....	....	....	....	....	211.8	222.9	Producer Prices	63
....	....	....	....	....	....	....	....	....	....	....	....	....	210.4	231.6	Consumer Prices	64
....	....	....	....	....	....	....	....	....	....	....	....	....	177.0	209.9	Wages	65
....	....	....	....	....	....	....	....	....	....	....	....	....	68.4	69.8	Industrial Production	66
....	....	....	....	....	....	....	....	....	....	....	....	....	77.3	73.6	Employment	67
Millions of Koruny															**International Transactions**	
....	....	....	....	....	....	....	....	....	....	....	....	....	384,966	411,457	Exports	70
....	....	....	....	....	....	....	....	....	....	....	....	....	370,397	423,964	Imports, fob	71.v
Minus Sign Indicates Debit															Balance of Payments	
....	....	....	....	....	....	....	....	....	....	....	....	....	12,729	....	Goods: Exports f.o.b.	78aa *d*
....	....	....	....	....	....	....	....	....	....	....	....	....	–13,002	....	Goods: Imports f.o.b.	78ab *d*
....	....	....	....	....	....	....	....	....	....	....	....	....	–273	....	Trade Balance	78ac *d*
....	....	....	....	....	....	....	....	....	....	....	....	....	4,733	....	Services: Credit	78ad *d*
....	....	....	....	....	....	....	....	....	....	....	....	....	–3,712	....	Services: Debit	78ae *d*
....	....	....	....	....	....	....	....	....	....	....	....	....	748	....	Balance on Goods and Services	78af *d*
....	....	....	....	....	....	....	....	....	....	....	....	....	827	....	Income: Credit	78ag *d*
....	....	....	....	....	....	....	....	....	....	....	....	....	–899	....	Income: Debit	78ah *d*
....	....	....	....	....	....	....	....	....	....	....	....	....	676	....	Balance on Goods, Serv., & Inc.	78ai *d*
....	....	....	....	....	....	....	....	....	....	....	....	....	182	....	Current Transfers, n.i.e.: Credit	78aj *d*
....	....	....	....	....	....	....	....	....	....	....	....	....	–658	....	Current Transfers: Debit	78ak *d*
....	....	....	....	....	....	....	....	....	....	....	....	....	201	....	Current Account, n.i.e.	78al *d*
....	....	....	....	....	....	....	....	....	....	....	....	....	—	....	Capital Account, n.i.e.: Credit	78ba *d*
....	....	....	....	....	....	....	....	....	....	....	....	....	—	....	Capital Account: Debit	78bb *d*
....	....	....	....	....	....	....	....	....	....	....	....	....	—	....	Capital Account, n.i.e.	78bc *d*
....	....	....	....	....	....	....	....	....	....	....	....	....	–51	....	Direct Investment Abroad	78bd *d*
....	....	....	....	....	....	....	....	....	....	....	....	....	569	....	Dir. Invest. in Rep. Econ., n.i.e.	78be *d*
....	....	....	....	....	....	....	....	....	....	....	....	....	–263	....	Portfolio Investment Assets	78bf *d*
....	....	....	....	....	....	....	....	....	....	....	....	....	1,900	....	Portfolio Investment Liab., n.i.e.	78bg *d*
....	....	....	....	....	....	....	....	....	....	....	....	....	–17	....	Other Investment Assets	78bh *d*
....	....	....	....	....	....	....	....	....	....	....	....	....	748	....	Other Investment Liab., n.i.e.	78bi *d*
....	....	....	....	....	....	....	....	....	....	....	....	....	2,884	....	Financial Account, n.i.e.	78bj *d*
....	....	....	....	....	....	....	....	....	....	....	....	....	–89	....	Net Errors and Omissions	78ca *d*
....	....	....	....	....	....	....	....	....	....	....	....	....	2,996	....	Overall Balance	78cb *d*
....	....	....	....	....	....	....	....	....	....	....	....	....	–2,996	....	Reserves and Related Items	79da *d*
....	....	....	....	....	....	....	....	....	....	....	....	....	–3,039	....	Reserve Assets	79db *d*
....	....	....	....	....	....	....	....	....	....	....	....	....	43	....	Use of Fund Credit and Loans	79dc *d*
....	....	....	....	....	....	....	....	....	....	....	....	....	—	....	Liabs.Constit.For.Auth.Reserves	79dd *d*
....	....	....	....	....	....	....	....	....	....	....	....	....	—	....	Exceptional Financing	79de *d*
Year Ending December 31															**Government Finance**	
....	....	....	....	....	....	....	....	....	....	....	....	....	1.1	10.4	Deficit (–) or Surplus	80
....	....	....	....	....	....	....	....	....	....	....	....	....	349.0	381.3	Revenue	81
....	....	....	....	....	....	....	....	....	....	....	....	....	351.9	373.1	Expenditure	82
....	....	....	....	....	....	....	....	....	....	....	....	....	–4.0	–2.2	Lending Minus Repayments	83
															Financing	
....	....	....	....	....	....	....	....	....	....	....	....	....	–1.1	–10.4	Domestic	84a
....	....	....	....	....	....	....	....	....	....	....	....	....	—	—	Foreign	85a
....	....	....	....	....	....	....	....	....	....	....	....	....	86.5	90.2	Debt: Domestic	88a
....	....	....	....	....	....	....	....	....	....	....	....	....	72.4	71.5	Foreign	89a
Billions of Koruny															**National Accounts**	
....	....	....	....	....	....	....	....	....	....	....	....	....	513.0	542.2	Exports of Goods & Services	90c
....	....	....	....	....	....	....	....	....	....	....	....	....	213.8	231.1	Government Consumption	91f
....	....	....	....	....	....	....	....	....	....	....	....	....	241.9	277.3	Gross Fixed Capital Formation	93e
....	....	....	....	....	....	....	....	....	....	....	....	....	–74.4	–66.0	Increase/Decrease(–) in Stocks	93i
....	....	....	....	....	....	....	....	....	....	....	....	....	512.6	597.8	Private Consumption	96f
....	....	....	....	....	....	....	....	....	....	....	....	....	–496.3	–544.9	Imports of Goods & Services	98c
....	....	....	....	....	....	....	....	....	....	....	....	....	910.6	1,037.5	Gross Domestic Product	99b
....	....	....	....	....	....	....	....	....	....	....	....	....	453.5	463.1	Gross Dom. Prod. 1990 Prices	99b.*p*
....	....	....	....	....	....	....	....	....	....	....	....	....	200.8	224.0	GDP Deflator (1990=100)	99bi *p*
Midyear Estimates																
....	....	....	....	....	....	....	....	....	....	....	....	....	10.33	10.33	**Population**	99z

Denmark
128

		1965	1966	1967	1968	1969	1970	1971	1972	1973	1974	1975	1976	1977	1978	1979
Exchange Rates															*Kroner*	*per SDR:*
Market Rate	aa	6.891	6.916	7.462	7.501	7.492	7.489	7.667	7.434	I7.588	6.918	7.232	6.724	7.018	6.631	7.067
														Kroner per US Dollar:		
Market Rate	ae	6.891	6.916	7.462	7.501	7.492	7.489	7.062	6.847	I6.290	5.650	6.178	5.788	5.778	5.090	5.365
Market Rate	rf	6.907	6.907	6.957	7.500	7.500	7.500	7.426	6.949	6.050	6.095	5.746	6.045	6.003	5.515	5.261
														Kroner	*per*	*ECU:*
ECU Rate	ea	....	....	....	....	....	....	....	....	....	....	....	....	....	....	7.7010
ECU Rate	eb	....	....	....	....	....	....	....	....	....	....	....	6.7627	6.8529	7.0188	7.2105
													Index Numbers	*(1990=100):*		
Market Rate	ahx	89.3	89.4	88.4	82.5	82.1	82.3	141.9	88.8	102.4	101.4	107.7	102.2	102.9	112.1	117.4
Nominal Effective Exchange Rate	neu	113.7	113.7	113.4	107.9	107.9	106.2	105.0	104.4	108.3	108.2	110.6	112.6	111.4	111.1	111.1
Real Effective Exchange Rate	reu	....	....	....	....	....	....	....	....	....	....	95.5	96.7	95.0	94.5	93.8
Fund Position															*Millions*	*of SDRs:*
Quota	2f.s	130.0	163.0	163.0	163.0	163.0	260.0	260.0	260.0	260.0	260.0	260.0	260.0	260.0	310.0	310.0
SDRs	1b.s	—	—	—	—	—	17.4	44.8	72.2	119.3	91.5	81.9	81.9	97.1	97.9	137.6
Reserve Position in the Fund	1c.s	58.4	66.8	61.9	85.3	1.0	26.4	52.3	65.0	119.1	72.9	61.1	67.0	72.8	68.7	76.8
International Liquidity											*Millions of US Dollars Unless Otherwise Indicated:*					
Total Reserves minus Gold	1l.d	490	489	427	335	357	419	653	786	1,247	858	803	841	1,589	3,129	3,236
SDRs	1b.d	—	—	—	—	—	17	49	78	144	112	96	95	118	128	181
Reserve Position in the Fund	1c.d	58	67	62	85	1	26	57	71	144	89	72	78	88	89	101
Foreign Exchange	1d.d	431	422	365	250	356	375	548	637	960	656	635	669	1,383	2,912	2,953
Gold (Million Fine Troy Ounces)	1ad	3	3	3	3	3	2	2	2	2	2	2	2	2	2	2
Gold (National Valuation)	1and	97	108	107	114	89	65	68[e]	69[e]	77	85	78	87	100	117	92
Monetary Authorities: Other Liab.	4..d	20	19	24	24	21	23	42	43	43	41	29	142	66	67	75
Deposit Money Banks: Assets	7a.d	181	248	289	435	348	364	398	449	723	1,289	1,068	1,764	2,734	3,832	4,812
Liabilities	7b.d	219	265	288	354	343	364	459	409	766	920	992	1,468	2,238	3,763	4,465
Monetary Authorities															*Billions*	*of Kroner:*
Foreign Assets	11	4.07	4.14	4.02	3.37	3.36	3.63	5.08	5.87	8.32	5.33	5.44	5.37	9.76	16.53	16.82
Claims on Central Government	12a	1.96	1.87	1.79	1.66	2.28	2.26	.50	.54	.58	1.07	4.03	8.49	11.33	12.09	24.00
Claims on Private Sector	12d	2.65	3.48	3.71	6.21	6.90	7.33	7.99	8.74	9.31	10.87	11.93	18.25	14.49	12.61	12.08
Claims on Deposit Money Banks	12e	.90	1.62	1.32	1.11	1.80	2.35	2.11	3.08	3.95	5.12	1.01	1.61	4.14	4.50	4.51
Claims on Other Financial Insts.	12f	....	....	....	....	....	....	....	....	....	....	....	....	....	....	....
Reserve Money	14	5.65	5.90	6.22	7.89	8.25	7.56	7.85	8.25	8.44	8.88	12.33	12.85	11.22	12.08	13.71
of which: Currency Outside DMBs	14a	4.14	4.53	4.72	4.85	5.23	4.87	4.92	5.56	5.99	6.04	7.63	8.44	9.91	10.75	11.57
Foreign Liabilities	16c	.14	.13	.18	.18	.16	.17	.29	.30	.27	.23	.19	.82	.38	.34	.40
Central Government Deposits	16d	3.26	4.21	3.39	3.06	5.05	6.46	5.42	6.87	10.74	10.03	7.20	16.46	24.41	29.91	37.98
Other Items (Net)	17r	.54	.87	1.04	1.22	.86	1.38	2.13	2.80	2.70	3.24	2.69	3.60	3.70	3.41	5.31
Deposit Money Banks															*Billions*	*of Kroner:*
Reserves	20	1.23	1.16	1.28	1.82	1.79	2.15	2.18	2.03	1.73	2.15	3.61	3.17	.82	.80	1.52
Foreign Assets	21	1.25	1.72	2.17	3.26	2.61	2.65	2.78	3.14	4.54	7.20	7.38	10.66	15.85	20.16	26.27
Claims on Central Government	22a	.81	.65	.60	1.70	1.66	1.64	1.77	1.72	3.47	4.25	4.82	8.55	9.50	10.65	15.74
Claims on Private Sector	22d	20.44	24.09	26.20	27.96	32.49	34.82	37.91	43.87	50.11	53.62	64.49	71.75	79.14	84.07	87.14
Claims on Other Banking Insts.	22f	....	....	....	....	....	....	....	....	....	....	....	....	....	....	....
Demand Deposits	24	10.17	11.75	13.08	15.84	17.71	17.26	19.10	21.92	24.13	26.09	31.46	32.66	34.58	40.64	44.23
Time and Savings Deposits	25	8.92	10.10	11.15	12.62	13.68	15.10	16.92	19.70	23.27	26.45	36.08	43.36	47.46	45.30	49.57
Foreign Liabilities	26c	1.51	1.83	2.16	2.66	2.57	2.76	3.21	2.86	4.81	5.14	6.50	8.67	12.99	19.06	23.81
Credit from Monetary Authorities	26g	.90	1.61	1.32	1.11	1.80	2.35	2.55	3.55	4.52	5.32	1.41	1.53	3.87	4.21	4.39
Capital Accounts	27a	2.77	3.11	3.47	3.96	4.21	4.57	4.94	5.47	6.58	7.09	7.66	10.67	11.47	12.91	14.48
Other Items (Net)	27r	-.54	-.77	-.92	-1.46	-1.42	-.78	-2.08	-2.73	-3.46	-2.87	-2.80	-2.77	-5.06	-6.45	-5.82
Other Monetary Institutions															*Billions*	*of Kroner:*
Reserves	20..h	.19	.24	.27	.36	.43	.39	.39	.31	.41	.53	1.04	1.25	.54	.56	.71
Claims on Central Govt. (Net)	22anh	.74	.80	.87	1.37	1.48	1.31	.90	1.20	1.12	.13	-.06	.28	1.60	4.06	7.44
Claims on Private Sector	22d.h	11.24	12.59	13.67	14.84	16.74	18.09	19.83	22.92	26.68	29.01	34.64	38.41	41.97	45.66	47.97
Demand Deposits	24..h	3.77	4.33	4.85	5.77	6.72	7.04	7.54	9.27	10.39	10.83	14.25	14.89	16.15	18.88	21.34
Time and Savings Deposits	25..h	7.78	8.58	9.35	10.24	11.08	11.82	12.68	13.79	15.42	16.88	19.04	21.60	24.66	26.08	28.93
Other Items (Net)	27r.h	.63	.72	.62	.56	.85	.95	.89	1.37	2.40	1.98	2.33	3.44	3.31	5.31	5.85
Monetary Survey															*Billions*	*of Kroner:*
Foreign Assets (Net)	31n	3.68	3.89	3.85	3.79	3.23	3.34	4.37	5.80	7.73	7.11	6.14	6.57	13.14	17.45	19.48
Domestic Credit	32	34.58	39.27	43.45	50.67	56.50	58.99	63.47	72.12	80.52	88.91	112.65	129.27	133.62	139.23	156.40
Claims on Central Govt. (Net)	32an	.26	-.89	-.14	1.66	.37	-1.25	-2.25	-3.40	-5.58	-4.59	1.59	.86	-1.98	-3.11	9.21
Claims on Local Government	32b	....	....	....	....	....	....	....	....	....	....	....	....	....	....	....
Claims on Private Sector	32d	34.33	40.16	43.58	49.01	56.13	60.24	65.72	75.52	86.09	93.49	111.06	128.41	135.60	142.34	147.19
Claims on Other Banking Insts.	32f	....	....	....	....	....	....	....	....	....	....	....	....	....	....	....
Money	34	16.97	19.34	21.12	24.06	27.13	27.47	29.61	33.64	37.59	39.36	49.86	52.34	56.08	65.06	71.88
Quasi-Money	35	16.70	18.68	20.49	22.87	24.76	26.92	29.60	33.48	38.68	43.34	55.12	64.96	72.11	71.38	78.50
Other Items (Net)	37r	4.60	5.16	5.68	7.54	7.84	7.96	8.63	10.79	11.98	13.34	13.81	18.53	18.58	20.24	25.49
Money plus Quasi-Money	35l	33.67	38.02	41.61	46.92	51.88	54.39	59.21	67.12	76.27	82.70	104.99	117.30	128.19	136.44	150.38
Money (National Definitions)															*Billions*	*of Kroner:*
Broad Money	38n	....	....	....	....	....	....	....	....	....	....	....	....	....	....	....
Interest Rates															*Percent*	*Per Annum*
Discount Rate (End of Period)	60	6.50	6.50	7.50	6.00	9.00	9.00	7.50	7.00	9.00	10.00	7.50	10.00	9.00	8.00	11.00
Money Market Rate	60b	....	....	....	....	....	....	....	6.26	8.10	13.34	6.47	10.28	14.48	15.42	12.63
Deposit Rate	60l	....	....	....	....	....	....	....	....	....	....	....	....	....	....	10.8
Lending Rate	60p	....	....	....	....	....	....	....	....	....	....	....	....	....	13.9	15.3
Government Bond Yield	61	7.35	7.86	8.17	8.43	9.34	10.57	10.67	10.37	11.08	14.55	13.10	13.21	13.38[e]	14.54	15.82
Mortgage Bond Yield	61a	8.62	8.74	9.06	8.69	9.66	10.92	10.96	10.57	11.83	15.12	12.96	15.03	15.74	16.51	16.91

Denmark

	1980	1981	1982	1983	1984	1985	1986	1987	1988	1989	1990	1991	1992	1993	1994		
End of Period																**Exchange Rates**	
	7.672	8.526	9.248	10.339	11.037	9.852	8.981	8.649	9.250	8.683	8.217	8.459	8.601	9.302	8.880	Market Rate	aa
End of Period (ae) Period Average (rf)																	
	6.015	7.325	8.384	9.875	11.260	8.969	7.343	6.097	6.874	6.608	5.776	5.914	6.256	6.773	6.083	Market Rate	ae
	5.636	7.123	8.332	9.145	10.357	10.596	8.091	6.840	6.732	7.310	6.189	6.396	6.036	6.484	6.361	Market Rate	rf
End of Period (ea) Period Average (eb)																	
	7.8494	7.9408	8.1149	8.1827	7.9881	7.9567	7.8619	7.9446	8.0298	7.8816	7.8826	7.9295	7.5748	7.5508	7.4823	ECU Rate	ea
	7.8283	7.9241	8.1544	8.1300	8.1457	8.0183	7.9360	7.8829	7.9517	8.0487	7.8561	7.9082	7.8119	7.5916	7.5415	ECU Rate	eb
Period Averages																	
	109.7	87.1	74.3	67.7	59.8	58.7	76.5	90.4	91.9	84.6	100.0	96.9	102.5	95.4	97.3	Market Rate	ahx
	101.0	95.5	92.0	92.7	90.4	91.7	95.7	98.4	96.8	94.6	100.0	98.7	101.1	105.3	105.4	Nominal Effective Exchange Rate	neu
	84.5	79.7	77.7	80.0	79.5	83.2	86.8	95.2	94.9	93.8	100.0	96.6	96.7	98.8	....	Real Effective Exchange Rate	reu
End of Period																**Fund Position**	
	465.0	465.0	465.0	711.0	711.0	711.0	711.0	711.0	711.0	711.0	711.0	711.0	1,069.9	1,069.9	1,069.9	Quota	2f.s
	137.6	172.6	176.4	118.7	158.1	178.7	207.2	214.5	167.0	213.1	151.6	169.0	66.7	62.4	124.6	SDRs	1b.s
	110.9	105.3	99.8	205.0	214.4	207.5	127.2	123.2	254.9	234.7	219.8	248.6	345.7	309.1	294.6	Reserve Position in the Fund	1c.s
End of Period																**International Liquidity**	
	3,387	2,548	2,266	3,621	3,009	5,429	4,964	10,066	10,765	6,397	10,591	7,404	11,044	10,301	9,056	Total Reserves minus Gold	1l.d
	175	201	195	124	155	196	253	304	225	280	216	242	92	86	182	SDRs	1b.d
	141	123	110	215	210	228	156	175	316	335	313	356	475	425	430	Reserve Position in the Fund	1c.d
	3,070	2,224	1,961	3,282	2,644	5,004	4,555	9,587	10,224	5,782	10,063	6,807	10,477	9,791	8,444	Foreign Exchange	1d.d
	2	2	2	2	2	2	2	2	2	2	2	2	2	2	2	Gold (Million Fine Troy Ounces)	1ad
	I542	784	568	573	545	631	650	767	713	711	780	638	580	478	703	Gold (National Valuation)	1and
	80	48	83	60	51	72	803	131	230	220	235	658	4,609	117	253	Monetary Authorities: Other Liab.	4..d
	4,833	5,265	5,865	6,654	7,975	14,158	16,033	24,155	28,781	34,661	45,546	I49,066	45,629	57,272	50,945	Deposit Money Banks: Assets	7a.d
	4,877	5,271	5,844	7,104	8,289	14,852	16,405	23,421	27,899	35,228	44,803	I47,379	36,845	27,128	30,141	Liabilities	7b.d
End of Period																**Monetary Authorities**	
	22.18	21.31	21.71	37.85	38.29	56.89	42.03	I67.07	74.07	49.77	67.64	46.44	72.32	70.88	63.18	Foreign Assets	11
	35.87	55.53	74.55	87.25	89.96	.64	.64	I6.40	5.93	8.06	10.35	16.48	6.79	10.04	20.05	Claims on Central Government	12a
	13.15	13.79	14.44	14.61	14.98	14.84	26.15	I.49	.77	1.27	1.43	.91	1.40	.24	2.86	Claims on Private Sector	12d
	1.75	1.27	6.18	5.42	9.71	22.63	42.42	I17.70	1.33	18.41	4.07	1.09	24.86	79.21	57.28	Claims on Deposit Money Banks	12e
	....	....	....	—	....	....	—	29.72	31.28	34.59	36.44	28.15	28.90	30.95	24.99	Claims on Other Financial Insts.	12f
	14.31	15.58	15.97	17.11	18.84	47.24	31.32	I36.60	38.17	36.62	44.79	43.55	38.18	62.70	63.15	Reserve Money	14
	12.36	13.57	14.18	15.42	16.37	17.57	18.82	I19.82	21.39	22.38	22.58	24.24	24.97	25.72	28.93	of which: Currency Outside DMBs	14a
	.48	.35	.70	.59	.57	.60	5.90	I.80	1.57	1.45	1.36	3.89	28.78	.79	1.54	Foreign Liabilities	16c
	47.17	59.41	81.47	105.39	102.92	18.33	49.92	I56.85	45.32	37.08	39.50	11.43	31.27	89.57	56.91	Central Government Deposits	16d
	10.99	16.57	18.74	22.03	30.60	28.83	24.11	I27.12	28.30	36.94	34.27	34.20	36.04	38.26	46.77	Other Items (Net)	17r
																Deposit Money Banks	
	1.14	1.74	1.59	1.27	2.09	25.80	11.23	I4.70	8.37	9.12	8.70	I19.38	16.31	35.33	32.69	Reserves	20
	31.33	41.53	53.17	72.90	104.60	144.27	137.42	I147.26	197.84	229.03	263.07	I290.15	285.43	387.88	309.90	Foreign Assets	21
	20.17	27.91	37.83	61.96	77.07	86.60	83.64	I92.90	104.77	96.39	82.18	I103.85	103.49	70.18	124.60	Claims on Central Government	22a
	94.04	99.41	111.53	132.85	162.01	190.41	251.92	I370.84	371.77	415.79	429.18	I371.95	361.76	317.67	297.74	Claims on Private Sector	22d
	....	....	....	....	....	....	....	....	....	....	....	49.92	46.51	136.53	108.44	Claims on Other Banking Insts.	22f
	47.78	55.15	56.74	72.88	80.10	99.81	106.45	I155.78	195.30	192.53	205.86	I233.09	229.77	255.44	248.31	Demand Deposits	24
	58.60	63.28	77.48	103.78	126.95	146.39	160.95	I238.86	225.83	230.79	242.24	I247.58	246.11	318.06	262.20	Time and Savings Deposits	25
	30.36	40.08	50.79	74.16	103.47	146.35	135.43	I142.79	191.78	232.77	258.78	I280.18	230.49	183.73	183.35	Foreign Liabilities	26c
	1.91	1.72	5.12	4.50	7.34	20.37	31.74	I17.73	3.32	19.79	4.72	I7.07	26.50	80.56	58.66	Credit from Monetary Authorities	26g
	16.39	19.18	21.62	25.57	35.44	40.86	53.00	I75.38	83.67	92.58	91.81	I78.01	86.11	72.13	79.54	Capital Accounts	27a
	−8.41	−8.81	−7.64	−11.90	−9.36	−6.69	−3.35	I−14.83	−17.14	−18.13	−20.30	I−10.67	−5.48	37.67	41.31	Other Items (Net)	27r
End of Period																**Other Monetary Institutions**	
	.78	.74	.66	.59	.80	3.93	2.45	.99	....	....	....	....	....	....	....	Reserves	20..h
	10.86	13.53	16.56	24.89	37.24	41.22	39.94	35.94	....	....	....	....	....	....	....	Claims on Central Govt. (Net)	22anh
	50.26	52.14	56.52	64.94	72.27	83.76	111.29	....	....	....	....	....	....	....	....	Claims on Private Sector	22d.h
	21.97	23.65	25.88	31.03	39.44	46.96	49.27	....	....	....	....	....	....	....	....	Demand Deposits	24..h
	31.88	34.90	37.68	47.22	54.76	63.78	72.28	....	....	....	....	....	....	....	....	Time and Savings Deposits	25..h
	8.03	7.86	10.19	12.17	16.11	18.18	32.09	....	....	....	....	....	....	....	....	Other Items (Net)	27r.h
End of Period																**Monetary Survey**	
	23.20	23.14	23.83	35.34	38.26	53.21	40.13	I70.74	78.56	44.58	70.57	I52.52	98.49	274.24	188.19	Foreign Assets (Net)	31n
	177.16	202.91	229.96	281.11	350.61	399.15	463.67	I443.50	469.19	519.00	520.07	I565.73	523.25	482.44	528.22	Domestic Credit	32
	19.72	37.57	47.47	68.71	101.34	110.14	74.31	I42.44	65.38	67.36	53.03	I108.90	79.00	−9.36	87.74	Claims on Central Govt. (Net)	32an
	....	....	....	....	....	....	....	....	....	....	....	5.90	5.67	6.40	6.44	Claims on Local Government	32b
	157.44	165.34	182.49	212.40	249.27	289.01	389.37	I371.34	372.54	417.06	430.61	I372.86	363.16	317.91	300.61	Claims on Private Sector	32d
	....	....	....	—	....	....	—	29.72	31.28	34.59	36.44	I78.07	75.41	167.48	133.43	Claims on Other Banking Insts.	32f
	77.51	88.03	91.67	113.30	128.08	156.49	167.97	I188.45	225.11	226.11	244.48	I258.27	256.00	283.00	279.05	Money	34
	90.48	98.18	115.16	151.00	181.71	210.18	233.23	I238.86	225.83	230.79	242.24	I247.58	246.11	318.06	262.20	Quasi-Money	35
	32.31	39.84	46.96	52.15	77.25	85.69	102.55	I86.93	96.81	106.68	103.92	I112.41	119.62	155.62	175.16	Other Items (Net)	37r
	167.99	186.21	206.83	264.31	309.79	366.67	401.19	I427.31	450.95	456.90	486.72	I505.85	502.11	601.06	541.22	Money plus Quasi-Money	35l
End of Period																**Money (National Definitions)**	
	....	156.58	172.27	217.41	259.45	306.49	333.74	343.57	358.25	368.16	391.73	379.42	373.90	416.42	394.59	Broad Money	38n
Percent Per Annum																**Interest Rates**	
	11.00	11.00	10.00	7.00	7.00	7.00	7.00	7.00	7.00	7.00	8.50	9.50	9.50	6.25	5.00	Discount Rate (End of Period)	60
	16.93	14.84	I16.92	12.81	11.77	10.33	9.22	10.20	8.52	9.66	10.97	9.78	11.35	10.73	6.21	Money Market Rate	60b
	10.8	13.0	12.9	10.0	9.0	8.2	6.6	7.1	7.8	8.3	7.9	7.2	7.5	6.5	....	Deposit Rate	60l
	17.2	17.7	18.6	14.5	13.4	14.7	13.0	13.6	12.6	13.4	14.1	11.4	11.6	10.5	....	Lending Rate	60p
	17.66	18.92	20.39	14.46	I13.96	11.31	9.91	11.06	9.78	9.75	10.74	9.59	9.47	7.08	7.41	Government Bond Yield	61
	19.03	I19.64	I21.35	15.34	14.63	12.19	10.50	12.54	11.28	10.16	10.97	10.09	10.14	8.17	8.34	Mortgage Bond Yield	61a

Denmark
128

		1965	1966	1967	1968	1969	1970	1971	1972	1973	1974	1975	1976	1977	1978	1979
Prices, Production, Employment																*Index Numbers (1990=100):*
Share Prices: Industrial	62a	⁑10	10	8	9	10	⁑9	8	11	18	13	15	19	20	19	18
Shipping	62b	⁑5	5	4	4	5	⁑5	4	5	9	8	9	11	12	13	11
Prices: Home & Import Goods	63	21.8	22.3	22.6	23.2	⁑24.0	25.9	26.7	28.3	32.4	39.5	⁑41.7	45.1	48.4	50.5	55.5
Home Goods	63a	21.9	22.7	23.1	23.6	⁑24.5	26.2	27.2	29.1	33.3	38.8	⁑41.9	45.2	48.6	51.5	54.8
Consumer Prices	64	16.0	17.1	18.5	20.0	20.7	22.0	23.3	24.9	27.2	31.3	⁑34.3	37.4	41.6	45.8	50.2
Wages: Hourly Earnings	65	9.1	10.2	11.1	12.4	13.8	15.3	17.5	19.5	22.4	26.8	31.7	35.3	38.8	42.8	47.7
Industrial Production	66..c	....	....	....	52.7	59.1	⁑60.7	62.0	66.3	68.8	⁑66.3	62.8	69.1	70.0	71.9	74.6
Agricultural Production	66bx	84.6	85.1	85.0	83.6	80.8	80.2	81.4	80.6	81.9	82.8	⁑82.5	82.7	84.7	88.2	92.7
Manufacturing Employment	67ey c	....	....	....	....	....	....	....	128.6	126.7	123.5	106.7	106.6	106.2	105.1	106.4
International Transactions																*Millions of Kroner*
Exports	70	16,023	16,946	17,661	19,799	22,640	25,171	27,303	30,789	37,549	46,920	50,030	55,035	60,436	65,314	77,321
Imports, cif	71	19,497	20,740	21,940	24,272	28,598	33,054	34,196	35,337	46,969	60,479	59,707	72,011	79,638	80,180	97,010
Imports, fob	71.v	18,428	19,603	20,737	22,941	27,030	30,974	32,329	33,451	44,539	57,768	57,235	72,120	76,438	77,857	92,578
																1990=100
Volume of Exports	72	⁑29	30	32	35	38	40	⁑42	45	48	⁑51	49	51	53	57	63
Volume of Imports	73	⁑43	45	47	49	58	63	⁑61	63	77	⁑72	67	80	78	82	86
Unit Value of Exports	74	⁑26	27	26	27	28	30	⁑30	32	36	⁑42	47	50	53	56	60
Unit Value of Imports	75	⁑24	24	24	25	26	27	⁑29	29	32	⁑44	46	49	54	54	61
Import Prices	76.x	22	22	22	23	⁑23	25	26	27	31	40	⁑42	44	48	49	57
Balance of Payments																*Millions of US Dollars:*
Goods: Exports f.o.b.	78aa d											8,652	9,053	10,011	11,807	....
Goods: Imports f.o.b.	78ab d											−9,956	−11,931	−12,725	−14,163	....
Trade Balance	78ac d											−1,304	−2,878	−2,715	−2,356	....
Services: Credit	78ad d											3,223	3,586	4,113	4,785	
Services: Debit	78ae d											−2,159	−2,480	−2,958	−3,596	
Balance on Goods and Services	78af d											−240	−1,771	−1,559	−1,167	
Income: Credit	78ag d											249	255	363	543	
Income: Debit	78ah d											−574	−616	−911	−1,429	
Balance on Goods, Serv., & Inc.	78ai d											−566	−2,132	−2,107	−2,053	
Current Transfers, n.i.e.: Credit	78aj d											448	641	944	1,196	
Current Transfers: Debit	78ak d											−373	−424	−559	−645	
Current Account, n.i.e.	78al d											−490	−1,914	−1,722	−1,502	
Capital Account, n.i.e.: Credit	78ba d															
Capital Account: Debit	78bb d															
Capital Account, n.i.e.	78bc d											—	—	—	—	
Direct Investment Abroad	78bd d											−79	−64	−161	−33	
Dir. Invest. in Rep. Econ., n.i.e.	78be d											267	−190	76	89	
Portfolio Investment Assets	78bf d											—	—	−18	−63	
Portfolio Investment Liab., n.i.e.	78bg d											—	—	283	541	
Other Investment Assets	78bh d											−172	−563	−1,420	−1,016	
Other Investment Liab., n.i.e.	78bi d											535	2,636	3,741	3,380	
Financial Account, n.i.e.	78bj d											552	1,819	2,501	2,899	
Net Errors and Omissions	78ca c											−104	114	−62	99	
Overall Balance	78cb d											−42	19	717	1,496	
Reserves and Related Items	79da d											42	−19	−717	−1,496	
Reserve Assets	79db d											42	−19	−717	−1,496	
Use of Fund Credit and Loans	79dc d											—	—	—	—	
Liabs.Constit.For.Auth.Reserves	79dd d											—	—	—	—	
Exceptional Financing	79de d											—	—	—	—	
Government Finance																*Millions of Kroner:*
Deficit (-) or Surplus	80	1,092	1,452	309	553	247	⁑2,950	3,569	4,089	6,140	1,335	−4,350	⁑−519	−2,730	−1,066	−2,584
Revenue	81	16,115	18,937	21,170	25,163	27,605	⁑41,605	47,319	53,380	58,268	66,918	69,810	⁑80,981	90,422	105,617	120,393
Grants Received	81z	....	....	....	....	....	⁑336	400	376	524	557	1,593	⁑3,189	1,491	1,804	2,307
Expenditure	82	14,762	17,246	20,552	24,142	26,851	⁑38,295	43,557	48,968	51,826	65,085	74,767	⁑83,604	93,654	107,137	124,520
Lending Minus Repayments	83	261	239	309	468	507	⁑696	593	699	826	1,055	986	⁑1,085	989	1,350	764
Net Borrowing: Kroner	84b	−897	−1,339	−422	−614	−905										
Foreign Currency	85b	−118	−74	102	83	688										
Finance from Foreign Aid	86a	—	—	—	—	—										
Use of Cash Balances	87	−77	−39	11	−21	−30										
Debt: Kroner	88b	7,011	6,832	6,477	6,099	5,944										
Debt: Foreign	89a						⁑3,699	5,292	6,106	6,517	7,243	10,429	⁑16,456	24,410	29,139	35,744
Foreign Currency	89b	1,877	1,989	1,920	2,140	2,413										
National Accounts																*Billions of Kroner*
Exports of Goods & Services	90c	21.4	22.2	23.5	26.3	29.4	33.1	36.2	40.8	49.3	61.5	65.0	72.5	80.5	86.5	101.4
Government Consumption	91f	10.5	13.2	15.1	17.6	20.3	23.7	27.9	32.1	36.8	45.3	53.2	60.5	66.8	76.2	86.8
Gross Fixed Capital Formation	93e	15.1	18.6	20.5	22.1	26.4	29.3	31.8	37.0	42.8	46.5	45.6	57.7	61.7	67.5	72.5
Increase/Decrease(-) in Stocks	93i	1.5	.5	−.4	.2	1.3	1.1	.8	.3	2.3	2.4	−.4	−2.6	2.2	−.5	1.6
Private Consumption	96f	43.7	46.0	50.8	55.5	61.7	68.1	73.2	80.4	94.2	105.2	119.9	142.1	158.9	174.9	195.8
Imports of Goods & Services	98c	−22.4	−23.1	−24.8	−27.3	−31.8	−36.7	−38.6	−39.9	−52.6	−67.2	−67.1	−84.1	−90.7	−93.2	−111.2
Gross Domestic Product	99b	69.7	77.2	84.8	94.4	107.3	118.6	131.1	150.7	172.9	193.6	216.3	251.2	279.3	311.4	346.9
Net Factor Inc/Pmts(-) Abroad	98.n	.1	—	−.1	−.1	−.1	−.2	−.4	−.7	−.8	−1.3	−1.7	−2.0	−3.1	−4.6	−6.6
Gross Nat'l Expenditure = GNP	99a	69.6	77.2	84.7	94.3	107.2	118.4	130.7	150.0	172.0	192.4	214.6	249.3	276.2	306.8	340.3
Nat'l Income, Market Prices	99e	64.0	71.7	78.8	87.7	99.9	110.3	121.6	139.5	159.9	177.0	196.7	229.0	253.2	280.7	310.9
Gross Dom. Prod. 1990 Prices	99b.p	436.6	⁑446.3	462.6	480.3	511.6	523.2	536.0	565.3	⁑586.9	581.4	577.6	615.0	625.0	634.2	656.7
GDP Deflator (1990=100)	99bi p	16.0	17.3	18.3	19.6	21.0	22.7	24.5	26.7	29.5	33.3	37.4	40.8	44.7	49.1	52.8
																Millions:
Population	99z	4.76	4.80	4.84	4.86	4.89	4.93	4.96	4.99	5.02	5.05	5.06	5.07	5.09	5.10	5.12

International Liquidity: *Gold (National Valuation) (line 1and):* ⁑ From 1980, official gold is revalued on the basis of the London market prices.

Monetary Authorities: ⁑ From 1987 through 1990, the accounts of the monetary authorities include the postal giro system. From 1991, comprises Danmarks Nationalbank.

Deposit Money Banks: ⁑ Beginning in 1987, the accounts of commercial banks and other monetary institutions were consolidated. ⁑ The accounts of the deposit money banks were completely restructured from 1991. The accounts of the postal giro system are included in the deposit money banks sector from 1991.

Interest Rates: *Mortgage Bond Yield:* ⁑ Before January 1981, data relate to the 5 percent bonds with a remaining period to maturity of about 40 years.

Government Finance: ⁑ Beginning in 1970, annual data are as reported in the *Government Finance Statistics Yearbook* and cover consolidated central government. Data are derived from Statsregnskabet (central government accounts), accounts of government agencies, parish funds accounts, and social security funds accounts. Data through 1975 relate to a fiscal year different from calendar year.

Denmark

1980	1981	1982	1983	1984	1985	1986	1987	1988	1989	1990	1991	1992	1993	1994		Prices, Production, Employment	
Period Averages																	
17	28	35	61	66	69	69	58	65	91	100	108	99	101	121		Share Prices: Industrial	62a
12	20	21	28	28	30	26	26	35	85	100	100	92	105	115		Shipping	62b
65.1	75.3	83.3	87.5	ⲓ94.0	96.8	90.2	90.0	93.7	99.0	100.0	101.0	99.8	ⲓ99.3	100.2		Prices: Home & Import Goods	63
62.8	71.1	78.7	83.1	ⲓ89.4	92.1	89.0	90.1	93.6	98.7	100.0	101.3	100.6	ⲓ100.1	....		Home Goods	63a
56.4	ⲓ63.0	69.3	74.1	78.8	82.5	85.5	88.9	93.0	97.4	100.0	102.4	104.5	105.9	108.0		Consumer Prices	64
53.2	57.9	64.1	68.3	71.6	75.1	79.4	87.0	92.6	96.2	100.0	103.9	106.9	....	....		Wages: Hourly Earnings	65
75.0	75.0	76.6	79.3	87.9	ⲓ91.7	98.6	95.7	97.6	100.0	100.0	101.8	103.7	101.3	....		Industrial Production	66..c
ⲓ94.7	94.8	95.5	99.8	98.6	ⲓ99.2	102.2	99.2	98.8	98.2	100.0	100.0	102.2	107.2	113.1		Agricultural Production	66bx
103.1	96.1	95.6	97.1	104.0	108.1	111.2	ⲓ105.3	ⲓ102.1	100.9	100.0	100.0	96.8	94.7	88.5		Manufacturing Employment	67ey c
Millions of Kroner																**International Transactions**	
94,359	114,263	128,194	146,761	165,335	179,578	171,720	175,187	185,819	205,300	216,444	229,764	247,254	241,034	262,365		Exports	70
109,086	124,611	138,813	148,897	171,826	191,563	184,733	174,033	174,429	195,328	195,781	206,798	212,087	191,325	148,394		Imports, cif	71
104,105	119,226	132,772	142,367	164,271	183,138	176,613	166,192	166,758	186,536	190,040	197,705	194,076	182,911	141,868		Imports, fob	71.v
1990=100																	
68	69	71	74	79	ⲓ84	84	87	91	98	100	108	113	113	....		Volume of Exports	72
79	75	77	81	86	ⲓ93	92	98	96	99	100	105	109	104	....		Volume of Imports	73
69	78	87	90	97	ⲓ101	98	96	96	102	100	100	100	99	96		Unit Value of Exports	74
75	87	96	99	108	ⲓ110	100	95	97	103	100	100	101	97	93		Unit Value of Imports	75
69	83	91	95	ⲓ102	105	92	90	93	99	100	100	100	98	ⲓ97		Import Prices	76.x
Minus Sign Indicates Debit																**Balance of Payments**	
16,790	16,136	15,685	16,226	16,090	17,123	21,307	25,695	27,537	28,728	36,072	36,783	40,650	37,070	....		Goods: Exports f.o.b.	78aa d
−18,798	−17,063	−16,479	−15,974	−16,285	−17,887	−22,357	−24,900	−25,654	−26,304	−31,197	−32,035	−33,446	−29,258	....		Goods: Imports f.o.b.	78ab d
−2,008	−927	−794	252	−195	−764	−1,050	795	1,883	2,425	4,875	4,748	7,204	7,812	....		Trade Balance	78ac d
6,114	5,853	5,410	5,131	5,049	5,487	6,372	7,848	9,623	9,570	12,830	14,264	14,495	12,744	....		Services: Credit	78ad d
−4,700	−4,663	−4,538	−4,501	−4,301	−4,794	−6,066	−7,302	−8,427	−8,638	−10,218	−10,420	−10,896	−10,558	....		Services: Debit	78ae d
−594	262	78	882	553	−71	−743	1,342	3,078	3,356	7,487	8,592	10,803	9,998	....		Balance on Goods and Services	78af d
1,252	1,187	1,146	909	1,227	1,409	1,995	2,627	3,677	4,718	6,011	8,855	15,569	22,666	....		Income: Credit	78ag d
−3,133	−3,164	−3,298	−2,984	−3,567	−3,970	−5,464	−6,750	−7,876	−9,049	−11,719	−14,599	−21,223	−27,446	....		Income: Debit	78ah d
−2,475	−1,715	−2,074	−1,194	−1,787	−2,632	−4,212	−2,781	−1,121	−975	1,779	2,848	5,148	5,219	....		Balance on Goods, Serv, & Inc.	78ai d
535	753	654	729	935	825	1,341	1,546	1,799	1,608	2,007	2,083	2,136	2,497	....		Current Transfers, n.i.e.: Credit	78aj d
−513	−914	−839	−917	−866	−960	−1,619	−1,766	−2,018	−1,750	−2,415	−2,948	−3,016	−3,005	....		Current Transfers: Debit	78ak d
−2,453	−1,875	−2,259	−1,382	−1,718	−2,767	−4,490	−3,002	−1,340	−1,118	1,372	1,983	4,268	4,711	....		Current Account, n.i.e.	78al d
—	—	—	—	—	—	—	—	—	—	—	—	—	—	....		Capital Account, n.i.e.: Credit	78ba d
—	—	—	—	—	—	—	—	—	—	—	—	—	—	....		Capital Account: Debit	78bb d
—	—	—	—	—	—	—	—	—	—	—	—	—	—	....		Capital Account, n.i.e.	78bc d
−197	−139	−82	−150	−289	−306	−654	−619	−720	−2,066	−1,482	−1,852	−2,236	−1,373	....		Direct Investment Abroad	78bd d
106	99	134	60	−15	111	163	85	503	1,090	1,132	1,553	1,017	1,713	....		Dir. Invest. in Rep. Econ., n.i.e.	78be d
−12	−18	−95	−61	−142	−346	−2,223	797	−585	−1,527	−1,168	−4,378	1,420	2	....		Portfolio Investment Assets	78bf d
−69	81	−46	363	823	1,579	144	2,886	1,815	−1,222	4,068	6,232	8,707	12,659	....		Portfolio Investment Liab., n.i.e.	78bg d
−403	−1,213	−1,102	−1,727	−2,270	−3,816	1,359	−4,174	−7,443	−4,242	−5,442	−3,012	395	−14,812	....		Other Investment Assets	78bh d
3,544	2,625	3,642	4,385	3,640	7,371	4,007	8,384	9,704	5,610	7,302	−1,645	−13,442	−268	....		Other Investment Liab., n.i.e.	78bi d
2,970	1,436	2,451	2,870	1,747	4,593	2,796	7,360	3,275	−2,357	4,409	−3,103	−4,138	−2,079	....		Financial Account, n.i.e.	78bj d
−462	−273	−489	−114	−396	−304	−285	85	−619	−347	−2,407	−2,183	−357	1,220	....		Net Errors and Omissions	78ca d
93	−713	−297	1,375	−367	1,522	−1,979	4,443	1,316	−3,821	3,374	−3,303	−226	3,851	....		Overall Balance	78cb d
−93	713	297	−1,375	367	−1,522	1,979	−4,443	−1,316	3,821	−3,374	3,303	226	−3,851	....		Reserves and Related Items	79da d
−182	735	257	−1,357	371	−1,532	1,329	−3,732	−1,436	3,838	−3,385	2,903	−4,075	567	....		Reserve Assets	79db d
														....		Use of Fund Credit and Loans	79dc d
89	−22	40	−18	−4	10	650	−712	120	−16	11	399	4,301	−4,419	....		Liabs.Constit.For.Auth.Reserves	79dd d
														....		Exceptional Financing	79de d
Year Ending December 31																**Government Finance**	
−10,002	−24,690	−37,522	−35,154	−22,241	−3,726	30,082	27,410	16,077	8,164	−5,550	−8,647	−13,283ᴾ	−20,591ᴾ	....		Deficit (−) or Surplus	80
136,398	145,706	163,129	188,365	218,810	246,846	281,324	291,516	303,078	312,992	314,135	328,397	343,577ᴾ	361,092ᴾ	....		Revenue	81
2,499	2,633	3,349	4,220	4,883	4,664	4,328	4,133	4,380	3,824	4,276	4,536	3,471ᴾ	5,728ᴾ	....		Grants Received	81z
147,376	171,020	202,363	225,514	243,895	253,940	255,127	266,843	289,116	307,738	321,978	337,897	356,631ᴾ	387,411ᴾ	....		Expenditure	82
1,523	2,009	1,637	2,225	2,039	1,296	443	1,396	2,265	914	1,983	3,683	3,700ᴾ	—ᴾ	....		Lending Minus Repayments	83
....	....	....	....	....	....	....	....	....	....	....	....	....	....	....		Net Borrowing: Kroner	84b
....	....	....	....	....	....	....	....	....	....	....	....	....	....	....		Foreign Currency	85b
....	....	....	....	....	....	....	....	....	....	....	....	....	....	....		Finance from Foreign Aid	86a
....	....	....	....	....	....	....	....	....	....	....	....	....	....	....		Use of Cash Balances	87
45,346	57,521	79,142	102,514	98,534	92,930	119,913	127,637	124,333	116,031	119,101	92,339	104,633ᴾ	....	....		Debt: Kroner	88b
....	....	....	....	....	....	....	....	....	....	....	....	....	....	....		Debt: Foreign	89a
....	....	....	....	....	....	....	....	....	....	....	....	....	....	....		Foreign Currency	89b
Billions of Kroner																**National Accounts**	
122.3	149.0	168.9	186.3	207.5	225.6	213.6	220.1	238.9	264.9	283.6	306.0	310.7	299.9	324.5		Exports of Goods & Services	90c
99.7	113.2	131.1	140.5	146.2	155.5	159.4	176.2	188.5	196.5	202.5	211.2	219.1	229.8	234.8		Government Consumption	91f
70.3	63.8	74.6	82.0	97.3	115.2	138.4	138.0	132.2	139.0	139.4	136.7	130.5	131.7	138.6		Gross Fixed Capital Formation	93e
−1.1	−.8	1.1	−.2	6.9	5.1	5.0	−5.1	−1.5	1.9	−.9	−.7	−.9	−7.3	−2.5		Increase/Decrease(−) in Stocks	93i
208.8	228.6	255.6	280.0	307.9	337.2	366.7	377.9	388.8	403.9	415.0	430.2	443.0	457.9	498.6		Private Consumption	96f
−126.2	−146.1	−166.9	−176.1	−200.4	−223.5	−216.6	−207.2	−214.9	−238.9	−240.4	−255.6	−251.0	−238.7	−264.7		Imports of Goods & Services	98c
373.8	407.8	464.5	512.5	565.3	615.1	666.5	699.9	732.1	767.2	799.1	827.9	851.3	873.2	929.3		Gross Domestic Product	99b
−9.3	−12.7	−17.8	−18.4	−23.9	−26.2	−27.5	−27.6	−27.7	−30.9	−34.3	−34.1	−31.9	−28.7	−31.4		Net Factor Inc/Pmts(−) Abroad	98.n
364.5	395.1	446.7	494.1	541.4	588.9	639.0	672.3	704.3	736.3	764.8	793.8	819.4	844.6	897.9		Gross Nat'l Expenditure = GNP	99a
330.8	357.1	404.1	447.2	491.2	534.1	581.4	610.7	639.5	667.3	692.7	717.4	739.8	760.8	812.1		Nat'l Income, Market Prices	99e
653.8	648.0	667.5	684.3	714.4	745.0	772.2	774.4	783.4	787.9	799.1	809.8	816.5	828.7	865.3		Gross Dom. Prod. 1990 Prices	99b.p
57.2	62.9	69.6	74.9	79.1	82.6	86.3	90.4	93.4	97.4	100.0	102.2	104.3	105.4	107.4		GDP Deflator (1990=100)	99bi p
Midyear Estimates																	
5.12	5.12	5.12	5.11	5.11	5.11	5.12	5.13	5.13	5.13	5.14	5.15	5.17	5.19	5.20		Population	99z

Djibouti

611

		1965	1966	1967	1968	1969	1970	1971	1972	1973	1974	1975	1976	1977	1978	1979
Exchange Rates															*Francs*	*per SDR*
Official Rate	aa	214.39	214.39	214.39	214.39	214.39	214.39	214.39	214.39	214.39	217.59	208.05	206.48	215.88	231.53	234.12
															Francs per US Dollar	
Official Rate	ae	214.39	214.39	214.39	214.39	214.39	214.39	197.47	197.47	177.72	177.72	177.72	177.72	177.72	177.72	177.72
Official Rate	rf	214.39	214.39	214.39	214.39	214.39	214.39	213.78	197.47	179.94	177.72	177.72	177.72	177.72	177.72	177.72
Fund Position															*Millions*	*of SDRs*
Quota	2f.s	....	....	....	....	....	....	....	....	....	....	....	....	....	3.80	3.80
SDRs	1b.s	....	....	....	....	....	....	....	....	....	....	....	....	....	—	.08
Reserve Position in the Fund	1c.s	....	....	....	....	....	....	....	....	....	....	....	....	....	—	.76
International Liquidity												*Millions of US Dollars Unless Otherwise Indicated*				
Total Reserves minus Gold	1l.d	....													....	.11
SDRs	1b.d	....													....	.11
Reserve Position in the Fund	1c.d	....													—	1.00
Foreign Exchange	1d.d	....														
Deposit Money Banks: Assets	7a.d	....														
Deposit Money Banks: Liabilities	7b.d	....														
of which: Liab. to Nonbanks	7bd.d	....														
Other Banking Insts.: Liabilities	7f.d	....														
Monetary Authorities															*Millions of Francs*	
Foreign Assets	11	....													....	....
Claims on Deposit Money Banks	12e	....														
Reserve Money	14	....														
of which: Currency Outside DMBs	14a	....														
Central Government Deposits	16d	....														
Capital Accounts	17a	....														
Other Items (Net)	17r	....														
Deposit Money Banks															*Millions of Francs*	
Reserves	20	....														
Foreign Assets	21	....														
Claims on Nonfin.Pub.Enterprises	22c	....														
Claims on Private Sector	22d	....														
Demand Deposits	24	....														
Time Deposits	25	....														
Foreign Liabilities	26c	....														
Central Government Deposits	26d	....														
Credit From Monetary Authorities	26g	....														
Capital Accounts	27a	....														
Other Items (Net)	27r	....														
Monetary Survey															*Millions of Francs*	
Foreign Assets (Net)	31n	....														
Domestic Credit	32	....														
Claims on Central Govt. (Net)	32an	....														
Claims on Nonfin.Pub.Enterprises	32c	....														
Claims on Private Sector	32d	....														
Money	34	....														
Quasi-Money	35	....														
Other Items (Net)	37r	....														
Money plus Quasi-Money	35l	....														
Other Banking Institutions															*Millions of Francs*	
Reserves	40	....														
Claims on Private Sector	42d	....														
Long-Term Foreign Liabilities	46cl	....														
Central Govt. Lending Funds	46f	....														
Capital Accounts	47a	....														
Other Items (Net)	47r	....														
International Transactions															*Millions of Francs*	
Exports	70	5,986	5,776	4,954	2,580	2,522	4,523	3,219	3,829	5,493	6,733	2,639	2,835	3,364	3,154	2,023
Imports, cif	71	13,117	12,629	12,290	10,753	10,475	10,593	11,335	12,935	12,935	14,496	24,933	21,284	18,949	29,117	33,454

Djibouti

1980	1981	1982	1983	1984	1985	1986	1987	1988	1989	1990	1991	1992	1993	1994		
End of Period (aa)															**Exchange Rates**	
226.67	206.86	196.05	186.07	174.20	195.21	217.39	252.13	239.16	233.55	252.84	254.22	244.37	244.11	259.45	Official Rate	aa
End of Period (ae) Period Average (rf)																
177.72	177.72	177.72	177.72	177.72	177.72	177.72	177.72	177.72	177.72	177.72	177.72	177.72	177.72	177.72	Official Rate	ae
177.72	177.72	177.72	177.72	177.72	177.72	177.72	177.72	177.72	177.72	177.72	177.72	177.72	177.72	177.72	Official Rate	rf
End of Period															**Fund Position**	
5.70	5.70	5.70	5.70	8.00	8.00	8.00	8.00	8.00	8.00	8.00	8.00	8.00	11.50	11.50	11.50 Quota	2f. s
.13	.50	.46	.43	.40	.37	.35	.33	.30	.27	.23	.19	.15	.15	.11	SDRs	1b. s
1.23	1.23	1.24	1.24	1.24	1.24	1.24	1.24	1.24	1.24	1.24	1.24	2.11	—	—	Reserve Position in the Fund	1c. s
End of Period															**International Liquidity**	
....	....	....	....	44.93	50.94	53.62	63.53	64.36	59.15	93.64	100.00	83.40	75.10	73.76	Total Reserves minus Gold	1l. d
.17	.58	.51	.45	.39	.41	.43	.47	.40	.35	.33	.27	.21	.21	.16	SDRs	1b. d
1.57	1.43	1.37	1.30	1.22	1.36	1.52	1.76	1.67	1.63	1.76	1.77	2.90	—	—	Reserve Position in the Fund	1c. d
....	....	....	....	43.33	49.17	51.67	61.30	62.29	57.17	91.55	97.95	80.29	74.89	73.60	Foreign Exchange	1d. d
....	....	....	....	170.13	195.86	186.92	198.14	198.39	238.27	209.40	225.35	200.09	219.26	211.53	Deposit Money Banks: Assets	7a. d
....	....	....	....	95.37	102.73	79.08	79.01	62.80	95.85	68.92	72.10	84.45	84.81	88.65	Deposit Money Banks: Liabilities	7b. d
....	....	....	....	67.58	36.21	32.46	30.69	30.70	38.01	31.10	25.53	31.17	36.84	31.62	of which: Liab. to Nonbanks	7bd d
....	....	....	....	—	—	.62	1.28	2.56	3.36	1.18	2.97	3.62	4.01	3.43	Other Banking Insts.: Liabilities	7f. d
End of Period															**Monetary Authorities**	
....	....	....	....	7,986	9,053	9,529	11,290	11,438	10,513	16,642	17,772	14,822	13,347	13,990	Foreign Assets	11
....	....	....	....	—	—	—	3,023	2,616	3,117	35	37	39	40	40	Claims on Deposit Money Banks	12e
....	....	....	....	7,471	7,237	7,994	9,366	9,301	8,960	9,875	9,899	12,187	11,250	11,869	Reserve Money	14
....	....	....	....	6,671	6,686	7,180	8,013	8,439	8,197	9,035	9,263	11,331	10,401	10,693	of which: Currency Outside DMBs	14a
....	....	....	....	225	1,357	992	4,366	3,690	3,545	2,637	2,490	114	582	797	Central Government Deposits	16d
....	....	....	....	357	470	593	792	861	935	1,037	1,244	1,436	1,425	1,390	Capital Accounts	17a
....	....	....	....	−70	−12	−52	−211	201	189	3,125	4,179	1,124	133	−23	Other Items (Net)	17r
End of Period															**Deposit Money Banks**	
....	....	....	....	800	551	790	1,432	929	748	894	647	868	925	1,148	Reserves	20
....	....	....	....	30,236	34,809	33,219	35,214	35,258	42,346	37,214	40,049	35,561	38,967	37,594	Foreign Assets	21
....	....	....	....	561	563	494	459	609	221	572	489	444	483	419	Claims on Nonfin.Pub.Enterprises	22c
....	....	....	....	29,114	32,965	35,701	35,684	36,529	38,062	36,165	35,105	34,712	32,057	33,382	Claims on Private Sector	22d
....	....	....	....	12,690	13,418	15,601	16,905	18,142	16,444	17,944	20,761	21,595	22,209	21,814	Demand Deposits	24
....	....	....	....	18,264	24,694	27,050	26,346	28,391	31,619	31,462	29,554	22,986	22,094	23,030	Time Deposits	25
....	....	....	....	16,949	18,257	14,055	14,041	11,161	17,034	12,249	12,814	15,008	15,073	15,755	Foreign Liabilities	26c
....	....	....	....	3,458	2,625	1,651	587	1,448	1,814	1,842	1,095	929	925	2,089	Central Government Deposits	26d
....	....	....	....	—	—	—	3,024	1,970	3,127	47	69	39	40	40	Credit From Monetary Authorities	26g
....	....	....	....	8,220	7,649	8,435	8,300	8,643	8,355	7,833	7,961	7,466	8,082	9,854	Capital Accounts	27a
....	....	....	....	1,129	2,245	3,411	3,584	3,569	2,984	3,468	4,035	3,562	4,010	−40	Other Items (Net)	27r
End of Period															**Monetary Survey**	
....	....	....	....	21,273	25,605	28,693	32,463	35,535	35,825	41,607	45,007	35,358	37,222	35,815	Foreign Assets (Net)	31n
....	....	....	....	26,565	29,975	34,061	31,603	32,485	33,467	32,641	33,634	36,168	35,580	39,075	Domestic Credit	32
....	....	....	....	−3,952	−4,490	−2,883	−5,251	−5,198	−5,259	−4,463	−2,307	739	2,292	5,180	Claims on Central Govt. (Net)	32an
....	....	....	....	561	563	494	459	609	221	572	489	444	483	419	Claims on Nonfin.Pub.Enterprises	32c
....	....	....	....	29,956	33,902	36,450	36,395	37,074	38,505	36,532	35,452	34,985	32,805	33,476	Claims on Private Sector	32d
....	....	....	....	19,934	20,533	23,290	25,331	27,066	25,184	27,362	31,649	34,981	36,404	37,608	Money	34
....	....	....	....	18,264	24,694	27,050	26,346	28,391	31,619	31,462	29,554	22,986	22,094	23,030	Quasi-Money	35
....	....	....	....	9,636	10,352	12,411	12,387	12,561	12,488	15,421	17,440	13,559	14,308	14,254	Other Items (Net)	37r
....	....	....	....	38,198	45,227	50,340	51,677	55,457	56,803	58,824	61,203	57,967	58,498	60,638	Money plus Quasi-Money	35l
End of Period															**Other Banking Institutions**	
....	....	....	....	195	295	184	310	721	561	656	510	251	261	167	Reserves	40
....	....	....	....	795	468	636	791	975	1,044	1,790	2,860	4,202	4,472	4,277	Claims on Private Sector	42d
....	....	....	....	—	—	111	228	455	597	210	527	644	712	610	Long-Term Foreign Liabilities	46cl
....	....	....	....	270	270	240	390	740	690	1,607	1,463	1,999	1,788	1,542	Central Govt. Lending Funds	46f
....	....	....	....	477	483	486	485	436	364	342	1,133	1,529	1,557	1,557	Capital Accounts	47a
....	....	....	....	243	10	−16	−2	63	−46	287	247	281	676	735	Other Items (Net)	47r
Millions of Francs															**International Transactions**	
2,221	1,554	2,232	1,919	2,362	2,488	3,628	4,976	4,116	4,423	4,420	3,083	2,800	....	....	Exports	70
37,920	39,865	40,197	39,307	39,425	35,670	32,731	36,487	35,771	34,920	38,174	38,103	38,860	....	....	Imports, cif	71

Djibouti
611

		1965	1966	1967	1968	1969	1970	1971	1972	1973	1974	1975	1976	1977	1978	1979
Balance of Payments															*Millions of US Dollars:*	
Goods: Exports f.o.b.	78aa d	....	....	....	....	....	....	....	....	....	....	....	....	....	....	....
Goods: Imports f.o.b.	78ab d	....	....	....	....	....	....	....	....	....	....	....	....	....	....	....
Trade Balance	78ac d	....	....	....	....	....	....	....	....	....	....	....	....	....	....	....
Services: Credit	78ad d	....	....	....	....	....	....	....	....	....	....	....	....	....	....	....
Services: Debit	78ae d	....	....	....	....	....	....	....	....	....	....	....	....	....	....	....
Balance on Goods and Services	78af d	....	....	....	....	....	....	....	....	....	....	....	....	....	....	....
Income: Credit	78ag d	....	....	....	....	....	....	....	....	....	....	....	....	....	....	....
Income: Debit	78ah d	....	....	....	....	....	....	....	....	....	....	....	....	....	....	....
Balance on Goods, Serv., & Inc.	78ai d	....	....	....	....	....	....	....	....	....	....	....	....	....	....	....
Current Transfers, n.i.e.: Credit	78aj d	....	....	....	....	....	....	....	....	....	....	....	....	....	....	....
Current Transfers: Debit	78ak d	....	....	....	....	....	....	....	....	....	....	....	....	....	....	....
Current Account, n.i.e.	78al d	....	....	....	....	....	....	....	....	....	....	....	....	....	....	....
Capital Account, n.i.e.: Credit	78ba d	....	....	....	....	....	....	....	....	....	....	....	....	....	....	....
Capital Account: Debit	78bb d	....	....	....	....	....	....	....	....	....	....	....	....	....	....	....
Capital Account, n.i.e.	78bc d	....	....	....	....	....	....	....	....	....	....	....	....	....	....	....
Direct Investment Abroad	78bd d	....	....	....	....	....	....	....	....	....	....	....	....	....	....	....
Dir. Invest. in Rep. Econ., n.i.e.	78be d	....	....	....	....	....	....	....	....	....	....	....	....	....	....	....
Portfolio Investment Assets	78bf d	....	....	....	....	....	....	....	....	....	....	....	....	....	....	....
Portfolio Investment Liab., n.i.e.	78bg d	....	....	....	....	....	....	....	....	....	....	....	....	....	....	....
Other Investment Assets	78bh d	....	....	....	....	....	....	....	....	....	....	....	....	....	....	....
Other Investment Liab., n.i.e.	78bi d	....	....	....	....	....	....	....	....	....	....	....	....	....	....	....
Financial Account, n.i.e.	78bj d	....	....	....	....	....	....	....	....	....	....	....	....	....	....	....
Net Errors and Omissions	78ca d	....	....	....	....	....	....	....	....	....	....	....	....	....	....	....
Overall Balance	78cb d	....	....	....	....	....	....	....	....	....	....	....	....	....	....	....
Reserves and Related Items	79da d	....	....	....	....	....	....	....	....	....	....	....	....	....	....	....
Reserve Assets	79db d	....	....	....	....	....	....	....	....	....	....	....	....	....	....	....
Use of Fund Credit and Loans	79dc d	....	....	....	....	....	....	....	....	....	....	....	....	....	....	....
Liabs.Constit.For.Auth.Reserves	79dd d	....	....	....	....	....	....	....	....	....	....	....	....	....	....	....
Exceptional Financing	79de d	....	....	....	....	....	....	....	....	....	....	....	....	....	....	....
Government Finance															*Millions of Francs:*	
Deficit (-) or Surplus	80	....	....	....	....	....	....	....	....	....	....	....	....	....	....	1,872
Revenue	81	....	....	....	....	....	....	....	....	....	....	....	....	....	....	13,918
Grants Received	81z	....	....	....	....	....	....	....	....	....	....	....	....	....	....	8,433
Expenditure	82	....	....	....	....	....	....	....	....	....	....	....	....	....	....	20,397
Lending Minus Repayments	83	....	....	....	....	....	....	....	....	....	....	....	....	....	....	82
Financing																
Domestic	84a	....	....	....	....	....	....	....	....	....	....	....	....	....	....	163
Foreign	85a	....	....	....	....	....	....	....	....	....	....	....	....	....	....	−2,035
National Accounts															*Billions of Francs:*	
Gross Domestic Product	99b	6	6	6	6	12	10	17	19	22	27	30	36	35	38	46
															Millions:	
Population	99z	.09	.09	.09	.09	.09	1.16	....	....	....	....	.21	.23	.25	.27	.29

Government Finance: ꭍ Data for 1979 cover budgetary central government and social security funds. ꭍ Data for 1981-85 and for 1988 cover budgetary central government only. ꭍ Data for 1980 and 1986 cover budgetary central government and operations of other Treasury accounts.

Djibouti

	1980	1981	1982	1983	1984	1985	1986	1987	1988	1989	1990	1991	1992	1993	1994	Balance of Payments	
Minus Sign Indicates Debit																	
	...	...	...	...	...	...	...	...	...	...	...	...	192.0	211.2	...	Goods: Exports f.o.b.	78aa *d*
	...	...	...	...	...	...	...	...	...	...	...	...	−383.4	−402.3	...	Goods: Imports f.o.b.	78ab *d*
	...	...	...	...	...	...	...	...	...	...	...	...	−191.4	−191.0	...	Trade Balance	78ac *d*
	...	...	...	...	...	...	...	...	...	...	...	...	150.6	164.7	...	Services: Credit	78ad *d*
	...	...	...	...	...	...	...	...	...	...	...	...	−85.9	−85.3	...	Services: Debit	78ae *d*
	...	...	...	...	...	...	...	...	...	...	...	...	−126.6	−111.6	...	Balance on Goods and Services	78af *d*
	...	...	...	...	...	...	...	...	...	...	...	...	23.8	19.2	...	Income: Credit	78ag *d*
	...	...	...	...	...	...	...	...	...	...	...	...	−10.0	−9.5	...	Income: Debit	78ah *d*
	...	...	...	...	...	...	...	...	...	...	...	...	−112.9	−101.9	...	Balance on Goods, Serv., & Inc.	78ai *d*
	...	...	...	...	...	...	...	...	...	...	...	...	117.7	106.4	...	Current Transfers, n.i.e.: Credit	78aj *d*
	...	...	...	...	...	...	...	...	...	...	...	...	−93.6	−92.8	...	Current Transfers: Debit	78ak *d*
	...	...	...	...	...	...	...	...	...	...	...	...	−88.7	−88.2	...	Current Account, n.i.e.	78al *d*
	...	...	...	...	...	...	...	...	...	...	...	...	—	—	...	Capital Account, n.i.e.: Credit	78ba *d*
	...	...	...	...	...	...	...	...	...	...	...	...	—	—	...	Capital Account: Debit	78bb *d*
	...	...	...	...	...	...	...	...	...	...	...	...	—	—	...	Capital Account, n.i.e.	78bc *d*
	...	...	...	...	...	...	...	...	...	...	...	...	—	—	...	Direct Investment Abroad	78bd *d*
	...	...	...	...	...	...	...	...	...	...	...	...	2.3	2.8	...	Dir. Invest. in Rep. Econ., n.i.e.	78be *d*
	...	...	...	...	...	...	...	...	...	...	...	...	—	—	...	Portfolio Investment Assets	78bf *d*
	...	...	...	...	...	...	...	...	...	...	...	...	—	—	...	Portfolio Investment Liab., n.i.e.	78bg *d*
	...	...	...	...	...	...	...	...	...	...	...	...	25.3	−21.8	...	Other Investment Assets	78bh *d*
	...	...	...	...	...	...	...	...	...	...	...	...	33.2	25.6	...	Other Investment Liab., n.i.e.	78bi *d*
	...	...	...	...	...	...	...	...	...	...	...	...	60.8	6.5	...	Financial Account, n.i.e.	78bj *d*
	...	...	...	...	...	...	...	...	...	...	...	...	11.4	73.3	...	Net Errors and Omissions	78ca *d*
	...	...	...	...	...	...	...	...	...	...	...	...	−16.5	−8.4	...	Overall Balance	78cb *d*
	...	...	...	...	...	...	...	...	...	...	...	...	16.5	8.4	...	Reserves and Related Items	79da *d*
	...	...	...	...	...	...	...	...	...	...	...	...	16.5	8.4	...	Reserve Assets	79db *d*
	...	...	...	...	...	...	...	...	...	...	...	...	—	—	...	Use of Fund Credit and Loans	79dc *d*
	...	...	...	...	...	...	...	...	...	...	...	...	—	—	...	Liabs.Constit.For.Auth.Reserves	79dd *d*
	...	...	...	...	...	...	...	...	...	...	...	...	—	—	...	Exceptional Financing	79de *d*
Year Ending December 31																**Government Finance**	
	ɪ4,062	ɪ5,268	2,798	4,587	2,729	922	ɪ−1,470	...	ɪ−733	...	...	...	...	...	...	Deficit (−) or Surplus	80
	ɪ17,922	ɪ23,058	24,904	26,706	23,644	22,485	ɪ21,024	...	ɪ20,101	...	...	...	...	...	...	Revenue	81
	13,460	ɪ96	2,896	1,916	1,473	1,445	ɪ2,404	...	ɪ1,400	...	...	...	...	...	...	Grants Received	81z
	26,916	ɪ16,396	24,190	24,035	22,182	22,918	ɪ24,383	...	ɪ22,234	...	...	...	...	...	...	Expenditure	82
	ɪ404	ɪ1,490	812	—	206	90	ɪ515	...	ɪ—	...	...	...	...	...	...	Lending Minus Repayments	83
																Financing	
	ɪ−241	...	...	...	...	...	ɪ1,693	...	...	...	...	...	...	...	...	Domestic	84a
	ɪ−3,821	...	...	...	...	...	ɪ−223	...	...	...	...	...	...	...	...	Foreign	85a
Billions of Francs																**National Accounts**	
	60	67	70	72	...	...	...	66	70	73	75	...	...	...	...	Gross Domestic Product	99b
Midyear Estimates																	
	.36	.37	.37	.38	.41	.43	.46	.44	.47	.50	.52	.53	.55	.56	...	Population	99z

Dominica

321

		1965	1966	1967	1968	1969	1970	1971	1972	1973	1974	1975	1976	1977	1978	1979
Exchange Rates												*E.Caribbean Dollars per SDR: End of Period (aa)*				
Official Rate	aa	1.7126	1.7203	1.9948	2.0131	1.9994	2.0053	2.0417	2.2194	2.4925	2.5024	2.7770	3.1369	3.2797	3.5175	3.5568
Official Rate	ae	1.7126	1.7203	1.9948	2.0131	1.9994	2.0053	1.8805	2.0442	2.0661	2.0439	2.3721	2.7000	2.7000	2.7000	2.7000
Fund Position															*Millions of SDRs:*	
Quota	2f. s	...	...	...	...	...	...	...	...	...	...	...	...	...	1.90	1.90
SDRs	1b. s	...	...	...	...	...	...	...	...	...	...	...	...	...	—	—
Reserve Position in the Fund	1c. s	...	...	...	...	...	...	...	...	...	...	...	...	...	—	—
Total Fund Cred.&Loans Outstg.	2tl	...	...	...	...	...	...	...	...	...	...	...	...	...	—	1.90
International Liquidity												*Millions of US Dollars Unless Otherwise Indicated:*				
Total Reserves minus Gold	1l. d	...	...	...	...	...	...	...	...	...	...	.35	1.17	2.23	1.93	9.84
SDRs	1b. d	...	...	...	...	...	...	...	...	...	...	...	...	...	—	—
Reserve Position in the Fund	1c. d	...	...	...	...	...	...	...	...	...	...	...	...	...	—	—
Foreign Exchange	1d. d	...	...	...	...	...	...	...	...	...	...	.35	1.17	2.23	1.93	9.84
Deposit Money Banks: Assets	7a. d	...	...	...	...	...	...	...	...	...	...	1.77	.86	1.43	1.50	6.40
of which: Claims on Nonbanks	7add	...	...	...	...	...	...	...	...	...	...	...	...	...	...	1.07
Deposit Money Banks: Liabilities	7b. d	...	...	...	...	...	...	...	...	...	...	3.96	3.88	5.00	5.44	6.69
of which: Liab. to Nonbanks	7bdd	...	...	...	...	...	...	...	...	...	...	3.00	2.84	3.69	3.75	3.90
Monetary Authorities												*Millions of E. Caribbean Dollars:*				
Foreign Assets	11	...	...	...	...	...	...	...	...	...	...	.82	3.17	6.02	5.20	26.56
Claims on Central Government	12a	...	...	...	...	...	...	...	...	...	...	3.30	3.30	3.70	3.70	11.08
Claims on Deposit Money Banks	12e	...	...	...	...	...	...	...	...	...	...	...	...	...	...	...
Reserve Money	14	...	...	...	...	...	...	...	...	...	...	4.12	6.47	9.72	8.90	30.88
of which: Currency Outside DMBs	14a	...	...	...	...	...	...	...	...	...	...	2.77	3.65	4.81	5.15	7.33
Foreign Liabilities	16c	...	...	...	...	...	...	...	...	...	...	—	—	—	—	6.76
Central Government Deposits	16d	...	...	...	...	...	...	...	...	...	...	...	...	...	...	...
Other Items (Net)	17r	...	...	...	...	...	...	...	...	...	...	—	—	—	—	—
Deposit Money Banks												*Millions of E. Caribbean Dollars:*				
Reserves	20	...	...	...	...	...	...	...	...	...	...	1.35	2.81	4.91	3.75	23.54
Foreign Assets	21	...	...	...	...	...	...	...	...	...	...	4.19	2.31	3.87	4.04	17.28
Claims on Central Government	22a	...	...	...	...	...	...	...	...	...	...	9.04	10.95	16.94	12.76	13.50
Claims on Local Government	22b															
Claims on Nonfin.Pub.Enterprises	22c	...	...	...	...	...	...	...	...	...	...	1.00	1.00	1.00	1.00	3.76
Claims on Private Sector	22d	...	...	...	...	...	...	...	...	...	...	25.53	28.82	25.86	34.27	36.76
Claims on Nonbank Financial Insts	22f	...	...	...	...	...	...	...	...	...	...	...	...	...	...	.01
Demand Deposits	24	...	...	...	...	...	...	...	...	...	...	5.77	5.70	6.72	12.34	22.75
Time, Savings,& Fgn.Currency Dep.	25	...	...	...	...	...	...	...	...	...	...	28.11	31.89	33.63	36.45	47.52
Foreign Liabilities	26c	...	...	...	...	...	...	...	...	...	...	9.39	10.48	13.51	14.69	18.07
Central Government Deposits	26d	...	...	...	...	...	...	...	...	...	...	—	—	—	—	—
Credit from Monetary Authorities	26g	...	...	...	...	...	...	...	...	...	...	—	—	—	—	—
Capital Accounts	27a	...	...	...	...	...	...	...	...	...	...	1.00	1.80	1.80	1.80	1.84
Other Items (Net)	27r	...	...	...	...	...	...	...	...	...	...	-3.16	-3.99	-3.07	-9.47	4.66
Monetary Survey												*Millions of E. Caribbean Dollars:*				
Foreign Assets (Net)	31n	...	...	...	...	...	...	...	...	...	...	-4.38	-5.01	-3.62	-5.45	19.00
Domestic Credit	32	...	...	...	...	...	...	...	...	...	...	38.87	44.07	47.50	51.72	65.10
Claims on Central Govt. (Net)	32an	...	...	...	...	...	...	...	...	...	...	12.34	14.25	20.64	16.46	24.57
Claims on Local Government	32b															
Claims on Nonfin.Pub.Enterprises	32c	...	...	...	...	...	...	...	...	...	...	1.00	1.00	1.00	1.00	3.76
Claims on Private Sector	32d	...	...	...	...	...	...	...	...	...	...	25.53	28.82	25.86	34.27	36.76
Claims on Nonbank Financial Inst	32f	...	...	...	...	...	...	...	...	...	...	—	—	—	—	.01
Money	34	...	...	...	...	...	...	...	...	...	...	8.54	9.36	11.53	17.49	30.09
Quasi-Money	35	...	...	...	...	...	...	...	...	...	...	28.11	31.89	33.63	36.45	47.52
Other Items (Net)	37r	...	...	...	...	...	...	...	...	...	...	-2.16	-2.19	-1.27	-7.67	6.50
Money plus Quasi-Money	35l	...	...	...	...	...	...	...	...	...	...	36.65	41.25	45.15	53.94	77.60
Interest Rates															*Percent Per Annum*	
Treasury Bill Rate	60c	...	...	...	...	...	...	...	...	...	...	...	...	...	...	...
Deposit Rate	60l	...	...	...	...	...	...	...	...	...	...	...	...	...	4.0	4.0
Lending Rate	60p	...	...	...	...	...	...	...	...	...	...	...	...	...	8.5	8.5
Prices														*Index Numbers (1990=100):*		
Consumer Prices	64	...	12.8	12.9	13.6	14.2	16.0	16.5	17.2	19.2	25.8	31.0	34.4	64.1	40.5	...
International Transactions												*Millions of E. Caribbean Dollars*				
Exports	70	9.51	10.05	10.77	12.37	14.15	11.81	12.28	13.50	16.74	20.95	24.65	29.05	32.30	42.89	25.39
Imports, cif	71	17.19	16.95	17.24	20.10	24.71	31.51	33.02	32.88	32.29	38.92	45.04	49.83	59.08	76.77	59.97

Dominica

	1980	1981	1982	1983	1984	1985	1986	1987	1988	1989	1990	1991	1992	1993	1994		
E.Caribbean Dollars per US Dollar: End of Period (ae)																**Exchange Rates**	
	3.4436	3.1427	2.9784	2.8268	2.6466	2.9657	3.3026	3.8304	3.6334	3.5482	3.8412	3.8622	3.7125	3.7086	3.9416	Official Rate	aa
	2.7000	2.7000	2.7000	2.7000	2.7000	2.7000	2.7000	2.7000	2.7000	2.7000	2.7000	2.7000	2.7000	2.7000	2.7000	Official Rate	ae
End of Period																**Fund Position**	
	2.90	2.90	2.90	4.00	4.00	4.00	4.00	4.00	4.00	4.00	4.00	4.00	4.00	6.00	6.00	6.00 Quota	2f. s
	—	.70	.26	.40	—	—	.81	.70	.55	.32	.21	.01	.07	—	—	SDRs	1b. s
	—	—	—	—	.01	.01	.01	.01	.01	.01	.01	.01	.01	.01	.01	Reserve Position in the Fund	1c. s
	1.65	6.47	9.32	11.00	10.66	9.17	8.63	8.23	6.57	4.99	4.00	3.32	2.78	2.26	1.71	Total Fund Cred.&Loans Outstg.	2tl
End of Period																**International Liquidity**	
	5.08	3.06	4.33	1.48	5.25	3.27	9.59	18.43	14.06	11.68	14.46	17.77	20.41	19.92	15.41	Total Reserves minus Gold	1l. d
	—	.81	.29	.42	—	—	.99	.99	.74	.42	.30	.01	.10	—	—	SDRs	1b. d
	—	—	—	—	.01	.01	.01	.01	.01	.01	.01	.01	.01	.01	.01	Reserve Position in the Fund	1c. d
	5.08	2.24	4.04	1.06	5.24	3.26	8.59	17.42	13.31	11.25	14.15	17.74	20.30	19.90	15.40	Foreign Exchange	1d. d
	4.41	6.28	6.79	7.77	5.53	6.87	14.88	28.64	40.19	32.54	23.16	22.88	28.13	24.13	26.62	Deposit Money Banks: Assets	7a. d
	1.10	2.64	2.46	3.10	4.18	3.32	7.36	2.42	5.04	3.93	2.48	2.87	6.41	9.47	9.98	of which: Claims on Nonbanks	7ad d
	7.64	10.18	8.86	7.61	8.21	8.76	13.95	15.42	16.77	18.63	20.40	23.08	27.73	30.94	39.39	Deposit Money Banks: Liabilities	7b. d
	4.29	7.77	7.10	7.30	7.01	7.99	10.30	11.43	13.25	15.01	18.28	20.96	23.91	25.75	28.46	of which: Liab. to Nonbanks	7bd d
End of Period																**Monetary Authorities**	
	13.71	8.25	11.69	3.99	19.85	10.63	25.91	47.77	37.96	31.54	39.04	47.93	55.10	53.71	41.71	Foreign Assets	11
	11.49	24.45	33.36	37.68	42.86	46.05	47.29	50.41	39.54	35.68	38.33	37.08	27.85	24.04	26.16	Claims on Central Government	12a
	—	—	—	—	—	—	—	.72	.38	1.30	.72	4.05	.02	.02	.37	2.04 Claims on Deposit Money Banks	12e
	19.52	12.37	17.29	10.58	34.49	29.48	45.42	67.04	54.94	50.23	66.06	72.21	72.64	69.73	63.18	Reserve Money	14
	7.48	7.73	6.58	6.39	12.22	9.64	6.64	20.77	22.83	20.69	24.96	30.76	31.13	27.86	24.49	of which: Currency Outside DMBs	14a
	5.68	20.33	27.76	31.09	28.21	27.20	28.50	31.52	23.87	17.71	15.36	12.82	10.32	8.38	6.72	Foreign Liabilities	16c
	—	—	—	—	—	—	—	—	—	—	—	—	—	—	—	Central Government Deposits	16d
	—	—	—	—	—	—	—	—	—	—	—	—	—	—	—	Other Items (Net)	17r
End of Period																**Deposit Money Banks**	
	12.04	4.64	10.71	4.19	23.00	25.33	39.31	46.46	29.19	29.98	38.33	41.65	41.68	42.78	33.46	Reserves	20
	11.92	16.96	18.32	20.97	14.93	18.55	40.18	77.34	108.51	87.86	62.53	61.78	75.95	65.16	71.88	Foreign Assets	21
	18.49	18.25	18.72	19.04	13.13	15.60	24.94	10.36	9.14	11.45	28.00	37.28	42.17	53.46	66.56	Claims on Central Government	22a
	—	—	—	—	—	—	—	—	—	—	—	—	—	.01	.05	.23 Claims on Local Government	22b
	2.20	8.87	4.82	3.31	9.02	7.36	2.38	1.03	6.01	8.27	18.47	24.65	21.40	26.40	29.07	Claims on Nonfin.Pub.Enterprises	22c
	49.78	60.50	67.49	79.07	81.32	89.03	86.16	93.59	128.73	171.49	211.13	234.43	263.99	289.57	312.48	Claims on Private Sector	22d
	.17	.13	.13	6.16	5.49	5.35	2.92	5.33	1.50	4.12	1.54	1.57	1.62	1.29	.42	Claims on Nonbank Financial Insts	22f
	19.63	18.71	18.83	19.01	20.18	21.58	30.39	37.89	34.37	35.39	44.96	42.81	54.96	47.87	49.88	Demand Deposits	24
	52.36	54.84	70.86	80.31	90.19	96.98	110.24	132.18	127.06	150.05	183.65	218.76	241.38	244.57	260.18	Time, Savings,& Fgn.Currency Dep.	25
	20.63	27.49	23.93	20.55	22.16	23.65	37.67	41.63	45.27	50.31	55.09	62.32	74.88	83.54	106.36	Foreign Liabilities	26c
	.22	3.76	2.98	5.50	4.19	2.17	3.35	8.07	52.55	43.81	29.63	24.72	29.81	43.14	55.43	Central Government Deposits	26d
	—	—	—	—	—	.47	.91	—	.42	1.90	2.68	1.54	—	9.68	2.00	Credit from Monetary Authorities	26g
	1.82	2.80	2.95	4.28	4.78	6.09	7.35	10.00	15.07	16.88	26.08	41.18	40.18	44.26	49.91	Capital Accounts	27a
	-.06	1.75	.66	3.09	5.39	10.29	5.99	4.33	8.32	14.85	17.92	10.02	5.61	5.66	-9.64	Other Items (Net)	27r
End of Period																**Monetary Survey**	
	-.69	-22.61	-21.68	-26.68	-15.59	-21.67	-.08	51.95	77.33	51.38	31.12	34.56	45.85	26.95	.51	Foreign Assets (Net)	31n
	81.92	108.45	121.55	139.76	147.62	161.22	160.34	152.65	132.36	187.21	267.84	310.29	327.23	351.67	379.50	Domestic Credit	32
	29.77	38.95	49.10	51.22	51.79	59.48	68.88	52.70	-3.87	3.32	36.70	49.64	40.21	34.36	37.30	Claims on Central Govt. (Net)	32an
	—	—	—	—	—	—	—	—	—	—	—	—	.01	.05	.23	Claims on Local Government	32b
	2.20	8.87	4.82	3.31	9.02	7.36	2.38	1.03	6.01	8.27	18.47	24.65	21.40	26.40	29.07	Claims on Nonfin.Pub.Enterprises	32c
	49.78	60.50	67.49	79.07	81.32	89.03	86.16	93.59	128.73	171.49	211.13	234.43	263.99	289.57	312.48	Claims on Private Sector	32d
	.17	.13	.13	6.16	5.49	5.35	2.92	5.33	1.50	4.12	1.54	1.57	1.62	1.29	.42	Claims on Nonbank Financial Inst	32f
	27.11	26.44	25.41	25.40	32.40	31.22	37.03	58.67	57.19	56.08	69.92	73.51	86.21	75.80	74.45	Money	34
	52.36	54.84	70.86	80.31	90.19	96.98	110.24	132.18	127.06	150.05	183.65	218.76	241.38	244.57	260.18	Quasi-Money	35
	1.76	4.56	3.60	7.37	9.44	11.36	12.99	13.75	25.44	32.46	45.39	52.58	45.48	58.24	45.38	Other Items (Net)	37r
	79.47	81.29	96.26	105.71	122.59	128.20	147.27	190.85	184.26	206.13	253.57	292.27	327.59	320.37	334.63	Money plus Quasi-Money	35l
Percent Per Annum																**Interest Rates**	
	6.5	6.5	6.5	6.5	6.5	6.5	6.5	6.5	6.5	6.5	6.5	6.5	6.5	6.4	6.4	Treasury Bill Rate	60c
	4.0	5.0	5.0	5.0	5.0	5.0	4.9	5.0	5.0	4.5	4.2	4.4	4.1	4.0	4.0	Deposit Rate	60l
	8.5	9.0	9.5	9.5	10.4	10.0	10.3	10.5	10.5	10.5	10.5	10.3	10.0	10.0	9.6	Lending Rate	60p
Period Averages																**Prices**	
	63.5	71.9	75.1	78.2	79.9	82.9	85.2	88.6	91.2	96.9	100.0	105.6	111.3	113.1	114.8	Consumer Prices	64
Millions of E. Caribbean Dollars																**International Transactions**	
	26.30	51.76	66.01	74.00	69.23	76.77	117.24	129.59	146.41	121.77	148.59	146.62	150.81	....	....	Exports	70
	128.73	134.10	128.19	121.71	156.10	149.38	150.69	179.22	236.34	289.09	318.39	295.98	300.02	....	....	Imports, cif	71

Dominica
321

		1965	1966	1967	1968	1969	1970	1971	1972	1973	1974	1975	1976	1977	1978	1979
Balance of Payments													\multicolumn{4}{l}{*Millions of US Dollars:*}			
Goods: Exports f.o.b.	78aa d	....	....	....	....	....	....	....	....	....	....	....	11.10	12.00	15.90	9.80
Goods: Imports f.o.b.	78ab d	....	....	....	....	....	....	....	....	....	....	....	−17.27	−19.91	−25.91	−35.82
Trade Balance	78ac d	....	....	....	....	....	....	....	....	....	....	....	−6.17	−7.91	−10.01	−26.02
Services: Credit	78ad d	....	....	....	....	....	....	....	....	....	....	....	2.50	3.00	3.10	9.50
Services: Debit	78ae d	....	....	....	....	....	....	....	....	....	....	....	−1.83	−2.29	−3.39	−4.48
Balance on Goods and Services	78af d	....	....	....	....	....	....	....	....	....	....	....	−5.50	−7.20	−10.30	−21.00
Income: Credit	78ag d	....	....	....	....	....	....	....	....	....	....	....	.40	.30	.20	.30
Income: Debit	78ah d	....	....	....	....	....	....	....	....	....	....	....	−.20	−.30	−.40	−.40
Balance on Goods, Serv., & Inc.	78ai d	....	....	....	....	....	....	....	....	....	....	....	−5.30	−7.20	−10.50	−21.10
Current Transfers, n.i.e.: Credit	78aj d	....	....	....	....	....	....	....	....	....	....	....	4.20	7.20	11.40	29.30
Current Transfers: Debit	78ak d	....	....	....	....	....	....	....	....	....	....	....	—	−1.50	−2.20	−1.90
Current Account, n.i.e.	78al d	....	....	....	....	....	....	....	....	....	....	....	−1.10	−1.50	−1.30	6.30
Capital Account, n.i.e.: Credit	78ba d	....	....	....	....	....	....	....	....	....	....	....	—	—	—	—
Capital Account: Debit	78bb d	....	....	....	....	....	....	....	....	....	....	....	—	—	—	—
Capital Account, n.i.e.	78bc d	....	....	....	....	....	....	....	....	....	....	....	—	—	—	—
Direct Investment Abroad	78bd d	....	....	....	....	....	....	....	....	....	....	....	—	—	—	—
Dir. Invest. in Rep. Econ., n.i.e.	78be d	....	....	....	....	....	....	....	....	....	....	....	—	—	—	—
Portfolio Investment Assets	78bf d	....	....	....	....	....	....	....	....	....	....	....	—	—	—	—
Portfolio Investment Liab., n.i.e.	78bg d	....	....	....	....	....	....	....	....	....	....	....	—	—	—	—
Other Investment Assets	78bh d	....	....	....	....	....	....	....	....	....	....	....	−.80	−.58	−.06	−3.84
Other Investment Liab., n.i.e.	78bi d	....	....	....	....	....	....	....	....	....	....	....	1.70	3.32	1.34	1.95
Financial Account, n.i.e.	78bj d	....	....	....	....	....	....	....	....	....	....	....	.90	2.74	1.27	−1.89
Net Errors and Omissions	78ca d	....	....	....	....	....	....	....	....	....	....	....	.60	−.29	.12	1.14
Overall Balance	78cb d	....	....	....	....	....	....	....	....	....	....	....	.40	.96	.10	5.56
Reserves and Related Items	79da d	....	....	....	....	....	....	....	....	....	....	....	−.40	−.96	−.10	−5.56
Reserve Assets	79db d	....	....	....	....	....	....	....	....	....	....	....	−.40	−.96	−.10	−8.05
Use of Fund Credit and Loans	79dc d	....	....	....	....	....	....	....	....	....	....	....	—	—	—	2.49
Liabs.Constit.For.Auth.Reserves	79dd d	....	....	....	....	....	....	....	....	....	....	....	—	—	—	—
Exceptional Financing	79de d	....	....	....	....	....	....	....	....	....	....	....	—	—	—	—
Government Finance													\multicolumn{4}{l}{*Millions of E. Caribbean Dollars:*}			
Deficit (−) or Surplus	80	....	....	....	....	....	....	....	....	....	....	....	−4.49	.20	−2.72	−8.11
Revenue	81	....	....	....	....	....	....	....	....	....	....	....	15.83	23.46	31.46	32.46
Grants Received	81z	....	....	....	....	....	....	....	....	....	....	....	5.85	7.54	11.84	19.67
Expenditure	82	....	....	....	....	....	....	....	....	....	....	....	23.21	27.74	44.20	53.40
Lending Minus Repayments	83	....	....	....	....	....	....	....	....	....	....	....	2.96	3.06	1.82	6.84
National Accounts													\multicolumn{4}{l}{*Millions of E. Caribbean Dollars*}			
Exports of Goods & Services	90c	....	....	....	....	....	....	....	....	....	29.4	30.8	36.6	40.5	49.1	32.4
Government Consumption	91f	....	....	....	....	....	....	....	....	....	14.9	18.1	23.4	33.4	27.0	41.1
Gross Fixed Capital Formation	93e	....	....	....	....	....	....	....	....	....	8.7	16.0	19.2	19.9	29.0	33.2
Increase/Decrease(−) in Stocks	93i	....	....	....	....	....	....	....	....	....	1.9	....	—	—	—	10.0
Private Consumption	96f	....	....	....	....	....	....	....	....	....	43.1	43.2	43.2	62.7	94.6	104.9
Imports of Goods & Services	98c	....	....	....	....	....	....	....	....	....	−41.8	−45.2	−49.9	−59.9	−79.1	−108.8
Gross Domestic Product	99b	....	....	....	....	....	....	....	....	....	56.5	62.9	72.5	96.6	120.6	112.8
Gross Dom. Prod. 1990 Prices	99b, p	....	....	....	....	....	....	....	....	....	....	....	254.5	263.3	294.9	244.1
GDP Deflator (1990=100)	99bi p	....	....	....	....	....	....	....	....	....	....	....	28.5	36.7	40.9	46.2
													\multicolumn{4}{l}{*Millions:*}			
Population	99z	.07	.07	.07	.07	.07	.07	.07	.07	.07	.07	.07	.07	.08	.08	.07

Government Finance: Annual data relate to a fiscal year different from calendar year.

Dominica

321

	1980	1981	1982	1983	1984	1985	1986	1987	1988	1989	1990	1991	1992	1993	1994		
Balance of Payments																	
Minus Sign Indicates Debit																	
Goods: Exports f.o.b.	10.10	19.70	25.10	27.80	25.60	28.40	44.57	49.29	57.03	46.30	56.06	55.56	54.57	48.27	….		78aa d
Goods: Imports f.o.b.	-48.36	-45.18	-43.18	-42.81	-50.72	-52.00	-49.16	-58.86	-77.24	-94.42	-103.95	-96.47	-97.51	-98.82	….		78ab d
Trade Balance	-38.26	-25.48	-18.08	-15.01	-25.12	-23.60	-4.59	-9.58	-20.21	-48.13	-47.89	-40.92	-42.94	-50.55	….		78ac d
Services: Credit	5.60	3.70	6.60	8.20	11.80	10.20	14.64	17.01	20.51	23.93	30.93	37.40	42.35	46.28	….		78ad d
Services: Debit	-6.34	-6.92	-6.92	-6.89	-9.48	-11.80	-19.91	-22.58	-22.97	-27.01	-30.91	-32.20	-33.01	-31.77	….		78ae d
Balance on Goods and Services	-39.00	-28.70	-18.40	-13.70	-22.80	-25.20	-9.86	-15.15	-22.68	-51.21	-47.86	-35.71	-33.60	-36.05	….		78af d
Income: Credit	.60	1.00	1.00	1.26	—	—	1.98	2.69	4.33	3.60	4.03	2.60	2.50	2.97	….		78ag d
Income: Debit	-.30	-.50	-.80	-1.70	-1.90	-1.90	-4.39	-5.03	-5.89	-7.59	-8.97	-10.27	-9.86	-9.58	….		78ah d
Balance on Goods, Serv., & Inc.	-38.70	-28.20	-18.20	-14.14	-24.70	-27.10	-12.27	-17.50	-24.24	-55.20	-52.80	-43.38	-40.96	-42.66	….		78ai d
Current Transfers, n.i.e.: Credit	26.70	18.09	12.86	16.71	21.97	25.27	23.43	19.17	23.79	25.82	25.42	26.02	22.15	23.63	….		78aj d
Current Transfers: Debit	-2.30	-2.70	-2.90	-4.40	-4.50	-4.60	-5.71	-4.78	-5.39	-3.17	-3.60	-3.86	-4.13	-3.87	….		78ak d
Current Account, n.i.e.	-14.30	-12.81	-8.24	-1.83	-7.23	-6.43	5.45	-3.10	-5.85	-32.55	-30.98	-21.21	-22.94	-22.90	….		78al d
Capital Account, n.i.e.: Credit	—	—	—	—	—	—	—	—	—	—	—	—	—	—	….		78ba d
Capital Account: Debit	—	—	—	—	—	—	—	—	—	—	—	—	—	—	….		78bb d
Capital Account, n.i.e.	—	—	—	—	—	—	—	—	—	—	—	—	—	—	….		78bc d
Direct Investment Abroad	—	—	—	—	—	—	—	—	—	—	—	—	—	—	….		78bd d
Dir. Invest. in Rep. Econ., n.i.e.	—	—	.20	.20	2.30	3.00	2.67	9.74	6.89	8.08	7.61	10.66	13.58	9.70	….		78be d
Portfolio Investment Assets	—	—	—	—	—	—	—	—	—	—	—	—	—	—	….		78bf d
Portfolio Investment Liab., n.i.e.	-.20	—	.09	.09	—	—	—	—	—	—	-.37	—	—	-.10	….		78bg d
Other Investment Assets	1.17	-1.87	-.50	-3.38	2.24	-1.31	-2.81	-11.41	-8.48	8.18	10.78	3.06	.90	5.61	….		78bh d
Other Investment Liab., n.i.e.	2.61	5.22	7.24	4.46	6.90	4.82	4.37	10.58	7.13	16.33	12.01	12.02	11.03	3.47	….		78bi d
Financial Account, n.i.e.	3.59	3.35	7.03	1.37	11.43	6.51	4.22	8.91	5.53	32.59	30.04	25.73	25.51	18.68	….		78bj d
Net Errors and Omissions	6.77	.94	-.76	-3.99	1.43	-.69	-3.10	2.59	-.72	.14	5.99	-.30	.79	4.84	….		78ca d
Overall Balance	-3.94	-8.52	-1.98	-4.46	5.64	-.61	6.57	8.39	-1.03	.18	5.05	4.22	3.36	.62	….		78cb d
Reserves and Related Items	3.94	8.52	1.98	4.46	-5.64	.61	-6.57	-8.39	1.03	-.18	-5.05	-4.22	-3.36	-.62	….		79da d
Reserve Assets	4.26	2.72	-1.60	2.56	-5.39	2.00	-6.04	-7.92	3.23	1.83	-3.70	-3.29	-2.60	.11	….		79db d
Use of Fund Credit and Loans	-.32	5.80	3.14	1.81	-.37	-1.52	-.61	-.53	-2.27	-2.03	-1.35	-.94	-.76	-.73	….		79dc d
Liabs.Constit.For.Auth.Reserves	—	—	—	—	—	—	—	—	—	—	—	—	—	—	….		79dd d
Exceptional Financing	—	.01	.44	.08	.12	.13	.09	.05	.07	.03	—	—	—	—	….		79de d
Government Finance																	
Year Ending June 30																	
Deficit (-) or Surplus	….	….	….	….	….	….	….	….	….	….	….	….	….	….	….		80
Revenue	….	….	….	….	….	….	….	….	….	….	….	….	….	….	….		81
Grants Received	….	….	….	….	….	….	….	….	….	….	….	….	….	….	….		81z
Expenditure	….	….	….	….	….	….	….	….	….	….	….	….	….	….	….		82
Lending Minus Repayments	….	….	….	….	….	….	….	….	….	….	….	….	….	….	….		83
National Accounts																	
Millions of E. Caribbean Dollars																	
Exports of Goods & Services	35.1	61.8	80.2	88.8	86.4	97.3	148.3	175.5	205.4	189.6	234.9	247.3	253.5	250.7	….		90c
Government Consumption	43.8	45.9	47.7	52.3	60.2	59.9	62.1	68.2	75.0	86.7	91.9	102.5	103.2	105.3	….		91f
Gross Fixed Capital Formation	79.7	57.0	60.1	60.6	89.4	75.8	67.5	79.3	120.6	164.2	178.2	148.8	154.9	158.6	….		93e
Increase/Decrease(-) in Stocks											6.5	5.0	5.2	6.1	7.1		93i
Private Consumption	148.2	154.5	141.8	144.9	172.5	192.8	188.9	229.8	257.8	295.0	303.3	331.5	354.3	383.2	….		96f
Imports of Goods & Services	-147.7	-140.5	-135.3	-130.7	-165.9	-159.6	-164.2	-211.7	-270.6	-327.9	-364.1	-348.0	-352.7	-374.2	….		98c
Gross Domestic Product	159.1	178.5	194.5	215.8	242.6	266.2	302.6	341.1	388.2	414.1	449.1	487.3	519.2	530.7	….		99b
Gross Dom. Prod. 1990 Prices	285.6	308.5	I318.6	325.3	342.7	348.7	372.4	397.9	427.1	422.3	449.1	459.3	472.3	480.9	….		99b.p
GDP Deflator (1990=100)	55.7	57.9	61.1	66.3	70.8	76.3	81.3	85.7	90.9	98.1	100.0	106.1	109.9	110.4	….		99bi p
Midyear Estimates																	
Population	.07	.07	.08	.08	.08	.08	.08	.08	.08	I.07	.07	.07	.07	.07	….		99z

Dominican Republic

243

		1965	1966	1967	1968	1969	1970	1971	1972	1973	1974	1975	1976	1977	1978	1979
Exchange Rates																*Pesos per SDR:*
Market Rate......aa=	wa	1.000	1.000	1.000	1.000	1.000	1.000	1.086	1.086	1.206	1.224	1.171	1.162	1.215	1.303	1.317
															Pesos per US Dollar:	
Market Rate......ae=	we	1.000	1.000	1.000	1.000	1.000	1.000	1.000	1.000	1.000	1.000	1.000	1.000	1.000	1.000	1.000
Market Rate......rf=	wf	1.000	1.000	1.000	1.000	1.000	1.000	1.000	1.000	1.000	1.000	1.000	1.000	1.000	1.000	1.000
Secondary Rate	xe	....	....	....	....	....	....	....	....	....	....	....	....	1.250	1.280	1.236
Secondary Rate	xf	....	....	....	....	....	1.137	1.131	1.112	1.124	1.130	1.170	1.190	1.213	1.245	1.217
														Index Numbers (1990=100):		
Market Rate......ah	x	800.0	800.0	800.0	800.0	800.0	800.0	311.1	800.0	311.1	800.0	800.0	800.0	800.0	800.0	800.0
Nominal Effective Exchange Rate	ne c	....	....	....	....	....	....	....	....	....	....	....	....	....	....	319.2
Real Effective Exchange Rate	re c	....	....	....	....	....	....	....	....	....	....	....	....	....	....	145.6
Fund Position																*Millions of SDRs:*
Quota	2f. s	25.0	26.4	27.8	29.2	32.0	43.0	43.0	43.0	43.0	43.0	43.0	43.0	43.0	55.0	55.0
SDRs	1b. s	—	—	—	—	—	—	—	6.9	6.8	7.2	6.5	6.0	5.2	4.7	7.2
Reserve Position in the Fund	1c. s	—	—	—	—	—	—	—	—	10.8	—	—	—	—	—	—
Total Fund Cred.&Loans Outstg.	2tl	13.8	20.0	16.7	9.3	14.6	6.6	10.8	3.8	—	—	—	21.5	36.5	36.5	94.3
International Liquidity													*Millions of US Dollars Unless Otherwise Indicated:*			
Total Reserves minus Gold	1l.d	47.8	40.6	29.4	32.6	36.8	29.1	52.8	55.3	84.3	87.1	112.6	123.5	180.1	154.0	238.6
SDRs	1b.d	—	—	—	—	—	—	—	7.5	8.2	8.8	7.6	7.0	6.3	6.1	9.5
Reserve Position in the Fund	1c.d	—	—	—	—	—	—	—	—	13.0	—	—	—	—	—	—
Foreign Exchange	1d.d	47.8	40.6	29.4	32.6	36.8	29.1	52.8	47.8	63.2	78.3	105.0	116.5	173.8	147.9	229.1
Gold (Million Fine Troy Ounces)	1ad	.086	.086	.086	.086	.086	.086	.086	.086	.086	.086	.086	.086	.104	.104	.113
Gold (National Valuation)	1an d	3.0	3.0	3.0	3.0	3.0	3.0	3.3	3.3	3.6	3.6	3.6	3.6	4.4	20.2	48.4
Monetary Authorities: Other Liab.	4..d	36.5	43.0	32.0	31.1	26.8	22.5	20.3	14.9	10.3	32.5	72.0	106.6	139.0	152.0	252.8
Deposit Money Banks: Assets	7a.d	3.8	5.5	6.4	4.9	5.3	7.4	11.4	9.2	8.1	9.8	17.0	36.1	40.4	25.3	56.9
Liabilities	7b.d	8.8	18.8	13.4	21.9	17.1	11.3	25.4	22.3	37.1	69.1	36.5	47.9	76.1	78.9	73.9
Other Banking Insts.: Liabilities	7f.d	....	....	....	....	....	42.0	35.0	34.2	36.2	39.6	48.2	51.1	51.5	46.1	
Monetary Authorities																*Millions of Pesos:*
Foreign Assets	11	51	44	32	36	40	32	56	58	88	92	119	129	184	174	282
Claims on Central Government	12a	86	87	I 101	111	123	139	157	173	189	249	256	260	270	295	335
Claims on Nonfin.Pub.Enterprises	12c	—	—	1	1	1	1	2	2	2	2	2	2	2	2	2
Claims on Deposit Money Banks	12e	44	54	44	48	54	55	46	53	65	97	120	114	135	199	215
Claims on Other Banking Insts.	12f	4	6	I 26	35	38	42	49	49	55	75	90	117	117	130	196
Reserve Money	14	127	117	117	138	161	181	211	229	288	422	389	390	500	542	587
of which: Currency Outside DMBs	14a	75	65	59	65	72	81	84	99	116	141	158	172	203	224	274
Bonds	16ab	—	—	1	1	1	—	—	—	—	—	—	—	—	—	—
Foreign Liabilities	16c	50	63	49	40	41	29	32	19	10	32	72	132	183	200	377
Long-Term Foreign Liabilities	16cl	—	—	17	17	9	15	20	18	35	19	29	35	3	57	78
Counterpart Funds	16e	6	7	—	—	—	—	—	—	—	—	—	—	—	—	—
Capital Accounts	17a	—	—	14	17	22	32	42	49	54	57	62	63	69	73	80
Other Items (Net)	17r	1	4	6	17	22	12	5	19	11	−16	34	3	−47	−72	−92
Deposit Money Banks																*Millions of Pesos:*
Reserves	20	53	55	54	72	88	98	124	126	161	280	215	220	306	316	323
Foreign Assets	21	4	6	6	5	5	7	11	9	8	10	17	36	40	25	57
Claims on Central Government	22a	74	83	I 28	35	33	31	39	57	58	63	102	95	86	78	102
Claims on Local Government	22b	1	—	2	3	2	2	2	3	3	2	2	3	6	12	13
Claims on Nonfin.Pub.Enterprises	22c	—	—	9	12	14	19	21	26	41	67	65	56	91	131	135
Claims on Private Sector	22d	68	72	78	113	152	180	217	282	386	578	685	789	851	885	990
Claims on Other Banking Insts.	22f	4	4	I 32	33	34	36	39	36	41	42	49	55	63	70	63
Demand Deposits	24	60	51	63	78	79	94	111	125	153	230	230	228	271	271	368
Time Deposits	25	61	49	32	49	74	101	130	181	245	360	454	458	540	527	510
Foreign Liabilities	26c	9	19	13	22	17	11	25	22	37	69	37	48	76	79	74
Central Government Deposits	26d	23	13	17	16	23	28	27	35	40	54	56	79	84	108	57
Credit from Monetary Authorities	26g	44	54	46	53	62	65	57	64	79	123	138	161	166	223	271
Capital Accounts	27a	46	—	17	21	23	23	26	32	44	64	108	124	136	148	163
Other Items (Net)	27r	−38	32	21	34	50	51	77	80	98	143	114	156	170	162	242
Monetary Survey																*Millions of Pesos:*
Foreign Assets (Net)	31n	−4	−33	−23	−22	−13	−1	10	26	48	—	27	−14	−35	−79	−112
Domestic Credit	32	217	224	I 254	311	353	409	493	582	715	1,022	1,133	1,236	1,362	1,492	1,774
Claims on Central Govt. (Net)	32an	141	141	I 105	114	112	129	162	184	188	256	241	213	232	261	374
Claims on Local Government	32b	—	—	2	3	2	2	2	3	3	2	2	3	6	12	13
Claims on Nonfin.Pub.Enterprises	32c	—	—	11	13	15	20	22	28	43	69	66	58	93	133	137
Claims on Private Sector	32d	68	72	78	113	152	180	217	282	386	578	685	789	851	885	990
Claims on Other Banking Insts.	32f	8	10	I 57	68	72	78	89	85	96	117	139	172	179	201	259
Money	34	135	116	124	147	154	178	198	231	274	378	399	403	475	496	643
Quasi-Money	35	61	49	32	49	74	101	130	181	245	360	454	458	540	527	510
Bonds	36ab	—	—	1	1	1	—	—	—	—	—	—	—	—	—	—
Other Items (Net)	37r	17	25	73	92	110	130	174	197	245	284	307	361	312	390	508
Money plus Quasi-Money	35l	196	165	156	196	228	278	329	411	518	738	853	861	1,015	1,023	1,154
Other Banking Institutions																*Millions of Pesos:*
Cash	40	....	....	....	....	....	....	—	—	—	2	1	2	2	4	4
Claims on Central Government	42a	....	....	....	....	....	....	43	43	42	46	69	75	81	94	39
Claims on Nonfin.Pub.Enterprises	42c	....	....	....	....	....	....	1	5	5	2	2	2	—	6	5
Claims on Private Sector	42d	....	....	....	....	....	....	133	137	153	206	259	332	403	538	702
Claims on Deposit Money Banks	42e	....	....	....	....	....	....	17	37	61	51	54	61	38	35	63
Time, Savings,& Fgn.Currency Dep.	45	....	....	....	....	....	....	23	32	55	75	101	124	208[e]	196	242
Bonds	46ab	....	....	....	....	....	....	6	5	5	5	14	23	41	65	112
Long-Term Foreign Liabilities	46cl	....	....	....	....	....	....	42	35	34	36	40	48	51	52	46
Credit from Monetary Authorities	46g	....	....	....	....	....	....	40	48	62	48	70	86	120[e]	127	145
Credit from Deposit Money Banks	46h	....	....	....	....	....	....	6	5	8	9	10	10	11	9	16
Capital Accounts	47a	....	....	....	....	....	....	101	116	119	123	129	139	151	180	207
Other Items (Net)	47r	....	....	....	....	....	....	−24	−20	−22	11	22	43	−59	48	44

Dominican Republic

	1980	1981	1982	1983	1984	1985	1986	1987	1988	1989	1990	1991	1992	1993	1994		
End of Period																**Exchange Rates**	
	1.275	1.164	1.103	1.047	.980	3.229	3.763	7.037	8.532	8.332	16.147	18.109	17.291	17.536	19.071	Market Rate........aa=	wa
End of Period (we) Period Average (wf)																	
	1.000	1.000	1.000	1.000	1.000	2.940	3.077	4.960	6.340	6.340	11.350	12.660	12.575	12.767	13.064	Market Rate........ae=	we
	1.000	1.000	1.000	1.000	1.000	3.113	2.904	3.845	6.113	6.340	8.525	12.692	12.774	12.679	13.160	Market Rate........rf=	wf
	1.232	1.315	1.536	1.800	3.105	....	....	....	....	....	....	....	....	....	....	Secondary Rate	xe
	1.255	1.278	1.457	....	2.737	....	....	....	....	....	....	....	....	....	....	Secondary Rate	xf
Period Averages																	
	800.0	800.0	800.0	800.0	800.0	257.2	275.0	213.0	133.1	124.2	100.0	62.7	62.6	63.1	60.8	Market Rate	ahx
	327.1	354.6	372.2	372.2	244.7	217.8	201.0	159.8	108.2	113.2	100.0	76.8	85.9	101.4	117.8	Nominal Effective Exchange Rate	ne c
	149.3	151.3	159.5	157.0	110.9	123.9	117.7	100.8	84.2	101.8	100.0	101.4	101.5	105.5	108.5	Real Effective Exchange Rate	re c
End of Period																**Fund Position**	
	82.5	82.5	82.5	112.1	112.1	112.1	112.1	112.1	112.1	112.1	112.1	112.1	158.8	158.8	158.8	Quota	2f. s
	—	1.6	.5	.2	.4	28.8	—	—	—	—	—	—	.1	10.3	2.5	SDRs	1b. s
	—	—	—	7.4	—	—	—	—	—	—	—	—	—	—	—	Reserve Position in the Fund	1c. s
	38.0	19.8	64.1	235.2	225.7	270.4	248.8	199.9	161.8	93.2	50.4	62.4	89.4	135.5	129.9	Total Fund Cred.&Loans Outstg.	2tl
End of Period																**International Liquidity**	
	201.8	225.2	129.0	171.3	253.5	340.1	376.3	182.2	254.0	164.0	61.6	441.9	499.8	651.2	252.1	Total Reserves minus Gold	1l. d
	—	1.9	.6	.2	.4	31.6	—	—	—	—	—	.1	.1	14.1	3.7	SDRs	1b. d
	—	—	—	7.7	—	—	—	—	—	—	—	—	—	—	—	Reserve Position in the Fund	1c. d
	201.8	223.3	128.4	163.3	253.1	308.5	376.3	182.2	254.0	164.0	61.6	441.8	499.7	637.1	248.4	Foreign Exchange	1d. d
	.131	.142	.091	.077	.018	.018	.018	.018	.018	.018	.018	.018	.018	.018	.018	Gold (Million Fine Troy Ounces)	1ad
	72.8	58.7	43.7	31.3	7.9	5.9	7.1	8.8	7.6	7.5	6.8	6.5	6.1	6.9	6.8	Gold (National Valuation)	1an d
	519.2	748.0	990.5	1,138.9	1,243.8	1,395.8	229.0	257.7	139.7	202.6	180.5	150.8	26.0	22.3	100.6	Monetary Authorities: Other Liab.	4..d
	127.4	272.5	292.0	42.8	58.7	123.1	171.0	122.3	205.3	123.5	122.6	129.2	136.4	155.4	138.6	Deposit Money Banks: Assets	7a. d
	154.8	341.3	314.1	93.7	85.1	39.1	80.2	91.8	32.5	28.8	68.6	64.1	54.0	40.5	61.6	Liabilities	7b. d
	38.9	30.6	26.9	23.3	21.0	24.0	22.4	60.9	107.8	12.9	28.1	41.8	49.3	62.7	91.2	Other Banking Insts.: Liabilities	7f. d
End of Period																**Monetary Authorities**	
	275	284	172	204	268	1,059	1,187	926	1,644	1,074	1,486	5,624	6,394	8,257	4,031	Foreign Assets	11
	364	492	660	867	938	953	941	1,046	1,087	1,104	1,146	1,972	1,953	938	639	Claims on Central Government	12a
	53	56	137	238	258	209	151	285	291	323	334	979	585	738	1,214	Claims on Nonfin.Pub.Enterprises	12c
	227	380	466	523	490	469	553	571	584	682	687	926	649	449	865	Claims on Deposit Money Banks	12e
	266	306	327	360	271	305	324	349	536	532	353	441	1,087	923	1,028	Claims on Other Banking Insts.	12f
	566	713	731	850	1,097	1,085	2,112	1,983	4,028	5,198	6,820	10,516	11,602	14,889	14,801	Reserve Money	14
	275	324	358	415	593	677	937	1,313	1,876	2,683	3,733	4,586	5,913	6,905	7,679	*of which:* Currency Outside DMBs	14a
	6	1	—	—	8	55	101	156	211	126	138	646	518	196	743	Bonds	16ab
	568	771	1,061	1,385	1,465	4,977	1,641	2,685	2,266	2,061	2,863	3,039	1,873	2,661	3,791	Foreign Liabilities	16c
	104	89	65	35	5	14	3,547	5,536	7,802	8,208	15,595	16,781	15,089	15,134	10,263	Long-Term Foreign Liabilities	16cl
	—	—	—	—	—	—	—	—	—	—	—	—	—	—	—	Counterpart Funds	16e
	80	66	72	112	130	174	−85	−90	−575	−1,069	−1,631	−892	500	−922	−491	Capital Accounts	17a
	−140	−121	−168	−190	−481	−3,310	−4,160	−7,092	−9,589	−10,809	−19,780	−20,147	−18,914	−20,652	−21,330	Other Items (Net)	17r
End of Period																**Deposit Money Banks**	
	268	388	362	449	528	543	1,266	816	2,267	2,423	2,660	5,452	5,253	7,476	6,757	Reserves	20
	127	272	292	43	59	362	526	607	1,302	783	1,392	1,636	1,715	1,984	1,811	Foreign Assets	21
	133	133	154	159	195	190	448	214	423	410	552	470	465	371	540	Claims on Central Government	22a
	15	17	16	17	16	17	16	17	17	17	10	7	6	3	5	Claims on Local Government	22b
	142	300	392	474	486	608	589	789	990	1,130	1,129	1,446	1,424	1,431	1,470	Claims on Nonfin.Pub.Enterprises	22c
	1,166	1,158	1,262	1,363	1,504	1,852	2,766	3,442	4,455	6,858	8,924	11,126	15,806	19,442	22,166	Claims on Private Sector	22d
	84	77	76	93	101	111	290	366	180	256	606	555	965	805	799	Claims on Other Banking Insts.	22f
	381	382	420	419	604	758	1,131	1,453	2,438	2,635	3,551	4,760	5,037	6,588	6,014	Demand Deposits	24
	544	610	650	812	897	1,037	2,256	2,287	3,301	4,580	6,262	9,610	13,322	17,226	19,975	Time Deposits	25
	155	341	314	94	85	115	247	455	206	183	779	812	679	517	804	Foreign Liabilities	26c
	54	39	51	96	86	182	423	324	498	556	733	1,535	2,774	2,568	1,746	Central Government Deposits	26d
	327	447	532	518	569	582	683	706	864	1,026	1,437	1,214	1,103	902	1,334	Credit from Monetary Authorities	26g
	183	212	219	252	281	371	504	640	1,188	1,575	2,122	2,951	3,028	3,388	4,050	Capital Accounts	27a
	291	313	368	408	366	638	658	386	1,137	1,315	385	−192	−309	325	−374	Other Items (Net)	27r
End of Period																**Monetary Survey**	
	−320	−556	−911	−1,232	−1,223	−3,671	−175	−1,607	474	−387	−764	3,408	5,557	7,063	1,247	Foreign Assets (Net)	31n
	2,159	2,494	2,964	3,445	3,680	3,996	5,051	5,721	7,368	9,805	12,119	13,966	17,207	19,907	25,959	Domestic Credit	32
	433	580	755	900	1,045	894	916	473	901	696	767	−588	−2,665	−3,438	−724	Claims on Central Govt. (Net)	32an
	15	17	16	17	16	17	16	17	17	17	10	7	6	3	5	Claims on Local Government	32b
	195	356	529	712	744	817	739	1,074	1,281	1,453	1,463	2,425	2,010	2,170	2,684	Claims on Nonfin.Pub.Enterprises	32c
	1,166	1,158	1,262	1,363	1,504	1,852	2,766	3,442	4,455	6,858	8,924	11,126	15,806	19,442	22,166	Claims on Private Sector	32d
	350	383	403	453	372	416	614	715	715	788	958	996	2,053	1,728	1,826	Claims on Other Banking Insts.	32f
	661	707	784	842	1,247	1,456	2,080	2,773	4,324	5,374	7,587	9,448	11,047	13,549	13,742	Money	34
	544	610	650	812	897	1,037	2,256	2,287	3,301	4,580	6,262	9,610	13,322	17,226	19,975	Quasi-Money	35
	6	1	—	—	8	55	101	156	211	126	138	646	518	196	743	Bonds	36ab
	627	620	619	559	304	−2,222	440	−1,102	5	−662	−2,632	−2,330	−2,122	−4,001	−7,254	Other Items (Net)	37r
	1,205	1,317	1,434	1,654	2,144	2,492	4,335	5,061	7,625	9,954	13,849	19,058	24,368	30,775	33,717	Money plus Quasi-Money	35l
End of Period																**Other Banking Institutions**	
	7	8	11	12	20	33	47	80	130	210	309	327	415	316	329	Cash	40
	51	94	74	82	145	161	164	173	80	13	200	311	277	474	522	Claims on Central Government	42a
	6	8	4	4	4	5	5	5	5	5	5	8	11	10	12	Claims on Nonfin.Pub.Enterprises	42c
	879	1,006	1,412	1,597	1,780	2,255	2,811	3,708	4,725	6,422	7,535	8,828	10,088	10,365	12,263	Claims on Private Sector	42d
	88	131	214	261	300	309	653	687	942	1,059	1,092	1,748	2,589	3,388	2,358	Claims on Deposit Money Banks	42e
	327	395	470	547	619	837	869	1,167	1,386	1,683	1,957	2,706	3,444	3,647	3,679	Time, Savings,& Fgn.Currency Dep.	45
	159	214	513	642	768	944	1,682	2,087	2,499	3,292	3,939	5,018	6,310	6,589	7,290	Bonds	46ab
	39	31	27	23	21	71	69	302	684	82	319	529	620	800	1,192	Long-Term Foreign Liabilities	46cl
	206	241	254	279	308	364	414	410	627	872	926	1,067	1,216	1,641	1,623	Credit from Monetary Authorities	46g
	7	9	15	18	26	20	28	78	68	177	311	298	354	429	424	Credit from Deposit Money Banks	46h
	234	300	319	361	431	529	652	812	1,115	1,429	1,823	2,122	2,554	2,543	2,667	Capital Accounts	47a
	58	58	117	87	76	−3	−33	−204	−497	174	−135	−517	−1,119	−1,096	−1,390	Other Items (Net)	47r

Dominican Republic
243

		1965	1966	1967	1968	1969	1970	1971	1972	1973	1974	1975	1976	1977	1978	1979
Banking Survey																*Millions of Pesos:*
Foreign Assets (Net)	51n	–4	–33	–23	–22	–13	–1	10	26	48	—	27	–14	–35	–79	–112
Domestic Credit	52	....	....	....	....	....	....	581	681	819	1,160	1,324	1,474	1,666	1,929	2,261
Claims on Central Govt. (Net)	52an	....	....	....	....	....	....	205	227	230	303	310	288	313	356	413
Claims on Local Government	52b	....	....	....	....	....	....	2	3	3	2	2	3	6	12	13
Claims on Nonfin.Pub.Enterprises	52c	....	....	....	....	....	....	24	32	47	71	69	61	93	138	142
Claims on Private Sector	52d	....	....	....	....	....	....	350	419	539	784	944	1,121	1,254	1,423	1,692
Liquid Liabilities	55l	....	....	....	....	....	....	352	443	573	811	953	983	1,221	1,215	1,391
Bonds	56ab	....	....	....	....	....	....	6	5	5	5	14	23	41	65	112
Long-Term Foreign Liabilities	56cl	....	....	....	....	....	....	62	53	69	55	69	83	54	109	124
Capital Accounts	57a	....	....	....	....	....	....	169	197	218	244	299	325	356	401	450
Other Items (Net)	57r	....	....	....	....	....	....	2	9	2	43	17	45	–40	60	72
Prices																*Index Numbers (1990=100):*
Consumer Prices	64	3.9	3.9	3.9	3.9	I4.0	4.1	4.3	4.6	5.3	6.0	6.9	7.4	8.4	I8.7	9.5
International Transactions																*Millions of US Dollars*
Exports	70..d	125.5	136.7	156.2	183.0	184.1	249.1	243.0	347.6	442.1	636.8	893.8	716.4	780.4	675.5	868.6
Imports, cif	71..d	97.1	181.5	197.3	222.5	246.4	304.2	357.8	388.4	489.4	807.6	888.6	878.1	975.0	986.9	1,212.8
Imports, fob	71.vd	86.7	160.8	174.7	196.9	217.2	266.8	311.1	337.7	421.9	673.0	772.7	763.6	847.8	859.7	1,054.6
																1990=100
Volume of Exports	72	61	65	69	67	71	83	92	123	134	137	121	131	138	113	133
																1990=100
Export Prices	74..d	40	43	43	36	34	34	22	36	44	67	102	70	78	71	77
Balance of Payments																*Millions of US Dollars:*
Goods: Exports f.o.b.	78aad	....	....	....	163.5	183.4	214.0	240.7	347.6	442.1	636.8	893.8	716.4	780.5	675.5	868.6
Goods: Imports f.o.b.	78abd	....	....	....	–196.8	–217.2	–278.0	–309.7	–337.7	–421.9	–673.0	–772.7	–763.6	–849.3	–862.4	–1,137.5
Trade Balance	78acd	....	....	....	–33.3	–33.8	–64.0	–69.0	9.9	20.2	–36.2	121.1	–47.2	–68.8	–186.9	–268.9
Services: Credit	78add	....	....	....	36.0	43.6	43.0	49.5	63.5	71.5	93.4	116.2	127.8	146.7	152.5	266.3
Services: Debit	78aed	....	....	....	–68.9	–79.5	–86.2	–98.5	–104.1	–142.0	–243.4	–236.3	–226.4	–247.7	–291.6	–346.8
Balance on Goods and Services	78afd	....	....	....	–66.2	–69.7	–107.2	–118.0	–30.7	–50.3	–186.2	1.0	–145.8	–169.8	–326.0	–349.4
Income: Credit	78agd	....	....	....	1.0	1.0	1.5	1.5	1.5	2.8	5.0	5.2	8.9	12.3	20.8	31.9
Income: Debit	78ahd	....	....	....	–20.0	–24.4	–27.4	–30.3	–48.4	–79.7	–94.8	–118.0	–118.1	–110.7	–156.5	–219.6
Balance on Goods, Serv., & Inc.	78aid	....	....	....	–85.2	–93.1	–133.1	–146.8	–77.6	–127.2	–276.0	–111.8	–255.0	–268.2	–461.7	–537.1
Current Transfers, n.i.e.: Credit	78ajd	....	....	....	14.1	11.1	35.4	21.0	34.3	34.0	37.9	41.3	127.5	141.5	150.2	207.5
Current Transfers: Debit	78akd	....	....	....	–4.1	–2.7	–4.2	–3.6	–3.7	–3.4	–2.9	–2.3	–1.7	–1.9	–.4	–1.7
Current Account, n.i.e.	78ald	....	....	....	–75.2	–84.7	–101.9	–129.4	–47.0	–96.6	–241.0	–72.8	–129.2	–128.6	–311.9	–331.3
Capital Account, n.i.e.: Credit	78bad	....	....	....	—	—	—	—	—	—	—	—	—	—	—	—
Capital Account: Debit	78bbd	....	....	....	—	—	—	—	—	—	—	—	—	—	—	—
Capital Account, n.i.e.	78bcd	....	....	....	—	—	—	—	—	—	—	—	—	—	—	—
Direct Investment Abroad	78bdd	....	....	....	—	—	—	—	—	—	—	—	—	—	—	—
Dir. Invest. in Rep. Econ., n.i.e.	78bed	....	....	....	23.0	40.9	71.6	65.0	43.5	34.5	53.6	63.9	60.0	71.5	63.6	17.1
Portfolio Investment Assets	78bfd	....	....	....	—	—	—	—	—	—	—	—	—	—	—	—
Portfolio Investment Liab., n.i.e.	78bgd	....	....	....	—	—	—	—	—	—	—	—	—	—	—	—
Other Investment Assets	78bhd	....	....	....	13.5	–1.6	–2.1	–4.7	–1.0	–1.4	–1.7	–7.2	–5.8	8.1	15.2	–17.3
Other Investment Liab., n.i.e.	78bid	....	....	....	40.4	39.6	39.7	41.8	51.1	36.8	183.5	88.3	104.5	107.5	45.4	267.3
Financial Account, n.i.e.	78bjd	....	....	....	76.9	78.9	109.2	102.1	93.6	69.9	235.4	145.0	158.7	187.1	124.2	267.1
Net Errors and Omissions	78cad	....	....	....	5.2	17.3	–16.8	40.3	–32.8	50.4	1.5	–68.8	–70.9	–16.8	69.2	–73.5
Overall Balance	78cbd	....	....	....	6.9	11.5	–9.5	13.0	13.8	23.7	–4.1	3.4	–41.4	41.7	–118.5	–137.7
Reserves and Related Items	79dad	....	....	....	–6.9	–11.5	9.5	–13.0	–13.8	–23.7	4.1	–3.4	41.4	–41.7	118.5	137.7
Reserve Assets	79dbd	....	....	....	–3.2	–4.2	13.1	–19.5	2.4	–28.4	–4.1	–27.5	–10.4	–66.9	39.0	–72.3
Use of Fund Credit and Loans	79dcd	....	....	....	–7.3	5.3	–8.0	4.2	–7.6	–4.5	—	—	24.8	17.4	—	75.4
Liabs.Constit.For.Auth.Reserves	79ddd	....	....	....	—	—	—	—	—	—	—	4.2	34.2	8.2	6.9	41.3
Exceptional Financing	79ded	....	....	....	3.6	–12.6	4.5	2.3	–8.6	9.2	4.0	–10.1	18.8	.9	82.1	93.2
Government Finance																*Millions of Pesos:*
Deficit (–) or Surplus	80	–31.6	–32.5	–28.0	I–13.3	–16.1	–10.1	–19.7	I–3.2	–20.6	–41.8	56.3	–10.6	–.1	–70.4	–315.0
Revenue	81	117.6	161.8	173.5	I189.6	214.7	244.4	276.4	I361.5	397.5	513.3	694.7	622.4	677.9	694.7	739.0
Grants Received	81z	....	....	....	.6	.1	....	....	I—	....	....	....	....	....	....	.7
Expenditure	82	149.2	194.3	201.5	I203.4	230.9	254.5	296.1	I359.4	412.7	548.2	631.7	632.7	669.3	744.8	968.8
Lending Minus Repayments	83	....	....	....	....	....	....	I5.3	....	5.4	6.9	6.7	.3	8.7	20.3	85.9
Financing																
Net Borrowing	84	31.6	32.5	28.0	I13.3	16.1	10.1	19.7	I3.2	20.6	41.8	–56.3	10.6	.1	70.4	315.0
Domestic	84a	....	....	....	5.2	8.3	–.1	11.3	I–.4	8.1	41.3	–63.6	17.8	–4.4	72.7	105.6
Foreign	85a	....	....	....	8.1	7.8	10.2	8.4	I3.6	12.5	.5	7.3	–7.2	4.5	–2.3	209.4
Debt: Foreign	89a	....	....	....	....	....	....	....	....	....	....	210.9	220.0	235.2	340.2	500.2
National Accounts																*Millions of Pesos*
Exports of Goods & Services	90c	145	161	187	202	227	256	292	411	513	730	1,009	840	918	828	1,135
Government Consumption	91f	173	152	140	149	161	172	169	178	194	292	222	152	189	271	420
Gross Fixed Capital Formation	93e	87	156	161	166	220	246	294	427	498	644	803	780	939	1,032	1,335
Increase/Decrease(–) in Stocks	93i	–2	15	7	–5	31	38	4	–35	20	45	79	101	60	98	60
Private Consumption	96f	719	821	866	904	1,002	1,138	1,318	1,449	1,685	2,139	2,496	3,083	3,589	3,659	4,034
Imports of Goods & Services	98c	–166	–230	–239	–266	–297	–365	–410	–442	–565	–917	–1,010	–1,005	–1,109	–1,154	–1,484
Gross Domestic Product	99b	954	1,074	1,122	1,149	1,345	1,486	1,667	1,987	2,345	2,931	3,599	3,952	4,587	4,734	5,499
Net Factor Inc/Pmts(–) Abroad	98.n	–12	–18	–20	–19	–23	–26	–29	–47	–77	–90	–113	–124	–123	–136	–188
Gross Nat'l Expenditure = GNP	99a	942	1,056	1,102	1,130	1,321	1,460	1,638	1,941	2,268	2,841	3,486	3,828	4,464	4,599	5,311
Nat'l Income, Market Prices	99e	885	992	1,035	1,061	1,242	1,371	1,538	1,821	2,127	2,666	3,270	3,591	4,191	4,323	4,984
Gross Dom. Prod. 1990 Prices	99b.p	17,964	20,319	21,009	21,111	23,689	I25,820	28,627	31,603	35,679	37,820	39,784	42,461	44,574	45,530	47,592
GDP Deflator (1990=100)	99bip	5.3	5.3	5.3	5.4	5.7	5.8	5.8	6.3	6.6	7.8	9.0	9.3	10.3	10.4	11.6
																Millions:
Population	99z	3.51	3.62	3.72	3.83	3.95	4.06	4.20	4.34	4.48	4.61	4.75	4.89	5.03	5.17	5.30

Monetary Authorities: I Beginning in 1967, the agricultural bank was reassigned the responsibility for credit extended by the government-owned commercial bank (Banco de Reservas) to certain government agencies. Also, part of the claims on government of the Banco de Reservas were taken over by the Central Bank. Central bank claims on government include the national currency subscription less obligations to international organizations other than IMF, formerly in *Other Items (Net).*

Deposit Money Banks: I See note to section 10.
Monetary Survey: I See note to section 10.

Prices: I Prior to 1978, data refer only to consumer prices in Santo Domingo.
Government Finance: I Beginning in 1968, data are shown on a cash basis, and comparable data for earlier periods are not available. I Beginning in 1972, data are as reported in the *Government Finance Statistics Yearbook* and cover consolidated central government (including extrabudgetary and social security funds).

Dominican Republic

	1980	1981	1982	1983	1984	1985	1986	1987	1988	1989	1990	1991	1992	1993	1994		
End of Period																**Banking Survey**	
	−320	−556	−911	−1,232	−1,223	−3,671	−175	−1,607	474	−387	−764	3,408	5,557	7,063	1,247	Foreign Assets (Net)	51n
	2,744	3,218	4,051	4,675	5,238	6,000	7,417	8,892	11,462	15,456	18,900	22,117	25,530	29,028	36,929	Domestic Credit	52
	484	674	829	981	1,190	1,055	1,080	646	980	709	967	−277	−2,388	−2,964	−202	Claims on Central Govt. (Net)	52an
	15	17	16	17	16	17	16	17	17	10	7	6	3	5	6	Claims on Local Government	52b
	201	363	533	716	748	821	744	1,079	1,285	1,458	1,468	2,433	2,020	2,180	2,696	Claims on Nonfin.Pub.Enterprises	52c
	2,045	2,164	2,673	2,960	3,283	4,107	5,576	7,150	9,179	13,280	16,459	19,954	25,894	29,807	34,429	Claims on Private Sector	52d
	1,524	1,703	1,893	2,189	2,743	3,297	5,157	6,148	8,881	11,427	15,497	21,437	27,398	34,106	37,066	Liquid Liabilities	55l
	165	214	513	642	776	998	1,783	2,243	2,710	3,418	4,077	5,664	6,828	6,785	8,033	Bonds	56ab
	143	119	92	58	26	85	3,616	5,838	8,485	8,289	15,914	17,310	15,709	15,934	11,455	Long-Term Foreign Liabilities	56cl
	497	578	609	724	843	1,075	1,071	1,362	1,727	1,936	2,314	4,180	6,082	5,009	6,225	Capital Accounts	57a
	94	47	32	−170	−373	−3,125	−4,385	−8,305	−9,868	−10,001	−19,666	−23,066	−24,929	−25,743	−24,603	Other Items (Net)	57r
Period Averages																**Prices**	
	11.1	11.9	12.8	13.4	17.1	23.5	25.8	29.9	43.1	62.7	100.0	153.9	160.9	169.4	183.4	Consumer Prices	64
Millions of US Dollars																**International Transactions**	
	961.9	1,188.0	767.7	785.2	868.1	735.2	717.6	711.3	889.7	924.4	734.5	658.3	562.4	511.0	633.4	Exports	70..d
	1,639.6	1,667.7	1,444.2	1,470.9	1,445.7	1,486.9	1,432.7	1,830.2	1,849.2	2,258.4	2,061.7	1,988.1	2,500.8	2,436.2	2,626.4	Imports, cif	71..d
	1,425.7	1,450.2	1,255.8	1,279.0	1,257.1	1,293.0	1,245.8	1,591.5	1,608.0	1,963.8	1,792.8	1,728.8	2,174.6	2,118.4	2,283.8	Imports, fob	71.vd
1990=100																	
	99	109	104	121	122	109	91	111	114	117	100	95	90	93	89	Volume of Exports	72
Indices of Unit Values in US Dollars																	
	92	118	76	72	83	71	76	63	90	104	100	95	82	75	87	Export Prices	74..d
Minus Sign Indicates Debit																**Balance of Payments**	
	961.9	1,188.0	767.7	785.2	868.1	738.5	722.1	711.3	889.7	924.4	734.5	658.3	562.5	511.5	....	Goods: Exports f.o.b.	78aad
	−1,519.7	−1,451.7	−1,257.3	−1,279.0	−1,257.1	−1,285.9	−1,351.7	−1,591.5	−1,608.0	−1,963.8	−1,792.8	−1,728.8	−2,174.3	−2,118.4	....	Goods: Imports f.o.b.	78abd
	−557.8	−263.7	−489.6	−493.8	−389.0	−547.4	−629.6	−880.2	−718.3	−1,039.4	−1,058.3	−1,070.5	−1,611.8	−1,606.9	....	Trade Balance	78acd
	309.4	324.6	374.1	456.6	501.5	584.3	692.9	852.0	1,013.4	1,152.8	1,270.6	1,320.3	1,530.8	1,827.9	....	Services: Credit	78add
	−399.0	−366.7	−277.3	−298.6	−299.5	−274.5	−283.1	−360.4	−397.0	−464.8	−440.4	−479.3	−577.4	−566.0	....	Services: Debit	78aed
	−647.4	−305.8	−392.8	−335.8	−187.0	−237.6	−219.8	−388.6	−101.9	−351.4	−228.1	−229.5	−658.4	−345.0	....	Balance on Goods and Services	78afd
	41.8	11.8	4.4	6.9	5.8	21.6	17.0	11.6	8.5	107.1	86.3	87.2	54.7	52.4	....	Income: Credit	78agd
	−318.8	−288.4	−259.2	−304.0	−247.2	−247.9	−266.7	−317.7	−279.1	−355.8	−335.0	−279.9	−273.3	−310.0	....	Income: Debit	78ahd
	−924.4	−582.4	−647.6	−632.9	−428.4	−463.9	−469.5	−694.7	−372.5	−600.1	−476.8	−422.2	−877.0	−602.6	....	Balance on Goods, Serv., & Inc.	78aid
	204.8	193.0	205.0	215.0	265.0	356.3	286.1	330.6	353.6	384.4	370.6	386.5	431.8	441.6	....	Current Transfers, n.i.e.: Credit	78ajd
	−.3	—	—	—	—	—	—	—	—	—	—	—	—	—	....	Current Transfers: Debit	78akd
	−719.9	−389.4	−442.6	−417.9	−163.4	−107.6	−183.4	−364.1	−18.9	−215.7	−106.2	−35.7	−445.2	−161.0	....	Current Account, n.i.e.	78ald
	—	—	—	—	—	—	—	—	—	—	—	—	—	—	....	Capital Account, n.i.e.: Credit	78bad
	—	—	—	—	—	—	—	—	—	—	—	—	—	—	....	Capital Account: Debit	78bbd
	—	—	—	—	—	—	—	—	—	—	—	—	—	—	....	Capital Account, n.i.e.	78bcd
	—	—	—	—	—	—	—	—	—	—	—	—	—	—	....	Direct Investment Abroad	78bdd
	92.7	79.7	−1.4	48.2	68.5	36.2	50.0	89.0	106.1	110.0	132.8	145.0	179.7	182.8	....	Dir. Invest. in Rep. Econ., n.i.e.	78bed
	—	—	—	—	—	—	—	—	—	—	—	—	—	—	....	Portfolio Investment Assets	78bfd
	—	—	—	—	—	—	—	—	—	—	—	—	—	—	....	Portfolio Investment Liab., n.i.e.	78bgd
	10.7	6.4	−19.1	−4.9	−19.6	−64.2	34.2	−34.7	−83.0	−98.0	89.3	−196.6	128.8	145.0	....	Other Investment Assets	78bhd
	445.0	319.2	66.2	−115.1	175.2	103.5	136.5	−11.4	−38.7	148.0	−239.3	−86.1	−232.2	−63.4	....	Other Investment Liab., n.i.e.	78bid
	548.4	405.3	45.7	−71.8	224.1	75.5	220.7	42.9	−15.6	160.0	−17.2	−137.7	76.3	264.4	....	Financial Account, n.i.e.	78bjd
	48.0	−54.5	−31.1	10.6	29.7	155.7	82.3	248.9	35.6	−185.2	−294.1	426.7	305.8	−69.1	....	Net Errors and Omissions	78cad
	−123.5	−38.6	−428.0	−479.1	90.4	123.6	119.6	−72.3	1.1	−240.9	−417.5	253.3	−63.1	34.3	....	Overall Balance	78cbd
	123.5	38.6	428.0	479.1	−90.4	−123.6	−119.6	72.3	−1.1	240.9	417.5	−253.3	63.1	−34.3	....	Reserves and Related Items	79ad
	39.5	−16.8	96.9	−46.3	−87.3	−91.9	−18.0	209.7	−58.9	90.0	49.0	−357.4	−63.5	−153.5	....	Reserve Assets	79dbd
	−72.1	−22.0	49.9	185.3	−9.8	49.2	−26.1	−62.9	−51.2	−88.0	−56.9	15.9	37.3	63.9	....	Use of Fund Credit and Loans	79dcd
	77.7	7.7	101.5	−20.9	7.8	−31.9	−49.6	−70.4	—	−22.1	−56.9	3.6	−.9	−9.1	....	Liabs.Constit.For.Auth.Reserves	79ddd
	78.4	69.7	179.7	361.1	−1.1	−49.0	−25.9	−4.1	109.0	261.0	482.0	84.6	90.2	64.4	....	Exceptional Financing	79ded
Year Ending December 31																**Government Finance**	
	−172.9	−181.4	−246.6	−216.4	−114.4	−262.0	76.9	−137.4	−563.4	18.7	347.6	....	....	....	....	Deficit (−) or Surplus	80
	954.0	987.7	823.5	998.9	1,263.1	1,726.9	2,249.2	3,019.4	4,658.7	6,112.3	7,334.3	....	....	....	....	Revenue	81
	1.5	6.6	2.8	1.4	18.7	2.4	208.1	65.7	156.0	67.5	50.0	....	....	....	....	Grants Received	81z
	1,121.9	1,173.9	1,077.2	1,205.3	1,385.1	1,971.0	2,370.0	3,218.3	5,368.5	6,161.3	7,029.1	....	....	....	....	Expenditure	82
	6.5	1.8	−4.3	11.4	11.1	20.3	10.4	4.2	9.6	—	7.6	....	....	....	....	Lending Minus Repayments	83
																Financing	
	172.9	181.4	246.6	216.4	114.4	262.0	−76.9	137.4	563.3	−18.7	−347.6	....	....	....	....	Net Borrowing	84
	76.9	92.6	195.9	172.5	....	....	....	....	....	....	....	....	....	....	....	Domestic	84a
	96.0	88.8	50.7	43.9	....	....	....	....	....	....	....	....	....	....	....	Foreign	85a
	650.4	778.4	871.6	934.9	1,113.5	....	....	....	....	....	....	....	....	....	....	Debt: Foreign	89a
Millions of Pesos																**National Accounts**	
	1,271	1,513	1,142	1,962	3,780	4,088	4,041	5,847	11,000	13,149	16,880	23,588	24,185	27,828	33,153	Exports of Goods & Services	90c
	504	693	779	786	871	1,112	1,297	1,205	1,783	1,824	2,308	4,074	5,681	6,805	9,588	Government Consumption	91f
	1,584	1,655	1,491	1,754	2,169	2,747	3,492	5,319	8,034	11,505	15,041	20,821	25,068	27,869	30,670	Gross Fixed Capital Formation	93e
	82	61	99	62	34	52	85	118	89	100	120	127	150	158	175	Increase/Decrease(−) in Stocks	93i
	5,109	5,163	5,986	6,583	7,906	10,832	11,606	14,543	19,096	31,236	51,309	79,613	91,815	91,684	99,544	Private Consumption	96f
	−1,919	−1,818	−1,533	−2,524	−4,405	−4,859	−4,741	−7,495	−11,649	−15,421	−20,791	−28,153	−34,531	−33,772	−37,005	Imports of Goods & Services	98c
	6,631	7,267	7,964	8,623	10,355	13,972	15,780	19,537	28,353	42,393	64,867	100,070	112,368	120,572	136,125	Gross Domestic Product	99b
	−210	−277	−254	−475	−683	−706	−722	−1,160	−1,651	−1,947	−1,878	−1,862	−3,895	−4,206	−4,616	Net Factor Inc/Pmts(−) Abroad	98.n
	6,421	6,990	7,710	8,148	9,672	13,266	15,058	18,377	26,702	40,446	62,989	98,208	108,473	116,366	131,509	Gross Nat'l Expenditure = GNP	99a
	6,025	6,558	7,236	7,635	9,056	12,435	14,119	17,215	25,015	37,924	59,129	92,254	101,787	109,192	123,341	Nat'l Income, Market Prices	99e
	50,472	52,525	53,347	57,011	57,741	56,507	58,505	64,415	65,806	68,969	64,867	65,406	70,499	72,636	75,748	Gross Dom. Prod. 1990 Prices	99b.p
	13.1	13.8	14.9	15.1	17.9	24.7	27.0	30.3	43.1	61.5	100.0	153.0	159.4	166.0	179.7	GDP Deflator (1990−100)	99bip
Midyear Estimates																	
	5.44	5.54	5.98	6.12	6.27	6.42	6.56	6.71	6.86	7.01	7.17	7.31	7.41	7.61	....	Population	99z

Ecuador

248		1965	1966	1967	1968	1969	1970	1971	1972	1973	1974	1975	1976	1977	1978	1979
Exchange Rates																*Sucres per SDR:*
Principal Rate	aa	18.0	18.0	18.0	18.0	18.0	25.0	27.1	27.1	30.2	30.6	29.3	29.0	30.4	32.6	32.9
																Sucres per US Dollar:
Principal Rate	ae	18.0	18.0	18.0	18.0	18.0	25.0	25.0	25.0	25.0	25.0	25.0	25.0	25.0	25.0	25.0
Principal Rate	rf	18.0	18.0	18.0	18.0	18.0	20.9	25.0	25.0	25.0	25.0	25.0	25.0	25.0	25.0	25.0
																Index Numbers (1990=100):
Principal Rate	ahx	4,229.6	4,229.6	4,229.6	4,229.6	4,229.6	3,676.5	275.6	3,045.3	275.6	3,045.3	3,045.3	3,045.3	3,045.3	3,045.3	3,045.3
Nominal Effective Exchange Rate	ne c	....	....	....	....	....	....	....	....	....	....	....	....	....	....	865.9
Real Effective Exchange Rate	re c	....	....	....	....	....	....	....	....	....	....	....	....	....	....	223.0
Fund Position																*Millions of SDRs:*
Quota	2f. s	20.0	25.0	25.0	25.0	25.0	33.0	33.0	33.0	33.0	33.0	33.0	33.0	33.0	70.0	70.0
SDRs	1b. s	—	—	—	—	—	.1	3.4	6.7	5.6	6.5	6.3	6.3	8.2	10.6	19.2
Reserve Position in the Fund	1c. s	—	—	—	.5	—	—	—	—	5.6	9.2	13.2	—	—	8.0	9.4
Total Fund Cred.&Loans Outstg.	2tl	6.0	11.0	10.2	—	12.3	13.8	5.5	8.3	—	—	—	—	—	—	—
International Liquidity																*Millions of US Dollars Unless Otherwise Indicated:*
Total Reserves minus Gold	1l. d	34.8	50.1	52.0	31.1	42.9	55.2	37.1	121.1	210.4	318.6	253.4	477.4	623.1	635.8	722.0
SDRs	1b. d	—	—	—	—	—	.1	3.6	7.3	6.7	7.9	7.4	7.3	10.0	13.8	25.2
Reserve Position in the Fund	1c. d	—	—	—	.5	—	—	—	—	6.8	11.3	15.5	—	—	10.4	12.4
Foreign Exchange	1d. d	34.8	50.1	52.0	30.6	42.9	55.1	33.5	113.8	196.9	299.4	230.5	470.1	613.1	611.5	684.4
Gold (Million Fine Troy Ounces)	1ad	.320	.314	.489	.749	.632	.546	.533	.355	.386	.386	.386	.386	.400	.407	.414
Gold (National Valuation)	1and	11.2	11.0	17.1	26.2	22.1	19.0	18.6	12.4	16.3	16.3	16.3	16.3	16.9	17.2	17.5
Monetary Authorities: Other Assets	3.. d	....	....	3.7	7.1	8.2	9.0	7.4	8.8	8.2	14.8	16.5	21.4	30.5	33.6	44.8
Other Liab.	4.. d	3.3	2.3	1.1	11.2	7.8	19.2	37.2	9.4	13.9	62.9	62.9	80.6	99.7	84.2	153.2
Deposit Money Banks: Assets	7a. d	....	4.5	4.0	6.4	6.6	.9	3.5	4.6	9.7	14.3	25.7	43.9	74.2	79.8	96.9
Liabilities	7b. d	—	—	—	—	—	—	1.9	4.4	6.4	10.7	14.2	21.8	31.8	33.2	43.0
Other Banking Insts.: Liabilities	7f. d	4.2	7.4	7.0	6.7	6.3	4.7	5.8	7.4	8.6	10.0	15.7	18.8	37.7	21.6	24.0
Monetary Authorities																*Millions of Sucres through 1978;*
Foreign Assets	11	827.2	1,100.5	1,244.5	1,031.9	1,169.4	2,082.0	1,577.5	3,557.8	5,871.3	8,743.8	7,154.8	11,669.8	15,916.0	16,666.4	I 19.2
Claims on Central Government	12a	860.1	1,120.7	1,006.1	1,426.0	2,488.0	3,269.0	3,430.7	4,236.7	4,434.6	6,280.2	6,003.9	5,958.0	5,206.0	4,163.0	I 4.1
Claims on Nonfin.Pub.Enterprises	12c	—	—	—	—	—	—	—	—	—	—	—	I—	—	—	I—
Claims on Private Sector	12d	562.2	584.6	549.1	711.7	824.8	1,094.2	1,154.0	1,055.9	1,057.0	1,406.2	2,178.5	3,329.0	4,050.0	5,867.0	I 8.6
Claims on Deposit Money Banks	12e	79.2	47.3	92.0	100.3	106.2	128.2	51.6	65.4	108.4	402.2	765.5	1,323.0	2,578.0	5,020.0	I 6.7
Claims on Other Banking Insts.	12f	216.7	216.5	228.3	267.0	479.2	473.2	514.1	502.1	748.3	1,852.3	3,504.5	I 4,318.0	3,913.0	4,008.0	I 5.3
Reserve Money	14	2,012.6	2,259.1	2,397.5	2,891.6	3,419.8	4,504.6	4,986.2	6,457.3	9,112.8	12,896.5	12,828.1	I 15715.0	19,105.0	22,294.0	I 28.6
of which: Currency Outside DMBs	14a	1,236.1	1,347.2	1,403.7	1,600.4	1,747.4	2,329.2	2,414.1	2,889.8	3,617.8	4,776.3	5,385.7	7,569.6	9,126.4	10,274.2	I 12.3
Private Sector Deposits	14d	230.5	236.3	264.2	424.0	507.8	704.3	801.8	1,355.2	2,178.5	3,897.8	3,060.0	I 1,664.0	3,838.0	3,146.0	I 6.4
Time & Foreign Currency Deposits	15	10.5	6.3	10.6	11.4	16.6	15.7	28.1	39.4	24.6	222.1	591.8	I 978.0	553.0	818.0	I 3.4
Bonds	16ab	—	—	—	—	—	—	—	3.0	360.0	183.4	327.5	474.0	1,679.0	1,613.0	I 1.5
Restricted Deposits	16b	189.0	310.1	365.7	435.9	952.1	1,180.5	693.0	1,148.9	13.5	7.5	859.0	2,643.0	2,846.0	2,459.0	I 2.9
Foreign Liabilities	16c	167.7	239.5	203.1	201.8	361.6	823.3	1,079.6	457.8	347.6	1,572.8	1,571.5	2,016.0	2,492.0	2,104.0	I 3.8
Long-Term Foreign Liabilities	16cl	—	—	—	—	—	—	—	—	—	—	—	—	—	—	I—
Central Government Deposits	16d	206.4	341.2	409.5	256.6	681.9	948.6	679.5	1,548.1	2,642.9	4,496.5	5,769.1	5,184.0	5,448.0	7,862.0	I 6.2
Central Govt. Lending Funds	16f	....	....	....	....	....	....	....	....	....	....	285.0	299.0	306.0	361.0	I .4
Capital Accounts	17a	90.6	93.2	94.4	106.0	95.7	205.3	298.8	399.6	508.1	1,035.5	1,009.2	1,141.0	1,020.0	1,442.0	I 1.8
Other Items (Net)	17r	-131.4	-179.8	-360.8	-366.4	-460.1	-631.4	-1,037.3	-636.2	-789.9	-1,729.6	-3,634.0	I -1852.2	-1,786.0	-3,228.6	I -4.7
Deposit Money Banks																*Millions of Sucres through 1978;*
Reserves	20	556.0	775.5	854.7	1,060.4	1,394.0	1,681.5	2,101.9	2,463.4	3,366.6	4,682.2	5,437.0	7,247.7	8,599.9	9,747.9	I 10.4
Foreign Assets	21	....	80.7	72.8	115.2	119.0	22.6	87.1	114.2	242.3	357.6	642.9	1,097.4	1,854.0	1,996.2	I 2.4
Claims on Central Government	22a	....	2.0	6.0	6.6	16.8	32.7	42.9	40.1	66.4	125.0	128.5	153.5	130.4	55.4	I .1
Claims on Private Sector	22d	2,646.0	I 2,707.2	3,281.4	3,889.3	4,094.8	4,873.8	5,418.4	6,260.5	7,615.8	9,826.6	12,195.5	16,024.4	21,883.6	26,848.3	I 33.8
Claims on Other Banking Insts.	22f	—	1.1	.3	.2	2.8	63.4	136.6	176.2	273.4	336.5	383.8	449.5	568.1	571.2	I .6
Demand Deposits	24	1,203.0	1,432.7	1,770.9	2,147.5	2,496.0	2,955.1	3,502.7	4,131.4	5,502.5	8,191.6	9,897.2	13,575.2	16,911.6	19,499.7	I 23.2
Time and Savings Deposits	25	605.0	824.7	1,010.4	1,379.9	1,530.6	1,730.2	2,147.3	2,555.5	3,107.0	3,944.7	4,148.7	5,028.0	5,534.0	6,002.3	I 6.9
Bonds	26ab	1,021.0	1,076.6	1,210.3	1,331.6	1,408.8	1,455.7	1,619.4	1,844.3	2,135.0	2,567.7	3,370.7	4,102.7	4,708.8	5,397.3	I 6.3
Foreign Liabilities	26c	—	—	.1	.4	.6	—	47.7	110.8	161.1	267.7	354.3	544.6	794.5	830.2	I 1.1
Credit from Monetary Authorities	26g	—	33.3	67.3	85.8	90.8	122.5	42.2	55.2	79.0	192.6	376.4	829.9	2,956.6	4,325.3	I 5.4
Capital Accounts	27a	....	413.0	485.0	548.3	633.6	764.4	900.9	991.1	1,172.7	1,412.2	1,879.2	2,348.6	3,085.2	4,207.9	I 5.5
Other Items (Net)	27r	373.0	I -213.8	-328.8	-421.8	-533.0	-353.9	-473.3	-633.9	-592.8	-1,248.6	-1,238.8	-1,456.5	-954.7	-1,043.7	I -1.1
Monetary Survey																*Millions of Sucres through 1978;*
Foreign Assets (Net)	31n	687.0	941.7	1,114.1	944.9	926.2	1,281.3	537.3	3,103.4	5,604.9	7,260.9	5,871.9	10,206.6	14,483.5	15,728.4	I 16.8
Domestic Credit	32	3,996.0	I 4,322.2	4,707.0	6,092.2	7,273.0	8,899.5	10,054.0	10,741.7	11,576.6	16,558.3	20,347.4	25,080.2	30,344.7	33,684.8	I 46.2
Claims on Central Govt. (Net)	32an	570.0	781.5	602.6	1,176.0	1,822.9	2,353.1	2,794.1	2,728.7	1,858.1	1,908.7	363.3	927.5	-111.6	-3,643.6	I -2.1
Claims on Local Government	32b	....	110.3	125.7	156.3	297.3	261.3	366.5	581.8	897.3	2,055.7	2,593.1	31.8	41.6	33.9	I—
Claims on Nonfin.Pub.Enterprises	32c	....	....	....	....	....	....	....	....	....	....	....	—	—	—	I—
Claims on Private Sector	32d	3,208.2	I 3,291.8	3,830.5	4,601.0	4,919.6	5,968.0	6,572.4	7,316.4	8,672.8	11,232.8	14,374.0	19,353.4	25,933.6	32,715.3	I 42.3
Claims on Other Banking Insts.	32f	....	217.6	228.6	267.2	482.0	536.6	650.7	678.3	1,021.7	2,188.8	3,888.3	4,767.5	4,481.1	4,579.2	I 5.9
Money	34	2,669.6	3,016.2	3,438.8	4,171.9	4,751.2	5,988.6	6,718.6	8,376.4	11,298.8	16,865.7	18,342.9	22,808.8	29,876.0	32,919.9	I 42.0
Quasi-Money	35	615.5	831.0	1,021.0	1,391.3	1,547.2	1,745.9	2,175.4	2,594.9	3,131.6	4,166.8	4,740.5	6,006.0	6,087.0	6,820.3	I 10.2
Bonds	36ab	1,021.0	1,076.6	1,210.3	1,331.6	1,408.8	1,455.7	1,619.4	1,847.3	2,495.0	2,751.1	3,698.2	4,576.7	6,387.8	7,010.3	I 7.8
Restricted Deposits	36b	189.0	310.1	365.7	435.9	952.1	1,180.5	693.0	1,148.9	13.5	7.5	859.0	2,643.0	2,846.0	2,459.0	I 2.9
Long-Term Foreign Liabilities	36cl	—	—	—	—	—	—	—	—	—	—	—	—	—	—	I—
Central Govt. Lending Funds	36f	....	....	....	....	....	....	....	....	....	....	285.0	299.0	306.0	361.0	I .4
Capital Accounts	37a	....	506.2	579.4	654.3	729.3	969.7	1,199.7	1,390.7	1,680.8	2,447.7	2,888.4	3,489.6	4,105.2	5,649.9	I 7.3
Other Items (Net)	37r	187.9	I -476.2	-794.1	-947.9	-1,189.4	-1,159.6	-1,814.8	-1,513.1	-1,438.2	-2,419.6	-4,594.7	-4,536.3	-4,779.8	-5,807.2	I -7.6
Money plus Quasi-Money	35l	3,285.1	3,847.2	4,459.8	5,563.2	6,298.4	7,734.5	8,894.0	10,971.3	14,430.4	21,032.5	23,083.4	28,814.8	35,963.0	39,740.2	I 52.2
Other Banking Institutions																*Millions of Sucres through 1978;*
Cash	40	....	91.8	83.4	106.7	109.4	153.7	179.4	238.8	271.1	451.5	339.9	634.5	745.4	994.3	I 1.0
Claims on Private Sector	42d	1,038.0	I 1,072.8	1,169.0	1,310.6	1,565.4	1,659.3	1,860.1	2,088.7	2,889.1	5,425.6	7,920.2	9,741.8	10,458.5	11,221.3	I 11.7
Claims on Deposit Money Banks	42e	—	1.1	.3	.2	2.8	3.6	6.5	8.0	293.4	434.5	638.7	748.7	1,111.1	1,249.2	I 1.3
Demand Deposits	44	64.0	73.0	73.0	77.0	79.0	105.0	133.0	179.0	264.0	505.0	531.0	804.0	879.0	1,006.0	I .9
Time and Savings Deposits	45	9.3	70.2	73.2	91.4	110.8	132.4	194.8	325.6	501.4	1,063.6	1,370.4	2,009.8	2,485.8	2,129.7	I 2.3
Bonds	46ab	....	56.0	45.0	34.6	25.0	17.4	10.8	6.4	3.7	1.6	.8	—	—	—	I—
Long-Term Foreign Liabilities	46cl	75.0	132.7	125.8	121.1	114.0	116.5	144.8	185.4	214.3	251.1	392.6	469.3	942.5	539.9	I .6
Central Government Deposits	46d	....	—	—	—	—	—	—	—	—	—	—	—	—	—	I—
Credit from Monetary Authorities	46g	201.6	222.3	228.5	267.4	525.2	452.5	519.4	530.3	854.6	1,981.8	3,418.9	4,453.9	3,304.1	3,042.2	I 3.8
Credit from Deposit Money Banks	46h	....	47.9	59.5	72.4	72.4	88.4	126.2	167.8	212.9	312.9	379.8	455.3	580.9	566.4	I .3
Capital Accounts	47a	540.0	499.4	557.0	573.4	642.2	694.3	732.7	693.2	838.8	1,631.9	1,991.9	2,348.8	2,591.6	4,830.5	I 4.8
Other Items (Net)	47r	148.1	I 64.2	90.7	180.2	109.3	210.2	184.1	247.6	564.1	563.4	813.3	583.8	1,531.4	1,349.9	I 1.2

Ecuador

	1980	1981	1982	1983	1984	1985	1986	1987	1988	1989	1990	1991	1992	1993	1994		
Exchange Rates																	
End of Period	31.9	29.1	36.6	56.6	65.8	105.2	179.2	314.2	582.0	852.1	1,249.4	1,817.5	2,535.8	2,807.3	3,312.4	Principal Rate	aa
End of Period (ae) Period Average (rf)	25.0	25.0	33.2	54.1	67.2	95.8	146.5	221.5	432.5	648.4	878.2	1,270.6	1,844.3	2,043.8	2,269.0	Principal Rate	ae
	25.0	25.0	30.0	44.1	62.5	69.6	122.8	170.5	301.6	526.3	767.8	1,046.2	1,534.0	1,919.1	2,196.7	Principal Rate	rf
Period Averages	3,045.3	3,045.3	2,583.6	1,770.4	1,223.3	1,105.1	634.4	455.2	267.9	146.6	100.0	73.1	50.9	39.5	34.7	Principal Rate	ahx
	915.4	1,022.5	974.2	715.4	506.3	469.3	342.1	228.5	133.4	114.5	100.0	86.6	68.1	65.2	68.2	Nominal Effective Exchange Rate	nec
	226.1	252.8	247.4	235.5	194.4	201.9	162.5	125.0	93.9	108.6	100.0	105.0	105.7	121.5	128.8	Real Effective Exchange Rate	rec
Fund Position																	
End of Period	105.0	105.0	105.0	150.7	150.7	150.7	150.7	150.7	150.7	150.7	150.7	150.7	219.2	219.2	219.2	Quota	2f. s
	19.0	28.9	—	.1	.5	26.2	45.7	.7	1.0	.7	10.3	28.9	.1	3.2	3.0	SDRs	1b. s
	21.8	24.8	—	11.4	—	—	—	—	—	—	—	—	17.1	17.1	17.1	Reserve Position in the Fund	1c. s
	—	—	—	203.5	242.9	327.3	397.7	345.2	300.7	247.2	186.0	127.5	72.6	51.8	135.7	Total Fund Cred.&Loans Outstg.	2tl
International Liquidity																	
End of Period	1,013.0	632.4	304.2	644.5	611.2	718.2	644.1	491.1	397.6	540.4	838.5	924.3	868.2	1,379.9	1,844.2	Total Reserves minus Gold	1l. d
	24.2	33.6	—	.1	.5	28.8	55.9	.9	1.3	.9	14.7	41.4	.1	4.3	4.3	SDRs	1b. d
	27.8	28.8	—	12.0	—	—	—	—	—	—	—	—	23.6	23.5	25.0	Reserve Position in the Fund	1c. d
	961.0	570.0	304.2	632.4	610.7	689.4	588.2	490.2	396.3	539.5	823.8	882.9	844.5	1,352.1	1,814.9	Foreign Exchange	1d. d
	.414	.414	.414	.414	.414	.414	.414	.414	.414	.414	.414	.443	.443	.443	.414	Gold (Million Fine Troy Ounces)	1ad
	17.5	17.5	124.3	124.3	124.3	124.3	124.3	165.7	165.7	165.7	165.7	165.7	165.7	165.6	165.6	Gold (National Valuation)	1and
	53.4	29.7	28.6	31.0	20.1	38.4	42.0	21.1	...	...	...	...	...	...	...	Monetary Authorities: Other Assets	3..d
	227.5	115.0	245.6	1,286.1	2,043.8	3,532.8	2,501.3	1,635.0	3,343.1	2,214.8	1,568.5	1,391.0	881.6	4,138.5	4,111.6	Other Liab.	4..d
	115.4	135.6	127.6	171.7	73.5	63.6	65.6	67.2	63.1	66.2	78.2	86.3	118.6	...	...	Deposit Money Banks: Assets	7a. d
	40.3	58.1	40.7	42.7	64.3	51.6	53.1	88.2	55.3	54.5	55.4	65.9	77.3	...	...	Liabilities	7b. d
	32.5	38.5	47.2	44.6	43.0	46.0	113.4	178.3	200.8	228.5	243.4	226.4	259.7	...	...	Other Banking Insts.: Liabilities	7f. d
Monetary Authorities																	
Billions of Sucres Beginning 1979: End of Period	26.8	16.7	14.8	42.6	49.3	82.2	73.7	57.4	229.2	282.3	389.4	447.8	422.1	3,037.0	4,488.7	Foreign Assets	11
	3.7	3.5	3.8	71.9	84.7	140.5	142.4	184.3	644.9	631.8	621.0	940.8	1,238.1	8,021.3	9,124.5	Claims on Central Government	12a
	—	—	.2	—	—	—	—	—	—	—	—	—	—	—	—	Claims on Nonfin.Pub.Enterprises	12c
	11.4	17.3	16.3	19.0	24.0	24.6	19.3	16.1	24.1	47.6	49.9	30.5	26.3	29.9	48.1	Claims on Private Sector	12d
	9.0	14.2	21.7	47.7	79.5	81.8	89.1	88.4	71.7	64.5	45.5	26.0	20.3	12.3	9.1	Claims on Deposit Money Banks	12e
	7.6	11.4	13.9	28.5	53.0	63.8	77.0	79.2	78.7	101.3	120.5	152.3	171.3	146.9	26.5	Claims on Other Banking Insts.	12f
	33.7	35.9	39.0	48.2	66.3	82.8	111.9	156.7	264.2	387.1	653.7	1,016.1	1,424.8	2,318.2	2,770.2	Reserve Money	14
	15.3	17.4	20.5	25.4	35.3	42.7	54.6	74.8	124.0	176.3	272.7	383.9	597.3	...	...	of which: Currency Outside DMBs	14a
	7.6	8.1	6.5	11.1	11.4	12.1	17.1	27.7	40.1	70.8	149.6	283.3	309.6	706.2	927.0	Private Sector Deposits	14d
	4.2	4.8	8.4	6.3	12.0	14.3	14.6	21.9	70.7	78.2	80.5	8.8	49.5	131.9	145.6	Time & Foreign Currency Deposits	15
	1.8	1.1	2.0	1.5	1.1	5.6	5.3	24.1	16.9	52.4	101.6	90.9	215.2	355.4	332.6	Bonds	16ab
	3.8	5.1	9.6	17.0	26.2	11.5	10.7	27.2	46.0	10.7	2.2	.8	.7	.7	.6	Restricted Deposits	16b
	5.7	2.9	8.1	34.5	38.8	67.0	107.2	141.0	331.3	299.7	301.1	297.9	248.9	621.4	717.4	Foreign Liabilities	16c
	—	—	—	46.6	114.5	305.7	330.5	329.6	1,289.6	1,347.0	1,308.7	1,701.2	1,561.1	7,982.1	9,061.5	Long-Term Foreign Liabilities	16cl
	7.5	11.4	6.5	83.1	124.2	99.6	92.4	85.5	182.1	265.1	496.0	517.0	772.7	1,349.9	1,869.2	Central Government Deposits	16d
	.3	.5	.7	1.9	1.5	1.5	2.3	3.7	11.2	22.5	27.0	36.7	68.3	84.4	94.5	Central Govt. Lending Funds	16f
	3.7	4.5	5.2	5.0	5.4	7.7	8.2	9.7	21.8	23.7	25.6	37.2	39.3	622.0	779.5	Capital Accounts	17a
	-2.2	-2.8	-9.0	-34.1	-99.5	-202.7	-281.5	-374.0	-1,185.3	-1,359.0	-1,774.2	-2,109.4	-2,502.5	-2,218.5	-2,074.2	Other Items (Net)	17r
Deposit Money Banks																	
Billions of Sucres Beginning 1979: End of Period	13.0	12.7	13.9	17.4	31.6	36.4	47.8	56.3	104.2	152.1	241.4	397.2	643.6	...	...	Reserves	20
	2.9	3.4	4.2	9.3	4.9	6.1	9.6	14.9	27.3	42.9	68.7	109.7	218.6	...	...	Foreign Assets	21
	—	—	—	—	—	2.0	3.7	.6	1.3	.3	11.4	9.8	19.6	...	...	Claims on Central Government	22a
	42.8	54.8	78.0	131.9	177.8	223.6	264.0	343.2	418.0	568.2	894.1	1,493.0	2,394.7	...	...	Claims on Private Sector	22d
	.7	.8	1.1	1.4	2.0	3.2	4.6	6.9	11.0	15.6	23.6	40.4	63.2	...	...	Claims on Other Banking Insts.	22f
	30.7	36.3	46.1	58.6	82.3	98.4	111.7	143.7	208.6	292.7	430.6	666.4	953.3	...	...	Demand Deposits	24
	8.3	9.1	12.1	16.5	28.2	49.5	70.2	115.8	178.3	264.4	423.8	704.2	1,321.2	...	...	Time and Savings Deposits	25
	8.8	11.4	13.8	17.2	25.8	67.0	89.8	117.6	139.0	210.0	395.5	606.5	861.7	...	...	Bonds	26ab
	1.0	1.5	1.3	2.3	4.3	4.9	7.8	19.5	23.9	35.4	48.6	83.7	142.5	...	...	Foreign Liabilities	26c
	7.0	9.8	15.4	53.4	70.2	65.6	69.6	68.0	53.3	38.5	20.3	8.3	6.1	...	...	Credit from Monetary Authorities	26g
	7.0	9.1	10.7	13.7	18.8	25.6	36.3	49.6	83.8	124.9	196.6	386.0	659.5	...	...	Capital Accounts	27a
	-3.4	-5.4	-2.2	-1.7	-13.3	-39.8	-55.7	-92.4	-125.0	-187.0	-276.3	-405.1	-604.9	...	...	Other Items (Net)	27r
Monetary Survey																	
Billions of Sucres Beginning 1979: End of Period	23.0	15.8	9.5	15.1	11.1	16.4	-31.6	-88.3	-98.7	-9.9	108.3	175.8	249.3	...	...	Foreign Assets (Net)	31n
	58.9	76.8	106.7	169.8	217.3	358.1	418.6	544.7	995.8	1,099.7	1,224.4	2,149.8	3,140.3	...	...	Domestic Credit	32
	-3.7	-7.8	-2.7	-11.1	-39.6	42.9	53.7	99.4	464.0	367.0	136.3	433.6	484.9	...	...	Claims on Central Govt. (Net)	32an
	—	.2	—	—	—	—	—	—	—	—	—	—	—	...	...	Claims on Local Government	32b
	—	—	—	—	—	—	—	—	—	—	—	—	—	...	...	Claims on Nonfin.Pub.Enterprises	32c
	54.2	72.2	94.3	151.0	201.8	248.2	283.3	359.3	442.1	615.8	944.0	1,523.5	2,421.0	...	...	Claims on Private Sector	32d
	8.4	12.3	15.0	29.9	55.0	66.9	81.6	86.1	89.7	116.9	144.1	192.7	234.5	...	...	Claims on Other Banking Insts.	32f
	53.6	61.8	73.1	95.1	129.1	153.2	183.4	246.2	372.6	539.8	852.9	1,333.6	1,860.2	...	...	Money	34
	12.6	13.9	20.5	22.9	40.2	63.8	84.8	137.7	249.0	342.6	504.3	713.1	1,370.7	...	...	Quasi-Money	35
	10.6	12.5	15.8	18.7	26.8	72.6	95.1	141.7	155.9	262.4	497.1	697.4	1,077.0	...	...	Bonds	36ab
	3.8	5.1	9.6	17.0	26.2	11.5	10.7	27.2	46.0	10.7	2.2	.8	.7	...	...	Restricted Deposits	36b
	—	—	—	46.6	114.5	305.7	330.5	329.6	1,289.6	1,347.0	1,308.7	1,701.2	1,561.1	...	...	Long-Term Foreign Liabilities	36cl
	.3	.5	.7	1.9	1.5	1.5	2.3	3.7	11.2	22.5	27.0	36.7	68.3	...	...	Central Govt. Lending Funds	36f
	10.7	13.6	15.9	18.7	24.2	33.3	44.6	59.3	105.6	148.6	222.2	423.2	698.8	...	...	Capital Accounts	37a
	-9.7	-14.8	-19.4	-35.9	-134.1	-267.0	-364.4	-488.9	-1,332.8	-1,583.8	-2,081.6	-2,580.4	-3,247.3	...	...	Other Items (Net)	37r
	66.2	75.7	93.6	118.0	169.3	217.0	268.2	383.9	621.6	882.4	1,357.2	2,046.7	3,231.0	...	...	Money plus Quasi-Money	35l
Other Banking Institutions																	
Billions of Sucres Beginning 1979: End of Period	1.4	2.1	1.0	1.9	1.6	2.5	4.8	12.3	5.9	9.6	12.4	11.2	44.5	...	...	Cash	40
	13.2	15.4	14.8	22.2	31.9	46.4	78.1	104.9	165.5	302.6	417.3	577.2	942.2	...	...	Claims on Private Sector	42d
	1.3	1.5	1.8	1.9	2.4	3.4	4.1	5.3	5.9	11.6	18.7	23.8	41.3	...	...	Claims on Deposit Money Banks	42e
	1.2	1.2	1.3	1.7	2.5	3.2	4.2	5.5	6.9	8.2	12.4	18.3	23.5	...	...	Demand Deposits	44
	3.1	4.4	4.1	5.7	7.0	10.1	15.3	19.4	22.1	30.2	44.9	57.7	95.4	...	...	Time and Savings Deposits	45
	—	.5	1.1	2.3	4.1	5.5	11.8	12.2	11.8	14.7	16.2	25.2	61.9	...	...	Bonds	46ab
	.8	1.0	1.6	2.4	2.9	4.4	16.6	39.5	86.9	148.1	213.7	287.7	478.9	...	...	Long-Term Foreign Liabilities	46cl
	—	—	—	—	—	—	—	—	—	—	—	—	—	...	...	Central Government Deposits	46d
	4.6	5.4	5.6	7.7	9.5	14.6	23.1	26.3	31.7	75.2	98.6	124.6	159.5	...	...	Credit from Monetary Authorities	46g
	.6	.8	.8	.9	1.2	1.9	1.8	1.6	1.6	6.4	7.2	14.8	32.6	...	...	Credit from Deposit Money Banks	46h
	4.7	5.0	4.3	4.5	8.0	14.8	15.3	15.9	13.9	35.8	45.7	69.0	190.4	...	...	Capital Accounts	47a
	.7	.8	-1.1	1.0	.6	-2.1	-1.0	2.1	2.4	5.3	9.7	14.9	-14.3	...	...	Other Items (Net)	47r

Ecuador
248

		1965	1966	1967	1968	1969	1970	1971	1972	1973	1974	1975	1976	1977	1978	1979
Banking Survey													*Millions of Sucres through 1978;*			
Foreign Assets (Net)	51n	687.0	941.7	1,114.1	944.9	926.2	1,281.3	537.3	3,103.4	5,604.9	7,260.9	5,871.9	10,206.6	14,483.5	15,728.4	I 16.8
Domestic Credit	52	....	5,177.4	5,647.4	7,135.6	8,356.4	10,022.2	11,263.4	12,152.1	13,444.0	19,795.1	24,379.3	30,054.5	36,322.1	40,326.9	I 52.0
Claims on Central Govt. (Net)	52an	570.0	781.5	602.6	1,176.0	1,822.9	2,353.1	2,794.1	2,728.7	1,858.1	1,908.7	363.3	927.5	–111.6	–3,643.6	I –2.1
Claims on Local Government	52b	....	110.3	125.7	156.3	297.3	261.3	366.5	581.8	897.3	2,055.7	2,593.1	31.8	41.6	33.9	I —
Claims on Nonfin.Pub.Enterprises	52c												—	—	—	I —
Claims on Private Sector	52d	4,246.2	4,364.6	4,999.5	5,911.6	6,485.0	7,627.3	8,432.5	9,405.1	11,561.9	16,658.4	22,294.2	29,095.2	36,392.1	43,936.6	I 54.0
Liquid Liabilities	55l	3,358.4	3,898.6	4,522.6	5,624.9	6,378.8	7,818.2	9,042.4	11,237.1	14,924.7	22,149.6	24,644.9	30,994.1	38,582.4	41,881.6	I 54.4
Bonds	56ab	....	1,132.6	1,255.3	1,366.2	1,433.8	1,473.1	1,630.2	1,853.7	2,498.7	2,752.7	3,699.0	4,576.7	6,387.8	7,010.3	I 7.8
Restricted Deposits	56b	189.0	310.1	365.7	435.9	952.1	1,180.5	693.0	1,148.9	13.5	7.5	859.0	2,643.0	2,846.0	2,459.0	I 2.9
Long-Term Foreign Liabilities	56cl	75.0	132.7	125.8	121.1	114.0	116.5	144.8	185.4	214.3	251.1	392.6	469.3	942.5	539.9	I .6
Central Govt. Lending Funds	56f											285.0	299.0	306.0	361.0	I .4
Capital Accounts	57a	....	1,005.6	1,136.4	1,227.7	1,371.5	1,664.0	1,932.4	2,083.9	2,519.6	4,079.6	4,880.3	5,838.4	6,696.8	10,480.4	I 12.1
Other Items (Net)	57r	....	–360.5	–644.3	–695.3	–967.6	–948.8	–1,642.1	–1,253.5	–1,121.9	–2,184.5	–4,509.6	–4,559.5	–4,955.6	–6,677.1	I –9.5
Interest Rates														*Percent Per Annum*		
Discount Rate (End of Period)	60						8.00	8.00	8.00	8.00	8.00	8.00	8.00	8.00	8.00	8.00
Deposit Rate	60l	....	....	....	....	....	....	....	....	....	....	....	....	....	....	....
Lending Rate	60p	....	....	....	....	....	....	....	....	....	....	....	....	....	....	....
Prices and Production													*Index Numbers (1990=100):*			
Wholesale Prices	63										3.0	3.4	3.9	4.3	5.0	5.5
Consumer Prices	64	1.1	I 1.1	1.2	1.2	1.3	1.4	1.5	1.6	I 1.8	2.2	2.6	2.9	3.2	3.6	4.0
Crude Petroleum Production	66aa	2.8	2.5	2.1	1.7	1.5	1.4	1.3	27.0	71.9	61.0	55.4	64.5	63.2	69.4	73.7
International Transactions													*Millions of US Dollars*			
Exports	70..d	164.1	154.6	189.6	226.3	193.0	189.9	199.1	326.3	532.0	1,123.5	973.9	1,257.5	1,436.3	1,557.5	2,104.2
Imports, cif	71..d	165.5	174.1	214.2	255.5	241.8	273.9	340.1	318.5	397.3	678.2	987.0	958.3	1,188.5	1,505.1	1,599.7
Imports, fob	71.vd	144.2	151.8	186.3	222.0	209.0	238.3	297.4	274.9	344.6	589.8	863.8	850.2	1,041.5	1,324.8	1,416.8
																1990=100
Volume of Exports	72	14.9	14.0	17.7	16.8	15.0	18.0	17.3	46.7	101.1	74.1	67.1	74.3	58.5	71.3	70.3
																1990=100:
Export Prices	74..d	24.2	21.6	24.4	20.8	16.1	21.9	22.7	19.0	24.1	61.5	60.9	66.0	74.6	70.6	115.5
Balance of Payments													*Millions of US Dollars:*			
Goods: Exports f.o.b.	78aa d												1,307.2	1,400.8	1,529.2	2,150.5
Goods: Imports f.o.b.	78ab d												–1,047.9	–1,360.5	–1,704.0	–2,096.8
Trade Balance	78ac d												259.3	40.3	–174.8	53.7
Services: Credit	78ad d												111.4	201.9	174.3	260.2
Services: Debit	78ae d												–268.2	–425.5	–474.9	–569.4
Balance on Goods and Services	78af d												102.5	–183.3	–475.4	–255.5
Income: Credit	78ag d												13.2	23.5	34.9	62.2
Income: Debit	78ah d												–153.0	–219.8	–303.7	–466.8
Balance on Goods, Serv., & Inc.	78ai d												–37.3	–379.6	–744.2	–660.1
Current Transfers, n.i.e.: Credit	78aj d												29.7	42.2	43.3	31.7
Current Transfers: Debit	78ak d												–2.0	–6.0	–2.4	–1.9
Current Account, n.i.e.	78al d												–9.6	–343.4	–703.3	–630.3
Capital Account, n.i.e.: Credit	78ba d												3.0	—	—	—
Capital Account: Debit	78bb d												—	—	—	—
Capital Account, n.i.e.	78bc d												3.0	—	—	—
Direct Investment Abroad	78bd d												—	—	—	—
Dir. Invest. in Rep. Econ., n.i.e.	78be d												–19.9	34.5	48.6	63.4
Portfolio Investment Assets	78bf d												—	—	—	—
Portfolio Investment Liab., n.i.e.	78bg d												5.7	52.0	—	—
Other Investment Assets	78bh d												–102.2	–41.0	–104.2	–33.8
Other Investment Liab., n.i.e.	78bi d												309.6	467.1	702.9	617.6
Financial Account, n.i.e.	78bj d												193.2	512.6	647.3	647.2
Net Errors and Omissions	78ca d												–13.2	–47.9	46.3	8.5
Overall Balance	78cb d												173.4	121.3	–9.7	25.4
Reserves and Related Items	79da d												–173.4	–121.3	9.7	–25.4
Reserve Assets	79db d												–203.2	–112.1	–5.5	–44.2
Use of Fund Credit and Loans	79dc d												—	—	—	—
Liabs.Constit.For.Auth.Reserves	79dd d												29.8	–9.2	15.2	18.8
Exceptional Financing	79de d												—	—	—	—
Government Finance													*Millions of Sucres through 1978;*			
Deficit (–) or Surplus	80	–626.0	–626.0	–378.0	–1,231.0	–1,255.0	–1,545.0	–1,733.0	–893.0	I 124.0	–3.0	–666.0	–2,160.0	–5,388.0	–2,296.0	I –1.5
Revenue	81	1,998.0	2,205.0	2,649.0	2,554.0	2,945.0	3,716.0	4,423.0	5,514.0	I 7,973.0	11,390.0	12,391.0	14,653.0	16,452.0	19,057.0	I 23.1
Exp. & Lending Minus Repay.	82z	2,624.0	2,831.0	3,027.0	3,785.0	4,200.0	5,261.0	6,156.0	6,407.0	I 7,849.0	11,393.0	13,057.0	16,813.0	21,840.0	21,353.0	I 24.6
Financing																
Net Borrowing: Domestic	84a	664.0	642.0	325.0	1,151.0	1,242.0	1,574.0	1,642.0	163.0	I –73.0	130.0	902.0	1,774.0	4,307.0	3,264.0	I 2.6
Foreign	85a	–17.0	30.0	34.0	66.0	17.0	11.0	–56.0	954.0	I –51.0	–127.0	–236.0	386.0	1,081.0	–968.0	I –1.1
Use of Cash Balances	87	–21.0	–46.0	19.0	14.0	–4.0	–40.0	147.0	–224.0	....	....	....	....	....	....	....
Debt: Sucres	88b	2,366.0	2,597.0	2,702.0	3,576.0	4,250.0	5,590.0	6,516.0	6,548.0							
Held by: Central Bank	88ba	452.0	652.0	652.0	1,068.0	1,500.0	2,545.0	2,665.0	3,333.0							
Nat'l Securities Comm.	88bc	229.0	126.0	110.0	188.0	70.0	51.0	33.0	78.0							
Others	88bd	1,685.0	1,819.0	1,940.0	2,320.0	2,680.0	2,994.0	3,818.0	3,137.0							
Intragovernmental Debt	88s	192.0	562.0	554.0	543.0	1,495.0	2,132.0	2,050.0	1,991.0							
Debt: Foreign Currency	89b	1,640.0	1,896.0	1,999.0	3,556.0											
National Accounts													*Millions of Sucres through 1978;*			
Exports of Goods & Services	90c	3,300	3,698	3,902	4,098	3,860	4,909	5,986	8,808	15,506	33,589	28,242	34,171	41,315	40,831	I 61
Government Consumption	91f	1,900	1,937	2,059	2,548	3,107	3,864	4,117	4,744	6,394	11,646	15,624	18,629	24,656	26,450	I 30
Gross Fixed Capital Formation	93e	2,300	2,653	3,433	3,937	4,827	5,842	8,704	8,441	10,885	16,859	24,907	29,470	39,285	50,085	I 55
Increase/Decrease(–) in Stocks	93i	600	814	946	997	450	529	574	936	1,230	3,991	3,890	2,109	4,852	4,347	I 4
Private Consumption	96f	16,600	17,753	19,778	21,474	23,584	26,375	30,436	34,429	41,711	55,506	70,298	84,517	102,578	121,244	I 143
Imports of Goods & Services	98c	–3,900	–4,259	–4,880	–5,642	–5,684	–6,500	–9,769	–10,499	–13,497	–28,828	–35,221	–35,983	–46,310	–51,612	I –59
Gross Domestic Product	99b	20,700	22,596	25,238	27,412	30,144	35,019	40,048	46,859	62,229	92,763	107,740	132,913	166,376	191,345	I 234
Net Factor Inc/Pmts(–) Abroad	98.n	–500	–460	–450	–500	–520	–670	–920	–1,680	–3,540	–5,670	–2,470	–4,060	–4,480	–5,520	I –10
Gross Nat'l Expenditure = GNP	99a	20,300	22,136	24,787	26,913	29,622	34,347	39,126	45,181	58,687	87,098	105,272	128,852	161,898	185,822	I 224
Nat'l Income, Market Prices	99e	19,000	20,619	23,035	23,920	27,294	32,865	35,726	40,943	53,303	80,484	96,423	117,776	147,764	169,110	I 202
GDP 1990 Prices (Billions)	99b.p	2,292	2,348	2,509	2,610	2,671	2,844	3,022	3,458	4,333	4,613	4,870	5,319	5,667	6,040	6,361
GDP Deflator (1990=100)	99bi p	I .9	1.0	1.0	1.1	1.1	1.2	1.3	1.4	1.4	2.0	2.2	2.5	2.9	3.2	3.7
																Millions:
Population	99z	5.07	5.22	5.40	5.58	5.77	5.96	6.17	6.38	6.60	6.82	7.03	7.24	7.45	7.67	7.89

Ecuador

248

1980	1981	1982	1983	1984	1985	1986	1987	1988	1989	1990	1991	1992	1993	1994		
Billions of Sucres Beginning 1979: End of Period															**Banking Survey**	
23.0	15.8	9.5	15.1	11.1	16.4	-31.6	-88.3	-98.7	-9.9	108.3	175.8	249.3	....	....	Foreign Assets (Net)	**51n**
63.7	80.0	106.5	162.1	194.2	337.5	415.1	563.5	1,071.6	1,285.4	1,497.6	2,534.3	3,848.1	....	....	Domestic Credit	**52**
-3.7	-7.8	-2.7	-11.1	-39.6	42.9	53.7	99.4	464.0	367.0	136.3	433.6	484.9	....	....	Claims on Central Govt. (Net)	**52an**
—	—	—	—	—	—	—	—	—	—	—	—	—	....	....	Claims on Local Government	**52b**
—	.2	—	—	—	—	—	—	—	—	—	—	—	....	....	Claims on Nonfin.Pub.Enterprises	**52c**
67.4	87.6	109.1	173.2	233.7	294.6	361.4	464.2	607.6	918.4	1,361.3	2,100.8	3,363.2	....	....	Claims on Private Sector	**52d**
69.1	79.2	98.1	123.4	177.2	227.8	282.8	396.5	644.6	911.2	1,402.0	2,111.5	3,305.5	....	....	Liquid Liabilities	**55l**
10.6	13.1	17.0	21.0	30.9	78.1	107.0	153.8	167.8	277.1	513.3	722.6	1,138.9	....	....	Bonds	**56ab**
3.8	5.1	9.6	17.0	26.2	11.5	10.7	27.2	46.0	10.7	2.2	.8	.7	....	....	Restricted Deposits	**56b**
.8	1.0	1.6	49.0	117.4	310.1	347.1	369.1	1,376.5	1,495.2	1,522.5	1,988.8	2,040.1	....	....	Long-Term Foreign Liabilities	**56cl**
.3	.5	.7	1.9	1.5	1.5	2.3	3.7	11.2	22.5	27.0	36.7	68.3	....	....	Central Govt. Lending Funds	**56f**
15.4	18.6	20.2	23.2	32.2	48.0	59.9	75.2	119.5	184.4	267.8	492.3	889.2	....	....	Capital Accounts	**57a**
-13.4	-21.7	-31.0	-58.2	-180.2	-323.1	-426.3	-550.2	-1,392.7	-1,625.6	-2,128.9	-2,642.6	-3,345.3	....	....	Other Items (Net)	**57r**
Percent Per Annum															**Interest Rates**	
8.00	15.00	15.00	19.00	23.00	23.00	23.00	23.00	23.00	32.00	35.00	49.00	49.00	33.57	44.88	Discount Rate *(End of Period)*	**60**
....	....	....	16.00	18.17	21.00	21.39	25.34	34.00	40.24	43.55	41.54	46.81	31.97	33.65	Deposit Rate	**60l**
9.00	9.00	9.25	12.33	16.17	18.00	18.00	18.42	23.00	30.08	37.50	46.67	60.17	47.83	43.99	Lending Rate	**60p**
Period Averages															**Prices and Production**	
5.9	6.5	7.6	8.7	10.7	13.5	17.4	I 22.9	38.2	68.7	100.0	148.0	228.9	318.3	376.4	Wholesale Prices	**63**
4.5	I 5.2	6.1	9.1	11.9	15.2	18.7	24.2	38.3	67.3	100.0	148.7	229.9	333.3	424.3	Consumer Prices	**64**
70.6	72.7	72.7	81.8	88.6	96.6	100.4	65.4	106.6	98.4	100.0	102.8	119.7	118.2	130.6	Crude Petroleum Production	**66aa**
Millions of US Dollars															**International Transactions**	
2,480.8	2,451.4	2,327.4	2,347.7	2,620.4	2,904.7	2,171.5	1,927.8	2,192.4	2,353.8	2,714.3	2,851.5	3,007.4	2,903.7	3,717.2	Exports	**70..*d***
2,253.3	I 2,246.1	2,168.9	1,487.4	1,616.3	1,766.6	1,810.2	2,251.5	1,713.5	1,854.8	1,861.8	2,398.7	2,500.5	2,561.9	3,642.2	Imports, cif	**71..*d***
1,989.8	I 1,895.2	1,897.7	1,304.6	1,395.5	1,543.9	1,575.0	1,981.7	1,517.4	1,634.1	1,644.5	2,115.5	1,975.5	2,223.0	3,209.2	Imports, fob	**71.v*d***
1990=100																
63.7	68.8	60.9	78.4	86.7	98.5	104.7	68.4	100.3	98.4	100.0	105.6	108.2	121.2	135.6	Volume of Exports	**72**
Indices of Unit Values in US Dollars																
161.8	157.0	149.3	129.0	125.5	127.8	76.3	86.1	72.4	85.2	100.0	87.5	96.6	75.0	83.7	Export Prices	**74..*d***
Minus Sign Indicates Debit															Balance of Payments	
2,520.0	2,527.0	2,327.0	2,348.0	2,621.0	2,905.0	2,186.0	2,021.0	2,202.0	2,354.0	2,714.0	2,851.0	3,008.0	3,062.0	3,717.0	Goods: Exports f.o.b.	**78aa*d***
-2,241.8	-2,353.0	-2,187.0	-1,421.0	-1,567.0	-1,611.0	-1,643.0	-2,054.0	-1,583.0	-1,693.0	-1,711.0	-2,207.0	-2,083.0	-2,474.0	-3,272.0	Goods: Imports f.o.b.	**78ab*d***
278.2	174.0	140.0	927.0	1,054.0	1,294.0	543.0	-33.0	619.0	661.0	1,003.0	644.0	925.0	588.0	445.0	Trade Balance	**78ac*d***
367.0	398.6	381.0	315.0	291.0	397.0	444.0	424.0	442.0	517.0	539.0	557.0	623.0	654.0	745.0	Services: Credit	**78ad*d***
-703.9	-834.3	-723.0	-491.0	-535.0	-636.0	-621.0	-665.0	-621.0	-639.0	-662.0	-718.0	-748.0	-799.0	-922.0	Services: Debit	**78ae*d***
-58.7	-261.7	-202.0	751.0	810.0	1,055.0	366.0	-274.0	440.0	539.0	880.0	483.0	800.0	443.0	268.0	Balance on Goods and Services	**78af*d***
88.0	69.4	26.0	23.0	59.0	29.0	29.0	25.0	15.0	19.0	24.0	30.0	29.0	26.0	52.0	Income: Credit	**78ag*d***
-701.1	-830.7	-1,026.0	-913.0	-1,162.0	-1,088.0	-1,036.0	-1,055.0	-1,163.0	-1,249.0	-1,221.0	-1,165.0	-1,022.0	-1,129.0	-1,162.0	Income: Debit	**78ah*d***
-671.8	-1,023.0	-1,202.0	-139.0	-293.0	-4.0	-641.0	-1,304.0	-708.0	-691.0	-317.0	-652.0	-193.0	-660.0	-842.0	Balance on Goods, Serv., & Inc.	**78ai*d***
36.3	35.0	30.0	38.0	25.0	85.0	51.0	135.0	104.0	106.0	119.0	123.0	134.0	145.0	164.0	Current Transfers, n.i.e.: Credit	**78aj*d***
-6.1	-10.0	-10.0	-14.0	-5.0	-5.0	-6.0	-3.0	-7.0	-9.0	-12.0	-13.0	-14.0	-15.0	-19.0	Current Transfers: Debit	**78ak*d***
-641.6	-998.0	-1,182.0	-115.0	-273.0	76.0	-596.0	-1,172.0	-611.0	-594.0	-210.0	-542.0	-73.0	-530.0	-697.0	Current Account, n.i.e.	**78al*d***
—	—	—	—	—	—	—	—	—	—	—	—	—	—	—	Capital Account, n.i.e.: Credit	**78ba*d***
—	—	—	—	—	—	—	—	—	—	—	—	—	—	—	Capital Account: Debit	**78bb*d***
—	—	—	—	—	—	—	—	—	—	—	—	—	—	—	Capital Account, n.i.e.	**78bc*d***
—	—	—	—	—	—	—	—	—	—	—	—	—	—	—	Direct Investment Abroad	**78bd*d***
70.0	60.0	40.0	50.0	50.0	62.0	81.0	123.0	155.0	200.0	126.0	160.0	178.0	469.0	531.0	Dir. Invest. in Rep. Econ., n.i.e.	**78be*d***
—	—	—	—	—	—	—	—	—	—	—	—	—	—	—	Portfolio Investment Assets	**78bf*d***
—	—	—	—	—	—	—	—	—	—	—	—	—	—	—	Portfolio Investment Liab., n.i.e.	**78bg*d***
-230.9	-449.4	503.0	-168.0	-26.0	54.0	-23.0	4.0	14.0	-68.0	-120.0	-14.0	64.0	-29.0	-9.0	Other Investment Assets	**78bh*d***
1,117.2	1,109.1	69.0	-2,443.0	-1,404.0	-1,167.0	-1,199.0	-312.0	-760.0	-599.0	-803.0	-628.0	-875.0	-284.0	-369.0	Other Investment Liab., n.i.e.	**78bi*d***
956.3	719.7	612.0	-2,561.0	-1,380.0	-1,051.0	-1,141.0	-185.0	-591.0	-467.0	-797.0	-482.0	-633.0	156.0	153.0	Financial Account, n.i.e.	**78bj*d***
-68.4	-89.3	-801.8	794.1	96.9	167.9	-432.5	-267.6	27.8	74.6	216.1	162.7	-99.2	-55.7	111.7	Net Errors and Omissions	**78ca*d***
246.3	-367.6	-1,371.8	-1,881.9	-1,556.1	-807.1	-2,169.5	-1,624.6	-1,174.2	-986.4	-790.9	-861.3	-805.2	-429.7	-432.3	Overall Balance	**78cb*d***
-246.3	367.6	1,371.8	1,881.9	1,556.1	807.1	2,169.5	1,624.6	1,174.2	986.4	790.9	861.3	805.2	429.7	645.3	Reserves and Related Items	**79da*d***
-270.1	370.4	338.8	-327.1	60.0	-96.6	124.1	185.4	25.9	-117.6	-195.0	-77.8	-22.4	-499.3	-452.9	Reserve Assets	**79db*d***
—	—	—	213.9	40.2	88.7	83.4	-68.8	-57.7	-68.9	-85.1	-78.9	-77.4	-29.0	122.2	Use of Fund Credit and Loans	**79dc*d***
23.8	-2.8	154.0	-10.0	-27.0	-71.0	133.0	-50.0	-44.0	-4.0	5.0	15.0	-19.0	-33.0	-4.0	Liabs.Constit.For.Auth.Reserves	**79dd*d***
—	—	879.0	2,005.0	1,483.0	886.0	1,829.0	1,558.0	1,250.0	1,177.0	1,066.0	1,003.0	924.0	991.0	980.0	Exceptional Financing	**79de*d***
Billions of Sucres Beginning 1979: Year Ending December 31															**Government Finance**	
-4.1	-16.8	-18.5	-14.0	-6.8	22.0	I -31.1	-41.8	-1.4	97.2	147.6	186.0	461.0	550.7	115.2	Deficit (-) or Surplus	**80**
37.5	39.3	46.0	60.2	99.9	189.5	I 186.9	236.8	415.5	835.4	1,355.2	1,820.1	3,008.6	4,314.6	5,647.6	Revenue	**81**
41.7	56.1	64.5	74.2	106.7	167.5	I 218.0	278.6	416.8	738.2	1,207.6	1,634.1	2,547.6	3,763.9	5,532.5	Exp. & Lending Minus Repay.	**82z**
															Financing	
2.6	9.2	8.5	16.3	10.8	-18.2	I 8.6	29.1	36.7	-5.7	4.8	91.9	29.9	-59.3	521.8	Net Borrowing: Domestic	**84a**
1.6	7.7	10.0	-2.3	-4.1	-3.8	I 22.5	12.7	-35.4	-91.5	-152.4	-277.9	-490.9	-491.4	-637.0	Foreign	**85a**
....	....	....	....	....	....	....	....	....	....	....	....	....	....	....	Use of Cash Balances	**87**
....	....	....	....	....	....	....	....	....	....	....	....	....	....	....	Debt: Sucres	**88b**
....	....	....	....	....	....	....	....	....	....	....	....	....	....	....	Held by: Central Bank	**88ba**
....	....	....	....	....	....	....	....	....	....	....	....	....	....	....	Nat'l Securities Comm.	**88bc**
....	....	....	....	....	....	....	....	....	....	....	....	....	....	....	Others	**88bd**
....	....	....	....	....	....	....	....	....	....	....	....	....	....	....	Intragovernmental Debt	**88s**
....	....	....	....	....	....	....	....	....	....	....	....	....	....	....	Debt: Foreign Currency	**89b**
Billions of Sucres Beginning 1979															**National Accounts**	
74	76	88	133	210	297	315	432	859	1,520	2,686	3,858	6,119	7,184	8,446	Exports of Goods & Services	**90c**
43	50	58	70	100	127	167	230	347	485	706	936	1,407	2,117	2,648	Government Consumption	**91f**
69	78	94	93	125	178	260	407	643	1,071	1,513	2,417	3,784	5,457	7,362	Gross Fixed Capital Formation	**93e**
7	3	11	5	15	23	28	—	6	-1	-77	309	333	330	635	Increase/Decrease(-) in Stocks	**93i**
175	215	262	369	521	716	926	1,269	2,087	3,706	5,622	8,432	13,148	19,375	26,816	Private Consumption	**96f**
-75	-72	-97	-111	-157	-232	-313	-544	-922	-1,611	-2,246	-3,655	-5,378	-7,011	-9,539	Imports of Goods & Services	**98c**
293	349	416	560	813	1,110	1,383	1,795	3,020	5,171	8,204	12,296	19,414	27,451	36,368	Gross Domestic Product	**99b**
-15	-18	-31	-42	-73	-82	-112	-122	-207	-384	-629	-737	-931	-1,098	....	Net Factor Inc/Pmts(-) Abroad	**98.n**
279	330	385	518	740	1,028	1,272	1,672	2,813	4,786	7,575	11,560	18,483	26,353	....	Gross Nat'l Expenditure = GNP	**99a**
230	294	340	456	643	893	1,072	1,357	2,271	3,851	6,159	9,436	15,446	21,311	....	Nat'l Income, Market Prices	**99e**
6,673	6,936	7,018	6,820	7,107	7,416	7,645	7,188	7,942	7,965	8,204	8,616	8,923	9,104	9,470	GDP 1990 Prices *(Billions)*	**99b.*p***
4.4	5.0	5.9	8.2	11.4	15.0	18.1	25.0	38.0	64.9	100.0	142.7	217.6	301.5	384.0	GDP Deflator (1990=100)	**99bi*p***
Midyear Estimates																
8.12	8.36	8.61	8.64	8.87	9.10	9.33	9.56	9.79	10.03	10.26	10.50	10.74	10.98	11.22	**Population**	**99z**

(Notes in the back of the book)

Egypt
469

		1965	1966	1967	1968	1969	1970	1971	1972	1973	1974	1975	1976	1977	1978	1979
Exchange Rates																*Pounds per SDR:*
Market Rate......aa=......	wa	.4348	.4348	.4348	.4348	.4348	.4348	.4720	.4720	.4720	.4791	.4581	.4546	.4753	.5098	.9221
																Pounds per US Dollar:
Market Rate......ae=......	we	.4348	.4348	.4348	.4348	.4348	.4348	.4348	.4348	.3913	.3913	.3913	.3913	.3913	.3913	.7000
Secondary Rate	xe	....	....	....	....	....	....	....	....	....	....	....	.7000	.7000	.7000	....
Secondary Rate	xf	....	....	....	....	....	....	....	....	....	....	....	....	.7000	....	....
Tertiary Rate	ye	....	....	....	....	....	....	....	....	....	....	....	....	....	....	....
Tertiary Rate	yf	....	....	....	....	....	....	....	....	....	....	....	....	....	....	....
Fund Position																*Millions of SDRs:*
Quota	2f.s	120	150	150	150	150	188	188	188	188	188	188	188	188	228	228
SDRs	1b.s	—	—	—	—	—	—	7	5	31	31	14	20	24	8	—
Reserve Position in the Fund	1c.s	—	—	—	—	—	—	—	—	—	—	—	—	—	—	—
Total Fund Cred.&Loans Outstg.	2tl	95	70	74	72	51	49	70	24	62	93	68	178	275	374	381
International Liquidity											*Millions of US Dollars Unless Otherwise Indicated:*					
Total Reserves minus Gold	1l.d	54	63	102	75	51	74	57	52	260	252	194	240	431	492	529
SDRs	1b.s	—	—	—	—	—	—	8	6	38	38	17	24	29	11	—
Reserve Position in the Fund	1c.d	—	—	—	—	—	—	—	—	—	—	—	—	—	—	—
Foreign Exchange	1d.d	54	63	102	75	51	74	49	46	222	214	177	216	402	481	529
Gold (Million Fine Troy Ounces)	1ad	3.980	2.666	2.671	2.674	2.674	2.434	2.432	2.432	2.432	2.432	2.432	2.432	2.432	2.473	2.472
Gold (National Valuation)	1an d	139	93	93	93	93	85	85	85	85	103	103	103	103	104	104
Monetary Authorities: Other Assets	3..d	115	157	65	111	123	101	90	75	132	265	631	300	347	510	409
Other Liab.	4..d	337	410	425	443	468	532	677	673	879	978	2,554	2,798	4,041	8,915	5,173
Deposit Money Banks: Assets	7a.d	132.9	110.9	110.4	106.3	115.0	108.3	97.5	138.7	415.5	1,042.4	1,265.3	1,965.5	3,406.6	4,420.6	2,745.1
Liabilities	7b.d	123.0	150.0	147.7	149.3	162.4	186.3	200.6	211.4	335.8	957.8	1,789.9	1,961.6	1,598.0	1,942.5	1,228.4
Other Banking Insts.: Assets	7e.d	2.3	2.3	2.3	2.3	2.3	2.3	2.3	2.3	2.6	2.6	2.6	2.6	2.6	2.6	5.7
Liabilities	7f.d	....	....	....	....	....	....	....	....	....	....	....	....	20.7	43.4	41.4
Monetary Authorities																*Millions of Pounds:*
Foreign Assets	11	119	117	99	106	102	102	100	92	185	201	265	251	344	590	763
Claims on Central Government	12a	438	450	448	475	496	517	592	668	819	982	1,511	1,594	1,878	4,178	6,211
Claims on Nonfin.Pub.Enterprises	12c	5	5	5	—	—	12	—	—	—	—	—	—	—	—	—
Claims on Deposit Money Banks	12e	181	203	285	278	320	417	390	383	395	580	775	1,105	1,544	1,633	1,153
Claims on Other Banking Insts.	12f	65	58	57	35	10	6	6	6	6	5	5	5	104	170	121
Reserve Money	14	553	549	600	608	656	751	703	802	1,000	1,270	1,446	1,730	2,083	2,655	3,402
of which: Currency Outside DMBs	14a	453	448	450	460	496	525	559	631	777	948	1,156	1,388	1,750	2,184	2,657
Foreign Liabilities	16c	188	209	217	224	226	253	327	304	373	427	1,031	1,176	1,712	3,679	3,972
Central Government Deposits	16d	18	19	17	10	12	15	18	18	20	34	38	40	47	101	693
Other Items (Net)	17r	50	57	60	53	35	35	40	26	13	37	43	9	30	136	181
Deposit Money Banks																*Millions of Pounds:*
Reserves	20	106	97	140	149	163	236	142	185	260	382	370	451	495	505	803
Foreign Assets	21	58	48	48	46	50	47	42	60	163	408	495	769	1,333	1,730	1,922
Claims on Central Government	22a	324	386	474	472	482	583	663	704	741	923	1,369	1,646	1,816	2,393	2,546
Claims on Nonfin.Pub.Enterprises	22c	....	....	....	....	....	....	....	....	....	....	....	....	....	....	....
Claims on Private Sector	22d	333	328	319	360	397	381	417	425	410	587	881	1,147	1,537	1,790	2,396
Claims on Other Banking Insts.	22f	59	49	66	89	111	123	126	122	115	196	207	174	102	67	136
Demand Deposits	24	199	234	245	255	250	258	287	357	425	553	706	849	1,194	1,369	1,697
Time, Savings,& Fgn.Currency Dep.	25	197	181	200	223	253	270	238	266	331	498	567	822	1,160	1,659	2,490
Restricted Deposits	26b	....	....	....	....	....	....	....	....	....	....	....	....	....	....	....
Foreign Liabilities	26c	54	65	64	65	71	81	87	92	131	375	700	768	625	760	860
Central Government Deposits	26d	120	81	88	88	90	105	126	130	128	184	211	247	366	596	821
Credit from Monetary Authorities	26g	172	192	284	280	318	416	385	383	395	578	771	1,105	1,530	1,589	1,078
Other Items (Net)	27r	137	155	166	205	223	240	268	268	278	308	367	397	409	512	857
Monetary Survey																*Millions of Pounds:*
Foreign Assets (Net)	31n	−64	−108	−134	−137	−145	−185	−272	−244	−157	−193	−971	−923	−660	−2,119	−2,148
Domestic Credit	32	1,085	1,175	1,264	1,332	1,394	1,502	1,660	1,777	1,943	2,475	3,725	4,279	5,024	7,901	9,897
Claims on Central Govt. (Net)	32an	624	735	818	849	876	980	1,111	1,224	1,412	1,686	2,632	2,953	3,282	5,874	7,243
Claims on Nonfin.Pub.Enterprises	32c	....	....	....	....	....	....	....	....	....	....	....	....	....	....	....
Claims on Private Sector	32d	338	333	324	360	398	394	418	426	411	587	881	1,147	1,537	1,790	2,396
Claims on Other Banking Insts.	32f	124	107	123	124	121	129	132	127	120	201	212	179	206	237	257
Money	34	655	684	707	722	746	783	846	989	1,205	1,503	1,863	2,239	2,943	3,553	4,354
of which: Foreign Currency Deps.	34a	....	....	....	....	....	....	....	....	....	....	....	....	....	....	....
Quasi-Money	35	197	181	209	223	253	270	238	266	331	498	567	822	1,160	1,659	2,490
of which: Foreign Currency Deps.	35a	....	....	....	....	....	....	....	....	....	....	....	....	....	....	....
Restricted Deposits	36b	....	....	....	....	....	....	....	....	....	....	....	....	....	....	....
Other Items (Net)	37r	169	202	214	251	251	265	304	278	251	281	325	295	262	570	904
Money plus Quasi-Money	35l	852	865	917	945	999	1,053	1,085	1,255	1,536	2,000	2,430	3,061	4,103	5,212	6,844
Other Banking Institutions																
Specialized Banks																*Millions of Pounds:*
Cash	40	....	....	....	....	....	....	....	....	....	....	....	....	....	1	1
Foreign Assets	41	1	1	1	1	1	1	1	1	1	1	1	1	1	1	4
Claims on Nonfin.Pub.Enterprises	42c	....	....	....	....	....	....	....	....	....	....	....	....	....	....	....
Claims on Private Sector	42d	91	98	100	113	115	122	154	140	153	154	137	138	185	210	243
Demand Deposits	44	17	19	20	18	17	17	20	23	25	28	29	36	40	54	93
Time and Savings Deposits	45	....	....	....	....	....	....	....	....	....	....	....	....	....	....	....
Restricted Deposits	46b	....	....	....	....	....	....	....	....	....	....	....	....	....	....	....
Foreign Liabilities	46c	....	....	....	....	....	....	....	....	....	....	....	....	8	17	29
Central Government Deposits	46d	4	3	7	2	2	3	9	12	13	23	23	28	48	58	70
Credit from Monetary Authorities	46g	68	72	58	35	10	6	6	6	6	6	6	7	106	175	125
Credit from Deposit Money Banks	46h	58	48	65	89	113	123	126	121	115	194	203	175	102	61	118
Other Items (Net)	47r	−55	−42	−49	−28	−25	−27	−6	−21	−6	−96	−123	−105	−117	−152	−187
Post Office: Savings Deposits	45..i	74	76	69	70	73	77	81	90	101	119	136	152	163	187	203

Egypt

469

1980	1981	1982	1983	1984	1985	1986	1987	1988	1989	1990	1991	1992	1993	1994	Series	Code
End of Period															**Exchange Rates**	
.8928	.8148	.7722	.7329	.6861	.7689	.8562	.9931	.9420	1.4456	2.8453	4.7633	4.5792	4.6294	4.9518	Market Rate aa=	wa
End of Period																
.7000	.7000	.7000	.7000	.7000	.7000	.7000	.7000	.7000	1.1000	2.0000	3.3300	3.3303	3.3704	3.3920	Market Rate ae=	we
....	.8317	.8317	.8317	.8317	1.3300	1.3600	1.8700	2.3529	2.5580	2.8736	....	....	....	....	Secondary Rate	xe
....	.7390	.8317	.8317	.8317	1.3010	1.3503	1.5183	2.2233	2.5171	2.7072	....	....	....	....	Secondary Rate	xf
....	1.0100	1.1300	1.1800	1.3800	1.7400	1.9325	2.2900	2.4700	2.7100	3.0500	....	....	....	....	Tertiary Rate	ye
....	....	....	1.1453	1.2543	1.5488	1.8838	2.1838	2.3731	2.6949	2.7978	....	....	....	....	Tertiary Rate	yf
End of Period															**Fund Position**	
342	342	342	463	463	463	463	463	463	463	463	463	678	678	678	Quota	2f.*s*
—	—	—	—	—	—	—	—	—	—	—	1	43	50	59	SDRs	1b.*s*
—	24	—	30	—	—	—	—	—	—	—	—	54	54	54	Reserve Position in the Fund	1c.*s*
322	269	236	228	210	167	118	185	141	122	88	89	147	147	132	Total Fund Cred.&Loans Outstg.	2tl
End of Period															**International Liquidity**	
1,046	716	698	771	736	792	829	1,378	1,263	1,520	2,684	5,325	10,810	12,904	13,481	Total Reserves minus Gold	1l.*d*
—	—	—	—	—	—	—	—	—	—	1	1	59	69	86	SDRs	1b.*d*
—	28	—	32	—	—	—	—	—	—	—	—	74	74	78	Reserve Position in the Fund	1c.*d*
1,046	688	698	739	736	792	829	1,378	1,263	1,520	2,683	5,324	10,677	12,761	13,316	Foreign Exchange	1d.*d*
2.432	2.432	2.432	2.432	2.432	2.432	2.432	2.432	2.432	2.432	2.432	2.432	2.432	2.432	2.432	Gold (Million Fine Troy Ounces)	1ad
103	775	578	757	679	578	622	814	794	679	641	656	616	616	694	Gold (National Valuation)	1an*d*
529	849	1,106	1,349	1,257	1,290	1,439	255	618	604	1,078	1,287	1,280	1,274	1,293	Monetary Authorities: Other Assets	3..*d*
I 5,082	4,768	5,126	4,487	4,403	4,133	4,732	9,136	12,620	16,108	15,622	11,860	12,488	11,847	12,545	Other Liab.	4..*d*
I 4,633.7	3,965.9	6,265.9	7,628.3	7,051.4	7,385.6	6,798.4	7,797.7	7,226.5	8,481.6	10,365.5	12,606.9	11,326.8	10,791.0	11,428.9	Deposit Money Banks: Assets	7a.*d*
I 2,598.9	3,116.3	4,292.3	5,288.4	5,262.8	5,251.5	4,834.6	4,370.2	3,621.1	3,485.4	3,714.3	3,423.6	2,343.2	1,782.7	1,464.9	Liabilities	7b.*d*
I 5.6	11.1	14.3	10.3	8.3	6.9	45.6	24.7	32.6	40.0	35.1	33.6	43.0	51.2	29.5	Other Banking Insts.: Assets	7e.*d*
I 63.1	99.4	149.0	377.1	388.9	501.3	594.9	790.7	1,100.7	770.5	530.7	423.6	437.2	486.7	457.0	Liabilities	7f.*d*
End of Period															**Monetary Authorities**	
I 1,187	1,639	1,667	2,030	1,888	1,888	2,128	2,646	2,704	3,639	11,029	26,086	45,911	55,894	60,523	Foreign Assets	11
I 6,184	8,093	10,393	12,627	14,377	15,966	17,841	21,058	24,588	34,263	52,238	56,562	56,993	52,849	50,974	Claims on Central Government	12a
I 625	676	329	351	334	425	492	545	559	694	722	725	823	820	799	Claims on Nonfin.Pub.Enterprises	12c
I 1,757	333	357	643	898	1,075	1,173	1,992	2,191	3,309	4,608	6,157	8,279	11,655	12,224	Claims on Deposit Money Banks	12e
I 213	314	518	551	665	837	1,078	1,155	1,256	1,425	1,624	1,823	1,974	2,134	2,040	Claims on Other Banking Insts.	12f
I 5,611	7,056	9,281	11,875	13,544	15,814	17,655	18,714	19,476	21,082	27,137	32,356	35,712	42,554	47,888	Reserve Money	14
I 3,398	4,291	5,503	6,475	7,098	8,285	8,803	9,537	10,406	10,934	12,410	13,524	15,241	17,818	20,612	*of which: Currency Outside DMBs*	14a
I 3,845	3,557	3,770	3,308	3,226	3,021	3,413	6,579	8,967	17,895	31,494	39,917	42,264	40,609	43,209	Foreign Liabilities	16c
I 362	406	300	847	1,062	933	1,209	1,626	1,289	2,308	9,211	18,634	35,109	38,481	33,617	Central Government Deposits	16d
I 148	36	-88	172	330	422	435	477	1,566	2,045	2,379	445	894	1,707	1,848	Other Items (Net)	17r
End of Period															**Deposit Money Banks**	
I 1,325	2,392	3,557	5,039	6,124	7,164	9,262	10,545	11,054	12,068	14,726	19,330	19,540	23,097	25,402	Reserves	20
I 3,244	3,298	5,211	6,344	5,864	6,142	9,246	14,581	17,004	21,696	29,786	41,980	37,722	36,370	38,767	Foreign Assets	21
I 2,775	1,335	1,785	1,206	1,973	2,684	3,911	5,233	7,302	7,360	6,747	17,699	40,681	41,262	42,398	Claims on Central Government	22a
2,685	3,809	3,950	5,576	7,145	8,529	9,683	11,148	13,091	16,615	23,026	28,214	23,928	29,283	29,998	Claims on Nonfin.Pub.Enterprises	22c
I 2,174	4,242	5,549	6,876	8,284	10,145	12,888	14,881	17,330	20,428	24,454	24,816	30,978	36,885	48,831	Claims on Private Sector	22d
I 119	304	272	309	391	686	1,123	1,284	1,629	1,695	2,095	2,056	1,250	1,432	1,284	Claims on Other Banking Insts.	22f
I 2,504	2,886	3,498	3,798	4,554	5,606	6,135	7,460	8,308	9,742	10,849	12,703	13,985	14,940	15,919	Demand Deposits	24
I 3,589	5,920	8,240	10,884	13,486	15,978	21,127	26,635	33,969	41,619	56,302	70,126	86,761	98,598	109,810	Time, Savings,& Fgn.Currency Dep.	25
897	1,279	1,478	1,677	1,753	1,942	3,108	5,079	5,070	6,023	7,423	8,152	7,076	8,239	9,182	Restricted Deposits	26b
I 1,819	2,592	3,570	4,398	4,377	4,368	6,575	8,172	8,520	8,916	10,673	11,400	7,804	6,009	4,969	Foreign Liabilities	26c
I 349	494	488	545	555	663	1,059	1,201	1,415	1,373	2,070	5,778	10,206	6,907	7,805	Central Government Deposits	26d
I 1,780	372	552	858	1,108	1,242	1,550	2,401	2,726	4,142	5,930	7,859	9,613	15,598	17,571	Credit from Monetary Authorities	26g
I 1,384	1,837	2,500	3,189	3,949	5,551	6,558	6,723	7,402	8,048	7,588	18,076	18,654	18,040	21,423	Other Items (Net)	27r
End of Period															**Monetary Survey**	
I -1,234	-1,211	-461	668	150	641	1,386	2,476	2,220	-1,476	-1,353	16,748	33,566	45,646	51,112	Foreign Assets (Net)	31n
I 14,065	17,871	22,008	26,104	31,553	37,674	44,747	52,476	63,052	78,798	99,625	107,483	111,311	119,278	134,902	Domestic Credit	32
I 8,248	8,527	11,390	12,441	14,733	17,053	19,484	23,464	29,186	37,941	47,705	49,848	52,358	48,724	51,949	Claims on Central Govt. (Net)	32an
3,310	4,485	4,279	5,927	7,479	8,953	10,175	11,692	13,651	17,309	23,748	28,940	24,751	30,103	30,797	Claims on Nonfin.Pub.Enterprises	32c
I 2,174	4,242	5,549	6,876	8,284	10,145	12,888	14,881	17,330	20,428	24,454	24,816	30,978	36,885	48,831	Claims on Private Sector	32d
I 333	617	790	860	1,056	1,523	2,200	2,439	2,885	3,120	3,720	3,879	3,224	3,566	3,324	Claims on Other Banking Insts.	32f
I 6,775	7,646	9,552	10,933	12,443	14,696	15,973	18,241	20,579	22,471	26,205	28,337	30,832	34,571	38,275	Money	34
874	1,030	1,361	1,612	1,913	2,454	2,848	3,878	4,484	5,588	8,249	11,104	10,253	10,918	9,892	*of which: Foreign Currency Deps.*	34a
I 3,589	5,920	8,240	10,885	13,486	15,980	21,129	26,637	33,970	41,623	56,303	70,127	86,762	98,602	109,834	Quasi-Money	35
1,493	2,524	3,640	4,301	4,616	5,230	8,645	12,214	17,124	21,749	29,802	36,093	27,608	25,964	30,851	*of which: Foreign Currency Deps.*	35a
897	1,279	1,478	1,677	1,753	1,942	3,108	5,079	5,070	6,023	7,423	8,152	7,076	8,239	9,182	Restricted Deposits	36b
I 1,571	1,815	2,277	3,277	4,020	5,697	5,922	4,994	5,654	7,206	8,342	17,616	20,207	23,512	28,724	Other Items (Net)	37r
I 10,364	13,566	17,792	21,817	25,929	30,676	37,102	44,878	54,549	64,094	82,508	98,464	117,594	133,174	148,109	Money plus Quasi-Money	35l
															Other Banking Institutions	
End of Period															Specialized Banks	
I 49	49	33	36	25	28	44	59	69	82	94	180	134	184	169	Cash	40
I 4	8	10	7	6	5	32	17	23	44	70	112	143	173	100	Foreign Assets	41
130	215	390	492	651	808	1,004	1,147	1,289	1,435	1,584	1,758	1,881	1,961	2,067	Claims on Nonfin.Pub.Enterprises	42c
I 327	511	674	1,182	1,490	1,794	2,472	2,983	3,596	4,047	4,950	5,442	5,458	6,361	7,425	Claims on Private Sector	42d
I 89	96	155	142	172	221	234	307	351	481	475	458	575	722	912	Demand Deposits	44
47	85	138	258	296	383	455	666	775	849	875	1,291	1,330	1,705	2,322	Time and Savings Deposits	45
8	12	16	23	26	2	10	27	25	27	21	19	19	32	20	Restricted Deposits	46b
I 44	70	104	264	272	351	416	554	771	848	1,061	1,411	1,456	1,640	1,550	Foreign Liabilities	46c
I 67	97	111	194	168	89	87	153	418	465	573	194	427	592	713	Central Government Deposits	46d
I 213	309	519	556	665	844	1,076	1,145	1,256	1,426	1,630	1,830	2,008	2,067	2,043	Credit from Monetary Authorities	46g
I 119	303	267	375	501	623	1,088	1,150	1,489	1,524	1,888	1,945	1,236	1,410	1,021	Credit from Deposit Money Banks	46h
I -78	-189	-203	-94	72	123	186	205	-109	-12	175	345	565	509	1,180	Other Items (Net)	47r
216	261	300	353	403	459	531	589	643	694	773	885	1,027	1,236	1,236	Post Office: Savings Deposits	45..*i*

Egypt
469

		1965	1966	1967	1968	1969	1970	1971	1972	1973	1974	1975	1976	1977	1978	1979
Banking Survey																*Millions of Pounds:*
Foreign Assets (Net)	51n	....	....	....	....	....	....	....	....	....	....	....	....	....	....	....
Domestic Credit	52	....	....	....	....	....	....	....	....	....	....	....	....	....	....	....
Claims on Central Govt. (Net)	52an	....	....	....	....	....	....	....	....	....	....	....	....	....	....	....
Claims on Nonfin.Pub.Enterprises	52c	....	....	....	....	....	....	....	....	....	....	....	....	....	....	....
Claims on Private Sector	52d	....	....	....	....	....	....	....	....	....	....	....	....	....	....	....
Liquid Liabilities	55l	....	....	....	....	....	....	....	....	....	....	....	....	....	....	....
Restricted Deposits	56b	....	....	....	....	....	....	....	....	....	....	....	....	....	....	....
Other Items (Net)	57r	....	....	....	....	....	....	....	....	....	....	....	....	....	....	....
Interest Rates																*Percent Per Annum*
Discount Rate *(End of Period)*	60	5.00	5.00	5.00	5.00	5.00	5.00	5.00	5.00	5.00	5.00	5.00	6.00	7.00	8.00	9.00
Deposit Rate	60l	....	....	....	....	....	....	....	....	....	....	....	3.0	4.7	5.9	7.0
Lending Rate	60p	....	....	....	....	....	....	....	....	....	....	....	8.0	8.8	10.2	12.0
Prices																*Index Numbers (1990=100):*
Wholesale Prices	63	8.2	8.9	9.5	9.3	9.3	I9.7	9.8	9.9	10.6	12.1	13.0	14.0	15.3	17.5	19.3
Consumer Prices	64	7.4	8.1	8.1	I8.0	8.3	8.6	8.8	9.0	9.5	10.4	11.5	12.6	14.2	15.8	17.4
International Transactions																*Millions of Pounds:*
Exports	70	263.1	263.1	246.1	270.3	323.9	331.2	343.2	358.8	444.2	593.3	548.6	595.5	668.5	679.8	1,287.8
Cotton	70f	146.3	143.4	121.6	120.1	130.8	147.9	175.0	162.0	191.9	279.1	201.0	154.8	182.3	131.5	267.3
Long Staple	70fa	92.6	91.6	74.6	72.5	78.9	86.8	126.7	100.0	109.3	154.1	124.3	119.0	136.5	99.5	174.7
Long-Medium Staple	70fb	42.2	51.8	46.9	48.8	51.8	61.1	48.3	61.9	82.6	125.0	76.8	35.7	45.8	32.0	92.6
Suez Canal Dues	70.s	86.2	95.3	47.0	—	—	—	—	—	—	—	33.2	121.7	167.4	201.1	412.1
Imports, cif	71	405.9	465.5	344.4	289.6	277.3	342.0	399.9	390.8	361.1	920.1	1,539.3	1,489.8	1,884.3	2,632.2	2,686.0
Imports, fob	71.v	369.3	423.6	313.4	263.7	252.2	311.3	363.8	355.5	328.5	837.2	1,400.9	1,355.7	1,695.8	2,369.0	2,417.4
Volume of Exports																*1990=100*
Cotton	72f	838	883	753	706	625	725	847	750	724	590	471	420	366	338	373
Long Staple	72fa	2,024	2,088	1,697	1,473	1,435	1,544	2,236	1,674	1,527	1,237	1,084	1,213	1,059	1,006	955
Long-Medium Staple	72fb	360	422	449	381	301	430	344	451	465	382	273	164	142	122	185
Export Prices																
Cotton (Unit Value)	74f	3	3	3	3	4	4	4	4	5	8	8	7	9	7	13
Long Staple (Unit Value)	74fa	3	3	3	3	4	4	4	4	5	8	7	6	8	6	12
Long-Medium Staple(Unit Val.)	74fb	3	3	3	3	4	3	3	3	4	8	7	5	8	6	12
Cotton (Wholesale Price)	76f	5	5	5	5	6	6	6	6	9	13	11	11	13	12	23
Balance of Payments																*Millions of US Dollars:*
Goods: Exports f.o.b.	78aa d	....	....	....	....	....	....	....	....	....	....	....	....	1,974	1,939	2,424
Goods: Imports f.o.b.	78ab d	....	....	....	....	....	....	....	....	....	....	....	....	−4,038	−4,743	−6,002
Trade Balance	78ac d	....	....	....	....	....	....	....	....	....	....	....	....	−2,064	−2,804	−3,578
Services: Credit	78ad d	....	....	....	....	....	....	....	....	....	....	....	....	1,601	1,633	1,788
Services: Debit	78ae d	....	....	....	....	....	....	....	....	....	....	....	....	−1,448	−1,548	−1,773
Balance on Goods and Services	78af d	....	....	....	....	....	....	....	....	....	....	....	....	−1,912	−2,719	−3,563
Income: Credit	78ag d	....	....	....	....	....	....	....	....	....	....	....	....	39	86	172
Income: Debit	78ah d	....	....	....	....	....	....	....	....	....	....	....	....	−315	−412	−420
Balance on Goods, Serv., & Inc.	78ai d	....	....	....	....	....	....	....	....	....	....	....	....	−2,188	−3,044	−3,811
Current Transfers, n.i.e.: Credit	78aj d	....	....	....	....	....	....	....	....	....	....	....	....	988	1,824	2,269
Current Transfers: Debit	78ak d	....	....	....	....	....	....	....	....	....	....	....	....	....	....	....
Current Account, n.i.e.	78al d	....	....	....	....	....	....	....	....	....	....	....	....	−1,200	−1,220	−1,542
Capital Account, n.i.e.: Credit	78ba d	....	....	....	....	....	....	....	....	....	....	....	....	....	....	....
Capital Account: Debit	78bb d	....	....	....	....	....	....	....	....	....	....	....	....	—	—	—
Capital Account, n.i.e.	78bc d	....	....	....	....	....	....	....	....	....	....	....	....	—	—	—
Direct Investment Abroad	78bd d	....	....	....	....	....	....	....	....	....	....	....	....	−7	−20	−5
Dir. Invest. in Rep. Econ., n.i.e.	78be d	....	....	....	....	....	....	....	....	....	....	....	....	105	318	1,216
Portfolio Investment Assets	78bf d	....	....	....	....	....	....	....	....	....	....	....	....	6	4	3
Portfolio Investment Liab., n.i.e.	78bg d	....	....	....	....	....	....	....	....	....	....	....	....	—	—	—
Other Investment Assets	78bh d	....	....	....	....	....	....	....	....	....	....	....	....	−136	−194	−407
Other Investment Liab., n.i.e.	78bi d	....	....	....	....	....	....	....	....	....	....	....	....	−705	76	709
Financial Account, n.i.e.	78bj d	....	....	....	....	....	....	....	....	....	....	....	....	−737	185	1,516
Net Errors and Omissions	78ca d	....	....	....	....	....	....	....	....	....	....	....	....	30	−29	10
Overall Balance	78cb d	....	....	....	....	....	....	....	....	....	....	....	....	−1,906	−1,064	−16
Reserves and Related Items	79da d	....	....	....	....	....	....	....	....	....	....	....	....	1,906	1,064	16
Reserve Assets	79db d	....	....	....	....	....	....	....	....	....	....	....	....	−130	22	−52
Use of Fund Credit and Loans	79dc d	....	....	....	....	....	....	....	....	....	....	....	....	114	125	10
Liabs.Constit.For.Auth.Reserves	79dd d	....	....	....	....	....	....	....	....	....	....	....	....	—	—	—
Exceptional Financing	79de d	....	....	....	....	....	....	....	....	....	....	....	....	1,922	917	58
Government Finance																*Millions of Pounds:*
Deficit (−) or Surplus	80	....	....	....	....	....	....	....	....	....	....	....	−938	−1,557	−1,114	−1,246	−1,964
Revenue	81												2,039	2,306	3,388	3,758	4,666
Grants Received	81z												250	223	60	62	20
Expenditure	82												2,912	3,774	3,911	4,151	5,590
Lending Minus Repayments	83												315	312	651	915	1,060
Financing																	
Domestic	84a	....	....	....	....	....	....	....	....	....	....	....	461	917	588	945	1,567
Foreign	85a												477	640	526	301	397
National Accounts																*Millions of Pounds:*
Exports of Goods & Services	90c	411	409	429	309	380	I439	447	457	531	890	894	1,034	1,470	1,945	3,251
Government Consumption	91f	437	482	488	562	645	I756	821	905	1,020	1,101	1,213	1,571	1,697	1,841	2,059
Gross Fixed Capital Formation	93e	358	377	359	292	333	I353	356	405	462	640	1,228	1,385	1,825	2,618	3,346
Increase/Decrease(−) in Stocks	93i	23	69	27	50	−15	I74	60	62	40	90	100	195	561	416	450
Private Consumption	96f	1,463	1,583	1,633	1,763	1,807	I2,011	2,119	2,237	2,339	2,871	3,281	3,863	4,917	6,279	8,623
Imports of Goods & Services	98c	−468	−532	−453	−444	−446	I−574	−600	−649	−729	−1,395	−1,831	−1,772	−2,260	−3,316	−5,254
Gross Domestic Product = GDP	99b	2,214	2,403	2,481	2,533	2,696	I2,971	3,203	3,417	3,663	4,197	4,886	6,276	8,210	9,783	12,475
Net Factor Inc/Pmts(−) Abroad	98.n	−15	−22	−23	−36	−39	I−44	−117	−14	−29	−112	−148	133	433	983	785
Gross National Product = GNP	99a	2,199	2,381	2,457	2,497	2,652	I3,059	3,086	3,403	3,634	4,085	4,738	6,409	8,643	10,766	13,260
Gross Dom. Prod. 1990 Prices	99b.p	....	....	....	....	....	....	....	....	....	....	....	....	....	....	....
GDP Deflator (1990=100)	99bi p	....	....	....	....	....	....	....	....	....	....	....	....	....	....	....
																Millions:
Population	99z	29.39	30.14	30.91	31.69	32.50	33.33	34.08	34.84	35.62	36.42	37.23	37.87	38.79	39.82	40.98

Monetary Authorities: I Beginning in 1980, data are based on improved classification and sectorization.
Deposit Money Banks: I See note to section 10.
Monetary Survey: I See note to section 10.
Other Banking Institutions: I See note to section 10.

Government Finance: I Beginning in 1980, data relate to a fiscal year different from calendar year.

Egypt
469

1980	1981	1982	1983	1984	1985	1986	1987	1988	1989	1990	1991	1992	1993	1994		
End of Period															**Banking Survey**	
-1,274	-1,273	-555	411	-117	295	1,001	1,940	1,473	-2,280	-2,344	15,450	32,253	44,178	49,662	Foreign Assets (Net)	**51n**
14,342	18,147	22,475	27,083	32,883	39,134	46,481	54,630	65,297	81,406	102,675	111,576	116,109	124,781	141,660	Domestic Credit	**52**
8,401	8,694	11,583	12,606	14,978	17,434	19,943	23,927	29,431	38,187	47,940	50,620	53,041	49,472	52,540	Claims on Central Govt. (Net)	**52an**
3,440	4,700	4,669	6,419	8,131	9,761	11,179	12,839	14,940	18,744	25,331	30,698	26,632	32,064	32,864	Claims on Nonfin.Pub.Enterprises	**52c**
2,501	4,753	6,223	8,058	9,774	11,940	15,360	17,864	20,926	24,475	29,404	30,258	36,436	43,246	56,256	Claims on Private Sector	**52d**
10,668	13,959	18,351	22,534	26,776	31,710	38,277	46,380	56,249	66,036	84,537	100,918	120,392	136,653	152,410	Liquid Liabilities	**55l**
905	1,291	1,494	1,700	1,779	1,944	3,118	5,106	5,095	6,050	7,443	8,171	7,095	8,271	9,202	Restricted Deposits	**56b**
1,496	1,624	2,075	3,260	4,211	5,775	6,087	5,083	5,425	7,041	8,352	17,937	20,876	24,035	29,711	Other Items (Net)	**57r**
Percent Per Annum															**Interest Rates**	
11.00	12.00	13.00	13.00	13.00	13.00	13.00	13.00	13.00	14.00	14.00	20.00	18.40	16.50	14.00	Discount Rate *(End of Period)*	**60**
8.3	10.0	11.0	11.0	11.0	11.0	11.0	11.0	11.0	11.7	12.0	....	....	....	....	Deposit Rate	**60l**
13.3	15.0	15.0	15.0	15.0	15.0	15.0	16.3	17.0	18.3	19.0	....	....	....	....	Lending Rate	**60p**
Period Averages															**Prices**	
23.4	25.3	27.7	32.1	35.3	40.0	46.9	53.3	67.3	85.6	100.0	117.9	132.2	I 143.5	....	Wholesale Prices	**63**
I 21.0	23.2	26.6	30.9	36.1	40.5	50.2	60.0	70.6	85.6	100.0	119.7	136.1	152.5	165.0	Consumer Prices	**64**
Millions of Pounds															**International Transactions**	
2,132.2	2,263.0	2,184.1	2,250.1	2,197.9	2,600.0	2,054.0	3,046.0	3,994.4	5,734.7	6,953.8	11,764.6	10,173.4	7,558.8	....	Exports	**70**
296.4	320.0	286.0	308.8	340.1	299.0	308.4	272.1	318.6	594.2	562.2	193.3	175.2	146.5	....	Cotton	**70f**
174.8	211.2	139.0	134.6	176.8	89.4	49.0	30.3	62.0	109.3	155.3	66.1	71.3	51.9	....	Long Staple	**70fa**
121.6	108.8	147.0	174.1	163.2	209.6	259.5	241.8	256.6	484.9	406.9	127.2	103.9	94.6	....	Long-Medium Staple	**70fb**
464.3	621.8	657.8	678.8	665.4	654.2	769.0	844.5	904.6	1,506.8	3,177.6	5,707.9	6,187.9	6,628.4	6,998.1	Suez Canal Dues	**70.s**
3,401.9	6,147.4	6,354.5	7,192.7	7,536.1	7,772.8	8,051.4	11,357.8	16,308.6	16,623.7	24,823.2	25,216.2	27,656.1	27,553.8	....	Imports, cif	**71**
3,061.7	5,532.7	5,719.1	6,473.5	6,782.5	6,996.2	7,247.0	10,223.0	14,679.2	14,962.8	22,343.1	22,696.8	24,893.0	24,800.9	....	Imports, fob	**71.v**
1990=100															Volume of Exports	
417	451	509	530	443	365	370	330	203	148	100	33	48	47	....	Cotton	**72f**
957	1,171	855	821	835	436	232	118	152	103	100	41	61	56	....	Long Staple	**72fa**
243	219	397	437	316	343	415	399	219	163	100	30	43	43	....	Long-Medium Staple	**72fb**
															Export Prices	
13	13	10	10	14	15	15	15	28	71	100	104	66	56	....	Cotton (Unit Value)	**74f**
12	12	10	11	14	13	14	17	26	69	100	103	75	59	....	Long Staple (Unit Value)	**74fa**
12	12	9	10	13	15	15	15	29	73	100	103	59	54	....	Long-Medium Staple(Unit Val.)	**74fb**
23	23	19	21	25	25	24	25	33	53	100	184	152	145	125	Cotton (Wholesale Price)	**76f**
Minus Sign Indicates Debit															Balance of Payments	
3,854	3,999	4,018	3,693	3,864	3,836	2,632	3,115	2,770	3,119	3,924	4,164	3,670	3,545	....	Goods: Exports f.o.b.	**78aa*d***
-6,814	-7,918	-7,733	-8,251	-10,080	-9,050	-7,170	-8,095	-9,378	-8,841	-10,303	-9,831	-8,901	-9,923	....	Goods: Imports f.o.b.	**78ab*d***
-2,960	-3,919	-3,715	-4,558	-6,216	-5,215	-4,538	-4,980	-6,608	-5,722	-6,379	-5,667	-5,231	-6,378	....	Trade Balance	**78ac*d***
2,393	2,537	2,800	3,133	2,990	3,024	3,358	3,627	4,408	4,203	5,971	6,783	7,716	7,895	....	Services: Credit	**78ad*d***
-2,343	-2,487	-2,727	-2,767	-3,096	-3,190	-3,012	-2,742	-3,082	-3,283	-3,788	-3,364	-4,867	-5,367	....	Services: Debit	**78ae*d***
-2,911	-3,869	-3,642	-4,192	-6,323	-5,381	-4,192	-4,095	-5,283	-4,802	-4,196	-2,248	-2,382	-3,850	....	Balance on Goods and Services	**78af*d***
270	401	402	437	522	418	406	503	575	709	857	860	915	1,110	....	Income: Credit	**78ag*d***
-589	-897	-1,092	-1,080	-1,092	-1,211	-1,126	-983	-776	-1,389	-1,879	-2,143	-2,797	-1,967	....	Income: Debit	**78ah*d***
-3,230	-4,366	-4,332	-4,835	-6,892	-6,174	-4,912	-4,575	-5,484	-5,482	-5,218	-3,531	-4,264	-4,707	....	Balance on Goods, Serv., & Inc.	**78ai*d***
2,791	2,230	2,481	4,505	4,904	4,007	3,101	4,329	4,436	4,183	5,417	5,434	7,076	7,006	....	Current Transfers, n.i.e.: Credit	**78aj*d***
—	—	—	—	—	—	—	—	—	-10	-14	—	—	—	....	Current Transfers: Debit	**78ak*d***
-438	-2,136	-1,851	-330	-1,988	-2,166	-1,811	-246	-1,048	-1,309	185	1,903	2,812	2,299	....	Current Account, n.i.e.	**78al*d***
—	—	—	—	—	—	—	—	—	—	—	—	—	—	....	Capital Account, n.i.e.: Credit	**78ba*d***
—	—	—	—	—	—	—	—	—	—	—	—	—	—	....	Capital Account: Debit	**78bb*d***
—	—	—	—	—	—	—	—	—	—	—	—	—	—	....	Capital Account, n.i.e.	**78bc*d***
-7	-6	-8	-19	-16	-3	-6	-19	-12	-23	-12	-62	-4	—	....	Direct Investment Abroad	**78bd*d***
548	753	294	490	729	1,178	1,217	948	1,190	1,250	734	253	459	493	....	Dir. Invest. in Rep. Econ., n.i.e.	**78be*d***
5	7	—	6	1	20	—	2	—	—	15	21	6	—	....	Portfolio Investment Assets	**78bf*d***
—	—	—	—	—	—	—	—	—	—	—	—	—	4	....	Portfolio Investment Liab., n.i.e.	**78bg*d***
-249	379	250	-389	488	-369	479	-909	546	-1,299	-1,921	-2,298	1,183	319	....	Other Investment Assets	**78bh*d***
715	933	938	196	516	555	245	-354	-416	432	-9,855	-2,620	-1,812	-1,578	....	Other Investment Liab., n.i.e.	**78bi*d***
1,012	2,065	1,474	285	1,718	1,381	1,936	-332	1,308	361	-11,039	-4,706	-168	-762	....	Financial Account, n.i.e.	**78bj*d***
36	124	132	131	24	585	-156	892	-362	414	630	730	716	-1,519	....	Net Errors and Omissions	**78ca*d***
610	53	-245	87	-247	-200	-31	315	-102	-533	-10,224	-2,073	3,360	18	....	Overall Balance	**78cb*d***
-610	-53	245	-87	247	200	31	-315	102	533	10,224	2,073	-3,360	-18	....	Reserves and Related Items	**79da*d***
-559	-105	-178	-152	55	-107	-282	-669	153	435	-2,508	-2,775	-6,330	-2,809	....	Reserve Assets	**79db*d***
-77	-63	-36	-9	-18	-43	-57	89	-59	-24	-48	—	81	—	....	Use of Fund Credit and Loans	**79dc*d***
—	—	—	—	—	—	—	—	—	—	—	—	—	—	....	Liabs.Constit.For.Auth.Reserves	**79dd*d***
26	115	460	74	210	350	370	266	7	122	12,781	4,849	2,889	2,791	....	Exceptional Financing	**79de*d***
Year Ending June 30															**Government Finance**	
....	I -1,096	-3,554	-2,364	-3,258	-3,439	-4,655	-2,613	-4,716	-4,126	-5,494	-1,067	-4,831	....	....	Deficit (-) or Surplus	**80**
....	I 8,072	9,711	10,977	12,345	13,681	15,508	16,764	19,916	22,601	23,435	35,430	49,678	....	....	Revenue	**81**
....	I 9	6	100	1	219	374	1,087	548	1,023	1,428	2,820	3,337	....	....	Grants Received	**81z**
....	I 7,892	11,595	11,195	13,361	14,945	17,552	18,091	22,548	23,913	26,738	35,499	54,649	....	....	Expenditure	**82**
....	I 1,285	1,676	2,246	2,243	2,394	2,985	2,373	2,632	3,837	3,619	3,818	3,197	....	....	Lending Minus Repayments	**83**
															Financing	
....	I 731	3,019	2,034	3,001	2,947	4,432	2,298	5,033	4,551	6,164	2,296	6,708	....	....	Domestic	**84a**
....	I 365	535	330	257	492	223	315	-317	-425	-670	-1,229	-1,877	....	....	Foreign	**85a**
Year Ending June 30															**National Accounts**	
I 4,322	5,307	5,810	6,159	6,387	6,598	6,034	6,500	10,700	13,800	19,400	31,000	40,400	43,500	40,100	Exports of Goods & Services	**90c**
I 2,549	2,841	3,584	4,160	4,957	5,668	6,134	7,350	8,600	9,700	10,850	12,450	14,500	16,000	18,000	Government Consumption	**91f**
I 4,062	5,108	6,150	8,233	9,084	10,555	12,928	14,100	20,150	23,100	26,500	27,850	28,700	25,500	29,000	Gross Fixed Capital Formation	**93e**
I 266	100	100	100	120	130	140	-650	300	900	1,800	-1,200	-1,200	—	—	Increase/Decrease(-) in Stocks	**93i**
I 11,023	11,155	13,285	16,224	21,356	24,927	27,895	35,900	43,550	54,100	68,950	80,900	101,000	115,000	130,500	Private Consumption	**96f**
I -6,410	-7,361	-8,176	-8,981	-10,357	-10,638	-10,568	-11,700	-21,700	-24,800	-31,400	-39,800	-44,300	-48,200	-49,200	Imports of Goods & Services	**98c**
I 15,470	17,150	20,753	25,895	31,547	37,240	42,563	51,500	61,600	76,800	96,100	111,200	139,100	157,300	175,000	Gross Domestic Product = GDP	**99b**
I 1,685	742	446	1,217	2,005	1,681	1,176	2,768	6,730	7,524	....	....	....	....	....	Net Factor Inc/Pmts(-) Abroad	**98.n**
I 17,231	17,892	21,327	26,051	30,605	35,892	39,397	46,818	....	....	....	....	....	....	....	Gross National Product = GNP	**99a**
....	....	55,951	59,553	63,130	70,785	77,203	I 82,144	86,610	90,916	96,100	97,137	I 101,443	104,360	108,517	Gross Dom. Prod. 1990 Prices	**99b.*p***
....	....	37.1	43.5	50.0	52.6	55.1	62.7	71.1	84.5	100.0	114.5	137.1	150.7	161.3	GDP Deflator (1990=100)	**99bi*p***
Midyear Estimates																
42.13	41.67	42.84	44.02	45.23	46.47	47.81	49.05	50.27	51.48	52.69	53.92	55.16	56.49	57.85	**Population**	**99z**

National Accounts: I Compilation procedures were revised in 1970. Data for 1970 to 1979 relate to calendar year.

El Salvador

253

		1965	1966	1967	1968	1969	1970	1971	1972	1973	1974	1975	1976	1977	1978	1979
Exchange Rates																*Colones per SDR: End of Period (aa)*
Principal Rate	aa	2.500	2.500	2.500	2.500	2.500	2.500	2.714	2.714	3.016	3.061	2.927	2.905	3.037	3.257	3.293
Principal Rate	ae	2.500	2.500	2.500	2.500	2.500	2.500	2.500	2.500	2.500	2.500	2.500	2.500	2.500	2.500	2.500
Fund Position																*Millions of SDRs:*
Quota	2f. s	20.0	25.0	25.0	25.0	25.0	35.0	35.0	35.0	35.0	35.0	35.0	35.0	35.0	43.0	43.0
SDRs	1b. s	—	—	—	—	—	—	2.2	3.7	3.8	3.6	3.9	4.0	7.8	7.6	13.2
Reserve Position in the Fund	1c. s	5.0	—	—	—	—	—	—	—	—	—	—	—	5.1	8.8	8.5
Total Fund Cred.&Loans Outstg.	2tl	—	13.7	13.7	16.7	14.0	6.5	10.2	8.8	—	17.9	17.9	12.8	—	—	—
International Liquidity														*Millions of US Dollars Unless Otherwise Indicated:*		
Total Reserves minus Gold	1l. d	38.4	38.9	37.0	44.2	46.5	45.4	46.2	63.9	41.3	77.6	107.0	185.4	211.2	268.1	142.6
SDRs	1b. d	—	—	—	—	—	—	2.4	4.1	4.6	4.4	4.6	4.7	9.5	9.9	17.4
Reserve Position in the Fund	1c. d	5.0	—	—	—	—	—	—	—	—	—	—	—	6.2	11.4	11.2
Foreign Exchange	1d. d	33.4	38.9	37.0	44.2	46.5	45.4	43.8	59.8	36.7	73.2	102.4	180.7	195.6	246.8	114.0
Gold (Million Fine Troy Ounces)	1ad	.516	.514	.508	.507	.494	.494	.492	.486	.486	.486	.486	.486	.501	.501	.508
Gold (National Valuation)	1an d	18.1	18.0	17.8	17.7	17.3	17.3	17.2	18.5	20.5	20.5	20.5	20.5	21.1	21.1	21.5
Monetary Authorities: Other Liab.	4..d	14.4	16.6	15.4	18.3	31.1	25.2	26.9	28.0	19.1	80.9	83.9	96.4	79.4	165.5	177.4
Deposit Money Banks. Asscts	7a. d	6.6	5.6	5.9	5.6	4.3	9.2	7.5	8.0	14.4	21.0	14.6	15.7	10.6	24.3	14.6
Liabilities	7b. d	12.6	10.4	11.2	9.9	5.5	13.5	8.7	7.6	22.2	33.3	9.9	21.5	37.7	55.8	43.9
Monetary Authorities																*Millions of Colones:*
Foreign Assets	11	138	142	137	155	141	157	158	206	154	245	319	515	581	723	404
Claims on Central Government	12a	70	73	77	102	124	116	136	152	131	253	281	295	391	401	688
Claims on Nonfin.Pub.Enterprises	12c	....	....	....	....	....	....	....	....	....	....	....	....	....	....	....
Claims on Private Sector	12d	9	25	26	31	48	44	65	77	90	128	194	231	275	306	360
Claims on Deposit Money Banks	12e	69	71	109	106	132	130	145	149	222	287	243	285	336	316	533
Claims on Other Banking Insts.	12f	....	....	....	....	....	....	....	....	....	....	....	....	....	....	....
Reserve Money	14	76	81	117	135	141	149	166	209	239	277	353	476	504	386	357
of which: Currency Outside DMBs	14a	112	115	122	116	133	136	145	175	201	241	253	380	432	500	743
Nonfin.Pub.Ent. Deps.	14e	1	2	2	5	2	2	3	7	2	2	3	25	7	7	11
Foreign Liabilities	16c	1	36	36	43	49	19	30	28	6	67	60	45	2	55	15
Long-Term Foreign Liabilities	16cl	35	40	37	45	64	60	65	66	42	190	202	233	196	358	429
Central Government Deposits	16d	51	29	25	34	29	35	40	31	47	72	85	131	235	213	195
Counterpart Funds	16e	....	....	....	....	....	....	....	....	....	....	....	....	....	....	....
Central Govt. Lending Funds	16f	....	....	....	....	....	....	....	....	....	....	....	....	....	....	....
Capital Accounts	17a	26	30	35	39	46	62	80	99	77	94	103	118	138	181	248
Other Items (Net)	17r	96	95	100	99	116	121	124	151	186	214	234	323	507	553	743
Deposit Money Banks																*Millions of Colones:*
Reserves	20	87	92	128	144	154	163	177	218	256	295	378	484	529	419	393
Foreign Assets	21	16	14	15	14	11	23	19	20	36	52	36	39	27	61	37
Claims on Central Government	22a	6	5	6	6	7	7	7	7	9	22	18	31	52	54	91
Claims on Private Sector	22d	431	463	472	493	545	588	640	720	909	1,072	1,128	1,350	1,647	1,914	2,128
Demand Deposits	24	121	129	129	144	152	157	167	208	263	314	392	512	550	579	567
Time, Savings,& Fgn.Currency Dep.	25	204	232	236	245	274	300	343	418	492	560	705	854	1,015	1,154	1,125
Bonds	26ab	96	97	97	114	119	126	124	120	121	135	117	123	139	149	162
Foreign Liabilities	26c	29	21	23	20	9	30	18	16	52	81	22	52	94	139	110
Central Government Deposits	26d	7	4	3	7	7	9	12	13	13	17	21	24	44	50	48
Credit from Monetary Authorities	26g	65	65	104	101	126	125	140	143	218	287	243	285	336	316	533
Capital Accounts	27a	49	51	53	54	58	59	62	70	83	79	90	107	131	149	164
Other Items (Net)	27r	−32	−24	−26	−28	−28	−25	−22	−23	−32	−30	−29	−52	−55	−90	−60
Monetary Survey																*Millions of Colones:*
Foreign Assets (Net)	31n	124	99	92	106	93	131	129	182	132	150	273	457	511	589	316
Domestic Credit	32	458	533	553	591	689	710	796	912	1,079	1,386	1,516	1,753	2,086	2,413	3,025
Claims on Central Govt. (Net)	32an	18	45	54	67	96	78	91	115	80	186	193	171	164	192	537
Claims on Nonfin.Pub.Enterprises	32c	....	....	....	....	....	....	....	....	....	....	....	....	....	....	....
Claims on Private Sector	32d	440	488	499	524	593	631	705	797	998	1,200	1,322	1,582	1,922	2,220	2,488
Claims on Other Banking Insts.	32f	....	....	....	....	....	....	....	....	....	....	....	....	....	....	....
Money	34	234	247	253	265	288	295	315	390	466	557	648	917	988	1,087	1,321
Quasi-Money	35	204	232	236	245	274	300	343	418	492	560	705	854	1,015	1,154	1,125
Bonds	36ab	96	97	97	114	119	127	124	120	121	135	117	123	221	230	243
Long-Term Foreign Liabilities	36cl	38	45	42	49	69	64	69	69	45	193	204	235	196	358	429
Counterpart Funds	36e	....	....	....	....	....	....	....	....	....	....	....	....	....	....	....
Central Govt. Lending Funds	36f	....	....	....	....	....	....	....	....	....	....	....	....	....	....	....
Other Items (Net)	37r	10	12	17	24	33	55	75	98	87	92	114	81	177	172	223
Money plus Quasi-Money	35l	439	479	489	509	562	595	658	807	958	1,116	1,353	1,770	2,004	2,241	2,446
Interest Rates																*Percent Per Annum*
Deposit Rate	60l	....	....	....	....	....	....	....	....	....	....	....	....	....	....	....
Lending Rate	60p	....	....	....	....	....	....	....	....	....	....	....	....	....	....	....
Prices																*Index Numbers (1990=100):*
Wholesale Prices	63	10.7	10.7	10.8	10.7	10.6	11.6	10.9	11.6	14.0	17.6	17.9	24.1	35.5	ⱡ28.5	30.6
Excl. Coffee	63a	10.6	10.3	10.9	10.7	10.6	10.6	10.7	11.2	13.3	17.4	18.6	20.7	23.1	ⱡ24.2	26.7
Consumer Prices	64	6.0	6.0	6.0	6.2	6.2	6.4	6.4	6.5	6.9	8.1	9.6	10.3	11.5	13.0	ⱡ14.9

El Salvador

	1980	1981	1982	1983	1984	1985	1986	1987	1988	1989	1990	1991	1992	1993	1994		
Colones per US Dollar: End of Period (ae)																**Exchange Rates**	
	3.189	2.910	2.758	2.617	2.451	2.746	6.116	7.093	6.729	6.571	11.424	11.558	12.609	11.909	12.774	Principal Rate	aa
	2.500	2.500	2.500	2.500	2.500	2.500	5.000	5.000	5.000	5.000	8.030	8.080	9.170	8.670	8.750	Principal Rate	ae
End of Period																**Fund Position**	
	64.5	64.5	64.5	89.0	89.0	89.0	89.0	89.0	89.0	89.0	89.0	89.0	125.6	125.6	125.6	Quota	2f. s
	—	.1	1.7	.1	—	—	—	—	—	—	—	—	—	—	.1	SDRs	1b. s
	—	—	—	—	—	—	—	—	—	—	—	—	—	—	—	Reserve Position in the Fund	1c. s
	25.0	57.3	117.1	132.6	127.2	100.6	50.9	15.8	8.0	4.1	.1	—	—	—	—	Total Fund Cred.&Loans Outstg.	2tl
End of Period																**International Liquidity**	
	77.7	71.9	108.5	160.2	165.8	179.6	169.7	186.1	161.6	265.9	414.8	287.2	422.1	536.2	649.4	Total Reserves minus Gold	1l. d
	—	.1	1.8	.1	—	—	—	—	—	—	—	—	—	—	.1	SDRs	1b. d
	—	—	—	—	—	—	—	—	—	—	—	—	—	—	—	Reserve Position in the Fund	1c. d
	77.7	71.8	106.7	160.1	165.8	179.6	169.7	186.1	161.6	265.9	414.8	287.2	422.1	536.2	649.3	Foreign Exchange	1d. d
	.516	.516	.516	.469	.469	.469	.469	.469	.469	.469	.469	.469	.469	.469	.469	Gold (Million Fine Troy Ounces)	1ad
	21.8	21.8	21.8	19.8	19.8	19.8	19.8	19.8	19.8	19.8	19.8	19.8	19.8	19.8	19.8	Gold (National Valuation)	1an d
	428.0	559.9	546.9	554.2	553.1	539.7	482.2	378.3	363.3	479.4	546.5	342.1	368.1	293.1	158.6	Monetary Authorities: Other Liab.	4..d
	43.0	67.5	39.0	87.0	104.7	148.4	94.5	81.8	72.3	93.1	86.9	65.8	81.1	94.0	59.3	Deposit Money Banks: Assets	7a. d
	9.1	22.4	22.5	37.0	47.0	42.2	23.7	17.0	29.1	51.8	17.1	18.0	31.4	48.5	140.8	Liabilities	7b. d
End of Period																**Monetary Authorities**	
	249	234	286	406	416	446	1,322	1,398	1,275	1,966	4,391	3,734	5,094	6,385	7,473	Foreign Assets	11
	1,158	1,781	1,546	1,474	1,883	2,026	1,974	2,083	2,295	3,287	5,125	6,287	6,827	6,782	6,271	Claims on Central Government	12a
	....	....	264	268	277	305	345	414	382	334	—	—	13	—	—	Claims on Nonfin.Pub.Enterprises	12c
	878	887	I 50	54	118	98	64	55	7	—	—	10	—	—	—	Claims on Private Sector	12d
	606	586	638	788	677	886	817	1,098	1,261	2,094	2,249	1,094	1,243	1,317	—	Claims on Deposit Money Banks	12e
	....	....	860	669	803	916	945	1,003	1,307	1,303	556	629	638	657	2,292	Claims on Other Banking Insts.	12f
	457	537	1,447	1,505	1,678	2,058	2,076	2,595	3,011	3,332	4,318	5,289	6,086	8,730	10,762	Reserve Money	14
	719	703	732	724	836	1,080	1,157	1,298	1,326	1,727	1,856	2,023	2,433	2,655	2,999	of which: Currency Outside DMBs	14a
	17	41	54	39	17	20	17	17	18	14	19	13	8	11	7	Nonfin.Pub.Ent. Deps.	14e
	499	823	874	583	537	477	639	243	303	656	1,428	356	551	300	63	Foreign Liabilities	16c
	651	743	816	1,149	1,158	1,149	2,083	1,760	1,567	1,768	2,962	2,407	2,825	2,242	1,325	Long-Term Foreign Liabilities	16cl
	260	305	158	216	590	610	1,093	907	1,213	1,137	1,521	1,772	1,446	1,496	2,009	Central Government Deposits	16d
	....	....	52	—	—	150	250	1,098	1,214	1,727	900	528	716	99	54	Counterpart Funds	16e
	....	....	97	103	52	52	105	105	105	362	105	517	22	20	1	Central Govt. Lending Funds	16f
	310	343	347	358	380	398	493	528	533	551	1,474	1,573	1,982	2,158	2,235	Capital Accounts	17a
	715	736	I –148	–255	–220	–217	–1,270	–1,185	–1,417	–549	–385	–691	188	98	–410	Other Items (Net)	17r
End of Period																**Deposit Money Banks**	
	508	567	I 624	693	784	902	833	1,193	1,577	1,525	2,874	3,175	4,252	6,341	8,383	Reserves	20
	108	169	I 97	218	262	371	473	409	362	465	698	532	744	815	519	Foreign Assets	21
	34	154	I 101	150	208	291	418	485	446	645	557	774	765	1,009	1,347	Claims on Central Government	22a
	2,124	2,244	I 2,574	2,848	3,081	3,977	4,917	5,345	6,063	6,604	7,345	8,598	12,267	14,405	19,638	Claims on Private Sector	22d
	693	693	I 810	785	937	1,151	1,528	1,370	1,567	1,568	2,190	2,288	3,220	3,682	3,808	Demand Deposits	24
	1,135	1,397	I 1,598	1,978	2,405	3,065	4,134	4,586	5,208	5,482	7,320	8,911	11,903	15,647	21,056	Time, Savings,& Fgn.Currency Dep.	25
	178	191	I 246	263	241	246	226	215	223	244	171	158	150	112	100	Bonds	26ab
	15	48	I 49	88	114	103	107	80	143	258	136	144	288	420	1,157	Foreign Liabilities	26c
	66	60	I 54	60	121	190	262	338	392	383	462	521	541	562	873	Central Government Deposits	26d
	606	586	I 638	788	677	886	817	1,098	1,261	2,094	2,249	1,094	1,238	1,317	—	Credit from Monetary Authorities	26g
	181	181	I 211	211	215	237	273	311	386	416	409	743	809	860	2,102	Capital Accounts	27a
	–100	–23	I –209	–264	–373	–335	–708	–565	–733	–1,204	–1,464	–778	–122	–31	791	Other Items (Net)	27r
End of Period																**Monetary Survey**	
	–157	–469	I –540	–47	27	238	1,049	1,484	1,190	1,518	3,525	3,765	4,999	6,480	6,772	Foreign Assets (Net)	31n
	3,868	4,700	I 5,344	5,341	5,818	6,966	7,457	8,290	9,110	10,859	11,667	14,065	18,579	20,852	26,749	Domestic Credit	32
	866	1,570	I 1,436	1,349	1,381	1,517	1,037	1,324	1,136	2,412	3,699	4,769	5,604	5,734	4,736	Claims on Central Govt. (Net)	32an
	....	....	290	289	299	323	360	429	393	347	12	1	13	—	—	Claims on Nonfin.Pub.Enterprises	32c
	3,002	3,130	I 2,624	2,902	3,199	4,075	4,981	5,400	6,070	6,604	7,345	8,608	12,267	14,405	19,638	Claims on Private Sector	32d
	....	....	865	672	806	919	947	1,005	1,310	1,305	560	633	643	659	2,320	Claims on Other Banking Insts.	32f
	1,429	1,437	I 1,633	1,596	1,830	2,306	2,758	2,762	2,996	3,370	4,153	4,872	6,284	7,353	7,802	Money	34
	1,135	1,397	I 1,600	1,979	2,405	3,068	4,147	4,609	5,223	5,760	7,867	9,684	12,597	16,500	21,897	Quasi-Money	35
	190	250	I 246	263	241	254	226	305	230	335	766	1,973	3,085	3,459	2,936	Bonds	36ab
	659	750	I 823	1,154	1,161	1,152	2,095	1,766	1,569	1,769	2,963	2,409	2,825	2,242	1,400	Long-Term Foreign Liabilities	36cl
	....	....	52	—	—	150	250	1,098	1,214	1,727	900	528	716	99	54	Counterpart Funds	36e
	....	....	97	103	52	52	105	105	105	362	105	517	22	20	1	Central Govt. Lending Funds	36f
	298	397	I 353	197	155	222	–1,074	–870	–1,035	–947	–1,562	–2,153	–1,949	–2,340	–569	Other Items (Net)	37r
	2,563	2,834	I 3,233	3,575	4,236	5,374	6,905	7,371	8,219	9,130	12,020	14,555	18,881	23,853	29,699	Money plus Quasi-Money	35l
Percent Per Annum																**Interest Rates**	
	....	....	....	12.50	12.50	12.50	15.00	15.00	15.00	16.25	18.00	16.11	11.51	15.27	13.57	Deposit Rate	60l
	....	....	....	15.00	14.00	14.00	17.00	17.00	17.00	18.50	21.17	19.67	16.43	19.42	19.03	Lending Rate	60p
Period Averages																**Prices**	
	35.5	39.0	42.3	45.2	47.8	54.5	72.2	72.7	76.7	84.1	100.0	106.9	109.3	117.5	126.7	Wholesale Prices	63
	31.6	35.5	38.5	41.6	44.6	52.5	64.6	70.1	73.5	82.8	100.0	103.4	106.0	111.5	117.2	Excl. Coffee	63a
	17.5	20.1	22.5	25.5	28.4	34.7	45.8	57.2	68.6	80.6	100.0	114.4	I 127.2	150.9	166.8	Consumer Prices	64

El Salvador
253

		1965	1966	1967	1968	1969	1970	1971	1972	1973	1974	1975	1976	1977	1978	1979
International Transactions														*Millions of US Dollars*		
Exports	70..d	188.7	188.9	207.2	212.5	201.8	229.4	228.2	273.3	352.0	462.6	531.4	743.3	972.4	848.4	1,223.2
Imports, cif	71..d	200.6	220.8	223.9	214.0	208.5	214.4	249.4	272.4	377.2	562.5	614.0	734.7	929.1	1,028.0	1,037.0
Imports, fob	71.vd	183.2	201.7	204.9	196.0	189.8	194.8	226.8	244.2	342.8	520.9	564.8	679.2	860.7	949.9	947.8
Balance of Payments														*Millions of US Dollars:*		
Goods: Exports f.o.b.	78aad	...	...	...	...	...	...	...	...	...	...	...	744.6	973.5	801.6	1,132.3
Goods: Imports f.o.b.	78abd	...	...	...	...	...	...	...	...	...	...	...	-681.0	-861.0	-951.1	-954.7
Trade Balance	78acd	...	...	...	...	...	...	...	...	...	...	...	63.7	112.5	-149.4	177.6
Services: Credit	78add	...	...	...	...	...	...	...	...	...	...	...	116.1	113.0	121.0	133.0
Services: Debit	78aed	...	...	...	...	...	...	...	...	...	...	...	-171.4	-208.6	-256.8	-300.6
Balance on Goods and Services	78afd	...	...	...	...	...	...	...	...	...	...	...	8.4	16.8	-285.3	10.0
Income: Credit	78agd	...	...	...	...	...	...	...	...	...	...	...	38.9	39.9	37.0	90.4
Income: Debit	78ahd	...	...	...	...	...	...	...	...	...	...	...	-52.8	-65.5	-88.8	-130.3
Balance on Goods, Serv., & Inc.	78aid	...	...	...	...	...	...	...	...	...	...	...	-5.6	-8.7	-337.2	-30.0
Current Transfers, n.i.e.: Credit	78ajd	...	...	...	...	...	...	...	...	...	...	...	38.1	50.0	61.8	65.6
Current Transfers: Debit	78akd	...	...	...	...	...	...	...	...	...	...	...	-8.9	-3.9	-3.4	-3.3
Current Account, n.i.e.	78ald	...	...	...	...	...	...	...	...	...	...	...	23.6	37.4	-278.7	32.2
Capital Account, n.i.e.: Credit	78bad	...	...	...	...	...	...	...	...	...	...	...	—	-6.5	-7.1	-10.8
Capital Account: Debit	78bbd	...	...	...	...	...	...	...	...	...	...	...	—	-6.5	-7.1	-10.8
Capital Account, n.i.e.	78bcd	...	...	...	...	...	...	...	...	...	...	...				
Direct Investment Abroad	78bdd	...	...	...	...	...	...	...	...	...	...	...				
Dir. Invest. in Rep. Econ., n.i.e.	78bed	...	...	...	...	...	...	...	...	...	...	...	13.0	18.6	23.4	-10.0
Portfolio Investment Assets	78bfd	...	...	...	...	...	...	...	...	...	...	...		-.8	-1.1	
Portfolio Investment Liab., n.i.e.	78bgd	...	...	...	...	...	...	...	...	...	...	...	17.8	1.5	5.1	-5.7
Other Investment Assets	78bhd	...	...	...	...	...	...	...	...	...	...	...	-30.2	-143.4	-33.0	7.3
Other Investment Liab., n.i.e.	78bid	...	...	...	...	...	...	...	...	...	...	...	85.0	167.9	346.0	-40.7
Financial Account, n.i.e.	78bjd	...	...	...	...	...	...	...	...	...	...	...	85.6	43.9	340.4	-49.0
Net Errors and Omissions	78cad	...	...	...	...	...	...	...	...	...	...	...	-24.9	-33.8	-29.1	-106.2
Overall Balance	78cbd	...	...	...	...	...	...	...	...	...	...	...	84.3	40.9	25.4	-133.8
Reserves and Related Items	79daad	...	...	...	...	...	...	...	...	...	...	...	-84.3	-40.9	-25.4	133.8
Reserve Assets	79dbd	...	...	...	...	...	...	...	...	...	...	...	-78.4	-26.0	-55.4	133.8
Use of Fund Credit and Loans	79dcd	...	...	...	...	...	...	...	...	...	...	...	-5.9	-14.9	—	—
Liabs.Constit.For.Auth.Reserves	79ddd	...	...	...	...	...	...	...	...	...	...	...				
Exceptional Financing	79ded	...	...	...	...	...	...	...	...	...	...	...	—	—	30.0	—
Government Finance														*Millions of Colones:*		
Deficit (-) or Surplus	80	2.7	-29.3	-16.1	-13.1	-30.1	.9	-30.2	-24.2	11.7	-54.3	-24.7	-21.4	179.7	-122.3	-121.9
Revenue	81	276.2	251.0	257.9	228.6	258.2	284.1	297.7	326.5	403.1	488.1	580.8	805.2	1,256.6	1,048.4	1,171.1
Expenditure	82	250.8	280.3	259.8	241.7	288.3	283.2	327.9	350.7	391.4	542.4	605.5	826.6	1,076.9	1,184.2	1,280.1
Lending Minus Repayments	83	22.7	—	14.2	—	—	—	—	—	—	—	—	—	—	-13.5	12.9
Financing																
Net Borrowing: Domestic	84a	-1.2	-1.2	4.8	11.6	23.5	-6.0	20.8	7.0	-39.8	4.7	3.2	25.4	-90.3	54.2	72.7
Foreign	85a	17.2	8.8	7.5	5.9	1.2	7.2	7.7	15.4	35.2	62.2	14.9	23.0	-.4	35.6	28.3
Use of Cash Balances	87	-18.7	21.6	3.7	-4.4	5.4	-2.1	1.5	1.7	-7.0	-12.8	6.7	-26.8	-88.8	32.6	21.0
Central Govt. & Official Entities																
Debt: Domestic	88a. i	58.0	57.1	54.8	67.7	94.1	97.6	117.2	129.5	138.5	160.3	194.2	289.2	299.0	459.9	581.0
Foreign	89a. i	146.6	182.6	204.9	212.3	217.7	223.4	228.4	276.2	320.9	444.6	623.0	713.3	700.9	847.8	996.4
National Accounts														*Millions of Colones*		
Exports of Goods & Services	90c	529	521	567	585	556	639	666	839	998	1,279	1,480	2,028	2,735	2,328	3,182
Government Consumption	91f	173	184	203	216	249	276	275	308	349	429	501	686	805	996	1,133
Gross Fixed Capital Formation	93e	296	326	324	248	274	308	359	474	521	719	1,031	1,145	1,521	1,652	1,512
Increase/Decrease(-) in Stocks	93i	11	36	3	7	30	33	62	-66	88	174	-40	-26	158	183	45
Private Consumption	96f	1,560	1,675	1,756	1,861	1,892	1,948	2,061	2,138	2,474	2,946	3,283	3,973	4,634	5,574	5,933
Imports of Goods & Services	98c	-577	-631	-637	-624	-618	-631	-720	-811	-1,099	-1,610	-1,711	-2,101	-2,686	-3,041	-3,197
Gross Domestic Product	99b	1,992	2,110	2,216	2,292	2,382	2,571	2,704	2,882	3,332	3,944	4,478	5,706	7,167	7,692	8,607
Net Factor Inc/Pmts(-) Abroad	98.n	-17	-17	-18	-18	-20	-21	-25	-27	-38	-53	-69	-17	-72	-130	-60
Gross Nat'l Expenditure = GNP	99a	1,975	2,093	2,197	2,274	2,362	2,550	2,679	2,855	3,294	3,891	4,409	5,689	7,095	7,562	8,547
Nat'l Income, Market Prices	99e	1,876	1,989	2,088	2,161	2,242	2,425	2,545	2,718	3,146	3,714	4,210	5,458	6,826	7,244	8,191
Gross Dom. Prod. 1990 Prices	99b.p	21,388	22,920	24,166	24,948	25,817	26,586	27,866	29,388	30,876	32,859	34,687	36,064	38,252	40,704	40,004
GDP Deflator (1990=100)	99bip	9.3	9.2	9.2	9.2	9.2	9.7	9.7	9.8	10.8	12.0	12.9	15.8	18.7	18.9	21.5
														Millions:		
Population	99z	2.93	3.04	3.15	3.27	3.36	3.44	3.55	I3.67	3.77	3.89	4.01	4.12	4.26	4.35	4.44

Monetary Authorities: I Beginning in March 1982, credit to certain institutions (mainly INCAFE and INAZUCAR) has been separately identified in *lines 12c* and *12f*. Prior to March 1982, data were included in *line 12d*. Also beginning in March 1982, *line 17r* reflects the transfer of several accounts from it, mainly to *lines 16e* and *16f*.

Deposit Money Banks: I Beginning in March 1982, data are based on an improved sectorization of accounts.
Monetary Survey: I See notes to sections 10 and 20.

El Salvador

1980	1981	1982	1983	1984	1985	1986	1987	1988	1989	1990	1991	1992	1993	1994		
Millions of US Dollars															**International Transactions**	
966.8	796.6	699.4	735.3	717.3	679.0	754.9	590.9	608.8	497.5	581.5	588.0	597.5	731.7	843.9	Exports	70..*d*
966.1	985.6	856.8	891.5	977.4	961.4	934.9	994.1	1,007.0	1,161.3	1,262.5	1,405.9	1,698.5	1,912.2	2,248.7	Imports, cif	71..*d*
878.3	887.6	771.9	803.1	880.6	866.1	842.3	895.5	907.2	1,046.2	1,137.4	1,266.6	1,530.2	1,722.7	2,025.9	Imports, fob	71.v*d*
Minus Sign Indicates Debit															**Balance of Payments**	
1,075.3	798.0	699.6	758.0	725.9	679.0	777.9	589.6	610.6	497.8	580.2	588.0	597.5	731.7	....	Goods: Exports f.o.b.	78aa*d*
−897.0	−898.4	−799.8	−832.2	−914.5	−895.0	−902.3	−938.7	−966.5	−1,089.5	−1,180.0	−1,294.1	−1,558.8	−1,766.9	....	Goods: Imports f.o.b.	78ab*d*
178.4	−100.3	−100.2	−74.3	−188.6	−216.0	−124.4	−349.1	−355.9	−591.7	−599.8	−706.1	−961.3	−1,035.2	....	Trade Balance	78ac*d*
138.8	124.7	117.4	135.8	165.4	223.9	241.1	318.1	328.0	313.4	296.7	311.6	376.7	406.4	....	Services: Credit	78ad*d*
−273.5	−263.4	−253.0	−246.3	−242.0	−290.8	−281.0	−280.1	−341.4	−350.1	−283.6	−323.5	−364.3	−382.2	....	Services: Debit	78ae*d*
43.7	−239.0	−235.9	−184.7	−265.1	−282.8	−164.4	−311.1	−369.3	−628.4	−586.7	−718.1	−948.9	−1,010.9	....	Balance on Goods and Services	78af*d*
56.6	47.5	50.9	37.0	62.9	48.5	36.9	42.9	24.2	23.3	26.6	30.3	31.7	30.8	....	Income: Credit	78ag*d*
−118.6	−119.3	−142.4	−151.6	−159.1	−137.9	−138.9	−134.9	−129.6	−113.7	−145.2	−151.4	−128.8	−142.4	....	Income: Debit	78ah*d*
−18.3	−310.9	−327.4	−299.3	−361.3	−372.3	−266.4	−403.1	−474.7	−718.9	−705.3	−839.1	−1,046.0	−1,122.5	....	Balance on Goods, Serv., & Inc.	78ai*d*
52.9	75.2	210.5	154.1	176.1	186.7	251.8	336.8	347.6	390.7	472.7	628.8	851.9	1,004.9	....	Current Transfers, n.i.e.: Credit	78aj*d*
−.6	−14.8	−3.1	−2.6	−3.5	−3.1	−2.5	−1.9	−2.1	−1.9	−2.4	−2.5	−.7	−.7	....	Current Transfers: Debit	78ak*d*
33.9	−250.5	−120.0	−147.8	−188.7	−188.7	−17.1	−68.2	−129.2	−330.1	−235.0	−212.8	−194.9	−118.3	....	Current Account, n.i.e.	78al*d*
														....	Capital Account, n.i.e.: Credit	78ba*d*
−3.3	—	—	—	—	—	—	—	—	—	—	—	—	—	....	Capital Account: Debit	78bb*d*
−3.3	—	—	—	—	—	—	—	—	—	—	—	—	—	....	Capital Account, n.i.e.	78bc*d*
														....	Direct Investment Abroad	78bd*d*
5.9	−5.7	−1.0	28.1	12.4	12.4	24.1	18.3	17.0	12.9	1.7	25.3	15.3	16.4	....	Dir. Invest. in Rep. Econ., n.i.e.	78be*d*
−1.0	—	−1.0	.1	—	—	−3.1	—	—	—	—	—	—	—	....	Portfolio Investment Assets	78bf*d*
−24.3	−22.4	−1.2	−45.2	−20.7	−51.6	54.4	9.7	10.6	−1.0	−18.8	15.1	—	4.1	....	Portfolio Investment Liab., n.i.e.	78bg*d*
44.8	179.4	177.8	109.5	27.4	36.0	−29.7	−86.9	24.7	93.6	6.8	−101.6	−19.6	66.1	....	Other Investment Assets	78bh*d*
25.3	151.3	174.5	92.6	19.0	−3.2	45.7	−59.0	52.3	105.5	−10.3	−61.3	−4.3	86.7	....	Other Investment Liab., n.i.e.	78bi*d*
−318.2	−58.6	−61.4	−50.5	−51.9	23.0	−141.8	6.9	−107.1	126.3	270.3	125.9	65.5	90.3	....	Financial Account, n.i.e.	78bj*d*
−262.3	−157.8	−6.9	−105.7	−221.5	−169.0	−113.2	−120.3	−184.1	−98.2	24.9	−148.2	−133.7	58.7	....	Net Errors and Omissions	78ca*d*
262.3	157.8	6.9	105.7	221.5	169.0	113.2	120.3	184.1	98.2	−24.9	148.2	133.7	−58.7	....	Overall Balance	78cb*d*
68.1	11.3	−36.5	−40.2	−1.4	—	14.1	−36.8	30.1	−98.2	−148.3	70.1	−91.5	−112.1	....	Reserves and Related Items	79da*d*
33.4	36.8	65.1	16.5	−5.3	−27.2	−57.9	−45.0	−10.5	−5.0	−5.2	−.2	—	—	....	Reserve Assets	79db*d*
5.3	36.2	−36.0	−5.6	13.6	6.2	−19.0	−1.3	—	—	—	—	—	—	....	Use of Fund Credit and Loans	79dc*d*
155.5	73.5	14.3	135.0	214.6	190.0	176.1	203.5	164.5	201.5	128.6	78.3	225.2	53.3	....	Liabs.Constit.For.Auth.Reserves	79dd*d*
														....	Exceptional Financing	79de*d*
Year Ending December 31															**Government Finance**	
−396.7	−549.2	−607.3	−324.4	−382.4	−192.6	42.1	85.8	−175.1	−730.5	−27.1	−1,184.9	−1,839.3	−1,284.4	−1,028.2	Deficit (-) or Surplus	80
1,028.9	1,068.2	1,091.3	1,258.2	1,573.9	1,901.9	2,821.9	2,981.0	2,927.6	2,631.2	3,852.7	4,072.1	5,715.6	7,215.7	9,082.4	Revenue	81
1,422.4	1,581.5	1,694.6	1,571.4	1,820.7	2,149.6	2,723.1	3,022.8	3,095.8	3,306.7	3,854.7	4,927.9	7,253.7	8,314.0	9,991.7	Expenditure	82
3.2	35.9	4.0	11.2	135.6	−55.1	56.7	−127.6	6.9	55.0	25.1	329.1	301.2	186.1	118.9	Lending Minus Repayments	83
															Financing	
429.3	501.3	436.6	296.2	341.5	142.0	33.3	−17.4	254.0	690.1	191.1	....	....	....	....	Net Borrowing: Domestic	84a
21.7	61.2	123.5	38.5	31.6	1.3	−84.1	103.9	302.4	258.9	−90.0	....	....	1,305.0	1,413.7	Foreign	85a
−54.2	−13.3	47.2	−10.3	9.3	49.3	8.7	−172.3	−381.3	−218.5	−74.0	....	....	....	....	Use of Cash Balances	87
															Central Govt. & Official Entities	
962.8	1,774.2	2,225.1	2,245.4	2,790.0	3,021.3	3,120.1	5,226.2	4,494.7	6,293.7	7,472.5	9,050.3	9,494.8	9,995.6	9,430.7	Debt: Domestic	88a.*i*
1,187.7	1,632.1	2,039.5	2,486.6	2,714.5	2,935.4	6,270.5	6,560.0	6,870.0	7,586.5	11,646.7	14,647.1	15,647.5	15,296.4	17,100.0	Foreign	89a.*i*
Millions of Colones															**National Accounts**	
3,046	2,307	2,042	2,486	2,536	3,199	4,875	4,395	4,327	4,261	6,771	7,332	8,019	11,822	14,250	Exports of Goods & Services	90c
1,247	1,369	1,415	1,607	1,869	2,220	2,803	3,181	3,484	3,930	3,618	4,236	4,670	5,237	5,855	Government Consumption	91f
1,210	1,173	1,130	1,180	1,336	1,723	2,594	3,158	3,456	4,293	5,004	6,456	6,561	10,818	13,149	Gross Fixed Capital Formation	93e
−27	58	56	44	59	−169	26	−297	45	646	54	107	673	452	175	Increase/Decrease(-) in Stocks	93i
6,405	6,644	6,877	7,871	9,184	11,640	15,206	18,744	22,153	26,729	32,435	37,463	44,062	52,782	62,441	Private Consumption	96f
−2,964	−2,904	−2,553	−3,036	−3,327	−4,283	−5,740	−6,040	−6,099	−7,636	−11,394	−13,000	−16,168	−20,588	−24,852	Imports of Goods & Services	98c
8,917	8,647	8,966	10,152	11,657	14,331	19,763	23,141	27,366	32,230	36,487	42,594	49,841	60,522	71,019	Gross Domestic Product	99b
−128	−149	−229	−370	−343	−354	−471	−525	−509	−568	−971	−1,145	−901	−1,051	−906	Net Factor Inc/Pmts(-) Abroad	98.n
8,789	8,498	8,737	9,782	11,314	13,977	19,292	22,616	26,857	31,662	35,516	41,449	48,840	59,471	70,113	Gross Nat'l Expenditure = GNP	99a
8,420	8,140	8,367	9,363	10,832	13,385	18,477	21,661	25,728	30,334	35,516	41,449	48,940	59,471	70,113	Nat'l Income, Market Prices	99e
36,535	33,508	31,630	31,882	32,606	33,250	33,460	34,360	34,919	35,287	36,487	37,791	40,643	43,643	46,258	Gross Dom. Prod. 1990 Prices	99b.*p*
24.4	25.8	28.3	31.8	35.8	43.1	59.1	67.3	78.4	91.3	100.0	112.7	122.6	138.7	153.5	GDP Deflator (1990=100)	99bi*p*
Midyear Estimates																
4.51	4.59	4.66	4.72	4.78	4.86	4.95	5.05	5.09	5.19	5.17	5.35	5.40	5.52	....	**Population**	99z

Equatorial Guinea
642

		1965	1966	1967	1968	1969	1970	1971	1972	1973	1974	1975	1976	1977	1978	1979
Exchange Rates																*Bipkwele per SDR through 1984;*
Official Rate	aa	245.07	247.59	245.42	247.40	277.91	276.02	283.61	278.00	284.00	272.08	262.55	288.70	285.76	272.28	264.78
													Bipkwele per US Dollar through 1984;			
Official Rate	ae	245.08	247.59	245.43	247.41	277.92	276.03	261.23	256.05	235.43	222.22	224.27	248.49	235.25	209.00	201.00
Official Rate	rf	245.06	245.68	246.00	247.56	259.96	276.40	275.59	252.03	222.89	240.70	214.31	238.95	245.68	225.66	212.72
													Index Numbers (1990=100):			
Nominal Effective Exchange Rate	ne c	....	....	....	....	....	....	....	....	....	....	....	....	....	....	798.60
Real Effective Exchange Rate	re c	....	....	....	....	....	....	....	....	....	....	....	....	....	....	....
Fund Position																*Millions of SDRs:*
Quota	2f. s	....	....	....	....	6.00	8.00	8.00	8.00	8.00	8.00	8.00	8.00	8.00	10.00	10.00
SDRs	1b. s	....	....	....	....	—	1.01	1.86	1.87	1.86	1.85	1.81	1.77	1.74	1.70	.65
Reserve Position in the Fund	1c. s	....	....	....	....	.50	1.00	1.00	.01	.01	.01	.01	1.76	—	—	.18
Total Fund Cred.&Loans Outstg.	2tl	....	....	....	....	—	—	—	—	—	—	—	—	—	—	—
International Liquidity												*Millions of US Dollars Unless Otherwise Indicated:*				
Total Reserves minus Gold	1l. d	....	....	....	....	....	1.01	2.02	2.03	2.24	2.27	2.12	2.06	2.11	2.21	.86
SDRs	1b. d	....	....	....	....	—	—	—	—	—	—	—	—	—	—	—
Reserve Position in the Fund	1c. d	....	....	....	....	.50	1.00	1.09	.01	.01	.01	.01	2.04	—	—	.24
Foreign Exchange	1d. d	....	....	....	....	....	....	....	....	....	....	....	....	....	....	....
Monetary Authorities: Other Liab.	4.. d	....	....	....	....	....	....	....	....	....	....	....	....	....	....	....
Deposit Money Banks: Assets	7a. d	....	....	....	....	....	....	....	....	....	....	....	....	....	....	....
Liabilities	7b. d	....	....	....	....	....	....	....	....	....	....	....	....	....	....	....
Monetary Authorities																*Billions of Francs:*
Foreign Assets	11	....	....	....	....	....	....	....	....	....	....	....	....	....	....	....
Claims on Central Government	12a	....	....	....	....	....	....	....	....	....	....	....	....	....	....	....
Claims on Deposit Money Banks	12e	....	....	....	....	....	....	....	....	....	....	....	....	....	....	....
Claims on Other Banking Insts.	12f	....	....	....	....	....	....	....	....	....	....	....	....	....	....	....
Reserve Money	14	....	....	....	....	....	....	....	....	....	....	....	....	....	....	....
of which: Currency Outside DMBs	14a	....	....	....	....	....	....	....	....	....	....	....	....	....	....	....
Foreign Liabilities	16c	....	....	....	....	....	....	....	....	....	....	....	....	....	....	....
Central Government Deposits	16d	....	....	....	....	....	....	....	....	....	....	....	....	....	....	....
Capital Accounts	17a	....	....	....	....	....	....	....	....	....	....	....	....	....	....	....
Other Items (Net)	17r	....	....	....	....	....	....	....	....	....	....	....	....	....	....	....
Deposit Money Banks																*Billions of Francs:*
Reserves	20	....	....	....	....	....	....	....	....	....	....	....	....	....	....	....
Foreign Assets	21	....	....	....	....	....	....	....	....	....	....	....	....	....	....	....
Claims on Central Government	22a	....	....	....	....	....	....	....	....	....	....	....	....	....	....	....
Claims on Nonfin.Pub.Enterprises	22c	....	....	....	....	....	....	....	....	....	....	....	....	....	....	....
Claims on Private Sector	22d	....	....	....	....	....	....	....	....	....	....	....	....	....	....	....
Claims on Other Banking Insts.	22f	....	....	....	....	....	....	....	....	....	....	....	....	....	....	....
Claims on Nonbank Financial Insts.	22g	....	....	....	....	....	....	....	....	....	....	....	....	....	....	....
Demand Deposits	24	....	....	....	....	....	....	....	....	....	....	....	....	....	....	....
Time and Savings Deposits	25	....	....	....	....	....	....	....	....	....	....	....	....	....	....	....
Foreign Liabilities	26c	....	....	....	....	....	....	....	....	....	....	....	....	....	....	....
Long-Term Foreign Liabilities	26cl	....	....	....	....	....	....	....	....	....	....	....	....	....	....	....
Central Government Deposits	26d	....	....	....	....	....	....	....	....	....	....	....	....	....	....	....
Credit from Monetary Authorities	26g	....	....	....	....	....	....	....	....	....	....	....	....	....	....	....
Capital Accounts	27a	....	....	....	....	....	....	....	....	....	....	....	....	....	....	....
Other Items (Net)	27r	....	....	....	....	....	....	....	....	....	....	....	....	....	....	....
Monetary Survey																*Billions of Francs:*
Foreign Assets (Net)	31n	....	....	....	....	....	....	....	....	....	....	....	....	....	....	....
Domestic Credit	32	....	....	....	....	....	....	....	....	....	....	....	....	....	....	....
Claims on Central Govt. (Net)	32an	....	....	....	....	....	....	....	....	....	....	....	....	....	....	....
Claims on Nonfin.Pub.Enterprises	32c	....	....	....	....	....	....	....	....	....	....	....	....	....	....	....
Claims on Private Sector	32d	....	....	....	....	....	....	....	....	....	....	....	....	....	....	....
Claims on Other Banking Insts.	32f	....	....	....	....	....	....	....	....	....	....	....	....	....	....	....
Claims on Nonbk.Financial Insts.	32g	....	....	....	....	....	....	....	....	....	....	....	....	....	....	....
Money	34	....	....	....	....	....	....	....	....	....	....	....	....	....	....	....
Quasi-Money	35	....	....	....	....	....	....	....	....	....	....	....	....	....	....	....
Other Items (Net)	37r	....	....	....	....	....	....	....	....	....	....	....	....	....	....	....
Money plus Quasi-Money	35l	....	....	....	....	....	....	....	....	....	....	....	....	....	....	....
Interest Rates																*Percent Per Annum*
Discount Rate (End of Period)	60	....	....	....	....	....	....	....	....	....	....	....	....	....	....	....
Deposit Rate	60l	....	....	....	....	....	....	....	....	....	....	....	....	....	....	....
Lending Rate	60p	....	....	....	....	....	....	....	....	....	....	....	....	....	....	....
Prices																*Index Numbers (1990=100):*
Consumer Prices	64	....	....	....	....	....	....	....	....	....	....	....	....	....	....	....

Equatorial Guinea

642

	1980	1981	1982	1983	1984	1985	1986	1987	1988	1989	1990	1991	1992	1993	1994		
																Exchange Rates	
Francs per SDR Beginning 1985: End of Period																	
	287.99	334.52	370.92	436.97	470.11	415.26	394.78	378.78	407.68	380.32	364.84	370.48	378.57	404.89	ℐ780.44	Official Rate	aa
Francs per US Dollar Beginning 1985: End of Period(ae) Period Average(rf)																	
	225.80	287.40	336.25	417.37	479.60	378.05	322.75	267.00	302.95	289.40	256.45	259.00	275.33	294.78	ℐ534.60	Official Rate	ae
	211.28	271.73	328.61	381.06	436.96	449.26	346.30	300.54	297.85	319.01	272.26	282.11	264.69	283.16	ℐ555.20	Official Rate	rf
Period Averages																	
	586.82	376.84	371.02	358.15	372.57	72.55	80.44	86.08	87.46	89.90	100.00	102.71	113.16	131.27	76.24	Nominal Effective Exchange Rate	ne c
	1,219.63	664.37	576.57	489.54	453.15	148.75	125.41	108.53	103.54	101.49	100.00	91.19	87.35	96.26	69.33	Real Effective Exchange Rate	re c
End of Period																**Fund Position**	
	15.00	15.00	15.00	18.40	18.40	18.40	18.40	18.40	18.40	18.40	18.40	18.40	24.30	24.30	24.30	Quota	2f. s
	.02	.12	.02	—	—	3.09	.61	.15	.03	.09	.05	5.57	5.52	.28	.01	SDRs	1b. s
	—	.24	.50	—	—	—	—	—	—	—	—	—	—	—	—	Reserve Position in the Fund	1c. s
	12.62	19.24	19.24	19.24	13.19	11.70	9.01	8.11	10.61	6.72	4.10	9.20	9.20	11.96	13.43	Total Fund Cred.&Loans Outstg.	2tl
End of Period																**International Liquidity**	
	....	....	2.77	1.30	1.38	3.47	2.68	.57	5.50	.82	.71	9.47	13.41	.48	.39	Total Reserves minus Gold	1l. d
	.03	.14	.02	—	—	3.39	.75	.21	.04	.12	.07	7.96	7.59	.38	.02	SDRs	1b. d
	—	.28	.55	—	—	—	—	—	—	—	—	—	—	—	—	Reserve Position in the Fund	1c. d
	....	....	2.20	1.30	1.38	.07	1.93	.36	5.46	.70	.64	1.51	5.82	.10	.37	Foreign Exchange	1d. d
	....	....	....	....	....	5.07	.34	11.01	14.79	5.69	20.13	17.50	24.32	12.78	11.57	Monetary Authorities: Other Liab.	4..d
	....	....	....	....	....	5.40	2.04	7.49	4.15	3.37	5.10	5.68	6.08	4.07	5.78	Deposit Money Banks: Assets	7a. d
	....	....	....	....	....	—	—	.30	1.17	1.72	3.49	2.34	2.96	2.17	2.67	Liabilities	7b. d
End of Period																**Monetary Authorities**	
	....	....	....	....	....	1.31	.86	.15	ℐ1.67	.24	.18	ℐ2.45	3.67	.14	.21	Foreign Assets	11
	....	....	....	....	....	6.46	5.11	4.62	ℐ6.06	4.25	3.09	ℐ11.06	11.46	12.18	17.84	Claims on Central Government	12a
	....	....	....	....	....	3.21	4.26	3.82	ℐ3.24	3.24	4.65	ℐ—	—	—	—	Claims on Deposit Money Banks	12e
	....	....	....	....	....	....	....	....	—	—	—	—	—	—	—	Claims on Other Banking Insts.	12f
	....	....	....	....	....	5.68	8.93	6.88	ℐ3.28	5.59	1.74	ℐ1.92	3.09	2.46	4.38	Reserve Money	14
	....	....	....	....	....	5.24	7.48	6.69	ℐ1.96	4.79	.90	ℐ1.09	1.62	1.21	3.77	of which: Currency Outside DMBs	14a
	....	....	....	....	....	6.78	3.67	6.01	ℐ8.81	4.20	6.66	7.94	10.18	8.09	15.38	Foreign Liabilities	16c
	....	....	....	....	....	1.02	.27	.72	ℐ1.74	.26	.07	ℐ.25	.35	.17	.06	Central Government Deposits	16d
	....	....	....	....	....	....	....	....	—	—	—	.25	.20	.20	.28	Capital Accounts	17a
	....	....	....	....	....	−2.49	−2.62	−5.02	−2.86	−2.32	−.56	ℐ3.15	1.31	1.40	−2.05	Other Items (Net)	17r
End of Period																**Deposit Money Banks**	
	....	....	....	....	....	.44	1.45	.20	ℐ1.31	.80	.84	.84	1.47	1.25	.62	Reserves	20
	....	....	....	....	....	2.04	.66	2.00	ℐ1.26	.98	1.31	ℐ1.47	1.67	1.20	3.09	Foreign Assets	21
	....	....	....	....	....	—	—	—	ℐ.57	.62	.78	ℐ1.08	2.76	.05	.23	Claims on Central Government	22a
	....	....	....	....	....	....	....	....	.24	.47	.64	.04	.29	.44	.72	Claims on Nonfin.Pub.Enterprises	22c
	....	....	....	....	....	6.53	8.36	7.52	ℐ7.37	7.79	7.87	ℐ12.45	7.92	1.99	2.25	Claims on Private Sector	22d
	....	....	....	....	....	....	....	....	—	—	—	—	—	—	—	Claims on Other Banking Insts.	22f
	....	....	....	....	....	....	....	....	—	—	—	—	—	—	—	Claims on Nonbank Financial Insts.	22g
	....	....	....	....	....	2.81	2.44	2.32	ℐ3.26	2.46	2.23	ℐ1.55	1.95	1.34	2.24	Demand Deposits	24
	....	....	....	....	....	.93	.62	.43	ℐ.38	.63	.67	ℐ.70	.80	.69	1.76	Time and Savings Deposits	25
	....	....	....	....	....	—	—	—	ℐ1.17	.25	.65	ℐ1.36	.56	.41	1.24	Foreign Liabilities	26c
	....	....	....	....	....	—	—	.08	ℐ.18	.25	.25	ℐ1.25	.25	.23	.19	Long-Term Foreign Liabilities	26cl
	....	....	....	....	....	.50	.18	.09	ℐ1.76	.75	1.07	ℐ1.10	1.05	.53	.46	Central Government Deposits	26d
	....	....	....	....	....	3.21	4.26	3.82	ℐ3.24	3.24	4.64	ℐ—	—	—	—	Credit from Monetary Authorities	26g
	....	....	....	....	....	.67	.71	1.16	ℐ2.36	2.54	2.70	ℐ10.49	9.63	1.67	1.36	Capital Accounts	27a
	....	....	....	....	....	.90	2.25	1.82	ℐ1.43	.53	−.77	ℐ1.48	−.13	.07	−.33	Other Items (Net)	27r
End of Period																**Monetary Survey**	
	....	....	....	....	....	−3.43	−2.14	−3.86	ℐ−6.23	−3.49	−6.07	ℐ−4.62	−5.65	−7.39	−13.51	Foreign Assets (Net)	31n
	....	....	....	....	....	11.47	13.02	11.33	ℐ11.74	12.12	11.24	ℐ23.34	21.04	13.96	20.53	Domestic Credit	32
	....	....	....	....	....	4.94	4.66	3.81	ℐ4.12	3.86	2.73	10.79	12.82	11.53	17.56	Claims on Central Govt. (Net)	32an
	....	....	....	....	....	....	....	....	.24	.47	.64	.04	.29	.44	.72	Claims on Nonfin.Pub.Enterprises	32c
	....	....	....	....	....	6.53	8.36	7.52	ℐ7.37	7.79	7.87	ℐ12.45	7.92	1.99	2.25	Claims on Private Sector	32d
	....	....	....	....	....	....	....	....	—	—	—	.06	—	—	—	Claims on Other Banking Insts.	32f
	....	....	....	....	....	....	....	....	—	—	—	—	—	—	—	Claims on Nonbk.Financial Insts.	32g
	....	....	....	....	....	8.05	9.92	9.00	ℐ5.22	7.25	3.12	2.64	3.57	2.55	6.00	Money	34
	....	....	....	....	....	.93	.62	.43	ℐ.38	.63	.67	.70	.80	.69	1.76	Quasi-Money	35
	....	....	....	....	....	−.93	.34	−1.97	−.10	.74	1.37	15.37	11.01	3.34	−.73	Other Items (Net)	37r
	....	....	....	....	....	8.97	10.54	9.43	ℐ5.60	7.88	3.79	3.34	4.37	3.24	7.76	Money plus Quasi-Money	35l
Percent Per Annum																**Interest Rates**	
	....	....	....	....	....	9.00	8.00	8.00	9.50	10.00	11.00	10.75	12.00	11.50	....	Discount Rate (End of Period)	60
	....	....	....	....	....	7.50	8.25	7.88	6.33	6.50	ℐ7.50	7.50	7.50	7.75	8.08	Deposit Rate	60l
	....	....	....	....	....	15.00	14.50	14.13	14.79	15.50	ℐ18.50	18.15	17.77	17.46	17.42	Lending Rate	60p
Period Averages																**Prices**	
	....	....	....	....	....	127.42	104.76	91.28	93.40	98.91	100.00	96.84	ℐ89.90	93.49	....	Consumer Prices	64

Equatorial Guinea

642

		1965	1966	1967	1968	1969	1970	1971	1972	1973	1974	1975	1976	1977	1978	1979
International Transactions																*Millions of Francs*
Exports	70	....	....	....	....	....	....	....	....	....	....	....	....	....	....	....
Imports, cif	71	....	....	....	....	....	....	....	....	....	....	....	....	....	....	....
Imports, fob	71.v	....	....	....	....	....	....	....	....	....	....	....	....	....	....	....
Balance of Payments																*Millions of US Dollars:*
Goods: Exports f.o.b.	78aa *d*	....	....	....	....	....	....	....	....	....	....	....	....	....	....	....
Goods: Imports f.o.b.	78ab *d*	....	....	....	....	....	....	....	....	....	....	....	....	....	....	....
Trade Balance	78ac *d*	....	....	....	....	....	....	....	....	....	....	....	....	....	....	....
Services: Credit	78ad *d*	....	....	....	....	....	....	....	....	....	....	....	....	....	....	....
Services: Debit	78ae *d*	....	....	....	....	....	....	....	....	....	....	....	....	....	....	....
Balance on Goods and Services	78af *d*	....	....	....	....	....	....	....	....	....	....	....	....	....	....	....
Income: Credit	78ag *d*	....	....	....	....	....	....	....	....	....	....	....	....	....	....	....
Income: Debit	78ah *d*	....	....	....	....	....	....	....	....	....	....	....	....	....	....	....
Balance on Goods, Serv., & Inc.	78ai *d*	....	....	....	....	....	....	....	....	....	....	....	....	....	....	....
Current Transfers, n.i.e.: Credit	78aj *d*	....	....	....	....	....	....	....	....	....	....	....	....	....	....	....
Current Transfers: Debit	78ak *d*	....	....	....	....	....	....	....	....	....	....	....	....	....	....	....
Current Account, n.i.e.	78al *d*	....	....	....	....	....	....	....	....	....	....	....	....	....	....	....
Capital Account, n.i.e.: Credit	78ba *d*	....	....	....	....	....	....	....	....	....	....	....	....	....	....	....
Capital Account: Debit	78bb *d*	....	....	....	....	....	....	....	....	....	....	....	....	....	....	....
Capital Account, n.i.e.	78bc *d*	....	....	....	....	....	....	....	....	....	....	....	....	....	....	....
Direct Investment Abroad	78bd *d*	....	....	....	....	....	....	....	....	....	....	....	....	....	....	....
Dir. Invest. in Rep. Econ., n.i.e.	78be *d*	....	....	....	....	....	....	....	....	....	....	....	....	....	....	....
Portfolio Investment Assets	78bf *d*	....	....	....	....	....	....	....	....	....	....	....	....	....	....	....
Portfolio Investment Liab., n.i.e.	78bg *d*	....	....	....	....	....	....	....	....	....	....	....	....	....	....	....
Other Investment Assets	78bh *d*	....	....	....	....	....	....	....	....	....	....	....	....	....	....	....
Other Investment Liab., n.i.e.	78bi *d*	....	....	....	....	....	....	....	....	....	....	....	....	....	....	....
Financial Account, n.i.e.	78bj *d*	....	....	....	....	....	....	....	....	....	....	....	....	....	....	....
Net Errors and Omissions	78ca *d*	....	....	....	....	....	....	....	....	....	....	....	....	....	....	....
Overall Balance	78cb *d*	....	....	....	....	....	....	....	....	....	....	....	....	....	....	....
Reserves and Related Items	79da *d*	....	....	....	....	....	....	....	....	....	....	....	....	....	....	....
Reserve Assets	79db *d*	....	....	....	....	....	....	....	....	....	....	....	....	....	....	....
Use of Fund Credit and Loans	79dc *d*	....	....	....	....	....	....	....	....	....	....	....	....	....	....	....
Liabs.Constit.For.Auth.Reserves	79dd *d*	....	....	....	....	....	....	....	....	....	....	....	....	....	....	....
Exceptional Financing	79de *d*	....	....	....	....	....	....	....	....	....	....	....	....	....	....	....
National Accounts																*Millions of Francs*
Exports of Goods & Services	90c	....	....	....	....	....	....	....	....	....	....	....	....	....	....	....
Government Consumption	91f	....	....	....	....	....	....	....	....	....	....	....	....	....	....	....
Gross Fixed Capital Formation	93e	....	....	....	....	....	....	....	....	....	....	....	....	....	....	....
Increase/Decrease(-) in Stocks	93i	....	....	....	....	....	....	....	....	....	....	....	....	....	....	....
Private Consumption	96f	....	....	....	....	....	....	....	....	....	....	....	....	....	....	....
Imports of Goods & Services	98c	....	....	....	....	....	....	....	....	....	....	....	....	....	....	....
Gross Domestic Product	99b	....	....	....	....	....	....	....	....	....	....	....	....	....	....	....
Gross Dom. Prod. 1985 Prices	99b.*p*	....	....	....	....	....	....	....	....	....	....	....	....	....	....	....
																Millions:
Population	99z	.27	.27	.28	.28	.29	.29	.29	.30	.31	.32	.32	.33	.33	.34	.35

Monetary Authorities: ℐ Beginning in March 1988, the sectorization and classification of accounts have been revised. ℐ Beginning in September 1991, *Claims on Central Government* include government assumption of certain nonperforming bank loans. ℐ Beginning in December 1992, the coverage of the banking system has been revised. Claims and deposits of nonactive banks or banks in the process of liquidation have been excluded from the monetary accounts.

Deposit Money Banks: ℐ Beginning in September 1991, the counterpart of government assumption of certain nonperforming bank loans was reclassified from *Credit from Monetary Authorities* to *Capital Accounts*. ℐ See note to section 10.

Monetary Survey: ℐ See notes to sections 10 and 20.

Interest Rates: *Deposit Rate:* ℐ Beginning in October 1990, minimum rate offered by deposit money banks on savings accounts.

Lending Rate: ℐ Beginning in October 1990, maximum rate charged by deposit money banks on all loans, excluding charges and fees.

Equatorial Guinea

International Transactions

	1980	1981	1982	1983	1984	1985	1986	1987	1988	1989	1990	1991	1992	1993	1994	
Millions of Francs																
Exports	....	3,067	3,797	5,074	6,526	7,441	12,100	12,600	14,719	12,925	16,806	23,463	10,857	17,666	....	70
Imports, cif	....	7,390	10,029	7,250	7,656	8,947	17,900	17,300	18,230	17,473	16,586	33,018	24,404	16,944	....	71
Imports, fob	....	....	....	....	....	....	....	....	....	....	....	....	....	....	....	71.v

Balance of Payments

Minus Sign Indicates Debit

	1980	1981	1982	1983	1984	1985	1986	1987	1988	1989	1990	1991	1992	1993	1994	
Goods: Exports f.o.b.	....	....	....	....	....	....	....	38.48	44.65	32.71	37.82	35.75	....	....	....	78aa d
Goods: Imports f.o.b.	....	....	....	....	....	....	....	−47.87	−56.51	−43.61	−53.17	−59.56	....	....	....	78ab d
Trade Balance	....	....	....	....	....	....	....	−9.38	−11.86	−10.91	−15.36	−23.81	....	....	....	78ac d
Services: Credit	....	....	....	....	....	....	....	6.11	5.87	5.84	4.51	6.19	....	....	....	78ad d
Services: Debit	....	....	....	....	....	....	....	−40.68	−48.69	−29.77	−35.23	−43.03	....	....	....	78ae d
Balance on Goods and Services	....	....	....	....	....	....	....	−43.96	−54.68	−34.84	−46.08	−60.65	....	....	....	78af d
Income: Credit	....	....	....	....	....	....	....						....	....	....	78ag d
Income: Debit	....	....	....	....	....	....	....	−6.51	−7.93	−10.00	−10.78	−9.41	....	....	....	78ah d
Balance on Goods, Serv., & Inc.	....	....	....	....	....	....	....	−50.46	−62.61	−44.84	−56.86	−70.06	....	....	....	78ai d
Current Transfers, n.i.e.: Credit	....	....	....	....	....	....	....	28.66	46.90	38.10	56.37	63.35	....	....	....	78aj d
Current Transfers: Debit	....	....	....	....	....	....	....	−3.64	−4.87	−14.25	−18.50	−17.94	....	....	....	78ak d
Current Account, n.i.e.	....	....	....	....	....	....	....	−25.44	−20.57	−21.00	−18.99	−24.66	....	....	....	78al d
Capital Account, n.i.e.: Credit	....	....	....	....	....	....	....	—	—	—	—	—	....	....	....	78ba d
Capital Account: Debit	....	....	....	....	....	....	....						....	....	....	78bb d
Capital Account, n.i.e.	....	....	....	....	....	....	....						....	....	....	78bc d
Direct Investment Abroad	....	....	....	....	....	....	....	—	—	−.14	−.13	−.11	....	....	....	78bd d
Dir. Invest. in Rep. Econ., n.i.e.	....	....	....	....	....	....	....	—	—	−.29	9.77	42.26	....	....	....	78be d
Portfolio Investment Assets	....	....	....	....	....	....	....	—	—	—	—	—	....	....	....	78bf d
Portfolio Investment Liab., n.i.e.	....	....	....	....	....	....	....	—	—	—	—	—	....	....	....	78bg d
Other Investment Assets	....	....	....	....	....	....	....	−4.91	−1.12	−1.08	−2.80	−1.49	....	....	....	78bh d
Other Investment Liab., n.i.e.	....	....	....	....	....	....	....	3.95	6.02	11.53	4.83	−8.48	....	....	....	78bi d
Financial Account, n.i.e.	....	....	....	....	....	....	....	−.95	4.90	10.02	11.68	32.19	....	....	....	78bj d
Net Errors and Omissions	....	....	....	....	....	....	....	.82	−1.70	−4.53	−2.39	−30.72	....	....	....	78ca d
Overall Balance	....	....	....	....	....	....	....	−25.58	−17.37	−15.50	−9.70	−23.19	....	....	....	78cb d
Reserves and Related Items	....	....	....	....	....	....	....	25.58	17.37	15.50	9.70	23.19	....	....	....	79da d
Reserve Assets	....	....	....	....	....	....	....	3.64	−7.11	4.51	.39	−8.64	....	....	....	79db d
Use of Fund Credit and Loans	....	....	....	....	....	....	....	−1.14	3.44	−5.01	−3.53	7.18	....	....	....	79cc d
Liabs.Constit.For.Auth.Reserves	....	....	....	....	....	....	....						....	....	....	79dd d
Exceptional Financing	....	....	....	....	....	....	....	23.08	21.05	16.00	12.84	24.65	....	....	....	79de d

National Accounts

Millions of Francs

	1980	1981	1982	1983	1984	1985	1986	1987	1988	1989	1990	1991	1992	1993	1994	
Exports of Goods & Services	....	....	....	1,477	1,886	10,388	12,092	18,568	19,187	17,083	26,483	13,174	....	....	....	90c
Government Consumption	....	....	....	7,080	8,505	5,909	7,240	5,210	7,804	9,397	6,765	6,696	....	....	....	91f
Gross Fixed Capital Formation	....	....	....	3,018	3,224	4,551	7,590	10,190	11,133	8,285	15,328	8,525	....	....	....	93e
Increase/Decrease(-) in Stocks	....	....	....	−158	418	−1,721	−624	654	−685	−7	−1,365	−1,091	....	....	....	93i
Private Consumption	....	....	....	16,083	17,511	30,566	28,754	26,630	29,096	22,956	23,593	35,225	....	....	....	96f
Imports of Goods & Services	....	....	....	−1,851	−2,012	−11,626	−17,847	−21,930	−23,786	−15,458	−26,455	−13,174	....	....	....	98c
Gross Domestic Product	....	....	....	25,649	29,532	38,067	37,205	39,700	35,900	39,600	39,500	41,500	48,000	53,100	....	99b
Gross Dom. Prod. 1985 Prices	....	....	....	....	....	38,067	36,623	39,362	41,439	40,296	....	....	....	....	....	99b.p

Midyear Estimates

	1980	1981	1982	1983	1984	1985	1986	1987	1988	1989	1990	1991	1992	1993	1994	
Population	.35	.23	.25	.27	.29	.31	.32	.33	.33	.34	.35	.36	.37	.38	....	99z

Estonia

939

		1965	1966	1967	1968	1969	1970	1971	1972	1973	1974	1975	1976	1977	1978	1979
Exchange Rates															*Kroons per SDR:*	
Official Rate	aa	...	...	...	...	...	...	...	...	...	...	...	...	...	...	...
															Kroons per US Dollar:	
Official Rate	ae	...	...	...	...	...	...	...	...	...	...	...	...	...	...	...
Official Rate	rf	...	...	...	...	...	...	...	...	...	...	...	...	...	...	...
Fund Position															*Millions of SDRs:*	
Quota	2f.s	...	...	...	...	...	...	...	...	...	...	...	...	...	...	...
SDRs	1b.s	...	...	...	...	...	...	...	...	...	...	...	...	...	...	...
Reserve Position in the Fund	1c.s	...	...	...	...	...	...	...	...	...	...	...	...	...	...	...
Total Fund Cred.&Loans Outstg.	2tl	...	...	...	...	...	...	...	...	...	...	...	...	...	...	...
International Liquidity												*Millions of US Dollars Unless Otherwise Indicated:*				
Total Reserves minus Gold	1l.d	...	...	...	...	...	...	...	...	...	...	...	...	...	...	...
SDRs	1b.d	...	...	...	...	...	...	...	...	...	...	...	...	...	...	...
Reserve Position in the Fund	1c.d	...	...	...	...	...	...	...	...	...	...	...	...	...	...	...
Foreign Exchange	1d.d	...	...	...	...	...	...	...	...	...	...	...	...	...	...	...
Gold (Million Fine Troy Ounces)	1ad	...	...	...	...	...	...	...	...	...	...	...	...	...	...	...
Gold (National Valuation)	1an d	...	...	...	...	...	...	...	...	...	...	...	...	...	...	...
Monetary Authorities: Other Liab.	4..d	...	...	...	...	...	...	...	...	...	...	...	...	...	...	...
Banks: Assets	7a.d	...	...	...	...	...	...	...	...	...	...	...	...	...	...	...
Liabilities	7b.d	...	...	...	...	...	...	...	...	...	...	...	...	...	...	...
of which: Liab. to Nonbanks	7bd d	...	...	...	...	...	...	...	...	...	...	...	...	...	...	...
Monetary Authorities															*Millions of Kroons:*	
Foreign Assets	11	...	...	...	...	...	...	...	...	...	...	...	...	...	...	...
Claims on Central Government	12a	...	...	...	...	...	...	...	...	...	...	...	...	...	...	...
Claims on Nonfin.Pub.Enterprises	12c	...	...	...	...	...	...	...	...	...	...	...	...	...	...	...
Claims on Private Sector	12d	...	...	...	...	...	...	...	...	...	...	...	...	...	...	...
Claims on Banks	12e	...	...	...	...	...	...	...	...	...	...	...	...	...	...	...
Reserve Money	14	...	...	...	...	...	...	...	...	...	...	...	...	...	...	...
of which: Currency Outside Banks	14a	...	...	...	...	...	...	...	...	...	...	...	...	...	...	...
Foreign Liabilities	16c	...	...	...	...	...	...	...	...	...	...	...	...	...	...	...
Central Government Deposits	16d	...	...	...	...	...	...	...	...	...	...	...	...	...	...	...
Capital Accounts	17a	...	...	...	...	...	...	...	...	...	...	...	...	...	...	...
Other Items (Net)	17r	...	...	...	...	...	...	...	...	...	...	...	...	...	...	...
Banking Institutions															*Millions of Kroons:*	
Reserves	20	...	...	...	...	...	...	...	...	...	...	...	...	...	...	...
Foreign Assets	21	...	...	...	...	...	...	...	...	...	...	...	...	...	...	...
Claims on Central Government	22a	...	...	...	...	...	...	...	...	...	...	...	...	...	...	...
Claims on Nonfin.Pub.Enterprises	22c	...	...	...	...	...	...	...	...	...	...	...	...	...	...	...
Claims on Private Sector	22d	...	...	...	...	...	...	...	...	...	...	...	...	...	...	...
Demand Deposits	24	...	...	...	...	...	...	...	...	...	...	...	...	...	...	...
Time,Savings,& Fgn.Currency Dep.	25	...	...	...	...	...	...	...	...	...	...	...	...	...	...	...
Foreign Liabilities	26c	...	...	...	...	...	...	...	...	...	...	...	...	...	...	...
Central Government Deposits	26d	...	...	...	...	...	...	...	...	...	...	...	...	...	...	...
Counterpart Funds	26e	...	...	...	...	...	...	...	...	...	...	...	...	...	...	...
Government Lending Funds	26f	...	...	...	...	...	...	...	...	...	...	...	...	...	...	...
Credit from Monetary Authorities	26g	...	...	...	...	...	...	...	...	...	...	...	...	...	...	...
Capital Accounts	27a	...	...	...	...	...	...	...	...	...	...	...	...	...	...	...
Other Items (Net)	27r	...	...	...	...	...	...	...	...	...	...	...	...	...	...	...
Banking Survey															*Millions of Kroons:*	
Foreign Assets (Net)	31n	...	...	...	...	...	...	...	...	...	...	...	...	...	...	...
Domestic Credit	32	...	...	...	...	...	...	...	...	...	...	...	...	...	...	...
Claims on Central Govt. (Net)	32an	...	...	...	...	...	...	...	...	...	...	...	...	...	...	...
Claims on Nonfin.Pub.Enterprises	32c	...	...	...	...	...	...	...	...	...	...	...	...	...	...	...
Claims on Private Sector	32d	...	...	...	...	...	...	...	...	...	...	...	...	...	...	...
Money	34	...	...	...	...	...	...	...	...	...	...	...	...	...	...	...
Quasi-Money	35	...	...	...	...	...	...	...	...	...	...	...	...	...	...	...
Government Lending Funds	36f	...	...	...	...	...	...	...	...	...	...	...	...	...	...	...
Other Items (Net)	37r	...	...	...	...	...	...	...	...	...	...	...	...	...	...	...
Money plus Quasi-Money	35l	...	...	...	...	...	...	...	...	...	...	...	...	...	...	...
Interest Rates															*Percent Per Annum*	
Discount Rate (End of Period)	60	...	...	...	...	...	...	...	...	...	...	...	...	...	...	...
Interbank Rate	60a	...	...	...	...	...	...	...	...	...	...	...	...	...	...	...
Deposit Rate	60l	...	...	...	...	...	...	...	...	...	...	...	...	...	...	...
Lending Rate	60p	...	...	...	...	...	...	...	...	...	...	...	...	...	...	...
Prices and Earnings															*Index Numbers (1992=100):*	
Producer Prices (Dec.93=100)	63	...	...	...	...	...	...	...	...	...	...	...	...	...	...	...
Consumer Prices	64	...	...	...	...	...	...	...	...	...	...	...	...	...	...	...
Monthly Earnings	65	...	...	...	...	...	...	...	...	...	...	...	...	...	...	...

Estonia

	1980	1981	1982	1983	1984	1985	1986	1987	1988	1989	1990	1991	1992	1993	1994		
End of Period																**Exchange Rates**	
	....	....	....	....	....	....	....	....	....	....	....	....	17.75	19.06	18.09	Official Rate	aa
End of Period (ae) Period Average (rf)																	
	....	....	....	....	....	....	....	....	....	....	....	....	12.91	13.88	12.39	Official Rate	ae
	....	....	....	....	....	....	....	....	....	....	....	....	....	13.22	12.99	Official Rate	rf
End of Period																**Fund Position**	
	....	....	....	....	....	....	....	....	....	....	....	....	46.50	46.50	46.50	Quota	2f. s
	....	....	....	....	....	....	....	....	....	....	....	....	7.72	41.56	1.09	SDRs	1b. s
	....	....	....	....	....	....	....	....	....	....	....	....	—	—	.01	Reserve Position in the Fund	1c. s
	....	....	....	....	....	....	....	....	....	....	....	....	7.75	41.85	41.85	Total Fund Cred.&Loans Outstg.	2tl
End of Period																**International Liquidity**	
	....	....	....	....	....	....	....	....	....	....	....	....	170.18	386.12	....	Total Reserves minus Gold	1l. d
	....	....	....	....	....	....	....	....	....	....	....	....	10.62	57.08	1.58	SDRs	1b. d
	....	....	....	....	....	....	....	....	....	....	....	....	—	—	.01	Reserve Position in the Fund	1c. d
	....	....	....	....	....	....	....	....	....	....	....	....	159.56	329.04	....	Foreign Exchange	1d. d
	....	....	....	....	....	....	....	....	....	....	....	....	.0820	.0080	....	Gold (Million Fine Troy Ounces)	1ad
	....	....	....	....	....	....	....	....	....	....	....	....	25.36	3.22	....	Gold (National Valuation)	1and
	....	....	....	....	....	....	....	....	....	....	....	....	42.44	I 8.08	12.00	Monetary Authorities: Other Liab.	4.. d
	....	....	....	....	....	....	....	....	....	....	....	....	122.81	103.10	243.80	Banks: Assets	7a. d
	....	....	....	....	....	....	....	....	....	....	....	....	7.95	14.34	55.98	Liabilities	7b. d
	....	....	....	....	....	....	....	....	....	....	....	....	2.80	11.12	33.92	of which: Liab. to Nonbanks	7bd d
End of Period																**Monetary Authorities**	
	....	....	....	....	....	....	....	....	....	....	....	1,782.8	3,596.7	I 5,290.1	5,511.0	Foreign Assets	11
	....	....	....	....	....	....	....	....	....	....	....	—	—	I 45.2	—	Claims on Central Government	12a
	....	....	....	....	....	....	....	....	....	....	....	651.9	—	I 63.5	14.8	Claims on Nonfin.Pub.Enterprises	12c
	....	....	....	....	....	....	....	....	....	....	....	14.6	—	I 4.6	8.2	Claims on Private Sector	12d
	....	....	....	....	....	....	....	....	....	....	....	275.4	583.7	I 576.7	480.9	Claims on Banks	12e
	....	....	....	....	....	....	....	....	....	....	....	732.7	1,862.8	I 3,884.3	4,321.6	Reserve Money	14
	....	....	....	....	....	....	....	....	....	....	....	212.4	1,040.7	I 2,440.6	3,131.3	of which: Currency Outside Banks	14a
	....	....	....	....	....	....	....	....	....	....	....	444.8	685.6	I 909.9	905.7	Foreign Liabilities	16c
	....	....	....	....	....	....	....	....	....	....	....	30.4	.3	I 5.1	.2	Central Government Deposits	16d
	....	....	....	....	....	....	....	....	....	....	....	1,094.9	1,672.7	I 2,101.9	1,822.3	Capital Accounts	17a
	....	....	....	....	....	....	....	....	....	....	....	454.3	–41.0	I –921.1	–10,512.8	Other Items (Net)	17r
End of Period																**Banking Institutions**	
	....	....	....	....	....	....	....	....	....	....	....	598.3	835.0	1,437.7	1,208.4	Reserves	20
	....	....	....	....	....	....	....	....	....	....	....	852.9	1,585.7	1,430.8	3,020.7	Foreign Assets	21
	....	....	....	....	....	....	....	....	....	....	....	1.8	14.5	294.6	405.3	Claims on Central Government	22a
	....	....	....	....	....	....	....	....	....	....	....	202.4	644.4	425.4	358.2	Claims on Nonfin.Pub.Enterprises	22c
	....	....	....	....	....	....	....	....	....	....	....	330.1	986.1	2,409.8	4,176.0	Claims on Private Sector	22d
	....	....	....	....	....	....	....	....	....	....	....	451.4	1,813.8	2,847.4	3,248.6	Demand Deposits	24
	....	....	....	....	....	....	....	....	....	....	....	696.0	1,123.1	852.6	1,818.9	Time,Savings,& Fgn.Currency Dep.	25
	....	....	....	....	....	....	....	....	....	....	....	19.4	102.6	199.0	693.5	Foreign Liabilities	26c
	....	....	....	....	....	....	....	....	....	....	....	60.5	154.9	916.9	1,711.1	Central Government Deposits	26d
	....	....	....	....	....	....	....	....	....	....	....	—	51.5	114.3	112.0	Counterpart Funds	26e
	....	....	....	....	....	....	....	....	....	....	....	—	9.8	151.8	487.1	Government Lending Funds	26f
	....	....	....	....	....	....	....	....	....	....	....	122.63	271.02	337.88	401.67	Credit from Monetary Authorities	26g
	....	....	....	....	....	....	....	....	....	....	....	228.8	493.9	776.8	994.4	Capital Accounts	27a
	....	....	....	....	....	....	....	....	....	....	....	406.9	45.1	–198.5	–309.7	Other Items (Net)	27r
End of Period																**Banking Survey**	
	....	....	....	....	....	....	....	....	....	....	....	2,171.5	4,394.2	I 5,612.0	6,932.5	Foreign Assets (Net)	31n
	....	....	....	....	....	....	....	....	....	....	....	1,110.0	1,438.2	I 2,321.2	3,251.2	Domestic Credit	32
	....	....	....	....	....	....	....	....	....	....	....	–89.0	–192.2	I –582.1	–1,306.0	Claims on Central Govt. (Net)	32an
	....	....	....	....	....	....	....	....	....	....	....	854.4	644.4	I 488.8	373.0	Claims on Nonfin.Pub.Enterprises	32c
	....	....	....	....	....	....	....	....	....	....	....	344.7	986.1	I 2,414.5	4,184.3	Claims on Private Sector	32d
	....	....	....	....	....	....	....	....	....	....	....	729.2	2,854.6	I 5,288.2	6,379.9	Money	34
	....	....	....	....	....	....	....	....	....	....	....	1,596.1	1,123.1	I 852.6	1,861.9	Quasi-Money	35
	....	....	....	....	....	....	....	....	....	....	....	—	9.8	151.8	487.1	Government Lending Funds	36f
	....	....	....	....	....	....	....	....	....	....	....	956.2	1,845.5	I 1,640.5	–8,034.2	Other Items (Net)	37r
	....	....	....	....	....	....	....	....	....	....	....	....	....	6,140.8	8,241.8	Money plus Quasi-Money	35l
Percent Per Annum																**Interest Rates**	
	....	....	....	....	....	....	....	....	....	....	....	....	....	....	....	Discount Rate (End of Period)	60
	....	....	....	....	....	....	....	....	....	....	....	....	....	....	....	Interbank Rate	60a
	....	....	....	....	....	....	....	....	....	....	....	....	....	....	....	Deposit Rate	60l
	....	....	....	....	....	....	....	....	....	....	....	....	30.5	27.3	....	Lending Rate	60p
Period Averages																**Prices and Earnings**	
	....	....	....	....	....	....	....	....	....	....	....	....	....	....	....	Producer Prices (Dec.93=100)	63
	....	....	....	....	....	....	....	....	....	....	....	8.5	100.0	189.8	280.3	Consumer Prices	64
	....	....	....	....	....	....	....	....	....	....	....	....	100.0	194.2	....	Monthly Earnings	65

Estonia

939

		1965	1966	1967	1968	1969	1970	1971	1972	1973	1974	1975	1976	1977	1978	1979
International Transactions																*Millions of Kroons*
Exports	70	....	....	....	....	....	....	....	....	....	....	....	....	....	....	....
Imports, cif	71	....	....	....	....	....	....	....	....	....	....	....	....	....	....	....
Imports, fob	71.v	....	....	....	....	....	....	....	....	....	....	....	....	....	....	....
Balance of Payments																*Millions of US Dollars:*
Goods: Exports f.o.b.	78aa *d*	....	....	....	....	....	....	....	....	....	....	....	....	....	....	....
Goods: Imports f.o.b.	78ab *d*	....	....	....	....	....	....	....	....	....	....	....	....	....	....	....
Trade Balance	78ac *d*	....	....	....	....	....	....	....	....	....	....	....	....	....	....	....
Services: Credit	78ad *d*	....	....	....	....	....	....	....	....	....	....	....	....	....	....	....
Services: Debit	78ae *d*	....	....	....	....	....	....	....	....	....	....	....	....	....	....	....
Balance on Goods and Services	78af *d*	....	....	....	....	....	....	....	....	....	....	....	....	....	....	....
Income: Credit	78ag *d*	....	....	....	....	....	....	....	....	....	....	....	....	....	....	....
Income: Debit	78ah *d*	....	....	....	....	....	....	....	....	....	....	....	....	....	....	....
Balance on Goods, Serv., & Inc.	78ai *d*	....	....	....	....	....	....	....	....	....	....	....	....	....	....	....
Current Transfers, n.i.e.: Credit	78aj *d*	....	....	....	....	....	....	....	....	....	....	....	....	....	....	....
Current Transfers: Debit	78ak *d*	....	....	....	....	....	....	....	....	....	....	....	....	....	....	....
Current Account, n.i.e.	78al *d*	....	....	....	....	....	....	....	....	....	....	....	....	....	....	....
Capital Account, n.i.e.: Credit	78ba *d*	....	....	....	....	....	....	....	....	....	....	....	....	....	....	....
Capital Account: Debit	78bb *d*	....	....	....	....	....	....	....	....	....	....	....	....	....	....	....
Capital Account, n.i.e.	78bc *d*	....	....	....	....	....	....	....	....	....	....	....	....	....	....	....
Direct Investment Abroad	78bd *d*	....	....	....	....	....	....	....	....	....	....	....	....	....	....	....
Dir. Invest. in Rep. Econ., n.i.e.	78be *d*	....	....	....	....	....	....	....	....	....	....	....	....	....	....	....
Portfolio Investment Assets	78bf *d*	....	....	....	....	....	....	....	....	....	....	....	....	....	....	....
Portfolio Investment Liab., n.i.e.	78bg *d*	....	....	....	....	....	....	....	....	....	....	....	....	....	....	....
Other Investment Assets	78bh *d*	....	....	....	....	....	....	....	....	....	....	....	....	....	....	....
Other Investment Liab., n.i.e.	78bi *d*	....	....	....	....	....	....	....	....	....	....	....	....	....	....	....
Financial Account, n.i.e.	78bj *d*	....	....	....	....	....	....	....	....	....	....	....	....	....	....	....
Net Errors and Omissions	78ca *d*	....	....	....	....	....	....	....	....	....	....	....	....	....	....	....
Overall Balance	78cb *d*	....	....	....	....	....	....	....	....	....	....	....	....	....	....	....
Reserves and Related Items	79da *d*	....	....	....	....	....	....	....	....	....	....	....	....	....	....	....
Reserve Assets	79db *d*	....	....	....	....	....	....	....	....	....	....	....	....	....	....	....
Use of Fund Credit and Loans	79dc *d*	....	....	....	....	....	....	....	....	....	....	....	....	....	....	....
Liabs.Constit.For.Auth.Reserves	79dd *d*	....	....	....	....	....	....	....	....	....	....	....	....	....	....	....
Exceptional Financing	79de *d*	....	....	....	....	....	....	....	....	....	....	....	....	....	....	....
Government Finance																*Millions of Kroons:*
Deficit (-) or Surplus	80	....	....	....	....	....	....	....	....	....	....	....	....	....	....	....
Revenue	81	....	....	....	....	....	....	....	....	....	....	....	....	....	....	....
Grants Received	81z	....	....	....	....	....	....	....	....	....	....	....	....	....	....	....
Expenditure	82	....	....	....	....	....	....	....	....	....	....	....	....	....	....	....
Lending Minus Repayments	83	....	....	....	....	....	....	....	....	....	....	....	....	....	....	....
Financing																
Domestic	84a	....	....	....	....	....	....	....	....	....	....	....	....	....	....	....
Foreign	85a	....	....	....	....	....	....	....	....	....	....	....	....	....	....	....
National Accounts																*Millions of Kroons*
Exports of Goods & Services	90c	....	....	....	....	....	....	....	....	....	....	....	....	....	....	....
Government Consumption	91f	....	....	....	....	....	....	....	....	....	....	....	....	....	....	....
Gross Fixed Capital Formation	93e	....	....	....	....	....	....	....	....	....	....	....	....	....	....	....
Increase/Decrease(-) in Stocks	93i	....	....	....	....	....	....	....	....	....	....	....	....	....	....	....
Private Consumption	96f	....	....	....	....	....	....	....	....	....	....	....	....	....	....	....
Imports of Goods & Services	98c	....	....	....	....	....	....	....	....	....	....	....	....	....	....	....
Gross Domestic Product = GDP	99b	....	....	....	....	....	....	....	....	....	....	....	....	....	....	....
Gross Dom. Prod. 1992 Prices	99b.*p*	....	....	....	....	....	....	....	....	....	....	....	....	....	....	....
GDP Deflator (1992=100)	99bi *p*	....	....	....	....	....	....	....	....	....	....	....	....	....	....	....
																Millions:
Population	99z	....	....	....	....	....	....	....	....	....	....	....	....	....	....	....

Monetary Authorities: ℓ Beginning in September 1993, data are based on improved sectorization and classification.

Government Finance: ℓ In 1992, data include European Union grants and oil purchase loans.

Estonia

1980	1981	1982	1983	1984	1985	1986	1987	1988	1989	1990	1991	1992	1993	1994		
Millions of Kroons															**International Transactions**	
....	....	....	....	....	....	....	....	....	....	....	....	5,549	10,642	ℐ16,872	Exports	70
....	....	....	....	....	....	....	....	....	....	....	....	5,128	11,848	ℐ21,561	Imports, cif	71
....	....	....	....	....	....	....	....	....	....	....	....	4,736	10,944	ℐ19,916	Imports, fob	71.v
Minus Sign Indicates Debit															**Balance of Payments**	
....	....	....	....	....	....	....	....	....	....	....	....	460.7	811.7	1,327.4	Goods: Exports f.o.b.	78aa *d*
....	....	....	....	....	....	....	....	....	....	....	....	−551.1	−956.6	−1,688.3	Goods: Imports f.o.b.	78ab *d*
....	....	....	....	....	....	....	....	....	....	....	....	−90.4	−144.9	−361.0	Trade Balance	78ac *d*
....	....	....	....	....	....	....	....	....	....	....	....	203.2	334.6	515.3	Services: Credit	78ad *d*
....	....	....	....	....	....	....	....	....	....	....	....	−160.5	−257.7	−410.8	Services: Debit	78ae *d*
....	....	....	....	....	....	....	....	....	....	....	....	−47.7	−68.0	−256.4	Balance on Goods and Services	78af *d*
....	....	....	....	....	....	....	....	....	....	....	....	.5	26.9	37.3	Income: Credit	78ag *d*
....	....	....	....	....	....	....	....	....	....	....	....	−13.7	−40.8	−65.6	Income: Debit	78ah *d*
....	....	....	....	....	....	....	....	....	....	....	....	−60.9	−81.9	−284.7	Balance on Goods, Serv., & Inc.	78ai *d*
....	....	....	....	....	....	....	....	....	....	....	....	97.4	108.4	120.3	Current Transfers, n.i.e.: Credit	78aj *d*
....	....	....	....	....	....	....	....	....	....	....	....	−.3	−3.2	−5.7	Current Transfers: Debit	78ak *d*
....	....	....	....	....	....	....	....	....	....	....	....	36.1	23.3	−170.0	Current Account, n.i.e.	78al *d*
....	....	....	....	....	....	....	....	....	....	....	....	27.4	—	.5	Capital Account, n.i.e.: Credit	78ba *d*
....	....	....	....	....	....	....	....	....	....	....	....	—	—	−1.1	Capital Account: Debit	78bb *d*
....	....	....	....	....	....	....	....	....	....	....	....	27.4	—	−.6	Capital Account, n.i.e.	78bc *d*
....	....	....	....	....	....	....	....	....	....	....	....	−1.9	−7.8	−2.4	Direct Investment Abroad	78bd *d*
....	....	....	....	....	....	....	....	....	....	....	....	82.3	162.2	213.2	Dir. Invest. in Rep. Econ., n.i.e.	78be *d*
....	....	....	....	....	....	....	....	....	....	....	....	—	−.4	−22.5	Portfolio Investment Assets	78bf *d*
....	....	....	....	....	....	....	....	....	....	....	....	—	.2	8.4	Portfolio Investment Liab., n.i.e.	78bg *d*
....	....	....	....	....	....	....	....	....	....	....	....	−122.4	−144.7	−146.9	Other Investment Assets	78bh *d*
....	....	....	....	....	....	....	....	....	....	....	....	40.7	182.8	121.5	Other Investment Liab., n.i.e.	78bi *d*
....	....	....	....	....	....	....	....	....	....	....	....	−1.3	192.3	171.3	Financial Account, n.i.e.	78bj *d*
....	....	....	....	....	....	....	....	....	....	....	....	−4.3	−50.9	16.8	Net Errors and Omissions	78ca *d*
....	....	....	....	....	....	....	....	....	....	....	....	57.9	164.6	17.5	Overall Balance	78cb *d*
....	....	....	....	....	....	....	....	....	....	....	....	−57.9	−164.6	−17.5	Reserves and Related Items	79da *d*
....	....	....	....	....	....	....	....	....	....	....	....	−69.2	−212.4	−17.5	Reserve Assets	79db *d*
....	....	....	....	....	....	....	....	....	....	....	....	11.3	47.7	—	Use of Fund Credit and Loans	79dc *d*
....	....	....	....	....	....	....	....	....	....	....	....	—	—	—	Liabs.Constit.For.Auth.Reserves	79dd *d*
....	....	....	....	....	....	....	....	....	....	....	....	—	—	—	Exceptional Financing	79de *d*
Year Ending December 31															**Government Finance**	
....	....	....	....	....	....	....	....	....	....	....	7.2	ℐ163.3	ℐ−458.5	....	Deficit (-) or Surplus	80
....	....	....	....	....	....	....	....	....	....	....	448.1	2,994.8	6,320.3	....	Revenue	81
....	....	....	....	....	....	....	....	....	....	....	14.9	ℐ219.9	ℐ243.7	....	Grants Received	81z
....	....	....	....	....	....	....	....	....	....	....	404.7	3,024.0	6,088.5	....	Expenditure	82
....	....	....	....	....	....	....	....	....	....	....	51.1	27.4	934.0	....	Lending Minus Repayments	83
															Financing	
....	....	....	....	....	....	....	....	....	....	....	−7.2	−172.1	....	....	Domestic	84a
....	....	....	....	....	....	....	....	....	....	....	—	ℐ8.8	....	....	Foreign	85a
Millions of Kroons															**National Accounts**	
....	....	....	....	....	....	....	....	....	....	....	584	7,893	15,196	....	Exports of Goods & Services	90c
....	....	....	....	....	....	....	....	....	....	....	241	1,775	3,776	....	Government Consumption	91f
....	....	....	....	....	....	....	....	....	....	....	357	2,755	4,975	....	Gross Fixed Capital Formation	93e
....	....	....	....	....	....	....	....	....	....	....	91	983	416	....	Increase/Decrease(-) in Stocks	93i
....	....	....	....	....	....	....	....	....	....	....	1,002	7,698	13,495	....	Private Consumption	96f
....	....	....	....	....	....	....	....	....	....	....	−495	−7,631	−15,908	....	Imports of Goods & Services	98c
....	....	....	....	....	....	....	....	....	....	....	1,832	14,255	22,845	....	Gross Domestic Product = GDP	99b
....	....	....	....	....	....	....	....	....	....	....	16,279	14,255	13,145	....	Gross Dom. Prod. 1992 Prices	99b.*p*
....	....	....	....	....	....	....	....	....	....	....	11.3	100.0	173.8	....	GDP Deflator (1992=100)	99bi *p*
Midyear Estimates																
....	....	....	....	....	....	....	....	....	....	....	....	1.54	1.52	1.50	Population	99z

Ethiopia

		1965	1966	1967	1968	1969	1970	1971	1972	1973	1974	1975	1976	1977	1978	1979
Exchange Rates															*Birr per SDR: End of Period*	*(aa)*
Market Rate	aa	2.5000	2.5000	2.5000	2.5000	2.5000	2.5000	2.4971	2.4971	2.4971	2.5344	2.4233	2.4050	2.5144	2.6968	2.7269
Market Rate	ae	2.5000	2.5000	2.5000	2.5000	2.5000	2.5000	2.3000	2.3000	2.0700	2.0700	2.0700	2.0700	2.0700	2.0700	2.0700
Fund Position																*Millions of SDRs:*	
Quota	2f. s	15.0	19.0	19.0	19.0	19.0	27.0	27.0	27.0	27.0	27.0	27.0	27.0	27.0	36.0	36.0
SDRs	1b. s	—	—	—	—	—	—	—	—	—	—	—	—	—	—	.4
Reserve Position in the Fund	1c. s	3.8	4.8	4.8	4.8	4.8	6.8	6.8	6.8	6.8	6.8	6.8	6.8	7.3		
Total Fund Cred.&Loans Outstg.	2tl	—	—	—	—	—	—	—	—	—	—	—	—	—	11.2	55.8
International Liquidity														*Millions of US Dollars Unless Otherwise Indicated:*		
Total Reserves minus Gold	1l. d	74.0	74.8	60.1	58.3	62.4	63.3	59.3	83.2	166.0	263.6	276.7	294.7	213.3	152.9	172.7
SDRs	1b. d	—	—	—	—	—	—	—	—	—	—	—	—	—	—	.5
Reserve Position in the Fund	1c. d	3.8	4.8	4.8	4.8	4.8	6.8	7.4	7.4	8.2	8.4	8.0	7.9	8.9		
Foreign Exchange	1d. d	70.2	70.0	55.3	53.5	57.6	56.5	51.9	75.8	157.8	255.2	268.7	286.8	204.4	152.9	172.2
Gold (Million Fine Troy Ounces)	1ad	.091	.111	.131	.231	.269	.226	.237	.249	.257	.275	.275	.275	.286	.286	.286
Gold (National Valuation)	1and	3.2	3.9	4.6	8.1	9.4	7.9	9.0	9.5	10.8	11.0	11.0	10.8	11.3	11.3	11.8
Monetary Authorities: Other Liab.	4..d	.1	.2	.5	.4	2.1	2.0	3.2	1.0	2.3	3.5	4.5	5.1	4.3	6.5	3.4
Deposit Money Banks: Assets	7a. d	14.6	11.8	7.7	15.3	14.1	12.1	13.6	21.1	52.5	48.1	40.3	38.8	57.9	45.4	70.0
of which: Claims on Nonbanks	7ad d	....	4.3	2.4	2.3	4.6	3.5	3.1	4.8	10.1	8.6	9.2	10.7	26.0	12.3	26.5
Deposit Money Banks: Liabilities	7b. d	6.0	7.6	6.8	13.0	11.5	25.6	27.7	24.5	23.6	21.4	23.0	22.4	25.0	22.2	23.8
of which: Liab. to Nonbanks	7bd d	....	3.0	2.2	7.9	6.5	16.3	19.7	22.1	18.4	18.2	19.6	18.4	21.3	17.5	21.0
Other Banking Insts.: Liabilities	7f. d	5.0	11.8	5.4	6.3	10.1	12.7	13.2	12.4	20.5	24.0	31.4	33.5	37.1	46.4	49.1
Monetary Authorities																*Millions of Birr:*
Foreign Assets	11	193	197	162	166	180	178	157	213	366	563	591	622	494	391	400
Claims on Central Government	12a	111	118	137	142	149	147	158	171	148	126	307	512	605	787	950
Claims on Other Financial Insts.	12f	—	—	—	—	—	—	—	—	—	—	83	105	167	282	441
Reserve Money	14	283	289	286	316	371	375	354	393	472	603	835	1,004	1,001	1,097	1,209
of which: Currency Outside DMBs	14a	254	268	251	274	319	323	304	340	404	533	689	575	769	895	1,012
Foreign Liabilities	16c	—	—	1	1	5	5	7	2	5	7	9	11	9	44	159
Central Government Deposits	16d	49	65	45	34	33	44	50	49	65	93	87	123	134	148	144
Capital Accounts	17a	22	25	27	31	34	38	37	49	47	65	77	97	122	151	174
Other Items (Net)	17r	–49	–65	–61	–73	–115	–137	–132	–109	–74	–79	–28	5	—	21	105
Deposit Money Banks																*Millions of Birr:*
Reserves	20	29	22	37	42	53	56	52	56	70	72	155	435	229	201	194
Foreign Assets	21	37	30	19	38	35	30	31	49	109	100	83	80	120	94	145
Claims on Central Government	22a	1	—	—	—	16	19	13	14	43	52	65	86	158	198	229
Claims on Official Entities	22bx	....	....	....	....	....	....	....	....	....	....	....	....	....	....	468
Claims on Private Sector	22d	170	207	220	260	298	387	419	444	473	545	464	467	568	732	411
Claims on Other Financial Insts.	22f	22	22	22	28	27	28	30	26	18	24	30	30	14	16	51
Demand Deposits	24	96	110	121	126	136	130	133	151	215	221	253	378	409	484	559
Time and Savings Deposits	25	71	86	100	125	150	187	215	265	363	381	302	450	473	483	536
Foreign Liabilities	26c	15	19	14	13	12	34	27	23	17	15	21	21	29	25	31
Long-Term Foreign Liabilities	26cl	—	—	3	20	16	30	37	34	32	29	27	25	23	21	18
Central Government Deposits	26d	17	13	14	12	12	13	13	13	14	21	25	31	24	28	39
Capital Accounts	27a	36	48	53	51	53	56	57	60	61	64	65	74	83	81	89
Other Items (Net)	27r	23	6	–7	22	49	70	63	43	11	63	105	119	48	119	227
Monetary Survey																*Millions of Birr:*
Foreign Assets (Net)	31n	214	207	166	190	197	169	155	237	453	640	645	671	575	416	355
Domestic Credit	32	239	270	320	384	444	524	557	594	604	635	837	1,047	1,355	1,840	2,368
Claims on Central Govt. (Net)	32an	47	41	78	97	120	109	109	124	113	65	259	445	606	809	996
Claims on Official Entities	32bx	....	....	....	....	....	....	....	....	....	....	....	....	....	....	468
Claims on Private Sector	32d	170	207	220	260	298	387	419	444	473	545	464	467	568	732	411
Claims on Other Financial Insts.	32f	22	22	22	28	27	28	30	26	19	24	113	135	181	299	492
Money	34	350	378	372	400	455	453	437	491	619	754	942	953	1,179	1,378	1,572
Quasi-Money	35	71	86	100	125	150	187	215	265	363	381	302	450	473	483	536
Long-Term Foreign Liabilities	36cl	—	—	3	20	16	30	37	34	32	29	27	25	23	21	18
Other Items (Net)	37r	32	14	11	30	20	24	23	41	43	111	210	290	256	373	596
Money plus Quasi-Money	35l	422	463	472	525	605	640	651	756	982	1,135	1,244	1,403	1,652	1,861	2,108
Other Banking Institutions																*Millions of Birr:*
Cash	40	1	2	2	3	1	2	6	8	15	9	9	31	43	41	30
Claims on Private Sector	42d	51	98	87	94	108	132	126	154	201	245	369	391	459	621	838
Time and Savings Deposits	45	3	7	5	7	7	11	14	28	34	42	58	77	86	124	144
Foreign Liabilities	46c	13	30	13	16	25	32	30	29	42	50	65	69	77	96	102
Central Govt. Lending Funds	46f	4	8	5	6	7	19	21	18	31	32	29	24	24	24	23
Credit from Monetary Authorities	46g	—	—	—	—	—	—	—	—	—	—	83	105	167	282	441
Credit from Deposit Money Banks	46h	1	21	25	26	26	27	29	23	22	29	34	29	31	35	40
Capital Accounts	47a	32	34	41	43	45	48	40	69	88	105	115	115	118	118	115
Other Items (Net)	47r	–1	1	–1	–1	–2	–2	–3	–3	–3	–3	–5	2	—	–16	2
Liquid Liabilities	55l	424	468	475	528	611	649	659	776	1,001	1,167	1,293	1,449	1,695	1,944	2,222
Interest Rates																*Percent Per Annum*
Discount Rate	60	....	....	....	....	....	....	....	....	....	....	....	....	....	....	....
Treasury Bill Rate	60c	....	....	....	....	....	....	....	....	....	....	....	....	....	2.03	2.02
Deposit Rate	60l	....	....	....	....	....	....	....	....	....	....	....	....	....	....	....
Lending Rate	60p	....	....	....	....	....	....	....	....	....	....	....	....	....	....	....
Government Bond Yield	61	....	....	....	....	....	....	....	....	....	....	....	....	....	....	....

Ethiopia
644

1980	1981	1982	1983	1984	1985	1986	1987	1988	1989	1990	1991	1992	1993	1994		
Birr per US Dollar: End of Period (ae)															**Exchange Rates**	
2.6401	2.4094	2.2834	2.1672	2.0290	2.2737	2.5320	2.9366	2.7856	2.7203	2.9449	2.9610	6.8750	6.8678	8.6861	Market Rate	aa
2.0700	2.0700	2.0700	2.0700	2.0700	2.0700	2.0700	2.0700	2.0700	2.0700	2.0700	2.0700	5.0000	5.0000	5.9500	Market Rate	ae
End of Period															**Fund Position**	
54.0	54.0	54.0	70.6	70.6	70.6	70.6	70.6	70.6	70.6	70.6	70.6	98.3	98.3	98.3	Quota	2f. s
—	10.4	3.2	2.3	3.0	.2	—	1.2	—	—	—	.2	.1	.2	.3	SDRs	1b. s
4.1	—	—	4.2	—	—	—	—	—	—	—	—	6.9	7.0	7.0	Reserve Position in the Fund	1c. s
62.3	124.4	145.6	127.6	100.2	64.8	68.8	53.4	40.8	23.0	4.5	—	14.1	35.3	49.4	Total Fund Cred.&Loans Outstg.	2tl
End of Period															**International Liquidity**	
80.1	266.7	181.8	125.9	44.3	148.0	250.5	122.7	64.2	46.1	20.2	54.5	232.4	455.8	544.2	Total Reserves minus Gold	1l. d
—	12.1	3.5	2.4	2.9	.2	—	1.7	—	.1	.3	.2	.1	.3	.4	SDRs	1b. d
5.2	—	—	4.4	—	—	—	—	—	—	—	—	9.5	9.6	10.2	Reserve Position in the Fund	1c. d
74.9	254.6	178.3	119.1	41.4	147.8	250.5	121.0	64.2	46.0	19.9	54.3	222.8	445.9	533.6	Foreign Exchange	1d. d
.309	.260	.209	.209	.209	.209	.209	.209	.209	.192	.091	.147	.113	.113	.113	Gold (Million Fine Troy Ounces)	1ad
24.5	23.3	21.3	21.3	21.3	21.3	21.3	21.3	21.3	17.3	9.4	15.1	11.4	11.4	11.4	Gold (National Valuation)	1and
5.2	9.6	7.4	10.4	6.0	12.9	12.5	18.1	37.8	48.8	60.8	18.9	174.0	161.5	146.5	Monetary Authorities: Other Liab.	4..d
50.8	63.8	90.1	71.9	64.9	57.4	72.6	52.3	71.6	64.1	43.6	151.4	192.2	236.2	532.9	Deposit Money Banks: Assets	7a. d
25.0	20.6	29.5	31.6	27.5	18.7	24.1	21.2	30.7	24.4	24.3	21.9	43.6	55.4	63.6	*of which:* Claims on Nonbanks	7ad d
40.7	60.0	71.6	66.7	62.1	59.2	57.0	56.2	62.3	60.9	67.9	77.5	65.9	91.4	134.8	Deposit Money Banks: Liabilities	7b. d
23.9	34.7	42.8	47.8	44.6	44.4	42.6	44.3	48.4	49.3	59.3	51.0	34.1	41.7	54.2	*of which:* Liab. to Nonbanks	7bd d
73.6	36.4	32.5	29.2	29.1	33.4	43.0	50.4	63.2	73.2	112.7	132.6	55.5	58.9	52.8	Other Banking Insts.: Liabilities	7f. d
End of Period															**Monetary Authorities**	
203	575	413	295	130	350	558	337	177	131	67	144	1,219	2,726	3,464	Foreign Assets	11
1,093	1,033	1,284	1,574	1,892	1,722	2,061	2,047	2,492	2,838	3,553	4,668	5,724	6,584	8,444	Claims on Central Government	12a
692	855	982	845	1,014	1,194	1,333	1,588	1,786	1,945	2,064	2,081	2,102	2,118	464	Claims on Other Financial Insts.	12f
1,355	1,554	1,690	1,690	2,027	2,117	2,638	2,596	3,085	3,515	4,028	5,137	6,120	6,421	7,084	Reserve Money	14
1,029	1,039	1,150	1,251	1,272	1,418	1,640	1,744	1,962	2,341	3,081	4,007	4,709	4,776	5,380	*of which:* Currency Outside DMBs	14a
175	319	348	298	216	174	200	194	192	163	139	39	967	1,050	1,301	Foreign Liabilities	16c
95	107	118	170	208	339	374	313	387	363	453	661	590	2,038	1,787	Central Government Deposits	16d
178	187	192	200	210	218	266	358	318	330	334	342	518	466	733	Capital Accounts	17a
185	295	331	355	375	419	473	510	473	543	729	715	850	1,453	1,464	Other Items (Net)	17r
End of Period															**Deposit Money Banks**	
325	514	540	I440	757	703	998	852	1,126	1,169	941	1,130	1,413	1,635	1,666	Reserves	20
105	132	187	I149	134	119	150	108	148	133	90	313	961	1,181	3,171	Foreign Assets	21
217	292	363	I914	951	1,451	1,449	1,476	1,498	1,869	2,639	2,630	2,617	2,617	....	Claims on Central Government	22a
586	636	677	I602	510	489	569	709	887	864	787	774	826	1,518	....	Claims on Official Entities	22bx
289	369	386	I386	360	373	374	515	384	388	407	410	623	1,347	....	Claims on Private Sector	22d
72	90	89	I84	84	91	91	89	119	118	116	115	144	141	....	Claims on Other Financial Insts.	22f
539	681	742	I892	1,037	1,285	1,633	1,597	1,759	1,981	2,192	2,192	2,433	2,674	3,646	Demand Deposits	24
628	718	797	I1,056	1,140	1,292	1,195	1,413	1,570	1,726	1,894	2,188	2,607	3,252	4,379	Time and Savings Deposits	25
68	110	136	I128	121	117	115	115	129	126	140	160	329	457	802	Foreign Liabilities	26c
16	14	12	10	8	5	3	1	—	—	—	—	—	—	—	Long-Term Foreign Liabilities	26cl
68	89	98	I117	89	81	123	130	150	149	153	178	243	412	619	Central Government Deposits	26d
85	232	223	I318	339	354	399	432	438	466	493	538	548	825	979	Capital Accounts	27a
188	190	234	I54	62	91	162	61	118	92	107	116	424	818	809	Other Items (Net)	27r
End of Period															**Monetary Survey**	
65	278	115	I18	−73	178	394	136	4	−26	−122	258	884	2,400	4,531	Foreign Assets (Net)	31n
2,785	3,079	3,565	I4,117	4,494	4,900	5,379	5,981	6,629	7,510	8,960	9,840	11,203	11,875	....	Domestic Credit	32
1,146	1,129	1,431	I2,201	2,546	2,753	3,012	3,080	3,453	4,195	5,586	6,460	7,508	6,751	....	Claims on Central Govt. (Net)	32an
586	636	677	I602	510	489	569	709	887	864	787	774	826	1,518	....	Claims on Official Entities	32bx
289	369	386	I386	360	373	374	515	384	388	407	410	623	1,347	....	Claims on Private Sector	32d
764	945	1,071	I930	1,098	1,286	1,423	1,677	1,905	2,063	2,180	2,196	2,246	2,259	....	Claims on Other Financial Insts.	32f
1,568	1,720	1,892	I2,142	2,309	2,702	3,273	3,341	3,722	4,322	5,273	6,199	7,142	7,450	9,027	Money	34
628	718	797	I1,056	1,140	1,292	1,195	1,413	1,570	1,726	1,894	2,188	2,607	3,252	4,379	Quasi-Money	35
16	14	12	10	8	5	3	1	—	—	—	—	—	—	—	Long-Term Foreign Liabilities	36cl
638	904	980	I928	985	1,078	1,301	1,361	1,342	1,436	1,670	1,711	2,338	3,573	4,024	Other Items (Net)	37r
2,196	2,438	2,689	I3,198	3,449	3,994	4,468	4,754	5,291	6,048	7,167	8,387	9,749	10,702	13,405	Money plus Quasi-Money	35l
End of Period															**Other Banking Institutions**	
49	53	34	75	64	38	217	211	208	351	331	308	297	369	234	Cash	40
1,161	1,149	1,262	1,138	1,347	1,553	1,705	2,013	2,335	2,479	3,067	3,113	2,701	954	1,206	Claims on Private Sector	42d
228	179	229	251	267	279	425	456	557	657	677	641	497	530	538	Time and Savings Deposits	45
152	75	67	61	60	69	89	104	131	152	233	274	278	295	314	Foreign Liabilities	46c
22	15	15	14	14	14	14	23	34	28	28	27	29	100	54	Central Govt. Lending Funds	46f
692	855	982	845	1,014	1,194	1,333	1,588	1,786	1,945	2,064	2,081	2,102	2,118	464	Credit from Monetary Authorities	46g
53	70	24	23	21	22	24	18	27	2	1	1	97	....	116	Credit from Deposit Money Banks	46h
115	104	91	73	81	95	125	142	128	154	87	61	....	....	101	Capital Accounts	47a
−52	−96	−113	−54	−46	−82	−88	−106	−121	−109	307	334	....	....	−148	Other Items (Net)	47r
2,375	2,565	2,884	3,374	3,652	4,235	4,676	4,999	5,640	6,354	7,514	8,721	9,949	10,863	13,710	Liquid Liabilities	55l
Percent Per Annum															**Interest Rates**	
....	....	....	....	....	6.00	6.00	3.00	3.00	3.00	3.00	3.00	5.25	12.00	12.00	Discount Rate	60
2.80	2.80	3.00	3.00	3.00	3.00	3.00	3.00	3.00	3.00	3.00	3.00	5.25	12.00	12.00	Treasury Bill Rate	60c
....	....	....	....	....	6.00	6.35	6.70	6.70	6.70	2.43	1.00	3.63	11.50	11.50	Deposit Rate	60l
....	....	....	....	....	8.50	7.25	6.00	6.00	6.00	6.00	6.00	8.00	14.00	14.33	Lending Rate	60p
....	....	....	....	....	....	6.00	5.00	5.00	5.00	5.00	5.00	7.00	13.00	13.00	Government Bond Yield	61

Ethiopia

644

		1965	1966	1967	1968	1969	1970	1971	1972	1973	1974	1975	1976	1977	1978	1979
Prices														*Index Numbers (1990=100):*		
Consumer Prices	64	23.6e	23.3	23.5	23.5	23.9	26.3	26.4	24.8	27.0	29.3	31.3	40.2	46.9	53.6	62.2
International Transactions														*Millions of Birr*		
Exports	70	289.8	277.5	252.7	266.0	298.1	305.9	314.4	384.1	502.4	556.2	497.8	580.6	689.0	633.6	864.3
Imports, cif	71	375.7	404.3	357.7	432.5	388.3	429.1	469.6	435.6	448.2	586.0	647.9	729.5	727.8	942.7	1,174.6
Imports, fob	71.v	318.4	342.6	303.1	367.3	326.3	360.6	394.6	366.1	376.2	487.9	534.7	591.5	580.5	787.6	982.1
														1990=100		
Volume of Exports	72	120.6	110.2	110.9	116.1	124.5	107.3	122.6	145.1	158.9	132.3	I118.8	115.3	84.7	93.1	142.3
Balance of Payments														*Millions of US Dollars:*		
Goods: Exports f.o.b.	78aa d	...	...	...	...	...	...	...	...	...	...	...	...	333.3	306.2	430.3
Goods: Imports f.o.b.	78ab d	...	...	...	...	...	...	...	...	...	...	...	...	-417.0	-436.5	-522.9
Trade Balance	78ac d	...	...	...	...	...	...	...	...	...	...	...	...	-83.7	-130.3	-92.5
Services: Credit	78ad d	...	...	...	...	...	...	...	...	...	...	...	...	83.9	79.5	86.3
Services: Debit	78ae d	...	...	...	...	...	...	...	...	...	...	...	...	-139.5	-151.1	-175.3
Balance on Goods and Services	78af d	...	...	...	...	...	...	...	...	...	...	...	...	-139.2	-201.9	-181.4
Income: Credit	78ag d	...	...	...	...	...	...	...	...	...	...	...	...	19.3	18.1	20.5
Income: Debit	78ah d	...	...	...	...	...	...	...	...	...	...	...	...	-19.1	-12.6	-12.5
Balance on Goods, Serv., & Inc.	78ai d	...	...	...	...	...	...	...	...	...	...	...	...	-139.1	-196.4	-173.5
Current Transfers, n.i.e.: Credit	78aj d	...	...	...	...	...	...	...	...	...	...	...	...	59.3	86.8	85.4
Current Transfers: Debit	78ak d	...	...	...	...	...	...	...	...	...	...	...	...	-2.8	-2.1	-3.2
Current Account, n.i.e.	78al d	...	...	...	...	...	...	...	...	...	...	...	...	-82.6	-111.7	-91.4
Capital Account, n.i.e.: Credit	78ba d	...	...	...	...	...	...	...	...	...	...	...	...	—	—	—
Capital Account: Debit	78bb d	...	...	...	...	...	...	...	...	...	...	...	...	-1.4	-.9	-.7
Capital Account, n.i.e.	78bc d	...	...	...	...	...	...	...	...	...	...	...	...	-1.4	-.9	-.7
Direct Investment Abroad	78bd d	...	...	...	...	...	...	...	...	...	...	...	...	—	—	—
Dir. Invest. in Rep. Econ., n.i.e.	78be d	...	...	...	...	...	...	...	...	...	...	...	...	5.8	—	—
Portfolio Investment Assets	78bf d	...	...	...	...	...	...	...	...	...	...	...	...	—	—	—
Portfolio Investment Liab., n.i.e.	78bg d	...	...	...	...	...	...	...	...	...	...	...	...	—	—	—
Other Investment Assets	78bh d	...	...	...	...	...	...	...	...	...	...	...	...	-26.7	-35.2	-23.6
Other Investment Liab., n.i.e.	78bi d	...	...	...	...	...	...	...	...	...	...	...	...	38.5	30.3	77.0
Financial Account, n.i.e.	78bj d	...	...	...	...	...	...	...	...	...	...	...	...	17.7	-4.9	53.4
Net Errors and Omissions	78ca d	...	...	...	...	...	...	...	...	...	...	...	...	3.3	29.2	19.5
Overall Balance	78cb d	...	...	...	...	...	...	...	...	...	...	...	...	-63.0	-88.4	-19.2
Reserves and Related Items	79da d	...	...	...	...	...	...	...	...	...	...	...	...	63.0	88.4	19.2
Reserve Assets	79db d	...	...	...	...	...	...	...	...	...	...	...	...	63.0	74.4	-39.0
Use of Fund Credit and Loans	79dc d	...	...	...	...	...	...	...	...	...	...	...	...	—	14.0	58.2
Liabs.Constit.For.Auth.Reserves	79dd d	...	...	...	...	...	...	...	...	...	...	...	...	—	—	—
Exceptional Financing	79de d	...	...	...	...	...	...	...	...	...	...	...	...	—	—	—
Government Finance														*Millions of Birr:*		
Deficit (-) or Surplus	80	-6.5	-38.4	-24.2	-52.0	-30.0	-46.8	-51.0	I-64.2	-49.2	-43.8	-226.2	-325.1	-232.5	-421.9	-254.5
Revenue	81	294.5	322.8	355.1	357.7	390.4	426.8	466.0	I494.1	561.0	619.7	710.4	777.9	1,013.7	1,184.3	1,410.1
Grants Received	81z	87.9	104.7	91.9	87.5	85.2	88.0	93.4	I92.9	91.7	97.5	96.1	77.2	82.6	71.8	26.7
Expenditure	82	388.8	468.6	477.7	503.8	506.6	550.4	603.8	I647.9	678.6	733.0	985.4	1,144.5	1,320.0	1,664.1	1,690.5
Lending Minus Repayments	83	.1	-2.7	-6.5	-6.6	-1.0	11.2	6.6	I3.3	23.3	28.4	47.3	35.7	8.8	13.9	.8
Financing																
Domestic	84	...	...	...	...	...	...	...	20.1	9.4	-3.1	127.9	220.9	145.7	348.2	83.7
Foreign	85	...	...	...	...	...	...	...	44.1	39.8	46.9	98.3	104.2	86.8	73.7	170.8
Financing																
Net Borrowing: Domestic	84a	11.1	.5	6.0	29.3	11.7	26.7	13.0	I20.3	-.7	8.1	146.1	203.8	131.0	338.0	85.6
Foreign	85a	—	34.0	9.7	6.1	-.4	27.3	39.8	I44.1	39.8	46.9	98.3	104.2	86.8	73.7	170.8
Use of Cash Balances	87	-4.7	3.9	8.7	16.5	18.8	-7.2	-1.7	I-.2	10.1	-11.2	-18.2	17.1	14.7	10.2	-1.9
Debt: Domestic	88a	...	...	...	...	...	...	205.7	225.9	225.1	237.1	383.2	587.0	732.4	1,080.6	1,164.3
Foreign	89a	...	...	...	...	...	...	305.7	335.4	367.9	410.0	508.3	612.5	699.3	773.0	943.8
National Accounts														*Millions of Birr:*		
Exports of Goods & Services	90c	390	398	376	399	400	489	469	491	654	828	682	760	822	866	943
Government Consumption	91f	336	376	384	403	411	443	461	508	538	586	730	866	967	1,240	1,168
Gross Capital Formation	93	399	448	511	538	544	512	554	603	569	549	579	578	606	545	699
Private Consumption	96f	2,588	2,658	2,787	2,969	3,188	3,519	3,782	3,720	3,797	4,244	4,428	4,618	5,461	5,885	6,544
Imports of Goods & Services	98c	-456	-497	-455	-473	-487	-504	-556	-578	-552	-655	-896	-818	-1,030	-1,271	-1,368
Gross Domestic Product	99b	3,258	3,383	3,604	3,837	4,056	4,461	4,710	4,744	5,006	5,552	5,523	6,004	6,826	7,265	7,988
Net Factor Inc/Pmts(-) Abroad	98.n	-9	-13	-17	-22	-20	-20	-19	-29	-47	-36	-35	-3	-6	-9	-8
Gross Nat'l Expenditure = GNP	99a	3,249	3,370	3,587	3,815	4,036	4,441	4,691	4,715	4,958	5,515	5,489	6,001	6,820	7,256	7,983
GDP at Factor Cost	99ba	...	...	...	...	...	...	...	...	...	...	...	5,530	6,146	6,487	7,087
Gross Dom. Prod. 1990 Prices	99b.p	9,026	9,380	9,804	10,097	10,707	11,093	11,591	12,144	12,472	12,652	12,665	12,958	13,035	12,887	13,572
GDP at Factor Cost, 1990 Prices	99ba.p	5,356	5,566	5,817	5,991	6,353	6,582	6,878	7,206	7,400	7,507	7,515	7,688	7,734	7,646	8,053
GDP Deflator (1990=100)	99bi.p	36.1	36.1	36.8	38.0	37.9	40.2	40.6	39.1	40.1	43.9	43.6	46.3	52.4	56.4	58.9
														Millions:		
Population	99z	22.17	22.49	I22.87	23.44	24.02	24.63	25.25	25.89	26.19	26.78	27.47	28.19	I35.92	36.76	37.63

Deposit Money Banks: I Beginning in December 1979, loans and advances of the commercial banks are separated into *Claims on Official Entities (line 22bx)*, *Claims on Private Sector (line 22d)*, and *Claims on Other Financial Institutions (line 22f)*. Previously, these loans and advances were all included in *line 22d*. I In July 1980 the Addis Bank was merged with the Commercial Bank of Ethiopia, and since then, owing to data reclassification, *IFS* time series on *Demand Deposits (line 24)*, *Other Items (Net) (line 27r)*, *Money (line 34)*, and *Other Items (Net) (line 37r)* have been revised. I Beginning in August 1983, revised data exclude the Djibouti branch of the Commercial Bank of Ethiopia.
Monetary Survey: I See note to section 20.
Government Finance: I Beginning in 1972, data are as reported in the *Government Finance Statistics Yearbook* and cover budgetary central government and some extrabudgetary accounts. I Beginning in 1982, data cover budgetary central government only. I Beginning in 1991, revenue data include loan repayments, and expenditure data include lending operations.

Ethiopia

644

	1980	1981	1982	1983	1984	1985	1986	1987	1988	1989	1990	1991	1992	1993	1994		
Period Averages																**Prices**	
	65.0	68.9	73.0	72.5	78.6	93.6	84.4	82.4	88.2	95.1	100.0	135.7	150.0	155.3	....	Consumer Prices	64
Millions of Birr																**International Transactions**	
	878.8	805.1	835.5	833.3	862.7	689.4	941.6	735.2	888.6	911.5	615.8	390.5	448.4	994.2	....	Exports	70
	1,494.7	1,528.9	1,627.8	1,813.3	1,921.4	2,056.4	2,280.4	2,205.9	2,336.2	1,967.7	2,238.5	976.8	2,604.3	3,936.7	....	Imports, cif	71
	1,270.6	1,304.9	1,397.3	1,534.2	1,631.1	1,733.9	1,922.8	1,859.9	1,969.8	1,659.1	1,887.4	823.6	2,195.9	3,319.3	....	Imports, fob	71.v
1990=100																	
	103.8	105.8	113.2	122.1	121.0	99.8	110.7	104.3	106.3	115.0	100.0	48.9	50.0	....	....	Volume of Exports	72
Minus Sign Indicates Debit																**Balance of Payments**	
	419.3	374.1	402.8	402.6	416.8	332.9	477.1	355.2	400.0	443.8	292.0	167.6	169.9	198.8	....	Goods: Exports f.o.b.	78aa d
	−649.6	−629.8	−675.2	−740.0	−798.4	−840.5	−932.6	−932.7	−956.0	−817.9	−912.1	−470.8	−992.7	−706.0	....	Goods: Imports f.o.b.	78ab d
	−230.3	−255.7	−272.4	−337.3	−381.5	−507.7	−455.4	−577.4	−556.0	−374.1	−620.1	−303.2	−822.9	−507.1	....	Trade Balance	78ac d
	125.4	132.4	135.1	138.9	186.5	288.8	243.9	296.9	271.7	289.2	304.6	268.3	267.9	278.1	....	Services: Credit	78ad d
	−208.3	−206.6	−212.4	−224.8	−252.6	−270.8	−271.7	−307.7	−330.1	−323.4	−358.5	−284.3	−368.3	−299.4	....	Services: Debit	78ae d
	−313.1	−329.9	−349.7	−423.2	−447.7	−489.6	−483.2	−588.3	−614.4	−408.3	−674.3	−319.3	−923.3	−528.5	....	Balance on Goods and Services	78af d
	28.1	24.8	41.4	30.7	23.8	24.7	34.0	21.9	17.1	12.7	9.2	14.4	22.3	21.5	....	Income: Credit	78ag d
	−13.5	−13.3	−27.4	−28.0	−37.5	−39.9	−61.1	−58.7	−72.8	−85.0	−77.7	−96.7	−104.1	−78.4	....	Income: Debit	78ah d
	−298.6	−318.4	−335.7	−420.6	−461.4	−504.7	−510.3	−625.1	−670.0	−480.6	−742.9	−401.5	−1,005.1	−585.4	....	Balance on Goods, Serv., & Inc.	78ai d
	74.3	70.3	143.4	254.3	332.5	612.5	184.2	412.9	443.2	337.5	451.3	505.9	887.4	532.6	....	Current Transfers, n.i.e.: Credit	78aj d
	−1.8	−1.4	−2.7	−3.6	−1.2	−1.4	−1.0	−4.6	−.7	−1.3	−2.2	−1.3	−2.0	−1.2	....	Current Transfers: Debit	78ak d
	−226.1	−249.5	−194.9	−169.9	−130.1	106.3	−327.1	−216.9	−227.5	−144.4	−293.8	103.1	−119.8	−54.0	....	Current Account, n.i.e.	78al d
	—	—	—	—	—	—	—	—	—	—	—	—	—	—	....	Capital Account, n.i.e.: Credit	78ba d
	−.6	−.4	−.3	−.5	−.3	−.4	−.1	—	−.6	−.3	−.1	—	—	—	....	Capital Account: Debit	78bb d
	−.6	−.4	−.3	−.5	−.3	−.4	−.1	—	−.6	−.3	−.1	—	—	—	....	Capital Account, n.i.e.	78bc d
	—	—	—	—	—	—	—	—	—	—	—	—	—	—	....	Direct Investment Abroad	78bd d
	—	—	—	—	—	—	—	—	—	—	—	—	—	—	....	Dir. Invest. in Rep. Econ., n.i.e.	78be d
	—	—	—	—	—	—	—	—	—	—	—	—	—	—	....	Portfolio Investment Assets	78bf d
	—	—	—	—	—	—	—	—	—	—	—	—	—	—	....	Portfolio Investment Liab., n.i.e.	78bg d
	63.9	21.1	17.6	−23.9	24.3	12.3	—	—	—	50.0	87.0	−166.7	−87.1	−31.7	....	Other Investment Assets	78bh d
	94.3	344.8	91.4	195.5	200.0	212.7	239.6	292.8	299.6	171.9	143.0	−37.4	21.7	111.2	....	Other Investment Liab., n.i.e.	78bi d
	158.2	365.9	109.0	171.6	224.2	225.0	239.6	292.8	299.6	222.0	230.0	−204.1	−65.4	79.4	....	Financial Account, n.i.e.	78bj d
	−33.4	−7.5	10.8	−54.1	−150.6	−168.8	201.6	−182.8	−94.0	−32.0	−134.6	−254.6	−81.1	66.3	....	Net Errors and Omissions	78ca d
	−101.9	108.4	−75.4	−52.9	−56.8	162.2	113.9	−107.4	−22.3	45.5	−198.3	−355.9	−266.2	91.7	....	Overall Balance	78cb d
	101.9	−108.4	75.4	52.9	56.8	−162.2	−113.9	107.4	22.3	−45.5	198.3	355.9	266.2	−91.7	....	Reserves and Related Items	79aa d
	93.4	−180.9	51.7	72.1	83.7	−126.0	−117.4	126.9	39.1	−22.7	34.7	−37.2	−95.9	−296.2	....	Reserve Assets	79db d
	8.5	72.6	23.7	−19.2	−28.0	−36.2	3.5	−19.9	−16.8	−22.8	−25.2	−6.5	19.6	29.7	....	Use of Fund Credit and Loans	79dc d
	—	—	—	—	—	—	—	—	—	—	—	—	—	2.5	18.2	Liabs.Constit.For.Auth.Reserves	79dd d
	.1	−.1	—	—	1.2	—	—	.4	—	—	188.8	399.6	340.0	156.6	....	Exceptional Financing	79de d
Year Ending July 7																**Government Finance**	
	−380.5	−334.2	I−491.5	−1,350.8	−621.5	−861.8	−805.0	−689.1	−784.2	−1,028.0	−1,739.1	I−1681.8	−1,419.8ᵖ	−1,881.4ᵖ	−2,362.1ᶠ	Deficit (−) or Surplus	80
	1,597.1	1,791.7	I 1,865.3	2,158.4	2,283.2	2,266.0	2,730.4	2,847.8	3,432.3	3,882.0	3,103.9	I 2,703.7	2,183.9ᵖ	3,091.6ᵖ	3,936.2ᶠ	Revenue	81
	6.9	3.0	13.1	30.0	20.7	79.4	51.2	79.8	46.4	190.9	66.8	I 19.3	—ᵖ	117.1ᵖ	1,364.8ᶠ	Grants Received	81z
	1,994.9	2,136.3	I 2,377.4	3,159.2	2,874.6	3,150.3	3,540.5	3,604.1	4,161.5	4,785.7	4,832.3	I 4,404.8	3,603.7ᵖ	5,090.1ᵖ	7,663.1ᶠ	Expenditure	82
	−10.4	−7.4	−7.5	380.0	50.8	56.9	46.1	12.6	101.4	315.2	77.5	....	....	....	....	Lending Minus Repayments	83
																Financing	
	230.0	203.7	16.6	929.8	413.0	533.1	334.8	362.3	382.2	426.4	1,243.2	I 1,340.1	1,170.5ᵖ	855.7ᵖ	240.0ᶠ	Domestic	84
	150.5	130.5	474.9	421.0	208.5	328.7	470.2	326.8	402.0	601.6	495.9	I 341.1	249.3ᵖ	1,025.7ᵖ	2,122.1ᶠ	Foreign	85
																Financing	
																Net Borrowing: Domestic	84a
	229.3	206.0	10.0	948.1	411.8	441.8	371.5	414.9	360.7	436.8	1,266.2	....	....	....	....		
	150.5	130.5	474.9	421.0	208.5	328.7	470.2	326.8	402.0	601.6	495.9	I 341.1	249.3ᵖ	1,025.7ᵖ	2,122.1ᶠ	Foreign	85a
	.7	−2.3	6.6	−18.3	1.2	91.3	−36.7	−52.6	21.5	−10.4	−23.0	....	....	....	....	Use of Cash Balances	87
	1,394.3	1,598.0	1,614.6	2,544.4	2,957.4	3,490.5	3,825.4	4,187.7	4,564.3	4,990.6	6,272.5	....	....	....	....	Debt: Domestic	88a
	1,094.3	1,224.8	1,699.7	2,122.2	2,330.7	2,666.4	3,091.2	3,483.4	3,939.3	4,526.5	5,913.7	....	....	....	....	Foreign	89a
Year Ending July 7																**National Accounts**	
	1,210	1,147	1,076	1,142	1,267	1,137	1,371	1,290	1,303	1,542	1,391	1,124	937	2,164	3,064	Exports of Goods & Services	90c
	1,293	1,443	1,690	2,035	1,920	2,001	2,152	2,288	2,757	3,129	3,296	3,048	2,108	2,819	3,246	Government Consumption	91f
	854	922	1,515	1,495	1,927	1,452	2,317	2,337	3,187	2,363	2,187	2,079	1,911	3,288	4,592	Gross Capital Formation	93
	6,795	6,851	9,149	9,858	9,047	11,527	11,161	12,127	11,342	12,324	13,211	16,103	17,661	22,307	23,645	Private Consumption	96f
	−1,652	−1,642	−1,959	−1,991	−2,311	−2,240	−2,508	−2,541	−2,592	−2,484	−2,213	−2,538	−2,223	−4,521	−7,150	Imports of Goods & Services	98c
	8,499	8,721	11,281	12,540	11,849	13,876	14,493	15,501	15,997	16,873	17,872	19,816	20,394	26,057	27,397	Gross Domestic Product	99b
	−14	−15	−18	−28	−40	−68	−65	−98	−134	−172	−139	−152	−175	−307	−518	Net Factor Inc/Pmts(−) Abroad	98.n
	8,514	8,706	11,263	12,512	11,810	13,808	14,429	15,403	15,863	16,702	17,733	19,664	20,219	25,749	26,879	Gross Nat'l Expenditure = GNP	99a
	7,625	7,913	10,400	11,835	10,784	12,882	13,404	14,329	14,718	15,582	16,661	18,528	19,416	24,537	25,295	GDP at Factor Cost	99ba
	14,324	I 15,204	15,355	16,544	15,727	14,803	15,828	17,340	17,665	17,950	17,872	16,793	....	....	....	Gross Dom. Prod. 1990 Prices	99b.p
	8,499	9,546	13,718	15,145	14,268	12,893	14,116	16,064	16,082	16,111	16,661	15,545	14,195	15,939	16,155	GDP at Factor Cost, 1990 Prices	99ba p
	59.3	62.4	73.5	75.8	75.3	93.7	91.6	89.4	90.6	94.0	100.0	118.0	122.5	140.6	....	GDP Deflator (1990=100)	99bi p
Midyear Estimates																	
	38.75	39.59	40.41	41.18	42.69	44.25	45.74	47.19	48.59	50.17	51.69	53.38	55.12	56.90	....	Population	99z

Fiji
819

		1965	1966	1967	1968	1969	1970	1971	1972	1973	1974	1975	1976	1977	1978	1979
Exchange Rates															*Fiji Dollars per SDR:*		
Official Rate	aa	.7921	.7956	.8686	.8765	1.8706	.8731	.8890	.9155	.9762	.9795	1.0104	1.0939	1.0575	1.0679	1.1077
														Fiji Dollars per US Dollar:		
Official Rate	ae	.7921	.7956	.8686	.8765	1.8706	.8731	.8188	.8432	.8092	.8000	.8631	.9415	.8705	.8197	.8409
Official Rate	rf	.7929	.7929	.8059	.8708	.8708	.8708	.8588	.8252	.7942	.8056	.8219	.8977	.9174	.8468	.8357
														Index Numbers (1990=100):		
Official Rate	ahx	186.3ᵉ	186.2ᵉ	184.1ᵉ	169.4ᵉ	169.2	169.6	173.0	179.5	186.4	183.7	180.2	165.0	161.4	174.8	177.1
Nominal Effective Exchange Rate	nec	....	....	....	....	....	....	....	....	....	....	....	....	....	....	112.9
Real Effective Exchange Rate	rec	....	....	....	....	....	....	....	....	....	....	....	....	....	....	139.5
Fund Position															*Millions of SDRs:*		
Quota	2f.s	....	....	....	....	....	....	13.00	13.00	13.00	13.00	13.00	13.00	13.00	18.00	18.00
SDRs	1b.s	....	....	....	....	....	....	—	1.38	1.38	1.37	1.33	1.33	1.27	1.30	3.10
Reserve Position in the Fund	1c.s	....	....	....	....	....	....	2.30	2.30	2.30	—	3.25	3.25	3.25	3.15	3.06
Total Fund Cred.&Loans Outstg.	2tl	....	....	....	....	....	....	—	—	—	.34	—	—	6.50	6.50	6.50
International Liquidity												*Millions of US Dollars Unless Otherwise Indicated:*					
Total Reserves minus Gold	1l.d	21.82	18.04	18.37	18.49	26.81	27.35	39.62	69.42	73.95	109.15	148.59	116.32	147.13	134.70	136.48
SDRs	1b.d	....	....	....	....	....	....	—	1.50	1.66	1.68	1.56	1.55	1.54	1.69	4.08
Reserve Position in the Fund	1c.d	....	....	....	....	....	....	2.50	2.50	2.77	—	3.80	3.78	3.95	4.10	4.03
Foreign Exchange	1d.d	21.82	18.04	18.37	18.49	26.81	27.35	37.12	65.42	69.51	107.47	143.23	111.00	141.64	128.90	128.37
Gold (Million Fine Troy Ounces)	1ad	....	....	....	....	....	....	....	....	....	....	....	.006	.008	.011
Gold (National Valuation)	1and	....	....	....	....	....	....	....	....	....	....	....	.24	.38	.51
Deposit Money Banks: Assets	7a.d	11.62	12.72	12.81	12.29	16.78	20.06	23.64	18.31	8.61	9.55	6.37	4.96	4.83	5.16	3.66
of which: Claims on Nonbanks	7add	3.17	3.20	2.65	2.85	2.83	3.49	5.09	5.48	5.44	4.95	1.57	1.03	1.74	1.93	1.86
Deposit Money Banks: Liabilities	7b.d	.86	.76	.82	.10	1.17	1.17	2.81	7.27	14.47	20.77	18.65	22.25	22.79	13.24	13.62
Monetary Authorities															*Millions of Fiji Dollars:*		
Foreign Assets	11	21.1	17.8	18.1	19.3	27.4	27.0	35.0	54.5	167.8	91.6	129.1	110.3	128.7	110.3	116.9
Claims on Central Government	12a	.1	.2	.4	1.5	3.8	3.5	3.5	3.6	2.6	2.8	3.0	2.8	1.6	5.1	10.4
Claims on Official Entities	12bx	—	—	—	—	—	—	—	—	.4	.1	—	.3	1.3	2.9	9.4
Reserve Money	14	12.9	12.7	13.6	13.5	15.6	17.3	20.4	24.9	37.6	48.5	63.4	54.5	56.4	64.1	72.0
of which: Currency Outside DMBs	14a	8.9	9.1	8.5	8.5	9.6	11.2	13.1	14.9	17.2	21.5	27.3	30.7	34.0	38.8	45.2
Bonds	16aa	—	—	—	—	—	—	—	—	—	—	—	—	—	—	—
Central Government Deposits	16d	7.1	4.4	5.3	5.7	11.9	8.4	12.3	12.7	22.0	13.4	27.5	20.6	21.3	15.1	16.1
Capital Accounts	17a	—	—	—	—	.3	.6	2.3	.8	9.1	10.8	10.8	20.4	18.1	19.3	24.8
Other Items (Net)	17r	1.2	1.0	-.4	1.6	3.4	4.1	3.5	19.8	12.1	21.8	30.5	18.0	35.8	19.8	23.9
Deposit Money Banks															*Millions of Fiji Dollars:*		
Reserves	20	1.9	1.5	2.1	1.9	2.3	2.3	3.0	12.6	16.7	18.6	25.3	18.1	20.8	19.1	20.4
Reserve Bank Bonds	20r	....	....	....	....	....	....	....	....	....	....	....	....	....	....	....
Foreign Assets	21	9.2	10.1	11.2	10.7	14.6	17.5	19.0	13.9	7.0	7.6	5.5	4.7	4.2	4.2	3.1
Claims on Central Government	22a	4.3	4.6	5.1	5.5	6.4	6.7	7.4	8.8	10.0	16.2	22.2	27.0	31.4	39.6	42.8
Claims on Official Entities	22bx	.6	.9	1.1	1.3	1.6	2.3	2.9	6.8	7.1	7.5	10.0	13.7	13.3	17.7	16.7
Claims on Private Sector	22d	11.6	12.3	12.8	16.4	17.8	23.8	30.8	40.4	57.7	75.5	78.2	102.3	119.5	127.2	167.9
Demand Deposits	24	11.7	12.8	12.9	14.7	18.5	22.4	25.3	31.5	35.4	39.4	47.3	47.9	48.4	53.5	61.8
Time Deposits	25	15.5	16.7	18.6	21.1	23.6	28.1	35.2	43.1	50.6	65.9	80.8	96.6	119.1	140.0	174.9
Foreign Liabilities	26c	.7	.6	.7	.1	1.0	1.0	2.3	5.5	11.7	16.6	16.1	21.0	19.8	10.8	11.5
Central Government Deposits	26d	1.7	1.5	2.7	2.5	3.0	5.3	4.2	3.7	4.0	5.3	2.7	5.0	5.1	5.3	7.1
Other Items (Net)	27r	-2.0	-2.3	-2.7	-2.4	-3.3	-4.3	-3.9	-1.3	-3.3	-1.8	-5.7	-4.7	-3.3	-1.9	-4.3
Monetary Survey															*Millions of Fiji Dollars:*		
Foreign Assets (Net)	31n	29.7	27.3	28.5	29.9	41.0	43.5	51.8	62.9	163.1	82.2	118.4	94.1	106.2	96.8	101.3
Domestic Credit	32	7.8	12.1	11.4	16.6	14.7	22.5	28.1	43.2	51.8	83.4	83.3	120.5	140.7	172.0	224.1
Claims on Central Govt. (Net)	32an	-4.4	-1.1	-2.5	-1.2	-4.7	-3.6	-5.6	-4.0	-13.4	.3	-4.9	4.2	6.7	24.2	30.0
Claims on Official Entities	32bx	.6	.9	1.1	1.3	1.6	2.3	2.9	6.8	7.5	7.6	10.0	14.0	14.6	20.5	26.2
Claims on Private Sector	32d	11.6	12.3	12.8	16.4	17.8	23.8	30.8	40.4	57.7	75.5	78.2	102.3	119.5	127.2	167.9
Money	34	22.8	24.1	24.4	26.3	31.8	37.3	42.7	52.3	56.5	69.1	84.0	85.4	84.1	98.4	112.3
Quasi-Money	35	15.5	16.7	18.6	21.1	23.6	28.1	35.2	43.1	51.6	81.4	107.2	108.5	146.0	149.0	186.0
Reserve Bank Bonds	36aa	....	....	....	....	....	....	....	....	....	....	....	....	....	....	....
Other Items (Net)	37r	-.9	-1.4	-3.1	-.9	.3	.5	1.9	10.8	16.8	15.1	10.5	20.7	16.8	21.3	27.1
Money plus Quasi-Money	35l	38.3	40.8	43.0	47.3	55.4	65.5	78.0	95.4	108.1	150.5	191.3	193.9	230.1	247.4	298.3
Nonbank Financial Institutions															*Millions of Fiji Dollars:*		
Claims on Central Government	42a.l	....	....	....	....	7.5	8.1	8.6	9.3	9.6	10.9	9.3	9.6	13.7	18.4	22.1
Claims on Official Entities	42bx.l	....	....	....	....	....	2.2	2.7	3.8	4.4	5.2	5.2	5.4	5.6	6.3	7.3	8.8
Claims on Private Sector	42d.l	....	....	....	....	2.3	2.9	3.1	3.3	4.7	5.7	6.7	5.6	8.0	9.4	10.7
Incr.in Total Assets(Within Per.)	49z.l	....	....	....	....	....	1.4	1.9	1.9	2.8	2.9	2.3	4.2	8.3	6.1	7.3
Interest Rates															*Percent Per Annum*		
Bank Rate (End of Period)	60	....	....	....	....	....	....	....	....	....	6.38	6.25	5.50	5.50	5.58	6.50
Money Market Rate	60b	....	....	....	....	....	....	....	....	....	....	....	....	....	....	....
Treasury Bill Rate	60c	....	....	....	....	....	....	....	....	....	....	4.34	4.34	4.34	4.50	5.32
Deposit Rate	60l	....	....	....	....	....	....	....	....	....	3.96	4.00	4.00	4.00	4.04	4.50
Lending Rate	60p	....	....	....	....	....	....	8.00	10.00	10.00	10.00	10.00	10.00	10.00	10.50	10.50
Prices, Production, Employment															*Index Numbers (1990=100):*		
Consumer Prices	64	....	....	....	....	16.7	17.3	18.9	23.1	25.7	29.4	33.2	37.0	39.6	42.0	45.3
Wage Rates	65	13.7	14.6	15.0	16.4	17.3	18.4	20.3	23.0	29.7	36.5	44.6	49.9	53.1	58.9	63.3
Industrial Production	66	....	....	....	....	....	....	....	....	....	....	....	....	....	....	....
Tourist Arrivals	66.t	....	....	....	....	....	....	....	....	....	....	....	....	....	....	....
Industrial Employment	67	....	....	....	....	....	....	....	....	....	....	....	....	....	85.1	87.2

Fiji

	1980	1981	1982	1983	1984	1985	1986	1987	1988	1989	1990	1991	1992	1993	1994		
End of Period																**Exchange Rates**	
	1.0089	1.0205	1.0450	1.0954	1.1204	1.2307	1.4010	2.0436	1.8906	1.9632	2.0760	2.1067	2.1511	2.1164	2.0570	Official Rate	aa
End of Period (ae) Period Average (rf)																	
	.7911	.8767	.9473	1.0462	1.1430	1.1204	1.1453	1.4405	1.4049	1.4939	1.4592	1.4728	1.5645	1.5408	1.4090	Official Rate	ae
	.8180	.8546	.9324	1.0170	1.0826	1.1536	1.1329	1.2439	1.4303	1.4833	1.4809	1.4756	1.5030	1.5418	1.4641	Official Rate	rf
Period Averages																	
	181.0	173.4	158.8	145.6	136.9	128.4	130.7	120.9	103.5	99.8	100.0	100.3	98.5	96.0	101.1	Official Rate	ah x
	117.1	120.8	124.8	125.1	128.3	134.8	127.2	110.5	91.0	94.9	100.0	104.4	108.1	114.8	124.5	Nominal Effective Exchange Rate	ne c
	145.3	149.1	149.9	149.0	150.7	152.8	137.4	117.0	99.1	99.2	100.0	103.6	105.3	108.8	108.2	Real Effective Exchange Rate	re c
End of Period																**Fund Position**	
	27.00	27.00	27.00	36.50	36.50	36.50	36.50	36.50	36.50	36.50	36.50	36.50	36.50	51.10	51.10	Quota	2f. s
	2.71	4.52	3.72	.28	6.31	5.14	5.82	9.90	15.08	15.90	16.48	9.26	5.97	6.26	7.39	SDRs	1b. s
	5.34	5.36	5.40	7.79	7.81	7.83	7.85	7.87	7.87	7.89	7.12	6.76	10.43	9.95	9.99	Reserve Position in the Fund	1c. s
	—	—	13.50	13.50	13.50	13.19	6.44	4.75	2.97	.59	—	—	—	—	—	Total Fund Cred.&Loans Outstg.	2tl
End of Period																**International Liquidity**	
	167.51	135.08	126.92	115.82	117.42	130.84	171.05	132.17	233.36	211.59	260.79	271.43	316.87	269.46	273.14	Total Reserves minus Gold	1l. d
	3.46	5.26	4.10	.29	6.19	5.65	7.12	14.04	20.29	20.90	23.45	13.25	8.21	8.59	10.79	SDRs	1b. d
	6.81	6.24	5.96	8.16	7.66	8.60	9.60	11.16	10.59	10.37	10.13	9.67	14.34	13.67	14.58	Reserve Position in the Fund	1c. d
	157.24	123.58	116.86	107.37	103.58	116.59	154.33	106.96	202.48	180.33	227.22	248.51	294.32	247.19	247.77	Foreign Exchange	1d. d
	.011	.011	.011	.011	.011	.011	.011	.001	.001	.001	.001	.001	.001	.001	.001	Gold (Million Fine Troy Ounces)	1ad
	.50	.45	.43	.41	.38	.43	.47	.41	.41	.30	.32	.29	.28	.33	.32	Gold (National Valuation)	1an d
	8.38	10.02	4.95	7.87	8.42	44.42	111.97	26.29	38.35	51.99	77.88	49.90	44.47	58.69	62.91	Deposit Money Banks: Assets	7a. d
	5.14	6.09	.84	1.79	2.22	22.97	103.42	20.25	30.43	37.98	42.43	30.06	28.10	26.51	26.09	of which: Claims on Nonbanks	7add d
	16.27	19.98	23.53	18.67	14.82	55.56	120.11	25.05	41.56	54.40	83.02	66.05	67.17	64.30	65.66	Deposit Money Banks: Liabilities	7b. d
End of Period																**Monetary Authorities**	
	132.5	116.0	123.4	122.5	130.0	146.5	195.9	190.2	326.8	316.1	380.5	399.7	498.0	414.8	384.8	Foreign Assets	11
	6.1	4.6	11.1	8.2	16.7	4.3	1.8	26.9	1.5	9.0	.1	.1	—	6.7	—	Claims on Central Government	12a
	2.9	1.0	2.8	11.4	6.5	6.2	.3	5.3	—	.1	.1	.1	.1	2.2	.1	Claims on Official Entities	12bx
	66.2	76.4	81.6	86.9	100.5	103.0	116.7	111.6	199.3	152.1	169.3	189.1	226.4	219.9	223.6	Reserve Money	14
	44.1	48.7	52.8	58.7	61.0	61.8	63.1	64.9	67.7	78.0	86.0	91.0	103.1	112.4	115.6	of which: Currency Outside DMBs	14a
	—	—	—	—	—	—	—	—	—	56.9	96.2	95.4	163.9	108.9	126.6	Bonds	16aa
	29.3	16.9	13.1	13.3	10.6	7.4	13.9	.9	49.0	42.9	36.2	31.7	21.8	14.3	14.8	Central Government Deposits	16d
	16.2	23.4	28.4	34.0	36.3	47.4	69.9	110.6	76.0	80.7	83.4	73.0	82.8	62.7	45.8	Capital Accounts	17a
	29.8	4.7	14.3	7.9	5.8	-.8	-2.5	-.7	4.0	-7.6	-4.4	10.7	3.2	17.9	-25.8	Other Items (Net)	17r
End of Period																**Deposit Money Banks**	
	22.2	23.3	28.2	28.3	39.5	41.4	53.4	46.7	131.5	73.1	83.2	97.8	123.3	107.5	107.9	Reserves	20
	....	....	....	....	....	....	....	....	....	20.3	60.7	39.9	60.2	44.6	44.0	Reserve Bank Bonds	20r
	6.6	8.8	4.7	8.2	9.6	49.8	128.2	37.9	53.9	77.7	113.6	73.5	69.6	90.4	88.6	Foreign Assets	21
	53.0	40.3	51.6	52.9	44.8	50.2	77.2	62.5	83.6	71.6	60.8	82.2	91.6	88.9	80.7	Claims on Central Government	22a
	18.3	25.0	46.4	61.8	52.0	53.4	56.1	60.9	70.4	67.9	68.0	75.2	97.5	118.4	144.4	Claims on Official Entities	22bx
	188.7	233.2	245.9	275.3	324.8	350.4	367.6	393.6	411.5	540.8	676.4	802.9	880.4	994.4	1,080.9	Claims on Private Sector	22d
	56.6	65.4	70.1	76.0	74.9	76.0	108.8	103.4	205.2	184.5	179.2	183.1	211.0	251.4	229.0	Demand Deposits	24
	205.4	234.1	257.5	297.5	344.1	351.6	402.9	429.9	448.4	525.6	722.9	855.4	977.4	1,013.7	1,069.7	Time Deposits	25
	12.9	17.5	22.3	19.5	16.9	62.2	137.6	36.1	58.4	81.3	121.1	97.3	105.1	99.1	92.5	Foreign Liabilities	26c
	8.1	7.7	11.1	14.9	21.7	17.3	17.7	7.5	26.4	18.2	13.6	15.1	6.8	21.5	40.5	Central Government Deposits	26d
	5.7	6.0	15.8	18.7	13.1	38.0	15.5	24.8	12.5	41.7	33.0	42.8	43.2	81.9	114.7	Other Items (Net)	27r
End of Period																**Monetary Survey**	
	126.3	107.3	91.7	96.4	107.6	117.7	177.6	182.3	316.7	311.3	373.0	376.0	462.5	406.2	381.0	Foreign Assets (Net)	31n
	231.5	279.4	333.7	381.5	412.6	439.9	471.3	540.9	491.8	628.2	762.7	935.9	1,061.9	1,198.2	1,250.7	Domestic Credit	32
	21.6	20.2	38.6	32.9	29.3	29.8	47.3	81.0	9.7	19.4	11.1	35.5	63.0	59.8	25.3	Claims on Central Govt. (Net)	32an
	21.2	25.9	49.3	73.3	58.5	59.6	56.4	66.2	70.4	68.0	75.2	97.6	118.5	144.1	144.5	Claims on Official Entities	32bx
	188.7	233.2	245.9	275.3	324.8	350.4	367.6	393.6	411.5	540.8	676.4	802.9	880.4	994.4	1,080.9	Claims on Private Sector	32d
	100.7	118.4	123.6	134.8	136.0	137.8	172.1	168.3	272.9	263.6	265.3	274.4	314.1	363.8	344.6	Money	34
	234.4	234.2	257.6	297.5	344.1	351.6	402.9	429.9	448.4	525.6	722.9	855.4	977.4	1,013.7	1,069.7	Quasi-Money	35
	....	....	....	....	....	....	....	....	....	36.6	35.5	55.6	103.7	64.4	82.5	Reserve Bank Bonds	36aa
	22.6	34.0	44.2	45.7	40.1	68.3	73.9	125.0	87.0	113.7	112.0	126.5	129.2	162.5	134.7	Other Items (Net)	37r
	335.1	352.6	381.2	432.2	480.1	489.4	575.0	598.2	721.3	789.2	988.2	1,129.8	1,291.5	1,377.5	1,414.4	Money plus Quasi-Money	35l
End of Period																**Nonbank Financial Institutions**	
	26.8	30.8	34.3	39.2	18.9	21.9	25.7	58.1	63.9	67.2	61.7	54.4	55.6	55.3	....	Claims on Central Government	42a. l
	10.8	14.0	14.2	17.3	8.9	21.9	25.7	24.9	25.8	23.8	26.6	30.0	28.3	30.0	....	Claims on Official Entities	42bx l
	12.1	14.2	19.4	21.8	24.2	28.1	32.5	37.2	32.8	36.1	29.1	33.0	37.6	42.6	....	Claims on Private Sector	42d. l
	7.7	9.5	11.4	12.1	13.5	15.2	16.4	10.5	5.0	11.4	12.2	14.0	19.9	22.1	....	Incr.in Total Assets(Within Per.)	49z. l
Percent Per Annum																**Interest Rates**	
	7.50	8.83	9.50	10.17	11.00	11.00	8.00	11.00	11.00	8.00	8.00	8.00	6.00	6.00	6.00	Bank Rate (End of Period)	60
	....	....	5.07	8.00	8.74	6.61	6.55	9.02	1.49	2.34	2.92	4.28	3.06	2.91	4.10	Money Market Rate	60b
	5.36	5.72	5.96	6.17	7.09	7.03	6.36	9.76	1.78	2.75	4.40	5.61	3.65	2.91	2.69	Treasury Bill Rate	60c
	4.50	6.00	6.00	6.00	6.00	6.00	6.00	6.00	4.88	4.00	4.00	4.06	4.10	3.69	3.15	Deposit Rate	60l
	12.00	13.50	13.50	13.50	13.50	13.50	13.50	13.50	20.46	11.64	11.86	12.25	12.35	11.74	11.28	Lending Rate	60p
Period Averages																**Prices, Production, Employment**	
	51.9	57.7	61.7	65.9	69.3	72.4	‡73.7	77.9	87.0	92.4	100.0	106.5	111.7	‡117.5	118.2	Consumer Prices	64
	69.3	75.8	81.8	87.2	88.4	89.6	89.6	94.3	96.7	94.3	100.0	105.0	110.2	....	....	Wage Rates	65
	73.2	76.0	79.0	70.7	84.7	81.4	‡89.4	80.9	85.1	93.3	100.0	102.8	104.6	110.7	116.1	Industrial Production	66
	70.2	68.1	72.9	68.7	84.3	81.8	92.4	68.1	74.6	89.8	100.0	93.0	99.8	103.0	114.3	Tourist Arrivals	66.t
	89.4	90.4	87.0	88.9	87.3	90.1	88.7	86.8	86.1	99.8	100.0	101.9	103.9	105.3	106.3	Industrial Employment	67

Fiji
819

		1965	1966	1967	1968	1969	1970	1971	1972	1973	1974	1975	1976	1977	1978	1979
International Transactions																*Millions of Fiji Dollars*
Exports	70	49.38	45.57	50.41	58.99	62.91	75.36	74.59	79.38	96.48	152.11	168.64	155.61	204.15	211.10	262.50
Imports, cif	71	58.16	50.54	57.29	68.39	77.51	90.52	110.80	131.55	176.34	219.33	220.97	238.04	281.01	300.00	392.87
Imports, fob	71.v	52.40	45.53	51.61	61.61	69.79	81.55	97.54	115.87	155.50	189.56	190.77	205.40	242.48	256.56	345.63
																1985=100
Unit Value of Exports	74	23.5	25.2	21.4	22.3	25.6	27.5	27.0	‖33.9	40.6	67.1	90.8	78.9	‖85.7	92.5	91.6
Balance of Payments																*Millions of US Dollars:*
Goods: Exports f.o.b.	78aa d	....	....	....	....	....	....	....	....	....	....	....	136.3	179.1	203.2	270.0
Goods: Imports f.o.b.	78ab d	....	....	....	....	....	....	....	....	....	....	....	−226.8	−258.5	−298.2	−412.4
Trade Balance	78ac d	....	....	....	....	....	....	....	....	....	....	....	−90.5	−79.4	−94.9	−142.4
Services: Credit	78ad d	....	....	....	....	....	....	....	....	....	....	....	122.2	138.5	156.9	191.4
Services: Debit	78ae d	....	....	....	....	....	....	....	....	....	....	....	−67.4	−75.3	−90.9	−106.6
Balance on Goods and Services	78af d	....	....	....	....	....	....	....	....	....	....	....	....	....	....	−57.6
Income: Credit	78ag d	....	....	....	....	....	....	....	....	....	....	....	6.3	8.0	8.9	14.1
Income: Debit	78ah d	....	....	....	....	....	....	....	....	....	....	....	−17.7	−16.8	−14.2	−27.4
Balance on Goods, Serv., & Inc.	78ai d	....	....	....	....	....	....	....	....	....	....	....	....	....	....	−70.9
Current Transfers, n.i.e.: Credit	78aj d	....	....	....	....	....	....	....	....	....	....	....	9.9	12.0	12.2	19.3
Current Transfers: Debit	78ak d	....	....	....	....	....	....	....	....	....	....	....	−13.4	−13.0	−14.2	−6.7
Current Account, n.i.e.	78al d	....	....	....	....	....	....	....	....	....	....	....	....	....	....	−58.3
Capital Account, n.i.e.: Credit	78ba d	....	....	....	....	....	....	....	....	....	....	....	....	....	....	.9
Capital Account: Debit	78bb d	....	....	....	....	....	....	....	....	....	....	....	....	....	....	−8.8
Capital Account, n.i.e.	78bc d	....	....	....	....	....	....	....	....	....	....	....	....	....	....	−7.9
Direct Investment Abroad	78bd d	....	....	....	....	....	....	....	....	....	....	....	—	—	—	—
Dir. Invest. in Rep. Econ., n.i.e.	78be d	....	....	....	....	....	....	....	....	....	....	....	—	—	—	10.2
Portfolio Investment Assets	78bf d	....	....	....	....	....	....	....	....	....	....	....	—	—	—	—
Portfolio Investment Liab., n.i.e.	78bg d	....	....	....	....	....	....	....	....	....	....	....	—	—	—	—
Other Investment Assets	78bh d	....	....	....	....	....	....	....	....	....	....	....	2.8	.5	—	1.4
Other Investment Liab., n.i.e.	78bi d	....	....	....	....	....	....	....	....	....	....	....	22.7	35.6	−9.4	44.9
Financial Account, n.i.e.	78bj d	....	....	....	....	....	....	....	....	....	....	....	....	....	....	56.5
Net Errors and Omissions	78ca d	....	....	....	....	....	....	....	....	....	....	....	....	....	....	15.3
Overall Balance	78cb d	....	....	....	....	....	....	....	....	....	....	....	....	....	....	5.5
Reserves and Related Items	79da d	....	....	....	....	....	....	....	....	....	....	....	....	....	....	−5.5
Reserve Assets	79db d	....	....	....	....	....	....	....	....	....	....	....	21.9	−23.9	21.4	−5.5
Use of Fund Credit and Loans	79dc d	....	....	....	....	....	....	....	....	....	....	....	—	—	—	—
Liabs.Constit.For.Auth.Reserves	79dd d	....	....	....	....	....	....	....	....	....	....	....	—	—	—	—
Exceptional Financing	79de d	....	....	....	....	....	....	....	....	....	....	....	—	—	—	—
Government Finance																*Millions of Fiji Dollars:*
Deficit (−) or Surplus	80	....	....	....	....	....	−5.25	−3.23	−4.02	−11.16	−16.04	−7.65	−23.62	−35.18	−30.57	−24.78
Revenue	81	....	....	....	....	....	40.22	48.19	53.21	64.92	76.71	107.38	122.71	131.63	152.79	188.68
Grants Received	81z	....	....	....	....	....	3.14	1.98	1.87	3.28	3.31	1.94	1.36	2.48	4.25	5.32
Expenditure	82	....	....	....	....	....	49.52	56.61	58.20	78.98	94.26	115.12	146.95	168.10	185.93	219.55
Lending Minus Repayments	83	....	....	....	....	....	−.91	−3.21	.90	.38	1.80	1.85	.74	1.19	1.68	−.77
Financing																
Domestic	84a	....	....	....	....	....	5.74	3.17	4.15	5.71	9.81	2.12	13.76	15.98	32.77	16.59
Foreign	85a	....	....	....	....	....	−.49	.06	−.13	5.45	6.23	5.53	9.86	19.20	−2.20	8.19
Debt: Domestic	88a	....	....	....	....	....	30.38	39.21	36.47	47.23	51.51	63.00	75.74	91.53	109.63	125.45
Foreign	89a	....	....	....	....	....	8.73	10.20	10.22	26.40	32.00	36.10	45.92	62.50	58.39	68.29
National Accounts																*Millions of Fiji Dollars*
Exports of Goods & Services	90c	54.5	52.4	58.7	69.1	78.9	92.8	105.5	119.9	153.2	221.1	241.8	235.1	289.9	299.5	385.8
Government Consumption	91f	15.7	17.2	18.5	19.4	22.1	26.8	30.7	37.9	42.4	54.0	67.5	85.3	102.3	115.1	143.9
Gross Fixed Capital Formation	93e	27.6	24.3	31.7	34.1	36.0	34.8	45.9	53.1	65.7	74.2	103.4	119.5	128.9	149.8	197.3
Increase/Decrease(−) in Stocks	93i	2.1	6.1	1.9	3.7	3.7	7.7	6.7	9.5	9.5	10.9	12.6	14.5	24.1	27.8	59.6
Private Consumption	96f	95.9	93.4	98.0	98.6	110.0	124.6	147.3	180.5	261.3	334.4	382.5	433.7	415.1	458.2	519.6
Imports of Goods & Services	98c	−63.2	−57.2	−61.7	−75.6	−85.8	−99.0	−122.0	−144.2	−198.8	−244.6	−245.4	−264.6	−308.1	−330.5	−432.1
Gross Domestic Product	99b	133.1	136.6	149.0	145.8	159.3	191.8	211.9	261.2	338.3	450.0	562.4	623.5	660.0	702.1	852.1
Net Factor Inc/Pmts(−) Abroad	98.n	−5.5	−3.3	−5.2	−6.8	−7.9	−8.2	−10.1	−9.1	−4.6	−1.8	−6.0	−1.0	−8.6	−4.5	−12.5
Gross Nat'l Expenditure = GNP	99a	127.9	133.3	143.8	139.1	151.4	183.6	201.8	252.2	333.7	448.2	556.4	622.5	651.4	697.6	839.6
Nat'l Income, Market Prices	99e	119.2	124.2	134.3	132.1	143.2	174.6	191.9	239.4	318.7	431.2	539.7	593.9	616.3	654.2	787.1
Gross Dom. Prod. 1990 Prices	99b.p	....	....	....	....	....	....	....	....	....	....	....	....	....	....	....
GDP Deflator (1990=100)	99bi p	....	15.6	15.0	14.5	15.4	16.5	17.0	19.5	22.7	29.4	36.8	40.1	43.9	45.9	49.7
																Millions:
Population	99z	.46	.47	.49	.50	.51	.55	.53	.54	.55	.56	.57	.58	.60	.61	.62

Exchange Rates: On January 13, 1969 the Fiji dollar, equal to one half the Fiji pound, was introduced.
Monetary Authorities: ‖ Data refer to the Currency Board through June 1973, to the Central Monetary Authority until December 1983, and to the Reserve Bank of Fiji thereafter. Prior to 1990, monetary data refer to the last Wednesday of the period.
Monetary Survey: ‖ See note to section 10.

Fiji

	1980	1981	1982	1983	1984	1985	1986	1987	1988	1989	1990	1991	1992	1993	1994		
																International Transactions	
Millions of Fiji Dollars																	
	381.45	344.21	353.92	312.04	362.40	352.23	383.02	483.12	531.19	658.62	731.87	664.60	666.98	692.40	800.49	Exports	70
	458.75	539.91	475.58	493.17	486.99	508.00	493.60	465.11	658.82	860.44	1,112.90	961.77	947.11	1,109.81	1,209.85	Imports, cif	71
	403.72	475.13	418.51	433.99	428.54	447.18	434.51	409.43	579.95	638.26	836.18	712.62	976.63	976.63	1,064.67	Imports, fob	71.v
1985=100																	
	123.1	108.4	106.2	112.3	111.1	100.0	134.3	183.5	175.4	....	....	....	....	....	....	Unit Value of Exports	74
																Balance of Payments	
Minus Sign Indicates Debit																	
	376.1	311.4	284.8	240.1	255.8	236.4	273.5	323.1	373.6	439.5	494.7	446.3	438.2	443.6	....	Goods: Exports f.o.b.	78aa d
	−493.0	−544.9	−440.2	−421.2	−390.7	−382.6	−378.7	−345.2	−389.9	−487.9	−644.6	−549.5	−539.5	−653.5	....	Goods: Imports f.o.b.	78ab d
	−116.9	−233.4	−155.5	−181.1	−134.9	−146.2	−105.2	−22.1	−16.3	−48.5	−149.9	−103.2	−101.3	−209.8	....	Trade Balance	78ac d
	200.9	219.2	236.2	250.5	249.5	272.9	262.4	206.6	244.9	336.2	378.9	403.2	429.1	491.5	....	Services: Credit	78ad d
	−124.6	−167.5	−154.8	−130.4	−128.3	−131.1	−157.3	−176.1	−183.3	−226.4	−258.0	−289.3	−299.2	−298.5	....	Services: Debit	78ae d
	−40.6	−181.7	−74.0	−61.0	−13.7	−4.5	−.1	8.4	45.3	61.4	−29.0	10.7	28.6	−16.8	....	Balance on Goods and Services	78af d
	23.1	30.8	22.5	20.7	20.9	35.2	41.3	40.4	46.3	55.8	63.4	70.9	65.9	65.8	....	Income: Credit	78ag d
	−40.2	−41.6	−58.8	−49.0	−49.1	−45.6	−49.6	−51.5	−61.5	−75.1	−62.7	−65.2	−72.3	−78.0	....	Income: Debit	78ah d
	−57.7	−192.5	−110.2	−89.3	−41.9	−14.9	−8.5	−2.7	30.0	42.0	−28.3	16.4	22.2	−29.0	....	Balance on Goods, Serv., & Inc.	78ai d
	48.8	44.1	42.3	47.1	36.6	51.5	37.5	28.6	53.5	55.3	41.5	63.9	63.0	70.7	....	Current Transfers, n.i.e.: Credit	78aj d
	−6.5	−16.1	−17.9	−14.4	−14.7	−17.5	−14.6	−24.8	−12.9	−22.3	−23.0	−27.9	−25.7	−28.6	....	Current Transfers: Debit	78ak d
	−15.4	−164.6	−85.8	−56.6	−20.0	19.1	14.4	1.2	70.7	75.0	−9.9	52.5	59.4	13.1	....	Current Account, n.i.e.	78al d
	.6	1.4	1.2	.7	1.3	.6	.7	.1	.1	.1	.6	.1	.1	.2	....	Capital Account, n.i.e.: Credit	78ba d
	−10.0	−12.3	−8.2	−8.7	−8.2	−11.0	−14.1	−14.4	−12.2	−21.1	−24.6	−30.7	−27.7	−26.3	....	Capital Account: Debit	78bb d
	−9.4	−10.9	−7.0	−8.0	−6.9	−10.4	−13.4	−14.3	−12.1	−21.0	−24.0	−30.7	−27.6	−26.1	....	Capital Account, n.i.e.	78bc d
	−2.2	1.5	−.8	−.1	−.5	−13.0	1.3	−25.9	−1.9	−26.5	−4.9	4.4	−1.7	−6.0	....	Direct Investment Abroad	78bd d
	36.4	36.1	36.7	32.1	23.6	21.2	8.0	11.4	32.0	8.0	80.4	15.0	50.4	29.1	....	Dir. Invest. in Rep. Econ., n.i.e.	78be d
	—	—	—	—	—	—	—	—	—	—	—	—	—	—	....	Portfolio Investment Assets	78bf d
	—	—	—	—	—	—	—	—	—	—	—	—	—	—	....	Portfolio Investment Liab., n.i.e.	78bg d
	−20.4	15.1	6.2	2.7	5.0	−48.3	−59.9	61.3	−7.0	−36.1	−12.3	39.1	9.2	−5.3	....	Other Investment Assets	78bh d
	56.5	88.0	44.2	32.7	6.6	37.7	50.6	−115.6	23.1	−17.8	−14.5	−56.1	−21.0	−31.7	....	Other Investment Liab., n.i.e.	78bi d
	70.3	140.7	86.3	67.5	34.7	−2.5	—	−68.7	46.3	−72.4	48.6	2.4	36.8	−13.9	....	Financial Account, n.i.e.	78bj d
	−5.2	11.2	−15.7	−9.1	−.3	−11.1	26.9	18.9	7.3	4.8	21.1	−14.6	−15.2	−15.2	....	Net Errors and Omissions	78ca d
	40.2	−23.6	−22.2	−6.3	7.5	−4.8	27.9	−62.9	112.1	−13.5	35.8	9.6	53.4	−42.1	....	Overall Balance	78cb d
	−40.2	23.6	22.2	6.3	−7.5	4.8	−27.9	62.9	−112.1	13.5	−35.8	−9.6	−53.4	42.1	....	Reserves and Related Items	79da d
	−31.6	23.6	6.9	6.3	−7.5	5.4	−19.9	65.1	−109.7	16.6	−35.0	−9.6	−53.4	42.1	....	Reserve Assets	79db d
	−8.6	—	15.3	—	—	−.6	−7.9	−2.1	−2.4	−3.1	−.8	—	—	—	....	Use of Fund Credit and Loans	79dc d
	—	—	—	—	—	—	—	—	—	—	—	—	—	—	....	Liabs.Constit.For.Auth.Reserves	79dd d
	—	—	—	—	—	—	—	—	—	—	—	—	—	—	....	Exceptional Financing	79de d
																Government Finance	
Year Ending December 31																	
	−29.54	−45.26	−70.33	−43.29	−38.73	−35.44	−70.57	−73.92	−11.89	−54.83	−46.49	−50.62	−23.34	−123.60	−117.10	Deficit (−) or Surplus	80
	220.42	255.16	254.70	283.68	319.06	329.17	330.61	324.79	367.62	447.88	530.38	499.05	574.37	636.14	645.13 f	Revenue	81
	3.93	7.69	10.10	9.97	10.10	10.52	9.45	11.39	22.22	11.94	8.68	11.21	10.78	8.31	10.32 f	Grants Received	81z
	255.34	292.24	323.88	329.50	366.06	371.70	383.34	398.24	397.19	477.92	522.10	577.33	646.23	754.40	758.90 f	Expenditure	82
	−1.45	15.87	11.25	7.44	1.83	3.43	27.29	11.86	4.54	36.73	63.45	−16.45	−37.74	13.65	13.65 f	Lending Minus Repayments	83
																Financing	
	4.77	13.37	52.36	38.14	34.44	33.39	73.73	88.83	29.38	83.73	66.90	65.59	39.47	131.33	....	Domestic	84a
	24.77	31.89	17.97	5.15	4.29	2.05	−3.16	−14.91	−17.49	−28.90	−20.41	−14.97	−16.13	−7.73	....	Foreign	85a
	157.07	168.80	215.95	250.81	289.39	318.98	389.32	....	....	....	....	546.32	571.91	732.88	....	Debt: Domestic	88a
	90.16	123.35	142.14	148.40	156.98	156.96	156.85	....	....	....	....	205.99	203.66	188.80	....	Foreign	89a
																National Accounts	
Millions of Fiji Dollars																	
	477.5	454.4	481.3	498.1	546.2	583.6	609.0	663.9	894.8	1,162.9	1,310.1	1,279.0	1,316.1	1,424.6	....	Exports of Goods & Services	90c
	156.7	173.1	203.8	231.6	244.8	252.4	252.6	255.1	263.4	296.1	339.6	396.5	449.0	513.9	....	Government Consumption	91f
	249.8	280.5	262.6	239.2	218.0	239.1	215.4	229.9	191.5	231.8	321.9	266.9	280.5	344.0	....	Gross Fixed Capital Formation	93e
	63.4	81.7	21.9	2.3	23.3	12.2	51.1	4.5	12.6	24.5	35.0	26.0	30.0	40.0	....	Increase/Decrease(−) in Stocks	93i
	574.7	660.0	684.7	748.2	794.1	838.1	873.3	959.6	1,093.5	1,210.2	1,366.0	1,484.0	1,580.1	1,688.8	....	Private Consumption	96f
	−510.8	−606.6	−552.6	−560.1	−559.8	−588.6	−577.0	−616.3	−814.6	−1,058.9	−1,329.7	−1,235.5	−1,258.6	−1,486.5	....	Imports of Goods & Services	98c
	983.7	1,056.1	1,113.4	1,142.2	1,275.3	1,316.5	1,461.7	1,465.2	1,587.6	1,860.6	2,045.3	2,176.1	2,377.2	2,540.0	....	Gross Domestic Product	99b
	−14.6	−9.2	−33.8	−28.2	−30.3	−36.3	−34.3	−47.9	−35.2	−36.3	−41.8	−40.4	−28.3	−32.0	....	Net Factor Inc/Pmts(−) Abroad	98.n
	969.2	1,046.9	1,079.6	1,114.0	1,245.0	1,280.2	1,427.4	1,417.3	1,552.6	1,825.1	2,048.1	2,158.9	2,094.3	2,220.0	....	Gross Nat'l Expenditure = GNP	99a
	903.7	969.4	991.7	1,034.4	1,156.7	1,185.2	1,324.5	1,306.2	1,433.7	1,686.4	1,855.9	1,980.3	2,153.5	2,343.6	....	Nat'l Income, Market Prices	99e
	1,552.5	1,656.4	1,638.1	1,520.9	1,629.8	1,675.5	1,663.0	1,702.1	1,793.5	1,916.5	2,045.3	....	....	....	....	Gross Dom. Prod. 1990 Prices	99b.p
	63.4	63.8	68.0	75.1	78.3	78.6	87.9	86.1	88.5	97.1	100.0	105.3	....	....	....	GDP Deflator (1990=100)	99bi p
Midyear Estimates																	
	.63	.65	.66	.67	.69	.70	.71	.72	.72	.72	.73	.74	.75	.76	....	Population	99z

Finland
172

		1965	1966	1967	1968	1969	1970	1971	1972	1973	1974	1975	1976	1977	1978	1979
Exchange Rates															*Markkaa per SDR:*	
Official Rate	aa	3.2200	3.2200	4.2000	4.2000	4.2000	4.1800	4.5057	4.5383	⁞4.6384	4.3477	4.5070	4.3766	4.8807	5.1148	4.8886
														Markkaa per US Dollar:		
Official Rate	ae	3.2200	3.2200	4.2000	4.2000	4.2000	4.1800	4.1500	4.1800	⁞3.8450	3.5510	3.8500	3.7670	4.0180	3.9260	3.7110
Official Rate	rf	3.2000	3.2000	3.4500	4.2000	4.2000	4.2000	4.1844	4.1463	3.8212	3.7738	3.6787	3.8644	4.0294	4.1173	3.8953
														Index Numbers (1990=100):		
Official Rate	ahx	118.4	118.4	112.2	91.1	90.8	91.3	147.6	92.0	100.0	101.2	103.9	98.8	94.8	92.8	98.0
Nominal Effective Exchange Rate	neu	143.4	143.4	135.2	112.1	112.1	110.8	109.1	102.5	101.1	103.6	102.7	105.0	99.5	89.6	90.7
Real Effective Exchange Rate	reu	....	....	....	....	....	....	....	....	....	....	100.1	106.3	100.6	87.4	85.8
Fund Position															*Millions of SDRs:*	
Quota	2f.s	57.0	125.0	125.0	125.0	125.0	190.0	190.0	190.0	190.0	190.0	190.0	190.0	190.0	262.0	262.0
SDRs	1b.s	—	—	—	—	—	23.3	47.0	67.5	67.8	68.1	66.2	56.1	41.8	61.8	88.1
Reserve Position in the Fund	1c.s	14.3	31.3	—	.1	41.3	66.8	63.8	63.8	63.8	63.8	—	—	—	46.1	44.7
Total Fund Cred.&Loans Outstg.	2tl	—	—	62.5	—	—	—	—	—	—	—	71.3	186.4	186.4	152.1	66.4
International Liquidity												*Millions of US Dollars Unless Otherwise Indicated:*				
Total Reserves minus Gold	1l.d	205.6	143.7	139.0	⁞293.0	281.9	424.6	623.1	667.6	574.3	595.9	433.2	462.1	531.1	1,222.9	1,540.0
SDRs	1b.d	—	—	—	—	—	23.3	51.0	73.2	81.8	83.4	77.5	65.2	50.8	80.4	116.1
Reserve Position in the Fund	1c.d	14.3	31.3	—	.1	41.3	66.7	69.2	69.2	76.9	78.1	—	—	—	60.0	58.8
Foreign Exchange	1d.d	191.3	112.4	139.0	⁞292.9	240.6	334.5	502.9	525.2	415.6	434.4	355.7	396.9	480.3	1,082.4	1,365.1
Gold (Million Fine Troy Ounces)	1ad	2.388	1.285	1.284	1.289	1.288	.825	1.396	1.397	.823	.823	.823	.823	.905	.945	.986
Gold (National Valuation)	1and	83.7	45.0	45.0	45.2	45.0	28.8	48.8	50.0ᵉ	31.0	34.1	31.4	32.1	33.1	43.0	289.1
Monetary Authorities: Other Assets	3..d	⁞25.8	22.4	18.7	12.2	6.2	6.5	7.0	25.5	92.7	4.6	129.0	125.5	143.1	132.4	45.5
Other Liab.	4..d	27.5	43.7	34.7	19.0	22.1	25.2	77.9	29.6	37.6	128.7	44.6	26.9	349.1	15.4	228.0
Deposit Money Banks: Assets	7a.d	84	81	90	71	146	218	300	418	531	686	593	718	1,136	1,401	2,026
Liabilities	7b.d	151	170	195	184	169	283	320	354	490	815	1,209	1,332	1,693	1,778	2,788
Monetary Authorities															*Millions of Markkaa:*	
Foreign Assets	11	1,008	674	852	1,560	1,400	1,932	2,798	3,047	2,710	2,258	2,290	2,339	2,848	5,501	6,970
Claims on Central Government	12a	81	298	360	225	133	140	167	196	223	300	335	442	391	633	884
Claims on Private Sector	12d	177	293	609	523	434	291	291	328	393	763	1,181	1,586	1,559	1,418	1,698
Claims on Deposit Money Banks	12e	666	990	984	634	946	1,110	1,137	946	2,792	3,558	4,260	3,845	4,979	2,220	4,229
Reserve Money	14	1,128	1,260	1,376	1,471	1,426	1,479	1,642	1,897	2,107	2,471	2,862	2,889	3,172	3,830	6,145
of which: Currency Outside DMBs	14a	933	1,026	959	1,088	1,205	1,286	1,476	1,546	1,782	2,150	2,508	2,544	2,843	3,483	3,908
Time Deposits	15	....	....	....	....	105	311	385	688	25	34	118	80	167	89	137
Restricted Deposits	16b	....	....	....	....	—	—	72	23	227	154	1,605	1,312	587	759	412
Foreign Liabilities	16c	88	140	408	80	93	106	327	122	147	457	493	917	2,312	838	1,171
Central Government Deposits	16d	2	41	19	364	200	323	291	189	1,985	1,598	408	62	368	1,153	2,069
Capital Accounts	17a	398	413	430	450	473	689	806	932	972	1,021	1,896	1,992	2,136	2,259	2,469
Other Items (Net)	17r	316	402	570	575	616	567	870	667	656	1,144	686	960	1,035	844	1,378
Deposit Money Banks															*Millions of Markkaa:*	
Reserves	20	178	211	389	399	339	216	165	366	335	319	351	345	342	342	486
Foreign Assets	21	270	259	376	300	611	916	1,261	1,714	2,072	2,436	2,282	2,706	4,565	5,502	7,519
Claims on Central Government	22a	747	855	844	969	932	781	634	568	494	242	461	127	148	392	347
Claims on Private Sector	22d	10,472	11,732	13,167	14,156	16,350	19,176	22,077	25,299	31,382	39,167	47,208	52,392	59,229	65,222	76,418
Demand Deposits	24	1,140	1,153	1,187	1,551	1,919	2,156	2,547	3,413	4,325	5,116	7,261	7,057	7,029	8,006	10,178
Time and Savings Deposits	25	8,847	10,062	11,121	12,291	13,769	15,728	17,846	20,712	23,555	27,601	32,854	37,010	42,068	48,388	56,524
Foreign Liabilities	26c	484	543	820	773	708	1,190	1,344	1,451	1,909	2,893	4,654	5,017	6,802	6,980	10,345
Central Government Deposits	26d	178	192	214	222	280	288	472	748	1,290	1,632	566	1,334	1,131	2,593	1,413
Central Govt. Lending Funds	26f	455	505	544	596	642	682	735	796	879	1,002	1,201	1,329	1,486	1,722	1,958
Credit from Monetary Authorities	26g	692	982	946	634	947	1,111	1,138	941	2,757	3,508	3,911	4,912	4,894	2,256	3,356
Other Items (Net)	27r	−129	−378	−56	−244	⁞406	392	664	600	251	1,037	635	−150	3,361	4,607	4,638
Monetary Survey															*Millions of Markkaa:*	
Foreign Assets (Net)	31n	706	250	—	1,007	1,210	1,552	2,388	3,188	2,727	1,345	−575	−889	−1,702	3,184	2,973
Domestic Credit	32	10,842	12,440	14,203	14,691	16,727	19,096	21,672	24,659	28,337	36,241	47,011	51,821	58,341	62,197	73,906
Claims on Central Govt. (Net)	32an	193	415	427	12	−57	−372	−696	−969	−3,438	−3,689	−1,378	−2,156	−2,447	−4,443	−4,209
Claims on Private Sector	32d	10,649	12,025	13,776	14,679	16,784	19,468	22,368	25,628	31,775	39,930	48,389	53,978	60,788	66,640	78,115
Money	34	2,085	2,222	2,184	2,668	3,126	3,445	4,025	4,959	6,114	7,267	9,772	9,601	9,872	11,496	14,087
Quasi-Money	35	8,847	10,062	11,121	12,291	13,783	16,039	17,956	20,750	23,559	27,635	32,927	37,074	42,123	48,427	56,659
Restricted Deposits	36b	....	....	....	....	—	—	72	23	227	154	1,605	1,312	587	759	412
Other Items (Net)	37r	616	409	896	736	1,029	1,163	2,007	2,115	1,163	2,530	2,133	2,945	4,057	4,699	5,722
Money plus Quasi-Money	35l	10,932	12,284	13,305	14,959	16,909	19,484	21,981	25,709	29,674	34,902	42,699	46,675	51,994	59,923	70,746
Unused Overdrafts	39b	396	376	418	474	550	634	702	872	934	1,213	1,372	1,375	1,493	2,033	2,385
Other Banking Institutions															*Millions of Markkaa:*	
Savings Deposits	45	357	381	431	465	522	574	642	720	805	921	1,094	1,265ᵉ	1,351	1,345	1,101
Liquid Liabilities	55l	11,289	12,665	13,736	15,424	17,431	20,058	22,623	26,429	30,479	35,823	43,793	47,940	53,345	61,268	71,847
Interest Rates															*Percent Per Annum*	
Discount Rate *(End of Period)*	60	7.00	7.00	7.00	7.00	7.00	7.00	8.50	7.75	9.25	9.25	9.25	9.25	8.25	7.25	8.50
Money Market Rate	60b	....	....	....	....	....	....	....	....	....	....	....	....	....	11.75	9.26
Deposit Rate	60l	....	....	....	....	....	....	....	....	....	....	....	....	....	....	....
Lending Rate	60p	....	....	....	....	....	....	....	....	....	....	....	....	8.85	8.22	8.03
Prices, Production, Employment															*Index Numbers (1990=100)*	
Industrial Share Prices	62	4.9	4.6	⁞4.1	5.2	7.0	8.1	9.1	12.2	18.9	18.3	16.5	14.8	12.1	11.8	14.3
Prices: Domestic Supply	63	17.2	17.6	18.1	20.1	20.8	21.7	22.8	24.7	29.0	36.1	⁞41.0	44.4	48.9	51.6	56.6
Producer, Manufacturing	63ey	16.4	17.3	17.4	17.6	19.2	22.0	23.1	24.4	29.5	37.1	⁞42.6	45.5	49.7	52.0	57.1
Consumer Prices	64	14.3	14.8	⁞15.7	17.1	17.5	18.0	19.1	⁞20.5	22.8	26.6	31.3	35.8	⁞40.3	43.4	46.7
Wages: Hourly Earnings	65ey	7.2	7.8	8.5	9.4	10.2	11.3	13.0	14.8	17.3	20.7	⁞24.7	28.8	31.6	33.9	37.5
Industrial Production	66..c	33.3	34.9	36.2	38.2	43.6	48.1	48.8	54.8	58.7	61.4	59.2	59.7	60.0	63.1	69.8
Industrial Employment	67ey c	....	....	....	....	....	....	....	....	....	....	....	....	108.3	107.1	104.2	108.2

Finland
172

1980	1981	1982	1983	1984	1985	1986	1987	1988	1989	1990	1991	1992	1993	1994		
End of Period															**Exchange Rates**	
4.8976	5.0714	5.8366	6.0828	6.4008	5.9501	5.8640	5.5980	5.6102	5.3342	5.1699	5.9120	7.2119	7.9454	6.9244	Official Rate	**aa**
End of Period (ae) Period Average (rf)																
3.8400	4.3570	5.2910	5.8100	6.5300	5.4170	4.7940	3.9460	4.1690	4.0590	3.6340	4.1330	5.2450	5.7845	4.7432	Official Rate	**ae**
3.7301	4.3153	4.8204	5.5701	6.0100	6.1979	5.0695	4.3956	4.1828	4.2912	3.8235	4.0440	4.4794	5.7123	5.2235	Official Rate	**rf**
Period Averages																
102.4	88.7	79.6	68.6	63.6	61.9	75.3	86.9	91.0	89.1	100.0	94.7	85.5	66.9	73.4	Official Rate	**ah x**
92.6	95.2	96.8	92.5	94.5	94.9	93.2	94.2	95.3	99.1	100.0	96.3	83.9	73.4	79.2	Nominal Effective Exchange Rate	**ne u**
89.7	93.6	95.4	91.6	93.8	93.4	90.4	89.7	92.4	96.6	100.0	92.2	75.8	63.5	....	Real Effective Exchange Rate	**re u**
End of Period															**Fund Position**	
393.0	393.0	393.0	574.9	574.9	574.9	574.9	574.9	574.9	574.9	574.9	574.9	861.8	861.8	861.8	Quota	**2f. s**
81.3	124.2	104.3	37.0	145.7	156.4	167.3	160.5	199.8	182.0	152.5	157.7	78.4	83.8	222.7	SDRs	**1b. s**
77.4	77.4	77.5	123.0	133.7	130.3	135.0	141.6	167.5	178.9	151.0	192.3	241.0	220.4	196.1	Reserve Position in the Fund	**1c. s**
66.4	52.1	14.4	—	—	—	—	—	—	—	—	—	—	—	—	Total Fund Cred.&Loans Outstg.	**2tl**
End of Period															**International Liquidity**	
1,870.2	1,483.7	1,517.5	1,237.7	2,754.3	3,749.9	1,787.1	6,417.5	6,369.2	5,111.2	9,644.1	7,608.7	5,213.4	5,410.8	10,662.0	Total Reserves minus Gold	**1l. d**
103.7	144.6	115.0	38.7	142.8	171.8	204.6	227.7	268.9	239.2	216.9	225.6	107.8	115.1	325.1	SDRs	**1b. d**
98.8	90.1	85.5	128.7	131.1	143.1	165.2	200.8	225.6	235.0	214.8	275.1	331.3	302.7	286.3	Reserve Position in the Fund	**1c. d**
1,667.7	1,249.0	1,317.0	1,070.3	2,480.4	3,435.0	1,417.4	5,989.0	5,874.7	4,636.9	9,212.4	7,108.0	4,774.3	4,993.0	10,050.6	Foreign Exchange	**1d. d**
.986	1.269	1.270	1.270	1.270	1.912	1.912	1.955	1.955	2.002	2.002	2.002	2.002	2.002	2.003	Gold (Million Fine Troy Ounces)	**1ad**
279.4	317.2	261.2	238.0	211.8	384.2	434.1	539.3	510.4	537.1	599.9	527.5	415.6	376.9	459.6	Gold (National Valuation)	**1an d**
58.7	476.0	306.0	101.3	62.5	47.2	716.6	325.4	257.4	22.7	20.6	8.2	....	....	....	Monetary Authorities: Other Assets	**3.. d**
255.9	21.9	504.9	356.4	123.9	106.3	6.4	34.1	59.3	171.8	270.6	11.2	452.7	33.4	27.5	Other Liab.	**4.. d**
2,762	3,231	4,154	4,777	6,258	7,671	14,310	18,825	20,542	22,242	27,000	24,272	21,500	21,608	22,295	Deposit Money Banks: Assets	**7a. d**
4,566	4,909	6,293	7,205	9,441	12,812	20,531	32,917	37,756	42,581	59,906	53,452	40,169	31,854	30,679	Liabilities	**7b. d**
End of Period															**Monetary Authorities**	
8,480	9,920	13,263	11,387	20,126	22,651	14,084	30,668	31,759	24,216	37,678	34,095	29,928	33,478	52,752	Foreign Assets	**11**
1,226	1,236	1,041	2,178	1,951	1,023	1,002	977	1,039	1,137	1,314	1,376	2,447	1,788	1,806	Claims on Central Government	**12a**
2,424	3,390	4,386	4,793	5,068	5,143	5,479	5,188	5,204	4,681	3,793	3,054	2,921	4,404	3,951	Claims on Private Sector	**12d**
6,035	3,769	4,542	8,464	6,727	7,596	13,314	3,639	12,095	36,542	13,075	15,648	11,547	7,575	1,718	Claims on Deposit Money Banks	**12e**
8,272	8,089	9,201	11,616	16,347	18,361	17,993	26,694	31,750	39,204	32,410	35,976	37,803	38,031	57,463	Reserve Money	**14**
4,305	4,824	5,170	5,628	5,876	6,143	6,357	7,259	8,418	8,772	9,555	8,813	9,404	10,394	10,810	of which: Currency Outside DMBs	**14a**
850	1,455	1,426	1,325	2,146	3,863	4,690	4,831	6,497	10,228	9,925	7,057	3,362	2,087	1,549	Time Deposits	**15**
191	201	492	566	1,413	1,063	591	209	349	773	—	—	—	—	—	Restricted Deposits	**16b**
1,308	359	2,755	2,071	809	576	31	135	247	697	983	46	2,375	193	130	Foreign Liabilities	**16c**
2,491	2,178	1,701	3,001	4,277	4,301	2,001	901	1,903	5,324	1,321	4	90	784	93	Central Government Deposits	**16d**
2,408	4,476	4,865	5,237	6,955	7,013	6,723	6,728	6,288	6,594	6,904	6,607	6,790	6,895	6,749	Capital Accounts	**17a**
2,645	1,556	2,792	3,006	1,925	1,236	1,851	975	3,064	3,756	4,317	4,483	-3,577	-745	-5,756	Other Items (Net)	**17r**
End of Period															**Deposit Money Banks**	
3,971	3,263	4,028	5,985	10,415	12,159	11,592	18,642	23,990	29,863	22,400	27,162	29,983	27,638	46,653	Reserves	**20**
10,605	14,077	21,979	27,754	40,865	41,553	68,603	74,283	85,641	90,280	98,117	100,315	112,765	124,993	105,751	Foreign Assets	**21**
1,110	976	1,958	3,485	3,662	2,050	2,624	2,662	2,487	2,205	1,993	ɪ 3,426	7,568	11,117	15,630	Claims on Central Government	**22a**
90,309	103,913	123,875	146,111	170,515	203,221	231,015	271,469	348,149	402,750	449,853	467,798	437,016	398,932	360,408	Claims on Private Sector	**22d**
10,673	12,361	14,746	15,798	19,007	21,483	21,425	23,047	27,472	32,634	34,837	ɪ 121,832	125,425	131,365	143,547	Demand Deposits	**24**
65,600	75,758	85,719	98,611	113,168	134,052	146,223	165,112	204,011	218,059	228,976	ɪ 158,200	154,861	153,618	145,670	Time and Savings Deposits	**25**
17,533	21,389	33,295	41,861	61,652	69,401	98,424	129,890	157,404	172,837	217,697	220,917	210,685	184,260	145,519	Foreign Liabilities	**26c**
1,122	2,028	2,927	2,078	2,397	2,498	10,025	11,830	10,865	10,456	14,237	4,280	2,911	3,358	4,644	Central Government Deposits	**26d**
2,298	2,741	3,267	3,881	4,423	4,969	5,485	5,885	6,204	6,429	6,820	7,034	6,933	6,816	6,607	Central Govt. Lending Funds	**26f**
6,044	3,722	4,493	8,432	6,670	7,572	13,140	2,843	10,844	36,011	12,419	ɪ 15,648	13,132	7,576	1,718	Credit from Monetary Authorities	**26g**
6,994	9,304	13,179	19,332	25,665	27,779	29,026	38,688	55,817	62,492	74,874	70,792	73,388	75,687	82,964	Other Items (Net)	**27r**
End of Period															**Monetary Survey**	
244	2,248	-809	-4,790	-1,471	-5,773	-15,768	-25,074	-40,251	-59,038	-82,886	-86,553	-70,367	-25,982	12,854	Foreign Assets (Net)	**31n**
89,158	102,567	123,365	147,606	170,100	199,670	222,610	261,680	337,909	388,565	434,574	ɪ 464,336	440,018	405,283	370,451	Domestic Credit	**32**
-3,575	-4,736	-4,896	-3,297	-5,483	-8,694	-13,884	-14,977	-15,445	-18,867	-19,072	ɪ -6,516	81	1,947	6,092	Claims on Central Govt. (Net)	**32an**
92,733	107,303	128,261	150,903	175,583	208,364	236,494	276,657	353,353	407,431	453,646	470,852	439,937	403,335	364,359	Claims on Private Sector	**32d**
14,979	17,186	19,917	21,427	24,945	27,694	27,838	30,342	35,921	41,444	44,428	ɪ 130,645	134,829	141,759	154,357	Money	**34**
66,431	77,190	87,140	99,912	115,300	137,895	150,895	169,911	210,458	228,315	238,901	ɪ 165,257	158,223	155,705	147,218	Quasi-Money	**35**
191	201	492	566	1,413	1,063	591	209	349	773	—	—	—	—	—	Restricted Deposits	**36b**
7,801	10,238	15,007	20,910	26,971	27,244	27,518	36,144	50,930	58,995	68,360	81,881	76,600	81,837	83,957	Other Items (Net)	**37r**
81,410	94,377	107,057	121,339	140,246	165,589	178,733	200,253	246,379	269,758	283,330	ɪ 295,902	293,052	297,464	301,576	Money plus Quasi-Money	**35l**
3,086	3,911	4,611	4,670	5,569	6,530	5,814	6,169	7,387	7,634	10,500	....	....	....	....	Unused Overdrafts	**39b**
End of Period															**Other Banking Institutions**	
1,074	1,028	1,033	1,090	1,129	1,144	1,156	1,152	1,252	1,347	1,360	1,947	2,734	3,096	1,685	Savings Deposits	**45**
82,484	95,405	108,090	122,429	141,375	166,733	179,889	201,405	247,631	271,105	284,690	ɪ 297,849	295,786	300,560	303,261	Liquid Liabilities	**55l**
Percent Per Annum															**Interest Rates**	
9.25	9.25	8.50	9.50	15.07	9.00	7.00	7.00	8.00	8.50	8.50	8.50	9.50	5.50	5.25	Discount Rate *(End of Period)*	**60**
12.35	11.46	11.66	14.67	16.50	13.46	11.90	10.03	9.97	12.56	14.00	13.08	13.25	7.77	5.35	Money Market Rate	**60b**
....	9.00	8.56	8.75	9.25	8.75	7.33	7.00	7.75	5.75	7.50	7.50	7.50	4.75	3.27	Deposit Rate	**60l**
9.77	9.84	9.32	9.56	10.49	10.41	9.08	8.91	9.72	10.31	11.62	11.80	12.14	9.92	7.91	Lending Rate	**60p**
Period Averages															**Prices, Production, Employment**	
15.3	15.7	21.0	32.1	45.1	38.7	59.0	ɪ 93.4	124.1	132.5	100.0	73.1	68.9	116.3	179.5	Industrial Share Prices	**62**
ɪ 65.9	74.3	79.7	84.1	88.6	92.6	87.8	88.6	92.1	ɪ 96.8	100.0	100.3	101.4	104.4	105.8	Prices: Domestic Supply	**63**
ɪ 66.1	71.8	79.3	83.3	88.0	91.6	87.7	88.5	92.4	ɪ 97.9	100.0	99.8	102.4	106.1	107.7	Producer, Manufacturing	**63ey**
52.1	58.3	63.9	69.3	74.2	ɪ 78.5	80.8	84.1	88.4	94.2	100.0	104.1	106.8	109.1	110.3	Consumer Prices	**64**
42.2	47.6	52.8	57.9	63.2	68.0	72.2	ɪ 77.2	83.5	91.1	100.0	106.4	108.7	....	....	Wages: Hourly Earnings	**65ey**
75.5	77.5	78.2	80.5	84.1	ɪ 87.4	88.9	93.7	ɪ 96.9	100.1	100.0	90.3	92.3	97.4	107.6	Industrial Production	**66.. c**
112.9	114.5	111.2	109.0	108.0	107.4	106.0	102.5	99.6	101.0	100.0	90.4	81.5	76.2	76.7	Industrial Employment	**67ey c**

Finland

		1965	1966	1967	1968	1969	1970	1971	1972	1973	1974	1975	1976	1977	1978	1979
International Transactions																*Millions of Markkaa*
Exports	70	4,565	4,817	5,230	6,869	8,344	9,687	9,898	12,082	14,609	20,687	20,246	24,506	30,931	35,206	43,430
Newsprint	70ul	437	479	501	596	594	631	647	751	816	1,114	993	1,089	1,201	1,679	2,200
Imports, cif	71	5,266	5,524	5,795	6,687	8,507	11,078	11,739	13,126	16,548	25,676	28,011	28,555	30,707	32,338	44,221
Imports, fob	71.v	4,921	5,163	5,416	6,250	7,952	10,351	10,974	12,274	15,472	24,007	26,695	27,212	29,262	30,816	42,140
																1990=100
Volume of Exports	72	32	34	36	39	Ɪ46	Ɪ49	47	55	59	59	48	57	Ɪ62	67	74
Newsprint	72ul	91	99	96	97	96	99	97	109	110	95	65	72	70	93	116
Volume of Imports	73	35	36	36	35	Ɪ43	Ɪ52	51	53	60	65	65	62	Ɪ57	54	64
Unit Value of Exports	74	14	14	15	17	Ɪ18	Ɪ19	20	22	25	35	41	42	Ɪ49	52	58
Newsprint	74ul	16	17	18	21	21	22	23	24	25	40	53	52	59	62	65
Unit Value of Imports	75	15	15	16	19	Ɪ20	Ɪ21	23	24	27	39	42	45	Ɪ52	58	67
Import Prices	76.x	21	21	22	25	26	28	29	31	37	46	Ɪ49	52	58	65	75
Balance of Payments																*Millions of US Dollars*
Goods: Exports f.o.b.	78aa d	....	....	....	....	....	....	....	....	....	....	5,508	6,295	7,609	8,504	11,100
Goods: Imports f.o.b.	78ab d	....	....	....	....	....	....	....	....	....	....	−7,241	−6,978	−7,182	−7,427	−10,755
Trade Balance	78ac d	....	....	....	....	....	....	....	....	....	....	−1,733	−684	427	1,077	345
Services: Credit	78ad d	....	....	....	....	....	....	....	....	....	....	1,100	1,253	1,455	1,861	2,249
Services: Debit	78ae d	....	....	....	....	....	....	....	....	....	....	−1,103	−1,208	−1,376	−1,614	−2,009
Balance on Goods and Services	78af d	....	....	....	....	....	....	....	....	....	....	−1,736	−639	506	1,324	584
Income: Credit	78ag d	....	....	....	....	....	....	....	....	....	....	134	132	147	225	368
Income: Debit	78ah d	....	....	....	....	....	....	....	....	....	....	−504	−566	−709	−823	−1,011
Balance on Goods, Serv., & Inc.	78ai d	....	....	....	....	....	....	....	....	....	....	−2,107	−1,073	−55	726	−59
Current Transfers, n.i.e.: Credit	78aj d	....	....	....	....	....	....	....	....	....	....	28	28	29	37	50
Current Transfers: Debit	78ak d	....	....	....	....	....	....	....	....	....	....	−61	−69	−73	−83	−154
Current Account, n.i.e.	78al d	....	....	....	....	....	....	....	....	....	....	−2,140	−1,114	−99	680	−163
Capital Account, n.i.e.: Credit	78ba d	....	....	....	....	....	....	....	....	....	....	—	—	—	—	—
Capital Account: Debit	78bb d	....	....	....	....	....	....	....	....	....	....	−2	−3	−6	−6	−6
Capital Account, n.i.e.	78bc d	....	....	....	....	....	....	....	....	....	....	−2	−3	−6	−6	−6
Direct Investment Abroad	78bd d	....	....	....	....	....	....	....	....	....	....	−26	−31	−72	−63	−125
Dir. Invest. in Rep. Econ., n.i.e.	78be d	....	....	....	....	....	....	....	....	....	....	68	58	48	34	28
Portfolio Investment Assets	78bf d	....	....	....	....	....	....	....	....	....	....	—	—	—	—	−13
Portfolio Investment Liab., n.i.e.	78bg d	....	....	....	....	....	....	....	....	....	....	233	174	224	694	162
Other Investment Assets	78bh d	....	....	....	....	....	....	....	....	....	....	−98	−428	−507	−691	−765
Other Investment Liab., n.i.e.	78bi d	....	....	....	....	....	....	....	....	....	....	1,981	955	802	−27	1,357
Financial Account, n.i.e.	78bj d	....	....	....	....	....	....	....	....	....	....	2,158	729	496	−52	644
Net Errors and Omissions	78ca d	....	....	....	....	....	....	....	....	....	....	−240	281	−348	89	−84
Overall Balance	78cb d	....	....	....	....	....	....	....	....	....	....	−225	−108	43	710	391
Reserves and Related Items	79da d	....	....	....	....	....	....	....	....	....	....	225	108	−43	−710	−391
Reserve Assets	79db d	....	....	....	....	....	....	....	....	....	....	129	−20	−45	−665	−274
Use of Fund Credit and Loans	79dc d	....	....	....	....	....	....	....	....	....	....	89	132	—	−44	−110
Liabs.Constit.For.Auth.Reserves	79dd d	....	....	....	....	....	....	....	....	....	....	7	−4	2	−1	−6
Exceptional Financing	79de d	....	....	....	....	....	....	....	....	....	....	—	—	—	—	—
Government Finance																*Millions of Markkaa*
Deficit (−) or Surplus	80	−226	−322	−555	91	−76	418	332	Ɪ715	2,044	755	−2,315	−32	−1,938	−2,645	−4,105
Revenue	81	5,843	6,337	7,063	8,391	9,065	10,231	11,340	Ɪ15,359	19,212	23,355	28,604	35,865	38,897	40,280	44,938
Grants Received	81z	....	....	....	....	....	....	....	Ɪ286	306	346	496	696	734	781	882
Expenditure	82	5,795	6,338	7,270	7,712	8,495	9,113	9,940	Ɪ14,073	16,275	21,465	28,920	33,305	37,679	41,275	47,702
Lending Minus Repayments	83	274	321	348	588	646	700	1,068	Ɪ857	1,199	1,481	2,495	3,288	3,890	2,431	2,223
Financing (By Residence of Lender)																	
Domestic	84a	....	....	....	....	....	....	....	Ɪ−679	−1,882	−567	1,927	−556	1,210	−358	1,822
Foreign	85a	....	....	....	....	....	....	....	Ɪ−36	−162	−188	388	588	728	3,003	2,283
Debt: Domestic	88a	....	....	....	....	....	....	Ɪ2,530	2,325	1,797	1,566	2,021	2,379	3,039	4,867	6,254
Foreign	89a	....	....	....	....	....	....	Ɪ1,524	1,517	1,395	1,152	1,609	2,248	3,679	7,360	8,964
Financing (By Currency)																	
Net Borrowing	84	266	351	580	227	−10	−486	−310	....	....	....	....	....	....	....	....
Markkaa	84b	276	346	495	96	−67	−434	−190	....	....	....	....	....	....	....	....
Foreign Currency	85b	−10	5	85	131	57	−52	−120	....	....	....	....	....	....	....	....
Use of Cash Balances	87	−40	−29	−25	−318	86	68	−22	....	....	....	....	....	....	....	....
Debt: Markkaa	88b	1,926	2,187	2,173	2,229	2,261	2,202	....	....	....	....	....	....	....	....	....
Foreign Currency	89b	1,040	1,040	1,450	1,670	1,646	1,548	....	....	....	....	....	....	....	....	....
National Accounts																*Billions of Markkaa*
Exports of Goods & Services	90c	5.39	5.68	6.18	8.14	9.90	11.75	12.22	14.95	18.15	24.79	24.76	29.54	36.97	43.04	52.55
Government Consumption	91f	3.64	4.09	4.66	5.48	5.93	6.61	7.62	8.97	10.70	13.70	17.59	21.02	23.74	26.04	29.41
Gross Fixed Capital Formation	93e	7.02	7.56	7.86	8.29	9.77	12.01	13.82	16.37	20.56	26.86	32.80	33.06	35.34	34.56	38.87
Increase/Decrease(−) in Stocks	93i	−.11	−.22	−.07	.64	1.23	1.79	1.64	.08	1.29	4.99	1.46	−.86	−5.43	−4.34	3.35
Private Consumption	96f	16.53	17.58	19.15	20.93	23.68	25.90	28.11	33.04	39.27	47.81	57.50	65.71	72.65	80.38	91.31
Imports of Goods & Services	98c	−5.84	−6.14	−6.46	−7.57	−9.52	−12.31	−13.15	−14.80	−18.60	−28.10	−30.92	−31.82	−34.73	−37.39	−49.95
Gross Domestic Product	99b	26.63	28.55	31.32	35.91	40.99	45.75	50.26	58.61	71.37	90.05	103.17	116.64	128.55	142.29	165.55
Net Factor Inc/Pmts(−) Abroad	98.n	−.15	−.17	−.24	−.31	−.37	−.42	−.49	−.65	−.82	−1.04	−1.53	−1.86	−2.48	−2.64	−2.72
Gross Nat'l Expenditure = GNP	99a	26.48	28.38	31.09	35.60	40.62	45.32	49.77	57.97	70.56	89.01	102.76	115.93	127.53	140.99	164.25
Nat'l Income, Market Prices	99e	23.43	25.01	27.35	31.24	35.85	39.80	43.32	50.44	61.22	76.75	87.79	98.50	107.19	118.65	139.48
Gross Dom. Prod. 1990 Prices	99b.p	214.52	219.62	224.39	229.55	251.57	270.36	276.01	297.05	317.00	326.61	Ɪ330.36	328.96	329.76	336.67	360.09
GDP Deflator (1990=100)	99bi p	12.4	13.0	14.0	15.6	16.3	16.9	18.2	19.7	22.5	27.6	31.2	35.5	39.0	42.3	46.0
																Millions
Population	99z	4.56	4.58	4.61	4.63	4.62	4.61	4.62	4.64	4.67	4.69	4.71	4.73	4.74	4.75	4.76

International Liquidity: Ɪ Beginning in 1968, data for *line 1d.d* exclude external bills discounted, which are reported in *line 7a.d*.
Deposit Money Banks: Ɪ Beginning in January 1991, data are based on improved sectorization.
Monetary Survey: Ɪ See note to section 20.

Government Finance: Ɪ Beginning in 1972 (1971 for debt data), annual data are as reported in the *Government Finance Statistics Yearbook* and cover consolidated central government.

Finland

172

1980	1981	1982	1983	1984	1985	1986	1987	1988	1989	1990	1991	1992	1993	1994		
Millions of Markkaa															**International Transactions**	
52,804	60,308	63,026	69,751	80,923	83,976	82,699	87,706	90,901	99,854	101,380	93,088	107,471	133,962	153,690	Exports	70
2,419	2,972	2,761	2,967	3,519	3,685	3,350	3,250	3,053	2,687	2,917	2,875	2,656	2,955	2,915	Newsprint	70ul
58,247	61,269	64,751	71,519	74,685	77,631	81,350	85,799	88,555	104,782	103,066	87,821	94,984	103,162	119,897	Imports, cif	71
55,507	58,398	61,675	68,235	71,325	77,851	74,288	82,104	84,742	100,270	98,628	84,039	90,894	98,720	114,734	Imports, fob	71.v
1990=100																
80	82	81	83	92	92	93	94	97	96	100	91	99	117	....	Volume of Exports	72
119	128	111	122	139	137	122	120	100	90	100	96	95	103	105	Newsprint	72ul
72	68	68	71	71	75	80	86	94	104	100	83	81	78	....	Volume of Imports	73
65	72	77	82	87	89	88	90	94	101	100	100	106	113	....	Unit Value of Exports	74
70	80	86	83	87	92	94	93	105	103	100	102	96	98	95	Newsprint	74ul
78	88	92	98	102	106	95	93	95	99	100	102	113	129	....	Unit Value of Imports	75
86	97	I 100	107	112	115	98	96	95	I 99	100	101	108	119	119	Import Prices	76.x
Minus Sign Indicates Debit															**Balance of Payments**	
14,070	13,662	12,842	12,172	13,087	13,351	16,005	19,079	21,826	22,882	26,101	22,516	23,571	23,135	29,333	Goods: Exports f.o.b.	78aa d
-14,752	-13,307	-12,641	-12,025	-11,607	-12,481	-14,371	-17,704	-20,694	-23,109	-25,383	-20,207	-19,627	-16,751	-21,682	Goods: Imports f.o.b.	78ab d
-683	354	201	147	1,480	870	1,634	1,375	1,132	-228	718	2,309	3,944	6,384	7,651	Trade Balance	78ac d
2,733	2,915	2,723	2,532	2,438	2,429	2,761	3,570	4,015	4,156	4,789	4,373	4,918	4,723	5,450	Services: Credit	78ad d
-2,555	-2,603	-2,523	-2,515	-2,672	-2,920	-3,380	-4,615	-5,587	-6,307	-7,808	-7,759	-7,633	-6,539	-7,377	Services: Debit	78ae d
-505	666	401	164	1,245	379	1,015	330	-441	-2,379	-2,302	-1,078	1,229	4,568	5,725	Balance on Goods and Services	78af d
530	683	571	520	872	999	1,023	1,488	2,348	2,455	3,404	2,546	1,457	1,268	1,707	Income: Credit	78ag d
-1,313	-1,716	-1,766	-1,670	-1,967	-2,014	-2,336	-3,056	-4,091	-5,109	-7,090	-7,158	-6,813	-6,265	-5,933	Income: Debit	78ah d
-1,288	-367	-794	-986	150	-635	-298	-1,239	-2,183	-5,033	-5,987	-5,689	-4,128	-429	1,498	Balance on Goods, Serv., & Inc.	78ai d
68	90	86	78	84	91	82	109	329	192	252	345	427	475	430	Current Transfers, n.i.e.: Credit	78aj d
-182	-201	-216	-216	-255	-262	-466	-587	-827	-940	-1,204	-1,397	-1,221	-1,005	-860	Current Transfers: Debit	78ak d
-1,403	-478	-923	-1,124	-21	-806	-682	-1,717	-2,681	-5,781	-6,939	-6,741	-4,922	-959	1,068	Current Account, n.i.e.	78al d
—	—	—	—	—	—	—	—	—	—	—	—	—	—	—	Capital Account, n.i.e.: Credit	78ba d
-7	-5	-6	-5	-4	-5	-9	-12	-14	-15	-22	-25	-24	-21	—	Capital Account: Debit	78bb d
-7	-5	-6	-5	-4	-5	-9	-12	-14	-15	-22	-25	-24	-21	—	Capital Account: Credit	78bc d
-137	-129	-78	-139	-492	-348	-818	-1,150	-2,624	-3,111	-3,313	-1,056	-407	-1,828	-3,782	Direct Investment Abroad	78bd d
28	100	1	84	136	113	348	265	532	490	812	-233	387	593	1,393	Dir. Invest. in Rep. Econ., n.i.e.	78be d
-120	13	-3	-31	-66	-191	-455	-519	-304	-40	-160	93	-75	-284	933	Portfolio Investment Assets	78bf d
154	317	517	364	1,339	1,534	1,811	1,931	3,465	3,441	5,965	9,240	8,070	6,105	6,135	Portfolio Investment Liab., n.i.e.	78bg d
-1,480	-1,812	-2,237	-1,332	-1,652	-177	-2,741	1,478	-2,162	-1,662	1,126	-3,614	-2,585	-2,060	-610	Other Investment Assets	78bh d
3,071	1,627	2,934	1,866	3,071	506	-165	5,268	3,236	4,343	8,830	774	-1,302	-2,198	217	Other Investment Liab., n.i.e.	78bi d
1,515	116	1,133	813	2,336	1,436	-2,020	7,273	2,143	3,462	13,262	5,204	4,089	329	4,286	Financial Account, n.i.e.	78bj d
175	143	-5	89	-495	-38	431	-1,523	807	1,276	-2,366	-328	-1,306	927	-633	Net Errors and Omissions	78ca d
280	-224	200	-228	1,817	586	-2,280	4,022	255	-1,058	3,935	-1,889	-2,163	276	4,721	Overall Balance	78cb d
-280	224	-200	228	-1,817	-586	2,280	-4,022	-255	1,058	-3,935	1,889	2,163	-276	-4,721	Reserves and Related Items	79da d
-280	237	-155	243	-1,824	-583	2,282	-4,033	-258	1,067	-3,931	1,886	2,150	-291	-4,714	Reserve Assets	79db d
—	-17	-42	-16	—	—	—	—	—	—	—	—	—	—	—	Use of Fund Credit and Loans	79dc d
—	4	-3	1	8	-3	-3	11	3	-10	-4	3	14	15	-7	Liabs.Constit.For.Auth.Reserves	79dd d
—	—	—	—	—	—	—	—	—	—	—	—	—	—	—	Exceptional Financing	79de d
Year Ending December 31															**Government Finance**	
-4,154	-1,968	-5,070	-7,965	-3,111	-2,702	394	-6,690	1,754	8,807	945	-34,096	-70,346	....	....	Deficit (-) or Surplus	80
52,050	61,518	68,775	77,049	87,235	98,617	111,091	114,733	134,761	151,922	160,241	154,141	156.114	....	....	Revenue	81
910	1,022	1,297	1,498	1,798	1,865	2,305	2,355	2,512	3,633	3,867	4,173	5,881	....	....	Grants Received	81z
53,858	61,878	72,671	84,892	90,321	100,887	110,383	121,278	132,038	143,593	158,673	184,225	203,201	....	....	Expenditure	82
3,256	2,630	2,471	1,620	1,823	2,297	2,619	2,500	3,481	3,155	4,490	8,185	29,140	....	....	Lending Minus Repayments	83
															Financing (By Residence of Lender)	
2,632	-349	2,297	5,541	414	1,096	-322	4,176	-59	-5,920	-4,377	11,301	19,449	....	....	Domestic	84a
1,522	2,317	2,773	2,424	2,697	1,606	-72	2,514	-1,695	-2,887	3,432	22,795	50,897	....	....	Foreign	85a
7,642	8,778	11,443	15,958	19,119	21,100	24,871	29,831	31,805	32,331	27,444	30,216	51,946	....	....	Debt: Domestic	88a
10,341	13,331	18,808	21,723	24,945	25,676	26,981	28,680	26,279	23,063	29,210	57,699	119,974	....	....	Foreign	89a
															Financing (By Currency)	
....	....	....	....	....	....	....	....	....	....	....	....	....	....	....	Net Borrowing	84
....	....	....	....	....	....	....	....	....	....	....	....	....	....	....	Markkaa	84b
....	....	....	....	....	....	....	....	....	....	....	....	....	....	....	Foreign Currency	85b
....	....	....	....	....	....	....	....	....	....	....	....	....	....	....	Use of Cash Balances	87
....	....	....	....	....	....	....	....	....	....	....	....	....	....	....	Debt: Markkaa	88b
....	....	....	....	....	....	....	....	....	....	....	....	....	....	....	Foreign Currency	89b
Billions of Markkaa															**National Accounts**	
63.49	72.36	75.80	82.74	94.19	98.03	95.63	100.05	108.75	116.70	118.83	109.29	128.27	159.44	181.22	Exports of Goods & Services	90c
34.39	40.18	45.84	52.45	58.84	66.97	72.85	80.05	87.20	97.02	108.54	118.72	118.45	112.54	114.63	Government Consumption	91f
48.70	54.78	61.65	69.55	73.01	79.42	82.91	92.54	109.26	136.15	139.14	110.06	87.95	71.35	77.53	Gross Fixed Capital Formation	93e
6.26	1.32	-.17	-1.39	-.46	.96	-.51	.46	6.42	8.54	5.77	-19.49	-8.14	-1.27	6.47	Increase/Decrease(-) in Stocks	93i
103.55	117.28	134.23	149.62	165.15	180.89	194.01	211.53	232.58	254.59	269.75	274.71	272.11	271.75	281.58	Private Consumption	96f
-65.02	-69.25	-73.76	-81.36	-86.14	-94.64	-89.90	-97.78	-109.87	-126.00	-126.60	-112.42	-121.88	-133.34	-149.83	Imports of Goods & Services	98c
191.38	216.66	243.59	271.61	304.60	331.63	354.99	386.86	434.34	487.00	515.43	480.87	476.78	480.47	511.60	Gross Domestic Product	99b
-3.13	-4.33	-5.29	-5.73	-8.74	-6.22	-2.25	-3.56	....	....	....	....	....	....	....	Net Factor Inc/Pmts(-) Abroad	98.n
189.43	214.13	239.88	268.71	300.82	330.60	355.30	388.03	....	....	....	....	....	....	....	Gross Nat'l Expenditure = GNP	99a
160.25	181.42	203.50	228.64	256.56	280.92	297.72	....	....	....	....	....	....	....	....	Nat'l Income, Market Prices	99e
379.29	386.36	398.91	409.69	422.05	436.26	446.61	464.92	487.72	515.36	515.43	479.01	462.00	454.63	472.26	Gross Dom. Prod. 1990 Prices	99b.p
50.5	56.1	61.1	66.3	72.2	76.0	79.5	83.2	89.1	94.5	100.0	100.4	103.2	105.7	108.3	GDP Deflator (1990=100)	99bi p
Midyear Estimates																
4.78	4.80	4.83	4.86	4.88	4.90	4.92	4.93	4.95	4.96	4.99	5.03	5.04	5.07	5.09	**Population**	99z

France

132

		1965	1966	1967	1968	1969	1970	1971	1972	1973	1974	1975	1976	1977	1978	1979
Exchange Rates																*Francs per SDR:*
Market Rate	aa	4.9371	4.9371	4.9371	4.9371	5.5542	5.5542	5.5542	5.5542	5.6801	5.4416	5.2510	5.7740	5.7152	5.4457	5.2957
																Francs per US Dollar:
Market Rate	ae	4.9371	4.9371	4.9371	4.9371	5.5542	5.5542	5.1157	5.1157	4.7085	4.4445	4.4855	4.9698	4.7050	4.1800	4.0200
Market Rate	rf	4.9371	4.9371	4.9371	4.9371	5.1942	5.5542	5.5406	5.0445	4.4528	4.8096	4.2878	4.8029	4.9052	4.5131	4.2544
																Francs per ECU
ECU Rate	ea	....	....	....	....	....	....	....	....	....	....	....	....	....	....	5.7931
ECU Rate	eb	....	....	....	....	....	....	....	....	....	....	....	5.3446	5.6060	5.7396	5.8288
																Index Numbers (1990=100):
Market Rate	ah x	110.8	110.5	110.4	109.7	104.7	98.2	98.6	107.7	122.4	113.0	126.8	113.3	110.7	120.6	127.7
Nominal Effective Exchange Rate	ne u	136.3	136.3	136.9	140.7	133.6	121.9	119.4	122.1	126.2	118.0	129.3	125.9	121.2	119.7	121.1
Real Effective Exchange Rate	re u	....	....	....	....	....	....	....	....	....	....	109.9	107.9	103.8	103.2	103.5
Fund Position																*Millions of SDRs:*
Quota	2f. s	788	985	985	985	985	1,500	1,500	1,500	1,500	1,500	1,500	1,500	1,500	1,919	1,919
SDRs	1b. s	—	—	—	—	—	171	348	581	73	202	244	227	233	286	644
Reserve Position in the Fund	1c. s	884	988	886	1	—	—	436	460	377	429	623	843	736	461	479
of which: Outstg.Fund Borrowing	2c	240	240	140	—	—	—	—	—	—	—	—	—	38	16	—
International Liquidity												*Millions of US Dollars Unless Otherwise Indicated:*				
Total Reserves minus Gold	1l. d	1,637	1,495	1,760	324	286	1,428	4,428	6,189	4,268	4,526	8,457	5,620	5,872	9,278	17,579
SDRs	1b. d	—	—	—	—	—	171	378	630	88	248	286	263	284	373	849
Reserve Position in the Fund	1c. d	884	988	886	1	—	—	473	499	455	525	729	979	895	600	630
Foreign Exchange	1d. d	753	507	874	323	286	1,257	3,577	5,059	3,725	3,753	7,442	4,377	4,694	8,305	16,100
Gold (Million Fine Troy Ounces)	1ad	134.46	149.66	149.54	110.77	101.34	100.91	100.66	100.69	100.91	100.93	100.93	101.02	101.67	101.99	81.92
Gold (National Valuation)	1an d	4,706	5,238	5,234	3,877	3,547	3,532	3,825	3,826	4,261	4,261	14,133	12,840	16,717	22,340	34,195
Monetary Authorities: Other Liab.	4.. d	28	43	51	679	1,766	437	240	221	356	605	934	942	453	849	8,570
Deposit Money Banks: Assets	7a. d	1,940	2,690	3,150	5,060	7,375	10,144	14,467	19,806	32,215	33,120	41,173	41,292	I72,689	I108,876	137,587
of which: Claims on Nonbanks	7ad d	....	....	....	....	918	1,575	2,346	2,832	4,224	6,464	9,854	14,967	22,336	I39,641	50,622
Deposit Money Banks: Liabilities	7b. d	....	....	....	....	8,412	10,833	16,553	23,090	33,516	35,691	41,924	51,500	66,835	I95,239	119,652
of which: Liab. to Nonbanks	7bd d	....	....	....	....	1,287	1,514	1,791	1,945	2,895	3,856	4,653	5,554	8,066	I16,603	20,672
Monetary Authorities																*Billions of Francs:*
Foreign Assets	11	31	33	35	21	21	29	47	54	44	44	101	94	I110	136	254
Claims on Central Government	12a	10	14	14	14	16	12	13	13	11	11	22	22	18	I23	24
Claims on Private Sector	12d	....	....	....	....	....	....	....	....	....	....	....	....	1	1	1
Claims on Banking Institutions	12e	25	23	26	48	59	51	41	66	86	98	51	54	I59	89	87
Reserve Money	14	69	72	78	83	82	86	95	125	135	152	119	128	140	I157	168
of which: Currency Outside Bks	14a	65	68	71	73	73	76	78	84	90	98	107	116	122	I132	139
Foreign Liabilities	16c	—	—	—	3	13	6	1	1	2	3	9	4	5	I2	34
Central Government Deposits	16d	....	....	....	....	....	....	....	....	....	....	....	....	3	27	23
Capital Accounts	17a	....	....	....	....	....	....	....	....	....	....	....	....	65	79	160
Other Items (Net)	17r	−2	−2	−4	−4	—	—	4	6	6	−2	50	37	−22	I−18	−18
Banking Institutions																*Billions of Francs:*
Reserves	20	3	4	6	9	I7	9	16	38	40	50	10	11	I16	I22	25
Foreign Assets	21	....	....	....	....	41	56	74	101	148	147	185	205	I342	I455	553
Claims on Central Government	22a	17	14	15	16	19	18	17	13	4	4	33	34	34	I268	297
Claims on Private Sector	22d	125	144	169	206	I236	271	321	396	468	551	629	767	I926	I1,623	1,848
Demand Deposits	24	87	96	100	111	I104	123	145	174	192	219	262	279	I313	I532	610
Time Deposits	25	29	37	57	71	I89	111	147	185	226	275	331	392	I465	I1,015	1,171
Money Market Instruments	26aa	....	....	....	....	....	....	....	....	....	....	....	....	....	....	1
Bonds	26ab	....	....	....	....	....	....	....	....	....	....	....	....	77	I177	200
Foreign Liabilities	26c	—	—	—	—	47	60	85	118	154	159	188	256	314	I398	481
Central Govt. Lending Funds	26e	....	....	....	....	....	....	....	....	....	....	....	....	....	58	61
Credit from Monetary Authorities	26g	25	23	26	48	59	51	41	66	86	98	51	54	59	89	87
Capital Accounts	27a	....	....	....	....	....	....	....	....	....	....	....	....	72	I112	146
Other Items (Net)	27r	4	4	6	1	I4	8	9	6	—	—	26	35	15	I−14	−34
Banking Survey																*Billions of Francs:*
Foreign Assets (Net)	31n	31	33	34	17	I2	20	35	36	37	30	94	39	I144	I189	291
Domestic Credit	32	175	195	224	265	303	335	388	463	524	618	734	888	1,043	1,888	2,147
Claims on Central Govt. (Net)	32an	50	51	55	60	67	64	67	66	56	68	104	120	121	I264	298
Claims on Private Sector	32d	125	144	169	206	I236	271	321	396	468	551	629	767	I922	I1,624	1,849
Money	34	176	189	198	214	I210	232	260	299	328	378	425	457	I508	I666	751
Quasi-Money	35	29	37	57	71	I90	112	148	185	227	276	332	393	I466	I1,015	1,171
Money Market Instruments	36aa	....	....	....	....	....	....	....	....	....	....	....	....	....	....	1
Bonds	36ab	....	....	....	....	....	....	....	....	....	....	....	....	....	177	200
Other Items (Net)	37r	2	2	3	−2	I3	6	9	8	3	−3	64	70	I213	I219	315
Money plus Quasi-Money	35l	204	226	256	285	300	344	407	484	555	654	757	850	I974	I2,360	2,701
Money (National Definitions)																*Billions of Francs: Average of*
M1	34n	....	....	....	....	....	....	....	....	....	....	....	....	602	665	750
M1, Seasonally Adjusted	34n. c	....	....	....	....	....	....	....	....	....	....	....	....	579	640	722
M2	38nb	....	....	....	....	....	....	....	....	....	....	....	....	1,071	1,212	1,370
M2, Seasonally Adjusted	38nb c	....	....	....	....	....	....	....	....	....	....	....	....	1,040	1,178	1,331
M3	38nc	....	....	....	....	....	....	....	....	....	....	....	....	1,405	1,583	1,805
M3, Seasonally Adjusted	38nc c	....	....	....	....	....	....	....	....	....	....	....	....	1,378	1,552	1,772
M4	38l	....	....	....	....	....	....	....	....	....	....	....	....	1,405	1,583	1,805
M4, Seasonally Adjusted	38l. c	....	....	....	....	....	....	....	....	....	....	....	....	1,378	1,556	1,775
Interest Rates																*Percent Per Annum*
Discount Rate (End of Period)	60	3.50	3.50	3.50	6.00	8.00	7.00	6.50	7.50	11.00	13.00	8.00	10.50	9.50	9.50	9.50
Money Market Rate	60b	4.21	4.78	4.80	6.15	8.96	8.68	5.84	4.95	8.91	12.91	7.92	8.56	9.07	7.98	9.04
Interbank Money Rate	60bs	....	....	....	....	8.93	6.29	5.51	9.13	13.02	7.84	8.69	9.22	8.16	9.48	
Deposit Rate	60l	....	....	....	....	4.06	4.11	3.89	3.82	4.81	5.78	7.50	7.00	6.75	5.81	
Lending Rate	60p	....	....	....	....	I7.64	12.88	12.10	11.80	14.30	17.65	15.97	15.05	15.50	15.12	15.90
Government Bond Yield	61	5.27	5.40	5.66	5.86	I7.64	8.06	7.74	7.35	8.25	10.49	9.49	9.16	9.61	8.96	9.48

France

1980	1981	1982	1983	1984	1985	1986	1987	1988	1989	1990	1991	1992	1993	1994		
End of Period															**Exchange Rates**	
5.7598	6.6904	7.4184	8.7394	9.4022	8.3052	7.8957	7.5756	8.1536	7.6064	7.2968	7.4096	7.5714	8.0978	7.8044	Market Rate	aa
End of Period (ae)	*Period Average (rf)*															
4.5160	5.7480	6.7250	8.3475	9.5920	7.5610	6.4550	5.3400	6.0590	5.7880	5.1290	5.1800	5.5065	5.8955	5.3460	Market Rate	ae
4.2256	5.4346	6.5721	7.6213	8.7391	8.9852	6.9261	6.0107	5.9569	6.3801	5.4453	5.6421	5.2938	5.6632	5.5520	Market Rate	rf
End of Period (ea)	*Period Average (eb)*															
5.9392	6.2018	6.5221	6.9036	6.8307	6.7047	6.8750	6.9834	7.0982	6.9204	6.9501	6.9534	6.6678	6.5742	6.5758	ECU Rate	ea
5.8694	6.0405	6.4255	6.7689	6.8714	6.7951	6.7981	6.9289	7.0361	7.0237	6.9141	6.9733	6.8496	6.6334	6.5796	ECU Rate	eb
Period Averages																
128.7	100.5	83.1	71.6	62.3	60.9	78.6	90.5	91.4	85.2	100.0	96.6	102.8	96.0	98.0	Market Rate	ah x
119.8	112.5	104.2	98.2	95.0	96.3	98.9	98.9	96.9	95.9	100.0	98.3	101.5	105.1	106.0	Nominal Effective Exchange Rate	ne u
105.5	102.8	103.9	101.2	99.9	102.8	104.5	102.4	99.3	97.0	100.0	95.9	96.9	98.9	....	Real Effective Exchange Rate	re u
End of Period															**Fund Position**	
2,879	2,879	2,879	4,483	4,483	4,483	4,483	4,483	4,483	4,483	4,483	4,483	7,415	7,415	7,415	Quota	2f. s
733	1,080	887	422	584	819	1,054	1,059	1,033	1,011	902	927	118	241	248	SDRs	1b. s
837	884	868	1,292	1,291	1,247	1,419	1,349	1,200	1,076	1,004	1,165	1,805	1,682	1,627	Reserve Position in the Fund	1c. s
—	—	—	—	—	—	—	—	—	—	—	—	—	—	—	of which: Outstg.Fund Borrowing	2c
End of Period															**International Liquidity**	
27,340	22,262	16,531	19,851	20,940	26,589	31,454	33,049	25,364	24,611	36,778	31,284	27,028	22,649	26,257	Total Reserves minus Gold	1l. d
935	1,257	979	442	572	900	1,290	1,502	1,390	1,329	1,283	1,326	163	331	362	SDRs	1b. d
1,067	1,029	958	1,352	1,265	1,370	1,736	1,914	1,615	1,414	1,428	1,666	2,482	2,310	2,375	Reserve Position in the Fund	1c. d
25,338	19,976	14,594	18,057	19,102	24,319	28,428	29,634	22,359	21,868	34,067	28,292	24,384	20,008	23,520	Foreign Exchange	1d. d
81.85	81.85	81.85	81.85	81.85	81.85	81.85	81.85	81.85	81.85	81.85	81.85	81.85	81.85	81.85	Gold (Million Fine Troy Ounces)	1ad
49,991	33,877	36,848	30,786	26,832	27,580	33,932	41,496	33,686	33,982	31,321	31,704	26,313	30,729	30,730	Gold (National Valuation)	1and
13,926	11,188	10,155	12,882	10,897	11,552	19,554	13,601	13,022	12,338	12,795	29,541	20,553	11,650		Monetary Authorities: Other Liab.	4..d
160,208	158,090	162,959	156,322	158,643	184,380	217,992	290,096	299,721	358,898	458,725	459,923	514,937	583,445	....	Deposit Money Banks: Assets	7a. d
56,754	60,230	65,859	64,558	64,231	78,323	93,035	110,657	103,930	118,314	147,748	148,842	158,159	179,730	....	of which: Claims on Nonbanks	7ad d
146,678	153,793	164,669	167,068	174,374	197,183	228,288	296,360	315,904	384,692	519,672	523,456	526,214	523,077	....	Deposit Money Banks: Liabilities	7b. d
25,443	26,775	34,810	38,335	45,152	53,908	59,597	75,067	82,169	98,618	137,434	158,514	176,283	187,024	....	of which: Liab. to Nonbanks	7bd d
End of Period															**Monetary Authorities**	
420	377	397	460	488	446	495	474	430	404	407	396	350	351	371	Foreign Assets	11
24	11	25	39	66	59	62	63	63	57	81	74	95	75	72	Claims on Central Government	12a
1	1	2	1	1	1	1	1	3	2	3	4	4	4	4	Claims on Private Sector	12d
90	116	221	175	154	159	130	212	238	271	162	166	294	372	200	Claims on Banking Institutions	12e
193	202	239	252	278	324	331	368	366	366	352	342	296	285	284	Reserve Money	14
144	161	177	192	199	207	214	222	236	246	259	255	256	253	....	of which: Currency Outside Bks	14a
63	64	68	108	105	82	75	104	82	75	63	66	163	121	62	Foreign Liabilities	16c
28	24	58	38	58	47	57	120	76	107	104	86	148	198	123	Central Government Deposits	16d
273	235	302	319	318	260	269	276	255	244	201	205	182	225	201	Capital Accounts	17a
-22	-19	-22	-40	-50	-49	-44	-116	-45	-57	-68	-59	-46	-26	-24	Other Items (Net)	17r
End of Period															**Banking Institutions**	
47	38	58	57	74	112	113	136	123	112	89	80	34	27	....	Reserves	20
724	909	1,096	1,305	1,522	1,394	1,407	1,549	1,816	2,077	2,353	2,382	2,836	3,440	....	Foreign Assets	21
308	374	478	529	584	670	724	760	746	740	676	630	687	754	....	Claims on Central Government	22a
2,107	2,383	2,739	3,065	3,398	3,646	4,056	4,599	5,142	5,656	6,314	6,588	6,816	6,556	....	Claims on Private Sector	22d
655	737	805	914	1,016	1,102	1,189	1,245	1,292	1,383	1,439	1,351	1,349	1,367	....	Demand Deposits	24
1,300	1,423	1,593	1,753	1,888	2,006	2,165	2,333	2,484	2,479	2,509	2,564	2,618	2,762	....	Time Deposits	25
1	1	1	1	1	9	39	163	274	426	780	851	1,128	1,174	....	Money Market Instruments	26aa
250	303	363	445	530	629	793	900	1,048	1,166	1,228	1,315	1,458	1,527	....	Bonds	26ab
662	884	1,107	1,395	1,673	1,491	1,474	1,583	1,914	2,227	2,665	2,712	2,898	3,084	....	Foreign Liabilities	26c
71	69	76	81	84	88	102	102	101	104	100	94	94	50	....	Central Govt. Lending Funds	26e
90	116	221	175	154	159	130	212	238	271	162	166	294	372	200	Credit from Monetary Authorities	26g
170	193	223	261	300	344	439	538	605	706	784	870	943	1,033	....	Capital Accounts	27a
-13	-22	-18	-69	-68	-6	-30	-31	-131	-178	-235	-244	-405	-588	....	Other Items (Net)	27r
															Banking Survey	
418	337	317	263	232	267	353	336	250	180	31	1	125	586	....	Foreign Assets (Net)	31n
2,413	2,746	3,186	3,597	3,991	4,329	4,787	5,305	5,877	6,349	6,971	7,210	7,455	7,192	....	Domestic Credit	32
304	361	445	531	592	682	729	703	733	690	653	618	634	632	....	Claims on Central Govt. (Net)	32an
2,109	2,385	2,741	3,067	3,399	3,647	4,057	4,602	5,144	5,659	6,318	6,592	6,820	6,560	....	Claims on Private Sector	32d
801	900	985	1,108	1,219	1,312	1,407	1,471	1,532	1,633	1,703	1,609	1,608	1,623	....	Money	34
1,300	1,423	1,593	1,753	1,888	2,006	2,165	2,333	2,484	2,479	2,509	2,564	2,618	2,762	....	Quasi-Money	35
1	1	1	1	1	9	39	163	274	426	780	851	1,128	1,174	....	Money Market Instruments	36aa
250	303	363	445	530	629	793	900	1,048	1,166	1,228	1,315	1,458	1,527	....	Bonds	36ab
479	457	562	553	585	639	737	774	788	824	782	870	772	697	....	Other Items (Net)	37r
2,967	3,280	3,651	4,050	4,412	4,688	5,025	5,334	5,612	5,761	5,850	5,783	5,793	5,983	....	Money plus Quasi-Money	35l
Figures for Last Month in Period															**Money (National Definitions)**	
800	899	983	1,103	1,215	1,294	1,386	1,446	1,506	1,622	1,685	1,606	1,602	1,626	1,676	M1	34n
771	864	943	1,055	1,158	1,230	1,315	1,369	1,423	1,531	1,590	1,517	1,513	1,536	1,584	M1, Seasonally Adjusted	34n. c
1,481	1,683	1,885	2,136	2,333	2,471	2,585	2,696	2,796	2,918	2,944	2,845	2,806	2,855	3,007	M2	38nb
1,439	1,633	1,826	2,066	2,252	2,382	2,489	2,594	2,689	2,803	2,826	2,734	2,694	2,741	2,890	M2, Seasonally Adjusted	38nb c
1,979	2,195	2,450	2,735	3,005	3,218	3,425	3,808	4,117	4,523	4,930	5,029	5,286	5,122	5,228	M3	38nc
1,946	2,157	2,406	2,682	2,944	3,152	3,354	3,740	4,048	4,454	4,869	4,984	5,249	5,080	5,185	M3, Seasonally Adjusted	38nc c
1,979	2,196	2,450	2,736	3,007	3,226	3,455	3,860	4,173	4,606	5,005	5,112	5,367	5,204	5,345	M4	38l
1,946	2,158	2,407	2,683	2,947	3,159	3,382	3,791	4,109	4,542	4,946	5,066	5,329	5,161	5,300	M4, Seasonally Adjusted	38l. c
Percent Per Annum															**Interest Rates**	
9.50	9.50	9.50	9.50	9.50	9.50	9.50	9.50	9.50	9.50	9.50	9.50	9.50	9.50	9.50	Discount Rate (End of Period)	60
11.85	15.30	14.87	12.53	11.74	9.93	7.74	7.98	7.52	9.07	9.85	9.49	10.35	8.75	5.69	Money Market Rate	60b
12.20	15.26	14.73	12.63	11.88	10.08	7.79	8.22	7.88	9.34	10.18	9.69	10.49	8.41	5.79	Interbank Money Rate	60bs
6.25	7.75	9.31	8.28	7.68	6.80	5.23	5.31	5.01	5.92	6.68	....	....	....	....	Deposit Rate	60l
18.73	20.77	20.33	18.95	18.85	17.77	16.28	15.82	15.65	16.01	....	....	....	....	....	Lending Rate	60p
13.03	15.79	15.69	13.63	12.54	10.94	8.62	9.43	9.06	8.79	9.96	9.05	8.60	6.91	7.35	Government Bond Yield	61

France

132		1965	1966	1967	1968	1969	1970	1971	1972	1973	1974	1975	1976	1977	1978	1979
Prices, Production, Employment																*Index Numbers (1990=100):*
Industrial Share Prices	**62**	14.1	13.1	12.0	12.7	15.2	16.7	16.0	I 17.9	19.8	14.8	16.3	15.7	12.6	16.5	20.9
Producer Prices																
Intermediate Indust. Goods	**63a**	....	....	....	....	....	....	....	....	....	....	....	....	....	....	....
Imported Raw Materials	**63b**	22.3	23.1	22.5	22.0	25.2	27.6	26.7	27.4	34.5	45.9	37.8	42.7	46.1	I 46.8	55.2
Consumer Prices	**64**	17.5	18.0	18.5	19.3	20.5	21.7	22.9	24.3	26.1	29.7	33.2	36.3	39.7	43.3	48.0
Labor Costs	**65**	7.4	7.8	8.4	9.3	10.1	11.3	12.6	14.1	I 16.0	19.1	23.0	26.8	30.6	35.0	40.3
Industrial Production	**66..*c***	50.9	53.5	54.9	56.8	62.8	66.1	70.1	74.0	79.3	81.3	76.0	82.0	83.3	85.3	88.6
Industrial Employment	**67..*c***	....	....	....	....	....	....	....	....	....	....	....	....	....	....	....
International Transactions																*Billions of Francs*
Exports	**70**	50.24	54.22	57.01	63.70	78.81	100.52	115.25	133.39	162.46	222.07	227.20	273.24	319.22	357.60	427.95
Imports, cif	**71**	51.27	58.55	61.43	69.21	90.06	106.26	118.15	136.19	167.25	254.20	231.18	308.12	346.36	368.59	454.69
Imports, fob	**71.v**	47.59	54.51	57.14	64.37	83.76	99.58	110.86	126.95	155.51	239.17	221.47	293.69	331.01	354.99	438.03
																1990=100
Volume of Exports	**72**	21.2	I 22.4	23.6[e]	26.5	30.3	35.2	38.1	43.5	I 48.0	52.6	I 50.4	55.0	58.6	62.1	68.4
Volume of Imports	**73**	19.6	I 22.2	23.2[e]	26.8	32.5	34.6	37.2	42.5	I 48.2	50.3	I 46.7	56.5	56.9	59.9	66.8
Unit Value of Exports	**74**	21.7	I 22.3	22.1[e]	21.9	23.6	26.0	27.5	27.8	I 30.6	38.6	I 40.7	44.5	48.8	51.3	56.2
Unit Value of Imports	**75**	22.4	I 22.9	23.0[e]	22.2	23.7	26.2	27.2	27.4	I 29.4	43.2	I 42.4	46.9	52.4	52.9	58.3
Balance of Payments																*Millions of US Dollars:*
Goods: Exports f.o.b.	**78aa*d***	....	....	....	....	....	....	....	....	....	....	50,425	54,054	61,989	75,186	95,513
Goods: Imports f.o.b.	**78ab*d***	....	....	....	....	....	....	....	....	....	....	-49,391	-59,048	-65,339	-75,219	-99,139
Trade Balance	**78ac*d***	....	....	....	....	....	....	....	....	....	....	1,033	-4,994	-3,350	-33	-3,626
Services: Credit	**78ad*d***	....	....	....	....	....	....	....	....	....	....	18,185	19,232	22,860	30,125	36,265
Services: Debit	**78ae*d***	....	....	....	....	....	....	....	....	....	....	-13,994	-15,387	-17,723	-21,015	-25,698
Balance on Goods and Services	**78af*d***	....	....	....	....	....	....	....	....	....	....	5,225	-1,149	1,787	9,077	6,941
Income: Credit	**78ag*d***	....	....	....	....	....	....	....	....	....	....	5,141	5,330	6,359	9,287	14,346
Income: Debit	**78ah*d***	....	....	....	....	....	....	....	....	....	....	-4,997	-5,095	-5,723	-8,026	-12,122
Balance on Goods, Serv., & Inc.	**78ai*d***	....	....	....	....	....	....	....	....	....	....	5,368	-914	2,422	10,337	9,165
Current Transfers, n.i.e.: Credit	**78aj*d***	....	....	....	....	....	....	....	....	....	....	2,580	2,657	3,215	4,080	5,538
Current Transfers: Debit	**78ak*d***	....	....	....	....	....	....	....	....	....	....	-5,208	-5,100	-6,043	-7,353	-9,561
Current Account, n.i.e.	**78al*d***	....	....	....	....	....	....	....	....	....	....	2,740	-3,356	-405	7,064	5,142
Capital Account, n.i.e.: Credit	**78ba*d***	....	....	....	....	....	....	....	....	....	....	—	—	—	—	—
Capital Account: Debit	**78bb*d***	....	....	....	....	....	....	....	....	....	....	—	—	—	—	—
Capital Account, n.i.e.	**78bc*d***	....	....	....	....	....	....	....	....	....	....	—	—	—	—	—
Direct Investment Abroad	**78bd*d***	....	....	....	....	....	....	....	....	....	....	-1,338	-1,638	-1,003	-1,901	-1,987
Dir. Invest. in Rep. Econ., n.i.e.	**78be*d***	....	....	....	....	....	....	....	....	....	....	1,564	977	1,896	2,471	2,588
Portfolio Investment Assets	**78bf*d***	....	....	....	....	....	....	....	....	....	....	-584	-680	-450	-1,022	-1,883
Portfolio Investment Liab., n.i.e.	**78bg*d***	....	....	....	....	....	....	....	....	....	....	1,694	1,994	1,412	930	281
Other Investment Assets	**78bh*d***	....	....	....	....	....	....	....	....	....	....	-9,713	-14,648	-17,986	-20,971	-28,161
Other Investment Liab., n.i.e.	**78bi*d***	....	....	....	....	....	....	....	....	....	....	7,318	13,305	16,295	16,488	25,215
Financial Account, n.i.e.	**78bj*d***	....	....	....	....	....	....	....	....	....	....	-1,058	-690	165	-4,005	-3,945
Net Errors and Omissions	**78ca*d***	....	....	....	....	....	....	....	....	....	....	1,826	1,003	925	-59	556
Overall Balance	**78cb*d***	....	....	....	....	....	....	....	....	....	....	3,508	-3,044	684	3,000	1,752
Reserves and Related Items	**79da*d***	....	....	....	....	....	....	....	....	....	....	-3,508	3,044	-684	-3,000	-1,752
Reserve Assets	**79db*d***	....	....	....	....	....	....	....	....	....	....	-3,991	2,832	-131	-3,296	-1,807
Use of Fund Credit and Loans	**79dc*d***	....	....	....	....	....	....	....	....	....	....	—	—	—	—	—
Liabs.Constit.For.Auth.Reserves	**79dd*d***	....	....	....	....	....	....	....	....	....	....	483	211	-553	297	55
Exceptional Financing	**79de*d***	....	....	....	....	....	....	....	....	....	....	—	—	—	—	—
Government Finance																*Billions of Francs:*
Deficit (-) or Surplus	**80**	.2	-2.0	-6.3	-9.5	-3.4	3.7	-3.5	I 6.8	4.7	5.8	-37.8	-17.1	-22.3	-29.6	-37.0
Revenue	**81**	105.8	112.0	120.8	129.8	153.2	169.9	180.2	I 331.3	372.0	455.9	512.6	625.5	695.6	787.1	935.4
Grants Received	**81z**	....	....	....	....	....	....	....	I 3.3	3.5	3.8	5.4	6.1	6.3	7.0	7.7
Exp. & Lending Minus Repay.	**82z**	105.6	114.0	127.2	139.3	156.6	166.2	183.7	I 329.1	366.0	453.3	555.5	642.4	719.8	835.4	970.0
Expenditure	**82**	....	....	....	....	....	....	....	I 320.2	356.7	440.4	536.9	620.7	701.2	818.6	945.4
Lending Minus Repayments	**83**	....	....	....	....	....	....	....	I 8.9	9.3	12.9	18.6	21.7	18.6	16.8	24.6
Overall Adj. to Cash Basis	**80x**	....	....	....	....	....	....	....	I 1.3	-4.8	-.6	-.3	-6.3	-4.4	11.7	-10.1
Financing																
Net Borrowing	**84**	-2.5	-5.5	10.5	4.3	2.6	-4.5	-2.5	I 1.8	.1	-4.0	46.3	20.8	35.7	56.0	40.0
Domestic	**84a**	....	....	....	....	....	....	....	I 1.7	-1.2	-4.9	46.2	19.4	34.0	56.2	38.5
Foreign	**85a**	....	....	....	....	....	....	....	I .1	1.3	.9	.1	1.4	1.7	-.2	1.5
Finance from Foreign Aid	**86a**	—	—	—	—	—	—	—	....	....	....	....	....	....	....	....
Use of Cash Balances	**87**	2.3	7.5	-4.2	5.1	.8	.7	5.9	I -8.3	-5.6	-.7	-8.6	-3.3	-13.1	-26.4	-3.0
Adj. to Total Financing	**84x**	....	....	....	....	....	....	....	I -.3	.8	-1.1	.1	-.4	-.3	—	—
Debt: Francs	**88b**	80.1	75.3	86.0	90.4	93.2	89.2	87.4	78.1	77.7	87.4	123.3	133.9	149.7	188.1	362.5
Foreign Currency	**89b**	4.8	4.8	4.6	6.9	7.6	9.7	8.8	8.3	8.3	8.2	5.9	4.8	5.7	9.6	10.3
National Accounts																*Billions of Francs*
Exports of Goods & Services	**90c.*c***	61.2	66.3	71.2	78.5	95.3	125.4	145.2	165.1	198.6	269.6	279.8	333.0	392.8	445.4	527.0
Government Consumption	**91f.*c***	64.6	69.2	74.7	84.7	95.4	119.0	134.6	149.8	171.1	204.2	247.9	292.9	335.2	390.1	443.8
Gross Fixed Capital Formation	**93e.*c***	112.6	124.0	134.7	143.4	164.3	192.9	218.3	244.4	285.2	336.1	354.3	407.2	439.4	488.5	555.1
Increase/Decrease(-) in Stocks	**93i.*c***	7.7	10.6	10.1	11.0	18.4	20.2	13.3	16.1	22.1	30.1	-10.0	24.5	29.4	17.5	32.5
Private Consumption	**96f.*c***	293.7	317.9	344.0	374.5	427.0	457.2	508.4	567.3	641.6	745.6	857.8	988.4	1,111.4	1,257.5	1,434.8
Imports of Goods & Services	**98c.*c***	-56.3	-64.6	-69.3	-77.6	-99.7	-121.2	-135.6	-154.9	-188.7	-282.7	-262.3	-345.4	-390.5	-416.4	-512.1
Gross Domestic Product	**99b.*c***	483.5	523.4	565.4	614.5	700.7	793.5	884.2	987.9	1,129.8	1,303.0	1,467.9	1,700.6	1,917.8	2,182.6	2,481.1
Net Factor Inc/Pmts(-) Abroad	**98.n*c***	3.8	3.5	4.0	3.8	3.9	3.3	2.9	2.2	2.4	4.1	2.4	2.9	3.9	4.7	8.6
Gross Nat'l Expenditure = GNP	**99a.*c***	487.3	526.9	569.4	618.3	704.6	796.8	887.1	990.1	1,132.2	1,307.1	1,470.3	1,703.5	1,921.7	2,187.3	2,489.7
Nat'l Income, Market Prices	**99e.*c***	440.1	475.5	513.5	559.7	639.3	724.4	804.1	894.4	1,021.1	1,168.8	1,306.7	1,510.9	1,699.6	1,934.3	2,197.3
Gross Dom. Prod. 1990 Prices	**99b.*r***	2,868.0	3,017.5	3,158.9	3,293.6	3,523.6	3,725.5	3,903.8	4,076.7	4,298.4	4,432.0	4,419.7	4,607.2	4,755.6	4,914.8	5,074.1
GDP Deflator (1990=100)	**99bi *r***	16.9	17.3	17.9	18.7	19.9	21.3	22.6	24.2	26.3	29.4	33.2	36.9	40.3	44.4	48.9
																Millions:
Population	**99z**	48.76	49.16	49.55	49.91	50.32	50.77	51.25	51.70	52.13	52.49	52.79	52.91	53.15	53.38	53.61

International Liquidity: I Beginning in December 1977, *line 7a.d* includes buyers' credits.

Banking Institutions: I Beginning in December 1969, data for deposit money banks are based on a new reporting system and include the accounts of the central institution for credit cooperatives and for the mutual credit banks. The new reporting system resulted mainly in the revision of *lines 22d, 24,* and *25* and also made it possible to separately report deposit money banks' foreign assets and liabilities, which were previously included in *line 27r*. These revisions affected sections 30 and 50. *Line 26c* includes, and *lines 24* and *25* exclude, liabilities to nonresidents. I Beginning in December 1977, data reflect institutional changes (see the deposit money bank notes on the page for France in the monthly issues of *IFS*). Data from this date are also based on a new reporting system by deposit money banks.

Interest Rates: *Government Bond Yield:* I Prior to 1969, current yield of the 5 percent perpetuity of 1949. Monthly yields are based on last Friday prices.

Government Finance: I Beginning in 1972, data are as reported in the *Government Finance Statistics Yearbook* and cover consolidated central government (including extrabudgetary and social security accounts).

1980	1981	1982	1983	1984	1985	1986	1987	1988	1989	1990	1991	1992	1993	1994		
															Prices, Production, Employment	
Period Averages																
24.2	I 21.4	20.7	I 28.0	I 37.8	I 44.2	67.7	78.4	71.6	103.7	100.0	97.5	107.8	116.2	....	Industrial Share Prices	62
															Producer Prices	
60.8	67.9	75.2	81.8	89.4	93.3	90.7	91.3	96.0	101.3	100.0	98.7	97.1	I 94.4	95.4	Intermediate Indust. Goods	63a
64.7	76.1	81.4	92.3	107.9	100.4	76.5	I 79.4	101.4	125.8	100.0	89.9	80.8	I 73.4	86.8	Imported Raw Materials	63b
I 54.4	61.7	69.0	75.6	81.2	85.9	88.1	91.0	93.5	96.7	I 100.0	103.2	105.7	107.9	109.7	Consumer Prices	64
46.7	53.5	64.3	72.5	78.6	83.4	87.1	91.2	94.1	98.5	100.0	104.4	108.4	111.7	115.0	Labor Costs	65
I 89.2	88.4	87.7	87.1	87.3	87.6	88.4	90.0	94.3	98.2	100.0	99.9	98.9	95.2	99.2	Industrial Production	66..c
116.7	113.1	112.1	109.9	106.9	104.0	102.1	99.7	98.6	99.4	100.0	98.2	95.5	90.8	88.9	Industrial Employment	67..c
															International Transactions	
Billions of Francs																
490.55	576.66	633.07	723.07	850.95	906.89	863.54	888.91	997.65	1,143.24	1,177.17	1,221.43	1,248.83	1,190.54	1,302.37	Exports	70
569.99	654.85	763.55	806.52	909.60	967.92	895.89	949.82	1,063.14	1,229.75	1,273.62	1,302.86	1,268.37	1,136.44	1,267.67	Imports, cif	71
550.97	635.77	704.99	757.54	870.72	930.93	863.17	920.52	1,030.47	1,187.18	1,226.74	1,250.98	1,217.81	1,088.87	1,214.60	Imports, fob	71.v
1990=100																
69.8	71.9	69.7	72.1	75.9	78.0	I 78.4	81.3	88.4	95.3	100.0	I 104.7	108.5	105.9	....	Volume of Exports	72
71.1	68.7	71.1	69.7	71.4	74.3	I 76.8	82.2	87.6	95.2	100.0	I 102.3	103.8	97.2	....	Volume of Imports	73
62.4	I 70.5	79.6	87.3	95.0	98.3	93.3	92.6	96.1	101.8	100.0	99.6	96.9	93.8	100.2	Unit Value of Exports	74
69.0	I 81.8	92.5	100.1	109.9	111.2	93.6	92.2	94.7	102.0	100.0	99.0	95.2	90.5	93.9	Unit Value of Imports	75
															Balance of Payments	
Minus Sign Indicates Debit																
109,691	102,583	93,384	91,317	93,374	97,102	120,533	143,004	161,603	172,011	208,597	208,880	226,988	196,816	222,733	Goods: Exports f.o.b.	78aad
-123,767	-112,722	-108,833	-99,730	-97,868	-101,916	-121,880	-150,779	-169,253	-182,251	-221,828	-218,474	-224,644	-189,067	-213,602	Goods: Imports f.o.b.	78abd
-14,076	-10,139	-15,449	-8,412	-4,494	-4,814	-1,347	-7,775	-7,649	-10,240	-13,230	-9,594	2,344	7,749	9,132	Trade Balance	78acd
43,506	41,239	35,842	34,246	34,327	35,557	43,078	50,492	54,116	60,054	76,838	80,445	99,590	97,053	91,625	Services: Credit	78add
-32,148	-33,285	-28,037	-25,663	-25,426	-25,891	-33,028	-40,109	-43,639	-46,659	-61,479	-64,174	-80,212	-79,492	-72,574	Services: Debit	78aed
-2,718	-2,185	-7,644	171	4,408	4,853	8,703	2,607	2,827	3,155	2,129	6,678	21,722	25,310	28,183	Balance on Goods and Services	78afd
20,921	26,161	25,439	20,216	20,420	21,791	24,240	27,561	34,016	41,282	55,734	69,770	80,247	88,787	110,222	Income: Credit	78agd
-18,241	-24,555	-25,255	-21,738	-22,807	-24,051	-25,924	-29,203	-34,964	-41,568	-59,626	-75,497	-89,132	-97,755	-121,286	Income: Debit	78ahd
-39	-579	-7,460	-1,351	2,021	2,593	7,019	965	1,879	2,870	-1,764	951	12,837	16,342	17,120	Balance on Goods, Serv., & Inc.	78aid
6,163	5,331	4,925	5,051	5,008	5,893	9,487	10,867	13,192	11,733	14,992	18,947	20,976	16,973	16,060	Current Transfers, n.i.e.: Credit	78ajd
-10,332	-9,563	-9,547	-8,866	-7,905	-8,520	-14,076	-16,278	-19,867	-19,329	-23,170	-26,366	-29,879	-23,014	-24,348	Current Transfers: Debit	78akd
-4,208	-4,811	-12,082	-5,166	-876	-35	2,430	-4,446	-4,795	-4,726	-9,942	-6,469	3,934	10,301	8,832	Current Account, n.i.e.	78ald
—	—	—	—	—	—	—	—	—	—	—	5	629	14	11	Capital Account, n.i.e.: Credit	78bad
—	—	—	—	—	—	—	—	—	-935	-5,294	-567	-225	-115	-4,797	Capital Account: Debit	78bbd
—	—	—	—	—	—	—	—	—	-935	-5,294	-561	403	-101	-4,786	Capital Account, n.i.e.	78bcd
-3,095	-4,549	-2,849	-1,713	-2,119	-2,243	-5,403	-9,210	-14,496	-19,503	-34,822	-23,932	-31,269	-20,604	-22,462	Direct Investment Abroad	78bdd
3,283	2,470	1,585	1,726	2,398	2,595	3,256	5,140	8,487	10,313	13,183	15,149	21,843	20,755	17,078	Dir. Invest. in Rep. Econ., n.i.e.	78bed
-2,068	-2,165	195	-1,631	-472	-2,469	-5,955	-3,269	-4,151	-6,653	-8,408	-15,718	-18,461	-30,760	-20,703	Portfolio Investment Assets	78bfd
2,373	1,835	7,000	7,401	7,457	8,948	7,829	8,711	11,949	32,045	43,217	29,535	52,496	34,515	-29,375	Portfolio Investment Liab., n.i.e.	78bgd
-31,463	-17,250	-11,508	-5,979	-13,538	-6,857	-9,871	-47,039	-33,225	-65,247	-66,963	-3,699	-62,248	-5,721	34,010	Other Investment Assets	78bhd
38,963	21,987	15,012	9,170	9,286	2,151	8,326	40,935	35,224	57,924	79,427	-5,019	18,098	-8,871	29,329	Other Investment Liab., n.i.e.	78bid
7,993	2,329	9,435	8,974	3,012	2,125	-1,818	-4,733	3,788	8,879	25,634	-3,683	-19,541	-10,686	7,877	Financial Account, n.i.e.	78bjd
2,275	-2,283	-958	358	650	290	807	850	940	-5,568	1,425	4,897	2,109	2,686	-6,893	Net Errors and Omissions	78cad
6,060	-4,766	-3,606	4,166	2,786	2,380	1,418	-8,329	-67	-2,350	11,823	-5,816	-13,094	2,201	5,029	Overall Balance	78cbd
-6,060	4,766	3,606	-4,166	-2,786	-2,380	-1,418	8,329	67	2,350	-11,823	5,816	13,094	-2,201	-5,029	Reserves and Related Items	79dad
-6,561	3,588	3,769	-3,605	-2,934	-2,696	-1,181	2,601	5,134	857	-10,910	5,151	1,575	5,017	-2,475	Reserve Assets	79dbd
—	—	—	—	—	—	—	—	—	—	—	—	—	—	—	Use of Fund Credit and Loans	79dcd
501	1,178	-163	-561	148	316	-237	5,727	-5,067	1,493	-913	665	11,519	-7,218	-2,554	Liabs.Constit.For.Auth.Reserves	79ddd
—	—	—	—	—	—	—	—	—	—	—	—	—	—	—	Exceptional Financing	79ded
															Government Finance	
Year Ending December 31																
-2.0	-73.2	-121.9	-140.7	-116.3	-127.7	-170.3	-64.5	-134.2	-118.6	-136.5	-84.6	-263.5	....	....	Deficit (-) or Surplus	80
1,112.9	1,275.5	1,482.4	1,652.5	1,817.7	1,962.4	2,076.5	2,206.9	2,342.8	2,495.2	2,638.7	2,765.5	2,846.7	....	....	Revenue	81
12.2	13.5	16.6	21.3	19.8	18.9	26.4	26.3	35.5	33.2	34.6	51.7	47.0	....	....	Grants Received	81z
1,121.9	1,353.1	1,638.8	1,805.3	1,971.6	2,122.8	2,268.7	2,313.9	2,480.3	2,612.8	2,761.6	2,999.2	3,154.7	....	....	Exp. & Lending Minus Repay.	82z
1,110.0	1,328.2	1,570.5	1,774.1	1,943.4	2,099.4	2,228.7	2,325.9	2,463.0	2,595.3	2,770.0	2,950.5	3,153.1	....	....	Expenditure	82
11.9	24.9	68.3	31.2	28.2	23.4	40.0	-12.0	17.4	17.5	-8.4	48.7	1.6	....	....	Lending Minus Repayments	83
-5.2	-9.1	17.9	-9.2	17.8	13.8	-4.5	16.2	-32.2	-34.2	-48.2	97.4	-2.5	....	....	Overall Adj. to Cash Basis	80x
															Financing	
31.6	83.8	185.3	119.8	160.4	164.3	135.5	128.5	84.0	151.9	152.7	....	....	....	....	Net Borrowing	84
31.5	82.5	185.5	117.7	161.9	163.5	135.3	121.1	60.3	105.8	81.9	65.2	291.5	....	....	Domestic	84a
.1	1.3	-.2	2.1	-1.5	.8	.2	7.4	23.7	46.1	70.8	....	....	....	....	Foreign	85a
....	....	....	....	....	....	....	....	....	....	....	....	....	....	....	Finance from Foreign Aid	86a
-29.6	-10.6	-63.4	20.9	-44.1	-36.6	34.8	-64.0	50.2	-33.3	-16.2	1.3	....	....	....	Use of Cash Balances	87
—	—	—	—	—	—	—	—	—	—	—	—	—	....	....	Adj. to Total Financing	84x
404.4	485.3	599.4	751.0	883.1	1,027.0	1,164.0	955.4	1,439.5	1,583.9	1,747.6	1,762.8	2,014.7	2,346.0	1,751.1	Debt: Francs	88b
13.9	15.1	17.3	29.4	31.7	40.0	31.9	33.4	36.7	40.4	38.4	37.8	55.4	57.9	62.6	Foreign Currency	89b
															National Accounts	
Billions of Francs																
604.4	714.2	790.4	900.6	1,053.3	1,123.9	1,074.1	1,101.4	1,221.3	1,411.1	1,468.0	1,538.1	1,587.9	1,558.7	1,684.1	Exports of Goods & Services	90c.c
517.5	604.3	711.8	793.5	866.4	923.0	972.8	1,018.6	1,073.3	1,122.0	1,187.7	1,257.1	1,339.1	1,423.9	1,462.4	Government Consumption	91f.c
645.8	694.6	774.3	809.7	840.4	905.3	977.5	1,054.8	1,188.3	1,314.6	1,391.4	1,436.9	1,401.9	1,319.2	1,351.2	Gross Fixed Capital Formation	93e.c
34.3	-7.5	18.9	-14.0	-12.4	-17.9	17.2	20.7	40.3	59.3	70.9	21.1	-14.9	-106.5	-27.6	Increase/Decrease(-) in Stocks	93i.c
1,645.0	1,897.8	2,190.4	2,424.1	2,639.2	2,858.4	3,049.5	3,235.6	3,429.5	3,655.8	3,861.3	4,037.5	4,189.8	4,291.6	4,433.9	Private Consumption	96f.c
-638.7	-744.8	-859.6	-907.4	-1,025.0	-1,092.6	-1,021.8	-1,094.3	-1,217.6	-1,403.1	-1,469.8	-1,514.5	-1,493.4	-1,404.2	-1,523.6	Imports of Goods & Services	98c.c
2,808.3	3,164.8	3,626.0	4,006.5	4,361.9	4,700.1	5,069.3	5,336.6	5,735.1	6,159.7	6,509.5	6,776.2	7,010.5	7,082.8	7,380.3	Gross Domestic Product	99b.c
12.6	10.3	2.0	-11.7	-23.5	-25.6	-16.6	-12.5	-31.8	-36.3	-57.3	-38.3	-57.1	-55.3	-50.7	Net Factor Inc/Pmts(-) Abroad	98.nc
2,820.9	3,175.1	3,628.0	3,994.8	4,338.4	4,674.5	5,052.7	5,324.2	5,703.3	6,123.4	6,452.2	6,737.9	6,953.4	7,027.5	7,325.3	Gross Nat'l Expenditure = GNP	99a.c
2,474.7	2,777.9	3,171.3	3,486.3	3,786.8	4,085.1	4,420.7	4,650.7	4,978.3	5,347.3	5,623.2	5,857.8	6,046.3	6,102.2	6,373.0	Nat'l Income, Market Prices	99e.c
5,156.6	5,217.2	5,350.1	5,387.2	5,458.1	5,560.7	5,700.7	5,829.0	6,091.2	6,350.3	6,509.5	6,560.4	6,648.7	6,551.4	6,726.4	Gross Dom. Prod. 1990 Prices	99b.r
54.5	60.7	67.8	74.4	79.9	84.5	88.9	91.6	94.2	97.0	100.0	103.3	105.4	108.1	109.7	GDP Deflator (1990=100)	99bir
Midyear Estimates																
53.88	54.18	54.48	54.73	54.95	55.17	55.39	55.63	55.88	56.16	56.73	57.05	57.37	57.66	....	**Population**	99z

Gabon
646

		1965	1966	1967	1968	1969	1970	1971	1972	1973	1974	1975	1976	1977	1978	1979
Exchange Rates															*Francs per SDR:*	
Official Rate	aa	245.07	247.59	245.42	247.40	277.91	276.02	283.61	278.00	284.00	272.08	262.55	288.70	285.76	272.28	264.78
															Francs per US Dollar:	
Official Rate	ae	245.08	247.59	245.43	247.41	277.92	276.03	261.23	256.05	235.43	222.22	224.27	248.49	235.25	209.00	201.00
Official Rate	rf	245.06	245.68	246.00	247.56	259.96	276.40	275.59	252.03	222.89	240.70	214.31	238.95	245.68	225.66	212.72
															Index Numbers (1990=100):	
Official Rate	ahx	110.8	110.5	110.4	109.7	104.8	98.2	98.6	107.8	122.3	112.8	126.9	113.8	110.5	120.6	127.7
Nominal Effective Exchange Rate	ne c	....	....	....	....	....	....	....	....	....	....	....	....	....	....	61.0
Real Effective Exchange Rate	re c	....	....	....	....	....	....	....	....	....	....	....	....	....	....	111.8
Fund Position															*Millions of SDRs:*	
Quota	2f. s	7.50	8.00	8.50	9.00	9.50	15.00	15.00	15.00	15.00	15.00	15.00	15.00	15.00	30.00	30.00
SDRs	1b. s	—	—	—	—	—	1.60	3.17	4.73	4.70	4.66	4.63	4.62	4.61	4.55	7.21
Reserve Position in the Fund	1c. s	.65	.77	.90	1.02	1.15	2.37	2.40	2.43	2.46	2.49	2.53	2.53	2.53	—	—
Total Fund Cred.&Loans Outstg.	2tl	—	—	—	—	—	—	—	—	—	—	—	—	—	7.61	15.22
International Liquidity											*Millions of US Dollars Unless Otherwise Indicated:*					
Total Reserves minus Gold	1l. d	17.63	11.56	9.43	5.47	8.29	14.74	25.39	23.23	47.86	103.29	146.07	116.16	9.91	22.57	20.13
SDRs	1b. d	—	—	—	—	—	1.60	3.44	5.14	5.67	5.71	5.42	5.37	5.60	5.93	9.50
Reserve Position in the Fund	1c. d	.65	.77	.90	1.02	1.15	2.37	2.61	2.64	2.97	3.05	2.97	2.94	3.08	—	—
Foreign Exchange	1d. d	16.98	10.79	8.53	4.44	7.13	10.77	19.34	15.45	39.22	94.53	137.68	107.84	1.23	16.65	10.64
Gold (Million Fine Troy Ounces)	1ad	....	....	....	....	....	....	....	....	....	....	....	....	.006	.010	.013
Gold (National Valuation)	1and	....	....	....	....	....	....	....	....	....	....	....	....	1.06	2.24	6.68
Monetary Authorities: Other Liab.	4. d	—	—	—	.04	.02	.04	.06	.08	.05	.02	.03	.04	.11	.35	.16
Deposit Money Banks: Assets	7a. d	.41	.81	1.86	4.16	.85	.60	3.17	6.97	6.48	10.31	11.31	30.26	25.39	18.61	32.81
Liabilities	7b. d	8.10	11.71	6.85	10.82	10.47	17.88	13.09	16.44	21.85	43.42	39.62	54.01	131.16	125.31	108.73
Monetary Authorities															*Billions of Francs:*	
Foreign Assets	11	4.35	2.86	2.33	1.35	2.30	4.09	6.49	5.94	11.02	22.95	32.76	28.86	2.58	5.19	5.40
Claims on Central Government	12a	1.03	.98	1.12	1.67	1.58	1.61	—	—	—	1.00	4.10	9.27	27.03	28.57	33.98
Claims on Deposit Money Banks	12e	.97	1.02	.88	1.41	1.07	1.16	2.48	4.39	5.37	7.02	6.84	4.81	17.15	11.88	12.07
Claims on Other Banking Insts.	12f	....	....	....	....	....	....	....	....	....	....	....	....	....	....	....
Reserve Money	14	5.23	4.06	3.82	4.14	4.76	5.73	6.95	7.93	10.26	18.95	24.44	40.27	40.94	35.72	37.91
of which: Currency Outside DMBs	14a	5.05	3.79	3.62	3.83	4.50	5.26	6.18	7.38	9.56	15.63	22.22	33.65	34.27	31.34	30.34
Foreign Liabilities	16c	—	—	—	.01	.01	.01	.02	.02	.01	.01	.01	.01	.03	2.15	4.06
Central Government Deposits	16d	1.04	.73	.48	.21	.14	.63	1.04	1.01	4.50	10.45	17.34	.21	3.21	3.15	2.15
Capital Accounts	17a	....	....	....	—	—	—	—	—	.02	.02	.03	.03	.04	.04	.05
Other Items (Net)	17r	.08	.07	.03	.07	.05	.49	.97	1.37	1.59	1.55	1.89	2.43	2.55	4.57	7.28
Deposit Money Banks															*Billions of Francs:*	
Reserves	20	.13	.19	.12	.32	.26	.48	.77	.55	.70	3.32	2.22	6.62	6.66	4.39	7.58
Foreign Assets	21	.10	.20	.46	1.03	.24	.17	.81	1.78	1.49	2.29	2.54	7.52	I 5.97	3.89	6.60
Claims on Central Government	22a	1.21	1.86	.53	1.14	1.88	1.94	2.06	3.38	4.95	13.22	11.61	34.80	39.63	27.45	27.07
Claims on Nonfin.Pub.Enterprises	22c	....	....	....	....	....	....	....	....	....	....	....	....	....	....	....
Claims on Private Sector	22d	7.74	8.74	9.48	10.75	12.94	15.90	19.49	24.78	33.13	48.77	66.63	99.75	I 124.71	129.98	123.35
Claims on Other Banking Insts.	22f	....	....	....	....	....	....	....	....	....	....	....	....	....	....	....
Claims on Nonbank.Financial Insts.	22g	....	....	....	....	....	....	....	....	....	....	....	....	....	....	....
Demand Deposits	24	3.58	4.60	4.95	5.91	7.18	7.55	8.70	11.41	13.70	22.82	37.26	71.33	I 65.26	59.37	55.56
Time and Savings Deposits	25	.57	.63	.92	.95	.99	.95	.83	1.30	3.27	5.89	11.98	28.43	33.82	22.94	36.94
Bonds	26ab	....	....	....	....	....	....	....	....	....	....	....	....	....	....	....
Foreign Liabilities	26c	2.00	2.30	.78	1.65	.81	2.73	1.06	1.80	2.40	6.80	5.43	9.42	26.77	22.45	17.68
Long-Term Foreign Liabilities	26cl	—	.60	.91	1.02	2.09	2.24	2.29	2.40	2.63	2.85	3.46	4.00	4.09	3.74	4.17
Central Government Deposits	26d	.39	.26	.32	.47	1.08	1.57	2.84	4.34	6.38	13.93	9.40	17.71	19.31	37.19	22.60
Credit from Monetary Authorities	26g	.97	1.02	.88	1.41	1.07	1.16	2.48	4.39	5.37	6.16	6.18	4.33	16.16	11.32	11.63
Capital Accounts	27a	1.71	1.73	1.99	2.10	2.26	2.47	2.87	3.36	4.27	5.20	7.01	10.19	14.40	19.36	23.72
Other Items (Net)	27r	-.04	-.14	-.16	-.28	-.18	-.18	2.06	1.50	2.26	3.95	2.28	3.28	I -2.82	-10.66	-7.70
Post Office: Checking Deposits	24.. i	.20	.23	.30	.30	.33	.48	.31	.62	.48	.15	.76	1.87	.84	2.46	1.83
Postal Debt	26c. i	....	....	....	.29	.28	.50	.61	.64	.70	1.47	1.05	1.88	2.26	2.71	2.17
Monetary Survey															*Billions of Francs:*	
Foreign Assets (Net)	31n	2.45	.77	2.01	.71	1.72	1.52	6.23	5.90	10.10	18.44	29.86	26.95	I -18.24	-15.52	-9.75
Domestic Credit	32	8.55	10.59	10.33	12.88	15.17	17.25	17.67	22.81	27.20	38.60	55.60	125.90	I 168.86	145.66	159.66
Claims on Central Govt. (Net)	32an	I .81	1.85	.85	2.13	2.24	1.35	-1.82	-1.96	-5.93	-10.17	-11.03	26.15	44.15	15.68	36.30
Claims on Nonfin.Pub.Enterprises	32c	....	....	....	....	....	....	....	....	....	....	....	....	....	....	....
Claims on Private Sector	32d	I7.74	8.74	9.48	10.75	12.94	15.90	19.49	24.78	33.13	48.77	66.63	99.75	I 124.71	129.98	123.35
Claims on Other Banking Insts.	32f	....	....	....	....	....	....	....	....	....	....	....	....	....	....	....
Claims on Nonbk.Financial Insts.	32g	....	....	....	....	....	....	....	....	....	....	....	....	....	....	....
Money	34	8.63	8.39	8.57	9.74	11.68	12.81	14.88	18.79	23.26	38.44	59.48	104.97	I 99.53	90.70	85.90
Quasi-Money	35	.57	.63	.92	.95	.99	.95	.83	1.30	3.27	5.89	11.98	28.43	33.82	22.94	36.94
Bonds	36ab	....	....	....	....	....	....	....	....	....	....	....	....	....	....	....
Other Items (Net)	37r	....	....	....	2.91	4.22	5.01	8.19	8.63	10.77	12.71	14.01	19.45	I 17.27	16.51	27.08
Money plus Quasi-Money	35l	9.20	9.02	9.49	10.69	12.67	13.76	15.71	20.09	26.53	44.33	71.46	133.40	I 133.35	113.64	122.83
Interest Rates															*Percent Per Annum*	
Discount Rate *(End of Period)*	60	....	....	....	4.50	4.50	4.50	4.50	4.50	4.50	4.50	5.50	5.50	6.50	6.50	8.50
Deposit Rate	60l	....	....	....	....	....	....	....	....	....	....	....	....	....	7.50	6.50
Lending Rate	60p	....	....	....	....	....	....	....	....	....	....	....	....	....	10.50	8.50
Prices															*Index Numbers (1990=100):*	
Wholesale Prices (1985=100)	63	16.3	I 17.2	17.5	18.1	19.3	21.5	22.4	23.5	25.1	30.8	35.4	41.5	47.5	51.8	54.8
Consumer Prices	64	16.3	16.8	17.2	17.6	18.1	18.8	19.5	20.2	21.5	24.0	I 30.9	37.1	42.3	46.8	50.5

Gabon

	1980	1981	1982	1983	1984	1985	1986	1987	1988	1989	1990	1991	1992	1993	1994		
																Exchange Rates	
End of Period	287.99	334.52	370.92	436.97	470.11	415.26	394.78	378.78	407.68	380.32	364.84	370.48	378.57	404.89	ⱡ780.44	Official Rate	aa
End of Period (ae) Period Average (rf)																	
	225.80	287.40	336.25	417.37	479.60	378.05	322.75	267.00	302.95	289.40	256.45	259.00	275.33	294.78	ⱡ534.60	Official Rate	ae
	211.28	271.73	328.61	381.06	436.96	449.26	346.30	300.54	297.85	319.01	272.26	282.11	264.69	283.16	ⱡ555.20	Official Rate	rf
Period Averages																	
	128.7	100.5	83.1	71.6	62.3	60.9	78.6	90.5	91.4	85.2	100.0	96.6	102.8	96.0	49.0	Official Rate	ah x
	63.1	59.0	57.1	56.2	56.4	59.7	65.0	69.5	74.1	80.9	100.0	106.2	119.8	131.8	76.0	Nominal Effective Exchange Rate	ne c
	113.4	100.7	101.7	99.8	95.3	98.3	107.0	105.3	90.7	92.0	100.0	87.9	87.6	81.0	53.3	Real Effective Exchange Rate	re c
End of Period																**Fund Position**	
	45.00	45.00	45.00	73.10	73.10	73.10	73.10	73.10	73.10	73.10	73.10	73.10	110.30	110.30	110.30	Quota	2f. s
	5.64	6.97	.74	.42	5.82	2.08	10.05	8.19	6.54	.17	.19	4.44	.08	.03	.17	SDRs	1b. s
	—	.03	.04	7.03	.03	.03	.03	.03	.03	.04	.04	.05	.05	.05	.05	Reserve Position in the Fund	1c. s
	11.36	11.34	9.35	1.85	—	—	27.41	42.50	98.68	102.69	98.49	84.34	58.55	32.89	61.04	Total Fund Cred.&Loans Outstg.	2tl
End of Period																**International Liquidity**	
	107.50	198.85	311.88	186.90	199.45	192.55	126.35	12.00	67.44	34.43	273.76	327.48	71.21	.75	175.19	Total Reserves minus Gold	1l. d
	7.19	8.11	.82	.44	5.70	2.28	12.29	11.62	8.80	.22	.27	6.35	.10	.03	.25	SDRs	1b. d
	—	.03	.04	7.36	.03	.03	.04	.04	.04	.05	.06	.07	.07	.07	.08	Reserve Position in the Fund	1c. d
	100.31	190.71	311.02	179.10	193.72	190.23	114.02	.34	58.59	34.15	273.44	321.05	71.04	.64	174.86	Foreign Exchange	1d. d
	.013	.013	.013	.013	.013	.013	.013	.013	.013	.013	.013	.013	.013	.013	....	Gold (Million Fine Troy Ounces)	1ad
	7.57	5.14	5.77	4.86	3.97	4.16	5.03	6.19	5.21	4.07	4.59	4.55	4.28	5.11	....	Gold (National Valuation)	1an d
	.20	.18	.35	.52	3.17	1.35	.65	64.52	56.64	6.66	3.99	5.50	14.82	4.42	.63	Monetary Authorities: Other Liab.	4.. d
	17.74	30.43	34.60	23.24	15.56	26.49	43.01	39.44	40.77	82.79	89.44	88.02	61.55	53.13	82.23	Deposit Money Banks: Assets	7a. d
	80.92	105.51	83.10	36.35	16.73	94.46	122.00	57.85	33.13	142.16	143.75	154.76	117.45	89.15	41.28	Liabilities	7b. d
End of Period																**Monetary Authorities**	
	25.99	58.63	106.81	80.05	97.56	74.38	42.40	4.87	ⱡ22.03	11.45	71.48	85.99	20.78	1.70	96.30	Foreign Assets	11
	23.90	3.79	5.16	.81	—	—	28.51	81.99	ⱡ90.14	101.00	40.26	ⱡ42.53	58.00	62.47	95.83	Claims on Central Government	12a
	8.83	7.14	6.21	7.27	8.03	26.98	22.83	28.82	ⱡ19.77	17.39	16.70	ⱡ11.77	23.54	19.82	.16	Claims on Deposit Money Banks	12e
	....	....	....	....	....	....	....	....	4.48	7.67	7.91	9.00	3.11	—	—	Claims on Other Banking Insts.	12f
	45.06	48.26	52.59	57.53	68.00	62.68	55.56	58.65	ⱡ54.63	63.28	69.02	88.44	63.58	58.38	133.91	Reserve Money	14
	35.85	37.82	45.45	50.24	54.29	57.39	49.12	51.46	ⱡ48.13	57.50	61.88	62.88	56.79	50.47	76.93	of which: Currency Outside DMBs	14a
	3.32	3.84	3.59	1.02	1.52	.51	11.03	33.33	ⱡ57.39	40.98	36.96	32.67	26.25	14.62	48.27	Foreign Liabilities	16c
	1.79	9.12	55.89	25.19	33.33	35.25	8.34	12.44	ⱡ11.34	31.05	23.87	22.41	7.97	3.11	18.51	Central Government Deposits	16d
	1.64	1.39	1.98	2.10	1.93	1.92	1.96	2.05	ⱡ1.92	1.74	1.76	1.94	1.64	1.89	1.49	Capital Accounts	17a
	6.92	6.94	4.12	2.29	.82	1.00	16.84	9.21	ⱡ11.14	.47	4.74	3.83	ⱡ6.00	5.99	-9.90	Other Items (Net)	17r
End of Period																**Deposit Money Banks**	
	9.21	10.44	7.15	7.29	13.72	5.29	6.44	7.19	ⱡ5.81	5.53	7.07	25.49	5.94	7.86	56.87	Reserves	20
	4.01	8.75	11.63	9.70	7.46	10.02	13.88	10.53	ⱡ12.38	23.96	22.94	22.80	16.95	15.66	43.96	Foreign Assets	21
	30.56	30.36	49.38	55.49	83.50	109.78	81.37	90.40	ⱡ102.34	102.20	101.17	95.20	ⱡ105.35	99.25	172.94	Claims on Central Government	22a
	....	....	....	....	....	....	....	....	22.49	22.84	19.06	19.90	8.78	9.88	10.17	Claims on Nonfin.Pub.Enterprises	22c
	142.59	170.99	184.98	229.11	251.83	303.20	336.33	293.33	ⱡ192.09	208.58	210.54	224.39	162.01	157.91	157.20	Claims on Private Sector	22d
	....	....	....	....	....	....	....	....	.17		.01		—	—	.88	Claims on Other Banking Insts.	22f
	....	....	....	....	....	....	....	2.18	2.64	4.06	4.04	4.65	4.22	7.07	Claims on Nonbank.Financial Insts.	22g
	59.03	77.76	81.58	94.20	115.11	120.78	105.00	83.80	ⱡ114.24	113.40	118.98	132.48	84.71	86.92	117.96	Demand Deposits	24
	58.11	61.67	74.08	92.73	105.05	129.41	122.51	105.46	ⱡ99.98	107.72	107.01	112.54	99.11	99.87	130.98	Time and Savings Deposits	25
	....	....	....	....	....	....	....	....	.23	.16	.11	1.01	.90	1.20	.30	Bonds	26ab
	10.91	25.06	19.75	7.86	1.56	29.99	33.77	-6.74	ⱡ9.43	4.76	12.45	ⱡ21.78	19.86	19.37	13.73	Foreign Liabilities	26c
	7.37	5.27	8.20	7.31	6.47	5.72	5.60	22.19	ⱡ34.97	36.44	24.42	ⱡ18.31	12.48	6.91	8.34	Long-Term Foreign Liabilities	26cl
	17.62	22.22	26.23	48.52	65.31	62.75	57.60	51.27	ⱡ39.59	35.32	34.31	39.42	ⱡ22.88	16.72	32.21	Central Government Deposits	26d
	8.48	6.65	6.21	7.27	8.03	26.98	22.83	28.82	ⱡ19.77	17.39	16.70	ⱡ11.77	23.54	19.82	.16	Credit from Monetary Authorities	26g
	25.68	36.40	36.83	46.75	49.41	58.20	62.56	77.28	ⱡ19.22	56.45	54.15	ⱡ58.91	54.68	54.55	133.44	Capital Accounts	27a
	-.83	-14.47	.26	-3.05	5.57	-5.54	28.15	39.37	ⱡ.02	-5.90	-3.27	-4.40	ⱡ-14.49	-10.58	11.97	Other Items (Net)	27r
	.57	1.26	1.78	1.63	1.95	1.45	1.08	.89	1.69	....	....	....	....	....	....	Post Office: Checking Deposits	24.. i
	1.08	.92	2.81	1.09	3.22	.26	3.10	....	....	....	....	....	....	....	....	Postal Debt	26c. i
End of Period																**Monetary Survey**	
	15.77	38.47	95.10	80.87	101.94	53.90	11.48	-11.18	ⱡ-67.39	-46.78	20.59	ⱡ36.04	-20.86	-23.54	69.92	Foreign Assets (Net)	31n
	177.64	173.81	157.39	211.69	236.69	314.98	380.27	402.00	ⱡ362.96	378.57	324.83	ⱡ333.22	ⱡ311.04	313.90	393.36	Domestic Credit	32
	35.05	2.82	-27.58	-17.41	-15.14	11.78	43.94	108.68	ⱡ141.55	136.83	83.25	ⱡ75.90	ⱡ132.50	141.89	218.05	Claims on Central Govt. (Net)	32an
	....	....	....	....	....	....	....	....	22.49	22.84	19.06	19.90	8.78	9.88	10.17	Claims on Nonfin.Pub.Enterprises	32c
	142.59	170.99	184.98	229.11	251.83	303.20	336.33	293.33	ⱡ192.09	208.58	210.54	224.39	162.01	157.91	157.20	Claims on Private Sector	32d
	....	....	....	....	....	....	....	....	4.65	7.67	7.92	9.00	3.11	—	.88	Claims on Other Banking Insts.	32f
	....	....	....	....	....	....	....	2.18	2.64	4.06	4.04	4.65	4.22	7.07	Claims on Nonbk.Financial Insts.	32g
	94.88	115.58	127.02	144.43	169.40	178.16	154.11	135.26	ⱡ163.06	171.16	180.93	195.43	142.35	137.44	195.01	Money	34
	58.11	61.67	74.08	92.73	105.05	129.41	122.51	105.46	ⱡ99.98	107.72	107.01	112.54	99.11	99.87	130.98	Quasi-Money	35
	....	....	....	....	....	....	....	....	.23	.16	.11	1.01	.90	1.20	.30	Bonds	36ab
	40.42	35.03	51.39	55.40	64.19	61.30	115.12	150.10	ⱡ32.31	52.76	57.37	ⱡ60.28	ⱡ47.83	51.85	137.00	Other Items (Net)	37r
	152.99	177.25	201.11	237.16	274.44	307.58	276.62	240.72	ⱡ263.04	278.87	287.94	307.97	241.46	237.31	325.98	Money plus Quasi-Money	35l
Percent Per Annum																**Interest Rates**	
	8.50	8.50	8.50	8.50	8.50	9.00	8.00	8.00	9.50	10.00	11.00	10.75	12.00	11.50	....	Discount Rate (End of Period)	60
	7.50	7.50	7.50	7.50	7.50	7.67	8.00	7.94	8.17	8.75	ⱡ7.50	7.50	7.50	7.75	8.08	Deposit Rate	60l
	12.50	12.50	12.46	13.00	13.00	12.67	11.50	11.13	11.79	12.50	ⱡ18.50	18.15	17.77	17.46	17.42	Lending Rate	60p
Period Averages																**Prices**	
	63.4	69.9	80.2	ⱡ86.7	92.8	100.0	102.3	104.6	109.7	....	....	....	....	....	....	Wholesale Prices (1985=100)	63
	56.8	61.7	ⱡ72.0	79.7	84.3	90.6	96.2	95.3	87.0	92.8	100.0	92.0	91.1	....	....	Consumer Prices	64

Gabon
646

		1965	1966	1967	1968	1969	1970	1971	1972	1973	1974	1975	1976	1977	1978	1979
International Transactions															*Billions of Francs*	
Exports	70	25.91	24.88	29.68	30.80	36.89	39.87	49.43	57.50	73.10	184.36	201.92	271.48	329.96	249.85	393.19
Imports, cif	71	15.43	16.38	16.65	15.93	20.16	22.23	25.31	35.00	42.29	79.89	100.56	120.24	176.00	139.17	113.11
Imports, fob	71.v	13.90	14.76	15.00	14.30	17.44	22.23	23.06	32.15	39.05	69.33	86.76	100.83	149.44	118.68	94.25
Imports, cif, from DOTS	71y	...	...	...	...	...	...	...	...	...	...	...	...	...	...	...
Balance of Payments															*Millions of US Dollars*	
Goods: Exports f.o.b.	78aa d	...	...	...	...	...	...	...	...	...	...	...	...	...	1,308.6	1,815.0
Goods: Imports f.o.b.	78ab d	...	...	...	...	...	...	...	...	...	...	...	...	...	−557.9	−554.8
Trade Balance	78ac d	...	...	...	...	...	...	...	...	...	...	...	...	...	750.7	1,260.2
Services: Credit	78ad d	...	...	...	...	...	...	...	...	...	...	...	...	...	169.9	208.8
Services: Debit	78ae d	...	...	...	...	...	...	...	...	...	...	...	...	...	−577.7	−741.9
Balance on Goods and Services	78af d	...	...	...	...	...	...	...	...	...	...	...	...	...	343.0	727.1
Income: Credit	78ag d	...	...	...	...	...	...	...	...	...	...	...	...	...	4.4	7.3
Income: Debit	78ah d	...	...	...	...	...	...	...	...	...	...	...	...	...	−231.1	−368.8
Balance on Goods, Serv., & Inc.	78ai d	...	...	...	...	...	...	...	...	...	...	...	...	...	116.2	365.6
Current Transfers, n.i.e.: Credit	78aj d	...	...	...	...	...	...	...	...	...	...	...	...	...	57.9	69.8
Current Transfers: Debit	78ak d	...	...	...	...	...	...	...	...	...	...	...	...	...	−100.2	−187.7
Current Account, n.i.e.	78al d	...	...	...	...	...	...	...	...	...	...	...	...	...	73.9	247.6
Capital Account, n.i.e.: Credit	78ba d	...	...	...	...	...	...	...	...	...	...	...	...	...		
Capital Account: Debit	78bb d	...	...	...	...	...	...	...	...	...	...	...	...	...	—	—
Capital Account, n.i.e.	78bc d	...	...	...	...	...	...	...	...	...	...	...	...	...		
Direct Investment Abroad	78bd d	...	...	...	...	...	...	...	...	...	...	...	...	...	—	−6.7
Dir. Invest. in Rep. Econ., n.i.e.	78be d	...	...	...	...	...	...	...	...	...	...	...	...	...	56.5	55.0
Portfolio Investment Assets	78bf d	...	...	...	...	...	...	...	...	...	...	...	...	...		
Portfolio Investment Liab., n.i.e.	78bg d	...	...	...	...	...	...	...	...	...	...	...	...	...	—	—
Other Investment Assets	78bh d	...	...	...	...	...	...	...	...	...	...	...	...	...	−17.8	−177.3
Other Investment Liab., n.i.e.	78bi d	...	...	...	...	...	...	...	...	...	...	...	...	...	−59.2	−105.1
Financial Account, n.i.e.	78bj d	...	...	...	...	...	...	...	...	...	...	...	...	...	−20.4	−234.1
Net Errors and Omissions	78ca d	...	...	...	...	...	...	...	...	...	...	...	...	...	−45.3	−29.9
Overall Balance	78cb d	...	...	...	...	...	...	...	...	...	...	...	...	...	8.2	−16.3
Reserves and Related Items	79da d	...	...	...	...	...	...	...	...	...	...	...	...	...	−8.2	16.3
Reserve Assets	79db d	...	...	...	...	...	...	...	...	...	...	...	...	...	−18.2	6.8
Use of Fund Credit and Loans	79dc d	...	...	...	...	...	...	...	...	...	...	...	...	...	9.8	9.7
Liabs.Constit.For.Auth.Reserves	79dd d	...	...	...	...	...	...	...	...	...	...	...	...	...		
Exceptional Financing	79de d	...	...	...	...	...	...	...	...	...	...	...	...	...	.2	−.2
Government Finance															*Billions of Francs:*	
Deficit (−) or Surplus	80	...	...	...	...	...	...	...	...	−17.6	−15.5	−37.0	ꞵ−158.1	...	...	ꞵ−3.5
Revenue	81	...	...	...	...	...	...	...	...	38.9	89.2	167.4	ꞵ189.1	...	...	ꞵ275.0
Grants Received	81z	...	...	...	...	...	...	...	...	—	—	—	ꞵ—	...	...	ꞵ—
Expenditure	82	...	...	...	...	...	...	...	...	54.9	98.9	195.4	ꞵ340.5	...	...	ꞵ276.9
Lending Minus Repayments	83	...	...	...	...	...	...	...	...	1.6	5.7	9.0	ꞵ6.7	...	...	ꞵ1.6
Financing																
Domestic	84a	...	...	...	...	...	...	...	...	1.7	−5.9	2.8	ꞵ22.8	...	...	...
Foreign	85a	...	...	...	...	...	...	...	...	15.9	21.4	34.2	ꞵ135.3	...	...	...
National Accounts															*Billions of Francs*	
Exports of Goods & Services	90c	26.4	26.9	...	33.2	39.5	44.5	...	79.3	94.8	213.9	229.0	327.8	356.1	333.0	376.9
Government Consumption	91f	8.4	10.6	...	12.9	14.9	17.6	...	19.2	25.1	34.4	56.5	76.0	124.9	73.8	77.9
Gross Capital Formation	93	12.7	16.7	...	22.2	25.4	27.6	...	52.2	60.4	192.4	289.7	528.5	400.8	188.8	211.0
Private Consumption	96f	25.4	27.7	...	32.2	35.3	37.4	...	36.3	73.6	91.8	108.7	118.3	162.1	196.6	213.0
Imports of Goods & Services	98c	−22.1	−25.4	...	−24.6	−30.0	−34.0	...	−78.4	−92.9	−160.4	−221.5	−331.5	−353.9	−253.0	−234.2
Gross Domestic Product	99b	50.8	56.5	58.8	75.9	85.1	93.1	100.8	108.5	161.1	371.7	462.4	719.1	690.2	539.2	644.6
Net Factor Inc/Pmts(−) Abroad	98.n	...	...	...	...	...	...	...	−9.6	−14.5	−27.2	−29.6	−33.8	−38.8	−76.6	−76.9
Gross Nat'l Expenditure = GNP	99a	...	...	...	...	...	...	...	98.9	146.6	344.5	432.8	685.3	651.4	462.6	567.7
Nat'l Income, Market Prices	99e	...	...	...	...	...	...	...	75.0	123.8	298.5	366.3	596.9	557.3	407.0	455.2
															Millions	
Population	99z	.46	.47	.47	.48	ꞵ.94	.95	.96	.97	.98	.99	1.00	1.02	ꞵ1.00	1.02	1.04

Monetary Authorities: ꞵ Beginning in March 1988, the sectorization and classification of accounts have been revised. ꞵ Beginning in September 1991, *Claims on Central Government* include government assumption of certain nonperforming bank loans. ꞵ Beginning in December 1992, the coverage of the banking system has been revised. Claims and deposits of nonactive banks or banks in the process of liquidation have been excluded from the monetary accounts.
Deposit Money Banks: ꞵ Beginning in September 1991, the counterpart of government assumption of certain nonperforming bank loans was reclassified from *Credit from Monetary Authorities* to *Capital Accounts*. ꞵ See note to section 10.
Monetary Survey: ꞵ Beginning in 1965, data for *line 32d* include Treasury claims on the private sector with the contra-entry reported in *line 32an*. ꞵ See notes to sections 10 and 20.

Interest Rates: *Deposit Rate:* ꞵ Beginning in October 1990, minimum rate offered by deposit money banks on savings accounts.
Lending Rate: ꞵ Beginning in October 1990, maximum rate charged by deposit money banks on all loans, excluding charges and fees.
Government Finance: ꞵ Prior to 1976, data cover Treasury accounts and the National Social Security Fund only. Data for 1976 also cover operations of the Autonomous Amortization Fund, which is responsible for most foreign borrowing and related investment expenditures. ꞵ Beginning in 1979, data cover the operations of the Treasury only. ꞵ Beginning in 1989, data are based on a revised budgetary nomenclature.
National Accounts: ꞵ Prior to 1972, data relate to the 1958 SNA.

Gabon

646

	1980	1981	1982	1983	1984	1985	1986	1987	1988	1989	1990	1991	1992	1993	1994		
International Transactions																	
Billions of Francs																	
Exports	459.06	598.00	710.00	762.20	878.90	876.70	440.00	386.60	356.10	509.60	670.80	641.20	616.50	....	....	70
Imports, cif	142.31	228.60	285.00	261.10	316.20	384.00	300.00	219.90	235.70	244.60	210.20	249.46	234.50	236.50	....	71
Imports, fob	118.52	189.98	236.96	215.70	261.12	317.09	247.73	181.59	194.63	201.98	173.58	205.99	193.64	195.29	....	71.v
Imports, cif, from DOTS	....	228.10	262.39	261.24	345.81	429.96	312.01	236.60	276.48	261.33	230.55	305.44	283.71	293.35	507.34	71y
Balance of Payments																	
Minus Sign Indicates Debit																	
Goods: Exports f.o.b.	2,084.4	2,200.2	2,160.4	2,000.1	2,017.8	1,951.4	1,074.2	1,286.4	1,195.6	1,626.0	2,488.8	2,227.9	2,259.2	2,149.7	....	78aa d
Goods: Imports f.o.b.	−686.1	−841.2	−722.6	−725.5	−733.2	−854.7	−979.1	−731.8	−791.2	−751.7	−805.1	−861.0	−886.3	−845.1	....	78ab d
Trade Balance	1,398.3	1,359.0	1,437.8	1,274.6	1,284.6	1,096.7	95.1	554.5	404.3	874.3	1,683.7	1,366.9	1,372.9	1,304.6	....	78ac d
Services: Credit	324.6	307.6	170.3	200.8	137.8	138.5	123.6	114.8	213.0	289.0	241.6	324.0	347.6	318.2	....	78ad d
Services: Debit	−789.4	−868.2	−926.1	−1,031.5	−1,018.5	−1,058.3	−882.7	−752.3	−811.0	−900.8	−1,006.6	−881.6	−924.9	−887.1	....	78ae d
Balance on Goods and Services	933.6	798.4	681.9	444.0	403.9	176.8	−664.0	−83.0	−193.7	262.5	918.7	809.3	795.6	735.6	....	78af d
Income: Credit	24.9	25.2	20.0	43.2	47.7	29.2	18.1	16.0	15.1	19.0	20.1	28.0	47.2	—	....	78ag d
Income: Debit	−450.5	−355.2	−333.3	−299.8	−271.8	−272.8	−264.7	−258.7	−292.7	−347.8	−636.7	−642.7	−868.9	−878.7	....	78ah d
Balance on Goods, Serv., & Inc.	507.9	468.4	368.6	187.4	179.8	−66.8	−910.6	−325.7	−471.2	−66.2	302.0	194.6	−26.1	−143.0	....	78ai d
Current Transfers, n.i.e.: Credit	72.7	61.6	36.8	43.0	50.3	42.0	52.8	57.1	53.8	42.3	59.0	44.0	51.4	49.1	....	78aj d
Current Transfers: Debit	−196.8	−126.7	−96.0	−132.4	−117.4	−137.7	−199.7	−180.5	−198.1	−168.3	−193.3	−163.8	−193.4	−174.8	....	78ak d
Current Account, n.i.e.	383.9	403.3	309.4	97.9	112.7	−162.5	−1,057.5	−449.1	−615.5	−192.2	167.7	74.8	−168.1	−268.8	....	78al d
Capital Account: Credit	—	—	—	—	—	—	—	—	—	—	—	—	—	—	....	78ba d
Capital Account: Debit	—	—	—	—	—	—	—	—	—	—	—	—	—	—	....	78bb d
Capital Account, n.i.e.	—	—	—	—	—	—	—	—	—	—	—	—	—	—	....	78bc d
Direct Investment Abroad	−8.0	−7.1	−4.8	−5.7	−3.4	−4.1	−6.6	−7.7	−9.7	−8.0	−28.8	−14.9	−25.7	−5.7	....	78bd d
Dir. Invest. in Rep. Econ., n.i.e.	31.5	54.6	131.7	111.8	8.1	15.1	110.2	89.8	132.5	−30.5	73.5	−54.6	126.9	97.1	....	78be d
Portfolio Investment Assets	—	—	—	—	—	—	—	—	—	—	—	—	—	—	....	78bf d
Portfolio Investment Liab., n.i.e.	—	—	—	—	—	—	—	—	—	—	—	—	—	—	....	78bg d
Other Investment Assets	−205.6	−239.1	−263.7	−175.7	−237.9	−184.2	−45.5	−113.1	42.1	−278.3	−285.1	−14.2	−27.2	3.2	....	78bh d
Other Investment Liab., n.i.e.	−83.8	−86.0	25.4	−21.9	217.3	337.3	852.7	395.8	551.7	378.0	−126.1	−220.1	−294.7	−241.2	....	78bi d
Financial Account, n.i.e.	−265.9	−277.7	−111.3	−91.5	−15.8	164.2	910.9	364.9	716.6	61.1	−366.5	−303.8	−220.6	−146.6	....	78bj d
Net Errors and Omissions	−22.0	−7.8	−51.4	−95.7	−83.8	−62.6	−48.9	−51.0	−101.9	35.0	−38.0	8.6	−55.1	−5.8	....	78ca d
Overall Balance	95.9	117.8	146.7	−89.3	13.1	−60.9	−195.4	−135.2	−.8	−96.1	−236.8	−220.4	−443.8	−421.2	....	78cb d
Reserves and Related Items	−95.9	−117.8	−146.7	89.3	−13.1	60.9	195.4	135.2	.8	96.1	236.8	220.4	443.8	421.2	....	79da d
Reserve Assets	−91.1	−117.8	−144.5	97.2	−11.2	60.9	99.3	115.6	−55.7	29.8	−219.3	−54.0	246.3	56.5	....	79db d
Use of Fund Credit and Loans	−4.9	—	−2.2	−8.0	−1.9	—	33.1	19.7	74.6	5.0	−5.9	−19.4	−36.3	−35.9	....	79dc d
Liabs.Constit.For.Auth.Reserves	—	—	—	—	—	—	—	—	—	—	−31.8	−2.9	1.9	16.2	....	79dd d
Exceptional Financing	—	—	—	—	—	—	63.0	−.1	−18.1	61.3	493.8	296.7	232.0	384.2	....	79de d
Government Finance																	
Year Ending December 31																	
Deficit (−) or Surplus	55.1	8.2	35.1	−16.3	3.1	1.1	....	....	....	‡−64.2	50.9	−25.2	....	....	....	80
Revenue	350.6	419.4	488.4	505.0	602.0	643.4	....	....	....	‡282.5	373.3	441.7	....	....	....	81
Grants Received	3.2	3.8	—	4.4	4.8	5.0	....	....	....	‡6.0	5.0	6.0	....	....	....	81z
Expenditure	330.3	415.6	451.0	516.3	594.9	637.2	....	....	....	‡351.7	326.7	465.5	....	....	....	82
Lending Minus Repayments	−31.6	−.6	2.3	9.4	8.8	10.1	....	....	....	‡1.0	.7	7.4	....	....	....	83
Financing																	
Domestic	−55.1	−8.1	−35.1	16.1	−2.8	−3.8	....	....	....	‡60.5	−94.0	25.5	....	....	....	84a
Foreign	—	−.1	—	.2	−.3	2.7	....	....	....	‡3.6	43.0	−.3	....	....	....	85a
National Accounts																	
Billions of Francs																	
Exports of Goods & Services	459.0	598.0	710.0	762.2	881.7	876.7	440.0	387.0	....	....	....	....	....	....	....	90c
Government Consumption	....	....	....	....	284.4	306.3	268.0	228.3	....	....	....	....	....	....	....	91f
Gross Capital Formation	....	....	....	....	476.5	596.8	550.3	333.2	....	....	....	....	....	....	....	93
Private Consumption	....	....	....	....	430.6	501.2	550.2	502.5	....	....	....	....	....	....	....	96f
Imports of Goods & Services	−142.3	−229.0	−285.0	−261.2	−320.4	−384.0	−300.0	−220.0	....	....	....	....	....	....	....	98c
Gross Domestic Product	904.5	1,049.0	1,188.9	1,320.0	1,455.6	1,576.0	1,590.0	1,044.0	1,140.9	1,344.4	1,494.5	1,533.1	1,565.2	....	....	99b
Net Factor Inc/Pmts(−) Abroad	....	....	....	....	....	....	....	....	....	....	....	....	....	....	....	98.n
Gross Nat'l Expenditure = GNP	....	....	....	....	....	....	....	....	....	....	....	....	....	....	....	99a
Nat'l Income, Market Prices	....	....	....	....	....	....	....	....	....	....	....	....	....	....	....	99e
Midyear Estimates																	
Population	‡.81	.84	.88	.91	.95	.99	1.02	1.05	1.08	1.11	1.15	1.18	1.21	‡1.01	....	99z

Gambia, The

		1965	1966	1967	1968	1969	1970	1971	1972	1973	1974	1975	1976	1977	1978	1979
Exchange Rates															*Dalasis per SDR:*	
Market Rate	aa	1.784	1.792	2.078	2.097	2.083	2.089	‡2.127	2.312	2.077	2.085	2.314	2.730	2.549	2.561	2.369
															Dalasis per US Dollar:	
Market Rate	ae	1.784	1.792	2.078	2.097	2.083	2.089	‡1.959	2.129	1.722	1.703	1.977	2.350	2.099	1.966	1.799
Market Rate	rf	1.786	1.786	1.835	2.083	2.083	2.083	2.055	2.001	1.702	1.711	1.808	2.226	2.293	2.086	1.888
														Index Numbers (1990=100):		
Market Rate	ah x	439.53	439.06	431.74	376.26	375.73	376.62	384.19	393.26	466.16	459.59	436.55	354.89	342.97	377.15	416.85
Nominal Effective Exchange Rate	ne c	....	....	....	....	....	....	....	....	....	....	....	....	....	....	184.43
Real Effective Exchange Rate	re c	....	....	....	....	....	....	....	....	....	....	....	....	....	....	135.53
Fund Position															*Millions of SDRs:*	
Quota	2f. s	....	....	5.00	5.00	5.00	7.00	7.00	7.00	7.00	7.00	7.00	7.00	7.00	9.00	9.00
SDRs	1b. s	....	....	—	—	—	.84	1.59	2.18	2.10	2.02	2.01	2.00	.86	1.13	.69
Reserve Position in the Fund	1c. s	....	....	.13	.13	.13	.26	.27	.44	.52	.59	1.75	1.74	—	—	—
Total Fund Cred.&Loans Outstg.	2tl	....	....	—	—	—	—	—	—	—	—	—	—	4.26	11.70	10.36
International Liquidity												*Millions of US Dollars Unless Otherwise Indicated:*				
Total Reserves minus Gold	1l. d	7.95	9.45	8.37	6.55	5.99	8.11	10.94	11.38	16.24	28.05	28.55	20.64	24.39	26.07	1.93
SDRs	1b. d	—	—	—	—	—	.84	1.73	2.37	2.53	2.47	2.35	2.32	1.04	1.47	.91
Reserve Position in the Fund	1c. d	....	....	.13	.13	.13	.26	.29	.48	.63	.72	2.05	2.02	—	—	—
Foreign Exchange	1d. d	7.95	9.45	8.24	6.42	5.86	7.01	8.92	8.54	13.08	24.85	24.15	16.29	23.35	24.60	1.02
Other Official Inst. Assets	3b. d	....	....	....	.68	2.28	3.62	7.79	12.39	2.03	.58	.32	.03	.02	.15	.05
Deposit Money Banks: Assets	7a. d	—	—	—	.11	.71	1.73	.18	.94	1.13	3.05	2.42	1.25	2.21	3.13	6.33
Liabilities	7b. d	4.48	3.47	3.33	2.36	1.91	2.01	3.11	—	.57	.72	.08	.37	2.13	2.63	6.63
Monetary Authorities															*Millions of Dalasis:*	
Foreign Assets	11	14.79	17.31	17.43	13.65	12.49	16.90	21.00	21.87	27.96	47.77	56.44	48.47	51.18	51.27	12.39
Claims on Central Government	12a	1.76	.76	.23	.73	.30	.03	.01	−.71	−1.08	.68	−2.34	3.64	20.59	16.96	41.92
Claims on Official Entities	12bx	....	....	....	....	....	....	....	....	....	....	....	....	....	3.09	3.09
Claims on Deposit Money Banks	12e	—	—	1.00	4.50	7.50	7.68	5.88	7.00	23.56	24.71	29.90	32.55	11.81	33.62	46.95
Reserve Money	14	8.72	9.54	9.84	11.47	11.99	14.28	14.94	16.26	48.33	69.44	82.25	68.96	58.96	‡42.72	50.40
of which: Currency Outside DMBs	14a	8.46	8.72	8.92	9.35	10.19	12.12	12.73	14.94	25.21	24.06	27.15	32.08	19.79	34.53	36.53
Restricted Deposits	16b	—	—	—	—	—	—	—	—	20.38	41.82	52.39	33.34	29.34	12.77	.02
Foreign Liabilities	16c	—	—	—	—	—	—	—	—	—	—	—	.63	20.37	53.08	38.30
Central Government Deposits	16d	7.62	7.96	8.31	6.55	6.78	8.63	9.66	8.10	2.78	3.28	5.55	13.06	9.21	‡3.51	2.26
Capital Accounts	17a	.01	.01	.27	.52	.75	2.75	4.56	6.11	6.11	6.11	6.77	10.88	10.94	12.21	13.73
Other Items (Net)	17r	.20	.56	.51	.62	1.03	−.49	−1.60	−1.35	−5.66	−4.39	−6.48	−4.03	−6.90	−.30	−1.37
of which: Valuation Adjustment	17rv	....	....	....	....	....	....	....	....	−7.18	−7.18	−6.62	−4.90	−7.19	4.15	1.82
Deposit Money Banks															*Millions of Dalasis:*	
Reserves	20	.26	.82	.92	2.12	1.80	2.05	2.05	1.30	2.78	2.77	2.66	3.43	8.31	7.16	5.56
Foreign Assets	21	—	—	.01	.22	1.48	3.60	.35	1.81	1.95	5.20	4.79	2.93	4.63	6.16	11.39
Claims on Central Government	22a	—	—	—	—	—	—	—	.50	—	.75	.75	3.50	5.40	12.18	4.75
Claims on Official Entities	22bx	—	—	—	—	—	—	—	—	3.97	12.20	14.80	25.25	13.68	13.08	27.77
Claims on Private Sector	22d	12.23	12.76	14.26	15.28	16.21	15.22	15.37	12.50	20.94	24.08	22.96	39.12	53.74	75.40	83.06
Demand Deposits	24	2.38	4.04	3.78	4.31	3.89	4.33	3.63	7.84	6.59	8.97	10.19	17.34	20.01	‡22.93	20.06
Time and Savings Deposits	25	1.68	1.40	2.12	2.37	2.67	2.91	3.08	4.29	6.62	9.21	10.56	20.49	21.65	31.90	24.41
Restricted Deposits	26b	....	....	....	....	....	....	....	....	....	....	....	....	....	....	....
Foreign Liabilities	26c	8.00	6.19	6.94	4.91	3.97	4.19	5.96	—	.98	1.22	.16	.86	4.46	5.18	11.93
Credit from Monetary Authorities	26g	—	—	1.00	4.50	7.50	7.68	5.88	7.00	23.56	23.22	29.90	32.55	17.86	33.12	46.96
Capital Accounts	27a	—	—	—	.06	.06	.98	.98	1.26	1.41	1.85	4.39	8.41	12.03	16.60	19.26
Other Items (Net)	27r	.44	1.93	1.36	1.47	1.44	.77	−1.78	−.28	−1.33	3.12	1.20	3.87	9.75	4.25	9.93
Monetary Survey															*Millions of Dalasis:*	
Foreign Assets (Net)	31n	6.79	11.12	10.50	8.96	10.00	16.31	15.39	23.68	28.93	51.75	61.07	49.91	30.98	−.82	−26.44
Domestic Credit	32	5.99	4.49	4.46	7.12	7.98	8.20	10.83	12.05	30.36	38.26	45.12	72.50	84.20	‡117.41	158.68
Claims on Central Govt. (Net)	32an	−6.24	−8.27	−9.80	−8.16	−8.23	−9.65	−9.09	−7.39	−2.78	−.62	−3.09	−1.17	16.78	25.54	44.32
Claims on Official Entities	32bx	—	—	—	—	—	2.63	4.55	6.94	12.20	14.80	25.25	34.55	13.68	16.17	30.86
Claims on Private Sector	32d	12.23	12.76	14.26	15.28	16.21	17.85	19.92	15.47	20.94	24.08	22.96	39.12	53.74	75.70	83.50
Money	34	10.84	12.76	12.70	13.66	14.08	16.45	16.36	22.78	31.80	33.03	37.34	49.42	39.80	‡57.78	57.78
Quasi-Money	35	1.68	1.40	2.12	2.37	2.67	2.91	3.08	4.29	6.62	9.21	10.56	20.49	21.65	31.90	24.41
Restricted Deposits	36b	....	....	....	....	....	....	....	....	....	....	....	....	....	....	....
Other Items (Net)	37r	.27	1.43	.15	.06	1.26	5.13	6.76	8.70	.44	5.94	5.88	19.13	31.83	33.18	49.03
Money plus Quasi-Money	35l	12.52	14.16	14.82	16.03	16.75	19.36	19.44	27.07	38.42	42.24	47.90	69.91	61.45	‡89.68	82.19
Other Banking Institutions															*Millions of Dalasis:*	
Deposits	45	1.10	1.10	1.10	1.07	1.09	1.06	.96	1.03	.83	.79	.97	1.16	1.34	1.09	1.19
Liquid Liabilities	55l	13.62	15.26	15.92	17.10	17.84	20.42	20.40	28.10	39.25	43.03	48.87	71.07	62.79	‡90.77	83.38
Interest Rates															*Percent Per Annum*	
Discount Rate (End of Period)	60	....	....	....	....	....	....	....	....	....	....	6.00	6.00	6.00	6.00	6.00
Deposit Rate	60l	....	....	....	....	....	....	....	....	....	....	....	....	....	5.00	5.00
Lending Rate	60p	....	....	....	....	....	....	....	....	....	....	....	....	....	15.00	15.00
Prices															*Index Numbers (1990=100):*	
Consumer Prices	64	7.0	7.0	7.1	7.4	7.7	7.6	7.8	8.5	9.1	‡9.9	12.5	14.6	16.4	17.9	19.0

Gambia, The
648

1980	1981	1982	1983	1984	1985	1986	1987	1988	1989	1990	1991	1992	1993	1994		
End of Period															**Exchange Rates**	
2.139	2.440	2.733	2.887	4.238	3.802	9.084	9.134	8.961	10.928	10.662	12.813	12.673	13.096	13.983	Market Rate............	**aa**
End of Period (ae)		*Period Average (rf)*														
1.677	2.096	2.478	2.757	4.323	3.461	7.426	6.439	6.659	8.315	7.495	8.957	9.217	9.535	9.579	Market Rate............	**ae**
1.721	1.990	2.290	2.639	3.584	3.894	6.938	7.074	6.709	7.585	7.883	8.803	8.888	9.129	9.576	Market Rate............	**rf**
Period Averages																
457.08	398.45	343.95	298.07	224.15	203.77	115.09	111.24	117.40	104.18	100.00	90.03	88.20	86.16	82.04	Market Rate............	**ah** x
203.01	207.55	209.90	210.61	183.65	185.70	92.72	83.83	91.28	95.86	100.00	97.86	103.65	117.29	125.51	Nominal Effective Exchange Rate...........	**ne** c
137.32	131.31	132.06	132.85	125.81	134.88	96.98	102.37	110.74	106.61	100.00	94.71	98.63	105.72	99.54	Real Effective Exchange Rate................	**re** c
End of Period															**Fund Position**	
13.50	13.50	13.50	17.10	17.10	17.10	17.10	17.10	17.10	17.10	17.10	17.10	22.90	22.90	22.90	Quota............	**2f.** s
—	.05	.12	.12	—	—	.59	3.24	.96	1.03	1.24	.54	.45	.23	.18	SDRs............	**1b.** s
—	—	.04	.04	.04	.04	.05	.05	.05	.05	.05	.03	.03	1.48	1.49	1.48 Reserve Position in the Fund................	**1c.** s
12.67	21.70	36.35	33.52	33.65	30.36	24.13	26.65	25.69	28.67	31.55	30.61	28.39	26.68	23.94	Total Fund Cred.&Loans Outstg.............	**2tl**
End of Period															**International Liquidity**	
5.67	3.95	8.39	2.92	2.26	1.73	13.56	25.76	19.05	20.59	55.39	67.62	94.03	....	98.02	Total Reserves minus Gold.................	**1l.** d
—	.06	.13	.13	—	—	.72	4.60	1.29	1.35	1.76	.77	.62	.31	.26	SDRs............	**1b.** d
—	—	.04	.04	.04	.04	.06	.07	.07	.07	.04	.04	2.04	2.04	2.17	Reserve Position in the Fund................	**1c.** d
5.67	3.89	8.21	2.75	2.22	1.69	12.78	21.09	17.69	19.17	53.58	66.80	91.38	....	95.59	Foreign Exchange............	**1d.** d
—	—	....	....	....	....	....	....	....	....	....	....	....	....	....	Other Official Inst. Assets................	**3b.** d
9.96	7.82	3.77	2.07	5.18	5.37	3.66	5.10	4.59	2.86	4.50	4.33	12.47	2.81	3.59	Deposit Money Banks: Assets................	**7a.** d
20.87	17.55	12.82	10.47	1.33	3.64	1.77	1.43	1.30	1.24	.37	.24	1.35	4.05	3.03	Liabilities............	**7b.** d
End of Period															**Monetary Authorities**	
9.53	8.27	23.19	8.04	15.37	10.66	102.57	134.66	187.06	228.92	397.70	582.84	861.03	1,008.27	935.76	Foreign Assets............	**11**
15.02	60.01	33.85	79.96	95.54	142.15	23.79	21.61	35.16	.89	29.99	21.60	258.76	270.72	297.93	Claims on Central Government................	**12a**
9.09	21.34	39.33	76.16	94.12	113.39	109.00	46.85	43.73	22.73	—	—	—	—	—	Claims on Official Entities................	**12bx**
86.41	138.41	129.61	132.18	131.81	154.64	151.71	84.11	86.05	50.20	50.08	51.27	—	—	—	Claims on Deposit Money Banks.............	**12e**
55.80	76.20	89.59	120.80	I57.35	103.57	101.63	121.21	150.55	192.35	204.62	278.28	287.44	319.64	307.08	Reserve Money............	**14**
36.76	42.62	55.92	57.18	58.38	85.67	91.18	95.02	111.99	134.78	152.17	182.28	207.08	224.49	207.36	of which: Currency Outside DMBs..........	**14a**
.29	—	—	.80	I78.60	124.24	110.97	97.06	81.81	32.38	14.67	14.67	—	—	—	Restricted Deposits............	**16b**
40.36	91.38	193.14	228.85	343.78	354.69	566.12	497.07	430.23	447.21	441.76	524.08	444.71	394.68	341.87	Foreign Liabilities............	**16c**
4.13	28.55	4.86	17.25	I13.67	26.83	112.74	165.69	189.20	181.63	361.69	475.00	383.29	553.08	597.69	Central Government Deposits................	**16d**
13.11	16.94	18.90	23.28	30.67	29.40	55.52	56.78	56.65	65.96	68.01	65.91	71.12	73.70	75.50	Capital Accounts............	**17a**
3.62	4.86	-10.07	-31.84	I -187.48	-219.83	-564.63	-658.24	-556.26	-616.77	-612.98	-701.93	-66.77	-62.12	-88.46	Other Items (Net)............	**17r**
9.49	5.48	-4.06	-21.49	-93.30	-72.55	-398.89	-450.87	-459.31	-532.64	-322.93	-482.57	250.32	199.13	217.01	of which: Valuation Adjustment..........	**17rv**
End of Period															**Deposit Money Banks**	
21.17	35.16	43.17	61.01	-1.78	14.71	14.04	23.52	20.87	55.97	38.03	98.21	83.15	97.28	97.09	Reserves............	**20**
16.70	16.39	9.34	5.72	22.41	18.59	27.21	32.86	30.55	23.81	33.73	38.83	114.93	26.80	34.41	Foreign Assets............	**21**
14.54	3.75	17.37	26.39	35.61	37.26	57.41	71.78	83.06	127.39	134.29	132.80	168.52	135.74	100.50	Claims on Central Government................	**22a**
62.12	73.75	101.53	65.06	60.14	51.74	95.78	48.42	61.44	13.55	11.91	12.45	1.54	3.81	.10	Claims on Official Entities................	**22bx**
98.46	104.44	102.91	137.59	158.17	212.37	192.34	184.14	208.53	231.31	265.45	300.52	222.85	361.90	385.44	Claims on Private Sector............	**22d**
23.95	33.50	30.34	41.43	40.45	74.98	73.14	100.32	97.86	120.03	137.90	211.30	228.09	236.89	200.17	Demand Deposits............	**24**
29.42	32.69	39.80	60.64	70.20	94.85	109.15	145.70	180.67	215.93	219.90	255.16	303.15	371.17	393.49	Time and Savings Deposits................	**25**
....	....	....	....	60.70	55.79	30.11	27.58	25.97	—	—	—	—	—	—	Restricted Deposits............	**26b**
35.01	36.79	31.76	28.87	I5.77	12.61	13.11	9.19	8.69	10.33	2.74	2.19	12.47	38.65	28.98	Foreign Liabilities............	**26c**
86.16	101.28	130.78	131.64	128.81	149.73	140.94	85.30	84.80	57.78	53.18	53.18	—	—	—	Credit from Monetary Authorities...........	**26g**
22.84	25.61	30.34	21.07	20.24	15.10	36.67	51.75	49.57	55.37	108.42	111.41	49.71	68.77	72.28	Capital Accounts............	**27a**
15.61	3.62	11.30	12.12	I -51.62	-68.39	-16.34	-59.12	-43.11	-7.41	-39.14	-50.37	-2.43	-88.48	-77.38	Other Items (Net)............	**27r**
End of Period															**Monetary Survey**	
-49.14	-103.51	-192.38	-243.96	I -311.77	-338.05	-449.44	-338.74	-221.13	-204.80	-13.07	95.40	518.78	601.74	599.31	Foreign Assets (Net)............	**31n**
195.59	235.52	291.41	369.22	I428.29	527.56	363.21	205.70	241.64	216.32	85.14	-.12	278.39	230.15	199.34	Domestic Credit............	**32**
25.34	35.12	46.27	89.01	I 114.38	148.49	-35.59	-76.35	-75.03	-57.40	-201.40	-324.65	40.03	-150.58	-203.22	Claims on Central Govt. (Net)..........	**32an**
71.21	95.09	140.86	141.22	154.26	165.13	204.78	95.27	105.17	36.28	11.91	12.45	1.54	3.81	.10	Claims on Official Entities................	**32bx**
99.04	105.31	104.28	138.99	159.65	213.94	194.02	186.78	211.50	237.44	274.63	312.08	236.82	376.92	402.46	Claims on Private Sector................	**32d**
61.28	76.97	87.22	100.32	99.58	162.10	166.49	197.83	213.62	260.25	296.19	393.58	435.17	461.38	407.53	Money............	**34**
29.42	32.69	39.80	60.64	70.20	94.85	109.15	145.70	180.67	215.93	219.90	255.16	303.15	371.17	393.49	Quasi-Money............	**35**
....	....	....	....	17.91	68.45	80.86	69.48	55.84	32.38	14.67	14.67	—	—	—	Restricted Deposits............	**36b**
52.72	40.18	42.46	26.30	I -71.41	-137.83	-447.46	-553.71	-429.52	-497.03	-459.10	-567.77	58.85	.80	-2.37	Other Items (Net)............	**37r**
90.70	109.66	127.02	160.96	169.78	256.95	275.64	343.53	394.19	476.18	516.09	648.74	738.32	832.55	801.02	Money plus Quasi-Money................	**35l**
End of Period															**Other Banking Institutions**	
1.11	1.04	1.04[e]	.88	.80	.72	1.22	.99	1.22	1.03	.93	....	....	....	....	Deposits............	**45**
91.81	110.70	128.06	161.84	170.58	257.67	276.86	344.52	395.41	477.21	517.02	....	....	....	....	Liquid Liabilities............	**55l**
Percent Per Annum															**Interest Rates**	
8.00	9.50	9.50	9.50	9.50	15.00	20.00	21.00	19.00	15.00	16.50	15.50	17.50	13.50	13.50	Discount Rate *(End of Period)*............	**60**
5.00	8.50	8.50	8.50	9.00	9.75	16.13	15.75	15.00	12.92	11.33	12.71	13.83	13.00	12.58	Deposit Rate............	**60l**
15.00	18.00	18.00	18.00	18.00	14.48	28.00	27.92	29.54	28.00	26.50	26.50	26.75	26.08	25.00	Lending Rate............	**60p**
Period Averages															**Prices**	
20.3	21.5	23.8	26.4	32.2	38.1	59.6	73.7	82.3	89.1	100.0	108.6	118.9	126.6	128.7	Consumer Prices............	**64**

Gambia, The

		1965	1966	1967	1968	1969	1970	1971	1972	1973	1974	1975	1976	1977	1978	1979
International Transactions															\multicolumn{2}{r}{*Millions of Dalasis*}	
Exports	70	24.42	28.40	31.92	26.86	34.35	35.12	27.70	37.38	39.98	72.21	77.00	74.67	110.19	82.91	109.82
Imports, cif	71	28.99	32.50	34.97	43.90	40.66	37.43	43.79	49.53	53.39	79.54	108.12	164.32	177.71	209.78	266.31
Imports, fob	71.v	27.35	30.66	32.99	41.42	38.36	35.30	41.30	45.64	48.10	66.47	92.59	140.80	152.28	179.78	228.22
Balance of Payments															*Millions of US Dollars: F.Y. Ending*	
Goods: Exports f.o.b.	78aa d	....	....	....	....	....	....	....	....	....	....	....	....	....	40.08	53.75
Goods: Imports f.o.b.	78ab d	....	....	....	....	....	....	....	....	....	....	....	....	....	−81.00	−94.74
Trade Balance	78ac d	....	....	....	....	....	....	....	....	....	....	....	....	....	−40.92	−40.99
Services: Credit	78ad d	....	....	....	....	....	....	....	....	....	....	....	....	....	13.27	22.51
Services: Debit	78ae d	....	....	....	....	....	....	....	....	....	....	....	....	....	−26.15	−37.27
Balance on Goods and Services	78af d	....	....	....	....	....	....	....	....	....	....	....	....	....	−53.80	−55.75
Income: Credit	78ag d	....	....	....	....	....	....	....	....	....	....	....	....	....	1.93	1.92
Income: Debit	78ah d	....	....	....	....	....	....	....	....	....	....	....	....	....	−4.68	−4.42
Balance on Goods, Serv., & Inc.	78ai d	....	....	....	....	....	....	....	....	....	....	....	....	....	−56.55	−58.25
Current Transfers, n.i.e.: Credit	78aj d	....	....	....	....	....	....	....	....	....	....	....	....	....	13.40	25.82
Current Transfers: Debit	78ak d	....	....	....	....	....	....	....	....	....	....	....	....	....	−1.57	−2.58
Current Account, n.i.e.	78al d	....	....	....	....	....	....	....	....	....	....	....	....	....	−44.72	−35.00
Capital Account, n.i.e.: Credit	78ba d	....	....	....	....	....	....	....	....	....	....	....	....	....	.33	.47
Capital Account: Debit	78bb d	....	....	....	....	....	....	....	....	....	....	....	....	....	−.25	−.24
Capital Account, n.i.e.	78bc d	....	....	....	....	....	....	....	....	....	....	....	....	....	.08	.23
Direct Investment Abroad	78bd d	....	....	....	....	....	....	....	....	....	....	....	....	....	—	—
Dir. Invest. in Rep. Econ., n.i.e.	78be d	....	....	....	....	....	....	....	....	....	....	....	....	....	2.00	11.68
Portfolio Investment Assets	78bf d	....	....	....	....	....	....	....	....	....	....	....	....	....	—	—
Portfolio Investment Liab., n.i.e.	78bg d	....	....	....	....	....	....	....	....	....	....	....	....	....	—	—
Other Investment Assets	78bh d	....	....	....	....	....	....	....	....	....	....	....	....	....	2.54	.68
Other Investment Liab., n.i.e.	78bi d	....	....	....	....	....	....	....	....	....	....	....	....	....	7.55	8.16
Financial Account, n.i.e.	78bj d	....	....	....	....	....	....	....	....	....	....	....	....	....	12.10	20.52
Net Errors and Omissions	78ca d	....	....	....	....	....	....	....	....	....	....	....	....	....	15.78	−5.33
Overall Balance	78cb d	....	....	....	....	....	....	....	....	....	....	....	....	....	−16.77	−19.58
Reserves and Related Items	79da d	....	....	....	....	....	....	....	....	....	....	....	....	....	16.77	19.58
Reserve Assets	79db d	....	....	....	....	....	....	....	....	....	....	....	....	....	12.23	14.47
Use of Fund Credit and Loans	79dc d	....	....	....	....	....	....	....	....	....	....	....	....	....	2.41	3.47
Liabs.Constit.For.Auth.Reserves	79dd d	....	....	....	....	....	....	....	....	....	....	....	....	....	—	—
Exceptional Financing	79de d	....	....	....	....	....	....	....	....	....	....	....	....	....	2.13	1.64
Government Finance															*Millions of Dalasis:*	
Deficit (−) or Surplus	80	....	2.54	−.07	−5.32	−2.75	−1.41	−1.00	⊺−4.58	.30	−2.79	−6.61	−6.65	−26.49	−35.85	−38.42
Revenue	81	....	13.86	16.34	15.16	19.48	17.47	26.70	⊺22.70	22.80	26.91	32.28	45.61	64.59	83.03	75.40
Grants Received	81z	....	7.16	2.27	.48	.10	.08	—	⊺—	.09	.04	2.76	1.89	—	19.74	13.46
Expenditure	82	....	17.97	18.74	20.92	20.63	20.81	27.57	⊺27.12	22.43	28.87	40.81	51.21	85.86	130.68	115.68
Lending Minus Repayments	83	....	.51	−.06	.04	1.70	−1.85	.13	.16	.16	.87	.84	2.94	5.22	7.94	11.60
Financing																
Domestic	84a	....	.13	−.03	.17	−3.89	−1.08	1.40	⊺1.17	−3.86	.12	1.35	1.39	20.48	8.47	18.41
Foreign	85a	....	−2.67	.09	5.15	6.64	2.50	−.39	⊺3.41	3.56	2.67	5.26	5.26	6.01	27.38	20.01
Debt: Domestic	88a	....	....	....	....	....	....	....	....	3.46	4.21	10.73	11.21	12.50	33.48	57.01
Foreign	89a	....	....	....	....	....	....	....	....	13.19	16.95	21.59	26.54	33.62	69.51	82.04
National Accounts															*Millions of Dalasis:*	
Gross Domestic Product	99b	62.7	69.7	76.7	61.9	77.4	81.9	81.4	108.8	109.8	158.4	221.2	278.3	355.1	360.7	425.0
Gross Dom. Prod. 1990 Prices	99b.p	....	....	....	....	....	910.2	1,052.5	1,129.2	1,180.3	1,816.0	1,741.5	1,856.0	1,722.6	1,822.7	1,655.9
GDP Deflator (1990=100)	99bi p	....	....	....	....	....	9.0	7.7	9.6	9.3	8.7	12.7	15.0	20.6	19.8	25.7
															Millions:	
Population	99z	.38	.40	.42	⊺.44	.45	.46	.48	.49	.49	.51	.52	.54	.55	.57	.58

Exchange Rates: On July 1, 1971 the dalasi, equal to one fifth the Gambian pound, was introduced.

Monetary Authorities: ⊺ Beginning in December 1978, revisions reflect improvement in the sector classification of domestic accounts. ⊺ Beginning in January 1984, domestic currency deposits made by the government in lieu of external debt service payments (i.e., special accounts) have been placed in *line 16b*, with a contra-entry in *line 16c*. From the same date, deposit money bank deposits with the central bank, arising from the receipt from the customers of domestic currency payments on account of external debt service (i.e., commercial arrears), have been treated similarly. In addition, *line 16b* includes the contra-entry of The Gambia Produce Marketing Board export proceeds, because access to that account is limited.

Deposit Money Banks: ⊺ See note to section 10. ⊺ Beginning in January 1984, a contra-entry to domestic currency payments received from customers to meet external debt service obligations (i.e., commercial arrears) is shown in *line 26b*.

Monetary Survey: ⊺ See note to section 10.

Government Finance: ⊺ Beginning in 1972, data are as reported in the *Government Finance Statistics Yearbook* and cover budgetary central government. ⊺ Beginning in 1990, data also cover all extrabudgetary and social security funds. Data relate to a fiscal year different from calendar year.

Gambia, The

648

	1980	1981	1982	1983	1984	1985	1986	1987	1988	1989	1990	1991	1992	1993	1994		
Millions of Dalasis																**International Transactions**	
	54.26	51.46	98.53	126.90	162.57	172.92	235.73	281.39	388.72	198.05	316.68	364.81	591.39	....	337.79	Exports	70
	285.40	246.76	235.63	304.60	354.16	362.27	733.39	897.24	919.36	1,221.01	1,573.90	1,932.74	2,072.18	....	2,002.89	Imports, cif	71
	244.59	211.47	201.91	261.01	303.48	310.43	628.44	768.84	787.79	1,046.28	1,348.67	1,656.16	1,775.64	....	1,716.27	Imports, fob	71.v
June 30: Minus Sign Indicates Debit																**Balance of Payments**	
	48.29	45.13	58.56	54.55	90.73	62.79	64.87	74.51	83.06	100.20	110.62	142.87	146.95	....	....	Goods: Exports f.o.b.	78aa *d*
	−137.69	−128.69	−94.41	−89.70	−99.43	−74.84	−84.57	−94.95	−105.92	−125.35	−140.51	−185.00	−177.76	....	....	Goods: Imports f.o.b.	78ab *d*
	−89.40	−83.57	−35.85	−35.15	−8.71	−12.05	−19.70	−20.43	−22.86	−25.16	−29.88	−42.13	−30.81	....	....	Trade Balance	78ac *d*
	17.96	20.16	24.32	27.19	27.73	24.42	28.69	49.37	62.21	65.73	69.78	80.53	80.86	....	....	Services: Credit	78ad *d*
	−41.56	−41.59	−36.17	−29.92	−25.88	−19.30	−21.48	−44.32	−48.17	−50.60	−51.83	−72.23	−66.93	....	....	Services: Debit	78ae *d*
	−113.00	−105.00	−47.70	−37.88	−6.86	−6.92	−12.49	−15.38	−8.83	−10.03	−11.93	−33.83	−16.89	....	....	Balance on Goods and Services	78af *d*
	—	—	.96	.22	—	—	—	.81	1.44	2.01	1.59	3.78	4.85	....	....	Income: Credit	78ag *d*
	−2.20	−2.72	−11.41	−17.66	−.01	−.05	−.86	−17.60	−13.24	−15.81	−13.04	−11.30	−7.31	....	....	Income: Debit	78ah *d*
	−115.21	−107.72	−58.15	−55.32	−6.86	−6.96	−13.35	−32.17	−20.62	−23.84	−23.38	−41.35	−19.35	....	....	Balance on Goods, Serv., & Inc.	78ai *d*
	29.09	60.79	39.01	24.53	16.12	14.87	18.57	42.85	54.45	46.36	59.98	58.58	60.51	....	....	Current Transfers, n.i.e.: Credit	78aj *d*
	−.81	−2.58	−3.40	−2.73	−1.19	−.61	−.93	−4.56	−7.33	−7.51	−2.67	−4.08	−4.00	....	....	Current Transfers: Debit	78ak *d*
	−86.93	−49.51	−22.54	−33.53	8.07	7.29	4.29	6.13	26.50	15.02	33.93	13.15	37.16	....	....	Current Account, n.i.e.	78al *d*
	—	—	.20	.75	—	—	—	—	—	—	—	—	—	....	....	Capital Account, n.i.e.: Credit	78ba *d*
	—	—	−.12	−.20	—	—	—	—	—	—	—	—	—	....	....	Capital Account: Debit	78bb *d*
	—	—	.07	.54	—	—	—	—	—	—	—	—	—	....	....	Capital Account, n.i.e.	78bc *d*
	—	—	—	—	—	—	—	—	—	—	—	—	—	....	....	Direct Investment Abroad	78bd *d*
	—	2.28	—	—	—	—	—	1.48	1.17	14.79	—	10.20	6.16	....	....	Dir. Invest. in Rep. Econ., n.i.e.	78be *d*
	—	—	—	—	—	—	—	—	—	—	—	—	—	....	....	Portfolio Investment Assets	78bf *d*
	—	—	—	—	—	—	—	—	—	—	—	—	—	....	....	Portfolio Investment Liab., n.i.e.	78bg *d*
	−6.19	3.35	−7.63	5.06	2.22	−6.53	4.26	−1.57	1.63	−2.42	−1.04	−.60	−1.52	....	....	Other Investment Assets	78bh *d*
	4.16	36.40	18.31	−10.19	−23.68	2.63	−13.60	−.51	6.83	−2.89	−5.05	11.17	14.07	....	....	Other Investment Liab., n.i.e.	78bi *d*
	−2.03	42.04	10.69	−5.13	−21.47	−3.90	−9.34	−.60	9.63	9.48	−6.09	20.76	18.71	....	....	Financial Account, n.i.e.	78bj *d*
	53.39	2.46	−17.52	15.79	−6.52	−9.15	−26.72	5.48	−11.29	−20.84	−24.01	−16.66	−36.65	....	....	Net Errors and Omissions	78ca *d*
	−35.57	−5.02	−29.30	−22.32	−19.92	−5.76	−31.77	11.00	24.83	3.65	3.83	17.26	19.22	....	....	Overall Balance	78cb *d*
	35.57	5.02	29.30	22.32	19.92	5.76	31.77	−11.00	−24.83	−3.65	−3.83	−17.26	−19.22	....	....	Reserves and Related Items	79da *d*
	4.12	−19.11	16.62	1.91	−2.71	3.69	.14	−11.61	−30.07	3.91	−2.86	−25.64	−35.34	....	....	Reserve Assets	79db *d*
	6.79	9.46	7.84	6.84	.36	−5.08	−3.06	−5.82	2.39	3.52	4.13	−1.76	.28	....	....	Use of Fund Credit and Loans	79dc *d*
	—	—	—	—	—	—	—	—	—	—	—	—	—	....	....	Liabs.Constit.For.Auth.Reserves	79dd *d*
	24.66	14.67	4.83	13.57	22.27	7.15	34.69	6.43	2.85	−11.08	−5.10	10.14	15.84	....	....	Exceptional Financing	79de *d*
Year Ending June 30																**Government Finance**	
	−18.32	−50.10	−33.86	....	....	....	....	....	....	....	‡−19.30	....	....	....	....	Deficit (-) or Surplus	80
	95.78	76.52	87.05	103.10	122.97	146.04	203.67	....	....	....	‡486.17	....	....	....	....	Revenue	81
	13.27	20.90	48.02	....	....	....	14.46	23.97	....	....	‡155.79	....	....	....	....	Grants Received	81z
	131.56	143.68	159.48	....	....	....	....	....	....	....	‡589.60	....	....	....	....	Expenditure	82
	−4.19	3.84	9.45	....	16.74	1.17	47.08	....	....	....	‡71.66	....	....	....	....	Lending Minus Repayments	83
																Financing	
	13.44	14.09	−1.80	....	....	....	....	....	....	....	‡−53.52	....	....	....	....	Domestic	84a
	4.88	36.01	35.66	....	....	....	....	....	....	....	‡72.82	....	....	....	....	Foreign	85a
	69.61	78.10	73.69	....	....	....	....	....	....	197.59	‡273.32	....	....	....	....	Debt: Domestic	88a
	92.00	111.03	144.80	....	....	....	....	....	....	....	....	....	....	....	....	Foreign	89a
Year Ending June 30																**National Accounts**	
	411.6	451.4	522.1	599.4	748.5	869.6	1,085.2	1,486.0	1,635.5	1,942.3	2,366.4	2,629.6	2,947.6	....	....	Gross Domestic Product	99b
	‡1,600.4	1,528.1	1,645.1	1,527.3	1,523.8	1,610.1	1,696.8	2,033.6	2,170.5	2,293.3	2,366.4	2,460.9	2,226.0	....	....	Gross Dom. Prod. 1990 Prices	99b. *p*
	25.7	29.5	31.7	39.2	49.1	54.0	64.0	73.1	75.4	84.7	100.0	106.9	132.4	....	....	GDP Deflator (1990=100)	99bi *p*
Midyear Estimates																	
	.60	.62	.64	.70	.72	.74	.77	.81	.85	.88	.92	.96	.88	‡1.03	....	Population	99z

Germany
134

		1965	1966	1967	1968	1969	1970	1971	1972	1973	1974	1975	1976	1977	1978	1979
Exchange Rates																*Deutsche Mark per SDR:*
Market Rate	aa	4.0056	3.9773	3.9990	3.9995	3.6899	3.6480	3.5486	3.4759	3.2608	2.9501	3.0698	2.7448	2.5570	2.3815	2.2810
																Deutsche Mark per US Dollar:
Market Rate	ae	4.0056	3.9773	3.9990	3.9995	3.6899	3.6480	3.2685	3.2015	2.7030	2.4095	2.6223	2.3625	2.1050	1.8280	1.7315
Market Rate	rf	4.0000	4.0000	4.0000	4.0000	3.9433	3.6600	3.5074	3.1886	2.6726	2.5878	2.4603	2.5180	2.3222	2.0086	1.8329
																Deutsche Mark per ECU:
ECU Rate	ea	....	....	....	....	....	....	....	....	....	....	....	....	....	....	2.4906
ECU Rate	eb	....	....	....	....	....	....	....	....	....	....	....	2.8165	2.6485	2.5557	2.5108
																Index Numbers (1990=100):
Market Rate	ah x	40.4	40.3	40.4	40.4	41.1	44.2	83.5	50.5	60.8	62.3	65.7	64.1	69.5	80.4	88.0
Nominal Effective Exchange Rate	ne u	42.9	42.9	43.1	44.3	45.3	49.3	50.7	51.9	57.4	60.7	61.6	66.1	71.6	75.5	80.1
Real Effective Exchange Rate	re u	....	....	....	....	....	....	....	....	....	....	80.1	81.1	85.3	87.3	88.1
Fund Position																*Millions of SDRs:*
Quota	2f. s	788	1,200	1,200	1,200	1,200	1,600	1,600	1,600	1,600	1,600	1,600	1,600	1,600	2,156	2,156
SDRs	1b. s	—	—	—	—	—	258	454	822	1,388	1,440	1,451	1,747	1,177	1,379	1,576
Reserve Position in the Fund	1c. s	1,076	1,257	1,052	1,515	302	917	1,078	1,140	1,207	1,290	1,581	2,133	2,185	3,302	2,372
of which: Outstg.Fund Borrowing	2c	348	348	168	521	—	—	—	—	—	—	150	600	1,031	1,278	948
International Liquidity												*Millions of US Dollars Unless Otherwise Indicated:*				
Total Reserves minus Gold	1l. d	3,020	3,737	3,925	5,409	3,050	9,630	14,231	19,326	28,206	27,359	26,216	30,019	34,708	48,474	52,549
SDRs	1b. d	—	—	—	—	—	258	493	893	1,674	1,763	1,698	2,030	1,429	1,796	2,076
Reserve Position in the Fund	1c. d	1,076	1,257	1,052	1,515	302	917	1,171	1,238	1,456	1,580	1,851	2,478	2,654	4,302	3,125
Foreign Exchange	1d. d	1,944	2,480	2,873	3,894	2,748	8,455	12,567	17,195	25,076	24,016	22,666	25,511	30,625	42,376	47,348
Gold (Million Fine Troy Ounces)	1ad	126.00	122.62	120.79	129.69	116.56	113.70	116.47	117.36	117.61	117.61	117.61	117.61	118.30	118.64	95.25
Gold (National Valuation)	1an d	4,404	4,317	4,229	4,541	3,984	3,994	4,494	4,364	5,179	5,810	5,339	5,926	6,684	9,344	7,906
Monetary Authorities: Other Assets	3.. d	877	728	699	676	624	689	771	772	919	1,511	1,442	1,569	1,683	1,360	1,433
Other Liab.	4.. d	169	142	279	348	389	768	892	917	710	914	713	1,160	939	3,757	2,839
Deposit Money Banks: Assets	7a. d	3,597	4,032	5,957	8,655	13,429	14,270	16,053	15,410	21,139	29,433	38,321	48,229	58,271	73,206	82,558
of which: Claims on Nonbanks	7ad d	2,482	2,682	3,530	4,782	8,085	8,374	9,198	8,298	8,898	11,372	13,126	17,752	23,924	33,594	40,785
Deposit Money Banks: Liabilities	7b. d	2,247	2,257	2,592	4,135	6,325	9,139	11,417	12,093	15,759	18,572	21,912	30,201	38,371	57,927	76,697
of which: Liab. to Nonbanks	7bd d	1,042	1,060	1,227	1,257	1,563	2,071	2,092	2,216	2,960	3,308	5,617	7,225	9,739	14,885	17,892
Monetary Authorities																*Billions of Deutsche Mark:*
Foreign Assets	11	33.5	35.2	35.6	43.3	28.7	52.6	62.4	77.6	92.5	83.5	86.4	88.5	90.2	107.2	107.0
Claims on Central Government	12a	14.4	14.9	15.3	13.6	14.7	14.6	14.8	13.6	16.4	15.3	18.4	15.2	16.0	17.8	17.0
Claims on Deposit Money Banks	12e	5.5	6.3	5.7	6.1	17.7	18.7	18.8	20.2	11.2	15.5	8.5	19.5	19.6	24.3	36.2
Reserve Money	14	48.9	52.0	50.5	54.0	55.7	67.8	78.0	98.6	105.9	104.7	107.7	118.6	128.1	144.9	152.4
of which: Currency Outside DMBs	14a	29.7	30.9	31.5	32.6	34.7	36.9	40.3	45.7	47.4	51.5	56.5	60.6	67.5	76.2	79.9
Foreign Liabilities	16c	.4	.6	.6	.5	1.4	2.8	2.9	3.0	1.9	2.2	1.9	2.7	2.0	6.9	5.0
Central Government Deposits	16d	1.2	.7	1.0	2.2	2.2	1.3	.9	2.8	2.8	.9	4.8	2.7	2.1	4.6	2.9
Other Items (Net)	17r	2.9	3.1	4.5	6.3	1.8	14.0	14.2	7.0	9.4	6.5	–1.0	–.8	–6.3	–7.1	–.1
Deposit Money Banks																*Billions of Deutsche Mark:*
Reserves	20	19.5	21.0	18.7	21.8	21.6	31.0	38.7	53.5	60.5	55.5	54.3	59.4	62.9	72.3	78.8
Foreign Assets	21	14.4	16.1	23.8	I 34.6	49.2	52.2	51.7	49.7	56.4	70.9	100.5	113.9	122.7	133.8	143.0
Claims on Central Government	22a	28.0	31.8	40.0	43.7	42.5	45.5	47.9	50.2	53.5	65.8	104.0	127.3	150.0	180.1	204.0
Claims on Official Entities	22bx	19.6	22.2	27.9	30.6	33.2	37.1	44.7	52.6	60.3	66.6	76.4	83.5	87.6	92.2	96.5
Claims on Private Sector	22d	261.2	283.0	301.3	337.5	389.7	434.3	496.3	576.2	638.6	680.5	712.6	779.8	851.7	940.0	1,053.5
Demand Deposits	24	42.9	43.0	49.7	I 57.6	60.3	66.3	76.0	87.1	87.7	98.2	114.6	116.2	130.6	150.7	153.6
Time Deposits	25	130.6	151.4	174.1	185.9	209.8	228.7	260.1	296.4	332.0	351.1	387.1	423.7	464.6	503.7	534.8
Bonds	26ab	47.4	51.6	53.7	I 80.3	93.4	112.4	133.3	169.0	213.8	240.7	277.5	322.1	355.1	397.5	467.4
Foreign Liabilities	26c	9.0	9.0	10.4	I 16.5	23.2	33.5	36.8	39.0	42.1	44.8	57.5	71.4	80.8	105.9	132.8
Central Government Deposits	26d	10.1	10.9	11.8	10.7	12.3	15.5	16.4	20.1	21.3	23.1	24.9	24.5	26.5	27.5	26.5
Central Govt. Lending Funds	26f	63.0	68.7	71.1	74.4	77.5	79.1	83.6	87.0	94.5	96.1	100.9	103.9	105.0	107.2	112.3
Credit from Monetary Authorities	26g	5.5	6.3	5.7	6.1	17.7	18.7	18.8	20.2	11.2	15.5	8.5	19.5	19.6	24.3	36.2
Capital Accounts	27a	28.6	28.4	31.0	31.0	33.0	37.2	40.8	46.7	52.1	57.6	63.5	70.9	77.9	85.0	92.9
Other Items (Net)	27r	5.6	4.8	4.2	5.7	9.0	9.4	13.4	16.8	14.9	12.3	13.4	11.9	14.8	16.6	19.4
Monetary Survey																*Billions of Deutsche Mark:*
Foreign Assets (Net)	31n	38.5	41.7	48.4	I 60.9	53.3	68.6	74.4	85.3	104.9	107.4	127.6	128.4	130.1	128.3	112.2
Domestic Credit	32	312.2	340.5	371.7	I 413.1	466.0	515.2	586.8	670.2	745.0	804.4	885.7	979.4	1,077.1	1,199.8	1,342.8
Claims on Central Govt. (Net)	32an	31.0	35.1	42.5	44.4	42.7	43.2	45.4	40.8	45.8	57.1	92.7	115.3	137.4	165.8	191.7
incl: Net Clms.on Laender Gov	32an x	3.9	5.3	7.4	8.0	6.9	9.7	14.1	12.5	13.2	20.8	37.6	49.2	57.9	67.7	78.9
Claims on Official Entities	32bx	19.6	22.2	27.9	I 30.6	33.2	37.1	44.7	52.6	60.3	66.2	76.4	83.5	87.6	92.2	96.5
Claims on Private Sector	32d	261.6	283.3	301.3	338.0	390.1	434.9	496.7	576.5	638.9	680.7	716.6	780.5	852.1	941.8	1,054.6
Money	34	72.8	74.2	81.6	I 90.6	95.4	103.7	116.9	133.4	135.7	150.2	171.7	177.3	198.6	227.5	234.1
Quasi-Money	35	130.6	151.4	174.1	185.9	209.8	228.7	260.1	296.4	332.0	351.1	387.1	423.7	464.6	503.7	534.8
Bonds	36ab	47.4	51.6	53.7	I 80.3	93.4	112.4	133.3	169.0	213.8	240.7	277.5	322.1	355.1	397.5	467.4
Central Govt. Lending Funds	36f	63.0	68.7	71.1	74.4	77.5	79.1	83.6	87.0	94.5	96.1	100.9	103.9	105.0	107.2	112.3
Other Items (Net)	37r	37.0	36.6	39.8	I 42.6	43.2	60.6	67.4	69.6	74.1	73.7	76.2	80.8	84.0	92.2	106.3
Money plus Quasi-Money	35l	210.7	233.7	264.9	I 284.2	313.7	341.5	387.4	441.7	480.6	515.2	574.3	617.6	681.5	751.4	790.2
Money (National Definitions)																*Billions of Deutsche Mark:*
Central Bank Money,Seas. Adj.	14n. c	45.2	47.7	50.9	55.6	60.9	65.0	72.9	82.5	88.8	94.4	103.8	112.5	123.6	134.0	141.7
M1, Seasonally Adjusted	34n. c	73.7	76.9	79.4	85.5	I 92.4	98.2	110.1	125.0	132.3	140.2	159.6	176.2	190.6	216.2	232.4
M2, Seasonally Adjusted	38na c	....	....	....	....	145.8	158.8	180.4	206.1	243.1	262.4	260.9	275.1	298.2	333.4	370.9
M3, Seasonally Adjusted	38nb c	....	....	....	....	251.3	270.6	304.3	344.3	385.8	419.5	450.9	495.9	542.2	600.0	653.6
Extended Money M3,Seas.Adj.	38nc c	....	....	....	....	....	....	....	....	....	429.0	459.6	502.5	549.1	606.4	664.4

Germany

1980	1981	1982	1983	1984	1985	1986	1987	1988	1989	1990	1991	1992	1993	1994		
End of Period															**Exchange Rates**	
2.4985	2.6245	2.6215	2.8517	3.0857	2.7035	2.3740	2.2436	2.3957	2.2312	2.1255	2.1685	2.2193	2.3712	2.2610	Market Rate	aa
End of Period (ae) Period Average (rf)																
1.9590	2.2548	2.3765	2.7238	3.1480	2.4613	1.9408	1.5815	1.7803	1.6978	1.4940	1.5160	1.6140	1.7263	1.5488	Market Rate	ae
1.8177	2.2600	2.4266	2.5533	2.8459	2.9440	2.1715	1.7974	1.7562	1.8800	1.6157	1.6595	1.5617	1.6533	1.6228	Market Rate	rf
End of Period (ea) Period Average (eb)																
2.5656	2.4444	2.3001	2.2575	2.2318	2.1839	2.0761	2.0603	2.0778	2.0241	2.0420	2.0355	1.9556	1.9357	1.9053	ECU Rate	ea
2.5244	2.5147	2.3770	2.2705	2.2380	2.2263	2.1287	2.0715	2.0744	2.0700	2.0519	2.0507	2.0210	1.9368	1.9248	ECU Rate	eb
Period Averages																
88.8	71.6	66.5	63.3	56.8	55.2	74.5	89.8	92.0	85.8	100.0	97.5	103.5	97.5	99.5	Market Rate	ah x
79.2	76.1	80.6	84.6	84.2	84.6	91.9	97.2	96.6	95.9	100.0	99.1	102.1	106.1	106.4	Nominal Effective Exchange Rate	ne u
85.1	78.7	80.6	83.7	82.5	82.6	90.0	96.1	96.1	94.6	100.0	99.5	102.3	110.6	....	Real Effective Exchange Rate	re u
End of Period															**Fund Position**	
3,234	3,234	3,234	5,404	5,404	5,404	5,404	5,404	5,404	5,404	5,404	5,404	8,242	8,242	8,242	Quota	2f. s
1,443	1,383	1,862	1,541	1,390	1,408	1,651	1,384	1,380	1,373	1,321	1,340	611	700	763	SDRs	1b. s
1,796	2,117	2,799	3,580	3,826	3,467	3,146	2,749	2,487	2,315	2,148	2,494	3,083	2,877	2,760	Reserve Position in the Fund	1c. s
629	929	1,205	878	853	723	424	173	—	—	—	—	—	—	—	of which: Outstg.Fund Borrowing	2c
End of Period															**International Liquidity**	
48,592	43,719	44,762	42,674	40,141	44,380	51,734	78,756	58,528	60,709	67,902	63,001	90,967	77,640	77,363	Total Reserves minus Gold	1l. d
1,840	1,609	2,054	1,613	1,362	1,547	2,020	1,964	1,857	1,804	1,880	1,917	841	962	1,114	SDRs	1b. d
2,291	2,465	3,088	3,748	3,750	3,808	3,848	3,900	3,346	3,043	3,056	3,567	4,239	3,951	4,030	Reserve Position in the Fund	1c. d
44,461	39,645	39,620	37,313	35,028	39,025	45,866	72,893	53,324	55,862	62,967	57,517	85,887	72,727	72,219	Foreign Exchange	1d. d
95.18	95.18	95.18	95.18	95.18	95.18	95.18	95.18	95.18	95.18	95.18	95.18	95.18	95.18	95.18	Gold (Million Fine Troy Ounces)	1ad
6,988	6,071	5,761	5,026	4,349	5,562	7,054	8,656	7,690	8,063	9,163	9,030	8,482	7,930	8,839	Gold (National Valuation)	1and
1,274	1,114	1,042	913	794	1,003	1,263	1,542	1,372	1,434	1,623	1,715	1,637	1,548	1,539	Monetary Authorities: Other Assets	3..d
5,214	5,064	6,475	5,177	4,813	7,451	12,137	12,794	15,306	30,417	34,979	27,925	16,423	22,909	15,620	Other Liab.	4..d
85,171	84,535	81,729	74,756	75,232	112,932	178,483	232,608	230,090	292,861	395,489	402,025	386,840	461,965	484,892	Deposit Money Banks: Assets	7a. d
41,276	39,352	38,292	35,495	32,357	45,313	57,997	74,404	70,471	81,164	112,095	124,505	134,926	152,048	166,187	of which: Claims on Nonbanks	7ad d
72,093	66,795	64,692	57,923	58,224	75,773	101,288	131,375	131,000	159,901	226,372	231,088	264,430	286,132	378,835	Deposit Money Banks: Liabilities	7b. d
15,115	16,068	15,342	15,952	17,465	21,919	29,467	41,467	36,438	44,293	61,727	64,017	80,397	96,078	119,028	of which: Liab. to Nonbanks	7bd d
End of Period															**Monetary Authorities**	
104.4	103.7	108.0	111.0	111.8	108.7	110.4	140.7	113.6	114.9	117.5	109.1	152.0	134.5	128.7	Foreign Assets	11
20.9	23.6	22.0	24.0	23.0	20.9	25.0	22.9	24.2	24.5	25.5	26.3	32.9	27.4	26.3	Claims on Central Government	12a
57.6	68.1	74.9	85.5	96.3	105.3	96.4	82.4	144.7	175.3	208.5	225.3	188.9	257.5	217.7	Claims on Deposit Money Banks	12e
146.8	144.4	152.1	160.6	166.7	172.2	182.9	199.7	221.1	234.6	262.9	276.9	317.0	312.9	307.8	Reserve Money	14
84.0	84.2	88.6	96.4	99.8	103.9	112.2	124.1	142.6	147.9	158.6	171.8	200.5	212.0	225.9	of which: Currency Outside DMBs	14a
14.4	11.4	15.4	14.1	15.2	18.3	23.6	20.2	27.3	51.6	52.3	42.3	26.5	23.2	19.6	Foreign Liabilities	16c
1.0	.7	1.2	2.1	.9	2.2	1.1	4.6	3.5	6.1	19.1	12.7	.4	13.4	.2	Central Government Deposits	16d
20.6	38.8	36.2	43.7	48.3	42.3	24.3	21.5	30.7	22.4	17.4	29.0	29.9	70.0	45.1	Other Items (Net)	17r
End of Period															**Deposit Money Banks**	
70.4	66.5	69.0	69.5	75.6	I 78.3	80.2	83.6	89.0	96.8	117.7	112.8	115.0	102.0	86.5	Reserves	20
166.9	190.6	194.2	203.6	236.8	I 278.0	346.4	367.9	409.6	497.2	590.9	609.5	624.4	797.5	751.0	Foreign Assets	21
218.7	258.2	290.5	306.7	322.0	I 338.0	337.3	361.3	397.7	399.7	449.8	459.7	549.7	627.2	690.8	Claims on Central Government	22a
103.0	110.6	118.2	121.2	124.8	129.1	134.5	139.2	143.7	147.5	153.8	169.5	189.6	213.3	235.5	Claims on Official Entities	22bx
1,155.2	1,238.7	1,306.3	1,399.4	1,489.0	I 1,594.6	1,665.5	1,726.1	1,818.5	1,952.6	2,311.0	2,559.0	2,788.4	3,045.5	3,281.7	Claims on Private Sector	22d
158.8	154.7	167.4	181.1	194.2	I 209.7	227.2	240.8	265.0	282.8	392.0	402.3	439.6	484.8	505.3	Demand Deposits	24
560.5	594.0	634.1	663.5	699.7	I 759.9	804.1	847.1	874.7	916.4	1,046.8	1,125.6	1,194.7	1,350.6	1,366.7	Time Deposits	25
524.3	600.5	634.1	687.8	739.6	I 796.2	843.3	894.7	917.1	1,003.4	1,130.9	1,266.3	1,370.0	1,467.6	1,612.5	Bonds	26ab
141.2	150.6	153.7	157.8	183.3	I 186.5	196.6	207.8	233.2	271.5	338.2	350.3	426.8	494.0	586.7	Foreign Liabilities	26c
28.3	32.9	34.6	34.2	32.7	I 35.9	42.0	41.2	40.6	46.6	64.2	63.2	60.8	60.9	58.6	Central Government Deposits	26d
121.0	128.4	129.8	136.8	144.2	I 152.2	157.5	162.8	168.1	172.5	177.0	188.7	176.7	182.0	191.0	Central Govt. Lending Funds	26f
57.6	68.1	74.9	85.5	96.3	105.3	96.4	82.4	144.7	175.3	208.5	225.3	188.9	257.5	217.7	Credit from Monetary Authorities	26g
98.9	107.1	115.8	126.1	137.4	I 153.9	169.2	183.0	190.2	202.5	257.0	304.3	343.4	382.2	400.3	Capital Accounts	27a
23.4	28.4	34.0	27.7	20.9	I 18.3	27.5	18.3	25.0	23.9	8.5	–15.3	66.0	105.9	106.7	Other Items (Net)	27r
End of Period															**Monetary Survey**	
115.6	132.3	133.1	142.7	150.2	I 181.8	236.7	280.6	262.8	289.0	317.9	326.0	323.1	414.9	273.3	Foreign Assets (Net)	31n
1,470.6	1,598.8	1,702.7	1,817.0	1,926.5	I 2,045.7	2,120.6	2,205.0	2,341.3	2,472.7	2,857.6	3,139.4	3,499.6	3,839.2	4,175.7	Domestic Credit	32
210.3	248.2	276.6	294.4	311.4	I 320.8	319.2	338.4	377.8	371.5	392.0	410.2	521.3	580.2	658.4	Claims on Central Govt. (Net)	32an
97.7	119.2	135.0	150.2	163.0	I 174.9	183.0	200.9	219.0	226.2	233.6	256.1	283.4	338.7	371.4	incl: Net Clms.on Laender Gov	32an x
103.0	110.6	118.2	121.2	124.8	I 129.1	134.4	139.2	143.7	147.5	153.8	169.5	189.6	213.3	235.5	Claims on Official Entities	32bx
1,156.7	1,240.1	1,307.8	1,401.3	1,490.3	I 1,595.9	1,667.0	1,727.4	1,819.7	1,953.6	2,311.8	2,559.7	2,788.7	3,045.8	3,281.9	Claims on Private Sector	32d
243.4	239.6	256.7	278.2	294.8	I 314.5	340.2	365.7	408.3	431.6	551.9	575.0	641.0	697.6	732.0	Money	34
560.5	594.0	634.1	663.5	699.7	I 759.9	804.1	847.1	874.7	916.4	1,046.8	1,125.6	1,194.7	1,350.6	1,366.7	Quasi-Money	35
524.3	600.5	634.1	687.8	739.6	I 796.2	843.3	894.7	917.1	1,003.4	1,130.9	1,266.3	1,370.0	1,467.6	1,612.5	Bonds	36ab
121.0	128.4	129.8	136.8	144.2	I 152.2	157.5	162.8	168.1	172.5	177.0	188.7	176.7	182.0	191.0	Central Govt. Lending Funds	36f
136.3	168.7	181.3	193.4	198.4	I 204.8	212.0	215.3	235.9	238.8	269.0	309.9	440.3	556.5	547.0	Other Items (Net)	37r
826.1	856.6	915.5	967.8	1,022.0	I 1,074.4	1,144.4	1,212.8	1,283.0	1,348.1	1,598.7	1,700.6	1,835.7	2,048.1	2,098.6	Money plus Quasi-Money	35l
End of Period															**Money (National Definitions)**	
149.6	154.3	163.6	174.5	182.7	I 190.8	206.6	223.5	242.4	254.3	I 290.9	328.5	363.4	399.7	434.0	Central Bank Money,Seas. Adj.	14n. c
237.9	240.7	249.3	274.9	284.0	296.5	325.9	355.1	389.8	414.4	432.9	547.6	586.1	641.2	702.8	M1, Seasonally Adjusted	34n. c
403.8	446.0	476.1	489.8	506.6	529.5	568.4	606.2	644.5	703.2	790.1	991.7	1,108.5	1,204.3	1,279.0	M2, Seasonally Adjusted	38na c
688.0	732.2	780.1	831.7	863.6	906.8	I 973.3	1,047.3	1,114.0	1,177.8	1,230.8	1,476.1	1,597.7	1,724.2	1,879.3	M3, Seasonally Adjusted	38nb c
708.0	767.1	823.4	877.4	916.3	960.7	1,041.2	1,112.5	1,187.6	1,287.2	I 1,373.1	1,651.7	1,802.3	1,988.7	2,173.4	Extended Money M3,Seas.Adj.	38nc c

Germany
134

		1965	1966	1967	1968	1969	1970	1971	1972	1973	1974	1975	1976	1977	1978	1979
Nonbank Financial Institutions																
Building Societies													*Billions of Deutsche Mark:*			
Claims on Central Government	42a. i	1.04	1.32	.37	1.40	1.42	1.40	1.49	1.77	.25	.24	.38	.71	1.09	1.09	.81
Claims on Private Sector	42d. i	15.61	19.72	22.12	24.01	28.31	34.70	39.65	45.49	56.20	61.54	67.47	74.37	82.37	91.13	103.90
Time and Savings Deposits	45.. i	21.04	25.73	28.61	31.22	35.30	40.71	46.47	53.58	61.86	67.71	75.22	82.51	89.04	96.22	104.12
Other Items (Net)	47r. i	−4.39	−4.69	−6.12	−5.81	−5.57	−4.61	−5.33	−6.32	−5.41	−5.93	−7.37	−7.43	−5.58	−4.00	.59
Liquid Liabilities	55l	224.4	251.3	284.3	ӏ307.8	340.5	373.0	423.4	483.4	529.5	569.1	634.0	683.5	752.2	827.4	873.0
Interest Rates														*Percent Per Annum*		
Discount Rate (End of Period)	60	4.0	5.0	3.0	3.0	6.0	6.0	4.0	4.5	7.0	6.0	3.5	3.5	3.0	3.0	6.0
Money Market Rate	60b	4.1	5.3	3.3	2.6	4.8	8.6	6.2	4.3	10.2	8.9	4.4	3.9	4.1	3.4	5.9
Interbank Deposit Rate	60bs	5.1	6.6	4.3	3.8	5.8	9.4	7.1	5.6	12.1	9.9	5.0	4.2	4.4	3.7	6.7
Treasury Bill Rate	60c	....	....	....	....	....	....	....	....	....	....	5.40	5.19	4.36	3.76	5.48
Deposit Rate	60l	....	....	....	....	....	....	....	....	....	....	....	....	....	3.06	5.14
Lending Rate	60p	....	....	....	....	....	....	....	....	....	....	....	....	....	7.33	8.63
Government Bond Yield	61	7.10	8.10	7.00	6.50	6.80	8.30	8.00	7.90	9.30	10.40	8.50	7.80	6.20	5.80	7.40
Mortgage Bond Yield	61a	6.7	7.6	7.0	6.8	7.0	8.2	8.3	8.4	9.6	10.7	9.0	8.2	6.6	6.4	7.7
Prices, Production, Employment														*Index Numbers (1990=100):*		
Industrial Share Prices	62	ӏ29.6	27.9	28.1	37.0	40.3	35.0	32.9	37.1	35.3	29.6	33.3	35.3	ӏ34.9	36.9	35.0
Prices: Industrial Products	63	46.1	46.9	46.5	46.2	47.0	49.3	51.4	52.8	56.3	63.8	66.8	69.2	71.1	72.0	75.4
Consumer Prices	64	41.8	43.3	44.0	44.7	45.5	47.1	49.6	52.3	55.9	59.8	63.4	66.1	68.5	70.4	73.3
Wages: Hourly Earnings	65.. c	15.5	17.1	18.1	18.9	20.8	24.5	27.7	30.6	34.6	39.6	44.1	46.7	50.7	54.1	57.9
Industrial Production	66.. c	55.1	55.7	54.0	59.0	66.6	70.7	71.7	74.3	78.4	76.7	71.5	76.6	78.5	80.0	84.0
Investment Goods	66iy c	46.8	46.8	43.8	47.8	56.3	61.5	61.2	62.5	66.9	65.2	62.1	66.6	69.7	69.8	72.9
Other Production Goods	66jy c	57.7	59.3	60.2	68.0	76.1	79.8	79.8	83.6	91.0	90.1	78.4	86.4	86.8	89.6	95.9
Consumer Goods	66hy c	67.0	67.4	63.8	69.8	77.3	79.7	82.4	87.0	88.5	84.4	79.8	85.5	88.2	88.3	91.2
Industrial Employment	67	117.9	116.9	109.3	110.1	115.8	119.9	119.1	116.4	116.9	113.8	106.4	103.9	103.0	102.3	102.6
International Transactions													*Billions of Deutsche Mark*			
Exports	70	71.65	80.63	87.05	99.55	113.56	125.28	136.01	149.02	178.40	230.58	221.59	256.64	273.61	284.91	314.47
Imports, cif	71	70.45	72.67	70.18	81.18	97.97	109.61	120.12	128.74	145.42	179.73	184.31	222.17	235.18	243.71	292.04
Imports, fob	71.v	65.96	68.04	65.59	76.15	92.82	102.87	112.72	121.72	137.73	171.88	177.06	214.56	227.69	235.75	282.66
															1990=100	
Volume of Exports	72	22.2	24.4	26.2	30.2	33.4	38.3	39.9	42.4	48.3	53.6	47.6	56.5	58.7	60.6	63.5
Volume of Imports	73	24.1	25.0	24.8	28.7	33.5	39.6	42.9	45.6	48.2	46.3	46.2	54.3	55.6	59.4	63.8
Unit Value of Exports	74	50.2	51.3	51.8	51.3	52.9	51.0	53.0	54.6	57.3	66.9	72.3	70.7	72.4	73.1	77.0
Export Prices	76	46.5	47.5	47.4	47.0	48.8	50.3	52.0	53.1	56.5	66.2	68.7	71.4	72.6	73.7	77.2
Unit Value of Imports	75	52.9	52.8	51.3	51.1	53.1	50.1	50.7	51.0	54.7	70.3	72.3	74.0	76.6	74.4	82.8
Import Prices	76.x	51.7	52.6	51.5	51.0	51.9	51.4	51.6	51.3	57.9	74.4	73.1	77.6	78.8	75.8	84.7
Balance of Payments													*Billions of US Dollars:*			
Goods: Exports f.o.b.	78aa d	....	....	....	....	....	....	....	....	....	....	....	101.70	117.27	141.15	170.23
Goods: Imports f.o.b.	78ab d	....	....	....	....	....	....	....	....	....	....	....	−86.42	−98.82	−117.90	−155.09
Trade Balance	78ac d	....	....	....	....	....	....	....	....	....	....	....	15.28	18.45	23.25	15.14
Services: Credit	78ad d	....	....	....	....	....	....	....	....	....	....	....	17.51	19.56	24.88	28.62
Services: Debit	78ae d	....	....	....	....	....	....	....	....	....	....	....	−21.65	−24.80	−30.67	−37.96
Balance on Goods and Services	78af d	....	....	....	....	....	....	....	....	....	....	....	11.14	13.21	17.46	5.79
Income: Credit	78ag d	....	....	....	....	....	....	....	....	....	....	....	5.98	6.47	9.47	12.07
Income: Debit	78ah d	....	....	....	....	....	....	....	....	....	....	....	−5.64	−7.61	−8.06	−11.62
Balance on Goods, Serv., & Inc.	78ai d	....	....	....	....	....	....	....	....	....	....	....	11.48	12.07	18.88	6.24
Current Transfers, n.i.e.: Credit	78aj d	....	....	....	....	....	....	....	....	....	....	....	3.50	5.16	7.13	7.65
Current Transfers: Debit	78ak d	....	....	....	....	....	....	....	....	....	....	....	−11.17	−13.29	−16.61	−19.24
Current Account, n.i.e.	78al d	....	....	....	....	....	....	....	....	....	....	....	3.82	3.93	9.39	−5.35
Capital Account, n.i.e.: Credit	78ba d	....	....	....	....	....	....	....	....	....	....	....	.09	.13	.10	.15
Capital Account: Debit	78bb d	....	....	....	....	....	....	....	....	....	....	....	−.09	−.12	−.14	−.40
Capital Account, n.i.e.	78bc d	....	....	....	....	....	....	....	....	....	....	....	—	.01	−.04	−.25
Direct Investment Abroad	78bd d	....	....	....	....	....	....	....	....	....	....	....	−2.61	−2.42	−3.94	−5.02
Dir. Invest. in Rep. Econ., n.i.e.	78be d	....	....	....	....	....	....	....	....	....	....	....	1.32	.95	1.60	1.73
Portfolio Investment Assets	78bf d	....	....	....	....	....	....	....	....	....	....	....	−.35	−2.36	−2.07	−1.82
Portfolio Investment Liab., n.i.e.	78bg d	....	....	....	....	....	....	....	....	....	....	....	1.86	1.05	1.62	3.18
Other Investment Assets	78bh d	....	....	....	....	....	....	....	....	....	....	....	−11.94	−7.45	−11.43	−12.66
Other Investment Liab., n.i.e.	78bi d	....	....	....	....	....	....	....	....	....	....	....	11.53	10.96	19.97	19.08
Financial Account, n.i.e.	78bj d	....	....	....	....	....	....	....	....	....	....	....	−.18	.74	5.75	4.49
Net Errors and Omissions	78ca d	....	....	....	....	....	....	....	....	....	....	....	.16	−.23	−2.19	−2.32
Overall Balance	78cb d	....	....	....	....	....	....	....	....	....	....	....	3.79	4.46	12.92	−3.44
Reserves and Related Items	79da d	....	....	....	....	....	....	....	....	....	....	....	−3.79	−4.46	−12.92	3.44
Reserve Assets	79db d	....	....	....	....	....	....	....	....	....	....	....	−3.79	−4.46	−12.92	3.44
Use of Fund Credit and Loans	79dc d	....	....	....	....	....	....	....	....	....	....	....	—	—	—	—
Liabs.Constit.For.Auth.Reserves	79dd d	....	....	....	....	....	....	....	....	....	....	....	....	....	....	....
Exceptional Financing	79de d	....	....	....	....	....	....	....	....	....	....	....	....	....	....	....

Germany

1980	1981	1982	1983	1984	1985	1986	1987	1988	1989	1990	1991	1992	1993	1994		
															Nonbank Financial Institutions	
End of Period															*Building Societies*	
.54	.36	.39	.55	.63	.54	.62	.77	2.15	3.49	4.44	5.99	6.97	8.92	11.13	Claims on Central Government	**42a.** *i*
115.77	126.91	133.18	139.23	145.09	145.88	143.12	139.40	131.64	129.84	135.08	140.60	150.74	160.95	169.75	Claims on Private Sector	**42d.** *i*
110.54	116.42	121.49	126.01	126.35	125.37	123.59	120.25	121.49	124.49	129.72	136.38	143.17	150.32	156.98	Time and Savings Deposits	**45..** *i*
5.77	10.85	12.08	13.77	19.37	21.05	20.15	19.92	12.30	8.84	9.80	10.21	14.54	19.55	23.90	Other Items (Net)	**47r.** *i*
914.4	950.0	1,012.4	1,067.8	1,120.8	1,199.7	1,268.0	1,333.1	1,404.5	1,472.5	1,728.4	1,837.0	1,978.9	2,198.5	2,255.6	Liquid Liabilities	**55***l*
															Interest Rates	
Percent Per Annum																
7.5	7.5	5.0	4.0	4.5	4.0	3.5	2.5	3.5	6.0	6.0	8.0	8.3	5.8	4.5	Discount Rate *(End of Period)*	**60**
9.1	11.3	8.7	5.4	5.5	5.2	4.6	3.7	4.0	6.6	7.9	8.8	9.4	7.5	5.3	Money Market Rate	**60b**
9.5	12.1	8.9	5.8	6.0	5.4	4.6	4.0	4.3	7.1	8.4	9.2	9.5	7.2	5.3	Interbank Deposit Rate	**60bs**
7.85	10.37	8.31	5.63	5.66	5.04	3.86	3.28	3.62	6.28	8.13	8.27	8.32	6.22	5.05	Treasury Bill Rate	**60c**
7.95	9.74	7.54	4.56	4.86	4.44	3.71	3.20	3.29	5.50	7.07	7.62	8.01	6.27	4.47	Deposit Rate	**60***l*
12.04	14.69	13.50	10.05	9.82	9.53	8.75	8.36	8.33	9.94	11.59	12.46	13.59	12.85	11.48	Lending Rate	**60p**
8.50	10.38	8.95	7.89	7.78	6.87	5.92	5.84	6.10	7.09	8.88	8.63	7.96	6.28	6.67	Government Bond Yield	**61**
8.7	10.6	9.1	8.0	7.8	7.0	6.1	5.9	6.1	7.2	9.0	8.9	8.3	6.5	6.8	Mortgage Bond Yield	**61a**
															Prices, Production, Employment	
Period Averages																
32.8	33.0	32.5	43.8	49.4	65.6	88.7	81.7	68.3	87.3	100.0	89.1	86.2	87.8	105.9	Industrial Share Prices	**62**
81.1	87.5	92.6	93.9	96.7	99.0	96.5	94.1	95.3	98.3	100.0	102.4	103.8	ɪ103.7	104.4	Prices: Industrial Products	**63**
77.3	82.1	86.5	89.3	91.5	ɪ93.5	93.3	93.6	94.8	97.4	100.0	103.5	107.6	112.0	115.4	Consumer Prices	**64**
62.8	67.4	70.9	73.8	76.2	79.3	83.5	87.6	91.0	94.9	100.0	107.2	114.8	121.7	123.6	Wages: Hourly Earnings	**65..** *c*
84.1	82.1	79.5	79.9	82.1	85.4	87.2	87.4	90.5	94.8	100.0	103.2	101.3	94.5	97.5	Industrial Production	**66..** *c*
75.0	74.8	73.6	72.8	74.8	81.8	85.2	85.6	88.5	94.8	100.0	102.8	99.0	87.9	91.4	Investment Goods	**66iy** *c*
92.2	88.5	84.1	86.4	89.9	90.6	89.8	89.7	95.5	97.6	100.0	101.2	102.5	99.1	105.2	Other Production Goods	**66jy** *c*
90.1	84.7	80.6	81.9	83.7	84.7	86.3	87.1	89.7	93.1	100.0	104.9	100.8	94.9	94.2	Consumer Goods	**66hy** *c*
103.3	101.0	97.5	93.5	92.5	93.7	95.3	95.2	95.0	97.3	100.0	101.4	99.0	91.9	85.9	Industrial Employment	**67**
															International Transactions	
Billions of Deutsche Mark																
350.33	396.90	427.74	432.28	488.22	537.16	526.36	527.38	567.65	641.04	661.88	665.81	658.47	628.39	677.81	Exports	**70**
341.38	369.18	376.46	390.19	434.26	463.81	413.74	409.64	439.61	506.47	556.58	643.91	628.19	576.50	603.30	Imports, cif	**71**
331.41	357.33	365.17	378.51	421.42	451.15	402.94	399.49	428.42	493.40	543.40	627.68	612.56	560.86	586.87	Imports, fob	**71.v**
1990=100																
64.6	68.9	71.1	70.9	77.4	82.0	83.1	85.5	91.2	98.5	100.0	100.0	102.2	98.5	111.7	Volume of Exports	**72**
63.8	60.6	61.5	63.9	67.2	70.0	74.3	78.3	83.3	89.3	100.0	112.7	115.3	104.3	113.5	Volume of Imports	**73**
84.3	89.6	93.5	94.8	98.1	101.9	98.5	96.0	96.7	101.1	100.0	99.4	98.7	94.2	93.3	Unit Value of Exports	**74**
82.0	86.8	90.6	92.1	95.3	97.9	96.1	95.2	ɪ97.2	100.0	100.0	101.3	102.3	102.6	ɪ103.6	Export Prices	**76**
96.8	110.2	110.9	110.5	117.0	120.0	100.9	94.7	95.5	102.6	100.0	101.7	98.6	93.2	95.0	Unit Value of Imports	**75**
97.4	110.7	113.2	112.8	119.6	121.3	102.3	96.7	ɪ97.9	102.3	100.0	100.4	97.2	95.2	ɪ95.9	Import Prices	**76.x**
Minus Sign Indicates Debit															**Balance of Payments**	
191.16	174.15	174.43	167.49	169.98	182.69	241.52	291.49	322.82	340.94	412.04	403.71	430.69	382.68	427.16	Goods: Exports f.o.b.	**78aa** *d*
−183.25	−158.72	−150.24	−148.01	−148.55	−154.16	−186.75	−223.38	−246.49	−265.90	−343.43	−385.20	−403.75	−343.00	−376.05	Goods: Imports f.o.b.	**78ab** *d*
7.92	15.43	24.19	19.48	21.43	28.53	54.77	68.11	76.33	75.04	68.62	18.51	26.94	39.68	51.10	Trade Balance	**78ac** *d*
33.12	31.44	32.20	30.51	29.61	30.76	39.44	45.98	47.32	49.51	63.08	63.92	67.31	62.12	61.17	Services: Credit	**78ad** *d*
−42.41	−38.27	−38.08	−35.86	−33.30	−33.63	−43.76	−53.70	−57.87	−58.66	−76.16	−81.04	−94.90	−93.54	−100.06	Services: Debit	**78ae** *d*
−1.37	8.61	18.31	14.13	17.74	25.65	50.45	60.39	65.78	65.90	55.54	1.39	−.66	8.26	12.20	Balance on Goods and Services	**78af** *d*
13.96	13.67	14.00	14.31	15.16	15.55	22.69	29.66	33.68	43.28	63.15	71.95	78.15	76.08	75.44	Income: Credit	**78ag** *d*
−13.04	−14.02	−15.98	−13.22	−12.15	−12.75	−18.64	−26.33	−30.01	−32.16	−46.05	−53.64	−63.78	−65.06	−70.67	Income: Debit	**78ah** *d*
−.45	8.27	16.33	15.23	20.75	28.46	54.51	63.72	69.46	77.02	72.64	19.70	13.71	19.28	16.97	Balance on Goods, Serv., & Inc.	**78ai** *d*
8.01	6.99	6.68	7.32	7.13	7.02	10.77	12.15	13.91	12.85	15.86	16.64	19.34	17.24	19.39	Current Transfers, n.i.e.: Credit	**78aj** *d*
−20.87	−18.66	−17.99	−17.80	−18.30	−17.70	−24.16	−29.21	−33.52	−32.54	−40.05	−54.96	−54.64	−51.96	−57.29	Current Transfers: Debit	**78ak** *d*
−13.31	−3.41	5.02	4.74	9.57	17.78	41.12	46.66	49.84	57.33	48.46	−18.62	−21.59	−15.44	−20.93	Current Account, n.i.e.	**78al** *d*
.15	.12	.13	.15	.12	.11	.21	.19	.27	.40	.40	.78	1.11	1.39	1.56	Capital Account, n.i.e.: Credit	**78ba** *d*
−1.07	−.19	−.19	−.23	−.16	−.29	−.23	−.28	−.28	−.32	−1.72	−1.44	−.43	−.84	−.87	Capital Account: Debit	**78bb** *d*
−.92	−.07	−.07	−.08	−.05	−.18	−.02	−.09	−.01	.08	−1.32	−.66	.68	.54	.69	Capital Account, n.i.e.	**78bc** *d*
−4.70	−4.48	−3.02	−3.67	−4.66	−5.30	−10.56	−9.76	−12.04	−15.29	−24.21	−23.72	−19.67	−14.48	−14.65	Direct Investment Abroad	**78bd** *d*
.33	.30	.75	1.72	.53	.49	1.02	1.82	1.07	7.07	2.49	4.07	2.44	.32	−3.02	Dir. Invest. in Rep. Econ., n.i.e.	**78be** *d*
−4.19	−2.67	−4.59	−4.20	−5.42	−11.03	−9.73	−13.76	−40.89	−26.73	−15.17	−17.79	−48.10	−33.11	−53.06	Portfolio Investment Assets	**78bf** *d*
.45	.42	1.07	5.11	5.87	12.85	33.15	17.60	4.11	24.35	13.42	42.79	80.25	139.71	27.22	Portfolio Investment Liab., n.i.e.	**78bg** *d*
−19.41	−17.34	−4.62	−8.33	−18.83	−22.92	−54.49	−24.01	−34.66	−90.35	−74.60	−23.89	−7.59	−130.88	−.02	Other Investment Assets	**78bh** *d*
33.18	24.77	10.92	3.02	10.34	7.61	3.63	4.10	14.69	41.90	43.61	23.98	44.20	50.77	67.93	Other Investment Liab., n.i.e.	**78bi** *d*
5.66	1.00	.50	−6.35	−12.16	−18.30	−36.98	−24.01	−67.72	−59.04	−54.47	5.43	51.54	12.32	24.40	Financial Account, n.i.e.	**78bj** *d*
−1.07	—	−2.61	−.27	2.28	2.93	1.31	−1.06	2.47	4.43	14.64	7.87	5.91	−12.88	−6.28	Net Errors and Omissions	**78ca** *d*
−9.64	−2.48	2.84	−1.95	−.35	2.23	5.43	21.49	−15.42	2.80	7.31	−5.98	36.54	−15.46	−2.12	Overall Balance	**78cb** *d*
9.64	2.48	−2.84	1.95	.35	−2.23	−5.43	−21.49	15.42	−2.80	−7.31	5.98	−36.54	15.46	2.12	Reserves and Related Items	**79da** *d*
9.64	2.48	−2.84	1.95	.35	−2.23	−5.43	−21.49	15.42	−2.80	−7.31	5.98	−36.54	15.46	2.12	Reserve Assets	**79db** *d*
—	—	—	—	—	—	—	—	—	—	—	—	—	—	—	Use of Fund Credit and Loans	**79dc** *d*
....	....	....	....	....	....	....	....	....	....	....	....	....	....	....	Liabs.Constit.For.Auth.Reserves	**79dd** *d*
....	....	....	....	....	....	....	....	....	....	....	....	....	....	....	Exceptional Financing	**79de** *d*

Germany

134

		1965	1966	1967	1968	1969	1970	1971	1972	1973	1974	1975	1976	1977	1978	1979
Government Finance															*Billions of Deutsche Mark:*	
Deficit (-) or Surplus	80	−1.93	−2.45	−8.27	−4.19	1.62	ℐ6.94	6.37	5.83	12.43	ℐ−6.43	ℐ−37.16	−31.21	−25.57	−26.49	−27.63
Revenue	81	61.27	64.80	66.63	70.70	82.42	ℐ166.51	186.03	208.63	241.96	ℐ258.86	ℐ271.79	303.47	326.52	349.83	377.18
Grants Received	81z	....	....	....	....	....	ℐ1.86	2.27	2.26	1.92	ℐ2.00	ℐ2.23	2.35	3.39	3.78	3.15
Adj. to Cash-Revenue & Grants	81x	....	....	....	....	....	ℐ−2.15	−1.51	−2.55	−1.49	ℐ−.38	ℐ−.93	−3.27	−.54	−1.09	−2.59
Expenditure	82	63.20	67.25	74.90	74.89	80.80	ℐ157.25	177.78	199.82	226.13	ℐ263.62	ℐ304.14	330.16	352.68	375.76	400.37
Lending Minus Repayments	83	....	....	....	....	....	ℐ2.03	2.64	2.69	3.83	ℐ3.29	ℐ6.11	3.60	2.26	3.25	5.00
Overall Cash Adjustment	80x	....	....	....	....	....	....	....	....	....	....	....	....	....	....	....
Financing																
Net Borrowing	84	1.70	2.55	7.89	3.73	−1.82	....	....	....	....	....	ℐ36.29	19.98	20.53	26.32	27.17
Domestic	84a	....	....	....	....	....	....	....	....	....	....	34.48	15.20	20.06	24.57	25.05
Foreign	85a	....	....	....	....	....	....	....	....	....	....	ℐ1.81	4.78	.47	1.75	2.12
Seigniorage	86d	.16	.18	.16	.18	.16	....	....	....	....	....	....	....	....	....	....
Pending Redemptions	87c	−.17	−.08	—	.27	.04	....	....	....	....	....	....	....	....	....	....
Use of Cash Balances	87	.24	−.20	.22	.01	—	....	....	....	....	....	ℐ.87	11.23	5.04	.17	.46
Debt	88	33.02	35.58	43.47	47.19	45.36	47.32	48.76	55.30	61.36	72.14	103.32	128.88	153.58	179.94	205.60
Domestic	88a	....	....	....	....	....	....	....	....	....	....	97.85	118.62	142.83	164.85	188.39
Foreign	89a	....	....	....	....	....	....	....	....	....	....	5.47	10.26	10.75	15.09	17.21
Intragovernmental Debt	88s	....	....	....	....	....	....	....	....	....	....	11.79	6.23	2.09	2.18	2.19
Other Deficits(-)or Surpluses																
Equalization of Burden Fund	80..*i*	−.52	−.24	−.22	−.31	−.21	.28	.23	.28	.47	.53	.29	.46	.98	.68	.16
Social Insurance System	80.*r*	2.26	1.77	−3.16	−2.08	−.51	2.99	4.51	5.35	5.92	1.52	−5.12	−5.97	−6.18		
National Accounts															*Billions of Deutsche Mark*	
Exports of Goods & Services	90c.*c*	....	....	....	....	....	....	....	....	....	....	....	....	....	329.6	349.2
Government Consumption	91f.*c*	69.7	75.4	80.1	82.7	93.0	106.5	126.8	141.0	163.1	190.1	210.1	221.9	235.1	253.1	273.5
Gross Fixed Capital Formation	93e.*c*	119.9	124.1	114.2	119.3	138.8	172.1	196.1	209.2	219.3	212.7	209.4	225.7	242.4	264.9	301.3
Increase/Decrease(-) in Stocks	93i.*c*	10.7	5.2	−.9	11.1	17.3	14.2	4.5	4.3	12.4	3.7	−6.4	15.7	7.0	7.2	43.0
Private Consumption	96f.*c*	257.6	275.1	282.6	300.7	330.9	368.9	409.0	452.0	495.6	533.6	583.5	631.9	682.1	725.9	781.3
Imports of Goods & Services	98c.*c*	....	....	....	....	....	....	....	....	....	....	....	....	....	....	−359.9
Gross Domestic Product	99b.*c*	459.2	488.2	494.4	533.3	597.0	675.3	749.8	823.1	917.3	983.9	1,026.6	1,120.5	1,195.3	1,283.6	1,388.4
Net Factor Inc/Pmts(-) Abroad	98.n*c*	−.9	−.8	−.8	.4	.7	.4	.7	1.5	1.6	−.2	1.1	3.3	.3	5.9	5.4
Gross Nat'l Expenditure = GNP	99a.*c*	458.3	487.4	493.6	533.7	597.7	675.7	750.4	824.6	918.8	983.7	1,027.7	1,123.8	1,195.6	1,289.4	1,393.8
Nat'l Income, Market Prices	99e.*c*	414.9	439.6	443.2	480.1	539.6	607.7	672.3	737.9	822.8	875.9	910.5	998.0	1,061.6	1,145.0	1,236.0
Gross Dom. Prod. 1990 Prices	99b.*r*	....	....	....	....	....	....	....	....	....	....	....	....	....	....	1,923.5
GDP Deflator (1990=100)	99bi*r*	....	....	....	....	....	....	....	....	....	....	....	....	....	....	72.2
															Millions:	
Population	99z	59.01	59.50	59.87	60.17	60.44	60.71	61.29	61.67	61.97	62.04	61.83	61.51	61.40	61.31	61.44

With the coming into effect on July 1, 1990 of the treaty on German Economic, Monetary, and Social Union (GEMSU) between the former Federal Republic of Germany (FRG) and the former German Democratic Republic (GDR), the deutsche mark became the sole currency of the GEMSU area, and customs borders between the two states were abolished. On October 3, 1990, the former GDR became part of the FRG under international law. The membership of the FRG in the Fund, under the designation Germany, remains unchanged. The presentation of exchange rates and Fund accounts shown for Germany in *IFS* is unaffected by the unification of the former FRG and the former GDR.

Stock data on international liquidity and money and banking cover the former FRG and the former GDR from 1990. Data on international transactions for 1990 reflect the transactions of the former FRG through June 1990 and unified Germany from July 1990. Data on national accounts refer only to the former Federal Republic of Germany.

Deposit Money Banks: ℐ Beginning in 1968, a new system of bank returns was introduced that led to changes in the coverage of deposit money bank data. ℐ Beginning in 1985, coverage of financial institutions was broadened to include all cooperative banks.

Monetary Survey: ℐ See note to section 20.

Government Finance: ℐ Beginning in 1970, data are as reported in the *Government Finance Statistics Yearbook* and cover consolidated central government, including extrabudgetary and social security accounts. ℐ Data for social security funds and the European Recovery Program are on a cash basis only beginning in 1974 and 1975 respectively. ℐ Beginning in 1990, central government extrabudgetary operations include operations of the German Unity Fund. ℐ Beginning in 1992, data refer to government operations on the territory of unified Germany; prior to 1992, data cover government operations on the territory of the former Federal Republic of Germany.

Germany

134

1980	1981	1982	1983	1984	1985	1986	1987	1988	1989	1990	1991	1992	1993	1994		
Year Ending December 31															**Government Finance**	
−26.91	−36.31	−32.02	−32.96	−32.31	−20.01	−17.56	−21.57	−35.54	−3.60	ɪ−39.55	−62.29	ɪ−73.10	−75.56ᴾ	....	Deficit (−) or Surplus	80
423.94	450.02	478.05	490.83	524.21	551.33	572.59	588.77	605.00	655.37	ɪ698.99	808.44	ɪ969.71	1,000.10ᴾ	....	Revenue	81
2.52	2.18	2.68	3.16	3.00	3.10	3.07	2.77	2.87	3.14	ɪ2.60	3.45	ɪ5.02	4.67ᴾ	....	Grants Received	81z
−.63	−.50	—	—	—	—	—	—	—	—	ɪ—	—	ɪ—	—ᴾ	....	Adj. to Cash-Revenue & Grants	81x
447.54	481.64	506.03	520.05	549.04	564.55	584.66	609.79	637.41	654.91	ɪ716.28	860.74	ɪ1022.95	1,062.38ᴾ	....	Expenditure	82
5.20	5.92	5.56	7.04	8.09	7.44	4.58	3.30	3.92	6.73	ɪ9.64	11.98	ɪ14.91	13.07ᴾ	....	Lending Minus Repayments	83
—	−.45	−1.16	.14	−2.39	−2.45	−3.98	−.02	−2.08	−.47	ɪ−15.22	−1.46	ɪ−9.97	−4.88ᴾ	....	Overall Cash Adjustment	80x
															Financing	
28.01	40.62	36.63	31.82	28.03	23.50	22.22	27.97	34.70	16.39	ɪ65.04	72.00	ɪ56.11	91.59ᴾ	....	Net Borrowing	84
7.17	19.45	29.15	18.32	18.56	5.42	−6.13	11.27	25.24	−2.81	ɪ51.73	26.95	ɪ−12.41	−69.55ᴾ	....	Domestic	84a
20.84	21.17	7.48	13.50	9.47	18.08	28.35	16.70	9.46	19.20	ɪ13.31	45.05	ɪ68.52	161.14ᴾ	....	Foreign	85a
....	....	....	....	....	....	....	....	....	....	....	....	....	....	....	Seigniorage	86d
....	....	....	....	....	....	....	....	....	....	....	....	....	....	....	Pending Redemptions	87c
−1.10	−4.31	−4.61	1.14	4.28	−3.49	−4.66	−6.40	.84	−12.79	ɪ−25.49	−9.71	ɪ16.99	−16.03ᴾ	....	Use of Cash Balances	87
235.77	277.99	314.44	347.27	373.91	399.15	421.99	446.56	481.26	497.66	ɪ599.14	680.81	ɪ801.57	902.52ᴾ	....	Debt	88
197.72	218.77	247.73	267.08	284.25	291.41	285.90	293.77	319.01	316.21	ɪ404.38	437.60	ɪ489.84	429.65ᴾ	....	Domestic	88a
38.05	59.22	66.71	80.19	89.66	107.74	136.09	152.79	162.25	181.45	ɪ194.76	243.21	ɪ311.73	472.87ᴾ	....	Foreign	89a
2.50	2.82	2.80	2.86	2.57	2.25	....	....	....	....	....	....	....	....	....	Intragovernmental Debt	88s
															Other Deficits(-)or Surpluses	
....	....	....	....	....	....	....	....	....	....	....	....	....	....	....	Equalization of Burden Fund	80..i
....	....	....	....	....	....	....	....	....	....	....	....	....	....	....	Social Insurance System	80.r
Billions of Deutsche Mark															**National Accounts**	
388.9	440.8	472.2	477.9	536.8	596.1	582.8	576.3	617.6	701.7	783.6	875.2	932.7	911.3	984.8	Exports of Goods & Services	90c.c
298.0	318.4	326.4	336.4	350.4	365.7	382.6	397.3	412.4	418.8	444.1	466.5	502.9	508.5	520.2	Government Consumption	91f.c
332.1	331.3	323.5	340.8	350.7	355.8	373.5	385.8	409.9	448.5	507.8	563.2	586.9	551.8	564.1	Gross Fixed Capital Formation	93e.c
37.0	26.3	26.1	34.2	40.6	41.4	48.9	48.9	66.8	77.1	89.1	123.1	120.4	131.4	166.1	Increase/Decrease(−) in Stocks	93i.c
837.0	883.5	916.1	959.3	1,001.2	1,036.5	1,066.4	1,108.0	1,153.7	1,221.0	1,318.7	1,448.8	1,536.3	1,588.9	1,644.5	Private Consumption	96f.c
−422.2	−464.8	−477.3	−481.6	−530.1	−569.5	−526.3	−525.0	−566.1	−643.5	−713.8	−829.3	−866.1	−838.1	−902.0	Imports of Goods & Services	98c.c
1,470.9	1,535.5	1,586.9	1,667.1	1,749.6	1,826.1	1,927.9	1,991.2	2,094.2	2,223.6	2,429.4	2,647.6	2,813.0	2,853.7	2,977.7	Gross Domestic Product	99b.c
6.5	4.1	3.4	8.6	13.7	8.4	8.2	11.8	13.8	25.5	18.8	20.4	6.8	−10.9	−32.4	Net Factor Inc/Pmts(−) Abroad	98.n c
1,477.4	1,539.6	1,590.3	1,675.7	1,763.3	1,834.5	1,936.1	2,003.0	2,108.0	2,249.1	2,448.2	2,668.0	2,819.8	2,842.8	2,945.3	Gross Nat'l Expenditure = GNP	99a.c
1,302.4	1,349.0	1,386.6	1,460.8	1,536.9	1,599.1	1,692.4	1,750.7	1,844.9	1,969.7	2,145.2	2,320.9	2,439.8	2,440.4	....	Nat'l Income, Market Prices	99e.c
1,942.4	1,945.1	1,924.8	1,958.3	2,013.6	2,059.4	2,107.3	2,136.3	2,213.0	2,294.3	2,429.4	2,548.6	2,593.5	2,549.5	2,608.3	Gross Dom. Prod. 1990 Prices	99b.r
75.7	78.9	82.4	85.1	86.9	88.7	91.5	93.2	94.6	96.9	100.0	103.9	108.5	111.9	114.2	GDP Deflator (1990=100)	99bi r
Midyear Estimates																
61.54	61.66	61.60	61.38	61.13	60.97	61.01	61.09	61.42	61.99	63.23	ɪ79.98	80.59	81.19	81.41	**Population**	99z

Ghana

652

		1965	1966	1967	1968	1969	1970	1971	1972	1973	1974	1975	1976	1977	1978	1979
Exchange Rates																*Cedis per SDR:*
Market Rate	aa	.71	.71	1.02	1.02	1.02	1.02	1.97	1.39	1.39	1.41	1.35	1.34	1.40	3.58	3.62
																Cedis per US Dollar:
Market Rate	ae	.71	.71	1.02	1.02	1.02	1.02	1.82	1.28	1.15	1.15	1.15	1.15	1.15	2.75	2.75
Market Rate	rf	.71	.71	.87	1.02	1.02	1.02	1.03	1.33	1.17	1.15	1.15	1.15	1.15	1.76	2.75
Fund Position																*Millions of SDRs:*
Quota	2f. s	55.0	69.0	69.0	69.0	69.0	87.0	87.0	87.0	87.0	87.0	87.0	87.0	87.0	106.0	106.0
SDRs	1b. s	—	—	—	—	—	—	3.1	10.0	9.7	9.6	7.5	6.7	10.1	9.5	13.7
Reserve Position in the Fund	1c. s	1.9	—	—	—	—	—	—	—	—	5.9	10.6	—	—	—	—
Total Fund Cred.&Loans Outstg.	2tl	—	45.0	63.9	74.7	69.3	46.1	18.3	1.7	—	—	38.6	38.6	38.6	34.4	82.5
International Liquidity												*Millions of US Dollars Unless Otherwise Indicated:*				
Total Reserves minus Gold	1l. d	110.2	105.5	77.1	90.3	66.2	36.6	36.1	93.7	176.1	71.5	124.7	91.7	148.6	277.2	289.1
SDRs	1b. d	—	—	—	—	—	—	3.3	10.9	11.7	11.8	8.8	7.7	12.3	12.4	18.0
Reserve Position in the Fund	1c. d	1.9	—	—	—	—	—	—	—	—	7.2	13.0	—	—	—	—
Foreign Exchange	1d. d	108.3	105.5	77.1	90.3	66.2	36.6	32.8	82.8	157.2	46.7	115.9	84.0	136.3	264.8	271.1
Gold (Million Fine Troy Ounces)	1ad	.160	.160	.160	.160	.160	.160	.160	.160	.160	.160	.160	.160	.200	.219	.219
Gold (National Valuation)	1and	5.6	5.6	5.6	5.6	5.6	5.6	5.6	5.6	5.6	5.6	5.6	5.6	7.2	8.1	8.1
Monetary Authorities: Other Assets	3.. d	2.0	2.3	5.9	5.2	4.3	15.7	5.5	7.6	6.1	15.3	18.5	5.9	6.8	2.3	2.5
Monetary Authorities: Other Liab.	4.. d	101.4	73.0	64.7	81.1	63.0	29.7	37.1	5.5	7.7	94.1	8.7	32.1	110.6	129.8	64.3
Deposit Money Banks: Assets	7a. d	1.1	2.8	1.0	.3	.4	4.2	4.7	1.4	12.2	.1	.1	8.9	6.3	2.1	.8
of which: Claims on Nonbanks	7ad d	....	....	.1	.1	.2	.2	—	.1	—	—	—	—	—	—	—
Deposit Money Banks: Liabilities	7b. d	26.2	34.4	16.3	13.1	29.1	21.8	1.7	9.5	2.1	11.9	3.9	15.1	14.5	7.0	11.0
of which: Liab. to Nonbanks	7bd d	....	....	1.2	1.5	1.3	.9	.8	1.3	1.9	2.1	3.0	15.0	14.5	7.0	9.3
Monetary Authorities													*Millions of Cedis through 1985;*			
Foreign Assets	11	86	83	96	108	82	75	97	148	230	145	213	129	247	784	817
Claims on Central Government	12a	139	143	228	271	266	255	349	305	339	574	881	1,513	2,528	4,287	4,413
Claims on Nonfin.Pub.Enterprises	12c	45	73	83	54	63	115	120	156	76	146	91	109	90	628	1,094
Claims on Deposit Money Banks	12e	....	....	—	—	—	—	—	11	—	—	3	5	6	6	6
Claims on Other Financial Insts.	12f	....	....	3	4	5	7	12	19	49	67	72	77	85	79	74
Reserve Money	14	151	156	161	168	201	231	238	352	437	594	879	1,246	2,017	3,721	4,396
of which: Currency Outside DMBs	14a	116	116	119	125	151	151	159	239	245	336	486	707	1,157	2,122	2,459
Nonfin.Pub.Ent. Deps.	14e	3	2	1	1	1	4	3	3	28	41	29	40	118	219	349
Restricted Deposits	16b	....	....	20	10	4	1	89	194	147	127	150	154	260	490	648
Foreign Liabilities	16c	72	84	131	159	135	77	104	9	9	108	62	88	181	480	476
Central Government Deposits	16d	27	21	45	31	33	62	28	13	31	40	58	112	84	132	217
Counterpart Funds	16e	—	—	—	—	15	6	3	11	—	—	—	—	—	1	1
Capital Accounts	17a	14	17	25	24	26	49	85	97	132	149	169	197	272	416	664
Other Items (Net)	17r	19	38	28	45	3	25	31	–38	–62	–86	–57	35	142	543	1
Deposit Money Banks													*Millions of Cedis through 1985;*			
Reserves	20	26	39	38	38	55	88	79	114	171	215	375	510	714	1,423	1,668
Foreign Assets	21	1	2	1	—	—	4	8	2	14	—	—	10	7	6	2
Claims on Central Government	22a	82	105	102	91	98	120	54	115	108	125	159	240	434	555	873
Claims on Nonfin.Pub.Enterprises	22c	....	....	16	15	11	1	1	11	⅃155	192	205	284	333	485	540
Claims on Private Sector	22d	125	128	114	147	184	186	315	283	⅃187	265	306	385	560	739	796
Demand Deposits	24	122	131	121	133	138	151	159	220	291	320	495	679	1,119	1,787	1,873
Time and Savings Deposits	25	60	67	78	93	99	121	154	205	230	308	377	474	651	1,005	1,262
Foreign Liabilities	26c	19	25	17	13	30	22	3	12	2	14	4	17	17	19	30
Central Government Deposits	26d	15	22	18	15	19	21	86	48	41	75	58	69	95	187	167
Credit from Monetary Authorities	26g	....	....	—	—	—	—	—	—	—	—	—	—	—	—	—
Capital Accounts	27a	....	....	7	10	13	19	24	29	32	35	40	44	55	77	114
Other Items (Net)	27r	18	29	29	27	51	65	31	11	39	45	70	147	111	132	434
Monetary Survey													*Millions of Cedis through 1985;*			
Foreign Assets (Net)	31n	–4	–24	–50	–64	–82	–20	–1	128	232	23	147	34	57	290	313
Domestic Credit	32	348	406	⅃481	537	577	600	736	828	⅃843	1,254	1,598	2,429	3,851	6,454	7,406
Claims on Central Govt. (Net)	32an	178	205	266	315	313	291	289	358	376	584	924	1,573	2,783	4,523	4,903
Claims on Nonfin.Pub.Enterprises	32c	45	73	99	69	74	115	120	168	⅃231	338	295	393	423	1,113	1,634
Claims on Private Sector	32d	125	128	⅃114	148	184	186	315	283	⅃187	265	306	385	560	739	796
Claims on Other Financial Insts.	32f	....	....	3	4	5	7	12	19	49	67	72	77	85	79	74
Money	34	240	248	241	259	290	306	321	463	564	697	1,009	1,426	2,394	4,128	4,680
Quasi-Money	35	60	67	78	93	99	121	154	205	230	308	377	474	651	1,005	1,262
Restricted Deposits	36b	....	....	20	10	4	1	89	194	147	127	150	154	260	490	648
Counterpart Funds	36e	—	—	—	—	15	6	3	11	—	—	—	—	—	1	1
Capital Accounts	37a	....	....	32	34	39	68	109	125	164	184	209	242	327	493	778
Other Items (Net)	37r	43	67	59	78	48	78	59	–42	–29	–39	—	167	275	626	350
Money plus Quasi-Money	35l	301	315	319	352	388	427	475	668	794	1,005	1,386	1,900	3,046	5,133	5,942
Other Banking Institutions																*Billions of Cedis:*
Reserves	40	....	....	....	....	....	....	....	....	....	....	....	....	....	....	....
Claims on Central Government	42a	....	....	....	....	....	....	....	....	....	....	....	....	....	....	....
Claims on Nonfin.Pub.Enterprises	42c	....	....	....	....	....	....	....	....	....	....	....	....	....	....	....
Claims on Deposit Money Banks	42e	....	....	....	....	....	....	....	....	....	....	....	....	....	....	....
Claims on Other Financial Insts	42f	....	....	....	....	....	....	....	....	....	....	....	....	....	....	....
Quasi-Monetary Liabilities	45	....	....	....	....	....	....	....	....	....	....	....	....	....	....	....
Credit from Monetary Authorities	46g	....	....	....	....	....	....	....	....	....	....	....	....	....	....	....
Capital Accounts	47a	....	....	....	....	....	....	....	....	....	....	....	....	....	....	....
Other Items (Net)	47r	....	....	....	....	....	....	....	....	....	....	....	....	....	....	....
Banking Survey																*Billions of Cedis:*
Foreign Assets (Net)	51n	....	....	....	....	....	....	....	....	....	....	....	....	....	....	....
Domestic Credit	52	....	....	....	....	....	....	....	....	....	....	....	....	....	....	....
Claims on Central Govt. (Net)	52an	....	....	....	....	....	....	....	....	....	....	....	....	....	....	....
Claims on Nonfin.Pub.Enterprises	52c	....	....	....	....	....	....	....	....	....	....	....	....	....	....	....
Claims on Private Sector	52d	....	....	....	....	....	....	....	....	....	....	....	....	....	....	....
Claims on Other Financial Insts	52f	....	....	....	....	....	....	....	....	....	....	....	....	....	....	....
Liquid Liabilities	55l	....	....	....	....	....	....	....	....	....	....	....	....	....	....	....
Restricted Deposits	56b	....	....	....	....	....	....	....	....	....	....	....	....	....	....	....
Counterpart Funds	56e	....	....	....	....	....	....	....	....	....	....	....	....	....	....	....
Capital Accounts	57a	....	....	....	....	....	....	....	....	....	....	....	....	....	....	....
Other Items (Net)	57r	....	....	....	....	....	....	....	....	....	....	....	....	....	....	....

Ghana

1980	1981	1982	1983	1984	1985	1986	1987	1988	1989	1990	1991	1992	1993	1994	652	
End of Period															**Exchange Rates**	
3.51	3.20	3.03	31.41	49.01	65.89	110.10	249.76	309.36	398.23	490.57	558.76	716.15[e]	1,125.87	1,536.68	Market Rate	aa
End of Period (ae) Period Average (rf)																
2.75	2.75	2.75	30.00	50.00	59.99	90.01	176.06	229.89	303.03	344.83	390.63	520.83[e]	819.67	1,052.63	Market Rate	ae
2.75	2.75	2.75	8.83	35.99	54.37	89.20	153.73	202.35	270.00	326.33	367.83	437.09[e]	649.06	956.71	Market Rate	rf
End of Period															**Fund Position**	
159.0	159.0	159.0	204.5	204.5	204.5	204.5	204.5	204.5	204.5	204.5	204.5	274.0	274.0	274.0	Quota	2f.s
—	.6	.2	2.1	.1	17.2	1.6	11.2	.2	22.8	3.1	8.8	3.2	.4	2.9	SDRs	1b.s
—	—	—	—	—	—	—	—	—	—	—	—	17.4	17.4	17.4	Reserve Position in the Fund	1c.s
82.5	73.2	68.4	316.6	525.1	638.0	642.3	610.9	566.4	561.2	523.4	583.1	537.8	537.3	479.7	Total Fund Cred.&Loans Outstg.	2tl
End of Period															**International Liquidity**	
180.4	145.6	138.9	144.8	301.6	478.5	513.0	195.1	221.3	347.3	218.8	550.2	319.9	409.7	583.9	Total Reserves minus Gold	1l.d
—	.7	.2	2.2	.1	18.9	2.0	15.9	.3	29.9	4.4	12.5	4.4	.5	4.2	SDRs	1b.d
—	—	—	—	—	—	—	—	—	—	—	—	23.9	23.9	25.4	Reserve Position in the Fund	1c.d
180.4	144.9	138.7	142.6	301.5	459.6	511.0	179.2	221.0	317.4	214.4	537.7	291.6	385.3	554.3	Foreign Exchange	1d.d
.253	.309	.384	.384	.440	.225	.284	.282	.217	.221	.235	.266	.275	.275	.275	Gold (Million Fine Troy Ounces)	1ad
19.0	48.2	68.8	72.5	91.7	46.1	76.6	81.5	77.5	78.3	63.3	74.0	78.1	77.2	77.2	Gold (National Valuation)	1and
16.2	2.4	3.5	1.2	11.5	7.4	15.1	50.5	....	....	....	....	....	....	....	Monetary Authorities: Other Assets	3..d
20.0	134.2	84.8	101.2	233.1	354.4	832.0	180.7	283.4	519.8	445.2	672.4	656.9	631.7	664.5	Monetary Authorities: Other Liab.	4..d
.8	3.2	3.7	30.7	9.2	7.5	4.3	27.2	28.0	112.9	289.9	306.3	311.1	313.8	405.4	Deposit Money Banks: Assets	7a.d
.1	2.1	—	1.6	—	—	—	3.5	3.8	16.7	100.2	127.1	100.6	104.5	122.1	*of which:* Claims on Nonbanks	7add
21.3	50.5	60.1	92.9	12.6	38.3	28.5	49.2	56.6	105.8	110.1	132.2	115.9	161.4	225.4	Deposit Money Banks: Liabilities	7b.d
11.6	13.8	18.1	38.9	3.9	3.1	4.3	3.6	12.6	17.3	32.9	82.7	94.8	126.1	192.9	*of which:* Liab. to Nonbanks	7bdd
Billions of Cedis Beginning 1986: End of Period															**Monetary Authorities**	
588	512	581	6,520	19,661	31,921	I92	58	77	141	113	I270	192	380	663	Foreign Assets	11
5,724	9,494	10,165	24,343	35,054	45,018	I79	162	160	134	167	I344	483	851	893	Claims on Central Government	12a
1,347	2,191	4,966	155	3,482	12,544	I16	15	1	25	6	I20	4	45	149	Claims on Nonfin.Pub.Enterprises	12c
6	6	6	6	6	6	I—	—	—	—	2	I8	4	7	7	Claims on Deposit Money Banks	12e
73	99	129	200	997	2,789	I4	5	6	9	9	I—	—	—	—	Claims on Other Financial Insts.	12f
5,744	8,926	10,213	14,641	21,828	29,570	I47	67	103	127	130	I130	246	258	461	Reserve Money	14
3,521	6,049	6,957	10,389	17,631	22,557	I32	49	68	83	80	I90	183	222	369	*of which: Currency Outside DMBs*	14a
476	56	200	853	440	2,510	I5	10	22	10	16	I13	2	3	3	*Nonfin.Pub.Ent. Deps.*	14e
458	699	1,817	3,536	5,735	8,313	I13	16	6	1	—	I1	1	1	1	Restricted Deposits	16b
344	603	440	12,981	37,386	63,299	I146	184	223	324	327	I429	522	800	1,017	Foreign Liabilities	16c
277	535	1,869	610	1,440	1,161	I7	9	14	17	34	I11	5	47	65	Central Government Deposits	16d
—	29	21	2	—	—	I—	—	—	—	—	I63	99	190	253	Counterpart Funds	16e
572	1,037	1,577	3,943	4,576	6,036	I14	15	17	16	22	I24	14	87	....	Capital Accounts	17a
342	474	–91	–4,490	–11,764	–16,100	I–36	–52	–118	–176	–216	I–15	–205	–101	....	Other Items (Net)	17r
Billions of Cedis Beginning 1986: End of Period															**Deposit Money Banks**	
1,854	2,802	3,366	4,341	8,757	10,848	I20	18	24	45	45	I139	135	305	458	Reserves	20
2	9	10	922	462	449	I—	5	6	34	100	I120	162	257	427	Foreign Assets	21
1,301	1,981	3,031	4,872	4,444	5,179	I6	6	5	6	3	I1	—	—	—	Claims on Central Government	22a
616	1,203	1,117	1,182	806	3,775	I4	5	7	16	24	I35	68	43	30	Claims on Nonfin.Pub.Enterprises	22c
940	1,342	1,558	2,838	5,978	10,663	I19	24	33	83	95	I89	139	187	273	Claims on Private Sector	22d
2,090	3,310	4,048	5,477	8,778	13,240	I18	25	32	93	111	I132	175	235	321	Demand Deposits	24
1,864	2,616	3,634	4,086	5,113	8,410	I14	22	33	53	65	I110	165	203	275	Time and Savings Deposits	25
59	139	165	255	632	2,298	I3	9	13	32	38	I52	60	132	237	Foreign Liabilities	26c
229	291	270	550	598	984	I1	2	3	13	17	I18	23	63	69	Central Government Deposits	26d
—	—	—	—	—	—	I—	—	—	3	1	I2	2	6	20	Credit from Monetary Authorities	26g
144	253	410	852	1,298	2,338	I5	7	7	–2	48	I76	90	132	250	Capital Accounts	27a
327	727	555	2,934	4,028	3,644	I9	–7	–14	–8	–13	I–6	–11	20	16	Other Items (Net)	27r
Billions of Cedis Beginning 1986: End of Period															**Monetary Survey**	
187	–221	–15	–5,795	–17,895	–33,227	I–56	–131	–153	–181	–152	I–91	–228	–295	–164	Foreign Assets (Net)	31n
9,493	15,483	18,827	32,429	48,723	77,823	I119	205	196	243	253	I460	666	1,015	1,211	Domestic Credit	32
6,518	10,649	11,057	28,055	37,459	48,052	I77	157	148	110	119	I316	455	740	759	Claims on Central Govt. (Net)	32an
1,962	3,394	6,083	1,337	4,288	16,319	I20	20	8	41	30	I55	72	88	178	Claims on Nonfin.Pub.Enterprises	32c
940	1,342	1,558	2,838	5,978	10,663	I19	24	33	83	95	I89	139	187	273	Claims on Private Sector	32d
73	99	129	200	997	2,789	I4	5	6	9	9	I—	—	—	—	Claims on Other Financial Insts.	32f
6,087	9,415	11,205	16,719	26,849	38,308	I55	84	122	186	206	I236	361	461	694	Money	34
1,864	2,616	3,634	4,086	5,113	8,410	I14	22	33	53	65	I110	165	203	275	Quasi-Money	35
458	699	1,817	3,536	5,735	8,313	I13	16	6	1	—	I1	1	1	1	Restricted Deposits	36b
—	29	21	2	—	—	I—	—	—	—	—	I63	99	190	253	Counterpart Funds	36e
716	1,290	1,986	4,795	5,874	8,374	I19	23	24	13	70	I100	105	219	....	Capital Accounts	37a
555	1,213	148	–2,504	–12,743	–18,809	I–37	–70	–142	–192	–241	I–139	–293	–354	....	Other Items (Net)	37r
7,951	12,031	14,839	20,805	31,962	46,718	I69	106	155	240	272	I345	526	665	969	Money plus Quasi-Money	35l
End of Period															**Other Banking Institutions**	
....	....	....	....	....	....	....	....	....	....	....	....	26	31	42	Reserves	40
....	....	....	....	....	....	....	....	....	....	....	....	—	—	—	Claims on Central Government	42a
....	....	....	....	....	....	....	....	....	....	....	....	7	1	—	Claims on Nonfin.Pub.Enterprises	42c
....	....	....	....	....	....	....	....	....	....	....	....	—	2	1	Claims on Deposit Money Banks	42e
....	....	....	....	....	....	....	....	....	....	....	....	—	—	—	Claims on Other Financial Insts	42f
....	....	....	....	....	....	....	....	....	....	....	....	32	31	38	Quasi-Monetary Liabilities	45
....	....	....	....	....	....	....	....	....	....	....	....	3	—	—	Credit from Monetary Authorities	46g
....	....	....	....	....	....	....	....	....	....	....	....	4	4	7	Capital Accounts	47a
....	....	....	....	....	....	....	....	....	....	....	....	–5	—	–2	Other Items (Net)	47r
End of Period															**Banking Survey**	
....	....	....	....	....	....	....	....	....	....	....	–91	–228	–295	–164	Foreign Assets (Net)	51n
....	....	....	....	....	....	....	....	....	....	....	....	676	1,016	1,211	Domestic Credit	52
....	....	....	....	....	....	....	....	....	....	....	....	455	740	759	Claims on Central Govt. (Net)	52an
....	....	....	....	....	....	....	....	....	....	....	....	79	89	178	Claims on Nonfin.Pub.Enterprises	52c
....	....	....	....	....	....	....	....	....	....	....	89	139	187	273	Claims on Private Sector	52d
....	....	....	....	....	....	....	....	....	....	....	....	—	—	—	Claims on Other Financial Insts	52f
....	....	....	....	....	....	....	....	....	....	....	....	532	664	965	Liquid Liabilities	55l
....	....	....	....	....	....	....	....	....	....	....	1	1	1	1	Restricted Deposits	56b
....	....	....	....	....	....	....	....	....	....	....	63	99	190	253	Counterpart Funds	56e
....	....	....	....	....	....	....	....	....	....	....	....	108	222	....	Capital Accounts	57a
....	....	....	....	....	....	....	....	....	....	....	....	–293	–356	....	Other Items (Net)	57r

Ghana
652

		1965	1966	1967	1968	1969	1970	1971	1972	1973	1974	1975	1976	1977	1978	1979
Interest Rates															*Percent Per Annum*	
Discount Rate *(End of Period)*	60	4.50	7.00	6.00	5.50	5.50	5.50	8.00	8.00	6.00	6.00	8.00	8.00	8.00	13.50	13.50
Treasury Bill Rate	60c	...	...	...	...	...	...	...	...	...	...	...	...	...	13.00	13.00
Deposit Rate	60l	...	...	...	...	...	...	...	...	...	...	...	...	...	11.50	11.50
Lending Rate	60p	...	...	...	...	...	...	...	...	...	...	...	...	...	19.00	19.00
Prices															*Index Numbers (1990=100)*	
Wholesale Prices	63	.1	.1	.1	.1	.1	.1	.1	.1	.1	.2	.2	.3	ⅠΙ.4	.7	1.1
Consumer Prices	64	.1	.1	Ⅰ.1	.1	.1	.1	.1	.1	.1	.2	.2	.3	.7	1.2	1.9
International Transactions															*Millions of Cedis through 1985;*	
Exports	70	227	191	245	339	333	467	496	565	730	840	928	951	1,166	1,581	2,737
Cocoa Beans	70r	135	117	131	181	221	301	203	275	397	466	556	516	680	988	1,846
Imports, cif	71	320	251	262	314	354	419	443	393	526	944	909	992	1,193	1,682	2,344
Imports, fob	71.v	288	226	235	284	312	365	390	351	465	832	804	877	1,120	1,550	2,194
Volume of Exports															*1990=100*	
Cocoa Beans	72r	198.9	163.1	137.3	137.5	127.5	150.6	134.8	163.8	184.3	127.8	120.1	122.2	94.3	79.6	70.6
Export Prices																
Cocoa Beans (Unit Value)	74r	.1	.1	.1	.1	.1	.2	.1	.1	.2	.3	.4	.3	.6	1.0	2.2
Cocoa Beans (Wholesale Price)	76r	.2	.3	.4	.5	.7	.5	.4	.6	1.1	1.6	1.2	1.9	3.7	4.5	6.5
Balance of Payments															*Millions of US Dollars:*	
Goods: Exports f.o.b.	78aa *d*	...	...	...	...	...	...	...	...	...	...	801.0	779.0	889.6	892.8	1,065.7
Goods: Imports f.o.b.	78ab *d*	...	...	...	...	...	...	...	...	...	...	−650.5	−690.3	−860.2	−780.3	−803.1
Trade Balance	78ac *d*	...	...	...	...	...	...	...	...	...	...	150.4	88.8	29.4	112.5	262.6
Services: Credit	78ad *d*	...	...	...	...	...	...	...	...	...	...	90.0	112.4	128.3	103.3	97.0
Services: Debit	78ae *d*	...	...	...	...	...	...	...	...	...	...	−231.0	−260.3	−261.0	−292.6	−260.9
Balance on Goods and Services	78af *d*	...	...	...	...	...	...	...	...	...	...	9.4	−59.0	−103.4	−76.8	98.7
Income: Credit	78ag *d*	...	...	...	...	...	...	...	...	...	...	4.4	2.5	2.5	1.3	1.9
Income: Debit	78ah *d*	...	...	...	...	...	...	...	...	...	...	−40.8	−44.3	−37.4	−28.7	−57.4
Balance on Goods, Serv., & Inc.	78ai *d*	...	...	...	...	...	...	...	...	...	...	−26.9	−100.8	−138.3	−104.2	43.2
Current Transfers, n.i.e.: Credit	78aj *d*	...	...	...	...	...	...	...	...	...	...	56.6	40.3	71.4	69.7	89.5
Current Transfers: Debit	78ak *d*	...	...	...	...	...	...	...	...	...	...	−12.1	−13.5	−12.9	−11.5	−9.2
Current Account, n.i.e.	78al *d*	...	...	...	...	...	...	...	...	...	...	17.6	−74.0	−79.7	−45.9	123.5
Capital Account, n.i.e.: Credit	78ba *d*	...	...	...	...	...	...	...	...	...	...	—	—	—	—	—
Capital Account: Debit	78bb *d*	...	...	...	...	...	...	...	...	...	...	—	—	—	—	−1.5
Capital Account, n.i.e.	78bc *d*	...	...	...	...	...	...	...	...	...	...	—	—	—	—	−1.5
Direct Investment Abroad	78bd *d*	...	...	...	...	...	...	...	...	...	...	—	—	—	—	—
Dir. Invest. in Rep. Econ., n.i.e.	78be *d*	...	...	...	...	...	...	...	...	...	...	70.9	−18.3	19.2	9.7	−2.8
Portfolio Investment Assets	78bf *d*	...	...	...	...	...	...	...	...	...	...	—	—	—	—	—
Portfolio Investment Liab., n.i.e.	78bg *d*	...	...	...	...	...	...	...	...	...	...	—	—	—	—	—
Other Investment Assets	78bh *d*	...	...	...	...	...	...	...	...	...	...	−3.1	3.9	1.7	10.8	20.7
Other Investment Liab., n.i.e.	78bi *d*	...	...	...	...	...	...	...	...	...	...	14.7	−22.2	38.1	82.5	36.0
Financial Account, n.i.e.	78bj *d*	...	...	...	...	...	...	...	...	...	...	82.4	−36.6	58.9	103.0	53.9
Net Errors and Omissions	78ca *d*	...	...	...	...	...	...	...	...	...	...	6.3	−26.7	12.4	−119.4	−106.1
Overall Balance	78cb *d*	...	...	...	...	...	...	...	...	...	...	106.3	−137.3	−8.4	−62.4	69.8
Reserves and Related Items	79da *d*	...	...	...	...	...	...	...	...	...	...	−106.3	137.3	8.4	62.4	−69.8
Reserve Assets	79db *d*	...	...	...	...	...	...	...	...	...	...	−45.6	59.3	−109.4	−80.2	3.1
Use of Fund Credit and Loans	79dc *d*	...	...	...	...	...	...	...	...	...	...	48.1	—	—	−5.3	62.1
Liabs.Constit.For.Auth.Reserves	79dd *d*	...	...	...	...	...	...	...	...	...	...	—	—	—	—	—
Exceptional Financing	79de *d*	...	...	...	...	...	...	...	...	...	...	−108.9	78.0	117.8	147.9	−135.0
Government Finance												*Millions of Cedis through 1985; Billions of Cedis Beginning 1986:*				
Deficit (−) or Surplus	80	−94.1	−76.6	−88.1	−104.0	−66.0	−49.9	−88.4	Ⅰ−161.2	−186.6	−196.1	−401.3	−736.2	−1,056.8	−1,896.7	−1,800.0
Revenue	81	284.0	230.9	253.8	297.9	332.0	437.3	450.7	Ⅰ418.7	391.1	578.9	809.0	869.8	1,146.9	1,392.1	2,600.0
Grants Received	81z	...	...	...	...	...	...	...	Ⅰ3.2	.5	4.7	.9	...	30.3	1.0	—
Expenditure	82	371.1	272.9	320.8	400.2	395.3	467.9	523.8	Ⅰ543.1	548.5	754.1	1,146.2	1,484.0	2,136.6	3,164.8	4,295.7
Lending Minus Repayments	83	7.0	34.6	21.1	1.7	2.7	19.3	15.3	Ⅰ40.0	29.7	25.6	65.0	122.0	91.4	125.0	104.3
Financing																
Net Borrowing: Domestic	84a	83.3	66.9	67.3	73.8	42.7	44.8	72.0	Ⅰ79.4	167.8	197.7	399.9	734.4	1,044.1	1,720.0	1,800.0
Foreign	85a	2.5	25.5	16.8	28.3	26.6	48.0	24.2	Ⅰ81.8	18.8	−1.6	1.4	1.8	12.7	67.2	—
Use of Cash Balances	87	8.4	−15.8	3.8	1.8	−3.3	−42.5	−7.8	Ⅰ—	—	—	—	—	—	—	—
Unallocable Financing	87c	...	...	...	...	...	...	...	Ⅰ—	—	—	—	—	—	109.5	—
Debt: Domestic	88a	...	...	...	...	605.5	681.1	710.5	Ⅰ928.1	1,055.9	1,275.5	1,486.0	2,269.5	3,208.2	5,136.0	6,154.0
Foreign	89a	...	...	...	...	428.5	487.6	509.3	Ⅰ228.3	261.4	263.9	482.2	482.2	...	...	2,741.7
National Accounts															*Millions of Cedis through 1985;*	
Exports of Goods & Services	90c	251.0	222.0	274.0	396.0	447.0	523.0	443.0	648.0	820.0	956.0	1,023.0	1,025.0	1,171.0	1,754.0	3,169.0
Government Consumption	91f	212.0	198.0	225.0	285.0	285.0	290.0	324.0	355.0	382.0	569.0	689.0	799.0	1,409.0	2,371.0	2,903.0
Gross Fixed Capital Formation	93e	266.0	197.0	174.0	187.0	195.0	271.0	311.0	244.0	267.0	555.0	614.0	641.0	1,049.0	1,355.0	1,899.0
Increase/Decrease(−) in Stocks	93i	−3.0	−14.0	−19.0	2.0	41.0	49.0	42.0	−44.0	48.0	53.0	59.0	−62.0	186.0	66.0	−54.0
Private Consumption	96f	1,133.0	1,201.0	1,165.0	1,198.0	1,459.0	1,664.0	1,917.0	2,096.0	2,619.0	3,588.0	3,873.0	5,171.0	8,638.0	17,473.0	23,455.0
Imports of Goods & Services	98c	−392.0	−298.0	−315.0	−369.0	−428.0	−539.0	−536.0	−484.0	−635.0	−1,061.0	−974.0	−1,047.0	−1,289.0	−2,033.0	−3,150.0
Gross Domestic Product	99b	1,466.0	1,518.0	1,504.0	1,700.0	1,999.0	2,259.0	2,501.0	2,815.0	3,502.0	4,660.0	5,283.0	6,526.0	11,163.0	20,986.0	28,222.0
Net Factor Inc/Pmts(−) Abroad	98.n	−20.0	−14.0	−25.0	−50.0	−58.0	−48.0	−52.0	−40.0	−30.0	−47.0	−42.0	−48.0	−40.0	−48.0	−98.0
Gross Nat'l Expenditure = GNP	99a	1,447.0	1,504.0	1,479.0	1,650.0	1,941.0	2,211.0	2,449.0	2,775.0	3,472.0	4,613.0	5,241.0	6,478.0	11,123.0	20,938.0	28,124.0
Nat'l Income, Market Prices	99e	...	...	...	1,540.0	1,811.0	2,077.0	2,304.0	2,605.0	3,255.0	4,378.0	4,918.0	6,100.0	10,599.0	20,213.0	27,071.0
Gross Dom. Prod. 1990 Prices	99b.p	Ⅰ1,254.6	1,255.8	1,218.2	1,296.4	1,372.6	1,465.4	1,547.0	1,508.4	1,738.5	1,797.5	1,566.2	1,511.1	1,545.2	1,676.2	1,623.2
GDP Deflator (1990=100)	99bi *p*	.1	.1	.1	.1	.1	.2	.2	.2	.2	.3	.3	.4	.7	1.3	1.7
															Millions:	
Population	99z	7.74	7.91	8.08	8.26	8.44	8.61	8.86	9.09	9.39	9.61	9.87	10.31	10.41	10.75	Ⅰ10.48

Exchange Rates: The cedi was introduced as a new monetary unit on July 19, 1965, replacing the Ghana pound at a rate of 2.40 cedis per pound. On February 23, 1967 the new cedi, equal to 1.2 old cedis, was introduced.
International Liquidity: Ⅰ Beginning in 1966, data for *line 1d.d* exclude the foreign assets of the sinking funds.
Monetary Authorities: Ⅰ Beginning in December 1991, data reflect the introduction of a new reporting system.
Deposit Money Banks: Ⅰ Beginning in 1973, the classification of claims on the private sector and claims on the public enterprises is revised. Ⅰ Beginning in December 1991, data reflect the introduction of a new reporting system.
Monetary Survey: Ⅰ Before 1967, data for *line 32d* include central bank claims on commercial banks.
Government Finance: Ⅰ For the period 1972-82, data relate to a fiscal year different from calendar year (ends June 30).

Ghana

	1980	1981	1982	1983	1984	1985	1986	1987	1988	1989	1990	1991	1992	1993	1994		
Percent Per Annum																**Interest Rates**	
	13.50	19.50	10.50	14.50	18.00	18.50	20.50	23.50	26.00	26.00	33.00	20.00	30.00	35.00	33.00	Discount Rate *(End of Period)*	60
	13.00	13.00	13.00	13.00	14.16	17.13	18.47	21.71	19.76	19.84	21.78	29.23	19.38	30.95	27.72	Treasury Bill Rate	60c
	11.50	11.50	11.50	11.50	15.00	15.75	17.00	17.58	16.50	....	....	21.32	16.32	23.63	23.15	Deposit Rate	60l
	19.00	19.00	19.00	19.00	21.17	21.17	20.00	25.50	25.58	....	....	....	....	....	....	Lending Rate	60p
Period Averages																**Prices**	
	1.6	2.3	3.2	7.3	13.4	20.6	33.7	47.7	64.2	81.5	100.0	....	....	....	....	Wholesale Prices	63
	2.8	6.1	7.4	16.5	23.1	25.4	31.7	44.3	58.2	72.9	100.0	118.0	129.9	162.3	202.7	Consumer Prices	64
Billions of Cedis Beginning 1986																**International Transactions**	
	3,458	2,924	2,402	10,225	19,396	33,490	‡78	143	206	275	....	....	....	....	....	Exports	70
	2,564	1,118	1,072	6,343	12,795	18,323	‡42	80	94	112	121	127	118	162	266	Cocoa Beans	70r
	3,104	3,041	1,939	11,022	21,887	47,155	‡93	175	186	347	....	....	....	....	....	Imports, cif	71
	2,904	2,845	1,814	10,310	20,475	44,112	‡87	163	174	325	....	....	....	....	....	Imports, fob	71.v
1990=100																Volume of Exports	
	96.0	67.7	83.3	64.9	56.8	62.4	79.9	81.2	82.5	101.0	100.0	90.6	83.4	95.7	88.7	Cocoa Beans	72r
																Export Prices	
	2.2	1.4	1.1	8.1	18.7	24.3	43.0	81.7	93.9	92.0	100.0	115.7	117.3	140.0	248.2	Cocoa Beans (Unit Value)	74r
	5.5	4.2	3.4	13.6	67.2	100.0	139.0	225.0	279.8	273.0	....	....	....	....	....	Cocoa Beans (Wholesale Price)	76r
Minus Sign Indicates Debit																Balance of Payments	
	1,103.6	710.7	607.0	439.1	565.9	632.4	773.4	826.8	881.0	807.2	890.6	997.6	986.4	....	....	Goods: Exports f.o.b.	78aa d
	−908.3	−954.3	−588.7	−499.7	−533.0	−668.5	−712.5	−951.5	−993.4	−1,002.2	−1,198.9	−1,318.7	−1,456.7	....	....	Goods: Imports f.o.b.	78ab d
	195.3	−243.6	18.3	−60.6	32.9	−36.3	60.9	−124.7	−112.4	−195.0	−308.3	−321.1	−470.3	....	....	Trade Balance	78ac d
	106.7	119.1	103.9	38.2	43.8	38.0	39.7	72.4	71.4	75.5	79.3	95.1	110.3	....	....	Services: Credit	78ad d
	−269.9	−295.3	−228.2	−134.7	−163.0	−167.5	−227.7	−237.6	−255.1	−270.9	−295.6	−319.3	−372.2	....	....	Services: Debit	78ae d
	32.1	−419.8	−106.0	−157.1	−86.3	−166.0	−127.1	−289.9	−296.1	−390.4	−524.6	−545.3	−732.2	....	....	Balance on Goods and Services	78af d
	2.8	2.0	3.0	.3	2.0	5.6	5.4	6.9	6.3	6.4	13.8	15.2	18.6	....	....	Income: Credit	78ag d
	−85.3	−86.0	−88.2	−89.7	−116.8	−115.9	−115.9	−138.7	−144.5	−136.9	−133.4	−143.5	−132.9	....	....	Income: Debit	78ah d
	−50.4	−503.8	−191.3	−246.5	−201.1	−276.3	−237.6	−421.7	−434.3	−520.9	−644.2	−673.6	−846.5	....	....	Balance on Goods, Serv., & Inc.	78ai d
	89.3	93.3	90.1	88.0	169.0	147.4	200.3	334.1	377.8	432.2	426.3	434.1	484.8	....	....	Current Transfers, n.i.e.: Credit	78aj d
	−8.7	−8.7	−6.1	−13.7	−6.7	−5.0	−5.2	−8.7	−8.6	−9.1	−10.1	−12.3	−15.1	....	....	Current Transfers: Debit	78ak d
	30.2	−419.2	−107.3	−172.2	−38.8	−133.9	−42.5	−96.3	−65.1	−97.8	−228.0	−251.8	−376.8	....	....	Current Account, n.i.e.	78al d
																Capital Account, n.i.e.: Credit	78ba d
	−1.0	−1.6	−1.5	−1.9	—	−.3	−.5	−.6	−.7	−.8	−.5	−.9	−1.0	....	....	Capital Account: Debit	78bb d
	−1.0	−1.6	−1.5	−1.9	—	−.3	−.5	−.6	−.7	−.8	−.5	−.9	−1.0	....	....	Capital Account, n.i.e.	78bc d
	—	—	—	—	—	—	—	—	—	—	—	—	—			Direct Investment Abroad	78bd d
	15.6	16.3	16.3	2.4	2.0	5.6	4.3	4.7	5.0	15.0	14.8	20.0	22.5	....	....	Dir. Invest. in Rep. Econ., n.i.e.	78be d
	—	—	—	—	—	—	—	—	—	—	—	—	—			Portfolio Investment Assets	78bf d
	—	—	—	—	—	—	—	—	—	—	—	—	—			Portfolio Investment Liab., n.i.e.	78bg d
	−6.3	14.9	−.3	−25.8	11.1	5.8	−2.2	−31.5	−.4	4.2	−11.8	−1.3	−3.5	....	....	Other Investment Assets	78bh d
	60.6	77.3	107.5	142.5	193.8	73.5	61.3	282.5	204.4	194.4	322.0	319.4	302.6	....	....	Other Investment Liab., n.i.e.	78bi d
	69.9	108.5	123.5	119.1	206.9	84.9	63.4	255.7	209.0	213.6	325.0	338.1	321.6	....	....	Financial Account, n.i.e.	78bj d
	−100.4	24.0	−32.6	−126.0	−132.5	63.4	−81.2	−18.7	37.9	40.6	8.8	23.8	−.4	....	....	Net Errors and Omissions	78ca d
	−1.3	−288.3	−17.9	−180.9	35.6	−14.1	−60.8	140.1	181.1	155.6	105.3	109.2	−56.6	....	....	Overall Balance	78cb d
	1.3	288.3	17.9	180.9	−35.6	14.1	60.8	−140.1	−181.1	−155.6	−105.3	−109.2	56.6	....	....	Reserves and Related Items	79da d
	124.1	47.2	6.6	−4.8	−146.7	−183.4	13.0	−41.5	−48.9	−52.4	−17.5	−220.5	166.3	....	....	Reserve Assets	79db d
	.4	−10.9	−5.4	260.5	212.9	115.7	5.9	−36.7	−59.1	−8.8	−53.8	83.8	−63.4	....	....	Use of Fund Credit and Loans	79dc d
																Liabs.Constit.For.Auth.Reserves	79dd d
	−123.3	252.0	16.6	−74.7	−101.8	53.5	41.9	−61.9	−73.2	−94.4	−34.0	27.5	−46.3	....	....	Exceptional Financing	79de d
Year Ending June 30 through 1982, December 31 Thereafter																**Government Finance**	
	−1,808.0	−4,706.8	−4,848.0	‡−4933.3	−4,843.0	−7,579.0	‡.3	4.1	3.9	10.3	3.3	39.0	−144.4	−97.3	....	Deficit (−) or Surplus	80
	2,951.0	3,234.1	4,804.0	‡10185.0	21,728.0	38,691.0	‡69.8	105.0	142.2	193.2	239.5	354.4	333.6	657.6	....	Revenue	81
	—	45.0	52.0	‡56.6	914.0	1,620.0	‡3.9	6.0	11.6	21.3	27.8	36.3	32.7	66.6	....	Grants Received	81z
	4,668.0	7,719.3	9,530.0	‡14755.5	26,694.0	45,763.0	‡70.7	102.1	143.9	196.5	254.5	340.3	498.8	813.5	....	Expenditure	82
	91.0	266.6	174.0	‡419.6	791.0	2,127.0	‡2.7	4.9	6.0	7.7	9.5	11.4	11.9	8.0	....	Lending Minus Repayments	83
																Financing	
	1,518.0	4,339.5	4,421.0	‡3,824.8	3,028.0	4,043.0	‡5.3	−2.9	−6.2	−15.3	−28.0	−51.7	144.1	45.4	....	Net Borrowing: Domestic	84a
	290.0	367.3	389.0	‡970.1	1,815.0	3,522.0	‡−5.6	−1.2	2.3	4.9	24.6	12.7	.3	51.9	....	Foreign	85a
	—	—	—	—	—	—	‡—	—	—	—	—	—	—	—	....	Use of Cash Balances	87
	—	—	38.0	‡138.4	—	14.0	‡—	—	—	—	—	—	—	—	....	Unallocable Financing	87c
	7,622.0	11,846.2	17,487.7	‡29315.5	32,908.0	37,766.0	....	....	....	....	....	....	....	....	....	Debt: Domestic	88a
	3,104.8	3,588.6	4,083.0	‡5,052.5	6,869.0	9,839.0	....	....	....	....	....	....	....	....	....	Foreign	89a
Billions of Cedis Beginning 1986																**National Accounts**	
	3,629.0	3,454.0	2,886.0	10,225.0	20,161.0	33,185.0	‡81.8	157.8	217.7	292.0	312.6	404.7	482.9	776.0	....	Exports of Goods & Services	90c
	4,784.0	6,384.0	5,603.0	10,787.0	19,641.0	32,241.0	‡56.6	74.7	104.8	145.5	222.0	294.2	400.1	559.6	....	Government Consumption	91f
	2,613.0	3,430.0	3,053.0	6,922.0	18,542.0	32,689.0	‡47.5	77.3	114.1	191.0	247.7	326.4	386.1	578.4	....	Gross Fixed Capital Formation	93e
	−203.0	−109.0	−132.0	−21.0	65.0	139.0	‡.3	.6	.8	1.0	1.4	1.6	1.9	3.4	....	Increase/Decrease(−) in Stocks	93i
	35,953.0	63,333.0	77,619.0	167,147.0	233,023.0	284,621.0	‡415.4	610.4	834.3	1,186.7	1,736.1	2,159.4	2,544.3	3,424.8	....	Private Consumption	96f
	−3,923.0	−3,966.0	−2,578.0	−11,022.0	−20,871.0	−39,826.0	‡−90.4	−174.7	−220.6	−398.9	−488.0	−611.5	−806.4	−1,049.8	....	Imports of Goods & Services	98c
	42,853.0	72,526.0	86,451.0	184,038.0	270,561.0	343,048.0	‡511.4	746.0	1,051.2	1,417.2	2,031.7	2,574.8	3,008.8	3,932.4	....	Gross Domestic Product	99b
	−182.0	−232.0	−225.0	−1,640.0	−3,643.0	−5,769.0	‡−12.6	−20.5	−26.5	−28.2	−36.7	−43.9	−46.4	−72.9	....	Net Factor Inc/Pmts(−) Abroad	98.n
	42,671.0	72,294.0	86,225.0	182,398.0	266,918.0	337,280.0	‡498.8	725.5	1,024.7	1,389.0	1,995.0	2,530.9	2,962.4	3,859.5	....	Gross Nat'l Expenditure = GNP	99a
	41,159.0	70,186.0	83,598.0	178,202.0	255,712.9	320,941.1	‡469.5	677.8	955.9	1,302.9	1,884.3	2,399.9	2,806.0	3,629.2	....	Nat'l Income, Market Prices	99e
	1,623.2	1,594.1	1,479.4	1,489.7	1,529.0	1,606.9	1,690.4	1,771.7	1,871.3	1,966.5	2,031.7	2,139.6	2,222.9	2,333.5	....	Gross Dom. Prod. 1990 Prices	99b.p
	2.6	4.5	5.8	12.4	17.7	21.3	30.3	42.1	56.2	72.1	100.0	120.3	135.4	168.5	....	GDP Deflator (1990=100)	99bi p
Midyear Estimates																	
	10.73	11.07	11.47	11.92	12.39	12.72	13.05	13.39	14.14	14.57	15.02	15.48	15.96	16.45	....	Population	99z

Greece
174

		1965	1966	1967	1968	1969	1970	1971	1972	1973	1974	1975	1976	1977	1978	1979
Exchange Rates															*Drachmas per SDR:*	
Market Rate	aa	30.00	30.00	30.00	30.00	30.00	30.00	32.57	32.57	35.83	36.73	41.73	43.02	43.13	46.91	50.43
														Drachmas per US Dollar:		
Market Rate	ae	30.00	30.00	30.00	30.00	30.00	30.00	30.00	30.00	29.70	30.00	35.65	37.03	35.51	36.01	38.28
Market Rate	rf	30.00	30.00	30.00	30.00	30.00	30.00	30.00	30.00	29.63	30.00	32.05ᵉ	36.52	36.84	36.75	37.04
														Drachmas per ECU:		
ECU Rate	ea	....	....	....	....	....	....	....	....	....	....	....	....	....	....	....
ECU Rate	eb	....	....	....	....	....	....	....	....	....	....	....	....	....	....	....
														Index Numbers (1990=100):		
Market Rate	ahx	527.9	527.9	527.9	527.9	527.9	527.9	459.0	527.9	534.9	527.9	496.4ᵉ	433.8	430.0	431.1	427.7
Nominal Effective Exchange Rate	nec	....	....	....	....	....	....	....	....	....	....	....	....	....	....	406.8
Real Effective Exchange Rate	rec	....	....	....	....	....	....	....	....	....	....	....	....	....	....	117.0
Fund Position															*Millions of SDRs:*	
Quota	2f.s	60.0	100.0	100.0	100.0	100.0	138.0	138.0	138.0	138.0	138.0	138.0	138.0	138.0	185.0	185.0
SDRs	1b.s	—	—	—	—	—	—	4.5	25.6	25.2	26.7	17.6	16.9	13.4	13.4	.8
Reserve Position in the Fund	1c.s	15.0	25.0	25.0	25.0	25.0	34.5	34.5	34.5	34.5	—	—	—	—	33.5	32.4
Total Fund Cred.&Loans Outstg.	2tl	—	—	—	—	—	—	—	—	—	36.2	189.8	247.8	176.5	185.2	147.3
International Liquidity													*Millions of US Dollars Unless Otherwise Indicated:*			
Total Reserves minus Gold	1l.d	172.8	152.9	156.0	182.2	187.2	193.6	412.4	898.8	898.9	781.7	ℐ963.6	880.6	1,048.3	1,305.0	1,342.8
SDRs	1b.d	—	—	—	—	—	—	4.9	27.8	30.4	32.7	20.6	19.6	16.3	17.4	1.1
Reserve Position in the Fund	1c.d	15.0	25.0	25.0	25.0	25.0	34.5	37.5	37.5	41.6	—	—	—	—	43.6	42.7
Foreign Exchange	1d.d	157.8	127.9	131.0	157.2	162.2	159.1	370.1	833.6	826.8	749.0	ℐ943.0	861.0	1,032.0	1,244.0	1,299.0
Gold (Million Fine Troy Ounces)	1ad	2.213	3.421	3.718	3.993	3.709	3.329	2.805	3.495	3.502	3.610	3.629	3.651	3.730	3.770	3.808
Gold (National Valuation)	1and	77.5	119.7	130.1	139.8	129.8	116.5	98.2	132.8	147.9	154.7	148.7	148.5	158.6	171.9	175.6
Deposit Money Banks: Assets	7a.d	46.3	51.7	45.0	53.2	77.2	103.2	112.7	159.6	253.0	236.9	280.4	348.7	445.2	407.1	738.9
Deposit Money Banks: Liabilities	7b.d	41.4	47.5	53.3	71.2	93.1	138.1	259.1	403.3	562.0	751.5	982.6	1,565.0	2,268.0	2,931.0	3,557.5
of which: Liab. to Nonbanks	7bd.d	41.4	47.5	53.3	71.2	93.1	138.1	259.1	403.3	539.2	700.9	924.7	1,423.6	2,001.1	2,506.1	2,992.5
Other Banking Insts.: Liabilities	7f.d	....	....	....	....	....	....	....	....	211.0	243.0	271.0	378.0	542.0	768.5	978.8
of which: Liab. to Nonbanks	7fd.d	....	....	....	....	....	....	....	....	156.0	179.0	198.0	281.0	410.0	599.9	710.8
Monetary Authorities															*Billions of Drachmas:*	
Foreign Assets	11	8.3	9.4	10.0	11.1	11.3	11.7	16.3	32.9	32.0	33.1	38.8	40.0	42.8	51.1	52.7
Claims on Central Government	12a	11.8	13.6	14.7	15.2	18.7	17.5	18.4	20.3	30.8	47.2	47.1	60.3	80.5	122.5	154.3
o/w: Cntrprt Gov.L/T.For.Liab.	12ae b	....	....	....	....	....	....	....	....	....	....	....	....	....	....	....
Claims on Deposit Money Banks	12e	2.4	2.3	3.5	3.0	4.1	2.5	1.2	.9	1.9	4.0	11.1	9.4	11.9	12.6	16.6
Claims on Other Banking Insts.	12f	12.5	15.4	18.5	24.6	27.7	35.3	43.8	53.8	67.4	82.2	97.4	116.5	138.5	139.5	159.8
Reserve Money	14	29.0	34.3	38.2	42.9	44.6	47.7	57.3	68.7	81.9	99.3	121.0	145.9	177.1	213.7	237.8
of which: Currency Outside DMBs	14a	23.4	26.3	33.7	33.3	35.7	39.1	43.3	50.8	65.3	80.6	92.2	112.3	133.4	161.8	184.7
Private Sector Deposits	14d	2.9	3.4	3.6	4.9	3.9	4.2	6.6	5.8	6.8	8.4	11.2	11.9	13.8	17.6	22.2
Restricted Deposits	16b	7.8	8.7	9.4	9.9	12.5	14.6	16.4	22.8	28.6	33.9	39.9	46.6	64.3	73.7	86.9
Foreign Liabilities	16c	....	....	....	....	....	....	....	....	....	....	....	....	....	....	....
Long-Term Foreign Liabilities	16cl	....	....	....	....	....	....	....	....	....	....	....	....	....	....	....
Central Government Deposits	16d	1.8	3.1	4.0	4.1	5.2	5.3	4.5	12.8	13.2	19.5	19.3	26.9	28.2	34.4	24.7
Other Items (Net)	17r	-3.7	-5.3	-4.9	-3.0	-.4	-.7	1.4	3.6	8.4	13.9	14.4	6.8	4.3	4.0	33.9
Deposit Money Banks															*Billions of Drachmas:*	
Reserves	20	2.7	4.8	1.4	5.1	5.7	5.3	8.9	14.9	14.8	15.0	20.6	34.1	36.7	43.7	58.7
Foreign Assets	21	1.4	1.6	1.3	1.6	2.3	3.1	3.4	4.8	7.5	7.1	10.0	12.9	15.8	14.7	28.3
Claims on Central Government	22a	4.9	5.9	7.0	9.5	13.1	17.8	23.3	33.2	40.8	48.3	62.9	81.9	106.9	141.6	168.6
Claims on Official Entities	22bx	....	....	....	....	....	....	....	....	....	....	....	....	....	....	....
Claims on Private Sector	22d	28.8	32.4	38.9	44.3	52.5	62.5	76.8	96.7	108.7	131.6	173.8	227.5	285.0	355.8	422.3
Claims on Other Banking Insts.	22f	....	....	....	....	....	....	....	....	....	....	....	....	....	....	....
Demand Deposits	24	6.0	6.9	6.8	8.3	9.3	11.3	13.8	19.3	21.6	23.2	27.2	35.4	39.4	48.8	58.6
Time, Savings, and Other Deposits	25	23.1	28.5	31.8	41.5	51.2	63.8	82.4	103.1	114.6	139.1	183.5	232.8	287.5	364.8	429.4
Restricted Deposits	26b	....	....	....	....	....	....	....	....	....	....	....	....	....	....	....
Foreign Liabilities	26c	1.2	1.4	1.6	2.1	2.8	4.1	7.8	12.1	16.7	22.5	35.0	57.7	80.2	105.5	136.2
Credit from Monetary Authorities	26g	2.4	2.3	3.4	3.0	4.1	2.5	1.2	1.0	2.0	4.2	11.2	10.7	12.8	16.2	34.0
Other Items (Net)	27r	5.1	5.5	5.1	5.5	6.2	7.0	7.2	14.1	16.8	13.1	10.3	19.8	24.6	20.4	19.7
Monetary Survey															*Billions of Drachmas:*	
Foreign Assets (Net)	31n	8.4	9.5	9.8	10.6	10.9	10.7	11.9	25.6	22.9	16.3	5.9	-15.5	-29.2	-48.5	-62.7
Domestic Credit	32	60.0	68.6	78.6	93.8	111.3	132.9	162.9	195.5	243.5	300.3	374.2	472.9	598.6	737.1	895.0
Claims on Central Govt. (Net)	32an	14.9	16.5	17.7	20.6	26.7	30.0	37.2	40.6	58.3	76.1	90.7	115.2	159.1	229.7	298.2
Claims on Official Entities	32bx	....	....	....	....	....	....	....	....	....	....	....	....	....	....	....
Claims on Private Sector	32d	32.5	36.6	42.4	48.6	57.0	67.6	81.9	101.0	117.8	142.1	186.1	241.2	301.0	367.9	437.1
Claims on Other Banking Insts.	32f	12.5	15.4	18.5	24.6	27.7	35.3	43.8	53.8	67.4	82.2	97.4	116.5	138.5	139.5	159.8
Money	34	32.3	36.6	44.0	46.5	48.9	54.6	63.6	75.9	93.7	112.2	130.6	159.6	186.6	228.2	265.4
Quasi-Money	35	30.9	37.3	41.1	51.4	63.7	78.4	98.8	125.9	143.3	173.0	223.3	279.5	351.8	438.5	516.3
Restricted Deposits	36b	....	....	....	....	....	....	....	....	....	....	....	....	....	....	....
Other Items (Net)	37r	5.1	4.2	3.1	6.5	9.6	10.5	12.3	19.3	29.4	31.5	26.2	18.4	31.2	22.0	50.6
Money plus Quasi-Money	35l	63.2	73.9	85.2	97.9	112.6	133.0	162.5	201.8	236.9	285.2	353.9	439.0	538.4	666.7	781.8
Other Banking Institutions															*Billions of Drachmas:*	
Cash	40	....	....	....	....	....	....	....	....	....	....	....	....	....	ℐ27.0	29.7
Claims on Central Government	42a	2.5	3.2	3.0	3.8	3.9	3.6	3.4	3.0	3.1	3.1	2.5	4.1	6.5	ℐ34.4	39.1
Claims on Nonfin.Pub.Enterprises	42c	....	....	....	....	....	....	....	....	....	....	....	....	....	ℐ57.6	78.2
Claims on Private Sector	42d	21.0	24.1	27.6	30.2	37.0	46.6	58.2	72.9	90.3	111.4	135.3	165.2	205.5	ℐ271.0	318.0
Demand Deposits	44	....	....	....	....	....	....	....	....	....	....	....	....	....	ℐ12.5	14.7
Time, Savings,& Fgn.Currency Dep.	45	2.8	3.1	3.4	4.0	4.8	5.9	8.0	10.3	13.0	16.2	21.5	33.1	47.8	ℐ145.1	180.6
Bonds	46ab	....	....	....	....	....	....	....	....	....	....	....	....	....	ℐ8.1	10.4
Foreign Liabilities	46c	....	....	....	....	....	....	....	....	....	....	....	....	....	ℐ27.7	37.5
of which: Natls.Residing Abroad	46cx	....	....	....	....	....	....	....	....	....	....	....	....	....	ℐ21.6	27.2
Credit from Monetary Authorities	46j	....	....	....	....	....	....	....	....	....	....	....	....	....	ℐ144.5	164.5
Capital Accounts	47a	8.7	9.0	9.1	9.3	9.6	9.9	11.2	12.5	13.0	15.8	17.6	19.1	20.5	ℐ43.8	48.3
Other Items (Net)	47r	....	....	....	....	....	....	....	....	....	....	....	....	....	ℐ8.5	9.0
Liquid Liabilities	55l	66.0	77.0	88.6	101.9	117.4	139.0	170.5	212.1	250.0	301.4	375.4	472.2	586.2	ℐ797.3	947.4

Greece
174

1980	1981	1982	1983	1984	1985	1986	1987	1988	1989	1990	1991	1992	1993	1994		
End of Period															**Exchange Rates**	
59.35	67.08	77.85	103.30	125.94	162.30	169.73	178.64	199.30	207.36	224.25	250.73	295.05	342.32	350.51	Market Rate	aa
End of Period (ae) Period Average (rf)																
46.54	57.63	70.57	98.67	128.48	147.76	138.76	125.93	148.10	157.79	157.63	175.28	214.58	249.22	240.10	Market Rate	ae
42.62	55.41	66.80	88.06	112.72	138.12	139.98	135.43	141.86	162.42	158.51	182.27	190.62	229.25	242.60	Market Rate	rf
End of Period (ea) Period Average (eb)																
....	62.18	68.54	81.78	91.04	131.20	148.53	164.48	172.91	188.23	214.07	235.07	260.20	278.20	294.78	ECU Rate	ea
59.24	61.62	65.30	78.09	88.44	105.66	137.41	156.19	167.55	178.88	201.43	225.22	246.60	267.99	287.21	ECU Rate	eb
Period Averages																
372.7	287.3	238.3	180.6	141.4	115.0	113.3	117.0	111.9	97.6	100.0	87.3	83.4	69.2	65.2	Market Rate	ahx
354.8	325.2	302.5	247.0	212.8	181.0	140.3	126.1	117.2	108.4	100.0	88.5	81.6	73.2	68.0	Nominal Effective Exchange Rate	nec
101.8	105.4	109.3	101.1	98.0	94.8	88.8	90.9	93.2	94.2	100.0	101.2	104.5	104.0	104.5	Real Effective Exchange Rate	rec
End of Period															**Fund Position**	
277.5	277.5	277.5	399.9	399.9	399.9	399.9	399.9	399.9	399.9	399.9	399.9	587.6	587.6	587.6	Quota	2f.s
—	.1	—	.6	1.1	—	—	—	.2	.3	.2	.3	—	.1	.2	SDRs	1b.s
55.6	55.6	55.6	86.2	81.4	75.0	70.1	70.1	71.1	89.2	74.7	74.7	116.9	113.7	113.7	Reserve Position in the Fund	1c.s
78.5	13.9	—	—	—	—	—	—	—	—	—	—	—	—	—	Total Fund Cred.&Loans Outstg.	2tl
End of Period															**International Liquidity**	
1,345.9	1,022.0	861.1	900.5	954.2	868.0	I1,518.7	2,681.4	3,619.4	3,223.5	3,412.1	5,188.9	4,793.6	7,790.3	14,487.9	Total Reserves minus Gold	1l.d
—	.1	—	.6	1.1	—	—	—	.3	.4	.3	.4	—	.2	.3	SDRs	1b.d
70.9	64.7	61.3	90.2	79.8	82.4	85.8	99.5	95.7	117.2	106.3	106.9	160.7	156.2	166.0	Reserve Position in the Fund	1c.d
1,275.0	957.2	799.8	809.7	873.3	785.6	I1,432.9	2,581.9	3,523.4	3,105.8	3,305.5	5,081.6	4,632.9	7,634.0	14,321.6	Foreign Exchange	1d.d
3.835	3.853	3.872	3.880	4.106	4.123	3.308	3.342	3.395	3.395	3.400	3.425	3.433	3.443	3.448	Gold (Million Fine Troy Ounces)	1ad
171.2	157.0	149.5	142.2	140.9	I862.8	841.3	1,057.2	925.0	902.1	834.4	807.2	746.5	856.3	850.9	Gold (National Valuation)	1and
1,187.9	1,666.2	1,408.0	1,386.0	1,598.0	1,980.0	1,788.0	1,876.3	2,593.4	2,974.7	3,456.5	4,001.5	4,707.1	5,358.7	....	Deposit Money Banks: Assets	7a.d
4,000.7	4,675.6	4,916.0	5,037.0	5,031.0	5,694.0	6,689.0	8,362.8	9,335.6	10,995.3	12,548.6	12,815.7	13,593.3	13,696.5	....	Deposit Money Banks: Liabilities	7b.d
3,377.9	3,874.8	4,099.7	4,313.3	4,503.1	5,184.3	6,105.2	7,520.5	8,098.5	9,552.9	11,498.7	12,454.9	13,073.0	13,581.7	....	*of which:* Liab. to Nonbanks	7bdd
1,150.1	1,247.1	1,394.5	1,558.2	1,564.6	1,894.2	2,434.0	3,048.2	2,964.3	3,370.0	3,913.0	4,395.5	4,533.4	4,539.0	....	Other Banking Insts.: Liabilities	7f.d
712.8	740.2	824.4	859.5	892.0	1,177.2	1,560.8	2,044.7	2,040.3	2,299.8	2,712.6	2,956.9	2,981.5	2,939.2	....	*of which:* Liab. to Nonbanks	7fdd
End of Period															**Monetary Authorities**	
74.1	72.5	79.2	114.9	152.9	265.1	331.8	I483.1	696.0	695.2	811.8	1,351.0	1,736.7	2,975.5	4,463.9	Foreign Assets	11
200.3	356.1	617.9	530.8	656.5	747.9	787.6	I1,999.3	2,256.7	2,610.8	3,171.1	3,703.3	4,537.0	5,899.3	5,073.6	Claims on Central Government	12a
....	....	....	....	....	....	....	1,012.9	1,160.0	1,319.9	1,451.2	1,819.7	2,440.9	3,596.3	3,294.5	*o/w:* Cntrprt Gov.L/T.For.Liab.	12aeb
24.5	31.7	35.5	18.5	15.3	5.8	6.5	I384.7	378.2	455.8	591.2	569.5	715.7	293.1	158.1	Claims on Deposit Money Banks	12e
173.6	254.6	264.1	289.0	274.8	276.5	291.8	I315.9	283.8	312.9	392.8	305.7	344.0	287.2	219.7	Claims on Other Banking Insts.	12f
304.0	440.4	563.4	617.8	806.3	856.1	1,015.0	I1,308.9	1,392.7	1,519.1	1,868.3	2,083.4	2,305.9	2,500.1	3,491.3	Reserve Money	14
211.8	263.7	305.2	348.2	408.2	513.5	550.1	I641.4	754.9	988.7	1,190.2	1,293.3	1,444.9	1,542.5	1,726.7	*of which: Currency Outside DMBs*	14a
21.1	24.3	29.1	55.0	56.9	31.3	123.5	I132.0	138.0	130.0	173.4	196.3	203.5	200.9	315.4	*Private Sector Deposits*	14d
92.5	106.5	127.2	174.5	170.7	179.0	157.9	I1,438.0	1,716.2	1,941.0	2,321.1	3,239.5	3,964.7	4,813.4	4,487.4	Restricted Deposits	16b
....	....	....	....	....	....	....	39.8	41.4	229.1	307.2	102.8	226.4	182.3	186.7	Foreign Liabilities	16c
....	....	....	....	....	....	....	999.5	1,145.4	1,304.0	1,436.9	1,817.9	2,482.5	3,626.6	3,342.7	Long-Term Foreign Liabilities	16cl
38.1	85.4	179.8	70.3	104.9	55.2	34.5	I43.7	120.5	69.8	117.8	143.5	83.0	234.9	210.9	Central Government Deposits	16d
38.0	82.6	126.3	90.7	17.7	205.0	210.5	I–646.9	–801.5	–988.5	–1,084.3	–1,457.5	–1,729.2	–1,902.1	–1,803.7	Other Items (Net)	17r
End of Period															**Deposit Money Banks**	
100.8	198.3	324.6	348.8	600.9	661.4	715.5	984.9	1,210.0	1,119.7	1,384.9	1,639.5	1,979.3	2,333.7	....	Reserves	20
55.3	96.0	99.3	136.8	205.4	292.6	248.1	I236.3	384.1	469.4	544.8	701.4	1,010.0	1,335.5	....	Foreign Assets	21
217.5	261.5	327.9	530.6	691.4	1,005.6	1,234.7	I1,505.5	1,996.9	2,629.5	3,220.5	3,321.3	4,216.3	4,888.2	....	Claims on Central Government	22a
....	....	....	....	....	....	....	413.5	515.3	620.6	526.9	674.7	415.0	478.3	....	Claims on Official Entities	22bx
516.8	671.7	831.3	933.5	1,143.1	1,355.4	1,670.9	I1,507.0	1,734.4	2,120.8	2,406.6	2,770.5	3,274.2	3,870.0	....	Claims on Private Sector	22d
....	....	....	....	....	....	....	11.3	30.8	16.4	19.9	106.0	112.9	104.1	....	Claims on Other Banking Insts.	22f
75.9	89.4	124.8	122.4	165.8	198.5	222.5	I284.2	312.8	367.8	484.6	608.0	728.6	901.0	....	Demand Deposits	24
544.7	757.9	990.3	1,208.5	1,587.1	2,031.6	2,483.3	I3,101.8	3,841.2	4,705.3	5,228.7	5,618.7	5,946.7	6,250.1	....	Time, Savings, and Other Deposits	25
....	....	....	....	....	....	....	51.7	58.4	63.5	71.2	86.1	99.6	81.8	....	Restricted Deposits	26b
186.2	269.5	346.9	497.0	646.4	841.4	927.2	I1,053.1	1,382.6	1,735.0	1,978.0	2,246.3	2,916.9	3,413.5	....	Foreign Liabilities	26c
46.3	68.4	78.1	115.5	177.1	249.7	248.5	I188.5	77.8	30.8	36.4	449.1	1,037.3	1,942.9	....	Credit from Monetary Authorities	26g
37.3	42.5	42.8	6.4	64.4	–6.2	–12.2	I–20.9	198.5	74.1	304.7	205.2	278.7	420.7	....	Other Items (Net)	27r
End of Period															**Monetary Survey**	
–61.4	–101.9	–168.4	–245.3	–288.1	–283.6	–347.2	I–1373.0	–1,489.3	–2,103.5	–2,365.4	–2,114.7	–2,879.0	–2,911.3	....	Foreign Assets (Net)	31n
1,091.5	1,485.0	1,877.9	2,225.0	2,671.7	3,342.6	3,963.3	I5,715.4	6,704.4	8,250.4	9,628.7	10,745.3	12,820.6	15,296.1	....	Domestic Credit	32
379.8	532.2	765.9	991.2	1,243.0	1,698.2	1,987.8	I3,461.1	4,133.1	5,170.5	6,273.8	6,881.1	8,670.2	10,552.6	....	Claims on Central Govt. (Net)	32an
....	....	....	....	....	....	....	413.7	515.4	620.6	526.9	674.7	415.0	478.3	....	Claims on Official Entities	32bx
538.1	698.2	847.9	944.9	1,153.9	1,368.0	1,683.6	I1,513.4	1,741.3	2,129.9	2,415.3	2,777.9	3,278.5	3,873.8	....	Claims on Private Sector	32d
173.6	254.6	264.1	289.0	274.8	276.5	291.8	I327.2	314.6	329.4	412.7	411.7	456.9	391.3	....	Claims on Other Banking Insts.	32f
308.8	377.4	459.1	525.6	630.9	743.3	896.0	I1,057.7	1,205.7	1,486.4	1,848.1	2,097.6	2,377.0	2,644.4	....	Money	34
637.2	864.4	1,117.5	1,383.0	1,757.8	2,210.6	2,641.2	I3,101.8	3,841.2	4,705.3	5,228.7	5,618.7	5,946.7	6,250.1	....	Quasi-Money	35
....	....	....	....	....	....	....	1,489.7	1,774.6	2,004.5	2,392.3	3,325.6	4,064.3	4,895.2	....	Restricted Deposits	36b
84.1	141.5	132.9	71.1	–5.0	105.3	79.0	I–1306.8	–1,606.6	–2,049.4	–2,205.8	–2,411.2	–2,446.4	–1,404.8	....	Other Items (Net)	37r
946.0	1,241.7	1,576.6	1,908.6	2,400.4	2,953.9	3,537.2	4,159.4	5,047.0	6,191.7	7,076.8	7,716.3	8,323.7	8,894.5	....	Money plus Quasi-Money	35l
End of Period															**Other Banking Institutions**	
33.3	45.9	60.0	102.5	82.3	49.8	84.0	119.8	115.0	229.8	153.1	181.3	211.0	245.4	....	Cash	40
34.0	34.6	11.2	.5	35.0	56.5	50.6	135.2	249.8	335.6	794.2	785.7	1,773.9	2,852.9	....	Claims on Central Government	42a
113.8	214.4	333.5	396.6	470.1	569.8	703.2	691.1	822.1	982.1	801.1	939.8	634.5	737.9	....	Claims on Nonfin.Pub.Enterprises	42c
372.3	445.0	560.8	690.6	827.1	1,032.0	1,209.9	1,500.9	1,733.4	2,113.7	2,416.8	2,848.2	3,081.9	2,774.9	....	Claims on Private Sector	42d
16.3	23.7	32.6	47.6	57.0	61.0	69.2	83.3	99.1	120.2	154.1	150.9	154.6	225.5	....	Demand Deposits	44
230.8	317.1	424.1	520.6	695.3	886.5	1,057.3	1,347.4	1,702.4	2,126.3	2,424.0	2,696.2	3,122.8	3,513.6	....	Time, Savings,& Fgn.Currency Dep.	45
17.2	30.6	48.3	77.1	127.4	184.6	244.3	251.6	399.5	481.2	594.0	663.2	744.5	767.6	....	Bonds	46ab
53.5	71.9	98.4	153.8	201.0	279.9	337.7	383.8	439.0	531.8	616.8	770.5	972.8	1,131.2	....	Foreign Liabilities	46c
33.2	42.7	58.2	84.8	114.6	174.0	216.6	257.5	302.2	362.9	427.6	518.3	639.8	732.5	....	*of which: Natls.Residing Abroad*	46cx
180.1	260.3	272.0	294.0	278.4	278.5	300.1	277.3	208.4	226.6	216.9	221.6	213.4	229.1	....	Credit from Monetary Authorities	46j
56.8	62.4	79.3	99.5	127.8	159.7	219.7	263.9	347.4	423.2	543.6	711.2	774.7	908.5	....	Capital Accounts	47a
–1.4	–26.2	10.7	–2.3	–72.3	–142.2	–180.8	–160.4	–275.5	–248.0	–384.2	–458.4	–281.4	–164.4	....	Other Items (Net)	47r
1,159.8	1,536.7	1,973.3	2,374.3	3,070.3	3,851.6	4,579.7	5,470.4	6,733.5	8,208.4	9,501.8	10,382.0	11,390.1	12,388.1	....	Liquid Liabilities	55l

Greece

174

		1965	1966	1967	1968	1969	1970	1971	1972	1973	1974	1975	1976	1977	1978	1979
Interest Rates																*Percent Per Annum*
Discount Rate (End of Period)	60	5.5	5.5	4.5	5.0	6.5	6.5	6.5	6.5	9.0	8.0	10.0	10.0	11.0	14.0	19.0
Treasury Bill Rate	60c	....	....	....	....	....	....	....	....	....	....	....	....	....	....	....
Deposit Rate	60l	5.30	5.30	5.80	5.80	5.80	5.80	5.80	5.80	5.80	5.80	9.83	9.58	8.92	8.50	9.96	11.88
Lending Rate	60p	9.00	9.00	9.00	8.75	8.00	8.00	8.00	8.00	9.00	11.83	11.88	11.50	12.00	13.46	16.71
Prices, Production, Employment																*Index Numbers (1990=100):*
Wholesale Prices	63	4.4	4.5	4.6	4.6	4.7	I4.9	5.1	5.4	6.7	8.8	9.5	10.8	12.3	13.6	16.4
Home and Import Goods	63a	4.3	4.4	4.5	4.5	4.6	I4.8	5.0	5.3	6.4	8.6	9.3	10.6	11.9	13.2	16.0
Consumer Prices	64	4.1	4.3	4.4	4.4	4.5	4.6	4.8	5.0	5.7	7.3	8.3	9.4	10.5	11.8	14.1
Wages: Hourly Earnings	65	1.5	1.7	1.9	2.1	2.3	2.4	2.6	2.9	3.3	4.2	5.3	6.8	8.2	10.1	12.2
Manufacturing Production	66ey	32.1	36.8	37.8	40.6	45.1	50.1	55.0	63.6	73.6	72.2	75.4	83.3	84.5	91.0	96.6
Industrial Employment	67ey	65.3	67.3	66.9	66.4	68.9	72.1	76.5	79.4	84.3	85.3	86.0	91.3	95.5	98.5	101.2
International Transactions																*Billions of Drachmas*
Exports	70	9.8	12.2	14.9	14.0	16.6	19.3	19.9	26.1	42.8	60.9	74.2	93.8	101.3	123.7	144.2
Imports, cif	71	34.0	36.7	35.6	41.8	47.8	58.8	62.9	70.4	102.7	131.6	172.0	221.8	252.2	287.7	356.8
Imports, fob	71.v	30.1	32.5	31.5	37.0	42.3	52.0	55.7	62.3	90.9	116.4	152.3	196.3	223.1	254.7	315.8
																1990=100
Volume of Exports	72	12.9	15.5	19.3	18.6	21.9	24.7	25.5	32.2	40.4	44.4	48.4	55.9	I54.9	63.5	66.9
Volume of Imports	73	19.3	19.9	20.7	22.4	25.5	27.0	28.9	33.0	41.7	38.0	37.2	40.1	I42.5	44.6	48.6
Unit Value of Exports	74	6.3	6.4	6.3	6.2	6.2	6.4	6.4	6.6	8.4	11.3	12.5	13.7	I15.1	15.8	17.0
Unit Value of Imports	75	4.9	4.9	4.9	4.9	4.9	5.1	5.3	5.8	6.9	10.2	12.0	13.4	I14.0	15.0	18.5
Export Prices	76	4.6	4.8	4.7	4.7	4.9	5.0	5.2	5.7	8.4	I9.9	10.2	12.1	14.5	15.2	19.1
Import Prices	76.x	3.2	3.2	3.2	3.2	3.3	3.6	3.9	4.4	5.4	I7.4	8.2	9.5	10.6	12.0	14.4
Balance of Payments																*Millions of US Dollars:*
Goods: Exports f.o.b.	78aa d	....	....	....	....	....	....	....	....	....	....	....	2,258	2,583	3,036	3,991
Goods: Imports f.o.b.	78ab d	....	....	....	....	....	....	....	....	....	....	....	−4,997	−5,728	−6,530	−8,997
Trade Balance	78ac d	....	....	....	....	....	....	....	....	....	....	....	−2,739	−3,145	−3,494	−5,006
Services: Credit	78ad d	....	....	....	....	....	....	....	....	....	....	....	1,808	2,133	2,705	3,436
Services: Debit	78ae d	....	....	....	....	....	....	....	....	....	....	....	−677	−829	−985	−1,308
Balance on Goods and Services	78af d	....	....	....	....	....	....	....	....	....	....	....	−1,608	−1,841	−1,774	−2,878
Income: Credit	78ag d	....	....	....	....	....	....	....	....	....	....	....	136	118	164	253
Income: Debit	78ah d	....	....	....	....	....	....	....	....	....	....	....	−267	−275	−327	−426
Balance on Goods, Serv., & Inc.	78ai d	....	....	....	....	....	....	....	....	....	....	....	−1,739	−1,998	−1,937	−3,051
Current Transfers, n.i.e.: Credit	78aj d	....	....	....	....	....	....	....	....	....	....	....	812	926	985	1,169
Current Transfers: Debit	78ak d	....	....	....	....	....	....	....	....	....	....	....	−2	−3	−3	−4
Current Account, n.i.e.	78al d	....	....	....	....	....	....	....	....	....	....	....	−929	−1,075	−955	−1,886
Capital Account, n.i.e.: Credit	78ba d	....	....	....	....	....	....	....	....	....	....	....	—	—	—	—
Capital Account: Debit	78bb d	....	....	....	....	....	....	....	....	....	....	....				
Capital Account, n.i.e.	78bc d	....	....	....	....	....	....	....	....	....	....	....				
Direct Investment Abroad	78bd d	....	....	....	....	....	....	....	....	....	....	....				
Dir. Invest. in Rep. Econ., n.i.e.	78be d	....	....	....	....	....	....	....	....	....	....	....	305	387	428	613
Portfolio Investment Assets	78bf d	....	....	....	....	....	....	....	....	....	....	....				
Portfolio Investment Liab., n.i.e.	78bg d	....	....	....	....	....	....	....	....	....	....	....	−1	−1	—	—
Other Investment Assets	78bh d	....	....	....	....	....	....	....	....	....	....	....	−4	−54	83	−332
Other Investment Liab., n.i.e.	78bi d	....	....	....	....	....	....	....	....	....	....	....	622	981	908	1,143
Financial Account, n.i.e.	78bj d	....	....	....	....	....	....	....	....	....	....	....	922	1,313	1,419	1,424
Net Errors and Omissions	78ca d	....	....	....	....	....	....	....	....	....	....	....	−127	−108	−270	470
Overall Balance	78cb d	....	....	....	....	....	....	....	....	....	....	....	−134	130	194	8
Reserves and Related Items	79da d	....	....	....	....	....	....	....	....	....	....	....	134	−130	−194	−8
Reserve Assets	79db d	....	....	....	....	....	....	....	....	....	....	....	5	−88	−144	92
Use of Fund Credit and Loans	79dc d	....	....	....	....	....	....	....	....	....	....	....	67	−83	10	−49
Liabs.Constit.For.Auth.Reserves	79dd d	....	....	....	....	....	....	....	....	....	....	....	—	—	—	—
Exceptional Financing	79de d	....	....	....	....	....	....	....	....	....	....	....	62	41	−60	−51
Government Finance																*Billions of Drachmas:*
Budgetary Central Government																
Deficit (−) or Surplus	80	−3.0	−2.5	−3.4	−4.5	−4.7	−5.2	−6.4	−9.8	−11.0	−18.0	−26.3	−31.2	−35.8	−42.4	−51.5
Revenue	81	28.9	34.0	38.6	43.8	49.1	54.3	59.4	69.4	83.9	100.8	134.2	170.4	205.2	242.0	306.2
Grants Received	81z	....	....	....	.3	.2	.2	.2	.9	1.4	1.7	.8	.8	.8	.6	.4
Expenditure	82	31.9	36.4	42.0	48.6	54.0	59.7	66.0	80.1	96.4	120.6	161.3	202.4	241.7	285.0	358.2
Financing																
Net Borrowing	84	3.0	2.5	3.4	4.5	4.7	5.2ᶠ	6.4ᶠ	9.8ᶠ	11.0	18.0	26.3	31.2	35.8	42.4	51.5
Borrowing: Domestic	84x	2.1	2.5	4.4	4.3	5.0	5.6ᶠ	7.3ᶠ	10.5ᶠ	7.3	17.0	16.0	35.8	39.3	36.6	41.4
Foreign	85x	1.6	1.1	.2	1.9	2.1	2.7	2.7	3.2	8.6	5.2	15.4	1.0	4.7	14.6	20.5
Amortization	84y	−.7	−1.1	−1.2	−1.7	−2.5	−3.2	−3.6	−3.9	−4.9	−4.2	−5.1	−5.6	−8.2	−8.6	−10.4
Social Security																
Deficit(−) or Surplus	80.r	1.1	1.2	−.2	1.3	2.8	2.8	3.6	8.2	7.7	7.1	8.7	15.6	23.2	24.6	28.2
Receipts	81.r	12.9	15.1	17.2	20.3	22.7	25.3	29.2	35.8	39.2	45.5	58.2	77.7	99.0	126.6	151.0
Payments	82.r	11.8	13.9	17.4	19.0	19.9	22.6	25.6	27.6	31.5	38.5	49.4	62.1	75.8	102.0	122.8
National Accounts																*Billions of Drachmas*
Exports of Goods & Services	90c	16.1	22.5	23.0	22.5	25.9	30.0	34.1	44.3	68.9	90.8	113.3	145.1	162.3	204.4	249.6
Government Consumption	91f	21.1	23.6	28.1	30.2	33.9	37.7	41.4	45.9	55.4	78.1	102.0	124.3	153.8	185.2	233.5
Gross Fixed Capital Formation	93e	38.8	43.3	43.9	54.4	65.6	70.7	83.3	104.8	135.7	125.5	139.9	175.0	221.4	278.0	369.2
Increase/Decrease(−) in Stocks	93i	8.5	1.3	4.4	−.2	3.5	13.3	9.0	6.8	37.5	39.9	41.4	41.7	33.3	43.4	61.6
Private Consumption	96f	130.8	144.5	156.5	168.5	184.3	206.8	224.5	248.1	307.1	381.9	454.0	542.5	634.9	756.8	904.9
Imports of Goods & Services	98c	−36.5	−37.5	−39.0	−43.1	−49.8	−55.0	−60.9	−75.7	−122.1	−144.7	−180.6	−213.1	−243.3	−286.1	−360.8
Gross Domestic Product	99b	179.8	200.0	216.1	234.6	266.5	298.9	330.3	377.7	484.4	564.4	672.2	825.0	963.7	1,161.4	1,428.7
Net Factor Inc/Pmts(−) Abroad	98.n	3.6	3.9	4.3	5.0	5.0	5.5	7.9	9.6	13.1	17.9	19.2	24.9	30.3	32.4	43.5
Gross Nat'l Expenditure = GNP	99a	183.4	203.9	220.4	239.6	271.5	304.4	338.2	387.3	497.2	582.1	691.4	849.9	994.0	1,193.8	1,472.2
Nat'l Income, Market Prices	99e	174.3	193.4	208.7	226.7	257.1	287.5	318.6	363.6	466.6	542.8	643.9	790.7	921.6	1,104.3	1,359.8
Gross Dom. Prod. 1990 Prices	99b.p	4,060.1	4,308.4	4,545.1	4,847.2	5,328.2	5,751.5	6,161.4	6,707.9	7,198.6	6,936.9	7,358.3	7,825.9	8,095.3	8,636.0	8,955.4
GDP Deflator (1990=100)	99bi p	4.4	4.6	4.8	4.8	5.0	5.2	5.4	5.6	6.7	8.1	9.1	10.5	11.9	13.4	16.0
																Millions:
Population	99z	8.55	8.61	8.72	8.74	8.77	8.79	8.83	8.89	8.93	8.96	9.05	9.17	9.27	9.36	9.45

International Liquidity: ℐ Beginning in 1975, data on *Foreign Exchange* (line 1d.d) exclude import documentary credit at time of payment. Earlier data exclude such credit at the time of opening of the account. ℐ Beginning in January 1986, data on *Gold* and *Foreign Exchange* exclude the deposits made with the European Monetary Institute (EMI) of gold and gross U.S. dollar holdings; the holdings of European currency units (ECUs) issued by the EMI against these deposits are included in line 1d.d.

Gold (National Valuation) (line 1and): ℐ Before December 1985, gold was valued at SDR 35 per fine troy ounce. Beginning in December 1985, gold is revalued each December at 65 percent of the average buying market price of gold during that month.

Monetary Authorities: ℐ Beginning in 1987, the data reflect improved classification in the report forms.

Deposit Money Banks: ℐ See note to section 10.

Monetary Survey: ℐ See note to section 10.

Greece

174

1980	1981	1982	1983	1984	1985	1986	1987	1988	1989	1990	1991	1992	1993	1994		
Percent Per Annum															**Interest Rates**	
20.5	20.5	20.5	20.5	20.5	20.5	20.5	20.5	19.0	19.0	19.0	19.0	19.0	21.5	20.5	Discount Rate *(End of Period)*	60
....	....	....	....	....	....	17.0	17.3	16.3	16.5	18.5	18.8	17.7	18.2	....	Treasury Bill Rate	60c
14.50	14.50	14.50	14.50	15.42	15.50	15.50	15.33	I 17.33	17.14	19.52	20.67	19.92	19.33	18.92	Deposit Rate	60l
21.25	21.33	20.50	20.50	20.50	20.50	20.50	21.82	22.89	23.26	27.62	29.45	28.71	28.56	27.44	Lending Rate	60p
Period Averages															**Prices, Production, Employment**	
I 21.1	....	....	36.9	44.8	54.1	62.9	69.1	76.0	86.3	100.0	116.7	130.0	145.4	158.1	Wholesale Prices	63
20.5	25.9	30.4	36.4	43.7	52.6	62.3	68.4	75.3	85.0	100.0	117.9	132.2	148.1	160.9	Home and Import Goods	63a
17.6	I 21.9	26.4	31.8	37.7	44.9	55.3	64.3	I 73.0	83.1	100.0	119.5	138.4	158.4	175.7	Consumer Prices	64
15.5	19.7	26.3	31.4	39.6	47.5	53.5	58.7	69.5	83.8	100.0	116.7	132.8	146.7	....	Wages: Hourly Earnings	65
I 97.5	....	96.1	94.7	96.0	98.4	97.8	95.8	100.6	102.9	100.0	99.1	97.9	94.6	95.7	Manufacturing Production	66ey
102.3	103.5	103.6	102.4	102.7	101.5	101.6	100.3	101.3	101.6	100.0	93.8	89.2	83.9	....	Industrial Employment	67ey
Billions of Drachmas															**International Transactions**	
221.1	237.9	286.3	392.7	542.7	629.1	790.0	881.0	776.4	1,231.0	1,281.0	1,584.6	1,880.8	1,933.4	....	Exports	70
452.9	493.8	665.9	846.7	1,083.9	1,412.8	1,587.4	1,773.4	1,758.0	2,629.4	3,137.9	3,921.9	4,442.3	5,050.5	....	Imports, cif	71
400.8	437.0	589.3	749.3	959.3	1,250.3	1,404.8	1,569.4	1,555.8	2,326.9	2,776.9	3,470.7	3,931.2	4,469.5	....	Imports, fob	71.v
1990=100																
73.8	62.2	62.4	71.2	86.5	86.3	100.9	114.0	76.6	105.5	100.0	114.5	118.4	115.3	....	Volume of Exports	72
45.0	45.1	49.9	54.6	54.9	62.3	58.4	72.6	57.8	77.9	100.0	98.7	105.1	115.3	....	Volume of Imports	73
24.5	30.1	36.2	43.4	50.1	57.4	61.7	65.9	79.8	91.9	100.0	109.5	116.9	120.1	....	Unit Value of Exports	74
25.2	29.0	36.2	41.9	52.1	60.3	68.0	66.4	81.7	91.4	100.0	109.9	117.1	118.5	....	Unit Value of Imports	75
24.2	30.3	32.7	I 39.1	50.8	62.0	67.6	72.7	83.1	95.0	100.0	110.7	117.8	131.2	142.6	Export Prices	76
18.5	24.2	I 27.9	33.8	41.9	51.7	62.3	69.2	79.0	88.9	100.0	114.6	129.0	144.7	158.0	Import Prices	76.x
Minus Sign Indicates Debit															Balance of Payments	
4,175	4,884	4,273	4,179	4,426	4,357	4,586	5,699	6,015	6,074	6,458	6,911	6,076	5,112	....	Goods: Exports f.o.b.	78aa*d*
-9,717	-10,221	-8,972	-8,449	-8,648	-9,370	-8,961	-11,134	-12,042	-13,401	-16,564	-16,933	-17,637	-15,611	....	Goods: Imports f.o.b.	78ab*d*
-5,542	-5,337	-4,699	-4,270	-4,222	-5,013	-4,375	-5,435	-6,027	-7,327	-10,106	-10,022	-11,561	-10,499	....	Trade Balance	78ac*d*
3,947	3,953	3,360	2,857	2,724	2,600	3,213	4,332	5,094	4,828	6,560	7,222	8,697	8,214	....	Services: Credit	78ad*d*
-1,428	-1,720	-1,562	-1,411	-1,309	-1,401	-1,574	-1,726	-2,164	-2,415	-3,000	-3,193	-3,701	-3,521	....	Services: Debit	78ae*d*
-3,023	-3,104	-2,901	-2,824	-2,807	-3,814	-2,736	-2,829	-3,097	-4,914	-6,546	-5,993	-6,565	-5,806	....	Balance on Goods and Services	78af*d*
252	346	258	130	183	154	106	185	269	283	315	421	555	927	....	Income: Credit	78ag*d*
-525	-887	-848	-951	-1,140	-1,282	-1,413	-1,614	-1,779	-1,913	-2,024	-2,185	-2,605	-2,367	....	Income: Debit	78ah*d*
-3,296	-3,645	-3,491	-3,645	-3,764	-4,942	-4,043	-4,258	-4,607	-6,544	-8,255	-7,757	-8,615	-7,246	....	Balance on Goods, Serv., & Inc.	78ai*d*
1,091	1,241	1,603	1,771	1,636	1,670	2,375	3,044	3,663	3,996	4,730	6,199	6,489	6,516	....	Current Transfers, n.i.e.: Credit	78aj*d*
-4	-4	-4	-4	-4	-4	-8	-9	-14	-13	-12	-16	-14	-17	....	Current Transfers: Debit	78ak*d*
-2,209	-2,408	-1,892	-1,878	-2,132	-3,276	-1,676	-1,223	-958	-2,561	-3,537	-1,574	-2,140	-747	....	Current Account, n.i.e.	78al*d*
—	—	—	—	—	—	—	—	—	—	—	—	—	—	....	Capital Account, n.i.e.: Credit	78ba*d*
—	—	—	—	—	—	—	—	—	—	—	—	—	—	....	Capital Account: Debit	78bb*d*
—	—	—	—	—	—	—	—	—	—	—	—	—	—	....	Capital Account, n.i.e.	78bc*d*
—	—	—	—	—	—	—	—	—	—	—	—	—	—	....	Direct Investment Abroad	78bd*d*
672	520	436	439	485	447	471	683	907	752	1,005	1,135	1,144	977	....	Dir. Invest. in Rep. Econ., n.i.e.	78be*d*
—	—	—	—	—	—	—	—	—	—	—	—	—	—	....	Portfolio Investment Assets	78bf*d*
—	—	—	—	—	—	—	—	—	—	—	—	—	—	....	Portfolio Investment Liab., n.i.e.	78bg*d*
-399	—	—	—	—	—	—	—	—	—	—	—	—	—	....	Other Investment Assets	78bh*d*
2,195	1,249	847	1,952	1,687	2,477	1,937	1,291	947	1,999	2,997	2,826	1,475	3,840	....	Other Investment Liab., n.i.e.	78bi*d*
2,468	1,769	1,283	2,391	2,172	2,924	2,408	1,974	1,854	2,751	4,002	3,961	2,619	4,817	....	Financial Account, n.i.e.	78bj*d*
-395	446	47	-313	-242	-44	-82	223	41	-538	-185	-183	-853	-631	....	Net Errors and Omissions	78ca*d*
-136	-193	-562	200	-202	-396	650	974	937	-348	280	2,204	-374	3,439	....	Overall Balance	78cb*d*
136	193	562	-200	202	396	-650	-974	-937	348	-280	-2,204	374	-3,439	....	Reserves and Related Items	79da*d*
227	234	128	-100	-131	141	-270	-806	-1,148	341	-40	-1,660	188	-3,019	....	Reserve Assets	79db*d*
-90	-75	-16	—	—	—	—	—	—	—	—	—	—	—	....	Use of Fund Credit and Loans	79dc*d*
—	—	—	—	—	—	—	—	—	—	—	—	—	—	....	Liabs.Constit.For.Auth.Reserves	79dd*d*
-1	35	450	-100	333	255	-380	-168	211	7	-240	-544	186	-420	....	Exceptional Financing	79de*d*
Year Ending December 31															**Government Finance**	
															Budgetary Central Government	
-53.4	-176.8	-174.5	-283.3	-351.0	-586.6	-519.9	-703.3	-1,045.1	-1,553.1	-1,814.3	-1,775.0	-1,358.4	-2,431.7	....	Deficit (-) or Surplus	80
341.3	404.2	590.4	721.0	936.5	1,114.4	1,464.9	1,707.4	1,936.0	2,134.8	2,888.0	3,679.6	4,617.6	4,989.1	....	Revenue	81
.6	8.3	7.7	5.7	7.5	7.9	30.1	10.7	56.0	63.0	103.3	137.3	204.0	292.6	....	Grants Received	81z
395.4	589.3	772.6	1,010.0	1,295.0	1,708.9	2,014.9	2,421.3	3,037.1	3,751.0	4,805.7	5,591.9	6,180.0	7,713.4	....	Expenditure	82
															Financing	
53.4	176.8	174.5	283.3	351.0	586.6	519.9	703.3	1,045.1	1,553.1	1,814.3	1,775.0	1,358.4	2,431.7	....	Net Borrowing	84
38.0	153.2	148.5	229.4	233.9	395.8	350.0	643.4	1,021.5	1,498.2	1,922.7	2,205.4	2,892.3	3,385.9	....	Borrowing: Domestic	84x
26.1	43.0	47.6	77.9	159.4	257.1	292.7	320.7	175.6	260.0	230.3	490.8	649.0	649.8	....	Foreign	85x
-10.6	-19.3	-21.7	-24.0	-42.2	-66.2	-122.8	-260.8	-152.0	-205.1	-338.7	-921.1	-2,182.9	-1,604.0	....	Amortization	84y
															Social Security	
31.6	28.4	22.2	24.1	4.2	-36.0	-74.1	-49.3	2.9	....	....	....	....	....	....	Deficit(-) or Surplus	80.r
189.7	243.9	350.1	446.2	557.7	681.7	783.2	955.1	1,189.0	....	....	....	....	....	....	Receipts	81.r
158.1	215.5	327.9	422.1	553.5	717.7	857.3	1,004.4	1,186.1	....	....	....	....	....	....	Payments	82.r
Billions of Drachmas															**National Accounts**	
357.7	422.4	473.0	609.5	824.6	977.6	1,233.1	1,536.8	1,800.9	2,018.8	2,279.1	2,905.6	3,438.2	3,709.4	....	Exports of Goods & Services	90c
280.0	368.5	471.2	579.4	742.8	942.0	1,067.2	1,224.8	1,529.5	1,819.1	2,250.7	2,555.0	2,925.3	3,200.6	....	Government Consumption	91f
413.7	456.4	513.5	624.0	702.9	880.4	1,018.1	1,074.7	1,318.4	1,690.3	2,071.7	2,375.7	2,695.7	2,910.0	....	Gross Fixed Capital Formation	93e
75.7	64.3	29.8	49.2	60.4	102.9	75.0	28.3	145.4	148.5	29.2	236.2	210.9	190.2	....	Increase/Decrease(-) in Stocks	93i
1,104.6	1,383.1	1,734.2	2,053.6	2,461.4	3,025.5	3,718.9	4,356.3	5,152.9	6,158.3	7,497.6	9,111.7	10,669.2	12,148.0	....	Private Consumption	96f
-448.9	-556.1	-738.3	-925.4	-1,139.1	-1,513.5	-1,703.3	-1,993.4	-2,290.7	-2,810.3	-3,445.3	-4,253.5	-4,897.9	-5,419.0	....	Imports of Goods & Services	98c
1,711.0	2,050.1	2,574.6	3,079.2	3,805.7	4,617.8	5,514.7	6,271.9	7,572.3	8,804.8	10,550.6	12,888.6	14,832.2	16,760.4	....	Gross Domestic Product	99b
56.6	59.0	57.8	30.4	1.9	-33.8	-67.8	-63.3	-56.7	-85.2	-46.1	50.4	51.7	94.2	....	Net Factor Inc/Pmts(-) Abroad	98.n
1,767.6	2,109.1	2,632.4	3,109.6	3,807.6	4,584.0	5,446.9	6,208.6	7,515.6	8,719.6	10,504.5	12,838.2	14,780.5	16,854.6	....	Gross Nat'l Expenditure = GNP	99a
1,625.5	1,933.6	2,417.0	2,837.0	3,478.2	4,181.0	4,941.8	5,630.5	6,854.0	7,926.2	9,562.1	11,730.0	13,504.8	15,408.0	....	Nat'l Income, Market Prices	99e
9,111.3	9,117.0	9,153.6	9,190.2	9,442.2	9,736.6	9,894.4	9,848.3	10,287.0	10,650.7	10,550.6	10,891.2	10,981.6	10,927.8	....	Gross Dom. Prod. 1990 Prices	99b.*p*
18.8	22.5	28.1	33.5	40.3	47.4	55.7	63.7	73.6	82.7	100.0	118.3	135.1	153.4	....	GDP Deflator (1990=100)	99bi*p*
Midyear Estimates																
9.64	9.73	9.79	9.85	9.90	9.93	9.96	9.98	10.00	10.04	10.09	10.20	10.31	10.35	10.43	**Population**	99z

Other Banking Institutions: I Beginning in 1978, data are based on improved classification and sectorization.

Interest Rates: *Deposit Rate:* I Before 1988, maximum rate offered by deposit money banks on three- to six-month drachma deposits by individuals and enterprises. Beginning in 1988, data refer to deposits with a maturity of three to twelve months.

Grenada

328

		1965	1966	1967	1968	1969	1970	1971	1972	1973	1974	1975	1976	1977	1978	1979
Exchange Rates												*E.Caribbean Dollars per SDR: End of Period (aa)*				
Official Rate	aa	1.7126	1.7203	1.9948	2.0131	1.9994	2.0053	2.0417	2.2194	2.4925	2.5024	2.7770	3.1369	3.2797	3.5175	3.5568
Official Rate	ae	1.7126	1.7203	1.9948	2.0131	1.9994	2.0053	1.8805	2.0442	2.0661	2.0439	2.3721	2.7000	2.7000	2.7000	2.7000
													Index Numbers (1990=100):			
Official Rate	ah x	157.3	157.1	154.5	134.6	134.5	134.8	137.3	140.7	137.9	131.6	125.0	100.0	100.0	100.0	100.0
Nominal Effective Exchange Rate	ne c	....	....	....	....	....	....	....	....	....	....	....	....	....	....	85.9
Real Effective Exchange Rate	re c	....	....	....	....	....	....	....	....	....	....	....	....	....	....	89.0
Fund Position														*Millions of SDRs:*		
Quota	2f. s											2.00	2.00	2.00	3.00	3.00
SDRs	1b. s											.07	.09	.02	—	.01
Reserve Position in the Fund	1c. s															
Total Fund Cred.&Loans Outstg.	2tl											.81	1.21	1.42	2.03	2.40
International Liquidity												*Millions of US Dollars Unless Otherwise Indicated:*				
Total Reserves minus Gold	1l. d	....	....	....	....	....	5.32	5.82	5.60	5.00	5.36	⅃5.04	8.11	7.65	9.70	12.22
SDRs	1b. d	....	....	....	....	....	....	....	....	....	....	.08	.10	.02	—	.01
Reserve Position in the Fund	1c. d	....	....	....	....	....	....	....	....	....	....	....	....	....	....	....
Foreign Exchange	1d. d	....	....	....	....	....	5.32	5.82	5.60	5.00	5.36	⅃4.95	8.01	7.63	9.70	12.21
Deposit Money Banks: Assets	7a. d	....	....	....	....	....	1.94	1.72	.68	1.40	4.33	6.03	5.26	4.99	5.44	11.08
of which: Claims on Nonbanks	7ad d															.24
Deposit Money Banks: Liabilities	7b. d	....	....	....	....	....	4.02	7.10	10.13	11.57	15.12	11.75	6.26	6.84	6.48	11.10
of which: Liab. to Nonbanks	7bd d								4.29	4.50	5.09	5.44	4.77	5.12	5.51	5.93
Monetary Authorities												*Millions of E. Caribbean Dollars:*				
Foreign Assets	11	....	....	....	....	....	10.63	10.72	10.32	10.34	10.96	⅃11.95	21.91	20.66	26.20	32.99
Claims on Central Government	12a						.60	.70	.70	1.59	1.89	5.53	8.36	9.44	12.56	14.89
Claims on Deposit Money Banks	12e						—	—	—	—	—	—	—	—	—	—
Reserve Money	14	....	....	....	....	....	11.24	11.43	11.03	11.92	12.85	⅃15.22	26.47	25.44	31.61	39.35
of which: Currency Outside DMBs	14a						6.09	6.90	8.28	8.39	9.71	12.65	15.32	18.33	23.67	28.50
Foreign Liabilities	16c												2.25	3.80	4.66	7.14	8.54
Central Government Deposits	16d												—	—	—	—
Other Items (Net)	17r	....	....	....	....	....										
Deposit Money Banks												*Millions of E. Caribbean Dollars:*				
Reserves	20	....	....	....	....	....	4.55	3.88	1.96	2.64	2.38	⅃2.57	11.15	7.11	7.95	10.85
Foreign Assets	21						3.88	3.17	1.39	2.89	8.86	⅃14.30	14.20	13.48	14.70	29.93
Claims on Central Government	22a						7.97	9.77	13.43	12.13	15.33	15.45	13.26	13.14	13.34	10.12
Claims on Local Government	22b						—	—	—	—	—	—	—	—	—	—
Claims on Nonfin.Pub.Enterprises	22c						—	—	—	—	—	.50	.50	.50	.40	.76
Claims on Private Sector	22d						31.33	38.54	46.32	50.72	45.94	⅃39.42	38.74	48.02	56.54	64.34
Claims on Nonbank Financial Insts	22f						.22	.12	.50	.50	.50	.50	.50	.49	.37	.27
Demand Deposits	24						4.72[e]	4.97[e]	6.03	7.23	6.07	6.73	11.38	11.18	14.37	17.15
Time, Savings,& Fgn.Currency Dep.	25						31.87[e]	33.54[e]	39.60	39.86	38.69	47.29	52.58	58.55	66.09	77.75
Foreign Liabilities	26c						8.05[e]	13.08[e]	20.70	23.90	30.90	⅃27.88	16.91	18.48	17.48	29.98
Central Government Deposits	26d						—	—	—	—	—	—	.10	.10	.40	.71
Credit from Monetary Authorities	26g						—	—	—	—	—	—	—	—	—	—
Capital Accounts	27a						.85	.88	.93	.95	1.00	.98	1.12	1.20	1.30	.88
Other Items (Net)	27r						2.45	3.02	-3.66	-3.07	-3.67	-10.15	-3.76	-6.78	-6.35	-10.21
Monetary Survey												*Millions of E. Caribbean Dollars:*				
Foreign Assets (Net)	31n						6.46	.82	-8.98	-10.67	-11.08	-3.89	15.40	11.00	16.27	⅃24.40
Domestic Credit	32						40.12	49.14	60.95	64.93	63.65	61.40	61.25	71.49	82.81	89.67
Claims on Central Govt. (Net)	32an						8.57	10.47	14.13	13.71	17.21	20.98	21.51	22.47	25.50	24.31
Claims on Local Government	32b						—	—	—	—	—	—	—	—	—	—
Claims on Nonfin.Pub.Enterprises	32c						—	—	—	—	—	.50	.50	.50	.40	.76
Claims on Private Sector	32d						31.33	38.54	46.32	50.72	45.94	39.42	38.74	48.02	56.54	64.34
Claims on Nonbank Financial Inst	32f						.22	.12	.50	.50	.50	.50	.50	.49	.37	.27
Money	34						10.81	11.87	14.31	15.62	15.79	19.38	26.70	29.51	38.04	45.65
Quasi-Money	35						31.87	33.54	39.60	39.86	38.69	47.29	52.58	58.55	66.09	77.75
Other Items (Net)	37r						3.90	4.55	-1.95	-1.23	-1.91	-9.16	-2.64	-5.57	-5.05	-9.33
Money plus Quasi-Money	35l						42.68	45.41	53.91	55.48	54.48	66.67	79.28	88.07	104.13	123.40
Interest Rates													*Percent Per Annum*			
Treasury Bill Rate	60c															
Deposit Rate	60l															
Lending Rate	60p															9.0	8.5
Prices													*Index Numbers (1990=100):*			
Consumer Prices	64												29.3	34.7	41.0	49.9
International Transactions												*Millions of E. Caribbean Dollars*				
Exports	70	10.87	10.20	8.58	9.84	16.00	12.08	10.19	10.53	14.51	19.27	26.84	33.82	38.75	45.58	57.80
Imports, cif	71	19.08	21.72	24.08	26.42	34.23	44.63	46.05	42.81	42.49	37.08	52.63	66.25	87.29	96.45	117.98
Imports, fob	71.v	17.34	19.75	21.89	24.02	31.11	40.57	41.86	38.92	38.62	33.71	47.84	60.22	79.36	87.67	106.37

Grenada

328

	1980	1981	1982	1983	1984	1985	1986	1987	1988	1989	1990	1991	1992	1993	1994		
Exchange Rates																	
E.Caribbean Dollars per US Dollar: End of Period (ae)																	
Official Rate	3.4436	3.1427	2.9784	2.8268	2.6466	2.9657	3.3026	3.8304	3.6334	3.5482	3.8412	3.8622	3.7125	3.7086	3.9416	aa
Official Rate	2.7000	2.7000	2.7000	2.7000	2.7000	2.7000	2.7000	2.7000	2.7000	2.7000	2.7000	2.7000	2.7000	2.7000	2.7000	ae
Period Averages																	
Official Rate	100.0	100.0	100.0	100.0	100.0	100.0	100.0	100.0	100.0	100.0	100.0	100.0	100.0	100.0	100.0	ahx
Nominal Effective Exchange Rate	83.7	90.4	96.3	101.5	108.9	111.9	107.2	101.5	99.0	104.3	100.0	101.2	101.9	111.5	113.6	nec
Real Effective Exchange Rate	92.6	107.1	113.6	119.8	127.8	127.9	119.1	107.1	104.0	108.7	100.0	98.5	98.1	106.1	106.8	rec
Fund Position																	
End of Period																	
Quota	4.50	4.50	4.50	6.00	6.00	6.00	6.00	6.00	6.00	6.00	6.00	6.00	8.50	8.50	8.50	2f.s
SDRs	—	—	.01	.14	.02	.01	—	—	—	—	—	—	—	—	.02	1b.s
Reserve Position in the Fund	—	—	—	—	—	—	—	—	—	—	—	—	—	—	—	1c.s
Total Fund Cred.&Loans Outstg.	2.21	7.10	6.27	7.32	6.30	3.83	2.13	1.47	.91	.35	.01	—	—	—	—	2tl
International Liquidity																	
End of Period																	
Total Reserves minus Gold	12.91	16.10	9.23	14.14	14.23	20.81	20.57	22.74	16.92	15.44	17.58	17.47	25.88	26.92	31.12	1l.d
SDRs	—	—	.01	.15	.02	.01	—	—	—	—	—	—	—	—	.03	1b.d
Reserve Position in the Fund	—	—	—	—	—	—	—	—	—	—	—	—	—	—	—	1c.d
Foreign Exchange	12.91	16.10	9.22	14.00	14.21	20.80	20.57	22.74	16.92	15.44	17.58	17.47	25.88	26.92	31.08	1d.d
Deposit Money Banks: Assets	10.89	12.71	6.49	7.47	8.04	7.55	9.21	14.25	21.33	10.31	18.52	18.05	27.93	35.68	51.88	7a.d
of which: Claims on Nonbanks	.72	3.44	.81	.74	.72	.88	1.19	2.04	2.31	3.20	3.96	3.63	3.57	8.17	16.41	7add
Deposit Money Banks: Liabilities	11.04	12.50	12.56	9.61	9.70	10.29	13.12	18.12	16.59	23.40	20.57	22.12	29.70	37.26	39.64	7b.d
of which: Liab. to Nonbanks	6.88	7.92	7.96	8.52	9.01	9.36	11.83	16.27	16.13	16.36	18.43	20.56	23.77	29.48	32.99	7bdd
Monetary Authorities																	
End of Period																	
Foreign Assets	34.85	43.46	24.93	38.18	38.43	56.19	55.53	61.40	45.69	41.69	47.46	47.18	69.25	72.68	84.01	11
Claims on Central Government	14.90	31.84	38.85	29.95	42.91	37.62	33.78	32.19	33.28	36.16	36.52	37.71	35.02	28.34	24.30	12a
Claims on Deposit Money Banks	—	—	—	—	—	.86	.24	1.90	1.43	3.22	1.15	.85	.64	.48	.27	12e
Reserve Money	42.15	52.98	45.09	47.45	64.66	83.30	82.50	89.86	77.10	79.84	85.09	85.74	104.91	100.79	107.24	14
of which: Currency Outside DMBs	32.58	37.41	39.95	41.36	20.58	25.07	30.69	33.07	35.13	31.40	38.05	40.35	46.68	46.56	52.96	14a
Foreign Liabilities	7.61	22.33	18.69	20.69	16.68	11.37	7.04	5.63	3.31	1.24	.04	—	—	—	—	16c
Central Government Deposits	—	—	—	—	—	—	—	—	—	—	—	—	—	.71	1.35	16d
Other Items (Net)	—	—	—	—	—	—	—	—	—	—	—	—	—	—	—	17r
Deposit Money Banks																	
End of Period																	
Reserves	9.57	15.56	5.14	6.08	43.27	44.69	49.72	53.80	44.15	54.19	45.53	43.15	55.55	53.14	56.10	20
Foreign Assets	29.39	34.32	17.52	20.17	21.71	20.39	24.85	38.49	57.60	27.83	50.00	48.74	75.42	96.33	140.08	21
Claims on Central Government	12.42	12.05	23.53	32.57	28.53	32.09	31.87	31.95	38.44	35.62	40.12	43.83	34.62	38.39	42.98	22a
Claims on Local Government	—	—	—	—	—	—	—	—	—	—	—	—	—	—	.06	22b
Claims on Nonfin.Pub.Enterprises	1.53	2.25	10.51	8.77	7.40	7.38	7.88	9.55	10.57	14.49	12.83	11.04	9.38	9.74	6.71	22c
Claims on Private Sector	72.34	75.11	78.80	76.17	81.27	109.67	152.02	188.60	212.70	272.99	270.74	287.52	315.02	413.64	414.60	22d
Claims on Nonbank Financial Insts	.29	.50	.53	.45	1.76	.52	.51	.42	.30	.32	.36	.32	2.22	4.82	4.24	22f
Demand Deposits	15.87	15.91	19.62	16.74	30.13	29.05	38.65	41.24	47.87	56.59	53.04	49.17	63.44	77.51	90.03	24
Time, Savings,& Fgn.Currency Dep.	82.51	87.83	87.03	88.86	97.71	123.09	157.61	179.24	216.63	234.26	263.32	283.35	290.62	364.42	409.15	25
Foreign Liabilities	29.80	33.75	33.90	25.95	26.20	27.80	35.41	48.93	44.80	63.18	55.54	59.72	80.19	100.60	107.03	26c
Central Government Deposits	3.31	2.28	1.12	2.49	4.73	2.65	1.25	4.80	10.35	14.89	13.08	6.98	17.03	20.35	24.37	26d
Credit from Monetary Authorities	—	—	2.54	6.41	—	—	—	3.21	1.42	2.86	1.21	.83	.79	.58	.25	26g
Capital Accounts	.70	3.03	3.10	9.54	17.87	19.43	22.38	27.18	28.32	30.94	35.18	43.33	47.02	64.73	68.28	27a
Other Items (Net)	-6.64	-3.01	-11.29	-5.78	7.29	12.72	11.55	18.20	14.38	2.71	-1.81	-8.78	-6.87	-12.14	-34.35	27r
Monetary Survey																	
End of Period																	
Foreign Assets (Net)	26.84	21.71	-10.15	11.72	17.26	37.42	37.92	45.33	55.18	5.10	41.88	36.19	64.48	68.41	117.06	31n
Domestic Credit	98.17	119.46	151.11	145.42	157.13	184.63	224.81	257.91	284.96	344.69	347.48	373.44	379.23	473.86	467.17	32
Claims on Central Govt. (Net)	24.01	41.61	61.27	60.04	66.71	67.05	64.40	59.34	61.38	56.89	63.56	74.56	52.61	45.65	41.55	32an
Claims on Local Government	—	—	—	—	—	—	—	—	—	—	—	—	—	—	.06	32b
Claims on Nonfin.Pub.Enterprises	1.53	2.25	10.51	8.77	7.40	7.38	7.88	9.55	10.57	14.49	12.83	11.04	9.38	9.74	6.71	32c
Claims on Private Sector	72.34	75.11	78.80	76.17	81.27	109.67	152.02	188.60	212.70	272.99	270.74	287.52	315.02	413.64	414.60	32d
Claims on Nonbank Financial Inst	.29	.50	.53	.45	1.76	.52	.51	.42	.30	.32	.36	.32	2.22	4.82	4.24	32f
Money	48.45	53.32	59.57	58.10	50.71	54.12	69.34	74.31	83.00	87.99	91.09	89.50	110.12	124.07	143.13	34
Quasi-Money	82.51	87.83	87.03	88.86	97.71	157.61	179.24	216.63	234.26	263.32	283.35	290.62	364.42	409.15		35
Other Items (Net)	-5.94	.02	-5.64	10.18	25.97	44.83	35.79	49.69	40.50	27.54	34.95	36.78	42.98	53.78	31.95	37r
Money plus Quasi-Money	130.95	141.16	146.61	146.96	148.42	177.21	226.95	253.55	299.63	322.25	354.42	372.86	400.74	488.49	552.28	35l
Interest Rates																	
Percent Per Annum																	
Treasury Bill Rate	6.5	6.5	6.5	6.5	6.5	6.5	6.5	6.5	6.5	6.5	6.5	6.5	6.5	6.5	6.5	60c
Deposit Rate	4.5	4.5	4.5	5.9	7.0	7.0	6.5	6.1	5.5	5.0	6.5	6.2	5.5	5.0	4.2	60l
Lending Rate	9.5	9.5	10.5	10.5	10.5	10.5	11.7	11.5	11.4	10.5	10.7	10.5	10.6	10.5	10.5	60p
Prices																	
Period Averages																	
Consumer Prices	60.4	71.8	77.4	82.1	86.7	89.0	89.4	88.6	92.2	97.3	100.0	102.6	106.5	109.5	....	64
International Transactions																	
Millions of E. Caribbean Dollars																	
Exports	46.95	51.36	50.09	51.09	49.11	61.33	84.36	86.10	88.50	75.40	71.60	61.50	53.90	....	....	70
Imports, cif	135.57	146.71	152.43	154.48	151.10	187.00	225.72	239.17	248.80	267.90	283.80	327.00	287.80	....	....	71
Imports, fob	122.29	131.80	138.36	138.32	135.27	167.41	202.08	214.12	222.74	239.84	254.07	292.75	257.65	....	....	71.v

Grenada

328

	1965	1966	1967	1968	1969	1970	1971	1972	1973	1974	1975	1976	1977	1978	1979
Balance of Payments													*Millions of US Dollars:*		
Goods: Exports f.o.b. .... 78aa d	....	....	....	....	....	....	....	....	....	....	....	....	14.26	16.90	21.40
Goods: Imports f.o.b. .... 78ab d	....	....	....	....	....	....	....	....	....	....	....	....	−28.54	−33.35	−42.64
Trade Balance .... 78ac d	....	....	....	....	....	....	....	....	....	....	....	....	−14.28	−16.45	−21.24
Services: Credit .... 78ad d	....	....	....	....	....	....	....	....	....	....	....	....	14.60	16.40	19.15
Services: Debit .... 78ae d	....	....	....	....	....	....	....	....	....	....	....	....	−4.35	−6.60	−12.42
Balance on Goods and Services .... 78af d	....	....	....	....	....	....	....	....	....	....	....	....	−4.03	−6.65	−14.51
Income: Credit .... 78ag d	....	....	....	....	....	....	....	....	....	....	....	....	.30	.30	.80
Income: Debit .... 78ah d	....	....	....	....	....	....	....	....	....	....	....	....	−.20	−.40	−.60
Balance on Goods, Serv., & Inc. ... 78ai d	....	....	....	....	....	....	....	....	....	....	....	....	−3.93	−6.75	−14.31
Current Transfers, n.i.e.: Credit ... 78aj d	....	....	....	....	....	....	....	....	....	....	....	....	5.24	7.80	14.90
Current Transfers: Debit .... 78ak d	....	....	....	....	....	....	....	....	....	....	....	....	—	—	−1.70
Current Account, n.i.e. .... 78al d	....	....	....	....	....	....	....	....	....	....	....	....	1.31	1.05	−1.11
Capital Account, n.i.e.: Credit ... 78ba d	....	....	....	....	....	....	....	....	....	....	....	....	—	—	—
Capital Account: Debit .... 78bb d	....	....	....	....	....	....	....	....	....	....	....	....	—	—	—
Capital Account, n.i.e. .... 78bc d	....	....	....	....	....	....	....	....	....	....	....	....	—	—	—
Direct Investment Abroad .... 78bd d	....	....	....	....	....	....	....	....	....	....	....	....	—	—	—
Dir. Invest. in Rep. Econ., n.i.e. 78be d	....	....	....	....	....	....	....	....	....	....	....	....	−.10	1.40	—
Portfolio Investment Assets .... 78bf d	....	....	....	....	....	....	....	....	....	....	....	....	—	—	—
Portfolio Investment Liab., n.i.e. 78bg d	....	....	....	....	....	....	....	....	....	....	....	....	—	—	—
Other Investment Assets .... 78bh d	....	....	....	....	....	....	....	....	....	....	....	....	.27	−.45	−5.40
Other Investment Liab., n.i.e. ... 78bi d	....	....	....	....	....	....	....	....	....	....	....	....	2.17	.51	6.84
Financial Account, n.i.e. .... 78bj d	....	....	....	....	....	....	....	....	....	....	....	....	2.34	1.46	1.44
Net Errors and Omissions .... 78ca d	....	....	....	....	....	....	....	....	....	....	....	....	−4.02	−1.48	1.41
Overall Balance .... 78cb d	....	....	....	....	....	....	....	....	....	....	....	....	−.37	1.03	1.74
Reserves and Related Items .... 79da d	....	....	....	....	....	....	....	....	....	....	....	....	.37	−1.03	−1.74
Reserve Assets .... 79db d	....	....	....	....	....	....	....	....	....	....	....	....	.13	−1.79	−2.22
Use of Fund Credit and Loans .... 79dc d	....	....	....	....	....	....	....	....	....	....	....	....	.24	.76	.47
Liabs.Constit.For.Auth.Reserves .. 79dd d	....	....	....	....	....	....	....	....	....	....	....	....	—	—	—
Exceptional Financing .... 79de d	....	....	....	....	....	....	....	....	....	....	....	....	—	—	—
Government Finance													*Millions of E. Caribbean Dollars:*		
Deficit (−) or Surplus 80	....	....	....	....	....	....	....	....	....	−5.25	−5.08	−6.37	−1.66	‡−10.60	−7.80
Revenue 81	....	....	....	....	....	....	....	....	....	15.76	18.41	28.18	33.65	‡44.80	55.10
Grants Received 81z	....	....	....	....	....	....	....	....	....	2.94	2.84	1.63	1.59	‡1.60	34.40
Expenditure 82	....	....	....	....	....	....	....	....	....	22.79	24.52	34.43	34.77	‡52.70	95.40
Lending Minus Repayments 83	....	....	....	....	....	....	....	....	....	1.16	1.81	1.75	2.13	‡4.30	1.90
Financing															
Domestic 84a	....	....	....	....	....	....	....	....	....	3.05	6.22	5.57	1.12	‡5.40	3.00
Foreign 85a	....	....	....	....	....	....	....	....	....	2.20	−1.14	.80	.54	‡5.20	4.80
National Accounts													*Millions of E. Caribbean Dollars*		
Exports of Goods & Services 90c	....	....	....	....	....	....	....	....	36.4	32.5	58.2	67.3	80.5	92.3	109.1
Government Consumption 91f	....	....	....	....	....	....	....	....	17.7	17.3	21.0	30.2	29.2	46.1	50.8
Gross Fixed Capital Formation 93e	....	....	....	....	....	....	....	....	15.2	13.6	6.3	13.7	14.8	13.8	31.3
Increase/Decrease(−) in Stocks ... 93i	....	....	....	....	....	....	....	....	....	....	—	1.6	6.2	.6	.7
Private Consumption 96f	....	....	....	....	....	....	....	....	41.5	48.7	69.5	75.6	97.0	132.1	156.0
Imports of Goods & Services 98c	....	....	....	....	....	....	....	....	−42.5	−38.1	−58.8	−72.3	−93.4	−112.6	−145.3
Gross Domestic Product 99b	....	....	....	....	....	....	....	....	68.3	74.0	96.2	116.1	134.3	172.3	202.6
Gross Dom. Prod. 1990 Prices 99b.p	....	....	....	....	....	....	....	....	....	....	268.5	292.8	309.5	334.6	342.6
GDP Deflator (1990=100) .... 99bi p	....	....	....	....	....	....	....	....	21.9	23.8	35.8	39.7	43.4	51.5	59.1
													Millions:		
Population 99z	.09	.09	.10	.10	.10	.09	.10	.10	.10	.10	.11	.11	.11	.11	.09

Exchange Rates: On October 6, 1965 the East Caribbean dollar, equal to the West Indian dollar, was introduced.
Monetary Authorities: ‡ For the period 1975 through 1978 *lines 11* and *14* include net local interbank claims of commercial banks as a proxy for banks' deposits with Eastern Caribbean Central Bank (ECCB).
Deposit Money Banks: ‡ For the period 1975 through 1978, *lines 20, 21,* and *26c* include net local interbank claims of commercial banks as a proxy for banks' deposits with ECCB. Beginning in 1979, the data reflect improved reporting of commercial bank accounts with the ECCB (*line 20*) and with branches in other member countries (*lines 20, 21,* and *26c*).
Monetary Survey: ‡ See note to section 20.
Government Finance: ‡ Prior to 1978, data are as reported in the *Government Finance Statistics Yearbook*. Beginning in 1978, data are as reported by the Ministry of Finance for publication in *IFS*.

Grenada

Balance of Payments

Minus Sign Indicates Debit

	1980	1981	1982	1983	1984	1985	1986	1987	1988	1989	1990	1991	1992	1993	1994	
Goods: Exports f.o.b.	17.40	19.00	18.50	19.30	18.20	22.30	28.70	31.89	32.78	28.19	26.59	23.19	19.93	20.42	....	78aa d
Goods: Imports f.o.b.	−48.79	−56.07	−59.03	−57.88	−51.12	−65.56	−80.89	−89.07	−92.19	−99.04	−106.26	−113.58	−103.18	−111.46	....	78ab d
Trade Balance	−31.39	−37.07	−40.53	−38.58	−32.92	−43.26	−52.19	−57.19	−59.41	−70.85	−79.67	−90.39	−83.25	−91.04	....	78ac d
Services: Credit	20.60	18.70	18.30	18.60	21.60	30.59	47.19	47.89	53.41	55.00	65.23	73.42	77.79	88.75	....	78ad d
Services: Debit	−11.07	−13.39	−17.37	−15.82	−18.38	−21.07	−25.81	−28.35	−29.19	−31.30	−34.17	−38.04	−38.70	−43.60	....	78ae d
Balance on Goods and Services	−21.86	−31.76	−39.60	−35.80	−29.70	−33.74	−30.81	−37.65	−35.19	−47.15	−48.62	−55.01	−44.16	−45.90	....	78af d
Income: Credit	1.10	1.30	1.50	1.70	1.40	1.39	1.82	1.73	2.73	2.43	2.51	2.89	3.41	2.80	....	78ag d
Income: Debit	−3.20	−6.30	−6.50	−6.10	−2.90	−3.10	−7.37	−8.37	−9.00	−11.96	−14.38	−9.77	−8.74	−11.16	....	78ah d
Balance on Goods, Serv., & Inc.	−23.96	−36.76	−44.60	−40.20	−31.20	−35.44	−36.37	−44.29	−41.46	−56.68	−60.49	−61.90	−49.50	−54.26	....	78ai d
Current Transfers, n.i.e.: Credit	26.10	25.11	30.19	29.61	37.20	41.96	41.29	32.59	33.44	27.15	34.87	29.88	29.77	29.72	....	78aj d
Current Transfers: Debit	−1.90	−2.30	−3.30	−4.50	−4.20	−4.30	−7.57	−8.24	−8.50	−.88	−2.38	−2.80	−4.05	−3.79	....	78ak d
Current Account, n.i.e.	.24	−13.95	−17.71	−15.09	1.80	2.22	−2.65	−19.93	−16.51	−30.41	−28.01	−34.81	−23.78	−28.33	....	78al d
Capital Account, n.i.e.: Credit	—	—	—	—	—	—	—	—	—	—	—	—	—	—	....	78ba d
Capital Account: Debit	—	—	—	—	—	—	—	—	—	—	—	—	—	—	....	78bb d
Capital Account, n.i.e.	—	—	—	—	—	—	—	—	—	—	—	—	—	—	....	78bc d
Direct Investment Abroad	—	—	—	—	—	—	—	—	—	—	—	—	—	—	....	78bd d
Dir. Invest. in Rep. Econ., n.i.e.	—	—	1.90	2.50	2.80	4.11	4.48	14.72	14.98	10.48	12.87	15.27	22.58	20.20	....	78be d
Portfolio Investment Assets	—	—	—	—	—	—	—	—	—	—	—	—	—	—	....	78bf d
Portfolio Investment Liab., n.i.e.	—	—	—	—	—	—	—	—	.15	—	.02	.05	−.16	.20	....	78bg d
Other Investment Assets	.49	−1.83	6.22	−.98	−.57	.49	1.19	−.01	−8.42	17.52	—	2.37	−1.93	−1.47	....	78bh d
Other Investment Liab., n.i.e.	1.14	9.09	8.90	10.47	5.34	1.39	3.30	6.22	3.91	.49	10.45	8.57	3.86	2.77	....	78bi d
Financial Account, n.i.e.	1.63	7.26	17.02	11.99	7.57	5.99	8.96	20.94	10.61	28.49	11.82	26.26	24.35	21.70	....	78bj d
Net Errors and Omissions	−.96	2.84	−1.31	2.76	−11.65	−1.99	−6.62	.07	−2.06	−5.32	11.33	8.51	7.97	5.82	....	78ca d
Overall Balance	.91	−3.85	−2.00	−.34	−2.28	6.22	−.30	1.07	−7.95	−7.25	−4.86	−.04	8.54	−.80	....	78cb d
Reserves and Related Items	−.91	3.85	2.00	.34	2.28	−6.22	.30	−1.07	7.95	7.25	4.86	.04	−8.54	.80	....	79da d
Reserve Assets	−.69	−1.98	2.90	−1.25	.31	−6.76	.01	−2.96	5.89	1.56	−2.07	−2.44	−8.10	−.44	....	79db d
Use of Fund Credit and Loans	−.25	5.75	−.91	1.10	−1.03	−2.51	−1.97	−.85	−.75	−.72	−.46	−.01	—	—	....	79dc d
Liabs.Constit.For.Auth.Reserves	—	—	—	—	—	—	—	—	—	—	—	—	—	—	....	79dd d
Exceptional Financing	.03	.08	.01	.49	3.00	3.06	2.26	2.74	2.81	6.41	7.39	2.50	−.44	1.24	....	79de d

Government Finance

Year Ending December 31

	1980	1981	1982	1983	1984	1985	1986	1987	1988	1989	1990	1991	1992	1993	1994	
Deficit (−) or Surplus	−4.60	....	....	....	....	....	....	....	....	....	....	....	....	....	....	80
Revenue	59.10	....	....	....	....	....	....	....	....	....	....	....	....	....	....	81
Grants Received	29.60	....	....	....	....	....	....	....	....	....	....	....	....	....	....	81z
Expenditure	91.00	....	....	....	....	....	....	....	....	....	....	....	....	....	....	82
Lending Minus Repayments	2.30	....	....	....	....	....	....	....	....	....	....	....	....	....	....	83
Financing																
Domestic	.40	....	....	....	....	....	....	....	....	....	....	....	....	....	....	84a
Foreign	4.20	....	....	....	....	....	....	....	....	....	....	....	....	....	....	85a

National Accounts

Millions of E. Caribbean Dollars

	1980	1981	1982	1983	1984	1985	1986	1987	1988	1989	1990	1991	1992	1993	1994	
Exports of Goods & Services	106.9	106.1	103.4	105.3	112.8	149.0	163.4	173.5	181.0	185.0	240.3	257.3	223.2	....	....	90c
Government Consumption	41.7	45.0	47.2	55.9	59.3	68.1	80.7	77.3	82.8	88.0	110.8	106.8	114.8	....	....	91f
Gross Fixed Capital Formation	52.7	91.1	107.2	106.8	80.0	97.1	117.1	141.6	160.5	181.4	210.5	226.8	187.4	....	....	93e
Increase/Decrease(−) in Stocks	3.2	4.9	−.1	−5.2	1.7	−5.2	−.6	8.4	7.4	15.0	17.0	20.9	12.1	....	....	93i
Private Consumption	161.1	154.6	195.0	183.9	213.2	240.1	261.6	295.0	320.0	340.0	355.1	392.6	384.1	....	....	96f
Imports of Goods & Services	−163.6	−185.0	−213.3	−193.8	−192.1	−237.9	−271.8	−289.7	−303.0	−318.0	−388.6	−437.2	−343.6	....	....	98c
Gross Domestic Product	202.0	216.7	239.4	252.9	274.9	311.2	350.4	406.1	448.7	491.4	541.1	567.2	578.0	....	....	99b
Gross Dom. Prod. 1990 Prices	343.1	350.2	368.9	373.3	394.1	413.5	436.3	462.4	486.8	514.3	541.1	557.0	560.2	....	....	99b.p
GDP Deflator (1990=100)	58.9	61.9	64.9	67.7	69.7	75.3	80.3	87.8	92.2	95.6	100.0	101.8	103.2	....	....	99bi p

Midyear Estimates

	1980	1981	1982	1983	1984	1985	1986	1987	1988	1989	1990	1991	1992	1993	1994	
Population	.11	.09	.09	.09	.09	.09	.10	.10	.09	.09	.09	.09	.09	.09	....	99z

Guatemala

		1965	1966	1967	1968	1969	1970	1971	1972	1973	1974	1975	1976	1977	1978	1979
Exchange Rates															*Quetzales per SDR:*	
Market Rate......aa=......wa		1.0000	1.0000	1.0000	1.0000	1.0000	1.0000	1.0857	1.0857	1.2064	1.2244	1.1707	1.1618	1.2147	1.3028	1.3173
														Quetzales per US Dollar:		
Market Rate......ae=......we		1.0000	1.0000	1.0000	1.0000	1.0000	1.0000	1.0000	1.0000	1.0000	1.0000	1.0000	1.0000	1.0000	1.0000	1.0000
Market Rate......rf=......wf		1.0000	1.0000	1.0000	1.0000	1.0000	1.0000	1.0000	1.0000	1.0000	1.0000	1.0000	1.0000	1.0000	1.0000	1.0000
Secondary Rate......xe		....	....	....	....	....	....	....	....	....	....	....	....	....	....	....
Secondary Rate......xf		....	....	....	....	....	....	....	....	....	....	....	....	....	....	....
Tertiary Rate......ye		....	....	....	....	....	....	....	....	....	....	....	....	....	....	....
Tertiary Rate......yf		....	....	....	....	....	....	....	....	....	....	....	....	....	....	....
Fund Position															*Millions of SDRs:*	
Quota......2f.s		20.0	25.0	25.0	25.0	25.0	36.0	36.0	36.0	36.0	36.0	36.0	36.0	36.0	51.0	51.0
SDRs......1b.s		—	—	—	—	—	2.1	7.8	7.6	11.5	11.5	11.5	11.4	11.5	11.6	18.4
Reserve Position in the Fund......1c.s		—	—	—	—	—	—	3.0	9.0	9.0	9.0	9.0	12.0	12.4	12.9	14.1
of which: Outstg.Fund Borrowing......2c		—	—	—	—	—	—	—	—	—	—	—	—	—	—	—
Total Fund Cred.&Loans Outstg.......2tl		—	5.3	15.3	13.4	11.1	—	—	—	—	—	—	—	—	—	—
International Liquidity												*Millions of US Dollars Unless Otherwise Indicated:*				
Total Reserves minus Gold......1l.d		46.1	40.7	45.1	45.4	54.1	60.8	74.7	116.2	191.3	181.3	283.8	491.0	668.9	741.5	696.3
SDRs......1b.d		—	—	—	—	—	2.1	8.5	8.3	13.8	14.1	13.4	13.3	14.0	15.1	24.2
Reserve Position in the Fund......1c.d		—	—	—	—	—	—	3.3	9.8	10.9	11.0	10.5	13.9	15.0	16.8	18.6
Foreign Exchange......1d.d		46.1	40.7	45.1	45.4	54.1	58.7	62.9	98.2	166.6	156.2	259.8	463.8	639.9	709.6	653.5
Gold (Million Fine Troy Ounces)......1ad		.619	.571	.571	.575	.572	.500	.495	.492	.492	.492	.492	.492	.507	.515	.522
Gold (National Valuation)......1and		21.7	20.0	20.0	20.1	20.0	17.5	17.3	18.7	20.8	20.8	20.8	20.8	21.4	21.7	22.1
Monetary Authorities: Other Liab.......4.d		25.1	20.2	20.0	25.0	26.3	27.1	24.1	22.2	19.2	24.2	50.1	69.8	101.5	111.4	104.6
Deposit Money Banks: Assets......7a.d		2.5	2.1	2.8	3.2	4.5	3.9	3.7	5.0	7.0	8.5	8.6	14.3	16.9	16.1	27.2
Liabilities......7b.d		13.6	15.6	16.5	17.5	19.8	9.5	13.0	9.2	11.7	9.8	12.7	23.5	26.4	27.5	51.6
Other Banking Insts.: Liabilities......7f.d		.1	—	.1	2.0	1.8	1.1	.8	.7	9.8	16.1	8.9	11.6	14.3	12.5	17.9
Monetary Authorities															*Millions of Quetzales:*	
Foreign Assets......11		70.1	63.0	66.1	67.9	76.7	85.8	99.9	142.6	222.9	204.1	311.9	522.5	703.9	777.0	755.3
Claims on Central Government......12a		51.9	52.3	48.2	44.8	53.7	50.8	63.7	70.0	55.5	125.3	102.7	203.0	254.8	291.0	268.8
Claims on Local Government......12b		—	—	.7	.3	.6	.4	2.0	4.6	1.6	3.7	3.1	3.3	3.3	3.4	3.4
Claims on Official Entities......12bx		3.4	4.2	3.8	—	—	4.0	6.1	5.6	5.7	14.1	24.4	9.9	9.0	9.4	13.6
Claims on Deposit Money Banks......12e		21.0	23.1	33.1	50.3	47.2	51.9	34.3	37.7	29.7	38.6	50.5	29.5	27.5	27.7	76.2
Claims on Other Banking Insts.......12f		17.8	19.7	14.5	—	—	—	—	—	—	—	.1	1.5	2.1	14.7	15.1
Reserve Money......14		121.4	132.4	132.8	126.5	140.7	158.5	167.8	213.6	252.0	291.5	344.1	527.5	595.2	652.4	681.7
of which: Currency Outside DMBs......14a		76.7	81.1	82.7	83.8	91.3	96.5	99.0	114.1	137.3	158.3	175.4	236.6	284.4	324.6	365.4
Private Sector Deposits......14d		1.5	2.2	2.3	1.3	.8	1.2	1.9	4.5	6.6	8.9	9.5	20.5	29.8	47.5	49.1
Bonds......16ab		—	—	—	—	—	—	—	—	—	—	—	—	—	—	—
Foreign Liabilities......16c		25.1	25.5	19.1	17.9	15.7	5.5	4.4	5.6	8.9	15.9	13.3	9.6	33.5	32.8	30.7
Long-Term Foreign Liabilities......16cl		—	—	16.2	20.5	21.7	21.6	19.7	16.6	10.3	8.3	36.8	60.2	68.0	78.6	73.9
Central Government Deposits......16d		23.5	15.0	9.6	14.8	17.4	22.2	25.1	31.1	38.4	62.6	82.8	141.8	264.2	288.9	206.1
Capital Accounts......17a		9.6ᵉ	9.8ᵉ	10.3	10.3	10.3	14.5	18.4	23.2	24.6	24.7	25.9	46.3	56.1	62.6	76.7
Other Items (Net)......17r		-15.4	-20.4	-21.6	-26.7	-27.6	-29.4	-29.4	-29.6	-18.8	-17.1	-10.2	-15.7	-16.4	7.9	63.3
Deposit Money Banks															*Millions of Quetzales:*	
Reserves......20		35.8	37.0	40.1	42.1	49.1	61.3	66.8	95.7	108.4	125.1	160.5	271.6	284.3	278.3	266.7
Foreign Assets......21		2.5	2.1	2.8	3.2	4.5	3.9	3.7	5.0	7.0	8.5	8.6	14.3	16.9	16.1	27.2
Claims on Central Government......22a		3.5	11.0	8.1	12.3	9.2	11.2	20.8	53.6	84.6	53.0	94.5	91.9	99.3	64.9	41.5
Claims on Private Sector......22d		134.2	147.9	175.7	193.9	210.5	218.1	238.6	261.3	296.0	386.2	433.1	502.8	651.1	826.9	998.4
Demand Deposits......24		57.4	59.7	63.3	66.0	68.8	75.1	78.0	95.8	120.4	138.2	168.7	236.7	279.9	291.9	320.4
Time and Savings Deposits......25		73.8	91.5	114.5	126.2	148.3	170.9	204.4	262.5	315.5	362.9	454.9	558.0	655.0	759.6	802.3
Foreign Liabilities......26c		13.6	15.6	14.2	15.1	17.9	7.7	11.2	7.9	11.5	9.6	12.5	23.4	26.3	27.5	51.6
Central Government Deposits......26d		—	—	—	3.6	3.5	3.8	2.3	1.6	2.0	3.2	3.1	5.3	3.3	3.3	4.6
Credit from Monetary Authorities......26g		20.3	21.6	24.0	23.3	20.2	16.6	12.0	19.4	15.5	19.6	17.1	7.8	8.2	31.0	80.8
Capital Accounts......27a		29.3	34.2	37.9	37.9	40.7	42.4	45.9	53.1	56.3	64.1	68.2	91.4	114.2	131.2	160.7
Other Items (Net)......27r		-18.4	-24.6	-27.2	-20.6	-26.1	-22.0	-23.9	-24.7	-25.2	-24.8	-27.8	-42.0	-35.2	-58.3	-86.6
Monetary Survey															*Millions of Quetzales:*	
Foreign Assets (Net)......31n		33.9	24.0	35.6	38.1	47.6	76.5	88.0	134.1	209.5	187.1	294.7	503.8	661.0	732.8	700.2
Domestic Credit......32		187.3	220.1	241.4	232.9	253.1	258.5	303.8	362.4	403.0	516.6	572.0	665.3	752.1	918.1	1,130.1
Claims on Central Govt. (Net)......32an		31.9	48.3	46.7	38.7	42.0	36.0	57.1	90.9	99.7	112.5	111.3	147.8	86.6	63.7	99.6
Claims on Local Government......32b		—	—	.7	.3	.6	.4	2.0	4.6	1.6	3.7	3.1	3.3	3.3	3.4	3.4
Claims on Official Entities......32bx		3.4	4.2	3.8	—	—	4.0	6.1	5.6	5.7	14.1	24.4	9.9	9.0	9.4	13.6
Claims on Private Sector......32d		134.2	147.9	175.7	193.9	210.5	218.1	238.6	261.3	296.0	386.2	433.1	502.8	651.1	826.9	998.4
Claims on Other Banking Insts.......32f		17.8	19.7	14.5	—	—	—	—	—	—	—	.1	1.5	2.1	14.7	15.1
Money......34		135.6	143.0	148.3	151.1	160.9	172.8	178.9	214.4	264.3	305.4	353.6	493.8	594.1	664.0	734.9
Quasi-Money......35		73.8	91.5	114.5	126.2	148.3	170.9	204.4	262.5	315.5	362.9	454.9	558.0	655.0	759.6	802.3
Bonds......36ab		5.3	5.7	4.4	.7	.3	.3	.2	.2	.6	.4	.6	.4	—	—	—
Long-Term Foreign Liabilities......36cl		—	—	18.5	22.9	23.6	23.4	21.5	17.9	10.5	8.5	37.0	60.3	68.1	78.6	73.9
Other Items (Net)......37r		6.5	3.9	-8.7	-29.9	-32.4	-32.4	-13.2	1.5	21.6	26.5	20.6	56.6	95.9	148.7	219.2
Money plus Quasi-Money......35l		209.4	234.5	262.8	277.3	309.2	343.7	383.3	476.9	579.8	668.3	808.5	1,051.8	1,249.1	1,423.6	1,537.2
Other Banking Institutions															*Millions of Quetzales:*	
Cash......40		1.8	2.5	1.5	1.7	1.2	1.6	2.4	4.9	7.3	9.9	10.7	21.9	31.2	49.1	50.7
Claims on Central Government......42a		—	—	—	.2	1.1	1.0	2.1	2.7	5.8	6.2	2.6	10.0	13.8	13.7	4.5
Claims on Private Sector......42d		36.3	35.9	29.7	25.3	24.4	23.6	12.5	10.8	9.9	14.0	23.7	32.7	40.5	41.0	45.0
Claims on Deposit Money Banks......42e		....	....	....	....	....	....	....	....	....	....	....	....	....	....	....
Bonds......46ab		2.6	2.5	2.5	—	—	—	—	—	—	—	—	—	—	—	—
Foreign Liabilities......46c		.1	—	.1	.7	.6	.3	.1	.2	9.3	15.7	8.5	11.2	14.3	.4	6.4
Long-Term Foreign Liabilities......46cl		—	—	—	1.3	1.2	.8	.7	.5	.5	.4	.4	.4	—	12.1	11.5
Credit from Monetary Authorities......46g		17.9	20.1	23.5	27.8	27.2	26.8	13.7	9.8	5.5	11.8	28.5	10.7	8.4	6.0	3.6
Credit from Deposit Money Banks......46h		—	—	—	—	—	.1	.1	.1	—	—	—	—	—	1.0	—
Capital Accounts......47a		21.7	21.0	19.1	9.1	8.6	7.3	4.5	5.6	11.9	18.1	28.6	32.9	39.4	39.5	37.8
Other Items (Net)......47r		-4.2	-5.2	-14.0	-11.7	-10.9	-9.1	-2.1	2.2	-4.2	-15.9	-29.0	9.4	23.4	44.8	40.9

Guatemala

258

1980	1981	1982	1983	1984	1985	1986	1987	1988	1989	1990	1991	1992	1993	1994		
End of Period															**Exchange Rates**	
1.2754	1.1640	1.1031	1.0470	.9802	1.0984	3.0580	3.5467	3.6401	4.4681	7.1341	7.2142	7.2522	7.9876	8.2460	Market Rate....................aa=	**wa**
End of Period (we) Period Average (wf)																
1.0000	1.0000	1.0000	1.0000	1.0000	1.0000	2.5000	2.5000	2.7050	3.4000	5.0146	5.0434	5.2743	5.8152	5.6485	Market Rate....................ae=	**we**
1.0000	1.0000	1.0000	1.0000	1.0000	1.0000	1.8750	2.5000	2.6196	2.8161	4.4858	5.0289	5.1706	5.6354	5.7512	Market Rate....................rf=	**wf**
....	....	....	....	1.47	2.93	1.00	1.00	1.00	1.00	1.00	1.00	1.00	1.00	1.00	Secondary Rate	**xe**
....	....	....	....	....	2.77	1.80	1.00	1.00	1.00	1.00	1.00	1.00	1.00	1.00	Secondary Rate	**xf**
....	....	....	....	....	2.65	2.57	2.51	2.71	....	....	....	....	....	....	Tertiary Rate	**ye**
....	....	....	....	....	....	2.85	2.70	2.65	....	....	....	....	....	....	Tertiary Rate	**yf**
End of Period															**Fund Position**	
76.5	76.5	76.5	108.0	108.0	108.0	108.0	108.0	108.0	108.0	108.0	108.0	153.8	153.8	153.8	Quota	**2f.*s***
17.7	2.2	—	.6	2.0	—	—	1.2	.1	.6	—	—	11.4	11.4	11.4	SDRs	**1b.*s***
21.7	8.4	—	7.9	—	—	—	—	—	—	—	—	—	—	—	Reserve Position in the Fund	**1c.*s***
—	8.4	—	—	—	—	—	—	—	—	—	—	—	—	—	*of which:* Outstg.Fund Borrowing	**2c**
—	95.6	95.6	133.9	153.0	105.2	57.2	41.7	65.4	55.5	46.8	44.8	22.4	—	—	Total Fund Cred.&Loans Outstg.	**2tl**
End of Period															**International Liquidity**	
444.7	149.7	112.2	210.0	274.4	300.9	362.1	287.8	201.2	306.0	282.0	807.3	765.2	867.8	863.1	Total Reserves minus Gold	**1l.*d***
22.6	2.6	—	.6	2.0	—	—	1.7	.2	.7	—	—	15.6	15.7	16.6	SDRs	**1b.*d***
27.7	9.7	—	8.2	—	—	—	—	—	—	—	—	—	—	—	Reserve Position in the Fund	**1c.*d***
394.4	137.4	112.2	201.2	272.4	300.9	362.1	286.1	201.0	305.3	282.0	807.3	749.6	852.1	846.5	Foreign Exchange	**1d.*d***
.522	.522	.522	.522	.522	.522	.522	.523	.523	.542	.207	.208	.122	.209	.209	Gold (Million Fine Troy Ounces)	**1ad**
22.1	22.1	22.1	22.1	22.1	22.1	22.1	22.1	22.1	22.9	8.8	8.8	5.1	8.8	8.8	Gold (National Valuation)	**1an*d***
183.7	296.5	361.7	784.1	1,124.2	1,259.6	437.4	436.7	257.8	209.3	93.0	76.6	90.2	89.6	66.5	Monetary Authorities: Other Liab.	**4..*d***
20.1	23.4	46.2	72.3	53.8	76.7	18.5	30.0	17.9	12.7	4.3	4.6	6.8	8.6	17.7	Deposit Money Banks: Assets	**7a.*d***
53.6	49.3	73.8	137.1	149.0	78.7	37.2	52.5	55.0	48.2	26.6	26.7	48.4	113.1	373.3	Liabilities	**7b.*d***
11.8	15.8	21.6	24.5	30.7	32.9	14.3	14.0	16.8	10.7	70.2	76.7	79.4	79.9	100.2	Other Banking Insts.: Liabilities	**7f.*d***
End of Period															**Monetary Authorities**	
530.2	305.8	254.1	307.5	366.0	402.8	491.8	391.1	363.2	401.3	358.2	905.3	840.4	955.1	939.6	Foreign Assets	**11**
461.4	860.4	1,362.1	1,619.1	1,791.8	1,931.7	1,528.2	1,441.2	1,571.4	1,615.3	1,551.1	117.3	452.4	112.5	357.6	Claims on Central Government	**12a**
3.8	2.7	3.9	8.5	7.7	8.8	7.9	7.1	6.2	5.3	4.4	—	—	2.6	2.0	Claims on Local Government	**12b**
15.3	37.9	35.0	25.6	17.3	12.2	11.4	9.4	10.6	8.4	7.4	7.4	7.4	7.4	7.4	Claims on Official Entities	**12bx**
121.2	138.1	85.8	146.7	144.3	121.1	133.9	122.0	156.2	162.4	159.4	154.6	184.6	184.8	61.3	Claims on Deposit Money Banks	**12e**
27.3	74.0	53.0	77.6	77.3	68.3	55.0	51.1	64.0	66.9	74.7	153.8	284.3	245.2	188.3	Claims on Other Banking Insts.	**12f**
680.4	720.1	838.3	773.7	805.6	1,302.0	1,569.6	1,578.6	1,932.7	2,301.8	3,079.7	3,946.2	4,263.2	5,255.3	5,494.3	Reserve Money	**14**
381.0	405.2	404.6	437.9	460.9	697.8	804.6	931.2	1,069.0	1,329.2	1,897.1	2,089.4	2,712.6	3,097.3	3,714.6	*of which: Currency Outside DMBs*	**14a**
51.3	45.4	42.3	49.7	26.9	34.2	55.2	26.5	34.4	43.0	2.9	1.2	5.2	22.8	22.8	*Private Sector Deposits*	**14d**
—	—	—	—	—	—	—	—	559.3	526.8	477.7	842.2	970.1	670.7	372.9	Bonds	**16ab**
53.8	152.9	154.3	464.3	730.6	735.1	669.0	639.9	303.7	230.7	174.8	169.9	175.9	69.7	97.9	Foreign Liabilities	**16c**
129.9	254.9	312.9	459.9	543.6	640.0	599.3	599.5	631.6	728.8	625.7	539.4	462.1	451.6	277.6	Long-Term Foreign Liabilities	**16cl**
171.0	171.7	420.2	443.0	284.7	355.4	568.5	683.7	746.7	694.7	687.6	1,416.3	1,555.4	1,421.5	1,566.3	Central Government Deposits	**16d**
124.2	149.0	138.1	123.9	122.1	125.3	128.8	134.2	132.1	131.3	134.2	134.4	133.0	133.0	135.3	Capital Accounts	**17a**
-.1	-29.7	-69.9	-79.8	-82.2	-612.9	-1,307.0	-1,614.0	-2,134.5	-2,354.5	-3,024.5	-5,710.0	-5,790.6	-6,494.2	-6,388.1	Other Items (Net)	**17r**
End of Period															**Deposit Money Banks**	
245.5	265.5	370.7	274.5	365.1	583.0	770.3	756.4	1,048.3	1,118.7	1,450.3	2,306.2	2,346.5	2,815.2	2,175.5	Reserves	**20**
20.1	23.4	46.2	72.3	53.8	76.7	46.2	74.9	48.3	43.1	21.4	23.0	35.7	50.0	100.1	Foreign Assets	**21**
55.2	74.6	123.6	56.1	47.8	137.1	295.7	239.1	65.7	148.5	240.3	1,994.1	1,732.4	1,794.1	2,869.7	Claims on Central Government	**22a**
1,222.2	1,374.4	1,476.4	1,670.3	1,867.8	2,037.1	2,242.1	2,711.2	3,109.2	3,427.1	4,299.9	5,010.6	6,624.8	7,434.4	9,156.9	Claims on Private Sector	**22d**
320.5	325.3	339.7	346.2	381.6	614.5	748.6	807.9	915.6	1,065.6	1,341.5	1,752.8	1,475.4	1,928.0	3,336.2	Demand Deposits	**24**
939.6	1,130.8	1,404.1	1,321.3	1,529.7	1,846.4	2,266.7	2,402.2	2,976.0	3,362.8	4,054.8	7,022.1	8,912.8	8,893.9	7,450.0	Time and Savings Deposits	**25**
53.6	49.3	73.8	137.1	149.0	78.7	93.0	131.3	148.9	164.0	133.6	134.8	255.5	657.9	2,108.7	Foreign Liabilities	**26c**
7.0	3.3	4.8	9.9	5.5	10.5	11.7	15.7	20.1	24.9	28.6	42.3	63.3	76.7	71.0	Central Government Deposits	**26d**
130.1	132.3	92.4	153.2	147.8	121.5	111.8	96.7	132.8	147.8	172.8	164.6	187.0	185.9	66.0	Credit from Monetary Authorities	**26g**
155.2	166.7	171.6	189.0	208.6	236.7	270.9	293.5	385.5	440.2	666.6	884.7	1,056.3	1,293.0	1,586.7	Capital Accounts	**27a**
-63.0	-69.8	-69.5	-83.5	-87.7	-74.4	-148.4	34.3	-307.4	-467.9	-386.0	-667.4	-1,210.9	-941.7	-316.4	Other Items (Net)	**27r**
End of Period															**Monetary Survey**	
442.9	127.0	72.2	-221.6	-459.8	-334.3	-224.0	-305.2	-41.1	49.7	71.2	623.6	444.7	277.5	-1,166.9	Foreign Assets (Net)	**31n**
1,607.2	2,249.0	2,629.0	3,004.3	3,519.5	3,829.3	3,560.1	3,759.7	4,060.3	4,551.9	5,461.6	5,824.6	7,482.6	8,098.0	10,944.6	Domestic Credit	**32**
338.6	760.0	1,060.7	1,222.3	1,549.4	1,702.9	1,243.7	980.9	870.3	1,044.2	1,075.2	652.8	566.1	408.4	1,590.0	Claims on Central Govt. (Net)	**32an**
3.8	2.7	3.9	8.5	7.7	8.8	7.9	7.1	6.2	5.3	4.4	—	—	2.6	2.0	Claims on Local Government	**32b**
15.3	37.9	35.0	25.6	17.3	12.2	11.4	9.4	10.6	8.4	7.4	7.4	7.4	7.4	7.4	Claims on Official Entities	**32bx**
1,222.2	1,374.4	1,476.4	1,670.3	1,867.8	2,037.1	2,242.1	2,711.2	3,109.2	3,427.1	4,299.9	5,010.6	6,624.8	7,434.4	9,156.9	Claims on Private Sector	**32d**
27.3	74.0	53.0	77.6	77.3	68.3	55.0	51.1	64.0	66.9	74.7	153.8	284.3	245.2	188.3	Claims on Other Banking Insts.	**32f**
752.8	775.9	786.6	833.8	869.4	1,346.5	1,608.4	1,765.6	2,019.0	2,437.8	3,241.5	3,843.4	4,193.2	5,048.1	7,073.6	Money	**34**
939.6	1,130.8	1,404.1	1,321.3	1,529.7	1,846.4	2,266.7	2,402.2	2,976.0	3,362.8	4,054.8	7,022.1	10,054.7	11,354.8	11,295.6	Quasi-Money	**35**
—	—	—	—	—	—	—	—	559.3	526.8	477.7	842.2	970.1	670.7	372.9	Bonds	**36ab**
129.9	254.9	312.9	459.9	543.6	640.0	599.3	599.5	631.6	728.8	625.7	539.4	462.1	451.6	277.6	Long-Term Foreign Liabilities	**36cl**
227.8	214.4	197.6	167.7	117.0	-337.9	-1,138.3	-1,312.8	-2,166.7	-2,454.6	-2,866.9	-5,798.9	-7,752.8	-9,149.7	-9,242.0	Other Items (Net)	**37r**
1,692.4	1,906.7	2,190.7	2,155.1	2,399.1	3,192.9	3,875.1	4,167.8	4,995.0	5,800.6	7,296.3	10,865.5	14,247.9	16,402.9	18,369.2	Money plus Quasi-Money	**35l**
End of Period															**Other Banking Institutions**	
53.0	47.2	44.5	51.9	29.9	37.1	58.5	31.1	40.1	49.2	I 11.7	51.4	51.7	66.1	31.5	Cash	**40**
6.2	7.5	1.4	5.2	1.6	14.1	31.8	22.7	11.1	48.1	I 8.4	109.0	36.0	36.2	48.4	Claims on Central Government	**42a**
56.2	60.3	60.4	69.2	68.6	97.5	108.5	214.3	236.0	255.7	I 565.5	641.3	1,188.9	1,489.9	2,055.3	Claims on Private Sector	**42d**
....	....	....	....	....	....	....	....	....	....	137.6	279.4	186.2	331.7	309.3	Claims on Deposit Money Banks	**42e**
—	—	—	9.8	—	—	—	—	—	—	I 200.2	463.6	942.2	1,326.4	1,710.5	Bonds	**46ab**
.9	.4	.3	.4	—	.7	.1	.9	12.1	5.8	I 2.0	8.4	9.0	26.4	99.7	Foreign Liabilities	**46c**
10.9	15.4	21.3	24.1	30.7	32.2	35.6	34.0	33.4	30.6	I 349.9	378.6	409.9	438.0	466.4	Long-Term Foreign Liabilities	**46cl**
3.0	14.1	8.6	6.8	.6	.5	.5	26.1	28.8	26.6	I 94.1	170.4	295.6	259.3	195.4	Credit from Monetary Authorities	**46g**
—	—	—	—	—	—	—	—	—	—	I 293.1	363.1	431.2	523.5	877.6	Credit from Deposit Money Banks	**46h**
40.2	36.4	32.4	37.5	30.5	47.4	51.6	55.7	58.8	65.2	I -73.3	-107.2	-107.0	-142.8	-107.4	Capital Accounts	**47a**
60.4	48.7	43.7	47.7	38.3	67.9	111.0	151.4	154.1	224.8	I -142.8	-195.8	-518.1	-506.9	-797.7	Other Items (Net)	**47r**

		1965	1966	1967	1968	1969	1970	1971	1972	1973	1974	1975	1976	1977	1978	1979
Banking Survey																*Millions of Quetzales:*
Foreign Assets (Net)	51n	34.0	24.0	35.8	37.6	47.3	76.5	87.9	134.2	200.5	174.3	286.4	492.9	648.1	733.0	700.7
Domestic Credit	52	205.8	236.3	256.6	257.7	277.8	282.1	317.3	374.0	417.2	534.6	595.1	704.4	803.4	957.1	1,161.7
Claims on Central Govt. (Net)	52an	31.9	48.3	46.7	38.2	42.3	36.0	58.1	91.7	104.0	116.5	110.7	154.2	98.3	75.5	100.7
Claims on Local Government	52b	—	—	.7	.3	.6	.4	2.0	4.6	1.6	3.7	3.1	3.3	3.3	3.4	3.4
Claims on Official Entities	52bx	3.4	4.2	3.8	—	—	4.0	6.1	5.6	5.7	14.1	24.4	9.9	9.0	9.4	13.6
Claims on Private Sector	52d	170.5	183.8	205.4	219.2	234.9	241.7	251.1	272.1	305.9	400.3	456.9	537.0	692.8	868.8	1,044.0
Liquid Liabilities	55l	227.4	248.7	268.4	280.7	315.2	350.1	389.2	483.0	591.3	674.4	827.0	1,081.9	1,284.6	1,461.0	1,568.0
Bonds	56ab	7.9	8.2	6.9	.7	.3	.3	.2	.2	.6	.4	.6	.4	—	—	—
Long-Term Foreign Liabilities	56cl	—	—	—	24.2	24.8	24.2	22.2	18.4	11.0	8.9	37.4	60.7	68.1	90.7	85.4
Capital Accounts	57a	60.6	65.0	67.3	57.3	59.6	64.2	68.8	81.9	92.8	106.9	122.7	170.6	209.7	233.3	275.2
Other Items (Net)	57r	–56.1	–61.6	–50.2	–67.6	–74.8	–80.2	–75.2	–75.3	–78.0	–81.7	–106.2	–116.3	–110.9	–94.9	–66.2
Interest Rates																*Percent Per Annum*
Discount Rate *(End of Period)*	60	4.0	4.0	4.0	4.0	4.0	4.0	4.0	4.0	4.0	5.0	5.0	5.0	7.0	5.0	9.0
Deposit Rate	60l	....	....	....	....	....	....	....	....	....	....	....	....	....	9.0	9.0
Lending Rate	60p	....	....	....	....	....	....	....	....	....	....	....	....	....	11.0	11.0
Prices																*Index Numbers (1990=100):*
Wholesale Prices (1985=100)	63	24.8	24.7	24.8	25.8	26.7	27.4	27.9	27.7	31.7	38.9	43.7	48.3	54.5	56.5	62.3
Home and Export Goods(1985=100)	63a	25.0	24.8	24.9	25.9	26.6	27.5	27.7	27.5	31.7	38.5	43.5	48.1	55.1	57.2	62.8
Consumer Prices	64	9.7	9.7	9.8	10.0	10.2	10.4	10.4	10.4	11.9	13.8	I 15.6	I 17.3	19.5	21.1	23.5
International Transactions																*Millions of US Dollars*
Exports	70..d	185.8	226.1	197.9	227.3	255.4	290.2	283.2	327.5	436.2	572.1	623.5	760.4	1,160.2	1,089.5	1,241.4
Imports, cif	71..d	229.3	206.9	247.3	249.4	250.2	284.3	296.6	324.0	431.0	700.5	732.7	838.9	1,052.5	1,285.7	1,503.9
Imports, fob	71.vd	210.6	188.1	226.5	228.3	229.3	261.0	278.1	289.5	389.0	624.1	669.8	766.8	926.5	1,178.9	1,395.4
Balance of Payments																*Millions of US Dollars:*
Goods: Exports f.o.b.	78aad	....	....	....	....	....	....	....	....	....	....	....	760.4	1,160.2	1,092.4	1,221.4
Goods: Imports f.o.b.	78abd	....	....	....	....	....	....	....	....	....	....	....	–950.7	–1,087.0	–1,283.8	–1,401.7
Trade Balance	78acd	....	....	....	....	....	....	....	....	....	....	....	–190.3	73.2	–191.4	–180.3
Services: Credit	78add	....	....	....	....	....	....	....	....	....	....	....	208.3	161.5	183.8	228.5
Services: Debit	78aed	....	....	....	....	....	....	....	....	....	....	....	–253.4	–339.5	–361.0	–383.1
Balance on Goods and Services	78afd	....	....	....	....	....	....	....	....	....	....	....	–235.4	–104.8	–368.6	–334.9
Income: Credit	78agd	....	....	....	....	....	....	....	....	....	....	....	39.0	47.9	72.9	102.1
Income: Debit	78ahd	....	....	....	....	....	....	....	....	....	....	....	–80.0	–74.2	–90.4	–99.4
Balance on Goods, Serv., & Inc.	78aid	....	....	....	....	....	....	....	....	....	....	....	–276.4	–131.1	–386.1	–332.2
Current Transfers, n.i.e.: Credit	78ajd	....	....	....	....	....	....	....	....	....	....	....	216.2	116.4	139.4	149.5
Current Transfers: Debit	78akd	....	....	....	....	....	....	....	....	....	....	....	–17.5	–20.6	–23.8	–22.9
Current Account, n.i.e.	78ald	....	....	....	....	....	....	....	....	....	....	....	–77.7	–35.3	–270.5	–205.6
Capital Account, n.i.e.: Credit	78bad	....	....	....	....	....	....	....	....	....	....	....	.8	—	—	—
Capital Account: Debit	78bbd	....	....	....	....	....	....	....	....	....	....	....	–.6	—	—	—
Capital Account, n.i.e.	78bcd	....	....	....	....	....	....	....	....	....	....	....	.2	—	—	—
Direct Investment Abroad	78bdd	....	....	....	....	....	....	....	....	....	....	....	—	—	—	—
Dir. Invest. in Rep. Econ., n.i.e.	78bed	....	....	....	....	....	....	....	....	....	....	....	12.5	97.5	127.2	117.0
Portfolio Investment Assets	78bfd	....	....	....	....	....	....	....	....	....	....	....	.1	.5	2.3	8.0
Portfolio Investment Liab., n.i.e.	78bgd	....	....	....	....	....	....	....	....	....	....	....	—	4.8	9.4	–2.7
Other Investment Assets	78bhd	....	....	....	....	....	....	....	....	....	....	....	–6.3	14.6	21.3	–217.2
Other Investment Liab., n.i.e.	78bid	....	....	....	....	....	....	....	....	....	....	....	218.3	105.0	217.0	300.4
Financial Account, n.i.e.	78bjd	....	....	....	....	....	....	....	....	....	....	....	224.6	222.4	377.2	205.5
Net Errors and Omissions	78cad	....	....	....	....	....	....	....	....	....	....	....	48.9	–26.5	–58.6	–44.4
Overall Balance	78cbd	....	....	....	....	....	....	....	....	....	....	....	196.0	160.6	48.1	–44.5
Reserves and Related Items	79dad	....	....	....	....	....	....	....	....	....	....	....	–196.0	–160.6	–48.1	44.5
Reserve Assets	79dbd	....	....	....	....	....	....	....	....	....	....	....	–219.5	–181.7	–68.3	25.7
Use of Fund Credit and Loans	79dcd	....	....	....	....	....	....	....	....	....	....	....	—	—	—	—
Liabs.Constit.For.Auth.Reserves	79ddd	....	....	....	....	....	....	....	....	....	....	....	—	—	—	—
Exceptional Financing	79ded	....	....	....	....	....	....	....	....	....	....	....	23.5	21.1	20.2	18.8
Government Finance																*Millions of Quetzales:*
Deficit (-) or Surplus	80	–5.9	–16.3	–23.4	–8.0	–15.3	–13.1	–30.1	I –45.2	–38.0	–45.6	–30.6	–111.2	–51.2	–71.2	–149.1
Revenue	81	122.6	122.5	126.6	138.5	151.9	165.2	173.4	I 182.3	211.3	278.8	327.0	404.4	588.2	657.4	664.9
Grants Received	81z	....	....	....	....	....	....	....	I .8	.9	.8	.4	5.3	1.3	4.1	1.6
Expenditure	82	128.5	138.8	150.0	146.5	167.2	178.3	203.5	I 204.3	245.1	318.4	348.2	437.8	594.0	666.9	785.1
Lending Minus Repayments	83	....	....	....	....	....	....	....	I 24.0	5.1	6.8	9.8	83.1	46.7	65.8	30.5
Financing (by Residence of Lender)																
Net Borrowing: Domestic	84a	....	....	....	....	....	....	....	I 19.3	20.2	48.6	24.5	126.2	95.8	12.7	–49.2
Foreign	85a	....	....	....	....	....	....	....	I 31.5	21.3	18.7	13.0	16.6	32.9	92.0	120.4
Use of Cash Balances	87	–10.5	7.3	9.8	–1.6	–.3	–4.9	–5.4	I –5.6	–3.5	–21.7	–6.9	–31.6	–77.5	–33.5	77.9
Debt: Domestic	88a	....	....	....	....	....	....	....	I 149.6	170.8	231.2	250.5	377.3	487.6	515.3	476.3
Foreign	89a	....	....	....	....	....	....	....	I 99.0	113.0	115.2	132.4	148.1	176.4	....	270.8
Financing (by Currency)																
Net Borrowing: Quetzales	84b	11.8	11.4	–4.1	–2.7	1.8	–6.4	28.1	....	....	....	....	....	....	....	....
Foreign Currency	85b	4.6	–2.4	17.8	12.2	13.8	24.4	7.4	....	....	....	....	....	....	....	....
Use of Cash Balances	87	–10.5	7.3	9.8	–1.6	–.3	–4.9	–5.4	I –5.6	–3.5	–21.7	–6.9	–31.6	–77.5	–33.5	77.9
National Accounts																*Millions of Quetzales*
Exports of Goods & Services	90c	224	263	236	270	305	354	343	397	537	708	792	942	1,340	1,304	1,474
Government Consumption	91f	98	105	113	115	135	151	139	157	167	207	250	297	354	435	488
Gross Fixed Capital Formation	93e	175	167	192	221	231	239	264	273	357	468	571	900	1,039	1,218	1,286
Increase/Decrease(-) in Stocks	93i	2	–18	–4	23	–35	6	22	–18	–5	120	16	34	60	95	8
Private Consumption	96f	1,094	1,139	1,201	1,279	1,379	1,493	1,588	1,682	2,034	2,470	2,875	3,396	4,127	4,675	5,432
Imports of Goods & Services	98c	–261	–266	–284	–297	–299	–338	–371	–389	–519	–811	–858	–1,204	–1,439	–1,655	–1,784
Gross Domestic Product = GDP	99b	1,331	1,391	1,454	1,611	1,715	1,904	1,985	2,102	2,569	3,162	3,646	4,365	5,481	6,071	6,903
Net Factor Inc/Pmts(-) Abroad	98.n	–18	–26	–28	–33	–38	–42	–44	–48	–48	–50	–69	–74	–33	–26	–12
Gross National Product = GNP	99a	1,314	1,365	1,426	1,578	1,678	1,862	1,941	2,054	2,521	3,111	3,577	4,292	5,448	6,044	6,891
Gross Dom. Prod. 1990 Prices	99b.p	13,718	14,475	15,069	16,391	17,168	18,147	19,161	20,566	21,961	23,361	23,816	25,576	27,574	28,951	30,315
GDP Deflator (1990=100)	99bip	9.7	9.6	9.6	9.8	10.0	10.5	10.4	10.2	11.7	13.5	15.3	17.1	19.9	21.0	22.8
																Millions:
Population	99z	4.41	4.50	4.70	4.84	5.02	5.27	5.42	5.58	5.74	I 6.05	6.24	I 6.19	6.36	6.54	6.73

Other Banking Institutions: I Beginning in January 1990, comprises Financiera Industrial y Agropecuaria S. A. (FIASA), Financiera Guatemalteca S. A. (FIGSA), Financiera Industrial S. A. (FISA), Financiera de Inversion S. A. (FIVSA), Financiera del Pais S. A. (FIPASA), and Corporacion Financiera Nacional (CORFINA).

Banking Survey: I See note to section 40.

Government Finance: I Beginning in 1972, data are as reported in the *Government Finance Statistics Yearbook* and cover budgetary central government. I Beginning in 1980, data include extrabudgetary and social security funds. I Beginning in 1984, data cover budgetary central government only; data do not exclude all intragovernmental transfers.

Guatemala

258

1980	1981	1982	1983	1984	1985	1986	1987	1988	1989	1990	1991	1992	1993	1994		
End of Period															**Banking Survey**	
442.3	127.3	72.5	-221.8	-459.6	-334.6	-223.9	-305.9	-52.9	44.2	I 69.7	616.6	435.9	251.5	-1,243.2	Foreign Assets (Net)	**51n**
1,640.6	2,243.7	2,665.4	3,034.5	3,538.4	3,897.7	3,653.2	3,973.9	4,273.1	4,816.8	I 5,960.8	6,421.1	8,423.2	9,378.9	12,860.0	Domestic Credit	**52**
343.1	755.1	1,050.3	1,221.6	1,537.7	1,702.8	1,244.0	992.6	871.8	1,081.0	I 1,083.6	761.8	602.1	444.6	1,638.4	Claims on Central Govt. (Net)	**52an**
3.8	2.7	3.9	8.5	7.7	8.8	7.9	7.1	6.2	5.3	4.4	—	—	2.6	2.0	Claims on Local Government	**52b**
15.3	37.9	35.0	25.6	17.3	12.2	11.4	9.4	10.6	8.4	7.4	7.4	7.4	7.4	7.4	Claims on Official Entities	**52bx**
1,278.4	1,448.0	1,576.2	1,778.8	1,975.7	2,173.9	2,389.9	2,964.8	3,384.5	3,722.1	I 4,865.4	5,651.9	7,813.7	8,924.3	11,212.2	Claims on Private Sector	**52d**
1,734.4	1,948.3	2,241.8	2,211.6	2,466.0	3,276.4	3,955.8	4,285.3	5,130.6	5,968.8	I 7,282.2	10,779.4	14,157.9	16,294.1	18,240.8	Liquid Liabilities	**55l**
—	—	—	9.8	—	—	—	—	559.3	526.8	I 677.9	1,305.8	1,912.3	1,997.1	2,083.4	Bonds	**56ab**
140.8	270.3	334.2	484.0	574.3	672.2	634.9	633.5	665.0	759.4	I 975.6	918.0	872.0	889.6	744.0	Long-Term Foreign Liabilities	**56cl**
319.6	352.1	342.1	350.4	361.2	409.4	451.3	483.4	576.4	636.7	I 727.5	911.9	1,082.3	1,283.2	1,614.6	Capital Accounts	**57a**
-111.9	-199.7	-180.2	-243.1	-322.7	-794.9	-1,612.7	-1,734.2	-2,711.1	-3,030.7	I -3632.7	-6,877.4	-9,165.4	-10,833.6	-11,066.0	Other Items (Net)	**57r**
Percent Per Annum															**Interest Rates**	
8.0	12.0	9.0	9.0	9.0	9.0	9.0	9.0	9.0	13.0	18.5	16.5	....	....	....	Discount Rate *(End of Period)*	**60**
9.0	10.0	12.0	9.0	9.0	9.0	10.2	11.0	12.2	13.0	18.2	24.4	10.4	12.6	9.7	Deposit Rate	**60l**
11.0	12.0	14.5	12.0	12.0	12.0	13.2	14.0	15.2	16.0	23.3	34.1	19.5	24.7	22.9	Lending Rate	**60p**
Period Averages															**Prices**	
72.3	80.8	75.9	76.8	81.1	100.0	142.9	....	....	....	....	....	....	....	....	Wholesale Prices (1985=100)	**63**
72.7	81.4	75.7	76.5	80.7	100.0	145.7	....	....	....	....	....	....	....	....	Home and Export Goods(1985=100)	**63a**
26.0	29.0	29.1	30.4	31.4	37.3	51.1	57.4	63.6	70.8	100.0	133.2	146.5	163.9	....	Consumer Prices	**64**
Millions of US Dollars															**International Transactions**	
1,519.8	1,226.1	1,119.8	1,158.8	1,128.5	1,057.0	1,043.8	987.3	1,021.7	1,108.0	1,163.0	1,202.2	1,295.3	1,340.4	....	Exports	**70..*d***
1,598.2	1,688.3	1,388.0	1,126.1	1,278.5	1,174.8	958.5	1,447.2	1,557.0	1,653.8	1,648.8	1,851.3	2,531.5	2,599.3	....	Imports, cif	**71..*d***
1,472.6	1,539.9	1,284.2	1,054.6	1,180.3	1,076.7	875.6	1,333.2	1,413.2	1,497.2	1,428.0	1,672.5	2,330.7	2,384.0	....	Imports, fob	**71.v*d***
Minus Sign Indicates Debit															Balance of Payments	
1,519.8	1,291.3	1,170.4	1,091.7	1,132.2	1,059.7	1,043.8	977.9	1,073.3	1,126.1	1,211.4	1,230.0	1,283.7	1,363.2	....	Goods: Exports f.o.b.	**78aa*d***
-1,472.6	-1,540.0	-1,284.3	-1,056.0	-1,182.2	-1,076.7	-875.7	-1,333.2	-1,413.2	-1,484.4	-1,428.0	-1,673.0	-2,327.8	-2,384.0	....	Goods: Imports f.o.b.	**78ab*d***
47.2	-248.7	-113.9	35.7	-50.0	-17.0	168.1	-355.3	-339.9	-358.3	-216.6	-443.0	-1,044.1	-1,020.8	....	Trade Balance	**78ac*d***
211.2	155.1	107.6	80.3	96.0	101.1	123.7	158.3	195.8	297.7	356.1	458.8	614.0	660.4	....	Services: Credit	**78ad*d***
-487.4	-484.3	-341.9	-257.8	-245.5	-180.0	-170.1	-259.5	-317.9	-376.9	-383.7	-356.4	-525.3	-586.1	....	Services: Debit	**78ae*d***
-229.0	-577.9	-348.2	-141.8	-199.5	-95.9	121.7	-456.5	-462.0	-437.5	-244.2	-340.6	-955.4	-946.5	....	Balance on Goods and Services	**78af*d***
103.0	79.5	34.2	33.0	33.0	30.5	35.7	31.1	31.6	31.0	20.9	63.9	69.1	61.1	....	Income: Credit	**78ag*d***
-147.1	-165.2	-147.8	-145.7	-239.6	-200.6	-250.1	-210.4	-207.9	-210.4	-216.6	-166.7	-210.1	-179.5	....	Income: Debit	**78ah*d***
-273.1	-663.6	-461.8	-254.5	-406.1	-266.0	-92.7	-635.8	-638.3	-616.9	-439.9	-443.4	-1,096.4	-1,064.9	....	Balance on Goods, Serv., & Inc.	**78ai*d***
125.3	96.9	66.1	34.2	31.6	21.0	76.2	195.9	227.7	255.1	217.6	276.7	406.2	371.4	....	Current Transfers, n.i.e.: Credit	**78aj*d***
-15.5	-6.0	-3.4	-3.6	-2.9	-1.3	-1.1	-2.6	-3.4	-5.3	-10.6	-17.0	-15.7	-8.2	....	Current Transfers: Debit	**78ak*d***
-163.3	-572.7	-399.1	-223.9	-377.4	-246.3	-17.6	-442.5	-414.0	-367.1	-232.9	-183.7	-705.9	-701.7	....	Current Account, n.i.e.	**78al*d***
—	—	—	—	—	—	—	—	—	—	—	—	—	—	....	Capital Account, n.i.e.: Credit	**78ba*d***
—	—	—	—	—	—	—	—	—	—	—	—	—	—	....	Capital Account: Debit	**78bb*d***
—	—	—	—	—	—	—	—	—	—	—	—	—	—	....	Capital Account, n.i.e.	**78bc*d***
—	—	—	—	—	—	—	—	—	—	—	—	—	—	....	Direct Investment Abroad	**78bd*d***
110.7	127.1	77.1	45.0	38.0	61.8	68.8	150.2	329.7	76.2	47.6	90.7	94.1	142.5	....	Dir. Invest. in Rep. Econ., n.i.e.	**78be*d***
4.2	-.4	—	-.1	.3	-1.1	-.2	—	—	—	-1.8	-.2	1.8	112.4	....	Portfolio Investment Assets	**78bf*d***
-.3	.7	.5	—	-9.9	-26.5	-11.4	-16.0	-372.2	-63.9	-19.5	71.3	9.6	-27.0	....	Portfolio Investment Liab., n.i.e.	**78bg*d***
-311.3	-149.1	-10.4	—	4.7	—	—	—	29.4	98.7	-78.0	68.1	57.2	-3.0	....	Other Investment Assets	**78bh*d***
52.8	132.3	-56.0	101.5	-142.5	-162.5	-390.2	52.5	93.6	114.3	5.5	502.9	447.8	564.3	....	Other Investment Liab., n.i.e.	**78bi*d***
-143.9	110.6	11.2	146.4	-109.4	-128.3	-333.0	186.7	80.5	225.3	-46.2	732.8	610.5	789.2	....	Financial Account, n.i.e.	**78bj*d***
-18.1	4.3	-18.0	-37.1	15.5	43.6	67.3	-72.7	-2.4	54.7	36.2	83.3	81.8	85.2	....	Net Errors and Omissions	**78ca*d***
-325.3	-457.8	-405.9	-114.6	-471.3	-331.0	-283.3	-328.5	-336.0	-87.1	-242.9	632.4	-13.6	172.7	....	Overall Balance	**78cb*d***
325.3	457.8	405.9	114.6	471.3	331.0	283.3	328.5	336.0	87.1	242.9	-632.4	13.6	-172.7	....	Reserves and Related Items	**79da*d***
257.9	189.8	38.4	-91.1	-30.9	-62.6	-56.2	73.2	110.6	-59.0	41.8	-551.3	51.6	-120.5	....	Reserve Assets	**79db*d***
—	111.5	—	40.1	20.2	-48.6	-56.7	-20.1	30.8	-12.7	-11.9	-2.8	-31.7	-31.3	....	Use of Fund Credit and Loans	**79dc*d***
—	—	—	41.4	-6.0	4.0	4.0	1.0	-2.5	3.0	—	-1.0	—	27.0	....	Liabs.Constit.For.Auth.Reserves	**79dd*d***
67.4	156.5	367.5	124.2	487.9	438.2	392.2	274.5	197.0	155.8	213.0	-77.3	-6.4	-47.9	....	Exceptional Financing	**79de*d***
Year Ending December 31															**Government Finance**	
I -307.3	-535.4	-416.9	-318.0	I -360.7	-201.6	-91.6	-133.7	-218.1	-408.3	....	....	....	....	....	Deficit (-) or Surplus	**80**
I 884.1	898.0	880.8	872.8	I 662.6	861.4	1,401.8	1,653.8	2,074.4	2,253.1	2,704.1	4,288.8	5,467.3	5,735.8	....	Revenue	**81**
I .5	.5	.7	1.2	I 2.0	1.1	60.1	198.2	216.9	174.1	84.8	16.0	267.0	18.3	....	Grants Received	**81z**
I 1,128.0	1,386.7	1,277.7	1,169.5	I 1,015.1	1,052.8	1,512.3	1,979.4	2,455.5	2,775.4	....	....	....	....	....	Expenditure	**82**
I 63.9	47.2	20.7	22.5	I 10.2	11.3	41.1	6.2	53.9	60.0	....	....	....	....	....	Lending Minus Repayments	**83**
															Financing (by Residence of Lender)	
I 189.4	435.5	321.7	237.7	I 307.5	102.4	-.4	50.0	65.6	307.9	....	....	....	....	....	Net Borrowing: Domestic	**84a**
I 117.9	99.9	95.2	80.3	I 53.2	99.3	92.0	83.8	152.5	100.3	....	....	....	....	....	Foreign	**85a**
....	....	....	....	....	....	....	....	....	....	....	....	....	....	....	Use of Cash Balances	**87**
725.1	1,187.5	1,627.2	1,887.3	2,044.3	2,252.7	2,388.1	2,308.9	....	....	....	....	....	....	....	Debt: Domestic	**88a**
334.1	393.7	436.8	513.9	539.9	584.5	666.3	711.4	....	....	....	....	....	....	....	Foreign	**89a**
															Financing (by Currency)	
....	....	....	....	....	....	....	....	....	....	....	....	....	....	....	Net Borrowing: Quetzales	**84b**
....	....	....	....	....	....	....	....	....	....	....	....	....	....	....	Foreign Currency	**85b**
....	....	....	....	....	....	....	....	....	....	....	....	....	....	....	Use of Cash Balances	**87**
Millions of Quetzales															**National Accounts**	
1,748	1,471	1,289	1,176	1,256	2,068	2,542	2,807	3,309	4,099	6,776	8,349	9,483	10,989	12,807	Exports of Goods & Services	**90c**
627	680	676	688	726	777	1,124	1,400	1,640	1,870	2,324	2,714	3,482	4,148	4,587	Government Consumption	**91f**
1,295	1,443	1,310	950	912	1,225	1,593	2,188	2,747	3,255	4,455	5,760	8,445	10,308	11,272	Gross Fixed Capital Formation	**93e**
-44	23	-76	52	184	61	43	275	67	-54	213	1,002	1,448	753	913	Increase/Decrease(-) in Stocks	**93i**
6,217	7,022	7,150	7,501	7,856	9,296	12,847	14,989	17,289	19,837	28,692	39,693	45,899	54,240	64,128	Private Consumption	**96f**
-1,963	-2,032	-1,629	-1,317	-1,464	-2,247	-2,311	-3,949	-4,507	-5,323	-8,143	-10,216	-14,771	-16,704	-19,216	Imports of Goods & Services	**98c**
7,879	8,608	8,717	9,050	9,470	11,180	15,838	17,711	20,545	23,685	34,317	47,302	53,985	63,733	74,491	Gross Domestic Product = GDP	**99b**
-71	-103	-121	-113	-207	-331	-436	-472	-471	-544	-828	-517	-426	-30	-117	Net Factor Inc/Pmts(-) Abroad	**98.n**
7,809	8,505	8,596	8,937	9,264	10,849	15,402	17,239	20,074	23,141	33,489	46,786	53,559	63,704	74,478	Gross National Product = GNP	**99a**
31,450	31,660	30,538	29,758	29,898	29,721	29,765	30,818	32,018	33,280	34,317	35,568	37,293	38,731	40,431	Gross Dom. Prod. 1990 Prices	**99b.*p***
25.1	27.2	28.5	30.4	31.7	37.6	53.2	57.5	64.2	71.2	100.0	133.0	144.8	164.6	179.1	GDP Deflator (1990=100)	**99bi*p***
Midyear Estimates																
6.92	7.11	7.32	7.52	7.74	7.96	8.19	8.43	8.68	8.94	9.20	9.47	9.74	10.03	10.32	**Population**	**99z**

Guinea
656

		1965	1966	1967	1968	1969	1970	1971	1972	1973	1974	1975	1976	1977	1978	1979
Exchange Rates																*Francs per SDR:*
Official Rate	aa	24.7	24.7	24.7	24.7	24.7	24.7	24.7	24.7	24.9	25.3	24.7	24.7	24.7	24.7	24.7
																Francs per US Dollar:
Official Rate	ae	24.7	24.7	24.7	24.7	24.7	24.7	22.7	22.7	20.7	20.7	21.1	21.2	20.3	18.9	18.7
Official Rate	rf	24.7	24.7	24.7	24.7	24.7	24.7	24.6	22.7	20.7	20.6	20.7	21.4	21.1	19.7	19.1
Fund Position																*Millions of SDRs:*
Quota	2f.s	15.00	19.00	19.00	19.00	19.00	24.00	24.00	24.00	24.00	24.00	24.00	24.00	24.00	30.00	30.00
SDRs	1b.s	—	—	—	—	—	.15	.11	2.88	1.43	3.41	3.14	2.86	2.17	—	—
Reserve Position in the Fund	1c.s	2.80	2.80	2.80	2.80	—	—	—	—	—	—	—	—	—	—	—
Total Fund Cred.&Loans Outstg.	2tl	—	—	—	—	.50	3.45	2.95	2.95	1.02	9.51	7.11	7.11	18.38	19.98	26.16
International Liquidity												*Millions of US Dollars Unless Otherwise Indicated:*				
Total Reserves minus Gold	1l.d	...	...	...	...	...	...	...	...	...	...	...	...	...	...	...
SDRs	1b.d	—	—	—	—	—	.15	.12	3.13	1.73	4.18	3.68	3.32	2.64	—	—
Reserve Position in the Fund	1c.d	2.80	2.80	2.80	2.80	—	—	—	—	—	—	—	—	—	—	—
Foreign Exchange	1d.d	...	...	...	...	...	...	...	...	...	...	...	...	...	...	...
Monetary Authorities: Other Liab.	4..d	...	...	...	...	...	...	...	...	...	...	...	...	...	...	...
Deposit Money Banks: Assets	7a.d	...	...	...	...	...	...	...	...	...	...	...	...	...	...	...
Liabilities	7b.d	...	...	...	...	...	...	...	...	...	...	...	...	...	...	...
Monetary Authorities																*Millions of Francs:*
Foreign Assets	11	...	...	...	...	...	...	...	...	...	...	...	...	...	...	...
Claims on Central Government	12a	...	...	...	...	...	...	...	...	...	...	...	...	...	...	...
Claims on Nonfin.Pub.Enterprises	12c	...	...	...	...	...	...	...	...	...	...	...	...	...	...	...
Claims on Private Sector	12d	...	...	...	...	...	...	...	...	...	...	...	...	...	...	...
Claims on Deposit Money Banks	12e	...	...	...	...	...	...	...	...	...	...	...	...	...	...	...
Claims on Other Banking Insts.	12f	...	...	...	...	...	...	...	...	...	...	...	...	...	...	...
Reserve Money	14	...	...	...	...	...	...	...	...	...	...	...	...	...	...	...
of which: Currency Outside DMBs	14a	...	...	...	...	...	...	...	...	...	...	...	...	...	...	...
Foreign Liabilities	16c	...	...	...	...	...	...	...	...	...	...	...	...	...	...	...
Central Government Deposits	16d	...	...	...	...	...	...	...	...	...	...	...	...	...	...	...
Capital Accounts	17a	...	...	...	...	...	...	...	...	...	...	...	...	...	...	...
Other Items (Net)	17r	...	...	...	...	...	...	...	...	...	...	...	...	...	...	...
Deposit Money Banks																*Millions of Francs:*
Reserves	20	...	...	...	...	...	...	...	...	...	...	...	...	...	...	...
Foreign Assets	21	...	...	...	...	...	...	...	...	...	...	...	...	...	...	...
Claims on Central Government	22a	...	...	...	...	...	...	...	...	...	...	...	...	...	...	...
Claims on Nonfin.Pub.Enterprises	22c	...	...	...	...	...	...	...	...	...	...	...	...	...	...	...
Claims on Private Sector	22d	...	...	...	...	...	...	...	...	...	...	...	...	...	...	...
Demand Deposits	24	...	...	...	...	...	...	...	...	...	...	...	...	...	...	...
Time,Savings,& Fgn.Currency Dep.	25	...	...	...	...	...	...	...	...	...	...	...	...	...	...	...
Foreign Liabilities	26c	...	...	...	...	...	...	...	...	...	...	...	...	...	...	...
Central Government Deposits	26d	...	...	...	...	...	...	...	...	...	...	...	...	...	...	...
Credit from Monetary Authorities	26g	...	...	...	...	...	...	...	...	...	...	...	...	...	...	...
Capital Accounts	27a	...	...	...	...	...	...	...	...	...	...	...	...	...	...	...
Other Items (Net)	27r	...	...	...	...	...	...	...	...	...	...	...	...	...	...	...
Monetary Survey																*Millions of Francs:*
Foreign Assets (Net)	31n	...	...	...	...	...	...	...	...	...	...	...	...	...	...	...
Domestic Credit	32	...	...	...	...	...	...	...	...	...	...	...	...	...	...	...
Claims on Central Govt. (Net)	32an	...	...	...	...	...	...	...	...	...	...	...	...	...	...	...
Claims on Nonfin.Pub.Enterprises	32c	...	...	...	...	...	...	...	...	...	...	...	...	...	...	...
Claims on Private Sector	32d	...	...	...	...	...	...	...	...	...	...	...	...	...	...	...
Claims on Other Banking Insts.	32f	...	...	...	...	...	...	...	...	...	...	...	...	...	...	...
Money	34	...	...	...	...	...	...	...	...	...	...	...	...	...	...	...
Quasi-Money	35	...	...	...	...	...	...	...	...	...	...	...	...	...	...	...
Capital Accounts	37a	...	...	...	...	...	...	...	...	...	...	...	...	...	...	...
Other Items (Net)	37r	...	...	...	...	...	...	...	...	...	...	...	...	...	...	...
Money plus Quasi-Money	35l	...	...	...	...	...	...	...	...	...	...	...	...	...	...	...
Interest Rates																*Percent Per Annum*
Refinancing Rate (End of Period)	60	...	...	...	...	...	...	...	...	...	...	...	...	...	...	...
Savings Rate	60k	...	...	...	...	...	...	...	...	...	...	...	...	...	...	...
Deposit Rate	60l	...	...	...	...	...	...	...	...	...	...	...	...	...	...	...
Lending Rate	60p	...	...	...	...	...	...	...	...	...	...	...	...	...	...	...

Guinea
656

	1980	1981	1982	1983	1984	1985	1986	1987	1988	1989	1990	1991	1992	1993	1994		
																Exchange Rates	
End of Period	24.7	24.7	24.7	24.7	24.7	24.7	288.2	624.2	740.1	814.8	967.4	1,148.6	1,268.3	1,335.7	1,432.1	Official Rate	aa
End of Period (ae) Period Average (rf)																	
	19.4	21.2	22.4	23.6	25.2	22.5	235.6	440.0	550.0	620.0	680.0	803.0	922.4	972.4	981.0	Official Rate	ae
	19.0	20.9	22.4	23.1	24.1	24.3	333.5	428.4	474.4	591.6	660.2	753.9	902.0	955.5	961.6	Official Rate	rf
																Fund Position	
End of Period	45.00	45.00	45.00	57.90	57.90	57.90	57.90	57.90	57.90	57.90	57.90	57.90	78.70	78.70	78.70	Quota	2f. s
	—	—	.17	.02	.03	—	.32	.21	.18	—	.16	9.44	7.93	8.49	3.79	SDRs	1b. s
	—	.55	1.45	—	—	—	—	—	—	—	—	—	.03	.07	.07	Reserve Position in the Fund	1c. s
	27.45	23.67	34.95	34.28	32.29	28.35	32.93	40.09	36.08	46.65	36.17	38.39	46.32	44.00	48.63	Total Fund Cred.&Loans Outstg.	2tl
																International Liquidity	
End of Period	....	....	....	....	....	....	....	....	....	....	....	80.05	86.96	132.12	87.85	Total Reserves minus Gold	1l. d
	....	....	.19	.02	.03	—	.39	.30	.24	—	.23	13.50	10.90	11.67	5.53	SDRs	1b. d
	—	.64	1.60	—	—	—	—	—	—	—	—	—	.04	.09	.10	Reserve Position in the Fund	1c. d
	....	....	....	....	....	....	....	....	....	....	....	66.55	76.01	120.36	82.22	Foreign Exchange	1d. d
	....	....	....	....	....	....	....	....	....	....	....	13.92	15.88	5.50	6.71	Monetary Authorities: Other Liab.	4..d
	....	....	....	....	....	....	....	....	....	56.79	70.36	81.27	87.24	85.47	86.27	Deposit Money Banks: Assets	7a. d
	....	....	....	....	....	....	....	....	....	45.42	48.79	51.31	45.68	46.81	52.39	Liabilities	7b. d
																Monetary Authorities	
End of Period	....	....	....	....	....	....	....	....	....	....	....	112,302	147,595	188,247	164,098	Foreign Assets	11
	....	....	....	....	....	....	....	....	....	....	....	131,239	163,336	178,636	226,413	Claims on Central Government	12a
	....	....	....	....	....	....	....	....	....	....	....	2,428	2,359	2,352	3,059	Claims on Nonfin.Pub.Enterprises	12c
	....	....	....	....	....	....	....	....	....	....	....	189	445	42	179	Claims on Private Sector	12d
	....	....	....	....	....	....	....	....	....	....	....	15,403	9,890	8,211	8,587	Claims on Deposit Money Banks	12e
	....	....	....	....	....	....	....	....	....	....	....	86	—	—	48	Claims on Other Banking Insts.	12f
	....	....	....	....	....	....	....	....	....	....	....	147,756	165,178	196,468	176,724	Reserve Money	14
	....	....	....	....	....	....	....	....	....	....	....	119,409	133,028	166,609	154,748	of which: Currency Outside DMBs	14a
	....	....	....	....	....	....	....	....	....	....	....	55,262	73,396	64,124	76,238	Foreign Liabilities	16c
	....	....	....	....	....	....	....	....	....	....	....	77,036	93,479	129,003	151,170	Central Government Deposits	16d
	....	....	....	....	....	....	....	....	....	....	....	31,512	41,609	51,848	57,608	Capital Accounts	17a
	....	....	....	....	....	....	....	....	....	....	....	-49,918	-50,038	-63,955	-59,356	Other Items (Net)	17r
																Deposit Money Banks	
End of Period	....	....	....	....	....	....	....	....	....	3,599	7,407	13,978	17,591	20,458	15,380	Reserves	20
	....	....	....	....	....	....	....	....	....	35,210	47,846	65,256	80,474	83,110	84,630	Foreign Assets	21
	....	....	....	....	....	....	....	....	....	156	4	16	20	12,596	13,210	Claims on Central Government	22a
	....	....	....	....	....	....	....	....	....	1	192	21	59	124	10	Claims on Nonfin.Pub.Enterprises	22c
	....	....	....	....	....	....	....	....	....	53,138	71,648	79,397	106,487	130,322	144,410	Claims on Private Sector	22d
	....	....	....	....	....	....	....	....	....	30,194	42,908	53,012	76,665	86,763	94,430	Demand Deposits	24
	....	....	....	....	....	....	....	....	....	17,703	14,623	26,059	38,624	54,794	52,180	Time,Savings,& Fgn.Currency Dep.	25
	....	....	....	....	....	....	....	....	....	28,163	33,175	41,199	42,135	45,523	51,400	Foreign Liabilities	26c
	....	....	....	....	....	....	....	....	....	8,422	10,360	13,515	13,934	15,267	17,100	Central Government Deposits	26d
	....	....	....	....	....	....	....	....	....	10,611	15,820	16,291	10,622	9,601	10,360	Credit from Monetary Authorities	26g
	....	....	....	....	....	....	....	....	....	16,272	23,652	26,760	39,613	47,601	46,400	Capital Accounts	27a
	....	....	....	....	....	....	....	....	....	-19,261	-13,441	-18,168	-16,962	-12,939	-14,230	Other Items (Net)	27r
																Monetary Survey	
End of Period	....	....	....	....	....	....	....	....	....	....	....	81,098	112,537	161,710	121,090	Foreign Assets (Net)	31n
	....	....	....	....	....	....	....	....	....	....	....	122,825	165,293	179,802	219,059	Domestic Credit	32
	....	....	....	....	....	....	....	....	....	....	....	40,704	55,943	46,962	71,353	Claims on Central Govt. (Net)	32an
	....	....	....	....	....	....	....	....	....	....	....	2,449	2,418	2,476	3,069	Claims on Nonfin.Pub.Enterprises	32c
	....	....	....	....	....	....	....	....	....	....	....	79,586	106,932	130,364	144,589	Claims on Private Sector	32d
	....	....	....	....	....	....	....	....	....	....	....	86	—	—	48	Claims on Other Banking Insts.	32f
	....	....	....	....	....	....	....	....	....	....	....	182,469	218,445	260,854	252,582	Money	34
	....	....	....	....	....	....	....	....	....	....	....	26,059	38,624	54,794	52,180	Quasi-Money	35
	....	....	....	....	....	....	....	....	....	....	....	58,272	81,222	99,449	104,008	Capital Accounts	37a
	....	....	....	....	....	....	....	....	....	....	....	-62,877	-60,461	-73,585	-68,621	Other Items (Net)	37r
	....	....	....	....	....	....	....	....	....	....	....	208,528	257,069	315,648	304,762	Money plus Quasi-Money	35l
																Interest Rates	
Percent Per Annum	....	....	....	....	....	....	9.00	10.00	10.00	13.00	15.00	19.00	19.00	17.00	17.00	Refinancing Rate (End of Period)	60
	....	....	....	....	....	....	....	....	12.00	12.67	16.08	19.00	21.00	17.00	16.00	Savings Rate	60k
	....	....	....	....	....	....	....	15.00	16.83	19.50	21.00	22.00	23.00	19.75	18.00	Deposit Rate	60l
	....	....	....	....	....	....	....	15.00	15.00	17.25	21.17	24.50	27.00	24.50	22.00	Lending Rate	60p

Guinea
656

		1965	1966	1967	1968	1969	1970	1971	1972	1973	1974	1975	1976	1977	1978	1979
Balance of Payments															*Millions of US Dollars:*	
Goods: Exports f.o.b.	78aa d	....	....	....	....	....	....	....	....	....	....	....	....	....	....	....
Goods: Imports f.o.b.	78ab d	....	....	....	....	....	....	....	....	....	....	....	....	....	....	....
Trade Balance	78ac d	....	....	....	....	....	....	....	....	....	....	....	....	....	....	....
Services: Credit	78ad d	....	....	....	....	....	....	....	....	....	....	....	....	....	....	....
Services: Debit	78ae d	....	....	....	....	....	....	....	....	....	....	....	....	....	....	....
Balance on Goods and Services	78af d	....	....	....	....	....	....	....	....	....	....	....	....	....	....	....
Income: Credit	78ag d	....	....	....	....	....	....	....	....	....	....	....	....	....	....	....
Income: Debit	78ah d	....	....	....	....	....	....	....	....	....	....	....	....	....	....	....
Balance on Goods, Serv., & Inc.	78ai d	....	....	....	....	....	....	....	....	....	....	....	....	....	....	....
Current Transfers, n.i.e.: Credit	78aj d	....	....	....	....	....	....	....	....	....	....	....	....	....	....	....
Current Transfers: Debit	78ak d	....	....	....	....	....	....	....	....	....	....	....	....	....	....	....
Current Account, n.i.e.	78al d	....	....	....	....	....	....	....	....	....	....	....	....	....	....	....
Capital Account, n.i.e.: Credit	78ba d	....	....	....	....	....	....	....	....	....	....	....	....	....	....	....
Capital Account: Debit	78bb d	....	....	....	....	....	....	....	....	....	....	....	....	....	....	....
Capital Account, n.i.e.	78bc d	....	....	....	....	....	....	....	....	....	....	....	....	....	....	....
Direct Investment Abroad	78bd d	....	....	....	....	....	....	....	....	....	....	....	....	....	....	....
Dir. Invest. in Rep. Econ., n.i.e.	78be d	....	....	....	....	....	....	....	....	....	....	....	....	....	....	....
Portfolio Investment Assets	78bf d	....	....	....	....	....	....	....	....	....	....	....	....	....	....	....
Portfolio Investment Liab., n.i.e.	78bg d	....	....	....	....	....	....	....	....	....	....	....	....	....	....	....
Other Investment Assets	78bh d	....	....	....	....	....	....	....	....	....	....	....	....	....	....	....
Other Investment Liab., n.i.e.	78bi d	....	....	....	....	....	....	....	....	....	....	....	....	....	....	....
Financial Account, n.i.e.	78bj d	....	....	....	....	....	....	....	....	....	....	....	....	....	....	....
Net Errors and Omissions	78ca d	....	....	....	....	....	....	....	....	....	....	....	....	....	....	....
Overall Balance	78cb d	....	....	....	....	....	....	....	....	....	....	....	....	....	....	....
Reserves and Related Items	79da d	....	....	....	....	....	....	....	....	....	....	....	....	....	....	....
Reserve Assets	79db d	....	....	....	....	....	....	....	....	....	....	....	....	....	....	....
Use of Fund Credit and Loans	79dc d	....	....	....	....	....	....	....	....	....	....	....	....	....	....	....
Liabs.Constit.For.Auth.Reserves	79dd d	....	....	....	....	....	....	....	....	....	....	....	....	....	....	....
Exceptional Financing	79de d	....	....	....	....	....	....	....	....	....	....	....	....	....	....	....
Government Finance															*Millions of Francs:*	
Deficit (-) or Surplus	80	....	....	....	....	....	....	....	....	....	....	....	....	....	....	....
Revenue	81	....	....	....	....	....	....	....	....	....	....	....	....	....	....	....
Grants Received	81z	....	....	....	....	....	....	....	....	....	....	....	....	....	....	....
Expenditure	82	....	....	....	....	....	....	....	....	....	....	....	....	....	....	....
Lending Minus Repayments	83	....	....	....	....	....	....	....	....	....	....	....	....	....	....	....
Financing																
Domestic	84a	....	....	....	....	....	....	....	....	....	....	....	....	....	....	....
Foreign	85a	....	....	....	....	....	....	....	....	....	....	....	....	....	....	....
																Millions:
Population	99z	3.51	3.61	3.70	3.75	3.84	3.92	4.02	4.11	....	....	4.34	4.43	I 5.06	5.17	5.29

Guinea

656

	1980	1981	1982	1983	1984	1985	1986	1987	1988	1989	1990	1991	1992	1993	1994		
Minus Sign Indicates Debit																**Balance of Payments**	
	....	....	....	....	....	....	506.6	544.6	511.9	595.6	671.2	687.1	517.2	561.1	....	Goods: Exports f.o.b.	78aa *d*
	....	....	....	....	....	....	−422.7	−380.3	−510.6	−531.6	−585.8	−694.9	−608.4	−582.7	....	Goods: Imports f.o.b.	78ab *d*
	....	....	....	....	....	....	83.9	164.4	1.3	64.0	85.5	−7.8	−91.2	−21.6	....	Trade Balance	78ac *d*
	....	....	....	....	....	....	55.6	53.6	52.6	103.7	157.8	144.7	159.7	308.5	....	Services: Credit	78ad *d*
	....	....	....	....	....	....	−137.4	−154.0	−230.8	−259.8	−367.3	−347.8	−322.6	−334.8	....	Services: Debit	78ae *d*
	....	....	....	....	....	....	2.2	64.0	−177.0	−92.1	−124.0	−210.9	−254.0	−47.8	....	Balance on Goods and Services	78af *d*
	....	....	....	....	....	....	4.9	4.6	11.2	8.6	12.6	15.5	7.9	9.3	....	Income: Credit...............................	78ag *d*
	....	....	....	....	....	....	−156.6	−128.8	−142.4	−178.5	−161.5	−181.4	−148.9	−92.6	....	Income: Debit................................	78ah *d*
	....	....	....	....	....	....	−149.6	−60.2	−308.1	−261.9	−272.9	−376.8	−395.0	−131.1	....	Balance on Goods, Serv., & Inc. ...	78ai *d*
	....	....	....	....	....	....	37.9	37.6	121.3	143.6	118.8	136.2	193.5	260.3	....	Current Transfers, n.i.e.: Credit	78aj *d*
	....	....	....	....	....	....	−12.3	−15.6	−34.7	−61.3	−48.6	−48.2	−61.2	−64.2	....	Current Transfers: Debit	78ak *d*
	....	....	....	....	....	....	−123.9	−38.3	−221.5	−179.7	−202.6	−288.8	−262.7	65.0	....	Current Account, n.i.e.	78al *d*
	....	....	....	....	....	....	—	—	—	198.7	—	—	8.0	5.0	....	Capital Account, n.i.e.: Credit	78ba *d*
	....	....	....	....	....	....	—	—	—	—	—	—	—	—	....	Capital Account: Debit	78bb *d*
	....	....	....	....	....	....	—	—	—	198.7	—	—	8.0	5.0	....	Capital Account, n.i.e.	78bc *d*
	....	....	....	....	....	....	—	—	—	—	—	—	—	—	....	Direct Investment Abroad	78bd *d*
	....	....	....	....	....	....	8.4	12.9	15.7	12.3	17.9	38.8	19.7	2.7	....	Dir. Invest. in Rep. Econ., n.i.e.	78be *d*
	....	....	....	....	....	....	—	—	—	—	—	—	—	—	....	Portfolio Investment Assets	78bf *d*
	....	....	....	....	....	....	—	—	—	—	—	—	—	—	....	Portfolio Investment Liab., n.i.e.	78bg *d*
	....	....	....	....	....	....	−29.1	−15.8	−5.2	−39.1	−52.7	−47.0	−27.5	−20.1	....	Other Investment Assets	78bh *d*
	....	....	....	....	....	....	25.4	14.0	64.3	−56.3	102.7	54.6	114.3	143.8	....	Other Investment Liab., n.i.e.	78bi *d*
	....	....	....	....	....	....	4.7	11.1	74.8	−83.1	67.8	46.4	106.4	126.5	....	Financial Account, n.i.e.	78bj *d*
	....	....	....	....	....	....	22.6	−9.3	−5.1	−44.9	52.1	112.3	18.6	−229.3	....	Net Errors and Omissions	78ca *d*
	....	....	....	....	....	....	−96.6	−36.5	−151.9	−109.0	−82.8	−130.2	−129.7	−32.9	....	Overall Balance	78cb *d*
	....	....	....	....	....	....	96.6	36.5	151.9	109.0	82.8	130.2	129.7	32.9	....	Reserves and Related Items	79da *d*
	....	....	....	....	....	....	−24.5	−15.0	35.3	−13.4	−3.4	10.5	1.6	−49.9	....	Reserve Assets	79db *d*
	....	....	....	....	....	....	5.2	8.9	−5.4	13.9	−14.3	3.2	11.0	−3.2	....	Use of Fund Credit and Loans......	79dc *d*
	....	....	....	....	....	....	−15.9	—	—	—	—	8.4	−5.7	−.1	....	Liabs.Constit.For.Auth.Reserves......	79dd *d*
	....	....	....	....	....	....	131.8	42.6	122.0	108.5	100.4	108.2	122.8	86.1	....	Exceptional Financing	79de *d*
Year Ending December 31																**Government Finance**	
	....	....	....	....	....	....	....	....	....	−50,145	−61,090	−76,955	−83,585	....	....	Deficit (−) or Surplus	80
	....	....	....	....	....	....	....	....	....	222,778	297,860	326,183	357,889	....	....	Revenue	81
	....	....	....	....	....	....	....	....	....	52,500	68,300	82,500	117,300	....	....	Grants Received............................	81z
	....	....	....	....	....	....	....	....	....	326,960	426,852	489,323	559,854	....	....	Expenditure...................................	82
	....	....	....	....	....	....	....	....	....	−1,537	398	−3,685	−1,080	....	....	Lending Minus Repayments	83
																Financing	
	....	....	....	....	....	....	....	....	....	−15,092	−14,654	478	−26,108	....	....	Domestic	84a
	....	....	....	....	....	....	....	....	....	65,237	75,744	76,477	109,693	....	....	Foreign	85a
Midyear Estimates																	
	5.41	4.55	4.64	4.41	4.53	4.66	4.79	4.93	5.07	5.59	5.75	5.93	6.12	6.31	....	**Population**...................................	99z

Guinea-Bissau

654

		1965	1966	1967	1968	1969	1970	1971	1972	1973	1974	1975	1976	1977	1978	1979
Exchange Rates																*Pesos per SDR:*
Official Rate	aa	29	29	29	29	29	29	30	29	31	30	32	37	42	44	44
																Pesos per US Dollar:
Official Rate	ae	29	29	29	29	29	29	28	27	26	25	27	32	34	34	33
Official Rate	rf	29	29	29	29	29	29	28	27	25	25	26	30	34	35	34
Fund Position																*Millions of SDRs:*
Quota	2f.s	....	....	....	....	....	....	....	....	....	....	....	....	3.20	3.90	3.90
SDRs	1b.s	....	....	....	....	....	....	....	....	....	....	....	....	—	—	.09
Reserve Position in the Fund	1c.s	....	....	....	....	....	....	....	....	....	....	....	....	.80	—	—
Total Fund Cred.&Loans Outstg.	2tl	....	....	....	....	....	....	....	....	....	....	....	....	—	—	1.10
International Liquidity																*Millions of US Dollars Unless Otherwise Indicated:*
Total Reserves minus Gold	1l.d	....	....	....	....	....	....	....	....	....	....	....	....	....	....	.12
SDRs	1b.d	....	....	....	....	....	....	....	....	....	....	....	....	—	—	.12
Reserve Position in the Fund	1c.d	....	....	....	....	....	....	....	....	....	....	....	....			
Foreign Exchange	1d.d	....	....	....	....	....	....	....	....	....	....	....	....			
Monetary Authorities: Other Liab.	4..d	....	....	....	....	....	....	....	....	....	....	....	....			
Deposit Money Banks: Assets	7a.d	....	....	....	....	....	....	....	....	....	....	....	....			
Liabilities	7b.d	....	....	....	....	....	....	....	....	....	....	....	....			
Monetary Authorities																*Billions of Pesos:*
Foreign Assets	11	....	....	....	....	....	....	....	....	....	....	....	....	....	....	....
Claims on Central Government	12a	....	....	....	....	....	....	....	....	....	....	....	....	....	....	....
Claims on Nonfin.Pub.Enterprises	12c	....	....	....	....	....	....	....	....	....	....	....	....	....	....	....
Claims on Private Sector	12d	....	....	....	....	....	....	....	....	....	....	....	....	....	....	....
Claims on Deposit Money Banks	12e	....	....	....	....	....	....	....	....	....	....	....	....	....	....	....
Reserve Money	14	....	....	....	....	....	....	....	....	....	....	....	....	....	....	....
of which: Currency Outside DMBs	14a	....	....	....	....	....	....	....	....	....	....	....	....	....	....	....
Time & Foreign Currency Dep.	15	....	....	....	....	....	....	....	....	....	....	....	....	....	....	....
Foreign Liabilities	16c	....	....	....	....	....	....	....	....	....	....	....	....	....	....	....
Long-Term Foreign Liabilities	16cl	....	....	....	....	....	....	....	....	....	....	....	....	....	....	....
Central Government Deposits	16d	....	....	....	....	....	....	....	....	....	....	....	....	....	....	....
Counterpart Funds	16e	....	....	....	....	....	....	....	....	....	....	....	....	....	....	....
Capital Accounts	17a	....	....	....	....	....	....	....	....	....	....	....	....	....	....	....
Other Items (Net)	17r	....	....	....	....	....	....	....	....	....	....	....	....	....	....	....
Deposit Money Banks																*Billions of Pesos:*
Reserves	20	....	....	....	....	....	....	....	....	....	....	....	....	....	....	....
Foreign Assets	21	....	....	....	....	....	....	....	....	....	....	....	....	....	....	....
Claims on Nonfin.Pub.Enterprises	22c	....	....	....	....	....	....	....	....	....	....	....	....	....	....	....
Claims on Private Sector	22d	....	....	....	....	....	....	....	....	....	....	....	....	....	....	....
Demand Deposits	24	....	....	....	....	....	....	....	....	....	....	....	....	....	....	....
Time & Foreign Currency Dep.	25	....	....	....	....	....	....	....	....	....	....	....	....	....	....	....
Foreign Liabilities	26c	....	....	....	....	....	....	....	....	....	....	....	....	....	....	....
Long-Term Foreign Liabilities	26cl	....	....	....	....	....	....	....	....	....	....	....	....	....	....	....
Central Government Deposits	26d	....	....	....	....	....	....	....	....	....	....	....	....	....	....	....
Credit from Monetary Authorities	26g	....	....	....	....	....	....	....	....	....	....	....	....	....	....	....
Capital Accounts	27a	....	....	....	....	....	....	....	....	....	....	....	....	....	....	....
Other Items (Net)	27r	....	....	....	....	....	....	....	....	....	....	....	....	....	....	....
Monetary Survey																*Billions of Pesos:*
Foreign Assets (Net)	31n	....	....	....	....	....	....	....	....	....	....	....	....	....	....	....
Domestic Credit	32	....	....	....	....	....	....	....	....	....	....	....	....	....	....	....
Claims on Central Govt. (Net)	32an	....	....	....	....	....	....	....	....	....	....	....	....	....	....	....
Claims on Nonfin.Pub.Enterprises	32c	....	....	....	....	....	....	....	....	....	....	....	....	....	....	....
Claims on Private Sector	32d	....	....	....	....	....	....	....	....	....	....	....	....	....	....	....
Money	34	....	....	....	....	....	....	....	....	....	....	....	....	....	....	....
Quasi-Money	35	....	....	....	....	....	....	....	....	....	....	....	....	....	....	....
Counterpart Funds	36e	....	....	....	....	....	....	....	....	....	....	....	....	....	....	....
Other Items (Net)	37r	....	....	....	....	....	....	....	....	....	....	....	....	....	....	....
Money plus Quasi-Money	35l	....	....	....	....	....	....	....	....	....	....	....	....	....	....	....
Interest Rates																*Percent Per Annum*
Discount Rate (End of Period)	60	....	....	....	....	....	....	....	....	....	....	....	....	....	....	....
Deposit Rate	60l	....	....	....	....	....	....	....	....	....	....	....	....	....	....	....
Lending Rate	60p	....	....	....	....	....	....	....	....	....	....	....	....	....	....	....
Prices																*Index Numbers (1990=100):*
Consumer Prices	64	....	....	....	....	....	....	....	....	....	....	....	....	....	....	....
International Transactions																*Millions of Pesos*
Exports	70	....	....	....	....	....	....	....	....	....	....	....	....	....	....	....
Imports, cif	71	....	....	....	....	....	....	....	....	....	....	....	....	....	....	....
Imports, fob	71.v	....	....	....	....	....	....	....	....	....	....	....	....	....	....	....

Guinea-Bissau

1980	1981	1982	1983	1984	1985	1986	1987	1988	1989	1990	1991	1992	1993	1994		
End of Period															**Exchange Rates**	
44	44	44	88	125	194	292	1,208	1,834	2,611	3,569	7,094	11,901	15,746	22,437	Official Rate	aa
End of Period (ae) Period Average (rf)																
34	38	40	84	127	176	239	851	1,363	1,987	2,509	4,959	8,656	11,464	15,369	Official Rate	ae
34	37	40	42	105	159	204	559	1,110	1,810	2,185	3,659	6,934	10,082	12,892	Official Rate	rf
End of Period															**Fund Position**	
5.90	5.90	5.90	7.50	7.50	7.50	7.50	7.50	7.50	7.50	7.50	7.50	10.50	10.50	10.50	Quota	2f. s
—	.07	.01	.01	.09	—	—	.05	—	—	—	—	—	.01	—	SDRs	1b. s
.50	—	—	—	—	—	—	—	—	—	—	—	—	—	—	Reserve Position in the Fund	1c. s
1.10	2.95	2.68	2.26	3.73	2.80	1.87	3.14	2.20	3.75	3.75	3.75	3.75	3.45	3.30	Total Fund Cred.&Loans Outstg.	2tl
End of Period															**International Liquidity**	
....	....	....	....	....	....	−.63	10.31	15.97	20.84	18.22	14.58	17.75	14.17	18.43	Total Reserves minus Gold	1l. d
....	.08	.01	.01	.09	—	—	.07	—	—	—	—	—	.01	—	SDRs	1b. d
....	....	....	....	....	....	....	....	....	....	....	....	....	....	....	Reserve Position in the Fund	1c. d
....	....	....	....	....	....	−.63	10.24	15.97	20.84	18.22	14.58	17.75	14.16	18.43	Foreign Exchange	1d. d
....	....	....	....	....	....	79.45	96.26	92.17	43.36	32.53	38.59	53.06	48.33	42.59	Monetary Authorities: Other Liab.	4.. d
....	....	....	....	....	....	....	....	....	....	4.48	2.80	12.09	10.84	12.08	Deposit Money Banks: Assets	7a. d
....	....	....	....	....	....	....	....	....	....	1.02	.21	1.74	.67	7.22	Liabilities	7b. d
End of Period															**Monetary Authorities**	
....	....	....	....	....	....	−.15	8.78	21.76	41.42	45.70	72.29	153.65	162.41	283.20	Foreign Assets	11
....	....	....	....	....	....	9.87	21.88	27.27	68.26	130.43	128.84	185.73	207.80	232.15	Claims on Central Government	12a
....	....	....	....	....	....	2.05	5.30	13.71	22.51	—	—	—	—	16.34	Claims on Nonfin.Pub.Enterprises	12c
....	....	....	....	....	....	9.45	16.25	30.85	68.05	—	—	—	—	20.84	Claims on Private Sector	12d
....	....	....	....	....	....	—	—	—	—	78.49	148.14	210.62	281.26	281.35	Claims on Deposit Money Banks	12e
....	....	....	....	....	....	8.65	16.80	30.89	42.07	51.62	119.02	197.00	260.34	344.48	Reserve Money	14
....	....	....	....	....	....	5.47	9.31	15.98	24.96	36.55	54.52	104.22	132.53	195.97	of which: Currency Outside DMBs	14a
....	....	....	....	....	....	.10	5.60	7.77	12.96	—	—	—	—	—	Time & Foreign Currency Dep.	15
....	....	....	....	....	....	7.13	32.07	42.80	93.26	71.49	168.80	279.68	422.17	728.55	Foreign Liabilities	16c
....	....	....	....	....	....	12.38	53.67	86.83	2.70	23.50	49.19	224.20	186.25	—	Long-Term Foreign Liabilities	16cl
....	....	....	....	....	....	−.81	9.16	13.14	23.25	33.05	33.22	33.15	36.60	145.19	Central Government Deposits	16d
....	....	....	....	....	....	.28	10.75	25.34	72.57	90.77	115.37	128.47	135.12	174.25	Counterpart Funds	16e
....	....	....	....	....	....	.64	2.86	4.37	7.88	11.23	19.15	30.85	72.31	69.81	Capital Accounts	17a
....	....	....	....	....	....	−7.15	−78.70	−117.55	−54.45	−27.04	−155.48	−343.35	−461.33	−628.40	Other Items (Net)	17r
End of Period															**Deposit Money Banks**	
....	....	....	....	....	....	....	....	....	....	14.92	61.69	96.48	133.41	157.33	Reserves	20
....	....	....	....	....	....	....	....	....	....	11.23	13.89	104.63	124.25	185.63	Foreign Assets	21
....	....	....	....	....	....	....	....	....	....	28.78	29.89	40.57	35.33	37.43	Claims on Nonfin.Pub.Enterprises	22c
....	....	....	....	....	....	....	....	....	....	98.64	116.13	113.82	185.81	300.08	Claims on Private Sector	22d
....	....	....	....	....	....	....	....	....	....	28.03	31.01	54.20	68.25	120.56	Demand Deposits	24
....	....	....	....	....	....	....	....	....	....	23.30	33.35	94.35	153.44	208.44	Time & Foreign Currency Dep.	25
....	....	....	....	....	....	....	....	....	....	2.55	1.04	14.81	7.41	110.52	Foreign Liabilities	26c
....	....	....	....	....	....	....	....	....	....	—	—	.21	.27	.37	Long-Term Foreign Liabilities	26cl
....	....	....	....	....	....	....	....	....	....	.11	.46	15.07	8.57	3.06	Central Government Deposits	26d
....	....	....	....	....	....	....	....	....	....	78.49	147.70	209.48	281.30	281.30	Credit from Monetary Authorities	26g
....	....	....	....	....	....	....	....	....	....	−.83	−14.15	−35.31	−66.52	−43.74	Capital Accounts	27a
....	....	....	....	....	....	....	....	....	....	21.92	22.19	2.69	26.08	−.04	Other Items (Net)	27r
End of Period															**Monetary Survey**	
....	....	....	....	....	....	−19.66	−76.96	−107.87	−54.54	−40.61	−132.85	−260.62	−329.45	−367.25	Foreign Assets (Net)	31n
....	....	....	....	....	....	22.18	34.27	58.69	135.57	224.69	241.18	291.90	383.77	458.59	Domestic Credit	32
....	....	....	....	....	....	10.68	12.72	14.13	45.01	97.27	95.16	137.51	162.63	83.90	Claims on Central Govt. (Net)	32an
....	....	....	....	....	....	2.05	5.30	13.71	22.51	28.78	29.89	40.57	35.33	53.77	Claims on Nonfin.Pub.Enterprises	32c
....	....	....	....	....	....	9.45	16.25	30.85	68.05	98.64	116.13	113.82	185.81	320.92	Claims on Private Sector	32d
....	....	....	....	....	....	8.65	16.73	30.80	40.29	64.73	86.58	158.61	201.91	319.27	Money	34
....	....	....	....	....	....	.10	5.60	7.77	12.96	23.30	33.35	94.35	153.44	208.44	Quasi-Money	35
....	....	....	....	....	....	.28	10.75	25.34	72.57	90.77	115.37	128.47	135.12	174.25	Counterpart Funds	36e
....	....	....	....	....	....	−6.51	−75.77	−113.09	−44.79	5.28	−126.97	−350.15	−436.15	−610.62	Other Items (Net)	37r
....	....	....	....	....	....	8.75	22.33	38.57	53.25	88.03	119.93	252.96	355.35	527.71	Money plus Quasi-Money	35l
Percent Per Annum															**Interest Rates**	
....	....	....	....	....	....	....	....	....	....	42.0	42.0	45.5	41.0	26.0	Discount Rate *(End of Period)*	60
....	....	....	....	....	....	....	....	23.0	28.0	32.7	36.0	39.3	53.9	28.7	Deposit Rate	60l
....	....	....	....	....	....	18.0	18.0	30.0	38.3	45.8	47.0	50.3	63.6	36.3	Lending Rate	60p
Period Averages															**Prices**	
....	....	....	....	....	....	....	25.9	41.6	75.2	100.0	157.6	267.3	395.8	455.9	Consumer Prices	64
Millions of Pesos															**International Transactions**	
....	....	....	....	....	....	....	17,644	25,704	42,092	74,782	44,862	161,109	416,257		Exports	70
....	....	....	....	....	....	....	73,532	140,309	187,351	277,702	661,773	620,137	815,814		Imports, cif	71
....	....	....	....	....	....	....	63,941	122,008	162,913	241,480	575,454	539,250	709,403		Imports, fob	71.v

Guinea-Bissau
654

		1965	1966	1967	1968	1969	1970	1971	1972	1973	1974	1975	1976	1977	1978	1979
Balance of Payments																*Millions of US Dollars:*
Goods: Exports f.o.b.	78aa d	....	....	....	....	....	....	....	....	....	....	....	....	....	....	....
Goods: Imports f.o.b.	78ab d	....	....	....	....	....	....	....	....	....	....	....	....	....	....	....
Trade Balance	78ac d	....	....	....	....	....	....	....	....	....	....	....	....	....	....	....
Services: Credit	78ad d	....	....	....	....	....	....	....	....	....	....	....	....	....	....	....
Services: Debit	78ae d	....	....	....	....	....	....	....	....	....	....	....	....	....	....	....
Balance on Goods and Services	78af d	....	....	....	....	....	....	....	....	....	....	....	....	....	....	....
Income: Credit	78ag d	....	....	....	....	....	....	....	....	....	....	....	....	....	....	....
Income: Debit	78ah d	....	....	....	....	....	....	....	....	....	....	....	....	....	....	....
Balance on Goods, Serv., & Inc.	78ai d	....	....	....	....	....	....	....	....	....	....	....	....	....	....	....
Current Transfers, n.i.e.: Credit	78aj d	....	....	....	....	....	....	....	....	....	....	....	....	....	....	....
Current Transfers: Debit	78ak d	....	....	....	....	....	....	....	....	....	....	....	....	....	....	....
Current Account, n.i.e.	78al d	....	....	....	....	....	....	....	....	....	....	....	....	....	....	....
Capital Account, n.i.e.: Credit	78ba d	....	....	....	....	....	....	....	....	....	....	....	....	....	....	....
Capital Account: Debit	78bb d	....	....	....	....	....	....	....	....	....	....	....	....	....	....	....
Capital Account, n.i.e.	78bc d	....	....	....	....	....	....	....	....	....	....	....	....	....	....	....
Direct Investment Abroad	78bd d	....	....	....	....	....	....	....	....	....	....	....	....	....	....	....
Dir. Invest. in Rep. Econ., n.i.e.	78be d	....	....	....	....	....	....	....	....	....	....	....	....	....	....	....
Portfolio Investment Assets	78bf d	....	....	....	....	....	....	....	....	....	....	....	....	....	....	....
Portfolio Investment Liab., n.i.e.	78bg d	....	....	....	....	....	....	....	....	....	....	....	....	....	....	....
Other Investment Assets	78bh d	....	....	....	....	....	....	....	....	....	....	....	....	....	....	....
Other Investment Liab., n.i.e.	78bi d	....	....	....	....	....	....	....	....	....	....	....	....	....	....	....
Financial Account, n.i.e.	78bj d	....	....	....	....	....	....	....	....	....	....	....	....	....	....	....
Net Errors and Omissions	78ca d	....	....	....	....	....	....	....	....	....	....	....	....	....	....	....
Overall Balance	78cb d	....	....	....	....	....	....	....	....	....	....	....	....	....	....	....
Reserves and Related Items	79da d	....	....	....	....	....	....	....	....	....	....	....	....	....	....	....
Reserve Assets	79db d	....	....	....	....	....	....	....	....	....	....	....	....	....	....	....
Use of Fund Credit and Loans	79dc d	....	....	....	....	....	....	....	....	....	....	....	....	....	....	....
Liabs.Constit.For.Auth.Reserves	79dd d	....	....	....	....	....	....	....	....	....	....	....	....	....	....	....
Exceptional Financing	79de d	....	....	....	....	....	....	....	....	....	....	....	....	....	....	....
Government Finance																*Billions of Pesos:*
Deficit (-) or Surplus	80	....	....	....	....	....	....	....	....	....	....	....	....	....	....	....
Revenue	81	....	....	....	....	....	....	....	....	....	....	....	....	....	....	....
Grants Received	81z	....	....	....	....	....	....	....	....	....	....	....	....	....	....	....
Expenditure	82	....	....	....	....	....	....	....	....	....	....	....	....	....	....	....
Lending Minus Repayments	83	....	....	....	....	....	....	....	....	....	....	....	....	....	....	....
Financing																	
Domestic	84a	....	....	....	....	....	....	....	....	....	....	....	....	....	....	....
Foreign	85a	....	....	....	....	....	....	....	....	....	....	....	....	....	....	....
Unallocated Financing	87c	....	....	....	....	....	....	....	....	....	....	....	....	....	....	....
National Accounts																*Billions of Pesos*
Exports of Goods & Services	90c	....	....	....	....	....	....	....	....	....	....	....	....	....	....	....
Government Consumption	91f	....	....	....	....	....	....	....	....	....	....	....	....	....	....	....
Gross Capital Formation	93	....	....	....	....	....	....	....	....	....	....	....	....	....	....	....
Private Consumption	96f	....	....	....	....	....	....	....	....	....	....	....	....	....	....	....
Imports of Goods & Services	98c	....	....	....	....	....	....	....	....	....	....	....	....	....	....	....
Gross Domestic Product	99b	....	....	....	....	....	....	....	....	....	....	....	....	....	....	....
Net Factor Inc/Pmts(-) Abroad	98.n	....	....	....	....	....	....	....	....	....	....	....	....	....	....	....
Gross National Product = GNP	99a	....	....	....	....	....	....	....	....	....	....	....	....	....	....	....
Gross Dom. Prod. 1990 Prices	99b.p	....	....	....	....	....	....	....	....	....	....	....	....	....	....	....
GDP Deflator (1990=100)	99bi p	....	....	....	....	....	....	....	....	....	....	....	....	....	....	....
																Millions:
Population	99z	.49	.49	.49	.48	.48	₤.53	.54	.55	.57	.60	.63	.66	.70	.74	.78

Government Finance: ₤ Beginning in 1987, data are derived from Ministry of Finance sources and cover budgetary central government. Prior to 1987, data are as reported in the *Government Finance Statistics Yearbook (GFSY)* and cover budgetary central government.

Guinea-Bissau

654

	1980	1981	1982	1983	1984	1985	1986	1987	1988	1989	1990	1991	1992	1993	1994		
Minus Sign Indicates Debit																	**Balance of Payments**
	....	....	11.80	8.60	17.40	11.60	9.70	15.40	15.90	14.20	19.26	20.44	6.47	15.96	....	....	Goods: Exports f.o.b. .... 78aa *d*
	....	....	−61.50	−58.40	−60.10	−59.50	−51.20	−44.70	−58.90	−68.90	−68.07	−67.47	−83.51	−53.82	....	....	Goods: Imports f.o.b. .... 78ab *d*
	....	....	−49.70	−49.80	−42.70	−47.90	−41.50	−29.30	−43.00	−54.70	−48.81	−47.03	−77.04	−37.86	....	....	Trade Balance .... 78ac *d*
	....	....	....	5.60	6.70	8.00	6.50	—	—	—	—	—	—	—	....	....	Services: Credit .... 78ad *d*
	....	....	....	−13.60	−13.20	−21.20	−25.10	−14.40	−15.30	−17.10	−20.95	−13.17	−14.35	−16.00	−11.38	....	....	Services: Debit .... 78ae *d*
	....	....	....	−57.70	−56.30	−55.90	−66.50	−55.90	−44.60	−60.10	−75.65	−61.98	−61.38	−93.04	−49.24	....	....	Balance on Goods and Services .... 78af *d*
	....	....	....	—	—	—	—	—	—	—	—	—	—	—	—	....	....	Income: Credit .... 78ag *d*
	....	....	....	−7.80	−4.80	−4.70	−5.90	−16.50	−17.90	−19.90	−28.05	−22.28	−32.91	−27.78	−28.98	....	....	Income: Debit .... 78ah *d*
	....	....	....	−65.50	−61.10	−60.60	−72.40	−72.40	−62.50	−80.00	−103.70	−84.26	−94.29	−120.82	−78.22	....	....	Balance on Goods, Serv., & Inc. .... 78ai *d*
	....	....	....	—	—	—	—	11.40	8.00	11.60	10.90	23.86	19.39	17.28	14.39	....	....	Current Transfers, n.i.e.: Credit .... 78aj *d*
	....	....	....	−14.00	−10.90	−4.90	−3.40	−1.50	−2.00	—	—	—	−4.14	−.64	−1.65	....	....	Current Transfers: Debit .... 78ak *d*
	....	....	....	−79.50	−72.00	−65.50	−75.80	−62.50	−56.50	−68.40	−92.80	−60.40	−79.04	−104.18	−65.48	....	....	Current Account, n.i.e. .... 78al *d*
	....	....	....	44.50	43.00	29.30	30.50	26.90	32.20	26.90	41.60	28.96	32.72	28.49	36.58	....	....	Capital Account, n.i.e.: Credit .... 78ba *d*
	....	....	....	—	—	—	—	—	—	—	—	—	—	—	—	....	....	Capital Account: Debit .... 78bb *d*
	....	....	....	44.50	43.00	29.30	30.50	26.90	32.20	26.90	41.60	28.96	32.72	28.49	36.58	....	....	Capital Account, n.i.e. .... 78bc *d*
	....	....	....	—	—	—	—	—	—	—	—	—	—	—	—	....	....	Direct Investment Abroad .... 78bd *d*
	....	....	....	—	—	—	—	—	—	—	—	—	—	—	—	....	....	Dir. Invest. in Rep. Econ., n.i.e. .... 78be *d*
	....	....	....	—	—	—	—	—	—	—	—	—	—	—	—	....	....	Portfolio Investment Assets .... 78bf *d*
	....	....	....	—	—	—	—	—	—	—	—	—	—	—	—	....	....	Portfolio Investment Liab., n.i.e. .... 78bg *d*
	....	....	....	23.80	16.66	36.63	62.96	6.67	1.48	−3.44	−7.00	1.22	−8.75	2.13	−13.55	....	....	Other Investment Assets .... 78bh *d*
	....	....	....	23.80	16.66	36.63	62.96	6.67	1.48	−3.44	−7.00	1.22	−8.75	2.13	−13.55	....	....	Other Investment Liab., n.i.e. .... 78bi *d*
	....	....	....	—	—	—	—	—	—	—	—	—	—	—	—	....	....	Financial Account, n.i.e. .... 78bj *d*
	....	....	....	−9.17	−5.35	−12.88	−9.64	−3.71	−7.70	3.50	−11.60	−1.47	−16.27	22.01	−15.98	....	....	Net Errors and Omissions .... 78ca *d*
	....	....	....	−20.37	−17.69	−12.45	8.01	−32.65	−30.52	−41.44	−69.81	−31.69	−71.34	−51.55	−58.43	....	....	Overall Balance .... 78cb *d*
	....	....	....	20.37	17.69	12.45	−8.01	32.65	30.52	41.44	69.81	31.69	71.34	51.55	58.43	....	....	Reserves and Related Items .... 79da *d*
	....	....	....	16.17	13.50	2.60	−15.61	−3.10	−2.36	−11.83	6.70	−5.20	8.89	−5.10	9.02	....	....	Reserve Assets .... 79db *d*
	....	....	....	−.29	−.45	1.48	−.94	−1.09	1.62	−1.26	1.97	—	—	—	−.42	....	....	Use of Fund Credit and Loans.......... 79dc *d*
	....	....	....	—	—	—	—	—	—	—	—	—	—	—	—	....	....	Liabs.Constit.For.Auth.Reserves .... 79dd *d*
	....	....	....	4.50	4.64	8.37	8.54	36.83	31.26	54.53	61.13	36.89	62.45	56.65	49.83	....	....	Exceptional Financing .... 79de *d*
Year Ending December 31																	**Government Finance**
	....	....	....	−2.22	−4.62	−7.16	−7.53	⌶−3.42	−21.16	−34.90	−72.18	−114.34	−237.63 ᵖ	....	....	....	Deficit (-) or Surplus 80
	....	....	....	1.02	1.99	2.94	3.83	⌶12.58	23.30	42.74	97.64	123.79	168.49 ᵖ	....	....	....	Revenue 81
	....	....	....	1.50	3.16	5.47	7.68	⌶25.49	48.83	105.35	96.73	137.80	216.34 ᵖ	....	....	....	Grants Received 81z
	....	....	....	4.73	9.76	14.52	19.23	⌶41.38	77.88	173.18	235.47	331.07	555.90 ᵖ	....	....	....	Expenditure 82
	....	....	....	—	—	1.06	−.20	⌶.11	15.41	9.81	31.08	44.86	66.56 ᵖ	....	....	....	Lending Minus Repayments 83
																	Financing
	....	....	....	1.26	1.25	1.76	....	⌶−9.54	−13.12	−12.76	30.45	−26.81	29.39 ᵖ	....	....	....	Domestic 84a
	....	....	....	.68	2.95	4.91	....	⌶14.70	32.40	53.58	57.48	130.09	208.21 ᵖ	....	....	....	Foreign 85a
	....	....	....	.28	.42	.49	....	⌶−1.74	1.87	−5.92	−15.74	11.06	.04 ᵖ	....	....	....	Unallocated Financing 87c
Billions of Pesos																	**National Accounts**
	....	....	....	....	....	....	2.21	11.81	24.38	37.34	57.02	122.56	125.01	292.63	....	....	Exports of Goods & Services 90c
	....	....	....	....	....	....	6.42	11.95	19.81	49.79	60.88	114.64	163.10	212.97	....	....	Government Consumption 91f
	....	....	....	....	....	....	9.97	30.75	58.80	123.07	125.78	231.50	405.66	540.29	....	....	Gross Capital Formation 93
	....	....	....	....	....	....	41.84	79.94	171.01	352.43	484.35	791.31	1,700.38	2,246.52	....	....	Private Consumption 96f
	....	....	....	....	....	....	−13.47	−42.07	−102.04	−203.75	−217.93	−405.03	−864.14	−926.69	....	....	Imports of Goods & Services 98c
	....	....	....	....	....	....	46.97	92.38	171.95	358.88	510.09	854.98	1,530.01	2,365.72	....	....	Gross Domestic Product 99b
	....	....	....	....	....	....	—	−.47	−2.46	−7.32	22.12	−7.76	.92	−8.54	....	....	Net Factor Inc/Pmts(-) Abroad 98.n
	....	....	....	....	....	....	46.97	91.90	169.49	351.55	532.21	847.23	1,530.92	2,357.18	....	....	Gross National Product = GNP 99a
	....	....	....	....	....	....	418.43	442.04	472.54	493.80	510.09	525.40	540.10	556.30	....	....	Gross Dom. Prod. 1990 Prices .... 99b. *p*
	....	....	....	....	....	....	11.2	20.9	36.4	72.7	100.0	162.7	283.3	425.3	....	....	GDP Deflator (1990=100) .... 99bi *p*
Midyear Estimates																	
	.78	.80	.81	.83	.85	.87	.89	.91	.93	.94	.96	.98	1.01	1.03	....	....	Population 99z

Guyana

		1965	1966	1967	1968	1969	1970	1971	1972	1973	1974	1975	1976	1977	1978	1979
Exchange Rates																
														Guyana Dollars per SDR:		
Market Rate	aa	1.7	1.7	2.0	2.0	2.0	2.0	2.2	2.4	2.7	2.7	3.0	3.0	3.1	3.3	3.4
													Guyana Dollars per US Dollar:			
Market Rate	ae	1.7	1.7	2.0	2.0	2.0	2.0	2.0	2.2	2.2	2.2	2.6	2.6	2.6	2.6	2.6
Market Rate	rf	1.7	1.7	1.7	2.0	2.0	2.0	2.0	2.1	2.1	2.2	2.4	2.6	2.6	2.6	2.6
													Index Numbers (1990=100):			
Market Rate	ahx	2,253.6	2,251.2	2,213.6	1,929.2	1,926.5	1,931.0	214.5	1,857.1	1,820.3	1,736.3	1,649.5	1,517.2	1,517.2	1,517.2	1,517.2
Nominal Effective Exchange Rate	nec	....	....	....	....	....	....	....	....	....	....	....	....	....	....	782.9
Real Effective Exchange Rate	rec	....	....	....	....	....	....	....	....	....	....	....	....	....	....	194.5
Fund Position														*Millions of SDRs:*		
Quota	2f.s	....	15.00	15.00	15.00	15.00	20.00	20.00	20.00	20.00	20.00	20.00	20.00	20.00	25.00	25.00
SDRs	1b.s	....	—	—	—	—	.07	2.17	4.10	4.04	3.91	3.77	3.54	2.73	2.76	2.83
Reserve Position in the Fund	1c.s	....	1.20	1.20	1.21	1.21	1.81	—	.57	—	1.76	5.00	—	—	—	—
Total Fund Cred.&Loans Outstg.	2tl	....	—	—	—	—	—	2.06	—	3.87	5.00	—	17.25	17.25	30.27	40.49
International Liquidity												*Millions of US Dollars Unless Otherwise Indicated:*				
Total Reserves minus Gold	1l.d	20.12	16.90	18.85	23.55	20.55	20.40	26.16	36.75	13.97	62.57	100.50	27.28	22.98	58.27	17.53
SDRs	1b.d	....	—	—	—	—	.07	2.36	4.45	4.87	4.79	4.41	4.11	3.32	3.60	3.73
Reserve Position in the Fund	1c.d	....	1.20	1.20	1.21	1.21	1.81	—	.62	—	2.15	5.85	—	—	—	—
Foreign Exchange	1d.d	20.12	15.70	17.65	22.34	19.34	18.52	23.80	31.68	9.10	55.63	90.23	23.17	19.66	54.67	13.80
Monetary Authorities: Other Liab.	4..d	....	....	....	....	....	....	.05	....	....	14.99	30.20	30.47	43.71	44.02	37.93
Deposit Money Banks: Assets	7a.d	9.62	6.30	7.14	1.78	2.14	2.08	2.31	1.12	5.99	6.27	17.20	10.28	8.31	13.25	21.91
of which: Claims on Nonbanks	7ad d	....	....	.47	.24	.36	.69	.38	.27	1.19	1.67	.92	.80	.63	1.85	1.51
Deposit Money Banks: Liabilities	7b.d	2.39	2.80	1.55	1.85	4.00	4.90	5.15	4.13	3.75	6.94	14.39	8.33	10.58	19.47	28.45
of which: Liab. to Nonbanks	7bd d	....	....	....	....	....	....	....	3.10	2.64	3.56	4.40	5.15	7.49	7.10	9.75
Other Banking Insts.: Assets	7e.d	....	....	.29	.30	.49	.52	.68	.70	.70	.78	.74	.81	.88	.97	.98
of which: Claims on Nonbanks	7ed d	....	....	....	....	....	....	....	....	....	....	....	....	....	....	....
Other Banking Insts.: Liabilities	7f.d	....	....	.03	—	—	—	—	.01	.01	.02	.02	.02	.02	.03	.03
of which: Liab. to Nonbanks	7fd d	....	....	....	....	....	....	....	....	....	....	....	....	....	....	....
Monetary Authorities												*Millions of Guyana Dollars:*				
Foreign Assets	11	34	29	37	46	40	40	57	74	28	138	256	70	60	149	45
Claims on Central Government	12a	3	12	7	4	17	21	20	29	89	29	44	254	346	396	589
Claims on Nonfin.Pub.Enterprises	12c	....	....	—	—	—	—	—	—	—	—	—	—	—	—	—
Reserve Money	14	37	39	41	46	52	50	55	72	75	86	127	143	183	259	268
of which: Currency Outside DMBs	14a	28	28	30	34	36	37	41	48	56	64	92	105	143	156	148
Time, Savings,& Fgn.Currency Dep.	15	....	....	....	....	....	....	....	....	....	....	....	....	....	....	....
Restricted Deposits	16b	....	....	....	....	....	....	....	....	....	....	....	....	....	....	....
Foreign Liabilities	16c	—	—	—	—	—	—	5	—	—	10	14	—	51	79	126	146
Long-Term Foreign Liabilities	16cl											33	77	78	86	87	87
Central Government Deposits	16d	—	—	—	—	—	—	—	—	6	1	—	42	2	2	4	41
Capital Accounts	17a	—	4	6	7	7	12	18	24	26	27	29	31	33	35	46
Other Items (Net)	17r	—	−2	−3	−2	−1	−1	−1	1	5	7	25	20	22	34	46
Deposit Money Banks												*Millions of Guyana Dollars:*				
Reserves	20	10	11	10	12	15	11	13	22	16	18	29	29	35	101	114
Foreign Assets	21	17	11	14	4	4	4	5	2	13	14	44	26	21	34	56
Claims on Central Government	22a	8	5	11	22	20	21	38	59	66	64	146	136	187	213	199
Claims on Local Government	22b	—	—	1	1	1	1	1	1	2	3	2	3	4	4	4
Claims on Nonfin.Pub.Enterprises	22c	12	12	8	8	10	12	13	12	20	56	57	76	119	122	173
Claims on Private Sector	22d	31	41	40	54	66	79	84	85	101	106	118	120	113	122	163
Claims on Other Banking Insts.	22f	—	—	3	3	3	3	2	1	2	2	1	4	1	2	2
Demand Deposits	24	17	19	19	21	23	22	26	32	34	60	102	97	127	127	122
Time, Savings,& Fgn.Currency Dep.	25	56	63	72	82	89	99	116	139	167	180	232	257	303	345	408
Restricted Deposits	26b	....	....	—	—	—	—	—	—	—	—	—	—	—	1	1
Foreign Liabilities	26c	4	5	3	4	8	10	10	8	8	15	37	21	27	50	73
Central Government Deposits	26d	—	—	1	1	—	—	—	—	4	4	7	9	9	11	17
Liab. to Other Banking Insts.	26i	....	....	1	3	5	7	10	12	14	10	17	23	19	28	24
Capital Accounts	27a	....	....	—	—	—	1	2	2	3	4	5	5	8	9	14
Other Items (Net)	27r	−2	−5	−9	−7	−7	−7	−9	−10	−9	−11	−1	−17	−15	29	50
Monetary Survey												*Millions of Guyana Dollars:*				
Foreign Assets (Net)	31n	47	35	48	46	37	35	46	68	23	123	263	23	−25	7	−118
Domestic Credit	32	54	71	69	92	116	137	158	182	276	255	321	584	758	845	1,071
Claims on Central Govt. (Net)	32an	11	17	17	26	37	42	58	82	151	88	142	380	522	595	729
Claims on Local Government	32b	—	—	1	1	1	1	1	1	2	3	2	3	4	4	4
Claims on Nonfin.Pub.Enterprises	32c	12	12	8	8	10	12	13	12	20	56	57	76	119	122	173
Claims on Private Sector	32d	31	41	40	54	66	79	84	85	101	106	118	120	113	122	163
Claims on Other Banking Insts.	32f	—	—	3	3	3	3	2	1	2	2	1	4	1	2	2
Money	34	45	47	51	56	61	61	69	83	93	127	199	207	276	290	277
Quasi-Money	35	56	63	72	82	89	99	116	139	167	180	232	257	303	345	408
Restricted Deposits	36b	....	....	—	—	—	—	—	—	—	—	—	—	—	1	1
Long-Term Foreign Liabilities	36cl											33	77	78	86	87	87
Liab. to Other Banking Insts.	36i	....	....	1	3	5	7	10	12	14	10	17	23	19	28	24
Capital Accounts	37a	....	4	6	7	7	13	20	26	29	31	35	36	41	44	60
Other Items (Net)	37r	−1	−4	−12	−10	−8	−8	−10	−10	−4	−4	24	6	7	57	96
Money plus Quasi-Money	35l	102	109	122	138	150	160	185	222	260	307	431	465	579	635	686
Other Banking Institutions												*Millions of Guyana Dollars.*				
Cash	40	....	....	—	—	—	—	1	1	1	—	2	1	1	4	3
Foreign Assets	41	....	....	1	1	1	1	1	1	2	2	2	2	2	4	3
Claims on Central Government	42a	....	....	—	—	—	—	—	1	1	2	5	8	9	7	9
Claims on Local Government	42b	....	....	—	—	—	—	—	—	1	1	1	1	2	1	1
Claims on Private Sector	42d	....	....	7	7	8	9	10	12	15	18	22	27	36	44	51
Claims on Deposit Money Banks	42e	....	....	—	—	—	—	—	—	—	—	—	—	—	—	—
Time, Savings,& Fgn.Currency Dep.	45	....	....	7	7	8	10	12	14	19	22	28	37	48	58	65
Foreign Liabilities	46c	....	....	—	—	—	—	—	—	—	—	—	—	—	—	—
Capital Accounts	47a	....	....	1	1	1	1	1	1	1	2	2	2	2	3	3
Other Items (Net)	47r	....	....	—	—	—	—	—	—	—	—	—	−1	−1	−1	−1

Guyana 336

1980	1981	1982	1983	1984	1985	1986	1987	1988	1989	1990	1991	1992	1993	1994		
End of Period															**Exchange Rates**	
3.3	3.5	3.3	3.1	4.1	4.6	5.4	14.2	13.5	43.4	64.0	174.5	173.3	179.6	208.0	Market Rate	aa
End of Period (ae)		*Period Average (rf)*														
2.6	3.0	3.0	3.0	4.2	4.2	4.4	10.0	10.0	33.0	45.0	122.0	126.0	130.8	142.5	Market Rate	ae
2.6	2.8	3.0	3.0	3.8	4.3	4.3	9.8	10.0	27.2	39.5	111.8	125.0	126.7	138.3	Market Rate	rf
Period Averages																
1,517.2	1,384.4	1,289.5	1,289.5	1,013.6	910.9	905.8	400.2	386.8	184.9	100.0	37.9	30.8	30.5	28.0	Market Rate	ah x
796.4	807.3	833.0	930.6	845.0	841.5	797.0	349.4	355.8	194.9	100.0	47.5	47.7	57.0	61.5	Nominal Effective Exchange Rate	ne c
192.6	208.2	235.9	276.7	282.2	291.6	276.5	142.3	178.8	141.3	100.0	86.2	95.4	104.3	104.5	Real Effective Exchange Rate	re c
End of Period															**Fund Position**	
37.50	37.50	37.50	49.20	49.20	49.20	49.20	49.20	49.20	49.20	49.20	49.20	67.20	67.20	67.20	Quota	2f. s
—	1.04	2.59	—	—	—	—	—	—	—	—	1.49	.99	.24	.05	SDRs	1b. s
—	—	—	—	—	—	—	—	—	—	—	—	—	—	—	Reserve Position in the Fund	1c. s
67.40	85.31	89.07	85.01	84.01	83.01	82.45	81.74	81.74	80.91	79.38	104.46	122.17	128.61	122.26	Total Fund Cred.&Loans Outstg.	2tl
End of Period															**International Liquidity**	
12.70	6.91	10.56	6.49	5.85	6.47	9.00	8.43	4.04	13.35	28.68	124.42	188.08	247.45	247.13	Total Reserves minus Gold	1l. d
—	1.21	2.86	—	—	—	—	—	—	—	—	2.12	1.42	.33	.08	SDRs	1b. d
—	—	—	—	—	—	—	—	—	—	—	—	—	—	—	Reserve Position in the Fund	1c. d
12.70	5.70	7.70	6.49	5.85	6.47	9.00	8.43	4.04	13.35	26.56	123.00	187.75	247.45	247.05	Foreign Exchange	1d. d
80.35	79.46	127.69	210.79	286.19	357.70	384.77	418.61	427.85	605.64	711.78	727.42	729.66	715.25	656.62	Monetary Authorities: Other Liab.	4.. d
23.12	12.16	10.24	9.13	6.93	8.19	9.17	16.05	16.42	23.06	53.38	19.74	29.83	24.40	24.88	Deposit Money Banks: Assets	7a. d
4.44	2.53	1.67	2.30	.40	.76	1.07	.09	.06	.18	.29	.05	2.45	3.81	7.54	of which: Claims on Nonbanks	7ad d
27.49	22.53	25.46	22.16	15.58	15.21	19.77	14.37	14.14	5.73	19.77	7.52	14.64	15.92	20.57	Deposit Money Banks: Liabilities	7b. d
12.77	13.05	15.82	16.94	14.74	14.83	18.94	13.85	11.92	4.79	7.05	3.43	8.90	13.82	17.72	of which: Liab. to Nonbanks	7bd d
1.10	1.05	.60	.66	.52	.58	.55	.27	.40	.12	.12	.16	.57	.87	1.04	Other Banking Insts.: Assets	7e. d
1.10	1.05	.60	.66	.52	.58	.55	.27	.40	.12	.12	.16	.57	.87	1.04	of which: Claims on Nonbanks	7ed d
.26	.26	.24	.23	.09	.12	.23	.22	.23	—	—	—	—	.04	—	Other Banking Insts.: Liabilities	7f. d
.26	.26	.24	.23	.09	.12	.23	.22	.23	—	—	—	—	.04	—	of which: Liab. to Nonbanks	7fd d
End of Period															**Monetary Authorities**	
32	21	32	19	21	27	38	84	40	470	1,328	15,277	23,488	ɪ31,557	35,741	Foreign Assets	11
828	934	1,467	2,026	2,421	3,228	4,252	6,664	10,445	24,199	31,301	68,417	100,839	ɪ109,080	118,849	Claims on Central Government	12a
—	—	—	—	—	—	—	41	94	318	671	801	898	ɪ762	1,098	Claims on Nonfin.Pub.Enterprises	12c
293	377	588	749	960	1,052	1,298	3,111	3,695	3,399	4,016	10,316	15,647	ɪ12,523	16,453	Reserve Money	14
167	186	231	269	336	422	509	726	1,058	1,506	2,211	3,711	5,095	ɪ6,480	8,167	of which: Currency Outside DMBs	14a
—	—	—	—	—	—	8	—	—	8	53	108	278	ɪ378	335	Time, Savings,& Fgn.Currency Dep.	15
—	—	—	—	—	—	8	—	1	30	—	—	84	ɪ—	—	Restricted Deposits	16b
229	265	260	433	909	1,230	1,466	3,806	3,843	18,420	25,171	73,028	78,533	ɪ81,295	79,699	Foreign Liabilities	16c
195	232	380	431	575	582	613	1,398	1,401	4,641	9,800	27,361	27,094	ɪ26,864	27,641	Long-Term Foreign Liabilities	16cl
2	8	13	400	26	5	8	7	-18	31	70	680	1,260	ɪ15,220	22,623	Central Government Deposits	16d
56	72	74	76	92	106	118	249	242	677	977	2,540	2,522	ɪ-1,455	2,345	Capital Accounts	17a
85	—	184	-42	-119	281	772	-1,782	1,413	-2,221	-6,789	-29,538	-193	ɪ6,574	6,591	Other Items (Net)	17r
End of Period															**Deposit Money Banks**	
126	187	361	482	617	628	791	2,433	2,697	1,865	1,802	6,629	10,548	5,503	8,171	Reserves	20
59	36	31	27	29	34	40	161	164	761	2,402	2,409	3,759	3,190	3,546	Foreign Assets	21
216	249	418	578	630	823	1,086	352	731	2,686	4,111	7,227	12,282	20,064	15,651	Claims on Central Government	22a
5	6	5	4	5	4	3	6	4	10	2	2	28	36	—	Claims on Local Government	22b
229	376	306	613	551	838	323	356	552	652	755	359	835	471	188	Claims on Nonfin.Pub.Enterprises	22c
196	263	314	377	463	520	674	987	1,591	2,566	4,160	6,672	8,735	10,254	13,900	Claims on Private Sector	22d
2	4	3	5	2	3	7	6	5	7	1	62	5	28	13	Claims on Other Banking Insts.	22f
136	144	184	219	251	286	337	558	934	1,165	1,918	3,126	3,897	4,902	4,941	Demand Deposits	24
478	584	738	899	1,035	1,270	1,507	2,173	2,733	4,479	6,742	12,003	21,483	25,271	28,764	Time, Savings,& Fgn.Currency Dep.	25
1	1	285	398	458	489	562	641	763	957	916	746	517	368	334	Restricted Deposits	26b
70	68	76	66	65	63	87	144	141	189	890	917	1,845	2,081	2,931	Foreign Liabilities	26c
25	34	32	32	35	60	154	194	248	356	515	1,064	1,612	3,161	3,246	Central Government Deposits	26d
59	63	95	125	166	155	129	356	676	975	1,437	2,840	3,200	2,895	1,356	Liab. to Other Banking Insts.	26i
18	24	39	63	69	93	132	170	247	388	797	1,397	4,045	3,660	3,968	Capital Accounts	27a
47	205	-12	284	217	435	16	64	2	38	20	1,265	-409	-2,792	-4,072	Other Items (Net)	27r
End of Period															**Monetary Survey**	
-208	-275	-274	-452	-924	-1,232	-1,475	-3,705	-3,780	-17,379	-22,331	-56,259	-53,131	ɪ-48,629	-43,344	Foreign Assets (Net)	31n
1,450	1,790	2,467	3,172	4,010	5,352	6,183	8,210	13,191	30,050	40,415	81,796	120,749	ɪ122,314	123,830	Domestic Credit	32
1,018	1,141	1,839	2,172	2,989	3,987	5,177	6,815	10,946	26,497	34,827	73,900	110,249	ɪ110,763	108,630	Claims on Central Govt. (Net)	32an
5	6	5	4	5	4	3	6	4	10	2	2	28	36	—	Claims on Local Government	32b
229	376	306	613	551	838	323	397	646	970	1,426	1,160	1,733	ɪ1,232	1,286	Claims on Nonfin.Pub.Enterprises	32c
196	263	314	377	463	520	674	987	1,591	2,566	4,160	6,672	8,735	10,254	13,900	Claims on Private Sector	32d
2	4	3	5	2	3	7	6	5	7	1	62	5	28	13	Claims on Other Banking Insts.	32f
309	336	421	494	594	714	852	1,291	1,999	2,677	4,136	6,844	8,999	ɪ11,881	13,115	Money	34
478	584	738	899	1,035	1,270	1,515	2,173	2,733	4,487	6,795	12,112	21,762	ɪ25,649	29,100	Quasi-Money	35
1	1	285	398	458	489	570	642	764	987	916	746	601	ɪ368	334	Restricted Deposits	36b
195	232	380	431	575	582	613	1,398	1,401	4,641	9,800	27,361	27,094	ɪ26,864	27,641	Long-Term Foreign Liabilities	36cl
59	63	95	125	166	155	129	356	676	975	1,437	2,840	3,200	2,895	1,356	Liab. to Other Banking Insts.	36i
75	97	113	138	161	199	250	419	489	1,065	1,774	3,937	6,567	ɪ2,205	6,313	Capital Accounts	37a
126	202	161	233	98	711	779	-1,773	1,350	-2,161	-6,773	-28,303	-605	ɪ3,822	2,627	Other Items (Net)	37r
787	920	1,159	1,393	1,629	1,984	2,367	3,464	4,732	7,164	10,930	18,956	30,760	ɪ37,531	42,214	Money plus Quasi-Money	35l
End of Period															**Other Banking Institutions**	
8	10	9	10	17	3	2	21	73	61	95	133	73	165	91	Cash	40
3	3	2	2	2	2	2	3	4	4	6	20	71	113	148	Foreign Assets	41
10	18	27	46	87	161	260	316	339	483	743	1,326	2,146	2,611	3,444	Claims on Central Government	42a
1	1	1	1	1	1	9	9	9	10	12	12	12	18	17	Claims on Local Government	42b
74	86	111	117	115	135	152	204	286	357	479	626	1,300	2,102	2,453	Claims on Private Sector	42d
—	3	5	9	6	8	9	5	7	5	82	178	390	503	73	Claims on Deposit Money Banks	42e
92	114	144	173	220	303	428	538	662	904	1,063	1,633	3,435	4,339	5,254	Time, Savings,& Fgn.Currency Dep.	45
1	1	1	1	—	1	1	2	2	—	—	—	—	5	—	Foreign Liabilities	46c
4	5	5	6	7	10	16	33	54	45	66	130	259	389	616	Capital Accounts	47a
—	2	6	6	2	-3	-11	-15	—	-28	287	531	299	779	357	Other Items (Net)	47r

Guyana

		1965	1966	1967	1968	1969	1970	1971	1972	1973	1974	1975	1976	1977	1978	1979
Banking Survey														*Millions of Guyana Dollars:*		
Foreign Assets (Net)	51n	....	....	49	47	38	36	48	69	24	125	265	25	−23	9	−115
Domestic Credit	52	....	....	73	96	122	144	166	193	291	274	347	616	804	896	1,129
Claims on Central Govt. (Net)	52an	....	....	18	26	37	42	58	83	152	90	147	388	531	602	738
Claims on Local Government	52b	....	....	1	1	1	1	1	1	3	4	3	4	5	6	5
Claims on Nonfin.Pub.Enterprises	52c	....	....	8	8	10	12	13	12	20	56	57	76	119	122	173
Claims on Private Sector	52d	....	....	47	62	74	88	94	97	116	125	139	147	149	166	214
Liquid Liabilities	55l	....	....	129	145	158	170	196	235	278	329	459	501	627	688	747
Restricted Deposits	56b	....	....	—	—	—	—	—	—	—	—	—	—	—	1	1
Long-Term Foreign Liabilities	56cl	....	....	—	—	—	—	—	—	—	33	77	78	86	87	87
Capital Accounts	57a	—	4	7	8	8	14	21	27	30	33	37	38	43	47	62
Other Items (Net)	57r	....	....	−14	−10	−7	−5	−3	—	7	4	39	25	25	82	117
Interest Rates														*Percent Per Annum*		
Discount Rate (End of Period)	60	....	6.0	6.5	6.5	6.5	6.5	6.5	6.5	6.5	6.5	6.5	6.5	6.5	8.5	10.5
Treasury Bill Rate	60c	....	....	....	....	....	....	5.9	5.9	5.9	5.9	5.9	5.9	5.9	7.0	9.1
Deposit Rate	60l	....	....	....	....	....	....	....	....	....	4.0	4.0	4.0	4.0	7.0	9.0
Lending Rate	60p	....	....	....	....	....	....	....	....	....	7.5	7.5	7.5	7.5	9.5	11.5
Prices														*Index Numbers (1990=100):*		
Consumer Prices	64	6.5	6.6	6.8	7.1	7.2	ɪ7.4	7.5	7.8	8.4	9.9	10.7	11.6	12.6	14.5	17.1
International Transactions														*Millions of Guyana Dollars:*		
Exports	70	166.6	186.4	197.5	229.0	252.9	271.9	298.4	306.5	288.0	600.0	858.0	711.3	661.2	753.8	746.4
Imports, cif	71	178.8	202.0	225.3	219.3	235.8	268.2	267.6	297.9	372.6	567.0	810.6	927.4	804.3	711.3	810.1
Imports, fob	71.v	161.7	182.8	204.6	199.3	212.4	241.6	241.6	269.2	336.4	515.4	732.2	843.0	731.1	646.6	736.4
														1990=100		
Volume of Exports	72	107	116	120	119	128	128	132	115	162	170	177	152	125	159	147
Balance of Payments														*Millions of US Dollars:*		
Goods: Exports f.o.b.	78aa d	....	....	....	....	....	....	....	....	....	....	....	....	259.3	295.6	292.7
Goods: Imports f.o.b.	78ab d	....	....	....	....	....	....	....	....	....	....	....	....	−286.7	−253.5	−288.8
Trade Balance	78ac d	....	....	....	....	....	....	....	....	....	....	....	....	−27.4	42.1	3.9
Services: Credit	78ad d	....	....	....	....	....	....	....	....	....	....	....	....	16.2	18.2	18.5
Services: Debit	78ae d	....	....	....	....	....	....	....	....	....	....	....	....	−60.7	−60.1	−71.4
Balance on Goods and Services	78af d	....	....	....	....	....	....	....	....	....	....	....	....	−72.0	.2	−48.9
Income: Credit	78ag d	....	....	....	....	....	....	....	....	....	....	....	....	....	....	3.7
Income: Debit	78ah d	....	....	....	....	....	....	....	....	....	....	....	....	−21.6	−23.3	−38.1
Balance on Goods, Serv., & Inc.	78ai d	....	....	....	....	....	....	....	....	....	....	....	....	−93.6	−23.1	−83.3
Current Transfers, n.i.e.: Credit	78aj d	....	....	....	....	....	....	....	....	....	....	....	....	3.6	3.8	10.2
Current Transfers: Debit	78ak d	....	....	....	....	....	....	....	....	....	....	....	....	−7.5	−10.3	−9.8
Current Account, n.i.e.	78al d	....	....	....	....	....	....	....	....	....	....	....	....	−97.5	−29.6	−82.9
Capital Account, n.i.e.: Credit	78ba d	....	....	....	....	....	....	....	....	....	....	....	....	....	....	....
Capital Account: Debit	78bb d	....	....	....	....	....	....	....	....	....	....	....	....	—	—	—
Capital Account, n.i.e.	78bc d	....	....	....	....	....	....	....	....	....	....	....	....	—	—	—
Direct Investment Abroad	78bd d	....	....	....	....	....	....	....	....	....	....	....	....	—	—	—
Dir. Invest. in Rep. Econ., n.i.e.	78be d	....	....	....	....	....	....	....	....	....	....	....	....	−1.8	—	.6
Portfolio Investment Assets	78bf d	....	....	....	....	....	....	....	....	....	....	....	....	−1.0	−1.5	3.5
Portfolio Investment Liab., n.i.e.	78bg d	....	....	....	....	....	....	....	....	....	....	....	....	—	—	—
Other Investment Assets	78bh d	....	....	....	....	....	....	....	....	....	....	....	....	−3.6	−12.7	−5.3
Other Investment Liab., n.i.e.	78bi d	....	....	....	....	....	....	....	....	....	....	....	....	37.1	48.9	30.3
Financial Account, n.i.e.	78bj d	....	....	....	....	....	....	....	....	....	....	....	....	30.7	34.7	29.2
Net Errors and Omissions	78ca d	....	....	....	....	....	....	....	....	....	....	....	....	9.6	21.4	−8.0
Overall Balance	78cb d	....	....	....	....	....	....	....	....	....	....	....	....	−57.3	26.6	−61.8
Reserves and Related Items	79da d	....	....	....	....	....	....	....	....	....	....	....	....	57.3	−26.6	61.8
Reserve Assets	79db d	....	....	....	....	....	....	....	....	....	....	....	....	11.4	−32.9	44.0
Use of Fund Credit and Loans	79dc d	....	....	....	....	....	....	....	....	....	....	....	....	—	16.4	13.0
Liabs.Constit.For.Auth.Reserves	79dd d	....	....	....	....	....	....	....	....	....	....	....	....	—	—	—
Exceptional Financing	79de d	....	....	....	....	....	....	....	....	....	....	....	....	45.8	−10.0	4.8
Government Finance														*Millions of Guyana Dollars:*		
Deficit (-) or Surplus	80	−18	−20	−17	−21	−28	ɪ−24	−33	−39	−105	−22	−78	−313	−133	−129	−232
Revenue	81	79	86	99	104	113	ɪ143	137	163	176	322	503	399	378	404	465
Grants Received	81z	5	11	8	6	4	ɪ1	4	—	3	1	—	—	2	1	16
Expenditure	82	102	117	124	131	144	ɪ169	173	202	280	340	560	685	513	533	689
Lending Minus Repayments	83	....	....	....	....	....	ɪ—	1	1	4	5	21	27	1	—	24
Financing																
Net Borrowing: Domestic	84a	18	19	5	6	13	ɪ18	−20	33	106	−46	9	225	153	138	173
Foreign	85a	1	6	10	12	13	ɪ7	64	7	41	63	152	126	14	45	52
Use of Cash Balances	87	−2	−5	2	2	1	ɪ—	−11	—	−42	5	−83	−38	−34	−55	7
Debt: Domestic	88a	....	....	....	....	....	ɪ83	113	157	210	189	304	511	692	810	1,014
Foreign	89a	....	....	....	....	....	ɪ70	127	129	241	414	588	700	722	789	879
Debt: Guyana Dollars	88b	42	58	63	73	88	....	....	....	....	....	....	....	....	....	....
Foreign Currency	89b	107	114	124	126	142	....	....	....	....	....	....	....	....	....	....
National Accounts														*Millions of Guyana Dollars:*		
Exports of Goods & Services	90c	200	213	241	264	292	302	329	344	337	652	890	751	711	800	793
Government Consumption	91f	54	59	67	70	80	91	102	117	160	162	233	320	290	296	348
Gross Fixed Capital Formation	93e	70	86	105	96	98	113	103	108	155	198	350	381	290	242	325
Private Consumption	96f	236	255	260	283	303	322	336	363	419	513	562	674	683	712	704
Imports of Goods & Services	98c	−209	−232	−254	−252	−274	−305	−309	−352	−444	−634	−890	−1,034	−886	−800	−930
Gross Domestic Product	99b	362	389	425	459	499	533	561	599	645	955	1,188	1,136	1,125	1,268	1,326
Net Factor Inc/Pmts(-) Abroad	98.n	−27	−33	−33	−30	−42	−43	−36	−22	−32	−49	−33	−61	−67	−56	−73
Gross Nat'l Expenditure = GNP	99a	335	356	392	429	457	491	525	577	613	906	1,155	1,075	1,058	1,212	1,253
Nat'l Income, Market Prices	99e	316	335	370	398	428	457	492	544	577	866	1,108	1,021	998	1,142	1,168
Gross Dom. Prod. 1990 Prices	99b.p	16,715	16,715	18,167	18,211	19,064	19,716	20,271	19,872	20,213	21,626	23,880	24,579	ɪ23,403	22,998	20,311
GDP Deflator (1990=100)	99bi p	2	2	2	3	3	3	3	3	3	4	5	5	5	6	7
														Millions:		
Population	99z	.63	.65	.67	.69	.69	.70	.73	.75	.76	.77	.78	.79	.81	.82	.85

Monetary Authorities: ɪ Beginning in August 1993, data are based on an improved reporting system.
Monetary Survey: ɪ See note to section 10.
Banking Survey: ɪ See note to section 10.

Government Finance: ɪ Data are as reported by the Central Bank of Guyana for publication in *IFS*. Beginning in 1970, data cover consolidated central government.

Guyana

336

	1980	1981	1982	1983	1984	1985	1986	1987	1988	1989	1990	1991	1992	1993	1994		
End of Period																**Banking Survey**	
	−206	−273	−273	−451	−922	−1,230	−1,474	−3,704	−3,778	−17,375	−22,325	−56,240	−53,059	I−48,520	−43,196	Foreign Assets (Net)	51n
	1,534	1,891	2,604	3,331	4,212	5,645	6,598	8,733	13,820	30,893	41,648	83,698	124,202	I127,017	129,731	Domestic Credit	52
	1,028	1,159	1,866	2,218	3,076	4,148	5,437	7,131	11,284	26,980	35,570	75,226	112,395	I113,374	112,074	Claims on Central Govt. (Net)	52an
	6	8	7	5	6	5	13	15	14	20	14	14	40	55	17	Claims on Local Government	52b
	229	376	306	613	551	838	323	397	646	970	1,426	1,160	1,733	I1,232	1,286	Claims on Nonfin.Pub.Enterprises	52c
	271	348	425	494	578	655	826	1,190	1,877	2,923	4,638	7,299	10,035	12,356	16,354	Claims on Private Sector	52d
	870	1,024	1,293	1,556	1,831	2,284	2,793	3,981	5,321	8,007	11,899	20,456	34,122	I41,705	47,377	Liquid Liabilities	55l
	1	1	285	398	458	489	570	642	764	987	916	746	601	I368	334	Restricted Deposits	56b
	195	232	380	431	575	582	613	1,398	1,401	4,641	9,800	27,361	27,094	I26,864	27,641	Long-Term Foreign Liabilities	56cl
	79	102	118	144	168	209	266	452	543	1,110	1,840	4,067	6,826	I2,594	6,930	Capital Accounts	57a
	183	260	254	350	259	852	883	−1,444	2,014	−1,227	−5,133	−25,171	2,499	I6,966	4,253	Other Items (Net)	57r
Percent Per Annum																**Interest Rates**	
	12.5	12.5	14.0	14.0	14.0	14.0	14.0	14.0	14.0	35.0	30.0	32.5	24.3	17.0	20.3	Discount Rate (End of Period)	60
	10.7	11.6	12.3	12.8	12.8	12.8	12.8	11.3	11.0	15.2	30.0	30.9	25.7	16.8	17.7	Treasury Bill Rate	60c
	11.0	11.0	11.6	12.0	12.0	12.0	12.0	11.1	12.0	15.8	29.2	29.5	22.5	12.3	11.4	Deposit Rate	60l
	13.5	13.5	14.4	15.0	15.0	15.0	15.0	15.0	15.1	18.9	32.8	33.6	28.7	19.4	18.4	Lending Rate	60p
Period Averages																**Prices**	
	19.5	23.8	28.8	33.1	41.5	47.7	51.5	66.3	I92.7	96.4	100.0	102.3	104.9	....	....	Consumer Prices	64
Millions of Guyana Dollars																**International Transactions**	
	992.4	974.3	724.0	566.5	807.7	705.6	953.2	2,596.3	2,295.6	6,123.2	10,207.7	28,107.2	36,567.2	52,506.9	63,389.8	Exports	70
	1,009.6	1,208.6	846.4	737.3	821.3	1,053.5	1,030.0	2,590.0	2,156.0	7,012.0	12,290.0	34,274.9	47,762.5	....	....	Imports, cif	71
	917.8	1,098.6	769.4	670.2	746.6	957.7	936.4	2,354.5	1,960.0	6,374.5	11,172.7	31,159.0	43,420.5	....	....	Imports, fob	71.v
1990 = 100																	
	144	142	108	102	110	120	115	117	98	104	100	83	119	172	188	Volume of Exports	72
Minus Sign Indicates Debit																Balance of Payments	
	388.9	346.4	241.4	193.3	216.9	214.0	....	....	....	....	....	....	....	....	....	Goods: Exports f.o.b.	78aa d
	−386.4	−399.6	−254.2	−225.7	−201.6	−209.1	....	....	....	....	....	....	....	....	....	Goods: Imports f.o.b.	78ab d
	2.4	−53.2	−12.7	−32.4	15.2	4.9	....	....	....	....	....	....	....	....	....	Trade Balance	78ac d
	19.8	23.0	22.6	31.5	29.2	48.0	....	....	....	....	....	....	....	....	....	Services: Credit	78ad d
	−107.3	−98.9	−94.5	−98.1	−99.0	−104.0	....	....	....	....	....	....	....	....	....	Services: Debit	78ae d
	−85.1	−129.1	−84.6	−99.0	−54.6	−51.1	....	....	....	....	....	....	....	....	....	Balance on Goods and Services	78af d
	1.9	3.1	.3	.3	.3	—	....	....	....	....	....	....	....	....	....	Income: Credit	78ag d
	−44.5	−57.6	−49.3	−57.8	−44.9	−40.3	....	....	....	....	....	....	....	....	....	Income: Debit	78ah d
	−127.7	−183.7	−133.5	−156.5	−99.3	−91.4	....	....	....	....	....	....	....	....	....	Balance on Goods, Serv., & Inc.	78ai d
	8.9	8.3	3.1	5.1	3.7	2.3	....	....	....	....	....	....	....	....	....	Current Transfers, n.i.e.: Credit	78aj d
	−9.7	−9.1	−11.9	−6.1	−3.4	−7.5	....	....	....	....	....	....	....	....	....	Current Transfers: Debit	78ak d
	−128.5	−184.5	−142.3	−157.5	−98.9	−96.6	....	....	....	....	....	....	....	....	....	Current Account, n.i.e.	78al d
	—	—	—	—	2.6	—	....	....	....	....	....	....	....	....	....	Capital Account, n.i.e.: Credit	78ba d
	—	—	—	—	—	—	....	....	....	....	....	....	....	....	....	Capital Account: Debit	78bb d
	—	—	—	—	2.6	—	....	....	....	....	....	....	....	....	....	Capital Account, n.i.e.	78bc d
	.6	−1.8	4.4	4.7	4.5	1.8	....	....	....	....	....	....	....	....	....	Direct Investment Abroad	78bd d
	2.5	—	—	—	—	—	....	....	....	....	....	....	....	....	....	Dir. Invest. in Rep. Econ.	78be d
	—	—	—	—	—	—	....	....	....	....	....	....	....	....	....	Portfolio Investment Assets	78bf d
	−1.1	9.8	−1.4	1.1	−.4	−1.2	....	....	....	....	....	....	....	....	....	Portfolio Investment Liab., n.i.e.	78bg d
	20.4	−25.8	−64.6	−137.3	−32.7	−38.2	....	....	....	....	....	....	....	....	....	Other Investment Assets	78bh d
	22.4	−17.7	−61.6	−131.4	−28.6	−37.6	....	....	....	....	....	....	....	....	....	Other Investment Liab., n.i.e.	78bi d
	.1	−10.8	43.4	58.1	−12.7	−4.3	....	....	....	....	....	....	....	....	....	Financial Account, n.i.e.	78bj d
	−106.0	−213.1	−160.5	−230.9	−137.6	−138.6	....	....	....	....	....	....	....	....	....	Net Errors and Omissions	78ca d
	106.0	213.1	160.5	230.9	137.6	138.6	....	....	....	....	....	....	....	....	....	Overall Balance	78cb d
	8.2	10.6	−3.5	4.0	−22.9	−3.5	....	....	....	....	....	....	....	....	....	Reserves and Related Items	79da d
	35.1	21.0	3.9	−4.4	−1.0	−1.0	....	....	....	....	....	....	....	....	....	Reserve Assets	79db d
	—	—	—	—	—	—	....	....	....	....	....	....	....	....	....	Use of Fund Credit and Loans	79dc d
	—	—	—	—	—	—	....	....	....	....	....	....	....	....	....	Liabs.Constit.For.Auth.Reserves	79dd d
	62.7	181.5	160.1	231.2	161.5	143.1	....	....	....	....	....	....	....	....	....	Exceptional Financing	79de d
Year Ending December 31																**Government Finance**	
	−440	−589	−958	−592	−693	−1,036	−1,234	−1,353	−1,235	−570	−3,584	−2,433	−3,975	....	....	Deficit (−) or Surplus	80
	527	644	624	630	714	846	1,094	1,293	1,804	3,383	5,671	11,930	17,192	....	....	Revenue	81
	13	3	3	1	51	31	26	70	59	1,065	1,982	1,067	165	....	....	Grants Received	81z
	906	1,154	1,509	1,141	1,457	1,913	2,353	2,716	3,098	5,017	11,237	15,430	21,332	....	....	Expenditure	82
	74	82	76	82	—	—	—	—	—	—	—	—	—	....	....	Lending Minus Repayments	83
Financing																	
	347	377	784	348	778	1,300	2,247	−2,017	4,419	2,619	852	1,050	1,784	....	....	Net Borrowing: Domestic	84a
	93	282	51	91	43	59	123	97	−167	609	−1,775	−256	1,889	....	....	Foreign	85a
	—	−70	122	153	−129	−323	−1,135	3,272	−3,017	−2,659	4,506	1,639	303	....	....	Use of Cash Balances	87
	1,637	1,808	2,763	3,810	4,531	5,359	6,215	7,030	7,378	9,824	9,743	12,272	18,198	....	....	Debt: Domestic	88a
	2,039	2,238	2,038	2,104	2,889	3,136	3,635	9,138	8,952	35,858	55,202	136,523	237,258	....	....	Foreign	89a
	....	....	....	....	....	....	....	....	....	....	....	....	....	....	....	Debt: Guyana Dollars	88b
	....	....	....	....	....	....	....	....	....	....	....	....	....	....	....	Foreign Currency	89b
Millions of Guyana Dollars																**National Accounts**	
	1,042	974	723	587	831	911	977	2,684	2,353	6,232	10,599	29,831	47,697	52,160	....	Exports of Goods & Services	90c
	436	470	435	488	550	700	876	952	1,162	1,701	2,133	4,610	6,357	7,377	....	Government Consumption	91f
	404	500	380	395	390	410	586	1,123	890	3,536	6,624	13,746	25,113	30,118	....	Gross Fixed Capital Formation	93e
	796	922	876	879	929	1,055	1,000	1,715	2,279	5,987	9,537	21,504	23,525	29,134	....	Private Consumption	96f
	−1,215	−1,375	−1,037	−973	−1,152	−1,243	−1,335	−3,518	−3,698	−11,603	−20,219	−28,196	−39,564	−61,376	....	Imports of Goods & Services	98c
	1,508	1,597	1,446	1,468	1,700	1,964	2,220	3,357	4,137	10,330	15,665	38,966	46,734	56,647	....	Gross Domestic Product	99b
	−83	−151	−156	−172	−182	−245	−283	−606	−869	−2,790	−4,239	−15,093	−8,257	9,982	....	Net Factor Inc/Pmts(−) Abroad	98.n
	1,425	1,446	1,290	1,296	1,518	1,719	1,936	2,551	3,269	7,540	11,426	23,873	38,447	46,665	....	Gross Nat'l Expenditure = GNP	99a
	1,330	1,343	1,172	1,166	1,393	1,731	1,802	2,411	3,127	7,739	11,206	23,873	38,447	46,665	....	Nat'l Income, Market Prices	99e
	20,644	20,581	18,438	16,731	17,085	17,252	I17,293	17,440	16,991	16,434	15,665	16,609	17,897	19,370	....	Gross Dom. Prod. 1990 Prices	99b.p
	7	8	8	9	10	11	13	19	24	63	100	235	261	292	....	GDP Deflator (1990=100)	99bi p
Midyear Estimates																	
	.87	.77	.77	.78	.79	.79	.79	.79	.79	.79	.80	.80	.81	.82	....	Population	99z

Haiti

		1965	1966	1967	1968	1969	1970	1971	1972	1973	1974	1975	1976	1977	1978	1979
Exchange Rates														*Gourdes per SDR: End of Period (aa)*		
Market Rate	aa	5.0000	5.0000	5.0000	5.0000	5.0000	5.0000	5.4285	5.4285	6.0317	6.1217	5.8533	5.8091	6.0736	6.5139	6.5866
Market Rate	ae	5.00	5.00	5.00	5.00	5.00	5.00	5.00	5.00	5.00	5.00	5.00	5.00	5.00	5.00	5.00
Fund Position															*Millions of SDRs:*	
Quota	2f. s	11.3	15.0	15.0	15.0	15.0	19.0	19.0	19.0	19.0	19.0	19.0	19.0	19.0	23.0	23.0
SDRs	1b. s	—	—	—	—	—	—	1.1	3.1	1.7	2.5	2.0	1.2	1.6	3.8	5.5
Reserve Position in the Fund	1c. s	—	—	—	—	—	2.5	2.9	.2	—	—	—	—	—	2.4	4.4
Total Fund Cred.&Loans Outstg.	2tl	6.2	6.4	7.7	5.7	5.1	2.2	.8	—	—	6.6	11.0	12.4	10.5	15.5	19.3
International Liquidity													*Millions of US Dollars Unless Otherwise Indicated:*			
Total Reserves minus Gold	1l. d	1.4	2.2	1.9	2.5	3.5	4.3	10.4	17.9	17.0	19.7	12.4	27.9	33.8	38.6	55.0
SDRs	1b. d	—	—	—	—	—	—	1.2	3.3	2.0	3.0	2.3	1.4	1.9	5.0	7.2
Reserve Position in the Fund	1c. d	—	—	—	—	—	—	2.7	3.2	.2	—	—	—	—	3.1	5.8
Foreign Exchange	1d. d	1.4	2.2	1.9	2.5	3.5	4.3	6.5	11.4	14.8	16.7	10.1	26.5	31.9	30.6	42.0
Gold (Million Fine Troy Ounces)	1ad	....	....	....	....	....	....	....	....	....	.002	.002	.002	.006	.010	.018
Gold (National Valuation)	1an d	.8	.1	.1	.1	.1	.1	.1	.1	.1	.1	.1	.1	.4	.4	9.3
Monetary Authorities: Other Liab.	4.. d	1.6	2.1	1.9	2.3	3.1	5.1	5.4	6.2	7.0	7.4	17.9	33.2	57.2	72.3	85.3
Deposit Money Banks: Assets	7a. d	.3	.2	.2	.1	.6	.5	1.2	3.5	2.4	3.0	5.5	5.3	8.9	6.0	8.8
Liabilities	7b. d	.3	.6	.8	1.8	.9	.5	—	—	4.7	17.0	23.0	19.6	16.8	16.2	13.3
Monetary Authorities															*Millions of Gourdes:*	
Foreign Assets	11	10.9	10.4	9.9	10.4	16.9	20.1	49.6	92.1	84.5	98.8	62.6	140.0	171.1	193.1	295.0
Claims on Central Government	12a	152.8	151.7	182.3	195.5	202.3	201.2	212.9	216.0	242.5	306.3	446.1	534.1	754.6	739.2	793.4
Claims on Nonfin.Pub.Enterprises	12c	4.7	7.0	7.4	8.0	11.8	22.5	26.5	32.2	46.0	61.9	161.4	243.8	298.6	358.8	421.1
Claims on Private Sector	12d	31.8	30.4	32.5	34.2	35.4	34.7	41.3	57.8	84.8	111.3	149.2	184.6	226.9	370.6	315.7
Claims on Deposit Money Banks	12e	—	.4	1.0	1.5	2.6	3.8	3.1	3.3	10.1	19.6	15.7	20.8	39.0	50.8	79.2
Claims on Other Banking Insts.	12f	7.3	7.4	6.8	6.5	6.2	9.0	9.0	9.8	11.2	12.8	11.0	12.4	12.4	10.2	16.6
Reserve Money	14	121.3	113.8	128.3	154.2	170.2	183.3	210.6	256.5	305.0	319.0	396.7	548.8	649.5	717.7	804.6
of which: Currency Outside DMBs	14a	83.5	79.4	88.1	94.0	105.0	114.6	126.1	147.7	172.9	182.7	189.5	243.2	265.5	311.4	418.5
Time and Savings Deposits	15	15.2	13.7	13.6	16.4	19.3	23.8	31.6	41.2	55.1	74.1	82.2	107.1	135.1	168.6	168.9
Foreign Liabilities	16c	31.0	33.3	38.5	28.8	26.9	11.2	4.4	2.0	2.7	45.6	66.4	76.0	56.3	55.9	46.7
Long-Term Foreign Liabilities	16cl	8.0	9.1	9.4	11.0	13.9	25.5	27.1	28.8	32.1	32.2	87.3	161.9	293.2	406.7	507.1
Central Government Deposits	16d	10.7	11.5	24.7	20.4	19.2	16.4	13.8	14.2	14.6	59.0	141.7	174.4	259.1	295.6	268.6
Capital Accounts	17a	17.1	17.3	17.3	18.6	19.9	33.6	47.6	62.1	71.3	75.7	77.0	87.5	103.3	120.8	156.0
Other Items (Net)	17r	4.2	8.5	8.1	6.7	5.8	-2.4	7.3	6.4	-1.7	5.1	-5.3	-20.1	6.1	-42.5	-30.9
Deposit Money Banks															*Millions of Gourdes:*	
Reserves	20	14.2	14.4	16.3	20.3	17.7	20.1	31.9	42.6	58.8	74.2	124.1	159.6	191.4	214.3	241.7
Foreign Assets	21	1.5	.9	.9	.7	2.8	2.4	6.1	17.7	12.2	14.9	27.5	26.4	44.3	30.0	44.1
Claims on Central Government	22a	.5	.8	—	—	2.5	3.6	2.5	2.5	2.5	22.0	27.2	27.1	26.3	25.5	—
Claims on Private Sector	22d	31.1	31.6	38.2	31.7	37.5	42.8	43.9	65.4	143.3	255.4	331.3	419.2	480.6	598.5	672.5
Demand Deposits	24	23.0	21.0	28.5	27.9	25.4	27.3	33.8	52.6	75.8	91.3	110.9	135.6	155.7	183.4	186.7
Time and Savings Deposits	25	22.6	24.4	22.9	24.4	29.5	34.2	43.8	69.1	99.4	167.1	250.1	358.5	452.6	545.1	602.9
Foreign Liabilities	26c	1.5	3.2	4.0	8.9	4.6	2.5	—	—	23.4	84.7	114.7	97.9	83.8	81.1	66.6
Central Government Deposits	26d	—	—	—	—	3.9	3.9	3.9	3.9	3.9	3.9	11.4	11.4	11.4	11.4	11.4
Credit from Monetary Authorities	26g	—	—	1.0	1.0	3.0	3.2	2.9	3.1	5.4	7.9	11.1	12.7	25.1	27.2	50.4
Capital Accounts	27a	3.1	3.6	3.4	6.7	7.6	7.7	7.7	6.8	18.5	24.1	28.9	29.4	30.9	40.4	31.5
Other Items (Net)	27r	-2.9	-4.6	-4.5	-16.1	-13.6	-10.0	-7.7	-7.4	-9.7	-12.6	-17.1	-13.2	-16.7	-20.4	8.8
Monetary Survey															*Millions of Gourdes:*	
Foreign Assets (Net)	31n	-20.1	-25.2	-31.7	-26.5	-11.8	8.8	51.3	107.7	70.5	-16.6	-91.1	-7.5	75.4	86.1	225.9
Domestic Credit	32	217.5	217.4	242.5	255.6	272.5	293.5	318.4	365.7	511.8	706.9	973.0	1,235.5	1,528.9	1,795.7	1,939.3
Claims on Central Govt. (Net)	32an	142.6	141.0	157.6	175.1	181.6	184.5	197.7	200.4	226.5	265.4	320.1	375.5	510.4	457.7	513.4
Claims on Nonfin.Pub.Enterprises	32c	4.7	7.0	7.4	8.0	11.8	22.5	26.5	32.2	46.0	61.9	161.4	243.8	298.6	358.8	421.1
Claims on Private Sector	32d	62.9	62.0	70.7	65.9	72.9	77.5	85.2	123.2	228.1	366.7	480.5	603.8	707.6	969.0	988.2
Claims on Other Banking Insts.	32f	7.3	7.4	6.8	6.5	6.2	9.0	9.0	9.8	11.2	12.8	11.0	12.4	12.4	10.2	16.6
Money	34	133.4	123.2	142.2	160.0	175.6	190.6	214.6	271.2	332.8	342.4	402.6	549.6	629.1	717.8	802.5
Quasi-Money	35	37.9	38.1	36.5	40.8	48.8	58.0	75.4	110.3	154.5	241.3	332.2	465.6	587.8	713.7	771.8
Long-Term Foreign Liabilities	36cl	8.0	9.1	9.4	11.4	14.0	25.6	27.2	28.9	32.2	32.3	87.4	161.9	293.2	406.7	507.1
Capital Accounts	37a	20.2	20.9	20.7	25.4	27.5	41.2	55.3	68.9	89.8	99.8	105.8	117.0	134.2	161.2	187.5
Other Items (Net)	37r	-2.1	.9	2.0	-8.5	-5.2	-13.3	-2.9	-6.0	-27.0	-25.6	-46.1	-66.2	-39.9	-117.5	-103.8
Money plus Quasi-Money	35l	171.2	161.4	178.7	200.8	224.4	248.6	290.0	381.6	487.3	583.7	734.8	1,015.2	1,216.8	1,431.5	1,574.4
Other Banking Institutions															*Millions of Gourdes:*	
Cash	40	11.0	10.0	11.1	10.5	5.6	5.4	3.7	4.4	5.4	7.8	3.8	11.3	11.7	11.5	11.1
Claims on Private Sector	42d	8.5	12.0	13.0	14.5	16.9	21.1	24.3	23.7	25.6	26.7	31.1	32.4	57.0	44.6	52.9
Credit from Monetary Authorities	46g	7.3	7.4	6.8	6.5	6.2	9.0	8.3	8.7	8.5	11.7	12.5	14.0	14.6	12.4	14.3
Capital Accounts	47a	13.2	12.5	14.1	15.3	12.9	13.6	14.9	17.1	18.0	21.0	22.7	28.2	41.1	47.3	63.0
Other Items (Net)	47r	-1.0	2.2	3.3	3.2	3.3	4.0	4.8	2.2	4.5	1.8	-.4	1.6	13.1	-3.6	-13.3
Prices															*Index Numbers (1990=100):*	
Consumer Prices	64	17.4	18.8	18.3	18.5	18.8	19.0	20.9	21.5	26.4	30.4	35.5	38.0	40.4	39.4	44.5
International Transactions															*Millions of Gourdes*	
Exports	70	183.7	177.5	168.3	178.1	186.1	201.8	236.6	220.0	263.6	357.7	398.8	621.7	742.8	776.7	926.9
Imports, cif	71	168.1	188.1	182.0	187.9	194.2	275.0	302.1	344.6	415.7	626.0	744.8	1,033.7	1,063.3	1,166.0	1,360.4
Imports, fob	71..v	149.8	169.2	159.6	164.8	170.4	241.2	260.4	297.1	358.4	539.7	639.3	872.3	915.1	1,000.0	1,180.9

Haiti

	1980	1981	1982	1983	1984	1985	1986	1987	1988	1989	1990	1991	1992	1993	1994		
	Gourdes per US Dollar: End of Period (ae)															**Exchange Rates**	
	6.3770	5.8198	5.5155	5.2347	4.9011	5.4921	6.1160	7.0933	6.7285	6.5708	7.1133	Ɪ11.7867	15.0604	17.5884	18.9001	Market Rate	aa
	5.00	5.00	5.00	5.00	5.00	5.00	5.00	5.00	5.00	5.00	5.00	Ɪ8.24	10.95	12.81	12.95	Market Rate	ae
	End of Period															**Fund Position**	
	34.5	34.5	34.5	44.1	44.1	44.1	44.1	44.1	44.1	44.1	44.1	44.1	44.1	44.1	44.1	Quota	2f. s
	—	—	1.0	1.0	—	—	5.4	—	—	.1	—	—	—	—	—	SDRs	1b. s
	—	—	.1	.1	.1	.1	.1	.1	.1	.1	.1	.1	.1	—	—	Reserve Position in the Fund	1c. s
	35.7	50.6	61.4	90.1	102.3	87.4	72.8	51.1	33.8	30.6	25.5	23.8	23.8	23.8	3.8	Total Fund Cred.&Loans Outstg.	2tl
	End of Period															**International Liquidity**	
	16.2	24.0	4.2	9.0	13.0	6.4	15.9	17.0	13.0	12.6	3.2	17.3	....	....	—	Total Reserves minus Gold	1l. d
	—	—	1.0	1.0	—	—	6.6	—	—	.1	—	—	—	—	—	SDRs	1b. d
	—	—	.1	.1	.1	.1	.1	.1	.1	.1	.1	.1	.1	.1	.1	Reserve Position in the Fund	1c. d
	16.2	24.0	3.1	7.9	12.9	6.3	9.2	16.9	12.9	12.4	3.1	17.2	....	....	....	Foreign Exchange	1d. d
	.018	.018	.018	.018	.018	.018	.018	.018	.018	.018	.018	.018	....	....	....	Gold (Million Fine Troy Ounces)	1ad
	9.3	7.1	6.2	6.2	6.2	6.2	7.5	7.5	7.1	6.6	....	....	....	....	....	Gold (National Valuation)	1and
	91.0	102.5	112.5	125.1	141.2	125.3	142.6	157.2	171.8	176.8	4.8	4.8	9.0	9.7	7.0	Monetary Authorities: Other Liab.	4..d
	20.7	46.5	19.4	26.5	29.8	30.0	30.2	23.4	23.1	17.1	42.4	32.4	54.0	78.3	....	Deposit Money Banks: Assets	7a. d
	13.2	12.3	15.4	11.9	8.7	....	2.4	1.6	1.6	8.5	20.3	.5	—	—	....	Liabilities	7b. d
	End of Period															**Monetary Authorities**	
	149.4	190.3	116.4	133.3	145.8	104.2	180.1	182.0	162.5	209.6	100.1	75.9	152.9	236.8	834.0	Foreign Assets	11
	1,094.1	1,382.3	1,549.0	2,183.1	2,204.3	2,199.9	2,700.0	2,769.8	2,848.8	2,876.1	3,243.4	3,397.2	3,985.1	4,394.6	5,860.7	Claims on Central Government	12a
	597.9	626.5	522.5	514.3	514.9	496.3	287.8	278.3	397.2	382.1	296.8	283.8	348.7	426.5	328.1	Claims on Nonfin.Pub.Enterprises	12c
	346.0	394.1	374.5	266.6	314.5	363.9	336.0	338.0	291.2	323.2	—	—	—	—	—	Claims on Private Sector	12d
	53.5	53.2	69.7	35.2	25.2	26.3	7.4	8.3	5.6	9.2	22.3	5.4	331.9	754.6	415.6	Claims on Deposit Money Banks	12e
	15.9	31.7	36.5	43.6	48.9	35.2	73.2	73.0	71.4	70.5	15.0	10.0	—	—	—	Claims on Other Banking Insts.	12f
	994.3	1,157.0	1,169.7	1,153.1	1,397.9	1,569.7	1,809.1	2,174.8	1,595.5	2,629.4	3,081.7	3,356.7	4,346.1	5,616.6	6,954.9	Reserve Money	14
	418.1	487.4	565.6	599.5	691.0	763.2	829.1	979.5	205.0	1,458.8	1,382.3	1,544.6	2,074.5	2,668.8	3,029.5	*of which:* Currency Outside DMBs	14a
	175.2	208.4	223.4	260.9	277.9	366.4	375.4	412.4	400.0	430.8	—	—	—	—	—	Time and Savings Deposits	15
	116.4	201.5	255.4	392.0	481.9	408.7	388.2	354.6	267.3	241.7	205.1	320.6	456.9	543.7	136.0	Foreign Liabilities	16c
	565.8	605.2	646.0	704.9	725.3	697.9	769.9	793.7	818.9	843.0	—	—	—	—	560.6	Long-Term Foreign Liabilities	16cl
	190.6	226.3	186.3	203.2	218.3	462.8	586.0	427.5	586.6	212.6	407.7	428.0	457.3	481.3	892.7	Central Government Deposits	16d
	237.8	229.7	210.6	167.4	286.5	181.1	165.0	216.9	227.0	259.1	232.5	316.4	411.4	472.2	564.0	Capital Accounts	17a
	-23.2	50.1	-22.8	294.6	-134.2	-460.6	-509.1	-730.4	-118.4	-746.0	-249.4	-649.4	-853.1	-1,301.3	-1,669.7	Other Items (Net)	17r
	End of Period															**Deposit Money Banks**	
	325.8	344.9	359.5	363.9	601.1	610.8	637.4	808.1	751.3	865.9	1,517.0	1,736.9	2,420.8	3,059.1	3,718.1	Reserves	20
	103.4	232.5	97.1	132.4	149.0	150.0	151.0	117.0	115.6	85.3	212.2	266.6	592.0	1,002.7	1,243.6	Foreign Assets	21
	.5	—	3.0	2.5	40.9	27.5	26.7	17.8	28.4	31.6	12.3	11.7	11.5	8.0	114.1	Claims on Central Government	22a
	726.0	816.4	858.1	850.2	884.6	885.4	886.0	957.1	1,250.5	1,503.3	1,800.6	1,862.2	2,100.2	2,516.3	3,253.2	Claims on Private Sector	22d
	224.0	295.2	318.2	357.2	384.4	512.6	544.2	658.6	715.7	767.2	920.2	1,062.5	1,199.9	1,429.6	1,578.0	Demand Deposits	24
	817.6	800.1	859.4	912.0	990.7	1,045.3	1,111.2	1,183.3	1,277.7	1,494.4	2,371.2	2,764.5	3,671.8	4,944.8	6,486.8	Time and Savings Deposits	25
	66.2	61.6	77.1	59.4	43.7	51.4	11.8	8.2	7.9	42.5	101.5	3.8	.5	.3	10.7	Foreign Liabilities	26c
	—	4.1	4.1	3.9	3.9	3.9	3.9	3.9	—	—	50.9	31.0	26.3	27.0	27.6	Central Government Deposits	26d
	23.9	41.8	10.6	42.5	33.7	17.7	25.0	18.6	33.6	73.5	—	—	—	—	—	Credit from Monetary Authorities	26g
	33.5	290.1	305.5	293.8	339.2	325.5	314.1	344.7	460.9	515.1	221.3	199.1	269.7	320.9	395.7	Capital Accounts	27a
	-9.7	-96.0	-257.6	-274.3	-120.0	-282.9	-309.0	-317.3	-350.1	-406.7	-123.0	-183.5	-43.7	-136.5	-169.7	Other Items (Net)	27r
	End of Period															**Monetary Survey**	
	70.1	159.8	-118.9	-185.7	-230.9	-205.9	-68.6	-63.9	2.9	10.7	5.7	18.1	287.5	695.5	1,370.3	Foreign Assets (Net)	31n
	2,589.7	3,023.7	3,152.7	3,698.6	3,786.0	3,541.5	3,719.8	4,002.7	4,301.0	4,974.2	4,909.5	5,105.9	5,961.9	6,837.1	8,441.0	Domestic Credit	32
	904.0	1,154.9	1,361.1	2,024.0	2,023.0	1,760.7	2,136.9	2,356.3	2,290.6	2,695.1	2,797.1	2,949.9	3,513.0	3,894.3	4,861.4	Claims on Central Govt. (Net)	32an
	597.9	626.5	522.5	514.3	514.9	496.3	287.8	278.3	397.2	382.1	296.8	283.8	348.7	426.5	326.3	Claims on Nonfin.Pub.Enterprises	32c
	1,071.9	1,210.6	1,232.6	1,116.7	1,199.1	1,249.3	1,222.0	1,295.2	1,541.7	1,826.5	1,800.6	1,862.2	2,100.2	2,516.3	3,253.2	Claims on Private Sector	32d
	15.9	31.7	36.5	43.6	48.9	35.2	73.2	73.0	71.4	70.5	15.0	10.0	—	—	—	Claims on Other Banking Insts.	32f
	945.4	1,166.5	1,164.3	1,174.7	1,388.0	1,588.7	1,789.9	2,097.9	1,635.2	2,633.6	2,302.5	2,464.4	3,150.1	3,866.4	5,095.5	Money	34
	992.8	1,008.5	1,082.7	1,172.9	1,268.6	1,411.7	1,486.7	1,595.7	1,677.0	1,925.3	2,371.2	2,764.5	3,671.8	4,944.8	6,486.8	Quasi-Money	35
	565.8	605.2	646.0	704.9	725.3	697.9	769.9	793.7	818.9	843.0	—	—	—	—	560.6	Long-Term Foreign Liabilities	36cl
	271.3	519.8	516.1	461.2	625.7	506.6	479.1	561.6	687.9	774.2	453.8	515.5	681.1	793.1	937.3	Capital Accounts	37a
	-115.5	-116.5	-375.3	-.8	-452.5	-869.3	-874.5	-1,110.1	-515.8	-1,191.2	-212.3	-620.4	-1,253.6	-2,071.7	-3,269.0	Other Items (Net)	37r
	1,938.2	2,175.0	2,247.0	2,347.6	2,656.6	3,000.4	3,276.5	3,693.6	3,312.9	4,558.8	4,673.7	5,228.9	6,821.9	8,811.2	11,582.4	Money plus Quasi-Money	35l
	End of Period															**Other Banking Institutions**	
	-2.8	8.8	9.9	14.8	4.5	4.5	3.3	....	....	....	....	....	....	....	....	Cash	40
	361.3	96.3	68.9	85.6	105.5	....	....	....	....	....	....	....	....	....	....	Claims on Private Sector	42d
	17.8	32.5	50.8	60.9	55.5	54.8	58.2	....	....	....	....	....	....	....	....	Credit from Monetary Authorities	46g
	52.2	51.6	31.0	40.5	58.2	87.8	28.6	5.3	3.2	....	....	....	....	....	....	Capital Accounts	47a
	288.5	34.8	-3.0	-1.0	-3.7	....	....	....	....	....	....	....	....	....	....	Other Items (Net)	47r
	Period Averages															**Prices**	
	Ɪ52.4	58.1	62.4	68.8	73.2	81.0	83.7	74.1	77.1	82.5	100.0	Ɪ115.4	137.8	168.8	240.7	Consumer Prices	64
	Millions of Gourdes															**International Transactions**	
	1,131.0	757.5	888.4	830.0	896.0	842.0	922.2	1,067.7	896.4	720.3	791.5	1,094.8	823.0	1,137.6	929.9	Exports	70
	1,770.7	2,239.8	1,936.4	2,202.6	2,360.7	2,207.8	1,799.9	1,995.9	1,721.3	1,455.0	1,394.7	2,532.2	3,208.1	2,925.5	4,315.0	Imports, cif	71
	1,539.7	1,947.7	1,683.8	1,915.3	2,052.8	1,919.8	1,565.1	1,735.6	1,496.8	1,265.2	1,212.7	2,201.9	2,789.6	2,543.9	3,752.2	Imports, fob	71.v

Haiti
263

		1965	1966	1967	1968	1969	1970	1971	1972	1973	1974	1975	1976	1977	1978	1979
Balance of Payments														*Millions of US Dollars: F.Y. Ending*		
Goods: Exports f.o.b.	78aa d	....	....	....	....	....	....	45.3	42.9	54.4	70.0	80.3	111.9	137.6	149.9	138.0
Goods: Imports f.o.b.	78ab d	....	....	....	....	....	....	-53.2	-57.6	-66.5	-96.5	-122.1	-158.7	-199.9	-207.5	-220.1
Trade Balance	78ac d	....	....	....	....	....	....	-7.9	-14.7	-12.1	-26.5	-41.8	-46.7	-62.3	-57.5	-82.1
Services: Credit	78ad d	....	....	....	....	....	....	18.8	21.0	21.6	21.8	25.6	28.8	36.4	61.3	74.9
Services: Debit	78ae d	....	....	....	....	....	....	-21.7	-22.2	-27.5	-34.2	-37.3	-52.8	-63.1	-101.6	-107.9
Balance on Goods and Services	78af d	....	....	....	....	....	....	-10.8	-15.9	-18.0	-38.9	-53.5	-70.8	-89.0	-97.9	-115.0
Income: Credit	78ag d	....	....	....	....	....	....	—	—	.2	.2	.3	1.0	1.3	2.0	2.6
Income: Debit	78ah d	....	....	....	....	....	....	-4.0	-5.4	-6.6	-8.1	-7.4	-8.1	-13.4	-16.7	-16.0
Balance on Goods, Serv., & Inc.	78ai d	....	....	....	....	....	....	-14.8	-21.3	-24.3	-46.7	-60.6	-77.9	-101.0	-112.5	-128.4
Current Transfers, n.i.e.: Credit	78aj d	....	....	....	....	....	....	25.1	32.7	33.3	36.5	76.9	111.8	107.4	114.9	126.3
Current Transfers: Debit	78ak d	....	....	....	....	....	....	-5.3	-3.1	-7.9	-10.8	-40.8	-46.5	-44.1	-47.3	-50.7
Current Account, n.i.e.	78al d	....	....	....	....	....	....	5.0	8.2	1.2	-21.0	-24.5	-12.5	-37.7	-44.9	-52.8
Capital Account, n.i.e.: Credit	78ba d	....	....	....	....	....	....	—	—	—	—	—	—	—	—	—
Capital Account: Debit	78bb d	....	....	....	....	....	....	-.8	-1.0	-1.1	-1.0	-.3	-.4	—	—	—
Capital Account, n.i.e.	78bc d	....	....	....	....	....	....	-.8	-1.0	-1.1	-1.0	-.3	-.4	—	—	—
Direct Investment Abroad	78bd d	....	....	....	....	....	....	—	—	—	—	—	—	—	—	—
Dir. Invest. in Rep. Econ., n.i.e.	78be d	....	....	....	....	....	....	3.4	4.1	7.0	7.9	2.6	7.8	8.0	10.0	12.0
Portfolio Investment Assets	78bf d	....	....	....	....	....	....	—	—	—	—	—	—	—	—	—
Portfolio Investment Liab., n.i.e.	78bg d	....	....	....	....	....	....	—	—	—	—	—	—	—	—	—
Other Investment Assets	78bh d	....	....	....	....	....	....	-1.0	-1.5	2.0	-1.8	-1.1	-2.7	.7	-3.0	3.5
Other Investment Liab., n.i.e.	78bi d	....	....	....	....	....	....	-.5	7.5	-1.6	14.9	32.3	21.4	58.6	29.4	44.3
Financial Account, n.i.e.	78bj d	....	....	....	....	....	....	1.9	10.0	7.4	21.1	33.8	26.5	67.3	36.4	59.8
Net Errors and Omissions	78ca d	....	....	....	....	....	....	-.3	-10.6	-10.7	-10.3	-17.7	-2.6	-19.7	15.5	-6.6
Overall Balance	78cb d	....	....	....	....	....	....	5.8	6.6	-3.2	-11.2	-8.6	11.0	9.8	7.0	.4
Reserves and Related Items	79da d	....	....	....	....	....	....	-5.8	-6.6	3.2	11.2	8.6	-11.0	-9.8	-7.0	-.4
Reserve Assets	79db d	....	....	....	....	....	....	-4.4	-5.7	3.2	3.2	3.3	-12.8	-7.9	-13.5	-5.7
Use of Fund Credit and Loans	79dc d	....	....	....	....	....	....	-1.4	-.9	—	7.9	5.3	1.7	-2.2	6.2	5.0
Liabs.Constit.For.Auth.Reserves	79dd d	....	....	....	....	....	....	—	—	—	—	—	—	—	—	—
Exceptional Financing	79de d	....	....	....	....	....	....	—	—	—	—	—	.1	.2	.2	.3
Government Finance														*Millions of Gourdes:*		
Deficit (-) or Surplus	80	....	....	-19.3	-.7	-12.7	-3.9	-9.8	2.5	1.2	-10.4	-42.2	-64.2	-143.3	-168.2	-168.0
Revenue	81	....	....	155.4	184.1	197.4	225.0	263.3	278.8	302.5	333.3	475.3	644.3	784.5	986.9	623.3
Grants Received	81z	....	....	....	....	....	....	....	....	....	....	....	....	....	....	....
Expenditure	82	....	....	174.7	184.8	210.1	228.9	273.1	276.3	301.3	343.7	517.5	708.5	927.8	1,155.1	791.3
Financing																
Net Domestic Borrowing	84a	....	....	28.4	10.3	11.4	6.3	15.4	2.8	5.0	20.7	54.5	31.8	45.0	36.1	68.2
Monetary Authorities	84aa	....	....	25.6	11.1	9.0	5.0	6.1	3.6	5.3	23.0	50.3	34.7	46.1	22.9	66.8
Other	84ac	....	....	2.8	-.8	2.4	1.3	9.3	-.8	-.3	-2.3	4.2	-2.9	-1.1	13.2	1.4
Net Foreign Borrowing	85a	....	....	-5.5	-1.2	-1.2	-5.9	-6.2	-6.7	-6.5	-9.0	-9.5	49.8	185.0	130.4	117.3
Use of Cash Balances	87	....	....	-3.8	-8.3	2.1	4.7	.9	1.4	.3	-2.3	-2.1	-17.3	-85.3	2.2	-17.5
Adjustment to Financing	84x	....	....	....	....	....	....	....	....	....	....	....	....	....	....	....
National Accounts														*Millions of Gourdes:*		
Exports of Goods & Services	90c	224	207	201	232	242	261	321	332	381	663	785	1,046	1,249	1,495	1,522
Gross Fixed Capital Formation	93e	112	96	96	93	124	161	186	207	258	I410	533	678	748	857	938
Increase/Decrease(-) in Stocks	93i	10	10	11	11	11	12	13	13	17	I19	23	26	28	—	—
Gov't and Private Consumption	96f	1,732	1,832	1,802	1,773	1,881	1,964	2,142	2,160	3,013	2,604	3,149	4,101	4,592	4,690	5,245
Imports of Goods & Services	98c	-311	-298	-264	-269	-298	-343	-395	-400	-508	-868	-1,082	-1,430	-1,692	-1,982	-2,105
Gross Domestic Product	99b	1,766	1,847	1,846	1,840	1,959	2,055	2,262	2,312	3,129	I2,828	3,408	4,395	4,897	5,060	5,600
Net Factor Inc/Pmts(-) Abroad	98.n	....	-19	-15	-16	-14	-15	-16	-20	I-21	-28	-34	-36	-63	-76	-70
Gross Nat'l Expenditure = GNP	99a	1,766	1,828	1,831	1,824	1,946	2,040	2,246	2,292	3,108	2,800	3,374	4,359	4,834	4,984	5,530
Nat'l Income, Market Prices	99e	....	1,789	1,771	1,770	1,884	1,993	2,190	2,241	3,062	2,739	3,300	4,251	4,715	4,847	5,380
Gross Dom. Prod. 1990 Prices	99b.p	....	7,276	7,122	7,349	7,628	7,678	8,176	8,251	8,646	9,148	9,248	10,028	10,076	10,567	11,369
GDP Deflator (1990=100)	99bi p	....	25.4	25.9	25.0	25.7	26.8	27.7	28.0	36.2	30.9	36.9	43.8	48.6	47.9	49.3
																Millions:
Population	99z	3.91	3.97	4.03	4.10	4.16	4.24	4.31	4.37	4.44	4.51	4.58	4.67	4.75	4.83	4.92

Government Finance: Data relate to a fiscal year different from calendar year.

Haiti

1980	1981	1982	1983	1984	1985	1986	1987	1988	1989	1990	1991	1992	1993	1994		
Sept 30; Minus Sign Indicates Debit															**Balance of Payments**	
215.8	151.1	177.1	186.6	214.6	223.0	190.8	210.1	180.4	148.3	265.8	202.0	75.6	81.6	....	Goods: Exports f.o.b.	78aa *d*
−319.0	−360.1	−301.9	−325.9	−337.9	−344.7	−303.2	−311.2	−283.9	−259.3	−442.6	−448.6	−214.1	−266.6	....	Goods: Imports f.o.b.	78ab *d*
−103.2	−209.0	−124.8	−139.3	−123.3	−121.7	−112.5	−101.1	−103.5	−111.0	−176.8	−246.6	−138.5	−185.0	....	Trade Balance	78ac *d*
89.9	90.4	97.7	103.3	104.5	114.2	101.3	110.3	94.5	88.5	52.2	57.6	38.5	35.8	....	Services: Credit	78ad *d*
−162.0	−156.5	−169.1	−171.3	−189.1	−212.4	−170.2	−190.5	−197.1	−188.8	−138.4	−150.5	−84.5	−91.5	....	Services: Debit	78ae *d*
−175.3	−275.1	−196.2	−207.4	−207.9	−219.9	−181.4	−181.3	−206.1	−211.4	−263.0	−339.5	−184.5	−240.7	....	Balance on Goods and Services	78af *d*
3.1	4.1	3.6	4.7	4.5	5.1	4.6	5.2	6.2	4.6	6.9	2.0	1.0	2.0	....	Income: Credit	78ag *d*
−17.4	−17.2	−17.6	−18.9	−22.6	−24.9	−19.9	−26.1	−33.4	−30.2	−25.1	−20.0	−12.9	−12.6	....	Income: Debit	78ah *d*
−189.6	−288.1	−210.2	−221.6	−226.0	−239.7	−196.8	−202.2	−233.2	−236.9	−281.2	−357.5	−196.4	−251.3	....	Balance on Goods, Serv., & Inc.	78ai *d*
158.5	201.2	159.0	153.9	168.0	192.3	205.3	228.0	253.6	237.7	192.9	234.2	155.0	173.4	....	Current Transfers, n.i.e.: Credit	78aj *d*
−70.0	−61.8	−47.3	−43.5	−45.0	−47.2	−53.4	−56.9	−60.7	−63.5	—	—	—	—	....	Current Transfers: Debit	78ak *d*
−101.1	−148.8	−98.5	−111.2	−103.0	−94.7	−44.9	−31.1	−40.4	−62.7	−88.3	−123.3	−41.4	−77.9	....	Current Account, n.i.e.	78al *d*
—	—	—	—	—	—	—	—	—	—	—	—	—	—	....	Capital Account, n.i.e.: Credit	78ba *d*
—	—	—	—	—	—	—	—	—	—	—	—	—	—	....	Capital Account: Debit	78bb *d*
—	—	—	—	—	—	—	—	—	—	—	—	—	—	....	Capital Account, n.i.e.	78bc *d*
—	—	—	—	—	—	—	—	—	—	8.0	13.6	—	—	....	Direct Investment Abroad	78bd *d*
13.0	8.3	7.1	8.4	4.5	4.9	4.8	4.7	10.1	9.4	—	—	—	—	....	Dir. Invest. in Rep. Econ., n.i.e.	78be *d*
—	—	—	—	—	—	—	—	—	—	—	—	—	—	....	Portfolio Investment Assets	78bf *d*
—	—	—	—	—	—	—	—	—	—	—	—	—	—	....	Portfolio Investment Liab., n.i.e.	78bg *d*
−7.5	−3.4	6.7	−.1	6.1	−7.1	−1.1	−7.8	−3.1	21.5	−23.1	−16.2	−12.6	−30.6	....	Other Investment Assets	78bh *d*
70.5	104.9	76.7	82.9	102.1	48.2	30.6	56.5	19.3	29.3	48.1	28.5	−8.0	−13.1	....	Other Investment Liab., n.i.e.	78bi *d*
76.0	109.8	90.5	91.2	112.7	46.0	34.4	53.4	26.3	60.1	33.0	25.9	−20.6	−43.7	....	Financial Account, n.i.e.	78bj *d*
−30.6	1.1	6.5	−17.2	−20.2	49.8	15.2	−13.5	11.8	−13.7	21.5	107.8	55.7	98.5	....	Net Errors and Omissions	78ca *d*
−55.6	−37.9	−1.5	−37.2	−10.5	1.1	4.6	8.8	−2.3	−16.2	−33.8	10.5	−6.3	−23.0	....	Overall Balance	78cb *d*
55.6	37.9	1.5	37.2	10.5	−1.1	−4.6	−8.8	2.3	16.2	33.8	−10.5	6.3	23.0	....	Reserves and Related Items	79da *d*
34.6	20.6	−10.3	6.6	−3.3	6.7	−7.8	19.3	.3	5.4	37.5	−20.0	−11.3	−19.1	....	Reserve Assets	79db *d*
20.7	17.3	11.8	30.4	12.9	−15.3	−17.1	−28.1	−23.1	−4.1	−6.9	−2.2	—	—	....	Use of Fund Credit and Loans	79dc *d*
														....	Liabs.Constit.For.Auth.Reserves	79dd *d*
.3			.2	.8	7.5	20.2	—	25.1	14.9	3.2	11.8	17.6	42.1	....	Exceptional Financing	79de *d*
Year Ending September 30															**Government Finance**	
−327.7	−446.3	−380.6	−277.1	−572.7	−217.5	−236.6	−151.2	....	....	−577.5	....	....	....	−947.1	Deficit (-) or Surplus	80
789.3	759.9	858.6	952.9	1,075.7	1,279.4	1,339.8	1,287.9	....	....	1,214.7	....	....	....	874.8	Revenue	81
151.0	157.7	593.0	640.8	341.9	515.8	385.9	564.6	....	....	7.6	....	....	....	2.2	Grants Received	81z
1,268.0	1,363.9	1,832.2	1,870.8	1,990.3	2,012.7	1,962.3	2,003.7	....	....	1,799.8	....	....	....	1,824.1	Expenditure	82
															Financing	
165.2	367.8	157.7	129.3	431.6	351.8	109.7	56.3	....	....	333.5	....	....	....	1,109.6	Net Domestic Borrowing	84a
161.0	364.8	154.4	109.5	435.9	356.6	111.7	60.0	....	....	328.4	....	....	....	1,109.6	Monetary Authorities	84aa
4.2	3.0	3.3	19.8	−4.3	−4.8	−2.0	−3.7	....	....	5.1	....	....	....	—	Other	84ac
156.6	105.6	171.8	150.8	159.6	33.6	229.8	134.4	....	....	30.2	....	....	....	—	Net Foreign Borrowing	85a
5.9	−27.1	51.1	−3.0	−18.5	−167.9	35.3	−1.3	....	....	−110.7	....	....	....	−88.1	Use of Cash Balances	87
....	....	....	....	....	....	−138.2	−38.2	....	....	324.5	....	....	....	−74.9	Adjustment to Financing	84x
Year Ending September 30															**National Accounts**	
2,148	1,944	2,139	2,302	2,598	2,716	2,340	2,860	2,542	2,145	2,511	3,682	1,701	2,416	3,011	Exports of Goods & Services	90c
1,238	1,252	1,230	1,331	1,441	1,673	1,614	1,546	1,501	1,692	1,161	1,156	776	817	850	Gross Fixed Capital Formation	93e
—	—	—	—	—	—	—	—	—	—	—	—	—	—	—	Increase/Decrease(-) in Stocks	93i
6,835	7,535	7,202	7,866	8,678	9,471	10,470	9,403	9,436	9,861	10,931	11,598	13,042	15,047	18,967	Gov't and Private Consumption	96f
−3,302	−3,650	−3,186	−3,381	−3,636	−3,813	−3,245	−3,767	−6,372	−3,201	−2,862	−3,073	−1,955	−2,565	−1,816	Imports of Goods & Services	98c
6,919	7,081	7,385	8,118	9,081	10,047	11,179	10,042	9,907	10,496	11,742	13,363	13,564	15,715	21,013	Gross Domestic Product	99b
−72	−66	−72	−73	−92	−101	−100	−105	−135	−128	−125	−131	−153	−211	−584	Net Factor Inc/Pmts(-) Abroad	98.n
6,847	7,015	7,299	8,045	8,990	9,946	11,081	9,937	9,773	10,467	12,401	14,624	14,871	....	....	Gross Nat'l Expenditure = GNP	99a
6,650	6,815	7,102	7,833	8,760	9,680	10,824	9,697	9,534	10,182	12,112	....	....	....	....	Nat'l Income, Market Prices	99e
12,204	11,856	11,450	11,537	11,572	11,601	11,715	11,728	11,836	11,879	11,742	11,667	9,935	9,415	8,173	Gross Dom. Prod. 1990 Prices	99b.*p*
56.7	59.7	64.5	70.4	78.5	86.6	95.4	85.6	83.7	88.4	100.0	114.5	136.5	166.9	257.1	GDP Deflator (1990=100)	99bi *p*
Midyear Estimates																
5.01	5.46	5.56	5.66	5.76	5.86	5.99	6.11	6.24	6.36	6.49	6.62	6.76	6.90	7.04	Population	99z

Honduras

		1965	1966	1967	1968	1969	1970	1971	1972	1973	1974	1975	1976	1977	1978	1979
Exchange Rates														*Lempiras per SDR: End of Period (aa)*		
Market Rate	aa	2.0000	2.0000	2.0000	2.0000	2.0000	2.0000	2.1714	2.1714	2.4127	2.4487	2.3413	2.3237	2.4294	2.6056	2.6347
Market Rate	ae	2.0000	2.0000	2.0000	2.0000	2.0000	2.0000	2.0000	2.0000	2.0000	2.0000	2.0000	2.0000	2.0000	2.0000	2.0000
Fund Position														*Millions of SDRs:*		
Quota	2f. s	15.00	19.00	19.00	19.00	19.00	25.00	25.00	25.00	25.00	25.00	25.00	25.00	25.00	34.00	34.00
SDRs	1b. s	—	—	—	—	—	.19	2.85	5.45	5.41	5.27	3.98	2.66	3.55	2.95	7.68
Reserve Position in the Fund	1c. s	—	—	2.26	2.26	4.75	—	—	—	—	6.25	—	—	—	6.25	6.06
Total Fund Cred.&Loans Outstg.	2tl	3.75	2.74	—	—	—	—	—	—	—	—	16.78	16.78	16.78	4.29	7.58
International Liquidity												*Millions of US Dollars Unless Otherwise Indicated:*				
Total Reserves minus Gold	1l. d	23.28	27.28	24.97	31.43	30.81	20.13	21.77	35.09	41.66	44.30	96.97	130.83	179.77	184.44	209.17
SDRs	1b. d	—	—	—	—	—	.19	3.09	5.92	6.53	6.45	4.66	3.09	4.31	3.84	10.12
Reserve Position in the Fund	1c. d	—	—	2.26	2.26	4.75	—	—	—	7.54	—	—	—	—	8.14	7.98
Foreign Exchange	1d. d	23.28	27.28	22.71	29.17	26.06	19.94	18.68	29.17	27.59	37.85	92.31	127.74	175.46	172.45	191.07
Gold (Million Fine Troy Ounces)	1ad	.003	.003	.003	.003	.003	.003	.003	.003	.003	.003	.003	.003	.014	.014	.014
Gold (National Valuation)	1and	.11	.11	.10	.10	.10	.10	.10	.10	.15	.15	.15	.15	.60	.60	.80
Monetary Authorities: Other Liab.	4..d	3.45	4.96	.70	1.30	2.80	1.70	1.30	1.50	3.75	6.41	91.36	101.65	129.29	129.20	151.31
Deposit Money Banks: Assets	7a. d	1.40	1.10	1.50	1.70	2.00	2.10	3.75	2.50	2.25	3.75	7.05	5.10	7.00	7.70	7.90
Deposit Money Banks: Liabilities	7b. d	2.10	4.15	9.15	4.90	7.15	10.30	17.70	20.35	27.75	29.75	32.50	43.50	67.05	52.40	67.25
of which: Liab. to Nonbanks	7bd d	....	....	....	.20	.40	.05	8.70	10.15	17.30	18.60	19.95	22.75	38.50	37.40	21.45
Other Banking Insts.: Liabilities	7f. d	10.05	13.60	20.40	23.55	24.85	27.15	16.15	20.95	22.55	27.70	44.60	56.25	72.70	87.10	101.90
of which: Liab. to Nonbanks	7fd d	....	....	15.65	20.95	23.50	23.60	14.00	18.50	19.15	23.90	39.10	41.15	60.15	74.00	77.50
Monetary Authorities														*Millions of Lempiras:*		
Foreign Assets	11	47	55	50	63	62	42	46	75	89	95	202	277	395	394	439
Claims on Central Government	12a	29	31	23	9	29	43	58	60	62	79	77	86	60	144	200
Claims on Local Government	12b	38	32	1	—	1	4	7	11	12	15	17	16	21	32	62
Claims on Deposit Money Banks	12e	4	6	5	10	16	20	20	19	30	47	68	62	75	80	97
Claims on Other Banking Insts.	12f	11	12	13	13	17	17	17	17	24	35	50	56	51	68	71
Reserve Money	14	69	71	78	87	101	112	122	125	151	147	165	229	270	323	377
of which: Currency Outside DMBs	14a	51	54	56	61	73	77	80	90	112	109	115	173	193	215	270
Private Sector Deposits	14d	6	7	2	1	2	1	1	1	1	1	3	4	4	8	6
Foreign Liabilities	16c	14	15	1	2	5	3	2	1	3	47	119	120	121	81	80
Long-Term Foreign Liabilities	16cl	—	—	1	1	1	1	—	2	4	7	103	123	148	178	243
Central Government Deposits	16d	12	17	27	22	30	17	22	55	47	57	43	61	74	124	167
Capital Accounts	17a	—	—	12	15	19	24	32	41	47	51	52	52	65	83	117
Other Items (Net)	17r	34	33	-27	-32	-30	-30	-30	-42	-35	-38	-70	-88	-76	-72	-115
Deposit Money Banks														*Millions of Lempiras:*		
Reserves	20	14	11	20	25	28	34	40	35	38	41	54	55	78	108	111
Foreign Assets	21	3	2	3	3	4	4	8	5	5	8	14	10	14	15	16
Claims on Central Government	22a	11	11	12	17	20	23	27	55	59	67	70	91	133	144	167
Claims on Local Government	22b	1	1	1	1	1	1	1	1	3	—	—	—	—	—	—
Claims on Private Sector	22d	82	102	130	158	199	234	279	305	378	427	504	637	774	859	931
Claims on Other Banking Insts.	22f	2	1	—	—	—	1	1	2	3	3	8	9	11	12	13
Demand Deposits	24	48	46	56	65	73	80	88	101	125	132	144	184	214	257	270
Time, Savings,& Fgn.Currency Dep.	25	46	58	66	85	102	127	149	170	202	214	241	301	379	472	490
Bonds	26ab	—	—	1	3	4	4	8	11	14	17	12	25	37	51	52
Foreign Liabilities	26c	4	8	18	10	14	21	18	21	25	25	30	43	65	34	97
Long-Term Foreign Liabilities	26cl	—	—	—	—	—	—	17	20	31	34	35	44	69	71	38
Central Government Deposits	26d	—	—	—	—	—	1	2	2	2	9	13	16	25	29	33
Credit from Monetary Authorities	26g	—	—	5	10	16	19	19	19	30	45	67	64	79	79	100
Capital Accounts	27a	24	27	34	39	41	46	52	57	61	69	80	92	105	122	144
Other Items (Net)	27r	-10	-11	-16	-6	2	-1	2	—	-5	—	29	35	37	25	13
Monetary Survey														*Millions of Lempiras:*		
Foreign Assets (Net)	31n	31	33	34	55	47	23	33	57	66	30	67	125	223	295	278
Domestic Credit	32	162	174	153	177	237	305	366	393	491	561	670	818	952	1,106	1,243
Claims on Central Govt. (Net)	32an	28	25	8	4	19	47	61	58	71	79	91	100	94	136	166
Claims on Local Government	32b	39	33	2	1	2	5	8	12	15	15	17	16	21	32	62
Claims on Private Sector	32d	82	102	130	158	199	235	279	305	378	428	505	638	774	859	931
Claims on Other Banking Insts.	32f	13	13	13	13	17	18	18	18	27	38	58	65	62	80	84
Money	34	105	107	114	127	148	159	169	193	238	242	263	361	411	480	545
Quasi-Money	35	47	59	69	86	104	130	152	173	207	218	245	311	385	482	495
Bonds	36ab	—	—	1	3	4	4	8	11	14	17	12	25	37	51	52
Long-Term Foreign Liabilities	36cl	—	—	1	1	1	1	17	22	35	41	139	167	217	248	281
Other Items (Net)	37r	41	41	1	15	27	35	53	52	62	72	80	79	124	139	148
Money plus Quasi-Money	35l	151	166	183	213	252	288	321	366	445	460	507	672	796	962	1,040
Other Banking Institutions														*Millions of Lempiras:*		
Cash	40	4	4	5	5	3	4	3	5	6	6	8	15	14	20	16
Foreign Assets	41	—	—	1	1	1	1	1	1	1	1	1	3	3	5	5
Claims on Central Government	42a	—	—	2	2	1	1	—	1	1	2	6	9	22	11	12
Claims on Local Government	42b	—	—	3	2	2	2	2	1	1	3	4	6	12	10	18
Claims on Private Sector	42d	53	68	84	84	100	113	90	109	129	155	193	201	264	342	429
Claims on Deposit Money Banks	42e	—	—	—	—	1	1	1	1	2	12	25	26	16	18	18
Demand Deposits	44	—	—	5	6	7	6	5	6	8	7	8	6	8	6	10
Deposits	45	21	27	8	4	7	9	10	11	14	14	25	29	49	60	73
Bonds	46ab	—	—	2	—	1	3	—	4	11	15	20	8	17	27	50
Foreign Liabilities	46c	—	—	10	5	3	7	4	5	7	8	11	30	25	26	49
Long-Term Foreign Liabilities	46cl	20	27	31	42	47	47	28	37	38	48	78	82	120	148	155
Central Government Deposits	46d	53	68	—	—	—	—	5	7	5	12	20	22	11	20	36
Credit from Monetary Authorities	46g	11	12	13	13	17	18	17	17	25	35	51	56	51	62	64
Credit from Deposit Money Banks	46h	—	—	—	—	—	2	—	1	2	7	7	3	4	4	3
Capital Accounts	47a	27	32	37	41	47	56	55	63	68	78	101	121	131	143	160
Other Items (Net)	47r	-76	-95	-12	-18	-21	-26	-27	-34	-37	-43	-82	-98	-86	-90	-102

Honduras

	1980	1981	1982	1983	1984	1985	1986	1987	1988	1989	1990	1991	1992	1993	1994		
																Exchange Rates	
Lempiras per US Dollar: End of Period (ae)																	
	2.5508	2.3279	2.2062	2.0939	1.9604	2.1968	2.4464	2.8373	2.6914	2.6283	2.8453	7.7243	8.0163	9.9720	13.7227	Market Rate	aa
	2.0000	2.0000	2.0000	2.0000	2.0000	2.0000	2.0000	2.0000	2.0000	2.0000	2.0000	5.4000	5.8300	7.2600	9.4001	Market Rate	ae
																Fund Position	
End of Period																	
	51.00	51.00	51.00	67.80	67.80	67.80	67.80	67.80	67.80	67.80	67.80	67.80	95.00	95.00	95.00	Quota	2f. s
	.02	1.39	1.63	2.12	.16	—	—	—	—	—	—	.01	—	.11	.11	.15 SDRs	1b. s
	—	—	—	4.20	—	—	—	—	—	—	—	—	—	—	—	Reserve Position in the Fund	1c. s
	25.73	46.46	108.16	154.06	152.47	133.72	89.54	54.37	27.29	26.96	22.66	23.55	81.35	86.01	74.81	Total Fund Cred.&Loans Outstg.	2tl
																International Liquidity	
End of Period																	
	149.83	101.02	112.23	113.62	128.16	105.80	111.30	106.00	50.00	21.10	40.41	104.90	197.45	97.15	171.01	Total Reserves minus Gold	1l. d
	.03	1.62	1.80	2.22	.16	—	—	—	—	—	.01	—	.15	.15	.21	SDRs	1b. d
	—	—	—	4.40	—	—	—	—	—	—	—	—	—	—	—	Reserve Position in the Fund	1c. d
	149.80	99.40	110.43	107.00	128.00	105.80	111.30	106.00	50.00	21.10	40.40	104.90	197.30	97.00	170.80	Foreign Exchange	1d. d
	.016	.016	.016	.016	.016	.016	.016	.016	.016	.016	.016	.021	.021	.021	.021	Gold (Million Fine Troy Ounces)	1ad
	1.05	1.05	1.05	1.05	1.05	1.05	1.05	1.05	1.05	1.05	2.80	7.78	7.79	8.47	8.30	Gold (National Valuation)	1an d
	162.83	208.82	253.09	221.71	281.10	376.87	477.23	547.28	582.46	626.79	1,820.21	614.87	587.71	565.17	596.99	Monetary Authorities: Other Liab.	4.. d
	9.15	12.65	5.10	2.85	2.85	3.30	4.60	4.30	9.55	14.95	65.95	29.11	66.52	75.65	84.32	Deposit Money Banks: Assets	7a. d
	46.95	19.50	13.45	19.75	23.45	31.20	51.90	45.15	24.40	43.75	17.28	16.95	28.71	68.89	Deposit Money Banks: Liabilities	7b. d
	20.80	10.05	7.50	8.90	4.90	9.70	13.60	13.85	14.65	10.30	19.95	11.52	5.92	19.39	42.80	of which: Liab. to Nonbanks	7bd d
	109.55	126.60	125.15	118.90	123.05	122.85	119.85	128.60	120.05	111.90	302.65	17.69	17.51	13.93	15.80	Other Banking Insts.: Liabilities	7f. d
	74.50	104.20	105.10	100.80	103.00	99.50	93.35	93.50	82.00	69.60	178.55	17.19	17.38	13.93	15.18	of which: Liab. to Nonbanks	7fd d
																Monetary Authorities	
End of Period																	
	324	238	262	257	297	204	221	196	153	95	357	748	1,343	954	1,930	Foreign Assets	11
	276	455	509	442	593	681	643	881	1,299	1,428	1,905	1,360	1,555	2,023	1,512	Claims on Central Government	12a
	66	66	61	65	69	67	64	62	59	54	80	75	67	63	60	Claims on Local Government	12b
	140	152	161	162	237	425	517	476	481	542	543	653	665	665	678	Claims on Deposit Money Banks	12e
	95	147	193	234	279	302	329	450	443	483	509	468	532	547	569	Claims on Other Banking Insts.	12f
	386	411	438	467	470	502	568	622	714	915	1,227	1,417	1,793	1,904	2,807	Reserve Money	14
	275	302	314	362	384	410	426	492	570	676	882	977	1,141	1,448	1,995	of which: Currency Outside DMBs	14a
	13	7	23	20	16	19	37	44	55	74	183	162	166	115	173	Private Sector Deposits	14d
	104	211	412	435	502	660	759	812	802	861	2,169	1,995	2,425	3,134	4,247	Foreign Liabilities	16c
	287	315	333	331	359	388	415	437	436	464	1,536	1,507	1,599	1,692	2,206	Long-Term Foreign Liabilities	16cl
	132	155	159	27	173	209	237	363	534	431	786	771	949	1,144	675	Central Government Deposits	16d
	170	199	220	246	271	333	353	331	398	474	594	737	890	1,123	1,415	Capital Accounts	17a
	−179	−233	−375	−345	−300	−414	−557	−499	−450	−543	−2,918	−3,124	−3,494	−4,744	−6,600	Other Items (Net)	17r
																Deposit Money Banks	
End of Period																	
	104	111	118	80	130	129	129	125	197	279	274	463	648	423	668	Reserves	20
	18	25	10	6	6	7	9	9	19	30	132	157	388	549	793	Foreign Assets	21
	193	182	276	371	449	518	691	699	715	836	919	1,202	1,045	968	1,287	Claims on Central Government	22a
	3	—	—	44	59	14	16	35	64	60	47	40	5	2	1	Claims on Local Government	22b
	945	992	1,095	1,253	1,414	1,617	1,795	2,131	2,386	2,604	3,026	3,481	4,341	5,009	6,364	Claims on Private Sector	22d
	13	17	33	32	36	35	30	33	31	30	28	3	6	6	37	Claims on Other Banking Insts.	22f
	323	328	380	431	444	424	490	581	625	774	903	1,138	1,276	1,313	1,761	Demand Deposits	24
	515	586	745	895	1,051	1,036	1,140	1,355	1,589	1,738	1,990	2,486	3,151	3,432	4,288	Time, Savings,& Fgn.Currency Dep.	25
	31	28	23	26	31	24	32	41	36	32	28	23	19	16	14	Bonds	26ab
	60	24	17	32	41	45	42	83	66	30	48	32	66	74	256	Foreign Liabilities	26c
	34	15	10	8	6	17	24	21	24	19	39	62	33	135	392	Long-Term Foreign Liabilities	26cl
	37	54	65	70	73	135	201	210	272	350	465	467	649	349	299	Central Government Deposits	26d
	180	166	174	177	255	429	522	479	497	554	545	656	679	704	691	Credit from Monetary Authorities	26g
	161	172	184	207	240	278	307	336	372	426	531	708	876	1,234	1,670	Capital Accounts	27a
	−65	−48	−66	−59	−47	−68	−87	−74	−69	−85	−123	−225	−315	−302	−222	Other Items (Net)	27r
																Monetary Survey	
End of Period																	
	179	29	−156	−204	−240	−495	−570	−690	−696	−767	−1,729	−1,122	−761	−1,705	−1,780	Foreign Assets (Net)	31n
	1,422	1,650	1,943	2,346	2,653	2,890	3,131	3,720	4,208	4,740	5,293	5,423	5,995	7,183	8,915	Domestic Credit	32
	299	428	561	717	795	855	896	1,007	1,207	1,483	1,573	1,324	1,002	1,497	1,826	Claims on Central Govt. (Net)	32an
	69	66	61	109	128	81	80	97	123	114	127	114	72	66	61	Claims on Local Government	32b
	946	992	1,095	1,254	1,415	1,618	1,795	2,134	2,404	2,630	3,055	3,513	4,383	5,068	6,422	Claims on Private Sector	32d
	107	164	226	267	315	337	359	483	474	513	537	471	538	553	606	Claims on Other Banking Insts.	32f
	610	637	717	813	844	853	953	1,117	1,250	1,524	1,968	2,277	2,582	2,876	3,929	Money	34
	517	589	761	919	1,065	1,015	1,095	1,377	1,617	1,778	2,046	2,461	3,228	3,696	4,501	Quasi-Money	35
	31	28	23	26	31	24	32	41	36	32	28	23	19	16	14	Bonds	36ab
	322	330	343	339	365	405	439	458	460	482	1,575	1,569	1,632	1,826	2,597	Long-Term Foreign Liabilities	36cl
	120	94	−58	46	108	99	42	38	149	158	−2,053	−2,029	−2,226	−2,935	−3,907	Other Items (Net)	37r
	1,128	1,226	1,478	1,731	1,909	1,868	2,047	2,494	2,867	3,301	4,014	4,738	5,810	6,572	8,430	Money plus Quasi-Money	35l
																Other Banking Institutions	
End of Period																	
	18	19	30	36	29	39	39	32	35	40	39	48	58	75	139	Cash	40
	3	4	2	1	5	2	4	3	4	4	8	23	38	64	96	Foreign Assets	41
	17	11	12	52	59	55	70	82	83	82	89	79	76	79	110	Claims on Central Government	42a
	25	41	45	54	62	75	80	67	73	73	76	73	76	80	86	Claims on Local Government	42b
	532	598	678	713	744	811	832	890	785	834	842	785	981	1,094	1,261	Claims on Private Sector	42d
	13	6	7	11	14	18	8	13	25	19	21	8	7	20	27	Claims on Deposit Money Banks	42e
	9	5	7	7	9	14	9	14	25	22	21	17	17	19	21	Demand Deposits	44
	94	108	124	148	165	164	183	229	226	231	258	355	557	675	744	Deposits	45
	38	40	44	49	58	60	61	65	68	65	63	4	1	1	1	Bonds	46ab
	70	45	40	36	40	47	53	70	76	85	248	3	1		6	Foreign Liabilities	46c
	149	208	210	202	206	199	187	187	164	139	357	93	101	101	143	Long-Term Foreign Liabilities	46cl
	64	78	85	101	105	119	121	102	122	120	142	147	194	217	326	Central Government Deposits	46d
	92	150	211	250	290	350	403	469	450	492	537	637	589	579	647	Credit from Monetary Authorities	46g
	3	7	21	22	24	20	13	17	13	10	7	2	4	5	36	Credit from Deposit Money Banks	46h
	153	181	302	303	312	328	329	321	310	368	373	328	345	301	407	Capital Accounts	47a
	−63	−143	−271	−250	−296	−300	−325	−387	−450	−478	−932	−570	−574	−487	−611	Other Items (Net)	47r

Honduras

268

		1965	1966	1967	1968	1969	1970	1971	1972	1973	1974	1975	1976	1977	1978	1979
Banking Survey															*Millions of Lempiras:*	
Foreign Assets (Net)	51n	31	33	26	50	45	17	29	53	60	24	57	97	201	273	234
Domestic Credit	52	149	160	228	252	322	402	436	478	591	671	795	947	1,176	1,369	1,582
Claims on Central Govt. (Net)	52an	−25	−43	10	6	19	48	57	52	67	70	77	86	104	127	143
Claims on Local Government	52b	39	33	4	4	5	6	10	13	16	19	21	22	34	41	80
Claims on Private Sector	52d	135	170	214	243	299	347	369	414	508	582	697	839	1,038	1,201	1,360
Liquid Liabilities	55l	168	188	192	219	263	300	333	378	461	474	532	693	839	1,008	1,107
Bonds	56ab	—	—	3	3	5	7	8	15	25	32	31	32	54	78	102
Long-Term Foreign Liabilities	56cl	20	27	32	43	48	48	45	59	74	89	217	249	338	396	436
Capital Accounts	57a	51	60	84	95	107	125	138	161	176	197	232	265	301	348	421
Other Items (Net)	57r	−60	−82	−57	−57	−55	−61	−59	−81	−85	−99	−160	−195	−156	−189	−250
Interest Rates															*Percent Per Annum*	
Discount Rate (End of Period)	60	....	....	....	....	....	....	....	....	....	....	....	....	....	13.0	13.5
Deposit Rate	60l	....	....	....	....	....	....	....	....	....	....	....	....	....	....	....
Lending Rate	60p	....	....	....	....	....	....	....	....	....	....	....	....	....	....	....
Government Bond Yield	61	....	....	....	....	....	....	....	....	....	....	....	....	....	....	....
Prices															*Index Numbers (1990=100):*	
Consumer Prices	64	19.8	‡20.1	20.5	20.9	21.2	21.8	22.3	23.1	24.3	27.4	29.7	31.1	33.8	‡35.7	40.0
International Transactions															*Millions of US Dollars*	
Exports	70..d	127.2	142.9	155.2	181.4	168.3	179.1	189.0	204.5	258.7	289.1	295.0	400.1	513.5	607.6	733.6
Imports, cif	71..d	121.9	149.0	164.5	185.8	184.3	220.7	193.7	193.3	262.3	382.2	400.1	455.9	574.7	693.0	825.9
Imports, fob	71.vd	110.9	135.3	148.9	167.2	166.1	199.1	172.4	171.3	235.2	348.0	364.5	414.3	520.6	628.9	748.8
																1990=100
Volume of Exports	72	55.6	66.8	69.6	78.7	78.4	77.5	93.0	93.5	96.7	74.6	76.7	89.4	101.3	104.3	121.4
Export Prices	74..d	....	....	....	....	....	....	....	....	....	....	53.3	74.4	121.1	104.1	93.9
Balance of Payments															*Millions of US Dollars:*	
Goods: Exports f.o.b.	78aad	....	....	....	....	....	....	....	....	....	303.9	313.1	415.5	534.4	631.2	763.8
Goods: Imports f.o.b.	78abd	....	....	....	....	....	....	....	....	....	−387.5	−372.4	−432.5	−550.1	−654.5	−783.5
Trade Balance	78acd	....	....	....	....	....	....	....	....	....	−83.5	−59.3	−17.0	−15.7	−23.3	−19.7
Services: Credit	78add	....	....	....	....	....	....	....	....	....	27.9	31.3	38.2	46.3	56.2	74.3
Services: Debit	78aed	....	....	....	....	....	....	....	....	....	−68.3	−73.8	−82.2	−105.4	−123.1	−148.2
Balance on Goods and Services	78afd	....	....	....	....	....	....	....	....	....	−123.9	−101.8	−60.9	−74.9	−90.2	−93.7
Income: Credit	78agd	....	....	....	....	....	....	....	....	....	5.0	6.5	9.7	13.2	19.1	21.2
Income: Debit	78ahd	....	....	....	....	....	....	....	....	....	−17.5	−34.6	−66.8	−81.2	−103.4	−140.1
Balance on Goods, Serv., & Inc.	78aid	....	....	....	....	....	....	....	....	....	−136.5	−129.8	−118.0	−142.8	−174.5	−212.6
Current Transfers, n.i.e.: Credit	78ajd	....	....	....	....	....	....	....	....	....	37.4	23.2	19.5	20.6	25.4	35.5
Current Transfers: Debit	78akd	....	....	....	....	....	....	....	....	....	−4.9	−5.5	−6.2	−6.5	−8.1	−15.0
Current Account, n.i.e.	78ald	....	....	....	....	....	....	....	....	....	−103.9	−112.1	−104.8	−128.7	−157.2	−192.1
Capital Account, n.i.e.: Credit	78bad	....	....	....	....	....	....	....	....	....	—	—	—	—	—	—
Capital Account: Debit	78bbd	....	....	....	....	....	....	....	....	....	—	—	—	—	—	—
Capital Account, n.i.e.	78bcd	....	....	....	....	....	....	....	....	....	—	—	—	—	—	—
Direct Investment Abroad	78bdd	....	....	....	....	....	....	....	....	....						
Dir. Invest. in Rep. Econ., n.i.e.	78bed	....	....	....	....	....	....	....	....	....	−1.2	7.0	5.3	8.9	13.2	28.2
Portfolio Investment Assets	78bfd	....	....	....	....	....	....	....	....	....	—	—	—	—	−.6	−.1
Portfolio Investment Liab., n.i.e.	78bgd	....	....	....	....	....	....	....	....	....	—	—	—	—	—	—
Other Investment Assets	78bhd	....	....	....	....	....	....	....	....	....	−5.8	−7.7	−1.6	−12.0	−12.0	−13.2
Other Investment Liab., n.i.e.	78bid	....	....	....	....	....	....	....	....	....	98.6	120.0	132.0	188.1	135.9	193.1
Financial Account, n.i.e.	78bjd	....	....	....	....	....	....	....	....	....	91.7	119.3	135.7	185.0	136.5	208.0
Net Errors and Omissions	78cad	....	....	....	....	....	....	....	....	....	−4.8	−.4	−1.6	−6.4	12.7	−18.5
Overall Balance	78cbd	....	....	....	....	....	....	....	....	....	−17.0	6.8	29.3	49.9	−8.0	−2.6
Reserves and Related Items	79dad	....	....	....	....	....	....	....	....	....	17.0	−6.8	−29.3	−49.9	8.0	2.6
Reserve Assets	79dbd	....	....	....	....	....	....	....	....	....	−3.2	−53.4	−37.9	−51.8	−4.0	−20.1
Use of Fund Credit and Loans	79dcd	....	....	....	....	....	....	....	....	....	20.2	—	—	−14.6	−5.7	9.9
Liabs.Constit.For.Auth.Reserves	79ddd	....	....	....	....	....	....	....	....	....	—	−.6	—	—	—	—
Exceptional Financing	79ded	....	....	....	....	....	....	....	....	....	—	47.1	8.6	16.6	17.6	12.9
Government Finance															*Millions of Lempiras:*	
Deficit (−) or Surplus	80	.6	−5.0	−4.1	−5.4	−27.8	−39.4	−44.6	−45.4	−16.0	−5.6	−48.0	−31.2	2.7	−29.7	−79.2
Revenue	81	109.1	120.4	129.3	148.1	155.0	177.8	181.0	192.9	219.5	257.0	272.0	352.7	457.1	549.5	655.9
Expenditure	82	108.5	125.4	133.4	153.5	182.8	217.2	225.6	238.3	235.5	262.6	320.0	383.9	454.4	579.2	735.1
Financing																
Net Borrowing: Lempiras	84b	−.2	5.3	5.6	−12.5	10.2	22.2	33.8	41.5	28.0	28.3	45.0	37.0	−15.9	139.8	102.6
Foreign Currency	85b	.7	3.9	6.8	13.2	17.6	34.6	38.1	20.7	16.9	7.9	24.9	16.3	22.7	38.6	13.7
Use of Cash Balances	87	−1.1	−4.2	−8.6	4.6	—	−17.4	−27.3	−16.8	−28.9	−30.6	−21.9	−22.1	−9.5	−148.7	−37.1
Debt: Lempiras	88b	38.1	45.6	52.7	43.7	72.1	86.1	105.3	136.0	141.3	153.2	162.4	198.8	218.0	296.9	347.2
Held by: Central Bank	88ba	14.5	15.8	19.5	4.0	25.1	36.2	52.0	53.4	52.7	66.2	65.3	73.6	43.1	115.2	151.4
Commercial Banks	88bb	10.9	11.1	11.9	17.1	19.7	22.8	26.6	54.5	59.1	63.2	70.3	90.7	126.7	143.8	166.6
Other Financial Inst.	88bc	2.1	2.1	2.4	2.2	1.7	2.9	3.3	3.7	4.3	3.9	5.1	9.5	19.3	11.8	10.9
Others	88bd	10.6	16.6	18.9	20.4	25.6	24.2	23.4	24.4	25.2	19.9	21.7	25.0	28.9	26.1	18.3
Intragovernmental Debt	88s	4.3	7.3	6.5	8.2	8.0	8.8	6.8	6.0	8.9	14.0	23.7	43.7	61.0	65.4	77.3
Debt: Foreign Currency	89b	48.8	54.2	61.9	76.6	98.5	136.8	176.5	197.0	214.2	257.3	344.1	416.4	480.5	645.4	834.8
National Accounts															*Millions of Lempiras*	
Exports of Goods & Services	90c	283	320	346	401	380	395	426	461	579	656	680	898	1,149	1,366	1,649
Government Consumption	91f	102	114	120	129	149	166	175	193	186	242	278	348	417	442	520
Gross Fixed Capital Formation	93e	132	159	213	226	244	268	253	245	325	433	476	550	711	941	1,004
Increase/Decrease(−) in Stocks	93i	16	17	22	13	14	34	−3	11	23	109	−50	−32	59	93	170
Private Consumption	96f	754	818	857	936	972	1,073	1,142	1,222	1,382	1,581	1,754	1,964	2,314	2,511	2,945
Imports of Goods & Services	98c	−270	−328	−362	−406	−411	−490	−442	−449	−600	−907	−890	−1,032	−1,311	−1,555	−1,863
Gross Domestic Product	99b	1,017	1,100	1,196	1,299	1,348	1,446	1,551	1,683	1,895	2,114	2,248	2,696	3,339	3,798	4,425
Net Factor Inc/Pmts(−) Abroad	98.n	−35	−28	−39	−47	−45	−40	−45	−50	−62	−22	−50	−102	−124	−157	−210
Gross Nat'l Expenditure = GNP	99a	982	1,072	1,157	1,252	1,303	1,406	1,506	1,633	1,833	2,092	2,198	2,594	3,215	3,641	4,215
Nat'l Income, Market Prices	99e	938	1,028	1,111	1,201	1,252	1,353	1,451	1,576	1,772	1,974	2,101	2,479	3,061	3,475	4,015
Gross Dom. Prod. 1990 Prices	99b.p	4,984	5,277	5,521	5,924	5,943	6,222	6,557	6,821	7,205	7,195	‡6,980	7,712	8,513	9,217	9,800
GDP Deflator (1990=100)	99bip	20.4	20.8	21.7	21.9	22.7	23.2	23.7	24.7	26.3	29.4	32.2	35.0	39.2	41.2	45.2
																Millions:
Population	99z	2.18	2.26	2.28	2.31	2.45	2.64	2.72	2.81	2.90	2.99	3.09	3.20	3.32	3.44	3.56

Honduras

1980	1981	1982	1983	1984	1985	1986	1987	1988	1989	1990	1991	1992	1993	1994		
End of Period															**Banking Survey**	
112	−12	−195	−239	−275	−539	−620	−757	−769	−847	−1,969	−1,101	−723	−1,641	−1,690	Foreign Assets (Net)	51n
1,824	2,058	2,365	2,797	3,098	3,376	3,632	4,173	4,554	5,096	5,621	5,741	6,396	7,665	9,440	Domestic Credit	52
253	361	487	669	749	791	845	986	1,169	1,445	1,520	1,256	884	1,358	1,610	Claims on Central Govt. (Net)	52an
94	107	106	162	190	156	160	163	196	187	203	187	148	146	146	Claims on Local Government	52b
1,477	1,590	1,773	1,966	2,159	2,429	2,627	3,024	3,189	3,464	3,897	4,298	5,364	6,161	7,683	Claims on Private Sector	52d
1,212	1,321	1,579	1,849	2,054	2,007	2,200	2,705	3,083	3,514	4,254	5,063	6,326	7,190	9,056	Liquid Liabilities	55l
69	68	67	75	89	85	94	105	104	97	91	27	20	17	14	Bonds	56ab
471	539	553	541	571	604	626	645	624	622	1,932	1,662	1,733	1,927	2,740	Long-Term Foreign Liabilities	56cl
484	552	706	756	822	939	988	988	1,080	1,267	1,498	1,773	2,111	2,659	3,493	Capital Accounts	57a
−300	−434	−734	−663	−713	−797	−895	−1,027	−1,106	−1,251	−4,124	−3,884	−4,518	−5,768	−7,554	Other Items (Net)	57r
Percent Per Annum															**Interest Rates**	
16.0	16.0	24.0	24.0	24.0	24.0	24.0	24.0	24.0	24.0	24.0	28.2	30.1	26.1	....	Discount Rate (End of Period)	60
....	....	10.6	11.3	10.3	9.9	9.7	9.6	8.6	8.6	8.8	11.5	12.3	11.6	11.6	Deposit Rate	60l
....	....	16.5	16.1	16.2	16.3	16.1	15.5	15.4	15.4	17.1	21.9	21.7	22.1	24.7	Lending Rate	60p
....	....	....	9.4	10.3	10.4	10.4	10.4	10.4	10.4	10.4	10.4	10.4	10.4	23.1	Government Bond Yield	61
Period Averages															**Prices**	
47.3	51.7	56.4	61.0	63.9	66.1	68.9	70.6	73.8	81.1	100.0	134.0	145.7	161.4	196.4	Consumer Prices	64
Millions of US Dollars															**International Transactions**	
829.5	760.7	659.5	671.8	725.4	780.1	854.2	791.4	841.9	858.5	831.0	792.4	801.5	814.0	842.5	Exports	70..d
1,008.7	949.1	700.5	802.6	893.4	888.1	875.1	827.4	940.1	968.6	934.8	955.1	1,036.6	1,130.0	1,055.9	Imports, cif	71..d
912.3	860.5	636.6	722.7	810.7	803.7	791.9	748.8	801.6	789.2	796.8	796.2	938.1	1,022.6	955.6	Imports, fob	71.vd
1990=100																
117.6	115.3	113.0	107.6	105.3	115.2	107.4	123.3	109.0	99.4	100.0	87.8	101.8	90.2	78.9	Volume of Exports	72
112.1	94.5	92.8	86.5	95.5	98.3	127.3	100.2	107.5	105.0	100.0	100.0	98.3	77.0	89.4	Export Prices	74..d
Minus Sign Indicates Debit															**Balance of Payments**	
860.1	793.0	685.1	707.2	746.2	805.7	902.1	830.5	889.5	911.2	895.2	840.6	839.3	853.0	....	Goods: Exports f.o.b.	78aad
−954.1	−898.6	−680.7	−756.3	−884.8	−891.7	−879.5	−871.4	−923.4	−955.7	−907.0	−912.5	−990.2	−943.9	....	Goods: Imports f.o.b.	78abd
−94.0	−105.7	4.4	−49.1	−138.6	−86.1	22.6	−40.9	−34.0	−44.5	−11.8	−71.9	−150.9	−90.9	....	Trade Balance	78acd
81.5	90.6	81.9	93.8	101.2	103.8	109.6	119.7	136.4	149.7	137.3	175.0	202.0	213.8	....	Services: Credit	78add
−174.0	−163.7	−144.3	−158.4	−183.2	−195.3	−198.6	−202.4	−217.5	−230.5	−219.8	−226.7	−243.2	−256.6	....	Services: Debit	78aed
−186.4	−178.7	−58.0	−113.6	−220.6	−177.6	−66.4	−123.7	−115.1	−125.3	−94.3	−123.6	−192.1	−133.7	....	Balance on Goods and Services	78afd
25.9	19.7	16.6	14.0	15.8	14.9	13.1	15.2	22.0	24.3	20.7	39.8	61.4	74.4	....	Income: Credit	78agd
−177.8	−171.2	−216.8	−164.1	−191.7	−203.0	−222.2	−247.9	−253.3	−261.9	−257.5	−285.9	−343.4	−330.4	....	Income: Debit	78ahd
−338.3	−330.2	−258.3	−263.7	−396.5	−365.7	−275.5	−356.4	−346.4	−362.9	−331.1	−369.7	−474.1	−389.7	....	Balance on Goods, Serv., & Inc.	78aid
37.7	38.1	40.0	42.9	33.7	69.0	63.4	96.2	168.4	159.6	106.2	114.3	126.1	84.1	....	Current Transfers, n.i.e.: Credit	78ajd
−16.2	−10.6	−10.0	−11.1	−11.5	−11.9	−12.5	−3.0	−3.0	−3.0	−3.0	−3.0	−3.0	−3.0	....	Current Transfers: Debit	78akd
−316.8	−302.7	−228.3	−232.0	−374.3	−308.6	−224.6	−263.2	−181.0	−206.3	−227.9	−258.4	−351.0	−308.6	....	Current Account, n.i.e.	78ald
							28.0	30.0	35.0	50.0	52.0	60.0	60.0	....	Capital Account, n.i.e.: Credit	78bad
							−10.0	−10.0	−9.0	−8.5	−7.0	−7.2	−7.2	....	Capital Account: Debit	78bbd
							18.0	20.0	26.0	41.5	45.0	52.8	52.8	....	Capital Account, n.i.e.	78bcd
—	—	—	—	—	—	—	—	—	—	—	—	—	—	....	Direct Investment Abroad	78bdd
5.8	−3.6	13.8	21.0	20.5	27.5	30.0	38.7	48.3	51.0	43.5	52.1	47.6	34.8	....	Dir. Invest. in Rep. Econ., n.i.e.	78bed
−.1	−.3	−.2	.2	−1.9	1.2	−1.0	.6	−.2	.1	.1	.1	.1	.1	....	Portfolio Investment Assets	78bfd
														....	Portfolio Investment Liab., n.i.e.	78bgd
−10.6	−18.1	−.9	−6.3	−2.5	−44.8	−41.2	−1.6	−12.5	−6.2	−39.5	−17.4	−63.4	−30.0	....	Other Investment Assets	78bhd
242.2	248.5	131.9	91.4	242.9	210.5	54.7	74.9	20.2	−110.1	−8.9	−131.8	38.2	149.5	....	Other Investment Liab., n.i.e.	78bid
237.4	226.6	144.6	106.2	259.0	194.4	42.6	112.5	55.8	−65.2	−4.8	−97.0	22.5	154.4	....	Financial Account, n.i.e.	78bjd
−38.9	−18.4	−.5	12.7	−8.6	−38.6	3.2	−33.4	−93.1	−138.9	−107.4	152.0	29.2	−81.8	....	Net Errors and Omissions	78cad
−118.4	−94.6	−84.2	−113.1	−123.8	−152.8	−178.9	−166.1	−198.3	−384.3	−298.6	−158.4	−246.5	−183.2	....	Overall Balance	78cbd
118.4	94.6	84.2	113.1	123.8	152.8	178.9	166.1	198.3	384.3	298.6	158.4	246.5	183.2	....	Reserves and Related Items	79dad
62.2	47.5	7.6	−1.6	−8.9	53.9	−7.9	−19.9	21.6	29.0	−20.1	−66.9	−92.0	99.6	....	Reserve Assets	79dbd
23.9	23.4	67.8	49.2	−1.6	−19.2	−51.9	−45.0	−36.0	−.4	−4.2	1.1	80.7	6.4	....	Use of Fund Credit and Loans	79dcd
—	2.9	8.8	−4.2	25.5	−19.4	26.8	−16.5	−10.4	16.6	−11.9	−1.3	−.5	—	....	Liabs.Constit.For.Auth.Reserves	79ddd
32.3	20.7		69.7	108.8	137.5	212.0	247.4	223.1	339.2	334.8	225.5	258.3	77.2	....	Exceptional Financing	79ded
Year Ending December 31															**Government Finance**	
−140.2	−144.5	−379.6	−603.8	−678.6	−653.6	−492.2	−298.7	−274.3	−339.2	−425.7	111.5	165.4	−51.2	−5.8ᴾ	Deficit (-) or Surplus	80
756.6	738.7	770.1	778.1	951.0	1,064.1	1,151.8	1,290.0	1,377.8	1,534.4	2,059.1	2,837.8	3,271.0	3,770.0	4,590.6ᴾ	Revenue	81
896.8	883.2	1,149.7	1,381.9	1,629.6	1,717.7	1,644.0	1,588.7	1,652.1	1,873.6	2,484.8	2,726.3	3,105.6	3,821.2	4,596.4ᴾ	Expenditure	82
															Financing	
83.8	217.6	152.6	301.9	167.3	210.3	193.8	407.9	708.4	518.0	42.1	−276.1	−45.8	337.9	120.1ᴾ	Net Borrowing: Lempiras	84b
124.1	12.1	189.2	327.3	514.6	444.6	219.0	82.0	64.7	193.5	1,539.7	721.4	949.2	1,573.9	913.4ᴾ	Foreign Currency	85b
−67.7	−85.2	37.7	−25.4	−3.3	−1.3	79.4	−191.2	−498.8	−372.3	−1,156.1	−556.8	−1,068.8	−1,860.6	−1,027.7ᴾ	Use of Cash Balances	87
451.0	649.3	817.5	1,101.6	1,250.5	1,438.0	1,640.6	2,043.3	2,433.8	3,017.4	3,427.1	3,176.9	3,131.1	3,469.0	3,589.9ᴾ	Debt: Lempiras	88b
232.8	414.1	457.9	566.1	585.2	704.4	695.0	969.0	1,391.1	1,535.7	1,837.7	1,300.8	1,443.2	1,921.9	1,353.6ᴾ	Held by: Central Bank	88ba
192.9	181.1	275.4	369.5	447.3	517.7	676.9	688.2	702.9	819.7	889.0	1,160.9	1,011.0	938.5	1,218.2ᴾ	Commercial Banks	88bb
9.8	12.3	12.9	33.5	34.5	42.1	55.9	81.4	56.5	46.3	50.0	47.6	62.0	52.9	69.4ᴾ	Other Financial Inst.	88bc
15.5	41.8	71.3	132.5	183.5	173.8	212.8	304.7	283.3	615.7	650.4	667.6	614.9	555.7	948.7ᴾ	Others	88bd
93.7	93.2	129.3	160.9	186.0	212.1	208.6	285.0	276.6	256.9	477.0	434.6	367.6	4,364.5	5,617.8ᴾ	Intragovernmental Debt	88s
1,081.1	1,323.4	1,721.2	1,890.2	2,259.5	2,615.8	2,891.2	3,153.5	3,524.4	3,801.8	11,360.0	10,883.7	13,760.0	19,095.3	29,215.2ᴾ	Debt: Foreign Currency	89b
Millions of Lempiras															**National Accounts**	
1,860	1,784	1,549	1,610	1,706	1,827	2,025	1,907	2,432	3,204	4,664	5,632	6,048	7,332	10,312	Exports of Goods & Services	90c
650	721	758	807	876	953	1,087	1,181	1,308	1,475	1,621	1,769	2,171	2,520	2,897	Government Consumption	91f
1,258	1,088	1,009	1,028	1,251	1,234	1,045	1,132	1,429	1,884	2,533	3,096	4,202	5,672	7,075	Gross Fixed Capital Formation	93e
13	100	−190	−176	−95	27	10	314	513	94	348	926	679	823	50	Increase/Decrease(-) in Stocks	93i
3,612	4,072	4,310	4,684	5,026	5,412	5,606	5,916	6,245	7,226	8,379	11,021	12,520	14,750	18,231	Private Consumption	96f
−2,261	−2,126	−1,629	−1,799	−2,126	−2,174	−2,156	−2,145	−2,676	−3,549	−5,008	−6,130	−6,820	−8,653	−11,206	Imports of Goods & Services	98c
5,132	5,639	5,807	6,154	6,638	7,279	7,617	8,305	9,251	10,334	12,537	16,314	18,800	22,444	27,359	Gross Domestic Product	99b
−275	−319	−429	−338	−373	−384	−420	−475	−570	−740	−1,136	−1,499	−1,859	−2,094	−2,774	Net Factor Inc/Pmts(-) Abroad	98.n
4,857	5,320	5,378	5,816	6,265	6,895	7,197	7,830	8,681	9,594	11,401	14,815	16,941	20,350	24,585	Gross Nat'l Expenditure = GNP	99a
4,536	4,960	4,984	5,389	5,803	6,408	6,663	7,259	8,073	8,940	10,529	13,700	15,727	18,978	22,878	Nat'l Income, Market Prices	99e
9,867	10,117	9,977	9,884	10,314	10,746	10,824	11,476	12,006	12,525	12,537	12,945	13,673	14,512	14,313	Gross Dom. Prod. 1990 Prices	99b.p
52.0	55.7	58.2	62.3	64.4	67.7	70.4	72.4	77.1	82.5	100.0	126.0	137.5	154.7	191.1	GDP Deflator (1990=100)	99bip
Midyear Estimates																
3.69	3.82	3.96	4.09	4.23	4.37	4.51	4.66	4.80	4.95	5.11	5.26	5.42	5.59	5.77	Population	99z

Hungary
944

		1965	1966	1967	1968	1969	1970	1971	1972	1973	1974	1975	1976	1977	1978	1979
Exchange Rates																*Forint per SDR:*
Official Rate	aa	....	....	....	60.000	60.000	60.000	59.996	59.996	56.400	57.241	50.934	47.984	49.317	46.351	46.868
																Forint per US Dollar:
Official Rate	ae				60.000	60.000	60.000	55.260	55.260	46.752	46.752	43.509	41.300	40.600	35.578	35.578
Official Rate	rf				60.000	60.000	60.000	59.822	55.260	48.966	46.752	43.971	41.575	40.961	37.911	35.578
Secondary Rate	xe				30.000	30.000	30.000	27.630	27.630	23.376	23.376	20.449	20.650	20.300	17.789	20.330
Secondary Rate	xf				30.000	30.000	30.000	29.911	27.630	24.483	23.376	20.666	20.788	20.480	18.956	20.013
															Index Numbers (1990=100):	
Official Rate	ah x				105.3	105.3	105.3	105.6	114.3	129.3	135.1	143.7	151.9	154.2	166.8	177.5
Nominal Effective Exchange Rate	ne c				....	....	....	....	....	....	....	....	....	....	....	137.6
Real Effective Exchange Rate	re c				....	....	....	....	....	....	....	....	....	....	....	96.7
Fund Position																*Millions of SDRs:*
Quota	2f. s															
SDRs	1b. s															
Reserve Position in the Fund	1c. s															
Total Fund Cred.&Loans Outstg.	2tl															
International Liquidity													*Millions of US Dollars Unless Otherwise Indicated:*			
Total Reserves minus Gold	1l. d															
SDRs	1b. d															
Reserve Position in the Fund	1c. d															
Foreign Exchange	1d. d															
Gold (Million Fine Troy Ounces)	1ad							1.446	1.671	1.820	1.330	.951	1.322	1.282	1.978	1.777
Gold (National Valuation)	1an d							61	71	77	56	67	66	70	249	402
Monetary Authorities: Other Assets	3.. d															
Other Liabs.	4.. d															
Deposit Money Banks: Assets	7a. d															
Liabilities	7b. d															
Monetary Authorities																*Billions of Forint*
Foreign Assets	11															
Claims on Consolidated Cent.Govt	12a															
Other Claims on Residents	12d															
Claims on Deposit Money Banks	12e															
Reserve Money	14															
of which: Currency Outside DMBs	14a															
Time Deposits	15															
Foreign Liabilities	16c															
Consolidated Centr.Govt.Deposits	16d															
Other Items (Net)	17r															
of which: Valuation Changes	17rv															
Deposit Money Banks																*Billions of Forint*
Reserves	20															
Foreign Assets	21															
Claims on Consolidated Cent.Govt	22a															
Claims on Local Government	22b															
Other Claims on Residents	22d															
Demand Deposits	24															
Time, Savings,& Fgn.Currency Dep.	25															
Bonds	26ab															
Foreign Liabilities	26c															
Consolidated Centr.Govt.Deposits	26d															
Credit from Monetary Authorities	26g															
Other Items (Net)	27r															
Monetary Survey																*Billions of Forint*
Foreign Assets (Net)	31n															
Domestic Credit	32															
Claims on Cons.Cent.Govt.(Net)	32an															
Other Claims on Residents	32d															
Money	34															
Quasi-Money	35															
Bonds	36ab															
Other Items (Net)	37r															
Money plus Quasi-Money	35l															
Interest Rates																*Percent Per Annum*
Discount Rate (End of Period)	60c															
Treasury Bill Rate	60c															
Deposit Rate	60l							3.0	3.0	3.0	3.0	3.0	3.0	3.0	3.0	3.0
Lending Rate	60p															
Prices, Production, Employment																*Index Numbers (1990=100):*
Producer Prices: Industry	63				28.9	30.6	31.2	31.9	32.5	33.5	34.6	38.2	40.0	40.8	42.3	43.2
Consumer Prices	64								24.3	25.1	25.5	26.5	27.9	29.0	30.4	33.1
Wages: Average Earnings	65						20.5	21.5	22.5	24.2	26.2	27.8	29.5	31.9	34.7	36.6
Industrial Production	66						59.9	64.1	67.4	72.4	79.1	83.2	87.1	92.8	97.4	100.7
Industrial Employment	67						129.7	131.2	133.1	134.9	137.2	138.5	137.4	137.2	137.0	134.8
International Transactions																*Billions of Forint*
Exports	70						103.6	110.5	132.8	164.2	184.3	198.7	204.8	238.6	240.7	282.1
Imports, cif	71						112.6	134.5	130.2	147.8	208.2	237.5	230.1	267.3	300.9	308.9
Imports, fob	71.v						110.6	132.1	127.9	145.2	204.5	233.2	225.4	262.9	295.8	304.0
																1990=100
Volume of Exports	72						34.9	37.1	43.6	50.5	51.4	53.9	58.2	65.6	66.5	74.8
Volume of Imports	73						55.3	64.7	61.3	64.2	74.2	78.1	81.1	88.0	99.1	95.8
Export Prices	76						47.6	47.7	48.6	52.0	57.4	59.0	56.3	58.2	57.9	60.3
Import Prices	76.x						36.0	36.8	37.5	40.7	49.6	53.8	50.2	53.8	53.8	57.0

Hungary

	1980	1981	1982	1983	1984	1985	1986	1987	1988	1989	1990	1991	1992	1993	1994		
End of Period																**Exchange Rates**	
	41.084	40.075	43.694	47.315	50.186	52.007	56.177	65.807	70.699	82.192	87.421	108.169	115.459	138.317	161.591	Official Rate	aa
End of Period (ae)	*Period Averages (rf)*																
	32.213	34.430	39.610	45.193	51.199	47.347	45.927	46.387	52.537	62.543	61.449	75.620	83.970	100.700	110.690	Official Rate	ae
	32.532	34.314	36.631	42.671	48.042	50.119	45.832	46.971	50.413	59.066	63.206	74.735	78.988	91.933	105.160	Official Rate	rf
	23.950	....	....	....	....	....	....	....	....	....	....	....	....	....	....	Secondary Rate	xe
	22.139	....	....	....	....	....	....	....	....	....	....	....	....	....	....	Secondary Rate	xf
Period Averages																	
	194.2	184.2	172.9	148.3	131.7	126.1	137.9	134.6	125.6	107.3	100.0	84.6	80.0	68.9	60.1	Official Rate	ah x
	151.1	171.8	180.3	169.1	168.6	171.0	151.2	130.3	121.2	113.4	100.0	88.7	83.9	81.3	73.9	Nominal Effective Exchange Rate	ne c
	104.6	112.7	116.5	109.9	111.4	114.9	103.4	93.3	94.8	96.1	100.0	113.4	122.4	134.8	134.7	Real Effective Exchange Rate	re c
End of Period																**Fund Position**	
	....	....	375	531	531	531	531	531	531	531	531	531	755	755	755	Quota	2f. s
	....	....	2	44	—	—	—	—	—	—	—	1	2	2	1	SDRs	1b. s
	....	....	—	39	—	—	—	—	—	—	—	—	56	56	56	Reserve Position in the Fund	1c. s
	....	....	215	547	972	884	843	570	471	347	232	880	876	896	782	Total Fund Cred.&Loans Outstg.	2tl
End of Period																**International Liquidity**	
	....	....	....	1,231	1,560	2,153	2,302	1,634	1,467	1,246	1,070	3,936	4,428	6,771	6,810	Total Reserves minus Gold	1l. d
	....	....	3	46	—	—	—	—	—	—	—	1	3	3	2	SDRs	1b. d
	....	....	—	41	—	—	—	—	—	—	—	—	77	77	82	Reserve Position in the Fund	1c. d
	....	....	....	1,144	1,560	2,153	2,302	1,634	1,467	1,246	1,069	3,935	4,348	6,691	6,727	Foreign Exchange	1d. d
	2.069	1.685	.646	1.532	2.063	2.327	2.346	1.641	1.593	1.497	.300	.258	.102	.114	.110	Gold (Million Fine Troy Ounces)	1ad
	468	381	146	346	466	640	751	525	510	479	97	83	33	45	42	Gold (National Valuation)	1an d
	....	....	....	....	436	342	855	426	821	661	876	....	....	....	....	Monetary Authorities: Other Assets	3.. d
	....	....	....	9,002	8,922	11,394	13,931	16,817	16,746	17,426	....	....	....	....	....	Other Liabs.	4.. d
	....	....	76	127	119	344	634	661	777	1,004	1,156	1,405	....	....	....	Deposit Money Banks: Assets	7a. d
	....	....	1,128	1,148	1,015	1,197	1,725	1,766	1,839	2,045	1,689	1,813	....	....	....	Liabilities	7b. d
End of Period																**Monetary Authorities**	
	....	....	57.8	91.2	121.3	172.7	159.8	138.3	138.6	162.7	130.4	362.5	....	....	....	Foreign Assets	11
	....	....	487.7	486.8	489.5	488.5	563.1	633.0	666.7	739.4	778.2	844.2	....	....	....	Claims on Consolidated Cent.Govt	12a
	....	....	276.2	283.2	299.7	322.5	353.8	2.6	5.3	1.7	5.2	2.8	....	....	....	Other Claims on Residents	12d
	....	....	....	....	....	....	....	253.8	225.4	252.1	351.1	416.7	....	....	....	Claims on Deposit Money Banks	12e
	....	....	360.9	324.2	289.2	330.1	352.2	313.4	299.3	358.0	523.8	798.9	....	....	....	Reserve Money	14
	....	....	84.9	94.8	105.4	116.8	130.9	153.8	164.4	180.6	209.8	260.2	....	....	....	*of which: Currency Outside DMBs*	14a
	....	....	51.4	44.4	44.3	27.8	22.5	.6	.7	.7	1.3	2.0	....	....	....	Time Deposits	15
	....	....	353.0	431.5	503.5	584.3	684.2	815.3	913.0	1,117.0	1,131.9	1,466.1	....	....	....	Foreign Liabilities	16c
	....	....	50.6	46.2	49.4	42.5	60.4	55.5	47.0	32.7	56.5	118.0	....	....	....	Consolidated Centr.Govt.Deposits	16d
	....	....	5.7	14.9	24.1	−.9	−42.5	−157.1	−224.0	−352.4	−448.7	−758.8	....	....	....	Other Items (Net)	17r
	....	....	37.8	31.3	40.9	43.2	106.2	196.3	249.5	460.7	519.2	777.9	....	....	....	*of which: Valuation Changes*	17rv
End of Period																**Deposit Money Banks**	
	....	....	181.5	143.0	103.2	117.7	120.0	151.9	126.8	168.8	300.0	524.8	....	....	....	Reserves	20
	....	....	3.0	5.8	6.1	16.3	29.1	30.7	40.8	62.8	71.0	106.3	....	....	....	Foreign Assets	21
	....	....	7.2	7.2	8.7	8.7	8.7	13.6	12.9	21.3	14.8	145.3	....	....	....	Claims on Consolidated Cent.Govt	22a
	....	....	6.7	6.3	6.0	6.7	7.3	10.9	15.7	18.2	21.9	22.9	....	....	....	Claims on Local Government	22b
	....	....	133.6	154.3	179.6	208.6	240.6	648.7	679.3	792.7	947.5	966.0	....	....	....	Other Claims on Residents	22d
	....	....	8.2	11.0	14.9	27.3	34.3	145.2	129.5	165.8	225.4	275.0	....	....	....	Demand Deposits	24
	....	....	178.9	190.8	204.1	230.8	253.1	287.0	310.1	350.6	462.6	619.4	....	....	....	Time, Savings,& Fgn.Currency Dep.	25
	....	....	8.2	11.6	26.9	30.6	34.8	53.1	58.7	66.8	93.3	185.7	....	....	....	Bonds	26ab
	....	....	44.7	51.9	52.0	56.7	79.2	81.9	96.6	127.9	103.8	137.1	....	....	....	Foreign Liabilities	26c
	....	....	—	—	—	—	—	1.5	2.9	2.2	6.0	18.2	....	....	....	Consolidated Centr.Govt.Deposits	26d
	....	....	—	—	—	—	—	253.8	225.4	252.1	351.1	416.7	....	....	....	Credit from Monetary Authorities	26g
	....	....	92.1	51.3	5.7	12.6	4.4	33.2	52.2	98.4	113.0	113.0	....	....	....	Other Items (Net)	27r
End of Period																**Monetary Survey**	
	....	....	−337.0	−386.4	−428.1	−452.0	−574.5	−728.3	−830.2	−1,019.4	−1,034.3	−1,134.5	....	....	....	Foreign Assets (Net)	31n
	....	....	860.9	891.6	934.0	992.5	1,113.1	1,251.7	1,329.9	1,538.4	1,704.9	1,844.9	....	....	....	Domestic Credit	32
	....	....	444.3	447.8	448.7	454.7	511.4	589.6	629.6	725.8	730.4	853.2	....	....	....	Claims on Cons.Cent.Govt.(Net)	32an
	....	....	416.6	443.9	485.3	537.8	601.7	662.1	700.2	812.6	974.5	991.7	....	....	....	Other Claims on Residents	32d
	....	....	187.6	192.2	200.9	239.7	266.5	306.0	302.0	355.0	449.1	549.2	....	....	....	Money	34
	....	....	230.3	235.2	248.4	258.6	275.5	287.6	310.8	351.2	463.9	621.4	....	....	....	Quasi-Money	35
	....	....	8.2	11.6	26.9	30.6	34.8	53.1	58.7	66.8	93.3	185.7	....	....	....	Bonds	36ab
	....	....	97.8	66.2	29.8	11.7	−38.2	−123.9	−171.8	−254.0	−335.7	−645.8	....	....	....	Other Items (Net)	37r
	....	....	417.9	427.4	449.3	498.3	542.0	594.3	612.8	706.2	913.0	1,170.6	....	....	....	Money plus Quasi-Money	35l
Percent Per Annum																**Interest Rates**	
	....	....	....	....	....	10.5	9.5	10.0	10.5	14.0	20.0	26.0	20.0	22.0	25.0	Discount Rate (End of Period)	60
	....	....	....	....	....	....	....	....	....	....	....	....	21.6	16.7	25.3	Treasury Bill Rate	60c
	3.0	3.0	3.5	5.0	5.0	5.0	4.5	4.0	5.3	9.4	19.1	I 23.8	19.1	13.4	18.2	Deposit Rate	60l
	....	....	....	....	....	....	....	....	....	....	....	35.2	33.1	25.4	27.4	Lending Rate	60p
Period Averages																**Prices, Production, Employment**	
	49.9	53.0	55.5	58.6	61.0	64.2	65.6	67.9	71.0	82.0	100.0	132.6	148.9	166.9	....	Producer Prices: Industry	63
	36.2	37.8	40.4	43.0	46.8	I 50.0	52.7	57.3	66.3	77.5	100.0	134.2	I 165.0	202.1	240.2	Consumer Prices	64
	38.9	41.7	44.3	46.5	49.7	54.8	59.0	64.2	70.7	84.5	100.0	130.0	163.8	....	....	Wages: Average Earnings	65
	98.5	101.3	103.2	104.6	107.0	107.8	109.3	112.5	111.7	109.3	100.0	78.2	70.6	73.3	80.1	Industrial Production	66
	131.1	128.3	125.7	123.2	122.7	121.4	120.6	117.6	114.3	109.7	100.0	....	....	....	....	Industrial Employment	67
Billions of Forint																**International Transactions**	
	281.0	299.5	324.5	374.1	414.0	424.6	420.3	450.1	504.1	571.3	615.0	764.3	843.6	819.9	1,114.1	Exports	70
	299.9	314.3	324.8	365.0	390.5	410.1	439.7	463.1	472.5	518.7	544.9	855.6	878.6	1,158.1	1,505.7	Imports, cif	71
	294.6	307.9	319.0	359.2	384.0	402.0	432.1	455.1	463.8	515.1	547.5	840.5	863.1	1,137.6	1,479.1	Imports, fob	71.v
1990=100																	
	75.7	77.6	80.1	85.4	91.5	96.2	94.0	97.2	103.8	104.1	100.0	95.0	96.0	83.4	94.6	Volume of Exports	72
	94.7	94.9	91.0	91.9	92.8	99.8	102.4	104.7	104.5	105.5	100.0	105.5	98.5	119.2	131.6	Volume of Imports	73
	59.5	61.7	62.4	65.7	68.7	70.7	71.6	73.8	78.6	90.9	100.0	130.8	....	....	....	Export Prices	76
	56.1	58.7	60.7	65.5	70.1	72.8	76.4	78.0	81.2	91.3	100.0	146.3	....	....	....	Import Prices	76.x

Hungary
944

		1965	1966	1967	1968	1969	1970	1971	1972	1973	1974	1975	1976	1977	1978	1979
Balance of Payments															*Millions of US Dollars:*	
Goods: Exports f.o.b.	78aa d	....	....	....	....	....	....	....	....	....	....	....	....	....	....	....
Goods: Imports f.o.b.	78ab d	....	....	....	....	....	....	....	....	....	....	....	....	....	....	....
Trade Balance	78ac d	....	....	....	....	....	....	....	....	....	....	....	....	....	....	....
Services: Credit	78ad d	....	....	....	....	....	....	....	....	....	....	....	....	....	....	....
Services: Debit	78ae d	....	....	....	....	....	....	....	....	....	....	....	....	....	....	....
Balance on Goods and Services	78af d	....	....	....	....	....	....	....	....	....	....	....	....	....	....	....
Income: Credit	78ag d	....	....	....	....	....	....	....	....	....	....	....	....	....	....	....
Income: Debit	78ah d	....	....	....	....	....	....	....	....	....	....	....	....	....	....	....
Balance on Goods, Serv., & Inc.	78ai d	....	....	....	....	....	....	....	....	....	....	....	....	....	....	....
Current Transfers, n.i.e.: Credit	78aj d	....	....	....	....	....	....	....	....	....	....	....	....	....	....	....
Current Transfers: Debit	78ak d	....	....	....	....	....	....	....	....	....	....	....	....	....	....	....
Current Account, n.i.e.	78al d	....	....	....	....	....	....	....	....	....	....	....	....	....	....	....
Capital Account, n.i.e.: Credit	78ba d	....	....	....	....	....	....	....	....	....	....	....	....	....	....	....
Capital Account: Debit	78bb d	....	....	....	....	....	....	....	....	....	....	....	....	....	....	....
Capital Account, n.i.e.	78bc d	....	....	....	....	....	....	....	....	....	....	....	....	....	....	....
Direct Investment Abroad	78bd d	....	....	....	....	....	....	....	....	....	....	....	....	....	....	....
Dir. Invest. in Rep. Econ., n.i.e.	78be d	....	....	....	....	....	....	....	....	....	....	....	....	....	....	....
Portfolio Investment Assets	78bf u	....	....	....	....	....	....	....	....	....	....	....	....	....	....	....
Portfolio Investment Liab., n.i.e.	78bg d	....	....	....	....	....	....	....	....	....	....	....	....	....	....	....
Other Investment Assets	78bh d	....	....	....	....	....	....	....	....	....	....	....	....	....	....	....
Other Investment Liab., n.i.e.	78bi d	....	....	....	....	....	....	....	....	....	....	....	....	....	....	....
Financial Account, n.i.e.	78bj d	....	....	....	....	....	....	....	....	....	....	....	....	....	....	....
Net Errors and Omissions	78ca d	....	....	....	....	....	....	....	....	....	....	....	....	....	....	....
Overall Balance	78cb d	....	....	....	....	....	....	....	....	....	....	....	....	....	....	....
Reserves and Related Items	79da d	....	....	....	....	....	....	....	....	....	....	....	....	....	....	....
Reserve Assets	79db d	....	....	....	....	....	....	....	....	....	....	....	....	....	....	....
Use of Fund Credit and Loans	79dc d	....	....	....	....	....	....	....	....	....	....	....	....	....	....	....
Liabs.Constit.For.Auth.Reserves	79dd d	....	....	....	....	....	....	....	....	....	....	....	....	....	....	....
Exceptional Financing	79de d	....	....	....	....	....	....	....	....	....	....	....	....	....	....	....
Government Finance															*Billions of Forint:*	
Deficit (-) or Surplus	80	....	....	....	....	....	....	....	....	....	....	....	....	....	....	....
Revenue	81	....	....	....	....	....	....	....	....	....	....	....	....	....	....	....
Grants Received	81z	....	....	....	....	....	....	....	....	....	....	....	....	....	....	....
Expenditure	82	....	....	....	....	....	....	....	....	....	....	....	....	....	....	....
Lending Minus Repayments	83	....	....	....	....	....	....	....	....	....	....	....	....	....	....	....
Financing																
Net Borrowing	84	....	....	....	....	....	....	....	....	....	....	....	....	....	....	....
Domestic	84a	....	....	....	....	....	....	....	....	....	....	....	....	....	....	....
Foreign	85a	....	....	....	....	....	....	....	....	....	....	....	....	....	....	....
Use of Cash Balances	87	....	....	....	....	....	....	....	....	....	....	....	....	....	....	....
National Accounts															*Billions of Forint*	
Exports of Goods & Services	90c	....	....	....	....	....	.1	.1	.1	.2	.2	.2	.2	.2	243.9	283.3
Government Consumption	91f	....	....	....	....	....	34.4	37.8	38.6	40.5	46.9	50.2	53.2	57.8	65.8	71.3
Gross Fixed Capital Formation	93e	....	....	....	....	....	113.1	116.8	123.1	139.2	161.0	161.0	168.2	197.7	214.4	220.8
Increase/Decrease(-) in Stocks	93i	....	....	....	....	....	11.4	22.8	7.3	4.1	21.3	21.4	21.5	18.8	45.5	11.3
Private Consumption	96f	....	....	....	....	....	194.1	209.6	223.5	241.7	261.4	286.1	307.3	334.0	361.7	401.2
Imports of Goods & Services	98c	....	....	....	....	....	–.1	–.1	–.1	–.1	–.2	–.2	–.2	–.3	–301.6	–305.6
Gross Domestic Product = GDP	99b	....	....	....	....	....	332.5	360.8	391.0	429.0	448.9	482.7	528.9	582.0	629.7	682.3
National Income, Market Prices	99e	....	....	....	....	....	295.9	320.6	347.8	382.9	398.8	427.8	467.1	513.4	553.6	598.9
Net Material Product = NMP	99m	....	....	....	....	....	275.5	296.9	321.5	354.5	368.7	395.0	432.9	476.7	514.6	556.3
Gross Dom. Prod. 1990 Prices	99b. p	....	....	....	....	....	1,076.8	1,143.9	1,214.2	1,297.4	1,373.5	1,458.7	1,510.6	1,626.1	1,698.4	1,743.9
GDP Deflator (1990=100)	99bi p	....	....	....	....	....	30.9	31.5	32.2	33.1	32.7	33.1	35.0	35.8	37.1	39.1
															Millions:	
Population	99z	....	....	....	....	....	10.34	10.37	10.40	10.43	10.48	10.53	10.59	10.64	10.67	10.70

Interest Rates: *Deposit Rate:* ℓ Beginning in May 1990, weighted average rate offered by commercial banks and specialized financial institutions on deposits of less than one month made by enterprises and entrepreneurs.

Hungary

Balance of Payments

	1980	1981	1982	1983	1984	1985	1986	1987	1988	1989	1990	1991	1992	1993	1994		
Minus Sign Indicates Debit																	
	....	....	9,038	8,978	9,090	8,578	9,198	9,967	9,989	10,493	9,151	9,688	10,097	8,119	7,648	Goods: Exports f.o.b.	78aa *d*
	....	....	−8,628	−8,544	−8,310	−8,130	−9,663	−9,887	−9,406	−9,450	−8,617	−9,330	−10,108	−12,140	−11,364	Goods: Imports f.o.b.	78ab *d*
	....	....	410	434	780	448	−465	80	583	1,043	534	358	−11	−4,021	−3,716	Trade Balance	78ac *d*
	....	....	633	589	595	622	729	980	1,047	1,291	2,884	2,526	3,405	2,836	3,117	Services: Credit	78ad *d*
	....	....	−524	−485	−552	−723	−713	−814	−1,227	−1,658	−2,400	−1,991	−2,641	−2,620	−2,958	Services: Debit	78ae *d*
	....	....	519	538	823	347	−449	246	403	676	1,019	892	753	−3,805	−3,557	Balance on Goods and Services	78af *d*
	....	....	109	117	139	195	261	247	240	231	280	322	424	465	676	Income: Credit	78ag *d*
	....	....	−1,222	−892	−989	−1,062	−1,252	−1,274	−1,332	−1,625	−1,707	−1,678	−1,684	−1,655	−2,082	Income: Debit	78ah *d*
	....	....	−594	−237	−27	−520	−1,440	−781	−689	−718	−408	−464	−506	−4,995	−4,963	Balance on Goods, Serv., & Inc.	78ai *d*
	....	....	63	56	66	65	75	105	117	130	1,595	2,604	2,866	2,694	2,871	Current Transfers, n.i.e.: Credit	78aj *d*
	....	....	—	—	—	—	—	—	—	—	−808	−1,737	−2,008	−1,961	−1,961	Current Transfers: Debit	78ak *d*
	....	....	−531	−181	39	−455	−1,365	−676	−572	−588	379	403	352	−4,262	−4,054	Current Account, n.i.e.	78al *d*
	....	....	—	—	—	—	—	—	—	—	—	—	—	—	—	Capital Account, n.i.e.: Credit	78ba *d*
	....	....	—	—	—	—	—	—	—	—	—	—	—	—	—	Capital Account: Debit	78bb *d*
	....	....	—	—	—	—	—	—	—	—	—	—	—	—	—	Capital Account, n.i.e.	78bc *d*
	....	....	—	—	—	—	—	—	—	—	—	—	—	−11	−49	Direct Investment Abroad	78bd *d*
	....	....	—	—	—	—	—	—	—	—	—	1,462	1,479	2,350	1,144	Dir. Invest. in Rep. Econ., n.i.e.	78be *d*
	....	....	—	—	—	—	—	—	—	—	—	—	—	−8	6	Portfolio Investment Assets	78bf *d*
	....	....	—	—	—	—	—	—	—	—	—	—	—	3,927	2,458	Portfolio Investment Liab., n.i.e.	78bg *d*
	....	....	−880	−429	−251	−424	180	−319	−83	−322	−524	−13	−421	881	362	Other Investment Assets	78bh *d*
	....	....	406	1,075	518	1,490	1,208	554	763	1,223	−278	25	−642	−1,055	−551	Other Investment Liab., n.i.e.	78bi *d*
	....	....	−474	646	267	1,066	1,388	235	680	901	−801	1,474	416	6,083	3,370	Financial Account, n.i.e.	78bj *d*
	....	....	465	−590	−240	−75	109	160	50	−141	10	−82	2	724	209	Net Errors and Omissions	78ca *d*
	....	....	−540	−125	66	536	132	−281	158	172	−413	1,795	770	2,545	−475	Overall Balance	78cb *d*
	....	....	540	125	−66	−536	−132	281	−158	−172	413	−1,795	−770	−2,545	475	Reserves and Related Items	79da *d*
	....	....	305	−228	−501	−441	−82	637	−25	−14	558	−2,700	−763	−2,574	640	Reserve Assets	79db *d*
	....	....	235	353	436	−95	−49	−356	−132	−158	−145	905	−7	30	−165	Use of Fund Credit and Loans	79dc *d*
	....	....	—	—	—	—	—	—	—	—	—	—	—	—	—	Liabs.Constit.For.Auth.Reserves	79dd *d*
	....	....	....	....	....	....	....	....	....	....	....	....	....	....	....	Exceptional Financing	79de *d*

Government Finance

	1980	1981	1982	1983	1984	1985	1986	1987	1988	1989	1990	1991	1992	1993	1994		
Year Ending December 31																	
	....	−22.1	−16.1	−6.4	15.7	−10.1	−30.9	−40.3	−3.2	−32.6	16.7	....	....	....	....	Deficit (-) or Surplus	80
	....	418.1	438.7	485.5	535.2	539.0	606.8	652.0	789.9	926.6	1,105.9	....	....	....	....	Revenue	81
	....	—	—	—	—	—	—	8.4	—	—	—	....	....	....	....	Grants Received	81z
	....	438.2	453.8	492.3	519.5	549.8	636.5	701.1	792.0	957.8	1,088.8	....	....	....	....	Expenditure	82
	....	2.0	1.0	−.4	—	−.7	1.2	.6	1.1	1.4	.4	....	....	....	....	Lending Minus Repayments	83
																Financing	
	....	16.3	17.8	7.6	−3.1	.1	31.2	40.3	4.4	32.0	−5.8	....	....	....	....	Net Borrowing	84
	....	—	14.9	3.5	−4.4	1.2	39.8	47.9	14.9	42.3	4.9	....	....	....	....	Domestic	84a
	....	16.3	2.9	4.1	1.3	−1.1	−8.6	−7.6	−10.5	−10.3	−10.7	....	....	....	....	Foreign	85a
	....	5.8	−1.7	−1.2	−12.6	10.0	−.3	....	−1.2	.6	−10.9	....	....	....	....	Use of Cash Balances	87

National Accounts

	1980	1981	1982	1983	1984	1985	1986	1987	1988	1989	1990	1991	1992	1993	1994		
Billions of Forint																	
	281.8	308.2	321.8	360.7	402.0	436.2	431.6	464.4	530.4	620.9	669.0	834.9	915.5	905.9	....	Exports of Goods & Services	90c
	74.1	79.1	84.2	90.9	95.3	104.6	116.0	126.3	168.5	177.7	221.8	289.3	350.0	433.4	....	Government Consumption	91f
	207.7	206.7	213.9	220.0	225.4	232.1	261.2	303.5	310.8	347.8	369.6	440.9	571.0	650.0	....	Gross Fixed Capital Formation	93e
	13.6	24.6	27.9	17.1	26.4	26.3	31.6	23.9	63.9	98.2	129.6	39.9	−24.0	100.9	....	Increase/Decrease(-) in Stocks	93i
	441.2	477.7	515.1	551.2	600.5	649.3	695.5	778.5	868.5	1,029.6	1,282.5	1,605.4	1,940.9	2,400.0	....	Private Consumption	96f
	−297.4	−316.4	−315.0	−343.6	−371.1	−414.8	−447.0	−470.3	−491.7	−563.5	−593.0	−902.0	−948.4	−1,170.2	....	Imports of Goods & Services	98c
	721.0	779.9	847.9	896.3	978.5	1,033.7	1,088.8	1,226.4	1,435.2	1,710.8	2,079.5	2,308.4	2,805.0	3,320.0	....	Gross Domestic Product = GDP	99b
	628.3	683.6	746.8	793.5	868.6	919.4	966.9	1,097.7	1,278.9	....	....	....	....	....	....	National Income, Market Prices	99e
	582.9	634.9	696.4	738.1	804.1	842.3	881.3	999.6	1,159.6	....	....	....	....	....	....	Net Material Product = NMP	99m
	⅋1,747.7	1,797.9	1,848.9	1,862.4	1,911.7	⅋1,906.8	1,953.2	2,026.8	⅋2,139.0	2,154.8	2,079.5	1,832.1	....	....	....	Gross Dom. Prod. 1990 Prices	99b.*p*
	41.3	43.4	45.9	48.1	51.2	54.2	55.7	60.5	67.1	79.4	100.0	126.0	....	....	....	GDP Deflator (1990=100)	99bi *p*
Midyear Estimates																	
	10.71	10.70	10.68	10.66	10.62	10.58	10.53	10.49	10.44	10.40	10.36	10.35	10.32	10.29	10.26	Population	99z

1995 INTERNATIONAL FINANCIAL STATISTICS YEARBOOK

Iceland

		1965	1966	1967	1968	1969	1970	1971	1972	1973	1974	1975	1976	1977	1978	1979
Exchange Rates																*Kronur per SDR:*
Official Rate	aa	.431	.431	.571	.881	.881	.881	.949	1.063	1.013	⁑1.451	1.999	2.204	2.589	4.144	5.202
																Kronur per US Dollar:
Official Rate	ae	.431	.431	.571	.881	.881	.881	.874	.979	.840	⁑1.185	1.708	1.897	2.131	3.181	3.949
Official Rate	rf	.430	.430	.442	.622	.880	.880	.880	.883	.901	1.000	1.537	1.822	1.989	2.711	3.526
																Index Numbers (1990=100):
Official Rate	ahx	13,511.3	13,511.3	13,234.9	9,713.7	6,603.8	6,603.8	4,714.6	6,632.7	6,477.7	5,920.1	3,819.6	3,197.8	2,930.3	2,174.1	1,660.1
Nominal Effective Exchange Rate	ne c	....	....	....	....	....	....	....	....	....	....	....	....	....	....	1,542.7
Real Effective Exchange Rate	re c	....	....	....	....	....	....	....	....	....	....	....	....	....	....	99.8
Fund Position																*Millions of SDRs:*
Quota	2f. s	11.3	15.0	15.0	15.0	15.0	23.0	23.0	23.0	23.0	23.0	23.0	23.0	23.0	29.0	29.0
SDRs	1b. s	—	—	—	—	—	.5	3.0	6.4	6.3	6.3	4.8	1.8	2.7	1.8	.2
Reserve Position in the Fund	1c. s	2.8	3.7	3.7	3.7	—	—	—	5.7	5.8	5.8	—	—	—	—	5.4
Total Fund Cred.&Loans Outstg.	2tl	—	—	3.8	7.5	11.3	1.8	—	—	—	—	15.5	31.4	56.4	56.4	47.3	34.7
International Liquidity												*Millions of US Dollars Unless Otherwise Indicated:*				
Total Reserves minus Gold	1l. d	52.9	57.0	34.2	26.7	37.5	52.7	68.8	83.0	98.4	47.3	45.6	79.4	98.3	135.8	161.9
SDRs	1b. d	—	—	—	—	—	.5	3.2	6.9	7.6	7.7	5.6	2.1	3.2	2.3	.2
Reserve Position in the Fund	1c. d	2.8	3.7	3.7	3.7	—	—	6.2	6.2	6.9	—	—	—	—	—	7.1
Foreign Exchange	1d. d	50.1	53.3	30.5	23.0	37.5	52.2	59.4	69.9	83.8	39.6	40.0	77.3	95.1	133.5	154.6
Gold (Million Fine Troy Ounces)	1ad	.029	.029	.029	.029	.029	.029	.029	.029	.029	.030	.030	.030	.039	.044	.049
Gold (National Valuation)	1and	1.0	1.0	1.0	1.0	1.0	1.0	1.0	1.1	1.2	1.2	1.2	1.2	1.7	2.0	2.2
Monetary Authorities: Other Liab.	4. d	9.7	9.7	8.7	11.1	5.8	11.9	15.6	18.3	21.4	28.5	56.5	54.0	31.1	39.5	32.0
Deposit Money Banks: Assets	7a. d	3.1	4.5	3.0	2.8	5.5	2.2	1.9	3.4	4.8	10.9	11.7	11.3	13.4	14.8	17.4
of which: Claims on Nonbanks	7ad d	....	....	....	1.1	.6	.3	.2	1.1	1.6	2.2	3.2	2.9	3.5	4.0	4.9
Deposit Money Banks: Liabilities	7b. d	7.1	13.3	13.2	13.7	6.9	5.9	8.2	13.8	21.4	39.6	60.8	60.3	78.1	102.9	126.5
Monetary Authorities												*Thousands of Kronur through 1974;*				
Foreign Assets	11	23,463	25,237	20,753	25,639	34,362	47,387	61,171	82,483	84,902	57,448	⁑80	153	213	438	648
Claims on Central Government	12a	10,320	7,653	12,067	17,804	18,794	20,448	20,819	28,800	43,530	77,820	⁑169	201	237	383	443
of which: Invest. Credit Funds	12ax	4,649	4,629	6,187	6,815	5,850	5,496	9,175	12,478	14,930	13,270	⁑32	38	36	36	33
Claims on Private Sector	12d	464	783	1,057	1,567	1,830	6,690	6,763	1,509	1,430	1,620	⁑1	2	3	4	4
Claims on Deposit Money Banks	12e	11,650	13,880	17,320	22,188	21,418	19,185	27,465	38,368	58,180	151,950	⁑182	245	333	460	683
Reserve Money	14	28,158	29,764	30,890	32,743	42,109	51,028	60,568	75,483	105,220	133,340	⁑179	244	378	587	866
of which: Currency Outside DMBs	14a	9,700	10,390	9,680	9,558	11,472	14,120	17,194	21,436	27,000	34,530	⁑44	57	88	124	160
Foreign Liabilities	16c	4,159	4,191	7,092	16,411	15,002	12,033	13,698	18,012	19,940	56,298	⁑159	227	212	322	307
Central Government Deposits	16d	8,395	8,903	6,718	9,319	12,002	19,260	25,056	32,579	46,710	66,190	⁑62	90	135	267	419
of which: Invest. Credit Funds	16dx	1,510	1,232	869	895	5,260	5,765	4,658	3,219	10,170	13,880	⁑19	26	32	30	73
Other Items (Net)	17r	5,155	4,686	6,583	8,706	7,270	11,368	16,876	25,023	16,182	32,980	⁑32	40	61	109	185
Deposit Money Banks												*Thousands of Kronur through 1974;*				
Reserves	20	15,199	15,452	20,720	24,670	29,710	35,640	42,250	53,120	76,980	99,560	⁑133	184	285	454	680
Foreign Assets	21	1,340	1,931	1,720	2,450	4,870	1,910	1,690	3,330	4,500	12,950	⁑20	21	29	47	69
Claims on Central Government	22a	....	....	6,680	6,090	7,200	12,500	15,380	17,200	21,410	27,450	⁑34	47	58	72	94
Claims on Private Sector	22d	73,715	86,318	99,490	113,390	123,630	142,800	176,150	215,240	293,230	465,430	⁑615	785	1,103	1,646	2,599
Demand Deposits	24	16,627	16,997	16,370	19,330	26,640	32,360	39,450	47,580	68,840	90,150	⁑123	151	217	306	469
Savings Deposits	25	50,844	58,958	77,990	84,170	101,340	126,240	151,980	177,740	230,970	295,680	⁑375	513	732	1,110	1,792
Bonds	26a	....	....	....	....	....	....	....	....	....	....	....	....	....	....	....
Restricted Deposits	26b	764	795	850	930	1,540	1,700	1,940	2,260	3,930	5,100	⁑6	7	9	16	8
Foreign Liabilities	26c	3,042	5,698	7,520	12,050	6,070	5,220	7,190	13,580	19,890	46,890	⁑104	114	166	327	499
Credit from Monetary Authorities	26g	11,651	13,128	17,330	22,230	21,320	18,900	27,410	38,330	58,160	151,170	⁑182	242	333	460	658
Other Items (Net)	27r	7,326	8,125	8,550	7,890	8,490	8,470	7,510	9,390	14,340	16,420	⁑14	11	17	1	16
Monetary Survey												*Thousands of Kronur through 1974;*				
Foreign Assets (Net)	31n	17,602	17,279	7,861	–372	18,160	32,044	41,973	54,221	49,572	–32,790	⁑–163	–167	–137	–164	–90
Domestic Credit	32	76,104	85,851	112,356	129,342	139,362	162,718	193,596	230,170	312,890	506,130	⁑758	945	1,266	1,839	2,722
Claims on Central Govt. (Net)	32an	1,925	–1,250	11,809	14,385	13,902	13,228	10,683	13,421	18,230	39,080	⁑141	157	160	188	118
Claims on Private Sector	32d	74,179	87,101	100,547	114,957	125,460	149,490	182,913	216,749	294,660	467,050	⁑616	788	1,106	1,650	2,604
Money	34	26,327	27,387	26,050	28,888	38,112	46,480	56,644	69,016	95,840	124,680	⁑167	208	305	430	629
Quasi-Money	35	50,844	58,958	77,990	84,170	101,340	126,240	151,980	177,740	230,970	295,680	⁑375	513	732	1,110	1,792
Bonds	36a	....	....	....	....	....	....	....	....	....	....	....	....	....	....	....
Other Items (Net)	37r	13,690	13,440	14,060	15,280	17,741	21,812	26,721	37,562	35,672	52,970	⁑52	57	91	135	210
Money plus Quasi-Money	35l	77,171	86,345	104,040	113,058	139,452	172,720	208,624	246,756	326,810	420,360	⁑542	720	1,038	1,540	2,421
Interest Rates																*Percent Per Annum*
Discount Rate *(End of Period)*	60	5.0	5.3	5.3	5.3	5.3	5.3	5.3	5.3	6.3	7.3	7.3	7.3	14.0	17.0	26.0
Money Market Rate	60b	....	....	....	....	....	....	....	....	....	....	....	....	....	....	....
Treasury Bill Rate	60c	....	....	....	....	....	....	....	....	....	....	....	....	....	....	....
Deposit Rate	60l	....	....	....	....	....	....	....	....	12.0	17.0	17.0	13.6	29.0	42.3	29.5
Lending Rate	60p	....	....	....	....	....	....	....	....	....	....	....	....	....	33.0	42.5
Prices and Production																*Index Numbers (1990=100):*
Consumer Prices	64	.2	.2	⁑.2	.2	.3	.3	.3	.4	.5	.6	1.0	1.3	1.7	2.4	3.5
Wages, Hourly	65	....	....	....	.2	.2	.3	.3	.4	.5	.7	.9	⁑1.2	1.7	2.6	3.7
Total Fish Catch	66al	80.3	83.2	59.0	36.6	43.7	47.5	45.6	47.9	60.0	63.2	68.6	65.3	91.9	104.9	110.0

Iceland

1980	1981	1982	1983	1984	1985	1986	1987	1988	1989	1990	1991	1992	1993	1994		
End of Period															**Exchange Rates**	
7.957	ⅰ9.513	18.339	30.016	39.743	46.200	49.221	50.589	62.198	80.387	78.801	79.561	87.890	99.899	99.708	Official Rate	aa
End of Period (ae) Period Average (rf)																
6.239	ⅰ8.173	16.625	28.670	40.545	42.060	40.240	35.660	46.220	61.170	55.390	55.620	63.920	72.730	68.300	Official Rate	ae
4.798	7.224	12.352	24.843	31.694	41.508	41.104	38.677	43.014	57.042	58.284	58.996	57.546	67.603	69.944	Official Rate	rf
Period Averages																
1,233.0	811.7	490.2	240.3	185.2	140.2	141.6	150.5	136.4	102.7	100.0	98.8	101.3	86.3	83.3	Official Rate	ah x
1,147.0	865.0	581.8	310.0	259.9	205.0	171.8	162.5	141.0	111.5	100.0	99.8	99.5	92.0	87.4	Nominal Effective Exchange Rate	ne c
104.3	110.8	101.0	92.8	98.8	98.1	97.8	105.6	110.6	100.9	100.0	102.1	102.8	96.3	90.9	Real Effective Exchange Rate	re c
End of Period															**Fund Position**	
43.5	43.5	43.5	59.6	59.6	59.6	59.6	59.6	59.6	59.6	59.6	59.6	59.6	85.3	85.3	Quota	2f. s
1.8	3.4	2.0	.2	.4	.4	.2	1.9	1.0	—	.3	.1	—	—	.1	SDRs	1b. s
9.0	9.0	—	4.0	4.0	4.0	4.0	4.0	4.0	4.0	4.0	4.0	4.0	10.5	10.5	Reserve Position in the Fund	1c. s
15.7	5.9	22.4	21.5	21.5	21.5	10.8	—	—	—	—	—	—	—	—	Total Fund Cred.&Loans Outstg.	2tl
End of Period															**International Liquidity**	
173.8	229.5	145.2	149.3	127.6	205.5	309.8	311.3	290.7	337.3	436.1	449.5	498.3	426.4	292.9	Total Reserves minus Gold	1l. d
2.3	4.0	2.2	.2	.4	.4	.2	2.7	1.3	—	.4	.1	—	.1	.1	SDRs	1b. d
11.5	10.5	—	4.2	4.0	4.4	4.9	5.7	5.4	5.3	5.7	5.8	14.4	14.4	15.3	Reserve Position in the Fund	1c. d
160.0	215.0	143.0	144.9	123.3	200.7	304.7	302.9	284.0	332.0	430.0	443.6	483.9	412.0	277.5	Foreign Exchange	1d. d
.049	.049	.049	.049	.049	.049	.049	.049	.049	.049	.049	.049	.049	.049	.049	Gold (Million Fine Troy Ounces)	1ad
2.1	2.0	1.9	1.8	1.7	1.9	2.1	2.4	2.3	2.2	2.4	2.5	2.4	2.4	2.5	Gold (National Valuation)	1an d
26.5	36.0	42.4	55.4	69.3	13.3	25.8	22.2	40.3	16.7	17.1	20.3	12.4	36.8	137.5	Monetary Authorities: Other Liab.	4.. d
25.0	20.2	24.5	26.7	27.6	40.9	43.6	63.9	63.7	62.3	81.0	83.5	70.8	94.0	118.7	Deposit Money Banks: Assets	7a. d
4.8	4.5	3.4	3.8	2.7	7.3	7.4	10.6	9.4	4.5	.8	2.7	5.6	5.8	12.1	*of which:* Claims on Nonbanks	7ad d
177.9	209.1	222.4	289.4	260.4	422.0	418.5	629.8	754.1	696.0	705.4	714.8	682.4	593.0	459.2	Deposit Money Banks: Liabilities	7b. d
Millions of Kronur Beginning 1975: End of Period															**Monetary Authorities**	
1,106	1,889	2,441	4,324	5,234	8,723	12,532	11,167	13,563	20,797	24,261	25,248	32,017	31,318	24,347	Foreign Assets	11
501	650	762	2,273	3,348	5,500	4,123	7,108	11,902	11,672	6,978	11,485	7,282	13,504	29,036	Claims on Central Government	12a
38	105	163	251	594	670	859	1,091	1,196	873	1,866	603	531	639	4,490	*of which:* Invest. Credit Funds	12ax
15	30	48	92	44	49	128	357	445	922	672	412	380	330	408	Claims on Private Sector	12d
1,105	1,589	4,514	6,934	10,256	5,673	5,955	5,153	4,565	4,726	4,319	3,342	3,983	2,630	2,226	Claims on Deposit Money Banks	12e
1,521	2,537	3,778	6,559	8,466	10,546	14,031	15,500	17,239	22,247	18,222	19,980	18,088	15,908	16,162	Reserve Money	14
224	406	527	770	966	1,251	1,734	2,244	2,631	2,975	3,057	3,239	3,593	3,906	4,695	*of which:* Currency Outside DMBs	14a
290	351	1,114	2,233	3,666	1,553	1,567	792	1,862	1,019	950	1,127	792	2,678	9,389	Foreign Liabilities	16c
436	735	1,261	2,546	3,623	4,000	2,719	3,340	4,276	3,530	5,323	6,775	9,751	11,775	12,206	Central Government Deposits	16d
56	75	281	684	1,543	1,816	1,432	989	1,848	1,303	2,875	1,657	4,239	4,424	4,787	*of which:* Invest. Credit Funds	16dx
480	536	1,613	2,284	3,126	3,845	4,421	4,154	7,099	11,321	11,735	12,605	15,031	17,421	18,259	Other Items (Net)	17r
Millions of Kronur Beginning 1975: End of Period															**Deposit Money Banks**	
1,255	2,134	3,177	5,241	7,368	9,139	12,151	13,141	14,510	19,525	15,042	16,706	14,474	11,747	11,472	Reserves	20
156	165	407	765	1,119	1,719	1,753	2,277	2,943	3,810	4,488	4,644	4,524	6,835	8,105	Foreign Assets	21
180	298	529	1,106	ⅰ1,384	1,712	2,025	3,897	5,110	10,543	21,058	22,075	23,739	31,011	22,438	Claims on Central Government	22a
4,294	7,313	14,261	26,034	ⅰ38,749	51,266	59,970	84,854	116,711	147,389	157,123	175,155	187,675	193,643	193,782	Claims on Private Sector	22d
786	1,222	1,549	2,928	ⅰ4,312	5,471	7,940	10,463	12,187	16,825	21,587	26,317	26,351	27,663	30,426	Demand Deposits	24
2,993	5,240	8,780	15,750	20,749	31,731	42,326	57,540	72,286	93,439	105,168	118,868	124,165	132,570	132,881	Savings Deposits	25
....	....	....	....	—	317	1,238	3,084	7,928	13,963	17,453	19,180	20,589	22,699	20,630	Bonds	26a
9	13	6	11	19	24	46	68	83	66	—	19	—	—	7	Restricted Deposits	26b
1,110	1,709	3,698	8,297	10,556	17,751	16,842	22,459	34,853	42,575	39,072	39,755	43,616	43,127	31,363	Foreign Liabilities	26c
994	1,507	4,463	6,939	10,251	5,656	6,035	5,038	4,578	4,737	3,625	3,335	2,520	1,600	3,104	Credit from Monetary Authorities	26g
−7	219	−122	ⅰ2,733	2,886	1,472	5,517	7,359	9,662	10,806	11,106	13,171	15,577	17,386	Other Items (Net)	27r
Millions of Kronur Beginning 1975: End of Period															**Monetary Survey**	
−138	−5	−1,964	−5,441	−7,869	−8,862	−4,124	−9,806	−20,208	−18,987	−11,272	−10,990	−7,867	−7,652	−8,301	Foreign Assets (Net)	31n
4,554	7,556	14,340	26,959	ⅰ39,902	54,526	63,527	92,877	129,893	166,996	180,508	202,352	209,325	226,713	233,457	Domestic Credit	32
245	212	31	833	ⅰ1,109	3,211	3,429	7,666	12,736	18,685	22,713	22,786	21,270	32,740	39,267	Claims on Central Govt. (Net)	32an
4,309	7,343	14,309	26,126	ⅰ38,793	51,315	60,098	85,211	117,156	148,311	157,795	175,567	188,055	193,973	194,190	Claims on Private Sector	32d
1,010	1,628	2,076	3,698	ⅰ5,278	6,722	9,674	12,707	14,818	19,800	24,644	29,556	29,944	31,569	35,121	Money	34
2,993	5,240	8,780	15,750	20,749	31,731	42,326	57,540	72,286	93,439	105,168	118,868	124,165	132,570	132,881	Quasi-Money	35
....	....	....	....	—	317	1,238	3,084	7,928	13,963	17,453	19,180	20,589	22,699	20,630	Bonds	36a
413	683	1,520	2,070	ⅰ6,005	6,894	6,164	9,740	14,652	20,807	21,970	23,759	26,761	32,224	36,525	Other Items (Net)	37r
4,003	6,868	10,856	19,448	ⅰ26,027	38,453	52,000	70,247	87,104	113,239	129,812	148,424	154,109	164,139	168,002	Money plus Quasi-Money	35l
Percent Per Annum															**Interest Rates**	
28.0	28.0	28.0	22.0	16.5	30.0	21.0	49.2	24.1	38.4	21.0	21.0	ⅰ10.5	5.5	5.4	Discount Rate *(End of Period)*	60
....	....	....	....	36.90	....	....	31.52	34.49	21.58	12.73	14.85	12.38	8.61	4.96	Money Market Rate	60b
....	....	....	....	....	....	....	....	26.39	23.00	12.92	14.25	9.96	8.88	5.40	Treasury Bill Rate	60c
38.8	38.8	38.3	39.5	18.1	24.7	12.2	15.5	17.4	12.3	4.3	4.9	1.4	ⅰ6.6	3.0	Deposit Rate	60l
45.0	40.0	46.0	42.8	22.8	32.6	18.8	26.6	30.3	28.0	16.2	17.5	13.1	14.1	10.6	Lending Rate	60p
Period Averages															**Prices and Production**	
5.6	8.4	12.7	23.3	30.2	39.7	48.4	57.0	71.7	86.6	100.0	106.8	111.0	115.6	117.4	Consumer Prices	64
5.8	8.8	13.8	21.0	23.4	30.8	38.7	64.6	82.0	92.9	100.0	108.6	112.9	115.0	115.5	Wages, Hourly	65
101.1	96.2	52.6	55.8	102.3	110.8	108.6	105.8	114.2	91.6	100.0	66.4	103.0	112.6	96.9	Total Fish Catch	66al

Iceland

		1965	1966	1967	1968	1969	1970	1971	1972	1973	1974	1975	1976	1977	1978	1979
International Transactions													*Thousands of Kronur through 1974;*			
Exports	70	55,600	60,400	43,000	50,900	94,700	129,000	131,800	167,000	260,200	328,800	I 474	735	1,019	1,763	2,786
Fish	70al	22,800	23,300	18,400	27,300	45,900	61,700	71,400	78,100	107,600	146,700	I 262	366	465	810	1,293
Fishmeal	70z	10,900	12,600	8,800	4,200	8,100	10,200	9,800	11,600	36,200	32,600	I 39	55	121	218	269
Imports, cif	71	59,000	68,500	71,200	82,300	108,600	138,400	184,500	204,200	318,600	525,700	I 751	857	1,210	1,843	2,913
Imports, fob	71.v	53,442	61,601	63,571	71,255	94,435	120,348	160,854	177,565	285,996	486,759	I 682	779	1,100	1,676	2,648
															1990=100	
Volume of Exports	72	39	42	33	31	38	44	37	44	48	44	48	55	60	70	76
Volume of Imports	73	61	71	72	66	59	73	89	95	111	121	103	104	116	127	128
Unit Value of Exports	74	.1	.2	.1	.2	.3	.3	.4	I.4	.6	.8	1.1	1.4	1.8	2.7	3.9
Unit Value of Imports	75	.2	.2	.2	.2	.3	.3	.4	I.4	.5	.7	1.2	1.4	1.6	2.4	3.8
Balance of Payments													*Millions of US Dollars:*			
Goods: Exports f.o.b.	78aa d	....	....	....	....	....	....	....	....	....	....	....	402.0	512.6	640.3	779.6
Goods: Imports f.o.b.	78ab d	....	....	....	....	....	....	....	....	....	....	....	−427.9	−564.7	−618.4	−754.1
Trade Balance	78ac d	....	....	....	....	....	....	....	....	....	....	....	−25.9	−52.1	21.9	25.5
Services: Credit	78ad d	....	....	....	....	....	....	....	....	....	....	....	172.5	212.1	262.0	292.8
Services: Debit	78ae d	....	....	....	....	....	....	....	....	....	....	....	−117.2	−149.8	−192.1	−253.5
Balance on Goods and Services	78af d	....	....	....	....	....	....	....	....	....	....	....	29.4	10.2	91.8	64.8
Income: Credit	78ag d	....	....	....	....	....	....	....	....	....	....	....	3.2	4.8	5.9	11.9
Income: Debit	78ah d	....	....	....	....	....	....	....	....	....	....	....	−55.7	−63.3	−77.7	−95.0
Balance on Goods, Serv., & Inc.	78ai d	....	....	....	....	....	....	....	....	....	....	....	−23.1	−48.3	20.0	−18.3
Current Transfers, n.i.e.: Credit	78aj d	....	....	....	....	....	....	....	....	....	....	....	—	.6	.8	1.0
Current Transfers: Debit	78ak d	....	....	....	....	....	....	....	....	....	....	....	−.8	−.7	−.8	−1.5
Current Account, n.i.e.	78al d	....	....	....	....	....	....	....	....	....	....	....	−23.9	−48.4	20.0	−18.8
Capital Account, n.i.e.: Credit	78ba d	....	....	....	....	....	....	....	....	....	....	....	1.4	1.2	1.0	.8
Capital Account: Debit	78bb d	....	....	....	....	....	....	....	....	....	....	....	−.3	−1.1	−2.1	−3.2
Capital Account, n.i.e.	78bc d	....	....	....	....	....	....	....	....	....	....	....	1.1	.1	−1.1	−2.4
Direct Investment Abroad	78bd d	....	....	....	....	....	....	....	....	....	....	....	—	—	—	—
Dir. Invest. in Rep. Econ., n.i.e.	78be d	....	....	....	....	....	....	....	....	....	....	....	4.5	4.2	8.1	3.1
Portfolio Investment Assets	78bf d	....	....	....	....	....	....	....	....	....	....	....	—	—	—	—
Portfolio Investment Liab., n.i.e.	78bg d	....	....	....	....	....	....	....	....	....	....	....	31.0	45.2	−4.7	—
Other Investment Assets	78bh d	....	....	....	....	....	....	....	....	....	....	....	−10.7	−20.0	−27.5	−34.4
Other Investment Liab., n.i.e.	78bi d	....	....	....	....	....	....	....	....	....	....	....	7.8	55.5	88.4	125.8
Financial Account, n.i.e.	78bj d	....	....	....	....	....	....	....	....	....	....	....	32.6	84.9	64.3	94.5
Net Errors and Omissions	78ca d	....	....	....	....	....	....	....	....	....	....	....	−6.3	−20.3	−31.9	−36.6
Overall Balance	78cb d	....	....	....	....	....	....	....	....	....	....	....	3.5	16.3	51.3	36.7
Reserves and Related Items	79da d	....	....	....	....	....	....	....	....	....	....	....	−3.5	−16.3	−51.3	−36.7
Reserve Assets	79db d	....	....	....	....	....	....	....	....	....	....	....	−32.6	−16.3	−39.7	−20.5
Use of Fund Credit and Loans	79dc d	....	....	....	....	....	....	....	....	....	....	....	29.0	—	−11.6	−16.2
Liabs.Constit.For.Auth.Reserves	79dd d	....	....	....	....	....	....	....	....	....	....	....	—	—	—	—
Exceptional Financing	79de d	....	....	....	....	....	....	....	....	....	....	....	—	—	—	—
Government Finance													*Thousands of Kronur through 1974;*			
Deficit (−) or Surplus	80	....	....	....	....	....	....	I −17,950	−29,960	−66,330	I −122	−69	−173	−156	−193	
Revenue	81	....	....	....	....	....	....	I 193,400	271,940	410,500	I 586	773	1,071	1,719	2,629	
Grants Received	81z	....	....	....	....	....	....	100	13,680	6,980	I 2	—	—	—	1	
Expenditure	82	....	....	....	....	....	....	I 188,920	286,160	451,460	I 638	741	1,086	1,720	2,644	
Lending Minus Repayments	83	....	....	....	....	....	....		22,530	29,420	32,350	I 72	100	159	155	179
Financing																
Domestic	84a	....	....	....	....	....	....		−1,780	14,480	49,250	I 84	15	51	115	47
Foreign	85a	....	....	....	....	....	....		19,700	15,480	17,080	I 38	54	122	42	146
Debt: Domestic	88a	....	....	....	....	....	....		36,600	42,360	57,280	I 137	200	286	411	777
Foreign	89a	....	....	....	....	....	....		72,920	80,100	134,900	I 222	316	522	920	1,304
National Accounts													*Thousands of Kronur through 1974;*			
Exports of Goods & Services	90c	82,600	90,000	77,900	94,300	159,700	208,100	220,300	259,000	369,300	474,750	I 718	1,048	1,443	2,482	3,810
Government Consumption	91f	23,450	28,720	32,070	36,850	43,850	56,840	74,750	104,170	141,660	229,200	I 335	449	653	1,074	1,638
Gross Fixed Capital Formation	93e	55,600	69,900	79,500	87,100	85,300	104,100	162,200	194,000	291,260	455,000	I 636	780	1,090	1,546	2,248
Increase/Decrease(−) in Stocks	93i	3,720	870	740	−3,000	2,050	−3,000	14,130	−10,000	−3,000	25,340	I 37	−18	66	−39	51
Private Consumption	96f	128,040	159,530	168,600	180,510	208,170	268,950	341,000	419,000	556,830	845,400	I 1,188	1,626	2,342	3,656	5,501
Imports of Goods & Services	98c	−78,400	−91,200	−98,000	−115,700	−149,600	−196,700	−253,900	−267,600	−383,850	−610,900	I −883	−1,019	−1,452	−2,242	−3,631
Gross Domestic Product	99b	214,330	256,970	259,840	279,390	348,080	438,000	558,000	698,000	972,000	1,418,000	I 2,031	2,866	4,142	6,477	9,617
Net Factor Inc/Pmts(−) Abroad	98.n	−1,800	−2,000	−2,501	−4,101	−6,101	−4,801	−5,101	−8,902	−11,803	−19,205	I −49	−73	−88	−161	−244
Gross Nat'l Expenditure = GNP	99a	212,570	254,950	257,320	275,300	341,960	433,000	553,000	689,000	960,000	1,399,000	I 1,982	2,793	4,054	6,316	9,373
Nat'l Income, Market Prices	99e	188,900	228,600	226,750	235,680	287,960	372,000	486,000	604,000	846,000	1,227,000	I 1,699	2,422	3,565	5,563	8,235
GNP 1990 Prices (Millions)	99a.p	139,116	150,908	148,001	138,968	143,365	155,286	175,155	185,218	199,420	206,466	201,977	207,717	231,798	245,522	I 257,866
GNP Deflator (1990=100)	99ai p	.2	.2	.2	.2	.2	.3	.3	.4	.5	.7	1.0	1.3	1.7	2.6	3.6
																Millions:
Population	99z	.19	.20	.20	.20	.20	.21	.21	.21	.21	.22	.22	.22	.22	.22	.23

Interest Rates: *Discount Rate (End of Period):* I Beginning in 1992, Central Bank's discount rate set for the purchase of Treasury bills from deposit money banks with a repurchase agreement. Data prior to 1992 refer to central bank rates on overdrafts to deposit money banks.

Government Finance: I Beginning in 1972, data are as reported in the *Government Finance Statistics Yearbook* and cover consolidated central government, including extrabudgetary and social security accounts.

Iceland

1980	1981	1982	1983	1984	1985	1986	1987	1988	1989	1990	1991	1992	1993	1994		
Millions of Kronur beginning 1975															**International Transactions**	
4,461	6,530	8,479	18,633	23,557	33,826	45,093	53,053	61,674	79,131	92,624	91,560	87,833	94,711	113,279	Exports	70
1,884	2,945	4,330	8,611	9,989	15,330	19,557	24,190	25,941	33,695	43,895	49,189	42,599	45,754	54,644	Fish	70al
361	423	235	335	1,547	1,879	2,671	2,222	3,699	3,934	3,369	1,700	4,415	5,015	4,757	Fishmeal	70z
4,802	7,485	11,647	20,596	26,780	37,600	45,910	61,237	68,996	80,284	97,559	104,129	96,895	90,775	102,499	Imports, cif	71
4,365	6,804	10,588	18,723	24,346	34,182	41,737	55,670	62,724	72,986	88,690	94,663	88,087	82,523	93,181	Imports, fob	71.v
1990=100																
82	81	67	76	79	I86	95	102	99	101	100	....	....	....	....	Volume of Exports	72
136	147	148	137	134	I161	170	117	112	101	100	....	....	....	....	Volume of Imports	73
I5.7	8.7	13.7	26.0	31.2	41.5	51.1	58.3	66.2	81.6	100.0	110.7	107.7	111.6	....	Unit Value of Exports	74
I5.8	8.6	13.6	26.8	33.2	43.7	49.5	53.5	63.5	83.3	100.0	103.1	104.9	114.5	....	Unit Value of Imports	75
Minus Sign Indicates Debit															**Balance of Payments**	
919.8	896.4	685.5	742.0	743.2	814.0	1,096.8	1,376.1	1,425.4	1,401.5	1,588.6	1,551.5	1,523.1	1,399.2	....	Goods: Exports f.o.b.	78aa d
−899.9	−925.1	−837.6	−721.6	−756.6	−814.3	−1,000.0	−1,428.2	−1,439.4	−1,267.3	−1,509.1	−1,598.9	−1,521.7	−1,217.9	....	Goods: Imports f.o.b.	78ab d
19.9	−29.1	−152.1	20.4	−13.4	−.3	96.8	−52.1	−14.0	134.2	79.5	−47.4	1.4	181.3	....	Trade Balance	78ac d
279.8	302.8	340.6	342.5	347.1	394.3	453.2	541.9	531.6	516.9	600.2	600.2	630.5	630.1	....	Services: Credit	78ad d
−262.8	−282.0	−308.5	−280.7	−310.9	−362.9	−373.6	−509.9	−535.6	−494.8	−557.8	−599.3	−599.2	−600.3	....	Services: Debit	78ae d
36.9	−8.3	−120.0	82.2	22.8	31.1	176.4	−20.1	−18.0	156.3	121.9	−46.5	32.7	211.1	....	Balance on Goods and Services	78af d
13.9	22.4	28.2	15.5	15.7	16.1	19.7	27.8	26.2	32.5	39.1	42.2	54.1	52.1	....	Income: Credit	78ag d
−125.7	−158.7	−166.3	−152.6	−170.6	−162.5	−182.9	−197.9	−228.5	−269.7	−295.1	−299.8	−288.6	−265.9	....	Income: Debit	78ah d
−74.9	−144.6	−258.1	−54.9	−132.1	−115.3	13.2	−190.2	−220.3	−80.9	−134.1	−304.1	−201.8	−2.7	....	Balance on Goods, Serv., & Inc.	78ai d
1.0	1.1	.9	1.3	2.0	2.7	6.2	6.5	9.0	10.5	16.5	14.5	17.7	18.0	....	Current Transfers, n.i.e.: Credit	78aj d
−2.4	−4.0	−3.6	−2.6	−2.5	−2.3	−3.3	−4.6	−19.9	−31.6	−28.9	−21.9	−22.3	−20.9	....	Current Transfers: Debit	78ak d
−76.3	−147.5	−260.8	−56.2	−132.6	−114.9	16.1	−188.3	−231.2	−102.0	−146.5	−311.5	−206.4	−5.6	....	Current Account, n.i.e.	78al d
.7	2.4	.5	1.4	5.5	3.4	5.6	10.0	18.4	25.9	25.1	13.1	11.1	11.0	....	Capital Account, n.i.e.: Credit	78ba d
−3.5	−2.8	−2.9	−2.1	−4.2	−3.6	−4.5	−12.7	−8.7	−7.8	−12.9	−10.9	−12.7	−10.2	....	Capital Account: Debit	78bb d
−2.8	−.4	−2.4	−.7	1.3	−.2	1.1	−2.7	9.7	18.1	12.2	2.2	−1.6	.8	....	Capital Account, n.i.e.	78bc d
—	—	—	—	—	—	−2.1	−.7	−1.1	−8.2	−9.1	−10.6	−5.2	−4.2	....	Direct Investment Abroad	78bd d
22.3	53.0	35.8	−23.4	13.7	23.6	8.5	2.4	−14.8	−27.4	6.0	34.7	14.4	7.5	....	Dir. Invest. in Rep. Econ., n.i.e.	78be d
—	—	—	—	—	—	—	—	—	—	.5	.3	—	−4.4	−31.1	....	Portfolio Investment Assets	78bf d
—	—	—	—	—	—	—	—	—	—	.1	—	26.5	−11.4	−9.2	....	Portfolio Investment Liab., n.i.e.	78bg d
−55.9	−20.6	−.8	−43.7	−26.2	40.9	−.3	−54.9	−65.3	11.8	−43.3	23.4	54.7	−22.6	....	Other Investment Assets	78bh d
190.6	201.9	179.4	133.3	157.1	168.0	94.1	284.9	308.0	148.2	257.0	225.9	228.1	10.2	....	Other Investment Liab., n.i.e.	78bi d
157.0	234.3	214.4	66.2	144.6	232.5	100.2	231.7	226.8	125.0	210.9	299.9	276.2	−49.4	....	Financial Account, n.i.e.	78bj d
−43.7	−14.5	−46.8	1.6	−28.5	−53.3	−18.5	−58.8	−4.1	13.5	−2.3	19.9	1.9	−5.9	....	Net Errors and Omissions	78ca d
34.2	71.9	−95.6	10.9	−15.2	64.1	98.9	−18.1	1.2	54.6	74.3	10.5	70.1	−60.1	....	Overall Balance	78cb d
−34.2	−71.9	95.6	−10.9	15.2	−64.1	−98.9	18.1	−1.2	−54.6	−74.3	−10.5	−70.1	60.1	....	Reserves and Related Items	79da d
−9.6	−60.4	77.7	−10.0	15.2	−64.1	−86.2	32.2	−1.2	−54.6	−74.3	−10.5	−70.1	60.1	....	Reserve Assets	79db d
−24.6	−11.5	17.9	−.9	—	—	−12.7	−14.1	—	—	—	—	—	—	....	Use of Fund Credit and Loans	79dc d
—	—	—	—	—	—	—	—	—	—	—	—	—	—	....	Liabs.Constit.For.Auth.Reserves	79dd d
—	—	—	—	—	—	—	—	—	—	—	—	—	—	....	Exceptional Financing	79de d
Millions of Kronur Beginning 1975: Year Ending December 31															**Government Finance**	
−193	−172	−958	−1,998	−1,610	−4,719	−7,639	−4,278	−9,702	−7,962	−8,952	−17,342	−12,489	....	....	Deficit (−) or Surplus	80
4,090	6,621	10,767	17,510	23,628	31,249	40,617	55,575	73,424	95,082	107,838	117,438	122,285	....	....	Revenue	81
1	3	5	4	6	8	1,321	—	—	—	—	—	575	....	....	Grants Received	81z
4,015	6,383	10,454	19,094	22,754	33,551	48,381	60,199	82,334	105,933	117,531	132,473	133,466	....	....	Expenditure	82
268	413	1,276	417	2,490	2,424	1,196	−347	792	−2,888	−740	2,308	1,883	....	....	Lending Minus Repayments	83
															Financing	
76	−22	−63	733	−810	1,508	3,859	3,678	4,878	2,913	6,281	9,633	2,118	....	....	Domestic	84a
117	194	1,021	1,265	2,421	3,211	3,780	600	4,823	5,050	2,672	7,709	10,371	....	....	Foreign	85a
1,530	2,284	3,515	6,525	7,513	10,348	15,122	22,071	28,068	38,671	53,005	59,703	66,139	....	....	Debt: Domestic	88a
2,118	2,756	6,741	12,487	19,498	25,631	29,304	29,955	40,205	58,512	59,779	67,953	87,273	....	....	Foreign	89a
Millions of Kronur Beginning 1975															**National Accounts**	
5,746	8,724	12,466	26,683	33,765	48,774	61,961	71,681	81,721	106,282	124,246	124,943	121,248	134,972	157,351	Exports of Goods & Services	90c
2,546	4,195	6,942	12,050	14,701	21,130	28,776	38,981	50,537	60,341	69,989	78,157	80,375	84,818	87,445	Government Consumption	91f
3,927	5,929	9,726	14,839	19,337	25,528	30,774	42,593	50,503	58,730	70,007	76,060	69,599	64,176	65,840	Gross Fixed Capital Formation	93e
80	253	913	−1,070	−661	−3,111	−3,748	−3,783	−3,085	−8,143	−4,546	−1,226	−406	557	−284	Increase/Decrease(−) in Stocks	93i
8,937	14,361	23,864	41,016	55,872	77,240	99,196	133,557	161,068	190,254	223,729	248,999	249,044	248,952	257,461	Private Consumption	96f
−5,648	−8,936	−14,329	−25,275	−33,871	−48,663	−55,880	−73,965	−84,100	−99,240	−119,595	−130,305	−121,943	−122,493	−134,525	Imports of Goods & Services	98c
15,588	24,526	39,582	68,243	89,143	120,898	161,083	209,064	256,644	308,224	363,830	396,628	397,917	410,982	433,288	Gross Domestic Product	99b
−411	−811	−1,247	−2,671	−4,024	−4,824	−5,302	−4,799	−6,506	−11,164	−12,401	−12,686	−11,305	−12,142	−12,706	Net Factor Inc/Pmts(−) Abroad	98.n
15,177	23,715	38,335	65,572	85,119	116,074	155,781	204,265	250,138	297,060	351,429	383,942	386,612	398,840	420,582	Gross Nat'l Expenditure = GNP	99a
13,367	20,817	33,235	56,242	73,710	100,591	136,085	180,792	221,137	259,793	307,615	335,595	335,189	344,258	363,933	Nat'l Income, Market Prices	99e
273,815	286,696	291,387	282,781	292,867	303,493	324,150	353,287	349,805	349,354	I351,429	355,599	343,457	347,221	358,351	GNP 1990 Prices (Millions)	99a.p
5.5	8.3	13.2	23.2	29.1	38.2	48.1	57.8	71.5	85.0	100.0	108.0	112.6	114.9	117.4	GNP Deflator (1990=100)	99ai p
Midyear Estimates																
.23	.23	.23	.24	.24	.24	.24	.25	.25	.25	.25	.25	.26	.26	.27	Population	99z

India

534

		1965	1966	1967	1968	1969	1970	1971	1972	1973	1974	1975	1976	1977	1978	1979
Exchange Rates																*Rupees per SDR:*
Market Rate	aa	4.775	7.576	7.547	7.628	7.559	7.576	7.903	8.773	9.896	ɪ9.978	10.462	10.318	9.971	10.668	10.416
																Rupees per US Dollar:
Market Rate	ae	4.775	7.576	7.547	7.628	7.559	7.576	7.279	8.080	8.203	ɪ8.150	8.937	8.881	8.209	8.188	7.907
Market Rate	rf	4.762	6.359	7.500	7.500	7.500	7.500	7.492	7.594	7.742	8.102	8.376	8.960	8.739	8.193	8.126
Fund Position																*Millions of SDRs:*
Quota	2f. s	600	750	750	750	750	940	940	940	940	940	940	940	940	1,145	1,145
SDRs	1b. s	—	—	—	—	—	44	148	246	245	240	212	189	149	226	371
Reserve Position in the Fund	1c. s	—	—	—	—	—	21	76	76	76	—	—	—	—	69	162
Total Fund Cred.&Loans Outstg.	2tl	287	361	456	374	240	10	—	—	—	497	698	406	125	—	—
International Liquidity											*Millions of US Dollars Unless Otherwise Indicated:*					
Total Reserves minus Gold	1l. d	319	365	419	439	683	763	942	916	849	1,028	1,089	2,792	4,872	6,426	7,432
SDRs	1b. d	—	—	—	—	—	44	161	268	296	294	248	220	181	294	489
Reserve Position in the Fund	1c. d	—	—	—	—	—	21	83	83	92	—	—	—	—	90	213
Foreign Exchange	1d. d	319	365	419	439	683	698	699	566	461	734	841	2,572	4,691	6,042	6,731
Gold (Million Fine Troy Ounces)	1ad	8.025	6.954	6.954	6.954	6.954	6.954	6.954	6.954	6.954	6.954	6.954	6.954	7.356	8.362	8.560
Gold (National Valuation)	1and	280	241	242	239	241	241	251	226	222	228	204	205	235	268	284
Other Banking Insts.: Liabilities	7f. d	78	96	103	103	103	119	137	145	162	176	215	234	273	303	306
of which: Liab. to Nonbanks	7fd d	78	96	103	103	103	119	137	145	162	176	215	234	273	303	306
Monetary Authorities																*Billions of Rupees:*
Foreign Assets	11	2.2	3.2	3.8	4.0	6.7	6.5	7.7	10.3	11.0	13.0	17.7	27.3	43.7	55.4	63.0
Claims on Central Government	12a	31.9	35.0	37.1	37.9	40.3	42.3	49.5	54.4	64.7	71.4	75.5	72.6	79.3	84.4	102.4
Claims on Deposit Money Banks	12e	2.0	2.0	2.4	3.3	4.1	6.2	5.3	3.6	6.7	7.5	11.4	15.9	10.9	10.3	13.9
Claims on Other Financial Insts.	12f	....	....	....	....	.2	1.0	1.7	1.3	1.9	3.4	4.6	6.3	7.9	10.4	13.6
Reserve Money	14	31.0	33.1	35.4	37.4	41.6	46.0	51.1	55.6	68.1	70.4	74.3	86.8	105.1	126.6	153.2
of which: Currency Outside DMBs	14a	28.7	30.1	32.1	33.7	37.6	41.6	45.6	49.1	57.8	61.4	64.4	73.2	84.2	94.6	108.0
Foreign Liabilities	16c	1.4	2.7	3.4	2.8	1.8	.1				5.0	7.3	4.2	1.2		
Central Government Deposits	16d	.6	.7	.6	.7	2.4	2.9	2.0	.8	.6	.6	.7	1.1	.7	.5	.6
Capital Accounts	17a	....	....	....	....	4.2	5.5	7.0	8.7	10.1	11.2	13.6	15.8	18.6	22.2	27.3
Other Items (Net)	17r	3.2	3.7	3.8	4.3	1.4	1.6	4.2	4.6	5.6	8.0	13.5	14.2	16.2	11.2	11.7
Deposit Money Banks																*Billions of Rupees:*
Reserves	20	2.1	2.6	2.9	2.8	3.3	3.6	4.5	5.3	9.4	8.9	8.8	12.0	23.0	28.6	41.6
Claims on Central Government	22a	8.7	9.9	10.5	11.7	12.8	13.9	16.9	22.2	24.5	28.7	32.5	1.2	49.9	63.3	76.7
Claims on Private Sector	22d	26.3	30.6	34.3	39.1	45.6	52.6	62.6	71.4	88.0	102.5	127.3	13.3	160.5	217.3	258.9
Demand Deposits	24	14.1	16.3	18.5	19.4	22.1	25.4	30.2	36.5	42.9	49.4	57.3	78.7	93.6	61.2	65.8
Time Deposits	25	16.1	18.9	20.8	24.8	28.9	32.4	40.7	49.0	60.5	70.0	84.4	104.6	128.2	213.9	260.5
Credit from Monetary Authorities	26g	2.0	1.9	2.4	3.2	4.0	6.2	5.3	3.6	6.6	7.5	11.4	15.5	14.4	13.3	13.9
Other Items (Net)	27r	4.8	5.9	6.0	6.2	6.7	4.6	6.6	9.7	11.9	13.1	15.4	17.0	23.6	24.6	37.0
Monetary Survey																*Billions of Rupees:*
Foreign Assets (Net)	31n	.8	.5	.3	1.2	4.9	6.5	7.7	10.3	11.0	8.0	10.4	23.1	42.5	55.4	63.0
Domestic Credit	32	66.3	74.8	81.3	88.0	96.6	107.0	128.8	148.5	178.6	205.4	239.3	92.3	296.1	374.9	451.0
Claims on Central Govt. (Net)	32an	40.0	44.2	47.0	48.9	50.8	53.4	64.5	75.9	88.6	99.5	107.4	72.6	127.8	147.2	178.5
Claims on Private Sector	32d	26.3	30.6	34.3	39.1	45.6	52.6	62.6	71.4	88.0	102.5	127.3	13.3	160.5	217.3	258.9
Claims on Other Financial Insts.	32f	....	....	....	....	.2	1.0	1.7	1.3	1.9	3.4	4.6	6.3	7.9	10.4	13.6
Money	34	43.0	46.8	51.0	53.9	60.4	67.6	76.5	86.2	101.0	111.3	122.3	152.8	178.5	157.6	176.9
Quasi-Money	35	16.1	18.9	20.8	24.8	28.9	32.4	40.7	49.0	60.5	70.0	84.4	104.6	128.2	213.9	260.5
Other Items (Net)	37r	8.0	9.5	9.8	10.5	12.2	11.9	18.0	23.6	28.0	32.1	42.9	47.2	59.1	62.5	76.6
Money plus Quasi-Money	35l	59.1	65.7	71.8	78.7	89.3	100.1	117.1	135.2	161.5	181.3	206.7	257.4	306.7	371.5	437.3
Other Banking Institutions																*Billions of Rupees:*
Claims on Private Sector	42d	3.06	4.25	4.95	5.31	5.75	6.39	7.36	8.20	9.35	11.57	14.03	17.57	21.72	27.37	34.51
Bonds	46ab	.65	.80	.91	1.01	1.23	1.40	1.54	2.14	2.47	3.07	4.13	5.78	7.70	10.40	14.27
Long-Term Foreign Liabilities	46cl	.37	.72	.77	.77	.77	.89	1.00	1.17	1.33	1.43	1.92	2.08	2.24	2.48	2.42
Central Govt. Lending Funds	46f	1.59	2.19	2.54	2.87	2.94	2.90	2.82	2.69	2.53	2.36	2.15	2.00	1.95	1.78	1.68
Capital Accounts	47a	.51	.55	.70	.76	.82	.90	1.09	1.30	1.41	1.61	1.76	1.92	2.27	2.73	3.38
Other Items (Net)	47r	−.08	−.02	.02	−.12	−.01	.31	.91	.90	1.61	3.10	4.06	5.79	7.57	9.98	12.75
Post Office: Savings Deposits	45.. i	6.12	6.70	7.15	7.78	8.41	9.12	9.88	10.37	11.31	11.62	11.66	14.34	15.23	16.78	18.53
Nonbank Financial Institutions																*Billions of Rupees:*
Claims on Central Government	42a. s	6.73	7.43	8.12	8.99	10.13	11.51	13.16	14.92	16.88	19.26	21.81	24.68	28.55	32.33	36.64
Claims on Local Government	42b. s	.15	.15	.18	.23	.32	.32	.37	.37	.37	.37	.35	.34	.33	.34	.43
Claims on Private Sector	42d. s	2.96	3.49	4.13	4.76	5.30	5.94	6.67	7.50	8.46	9.86	10.94	12.25	13.42	14.46	19.35
Incr.in Total Assets(Within Per.)	49z. s	.90	1.43	1.46	1.71	1.90	2.09	2.50	3.06	3.66	3.61	4.05	5.21	5.80	6.78	7.56
Liquid Liabilities	55l	65.16	72.32	78.91	86.36	97.55	109.03	126.87	145.33	172.57	192.81	218.15	271.53	322.09	ɪ385.92	455.88
Interest Rates																*Percent Per Annum*
Bank Rate *(End of Period)*	60	6.00	6.00	6.00	5.00	5.00	5.00	6.00	6.00	7.00	9.00	9.00	9.00	9.00	9.00	9.00
Money Market Rate	60b	6.28	4.37	5.36	3.90	3.92	5.68	6.30	4.69	6.64	13.52	10.40	11.28	10.18	8.05	8.47
Lending Rate	60p	....	....	....	....	....	....	....	....	....	....	....	....	....	13.50	14.50
Government Bond Yield	61	5.32	5.54	5.52	5.07	5.00	5.00	ɪ5.64	5.65	5.65	6.04	6.35	6.29	6.32	6.37	6.45
Prices and Production																*Index Numbers (1990=100):*
Share Prices	62	11.1	10.9	11.0	11.0	12.8	13.9	13.4	13.2	ɪ14.6	16.1	13.2	14.1	14.4	16.8	19.2
Wholesale Prices	63	14.5	16.2	18.6	18.6	18.9	20.1	21.1	23.0	26.8	34.4	35.7	35.0	37.7	37.6	42.0
Consumer Prices	64	14.8	16.4	18.6	ɪ19.1	19.2	20.2	20.8	22.2	25.9	33.3	35.3	32.6	35.3	36.2	38.4
Industrial Production	66	27.1	26.9	26.6	28.3	ɪ30.3	31.9	33.3	35.2	35.8	36.5	38.2	42.0	44.2	47.2	47.7

India

	1980	1981	1982	1983	1984	1985	1986	1987	1988	1989	1990	1991	1992	1993	1994		
Exchange Rates																	
End of Period	10.114	10.591	10.627	10.986	12.205	13.363	16.051	18.268	20.117	22.387	25.712	36.953	36.025	43.102	45.810	Market Rate	aa
End of Period (ae) Period Average (rf)	7.930	9.099	9.634	10.493	12.451	12.166	13.122	12.877	14.949	17.035	18.073	25.834	26.200	31.380	31.380	Market Rate	ae
	7.863	8.659	9.455	10.099	11.363	12.369	12.611	12.962	13.917	16.226	17.504	22.742	25.918	30.493	31.374	Market Rate	rf
Fund Position																	
End of Period	1,718	1,718	1,718	2,208	2,208	2,208	2,208	2,208	2,208	2,208	2,208	2,208	3,056	3,056	3,056	Quota	2f. s
	377	468	339	105	338	306	291	112	71	86	222	32	3	73	1	SDRs	1b. s
	330	330	364	487	487	487	487	487	487	487	—	—	213	213	213	Reserve Position in the Fund	1c. s
	791	1,095	2,595	4,062	4,529	4,354	3,918	3,175	2,282	1,440	804	2,426	3,260	3,585	2,763	Total Fund Cred.&Loans Outstg.	2tl
International Liquidity																	
End of Period	6,944	4,693	4,315	4,937	5,842	6,420	6,396	6,454	4,899	3,859	1,521	3,627	5,757	10,199	19,698	Total Reserves minus Gold	1l. d
	480	545	374	110	331	336	356	159	96	113	316	46	4	100	2	SDRs	1b. d
	420	384	402	510	477	535	596	691	656	640	—	—	292	292	310	Reserve Position in the Fund	1c. d
	6,043	3,764	3,539	4,318	5,034	5,549	5,444	5,603	4,148	3,105	1,205	3,580	5,461	9,807	19,386	Foreign Exchange	1d. d
	8.594	8.594	8.594	8.594	8.737	9.397	10.449	10.449	10.449	10.449	10.692	11.282	11.348	11.457	11.800	Gold (Million Fine Troy Ounces)	1ad
	284	248	234	215	184	203	209	213	183	161	3,667	3,168	2,908	3,325	3,355	Gold (National Valuation)	1and d
	293	371	422	447	470	623	826	1,268	1,566	1,641	1,926	1,718	....	....	....	Other Banking Insts.: Liabilities	7f. d
	293	371	422	447	470	623	826	1,268	1,566	1,641	1,926	1,718	....	....	....	of which: Liab. to Nonbanks	7fd d
Monetary Authorities																	
Last Friday of Period	57.2	46.6	44.1	54.3	76.2	79.2	88.0	83.8	77.1	68.4	96.4	177.9	230.6	413.0	721.3	Foreign Assets	11
	144.3	187.1	237.9	273.7	330.7	406.4	480.7	552.2	649.2	758.7	896.5	1,056.0	1,020.6	1,155.7	1,034.4	Claims on Central Government	12a
	10.9	13.6	8.3	8.7	16.5	6.2	5.8	16.7	16.5	24.4	18.2	4.1	37.7	13.2	25.2	Claims on Deposit Money Banks	12e
	15.9	18.4	29.9	33.9	49.0	52.7	56.5	65.4	76.4	86.4	91.6	97.8	105.4	103.8	120.7	Claims on Other Financial Insts.	12f
	176.5	195.1	230.3	260.2	303.9	375.3	436.5	516.0	599.9	712.1	809.7	961.1	1,042.2	1,268.0	1,543.3	Reserve Money	14
	126.3	137.4	157.4	181.3	218.1	239.4	268.0	315.6	356.4	434.5	501.9	591.3	645.8	783.3	948.2	of which: Currency Outside DMBs	14a
	2.7	6.0	22.0	38.8	48.8	51.1	56.1	52.2	41.6	29.8	20.6	89.7	117.5	154.5	126.6	Foreign Liabilities	16c
	.8	.7	.6	18.9	30.7	.7	.6	.6	1.6	.8	2.1	1.1	.6	.7	.7	Central Government Deposits	16d
	32.9	38.9	34.2	36.6	39.3	42.3	46.8	51.2	57.0	63.8	135.3	148.7	148.1	152.9	154.8	Capital Accounts	17a
	15.4	25.0	33.1	16.1	49.8	75.0	91.2	98.1	119.2	131.3	135.0	135.1	86.0	109.5	76.4	Other Items (Net)	17r
Deposit Money Banks																	
Last Friday of Period	47.7	54.8	70.4	76.3	81.9	130.7	143.3	194.8	239.1	263.5	287.4	352.0	379.9	483.9	624.1	Reserves	20
	92.5	103.9	114.5	148.8	188.7	194.2	245.0	308.4	366.1	422.3	508.0	617.1	761.2	922.1	1,197.2	Claims on Central Government	22a
	302.1	366.7	438.5	515.3	612.4	698.9	821.4	918.5	1,085.2	1,311.6	1,435.5	1,577.6	1,880.5	2,087.7	2,252.5	Claims on Private Sector	22d
	76.1	93.2	113.8	125.7	144.5	170.1	207.8	224.1	272.7	307.0	337.4	445.8	466.4	530.6	669.1	Demand Deposits	24
	302.3	362.9	424.0	507.0	596.7	712.3	847.7	999.6	1,192.2	1,365.1	1,576.7	1,829.3	2,239.4	2,601.5	2,932.0	Time Deposits	25
	10.9	13.5	18.0	8.8	16.5	6.2	7.7	16.5	16.5	25.7	18.1	4.0	37.4	16.2	77.6	Credit from Monetary Authorities	26g
	53.0	55.9	67.6	99.2	125.3	135.2	146.6	181.4	209.1	299.6	298.6	267.7	277.9	345.3	395.1	Other Items (Net)	27r
Monetary Survey																	
Last Friday of Period	54.5	40.6	22.1	15.5	27.4	28.1	31.9	31.6	35.5	38.6	75.9	88.3	113.2	258.4	594.8	Foreign Assets (Net)	31n
	554.1	675.5	820.1	952.7	1,150.1	1,351.4	1,603.0	1,843.8	2,175.4	2,578.2	2,929.5	3,347.1	3,766.6	4,268.6	4,604.2	Domestic Credit	32
	236.1	290.3	351.8	403.5	488.7	599.9	725.0	859.9	1,013.7	1,180.2	1,402.4	1,672.0	1,781.2	2,077.1	2,230.9	Claims on Central Govt. (Net)	32an
	302.1	366.7	438.5	515.3	612.4	698.9	821.4	918.5	1,085.2	1,311.6	1,435.5	1,577.6	1,880.5	2,087.7	2,252.5	Claims on Private Sector	32d
	15.9	18.4	29.9	33.9	49.0	52.7	56.5	65.4	76.4	86.4	91.6	97.8	105.4	103.8	120.7	Claims on Other Financial Insts.	32f
	204.6	232.5	273.7	308.6	365.6	412.4	478.5	543.2	632.8	746.9	853.6	1,046.1	1,120.9	1,330.2	1,653.2	Money	34
	302.3	362.9	424.0	507.0	596.7	712.3	847.7	999.6	1,192.2	1,365.1	1,576.7	1,829.3	2,239.4	2,601.5	2,932.0	Quasi-Money	35
	101.7	120.7	144.5	152.6	215.3	254.8	308.7	332.7	385.9	504.7	575.1	560.2	519.5	595.3	613.8	Other Items (Net)	37r
	506.9	595.3	697.7	815.6	962.3	1,124.7	1,326.3	1,542.8	1,825.0	2,112.0	2,430.2	2,875.4	3,360.3	3,931.8	4,585.2	Money plus Quasi-Money	35l
Other Banking Institutions																	
End of Period	42.81	55.58	68.35	85.02	102.69	124.35	151.36	186.09	228.99	....	....	....	....	....	....	Claims on Private Sector	42d
	20.15	27.34	35.93	43.94	56.81	71.00	86.24	107.16	127.26	....	....	....	....	....	....	Bonds	46ab
	2.33	3.38	4.06	4.69	5.85	7.58	10.84	16.33	23.41	27.95	34.80	44.39	....	....	....	Long-Term Foreign Liabilities	46cl
	1.57	2.10	3.97	4.15	4.99	5.13	5.56	5.28	5.11	....	....	....	....	....	....	Central Govt. Lending Funds	46f
	4.01	5.25	6.92	8.39	11.12	13.10	15.87	19.08	23.91	....	....	....	....	....	....	Capital Accounts	47a
	14.75	17.52	17.47	23.86	23.92	27.54	32.86	38.25	49.15	....	....	....	....	....	....	Other Items (Net)	47r
	20.83	22.68	23.20	24.86	26.14	27.76	29.62	32.63	34.02	37.36	39.92	42.45	....	....	....	Post Office: Savings Deposits	45.. i
Nonbank Financial Institutions																	
Year Beginning April 1	43.11	50.14	57.25	65.71	....	....	....	....	....	....	....	....	....	....	....	Claims on Central Government	42a. s
	.53	.62	.62	.57	....	....	....	....	....	....	....	....	....	....	....	Claims on Local Government	42b. s
	20.58	22.74	26.62	28.37	....	....	....	....	....	....	....	....	....	....	....	Claims on Private Sector	42d. s
	9.14	9.77	10.34	11.54	....	....	....	....	....	....	....	....	....	....	....	Incr.in Total Assets(Within Per.)	49z. s
	527.71	618.01	720.95	840.44	988.40	1,152.48	1,346.51	1,564.04	1,844.95	2,133.28	2,452.97	2,898.59	....	....	....	Liquid Liabilities	55l
Interest Rates																	
Percent Per Annum	9.00	10.00	10.00	10.00	10.00	10.00	10.00	10.00	10.00	10.00	10.00	10.00	12.00	12.00	12.00	Bank Rate (End of Period)	60
	7.24	8.61	7.27	8.30	9.95	10.00	9.97	9.83	....	....	....	15.57	19.35	15.23	8.64	Money Market Rate	60b
	16.50	16.50	16.50	16.50	16.50	16.50	16.50	16.50	16.50	16.50	16.50	16.50	17.88	18.92	16.25	Lending Rate	60p
	6.71	7.15	7.59	7.99	8.65	8.99	....	....	....	....	....	....	....	....	....	Government Bond Yield	61
Prices and Production																	
Period Averages	20.7	25.4	24.9	26.1	ⅼ27.9	41.4	50.6	46.4	47.7	72.1	100.0	134.8	247.3	202.9	322.1	Share Prices	62
	50.4	56.6	58.0	ⅼ62.5	66.9	70.0	73.9	79.0	85.9	91.7	100.0	113.5	127.0	136.4	150.7	Wholesale Prices	63
	42.8	48.4	52.2	58.4	63.3	66.8	72.6	79.0	ⅼ86.4	91.8	100.0	113.9	127.3	135.4	149.2	Consumer Prices	64
	48.1	ⅼ52.4	53.5	56.2	61.5	67.0	71.5	79.5	85.4	90.1	100.0	101.6	104.5	106.5	....	Industrial Production	66

India

534

		1965	1966	1967	1968	1969	1970	1971	1972	1973	1974	1975	1976	1977	1978	1979
International Transactions																*Millions of Rupees*
Exports	70	8,032	11,714	12,097	13,209	13,763	15,198	15,256	18,568	22,591	31,786	36,412	49,702	55,734	54,564	63,445
Imports, cif	71	13,516	20,373	20,796	19,273	16,589	15,933	18,155	16,844	24,893	41,596	53,388	50,738	57,937	64,387	79,820
Imports, fob	71.v	11,454	17,265	17,624	16,333	14,013	13,518	15,600	14,745	21,948	36,408	47,160	44,991	51,254	57,347	71,231
																1990=100
Export Prices	74	9	12	14	I13	14	14	14	I16	17	21	27	29	30	34	34
Unit Value of Imports	75	8	11	13	I12	12	12	12	I12	13	18	32	37	36	33	37
Balance of Payments																*Millions of US Dollars*
Goods: Exports f.o.b.	78aa d	....	....	....	....	....	....	....	....	....	....	4,666	5,410	6,249	6,518	7,597
Goods: Imports f.o.b.	78ab d	....	....	....	....	....	....	....	....	....	....	−4,952	−4,623	−5,317	−7,402	−9,819
Trade Balance	78ac d	....	....	....	....	....	....	....	....	....	....	−286	787	932	−884	−2,222
Services: Credit	78ad d	....	....	....	....	....	....	....	....	....	....	841	1,056	1,316	1,607	2,083
Services: Debit	78ae d	....	....	....	....	....	....	....	....	....	....	−1,054	−1,140	−1,286	−1,555	−2,120
Balance on Goods and Services	78af d	....	....	....	....	....	....	....	....	....	....	−500	703	962	−832	−2,258
Income: Credit	78ag d	....	....	....	....	....	....	....	....	....	....	130	195	275	390	749
Income: Debit	78ah d	....	....	....	....	....	....	....	....	....	....	−388	−355	−425	−492	−485
Balance on Goods, Serv., & Inc.	78ai d	....	....	....	....	....	....	....	....	....	....	−758	543	813	−935	−1,995
Current Transfers, n.i.e.: Credit	78aj d	....	....	....	....	....	....	....	....	....	....	636	1,043	1,306	1,637	2,065
Current Transfers: Debit	78ak d	....	....	....	....	....	....	....	....	....	....	−26	−16	−11	−20	−23
Current Account, n.i.e.	78al d	....	....	....	....	....	....	....	....	....	....	−148	1,571	2,108	683	48
Capital Account, n.i.e.: Credit	78ba d	....	....	....	....	....	....	....	....	....	....	—	—	—	—	—
Capital Account: Debit	78bb d	....	....	....	....	....	....	....	....	....	....	—	—	—	—	—
Capital Account, n.i.e.	78bc d	....	....	....	....	....	....	....	....	....	....	—	—	—	—	—
Direct Investment Abroad	78bd d	....	....	....	....	....	....	....	....	....	....	—	—	—	—	—
Dir. Invest. in Rep. Econ., n.i.e.	78be d	....	....	....	....	....	....	....	....	....	....	−10	−8	—	—	—
Portfolio Investment Assets	78bf d	....	....	....	....	....	....	....	....	....	....	—	—	—	—	—
Portfolio Investment Liab., n.i.e.	78bg d	....	....	....	....	....	....	....	....	....	....	—	—	—	—	—
Other Investment Assets	78bh d	....	....	....	....	....	....	....	....	....	....	3	−51	−210	95	−19
Other Investment Liab., n.i.e.	78bi d	....	....	....	....	....	....	....	....	....	....	952	989	640	711	502
Financial Account, n.i.e.	78bj d	....	....	....	....	....	....	....	....	....	....	944	930	430	806	483
Net Errors and Omissions	78ca d	....	....	....	....	....	....	....	....	....	....	−439	−291	−456	431	301
Overall Balance	78cb d	....	....	....	....	....	....	....	....	....	....	357	2,210	2,081	1,920	832
Reserves and Related Items	79da d	....	....	....	....	....	....	....	....	....	....	−357	−2,210	−2,081	−1,920	−832
Reserve Assets	79db d	....	....	....	....	....	....	....	....	....	....	−597	−1,881	−2,090	−1,772	−835
Use of Fund Credit and Loans	79dc d	....	....	....	....	....	....	....	....	....	....	239	−337	−330	−158	—
Liabs.Constit.For.Auth.Reserves	79dd d	....	....	....	....	....	....	....	....	....	....	—	—	—	—	—
Exceptional Financing	79de d	....	....	....	....	....	....	....	....	....	....	—	8	338	9	3
Government Finance																*Billions of Rupees:*
Deficit (−) or Surplus	80	−12.4	−17.2	−14.6	−10.8	−10.2	−13.6	−16.0	−21.8	−17.0	I−23.6	−32.0	−36.9	−37.9	−50.8	−63.0
Revenue	81	23.8	25.3	25.5	27.8	30.5	33.3	40.6	45.7	49.7	I75.3	91.7	102.6	113.5	129.6	144.0
Grants Received	81z	....	....	....	....	....	....	....	....	....	I1.0	2.8	2.7	3.2	2.7	3.9
Expenditure	82	26.6	30.4	31.5	30.4	35.3	39.3	49.3	55.2	58.1	I77.0	93.3	104.1	114.8	133.5	159.0
Lending Minus Repayments	83	9.7	12.1	8.6	8.0	5.5	7.6	7.2	12.3	8.6	I22.9	33.3	38.1	39.9	49.6	51.8
Financing																	
Net Borrowing: Domestic	84a	....	....	....	....	....	....	....	....	....	I17.6	22.0	20.9	58.3	21.2	60.0
Rupees	84b	7.3	10.0	8.0	5.6	5.5	10.6	10.6	19.4	−3.3	....	....	....	....	....	....
Foreign	85a	....	....	....	....	....	....	....	....	....	I6.5	14.7	11.2	3.8	4.5	5.0
Foreign Currency	85b	4.8	7.0	6.0	4.8	4.5	3.3	3.5	2.9	4.7	....	....	....	....	....	....
Finance from Foreign Aid	86a	.7	.8	.2	.9	.4	.4	.2	.3	16.7	....	....	....	....	....	....
Use of Cash Balances	87	−.5	−.6	.4	−.5	−.2	−.7	1.7	−.9	−1.1	I−.6	−4.8	4.7	−24.2	25.2	−2.1
Debt: Domestic	88a	....	....	....	....	....	....	....	....	....	I174.0	201.3	221.6	281.1	305.8	367.8
Rupees	88b	91.4	105.8	109.6	115.8	122.3	133.8	145.9	168.2	184.0	....	....	....	....	....	....
Foreign	89a	....	....	....	....	....	....	....	....	....	I64.2	76.0	86.1	89.9	93.8	99.6
Foreign Currency	89b	26.1	46.3	51.3	56.4	61.5	64.9	68.3	71.2	58.7	....	....	....	....	....	....
National Accounts																*Billions of Rupees:*
Exports of Goods & Services	90c	9.3	13.3	15.1	16.0	16.3	16.4	17.9	21.5	26.6	36.9	49.5	61.3	64.0	71.2	83.4
Government Consumption	91f	22.9	25.0	27.9	30.6	34.4	38.4	44.6	47.3	51.6	62.4	73.0	82.3	87.6	97.2	111.7
Gross Fixed Capital Formation	93e	41.3	46.0	50.8	53.8	59.0	63.1	70.8	81.3	90.7	110.0	133.3	153.0	172.2	188.8	213.1
Increase/Decrease(−) in Stocks	93i	3.0	7.2	6.2	1.6	5.8	10.7	14.6	5.9	22.6	34.7	30.8	24.7	18.0	41.1	48.4
Private Consumption	96f	204.2	237.9	283.4	283.9	307.8	325.5	351.0	386.9	434.3	565.1	578.2	600.8	691.8	752.4	817.0
Imports of Goods & Services	98c	−14.6	−21.2	−22.0	−19.0	−17.5	−18.2	−21.8	−20.5	−31.8	−47.8	−56.6	−56.1	−65.2	−74.2	−100.9
Gross Domestic Product	99b	261.5	295.7	346.1	366.7	403.9	431.6	462.6	510.1	620.1	732.4	787.6	848.9	960.7	1,041.9	1,143.6
Net Factor Inc/Pmts(-) Abroad	98.n	−1.7	−2.3	−2.6	−2.5	−2.7	−2.8	−2.9	−3.1	−3.0	−2.5	−2.6	−2.3	−2.4	−1.6	1.5
Gross Nat'l Expenditure = GNP	99a	259.8	293.4	343.5	364.2	401.2	428.8	459.7	507.0	616.8	729.4	785.1	846.6	958.3	1,040.3	1,145.1
Nat'l Income, Market Prices	99e	241.9	272.5	320.2	338.9	373.2	398.2	425.9	469.1	572.9	673.9	720.9	777.7	883.9	955.7	1,042.3
Gross Dom. Prod. 1990 Prices	99b.p	1,744.3	1,764.0	1,907.9	1,961.8	2,087.0	I2,207.6	2,258.8	2,242.6	2,323.2	2,326.8	2,553.7	2,592.9	2,805.3	2,991.7	2,847.7
GDP Deflator (1990=100)	99bi.p	15.0	16.8	18.1	18.7	19.4	19.6	20.5	22.7	26.7	31.5	30.8	32.7	34.2	34.8	40.2
																Millions:
Population	99z	482.71	493.39	504.34	515.60	527.18	539.08	551.23	563.53	575.89	588.30	600.76	613.27	625.82	I646.00	660.00

Deposit Money Banks: I Since March 1978, a new classification of *Demand* and *Time Deposits* has reduced *lines 24* and *34* and increased *lines 25* and *35*.

Interest Rates: *Government Bond Yield:* I Beginning in 1971, the average yield on government 5 1/2 percent bonds maturing in the years 1999 and 2000.

Government Finance: I Beginning in 1974, data are as reported in the *Government Finance Statistics Yearbook* and cover consolidated central government. Data are reported by the Ministry of Finance.

India

International Transactions

	1980	1981	1982	1983	1984	1985	1986	1987	1988	1989	1990	1991	1992	1993	1994		
Millions of Rupees																	
	67,517	71,780	88,416	92,430	107,464	113,192	118,524	146,417	184,099	257,553	314,394	401,230	508,706	656,894	785,935	Exports	70
	116,771	133,379	139,691	142,012	172,799	196,768	194,502	216,134	266,059	334,011	413,566	459,378	611,131	694,463	839,641	Imports, cif	71
	104,500	119,462	125,257	127,163	154,699	176,158	174,129	193,495	238,191	299,025	370,247	411,261	547,118	618,951	751,693	Imports, fob	71.v
1990=100																	
	36	37	42	45	52	58	58	61	79	95	100	126	144	162	....	Export Prices	74
	43	49	50	51	47	60	60	52	69	85	100	115	124	122	....	Unit Value of Imports	75

Balance of Payments

Minus Sign Indicates Debit

1980	1981	1982	1983	1984	1985	1986	1987	1988	1989	1990	1991	1992	1993	1994		
8,303	8,437	9,226	9,770	10,192	9,465	10,248	11,884	13,510	16,144	18,286	....	....	....	....	Goods: Exports f.o.b.	78aa d
−13,947	−14,149	−14,046	−13,868	−14,216	−15,081	−15,686	−17,661	−20,091	−22,254	−23,437	....	....	....	....	Goods: Imports f.o.b.	78ab d
−5,644	−5,711	−4,820	−4,098	−4,025	−5,616	−5,438	−5,777	−6,581	−6,110	−5,151	....	....	....	....	Trade Balance	78ac d
2,971	2,797	2,933	3,290	3,232	3,384	3,228	3,363	3,791	4,140	4,625	....	....	....	....	Services: Credit	78ad d
−2,981	−3,249	−3,471	−3,705	−3,641	−3,903	−3,945	−4,629	−5,326	−5,874	−6,090	....	....	....	....	Services: Debit	78ae d
−5,654	−6,163	−5,359	−4,513	−4,434	−6,135	−6,156	−7,043	−8,116	−7,844	−6,616	....	....	....	....	Balance on Goods and Services	78af d
1,058	972	608	480	487	528	518	450	427	446	436	....	....	....	....	Income: Credit	78ag d
−523	−513	−690	−982	−1,166	−1,347	−1,581	−1,605	−2,211	−2,498	−3,693	....	....	....	....	Income: Debit	78ah d
−5,119	−5,704	−5,441	−5,014	−5,113	−6,953	−7,219	−8,198	−9,900	−9,896	−9,873	....	....	....	....	Balance on Goods, Serv., & Inc.	78ai d
3,347	3,026	2,939	3,075	2,789	2,799	2,638	3,034	2,768	3,093	2,853	....	....	....	....	Current Transfers, n.i.e.: Credit	78aj d
−14	−21	−22	−13	−19	−23	−17	−28	−16	−23	−17	....	....	....	....	Current Transfers: Debit	78ak d
−1,785	−2,698	−2,524	−1,953	−2,343	−4,177	−4,598	−5,192	−7,148	−6,826	−7,037	....	....	....	....	Current Account, n.i.e.	78al d
—	—	—	—	—	—	—	—	—	—	—	....	....	....	....	Capital Account, n.i.e.: Credit	78ba d
—	—	—	—	—	—	—	—	—	—	—	....	....	....	....	Capital Account: Debit	78bb d
—	—	—	—	—	—	—	—	—	—	—	....	....	....	....	Capital Account, n.i.e.	78bc d
—	—	—	—	—	—	—	—	—	—	—	....	....	....	....	Direct Investment Abroad	78bd d
—	—	—	—	—	—	—	—	—	—	—	....	....	....	....	Dir. Invest. in Rep. Econ., n.i.e.	78be d
—	—	—	—	—	—	—	—	—	—	—	....	....	....	....	Portfolio Investment Assets	78bf d
—	—	—	—	—	—	—	—	—	—	—	....	....	....	....	Portfolio Investment Liab., n.i.e.	78bg d
−318	−47	−691	541	−254	53	−250	125	276	74	−611	....	....	....	....	Other Investment Assets	78bh d
802	893	1,147	1,510	3,298	3,228	4,242	5,609	6,967	7,275	6,281	....	....	....	....	Other Investment Liab., n.i.e.	78bi d
483	845	456	2,051	3,044	3,281	3,992	5,734	7,243	7,349	5,670	....	....	....	....	Financial Account, n.i.e.	78bj d
−361	−325	369	−850	368	500	197	−409	−112	−285	−571	....	....	....	....	Net Errors and Omissions	78ca d
−1,663	−2,178	−1,698	−752	1,070	−397	−409	133	−16	239	−1,937	....	....	....	....	Overall Balance	78cb d
1,663	2,178	1,698	752	−1,070	397	409	−133	16	−239	1,937	....	....	....	....	Reserves and Related Items	79da d
624	1,824	43	−840	−1,595	538	891	800	1,184	835	2,794	....	....	....	....	Reserve Assets	79db d
1,039	354	1,656	1,576	494	−177	−512	−954	−1,197	−1,086	−858	....	....	....	....	Use of Fund Credit and Loans	79dc d
—	—	—	—	—	—	—	—	—	—	—	....	....	....	....	Liabs.Constit.For.Auth.Reserves	79dd d
—	—	—	16	31	37	30	21	29	13	1	....	....	....	....	Exceptional Financing	79de d

Government Finance

Year Beginning April 1

1980	1981	1982	1983	1984	1985	1986	1987	1988	1989	1990	1991	1992	1993	1994		
−88.6	−87.3	−107.3	−133.3	−175.8	−222.5	−272.0	−278.8	−320.6	−361.8	−434.6	−358.2	−366.5ᵖ	−372.0	....	Deficit (−) or Surplus	80
161.1	195.9	225.1	255.2	296.1	361.2	420.7	480.8	557.4	675.4	723.6	892.1	1,058.8ᵖ	1,162.6 f	....	Revenue	81
4.4	3.8	4.0	3.3	4.8	4.9	4.4	4.9	6.0	7.5	5.9	9.5	11.0ᵖ	13.7 f	....	Grants Received	81z
180.3	208.4	244.2	287.2	351.3	430.7	518.1	597.1	694.9	818.3	924.6	1,050.5	1,209.6ᵖ	1,310.7 f	....	Expenditure	82
73.9	78.7	92.1	104.6	125.3	157.9	178.9	167.4	189.0	226.4	239.5	209.3	226.7ᵖ	237.6 f	....	Lending Minus Repayments	83
															Financing	
83.4	73.5	133.0	85.5	161.5	208.9	258.5	244.4	302.0	335.8	407.0	304.4	300.9ᵖ	316.2	....	Net Borrowing: Domestic	84a
															Rupees	84b
7.0	9.2	11.9	12.9	13.8	13.7	19.4	32.7	24.6	26.0	31.8	54.2	46.8ᵖ	55.8 f	....	Foreign	85a
															Foreign Currency	85b
....	....	....	....	....	....	....	....	....	....	....	....	....	....	....	Finance from Foreign Aid	86a
−1.8	4.7	−37.6	34.9	.5	—	−6.0	1.6	−6.0	....	−4.2	−.3	18.7ᵖ	— f	....	Use of Cash Balances	87
453.4	527.7	673.6	746.8	887.8	1,083.6	1,315.4	1,532.9	1,830.4	2,202.6	2,610.4	2,942.5	3,301.8ᵖ	3,672.1 f	....	Debt: Domestic	88a
															Rupees	88b
107.6	117.9	131.4	145.8	161.0	181.5	203.0	232.2	257.5	283.4	315.3	369.5	412.2ᵖ	464.5 f	....	Foreign	89a
															Foreign Currency	89b

National Accounts

Year Beginning April 1

1980	1981	1982	1983	1984	1985	1986	1987	1988	1989	1990	1991	1992	1993	1994		
90.3	102.6	115.6	131.4	158.5	149.5	165.4	202.8	259.1	346.1	406.4	562.5	673.1	....	....	Exports of Goods & Services	90c
130.8	153.6	182.7	211.4	243.5	291.7	346.3	408.4	473.3	542.0	617.8	694.6	785.9	910.5	....	Government Consumption	91f
262.8	314.6	357.7	399.9	455.7	542.6	620.5	721.9	856.7	1,027.8	1,240.0	1,367.8	1,511.8	1,643.8	....	Gross Fixed Capital Formation	93e
21.8	85.6	50.2	38.0	34.4	91.9	58.5	26.9	113.9	80.2	133.9	40.9	125.8	31.7	....	Increase/Decrease(−) in Stocks	93i
992.9	1,137.7	1,251.7	1,469.5	1,620.9	1,777.6	1,986.0	2,225.5	2,574.2	2,882.4	3,323.6	3,848.0	4,245.6	4,795.9	....	Private Consumption	96f
−136.0	−148.1	−157.4	−176.8	−194.8	−217.5	−223.6	−252.6	−320.1	−402.1	−487.0	−562.5	−730.0	....	....	Imports of Goods & Services	98c
1,360.1	1,597.6	1,781.3	2,075.9	2,313.4	2,622.4	2,929.5	3,332.0	3,957.8	4,568.2	5,355.2	6,160.6	7,028.3	7,863.6	....	Gross Domestic Product	99b
3.5	.4	−6.3	−9.4	−14.2	−14.3	−18.1	−26.2	−44.9	−57.3	−75.5	−100.8	−118.0	−118.1	....	Net Factor Inc/Pmts(−) Abroad	98.n
1,363.6	1,598.0	1,775.0	2,066.5	2,299.2	2,608.1	2,911.4	3,305.8	3,912.9	4,510.9	5,279.7	6,059.8	6,910.3	7,745.5	....	Gross Nat'l Expenditure = GNP	99a
1,242.7	1,453.4	1,601.1	1,874.2	2,078.3	2,345.8	2,613.2	2,972.4	3,523.6	4,054.4	4,757.8	5,430.3	6,187.6	6,944.8	....	Nat'l Income, Market Prices	99e
3,031.6	3,229.7	3,351.8	3,600.8	3,733.2	3,937.4	4,129.1	4,326.1	4,755.4	5,067.9	5,355.2	5,381.3	5,629.1	5,824.6	....	Gross Dom. Prod. 1990 Prices	99b.p
44.9	49.5	53.1	57.7	62.0	66.6	70.9	77.0	83.2	90.1	100.0	114.5	124.9	135.0	....	GDP Deflator (1990=100)	99bi p
Midyear Estimates																
675.00	690.00	705.00	720.00	736.00	750.86	766.14	781.37	796.60	811.82	827.06	849.64	870.00	901.46	....	Population	99z

Indonesia
536

		1965	1966	1967	1968	1969	1970	1971	1972	1973	1974	1975	1976	1977	1978	1979
Exchange Rates																*Rupiah per SDR:*
Market Rate	aa	....	....	235.0	326.0	326.0	378.0	450.6	450.6	500.6	508.1	485.8	482.2	504.1	814.2	826.0
																Rupiah per US Dollar:
Market Rate	ae	....	....	235.0	326.0	326.0	378.0	415.0	415.0	415.0	415.0	415.0	415.0	415.0	625.0	627.0
Market Rate	rf	....	....	149.6ᵉ	296.3	326.0	362.8	391.9	415.0	415.0	415.0	415.0	415.0	415.0	442.0	623.1
Fund Position																*Millions of SDRs:*
Quota	2f.s	—	—	207	207	207	260	260	260	260	260	260	260	260	480	480
SDRs	1b.s	—	—	—	—	—	—	—	36	43	56	6	4	22	57	129
Reserve Position in the Fund	1c.s	—	—	—	—	—	—	—	—	—	29	—	—	68	69	74
Total Fund Cred.&Loans Outstg.	2tl	63	63	49	64	112	138	125	107	19	—	—	—	—	—	—
International Liquidity											*Millions of US Dollars Unless Otherwise Indicated:*					
Total Reserves minus Gold	1l.d	17	19	2	I 83	118	156	I 185	572	805	1,490	584	1,497	2,509	2,626	4,062
SDRs	1b.d	—	—	—	—	—	—	—	39	52	68	7	5	26	75	170
Reserve Position in the Fund	1c.d	—	—	—	—	—	—	—	—	—	35	—	—	83	90	97
Foreign Exchange	1d.d	17	19	2	I 83	118	156	I 185	533	753	1,386	577	1,492	2,400	2,461	3,795
Gold (Million Fine Troy Ounces)	1ad	.114	.114	.114	.114	.114	.114	.057	.121	.057	.057	.057	.057	.169	.224	.280
Gold (National Valuation)	1and	4	4	4	4	4	4	2	5	2	2	2	2	7	37	105
Monetary Authorities: Other Liab.	4..d	—	10	358	—	14	17	—	—	—	—	301	468	70	73	2
Deposit Money Banks: Assets	7a.d	—	—	1	67	192	227	263	377	521	722	475	690	761	1,097	2,098
Liabilities	7b.d	—	—	1	66	174	221	285	323	610	622	612	650	663	710	687
Monetary Authorities																*Billions of Rupiah:*
Foreign Assets	11	....	....	....	....	....	....	....	....	....	....	....	....	....	....	....
Claims on Central Government	12a	....	....	....	....	....	....	....	....	....	....	....	....	....	....	....
Claims on Official Entities	12bx	....	....	....	....	....	....	....	....	....	....	....	....	....	....	....
Claims on Private Sector	12d	....	....	....	....	....	....	....	....	....	....	....	....	....	....	....
Claims on Deposit Money Banks	12e	....	....	....	....	....	....	....	....	....	....	....	....	....	....	....
Claims on Other Financial Insts.	12f	....	....	....	....	....	....	....	....	....	....	....	....	....	....	....
Reserve Money	14	....	....	....	....	....	....	....	....	....	....	....	....	....	....	....
of which: Currency Outside DMBs	14a	....	....	....	....	....	....	....	....	....	....	....	....	....	....	....
Foreign Currency & Time Deposits	15	....	....	....	....	....	....	....	....	....	....	....	....	....	....	....
Restricted Deposits	16b	....	....	....	....	....	....	....	....	....	....	....	....	....	....	....
Foreign Liabilities	16c	....	....	....	....	....	....	....	....	....	....	....	....	....	....	....
Long-Term Foreign Liabilities	16cl	....	....	....	....	....	....	....	....	....	....	....	....	....	....	....
Central Government Deposits	16d	....	....	....	....	....	....	....	....	....	....	....	....	....	....	....
Counterpart Funds	16e	....	....	....	....	....	....	....	....	....	....	....	....	....	....	....
Capital Accounts	17a	....	....	....	....	....	....	....	....	....	....	....	....	....	....	....
Other Items (Net)	17r	....	....	....	....	....	....	....	....	....	....	....	....	....	....	....
Deposit Money Banks																*Billions of Rupiah:*
Reserves	20	....	....	....	....	....	....	....	....	....	....	....	....	....	....	....
Foreign Assets	21	....	....	....	....	....	....	....	....	....	....	....	....	....	....	....
Claims on Central Government	22a	....	....	....	....	....	....	....	....	....	....	....	....	....	....	....
Claims on Official Entities	22bx	....	....	....	....	....	....	....	....	....	....	....	....	....	....	....
Claims on Private Sector	22d	....	....	....	....	....	....	....	....	....	....	....	....	....	....	....
Claims on Other Financial Insts.	22f	....	....	....	....	....	....	....	....	....	....	....	....	....	....	....
Demand Deposits	24	....	....	....	....	....	....	....	....	....	....	....	....	....	....	....
Time and Savings Deposits	25a	....	....	....	....	....	....	....	....	....	....	....	....	....	....	....
Foreign Currency Deposits	25b	....	....	....	....	....	....	....	....	....	....	....	....	....	....	....
Restricted Deposits	26b	....	....	....	....	....	....	....	....	....	....	....	....	....	....	....
Foreign Liabilities	26c	....	....	....	....	....	....	....	....	....	....	....	....	....	....	....
Central Government Deposits	26d	....	....	....	....	....	....	....	....	....	....	....	....	....	....	....
Credit from Monetary Authorities	26g	....	....	....	....	....	....	....	....	....	....	....	....	....	....	....
Capital Accounts	27a	....	....	....	....	....	....	....	....	....	....	....	....	....	....	....
Other Items (Net)	27r	....	....	....	....	....	....	....	....	....	....	....	....	....	....	....
Monetary Survey																*Billions of Rupiah:*
Foreign Assets (Net)	31n	....	....	....	I —	46	−43	−58	117	296	659	−345	525	1,061	1,844	3,483
Domestic Credit	32	....	....	....	I 135	244	378	517	I 633	1,086	1,388	2,803	3,283	3,299	4,522	4,616
Claims on Central Govt. (Net)	32an	....	....	....	I 41	35	29	37	−12	−32	−151	18	−279	−613	−878	−1,711
Claims on Official Entities	32bx	....	....	....	I 23	53	55	69	105	70	146	125	84	84	140	133
Claims on Private Sector	32d	....	....	....	I 71	156	294	411	I 540	1,048	1,394	2,660	3,477	3,828	5,260	6,194
Claims on Other Financial Insts.	32f	....	....	....	....	....	....	....	....	....	....	....	....	....	....	....
Money	34	....	....	....	I 114	180	241	313	471	669	940	1,250	1,601	2,006	2,488	3,379
Quasi-Money	35	....	....	....	I 12	50	80	145	190	319	515	747	1,019	1,125	1,320	1,837
Restricted Deposits	36b	....	....	....	....	....	....	....	....	....	....	....	....	....	....	....
Other Items (Net)	37r	....	....	....	I 9	−28	15	2	90	394	592	460	1,188	1,228	2,557	2,883
Money plus Quasi-Money	35l	....	....	....	I 126	230	321	458	661	988	1,455	1,997	2,620	3,131	3,808	5,216
Other Banking Institutions											*Millions of Rupiah through 1967;*					
Cash	40	10	10	40	I —	—	1	1	1	2	6	8	10	16	22	30
Savings Deposits	45	10	20	110	I —	—	1	1	1	2	3	5	8	13	17	20
Credit from Monetary Authorities	46g	10	40	110	I —	—	1	1	1	1	—	3	5	6	6	11
Other Items (Net)	47r	—	−50	−170	I —	—	−1	−1	−1	−1	3	—	−3	−3	—	−2
Liquid Liabilities	55l	2,680	22,530	54,020	I 126	230	321	458	661	988	1,452	1,994	2,618	3,127	3,802	5,206
Interest Rates																*Percent Per Annum*
Money Market Rate	60b	....	....	....	....	....	....	....	....	....	11.42	13.41	14.17	7.23	7.29	13.23
Deposit Rate	60l	....	....	....	....	....	21.00	21.00	15.00	12.00	12.00	12.00	12.00	9.00	6.00	6.00
Lending Rate	60p	....	....	....	....	....	....	....	....	....	....	....	....	....	....	....

Indonesia

	1980	1981	1982	1983	1984	1985	1986	1987	1988	1989	1990	1991	1992	1993	1994		
Exchange Rates																	
End of Period	799.4	749.6	763.9	1,040.7	1,052.7	1,235.7	2,007.3	2,340.8	2,329.4	2,361.5	2,704.5	2,849.4	2,835.3	2,898.2	3,211.7	Market Rate	aa
End of Period (ae) Period Average (rf)	626.8	644.0	692.5	994.0	1,074.0	1,125.0	1,641.0	1,650.0	1,731.0	1,797.0	1,901.0	1,992.0	2,062.0	2,110.0	2,200.0	Market Rate	ae
	627.0	631.8	661.4	909.3	1,025.9	1,110.6	1,282.6	1,643.8	1,685.7	1,770.1	1,842.8	1,950.3	2,029.9	2,087.1	2,160.8	Market Rate	rf
Fund Position																	
End of Period	720	720	720	1,010	1,010	1,010	1,010	1,010	1,010	1,010	1,010	1,010	1,498	1,498	1,498	Quota	2f. s
	137	227	282	4	1	51	36	4	2	1	2	3	—	—	—	SDRs	1b. s
	161	196	218	72	72	72	72	72	72	72	72	72	194	200	214	Reserve Position in the Fund	1c. s
	—	—	—	425	421	42	42	505	463	463	347	116	—	—	—	Total Fund Cred.&Loans Outstg.	2tl
International Liquidity																	
End of Period	5,392	5,014	3,144	3,718	4,773	4,974	4,051	5,592	5,048	5,454	7,459	9,258	10,449	11,263	12,133	Total Reserves minus Gold	1l. d
	175	264	311	4	1	56	43	6	3	1	3	4	—	—	—	SDRs	1b. d
	205	228	241	76	71	80	89	103	97	95	103	104	267	274	312	Reserve Position in the Fund	1c. d
	5,012	4,521	2,593	3,639	4,702	4,838	3,919	5,483	4,948	5,357	7,353	9,151	10,181	10,988	11,820	Foreign Exchange	1d. d
	2.394	3.104	3.104	3.104	3.104	3.104	3.104	3.104	3.104	3.107	3.111	3.111	3.101	3.101	3.101	Gold (Million Fine Troy Ounces)	1ad
	1,108	1,062	1,052	1,096	947	906	1,360	1,319	1,158	1,044	1,061	992	946	1,092	1,067	Gold (National Valuation)	1an d
	—	—	—	1	—	—	—	—	—	—	—	—	—	...	...	Monetary Authorities: Other Liab.	4.. d
	4,364	5,059	3,776	4,548	4,777	5,546	4,993	4,731	4,851	6,025	6,223	5,591	6,338	5,367	5,843	Deposit Money Banks: Assets	7a. d
	618	676	966	973	712	523	329	456	669	1,793	6,737	6,025	7,894	9,252	10,766	Liabilities	7b. d
Monetary Authorities																	
End of Period	4,217	4,037	3,685	5,309	8,041	8,507	8,352	12,458	11,732	11,835	17,950	25,155	34,751	....	....	Foreign Assets	11
	716	925	1,154	1,521	1,670	1,237	3,106	3,518	4,427	4,589	5,221	6,258	7,896			Claims on Central Government	12a
	2,370	2,467	2,453	1,864	203	32	24	36	58	830	759	35	25			Claims on Official Entities	12bx
	69	107	409	444	652	823	1,133	1,676	1,724	1,307	1,732	953	951			Claims on Private Sector	12d
	1,722	2,548	5,050	5,866	9,521	10,041	12,552	14,562	20,375	15,240	20,990	14,867	13,532			Claims on Deposit Money Banks	12e
	44	117	215	366	518	729	877	978	950	988	992	1,012	1,050			Claims on Other Financial Insts.	12f
	3,375	3,920	4,107	5,138	5,701	6,721	8,170	9,032	8,381	10,788	12,549	12,961	15,509			Reserve Money	14
	2,169	2,546	2,934	3,340	3,712	4,460	5,338	5,802	6,245	7,908	9,094	9,346	11,478			of which: Currency Outside DMBs	14a
	41	104	57	110	25	69	42	305	143	11	18	21	21			Foreign Currency & Time Deposits	15
	119	134	46	74	33	23	24	24	25	26	26	24	25			Restricted Deposits	16b
	—	—	—	443	444	52	84	1,182	1,078	1,093	939	330	—			Foreign Liabilities	16c
	30	27	22	28	23	22	27	2,126	4,141	5,711	5,388	6,683	3,569			Long-Term Foreign Liabilities	16cl
	2,755	4,770	5,796	5,946	8,745	8,970	10,643	9,713	10,435	10,545	13,462	14,509	17,770			Central Government Deposits	16d
	89	26	15	58	222	162	144	74	18	1	−1	2	2			Counterpart Funds	16e
	1,182	1,040	601	596	1,179	1,192	2,409	3,715	3,624	3,825	3,587	4,594	6,015			Capital Accounts	17a
	1,547	180	2,321	2,976	4,233	4,158	4,500	7,057	11,420	2,788	11,677	9,156	15,295			Other Items (Net)	17r
Deposit Money Banks																	
	1,262	1,430	1,988	1,815	2,273	2,940	2,935	3,433	5,151	5,615	4,893	12,300	15,879	....	....	Reserves	20
	2,741	3,233	2,591	4,520	5,107	6,239	8,193	7,807	8,397	10,731	11,681	11,076	13,011			Foreign Assets	21
	28	69	139	266	440	530	683	1,093	1,069	960	933	1,027	1,111			Claims on Central Government	22a
	1,359	1,791	2,427	2,819	4,515	4,981	5,080	4,782	6,292	7,730	6,950	9,671	11,317			Claims on Official Entities	22bx
	4,254	5,942	8,106	10,490	14,086	17,281	21,731	28,034	38,809	58,404	97,145	114,453	123,553			Claims on Private Sector	22d
	19	26	20	25	37	41	25	115	170	246	345	590	1,530			Claims on Other Financial Insts.	22f
	2,795	3,847	4,133	4,177	4,817	5,560	6,082	6,776	8,032	12,477	14,532	17,103	16,997			Demand Deposits	24
	1,480	2,032	2,491	4,694	6,387	9,607	11,355	16,230	21,015	29,895	46,150	52,633	67,560			Time and Savings Deposits	25a
	1,174	1,094	1,406	2,289	2,944	3,378	4,587	4,665	6,524	8,061	14,643	20,064	22,693			Foreign Currency Deposits	25b
	366	298	300	242	218	268	402	425	684	632	1,048	966	890			Restricted Deposits	26b
	388	432	663	968	762	588	541	752	1,159	3,193	12,645	11,935	16,206			Foreign Liabilities	26c
	735	914	691	779	1,397	1,884	1,687	1,779	2,227	3,943	4,719	5,487	6,500			Central Government Deposits	26d
	1,636	2,596	3,890	4,264	7,045	7,039	7,747	8,100	11,711	12,936	11,144	11,692	10,006			Credit from Monetary Authorities	26g
	803	1,014	1,268	1,630	2,211	2,541	3,049	3,650	4,464	7,376	11,255	9,075	8,840			Capital Accounts	27a
	285	262	427	893	677	1,146	3,197	2,888	4,072	5,171	5,811	20,161	16,708			Other Items (Net)	27r
Monetary Survey																	
End of Period	6,540	6,811	5,590	8,391	11,919	14,083	15,892	16,206	13,751	12,568	10,659	17,283	27,987	....	....	Foreign Assets (Net)	31n
	5,369	5,759	8,434	11,069	11,978	14,799	20,329	28,739	40,835	60,564	95,896	114,002	123,164			Domestic Credit	32
	−2,746	−4,691	−5,195	−4,938	−8,031	−9,087	−8,541	−6,882	−7,167	−8,941	−12,026	−12,711	−15,262			Claims on Central Govt. (Net)	32an
	3,729	4,258	4,879	4,682	4,717	5,013	5,104	4,818	6,350	8,560	7,709	9,706	11,342			Claims on Official Entities	32bx
	4,323	6,049	8,515	10,934	14,737	18,104	22,864	29,710	40,532	59,711	98,877	115,406	124,505			Claims on Private Sector	32d
	62	143	235	391	555	770	902	1,093	1,120	1,234	1,337	1,601	2,579			Claims on Other Financial Insts.	32f
	5,011	6,474	7,120	7,576	8,581	10,124	11,631	12,705	14,392	20,559	23,819	26,693	28,801			Money	34
	2,696	3,231	3,954	7,093	9,356	13,054	15,984	21,200	27,681	37,967	60,811	72,717	90,274			Quasi-Money	35
	484	432	346	316	251	291	426	449	709	658	1,074	990	915			Restricted Deposits	36b
	3,717	2,433	2,604	4,475	5,709	5,414	8,180	10,592	11,805	13,948	20,852	30,885	31,161			Other Items (Net)	37r
	7,707	9,705	11,074	14,670	17,937	23,177	27,615	33,904	42,073	58,526	84,630	99,410	119,075			Money plus Quasi-Money	35l
Other Banking Institutions																	
Billions of Rupiah Beginning 1968: End of Period	42	61	75	101	130	74	63	72	76	65	162	99	296	....	....	Cash	40
	36	46	54	75	98	134	220	348	492	289	740	919	1,325			Savings Deposits	45
	44	122	222	389	523	734	882	1,157	951	1,827	1,412	1,338	1,443			Credit from Monetary Authorities	46g
	−38	−107	−200	−362	−492	−793	−1,038	−1,433	−1,368	−2,051	−1,990	−2,158	−2,471			Other Items (Net)	47r
	7,701	9,690	11,052	14,643	17,905	23,237	27,772	34,181	42,489	58,750	85,208	100,230	120,103			Liquid Liabilities	55l
Interest Rates																	
Percent Per Annum	12.87	16.26	17.24	13.17	18.63	10.33	13.00e	14.52	15.00	12.57	14.37	15.12	12.14	....	....	Money Market Rate	60b
	6.00	6.00	6.00	6.00	16.00	18.00	15.39	16.78	17.72	18.63	17.30	23.27	20.37			Deposit Rate	60l
	....	....	....	....	....	....	21.49	21.67	22.10	21.70	20.61	....	24.03	20.24	....	Lending Rate	60p

Indonesia

536

	1965	1966	1967	1968	1969	1970	1971	1972	1973	1974	1975	1976	1977	1978	1979
Prices and Production													*Index Numbers (1990=100):*		
Wholesale Prices: Incl. Petroleum 63	....	....	....	....	....	....	5.9	6.8	9.3	13.8	14.7	16.9	19.2	‡21.1	31.5
Excl. Petroleum 63a	....	....	....	....	....	....	7.5	8.4	11.4	14.7	16.3	19.2	21.9	‡24.1	32.2
Consumer Prices 64	.1	‡1.5	3.1	7.0	8.1	9.1	9.5	10.1	13.3	18.7	22.2	26.7	29.6	32.0	‡37.2
Crude Petroleum Production 66aa	33.0	32.0	34.9	41.2	54.5	58.5	60.9	74.3	91.6	94.1	89.4	103.2	115.3	111.9	108.8
International Transactions													*Millions of US Dollars*		
Exports .... 70..d	708	679	665	731	854	1,108	1,234	1,777	3,211	7,426	7,102	8,547	10,853	11,643	15,591
Crude Petroleum & Products 70a.d	272	203	240	298	383	446	565	913	1,609	5,211	5,311	6,004	7,298	7,439	8,871
Crude Petroleum .... 70aa d	169	164	188	245	333	409	468	834	1,383	4,680	4,933	5,652	6,827	7,015	8,124
Imports, cif. .... 71..d	695	527	649	716	781	1,002	1,103	1,562	2,729	3,842	4,770	5,673	6,230	6,690	7,202
Imports, fob. .... 71.v d	631	468	586	644	692	889	984	1,401	2,447	3,402	4,210	5,020	5,484	5,910	6,425
														1990=100	
Volume of Exports 72	27	26	27	31	‡30	37	‡45	53	64	66	69	79	90	95	92
Crude Petroleum 72aa	28	28	47	61	78	94	99	124	152	157	158	180	205	210	182
Export Prices														*1990=100:*	
Exports (Unit Value) .... 74..d	11.1	10.6	10.1	10.1	‡11.7	‡17.2	17.1	20.6	29.9	65.4	69.1	72.6	81.1	82.2	115.5
Crude Petroleum (Unit Value) .... 74aa d	5.8	5.3	5.3	5.3	5.8	5.8	8.0	12.7	17.3	53.0	58.2	59.0	62.1	62.4	84.3
Crude Petroleum (Ofc.Price) .... 76aa d	7.5	7.5	7.5	7.5	7.5	7.5	9.4	12.5	18.0	53.7	56.9	57.9	61.0	61.0	82.8
Balance of Payments													*Millions of US Dollars:*		
Goods: Exports f.o.b. .... 78aa d	....	....	....	....	....	....	....	....	....	....	....	....	....	....	....
Goods: Imports f.o.b. .... 78ab d	....	....	....	....	....	....	....	....	....	....	....	....	....	....	....
Trade Balance .... 78ac d	....	....	....	....	....	....	....	....	....	....	....	....	....	....	....
Services: Credit .... 78ad d	....	....	....	....	....	....	....	....	....	....	....	....	....	....	....
Services: Debit .... 78ae d	....	....	....	....	....	....	....	....	....	....	....	....	....	....	....
Balance on Goods and Services .... 78af d	....	....	....	....	....	....	....	....	....	....	....	....	....	....	....
Income: Credit .... 78ag d	....	....	....	....	....	....	....	....	....	....	....	....	....	....	....
Income: Debit .... 78ah d	....	....	....	....	....	....	....	....	....	....	....	....	....	....	....
Balance on Goods, Serv., & Inc. .... 78ai d	....	....	....	....	....	....	....	....	....	....	....	....	....	....	....
Current Transfers, n.i.e.: Credit .... 78aj d	....	....	....	....	....	....	....	....	....	....	....	....	....	....	....
Current Transfers: Debit .... 78ak d	....	....	....	....	....	....	....	....	....	....	....	....	....	....	....
Current Account, n.i.e. .... 78al d	....	....	....	....	....	....	....	....	....	....	....	....	....	....	....
Capital Account, n.i.e.: Credit .... 78ba d	....	....	....	....	....	....	....	....	....	....	....	....	....	....	....
Capital Account: Debit .... 78bb d	....	....	....	....	....	....	....	....	....	....	....	....	....	....	....
Capital Account, n.i.e. .... 78bc d	....	....	....	....	....	....	....	....	....	....	....	....	....	....	....
Direct Investment Abroad .... 78bd d	....	....	....	....	....	....	....	....	....	....	....	....	....	....	....
Dir. Invest. in Rep. Econ., n.i.e. .... 78be d	....	....	....	....	....	....	....	....	....	....	....	....	....	....	....
Portfolio Investment Assets .... 78bf d	....	....	....	....	....	....	....	....	....	....	....	....	....	....	....
Portfolio Investment Liab., n.i.e. .... 78bg d	....	....	....	....	....	....	....	....	....	....	....	....	....	....	....
Other Investment Assets .... 78bh d	....	....	....	....	....	....	....	....	....	....	....	....	....	....	....
Other Investment Liab., n.i.e. .... 78bi d	....	....	....	....	....	....	....	....	....	....	....	....	....	....	....
Financial Account, n.i.e. .... 78bj d	....	....	....	....	....	....	....	....	....	....	....	....	....	....	....
Net Errors and Omissions .... 78ca d	....	....	....	....	....	....	....	....	....	....	....	....	....	....	....
Overall Balance .... 78cb d	....	....	....	....	....	....	....	....	....	....	....	....	....	....	....
Reserves and Related Items .... 79da d	....	....	....	....	....	....	....	....	....	....	....	....	....	....	....
Reserve Assets .... 79db d	....	....	....	....	....	....	....	....	....	....	....	....	....	....	....
Use of Fund Credit and Loans .... 79dc d	....	....	....	....	....	....	....	....	....	....	....	....	....	....	....
Liabs.Constit.For.Auth.Reserves .... 79dd d	....	....	....	....	....	....	....	....	....	....	....	....	....	....	....
Exceptional Financing .... 79de d	....	....	....	....	....	....	....	....	....	....	....	....	....	....	....
Government Finance													*Billions of Rupiah:*		
Deficit (-) or Surplus 80	....	....	....	....	−76	−101	−91	‡−117	−163	−168	−468	−693	−393	−754	−764
Revenue 81	....	....	....	....	271	360	442	‡644	1,020	1,832	2,300	2,968	3,634	4,378	7,050
Expenditure 82	....	....	....	....	347	461	534	‡718	1,103	1,857	2,592	3,375	3,707	4,870	7,284
Lending Minus Repayment 83	....	....	....	....	....	....	....	43	80	143	176	286	320	262	530
Financing															
Net Borrowing: Domestic 84a	....	....	....	....	7	5	5	‡5	−2	−15	28	−37	64	42	41
Foreign 85a	....	....	....	....	77	88	92	‡112	165	182	454	750	460	701	868
Use of Cash Balances 87	....	....	....	....	−7	8	−5	‡—	—	—	−14	−20	−131	11	−145
Debt: Domestic 88a	....	....	....	....	....	....	....	111	115	115	143	106	170	212	252
Foreign 89a	....	....	....	....	....	....	....	1,890	2,170	2,358	2,671	3,317	3,831	7,144	7,392
National Accounts												*Millions of Rupiah through 1967;*			
Exports of Goods & Services 90c	1,300	40,300	74,400	‡228	245	429	530	754	1,354	3,105	2,851	3,430	4,466	4,935	9,629
Government Consumption 91f	1,300	27,800	62,500	‡156	199	293	341	414	716	841	1,254	1,591	2,077	2,659	3,733
Gross Capital Formation 93	1,600	14,300	67,900	‡185	317	455	580	857	1,208	1,797	2,572	3,205	3,826	4,671	6,704
Private Consumption 96f	20,900	303,300	786,000	‡1,854	2,360	2,693	2,833	3,402	4,791	7,259	8,745	10,464	12,458	13,850	19,514
Imports of Goods & Services 98c	−1,400	−69,800	−143,000	‡−327	−403	−529	−611	−862	−1,316	−2,294	−2,778	−3,222	−3,817	−3,370	−7,555
Gross Domestic Product 99b	23,710	315,900	847,800	‡2,097	2,718	3,340	3,672	4,564	6,753	10,708	12,643	15,467	19,011	22,746	32,025
Net Factor Inc/Pmts(-) Abroad 98.n	−200	−4,900	−9,600	‡−29	−35	−50	−67	−159	−246	−507	−556	−432	−679	−892	−1,484
Gross Nat'l Expenditure = GNP 99a	23,500	311,000	838,200	‡2,068	2,683	3,290	3,605	4,405	6,508	10,201	12,087	15,035	18,332	21,854	30,541
Nat'l Income, Market Prices 99e	22,100	293,800	783,500	‡1,937	2,507	3,071	3,367	4,109	6,069	9,505	11,266	14,028	17,097	20,371	28,452
GDP 1990 Prices *(Billions)* 99b.p	40,116	41,040	41,979	46,643	49,445	53,170	‡56,895	62,257	69,298	74,588	78,301	83,693	91,026	98,163	104,304
GDP Deflator (1990=100) .... 99bi p	.1	.8	2.0	4.5	5.5	6.3	6.5	7.3	9.7	14.4	16.1	18.5	20.9	23.2	30.7
															Millions:
Population 99z	105.07	107.83	110.61	113.49	116.46	119.47	122.53	125.64	128.80	132.00	135.67	‡133.53	136.63	139.80	143.04

Exchange Rates: In 1965 a new rupiah, equal to 1,000 old rupiahs, was introduced.
International Liquidity: ‡ Beginning in 1968, the foreign accounts were restructured to eliminate backlogs and other inactive accounts. The net of both assets and liabilities accounts is recorded as a special correction account and shown in nominal book values in *Other Items (Net)(line 17r)*. Foreign Assets (line 11) and Foreign Liabilities (line 16c) were revalued from Rp 25 to Rp 250 per U.S. dollar in December 1967, to Rp 325 in January 1969, to Rp 378 in May 1970, and to Rp 415 in August 1971. ‡ Beginning in December 1971, line 1d.d includes the foreign exchange holdings of the West Irian branch of Bank Indonesia and excludes foreign currency accounts of residents.

Monetary Survey: ‡ Prior to 1980, the data are from the monetary survey published in the monthly *Bulletin of Bank Indonesia*.
Other Banking Institutions: ‡ Beginning in 1968, the data are based on an improved classification.
Prices and Production: ‡ Prior to March 1979, the CPI series is based on an index that covered Djakarta only.
Government Finance: ‡ Beginning in 1972, data are as reported in the *Government Finance Statistics Yearbook* and cover consolidated central government, including extrabudgetary accounts. Prior to 1972, data are as reported to *IFS*. Data relate to a fiscal year different from calendar year.

Indonesia

536

	1980	1981	1982	1983	1984	1985	1986	1987	1988	1989	1990	1991	1992	1993	1994		
Period Averages																**Prices and Production**	
	39.9	44.4	47.6	ɪ56.2	62.4	65.4	66.9	79.8	83.7	90.9	100.0	105.1	110.6	114.7	120.9	Wholesale Prices: Incl. Petroleum	63
	38.2	42.0	45.5	54.5	61.6	ɪ64.3	69.7	80.2	88.5	94.5	100.0	106.0	116.1	137.4		Excl. Petroleum	63a
	43.9	49.3	53.9	60.3	66.6	69.8	73.8	80.7	87.2	92.8	100.0	109.4	ɪ117.7	128.5	139.5	Consumer Prices	64
	108.2	109.6	91.5	92.0	95.3	90.7	96.5	96.1	92.1	96.4	100.0	108.9	103.2	103.0	110.3	Crude Petroleum Production	66aa
Millions of US Dollars																**International Transactions**	
	21,909	22,260	22,293	21,152	21,902	18,590	16,075	17,135	19,465	22,160	25,674	29,543	33,861	36,825	40,054	Exports	70..d
	12,850	14,390	14,861	13,478	12,097	7,670	5,167	5,919	....	4,964	6,481	5,745	5,850	5,009	6,006	Crude Petroleum & Products	70a.d
	11,671	13,183	14,002	11,646	10,214	7,217	4,721	4,575	5,400	4,349	5,313	4,999	4,648	4,259	5,073	Crude Petroleum	70aa d
	10,834	13,272	16,859	16,352	13,882	10,262	10,718	12,891	13,249	16,360	21,837	25,869	27,280	28,086	31,985	Imports, cif	71..d
	9,674	11,850	15,053	14,600	12,395	9,162	9,570	11,510	11,829	14,607	19,497	23,097	24,357	25,077	28,558	Imports, fob	71.v d
1990 = 100																	
	87	71	68	82	82	91	98	95	93	102	100	128	117	126	213	Volume of Exports	72
	150	157	128	151	141	105	123	120	96	101	100	107	104	87	96	Crude Petroleum	72aa
Indices of Unit Values in US Dollars																Export Prices	
	168.8	169.0	165.0	146.4	144.6	124.5	82.9	81.4	77.4	82.2	100.0	87.9	84.3	77.3	47.8	Exports (Unit Value)	74..d
	141.6	162.4	162.8	141.9	135.2	128.5	83.1	77.9	72.9	76.0	100.0	87.7	83.6	76.1	50.5	Crude Petroleum (Unit Value)	74aa d
	137.5	157.5	157.2	136.3	132.9	128.8	128.4	83.1	69.6	78.9	100.0	85.2	85.2	78.6	....	Crude Petroleum (Ofc.Price)	76aa d
																Balance of Payments	
	....	23,348	19,747	18,689	20,754	18,527	14,396	17,206	19,509	22,974	26,807	29,635	33,796	36,607	....	Goods: Exports f.o.b.	78aa d
	....	−16,542	−17,854	−17,726	−15,047	−12,705	−11,938	−12,532	−13,831	−16,310	−21,455	−24,834	−26,774	−28,376	....	Goods: Imports f.o.b.	78ab d
	....	6,806	1,893	963	5,707	5,822	2,458	4,674	5,678	6,664	5,352	4,801	7,022	8,231	....	Trade Balance	78ac d
	....	449	504	546	570	844	844	1,065	1,369	1,875	2,488	2,822	3,391	4,040	....	Services: Credit	78ad d
	....	−4,998	−4,862	−4,311	−4,239	−5,135	−4,256	−4,440	−4,606	−5,439	−6,056	−6,564	−8,100	−8,934	....	Services: Debit	78ae d
	....	2,257	−2,465	−2,802	2,038	1,531	−954	1,299	2,441	3,100	1,784	1,059	2,313	3,337	....	Balance on Goods and Services	78af d
	....	1,081	1,023	631	828	768	732	561	492	562	409	917	818	883	....	Income: Credit	78ag d
	....	−4,154	−4,016	−4,281	−4,889	−4,310	−3,948	−4,215	−4,584	−5,109	−5,599	−6,498	−6,482	−6,864	....	Income: Debit	78ah d
	....	−816	−5,458	−6,452	−2,023	−2,011	−4,170	−2,355	−1,651	−1,447	−3,406	−4,522	−3,351	−2,644	....	Balance on Goods, Serv., & Inc.	78ai d
	....	250	134	114	167	88	259	257	254	339	418	262	571	628	....	Current Transfers, n.i.e.: Credit	78aj d
	....	—	—	—	—	—	—	—	—	—	—	—	—	—	....	Current Transfers: Debit	78ak d
	....	−566	−5,324	−6,338	−1,856	−1,923	−3,911	−2,098	−1,397	−1,108	−2,988	−4,260	−2,780	−2,016	....	Current Account, n.i.e.	78al d
	....	—	—	—	—	—	—	—	—	—	—	—	—	—	....	Capital Account, n.i.e.: Credit	78ba d
	....	—	—	—	—	—	—	—	—	—	—	—	—	—	....	Capital Account: Debit	78bb d
	....	—	—	—	—	—	—	—	—	—	—	—	—	—	....	Capital Account, n.i.e.	78bc d
	....	—	—	—	—	—	—	—	—	—	—	—	—	—	....	Direct Investment Abroad	78bd d
	....	133	225	292	222	310	258	385	576	682	1,093	1,482	1,777	2,004	....	Dir. Invest. in Rep. Econ., n.i.e.	78be d
	....	—	—	—	—	—	—	—	—	—	—	—	—	—	....	Portfolio Investment Assets	78bf d
	....	47	315	368	−10	−35	268	−88	−98	−173	−93	−12	−88	−201	....	Portfolio Investment Liab., n.i.e.	78bg d
	....	—	—	—	—	—	—	—	—	—	—	—	—	—	....	Other Investment Assets	78bh d
	....	1,681	5,082	5,394	3,245	1,507	3,651	3,184	1,739	2,409	3,495	4,227	4,440	3,878	....	Other Investment Liab., n.i.e.	78bi d
	....	1,861	5,622	6,054	3,457	1,782	4,177	3,481	2,217	2,918	4,495	5,697	6,129	5,681	....	Financial Account, n.i.e.	78bj d
	....	−1,669	−2,151	467	−620	651	−1,269	−753	−933	−1,315	744	91	−1,279	−3,078	....	Net Errors and Omissions	78ca d
	....	−374	−1,853	183	981	510	−1,003	630	−113	495	2,251	1,528	2,070	587	....	Overall Balance	78cb d
	....	374	1,853	−183	−981	−510	1,003	−630	113	−495	−2,251	−1,528	−2,070	−587	....	Reserves and Related Items	79da d
	....	374	1,853	−633	−977	−126	1,003	−1,233	167	−495	−2,088	−1,210	−1,909	−587	....	Reserve Assets	79db d
	....	—	—	450	−4	−385	—	604	−54	—	−163	−319	−161	—	....	Use of Fund Credit and Loans	79dc d
	....	—	—	—	—	—	—	—	—	—	—	—	—	—	....	Liabs.Constit.For.Auth.Reserves	79dd d
	....	—	—	—	—	—	—	—	—	—	—	—	—	—	....	Exceptional Financing	79de d
Year Beginning April 1																**Government Finance**	
	−1,102	−1,172	−1,191	−1,862	1,219	−948	−3,621	−1,037	−4,388	−3,362	798	982	−1,096	2,018	....	Deficit (−) or Surplus	80
	10,406	13,763	12,815	15,511	18,724	20,347	21,324	24,781	24,088	29,093	39,566	42,415	50,645	56,318	....	Revenue	81
	10,827	14,246	13,568	16,359	16,803	20,770	24,844	26,056	28,691	32,545	38,720	41,319	52,200	54,983	....	Expenditure	82
	681	689	438	1,014	702	525	101	−238	−215	−90	48	114	−459	−683	....	Lending Minus Repayment	83
																Financing	
	43	145	−155	960	−1,088	348	836	610	1,424	336	−147	594	−1,225	444	....	Net Borrowing: Domestic	84a
	1,024	1,094	1,277	1,082	207	705	2,889	456	3,354	2,882	1,515	1,798	1,159	−451	....	Foreign	85a
	35	−67	69	−180	−338	−105	−104	−29	−390	144	−2,166	−3,374	1,162	−2,011	....	Use of Cash Balances	87
	229	371	216	1,176	115	462	1,298	1,908	3,343	3,686	3,578	4,172	5,449	4,861	....	Debt: Domestic	88a
	8,211	9,462	17,254	21,018	22,972	30,747	52,298	63,297	76,902	74,817	85,891	87,435	105,546	118,797	....	Foreign	89a
Billions of Rupiah Beginning 1968																**National Accounts**	
	13,849	16,177	15,103	19,847	22,999	21,534	20,010	29,874	34,666	42,505	51,953	62,264	76,385	85,296	94,537	Exports of Goods & Services	90c
	4,688	6,452	7,229	8,077	9,122	10,893	11,329	11,764	12,756	15,698	17,573	20,785	24,731	29,757	31,014	Government Consumption	91f
	9,485	17,324	17,406	22,261	23,543	27,204	29,025	39,146	44,810	58,831	70,705	80,742	93,225	109,575	128,327	Gross Capital Formation	93
	27,503	32,293	37,924	47,063	54,067	57,201	63,355	71,989	81,045	88,752	106,312	125,035	135,880	183,531	213,256	Private Consumption	96f
	−10,080	−14,119	−15,186	−19,626	−19,845	−19,835	−21,036	−27,956	−31,171	−38,601	−50,946	−61,376	−70,337	−78,383	−89,780	Imports of Goods & Services	98c
	45,446	58,127	62,476	77,623	89,885	96,997	102,683	124,817	142,105	167,185	195,597	227,450	259,884	329,776	377,354	Gross Domestic Product	99b
	−2,011	−1,930	−1,980	−3,283	−4,183	−3,941	−4,193	−6,022	−6,922	−8,074	−9,616	−10,899	−12,447	−12,553	−14,349	Net Factor Inc/Pmts(−) Abroad	98.n
	43,435	56,197	60,496	74,340	85,702	93,056	98,490	118,795	135,183	159,111	185,982	216,551	247,437	317,223	363,005	Gross Nat'l Expenditure = GNP	99a
	40,473	52,685	56,620	70,459	81,208	88,206	93,356	112,554	128,078	150,746	176,198	205,171	234,392	300,734	344,137	Nat'l Income, Market Prices	99e
	114,609	123,694	126,473	ɪ131,776	140,967	144,439	152,925	160,458	169,732	182,389	195,597	209,192	222,705	237,172	254,574	GDP 1990 Prices (Billions)	99b.p
	39.7	47.0	49.4	58.9	63.8	67.2	67.1	77.8	83.7	91.7	100.0	108.7	116.7	139.0	148.2	GDP Deflator (1990=100)	99bi p
Midyear Estimates																	
	147.49	151.31	154.66	158.08	161.58	164.63	168.35	172.01	175.59	179.14	ɪ179.83	182.94	186.04	189.14	192.22	Population	99z

Iran, I.R. of
429

		1965	1966	1967	1968	1969	1970	1971	1972	1973	1974	1975	1976	1977	1978	1979
Exchange Rates																*Rials per SDR:*
Market Rate	aa	75.75	75.75	75.25	75.09	76.38	76.38	82.93	82.93	81.58	82.80	81.10	82.05	85.61	91.81	92.84
																Rials per US Dollar:
Market Rate	ae	75.75	75.75	75.25	75.09	76.38	76.38	76.38	76.38	67.63	67.63	69.28	70.63	70.48	70.48	70.48
Market Rate	rf	75.75	75.75	75.75	75.75	75.75	75.75	75.75	75.75	68.88	67.63	67.64	70.22	70.62	70.48	70.48
																Rials per US Dollar:
Weighted Average	yf	....	....	....	....	....	....	....	....	....	....	....	....	....	....	....
Fund Position																*Millions of SDRs:*
Quota	2f. s	70	125	125	125	125	192	192	192	192	192	192	192	192	660	660
SDRs	1b. s	—	—	—	—	—	1	1	34	37	45	56	64	70	96	167
Reserve Position in the Fund	1c. s	3	17	31	—	—	—	—	19	48	422	959	998	986	725	325
International Liquidity													*Millions of US Dollars Unless Otherwise Indicated:*			
Total Reserves minus Gold	1l. d	105	138	180	133	152	77	479	818	1,078	8,223	8,744	8,681	12,106	11,977	15,210
SDRs	1b. d	—	—	—	—	—	1	1	37	45	55	65	75	85	125	220
Reserve Position in the Fund	1c. d	3	17	31	—	—	—	—	21	58	517	1,122	1,160	1,197	945	428
Foreign Exchange	1d. d	102	121	149	133	152	76	478	760	976	7,652	7,556	7,447	10,824	10,907	14,561
Gold (Million Fine Troy Ounces)	1ad	4.171	3.714	4.114	4.514	4.514	3.743	3.743	3.743	3.743	3.738	3.738	3.738	3.779	3.820	3.903
Gold (National Valuation)	1and	146	130	144	158	158	131	142	142	158	160	153	152	161	174	180
Monetary Authorities: Other Assets	3..d	—	—	—	−4	12	17	35	33	48	28	27	51	58	....	209
Deposit Money Banks: Assets	7a. d	60	40	38	57	61	108	100	183	233	458	637	583	618	969	1,409
Liabilities	7b. d	23	22	32	39	38	71	102	161	321	639	1,069	1,419	1,830	1,500	653
Other Banking Insts.: Liabilities	7f. d	6	13	23	34	43	55	83	206	305	383	578	1,192	1,913	2,200	2,133
Monetary Authorities																*Billions of Rials:*
Foreign Assets	11	19	20	25	22	24	17	48	75	87	569	628	660	903	....	1,109
Claims on Central Government	12a	35	42	54	64	80	118	141	149	208	124	156	101	176	....	480
Claims on Official Entities	12bx	5	6	8	14	14	12	9	15	32	128	268	445	473	....	723
Claims on Deposit Money Banks	12e	10	10	9	10	11	17	15	20	38	37	82	101	80	....	80
Reserve Money	14	56	59	68	76	87	106	131	179	246	330	412	573	733	....	1,444
of which: Currency Outside DMBs	14a	23	24	27	31	32	37	42	56	70	102	148	206	252	....	769
Nonfin.Pub.Ent. Deps.	14e	15	15	19	17	20	23	34	57	82	96	77	102	139	....	220
Restricted Deposits	16b	3	6	8	6	6	11	15	25	46	147	131	124	151	....	163
Foreign Liabilities	16c	1	1	3	9	18	33	41	20	2	12	11	12	12	....	14
Central Government Deposits	16d	3	9	10	13	10	8	17	22	48	296	423	408	513	....	528
Capital Accounts	17a	4	4	4	4	4	6	8	12	12	14	39	54	61	....	106
Other Items (Net)	17r	2	1	2	1	4	−1	—	1	10	59	117	137	162	....	136
Deposit Money Banks																*Billions of Rials:*
Reserves	20	17	19	22	29	35	47	53	66	86	132	187	265	342	....	455
Foreign Assets	21	5	3	3	4	5	8	8	14	16	31	44	41	44	....	99
Claims on Central Government	22a	1	3	3	3	9	5	11	18	32	83	148	229	349	....	479
Claims on Private Sector	22d	75	89	102	124	143	174	205	266	369	480	738	1,041	1,223	....	1,639
Demand Deposits	24	36	43	51	58	60	69	79	101	126	183	233	360	431	....	700
Time and Savings Deposits	25	40	48	59	75	100	121	155	204	268	398	592	843	1,083	....	1,497
Foreign Liabilities	26c	2	2	2	3	3	5	8	12	22	43	74	100	129	....	46
Credit from Monetary Authorities	26g	10	10	9	10	11	17	15	20	38	37	82	101	80	....	80
Capital Accounts	27a	8	9	9	11	12	14	15	17	26	33	73	96	129	....	162
Other Items (Net)	27r	3	2	1	4	5	8	5	10	24	32	63	76	105	....	188
Monetary Survey																*Billions of Rials:*
Foreign Assets (Net)	31n	21	21	22	14	8	−13	7	57	79	544	587	590	805	....	1,147
Domestic Credit	32	113	131	157	191	236	304	348	427	594	520	838	1,368	1,661	....	2,724
Claims on Central Govt. (Net)	32an	33	36	48	53	79	115	135	146	193	−88	−168	−124	−44	....	352
Claims on Official Entities	32bx	5	6	8	14	14	14	9	15	32	128	268	450	482	....	732
Claims on Private Sector	32d	75	89	102	124	143	174	205	266	369	480	738	1,041	1,223	....	1,639
Money	34	74	82	97	105	112	128	155	214	278	381	458	668	822	1,078[e]	1,689
Quasi-Money	35	40	48	59	75	100	121	155	204	268	398	592	843	1,083	1,273	1,497
Restricted Deposits	36b	3	6	8	6	6	11	15	25	46	147	131	124	151	....	163
Other Items (Net)	37r	17	15	16	20	25	30	31	39	81	138	244	323	411	....	522
Money plus Quasi-Money	35l	114	131	156	180	212	250	310	419	546	779	1,050	1,511	1,905	2,351	3,186
Other Banking Institutions																*Billions of Rials:*
Cash	40	3	1	2	1	2	2	3	4	5	7	19	25	28	....	26
Claims on Central Government	42a	2	1	1	1	1	1	2	4	5	6	14	13	13	....	7
Claims on Official Entities	42bx	1	—	—	1	2	2	8	13	17	20	22	22	20	....	18
Claims on Private Sector	42d	22	27	30	36	39	47	54	68	83	134	233	360	497	....	697
Demand Deposits	44	4	5	4	5	7	9	10	11	14	35	45	51	50	....	50
Private Sector	44x	3	4	4	3	2	2	3	4	5	9	14	18	21	....	27
Official Entities	44y	1	1	—	2	4	6	7	7	9	26	32	33	30	....	23
Time and Savings Deposits	45	2	2	3	4	4	5	6	11	15	20	30	48	67	....	99
Foreign Liabilities	46c	—	1	2	3	3	4	6	16	21	26	40	84	135	....	150
Central Government Deposits	46d	7	5	5	4	4	5	14	20	26	31	64	75	83	....	78
Credit from Monetary Authorities	46g	1	2	1	3	3	3	2	1	2	11	23	42	95	....	163
Capital Accounts	47a	17	18	20	22	22	26	27	33	39	53	79	98	118	....	171
Other Items (Net)	47r	−3	−2	−1	—	1	2	1	−1	−5	−8	7	21	11	....	37
Liquid Liabilities	55l	116	135	160	187	220	261	322	435	568	825	1,106	1,584	1,993	....	3,308

Iran, I.R. of

1980	1981	1982	1983	1984	1985	1986	1987	1988	1989	1990	1991	1992	1993	1994		
															Exchange Rates	
End of Period																
92.30	92.30	92.30	92.30	92.30	92.30	92.30	92.30	92.30	92.30	92.30	92.30	92.30	2,415.49	2,534.26	Market Rate	aa
End of Period (ae) Period Average (rf)																
72.32	79.45	83.43	88.16	93.99	84.23	75.64	65.62	68.59	70.24	65.31	64.59	67.04	1,758.56	1,735.97	Market Rate	ae
70.61	78.33	83.60	86.36	90.03	91.05	78.76	71.46	68.68	72.01	68.10	67.51	65.55	1,267.77	1,748.75	Market Rate	rf
Year Ending December 20																
....	....	....	....	....	207.300	217.500	221.600	236.600	302.800	415.600	511.200	579.000	1,224.200	....	Weighted Average	yf
															Fund Position	
End of Period																
660	660	660	660	660	660	660	660	660	660	660	660	1,079	1,079	1,079	Quota	2f. s
240	291	300	309	320	328	335	342	116	305	310	216	7	105	98	SDRs	1b. s
235	141	76	71	71	71	71	71	—	—	—	—	105	—	—	Reserve Position in the Fund	1c. s
															International Liquidity	
End of Period																
10,223	1,605	5,701	....	....	....	....	....	....	....	....	....	....	....	....	Total Reserves minus Gold	1l. d
307	339	331	324	314	361	410	486	156	400	442	309	10	144	143	SDRs	1b. d
299	165	84	74	69	78	87	100	—	—	—	—	144	—	—	Reserve Position in the Fund	1c. d
9,617	1,102	5,287	....	....	....	....	....	....	....	....	....	....	....	....	Foreign Exchange	1d. d
4.343	4.343	4.343	4.343	4.343	4.343	4.343	4.343	4.343	4.343	4.343	4.343	4.343	....	....	Gold (Million Fine Troy Ounces)	1ad
194	177	168	159	149	167	186	216	205	200	216	217	209	....	....	Gold (National Valuation)	1an d
203	185	176	1,143	....	....	....	....	....	....	....	....	....	....	....	Monetary Authorities: Other Assets	3..d
2,218	1,824	3,090	2,191	1,626	2,004	2,083	1,518	1,448	2,029	3,110	2,912	3,070	1,459	....	Deposit Money Banks: Assets	7a. d
693	743	798	730	622	....	997	1,067	1,077	1,242	1,860	2,262	4,053	3,397	....	Liabilities	7b. d
1,778	1,473	1,363	1,197	—	—	—	—	10	3	5	227	71			Other Banking Insts.: Liabilities	7f. d
															Monetary Authorities	
Year Ending December 20																
837	479	1,232	720	....	....	569	758	602	731	696	1,238	1,349	7,916	....	Foreign Assets	11
1,636	3,003	4,003	3,758	....	....	6,290	8,095	10,156	11,954	12,818	14,267	14,651	15,078	....	Claims on Central Government	12a
720	892	954	1,005	....	....	942	1,036	1,072	1,137	1,651	2,384	2,520	3,792	....	Claims on Official Entities	12bx
100	127	110	120	....	....	82	99	128	162	194	379	742	3,751	....	Claims on Deposit Money Banks	12e
1,833	2,421	3,408	3,823	....	....	5,798	7,240	9,063	10,254	10,577	12,293	13,901	16,511	....	Reserve Money	14
1,108	1,248	1,465	1,757	....	....	2,354	2,712	3,068	3,225	3,518	3,862	4,088	4,925	....	of which: Currency Outside DMBs	14a
169	167	329	335	....	....	290	281	214	151	183	553	559	862	....	Nonfin.Pub.Ent. Deps.	14e
201	185	201	335	....	....	241	364	289	377	611	568	352	1,158	....	Restricted Deposits	16b
53	56	26	92	....	....	51	26	28	64	148	129	166	2,924	....	Foreign Liabilities	16c
588	796	836	1,005	....	....	1,164	1,269	1,515	1,788	2,426	2,779	3,077	4,965	....	Central Government Deposits	16d
112	117	178	218	....	....	244	261	261	265	275	281	294	801	....	Capital Accounts	17a
507	926	1,649	130	....	....	385	828	800	1,236	1,322	2,220	1,472	4,180	....	Other Items (Net)	17r
															Deposit Money Banks	
Year Ending December 20																
556	1,006	1,614	1,731	2,056	2,909	3,068	4,207	5,715	6,797	6,780	7,764	9,134	10,586	....	Reserves	20
160	145	258	193	153	169	158	100	99	143	203	188	206	2,566	....	Foreign Assets	21
496	543	763	943	1,179	1,194	1,194	1,249	1,247	1,347	1,346	1,338	1,343	1,236	....	Claims on Central Government	22a
2,006	2,104	2,199	2,703	2,730	3,045	3,647	4,184	4,672	6,184	8,729	12,059	16,665	22,131	....	Claims on Private Sector	22d
981	1,222	1,499	1,830	2,296	....	2,865	3,469	3,836	4,862	6,028	7,851	9,434	12,519	....	Demand Deposits	24
1,767	2,046	2,591	3,061	2,986	....	4,339	5,283	6,988	9,045	10,663	13,342	17,770	23,181	....	Time and Savings Deposits	25
50	59	67	64	59	....	75	70	74	87	122	146	272	5,973	....	Foreign Liabilities	26c
100	127	110	120	116	....	82	99	128	162	194	379	742	3,751	....	Credit from Monetary Authorities	26g
—	—	—	—	85	100	84	134	134	134	134	134	134	3,719	....	Capital Accounts	27a
320	344	567	495	576	....	620	685	573	180	−83	−502	−1,003	−12,625	....	Other Items (Net)	27r
															Monetary Survey	
Year Ending December 20																
895	509	1,397	756	....	....	600	762	599	723	629	1,152	1,118	1,585	....	Foreign Assets (Net)	31n
4,236	5,689	7,132	7,141	....	....	10,874	13,414	15,807	19,199	22,751	28,030	33,915	42,461	....	Domestic Credit	32
1,504	2,688	3,916	3,414	....	....	6,257	7,972	9,746	11,367	11,636	12,727	12,816	11,287	....	Claims on Central Govt. (Net)	32an
726	898	1,017	1,024	17	28	971	1,258	1,389	1,647	2,386	3,244	4,434	9,043	....	Claims on Official Entities	32bx
2,006	2,104	2,199	2,703	2,730	3,045	3,647	4,184	4,672	6,184	8,729	12,059	16,665	22,131	....	Claims on Private Sector	32d
2,258	2,637	3,293	3,922	....	....	5,509	6,462	7,118	8,238	9,729	12,266	14,081	18,305	....	Money	34
1,767	2,046	2,591	3,061	2,986	....	4,339	5,283	6,988	9,045	10,663	13,342	17,770	23,181	....	Quasi-Money	35
201	185	201	335	....	....	241	364	289	377	611	568	352	1,158	....	Restricted Deposits	36b
906	1,330	2,444	579	....	....	1,385	2,066	2,011	2,262	2,377	3,007	2,829	1,402	....	Other Items (Net)	37r
4,025	4,683	5,884	6,983	8,045	10,965	9,848	11,745	14,106	17,283	20,392	25,607	31,851	41,486	....	Money plus Quasi-Money	35l
															Other Banking Institutions	
Year Ending December 20																
16	22	29	33	33	37	40	46	75	93	109	132	147	166	....	Cash	40
7	4	4	3	122	2	2	2	2	2	2	2	2	2	....	Claims on Central Government	42a
17	17	14	12	19	13	16	17	16	21	67	75	58	113	....	Claims on Official Entities	42bx
896	1,014	1,174	1,403	1,594	1,765	1,874	1,948	2,130	2,577	3,191	4,214	5,134	6,159	....	Claims on Private Sector	42d
54	74	83	111	103	143	184	157	155	213	281	408	476	767	....	Demand Deposits	44
43	63	83	111	103	143	184	157	155	213	281	408	476	767	....	Private Sector	44x
11	11	—	—	—	—	—	—	—	—	—	—	—	—	....	Official Entities	44y
166	203	236	302	385	345	336	342	408	484	549	682	729	914	....	Time and Savings Deposits	45
129	117	114	106	—	—	—	—	—	—	1	—	15	125	....	Foreign Liabilities	46c
109	139	83	139	269	160	118	177	148	144	65	95	138	139	....	Central Government Deposits	46d
214	299	365	336	332	319	248	270	257	275	307	307	509	215	....	Credit from Monetary Authorities	46g
200	153	....	231	273	270	212	259	260	260	280	300	567	870	....	Capital Accounts	47a
65	72	....	228	404	582	835	807	995	1,316	1,888	2,632	2,907	3,409	....	Other Items (Net)	47r
4,228	4,937	6,173	7,362	8,501	11,416	10,327	12,197	14,594	17,887	21,112	26,565	32,908	43,001	....	Liquid Liabilities	55l

Iran, I.R. of

429

		1965	1966	1967	1968	1969	1970	1971	1972	1973	1974	1975	1976	1977	1978	1979
Interest Rates															*Percent Per Annum*	
Discount Rate (End of Period)	60	4.00	5.00	5.00	7.00	8.00	8.00	7.00	7.50	9.00	9.00	8.00	8.00	8.00	10.00	9.00
Prices and Production														*Index Numbers (1990=100):*		
Wholesale Prices	63	5.7	5.6	5.6	5.6	5.8	6.0	6.3	6.7	7.4	8.7	9.4	10.2	12.0	13.2	15.1
Home Goods	63a	5.4	5.2	5.2	5.3	5.4	5.5	5.9	6.2	6.8	8.0	8.7	9.7	11.5	12.6	14.5
Consumer Prices	64	5.3	5.2	5.3	5.4	5.6	5.6	5.9	6.3	6.9	7.9	8.9	9.9	12.6	14.0	15.5
Wages	65ey	....	....	....	....	....	3.4	4.1	5.0	6.3	8.3	‡11.7	16.3	21.1	27.7	41.0
Crude Petroleum Production	66aa	59.0	66.2	81.3	89.1	105.5	119.6	141.9	157.4	183.2	188.2	167.2	184.3	177.0	167.5	96.7
International Transactions															*Billions of Rials:*	
Exports	70	98.8	99.2	146.1	142.5	159.1	198.7	289.7	199.7	258.8	841.3	1,367.1	889.2	924.7	1,557.6	1,407.8
Petroleum	70a	86.2	87.0	132.4	127.9	140.7	178.6	264.7	169.3	219.7	796.2	1,328.0	847.2	878.0	1,528.2	1,352.1
Crude Petroleum	70aa	22.9	26.9	33.7	36.8	45.5	52.0	78.0	97.4	138.8	507.8	473.2	585.0	605.5	558.8	466.6
Imports, cif	71	65.1	70.5	84.8	104.8	115.7	125.9	141.9	182.5	233.0	367.4	700.3	905.2	1,034.2	954.9	684.5
Imports, fob	71.v	57.6	62.4	75.0	92.7	101.7	110.7	123.0	158.8	200.9	308.6	577.3	762.2	891.0	823.2	590.1
Imports, cif, from DOTS	71y	....	....	....	....	....	....	....	....	....	....	....	....	....	....	....
Volume of Exports															*1985=100:*	
Petroleum	72a	153.5	168.6	195.0	209.2	245.7	270.9	307.7	338.5	378.0	383.6	342.7	359.0	336.0	308.9	188.2
Crude Petroleum(1990=100)	72aa	69.9	81.6	102.4	112.0	138.3	157.6	189.8	215.1	251.7	256.1	222.9	248.8	232.7	215.2	111.0
																1990=100
Export Prices	76	....	....	....	....	....	1.6	2.3	2.6	2.7	3.0	3.7	3.8	4.4		
Import Prices	76.x	7.5	7.6	7.7	7.7	8.0	8.4	8.5	‡9.1	10.3	11.8	12.4	13.0	14.5	16.2	18.0
Balance of Payments														*Millions of US$: Year Beginning*		
Goods: Exports f.o.b.	78aa d											....	24,719	24,076	17,675	24,171
Goods: Imports f.o.b.	78ab d											....	-13,860	-16,718	-11,803	-8,521
Trade Balance	78ac d											....	10,859	7,358	5,872	15,650
Services: Credit	78ad d											....	2,651	3,699	3,104	1,580
Services: Debit	78ae d											....	-5,773	-8,201	-9,177	-5,690
Balance on Goods and Services	78af d											....	7,737	2,856	-201	11,540
Income: Credit	78ag d											....	610	769	1,100	1,240
Income: Debit	78ah d											....	-670	-684	-780	-797
Balance on Goods, Serv., & Inc.	78ai d											....	7,677	2,941	119	11,983
Current Transfers, n.i.e.: Credit	78aj d											....	—	—	—	—
Current Transfers: Debit	78ak d											....	-17	-125	-15	-15
Current Account, n.i.e.	78al d											....	7,660	2,816	104	11,968
Capital Account, n.i.e.: Credit	78ba d											....	—	—	—	—
Capital Account: Debit	78bb d											....	—	—	—	—
Capital Account, n.i.e.	78bc d											....	—	—	—	—
Direct Investment Abroad	78bd d											....	—	—	—	—
Dir. Invest. in Rep. Econ., n.i.e.	78be d											....	—	—	—	—
Portfolio Investment Assets	78bf d											....	—	—	—	—
Portfolio Investment Liab., n.i.e.	78bg d											....	—	—	—	—
Other Investment Assets	78bh d											....	-5,623	-3,663	-879	-4,396
Other Investment Liab., n.i.e.	78bi d											....	666	3,297	714	-3,627
Financial Account, n.i.e.	78bj d											....	-4,957	-366	-165	-8,023
Net Errors and Omissions	78ca d											....	-290	-360	-654	-876
Overall Balance	78cb d											....	2,413	2,090	-715	3,069
Reserves and Related Items	79da d											....	-2,413	-2,090	715	-3,069
Reserve Assets	79db d											....	-2,413	-2,090	715	-3,069
Use of Fund Credit and Loans	79dc d											....	—	—	—	—
Liabs.Constit.For.Auth.Reserves	79dd d											....	—	—	—	—
Exceptional Financing	79de d											....	—	—	—	—
Government Finance															*Billions of Rials:*	
Deficit (-) or Surplus	80	....	....	....	....	....	-54	-26	-54	-13	140	12	-38	-262	-450	-231
Revenue	81	....	....	....	....	....	187	275	323	491	1,427	1,627	1,896	2,193	1,736	1,781
Expenditure	82	....	....	....	....	....	241	301	378	504	1,287	1,615	1,933	2,455	2,286	2,104
Lending Minus Repayments	83	....	....	....	....	....	—	—	—	—	—	—	—	—	-100	-92
Financing																
Net Borrowing: Domestic	84a	....	....	....	....	28	35	11	44	16	34	124	130	331	505	267
Foreign	85a	....	....	....	....	17	19	15	11	-3	-174	-136	-93	-69	-56	-35
Debt: Domestic	88a	....	....	....	....	....	....	....	....	....	....	368	391	738	....	....
National Accounts															*Billions of Rials:*	
Exports of Goods & Services	90c	76	84	99	114	133	154	241	299	642	1,478	1,440	1,787	1,751	1,189	1,762
Government Consumption	91f	66	75	86	100	120	141	189	243	313	639	818	1,004	1,134	1,245	1,223
Gross Fixed Capital Formation	93e	86	90	119	136	163	185	220	293	387	530	999	1,589	1,790	1,628	1,197
Increase/Decrease(-) in Stocks	93i	—	—	—	72	89	82	58	113	106	35	14	-251	-169	-479	99
Private Consumption	96f	320	355	374	381	439	493	597	679	852	1,180	1,430	1,869	2,697	2,503	3,027
Imports of Goods & Services	98c	-70	-81	-101	-120	-140	-158	-199	-251	-345	-676	-1,127	-1,295	-1,491	-1,103	-923
Gross Domestic Product	99b	478	523	577	624	804	771	969	1,208	1,764	3,090	3,512	4,697	5,948	5,179	5,970
Net Factor Inc/Pmts(-) Abroad	98.n	-20	-18	-21	-29	-34	-40	-46	-29	-36	-11	-15	-5	-98	-186	56
Gross National Expenditure=GNP	99a	458	505	557	595	770	732	923	1,179	1,728	3,079	3,497	4,692	5,850	4,993	6,025
Gross Dom. Prod. 1990 Prices	99b.p	14,625	‡16,091	17,903	20,597	23,268	25,729	28,913	33,615	36,501	39,735	40,847	48,326	51,995	41,040	37,227
GDP Deflator (1990=100)	99bi p	3.3	3.2	3.2	3.0	3.5	3.0	3.4	3.6	4.8	7.8	8.6	9.7	11.4	12.6	16.0
																Millions:
Population	99z	24.81	25.54	26.30	27.08	27.89	28.66	29.61	30.41	31.23	32.50	33.38	33.71	34.69	36.11	37.20

International Transactions: ‡ Beginning in October 1980, data on the value and volume of oil exports and on the value of total exports are rough estimates based on information published in various petroleum industry journals.

Balance of Payments: ‡ Prior to 1976, year ending December 31.

Government Finance: ‡ During the period 1988-92, data included, within the extrabudgetary accounts, the operations of the Organization for Protection of Consumers and Producers. Data relate to a fiscal year different from calendar year.

Iran, I.R. of

1980	1981	1982	1983	1984	1985	1986	1987	1988	1989	1990	1991	1992	1993	1994		
															Interest Rates	
Year Ending December 20															Discount Rate *(End of Period)*	60
....	....	....	....	....	....	....	....	....	....	....	....	....	....	....		
Year Ending December 20															**Prices and Production**	
19.8	24.4	27.6	31.6	34.0	‡35.8	42.6	56.4	68.9	82.9	‡100.0	125.8	167.4	210.2	289.3	Wholesale Prices	63
19.4	24.7	28.1	32.6	35.2	‡37.1	43.5	56.1	68.1	83.3	‡100.0	123.3	168.2	211.3	290.1	Home Goods	63a
18.7	23.2	27.6	33.0	37.1	‡38.8	45.9	59.0	75.9	92.9	100.0	‡117.1	147.2	178.4	234.6	Consumer Prices	64
‡55.5	60.2	66.0	76.9	88.1	100.0	....	....	....	....	....	....	....	....	....	Wages	65ey
52.2	44.9	76.0	85.1	74.1	78.3	68.0	76.9	79.9	92.1	100.0	104.6	107.5	114.1	112.4	Crude Petroleum Production	66aa
Year Ending December 20															**International Transactions**	
994.4	‡980.8	968.6	1,684.7	1,127.8	1,218.6	....	....	....	....	....	....	....	....	....	Exports	70
938.2	‡944.1	944.1	762.1	1,319.0	725.2	202.0	274.2	240.4	778.4	....	....	....	....	....	Petroleum	70a
259.9	‡278.0	573.2	616.0	1,065.9	518.4	185.7	274.2	240.4	305.0	....	....	....	....	....	Crude Petroleum	70aa
863.3	985.3	1,002.3	1,582.7	....	....	....	....	....	....	....	....	....	....	....	Imports, cif	71
744.2	849.4	864.1	1,364.4	....	....	....	....	....	....	....	....	....	....	....	Imports, fob	71.v
....	1,058.6	990.3	1,563.3	1,304.9	1,038.7	736.8	669.5	561.2	922.3	1,082.0	1,472.3	1,516.0	....	....	Imports, cif, from DOTS	71y
Year Ending December 20															Volume of Exports	
95.4	‡47.7	118.5	117.2	110.9	100.0	74.9	91.1	97.0	119.7	138.4	167.2	159.2	177.9	....	Petroleum	72a
38.0	‡34.0	77.4	87.2	76.6	70.4	59.6	73.7	78.6	89.7	100.0	117.9	112.3	120.5	....	Crude Petroleum(1990=100)	72aa
1990=100																
5.8	7.0	8.2	8.5	9.4	11.3	33.4	76.1	90.5	93.6	100.0	154.0	174.8	180.4	....	Export Prices	76
22.2	25.1	27.5	29.2	30.2	32.5	38.8	53.9	68.0	77.9	100.0	124.3	165.4	217.2	....	Import Prices	76.x
March 21:Minus Sign Indicates Debit															Balance of Payments	
12,338	11,831	20,452	21,507	17,087	14,175	7,171	11,916	10,709	13,081	19,305	18,661	19,868	....	....	Goods: Exports f.o.b.	78aa d
-10,888	-13,138	-12,552	-18,027	-14,729	-12,006	-10,585	-12,005	-10,608	-13,448	-18,330	-25,190	-23,274	....	....	Goods: Imports f.o.b.	78ab d
1,450	-1,307	7,900	3,480	2,358	2,169	-3,414	-89	101	-367	975	-6,529	-3,406	....	....	Trade Balance	78ac d
731	556	509	540	475	370	242	231	244	446	436	668	559	....	....	Services: Credit	78ad d
-5,223	-3,315	-3,061	-4,273	-3,698	-3,308	-2,282	-2,372	-2,355	-3,018	-3,962	-5,715	-5,783	....	....	Services: Debit	78ae d
-3,042	-4,066	5,348	-253	-865	-769	-5,454	-2,230	-2,010	-2,939	-2,551	-11,576	-8,630	....	....	Balance on Goods and Services	78af d
1,004	895	612	795	594	393	365	206	223	352	456	213	287	....	....	Income: Credit	78ag d
-398	-275	-227	-184	-143	-100	-66	-66	-82	-104	-78	-85	-157	....	....	Income: Debit	78ah d
-2,436	-3,446	5,733	358	-414	-476	-5,155	-2,090	-1,869	-2,691	-2,173	-11,448	-8,500	....	....	Balance on Goods, Serv., & Inc.	78ai d
—	—	—	—	—	—	—	—	—	2,500	2,500	2,000	1,996	....	....	Current Transfers, n.i.e.: Credit	78aj d
-2	—	—	—	—	—	—	—	—	—	—	—	—	....	....	Current Transfers: Debit	78ak d
-2,438	-3,446	5,733	358	-414	-476	-5,155	-2,090	-1,869	-191	327	-9,448	-6,504	....	....	Current Account, n.i.e.	78al d
—	—	—	—	—	—	—	—	—	—	—	—	—	....	....	Capital Account, n.i.e.: Credit	78ba d
—	—	—	—	—	—	—	—	—	—	—	—	—	....	....	Capital Account: Debit	78bb d
—	—	—	—	—	—	—	—	—	—	—	—	—	....	....	Capital Account, n.i.e.	78bc d
—	—	—	—	—	—	—	—	—	—	—	—	—	....	....	Direct Investment Abroad	78bd d
—	—	—	—	—	—	—	—	—	—	—	—	—	....	....	Dir. Invest. in Rep. Econ., n.i.e.	78be d
—	—	—	—	—	—	—	—	—	—	—	—	—	....	....	Portfolio Investment Assets	78bf d
—	—	—	—	—	—	—	—	—	—	—	—	—	....	....	Portfolio Investment Liab., n.i.e.	78bg d
91	1,968	-157	-915	504	-249	532	287	10	539	-1,510	1,082	1,000	....	....	Other Investment Assets	78bh d
-8,329	-527	-1,690	-1,559	-3,322	793	2,595	1,424	312	2,722	1,805	4,951	3,703	....	....	Other Investment Liab., n.i.e.	78bi d
-8,238	1,441	-1,847	-2,474	-2,818	544	3,127	1,711	322	3,261	295	6,033	4,703	....	....	Financial Account, n.i.e.	78bj d
829	1,635	1,001	867	-904	487	814	155	537	-770	-946	1,321	1,636	....	....	Net Errors and Omissions	78ca d
-9,847	-370	4,887	-1,249	-4,136	555	-1,214	-224	-1,010	2,300	-324	-2,094	-165	....	....	Overall Balance	78cb d
9,847	370	-4,887	1,249	4,136	-555	1,214	224	1,010	-2,300	324	2,094	165	....	....	Reserves and Related Items	79da d
9,847	370	-4,887	1,249	4,136	-555	1,214	224	1,010	-2,300	324	2,094	165	....	....	Reserve Assets	79db d
—	—	—	—	—	—	—	—	—	—	—	—	—	....	....	Use of Fund Credit and Loans	79dc d
—	—	—	—	—	—	—	—	—	—	—	—	—	....	....	Liabs.Constit.For.Auth.Reserves	79dd d
....	....	....	....	....	....	....	....	....	....	....	....	....	....	....	Exceptional Financing	79de d
Year Beginning March 21															**Government Finance**	
-915	-841	-603	-842	-597	-594	-1,353	-1,419	‡-2,041	-1,089	-665	-1,126	-950	‡-242	....	Deficit (-) or Surplus	80
1,430	1,923	2,698	2,994	2,989	2,964	2,017	2,511	‡2,656	3,830	6,617	8,392	12,412	‡25,184	....	Revenue	81
2,368	2,814	3,317	3,857	3,598	3,583	3,438	3,966	‡4,703	4,924	7,288	9,518	13,362	‡25,426	....	Expenditure	82
-23	-51	-16	-21	-12	-25	-68	-36	‡-6	-5	-6	—	—	‡—	....	Lending Minus Repayments	83
															Financing	
952	886	641	878	627	625	1,375	1,430	‡2,048	1,093	670	....	....	....	....	Net Borrowing: Domestic	84a
-37	-45	-38	-36	-30	-31	-22	-11	‡-7	-4	-5	....	....	....	....	Foreign	85a
....	....	....	....	....	....	....	....	....	....	....	....	....	....	....	Debt: Domestic	88a
Year Beginning March 21															**National Accounts**	
883	945	1,726	1,878	1,570	1,251	553	837	1,514	2,773	5,395	7,439	9,864	22,617	....	Exports of Goods & Services	90c
1,380	1,676	1,910	2,151	2,190	2,443	2,371	2,707	3,199	3,294	4,054	5,367	6,927	13,644	....	Government Consumption	91f
1,442	1,528	1,842	2,870	3,096	2,759	2,494	2,662	2,957	3,709	5,663	10,844	14,640	20,657	....	Gross Fixed Capital Formation	93e
520	295	-165	226	508	562	1,099	2,417	1,296	2,891	4,827	5,806	8,867	6,690	....	Increase/Decrease(-) in Stocks	93i
3,531	4,653	5,943	7,771	8,927	9,627	10,439	12,226	14,906	18,448	24,071	31,677	41,187	51,623	....	Private Consumption	96f
-1,089	-1,260	-1,251	-1,851	-1,605	-1,266	-935	-950	-1,756	-3,594	-6,792	-9,749	-12,319	-21,431	....	Imports of Goods & Services	98c
6,632	8,009	10,540	13,376	14,804	15,775	16,227	19,949	22,304	27,787	36,645	50,107	66,463	93,801	....	Gross Domestic Product	99b
26	33	—	-7	-11	-34	-19	-39	-116	-212	-263	463	-67	-2,485	....	Net Factor Inc/Pmts(-) Abroad	98.n
6,658	8,042	10,540	13,370	14,793	15,742	16,208	19,910	22,188	27,575	36,381	50,570	66,396	91,315	....	Gross National Expenditure=GNP	99a
‡32,036	31,249	35,336	40,012	40,378	40,474	34,360	34,760	31,742	32,793	36,645	40,839	43,178	43,965	....	Gross Dom. Prod. 1990 Prices	99b.p
20.7	25.6	29.8	33.4	36.7	39.0	47.2	57.4	70.3	84.7	100.0	122.7	153.9	213.4	....	GDP Deflator (1990=100)	99bi p
Midyear Estimates																
39.30	40.85	42.48	44.08	45.80	47.82	49.44	50.66	51.91	53.19	54.50	55.84	57.15	58.49	59.78	**Population**	99z

Iraq

433

		1965	1966	1967	1968	1969	1970	1971	1972	1973	1974	1975	1976	1977	1978	1979
Exchange Rates																*SDRs per Dinar:*
Principal Rate	ac	2.8000	2.8000	2.8000	2.8000	2.7942	2.7849	2.7307	2.7440	2.8070	2.7657	2.8926	2.9145	2.7877	2.5992	2.5705
																US Dollars per Dinar:
Principal Rate	ag	2.8000	2.8000	2.8000	2.8000	2.7942	2.7849	2.9647	2.9792	3.3862	3.3862	3.3862	3.3862	3.3862	3.3862	3.3862
Principal Rate	rh	2.8000	2.8000	2.8000	2.8000	2.8000	2.8000	2.8305	3.0039	3.3064	3.3862	3.3862	3.3862	3.3862	3.3862	3.3862
																Index Numbers (1990=100):
Principal Rate	ah x	87.0	87.0	87.0	87.0	86.5	86.9	88.2	93.4	102.8	105.3	105.3	105.3	105.3	105.3	105.3
Nominal Effective Exchange Rate	ne c	....	....	....	....	....	....	....	....	....	....	....	....	....	....	97.9
Fund Position																*Millions of SDRs:*
Quota	2f. s	64.0	80.0	80.0	80.0	80.0	109.0	109.0	109.0	109.0	109.0	109.0	109.0	109.0	141.0	141.0
SDRs	1b. s	—	—	—	—	—	—	11.7	23.2	20.1	23.0	23.0	28.0	34.2	45.5	82.2
Reserve Position in the Fund	1c. s	16.0	20.0	—	20.0	20.0	—	—	17.3	27.3	27.3	27.3	27.3	27.5	27.7	47.8
Total Fund Cred.&Loans Outstg.	2tl	—	—	20.0	—	—	—	—	—	—	—	—	—	—	—	—
International Liquidity														*Millions of US Dollars Unless Otherwise Indicated:*		
Total Reserves minus Gold	1l. d	124.9	218.8	253.7	260.0	283.7	318.7	444.6	625.7	1,380.0	3,097.5	2,559.3	4,434.0	6,819.6	....	....
SDRs	1b. d	—	—	—	—	—	—	12.7	25.2	24.2	28.2	26.9	32.5	41.5	59.3	108.3
Reserve Position in the Fund	1c. d	16.0	20.0	—	20.0	20.0	—	—	18.7	32.9	33.4	31.9	31.7	33.4	36.0	63.0
Foreign Exchange	1d. d	108.9	198.8	253.7	240.0	263.7	318.7	431.9	581.8	1,322.9	3,035.9	2,500.5	4,369.8	6,744.7	....	....
Gold (Million Fine Troy Ounces)	1ad	3.136	3.016	3.280	5.504	5.507	4.099	4.099	4.099	4.099	4.099	4.099	4.099	4.144	....	....
Monetary Authorities: Other Assets	3.. d	2.5	1.7	.1	—	—	—	—	9.1	7.9	13.3	12.5	10.0	....	....	....
Other Liab.	4.. d	11.8	23.5	18.6	37.4	43.4	31.7	34.4	49.6	176.0	284.3	43.3	1.4	....	....	....
Deposit Money Banks: Assets	7a. d	28.0	19.6	16.1	25.1	25.8	24.5	30.7	26.4	121.4	348.7	269.3	333.8	....	....	....
Liabilities	7b. d	2.7	3.8	1.9	2.9	4.0	3.2	5.3	2.4	4.5	47.1	42.0	54.6	....	....	....
Monetary Authorities																*Millions of Dinars:*
Foreign Assets	11	84.7	116.5	131.6	161.7	170.2	165.1	197.5	260.1	462.1	993.9	805.7	1,356.8	....	....	....
Claims on Central Government	12a	89.6	74.9	88.0	83.5	110.3	138.5	120.9	110.7	69.5	90.0	130.5	64.2	....	....	....
Claims on Deposit Money Banks	12e	2.1	6.3	.4	.3	3.8	1.9	.5	.4	27.5	—	295.7	—	....	....	....
Reserve Money	14	130.7	145.4	166.1	174.7	186.9	217.3	217.5	257.2	344.5	444.6	571.5	726.6	....	....	....
of which: Currency Outside DMBs	14a	112.5	120.6	128.6	137.9	161.3	173.0	179.4	206.9	252.2	358.2	472.6	565.9	....	....	....
Foreign Liabilities	16c	4.2	8.4	13.8	13.4	15.5	11.3	11.3	16.3	52.1	84.0	12.8	.4	....	....	....
Central Government Deposits	16d	22.6	19.4	16.0	22.3	41.5	32.1	38.8	43.8	73.7	393.9	480.6	486.5	....	....	....
Capital Accounts	17a	29.8	33.6	35.7	40.0	45.8	50.4	56.3	59.7	68.1	132.9	130.7	145.0	....	....	....
Other Items (Net)	17r	-10.9	-9.1	-11.8	-4.8	-5.4	-5.5	-5.0	-5.9	-6.7	28.6	36.0	62.6	....	....	....
Deposit Money Banks																*Millions of Dinars:*
Reserves	20	17.3	23.8	35.4	34.6	24.3	42.6	36.6	46.3	78.8	65.6	95.8	150.0	....	....	....
Foreign Assets	21	10.0	7.0	5.8	9.0	9.2	8.8	10.1	8.7	36.0	103.0	79.5	98.6	....	....	....
Claims on Central Government	22a	18.1	35.7	39.9	55.0	83.2	63.1	94.8	114.5	151.3	316.2	621.4	620.4	....	....	....
Claims on Private Sector	22d	62.5	64.2	57.9	63.1	62.1	87.2	85.4	82.5	81.1	102.5	118.2	132.8	....	....	....
Demand Deposits	24	31.0	34.3	35.9	39.4	42.8	43.5	46.4	50.5	64.3	92.7	149.5	184.9	....	....	....
Time and Savings Deposits	25	48.5	51.9	54.6	64.3	70.6	73.9	85.8	95.2	122.4	172.8	257.0	315.0	....	....	....
Central Government Deposits	26d	16.7	20.9	31.4	37.7	40.9	57.6	66.1	75.1	118.7	201.4	301.2	399.4	....	....	....
Credit from Monetary Authorities	26g	2.1	6.3	.4	.3	3.8	1.9	.5	.4	.1	—	130.5	—	....	....	....
Capital Accounts	27a	18.2	20.8	22.5	23.7	24.9	28.5	27.8	28.7	33.1	51.1	74.5	89.9	....	....	....
Other Items (Net)	27r	-8.5	-3.4	-5.7	-3.8	-4.2	-3.8	.3	2.2	8.4	69.3	2.3	12.6	....	....	....
Monetary Survey																*Millions of Dinars:*
Foreign Assets (Net)	31n	89.5	113.7	122.9	156.3	162.4	161.4	194.5	251.7	444.7	999.0	860.0	1,438.8	....	....	....
Domestic Credit	32	140.0	141.9	144.6	148.6	181.9	208.2	206.0	197.8	117.5	-74.4	107.8	-37.7	....	....	....
Claims on Central Govt. (Net)	32an	68.5	70.4	80.5	78.5	111.1	111.9	110.8	106.3	28.3	-189.1	-29.9	-201.3	....	....	....
Claims on Private Sector	32d	62.5	64.2	57.9	63.1	62.1	87.2	85.4	82.5	81.1	102.5	118.2	132.8	....	....	....
Claims on Other Banking Insts.	32f	9.1	7.4	6.2	7.0	8.7	9.1	9.7	9.0	8.3	12.3	19.5	30.8	....	....	....
Money	34	144.9	156.2	166.1	178.9	205.4	217.7	227.1	259.7	322.7	462.3	625.5	754.8	....	....	....
Quasi-Money	35	48.5	51.9	54.6	64.3	70.6	73.9	85.8	95.2	122.4	172.8	257.0	315.0	....	....	....
Other Items (Net)	37r	36.1	47.6	46.8	61.6	68.3	78.0	87.6	94.5	117.3	289.5	85.3	331.4	....	....	....
Money plus Quasi-Money	35l	193.4	208.0	220.6	243.2	276.0	291.6	312.9	354.9	445.1	635.1	882.6	1,069.8	....	....	....
Other Banking Institutions																
Specialized Banks																*Millions of Dinars:*
Cash	40	1.9	1.9	2.1	2.6	1.9	1.8	2.4	4.1	7.9	14.2	12.6	14.8	....	....	....
Claims on Private Sector	42d	60.6	65.2	68.2	72.8	78.6	71.8	79.0	84.1	96.6	122.0	150.9	189.5	....	....	....
Central Government Deposits	46d	16.3	18.9	26.9	29.9	35.7	29.8	34.5	38.2	44.4	52.3	64.2	79.4	....	....	....
Credit from Monetary Authorities	46g	7.1	5.6	4.7	3.5	3.9	4.0	4.2	3.5	1.9	1.2	2.9	10.5	....	....	....
Credit from Deposit Money Banks	46h	2.4	1.7	1.4	3.6	4.5	5.4	4.8	5.5	5.7	10.6	17.3	17.4	....	....	....
Capital Accounts	47a	34.7	35.7	36.6	38.3	39.6	37.3	40.2	43.4	52.7	70.7	74.5	87.7	....	....	....
Other Items (Net)	47r	2.0	5.2	.7	.1	-3.2	-2.8	-2.4	-2.0	-.1	1.4	4.6	9.2	....	....	....
Post Office: Savings Deposits	45.. i	3.9	4.3	4.5	5.2	5.6	5.8	6.1	6.9	8.4	12.4	16.6	21.3	....	....	....
Nonbank Financial Institutions																*Millions of Dinars:*
Cash	40.. s	.31	.38	1.27	1.54	1.43	1.37	1.50	1.60	2.04	2.68	3.80	4.61	....	....	....
Claims on Central Government	42a. s	.23	.23	.30	.23	.48	.68	.68	1.11	1.09	.86	.86	.86	....	....	....
Claims on Private Sector	42d. s	.74	.68	.77	.76	.78	.81	.87	.96	1.07	1.18	1.25	1.40	....	....	....
Incr.in Total Assets(Within Per.)	49z. s	—	-.04	1.28	.18	.21	.34	.39	.52	.58	.81	1.11	1.31	....	....	....

Iraq

	1980	1981	1982	1983	1984	1985	1986	1987	1988	1989	1990	1991	1992	1993	1994	Exchange Rates	
End of Period	2.6550	2.9092	2.9162	3.0726	3.2818	2.9287	2.6299	2.2676	2.3905	2.4479	2.2612	2.2489	2.3396	2.3420	2.2036	Principal Rate	ac
End of Period (ag) Period Average (rh)																	
	3.3862	3.3862	3.2169	3.2169	3.2169	3.2169	3.2169	3.2169	3.2169	3.2169	3.2169	3.2169	3.2169	3.2169	3.2169	Principal Rate	ag
	3.3862	3.3862	3.3513	3.2169	3.2169	3.2169	3.2169	3.2169	3.2169	3.2169	3.2169	3.2169	3.2169	3.2169	3.2169	Principal Rate	rh
Period Averages																	
	105.3	105.3	104.2	100.0	100.0	100.0	100.0	100.0	100.0	100.0	100.0	100.0	100.0	100.0	100.0	Principal Rate	ah x
	100.2	115.9	130.2	133.5	146.6	152.0	118.8	103.8	100.3	107.8	100.0	101.0	98.1	104.3	103.5	Nominal Effective Exchange Rate	ne c
End of Period																**Fund Position**	
	234.1	234.1	234.1	234.1	504.0	504.0	504.0	504.0	504.0	504.0	504.0	504.0	504.0	504.0	504.0	Quota	2f. s
	87.2	113.7	74.2	8.6	.1	—	—	5.1	—	—	—	—	—	—	—	SDRs	1b. s
	111.9	111.9	111.9	—	—	—	—	—	—	—	—	—	—	—	—	Reserve Position in the Fund	1c. s
	—	—	—	—	—	—	—	—	—	—	—	—	—	—	—	Total Fund Cred.&Loans Outstg.	2tl
End of Period																**International Liquidity**	
	111.2	132.3	81.9	9.0	—	—	—	—	—	—	—	—	—	—	....	Total Reserves minus Gold	1l. d
	—	—	—	—	—	—	—	7.2	—	—	—	—	—	—	....	SDRs	1b. d
	142.7	130.3	123.5	—	—	—	—	—	—	—	—	—	—	—	....	Reserve Position in the Fund	1c. d
	....	....	....	....	....	....	....	....	....	....	....	....	....	....	....	Foreign Exchange	1d. d
	....	....	....	....	....	....	....	....	....	....	....	....	....	....	....	Gold (Million Fine Troy Ounces)	1ad
	....	....	....	....	....	....	....	....	....	....	....	....	....	....	....	Monetary Authorities: Other Assets	3..d
	....	....	....	....	....	....	....	....	....	....	....	....	....	....	....	Other Liab.	4..d
	....	....	....	....	....	....	....	....	....	....	....	....	....	....	....	Deposit Money Banks: Assets	7a. d
	....	....	....	....	....	....	....	....	....	....	....	....	....	....	....	Liabilities	7b. d
End of Period																**Monetary Authorities**	
	....	....	....	....	....	....	....	....	....	....	....	....	....	....	....	Foreign Assets	11
	....	....	....	....	....	....	....	....	....	....	....	....	....	....	....	Claims on Central Government	12a
	....	....	....	....	....	....	....	....	....	....	....	....	....	....	....	Claims on Deposit Money Banks	12e
	....	....	....	....	....	....	....	....	....	....	....	....	....	....	....	Reserve Money	14
	....	....	....	....	....	....	....	....	....	....	....	....	....	....	....	of which: Currency Outside DMBs	14a
	....	....	....	....	....	....	....	....	....	....	....	....	....	....	....	Foreign Liabilities	16c
	....	....	....	....	....	....	....	....	....	....	....	....	....	....	....	Central Government Deposits	16d
	....	....	....	....	....	....	....	....	....	....	....	....	....	....	....	Capital Accounts	17a
	....	....	....	....	....	....	....	....	....	....	....	....	....	....	....	Other Items (Net)	17r
End of Period																**Deposit Money Banks**	
	....	....	....	....	....	....	....	....	....	....	....	....	....	....	....	Reserves	20
	....	....	....	....	....	....	....	....	....	....	....	....	....	....	....	Foreign Assets	21
	....	....	....	....	....	....	....	....	....	....	....	....	....	....	....	Claims on Central Government	22a
	....	....	....	....	....	....	....	....	....	....	....	....	....	....	....	Claims on Private Sector	22d
	....	....	....	....	....	....	....	....	....	....	....	....	....	....	....	Demand Deposits	24
	....	....	....	....	....	....	....	....	....	....	....	....	....	....	....	Time and Savings Deposits	25
	....	....	....	....	....	....	....	....	....	....	....	....	....	....	....	Central Government Deposits	26d
	....	....	....	....	....	....	....	....	....	....	....	....	....	....	....	Credit from Monetary Authorities	26g
	....	....	....	....	....	....	....	....	....	....	....	....	....	....	....	Capital Accounts	27a
	....	....	....	....	....	....	....	....	....	....	....	....	....	....	....	Other Items (Net)	27r
End of Period																**Monetary Survey**	
	....	....	....	....	....	....	....	....	....	....	....	....	....	....	....	Foreign Assets (Net)	31n
	....	....	....	....	....	....	....	....	....	....	....	....	....	....	....	Domestic Credit	32
	....	....	....	....	....	....	....	....	....	....	....	....	....	....	....	Claims on Central Govt. (Net)	32an
	....	....	....	....	....	....	....	....	....	....	....	....	....	....	....	Claims on Private Sector	32d
	....	....	....	....	....	....	....	....	....	....	....	....	....	....	....	Claims on Other Banking Insts.	32f
	....	....	....	....	....	....	....	....	....	....	....	....	....	....	....	Money	34
	....	....	....	....	....	....	....	....	....	....	....	....	....	....	....	Quasi-Money	35
	....	....	....	....	....	....	....	....	....	....	....	....	....	....	....	Other Items (Net)	37r
	....	....	....	....	....	....	....	....	....	....	....	....	....	....	....	Money plus Quasi-Money	35l
End of Period																**Other Banking Institutions**	
																Specialized Banks	
	....	....	....	....	....	....	....	....	....	....	....	....	....	....	....	Cash	40
	....	....	....	....	....	....	....	....	....	....	....	....	....	....	....	Claims on Private Sector	42d
	....	....	....	....	....	....	....	....	....	....	....	....	....	....	....	Central Government Deposits	46d
	....	....	....	....	....	....	....	....	....	....	....	....	....	....	....	Credit from Monetary Authorities	46g
	....	....	....	....	....	....	....	....	....	....	....	....	....	....	....	Credit from Deposit Money Banks	46h
	....	....	....	....	....	....	....	....	....	....	....	....	....	....	....	Capital Accounts	47a
	....	....	....	....	....	....	....	....	....	....	....	....	....	....	....	Other Items (Net)	47r
	....	....	....	....	....	....	....	....	....	....	....	....	....	....	....	Post Office: Savings Deposits	45.. i
End of Period																Nonbank Financial Institutions	
	....	....	....	....	....	....	....	....	....	....	....	....	....	....	....	Cash	40.. s
	....	....	....	....	....	....	....	....	....	....	....	....	....	....	....	Claims on Central Government	42a. s
	....	....	....	....	....	....	....	....	....	....	....	....	....	....	....	Claims on Private Sector	42d. s
	....	....	....	....	....	....	....	....	....	....	....	....	....	....	....	Incr.in Total Assets(Within Per.)	49z. s

Iraq

433

		1965	1966	1967	1968	1969	1970	1971	1972	1973	1974	1975	1976	1977	1978	1979
Production															*Index Numbers (1990=100):*	
Wholesale Prices (1975=100)	63	65.6	65.3	70.1	66.8	68.6	75.2	80.0	76.9	80.5	90.6	100.0	111.2	118.6[e]	....	....
Consumer Prices (1975=100)	64	62.4	63.7	65.7	67.2	71.0	74.1	76.8	80.8	84.7[e]	91.3[e]	100.0[e]	112.8[e]	123.1[e]	128.8	....
Crude Petroleum Production	66aa	64.3	67.8	59.9	73.6	74.5	76.5	83.8	73.2	100.6	98.1	112.6	120.5	114.4	130.9	171.9
International Transactions															*Millions of Dinars*	
Exports	70	315.0	333.6	293.7	371.0	373.3	392.3	549.4	362.0	251.4	706.5	4,705.5	5,389.5	5,614.6	6,422.7	12,522.0
Crude Petroleum	70aa	442.4	467.9	409.2	506.4	510.2	525.4	712.2	658.6	1,102.3	3,813.8	4,669.9	5,342.9	5,571.9	6,360.5	12,480.0
Imports, cif	71	162.6	176.1	151.2	144.5	157.1	181.6	247.9	234.6	270.3	700.1	1,244.7	1,150.9	1,323.2	1,244.1	1,738.9
Imports, fob	71.v	145.2	157.2	135.0	129.5	142.1	164.1	224.0	211.7	244.9	621.7	1,118.7	1,036.8	1,192.1	1,120.8	1,566.6
Imports, cif, from DOTS	71y	....	....	....	....	....	....	....	....	....	....	....	....	....	....	....
Volume of Exports															*1985=100*	
Crude Petroleum	72aa	91.4	96.7	84.6	104.6	105.4	108.6	118.5	103.1	142.4	138.7	149.8	166.7	161.0	184.2	241.7
Export Prices															*1985=100:*	
Crude Petroleum	76aa d	5.2	5.2	5.2	5.2	5.2	5.2	6.5	7.3	9.8	35.6	38.1	40.7	44.7	44.6	65.9
Balance of Payments															*Millions of US Dollars:*	
Goods: Exports f.o.b.	78aa d	....	....	....	....	....	....	....	....	....	....	....	7,854	10,838	....	....
Goods: Imports f.o.b.	78ab d	....	....	....	....	....	....	....	....	....	....	....	−4,269	−5,867	....	....
Trade Balance	78ac d	....	....	....	....	....	....	....	....	....	....	....	3,585	4,971	....	....
Services: Credit	78ad d	....	....	....	....	....	....	....	....	....	....	....	582	760	....	....
Services: Debit	78ae d	....	....	....	....	....	....	....	....	....	....	....	−1,540	−2,708	....	....
Balance on Goods and Services	78af d	....	....	....	....	....	....	....	....	....	....	....	2,627	3,023	....	....
Income: Credit	78ag d	....	....	....	....	....	....	....	....	....	....	....	—	—	....	....
Income: Debit	78ah d	....	....	....	....	....	....	....	....	....	....	....	—	—	....	....
Balance on Goods, Serv., & Inc.	78ai d	....	....	....	....	....	....	....	....	....	....	....	2,627	3,023	....	....
Current Transfers, n.i.e.: Credit	78aj d	....	....	....	....	....	....	....	....	....	....	....	—	—	....	....
Current Transfers: Debit	78ak d	....	....	....	....	....	....	....	....	....	....	....	−132	−35	....	....
Current Account, n.i.e.	78al d	....	....	....	....	....	....	....	....	....	....	....	2,495	2,988	....	....
Capital Account, n.i.e.: Credit	78ba d	....	....	....	....	....	....	....	....	....	....	....	—	—	....	....
Capital Account: Debit	78bb d	....	....	....	....	....	....	....	....	....	....	....	—	—	....	....
Capital Account, n.i.e.	78bc d	....	....	....	....	....	....	....	....	....	....	....	—	—	....	....
Direct Investment Abroad	78bd d	....	....	....	....	....	....	....	....	....	....	....	—	—	....	....
Dir. Invest. in Rep. Econ., n.i.e.	78be d	....	....	....	....	....	....	....	....	....	....	....	—	—	....	....
Portfolio Investment Assets	78bf d	....	....	....	....	....	....	....	....	....	....	....	—	—	....	....
Portfolio Investment Liab., n.i.e.	78bg d	....	....	....	....	....	....	....	....	....	....	....	—	—	....	....
Other Investment Assets	78bh d	....	....	....	....	....	....	....	....	....	....	....	−201	−152	....	....
Other Investment Liab., n.i.e.	78bi d	....	....	....	....	....	....	....	....	....	....	....	−852	145	....	....
Financial Account, n.i.e.	78bj d	....	....	....	....	....	....	....	....	....	....	....	−1,053	−7	....	....
Net Errors and Omissions	78ca d	....	....	....	....	....	....	....	....	....	....	....	423	−508	....	....
Overall Balance	78cb d	....	....	....	....	....	....	....	....	....	....	....	1,865	2,473	....	....
Reserves and Related Items	79da d	....	....	....	....	....	....	....	....	....	....	....	−1,865	−2,473	....	....
Reserve Assets	79db d	....	....	....	....	....	....	....	....	....	....	....	−1,865	−2,473	....	....
Use of Fund Credit and Loans	79dc d	....	....	....	....	....	....	....	....	....	....	....	—	—	....	....
Liabs.Constit.For.Auth.Reserves	79dd d	....	....	....	....	....	....	....	....	....	....	....	—	—	....	....
Exceptional Financing	79de d	....	....	....	....	....	....	....	....	....	....	....	....	....	....	....
National Accounts															*Millions of Dinars*	
Exports of Goods & Services	90c	344.3	366.1	326.1	402.7	412.3	437.5	596.5	505.7	720.5	2,075.9	2,329.0	2,491.0	3,425.6	3,977.1	6,974.3
Government Consumption	91f	178.6	189.1	201.8	220.4	242.5	268.9	301.6	....	....	....	755.6	870.6	1,223.3	1,584.1	1,646.3
Gross Fixed Capital Formation	93e	129.8	149.5	143.6	143.0	157.2	185.1	194.7	217.1	288.6	628.6	1,067.9	1,336.4	1,478.6	1,993.0	2,714.3
Increase/Decrease(−) in Stocks	93i	13.5	9.3	14.0	11.5	8.2	17.7	14.7	56.2	70.6	320.2	150.8	−301.2	—	−537.4	564.3
Private Consumption	96f	455.1	496.8	495.9	547.7	565.1	609.9	633.2	956.1	929.4	1,427.1	2,266.7	2,611.9	3,669.9	2,628.9	2,971.8
Imports of Goods & Services	98c	−207.5	−221.0	−183.2	−192.1	−205.3	−236.6	−314.2	−294.2	−382.7	−1,073.8	−1,792.0	−1,479.0	−2,532.0	−2,220.8	−3,480.1
Gross Domestic Product	99b	908.6	985.0	994.0	1,128.8	1,180.0	1,282.5	1,433.8	1,440.9	1,626.4	3,378.0	4,022.4	4,659.1	6,042.1	7,224.9	11,390.9
Net Factor Inc/Pmts(−) Abroad	98.n	−129.4	−138.6	−122.6	−156.8	−154.7	−166.0	−214.9	−136.5	−82.0	−242.0	−115.0	37.7	80.7	139.0	90.4
Gross Nat'l Expenditure = GNP	99a	779.2	846.4	871.4	972.0	995.7	1,085.2	1,218.9	1,304.4	1,544.4	3,136.0	3,907.4	....	....	7,363.9	11,481.3
Nat'l Income, Market Prices	99e	742	806	811	907	926	1,011	1,140	1,219	1,451	3,033	3,802	....	....	....	....
															Millions:	
Population	99z	8.05	8.31	8.58	8.86	9.15	9.44	9.75	10.07	10.41	10.77	11.12	11.51	12.03	12.41	12.82

Iraq

	1980	1981	1982	1983	1984	1985	1986	1987	1988	1989	1990	1991	1992	1993	1994	
Period Averages																**Production**
	....	....	....	....	....	....	....	....	....	....	....	....	....	....	....	Wholesale Prices (1975=100) 63
	....	....	....	....	....	....	....	....	....	....	....	....	....	....	....	Consumer Prices (1975=100) 64
	132.2	44.7	45.9	50.1	60.1	71.4	84.1	103.5	130.5	140.6	100.0	13.6	20.6	....	....	Crude Petroleum Production 66aa
Millions of Dinars																**International Transactions**
	....	....	....	....	....	....	....	....	....	....	....	....	....	....	....	Exports 70
	15,321.3	6,089.6	5,982.4	5,954.8	6,937.0	8,142.5	5,126.2	6,988.9	7,245.8	....	....	....	....	....	....	Crude Petroleum 70aa
	2,208.1	2,333.8	....	....	....	....	....	....	....	....	....	....	....	....	....	Imports, cif 71
	1,989.3	2,102.5	....	....	....	....	....	....	....	....	....	....	....	....	....	Imports, fob 71.v
	....	6,013.0	6,309.0	3,086.2	3,032.4	3,285.7	2,773.0	2,268.7	2,888.8	3,074.5	2,028.5	....	....	....	....	Imports, cif, from DOTS 71y
1985=100																Volume of Exports
	187.7	62.9	64.6	70.4	84.5	100.0	117.7	143.5	180.5	197.2	....	....	....	....	....	Crude Petroleum 72aa
Index of Prices in US Dollars																Export Prices
	107.2	125.5	118.4	104.4	100.7	100.0	54.0	59.8	49.2	....	....	....	....	....	....	Crude Petroleum .... 76aa *d*
Minus Sign Indicates Debit																Balance of Payments
	....	....	....	....	....	....	....	....	....	....	....	....	....	....	....	Goods: Exports f.o.b. .... 78aa *d*
	....	....	....	....	....	....	....	....	....	....	....	....	....	....	....	Goods: Imports f.o.b. .... 78ab *d*
	....	....	....	....	....	....	....	....	....	....	....	....	....	....	....	Trade Balance .... 78ac *d*
	....	....	....	....	....	....	....	....	....	....	....	....	....	....	....	Services: Credit .... 78ad *d*
	....	....	....	....	....	....	....	....	....	....	....	....	....	....	....	Services: Debit .... 78ae *d*
	....	....	....	....	....	....	....	....	....	....	....	....	....	....	....	Balance on Goods and Services .... 78af *d*
	....	....	....	....	....	....	....	....	....	....	....	....	....	....	....	Income: Credit .... 78ag *d*
	....	....	....	....	....	....	....	....	....	....	....	....	....	....	....	Income: Debit .... 78ah *d*
	....	....	....	....	....	....	....	....	....	....	....	....	....	....	....	Balance on Goods, Serv., & Inc. .... 78ai *d*
	....	....	....	....	....	....	....	....	....	....	....	....	....	....	....	Current Transfers, n.i.e.: Credit .... 78aj *d*
	....	....	....	....	....	....	....	....	....	....	....	....	....	....	....	Current Transfers: Debit .... 78ak *d*
	....	....	....	....	....	....	....	....	....	....	....	....	....	....	....	Current Account, n.i.e. .... 78al *d*
	....	....	....	....	....	....	....	....	....	....	....	....	....	....	....	Capital Account, n.i.e.: Credit .... 78ba *d*
	....	....	....	....	....	....	....	....	....	....	....	....	....	....	....	Capital Account: Debit .... 78bb *d*
	....	....	....	....	....	....	....	....	....	....	....	....	....	....	....	Capital Account, n.i.e. .... 78bc *d*
	....	....	....	....	....	....	....	....	....	....	....	....	....	....	....	Direct Investment Abroad .... 78bd *d*
	....	....	....	....	....	....	....	....	....	....	....	....	....	....	....	Dir. Invest. in Rep. Econ., n.i.e. .... 78be *d*
	....	....	....	....	....	....	....	....	....	....	....	....	....	....	....	Portfolio Investment Assets .... 78bf *d*
	....	....	....	....	....	....	....	....	....	....	....	....	....	....	....	Portfolio Investment Liab., n.i.e. .... 78bg *d*
	....	....	....	....	....	....	....	....	....	....	....	....	....	....	....	Other Investment Assets .... 78bh *d*
	....	....	....	....	....	....	....	....	....	....	....	....	....	....	....	Other Investment Liab., n.i.e. .... 78bi *d*
	....	....	....	....	....	....	....	....	....	....	....	....	....	....	....	Financial Account, n.i.e. .... 78bj *d*
	....	....	....	....	....	....	....	....	....	....	....	....	....	....	....	Net Errors and Omissions .... 78ca *d*
	....	....	....	....	....	....	....	....	....	....	....	....	....	....	....	Overall Balance .... 78cb *d*
	....	....	....	....	....	....	....	....	....	....	....	....	....	....	....	Reserves and Related Items .... 79da *d*
	....	....	....	....	....	....	....	....	....	....	....	....	....	....	....	Reserve Assets .... 79db *d*
	....	....	....	....	....	....	....	....	....	....	....	....	....	....	....	Use of Fund Credit and Loans .... 79dc *d*
	....	....	....	....	....	....	....	....	....	....	....	....	....	....	....	Liabs.Constit.For.Auth.Reserves .... 79dd *d*
	....	....	....	....	....	....	....	....	....	....	....	....	....	....	....	Exceptional Financing .... 79de *d*
Millions of Dinars																**National Accounts**
	10,012.4	3,587.8	3,350.5	3,107.9	3,734.3	3,774.7	2,417.8	4,087.1	3,825.7	5,342.7	....	....	....	....	....	Exports of Goods & Services 90c
	2,451.2	3,446.2	4,468.2	5,475.3	4,989.1	4,431.8	5,252.8	5,673.8	6,260.0	6,578.7	....	....	....	....	....	Government Consumption 91f
	3,807.1	5,708.1	6,536.5	5,513.2	4,433.4	4,301.2	3,859.2	3,657.5	4,396.8	5,738.0	....	....	....	....	....	Gross Fixed Capital Formation 93e
	1,053.3	1,313.6	833.6	−3,533.3	−1,733.2	−636.5	−990.9	−124.1	−118.3	−4,123.9	....	....	....	....	....	Increase/Decrease(−) in Stocks 93i
	3,601.9	4,156.2	6,035.6	6,848.9	7,815.2	8,098.7	8,397.7	9,204.4	10,101.4	11,232.4	....	....	....	....	....	Private Consumption 96f
	−4,977.6	−7,068.3	−8,447.4	−4,156.3	−4,316.4	−4,476.0	−3,873.6	−4,598.4	−4,432.9	−4,755.9	....	....	....	....	....	Imports of Goods & Services 98c
	15,948.4	11,143.6	12,777.0	13,255.7	14,922.4	15,493.8	15,063.0	17,900.6	20,032.5	20,009.8	....	....	....	....	....	Gross Domestic Product 99b
	474.2	−401.0	−729.1	−589.6	−470.5	−558.5	−692.4	−704.7	−700.4	−678.2	....	....	....	....	....	Net Factor Inc/Pmts(−) Abroad 98,n
	16,422.6	10,742.6	12,051.9	12,666.1	14,451.9	14,935.0	14,370.6	17,195.9	19,332.1	19,331.6	....	....	....	....	....	Gross Nat'l Expenditure = GNP 99a
	....	....	....	....	....	....	....	....	....	....	....	....	....	....	....	Nat'l Income, Market Prices 99e
Midyear Estimates																
	13.24	13.67	14.11	14.59	15.08	15.58	16.11	16.33	17.25	17.55	18.08	18.56	19.01	19.45	....	Population 99z

Ireland

		1965	1966	1967	1968	1969	1970	1971	1972	1973	1974	1975	1976	1977	1978	1979
Exchange Rates															*SDRs per*	*Pound:*
Market Rate	ac	2.8028	2.7902	2.4063	2.3844	2.4007	2.3937	2.3510	2.1627	1.9258	1.9182	1.7285	1.4653	1.5691	1.5616	1.6283
															US Dollars per	*Pound:*
Market Rate	ag	2.8028	2.7902	2.4063	2.3844	2.4007	2.3937	2.5525	2.3481	2.3232	2.3485	2.0235	1.7024	1.9060	2.0345	2.1450
Market Rate	rh	2.8000	2.8000	2.7667	2.4000	2.4000	2.4000	2.4344	2.5018	2.4522	2.3390	2.2218	1.8062	1.7455	1.9195	2.0475
															ECUs per	*Pound:*
ECU Rate	ec	....	....	....	....	....	....	....	....	....	....	....	....	....	....	1.4913
ECU Rate	ed	....	....	....	....	....	....	....	....	....	....	....	....	....	1.5063	1.4938
															Index Numbers (1990=100):	
Market Rate	ah x	262.4	262.1	257.7	224.6	224.3	144.5	147.4	150.9	147.9	141.0	134.0	108.9	105.2	115.7	123.5
Nominal Effective Exchange Rate	ne u	177.35	177.35	175.96	160.69	161.08	160.18	159.61	154.77	142.46	139.16	130.46	117.66	113.41	113.80	114.77
Fund Position															*Millions of*	*SDRs:*
Quota	2f. s	45	80	80	80	80	121	121	121	121	121	121	121	121	155	155
SDRs	1b. s	—	—	—	—	—	13	26	39	39	41	41	45	46	48	71
Reserve Position in the Fund	1c. s	11	—	11	48	58	30	35	40	40	42	39	69	66	60	61
Total Fund Cred.&Loans Outstg.	2tl	—	1	—	—	—	—	—	—	—	—	—	—	—	—	—
International Liquidity												*Millions of US Dollars Unless Otherwise Indicated:*				
Total Reserves minus Gold	1l. d	388	471	414	466	652	681	978	1,109	1,007	1,247	1,513	1,818	2,351	2,668	2,212
SDRs	1b. d	—	—	—	—	—	13	29	43	48	50	48	53	55	63	93
Reserve Position in the Fund	1c. d	11	—	11	48	58	30	38	44	49	52	46	80	80	78	80
Foreign Exchange	1d. d	377	471	403	418	594	637	911	1,023	911	1,146	1,419	1,686	2,216	2,528	2,039
Gold (Million Fine Troy Ounces)	1ad	.600	.657	.714	2.257	1.114	.457	.457	.457	.429	.447	.447	.447	.473	.447	.383
Gold (National Valuation)	1an d	21	23	25	79	39	16	17	17	18	19	18	18	20	20	18
Deposit Money Banks: Assets	7a. d	905	786	836	759	668	954	1,115	1,348	1,918	2,302	2,371	2,350	3,165	3,966	5,314
of which: Claims on Nonbanks	7ad d	....	....	....	....	....	....	....	....	....	....	....	....	....	....	....
Deposit Money Banks: Liabilities	7b. d	655	547	523	580	623	804	1,069	1,417	1,954	2,326	2,387	2,383	3,321	4,056	5,601
of which: Liab. to Nonbanks	7bd d	....	....	....	....	....	....	....	....	....	....	....	....	....	....	....
Other Banking Insts.: Assets	7k. d	....	....	....	....	....	....	393	379	706	1,026	767	682	1,051	1,356	1,769
of which: Claims on Nonbanks	7kd d	....	....	....	....	....	....	....	....	....	....	....	....	....	....	....
Other Banking Insts.: Liab.	7m. d	....	....	....	....	....	....	671	757	1,009	1,410	1,186	1,195	2,010	2,472	2,949
of which: Liab. to Nonbanks	7md d	....	....	....	....	....	....	....	....	....	....	....	....	....	....	....
Nonbank Fin. Insts.: Assets	7e. d	....	86	100	174	291	310^e	4	2	3	2	1	1	2	2	1
Nonbank Fin. Insts.: Liabilities	7f. d	....	117	146	198	422	500^e	34	43	43	69	49	49	64	90	81
of which: Liab. to Nonbanks	7fd d	....	....	....	....	....	....	....	....	....	....	....	....	....	....	....
Monetary Authorities															*Millions of*	*Pounds:*
Foreign Assets	11	146	176	179	I227	288	290	381	432	443	504	689	978	1,218	1,270	989
Claims on Central Government	12a	26	32	34	27	24	47	27	33	61	63	114	108	111	136	278
Reserve Money	14	141	167	155	I169	208	240	305	343	428	533	620	726	827	1,036	1,142
of which: Currency Outside DMBs	14a	110	116	124	131	137	155	173	191	219	244	292	342	390	476	582
Foreign Liabilities	16c	—	1	—	—	—	—	—	—	—	—	—	—	—	—	—
Central Government Deposits	16d	11	21	31	18	28	30	58	85	40	28	135	232	297	193	117
Capital Accounts	17a	9	9	12	15	13	28	39	43	41	62	84	183	202	183	203
Other Items (Net)	17r	11	12	13	11	9	13	−23	−7	−4	−56	−37	−55	5	−7	−195
Deposit Money Banks															*Millions of*	*Pounds:*
Reserves	20	33	53	33	I79	124	86^e	152	134	161	222	254	285	329	413	410
Foreign Assets	21	323	281	349	I316	278	397^e	428	517	826	980	1,172	1,380	1,660	1,949	2,477
Claims on Central Government	22a	59	82	91	130	167	170^e	242	265	314	412	540	578	722	756	785
Claims on Other Financial Insts.	22f	....	....	....	....	....	....	....	....	....	....	....	....	....	....	....
Claims on Private Sector	22d	309	325	349	413	446	461^e	476	646	758	852	1,015	1,221	1,552	1,990	2,579
Demand Deposits	24	189	199	217	233	249	234^e	256	302	303	310	379	431	570	739	740
Time Deposits	25	274	305	352	429	484	541^e	598	654	824	1,042	1,280	1,417	1,693	2,047	2,400
Foreign Liabilities	26c	234	196	218	242	259	335^e	410	544	841	990	1,180	1,400	1,743	1,994	2,611
Central Government Deposits	26d	11	23	19	19	8	23^e	37	9	17	13	15	27	34	30	38
Capital Accounts	27a	....	....	....	....	....	....	....	....	....	....	....	....	....	....	....
Other Items (Net)	27r	18	18	16	17	15	−19^e	−4	53	75	111	128	189	225	298	462
Monetary Survey															*Millions of*	*Pounds:*
Foreign Assets (Net)	31n	236	261	310	I302	307	353	399	406	428	493	681	959	1,136	1,225	855
Domestic Credit	32	372	395	424	532	601	625	650	853	1,077	1,286	1,519	1,715	2,065	2,685	3,502
Claims on Central Govt. (Net)	32an	63	70	75	120	155	164	174	204	319	434	504	427	502	669	908
Claims on Other Financial Insts.	32f	....	....	....	....	....	....	....	....	....	....	....	....	....	....	....
Claims on Private Sector	32d	309	325	349	413	446	461	476	646	758	852	1,015	1,288	1,562	2,016	2,594
Money	34	298	315	341	364	389	415	440	518	572	624	748	875	1,072	1,367	1,479
Quasi-Money	35	274	305	352	429	484	541	598	654	824	1,042	1,280	1,417	1,693	2,047	2,400
Other Items (Net)	37r	36	37	40	1	−20	22^e	−20	82	109	114	171	381	437	496	479
Money plus Quasi-Money	35l	572	620	693	793	874	956	1,038	1,172	1,396	1,666	2,028	2,292	2,764	3,415	3,878
Other Banking Institutions															*Millions of*	*Pounds:*
Reserves	40	....	....	....	....	....	....	19	31	57	81	87	117	147	207	212
Foreign Assets	41	....	....	....	....	....	....	151	146	304	437	379	401	552	666	825
Claims on Central Government	42a	....	....	....	....	....	....	17	27	34	77	116	144	157	174	271
Claims on Other Financial Insts.	42f	....	....	....	....	....	....	....	....	....	....	....	....	....	....	....
Claims on Private Sector	42d	....	....	....	....	....	....	210	271	330	404	455	526	752	1,047	1,090
Liquid Liabilities	45	....	....	....	....	....	....	158	210	342	448	515	594	644	934	1,248
Foreign Liabilities	46c	....	....	....	....	....	....	258	291	435	601	586	702	1,055	1,215	1,375
Credit from Deposit Money Banks	46h	....	....	....	....	....	....	12	15	30	34	29	25	20	79	97
Capital Accounts	47a	....	....	....	....	....	....	26	16	23	36	38	49	68	91	115
Other Items (Net)	47r	....	....	....	....	....	....	−57	−58	−105	−120	−131	−182	−179	−225	−436
Banking Survey															*Millions of*	*Pounds:*
Foreign Assets (Net)	51n	....	....	....	....	....	....	292	261	298	330	474	658	633	677	306
Domestic Credit	52	....	....	....	....	....	....	877	1,151	1,441	1,767	2,090	2,385	2,974	3,906	4,863
Claims on Central Govt. (Net)	52an	....	....	....	....	....	....	191	235	352	510	620	571	659	843	1,179
Claims on Private Sector	52d	....	....	....	....	....	....	686	917	1,089	1,257	1,470	1,814	2,315	3,063	3,684
Liquid Liabilities	55l	....	....	....	....	....	....	1,177	1,352	1,682	2,033	2,456	2,770	3,261	4,142	4,914
Other Items (Net)	57r	....	....	....	....	....	....	−9	60	57	64	108	273	346	441	255

Ireland

1980	1981	1982	1983	1984	1985	1986	1987	1988	1989	1990	1991	1992	1993	1994		
End of Period															**Exchange Rates**	
1.4878	1.3574	1.2660	1.0841	1.0115	1.1321	1.1441	1.1810	1.1202	1.1843	1.2480	1.2233	1.1850	1.0271	1.0598	Market Rate	**ac**
End of Period (ag)		*Period Average (rh)*														
1.8975	1.5800	1.3965	1.1350	.9915	1.2435	1.3995	1.6755	1.5075	1.5563	1.7755	1.7498	1.6294	1.4108	1.5471	Market Rate	**ag**
2.0580	1.6167	1.4222	1.2482	1.0871	1.0656	1.3415	1.4881	1.5261	1.4190	1.6585	1.6155	1.7053	1.4671	1.4978	Market Rate	**rh**
End of Period (ec)		*Period Average (ed)*														
1.4537	1.4560	1.4432	1.3718	1.3986	1.4005	1.3075	1.2855	1.2846	1.3002	1.3024	1.3049	1.3456	1.2630	1.2578	ECU Rate	**ec**
1.4793	1.4470	1.4502	1.3996	1.3773	1.3982	1.3661	1.2896	1.2892	1.2873	1.3026	1.3024	1.3146	1.2514	1.2604	ECU Rate	**ed**
Period Averages																
124.1	97.5	85.8	75.3	65.5	64.3	80.9	89.7	92.0	85.6	100.0	97.4	102.8	88.5	90.3	Market Rate	**ah x**
111.50	102.14	101.00	97.43	93.82	94.60	98.89	97.05	95.35	94.34	100.00	98.63	101.71	96.45	96.77	Nominal Effective Exchange Rate	**ne u**
End of Period															**Fund Position**	
233	233	233	343	343	343	343	343	343	343	343	343	343	525	525	525	Quota	**2f. s**
71	91	96	65	89	99	113	126	134	145	158	170	90	97	101	SDRs	**1b. s**
77	75	75	116	124	121	131	131	134	125	105	124	171	155	152	Reserve Position in the Fund	**1c. s**
—	—	—	—	—	—	—	—	—	—	—	—	—	—	—	Total Fund Cred.&Loans Outstg.	**2tl**
End of Period															**International Liquidity**	
2,860	2,651	2,622	2,640	2,352	2,940	3,236	4,796	5,087	4,057	5,223	5,740	3,440	5,925	6,115	Total Reserves minus Gold	**1l. d**
91	106	106	68	88	109	139	179	181	191	225	243	124	133	148	SDRs	**1b. d**
98	87	83	121	122	133	160	186	181	165	149	177	236	213	222	Reserve Position in the Fund	**1c. d**
2,672	2,458	2,433	2,450	2,143	2,698	2,938	4,431	4,725	3,702	4,849	5,320	3,080	5,579	5,745	Foreign Exchange	**1d. d**
.357	.359	.360	.360	.360	.359	.359	.359	.359	.359	.359	.359	.360	.360	.360	Gold (Million Fine Troy Ounces)	**1ad**
16	117	96	106	88	95	105	139	114	109	109	109	104	109	141	Gold (National Valuation)	**1an d**
6,868	6,858	I 1,020	1,044	1,164	1,352	2,119	2,961	3,125	5,298	6,843	8,027	7,784	8,024	8,327	Deposit Money Banks: Assets	**7a. d**
....	415	I 168	180	211	246	339	324	424	412	844	1,332	1,436	1,166	2,075	of which: Claims on Nonbanks	**7ad d**
7,272	7,168	I 2,082	2,266	2,326	2,922	3,933	4,796	4,960	5,345	7,599	7,549	6,267	5,923	7,261	Deposit Money Banks: Liabilities	**7b. d**
....	2,570	I 1,211	1,269	1,220	1,713	1,753	1,916	1,656	1,849	2,508	2,805	2,120	2,147	2,361	of which: Liab. to Nonbanks	**7bd d**
1,913	1,725	1,754	1,535	1,467	1,862	1,709	2,901	2,978	4,405	6,602	6,311	10,644	13,357	21,760	Other Banking Insts.: Assets	**7k. d**
....	378[e]	376	379	327	346	347	411	372	446	1,214	1,876	3,064	3,356	9,462	of which: Claims on Nonbanks	**7kd d**
3,448	3,196	2,993	2,850	2,801	3,401	4,385	5,958	5,790	7,478	10,141	9,505	12,460	13,222	20,866	Other Banking Insts.: Liab.	**7m. d**
....	....	1,266	1,220	1,201	1,638	1,740	2,163	2,219	2,514	3,101	2,979	2,757	2,987	4,744	of which: Liab. to Nonbanks	**7md d**
—	—	I 16	11	15	6	7	39	155	160	98	35	182	340	1,089	Nonbank Fin. Insts.: Assets	**7e. d**
68	52	I 642	553	523	659	765	1,021	1,016	1,321	1,590	1,950	2,373	2,384	3,455	Nonbank Fin. Insts.: Liabilities	**7f. d**
....	....	189	174	176	217	254	484	551	801	1,185	1,567	1,856	1,974	2,804	of which: Liab. to Nonbanks	**7fd d**
Approximately End of Period															**Monetary Authorities**	
1,369	1,507	1,637	2,061	2,160	2,326	2,259	2,868	3,220	2,565	2,926	3,294	2,158	4,283	....	Foreign Assets	**11**
342	334	398	412	513	454	442	439	492	484	496	361	361	315	....	Claims on Central Government	**12a**
1,324	1,281	1,396	1,549	1,670	1,801	1,861	2,058	2,122	2,224	2,462	2,247	2,062	2,485	....	Reserve Money	**14**
663	739	811	907	923	970	1,024	1,107	1,212	1,310	1,317	1,382	1,411	1,572	....	of which: Currency Outside DMBs	**14a**
—	—	—	—	—	—	—	—	—	—	—	—	716	—	....	Foreign Liabilities	**16c**
138	130	186	222	198	193	274	648	883	1,133	979	1,248	639	1,426	....	Central Government Deposits	**16d**
248	382	434	654	796	793	824	864	863	933	807	822	999	1,366	....	Capital Accounts	**17a**
1	48	18	47	9	–7	–257	–263	–156	–1,241	–827	–662	–1,897	–679	....	Other Items (Net)	**17r**
Approximately End of Period															**Deposit Money Banks**	
456	383	I 388	409	474	545	556	616	623	645	767	566	490	654	....	Reserves	**20**
3,620	4,340	I 730	919	1,174	1,087	1,514	1,767	2,073	3,404	3,854	4,587	4,777	5,688	....	Foreign Assets	**21**
907	1,000	I 1,294	1,494	1,827	2,066	2,111	2,147	2,140	1,885	1,930	1,815	2,120	2,473	....	Claims on Central Government	**22a**
....	....	639	815	836	1,026	1,771	1,787	1,712	1,739	2,291	3,782	3,591	3,597	....	Claims on Other Financial Insts.	**22f**
2,948	3,490	I 3,740	4,117	4,479	4,342	4,685	5,015	6,331	7,737	7,804	7,008	8,967	9,545	....	Claims on Private Sector	**22d**
817	845	I 844	907	1,049	1,033	1,077	1,198	1,327	1,533	1,651	1,709	1,681	2,166	....	Demand Deposits	**24**
2,993	3,439	I 3,696	3,855	4,188	4,464	5,459	5,892	6,258	7,245	7,934	9,181	10,911	12,880	....	Time Deposits	**25**
3,832	4,537	I 1,491	1,997	2,346	2,350	2,810	2,862	3,290	3,434	4,280	4,314	3,846	4,198	....	Foreign Liabilities	**26c**
22	43	I 46	60	84	55	93	83	99	110	124	125	121	103	....	Central Government Deposits	**26d**
....	....	814	978	1,191	1,275	1,163	1,262	1,736	2,456	2,525	2,512	2,471	2,735	....	Capital Accounts	**27a**
266	349	I –100	–42	–67	–112	36	36	170	632	134	–82	915	–126	....	Other Items (Net)	**27r**
Approximately End of Period															**Monetary Survey**	
1,156	1,310	I 876	984	987	1,063	963	1,773	2,002	2,535	2,500	3,567	2,373	5,772	....	Foreign Assets (Net)	**31n**
4,037	4,651	I 5,923	6,589	7,420	7,700	8,696	8,707	9,741	10,643	11,448	11,661	14,335	14,440	....	Domestic Credit	**32**
1,089	1,162	I 1,460	1,623	2,058	2,272	2,187	1,856	1,650	1,126	1,323	803	1,721	1,259	....	Claims on Central Govt. (Net)	**32an**
....	....	639	815	836	1,026	1,771	1,787	1,712	1,739	2,291	3,782	3,591	3,597	....	Claims on Other Financial Insts.	**32f**
2,948	3,490	I 3,795	4,118	4,483	4,344	4,685	5,020	6,331	7,737	7,804	7,008	8,967	9,545	....	Claims on Private Sector	**32d**
1,686	1,743	I 1,838	2,048	2,245	2,288	2,382	2,640	2,826	3,112	3,346	3,390	3,253	3,996	....	Money	**34**
2,993	3,439	I 3,696	3,855	4,188	4,464	5,459	5,892	6,258	7,245	7,934	9,181	10,911	12,880	....	Quasi-Money	**35**
514	779	I 1,265	1,670	1,975	2,010	1,818	1,948	2,659	2,821	2,668	2,637	2,544	3,336	....	Other Items (Net)	**37r**
4,679	5,183	I 5,534	5,903	6,433	6,753	7,841	8,532	9,084	10,357	11,280	12,571	14,164	16,876	....	Money plus Quasi-Money	**35l**
Approximately End of Period															**Other Banking Institutions**	
314	570	443	447	543	528	1,444	1,423	2,051	2,298	2,659	3,744	5,262	4,792	....	Reserves	**40**
1,008	1,092	1,256	1,353	1,479	1,497	1,221	1,731	1,975	2,831	3,718	3,607	6,533	9,468	....	Foreign Assets	**41**
368	443	490	600	834	772	843	1,011	755	758	803	900	1,061	656	....	Claims on Central Government	**42a**
....	....	146	174	141	127	124	147	203	246	170	279	194	287	....	Claims on Other Financial Insts.	**42f**
1,352	1,734	2,683	3,112	3,412	3,855	4,120	4,207	4,220	4,462	5,811	6,268	5,354	5,289	....	Claims on Private Sector	**42d**
1,589	2,219	2,002	2,067	2,417	2,574	2,277	2,528	2,690	2,786	3,845	4,279	5,080	5,441	....	Liquid Liabilities	**45**
1,817	2,023	2,143	2,511	2,825	2,735	3,133	3,556	3,841	4,805	5,711	5,432	7,647	9,372	....	Foreign Liabilities	**46c**
39	55	491	713	714	909	1,618	1,595	2,053	1,756	2,191	3,638	3,406	3,460	....	Credit from Deposit Money Banks	**46h**
142	184	374	394	416	411	421	506	557	674	865	997	1,463	1,587	....	Capital Accounts	**47a**
–546	–642	9	–1	38	151	303	334	65	575	548	452	808	633	....	Other Items (Net)	**47r**
Approximately End of Period															**Banking Survey**	
347	380	I –11	–175	–358	–174	–949	–51	137	560	507	1,742	1,258	5,867	....	Foreign Assets (Net)	**51n**
5,757	6,828	I 8,660	9,717	11,025	11,487	12,096	12,367	13,259	14,422	15,997	15,393	17,482	17,166	....	Domestic Credit	**52**
1,457	1,605	I 1,950	2,223	2,893	3,044	3,031	2,867	2,406	1,884	2,125	1,703	2,781	1,899	....	Claims on Central Govt. (Net)	**52an**
4,300	5,224	I 6,710	7,494	8,132	8,443	9,065	9,500	10,853	12,538	13,872	13,691	14,701	15,267	....	Claims on Private Sector	**52d**
5,954	6,832	I 7,043	7,486	8,257	8,750	8,620	9,559	9,654	10,751	12,259	12,999	13,845	17,324	....	Liquid Liabilities	**55l**
150	376	I 1,606	2,057	2,410	2,563	2,528	2,756	3,742	4,232	4,246	4,137	4,895	5,710	....	Other Items (Net)	**57r**

Ireland

178

		1965	1966	1967	1968	1969	1970	1971	1972	1973	1974	1975	1976	1977	1978	1979
Nonbank Financial Institutions																*Millions of Pounds*
Cash	40..k	...	...	...	...	...	6	5	7	9	13	26	28	30	38	74
Foreign Assets	41..k	...	...	...	...	...	...	2	1	2	1	1	1	1	1	1
Claims on Central Government	42a.k	...	...	...	...	...	8	226	270	306	363	444	544	721	868	1,024
Claims on Private Sector	42d.k	...	...	...	...	...	436	116	152	191	218	266	354	458	585	776
Quasi-Monetary Liabilities	45..k	...	...	...	...	...	...	313	386	458	535	673	847	1,108	1,357	1,699
Foreign Liabilities	46c.k	...	...	...	...	...	...	13	16	18	29	24	29	34	44	38
Cred.from Deposit Money Banks	46h.k	...	...	...	...	...	...	13	16	19	24	20	23	30	41	70
Capital Accounts	47a.k	...	...	...	...	...	4	5	7	8	11	15	16	20	30	39
Other Items (Net)	47r.k	...	...	...	...	...	...	4	5	5	−3	6	11	19	21	29
Interest Rates																*Percent Per Annum*
Discount Rate *(End of Period)*	60	5.88	6.87	7.78	7.17	8.25	7.31	4.81	8.00	12.75	12.00	10.00	14.75	6.75	11.85	I16.50
Money Market Rate	60b	...	...	...	...	...	...	4.81	8.75	12.12	13.81	10.71	14.94	8.27	12.44	16.11
Treasury Bill Rate	60c	...	...	...	...	...	7.27	4.58	7.98	9.52	11.58	10.33	14.28	8.15	11.83	12.96
Deposit Rate	60l	2.50	2.92	3.08	4.06	4.33	4.50	3.69	3.33	7.06	9.63	7.75	7.54	6.17	6.33	10.96
Lending Rate	60p	...	...	...	...	...	...	...	...	...	...	...	11.25	13.25	9.65	13.00	15.50
Government Bond Yield	61	6.24	6.96	6.99	7.36	I9.71	9.86	8.48	9.46	12.33	16.86	14.64	15.49	11.30	12.83	15.07
Prices, Production, Employment																*Index Numbers (1990=100):*
Share Prices	62	9.7	9.0	9.0	12.8	13.6	11.9	11.6	17.0	I20.1	13.5	13.3	13.9	17.5	26.5	28.3
Wholesale Prices	63	13.5	13.8	14.1	15.0	16.0	16.9	17.8	19.7	23.1	26.2	I32.7	39.1	45.8	49.9	55.9
Output Manufacturing Industry	63a	13.0	13.3	13.7	14.5	15.6	16.4	17.3	19.2	22.7	25.3	I31.7	37.6	44.2	48.2	53.9
Consumer Prices	64	10.2	10.5	10.9	11.4	12.2	13.2	14.4	15.7	17.5	20.4	24.7	I29.1	33.1	35.6	40.3
Wages: Weekly Earnings	65ey	4.9	5.4	5.8	6.3	7.1	8.1	9.4	10.8	13.0	15.3	20.0	24.0	28.2	32.6	37.2
Industrial Production	66..c	23.7	24.9	26.3	29.7	31.8	33.2	34.4	35.9	39.5	40.6	39.0	42.4	45.8	49.5	53.3
Manufacturing Employment	67ey	90.6	91.4	92.4	95.9	101.4	102.8	102.4	102.9	107.8	109.7	102.9	102.5	105.8	107.8	118.2
International Transactions																*Millions of Pounds*
Exports	70	221	244	285	333	371	467	539	645	869	1,136	1,447	1,859	2,518	2,963	3,483
Imports, cif	71	371.8	372.6	392.3	489.5	589.8	675.6	754.9	842.6	1,137.2	1,627.2	1,703.9	2,340.6	3,090.9	3,713.1	4,827.9
Imports, fob	71.v	354.0	354.8	373.8	466.2	561.8	643.6	719.5	802.8	1,083.2	1,549.1	1,622.1	2,228.3	2,942.6	3,534.8	4,596.1
																1990=100
Volume of Exports	72	12.4	13.5	15.8	16.9	17.9	19.4	20.7	21.8	23.0	25.7	I27.6	28.7	33.8	37.8	40.9
Volume of Imports	73	22.9	23.0	24.2	28.1	31.8	32.9	34.6	37.5	42.6	43.1	I38.7	44.6	50.3	58.8	67.0
Unit Value of Exports	74	13.6	13.8	13.9	I15.0	15.7	16.9	18.1	20.7	26.3	30.8	I36.6	45.2	52.0	54.5	59.6
Unit Value of Imports	75	13.4	13.4	13.3	I14.4	14.9	16.0	16.9	17.7	20.0	29.2	I35.3	42.0	49.2	50.5	57.8
Balance of Payments																*Millions of US Dollars:*
Goods: Exports f.o.b.	78aa d	...	...	...	...	...	...	...	...	...	2,479	3,032	3,326	4,229	5,604	6,949
Goods: Imports f.o.b.	78ab d	...	...	...	...	...	...	...	...	...	−3,561	−3,518	−3,935	−5,049	−6,669	−9,269
Trade Balance	78ac d	...	...	...	...	...	...	...	...	...	−1,082	−486	−609	−820	−1,065	−2,320
Services: Credit	78ad d	...	...	...	...	...	...	...	...	...	508	568	561	715	896	1,169
Services: Debit	78ae d	...	...	...	...	...	...	...	...	...	−407	−550	−572	−739	−1,024	−1,372
Balance on Goods and Services	78af d	...	...	...	...	...	...	...	...	...	−982	−467	−620	−844	−1,193	−2,523
Income: Credit	78ag d	...	...	...	...	...	...	...	...	...	331	347	360	343	442	565
Income: Debit	78ah d	...	...	...	...	...	...	...	...	...	−342	−395	−485	−608	−984	−1,288
Balance on Goods, Serv., & Inc.	78ai d	...	...	...	...	...	...	...	...	...	−992	−515	−744	−1,109	−1,735	−3,246
Current Transfers, n.i.e.: Credit	78aj d	...	...	...	...	...	...	...	...	...	335	468	431	736	1,039	1,336
Current Transfers: Debit	78ak d	...	...	...	...	...	...	...	...	...	−31	−77	−114	−149	−153	−190
Current Account, n.i.e.	78al d	...	...	...	...	...	...	...	...	...	−688	−124	−428	−522	−849	−2,100
Capital Account, n.i.e.: Credit	78ba d	...	...	...	...	...	...	...	...	...	—	—	—	—	—	—
Capital Account: Debit	78bb d	...	...	...	...	...	...	...	...	...	—	—	—	—	—	—
Capital Account, n.i.e.	78bc d	...	...	...	...	...	...	...	...	...	—	—	—	—	—	—
Direct Investment Abroad	78bd d	...	...	...	...	...	...	...	...	...	—	—	—	—	—	—
Dir. Invest. in Rep. Econ., n.i.e.	78be d	...	...	...	...	...	...	...	...	...	51	158	173	136	375	337
Portfolio Investment Assets	78bf d	...	...	...	...	...	...	...	...	...	2	−1	9	56	−58	−32
Portfolio Investment Liab., n.i.e.	78bg d	...	...	...	...	...	...	...	...	...	155	114	139	275	537	−86
Other Investment Assets	78bh d	...	...	...	...	...	...	...	...	...	−519	−452	−9	−22	−301	−117
Other Investment Liab., n.i.e.	78bi d	...	...	...	...	...	...	...	...	...	1,029	666	679	951	611	1,569
Financial Account, n.i.e.	78bj d	...	...	...	...	...	...	...	...	...	717	485	990	1,397	1,164	1,671
Net Errors and Omissions	78ca d	...	...	...	...	...	...	...	...	...	103	−12	−233	−467	−172	−157
Overall Balance	78cb d	...	...	...	...	...	...	...	...	...	132	350	329	408	142	−586
Reserves and Related Items	79da d	...	...	...	...	...	...	...	...	...	−132	−350	−329	−408	−142	586
Reserve Assets	79db d	...	...	...	...	...	...	...	...	...	−132	−350	−329	−408	−142	586
Use of Fund Credit and Loans	79dc d	...	...	...	...	...	...	...	...	...	—	—	—	—	—	—
Liabs.Constit.For.Auth.Reserves	79dd d	...	...	...	...	...	...	...	...	...	—	—	—	—	—	—
Exceptional Financing	79de d	...	...	...	...	...	...	...	...	...	—	—	—	—	—	—
Government Finance																*Millions of Pounds*
Deficit (−) or Surplus	80	−70.2	−47.7	−44.9	−75.4	−89.8	−103.6	−100.5	−127.6	−170.5	−352.2	−499.4	−491.3	−555.6	−856.3	−1,055.2
Revenue	81	236.5	274.8	301.4	342.1	399.8	427.0	581.7	634.0	758.6	911.7	1,295.5	1,550.9	1,779.3	2,076.1	2,483.6
Expenditure	82	306.7	322.5	346.3	417.5	489.6	530.6	682.2	761.6	929.1	1,263.9	1,794.9	2,042.2	2,334.9	2,932.4	3,538.8
Financing																
Net Borrowing	84	70.0	47.4	43.6	75.7	89.7	104.0	100.5	127.6	170.5	352.2	499.4	491.3	555.2	856.2	1,055.1
Use of Cash Balances	87	.2	.3	1.2	−.3	.1	−.2	—	—	—	—	—	—	—	—	—
Total Debt *(Yr. Beg. April 1)*	88	714.9	770.8	823.2	914.0	1,008.9	1,105.9	1,251.4	1,421.1	1,622.2	1,957.9	2,743.8	3,612.0	4,208.2	...	...
National Accounts																*Millions of Pounds*
Exports of Goods & Services	90c	334	376	418	484	537	599	669	773	1,026	1,272	1,619	2,152	2,817	3,374	3,936
Government Consumption	91f	130	137	147	167	195	237	283	342	422	512	703	838	970	1,156	1,431
Gross Fixed Capital Formation	93e	200	200	221	258	332	362	430	497	671	753	885	1,157	1,414	1,862	2,430
Increase/Decrease(−) in Stocks	93i	27	8	−4	16	37	35	15	64	83	118	—	24	178	99	184
Private Consumption	96f	688	725	774	884	1,003	1,116	1,261	1,455	1,738	2,045	2,434	3,004	3,661	4,309	5,170
Imports of Goods & Services	98c	−420	−436	−451	−563	−666	−728	−804	−893	−1,211	−1,708	−1,849	−2,522	−3,337	−4,043	−5,235
Gross Domestic Product	99b	959	1,010	1,104	1,245	1,438	1,621	1,853	2,238	2,729	2,991	3,792	4,653	5,703	6,757	7,917
Net Factor Inc/Pmts(−) Abroad	98.n	26	23	25	32	28	28	27	30	12	19	4	−36	−108	−228	−283
Gross Nat'l Expenditure = GNP	99a	984	1,034	1,128	1,277	1,467	1,648	1,880	2,267	2,742	3,010	3,796	4,617	5,595	6,529	7,634
Nat'l Income, Market Prices	99e	911	954	1,040	1,175	1,344	1,514	1,724	2,083	2,527	2,751	3,493	4,223	5,095	5,872	6,835
Gross Dom. Prod. 1990 Prices	99b.p	9,135	9,225	9,702	10,489	11,125	11,511	11,904	12,680	I13,471	14,017	14,346	14,547	15,742	16,872	17,391
GDP Deflator (1990=100)	99bi p	10.5	10.9	11.4	11.9	12.9	14.1	15.6	17.6	20.3	21.3	26.4	32.0	36.2	40.0	45.5
																Millions:
Population	99z	2.88	2.88	2.90	2.91	2.93	2.95	2.98	3.02	3.07	3.12	3.18	3.23	3.27	3.31	3.37

Ireland
178

1980	1981	1982	1983	1984	1985	1986	1987	1988	1989	1990	1991	1992	1993	1994	Series	Code
Approximately End of Period															**Nonbank Financial Institutions**	
91	111	I 300	319	402	463	437	632	607	676	679	830	915	1,559	1,676	Cash	**40..k**
—	—	I 11	10	15	5	5	23	103	103	55	20	112	241	704	Foreign Assets	**41..k**
1,155	1,285	I 923	980	1,560	1,383	1,344	1,498	1,598	1,592	1,882	2,022	2,147	1,801	1,782	Claims on Central Government	**42a.k**
987	1,264	I 2,342	2,680	3,021	3,325	3,577	3,626	4,006	4,627	5,251	5,894	6,836	7,634	8,438	Claims on Private Sector	**42d.k**
2,061	2,442	I 2,794	3,163	3,697	4,280	4,393	4,793	5,103	5,385	6,175	6,894	7,927	8,682	9,279	Quasi-Monetary Liabilities	**45..k**
36	33	I 460	487	528	530	547	610	674	849	895	1,114	1,456	1,690	2,233	Foreign Liabilities	**46c.k**
67	89	I 203	183	184	185	198	176	278	383	475	627	653	1,009	1,285	Cred.from Deposit Money Banks	**46h.k**
50	66	I 131	159	184	209	268	282	334	382	426	495	607	795	928	Capital Accounts	**47a.k**
22	31	-11	-2	18	-28	-43	-81	-75	—	-104	-365	-634	-941	-1,125	Other Items (Net)	**47r.k**
Percent Per Annum															**Interest Rates**	
14.00	16.50	14.00	12.25	14.00	10.25	13.25	9.25	8.00	12.00	11.25	10.75	....	7.00	6.25	Discount Rate *(End of Period)*	**60**
16.39	16.20	17.65	14.45	12.93	11.87	12.28	10.84	7.84	9.55	11.10	10.45	15.12	10.49	5.66	Money Market Rate	**60b**
15.13	15.20	16.33	13.26	13.13	11.78	11.85	10.70	7.81	9.70	10.90	10.12	....	....	....	Treasury Bill Rate	**60c**
12.00	11.33	12.73	9.27	7.83	6.98	6.50	6.21	3.63	4.54	6.29	5.21	5.42	2.27	.33	Deposit Rate	**60l**
15.96	15.50	17.04	14.13	12.92	12.44	12.23	11.15	8.29	9.42	11.29	10.63	....	....	....	Lending Rate	**60p**
15.35	17.26	17.06	13.90	14.62	12.64	11.07	11.27	9.49	8.95	10.08	9.17	9.11	7.72	8.19	Government Bond Yield	**61**
Period Averages															**Prices, Production, Employment**	
27.9	28.9	23.6	29.4	38.9	I 41.6	65.3	94.3	92.6	I 109.9	100.0	92.0	85.6	106.9	121.9	Share Prices	**62**
61.8	72.5	80.7	85.6	92.2	I 95.1	93.0	93.6	97.5	102.8	100.0	101.2	102.1	106.9	....	Wholesale Prices	**63**
59.8	69.8	78.0	83.2	89.3	I 92.8	91.7	93.2	97.0	101.6	100.0	100.9	102.5	107.2	108.4	Output Manufacturing Industry	**63a**
I 47.7	57.4	67.2	74.3	80.7	I 85.0	88.3	91.0	93.0	96.8	100.0	103.2	106.4	107.9	110.4	Consumer Prices	**64**
43.9	51.2	57.8	64.6	72.5	78.2	84.1	88.4	92.6	96.3	100.0	104.4	108.6	114.4	....	Wages: Weekly Earnings	**65ey**
I 52.6	55.5	55.0	59.5	65.2	67.5	69.0	75.1	85.4	95.7	100.0	102.8	112.9	119.2	134.1	Industrial Production	**66..c**
118.5	115.1	111.5	104.8	101.7	97.4	96.0	95.1	95.3	97.4	100.0	100.5	100.2	100.2	....	Manufacturing Employment	**67ey**
Millions of Pounds															**International Transactions**	
4,082	4,778	5,691	6,944	8,898	9,743	9,374	10,723	12,305	14,597	14,337	15,019	16,629	19,656	....	Exports	**70**
5,420.7	6,578.4	6,816.2	7,366.8	8,912.2	9,428.2	8,621.3	9,155.2	10,214.8	12,284.3	12,469.0	12,851.0	13,195.0	14,798.0	....	Imports, cif	**71**
5,160.6	6,262.4	6,489.2	7,013.8	8,485.3	8,979.2	8,210.8	8,719.2	9,728.4	11,699.3	11,875.2	12,239.0	12,566.7	14,093.3	....	Imports, fob	**71.v**
1990=100																
43.1	44.1	46.8	52.6	62.0	I 65.2	67.8	77.5	82.9	I 92.2	100.0	105.6	120.1	132.2	....	Volume of Exports	**72**
63.7	64.5	61.9	64.0	70.0	I 72.4	74.6	79.2	82.9	I 93.6	100.0	100.8	105.6	112.3	....	Volume of Imports	**73**
66.3	76.1	84.7	91.9	100.1	I 104.3	96.7	96.7	103.5	110.4	100.0	99.3	I 96.6	103.9	....	Unit Value of Exports	**74**
68.5	81.7	88.4	92.2	102.1	I 104.6	92.9	92.9	98.9	I 105.3	100.0	102.3	100.2	105.4	....	Unit Value of Imports	**75**
Minus Sign Indicates Debit															Balance of Payments	
8,229	7,696	7,933	8,438	9,421	10,131	12,366	15,566	18,389	20,356	23,356	23,660	27,905	28,729	....	Goods: Exports f.o.b.	**78aad**
-10,452	-9,950	-9,096	-8,690	-9,183	-9,500	-11,221	-12,952	-14,567	-16,352	-19,387	-19,493	-21,092	-20,557	....	Goods: Imports f.o.b.	**78abd**
-2,222	-2,255	-1,162	-252	237	631	1,145	2,614	3,822	4,003	3,969	4,167	6,813	8,172	....	Trade Balance	**78acd**
1,381	1,209	1,219	1,174	1,166	1,302	1,595	2,069	2,414	2,533	3,332	3,515	3,958	3,561	....	Services: Credit	**78add**
-1,593	-1,435	-1,375	-1,372	-1,372	-1,471	-2,057	-2,844	-3,491	-3,920	-4,572	-4,707	-5,566	-5,198	....	Services: Debit	**78aed**
-2,434	-2,481	-1,318	-450	31	461	684	1,838	2,744	2,616	2,729	2,975	5,205	6,535	....	Balance on Goods and Services	**78afd**
808	776	712	584	663	756	934	1,085	1,411	1,795	2,627	2,750	2,699	2,313	....	Income: Credit	**78agd**
-1,710	-1,734	-2,162	-2,179	-2,531	-2,954	-3,732	-4,322	-5,626	-6,497	-7,928	-7,467	-8,415	-8,019	....	Income: Debit	**78ahd**
-3,336	-3,439	-2,768	-2,045	-1,837	-1,736	-2,114	-1,399	-1,471	-2,086	-2,572	-1,742	-511	830	....	Balance on Goods, Serv., & Inc.	**78aid**
1,442	1,064	1,082	1,113	1,163	1,422	1,850	1,968	2,155	2,176	3,324	3,984	3,833	3,718	....	Current Transfers, n.i.e.: Credit	**78ajd**
-238	-226	-248	-286	-276	-314	-465	-469	-460	-471	-607	-701	-767	-813	....	Current Transfers: Debit	**78akd**
-2,132	-2,601	-1,935	-1,219	-950	-628	-728	100	224	-381	146	1,541	2,555	3,735	....	Current Account, n.i.e.	**78ald**
—	—	—	—	—	—	—	—	—	—	—	—	—	—	....	Capital Account, n.i.e.: Credit	**78bad**
—	—	—	—	-87	-62	-93	-195	-152	-127	-101	-97	-102	-89	....	Capital Account: Debit	**78bbd**
—	—	—	—	-87	-62	-93	-195	-152	-127	-101	-97	-102	-89	....	Capital Account, n.i.e.	**78bcd**
—	—	—	—	—	—	—	—	—	—	—	—	—	—	....	Direct Investment Abroad	**78bdd**
286	203	242	170	121	164	-40	89	92	85	99	97	102	89	....	Dir. Invest. in Rep. Econ., n.i.e.	**78bed**
-44	-116	-108	-90	-91	-134	-239	-316	-485	-1,120	-465	-1,717	-439	-273	....	Portfolio Investment Assets	**78bfd**
224	605	279	467	1,268	1,104	1,986	109	1,475	1,770	266	648	-2,750	2,724	....	Portfolio Investment Liab., n.i.e.	**78bgd**
-500	-229	-649	-423	-634	44	-443	-1,906	-1,941	-4,483	-5,014	-1,998	-8,490	-10,569	....	Other Investment Assets	**78bhd**
2,757	1,927	2,605	1,628	545	-50	526	2,655	1,060	2,175	3,209	-231	5,113	7,639	....	Other Investment Liab., n.i.e.	**78bid**
2,724	2,390	2,369	1,752	1,208	1,127	1,790	632	200	-1,574	-1,905	-3,202	-6,464	-390	....	Financial Account, n.i.e.	**78bjd**
120	203	-313	-345	-213	-389	-1,063	350	320	1,145	2,608	2,221	470	659	....	Net Errors and Omissions	**78cad**
712	-8	121	188	-43	48	-94	886	592	-937	748	464	-3,542	3,915	....	Overall Balance	**78cbd**
-712	8	-121	-188	43	-48	94	-886	-592	937	-748	-464	3,542	-3,915	....	Reserves and Related Items	**79dad**
-712	8	-121	-188	43	-48	94	-886	-592	937	-748	-464	2,166	-2,660	....	Reserve Assets	**79dbd**
—	—	—	—	—	—	—	—	—	—	—	—	—	—	....	Use of Fund Credit and Loans	**79dcd**
—	—	—	—	—	—	—	—	—	—	—	—	1,376	-1,255	....	Liabs.Constit.For.Auth.Reserves	**79ddd**
—	—	—	—	—	—	—	—	—	—	—	—	—	—	....	Exceptional Financing	**79ded**
Year Ending December 31															**Government Finance**	
-1,284.7	-1,789.1	-2,027.8	-1,835.3	-1,821.7	-2,129.1	-2,115.2	-1,803.4	-640.3	-484.7	-471.9	-235.4	-700.5	-260.4	-322.6	Deficit (-) or Surplus	**80**
3,256.2	4,064.2	5,158.7	5,878.2	6,138.7	6,601.7	6,936.7	7,467.5	8,160.2	8,145.2	8,586.2	9,457.5	9,812.9	10,872.8	11,676.6	Revenue	**81**
4,540.9	5,853.3	7,186.5	7,713.5	7,960.4	8,730.8	9,051.9	9,270.9	8,800.5	8,629.9	9,058.1	9,692.9	10,513.4	11,133.2	11,999.2	Expenditure	**82**
															Financing	
1,284.9	1,789.1	2,027.8	1,835.3	1,821.7	2,129.0	2,192.0	2,042.2	1,045.5	737.8	347.0	527.3	-440.0	850.2	-18.6	Net Borrowing	**84**
—	—	—	—	—	—	-76.8	-238.8	-405.2	-252.9	125.0	-292.0	1,140.5	-589.8	341.2	Use of Cash Balances	**87**
....	....	....	....	....	....	....	....	....	....	....	....	....	....	....	Total Debt *(Yr. Beg. April 1)*	**88**
Millions of Pounds															**National Accounts**	
4,639	5,504	6,433	7,752	9,770	10,738	10,377	11,855	13,634	16,137	16,116	16,893	18,707	21,871	....	Exports of Goods & Services	**90c**
1,860	2,260	2,646	2,857	3,067	3,301	3,542	3,575	3,540	3,686	4,082	4,480	4,842	5,167	....	Government Consumption	**91f**
2,718	3,350	3,531	3,414	3,506	3,377	3,456	3,453	3,567	4,277	4,887	4,642	4,661	4,808	....	Gross Fixed Capital Formation	**93e**
-114	-128	185	106	228	173	118	28	26	275	722	639	-79	-179	....	Increase/Decrease(-) in Stocks	**93i**
6,158	7,490	8,001	8,950	9,801	10,777	12,138	12,845	13,811	15,378	15,800	16,607	17,575	18,065	....	Private Consumption	**96f**
-5,900	-7,117	-7,414	-8,164	-9,815	-10,397	-9,928	-10,681	-11,921	-14,360	-14,514	-15,072	-15,718	-17,442	....	Imports of Goods & Services	**98c**
9,361	11,359	13,382	14,916	16,556	17,969	19,703	21,075	22,657	25,393	27,093	28,189	29,987	32,290	....	Gross Domestic Product	**99b**
-358	-505	-928	-1,184	-1,639	-1,966	-2,017	-2,112	-2,662	-3,233	-3,131	-2,865	-3,295	-3,727	....	Net Factor Inc/Pmts(-) Abroad	**98.n**
9,003	10,854	12,455	13,732	14,917	16,003	17,686	18,962	19,995	22,161	23,962	25,324	26,693	28,563	....	Gross Nat'l Expenditure = GNP	**99a**
7,969	9,690	11,089	12,203	13,320	14,279	15,801	16,899	17,833	19,781	21,403	22,601	23,815	25,519	....	Nat'l Income, Market Prices	**99e**
I 17,928	18,523	18,943	19,087	19,916	20,533	21,289	22,282	23,233	24,954	27,093	27,872	29,269	30,432	....	Gross Dom. Prod. 1990 Prices	**99b.p**
52.2	61.3	70.6	78.1	83.1	87.5	92.5	94.6	97.5	101.8	100.0	101.1	102.5	106.1	....	GDP Deflator (1990=100)	**99bip**
Midyear Estimates																
3.40	3.44	3.48	3.50	3.53	3.54	3.54	3.54	3.54	3.51	3.50	3.52	3.55	3.56	3.57	**Population**	**99z**

(Notes in the back of the book)

Israel
436

		1965	1966	1967	1968	1969	1970	1971	1972	1973	1974	1975	1976	1977	1978	1979
Exchange Rates															*New Sheqalim per Thousand SDRs through 1980*	
Market Rate	aa	.2997	.2997	.3496	.3496	.3496	.3496	.4555	.4555	.5061	.7338	.8303	1.0158	1.8672	2.4746	4.6517
												New Sheqalim per Thousand US Dollars through 1980					
Market Rate	ae	.2997	.2997	.3496	.3496	.3496	.3496	.4195	.4195	.4195	.5994	.7092	.8743	1.5372	1.8995	3.5311
Market Rate	rf	.3000	.3000	.3083	.3500	.3500	.3500	.4200	.4180	.4195	.4452	.6336	.7926	1.0445	1.7435	2.5406
Fund Position															*Millions of SDRs*	
Quota	2f.s	50.0	90.0	90.0	90.0	90.0	130.0	130.0	130.0	130.0	130.0	130.0	130.0	130.0	205.0	205.0
SDRs	1b.s	—	—	—	—	—	—	13.1	29.2	27.9	2.5	2.0	8.7	22.2	21.0	4.8
Reserve Position in the Fund	1c.s	12.5	22.5	22.5	22.5	—	—	—	—	32.5	—	—	—	—	—	31.6
Total Fund Cred.&Loans Outstg.	2tl	—	—	—	—	22.5	12.5	32.5	—	—	32.5	208.3	285.3	285.2	271.3	224.2
International Liquidity											*Millions of US Dollars Unless Otherwise Indicated:*						
Total Reserves minus Gold	1l.d	587.2	575.2	668.7	616.8	366.7	405.2	689.8	1,178.8	1,768.3	1,153.4	1,137.1	1,328.3	1,521.6	2,625.1	3,063.5
SDRs	1b.d	—	—	—	—	—	—	14.3	31.7	33.6	3.1	2.4	10.0	27.0	27.3	6.3
Reserve Position in the Fund	1c.d	12.5	22.5	22.5	22.5	—	—	—	—	39.2	—	—	—	—	—	41.6
Foreign Exchange	1d.d	574.7	552.7	646.2	594.3	366.7	405.2	675.5	1,147.1	1,695.4	1,150.3	1,134.7	1,318.3	1,494.6	2,597.8	3,015.6
Gold (Million Fine Troy Ounces)	1ad	1.594	1.311	1.311	1.317	1.306	1.240	1.240	1.143	1.097	1.099	1.101	1.103	1.164	1.171	1.231
Gold (National Valuation)	1and	55.8	45.9	45.9	46.1	45.7	43.4	47.1	43.4	46.3	47.1	45.1	44.9	49.5	53.4	56.8
Monetary Authorities: Other Assets	3..d	33.3	33.3	28.6	28.6	28.6	28.6	47.6	95.2	119.0	100.1	84.6	228.8	214.7	279.0	36.8
Monetary Authorities: Other Liab.	4..d	30.0	33.3	40.0	37.1	48.6	62.9	150.0	150.0	116.7	133.5	145.2	209.3	214.7	7.9	25.2
Deposit Money Banks: Assets	7a.d	137	157	189	231	320	514	795	1,251	1,695	1,819	1,877	1,989	2,473	3,452	4,319
of which: Claims on Nonbanks	7ad d	....	....	....	....	....	....	....	8	11	15	13	15	485	482	867
Deposit Money Banks: Liabilities	7b.d	187	210	211	254	309	563	898	1,357	1,876	2,231	2,638	2,918	3,190	4,679	6,216
of which: Liab. to Nonbanks	7bdd d	....	....	....	....	....	....	....	—	—	—	—	—	—	1,910	2,786
Monetary Authorities											*Thousands of New Sheqalim through 1982;*						
Foreign Assets	11	200	195	259	242	155	168	331	570	826	778	902	1,416	2,784	5,673	11,332
Claims on Central Government	12a	30	32	92	113	230	319	445	424	428	695	829	1,249	2,558	3,540	5,688
Claims on Deposit Money Banks	12e	14	27	41	45	82	101	129	172	279	460	639	796	1,809	3,308	7,989
Reserve Money	14	131	131	171	202	190	242	364	760	957	1,157	1,378	2,021	6,492	11,189	21,741
of which: Currency Outside DMBs	14a	66	75	97	109	113	128	159	198	271	317	397	477	632	878	1,205
Foreign Cur.Deps.	14cf	....	....	....	....	....	....	....	220	268	435	554	898	4,891	9,142	19,461
Foreign Liabilities	16c	9	10	14	13	25	26	78	63	49	104	276	473	863	686	1,132
Central Government Deposits	16d	9	2	54	1	4	19	21	48	103	30	32	46	223	644	1,040
Other Items (Net)	17r	100	116	160	191	238	287	432	283	426	640	682	904	−483	−73	926
Deposit Money Banks											*Thousands of New Sheqalim through 1982;*						
Reserves	20	64	55	72	86	74	93	173	ℓ825	1,021	1,472	1,721	2,743	5,822	10,321	20,540
Foreign Assets	21	41	47	66	81	112	180	334	ℓ48	61	143	124	141	1,143	1,863	5,294
Claims on Central Government	22a	14	20	37	44	63	91	101	ℓ225	506	1,220	2,233	3,388	6,502	10,730	24,402
Claims on Other Banking Insts.	22f	....	....	....	....	....	....	....	51	84	134	297	531	899	1,462	3,176
Claims on Private Sector	22d	216	275	310	375	454	563	695	ℓ1,027	1,424	2,254	3,172	4,260	7,379	15,313	33,051
Demand Deposits	24	124	126	157	181	184	210	276	ℓ359	470	554	666	871	1,240	1,818	2,343
Time and Savings Deposits	25	197	252	319	406	508	627	851	ℓ557	624	1,063	1,590	2,383	4,217	3,553	5,985
Restricted Deposits	26b	....	....	....	....	....	....	....	459	904	1,786	2,905	4,632	7,932	13,010	29,072
Foreign Liabilities	26c	56	63	74	89	108	197	377	ℓ—	—	—	—	—	—	3,628	9,838
Central Government Deposits	26d	1	1	1	2	2	4	5	ℓ245	302	415	604	816	1,208	1,701	3,115
Credit from Monetary Authorities	26g	....	....	....	....	....	....	....	138	243	421	623	795	1,834	3,341	7,964
Other Items (Net)	27r	−44	−44	−64	−93	−99	−111	−208	ℓ418	552	985	1,160	1,566	5,314	12,638	28,147
Monetary Survey											*Thousands of New Sheqalim through 1982;*						
Foreign Assets (Net)	31n	176	169	237	221	134	125	210	ℓ555	837	817	750	1,084	3,065	3,221	5,656
Domestic Credit	32	250	324	384	529	741	950	1,215	ℓ1,434	2,037	3,859	5,895	8,567	15,907	28,700	62,163
Claims on Central Govt. (Net)	32an	34	49	74	154	287	387	520	ℓ356	529	1,471	2,426	3,776	7,629	11,925	25,935
Claims on Other Banking Insts.	32f	....	....	....	....	....	....	....	51	84	134	297	531	899	1,462	3,176
Claims on Private Sector	32d	216	275	310	375	454	563	695	ℓ1,027	1,424	2,254	3,172	4,260	7,379	15,313	33,051
Money	34	190	201	254	290	297	338	435	ℓ557	741	871	1,063	1,348	1,872	2,696	3,548
Quasi-Money	35	197	252	319	406	508	627	851	ℓ557	624	1,063	1,590	2,383	4,217	3,631	6,432
Restricted Deposits	36b	....	....	....	....	....	....	....	459	904	1,786	2,905	4,632	7,932	13,010	29,072
Other Items (Net)	37r	66	59	71	61	63	92	106	ℓ491	666	1,052	1,195	1,548	5,359	12,325	28,260
Money plus Quasi-Money	35l	387	453	573	696	805	965	1,286	ℓ1,114	1,366	1,935	2,652	3,732	6,089	6,327	9,979
Interest Rates															*Percent Per Annum*	
Discount Rate	60	....	....	....	....	....	....	....	....	....	....	....	....	....	....	....
Treasury Bill Rate	60c	....	....	....	....	....	....	....	....	....	....	....	....	....	....	....
Deposit Rate	60l	....	....	....	....	....	....	....	....	....	....	....	....	....	....	....
Lending Rate	60p	....	....	....	....	....	....	....	....	....	....	....	....	....	....	89.2
Prices, Production, Employment															*Index Numbers (1990=100):*	
Share Prices	62	—	—	—	—	ℓ—	—	—	—	—	—	—	—	—	—	.1
Prices: Industrial Products	63	—	ℓ—	—	—	—	—	—	—	—	—	ℓ—	—	—	—	.1
Consumer Prices	64	—	ℓ—	—	—	—	—	—	—	—	—	ℓ—	—	—	—	.1
Wages: Daily Earnings	65	—	—	—	—	—	—	—	—	—	—	—	—	—	ℓ—	
Industrial Production	66..c	28.3	28.6	27.8	35.7	ℓ41.3	45.5	49.9	55.9	58.3	61.5	ℓ63.3	65.7	69.0	73.9	77.9
Industrial Employment	67	66.5	65.2	61.7	70.9	78.3	83.3	86.4	91.2	92.2	94.8	95.5	97.9	99.8	ℓ101.7	105.1

Israel

1980	1981	1982	1983	1984	1985	1986	1987	1988	1989	1990	1991	1992	1993	1994		
and per SDR thereafter: End of Period															**Exchange Rates**	
9.6268	₪.0182	.0371	.1128	.6261	1.6471	1.8181	2.1828	2.2675	2.5797	2.9136	3.2657	3.8005	4.1015	4.4058	Market Rate	aa
and per US Dollar thereafter: End of Period (ae) Period Average (rf)																
7.5480	₪.0156	.0337	.1078	.6387	1.4995	1.4864	1.5386	1.6850	1.9630	2.0480	2.2830	2.7640	2.9860	3.0180	Market Rate	ae
5.1243	₪.0114	.0243	.0562	.2932	1.1788	1.4878	1.5946	1.5989	1.9164	2.0162	2.2791	2.4591	2.8301	3.0111	Market Rate	rf
End of Period															**Fund Position**	
307.5	307.5	307.5	446.6	446.6	446.6	446.6	446.6	446.6	446.6	446.6	446.6	666.2	666.2	666.2	Quota	2f. s
8.8	.6	.5	1.6	.1	.1	—	.1	.1	.1	.2	.3	.2	.4	.2	SDRs	1b. s
25.6	—	—	34.8	—	—	—	—	—	—	—	—	—	—	—	Reserve Position in the Fund	1c. s
156.4	87.5	27.2	—	—	—	—	—	—	—	—	—	178.6	178.6	178.6	Total Fund Cred.&Loans Outstg.	2tl
End of Period															**International Liquidity**	
3,351.4	3,496.7	3,839.3	3,651.2	3,060.3	3,680.2	4,659.6	5,876.1	4,015.6	5,276.2	6,275.1	6,279.1	5,127.4	6,382.6	6,792.4	Total Reserves minus Gold	1l. d
11.2	.7	.6	1.7	.1	.1	—	.1	.1	.1	.2	.4	.3	.5	.4	SDRs	1b. d
32.7	—	—	36.4	—	—	—	—	—	—	—	—	—	—	—	Reserve Position in the Fund	1c. d
3,307.5	3,496.0	3,838.7	3,613.1	3,060.2	3,680.1	4,659.6	5,876.0	4,015.5	5,276.1	6,274.9	6,278.7	5,127.1	6,382.1	6,792.0	Foreign Exchange	1d. d
1.194	1.193	1.084	1.015	1.017	1.017	1.017	1.017	1.018	1.017	.839	.421	.009	.009	.009	Gold (Million Fine Troy Ounces)	1ad
53.3	48.6	41.9	37.2	34.9	39.1	43.5	50.5	47.9	46.8	41.8	21.1	.4	.4	.4	Gold (National Valuation)	1and
90.1	6.4	218.4	70.0	1.6	1.3	161.5	....	....	....	....	....	....	....	....	Monetary Authorities: Other Assets	3..d
17.2	17.2	14.6	13.5	17.4	17.3	19.5	29.2	36.2	32.6	28.8	28.9	37.7	38.5	37.8	Monetary Authorities: Other Liab.	4..d
5,523	6,271	7,193	6,849	6,637	6,256	6,575	6,447	7,264	7,361	8,317	8,897	10,609	10,138	11,330	Deposit Money Banks: Assets	7a. d
1,004	1,067	1,035	1,045	853	1,125	1,210	1,240	793	983	1,545	1,400	1,817	2,780	3,635	*of which:* Claims on Nonbanks	7ad d
7,593	8,662	10,965	10,631	10,309	10,038	10,313	10,264	10,676	9,982	11,025	11,480	12,093	12,159	13,099	Deposit Money Banks: Liabilities	7b. d
3,400	3,940	5,360	5,611	5,558	5,952	6,454	6,968	7,972	8,160	9,344	9,902	10,618	10,829	12,157	*of which:* Liab. to Nonbanks	7bd d
Millions of New Sheqalim Beginning 1983: End of Period															**Monetary Authorities**	
26,625	55,386	136,370	₪410	1,980	5,578	7,230	9,377	7,391	10,464	12,935	14,380	14,186	19,065	20,508	Foreign Assets	11
9,383	34,104	104,040	₪493	3,104	8,498	8,144	8,029	9,905	10,086	10,300	10,285	10,419	10,338	9,976	Claims on Central Government	12a
19,283	27,378	18,360	₪83	294	392	500	1,205	3,853	4,711	3,066	5,475	11,053	16,972	15,555	Claims on Deposit Money Banks	12e
46,832	96,666	224,030	₪832	4,596	11,366	11,926	14,128	15,059	16,530	18,815	20,488	21,901	28,051	26,166	Reserve Money	14
2,100	4,413	8,430	₪25	123	481	974	1,365	1,643	2,225	2,817	3,228	₪4,113	4,852	5,467	*of which:* Currency Outside DMBs	14a
42,288	86,042	199,000	₪775	4,288	9,158	8,978	9,919	11,796	12,700	14,442	15,364	15,893	20,203	16,413	Foreign Cur.Deps.	14cf
1,636	1,858	1,498	₪1	11	26	29	45	61	64	59	66	783	848	901	Foreign Liabilities	16c
2,334	4,281	14,870	₪87	473	1,369	2,620	3,469	5,025	7,503	6,108	8,383	11,694	16,165	17,456	Central Government Deposits	16d
4,158	14,051	17,612	₪65	297	1,707	1,299	969	1,004	1,164	1,319	1,203	1,280	1,311	1,516	Other Items (Net)	17r
Millions of New Sheqalim Beginning 1983: End of Period															**Deposit Money Banks**	
44,756	96,171	228,692	₪836	4,601	11,107	11,227	13,026	13,313	14,223	15,911	17,053	₪17,854	23,223	20,743	Reserves	20
12,617	97,851	242,053	₪738	4,239	9,381	9,773	9,920	12,241	14,449	17,033	20,311	29,322	30,271	34,194	Foreign Assets	21
64,023	173,753	456,180	₪1,353	9,000	25,939	30,034	34,588	40,937	46,860	49,814	56,836	₪62,094	65,080	66,289	Claims on Central Government	22a
7,356	15,712	39,723	₪119	777	2,361	2,971	3,661	4,299	5,289	5,605	7,515	....	....	....	Claims on Other Banking Insts.	22f
79,029	164,099	409,170	₪1,097	6,236	17,051	23,267	31,698	40,720	49,464	60,957	75,468	₪94,092	121,800	154,285	Claims on Private Sector	22d
4,879	8,101	17,880	₪38	154	508	1,203	1,922	2,012	3,079	4,133	4,680	₪6,324	8,526	8,946	Demand Deposits	24
15,346	205,775	496,798	₪1,554	9,640	24,243	27,989	34,595	45,136	52,273	60,780	71,643	₪89,564	104,678	139,900	Time and Savings Deposits	25
76,059	175,826	435,335	₪1,227	7,115	20,518	24,625	27,206	29,937	32,830	35,500	37,855	₪29,879	28,775	28,730	Restricted Deposits	26b
25,663	135,170	368,976	₪1,146	6,584	15,052	15,329	15,793	17,990	19,595	22,578	26,210	33,425	36,307	39,533	Foreign Liabilities	26c
6,595	16,713	47,388	₪149	922	2,661	3,974	4,781	5,648	6,606	8,145	12,149	₪15,147	19,604	23,211	Central Government Deposits	26d
19,181	26,716	33,340	₪111	433	665	832	1,546	3,828	4,685	3,056	5,453	₪11,053	16,896	15,569	Credit from Monetary Authorities	26g
60,056	−20,755	−23,900	₪−3	5	2,192	3,321	7,051	6,960	11,215	15,127	19,194	₪17,972	25,587	19,622	Other Items (Net)	27r
Millions of New Sheqalim Beginning 1983: End of Period															**Monetary Survey**	
11,943	16,209	7,950	₪1	−376	−119	1,645	3,459	1,581	5,254	7,331	8,415	9,300	12,181	14,268	Foreign Assets (Net)	31n
150,861	366,674	946,854	₪2,827	17,722	49,819	57,822	69,726	85,188	97,589	112,424	129,573	₪139,765	161,448	189,882	Domestic Credit	32
64,477	186,864	497,961	₪1,611	10,709	30,406	31,584	34,368	40,169	42,837	45,861	46,589	₪45,673	39,649	35,598	Claims on Central Govt. (Net)	32an
7,356	15,712	39,723	₪119	777	2,361	2,971	3,661	4,299	5,289	5,605	7,515	....	....	....	Claims on Other Banking Insts.	32f
79,029	164,099	409,170	₪1,097	6,236	17,051	23,267	31,698	40,720	49,464	60,957	75,468	₪94,092	121,800	154,285	Claims on Private Sector	32d
6,979	13,354	27,930	₪67	304	1,052	2,238	3,346	3,723	5,376	7,022	7,988	₪10,541	13,486	14,523	Money	34
17,230	211,629	516,186	₪1,602	9,884	26,309	30,800	38,691	47,668	56,842	67,280	79,486	₪100,085	121,441	153,587	Quasi-Money	35
76,059	175,826	435,335	₪1,227	7,115	20,518	24,625	27,206	29,937	32,830	35,500	37,855	₪29,879	28,775	28,730	Restricted Deposits	36b
61,505	−19,082	−26,429	₪−70	42	1,821	1,804	3,943	5,441	7,796	9,952	12,660	₪8,560	9,928	7,310	Other Items (Net)	37r
24,210	224,983	544,116	₪1,670	10,188	27,361	33,038	42,037	51,391	62,218	74,303	87,473	₪110,626	134,926	168,110	Money plus Quasi-Money	35l
Percent Per Annum															**Interest Rates**	
....	....	108.2	₪311.0	690.3	79.6	31.4	26.8	30.9	15.0	13.0	14.2	10.4	9.8	17.0	Discount Rate	60
....	....	....	....	217.3	210.1	19.9	20.0	16.0	12.9	15.1	14.5	11.8	10.5	11.8	Treasury Bill Rate	60c
....	....	....	132.9	438.4	178.8	18.6	19.4	14.5	14.1	14.4	13.9	11.3	10.4	12.2	Deposit Rate	60l
176.9	170.6	140.2	186.2	823.0	503.4	60.3	61.4	41.7	31.6	26.4	26.4	19.9	16.4	17.3	Lending Rate	60p
Period Averages															**Prices, Production, Employment**	
₪—	₪—	₪1	2	₪7	₪32	40	49	49	87	100	155	297	418	257	Share Prices	62
.2	.4	.8	2.0	₪10.0	36.6	₪53.2	63.0	74.0	89.6	100.0	₪116.1	127.9	₪138.3	149.2	Prices: Industrial Products	63
₪.2	.3	.7	1.8	₪8.5	₪34.4	₪50.9	61.0	71.0	85.3	100.0	119.0	133.2	₪147.8	166.0	Consumer Prices	64
.1	.3	.6	₪1.6	7.7	27.3	44.0	57.9	70.4	₪85.2	100.0	116.1	129.6	144.8	160.2	Wages: Daily Earnings	65
75.3	80.2	81.1	84.3	87.8	90.7	93.8	98.4	95.3	₪93.9	100.0	107.4	116.3	123.7	133.4	Industrial Production	66..c
101.0	103.7	105.6	₪107.5	108.5	108.2	109.2	111.4	107.4	₪100.8	100.0	104.1	108.3	112.9	116.9	Industrial Employment	67

Israel

		1965	1966	1967	1968	1969	1970	1971	1972	1973	1974	1975	1976	1977	1978	1979
International Transactions																*Thousands of New Sheqalim through 1982;*
Exports	70	129	151	171	224	255	273	402	479	608	812	1,230	1,914	3,219	6,837	11,551
Imports, cif	71	251	250	239	458	578	728	993	1,034	1,779	2,420	3,800	4,493	6,045	12,928	21,789
Imports, fob	71.v	232	232	220	424	533	674	922	966	1,665	2,247	3,513	4,176	5,643	12,082	20,377
																Millions of US Dollars
Exports	70..d	430	503	555	639	729	779	958	1,147	1,449	1,825	1,941	2,415	3,082	3,921	4,546
Imports, cif	71..d	838	833	774	1,307	1,653	2,079	2,363	2,473	4,240	5,437	5,997	5,669	5,787	7,415	8,576
Imports, fob	71.vd	774	772	715	1,211	1,523	1,927	2,195	2,311	3,969	5,048	5,545	5,269	5,403	6,930	8,021
																1990=100
Volume of Exports	72	15.2	17.0	19.0	22.1	23.7	26.0	31.0	‡34.1	34.8	37.1	37.8	46.4	50.8	50.8	52.1
Volume of Imports	73	‡24.1	23.4	21.8	32.1	36.3	38.9	46.7	‡48.8	57.5	59.0	56.1	56.6	60.9	63.4	66.3
Unit Value of Exports (US$)	74..d	‡21.3	22.6	22.2	21.9	22.9	22.6	23.4	‡25.5	31.8	37.2	38.8	‡39.5	46.7	‡61.8	‡70.9
Unit Value of Imports (US$)	75..d	‡21.1	21.5	21.5	21.1	21.9	22.3	22.8	‡24.3	31.4	42.6	44.5	‡43.5	47.4	‡58.2	‡72.3
Balance of Payments																*Millions of US Dollars*
Goods: Exports f.o.b.	78aad	408	480	535	657	758	814	1,012	1,227	1,571	2,029	2,192	2,688	3,422	4,104	4,841
Goods: Imports f.o.b.	78abd	−840	−865	−977	−1,265	−1,528	−1,944	−2,224	−2,307	−3,987	−5,060	−5,600	−5,345	−5,484	−6,814	−8,088
Trade Balance	78acd	−432	−385	−442	−608	−770	−1,130	−1,212	−1,080	−2,416	−3,031	−3,408	−2,657	−2,062	−2,710	−3,247
Services: Credit	78add	264	301	317	425	455	496	702	727	848	1,140	1,126	1,338	1,606	1,954	2,318
Services: Debit	78aed	−288	−305	−340	−342	−423	−453	−632	−634	−880	−1,092	−1,198	−1,365	−1,538	−1,851	−2,133
Balance on Goods and Services	78afd	−456	−389	−465	−525	−738	−1,087	−1,142	−987	−2,448	−2,983	−3,480	−2,684	−1,994	−2,607	−3,062
Income: Credit	78agd	39	50	59	79	91	92	160	166	278	394	370	371	431	561	916
Income: Debit	78ahd	−94	−113	−130	−146	−169	−217	−240	−278	−396	−604	−739	−756	−796	−1,047	−1,369
Balance on Goods, Serv., & Inc.	78aid	−511	−452	−536	−592	−816	−1,212	−1,222	−1,099	−2,566	−3,193	−3,849	−3,069	−2,359	−3,093	−3,515
Current Transfers, n.i.e.: Credit	78ajd	330	298	524	421	439	628	691	933	2,101	1,651	2,065	2,492	2,103	2,212	2,733
Current Transfers: Debit	78akd	−9	−6	−8	−13	−18	−33	−14	−50	−60	−21	−38	−99	−100	−128	−138
Current Account, n.i.e.	78ald	−190	−160	−20	−184	−395	−617	−545	−216	−525	−1,563	−1,822	−676	−356	−1,009	−920
Capital Account, n.i.e.: Credit	78bad	—	—	17	31	40	55	113	166	148	100	64	40	69	141	242
Capital Account: Debit	78bbd															
Capital Account, n.i.e.	78bcd	—	—	17	31	40	55	113	166	148	100	64	40	69	141	242
Direct Investment Abroad	78bdd	−4	−7	−6	−3	3	−9	−4	—	—	—	2	−6	−6	−7	−1
Dir. Invest. in Rep. Econ., n.i.e.	78bed	5	43	4	14	30	49	57	114	149	84	45	47	81	39	11
Portfolio Investment Assets	78bfd	−14	−5	−12	−15	−20	−14	−7	—	−14	−9	14	−6	−2	−107	−149
Portfolio Investment Liab., n.i.e.	78bgd	60	45	192	90	80	148	200	221	399	187	162	169	193	248	127
Other Investment Assets	78bhd	−25	−48	−48	−49	−137	−60	−240	−484	−301	−55	−301	−819	−1,122	−1,015	−1,607
Other Investment Liab., n.i.e.	78bid	204	124	86	103	178	577	585	730	878	701	1,806	1,033	1,237	2,173	3,287
Financial Account, n.i.e.	78bjd	226	152	216	140	134	691	591	581	1,111	908	1,728	418	381	1,331	1,668
Net Errors and Omissions	78cad	62	−27	−20	−81	−122	−122	52	17	−186	−287	−126	402	120	482	−779
Overall Balance	78cbd	98	−35	193	−94	−343	7	211	548	548	−842	−156	184	214	945	211
Reserves and Related Items	79dad	−98	35	−193	94	343	−7	−211	−548	−548	842	156	−184	−214	−945	−211
Reserve Assets	79dbd	−98	35	−193	94	321	3	−231	−513	−548	802	−57	−273	−214	−929	−151
Use of Fund Credit and Loans	79dcd	—	—	—	—	22	−10	20	−35	—	39	213	88	—	−16	−61
Liabs.Constit.For.Auth.Reserves	79ddd															
Exceptional Financing	79ded															
Government Finance										*Thousands of New Sheqalim through 1982; Millions Beginning 1983*						
Deficit (−) or Surplus	80	−74	−108	−187	−278	−279	−383	−437	‡−463	−745	‡−1,329	−1,561	−1,818	−2,798	−2,990	−6,730
Revenue	81	291	339	326	417	520	659	916	‡1,018	1,442	‡2,369	3,588	5,206	7,700	12,300	25,900
Grants Received	81z	29	18	92	57	57	76	61	‡22	500	‡206	609	1,005	1,318	2,132	4,631
Expenditure	82	344	415	534	666	764	996	1,274	‡1,403	2,521	‡3,611	5,251	7,356	10,900	16,055	34,037
Lending Minus Repayments	83	50	50	71	86	92	122	140	‡100	166	‡293	507	673	916	1,367	3,226
Financing																
Domestic	84a	19	59	116	194	229	209	255	‡341	560	‡700	896	1,500	1,900	1,600	2,800
Foreign	85a	55	50	71	86	50	174	183	‡178	236	‡553	665	417	925	1,461	3,922
Debt: Domestic	88a	....	....	....	....	....	....	....	‡2,500	3,700	5,300	7,600	10,500	16,774	26,100	51,700
Foreign	89a	....	....	....	....	....	....	....	‡1,500	1,700	3,000	4,532	6,900	13,810	20,200	46,200
National Accounts															*Thousands of New Sheqalim through 1982*	
Exports of Goods & Services	90c	207	238	286	413	466	508	720	939	1,165	1,683	2,551	3,851	6,413	11,771	21,104
Government Consumption	91f	219	259	360	409	492	673	794	924	1,640	2,207	3,393	4,027	5,101	9,022	15,187
Gross Capital Formation	93	286	252	204	322	425	535	748	938	1,000	2,000	2,444	2,698	3,512	6,423	12,056
Gross Fixed Capital Formation	93e	297	241	200	290	400	500	690	920	1,260	1,750	2,300	2,550	3,100	5,540	11,510
Increase/Decrease(−) in Stocks	93i	9	11	—	30	40	40	50	50	30	20	190	140	320	660	750
Private Consumption	96f	719	800	811	904	1,029	1,132	1,328	1,669	2,182	3,264	4,628	6,192	8,795	14,576	27,956
Imports of Goods & Services	98c	−351	−354	−453	−663	−814	−970	−1,244	−1,512	−2,182	−3,264	−5,262	−6,816	−9,431	−18,047	−31,813
Gross Domestic Product	99b	1,099	1,194	1,209	1,386	1,599	1,880	2,341	2,999	3,877	5,595	7,817	9,888	14,390	23,745	44,490
Net Factor Inc/Pmts(−) Abroad	98.n	−6	−8	−19	−13	−19	−31	−38	−52	−115	−167	−284	−356	−361	−710	−1,758
Gross Nat'l Expenditure = GNP	99a	1,093	1,186	1,197	1,373	1,580	1,849	2,303	2,947	3,762	5,427	7,533	9,532	14,029	23,035	42,732
Nat'l Income, Market Prices	99e	828	911	1,077	1,239	1,430	1,667	2,075	2,656	3,375	4,820	6,556	8,330	12,105	20,970	39,117
GDP 1990 Prices *(Millions)*	99b.p	....	....	....	27,032	27,032	36,043	36,043	36,043	54,065	54,065	‡63,075	65,412	51,395	58,403	72,420
GDP Deflator (1990=100)	99bip	—	—	—	—	—	—	—	—	—	—	—	—	—	—	—
																Millions
Population	99z	2.56	2.63	2.68	2.80	2.88	2.97	3.07	3.15	3.28	3.38	3.46	3.53	3.61	3.69	3.79

Exchange Rates: On February 22, 1980 the shekel, equal to 10 Israel pounds, was introduced. On September 4, 1985 the new sheqel, equal to 1,000 old sheqalim, was introduced.
Deposit Money Banks: ‡ Beginning in December 1992, other deposits, which were previously included in *Time and Savings Deposits (line 25)*, are included in *Demand Deposits (line 24)*. Earmarked government deposits, which were previously included in *Restricted Deposits (line 26b)*, are included in *Central Government Deposits (line 26d)*. A new reporting procedure was also introduced, which resulted in other changes in the classification of accounts.
Prices, Production, Employment: ‡ The indices for wages, industrial production, and industrial employment exclude the diamond sector as of January 1979.

International Transactions: ‡ *Export* and *Import Unit Value* indices are source S data, base 1984; prior to 1976, they are Paasche indices; beginning in 1976, they are Laspeyres indices; from 1984 onwards they are compiled using Fischer's ideal formula. The weights are revised every two years. For example, for 1981 the weights are calculated on the basis of Israel's trade in 1979.
Government Finance: ‡ Beginning in 1972, data are as reported in the *Government Finance Statistics Yearbook* and cover budgetary central government. ‡ Beginning in 1974, data also include social security funds. ‡ Prior to 1991, data relate to a fiscal year different from calendar year. ‡ Break symbols in 1991 data indicate that data refer to period April 1—December 31.

Israel

	1980	1981	1982	1983	1984	1985	1986	1987	1988	1989	1990	1991	1992	1993	1994	International Transactions	
Millions of New Sheqalim Beginning 1983																	
	28,376	64,813	127,530	ℐ287	1,703	7,380	10,644	13,482	13,108	20,578	23,339	27,169	32,260	41,957	50,839	Exports	70
	50,137	116,993	234,305	ℐ538	2,879	11,641	16,077	22,880	24,013	27,495	33,853	42,524	49,803	64,028	37,517	Imports, cif	71
	47,158	108,543	216,893	ℐ498	2,665	10,777	14,886	21,185	22,235	25,458	31,345	39,374	46,114	59,285	34,738	Imports, fob	71.v
Millions of US Dollars																	
	5,538	5,670	5,255	5,108	5,807	6,260	7,154	8,454	8,198	10,738	11,576	11,921	13,119	14,826	16,884	Exports	70..d
	9,784	10,235	9,655	9,574	9,819	9,875	10,806	14,348	15,018	14,347	16,791	18,658	20,253	22,624	....	Imports, cif	71..d
	9,203	9,496	8,938	8,851	9,088	9,142	10,005	13,285	13,906	13,284	15,547	17,276	18,752	20,948	....	Imports, fob	71.v d
1990=100																	
	ℐ56.9	60.3	59.2	59.8	68.9	75.1	83.2	92.2	95.2	99.5	ℐ100.0	97.9	107.1	120.8	139.7	Volume of Exports	72
	ℐ59.0	60.2	66.7	73.1	72.7	74.1	86.4	97.0	97.2	92.9	ℐ100.0	116.0	129.6	146.3	166.0	Volume of Imports	73
	ℐ79.9	ℐ77.1	73.0	ℐ71.1	ℐ69.9	69.1	71.4	76.1	86.8	92.3	ℐ100.0	100.4	101.2	101.7	100.2	Unit Value of Exports(US$)	74..d
	ℐ88.8	ℐ85.9	78.6	ℐ75.0	ℐ75.0	73.4	73.0	80.3	87.0	92.9	ℐ100.0	95.1	95.2	92.0	93.8	Unit Value of Imports(US$)	75..d
Minus Sign Indicates Debit																**Balance of Payments**	
	5,946	6,095	5,733	5,718	6,375	6,820	7,890	9,306	10,334	11,123	12,214	12,092	13,382	14,888	16,598	Goods: Exports f.o.b.	78aa d
	−9,201	−9,694	−8,986	−8,971	−8,959	−9,202	−9,727	−13,008	−13,231	−13,049	−15,305	−17,117	−18,412	−20,549	−22,740	Goods: Imports f.o.b.	78ab d
	−3,255	−3,599	−3,253	−3,253	−2,584	−2,382	−1,838	−3,702	−2,897	−1,926	−3,091	−5,025	−5,030	−5,661	−6,141	Trade Balance	78ac d
	2,722	2,724	2,572	2,697	2,788	3,004	2,986	3,677	4,017	4,220	4,493	4,665	5,818	6,039	6,414	Services: Credit	78ad d
	−2,310	−2,663	−2,980	−3,226	−3,221	−2,752	−3,201	−4,027	−4,458	−4,879	−5,616	−5,951	−6,476	−7,288	−8,267	Services: Debit	78ae d
	−2,843	−3,538	−3,662	−3,781	−3,018	−2,130	−2,053	−4,052	−3,338	−2,585	−4,214	−6,311	−5,688	−6,910	−7,995	Balance on Goods and Services	78af d
	1,190	1,735	1,897	1,588	1,362	1,023	939	975	1,132	1,410	1,628	1,803	1,579	1,216	1,140	Income: Credit	78ag d
	−1,947	−2,253	−2,683	−2,616	−2,925	−2,774	−2,568	−2,501	−2,690	−2,689	−2,763	−2,583	−2,558	−2,426	−2,858	Income: Debit	78ah d
	−3,600	−4,056	−4,448	−4,809	−4,580	−3,881	−3,681	−5,578	−4,896	−3,865	−5,349	−7,091	−6,667	−8,120	−9,713	Balance on Goods, Serv., & Inc.	78ai d
	2,864	2,894	2,547	2,957	3,376	5,019	5,130	4,591	4,607	4,564	5,472	6,223	6,255	6,152	6,002	Current Transfers, n.i.e.: Credit	78aj d
	−135	−199	−224	−247	−218	−115	−110	−196	−185	−141	−189	−236	−294	−354	−297	Current Transfers: Debit	78ak d
	−871	−1,361	−2,125	−2,099	−1,423	1,023	1,339	−1,183	−474	558	−66	−1,104	−706	−2,322	−4,008	Current Account, n.i.e.	78al d
	296	403	129	120	125	120	349	503	433	677	624	688	924	949	1,251	Capital Account, n.i.e.: Credit	78ba d
	—	—	—	—	—	—	—	—	—	—	—	—	—	—	—	Capital Account: Debit	78bb d
	296	403	129	120	125	120	349	503	433	677	624	688	924	949	1,251	Capital Account, n.i.e.	78bc d
	3	−114	−189	−100	−24	−55	−57	−80	−62	−38	−165	−424	−651	−929	−826	Direct Investment Abroad	78bd d
	51	114	51	88	53	99	137	233	235	125	101	351	539	555	406	Dir. Invest. in Rep. Econ., n.i.e.	78be d
	−173	−155	−32	−269	144	118	131	68	−39	−102	−345	−262	−1,268	−730	−287	Portfolio Investment Assets	78bf d
	148	93	74	883	66	204	261	100	4,211	1,124	134	811	528	2,480	2,666	Portfolio Investment Liab., n.i.e.	78bg d
	−1,694	−347	−502	−244	215	320	−929	855	−217	−1,408	−935	−698	−2,065	1,016	−1,938	Other Investment Assets	78bh d
	2,747	2,685	3,847	1,453	978	−776	331	157	−4,718	−765	895	133	796	−392	1,127	Other Investment Liab., n.i.e.	78bi d
	1,082	2,277	3,248	1,809	1,432	−92	−127	1,332	−590	−1,064	−315	−89	−2,120	2,001	1,147	Financial Account, n.i.e.	78bj d
	34	−768	−338	−330	−681	−653	−568	9	−539	1,227	272	332	445	854	1,679	Net Errors and Omissions	78ca d
	541	550	914	−500	−547	399	993	661	−1,170	1,398	515	−173	−1,457	1,481	69	Overall Balance	78cb d
	−541	−550	−914	500	547	−399	−993	−661	1,170	−1,398	−515	173	1,457	−1,481	−69	Reserves and Related Items	79da d
	−453	−468	−847	529	547	−399	−993	−661	1,170	−1,398	−515	173	1,212	−1,481	−69	Reserve Assets	79db d
	−89	−82	−67	−29	—	—	—	—	—	—	—	—	245	—	—	Use of Fund Credit and Loans	79dc d
	—	—	—	—	—	—	—	—	—	—	—	—	—	—	—	Liabs.Constit.For.Auth.Reserves	79dd d
	—	—	—	—	—	—	—	—	—	—	—	—	—	—	—	Exceptional Financing	79de d
Year Ending March 31 through 1991, December 31 Thereafter																**Government Finance**	
	−18,107	−58,218	−100,501	ℐ−412	−1,440	−951	333	−2,000	−5,897	−3,512	−4,778	ℐ−8,514	ℐ−6,232	−3,326	....	Deficit (-) or Surplus	80
	58,300	133,800	354,800	ℐ954	4,490	15,503	23,094	27,862	29,582	34,520	43,148	ℐ40,404	ℐ64,012	74,831	....	Revenue	81
	11,437	24,181	26,605	ℐ154	1,301	5,446	6,010	5,193	5,020	5,816	6,941	ℐ6,458	ℐ9,074	8,229	....	Grants Received	81z
	81,229	198,568	443,100	ℐ1,373	6,803	19,817	26,696	32,487	35,010	42,649	53,702	ℐ50,818	ℐ78,163	86,273	....	Expenditure	82
	6,615	17,631	38,806	ℐ148	429	2,083	2,076	2,568	5,488	1,199	1,165	ℐ4,558	ℐ1,155	113	....	Lending Minus Repayments	83
																Financing	
	9,000	46,900	48,400	ℐ280	1,137	807	−11	2,056	4,196	3,973	3,974	ℐ7,661	ℐ4,147	−1,621	....	Domestic	84a
	9,100	11,277	52,111	ℐ132	302	144	−322	−56	1,701	−461	804	ℐ853	ℐ2,085	4,948	....	Foreign	85a
	190,000	491,400	884,500	ℐ4,328	20,321	47,205	58,138	68,827	87,275	103,729	123,837	147,861	168,248	....	....	Debt: Domestic	88a
	107,200	251,600	588,100	ℐ2,396	13,838	25,314	27,992	26,701	32,655	35,659	41,362	42,638	54,742	....	....	Foreign	89a
Millions of New Sheqalim Beginning 1983																**National Accounts**	
	48,863	112,684	227,483	ℐ546	3,099	12,577	17,313	22,161	24,646	31,358	35,816	40,610	50,124	61,836	....	Exports of Goods & Services	90c
	44,701	109,973	228,133	ℐ545	2,919	10,461	13,922	19,802	22,761	25,934	31,912	40,182	45,180	53,010	....	Government Consumption	91f
	25,000	56,000	140,000	ℐ360	1,656	5,264	8,629	10,894	12,140	13,621	19,675	32,897	39,246	44,204	....	Gross Capital Formation	93
	24,543	59,002	136,006	ℐ360	1,568	5,331	7,962	11,105	12,610	14,299	20,092	32,575	37,580	41,615	....	Gross Fixed Capital Formation	93e
	840	−2,768	4,968	ℐ5	100	103	758	−64	102	−157	405	1,258	2,234	2,589	....	Increase/Decrease(-) in Stocks	93i
	ℐ58,891	145,250	342,832	ℐ910	4,160	16,552	27,739	36,205	43,920	53,234	65,051	82,177	98,513	116,315	....	Private Consumption	96f
	−66,226	−158,993	−343,990	ℐ−824	−4,210	−16,570	−23,131	−32,304	−33,814	−39,026	−48,060	−61,167	−72,352	−91,287	....	Imports of Goods & Services	98c
	ℐ111,612	265,148	596,306	ℐ1,542	7,636	28,454	44,563	56,906	70,225	85,642	105,216	135,635	161,279	184,078	....	Gross Domestic Product	99b
	−3,802	−6,350	−17,747	ℐ−48	−333	−1,130	−1,522	−1,811	−1,790	−2,192	−2,534	−2,314	−3,157	....	....	Net Factor Inc/Pmts(-) Abroad	98.n
	107,809	258,755	578,559	ℐ1,494	7,303	27,324	43,041	55,095	68,435	83,450	102,682	133,321	158,122	....	....	Gross Nat'l Expenditure = GNP	99a
	90,941	217,995	486,351	ℐ1,261	6,093	22,580	35,905	46,239	57,997	70,352	86,729	114,556	134,893	....	....	Nat'l Income, Market Prices	99e
	ℐ74,756	78,131	79,154	81,165	82,900	86,222	ℐ89,789	95,306	98,246	99,483	ℐ105,216	111,787	119,157	122,736	130,711	GDP 1990 Prices (Millions)	99b.p
	—	—	1	2	9	33	50	60	71	86	100	121	135	150	....	GDP Deflator (1990=100)	99bi p
Midyear Estimates																	
	3.88	3.95	4.03	4.11	4.16	4.23	4.30	4.37	4.44	4.52	4.66	4.95	5.19	5.26	....	Population	99z

Italy
136

		1965	1966	1967	1968	1969	1970	1971	1972	1973	1974	1975	1976	1977	1978	1979
Exchange Rates																*Lire per SDR:*
Market Rate	aa	624.7	624.4	623.9	623.5	625.5	623.0	644.9	632.4	733.4	795.1	800.2	1,016.6	1,058.7	1,081.0	1,059.1
																Lire per US Dollar:
Market Rate	ae	624.7	624.5	623.9	623.5	625.5	623.0	594.0	582.5	607.9	649.4	683.6	875.0	871.6	829.8	804.0
Market Rate	rf	625.0	625.0	625.0	625.0	625.0	625.0	620.4	583.2	583.0	650.3	652.8	832.3	882.1	848.7	830.9
																Lire per ECU:
ECU Rate	ea	....	....	....	....	....	....	....	....	....	....	....	....	....	....	1,157.2
ECU Rate	eb	....	....	....	....	....	....	....	....	....	....	....	929.8	1,006.9	1,080.6	1,138.5
															Index Numbers (1990=100):	
Market Rate	ah x	191.4	191.5	191.6	191.8	190.6	190.7	307.5	205.0	205.2	183.4	183.4	144.2	135.5	141.0	144.0
Nominal Effective Exchange Rate	ne u	260.5	260.5	261.4	267.7	269.0	266.4	262.4	258.6	230.9	208.5	198.4	166.3	153.3	143.4	139.9
Real Effective Exchange Rate	re u	....	....	....	....	....	....	....	....	....	....	104.5	96.2	92.8	88.7	90.4
Fund Position																*Millions of SDRs:*
Quota	2f. s	500	625	625	625	625	1,000	1,000	1,000	1,000	1,000	1,000	1,000	1,000	1,240	1,240
SDRs	1b. s	—	—	—	—	—	77	228	341	343	181	83	78	119	226	449
Reserve Position in the Fund	1c. s	549	885	842	894	863	276	349	330	297	—	—	—	—	243	237
of which: Outstg.Fund Borrowing	2c	70	320	315	501	551	—	—	—	—	—	—	—	—	—	—
Total Fund Cred.&Loans Outstg.	2tl	—	—	—	—	—	—	—	—	—	1,377	2,457	2,457	1,581	880	—
International Liquidity														*Millions of US Dollars Unless Otherwise Indicated:*		
Total Reserves minus Gold	1l. d	2,396	2,497	3,063	2,418	2,089	2,465	3,689	2,954	2,953	3,406	1,306	3,223	8,104	11,109	18,197
SDRs	1b. d	—	—	—	—	—	77	247	371	414	221	97	91	144	294	592
Reserve Position in the Fund	1c. d	549	885	842	894	863	276	378	359	359	—	—	—	—	316	312
Foreign Exchange	1d. d	1,847	1,612	2,221	1,524	1,226	2,113	3,063	2,225	2,181	3,185	1,209	3,132	7,960	10,499	17,294
Gold (Million Fine Troy Ounces)	1ad	68.68	68.97	68.57	83.52	84.46	82.48	82.40	82.37	82.48	82.48	82.48	82.48	82.91	83.12	66.71
Gold (National Valuation)	1an d	2,403	2,414	2,400	2,923	2,957	2,887	2,884	3,130	3,482	3,482	3,482	9,321	11,260	14,334	20,125
Monetary Authorities: Other Liab.	4. d	78	53	53	26	181	35	107	100	390	584	−2,327	−1,458	802	−553	1,348
Deposit Money Banks: Assets	7a. d	2,474	3,307	3,597	5,160	7,240	10,118	13,266	19,866	25,294	13,296	15,699	12,645	15,260	23,061	30,418
Liabilities	7b. d	2,651	3,059	3,534	4,430	7,186	9,890	13,078	19,948	25,123	15,101	16,327	16,275	23,096	30,028	38,612
Other Banking Insts.: Assets	7e. d	173	357	538	710	1,154	1,400	1,534	1,441	1,642	1,645	1,885	2,024	2,320	2,514	2,681
Liabilities	7f. d	696	645	638	678	838	1,522	1,972	2,690	5,551	7,419	6,463	6,494	6,203	6,124	3,986
Monetary Authorities																*Trillions of Lire:*
Foreign Assets	11	3.02	3.14	3.19	3.40	3.15	3.69	4.26	3.84	3.96	4.37	3.22	11.74	17.97	22.41	32.12
Claims on Central Govt. (Net)	12an	5.16	5.28	5.19	5.84	6.79	9.13	10.56	13.19	18.76	25.28	30.57	39.75	35.50	40.69	41.08
Claims on Deposit Money Banks	12e	.22	.77	1.41	1.62	2.11	.86	.87	1.84	2.10	3.19	2.53	1.02	1.00	.31	3.60
Reserve Money	14	8.37	9.06	9.97	10.68	11.79	12.89	15.04	18.00	22.90	27.04	31.18	36.57	41.80	50.39	55.53
of which: Currency Outside DMBs	14a	4.21	4.59	5.07	5.28	5.97	6.48	7.15	8.02	9.62	10.78	12.56	14.25	16.08	19.02	21.65
Foreign Liabilities	16c	.05	.03	.03	.02	.11	.02	.06	.06	.24	1.47	.38	1.22	2.37	.49	1.08
Other Items (Net)	17r	−.03	.10	−.22	.16	.16	.78	.59	.80	1.68	4.33	4.77	14.72	10.29	12.53	20.19
Deposit Money Banks																*Trillions of Lire:*
Reserves	20	2.02	2.23	2.52	2.88	3.25	3.88	5.00	5.55	6.54	8.25	14.06	18.05	22.36	28.81	33.23
Foreign Assets	21	1.55	2.07	2.25	3.23	4.53	6.32	7.71	11.55	15.38	8.64	10.73	11.06	13.30	19.14	24.46
Claims on Central Government	22a	.72	1.04	1.18	1.66	1.77	1.73	2.16	2.57	3.02	7.05	12.28	11.77	28.52	41.98	50.24
Claims on Private Sector	22d	15.41	17.69	20.52	22.83	26.35	29.77	33.59	39.92	47.73	57.09	65.36	80.16	88.41	97.70	117.60
Claims on Other Banking Insts.	22f	2.12	2.52	3.14	3.71	4.40	5.10	5.77	6.87	11.56	14.67	19.03	23.51	29.16	34.06	38.45
Demand Deposits	24	7.97	9.01	10.61	12.90	15.58	22.17	27.14	32.30	38.90	I44.10	50.71	62.09	76.31	98.74	122.54
Time and Savings Deposits	25	....	....	....	....	....	....	....	....	....	36.45	50.63	61.54	75.27	89.43	103.21
Foreign Liabilities	26c	1.66	1.91	2.21	2.77	4.49	6.18	7.61	11.60	15.27	9.81	11.16	14.24	20.13	24.92	31.04
Credit from Monetary Authorities	26g	.22	.77	1.41	1.62	2.11	.86	.87	1.84	2.10	3.19	2.53	1.02	1.00	.31	3.60
Other Items (Net)	27r	−.06	−.14	−.46	−.79	−1.35	−1.83	−2.87	−4.13	−3.17	2.16	6.42	5.66	9.04	8.29	3.58
Post Office: Checking Deposits	24.. i	.37	.42	.52	.54	.59	.66	.72	1.06	.99	1.21	1.47	1.84	2.53	3.60	5.93
Treasury: Checking Deposits	24.. r	.04	.04	.06	.02	.05	.07	.09	.18	.14	.20	.23	.01	−.04	.20	.26
Post Office: Savings Deposits	25.. i	....	....	....	....	....	....	....	....	....	2.30	2.84	3.36	3.87	4.56	5.43
Savings Certif.	26ab	2.80	3.07	3.33	3.56	3.76	3.78	4.73	5.87	7.12	7.49	9.01	10.73	12.67	15.74	19.31
Monetary Survey																*Trillions of Lire:*
Foreign Assets (Net)	31n	2.86	3.26	3.19	3.84	3.08	3.81	4.31	3.73	3.83	1.73	2.42	7.34	8.76	16.14	24.45
Domestic Credit	32	24.22	27.41	31.03	35.00	40.19	46.67	53.78	64.75	83.08	115.51	140.98	171.34	200.86	238.81	278.60
Claims on Central Govt. (Net)	32an	6.64	7.13	7.31	8.38	9.31	11.64	14.25	17.79	23.59	43.52	56.39	67.45	83.06	106.77	122.25
Claims on Private Sector	32d	15.41	17.69	20.52	22.83	26.35	29.77	33.59	39.92	47.73	57.09	65.36	80.16	88.41	97.70	117.60
Claims on Other Financial Insts.	32f	2.18	2.59	3.20	3.79	4.53	5.26	5.95	7.04	11.76	14.90	19.22	23.73	29.40	34.34	38.74
Money (M1)	34	12.67	14.15	16.43	18.97	22.48	29.89	35.57	42.23	52.46	I56.29	64.97	78.19	94.89	121.55	150.37
Quasi-Money	35	....	....	....	....	....	....	....	....	....	38.75	53.47	64.90	79.14	94.00	108.63
Bonds	36ab	2.80	3.07	3.33	3.56	3.76	3.78	4.73	5.87	7.12	7.49	9.01	10.73	12.67	15.74	19.31
Other Items (Net)	37r	.10	.10	−.22	−.47	−.96	−1.12	−2.28	−3.33	−1.44	14.71	15.94	24.87	22.93	23.67	24.72
Money plus Quasi-Money	35l	27.12	30.65	34.83	39.39	44.32	51.38	60.19	71.64	88.19	100.07	125.75	152.26	185.26	229.65	276.57
Money (National Definitions)																*Trillions of Lire:*
M2	38n	....	....	....	....	....	....	....	....	....	94.61	118.13	142.63	173.56	214.95	258.48
Other Banking Institutions																*Trillions of Lire:*
Specialized Credit Institutions																
Cash	40.. g	.71	.87	.92	.93	.96	1.49	1.95	2.47	4.73	3.66	5.03	5.26	5.21	5.89	5.02
Foreign Assets	41.. g	.11	.22	.34	.44	.72	.88	.89	1.48	3.33	4.82	4.54	5.62	5.34	4.58	2.74
Claims on Central Government	42a. g	1.40	2.27	2.83	3.31	4.41	5.11	6.35	8.09	10.76	11.53	14.31	13.69	14.15	14.40	14.26
Claims on Private Sector	42d. g	8.22	9.35	10.85	12.91	14.66	16.61	19.98	23.30	28.41	31.48	37.50	42.50	54.13	60.56	65.50
Time and Savings Deposits	45.. g	.69	.85	1.03	1.32	1.44	1.61	2.13	2.53	2.92	3.15	4.08	4.27	5.19	6.42	6.70
Bonds	46ab g	5.69	6.64	7.65	8.92	10.23	11.86	14.38	17.16	23.86	26.36	32.78	38.17	43.73	49.44	54.69
Foreign Liabilities	46c. g	.25	.24	.22	.22	.33	.76	.95	1.31	3.11	I4.82	4.42	5.68	5.41	5.08	3.21
Central Government Deposits	46d. g	.79	.87	.99	1.20	1.33	1.44	1.64	1.83	2.09	14.36	16.74	16.81	16.68	16.43	16.30
Cred.from Deposit Money Banks	46h. g	.67	.73	.94	1.10	1.17	1.23	1.33	1.33	1.31	1.36	1.38	1.38	1.56	2.25	2.58
Capital Accounts	47a. g	.50	.61	.72	.85	.98	1.13	1.29	1.46	1.83	2.08	2.40	2.89	3.48	1.74	5.65
Other Items (Net)	47r. g	1.85	2.79	3.39	3.99	5.28	6.05	7.46	.91	1.08	−.40	−.18	−1.91	2.99	4.16	−1.22
Nonbank Financial Institutions																*Trillions of Lire:*
Foreign Assets	41.. s	144	158	189	230	260	313	378	422	528	614	708	907	881	899	981
Claims on Central Government	42a. s	35	42	43	46	45	41	41	40	39	112	71	185	328	548	1,071
Claims on Private Sector	42d. s	558	643	776	905	1,011	1,111	1,197	1,352	1,507	1,552	1,775	1,873	2,209	2,665	3,086
Incr.in Total Assets(Within Per.)	49z. s	259	339	412	28	358	392	547	656	895	955	1,349	1,588	1,390	1,797	4,543
Liquid Liabilities	55l	30.73	34.64	39.30	44.48	49.82	56.68	66.63	79.31	95.56	109.34	136.65	165.36	201.78	250.59	303.00

Italy
136

1980	1981	1982	1983	1984	1985	1986	1987	1988	1989	1990	1991	1992	1993	1994		
End of Period															**Exchange Rates**	
1,186.8	1,396.8	1,511.3	1,737.4	1,897.6	1,843.7	1,661.3	1,658.8	1,757.2	1,669.6	1,607.8	1,646.5	2,022.4	2,340.5	2,379.2	Market Rate	**aa**
End of Period (ae) Period Average (rf)																
930.5	1,200.0	1,370.0	1,659.5	1,935.9	1,678.5	1,358.1	1,169.3	1,305.8	1,270.5	1,130.2	1,151.1	1,470.9	1,704.0	1,629.7	Market Rate	**ae**
856.4	1,136.8	1,352.5	1,518.8	1,757.0	1,909.4	1,490.8	1,296.1	1,301.6	1,372.1	1,198.1	1,240.6	1,232.4	1,573.7	1,612.4	Market Rate	**rf**
End of Period (ea) Period Average (eb)																
1,215.0	1,303.6	1,325.7	1,372.0	1,371.1	1,489.9	1,446.2	1,521.7	1,531.1	1,517.6	1,540.3	1,542.4	1,787.4	1,908.4	1,997.5	ECU Rate	**ea**
1,189.1	1,263.1	1,323.6	1,349.7	1,376.0	1,430.7	1,462.1	1,494.7	1,537.3	1,510.7	1,521.9	1,533.3	1,587.5	1,841.6	1,913.9	ECU Rate	**eb**
Period Averages																
139.9	105.9	88.7	79.0	68.3	62.8	80.5	92.4	92.1	87.2	100.0	96.7	97.5	76.1	74.2	Market Rate	**ah*x***
132.2	119.7	112.4	109.8	105.2	99.8	101.3	101.0	97.6	98.4	100.0	98.6	95.5	80.4	76.9	Nominal Effective Exchange Rate	**ne*u***
89.6	87.5	87.0	92.0	93.6	90.9	92.3	93.2	92.3	96.3	100.0	101.1	99.2	82.5	....	Real Effective Exchange Rate	**re*u***
End of Period															**Fund Position**	
1,860	1,860	1,860	2,909	2,909	2,909	2,909	2,909	2,909	2,909	2,909	2,909	4,591	4,591	4,591	Quota	**2f.*s***
521	673	711	565	645	297	480	668	705	759	729	650	173	175	86	SDRs	**1b.*s***
646	631	631	945	1,096	1,056	1,037	1,020	941	1,099	1,205	1,576	1,774	1,575	1,393	Reserve Position in the Fund	**1c.*s***
—	—	—	—	—	—	—	—	—	—	—	—	—	—	—	*of which:* Outstg.Fund Borrowing	**2c**
—	—	—	—	—	—	—	—	—	—	—	—	—	—	—	Total Fund Cred.&Loans Outstg.	**2tl**
End of Period															**International Liquidity**	
23,126	20,134	14,091	20,105	20,795	15,595	19,987	30,214	34,715	46,720	62,927	48,679	27,643	27,545	32,265	Total Reserves minus Gold	**1l.*d***
665	783	785	591	633	326	587	948	949	998	1,037	930	238	241	125	SDRs	**1b.*d***
823	734	696	990	1,074	1,160	1,268	1,447	1,266	1,444	1,714	2,255	2,439	2,164	2,033	Reserve Position in the Fund	**1c.*d***
21,638	18,617	12,611	18,524	19,088	14,109	18,132	27,819	32,500	44,278	60,176	45,495	24,966	25,140	30,107	Foreign Exchange	**1d.*d***
66.67	66.67	66.67	66.67	66.67	66.67	66.67	66.67	66.67	66.67	66.67	66.67	66.67	66.67	66.67	Gold (Million Fine Troy Ounces)	**1ad**
36,722	28,993	23,685	26,152	21,637	23,558	26,055	34,050	28,521	26,496	24,913	23,230	23,175	23,593	26,342	Gold (National Valuation)	**1an*d***
1,430	1,153	566	514	136	122	210	109	147	315	354	363	5,316	578	....	Monetary Authorities: Other Liab.	**4..*d***
31,467	35,893	32,982	32,973	37,515	47,855	57,718	63,802	62,019	79,981	94,613	99,660	102,141	123,820	114,620	Deposit Money Banks: Assets	**7a.*d***
46,810	48,785	44,477	46,473	51,733	59,737	73,131	88,799	94,197	120,427	139,948	163,721	173,116	147,598	163,664	Liabilities	**7b.*d***
3,027	3,031	3,182	3,381	2,623	2,590	2,814	4,712	4,839	7,634	9,441	11,109	12,428	11,711	12,568	Other Banking Insts.: Assets	**7e.*d***
4,601	5,497	7,528	9,035	10,078	13,094	17,826	25,622	27,974	41,346	65,428	79,344	76,735	69,531	66,874	Liabilities	**7f.*d***
End of Period															**Monetary Authorities**	
57.15	60.49	53.09	78.12	83.45	66.38	62.58	75.45	84.20	94.81	104.94	96.02	76.72	86.57	93.90	Foreign Assets	**11**
50.89	64.33	75.97	77.31	91.14	118.77	129.68	136.41	138.75	145.34	146.35	165.52	204.48	187.00	....	Claims on Central Govt. (Net)	**12an**
.50	.97	2.02	4.79	1.24	6.91	3.55	3.88	4.36	5.28	6.90	7.95	8.51	2.23	2.54	Claims on Deposit Money Banks	**12e**
62.57	70.27	81.37	94.76	108.39	127.59	137.85	150.03	164.03	185.10	200.56	211.28	221.01	201.09	....	Reserve Money	**14**
25.31	29.74	33.26	37.34	41.19	45.20	48.34	52.72	57.17	67.64	69.45	76.35	85.62	89.77	96.22	*of which: Currency Outside DMBs*	**14a**
1.33	1.38	.78	.85	.26	.21	.29	.13	.19	.40	.40	.42	7.82	.99	....	Foreign Liabilities	**16c**
44.64	54.13	48.93	64.59	67.17	64.27	57.68	65.58	63.09	59.93	57.23	57.80	60.88	73.73	....	Other Items (Net)	**17r**
End of Period															**Deposit Money Banks**	
36.49	39.83	47.58	57.08	67.01	81.87	89.41	97.20	106.77	117.38	130.97	134.82	135.33	111.32	....	Reserves	**20**
29.28	43.07	45.19	54.72	72.63	80.32	78.39	74.60	80.98	101.62	106.93	114.72	150.24	210.99	186.80	Foreign Assets	**21**
56.22	60.37	85.59	109.31	118.75	138.03	148.02	149.60	144.81	143.57	146.68	201.26	255.29	274.63	311.34	Claims on Central Government	**22a**
141.11	158.63	176.14	201.93	241.60	269.95	297.24	321.61	375.38	455.28	523.44	607.08	679.54	....	....	Claims on Private Sector	**22d**
43.45	48.36	54.41	57.86	58.96	60.78	63.00	65.83	61.35	58.31	52.12	51.90	53.81	45.75	....	Claims on Other Banking Insts.	**22f**
140.07	153.71	181.73	203.93	230.10	253.80	285.07	308.00	334.81	372.91	402.31	450.37	447.50	477.07	491.91	Demand Deposits	**24**
114.59	126.85	150.84	172.30	190.75	211.30	220.84	234.25	250.24	271.01	301.81	320.43	359.19	393.11	....	Time and Savings Deposits	**25**
43.56	58.54	60.93	77.12	100.15	100.27	99.32	103.83	123.00	153.00	158.16	188.45	254.63	251.50	266.73	Foreign Liabilities	**26c**
.50	.97	2.02	4.79	1.24	6.91	3.55	3.88	4.36	5.28	6.90	7.95	8.51	2.23	2.54	Credit from Monetary Authorities	**26g**
7.85	10.19	13.39	22.76	36.70	58.68	67.26	58.88	56.89	73.96	90.96	142.57	204.39	....	....	Other Items (Net)	**27r**
4.34	5.10	5.86	7.12	7.44	8.76	9.44	10.21	7.70	9.39	7.83	7.02	9.52	9.78	8.49	Post Office: Checking Deposits	**24.. *i***
.11	.25	.56	1.46	1.68	2.56	1.45	1.30	1.46	2.14	3.17	4.21	3.34	2.76	—	Treasury: Checking Deposits	**24.. *r***
6.12	6.70	7.30	7.91	8.57	9.51	11.05	13.43	16.37	19.73	23.59	26.92	29.05	30.83	38.47	Post Office: Savings Deposits	**25.. *i***
22.32	23.65	25.96	29.03	34.36	41.19	50.13	59.87	70.43	80.66	91.01	100.37	107.21	117.68	135.66	Savings Certif.	**26ab**
End of Period															**Monetary Survey**	
41.54	43.63	36.56	54.86	55.66	46.23	41.36	46.09	41.99	43.03	53.31	21.87	-35.50	45.06	....	Foreign Assets (Net)	**31n**
324.88	367.80	432.15	492.02	562.60	650.32	710.81	759.15	817.19	915.36	995.09	1,165.17	1,343.08	....	....	Domestic Credit	**32**
140.01	160.39	201.23	232.14	261.94	318.82	349.77	370.81	379.51	400.84	418.62	505.30	608.89	622.70	....	Claims on Central Govt. (Net)	**32an**
141.11	158.63	176.14	201.93	241.60	269.95	297.24	321.61	375.38	455.28	523.44	607.08	679.54	....	....	Claims on Private Sector	**32d**
43.76	48.78	54.77	57.95	59.07	61.54	63.81	66.72	62.29	59.24	53.03	52.79	54.65	46.54	....	Claims on Other Financial Insts.	**32f**
169.82	188.80	221.42	249.85	280.41	310.31	344.30	372.23	401.13	452.09	482.75	537.95	545.97	579.38	596.61	Money (M1)	**34**
120.72	133.54	158.13	180.21	199.32	220.81	231.89	247.68	266.61	290.75	325.40	347.36	388.23	423.95	....	Quasi-Money	**35**
22.32	23.65	25.96	29.03	34.36	41.19	50.13	59.87	70.43	80.66	91.01	100.37	107.21	117.68	135.66	Bonds	**36ab**
53.56	65.44	63.20	87.79	104.18	124.24	125.86	125.46	121.01	134.89	149.23	201.36	266.17	....	....	Other Items (Net)	**37r**
310.99	343.68	406.96	457.01	511.49	568.95	623.04	677.03	734.90	738.40	801.99	878.10	920.03	968.28	983.70	Money plus Quasi-Money	**35l**
End of Period															**Money (National Definitions)**	
290.05	321.54	378.50	428.99	478.72	529.57	574.86	617.58	663.85	738.40	801.99	878.14	921.03	986.27	1,006.12	*M2*	**38n**
End of Period															**Other Banking Institutions**	
															Specialized Credit Institutions	
5.57	4.30	5.02	4.93	4.96	4.41	4.57	5.15	5.44	5.08	5.48	7.34	5.88	6.85	6.57	Cash	**40..*g***
3.37	4.19	4.80	I 5.61	5.08	4.35	3.82	5.51	6.32	9.70	10.67	12.79	18.28	19.96	20.48	Foreign Assets	**41..*g***
13.61	13.43	18.06	20.53	23.18	23.59	20.60	15.45	16.21	10.81	10.89	11.55	6.74	20.18	14.16	Claims on Central Government	**42a.*g***
74.12	90.89	106.14	113.87	129.90	141.49	158.41	182.12	209.52	246.95	287.53	322.67	358.43	384.23	....	Claims on Private Sector	**42d.*g***
7.44	9.52	18.06	19.26	23.48	25.55	28.26	30.88	43.84	52.80	64.84	72.51	77.15	82.82	74.64	Time and Savings Deposits	**45..*g***
60.98	68.86	77.17	85.13	89.55	95.02	102.19	113.68	121.24	129.58	135.79	153.05	166.22	193.66	212.87	Bonds	**46ab*g***
4.28	6.60	10.31	14.99	19.51	21.98	24.21	I 29.96	36.53	52.53	73.94	91.33	112.87	118.48	108.99	Foreign Liabilities	**46c.*g***
15.86	16.12	16.15	15.70	14.91	14.39	14.84	15.41	15.22	15.82	13.32	12.31	9.58	12.05	....	Central Government Deposits	**46d.*g***
3.44	4.86	4.01	4.31	4.91	5.51	5.37	5.63	5.97	7.33	7.96	6.83	9.37	15.55	20.69	Cred.from Deposit Money Banks	**46h.*g***
6.77	8.36	10.03	12.59	15.32	18.11	21.23	23.61	25.96	28.47	30.87	35.95	36.40	39.52	39.65	Capital Accounts	**47a.*g***
-1.66	-.65	-.83	-7.05	-4.57	-6.73	-8.69	-10.94	-11.26	-13.99	-12.15	-17.62	-22.26	-30.87	....	Other Items (Net)	**47r.*g***
End of Period															Nonbank Financial Institutions	
....	....	....	....	....	....	....	....	....	....	....	....	....	....	....	Foreign Assets	**41.. *s***
....	....	....	....	....	....	....	....	....	....	....	....	....	....	....	Claims on Central Government	**42a. *s***
....	....	....	....	....	....	....	....	....	....	....	....	....	....	....	Claims on Private Sector	**42d. *s***
....	....	....	....	....	....	....	....	....	....	....	....	....	....	....	*Incr.in Total Assets(Within Per.)*	**49z. *s***
341.32	379.26	453.27	508.30	572.93	640.80	707.99	776.16	860.20	886.71	976.02	1,070.65	1,127.86	....	....	Liquid Liabilities	**55l**

Italy

136

		1965	1966	1967	1968	1969	1970	1971	1972	1973	1974	1975	1976	1977	1978	1979
Interest Rates															*Percent Per Annum*	
Discount Rate (End of Period)	60	3.50	3.50	3.50	3.50	4.00	5.50	4.50	4.00	6.50	8.00	6.00	15.00	11.50	10.50	15.00
Money Market Rate	60b	....	....	....	....	5.00	7.38	5.76	5.18	6.93	14.57	10.64	15.68	14.03	11.49	11.86
Treasury Bill Rate	60c	....	....	....	....	....	....	....	....	....	....	....	....	12.34	11.99	12.51
Deposit Rate	60l	....	....	....	....	....	....	....	....	....	....	....	....	....	10.82	10.59
Lending Rate	60p	....	....	....	....	....	....	....	....	....	....	....	....	....	16.05	14.64
Govt. Bond Yield: Long-Term	61	6.94	6.54	6.61	6.70	6.85	9.01	8.34	7.47	7.42	9.87	11.54	13.08	14.62	13.70	14.05
Medium-Term	61b	5.39	5.49	5.59	5.61	5.80	7.73	7.00	6.59	6.92	9.61	10.04	12.66	14.71	13.05	13.02
Prices, Production, Employment															*Index Numbers (1990=100):*	
Share Prices	62	12.3	14.6	13.4	13.2	14.8	14.4	11.2	10.7	13.8	12.6	9.4	8.9	7.2	7.9	10.0
Producer Prices	63	10.0	10.2	10.1	10.1	10.5	11.3	11.7	12.2	14.3	20.1	21.8	26.8	31.4	34.1	39.4
Wholesale Prices	63a	....	....	....	....	....	....	....	....	....	....	....	....	....	....	....
Consumer Prices	64	9.4	9.7	9.8	9.9	10.1	10.7	11.2	11.8	13.1	15.6	18.2	21.3	25.2	28.2	32.4
Wages: Contractual	65ey	4.0	4.2	4.4	4.6	4.9	6.0	6.6	7.3	8.9	10.7	13.8	16.6	21.2	24.7	29.5
Industrial Production	66..c	43.0	48.8	52.8	56.2	58.3	62.3	62.0	64.7	71.0	74.1	67.3	75.7	76.5	78.3	83.3
Industrial Employment	67	104.2	102.8	105.6	106.9	110.6	113.1	114.7	113.0	113.2	116.2	116.2	114.5	115.5	114.3	114.5
International Transactions															*Billions of Lire*	
Exports	70	4,499	5,024	5,441	6,366	7,330	8,253	9,363	10,850	12,971	19,825	22,867	31,170	39,968	47,506	59,927
Imports, cif	71	4,611	5,369	6,143	6,428	7,794	9,359	9,902	11,265	16,225	26,715	25,199	36,730	42,430	47,867	64,598
Imports, fob	71.v	4,196	4,885	5,590	5,849	7,092	8,771	9,010	10,250	15,005	25,038	23,325	34,311	39,639	44,686	60,070
															1990=100	
Volume of Exports	72	21.1	23.8	25.6	30.1	33.3	36.0	38.8	43.6	44.2	47.5	49.3	55.1	59.3	65.7	70.7
Volume of Imports	73	23.1	26.6	30.1	31.3	37.5	43.3	43.5	48.2	53.7	50.7	45.3	52.4	52.2	56.1	63.5
Unit Value of Exports	74	10.5	10.4	10.5	10.4	10.9	11.3	11.9	12.2	14.5	20.5	22.8	27.8	33.2	35.6	41.7
Unit Value of Imports	75	9.4	9.5	9.6	9.7	9.8	10.1	10.6	10.9	14.2	24.4	25.8	32.5	37.7	39.5	47.2
Balance of Payments															*Millions of US Dollars:*	
Goods: Exports f.o.b.	78aa d	....	....	....	....	....	13,216	15,116	18,633	22,259	30,494	35,000	37,271	45,310	56,051	72,217
Goods: Imports f.o.b.	78ab d	....	....	....	....	....	–13,469	–14,819	–18,395	–26,019	–38,559	–35,657	–41,013	–44,928	–52,596	–72,372
Trade Balance	78ac d	....	....	....	....	....	–253	297	238	–3,760	–8,065	–657	–3,742	381	3,455	–155
Services: Credit	78ad d	....	....	....	....	....	4,146	4,558	5,339	6,277	6,910	8,167	8,343	10,630	13,339	17,129
Services: Debit	78ae d	....	....	....	....	....	–3,792	–4,045	–4,613	–5,848	–6,736	–7,970	–7,323	–8,797	–10,615	–13,175
Balance on Goods and Services	78af d	....	....	....	....	....	101	809	964	–3,331	–7,891	–460	–2,722	2,215	6,179	3,798
Income: Credit	78ag d	....	....	....	....	....	1,581	1,799	2,115	2,540	3,329	2,564	2,081	2,585	3,787	5,849
Income: Debit	78ah d	....	....	....	....	....	–1,032	–1,190	–1,470	–2,138	–3,632	–3,059	–2,594	–2,671	–3,429	–4,546
Balance on Goods, Serv., & Inc.	78ai d	....	....	....	....	....	650	1,419	1,609	–2,929	–8,194	–955	–3,236	2,129	6,537	5,101
Current Transfers, n.i.e.: Credit	78aj d	....	....	....	....	....	885	1,241	1,588	1,656	1,277	1,917	1,879	2,299	2,896	4,469
Current Transfers: Debit	78ak d	....	....	....	....	....	–725	–1,047	–1,218	–1,575	–1,362	–1,596	–1,494	–2,085	–3,379	–3,657
Current Account, n.i.e.	78al d	....	....	....	....	....	810	1,613	1,978	–2,848	–8,279	–634	–2,850	2,343	6,054	5,913
Capital Account, n.i.e.: Credit	78ba d	....	....	....	....	....	56	37	15	12	12	14	125	118	88	223
Capital Account: Debit	78bb d	....	....	....	....	....	–24	–24	–15	–19	–67	–98	–77	–86	–82	–260
Capital Account, n.i.e.	78bc d	....	....	....	....	....	32	13	—	–7	–55	–84	48	32	7	–38
Direct Investment Abroad	78bd d	....	....	....	....	....	–114	–405	–221	–275	–204	–342	–160	–560	–160	–539
Dir. Invest. in Rep. Econ., n.i.e.	78be d	....	....	....	....	....	624	552	675	664	597	646	109	1,129	477	416
Portfolio Investment Assets	78bf d	....	....	....	....	....	–523	–189	–708	–715	126	194	271	317	21	49
Portfolio Investment Liab., n.i.e.	78bg d	....	....	....	....	....	....	....	....	....	....	....	....	....	....	....
Other Investment Assets	78bh d	....	....	....	....	....	–4,536	–3,873	–9,492	–7,662	7,050	–4,404	–2,473	–2,998	–9,320	–12,116
Other Investment Liab., n.i.e.	78bi d	....	....	....	....	....	4,200	3,425	5,745	6,616	–881	2,408	7,171	4,895	5,381	7,490
Financial Account, n.i.e.	78bj d	....	....	....	....	....	–349	–492	–4,001	–1,372	6,689	–1,498	4,919	2,781	–3,601	–4,701
Net Errors and Omissions	78ca d	....	....	....	....	....	–265	–236	–531	–535	–1,635	–1,752	–266	420	826	–756
Overall Balance	78cb d	....	....	....	....	....	228	899	–2,553	–4,762	–3,280	–3,968	1,851	5,576	3,286	419
Reserves and Related Items	79da d	....	....	....	....	....	–232	–1,012	2,501	5,148	3,454	4,077	–1,718	–5,598	–3,180	–485
Reserve Assets	79db d	....	....	....	....	....	–232	–1,012	850	122	–375	1,811	–2,075	–5,189	–3,139	–1,830
Use of Fund Credit and Loans	79dc d	....	....	....	....	....	—	—	—	—	1,646	1,295	—	–1,024	–885	–1,142
Liabs.Constit.For.Auth.Reserves	79dd d	....	....	....	....	....	....	....	....	....	....	....	....	....	....	....
Exceptional Financing	79de d	....	....	....	....	....	....	....	1,651	5,026	2,184	971	356	615	844	2,488
Government Finance															*Trillions of Lire:*	
Deficit (–) or Surplus	80	–1.55	–1.83	–1.27	–2.03	–1.72	–3.23	–4.78	–5.89	–8.02	–8.97	–16.47	–14.87	–22.57	–34.31	–30.40
Revenue	81	6.55	6.88	8.05	8.68	9.13	10.37	11.66	12.06	14.08	18.27	23.36	31.55	41.36	52.68	63.49
Expenditure	82	7.39	7.94	8.46	9.46	9.92	12.68	14.88	16.39	19.90	24.95	36.99	42.19	52.87	79.86	90.26
Lending Minus Repayments	83	.71	.77	.86	1.25	.93	.93	1.56	1.56	2.20	2.28	2.83	4.23	11.05	7.12	3.64
Financing																
Net Borrowing: Lire	84b	1.54	1.79	1.23	2.04	1.65	3.14	4.74	5.82	7.91	8.88	16.38	14.85	22.49	33.65	29.67
From: Bank of Italy	84ba	.29	–.08	–.14	.50	1.12	2.74	1.05	1.57	5.03	8.77	7.15	9.93	–4.89	5.05	.37
Coml. & Savings Banks	84bb	.62	.80	.38	.95	–.02	.04	2.47	2.40	1.44	1.83	3.47	–.50	16.99	13.07	8.57
Post Office	84bc	.41	.44	.46	.35	.38	.24	1.14	1.72	1.53	.83	2.31	2.64	3.21	4.87	6.75
Others	84bd	.22	.64	.57	.22	.21	.14	.11	.23	–.12	–.23	1.80	2.56	6.25	10.92	14.07
Net Borrowing: Foreign Currency	85b	—	–.01	—	.01	.03	.06	—	–.03	.13	.02	.03	.20	.08	.27	.58
Monetary Operations	86c	.01	.04	.01	.01	.01	.01	.01	.02	.02	.02	.03	.04	.05	.15	.09
Debt: Lire & Foreign Currency	88	13.38	15.03	16.44	18.46	19.89	22.93	27.94	33.93	42.48	53.71	69.06	85.18	109.92	144.55	175.26
National Accounts															*Trillions of Lire*	
Exports of Goods & Services	90c.c	5.44	6.04	6.65	7.70	8.88	10.00	11.16	12.70	15.23	22.87	26.31	35.89	45.62	54.03	68.32
Government Consumption	91f.c	6.09	6.48	6.93	7.54	8.18	8.88	10.84	12.32	14.18	17.12	19.94	23.96	30.08	36.49	45.73
Gross Fixed Capital Formation	93e.c	7.54	7.97	9.10	10.28	11.75	16.53	17.48	18.47	24.06	31.67	34.57	41.78	50.32	57.66	70.77
Increase/Decrease(–) in Stocks	93i.c	.28	.36	.49	.02	.39	1.88	.72	.72	2.21	5.16	–1.38	5.30	3.04	3.51	5.63
Private Consumption	96f.c	24.88	27.47	30.30	32.27	35.37	40.36	44.09	48.61	59.18	74.46	87.08	107.80	131.90	154.34	189.67
Imports of Goods & Services	98c.c	–5.10	–5.93	–6.78	–7.19	–8.69	–10.49	–11.30	–13.00	–18.13	–29.08	–27.88	–39.86	–46.55	–52.49	–70.29
Gross Domestic Product	99b.c	39.1	42.4	46.7	50.6	55.9	67.2	73.0	79.8	96.7	122.2	138.6	174.9	214.4	253.5	309.8
Net Factor Inc/Pmts(–) Abroad	98.n	.14	.19	.17	.20	.26	.31	.34	.34	.27	–.10	–.42	–.51	–.22	–.02	.85
Gross Nat'l Expenditure = GNP	99a	39.26	42.58	46.86	50.82	56.14	67.49	73.33	80.15	97.01	122.09	138.21	174.36	214.18	253.52	310.68
Nat'l Income, Market Prices	99e	35.98	39.12	43.16	46.85	51.74	58.00	55.51	61.03	75.25	101.71	129.19	157.93	194.42	223.64	264.34
Gross Dom. Prod. 1990 Prices	99b.r	538.38	570.60	611.57	651.60	691.33	728.06	728.32	759.71	813.72	857.90	835.13	887.37	920.12	953.94	1,012.44
GDP Deflator (1990=100)	99bi r	7.3	7.4	7.6	7.8	8.1	9.2	10.0	10.5	11.9	14.2	16.6	19.7	23.3	26.6	30.6
															Millions:	
Population	99z	51.99	52.33	52.67	52.99	53.32	53.66	54.01	54.41	54.80	55.10	55.40	55.70	55.93	56.13	56.29

1980	1981	1982	1983	1984	1985	1986	1987	1988	1989	1990	1991	1992	1993	1994		
Percent Per Annum															**Interest Rates**	
16.50	19.00	18.00	17.00	16.50	15.00	12.00	12.00	12.50	13.50	12.50	12.00	12.00	8.00	7.50	Discount Rate *(End of Period)*	**60**
17.17	19.60	20.16	18.44	17.27	15.25	13.41	11.51	11.29	12.69	12.38	12.18	13.97	10.20	....	Money Market Rate	**60b**
15.92	19.70	19.44	17.90	15.37	13.71	11.40	10.73	11.13	12.58	12.38	12.54	14.32	10.58	9.17	Treasury Bill Rate	**60c**
12.70	14.31	15.28	12.91	10.77	8.09	8.89	7.01	6.69	6.93	6.80	6.64	7.11	6.12	4.78	Deposit Rate	**60l**
19.03	18.36	17.37	22.27	20.38	13.36	15.93	13.58	13.57	14.21	14.08	13.89	15.77	13.86	11.23	Lending Rate	**60p**
16.11	20.56	20.90	18.02	14.95	13.00	10.52	9.68	10.16	10.72	11.51	I 13.18	13.27	11.31	10.56	Govt. Bond Yield: Long-Term	**61**
15.25	19.36	20.22	18.30	15.60	13.71	11.47	10.58	10.54	11.61	11.87	I 13.37	13.67	11.21	10.57	Medium-Term	**61b**
Period Averages															**Prices, Production, Employment**	
16.2	31.1	26.5	28.7	31.6	49.6	104.8	99.6	80.3	99.3	100.0	84.7	70.5	83.5	104.1	Share Prices	**62**
47.3	55.5	63.2	69.3	76.5	82.1	81.4	83.6	87.5	I 93.1	100.0	105.2	107.4	....	....	Producer Prices	**63**
....	....	....	....	....	....	....	....	....	93.1	100.0	105.2	107.4	....	....	Wholesale Prices	**63a**
39.3	47.0	54.7	62.7	69.5	75.9	80.3	84.1	88.4	93.9	100.0	106.3	111.8	116.8	121.5	Consumer Prices	**64**
35.9	44.5	52.3	60.1	66.8	74.2	77.8	82.9	87.9	93.2	100.0	109.8	115.4	119.8	....	Wages: Contractual	**65ey**
87.3	85.5	82.9	80.9	83.5	84.7	88.2	90.5	96.8	100.6	100.0	97.8	97.2	94.4	....	Industrial Production	**66..c**
115.1	113.9	111.4	108.3	103.6	101.3	99.7	98.1	98.5	98.5	100.0	100.8	....	97.2	95.1	Industrial Employment	**67**
Billions of Lire															**International Transactions**	
66,869	87,716	99,596	110,600	130,836	145,888	145,015	150,441	166,380	192,888	203,598	209,739	219,441	263,967	305,758	Exports	**70**
86,215	106,574	117,802	121,078	149,469	167,095	148,196	162,353	180,014	209,910	217,704	225,751	232,200	231,227	270,273	Imports, cif	**71**
80,420	99,752	110,198	113,263	139,821	156,310	138,630	151,874	168,395	196,361	203,652	211,180	217,212	216,302	252,828	Imports, fob	**71.v**
1990=100																
I 65.2	68.0	68.3	70.7	75.3	81.0	82.4	84.1	89.1	96.7	100.0	100.1	103.8	112.3	....	Volume of Exports	**72**
I 65.2	60.9	60.9	60.9	66.4	72.3	75.5	82.7	88.4	95.7	100.0	104.5	108.0	96.0	....	Volume of Imports	**73**
I 50.4	62.0	71.5	76.8	84.1	91.0	86.7	87.7	92.1	97.9	100.0	102.9	103.7	115.4	....	Unit Value of Exports	**74**
I 60.8	78.6	88.5	92.7	103.2	110.9	91.2	90.0	93.6	100.7	100.0	99.2	98.7	....	....	Unit Value of Imports	**75**
Minus Sign Indicates Debit															Balance of Payments	
78,106	77,071	73,791	72,878	74,564	76,717	97,205	116,712	127,859	140,556	170,304	169,465	178,155	169,153	189,805	Goods: Exports f.o.b.	**78aa*d***
-94,018	-88,385	-81,771	-74,588	-79,695	-82,085	-92,158	-116,629	-128,782	-142,219	-168,931	-169,911	-175,070	-136,328	-154,308	Goods: Imports f.o.b.	**78ab*d***
-15,911	-11,314	-7,980	-1,710	-5,132	-5,367	5,047	83	-924	-1,664	1,373	-445	3,085	32,825	35,497	Trade Balance	**78ac*d***
19,192	16,359	16,891	17,723	18,010	19,818	23,669	29,797	30,544	32,452	50,237	49,920	62,743	57,283	59,594	Services: Credit	**78ad*d***
-16,249	-14,488	-14,598	-14,090	-14,726	-16,406	-20,213	-26,334	-29,417	-32,782	-51,391	-50,104	-67,181	-57,233	-58,146	Services: Debit	**78ae*d***
-12,968	-9,443	-5,687	1,922	-1,848	-1,955	8,503	3,546	204	-1,995	219	-629	-1,353	32,875	36,945	Balance on Goods and Services	**78af*d***
7,681	7,842	7,694	6,069	6,648	6,960	8,159	9,193	11,025	14,585	18,684	21,345	27,399	30,310	28,667	Income: Credit	**78ag*d***
-6,402	-9,470	-10,148	-8,579	-9,196	-9,692	-12,398	-14,108	-16,536	-21,906	-33,324	-38,497	-48,006	-46,602	-43,920	Income: Debit	**78ah*d***
-11,690	-11,071	-8,141	-587	-4,395	-4,687	4,263	-1,370	-5,307	-9,315	-14,421	-17,781	-21,960	16,582	21,692	Balance on Goods, Serv., & Inc.	**78ai*d***
5,457	4,839	5,080	5,655	5,775	5,398	6,716	8,790	10,037	10,552	11,386	11,990	11,677	11,179	9,123	Current Transfers, n.i.e.: Credit	**78aj*d***
-4,356	-4,233	-4,317	-4,369	-4,570	-4,795	-8,517	-10,056	-11,910	-14,048	-14,551	-18,857	-18,444	-18,350	-16,222	Current Transfers: Debit	**78ak*d***
-10,589	-10,466	-7,379	699	-3,190	-4,084	2,461	-2,635	-7,180	-12,812	-17,586	-24,649	-28,727	9,411	14,593	Current Account, n.i.e.	**78al*d***
497	380	484	461	530	526	751	984	1,514	1,608	1,822	1,717	2,265	2,801	2,217	Capital Account, n.i.e.: Credit	**78ba*d***
-287	-211	-229	-259	-240	-258	-667	-717	-934	-696	-1,063	-1,129	-1,445	-1,149	-1,188	Capital Account: Debit	**78bb*d***
210	170	255	202	290	268	84	267	580	912	759	588	820	1,652	1,029	Capital Account, n.i.e.	**78bc*d***
-740	-1,392	-1,038	-2,136	-1,979	-1,870	-2,694	-2,366	-5,583	-2,160	-7,585	-7,222	-5,891	-7,409	-5,106	Direct Investment Abroad	**78bd*d***
577	1,127	617	1,190	1,321	1,072	-172	4,175	6,801	2,166	6,411	2,401	3,105	3,749	2,199	Dir. Invest. in Rep. Econ., n.i.e.	**78be*d***
-410	-561	57	-163	-222	-780	-2,216	-3,642	-5,514	-9,098	-19,616	-25,206	-25,480	6,871	-31,400	Portfolio Investment Assets	**78bf*d***
....	....	....	....	....	....	....	....	....	....	....	....	....	....	....	Portfolio Investment Liab., n.i.e.	**78bg*d***
-8,218	-16,114	-1,514	-9,285	-9,572	-5,676	-972	2,076	-10,040	-21,462	-13,373	-14,907	-18,613	-38,809	-4,220	Other Investment Assets	**78bh*d***
21,347	25,374	4,831	13,904	12,970	6,342	6,908	12,343	25,239	43,047	57,542	49,979	36,435	-24,256	-1,293	Other Investment Liab., n.i.e.	**78bi*d***
12,556	8,434	2,953	3,508	2,518	-912	853	12,586	10,902	12,493	23,379	5,044	-10,444	-59,854	-39,820	Financial Account, n.i.e.	**78bj*d***
-859	742	-89	1,071	2,640	-3,891	-2,187	-1,048	-1,695	-1,568	-14,188	-6,871	-7,637	-19,458	243	Net Errors and Omissions	**78ca*d***
1,318	-1,120	-4,259	5,479	2,258	-8,619	1,211	9,169	2,607	-975	-7,636	-25,887	-45,989	-68,249	-23,955	Overall Balance	**78cb*d***
-793	961	4,707	-5,883	-2,578	7,590	-2,329	-5,493	-8,416	-11,270	-11,623	6,718	23,992	3,135	-1,575	Reserves and Related Items	**79da*d***
-793	961	4,707	-5,883	-2,578	7,590	-2,329	-5,493	-8,416	-11,270	-11,623	6,718	23,992	3,135	-1,575	Reserve Assets	**79db*d***
—	—	—	—	—	—	—	—	—	—	—	—	—	—	—	Use of Fund Credit and Loans	**79dc*d***
....	....	....	....	....	....	....	....	....	....	....	....	....	....	....	Liabs.Constit.For.Auth.Reserves	**79dd*d***
....	....	....	....	....	....	....	....	....	....	....	....	....	....	....	Exceptional Financing	**79de*d***
Year Ending December 31															**Government Finance**	
-37.02	-53.30	-72.80	-88.26	-95.69	-122.62	-110.16	-114.25	-125.64	-133.86	-145.27	-152.30	....	....	....	Deficit (-) or Surplus	**80**
89.24	106.83	151.73	177.24	199.26	221.27	253.15	281.15	311.52	353.18	405.98	444.82	....	....	....	Revenue	**81**
118.29	150.93	210.81	249.10	281.76	328.57	350.63	383.42	422.52	471.33	532.46	583.62	....	....	....	Expenditure	**82**
7.97	9.20	13.72	16.40	13.19	15.31	12.68	11.98	14.64	15.71	18.79	13.50	....	....	....	Lending Minus Repayments	**83**
															Financing	
36.32	50.59	69.83	86.02	93.10	118.76	110.39	108.25	121.57	124.68	129.18	145.55	....	....	....	Net Borrowing: Lire	**84b**
12.40	12.66	12.98	2.97	10.99	22.56	9.09	11.19	3.73	2.42	-1.35	1.63	21.69	-22.92	-3.51	From: Bank of Italy	**84ba**
7.45	3.01	26.77	24.67	5.31	11.36	7.29	7.85	....	....	....	....	....	....	....	Coml. & Savings Banks	**84bb**
2.19	2.59	3.68	4.94	6.37	9.07	11.27	12.92	11.00	15.36	12.77	11.70	....	13.12	24.08	Post Office	**84bc**
16.61	31.43	27.10	56.05	67.93	71.75	79.75	80.30	....	....	....	....	....	....	....	Others	**84bd**
.79	2.52	2.57	1.26	2.27	2.94	.86	6.07	4.23	8.40	14.92	5.51	.18	14.44	....	Net Borrowing: Foreign Currency	**85b**
.05	.06	.09	.09	.10	.04	.02	.09	.08	.09	.09	.10	....	....	.10	Monetary Operations	**86c**
212.56	267.51	341.71	432.29	530.82	654.90	766.63	883.94	1,011.74	1,146.28	1,294.86	1,451.56	1,636.78	1,768.06	1,937.35	Debt: Lire & Foreign Currency	**88**
Trillions of Lire															**National Accounts**	
77.26	100.00	114.19	126.87	150.69	169.00	167.19	176.39	193.82	226.60	249.20	256.19	273.30	329.63	378.06	Exports of Goods & Services	**90c. c**
58.06	75.35	88.81	105.17	120.01	135.50	148.36	166.34	186.96	201.38	231.58	253.42	266.93	275.32	284.01	Government Consumption	**91f. c**
94.06	110.68	121.73	134.84	152.60	167.59	177.65	194.10	219.25	241.02	265.95	281.77	288.05	261.95	269.54	Gross Fixed Capital Formation	**93e. c**
10.46	4.15	6.45	3.35	13.90	14.97	10.72	12.40	15.41	13.78	9.42	10.30	4.42	-1.51	9.53	Increase/Decrease(-) in Stocks	**93i. c**
241.36	289.14	342.50	396.14	452.43	507.81	559.55	614.02	676.18	744.55	810.46	885.99	951.01	968.28	1,030.30	Private Consumption	**96f. c**
-93.52	-115.29	-128.56	-132.93	-163.87	-184.29	-163.57	-179.44	-199.78	-233.86	-254.55	-261.09	-276.52	-285.10	-330.65	Imports of Goods & Services	**98c. c**
387.7	464.0	545.1	633.4	725.8	810.6	899.9	983.8	1,091.8	1,193.5	1,312.1	1,426.6	1,507.2	1,550.2	1,641.1	Gross Domestic Product	**99b. c**
.79	-2.19	-4.43	-5.08	-5.48	-6.77	-9.35	-8.75	-10.15	-14.97	-17.46	-25.49	....	....	....	Net Factor Inc/Pmts(-) Abroad	**98.n**
388.46	461.84	542.37	630.96	723.14	806.41	890.49	975.20	1,081.69	1,178.21	1,291.48	1,399.10	....	....	....	Gross Nat'l Expenditure = GNP	**99a**
343.92	405.38	474.21	552.48	633.98	706.32	782.83	858.70	954.49	1,037.65	1,137.23	1,231.56	....	....	....	Nat'l Income, Market Prices	**99e**
1,053.96	1,059.77	1,062.03	1,072.32	1,101.12	1,129.75	1,162.76	1,199.22	1,247.96	1,284.65	1,312.07	1,328.50	1,340.84	....	....	Gross Dom. Prod. 1990 Prices	**99b. *r***
36.8	43.8	51.3	59.1	65.9	71.7	77.4	82.0	87.5	92.9	100.0	107.4	112.4	....	....	GDP Deflator (1990=100)	**99bi *r***
Midyear Estimates																
56.43	56.51	56.64	56.84	57.00	57.14	57.25	57.34	57.44	57.54	57.66	I 57.76	56.86	57.07	57.19	**Population**	**99z**

Jamaica

343

		1965	1966	1967	1968	1969	1970	1971	1972	1973	1974	1975	1976	1977	1978	1979
Exchange Rates																
Market Rate ......aa= ......wa		.714	.717	.831	.839	.833	.836	.851	.925	1.097	1.113	1.064	1.056	1.104	2.208	2.347
															Jamaica Dollars per US Dollar:	
Market Rate ......ae= ......we		.714	.717	.831	.839	.833	.836	.784	.852	.909	.909	.909	.909	.909	1.695	1.781
Market Rate ......rf= ......wf		.714	.714	.724	.833	.833	.833	.833	.767	.902	.909	.909	.909	.909	1.413	1.765
Fund Position															*Millions of SDRs:*	
Quota	2f.s	20.0	30.0	30.0	30.0	38.0	53.0	53.0	53.0	53.0	53.0	53.0	53.0	53.0	74.0	74.0
SDRs	1b.s	—	—	—	—	—	6.4	12.8	6.9	6.4	5.1	4.3	.8	14.3	4.5	.4
Reserve Position in the Fund	1c.s	4.8	7.3	7.3	7.3	9.3	9.5	13.3	—	—	—	—	—	—	—	—
Total Fund Cred.&Loans Outstg.	2tl	—	—	—	—	—	—	—	—	13.3	13.3	13.3	68.9	88.1	138.6	266.8
International Liquidity											*Millions of US Dollars Unless Otherwise Indicated:*					
Total Reserves minus Gold	1l.d	95.8	87.6	85.0	120.2	117.9	139.2	179.1	159.7	127.4	190.4	125.6	32.4	47.8	58.8	63.8
SDRs	1b.d	—	—	—	—	—	6.4	13.9	7.5	7.7	6.3	5.0	.9	17.4	5.8	.5
Reserve Position in the Fund	1c.d	4.8	7.3	7.3	7.3	9.3	9.5	14.4	—	—	—	—	—	—	—	—
Foreign Exchange	1d.d	91.0	80.3	77.7	112.9	108.6	123.3	150.8	152.2	119.7	184.1	120.6	31.5	30.4	53.0	63.3
Other Official Insts.: Assets	3b.d	....	3.2	1.9	2.2	2.0	1.8	2.1	2.8	5.3	14.1	33.5	1.4	.8	1.2	1.1
Monetary Authorities: Other Liab.	4..d										20.0	51.2	116.6	132.7	205.8	161.8
Deposit Money Banks: Assets	7a.d	14.6	16.1	11.0	2.9	8.8	19.6	22.9	30.4	51.4	44.0	38.2	36.3	40.1	32.2	28.4
of which: Claims on Nonbanks	7ad d	....	....	....	....	....	....	....	....	1.3	1.3	2.6	1.4	1.2	4.4	5.3
Deposit Money Banks: Liabilities	7b.d	45.4	33.6	19.9	17.6	34.7	45.5	31.8	71.1	125.9	111.4	109.7	115.2	119.0	73.5	67.1
of which: Liab. to Nonbanks	7bd d	....	....	....	....	....	....	....	....	44.3	52.2	55.0	56.2	58.2	38.6	38.2
Other Banking Insts.: Liabilities	7f.d	....	....	....	....	....	.9	13.2	22.6	24.5	45.1	63.3	49.5	38.9	31.4	31.3
Monetary Authorities														*Millions of Jamaica Dollars:*		
Foreign Assets	11	50	63	71	100	98	116	138	118	117	174	115	35	44	99	122
Claims on Central Government	12a	10	8	5	5	5	7	11	33	51	72	204	505	469	616	1,347
Claims on Deposit Money Banks	12e	—	—	—	2	5	6	7	10	32	46	11	16	6	10	18
Reserve Money	14	37	43	46	66	63	75	96	109	140	170	202	234	273	302	362
of which: Currency Outside DMBs	14a	24	26	28	32	37	46	58	72	82	102	127	138	182	173	220
Foreign Liabilities	16c	—	—	—	—	—	—	—	—	15	33	61	179	218	655	914
Central Government Deposits	16d	19	22	24	37	42	40	39	27	21	74	58	138	50	15	119
Capital Accounts	17a	5	6	7	7	7	12	17	23	26	28	27	35	36	44	65
Other Items (Net)	17r	—	–1	–1	–2	–3	2	4	3	–2	–12	–18	–30	–57	–290	27
Deposit Money Banks														*Millions of Jamaica Dollars:*		
Reserves	20	13	17	19	37	29	30	39	40	58	70	70	95	93	198	156
Foreign Assets	21	10	12	9	2	7	16	18	23	47	40	35	33	36	55	51
Claims on Central Government	22a	23	26	33	50	49	63	76	79	74	77	107	133	288	355	384
Claims on Nonfin.Pub.Enterprises	22c	....	....	....	....	....	....	....	....	35	33	47	58	92	105	129
Claims on Private Sector	22d	127	135	146	174	245	280	326	416	471	549	641	622	544	654	775
Claims on Other Banking Insts.	22f	2	—	1	—	—	1	—	9	5	9	4	16	3	13	—
Demand Deposits	24	40	46	48	63	74	80	102	101	I 136	156	195	200	292	397	410
Time and Savings Deposits	25	104	122	137	176	214	252	311	356	I 359	428	506	558	570	665	793
Foreign Liabilities	26c	32	24	17	15	29	38	24	55	I 114	101	100	105	108	125	120
Central Government Deposits	26d	4	5	4	4	6	5	4	3	9	10	10	13	13	17	32
Capital Accounts	27a	—	—	9	10	11	16	22	36	69	109	119	115	104	141	158
Other Items (Net)	27r	....	....	....	....	....	....	....	....	2	–26	–25	–34	–32	35	–18
Monetary Survey														*Millions of Jamaica Dollars:*		
Foreign Assets (Net)	31n	28	50	63	88	77	94	131	87	I 34	80	–11	–215	–246	–626	–861
Domestic Credit	32	143	146	165	203	265	318	385	528	610	667	950	1,201	1,348	1,735	2,527
Claims on Central Govt. (Net)	32an	11	7	11	14	5	25	44	82	95	66	243	487	693	939	1,581
Claims on Local Government	32b	....	....	....	....	....	....	....	....	—	1	3	3	3	3	10
Claims on Nonfin.Pub.Enterprises	32c	....	....	....	....	....	....	....	....	35	33	47	58	92	105	129
Claims on Private Sector	32d	127	135	146	174	245	281	329	420	475	558	650	630	552	663	785
Claims on Other Banking Insts.	32f	2	—	1	—	—	1	—	9	5	9	7	23	8	25	22
Money	34	64	71	76	95	111	127	160	173	I 218	258	322	339	474	570	629
Quasi-Money	35	104	122	137	176	214	252	311	356	I 359	428	506	558	570	665	793
Other Items (Net)	37r	4	3	16	19	17	34	45	87	67	60	111	89	58	–125	243
Money plus Quasi-Money	35l	168	193	212	271	325	379	471	528	I 578	687	828	897	1,044	1,235	1,422
Other Banking Institutions														*Millions of Jamaica Dollars:*		
Reserves	40	....	....	....	....	....	—	—	1	—	—	—	—	—	—	—
Claims on Central Government	42a	....	....	....	....	....	....	....	....	....	....	....	—	8	5	23
Claims on Private Sector	42d	....	....	....	....	....	11	23	43	92	136	160	159	141	168	169
Claims on Deposit Money Banks	42e	....	....	....	....	....	6	10	31	29	98	73	61	54	66	50
Demand Deposits	44	....	....	....	....	....	—	—	—	7	95	—	—	—	—	—
Time and Savings Deposits	45	....	....	....	....	....	14	21	53	81	86	135	133	101	119	116
Foreign Liabilities	46c	....	....	....	....	....	1	10	17	21	41	56	44	34	52	54
Credit from Deposit Money Banks	46h	....	....	....	....	....	1	—	2	3	—	6	10	27	24	39
Capital Accounts	47a	....	....	....	....	....	2	3	5	6	6	14	14	15	15	17
Other Items (Net)	47r	....	....	....	....	....	–1	–1	–2	2	6	22	20	26	29	17
Banking Survey														*Millions of Jamaica Dollars:*		
Foreign Assets (Net)	51n	....	....	....	....	....	94	122	70	13	39	–66	–259	–278	–676	–911
Domestic Credit	52	....	....	....	....	....	....	....	....	698	795	1,103	1,338	1,488	1,883	2,697
Claims on Central Govt. (Net)	52an	....	....	....	....	....	25	44	82	95	66	243	487	701	944	1,604
Claims on Local Government	52b	....	....	....	....	....	....	....	....	—	1	3	3	3	3	10
Claims on Nonfin.Pub.Enterprises	52c	....	....	....	....	....	....	....	....	35	33	47	58	92	105	129
Claims on Private Sector	52d	....	....	....	....	....	292	352	463	567	694	810	789	692	831	954
Liquid Liabilities	55l	....	....	....	....	....	393	492	581	I 667	868	962	1,030	1,145	1,353	1,538
Capital Accounts	57a	....	....	....	....	....	30	41	64	101	142	161	163	154	200	240
Other Items (Net)	57r	....	....	....	....	....	....	....	....	–56	–176	–86	–114	–89	–347	7

Jamaica

343

1980	1981	1982	1983	1984	1985	1986	1987	1988	1989	1990	1991	1992	1993	1994		
End of Period															**Exchange Rates**	
2.272	2.074	1.965	3.432	4.832	6.019	6.703	7.803	7.374	8.516	11.435	30.744	30.504	44.606	48.469	Market Rate aa=	**wa**
End of Period (we) Period Average (wf)																
1.781	1.781	1.781	3.278	4.930	5.480	5.480	5.500	5.480	6.480	8.038	21.493	22.185	32.475	33.202	Market Rate ae=	**we**
1.781	1.781	1.781	1.932	3.943	5.559	5.478	5.487	5.489	5.745	7.184	12.116	22.960	24.949	33.086	Market Rate rf=	**wf**
End of Period															**Fund Position**	
111.0	111.0	111.0	111.0	145.5	145.5	145.5	145.5	145.5	145.5	145.5	145.5	200.9	200.9	200.9	Quota	**2f.*s***
—	1.1	.1	—	—	—	.3	1.0	—	—	.3	—	9.0	9.1	—	SDRs	**1b.*s***
—	2.4	3.8	—	—	—	—	—	—	—	—	—	—	—	—	Reserve Position in the Fund	**1c.*s***
242.5	403.5	528.4	599.1	641.4	631.1	554.4	478.2	358.8	291.8	250.7	273.6	259.7	244.2	217.6	Total Fund Cred.&Loans Outstg.	**2tl**
End of Period															**International Liquidity**	
105.0	85.2	109.0	63.2	96.9	161.3	98.4	174.3	147.2	107.5	168.2[e]	106.1	324.1	417.0	735.9	Total Reserves minus Gold	**1l.*d***
—	1.3	.1	—	—	—	.4	1.4	—	—	.5	.1	12.3	12.4	—	SDRs	**1b.*d***
—	2.8	4.1	—	—	—	—	—	—	—	—	—	—	—	—	Reserve Position in the Fund	**1c.*d***
105.0	81.1	104.7	63.2	96.9	161.3	98.0	172.9	147.2	107.5	167.7[e]	106.0	311.8	404.6	735.9	Foreign Exchange	**1d.*d***
.8	10.8	14.5	—	37.1	37.6	49.4	54.1	59.7	52.9	....	....	14.9	17.5	8.3	Other Official Insts.: Assets	**3b.*d***
320.2	411.4	415.0	834.6	529.7	668.4	611.3	493.9	535.1	523.4	492.1	232.0	109.8	65.1	58.2	Monetary Authorities: Other Liab.	**4..*d***
37.8	45.8	60.8	82.4	56.7	59.9	62.1	66.1	99.0	122.2	113.0	236.2	307.0	292.6	449.5	Deposit Money Banks: Assets	**7a.*d***
13.1	11.7	10.2	16.0	1.8	1.4	1.6	1.5	5.2	12.1	14.3	9.5	53.2	69.6	104.1	*of which:* Claims on Nonbanks	**7ad*d***
65.1	91.5	94.7	53.7	48.2	71.1	81.0	104.1	155.4	161.5	138.4	204.0	253.4	238.3	393.2	Deposit Money Banks: Liabilities	**7b.*d***
44.1	59.6	74.9	46.6	41.7	50.2	62.0	85.2	103.9	86.0	91.5	115.3	155.5	182.0	206.3	*of which:* Liab. to Nonbanks	**7bd*d***
8.0	12.8	12.6	4.7	.1	.1	—	—	.6	.3	3.5	.7	.1	3.9	53.8	Other Banking Insts.: Liabilities	**7f.*d***
End of Period															**Monetary Authorities**	
200	324	203	244	475	1,087	573	930	806	692	1,352	2,311	6,912	12,618	24,506	Foreign Assets	**11**
1,539	1,989	2,235	3,164	3,919	3,598	4,294	2,829	2,940	3,343	3,316	2,614	2,562	7,055	7,466	Claims on Central Government	**12a**
64	10	15	—	49	47	38	—	150	127	12	—	—	—	—	Claims on Deposit Money Banks	**12e**
510	489	433	744	1,427	1,926	2,285	2,736	3,752	4,604	5,321	6,820	12,859	18,588	24,969	Reserve Money	**14**
260	282	316	375	436	540	729	844	1,288	1,378	1,640	2,632	3,741	5,228	7,118	*of which: Currency Outside DMBs*	**14a**
1,121	1,570	1,778	4,792	5,711	7,462	7,066	6,448	5,578	5,876	6,822	13,398	10,357	13,007	12,480	Foreign Liabilities	**16c**
406	243	349	448	833	1,349	1,855	2,261	3,707	4,452	6,410	9,188	12,682	17,255	26,532	Central Government Deposits	**16d**
79	88	84	143	200	248	276	321	303	350	468	1,252	1,243	1,815	1,972	Capital Accounts	**17a**
-314	-66	-192	-2,719	-3,730	-6,253	-6,577	-8,007	-9,444	-11,121	-14,341	-25,734	-27,668	-30,993	-33,981	Other Items (Net)	**17r**
End of Period															**Deposit Money Banks**	
392	302	59	372	1,015	1,304	2,340	2,323	3,270	3,838	4,273	5,059	11,113	13,681	18,794	Reserves	**20**
67	82	108	270	280	328	340	364	543	792	908	5,076	6,810	9,501	14,924	Foreign Assets	**21**
378	553	705	794	744	1,069	1,920	2,049	1,977	1,150	1,539	1,843	8,134	7,580	16,967	Claims on Central Government	**22a**
195	274	330	368	380	558	157	276	285	423	335	222	159	730	1,016	Claims on Nonfin.Pub.Enterprises	**22c**
904	1,231	1,683	2,123	2,483	2,602	3,109	4,046	5,549	7,290	8,583	11,940	14,358	23,326	32,164	Claims on Private Sector	**22d**
—	11	21	74	123	125	71	10	82	86	66	233	488	281	686	Claims on Other Banking Insts.	**22f**
457	492	560	691	882	980	1,410	1,407	2,157	1,775	2,376	5,185	9,650	11,675	14,134	Demand Deposits	**24**
996	1,422	1,897	2,461	2,878	3,718	4,548	5,275	6,513	7,460	8,875	11,698	20,908	29,725	44,300	Time and Savings Deposits	**25**
116	163	169	176	237	390	444	572	852	1,046	1,113	4,384	5,622	7,740	13,055	Foreign Liabilities	**26c**
35	45	44	88	101	141	139	206	262	366	378	563	1,814	2,304	6,529	Central Government Deposits	**26d**
182	205	224	327	490	522	788	958	1,232	1,560	1,876	2,510	3,902	5,139	8,615	Capital Accounts	**27a**
151	125	13	257	435	235	609	649	690	1,371	1,087	32	-834	-1,484	-2,080	Other Items (Net)	**27r**
End of Period															**Monetary Survey**	
-970	-1,327	-1,635	-4,454	-5,194	-6,436	-6,596	-5,727	-5,081	-5,440	-5,675	-10,396	-2,257	1,372	13,895	Foreign Assets (Net)	**31n**
2,649	3,797	4,605	6,012	6,736	6,482	7,597	6,808	7,006	7,616	7,227	7,273	11,378	19,442	25,473	Domestic Credit	**32**
1,476	2,255	2,548	3,422	3,729	3,178	4,220	2,411	948	-325	-1,932	-5,294	-3,800	-4,924	-8,627	Claims on Central Govt. (Net)	**32an**
6	2	7	6	5	4	—	—	—	—	—	—	—	—	6	Claims on Local Government	**32b**
195	274	330	368	380	558	157	276	285	423	335	222	159	730	1,016	Claims on Nonfin.Pub.Enterprises	**32c**
914	1,241	1,692	2,135	2,494	2,613	3,146	4,046	5,689	7,430	8,756	12,113	14,531	23,355	32,391	Claims on Private Sector	**32d**
59	26	29	81	128	129	74	76	84	88	68	233	488	281	686	Claims on Other Banking Insts.	**32f**
717	775	876	1,066	1,319	1,520	2,140	2,252	3,445	3,153	4,016	7,818	13,391	16,903	21,252	Money	**34**
996	1,422	1,897	2,461	2,878	3,718	4,548	5,275	6,513	7,460	8,875	11,698	20,908	29,725	44,300	Quasi-Money	**35**
-32	273	197	-1,969	-2,656	-5,192	-5,687	-6,446	-8,032	-8,436	-11,338	-22,638	-25,178	-25,814	-26,184	Other Items (Net)	**37r**
1,712	2,197	2,773	3,527	4,197	5,238	6,687	7,527	9,958	10,612	12,891	19,516	34,299	46,628	65,552	Money plus Quasi-Money	**35l**
End of Period															**Other Banking Institutions**	
—	—	—	2	—	12	45	71	187	196	257	406	870	1,396	1,276	Reserves	**40**
9	7	10	7	9	52	103	214	328	334	323	471	832	312	1,681	Claims on Central Government	**42a**
134	170	258	347	476	615	768	1,122	1,843	2,724	3,149	4,257	6,902	7,468	7,627	Claims on Private Sector	**42d**
55	57	42	77	130	96	103	100	115	153	409	332	1,019	686	1,148	Claims on Deposit Money Banks	**42e**
1	3	—	10	12	—	19	—	—	—	—	—	—	—	—	Demand Deposits	**44**
129	158	242	362	483	771	917	1,403	2,140	2,635	2,929	3,229	6,580	7,306	6,998	Time and Savings Deposits	**45**
14	22	10	—	—	—	—	—	—	—	—	—	—	—	—	Foreign Liabilities	**46c**
17	22	36	30	113	65	120	41	117	336	402	661	843	949	1,312	Credit from Deposit Money Banks	**46h**
18	19	25	29	54	67	90	125	198	202	252	491	1,189	1,738	2,521	Capital Accounts	**47a**
18	10	-3	2	-47	-129	-127	-61	19	233	555	1,085	1,011	-132	902	Other Items (Net)	**47r**
End of Period															**Banking Survey**	
-983	-1,348	-1,645	-4,453	-5,193	-6,434	-6,594	-5,727	-5,068	-5,424	-5,651	-10,341	-2,090	1,432	15,028	Foreign Assets (Net)	**51n**
2,733	3,948	4,845	6,285	7,092	7,020	8,395	8,069	9,093	10,586	10,631	11,768	18,624	26,940	34,095	Domestic Credit	**52**
1,485	2,262	2,558	3,429	3,737	3,230	4,324	2,626	1,276	9	-1,609	-4,824	-2,968	-4,612	-6,946	Claims on Central Govt. (Net)	**52an**
6	2	7	6	5	4	—	—	—	—	—	—	—	—	6	Claims on Local Government	**52b**
195	274	330	368	380	558	157	276	285	423	335	222	159	730	1,016	Claims on Nonfin.Pub.Enterprises	**52c**
1,047	1,411	1,950	2,482	2,971	3,228	3,914	5,167	7,532	10,154	11,904	16,370	21,433	30,823	40,018	Claims on Private Sector	**52d**
1,842	2,358	3,015	3,897	4,692	5,997	7,579	8,859	11,910	13,051	15,563	22,339	40,008	52,538	71,273	Liquid Liabilities	**55l**
279	312	333	500	744	838	1,154	1,403	1,733	2,113	2,596	4,254	6,334	8,692	13,108	Capital Accounts	**57a**
-371	-70	-148	-2,564	-3,537	-6,249	-6,932	-7,920	-9,618	-10,003	-13,180	-25,166	-29,808	-32,859	-35,259	Other Items (Net)	**57r**

Jamaica
343

		1965	1966	1967	1968	1969	1970	1971	1972	1973	1974	1975	1976	1977	1978	1979
Interest Rates															*Percent Per Annum*	
Bank Rate *(End of Period)*	60	5.00	5.50	6.00	5.00	6.00	6.00	5.00	6.00	7.00	9.00	8.00	9.00	9.00	9.00	9.00
Treasury Bill Rate	60c	4.39	4.65	4.68	4.47	3.52	4.03	3.81	4.32	5.54	7.19	6.94	7.23	7.21	8.26	9.25
Deposit Rate	60l	...	...	...	...	...	...	...	...	...	...	...	10.78	7.08	5.68	8.28
Lending Rate	60p	...	...	...	...	...	...	...	...	...	...	...	13.76	13.86	13.68	13.81
Government Bond Yield	61	6.95	7.08	7.21	7.25	7.40	7.83	8.35	8.35	8.81	10.41	11.10	11.60	11.70	11.70	12.28
Prices and Production															*Index Numbers (1990=100):*	
Industrial Share Prices	62	...	...	...	...	4.4	3.8	3.7	4.8	4.5	3.6	3.5	2.5	1.9	1.7	2.2
Consumer Prices	64	3.5	3.6	3.7	3.9	4.1	4.7	5.0	5.3	6.2	7.9	9.3	10.2	11.3	15.3	19.7
Industrial Production	66	...	...	...	...	...	...	...	...	...	...	...	...	...	...	...
International Transactions															*Millions of Jamaica Dollars*	
Exports	70	153.1	162.9	163.3	183.0	211.8	284.8	282.7	300.1	354.6	549.1	690.2	572.8	698.6	1,142.5	1,445.8
Imports, cif	71	206.5	233.7	252.6	320.3	363.3	437.8	459.8	489.3	615.1	850.8	1,021.4	829.8	781.6	1,260.0	1,754.4
Imports, fob	71.v	182.0	203.6	218.1	275.9	312.5	376.5	395.5	420.8	529.0	737.5	881.5	719.6	606.1	1,092.9	1,544.1
															1990=100	
Volume of Exports	72	81.0	84.3	82.3	79.5	90.8	107.4	107.4	113.9	123.5	82.6	109.6	96.5	104.4	105.5	103.2
Balance of Payments															*Millions of US Dollars:*	
Goods: Exports f.o.b.	78aa d	...	...	...	...	...	...	...	...	...	...	...	656.4	737.8	831.1	818.2
Goods: Imports f.o.b.	78ab d	...	...	...	...	...	...	...	...	...	...	...	−791.6	−666.7	−750.1	−882.5
Trade Balance	78ac d	...	...	...	...	...	...	...	...	...	...	...	−135.2	71.1	81.0	−64.3
Services: Credit	78ad d	...	...	...	...	...	...	...	...	...	...	...	232.7	217.2	285.4	351.8
Services: Debit	78ae d	...	...	...	...	...	...	...	...	...	...	...	−332.8	−257.0	−299.7	−339.5
Balance on Goods and Services	78af d	...	...	...	...	...	...	...	...	...	...	...	−235.3	31.3	66.7	−52.0
Income: Credit	78ag d	...	...	...	...	...	...	...	...	...	...	...	53.8	52.0	53.3	50.9
Income: Debit	78ah d	...	...	...	...	...	...	...	...	...	...	...	−127.0	−145.5	−195.8	−217.9
Balance on Goods, Serv., & Inc.	78ai d	...	...	...	...	...	...	...	...	...	...	...	−308.5	−62.2	−75.8	−219.0
Current Transfers, n.i.e.: Credit	78aj d	...	...	...	...	...	...	...	...	...	...	...	94.2	92.3	93.3	152.7
Current Transfers: Debit	78ak d	...	...	...	...	...	...	...	...	...	...	...	−49.5	−42.8	−39.2	−40.2
Current Account, n.i.e.	78al d	...	...	...	...	...	...	...	...	...	...	...	−263.8	−12.7	−21.7	−106.5
Capital Account, n.i.e.: Credit	78ba d	...	...	...	...	...	...	...	...	...	...	...	...	...	...	...
Capital Account: Debit	78bb d	...	...	...	...	...	...	...	...	...	...	...	−38.8	−29.4	−28.3	−32.4
Capital Account, n.i.e.	78bc d	...	...	...	...	...	...	...	...	...	...	...	−38.8	−29.4	−28.3	−32.4
Direct Investment Abroad	78bd d	...	...	...	...	...	...	...	...	...	...	...	...	...	...	...
Dir. Invest. in Rep. Econ., n.i.e.	78be d	...	...	...	...	...	...	...	...	...	...	...	−.6	−9.7	−26.6	−26.4
Portfolio Investment Assets	78bf d	...	...	...	...	...	...	...	...	...	...	...	3.8	—	—	—
Portfolio Investment Liab., n.i.e.	78bg d	...	...	...	...	...	...	...	...	...	...	...	—	—	—	—
Other Investment Assets	78bh d	...	...	...	...	...	...	...	...	...	...	...	13.1	.1	2.5	.1
Other Investment Liab., n.i.e.	78bi d	...	...	...	...	...	...	...	...	...	...	...	19.7	−17.1	−118.3	18.4
Financial Account, n.i.e.	78bj d	...	...	...	...	...	...	...	...	...	...	...	36.0	−26.7	−142.4	−7.9
Net Errors and Omissions	78ca d	...	...	...	...	...	...	...	...	...	...	...	43.5	−1.1	35.8	−4.2
Overall Balance	78cb d	...	...	...	...	...	...	...	...	...	...	...	−223.1	−69.9	−156.6	−151.0
Reserves and Related Items	79da d	...	...	...	...	...	...	...	...	...	...	...	223.1	69.9	156.6	151.0
Reserve Assets	79db d	...	...	...	...	...	...	...	...	...	...	...	119.9	−8.4	−9.8	−.4
Use of Fund Credit and Loans	79dc d	...	...	...	...	...	...	...	...	...	...	...	64.4	22.5	63.3	165.8
Liabs.Constit.For.Auth.Reserves	79dd d	...	...	...	...	...	...	...	...	...	...	...	22.0	20.0	3.0	−6.2
Exceptional Financing	79de d	...	...	...	...	...	...	...	...	...	...	...	16.8	35.8	100.1	−8.2
Government Finance															*Millions of Jamaica Dollars:*	
Deficit (−) or Surplus	80	...	...	...	...	...	...	...	...	...	...	−253.0	−394.9	−496.5	−514.1	−542.6
Revenue	81	...	...	...	...	...	...	...	...	...	...	682.0	709.9	734.1	1,129.7	1,149.9
Grants Received	81z	...	...	...	...	...	...	...	...	...	...	—	—	—	—	—
Expenditure	82	...	...	...	...	...	...	...	...	...	...	805.6	946.2	1,064.5	1,427.7	1,426.4
Lending Minus Repayments	83	...	...	...	...	...	...	...	...	...	...	129.4	158.6	166.1	216.1	266.1
Debt: Domestic	88a	...	...	...	...	...	...	...	...	...	...	...	...	...	...	...
Foreign	89a	...	...	...	...	...	...	...	...	...	...	...	...	...	...	...
National Accounts															*Millions of Jamaica Dollars*	
Exports of Goods & Services	90c	258	306	315	345	365	389	434	472	543	770	917	783	928	1,575	2,065
Government Consumption	91f	70	77	90	105	103	137	159	197	280	386	477	562	612	750	825
Gross Fixed Capital Formation	93e	124	146	170	221	315	367	356	367	448	478	610	451	350	499	748
Increase/Decrease(−) in Stocks	93i	5	6	7	9	34	2	56	27	94	47	60	40	12	63	74
Private Consumption	96f	469	500	532	571	608	713	803	968	1,063	1,469	1,723	1,887	2,030	2,387	2,714
Imports of Goods & Services	98c	−290	−344	−369	−430	−432	−438	−525	−591	−707	−991	−1,186	−1,022	−972	−1,525	−2,133
Gross Domestic Product	99b	636	691	745	820	993	1,171	1,282	1,439	1,720	2,159	2,601	2,702	2,960	3,749	4,293
Net Factor Inc/Pmts(−) Abroad	98.n	−19	−56	−52	−46	−51	−51	−74	−25	−27	52	20	−69	−98	−152	−257
Gross Nat'l Expenditure = GNP	99a	617	635	693	774	941	1,120	1,208	1,414	1,693	2,211	2,620	2,632	2,862	3,598	4,037
Gross Dom. Prod. 1990 Prices	99b.p	20,002	20,786	21,317	22,607	24,077	25,941	27,075	29,200	30,013	28,393	28,055	26.298	25,674	25,859	25,388
GDP Deflator (1990=100)	99bi p	3.2	3.3	3.5	3.6	4.1	4.5	4.7	4.9	5.7	7.6	9.3	10.3	11.5	14.5	16.9
															Millions:	
Population	99z	1.76	1.78	1.81	1.83	1.84	1.87	1.90	1.93	1.97	2.01	2.04	2.07	2.09	2.10	2.11

Exchange Rates: On September 8, 1969 the Jamaican dollar, equal to one half the Jamaican pound, was introduced.
International Liquidity: ⌶ Beginning in 1966, data for *line 1d.d* exclude foreign assets of sinking funds.
Deposit Money Banks: ⌶ Prior to November 1973, *Demand Deposits* and *Time and Savings Deposits* include nonresident deposits. Beginning with that date, nonresident deposits are included in *Foreign Liabilities*.
Monetary Survey: ⌶ See note to section 20.
Banking Survey: ⌶ See note to section 20.

Jamaica

343

1980	1981	1982	1983	1984	1985	1986	1987	1988	1989	1990	1991	1992	1993	1994		
Percent Per Annum															**Interest Rates**	
11.00	11.00	11.00	11.00	16.00	21.00	21.00	21.00	21.00	21.00	21.00	....	....	....	....	Bank Rate (End of Period)	60
9.97	9.83	8.61	12.38	13.29	19.03	20.88	18.16	18.50	19.10	26.21	25.56	34.36	28.85	42.98	Treasury Bill Rate	60c
9.53	10.55	10.71	13.60	15.86	19.58	18.76	15.64	15.80	15.95	23.88	24.67	33.63	27.59	36.41	Deposit Rate	60l
15.63	16.07	16.44	16.97	18.53	24.92	27.34	25.45	25.19	25.22	30.50	31.51	44.81	43.71	49.46	Lending Rate	60p
13.61	13.68	13.68	15.16	17.14	22.48	22.62	20.83	20.40	20.17	25.46	26.33	30.50	23.76	26.82	Government Bond Yield	61
Period Averages															**Prices and Production**	
2.7	5.4	8.3	10.7	16.5	27.0	51.3	78.9	64.2	92.6	100.0	232.6	540.3	973.4	663.5	Industrial Share Prices	62
25.1	28.3	30.1	33.6	42.9	54.0	62.1	66.2	‡71.7	82.0	100.0	151.1	267.8	327.0	441.6	Consumer Prices	64
....	....	....	....	....	....	75.2	80.2	80.1	93.0	100.0	....	....	....	....	Industrial Production	66
Millions of Jamaica Dollars															**International Transactions**	
1,715.0	1,735.1	1,367.0	1,392.1	2,732.5	3,128.3	3,225.9	3,873.6	4,830.3	5,746.6	8,305.0	13,079.0	24,099.0	26,361.0	....	Exports	70
2,086.6	2,623.4	2,460.3	2,841.0	4,509.5	6,146.7	5,322.4	6,790.5	7,983.2	10,668.3	13,923.0	20,830.0	38,267.0	52,847.0	....	Imports, cif	71
1,840.4	2,270.2	2,153.5	2,493.4	3,952.3	5,396.6	4,672.9	5,961.8	7,009.0	9,366.4	12,223.9	18,288.0	33,597.0	46,397.7	....	Imports, fob	71.v
1990=100																
102.1	100.2	74.8	75.6	74.7	60.7	62.6	67.5	69.8	84.7	100.0	105.6	101.5	100.9	....	Volume of Exports	72
															Balance of Payments	
Minus Sign Indicates Debit																
962.7	974.0	767.4	685.7	702.3	568.6	589.5	725.2	898.4	1,028.9	1,190.6	1,196.7	1,116.5	1,074.5	....	Goods: Exports f.o.b.	78aa d
−1,038.2	−1,296.7	−1,208.9	−1,124.2	−1,037.0	−1,004.2	−837.4	−1,077.3	−1,255.3	−1,618.7	−1,692.7	−1,588.3	−1,541.1	−1,896.5	....	Goods: Imports f.o.b.	78ab d
−75.5	−322.7	−441.5	−438.5	−334.7	−435.6	−247.9	−352.1	−356.9	−589.8	−502.1	−391.6	−424.6	−822.0	....	Trade Balance	78ac d
400.7	430.9	493.0	540.1	566.3	609.5	753.5	837.5	785.3	876.1	1,026.5	992.1	1,104.0	1,268.9	....	Services: Credit	78ad d
−369.9	−407.1	−430.0	−403.3	−418.0	−414.9	−411.4	−455.0	−567.6	−720.8	−697.4	−670.3	−714.4	−842.3	....	Services: Debit	78ae d
−44.7	−298.9	−378.5	−301.7	−186.4	−241.0	94.2	30.4	−139.2	−434.5	−173.0	−69.8	−35.0	−395.4	....	Balance on Goods and Services	78af d
58.2	94.9	110.7	106.4	66.6	88.1	68.0	71.5	88.0	104.0	107.6	59.7	75.0	117.0	....	Income: Credit	78ag d
−270.2	−257.1	−285.9	−261.3	−332.9	−369.9	−348.7	−414.8	−423.2	−454.1	−537.6	−498.5	−368.9	−319.9	....	Income: Debit	78ah d
−256.7	−461.1	−553.7	−456.6	−452.7	−522.8	−186.5	−312.9	−474.4	−784.6	−603.0	−508.6	−328.9	−598.3	....	Balance on Goods, Serv., & Inc.	78ai d
162.7	199.3	219.0	174.8	178.5	294.4	209.4	217.7	587.8	523.8	314.9	294.8	387.2	410.9	....	Current Transfers, n.i.e.: Credit	78aj d
−42.1	−45.0	−48.6	−56.8	−41.0	−45.0	−40.8	−30.5	−66.8	−21.8	−24.0	−26.3	−29.8	−26.1	....	Current Transfers: Debit	78ak d
−136.1	−306.8	−383.3	−338.6	−315.2	−273.4	−17.9	−125.7	46.6	−282.6	−312.1	−240.1	28.5	−213.5	....	Current Account, n.i.e.	78al d
															Capital Account, n.i.e.: Credit	78ba d
−29.9	−30.0	−25.2	−20.0	−20.0	−31.0	−22.3	−16.5	−15.4	−15.0	−15.9	−15.7	−17.6	−12.9	....	Capital Account: Debit	78bb d
−29.9	−30.0	−25.2	−20.0	−20.0	−31.0	−22.3	−16.5	−15.4	−15.0	−15.9	−15.7	−17.6	−12.9	....	Capital Account, n.i.e.	78bc d
															Direct Investment Abroad	78bd d
27.7	−11.5	−15.8	−18.7	12.2	−9.0	−4.6	53.4	−12.0	57.1	137.9	133.2	142.4	77.9	....	Dir. Invest. in Rep. Econ., n.i.e.	78be d
—	—	—	—	—	—	—	—	—	—	—	—	—	—	....	Portfolio Investment Assets	78bf d
—	—	—	—	—	—	—	—	—	—	—	—	—	—	....	Portfolio Investment Liab., n.i.e.	78bg d
−11.6	−16.7	−21.6	−14.7	−33.9	−5.2	−8.4	1.6	1.3	12.0	−2.5	105.7	10.2	1.1	....	Other Investment Assets	78bh d
91.8	72.5	304.4	31.0	572.8	241.5	−92.6	305.5	98.7	29.1	269.1	32.5	201.9	217.4	....	Other Investment Liab., n.i.e.	78bi d
107.9	44.3	267.0	−2.4	551.1	227.3	−105.6	360.5	88.0	98.2	404.5	271.4	354.5	296.4	....	Financial Account, n.i.e.	78bj d
−28.4	3.9	18.0	−.9	−64.0	17.0	80.0	84.6	−46.0	10.0	29.3	−20.4	−59.9	79.2	....	Net Errors and Omissions	78ca d
−86.5	−288.5	−123.5	−361.9	151.8	−60.0	−65.8	302.9	73.2	−189.4	105.8	−4.8	305.5	149.2	....	Overall Balance	78cb d
86.5	288.5	123.5	361.9	−151.8	60.0	65.8	−302.9	−73.2	189.4	−105.8	4.8	−305.5	−149.2	....	Reserves and Related Items	79da d
−41.6	25.1	−19.7	56.6	−65.9	−18.7	−14.1	−69.3	25.2	39.9	−65.3	52.9	−192.2	−92.9	....	Reserve Assets	79db d
−31.0	190.3	137.3	76.6	44.3	−10.5	−88.6	−96.5	−160.2	−86.0	−53.2	32.6	−19.4	−21.3	....	Use of Fund Credit and Loans	79dc d
10.0	50.7	−67.3	−24.8	1.5	−10.8	−12.4	−3.0	4.8	17.6	23.7	−16.5	−57.2	−39.3	....	Liabs.Constit.For.Auth.Reserves	79dd d
149.1	22.4	73.3	253.5	−131.7	100.1	180.9	−134.1	57.0	217.9	−11.1	−64.2	−36.7	4.4	....	Exceptional Financing	79de d
Year Ending December 31															**Government Finance**	
−739.3	−720.6	−893.3	−1,389.9	−547.0	−963.4	....	....	....	....	....	....	....	....	....	Deficit (-) or Surplus	80
1,381.9	1,671.7	1,719.4	1,840.8	2,882.2	3,740.8	....	....	....	....	....	....	....	....	....	Revenue	81
															Grants Received	81z
1,980.9	2,116.3	2,263.2	2,847.3	3,168.2	4,492.6	....	....	....	....	....	....	....	....	....	Expenditure	82
140.3	275.7	349.5	383.4	261.0	211.6	....	....	....	....	....	....	....	....	....	Lending Minus Repayments	83
2,253.1	2,585.3	3,158.4	6,178.1	5,871.8	6,831.0	....	....	....	....	....	....	....	....	....	Debt: Domestic	88a
1,700.1	2,232.1	2,605.9	4,681.2	8,417.5	10,404.4	....	....	....	....	....	....	....	....	....	Foreign	89a
Millions of Jamaica Dollars															**National Accounts**	
2,426	2,510	2,240	2,621	4,956	6,521	7,294	8,405	9,197	10,769	15,873	19,912	51,087	57,050	....	Exports of Goods & Services	90c
966	1,095	1,288	1,406	1,548	1,742	2,136	2,492	3,028	3,241	4,308	5,554	6,878	12,576	....	Government Consumption	91f
690	954	1,168	1,436	1,981	2,581	2,432	3,545	4,865	6,538	8,362	11,850	20,494	32,813	....	Gross Fixed Capital Formation	93e
69	12	3	57	120	183	256	142	160	133	188	171	260	200	454	Increase/Decrease(-) in Stocks	93i
3,147	3,682	4,034	4,874	6,271	7,772	8,897	10,372	12,143	15,870	18,913	30,207	43,325	57,979	....	Private Consumption	96f
−2,525	−3,058	−2,919	−3,465	−5,580	−7,669	−7,001	−8,344	−9,930	−13,253	−17,115	−23,656	−49,445	−65,087	....	Imports of Goods & Services	98c
4,773	5,307	5,867	6,993	9,358	11,203	13,899	16,629	19,436	23,354	30,513	44,128	72,539	95,785	....	Gross Domestic Product	99b
−318	−293	−289	−248	−902	−1,466	−1,552	−1,898	−1,884	−2,300	−3,122	−5,057	−6,843	−6,326	....	Net Factor Inc/Pmts(-) Abroad	98.n
4,455	5,014	5,578	6,745	8,456	9,736	12,347	14,731	17,552	21,054	27,355	39,101	65,744	89,495	....	Gross Nat'l Expenditure = GNP	99a
23,933	24,544	24,848	25,417	25,192	24,029	‡24,436	26,322	27,082	28,934	30,513	30,670	31,252	31,465	....	Gross Dom. Prod. 1990 Prices	99b.p
19.9	21.6	23.6	27.5	37.1	46.6	56.9	63.2	71.8	80.7	100.0	143.9	232.1	304.4	....	GDP Deflator (1990=100)	99bi p
Midyear Estimates																
2.13	2.18	2.19	2.24	2.28	2.31	2.34	2.35	2.36	2.39	2.41	‡2.37	2.39	2.41	2.50	Population	99z

Japan

158		1965	1966	1967	1968	1969	1970	1971	1972	1973	1974	1975	1976	1977	1978	1979
Exchange Rates																*Yen per SDR:*
Market Rate	aa	360.90	362.47	361.91	357.70	357.80	357.65	341.78	327.88	337.78	368.47	357.23	340.18	291.53	253.52	315.76
																Yen per US Dollar:
Market Rate	ae	360.90	362.47	361.91	357.70	357.80	357.65	314.80	302.00	280.00	300.95	305.15	292.80	240.00	194.60	239.70
Market Rate	rf	360.00	360.00	360.00	360.00	360.00	360.00	350.68	303.17	271.70	292.08	296.79	296.55	268.51	210.44	219.14
																Index Numbers (1990=100):
Market Rate	ahx	39.9	39.8	39.8	40.0	40.2	40.2	67.9	47.5	53.1	49.4	48.6	48.6	53.8	69.1	66.0
Nominal Effective Exchange Rate	neu	44.0	44.0	44.0	44.7	44.7	44.4	45.0	50.4	53.6	50.0	48.6	50.6	55.8	68.4	64.3
Real Effective Exchange Rate	reu	....	....	....	....	....	....	....	....	....	....	88.0	87.1	93.3	108.0	93.5
Fund Position																*Millions of SDRs:*
Quota	2f. s	500	725	725	725	725	1,200	1,200	1,200	1,200	1,200	1,200	1,200	1,200	1,659	1,659
SDRs	1b. s	—	—	—	—	—	146	283	424	425	432	444	460	494	1,053	1,281
Reserve Position in the Fund	1c. s	255	321	239	289	627	973	490	571	529	603	686	1,143	1,329	1,642	1,121
of which: Outstg.Fund Borrowing	2c	45	45	25	15	158	440	—	—	—	—	—	—	339	369	236
International Liquidity																*Millions of US Dollars Unless Otherwise Indicated*
Total Reserves minus Gold	1l. d	1,824	1,790	1,692	2,550	3,241	4,308	14,622	17,564	11,355	12,614	11,950	15,746	22,341	32,407	19,52[illegible]
SDRs	1b. d	—	—	—	—	—	146	307	461	513	529	520	535	600	1,372	1,68[illegible]
Reserve Position in the Fund	1c. d	255	321	239	289	627	973	532	620	639	739	804	1,329	1,615	2,139	1,47[illegible]
Foreign Exchange	1d. d	1,569	1,469	1,453	2,261	2,614	3,188	13,783	16,483	10,203	11,347	10,627	13,883	20,126	28,896	16,35[illegible]
Gold (Million Fine Troy Ounces)	1ad	9.38	9.42	9.68	10.17	11.81	15.22	19.42	21.10	21.11	21.11	21.11	21.11	21.62	23.97	24.2[illegible]
Gold (National Valuation)	1and	328	330	339	356	413	533	680	802	891	905	865	858	919	1,093	1,11[illegible]
Deposit Money Banks: Assets	7a. d	2,549	2,661	3,105	3,829	5,224	6,599	6,020	8,864	I 17,110	20,610	20,360	21,647	21,694	33,691	45,43[illegible]
of which: Claims on Nonbanks	7ad d	....	....	....	....	....	....	....	....	....	....	....	7,444	7,045	11,098	14,01[illegible]
Deposit Money Banks: Liabilities	7b. d	3,452	3,179	4,133	4,618	4,530	5,539	7,491	8,356	I 13,620	24,950	26,690	29,037	28,581	39,013	50,48[illegible]
of which: Liabilities to Nonbanks	7bd d	....	....	....	....	....	....	....	....	....	....	....	1,172	1,798	2,365	1,636
Monetary Authorities																*Trillions of Yen:*
Foreign Assets	11	.78	.76	.73	1.05	1.32	I 1.68	4.58	5.43	3.55	3.97	3.73	4.82	6.69	6.96	3.4[illegible]
Claims on Central Government	12a	.91	.74	1.24	1.57	2.03	2.57	1.82	1.22	1.74	4.05	7.49	7.29	6.90	8.73	9.0[illegible]
Claims on Deposit Money Banks	12e	1.27	1.65	1.48	1.60	1.92	2.25	.62	2.79	6.24	5.80	4.03	4.38	5.15	5.42	5.46
Reserve Money	14	2.79	3.16	3.74	4.44	5.31	6.20	7.10	9.15	12.29	14.28	14.86	16.13	17.48	20.08	21.58
of which: Currency Outside DMBs	14a	2.26	2.59	3.11	3.60	4.32	5.10	5.96	7.71	9.11	10.73	11.58	12.86	14.12	16.26	17.05
Central Government Deposits	16d	.27	.17	.16	.16	.14	.23	.31	.68	1.27	.93	.66	.76	1.01	1.42	1.88
Other Items (Net)	17r	-.04	.21	.17	.38	.45	I .08	-.38	-.40	-2.03	-1.38	-.27	-.40	.24	I -.40	-5.46
Deposit Money Banks																*Trillions of Yen:*
Reserves	20	.52	.57	.62	.85	1.00	1.10	1.14	1.45	3.18	3.55	3.28	3.28	3.36	3.82	4.53
Foreign Assets	21	.92	.96	1.12	1.38	1.88	2.38	1.85	2.73	3.08	4.03	3.99	4.40	4.45	5.00	6.17
Claims on Central Government	22a	.03	.63	.67	.76	.82	.63	1.11	2.61	1.99	1.50	3.84	8.53	12.50	18.49	20.08
Claims on Local Government	22b	.59	.69	.76	.95	1.11	1.31	1.65	2.16	2.78	3.99	4.79	5.27	6.59	8.20	9.65
Claims on Nonfin.Pub.Enterprises	22c	.74	.73	.82	1.01	1.10	1.38	1.86	1.99	2.33	2.59	2.99	3.70	4.26	4.94	6.12
Claims on Private Sector	22d	26.79	31.23	36.31	41.22	48.39	56.83	69.40	87.24	103.25	116.12	130.04	145.04	157.78	173.74	187.49
Demand Deposits	24	8.02	9.13	10.26	11.56	13.96	16.26	21.74	26.82	31.20	34.22	38.37	43.32	46.66	52.67	53.97
Time Deposits	25	15.11	17.81	20.73	24.00	28.12	32.88	39.71	49.51	57.88	64.54	75.38	86.07	97.25	109.79	122.70
Certificates of Deposit	26aa	—	—	—	—	—	—	—	—	—	—	—	—	—	—	1.29
Bonds	26ab	1.39	1.69	2.25	2.72	3.29	3.93	4.45	6.12	7.22	8.45	10.89	13.51	15.26	17.28	18.69
Foreign Liabilities	26c	1.24	1.14	1.49	1.66	1.63	1.99	2.31	2.57	4.15	7.60	8.14	8.74	8.27	8.60	10.34
Credit from Monetary Authorities	26g	1.27	1.65	1.48	1.60	1.92	2.25	.62	2.79	6.24	5.80	4.03	4.38	5.15	5.42	5.46
Other Items (Net)	27r	2.55	3.37	4.09	4.62	5.37	6.31	8.19	10.37	9.92	11.18	12.12	14.20	16.35	20.42	21.58
Monetary Survey																*Trillions of Yen:*
Foreign Assets (Net)	31n	.45	.57	.36	.76	1.56	2.06	4.13	5.59	2.49	.40	-.42	.48	2.86	3.36	-.72
Domestic Credit	32	28.77	33.84	39.64	45.34	53.30	62.50	75.53	94.54	110.82	127.33	148.49	169.07	187.02	212.67	230.55
Claims on Central Govt. (Net)	32an	.66	1.20	1.75	2.17	2.70	2.98	2.62	3.15	2.46	4.62	10.67	15.06	18.39	25.80	27.28
Claims on Local Government	32b	.59	.69	.76	.95	1.11	1.31	1.65	2.16	2.78	3.99	4.79	5.27	6.59	8.20	9.65
Claims on Nonfin.Pub.Enterprises	32c	.74	.73	.82	1.01	1.10	1.38	1.86	1.99	2.33	2.59	2.99	3.70	4.26	4.94	6.12
Claims on Private Sector	32d	26.79	31.23	36.31	41.22	48.39	56.83	69.40	87.24	103.25	116.12	130.04	145.04	157.78	173.74	187.49
Money	34	10.29	11.72	13.37	15.16	18.28	21.36	27.69	34.53	40.31	44.95	49.95	56.18	60.79	68.93	71.02
Quasi-Money	35	15.11	17.81	20.73	24.00	28.12	32.88	39.71	49.51	57.88	64.54	75.38	86.07	97.25	109.79	122.70
Certificates of Deposit	36aa	—	—	—	—	—	—	—	—	—	—	—	—	—	—	1.29
Bonds	36ab	1.39	1.69	2.25	2.72	3.29	3.93	4.45	6.12	7.22	8.45	10.89	13.51	15.26	17.28	18.69
Other Items (Net)	37r	2.44	3.20	3.64	4.23	5.17	6.39	7.82	9.98	7.89	9.79	11.85	13.80	16.59	20.03	16.13
Money plus Quasi-Money	35l	25.39	29.52	34.10	39.15	46.40	54.24	67.40	84.04	98.19	109.49	125.33	142.25	158.03	178.72	193.72
Other Banking Institutions																*Trillions of Yen:*
Cash	40	....	....	....	....	....	3.73	4.32	5.43	5.35	6.93	8.40	9.66	12.06	15.17	16.60
Claims on Central Government	42a	....	....	....	....	....	2.42	3.46	5.59	5.72	5.68	7.24	10.05	15.55	20.73	25.52
Claims on Local Government	42b	....	....	....	....	....	3.93	4.61	5.59	7.31	9.23	11.44	14.39	16.90	19.78	23.54
Claims on Nonfin.Pub.Enterprises	42c	....	....	....	....	....	3.66	4.63	5.78	7.81	10.14	12.99	15.90	18.52	21.98	24.63
Claims on Private Sector	42d	....	....	....	....	....	20.27	24.31	28.82	36.72	43.52	50.90	59.02	65.64	71.19	80.99
Demand and Time Deposits	45a	....	....	....	....	....	23.42	29.04	36.47	45.16	54.01	65.92	78.68	93.24	108.75	124.52
Trust Funds	46ab	....	....	....	....	....	5.39	6.59	8.42	9.99	11.65	13.59	16.09	18.76	21.58	24.43
Insurance Reserves	47d	....	....	....	....	....	2.41	2.88	3.50	4.29	5.22	6.37	7.73	9.23	10.86	12.68
Other Items (Net)	47r	....	....	....	....	....	2.80	2.81	2.83	3.47	4.62	5.10	6.52	7.46	7.65	9.65
Nonbank Financial Institutions																*Trillions of Yen:*
Cash	40.. s	....	....	....	....	....	.74	.85	1.11	1.22	1.56	1.73	2.07	2.69	3.48	3.94
Claims on Central Government	42a. s	....	....	....	....	....	.02	.03	.05	.05	.03	.19	.44	.50	.88	1.02
Claims on Local Government	42b. s	....	....	....	....	....	.06	.06	.07	.08	.13	.20	.30	.49	.74	1.11
Claims on Nonfin.Pub.Enterprise	42c. s	....	....	....	....	....	.52	.54	.60	.64	.72	.83	.95	1.20	1.46	1.65
Claims on Private Sector	42d. s	....	....	....	....	....	I 5.76	7.25	8.63	10.41	12.05	13.97	15.95	17.72	19.01	20.99
Insurance Reserves	47d. s	....	....	....	....	....	6.64	7.97	9.44	10.96	12.82	15.01	17.52	20.13	23.04	26.57
Other Items (Net)	47r. s	....	....	....	....	....	.46	.75	1.01	1.43	1.67	1.92	2.17	2.47	2.53	2.14
Financial Survey																*Trillions of Yen:*
Foreign Assets (Net)	51n	.45	.57	.36	.76	1.56	2.06	4.13	5.59	2.49	.40	-.42	.48	2.86	3.36	-.72
Domestic Credit	52	....	....	....	....	....	99.14	120.41	149.67	179.55	208.83	246.25	286.06	323.54	368.43	409.99
Claims on Central Govt. (Net)	52an	....	....	....	....	....	5.42	6.11	8.79	8.23	10.33	18.10	25.55	34.44	47.41	53.82
Claims on Local Government	52b	....	....	....	....	....	5.29	6.32	7.82	10.17	13.36	16.43	19.96	23.98	28.71	34.29
Claims on Nonfin.Pub.Enterprises	52c	....	....	....	....	....	5.56	7.03	8.37	10.77	13.46	16.81	20.55	23.98	28.37	32.40
Claims on Private Sector	52d	....	....	....	....	....	82.87	100.95	124.69	150.37	171.69	194.91	220.01	241.14	263.94	289.48
Liquid Liabilities	55l	....	....	....	....	....	74.89	92.74	115.73	139.02	158.67	185.19	213.63	242.07	275.57	306.50
Bonds and Trust Funds	56ab	....	....	....	....	....	9.32	11.04	14.53	17.21	20.09	24.48	29.60	34.03	38.86	43.12
Insurance Reserves	57d	....	....	....	....	....	9.05	10.85	12.93	15.25	18.04	21.38	25.24	29.35	33.90	39.25
Other Items (Net)	57r	....	....	....	....	....	7.94	9.91	12.06	10.55	12.44	14.79	18.07	20.97	23.46	20.41

Japan
158

1980	1981	1982	1983	1984	1985	1986	1987	1988	1989	1990	1991	1992	1993	1994		
End of Period															**Exchange Rates**	
258.91	255.95	259.23	243.10	246.13	220.23	194.61	175.20	169.36	188.52	191.21	179.09	171.53	153.63	145.61	Market Rate	aa
End of Period (ae) Period Average (rf)																
203.00	219.90	235.00	232.20	251.10	200.50	159.10	123.50	125.85	143.45	134.40	125.20	124.75	111.85	99.74	Market Rate	ae
226.74	220.54	249.08	237.51	237.52	238.54	168.52	144.64	128.15	137.96	144.79	134.71	126.65	111.20	102.21	Market Rate	rf
Period Averages																
63.8	65.5	58.1	60.7	60.7	60.9	86.1	99.9	112.6	104.7	100.0	107.2	113.9	130.0	141.2	Market Rate	ahx
61.0	68.3	64.0	70.0	73.8	75.5	96.4	104.7	116.0	111.0	100.0	108.4	113.7	136.5	147.1	Nominal Effective Exchange Rate	neu
85.8	90.9	79.9	84.8	86.7	85.8	108.1	113.2	119.1	111.9	100.0	105.8	109.1	127.5	....	Real Effective Exchange Rate	reu
End of Period															**Fund Position**	
2,489	2,489	2,489	4,223	4,223	4,223	4,223	4,223	4,223	4,223	4,223	4,223	8,242	8,242	8,242	Quota	2f. s
1,363	1,662	1,895	1,848	1,966	1,926	1,813	1,736	2,182	1,862	2,138	1,803	795	1,123	1,427	SDRs	1b. s
1,044	1,339	1,878	2,199	2,264	2,071	1,947	2,011	2,436	2,677	4,197	5,398	6,284	6,015	5,912	Reserve Position in the Fund	1c. s
381	641	825	839	793	663	487	294	154	134	1,866	3,000	2,985	2,985	2,913	*of which:* Outstg.Fund Borrowing	2c
End of Period															**International Liquidity**	
24,636	28,208	23,334	24,602	26,429	26,719	42,257	80,973	96,728	83,957	78,501	72,059	71,623	98,524	125,860	Total Reserves minus Gold	1l. d
1,738	1,934	2,091	1,935	1,927	2,116	2,218	2,463	2,936	2,447	3,042	2,579	1,094	1,543	2,083	SDRs	1b. d
1,331	1,558	2,071	2,303	2,219	2,275	2,382	2,853	3,278	3,518	5,971	7,722	8,641	8,261	8,631	Reserve Position in the Fund	1c. d
21,567	24,716	19,172	20,364	22,283	22,328	37,657	75,657	90,514	77,992	69,487	61,758	61,888	88,720	115,146	Foreign Exchange	1d. d
24.23	24.23	24.23	24.23	24.23	24.23	24.23	24.23	24.23	24.23	24.23	24.23	24.23	24.23	24.23	Gold (Million Fine Troy Ounces)	1ad
1,082	987	935	888	831	931	1,037	1,203	1,141	1,114	1,206	1,213	1,166	1,165	1,238	Gold (National Valuation)	1and
65,666	84,607	90,949	109,063	126,921	194,620	345,327	576,828	733,688	842,055	950,578	942,431	879,191	918,559	1,007,605	Deposit Money Banks: Assets	7a. d
18,049	21,074	23,867	28,123	36,985	58,534	85,316	125,248	139,892	159,714	181,143	191,347	200,555	235,788	243,226	*of which:* Claims on Nonbanks	7ad d
80,209	100,391	100,018	106,645	127,046	179,306	345,987	592,027	772,423	879,721	958,478	845,674	708,623	688,436	723,697	Deposit Money Banks: Liabilities	7b. d
2,110	2,435	2,486	2,356	3,576	6,203	6,862	7,168	9,911	13,481	13,344	15,162	17,713	19,030	19,784	*of which:* Liabilities to Nonbanks	7bd d
End of Period															**Monetary Authorities**	
5.27	5.32	4.76	5.17	5.47	5.87	6.70	11.82	11.78	8.86	7.63	4.11	3.40	5.16	4.07	Foreign Assets	11
10.25	13.35	14.72	14.57	14.50	12.83	11.30	12.28	12.12	13.27	21.33	15.27	19.13	21.40	21.98	Claims on Central Government	12a
5.25	2.24	3.43	5.97	5.35	9.01	10.62	10.82	11.68	15.68	12.89	20.76	20.01	14.17	12.92	Claims on Deposit Money Banks	12e
22.96	23.57	25.03	26.39	28.63	29.71	32.12	34.92	39.46	44.57	47.86	47.19	45.40	48.07	49.44	Reserve Money	14
17.48	18.58	19.78	20.58	22.11	23.41	26.20	28.58	31.52	36.68	37.25	37.97	38.10	40.85	42.35	*of which: Currency Outside DMBs*	14a
.95	1.49	1.37	3.48	1.33	2.52	1.41	6.07	5.03	2.25	2.02	3.14	5.61	2.07	5.03	Central Government Deposits	16d
–3.14	–4.15	–3.50	–4.16	–4.63	–4.52	–4.90	–6.07	–8.92	–9.01	–8.03	–10.21	–8.47	–9.40	–15.49	Other Items (Net)	17r
End of Period															**Deposit Money Banks**	
5.48	4.99	5.26	5.81	6.51	6.30	5.92	6.34	7.94	7.89	10.61	9.22	7.29	7.22	7.09	Reserves	20
10.93	12.83	14.24	17.09	17.92	25.33	36.02	48.35	63.79	81.62	96.68	86.51	77.99	71.72	71.74	Foreign Assets	21
20.24	21.27	22.05	25.08	26.12	27.91	31.12	34.26	38.71	41.48	40.02	36.76	40.25	42.89	40.14	Claims on Central Government	22a
10.33	11.22	10.89	10.56	10.45	10.51	10.47	10.54	10.26	10.75	10.73	10.98	12.01	14.95	17.38	Claims on Local Government	22b
7.08	8.71	9.55	10.46	11.24	11.71	13.09	13.69	13.95	13.88	14.12	14.04	13.58	13.47	12.55	Claims on Nonfin.Pub.Enterprises	22c
203.02	221.84	241.72	262.70	287.37	318.50	348.73	387.70	430.13	480.17	524.38	552.11	564.98	558.67	559.81	Claims on Private Sector	22d
52.10	57.93	61.12	60.23	64.26	65.57	72.02	74.39	80.32	77.79	82.37	93.07	98.04	104.77	109.31	Demand Deposits	24
137.42	152.70	165.68	182.78	195.43	217.82	237.09	269.72	297.53	343.15	375.38	376.48	370.66	372.57	382.44	Time Deposits	25
2.00	2.84	3.88	5.11	7.91	8.14	8.58	8.17	10.36	12.40	9.96	8.82	8.69	8.65	7.32	Certificates of Deposit	26aa
20.19	22.03	24.40	27.72	31.26	33.69	37.82	39.94	44.14	47.43	55.30	61.86	65.89	64.39	63.90	Bonds	26ab
18.87	21.13	23.32	25.43	30.05	40.89	59.60	80.04	97.18	116.31	134.83	108.48	89.01	77.84	72.65	Foreign Liabilities	26c
5.25	2.24	3.43	5.97	5.35	9.01	10.62	10.82	11.68	15.68	12.89	20.76	20.01	14.17	12.92	Credit from Monetary Authorities	26g
21.26	21.99	21.85	24.45	25.33	25.14	19.63	17.79	23.56	23.02	25.81	40.15	63.81	66.53	60.16	Other Items (Net)	27r
End of Period															**Monetary Survey**	
–2.67	–2.99	–4.32	–3.18	–6.67	–9.70	–16.88	–19.88	–21.61	–25.83	–30.52	–17.86	–7.62	–.95	3.17	Foreign Assets (Net)	31n
249.97	274.90	297.55	319.88	348.34	378.94	413.31	452.40	500.13	557.29	608.57	626.01	644.34	649.31	646.82	Domestic Credit	32
29.54	33.13	35.39	36.16	39.29	38.22	41.02	40.48	45.80	52.50	59.34	48.88	53.77	62.22	57.09	Claims on Central Govt. (Net)	32an
10.33	11.22	10.89	10.56	10.45	10.51	10.47	10.54	10.26	10.75	10.73	10.98	12.01	14.95	17.38	Claims on Local Government	32b
7.08	8.71	9.55	10.46	11.24	11.71	13.09	13.69	13.95	13.88	14.12	14.04	13.58	13.47	12.55	Claims on Nonfin.Pub.Enterprises	32c
203.02	221.84	241.72	262.70	287.37	318.50	348.73	387.70	430.13	480.17	524.38	552.11	564.98	558.67	559.81	Claims on Private Sector	32d
69.57	76.51	80.90	80.80	86.38	88.98	98.21	102.97	111.84	114.47	119.63	131.04	136.14	145.61	151.67	Money	34
137.42	152.70	165.68	182.78	195.43	217.82	237.09	269.72	297.53	343.15	375.38	376.48	370.66	372.57	382.44	Quasi-Money	35
2.00	2.84	3.88	5.11	7.91	8.14	8.58	8.17	10.36	12.40	9.96	8.82	8.69	8.65	7.32	Certificates of Deposit	36aa
20.19	22.03	24.40	27.72	31.26	33.69	37.82	39.94	44.14	47.43	55.30	61.86	65.89	64.39	63.90	Bonds	36ab
18.12	17.84	18.36	20.28	20.70	20.61	14.72	11.72	14.65	14.01	17.78	29.94	55.34	57.13	44.67	Other Items (Net)	37r
206.99	229.21	246.58	263.59	281.81	306.80	335.31	372.70	409.38	457.62	495.01	507.53	506.79	518.19	534.10	Money plus Quasi-Money	35l
End of Period															**Other Banking Institutions**	
16.46	18.20	20.40	24.06	28.32	31.82	40.35	46.95	53.30	55.14	56.73	65.19	76.47	82.85	76.56	Cash	40
32.09	36.51	44.59	53.03	60.71	71.90	83.82	90.68	94.40	97.70	93.59	103.51	111.09	117.65	126.45	Claims on Central Government	42a
27.44	31.15	35.65	39.59	43.55	46.78	49.80	53.19	57.44	60.41	62.97	66.01	69.31	74.34	82.91	Claims on Local Government	42b
28.09	31.09	34.58	37.11	39.83	40.20	42.25	29.35	29.79	31.52	33.43	36.62	39.17	43.44	47.27	Claims on Nonfin.Pub.Enterprises	42c
91.32	100.67	110.84	118.62	125.01	132.22	143.79	177.81	204.74	226.60	249.06	265.12	289.22	307.76	324.62	Claims on Private Sector	42d
141.38	159.59	177.56	195.66	211.15	229.72	250.76	269.78	289.98	317.64	336.54	371.75	401.74	430.84	456.40	Demand and Time Deposits	45a
26.96	30.91	36.00	40.32	46.12	54.06	67.21	84.22	98.50	116.38	124.10	129.05	138.86	147.58	153.18	Trust Funds	46ab
14.70	16.96	19.50	22.22	25.00	27.98	31.29	35.31	39.93	44.78	49.94	55.56	62.81	71.34	79.86	Insurance Reserves	47d
12.35	10.16	13.00	14.20	15.09	11.16	10.75	8.68	11.26	–7.43	–14.79	–19.91	–18.16	–23.73	–31.64	Other Items (Net)	47r
End of Period															**Nonbank Financial Institutions**	
4.33	4.75	5.57	6.62	8.61	11.34	10.29	11.03	11.95	12.36	19.45	22.14	24.62	27.30	30.88	Cash	40.. s
1.00	1.34	1.76	2.64	3.09	3.86	5.20	5.60	7.13	6.86	5.36	6.14	10.39	14.86	20.86	Claims on Central Government	42a. s
1.41	1.49	1.72	1.75	1.80	1.79	2.07	2.35	2.02	1.89	2.08	2.09	2.19	2.98	4.44	Claims on Local Government	42b. s
1.75	1.93	2.37	2.79	3.17	3.46	4.07	3.38	2.56	2.78	3.30	3.42	4.38	3.62	4.42	Claims on Nonfin.Pub.Enterprise	42c. s
24.50	27.60	30.03	32.11	34.30	37.04	39.77	48.89	60.06	73.60	89.13	100.04	105.59	111.33	114.86	Claims on Private Sector	42d. s
30.56	35.04	40.13	45.67	52.22	60.69	73.50	87.58	106.50	126.94	144.16	157.62	171.50	186.38	199.49	Insurance Reserves	47d. s
2.43	2.06	1.31	.24	–1.24	–3.20	–12.11	–16.34	–22.78	–29.45	–24.85	–23.79	–24.34	–26.30	–24.04	Other Items (Net)	47r. s
End of Period															**Financial Survey**	
–2.67	–2.99	–4.32	–3.18	–6.67	–9.70	–16.88	–19.88	–21.61	–25.83	–30.52	–17.86	–7.62	–.95	3.17	Foreign Assets (Net)	51n
457.56	506.68	559.08	607.51	659.80	716.19	784.07	863.64	958.27	1,058.65	1,147.49	1,208.95	1,275.67	1,325.28	1,372.64	Domestic Credit	52
62.63	70.98	81.74	91.82	103.10	113.98	130.04	136.75	147.33	157.06	158.29	158.53	175.25	194.73	204.40	Claims on Central Govt. (Net)	52an
39.18	43.87	48.25	51.90	55.80	59.08	62.34	66.08	69.73	73.04	75.78	79.08	83.51	92.27	104.72	Claims on Local Government	52b
36.92	41.73	46.50	50.36	54.23	55.37	59.41	46.41	46.29	48.18	50.85	54.08	57.12	60.53	64.24	Claims on Nonfin.Pub.Enterprises	52c
318.83	350.10	382.59	413.43	446.67	487.77	532.28	614.40	694.93	780.37	862.57	917.27	959.79	977.75	999.29	Claims on Private Sector	52d
337.43	376.89	411.56	443.74	477.58	519.33	567.36	619.43	675.85	756.28	806.12	847.89	868.82	900.42	945.09	Liquid Liabilities	55l
47.15	52.95	60.41	68.04	77.38	87.75	105.03	124.16	142.64	163.81	179.40	190.91	204.76	211.97	217.08	Bonds and Trust Funds	56ab
45.26	52.00	59.63	67.89	77.22	88.66	104.79	122.89	146.43	171.72	194.10	213.18	234.31	257.73	279.35	Insurance Reserves	57d
25.06	21.86	23.16	24.65	20.91	10.75	–9.99	–22.70	–28.26	–58.99	–62.65	–60.89	–39.84	–45.79	–65.72	Other Items (Net)	57r

Japan

		1965	1966	1967	1968	1969	1970	1971	1972	1973	1974	1975	1976	1977	1978	1979
Interest Rates															*Percent Per Annum*	
Discount Rate *(End of Period)*	60	5.48	5.48	5.84	5.84	6.25	6.00	4.75	4.25	9.00	9.00	6.50	6.50	4.25	3.50	6.25
Money Market Rate	60b	6.97	5.84	6.39	7.88	7.70	8.28	6.41	4.72	7.16	12.54	10.67	6.98	5.68	4.36	5.86
Private Bill Rate	60bs	....	....	....	....	....	....	....	....	....	....	....	....	....	....	....
Deposit Rate	60l	4.00	4.00	4.00	4.00	4.00	4.00	4.00	3.88	4.00	5.33	5.33	4.50	3.83	2.69	3.31
Lending Rate	60p	7.80	7.48	7.31	7.46	7.41	7.66	7.59	7.05	7.19	9.11	9.10	8.26	7.56	6.42	6.37
Government Bond Yield	61	....	6.86	6.91	7.03	7.09	7.19	7.28	6.70	7.26	9.26	9.20	8.72	7.33	6.09	7.69
Prices, Production, Employment															*Index Numbers (1990=100)*:	
Share Prices	62	4.2	5.0	5.1	5.5	6.9	7.5	8.2	13.0	16.6	14.1	14.3	15.9	17.3	19.0	20.6
Wholesale Prices	63	48.2	49.3	50.2	50.6	51.7	53.6	53.2	53.6	62.1	81.6	84.1	88.4	90.0	87.7	94.1
Consumer Prices	64	26.5	28.1	27.8	28.9	30.5	32.1	ⅼ34.6	36.8	38.5	43.0	53.0	59.2	64.8	70.1	73.0
Consumer Prices (cont)																75.7
Wages: Monthly Earnings	65	12.9	14.2	15.9	17.8	20.2	20.7	23.7	27.4	32.6	40.7	48.0	54.0	59.0	63.2	66.9
Industrial Production	66..c	22.0	24.9	29.8	34.4	39.8	45.3	46.5	49.8	57.3	55.2	49.0	54.4	56.7	60.3	64.7
Manufacturing Employment	67ey c	86.0	86.4	89.2	92.9	96.3	100.0	100.6	98.7	99.0	98.6	93.4	91.5	90.7	88.7	88.3
International Transactions															*Billions of Yen*	
Exports	70	3,042	3,520	3,759	4,670	5,756	6,954	8,393	8,806	10,031	16,220	16,572	19,930	21,648	20,526	22,532
Imports, cif	71	2,941	3,428	4,199	4,676	5,408	6,797	6,910	7,229	10,404	18,067	17,176	19,229	19,132	16,728	24,245
Imports, fob	71.v	2,423	2,805	3,439	3,842	4,496	5,664	5,821	6,142	8,977	15,904	15,173	17,184	17,298	15,097	21,941
															1990=100	
Volume of Exports	72	12.0	13.8	14.1	17.5	20.7	23.9	28.3	30.1	32.2	38.8	38.7	46.9	50.8	51.2	51.3
Volume of Imports	73	15.6	18.2	22.4	25.2	29.3	34.8	34.7	39.5	51.5	51.1	44.9	48.9	50.1	53.5	59.5
Unit Value of Exports	74	61.1	61.3	64.3	63.8	66.7	69.8	71.2	70.2	74.6	100.1	102.5	101.9	102.1	96.4	105.3
Unit Value of Imports	75	55.1	55.4	55.1	54.6	54.3	57.6	58.6	53.8	59.4	103.9	112.4	115.0	111.5	91.5	119.1
Export Prices	76	78.8	78.6	78.8	78.8	81.0	84.5	83.3	80.7	88.9	119.0	114.2	113.4	108.0	100.9	111.8
Import Prices	76.x	46.4	47.4	46.9	47.0	48.0	49.6	49.6	47.4	57.6	96.5	103.6	109.0	104.0	85.8	110.4
Balance of Payments															*Billions of US Dollars:*	
Goods: Exports f.o.b.	78aa d													79.16	95.32	101.12
Goods: Imports f.o.b.	78ab d													-62.00	-71.02	-99.38
Trade Balance	78ac d													17.16	24.30	1.74
Services: Credit	78ad d													11.77	13.55	16.01
Services: Debit	78ae d													-17.68	-21.51	-27.35
Balance on Goods and Services	78af d													11.25	16.34	-9.60
Income: Credit	78ag d													3.82	5.41	9.13
Income: Debit	78ah d													-3.76	-4.54	-7.15
Balance on Goods, Serv., & Inc.	78ai d													11.31	17.21	-7.62
Current Transfers, n.i.e.: Credit	78aj d													.26	.30	.37
Current Transfers: Debit	78ak d													-.66	-.98	-1.49
Current Account, n.i.e.	78al d													10.91	16.53	-8.74
Capital Account, n.i.e.: Credit	78ba d													—	—	—
Capital Account: Debit	78bb d													—	—	—
Capital Account, n.i.e.	78bc d													—	—	—
Direct Investment Abroad	78bd d													-1.65	-2.37	-2.90
Dir. Invest. in Rep. Econ., n.i.e.	78be d													.02	.01	.24
Portfolio Investment Assets	78bf d													-1.72	-5.30	-5.87
Portfolio Investment Liab., n.i.e.	78bg d													2.36	2.49	4.28
Other Investment Assets	78bh d													-2.13	-13.65	-16.18
Other Investment Liab., n.i.e.	78bi d													-1.84	12.12	13.61
Financial Account, n.i.e.	78bj d													-4.96	-6.70	-6.82
Net Errors and Omissions	78ca d													.54	.13	2.42
Overall Balance	78cb d													6.49	9.96	-13.14
Reserves and Related Items	79da d													-6.49	-9.96	13.14
Reserve Assets	79db d													-6.49	-9.96	13.14
Use of Fund Credit and Loans	79dc d													—	—	—
Liabs.Constit.For.Auth.Reserves	79dd d															
Exceptional Financing	79de d															
Government Finance															*Billions of Yen:*	
Deficit (-) or Surplus	80	-515	-827	-722	-703	-609	-319	-181	-1,457	-1,825	-1,798	ⅼ-7,666	-9,417	-11,916	-15,236	-16,318
Revenue	81	3,536	3,955	4,738	5,648	6,666	8,053	9,320	9,681	9,868	12,200	ⅼ14,608	16,509	18,469	20,606	24,113
Grants Received	81z	....	....	....	....	....	....	....	....	....	....	ⅼ93	146	124	134	157
Expenditure	82	4,050	4,782	5,460	6,351	7,275	8,372	9,501	11,138	11,693	13,997	ⅼ21,827	25,534	29,841	35,207	39,728
Lending Minus Repayments	83	....	....	....	....	....	....	....	....	....	....	ⅼ540	538	668	769	860
Financing																
Net Borrowing: Yen	84b	299	782	747	701	578	318	307	1,457	1,570	2,009	5,570	3,191	11,434	13,422	11,818
Foreign Currency	85b	-3	-3	-5	8	—	-5	-11	-4	-33	-4	-11	-3	-4	-2	-10
Use of Cash Balances	87	219	48	-20	-6	31	6	-115	4	288	-207	1,493	102	-8	-31	-38
Debt: Domestic	88a	....	....	....	....	....	....	....	....	....	....	ⅼ23,448	33,542	46,932	63,098	78,367
Foreign	89a	....	....	....	....	....	....	....	....	....	....	ⅼ517	528	587	518	408
National Accounts															*Billions of Yen*	
Exports of Goods & Services	90c. c	3,451	4,031	4,311	5,348	6,558	7,926	9,452	9,779	11,291	18,258	18,982	22,582	24,308	22,729	25,627
Government Consumption	91f. c	2,690	3,054	3,410	3,934	4,558	5,455	6,422	7,537	9,336	12,240	14,890	16,417	18,243	19,753	21,486
Gross Fixed Capital Formation	93e. c	9,782	11,562	14,288	17,567	21,441	26,043	27,637	31,524	40,938	46,695	48,136	51,945	55,982	62,147	70,171
Increase/Decrease(-) in Stocks	93i. c	695	815	1,528	1,910	1,938	2,573	1,215	1,299	1,885	3,396	476	1,092	1,280	1,027	1,813
Private Consumption	96f. c	19,239	22,142	25,405	28,974	33,300	38,333	43,220	49,901	60,308	72,912	84,763	95,784	107,076	117,923	130,078
Imports of Goods & Services	98c. c	-2,991	-3,434	-4,211	-4,757	-5,567	-6,985	-7,254	-7,645	-11,261	-19,257	-18,919	-21,247	-21,267	-19,174	-27,629
Gross Domestic Product	99b. c	32,866	38,170	44,731	52,975	62,229	73,345	80,701	92,394	112,498	134,244	148,327	166,573	185,622	204,404	221,547
Net Factor Inc/Pmts(-) Abroad	98.n c	-93	-97	-104	-150	-163	-157	-109	6	21	-247	-157	-156	-92	70	278
Gross Nat'l Expenditure = GNP	99a. c	32,773	38,073	44,626	52,825	62,066	73,188	80,592	92,401	112,520	133,997	148,170	166,417	185,530	204,475	221,825
Nat'l Income, Market Prices	99e	28,233	32,798	38,754	45,651	53,534	63,549	69,452	80,026	98,532	116,191	128,554	145,809	161,816	178,770	193,965
Gross Nat'l Prod. 1990 Prices	99a. r	107,259	118,404	131,436	147,438	165,327	182,230	190,149	206,077	221,830	220,011	226,469	236,036	247,272	259,530	274,150
GNP Deflator (1990=100)	99ai r	30.6	32.2	34.0	35.8	37.5	40.2	42.4	44.8	50.7	60.9	65.4	70.5	75.0	78.8	80.9
															Millions:	
Population	99z	98.88	99.79	100.83	101.96	103.17	104.34	105.70	107.19	108.71	110.16	111.57	112.77	113.86	114.90	115.87

International Liquidity: ⅼ Beginning in December 1973, data for lines 7a.d and 7b.d include long-term foreign accounts and therefore are not the U.S. dollar equivalents of lines 21 and 26c, which comprise only short-term accounts; data are from the Bank for International Settlement's *Annual Report* and *Quarterly Press Release*.

Monetary Authorities: ⅼ Beginning in 1970, data are based on an improved sectorization of accounts. ⅼ Beginning in August 1978, data for line 11 are provided net of foreign liabilities. Prior to this date, line 11 was reported on a gross basis with foreign liabilities being included in line 17r.

Deposit Money Banks: ⅼ See note to section 10.

Monetary Survey: ⅼ See note to section 10.

Interest Rates: *Money Market Rate:* ⅼ From November 1990, lending rate for collateral and overnight loans in the Tokyo Call Money Market.

Private Bill Rate: ⅼ Beginning in January 1991, rate on newly issued certificates of three-month deposits.

Deposit Rate: ⅼ From June 1992, average interest rate for the last week of the month on unregulated three-month time deposits, ranging in size from three million yen to under ten million yen.

Lending Rate: ⅼ From April 1993, weighted average of contrated interest rates charged by all banks on short- and long-term loans, discounts, and overdrafts. Previously, overdrafts were excluded.

Japan

158

	1980	1981	1982	1983	1984	1985	1986	1987	1988	1989	1990	1991	1992	1993	1994	
Percent Per Annum																**Interest Rates**
	7.25	5.50	5.50	5.00	5.00	5.00	3.00	2.50	2.50	4.25	6.00	4.50	3.25	1.75	1.75	Discount Rate *(End of Period)* 60
	10.93	7.43	6.94	6.39	6.10	6.46	4.79	3.51	3.62	4.87	7.24	7.46	4.58	I 3.06	2.20	Money Market Rate 60b
	....	7.69	7.12	6.72	6.32	6.70	4.99	3.88	4.08	5.37	7.67	I 7.31	4.40	2.97	2.24	Private Bill Rate 60bs
	5.50	4.44	3.75	3.75	3.50	3.50	2.32	1.76	1.76	1.97	3.56	I 4.14	3.35	2.14	1.70	Deposit Rate 60l
	8.35	7.86	7.31	7.13	6.75	6.60	6.02	5.21	5.03	5.29	6.95	7.53	6.15	I 4.41	4.13	Lending Rate 60p
	9.22	8.66	8.06	7.42	6.81	6.34	4.94	4.21	4.27	5.05	7.36	6.53	4.94	3.69	3.71	Government Bond Yield 61
Period Averages																**Prices, Production, Employment**
	21.7	25.3	25.2	29.7	37.4	45.7	60.7	89.8	97.8	117.8	100.0	84.5	62.6	69.9	73.3	Share Prices 62
	110.8	112.4	114.4	111.9	111.6	110.3	100.2	96.5	95.5	98.0	100.0	100.2	I 98.7	95.0	93.0	Wholesale Prices 63
	81.6	85.6	88.0	89.7	91.7	93.5	94.1	94.2	94.9	97.0	100.0	103.3	105.1	106.4	107.1	Consumer Prices 64
	70.7	74.3	78.1	80.6	83.3	85.9	88.4	90.2	93.4	96.3	100.0	103.4	105.6	107.8	....	Wages: Monthly Earnings 65
	67.8	68.5	68.7	70.7	77.4	80.3	80.1	82.8	90.8	96.1	100.0	101.8	95.6	91.2	91.8	Industrial Production 66..c
	89.2	90.2	91.3	91.8	93.6	95.9	96.9	95.6	96.2	97.9	100.0	102.1	102.8	102.4	....	Manufacturing Employment 67ey c
Billions of Yen																**International Transactions**
	29,382	33,469	34,433	34,910	40,325	41,959	35,291	33,316	33,928	37,823	41,457	42,359	43,011	40,200	40,470	Exports 70
	31,995	31,464	32,656	30,015	32,320	31,076	21,551	21,739	24,007	28,981	33,854	31,900	29,527	26,824	28,051	Imports, cif 71
	29,408	29,133	30,293	27,947	29,954	28,721	19,772	21,209	22,025	26,588	31,059	29,266	27,089	24,609	25,734	Imports, fob 71.v
1990=100																
	60.1	66.4	64.9	I 70.6	81.7	86.3	85.7	I 86.0	91.1	95.0	100.0	102.5	104.0	101.5	103.2	Volume of Exports 72
	56.5	55.3	55.0	I 55.7	61.5	62.2	68.1	I 74.4	87.7	94.6	100.0	104.0	103.6	106.6	121.1	Volume of Imports 73
	117.3	120.8	127.1	I 118.5	118.4	117.5	99.4	I 93.4	89.9	96.1	100.0	99.7	99.7	95.6	94.7	Unit Value of Exports 74
	165.5	166.3	173.6	157.5	153.2	I 147.8	93.5	I 86.3	80.9	90.5	100.0	90.6	84.2	74.5	68.6	Unit Value of Imports 75
	121.5	122.9	127.7	120.0	120.8	119.0	I 101.1	96.0	93.8	97.9	100.0	94.6	91.2	83.9	81.6	Export Prices 76
	159.8	162.4	175.2	161.5	156.1	152.2	I 97.7	89.7	85.6	92.0	100.0	91.8	86.2	77.3	73.0	Import Prices 76.x
Minus Sign Indicates Debit																Balance of Payments
	126.74	149.52	137.66	145.47	168.29	174.02	205.59	224.62	259.77	269.55	280.35	306.58	330.87	351.31	384.18	Goods: Exports f.o.b. 78aa d
	-124.61	-129.56	-119.58	-114.01	-124.03	-118.03	-112.77	-128.20	-164.77	-192.66	-216.77	-203.49	-198.47	-209.74	-238.25	Goods: Imports f.o.b. 78ab d
	2.13	19.96	18.08	31.46	44.26	55.99	92.82	96.42	95.00	76.89	63.58	103.09	132.40	141.57	145.93	Trade Balance 78ac d
	20.24	23.83	22.56	21.81	23.12	23.19	24.45	30.15	36.67	41.72	43.33	47.52	51.37	55.39	60.52	Services: Credit 78ad d
	-32.36	-36.59	-34.01	-33.86	-35.02	-35.10	-38.69	-52.24	-68.55	-80.33	-88.03	-91.11	-96.94	-99.93	-110.06	Services: Debit 78ae d
	-9.99	7.20	6.63	19.41	32.36	44.08	78.58	74.33	63.12	38.28	18.88	59.50	86.83	97.03	96.39	Balance on Goods and Services 78af d
	11.25	15.95	18.53	15.78	18.98	22.32	29.25	49.51	75.11	102.19	122.64	141.07	142.69	148.26	155.41	Income: Credit 78ag d
	-10.48	-16.76	-16.93	-12.84	-14.83	-15.58	-19.94	-33.14	-54.50	-79.20	-100.14	-115.17	-107.25	-107.66	-115.08	Income: Debit 78ah d
	-9.22	6.39	8.23	22.35	36.51	50.82	87.89	90.70	83.73	61.27	41.38	85.40	122.27	137.63	136.72	Balance on Goods, Serv., & Inc. 78ai d
	.39	.44	.47	.48	.56	.43	.41	.62	1.09	1.01	1.00	1.24	1.46	1.40	1.52	Current Transfers, n.i.e.: Credit 78aj d
	-1.92	-2.06	-1.85	-2.03	-2.07	-2.08	-2.47	-4.30	-5.21	-5.29	-6.52	-13.74	-6.08	-7.49	-9.00	Current Transfers: Debit 78ak d
	-10.75	4.77	6.85	20.80	35.00	49.17	85.83	87.02	79.61	56.99	35.86	72.91	117.65	131.54	129.24	Current Account, n.i.e. 78al d
	—	—	—	—	—	—	—	—	—	—	—	—	—	—	—	Capital Account, n.i.e.: Credit 78ba d
	—	—	—	—	—	—	—	—	—	—	—	—	—	—	—	Capital Account: Debit 78bb d
	—	—	—	—	—	—	—	—	—	—	—	—	—	—	—	Capital Account, n.i.e. 78bc d
	-2.39	-4.90	-4.54	-3.61	-5.96	-6.45	-14.48	-19.52	-34.21	-44.16	-48.05	-30.74	-17.24	-13.74	-17.97	Direct Investment Abroad 78bd d
	.28	.19	.44	.41	-.01	.64	.23	1.17	-.52	-1.06	1.76	1.37	2.72	.10	.89	Dir. Invest. in Rep. Econ., n.i.e. 78be d
	-3.75	-8.77	-9.74	-16.02	-30.63	-59.78	-101.98	-88.08	-87.12	-113.24	-40.20	-74.35	-34.96	-52.15	-83.21	Portfolio Investment Assets 78bf d
	13.11	13.22	11.86	14.15	7.03	16.71	.60	-6.29	21.01	84.48	35.39	114.01	6.24	-11.62	34.43	Portfolio Investment Liab., n.i.e. 78bg d
	-20.14	-25.53	-14.64	-24.41	-29.33	-42.41	-101.35	-141.26	-189.99	-171.54	-89.14	14.23	40.97	1.64	-46.45	Other Investment Assets 78bh d
	31.77	24.23	.42	8.16	22.33	37.76	143.50	208.61	224.61	197.59	118.70	-96.37	-104.28	-27.83	26.12	Other Investment Liab., n.i.e. 78bi d
	18.88	-1.56	-16.20	-21.32	-36.57	-53.53	-73.48	-45.37	-66.22	-47.93	-21.54	-71.85	-106.55	-103.60	-86.19	Financial Account, n.i.e. 78bj d
	-3.10	.43	4.65	2.07	3.69	3.78	2.49	-3.71	3.13	-21.82	-20.91	-7.67	-10.47	-.28	-17.77	Net Errors and Omissions 78ca d
	5.03	3.64	-4.70	1.55	2.12	-.58	14.84	37.94	16.52	-12.76	-6.59	-6.62	.63	27.66	25.28	Overall Balance 78cb d
	-5.03	-3.64	4.70	-1.55	-2.12	.58	-14.84	-37.94	-16.52	12.76	6.59	6.62	-.63	-27.66	-25.28	Reserves and Related Items 79da d
	-5.03	-3.64	4.70	-1.55	-2.12	.58	-14.84	-37.94	-16.52	12.76	6.59	6.62	-.63	-27.66	-25.28	Reserve Assets 79db d
	—	—	—	—	—	—	—	—	—	—	—	—	—	—	—	Use of Fund Credit and Loans 79dc d
	—	—	—	—	—	—	—	—	—	—	—	—	—	—	—	Liabs.Constit.For.Auth.Reserves 79dd d
	—	—	—	—	—	—	—	—	—	—	—	—	—	—	—	Exceptional Financing 79de d
Year Beginning April 1																**Government Finance**
	-16,872	-16,826	-17,583	-18,843	-17,290	-15,603	-15,965	-12,195	-9,657	-11,645	-6,781	....	....	....	....	Deficit (-) or Surplus 80
	27,907	31,429	32,826	33,776	36,738	40,262	41,685	47,176	52,082	55,762	62,146	....	....	....	....	Revenue 81
	198	212	212	139	97	99	108	134	148	160	166	....	....	....	....	Grants Received 81z
	44,137	47,619	49,831	52,012	53,148	55,214	56,962	58,641	60,863	66,695	67,533	....	....	....	....	Expenditure 82
	840	848	790	746	977	750	796	864	1,024	872	1,560	....	....	....	....	Lending Minus Repayments 83
																Financing
	....	....	....	....	....	....	....	....	....	....	....	....	....	....	....	Net Borrowing: Yen 84b
	....	....	....	....	....	....	....	....	....	....	....	....	....	....	....	Foreign Currency 85b
	....	....	....	....	....	....	....	....	....	....	....	....	....	....	....	Use of Cash Balances 87
	97,528	113,209	127,646	144,679	159,356	173,660	196,148	210,407	220,644	231,008	238,746	....	....	....	....	Debt: Domestic 88a
	621	691	735	704	925	991	1,036	1,144	1,200	1,149	1,186	....	....	....	....	Foreign 89a
Billions of Yen																**National Accounts**
	32,887	37,977	39,391	39,275	45,066	46,307	38,090	36,210	37,483	42,352	45,920	46,810	47,409	44,244	44,431	Exports of Goods & Services 90c. c
	23,568	25,585	26,796	27,996	29,449	30,685	32,388	32,975	34,184	36,275	38,807	41,232	43,258	44,666	46,108	Government Consumption 91f. c
	75,821	78,908	79,735	78,881	83,251	88,040	91,310	99,160	111,074	122,766	136,733	143,429	142,207	138,815	134,127	Gross Fixed Capital Formation 93e. c
	1,613	1,424	1,187	187	1,011	2,159	1,643	690	2,630	3,089	2,322	3,271	1,631	661	1,278	Increase/Decrease(-) in Stocks 93i. c
	141,324	149,997	160,834	169,687	178,631	188,760	195,969	204,585	215,122	228,483	243,628	255,084	264,824	270,919	277,677	Private Consumption 96f. c
	-35,036	-35,927	-37,341	-34,258	-36,866	-35,532	-24,791	-25,195	-29,065	-36,768	-42,872	-38,529	-36,184	-33,333	-34,381	Imports of Goods & Services 98c. c
	240,176	257,963	270,601	281,767	300,543	320,419	334,609	348,425	371,429	396,197	424,537	451,297	463,145	465,972	469,240	Gross Domestic Product 99b. c
	-78	-546	69	311	505	1,137	1,229	2,054	2,302	2,849	2,932	3,190	4,268	4,381	3,937	Net Factor Inc/Pmts(-) Abroad 98.n c
	240,098	257,417	270,669	282,078	301,048	321,556	335,838	350,479	373,731	399,046	427,469	454,487	467,413	470,353	473,177	Gross Nat'l Expenditure = GNP 99a. c
	209,172	222,985	234,349	243,564	260,157	277,779	289,509	302,708	323,132	342,855	....	....	....	....	....	Nat'l Income, Market Prices 99e
	283,659	293,282	303,273	311,733	325,216	342,063	351,094	366,319	389,182	407,932	427,469	445,742	451,797	452,311	455,027	Gross Nat'l Prod. 1990 Prices 99a. r
	84.6	87.8	89.2	90.5	92.6	94.0	95.7	95.7	96.0	97.8	100.0	102.0	103.5	104.0	104.0	GNP Deflator (1990=100) 99ai r
Midyear Estimates																
	116.81	117.66	118.48	119.31	120.08	120.84	121.49	122.09	122.61	123.12	123.54	123.92	124.32	124.70	124.96	**Population** 99z

Government Finance: I Beginning in 1975, data are as reported in the *Government Finance Statistics Yearbook* and cover budgetary central government. Data prior to 1975 also cover budgetary central government. Data relate to a fiscal year different from calendar year.

Jordan
439

		1965	1966	1967	1968	1969	1970	1971	1972	1973	1974	1975	1976	1977	1978	1979
Exchange Rates																*SDRs per Dinar:*
Official Rate	ac	2.8000	2.8000	2.8000	2.8000	2.8000	2.8000	2.5790	2.5790	2.5192	2.5929	2.5790	2.5790	2.5790	2.5790	2.5790
																US Dollars per Dinar:
Official Rate	ag	2.8000	2.8000	2.8000	2.8000	2.8000	2.8000	2.8000	2.8000	3.0390	3.1746	3.0303	3.0211	3.1746	3.4130	3.3898
Official Rate	rh	2.8000	2.8000	2.8000	2.8000	2.8000	2.8000	2.8000	2.8000	3.0462	3.1113	3.1393	3.0122	3.0375	3.2733	3.3299
Fund Position																*Millions of SDRs:*
Quota	2f. s	12.3	13.0	13.8	16.0	16.0	23.0	23.0	23.0	23.0	23.0	23.0	23.0	23.0	30.0	30.0
SDRs	1b. s	—	—	—	—	—	2.7	5.1	7.6	7.5	7.4	7.4	7.4	7.4	7.4	11.0
Reserve Position in the Fund	1c. s	2.7	3.0	3.2	4.0	4.0	5.8	5.8	5.8	5.8	5.8	5.8	5.8	5.8	5.6	10.3
Total Fund Cred.&Loans Outstg.	2tl	—	—	—	—	—	—	4.5	4.5	1.6	—	—	—	—	—	—
International Liquidity												*Millions of US Dollars Unless Otherwise Indicated:*				
Total Reserves minus Gold	1l. d	136.4	164.3	240.7	254.8	232.9	227.7	222.9	241.0	270.7	312.8	458.9	471.5	643.1	885.6	1,166.1
SDRs	1b. d	—	—	—	—	—	2.7	5.6	8.2	9.1	9.1	8.7	8.6	9.0	9.6	14.4
Reserve Position in the Fund	1c. d	2.7	3.0	3.2	4.0	4.0	5.8	6.2	6.2	6.9	7.1	6.7	6.7	7.0	7.3	13.6
Foreign Exchange	1d. d	133.7	161.3	237.5	250.8	228.9	219.3	211.1	226.5	254.7	296.7	443.5	456.2	627.2	868.7	1,138.1
Gold (Million Fine Troy Ounces)	1ad	.097	.097	.097	.846	.846	.797	.797	.797	.797	.797	.797	.797	.806	.811	.816
Gold (National Valuation)	1an d	3.4	3.4	3.4	29.6	29.6	27.9	27.9	30.3	33.6	34.3	32.8	79.7	80.6	81.1	81.6
Monetary Authorities: Other Liab.	4.. d	—	.2	.2	.2	.3	.4	.5	.5	1.2	1.8	1.5	.5	1.2	.8	11.2
Deposit Money Banks: Assets	7a. d	28.1	20.3	14.9	17.7	13.5	17.0	8.6	9.5	20.4	25.3	37.7	58.1	116.6	254.7	271.4
of which: Claims on Nonbanks	7ad d	.7	.1	.2	.1	.1	1.6	2.0	2.0	2.4	2.9	3.6	4.8	5.7	7.9	11.3
Deposit Money Banks: Liabilities	7b. d	9.3	8.1	7.4	7.2	9.2	9.9	7.0	6.8	8.1	13.5	31.4	80.4	67.4	204.6	283.6
of which: Liab. to Nonbanks	7bd d	5.6	6.0	6.0	5.2	7.1	7.1	5.8	5.7	6.7	11.5	26.2	61.5	60.1	162.0	227.4
Other Banking Insts.: Liabilities	7f. d	....	9.6	10.4	9.2	9.7	10.0	10.4	10.4	11.9	13.2	14.9	12.8	42.6	34.3	48.1
Monetary Authorities																*Millions of Dinars:*
Foreign Assets	11	49.4	59.9	87.2	101.6	93.8	91.3	89.6	96.9	100.4	110.2	162.3	182.2	229.1	286.1	370.8
Claims on Central Government	12a	—	.1	—	—	3.9	10.8	19.5	11.5	28.8	30.4	27.2	44.9	58.9	56.5	60.3
Reserve Money	14	35.5	45.4	70.0	80.9	85.7	97.3	99.5	100.7	117.2	140.5	173.5	216.4	255.2	299.9	380.3
of which: Currency Outside DMBs	14a	26.5	30.3	51.5	63.5	71.3	82.4	83.0	81.5	97.5	115.5	139.0	161.5	188.2	219.5	275.4
Central Government Deposits	16d	10.4	10.0	18.4	21.2	10.5	2.5	1.7	2.4	6.7	4.2	14.1	10.0	23.9	31.4	31.5
Other Items (Net)	17r	3.5	4.6	-1.2	-.6	1.5	2.4	7.8	5.3	5.4	-4.0	1.7	.7	8.9	11.3	19.3
Deposit Money Banks																*Millions of Dinars:*
Reserves	20	8.9	14.8	18.4	17.5	14.4	14.8	16.4	19.2	18.8	24.5	35.9	54.2	67.6	81.7	101.6
Foreign Assets	21	10.0	7.3	5.3	6.3	4.8	6.1	3.1	3.4	6.6	8.0	12.5	19.2	36.7	74.6	80.1
Claims on Central Government	22a	—	—	—	—	3.8	3.3	8.6	16.2	16.9	14.9	24.5	23.0	32.9	68.6	73.8
Claims on Private Sector	22d	31.6	37.2	36.9	38.3	43.5	43.6	44.8	47.9	59.3	80.3	115.6	177.2	196.7	313.8	444.0
Demand Deposits	24	20.8	25.7	23.7	24.4	24.9	23.0	25.0	33.5	40.9	55.7	84.5	113.9	139.8	150.0	182.0
Time and Savings Deposits	25	17.0	19.8	18.7	20.5	22.4	23.4	26.5	31.1	36.6	47.3	63.6	99.1	135.1	226.8	298.2
Foreign Liabilities	26c	3.3	2.9	2.6	2.6	3.3	3.5	2.5	2.4	2.6	4.3	10.3	26.6	21.2	60.0	83.7
Central Government Deposits	26d	4.4	5.2	8.8	7.4	7.5	8.7	6.1	6.2	6.1	8.4	12.0	16.6	21.0	24.3	45.8
Capital Accounts	27a	5.0	6.0	6.2	7.1	7.9	8.0	8.0	8.0	8.0	11.6	14.9	21.0	32.7	54.7	67.9
Other Items (Net)	27r	.2	-.3	.5	.1	.5	1.2	4.8	5.3	7.4	.4	3.2	-3.6	-16.0	23.0	21.9
Monetary Survey																*Millions of Dinars:*
Foreign Assets (Net)	31n	56.1	64.2	89.8	105.3	95.2	93.7	88.2	95.9	103.4	113.3	163.8	174.7	244.2	300.6	363.9
Domestic Credit	32	18.9	24.6	12.6	13.4	36.1	49.4	68.4	71.4	98.1	122.0	152.6	240.0	275.7	425.2	545.9
Claims on Central Govt. (Net)	32an	-14.8	-15.1	-27.2	-28.6	-10.3	3.0	20.2	19.1	32.9	32.8	25.5	41.3	46.8	69.4	56.7
Claims on Nonfin.Pub.Enterprises	32c	2.1	2.6	2.9	3.7	2.9	2.8	3.3	4.4	5.8	9.0	11.5	21.4	31.6	42.0	44.2
Claims on Private Sector	32d	31.6	37.2	36.9	38.3	43.5	43.6	44.9	47.9	59.3	80.3	115.6	177.2	197.3	313.8	445.0
Money	34	47.3	56.0	75.2	88.0	96.2	105.5	108.0	115.0	139.2	172.0	224.7	276.7	329.0	370.5	465.6
Quasi-Money	35	17.0	20.0	18.9	20.9	22.6	23.8	27.1	31.6	37.2	48.5	67.5	110.8	144.9	237.1	301.6
Other Items (Net)	37r	10.7	12.8	8.2	9.8	12.5	13.8	21.4	20.7	25.0	14.8	24.4	27.2	46.0	118.2	142.7
Money plus Quasi-Money	35l	64.3	76.0	94.1	108.8	118.8	129.3	135.1	146.6	176.4	220.5	292.1	387.5	473.9	607.6	767.2
Other Banking Institutions																*Millions of Dinars:*
Cash	40	....	2.3	1.9	1.7	2.1	1.6	1.4	.8	1.3	1.3	.9	2.1	2.3	3.4	7.0
Claims on Private Sector	42d	....	10.4	12.1	13.4	13.4	14.1	14.9	16.2	17.5	21.5	25.1	30.5	36.0	43.4	50.0
Deposits	45	....	—	—	—	—	—	—	—	—	—	—	2.1	—	—	—
Foreign Liabilities	46c	....	3.4	3.7	3.3	3.5	3.6	3.7	3.7	3.8	4.2	4.9	4.2	13.4	10.0	14.2
Central Govt. Lending Funds	46f	....	.5	.5	1.2	1.8	1.9	1.8	1.8	1.7	1.6	1.7	1.7	1.5	1.5	1.5
Capital Accounts	47a	....	8.0	9.4	10.3	11.1	11.4	12.1	13.0	14.1	15.0	17.9	19.5	22.4	24.4	28.1
Other Items (Net)	47r	....	.8	.4	.3	-.9	-1.1	-1.4	-1.5	-.8	2.0	1.5	5.1	1.0	10.9	13.2
Liquid Liabilities	55l	....	73.68	92.24	107.16	116.78	127.64	133.73	145.75	175.09	218.57	287.48	387.54	471.58	604.21	760.20
Interest Rates																*Percent Per Annum*
Discount Rate (End of Period)	60	....	5.50	5.25	5.25	5.25	5.25	5.25	5.00	5.00	5.00	5.00	5.50	5.50	5.50	6.00
Deposit Rate (End of Period)	60l	....	....	....	....	....	....	....	....	....	....	....	....	....	....	....
Lending Rate (End of Period)	60p	....	....	....	....	....	....	....	....	....	....	....	....	....	....	....
Prices and Production																*Index Numbers (1990=100):*
Consumer Prices	64	....	....	....	....	16.1	17.0	17.8	19.2	21.4	25.5	I28.6	31.8	36.5	39.0	I44.6
Industrial Production	66	....	15.4	14.0	14.3	17.1	14.8	17.5	21.4	23.5	24.5	I26.3	32.9	34.2	41.9	50.2

Jordan

	1980	1981	1982	1983	1984	1985	1986	1987	1988	1989	1990	1991	1992	1993	1994		
End of Period																**Exchange Rates**	
	2.5790	2.5790	2.5790	2.5790	2.5790	2.5790	2.5790	2.5790	1.5579	1.1743	1.0570	1.0357	1.0525	1.0341	.9772	Official Rate	ac
End of Period (ag) Period Average (rh)																	
	3.2415	2.9498	2.8450	2.6918	2.4691	2.7192	2.9061	3.0395	2.0964	1.5432	1.5038	1.4815	1.4472	1.4205	1.4265	Official Rate	ag
	3.3543	3.0293	2.8384	2.7550	2.6036	2.5379	2.8583	2.9522	2.6916	1.7532	1.5069	1.4689	1.4712	1.4434	1.4312	Official Rate	rh
End of Period																**Fund Position**	
	45.0	45.0	45.0	73.9	73.9	73.9	73.9	73.9	73.9	73.9	73.9	73.9	121.7	121.7	121.7	Quota	2f. s
	11.7	15.5	16.5	17.4	15.8	21.9	19.6	8.5	—	8.4	.7	.8	.4	4.0	.5	SDRs	1b. s
	16.6	16.6	16.6	7.2	—	—	—	—	—	—	—	—	12.0	—	—	Reserve Position in the Fund	1c. s
	—	—	—	—	—	57.4	57.4	57.4	35.9	73.4	66.2	66.2	81.2	59.2	98.9	Total Fund Cred.&Loans Outstg.	2tl
End of Period																**International Liquidity**	
	1,142.8	1,086.7	884.1	824.2	515.0	422.8	437.1	424.7	109.6	470.7	848.8	825.8	767.2	⅃1,637.4	1,692.6	Total Reserves minus Gold	1l. d
	14.9	18.0	18.2	18.2	15.5	24.1	23.9	12.1	.1	11.0	1.0	1.1	.6	5.5	.7	SDRs	1b. d
	21.1	19.3	18.3	7.6	—	—	—	—	—	—	—	—	16.4	—	—	Reserve Position in the Fund	1c. d
	1,106.8	1,049.4	847.6	798.4	499.5	398.7	413.2	412.6	109.5	459.7	847.8	824.7	750.2	⅃1,631.9	1,691.9	Foreign Exchange	1d. d
	1.021	1.067	1.080	1.090	1.060	1.061	1.064	1.002	.743	.748	.753	.789	.789	.791	.794	Gold (Million Fine Troy Ounces)	1ad
	204.2	213.4	216.0	199.5	172.2	189.8	203.5	200.1	138.3	102.5	100.6	103.8	101.4	99.8	198.5	Gold (National Valuation)	1an d
	1.3	3.6	1.5	.7	1.1	1.0	1.0	176.2	25.5	15.4	10.6	.5	.8	1.8	....	Monetary Authorities: Other Liab.	4..d
	665.2	688.2	726.6	819.3	816.1	1,046.6	1,172.1	1,374.0	1,200.4	976.0	986.9	1,922.5	2,137.9	2,216.3	2,399.3	Deposit Money Banks: Assets	7a. d
	12.1	14.2	25.0	51.1	40.2	38.9	46.9	54.2	46.0	28.0	27.0	35.1	30.3	75.8	....	of which: Claims on Nonbanks	7ad d
	480.5	523.3	572.1	664.2	779.3	917.9	1,011.6	1,160.0	1,157.8	779.2	691.5	1,367.1	2,310.5	2,166.6	2,518.5	Deposit Money Banks: Liabilities	7b. d
	431.9	423.5	488.1	583.2	683.6	800.2	887.8	914.3	885.8	617.9	581.9	1,197.3	2,204.0	1,895.9	....	of which: Liab. to Nonbanks	7bd d
	53.1	56.4	59.0	57.0	71.0	81.0	101.0	110.0	77.0	61.0	75.0	85.6	97.6	112.3	....	Other Banking Insts.: Liabilities	7f. d
End of Period																**Monetary Authorities**	
	416.9	433.7	372.9	380.3	278.3	379.3	402.0	391.7	346.9	601.4	788.0	949.5	999.7	⅃1,688.7	1,904.3	Foreign Assets	11
	126.7	150.3	195.4	200.4	181.1	204.7	225.9	351.6	663.7	741.3	747.5	685.9	688.9	772.5	905.3	Claims on Central Government	12a
	467.3	534.1	596.5	663.6	676.2	701.7	747.2	779.9	959.1	1,135.9	1,279.7	1,665.6	1,771.3	⅃2,236.0	2,349.5	Reserve Money	14
	351.6	412.3	470.0	516.0	530.5	531.8	583.9	655.8	811.2	871.1	1,006.2	992.4	1,003.9	1,047.9	1,072.6	of which: Currency Outside DMBs	14a
	51.1	39.3	23.6	40.3	17.5	6.7	10.4	1.7	—	21.4	5.7	210.7	137.6	101.3	225.1	Central Government Deposits	16d
	25.1	10.6	-51.8	-123.2	-234.2	-124.4	-129.6	-38.3	51.4	185.4	250.0	-240.9	-220.2	⅃123.9	235.0	Other Items (Net)	17r
End of Period																**Deposit Money Banks**	
	116.6	115.1	118.5	134.0	136.2	161.9	180.6	181.0	248.8	456.4	566.6	1,318.2	1,584.9	1,477.1	1,576.9	Reserves	20
	205.2	233.3	255.4	304.4	330.5	384.9	403.3	452.0	572.6	632.4	656.3	1,297.3	1,477.3	1,560.3	1,681.9	Foreign Assets	21
	59.8	80.8	102.8	147.2	208.5	228.3	275.7	345.9	334.9	369.0	388.8	424.1	457.9	358.7	307.0	Claims on Central Government	22a
	541.6	689.7	843.0	993.3	1,133.5	1,193.4	1,291.5	1,349.9	1,461.5	1,565.0	1,716.1	1,841.0	2,013.7	2,310.5	2,763.4	Claims on Private Sector	22d
	225.2	280.1	305.1	338.7	336.9	308.4	310.7	322.8	353.7	425.4	413.8	640.3	685.9	⅃669.6	666.0	Demand Deposits	24
	386.4	476.8	614.5	745.2	877.4	1,023.2	1,173.8	1,391.4	1,459.3	1,638.5	1,673.0	2,361.1	2,448.8	⅃2,510.0	2,782.4	Time and Savings Deposits	25
	148.2	177.4	201.1	246.7	315.6	337.6	348.1	381.6	552.3	504.9	459.8	922.8	1,596.5	1,525.3	1,765.5	Foreign Liabilities	26c
	63.6	77.2	78.3	97.2	111.9	121.3	156.2	127.3	110.6	161.1	168.8	212.4	91.5	⅃424.8	499.8	Central Government Deposits	26d
	76.8	91.7	131.2	140.3	152.9	164.4	177.5	185.6	194.4	204.2	75.9	88.7	348.5	492.6	582.8	Capital Accounts	27a
	23.0	15.7	-10.5	10.7	14.1	13.6	-15.3	-80.0	-52.5	88.8	536.4	655.6	362.7	⅃84.3	32.9	Other Items (Net)	27r
End of Period																**Monetary Survey**	
	473.4	488.4	426.7	437.7	292.8	403.1	432.7	377.4	332.0	656.5	914.7	1,260.1	802.7	⅃1,578.0	1,637.2	Foreign Assets (Net)	31n
	666.7	883.9	1,162.1	1,360.4	1,587.7	1,743.0	1,833.6	2,190.5	2,637.3	2,780.7	2,935.1	2,759.1	3,220.9	⅃3,324.8	3,723.1	Domestic Credit	32
	71.8	114.6	196.3	210.1	260.2	305.0	335.0	568.5	888.0	927.7	961.7	686.9	917.8	⅃605.1	487.4	Claims on Central Govt. (Net)	32an
	53.3	78.2	122.8	157.0	173.5	218.7	175.1	237.7	253.0	251.4	250.5	225.2	235.0	⅃296.8	341.9	Claims on Nonfin.Pub.Enterprises	32c
	541.6	691.1	843.0	993.3	1,133.5	1,197.1	1,296.2	1,354.7	1,467.4	1,568.4	1,719.5	1,844.7	2,018.1	2,316.1	2,769.9	Claims on Private Sector	32d
	580.7	701.7	787.5	869.4	878.4	848.2	897.1	979.8	1,168.6	1,302.3	1,425.3	1,646.6	1,716.0	⅃1,719.4	1,741.6	Money	34
	399.5	482.0	619.4	748.5	883.8	1,030.9	1,181.7	1,424.4	1,611.2	1,935.3	2,080.1	2,412.8	2,479.0	⅃2,664.7	2,788.6	Quasi-Money	35
	159.9	188.6	181.9	180.2	118.3	267.0	187.6	163.7	191.3	199.5	344.4	-40.2	-171.4	⅃518.8	830.1	Other Items (Net)	37r
	980.3	1,183.6	1,406.9	1,617.9	1,762.2	1,879.1	2,078.8	2,404.2	2,778.0	3,237.6	3,505.4	4,059.4	4,195.0	⅃4,384.1	4,530.2	Money plus Quasi-Money	35l
End of Period																**Other Banking Institutions**	
	9.2	18.3	12.5	12.2	13.6	22.9	19.8	26.8	25.1	42.3	39.1	65.9	49.8	⅃70.6	....	Cash	40
	59.9	71.5	95.9	119.9	128.0	138.4	144.0	191.2	213.0	210.5	209.8	219.8	256.2	⅃294.9	....	Claims on Private Sector	42d
	—	10.2	10.4	12.4	16.5	18.6	28.7	35.9	29.4	32.2	35.4	58.9	44.9	⅃66.5	....	Deposits	45
	16.4	19.1	20.6	25.3	28.8	30.0	34.6	36.3	36.8	39.8	50.0	57.8	67.5	⅃79.0	....	Foreign Liabilities	46c
	1.3	1.2	2.1	2.0	2.1	2.2	2.3	2.2	3.0	2.8	2.9	3.1	.9	⅃17.1	....	Central Govt. Lending Funds	46f
	31.7	39.5	48.5	55.4	62.3	63.9	69.1	70.7	76.6	80.9	88.1	78.5	104.0	⅃90.9	....	Capital Accounts	47a
	19.7	19.8	26.7	37.0	31.8	46.7	29.1	73.0	92.4	97.1	72.9	87.4	88.7	⅃111.9	....	Other Items (Net)	47r
	971.01	1,175.50	1,404.83	1,618.06	1,765.12	1,874.79	2,087.65	2,413.28	2,782.24	3,227.50	3,501.62	4,052.39	4,190.08	⅃4379.98	....	Liquid Liabilities	55l
Percent Per Annum																**Interest Rates**	
	6.00	6.50	6.50	6.25	6.25	6.25	6.25	6.25	6.25	8.00	8.50	8.50	8.50	8.50	8.50	Discount Rate *(End of Period)*	60
	....	....	....	....	....	....	....	....	....	....	6.75	3.25	3.25	3.25	3.25	Deposit Rate *(End of Period)*	60l
	....	....	....	....	....	....	....	....	....	....	10.00	10.00	9.75	9.00	9.00	Lending Rate *(End of Period)*	60p
Period Averages																**Prices and Production**	
	49.5	53.3	57.3	60.2	62.5	⅃64.3	64.3	64.2	68.5	86.1	100.0	108.2	112.5	⅃117.8	122.0	Consumer Prices	64
	60.0	69.9	72.2	75.8	86.9	93.1	94.3	103.1	94.7	99.4	100.0	98.8	106.5	108.3	113.4	Industrial Production	66

Jordan

439

		1965	1966	1967	1968	1969	1970	1971	1972	1973	1974	1975	1976	1977	1978	1979
International Transactions																*Millions of Dinars*
Exports	70	9.9	10.4	11.3	14.3	14.7	12.2	11.4	17.0	24.0	49.8	48.9	68.7	82.1	90.9	120.9
Imports, cif	71	56.1	68.2	55.0	56.6	67.7	65.8	76.6	97.7	108.2	156.8	234.0	334.1	454.4	458.8	589.5
Imports, fob	71.v	50.1	60.9	49.1	50.6	60.4	58.8	68.4	87.0	96.2	139.6	208.3	297.3	404.5	408.4	524.7
																1990=100
Volume of Exports	72	....	....	....	....	11.5	11.5	10.5	13.0	14.1	20.0	‡17.2	20.8	25.1	27.0	33.4
Volume of Imports	73	....	....	....	....	22.6	20.4	19.6	25.0	24.4	27.2	‡34.6	51.9	60.6	69.1	81.2
Export Prices	74	....	....	....	....	20.3	17.1	15.9	19.2	19.3	39.3	‡44.5	41.4	41.4	39.9	40.2
Unit Value of Imports	75	....	....	....	....	15.7	17.1	19.9	21.7	22.7	28.9	‡39.7	38.6	39.4	38.3	41.0
Balance of Payments																*Millions of US Dollars:*
Goods: Exports f.o.b.	78aa d	....	....	....	....	....	....	....	47.6	73.7	154.3	152.9	206.9	248.9	297.4	402.2
Goods: Imports f.o.b.	78ab d	....	....	....	....	....	....	....	−236.6	−291.9	−430.3	−648.2	−907.9	−1,225.2	−1,339.2	−1,743.2
Trade Balance	78ac d	....	....	....	....	....	....	....	−189.0	−218.2	−276.0	−495.3	−700.9	−976.3	−1,041.8	−1,341.0
Services: Credit	78ad d	....	....	....	....	....	....	....	65.0	96.2	98.1	226.4	344.3	442.5	572.4	731.3
Services: Debit	78ae d	....	....	....	....	....	....	....	−90.7	−122.0	−172.3	−293.3	−387.4	−426.0	−650.5	−1,001.7
Balance on Goods and Services	78af d	....	....	....	....	....	....	....	−214.8	−244.1	−350.2	−562.2	−744.0	−959.8	−1,119.9	−1,611.3
Income: Credit	78ag d	....	....	....	....	....	....	....	12.3	19.2	27.3	35.3	39.2	40.4	51.5	88.1
Income: Debit	78ah d	....	....	....	....	....	....	....	−2.8	−4.0	−6.5	−9.7	−14.2	−18.2	−24.7	−49.0
Balance on Goods, Serv., & Inc.	78ai d	....	....	....	....	....	....	....	−205.2	−228.9	−329.4	−536.6	−719.0	−937.6	−1,093.1	−1,572.2
Current Transfers, n.i.e.: Credit	78aj d	....	....	....	....	....	....	....	211.7	241.3	333.1	583.2	779.6	975.5	872.4	1,666.3
Current Transfers: Debit	78ak d	....	....	....	....	....	....	....	—	—	−.3	−1.9	−24.4	−54.4	−67.7	−100.6
Current Account, n.i.e.	78al d	....	....	....	....	....	....	....	6.4	12.5	3.4	44.7	36.1	−16.5	−288.4	−6.5
Capital Account, n.i.e.: Credit	78ba d	....	....	....	....	....	....	....	—	—	—	—	—	—	—	—
Capital Account: Debit	78bb d	....	....	....	....	....	....	....	—	—	—	—	—	—	—	—
Capital Account, n.i.e.	78bc d	....	....	....	....	....	....	....	—	—	—	—	—	—	—	—
Direct Investment Abroad	78bd d	....	....	....	....	....	....	....	−1.7	−5.5	−3.4	−6.3	−2.7	—	—	—
Dir. Invest. in Rep. Econ., n.i.e.	78be d	....	....	....	....	....	....	....	.6	2.1	6.8	25.6	−7.5	11.2	56.4	26.4
Portfolio Investment Assets	78bf d	....	....	....	....	....	....	....								
Portfolio Investment Liab., n.i.e.	78bg d	....	....	....	....	....	....	....								
Other Investment Assets	78bh d	....	....	....	....	....	....	....	.3	.3	.6	−1.9	.3	−7.8	−2.6	−38.0
Other Investment Liab., n.i.e.	78bi d	....	....	....	....	....	....	....	18.2	26.2	35.4	147.0	25.9	131.4	372.6	279.8
Financial Account, n.i.e.	78bj d	....	....	....	....	....	....	....	17.4	23.1	39.4	164.5	16.0	134.8	426.5	268.2
Net Errors and Omissions	78ca d	....	....	....	....	....	....	....	−5.1	3.8	−16.9	−36.3	−24.7	67.6	113.9	59.2
Overall Balance	78cb d	....	....	....	....	....	....	....	18.7	39.4	26.0	172.9	27.4	185.9	251.9	320.9
Reserves and Related Items	79da d	....	....	....	....	....	....	....	−18.7	−39.4	−26.0	−172.9	−27.4	−185.9	−251.9	−320.9
Reserve Assets	79db d	....	....	....	....	....	....	....	−18.7	−35.6	−24.1	−172.9	−27.4	−185.9	−251.9	−320.9
Use of Fund Credit and Loans	79dc d	....	....	....	....	....	....	....	—	−3.8	−1.9	—	—	—	—	—
Liabs.Constit.For.Auth.Reserves	79dd d	....	....	....	....	....	....	....	—	—	—	—	—	—	—	—
Exceptional Financing	79de d	....	....	....	....	....	....	....	—	—	—	—	—	—	—	—
Government Finance																*Millions of Dinars:*
Deficit (−) or Surplus	80	−4.99	−5.41	−2.24	−14.14	−17.50	−15.03	−15.10	21.99	−23.10	−15.13	−14.83	−81.41	−61.08	−110.80	−104.07
Revenue	81	26.73	31.19	25.50	26.27	32.52	30.26	35.74	42.56	46.18	65.74	82.63	107.59	142.25	158.49	187.90
Grants Received	81z	15.27	15.73	40.41	40.11	38.38	35.42	35.12	45.56	43.57	57.65	97.11	66.24	122.20	81.70	210.30
Expenditure	82	46.99	52.33	66.15	78.49	87.87	80.40	85.68	66.08	112.65	138.23	183.62	243.98	307.93	340.10	475.37
Lending Minus Repayments	83	—	—	2.00	2.03	.53	.31	.28	.05	.20	.29	10.95	11.26	17.60	10.89	26.90
Financing																
Net Borrowing: Dinars	84b	—	—	—	—	8.40	4.20	12.10	4.25	9.32	8.08	9.75	12.89	9.62	13.29	26.89
Foreign Currency	85b	2.56	3.71	2.92	3.11	3.58	1.45	3.58	3.94	8.22	9.36	9.25	12.76	51.58	82.89	29.69
Use of Cash Balances	87	2.43	1.70	−.68	11.03	5.52	9.38	−.58	−30.18	5.56	−2.31	−4.17	55.76	−.12	14.62	47.49
Debt: Domestic	88a					8.40	14.30	29.40	37.70	50.40	56.00	65.40	89.30	105.90	135.20	139.40
Foreign	89a	23.70	26.90	31.10	36.90	39.90	41.80	48.00	59.50	67.70	79.80	91.70	114.10	147.30	187.80	233.70
National Accounts																*Millions of Dinars*
Exports of Goods & Services	90c	28.5	32.1	20.8	18.9	20.6	17.6	17.8	37.0	52.4	80.3	118.9	192.1	242.0	264.3	339.5
Government Consumption	91f	36.8	39.2	44.0	55.9	64.0	58.7	60.4	68.3	80.0	97.7	110.1	155.9	156.6	190.0	235.3
Gross Fixed Capital Formation	93e	23.9	27.7	24.0	27.0	35.8	25.2	30.7	36.3	47.2	63.2	87.9	138.0	201.0	229.1	294.5
Increase/Decrease(−) in Stocks	93i	3.9	4.1	−1.6	.5	3.9	−3.1	4.5	6.0	−8.0	2.4	.9	12.2	5.5	−6.1	−14.5
Private Consumption	96f	138.0	149.5	103.8	127.4	156.8	152.8	161.7	177.4	183.1	199.8	261.9	325.5	412.8	517.4	736.8
Imports of Goods & Services	98c	−63.6	−76.6	−59.8	−73.6	−97.7	−76.8	−88.9	−117.8	−136.4	−196.1	−301.1	−422.0	−540.3	−605.6	−824.5
Gross Domestic Product	99b	167.6	139.4	159.2	189.6	222.8	211.8	226.2	251.7	265.2	300.4	379.1	512.1	624.6	767.9	914.6
Net Factor Inc/Pmts(−) Abroad	98.n	12.9	15.2	11.3	10.3	14.0	12.6	13.2	13.8	23.2	32.0	63.9	140.8	145.9	148.8	168.3
Gross Nat'l Expenditure = GNP	99a	180.5	128.9	143.0	167.0	198.2	187.7	200.2	221.9	242.4	280.4	377.5	564.6	662.7	784.0	924.9
Nat'l Income, Market Prices	99e	173.9	119.7	134.3	156.6	187.6	177.1	189.3	210.7	231.0	268.7	360.2	545.0	639.1	754.0	882.8
Gross Dom. Prod. 1990 Prices	99b.p	....	....	....	....	1,294.3	1,162.6	1,179.5	1,224.3	1,158.2	1,098.1	1,236.9	1,499.4	‡1,595.5	1,832.3	1,914.4
GDP Deflator (1990=100)	99bi p	....	....	....	....	17.2	18.2	19.2	20.6	22.9	27.4	30.6	34.2	39.1	41.9	47.8
																Millions:
Population	99z	1.91	1.97	2.04	2.10	2.19	2.30	2.38	2.46	2.54	2.62	2.70	2.78	‡2.71	2.77	2.84

Monetary Authorities: ‡ Beginning in 1993, *lines 11* and *14* reflect foreign currency deposits of licensed banks.
Deposit Money Banks: ‡ Beginning in 1993, *line 26d* includes deposits of the Social Security Corporation, which previously were included in *lines 24* and *25*.
Monetary Survey: ‡ See notes to sections 10 and 20.
Other Banking Institutions: ‡ Beginning in 1993, comprises Cities and Villages Development Bank, Agricultural Credit Corporation, Industrial Development Bank, the Housing Corporation, and Jordan Cooperative Organization. Prior to 1993, comprises the Industrial Development Bank, the Agricultural Credit Corporation, and the Municipal Loan Fund.
National Accounts: ‡ Beginning 1967, data refer to the East Bank only.

Jordan

	1980	1981	1982	1983	1984	1985	1986	1987	1988	1989	1990	1991	1992	1993	1994		
Millions of Dinars																**International Transactions**	
	171.4	242.6	264.5	210.6	290.7	310.9	256.0	315.7	381.5	637.6	706.1	770.7	829.3	864.7	995.2	Exports	70
	716.1	1,047.5	1,142.5	1,103.3	1,071.4	1,074.4	850.2	915.6	1,022.5	1,230.0	1,725.8	1,710.5	2,214.0	2,453.6	2,362.6	Imports, cif	71
	637.4	932.7	1,016.6	982.2	953.5	955.9	756.4	814.5	909.7	1,094.3	1,535.4	1,521.8	1,969.8	2,182.9	2,101.9	Imports, fob	71.v
1990=100																	
	41.7	48.6	49.7	‡49.4	69.3	72.2	74.0	88.0	98.6	103.9	100.0	87.9	96.5	104.3	....	Volume of Exports	72
	79.7	94.5	103.8	‡104.7	98.2	100.5	105.6	109.5	115.7	95.9	100.0	98.8	135.5	147.7	....	Volume of Imports	73
	47.7	54.8	59.8	‡54.7	59.6	57.8	49.8	46.2	53.8	84.0	100.0	100.0	111.3	107.2	108.3	....	Export Prices	74
	50.9	61.9	62.9	‡57.5	63.6	61.9	46.6	48.4	51.2	74.3	100.0	100.2	94.7	96.2	....	Unit Value of Imports	75
Minus Sign Indicates Debit																**Balance of Payments**	
	575.2	733.2	751.6	580.0	751.9	788.9	732.0	933.1	1,007.4	1,109.4	1,063.8	1,129.5	1,218.9	1,246.3	....	Goods: Exports f.o.b.	78aa d
	−2,136.1	−2,815.3	−2,878.6	−2,700.1	−2,472.6	−2,426.7	−2,158.4	−2,400.1	−2,418.7	−1,882.5	−2,300.7	−2,302.2	−2,998.7	−3,145.2	....	Goods: Imports f.o.b.	78ab d
	−1,560.9	−2,082.1	−2,127.0	−2,120.1	−1,720.7	−1,637.9	−1,426.4	−1,467.0	−1,411.3	−773.1	−1,236.9	−1,172.7	−1,779.7	−1,898.8	....	Trade Balance	78ac d
	1,002.9	1,160.0	1,112.1	1,124.5	1,131.0	1,167.1	1,058.8	1,291.7	1,420.6	1,239.2	1,447.2	1,351.2	1,449.2	1,573.7	....	Services: Credit	78ad d
	−1,094.3	−1,386.1	−1,376.9	−1,159.5	−1,330.2	−1,286.9	−1,150.5	−1,298.3	−1,340.5	−1,063.3	−1,267.9	−1,122.5	−1,324.7	−1,347.2	....	Services: Debit	78ae d
	−1,652.4	−2,308.2	−2,391.8	−2,155.1	−1,920.0	−1,757.7	−1,518.1	−1,473.6	−1,331.1	−597.1	−1,057.6	−944.0	−1,655.2	−1,672.3	....	Balance on Goods and Services	78af d
	126.1	200.4	204.7	173.0	100.7	101.1	100.1	58.3	40.6	39.0	67.3	114.3	112.4	99.0	....	Income: Credit	78ag d
	−78.9	−113.0	−112.0	−127.9	−161.4	−189.6	−240.4	−278.6	−354.8	−235.6	−281.8	−447.7	−460.0	−409.4	....	Income: Debit	78ah d
	−1,605.1	−2,220.8	−2,299.1	−2,110.0	−1,980.6	−1,846.2	−1,658.4	−1,693.8	−1,645.2	−793.7	−1,272.1	−1,277.4	−2,002.8	−1,982.8	....	Balance on Goods, Serv., & Inc.	78ai d
	2,140.8	2,344.2	2,149.3	1,925.0	1,979.5	1,828.3	1,872.7	1,547.1	1,532.0	1,284.5	1,123.1	949.5	1,263.6	1,441.1	....	Current Transfers, n.i.e.: Credit	78aj d
	−161.8	−162.3	−183.0	−205.7	−263.7	−242.5	−254.1	−205.1	−180.5	−105.8	−78.2	−65.7	−96.1	−87.4	....	Current Transfers: Debit	78ak d
	373.9	−38.9	−332.7	−390.7	−264.7	−260.5	−39.8	−351.8	−293.7	384.9	−227.1	−393.5	−835.2	−629.1	....	Current Account, n.i.e.	78al d
	—	—	—	—	—	—	—	—	—	—	—	—	—	—	....	Capital Account, n.i.e.: Credit	78ba d
	—	—	—	—	—	—	—	—	—	—	—	—	—	—	....	Capital Account: Debit	78bb d
	—	—	—	—	—	—	—	—	—	—	—	—	—	—	....	Capital Account, n.i.e.	78bc d
	−3.1	7.0	−3.4	−4.8	−2.7	.7	−3.9	−1.2	.1	−16.7	31.5	−13.7	3.4	53.0	....	Direct Investment Abroad	78bd d
	33.8	140.8	59.4	34.9	77.5	24.9	22.8	39.5	23.7	−1.3	37.6	−11.9	40.7	−33.5	....	Dir. Invest. in Rep. Econ., n.i.e.	78be d
	—	—	—	—	—	—	—	—	—	—	—	—	—	—	....	Portfolio Investment Assets	78bf d
	—	—	—	—	—	—	—	—	—	—	—	—	—	—	....	Portfolio Investment Liab., n.i.e.	78bg d
	−170.8	−244.4	−104.2	−198.1	−246.2	−190.2	−84.9	−9.0	—	—	222.2	561.5	609.2	384.8	....	Other Investment Assets	78bh d
	468.3	396.1	433.7	651.7	295.0	412.7	165.6	435.9	350.4	97.6	281.4	1,561.6	−38.3	−934.3	....	Other Investment Liab., n.i.e.	78bi d
	328.2	299.5	385.5	483.7	123.7	248.2	99.5	465.2	374.2	79.5	572.7	2,097.3	615.1	−530.0	....	Financial Account, n.i.e.	78bj d
	−257.3	−99.6	−152.3	−40.0	−47.9	−29.6	−17.2	27.9	123.4	.3	75.4	321.4	83.1	298.0	....	Net Errors and Omissions	78ca d
	444.8	161.0	−99.5	53.0	−189.0	−41.9	42.5	141.3	203.9	464.7	421.0	2,025.2	−137.1	−861.1	....	Overall Balance	78cb d
	−444.8	−161.0	99.5	−53.0	189.0	41.9	−42.5	−141.3	−203.9	−464.7	−421.0	−2,025.2	137.1	861.1	....	Reserves and Related Items	79a d
	−444.8	−161.0	99.5	−53.0	189.0	−14.1	−42.5	−141.3	−175.2	−512.0	−411.5	−2,025.2	−432.0	402.9	....	Reserve Assets	79b d
	—	—	—	—	—	56.0	—	—	−28.7	47.2	−9.5	—	21.1	−31.0	....	Use of Fund Credit and Loans	79c d
	—	—	—	—	—	—	—	—	—	—	—	—	—	—	....	Liabs.Constit.For.Auth.Reserves	79dd d
	—	—	—	—	—	—	—	—	—	—	—	—	548.0	489.1	....	Exceptional Financing	79de d
Year Ending December 31																**Government Finance**	
	−103.93	−100.77	−113.00	−68.21	−141.99	−111.74	−153.13	−198.21	−204.57	−137.10	−95.05	−5.94	144.20	26.40	55.10	Deficit (−) or Surplus	80
	226.15	309.20	362.04	400.58	415.01	440.81	514.39	531.53	544.34	565.40	744.07	829.43	1,100.00	1,176.30	1,270.00	Revenue	81
	209.30	206.31	199.58	197.01	106.11	187.84	143.71	127.54	155.43	261.72	164.28	230.27	198.40	142.00	167.30	Grants Received	81z
	512.54	576.17	643.65	630.04	640.64	713.44	770.13	825.71	910.87	947.92	1,000.93	1,101.43	1,167.01	1,310.70	1,401.60	Expenditure	82
	26.84	40.11	30.97	35.76	22.47	26.95	41.10	31.57	−6.53	16.30	2.47	−35.79	−12.81	−18.80	−19.40	Lending Minus Repayments	83
																Financing	
	11.21	16.06	19.19	8.04	14.24	25.89	−8.90	95.13	115.32	22.32	14.43	−5.59	−28.50	−35.70	−15.50	Net Borrowing: Dinars	84b
	54.60	54.73	55.50	60.38	85.38	124.97	86.11	7.24	−10.91	96.01	129.70	313.70	242.90	9.30	−39.70	Foreign Currency	85b
	38.12	29.98	38.31	−.21	42.37	−39.12	75.92	95.84	100.16	18.77	−49.08	−302.17	−358.60	—	.10	Use of Cash Balances	87
	177.80	209.50	250.00	287.90	316.50	370.16	416.80	630.80	926.30	....	....	....	....	....	....	Debt: Domestic	88a
	255.90	350.20	441.50	536.50	653.60	727.24	836.30	898.20	3,814.20	....	....	....	....	....	....	Foreign	89a
Millions of Dinars																**National Accounts**	
	448.0	588.5	670.2	‡639.6	746.3	781.5	634.1	756.2	1,020.8	1,359.5	1,652.1	1,697.5	1,819.9	1,962.1	2,151.4	Exports of Goods & Services	90c
	342.7	455.5	477.9	473.4	534.4	531.7	566.5	586.7	604.3	618.8	663.9	742.0	790.6	852.1	904.4	Government Consumption	91f
	452.9	672.6	626.9	535.9	526.8	384.8	409.3	448.5	513.4	554.1	694.0	678.0	1,049.2	1,235.0	1,220.1	Gross Fixed Capital Formation	93e
	11.0	28.4	23.9	‡53.9	44.4	30.1	35.0	67.1	19.1	9.1	156.2	60.5	159.6	—	−42.7	Increase/Decrease(−) in Stocks	93i
	858.3	1,074.5	1,457.9	‡1,579.1	1,648.4	1,794.8	1,718.2	1,669.8	1,626.5	1,635.1	1,976.4	2,039.6	2,648.4	2,985.0	3,237.7	Private Consumption	96f
	−961.7	−1,392.7	−1,555.7	‡−1453.2	−1,519.1	−1,502.7	−1,199.5	−1,319.7	−1,519.7	−1,804.4	−2,474.3	−2,362.6	−2,974.7	−3,151.7	−3,204.7	Imports of Goods & Services	98c
	1,151.2	1,426.7	1,701.1	‡1,828.7	1,981.4	2,020.2	2,163.6	2,208.6	2,264.4	2,372.1	2,668.3	2,855.1	3,493.0	3,882.5	4,266.2	Gross Domestic Product	99b
	32.4	57.5	64.4	‡49.2	13.6	−4.7	−17.3	−50.2	−88.5	−191.4	−239.5	−221.4	−186.2	−149.1	−149.1	Net Factor Inc/Pmts(−) Abroad	98.n
	1,183.6	1,484.2	1,765.5	1,877.9	1,995.0	2,015.5	2,146.3	2,158.4	2,175.9	2,180.7	2,428.8	2,634.0	3,306.8	3,733.4	4,117.1	Gross Nat'l Expenditure = GNP	99a
	1,096.3	1,371.2	1,608.1	1,699.2	1,795.3	1,809.0	1,949.1	1,955.1	1,955.3	1,942.5	2,195.4	2,331.3	2,983.0	....	....	Nat'l Income, Market Prices	99e
	2,251.9	2,473.5	2,611.6	2,676.9	2,714.9	‡2,825.2	3,023.4	3,140.3	3,053.2	2,642.6	2,668.3	2,717.0	3,153.7	3,335.4	3,525.4	Gross Dom. Prod. 1990 Prices	99b.p
	51.1	57.7	65.1	68.3	73.0	71.5	71.6	70.3	74.2	89.8	100.0	105.1	110.8	116.4	121.0	GDP Deflator (1990=100)	99bi p
Midyear Estimates																	
	2.92	3.01	3.10	3.20	‡3.36	3.83	3.94	4.00	4.06	4.13	4.26	4.44	4.67	4.94	....	Population	99z

Kenya
664

		1965	1966	1967	1968	1969	1970	1971	1972	1973	1974	1975	1976	1977	1978	1979
Exchange Rates																*Shillings per SDR:*
Principal Rate	aa	7.143	7.143	7.143	7.143	7.143	7.143	7.755	7.755	8.324	8.745	9.660	9.660	9.660	9.660	9.660
																Shillings per US Dollar:
Principal Rate	ae	7.143	7.143	7.143	7.143	7.143	7.143	7.143	7.143	6.900	7.143	8.260	8.310	7.947	7.404	7.328
Principal Rate	rf	7.143	7.143	7.143	7.143	7.143	7.143	7.143	7.143	7.020	7.143	7.343	8.367	8.277	7.729	7.475
Fund Position																*Millions of SDRs:*
Quota	2f. s	25.0	32.0	32.0	32.0	32.0	48.0	48.0	48.0	48.0	48.0	48.0	48.0	48.0	69.0	69.0
SDRs	1b. s	—	—	—	—	—	5.8	12.0	17.1	17.1	1.9	3.8	2.8	14.4	11.0	82.1
Reserve Position in the Fund	1c. s	2.3	4.0	4.0	4.1	4.1	12.0	12.0	12.0	12.3	—	—	—	—	—	—
Total Fund Cred.&Loans Outstg.	2tl	—	—	—	—	—	—	—	—	—	32.1	68.6	85.0	52.8	72.2	142.7
International Liquidity											*Millions of US Dollars Unless Otherwise Indicated:*					
Total Reserves minus Gold	1l. d	20.0[e]	52.4	75.8	100.1	169.7	219.8	170.9	202.0	233.0	193.3	173.4	275.5	522.4	352.6	627.7
SDRs	1b. d						5.8	13.0	18.5	20.6	2.3	4.4	3.2	17.5	14.3	108.1
Reserve Position in the Fund	1c. d	2.3	4.0	4.0	4.1	4.1	12.0	13.1	13.1	14.8	—	—	—	—	—	—
Foreign Exchange	1d. d	17.7[e]	48.4	71.8	96.0	165.6	202.0	144.9	170.4	197.6	191.0	169.0	272.3	504.9	338.3	519.6
Gold (Million Fine Troy Ounces)	1ad	....	....	....	....	....	....	....	....	....	—	—	—	.021	.072	.080
Gold (National Valuation)	1and	....	....	....	....	....	....	....	....	—[e]	—	—	—	.9	9.4	9.7
Monetary Authorities: Other Liab.	4..d	....	.6	.7	.7	1.3	1.3	1.1	2.9	.8	1.3	10.5	2.8	7.6	9.0	13.4
Deposit Money Banks: Assets	7a. d	54.6	44.2	23.9	22.3	22.1	25.2	22.0	16.4	32.1	42.6	40.7	48.3	42.0	50.4	68.8
of which: Claims on Nonbanks	7ad d	....	....	....	....	7.2	8.7	10.4	9.1	17.4	25.3	20.1	28.9	27.3	24.7	28.3
Deposit Money Banks: Liabilities	7b. d	30.7	10.4	20.3	14.3	16.4	19.6	25.0	25.4	39.5	56.0	58.1	49.7	52.0	52.5	72.7
of which: Liab. to Nonbanks	7bd d	....	....	....	....	....	....	.8	....	....	....	....	....	....	....	....
Other Banking Insts.: Liabilities	7f. d	....	....	....	....	....	3.6	2.3	1.9	2.7	7.5	6.2	8.3	8.7	11.1	11.3
of which: Liab. to Nonbanks	7fd d	....	....	....	....	....	3.6	2.3	1.9	2.7	7.5	6.2	8.3	8.7	11.1	11.3
Monetary Authorities															*Millions of Shillings:*	
Foreign Assets	11	....	537	573	737	1,225	1,586	1,230	1,416	1,603	1,347	1,427	2,301	4,259	2,732	4,780
Claims on Central Government	12a	....	70	65	82	35	75	158	194	367	661	1,171	833	1,217	1,638	1,783
Reserve Money	14	....	490	624	785	1,121	1,248	1,143	1,264	1,395	1,789	1,613	2,001	3,233	3,466	4,325
of which: Currency Outside DMBs	14a	....	399	452	492	570	697	740	894	982	1,086	1,235	1,625	2,182	2,305	2,673
Restricted Deposits	16b	....	—	—	—	—	—	—	—	—	—	—	—	—	—	457
Foreign Liabilities	16c	....	4	5	5	9	9	8	21	6	289	750	845	570	763	1,476
Long-Term Foreign Liabilities	16cl	....	....	....	....	....	....	....	....	....	....	....	....	....	....	....
Central Government Deposits	16d	....	131	90	83	135	339	190	241	330	37	—	55	1,253	—	—
Counterpart Funds	16e	....	....	....	....	....	....	....	....	....	....	....	....	....	....	....
Capital Accounts	17a	....	13	15	19	26	52	52	52	182	186	186	186	186	186	312
Other Items (Net)	17r	....	−31	−98	−73	−44	−2	−15	32	57	−293	47	48	233	−45	−7
Deposit Money Banks															*Millions of Shillings:*	
Reserves	20	55	81	159	287	550	515	391	343	372	514	298	313	972	833	1,184
Foreign Assets	21	390	316	171	159	158	180	157	117	222	304	336	401	334	373	504
Claims on Central Government	22a	169	44	56	55	192	357	233	452	650	510	677	1,192	1,963	1,805	2,216
Claims on Local Government	22b	21	30	47	54	18	15	21	26	42	38	34	25	24	29	33
Claims on Nonfin.Pub.Enterprises	22c	....	....	....	....	29	86	152	157	188	185	269	190	235	182	207
Claims on Private Sector	22d	981	1,049	1,284	1,246	1,326	1,732	2,214	2,481	3,143	3,814	4,149	4,892	6,513	8,901	9,774
Claims on Other Financial Insts.	22f	....	....	....	....	....	....	....	....	....	....	196	471	684	235	692
Demand Deposits	24	830	934	949	1,133	1,219	1,489	1,616	1,880	2,413	2,620	2,851	3,525	5,095	5,445	6,327
Time & Foreign Currency Deposits	25	383	552	676	690	947	1,279	1,398	1,492	1,907	2,064	2,672	3,335	5,193	6,277	6,833
Foreign Liabilities	26c	219	74	145	102	117	140	178	181	273	400	480	413	413	388	533
Central Government Deposits	26d	178	62	77	21	22	54	67	58	76	70	81	72	128	219	353
Credit from Monetary Authorities	26g	42	—	—	—	6	—	5	—	—	254	19	—	—	120	—
Credit from Other Financial Insts.	26i	....	....	....	....	....	....	....	....	....	....	....	....	....	....	....
Capital Accounts	27a	3	3	9	35	155	185	212	273	307	373	433	537	750	983	1,056
Other Items (Net)	27r	−35	−105	−139	−181	−203	−261	−309	−308	−359	−416	−578	−398	−855	−1,074	−493
Monetary Survey															*Millions of Shillings:*	
Foreign Assets (Net)	31n	....	775	594	789	1,256	1,617	1,200	1,331	1,546	962	534	1,446	3,610	1,954	3,275
Domestic Credit	32	....	1,000	1,293	1,341	1,440	1,879	2,527	3,019	3,990	5,101	6,414	7,475	9,254	12,570	14,352
Claims on Central Govt. (Net)	32an	....	−79	−46	33	70	39	133	347	610	1,064	1,766	1,898	1,799	3,224	3,646
Claims on Local Government	32b	....	30	55	62	18	15	21	26	42	38	34	25	24	29	33
Claims on Nonfin.Pub.Enterprises	32c	....	....	....	....	29	86	152	157	188	185	269	190	235	182	207
Claims on Private Sector	32d	981	1,049	1,284	1,246	1,326	1,732	2,214	2,481	3,143	3,814	4,149	4,892	6,513	8,901	9,774
Claims on Other Financial Insts.	32f	....	....	....	....	7	7	7	8	7	....	196	471	684	235	692
Money	34	....	1,333	1,410	1,627	1,801	2,226	2,371	2,804	3,449	3,755	4,143	5,120	7,333	7,879	9,178
Quasi-Money	35	383	552	676	690	947	1,279	1,398	1,492	1,907	2,064	2,672	3,335	5,193	6,277	6,833
Restricted Deposits	36b	....	—	—	—	—	—	—	—	—	—	—	—	—	—	457
Long-Term Foreign Liabilities	36cl	....	....	....	....	....	....	....	....	....	....	....	....	....	....	....
Counterpart Funds	36e	....	....	....	....	....	....	....	....	....	....	....	....	....	....	....
Other Items (Net)	37r	....	−109	−202	−188	−52	−9	−42	55	180	243	133	466	337	369	1,159
Money plus Quasi-Money	35l	....	1,885	2,086	2,317	2,748	3,505	3,769	4,295	5,356	5,819	6,814	8,455	12,527	14,155	16,011
Other Banking Institutions															*Millions of Shillings:*	
Cash	40	....	....	....	....	....	....	....	....	40	44	163	206	458	527	682
Claims on Central Government	42a	....	....	....	....	....	....	....	....	131	173	166	166	191	257	286
Claims on Local Government	42b	....	....	....	....	....	....	....	....	2	2	—	13	—	—	—
Claims on Nonfin.Pub.Enterprises	42c	....	....	....	....	....	....	....	....	33	17	16	—	13	13	39
Claims on Private Sector	42d	....	....	....	....	....	....	....	....	712	842	1,059	1,409	1,772	2,406	2,935
Claims on Deposit Money Banks	42e	....	....	....	....	....	....	....	....	....	....	....	....	....	....	....
Claims on Other Financial Insts.	42f	....	....	....	....	....	....	....	....	19	20	3	31	124	153	193
Demand Deposits	44	....	....	....	....	....	....	....	....	14	3	105	35	450	307	376
Time and Savings Deposits	45	....	....	....	....	....	....	....	....	790	952	1,295	1,536	1,837	2,636	3,548
Foreign Liabilities	46c	....	....	....	....	....	....	26	16	14	19	54	51	69	82	83
Central Government Deposits	46d	....	....	....	....	....	....	....	....	22	63	73	116	118	220	172
Credit from Deposit Money Banks	46h	....	....	....	....	....	....	....	....	122	51	8	26	36	112	214
Capital Accounts	47a	....	....	....	....	....	....	....	....	91	90	117	136	171	233	293
Other Items (Net)	47r	....	....	....	....	....	....	....	....	−126	−116	−242	−91	−124	−235	−551

Kenya

664

1980	1981	1982	1983	1984	1985	1986	1987	1988	1989	1990	1991	1992	1993	1994		
End of Period															**Exchange Rates**	
9.660	11.950	14.060	14.417	15.187	17.738	19.135	23.429	25.029	28.387	34.263	40.158	49.797	93.626	65.458	Principal Rate	aa
End of Period (ae) Period Average (rf)																
7.569	10.286	12.725	13.796	15.781	16.284	16.042	16.515	18.599	21.601	24.084	28.074	36.216	68.163	44.839	Principal Rate	ae
7.420	9.047	10.922	13.312	14.414	16.432	16.226	16.454	17.747	20.572	22.915	27.508	32.217	58.001	56.051	Principal Rate	rf
End of Period															**Fund Position**	
103.5	103.5	103.5	142.0	142.0	142.0	142.0	142.0	142.0	142.0	142.0	142.0	199.4	199.4	199.4	Quota	2f. *s*
20.2	9.4	14.0	16.6	2.2	.8	9.9	11.4	.4	8.7	2.8	1.0	.6	.8	.5	SDRs	1b. *s*
—	.2	1.5	9.6	10.9	12.2	12.2	12.2	12.2	12.2	12.2	12.2	12.2	12.2	12.3	Reserve Position in the Fund	1c. *s*
199.1	222.2	356.7	443.5	428.3	474.7	375.9	282.9	338.4	316.1	338.9	344.8	286.1	264.3	277.2	Total Fund Cred.&Loans Outstg.	2tl
End of Period															**International Liquidity**	
491.7	231.1	211.7	376.0	389.8	390.6	413.3	255.8	263.7	284.6	205.4	116.9	53.0	405.6	557.6	Total Reserves minus Gold	1l. *d*
25.7	10.9	15.4	17.4	2.1	.9	12.1	16.2	.6	11.5	3.9	1.4	.8	1.1	.7	SDRs	1b. *d*
—	.2	1.6	10.1	10.7	13.4	14.9	17.3	16.4	16.1	17.4	17.5	16.8	16.8	18.0	Reserve Position in the Fund	1c. *d*
466.0	220.0	194.6	348.5	377.0	376.4	386.3	222.3	246.7	257.1	184.1	98.1	35.4	387.7	538.9	Foreign Exchange	1d. *d*
.080	.080	.080	.080	.080	.080	.080	.080	.080	.080	.080	.080	.080	.080	.080	Gold (Million Fine Troy Ounces)	1ad
9.4	18.6	17.4	16.6	13.6	12.6	14.0	17.8	16.9	14.5	13.5	15.0	12.2	14.3	15.2	Gold (National Valuation)	1an *d*
6.0	4.2	14.4	4.7	.8	7.1	2.1	2.7	1.9	69.4	174.0	208.5	200.7	230.8	277.5	Monetary Authorities: Other Liab.	4.. *d*
70.4	67.5	49.3	44.2	40.1	39.3	45.9	39.8	46.1	64.8	68.7	70.4	108.2	348.9	....	Deposit Money Banks: Assets	7a. *d*
29.1	21.3	19.4	15.1	15.8	19.9	22.2	19.6	22.4	39.2	35.1	34.2	37.5	185.3	....	*of which:* Claims on Nonbanks	7ad *d*
68.7	42.8	44.1	45.3	51.5	50.0	53.2	54.4	83.8	77.9	70.5	49.5	53.1	49.8	....	Deposit Money Banks: Liabilities	7b. *d*
—	.5	.5	.6	11.1	9.7	6.7	45.5	41.1	38.9	46.1	40.1	33.6	28.0	....	*of which:* Liab. to Nonbanks	7bd *d*
17.8	14.5	11.1	9.9	7.5	8.7	7.9	17.1	14.5	19.8	15.3	16.5	13.4	10.2	11.0	Other Banking Insts.: Liabilities	7f. *d*
17.8	14.5	11.1	9.9	7.5	8.7	7.9	17.1	14.5	19.7	8.9	16.5	13.4	10.2	11.0	*of which:* Liab. to Nonbanks	7fd *d*
End of Period															**Monetary Authorities**	
3,784	2,577	2,957	5,459	6,444	6,807	7,115	4,753	5,558	7,310	6,630	5,339	6,315	34,527	28,294	Foreign Assets	11
2,663	4,955	8,725	7,028	7,091	8,884	11,260	14,491	15,078	13,225	20,963	24,900	16,074	49,274	....	Claims on Central Government	12a
4,422	4,605	5,787	5,659	6,304	7,257	10,132	12,093	12,342	14,434	17,585	20,341	31,230	47,628	....	Reserve Money	14
3,032	3,569	3,724	4,083	4,370	5,038	6,371	7,688	8,536	9,655	10,829	12,761	17,205	21,355	....	*of which: Currency Outside DMBs*	14a
125	127	11	—	—	10	8	1	1	10	—	1	1	1	1	Restricted Deposits	16b
1,967	2,704	5,190	6,470	6,637	8,607	7,410	6,673	8,507	9,399	12,035	13,871	14,286	24,771	18,252	Foreign Liabilities	16c
....	....	....	....	....	68	78	53	23	62	42	89	81	83	25	Long-Term Foreign Liabilities	16cl
—	103	—	—	—	—	—	—	—	—	—	—	—	38,289	-20,555	Central Government Deposits	16d
....	....	....	....	....	34	33	38	46	49	42	58	73	73	127	Counterpart Funds	16e
364	391	431	525	618	708	805	898	1,049	1,229	1,479	1,820	2,278	720	813	Capital Accounts	17a
-431	-397	263	-167	-26	-992	-91	-511	-1,332	-4,647	-3,591	-5,940	-25,560	-27,764	....	Other Items (Net)	17r
End of Period															**Deposit Money Banks**	
1,204	985	1,834	1,323	1,635	2,272	3,420	3,475	3,430	4,119	5,353	6,571	8,956	20,870	....	Reserves	20
533	695	627	609	632	640	737	658	857	1,401	1,653	1,975	3,919	23,783	....	Foreign Assets	21
1,542	2,133	2,544	2,121	3,093	2,407	5,252	7,046	5,383	7,737	9,548	11,562	18,010	21,136	....	Claims on Central Government	22a
28	15	25	23	24	25	33	49	80	50	62	64	148	219	....	Claims on Local Government	22b
337	333	540	1,138	1,526	1,735	1,757	3,516	3,372	2,735	3,198	3,960	4,003	3,885	....	Claims on Nonfin.Pub.Enterprises	22c
11,759	13,025	14,357	15,380	16,944	19,491	22,684	24,154	28,064	32,759	36,648	44,752	58,587	61,705	....	Claims on Private Sector	22d
147	117	434	693	563	560	1,000	1,507	2,638	2,725	3,036	3,907	4,809	3,793	....	Claims on Other Financial Insts.	22f
5,814	6,374	6,798	7,640	8,901	9,219	11,314	11,281	11,551	14,931	16,773	19,155	26,621	33,664	....	Demand Deposits	24
7,702	8,872	10,735	10,953	12,198	13,976	18,172	20,750	23,696	26,746	30,571	37,804	50,003	64,332	....	Time & Foreign Currency Deposits	25
520	440	561	626	813	814	854	898	1,558	1,682	1,698	1,388	1,922	3,392	....	Foreign Liabilities	26c
246	212	566	440	613	928	961	1,624	2,086	3,470	3,098	5,323	3,078	4,790	....	Central Government Deposits	26d
197	75	—	4	165	165	1	—	183	864	25	1,342	4,921	252	....	Credit from Monetary Authorities	26g
....	....	....	....	....	....	....	6	—	—	—	—	—	—	....	Credit from Other Financial Insts.	26i
1,360	1,718	1,964	2,099	2,454	2,806	3,386	5,572	6,456	8,465	10,098	12,360	17,398	24,328	....	Capital Accounts	27a
-289	-387	-263	-474	-727	-779	196	275	-1,706	-4,633	-2,764	-4,583	-5,510	4,634	....	Other Items (Net)	27r
End of Period															**Monetary Survey**	
1,830	128	-2,167	-1,027	-374	-1,975	-411	-2,159	-3,651	-2,370	-5,450	-7,945	-5,974	30,146	....	Foreign Assets (Net)	31n
16,230	20,264	26,058	25,944	28,628	32,173	41,025	49,139	52,529	55,761	70,356	83,821	98,554	96,934	....	Domestic Credit	32
3,959	6,773	10,703	8,710	9,571	10,363	15,552	19,912	18,375	17,492	27,412	31,138	31,007	27,331	....	Claims on Central Govt. (Net)	32an
28	15	25	23	24	25	33	49	80	50	62	64	148	219	....	Claims on Local Government	32b
337	333	540	1,138	1,526	1,735	1,757	3,516	3,372	2,735	3,198	3,960	4,003	3,885	....	Claims on Nonfin.Pub.Enterprises	32c
11,759	13,025	14,357	15,380	16,944	19,491	22,684	24,154	28,064	32,759	36,648	44,752	58,587	61,705	....	Claims on Private Sector	32d
147	117	434	693	563	560	1,000	1,507	2,638	2,725	3,036	3,907	4,809	3,793	....	Claims on Other Financial Insts.	32f
8,434	9,409	10,635	11,473	13,095	12,923	17,522	18,917	19,160	21,647	27,529	31,667	46,577	59,322	....	Money	34
7,702	8,872	10,735	10,953	12,198	13,976	18,172	20,750	23,696	26,746	30,571	37,804	50,003	64,332	....	Quasi-Money	35
125	127	11	—	—	10	8	1	1	10	—	1	1	1	1	Restricted Deposits	36b
....	....	....	....	....	68	78	53	23	62	42	89	81	83	25	Long-Term Foreign Liabilities	36cl
....	....	....	....	....	34	33	38	46	49	42	58	73	73	127	Counterpart Funds	36e
1,799	1,984	2,511	2,490	2,961	3,188	4,801	7,222	5,953	4,877	6,723	6,258	-4,156	3,270	....	Other Items (Net)	37r
16,136	18,281	21,370	22,426	25,293	26,898	35,694	39,667	42,856	48,393	58,099	69,471	96,579	123,654	....	Money plus Quasi-Money	35l
End of Period															**Other Banking Institutions**	
847	642	1,390	1,281	2,065	1,978	2,470	1,325	2,287	2,845	4,033	4,196	5,502	5,781	8,762	Cash	40
577	854	1,073	2,340	2,464	3,420	4,021	4,206	3,906	4,734	4,507	5,971	8,915	20,933	....	Claims on Central Government	42a
—	1	—	1	1	—	—	11	12	37	44	39	47	39	35	Claims on Local Government	42b
34	35	118	79	70	71	152	184	314	133	583	601	434	348	1,031	Claims on Nonfin.Pub.Enterprises	42c
4,136	5,209	6,710	7,978	10,324	12,290	12,856	13,819	17,655	20,715	27,523	30,921	33,557	35,734	37,808	Claims on Private Sector	42d
....	....	....	....	....	....	....	67	133	83	82	68	92	150	446	Claims on Deposit Money Banks	42e
169	320	714	683	1,714	1,506	1,980	1,139	671	1,212	1,375	1,336	2,083	578	1,024	Claims on Other Financial Insts.	42f
104	324	323	488	919	1,455	1,976	2,199	2,019	2,979	5,578	6,421	6,062	7,763	12,738	Demand Deposits	44
5,037	5,745	7,281	8,623	11,714	13,112	14,779	15,111	17,476	20,266	25,111	28,355	32,764	37,939	....	Time and Savings Deposits	45
134	149	141	137	119	142	126	282	269	428	368	462	484	697	494	Foreign Liabilities	46c
166	169	185	229	238	258	280	388	412	441	937	724	511	403	908	Central Government Deposits	46d
124	377	854	1,150	1,046	1,047	899	724	1,283	1,852	1,626	1,489	1,687	661	674	Credit from Deposit Money Banks	46h
455	589	742	878	1,003	1,082	1,350	1,525	1,988	2,308	2,996	3,393	4,154	6,315	7,773	Capital Accounts	47a
-258	-293	478	857	1,600	2,171	2,068	520	1,531	1,484	1,532	2,288	4,968	9,785	7,318	Other Items (Net)	47r

Kenya

664

		1965	1966	1967	1968	1969	1970	1971	1972	1973	1974	1975	1976	1977	1978	1979
Banking Survey															*Millions of Shillings:*	
Foreign Assets (Net)	51n	....	....	....	....	....	1,594	1,191	1,322	1,531	911	483	1,377	3,541	1,871	3,193
Domestic Credit	52	....	....	....	....	....	....	....	....	4,863	6,091	7,585	8,980	11,235	15,180	17,633
Claims on Central Govt. (Net)	52an	....	....	....	....	....	....	....	....	718	1,174	1,859	1,948	1,872	3,262	3,760
Claims on Local Government	52b									43	40	35	38	24	30	33
Claims on Nonfin.Pub.Enterprises	52c									221	203	284	192	247	195	245
Claims on Private Sector	52d									3,855	4,655	5,208	6,301	8,285	11,306	12,709
Claims on Nonbank Financ.Insts.	52f									26	20	199	502	807	388	885
Liquid Liabilities	55l	....	....	....	....	....	....	....	....	6,120	6,731	8,051	9,820	14,355	16,571	19,253
Restricted Deposits	56b	....	—	—	—	—	—	—	—	—	—	—	—	—	—	457
Long-Term Foreign Liabilities	56cl	....								....	....	....	....	....	....	....
Counterpart Funds	56e															
Capital Accounts	57a	....	....	....	....	....	....	....	....	580	649	737	859	1,108	1,402	1,661
Other Items (Net)	57r	....	....	....	....	....	....	....	....	−307	−377	−720	−322	−686	−922	−546
Interest Rates															*Percent Per Annum*	
Discount Rate (End of Period)	60	....	....	6.50	6.50	6.50	6.50	6.50	6.50	6.50	6.50	7.00	7.00	6.50	7.50	7.50
Treasury Bill Rate	60c	....	....	....	....	3.95	2.00	1.42	3.45	1.92	4.63	6.08	5.54	2.13	4.29	6.01
Deposit Rate	60l	....	....	3.50	3.50	3.50	3.50	3.50	3.50	3.50	4.32	5.13	5.13	5.13	5.13	5.13
Lending Rate	60p	....	....	....	....	....	....	....	9.00	9.00	9.00	9.50	10.00	10.00	10.00	10.00
Prices and Production															*Index Numbers (1990=100):*	
Consumer Prices	64	9.6	10.1	10.3	10.3	10.3	10.5	ɪ10.9	11.6	12.7	ɪ14.9	17.8	19.8	22.7	26.6	28.7
Industrial Production	66	17.3	18.1	19.6	21.0	23.1	25.4	28.1	29.6	33.8	35.8	ɪ35.6	42.4	49.1	55.4	59.6
International Transactions															*Millions of Shillings*	
Exports	70	1,629	1,855	1,732	1,798	1,933	2,179	2,244	2,567	3,335	4,305	4,464	6,610	9,824	7,914	8,144
Imports, cif	71	2,015	2,471	2,404	2,543	2,581	3,159	3,999	3,822	4,316	7,327	6,948	8,113	10,663	13,225	12,228
Imports, fob	71.v	1,768	2,168	2,109	2,229	2,265	2,764	3,489	3,338	3,747	6,371	6,059	7,103	9,282	11,340	10,470
															1990=100	
Volume of Exports	72	48	ɪ59	57	60	71	75	57	86	100	95	ɪ87	92	96	88	87
Volume of Imports	73	78	ɪ98	93	99	102	119	140	121	117	133	ɪ99	95	116	135	111
Export Prices	74	12	ɪ12	12	12	12	13	13	13	16	20	ɪ24	32	45	38	41
Unit Value of Imports	75	5	ɪ5	5	5	5	5	6	6	8	11	ɪ14	17	18	19	22
Balance of Payments															*Millions of US Dollars:*	
Goods: Exports f.o.b.	78aa d									....	....	688.0	811.4	1,222.5	1,056.4	1,120.2
Goods: Imports f.o.b.	78ab d											−846.9	−809.7	−1,112.8	−1,631.8	−1,594.2
Trade Balance	78ac d											−158.9	1.7	109.7	−575.5	−474.0
Services: Credit	78ad d											266.8	296.2	330.6	439.9	448.7
Services: Debit	78ae d											−283.8	−294.6	−320.9	−428.4	−376.6
Balance on Goods and Services	78af d											−175.9	3.2	119.4	−564.0	−401.9
Income: Credit	78ag d											56.4	35.4	40.8	47.4	60.5
Income: Debit	78ah d											−149.3	−177.4	−199.1	−234.9	−248.3
Balance on Goods, Serv., & Inc.	78ai d											−268.8	−138.8	−38.9	−751.5	−589.7
Current Transfers, n.i.e.: Credit	78aj d											91.1	67.8	93.8	115.4	114.6
Current Transfers: Debit	78ak d											−42.5	−49.2	−19.8	−24.8	−19.5
Current Account, n.i.e.	78al d											−220.2	−120.2	35.1	−661.0	−494.6
Capital Account, n.i.e.: Credit	78ba d											1.9	1.7	3.6	7.8	8.0
Capital Account: Debit	78bb d											−5.4	−7.4	−12.8	−9.1	−13.6
Capital Account, n.i.e.	78bc d											−3.5	−5.7	−9.2	−1.3	−5.6
Direct Investment Abroad	78bd d											−1.4	−4.3	−2.7	−2.3	−5.9
Dir. Invest. in Rep. Econ., n.i.e.	78be d											17.2	46.4	56.5	34.4	84.0
Portfolio Investment Assets	78bf d											−2.2	—	—	—	—
Portfolio Investment Liab., n.i.e.	78bg d											−.5	−4.3	.7	—	—
Other Investment Assets	78bh d											−13.9	−31.2	11.5	−18.8	−41.5
Other Investment Liab., n.i.e.	78bi d											198.1	202.7	174.1	422.0	530.3
Financial Account, n.i.e.	78bj d											197.3	209.3	240.2	435.4	566.9
Net Errors and Omissions	78ca d											−16.6	.6	.0	6.8	4.8
Overall Balance	78cb d											−43.0	83.9	269.1	−220.2	71.6
Reserves and Related Items	79da d											43.0	−83.9	−269.1	220.2	−71.6
Reserve Assets	79db d											−6.3	−104.5	−233.2	194.3	−263.2
Use of Fund Credit and Loans	79dc d											44.0	18.8	−37.6	24.1	91.5
Liabs.Constit.For.Auth.Reserves	79dd d											—	—	—	—	—
Exceptional Financing	79de d											5.3	1.7	1.6	1.8	100.1
Government Finance															*Millions of Shillings*	
Deficit (-) or Surplus	80							−566	−902	−587	−1,151	−1,709	−1,327	−1,627	−3,015
Revenue	81									2,631	2,817	3,625	4,347	5,124	6,149	9,182	9,835
Grants Received	81z									81	11	71	175	201	234	183	267
Expenditure	82									3,077	3,428	3,937	5,179	6,164	7,240	9,909	11,935
Lending Minus Repayments	83									201	302	346	494	870	470	1,083	1,182
Financing																	
Net Borrowing: Domestic	84a									229	503	266	356	1,574	979	594	2,803
Foreign	85a									167	429	209	425	774	464	466	1,107
Use of Cash Balances	87									170	−30	112	370	−639	−116	567	−895
Adjustment to Total Financing	84.x									—	—	—	—	—	—	—	—
National Accounts															*Millions of Shillings*	
Exports of Goods & Services	90c	2,370	2,710	2,506	2,644	2,881	3,207	3,423	4,002	4,812	7,144	7,138	9,434	13,004	11,862	12,002
Government Consumption	91f	1,058	1,112	1,245	1,470	1,711	1,885	2,285	2,573	2,796	3,530	4,386	5,075	6,441	7,972	8,946
Gross Fixed Capital Formation	93e	930	1,224	1,644	1,790	1,875	2,254	2,884	3,302	3,645	4,075	4,837	5,808	7,800	10,280	10,809
Increase/Decrease(-) in Stocks	93i	110	324	133	51	170	268	360	−111	−304	1,715	−496	79	1,024	1,932	−484
Private Consumption	96f	4,972	5,574	5,810	6,347	6,593	7,292	8,153	9,003	10,848	12,554	16,240	17,908	20,680	24,977	28,896
Imports of Goods & Services	98c	−2,300	−2,720	−2,586	−2,709	−2,814	−3,407	−4,259	−4,323	−5,036	−8,676	−8,260	−9,232	−11,752	−15,860	−14,732
Gross Domestic Product	99b	7,139	8,224	8,751	9,595	10,416	11,499	12,845	14,447	16,761	20,342	23,846	29,072	37,197	41,163	45,437
Net Factor Inc/Pmts(-) Abroad	98.n	−133	−128	−271	−282	−196	−230	−187	−434	−879	−846	−1,271	−1,362	−1,574	−1,812	−1,672
Gross Nat'l Expenditure = GNP	99a	7,006	8,096	8,480	9,313	10,220	11,269	12,658	14,013	15,882	19,496	22,575	27,710	35,623	39,351	43,765
Gross Dom. Prod. 1990 Prices	99b.p	....	....	56,933	61,829	65,236	70,052	74,851	ɪ81,939	87,534	ɪ88,837	91,869	98,325	107,587	119,211	123,661
GDP Deflator (1990=100)	99bi p	19.5	22.1	15.4	15.5	16.0	16.4	17.2	17.6	19.1	22.9	26.0	29.6	34.6	34.5	36.7
															Millions:	
Population	99z	9.53	9.78	10.12	10.48	10.88	11.23	11.67	12.07	12.48	12.91	13.41	13.85	14.35	14.88	15.33

Exchange Rates: On September 14, 1966 the Kenya shilling, equal to the East African shilling, was introduced.
Deposit Money Banks: ɪ Before 1965, data for *line 21* are net of foreign liabilities and exclude intraterritorial claims. ɪ Beginning in 1969, data are based on improved classification.

Monetary Survey: ɪ Beginning in 1969, data are based on improved classification.

Kenya
664

1980	1981	1982	1983	1984	1985	1986	1987	1988	1989	1990	1991	1992	1993	1994		
End of Period															**Banking Survey**	
1,695	-21	-2,308	-1,164	-492	-2,117	-537	-2,441	-3,919	-2,798	-5,817	-8,407	-6,458	29,450	....	Foreign Assets (Net)	51n
20,981	26,513	34,488	36,796	42,963	49,204	59,755	68,109	74,675	82,151	103,450	121,965	143,079	154,163	....	Domestic Credit	52
4,370	7,458	11,591	10,821	11,797	13,525	19,293	23,730	21,870	21,785	30,982	36,386	39,411	47,861	....	Claims on Central Govt. (Net)	52an
28	16	25	24	25	25	33	60	91	86	106	103	195	258	....	Claims on Local Government	52b
371	368	658	1,217	1,596	1,806	1,909	3,700	3,686	2,869	3,781	4,561	4,438	4,233	....	Claims on Nonfin.Pub.Enterprises	52c
15,895	18,234	21,067	23,358	27,268	31,781	35,540	37,973	45,719	53,475	64,171	75,673	92,144	97,440	....	Claims on Private Sector	52d
316	437	1,148	1,376	2,277	2,066	2,980	2,646	3,308	3,936	4,411	5,242	6,892	4,371	....	Claims on Nonbank Financ.Insts.	52f
20,431	23,708	27,585	30,256	35,862	39,488	49,979	55,653	60,064	68,794	84,755	100,051	129,903	163,575	....	Liquid Liabilities	55l
125	127	11	—	—	10	8	1	1	10	—	1	1	1	1	Restricted Deposits	56b
....	....	....	....	....	68	78	53	23	62	42	89	81	83	25	Long-Term Foreign Liabilities	56cl
....	....	....	....	....	34	33	38	46	49	42	58	73	73	127	Counterpart Funds	56e
2,179	2,697	3,137	3,503	4,075	4,596	5,541	7,994	9,492	12,001	14,573	17,573	23,830	31,364	....	Capital Accounts	57a
-59	-40	1,448	1,873	2,534	2,892	3,578	1,930	1,130	-1,563	-1,778	-4,213	-17,268	-11,482	....	Other Items (Net)	57r
Percent Per Annum															**Interest Rates**	
8.00	12.50	15.00	15.00	12.50	12.50	12.50	12.50	16.02	16.50	19.43	20.27	20.46	45.50	21.50	Discount Rate *(End of Period)*	60
5.26	7.61	12.58	14.15	13.24	13.90	13.23	12.86	13.48	13.86	14.78	16.59	16.53	49.80	23.32	Treasury Bill Rate	60c
5.75	8.85	12.20	13.27	11.77	11.25	11.25	10.31	10.33	12.00	13.67	....	....	....	....	Deposit Rate	60l
10.58	12.42	14.50	15.83	14.42	14.00	14.00	14.00	15.00	17.25	18.75	....	....	....	....	Lending Rate	60p
Period Averages															**Prices and Production**	
Ɪ32.7	36.5	44.0	49.0	54.0	61.1	64.0	68.9	76.6	86.5	100.0	119.8	155.2	226.3	292.0	Consumer Prices	64
62.7	65.8	66.4	69.4	72.3	75.6	80.1	84.6	89.7	95.0	100.0	103.8	105.1	107.0	....	Industrial Production	66
Millions of Shillings															**International Transactions**	
9,248	10,243	11,109	11,676	15,507	15,725	19,460	15,790	19,012	19,904	23,677	30,376	44,494	77,915	87,142	Exports	70
15,747	17,413	17,809	17,802	21,180	23,589	26,163	28,904	35,072	44,235	48,661	49,147	58,635	97,521	120,929	Imports, cif	71
13,700	14,977	15,361	15,292	18,385	20,283	22,496	24,853	30,156	38,035	41,841	42,259	50,417	83,853	103,980	Imports, fob	71.v
1990=100																
Ɪ89	84	82	79	78	81	93	90	95	94	100	103	103	121	137	Volume of Exports	72
Ɪ127	99	84	66	78	72	85	89	100	105	100	93	90	97	121	Volume of Imports	73
Ɪ49	54	59	71	85	84	90	75	86	92	100	128	144	259	266	Export Prices	74
Ɪ29	37	42	54	55	65	62	63	69	83	100	111	129	208	187	Unit Value of Imports	75
Minus Sign Indicates Debit															Balance of Payments	
1,430.7	1,192.7	1,045.7	984.0	1,081.7	991.0	1,219.4	962.5	1,072.7	1,001.5	1,090.2	1,185.3	1,099.4	1,253.6	....	Goods: Exports f.o.b.	78aad
-2,344.8	-1,834.0	-1,467.7	-1,197.9	-1,348.2	-1,269.8	-1,454.6	-1,622.6	-1,802.2	-1,963.4	-2,005.3	-1,697.3	-1,594.3	-1,492.8	....	Goods: Imports f.o.b.	78abd
-914.1	-641.3	-422.0	-214.0	-266.5	-278.7	-235.2	-660.1	-729.5	-961.9	-915.2	-511.9	-494.9	-239.2	....	Trade Balance	78acd
576.7	568.9	562.3	512.2	542.4	577.3	646.0	738.7	798.9	921.4	1,138.3	1,014.4	1,051.2	1,072.6	....	Services: Credit	78add
-501.6	-503.0	-398.4	-341.5	-377.0	-359.5	-415.2	-504.7	-530.0	-603.1	-699.7	-632.7	-578.1	-586.3	....	Services: Debit	78aed
-839.1	-575.4	-258.0	-43.3	-101.1	-60.9	-4.4	-426.1	-460.5	-643.7	-476.5	-130.2	-21.8	247.1	....	Balance on Goods and Services	78afd
53.9	37.0	21.9	28.7	39.0	38.2	36.9	37.4	20.1	11.8	4.8	5.9	1.7	3.3	....	Income: Credit	78agd
-248.2	-238.1	-201.4	-213.2	-240.8	-281.8	-277.8	-319.9	-365.5	-330.1	-423.2	-434.7	-359.6	-339.0	....	Income: Debit	78ahd
-1,033.4	-776.5	-437.5	-227.8	-302.9	-304.5	-245.3	-708.6	-805.9	-962.0	-894.9	-559.0	-379.6	-88.5	....	Balance on Goods, Serv., & Inc.	78aid
163.0	241.4	157.2	209.2	208.4	214.4	232.0	246.1	372.9	420.6	422.9	396.7	392.9	276.0	....	Current Transfers, n.i.e.: Credit	78ajd
-7.3	-28.4	-27.6	-31.9	-35.3	-27.4	-33.5	-40.4	-39.1	-49.1	-55.1	-51.1	-193.4	-63.0	....	Current Transfers: Debit	78akd
-877.7	-563.4	-307.9	-50.4	-129.8	-117.6	-46.8	-503.0	-472.1	-590.6	-527.1	-213.3	-180.2	124.5	....	Current Account, n.i.e.	78ald
2.4	7.1	6.8	5.5	5.6	6.1	9.8	10.3	11.8	11.2	7.6	3.6	83.5	28.5	....	Capital Account, n.i.e.: Credit	78bad
-12.1	-3.9	-3.6	-3.2	-2.1	-1.5	-1.4	-2.2	-.3	-.2	-.8	-.4	-.4	-.4	....	Capital Account: Debit	78bbd
-9.7	3.2	3.2	2.3	3.5	4.7	8.4	8.0	11.5	11.0	6.8	3.2	83.1	28.0	....	Capital Account, n.i.e.	78bcd
-1.1	-5.9	-9.6	-14.5	-6.9	-5.4	-4.9	2.1	-2.2	-1.4	—	—	—	—	....	Direct Investment Abroad	78bdd
79.0	14.1	13.0	23.7	10.8	18.1	32.7	42.8	.4	62.2	57.1	18.8	6.4	1.5	....	Dir. Invest. in Rep. Econ., n.i.e.	78bed
—	—	—	—	—	—	—	—	—	—	—	—	—	—	....	Portfolio Investment Assets	78bfd
.8	—	—	—	—	—	—	—	—	—	—	—	—	—	....	Portfolio Investment Liab., n.i.e.	78bgd
-15.4	-94.7	-77.7	-61.5	-64.1	-58.5	-83.1	-5.5	-14.4	-56.5	72.7	-77.5	-125.0	-84.7	....	Other Investment Assets	78bhd
443.3	272.3	174.0	182.9	239.4	67.1	187.9	322.2	398.4	629.6	231.1	155.3	-151.5	85.0	....	Other Investment Liab., n.i.e.	78bid
506.6	185.9	99.6	130.7	179.1	21.3	132.6	361.7	382.3	633.9	360.9	96.6	-270.1	1.9	....	Financial Account, n.i.e.	78bjd
9.4	68.4	45.2	15.0	8.6	39.6	43.2	107.9	34.7	67.7	66.9	69.6	110.3	257.5	....	Net Errors and Omissions	78cad
-371.4	-305.9	-159.9	97.6	61.5	-52.1	137.4	-25.3	-43.6	121.9	-92.5	-43.9	-256.9	411.8	....	Overall Balance	78cbd
371.4	305.9	159.9	-97.6	-61.5	52.1	-137.4	25.3	43.6	-121.9	92.5	43.9	256.9	-411.8	....	Reserves and Related Items	79dad
144.8	160.6	5.8	-194.0	-48.9	-.9	-23.0	145.1	-30.8	-92.9	58.8	36.9	-27.4	-477.4	....	Reserve Assets	79dbd
72.7	28.7	151.6	93.2	-15.5	48.6	-116.2	-120.7	73.6	-29.2	33.7	7.0	-82.9	-30.6	....	Use of Fund Credit and Loans	79dcd
—	—	—	—	—	—	—	—	—	—	—	—	—	—	....	Liabs.Constit.For.Auth.Reserves	79ddd
154.0	116.6	2.5	3.2	2.9	4.5	1.8	.9	.8	.2	—	—	367.1	96.2	....	Exceptional Financing	79ded
Year Ending June 30															**Government Finance**	
-2,409	-4,002	-5,463	-3,838	-4,281	-6,245	-5,144	-8,329	-6,242	-11,193	-7,412	-5,755	-1,047	-11,543	-13,091	Deficit (-) or Surplus	80
11,825	13,582	14,885	16,159	18,019	20,185	23,899	27,590	31,964	37,396	43,758	54,591	55,671	67,491	90,211	Revenue	81
383	392	396	463	212	163	232	1,537	2,206	4,112	3,761	5,060	7,550	9,115	11,792	Grants Received	81z
13,615	16,731	19,410	19,961	22,014	25,981	28,606	36,654	39,968	51,801	53,701	63,913	63,863	86,720	113,721	Expenditure	82
1,002	1,245	1,334	499	498	612	669	802	444	900	1,230	1,493	405	1,429	1,373	Lending Minus Repayments	83
															Financing	
90	993	3,163	3,353	2,997	4,403	6,012	7,926	3,747	3,577	....	....	....	....	....	Net Borrowing: Domestic	84a
1,268	1,876	2,063	1,825	1,548	1,842	-868	403	2,181	3,968	....	....	....	....	....	Foreign	85a
1,051	1,133	237	-1,340	-264	....	....	....	314	3,648	....	....	....	....	....	Use of Cash Balances	87
—	—	—	—	—	—	—	—	—	—	....	....	....	....	....	Adjustment to Total Financing	84.x
Millions of Shillings															**National Accounts**	
15,066	15,474	17,552	19,927	23,410	25,524	30,334	27,992	33,084	39,554	51,186	60,512	69,287	134,918	....	Exports of Goods & Services	90c
10,675	11,528	12,949	14,662	15,512	17,602	21,518	24,354	27,293	30,769	36,620	37,606	41,475	42,178	....	Government Consumption	91f
12,451	14,508	13,364	14,349	16,143	17,631	23,064	25,735	30,359	33,156	40,560	42,671	43,780	49,474	....	Gross Fixed Capital Formation	93e
3,333	2,663	1,990	2,237	2,372	8,119	2,504	6,116	7,417	9,209	6,906	1,351	898	2,245	....	Increase/Decrease(-) in Stocks	93i
32,178	37,203	44,612	48,734	56,481	58,435	70,385	81,654	94,127	111,149	121,655	139,437	169,346	212,980	....	Private Consumption	96f
-21,054	-20,914	-20,188	-20,284	-24,639	-26,540	-30,129	-34,682	-41,086	-52,247	-61,390	-63,326	-69,041	-118,783	....	Imports of Goods & Services	98c
52,649	60,462	70,279	79,626	89,279	100,831	117,472	131,169	151,194	171,589	195,537	221,251	255,745	323,012	....	Gross Domestic Product	99b
-1,680	-1,942	-2,787	-2,544	-3,043	-3,665	-4,183	-5,030	-6,412	-7,097	-10,179	-12,452	-12,493	-21,271	....	Net Factor Inc/Pmts(-) Abroad	98.n
50,969	58,520	68,085	73,860	86,170	97,062	113,287	126,139	144,782	164,492	185,358	208,799	243,252	301,741	....	Gross Nat'l Expenditure = GNP	99a
130,552	136,212	138,257	140,074	142,577	148,709	159,332	168,791	179,260	187,669	195,537	198,349	199,212	198,809	....	Gross Dom. Prod. 1990 Prices	99b.p
40.3	44.4	50.8	56.8	62.6	67.8	73.7	77.7	84.3	91.4	100.0	111.5	128.4	162.5	....	GDP Deflator (1990=100)	99bip
Midyear Estimates																
16.67	17.34	18.04	18.77	19.54	20.33	21.16	22.94	23.88	24.87	Ɪ24.03	25.91	25.70	Ɪ28.11	29.29	**Population**	99z

Government Finance: Data relate to a fiscal year different from calendar year.

Korea
542

		1965	1966	1967	1968	1969	1970	1971	1972	1973	1974	1975	1976	1977	1978	1979
Exchange Rates															*Won per SDR:*	
Market Rate	aa	271.78	271.18	274.60	281.50	304.45	316.65	405.30	433.09	479.52	592.59	566.60	562.33	587.92	630.55	637.59
															Won per US Dollar:	
Market Rate	ae	271.78	271.18	274.60	281.50	304.45	316.65	373.30	398.90	397.50	484.00	484.00	484.00	484.00	484.00	484.00
Market Rate	rf	266.40	271.34	270.52	276.65	288.16	310.56	347.15	392.89	398.32	404.47	484.00	484.00	484.00	484.00	484.00
Fund Position															*Millions of SDRs:*	
Quota	2f.s	18.8	24.0	24.0	50.0	50.0	50.0	80.0	80.0	80.0	80.0	80.0	80.0	80.0	160.0	160.0
SDRs	1b.s	—	—	—	—	—	10.3	17.6	26.1	26.1	1.4	3.4	6.8	10.0	11.4	18.9
Reserve Position in the Fund	1c.s	4.7	6.0	6.0	—	—	12.5	12.5	12.5	20.0	—	—	—	—	10.4	18.8
Total Fund Cred.&Loans Outstg.	2tl	—	—	—	—	—	—	—	—	—	110.0	217.3	301.7	280.4	201.8	104.4
International Liquidity													*Millions of US Dollars Unless Otherwise Indicated:*			
Total Reserves minus Gold	1l.d	143.0	241.8	353.2	387.7	549.5	606.3	433.5	523.0	884.8	277.2	781.3	1,970.0	2,967.1	2,763.9	2,959.2
SDRs	1b.d	—	—	—	—	—	10.3	19.1	28.3	31.5	1.7	3.9	7.9	12.2	14.9	24.9
Reserve Position in the Fund	1c.d	4.7	6.0	6.0	—	—	12.5	13.6	13.6	24.1	—	—	—	—	13.6	24.8
Foreign Exchange	1d.d	138.3	235.8	347.2	387.7	549.5	583.5	400.8	481.1	829.2	275.5	777.4	1,962.1	2,954.9	2,735.5	2,909.5
Gold (Million Fine Troy Ounces)	1ad	.094	.097	.096	.097	.097	.097	.099	.107	.110	.110	.111	.112	.147	.275	.295
Gold (National Valuation)	1an d	3.3	3.4	3.3	3.4	3.4	3.4	3.5	4.0	4.6	4.7	4.7	4.7	6.2	29.7	30.6
Monetary Authorities: Other Liab.	4..d	....	....	....	....	....	....	....	....	....	100.0	201.7	208.5	151.3	10.1	9.3
Deposit Money Banks: Assets	7a.d	4.8	8.5	99.9	7.5	60.4	79.9	133.7	212.7	204.9	773.8	764.2	986.0	1,333.4	2,143.8	2,718.6
Deposit Money Banks: Liabilities	7b.d	—	—	47.0	66.1	159.9	233.1	387.1	447.0	376.4	1,073.1	1,514.1	1,740.7	2,295.7	3,217.1	5,106.8
of which: Liab. to Nonbanks	7bd d	....	....	....	....	....	....	....	....	....	30.6	56.9	84.1	59.5	96.7	98.9
Other Banking Insts.: Assets	7e.d	....	....	....	....	....	....	....	....	....	....	....	....	....	111.0	232.0
Liabilities	7f.d	....	....	....	....	....	....	....	....	....	....	....	....	....	1,255.0	2,375.0
Monetary Authorities													*Millions of Won through 1965;*			
Foreign Assets	11	38,700	I 65	69	105	149	171	147	130	266	102	367	927	1,514	1,313	1,434
Claims on Central Government	12a	45,104	I 42	48	40	46	51	47	189	208	402	674	799	910	1,172	1,155
Claims on Official Entities	12bx	12,300	I 19	20	28	32	30	32	34	43	20	110	110	210	240	240
Claims on Deposit Money Banks	12e	6,900	I 6	12	19	35	90	112	179	280	667	686	686	849	1,493	2,339
Reserve Money	14	48,348	I 80	111	157	216	300	288	428	624	775	1,077	1,438	2,072	2,802	3,468
of which: Currency Outside DMBs	14a	31,630	I 43	58	83	111	134	162	218	311	411	507	677	953	1,364	1,604
Bonds	16ab	—	I —	—	—	6	4	1	8	18	1	94	150	429	426	532
Foreign Liabilities	16c	21,384	I 16	3	2	11	9	4	5	5	94	187	272	233	121	59
Central Government Deposits	16d	24,700	I 26	31	33	36	42	38	88	104	154	217	388	711	914	902
Other Items (Net)	17r	8,588	I 5	−10	−16	−23	−11	−18	−34	2	166	261	275	38	−45	208
Deposit Money Banks													*Millions of Won through 1965;*			
Reserves	20	14,563	I 32	45	64	80	162	102	158	258	352	557	755	1,110	1,401	1,815
Central Bank Bonds	20r		I 5	15	15	27	5	26	52	79	65	284	327	571	447	493
Foreign Assets	21	1,317	I 2	27	2	18	25	44	163	195	483	698	767	1,313	1,427	1,657
Claims on Central Government	22a	1,620	I —	4	3	4	5	3	4	28	47	104	228	371	518	632
Claims on Private Sector	22d	82,180	I 114	221	432	706	919	1,201	1,453	1,890	2,853	3,544	4,424	5,532	8,198	11,424
Demand Deposits	24	34,930	I 43	66	98	152	185	220	332	440	533	668	866	1,233	1,325	1,648
Time, Savings,& Fgn.Currency Dep.	25	30,900	I 70	131	259	453	589	725	929	1,245	1,506	1,965	2,660	3,699	5,211	6,603
Bonds	26ab	—	I —	—	2	4	7	10	11	24	36	52	82	151	176	235
Restricted Deposits	26b	7,643	I 7	28	24	28	35	52	77	168	173	258	327	298	329	370
Foreign Liabilities	26c	2	I —	13	19	49	74	145	178	150	519	733	842	1,111	1,557	2,472
Central Government Deposits	26d	662	I —	2	1	1	1	5	2	1	13	31	57	—	—	33
Central Govt. Lending Funds	26f	18,748	I 23	28	38	65	93	102	116	127	168	209	299	394	531	738
Credit from Monetary Authorities	26g	6,930	I 6	12	19	35	90	112	179	280	666	673	686	849	1,496	2,340
Capital Accounts	27a	9,702	I 15	34	46	65	71	95	126	173	215	348	445	545	829	1,134
Other Items (Net)	27r	−9,843	I −13	−1	11	−17	−28	−89	−121	−159	−29	249	235	618	535	449
Monetary Survey													*Millions of Won through 1965;*			
Foreign Assets (Net)	31n	18,631	I 52	80	85	108	113	42	110	307	−27	145	579	1,482	1,063	561
Domestic Credit	32	118,742	I 153	260	469	751	962	1,240	1,600	2,074	3,164	4,193	5,146	6,379	9,275	12,584
Claims on Central Govt. (Net)	32an	21,362	I 16	19	9	13	13	6	103	131	282	529	583	570	775	852
Claims on Official Entities	32bx	12,300	I 19	20	28	32	30	32	34	43	20	110	110	210	240	240
Claims on Private Sector	32d	85,080	I 119	221	432	706	919	1,201	1,463	1,900	2,863	3,554	4,454	5,599	8,260	11,491
Money	34	65,617	I 85	123	179	252	308	358	519	730	946	1,182	1,544	2,173	2,714	3,275
Quasi-Money	35	31,488	I 72	131	259	453	590	727	932	1,250	1,511	1,968	2,661	3,702	5,215	6,603
Bonds	36ab	—	I −5	−15	−13	−12	9	−13	−24	−19	36	78	164	199	264	448
Restricted Deposits	36b	7,643	I 7	28	24	28	35	52	77	168	173	258	327	298	329	370
Central Govt. Lending Funds	36f	18,748	I 23	28	39	67	96	105	121	133	178	219	310	402	534	738
Other Items (Net)	37r	13,887	I 18	31	52	54	40	30	47	74	294	632	719	1,089	1,283	1,711
Money plus Quasi-Money	35l	97,105	I 157	254	438	705	898	1,085	1,452	1,980	2,457	3,150	4,205	5,874	7,929	9,878
Other Banking Institutions													*Millions of Won through 1965;*			
Development Institutions																
Claims on Private Sector	42d	38,600	I 49	58	85	131	185	215	311	386	502	723	918	1,249	1,743	2,470
Bonds	46ab	270	I —	—	—	16	28	26	51	82	88	67	115	176	235	299
Counterpart Funds	46e	18,380	I 18	15	16	17	17	17	17	16	16	15	15	14	14	13
Central Govt. Lending Funds	46f	5,910	I 12	21	25	42	52	69	85	100	162	251	361	486	786	1,108
Credit from Deposit Money Banks	46h		I —	—	15	21	25	38	40	40	34	36	23	35	29	32
Capital Accounts	47a	14,170	I 18	22	28	37	61	67	125	129	143	237	330	365	449	480
Other Items (Net)	47r	−130	I 1	1	—	−3	1	−2	−7	18	60	117	75	172	231	538
Trust Accounts of Coml. Banks																
Claims on Private Sector	42d.g	6,240	I 11	15	25	51	73	115	131	167	149	160	256	507	765	1,062
Claims on Deposit Money Banks	42e.g	1,250	I 5	16	29	19	10	5	18	5	21	27	46	23	7	24
Quasi-Monetary Liabilities	45..g	7,600	I 16	30	52	67	79	125	158	183	191	186	251	355	429	588
Other Items (Net)	47r.g	−100	I 1	1	3	3	4	−4	−9	−10	−20	—	51	175	344	498
Postal Savings Deposits	45..h	2,008	I 4	6	8	12	15	16	25	32	40	47	62	35	30	41
Nonbank Financial Institutions													*Millions of Won through 1965;*			
Cash	40..s	290	I —	1	1	2	2	2	3	4	5	5	7	8	14	22
Claims on Central Government	42a.s	70	I —	—	—	1	—	1	1	1	5	13	21	25	44	52
Claims on Private Sector	42d.s	1,400	I 2	3	5	6	8	12	16	29	39	50	70	137	227	494
Real Estate	42h.s	1,430	I 2	3	4	7	10	13	15	17	21	23	35	28	48	71
Incr.in Total Assets(Within Per.)	49z.s	710	I 1	3	3	8	5	8	8	17	22	25	38	70	141	314
Liquid Liabilities	55l	106,423	I 176	289	497	782	990	1,224	1,632	2,191	2,682	3,379	4,511	6,256	8,374	10,484

Korea

1980	1981	1982	1983	1984	1985	1986	1987	1988	1989	1990	1991	1992	1993	1994	Korea 542
End of Period															**Exchange Rates**
841.64	815.35	826.01	832.85	811.03	977.81	1,053.66	1,124.00	920.59	893.10	1,019.19	1,088.27	1,084.05	1,109.97	1,151.38	Market Rate **aa**
End of Period (ae) Period Average (rf)															
659.90	700.50	748.80	795.50	827.40	890.20	861.40	792.30	684.10	679.60	716.40	760.80	788.40	808.10	788.70	Market Rate **ae**
607.43	681.03	731.08	775.75	805.98	870.02	881.45	822.57	731.47	671.46	707.76	733.35	780.65	802.67	803.45	Market Rate **rf**
End of Period															**Fund Position**
255.9	255.9	255.9	462.8	462.8	462.8	462.8	462.8	462.8	462.8	462.8	462.8	799.6	799.6	799.6	Quota **2f. s**
9.9	54.1	57.8	60.2	30.9	36.2	14.4	11.6	4.2	1.2	10.1	20.9	30.6	42.3	52.3	SDRs **1b. s**
—	—	—	51.7	—	.7	.7	.7	.7	178.2	224.5	255.4	319.1	339.2	363.6	Reserve Position in the Fund **1c. s**
535.4	1,070.6	1,141.7	1,292.8	1,598.9	1,373.0	1,266.3	369.8	—	—	—	—	—	—	—	Total Fund Cred.&Loans Outstg. **2tl**
End of Period															**International Liquidity**
2,924.9	2,681.7	2,807.3	2,346.7	2,753.6	2,869.3	3,319.6	3,583.7	12,346.7	15,213.6	14,793.0	13,701.1	17,120.6	20,228.2	25,639.3	Total Reserves minus Gold **1l. d**
12.6	63.0	63.7	63.0	30.3	39.8	17.7	16.4	5.7	1.6	14.4	29.8	42.0	58.1	76.3	SDRs **1b. d**
—	—	—	54.1	—	.7	.8	1.0	.9	234.2	319.4	365.3	438.7	465.9	530.8	Reserve Position in the Fund **1c. d**
2,912.3	2,618.7	2,743.6	2,229.5	2,723.3	2,828.8	3,301.1	3,566.3	12,340.1	14,977.8	14,459.2	13,306.0	16,639.9	19,704.2	25,032.1	Foreign Exchange **1d. d**
.299	.303	.303	.304	.309	.313	.317	.320	.320	.320	.320	.321	.323	.324	.325	Gold (Million Fine Troy Ounces) **1ad**
30.8	32.2	30.9	31.0	31.1	31.4	31.5	31.6	31.6	31.6	31.6	32.2	32.6	33.3	33.6	Gold (National Valuation) **1and**
7.5	7.6	7.4	7.8	7.4	6.2	6.4	18.3	35.7	33.7	45.6	46.9	46.4	50.9	54.5	Monetary Authorities: Other Liab. **4.. d**
3,615.8	4,176.2	4,146.9	4,531.0	4,865.0	4,848.0	4,692.0	5,578.0	I 8,513.0	7,868.0	9,532.0	10,705.0	12,905.0	16,211.0	20,938.0	Deposit Money Banks: Assets **7a. d**
7,145.9	9,288.9	11,976.0	12,514.8	14,187.9	15,866.6	14,535.5	11,591.1	10,245.6	9,781.4	10,181.2	13,794.4	14,652.6	14,795.8	21,170.3	Deposit Money Banks: Liabilities **7b. d**
92.7	141.9	252.1	438.2	555.5	794.7	576.3	495.3	402.6	297.0	296.2	267.0	260.8	329.5	529.4	*of which:* Liab. to Nonbanks **7bd d**
144.0	210.0	402.0	306.0	389.0	385.0	179.0	150.0	357.0	659.0	1,064.0	1,788.0	1,963.0	5,365.0	7,897.0	Other Banking Insts.: Assets **7e. d**
2,821.0	3,636.0	4,628.0	5,353.0	6,322.0	8,396.0	8,606.0	5,204.0	3,803.0	3,368.0	4,653.0	7,609.0	9,780.0	15,834.0	21,692.0	Liabilities **7f. d**
Billions of Won Beginning 1966: End of Period															**Monetary Authorities**
1,938	1,897	2,161	1,826	2,288	2,476	2,805	2,801	8,458	10,348	10,791	10,673	13,647	16,632	20,830	Foreign Assets **11**
1,147	1,680	1,883	2,176	2,130	2,130	2,127	2,237	2,767	2,813	2,151	2,397	2,407	2,623	2,323	Claims on Central Government **12a**
270	370	470	570	570	570	570	570	570	570	570	570	570	570	570	Claims on Official Entities **12bx**
2,917	3,627	4,193	5,244	7,095	9,078	10,849	14,890	15,958	16,144	19,553	21,122	25,571	29,169	28,971	Claims on Deposit Money Banks **12e**
3,244	2,802	3,825	4,095	4,248	4,319	5,017	7,469	9,728	12,819	13,811	16,322	18,107	23,080	25,204	Reserve Money **14**
1,856	2,025	2,574	2,874	3,109	3,286	3,679	4,443	5,133	6,140	7,011	7,913	8,581	12,109	13,127	*of which: Currency Outside DMBs* **14a**
580	1,934	2,538	3,737	5,651	8,418	9,677	13,635	20,470	19,371	18,403	17,651	23,614	27,148	29,114	Bonds **16ab**
417	880	939	1,041	1,345	1,187	1,328	422	29	23	33	36	37	41	43	Foreign Liabilities **16c**
780	544	627	764	1,121	1,187	1,447	3,408	5,766	7,276	7,424	5,770	4,524	5,059	6,477	Central Government Deposits **16d**
1,250	1,414	778	179	–281	–857	–1,118	–4,436	–8,240	–9,612	–6,606	–5,015	–4,086	–6,333	–8,145	Other Items (Net) **17r**
Billions of Won Beginning 1966: End of Period															**Deposit Money Banks**
1,324	738	1,196	1,129	856	1,016	1,307	3,017	4,535	6,613	6,717	8,304	9,399	10,836	11,947	Reserves **20**
936	1,987	2,409	2,836	4,126	5,558	5,023	4,474	4,606	3,296	2,761	4,052	7,068	8,865	12,700	Central Bank Bonds **20r**
3,074	3,601	3,659	4,336	4,861	5,139	4,928	5,206	5,824	5,400	6,829	8,145	10,174	13,100	16,514	Foreign Assets **21**
1,030	1,407	2,229	2,395	2,897	2,968	3,595	4,426	5,120	4,927	5,131	5,394	4,921	4,912	5,196	Claims on Central Government **22a**
15,937	20,114	25,249	29,693	33,946	40,376	46,474	53,016	59,724	75,118	95,064	114,969	130,056	147,131	176,517	Claims on Private Sector **22d**
1,920	1,969	3,306	3,872	3,777	4,302	5,223	5,829	7,112	8,419	9,218	14,009	16,182	17,344	19,593	Demand Deposits **24**
8,727	11,688	14,105	16,154	17,885	21,001	25,023	30,172	36,786	44,308	52,800	61,984	71,660	83,178	100,668	Time, Savings,& Fgn.Currency Dep. **25**
316	44	90	180	200	218	96	24	70	794	1,533	1,381	1,896	2,270	2,923	Bonds **26ab**
617	592	281	306	287	359	725	1,305	1,694	1,286	1,052	1,723	1,693	635	792	Restricted Deposits **26b**
4,716	6,507	8,968	9,956	11,739	14,124	12,521	9,184	7,009	6,647	7,294	10,495	11,552	11,957	16,697	Foreign Liabilities **26c**
23	4	321	569	521	240	187	67	356	23	305	123	400	424	286	Central Government Deposits **26d**
882	1,130	1,434	1,742	1,928	2,172	2,554	3,132	3,925	4,553	5,300	6,904	7,708	9,234	11,032	Central Govt. Lending Funds **26f**
2,918	3,627	4,197	5,245	7,098	9,112	10,860	14,858	15,948	16,103	19,664	21,207	25,874	29,420	29,256	Credit from Monetary Authorities **26g**
1,404	1,689	1,907	2,383	2,706	3,031	3,462	4,069	6,205	11,803	12,939	14,504	15,641	17,110	20,406	Capital Accounts **27a**
779	596	134	–18	546	499	677	1,499	704	1,415	6,397	8,534	9,012	13,272	21,219	Other Items (Net) **27r**
Billions of Won Beginning 1966: End of Period															**Monetary Survey**
–121	–1,889	–4,086	–4,835	–5,935	–7,696	–6,116	–1,598	7,244	9,078	10,293	8,287	12,233	17,734	20,603	Foreign Assets (Net) **31n**
17,690	23,184	29,005	33,642	38,042	44,789	51,318	59,693	66,611	81,807	102,108	124,974	139,537	157,322	186,214	Domestic Credit **32**
1,373	2,540	3,165	3,238	3,385	3,671	4,087	3,188	1,765	442	–447	1,899	2,404	2,053	755	Claims on Central Govt. (Net) **32an**
270	370	470	570	570	570	570	570	570	570	570	570	570	570	570	Claims on Official Entities **32bx**
16,047	20,273	25,371	29,834	34,086	40,548	46,661	55,935	64,276	80,795	101,985	122,505	136,564	154,699	184,888	Claims on Private Sector **32d**
3,807	3,982	5,799	6,783	6,821	7,558	8,809	10,107	12,152	14,328	15,905	21,752	24,586	29,041	32,511	Money **34**
8,727	11,689	14,105	16,155	17,885	21,007	25,024	30,172	36,787	44,309	52,802	61,994	71,672	83,178	100,668	Quasi-Money **35**
341	412	243	1,086	1,725	3,078	4,750	9,185	15,934	16,869	17,174	14,980	18,442	20,553	19,338	Bonds **36ab**
617	592	281	306	287	359	725	1,305	1,694	1,286	1,052	1,723	1,693	635	792	Restricted Deposits **36b**
882	1,130	1,435	1,742	1,928	2,173	2,554	3,133	3,925	4,553	5,300	6,906	7,713	9,234	11,032	Central Govt. Lending Funds **36f**
3,194	3,488	3,057	2,736	3,461	2,918	3,340	4,192	3,364	9,538	20,166	25,906	27,664	32,415	42,476	Other Items (Net) **37r**
12,534	15,671	19,904	22,938	24,706	28,565	33,833	40,280	48,939	58,637	68,708	83,746	96,259	112,219	133,179	Money plus Quasi-Money **35l**
Billions of Won Beginning 1966: End of Period															**Other Banking Institutions**
															Development Institutions
3,620	4,449	5,311	6,049	6,699	7,740	8,315	9,760	10,447	12,403	15,187	18,665	21,102	23,874	26,771	Claims on Private Sector **42d**
510	610	786	900	1,160	1,710	2,229	2,688	2,896	3,404	4,612	7,974	10,412	13,921	16,617	Bonds **46ab**
12	12	3	2	2	2	2	2	1	1	1	1	1	1	1	Counterpart Funds **46e**
1,468	1,925	2,333	2,728	2,779	2,948	2,650	2,661	2,829	2,927	3,085	3,117	3,121	3,045	2,967	Central Govt. Lending Funds **46f**
31	39	12	20	9	36	55	2,328	3,640	4,663	5,183	5,480	4,910	5,110	5,450	Credit from Deposit Money Banks **46h**
618	666	685	781	768	786	825	946	1,023	1,059	1,242	1,387	1,285	1,382	1,615	Capital Accounts **47a**
981	1,197	1,493	1,617	1,982	2,256	2,554	1,135	58	348	1,064	706	1,373	415	121	Other Items (Net) **47r**
															Trust Accounts of Coml. Banks
1,826	2,873	4,044	5,190	6,493	9,425	13,358	18,008	27,344	38,990	47,578	56,964	79,724	112,416	143,539	Claims on Private Sector **42d. g**
36	28	117	120	100	375	259	356	356	879	854	833	1,259	1,000	1,118	Claims on Deposit Money Banks **42e. g**
1,043	1,448	1,581	1,721	2,236	3,928	5,095	8,741	13,453	22,119	29,175	36,619	53,022	71,319	93,415	Quasi-Monetary Liabilities **45.. g**
819	1,453	2,580	3,589	4,356	5,872	8,522	9,622	14,246	17,750	19,257	21,178	27,961	42,096	51,242	Other Items (Net) **47r. g**
85	93	282	439	586	475	512	1,052	1,566	1,710	1,973	2,346	3,578	4,078	5,948	Postal Savings Deposits **45.. h**
Billions of Won Beginning 1966: End of Period															**Nonbank Financial Institutions**
40	59	87	127	208	328	549	870	1,324	1,850	2,304	3,247	4,496	3,186	3,633	Cash **40.. s**
72	113	152	172	252	286	213	137	22	63	108	324	401	452	269	Claims on Central Government **42a. s**
728	1,061	1,519	2,356	3,447	4,575	5,653	7,937	10,608	14,411	19,279	24,337	28,656	33,091	38,931	Claims on Private Sector **42d. s**
111	176	332	484	644	748	839	917	1,147	1,489	2,210	2,798	3,333	3,842	4,504	Real Estate **42h. s**
322	479	817	1,138	1,455	1,703	1,901	3,163	3,933	5,223	7,657	8,196	6,528	5,607	7,230	*Incr.in Total Assets(Within Per.)* **49z. s**
13,622	17,153	21,680	24,972	27,320	32,640	38,892	49,202	62,634	80,616	97,551	119,465	148,364	184,430	228,909	Liquid Liabilities **55l**

Korea
542

		1965	1966	1967	1968	1969	1970	1971	1972	1973	1974	1975	1976	1977	1978	1979
Interest Rates																*Percent Per Annum*
Discount Rate *(End of Period)*	60	28.0	28.0	28.0	23.0	22.0	19.0	16.0	11.0	11.0	11.0	14.0	14.0	14.0	15.0	15.0
Money Market Rate	60b	....	....	....	....	....	....	....	....	....	....	....	....	18.1	19.3	18.9
Corporate Bond Rate	60bc	....	....	....	....	....	....	....	....	....	....	....	....	....	....	....
Deposit Rate	60l	....	....	....	....	22.8	22.8	20.4	12.0	12.0	15.0	15.0	16.2	14.4	18.6	18.6
Lending Rate	60p	....	....	....	....	....	....	....	....	....	....	....	....	....	....	....
Government Bond Yield	61	....	....	....	....	....	....	....	....	....	21.0	21.1	21.6	21.5	21.6	25.2
Prices, Production, Employment																*Index Numbers (1990=100)*:
Share Prices	62	....	....	....	....	....	....	....	5.6	10.7	10.5	11.7	14.4	I15.2	19.2	16.1
Producer Prices	63	9.3	10.1	10.8	11.6	12.4	13.6	I14.7	16.8	17.9	25.5	32.2	I36.1	39.4	43.9	52.2
Consumer Prices	64	....	7.5	I8.3	9.3	10.4	12.1	13.7	15.3	15.8	19.6	24.6	I28.4	31.3	35.8	42.3
Wages: Monthly Earnings	65ey	.8	.9	1.1	I1.4	1.9	2.4	2.8	3.4	3.8	5.1	6.5	8.7	11.7	15.8	20.3
Industrial Production	66..c	2.2	2.7	3.4	4.5	5.3	6.0	6.9	7.9	10.5	13.4	16.0	20.7	24.9	30.6	34.2
Manufacturing Employment	67ey	16.3	17.5	21.2	24.1	24.9	25.7	27.2	29.4	36.1	41.0	44.9	54.5	57.0	61.4	63.7
International Transactions															*Millions of Won through 1965;*	
Exports	70	46,087	I68	87	126	180	260	370	638	1,283	1,805	2,393	3,735	4,863	6,157	7,288
Imports, cif	71	123,344	I194	269	405	526	616	831	991	1,689	2,771	3,521	4,247	5,233	7,246	9,844
Imports, fob	71.v	112,952	I178	247	371	482	561	756	898	1,528	2,533	3,268	3,988	4,905	6,773	9,136
															1990 – 100	
Volume of Exports	72	1.0	1.2	1.5	2.3	3.2	4.0	5.1	7.7	12.0	13.1	16.1	21.8	26.1	29.8	29.5
Volume of Imports	73	2.3	3.6	5.0	7.4	9.4	9.9	12.0	12.3	15.8	16.3	16.8	20.7	25.1	32.7	36.4
Unit Value of Exports	74	10.6	11.7	12.2	12.9	12.8	14.4	15.9	18.2	23.3	29.9	33.2	37.2	40.6	45.0	53.8
Unit Value of Imports	75	10.8	10.8	10.8	11.0	11.3	12.6	14.0	16.1	21.7	34.3	42.2	41.4	42.3	44.7	54.6
Export Prices	76	....	....	....	....	....	....	18.6	20.7	23.7	25.6	30.5	34.4	37.0	41.9	49.2
Import Prices	76.x	....	....	....	....	....	....	13.5	16.3	20.7	29.3	33.9	34.9	35.3	36.8	46.6
Balance of Payments															*Millions of US Dollars:*	
Goods: Exports f.o.b.	78aa d	....	....	....	....	....	....	....	....	....	....	....	7,814	10,046	12,711	14,705
Goods: Imports f.o.b.	78ab d	....	....	....	....	....	....	....	....	....	....	....	-8,404	-10,523	-14,491	-19,100
Trade Balance	78ac d	....	....	....	....	....	....	....	....	....	....	....	-590	-477	-1,780	-4,395
Services: Credit	78ad d	....	....	....	....	....	....	....	....	....	....	....	1,527	2,784	4,059	4,392
Services: Debit	78ae d	....	....	....	....	....	....	....	....	....	....	....	-1,191	-2,025	-3,195	-3,503
Balance on Goods and Services	78af d	....	....	....	....	....	....	....	....	....	....	....	-254	282	-916	-3,506
Income: Credit	78ag d	....	....	....	....	....	....	....	....	....	....	....	116	243	391	433
Income: Debit	78ah d	....	....	....	....	....	....	....	....	....	....	....	-518	-736	-1,031	-1,517
Balance on Goods, Serv., & Inc.	78ai d	....	....	....	....	....	....	....	....	....	....	....	-656	-211	-1,556	-4,590
Current Transfers, n.i.e.: Credit	78aj d	....	....	....	....	....	....	....	....	....	....	....	461	388	574	560
Current Transfers: Debit	78ak d	....	....	....	....	....	....	....	....	....	....	....	-115	-165	-103	-121
Current Account, n.i.e.	78al d	....	....	....	....	....	....	....	....	....	....	....	-310	12	-1,085	-4,151
Capital Account, n.i.e.: Credit	78ba d	....	....	....	....	....	....	....	....	....	....	....	—	—	—	—
Capital Account: Debit	78bb d	....	....	....	....	....	....	....	....	....	....	....	—	—	—	—
Capital Account, n.i.e.	78bc d	....	....	....	....	....	....	....	....	....	....	....	—	—	—	—
Direct Investment Abroad	78bd d	....	....	....	....	....	....	....	....	....	....	....	-6	-21	-28	-19
Dir. Invest. in Rep. Econ., n.i.e.	78be d	....	....	....	....	....	....	....	....	....	....	....	81	94	89	35
Portfolio Investment Assets	78bf d	....	....	....	....	....	....	....	....	....	....	....	....	....	....	....
Portfolio Investment Liab., n.i.e.	78bg d	....	....	....	....	....	....	....	....	....	....	....	74	70	42	8
Other Investment Assets	78bh d	....	....	....	....	....	....	....	....	....	....	....	-289	-924	-175	-687
Other Investment Liab., n.i.e.	78bi d	....	....	....	....	....	....	....	....	....	....	....	2,006	2,171	2,201	6,016
Financial Account, n.i.e.	78bj d	....	....	....	....	....	....	....	....	....	....	....	1,866	1,390	2,129	5,353
Net Errors and Omissions	78ca d	....	....	....	....	....	....	....	....	....	....	....	-243	-32	-313	-328
Overall Balance	78cb d	....	....	....	....	....	....	....	....	....	....	....	1,313	1,370	731	874
Reserves and Related Items	79da d	....	....	....	....	....	....	....	....	....	....	....	-1,313	-1,370	-731	-874
Reserve Assets	79db d	....	....	....	....	....	....	....	....	....	....	....	-1,410	-1,345	-630	-749
Use of Fund Credit and Loans	79dc d	....	....	....	....	....	....	....	....	....	....	....	97	-25	-100	-125
Liabs.Constit.For.Auth.Reserves	79dd d	....	....	....	....	....	....	....	....	....	....	....	....	....	....	....
Exceptional Financing	79de d	....	....	....	....	....	....	....	....	....	....	....	....	....	....	....
Government Finance															*Millions of Won through 1965;*	
Deficit (-) or Surplus	80	-1,100	I-6	-7	6	-44	I-21	-10	-161	-27	-164	-202	-192	-316	-300	-545
Revenue	81	61,800	I134	190	282	383	I419	514	558	679	1,026	1,549	2,325	2,958	4,108	5,446
Grants Received	81z	27,500	I31	25	36	22	I29	24	27	16	13	15	2	—	—	—
Expenditure	82	89,300	I160	208	288	417	I443	542	751	707	1,065	1,601	2,294	2,804	3,781	5,225
Lending Minus Repayments	83	1,100	I10	14	24	33	I26	7	-5	14	138	165	225	470	627	766
Financing																
Domestic	84a	....	....	....	....	....	I7	4	105	-38	69	46	-22	38	-65	272
Foreign	85a	....	....	....	....	....	I14	7	56	64	95	156	215	278	365	273
Net Borrowing	84	1,700	I8	16	—	50	....	....	....	....	....	....	....	....	....	....
Use of Cash Balances	87	-600	I-2	-9	-6	-6	....	....	....	....	....	....	....	....	....	....
Debt	88	49,900	I46	55	58	57	I280	409	647	775	1,107	1,505	1,867	2,347	2,980	3,530
Domestic	88a	....	....	....	....	....	82	92	190	195	276	384	539	652	861	1,183
Foreign	89a	....	....	....	....	....	198	317	456	580	831	1,121	1,328	1,695	2,119	2,347
National Accounts															*Millions of Won through 1965;*	
Exports of Goods & Services	90c	68,600	I107	145	209	288	382	517	819	1,578	2,071	2,855	4,446	5,707	7,227	8,739
Government Consumption	91f	74,800	I103	130	173	221	265	335	412	448	688	1,121	1,521	1,937	2,530	3,109
Gross Fixed Capital Formation	93e	119,000	I210	275	414	556	627	726	831	1,258	1,899	2,550	3,365	5,100	7,909	10,576
Increase/Decrease(-) in Stocks	93i	1,900	I14	6	14	66	66	122	92	124	476	217	181	60	132	702
Private Consumption	96f	671,500	I811	1,005	1,231	1,529	2,041	2,548	3,055	3,705	5,323	7,248	9,235	11,250	14,786	19,367
Imports of Goods & Services	98c	-127,800	I-208	-279	-417	-542	-643	-867	-1,015	-1,740	-2,916	-3,728	-4,621	-5,813	-8,063	-10,831
Gross Domestic Product	99b	798,100	I1,024	1,259	1,630	2,130	2,724	3,379	4,170	5,416	7,569	10,224	13,996	18,074	24,327	31,323
Net Factor Inc/Pmts(-) Abroad	98.n	7,700	I13	22	23	25	12	-4	-16	-37	-66	-159	-178	-268	-326	-521
Gross Nat'l Expenditure = GNP	99a	805,700	I1,037	1,281	1,653	2,155	2,736	3,375	4,154	5,379	7,503	10,065	13,818	17,807	24,002	30,802
Nat'l Income, Market Prices	99e	760,200	I978	1,204	1,547	2,019	2,574	3,172	3,878	4,954	6,916	9,362	12,819	16,461	22,286	28,424
GDP 1990 Prices *(Billions)*	99b.p	20,671	23,189	24,557	27,340	31,126	I33,853	36,966	39,164	44,812	I48,358	51,806	58,485	64,376	70,627	75,988
GDP Deflator (1990=100)	99bi p	3.9	4.4	5.1	6.0	6.8	8.0	9.1	10.6	12.1	15.7	19.7	23.9	28.1	34.4	41.2
																Millions:
Population	99z	28.33	28.96	30.13	30.84	31.54	32.24	32.88	33.51	34.10	34.69	35.28	35.85	36.41	36.97	37.53

Prices, Production, Employment: I Prior to 1967, data refer to consumer prices in Seoul.
Government Finance: I Beginning in 1966, revenues and expenditures are on a gross basis. I Beginning in 1970, data are as reported in the *Government Finance Statistics Yearbook* and cover consolidated central government.

Korea
542

1980	1981	1982	1983	1984	1985	1986	1987	1988	1989	1990	1991	1992	1993	1994		
Percent Per Annum															**Interest Rates**	
16.0	11.0	5.0	5.0	5.0	5.0	7.0	7.0	8.0	7.0	7.0	7.0	7.0	5.0	5.0	Discount Rate (*End of Period*)	60
22.9	18.1	14.2	13.0	11.4	9.4	9.7	8.9	9.6	13.3	14.0	17.0	14.3	12.1	12.5	Money Market Rate	60b
....	17.4	19.3	14.4	13.6	13.4	13.3	12.9	12.8	15.7	13.3	13.4	16.0	12.6	12.9	Corporate Bond Rate	60bc
19.5	16.2	8.0	8.0	9.2	10.0	10.0	10.0	10.0	10.0	10.0	10.0	10.0	8.6	8.5	Deposit Rate	60l
18.0	17.4	11.8	10.0	10.0	10.0	10.0	10.0	10.1	11.3	10.0	10.0	10.0	8.6	8.5	Lending Rate	60p
28.8	23.6	17.4	13.1	14.3	13.6	11.6	12.4	13.0	14.7	15.0	16.5	15.1	12.1	12.3	Government Bond Yield	61
Period Averages															**Prices, Production, Employment**	
14.6	16.9	16.3	16.3	17.7	18.6	30.5	55.9	92.8	123.0	100.0	88.0	78.6	98.2	129.6	Share Prices	62
72.5	87.3	91.4	I91.6	92.2	93.0	91.7	92.1	94.6	I96.0	100.0	104.7	107.0	108.6	111.6	Producer Prices	63
54.5	66.1	70.8	I73.3	75.0	76.8	78.9	81.3	87.1	I92.1	100.0	109.3	116.1	121.7	129.3	Consumer Prices	64
24.9	29.8	34.2	38.3	41.5	45.7	49.8	55.6	66.5	83.2	100.0	116.9	135.2	149.9	173.1	Wages: Monthly Earnings	65ey
33.5	37.8	39.7	I45.9	52.8	55.2	66.5	I78.6	89.0	91.9	100.0	109.6	116.0	121.1	134.5	Industrial Production	66..c
60.5	58.5	61.6	66.7	68.2	71.5	77.9	89.9	95.0	99.4	100.0	101.7	98.3	94.7	95.6	Manufacturing Employment	67ey
Billions of Won Beginning 1966															**International Transactions**	
10,637	14,484	15,976	18,964	23,571	26,346	30,600	38,892	44,397	41,883	46,016	52,706	59,823	66,008	77,141	Exports	70
13,541	17,796	17,730	20,318	24,688	27,089	27,841	33,742	37,898	41,271	49,433	59,787	63,838	67,264	82,231	Imports, cif	71
12,384	16,624	16,569	19,114	23,214	25,641	26,364	31,952	35,888	39,082	46,812	56,616	60,452	63,697	77,870	Imports, fob	71.v
1990=100																
32.9	38.6	41.2	47.9	55.4	59.5	66.8	82.7	I93.4	94.2	100.0	109.9	119.1	127.2	146.1	Volume of Exports	72
33.1	36.8	37.1	42.1	48.6	51.5	55.6	67.3	I76.9	89.3	100.0	116.7	119.0	126.7	153.9	Volume of Imports	73
70.4	81.5	84.5	86.3	92.7	96.4	99.7	102.4	103.5	96.7	100.0	104.2	109.2	112.7	114.8	Unit Value of Exports	74
82.4	97.4	96.8	97.9	103.0	106.5	101.2	101.5	99.7	93.4	100.0	103.6	108.5	107.4	108.1	Unit Value of Imports	75
64.1	74.5	77.0	79.4	84.0	88.5	92.6	94.8	98.8	97.2	100.0	103.8	106.5	109.2	112.2	Export Prices	76
74.0	86.7	88.3	89.7	93.2	96.6	92.5	99.0	104.8	101.0	100.0	99.7	101.1	104.7	108.9	Import Prices	76.x
Minus Sign Indicates Debit															Balance of Payments	
17,214	20,671	20,879	23,204	26,335	26,442	33,913	46,244	59,648	61,408	63,123	69,581	75,169	80,950	93,676	Goods: Exports f.o.b.	78aa*d*
-21,598	-24,299	-23,473	-24,967	-27,371	-26,461	-29,707	-38,585	-48,203	-56,811	-65,127	-76,561	-77,315	-79,090	-96,822	Goods: Imports f.o.b.	78ab*d*
-4,384	-3,628	-2,594	-1,763	-1,036	-19	4,206	7,659	11,445	4,597	-2,004	-6,980	-2,146	1,860	-3,146	Trade Balance	78ac*d*
4,710	5,760	6,679	6,477	6,456	5,596	6,882	8,807	9,706	10,349	11,208	12,222	12,750	15,545	19,814	Services: Credit	78ad*d*
-4,089	-4,456	-4,194	-4,186	-4,231	-4,118	-4,645	-5,454	-6,911	-9,466	-11,287	-13,482	-14,858	-16,784	-20,656	Services: Debit	78ae*d*
-3,763	-2,324	-109	528	1,189	1,459	6,443	11,012	14,240	5,480	-2,083	-8,240	-4,254	621	-3,988	Balance on Goods and Services	78af*d*
653	838	798	702	861	1,068	1,170	1,204	1,546	2,294	3,061	3,309	3,260	2,708	2,738	Income: Credit	78ag*d*
-2,660	-3,661	-3,838	-3,428	-3,963	-3,992	-4,035	-3,580	-3,073	-2,966	-3,425	-3,642	-3,767	-3,436	-3,886	Income: Debit	78ah*d*
-5,770	-5,147	-3,149	-2,198	-1,913	-1,465	3,578	8,636	12,713	4,808	-2,447	-8,573	-4,761	-107	-5,136	Balance on Goods, Serv., & Inc.	78ai*d*
587	652	692	743	715	799	1,218	1,495	2,021	1,488	1,823	2,072	2,653	2,948	3,322	Current Transfers, n.i.e.: Credit	78aj*d*
-142	-154	-194	-153	-179	-227	-185	-282	-579	-1,249	-1,555	-1,897	-2,014	-1,982	-2,281	Current Transfers: Debit	78ak*d*
-5,325	-4,649	-2,651	-1,608	-1,377	-893	4,611	9,849	14,155	5,047	-2,179	-8,398	-4,122	859	-4,095	Current Account, n.i.e.	78al*d*
4	3	4	6	8	7	6	5	6	9	7	7	5	2	8	Capital Account, n.i.e.: Credit	78ba*d*
—	—	-3	-4	-3	-1	—	—	—	—	—	-335	-412	-477	-445	Capital Account: Debit	78bb*d*
4	3	1	2	5	6	6	5	6	9	7	-328	-407	-475	-437	Capital Account, n.i.e.	78bc*d*
-13	-42	-145	-126	-37	-34	-110	-183	-151	-305	-820	-1,357	-1,047	-1,056	-2,075	Direct Investment Abroad	78bd*d*
6	102	69	69	110	234	435	601	871	758	715	1,116	550	516	758	Dir. Invest. in Rep. Econ., n.i.e.	78be*d*
—	—	—	—	—	—	—	—	-22	-58	-88	-38	-19	-297	-470	Portfolio Investment Assets	78bf*d*
40	60	15	188	333	982	301	-113	-460	29	899	3,154	5,761	11,022	7,276	Portfolio Investment Liab., n.i.e.	78bg*d*
-462	-21	-794	-521	300	-1,664	-1,797	-444	-2,441	-1,684	-2,585	-6,450	-2,550	-4,378	-8,161	Other Investment Assets	78bh*d*
6,399	4,628	4,811	2,705	2,117	2,444	-2,822	-8,795	-2,051	-1,366	4,848	10,400	4,459	-2,467	13,523	Other Investment Liab., n.i.e.	78bi*d*
5,970	4,727	3,956	2,315	2,823	1,962	-3,993	-8,934	-4,254	-2,626	2,969	6,825	7,154	3,340	10,851	Financial Account, n.i.e.	78bj*d*
-338	-410	-1,301	-945	-891	-883	-547	1,184	-591	690	-2,005	753	1,099	-715	-1,705	Net Errors and Omissions	78ca*d*
311	-329	5	-236	560	192	77	2,104	9,316	3,120	-1,208	-1,148	3,724	3,009	4,614	Overall Balance	78cb*d*
-311	329	-5	236	-560	-192	-77	-2,104	-9,316	-3,120	1,208	1,148	-3,724	-3,009	-4,614	Reserves and Related Items	79da*d*
-875	-300	-89	76	-878	41	50	-886	-8,826	-3,120	1,208	1,148	-3,724	-3,009	-4,614	Reserve Assets	79db*d*
564	629	84	160	318	-232	-127	-1,218	-490	—	—	—	—	—	—	Use of Fund Credit and Loans	79dc*d*
—	—	—	—	—	—	—	—	—	—	—	—	—	—	—	Liabs.Constit.For.Auth.Reserves	79dd*d*
—	—	—	—	—	—	—	—	—	—	—	—	—	—	—	Exceptional Financing	79de*d*
Billions of Won Beginning 1966: Year Ending December 31															**Government Finance**	
-849	-1,585	-1,656	-663	-841	-943	-86	478	2,009	285	-1,207	-3,494	-1,188	1,704	-1,602	Deficit (-) or Surplus	80
6,834	8,605	9,983	11,538	12,604	13,923	15,840	18,658	22,890	25,962	32,089	36,818	43,805	50,750	58,824	Revenue	81
—	—	—	—	—	—	—	—	—	—	—	—	—	—	—	Grants Received	81z
6,563	8,045	10,115	10,682	11,875	13,336	14,948	16,944	19,454	23,776	29,004	35,619	40,776	45,010	53,952	Expenditure	82
1,120	2,145	1,524	1,519	1,570	1,530	978	1,236	1,427	1,901	4,292	4,693	4,217	4,036	6,474	Lending Minus Repayments	83
															Financing	
524	1,046	974	260	527	501	233	-489	-1,297	315	1,535	3,776	1,499	-1,257	....	Domestic	84a
325	539	682	403	314	442	-147	11	-712	-600	-328	-282	-311	-447	....	Foreign	85a
....	....	....	....	....	....	....	....	....	....	....	....	....	....	....	Net Borrowing	84
....	....	....	....	....	....	....	....	....	....	....	....	....	....	....	Use of Cash Balances	87
5,328	7,346	9,343	10,715	11,614	12,751	13,576	14,417	13,516	14,144	14,927	16,107	17,082	18,007	....	Debt	88
1,511	2,851	4,020	4,743	5,241	5,422	5,759	6,562	7,548	9,034	9,369	10,407	11,561	12,513	....	Domestic	88a
3,817	4,495	5,323	5,972	6,373	7,329	7,817	7,855	5,968	5,110	5,558	5,700	5,521	5,494	....	Foreign	89a
Billions of Won Beginning 1966															**National Accounts**	
12,944	17,341	18,770	22,749	26,126	27,968	36,034	45,051	51,132	48,829	53,467	60,735	69,433	78,163	91,780	Exports of Goods & Services	90c
4,387	5,515	6,255	6,935	7,354	8,305	9,575	10,843	12,660	15,237	18,187	22,170	26,110	28,746	32,483	Government Consumption	91f
12,226	13,276	15,446	18,944	21,381	23,435	26,969	32,587	39,425	47,625	66,569	82,947	87,907	96,219	109,374	Gross Fixed Capital Formation	93e
-154	718	117	-346	778	849	505	841	1,932	2,539	-270	973	35	-2,512	199	Increase/Decrease(-) in Stocks	93i
24,585	30,633	34,554	38,892	43,443	48,027	52,822	59,031	67,963	79,424	96,388	115,043	129,735	143,722	164,212	Private Consumption	96f
-15,774	-19,719	-20,174	-23,049	-26,040	-26,923	-30,366	-36,356	-40,567	-44,785	-54,417	-66,050	-71,840	-76,971	-94,313	Imports of Goods & Services	98c
38,041	47,482	54,443	64,197	73,605	82,062	95,736	112,130	133,134	149,165	179,539	215,734	240,392	267,146	305,008	Gross Domestic Product	99b
-1,291	-1,954	-2,261	-2,111	-2,561	-2,761	-2,827	-2,404	-1,763	-1,223	-1,277	-1,495	-1,688	-1,628	2,141	Net Factor Inc/Pmts(-) Abroad	98.n
36,750	45,528	52,182	62,086	71,045	79,301	92,909	109,727	131,371	147,942	178,262	214,240	238,705	265,518	302,867	Gross Nat'l Expenditure = GNP	99a
33,770	41,726	47,454	55,972	63,753	71,096	83,443	98,136	117,319	132,254	159,675	192,650	214,779	238,554	272,957	Nat'l Income, Market Prices	99e
74,345	79,339	85,130	95,155	104,113	I111,330	124,194	138,499	154,111	163,950	179,539	195,936	205,860	217,699	235,931	GDP 1990 Prices (*Billions*)	99b.*p*
51.2	59.8	64.0	67.5	70.7	73.7	77.1	81.0	86.4	91.0	100.0	110.1	116.8	122.7	129.3	GDP Deflator (1990=100)	99bi*p*
Midyear Estimates																
38.12	38.72	39.33	39.91	40.41	40.81	41.21	41.62	42.03	42.45	42.87	43.27	43.66	44.06	44.45	**Population**	99z

Kuwait

443		1965	1966	1967	1968	1969	1970	1971	1972	1973	1974	1975	1976	1977	1978	1979
Exchange Rates															*SDRs per Dinar:*	
Official Rate	ac	2.8000	2.8000	2.8000	2.8000	2.8000	2.8000	2.8000	2.8102	2.7940	2.8199	2.9040	2.9995	2.9392	2.8241	2.7795
															US Dollars per Dinar:	
Official Rate	ag	2.8000	2.8000	2.8000	2.8000	2.8000	2.8000	3.0400	3.0511	3.3705	3.4526	3.3996	3.4849	3.5703	3.6792	3.6615
Official Rate	rh	2.8000	2.8000	2.8000	2.8000	2.8000	2.8000	2.8085	3.0400	3.3770e	3.4115	3.4483	3.4203	3.4898	3.6362	3.6203
Fund Position															*Millions of SDRs:*	
Quota	2f.s	50.0	50.0	50.0	50.0	50.0	65.0	65.0	65.0	65.0	65.0	65.0	65.0	65.0	235.0	235.0
SDRs	1b.s	—	—	—	—	—	—	—	—	—	—	—	—	—	—	—
Reserve Position in the Fund	1c.s	12.5	12.5	12.5	12.5	12.5	21.3	20.7	20.7	19.7	255.8	573.6	742.7	722.2	588.4	389.7
of which: Outstg.Fund Borrowing	2c	—	—	—	—	—	—	—	—	—	225.0	523.9	685.0	676.2	543.9	339.6
International Liquidity											*Millions of US Dollars Unless Otherwise Indicated:*					
Total Reserves minus Gold	1l.d	72.1	97.1	47.5	51.1	95.9	117.1	193.7	269.0	380.8	1,249.2	1,491.5	1,701.8	2,883.1	2,500.4	2,870.1
SDRs	1b.d	—	—	—	—	—	—	—	—	—	—	—	—	—	—	—
Reserve Position in the Fund	1c.d	12.5	12.5	12.5	12.5	12.5	21.3	22.5	22.5	23.8	313.2	671.5	862.9	877.2	766.6	513.4
Foreign Exchange	1d.d	59.6	84.6	35.0	38.6	83.4	95.8	171.2	246.5	357.0	936.0	820.0	838.9	2,005.9	1,733.8	2,356.7
Gold (Million Fine Troy Ounces)	1ad	1.480	1.920	3.897	3.471	2.463	2.463	2.480	2.480	2.846	3.504	3.988	5.578	2.511	2.525	2.539
Gold (National Valuation)	1and	51.8	67.2	136.4	121.5	86.2	86.2	94.2	94.2	....	150.5	169.6	242.9	112.1	116.3	116.1
Deposit Money Banks: Assets	7a.d	535.6	738.1	728.3	882.3	1,033.8	1,230.9	1,452.8	1,560.7	1,618.0	1,938.3	2,088.7	2,352.0	2,936.2	4,468.0	5,154.3
of which: Claims on Nonbanks	7add	....	....	....	....	....	239.4	253.2	437.8	625.2	612.1	721.1	752.0	700.8	1,059.6	1,387.0
Deposit Money Banks: Liabilities	7b.d	24.4	27.2	24.4	48.4	219.5	323.7	316.8	314.9	459.7	495.1	574.5	1,129.5	1,498.5	2,213.0	2,943.5
Other Banking Insts.: Assets	7e.d	....	....	....	....	....	....	....	....	....	....	....	1,191.8	1,680.5	2,118.9	2,392.8
of which: Claims on Nonbanks	7edd	....	....	....	....	....	....	....	....	....	....	....	677.5	1,016.1	1,277.4	1,537.5
Other Banking Insts.: Liabilities	7f.d	....	....	....	....	....	....	....	....	....	....	....	426.6	805.8	1,187.6	1,341.9
Monetary Authorities															*Millions of Dinars:*	
Foreign Assets	11	44.3	58.7	65.7	61.7	I65.2	72.5	94.7	119.6	148.5	395.0	482.4	547.0	821.9	709.8	814.4
Claims on Central Government	12a	....	....	....	....	....	....	....	....	....	....	....	....	....	....	....
Reserve Money	14	37.0	50.1	58.9	54.4	I50.8	51.1	59.0	71.0	95.8	129.2	169.2	224.8	431.5	318.7	379.2
of which: Currency Outside DMBs	14a	32.1	44.2	52.5	47.0	I44.3	44.8	50.4	57.1	71.1	81.7	101.7	129.1	150.9	177.0	215.9
Central Government Deposits	16d	....	....	....	7.1	14.7	30.9	36.5	28.4	27.1	213.1	271.5	270.8	325.1	274.8	446.1
Capital Accounts	17a	....	....	....	....	5.0	5.0	5.0	5.0	5.0	5.0	5.0	5.0	8.0	27.9	27.9
Other Items (Net)	17r	7.3	8.6	6.8	7.3	I2.3	1.7	−.2	7.1	19.2	47.7	36.7	46.4	57.3	88.4	−39.0
Deposit Money Banks															*Millions of Dinars:*	
Reserves	20	4.9	5.9	6.4	7.4	I4.4	6.2	8.5	13.8	26.9	57.9	67.2	92.4	271.0	122.7	143.3
Foreign Assets	21	191.3	263.6	260.1	315.1	I369.2	439.6	477.9	513.4	479.0	561.4	614.4	674.9	822.4	1,214.4	1,407.7
Claims on Central Government	22a	....	....	....	....	....	—	.1	.7	1.9	3.6	5.9	12.5	15.2	20.6	35.3
Claims on Private Sector	22d	74.3	86.2	96.7	134.3	I135.0	137.1	146.9	175.7	247.6	351.7	500.8	921.8	1,221.5	1,543.5	2,088.3
Demand Deposits	24	49.3	80.3	81.9	73.0	I63.3	50.4	57.3	84.9	101.3	113.9	188.6	264.6	339.8	459.4	453.5
Time and Savings Deposits	25	134.5	180.7	187.2	266.4	I271.5	266.9	311.1	351.6	363.9	489.0	600.8	826.4	1,078.0	1,314.0	1,593.3
Foreign Liabilities	26c	8.7	9.7	8.7	17.3	I78.4	115.6	104.2	103.6	136.1	143.4	169.0	324.1	419.8	601.5	803.9
Central Government Deposits	26d	46.9	49.6	48.7	57.4	I54.2	80.9	83.1	71.2	58.2	83.7	87.3	71.0	114.9	99.2	139.9
Capital Accounts	27a	16.0	18.7	20.3	23.9	I27.1	31.6	36.4	40.8	45.6	51.0	63.8	89.2	197.4	218.4	268.6
Other Items (Net)	27r	15.1	16.5	16.2	18.8	I14.1	37.4	41.3	51.6	50.4	93.6	78.8	126.3	180.2	208.6	415.4
Monetary Survey															*Millions of Dinars:*	
Foreign Assets (Net)	31n	226.9	312.6	317.1	359.5	I356.0	396.5	468.4	529.4	491.4	813.0	927.8	897.8	1,224.5	1,322.7	1,417.9
Domestic Credit	32	22.9	32.1	43.5	72.4	73.7	41.5	33.0	68.7	162.9	58.5	147.9	592.5	796.7	1,190.1	1,537.6
Claims on Central Govt. (Net)	32an	−51.4	−54.1	−53.2	−61.9	−61.3	−95.6	−113.9	−107.0	−84.7	−293.2	−352.9	−329.3	−424.8	−353.4	−550.7
Claims on Private Sector	32d	74.3	86.2	96.7	134.3	I135.0	137.1	146.9	175.7	247.6	351.7	500.8	921.8	1,221.5	1,543.5	2,088.3
Money	34	81.4	124.5	134.4	120.0	I107.6	95.2	107.7	142.0	172.4	195.6	290.3	393.7	490.7	636.4	669.4
Quasi-Money	35	134.5	180.7	187.2	266.4	I271.5	266.9	311.1	351.6	363.9	489.0	600.8	826.4	1,078.0	1,314.0	1,593.3
Other Items (Net)	37r	33.9	39.5	39.0	45.5	I50.6	75.8	82.6	104.6	118.0	186.9	184.6	270.2	452.5	562.3	692.9
Money plus Quasi-Money	35l	215.9	305.2	321.6	386.4	I379.1	362.1	418.8	493.6	536.3	684.6	891.1	1,220.1	1,568.7	1,950.4	2,262.7
Other Banking Institutions															*Millions of Dinars:*	
Foreign Assets	41	....	....	....	....	....	....	....	....	....	....	....	342.0	470.7	575.9	653.5
Claims on Private Sector	42d	....	....	....	....	....	....	....	....	....	....	....	251.8	406.6	572.2	698.8
Claims on Deposit Money Banks	42e	....	....	....	....	....	....	....	....	....	....	....	78.3	126.3	141.5	171.7
Time and Savings Deposits	45	....	....	....	....	....	....	....	....	....	....	....	83.9	110.5	163.5	154.6
Foreign Liabilities	46c	....	....	....	....	....	....	....	....	....	....	....	122.4	225.7	322.8	366.5
Central Government Deposits	46d	....	....	....	....	....	....	....	....	....	....	....	98.7	141.5	205.8	242.6
Credit from Deposit Money Banks	46h	....	....	....	....	....	....	....	....	....	....	....	99.6	225.6	225.8	257.4
Capital Accounts	47a	....	....	....	....	....	....	....	....	....	....	....	210.3	293.8	385.3	507.3
Other Items (Net)	47r	....	....	....	....	....	....	....	....	....	....	....	57.2	6.5	−13.6	−4.4
Liquid Liabilities	55l	....	....	....	....	....	....	....	....	....	....	....	1,304.0	1,679.2	2,113.9	2,417.5
Interest Rates															*Percent Per Annum*	
Discount Rate *(End of Period)*	60											5.5	5.5	5.5	5.5	6.0
Money Market Rate	60b															8.58
Treasury Bill Rate	60c															....
Deposit Rate	60l															....
Lending Rate	60p															....
Prices and Production															*Index Numbers (1990=100):*	
Wholesale Prices (1985=100)	63	....	....	....	....	....	....	....	47.8	58.3	64.4	69.2	74.5	79.7	78.8	83.9
Consumer Prices	64	....	....	....	....	....	....	....	38.8	42.0	47.5	51.5	54.2	59.5	I64.7	69.2
Crude Petroleum Production	66aa	195.5	205.8	207.2	217.2	229.8	247.7	253.5	272.9	250.4	211.1	172.7	178.3	163.1	176.5	206.9

Kuwait

1980	1981	1982	1983	1984	1985	1986	1987	1988	1989	1990	1991	1992	1993	1994		
End of Period															**Exchange Rates**	
2.8901	3.0529	3.1400	3.2648	3.3508	3.1501	2.7965	2.6117	2.6294	2.6062	....	2.4593	2.4026	2.4396	2.2824	Official Rate	ac
End of Period (ag)	*Period Average (rh)*															
3.6860	3.5535	3.4638	3.4181	3.2845	3.4601	3.4206	3.7051	3.5384	3.4250	....	3.5178	3.3036	3.3510	3.3320	Official Rate	ag
3.6993	3.5878	3.4737	3.4309	3.3785	3.3261	3.4412	3.5896	3.5848	3.4049	....	....	3.4087	3.3147	3.3600	Official Rate	rh
End of Period															**Fund Position**	
393.3	393.3	393.3	635.3	635.3	635.3	635.3	635.3	635.3	635.3	635.3	635.3	635.3	995.2	995.2	Quota	2f. s
—	35.4	62.3	35.6	76.0	104.3	128.4	148.8	166.2	97.8	113.9	128.3	130.4	49.1	55.0	SDRs	1b. s
410.5	409.7	461.0	696.7	716.4	639.4	515.8	378.0	247.3	158.2	123.5	111.1	96.7	167.8	142.6	Reserve Position in the Fund	1c. s
313.0	287.4	291.2	358.7	362.1	309.2	228.8	140.2	70.9	23.9	4.3	—	—	—	—	*of which:* Outstg.Fund Borrowing	2c
End of Period															**International Liquidity**	
3,928.5	4,067.5	5,913.2	5,192.1	4,590.2	5,470.7	5,501.1	4,141.6	1,923.5	3,101.9	1,951.7	3,409.0	5,146.9	4,214.1	3,500.7	Total Reserves minus Gold	1l. d
—	41.2	68.7	37.3	74.5	114.6	157.1	211.1	224.4	128.6	162.1	183.5	179.2	67.4	80.3	SDRs	1b. d
523.6	476.9	508.6	729.4	702.3	702.3	631.0	536.2	332.8	207.9	175.7	158.9	132.9	230.5	208.2	Reserve Position in the Fund	1c. d
3,404.9	3,549.4	5,335.9	4,425.4	3,813.4	4,653.8	4,713.1	3,394.3	1,366.3	2,765.4	1,613.9	3,066.6	4,834.8	3,916.3	3,212.2	Foreign Exchange	1d. d
2.539	2.539	2.539	2.539	2.539	2.539	2.539	2.539	2.539	2.539	2.539	2.539	2.539	2.539	2.539	Gold (Million Fine Troy Ounces)	1ad
116.8	112.6	109.8	108.4	104.1	109.7	108.4	117.5	112.2	108.6	....	111.5	104.7	106.2	105.6	Gold (National Valuation)	1an d
6,930.0	7,979.4	7,797.4	7,865.7	8,236.2	7,714.6	7,453.8	8,455.0	8,762.5	9,723.6	....	6,219.1	4,380.2	4,904.5	5,288.2	Deposit Money Banks: Assets	7a. d
1,634.4	1,801.6	1,999.7	2,721.5	3,301.9	2,985.0	3,315.2	3,643.2	3,826.1	4,220.6	....	3,224.1	2,849.4	2,860.4	3,117.1	*of which:* Claims on Nonbanks	7ad d
4,181.0	4,485.6	5,287.5	5,299.4	5,126.1	4,706.8	4,152.6	4,467.6	4,465.1	5,067.6	....	1,067.3	1,856.3	1,707.3	2,290.4	Deposit Money Banks: Liabilities	7b. d
2,854.4	3,479.6	3,704.2	4,483.9	4,535.6	....	....	3,938.5	4,994.8	5,759.1	....	4,081.0	....	....	....	Other Banking Insts.: Assets	7e. d
1,799.9	1,958.0	2,168.3	2,420.4	2,424.5	....	....	2,415.4	3,068.9	3,793.9	....	3,006.0	....	....	....	*of which:* Claims on Nonbanks	7ed d
1,913.8	2,502.0	2,992.0	3,493.0	2,728.4	....	....	1,992.2	2,457.1	2,880.8	....	2,194.4	....	....	....	Other Banking Insts.: Liabilities	7f. d
End of Period															**Monetary Authorities**	
1,092.0	1,162.6	1,720.1	1,537.2	1,405.6	1,579.6	1,564.4	1,048.3	511.8	853.2	....	963.7	1,564.5	1,151.4	1,168.2	Foreign Assets	11
....	....	....	....	....	....	1.8	81.3	304.4	335.4	....	72.0	169.8	104.0	61.9	Claims on Central Government	12a
506.2	679.3	1,097.6	841.0	743.9	729.6	667.8	547.5	394.4	389.9	....	570.4	537.4	503.4	504.1	Reserve Money	14
251.3	284.7	342.7	340.6	325.1	327.9	337.1	338.3	342.5	334.1	....	446.0	389.7	365.7	365.3	*of which:* Currency Outside DMBs	14a
668.7	671.3	796.1	754.6	900.8	859.1	571.0	516.4	655.8	972.3	....	322.7	863.7	497.2	368.8	Central Government Deposits	16d
30.0	44.2	53.3	149.3	211.4	225.9	236.1	248.2	254.7	234.7	....	204.1	208.0	210.3	209.7	Capital Accounts	17a
–112.9	–232.2	–226.9	–207.8	–450.5	–235.0	91.4	–186.2	–488.6	–408.3	....	–61.6	125.3	44.5	147.8	Other Items (Net)	17r
End of Period															**Deposit Money Banks**	
221.7	321.6	625.9	372.5	323.0	329.9	288.0	160.9	42.1	38.4	....	33.6	46.9	48.2	69.1	Reserves	20
1,880.1	2,245.5	2,251.1	2,301.2	2,507.6	2,229.6	2,179.1	2,282.0	2,476.4	2,839.0	....	1,767.9	1,325.9	1,463.6	1,587.1	Foreign Assets	21
47.4	35.0	54.2	522.2	643.6	655.8	662.8	805.2	1,017.1	753.5	....	607.6	4,919.5	3,435.1	3,272.9	Claims on Central Government	22a
2,629.1	3,424.0	4,223.5	4,220.9	4,392.2	4,396.7	4,491.5	4,791.4	4,962.3	4,950.9	....	5,557.8	817.8	931.8	1,369.8	Claims on Private Sector	22d
469.5	1,005.5	904.9	839.0	643.0	616.0	642.2	697.4	615.5	604.7	....	784.0	652.6	731.6	699.6	Demand Deposits	24
2,136.8	2,575.8	2,935.1	3,188.2	3,507.5	3,491.4	3,567.6	3,726.4	4,109.5	4,338.0	....	4,087.6	4,250.0	4,538.4	4,862.4	Time and Savings Deposits	25
1,134.3	1,262.3	1,526.5	1,550.4	1,560.7	1,360.3	1,214.0	1,205.8	1,261.9	1,479.6	....	303.4	561.9	509.5	687.4	Foreign Liabilities	26c
164.9	163.9	393.8	362.4	387.8	385.5	376.6	595.7	646.0	819.7	....	861.5	821.2	61.0	88.0	Central Government Deposits	26d
337.0	411.0	576.9	664.4	823.8	846.6	898.8	1,000.9	1,049.5	1,087.5	....	1,087.5	786.2	878.1	888.1	Capital Accounts	27a
535.8	607.6	817.5	812.5	944.0	912.2	922.2	813.1	815.4	252.5	....	843.0	38.8	–839.7	–926.6	Other Items (Net)	27r
End of Period															**Monetary Survey**	
1,837.8	2,145.2	2,444.7	2,288.0	2,352.5	2,448.9	2,529.5	2,124.5	1,726.3	2,212.6	....	2,428.2	2,328.5	2,105.5	2,067.9	Foreign Assets (Net)	31n
1,842.9	2,623.8	3,087.8	3,626.1	3,747.2	3,807.9	4,208.5	4,565.8	4,982.0	4,247.9	....	5,053.4	4,222.9	3,912.7	4,247.8	Domestic Credit	32
–786.2	–800.2	–1,135.7	–594.8	–645.0	–588.8	–283.0	–225.6	19.7	–703.1	....	–504.6	3,404.9	2,980.9	2,878.0	Claims on Central Govt. (Net)	32an
2,629.1	3,424.0	4,223.5	4,220.9	4,392.2	4,396.7	4,491.5	4,791.4	4,962.3	4,950.9	....	5,557.8	817.8	931.8	1,369.8	Claims on Private Sector	32d
720.8	1,290.2	1,247.6	1,179.6	968.1	943.9	979.3	1,035.7	958.0	938.8	....	1,230.0	1,042.3	1,097.3	1,064.9	Money	34
2,136.8	2,575.8	2,935.1	3,188.2	3,507.5	3,491.4	3,567.6	3,726.4	4,109.5	4,338.0	....	4,087.6	4,250.0	4,538.4	4,862.4	Quasi-Money	35
823.1	903.6	1,349.8	1,546.3	1,624.0	1,821.5	2,191.2	1,927.9	1,640.8	1,183.7	....	2,163.7	1,259.0	382.7	388.7	Other Items (Net)	37r
2,857.6	3,866.0	4,182.7	4,367.8	4,475.8	4,435.3	4,546.9	4,762.1	5,067.5	5,276.8	....	5,317.6	5,292.3	5,635.7	5,927.3	Money plus Quasi-Money	35l
End of Period															**Other Banking Institutions**	
774.4	979.2	1,069.4	1,311.8	1,380.9	....	....	1,063.0	1,411.6	1,681.5	....	1,160.1	....	....	....	Foreign Assets	41
590.1	812.0	1,257.9	1,165.5	1,097.6	....	....	1,094.7	1,176.7	1,293.8	....	1,423.2	....	....	....	Claims on Private Sector	42d
153.1	223.1	294.4	309.5	214.0	172.2	171.0	220.3	191.4	179.1	....	1.7	1.0	29.9	37.9	Claims on Deposit Money Banks	42e
124.4	134.2	139.8	123.9	143.4	187.2	176.5	164.4	150.3	168.8	....	143.0	129.5	182.1	201.6	Time and Savings Deposits	45
519.2	704.1	863.8	1,021.9	830.7	....	....	537.0	694.4	841.1	....	623.8	....	....	....	Foreign Liabilities	46c
249.6	349.0	421.0	401.5	526.3	....	....	469.5	555.5	448.7	....	300.3	....	....	....	Central Government Deposits	46d
334.6	426.6	631.0	580.9	478.8	....	....	314.6	274.0	308.8	....	216.3	....	....	....	Credit from Deposit Money Banks	46h
217.3	271.4	490.8	514.9	422.0	....	....	399.7	628.1	729.5	....	630.4	....	....	....	Capital Accounts	47a
72.5	129.1	75.3	143.6	291.3	....	....	492.2	477.4	657.6	....	671.0	....	....	....	Other Items (Net)	47r
2,982.0	4,000.2	4,322.5	4,491.7	4,619.2	4,622.5	4,723.4	4,926.5	5,217.8	5,445.6	....	5,460.6	5,421.8	5,817.8	6,128.9	Liquid Liabilities	55l
Percent Per Annum															**Interest Rates**	
6.0	6.0	6.0	6.0	6.0	6.0	6.0	6.0	7.5	7.5	....	7.5	7.5	5.8	7.0	Discount Rate *(End of Period)*	60
10.94	10.13	10.22	6.78	8.90	....	7.53	6.08	6.12	8.70	....	....	....	7.43	6.27	Money Market Rate	60b
6.50	6.50	6.42	5.68	5.68	5.68	5.69	5.48	6.01	8.28	....	....	....	....	....	Treasury Bill Rate	60c
....	9.2	9.2	7.1	7.7	7.2	6.8	5.7	5.3	7.4	....	....	....	7.6	7.1	Deposit Rate	60l
....	9.2	9.4	9.2	8.8	9.1	9.0	8.3	7.1	8.3	....	....	....	7.9	7.9	Lending Rate	60p
															Prices and Production	
92.7	99.0	100.1	101.9	101.3	100.0	100.6	103.9	108.7	118.2	....	....	....	....	....	Wholesale Prices (1985=100)	63
74.0	79.5	85.7	89.7	90.8	92.1	93.0	93.6	95.0	98.2	100.0	116.9	....	....	....	Consumer Prices	64
137.9	93.4	68.2	87.2	96.4	88.0	116.8	110.7	115.9	147.7	100.0	15.2	85.5	155.1	168.4	Crude Petroleum Production	66aa

Kuwait
443

		1965	1966	1967	1968	1969	1970	1971	1972	1973	1974	1975	1976	1977	1978	1979
International Transactions																*Millions of Dinars*
Exports	70	458.4	479.4	307.6	331.5	355.9	604.7	808.6	841.3	1,129.7	3,214.8	2,663.0	2,874.4	2,792.6	2,864.1	5,088.5
Oil Exports	70a	174.6	189.1	186.9	201.8	214.1	578.3	774.2	791.7	1,059.9	3,098.0	2,492.6	2,658.7	2,557.1	2,628.7	4,781.0
Imports, cif	71	134.7	165.3	211.9	218.3	230.8	223.3	232.3	262.2	310.6	455.1	693.2	972.0	1,387.1	1,263.9	1,437.0
Imports, fob	71.v	118.2	145.0	185.9	191.5	202.5	196.0	204.0	230.2	272.7	399.6	608.6	856.1	1,207.5	1,090.1	1,244.7
Volume of Exports																*1985=100*
Petroleum	72a	....	....	194.4	204.9	217.1	237.1	242.3	258.0	238.4	201.6	164.9	174.8	161.1	172.3	200.2
Refined Petroleum	72ab	....	....	51.8	59.3	64.0	83.1	83.1	77.3	78.2	68.8	55.6	78.1	76.8	74.4	78.8
Export Prices																*1985=100:*
Crude Petroleum	76aa *d*	5.1	5.1	5.1	5.1	5.1	5.1	6.6	7.0	9.7	38.4	38.8	41.2	45.3	44.8	67.7
Balance of Payments																*Millions of US Dollars:*
Goods: Exports f.o.b.	78aa *d*	....	....	....	....	....	....	....	....	....	....	8,485	9,621	9,561	10,234	18,114
Goods: Imports f.o.b.	78ab *d*	....	....	....	....	....	....	....	....	....	....	–2,400	–3,300	–4,735	–4,326	–4,870
Trade Balance	78ac *d*	....	....	....	....	....	....	....	....	....	....	6,086	6,320	4,826	5,908	13,243
Services: Credit	78ad *d*	....	....	....	....	....	....	....	....	....	....	521	612	625	702	1,183
Services: Debit	78ae *d*	....	....	....	....	....	....	....	....	....	....	–759	–975	–1,406	–1,854	–2,265
Balance on Goods and Services	78af *d*	....	....	....	....	....	....	....	....	....	....	5,848	5,958	4,044	4,755	12,161
Income: Credit	78ag *d*	....	....	....	....	....	....	....	....	....	....	1,283	1,631	1,965	2,901	3,575
Income: Debit	78ah *d*	....	....	....	....	....	....	....	....	....	....	–131	–123	–199	–294	–416
Balance on Goods, Serv., & Inc.	78ai *d*	....	....	....	....	....	....	....	....	....	....	6,999	7,466	5,810	7,362	15,320
Current Transfers, n.i.e.: Credit	78aj *d*	....	....	....	....	....	....	....	....	....	....	—	—	—	—	—
Current Transfers: Debit	78ak *d*	....	....	....	....	....	....	....	....	....	....	–1,069	–537	–1,249	–1,232	–1,288
Current Account, n.i.e.	78al *d*	....	....	....	....	....	....	....	....	....	....	5,930	6,929	4,561	6,130	14,032
Capital Account, n.i.e.: Credit	78ba *d*	....	....	....	....	....	....	....	....	....	....	—	—	—	—	—
Capital Account: Debit	78bb *d*	....	....	....	....	....	....	....	....	....	....	—	—	—	—	—
Capital Account, n.i.e.	78bc *d*	....	....	....	....	....	....	....	....	....	....	—	—	—	—	—
Direct Investment Abroad	78bd *d*	....	....	....	....	....	....	....	....	....	....	–93	–109	–52	–95	188
Dir. Invest. in Rep. Econ., n.i.e.	78be *d*	....	....	....	....	....	....	....	....	....	....	—	—	—	—	—
Portfolio Investment Assets	78bf *d*	....	....	....	....	....	....	....	....	....	....	–90	–174	–157	–80	–586
Portfolio Investment Liab., n.i.e.	78bg *d*	....	....	....	....	....	....	....	....	....	....	—	—	—	15	—
Other Investment Assets	78bh *d*	....	....	....	....	....	....	....	....	....	....	–6,368	–8,920	–4,086	–5,526	–10,334
Other Investment Liab., n.i.e.	78bi *d*	....	....	....	....	....	....	....	....	....	....	–97	451	265	538	803
Financial Account, n.i.e.	78bj *d*	....	....	....	....	....	....	....	....	....	....	–6,648	–8,752	–4,030	–5,148	–9,929
Net Errors and Omissions	78ca *d*	....	....	....	....	....	....	....	....	....	....	1,032	2,070	412	–1,424	–3,737
Overall Balance	78cb *d*	....	....	....	....	....	....	....	....	....	....	315	247	943	–443	366
Reserves and Related Items	79da *d*	....	....	....	....	....	....	....	....	....	....	–315	–247	–943	443	–366
Reserve Assets	79db *d*	....	....	....	....	....	....	....	....	....	....	–315	–247	–943	443	–366
Use of Fund Credit and Loans	79dc *d*	....	....	....	....	....	....	....	....	....	....	—	—	—	—	—
Liabs.Constit.For.Auth.Reserves	79dd *d*	....	....	....	....	....	....	....	....	....	....	....	....	....	....	....
Exceptional Financing	79de *d*	....	....	....	....	....	....	....	....	....	....	....	....	....	....	....
Government Finance																*Millions of Dinars:*
Deficit (-) or Surplus	80	–63	–111	–105	7	44	60	67	ɪ192	162	1,588	....	ɪ1,514	1,134	1,753
Revenue	81	258	272	281	290	336	374	424	ɪ609	696	2,729	....	ɪ2,996	3,050	3,647
Expenditure	82	321	382	386	283	284	303	347	ɪ379	458	895	....	ɪ1,272	1,612	1,632
Lending Minus Repayments	83	....	....	....	....	8	11	10	ɪ38	76	246	....	ɪ210	304	262
Financing																
Use of Cash Balances	87	63	111	105	–7	–44	–60	–67	ɪ–192	–162	–1,588	....	ɪ–1,514	–1,134	–1,753
National Accounts																*Millions of Dinars*
Exports of Goods & Services	90c	516	561	519	587	628	614	917	1,004	1,154	3,239	2,806	2,992	2,918	3,008	5,333
Government Consumption	91f	101	118	135	144	152	139	173	199	215	279	386	432	586	616	764
Gross Capital Formation	93	110	151	186	171	189	124	130	136	153	259	444	635	944	863	934
Gross Fixed Capital Formation	93e	95	135	163	157	170	126	127	127	146	222	418	563	815	794	790
Increase/Decrease(-) in Stocks	93i	15	16	23	14	19	–2	3	9	7	37	26	72	129	69	144
Private Consumption	96f	191	232	280	297	306	396	420	427	439	563	756	1,027	1,363	1,478	1,734
Imports of Goods & Services	98c	–167	–208	–248	–248	–286	–248	–258	–303	–356	–528	–907	–1,250	–1,760	–1,700	–1,902
Gross Domestic Product	99b	751	854	962	951	989	1,026	1,382	1,464	1,604	3,812	3,485	3,837	4,052	4,264	6,862
Net Factor Inc/Pmts(-) Abroad	98.n	–198	–172	138	–158	–149	–175	–265	–362	–342	–281	224	441	506	717	873
Gross Nat'l Expenditure = GNP	99a	553	682	824	793	840	851	1,117	1,103	1,262	3,532	3,709	4,277	4,558	4,981	7,735
Nat'l Income, Market Prices	99e	526	642	692	748	790	808	1,053	1,032	1,186	3,451	3,616	4,170	4,428	4,812	7,518
Gross Dom. Prod. 1985 Prices	99b.*p*	....	....	....	....	....	9,043	9,758	10,306	10,009	ɪ9,357	8,207	8,749	8,535	9,153	10,449
GDP Deflator (1985=100)	99bi *p*	....	....	....	....	....	11.3	14.2	14.2	16.0	40.7	42.5	43.9	47.5	46.6	65.9
																Millions:
Population	99z	.48	.52	.57	.62	.68	.74	.79	.84	.89	.94	1.01	1.07	1.14	1.21	1.29

Monetary Authorities: ɪ The Central Bank began operations on April 1, 1969. Prior to this date, data refer to a consolidation of the Currency Board and Treasury IMF accounts. ɪ Beginning in 1969, data are based on fully sectored and consolidated accounts.
Deposit Money Banks: ɪ See note to section 10.
Monetary Survey: ɪ See note to section 10.
Government Finance: ɪ Beginning in 1972, data include end-year adjustments that were not available for earlier years and also adjustments resulting from the treatment on a net basis of nonfinancial public enterprises. Data relate to a fiscal year different from calendar year (fiscal year ends March 31 through 1974; ends June 30 beginning in 1975).

Kuwait

1980	1981	1982	1983	1984	1985	1986	1987	1988	1989	1990	1991	1992	1993	1994		
Millions of Dinars																**International Transactions**
5,368.9	4,530.8	3,156.4	3,373.6	3,632.4	3,185.0	2,105.0	2,304.4	2,166.0	3,378.0	2,031.4	309.4	1,931.1	3,179.4	....	Exports	70
4,960.8	3,969.2	2,611.5	2,938.2	3,256.9	2,843.0	1,853.4	2,096.7	1,908.4	3,064.9	1,842.0	248.6	1,824.9	3,017.9	....	Oil Exports	70a
1,764.9	1,945.4	2,384.6	2,149.1	2,041.7	1,806.0	1,661.2	1,530.7	1,714.2	1,849.4	1,145.7	1,353.3	2,129.2	2,123.8	....	Imports, cif	71
1,531.2	1,685.0	2,064.9	1,860.6	1,770.5	1,566.9	1,440.8	1,327.6	1,486.7	1,604.0	993.7	1,173.7	1,846.7	1,842.0	....	Imports, fob	71.v
1985=100																Volume of Exports
136.3	94.6	77.1	95.4	104.7	100.0	....	....	....	....	....	....	....	....	....	Petroleum	72a
65.2	54.6	75.7	82.5	87.6	100.0	....	....	....	....	....	....	....	....	....	Refined Petroleum	72ab
Index of Prices in US Dollars																Export Prices
109.2	128.4	118.2	101.8	99.9	100.0	73.5	60.8	46.7	....	....	....	....	....	....	Crude Petroleum	76aa d
Minus Sign Indicates Debit																Balance of Payments
20,633	16,023	10,819	11,473	12,156	10,374	7,216	8,221	7,709	11,396	6,989	869	6,548	10,456	11,891	Goods: Exports f.o.b.	78aa d
−6,756	−6,736	−7,811	−6,889	−6,549	−5,719	−5,262	−4,941	−5,999	−6,410	−3,810	−5,073	−7,237	−6,957	−6,670	Goods: Imports f.o.b.	78ab d
13,877	9,287	3,008	4,584	5,607	4,655	1,955	3,280	1,709	4,987	3,179	−4,204	−689	3,499	5,221	Trade Balance	78ac d
1,225	1,392	941	868	888	1,137	1,053	1,030	1,158	1,345	1,279	992	1,494	1,269	1,529	Services: Credit	78ad d
−3,067	−2,905	−3,491	−3,620	−3,705	−4,086	−3,861	−4,077	−4,204	−4,119	−3,359	−5,090	−4,590	−4,542	−4,648	Services: Debit	78ae d
12,035	7,773	458	1,832	2,790	1,706	−853	233	−1,337	2,213	1,099	−8,302	−3,786	225	2,102	Balance on Goods and Services	78af d
5,487	8,325	6,780	5,712	5,854	5,330	8,352	6,129	7,863	9,211	8,584	6,093	5,907	4,486	4,507	Income: Credit	78ag d
−640	−739	−754	−683	−838	−665	−613	−545	−606	−793	−846	−682	−662	−679	−943	Income: Debit	78ah d
16,881	15,359	6,485	6,862	7,806	6,371	6,886	5,817	5,921	10,630	8,837	−2,892	1,460	4,032	5,666	Balance on Goods, Serv., & Inc.	78ai d
—	—	—	—	—	—	—	—	—	—	—	—	—	—	—	Current Transfers, n.i.e.: Credit	78aj d
−1,580	−1,661	−1,521	−1,551	−1,378	−1,573	−1,266	−1,260	−1,319	−1,494	−4,951	−23,798	−1,927	−1,620	−1,903	Current Transfers: Debit	78ak d
15,302	13,699	4,963	5,311	6,428	4,798	5,620	4,557	4,602	9,136	3,886	−26,690	−467	2,412	3,763	Current Account, n.i.e.	78al d
—	—	—	—	—	—	—	—	—	—	—	—	—	—	—	Capital Account, n.i.e.: Credit	78ba d
—	—	—	—	—	—	—	—	—	—	—	—	—	—	—	Capital Account: Debit	78bb d
—	—	—	—	—	—	—	—	—	—	—	—	—	—	—	Capital Account, n.i.e.	78bc d
−407	151	−108	−240	−95	−70	−248	−775	−477	−994	−239	186	−1,211	−848	−1,075	Direct Investment Abroad	78bd d
—	—	—	—	—	—	—	—	—	—	—	—	—	—	—	Dir. Invest. in Rep. Econ., n.i.e.	78be d
−329	−140	—	−213	−7	−392	−506	−179	−720	−623	−919	−813	−3	−89	−451	Portfolio Investment Assets	78bf d
—	14	184	—	216	47	21	219	280	24	537	211	276	252	451	Portfolio Investment Liab., n.i.e.	78bg d
−12,198	−8,810	−4,088	628	−7,431	−1,184	−6,235	−4,389	−6,042	−7,295	829	43,061	11,261	−2,511	1,236	Other Investment Assets	78bh d
1,628	484	979	−51	−135	−735	−537	−441	−380	565	205	−3,880	743	−315	724	Other Investment Liab., n.i.e.	78bi d
−11,306	−8,300	−3,032	124	−7,451	−2,334	−7,505	−5,566	−7,340	−8,323	413	38,766	11,067	−3,512	886	Financial Account, n.i.e.	78bj d
−2,950	−5,116	44	−4,432	1,140	−1,919	1,802	−839	810	462	−5,196	−10,801	−8,748	−385	−4,595	Net Errors and Omissions	78ca d
1,045	283	1,975	1,002	117	545	−83	−1,847	−1,928	1,275	−897	1,276	1,851	−1,485	53	Overall Balance	78cb d
−1,045	−283	−1,975	−1,002	−117	−545	83	1,847	1,928	−1,275	897	−1,276	−1,851	1,485	−53	Reserves and Related Items	79da d
−1,045	−283	−1,975	−1,002	−117	−545	83	1,847	1,928	−1,275	897	−1,276	−1,851	1,485	−53	Reserve Assets	79db d
—	—	—	—	—	—	—	—	—	—	—	—	—	—	—	Use of Fund Credit and Loans	79dc d
—	—	—	—	—	—	—	—	—	—	—	—	—	—	—	Liabs.Constit.For.Auth.Reserves	79dd d
....	....	....	....	....	....	....	....	....	....	....	....	....	....	....	Exceptional Financing	79de d
Year Ending June 30																**Government Finance**
4,545	3,025	566	492	780	501	1,690	....	....	....	....	....	....	....	....	Deficit (−) or Surplus	80
6,923	6,351	4,280	4,155	4,367	3,806	4,751	....	....	....	....	....	....	....	....	Revenue	81
2,147	2,577	3,028	3,089	3,047	3,077	2,975	2,646	2,698	2,901	2,933	6,638	5,884	4,377	....	Expenditure	82
231	749	686	574	540	228	86	....	....	....	....	....	....	....	....	Lending Minus Repayments	83
															Financing	
−4,545	−3,025	−566	−492	−780	−501	−1,690	....	....	....	....	....	....	....	....	Use of Cash Balances	87
Millions of Dinars																**National Accounts**
6,065	4,855	3,386	3,597	3,862	3,462	2,403	3,275	2,746	3,743	2,385	529	2,358	3,600	....	Exports of Goods & Services	90c
865	993	1,190	1,287	1,345	1,445	1,403	1,374	1,517	1,814	2,057	6,294	2,244	2,175	....	Government Consumption	91f
1,078	1,162	1,426	1,508	1,351	1,216	1,150	1,093	906	879	935	1,239	1,056	1,548	....	Gross Capital Formation	93
973	1,073	1,297	1,527	1,359	1,277	1,127	1,056	790	773	956	1,083	926	....	....	Gross Fixed Capital Formation	93e
105	89	129	−19	−8	−61	23	37	116	106	−21	156	130	....	....	Increase/Decrease(−) in Stocks	93i
2,325	2,630	3,344	2,694	2,735	3,084	2,744	2,805	3,014	3,662	3,012	2,911	3,020	2,537	....	Private Consumption	96f
−2,577	−2,601	−3,132	−3,002	−2,868	−2,757	−2,498	−2,314	−2,479	−2,955	−3,082	−7,843	−3,159	−3,094	....	Imports of Goods & Services	98c
7,755	7,039	6,214	6,083	6,425	6,450	5,203	6,233	5,773	7,143	5,307	3,130	5,518	6,766	....	Gross Domestic Product	99b
1,310	2,137	1,709	1,459	1,470	1,388	2,182	1,504	1,992	2,419	2,196	1,544	1,491	1,250	....	Net Factor Inc/Pmts(−) Abroad	98.n
9,065	9,176	7,923	7,542	7,895	7,838	7,385	7,737	7,765	9,562	7,503	4,674	7,009	8,016	....	Gross Nat'l Expenditure = GNP	99a
8,802	8,886	7,586	7,197	7,492	7,407	6,921	7,216	7,211	8,989	7,098	4,284	6,509	7,494	....	Nat'l Income, Market Prices	99e
8,289	6,721	5,931	6,401	6,737	6,450	7,000	6,718	6,956	....	....	....	....	....	....	Gross Dom. Prod. 1985 Prices	99b.p
93.6	104.7	104.8	95.0	95.4	100.0	74.3	92.8	83.0	....	....	....	....	....	....	GDP Deflator (1985=100)	99bi p
Midyear Estimates																
1.37	1.43	1.50	1.57	1.64	1.72	1.80	1.88	1.96	2.04	2.13	‡2.07	‡1.42	1.46	1.62	Population	99z

Lebanon

446

		1965	1966	1967	1968	1969	1970	1971	1972	1973	1974	1975	1976	1977	1978	1979
Exchange Rates																*Pounds per SDR:*
Market Rate	aa	3.1	3.2	3.1	3.2	3.3	3.3	3.4	3.3	3.0	2.8	2.8	3.4	3.6	3.9	4.3
																Pounds per US Dollar:
Market Rate	ae	3.1	3.2	3.1	3.2	3.3	3.3	3.2	3.0	2.5	2.3	2.4	2.9	3.0	3.0	3.3
Market Rate	rf	3.1	3.1	3.2	3.2	3.3	3.3	3.2	3.1	2.6	2.3	2.3[e]	2.9	3.1	3.0	3.2
																Index Numbers (1990=100):
Market Rate	ah x	21,882.58	21,473.46	20,978.01	21,293.78	20,655.34	20,563.21	20,829.85	22,040.86	25,856.36	28,902.85	29,224.64[e]	23,687.29	21,906.06	22,747.95	20,746.80
Nominal Effective Exchange Rate	ne c	....	....	....	....	....	....	....	....	....	....	....	....	....	....	19,014.51
Fund Position																*Millions of SDRs:*
Quota	2f. s	6.8	6.8	9.0	9.0	9.0	9.0	9.0	9.0	9.0	9.0	9.0	9.0	9.0	12.0	12.0
SDRs	1b. s	—	—	—	—	—	—	—	—	—	—	—	—	—	—	1.3
Reserve Position in the Fund	1c. s	1.7	1.7	2.3	2.3	2.3	2.3	2.3	2.3	2.3	2.3	2.3	2.3	2.3	2.3	2.1
International Liquidity												*Millions of US Dollars Unless Otherwise Indicated:*				
Total Reserves minus Gold	1l. d	68.8	88.7	88.1	44.4	59.8	98.0	197.0	324.9	472.4	1,278.8	1,201.7	1,302.6	1,568.8	1,834.9	1,531.5
SDRs	1b. d	—	—	—	—	—	—	—	—	—	—	—	—	—	—	1.6
Reserve Position in the Fund	1c. d	1.7	1.7	2.3	2.3	2.3	2.3	2.5	2.5	2.7	2.8	2.7	2.6	2.8	3.0	2.8
Foreign Exchange	1d. d	67.1	87.0	85.8	42.1	57.5	95.7	194.5	322.4	469.7	1,276.0	1,199.0	1,300.0	1,566.0	1,831.9	1,527.0
Gold (Million Fine Troy Ounces)	1ad	5.206	5.514	5.514	8.214	8.214	8.214	9.211	9.211	9.217	9.215	9.215	9.215	9.218	9.218	9.222
Gold (National Valuation)	1an d	182.8	187.5	189.9	278.5	272.5	272.5	349.6	350.2	389.1	386.1	389.1	389.0	389.2	389.2	389.4
Monetary Authorities: Other Liab.	4.. d	1.1	1.2	1.2	2.2	2.7	3.1	1.6	1.6	2.1	2.5	2.7	19.7	21.5	24.8	21.4
Deposit Money Banks: Assets	7a. d	601.9	499.6	420.9	495.1	504.8	642.4	825.0	1,056.0	1,443.8	1,730.5	2,103.8	1,544.2	1,923.5	2,017.6	2,879.3
of which: Claims on Nonbanks	7ad d	....	....	....	....	....	....	133.8	224.1	348.2	431.0	486.5	352.0	406.5	408.7	471.3
Deposit Money Banks: Liabilities	7b. d	376.4	258.8	195.5	283.9	256.7	279.7	332.8	389.9	605.4	881.5	1,178.1	958.0	852.5	1,030.3	1,200.1
of which: Liab. to Nonbanks	7bd d	....	....	....	....	....	....	247.4	302.5	400.2	532.3	513.9	416.0	432.2	398.7	525.0
Monetary Authorities												*Millions of Pounds through 1985;*				
Foreign Assets	11	779	874	869	1,027	1,081	1,194	1,733	2,048	2,166	3,811	3,865	4,957	5,873	6,683	6,252
Claims on Central Government	12a	79	73	65	62	57	55	15	13	197	301	145	803	891	843	1,476
Claims on Private Sector	12d	83	82	76	74	69	66	57	52	51	38	45	45	33	76	110
Claims on Deposit Money Banks	12e	24	166	219	227	311	173	103	100	173	71	109	165	101	77	72
Reserve Money	14	659	834	945	1,127	1,172	1,199	1,462	1,643	1,877	3,131	3,172	4,229	4,751	5,384	5,209
of which: Currency Outside DMBs	14a	547	645	786	838	868	845	919	1,033	1,226	1,353	2,241	3,084	2,729	3,286	3,506
Foreign Liabilities	16c	3	4	4	7	9	10	5	5	5	6	7	58	64	76	70
Central Government Deposits	16d	260	308	209	177	256	202	360	466	593	978	902	1,491	1,843	1,716	1,829
Capital Accounts	17a	17	20	25	28	28	34	41	41	59	59	126	161	213	213	278
Other Items (Net)	17r	26	28	46	51	54	43	40	59	53	46	-42	31	26	293	525
of which: Valuation Adjustment	17rv	....	....	....	....	....	....	....	....	....	....	....	....	....	....	....
Deposit Money Banks												*Millions of Pounds through 1985;*				
Reserves	20	108	189	149	287	297	345	542	577	626	1,667	808	1,074	1,898	2,032	1,390
Foreign Assets	21	1,848	1,584	1,317	1,574	1,641	2,088	2,607	3,179	3,624	3,980	5,112	4,525	5,770	6,063	9,379
Claims on Central Government	22a	—	—	40	69	118	101	60	78	60	36	16	10	475	982	1,066
Claims on Private Sector	22d	2,310	2,336	2,285	2,028	2,132	2,145	2,673	3,272	4,671	5,733	6,855	7,247	8,031	10,009	13,030
Demand Deposits	24	962	894	782	909	787	830	1,080	1,239	1,390	1,642	1,588	1,804	2,300	2,838	3,152
Time & Foreign Currency Deposits	25	1,705	1,891	1,784	1,721	2,062	2,590	3,273	4,106	5,112	6,578	6,814	6,299	9,309	11,078	15,182
Foreign Liabilities	26c	1,156	820	612	903	834	909	1,052	1,174	1,520	2,027	2,863	2,807	2,558	3,096	3,909
Central Government Deposits	26d	5	5	6	9	12	15	111	176	259	344	407	419	490	517	585
Credit from Monetary Authorities	26g	24	166	219	227	311	173	103	100	173	71	109	165	101	77	72
Capital Accounts	27a	389	391	410	340	345	359	379	413	437	496	551	583	619	683	878
Other Items (Net)	27r	25	-58	-20	-152	-163	-198	-117	-103	90	258	460	780	798	797	1,088
Monetary Survey												*Millions of Pounds through 1985;*				
Foreign Assets (Net)	31n	1,468	1,633	1,571	1,691	1,878	2,362	3,283	4,049	4,265	5,758	6,108	6,617	9,021	9,576	11,652
Domestic Credit	32	2,207	2,178	2,251	2,047	2,110	2,150	2,333	2,773	4,127	4,786	5,751	6,195	7,097	9,677	13,269
Claims on Central Govt. (Net)	32an	-186	-240	-110	-54	-92	-61	-397	-552	-595	-985	-1,148	-1,097	-967	-408	129
Claims on Private Sector	32d	2,393	2,418	2,361	2,102	2,202	2,210	2,730	3,324	4,722	5,771	6,900	7,293	8,064	10,085	13,141
Money	34	1,510	1,541	1,570	1,749	1,657	1,677	2,002	2,275	2,619	2,998	3,836	4,905	5,062	6,148	6,684
Quasi-Money	35	1,706	1,892	1,784	1,722	2,062	2,592	3,275	4,108	5,114	6,580	6,816	6,302	9,311	11,081	15,184
Other Items (Net)	37r	460	379	467	268	269	243	340	439	659	966	1,207	1,606	1,745	2,025	3,053
Money plus Quasi-Money	35l	3,216	3,433	3,354	3,471	3,719	4,269	5,276	6,382	7,733	9,578	10,652	11,207	14,373	17,229	21,868
Interest Rates																*Percent Per Annum*
Discount Rate (End of Period)	60	3.00	3.00	3.00	3.00	3.00	3.00	3.00	3.00	5.00	7.00	7.00	6.00	6.00	6.00	8.50
Treasury Bill Rate	60c	....	....	....	....	....	....	....	....	....	....	....	....	....	....	9.50
Deposit Rate	60l	....	....	....	....	....	....	....	....	....	....	....	....	....	....	....
Lending Rate	60p	....	....	....	....	....	....	....	....	....	....	....	....	....	....	....
International Transactions																*Millions of Pounds*
Exports	70	268	323	380	466	538	628	796	1,149	1,587	3,386[e]	....	....	....	....	....
Imports, cif	71	1,668	1,902	1,760	1,875	1,898	2,135	2,357	2,818	3,355	5,580[e]	....	....	....	....	....
Imports, fob	71.v	1,545	1,761	1,630	1,736	1,758	1,977	2,182	2,609	3,107	5,166	....	....	....	....	....
																Millions:
Population	99z	2.15	2.21	2.27	2.34	2.40	2.47	2.53	2.60	2.66	2.73	2.77	2.77	2.76	2.73	2.70

Interest Rates: *Treasury Bill Rate:* ℓ Beginning in January 1987, secondary market yield on three-month treasury bills determined by the Central Bank of Lebanon.

Lebanon

1980	1981	1982	1983	1984	1985	1986	1987	1988	1989	1990	1991	1992	1993	1994		
End of Period															**Exchange Rates**	
4.7	5.4	4.2	5.7	8.7	19.9	106.4	645.5	713.2	663.7	1,197.9	1,257.3	2,527.3	2,350.2	2,404.4	Market Rate	aa
End of Period (ae) Period Average (rf)																
3.6	4.6	3.8	5.5	8.9	18.1	87.0	455.0	530.0	505.0	842.0	879.0	1,838.0	1,711.0	1,647.0	Market Rate	ae
3.4	4.3	4.7	4.5	6.5	16.4	38.4	224.6	409.2	496.7	695.1	928.2	1,712.8	1,741.4	1,680.1	Market Rate	rf
Period Averages																
19,580.87	15,667.04	14,263.57	15,028.01	10,541.12	4,195.61	2,076.37	426.34	167.48	136.00	100.00	72.65	43.83	38.56	39.95	Market Rate	ahx
17,963.63	16,942.83	17,370.82	19,690.54	15,161.58	6,326.09	2,549.96	459.68	174.13	149.09	100.00	73.31	43.02	40.90	41.72	Nominal Effective Exchange Rate	nec
End of Period															**Fund Position**	
27.9	27.9	27.9	78.7	78.7	78.7	78.7	78.7	78.7	78.7	78.7	78.7	78.7	78.7	146.0	Quota	2f.s
—	1.9	2.0	—	.8	1.8	2.6	3.4	4.2	5.4	6.9	8.3	9.5	10.5	11.4	SDRs	1b.s
6.1	6.1	6.1	18.8	18.8	18.8	18.8	18.8	18.8	18.8	18.8	18.8	18.8	18.8	18.8	Reserve Position in the Fund	1c.s
End of Period															**International Liquidity**	
1,588.2	1,516.4	2,608.1	1,902.5	671.6	1,073.8	488.0	367.9	977.8	938.2	659.9	1,275.5	1,496.4	2,260.3	3,884.2	Total Reserves minus Gold	1l.d
. . .	2.2	2.3	. . .	.8	1.9	3.2	4.8	5.7	7.1	9.8	11.8	13.0	14.4	16.6	SDRs	1b.d
7.8	7.1	6.8	19.7	18.5	20.7	23.0	26.7	25.3	24.7	26.8	26.9	25.9	25.9	27.5	Reserve Position in the Fund	1c.d
1,580.4	1,507.0	2,599.1	1,882.8	652.3	1,051.2	461.8	336.4	946.8	906.3	623.3	1,236.7	1,457.5	2,220.0	3,840.1	Foreign Exchange	1d.d
9.222	9.222	9.222	9.222	9.222	9.222	9.222	9.222	9.222	9.222	9.222	9.222	9.222	9.222	9.222	Gold (Million Fine Troy Ounces)	1ad
389.4	389.4	1389.4	389.4	389.4	389.4	389.4	389.4	3,781.2	3,696.8	3,554.0	3,260.1	3,066.4	3,603.6	3,534.5	Gold (National Valuation)	1and
21.9	22.0	17.1	1.6	1.3	1.1	1.1	3.3	1.8	3.0	3.2	3.2	3.3	5.8	30.0	Monetary Authorities: Other Liab.	4..d
3,673.9	4,336.7	3,695.9	3,284.8	2,948.0	2,559.0	2,753.2	3,153.1	3,198.9	2,887.6	2,820.1	3,482.6	3,169.1	4,114.9	3,806.5	Deposit Money Banks: Assets	7a.d
501.1	430.7	413.9	554.6	328.5	332.9	226.0	209.4	260.1	188.3	227.8	297.2	227.5	254.5	297.3	of which: Claims on Nonbanks	7add
1,577.1	1,594.8	1,782.6	1,603.7	1,390.4	1,019.0	745.6	899.9	943.0	887.5	901.3	1,019.1	950.5	1,198.6	1,579.7	Deposit Money Banks: Liabilities	7b.d
518.8	687.6	652.5	606.4	565.7	478.9	316.7	343.7	343.6	337.5	381.5	593.8	624.6	815.1	1,009.9	of which: Liab. to Nonbanks	7bdd
Billions of Pounds Beginning 1986: End of Period															**Monetary Authorities**	
7,213	8,803	11,412	12,582	9,424	26,450	₹76	342	2,519	2,337	3,540	3,976	8,363	10,026	12,209	Foreign Assets	11
1,924	1,957	3,090	5,198	12,481	15,642	₹35	119	98	151	589	253	236	428	32	Claims on Central Government	12a
129	148	267	323	516	371	₹—	1	1	1	7	18	20	95	44	73	Claims on Private Sector	12d
60	126	116	127	1,122	1,262	₹1	1	1	2	93	169	189	164	187	Claims on Deposit Money Banks	12e
6,197	7,156	10,147	11,584	13,170	18,642	₹25	58	196	332	509	800	1,522	2,160	3,817	Reserve Money	14
3,982	4,625	5,582	7,058	7,669	10,267	₹15	39	116	192	333	485	798	715	939	of which: Currency Outside DMBs	14a
80	102	65	9	11	21	₹—	1	1	2	3	3	6	10	49	Foreign Liabilities	16c
1,449	1,544	3,863	3,143	4,020	9,561	₹19	97	187	104	201	289	927	1,237	2,384	Central Government Deposits	16d
370	494	665	859	859	1,267	₹2	3	15	15	27	60	80	96	89	Capital Accounts	17a
1,231	1,738	146	2,638	5,483	14,235	₹67	305	2,222	2,136	3,577	3,286	6,323	7,183	6,143	Other Items (Net)	17r
604	1,430	−1,366	1,927	4,102	12,278	₹62	290	2,236	2,104	3,429	3,228	6,252	6,630	6,094	of which: Valuation Adjustment	17rv
Billions of Pounds Beginning 1986: End of Period															**Deposit Money Banks**	
2,168	2,535	4,568	4,396	5,292	8,848	₹10	19	73	131	178	283	669	1,435	2,786	Reserves	20
13,400	20,057	14,081	18,033	26,208	46,317	₹240	1,435	1,695	1,458	2,375	3,061	5,825	7,041	6,269	Foreign Assets	21
2,027	4,176	11,049	14,712	15,241	28,057	₹37	52	302	558	688	1,309	3,098	4,013	6,909	Claims on Central Government	22a
16,166	21,292	25,729	33,604	43,268	57,707	₹127	530	738	878	1,548	1,971	4,804	5,898	7,800	Claims on Private Sector	22d
3,668	4,360	5,468	5,868	6,089	9,852	₹16	30	66	93	115	202	394	422	493	Demand Deposits	24
21,158	31,389	37,485	48,773	62,492	98,948	₹294	1,402	1,992	2,178	3,372	4,810	10,575	13,987	18,194	Time & Foreign Currency Deposits	25
5,752	7,376	6,792	8,805	12,361	18,445	₹65	409	500	448	759	896	1,747	2,051	2,602	Foreign Liabilities	26c
586	803	826	734	745	705	₹1	3	6	11	26	40	106	152	255	Central Government Deposits	26d
60	126	116	127	1,122	1,262	₹1	1	2	93	169	189	164	187	167	Credit from Monetary Authorities	26g
1,180	1,668	2,162	2,978	3,384	3,783	₹4	5	11	24	59	94	215	444	676	Capital Accounts	27a
1,357	2,338	2,578	3,461	3,815	7,935	₹33	184	232	179	288	393	1,195	1,144	1,378	Other Items (Net)	27r
Billions of Pounds Beginning 1986: End of Period															**Monetary Survey**	
14,782	21,382	18,636	21,802	23,259	54,302	₹251	1,366	3,714	3,346	5,153	6,139	12,434	15,006	15,827	Foreign Assets (Net)	31n
18,212	25,226	35,447	49,961	66,741	91,512	₹180	602	948	1,478	2,617	3,224	7,200	8,995	12,175	Domestic Credit	32
1,917	3,786	9,450	16,034	22,958	33,434	₹52	71	208	594	1,051	1,233	2,301	3,052	4,302	Claims on Central Govt. (Net)	32an
16,295	21,440	25,996	33,927	43,783	58,078	₹128	531	740	885	1,566	1,991	4,899	5,942	7,873	Claims on Private Sector	32d
7,667	9,005	11,070	12,945	13,784	20,154	₹30	69	183	287	450	689	1,199	1,143	1,437	Money	34
21,160	31,392	37,487	48,775	62,494	98,948	₹294	1,402	1,992	2,178	3,372	4,810	10.576	14,535	18,214	Quasi-Money	35
4,167	6,211	5,526	10,044	13,723	26,712	₹107	497	2,487	2,359	3,947	3,863	7,859	8,322	8,350	Other Items (Net)	37r
28,826	40,397	48,557	61,720	76,277	119,102	₹324	1,471	2,175	2,465	3,822	5,499	11,776	15,678	19,651	Money plus Quasi-Money	35l
Percent Per Annum															**Interest Rates**	
10.00	13.00	12.00	12.00	12.00	19.70	21.85	21.85	21.84	21.84	21.84	18.04	16.00	20.22	16.49	Discount Rate (End of Period)	60
10.40	14.00	14.02	9.52	13.08	14.96	₹18.67	26.91	25.17	18.84	18.84	17.47	22.40	18.27	15.09	Treasury Bill Rate	60c
. . .	. . .	12.94	10.01	11.53	13.24	16.42	21.18	21.96	17.54	16.86	16.76	17.09	15.56	14.80	Deposit Rate	60l
. . .	. . .	16.83	14.53	15.58	17.29	22.21	36.54	44.46	39.86	39.94	38.01	40.21	28.53	. . .	Lending Rate	60p
Millions of Pounds															**International Transactions**	
. . .	. . .	. . .	. . .	. . .	. . .	. . .	. . .	. . .	. . .	. . .	. . .	. . .	. . .	. . .	Exports	70
. . .	. . .	. . .	. . .	. . .	. . .	. . .	. . .	. . .	. . .	. . .	. . .	. . .	. . .	. . .	Imports, cif	71
. . .	. . .	. . .	. . .	. . .	. . .	. . .	. . .	. . .	. . .	. . .	. . .	. . .	. . .	. . .	Imports, fob	71.v
Midyear Estimates																
2.67	2.66	2.66	2.66	2.68	2.67	2.64	2.60	2.56	2.54	2.55	2.61	2.70	2.81	. . .	Population	99z

Lesotho
666

		1965	1966	1967	1968	1969	1970	1971	1972	1973	1974	1975	1976	1977	1978	1979
Exchange Rates															*SDRs per Loti*	
Principal Rate	ac	1.3998	1.3933	1.4018	1.3898	1.3988	1.3943	1.2036	1.1765	1.2351	1.1843	.9824	.9898	.9467	.8827	.9181
															US Dollars per Loti	
Principal Rate	ag	1.3998	1.3933	1.4018	1.3898	1.3988	1.3943	1.3068	1.2773	1.4900	1.4501	1.1500	1.1500	1.1500	1.1500	1.2094
Principal Rate	rh	1.4000	1.4000	1.4000	1.4000	1.4000	1.4000	1.3982	1.3018	1.4441	1.4722	1.3663	1.1500	1.1500	1.1500	1.1879
														Index Numbers (1990=100)		
Principal Rate	ahx	361.1	360.7	360.7	360.7	360.2	361.0	306.4	334.9	373.4	380.7	353.4	297.4	297.4	297.4	307.2
Nominal Effective Exchange Rate	nec	....	....	....	....	....	....	....	....	....	....	....	....	....	....	104.8
Real Effective Exchange Rate	rec	....	....	....	....	....	....	....	....	....	....	....	....	....	....	110.9
Fund Position															*Millions of SDRs*	
Quota	2f.s	....	....	....	3.00	3.00	5.00	5.00	5.00	5.00	5.00	5.00	5.00	5.00	7.00	7.00
SDRs	1b.s	....	....	....	—	—	—	.44	.86	.66	.58	.54	.50	.45	.41	1.09
Reserve Position in the Fund	1c.s	....	....	....	.10	.11	.03	.13	.23	.43	.63	1.25	1.25	1.25	1.14	1.14
Total Fund Cred.&Loans Outstg.	2tl	....	....	....	—	—	—	—	—	—	—	—	—	.54	2.08	3.59
International Liquidity										*Millions of US Dollars Unless Otherwise Indicated*						
Total Reserves minus Gold	1l.d	....	....	....	....	....	....	....	....	....	....	....	....	....	....	....
SDRs	1b.d	....	....	....	—	—	—	.48	.93	.80	.71	.63	.58	.55	.53	1.44
Reserve Position in the Fund	1c.d	....	....	....	.10	.11	.03	.14	.25	.52	.77	1.46	1.45	1.52	1.49	1.50
Foreign Exchange	1d.d	....	....	....	....	....	....	....	....	....	....	....	....	....	....	....
Deposit Money Banks: Assets	7a.d	....	....	....	....	....	....	....	....	20.72	22.11	20.87	21.56	28.22	48.42	61.89
Deposit Money Banks: Liabilities	7b.d	....	....	....	....	....	....	....	....	6.68	1.83	.87	1.54	1.58	3.02	2.08
of which: Liab. to Nonbanks	7bd.d	....	....	....	....	....	....	....	....	—	1.09	.80	1.39	1.41	2.94	1.99
Monetary Authorities															*Millions of Maloti*	
Foreign Assets	11	....														
Claims on Central Government	12a	....														
Claims on Deposit Money Banks	12e	....														
Reserve Money	14	....														
of which: Currency Outside DMBs	14a	....														
Foreign Liabilities	16c	....														
Central Government Deposits	16d	....														
Capital Accounts	17a	....														
Other Items (Net)	17r	....														
Deposit Money Banks															*Millions of Maloti*	
Reserves	20	....	....	....	....	....	....	....	....	1.16	1.67	1.20	2.69	3.55	4.72	6.67
Foreign Assets	21	....	....	....	....	....	....	....	....	14.60	15.25	18.15	18.74	24.54	42.11	51.17
Claims on Central Government	22a	....	....	....	....	....	....	....	....	1.48	1.04	1.75	4.14	9.45	10.79	17.55
Claims on Official Entities	22bx	....	....	....	....	....	....	....	....	.95	1.57	1.40	2.34	4.29	10.21	8.55
Claims on Private Sector	22d	....	....	....	....	....	....	....	....	5.74	8.61	8.43	11.57	13.64	18.44	23.85
Demand Deposits	24	....	....	....	....	....	....	....	....	4.71	5.46	7.41	11.37	18.78	28.08	39.81
Time and Savings Deposits	25	....	....	....	....	....	....	....	....	13.39	14.73	18.70	23.24	29.24	47.83	55.77
Foreign Liabilities	26c	....	....	....	....	....	....	....	....	4.71	1.26	.76	1.34	1.38	2.62	1.72
Central Government Deposits	26d	....	....	....	....	....	....	....	....	2.70	7.18	2.56	2.67	3.16	7.09	9.36
Other Items (Net)	27r	....	....	....	....	....	....	....	....	−1.58	−.50	1.51	.87	2.91	.65	1.13
Monetary Survey															*Millions of Maloti*	
Foreign Assets (Net)	31n	....														
Domestic Credit	32	....														
Claims on Central Govt. (Net)	32an	....														
Claims on Official Entities	32bx	....	....	....	....	....	....	....	....	.95	1.57	1.40	2.34	4.29	10.21	8.55
Claims on Private Sector	32d	....	....	....	....	....	....	....	....	5.74	8.61	8.43	11.57	13.64	18.44	23.85
Money	34	....														
Quasi-Money	35	....	....	....	....	....	....	....	....	13.39	14.73	18.70	23.24	29.24	47.83	55.77
Other Items (Net)	37r	....														
Money plus Quasi-Money	35l	....														
Other Banking Institutions															*Millions of Maloti*	
Cash	40	....	....	....	....	....	....	....	....	....	....	....	....	.33	.99	1.33
Claims on Private Sector	42d	....	....	....	....	....	....	....	....	....	....	....	....	.01	.50	1.79
Time and Savings Deposits	45	....	....	....	....	....	....	....	....	....	....	....	....	.01	.03	.58
Capital Accounts	47a	....	....	....	....	....	....	....	....	....	....	....	....	.25	1.25	2.25
Other Items (Net)	47r	....	....	....	....	....	....	....	....	....	....	....	....	.08	.20	.29
Liquid Liabilities	55l	....														
Interest Rates															*Percent Per Annum*	
Discount Rate *(End of Period)*	60	....														
Treasury Bill Rate	60c	....														
Deposit Rate	60l	....														
Lending Rate	60p	....														
Prices															*Index Numbers (1990=100)*	
Consumer Prices	64	....	....	....	....	....	....	....	....	11.2	12.7	14.5	16.2	18.9	21.3	24.7

Lesotho

	1980	1981	1982	1983	1984	1985	1986	1987	1988	1989	1990	1991	1992	1993	1994		
Exchange Rates																	
End of Period																	
	1.0519	.8981	.8423	.7817	.5140	.3560	.3744	.3652	.3125	.3001	.2743	.2549	.2382	.2143	.1933	Principal Rate	ac
End of Period (ag) Period Average (rh)																	
	1.3416	1.0454	.9291	.8184	.5038	.3910	.4580	.5182	.4206	.3943	.3902	.3646	.3275	.2943	.2822	Principal Rate	ag
	1.2854	1.1491	.9245	.8991	.6954	.4564	.4408	.4914	.4423	.3822	.3866	.3628	.3509	.3064	.2818	Principal Rate	rh
Period Averages																	
	332.5	297.2	239.1	232.5	179.8	118.0	114.0	127.1	114.4	98.8	100.0	93.8	90.8	79.2	72.9	Principal Rate	ah x
	105.1	105.3	104.8	105.1	104.3	102.5	101.4	101.3	100.7	100.4	100.0	99.9	99.6	99.4	99.0	Nominal Effective Exchange Rate	ne c
	112.8	110.5	108.3	113.1	112.2	108.6	106.9	103.5	102.2	102.3	100.0	102.1	105.5	107.9	107.2	Real Effective Exchange Rate	re c
Fund Position																	
End of Period																	
	10.50	10.50	10.50	15.10	15.10	15.10	15.10	15.10	15.10	15.10	15.10	15.10	15.10	23.90	23.90	Quota	2f. s
	.85	1.41	1.10	1.04	.97	.99	.80	.62	.97	.74	.46	.20	.48	.41	.33	SDRs	1b. s
	1.98	2.01	.08	1.24	1.25	1.25	1.26	1.27	1.29	1.29	1.30	1.31	3.51	3.51	3.51	Reserve Position in the Fund	1c. s
	4.87	4.89	4.89	4.75	4.33	3.51	2.54	1.56	3.75	7.72	10.59	12.84	18.12	24.92	27.63	Total Fund Cred.&Loans Outstg.	2tl
International Liquidity																	
End of Period																	
	50.27	43.40	47.54	66.68	48.58	43.52	60.26	67.53	56.28	49.00	72.37	115.04	157.49	252.69	372.62	Total Reserves minus Gold	1l. d
	1.08	1.64	1.21	1.09	.95	1.09	.98	.88	1.31	.97	.65	.29	.66	.56	.47	SDRs	1b. d
	2.53	.24	.09	1.30	1.23	1.37	1.54	1.80	1.74	1.70	1.85	1.87	4.83	4.82	5.13	Reserve Position in the Fund	1c. d
	46.66	39.41	46.23	64.29	46.40	41.06	57.74	64.85	53.24	46.33	69.87	112.88	152.00	247.30	367.02	Foreign Exchange	1d. d
	45.21	37.33	51.03	58.95	44.79	43.93	38.17	35.31	41.23	43.40	79.88	71.89	95.26	65.84	48.52	Deposit Money Banks: Assets	7a. d
	8.25	5.89	3.23	18.98	3.78	3.09	4.54	6.85	13.78	16.36	9.60	11.34	7.99	9.64	10.29	Deposit Money Banks: Liabilities	7b. d
	2.57	2.33	1.30	1.82	1.10	.76	1.17	2.55	2.83	3.76	1.28	2.81	3.42	4.94	6.45	of which: Liab. to Nonbanks	7bd d
Monetary Authorities																	
End of Period																	
	41.23	45.58	52.62	83.40	100.20	116.06	135.48	135.64	140.21	129.85	197.29	322.48	483.08	869.28	1,337.58	Foreign Assets	11
	4.63	26.45	34.60	24.94	13.82	36.15	44.33	92.18	262.71	294.02	295.68	592.84	137.31	259.58	238.68	Claims on Central Government	12a
	—	—	—	—	—	—	—	—	—	—	—	—	6.25	.39	.44	Claims on Deposit Money Banks	12e
	40.20	42.59	46.07	72.57	85.35	110.61	137.09	161.05	236.47	222.20	208.59	245.81	191.77	233.68	249.15	Reserve Money	14
	6.92	10.62	17.77	23.14	23.67	25.23	32.55	33.19	41.87	53.36	59.79	37.01	39.86	43.75	52.57	of which: Currency Outside DMBs	14a
	4.69	25.69	31.12	22.22	11.25	11.89	8.87	6.45	14.43	28.24	40.48	56.14	81.55	121.82	149.49	Foreign Liabilities	16c
	.01	.74	5.38	6.09	2.33	2.93	7.19	29.36	125.94	155.88	210.11	593.50	349.19	790.87	1,134.25	Central Government Deposits	16d
	3.89	5.40	5.72	7.62	15.79	27.28	20.82	21.62	23.35	24.69	54.14	53.10	54.30	77.86	82.34	Capital Accounts	17a
	-2.92	-2.39	-1.08	-.15	-.70	-.50	5.85	9.33	2.72	-7.15	-20.36	-33.22	-50.17	-94.97	-38.53	Other Items (Net)	17r
Deposit Money Banks																	
End of Period																	
	32.87	28.60	28.48	48.85	54.03	77.94	97.55	118.47	189.37	161.57	136.40	189.68	135.95	179.47	180.45	Reserves	20
	33.70	35.71	54.92	72.03	88.91	112.36	83.34	68.15	98.04	110.05	204.69	197.19	290.84	223.69	171.94	Foreign Assets	21
	38.40	42.65	54.50	64.91	62.28	74.00	126.06	135.02	128.54	189.66	153.29	131.07	108.45	99.72	103.95	Claims on Central Government	22a
	9.24	10.44	10.92	14.30	13.38	11.26	11.07	7.61	24.05	24.62	26.24	35.86	28.91	29.31	30.92	Claims on Official Entities	22bx
	21.45	37.15	46.97	51.75	68.34	89.16	90.47	112.70	145.32	170.85	204.78	273.79	316.37	502.61	699.24	Claims on Private Sector	22d
	41.55	48.00	59.40	61.52	79.60	107.91	122.09	123.62	178.01	191.82	204.43	275.77	311.29	389.43	434.02	Demand Deposits	24
	68.17	85.58	108.24	132.36	147.04	177.58	197.47	230.26	270.12	310.63	338.41	345.45	371.62	501.99	550.42	Time and Savings Deposits	25
	6.15	5.63	3.48	23.20	7.51	7.91	9.90	13.22	32.76	41.50	24.60	31.11	24.40	32.74	36.47	Foreign Liabilities	26c
	15.57	12.41	12.47	13.14	12.43	20.62	24.19	19.28	17.24	23.08	32.21	26.85	39.85	48.30	39.59	Central Government Deposits	26d
	4.22	2.92	12.20	21.60	40.36	50.70	54.83	55.56	87.17	89.72	130.55	148.41	132.65	62.33	126.00	Other Items (Net)	27r
Monetary Survey																	
End of Period																	
	64.09	49.96	72.94	110.01	170.35	208.62	200.05	184.12	191.05	170.16	336.90	432.43	667.97	938.41	1,323.56	Foreign Assets (Net)	31n
	58.13	103.54	129.14	136.67	143.07	187.02	240.54	298.86	417.42	500.19	437.68	413.20	202.00	52.06	-101.04	Domestic Credit	32
	27.44	55.95	71.25	70.62	61.34	86.60	139.01	178.55	248.06	304.72	206.66	103.55	-143.27	-479.86	-831.21	Claims on Central Govt. (Net)	32an
	9.24	10.44	10.92	14.30	13.38	11.26	11.07	7.61	24.05	24.62	26.24	35.86	28.91	29.31	30.92	Claims on Official Entities	32bx
	21.45	37.15	46.97	51.75	68.34	89.16	90.47	112.70	145.32	170.85	204.78	273.79	316.37	502.61	699.24	Claims on Private Sector	32d
	48.47	58.62	77.17	84.67	103.28	133.14	154.64	156.81	219.88	245.18	264.22	312.78	351.15	433.18	486.59	Money	34
	68.17	85.58	108.24	132.36	147.04	177.58	197.47	230.26	270.12	310.63	338.41	345.45	371.62	501.99	550.42	Quasi-Money	35
	5.59	9.30	16.67	29.64	63.10	84.92	88.48	95.89	118.48	114.54	176.74	187.41	146.49	55.29	185.51	Other Items (Net)	37r
	116.64	144.20	185.41	217.03	250.32	310.72	352.11	387.08	490.00	555.82	602.64	658.23	722.77	935.17	1,037.01	Money plus Quasi-Money	35l
Other Banking Institutions																	
End of Period																	
	—	.52	.53	1.24	1.99	2.64	2.26	2.12	2.88	2.95	2.86	2.48	8.00	....	....	Cash	40
	6.61	7.99	8.08	7.93	11.68	12.49	13.70	17.63	24.04	31.65	42.57	52.08	64.91	....	....	Claims on Private Sector	42d
	1.97	1.96	2.26	4.37	3.18	3.17	5.54	7.77	10.09	15.11	24.38	32.29	41.52	....	....	Time and Savings Deposits	45
	3.52	5.29	5.44	5.44	6.97	7.63	8.43	8.54	9.34	9.59	9.23	9.46	9.23	....	....	Capital Accounts	47a
	1.12	1.26	.92	-.64	3.51	4.33	1.99	3.44	7.50	9.89	11.83	12.80	21.64	....	....	Other Items (Net)	47r
	118.60	145.64	187.14	220.16	251.52	311.25	355.39	392.73	497.21	567.98	624.16	688.04	756.29	....	....	Liquid Liabilities	55l
Interest Rates																	
Percent Per Annum																	
	8.00	12.00	12.00	12.00	15.00	12.00	9.50	9.00	15.50	17.00	15.75	18.00	15.00	13.50	13.50	Discount Rate (End of Period)	60
	....	7.00	10.67	18.00	18.42	17.60	11.21	10.75	11.42	15.75	16.33	15.75	14.20	....	19.44	Treasury Bill Rate	60c
	....	9.6	11.8	9.4	....	10.4	10.0	7.0	9.6	12.8	13.0	13.0	10.6	8.1	8.4	Deposit Rate	60l
	11.0	15.0	17.0	15.4	17.6	19.7	13.4	11.1	13.7	18.8	20.4	20.0	18.3	15.8	14.3	Lending Rate	60p
Prices																	
Period Averages																	
	28.5	32.1	35.9	42.2	46.9	53.1	62.7	70.1	78.1	89.6	100.0	117.7	137.9	156.0	168.9	Consumer Prices	64

Lesotho
666

		1965	1966	1967	1968	1969	1970	1971	1972	1973	1974	1975	1976	1977	1978	1979
International Transactions																*Millions of Maloti*
Exports	70	4.7	4.4	4.2	3.4	4.9	4.2	3.0	6.1	8.8	9.8	9.2	14.6	12.2	28.7	38.9
Imports, cif	71	17.5	22.9	23.8	23.9	23.9	22.9	28.0	43.0	60.5	81.7	122.2	184.4	203.3	244.2	275.3
Imports, fob	71.v	16.8	22.0	22.9	23.0	23.0	22.0	26.9	41.3	58.1	78.5	117.4	177.4	195.7	235.0	265.8
Balance of Payments																*Millions of US Dollars:*
Goods: Exports f.o.b.	78aa d	….	….	….	….	….	….	….	….	….	….	13.5	17.9	15.2	33.0	39.1
Goods: Imports f.o.b.	78ab d	….	….	….	….	….	….	….	….	….	….	−151.5	−189.4	−210.8	−243.1	−316.7
Trade Balance	78ac d	….	….	….	….	….	….	….	….	….	….	−137.9	−171.5	−195.6	−210.1	−277.7
Services: Credit	78ad d	….	….	….	….	….	….	….	….	….	….	12.0	12.0	14.1	16.8	18.6
Services: Debit	78ae d	….	….	….	….	….	….	….	….	….	….	−19.1	−20.9	−24.8	−29.9	−35.3
Balance on Goods and Services	78af d	….	….	….	….	….	….	….	….	….	….	−145.0	−180.4	−206.3	−223.2	−294.3
Income: Credit	78ag d	….	….	….	….	….	….	….	….	….	….	127.0	142.7	170.7	183.5	219.7
Income: Debit	78ah d	….	….	….	….	….	….	….	….	….	….	−4.5	−4.1	−5.1	−5.8	−6.1
Balance on Goods, Serv., & Inc.	78ai d	….	….	….	….	….	….	….	….	….	….	−22.4	−41.9	−40.7	−45.4	−80.6
Current Transfers, n.i.e.: Credit	78aj d	….	….	….	….	….	….	….	….	….	….	21.4	16.2	31.5	53.9	80.8
Current Transfers: Debit	78ak d	….	….	….	….	….	….	….	….	….	….	—	−8.5	—	—	−.1
Current Account, n.i.e.	78al d	….	….	….	….	….	….	….	….	….	….	−1.1	−34.2	−9.2	8.5	—
Capital Account, n.i.e.: Credit	78ba d	….	….	….	….	….	….	….	….	….	….	—	—	—	—	—
Capital Account: Debit	78bb d	….	….	….	….	….	….	….	….	….	….	—	—	—	—	—
Capital Account, n.i.e.	78bc d	….	….	….	….	….	….	….	….	….	….	—	—	—	—	—
Direct Investment Abroad	78bd d	….	….	….	….	….	….	….	….	….	….	—	—	—	—	—
Dir. Invest. in Rep. Econ., n.i.e.	78be d	….	….	….	….	….	….	….	….	….	….	—	—	—	—	—
Portfolio Investment Assets	78bf d	….	….	….	….	….	….	….	….	….	….	—	—	—	—	—
Portfolio Investment Liab., n.i.e.	78bg d	….	….	….	….	….	….	….	….	….	….	—	—	—	—	—
Other Investment Assets	78bh d	….	….	….	….	….	….	….	….	….	….	−3.8	−1.6	−9.7	−7.5	−13.7
Other Investment Liab., n.i.e.	78bi d	….	….	….	….	….	….	….	….	….	….	3.7	3.2	9.9	10.6	21.9
Financial Account, n.i.e.	78bj d	….	….	….	….	….	….	….	….	….	….	−.1	1.6	.2	3.1	8.3
Net Errors and Omissions	78ca d	….	….	….	….	….	….	….	….	….	….	1.9	32.5	8.3	−13.7	−11.1
Overall Balance	78cb d	….	….	….	….	….	….	….	….	….	….	.7	—	−.7	−2.1	−2.9
Reserves and Related Items	79da d	….	….	….	….	….	….	….	….	….	….	−.7	—	.7	2.1	2.9
Reserve Assets	79db d	….	….	….	….	….	….	….	….	….	….	−.7	—	.1	.2	.9
Use of Fund Credit and Loans	79dc d	….	….	….	….	….	….	….	….	….	….	—	—	.6	1.9	2.0
Liabs.Constit.For.Auth.Reserves	79dd d	….	….	….	….	….	….	….	….	….	….	—	—	—	—	—
Exceptional Financing	79de d	….	….	….	….	….	….	….	….	….	….	….	….	….	….	….
Government Finance																*Thousands of Maloti:*
Deficit (−) or Surplus	80	….	….	….	….	….	….	−543	−847	4,697	8,720	−8,698	−12,854	−2,994	….	….
Revenue	81	….	….	….	….	….	….	10,289	11,183	20,430	28,500	28,425	38,133	60,180	….	….
Grants Received	81z	….	….	….	….	….	….	4,605	3,778	3,485	3,543	3,993	2,247	9,957	….	….
Expenditure	82	….	….	….	….	….	….	15,254	15,938	19,197	23,088	40,641	53,215	71,174	….	….
Lending Minus Repayments	83	….	….	….	….	….	….	183	−130	21	235	475	19	1,957	….	….
Financing																
Net Borrowing: Domestic	84a	….	….	….	….	….	….	….	….	….	….	1,733	971	1,175	2,292	….
Foreign	85a	….	….	….	….	….	….	….	….	….	….	1,315	3,148	2,311	4,546	….
Use of Cash Balances	87	….	….	….	….	….	….	….	….	….	….	−11,768	4,579	9,368	−3,844	….
Debt: Domestic	88a	….	….	….	….	….	….	….	….	….	….	….	….	….	….	….
Foreign	89a	….	….	….	….	….	….	….	….	….	….	….	….	….	….	….
National Accounts																*Millions of Maloti:*
Exports of Goods & Services	90c	6.1	4.4	4.2	3.2	3.8	3.4	2.6	5.8	9.0	14.1	14.6	21.3	18.0	36.4	50.0
Government Consumption	91f	6.9	5.1	6.8	6.2	6.1	6.2	8.3	9.3	9.6	15.8	21.3	24.9	29.2	40.9	52.4
Gross Fixed Capital Formation	93e	4.4	4.1	4.7	4.7	4.9	5.0	6.6	6.0	10.4	14.5	20.7	45.5	40.3	51.0	73.7
Increase/Decrease(−) in Stocks	93i	.1	.2	—	—	—	—	—	1.2	5.6	2.8	—	.9	1.7	9.1	10.9
Private Consumption	96f	41.8	49.8	50.5	53.8	55.3	58.6	67.7	86.4	115.5	146.9	167.2	210.5	264.2	300.7	353.7
Imports of Goods & Services	98c	−20.9	−22.9	−23.9	−24.0	−23.1	−24.3	−30.6	−46.2	−66.1	−91.6	−113.2	−174.7	−185.3	−206.3	−296.4
Gross Domestic Product = GDP	99b	39.2	40.5	42.3	43.9	47.1	49.1	54.7	62.2	84.1	102.5	110.6	128.4	168.1	231.8	244.3
Net Factor Inc/Pmts(−) Abroad	98.n	….	10.8	10.6	11.7	12.5	14.1	15.5	20.7	29.7	60.1	89.1	119.3	139.9	153.3	178.2
Gross National Product = GNP	99a	43.3	51.3	53.0	55.6	59.6	63.1	70.2	82.9	113.8	162.6	199.7	247.7	308.0	385.1	422.5
Nat'l Income, Market Prices	99e	41.0	51.1	50.4	55.6	59.6	63.1	70.2	81.7	112.9	153.2	210.7	260.8	326.5	413.9	492.1
Gross Dom. Prod. 1990 Prices	99b.p	….	….	….	….	….	….	….	….	….	….	….	….	….	….	….
GDP Deflator (1990=100)	99bi.p	….	….	….	….	….	….	….	….	….	….	….	….	….	….	….
																Millions:
Population	99z	.95	.97	.99	1.02	1.04	1.06	1.09	1.11	1.14	1.16	1.19	1.21	1.24	1.28	1.31

Government Finance: Data relate to a fiscal year different from calendar year.

Lesotho

	1980	1981	1982	1983	1984	1985	1986	1987	1988	1989	1990	1991	1992	1993	1994			
Millions of Maloti																	**International Transactions**	
	46.6	44.6	40.6	34.6	41.8	50.0	58.0	94.7	144.9	173.0	153.0	186.0	310.0	433.0	….	….	Exports	70
	331.5	405.5	497.8	539.7	634.5	751.0	803.3	954.8	1,327.5	1,552.0	1,738.0	2,242.0	2,784.0	2,975.0	….	….	Imports, cif	71
	321.3	390.2	480.1	520.1	610.9	724.1	774.6	920.7	1,280.1	1,496.6	1,676.0	2,162.0	2,684.7	2,868.9	….	….	Imports, fob	71.v
Minus Sign Indicates Debit																	Balance of Payments	
	58.2	45.2	37.4	31.1	28.3	22.4	25.4	46.5	63.7	66.4	59.5	67.2	109.2	134.0	….	….	Goods: Exports f.o.b.	78aa d
	−424.5	−448.6	−446.9	−482.5	−433.2	−324.0	−341.5	−451.5	−559.4	−592.6	−672.6	−803.5	−932.6	−911.6	….	….	Goods: Imports f.o.b.	78ab d
	−366.3	−403.4	−409.6	−451.4	−404.9	−301.6	−316.2	−405.0	−495.7	−526.2	−613.2	−736.4	−823.4	−777.6	….	….	Trade Balance	78ac d
	32.2	34.3	26.2	27.9	24.4	18.3	20.2	27.5	32.1	32.9	40.6	40.9	41.3	36.7	….	….	Services: Credit	78ad d
	−50.3	−55.2	−46.7	−50.2	−45.1	−35.5	−46.2	−60.7	−69.1	−70.9	−81.4	−83.9	−82.8	−72.3	….	….	Services: Debit	78ae d
	−384.4	−424.3	−430.0	−473.7	−425.6	−318.8	−342.1	−438.2	−532.7	−564.2	−654.0	−779.5	−864.9	−813.2	….	….	Balance on Goods and Services	78af d
	273.1	301.9	361.4	395.0	343.5	242.0	268.6	364.8	384.9	380.0	455.0	476.8	496.3	457.0	….	….	Income: Credit	78ag d
	−7.6	−9.1	−15.1	−12.4	−11.1	−9.0	−10.3	−15.0	−14.9	−20.3	−21.8	−20.4	−32.6	−22.8	….	….	Income: Debit	78ah d
	−118.9	−131.5	−83.8	−91.2	−93.2	−85.8	−83.8	−88.4	−162.8	−204.5	−220.9	−323.1	−401.1	−379.0	….	….	Balance on Goods, Serv., & Inc.	78ai d
	222.1	184.8	163.1	192.8	147.5	104.4	116.9	160.8	197.0	281.7	362.3	492.8	542.1	401.8	….	….	Current Transfers, n.i.e.: Credit	78aj d
	−46.9	−49.0	−57.3	−60.9	−47.8	−30.7	−35.8	−48.7	−58.8	−66.6	−76.4	−86.6	−103.3	−1.3	….	….	Current Transfers: Debit	78ak d
	56.3	4.3	22.1	40.7	6.5	−12.1	−2.8	23.6	−24.6	10.4	65.0	83.1	37.6	21.6	….	….	Current Account, n.i.e.	78al d
	—	—	—	—	—	—	—	—	—	—	—	—	—	—	….	….	Capital Account, n.i.e.: Credit	78ba d
	—	—	—	—	—	—	—	—	—	—	—	—	—	—	….	….	Capital Account: Debit	78bb d
	—	—	—	—	—	—	—	—	—	—	—	—	—	—	….	….	Capital Account, n.i.e.	78bc d
	—	—	—	—	—	—	—	—	−.1	—	—	—	—	—	….	….	Direct Investment Abroad	78bd d
	4.5	4.8	3.0	4.8	2.3	4.8	2.1	5.7	21.0	13.4	17.1	7.5	2.7	15.0	….	….	Dir. Invest. in Rep. Econ., n.i.e.	78be d
	—	—	—	—	—	—	—	—	—	—	—	—	—	—	….	….	Portfolio Investment Assets	78bf d
	—	—	—	—	—	—	—	—	—	—	—	—	—	—	….	….	Portfolio Investment Liab., n.i.e.	78bg d
	−41.9	−53.4	−31.2	−53.0	−17.9	−9.0	−1.6	−39.0	−80.0	−64.8	−109.7	−103.6	−106.4	8.9	….	….	Other Investment Assets	78bh d
	33.7	55.8	35.4	46.5	−12.8	24.9	16.3	36.6	51.0	31.3	47.6	35.4	41.2	40.9	….	….	Other Investment Liab., n.i.e.	78bi d
	−3.7	7.2	7.2	−1.7	−28.4	20.7	16.8	3.3	−8.0	−20.2	−45.0	−60.8	−62.6	64.8	….	….	Financial Account, n.i.e.	78bj d
	−11.2	−10.9	−21.3	−12.9	30.5	−3.1	−1.4	−26.0	26.5	1.9	−2.8	20.1	74.8	16.1	….	….	Net Errors and Omissions	78ca d
	41.4	.6	8.0	26.1	8.6	5.6	12.6	.9	−6.1	−7.9	17.2	42.4	49.9	102.4	….	….	Overall Balance	78cb d
	−41.4	−.6	−8.0	−26.1	−8.6	−5.6	−12.6	−.9	6.1	7.9	−17.2	−42.4	−49.9	−102.4	….	….	Reserves and Related Items	79da d
	−43.1	−.6	−8.0	−26.0	−8.1	−4.8	−11.5	.3	3.3	3.0	−21.0	−45.4	−57.3	−111.9	….	….	Reserve Assets	79db d
	1.7	—	—	−.2	−.4	−.8	−1.1	−1.2	2.8	4.9	3.8	3.0	7.5	9.5	….	….	Use of Fund Credit and Loans	79dc d
	—	—	—	—	—	—	—	—	—	—	—	—	—	—	….	….	Liabs.Constit.For.Auth.Reserves	79dd d
	—	—	—	—	—	—	—	—	—	—	—	—	—	—	….	….	Exceptional Financing	79de d
Year Beginning April 1																	**Government Finance**	
	….	….	….	….	….	….	….	−160,540	−181,235	−103,368	−16,797	−9,853	….	….	….	….	Deficit (−) or Surplus	80
	….	….	135,835	167,892	216,381	238,163	260,213	300,051	369,191	525,193	627,679	819,955	….	….	….	….	Revenue	81
	….	….	….	….	23,095	….	27,123	62,600	96,632	151,925	188,000	149,200	….	….	….	….	Grants Received	81z
	….	….	….	….	….	….	….	517,991	636,908	770,173	823,526	969,958	….	….	….	….	Expenditure	82
	….	….	….	….	….	….	….	5,200	10,150	10,313	8,950	9,050	….	….	….	….	Lending Minus Repayments	83
																	Financing	
	….	….	55,027	−14,298	4,433	34,741	32,475	90,240	110,035	−8,432	−110,603	−116,647	….	….	….	….	Net Borrowing: Domestic	84a
	….	….	….	….	….	….	….	70,300	71,200	111,800	127,400	126,500	….	….	….	….	Foreign	85a
	….	….	−36,979	….	2,203	−1,518	17,667	….	….	….	….	….	….	….	….	….	Use of Cash Balances	87
	….	….	….	….	51,950	….	….	271,700	381,400	372,800	262,200	145,500	….	….	….	….	Debt: Domestic	88a
	….	….	….	398,641	….	….	….	522,600	685,300	815,040	978,100	1,070,550	….	….	….	….	Foreign	89a
Year Beginning April 1																	**National Accounts**	
	58.0	58.2	55.4	50.8	60.5	70.2	80.4	122.8	185.3	227.0	216.0	250.1	378.9	512.2	….	….	Exports of Goods & Services	90c
	74.0	81.0	89.9	91.7	98.6	135.9	159.3	171.5	215.8	222.2	234.6	332.7	394.0	458.1	….	….	Government Consumption	91f
	115.8	133.2	186.8	130.9	184.7	273.3	277.3	337.2	504.2	823.7	1,148.5	1,460.5	1,787.9	2,019.0	….	….	Gross Fixed Capital Formation	93e
	6.3	8.3	−2.9	.6	5.2	−.9	13.6	5.1	2.0	5.2	−10.3	−6.9	−7.7	—	….	….	Increase/Decrease(−) in Stocks	93i
	387.2	471.0	557.1	686.2	783.4	837.9	935.9	1,109.2	1,495.1	1,678.9	1,911.2	2,156.1	2,575.1	2,799.7	….	….	Private Consumption	96f
	−350.2	−423.3	−513.4	−569.6	−676.8	−765.2	−835.3	−992.5	−1,375.6	−1,658.3	−1,850.2	−2,371.8	−2,943.2	−3,128.8	….	….	Imports of Goods & Services	98c
	287.0	328.4	372.9	390.6	455.5	551.1	631.2	753.2	1,026.4	1,299.4	1,649.8	1,820.7	2,184.4	2,587.0	….	….	Gross Domestic Product = GDP	99b
	205.0	254.8	372.9	423.1	487.2	514.3	583.3	705.9	829.7	927.8	1,101.8	1,161.2	1,292.5	1,393.0	….	….	Net Factor Inc/Pmts(−) Abroad	98.n
	492.0	583.2	745.8	813.7	942.6	1,065.4	1,214.6	1,459.1	1,856.2	2,227.2	2,751.6	2,981.9	3,476.9	3,980.0	….	….	Gross National Product = GNP	99a
	570.5	650.6	789.2	897.8	1,073.5	1,229.8	1,366.1	1,603.7	2,062.6	2,673.6	3,173.9	3,830.0	4,465.8	5,276.0	….	….	Nat'l Income, Market Prices	99e
	1,069.8	1,080.2	1,119.0	1,022.8	1,109.3	1,148.1	1,170.8	1,230.5	1,388.9	1,552.5	1,649.8	1,684.8	1,709.1	1,794.1	….	….	Gross Dom. Prod. 1990 Prices	99b.p
	26.8	30.4	33.3	38.2	41.1	48.0	53.9	61.2	73.9	83.7	100.0	108.1	127.8	144.2	….	….	GDP Deflator (1990=100)	99bi p
Midyear Estimates																		
	1.34	1.37	1.41	1.43	1.47	1.50	1.58	1.62	1.70	1.70	1.79	1.84	1.89	1.94	….	….	**Population**	99z

Liberia
668

		1965	1966	1967	1968	1969	1970	1971	1972	1973	1974	1975	1976	1977	1978	1979
Exchange Rates														*Liberian Dollars per SDR End of Period (aa)*		
Official Rate	aa	1.0000	1.0000	1.0000	1.0000	1.0000	1.0000	1.0857	1.0857	1.2064	1.2244	1.1707	1.1618	1.2147	1.3028	1.3173
Official Rate	ae	1.0000	1.0000	1.0000	1.0000	1.0000	1.0000	1.0000	1.0000	1.0000	1.0000	1.0000	1.0000	1.0000	1.0000	1.0000
Fund Position														*Millions of SDRs:*		
Quota	2f. s	16.00	20.00	20.00	20.00	20.00	29.00	29.00	29.00	29.00	29.00	29.00	29.00	29.00	37.00	37.00
SDRs	1b. s	—	—	—	—	—	1.03	.09	1.63	3.28	3.18	2.90	3.52	3.33	3.34	6.52
Reserve Position in the Fund	1c. s	—	—	—	—	—	—	—	.31	—	1.36	1.78	—	—	—	—
Total Fund Cred.&Loans Outstg.	2tl	9.05	9.64	10.60	10.60	7.61	4.35	1.52	—	.06				3.11	12.02	50.98
International Liquidity														*Millions of US Dollars:*		
Total Reserves minus Gold	1l. d	....	....	....	....	....	....	....	....	....	18.72	19.19	17.17	27.34	18.02	54.98
SDRs	1b. d	—	—	—	—	—	1.03	.10	1.77	3.96	3.89	3.39	4.09	4.04	4.35	8.59
Reserve Position in the Fund	1c. d	—	—	—	—	—	—	—	.34	—	1.67	2.08	—	—	—	—
Foreign Exchange	1d. d	....	....	....	....	....	....	....	....	....	13.16	13.71	13.08	23.30	13.67	46.39
Monetary Authorities: Other Liab.	4.. d	....	....	....	....	....	....	....	....	....	—	.03	3.61	.94	5.03	27.67
Deposit Money Banks: Assets	7a. d	4.82	4.89	6.79	24.41	10.72	11.16	9.44	11.86	16.80	33.68	33.98	54.98	38.77	35.36	49.34
Deposit Money Banks: Liabilities	7b. d	10.57	10.93	9.52	11.02	15.16	15.30	15.81	16.31	14.38	27.38	25.03	15.65	20.31	29.58	62.75
of which: Liab. to Nonbanks	7bd d	....	....	1.56	20.93	5.65	3.43	2.19	5.40	1.69	1.25	3.98	3.02	2.97	3.40	2.57
Monetary Authorities														*Millions of Liberian Dollars:*		
Foreign Assets	11	....	....	....	....	....	....	....	....	....	13.62	13.93	17.17	27.34	18.02	54.97
Claims on Central Government	12a	....	....	....	....	....	....	....	....	....	21.26	20.97	27.91	30.75	75.37	118.39
Claims on Nonfin.Pub.Enterprises	12c	....	....	....	....	....	....	....	....	....	....	....	....	....	....	....
Claims on Private Sector	12d	....	....	....	....	....	....	....	....	....	.01	1.88	1.48	1.46	.27	.34
Claims on Deposit Money Banks	12e	....	....	....	....	....	....	....	....	....	2.69	2.90	3.65	2.73	3.02	2.37
Claims on Other Financial Insts.	12f	....	....	....	....	....	....	....	....	....	....	....	....	....	....	....
Monetary Liabilities	14m	....	....	....	....	....	....	....	....	....	12.40	13.13	15.47	18.52	31.79	30.51
of which: Cur. Outside DMBs	14ac	....	....	....	....	....	....	....	....	....	8.48	7.97	8.36	9.24	10.19	11.00
Foreign Liabilities	16c	....	....	....	....	....	....	....	....	....	—	.03	3.61	4.72	20.69	94.83
Central Government Deposits	16d	....	....	....	....	....	....	....	....	....	5.84	8.90	12.93	19.85	22.83	28.84
Capital Accounts	17a	....	....	....	....	....	....	....	....	....	16.69	16.49	16.16	16.93	17.77	22.92
Other Items (Net)	17r	....	....	....	....	....	....	....	....	....	2.64	1.13	2.04	2.26	3.60	-1.02
Deposit Money Banks														*Millions of Liberian Dollars:*		
Reserves	20	—	—	.63	.48	.52	.54	.60	.70	1.06	3.50	4.65	6.19	9.06	19.08	14.40
Foreign Assets	21	4.82	4.89	6.79	24.41	10.72	11.16	9.44	11.86	16.80	33.68	33.98	54.98	38.77	35.36	49.34
Claims on Central Government	22a	20.12	21.27	23.52	21.93	15.74	19.47	18.76	17.43	8.26	3.96	2.24	1.04	4.80	9.41	2.84
Claims on Nonfin.Pub.Enterprises	22c	....	....	....	....	....	—	—	.03	.80	.84	1.79	.68	1.14	11.33	38.01
Claims on Private Sector	22d	18.25	17.84	21.58	24.05	29.40	35.30	38.76	47.35	54.28	72.67	76.77	83.13	109.23	132.17	146.27
Claims on Other Financial Insts.	22f	....	....	....	....	....	....	....	....	....	....	....	.50	.85	—	—
Demand Deposits	24	14.85	13.70	13.57	12.57	16.17	20.11	18.28	21.45	27.89	37.21	30.67	50.42	43.19	60.01	58.54
Time and Savings Deposits	25	9.57	12.94	12.57	14.98	11.64	13.65	19.04	28.45	31.01	30.14	34.96	49.62	69.10	77.51	82.17
Foreign Liabilities	26c	10.57	10.93	9.52	11.02	15.16	15.30	15.81	16.31	14.38	27.38	25.03	15.65	20.31	29.58	62.75
Central Government Deposits	26d	5.96	5.41	13.22	11.03	8.90	12.10	8.84	11.93	5.59	2.86	4.20	1.00	.80	—	—
Credit from Monetary Authorities	26g	....	....	....	....	....	....	....	....	....	2.55	2.40	3.10	2.12	1.43	1.53
Capital Accounts	27a	5.87	4.26	5.83	5.94	5.63	5.67	5.87	4.86	8.74	8.89	5.76	8.80	14.48	17.16	18.59
Other Items (Net)	27r	-3.64	-3.25	-3.75	-5.59	-2.09	-7.64	-5.01	-5.65	-5.93	6.42	16.42	17.94	13.84	21.67	27.28
Monetary Survey														*Millions of Liberian Dollars:*		
Foreign Assets (Net)	31n	....	....	....	....	....	....	....	....	....	19.92	22.86	52.90	41.08	3.11	-53.27
Domestic Credit	32	....	....	....	....	....	....	....	....	....	89.19	88.77	99.63	125.59	194.40	239.00
Claims on Central Govt. (Net)	32an	....	....	....	....	....	....	....	....	....	16.51	10.12	15.02	14.90	61.95	92.39
Claims on Nonfin.Pub.Enterprises	32c	....	....	....	....	....	....	....	....	....	....	....	....	....	....	....
Claims on Private Sector	32d	....	....	....	....	....	....	....	....	....	72.68	78.65	84.61	110.69	132.44	146.61
Claims on Other Financial Insts.	32f	....	....	....	....	....	....	....	....	....	....	....	....	....	....	....
Monetary Liabilities	34m	....	....	....	....	....	....	....	....	....	44.89	38.96	59.25	53.17	72.47	72.56
Quasi-Money	35	....	....	....	....	....	....	....	....	....	30.14	34.96	49.62	69.10	78.51	82.17
Other Items (Net)	37r	....	....	....	....	....	....	....	....	....	34.08	37.70	43.65	44.41	46.53	31.00
Money plus Quasi-Money	35l	....	....	....	....	....	....	....	....	....	75.03	73.92	108.88	122.27	150.97	154.73
Interest Rates														*Percent Per Annum*		
Deposit Rate	60l	....	....	....	....	....	....	....	....	....	....	....	....	....	....	....
Lending Rate	60p	....	....	....	....	....	....	....	....	....	....	....	....	....	....	....
Prices														*Index Numbers (1985=100):*		
Consumer Prices	64	26.6	27.2	28.8	29.2	32.5	33.0	32.8	34.1	40.8	48.5	55.3	58.4	62.0	66.6	74.3

Liberia

668

	1980	1981	1982	1983	1984	1985	1986	1987	1988	1989	1990	1991	1992	1993	1994		
Exchange Rates																	
Liberian Dollars per US Dollar: End of Period (ae)																	
Official Rate	1.2754	1.1640	1.1031	1.0470	.9802	1.0984	1.2232	1.4187	1.3457	1.3142	1.4227	1.4304	1.3750	1.3736	1.4599	aa
Official Rate	1.0000	1.0000	1.0000	1.0000	1.0000	1.0000	1.0000	1.0000	1.0000	1.0000	1.0000	1.0000	1.0000	1.0000	1.0000	ae
Fund Position *End of Period*																	
Quota	55.50	55.50	55.50	71.30	71.30	71.30	71.30	71.30	71.30	71.30	71.30	71.30	71.30	71.30	71.30	2f. s
SDRs	—	1.08	.01	—	.03	—	—	—	—	—	—	—	—	—	—	1b. s
Reserve Position in the Fund	—	.01	—	—	—	.02	.02	.03	.03	.03	.03	.03	.03	.03	.03	1c. s
Total Fund Cred.&Loans Outstg.	69.78	115.27	176.82	223.75	237.25	230.40	230.40	230.40	229.36	227.20	226.52	226.52	226.52	226.52	225.83	2tl
International Liquidity *End of Period*																	
Total Reserves minus Gold	5.48	9.60	6.50	20.41	3.51	1.52	2.66	.51	.38	7.88	....	1.31	.98	2.37	5.07	1l. d
SDRs	—	1.26	.01	—	.03	—	—	—	—	—	—	—	—	—	—	1b. d
Reserve Position in the Fund	—	.01	—	—	—	.02	.02	.04	.04	.04	.04	.04	.04	.04	.04	1c. d
Foreign Exchange	5.48	8.33	6.49	20.41	3.48	1.50	2.64	.47	.34	7.84	....	1.27	.94	2.33	5.03	1d. d
Monetary Authorities: Other Liab.	25.63	13.44	7.53	16.69	.14	11.50	35.57	65.05	87.51	115.77	....	216.88	232.46	260.40	292.67	4.. d
Deposit Money Banks: Assets	24.27	15.53	26.37	24.50	11.66	14.71	18.50	18.57	23.05	34.05	....	17.53	13.78	49.05	9.46	7a. d
Deposit Money Banks: Liabilities	49.36	56.35	54.55	40.59	35.61	46.22	34.45	39.32	39.47	43.17	....	48.32	36.97	17.86	46.33	7b. d
of which: Liab. to Nonbanks	.08	.12	.08	.03	.11	.60	.32	.16	.14	.14	....	—	.05	.14	—	7bd d
Monetary Authorities *End of Period*																	
Foreign Assets	5.48	8.34	6.49	20.41	3.48	1.52	2.66	.51	.38	7.88	....	1.31	.98	2.37	5.07	11
Claims on Central Government	173.52	214.23	284.17	352.11	347.73	427.99	477.03	562.98	733.84	841.07	....	985.30	1,072.93	1,264.09	1,284.92	12a
Claims on Nonfin.Pub.Enterprises	2.32	4.16	4.38	5.61	5.26	.98	—	—	—	4.12	....	4.83	4.83	4.83	4.83	12c
Claims on Private Sector	1.46	.53	.56	.74	1.81	.74	.81	1.05	1.03	1.07	....	11.05	12.03	17.82	15.48	12d
Claims on Deposit Money Banks	1.71	1.07	1.22	2.32	.85	.81	1.96	.93	1.89	2.47	....	24.41	23.83	23.39	51.36	12e
Claims on Other Financial Insts.	.50	1.56	1.96	2.13	2.05	2.05	2.05	3.77	3.62	3.84	....	3.84	3.84	.71	.71	12f
Monetary Liabilities	41.81	40.69	57.05	71.33	86.47	121.24	152.18	192.73	220.98	275.99	....	336.07	322.86	503.44	531.67	14m
of which: Cur. Outside DMBs	11.35	11.59	15.74	19.83	28.59	46.17	66.06	82.52	96.50	101.59	....	189.28	154.94	274.11	302.95	14c
Foreign Liabilities	114.63	147.61	202.59	250.94	232.69	264.57	317.39	391.91	396.16	414.34	....	540.90	543.92	571.54	622.35	16c
Central Government Deposits	25.54	25.29	28.30	25.78	7.67	9.37	15.37	17.18	16.99	25.26	....	15.87	7.75	71.59	74.22	16d
Capital Accounts	29.99	35.95	43.68	48.87	63.42	75.71	19.79	20.05	-9.49	80.72	....	100.06	69.03	68.59	58.42	17a
Other Items (Net)	-27.97	-19.63	-32.83	-13.61	-29.08	-36.80	-20.22	-52.64	116.11	64.11	....	37.82	174.88	98.05	75.71	17r
Deposit Money Banks *End of Period*																	
Reserves	29.56	27.66	39.87	53.33	57.24	70.56	79.16	106.42	126.06	190.10	....	113.90	143.92	217.30	215.40	20
Foreign Assets	24.27	15.53	26.37	24.50	11.66	14.71	18.50	18.57	23.05	34.05	....	17.53	13.78	49.05	9.46	21
Claims on Central Government	2.85	3.86	4.06	2.83	3.52	4.22	10.01	10.87	17.59	9.84	....	7.24	3.10	8.78	5.37	22a
Claims on Nonfin.Pub.Enterprises	40.93	33.15	42.39	44.43	47.91	45.90	52.93	38.67	49.71	42.04	....	47.86	55.60	82.72	63.14	22c
Claims on Private Sector	88.69	91.48	74.95	71.27	74.80	77.55	74.30	89.89	74.36	123.33	....	96.59	152.83	127.24	222.70	22d
Claims on Other Financial Insts.	—	—	1.25	.21	.40	.35	1.42	.10	1.21	.32	....	6.29	.30	.30	—	22f
Demand Deposits	53.85	37.84	45.69	52.89	60.76	67.46	82.05	93.45	92.55	124.99	....	92.32	111.12	149.95	154.32	24
Time and Savings Deposits	48.95	51.05	64.19	68.63	54.46	56.17	53.75	56.74	66.40	73.90	....	72.00	156.29	274.49	324.44	25
Foreign Liabilities	49.36	56.35	54.55	40.59	35.61	46.22	34.45	39.32	39.47	43.17	....	48.32	36.97	17.86	46.33	26c
Central Government Deposits	.06	.06	.06	1.52	6.31	10.62	18.82	13.14	20.29	26.00	....	35.13	29.87	30.46	35.34	26d
Credit from Monetary Authorities	.51	.51	.63	1.13	.49	1.86	.17	.59	1.11	1.21	....	14.22	20.67	20.02	23.66	26g
Capital Accounts	17.85	18.28	19.70	22.60	25.09	22.04	25.01	29.77	34.99	48.74	....	44.65	48.26	22.67	33.46	27a
Other Items (Net)	15.73	7.57	4.06	9.22	12.82	8.92	22.07	31.50	37.16	81.68	....	-17.22	-33.65	-30.05	-101.47	27r
Monetary Survey *End of Period*																	
Foreign Assets (Net)	-134.23	-180.09	-224.29	-246.62	-253.16	-294.56	-330.67	-412.15	-412.20	-415.58	....	-570.39	-566.13	-537.98	-654.15	31n
Domestic Credit	283.68	323.62	385.35	452.02	469.50	539.79	584.35	677.01	844.07	974.36	....	1,111.99	1,267.84	1,404.45	1,487.59	32
Claims on Central Govt. (Net)	150.77	192.74	259.86	327.64	337.27	412.23	452.85	543.53	714.14	799.65	....	941.54	1,038.41	1,170.83	1,180.73	32an
Claims on Nonfin.Pub.Enterprises	43.25	37.31	46.77	50.04	53.17	46.88	52.93	38.67	49.71	46.16	....	52.69	60.43	87.55	67.97	32c
Claims on Private Sector	89.15	92.01	75.51	72.01	76.62	78.29	75.11	90.94	75.39	124.39	....	107.64	164.87	145.05	238.18	32d
Claims on Other Financial Insts.	.50	1.56	3.21	2.34	2.44	2.40	3.47	3.87	4.83	4.16	....	10.13	4.14	1.01	.71	32f
Monetary Liabilities	65.59	49.89	61.65	72.98	89.43	113.71	148.21	176.06	189.08	226.71	....	281.67	266.11	424.14	457.34	34m
Quasi-Money	48.95	51.05	65.04	69.13	54.96	57.04	53.94	57.48	67.47	75.43	....	72.42	157.69	276.67	326.54	35
Other Items (Net)	34.91	42.59	34.37	63.29	71.95	74.48	51.53	31.31	175.32	256.65	....	187.52	277.91	165.66	49.57	37r
Money plus Quasi-Money	114.54	100.94	126.69	142.12	144.39	170.75	202.15	233.54	256.54	302.14	....	354.09	423.80	700.81	783.88	35l
Interest Rates *Percent Per Annum*																	
Deposit Rate	10.30	11.50	10.21	10.25	9.81	9.34	7.25	5.88	5.43	6.77	....	....	....	....	6.34	60l
Lending Rate	18.40	21.50	18.23	20.69	20.63	19.34	14.45	13.63	13.36	13.82	....	....	....	....	14.53	60p
Prices *Period Averages*																	
Consumer Prices	85.2	91.7	97.1	99.8	101.0	100.0	104.0	109.2	119.8	130.6	....	....	....	....	....	64

Liberia
668

		1965	1966	1967	1968	1969	1970	1971	1972	1973	1974	1975	1976	1977	1978	1979
International Transactions														*Millions of Liberian Dollars*		
Exports	70	135.40	150.46	158.77	169.03	195.93	213.73	222.13	244.40	324.00	400.27	393.83	459.96	447.42	504.05	536.56
Imports, cif	71	104.60	113.60	125.17	108.43	114.65	149.70	157.37	178.68	193.45	288.44	331.20	399.22	463.53	480.87	506.55
Imports, fob	71.v	91.75	99.65	109.80	95.11	100.57	131.32	138.04	156.74	169.69	253.02	290.40	351.31	407.91	415.36	437.64
															1985=100	
Unit Value of Exports	74	44.7	40.2	40.3	38.6	42.2	38.5	ɪ42.8	42.8	47.5	62.5	ɪ81.8	84.2	98.1	88.3	103.9
Unit Value of Imports	75	....	....	....	....	....	....	33	37	42	62	ɪ67	64	79	81	94
Balance of Payments														*Millions of US Dollars:*		
Goods: Exports f.o.b.	78aa d	....	....	....	....	....	....	....	....	....	....	....	....	....	....	536.6
Goods: Imports f.o.b.	78ab d	....	....	....	....	....	....	....	....	....	....	....	....	....	....	-457.5
Trade Balance	78ac d	....	....	....	....	....	....	....	....	....	....	....	....	....	....	79.1
Services: Credit	78ad d	....	....	....	....	....	....	....	....	....	....	....	....	....	....	17.0
Services: Debit	78ae d	....	....	....	....	....	....	....	....	....	....	....	....	....	....	-68.9
Balance on Goods and Services	78af d	....	....	....	....	....	....	....	....	....	....	....	....	....	....	27.2
Income: Credit	78ag d	....	....	....	....	....	....	....	....	....	....	....	....	....	....	—
Income: Debit	78ah d	....	....	....	....	....	....	....	....	....	....	....	....	....	....	-13.7
Balance on Goods, Serv., & Inc.	78ai d	....	....	....	....	....	....	....	....	....	....	....	....	....	....	13.5
Current Transfers, n.i.e.: Credit	78aj d	....	....	....	....	....	....	....	....	....	....	....	....	....	....	37.7
Current Transfers: Debit	78ak d	....	....	....	....	....	....	....	....	....	....	....	....	....	....	-35.0
Current Account, n.i.e.	78al d	....	....	....	....	....	....	....	....	....	....	....	....	....	....	16.2
Capital Account, n.i.e.: Credit	78ba d	....	....	....	....	....	....	....	....	....	....	....	....	....	....	—
Capital Account: Debit	78bb d	....	....	....	....	....	....	....	....	....	....	....	....	....	....	—
Capital Account, n.i.e.	78bc d	....	....	....	....	....	....	....	....	....	....	....	....	....	....	—
Direct Investment Abroad	78bd d	....	....	....	....	....	....	....	....	....	....	....	....	....	....	—
Dir. Invest. in Rep. Econ., n.i.e.	78be d	....	....	....	....	....	....	....	....	....	....	....	....	....	....	—
Portfolio Investment Assets	78bf d	....	....	....	....	....	....	....	....	....	....	....	....	....	....	—
Portfolio Investment Liab., n.i.e.	78bg d	....	....	....	....	....	....	....	....	....	....	....	....	....	....	—
Other Investment Assets	78bh d	....	....	....	....	....	....	....	....	....	....	....	....	....	....	-14.0
Other Investment Liab., n.i.e.	78bi d	....	....	....	....	....	....	....	....	....	....	....	....	....	....	136.1
Financial Account, n.i.e.	78bj d	....	....	....	....	....	....	....	....	....	....	....	....	....	....	122.1
Net Errors and Omissions	78ca d	....	....	....	....	....	....	....	....	....	....	....	....	....	....	-211.1
Overall Balance	78cb d	....	....	....	....	....	....	....	....	....	....	....	....	....	....	-72.8
Reserves and Related Items	79da d	....	....	....	....	....	....	....	....	....	....	....	....	....	....	72.8
Reserve Assets	79db d	....	....	....	....	....	....	....	....	....	....	....	....	....	....	-.5
Use of Fund Credit and Loans	79dc d	....	....	....	....	....	....	....	....	....	....	....	....	....	....	50.7
Liabs.Constit.For.Auth.Reserves	79dd d	....	....	....	....	....	....	....	....	....	....	....	....	....	....	—
Exceptional Financing	79de d	....	....	....	....	....	....	....	....	....	....	....	....	....	....	22.6
Government Finance														*Millions of Liberian Dollars:*		
Deficit (-) or Surplus	80	-18.0	-21.9	-22.3	-10.7	-8.2	-6.2	10.4	13.2	10.5	6.8	3.4	-16.0	ɪ-24.2	-56.2	-141.2
Revenue	81	42.4	46.7	48.1	51.8	61.8	66.5	67.6	75.1	88.8	104.6	121.0	147.9	ɪ165.4	181.7	201.3
Grants Received	81z	12.4	13.4	13.4	11.6	9.0	10.8	13.2	11.3	11.0	12.3	11.3	16.0	ɪ16.0	16.0	23.0
Exp. & Lending Minus Repay.	82z	72.8	82.0	83.8	74.1	79.0	83.5	70.4	73.2	89.3	110.1	128.9	179.9	ɪ205.6	253.9	365.5
Expenditure	82	....	....	....	....	....	....	....	....	....	102.3	119.9	178.4	ɪ182.6	232.7	344.3
Lending Minus Repayments	83	....	....	....	....	....	....	....	....	....	7.8	9.0	1.5	ɪ23.0	21.2	21.2
Financing	84x	18.0	21.9	22.3	10.7	8.2	6.2	-10.4	-13.2	-10.5	-6.8	-3.4	16.0	ɪ24.2	56.2	141.2
Domestic	84a	....	....	....	....	....	....	....	....	....	-1.6	-5.7	....	ɪ-13.5	41.3	30.8
Foreign	85a	....	....	....	....	....	....	....	....	....	-5.2	2.3	....	ɪ37.7	14.9	110.4
Debt: Domestic	88a	....	....	....	....	....	....	....	....	....	7.7	13.2	10.9	ɪ35.9	63.5	95.1
Foreign	89a	....	....	....	....	....	....	....	....	143.2	138.7	141.9	....	ɪ215.2	223.7	350.5
National Accounts														*Millions of Liberian Dollars*		
Exports of Goods & Services	90c	144.2	166.2	183.9	203.0	237.0	240.1	251.8	274.8	329.9	407.2	403.7	467.1	459.0	500.0	553.6
Government Consumption	91f	35.6	39.5	41.4	42.5	45.3	45.1	53.1	55.4	56.9	64.5	73.2	89.3	120.0	139.0	156.6
Gross Fixed Capital Formation	93e	49.4	58.8	73.6	53.5	61.1	77.8	73.4	88.7	85.5	116.7	161.2	206.4	234.3	260.1	277.6
Increase/Decrease(-) in Stocks	93i	3.1	14.1	4.7	11.3	-7.5	8.4	14.8	15.4	-13.9	5.1	85.8	33.4	51.7	20.4	43.9
Private Consumption	96f	131.7	142.8	153.0	148.6	146.0	152.4	166.8	176.4	197.1	245.8	257.6	281.7	363.1	402.8	436.2
Imports of Goods & Services	98c	-116.8	-130.4	-148.3	-135.7	-143.6	-172.2	-187.4	-204.8	-240.9	-332.1	-371.9	-446.2	-521.9	-548.6	-587.4
Gross Domestic Product	99b	247.2	291.1	308.3	323.2	338.7	351.6	372.5	405.9	414.6	507.2	609.6	631.7	706.2	773.7	880.5
Net Factor Inc/Pmts(-) Abroad	98.n	-51.8	-88.3	-95.5	-97.5	-90.6	-93.5	-91.0	-68.0	-92.0	-85.4	-122.8	-86.0	-80.0	-95.9	-87.7
Gross Nat'l Expenditure = GNP	99a	195.4	202.8	212.8	225.7	248.1	258.1	281.5	337.9	322.6	421.8	486.8	545.7	626.2	677.8	792.8
Gross Dom. Prod. 1985 Prices	99b.p	760.1	904.4	898.3	941.0	1,009.5	1,075.6	1,128.9	1,171.7	1,142.0	1,226.5	1,041.0	1,082.6	1,073.5	1,115.9	1,165.0
GDP Deflator (1985=100)	99bi p	32.5	32.2	34.3	34.3	33.6	32.7	33.0	34.6	36.3	41.4	58.6	58.4	65.8	69.3	75.6
																Millions:
Population	99z	1.38	1.40	1.25	1.26	1.29	1.37	1.38	1.42	1.47	1.50	1.55	1.61	1.67	1.72	1.78

Monetary Authorities: ɪ Beginning in December 1980, revisions reflect improvements in the sector classification of the accounts.
Monetary Survey: ɪ See note to section 10.
Government Finance: ɪ During the period 1977-87, data relate to a fiscal year different from calendar year (fiscal year ends June 30).

Liberia

668

	1980	1981	1982	1983	1984	1985	1986	1987	1988	1989	1990	1991	1992	1993	1994		
International Transactions																	
Millions of Liberian Dollars																	
Exports	600.40	529.16	477.44	427.60	452.12	435.60	408.37	382.20	396.33	460.11	....	....	....	....	....		70
Imports, cif	534.62	447.38	428.32	411.58	363.21	284.40	259.04	307.60	272.32	....	....	....	....	....	....		71
Imports, fob	461.82	382.64	370.02	353.78	314.51	246.23	224.28	266.32	235.77	....	....	....	....	....	....		71.v
1985=100																	
Unit Value of Exports	121.1	ⲓ100.6	109.1	101.9	100.5	100.0	98.2	93.6	....	....	....	....	....	....	....		74
Unit Value of Imports	109	ⲓ98	104	99	108	100	105	112	....	....	....	....	....	....	....		75
Balance of Payments																	
Minus Sign Indicates Debit																	
Goods: Exports f.o.b.	600.4	529.2	477.4	420.8	446.7	430.4	407.9	374.9	....	....	....	....	....	....	....		78aa d
Goods: Imports f.o.b.	−478.0	−423.9	−390.2	−374.8	−325.4	−263.8	−258.8	−311.7	....	....	....	....	....	....	....		78ab d
Trade Balance	122.4	105.3	87.2	46.0	121.3	166.6	149.1	63.2	....	....	....	....	....	....	....		78ac d
Services: Credit	13.1	11.5	32.7	38.5	36.9	34.6	56.9	52.5	....	....	....	....	....	....	....		78ad d
Services: Debit	−72.7	−58.7	−92.0	−108.7	−92.5	−80.2	−80.5	−74.2	....	....	....	....	....	....	....		78ae d
Balance on Goods and Services	62.8	58.1	27.9	−24.2	65.7	121.0	125.5	41.5	....	....	....	....	....	....	....		78af d
Income: Credit	—	—	1.8	1.8	2.6	3.7	2.1	5.2	....	....	....	....	....	....	....		78ag d
Income: Debit	−24.0	−21.1	−74.1	−155.4	−129.4	−131.8	−183.3	−188.3	....	....	....	....	....	....	....		78ah d
Balance on Goods, Serv., & Inc.	38.8	37.0	−44.4	−177.8	−61.1	−7.1	−55.7	−141.6	....	....	....	....	....	....	....		78ai d
Current Transfers, n.i.e.: Credit	39.2	71.1	124.9	146.5	142.6	130.0	97.9	50.0	....	....	....	....	....	....	....		78aj d
Current Transfers: Debit	−32.0	−33.0	−78.0	−72.7	−83.6	−67.6	−59.9	−53.5	....	....	....	....	....	....	....		78ak d
Current Account, n.i.e.	46.0	75.1	2.5	−104.0	−2.1	55.3	−17.7	−145.1	....	....	....	....	....	....	....		78al d
Capital Account, n.i.e.: Credit	—	—	—	—	—	—	—	—	....	....	....	....	....	....	....		78ba d
Capital Account: Debit	—	—	—	—	—	—	—	—	....	....	....	....	....	....	....		78bb d
Capital Account, n.i.e.	—	—	—	—	—	—	—	—	....	....	....	....	....	....	....		78bc d
Direct Investment Abroad	—	—	—	—	—	—	—	—	....	....	....	....	....	....	....		78bd d
Dir. Invest. in Rep. Econ., n.i.e.	—	—	34.8	49.1	36.2	−16.2	−16.5	38.5	....	....	....	....	....	....	....		78be d
Portfolio Investment Assets	—	—	—	5.0	6.8	4.4	5.6	—	....	....	....	....	....	....	....		78bf d
Portfolio Investment Liab., n.i.e.	—	—	—	—	—	—	—	—	....	....	....	....	....	....	....		78bg d
Other Investment Assets	25.1	8.7	10.8	−3.3	−28.7	−9.3	7.1	4.3	....	....	....	....	....	....	....		78bh d
Other Investment Liab., n.i.e.	57.1	50.0	94.0	−67.4	−30.7	−128.9	−199.1	−228.1	....	....	....	....	....	....	....		78bi d
Financial Account, n.i.e.	82.2	58.7	139.6	−16.6	−16.4	−150.0	−202.9	−185.3	....	....	....	....	....	....	....		78bj d
Net Errors and Omissions	−175.0	−182.7	−265.8	−7.0	−134.3	−108.7	−73.4	30.3	....	....	....	....	....	....	....		78ca d
Overall Balance	−46.8	−48.9	−123.7	−127.6	−152.8	−203.4	−294.0	−300.1	....	....	....	....	....	....	....		78cb d
Reserves and Related Items	46.8	48.9	123.7	127.6	152.8	203.4	294.0	300.1	....	....	....	....	....	....	....		79da d
Reserve Assets	25.9	1.4	1.2	−14.2	16.9	2.0	2.6	.5	....	....	....	....	....	....	....		79db d
Use of Fund Credit and Loans	24.4	53.0	67.1	50.1	14.1	−7.0	—	—	....	....	....	....	....	....	....		79dc d
Liabs.Constit.For.Auth.Reserves	—	—	—	—	—	—	—	—	....	....	....	....	....	....	....		79dd d
Exceptional Financing	−3.5	−5.5	55.5	91.6	121.8	208.4	291.4	299.6	....	....	....	....	....	....	....		79de d
Government Finance																	
Year Ending December 31																	
Deficit (-) or Surplus	−88.3	−110.3	−116.6	−102.9	−61.0	−87.1	−90.9	−83.9	ⲓ−91.9	....	....	....	....	....	....		80
Revenue	202.3	218	236.9	229.7	223.7	206.8	180.7	180.6	ⲓ212.8	....	....	....	....	....	....		81
Grants Received	23.0	24.5	41.4	33.0	36.0	22.5	25.0	18.0	ⲓ—	....	....	....	....	....	....		81z
Exp. & Lending Minus Repay.	313.6	352.8	394.9	365.6	320.7	316.4	296.6	282.5	ⲓ304.7	....	....	....	....	....	....		82z
Expenditure	281.0	323.2	371.0	338.3	298.4	291.0	273.9	263.5	ⲓ283.4	....	....	....	....	....	....		82
Lending Minus Repayments	32.6	29.6	23.9	27.3	22.3	25.4	22.7	19.0	ⲓ21.3	....	....	....	....	....	....		83
Financing	88.3	110.3	116.6	102.9	61.0	87.1	90.9	83.9	ⲓ91.9	....	....	....	....	....	....		84x
Domestic	58.0	48.9	75.6	63.2	41.1	34.8	22.1	42.3	ⲓ71.9	....	....	....	....	....	....		84a
Foreign	30.3	61.4	41.0	39.7	19.9	52.3	68.8	41.6	ⲓ20.0	....	....	....	....	....	....		85a
Debt: Domestic	156.0	206.1	258.3	335.0	363.0	378.5	412.6	459.4	ⲓ507.0	....	....	....	....	....	....		88a
Foreign	435.8	498.2	511.4	559.7	585.1	982.1	1,121.0	1,306.4	ⲓ1,427.1	....	....	....	....	....	....		89a
National Accounts																	
Millions of Liberian Dollars																	
Exports of Goods & Services	613.5	540.7	487.4	466.1	489.0	470.2	462.2	427.4	448.9	521.9	....	....	....	....	....		90c
Government Consumption	182.0	229.5	231.1	197.0	152.2	149.9	131.0	163.2	142.8	160.0	....	....	....	....	....		91f
Gross Fixed Capital Formation	196.1	179.6	193.1	183.1	168.9	126.5	115.0	120.4	115.3	96.8	....	....	....	....	....		93e
Increase/Decrease(-) in Stocks	109.0	18.5	42.9	47.2	25.7	7.8	7.8	7.0	3.5	4.0	....	....	....	....	....		93i
Private Consumption	430.0	647.2	650.4	723.0	710.2	706.8	662.6	713.9	733.3	656.8	....	....	....	....	....		96f
Imports of Goods & Services	−614.0	−560.9	−478.5	−479.2	−411.5	−322.8	−299.7	−356.8	−321.5	−275.2	....	....	....	....	....		98c
Gross Domestic Product	916.6	1,022.3	1,119.5	1,128.9	1,058.0	1,069.2	1,051.2	1,120.9	1,174.4	1,182.8	....	....	....	....	....		99b
Net Factor Inc/Pmts(-) Abroad	−83.7	−125.2	−145.9	−153.6	−126.8	−123.6	−180.5	−183.1	−193.8	−199.1	....	....	....	....	....		98.n
Gross Nat'l Expenditure = GNP	832.9	942.1	973.6	975.3	931.2	945.6	820.7	937.8	980.6	983.8	....	....	....	....	....		99a
Gross Dom. Prod. 1985 Prices	ⲓ1,109.8	1,134.7	1,102.0	1,094.3	1,084.5	1,069.2	1,100.5	1,130.3	1,130.3	....	....	....	....	....	....		99b.p
GDP Deflator (1985=100)	82.6	90.1	101.6	103.2	97.6	100.0	95.5	99.2	103.9	....	....	....	....	....	....		99bi.p
Midyear Estimates																	
Population	1.85	1.91	1.98	2.04	2.11	2.16	2.22	2.28	2.34	2.40	2.46	2.52	2.58	2.64	2.70		99z

Libya

672

		1965	1966	1967	1968	1969	1970	1971	1972	1973	1974	1975	1976	1977	1978	1979
Exchange Rates																*SDRs per Dinar: End of Period (ac)*
Official Rate	ac	2.8000	2.8000	2.8000	2.8000	2.8000	2.8000	2.8000	2.8000	2.8000	2.7589	2.8854	2.9073	2.7807	2.5927	2.5641
Official Rate	ag	2.8000	2.8000	2.8000	2.8000	2.8000	2.8000	3.0400	3.0400	3.3778	3.3778	3.3778	3.3778	3.3778	3.3778	3.3778
Fund Position																*Millions of SDRs:*
Quota	2f.s	15	19	19	19	19	24	24	24	24	24	24	24	24	185	185
SDRs	1b.s	—	—	—	—	—	—	—	—	—	—	—	—	—	—	31
Reserve Position in the Fund	1c.s	4	5	5	5	5	6	6	6	6	6	6	6	6	6	42
International Liquidity														*Millions of US Dollars Unless Otherwise Indicated:*
Total Reserves minus Gold	1l.d	178	271	317	453	832	1,505	2,573	2,832	2,024	3,511	2,095	3,106	4,786	4,105	6,344
SDRs	1b.d	—	—	—	—	—	—	—	—	—	—	—	—	—	—	40
Reserve Position in the Fund	1c.d	4	5	5	5	5	6	7	7	7	7	7	7	7	8	56
Foreign Exchange	1d.d	174	267	313	449	828	1,499	2,566	2,826	2,017	3,504	2,088	3,099	4,779	4,097	6,248
Gold (Million Fine Troy Ounces)	1ad	1.934	1.934	1.934	2.437	2.437	2.437	2.437	2.437	2.437	2.438	2.438	2.438	2.448	2.448	2.464
Gold (National Valuation)	1and	68	68	68	86	86	88	94	95	107	103	103	103	103	103	104
Deposit Money Banks: Assets	7a.d	5	4	6	7	10	22	26	47	128	141	152	215	269	273	508
Liabilities	7b.d	—	—	8	12	13	5	7	19	40	15	82	52	148	156	120
Monetary Authorities																*Millions of Dinars:*
Foreign Assets	11	87.8	121.1	137.6	192.4	327.7	567.9	876.8	962.3	629.6	1,244.7	753.0	1,064.2	1,623.6	1,492.4	2,207.2
Claims on Central Government	12a									163.8	249.3	584.2	533.5	353.8	1,106.6	1,129.1
Claims on Private Sector	12d	7.1	10.5	14.0	22.4	30.7	.4	—	.9	4.3	3.5	.7	.8	23.3	25.4	23.3
Reserve Money	14	57.8	78.2	107.1	130.6	175.7	199.5	314.6	367.8	402.0	590.1	673.4	829.6	1,051.5	1,355.9	1,793.9
of which: Currency Outside DMBs	14a	33.6	47.7	61.0	70.4	102.4	112.3	120.7	147.4	202.6	262.2	346.0	436.0	585.0	868.5	1,053.7
Private Sector Deposits	14d	10.0	14.2	23.2	34.8	51.6	52.3	102.5	112.3	133.0	180.6	185.8	210.5	265.9	260.0	488.7
Quasi-Monetary Liabilities	15	12.9	13.2	13.9	19.4	25.5	40.5	45.0	80.4	143.7	322.8	246.0	261.1	286.1	299.9	334.7
of which: Coml. Prepayments	15c	1.4	.6	1.3	1.5	1.4	13.9	13.3	39.8	75.1	170.9	144.8	140.2	144.1	133.0	150.4
Foreign Liabilities	16c	.1	1.0	.8	.4	.4	.4	.4	.7	1.0	.5	1.5	.9	.6	1.1	2.6
Central Government Deposits	16d	17.9	30.2	20.8	45.2	118.8	280.9	482.1	523.0	327.9	378.5	310.4	323.7	314.2	425.6	506.5
Other Items (Net)	17r	6.2	9.1	8.8	19.4	38.0	47.0	35.7	−5.2	−77.8	202.8	106.7	205.7	349.0	541.9	722.0
Deposit Money Banks																*Millions of Dinars:*
Reserves	20	14.3	14.9	22.0	25.6	22.6	27.1	124.5	135.0	97.9	148.7	157.1	186.5	225.9	234.0	291.7
Foreign Assets	21	1.7	1.4	2.2	2.4	3.7	6.0	8.7	15.3	38.0	41.7	45.0	63.8	79.7	80.7	150.3
Claims on Private Sector	22d	28.1	36.9	40.3	51.1	62.0	95.5	107.5	148.0	274.1	451.2	644.5	741.7	855.9	928.6	1,049.0
Demand Deposits	24	23.1	29.0	32.6	45.0	47.9	76.5	141.3	153.3	178.4	311.1	335.7	492.9	592.9	559.3	705.0
Quasi-Monetary Deposits	25	15.9	18.6	23.1	25.0	28.2	39.2	53.5	95.3	153.2	257.8	246.9	294.5	398.2	386.0	617.8
Foreign Liabilities	26c	.2	.1	3.0	4.4	4.5	1.9	2.3	6.2	11.9	4.4	24.3	15.5	43.7	46.3	35.5
Central Government Deposits	26d	—	.1	.1	—	—	1.0	12.6	10.3	30.0	27.3	27.8	33.7	45.0	41.5	78.2
Capital Accounts	27a	7.0	6.8	7.7	7.1	8.5	9.9	10.3	20.2	24.2	31.1	43.6	47.9	65.3	90.5	117.7
Other Items (Net)	27r	−1.7	−1.4	−2.0	−2.5	−.6	2.0	20.7	13.1	12.4	10.0	168.5	107.7	16.5	119.9	−63.2
Monetary Survey																*Millions of Dinars:*
Foreign Assets (Net)	31n	89.2	121.4	135.9	190.0	326.5	573.7	882.8	970.7	654.6	1,281.5	772.2	1,111.5	1,659.0	1,525.7	2,319.4
Domestic Credit	32	17.2	17.0	33.4	28.3	−26.1	−186.1	−386.3	−381.0	83.6	298.4	901.7	1,037.0	1,093.7	1,776.6	2,071.9
Claims on Central Govt. (Net)	32an	−18.0	−30.3	−20.9	−45.2	−118.8	−281.9	−494.7	−533.3	−194.1	−153.4	256.4	271.9	213.8	822.6	999.6
Claims on Private Sector	32d	35.2	47.3	54.3	73.5	92.7	95.9	108.4	152.3	277.6	451.8	645.3	765.0	879.9	954.1	1,072.4
Money	34	66.8	90.9	116.8	150.2	201.9	241.1	364.5	413.0	514.0	753.8	867.6	1,139.4	1,443.8	1,687.8	2,247.3
Quasi-Money	35	28.7	31.7	37.1	44.4	53.6	79.7	98.4	175.7	296.9	580.5	492.9	555.6	684.3	685.9	952.5
Other Items (Net)	37r	11.4	15.8	15.4	23.7	44.9	66.8	33.6	1.1	−72.7	245.5	313.5	453.7	624.6	928.7	1,191.5
Money plus Quasi-Money	35l	95.5	122.7	153.9	194.6	255.5	320.8	462.9	588.7	810.9	1,334.3	1,360.5	1,694.9	2,128.1	2,373.7	3,199.8
Other Banking Institutions																*Millions of Dinars:*
Cash	40	2.65	2.68	4.58	7.46	8.13	9.77	8.94	6.48	6.45	9.06	16.38	17.02	22.66	20.66	19.97
Claims on Private Sector	42d	4.34	7.38	6.46	7.56	8.89	11.38	16.18	22.11	25.26	29.50	30.54	32.24	38.66	40.62	45.17
Capital Accounts	47a	4.00	4.50	5.60	7.00	7.20	7.20	8.37	8.37	11.81	12.75	12.76	44.98	45.98	45.98	45.98
Other Items (Net)	47r	2.99	5.55	5.44	8.02	9.82	13.95	16.74	20.22	19.88	25.81	34.17	4.28	15.35	15.30	19.16
Interest Rates																*Percent Per Annum:*
Discount Rate (End of Period)	60	5.0	5.0	5.0	5.0	5.0	5.0	5.0	5.0	5.0	5.0	5.0	5.0	5.0	5.0	5.0
Money Market Rate	60b	....	....	....	4.0	4.0	4.0	4.0	4.0	4.0	4.0	4.0	4.0	4.0	4.0	4.0
Deposit Rate	60l	....	....	....	3.5	3.5	4.0	4.0	4.0	4.0	4.0	4.0	4.0	4.0	4.0	4.0
Lending Rate	60p	7.0	7.0	7.0	7.0	7.0	7.0	7.0	7.0	7.0	7.0	7.0	7.0	7.0	7.0	7.0

Libya

672

	1980	1981	1982	1983	1984	1985	1986	1987	1988	1989	1990	1991	1992	1993	1994		
Exchange Rates																	
US Dollars per Dinar: End of Period (ag)																	
Official Rate	2.6484	2.9020	3.0621	3.2263	3.4460	3.0751	2.6046	2.6046	2.6046	2.6046	2.6046	2.6046	2.4138^e	2.2400	1.9048	ac	
Official Rate	3.3778	3.3778	3.3778	3.3778	3.3778	3.3778	3.1860^e	3.6951^e	3.5051^e	3.4229^e	3.7055^e	3.7258^e	3.3190^e	3.0768	2.7807	ag	
Fund Position																	
End of Period																	
Quota	298	298	298	298	516	516	516	516	516	516	516	516	818	818	818	2f. s	
SDRs	47	104	129	158	133	156	178	198	219	249	287	323	278	303	325	1b. s	
Reserve Position in the Fund	148	189	189	189	244	244	244	244	244	244	244	244	319	319	319	1c. s	
International Liquidity																	
End of Period																	
Total Reserves minus Gold	13,091	9,003	7,059	5,219	3,634	5,904	5,953^e	5,838^e	4,322^e	4,333^e	5,839^e	5,695^e	6,182^e	....	....	1l. d	
SDRs	59	121	143	165	130	172	217	280	294	328	409	461	383	417	474	1b. d	
Reserve Position in the Fund	189	220	209	198	239	267	298	345	328	320	346	348	439	438	466	1c. d	
Foreign Exchange	12,842	8,662	6,708	4,856	3,266	5,465	5,438^e	5,212^e	3,699^e	3,685^e	5,084^e	4,885^e	5,361^e	....	....	1d. d	
Gold (Million Fine Troy Ounces)	3.078	3.578	3.578	3.578	3.648	3.600	3.600	3.600	3.600	3.600	3.600	3.600	3.600	....	....	1ad	
Gold (National Valuation)	130	151	151	151	154	152	152	152	152	152	152	152	152	....	....	1an d	
Deposit Money Banks: Assets	1,131	977	929	722	701	551	480	371	378	178	287	278	456	....	....	7a. d	
Liabilities	113	256	239	203	146	1	171	46	540	906	1,017	1,103	694	....	....	7b. d	
Monetary Authorities																	
End of Period																	
Foreign Assets	4,205.6	2,772.3	2,115.8	1,594.2	1,075.7	1,846.7	1,910.4	1,620.7	1,274.5	1,379.9	1,762.1	1,621.3	1,922.5	....	....	11	
Claims on Central Government	340.3	1,192.0	1,825.2	932.3	1,151.4	828.2	686.4	650.8	625.1	3,728.8	4,216.0	4,630.9	4,726.5	....	....	12a	
Claims on Private Sector	21.1	18.0	15.0	12.3	39.0	36.0	34.1	35.0	35.6	53.0	6.2	6.4	6.3	....	....	12d	
Reserve Money	2,297.2	2,166.8	2,261.1	1,798.9	1,717.9	2,221.6	2,113.2	2,250.7	1,912.9	2,371.1	3,185.9	3,185.5	4,092.3	....	....	14	
of which: Currency Outside DMBs	685.7	791.1	889.9	838.2	767.5	985.0	1,023.7	1,068.2	899.6	1,131.6	1,461.0	1,620.8	1,982.2	....	....	14a	
Private Sector Deposits	783.1	833.4	748.0	377.6	308.1	394.9	182.0	162.1	131.4	298.2	751.6	392.9	312.0	....	....	14d	
Quasi-Monetary Liabilities	448.0	414.8	462.0	508.5	642.0	605.4	573.5	645.1	624.1	731.6	803.5	578.0	595.4	....	....	15	
of which: Coml. Prepayments	221.0	226.7	259.1	269.6	354.8	307.8	284.3	356.9	290.7	210.8	341.4	240.6	175.6	....	....	15c	
Foreign Liabilities	2.9	3.2	7.1	—	—	—	—	—	—	—	—	—	—	....	....	16c	
Central Government Deposits	903.2	782.0	742.9	712.3	719.1	720.8	732.5	755.7	759.1	774.7	789.6	980.4	826.3	....	....	16d	
Other Items (Net)	915.7	615.2	483.0	−481.0	−812.9	−837.0	−788.2	−1,345.1	−1,360.8	1,284.4	1,204.9	1,514.7	1,141.4	....	....	17r	
Deposit Money Banks																	
End of Period																	
Reserves	875.6	563.2	597.6	595.0	632.3	851.9	902.7	1,025.4	846.9	944.7	1,073.1	1,232.2	1,786.3	....	....	20	
Foreign Assets	334.8	289.4	275.0	213.7	207.6	163.2	150.7	100.5	107.8	51.9	77.3	74.6	137.4	....	....	21	
Claims on Private Sector	1,123.8	2,173.9	1,570.7	2,214.7	2,163.7	2,044.6	2,040.4	2,430.9	2,325.6	2,460.4	2,553.9	2,645.6	2,840.3	....	....	22d	
Demand Deposits	1,430.1	1,887.6	1,594.4	1,668.6	1,635.7	2,112.3	1,835.7	2,208.3	1,980.6	2,091.6	2,239.6	2,279.1	2,693.0	....	....	24	
Quasi-Monetary Deposits	757.7	719.8	611.2	733.8	822.0	956.0	1,196.5	989.4	1,118.8	903.5	945.4	1,120.4	1,256.2	....	....	25	
Foreign Liabilities	33.4	75.7	70.8	60.1	43.3	.3	53.6	12.5	154.1	264.7	274.5	296.0	209.0	....	....	26c	
Central Government Deposits	195.1	198.7	286.5	160.4	387.6	164.8	437.2	355.1	136.6	160.4	193.1	149.8	181.0	....	....	26d	
Capital Accounts	148.6	164.3	220.5	237.1	188.9	208.8	225.6	249.8	293.0	287.3	311.8	356.1	373.3	....	....	27a	
Other Items (Net)	−230.5	−19.8	−339.9	163.3	−73.9	−382.5	−654.8	−258.2	−402.7	−251.2	−260.0	−249.0	51.4	....	....	27r	
Monetary Survey																	
End of Period																	
Foreign Assets (Net)	4,504.2	2,982.7	2,312.9	1,747.8	1,240.0	2,009.5	2,007.5	1,708.7	1,228.3	1,167.1	1,564.9	1,399.8	1,850.9	....	....	31n	
Domestic Credit	1,215.3	2,938.6	2,706.7	2,848.0	3,344.8	3,429.6	3,137.7	3,325.0	3,688.3	6,744.8	7,229.8	7,589.1	8,009.9	....	....	32	
Claims on Central Govt. (Net)	70.4	746.7	1,120.9	621.0	1,142.1	1,349.6	1,063.2	859.0	1,327.2	4,231.4	4,669.7	4,937.1	5,163.3	....	....	32an	
Claims on Private Sector	1,144.9	2,191.8	1,585.8	2,227.0	2,202.7	2,080.6	2,074.5	2,466.0	2,361.1	2,513.4	2,560.1	2,651.9	2,846.6	....	....	32d	
Money	2,898.9	3,512.2	3,232.3	2,884.5	2,711.3	3,492.2	3,041.4	3,438.6	3,011.6	3,521.6	4,452.2	4,292.8	4,987.2	....	....	34	
Quasi-Money	1,205.7	1,134.7	1,073.1	1,242.3	1,464.0	1,561.4	1,770.0	1,634.5	1,742.9	1,635.0	1,748.9	1,698.3	1,851.6	....	....	35	
Other Items (Net)	1,615.0	1,274.4	714.1	469.0	409.5	385.6	333.7	−39.5	162.1	2,754.8	2,593.3	2,997.8	3,022.1	....	....	37r	
Money plus Quasi-Money	4,104.6	4,646.8	4,305.4	4,126.8	4,175.3	5,053.6	4,811.4	5,073.2	4,754.5	5,156.5	6,201.1	5,991.1	6,838.7	....	....	35l	
Other Banking Institutions																	
End of Period																	
Cash	48.25	25.72	28.69	....	....	....	....	....	....	....	....	....	....	....	....	40	
Claims on Private Sector	38.25	46.00	46.09	....	....	....	....	....	....	....	....	....	....	....	....	42d	
Capital Accounts	45.98	46.07	46.60	....	....	....	....	....	....	....	....	....	....	....	....	47a	
Other Items (Net)	40.51	25.64	28.19	....	....	....	....	....	....	....	....	....	....	....	....	47r	
Interest Rates																	
Percent Per Annum																	
Discount Rate (End of Period)	5.0	5.0	5.0	5.0	5.0	5.0	5.0	5.0	5.0	....	....	....	....	....	....	60	
Money Market Rate	4.0	4.0	4.0	4.0	4.0	4.0	4.0	4.0	4.0	....	....	....	....	....	....	60b	
Deposit Rate	5.1	5.5	5.5	5.5	5.5	5.5	5.5	5.5	5.5	....	....	....	....	....	....	60l	
Lending Rate	7.0	7.0	7.0	7.0	7.0	7.0	7.0	7.0	7.0	....	....	....	....	....	....	60p	

Libya
672

		1965	1966	1967	1968	1969	1970	1971	1972	1973	1974	1975	1976	1977	1978	1979
Production														*Index Numbers (1990=100)*		
Consumer Prices (1975=100)	64	65.0	73.0	78.3	78.6	86.3	ɪ81.7	79.2	79.0	85.3	91.6	100.0	105.5	112.1	145.0	136.3
Foodstuffs (1975=100)	64a	72.0	82.3	83.9	88.8	98.3	118.4	96.6	95.9	87.8	93.9	100.0	113.5	127.3	142.2	180.7
Crude Petroleum Production	66aa	90.1	111.6	128.2	192.6	230.3	245.8	204.5	166.3	160.5	112.7	109.6	143.8	152.8	146.5	152.6
International Transactions														*Millions of Dinars*		
Exports	70	282.0	355.3	417.3	668.1	772.8	841.8	959.9	966.3	1,196.4	2,445.2	2,023.2	2,828.5	3,378.2	2,929.3	4,759.3
Crude Petroleum	70aa	280.3	351.1	416.4	667.3	771.9	841.1	956.9	949.2	1,161.7	2,388.3	1,925.3	2,711.2	3,189.7	2,719.5	4,419.2
Imports, cif	71	114.4	144.7	170.2	230.2	241.3	198.0	250.4	343.2	539.9	817.6	1,048.7	950.8	1,117.1	1,362.6	1,572.4
Imports, fob	71.v	101.2	128.1	150.6	203.7	214.2	171.9	214.1	296.4	473.3	694.2	904.3	855.6	1,005.4	1,226.3	1,415.4
Imports, cif, from DOTS	71y	....	....	....	....	....	....	....	....	....	....	....	....	....	....	....
Export Prices															*1985=100:*	
Crude Petroleum	76aa d	7.8	7.8	7.8	7.8	7.8	7.8	9.6	10.2	14.5	43.3	38.8	41.0	46.0	45.5	70.0
Balance of Payments														*Millions of US Dollars:*		
Goods: Exports f.o.b.	78aa d	....	....	....	....	....	....	....	....	....	....	....	....	10,406	9,900	15,981
Goods: Imports f.o.b.	78ab d	....	....	....	....	....	....	....	....	....	....	....	....	−4,929	−5,764	−8,647
Trade Balance	78ac d	....	....	....	....	....	....	....	....	....	....	....	....	5,476	4,136	7,334
Services: Credit	78ad d	....	....	....	....	....	....	....	....	....	....	....	....	136	153	143
Services: Debit	78ae d	....	....	....	....	....	....	....	....	....	....	....	....	−1,301	−1,448	−1,953
Balance on Goods and Services	78af d	....	....	....	....	....	....	....	....	....	....	....	....	4,311	2,841	5,523
Income: Credit	78ag d	....	....	....	....	....	....	....	....	....	....	....	....	244	317	424
Income: Debit	78ah d	....	....	....	....	....	....	....	....	....	....	....	....	−1,459	−1,370	−1,273
Balance on Goods, Serv., & Inc.	78ai d	....	....	....	....	....	....	....	....	....	....	....	....	3,096	1,788	4,673
Current Transfers, n.i.e.: Credit	78aj d	....	....	....	....	....	....	....	....	....	....	....	....	15	17	18
Current Transfers: Debit	78ak d	....	....	....	....	....	....	....	....	....	....	....	....	−952	−1,067	−920
Current Account, n.i.e.	78al d	....	....	....	....	....	....	....	....	....	....	....	....	2,159	738	3,771
Capital Account, n.i.e.: Credit	78ba d	....	....	....	....	....	....	....	....	....	....	....	....	—	—	—
Capital Account: Debit	78bb d	....	....	....	....	....	....	....	....	....	....	....	....	—	—	—
Capital Account, n.i.e.	78bc d	....	....	....	....	....	....	....	....	....	....	....	....	—	—	—
Direct Investment Abroad	78bd d	....	....	....	....	....	....	....	....	....	....	....	....	−60	−28	−21
Dir. Invest. in Rep. Econ., n.i.e.	78be d	....	....	....	....	....	....	....	....	....	....	....	....	−451	−692	−588
Portfolio Investment Assets	78bf d	....	....	....	....	....	....	....	....	....	....	....	....	−220	−146	−23
Portfolio Investment Liab., n.i.e.	78bg d	....	....	....	....	....	....	....	....	....	....	....	....	—	—	—
Other Investment Assets	78bh d	....	....	....	....	....	....	....	....	....	....	....	....	−232	−716	−839
Other Investment Liab., n.i.e.	78bi d	....	....	....	....	....	....	....	....	....	....	....	....	446	177	173
Financial Account, n.i.e.	78bj d	....	....	....	....	....	....	....	....	....	....	....	....	−518	−1,406	−1,298
Net Errors and Omissions	78ca d	....	....	....	....	....	....	....	....	....	....	....	....	33	47	−253
Overall Balance	78cb d	....	....	....	....	....	....	....	....	....	....	....	....	1,674	−621	2,220
Reserves and Related Items	79da d	....	....	....	....	....	....	....	....	....	....	....	....	−1,674	621	−2,220
Reserve Assets	79db d	....	....	....	....	....	....	....	....	....	....	....	....	−1,674	621	−2,220
Use of Fund Credit and Loans	79dc d	....	....	....	....	....	....	....	....	....	....	....	....	—	—	—
Liabs.Constit.For.Auth.Reserves	79dd d	....	....	....	....	....	....	....	....	....	....	....	....	—	—	—
Exceptional Financing	79de d	....	....	....	....	....	....	....	....	....	....	....	....	....	....	....
National Accounts														*Millions of Dinars*		
Exports of Goods & Services	90c	299	370	431	680	788	870	975	998	1,240	2,490	2,053	2,881	3,431	2,978	4,801
Government Consumption	91f	80	107	132	193	257	260	318	359	465	865	1,044	1,185	1,400	1,692	2,007
Gross Fixed Capital Formation	93e	147	191	210	290	315	243	288	437	636	979	1,055	1,226	1,383	1,532	1,855
Increase/Decrease(-) in Stocks	93i	5	4	8	6	8	4	13	14	28	50	100	−50	58	20	110
Private Consumption	96f	201	253	301	335	383	464	469	543	703	927	1,194	1,337	1,482	1,665	1,895
Imports of Goods & Services	98c	−183	−223	−253	−333	−419	−403	−436	−552	−826	−1,428	−1,666	−1,671	−1,948	−2,199	−2,822
Gross Domestic Product	99b	560	717	845	1,194	1,358	1,426	1,627	1,798	2,246	3,883	3,780	4,907	5,763	5,688	7,846
Net Factor Inc/Pmts(-) Abroad	98.n	−81	−105	−129	−228	−214	−216	−211	−275	−318	−439	−400	−517	−517	−505	....
Gross Nat'l Expenditure = GNP	99a	478	612	716	965	1,144	1,210	1,416	1,524	1,928	3,444	3,380	4,390	5,304	5,183	....
Nat'l Income, Market Prices	99e	430	553	643	878	1,046	1,101	1,316	1,412	1,816	3,296	3,214	4,198	5,096	4,946	7,030
Gross Dom. Prod. 1980 Prices	99b.p	2,552.2	3,022.4	3,363.0	4,490.4	5,075.7	5,272.3	4,994.1	5,449.8	5,555.4	6,788.3	ɪ7,061.8	8,661.0	9,429.8	9,672.0	10,471.6
GDP Deflator (1980=100)	99bi p	21.9	23.7	25.1	26.6	26.8	27.0	32.6	33.0	40.4	57.2	53.5	56.7	61.1	58.8	74.9
																Millions:
Population	99z	1.62	1.69	1.76	1.84	1.91	1.98	2.07	2.15	2.24	2.33	2.43	ɪ2.56	2.67	2.79	2.91

Exchange Rates: On September 1, 1971 the Libyan dinar, equal to the Libyan pound, was introduced.

Libya

672

	1980	1981	1982	1983	1984	1985	1986	1987	1988	1989	1990	1991	1992	1993	1994		
Period Averages																**Production**	
	....	....	....	....	....	....	....	....	....	....	....	....	....	....	....	Consumer Prices (1975=100)	64
	....	....	....	....	....	....	....	....	....	....	....	....	....	....	....	Foodstuffs (1975=100)	64a
	132.8	82.2	85.2	79.7	79.7	78.2	76.6	72.0	75.3	81.2	100.0	110.2	110.2	102.0	102.2	Crude Petroleum Production	66aa
Millions of Dinars																**International Transactions**	
	6,486.4	4,609.8	3,908.8	3,616.6	3,300.4	3,645.6	2,432.0	2,372.0	1,907.0	2,407.0	3,745.0	3,154.0	....	....	....	Exports	70
	6,287.3	4,384.3	3,718.0	3,370.7	3,020.8	3,184.3	1,572.0	....	....	....	....	....	....	....	....	Crude Petroleum	70aa
	2,006.2	2,481.4	2,124.3	1,785.0	1,842.0	1,214.0	1,316.0	1,278.0	1,677.0	1,475.0	1,511.0	1,505.0	....	....	....	Imports, cif	71
	1,805.6	2,233.3	1,911.9	1,606.5	1,657.8	1,092.7	1,184.5	1,150.3	1,509.5	1,327.6	1,360.0	1,354.6	....	....	....	Imports, fob	71.v
	....	2,481.4	2,548.4	2,287.1	2,148.6	1,658.9	1,121.8	1,184.0	1,689.0	1,316.1	1,603.6	1,498.9	1,469.2	1,644.1	1,407.3	Imports, cif, from DOTS	71y
Index of Prices in US Dollars																**Export Prices**	
	119.5	132.8	117.8	102.5	100.0	100.0	....	....	....	....	....	....	....	....	....	Crude Petroleum	76aa *d*
Minus Sign Indicates Debit																**Balance of Payments**	
	21,919	14,731	13,701	12,348	11,028	10,353	6,186	6,292	5,653	7,274	11,352	....	....	....	....	Goods: Exports f.o.b.	78aa *d*
	−10,368	−14,563	−10,976	−8,978	−8,464	−5,754	−4,718	−5,820	−5,762	−6,509	−7,575	....	....	....	....	Goods: Imports f.o.b.	78ab *d*
	11,551	168	2,725	3,370	2,564	4,599	1,468	472	−109	765	3,777	....	....	....	....	Trade Balance	78ac *d*
	164	163	163	161	170	63	87	123	128	117	117	....	....	....	....	Services: Credit	78ad *d*
	−2,303	−2,757	−2,265	−2,315	−2,202	−1,775	−1,114	−1,552	−1,637	−1,481	−1,385	....	....	....	....	Services: Debit	78ae *d*
	9,413	−2,427	624	1,216	532	2,887	442	−957	−1,617	−598	2,508	....	....	....	....	Balance on Goods and Services	78af *d*
	1,282	1,627	868	676	550	463	582	789	762	447	666	....	....	....	....	Income: Credit	78ag *d*
	−1,347	−1,517	−1,376	−1,433	−1,218	−540	−629	−393	−437	−388	−493	....	....	....	....	Income: Debit	78ah *d*
	9,348	−2,317	115	459	−135	2,811	395	−560	−1,292	−539	2,682	....	....	....	....	Balance on Goods, Serv., & Inc.	78ai *d*
	20	26	32	29	14	9	7	5	7	6	7	....	....	....	....	Current Transfers, n.i.e.: Credit	78aj *d*
	−1,154	−1,672	−1,706	−2,131	−1,335	−913	−567	−574	−541	−493	−488	....	....	....	....	Current Transfers: Debit	78ak *d*
	8,214	−3,963	−1,560	−1,643	−1,456	1,906	−166	−1,128	−1,826	−1,026	2,201	....	....	....	....	Current Account, n.i.e.	78al *d*
	—	—	—	—	—	—	—	—	—	—	—	....	....	....	....	Capital Account, n.i.e.: Credit	78ba *d*
	—	—	—	—	—	—	—	—	—	—	—	....	....	....	....	Capital Account: Debit	78bb *d*
	—	—	—	—	—	—	—	—	—	—	—	....	....	....	....	Capital Account, n.i.e.	78bc *d*
	−47	−25	−19	—	—	—	—	−124	−56	−35	−105	....	....	....	....	Direct Investment Abroad	78bd *d*
	−1,089	−744	−392	−327	−17	119	−188	−106	98	125	159	....	....	....	....	Dir. Invest. in Rep. Econ., n.i.e.	78be *d*
	−113	−430	−255	−107	47	55	−72	−3,213	−222	−52	−115	....	....	....	....	Portfolio Investment Assets	78bf *d*
																Portfolio Investment Liab., n.i.e.	78bg *d*
	−1,275	52	−578	38	324	505	−404	3,777	−670	320	−715	....	....	....	....	Other Investment Assets	78bh *d*
	821	637	619	488	477	105	206	−472	1,013	830	−230	....	....	....	....	Other Investment Liab., n.i.e.	78bi *d*
	−1,703	−511	−625	93	831	784	−458	−137	163	1,188	−1,006	....	....	....	....	Financial Account, n.i.e.	78bj *d*
	−104	329	172	−236	−1,096	−328	847	184	271[e]	130	−37	....	....	....	....	Net Errors and Omissions	78ca *d*
	6,407	−4,145	−2,013	−1,786	−1,721	2,362	224	−1,082	−1,392[e]	292	1,158	....	....	....	....	Overall Balance	78cb *d*
	−6,407	4,145	2,013	1,786	1,721	−2,362	−224	1,082	1,392[e]	−292	−1,158	....	....	....	....	Reserves and Related Items	79da *d*
	−6,407	4,145	2,013	1,786	1,721	−2,362	−224	1,082	1,392[e]	−292	−1,158	....	....	....	....	Reserve Assets	79db *d*
	—	—	—	—	—	—	—	—	—	—	—	....	....	....	....	Use of Fund Credit and Loans	79dc *d*
	—	—	—	—	—	—	—	—	—	—	—	....	....	....	....	Liabs.Constit.For.Auth.Reserves	79dd *d*
	....	....	....	....	....	....	....	....	....	....	....	....	....	....	....	Exceptional Financing	79de *d*
Millions of Dinars																**National Accounts**	
	6,737	4,868	4,105	....	....	....	....	....	....	....	....	....	....	....	....	Exports of Goods & Services	90c
	2,351	2,721	2,966	....	....	....	....	....	....	....	....	....	....	....	....	Government Consumption	91f
	2,424	2,811	2,362	....	....	....	....	....	....	....	....	....	....	....	....	Gross Fixed Capital Formation	93e
	95	120	−50	....	....	....	....	....	....	....	....	....	....	....	....	Increase/Decrease(-) in Stocks	93i
	2,328	3,127	3,384	....	....	....	....	....	....	....	....	....	....	....	....	Private Consumption	96f
	−3,399	−4,306	−3,920	....	....	....	....	....	....	....	....	....	....	....	....	Imports of Goods & Services	98c
	10,535	9,341	8,846	8,531	7,574	7,203	6,473	....	....	....	....	....	....	....	....	Gross Domestic Product	99b
	....	....	....	....	....	....	....	....	....	....	....	....	....	....	....	Net Factor Inc/Pmts(-) Abroad	98.n
	....	....	....	....	....	....	....	....	....	....	....	....	....	....	....	Gross Nat'l Expenditure = GNP	99a
	9,908	8,570	7,790	....	....	....	....	....	....	....	....	....	....	....	....	Nat'l Income, Market Prices	99e
	10,535.0	....	....	....	....	....	....	....	....	....	....	....	....	....	....	Gross Dom. Prod. 1980 Prices	99b.*p*
	100.0	....	....	....	....	....	....	....	....	....	....	....	....	....	....	GDP Deflator (1980=100)	99bi *p*
Midyear Estimates																	
	2.76	2.87	2.99	3.11	3.24	3.37	3.52	3.67	3.82	3.98	4.15	4.33	4.51	4.70	4.90	Population	99z

Luxembourg

137

		1965	1966	1967	1968	1969	1970	1971	1972	1973	1974	1975	1976	1977	1978	1979
Exchange Rates																*Francs per SDR:*
Market Rate	aa	49.642	50.052	49.627	50.140	49.666	49.675	48.591	47.839	49.846	44.227	46.273	41.806	40.013	37.520	36.948
																Francs per US Dollar:
Market Rate	ae	49.643	50.053	49.628	50.140	49.666	49.675	44.755	44.063	41.320	36.123	39.528	35.983	32.940	28.800	28.048
Market Rate	rf	50.000	50.000	50.000	50.000	50.000	50.000	48.870	44.015	38.977	38.952	36.779	38.605	35.843	31.492	29.319
																Francs per ECU:
ECU Rate	ea	....	....	....	....	....	....	....	....	....	....	....	....	....	....	40.318
ECU Rate	eb	....	....	....	....	....	....	....	....	....	....	....	42.913	40.884	40.059	40.164
														Index Numbers (1990=100):		
Market Rate	ah x	67.1	66.9	67.1	66.7	66.5	67.1	120.9	75.7	85.8	85.7	90.9	86.5	93.0	106.0	113.7
Nominal Effective Exchange Rate	ne c	....	....	....	....	....	....	....	....	....	....	....	....	....	....	108.7
Real Effective Exchange Rate	re c	....	....	....	....	....	....	....	....	....	....	....	....	....	....	109.8
Fund Position																*Millions of SDRs:*
Quota	2f. s	15.00	15.80	16.60	17.40	19.00	19.00	20.00	20.00	20.00	20.00	20.00	20.00	20.00	31.00	31.00
SDRs	1b. s	—	—	—	—	—	3.19	5.22	7.34	7.34	7.34	7.34	7.34	7.44	7.58	11.59
Reserve Position in the Fund	1c. s	3.01	3.22	3.42	3.62	4.02	4.02	4.27	5.01	5.01	5.01	5.01	9.01	8.72	9.57	9.42
International Liquidity												*Millions of US Dollars Unless Otherwise Indicated:*				
Total Reserves minus Gold	1l. d	....	....	....	....	....	....	....	....	....	....	....	....	....	....	....
SDRs	1b. d	....	....	....	....	....	3.19	5.67	7.97	8.85	8.99	8.59	8.53	9.04	9.88	15.27
Reserve Position in the Fund	1c. d	3.01	3.22	3.42	3.62	4.02	4.02	4.64	5.44	6.04	6.13	5.87	10.47	10.59	12.47	12.41
Foreign Exchange	1d. d	....	....	....	....	....	....	....	....	....	....	....	....	....	....	....
Gold (Million Fine Troy Ounces)	1ad	.298	.343	.343	.440	.440	.440	.442	.442	.442	.442	.442	.442	.451	.455	.455
Gold (National Valuation)	1an d	12.60	14.49	14.49	18.56	18.56	18.56	18.67	18.67	18.67	18.67	18.67	18.67	19.04	19.22	19.22
Deposit Money Banks: Assets	7a. d	402	516	712	1,106	1,920	3,709	6,287	9,601	17,264	24,608	30,369	38,174	51,191	68,898	95,095
of which: Claims on Nonbanks	7ad d	141	179	240	383	564	1,734	2,869	4,128	7,842	11,898	15,493	18,726	26,915	36,750	45,255
Deposit Money Banks: Liabilities	7b. d	515	656	763	1,110	1,830	3,589	5,942	8,954	15,608	22,108	27,890	35,123	48,206	64,010	89,507
of which: Liab. to Nonbanks	7bd d	403	471	516	614	960	1,217	1,691	2,248	3,498	6,241	5,776	6,910	8,804	11,661	16,768
Monetary Authorities																*Billions of Francs:*
Foreign Assets	11	....	....	....	....	....	....	....	....	....	....	....	....	....	....	....
Claims on Central Government	12a	....	....	....	....	....	....	....	....	....	....	....	....	....	....	....
Claims on Deposit Money Banks ...	12e	....	....	....	....	....	....	....	....	....	....	....	....	....	....	....
Reserve Money	14	....	....	....	....	....	....	....	....	....	....	....	....	....	....	....
Foreign Liabilities	16c	....	....	....	....	....	....	....	....	....	....	....	....	....	....	....
Central Government Deposits	16d	....	....	....	....	....	....	....	....	....	....	....	....	....	....	....
Capital Accounts	17a	....	....	....	....	....	....	....	....	....	....	....	....	....	....	....
Other Items (Net)	17r	....	....	....	....	....	....	....	....	....	....	....	....	....	....	....
Deposit Money Banks																*Billions of Francs:*
Foreign Assets	21	20.0	25.7	35.5	55.2	95.7	183.9	280.0	428.2	692.9	879.9	1,192.0	1,362.2	ɪ 1,686.2	1,984.3	2,667.2
Claims on Private Sector	22d	21.6	24.3	23.6	24.5	27.8	33.6	34.6	38.6	48.1	64.8	74.3	86.3	ɪ 58.0	117.2	135.9
Demand Deposits	24	3.9	4.0	4.9	5.6	8.9	9.4	10.6	12.7	15.6	16.8	22.1	20.2	23.0	25.6	23.6
Time and Savings Deposits	25	11.8	13.0	14.5	16.0	19.6	23.1	28.6	37.9	54.6	76.7	85.8	103.6	112.4	141.7	160.7
Foreign Liabilities	26c	25.8	32.8	38.1	55.5	91.5	179.4	266.3	401.3	629.5	798.6	1,102.4	1,263.8	1,587.9	1,843.5	2,510.5
Capital Accounts	27a	3.1	3.2	4.3	5.7	6.6	8.5	11.2	17.4	25.0	36.0	47.3	59.3	76.5	95.4	119.5
Other Items (Net)	27r	–3.0	–3.1	–2.7	–3.2	–3.2	–3.0	–2.2	–2.6	16.3	16.5	8.7	1.6	ɪ –55.5	–4.7	–11.1
Luxembourg Notes and Coins	24a	.3	.3	.4	.4	.4	.4	.5	.5	.5	.5	.5	.5	.6	.6	.6
Post Office: Checking Deposits	24.. i	1.4	1.4	1.4	1.6	1.5	1.5	1.7	2.2	2.6	ɪ 1.8	2.0	2.3	2.6	2.8	3.0
Money (National Definitions)																*Billions of Francs:*
Money	34n	....	....	....	....	....	....	....	....	....	23.5	26.4	28.2	32.1	34.1	36.3
Quasi-Money	35n	....	....	....	....	....	....	....	....	....	40.3	42.2	51.5	57.2	68.1	80.8
Broad Money	38n	....	....	....	....	....	....	....	....	....	63.8	68.6	79.7	89.3	102.2	117.1
Interest Rates																*Percent Per Annum*
Deposit Rate	60l	....	....	....	....	....	....	....	....	....	....	....	....	....	....	....
Lending Rate	60p	....	....	....	....	....	....	....	....	....	....	....	....	....	....	....
Government Bond Yield	61	....	....	....	....	....	7.52	7.58	7.25	6.80	7.27	6.73	7.23	7.03ᵉ	ɪ 6.64	6.78
Prices, Production, Employment														*Index Numbers (1990=100):*		
Share Prices	62	....	....	....	....	....	9.0	10.1	12.8	15.6	16.0	20.7	21.4	23.0	30.6	47.1
Producer Prices in Industry	63a	....	....	....	....	....	....	....	....	....	....	....	....	....	....	....
Consumer Prices	64	29.5	30.4	31.1	31.9	32.6	34.2	35.8	37.6	39.9	43.7	48.4	53.1	56.7	58.5	61.1
Industrial Production	66.. b	56.9	54.8	55.0	58.3	65.7	66.1	65.2	67.9	76.0	78.6	61.4	62.8	63.1	66.1	68.3
Steel Production	66rr	96.8	96.8	ɪ 96.8	102.4	117.2	ɪ 115.7	110.5	115.8	128.5	135.4	93.7	96.7	95.6	ɪ 104.9	108.6
Industrial Empl. (1985=100)	67	92.3	91.2	86.9	86.9	89.2	94.2	ɪ 97.3	100.3	103.1	107.2	107.7	105.5	104.0	102.7	103.5
Empl. in Steel Ind.(1985=100) ...	67rr	203.0	201.9	197.5	192.9	192.9	197.3	205.3	201.4	203.5	207.1	198.1	188.4	178.1	161.9	153.5
International Transactions																*Billions of Francs*
Exports	70	....	....	....	28.58	34.96	42.75	36.25	44.03	57.63	82.54	65.29	70.64	68.56	72.31	85.80
Imports	71	....	....	....	25.47	28.91	37.37	33.99	42.26	51.95	67.51	66.85	71.84	73.01	79.57	91.20

Luxembourg

	1980	1981	1982	1983	1984	1985	1986	1987	1988	1989	1990	1991	1992	1993	1994		
Exchange Rates																	
End of Period																Market Rate	aa
	40.205	44.766	51.758	58.252	61.832	55.316	49.429	47.032	50.255	46.994	44.078	44.730	45.623	49.599	46.478		
End of Period (ae) Period Average (rf)																Market Rate	ae
	31.523	38.460	46.920	55.640	63.080	50.360	40.410	33.153	37.345	35.760	30.983	31.270	33.180	36.110	31.838	Market Rate	rf
	29.242	37.129	45.691	51.132	57.784	59.378	44.672	37.334	36.768	39.404	33.418	34.148	32.150	34.597	33.456		
End of Period (ea) Period Average (eb)																ECU Rate	ea
	41.335	41.747	45.321	46.097	44.717	44.645	43.233	43.154	43.576	42.592	42.184	41.931	40.178	40.266	39.161	ECU Rate	eb
	40.601	41.301	44.680	45.430	45.438	44.913	43.803	43.039	43.427	43.378	42.506	42.222	41.604	40.468	39.661		
Period Averages																Market Rate	ah x
	114.1	90.2	73.3	65.4	57.8	56.5	74.9	89.4	90.8	84.7	100.0	98.0	103.9	96.5	99.9	Nominal Effective Exchange Rate	nec
	108.3	106.0	98.5	96.1	95.3	95.7	97.3	98.8	98.4	98.1	100.0	100.4	101.0	101.0	102.2	Real Effective Exchange Rate	rec
	107.2	104.4	98.2	98.3	98.1	98.5	99.3	99.0	98.3	98.0	100.0	99.8	100.4	100.8	101.7		
Fund Position																	
End of Period																Quota	2f. s
	46.50	46.50	46.50	77.00	77.00	77.00	77.00	77.00	77.00	77.00	77.00	77.00	77.00	135.50	135.50	SDRs	1b. s
	11.32	14.88	15.41	15.98	16.58	17.08	17.54	17.96	18.41	19.05	19.86	20.60	6.62	6.98	7.22	Reserve Position in the Fund	1c. s
	12.19	12.20	12.21	12.21	12.21	12.21	12.23	12.23	12.23	12.23	12.25	12.25	12.27	25.85	23.58		
International Liquidity																	
End of Period																Total Reserves minus Gold	1l. d
	....	....	....	....	28.56	32.71	36.43	42.84	41.24	75.24	80.53	80.42	74.13	67.38	75.73	SDRs	1b. d
	14.44	17.32	17.00	16.73	18.76	21.45	25.48	24.77	25.03	28.25	29.47	9.10	9.59	10.54	Reserve Position in the Fund	1c. d
	15.55	14.20	13.47	12.78	11.97	13.41	14.96	17.35	16.46	16.10	17.43	17.55	35.54	32.38	34.46	Foreign Exchange	1d. d
	....	....	....	.34	.53	.01	.01	.01	34.11	34.85	33.40	29.48	25.40	30.73	Gold (Million Fine Troy Ounces)	1ad
	.455	.455	.455	.455	.429	.429	.429	.429	.429	I.343	.343	.343	.343	.305	.305	Gold (National Valuation)	1an d
	19.22	19.22	19.22	19.22	18.12	18.12	18.11	18.11	18.11	I16.79	19.38	19.20	19.25	14.90	16.90	Deposit Money Banks: Assets	7a. d
	104,828	114,204	109,711	103,235	101,708	130,949	171,691	226,519	232,010	280,189	355,119	358,711	376,499	....	....	*of which:* Claims on Nonbanks	7ad d
	53,647	60,208	57,645	54,462	53,138	64,099	79,920	99,079	98,638	115,203	143,242	148,079	158,909	....	....	Deposit Money Banks: Liabilities	7b. d
	98,454	106,698	102,572	94,967	93,349	117,205	151,901	197,771	199,238	241,426	308,087	309,656	320,644	....	....	*of which:* Liab. to Nonbanks	7bd d
	20,967	24,430	23,626	22,551	23,840	31,654	47,378	66,955	77,946	109,603	151,711	160,306	171,552	....	....		
Monetary Authorities																	
End of Period																Foreign Assets	11
	....	....	....	2.4	3.2	3.4	5.3	5.4	5.7	7.1	7.0	7.1	7.0	8.3	8.5	Claims on Central Government	12a
	....	....	....	—	—	2.3	2.5	2.8	3.0	3.0	3.5	3.4	3.2	5.5	5.5	Claims on Deposit Money Banks	12e
	....	....	....	.5	.5	.3	.3	.3	.3	.2	.2	.3	.3	.1	.1	Reserve Money	14
	....	....	....	—	—	2.3	2.5	2.8	3.0	3.0	3.5	3.4	3.2	5.5	5.5	Foreign Liabilities	16c
	....	....	....	—	—	—	—	—	—	1.2	1.1	1.0	.9	.9	1.0	Central Government Deposits	16d
	....	....	....	1.2	.7	.7	2.7	2.7	2.7	2.7	2.7	2.8	2.9	3.2	3.4	Capital Accounts	17a
	....	....	....	1.7	2.5	2.5	2.4	2.4	2.6	2.8	2.8	3.1	3.3	4.1	4.2	Other Items (Net)	17r
	....	....	....	.1	.6	.4	.5	.6	.7	.6	.5	.6	.2	.2	.1		
Deposit Money Banks																	
End of Period																Foreign Assets	21
	3,304.5	4,392.3	5,147.7	5,744.0	6,415.8	6,594.6	6,938.0	7,509.7	8,664.4	10,019.5	11,002.5	11,216.9	12,492.3	....	....	Claims on Private Sector	22d
	160.8	180.4	202.5	204.5	218.4	224.9	259.7	280.2	323.6	372.4	446.4	476.4	578.5	....	....	Demand Deposits	24
	25.1	27.1	29.6	34.9	38.9	38.4	45.1	60.9	83.5	96.6	106.9	98.1	101.8			Time and Savings Deposits	25
	191.0	222.6	246.1	272.2	300.4	402.5	470.3	604.3	838.4	930.4	1,075.0	1,052.7	1,384.6			Foreign Liabilities	26c
	3,103.6	4,103.6	4,812.7	5,284.0	5,888.4	5,902.4	6,138.3	6,556.6	7,440.6	8,633.4	9,545.3	9,682.9	10,639.0			Capital Accounts	27a
	147.4	190.0	252.7	315.8	388.7	451.7	513.2	545.9	599.0	636.0	686.7	750.2	860.3			Other Items (Net)	27r
	−1.7	29.5	9.1	41.6	17.7	24.5	30.8	22.2	26.5	95.6	35.1	109.5	85.2				
	.7	.8	.8	.8	.8	3.1	3.0	3.2	3.3	3.3	3.8	3.7	3.5			Luxembourg Notes and Coins	24a
	3.2	3.5	3.6	3.9	4.5	4.7	4.7	5.7	6.5	7.3	8.1	7.3	8.9			Post Office: Checking Deposits	24.. i
Money (National Definitions)																	
End of Period																Money	34n
	38.1	40.2	41.1	45.8	47.5	44.9	49.2	54.3	58.6	66.7	72.8	80.4	81.8	....	....	Quasi-Money	35n
	101.7	114.5	113.5	122.8	122.8	152.8	170.9	200.1	235.9	286.1	338.6	378.1	406.8	....	....	Broad Money	38n
	139.8	154.7	154.6	168.6	170.3	197.7	220.1	254.4	294.5	352.8	411.4	458.5	488.6	....	....		
Interest Rates																	
Percent Per Annum																Deposit Rate	60l
	6.50	6.75	7.50	7.17	7.00	6.50	5.50	4.94	4.46	5.04	6.00	6.00	6.00	5.33	5.00	Lending Rate	60p
	9.25	9.63	10.00	9.38	9.25	8.75	7.75	7.19	6.71	7.25	8.23	8.25	8.75	7.65	6.58	Government Bond Yield	61
	7.50	8.68	10.50	9.83	10.22	9.53	8.67	7.96	7.13	7.68	8.51	8.15	7.90	6.93	6.38		
Prices, Production, Employment																	
Period Averages																Share Prices	62
	43.1	37.5	33.5	37.7	44.1	65.4	99.0	I90.2	89.9	108.7	100.0	95.5	90.7	127.5	179.7	Producer Prices in Industry	63a
	67.7	75.0	88.4	92.7	98.5	101.4	I98.8	92.4	94.8	102.1	100.0	97.4	94.8	93.6	94.9	Consumer Prices	64
	65.0	70.2	76.8	83.4	I88.1	91.7	92.0	91.9	93.3	96.4	I100.0	103.1	106.4	110.2	112.6	Industrial Production	66..b
	66.1	62.3	62.9	66.3	75.1	80.2	82.4	82.8	92.6	99.7	100.0	99.6	98.8	96.1	....	Steel Production	66rr
	I104.1	88.2	83.3	80.2	94.0	102.4	97.5	89.7	I101.2	97.6	100.0	95.9	89.6	....	....	Industrial Empl. (1985=100)	67
	104.3	103.7	102.5	100.2	99.0	100.0	102.0	103.2	107.1	110.0	114.4	109.5	....	....	....	Empl. in Steel Ind.(1985=100)	67rr
	144.8	128.3	129.7	115.6	104.9	100.0	99.0	91.7	79.4	74.4	....	63.7	....	....	....		
International Transactions																	
Billions of Francs																Exports	70
	87.88	88.56	101.90	111.47	145.56	168.07	....	....	....	212.81	210.70	214.15	208.13	....	....	Imports	71
	105.62	111.33	124.64	136.22	160.06	186.70	....	....	....	244.70	253.83	274.68	265.18	....	....		

Luxembourg

137

		1965	1966	1967	1968	1969	1970	1971	1972	1973	1974	1975	1976	1977	1978	1979
Government Finance																*Millions of Francs:*
Deficit (-) or Surplus	80	....	....	....	....	....	....	....	....	2,125	4,067	1,008	314	706	3,801	−294
Revenue	81	....	....	....	....	....	....	....	....	27,374	34,187	38,341	44,671	50,421	56,060	58,148
Grants Received	81z	....	....	....	....	....	....	....	....	140	170	222	115	111	89	102
Expenditure	82	....	....	....	....	....	....	....	....	25,077	29,439	36,761	43,137	47,958	51,058	56,921
Lending Minus Repayments	83	....	....	....	....	....	....	....	....	312	851	794	1,335	1,868	1,290	1,623
Adjustment for Complem. Period	80x	....	....	....	....	....	....	....	....	—	—	—	—	—	—	—
Financing																
Total Financing	84	....	....	....	....	....	....	....	....	−2,125	−4,067	−1,008	−314	−706	−3,801	294
Net Borrowing: Domestic	84a	....	....	....	....	....	....	....	....	....	....	....	....	....	....	....
Foreign	85a	....	....	....	....	....	....	....	....	....	....	....	....	....	....	....
Use of Cash Balances	87	....	....	....	....	....	....	....	....	....	....	....	....	....	....	....
Debt: Domestic	88a	....	....	....	....	....	....	....	....	....	8,496	8,007	8,571	8,718	8,798	8,322
Foreign	89a	....	....	....	....	....	....	....	....	....	763	677	609	522	442	375
National Accounts																*Billions of Francs*
Exports of Goods & Services	90c	27.6	27.7	28.5	32.0	39.3	48.9	49.4	52.4	68.6	96.1	80.2	87.9	89.1	94.0	111.0
Government Consumption	91f	3.8	4.2	4.5	4.9	5.2	5.8	6.6	7.4	8.7	10.7	13.0	14.7	16.3	17.6	19.5
Gross Fixed Capital Formation	93e	9.8	9.8	8.9	9.0	10.5	12.7	15.9	17.6	21.0	23.0	24.1	24.9	25.7	27.0	29.8
Increase/Decrease(-) in Stocks	93i	.6	.5	−1.3	−.9	−.6	1.5	.7	.4	.2	−3.2	−4.2	−2.1	−4.8	1.0	−2.8
Private Consumption	96f	20.6	21.6	22.0	23.6	25.3	27.8	30.7	33.9	37.6	43.2	50.1	56.5	61.1	65.0	70.6
Imports of Goods & Services	98c	−27.2	−26.8	−25.3	−27.6	−31.7	−41.7	−47.3	−48.5	−58.8	−76.2	−76.4	−82.1	−84.8	−92.3	−106.0
Gross Domestic Product = GDP	99b	35.2	37.0	37.3	41.0	47.9	55.0	56.1	63.2	76.8	93.6	86.7	99.8	102.6	112.2	122.1
Net Factor Inc/Pmts(-) Abroad	98.n	−.2	.4	1.8	2.1	−.7	1.9	2.2	3.4	3.5	5.7	11.9	16.7	19.4	21.3	23.2
Gross National Product = GNP	99a	35.0	37.4	39.1	43.0	49.1	57.0	58.3	66.6	80.3	99.3	98.6	116.5	122.0	133.5	145.3
Nat'l Income, Market Prices	99e	29.8	31.3	31.1	33.8	39.4	49.1	49.7	57.8	69.1	87.2	86.2	104.2	110.0	120.7	130.7
Gross Dom. Prod. 1990 Prices	99b.*p*	133.7	135.2	136.0	142.3	158.0	I 163.8	168.2	179.3	194.2	202.4	189.1	193.9	196.9	204.9	209.5
GDP Deflator (1990=100)	99bi *p*	26.4	27.4	27.4	28.8	30.3	33.6	33.3	35.3	39.6	46.3	45.9	51.5	52.1	54.8	58.3
																Millions:
Population	99z	.33	.33	.34	.34	.34	.34	.34	.35	.35	.36	.36	.36	.36	.36	.36

International Liquidity: ℐ Beginning in March 1989, data on gold holdings exclude the gold deposits made with the European Monetary Institute (EMI); the holdings of European currency units (ECUs) issued by the EMI against these gold deposits are included in *line 1d.d*.

Deposit Money Banks: ℐ *Line 24..i* refers to the deposits of the government and private sectors through July 1974 and to private sector deposits only thereafter. The bulk of these deposits is maintained with the Caisse d'Epargne de l'Etat for account of the government.

Interest Rates: *Government Bond Yield:* ℐ Weighted average yield to final maturity of all government bonds quoted in the Luxembourg Stock Exchange. Before July 1977, data referred to the average weighted yield to average maturity as then calculated by the Luxembourg stock exchange.

Luxembourg

	1980	1981	1982	1983	1984	1985	1986	1987	1988	1989	1990	1991	1992	1993	1994		
	Year Ending December 31															**Government Finance**	
	1,673	−3,016	1,190	−3,538	10,279	21,504	16,390	8,081	7,610	9,209	16,913	−37,189	....	....	....	Deficit (−) or Surplus	80
	66,251	72,070	79,285	90,245	96,694	104,637	109,616	113,922	120,852	135,738	149,854	165,523	179,533	....	....	Revenue	81
	101	161	314	144	366	543	417	253	264	1,403	954	613	525	....	....	Grants Received	81z
	64,818	70,985	81,389	88,971	92,095	93,197	97,962	106,519	115,421	119,200	139,122	153,408	175,510	....	....	Expenditure	82
	333	1,803	601	4,176	97	3,032	3,465	1,044	733	3,534	3,022	8,514	1,385	....	....	Lending Minus Repayments	83
	472	−2,459	3,581	−780	5,411	12,553	7,784	1,469	2,648	−5,198	8,249	−41,403	....	....	....	Adjustment for Complem. Period	80x
																Financing	
	−1,673	3,016	−1,190	3,538	−10,279	−21,504	−16,390	−8,081	−7,610	−9,209	−16,913	37,189	....	....	....	Total Financing	84
	−2,238	−1,043	−739	−121	−1,761	−3,868	−6,488	−5,619	−6,855	−8,024	−8,473	1,922	....	....	....	Net Borrowing: Domestic	84a
	−82	−87	−98	−97	661	−34	−70	−1,591	−968	−534	−770	−329	....	....	....	Foreign	85a
	647	4,146	−353	3,756	−9,179	−17,602	−9,832	−871	213	−651	−7,670	35,596	....	....	....	Use of Cash Balances	87
	8,155	9,340	10,774	12,834	14,089	14,110	15,469	14,739	13,035	11,774	9,473	8,190	12,181	....	....	Debt: Domestic	88a
	294	212	129	62	750	750	4,997	3,316	2,402	1,951	1,289	1,053	902	....	....	Foreign	89a
	Billions of Francs															**National Accounts**	
	117.7	122.8	141.3	157.6	195.8	222.9	224.8	223.8	249.2	285.9	291.0	300.6	302.4	....	....	Exports of Goods & Services	90c
	22.2	24.7	26.1	27.6	29.8	32.3	35.0	38.2	40.3	43.6	49.3	54.4	58.0	....	....	Government Consumption	91f
	36.0	36.0	39.7	37.1	38.8	36.3	49.3	58.1	67.6	76.6	80.7	92.4	94.1	....	....	Gross Fixed Capital Formation	93e
	−2.5	−1.3	−.2	5.4	9.1	5.3	3.1	−1.7	.1	1.4	4.2	7.7	8.4	....	....	Increase/Decrease(−) in Stocks	93i
	78.1	86.3	95.8	104.2	112.6	120.5	126.2	134.7	143.7	154.6	166.5	182.6	191.0	....	....	Private Consumption	96f
	−118.5	−126.8	−143.8	−157.2	−192.3	−212.1	−215.0	−225.7	−250.7	−279.3	−291.3	−318.9	−314.6	....	....	Imports of Goods & Services	98c
	132.9	141.7	158.8	174.7	193.7	205.3	223.3	227.5	250.2	282.8	300.4	318.8	339.2	....	....	Gross Domestic Product = GDP	99b
	28.0	36.6	60.2	72.2	76.7	83.5	82.3	68.2	85.7	96.0	109.1	114.3	....	....	....	Net Factor Inc/Pmts(−) Abroad	98.n
	160.9	178.3	218.9	246.9	270.4	288.8	305.6	304.7	336.0	378.8	409.5	433.1	....	....	....	Gross National Product = GNP	99a
	145.0	161.3	200.8	226.7	247.8	264.8	280.5	278.3	308.2	348.5	377.8	399.1	....	....	....	Nat'l Income, Market Prices	99e
	211.5	210.3	212.7	219.1	232.6	239.4	250.8	258.2	273.0	291.1	300.4	309.6	315.3	....	....	Gross Dom. Prod. 1990 Prices	99b.p
	62.9	67.4	74.7	79.7	83.3	85.7	89.0	88.1	91.7	97.1	100.0	103.0	107.6	....	....	GDP Deflator (1990=100)	99bi p
	Midyear Estimates																
	.36	.37	.37	.37	.37	.37	.37	.37	.37	.38	.38	.39	.39	I.40	.40	**Population**	99z

Madagascar

674

		1965	1966	1967	1968	1969	1970	1971	1972	1973	1974	1975	1976	1977	1978	1979
Exchange Rates															*Francs per SDR:*	
Official Rate	aa	245.1	247.6	245.4	247.4	277.9	276.0	283.6	278.0	284.0	272.1	262.5	288.7	285.8	272.3	264.8
															Francs per US Dollar:	
Official Rate	ae	245.1	247.6	245.4	247.4	277.9	276.0	261.2	256.1	235.4	222.2	224.3	248.5	235.2	209.0	201.0
Official Rate	rf	246.9	246.9	246.9	246.9	259.7	277.7	276.9	252.0	222.9	240.7	214.3	238.9	245.7	225.7	212.7
Fund Position															*Millions of SDRs:*	
Quota	2f. s	15.0	19.0	19.0	19.0	19.0	26.0	26.0	26.0	26.0	26.0	26.0	26.0	26.0	34.0	34.0
SDRs	1b. s	—	—	—	—	—	3.2	6.0	8.7	8.7	.2	.9	1.9	6.9	8.7	—
Reserve Position in the Fund	1c. s	2.3	3.3	3.3	3.3	3.3	5.0	5.0	5.0	5.0	—	—	—	—	—	—
Total Fund Cred.&Loans Outstg.	2tl	—	—	—	—	—	—	—	—	—	3.5	14.3	14.3	15.7	24.2	20.7
International Liquidity											*Millions of US Dollars Unless Otherwise Indicated:*					
Total Reserves minus Gold	1l. d	49.9	51.5	42.9	30.6	19.4	37.1	46.3	52.2	67.9	49.4	35.6	42.2	68.9	59.2	5.0
SDRs	1b. d	—	—	—	—	—	3.2	6.5	9.5	10.5	.2	1.1	2.2	8.3	11.3	—
Reserve Position in the Fund	1c. d	2.3	3.3	3.3	3.3	3.3	5.0	5.5	5.5	6.1	—	—	—	—	—	—
Foreign Exchange	1d. d	47.6	48.2	39.6	27.3	16.1	28.9	34.4	37.3	51.3	49.2	34.5	40.0	60.6	47.9	5.0
Deposit Money Banks: Assets	7a. d	4.5	6.0	10.3	11.0	12.4	21.7	13.2	20.0	24.1	46.3	38.9	29.6	44.5	45.6	46.7
Liabilities	7b. d	3.2	4.1	6.2	6.5	6.9	10.2	8.7	8.8	11.2	6.5	7.1	4.1	5.7	6.2	67.4
Monetary Authorities															*Billions of Francs:*	
Foreign Assets	11	14.5	15.0	13.5	10.7	8.5	13.4	14.9	16.8	19.0	13.4	9.6	12.5	16.3	12.0	ɪ.3
Claims on Central Government	12a	-2.2	-2.3	-2.9	-3.1	-.1	-3.1	-3.0	-1.8	-.7	10.2	17.1	26.7	46.9	82.8	ɪ139.5
Claims on Nonfin.Pub.Enterprises	12c															9.8
Claims on Deposit Money Banks	12e	12.5	13.6	15.5	14.4	14.0	17.2	19.5	18.0	14.5	19.1	18.9	12.0	12.4	8.3	ɪ9.0
Reserve Money	14	15.8	16.8	18.3	18.4	19.2	22.9	22.6	26.0	27.4	32.4	34.7	39.5	44.3	59.0	ɪ57.4
of which: Currency Outside DMBs	14a	15.6	16.5	18.1	18.1	19.0	22.5	22.2	25.4	27.0	31.9	34.0	35.5	42.1	48.2	ɪ53.5
Foreign Liabilities	16c	—	—	—	—	—	—	—	—	.4	.1	3.2	4.3	4.0	9.7	8.7 ɪ53.9
Central Government Deposits	16d	8.0	8.4	6.5	2.5	1.4	2.6	5.1	2.2	.5	2.2	2.1	2.1	17.7	32.6	ɪ43.1
Counterpart Funds	16e	....	....	....	....	....	....	....	....	....	....	....	....	....	....	....
Capital Accounts	17a	.8	1.0	1.1	1.3	1.3	2.4	3.4	4.2	5.0	6.0	5.8	6.0	5.7	5.3	ɪ6.2
Other Items (Net)	17r	8.2	8.5	6.6	2.4	1.8	2.3	5.4	2.5	.1	1.1	.8	1.7	15.9	30.1	ɪ-2.1
Deposit Money Banks															*Billions of Francs:*	
Reserves	20	.2	.3	.2	.4	.2	.3	.3	.6	.4	.7	.6	2.0	2.7	10.8	ɪ3.8
Foreign Assets	21	1.1	1.5	2.5	2.7	3.5	6.0	3.4	5.1	5.6	10.3	8.6	7.4	10.5	9.5	ɪ9.4
Claims on Central Government	22a	1.9	2.4	2.2	2.0	1.7	2.6	3.4	5.4	5.7	8.5	9.7	9.7	9.9	10.0	ɪ13.2
Claims on Private Sector	22d	27.9	31.2	36.7	39.1	41.3	48.8	55.0	55.7	55.8	65.6	67.0	70.9	86.5	91.0	ɪ120.3
Demand Deposits	24	11.7	13.3	14.7	16.9	18.5	19.5	20.3	23.5	26.3	31.7	30.5	39.6	51.8	56.0	ɪ70.7
Time Deposits	25	1.6	2.4	4.2	4.3	6.2	9.0	11.6	12.1	10.7	14.2	14.4	17.4	16.5	23.5	ɪ16.4
Bonds	26ab	....	....	2.2	2.8	3.4	4.8	5.4	5.4	5.1	11.1	11.0	—	—	—	14.6
Foreign Liabilities	26c	.8	1.0	1.5	1.6	1.9	2.8	2.2	2.2	2.6	1.5	1.6	1.0	1.3	1.3	ɪ10.6
Long-Term Foreign Liabilities	26cl															2.9
Central Government Deposits	26d	1.6	1.8	3.7	4.8	4.3	5.0	4.1	4.7	8.0	10.5	11.5	13.4	14.3	14.7	ɪ11.8
Central Govt. Lending Funds	26f															3.8
Credit from Monetary Authorities	26g	9.9	10.8	ɪ12.3	12.1	10.2	11.9	13.1	11.2	10.5	11.0	11.1	—	—	—	9.0
Capital Accounts	27a	2.0	2.1	2.3	2.5	2.7	3.1	3.3	3.7	3.8	5.2	5.4	5.7	12.5	13.5	ɪ15.4
Other Items (Net)	27r	13.5	14.7	15.3	14.0	13.1	18.3	20.5	20.6	16.1	21.9	22.6	12.8	13.2	12.4	ɪ-8.5
Treasury Claims: Private Sector	22d. i	1.9	2.1	2.2	2.5	3.9	4.1	4.7	3.8	3.9	4.4	5.5	5.3	4.9	5.1	4.7
Post Office: Checking Deposits	24.. i	1.9	1.8	2.0	2.1	2.0	2.0	2.0	2.0	2.2	1.9	2.1	2.2	2.4	3.0	3.9
Treasury: Checking Deposits	24.. r	1.6	1.1	1.7	2.4	2.1	2.1	2.4	2.6	1.8	2.5	2.8	2.4	3.8	5.7	10.1ᵉ
Monetary Survey															*Billions of Francs:*	
Foreign Assets (Net)	31n	14.9	15.4	14.5	11.8	10.0	16.6	16.0	19.3	21.8	19.0	12.2	14.8	15.7	11.5	ɪ-54.9
Domestic Credit	32	21.5	24.0	29.6	35.1	41.2	44.9	50.6	56.8	56.3	76.0	85.1	96.4	117.4	145.2	ɪ227.8
Claims on Central Govt. (Net)	32an	-8.4	-9.3	-9.3	-6.5	-3.9	-7.9	-9.1	-2.7	-3.5	6.0	12.6	20.2	26.1	49.1	ɪ97.8
Claims on Private Sector	32d	29.9	33.3	38.9	41.6	45.1	52.8	59.7	59.5	59.8	70.0	72.5	76.2	91.3	96.1	ɪ130.1
Money	34	30.8	32.8	36.5	39.4	41.5	46.2	47.0	53.3	57.3	67.9	69.4	79.7	100.0	112.8	ɪ124.3
Quasi-Money	35	1.6	2.4	4.2	4.3	6.2	9.0	11.6	12.1	10.7	14.2	14.4	17.4	16.5	23.5	ɪ16.4
Bonds	36ab	....	....	2.2	2.8	3.4	4.8	5.4	5.4	5.1	11.1	11.0	—	—	—	14.6
Long-Term Foreign Liabilities	36cl	....	....	....	....	....	....	....	....	....	....	....	....	....	....	2.9
Other Items (Net)	37r	4.0	4.3	4.9	5.2	3.7	6.4	7.8	11.4	10.1	12.7	13.6	14.2	17.9	24.0	ɪ14.8
Money plus Quasi-Money	35l	32.4	35.2	40.7	43.6	47.7	55.2	58.6	65.4	68.0	82.2	83.7	97.1	116.4	136.3	ɪ140.7
Liquid Liabilities	55l	33.7	36.5	42.1	45.3	49.5	57.1	60.6	67.5	70.2	85.0	86.7	100.2	122.4	....	....
Interest Rates															*Percent Per Annum*	
Discount Rate (End of Period)	60	....	....	....	....	5.50	5.50	5.50	5.50	5.50	5.50	5.50	5.50	5.50	5.50	5.50
Prices															*Index Numbers (1990=100):*	
Consumer Prices	64	7.2	7.5	7.5	7.6	7.9	8.1	8.6	9.0	9.6	11.7	12.7	13.3	13.7	14.6	16.7

Madagascar

674

	1980	1981	1982	1983	1984	1985	1986	1987	1988	1989	1990	1991	1992	1993	1994		
Exchange Rates																	
End of Period	288.0	334.5	405.6	515.3	645.0	698.4	941.6	1,751.0	2,054.1	2,014.0	2,085.4	2,621.5	2,626.5	2,695.8	5,651.2	Official Rate	aa
End of Period (ae) Period Average (rf)	225.8	287.4	367.7	492.2	658.0	635.8	769.8	1,234.3	1,526.4	1,532.5	1,465.8	1,832.7	1,910.2	1,962.7	3,871.1	Official Rate	ae
	211.3	271.7	349.7	430.4	576.6	662.5	676.3	1,069.2	1,407.1	1,603.4	1,494.1	1,835.4	1,864.0	1,913.8	3,067.3	Official Rate	rf
Fund Position																	
End of Period	51.0	51.0	51.0	66.4	66.4	66.4	66.4	66.4	66.4	66.4	66.4	66.4	90.4	90.4	90.4	Quota	2f. s
	—	.3	1.1	.1	1.5	—	—	.1	.1	.1	.1	—	—	.1	—	SDRs	1b. s
	—	.3	1.2	—	—	—	—	—	—	—	—	—	—	—	—	Reserve Position in the Fund	1c. s
	68.2	100.2	152.0	158.1	173.8	167.6	166.0	167.7	141.4	125.8	101.0	88.7	77.1	67.0	58.9	Total Fund Cred.&Loans Outstg.	2tl
International Liquidity																	
End of Period	9.1	26.5	20.0	29.2	58.9	48.4	114.5	185.2	223.7	245.3	92.1	88.9	....	....	71.6	Total Reserves minus Gold	1l. d
	—	.3	1.3	.1	1.5	—	—	.1	.1	.1	.2	.1	—	.1	—	SDRs	1b. d
	—	.4	1.3	—	—	—	—	—	—	—	—	—	—	—	—	Reserve Position in the Fund	1c. d
	9.1	25.8	17.4	29.1	57.4	48.4	114.5	185.1	223.6	245.2	91.9	88.8	....	....	71.6	Foreign Exchange	1d. d
	75.3	46.0	45.1	31.5	44.6	46.9	52.0	58.6	61.6	79.5	93.0	97.0	102.8	126.7	157.6	Deposit Money Banks: Assets	7a. d
	111.5	103.6	68.8	42.5	33.5	27.8	31.3	21.0	22.7	20.8	48.3	26.6	22.9	22.2	37.0	Liabilities	7b. d
Monetary Authorities																	
End of Period	4.0	6.7	10.0	17.4	47.7	31.5	87.8	236.7	342.4	379.0	136.3	163.0	159.8	156.8	276.2	Foreign Assets	11
	215.1	278.8	361.7	460.1	572.2	664.1	802.6	1,083.7	1,251.9	1,310.2	1,275.8	1,265.6	1,246.9	1,252.9	1,412.3	Claims on Central Government	12a
	8.6	8.6	8.3	26.9	35.9	32.4	29.7	32.7	26.7	26.6	21.2	22.2	9.3	8.1	7.3	Claims on Nonfin.Pub.Enterprises	12c
	2.3	1.5	—	8.2	8.9	4.8	.2	5.4	10.6	11.9	127.5	84.1	46.4	49.5	134.7	Claims on Deposit Money Banks	12e
	77.5	104.0	102.8	97.8	106.9	111.4	189.8	229.1	237.6	327.5	296.6	460.6	556.5	519.9	893.9	Reserve Money	14
	70.2	83.1	90.4	75.8	89.9	96.2	113.2	140.3	171.2	216.6	214.9	287.3	317.2	378.7	614.5	of which: Currency Outside DMBs	14a
	117.0	161.9	215.3	454.5	671.3	752.3	1,031.0	2,008.0	2,363.4	2,465.4	2,404.4	3,100.2	452.1	378.8	719.5	Foreign Liabilities	16c
	31.3	42.9	82.4	116.2	169.3	228.5	307.3	438.3	599.1	784.1	795.7	690.6	327.3	389.7	283.4	Central Government Deposits	16d
	.2	.6	1.3	1.5	.3	.4	.1	.1	.1	.1	.1	.1	—	—	—	Counterpart Funds	16e
	7.2	8.2	8.2	8.2	8.2	9.2	9.2	9.2	9.2	9.2	9.2	9.2	42.7	42.2	77.3	Capital Accounts	17a
	−3.2	−21.9	−29.9	−165.5	−291.2	−369.2	−617.2	−1,326.3	−1,577.9	−1,858.7	−1,945.2	−2,725.8	83.8	136.7	−143.7	Other Items (Net)	17r
Deposit Money Banks																	
End of Period	7.3	20.5	12.0	20.8	14.8	12.3	76.5	88.8	66.3	110.8	80.9	173.3	239.2	141.1	279.4	Reserves	20
	17.0	13.2	16.6	15.5	29.4	29.8	40.1	72.3	94.1	121.8	136.3	177.9	196.3	248.6	610.3	Foreign Assets	21
	12.4	17.0	16.8	9.0	9.4	9.8	10.7	10.7	15.0	78.6	61.1	25.9	19.0	220.1	250.6	Claims on Central Government	22a
	155.1	171.9	208.1	245.6	303.0	362.7	424.7	499.4	524.5	582.2	757.2	851.7	918.5	1,061.6	1,338.5	Claims on Private Sector	22d
	81.1	110.4	117.3	116.7	149.7	142.3	176.3	231.5	283.7	381.7	358.7	465.3	598.1	645.7	986.8	Demand Deposits	24
	18.3	16.4	20.9	14.3	16.3	51.0	77.7	63.2	77.6	113.7	169.5	222.8	277.1	456.8	658.2	Time Deposits	25
	17.7	21.0	27.8	42.9	46.0	52.8	61.1	71.4	80.0	89.2	59.7	37.3	36.5	39.7	42.6	Bonds	26ab
	14.0	15.1	9.3	6.4	10.3	9.6	18.4	18.6	29.8	28.5	69.7	47.6	37.4	37.4	129.2	Foreign Liabilities	26c
	11.1	14.7	16.0	14.5	11.7	8.1	5.7	7.3	4.9	3.4	1.1	1.1	6.3	6.3	13.9	Long-Term Foreign Liabilities	26cl
	19.2	12.2	15.0	18.1	24.0	28.7	33.4	45.3	43.8	69.4	111.5	125.4	137.9	155.5	141.3	Central Government Deposits	26d
	4.7	5.3	5.1	6.9	8.8	9.2	11.1	16.3	18.6	19.6	1.3	1.2	1.2	1.1	1.4	Central Govt. Lending Funds	26f
	2.3	1.5	—	8.2	8.9	4.8	.2	5.4	10.6	11.9	127.5	84.1	46.4	49.5	134.7	Credit from Monetary Authorities	26g
	23.7	27.4	33.3	47.0	64.1	86.6	131.3	152.1	144.9	149.5	174.1	198.0	226.9	106.6	104.7	Capital Accounts	27a
	−.5	−1.4	8.9	16.1	16.6	21.5	36.8	60.0	6.0	26.6	−37.5	46.1	5.2	173.1	266.0	Other Items (Net)	27r
	5.6	....	....	....	....	....	3.5	5.9	6.8	8.3	11.8	5.6	9.2	10.0	10.2	Treasury Claims: Private Sector	22d. i
	3.8	....	....	....	....	....	4.8	5.1	5.0	5.0	5.2	5.7	5.7	5.3	4.5	Post Office: Checking Deposits	24.. i
	....	....	....	....	....	....	9.7	9.7	9.7	9.7	9.7	9.7	9.7	9.7	9.7	Treasury: Checking Deposits	24.. r
Monetary Survey																	
End of Period	−110.0	−157.1	−198.0	−427.9	−604.6	−700.8	−921.5	−1,717.6	−1,956.7	−1,993.1	−2,201.5	−2,807.1	−133.5	−10.7	37.8	Foreign Assets (Net)	31n
	340.6	421.1	497.6	607.5	727.1	811.8	927.0	1,142.7	1,175.2	1,144.1	1,208.2	1,349.5	1,728.4	1,997.5	2,584.0	Domestic Credit	32
	176.9	240.6	281.1	334.9	388.3	416.7	472.6	610.7	624.0	535.3	429.7	475.6	800.6	927.8	1,238.2	Claims on Central Govt. (Net)	32an
	163.7	180.5	216.5	272.6	338.8	395.1	454.4	532.1	551.2	608.8	778.4	873.9	927.8	1,069.7	1,345.8	Claims on Private Sector	32d
	151.3	193.8	208.0	192.7	239.9	238.6	289.6	371.8	455.0	598.3	574.5	752.6	915.3	1,024.4	1,601.3	Money	34
	18.3	16.4	20.9	15.4	18.2	53.7	77.7	63.2	77.6	113.7	169.5	222.8	277.1	456.8	658.2	Quasi-Money	35
	17.7	21.0	27.8	42.9	46.0	52.8	61.1	71.4	80.0	89.2	59.7	37.3	36.5	39.7	42.6	Bonds	36ab
	11.1	14.7	16.0	14.5	11.7	8.1	5.7	7.3	4.9	3.4	1.1	1.1	6.3	6.3	13.9	Long-Term Foreign Liabilities	36cl
	32.2	18.1	26.9	−86.0	−193.3	−242.2	−428.6	−1,088.6	−1,399.0	−1,653.6	−1,798.0	−2,471.2	359.8	459.6	305.7	Other Items (Net)	37r
	169.6	210.2	228.9	208.1	258.1	292.3	367.2	435.0	532.6	712.0	743.9	975.3	1,192.4	1,481.3	2,259.5	Money plus Quasi-Money	35l
	....	....	....	....	363.3	419.3	511.0	625.4	760.2	984.8	819.6	1,044.4	1,266.7	1,636.3	2,473.0	Liquid Liabilities	55l
Interest Rates																	
Percent Per Annum	5.50	8.00	12.50	13.00	13.00	11.50	11.50	11.50	11.50	....	....	....	....	....	....	Discount Rate (End of Period)	60
Prices																	
Period Averages	19.7	25.7	33.9	40.5	44.4	49.1	56.3	64.7	82.1	89.5	100.0	108.6	124.4	136.8	190.1	Consumer Prices	64

Madagascar
674

		1965	1966	1967	1968	1969	1970	1971	1972	1973	1974	1975	1976	1977	1978	1979
International Transactions																*Billions of Francs*
Exports	70	22.63	24.13	25.71	28.61	29.15	40.22	40.81	41.86	44.75	58.50	64.64	66.04	82.93	87.21	83.83
Imports, cif	71	34.16	35.97	35.89	42.02	47.20	47.35	59.26	51.75	45.16	67.26	78.05	68.43	85.22	99.63	135.32
Imports, fob	71.v	28.70	30.23	30.16	35.31	39.64	39.09	49.02	42.44	36.12	54.06	61.69	53.76	67.25	79.61	110.11
Balance of Payments																*Millions of US Dollars:*
Goods: Exports f.o.b.	78aa d	...	...	...	...	...	...	...	...	...	240	320	289	351	405	414
Goods: Imports f.o.b.	78ab d	...	...	...	...	...	...	...	...	...	−238	−332	−262	−312	−404	−662
Trade Balance	78ac d	...	...	...	...	...	...	...	...	...	2	−12	27	39	1	−249
Services: Credit	78ad d	...	...	...	...	...	...	...	...	...	40	62	41	35	35	74
Services: Debit	78ae d	...	...	...	...	...	...	...	...	...	−107	−148	−132	−136	−169	−267
Balance on Goods and Services	78af d	...	...	...	...	...	...	...	...	...	−65	−98	−63	−63	−133	−441
Income: Credit	78ag d	...	...	...	...	...	...	...	...	...	7	5	4	2	5	2
Income: Debit	78ah d	...	...	...	...	...	...	...	...	...	−25	−22	−21	−8	−12	−30
Balance on Goods, Serv., & Inc.	78ai d	...	...	...	...	...	...	...	...	...	−83	−115	−80	−68	−140	−469
Current Transfers, n.i.e.: Credit	78aj d	...	...	...	...	...	...	...	...	...	64	99	87	81	94	76
Current Transfers: Debit	78ak d	...	...	...	...	...	...	...	...	...	−20	−39	−34	−28	−33	−34
Current Account, n.i.e.	78al d	...	...	...	...	...	...	...	...	...	−40	−56	−28	−15	−79	−426
Capital Account, n.i.e.: Credit	78ba d	...	...	...	...	...	...	...	...	...	—	—	—	—	—	—
Capital Account: Debit	78bb d	...	...	...	...	...	...	...	...	...	—	—	—	−1	−1	−1
Capital Account, n.i.e.	78bc d	...	...	...	...	...	...	...	...	...	—	—	—	−1	−1	−1
Direct Investment Abroad	78bd d	...	...	...	...	...	...	...	...	...	—	—	—	—	—	—
Dir. Invest. in Rep. Econ., n.i.e.	78be d	...	...	...	...	...	...	...	...	...	14	5	1	−3	−4	−7
Portfolio Investment Assets	78bf d	...	...	...	...	...	...	...	...	...	—	—	—	—	—	—
Portfolio Investment Liab., n.i.e.	78bg d	...	...	...	...	...	...	...	...	...	—	—	—	—	—	—
Other Investment Assets	78bh d	...	...	...	...	...	...	...	...	...	−18	7	3	−15	3	—
Other Investment Liab., n.i.e.	78bi d	...	...	...	...	...	...	...	...	...	6	28	15	26	20	231
Financial Account, n.i.e.	78bj d	...	...	...	...	...	...	...	...	...	1	39	20	9	20	225
Net Errors and Omissions	78ca d	...	...	...	...	...	...	...	...	...	−3	−9	9	−8	49	71
Overall Balance	78cb d	...	...	...	...	...	...	...	...	...	−42	−26	1	−16	−11	−131
Reserves and Related Items	79da d	...	...	...	...	...	...	...	...	...	42	26	−1	16	11	131
Reserve Assets	79db d	...	...	...	...	...	...	...	...	...	29	20	−3	−8	19	60
Use of Fund Credit and Loans	79dc d	...	...	...	...	...	...	...	...	...	4	13	—	2	10	−5
Liabs.Constit.For.Auth.Reserves	79dd d	...	...	...	...	...	...	...	...	...	9	−8	2	22	−18	75
Exceptional Financing	79de d	...	...	...	...	...	...	...	...	...	—	—	—	—	—	—
Government Finance																*Billions of Francs:*
Deficit (−) or Surplus	80	−3.1	−3.5	−5.2	−6.9	−7.1	−6.4	...	Ⅰ−6.7	−7.3	−9.0	...	...	...	...	...
Revenue	81	34.7	36.4	38.8	43.3	47.6	51.3	...	Ⅰ48.7	54.2	58.2	...	...	...	129.9	168.4
Grants Received	81z	...	...	...	...	...	...	...	Ⅰ1.2	—	—	...	...	...	...	...
Expenditure	82	37.3	39.1	41.9	49.3	54.4	55.9	...	Ⅰ55.2	59.5	63.2	...	...	...	...	...
Lending Minus Repayments	83	.5	.8	2.1	.9	.3	1.8	...	Ⅰ1.3	2.1	4.1	...	...	...	...	...
Financing																
Domestic Financing	84	.8	−.9	3.0	4.1	3.4	1.6	...	Ⅰ5.0	3.3	5.7	...	...	...	...	...
Financing Abroad	85	2.2	4.4	2.2	2.8	3.6	4.8	...	Ⅰ1.8	4.0	3.4	...	...	...	...	...
Unclassified Financing	84x															
Debt: Domestic	88a	...	...	...	...	...	8.9	10.0	15.2	15.8	...	...	...	...	...	...
Foreign	89a	...	...	...	...	...	18.7	20.5	24.5	27.9	...	...	...	...	...	...
National Accounts																*Billions of Francs*
Exports of Goods & Services	90c	25.0	27.4	27.8	31.2	32.2	43.5	46.1	46.3	42.2	65.8	74.5	73.9	97.6	96.1	95.3
Government Consumption	91f	37.5	39.3	41.3	45.7	48.3	50.3	56.1	52.6	51.0	59.0	60.4	66.6	72.8	81.6	103.0
Gross Capital Formation	93	17.0	24.4	28.1	33.8	37.9	38.9	48.4	37.9	42.6	50.8	50.6	53.9	60.2	70.4	150.8
Gross Fixed Capital Formation	93e	16.0	22.4	25.4	29.8	33.6	36.4	42.7	36.0	39.7	47.0	49.4	54.1	58.0	64.8	...
Increase/Decrease(−) in Stocks	93i	1.0	2.0	2.7	4.0	4.3	2.5	4.7	1.9	5.8	6.8	2.2	1.8	2.2	5.0	...
Private Consumption	96f	122.5	129.6	135.8	144.3	156.4	169.6	181.4	191.7	206.7	277.7	301.1	305.2	343.1	360.6	444.3
Imports of Goods & Services	98c	−35.7	−39.1	−40.2	−46.7	−50.5	−52.5	−62.5	−55.4	−47.7	−83.4	−91.4	−81.7	−105.6	−122.1	−198.3
Gross Domestic Product	99b	166.2	181.6	192.9	208.3	224.3	249.4	268.5	273.1	297.6	372.9	395.2	419.9	468.1	486.6	595.1
Net Factor Inc/Pmts(−) Abroad	98.n	−3.9	−2.3	.3	.5	−2.7	−6.3	−6.6	−2.8	−1.9	−3.7	−3.2	−1.9	−.6	−.6	−.9
Gross Nat'l Expenditure = GNP	99a	162.3	179.3	193.2	208.7	221.6	243.1	261.9	270.3	295.7	369.2	392.0	418.0	467.5	486.0	594.2
Gross Dom. Prod. 1990 Prices	99b.p	3,143.9	3,207.9	3,384.5	3,615.8	3,748.6	3,897.0	3,989.2	3,861.1	3,783.0	3,906.4	4,022.0	3,861.1	3,990.8	3,886.1	4,267.3
GDP Deflator (1990=100)	99bi p	5.3	5.7	5.7	5.8	6.0	6.4	6.7	7.1	7.9	9.5	9.8	10.9	11.7	12.5	13.9
																Millions:
Population	99z	6.08	6.20	6.41	6.58	6.65	6.80	6.96	7.13	7.30	7.49	Ⅰ7.60	7.81	8.02	8.24	8.47

Monetary Authorities: Ⅰ Beginning with 1979, claims on public enterprises are separately identified.
Deposit Money Banks: Ⅰ Beginning with 1967, data are based on improved classification. Ⅰ Beginning with 1979, data are based on an improved classification; as a result, bonds, central government lending funds, and credit from the Central Bank are separately identified.
Monetary Survey: Ⅰ See notes to sections 10 and 20.
Government Finance: Ⅰ Beginning in 1972, data are as reported in the *Government Finance Statistics Yearbook* and cover the general budget, the *Caisse nationale de prevoyance sociale* (National Social Security Fund), and the *Office des anciens combattants* (Veterans' Office). Prior to 1972, data are as reported by the Central Bank of the Republic of Madagascar for publication in *IFS*. Ⅰ Beginning in 1988, data cover the general budget and extrabudgetary units excluding social security.

Madagascar
674

	1980	1981	1982	1983	1984	1985	1986	1987	1988	1989	1990	1991	1992	1993	1994		
Billions of Francs																**International Transactions**	
	84.78	85.74	107.64	113.39	192.33	181.63	212.74	353.98	385.10	514.85	476.68	559.07	516.82	499.00	849.96	Exports	70
	126.78	147.98	148.60	166.75	213.53	265.92	238.46	323.05	538.36	595.64	969.54	785.69	833.77	895.69	1,386.69	Imports, cif	71
	101.92	123.52	126.90	138.38	177.20	220.68	197.89	268.09	446.77	494.31	804.60	652.02	691.93	743.31	1,150.77	Imports, fob	71.v
Minus Sign Indicates Debit																**Balance of Payments**	
	436	332	327	310	337	291	323	327	284	321	319	338	328	....	....	Goods: Exports f.o.b.	78aa d
	−764	−511	−452	−378	−360	−336	−331	−315	−319	−320	−566	−440	−466	....	....	Goods: Imports f.o.b.	78ab d
	−328	−179	−124	−68	−23	−44	−8	11	−34	1	−248	−102	−138	....	....	Trade Balance	78ac d
	79	62	49	45	53	59	75	96	118	143	194	147	172	....	....	Services: Credit	78ad d
	−311	−224	−200	−172	−155	−167	−205	−226	−250	−229	−274	−239	−266	....	....	Services: Debit	78ae d
	−559	−341	−275	−195	−125	−153	−138	−119	−166	−86	−328	−194	−232	....	....	Balance on Goods and Services	78af d
	2	4	6	3	5	4	5	9	13	18	15	4	6	....	....	Income: Credit	78ag d
	−46	−92	−101	−121	−151	−133	−160	−184	−193	−208	−176	−178	−145	....	....	Income: Debit	78ah d
	−603	−430	−370	−313	−271	−282	−293	−294	−345	−275	−489	−367	−372	....	....	Balance on Goods, Serv., & Inc.	78ai d
	86	103	102	89	95	124	183	179	225	235	270	195	255	....	....	Current Transfers, n.i.e.: Credit	78aj d
	−39	−36	−31	−23	−18	−25	−32	−26	−30	−34	−36	−20	−22	....	....	Current Transfers: Debit	78ak d
	−556	−363	−299	−247	−193	−184	−143	−141	−150	−74	−255	−192	−139	....	....	Current Account, n.i.e.	78al d
	—	—	—	—	—	—	2	1	1	2	3	4	3	....	....	Capital Account, n.i.e.: Credit	78ba d
	—	—	—	—	—	—	—	—	—	—	—	—	—	....	....	Capital Account: Debit	78bb d
	—	—	—	—	—	—	2	1	1	2	3	4	3	....	....	Capital Account, n.i.e.	78bc d
	—	—	—	—	—	—	—	—	—	—	—	—	—	....	....	Direct Investment Abroad	78bd d
	—	—	—	—	—	—	—	—	—	13	22	14	21	....	....	Dir. Invest. in Rep. Econ., n.i.e.	78be d
	—	—	—	—	—	—	—	—	—	—	—	—	—	....	....	Portfolio Investment Assets	78bf d
	—	—	—	—	—	—	—	—	—	—	—	—	—	....	....	Portfolio Investment Liab., n.i.e.	78bg d
	7	−21	−2	8	10	42	27	37	9	−18	−7	−3	−11	....	....	Other Investment Assets	78bh d
	375	217	5	−29	−33	−36	−5	−48	−31	−50	−33	−53	−98	....	....	Other Investment Liab., n.i.e.	78bi d
	381	196	2	−21	−22	6	22	−11	−22	−56	−18	−42	−88	....	....	Financial Account, n.i.e.	78bj d
	−73	3	88	−1	13	10	4	−11	53	−46	−9	−4	−52	....	....	Net Errors and Omissions	78ca d
	−248	−165	−209	−269	−203	−167	−116	−163	−118	−174	−278	−235	−276	....	....	Overall Balance	78cb d
	248	165	209	269	203	167	116	163	118	174	278	235	276	....	....	Reserves and Related Items	79da d
	−100	−6	−10	13	−40	28	−59	−51	−42	−26	167	4	1	....	....	Reserve Assets	79db d
	63	38	56	7	16	−6	−2	3	−35	−20	−34	−16	−16	....	....	Use of Fund Credit and Loans	79dc d
	—	—	—	—	−1	—	−1	—	—	1	13	—	−4	−2	....	Liabs.Constit.For.Auth.Reserves	79dd d
	285	133	163	249	228	146	177	211	195	207	145	251	293	....	....	Exceptional Financing	79de d
Year Ending December 31																**Government Finance**	
	....	....	....	....	....	....	....	....	I−119.5	−163.3	−34.9	−272.4	....	....	....	Deficit (−) or Surplus	80
	133.0	....	....	....	....	....	....	....	I 449.1	460.8	547.0	429.2	....	....	....	Revenue	81
	....	....	....	....	....	....	....	....	I 24.5	55.8	66.8	38.2	....	....	....	Grants Received	81z
	....	....	....	....	....	....	....	....	I 593.1	679.9	648.7	739.8	....	....	....	Expenditure	82
	....	....	....	....	....	....	....	....	I —	....	....	....	....	....	....	Lending Minus Repayments	83
																Financing	
	....	....	....	....	....	....	....	....	I −14.1	−19.1	−54.0	60.6	....	....	....	Domestic Financing	84
	....	....	....	....	....	....	....	....	I 134.6	185.3	97.2	190.7	....	....	....	Financing Abroad	85
	....	....	....	....	....	....	....	....	I −1.0	−2.9	−8.3	21.1	....	....	....	Unclassified Financing	84x
	....	....	....	....	....	....	....	....	....	....	....	....	....	....	....	Debt: Domestic	88a
	....	....	....	....	....	....	....	....	....	....	....	....	....	....	....	Foreign	89a
Billions of Francs																**National Accounts**	
	96.8	96.4	125.7	139.7	223.1	220.5	263.4	453.0	559.8	720.9	730.2	846.4	929.9	987.9	1,894.6	Exports of Goods & Services	90c
	117.8	129.1	149.5	165.3	166.8	184.8	194.9	250.5	279.6	350.9	367.3	422.0	463.4	506.5	603.9	Government Consumption	91f
	162.4	142.5	133.0	160.7	182.4	217.7e	....	....	....	....	....	....	....	....	....	Gross Capital Formation	93
	157.6	148.3	129.4	160.7	146.1	161.8	199.2	277.2	456.9	536.3	781.4	401.5	631.9	738.5	1,009.4	Gross Fixed Capital Formation	93e
	4.8	−5.8	3.6	—	—	—	—	—	—	—	—	—	—	—	—	Increase/Decrease(−) in Stocks	93i
	526.1	604.6	799.0	973.4	1,429.4	1,684.4	1,856.4	2,330.1	2,869.2	3,254.8	3,960.6	4,529.1	4,973.0	5,798.0	8,245.0	Private Consumption	96f
	−213.3	−183.6	−211.1	−218.0	−270.3	−358.3	−310.1	−567.7	−728.8	−857.6	−1,235.6	−1,285.4	−1,405.1	−1,580.0	−2,684.0	Imports of Goods & Services	98c
	689.8	789.0	996.1	1,221.1	1,695.0	1,893.2	2,203.8	2,743.1	3,436.7	4,005.3	4,603.9	4,913.6	5,593.1	6,450.9	9,068.9	Gross Domestic Product	99b
	....	....	....	....	....	....	....	....	....	....	....	....	....	....	....	Net Factor Inc/Pmts(−) Abroad	98.n
	....	....	....	....	....	....	....	....	....	....	....	....	....	....	....	Gross Nat'l Expenditure = GNP	99a
	4,301.7	3,929.8	3,858.0	3,889.2	I 3,975.1	4,021.1	4,099.9	4,148.2	4,289.4	4,464.4	4,603.9	4,313.6	4,364.7	4,456.2	4,465.3	Gross Dom. Prod. 1990 Prices	99b.p
	16.0	20.1	25.8	31.4	42.6	47.1	53.8	66.1	80.1	89.7	100.0	113.9	128.1	144.8	203.1	GDP Deflator (1990=100)	99bi p
Midyear Estimates																	
	8.78	8.96	9.34	9.40	I 10.29	9.98	10.99	11.37	11.76	12.16	I 11.20	11.49	13.42	13.85	....	Population	99z

Malawi

		1965	1966	1967	1968	1969	1970	1971	1972	1973	1974	1975	1976	1977	1978	1979
Exchange Rates																Kwacha per SDR:
Official Rate	aa	.7143	.7143	.8333	.8333	.8333	.8333	.8334	.9280	1.0224	1.0291	1.0541	1.0541	1.0541	1.0541	1.0541
																Kwacha per US Dollar:
Official Rate	ae	.7143	.7143	.8333	.8333	.8333	.8333	.7676	.8547	.8475	.8405	.8998	.9074	.8678	.8091	.7996
Official Rate	rf	.7143	.7143	.7242	.8333	.8333	.8333	.8309	.8016	.8193	.8412	.8638	.9130	.9029	.8437	.8169
															Index Numbers	(1990=100):
Official Rate	ahx	381.5	381.5	375.0	327.0	327.0	327.0	205.3	339.7	332.9	323.9	315.7	298.6	301.8	323.1	333.6
Nominal Effective Exchange Rate	nec	....	....	....	....	....	....	....	....	....	....	....	....	....	....	146.3
Real Effective Exchange Rate	rec	....	....	....	....	....	....	....	....	....	....	....	....	....	....	105.5
Fund Position																Millions of SDRs:
Quota	2f.s	11.25	11.25	11.25	11.25	11.25	15.00	15.00	15.00	15.00	15.00	15.00	15.00	15.00	19.00	19.00
SDRs	1b.s	—	—	—	—	—	1.89	3.49	4.60	4.60	4.59	4.56	4.31	3.87	3.29	3.05
Reserve Position in the Fund	1c.s	1.38	1.38	1.38	1.39	1.40	1.40	1.41	1.90	3.75	3.75	—	—	—	—	—
Total Fund Cred.&Loans Outstg.	2tl	—	—	—	—	—	—	—	—	—	—	2.37	3.73	10.77	11.75	37.70
International Liquidity												Millions of US Dollars	Unless Otherwise	Indicated:		
Total Reserves minus Gold	1l.d	25.23	21.41	22.50	22.51	21.01	29.20	31.92	36.24	66.64	81.79	61.46	26.22	87.49	74.80	69.51
SDRs	1b.d	—	—	—	—	—	1.89	3.79	4.99	5.55	5.62	5.34	5.01	4.70	4.29	4.02
Reserve Position in the Fund	1c.d	1.38	1.38	1.38	1.39	1.40	1.40	1.53	2.06	4.52	4.59	—	—	—	—	—
Foreign Exchange	1d.d	23.85	20.03	21.12	21.12	19.61	25.91	26.60	29.18	56.57	71.58	56.12	21.21	82.79	70.51	65.49
Gold (Million Fine Troy Ounces)	1ad	....	....	....	....	....	....	....	....	....	....	....	....	.006	.010	.013
Gold (National Valuation)	1and	....	....	....	....	....	....	....	....	....	....	....	.27	.27	.44	.59
Monetary Authorities: Other Liab.	4..d	.01	.06	.11	.06	.02	.08	.14	.30	.18	.21	27.87	30.28	32.55	42.39	56.52
Deposit Money Banks: Assets	7a.d	2.25	2.77	1.33	1.08	.63	.80	2.46	3.44	4.07	2.58	5.80	6.27	6.53	13.36	8.30
of which: Claims on Nonbanks	7add	.45	.28	.09	.08	.07	.02	.12	.10	.87	.15	2.77	2.00	.63	1.48	3.13
Deposit Money Banks: Liabilities	7b.d	2.54	5.99	8.70	6.69	4.81	5.51	6.99	6.94	9.26	8.23	12.59	24.71	36.61	39.81	69.18
of which: Liab. to Nonbanks	7bdd	.99	1.25	1.32	1.50	1.20	1.68	2.27	2.47	7.65	4.78	7.61	10.15	14.28	21.94	14.76
Monetary Authorities																Millions of Kwacha:
Foreign Assets	11	18.03	15.31	18.75	18.76	17.50	24.34	24.50	28.43	56.47	72.59	55.30	23.79	76.18	60.87	51.57
Claims on Central Government	12a	.46	1.84	1.78	3.72	5.12	2.62	1.88	6.57	6.66	7.99	22.55	27.08	14.33	17.24	48.64
Claims on Official Entities	12bx	—	—	—	—	—	—	—	—	—	—	25.43	27.73	28.18	33.79	30.68
Reserve Money	14	11.28	12.57	13.62	13.60	15.20	16.57	18.71	21.68	45.42	59.16	52.50	34.58	63.65	41.70	38.55
of which: Currency Outside DMBs	14a	8.88	10.57	11.82	11.57	12.54	13.28	14.80	17.30	21.31	28.31	27.84	23.07	24.58	29.80	32.29
Nonfin.Pub.Ent. Deps.	14e	.01	.08	.06	.12	.04	.04	1.05	.58	1.95	4.23	4.24	6.39	21.60	1.91	1.47
Restricted Deposits	16b	—	—	—	—	—	—	—	—	—	—	—	—	—	—	—
Foreign Liabilities	16c	.01	.04	.09	.05	.02	.07	.11	.23	.16	.17	27.58	31.41	39.60	46.69	84.91
Central Government Deposits	16d	3.91	1.05	2.84	3.83	2.52	4.28	2.70	3.40	5.24	5.51	7.94	2.72	5.75	7.69	8.40
Other Items (Net)	17r	2.31	2.51	2.76	3.54	3.70	4.85	3.62	7.90	8.61	12.03	42.69	41.32	49.32	15.79	-.96
Deposit Money Banks																Millions of Kwacha:
Reserves	20	2.39	1.92	1.75	1.91	2.62	3.26	2.86	3.80	22.16	26.62	20.67	5.13	17.47	9.86	4.81
Foreign Assets	21	1.61	1.98	1.11	.90	.53	.67	1.89	2.64	3.45	2.17	5.22	5.69	5.67	10.81	6.64
Claims on Central Government	22a	2.54	2.67	3.17	4.20	3.48	4.02	4.20	7.12	12.20	14.50	20.07	21.17	26.29	37.01	29.90
Claims on Official Entities	22bx	.13	3.71	7.59	2.44	.97	.45	1.23	1.37	.71	2.48	7.35	14.68	19.76	16.91	25.77
Claims on Private Sector	22d	10.10	11.20	13.57	17.06	21.44	26.44	35.13	35.62	32.96	49.44	56.09	76.55	87.79	122.38	170.99
Demand Deposits	24	10.13	10.98	12.66	13.41	15.90	19.37	22.96	22.73	31.85	40.88	41.56	43.34	53.86	62.07	56.83
Time and Savings Deposits	25	6.25	7.80	8.57	10.38	12.22	14.44	17.84	22.32	29.68	42.45	48.73	48.22	60.86	74.77	79.50
Foreign Liabilities	26c	1.81	4.28	7.25	5.58	4.01	4.59	5.36	5.33	7.84	6.92	11.33	22.42	31.77	32.21	55.32
Other Items (Net)	27r	-1.42	-1.59	-1.30	-2.87	-3.10	-3.56	-.86	.23	2.12	4.95	7.78	9.23	10.46	27.92	46.45
Monetary Survey																Millions of Kwacha:
Foreign Assets (Net)	31n	17.81	12.97	12.52	14.03	14.00	20.35	20.91	25.51	51.92	67.66	21.61	-24.36	10.47	-7.23	-82.01
Domestic Credit	32	8.95	18.26	23.26	23.59	28.49	29.25	39.74	47.28	47.30	68.90	123.56	164.48	170.60	219.65	297.58
Claims on Central Govt. (Net)	32an	-1.27	3.35	2.11	4.09	6.08	2.36	3.38	10.29	13.62	16.98	34.68	45.52	34.87	46.57	70.14
Claims on Official Entities	32bx	.13	3.71	7.59	2.44	.97	.45	1.23	1.37	.71	2.48	32.79	42.41	47.93	50.70	56.45
Claims on Private Sector	32d	10.10	11.20	13.57	17.06	21.44	26.44	35.13	35.62	32.96	49.44	56.09	76.55	87.79	122.38	170.99
Money	34	19.02	21.63	24.53	25.11	28.48	32.68	38.81	40.61	55.12	73.43	73.63	72.80	100.06	93.79	90.59
Quasi-Money	35	6.25	7.80	8.65	10.67	12.24	14.47	17.92	22.33	29.71	42.46	48.73	48.24	60.94	74.77	79.50
Restricted Deposits	36b	—	—	—	—	—	—	—	—	—	—	—	—	—	—	—
Other Items (Net)	37r	.53	.82	1.46	.67	.60	1.29	2.76	8.13	10.73	16.99	50.22	50.55	59.78	43.83	45.47
Money plus Quasi-Money	35l	25.27	29.42	33.18	35.78	40.72	47.15	56.73	62.94	84.82	115.89	122.36	121.04	161.00	168.55	170.09
Other Banking Institutions																Millions of Kwacha:
Cash	40	.20	.14	.12	.17	.13	.10	.11	.11	.14	.31	.25	.47	.37	.72	1.62
Claims on Central Government	42a	2.00	3.06	3.49	4.36	4.88	6.10	7.40	8.45	2.14	1.25	1.95	1.84	2.75	2.50	2.08
Claims on Private Sector	42d	1.19	1.25	1.99	2.43	3.17	3.15	3.30	3.58	5.55	8.35	8.82	10.95	12.20	16.44	17.67
Shares, Time and Savings Deposits	45	3.94	4.66	5.71	6.89	8.10	9.21	10.48	11.72	8.63	10.26	11.18	14.19	16.94	18.77	22.66
Other Items (Net)	47r	-.55	-.21	-.11	.07	.08	.14	.33	.42	-.87	-.52	-.28	-.97	-1.72	.78	-1.32
Nonbank Financial Institutions																Millions of Kwacha:
Claims on Central Government	42a.s	.53	.59	.72	.80	1.06	1.68	2.03	3.92	4.88	6.03	7.17	7.16	6.61	6.88	8.23
Claims on Private Sector	42d.s	.12	.13	.13	.14	.26	.64	1.07	1.09	1.31	2.24	3.32	4.31	7.28	7.88	8.96
of which: Policy Loans	42dx s	.12	.12	.13	.14	.16	.17	.21	.25	.44	.94	1.54	1.85	2.70	2.75	2.42
Incr.in Total Assets(Within Per.)	49z.s	.71	.15	.12	.16	.46	1.14	.79	3.31	2.15	2.79	2.32	2.49	5.12	4.46	4.62
Liquid Liabilities	55l	28.95	33.94	38.76	42.50	48.69	56.26	67.10	74.55	99.26	133.89	139.60	137.91	178.70	190.70	193.43
Interest Rates																Percent Per Annum
Discount Rate (End of Period)	60	4.50	4.50	4.50	5.50	5.50	6.00	6.00	6.00	6.00	6.00	6.00	7.00	7.00	7.00	8.00
Treasury Bill Rate	60c	....	....	....	....	....	....	....	....	....	....	....	....	....	....	....
Deposit Rate	60l	....	....	....	....	....	....	....	....	....	....	....	....	....	....	....
Lending Rate	60p	....	....	....	....	....	....	....	....	....	....	....	....	....	....	....
Government Bond Yield	61	....	....	....	....	....	....	....	....	....	....	....	....	....	....	....

Malawi

1980	1981	1982	1983	1984	1985	1986	1987	1988	1989	1990	1991	1992	1993	1994		
End of Period															**Exchange Rates**	
1.0541	1.0541	1.2122	1.3577	1.5339	1.8445	2.3882	2.9136	3.4120	3.5204	3.7656	3.8104	6.0442	6.1733	22.3337	Official Rate	aa
End of Period (ae)	*Period Average (rf)*															
.8258	.9074	1.0970	1.2992	1.5649	1.6792	1.9524	2.0538	2.5355	2.6788	2.6469	2.6638	4.3958	4.4944	15.2986	Official Rate	ae
.8121	.8953	1.0555	1.1748	1.4134	1.7191	1.8611	2.2087	2.5613	2.7595	2.7289	2.8033	3.6033	4.4028	8.7364	Official Rate	rf
Period Averages																
335.6	304.7	259.9	232.8	193.4	159.7	146.8	123.7	106.6	98.8	100.0	97.4	77.7	61.8	35.5	Official Rate	ahx
147.8	152.2	148.4	147.8	144.1	139.2	119.0	94.6	86.0	92.4	100.0	108.1	94.7	90.0	58.7	Nominal Effective Exchange Rate	nec
110.1	109.9	105.4	107.3	106.2	106.3	95.5	88.8	93.9	99.6	100.0	104.5	96.9	99.0	72.4	Real Effective Exchange Rate	rec
End of Period															**Fund Position**	
28.50	28.50	28.50	37.20	37.20	37.20	37.20	37.20	37.20	37.20	37.20	37.20	50.90	50.90	50.90	Quota	2f. s
.03	5.66	3.59	.83	2.85	.02	.37	—	2.38	.28	2.23	.18	.06	.17	4.25	SDRs	1b. s
—	3.76	.01	2.18	2.20	2.20	2.20	2.20	2.20	2.21	2.22	2.22	2.22	2.22	2.22	Reserve Position in the Fund	1c. s
62.49	89.94	88.24	111.76	127.92	132.47	108.96	82.43	78.55	76.45	80.83	80.45	66.86	62.62	76.90	Total Fund Cred.&Loans Outstg.	2tl
End of Period															**International Liquidity**	
68.39	49.05	22.66	15.40	56.60	44.95	24.60	51.83	145.57	100.31	137.16	153.20	39.95	56.88	42.79	Total Reserves minus Gold	1l. d
.04	6.59	3.96	.87	2.79	.02	.45	—	3.20	.37	3.17	.26	.08	.23	6.20	SDRs	1b. d
—	4.38	.01	2.28	2.16	2.42	2.69	3.12	2.96	2.90	3.16	3.18	3.05	3.05	3.25	Reserve Position in the Fund	1c. d
68.35	38.09	18.69	12.25	51.65	42.51	21.46	48.71	139.41	97.04	130.83	149.77	36.82	53.59	33.35	Foreign Exchange	1d. d
.013	.013	.013	.013	.013	.013	.013	.013	.013	.013	.013	.013	.013	.013	.013	Gold (Million Fine Troy Ounces)	1ad
.57	.52	.50	.49	.30	.53	.56	.62	.50	.48	.55	.54	.54	.54	.55	Gold (National Valuation)	1and
36.75	50.72	57.42	40.64	-.63	11.50	36.65	35.49	30.18	17.24	14.58	14.84	55.42	36.81	21.92	Monetary Authorities: Other Liab.	4..d
6.84	7.18	8.23	10.51	6.06	7.76	5.31	3.07	5.83	8.28	11.33	4.56	10.06	17.34	25.61	Deposit Money Banks: Assets	7a. d
1.15	.62	.01	4.97	1.54	1.69	1.47	.03	.06	.07	1.75	1.96	1.19	.75	.53	of which: Claims on Nonbanks	7ad d
56.39	32.69	29.85	37.03	32.75	40.85	50.86	27.89	17.96	18.57	21.59	19.97	29.15	24.47	27.22	Deposit Money Banks: Liabilities	7b. d
12.44	10.28	10.53	7.44	5.87	6.84	7.02	8.97	8.71	9.53	11.86	8.86	7.35	8.83	24.01	of which: Liab. to Nonbanks	7bd d
End of Period															**Monetary Authorities**	
56.46	44.50	24.87	20.01	92.37	76.85	42.24	106.49	370.32	277.12	367.92	399.84	215.75	255.63	613.64	Foreign Assets	11
67.25	152.21	223.73	282.18	240.01	297.73	383.69	498.33	417.33	491.00	440.48	459.19	803.27	958.66	1,309.48	Claims on Central Government	12a
34.52	39.33	36.35	40.12	50.63	63.45	72.21	78.11	83.35	86.81	81.26	131.82	119.72	117.51	115.47	Claims on Official Entities	12bx
53.31	71.79	84.80	89.63	158.06	165.97	286.42	445.33	495.67	447.50	374.50	462.12	541.75	880.71	1,244.79	Reserve Money	14
35.34	39.36	49.47	50.03	56.85	65.99	79.30	107.62	134.62	156.60	159.38	222.69	289.79	414.17	624.74	of which: Currency Outside DMBs	14a
.40	1.52	.90	6.17	9.66	3.44	17.40	33.95	70.34	65.23	38.49	65.17	22.01	45.58	14.75	Nonfin.Pub.Ent. Deps.	14e
—	—	—	8.12	10.00	19.55	15.43	10.40	6.57	6.57	2.74	2.74	—	—	—	Restricted Deposits	16b
96.16	141.02	169.77	204.81	195.23	263.65	331.76	313.06	325.49	262.93	251.92	211.43	434.13	333.85	1,176.16	Foreign Liabilities	16c
.29	.78	26.84	36.59	31.87	33.23	-4.61	82.20	167.50	222.92	290.14	351.24	234.99	351.72	349.54	Central Government Deposits	16d
8.47	22.45	3.52	3.15	-12.15	-44.36	-128.26	-168.06	-124.23	-85.00	-29.46	-36.67	-72.13	-234.52	-731.91	Other Items (Net)	17r
End of Period															**Deposit Money Banks**	
17.63	30.94	34.43	33.44	91.55	96.42	189.72	303.76	288.21	225.61	221.66	174.33	209.46	380.18	591.37	Reserves	20
5.65	6.51	9.03	13.66	9.48	13.03	10.37	6.31	14.79	22.18	29.99	12.14	44.24	77.95	391.74	Foreign Assets	21
25.27	24.68	24.69	27.92	86.67	97.86	97.49	94.02	93.25	82.88	80.84	71.38	153.47	335.28	387.86	Claims on Central Government	22a
22.39	22.70	29.12	24.38	32.02	46.78	41.09	53.44	23.79	30.50	45.57	84.15	22.54	154.34	47.63	Claims on Official Entities	22bx
184.23	191.97	219.11	254.72	228.80	212.67	236.33	205.09	262.38	383.16	519.05	662.63	888.56	785.11	1,207.90	Claims on Private Sector	22d
61.45	73.87	80.44	71.56	87.74	97.51	124.07	156.46	230.96	230.88	284.25	346.00	444.90	560.15	895.94	Demand Deposits	24
94.33	126.66	145.57	165.02	234.04	217.50	268.03	370.44	376.57	408.98	475.00	566.73	633.51	924.45	1,119.48	Time and Savings Deposits	25
46.56	29.66	32.74	48.11	51.24	68.59	99.30	57.29	45.53	49.75	57.15	53.19	128.14	110.00	416.48	Foreign Liabilities	26c
52.83	46.61	57.63	69.43	75.49	83.17	83.60	78.43	30.23	54.73	80.25	38.70	111.61	138.35	193.82	Other Items (Net)	27r
End of Period															**Monetary Survey**	
-80.62	-119.67	-168.61	-219.25	-144.62	-242.35	-378.45	-257.55	14.09	-13.38	88.84	147.37	-302.29	-110.27	-587.26	Foreign Assets (Net)	31n
333.37	430.12	506.15	592.73	606.25	685.27	835.43	846.79	712.61	851.43	876.61	1,057.92	1,747.78	1,997.96	2,716.15	Domestic Credit	32
92.23	176.12	221.57	273.51	294.81	362.37	485.80	510.15	343.09	350.96	230.73	179.32	716.96	941.00	1,345.15	Claims on Central Govt. (Net)	32an
56.91	62.03	65.46	64.50	82.64	110.23	113.30	131.55	107.14	117.31	126.83	215.97	142.26	271.85	163.10	Claims on Official Entities	32bx
184.23	191.97	219.11	254.72	228.80	212.67	236.33	205.09	262.38	383.16	519.05	662.63	888.56	785.11	1,207.90	Claims on Private Sector	32d
97.20	114.75	130.81	127.76	154.25	166.93	220.78	298.02	435.92	452.71	482.12	633.86	756.70	1,019.90	1,535.43	Money	34
94.33	126.66	145.57	165.02	234.04	217.50	268.03	370.44	376.57	408.98	475.00	566.73	633.51	924.45	1,119.48	Quasi-Money	35
—	—	—	8.12	10.00	19.55	15.43	10.40	6.57	6.57	2.74	2.74	—	—	—	Restricted Deposits	36b
61.23	69.03	61.15	72.58	63.33	38.93	-44.67	-89.62	-91.50	-30.21	5.31	1.95	55.17	-56.61	-526.82	Other Items (Net)	37r
191.52	241.41	276.38	292.78	388.29	384.43	488.81	668.47	812.49	861.69	957.12	1,200.59	1,390.22	1,944.34	2,654.90	Money plus Quasi-Money	35l
End of Period															**Other Banking Institutions**	
1.36	4.00	2.38	2.00	7.08	2.40	1.50	7.75	‡14.99	14.84	4.11	3.74	32.57	79.11	98.87	Cash	40
2.40	2.82	5.93	7.69	7.47	11.74	11.07	15.20	‡26.13	26.64	24.22	23.79	23.74	29.23	8.88	Claims on Central Government	42a
23.50	27.00	30.87	33.16	33.36	41.42	47.91	51.53	‡57.19	75.66	109.88	167.40	248.91	324.66	394.85	Claims on Private Sector	42d
26.70	32.71	37.42	42.86	47.38	54.92	58.93	71.28	‡97.04	110.84	129.25	200.54	278.47	379.50	457.64	Shares, Time and Savings Deposits	45
.49	1.10	1.63	-.07	.53	.07	1.55	3.20	‡1.27	6.31	8.04	-5.59	26.40	53.51	44.97	Other Items (Net)	47r
End of Period															**Nonbank Financial Institutions**	
10.11	8.29	10.63	14.69	23.58	36.53	45.15	42.81	57.80	63.25	69.12	60.92	84.91	71.06	93.51	Claims on Central Government	42a. s
11.31	10.67	14.36	19.40	23.09	26.28	32.73	35.06	44.60	46.67	80.71	112.26	138.82	208.70	269.01	Claims on Private Sector	42d. s
2.88	2.16	1.08	4.61	7.08	7.63	10.09	8.97	9.40	7.47	8.69	10.19	12.34	11.05	12.48	of which: Policy Loans	42dx s
14.23	-2.57	-5.84	25.40	22.33	9.92	27.57	14.09	38.10	41.94	68.70	-43.13	45.49	70.20	103.28	Incr.in Total Assets(Within Per.)	49z. s
219.48	273.73	317.94	348.52	454.12	408.20	581.17	782.13	894.54	957.68	1,082.25	1,397.39	1,636.11	2,244.73	3,013.67	Liquid Liabilities	55l
Percent Per Annum															**Interest Rates**	
10.00	10.00	10.00	10.00	10.00	11.00	11.00	14.00	11.00	11.00	14.00	13.00	20.00	25.00	40.00	Discount Rate (End of Period)	60
....	9.00	9.00	11.00	11.00	12.31	12.75	14.25	15.75	15.75	12.92	11.50	15.62	23.54	27.68	Treasury Bill Rate	60c
7.92	9.75	9.75	9.92	11.75	12.50	12.75	14.25	13.50	12.73	12.10	12.50	16.50	21.75	25.00	Deposit Rate	60l
16.67	18.50	18.50	18.33	16.50	18.38	19.00	19.50	22.25	23.00	21.00	20.00	22.00	29.50	31.00	Lending Rate	60p
....	9.25	9.73	10.27	10.58	11.50	11.50	11.50	11.50	11.50	11.50	11.50	....	....	23.50	Government Bond Yield	61

Malawi
676

		1965	1966	1967	1968	1969	1970	1971	1972	1973	1974	1975	1976	1977	1978	1979
Prices and Production														*Index Numbers (1990=100):*		
Consumer Prices	64	....	....	....	....	....	....	....	....	....	....	....	....	....	....	....
Industrial Production	66	....	....	....	....	....	29.6	32.7	36.1	43.6	46.1	53.2	52.7	58.9	65.1	65.3
International Transactions														*Millions of Kwacha*		
Exports	70	28.82	34.81	41.04	40.04	43.97	49.70	59.30	64.49	79.92	101.31	122.12	151.62	180.33	155.66	189.83
Imports, cif	71	46.17	61.19	57.39	66.66	69.29	82.49	89.75	102.91	114.66	157.74	218.66	188.45	211.80	284.75	325.76
Imports, fob	71.v	39.93	52.93	50.94	59.16	61.49	71.35	77.65	90.45	100.75	138.60	192.16	165.31	186.12	250.60	289.43
														1985=100		
Volume of Exports	72	37.3	39.4	ɪ49.7	49.1	45.2	45.6	50.6	58.0	61.6	59.6	61.5	68.7	75.0	71.4	94.7
Volume of Imports	73	....	....	80.6	83.7	73.1	76.7	80.7	89.5	83.2	87.7	98.7	75.8	84.3	112.1	113.9
Export Prices	74	23.7	22.9	ɪ21.7	24.1	25.3	26.9	29.2	27.8	31.1	39.4	46.2	51.7	68.1	61.3	55.2
Unit Value of Imports	75	....	....	14.3	15.3	15.5	15.3	16.3	17.0	19.8	26.7	32.5	37.1	41.3	41.5	47.3
Balance of Payments														*Millions of US Dollars:*		
Goods: Exports f.o.b.	78aa d	....	....	....	....	....	....	....	....	....	....	....	....	199.8	184.5	222.4
Goods: Imports f.o.b.	78ab d	....	....	....	....	....	....	....	....	....	....	....	....	-183.0	-263.9	-317.6
Trade Balance	78ac d	....	....	....	....	....	....	....	....	....	....	....	....	16.8	-79.4	-95.1
Services: Credit	78ad d	....	....	....	....	....	....	....	....	....	....	....	....	13.4	25.6	34.8
Services: Debit	78ae d	....	....	....	....	....	....	....	....	....	....	....	....	-117.5	-119.3	-133.2
Balance on Goods and Services	78af d	....	....	....	....	....	....	....	....	....	....	....	....	-87.3	-173.2	-193.5
Income: Credit	78ag d	....	....	....	....	....	....	....	....	....	....	....	....	—	1.1	1.3
Income: Debit	78ah d	....	....	....	....	....	....	....	....	....	....	....	....	—	-49.4	-127.2
Balance on Goods, Serv., & Inc.	78ai d	....	....	....	....	....	....	....	....	....	....	....	....	-87.3	-221.5	-319.4
Current Transfers, n.i.e.: Credit	78aj d	....	....	....	....	....	....	....	....	....	....	....	....	26.0	60.2	71.4
Current Transfers: Debit	78ak d	....	....	....	....	....	....	....	....	....	....	....	....	-.6	-13.7	-17.6
Current Account, n.i.e.	78al d	....	....	....	....	....	....	....	....	....	....	....	....	-61.8	-175.1	-265.6
Capital Account, n.i.e.: Credit	78ba d	....	....	....	....	....	....	....	....	....	....	....	....	—	—	—
Capital Account: Debit	78bb d	....	....	....	....	....	....	....	....	....	....	....	....	—	—	—
Capital Account, n.i.e.	78bc d	....	....	....	....	....	....	....	....	....	....	....	....	—	—	—
Direct Investment Abroad	78bd d	....	....	....	....	....	....	....	....	....	....	....	....	—	—	—
Dir. Invest. in Rep. Econ., n.i.e.	78be d	....	....	....	....	....	....	....	....	....	....	....	....	5.5	9.1	-1.2
Portfolio Investment Assets	78bf d	....	....	....	....	....	....	....	....	....	....	....	....	—	—	—
Portfolio Investment Liab., n.i.e.	78bg d	....	....	....	....	....	....	....	....	....	....	....	....	—	16.5	19.8
Other Investment Assets	78bh d	....	....	....	....	....	....	....	....	....	....	....	....	—	28.3	5.1
Other Investment Liab., n.i.e.	78bi d	....	....	....	....	....	....	....	....	....	....	....	....	63.5	73.0	108.5
Financial Account, n.i.e.	78bj d	....	....	....	....	....	....	....	....	....	....	....	....	69.0	126.9	132.2
Net Errors and Omissions	78ca d	....	....	....	....	....	....	....	....	....	....	....	....	42.3	35.4	50.3
Overall Balance	78cb d	....	....	....	....	....	....	....	....	....	....	....	....	49.5	-12.7	-83.1
Reserves and Related Items	79da d	....	....	....	....	....	....	....	....	....	....	....	....	-49.5	12.7	83.1
Reserve Assets	79db d	....	....	....	....	....	....	....	....	....	....	....	....	-57.7	11.6	49.4
Use of Fund Credit and Loans	79dc d	....	....	....	....	....	....	....	....	....	....	....	....	8.2	1.1	33.7
Liabs.Constit.For.Auth.Reserves	79dd d	....	....	....	....	....	....	....	....	....	....	....	....			
Exceptional Financing	79de d	....	....	....	....	....	....	....	....	....	....	....	....			
Government Finance														*Millions of Kwacha:*		
Deficit (-) or Surplus	80	1.9	-11.2	-9.3	-13.7	-13.1	-25.5	ɪ-24.9	-20.0	-20.6	-29.5	-48.6	-37.6	-45.2	-74.3	-75.5
Revenue	81	18.4	22.8	26.7	29.5	32.1	38.6	ɪ48.0	51.8	59.9	70.7	81.3	87.7	109.1	142.4	176.2
Grants Received	81z	21.1	11.4	11.1	9.2	6.1	9.4	ɪ3.2	3.4	2.6	2.3	12.4	10.0	16.5	26.9	35.4
Exp. & Lending Minus Repay.	82z	37.7	45.4	47.1	52.4	51.3	73.5	ɪ76.1	75.3	83.1	102.5	142.3	135.3	170.7	243.7	287.1
Expenditure	82	37.0	44.7	45.9	51.2	47.0	73.5	ɪ67.9	71.1	79.6	103.9	140.5	129.2	159.8	214.8	279.6
Lending Minus Repayments	83	.7	.7	1.2	1.2	4.3	—	ɪ8.2	4.1	3.5	-1.5	1.8	6.1	10.9	28.9	7.5
Financing																
Net Borrowing: Domestic	84a	1.0	6.4	3.1	5.6	4.6	-2.7	ɪ4.2	6.0	5.5	11.8	13.4	.5	14.3	2.2	30.9
Foreign	85a	-.2	5.4	6.1	8.0	13.9	30.9	ɪ20.1	16.8	15.5	19.9	33.3	24.1	41.8	60.1	40.1
Use of Cash Balances	87	-2.7	-.6	.1	.1	-5.4	-2.7	ɪ.6	-2.9	-.4	-2.2	1.9	13.0	-10.9	12.0	4.5
Debt: Domestic	88a	....	....	....	....	....	....	ɪ37.8	40.4	47.4	53.4	67.1	81.7	92.0	....	....
Debt: Foreign	89a	....	....	....	....	....	....	ɪ105.4	127.7	157.6	179.0	218.6	241.5	251.6	195.1	274.0
National Accounts														*Millions of Kwacha*		
Exports of Goods & Services	90c	33.2	41.7	49.0	49.1	52.9	60.5	72.7	79.4	100.6	126.2	155.4	185.6	218.4	168.9	200.5
Government Consumption	91f	26.8	31.6	34.5	36.7	37.9	41.0	46.6	46.4	48.7	65.7	74.7	86.3	98.6	134.2	164.2
Gross Fixed Capital Formation	93e	19.3	29.4	25.4	37.4	47.7	61.1	54.4	72.4	74.3	87.3	131.8	135.3	161.6	247.1	231.9
Increase/Decrease(-) in Stocks	93i	5.8	6.0	4.0	-.7	-2.2	8.5	10.6	16.4	7.2	41.0	48.6	10.9	18.0	60.7	95.4
Private Consumption	96f	150.1	166.0	171.4	182.5	193.4	190.5	257.1	268.4	270.0	320.2	365.2	416.6	483.4	502.2	525.6
Imports of Goods & Services	98c	-55.0	-70.2	-68.9	-79.7	-85.3	-94.5	-106.5	-124.3	-136.8	-178.9	-246.0	-222.7	-252.0	-312.4	-353.1
Gross Domestic Product	99b	180.2	204.4	215.5	225.4	244.4	267.1	334.9	359.1	364.0	461.5	529.7	612.0	728.0	800.7	864.5
Net Factor Inc/Pmts(-) Abroad	98.n	-4.3	-5.6	-7.8	-7.0	-5.7	-6.1	-3.2	-3.7	.8	12.4	10.7	-17.5	-23.0	-4.0	-34.8
Gross Nat'l Expenditure = GNP	99a	175.9	198.8	207.7	218.4	238.7	261.0	331.7	355.4	364.8	473.9	540.4	594.5	705.0	796.7	829.7
Gross Dom. Prod. 1990 Prices	99b.p	1,585.9	1,742.2	1,945.8	1,836.9	1,954.5	1,983.5	ɪ2,268.8	2,439.0	ɪ2,740.3	2,944.2	3,107.0	3,300.4	3,443.5	3,729.9	3,854.4
GDP Deflator (1990=100)	99bi p	11.4	11.7	11.1	12.3	12.5	13.5	14.8	14.7	13.3	15.7	17.0	18.5	21.1	21.5	22.4
														Millions:		
Population	99z	3.91	4.02	4.12	4.23	4.33	4.44	4.55	4.67	4.79	5.10	5.24	5.37	5.54	5.68	5.86

Exchange Rates: On February 15, 1971, the kwacha, equal to one half the Malawi pound, was introduced.
Other Banking Institutions: ɪ Beginning in 1988, data exclude the accounts for the Post Office Savings Bank.
Government Finance: ɪ Beginning in 1971, data are as reported in the *Government Finance Statistics Yearbook* and cover budgetary central government. Prior to 1971, data are as reported by the Reserve Bank of Malawi for publication in *IFS*. Data relate to a fiscal year different from calendar year.

Malawi

	1980	1981	1982	1983	1984	1985	1986	1987	1988	1989	1990	1991	1992	1993	1994		
Period Averages																**Prices and Production**	
	22.5	25.2	27.6	31.4	37.6	41.6	47.5	59.4	79.5	89.4	100.0	ⅈ112.6	138.2	165.3	....	Consumer Prices	64
	66.2	73.0	68.7	78.8	78.0	78.2	79.4	ⅈ76.5	80.9	87.9	100.0	105.2	103.9	97.2	....	Industrial Production	66
Millions of Kwacha																**International Transactions**	
	239.25	255.77	256.59	270.61	446.24	421.96	462.10	615.06	751.69	743.22	1,123.52	1,326.36	1,488.90	1,410.91	....	Exports	70
	356.21	321.14	322.12	363.77	381.57	506.19	477.97	653.94	1,080.15	1,398.80	1,572.47	1,975.81	2,653.83	2,404.86	....	Imports, cif	71
	313.00	282.91	283.04	318.61	339.53	303.72	286.78	392.36	648.09	839.28	943.47	1,185.46	1,592.30	1,439.93	....	Imports, fob	71.v
1985=100																	
	ⅈ105.5	83.6	86.9	115.2	83.8	100.0	104.3	109.9	109.3	86.8	....	....	....	....	....	Volume of Exports	72
	ⅈ101.2	75.1	75.9	77.8	83.3	100.0	73.2	96.7	76.4	109.1	....	....	....	....	....	Volume of Imports	73
	ⅈ57.1	80.0	87.7	89.5	110.7	100.0	111.9	146.5	176.1	206.3	....	....	....	....	....	Export Prices	74
	ⅈ57.6	66.0	71.6	79.7	94.5	100.0	128.5	174.3	216.5	248.5	....	....	....	....	....	Unit Value of Imports	75
Minus Sign Indicates Debit																**Balance of Payments**	
	280.8	272.5	239.7	246.2	311.8	245.5	248.4	277.6	293.5	268.8	415.7	475.5	399.9	327.7	....	Goods: Exports f.o.b.	78aa *d*
	−308.0	−244.3	−214.0	−216.2	−162.0	−176.7	−154.1	−177.6	−253.0	−304.1	−348.3	−422.9	−431.6	−327.7	....	Goods: Imports f.o.b.	78ab *d*
	−27.2	28.3	25.7	30.0	149.8	68.8	94.3	100.0	40.4	−35.4	67.4	52.6	−31.7	—	....	Trade Balance	78ac *d*
	31.8	43.7	27.9	28.8	27.0	25.9	20.1	28.4	38.5	30.5	36.6	38.5	28.5	30.0	....	Services: Credit	78ad *d*
	−178.6	−146.8	−123.0	−127.8	−141.6	−143.3	−130.5	−143.6	−197.9	−231.3	−268.4	−356.5	−338.8	−260.1	....	Services: Debit	78ae *d*
	−174.0	−74.8	−69.4	−69.0	35.2	−48.5	−16.1	−15.3	−119.0	−236.1	−164.4	−265.3	−342.0	−230.1	....	Balance on Goods and Services	78af *d*
	2.2	1.3	1.5	1.1	2.6	4.7	3.3	3.3	9.6	10.5	9.3	7.4	6.3	2.2	....	Income: Credit	78ag *d*
	−151.3	−131.5	−92.9	−101.6	−116.3	−118.9	−114.9	−92.7	−92.9	−85.4	−78.4	−83.7	−74.8	−10.5	....	Income: Debit	78ah *d*
	−323.1	−205.0	−160.9	−169.6	−78.5	−162.7	−127.7	−104.7	−202.3	−311.0	−233.4	−341.6	−410.5	−238.4	....	Balance on Goods, Serv., & Inc.	78ai *d*
	82.6	74.7	64.6	54.6	53.6	47.9	57.2	70.8	169.2	208.0	134.1	159.0	155.2	170.0	....	Current Transfers, n.i.e.: Credit	78aj *d*
	−19.5	−16.5	−16.5	−16.8	−17.6	−12.3	−14.9	−26.9	−38.6	−33.9	−35.1	−42.9	−37.7	−27.4	....	Current Transfers: Debit	78ak *d*
	−259.9	−146.8	−112.7	−131.8	−42.6	−127.1	−85.3	−60.8	−71.6	−136.8	−134.4	−225.5	−293.0	−95.8	....	Current Account, n.i.e.	78al *d*
	—	—	—	—	—	—	—	—	—	—	—	—	—	—	....	Capital Account, n.i.e.: Credit	78ba *d*
	—	—	—	—	—	—	—	—	—	—	—	—	—	—	....	Capital Account: Debit	78bb *d*
	—	—	—	—	—	—	—	—	—	—	—	—	—	—	....	Capital Account, n.i.e.	78bc *d*
	—	—	—	—	—	—	—	—	—	—	—	—	—	—	....	Direct Investment Abroad	78bd *d*
	9.5	1.1	—	2.6	—	.5	—	.1	—	—	—	—	—	—	....	Dir. Invest. in Rep. Econ., n.i.e.	78be *d*
	—	—	—	—	—	—	—	—	—	—	—	—	—	—	....	Portfolio Investment Assets	78bf *d*
	.5	1.9	3.3	.4	1.0	.4	1.3	4.2	.8	2.6	.8	−5.8	11.9	−11.8	....	Portfolio Investment Liab., n.i.e.	78bg *d*
	1.5	−.9	−2.4	−1.9	−4.4	−2.6	13.8	6.6	6.7	42.8	33.9	−5.8	11.9	−11.8	....	Other Investment Assets	78bh *d*
	140.5	29.4	−9.7	34.0	48.7	−2.0	30.7	48.6	61.4	46.7	93.9	110.0	81.7	194.4	....	Other Investment Liab., n.i.e.	78bi *d*
	152.0	31.5	−8.7	35.2	45.3	−3.7	45.8	59.5	68.9	92.0	128.6	104.3	93.6	182.7	....	Financial Account, n.i.e.	78bj *d*
	86.0	88.7	83.5	−1.4	.8	105.1	38.9	46.8	62.9	−6.9	34.5	137.0	152.9	−62.8	....	Net Errors and Omissions	78ca *d*
	−22.0	−26.5	−37.9	−98.0	3.5	−25.6	−.6	45.4	60.2	−51.7	28.7	15.7	−46.5	24.0	....	Overall Balance	78cb *d*
	22.0	26.5	37.9	98.0	−3.5	25.6	.6	−45.4	−60.2	51.7	−28.7	−15.7	46.5	−24.0	....	Reserves and Related Items	79da *d*
	−10.4	−6.1	20.5	12.5	−44.4	13.0	25.0	−33.6	−102.1	36.7	−34.3	−15.8	65.7	−18.1	....	Reserve Assets	79db *d*
	32.1	31.4	−2.3	25.4	16.5	5.1	−27.7	−34.6	−5.4	−2.6	5.6	.1	−19.2	−5.9	....	Use of Fund Credit and Loans	79dc *d*
	—	—	—	—	—	—	—	—	—	—	—	—	—	—	....	Liabs.Constit.For.Auth.Reserves	79dd *d*
	.3	1.2	19.7	60.1	24.4	7.5	3.3	22.8	47.4	17.7	—	—	—	—	....	Exceptional Financing	79de *d*
Year Beginning April 1																**Government Finance**	
	−160.3	−137.7	−95.0	−101.8	−88.3	−162.6	−217.7	−226.1	−204.7	−118.7	−81.4	....	....	....	....	Deficit (−) or Surplus	80
	192.2	214.1	232.0	276.5	339.7	431.6	479.2	542.8	722.9	945.5	1,018.5	....	....	....	....	Revenue	81
	43.9	43.5	39.8	34.4	41.0	29.8	52.1	83.7	82.3	91.5	204.3	....	....	....	....	Grants Received	81z
	396.4	395.3	366.8	412.7	469.1	623.9	749.1	852.5	1,010.0	1,155.7	1,304.1	....	....	....	....	Exp. & Lending Minus Repay.	82z
	347.7	393.4	359.8	415.4	473.4	608.5	742.6	841.5	1,006.5	1,159.4	1,306.1	....	....	....	....	Expenditure	82
	48.7	1.9	7.0	−2.7	−4.3	15.4	6.5	11.1	3.5	−3.8	−2.0	....	....	....	....	Lending Minus Repayments	83
																Financing	
	58.0	80.8	−6.6	56.4	73.5	96.0	−30.9	81.6	....	....	....	....	....	....	....	Net Borrowing: Domestic	84a
	83.6	33.6	62.6	95.0	56.1	68.9	165.5	184.1	....	....	....	....	....	....	....	Foreign	85a
	18.7	23.4	39.1	−49.7	−41.3	−2.3	83.1	−39.6	....	....	....	....	....	....	....	Use of Cash Balances	87
	....	....	....	408.5	433.8	514.8	741.5	....	....	....	....	....	....	....	....	Debt: Domestic	88a
	366.7	426.9	630.0	798.7	915.3	1,196.8	1,918.4	2,266.6	....	....	....	....	....	....	....	Debt: Foreign	89a
Millions of Kwacha																**National Accounts**	
	249.7	284.4	280.2	298.2	484.4	470.5	504.7	665.1	824.3	824.1	1,220.6	1,437.2	1,504.3	1,472.1	....	Exports of Goods & Services	90c
	193.9	198.0	218.3	235.9	268.0	344.0	433.8	499.2	555.3	716.8	772.9	852.4	1,240.9	1,487.4	....	Government Consumption	91f
	223.1	167.8	181.7	197.3	222.7	259.5	264.1	352.9	524.0	699.6	820.0	1,030.0	1,077.0	890.0	....	Gross Fixed Capital Formation	93e
	97.3	89.0	112.2	193.8	−2.8	102.2	5.3	49.2	116.5	189.0	150.0	200.0	180.0	200.0	....	Increase/Decrease(−) in Stocks	93i
	631.2	716.2	812.0	918.8	1,186.3	1,350.2	1,541.5	1,774.3	2,548.0	3,284.4	3,821.7	4,770.8	5,323.3	7,236.2	....	Private Consumption	96f
	−390.1	−348.6	−359.3	−407.1	−451.2	−581.5	−551.8	−726.7	−1,150.2	−1,514.7	−1,715.3	−2,184.8	−2,631.6	−2,404.4	....	Imports of Goods & Services	98c
	1,005.1	1,108.1	1,245.1	1,436.9	1,707.4	1,944.9	2,197.6	2,614.0	3,417.9	4,199.2	4,919.9	6,105.5	6,693.9	8,881.6	....	Gross Domestic Product	99b
	−81.1	−74.3	−101.3	−139.0	−78.8	−90.9	−112.9	−125.7	−137.9	−137.6	−118.2	−130.4	−140.5	−184.0	....	Net Factor Inc/Pmts(−) Abroad	98.n
	924.0	1,033.8	1,143.8	1,297.9	1,628.6	1,854.0	2,084.7	2,488.0	3,280.0	4,062.0	4,961.0	5,976.0	6,554.0	8,702.0	....	Gross Nat'l Expenditure = GNP	99a
	3,839.9	3,638.9	3,741.9	3,874.0	4,046.3	4,226.7	4,272.9	4,363.8	4,512.5	4,695.9	4,919.9	5,303.7	4,883.2	5,410.7	....	Gross Dom. Prod. 1990 Prices	99b. *p*
	26.2	30.5	33.3	37.1	42.2	46.0	51.4	59.9	75.7	89.4	100.0	115.1	137.1	164.1	....	GDP Deflator (1990=100)	99bi *p*
Midyear Estimates																	
	6.05	6.23	6.45	6.62	6.84	7.06	7.28	7.55	7.75	8.02	8.29	8.56	ⅈ10.16	9.13	....	**Population**	99z

Malaysia
548

		1965	1966	1967	1968	1969	1970	1971	1972	1973	1974	1975	1976	1977	1978	1979
Exchange Rates																*Ringgit per SDR:*
Official Rate	aa	3.0592	3.0710	3.0563	3.0650	3.0750	3.0775	3.1334	3.0584	2.9580	2.8317	3.0300	2.9452	2.8734	2.8740	2.8836
																Ringgit per US Dollar:
Official Rate	ae	3.0592	3.0710	3.0563	3.0650	3.0750	3.0775	2.8860	2.8170	2.4520	2.3128	2.5883	2.5350	2.3655	2.2060	2.1890
Official Rate	rf	3.0612	3.0612	3.0612	3.0612	3.0612	3.0612	3.0523	2.8196	2.4433	2.4071	2.3938	2.5416	2.4613	2.3160	2.1884
																Index Numbers (1990=100):
Official Rate	ahx	88.2	88.1	88.2	88.3	88.4	87.8	82.1	96.4	111.1	112.4	113.4	106.4	109.9	116.9	123.6
Nominal Effective Exchange Rate	nec	....	....	....	....	....	....	....	....	....	....	....	....	....	....	119.7
Real Effective Exchange Rate	rec	....	....	....	....	....	....	....	....	....	....	....	....	....	....	138.3
Fund Position																*Millions of SDRs:*
Quota	2f.s	58	84	110	115	125	186	186	186	186	186	186	186	186	253	253
SDRs	1b.s	—	—	—	—	—	23	43	63	61	62	62	65	27	39	87
Reserve Position in the Fund	1c.s	14	20	32	33	36	51	39	39	47	50	54	54	52	54	67
Total Fund Cred.&Loans Outstg.	2tl	—	—	—	—	—	—	7	7	—	—	—	93	—	—	—
International Liquidity														*Millions of US Dollars Unless Otherwise Indicated:*		
Total Reserves minus Gold	1l.d	468	493	426	450	557	616	755	907	1,275	1,547	1,456	2,404	2,784	3,243	3,915
SDRs	1b.d	—	—	—	—	—	23	47	69	73	75	72	76	32	50	115
Reserve Position in the Fund	1c.d	14	20	32	33	36	51	43	43	56	61	63	62	64	70	89
Foreign Exchange	1d.d	454	473	394	417	521	542	665	796	1,146	1,411	1,321	2,266	2,688	3,123	3,711
Gold (Million Fine Troy Ounces)	1ad	.060	.030	.890	1.890	1.800	1.370	1.660	1.660	1.660	1.660	1.660	1.660	1.740	1.890	2.130
Gold (National Valuation)	1and	2	1	31	66	63	48	63	63	70	71	68	68	74	86	98
Government Assets	3bad	272	206	131	110	142	136	150	42	41	42	41	30	36	39	35
Other Official Inst. Assets	3bbd	41	40	36	28	26	23	20	17	14	15	13	14	8	8	8
Deposit Money Banks: Assets	7a.d	162	170	86	96	132	121	128	164	235	250	258	444	436	460	774
of which: Claims on Nonbanks	7ad.d	19	22	26	43	69	58	62	82	117	122	151	200	229	282	280
Deposit Money Banks: Liabilities	7b.d	77	90	69	116	111	94	123	154	326	378	330	543	626	771	826
of which: Liab. to Nonbanks	7bd.d	5	7	6	9	11	11	14	17	28	34	37	44	61	60	80
Monetary Authorities																*Millions of Ringgit:*
Foreign Assets	11	1,439	1,512	1,400	1,579	1,896	2,034	2,307	2,735	3,319	3,763	3,943	6,272	6,772	7,404	9,247
Claims on Central Government	12a	66	83	141	103	123	124	128	171	277	253	445	325	422	386	742
Claims on Private Sector	12d	....	....	....	....	....	....	....	....	....	....	....	....	....	....	....
Claims on Deposit Money Banks	12e	....	....	....	....	....	....	....	....	....	....	....	....	....	....	....
Claims on Nonmonetary Fin. Insts.	12f	....	....	....	....	....	....	....	....	....	....	....	....	....	....	....
Reserve Money	14	1,300	1,119	983	1,047	1,233	1,349	1,456	1,903	2,582	2,931	3,004	3,567	4,126	4,755	5,498
of which: Currency Outside DMBs	14a	1,136	935	772	806	930	1,000	1,061	1,269	1,718	2,030	2,239	2,628	3,112	3,578	4,094
Foreign Liabilities	16c	65	72	—	3	10	16	48	26	12	6	13	297	33	40	20
Central Government Deposits	16d	202	209	418	498	709	585	662	627	647	529	792	1,650	2,063	1,703	3,386
Other Items (Net)	17r	−62	195	141	134	67	208	270	350	356	551	580	1,083	973	1,291	1,085
Deposit Money Banks																*Millions of Ringgit:*
Reserves	20	138	167	184	198	251	285	300	575	750	858	731	869	938	1,049	1,246
Foreign Assets	21	495	519	264	294	406	370	361	462	597	579	669	1,126	1,032	1,014	1,695
Claims on Central Government	22a	183	304	575	854	909	833	1,045	1,186	1,375	1,746	2,148	3,036	3,583	3,379	3,843
Claims on Private Sector	22d	1,119	1,270	1,398	1,672	1,839	2,245	2,572	3,012	4,583	5,275	6,077	7,471	8,971	11,626	14,641
Claims on Other Banking Insts.	22f	....	....	....	....	....	....	....	....	....	....	....	....	....	....	....
Demand Deposits	24	652	728	732	869	931	1,007	1,018	1,393	1,928	1,982	2,083	2,572	2,953	3,548	4,252
Time and Savings Deposits	25	940	1,080	1,289	1,543	1,806	2,043	2,480	2,949	3,710	4,536	5,541	7,384	8,580	10,162	13,166
Bonds and Money Market Instr.	26a	....	....	....	....	....	....	....	....	....	....	....	....	....	....	....
Foreign Liabilities	26c	237	276	211	355	339	287	347	433	826	874	855	1,378	1,481	1,700	1,808
Central Government Deposits	26d	153	174	217	252	293	343	340	271	440	512	495	574	729	1,045	1,899
Credit from Central Bank	26g	....	....	....	....	....	....	....	....	....	....	....	....	....	....	....
Capital Accounts	27a	—	101	107	129	134	141	192	209	252	255	337	375	556	613	714
Other Items (Net)	27r	−46	−98	−136	−132	−99	−88	−99	−20	150	299	313	218	225	1	−412
Monetary Survey																*Millions of Ringgit:*
Foreign Assets (Net)	31n	1,632	1,683	1,453	1,515	1,953	2,101	2,296	2,760	3,078	3,462	3,745	5,723	6,290	6,678	9,114
Domestic Credit	32	1,017	1,275	1,487	1,894	1,868	2,275	2,714	3,451	5,152	6,237	7,390	8,607	10,184	12,644	13,942
Claims on Central Govt. (Net)	32an	−106	5	81	206	29	30	172	460	566	959	1,306	1,136	1,214	1,017	−699
Claims on Private Sector	32d	1,119	1,270	1,398	1,672	1,839	2,245	2,572	3,012	4,583	5,275	6,077	7,471	8,971	11,626	14,641
Claims on Nonmonetary Fin. Insts.	32f	....	....	....	....	....	....	....	....	....	....	....	....	....	....	....
Money	34	1,801	1,681	1,529	1,717	1,913	2,071	2,172	2,715	3,735	4,055	4,349	5,257	6,127	7,243	8,487
Quasi-Money	35	940	1,080	1,289	1,543	1,806	2,051	2,488	3,047	3,817	4,659	5,652	7,514	8,734	10,278	13,252
Bonds and Money Market Instr.	36a	....	....	....	....	....	....	....	....	....	....	....	....	....	....	....
Other Items (Net)	37r	−91	196	123	149	102	253	349	449	678	985	1,133	1,558	1,613	1,799	1,319
Money plus Quasi-Money	35l	2,741	2,761	2,818	3,260	3,719	4,123	4,661	5,763	7,552	8,714	10,001	12,771	14,861	17,521	21,739
Other Banking Institutions																*Millions of Ringgit:*
Reserves	40	....	....	....	....	111	186	ℐ272	228	368	ℐ671	674	802	943	1,183	1,209
Foreign Assets	41	....	....	....	....	45	35	ℐ23	17	5	35	35	35	19	19	21
Claims on Central Government	42a	134	151	173	213	ℐ246	273	ℐ304	416	512	ℐ4,086	4,651	5,410	6,398	7,430	8,747
Claims on Private Sector	42d	....	....	....	220	273	ℐ351	433	617	ℐ1,176	1,579	2,073	2,615	3,222	4,614	
Claims on Deposit Money Banks	42e	....	....	....	....	....	....	....	....	....	....	....	....	....	....	....
Time and Savings Deposits	45	192	206	223	239	ℐ566	709	ℐ867	1,021	1,401	ℐ4,983	5,872	7,254	8,285	10,220	12,546
Money Market Instruments	46aa	....	....	....	....	....	....	....	....	....	....	....	....	....	....	....
Central Government Deposits	46d	....	....	....	....	....	....	....	....	....	....	....	....	....	....	....
Credit from Deposit Money Banks	46h	....	....	....	....	....	....	....	....	....	....	....	....	....	....	....
Other Items (Net)	47r	−58	−55	−50	−26	ℐ57	59	ℐ83	74	101	ℐ985	1,067	1,067	1,690	1,634	2,046
Banking Survey																*Millions of Ringgit:*
Foreign Assets (Net)	51n	....	....	....	....	....	....	....	....	....	....	....	....	....	....	....
Domestic Credit	52	....	....	....	....	....	....	....	....	....	....	....	....	....	....	....
Claims on Central Govt. (Net)	52an	....	....	....	....	....	....	....	....	....	....	....	....	....	....	....
Claims on Private Sector	52d	....	....	....	....	....	....	....	....	....	....	....	....	....	....	....
Claims on Nonbank Fin. Insts.	52f	....	....	....	....	....	....	....	....	....	....	....	....	....	....	....
Liquid Liabilities	55l	2,636	2,962	3,041	3,499	ℐ4,180	4,654	ℐ5,261	6,563	8,606	ℐ13,027	15,199	19,222	22,204	26,558	33,075
Monetary Liabilities	54	....	....	....	....	....	....	....	....	....	....	....	....	....	....	....
Quasi-Monetary Liabilities	55	....	....	....	....	....	....	....	....	....	....	....	....	....	....	....
Bonds and Money Market Instr.	56a	....	....	....	....	....	....	....	....	....	....	....	....	....	....	....
Other Items (Net)	57r	....	....	....	....	....	....	....	....	....	....	....	....	....	....	....
Nonbank Financial Institutions																*Millions of Ringgit:*
Cash	40..s	11.3	15.9	18.7	19.2	18.5	16.4	16.6	22.1	25.9	42.0	91.6	....	....	....	....
Foreign Assets	41.s	56.6	57.7	61.3	53.3	60.0	57.0	58.5	62.6	58.2	85.6	23.1	26.2	20.3	13.6	12.2
Claims on Central Government	42a.s	19.0	19.3	22.3	23.7	26.2	48.9	69.4	104.6	123.6	136.6	156.6	179.3	212.8	250.4	279.0
Claims on Private Sector	42d.s	57.3	67.9	83.0	121.1	146.8	163.2	181.3	216.9	251.9	273.5	349.1	393.7	439.1	473.2	577.0
Real Estate	42h.s	24.5	25.7	27.3	29.1	27.0	27.6	30.0	31.0	36.7	40.0	46.7	....	....	....	....

Malaysia

548

1980	1981	1982	1983	1984	1985	1986	1987	1988	1989	1990	1991	1992	1993	1994	
End of Period															**Exchange Rates**
2.8345	2.6099	2.5606	2.4481	2.3770	2.6653	3.1840	3.5364	3.6540	3.5526	3.8433	3.8965	3.5915	3.7107	3.7372	Official Rate **aa**
End of Period (ae) Period Average (rf)															
2.2224	2.2423	2.3213	2.3383	2.4250	2.4265	2.6030	2.4928	2.7153	2.7033	2.7015	2.7240	2.6120	2.7015	2.5600	Official Rate **ae**
2.1769	2.3041	2.3354	2.3213	2.3436	2.4830	2.5814	2.5196	2.6188	2.7088	2.7049	2.7501	2.5474	2.5741	2.6243	Official Rate **rf**
Period Averages															
124.3	117.5	115.9	116.6	115.4	109.0	104.8	107.4	103.3	99.9	100.0	98.4	106.2	105.1	103.1	Official Rate **ahx**
120.9	120.9	128.6	135.1	140.6	137.2	116.0	111.7	102.6	102.2	100.0	97.3	102.1	101.0	97.3	Nominal Effective Exchange Rate **nec**
133.2	133.8	142.2	149.0	154.7	147.0	123.4	117.0	106.1	104.2	100.0	97.2	103.3	102.3	98.7	Real Effective Exchange Rate **rec**
End of Period															**Fund Position**
380	380	380	551	551	551	551	551	551	551	551	551	833	833	833	Quota **2f.s**
98	126	118	103	99	105	111	115	120	127	136	145	82	88	93	SDRs **1b.s**
116	117	117	159	159	159	159	153	172	170	164	180	240	229	274	Reserve Position in the Fund **1c.s**
—	190	248	315	263	107	—	—	—	—	—	—	—	—	—	Total Fund Cred.&Loans Outstg. **2tl**
End of Period															**International Liquidity**
4,387	4,098	3,768	3,784	3,723	4,912	6,027	7,435	6,527	7,783	9,754	10,886	17,228	27,249	25,423	Total Reserves minus Gold **1l.d**
125	146	130	108	97	116	135	163	161	167	194	207	113	121	135	SDRs **1b.d**
149	136	129	167	156	175	195	217	231	223	233	257	330	315	400	Reserve Position in the Fund **1c.d**
4,114	3,816	3,509	3,509	3,470	4,621	5,697	7,055	6,134	7,393	9,327	10,421	16,784	26,814	24,888	Foreign Exchange **1d.d**
2.320	2.330	2.330	2.330	2.330	2.340	2.340	2.350	2.350	2.370	2.350	2.350	2.390	2.390	2.390	Gold (Million Fine Troy Ounces) **1ad**
104	95	90	85	80	90	100	117	111	109	117	118	115	115	122	Gold (National Valuation) **1and**
38	33	31	32	363	238	31	42	44	39	....	....	....	....	....	Government Assets **3bad**
8	7	2	—	1	1	2	1	1	1	....	....	....	....	....	Other Official Inst. Assets **3bbd**
873	893	1,240	2,312	1,081	1,247	1,487	2,009	2,802	2,938	2,804	2,366	2,009	3,880	4,118	Deposit Money Banks: Assets **7a.d**
421	360	327	1,663	444	559	613	787	919	....	....	....	....	....	....	*of which:* Claims on Nonbanks **7add**
1,303	1,606	1,690	2,965	2,470	2,633	2,371	1,999	1,874	2,783	3,500	4,957	7,153	11,656	6,641	Deposit Money Banks: Liabilities **7b.d**
131	131	155	1,192	213	279	250	182	196	327	343	406	477	1,197	959	*of which:* Liab. to Nonbanks **7bdd**
End of Period															**Monetary Authorities**
10,316	9,805	9,338	9,456	9,655	12,479	16,358	19,516	18,340	21,673	27,040	30,463	47,233	76,485	68,200	Foreign Assets **11**
1,681	708	2,001	3,525	4,809	2,468	2,058	1,961	2,164	1,529	2,681	1,611	561	454	980	Claims on Central Government **12a**
....	....	....	....	....	....	....	....	....	....	....	....	410	1,296	1,601	Claims on Private Sector **12d**
....	....	....	....	....	....	....	....	....	....	....	....	-11,566	3,597	3,443	Claims on Deposit Money Banks **12e**
....	....	....	....	....	....	....	....	....	....	....	....	698	1,104	1,718	Claims on Nonmonetary Fin. Insts. **12f**
6,493	7,164	8,360	8,718	9,038	9,729	10,134	10,664	11,894	14,783	18,145	20,771	I 25,306	28,253	38,482	Reserve Money **14**
4,758	5,100	5,727	6,025	5,974	6,773	7,146	7,965	9,031	9,904	11,224	12,070	12,124	13,506	15,884	*of which: Currency Outside DMBs* **14a**
4	506	643	784	652	304	34	84	10	23	20	15	22	39	30	Foreign Liabilities **16c**
2,426	998	1,327	1,808	2,267	703	601	1,053	1,112	1,068	5,233	5,989	I 5,679	2,912	8,469	Central Government Deposits **16d**
3,075	1,845	1,010	1,670	2,507	4,211	7,648	9,677	7,487	7,328	6,323	5,299	I 6,328	51,732	28,961	Other Items (Net) **17r**
End of Period															**Deposit Money Banks**
1,587	1,834	2,323	2,451	2,816	2,552	2,440	2,472	2,598	4,204	6,205	7,807	I 8,604	9,242	15,810	Reserves **20**
1,940	2,003	2,880	5,390	2,451	2,995	3,821	4,863	7,267	6,841	6,672	5,500	I 5,247	10,482	10,542	Foreign Assets **21**
3,972	5,552	6,301	7,588	8,333	7,823	7,644	10,544	10,384	11,811	11,851	12,376	I 11,324	10,683	11,127	Claims on Central Government **22a**
20,353	24,976	29,197	35,403	41,976	47,849	51,275	51,308	55,763	68,219	82,657	99,668	I 110,418	122,344	141,965	Claims on Private Sector **22d**
1,473	2,452	2,912	3,016	3,755	3,941	4,137	4,228	4,047	3,459	3,563	5,242	I 8,252	8,770	14,463	Claims on Other Banking Insts. **22f**
4,875	5,714	6,479	7,216	7,210	7,088	7,003	8,342	9,627	11,979	14,106	15,758	I 18,931	29,128	31,724	Demand Deposits **24**
16,549	21,309	25,136	27,725	32,500	34,786	39,779	39,970	41,404	47,314	51,255	61,670	I 80,172	98,447	108,977	Time and Savings Deposits **25**
....	....	....	....	....	....	....	....	....	....	....	....	15,251	14,933	26,529	Bonds and Money Market Instr. **26a**
2,896	3,601	3,924	6,924	5,968	6,358	6,157	4,981	5,084	6,317	8,129	11,755	I 18,684	31,488	17,000	Foreign Liabilities **26c**
2,678	2,475	2,358	5,100	6,104	7,934	6,300	6,491	7,552	7,576	5,415	6,137	I 1,495	1,903	2,795	Central Government Deposits **26d**
....	....	....	....	....	....	....	....	....	....	....	....	-12,943	-40,080	-18,079	Credit from Central Bank **26g**
965	1,595	1,997	2,995	3,588	4,143	4,431	5,344	5,713	6,163	6,916	7,670	I 14,843	16,884	23,813	Capital Accounts **27a**
I 1,361	2,123	3,719	3,887	3,960	4,851	5,648	8,288	10,679	15,186	25,127	27,602	I 7,411	8,819	1,146	Other Items (Net) **27r**
End of Period															**Monetary Survey**
9,357	7,701	7,651	7,138	5,486	8,812	13,989	19,315	20,513	22,174	25,563	24,192	I 33,773	55,440	61,712	Foreign Assets (Net) **31n**
22,375	30,214	36,726	42,623	50,501	53,444	58,213	60,497	63,694	76,375	90,103	106,771	I 124,488	139,837	160,591	Domestic Credit **32**
549	2,786	4,617	4,204	4,771	1,654	2,801	4,961	3,884	4,696	3,883	1,861	I 4,710	6,323	844	Claims on Central Govt. (Net) **32an**
20,353	24,976	29,197	35,403	41,976	47,849	51,275	51,308	55,763	68,219	82,657	99,668	I 110,828	123,640	143,566	Claims on Private Sector **32d**
1,473	2,452	2,912	3,016	3,755	3,941	4,137	4,228	4,047	3,459	3,563	5,242	I 8,950	9,874	16,181	Claims on Nonmonetary Fin. Insts. **32f**
9,757	11,015	12,477	13,432	13,357	14,132	14,523	16,375	18,730	21,978	25,405	27,928	I 35,544	48,077	56,175	Money **34**
17,680	21,325	25,141	27,731	32,502	34,788	39,779	39,977	41,405	47,315	51,256	61,671	I 80,177	98,472	108,993	Quasi-Money **35**
....	....	....	....	....	....	....	....	....	....	....	....	15,251	14,933	26,529	Bonds and Money Market Instr. **36a**
I 4,295	5,576	6,759	8,597	10,129	13,336	17,900	23,460	24,072	29,255	39,005	41,364	I 27,289	33,795	30,605	Other Items (Net) **37r**
27,436	32,339	37,618	41,163	45,858	48,920	54,302	56,352	60,136	69,294	76,661	89,599	I 115,721	146,549	165,168	Money plus Quasi-Money **35l**
End of Period															**Other Banking Institutions**
1,678	2,150	2,746	3,111	4,053	4,080	4,335	3,637	2,816	....	....	....	I 4,436	8,421	10,394	Reserves **40**
2	3	2	2	—	—	2	2	2	....	....	....	I 129	137	167	Foreign Assets **41**
9,881	11,507	13,677	15,831	18,654	22,204	25,793	30,846	35,945	....	....	....	I 4,209	3,703	3,010	Claims on Central Government **42a**
6,253	8,302	....	13,856	17,599	20,460	21,368	21,325	24,102	....	....	....	I 52,706	59,678	70,911	Claims on Private Sector **42d**
....	....	....	....	....	....	....	....	....	....	....	....	5,482	7,020	9,136	Claims on Deposit Money Banks **42e**
15,552	19,183	....	28,683	35,366	40,276	46,475	46,648	51,706	....	....	....	I 47,395	58,657	64,399	Time and Savings Deposits **45**
....	....	....	....	....	....	....	....	....	....	....	....	5,091	5,039	7,556	Money Market Instruments **46aa**
....	....	....	....	....	....	....	....	....	....	....	....	453	722	707	Central Government Deposits **46d**
....	....	....	....	....	....	....	....	....	....	....	....	6,085	6,981	13,267	Credit from Deposit Money Banks **46h**
2,262	2,778	....	4,117	4,941	6,467	5,023	9,161	11,160	....	....	....	I 7,939	7,560	7,689	Other Items (Net) **47r**
End of Period															**Banking Survey**
....	....		....	....	....	....	....	....	....	....	....	33,902	55,577	61,849	Foreign Assets (Net) **51n**
....	....	....	....	....	....	....	....	....	....	....	....	172,698	193,725	219,341	Domestic Credit **52**
....	....	....	....	....	....	....	....	....	....	....	....	8,466	9,304	3,146	Claims on Central Govt. (Net) **52an**
....	....	....	....	....	....	....	....	....	....	....	....	163,534	183,317	214,477	Claims on Private Sector **52d**
....	....	....	....	....	....	....	....	....	....	....	....	698	1,104	1,718	Claims on Nonbank Fin. Insts. **52f**
41,310	49,372	....	66,735	77,171	85,116	96,442	99,363	109,025	....	....	....	I 158,787	196,785	219,173	Liquid Liabilities **55l**
....	....	....	....	....	....	....	....	....	....	....	....	31,625	42,178	48,108	Monetary Liabilities **54**
....	....	....	....	....	....	....	....	....	....	....	....	127,162	154,607	171,064	Quasi-Monetary Liabilities **55**
....	....	....	....	....	....	....	....	....	....	....	....	20,342	19,972	34,085	Bonds and Money Market Instr. **56a**
....	....	....	....	....	....	....	....	....	....	....	....	27,472	32,545	27,932	Other Items (Net) **57r**
End of Period															**Nonbank Financial Institutions**
....	....	....	825.9	834.0	865.9	960.6	....	1,058.1	....	....	....	....	....	....	Cash **40..s**
11.5	2.9	2.7	1.7	.9	.1	.1	.1	—	—	....	....	....	....	....	Foreign Assets **41..s**
327.8	395.0	442.2	421.4	452.3	489.7	....	990.9	1,547.5	1,816.3	....	....	....	....	....	Claims on Central Government **42a.s**
759.4	829.1	1,042.5	1,282.7	1,701.5	2,033.5	2,325.6	2,380.4	2,323.2	2,497.8	....	....	....	....	....	Claims on Private Sector **42d.s**
....	....	....	132.0	176.6	206.6	228.7	253.8	251.0	269.8	....	....	....	....	....	Real Estate **42h.s**

Malaysia

548

		1965	1966	1967	1968	1969	1970	1971	1972	1973	1974	1975	1976	1977	1978	1979
Interest Rates																*Percent Per Annum*
Discount Rate (End of Period)	60	5.00	5.00	5.50	4.00	4.00	5.13	4.25	3.75	3.78	4.89	4.97	4.38	3.56	4.21	3.47
Money Market Rate	60b	....	....	....	3.31	3.63	3.81	3.30	3.20	2.80	2.70	4.20	2.60	4.83	2.47	4.37
Deposit Rate	60l	....	....	....	....	....	....	....	....	....	....	....	5.50	5.21	5.13	5.50
Lending Rate	60p	....	....	....	....	....	....	....	....	....	....	....	8.50	7.92	7.50	7.50
Prices, Production, Employment																*Index Numbers (1990=100):*
Producer Prices	63	....	....	....	....	....	....	....	....	....	....	....	....	....	....	....
Consumer Prices	64	38.4	38.8	40.6	40.5	40.4	41.1	41.8	43.1	47.7	55.9	58.4	60.0	62.9	65.9	68.3
Industrial Production	66	....	....	....	16.0	17.5	18.9	19.3	21.2	24.1	26.8	26.8	31.0	33.6	36.9	40.1
Total Employment	67	....	....	....	....	....	....	....	....	....	....	....	....	....	....	....
International Transactions																*Millions of Ringgit*
Exports	70	3,783	3,846	3,724	4,123	5,055	5,163	5,017	4,854	7,372	10,195	9,231	13,442	14,959	17,074	24,222
Rubber	70l	1,462	1,474	1,275	1,353	2,031	1,724	1,460	1,298	2,507	2,887	2,026	3,117	3,380	3,601	4,482
Palm Oil	70dg	107	120	116	125	153	264	380	368	467	1,086	1,320	1,155	1,680	1,871	2,471
Tin	70q	872	793	756	830	940	1,006	901	924	897	1,515	1,206	1,527	1,704	2,022	2,316
Imports, cif	71	3,356	3,380	3,325	3,552	3,605	4,288	4,416	4,543	5,934	9,891	8,530	9,713	11,165	13,646	17,161
Imports, fob	71.v	3,178	3,201	3,149	3,362	3,354	3,981	4,080	4,206	5,467	9,070	7,808	8,792	10,078	12,262	15,444
																1990=100
Volume of Exports	72	32	29	31	37	40	42	49	42	44	42	42	54	55	61	68
Rubber	72l	73	76	79	89	103	102	105	103	124	119	110	123	125	122	125
Palm Oil	72dg	3	3	3	5	6	7	10	12	14	16	20	22	23	27	33
Tin	72q	143	140	143	167	175	176	165	170	157	161	148	155	126	133	137
Export Prices																
All Exports (Unit Value)	74	42	39	37	33	35	39	39	34	45	76	68	75	87	85	110
Rubber (Wholesale Price)	76l	67	63	52	51	67	54	44	41	72	78	60	87	89	100	122
Palm Oil (Unit Value)	74dg	96	84	79	56	55	85	85	68	75	155	146	118	166	159	167
Tin (Wholesale Price)	76q	68	62	58	55	60	64	61	61	66	110	93	111	154	168	189
Unit Value of Imports (1985=100)	75	34	35	34	35	36	36	38	40	46	66	69	71	72	74	80
Balance of Payments																*Millions of US Dollars:*
Goods: Exports f.o.b.	78aa d	....	....	....	....	....	....	....	....	....	4,199	3,826	5,293	6,093	7,380	11,074
Goods: Imports f.o.b.	78ab d	....	....	....	....	....	....	....	....	....	−3,959	−3,551	−3,812	−4,552	−5,760	−7,914
Trade Balance	78ac d	....	....	....	....	....	....	....	....	....	241	275	1,481	1,541	1,620	3,160
Services: Credit	78ad d	....	....	....	....	....	....	....	....	....	372	410	398	491	628	790
Services: Debit	78ae d	....	....	....	....	....	....	....	....	....	−698	−848	−832	−1,050	−1,359	−2,108
Balance on Goods and Services	78af d	....	....	....	....	....	....	....	....	....	−86	−163	1,047	982	889	1,842
Income: Credit	78ag d	....	....	....	....	....	....	....	....	....	162	156	175	257	378	555
Income: Debit	78ah d	....	....	....	....	....	....	....	....	....	−576	−456	−602	−771	−1,114	−1,460
Balance on Goods, Serv., & Inc.	78ai d	....	....	....	....	....	....	....	....	....	−500	−463	619	468	152	937
Current Transfers, n.i.e.: Credit	78aj d	....	....	....	....	....	....	....	....	....	47	59	58	70	76	75
Current Transfers: Debit	78ak d	....	....	....	....	....	....	....	....	....	−86	−87	−91	−91	−101	−71
Current Account, n.i.e.	78al d	....	....	....	....	....	....	....	....	....	−538	−491	586	447	127	941
Capital Account, n.i.e.: Credit	78ba d	....	....	....	....	....	....	....	....	....	—	—	—	—	—	—
Capital Account: Debit	78bb d	....	....	....	....	....	....	....	....	....	−5	−5	−6	−11	−19	−12
Capital Account, n.i.e.	78bc d	....	....	....	....	....	....	....	....	....	−5	−5	−6	−11	−19	−12
Direct Investment Abroad	78bd d	....	....	....	....	....	....	....	....	....	—	—	—	—	—	—
Dir. Invest. in Rep. Econ., n.i.e.	78be d	....	....	....	....	....	....	....	....	....	571	350	381	406	500	573
Portfolio Investment Assets	78bf d	....	....	....	....	....	....	....	....	....	—	—	—	—	—	—
Portfolio Investment Liab., n.i.e.	78bg d	....	....	....	....	....	....	....	....	....	12	268	52	63	79	194
Other Investment Assets	78bh d	....	....	....	....	....	....	....	....	....	130	−82	−282	−449	−166	−777
Other Investment Liab., n.i.e.	78bi d	....	....	....	....	....	....	....	....	....	107	121	360	234	214	211
Financial Account, n.i.e.	78bj d	....	....	....	....	....	....	....	....	....	820	658	511	253	627	202
Net Errors and Omissions	78ca d	....	....	....	....	....	....	....	....	....	−79	−96	−293	−381	−455	−329
Overall Balance	78cb d	....	....	....	....	....	....	....	....	....	198	65	798	308	279	802
Reserves and Related Items	79da d	....	....	....	....	....	....	....	....	....	−198	−65	−798	−308	−279	−802
Reserve Assets	79db d	....	....	....	....	....	....	....	....	....	−195	−68	−909	−204	−282	−792
Use of Fund Credit and Loans	79dc d	....	....	....	....	....	....	....	....	....	—	—	107	−108	—	—
Liabs.Constit.For.Auth.Reserves	79dd d	....	....	....	....	....	....	....	....	....	−2	3	4	3	3	−9
Exceptional Financing	79de d	....	....	....	....	....	....	....	....	....	—	—	—	—	—	—
Government Finance																*Millions of Ringgit:*
Deficit (-) or Surplus	80	I−482	−518	−524	−478	−414	−458	−1,010	−1,305	−1,040	−1,371	−1,892	−1,996	−2,766	−2,896	−3,683
Revenue	81	I 1,640	1,746	1,884	1,928	2,117	2,417	2,458	2,929	3,408	4,799	5,126	6,166	7,770	8,844	10,507
Expenditure	82	I 2,056	2,166	2,308	2,292	2,434	2,728	3,152	3,869	4,094	5,425	6,166	7,413	9,412	10,439	12,867
Lending Minus Repayments	83	I 66	98	100	114	97	147	316	365	354	745	852	749	1,124	1,301	1,323
Financing																
Net Borrowing: Domestic	84a	I 420	286	351	425	377	306	677	836	876	828	1,209	1,901	1,619	1,164	2,508
Foreign	85a	I 72	−10	83	63	155	−2	344	354	69	227	904	369	534	541	679
Use of Cash Balances	87	I −10	242	90	−10	−118	154	−11	115	95	316	−221	−274	613	1,191	496
Debt: Ringgits	88b	I 2,183	2,511	2,997	3,490	3,906	4,272	5,000	5,835	6,712	7,544	8,755	10,391	12,277	13,783	16,281
Foreign Currency	89b	I 510	504	530	592	747	745	1,089	1,396	1,295	1,497	2,424	2,806	3,352	3,859	4,543
National Accounts																*Millions of Ringgit*
Exports of Goods & Services	90c	4,202	4,306	4,152	4,586	5,505	5,602	5,208	5,083	7,738	11,004	10,150	14,474	16,216	18,585	26,004
Government Consumption	91f	1,441	1,637	1,677	1,707	1,815	1,997	2,170	2,738	2,934	3,516	3,924	4,301	5,388	6,090	6,475
Gross Fixed Capital Formation	93e	1,388	1,456	1,480	1,479	1,630	2,152	2,701	3,211	4,219	5,798	5,602	6,206	7,465	9,381	12,250
Increase/Decrease(-) in Stocks	93i	2	20	92	123	68	315	2	−179	206	974	101	192	247	723	1,173
Private Consumption	96f	5,622	5,915	6,274	6,518	6,960	7,486	7,911	8,613	10,308	12,776	13,086	14,715	16,812	19,584	22,406
Imports of Goods & Services	98c	−3,818	−3,940	−3,901	−4,253	−4,349	−5,397	−5,037	−5,246	−6,682	−11,210	−10,531	−11,803	−13,788	−16,477	−21,884
Gross Domestic Product	99b	8,837	9,394	9,774	10,160	11,629	12,155	12,955	14,220	18,723	22,858	22,332	28,085	32,340	37,886	46,424
Net Factor Inc/Pmts(-) Abroad	98.n	−255	−268	−144	−154	−334	−355	−363	−378	−659	−997	−727	−1,097	−1,276	−1,700	−2,070
Gross Nat'l Expenditure = GNP	99a	8,582	9,126	9,630	10,006	11,295	11,800	12,592	13,842	18,064	21,861	21,605	26,988	31,064	36,186	44,354
Gross Dom. Prod. 1990 Prices	99b.p	....	....	....	....	....	30,149	32,285	35,317	39,449	42,731	43,073	48,054	51,779	I 55,225	60,388
GDP Deflator (1990=100)	99bi p	....	....	....	....	....	40.3	40.1	40.3	47.5	53.5	51.8	58.4	62.5	68.6	76.9
																Millions:
Population	99z	9.24	9.47	9.71	9.94	10.15	10.39	10.70	11.00	11.31	11.65	11.90	12.30	12.58	12.91	13.45

Monetary Authorities: I Beginning in January 1992, lines *12d, 12e,* and *12f,* which were previously included in *line 17r,* are shown separately. Revised data for *Central Government Deposits (line 16d)* and *Reserve Money (line 14)* reflect an improved classification of accounts.

Deposit Money Banks: I Beginning in December 1980, claims on financial institutions *(line 22f)*, which were previously included in *line 27r,* are shown separately. I Beginning in January 1992, revised data reflect an improved classification of accounts.

Monetary Survey: I See notes to sections 10 and 20.

Other Banking Institutions: I Prior to December 1969, savings institutions' data relate to the national savings banks; beginning in December 1969, finance companies' data are included. Data for the Employees Provident Fund and the merchant banks are also included beginning in January 1971 and January 1974, respectively. I Beginning in January 1992, comprises finance companies, merchant banks, and discount houses. The revised data exclude accounts of the National Savings Bank and the Employees Provident Fund.

Banking Survey: I See notes to sections 10, 20, and 40.

Government Finance: I Data are as reported for publication in *IFS*.

Malaysia
548

1980	1981	1982	1983	1984	1985	1986	1987	1988	1989	1990	1991	1992	1993	1994		
Percent Per Annum															**Interest Rates**	
4.46	4.50	5.12	5.20	5.06	4.13	3.89	3.20	3.33	4.44	6.79	7.38	....	....	5.07	Discount Rate *(End of Period)*	60
3.31	3.47	7.90	8.97	8.96	7.57	8.03	2.85	3.22	4.72	6.81	7.83	....	....	....	Money Market Rate	60b
6.23	9.67	9.75	8.02	9.54	8.81	7.17	3.00	....	4.60	5.90	7.18	....	....	....	Deposit Rate	60l
7.75	8.50	8.79	11.08	11.35	11.54	10.80	8.19	7.25	7.00	7.17	8.13	....	....	7.62	Lending Rate	60p
Period Averages															**Prices, Production, Employment**	
....	....	....	93.4	91.5	85.8	89.0	95.5	99.1	100.0	104.0	105.2	106.7	111.9		Producer Prices	63
I72.9	80.0	84.6	87.7	91.2	91.5	92.2	92.4	94.8	97.4	I100.0	104.4	109.3	113.2	I117.4	Consumer Prices	64
42.4	I43.8	46.2	51.9	60.3	58.8	64.4	69.8	I79.7	89.2	100.0	111.2	120.9	132.4	148.3	Industrial Production	66
72.3	75.7	78.5	81.2	83.2	84.1	85.3	88.0	91.0	95.6	100.0	103.1	106.1	110.6	113.9	Total Employment	67
Millions of Ringgit															**International Transactions**	
28,172	27,109	28,108	32,771	38,647	38,017	35,319	45,225	55,260	67,824	79,646	94,497	103,657	121,238	153,688	Exports	70
4,618	3,713	2,655	3,664	3,672	2,872	3,183	3,915	5,256	3,949	3,028	2,690	2,357	2,144	2,927	Rubber	70l
2,603	2,836	2,742	2,995	4,547	3,963	3,019	3,292	4,540	4,691	4,411	5,045	5,437	5,797	6,570	Palm Oil	70dg
2,505	2,138	1,484	1,718	1,162	1,648	650	839	910	1,161	902	684	730	489	507	Tin	70q
23,451	26,604	29,023	30,795	32,926	30,438	27,921	31,934	43,293	60,858	79,119	100,831	101,441	117,422	155,871	Imports, cif	71
21,144	24,015	26,286	27,819	29,772	27,596	25,268	28,900	39,179	55,075	71,601	91.250	91,802	106,264	141,060	Imports, fob	71.v
1990=100																
66	63	67	75	77	81	86	89	92	98	100	97	96	86	84	Volume of Exports	72
115	112	104	118	120	113	115	123	122	113	100	86	78	71	77	Rubber	72l
40	44	50	52	53	57	76	72	73	87	100	98	98	104	116	Palm Oil	72dg
132	126	92	108	75	109	77	94	93	94	100	81	86	67	67	Tin	72q
															Export Prices	
127	126	118	112	122	109	75	90	99	101	100	102	....	....	....	All Exports (Unit Value)	74
136	113	88	108	98	82	91	109	135	116	100	104	100	99	124	Rubber (Wholesale Price)	76l
148	146	125	131	196	158	90	103	140	122	100	117	125	127	129	Palm Oil (Unit Value)	74dg
209	189	176	176	170	173	90	98	108	137	100	94	93	80	84	Tin (Wholesale Price)	76q
95	109	104	101	100	88	89	....	....	....						Unit Value of Imports (1985=100)	75
Minus Sign Indicates Debit															Balance of Payments	
12,963	11,771	12,070	13,804	16,521	15,251	13,655	17,877	20,980	24,776	28,806	33,712	39,828	46,220	....	Goods: Exports f.o.b.	78aa*d*
−10,569	−11,886	−12,801	−13,366	−13,590	−11,677	−10,441	−12,093	−15,553	−20,498	−26,280	−33,321	−36,678	−43,209	....	Goods: Imports f.o.b.	78ab*d*
2,393	−115	−731	438	2,931	3,573	3,214	5,783	5,427	4,277	2,525	391	3,150	3,011	....	Trade Balance	78ac*d*
1,135	1,315	1,579	1,851	1,932	1,934	1,981	2,273	2,379	2,870	3,859	4,374	5,223	5,371	....	Services: Credit	78ad*d*
−2,957	−2,856	−3,269	−3,964	−4,254	−3,927	−3,575	−3,595	−4,205	−4,792	−5,485	−6,564	−7,197	−7,800	....	Services: Debit	78ae*d*
572	−1,655	−2,421	−1,675	609	1,581	1,621	4,461	3,600	2,356	900	−1,799	1,176	582	....	Balance on Goods and Services	78af*d*
739	792	650	562	614	591	548	834	1,090	1,172	1,849	1,425	1,605	1,987	....	Income: Credit	78ag*d*
−1,575	−1,589	−1,797	−2,375	−2,856	−2,779	−2,329	−2,797	−3,032	−3,351	−3,721	−3,898	−4,748	−5,194	....	Income: Debit	78ah*d*
−264	−2,452	−3,569	−3,488	−1,633	−607	−160	2,498	1,659	177	−972	−4,271	−1,968	−2,625	....	Balance on Goods, Serv., & Inc.	78ai*d*
73	74	79	77	70	93	149	173	288	212	249	215	296	345	....	Current Transfers, n.i.e.: Credit	78aj*d*
−75	−91	−95	−72	−94	−86	−91	−96	−80	−74	−147	−126	−116	−131	....	Current Transfers: Debit	78ak*d*
−266	−2,469	−3,585	−3,482	−1,657	−600	−101	2,575	1,867	315	−870	−4,183	−1,788	−2,411	....	Current Account, n.i.e.	78al*d*
														....	Capital Account, n.i.e.: Credit	78ba*d*
−19	−17	−15	−15	−15	−13	−21	−33	−58	−57	−48	−51	−47	−56	....	Capital Account: Debit	78bb*d*
−19	−17	−15	−15	−15	−13	−21	−33	−58	−57	−48	−51	−47	−56	....	Capital Account, n.i.e.	78bc*d*
—	—	—	—	—	—	—	—	—	—	—	—	—	—	....	Direct Investment Abroad	78bd*d*
934	1,265	1,397	1,261	797	695	489	423	719	1,668	2,332	3,998	5,183	5,206	....	Dir. Invest. in Rep. Econ., n.i.e.	78be*d*
														....	Portfolio Investment Assets	78bf*d*
−11	1,131	601	668	1,108	1,942	30	140	−448	−107	−255	170	−1,108	−984	....	Portfolio Investment Liab., n.i.e.	78bg*d*
−101	−276	−136	−1,471	262	155	58	−529	−1,083	32	−205	957	1,542	−938	....	Other Investment Assets	78bh*d*
613	496	1,883	3,395	853	−858	525	−1,571	−1,162	−262	−87	497	3,166	7,723	....	Other Investment Liab., n.i.e.	78bi*d*
1,435	2,616	3,745	3,853	3,021	1,933	1,102	−1,537	−1,973	1,330	1,786	5,623	8,784	11,007	....	Financial Account, n.i.e.	78bj*d*
−682	−582	−406	−371	−863	−168	476	114	−267	−358	1,085	−151	−292	2,802	....	Net Errors and Omissions	78ca*d*
468	−452	−262	−15	486	1,151	1,455	1,119	−430	1,230	1,953	1,238	6,655	11,343	....	Overall Balance	78cb*d*
−468	452	262	15	−486	−1,151	−1,455	−1,119	430	−1,230	−1,953	−1,238	−6,655	−11,343	....	Reserves and Related Items	79da*d*
−464	235	199	−60	−438	−987	−1,340	−1,139	458	−1,235	−1,951	−1,236	−6,658	−11,350	....	Reserve Assets	79db*d*
—	217	64	73	−54	−161	−121	—	—	—	—	—	—	—	....	Use of Fund Credit and Loans	79dc*d*
−4	—	−2	3	6	−4	6	20	−28	5	−1	−1	3	7	....	Liabs.Constit.For.Auth.Reserves	79dd*d*
														....	Exceptional Financing	79de*d*
Year Ending December 31															**Government Finance**	
−7,104	−11,015	−11,171	−9,183	−7,075	−5,708	−7,506	−6,153	−3,891	−5,260	−5,515	−5,640	−6,243	−8,646	4,409	Deficit (-) or Surplus	80
13,926	15,806	16,690	18,608	20,805	21,114	19,518	18,143	21,967	25,273	29,521	34,053	39,250	41,691	49,446	Revenue	81
18,971	24,550	23,751	24,166	24,085	23,902	24,444	23,379	25,207	30,838	36,264	39,812	45,711	50,209	45,013	Expenditure	82
2,059	2,271	4,110	3,625	3,795	2,920	2,580	917	651	−305	−1,228	−119	−218	128	24	Lending Minus Repayments	83
															Financing	
2,311	4,072	6,047	4,503	3,156	3,591	4,930	8,693	7,854	2,492	3,816	3,157	1,480	375	1,848	Net Borrowing: Domestic	84a
310	3,419	4,894	4,569	3,093	957	1,348	−2,438	−3,095	−1,038	−787	106	−3,170	−3,134	−4,757	Foreign	85a
4,483	3,524	230	111	826	1,160	1,228	−102	−868	3,806	2,486	2,377	7,933	11,405	−1,500	Use of Cash Balances	87
18,578	22,851	28,711	33,955	37,075	40,812	45,698	54,796	63,097	65,763	69,988	73,655	76,083	76,536	78,260	Debt: Ringgits	88b
4,861	8,278	13,158	17,728	20,848	23,070	28,310	27,629	25,922	24,182	24,182	25,145	20,922	19,362	14,818	Foreign Currency	89b
Millions of Ringgit															**National Accounts**	
30,676	30,154	31,846	35,795	43,171	42,537	40,305	50,838	61,435	75,151	88,354	104,740	114,760	132,800	166,467	Exports of Goods & Services	90c
8,811	10,425	11,469	11,015	11,741	11,844	12,127	12,239	12,997	14,769	16,190	18,391	19,304	21,590	24,026	Government Consumption	91f
16,597	20,759	22,745	25,213	25,391	23,124	18,865	18,280	21,922	30,063	37,490	46,181	50,697	57,355	70,748	Gross Fixed Capital Formation	93e
−380	−602	593	1,253	1,306	−1,757	−261	175	1,662	−769	−1,189	324	−1,257	−313	628	Increase/Decrease(-) in Stocks	93i
26,946	30,594	33,226	36,458	39,594	40,360	36,499	37,685	44,856	52,165	60,903	69,609	76,046	62,913	92,857	Private Consumption	96f
−29,342	−33,717	−37,300	−39,793	−41,653	−38,561	−35,941	−39,592	−52,011	−68,792	−85,920	−109,686	−111,756	−131,302	−169,382	Imports of Goods & Services	98c
53,308	57,613	62,579	69,941	79,550	77,547	71,594	79,625	90,861	102,587	115,828	129,559	147,784	163,039	185,344	Gross Domestic Product	99h
−1,918	−2,011	−2,889	−4,411	−5,368	−5,508	−4,780	−4,946	5,084	5,903	−5,064	−6,800	−8,008	−6,256	−9,067	Net Factor Inc/Pmts(-) Abroad	98.n
51,390	55,602	59,690	65,530	74,182	72,039	66,814	74,679	85,777	96,684	110,764	122,759	139,778	154,788	176,257	Gross Nat'l Expenditure = GNP	99a
64,883	69,387	73,509	78,104	84,166	83,305	84,179	88,717	96,647	105,547	115,828	125,861	135,667	146,987	159,848	Gross Dom. Prod. 1990 Prices	99b.*p*
82.2	83.0	85.1	89.5	94.5	93.1	85.0	89.8	94.0	97.2	100.0	102.9	108.9	110.9	116.0	GDP Deflator (1990=100)	99bi*p*
Midyear Estimates																
13.70	14.11	14.51	14.89	15.27	15.68	16.11	16.53	16.94	17.35	17.76	18.18	18.61	19.25	....	Population	99z

Maldives

		1965	1966	1967	1968	1969	1970	1971	1972	1973	1974	1975	1976	1977	1978	1979
Exchange Rates																*Rufiyaa per SDR:*
Market Rate	aa	4.775	4.775	4.750	4.750	4.750	4.750	4.750	4.750	4.741	4.812	7.170	10.021	10.841	11.237	9.946
																Rufiyaa per US Dollar:
Market Rate	ae	4.775	4.775	4.750	4.750	4.750	4.750	4.375	4.375	3.930	3.930	6.125	8.625	8.925	8.625	7.550
Market Rate	rf	4.762	4.762	4.761^e	4.750^e	4.750^e	4.750^e	4.734^e	4.375^e	3.986^e	3.930^e	5.765^e	8.365^e	8.767^e	8.969^e	7.489
Fund Position																*Millions of SDRs:*
Quota	2f. s	....	....	....	....	....	....	....	....	....	....	....	....	....	.9	.9
SDRs	1b. s	....	....	....	....	....	....	....	....	....	....	....	....	....	—	.1
Reserve Position in the Fund	1c. s	....	....	....	....	....	....	....	....	....	....	....	....	....	.2	.2
International Liquidity													*Millions of US Dollars Unless Otherwise Indicated:*			
Total Reserves minus Gold	1l. d	....	....	....	....	....	....	....	....	....	....	....	.01	.08	.57	.71
SDRs	1b. d	....	....	....	....	....	....	....	....	....	....	....	....	....	—	.12
Reserve Position in the Fund	1c. d	....	....	....	....	....	....	....	....	....	....	....	....	....	.22	.22
Foreign Exchange	1d. d	....	....	....	....	....	....	....	....	....	....	....	.01	.08	.35	.37
Gold (Million Fine Troy Ounces)	1ad	....	....	....	....	....	....	....	....	....	....	....	....	....	....	....
Gold (National Valuation)	1and	....	....	....	....	....	....	....	....	....	....	....	....	....	....	....
Monetary Authorities: Other Liab.	4..d	....	....	....	....	....	....	....	....	....	....	....	—	—	—	—
Deposit Money Banks: Assets	7a. d	....	....	....	....	....	....	....	....	....	....	....	.23	.27	2.38	1.81
of which: Claims on Nonbanks	7ad d	....	....	....	....	....	....	....	....	....	....	....	....	....	....	....
Deposit Money Banks: Liabilities	7b. d	....	....	....	....	....	....	....	....	....	....	....	.06	.93	.54	.24
Monetary Authorities																*Millions of Rufiyaa:*
Foreign Assets	11	....	....	....	....	....	....	....	....	....	....	....	.02	.31	2.41	2.96
Claims on Central Government	12a	....	....	....	....	....	....	....	....	....	....	....	111.29	121.52	90.70	111.16
Claims on Nonfin.Pub.Enterprises	12c	....	....	....	....	....	....	....	....	....	....	....	....	....	....	....
Claims on Deposit Money Banks	12e	....	....	....	....	....	....	....	....	....	....	....	—	.01	2.57	2.24
Reserve Money	14	....	....	....	....	....	....	....	....	....	....	....	57.44	53.71	37.72	63.10
of which: Currency Outside DMBs	14a	....	....	....	....	....	....	....	....	....	....	....	13.22	14.18	17.53	23.12
Foreign Liabilities	16c	....	....	....	....	....	....	....	....	....	....	....	....	....	....	....
Central Government Deposits	16d	....	....	....	....	....	....	....	....	....	....	....	53.87	68.14	57.96	51.97
Capital Accounts	17a	....	....	....	....	....	....	....	....	....	....	....	—	—	—	.45
Other Items (Net)	17r	....	....	....	....	....	....	....	....	....	....	....	—	—	—	.84
Deposit Money Banks																*Millions of Rufiyaa:*
Reserves	20	....	....	....	....	....	....	....	....	....	....	....	23.71	22.68	4.25	12.08
Foreign Assets	21	....	....	....	....	....	....	....	....	....	....	....	1.97	2.42	20.56	13.64
Claims on Central Government	22a	....	....	....	....	....	....	....	....	....	....	....	—	—	—	—
Claims on Nonfin.Pub.Enterprises	22c	....	....	....	....	....	....	....	....	....	....	....	—	2.10	—	3.02
Claims on Private Sector	22d	....	....	....	....	....	....	....	....	....	....	....	2.20	16.43	13.66	17.55
Demand Deposits	24	....	....	....	....	....	....	....	....	....	....	....	16.16	18.16	3.91	6.23
Time and Savings Deposits	25	....	....	....	....	....	....	....	....	....	....	....	8.05	16.98	29.28	37.01
Foreign Liabilities	26c	....	....	....	....	....	....	....	....	....	....	....	.54	8.27	4.69	1.80
Central Government Deposits	26d	....	....	....	....	....	....	....	....	....	....	....	—	—	—	—
Capital Accounts	27a	....	....	....	....	....	....	....	....	....	....	....	—	—	.84	.14
Other Items (Net)	27r	....	....	....	....	....	....	....	....	....	....	....	3.12	.21	−.26	1.13
Monetary Survey																*Millions of Rufiyaa:*
Foreign Assets (Net)	31n	....	....	....	....	....	....	....	....	....	....	....	1.45	−5.55	18.28	14.81
Domestic Credit	32	....	....	....	....	....	....	....	....	....	....	....	59.62	71.91	46.40	79.76
Claims on Central Govt. (Net)	32an	....	....	....	....	....	....	....	....	....	....	....	57.42	53.38	32.74	59.19
Claims on Nonfin.Pub.Enterprises	32c	....	....	....	....	....	....	....	....	....	....	....	—	2.10	—	3.02
Claims on Private Sector	32d	....	....	....	....	....	....	....	....	....	....	....	2.20	16.43	13.66	17.55
Money	34	....	....	....	....	....	....	....	....	....	....	....	53.76	46.19	37.52	53.41
Quasi-Money	35	....	....	....	....	....	....	....	....	....	....	....	8.05	16.98	29.28	37.01
Other Items (Net)	37r	....	....	....	....	....	....	....	....	....	....	....	−.75	3.19	−2.13	4.15
Money plus Quasi-Money	35l	....	....	....	....	....	....	....	....	....	....	....	61.82	63.17	66.81	90.42
Interest Rates																*Percent Per Annum*
Money Market Rate	60b	....	....	....	....	....	....	....	....	....	....	....	....	....	....	....
Prices and Production																*Index Numbers (1990=100):*
Consumer Prices	64	....	....	....	....	....	....	....	....	....	....	....	....	30.2	34.0	43.4
Total Fish Catch	66al	....	....	....	....	....	....	....	....	....	....	....	....	34.4	33.8	36.3
Tourist Bed Night Index	66.t	....	....	....	....	....	....	....	....	....	....	....	....	7.8	12.2	12.8
International Transactions																*Millions of US Dollars*
Exports	70..d	2.5	2.2	2.6	2.4	2.8	3.9	4.3	3.5	3.5	4.0	2.5	3.0	3.4	4.1	4.6
Imports, cif	71..d	1.8	2.3	3.5	2.2	3.1	2.4	3.5	5.4	7.5	7.5	7.4	6.0	10.0	14.4	21.5
Imports, fob	71.v d	1.6	2.1	3.2	2.0	2.8	2.2	3.2	4.9	6.8	6.8	6.8	5.5	9.1	13.1	19.5

Maldives 556

	1980	1981	1982	1983	1984	1985	1986	1987	1988	1989	1990	1991	1992	1993	1994		
End of Period																**Exchange Rates**	
	9.629	8.788	7.777	7.381	6.910	7.830	8.861	13.328	11.472	12.097	13.686	14.762	14.486	15.253	17.182	Market Rate	aa
End of Period (ae)	*Period Average (rf)*																
	7.550	7.550	7.050	7.050	7.050	7.129	7.244	9.395	8.525	9.205	9.620	10.320	10.535	11.105	11.770	Market Rate	ae
	7.550	7.550	7.174	7.050	7.050	7.050	7.098	7.151	9.223	8.785	9.041	9.552	10.253	10.569	10.957	11.586	Market Rate	rf
End of Period																**Fund Position**	
	1.4	1.4	1.4	2.0	2.0	2.0	2.0	2.0	2.0	2.0	2.0	2.0	2.0	5.5	5.5	5.5	Quota	2f. s
	.1	.2	.2	—	—	—	—	—	—	—	—	—	—	—	—	—	SDRs	1b. s
	.3	.3	.3	.5	—	—	—	—	—	—	—	—	—	.9	.9	.9	Reserve Position in the Fund	1c. s
End of Period																**International Liquidity**	
	.95	1.15	8.41	4.54	5.13	4.59	6.91	8.19	21.59	24.77	24.38	23.47	28.19	26.15	31.22	Total Reserves minus Gold	1l. d
	.08	.19	.17	—	.01	.02	.02	.01	.03	.03	.03	.03	.01	.03	.05	SDRs	1b. d
	.38	.35	.33	.47	—	—	—	—	—	—	—	—	1.21	1.21	1.28	Reserve Position in the Fund	1c. d
	.49	.61	7.91	4.07	5.12	4.57	6.89	8.18	21.56	24.74	24.35	23.44	26.97	24.92	29.89	Foreign Exchange	1d. d
	....	—	—	—	—	—	—	—	—	—	—	—	—	—	.01	Gold (Million Fine Troy Ounces)	1ad
	....	.055	.042	.042	.042	.042	.042	.042	.042	.042	.042	.042	.042	.042	.042	Gold (National Valuation)	1and
	—	.23	8.20	7.71	7.21	3.48	1.87	.13	.20	.19	.18	.17	.17	15.39	14.52	Monetary Authorities: Other Liab.	4.. d
	2.44	2.75	1.94	1.72	3.56	2.24	2.30	7.22	5.60	8.62	10.66	12.84	14.62	10.30	10.23	Deposit Money Banks: Assets	7a. d
	—	.99	.66	.30	2.33	.63	.65	1.54	2.05	2.01	4.90	2.75	2.79	.64	2.45	*of which:* Claims on Nonbanks	7ad d
	1.58	10.43	14.31	18.32	25.55	30.66	24.84	21.29	19.08	28.83	27.95	17.81	22.08	18.37	13.61	Deposit Money Banks: Liabilities	7b. d
End of Period																**Monetary Authorities**	
	3.88	I 6.03	63.39	36.38	36.27	33.77	51.45	78.45	187.13	226.53	230.39	237.17	292.60	293.92	376.86	Foreign Assets	11
	142.95	I 152.95	156.21	167.39	185.21	I 244.78	286.44	297.26	228.24	288.13	318.43	448.23	618.97	910.65	999.33	Claims on Central Government	12a
	....	....	....	....	9.10	3.36	11.92	14.84	20.06	4.45	40.68	8.86	9.75	6.16	Claims on Nonfin.Pub.Enterprises	12c
	3.32	1.96	1.15	.15	.40	.17	.23	.95	.54	4.06	9.14	9.56	8.80	7.91	6.57	Claims on Deposit Money Banks	12e
	99.87	I 106.77	97.18	117.34	155.69	209.98	239.76	246.48	301.26	358.53	445.80	544.00	732.37	870.49	998.59	Reserve Money	14
	27.46	32.37	41.70	50.31	56.77	68.52	91.97	116.54	140.08	158.32	206.73	253.46	300.91	330.38	382.27	*of which:* Currency Outside DMBs	14a
	—	1.76	57.79	54.33	50.86	I 24.80	13.54	1.27	1.70	1.71	1.70	1.80	1.81	170.90	189.90	Foreign Liabilities	16c
	48.47	45.82	26.74	22.37	30.32	29.63	61.39	98.89	89.70	112.07	45.60	95.13	93.65	70.28	66.47	Central Government Deposits	16d
	1.86	2.34	7.18	6.06	9.62	11.22	13.16	26.58	17.81	36.72	42.23	51.57	46.63	74.49	90.52	Capital Accounts	17a
	—	I 4.26	31.86	3.82	−24.61	12.19	13.62	15.35	20.28	29.75	27.08	43.14	54.79	36.06	43.43	Other Items (Net)	17r
End of Period																**Deposit Money Banks**	
	10.31	3.87	20.05	47.29	71.24	72.38	91.08	98.56	135.98	161.75	199.35	252.79	383.00	454.02	498.55	Reserves	20
	18.43	20.80	13.71	12.13	25.12	15.99	16.68	67.82	47.75	79.33	102.54	132.52	154.02	114.43	120.46	Foreign Assets	21
	—	22.83	34.40	20.14	—	4.80	2.32	2.97	1.62	2.44	5.60	8.73	9.95	4.21	—	Claims on Central Government	22a
	40.66	38.58	13.61	42.63	65.70	84.64	88.42	101.61	106.91	191.47	155.09	161.55	154.31	177.04	137.24	Claims on Nonfin.Pub.Enterprises	22c
	16.47	51.16	97.92	126.51	187.07	184.00	181.51	180.59	159.15	195.55	255.30	247.80	256.75	398.53	507.38	Claims on Private Sector	22d
	7.29	6.31	14.28	18.60	29.37	26.23	39.45	51.24	57.27	66.95	68.21	112.98	117.02	281.13	356.06	Demand Deposits	24
	62.16	48.02	47.13	49.27	68.67	72.39	107.05	132.17	156.26	189.75	224.67	269.48	293.80	340.13	429.26	Time and Savings Deposits	25
	11.90	78.78	100.86	129.18	180.11	I 218.54	179.98	199.99	162.68	265.41	268.85	183.76	232.62	203.95	160.22	Foreign Liabilities	26c
	—	.16	.63	6.55	13.99	1.73	1.09	1.89	3.90	11.04	13.27	21.31	51.06	60.40	31.52	Central Government Deposits	26d
	.39	.47	5.63	26.61	26.83	27.81	32.57	43.76	44.14	38.66	48.04	62.15	91.72	122.32	143.77	Capital Accounts	27a
	4.12	I 3.49	11.16	18.50	30.17	15.12	19.86	22.51	27.16	58.75	94.84	153.73	171.82	140.32	142.80	Other Items (Net)	27r
End of Period																**Monetary Survey**	
	10.41	I −53.72	−81.55	−135.00	−169.58	I −193.58	−125.38	−54.99	70.50	38.74	62.38	184.13	212.19	33.50	147.20	Foreign Assets (Net)	31n
	151.61	I 219.55	274.77	327.75	393.67	I 495.95	499.56	493.57	417.15	574.54	679.99	790.55	904.13	1,369.50	1,552.12	Domestic Credit	32
	94.48	I 129.80	163.24	158.61	140.90	I 218.21	226.27	199.45	136.25	167.46	265.16	340.52	484.21	784.18	901.34	Claims on Central Govt. (Net)	32an
	40.66	38.58	13.61	42.63	65.70	93.74	91.78	113.53	121.75	211.53	159.54	202.23	163.17	186.79	143.40	Claims on Nonfin.Pub.Enterprises	32c
	16.47	51.16	97.92	126.51	187.07	184.00	181.51	180.59	159.15	195.55	255.30	247.80	256.75	398.53	507.38	Claims on Private Sector	32d
	80.75	I 109.33	92.74	88.80	113.90	163.69	188.80	198.45	221.67	263.14	312.86	402.05	463.88	694.54	850.87	Money	34
	62.16	48.47	47.82	49.35	68.91	72.47	107.12	132.86	157.01	190.33	225.31	270.20	295.43	340.76	434.76	Quasi-Money	35
	19.11	I 8.04	52.66	54.60	41.29	66.22	78.23	107.28	108.97	159.82	204.21	302.44	357.04	367.71	413.68	Other Items (Net)	37r
	142.91	I 157.79	140.56	138.16	182.81	236.15	295.92	331.31	378.68	453.47	538.17	672.25	759.31	1,035.30	1,285.63	Money plus Quasi-Money	35l
Percent Per Annum																**Interest Rates**	
	....	....	....	....	11.00	9.00	9.00	8.67	8.50	7.33	7.00	....	....	....	....	Money Market Rate	60b
Period Averages																**Prices and Production**	
	53.8	66.5	81.1	—	—	—	—	—	90.0	I 96.5	100.0	114.7	134.0	161.1	....	Consumer Prices	64
	45.3	45.7	39.7	50.5	72.1	81.1	77.6	74.5	93.6	93.3	100.0	105.7	107.2	117.8	....	Total Fish Catch	66al
	17.8	26.5	35.3	38.5	47.1	62.5	61.5	75.4	98.8	86.9	100.0	102.6	117.4	124.4	....	Tourist Bed Night Index	66.t
Millions of US Dollars																**International Transactions**	
	7.8	8.6	9.8	13.4	17.6	23.0	24.5	30.8	40.2	44.7	52.1	53.7	40.0	34.6	45.9	Exports	70. d
	28.6	30.6	43.2	56.9	53.3	52.7	44.6	81.0	90.1	112.6	137.8	161.2	189.3	185.1	221.7	Imports, cif	71.. d
	26.0	27.9	39.3	51.7	48.5	47.9	40.5	73.7	81.9	95.7	117.1	137.0	166.6	168.3	195.1	Imports, fob	71.v d

Maldives

556

		1965	1966	1967	1968	1969	1970	1971	1972	1973	1974	1975	1976	1977	1978	1979
Balance of Payments														\multicolumn{3}{r}{*Millions of US Dollars:*}		
Goods: Exports f.o.b.	78aa d	....	....	....	....	....	....	....	....	....	....	....	....	5.0	7.2	10.7
Goods: Imports f.o.b.	78ab d	....	....	....	....	....	....	....	....	....	....	....	....	-9.9	-14.8	-21.7
Trade Balance	78ac d	....	....	....	....	....	....	....	....	....	....	....	....	-4.9	-7.6	-11.0
Services: Credit	78ad d	....	....	....	....	....	....	....	....	....	....	....	....	5.0	5.6	31.1
Services: Debit	78ae d	....	....	....	....	....	....	....	....	....	....	....	....	-1.0	-1.4	-25.0
Balance on Goods and Services	78af d	....	....	....	....	....	....	....	....	....	....	....	....	-.9	-3.4	-4.9
Income: Credit	78ag d	....	....	....	....	....	....	....	....	....	....	....	....	—	—	—
Income: Debit	78ah d	....	....	....	....	....	....	....	....	....	....	....	....	—	—	-1.6
Balance on Goods, Serv., & Inc.	78ai d	....	....	....	....	....	....	....	....	....	....	....	....	-.9	-3.4	-6.5
Current Transfers, n.i.e.: Credit	78aj d	....	....	....	....	....	....	....	....	....	....	....	....	.9	5.0	1.7
Current Transfers: Debit	78ak d	....	....	....	....	....	....	....	....	....	....	....	....	—	—	—
Current Account, n.i.e.	78al d	....	....	....	....	....	....	....	....	....	....	....	....	—	1.6	-4.8
Capital Account, n.i.e.: Credit	78ba d	....	....	....	....	....	....	....	....	....	....	....	....	—	—	—
Capital Account: Debit	78bb d	....	....	....	....	....	....	....	....	....	....	....	....	—	—	—
Capital Account, n.i.e.	78bc d	....	....	....	....	....	....	....	....	....	....	....	....	—	—	—
Direct Investment Abroad	78bd d	....	....	....	....	....	....	....	....	....	....	....	....	—	—	—
Dir. Invest. in Rep. Econ., n.i.e.	78be d	....	....	....	....	....	....	....	....	....	....	....	....	—	—	—
Portfolio Investment Assets	78bf d	....	....	....	....	....	....	....	....	....	....	....	....	—	—	—
Portfolio Investment Liab., n.i.e.	78bg d	....	....	....	....	....	....	....	....	....	....	....	....	—	—	—
Other Investment Assets	78bh d	....	....	....	....	....	....	....	....	....	....	....	....	—	-2.1	.6
Other Investment Liab., n.i.e.	78bi d	....	....	....	....	....	....	....	....	....	....	....	....	2.5	2.0	7.3
Financial Account, n.i.e.	78bj d	....	....	....	....	....	....	....	....	....	....	....	....	2.5	-.1	7.9
Net Errors and Omissions	78ca d	....	....	....	....	....	....	....	....	....	....	....	....	-2.4	-1.3	-3.1
Overall Balance	78cb d	....	....	....	....	....	....	....	....	....	....	....	....	.1	.2	—
Reserves and Related Items	79da d	....	....	....	....	....	....	....	....	....	....	....	....	-.1	-.2	—
Reserve Assets	79db d	....	....	....	....	....	....	....	....	....	....	....	....	-.1	-.2	—
Use of Fund Credit and Loans	79dc d	....	....	....	....	....	....	....	....	....	....	....	....	—	—	—
Liabs.Constit.For.Auth.Reserves	79dd d	....	....	....	....	....	....	....	....	....	....	....	....	—	—	—
Exceptional Financing	79de d	....	....	....	....	....	....	....	....	....	....	....	....	—	—	—
Government Finance																*Millions of Rufiyaa:*
Deficit (-) or Surplus	80													....	....	-27.9
Revenue	81													....	....	16.5
Grants Received	81z													....	....	7.9
Expenditure	82													....	....	48.6
Lending Minus Repayments	83													....	....	3.7
Financing																
Domestic	84a													....	....	16.4
Foreign	85a													....	....	11.5
Debt: Domestic	88a													....	....	....
Debt: Foreign	89a													....	....	23.2
National Accounts																*Millions of Rufiyaa*
Exports of Goods & Services	90c	....	....	....	....	....	....	....	....	....	....	....	....	....	....	....
Government Consumption	91f	....	....	....	....	....	....	....	....	....	....	....	....	....	....	....
Gross Fixed Capital Formation	93e	....	....	....	....	....	....	....	....	....	....	....	....	....	....	....
Increase/Decrease(-) in Stocks	93i	....	....	....	....	....	....	....	....	....	....	....	....	....	....	....
Private Consumption	96f	....	....	....	....	....	....	....	....	....	....	....	....	....	....	....
Imports of Goods & Services	98c	....	....	....	....	....	....	....	....	....	....	....	....	....	....	....
Gross Domestic Product	99b	....	....	....	....	....	....	....	....	....	....	....	....	142	170	224
Gross Dom. Prod. 1990 Prices	99b. p	....	....	....	....	....	....	....	....	....	172.2	168.6	212.4	246.5	283.4	313.0
GDP Deflator (1990=100)	99bi p	....	....	....	....	....	....	....	....	....	....	....	....	57.7	59.9	71.5
																Millions:
Population	99z	.10	.10	.10	.11	.11	.11	.11	.11	.12	.13	.13	.13	.14	.15	.15

Monetary Authorities: ℹ Beginning in 1981, comprises the Maldives Monetary Authority only, which was established in June 1981. Before that date, the data relate to the monetary authority functions of the Department of Finance (Treasury) and the State Trading Organization, which managed a large part of the official foreign exchange holdings.

Claims on Central Government (line 12a): ℹ Prior to January 1985, data include claims on nonfinancial public enterprises.

Foreign Liabilities (line 16c): ℹ Prior to January 1985, data include amounts of government foreign borrowing, with a contra-entry in *Claims on Government (line 12a)*.

Deposit Money Banks: ℹ Beginning in 1981, data are based on an improved sectorization of accounts.

Foreign Liabilities (line 26c): ℹ Prior to January 1985, data exclude nonresident deposits with domestic banks.

Monetary Survey: ℹ See notes to sections 10 and 20.

Maldives

556

1980	1981	1982	1983	1984	1985	1986	1987	1988	1989	1990	1991	1992	1993	1994		
Minus Sign Indicates Debit																**Balance of Payments**
12.8	15.8	17.3	19.8	23.1	25.5	26.9	34.9	44.6	51.3	58.1	59.2	51.1	38.5	....	....	Goods: Exports f.o.b. .... 78aa *d*
−44.0	−41.7	−46.0	−57.6	−61.0	−58.0	−63.0	−66.5	−87.3	−111.3	−121.2	−141.8	−167.9	−177.8	....	....	Goods: Imports f.o.b. .... 78ab *d*
−31.2	−25.9	−28.7	−37.8	−37.9	−32.5	−36.1	−31.6	−42.7	−60.0	−63.1	−82.6	−116.8	−139.3	....	....	Trade Balance .... 78ac *d*
52.4	58.7	59.3	56.9	61.4	65.6	69.7	76.3	83.3	98.8	119.7	125.1	168.2	178.2	....	....	Services: Credit .... 78ad *d*
−43.1	−51.9	−47.7	−38.9	−34.2	−27.0	−23.2	−28.4	−28.5	−28.9	−38.0	−42.1	−49.4	−55.8	....	....	Services: Debit .... 78ae *d*
−21.9	−19.1	−17.1	−19.8	−10.7	6.1	10.4	16.3	12.1	9.9	18.6	.4	2.0	−16.9	....	....	Balance on Goods and Services .... 78af *d*
—	—	.4	.6	.4	.3	1.4	1.3	2.0	3.8	4.7	3.8	2.9	3.0	....	....	Income: Credit .... 78ag *d*
−2.7	−3.5	−5.7	−10.1	−12.6	−13.5	−19.9	−16.9	−11.7	−16.3	−18.5	−18.7	−20.0	−22.0	....	....	Income: Debit .... 78ah *d*
−24.6	−22.6	−22.4	−29.3	−22.9	−7.1	−8.1	.7	2.4	−2.6	4.8	−14.5	−15.1	−35.9	....	....	Balance on Goods, Serv., & Inc. .... 78ai *d*
2.6	2.7	4.6	7.1	10.0	3.6	9.3	9.7	11.5	18.3	11.2	22.1	14.3	8.3	....	....	Current Transfers, n.i.e.: Credit .... 78aj *d*
−.2	−.3	−1.3	−2.0	−3.4	−2.0	−1.5	−2.4	−5.0	−5.1	−7.4	−16.6	−18.9	−20.0	....	....	Current Transfers: Debit .... 78ak *d*
−22.2	−20.2	−19.1	−24.2	−16.3	−5.5	−.3	8.0	8.9	10.6	8.6	−9.0	−19.7	−47.6	....	....	Current Account, n.i.e. .... 78al *d*
—	—	—	—	—	—	—	—	—	—	—	—	—	—	....	....	Capital Account, n.i.e.: Credit .... 78ba *d*
—	—	—	—	—	—	—	—	—	—	—	—	—	—	....	....	Capital Account: Debit .... 78bb *d*
—	—	—	—	—	—	—	—	—	—	—	—	—	—	....	....	Capital Account, n.i.e. .... 78bc *d*
—	—	—	—	—	—	—	—	—	—	—	—	—	—	....	....	Direct Investment Abroad .... 78bd *d*
—	—	—	—	—	—	5.4	5.1	1.2	4.4	5.6	6.5	6.6	6.9	....	....	Dir. Invest. in Rep. Econ., n.i.e. .... 78be *d*
—	—	—	—	—	—	—	—	—	—	—	—	—	—	....	....	Portfolio Investment Assets .... 78bf *d*
—	—	—	—	—	—	—	—	—	—	—	—	—	—	....	....	Portfolio Investment Liab., n.i.e. .... 78bg *d*
−.6	−.3	.8	.2	−1.9	1.4	−.1	−4.9	1.6	−2.9	−2.2	−2.2	−1.8	4.3	....	....	Other Investment Assets .... 78bh *d*
16.5	22.3	16.2	6.5	3.4	−5.7	−10.8	−5.6	−4.3	10.3	4.7	1.1	20.7	13.7	....	....	Other Investment Liab., n.i.e. .... 78bi *d*
15.9	22.0	17.0	6.7	1.5	−4.3	−5.5	−5.4	−1.5	11.8	8.1	5.4	25.5	24.9	....	....	Financial Account, n.i.e. .... 78bj *d*
6.3	−2.9	8.2	13.7	9.5	11.3	1.6	−1.4	6.2	−20.1	−17.8	2.6	−1.0	22.6	....	....	Net Errors and Omissions .... 78ca *d*
—	−1.1	6.1	−3.8	−5.3	1.5	−4.2	1.2	13.6	2.3	−1.1	−1.0	4.8	−.1	....	....	Overall Balance .... 78cb *d*
—	1.1	−6.1	3.8	5.3	−1.5	4.2	−1.2	−13.6	−2.3	1.1	1.0	−4.8	.1	....	....	Reserves and Related Items .... 79da *d*
—	−.2	−6.9	3.8	−.5	−3.0	−2.3	−1.2	−13.6	−2.3	.3	1.0	−4.8	.1	....	....	Reserve Assets .... 79db *d*
—	—	—	—	—	—	—	—	—	—	—	—	—	—	....	....	Use of Fund Credit and Loans .... 79dc *d*
—	—	—	—	—	—	—	—	—	—	—	—	—	—	....	....	Liabs.Constit.For.Auth.Reserves .... 79dd *d*
—	1.3	.8	—	5.8	1.5	6.5	—	—	—	.8	—	—	—	....	....	Exceptional Financing .... 79de *d*
Year Ending December 31																**Government Finance**
−76.4	−26.4	−19.6	−72.8	−25.1	−30.6	−83.7	19.1	25.6	−42.7	−164.8	−238.2	−355.6	....	....	....	Deficit (−) or Surplus 80
46.3	74.5	96.4	109.5	128.5	155.9	179.8	273.6	315.0	406.8	466.3	569.2	685.5	....	....	....	Revenue 81
11.5	8.3	23.4	12.4	35.2	9.7	66.3	89.5	101.3	165.7	85.0	226.2	151.4	....	....	....	Grants Received 81z
102.9	108.4	138.8	192.9	192.7	187.0	312.3	327.0	377.8	600.7	699.5	1,014.4	1,166.9	....	....	....	Expenditure 82
31.3	.8	.6	1.8	−3.9	9.2	17.5	17.0	12.9	14.5	16.6	19.2	25.6	....	....	....	Lending Minus Repayments 83
																Financing
6.0	−9.9	2.7	42.6	27.3	32.3	52.9	−20.2	−21.7	2.6	88.5	114.2	187.7	....	....	....	Domestic 84a
70.4	36.3	16.9	30.2	−2.2	−1.7	30.8	1.1	−3.9	40.1	76.3	124.0	167.9	....	....	....	Foreign 85a
....	155.5	154.3	184.1	206.7	237.4	246.6	245.0	178.2	183.0	200.1	331.5	526.1	....	....	....	Debt: Domestic 88a
93.6	130.2	246.4	272.8	259.1	253.7	276.7	321.0	325.8	358.7	432.2	562.1	729.1	....	....	....	Debt: Foreign 89a
Millions of Rufiyaa																**National Accounts**
59	65	74	101	124	164	179	289	351	401	503	544	417	....	....	....	Exports of Goods & Services 90c
39	50	61	76	99	111	137	230	263	347	422	....	....	....	....	....	Government Consumption 91f
76	99	106	115	165	234	253	511	545	685	755	....	....	....	....	....	Gross Fixed Capital Formation 93e
....	....	....	....	....	....	....	....	....	....	....	....	....	....	....	....	Increase/Decrease(−) in Stocks 93i
267	344	366	385	336	498	546	528	523	613	621	....	....	....	....	....	Private Consumption 96f
−186	−195	−275	−362	−364	−340	−302	−726	−843	−1,020	−1,315	−1,654	−2,002	....	....	....	Imports of Goods & Services 98c
321	376	432	466	537	600	691	845	949	1,045	1,164	....	....	....	....	....	Gross Domestic Product 99b
339.8	1437.2	424.6	493.1	627.4	713.3	774.7	843.6	916.8	1,001.9	1,164.4	1,253.3	1,332.0	1,414.2	....	....	Gross Dom. Prod. 1990 Prices 99b.*p*
94.3	85.9	101.7	94.6	85.5	84.2	89.2	100.1	103.5	104.3	100.0	....	....	....	....	....	GDP Deflator (1990=100) .... 99bi *p*
Midyear Estimates																
.15	.16	.16	.17	.18	.18	.19	.20	.20	.21	.22	.22	.23	.24	.25		Population 99z

Mali

678

		1965	1966	1967	1968	1969	1970	1971	1972	1973	1974	1975	1976	1977	1978	1979
Exchange Rates																*Francs per SDR*
Official Rate	aa	245.07	247.59	245.42	247.40	277.91	276.02	283.61	278.00	284.00	272.08	262.55	288.70	285.76	272.28	264.78
																Francs per US Dollar
Official Rate	ae	245.07	247.59	245.42	247.40	277.91	276.02	261.22	256.05	235.42	222.22	224.27	248.48	235.25	209.00	201.00
Official Rate	rf	245.06	245.68	246.00	247.56	259.96	276.40	275.59	252.03	222.89	240.70	214.31	238.95	245.68	225.66	212.72
Fund Position																*Millions of SDRs*
Quota	2f. s	13.0	17.0	17.0	17.0	17.0	22.0	22.0	22.0	22.0	22.0	22.0	22.0	22.0	27.0	27.0
SDRs	1b. s	—	—	—	—	—	—	1.3	2.4	2.3	3.0	2.7	2.8	2.7	2.6	1.3
Reserve Position in the Fund	1c. s	—	—	—	—	—	—	—	—	—	—	—	—	—	—	—
Total Fund Cred.&Loans Outstg.	2tl	9.7	9.9	11.3	11.7	10.7	8.6	7.5	8.3	7.3	10.4	10.6	12.7	11.2	19.2	22.1
International Liquidity														*Millions of US Dollars Unless Otherwise Indicated*		
Total Reserves minus Gold	1l. d	2.8	.4	1.0	.6	1.1	.9	2.1	3.7	4.2	6.1	4.2	6.9	5.4	8.2	6.0
SDRs	1b. d	—	—	—	—	—	—	1.4	2.6	2.7	3.7	3.2	3.2	3.3	3.4	1.7
Reserve Position in the Fund	1c. d	—	—	—	—	—	—	—	—	—	—	—	—	—	—	—
Foreign Exchange	1d. d	2.8	.4	1.0	.6	1.1	.9	.7	1.1	1.5	2.4	1.0	3.7	2.1	4.8	4.3
Gold (Million Fine Troy Ounces)	1ad	....	....	....	....	....	....	....	....	....	....	....	....	.010	.014	.019
Gold (National Valuation)	1and	....	....	....	....	....	....	....	....	....	....	....	....	.4	.6	.9
Monetary Authorities: Other Liab.	4.. d	1.2	4.1	23.2	38.0	49.1	49.0	58.2	64.4	88.2	127.0	—	—	—	—	—
Deposit Money Banks: Assets	7a. d	—	—	.1	2.2	9.8	7.7	6.2	9.9	10.3	14.3	12.1	12.7	21.6	11.2	10.9
Deposit Money Banks: Liabilities	7b. d	.1	—	—	6.4	12.8	12.0	11.4	17.4	19.5	24.6	21.6	22.6	33.1	23.6	33.9
of which: Liab. to Nonbanks	7bd d	....	....	....	....	....	....	....	....	....	....	....	....	....	....	....
Monetary Authorities																*Billions of Francs*
Foreign Assets	11	.86	.74	1.75	.15	.31	.25	.54	.96	.99	1.37	I.93	1.71	1.35	1.84	1.80
Claims on Central Government	12a	8.08	11.92	19.42	I17.52	18.46	19.35	20.74	21.62	24.15	27.18	I31.55	34.94	46.42	50.36	53.80
Claims on Deposit Money Banks	12e	.74	—	—	2.16	5.67	6.52	7.28	9.33	11.70	21.04	I32.38	40.86	29.37	36.44	47.67
Claims on Other Financial Insts.	12f	....	....	....	....	....	....	....	....	....	....	....	....	....	....	....
Reserve Money	14	7.86	9.69	10.71	I7.07	7.65	9.04	9.80	10.76	11.55	15.33	I18.70	22.49	27.40	30.70	38.16
of which: Currency Outside DMBs	14a	5.86	6.35	7.40	6.89	7.47	8.89	9.69	10.52	11.13	15.07	I18.70	22.49	27.40	30.70	38.16
Foreign Liabilities	16c	2.70	3.46	8.50	I12.27	16.61	15.88	16.96	18.77	22.33	31.04	I2.79	3.68	3.19	5.23	5.84
Central Government Deposits	16d	.59	.85	1.03	.11	.08	.15	.10	—	.44	.03	.65	.27	.28	1.11	.13
Other Items (Net)	17r	-1.46	-1.34	.93	.37	.09	1.05	1.68	2.37	2.52	3.19	I42.72	51.08	46.27	54.09	63.32
Deposit Money Banks																*Billions of Francs*
Reserves	20	.47	.93	1.15	.18	I.18	.15	.13	.19	.33	.28	.42	.71	.51	1.27	.56
Foreign Assets	21	.01	.01	.02	.56	2.73	2.13	1.60	2.54	2.37	3.18	2.71	3.16	5.08	2.35	I2.19
Claims on Central Government	22a	.84	.58	.81	I.26	1.88	1.76	1.71	1.84	1.61	1.82	1.21	.84	.56	1.14	1.88
Claims on Private Sector	22d	1.11	.41	.49	I6.50	I9.79	11.74	13.84	16.96	21.64	34.12	51.08	61.30	53.34	65.78	76.09
Claims on Other Financial Insts.	22f	....	....	....	....	....	....	....	....	....	....	....	....	....	....	....
Demand Deposits	24	1.50	1.79	2.32	I3.71	3.59	4.05	4.28	5.09	5.57	11.26	12.46	12.63	12.76	17.29	I18.1
Time Deposits	25	.13	.09	.10	.51	.25	.23	.24	.42	.31	.14	.57	.64	1.17	3.00	I3.34
Foreign Liabilities	26c	.02	.01	.01	I1.58	1.52	1.40	1.54	1.73	2.93	3.23	4.62	4.35	5.83	6.56	4.28
Long-Term Foreign Liabilities	26cl	....	....	....	....	.82	1.19	1.33	1.91	2.13	2.29	2.13	2.46	2.72	2.58	I2.54
Central Government Deposits	26d	....	....	....	....	....	....	....	....	....	....	....	....	....	....	....
Credit from Monetary Authorities	26g	.72	—	—	2.13	5.66	6.51	7.27	9.27	11.68	21.02	32.34	40.83	29.34	36.39	I47.67
Other Items (Net)	27r	.05	.04	.04	-.43	2.75	2.40	2.60	3.12	3.33	1.47	3.29	5.09	7.68	4.72	I3.79
Treasury Claims: Private Sector	22d. i	....	....	....	....	....	....	....	....	....	....	....	....	....	....	....
Post Office: Checking Deposits	24.. i	.36	.77	.33	.67	—	—	—	.01	.01	.01	.01	.50	.50	.50	.50
Monetary Survey																*Billions of Francs*
Foreign Assets (Net)	31n	-1.86	-2.72	-6.74	-13.15	-15.09	-14.90	-16.36	-17.00	-21.89	-29.73	-42.73	-50.32	-46.40	-51.86	I-6.14
Domestic Credit	32	14.66	18.94	27.09	I24.84	30.94	33.17	36.65	40.79	47.80	63.77	83.99	97.31	100.55	116.68	131.14
Claims on Central Govt. (Net)	32an	8.69	12.41	19.52	I18.34	20.26	20.97	22.34	23.46	26.16	29.65	32.91	36.01	47.20	50.90	I55.05
Claims on Private Sector	32d	5.97	6.53	7.57	6.50	I9.79	11.74	13.84	16.96	21.64	34.12	51.08	61.30	53.34	65.78	76.09
Claims on Other Financial Insts.	32f	....	....	....	....	....	....	....	....	....	....	....	....	....	....	....
Money	34	9.19	11.19	12.25	I11.27	11.95	13.41	14.44	15.99	17.54	27.00	31.95	35.62	40.66	48.49	56.77
Quasi-Money	35	.13	.09	.10	.51	.25	.23	.24	.42	.31	.14	.57	.64	1.17	3.00	I3.34
Long-Term Foreign Liabilities	36cl	....	....	....	....	.82	1.19	1.33	1.91	2.13	2.29	2.13	2.46	2.72	2.58	I2.54
Other Items (Net)	37r	4.76	7.07	10.04	-.09	2.84	3.45	4.27	5.47	5.92	4.62	6.60	8.27	9.61	10.74	I66.54
Money plus Quasi-Money	35l	9.32	11.27	12.34	11.78	12.20	13.64	14.68	16.41	17.85	27.13	32.53	36.25	41.82	51.49	I60.1
Other Banking Institutions																*Billions of Francs*
Savings Deposits	45	.14	.15	.19	.21	.24	.28	.29	.30	.34	.41	.47	.49	.49	.49	.49
Liquid Liabilities	55l	9.46	11.42	12.53	11.98	12.44	13.92	14.97	16.71	18.19	27.54	33.00	36.74	42.31	51.98	I60.60
Interest Rates																*Percent Per Annum*
Discount Rate *(End of Period)*	60	3.50	3.50	3.50	3.50	3.50	3.50	3.50	3.50	5.50	5.50	8.00	8.00	8.00	8.00	8.00
Money Market Rate	60b	....	....	....	....	....	....	....	....	....	....	....	7.28	7.38	7.40	7.72
Deposit Rate	60l	....	....	....	....	....	3.00	3.00	3.00	5.75	5.75	5.88	6.00	6.00	6.00	6.00
Lending Rate	60p	....	....	....	....	....	....	....	....	....	....	....	12.00	12.00	12.00	12.00
Prices															*Index Numbers (1990=100)*	
Consumer Prices	64	....	....	....	....	....	....	....	....	....	....	....	....	....	....	....
International Transactions																*Billions of Francs*
Exports	70	2.12	2.23	2.04	2.65	4.38	9.65	10.00	10.53	11.65	15.41	11.49	20.56	30.61	25.20	31.35
Imports, cif	71	8.09	7.06	6.36	9.13	6.61	9.47	16.47	19.81	28.13	43.04	37.71	36.85	39.00	64.30	76.45
Imports, fob	71.v	6.52	5.69	5.13	7.36	5.33	7.63	13.28	15.96	23.67	31.04	27.21	26.59	27.30	45.00	57.50

Mali

1980	1981	1982	1983	1984	1985	1986	1987	1988	1989	1990	1991	1992	1993	1994		
															Exchange Rates	
End of Period																
287.99	334.52	370.92	436.97	470.11	415.26	394.78	378.78	407.68	380.32	364.84	370.48	378.57	404.89	I 780.44	Official Rate	aa
End of Period (ae) Period Average (rf)																
225.80	287.40	336.24	417.37	479.59	378.04	322.74	267.00	302.94	289.40	256.45	259.00	275.32	294.77	I 534.60	Official Rate	ae
211.28	271.73	328.61	381.06	436.96	449.26	346.30	300.54	297.85	319.01	272.26	282.11	264.69	283.16	I 555.20	Official Rate	rf
															Fund Position	
End of Period																
40.5	40.5	40.5	50.8	50.8	50.8	50.8	50.8	50.8	50.8	50.8	50.8	50.8	68.9	68.9	68.9	Quota	2f. s
—	.2	.5	.1	1.7	1.7	—	.2	.2	.1	.3	.3	.3	.1	.1	SDRs	1b. s
5.4	7.6	8.7	8.7	8.7	8.7	8.7	8.7	8.7	8.7	8.7	8.7	8.7	8.7	8.7	Reserve Position in the Fund	1c. s
30.3	28.2	52.5	65.3	84.3	89.2	80.8	60.0	54.9	41.9	48.7	42.0	47.5	51.4	74.1	Total Fund Cred.&Loans Outstg.	2tl
															International Liquidity	
End of Period																
14.5	17.4	16.7	16.2	26.6	22.5	12.3	15.8	36.0	115.8	190.5	319.3	307.9	332.4	221.4	Total Reserves minus Gold	1l. d
—	.2	.6	.1	1.7	1.8	—	.3	.2	.2	.5	.4	.1	.1	.2	SDRs	1b. d
6.8	8.8	9.6	9.1	8.5	9.5	10.6	12.3	11.7	11.4	12.4	12.4	11.9	12.0	12.7	Reserve Position in the Fund	1c. d
7.7	8.4	6.6	7.0	16.5	11.2	1.7	3.3	24.1	104.2	177.7	306.5	295.9	320.3	208.5	Foreign Exchange	1d. d
.019	.019	.019	.019	.019	.019	.019	.019	.019	.019	.019	.019	.019	.019	.019	Gold (Million Fine Troy Ounces)	1ad
.9	7.9	8.0	7.3	6.3	6.1	7.6	8.9	7.8	7.3	7.1	6.7	6.5	7.0	7.0	Gold (National Valuation)	1an d
				3.9	2.7	34.3	51.9	6.9	7.6	4.9	16.2	2.5	6.0	9.7	Monetary Authorities: Other Liab.	4..d
9.7	10.9	13.4	19.0	24.3	15.4	24.8	27.2	19.4	63.7	72.1	60.8	40.4	26.3	118.7	Deposit Money Banks: Assets	7a. d
34.4	27.4	26.4	23.9	33.5	51.2	72.6	87.4	87.0	93.1	113.0	78.4	47.3	42.2	34.3	Deposit Money Banks: Liabilities	7b. d
....	....	....	....	13.0	14.5	18.2	30.1	37.5	34.3	40.5	45.9	24.4	18.9	18.0	*of which:* Liab. to Nonbanks	7bd d
															Monetary Authorities	
End of Period																
3.46	4.78	5.82	6.77	12.78	8.51	3.97	4.23	10.90	33.52	48.86	82.71	84.78	97.99	118.37	Foreign Assets	11
55.34	60.87	78.31	93.06	47.22	51.22	48.84	46.79	52.10	42.14	34.05	34.51	37.25	40.98	58.70	Claims on Central Government	12a
48.43	50.02	54.14	54.28	12.51	20.62	38.14	32.22	30.41	23.90	23.90	23.90	23.90	23.90	—	Claims on Deposit Money Banks	12e
															Claims on Other Financial Insts.	12f
40.60	40.90	45.00	50.15	63.59	71.75	80.69	78.10	86.37	98.87	100.26	131.95	131.65	143.78	118.90	Reserve Money	14
40.60	40.90	45.00	50.15	50.48	59.77	66.92	60.77	62.19	54.77	46.88	59.97	60.84	65.07	94.18	*of which:* Currency Outside DMBs	14a
8.73	9.42	19.46	28.54	49.94	45.43	47.63	39.38	25.71	18.47	19.05	19.76	18.69	22.60	63.04	Foreign Liabilities	16c
.90	.81	3.94	3.34	I 5.92	3.71	.55	.98	12.29	6.09	8.90	3.06	6.03	5.54	9.74	Central Government Deposits	16d
63.17	70.74	77.85	81.31	-46.93	-40.53	-37.92	-35.22	-30.97	-23.86	-21.40	-13.65	-10.44	-9.05	-14.61	Other Items (Net)	17r
															Deposit Money Banks	
End of Period																
.52	.43	1.40	.87	I 10.93	12.78	13.97	17.26	24.60	43.79	54.03	71.82	70.51	79.43	25.29	Reserves	20
2.18	3.12	4.50	7.92	11.66	5.83	7.99	7.26	5.88	18.45	18.48	15.76	11.12	7.75	63.44	Foreign Assets	21
1.06	1.09	1.12	1.19	2.60	2.62	3.42	2.83	4.19	2.47	3.83	2.57	3.38	3.44	27.98	Claims on Central Government	22a
81.99	87.38	94.99	101.64	I 70.25	83.20	99.48	95.24	70.21	84.12	84.12	86.23	91.87	93.79	84.85	Claims on Private Sector	22d
															Claims on Other Financial Insts.	22f
18.47	18.90	22.87	30.65	53.39	49.69	47.48	44.95	48.89	47.82	47.30	47.40	47.36	52.72	82.99	Demand Deposits	24
3.28	4.45	3.98	6.02	10.30	13.81	17.80	20.62	26.04	31.56	36.57	45.35	48.96	52.62	63.05	Time Deposits	25
5.29	5.39	5.74	6.71	I 12.62	16.97	19.76	18.07	19.01	19.60	21.17	13.95	8.71	8.83	11.46	Foreign Liabilities	26c
2.47	2.49	3.14	3.29	3.47	2.40	3.68	5.28	7.35	7.33	7.80	6.34	4.32	3.62	6.89	Long-Term Foreign Liabilities	26cl
				5.98	10.49	9.86	11.08	16.91	21.45	27.24	32.72	37.14	32.96	39.26	Central Government Deposits	26d
48.43	50.02	54.14	54.28	6.89	20.73	38.34	32.88	30.54	24.37	24.42	24.18	24.13	23.90	—	Credit from Monetary Authorities	26g
7.81	10.77	12.15	10.68	2.81	-9.66	-12.06	-10.28	-43.87	-3.30	-4.04	6.43	6.26	9.77	-2.08	Other Items (Net)	27r
—	—	—	—	.34	.34	.34	.36	.22	.21	.29	.14	.28	1.51	—	Treasury Claims: Private Sector	22d. i
.45	.45	.45	.45	3.22	4.31	3.11	3.58	3.35	7.85	4.30	—	—	—	—	Post Office: Checking Deposits	24.. i
															Monetary Survey	
End of Period																
-8.38	-6.91	-14.88	-20.56	-38.11	-48.07	-55.54	-45.96	-27.94	13.89	27.11	64.76	68.51	74.32	107.31	Foreign Assets (Net)	31n
137.94	147.98	170.93	193.00	I 111.40	127.16	144.43	136.38	100.64	109.04	90.15	87.53	89.32	99.71	122.53	Domestic Credit	32
55.94	60.60	75.94	91.36	40.80	43.62	44.61	40.78	30.22	24.72	5.75	1.16	-2.83	4.41	37.68	Claims on Central Govt. (Net)	32an
81.99	87.38	94.99	101.64	I 70.60	83.55	99.82	95.61	70.42	84.32	84.40	86.37	92.15	95.30	84.85	Claims on Private Sector	32d
															Claims on Other Financial Insts.	32f
59.52	60.25	68.32	81.25	I 107.09	113.77	117.51	109.30	114.44	110.43	98.48	107.37	108.20	117.79	177.21	Money	34
3.28	4.45	3.98	6.02	10.30	13.81	17.80	20.62	26.04	31.56	36.57	45.35	48.96	52.62	63.05	Quasi-Money	35
2.47	2.49	3.14	3.29	3.47	2.40	3.68	5.28	7.35	7.33	7.80	6.34	4.32	3.62	6.89	Long-Term Foreign Liabilities	36cl
70.46	81.08	88.60	91.12	-47.57	-50.88	-49.99	-44.77	-75.12	-26.39	-25.57	-6.77	-3.65	—	-17.30	Other Items (Net)	37r
62.80	64.70	72.30	87.27	117.39	127.58	135.31	129.92	140.47	141.99	135.04	152.72	157.16	170.41	240.26	Money plus Quasi-Money	35l
															Other Banking Institutions	
End of Period																
.43	.36	....	....	....	....	....	....	....	....	....	....	....	....	....	Savings Deposits	45
63.23	65.06	....	....	....	....	....	....	....	....	....	....	....	....	....	Liquid Liabilities	55l
															Interest Rates	
Percent Per Annum																
10.50	10.50	12.50	10.50	10.50	10.50	8.50	8.50	9.50	11.00	11.00	11.00	12.50	10.50	10.00	Discount Rate (End of Period)	60
10.13	13.68	14.66	12.23	11.84	10.66	8.58	8.37	8.72	10.07	10.98	10.94	11.44	....	....	Money Market Rate	60b
6.19	6.25	7.75	7.50	7.25	7.25	6.08	5.25	5.25	6.42	7.00	7.00	7.75	....	....	Deposit Rate	60l
14.50	14.50	16.00	14.50	14.50	14.50	13.50	13.50	13.58	15.08	16.00	16.00	16.75	....	....	Lending Rate	60p
															Prices	
Period Averages																
....	....	....	....	....	....	....	....	....	99.5	99.4	100.0	101.8	95.4	95.4	Consumer Prices	64
															International Transactions	
Billions of Francs																
43.31	41.92	47.90	62.90	57.97	55.56	73.34	53.79	63.89	78.78	97.68	....	....	....	....	Exports	70
93.05	104.75	109.20	134.60	121.69	134.54	153.71	112.44	150.23	108.47	164.02	....	....	....	....	Imports, cif	71
65.15	73.31	76.45	94.21	85.18	94.15	107.56	78.68	105.13	75.91	114.78	....	....	....	....	Imports, fob	71.v

Mali
678

		1965	1966	1967	1968	1969	1970	1971	1972	1973	1974	1975	1976	1977	1978	1979
Balance of Payments															*Millions of US Dollars:*	
Goods: Exports f.o.b.	78aa d	....	....	....	....	....	....	....	....	....	....	71.9	94.4	124.6	94.2	145.7
Goods: Imports f.o.b.	78ab d	....	....	....	....	....	....	....	....	....	....	−136.2	−111.3	−111.1	−199.4	−270.3
Trade Balance	78ac d	....	....	....	....	....	....	....	....	....	....	−64.3	−16.9	13.5	−105.2	−124.6
Services: Credit	78ad d	....	....	....	....	....	....	....	....	....	....	22.9	17.8	23.9	37.2	45.6
Services: Debit	78ae d	....	....	....	....	....	....	....	....	....	....	−102.5	−78.7	−95.4	−150.7	−163.8
Balance on Goods and Services	78af d	....	....	....	....	....	....	....	....	....	....	−143.9	−77.8	−58.1	−218.7	−242.8
Income: Credit	78ag d	....	....	....	....	....	....	....	....	....	....					
Income: Debit	78ah d	....	....	....	....	....	....	....	....	....	....	−21.7	−16.6	−19.8	−13.3	−11.8
Balance on Goods, Serv., & Inc.	78ai d	....	....	....	....	....	....	....	....	....	....	−165.6	−94.4	−77.9	−232.0	−254.6
Current Transfers, n.i.e.: Credit	78aj d	....	....	....	....	....	....	....	....	....	....	119.9	62.6	91.3	101.0	165.6
Current Transfers: Debit	78ak d	....	....	....	....	....	....	....	....	....	....	−15.5	−10.5	−8.3	−15.3	−24.7
Current Account, n.i.e.	78al d	....	....	....	....	....	....	....	....	....	....	−61.1	−42.2	5.2	−146.3	−113.6
Capital Account, n.i.e.: Credit	78ba d	....	....	....	....	....	....	....	....	....	....	4.5	—	—	47.2	—
Capital Account: Debit	78bb d	....	....	....	....	....	....	....	....	....	....					
Capital Account, n.i.e.	78bc d	....	....	....	....	....	....	....	....	....	....	4.5	—	—	47.2	—
Direct Investment Abroad	78bd d	....	....	....	....	....	....	....	....	....	....	−.6	−7.6	−8.0	−8.9	3.1
Dir. Invest. in Rep. Econ., n.i.e.	78be d	....	....	....	....	....	....	....	....	....	....	2.6	2.6	3.1	−.9	—
Portfolio Investment Assets	78bf d	....	....	....	....	....	....	....	....	....	....					
Portfolio Investment Liab., n.i.e.	78bg d	....	....	....	....	....	....	....	....	....	....	—	—	—	—	—
Other Investment Assets	78bh d	....	....	....	....	....	....	....	....	....	....	−13.6	−12.8	−7.5	5.8	26.7
Other Investment Liab., n.i.e.	78bi d	....	....	....	....	....	....	....	....	....	....	15.9	24.5	35.4	53.8	91.0
Financial Account, n.i.e.	78bj d	....	....	....	....	....	....	....	....	....	....	4.3	6.7	22.9	49.8	120.8
Net Errors and Omissions	78ca d	....	....	....	....	....	....	....	....	....	....	−9.9	−7.5	−13.0	31.6	−27.2
Overall Balance	78cb d	....	....	....	....	....	....	....	....	....	....	−62.1	−43.0	15.0	−17.7	−20.1
Reserves and Related Items	79da d	....	....	....	....	....	....	....	....	....	....	62.1	43.0	−15.0	17.7	20.1
Reserve Assets	79db d	....	....	....	....	....	....	....	....	....	....	7.6	−4.6	.4	5.5	−1.2
Use of Fund Credit and Loans	79dc d	....	....	....	....	....	....	....	....	....	....	.3	2.4	−1.8	9.9	3.8
Liabs.Constit.For.Auth.Reserves	79dd d	....	....	....	....	....	....	....	....	....	....					
Exceptional Financing	79de d	....	....	....	....	....	....	....	....	....	....	54.2	45.2	−13.7	2.3	17.5
Government Finance															*Billions of Francs:*	
Deficit (-) or Surplus	80	....	....	....	....	....	....	....	....	....	....	....	.02	.24	−4.02	−9.08
Revenue	81	....	....	....	....	....	....	....	....	....	....	18.38	24.41	32.13	33.10	32.80
Grants Received	81z	....	....	....	....	....	....	....	....	....	....	5.78	2.69	2.61	2.09	3.22
Expenditure	82	....	....	....	....	....	....	....	....	....	....	....	27.10	34.49	39.20	45.10
Lending Minus Repayments	83	....	....	....	....	....	....	....	....	....	....	....	−.03	—	.01	—
Financing	84	....	....	....	....	....	....	....	....	....	....	....	−.02	−.24	4.02	9.10
Domestic	84a	....	....	....	....	....	....	....	....	....	....		.38	.32	....	....
Foreign	85a	....	....	....	....	....	....	....	....	....	....		−.40	−.56	....	....
Debt: Domestic	88a	....	....	....	....	....	....	....	....	....	....					
Debt: Foreign	89a	....	....	....	....	....	....	....	....	....	....					
National Accounts															*Billions of Francs*	
Exports of Goods & Services	90c	....	....	....	....	....	....	....	....	....	....	....	30.4	39.2	30.0	37.2
Government Consumption	91f	....	....	....	....	....	....	....	....	....	....	....	6.5	8.3	9.4	11.3
Gross Fixed Capital Formation	93e	....	....	....	....	....	....	....	....	....	....					
Increase/Decrease(-) in Stocks	93i	....	....	....	....	....	....	....	....	....	....					
Private Consumption	96f	....	....	....	....	....	....	....	....	....	....	....	135.4	149.9	172.8	213.6
Imports of Goods & Services	98c	....	....	....	....	....	....	....	....	....	....	....	−46.2	−51.3	−65.4	−76.9
Gross Domestic Product	99b	45.2	47.3	52.0	65.3	67.8	76.3	83.5	88.4	92.1	97.7	129.5	178.6	204.5	217.8	259.6
Gross Dom. Prod. 1990 Prices	99b.p	328.7	327.0	341.4	403.9	403.1	456.3	435.2	403.9	464.7	456.3	452.1	456.3	460.5	463.9	460.5
GDP Deflator (1990=100)	99bi p	13.8	14.5	15.2	16.2	16.8	16.7	19.2	21.9	19.8	21.4	28.6	39.1	44.4	46.9	56.4
																Millions:
Population	99z	4.58	4.65	4.74	4.83	4.93	5.05	5.14	5.26	5.38	5.66	ɪ6.29	6.32	ɪ6.51	6.70	6.90

Monetary Authorities: ɪ In March 1968 the Bank of the Republic of Mali was liquidated by transferring mainly its claims on and demand deposit liabilities to the private sector and certain of its foreign assets and liabilities to the new development bank. Its remaining assets, including a claim on the government, owing to government assumption of claims on state enterprises, and its other liabilities were assumed by the new Central Bank of Mali. ɪ Beginning in June 1984, data reflect Mali's re-entry into the West African Monetary Union and the compilation of the data on the Central Bank of West African States' (BCEAO's) basis. At the end of May 1984, data reflect the consolidation and transfer to the government of the central bank's liabilities under the operations account and the cancellation of certain loans to the government and to state enterprises.
Deposit Money Banks: ɪ See note to section 10.
Monetary Survey: ɪ See note to section 10.
Government Finance: ɪ Beginning in 1980, data also cover extrabudgetary foreign grants and loans not recorded in the treasury accounts. ɪ Data for 1980 and 1981 do not cover social security operations.

Mali

678

	1980	1981	1982	1983	1984	1985	1986	1987	1988	1989	1990	1991	1992	1993	1994		
	Minus Sign Indicates Debit															**Balance of Payments**	
	204.9	154.2	145.8	166.8	192.0	176.1	205.6	255.9	251.5	269.3	337.9	354.5	339.3	343.6	....	Goods: Exports f.o.b.	78aa *d*
	−308.4	−269.0	−232.7	−240.9	−257.8	−328.5	−339.0	−335.4	−359.1	−338.8	−432.4	−447.1	−484.0	−463.5	....	Goods: Imports f.o.b.	78ab *d*
	−103.4	−114.8	−86.9	−74.1	−65.8	−152.4	−133.4	−79.5	−107.6	−69.5	−94.5	−92.7	−144.7	−119.9	....	Trade Balance	78ac *d*
	57.7	46.2	44.4	42.0	40.7	57.3	68.1	82.5	83.6	69.0	80.1	85.4	74.4	78.4	....	Services: Credit	78ad *d*
	−211.8	−168.9	−162.7	−166.9	−172.9	−263.7	−306.7	−327.1	−344.6	−317.0	−395.1	−378.4	−406.5	−394.5	....	Services: Debit	78ae *d*
	−257.5	−237.6	−205.1	−199.0	−198.0	−358.8	−371.9	−324.1	−368.6	−317.5	−409.5	−385.7	−476.8	−435.9	....	Balance on Goods and Services	78af *d*
	—	—	—	—	—	4.9	3.2	3.1	4.4	6.6	19.5	20.9	24.6	24.4	....	Income: Credit	78ag *d*
	−16.9	−32.6	−24.2	−27.5	−19.2	−18.7	−24.8	−28.0	−27.5	−36.7	−61.0	−59.2	−54.8	−47.0	....	Income: Debit	78ah *d*
	−274.4	−270.1	−229.3	−226.5	−217.2	−372.6	−393.6	−349.0	−391.8	−347.6	−451.0	−424.0	−507.0	−458.5	....	Balance on Goods, Serv., & Inc.	78ai *d*
	169.3	147.2	133.7	131.7	111.9	207.5	198.4	209.3	235.7	232.1	291.5	333.0	344.9	296.7	....	Current Transfers, n.i.e.: Credit	78aj *d*
	−24.8	−20.1	−19.6	−18.4	−16.2	−44.5	−58.9	−79.5	−77.6	−75.0	−90.6	−87.7	−87.6	−81.9	....	Current Transfers: Debit	78ak *d*
	−129.9	−143.0	−115.3	−113.2	−121.5	−209.7	−254.1	−219.2	−233.7	−190.6	−250.1	−178.7	−249.7	−243.8	....	Current Account, n.i.e.	78al *d*
	—	—	—	—	52.9	80.8	92.7	116.8	142.0	107.8	105.8	137.5	143.6	141.3	....	Capital Account, n.i.e.: Credit	78ba *d*
	—	—	—	—	—	—	—	—	—	—	—	—	—	—	....	Capital Account: Debit	78bb *d*
	—	—	—	—	52.9	80.8	92.7	116.8	142.0	107.8	105.8	137.5	143.6	141.3	....	Capital Account, n.i.e.	78bc *d*
	—	—	—	—	—	—	—	—	—	—	—	—	—	—	....	Direct Investment Abroad	78bd *d*
	2.4	3.7	1.5	3.1	10.1	2.9	−8.4	−6.0	.7	15.0	−6.6	3.5	−7.6	—	....	Dir. Invest. in Rep. Econ., n.i.e.	78be *d*
	—	—	—	—	—	—	—	—	—	—	—	—	—	—	....	Portfolio Investment Assets	78bf *d*
	—	—	—	—	—	—	—	—	—	—	—	—	—	—	....	Portfolio Investment Liab., n.i.e.	78bg *d*
	6.2	4.2	—	—	−8.6	13.0	−6.2	2.4	4.6	−39.4	−.1	9.6	17.5	11.9	....	Other Investment Assets	78bh *d*
	119.4	99.8	75.2	85.5	66.9	104.7	142.0	90.2	133.5	121.3	84.4	39.6	−7.0	−17.6	....	Other Investment Liab., n.i.e.	78bi *d*
	127.9	107.8	76.7	88.7	68.4	120.6	127.4	86.6	138.8	96.9	77.6	52.8	3.0	−5.7	....	Financial Account, n.i.e.	78bj *d*
	−30.8	22.7	12.6	−7.3	.7	−18.4	−15.6	1.5	−1.5	−1.5	1.1	29.0	−22.7	22.7	....	Net Errors and Omissions	78ca *d*
	−32.8	−12.6	−26.0	−31.9	.5	−26.6	−49.5	−14.3	45.7	12.6	−65.6	40.7	−125.8	−85.5	....	Overall Balance	78cb *d*
	32.8	12.6	26.0	31.9	−.5	26.6	49.5	14.3	−45.7	−12.6	65.6	−40.7	125.8	85.5	....	Reserves and Related Items	79da *d*
	4.7	9.5	−1.1	−1.5	−33.7	3.5	47.2	7.5	−61.9	−71.9	−54.8	−119.8	−7.6	−45.8	....	Reserve Assets	79db *d*
	10.6	−2.6	27.0	13.5	19.3	5.1	−9.8	−26.8	−7.6	−16.6	8.3	−9.2	8.4	5.6	....	Use of Fund Credit and Loans	79dc *d*
	—	—	—	—	—	—	—	—	—	—	—	—	—	—	....	Liabs.Constit.For.Auth.Reserves	79dd *d*
	17.6	5.7	.1	19.8	13.9	18.0	12.1	33.6	23.9	75.9	112.0	88.3	125.1	125.7	....	Exceptional Financing	79de *d*
	Year Ending December 31															**Government Finance**	
	ⅰ−16.03	−14.70	ⅰ−31.60	−34.54	−35.00	−46.50	−43.20	−30.90	−27.60 ᴾ	....	....	....	....	....	....	Deficit (-) or Surplus	80
	ⅰ37.50	43.70	ⅰ52.64	54.61	66.10	79.70	87.60	89.40	114.30 ᴾ	....	....	....	....	....	....	Revenue	81
	ⅰ23.89	28.26	ⅰ30.58	40.51	41.80	39.60	29.10	37.80	35.50 ᴾ	....	....	....	....	....	....	Grants Received	81z
	ⅰ73.38	86.80	ⅰ114.80	129.53	142.80	165.70	159.60	157.90	174.80 ᴾ	....	....	....	....	....	....	Expenditure	82
	ⅰ4.04	−.14	ⅰ.02	.13	.10	.10	.30	.20	2.60 ᴾ	....	....	....	....	....	....	Lending Minus Repayments	83
	ⅰ16.03	14.70	ⅰ31.60	34.54	35.00	46.50	43.20	30.90	27.60 ᴾ	....	....	....	....	....	....	Financing	84
	ⅰ1.30	−1.40	ⅰ3.30	4.69	2.50	5.40	....	....	4.70 ᴾ	....	....	....	....	....	....	Domestic	84a
	ⅰ14.73	16.10	ⅰ28.30	29.85	32.50	41.10	....	....	22.90 ᴾ	....	....	....	....	....	....	Foreign	85a
	ⅰ26.51	28.18	ⅰ43.24	44.45	....	....	23.60	....	....	....	....	....	....	....	....	Debt: Domestic	88a
	ⅰ137.21		ⅰ264.92	289.64	....	....	546.80	604.00	726.80 ᴾ	....	....	....	....	....	....	Debt: Foreign	89a
	Billions of Francs															**National Accounts**	
	50.3	55.6	62.6	78.6	107.2	103.8	87.3	94.3	95.1	106.6	114.8	120.0	....	....	....	Exports of Goods & Services	90c
	12.6	36.6	39.6	44.9	50.1	78.6	86.9	88.2	91.2	98.4	96.1	117.2	....	....	....	Government Consumption	91f
	....	93.0	71.4	75.0	84.6	80.4	106.7	126.5	119.6	148.6	139.4	118.6	....	....	....	Gross Fixed Capital Formation	93e
	—	—	—	−15	−14	−12	10	5	7	13	15	−17	....	....	....	Increase/Decrease(-) in Stocks	93i
	246.5	315.6	360.4	386.5	423.8	522.2	518.6	464.7	475.5	495.1	534.3	556.6	....	....	....	Private Consumption	96f
	−90.0	−120.6	−130.0	−158.6	−188.1	−227.2	−207.2	−183.3	−192.3	−206.4	−218.3	−226.9	....	....	....	Imports of Goods & Services	98c
	300.5	380.2	403.6	411.3	463.5	557.8	592.3	594.4	589.1	642.3	666.2	685.3	....	....	....	Gross Domestic Product	99b
	ⅰ463.9	483.9	514.0	487.4	490.7	532.4	618.3	603.7	605.2	650.5	666.2	664.9	....	....	....	Gross Dom. Prod. 1990 Prices	99b.*p*
	64.8	78.6	78.5	84.4	94.5	104.8	95.8	98.5	97.3	98.7	100.0	103.1	....	....	....	GDP Deflator (1990=100)	99bi *p*
	Midyear Estimates																
	7.10	7.29	7.51	7.74	7.97	8.21	ⅰ7.57	7.70	7.83	7.96	8.16	ⅰ9.51	9.82	10.13	....	Population	99z

Malta

		1965	1966	1967	1968	1969	1970	1971	1972	1973	1974	1975	1976	1977	1978	1979
Exchange Rates																*SDRs per Lira:*
Official Rate	ac	2.8000	2.8000	2.4000	2.4000	2.4000	2.4000	2.4110	2.3220	2.1437	2.1754	2.1161	2.0175	2.0864	2.1105	2.2076
																US Dollars per Lira:
Official Rate	ag	2.8000	2.8000	2.4000	2.4000	2.4000	2.4000	2.6176	2.5210	2.5860	2.6635	2.4772	2.3440	2.5344	2.7495	2.9082
Official Rate	rh	2.8000	2.8000	2.7667	2.4000	2.4000	2.4000	2.4496	2.6095	2.7232	2.5947	2.6202	2.3534	2.3688	2.5974	2.7911
																Index Numbers (1990=100):
Official Rate	ah x	88.8	88.8	87.3	76.1	76.1	76.1	114.5	82.8	86.4	82.3	83.1	74.6	75.1	82.4	88.5
Nominal Effective Exchange Rate	ne c	....	....	....	....	....	....	....	....	....	....	....	....	....	....	81.5
Real Effective Exchange Rate	re c	....	....	....	....	....	....	....	....	....	....	....	....	....	....	107.9
Fund Position																*Millions of SDRs:*
Quota	2f. s	....	....	....	10.0	10.0	16.0	16.0	16.0	16.0	16.0	16.0	16.0	16.0	20.0	20.0
SDRs	1b. s	....	....	....	—	—	1.7	3.4	5.1	5.1	5.1	5.1	5.2	5.5	5.8	9.4
Reserve Position in the Fund	1c. s	....	....	....	2.5	2.5	4.0	4.0	4.0	4.0	4.0	7.8	13.8	12.2	13.2	13.3
International Liquidity												*Millions of US Dollars Unless Otherwise Indicated:*				
Total Reserves minus Gold	1l. d	78.9	90.2	89.5	ɪ138.7	127.0	148.2	184.7	261.7	310.4	386.7	485.8	607.8	719.6	925.1	1,012.7
SDRs	1b. d	....	....	....	—	—	1.7	3.7	5.5	6.1	6.2	6.0	6.0	6.7	7.6	12.4
Reserve Position in the Fund	1c. d	....	....	....	2.5	2.5	4.0	4.4	4.4	4.9	4.9	9.1	16.0	14.8	17.2	17.5
Foreign Exchange	1d. d	78.9	90.2	89.5	ɪ136.2	124.5	142.5	176.7	251.8	299.4	375.5	470.7	585.8	698.1	900.4	982.8
Gold (Million Fine Troy Ounces)	1ad	—	—	—	.349	.349	.277	.353	.353	.353	.353	.353	.353	.360	.360	.366
Gold (National Valuation)	1an d	....	....	....	12.2	12.2	9.7	12.3	12.3	12.3	12.3	12.3	12.3	12.6	12.7	12.8
Monetary Authorities: Other Assets	3.. d	....	....	....	....	....	....	....	....	....	....	....	....	....	....	....
Other Official Insts.: Assets	3b. d	6.9	6.8	5.2	4.8	3.9	2.7	.3e	.2	.2	9.3	.1	.1	.1	4.9	5.4
Deposit Money Banks: Assets	7a. d	106.3	118.1	105.3	63.9	78.3	76.7	94.7	70.6	95.9	102.8	102.0	117.7	130.7	134.6	162.2
of which: Claims on Nonbanks	7ad d	102.6	111.4	95.9	55.6	72.9	68.4	66.5	49.9	89.0	95.3	89.0	102.0	107.5	96.3	135.0
Deposit Money Banks: Liabilities	7b. d	.1	.7	.8	1.1	2.3	8.0	7.6	15.2	2.9	1.5	4.7	8.7	13.9	17.6	18.3
of which: Liab. to Nonbanks	7bd d	—	—	—	—	—	5.7	4.4	6.3	2.6	1.3	4.1	7.5	12.2	12.7	10.2
Other Banking Insts.: Assets	7e. d	27.2	27.2	23.7	22.4	24.5	28.6	32.5	26.0	16.4	15.5	14.8	5.4	3.2	3.1	3.7
Liabilities	7f. d	4.6	4.5	3.1	1.1	.2	.3	.4	.1	.1	.1	.1	.1	.1	.1	.2
Monetary Authorities																*Millions of Liri:*
Foreign Assets	11	28.17	32.20	37.30	ɪ62.87	57.93	65.77	74.32	103.14	118.32	131.08	183.93	238.61	271.51	322.59	342.74
Claims on Central Government	12a	3.00	1.92	.87	.88	5.03	7.17	5.22	2.05	.23	.37	.06	8.77	.04	.04	.02
Reserve Money	14	28.18	30.59	34.07	ɪ59.99	58.46	62.71	73.27	98.65	95.05	110.30	158.04	200.86	222.03	267.66	297.45
of which: Currency Outside DMBs	14a	27.35	29.69	33.05	36.20	40.33	45.87	55.66	62.25	72.67	79.55	98.88	119.64	137.83	155.02	176.25
Central Government Deposits	16d	.27	.29	1.57	.45	.64	4.38	.48	.56	11.31	3.25	3.34	3.22	6.25	16.15	19.52
Other Items (Net)	17r	2.72	3.24	2.53	3.32	3.87	5.85	5.78	5.98	12.19	17.90	22.61	43.30	43.26	38.83	25.79
Deposit Money Banks																*Millions of Liri:*
Reserves	20	.83	.90	1.02	ɪ23.14	18.14	16.82	16.76	30.82	18.24	24.13	51.75	74.90	77.78	100.15	96.08
Foreign Assets	21	37.98	42.16	43.89	ɪ26.61	32.63	31.96	35.44	26.43	37.09	38.61	41.19	50.20	51.57	48.95	55.77
Claims on Central Government	22a	2.20	1.28	1.31	2.16	2.76	8.18	10.22	9.41	8.83	8.49	6.22	6.22	6.23	6.23	6.23
Claims on Private Sector	22d	9.59	13.29	17.71	23.39	36.79	45.72	49.88	52.97	50.74	55.15	52.41	55.60	56.62	60.92	74.15
Demand Deposits	24	7.08	9.00	10.24	13.42	15.58	11.05	10.84	12.01	10.29	13.00	17.51	22.73	21.35	27.05	30.58
Time and Savings Deposits	25	42.37	46.55	51.33	57.58	67.31	78.63	89.99	94.70	94.45	99.13	116.02	139.12	146.31	162.32	173.05
Foreign Liabilities	26c	.03	.24	.33	.45	.95	3.33	2.84	5.67	1.12	.57	1.90	3.71	5.47	6.41	6.29
Other Items (Net)	27r	1.10	1.85	2.02	3.85	6.49	9.67	8.62	7.25	9.03	13.67	16.15	21.37	19.07	20.47	22.30
Monetary Survey																*Millions of Liri:*
Foreign Assets (Net)	31n	66.43	74.45	81.24	ɪ89.46	90.20	95.12	107.44	124.10	154.29	169.12	223.22	285.11	317.61	365.14	392.22
Domestic Credit	32	13.77	15.15	17.20	24.86	43.43	56.41	64.48	63.71	48.43	60.31	54.97	67.37	56.64	50.90	60.82
Claims on Central Govt. (Net)	32an	4.18	1.86	-.52	1.47	6.64	10.69	14.60	10.74	-2.31	5.16	2.57	11.77	.02	-10.02	-13.33
Claims on Private Sector	32d	9.59	13.29	17.71	23.39	36.79	45.72	49.88	52.97	50.74	55.15	52.41	55.60	56.62	60.92	74.15
Money	34	34.76	39.01	43.68	50.06	56.64	57.71	67.88	80.06	87.15	99.02	123.75	148.34	165.64	194.57	231.64
Quasi-Money	35	42.37	46.55	51.33	57.58	67.31	78.63	89.99	94.70	99.49	106.17	123.06	157.07	170.31	187.32	198.05
Other Items (Net)	37r	3.07	4.04	3.43	6.68	9.68	15.19	14.05	13.05	16.08	24.23	31.38	47.07	38.29	34.15	23.35
Money plus Quasi-Money	35l	77.12	85.56	95.01	107.63	123.94	136.34	157.87	174.76	186.64	205.20	246.81	305.42	335.95	381.89	429.69
Other Banking Institutions																*Millions of Liri:*
Foreign Assets	41	9.72	9.70	9.87	9.33	10.22	11.93	12.19	9.74	6.35	5.83	5.98	2.29	1.25	1.13	1.27
Claims on Private Sector	42d	—	—	—	.87	3.10	4.14	4.72	4.86	4.47	4.74	6.45	7.01	8.15	9.09	10.97
Claims on Deposit Money Banks	42e	—	—	—	1.38	2.18	1.26	.81	.61	.54	.62	.87	1.20	1.56	1.94	.29
Foreign Liabilities	46c	1.63	1.60	1.31	.45	.09	.14	.14	.05	.04	.04	.04	.02	.04	.04	.09
Credit from Deposit Money Banks	46h	—	—	—	.79	1.94	2.19	3.02	3.23	2.36	4.06	5.74	6.15	4.33	5.15	7.03
Other Items (Net)	47r	8.09	8.10	8.56	10.34	13.47	15.00	14.55	11.93	8.96	7.09	7.52	4.32	6.60	6.97	5.41
Banking Survey																*Millions of Liri:*
Foreign Assets (Net)	51n	74.52	82.55	89.80	98.34	100.33	106.91	119.48	133.79	160.60	174.91	229.16	287.37	318.82	366.23	393.40
Domestic Credit	52	13.77	15.15	17.20	25.78	46.71	62.37	73.32	72.40	60.16	72.81	71.79	84.75	75.16	70.58	82.51
Claims on Central Govt. (Net)	52an	4.18	1.86	-.52	1.52	6.82	12.51	18.72	14.57	4.95	12.92	12.94	22.14	10.39	.57	-2.61
Claims on Private Sector	52d	9.59	13.29	17.71	24.26	39.89	49.86	54.60	57.83	55.21	59.89	58.86	62.61	64.77	70.01	85.12
Liquid Liabilities	55l	84.96	93.41	103.34	119.85	136.63	152.03	174.32	189.52	202.45	220.38	264.46	319.02	349.12	395.28	441.10
Other Items (Net)	57r	3.32	4.29	3.67	4.26	10.41	17.24	18.48	16.67	18.32	27.34	36.50	53.11	44.86	41.53	34.81
Interest Rates																*Percent Per Annum*
Discount Rate (End of Period)	60	....	....	....	....	5.0	5.5	5.5	5.5	5.5	5.5	5.5	5.5	5.5	5.5	5.5
Deposit Rate	60l	....	....	....	....	....	....	....	....	....	....	....	....	5.0	5.0	5.0
Lending Rate	60p	....	....	....	....	....	....	....	....	....	....	....	8.0	8.0	8.0	8.0

Malta

1980	1981	1982	1983	1984	1985	1986	1987	1988	1989	1990	1991	1992	1993	1994		
End of Period															**Exchange Rates**	
2.2140	2.2185	2.1821	2.1440	2.0744	2.1479	2.2147	2.2614	2.2373	2.2589	2.3371	2.2877	1.9436	1.8426	1.8609	Official Rate	ac
End of Period (ag) Period Average (rh)																
2.8237	2.5823	2.4071	2.2447	2.0333	2.3593	2.7090	3.2081	3.0107	2.9686	3.3249	3.2724	2.6725	2.5309	2.7166	Official Rate	ag
2.8962	2.5894	2.4282	2.3135	2.1718	2.1385	2.5481	2.8981	3.0251	2.8712	3.1527	3.1002	3.1462	2.6171	2.6486	Official Rate	rh
Period Averages																
91.9	82.1	77.0	73.4	68.9	67.8	80.8	91.9	96.0	91.1	100.0	98.3	99.8	83.0	84.0	Official Rate	ah x
83.4	89.6	95.2	99.6	104.1	106.2	100.9	99.8	100.6	101.8	100.0	99.9	98.2	90.8	90.5	Nominal Effective Exchange Rate	ne c
113.7	122.9	127.1	123.8	122.1	118.4	112.1	108.6	107.1	104.3	100.0	97.8	94.2	87.9	88.8	Real Effective Exchange Rate	re c
End of Period															**Fund Position**	
30.0	30.0	30.0	45.1	45.1	45.1	45.1	45.1	45.1	45.1	45.1	45.1	67.5	67.5	67.5	Quota	2f. s
11.3	14.6	21.2	31.0	35.7	39.6	43.1	46.6	50.1	53.6	59.1	64.2	33.1	35.3	35.6	SDRs	1b. s
15.8	23.7	25.8	28.8	30.9	29.7	32.4	31.2	27.3	23.5	19.6	20.8	25.3	25.3	25.4	Reserve Position in the Fund	1c. s
End of Period															**International Liquidity**	
990.1	1,073.8	1,083.6	1,112.3	990.2	986.9	1,145.4	1,414.6	1,364.7	1,355.1	1,431.8	1,333.3	1,268.3	1,362.4	1,849.6	Total Reserves minus Gold	1l. d
14.5	17.0	23.4	32.4	35.0	43.5	52.8	66.1	67.5	70.4	84.1	91.8	45.5	48.4	52.0	SDRs	1b. d
20.1	27.6	28.4	30.2	30.3	32.6	39.6	44.3	36.7	30.9	27.9	29.8	34.8	34.7	37.1	Reserve Position in the Fund	1c. d
955.5	1,029.3	1,031.8	1,049.7	925.0	910.9	1,053.0	1,304.2	1,260.5	1,253.8	1,319.8	1,211.7	1,188.0	1,279.3	1,760.5	Foreign Exchange	1d. d
.434	.456	.462	.472	.466	.466	.466	.466	.466	.226	.157	.117	.120	.100	.105	Gold (Million Fine Troy Ounces)	1ad
51.4	60.8	62.9	66.7	64.5	134.8	163.9	163.9	200.0	93.7	59.4	42.4	40.3	38.5	40.0	Gold (National Valuation)	1an d
....	45.7	47.8	62.4	75.4	90.1	84.8	84.4	84.4	80.4	78.5	30.5	33.4	29.6	27.2	Monetary Authorities: Other Assets	3.. d
6.1	39.3	33.5	40.2	37.4	52.7	65.5	84.4	84.4	80.4	78.5	30.5	33.4	29.6	26.8	Other Official Insts.: Assets	3b. d
158.9	145.1	140.6	125.0	118.2	157.3	198.7	260.0	308.3	425.1	657.6	806.6	860.1	939.9	1,116.1	Deposit Money Banks: Assets	7a. d
140.5	128.7	122.3	106.6	94.9	122.0	173.7	215.5	263.2	364.5	600.2	726.4	728.1	805.2	1,011.3	of which: Claims on Nonbanks	7ad d
19.0	24.6	25.4	30.3	26.5	42.1	49.2	76.5	103.2	124.3	219.8	301.4	164.1	262.6	255.2	Deposit Money Banks: Liabilities	7b. d
10.4	15.8	18.5	25.3	20.4	31.6	39.3	60.1	79.5	109.9	200.7	258.8	117.7	107.5	96.7	of which: Liab. to Nonbanks	7bd d
3.7	3.5	3.6	2.7	2.7	52.4	51.0	110.9	181.8	220.0	298.5	321.0	303.1	294.0	13.7	Other Banking Insts.: Assets	7e. d
.1	—	—	—	.1	25.3	15.8	65.9	151.4	197.1	271.3	273.0	467.8	496.3	366.3	Liabilities	7f. d
End of Period															**Monetary Authorities**	
370.66	416.41	444.09	489.92	529.57	513.86	514.57	529.59	534.00	509.97	452.63	423.81	494.46	559.11	698.01	Foreign Assets	11
.16	.18	.23	.62	.67	.25	.30	4.12	1.85	2.88	22.21	58.17	62.30	18.08	39.22	Claims on Central Government	12a
302.84	338.76	347.23	369.75	409.77	413.36	417.22	429.05	430.10	412.82	389.84	416.51	442.60	443.58	584.20	Reserve Money	14
206.08	239.16	259.73	279.63	283.69	273.34	273.79	300.24	314.31	319.41	330.32	344.34	337.64	353.26	365.91	of which: Currency Outside DMBs	14a
28.45	35.34	31.82	37.42	35.44	56.91	32.86	33.73	47.25	25.98	22.96	16.74	17.00	21.04	22.25	Central Government Deposits	16d
39.54	42.50	65.27	83.38	85.03	43.84	64.79	70.94	58.50	74.05	62.04	48.73	97.17	112.56	130.78	Other Items (Net)	17r
End of Period															**Deposit Money Banks**	
76.52	76.76	70.21	75.17	114.32	127.18	127.55	113.21	103.61	86.40	58.35	62.79	93.82	83.25	194.50	Reserves	20
56.29	56.18	58.43	55.69	58.13	66.67	73.34	81.04	102.39	143.19	197.79	246.50	321.83	371.36	410.85	Foreign Assets	21
6.23	6.23	6.23	6.23	18.74	19.42	19.47	43.70	70.38	79.23	88.68	79.50	78.25	142.65	135.88	Claims on Central Government	22a
104.51	121.32	144.67	164.39	187.45	212.81	244.69	276.42	311.23	376.12	470.85	548.04	608.20	697.77	782.02	Claims on Private Sector	22d
32.62	31.94	29.60	30.39	30.93	35.48	36.66	39.01	38.62	42.04	49.75	53.22	57.43	59.42	72.15	Demand Deposits	24
180.07	195.03	209.65	230.88	303.57	341.32	377.60	416.04	473.85	555.48	642.83	723.33	827.13	940.86	1,105.35	Time and Savings Deposits	25
6.72	9.51	10.54	13.50	13.06	17.83	18.15	23.86	34.28	41.87	66.11	92.11	61.41	103.75	93.94	Foreign Liabilities	26c
24.13	24.01	29.74	26.70	31.07	31.46	32.64	35.45	40.86	45.57	56.98	68.18	156.12	190.99	251.81	Other Items (Net)	27r
End of Period															**Monetary Survey**	
420.22	463.08	491.97	532.12	574.64	562.70	569.76	586.77	602.11	611.29	584.31	578.20	754.88	826.72	1,014.92	Foreign Assets (Net)	31n
82.41	92.25	119.16	133.69	171.24	175.39	231.46	290.37	336.07	431.10	556.97	667.58	729.79	835.10	932.65	Domestic Credit	32
−22.10	−29.07	−25.51	−30.70	−16.21	−37.42	−13.23	13.95	24.84	54.98	86.12	119.54	121.59	137.33	150.63	Claims on Central Govt. (Net)	32an
104.51	121.32	144.67	164.39	187.45	212.81	244.69	276.42	311.23	376.12	470.85	548.04	608.20	697.77	782.02	Claims on Private Sector	32d
258.80	293.73	306.28	324.63	325.92	321.21	323.25	354.59	363.95	368.64	384.63	406.70	408.56	425.07	463.55	Money	34
205.07	220.03	238.65	262.88	303.57	341.32	377.60	416.04	473.85	555.48	642.83	723.33	827.13	940.86	1,105.35	Quasi-Money	35
38.75	41.58	66.20	78.30	116.38	75.56	100.37	106.51	100.39	118.27	113.82	115.75	248.98	295.88	378.67	Other Items (Net)	37r
463.88	513.76	544.93	587.51	629.49	662.53	700.85	770.63	837.80	924.12	1,027.46	1,130.03	1,235.69	1,365.93	1,568.90	Money plus Quasi-Money	35l
End of Period															**Other Banking Institutions**	
1.30	1.34	1.49	1.20	1.33	22.21	18.81	34.58	60.39	74.11	89.77	98.10	113.40	116.16	5.04	Foreign Assets	41
12.93	17.89	24.10	40.06	42.82	49.49	54.13	63.24	77.58	88.66	104.54	138.21	164.00	181.76	203.49	Claims on Private Sector	42d
.26	.24	5.28	.27	.35	.22	.21	.24	.73	1.01	.70	.01	79.26	96.77	134.83	Claims on Deposit Money Banks	42e
.03	.01	.01	.01	.03	10.72	5.82	20.55	50.30	66.41	81.59	83.44	175.06	196.11	134.84	Foreign Liabilities	46c
8.40	12.85	18.62	28.07	33.01	44.85	50.26	59.02	67.39	75.96	87.00	62.17	88.93	106.32	121.85	Credit from Deposit Money Banks	46h
6.06	6.60	12.26	13.44	11.46	16.35	17.07	18.50	21.01	21.42	26.43	90.71	92.68	92.26	86.67	Other Items (Net)	47r
End of Period															**Banking Survey**	
421.49	464.40	493.46	533.31	575.94	574.19	582.75	600.80	612.20	618.99	592.49	592.87	693.22	746.77	885.12	Foreign Assets (Net)	51n
106.75	122.47	156.01	186.54	214.70	225.54	286.24	354.97	417.07	523.05	666.57	805.79	893.80	1,016.85	1,136.14	Domestic Credit	52
−10.69	−16.74	−12.77	−17.91	−15.57	−36.76	−12.57	15.31	28.26	58.27	91.18	119.54	121.59	137.33	150.63	Claims on Central Govt. (Net)	52an
117.44	139.20	168.78	204.45	230.26	262.30	298.82	339.66	388.81	464.78	575.39	686.25	772.21	879.53	985.51	Claims on Private Sector	52d
475.73	526.57	562.78	601.96	631.35	664.54	702.87	773.78	844.25	930.60	1,035.92	1,130.03	1,235.68	1,365.93	1,568.90	Liquid Liabilities	55l
52.52	60.30	86.69	117.89	159.29	135.19	166.13	182.00	185.02	211.43	223.14	268.63	351.34	397.70	452.35	Other Items (Net)	57r
Percent Per Annum															**Interest Rates**	
5.5	5.5	6.5	6.5	6.5	6.0	6.0	5.5	5.5	5.5	5.5	5.5	5.5	5.5	5.5	Discount Rate *(End of Period)*	60
5.0	5.0	5.0	5.0	5.0	5.0	4.5	4.5	4.5	4.5	4.5	4.5	4.5	4.5	4.5	Deposit Rate	60l
8.0	8.0	8.0	8.0	8.0	8.0	8.0	8.0	8.5	8.5	8.5	8.5	8.5	8.5	8.5	Lending Rate	60p

Malta

181		1965	1966	1967	1968	1969	1970	1971	1972	1973	1974	1975	1976	1977	1978	1979
Prices and Production																*Index Numbers (1990=100):*
Consumer Prices	64	38.3	38.5	38.7	39.5	40.5	42.0	42.9	44.4	47.8	ɪ51.3	55.8	56.1	61.7	64.6	69.2
Industrial Production	66	....	....	....	....	....	....	....	....	....	....	29.0	33.6	39.8	41.7	44.4
International Transactions																*Millions of Liri*
Exports	70	8.65	10.75	9.89	14.15	15.96	16.07	18.82	25.72	35.96	51.58	63.90	97.41	121.79	131.95	152.17
Imports, cif	71	35.14	38.88	40.51	51.40	61.52	67.12	65.38	67.21	88.10	138.97	144.45	179.92	217.68	221.50	271.96
Imports, fob	71.v	31.43	34.77	36.24	45.98	55.06	60.04	58.48	60.11	79.20	125.07	130.04	162.12	195.88	199.30	244.76
																1985=100
Volume of Exports	72	10.6	13.4	13.0	17.4	20.4	17.4	22.3	28.6	38.3	40.2	44.8	63.9	80.1	83.0	89.7
Volume of Imports	73	ɪ39.0	44.5	43.4	52.7	61.9	63.7	60.4	56.8	59.9	69.3	67.4	77.3	86.0	82.4	89.7
Unit Value of Exports	74	34.7	33.9	32.6	35.0	36.4	40.9	40.2	44.7	49.4	62.7	66.7	74.3	77.1	83.8	90.5
Unit Value of Imports	75	ɪ25.4	24.8	26.4	27.5	28.1	29.7	30.6	33.3	41.5	56.7	60.5	65.7	71.5	75.9	85.6
Balance of Payments																*Millions of US Dollars:*
Goods: Exports f.o.b.	78aa d	....	....	....	....	....	....	51.3	81.5	113.9	171.0	199.3	254.7	319.0	362.2	462.2
Goods: Imports f.o.b.	78ab d	....	....	....	....	....	....	−142.0	−155.9	−212.9	−313.6	−332.4	−376.6	−456.8	−507.3	−674.3
Trade Balance	78ac d	....	....	....	....	....	....	−90.6	−74.4	−99.0	−142.7	−133.1	−121.8	−137.8	−145.1	−212.0
Services: Credit	78ad d	....	....	....	....	....	....	81.8	90.4	133.7	151.0	188.9	178.8	197.0	264.2	344.8
Services: Debit	78ae d	....	....	....	....	....	....	−41.8	−44.6	−51.8	−73.2	−80.0	−85.9	−114.8	−140.1	−184.1
Balance on Goods and Services	78af d	....	....	....	....	....	....	−50.6	−28.6	−17.1	−64.9	−24.2	−28.9	−55.6	−21.0	−51.3
Income: Credit	78ag d	....	....	....	....	....	....	28.5	32.2	35.0	48.0	63.7	61.6	70.1	78.9	102.1
Income: Debit	78ah d	....	....	....	....	....	....	−10.1	−10.7	−13.3	−15.0	−14.6	−16.0	−19.7	−31.7	−61.4
Balance on Goods, Serv., & Inc.	78ai d	....	....	....	....	....	....	−32.2	−7.1	4.6	−31.9	24.9	16.7	−5.2	26.2	−10.6
Current Transfers, n.i.e.: Credit	78aj d	....	....	....	....	....	....	37.8	34.9	31.5	41.2	39.0	44.0	49.0	52.7	64.7
Current Transfers: Debit	78ak d	....	....	....	....	....	....	−4.4	−5.2	−5.7	−4.2	−4.7	−5.6	−3.8	−6.2	−7.5
Current Account, n.i.e.	78al d	....	....	....	....	....	....	1.2	22.5	30.4	5.2	59.3	55.0	40.0	72.7	46.6
Capital Account, n.i.e.: Credit	78ba d	....	....	....	....	....	....	4.7	2.6	6.2	7.5	6.8	7.5	6.4	7.0	6.1
Capital Account: Debit	78bb d	....	....	....	....	....	....	—	—	—	—	—	—	—	—	—
Capital Account, n.i.e.	78bc d	....	....	....	....	....	....	4.7	2.6	6.2	7.5	6.8	7.5	6.4	7.0	6.1
Direct Investment Abroad	78bd d	....	....	....	....	....	....	—	—	—	—	—	—	—	—	—
Dir. Invest. in Rep. Econ., n.i.e.	78be d	....	....	....	....	....	....	11.5	4.5	5.2	10.6	15.9	14.1	18.5	21.5	16.2
Portfolio Investment Assets	78bf d	....	....	....	....	....	....	−30.2	14.9	22.2	7.3	−9.1	−1.9	−13.7	−18.9	−30.4
Portfolio Investment Liab., n.i.e.	78bg d	....	....	....	....	....	....	—	—	—	—	—	—	—	—	—
Other Investment Assets	78bh d	....	....	....	....	....	....	22.6	12.8	−32.0	−13.5	1.8	−15.5	4.3	18.9	.8
Other Investment Liab., n.i.e.	78bi d	....	....	....	....	....	....	−1.0	13.1	1.4	22.8	26.2	44.5	9.2	29.3	12.6
Financial Account, n.i.e.	78bj d	....	....	....	....	....	....	2.9	45.3	−3.3	27.2	34.8	41.2	18.2	50.9	−.8
Net Errors and Omissions	78ca d	....	....	....	....	....	....	8.4	1.6	6.0	2.1	12.0	−9.5	−4.6	−5.3	3.5
Overall Balance	78cb d	....	....	....	....	....	....	17.2	72.1	39.3	42.0	112.8	94.2	60.1	125.2	55.4
Reserves and Related Items	79da d	....	....	....	....	....	....	−17.2	−72.1	−39.3	−42.0	−112.8	−94.2	−60.1	−125.2	−55.4
Reserve Assets	79db d	....	....	....	....	....	....	−17.2	−72.1	−39.3	−42.0	−112.8	−94.2	−60.1	−125.2	−55.4
Use of Fund Credit and Loans	79dc d	....	....	....	....	....	....	—	—	—	—	—	—	—	—	—
Liabs.Constit.For.Auth.Reserves	79dd d	....	....	....	....	....	....	—	—	—	—	—	—	—	—	—
Exceptional Financing	79de d	....	....	....	....	....	....	—	—	—	—	—	—	—	....	....
Government Finance																*Millions of Liri:*
Deficit (-) or Surplus	80	−2.31	−.74	−3.71	−3.41	−11.48	−6.31	10.11	−4.76	3.07	4.83	−6.22	4.50	3.47	11.75	....
Revenue	81	13.80	16.85	17.10	19.40	22.98	33.83	50.74	37.75	57.35	74.08	91.79	104.78	105.24	125.29	....
Grants Received	81z	4.60	4.13	4.02	5.26	.10	8.50	2.59	3.10	.25	.17	.44	.32	.32	.25	....
Expenditure	82	19.47	21.26	24.37	27.70	32.31	48.16	43.04	43.42	47.19	67.57	83.35	92.46	96.30	106.44	....
Lending Minus Repayments	83	1.24	.46	.46	.37	2.25	.48	.18	2.19	7.34	1.85	15.10	8.14	5.79	7.35	....
Financing																
Domestic	84a	.66	.63	2.03	1.00	8.98	7.89	−5.00	2.35	−3.66	−2.71	−5.54	−7.56	−3.04	−13.83	....
Foreign	85a	1.65	.11	1.68	2.41	2.50	−1.58	−5.11	2.41	.59	−2.12	11.76	3.06	−.43	2.08	....
Debt: Domestic	88a	5.76	7.00	9.40	9.88	11.30	20.90	30.34	27.46	27.46	27.46	27.46	27.46	27.46	27.46	....
Foreign	89a	3.28	4.81	5.66	7.70	10.64	13.03	7.08	8.91	9.44	10.44	16.50	19.06	18.92	23.06	....
National Accounts																*Millions of Liri*
Exports of Goods & Services	90c	28.4	33.4	33.3	40.8	46.6	47.1	50.0	53.5	75.3	110.4	137.3	172.7	207.4	229.6	290.8
Government Consumption	91f	9.1	9.7	11.2	12.2	13.7	18.3	19.5	19.8	22.8	26.9	30.5	35.9	39.7	46.1	53.7
Gross Fixed Capital Formation	93e	11.8	13.1	15.6	19.9	25.5	27.8	25.5	22.5	22.3	31.2	37.5	54.1	60.0	60.3	78.2
Increase/Decrease(-) in Stocks	93i	1.7	2.2	3.0	3.1	1.3	3.2	2.9	3.0	3.3	4.5	1.5	1.9	2.3	4.8	4.8
Private Consumption	96f	39.2	41.9	45.9	53.2	64.0	73.9	75.1	80.4	90.1	107.0	118.7	135.7	172.4	186.4	206.0
Imports of Goods & Services	98c	−37.4	−41.5	−45.4	−57.9	−69.0	−75.5	−75.2	−76.9	−98.0	−148.4	−159.7	−196.6	−242.0	−249.5	−307.7
Gross Domestic Product	99b	52.7	58.8	63.7	71.3	82.0	94.8	97.9	102.2	115.7	131.6	165.8	203.7	239.8	277.6	325.8
Net Factor Inc/Pmts(-) Abroad	98.n	4.3	4.4	4.8	5.8	6.5	7.3	7.5	8.3	7.5	12.5	18.3	18.1	19.1	16.9	13.0
Gross Nat'l Expenditure = GNP	99a	57.0	63.2	68.5	77.1	88.5	102.1	105.3	110.5	123.2	144.0	184.0	221.9	258.9	294.6	338.7
Nat'l Income, Market Prices	99e	54.8	60.9	66.1	74.5	85.7	99.2	101.9	106.8	119.2	139.4	178.6	215.0	250.4	284.6	327.6
Gross Dom. Prod. 1990 Prices	99b.p	118.6	131.4	140.5	154.7	164.7	185.4	190.0	201.1	ɪ220.7	242.8	290.3	339.7	381.1	423.6	468.1
GDP Deflator (1990=100)	99bi p	44.4	44.8	45.3	46.1	49.8	51.1	51.5	50.8	52.4	54.2	57.1	60.0	62.9	65.5	69.6
																Millions:
Population	99z	.32	.32	.32	ɪ.30	.30	.30	.30	.30	.30	.30	ɪ.33	.33	.33	.34	ɪ.32

Monetary Authorities: ɪ Beginning in 1968, *line 11* and *line 1d.d* increased and *line 21* decreased as a result of the transfer of foreign assets, following the Basle Agreement for the support of sterling. Offsetting items affect *line 14* and *line 20*.
Deposit Money Banks: ɪ See note to section 10.
Monetary Survey: ɪ See note to section 10.

Government Finance: ɪ Prior to 1979, data relate to a fiscal year different from calendar year (fiscal year ends April 1 through 1978).

Malta

181

	1980	1981	1982	1983	1984	1985	1986	1987	1988	1989	1990	1991	1992	1993	1994	Prices and Production	
Period Averages																	
	80.1	89.4	94.6	ℐ93.7	93.3	93.1	95.0	95.4	96.3	97.1	100.0	ℐ102.5	104.2	108.5	113.0	Consumer Prices	64
	52.8	53.7	56.3	57.9	ℐ62.4	63.3	67.0	69.6	75.4	88.6	100.0	....	....	....	....	Industrial Production	66
Millions of Liri																**International Transactions**	
	166.72	173.73	169.04	156.75	181.36	187.10	194.67	208.59	235.92	294.41	357.90	405.50	490.90	515.70	577.40	Exports	70
	323.74	332.27	325.07	316.63	330.49	354.14	348.11	392.88	447.40	515.80	620.50	684.00	747.80	827.90	927.00	Imports, cif	71
	291.33	299.07	292.71	287.98	297.49	318.76	313.33	353.62	402.70	464.27	558.51	615.66	673.09	745.18	834.38	Imports, fob	71.v
1985=100																	
	ℐ93.6	92.3	85.3	85.5	97.7	100.0	104.4	105.4	108.4	130.4	....	....	....	....	....	Volume of Exports	72
	ℐ98.8	88.8	88.8	86.5	92.0	100.0	102.1	114.6	129.1	144.2	....	....	....	....	....	Volume of Imports	73
	ℐ94.5	101.3	104.3	98.0	99.7	100.0	102.5	107.4	118.8	124.3	....	....	....	....	....	Unit Value of Exports	74
	ℐ92.5	102.2	103.3	103.3	101.4	100.0	96.2	96.8	97.9	101.0	....	....	....	....	....	Unit Value of Imports	75
Minus Sign Indicates Debit																**Balance of Payments**	
	537.6	499.9	445.5	406.1	426.4	435.5	534.1	653.0	780.1	891.3	1,192.0	1,324.4	1,603.5	1,398.7	....	Goods: Exports f.o.b.	78aa d
	–884.7	–778.1	–709.2	–659.5	–639.2	–672.1	–786.5	–1,024.6	–1,222.3	–1,327.7	–1,753.0	–1,897.3	–2,104.0	–1,953.2	....	Goods: Imports f.o.b.	78ab d
	–347.1	–278.3	–263.7	–253.4	–212.8	–236.6	–252.4	–371.6	–442.2	–436.5	–561.1	–572.9	–500.4	–554.6	....	Trade Balance	78ac d
	481.1	411.9	306.0	282.6	250.5	273.7	370.5	557.2	653.2	644.5	758.4	819.8	889.9	899.1	....	Services: Credit	78ad d
	–242.9	–243.6	–246.0	–207.2	–209.7	–218.5	–280.4	–358.9	–412.3	–433.3	–530.5	–544.5	–607.0	–619.9	....	Services: Debit	78ae d
	–108.9	–109.9	–203.8	–178.1	–172.0	–181.4	–162.3	–173.4	–201.3	–225.3	–333.2	–297.6	–217.6	–275.4	....	Balance on Goods and Services	78af d
	153.1	161.6	174.0	133.0	138.6	126.6	146.3	139.5	156.6	190.5	269.0	268.5	271.2	244.8	....	Income: Credit	78ag d
	–57.6	–50.9	–28.6	–22.9	–20.0	–22.8	–44.0	–25.8	–53.5	–73.2	–79.0	–94.0	–117.0	–97.8	....	Income: Debit	78ah d
	–13.3	.8	–58.5	–68.0	–53.4	–77.6	–60.1	–59.6	–98.2	–107.9	–143.2	–123.1	–63.3	–128.4	....	Balance on Goods, Serv., & Inc.	78ai d
	60.5	93.9	76.7	68.2	68.5	57.1	73.5	91.2	170.5	114.5	105.1	114.5	94.1	62.5	....	Current Transfers, n.i.e.: Credit	78aj d
	–8.4	–8.3	–5.8	–5.1	–6.9	–5.3	–6.6	–9.0	–11.2	–16.1	–23.3	–4.9	–4.7	–4.2	....	Current Transfers: Debit	78ak d
	38.8	86.4	12.4	–4.9	8.2	–25.8	6.9	22.6	61.1	–9.5	–61.4	–13.6	26.0	–70.1	....	Current Account, n.i.e.	78al d
	5.8	4.7	3.9	3.2	3.0	3.0	4.3	4.3	7.0	6.0	5.7	6.2	4.4	2.6	....	Capital Account, n.i.e.: Credit	78ba d
	—	—	—	—	—	—	—	—	—	—	—	—	—	—	....	Capital Account: Debit	78bb d
	5.8	4.7	3.9	3.2	3.0	3.0	4.3	4.3	7.0	6.0	5.7	6.2	4.4	2.6	....	Capital Account, n.i.e.	78bc d
	—	—	—	—	—	—	—	—	—	—	—	—	—	....	....	Direct Investment Abroad	78bd d
	26.6	39.0	20.9	24.5	26.2	19.0	21.9	19.4	40.8	51.7	45.6	77.0	39.5	....	....	Dir. Invest. in Rep. Econ., n.i.e.	78be d
	—	—	—	—	—	—	—	—	—	—	—	—	—	....	....	Portfolio Investment Assets	78bf d
	–8.7	3.9	–3.4	–27.1	.9	–32.8	44.0	–7.5	–38.4	–57.7	–1.9	–241.3	–209.5	....	....	Portfolio Investment Liab., n.i.e.	78bg d
	–13.6	–17.3	–21.6	–13.6	3.7	–1.1	–59.0	–62.5	–105.5	–100.1	–227.5	75.2	–100.3	....	....	Other Investment Assets	78bh d
	20.6	16.3	28.4	105.0	–8.7	–9.8	–25.2	48.0	120.3	59.4	140.3	105.8	347.4	—	....	Other Investment Liab., n.i.e.	78bi d
	24.9	41.9	24.3	88.8	22.1	–24.7	–18.3	–2.6	17.2	–46.8	–43.4	16.7	77.1	....	....	Financial Account, n.i.e.	78bj d
	–18.1	14.9	11.6	17.0	–1.5	–19.6	2.6	–28.8	–50.4	64.4	24.2	–93.9	–62.8	70.4	....	Net Errors and Omissions	78ca d
	51.4	147.8	52.1	104.2	31.9	–67.1	–4.6	–4.5	34.8	14.2	–74.9	–84.6	44.8	2.9	....	Overall Balance	78cb d
	–51.4	–147.8	–52.1	–104.2	–31.9	67.1	4.6	4.5	–34.8	–14.2	74.9	84.6	–44.8	–2.9	....	Reserves and Related Items	79da d
	–51.4	–147.8	–52.1	–104.2	–31.9	67.1	4.6	4.5	–34.8	–14.2	74.9	84.6	–44.8	–2.9	....	Reserve Assets	79db d
	—	—	—	—	—	—	—	—	—	—	—	—	—	—	....	Use of Fund Credit and Loans	79dc d
	....	....	....	....	....	....	....	....	....	....	....	....	....	....	....	Liabs.Constit.For.Auth.Reserves.	79dd d
	—	—	—	—	—	—	—	—	—	—	—	—	—	—	....	Exceptional Financing	79de d
Year Ending December 31																**Government Finance**	
	ℐ4.29	5.55	–7.63	7.33	2.06	–19.21	–19.50	–36.68	–.18	–31.13	–38.06	–40.76	–27.19	....	....	Deficit (–) or Surplus	80
	ℐ139.92	167.40	186.35	192.88	186.83	196.81	189.59	188.87	219.82	230.76	280.54	302.81	292.91	....	....	Revenue	81
	ℐ3.45	15.75	7.03	6.78	6.95	.25	.29		14.25	8.19	7.68	16.37	16.39	....	....	Grants Received	81z
	ℐ131.29	155.54	175.02	180.31	187.40	190.77	204.00	223.71	229.85	274.41	327.20	360.38	333.79	....	....	Expenditure	82
	ℐ7.79	22.06	25.99	12.02	4.32	25.50	5.38	1.84	4.40	–4.33	–.92	–.44	2.70	....	....	Lending Minus Repayments	83
																Financing	
	ℐ–11.11	–7.63	6.30	–17.23	–3.66	20.34	24.45	38.89	2.64	34.34	27.27	34.95	33.64	....	....	Domestic	84a
	ℐ6.82	2.08	1.33	9.90	1.60	–1.13	–4.95	–2.21	–2.46	–3.21	10.79	5.81	–6.45	....	....	Foreign	85a
	ℐ25.21	25.22	25.24	25.23	25.24	25.26	25.25	54.89	80.40	90.95	125.54	157.28	186.93	....	....	Debt: Domestic	88a
	ℐ33.06	32.69	32.56	42.41	45.31	42.52	35.44	29.84	28.14	26.89	37.49	44.71	48.40	....	....	Foreign	89a
Millions of Liri																**National Accounts**	
	356.6	355.9	319.8	307.6	323.5	345.2	370.2	429.6	480.0	543.5	626.4	701.9	804.1	897.3	....	Exports of Goods & Services	90c
	63.4	75.4	85.2	82.3	80.3	84.3	89.5	98.2	105.2	119.6	129.2	147.1	164.3	188.9	....	Government Consumption	91f
	87.1	105.6	120.1	131.6	126.5	125.9	122.3	153.5	166.4	188.4	232.6	239.1	240.9	272.9	....	Gross Fixed Capital Formation	93e
	9.4	12.6	25.5	5.5	6.8	7.9	8.2	–2.4	8.2	9.9	12.7	15.6	.1	8.2	....	Increase/Decrease(–) in Stocks	93i
	253.5	279.4	305.7	306.7	317.5	333.2	343.4	351.2	387.6	425.5	460.8	494.5	531.4	569.1	....	Private Consumption	96f
	–378.0	–392.5	–394.6	–376.1	–393.5	–420.5	–421.7	–480.9	–540.9	–616.8	–726.9	–791.2	–866.0	–998.3	....	Imports of Goods & Services	98c
	392.0	436.5	461.8	457.6	461.1	476.0	511.9	549.2	606.5	670.1	734.7	806.9	874.8	938.2	....	Gross Domestic Product	99b
	30.6	41.2	52.0	38.1	45.5	38.8	28.1	30.7	28.3	35.8	55.0	49.7	42.7	37.8	....	Net Factor Inc/Pmts(–) Abroad	98.n
	422.5	477.7	513.8	495.7	506.5	514.8	539.9	579.8	634.8	705.9	789.8	856.5	916.4	976.0	....	Gross Nat'l Expenditure = GNP	99a
	409.6	463.3	498.1	475.9	485.5	493.4	516.7	553.8	605.9	673.9	754.5	818.8	....	....	....	Nat'l Income, Market Prices	99e
	501.1	517.6	529.5	526.2	531.2	544.9	566.1	589.4	639.0	691.2	734.7	780.7	814.6	....	....	Gross Dom. Prod. 1990 Prices	99b.p
	78.2	84.3	87.2	87.0	86.8	87.4	90.4	93.2	94.9	96.9	100.0	103.4	107.4	....	....	GDP Deflator (1990=100)	99bi p
Midyear Estimates																	
	.32	.32	.32	.33	.33	.34	.34	.34	.35	.35	.35	.36	.36	.36	....	Population	99z

1995 INTERNATIONAL FINANCIAL STATISTICS YEARBOOK   529

Mauritania

		1965	1966	1967	1968	1969	1970	1971	1972	1973	1974	1975	1976	1977	1978	1979
Exchange Rates														*Ouguiyas per SDR:*		
Official Rate	aa	49.015	49.518	49.085	49.481	55.583	55.205	56.723	55.599	56.801	53.014	52.855	50.702	55.937	60.130	60.393
														Ouguiyas per US Dollar		
Official Rate	ae	49.015	49.518	49.085	49.481	55.583	55.205	52.245	51.210	47.085	43.300	45.150	43.640	46.050	46.155	45.845
Official Rate	rf	49.370	49.370	49.370	49.370	51.942	55.542	55.426	50.405	44.578	45.333ᵉ	43.104ᵉ	45.022ᵉ	45.587	46.163	45.893
Fund Position														*Millions of SDRs:*		
Quota	2f.s	7.5	8.0	8.5	9.0	10.0	13.0	13.0	13.0	13.0	13.0	13.0	13.0	13.0	17.0	17.0
SDRs	1b.s	—	—	—	—	—	1.7	.9	2.2	2.1	2.0	1.7	1.2	.6	.7	1.3
Reserve Position in the Fund	1c.s	.8	.9	1.0	1.1	1.4	1.5	.6	.8	.9	—	—	—	—	—	—
Total Fund Cred.&Loans Outstg.	2tl	—	—	—	—	—	—	—	—	—	—	—	11.8	17.9	22.0	25.1
International Liquidity													*Millions of US Dollars Unless Otherwise Indicated:*			
Total Reserves minus Gold	1l.d	9.9	7.8	8.8	7.4	3.6	3.2	7.5	13.5	42.2	103.8	47.7	82.0	50.0	79.5	113.7
SDRs	1b.d	—	—	—	—	—	1.7	1.0	2.3	2.6	2.4	2.0	1.4	.7	.9	1.7
Reserve Position in the Fund	1c.d	.8	.9	1.0	1.1	1.4	1.5	.7	.8	1.1	—	—	—	—	—	—
Foreign Exchange	1d.d	9.1	6.9	7.8	6.3	2.2	—	5.8	10.3	38.6	101.4	45.7	80.6	49.3	78.6	112.0
Gold (Million Fine Troy Ounces)	1ad	....	....	....	....	....	....	....	....	....	....	....	....	.006	.008	.008
Gold (National Valuation)	1and	....	....	....	....	....	....	....	....	....	....	....	....	.2	.2	1.7
Monetary Authorities: Other Liab.	4..d	2.8	4.9	—	.3	6.5	.7	—	—	19.8	35.9	36.8	55.9	57.5	81.0	88.1
Deposit Money Banks: Assets	7a.d	2.8	5.4	3.8	1.6	.5	.5	2.4	.6	1.1	1.0	.4	18.5	21.9	11.5	3.1
Liabilities	7b.d	2.3	1.7	2.2	2.8	2.3	3.9	6.6	5.5	7.9	24.1	11.4	29.5	40.0	67.7	70.1
Monetary Authorities														*Millions of Ouguiyas:*		
Foreign Assets	11	482	384	435	367	202	164	393	691	1,948	4,500	2,159	3,582	2,519	3,655	5,330
Claims on Central Government	12a	—	—	—	—	—	—	6	10	334	25	749	369	1,749	1,459	1,752
Claims on Nonfin.Pub.Enterprises	12c															
Claims on Private Sector	12d	....	....	....	....	....	....	....	....	....	....	921	788	766	766	766
Claims on Deposit Money Banks	12e	—	—	—	67	270	491	346	280	822	490	1,348	1,428	2,255	2,103	1,781
Claims on Nonbank Financial Insts	12g															
Reserve Money	14	266	263	299	340	390	475	480	662	788	1,833	1,653	1,796	2,038	2,210	2,963
of which: Currency Outside DMBs	14a	246	249	285	312	358	445	461	618	630	954	1,214	1,464	1,529	1,729	2,311
Restricted Deposits	16b															
Foreign Liabilities	16c	14	24	—	1	36	4	2	—	933	1,555	1,663	3,040	3,574	4,738	4,990
Long-Term Foreign Liabilities	16cl															
Central Government Deposits	16d	202	97	133	93	45	82	89	62	512	599	1,161	320	153	128	177
Capital Accounts	17a	....	....	....	—	—	—	171	247	454	506	552	751	869	871	1,131
Other Items (Net)	17r	—	—	3	—	1	94	3	10	417	522	148	260	654	38	367
Deposit Money Banks														*Millions of Ouguiyas:*		
Reserves	20	20	15	24	35	77	32	38	432	1,106	7,964	3,202	344	504	476	638
Foreign Assets	21	139	268	190	80	25	25	122	29	50	44	19	808	1,008	533	142
Claims on Central Government	22a	3	4	2	12	10	17	6	116	20	74	48	111	26	59	57
Claims on Nonfin.Pub.Enterprises	22c															
Claims on Private Sector	22d	305	278	519	800	1,010	1,526	1,544	1,789	2,740	3,041	4,616	5,488	7,112	7,712	7,835
Claims on Nonbank Financial Insts	22g															
Demand Deposits	24	154	301	351	443	412	600	598	708	778	1,407	1,564	2,068	2,386	2,226	2,598
Time Deposits	25	32	40	56	80	125	143	125	160	531	694	1,052	1,131	964	1,025	1,212
Foreign Liabilities	26c	113	85	110	136	126	213	346	281	370	1,045	513	1,225	1,783	2,242	2,610
Long-Term Foreign Liabilities	26cl	....	....	....	....	....	....	....	....	....	....	....	62	57	882	604
Central Government Deposits	26d	131	90	147	134	96	90	159	317	89	162	277	267	217	143	75
Central Govt. Lending Funds	26f															69
Credit from Monetary Authorities	26g	—	—	—	67	270	491	347	281	822	161	1,296	1,428	2,255	2,109	1,781
Capital Accounts	27a	....	....	—	109	124	136	172	204	367	562	626	752	832	855	888
Other Items (Net)	27r	37	49	72	–42	–31	–73	–37	414	960	7,092	2,557	–182	157	–701	–1,164
Monetary Survey														*Millions of Ouguiyas:*		
Foreign Assets (Net)	31n	494	543	515	310	65	–28	167	439	695	1,944	1	63	–1,888	–3,674	–2,732
Domestic Credit	32	4	127	298	630	931	1,436	1,381	1,638	2,580	2,470	5,043	6,320	9,464	9,907	10,330
Claims on Central Govt. (Net)	32an	–304	–160	–224	–178	–85	–117	–224	–216	–279	–709	–719	–241	1,394	1,052	1,443
Claims on Nonfin.Pub.Enterprises	32c															
Claims on Private Sector	32d	308	287	522	807	1,016	1,553	1,605	1,854	2,858	3,179	5,762	6,561	8,071	8,855	8,887
Claims on Nonbank Fin. Insts	32g															
Money	34	429	582	693	799	822	1,110	1,132	1,428	1,494	2,451	2,926	3,683	4,095	4,134	5,081
Quasi-Money	35	32	40	56	80	125	143	125	160	531	694	1,052	1,131	964	1,025	1,212
Restricted Deposits	36b															
Central Govt. Lending Funds	36f	....	....	....	—	—	—	—	—	—	—	—	—	—	—	69
Other Items (Net)	37r	37	48	64	61	49	155	291	489	1,250	1,268	1,066	1,569	2,518	1,073	1,236
Money plus Quasi-Money	35l	461	622	749	879	947	1,252	1,257	1,588	2,024	3,145	3,979	4,964	5,239	5,340	6,465
Interest Rates														*Percent Per Annum*		
Discount Rate (End of Period)	60	3.50	3.50	3.50	3.50	3.50	3.50	3.50	3.50	5.50	5.50	5.00	5.00	5.00	5.00	5.00
Deposit Rate	60l															
Lending Rate	60p															
Prices														*Index Numbers (1990=100):*		
Consumer Prices	64															
International Transactions														*Millions of Ouguiyas*		
Exports	70	2,844	3,418	3,556	3,543	3,912	4,936	5,026	5,991	6,918	8,175	7,527	8,013	7,156	5,692	6,733
Imports, cif	71	1,173	1,136	1,843	1,743	2,193	3,103	3,156	3,475	5,692	5,453	6,934	8,049	9,414	8,361	11,869
Imports, fob	71.v	1,066	1,005	1,631	1,542	1,941	2,746	2,793	3,075	5,037	4,826	6,136	7,123	8,331	7,399	10,504

Mauritania

682

	1980	1981	1982	1983	1984	1985	1986	1987	1988	1989	1990	1991	1992	1993	1994		
	\multicolumn{15}{l	}{}	**Exchange Rates**	
End of Period	58.707	56.964	58.421	59.708	65.958	84.655	90.614	101.576	101.910	109.798	110.740	111.316	158.263	170.541	187.401	Official Rate	aa
End of Period (ae) Period Average (rf)																Official Rate	
	46.030	48.940	52.960	57.030	67.290	77.070	74.080	71.600	75.730	83.550	77.840	77.820	115.100	124.160	128.370	Official Rate	ae
	45.914	48.296	51.769	54.812	63.803	77.085	74.375	73.878	75.261	83.051	80.609	81.946	87.027	120.806	123.575	Official Rate	rf
																Fund Position	
End of Period																	
	25.5	25.5	25.5	33.9	33.9	33.9	33.9	33.9	33.9	33.9	33.9	33.9	47.5	47.5	47.5	Quota	2f. s
	—	1.1	—	.7	—	3.9	2.6	12.1	.1	.1	.6	.1	.1	.1	—	SDRs	1b. s
	—	—	—	—	—	—	—	—	—	—	—	—	—	—	—	Reserve Position in the Fund	1c. s
	39.1	42.5	56.4	51.7	41.4	36.5	42.7	54.1	52.5	52.3	49.2	39.5	42.0	46.1	58.8	Total Fund Cred.&Loans Outstg.	2tl
																International Liquidity	
End of Period																	
	139.9	161.8	139.1	105.9	77.5	59.2	48.2	71.8	55.6	82.4	54.1	67.6	61.2	44.6	39.7	Total Reserves minus Gold	1l. d
	—	1.3	—	.7	—	4.3	3.1	17.2	.1	.1	.8	.1	.1	.1	—	SDRs	1b. d
	—	—	—	—	—	—	—	—	—	—	—	—	—	—	—	Reserve Position in the Fund	1c. d
	139.9	160.5	139.1	105.2	77.5	54.9	45.1	54.6	55.5	82.3	53.3	67.5	61.1	44.4	39.7	Foreign Exchange	1d. d
	.011	.011	.011	.011	.011	.011	.012	.012	.012	.012	.012	.012	.012	.012	.012	Gold (Million Fine Troy Ounces)	1ad
	6.9	4.5	4.1	4.5	3.6	3.7	4.5	5.7	4.8	4.6	4.4	4.2	3.8	4.5	....	Gold (National Valuation)	1and
	79.2	98.2	93.9	88.5	89.3	89.6	89.9	94.2	91.1	11.0	20.8	24.2	85.4	61.0	....	Monetary Authorities: Other Liab.	4..d
	9.2	14.5	4.4	4.8	1.5	3.3	11.0	23.0	32.6	30.0	28.7	14.1	15.7	25.8	....	Deposit Money Banks: Assets	7a. d
	81.3	79.3	98.0	78.7	93.4	56.8	77.5	79.9	87.6	106.0	120.6	181.8	110.0	106.4	....	Liabilities	7b. d
																Monetary Authorities	
End of Period																	
	6,953	8,650	6,545	5,018	4,929	3,954	3,714	5,461	4,616	I 7,386	4,136	5,308	7,598	6,218	....	Foreign Assets	11
	1,965	2,726	4,515	4,535	5,052	3,839	4,476	4,811	4,779	I 10,779	11,474	12,990	14,057	18,979	....	Claims on Central Government	12a
	....	....	....	....	....	....	....	....	....	60	60	60	60	60	....	Claims on Nonfin.Pub.Enterprises	12c
	926	926	926	926	926	925	—	—	—	I 306	339	398	450	516	....	Claims on Private Sector	12d
	1,770	1,679	1,952	3,105	4,029	6,471	4,303	5,122	6,396	I 3,269	3,682	2,858	5,980	2,353	....	Claims on Deposit Money Banks	12e
	....	....	....	....	....	....	....	....	....	49	49	49	49	49	....	Claims on Nonbank Financial Insts	12g
	3,163	4,178	4,138	4,023	4,045	5,636	5,386	6,615	7,537	I 9,356	8,961	12,102	14,706	22,810	....	Reserve Money	14
	2,376	2,678	2,950	3,024	3,658	4,700	4,418	5,648	5,845	I 6,040	6,139	7,335	7,898	9,097	....	of which: Currency Outside DMBs	14a
	....	....	....	....	....	....	....	....	....	92	5	39	86	29	....	Restricted Deposits	16b
	5,195	6,500	7,528	7,394	8,009	9,236	9,951	11,842	12,081	I 6,054	5,559	4,767	13,533	10,813	....	Foreign Liabilities	16c
	....	....	....	....	....	....	....	....	....	7,028	6,975	11,222	15,031	15,663	....	Long-Term Foreign Liabilities	16cl
	277	135	155	164	167	191	425	191	366	I 1,645	1,767	2,760	4,200	7,573	....	Central Government Deposits	16d
	1,818	2,230	2,708	3,130	3,380	3,403	3,813	3,574	3,663	I 4,475	4,149	4,177	4,496	4,946	....	Capital Accounts	17a
	1,162	939	-591	-1,126	-663	-3,277	-7,081	-6,829	-7,855	I -6,801	-7,676	-13,404	-23,858	-33,659	....	Other Items (Net)	17r
																Deposit Money Banks	
End of Period																	
	719	890	697	999	627	1,226	938	1,412	728	I 2,845	2,291	4,031	5,191	10,799	....	Reserves	20
	424	708	235	276	100	256	815	1,643	2,465	I 2,503	2,232	1,100	1,809	3,201	....	Foreign Assets	21
	31	24	85	17	50	154	213	130	166	I 252	198	152	193	1,083	....	Claims on Central Government	22a
	....	....	....	....	....	....	....	....	....	—	—	—	—	—	....	Claims on Nonfin.Pub.Enterprises	22c
	8,869	10,051	11,425	12,735	13,855	15,519	17,202	18,959	20,598	I 31,202	35,411	39,316	40,101	41,191	....	Claims on Private Sector	22d
	....	....	....	....	....	....	....	....	....	....	....	....	....	....	....	Claims on Nonbank Financial Insts	22g
	2,990	4,845	4,049	4,941	5,891	7,376	6,853	7,630	8,068	I 10,813	11,178	11,646	11,986	11,508	....	Demand Deposits	24
	1,403	1,777	2,437	1,995	1,682	1,674	3,471	4,244	3,971	I 3,947	5,769	6,181	7,187	6,635	....	Time Deposits	25
	3,326	3,681	5,114	4,374	6,187	4,321	5,662	5,623	6,070	I 8,858	9,387	14,145	12,656	13,216	....	Foreign Liabilities	26c
	414	201	74	116	100	55	78	99	563	I —	—	—	—	—	....	Long-Term Foreign Liabilities	26cl
	115	25	491	89	105	130	160	254	273	I 580	778	815	1,093	1,330	....	Central Government Deposits	26d
	1,162	1,223	605	820	1,448	608	159	1,159	1,789	I 617	719	978	1,179	1,208	....	Central Govt. Lending Funds	26f
	1,770	1,574	2,036	2,406	3,784	4,879	5,331	6,384	5,855	I 2,417	2,668	1,801	4,380	3,351	....	Credit from Monetary Authorities	26g
	908	924	957	1,023	1,405	1,759	1,960	1,758	4,294	I 12,226	12,597	13,905	14,018	20,802	....	Capital Accounts	27a
	-2,045	-2,575	-3,322	-1,737	-5,970	-3,648	-4,505	-5,006	-6,927	I -2,656	-2,964	-4,872	-5,204	-1,776	....	Other Items (Net)	27r
																Monetary Survey	
End of Period																	
	-1,558	-1,025	-5,937	-6,590	-9,267	-9,402	-11,162	-10,460	-11,633	I -12,051	-15,553	-23,726	-31,813	-30,273	....	Foreign Assets (Net)	31n
	11,711	13,699	16,441	18,085	19,703	20,212	21,428	23,574	25,022	I 40,423	44,986	49,390	49,617	52,975	....	Domestic Credit	32
	1,630	2,436	3,683	4,216	4,715	3,561	3,966	4,355	4,165	I 8,806	9,127	9,567	8,957	11,159	....	Claims on Central Govt. (Net)	32an
	....	....	....	....	....	....	....	....	....	60	60	60	60	60	....	Claims on Nonfin.Pub.Enterprises	32c
	10,081	11,263	12,758	13,869	14,989	16,651	17,462	19,219	20,858	I 31,508	35,750	39,714	40,551	41,707	....	Claims on Private Sector	32d
	....	....	....	....	....	....	....	....	....	49	49	49	49	49	....	Claims on Nonbank Fin. Insts	32g
	5,677	7,653	7,135	8,090	9,641	12,173	11,393	13,397	14,032	I 17,028	17,622	19,376	20,202	20,938	....	Money	34
	1,403	1,777	2,437	1,995	1,682	1,674	3,471	4,244	3,971	I 3,947	5,769	6,181	7,187	6,635	....	Quasi-Money	35
	....	....	....	....	....	....	....	....	....	92	5	39	86	29	....	Restricted Deposits	36b
	1,162	1,223	605	820	1,448	608	159	1,159	1,789	I 617	719	978	1,179	1,208	....	Central Govt. Lending Funds	36f
	1,911	2,021	327	590	-2,334	-3,645	-4,757	-5,686	-6,403	I 6,688	5,318	-910	-10,849	-6,108	....	Other Items (Net)	37r
	7,392	9,560	9,708	10,209	11,414	13,944	14,985	17,761	18,122	I 20,975	23,391	25,557	27,389	27,573	....	Money plus Quasi-Money	35l
																Interest Rates	
Percent Per Annum																	
	6.00	6.00	6.00	6.00	6.00	6.50	6.50	6.50	6.50	7.00	7.00	7.00	7.00	....	....	Discount Rate (End of Period)	60
	....	5.50	5.50	5.50	5.50	7.17	6.58	6.00	6.00	5.00	5.00	5.00	5.00	....	....	Deposit Rate	60l
	12.00	12.00	12.00	12.00	12.00	12.00	12.00	12.00	12.00	10.00	10.00	10.00	10.00	....	....	Lending Rate	60p
																Prices	
Period Averages																	
	....	....	....	....	....	70.6	75.8	82.0	83.1	93.8	100.0	105.6	116.3	127.2	....	Consumer Prices	64
																International Transactions	
Millions of Ouguiyas																	
	8,916	12,622	12,050	15,982	18,715	28,887	25,956	31,608	26,655	36,332	....	....	....	....	....	Exports	70
	13,118	12,793	14,213	12,411	13,201	17,806	16,429	17,392	18,029	18,462	....	....	....	....	....	Imports, cif	71
	11,609	11,321	12,578	10,983	11,682	15,758	14,539	15,391	15,955	16,338	....	....	....	....	....	Imports, fob	71.v

Mauritania
682

		1965	1966	1967	1968	1969	1970	1971	1972	1973	1974	1975	1976	1977	1978	1979
Balance of Payments														*Millions of US Dollars:*		
Goods: Exports f.o.b.	78aa d	....	....	....	....	....	....	....	....	....	....	167.3	181.9	157.2	118.6	147.2
Goods: Imports f.o.b.	78ab d	....	....	....	....	....	....	....	....	....	....	−208.5	−272.0	−295.5	−267.1	−286.0
Trade Balance	78ac d	....	....	....	....	....	....	....	....	....	....	−41.2	−90.2	−138.3	−148.5	−138.8
Services: Credit	78ad d	....	....	....	....	....	....	....	....	....	....	18.0	19.5	21.5	33.9	45.5
Services: Debit	78ae d	....	....	....	....	....	....	....	....	....	....	−69.2	−80.9	−67.2	−75.3	−83.2
Balance on Goods and Services	78af d	....	....	....	....	....	....	....	....	....	....	−92.3	−151.6	−184.0	−189.9	−176.6
Income: Credit	78ag d	....	....	....	....	....	....	....	....	....	....	5.0	4.4	4.3	3.1	11.4
Income: Debit	78ah d	....	....	....	....	....	....	....	....	....	....	−35.1	−62.9	−47.7	−30.2	−42.8
Balance on Goods, Serv., & Inc.	78ai d	....	....	....	....	....	....	....	....	....	....	−122.4	−210.2	−227.4	−217.0	−208.0
Current Transfers, n.i.e.: Credit	78aj d	....	....	....	....	....	....	....	....	....	....	87.5	159.1	130.3	163.2	131.6
Current Transfers: Debit	78ak d	....	....	....	....	....	....	....	....	....	....	−28.3	−35.0	−25.5	−24.8	−38.3
Current Account, n.i.e.	78al d	....	....	....	....	....	....	....	....	....	....	−63.2	−86.0	−122.5	−78.5	−114.7
Capital Account, n.i.e.: Credit	78ba d	....	....	....	....	....	....	....	....	....	....	—	—	—	—	—
Capital Account: Debit	78bb d	....	....	....	....	....	....	....	....	....	....	—	—	—	—	—
Capital Account, n.i.e.	78bc d	....	....	....	....	....	....	....	....	....	....	—	—	—	—	—
Direct Investment Abroad	78bd d	....	....	....	....	....	....	....	....	....	....	—	—	—	—	—
Dir. Invest. in Rep. Econ., n.i.e.	78be d	....	....	....	....	....	....	....	....	....	....	−122.7	1.6	4.1	2.9	63.2
Portfolio Investment Assets	78bf d	....	....	....	....	....	....	....	....	....	....	—	—	—	—	—
Portfolio Investment Liab., n.i.e.	78bg d	....	....	....	....	....	....	....	....	....	....	—	—	—	—	—
Other Investment Assets	78bh d	....	....	....	....	....	....	....	....	....	....	−2.7	.9	−4.5	9.1	16.6
Other Investment Liab., n.i.e.	78bi d	....	....	....	....	....	....	....	....	....	....	135.7	94.8	53.6	86.5	67.0
Financial Account, n.i.e.	78bj d	....	....	....	....	....	....	....	....	....	....	10.3	97.3	53.2	98.5	146.8
Net Errors and Omissions	78ca d	....	....	....	....	....	....	....	....	....	....	−2.5	1.0	14.5	−9.9	−26.5
Overall Balance	78cb d	....	....	....	....	....	....	....	....	....	....	−55.4	12.3	−54.8	10.1	5.6
Reserves and Related Items	79da d	....	....	....	....	....	....	....	....	....	....	55.4	−12.3	54.8	−10.1	−5.6
Reserve Assets	79db d	....	....	....	....	....	....	....	....	....	....	55.3	−29.6	34.9	−30.7	−29.0
Use of Fund Credit and Loans	79dc d	....	....	....	....	....	....	....	....	....	....	—	13.7	7.1	5.1	4.0
Liabs.Constit.For.Auth.Reserves	79dd d	....	....	....	....	....	....	....	....	....	....	−.1	3.3	10.1	14.8	1.6
Exceptional Financing	79de d	....	....	....	....	....	....	....	....	....	....	.3	.3	2.7	.7	17.8
Government Finance															*Millions of Ouguiyas:*	
Deficit (−) or Surplus	80	....	....	....	....	....	....	....	....	....	....	−532	−2,321	−1,685	I−871	−1,464
Revenue	81	....	....	....	....	....	....	....	....	....	....	4,100	5,662	5,543	I 6,429	6,481
Grants Received	81z	....	....	....	....	....	....	....	....	....	....	3,542	6,398	3,862	I 3,341	3,182
Expenditure	82	....	....	....	....	....	....	....	....	....	....	8,126	14,125	10,406	I 9,071	11,013
Lending Minus Repayments	83	....	....	....	....	....	....	....	....	....	....	48	256	684	I 1,570	114
Financing																
Net Borrowing: Domestic	84a	....	....	....	....	....	....	....	....	....	....	−7	501	549	I 553	103
Foreign	85a	....	....	....	....	....	....	....	....	....	....	613	2,052	−56	I 1,047	1,037
Use of Cash Balances	87	....	....	....	....	....	....	....	....	....	....	−74	−232	1,192	I−729	324
Debt: Foreign	89a	....	....	....	....	....	....	....	....	....	....	....	....	28,713	....	....
National Accounts															*Millions of Ouguiyas:*	
Gross Domestic Product	99b	....	....	....	9,420	....	11,209	12,140	12,884	12,919	16,660	20,595	24,105	24,998	24,908	30,853
															Millions:	
Population	99z	1.08	1.11	1.14	1.18	I 1.21	1.25	1.28	1.31	1.35	1.38	1.42	1.46	1.50	1.54	1.51

Exchange Rates: On June 29, 1973 the ouguiya, equal to five CFA francs, was introduced.
Monetary Authorities: I The sectorization and classification of accounts have been revised from March 1989.
Deposit Money Banks: I See note to section 10.
Monetary Survey: I See note to section 10.

Government Finance: I Prior to 1978, data cover budgetary and social security operations. Beginning in 1978, data also cover extrabudgetary operations.

Mauritania

682

	1980	1981	1982	1983	1984	1985	1986	1987	1988	1989	1990	1991	1992	1993	1994		
Minus Sign Indicates Debit																**Balance of Payments**	
	196.3	269.9	240.0	315.4	293.8	371.5	418.8	402.4	437.6	447.9	443.9	435.8	406.8	403.0	....	Goods: Exports f.o.b.	78aa *d*
	−321.3	−386.2	−426.6	−378.2	−302.1	−333.9	−401.2	−359.2	−348.9	−349.3	−382.9	−399.1	−461.3	−400.4	....	Goods: Imports f.o.b.	78ab *d*
	−125.0	−116.3	−186.5	−62.9	−8.3	37.6	17.6	43.2	88.8	98.6	61.0	36.7	−54.5	2.6	....	Trade Balance	78ac *d*
	56.5	48.9	47.2	30.2	28.0	27.1	23.7	34.5	35.3	33.6	26.8	31.2	20.2	17.0	....	Services: Credit	78ad *d*
	−127.8	−128.1	−157.5	−177.2	−177.8	−201.8	−211.1	−214.5	−217.0	−196.0	−136.8	−151.0	−179.1	−145.2	....	Services: Debit	78ae *d*
	−196.3	−195.5	−296.8	−209.8	−158.1	−137.1	−169.9	−136.8	−93.0	−63.9	−49.1	−83.1	−213.4	−125.6	....	Balance on Goods and Services	78af *d*
	17.0	20.1	18.5	9.1	8.5	4.0	2.3	2.5	4.1	5.6	3.8	2.0	1.1	.8	....	Income: Credit	78ag *d*
	−43.8	−70.7	−64.1	−71.4	−47.6	−96.1	−118.6	−91.7	−89.7	−55.6	−50.2	−34.9	−29.9	−97.6	....	Income: Debit	78ah *d*
	−223.1	−246.1	−342.4	−272.1	−197.2	−229.2	−286.1	−226.0	−178.6	−113.9	−95.5	−115.9	−242.2	−222.4	....	Balance on Goods, Serv., & Inc.	78ai *d*
	132.4	125.8	101.4	89.6	111.9	140.1	128.9	115.8	123.3	130.0	120.2	118.9	157.4	110.3	....	Current Transfers, n.i.e.: Credit	78aj *d*
	−42.8	−27.2	−35.9	−31.1	−25.9	−27.4	−37.3	−37.2	−40.8	−34.7	−34.3	−32.8	−33.4	−26.5	....	Current Transfers: Debit	78ak *d*
	−133.6	−147.5	−277.0	−213.6	−111.2	−116.5	−194.6	−147.4	−96.0	−18.6	−9.6	−29.9	−118.3	−138.5	....	Current Account, n.i.e.	78al *d*
	—	—	—	—	—	—	—	—	—	—	—	—	—	—	....	Capital Account, n.i.e.: Credit	78ba *d*
	—	—	—	—	—	—	—	—	—	—	—	—	—	—	....	Capital Account: Debit	78bb *d*
	—	—	—	—	—	—	—	—	—	—	—	—	—	—	....	Capital Account, n.i.e.	78bc *d*
	—	—	—	—	—	—	−1.4	−.2	−.9	—	—	—	—	—	....	Direct Investment Abroad	78bd *d*
	27.1	12.4	15.0	1.4	8.5	7.0	4.5	1.7	1.9	3.5	6.7	2.3	7.5	16.1	....	Dir. Invest. in Rep. Econ., n.i.e.	78be *d*
	—	—	—	—	—	—	—	—	—	—	—	—	—	—	....	Portfolio Investment Assets	78bf *d*
	—	—	—	—	—	—	—	—	—	—	—	—	—	—	....	Portfolio Investment Liab., n.i.e.	78bg *d*
	−24.4	−13.8	7.4	1.7	−7.9	−6.8	−7.5	8.1	2.2	−9.9	205.8	194.0	168.7	171.3	....	Other Investment Assets	78bh *d*
	120.5	124.1	202.6	155.1	77.8	90.3	186.7	82.0	36.2	23.3	−213.0	−169.6	−98.3	−321.3	....	Other Investment Liab., n.i.e.	78bi *d*
	123.1	122.8	225.0	158.1	78.4	90.5	182.3	91.6	39.4	16.9	−.5	26.7	77.9	−133.9	....	Financial Account, n.i.e.	78bj *d*
	−32.2	−.7	−4.6	12.7	−.8	−5.6	−5.7	−101.5	−16.0	−3.6	−62.3	19.5	57.4	−27.6	....	Net Errors and Omissions	78ca *d*
	−42.6	−25.4	−56.6	−42.7	−33.6	−31.6	−17.9	−157.3	−72.6	−5.3	−72.5	16.3	17.0	−300.1	....	Overall Balance	78cb *d*
	42.6	25.4	56.6	42.7	33.6	31.6	17.9	157.3	72.6	5.3	72.5	−16.3	−17.0	300.1	....	Reserves and Related Items	79da *d*
	−19.0	−27.5	17.3	24.6	18.7	27.8	11.0	−12.8	10.6	−16.8	40.6	−3.1	−20.4	87.0	....	Reserve Assets	79db *d*
	18.6	3.6	15.7	−5.1	−10.5	−4.8	7.8	15.4	−1.9	−.7	−4.5	−13.2	3.4	5.6	....	Use of Fund Credit and Loans	79dc *d*
	28.2	25.1	−5.5	8.0	19.5	.9	−11.3	25.5	9.4	−.6	—	—	—	—	....	Liabs.Constit.For.Auth.Reserves	79dd *d*
	14.7	24.1	29.2	15.2	5.9	7.7	10.4	129.2	54.5	23.3	36.4	—	—	207.5	....	Exceptional Financing	79de *d*
Year Ending December 31																**Government Finance**	
	....	....	....	....	....	....	....	....	....	....	....	....	....	....	....	Deficit (-) or Surplus	80
	....	....	....	....	....	....	....	....	....	....	....	....	....	....	....	Revenue	81
	....	....	....	....	....	....	....	....	....	....	....	....	....	....	....	Grants Received	81z
	....	....	....	....	....	....	....	....	....	....	....	....	....	....	....	Expenditure	82
	....	....	....	....	....	....	....	....	....	....	....	....	....	....	....	Lending Minus Repayments	83
																Financing	
	....	....	....	....	....	....	....	....	....	....	....	....	....	....	....	Net Borrowing: Domestic	84a
	....	....	....	....	....	....	....	....	....	....	....	....	....	....	....	Foreign	85a
	....	....	....	....	....	....	....	....	....	....	....	....	....	....	....	Use of Cash Balances	87
	....	....	....	....	....	....	....	....	....	....	....	....	....	....	....	Debt: Foreign	89a
Millions of Ouguiyas																**National Accounts**	
	31,728	36,125	38,838	43,014	46,068	53,230	62,699	69,171	72,053	81,517	84,615	93,050	....	....	....	Gross Domestic Product	99b
Midyear Estimates																	
	1.55	1.59	1.63	1.68	1.72	1.77	1.81	1.86	1.90	1.95	2.00	2.04	2.11	2.16	2.21	**Population**	99z

Mauritius

684

		1965	1966	1967	1968	1969	1970	1971	1972	1973	1974	1975	1976	1977	1978	1979
Exchange Rates																*Rupees per SDR:*
Official Rate	aa	4.757	4.779	5.541	5.592	5.554	5.570	5.671	6.165	6.923	6.951	7.714	7.714	7.714	7.714	↕10.000
																Rupees per US Dollar:
Official Rate	ae	4.757	4.779	5.541	5.592	5.554	5.570	5.224	5.678	5.739	5.677	↕6.589	6.639	6.350	5.921	7.586
Official Rate	rf	4.762	4.762	4.828	5.556	5.556	5.556	5.486	5.339	5.442	5.703	6.027	6.682ᵉ	6.607ᵉ	6.163ᵉ	6.308ᵉ
Fund Position																*Millions of SDRs:*
Quota	2f.s	....	....	....	16.0	16.0	22.0	22.0	22.0	22.0	22.0	22.0	22.0	22.0	27.0	27.0
SDRs	1b.s	....	....	....	—	—	2.6	5.0	7.3	7.3	2.8	2.6	2.7	2.3	1.6	.6
Reserve Position in the Fund	1c.s	....	....	....	.3	—	1.8	2.5	2.5	2.5	—	—	5.5	5.5	—	—
Total Fund Cred.&Loans Outstg.	2tl	....	....	....	—	3.7	—	—	—	—	—	—	—	11.0	20.3	48.4
International Liquidity												*Millions of US Dollars Unless Otherwise Indicated:*					
Total Reserves minus Gold	1l.d	20.0	19.3	13.3	16.3	33.1	46.2	51.7	70.1	66.8	131.1	166.0	89.5	66.3	45.8	29.2
SDRs	1b.d	....	....	....	—	—	2.6	5.4	7.9	8.8	3.4	3.0	3.1	2.8	2.1	.8
Reserve Position in the Fund	1c.d	....	....	....	.3	—	1.8	2.7	2.7	3.0	—	—	6.4	—	—	—
Foreign Exchange	1d.d	20.0	19.3	13.3	16.0	33.1	41.7	43.6	59.5	55.0	127.7	156.5	80.0	63.5	43.7	28.4
Gold (Million Fine Troy Ounces)	1ad	....	....	....	....	....	....	....	....	....	....	....	—	.009	.033	.038
Gold (National Valuation)	1and	....	....	....	....	....	....	....	....	....	....	....	—	1.6	5.8	4.8
Government Assets	3ba.d	1.1	7.7	2.9	5.6	2.3	2.7	1.4ᵉ	.7	.8	.3	1.4	.5	.7	1.1	1.6
Other Official Inst. Assets	3bb.d	3.7	3.9	3.2	2.8	2.6	1.5	2.4	2.7	3.3	4.1ᵉ	1.4	1.3	—	.3	.4
Deposit Money Banks: Assets	7a.d	13.1	12.3	9.8	7.3	8.6	6.3	3.5	3.3	4.4	6.3	8.2	5.3	6.9	8.3	8.4
of which: Claims on Nonbanks	7ad.d	.9	.4	.4	.4	.4	.5	.7	1.0	1.5	1.4	1.3	2.6	3.1	3.5	2.6
Deposit Money Banks: Liabilities	7b.d	2.9	.7	2.9	3.5	1.1	1.9	2.8	1.5	2.0	1.7	1.8	1.4	15.8	15.4	16.1
of which: Liab. to Nonbanks	7bd.d	—	—	—	—	—	—	—	—	—	—	—	—	12.4	12.1	13.7
Monetary Authorities																*Millions of Rupees:*
Foreign Assets	11	95.0	91.8	73.8	90.8	183.6	256.6	264.8	393.4	383.4	743.6	1,093.5	594.2	431.1	305.5	257.9
Claims on Central Government	12a	—	—	40.9	37.3	22.8	5.2	2.9	33.4	13.7	17.6	−26.0	338.7	823.0	1,111.8	1,541.5
Claims on Deposit Money Banks	12e	—	—	—	.9	9.2	1.4	31.7	31.6	66.4	10.9	3.0	42.9	34.8	42.0	80.0
Reserve Money	14	99.0	98.3	100.8	98.8	111.7	144.8	145.6	217.3	258.3	475.5	653.1	774.1	917.5	1,077.8	1,041.6
of which: Currency Outside DMBs	14a	93.1	93.0	93.3	89.2	97.2	104.7	126.3	156.3	200.7	314.2	438.1	587.9	693.6	824.1	724.8
Money Market Instruments	16aa	....	....	....	....	....	....	....	....	....	....	....	....	....	....	....
Foreign Liabilities	16c	—	—	—	—	20.6	—	—	—	—	—	—	—	84.9	156.5	498.9
Central Government Deposits	16d	—	—	—	1.5	9.8	29.2	34.1	132.2	73.3	86.4	118.7	—	.6	1.9	3.1
Capital Accounts	17a	—	—	5.0	6.0	7.2	24.4	42.5	57.5	70.7	75.9	84.9	89.8	89.9	89.9	134.7
Other Items (Net)	17r	−4.0	−6.5	8.9	1.8	5.5	4.3	6.7	9.5	23.2	87.8	153.3	90.5	196.1	133.2	201.0
Deposit Money Banks																*Millions of Rupees:*
Reserves	20	5.9	5.3	7.5	9.5	13.0	39.1	18.4	42.9	56.7	160.6	190.1	182.0	213.0	243.2	294.4
Foreign Assets	21	62.2	58.7	54.3	40.7	47.9	34.8	18.0	17.1	25.3	35.8	54.3	34.9	43.9	49.4	63.6
Claims on Central Government	22a	3.2	4.2	3.5	8.5	21.1	50.1	78.5	127.6	145.4	479.4	518.7	247.0	338.6	502.7	637.0
Claims on Private Sector	22d	166.1	169.9	195.3	201.0	209.0	209.9	311.1	356.5	545.4	594.3	746.6	1,157.2	1,352.2	1,508.1	1,721.6
Demand Deposits	24	95.6	126.9	130.2	102.1	118.8	123.8	134.4	201.9	265.0	468.8	530.2	506.5	525.3	615.5	683.8
Time and Savings Deposits	25	57.1	57.5	71.2	102.0	126.5	171.1	203.2	259.3	375.9	755.5	892.8	964.5	1,124.9	1,410.0	1,687.4
Foreign Liabilities	26c	13.9	3.5	16.3	19.2	6.0	10.6	14.3	7.9	11.5	9.7	11.8	9.1	100.4	91.3	122.1
Credit from Monetary Authorities	26g	—	—	—	.9	9.2	1.4	31.7	31.6	66.4	10.9	3.0	25.6	33.2	35.4	71.5
Capital Accounts	27a	14.7	15.2	15.7	16.1	16.7	17.8	30.7	31.9	40.0	45.1	53.1	71.4	111.8	154.7	166.8
Other Items (Net)	27r	56.1	35.0	27.2	19.4	13.8	9.2	11.7	11.5	13.8	−19.9	18.8	44.0	52.1	−3.5	−15.0
Monetary Survey																*Millions of Rupees:*
Foreign Assets (Net)	31n	143.3	147.0	111.8	112.3	204.9	280.8	268.5	402.6	397.2	769.7	1,136.0	620.0	289.7	107.1	−299.5
Domestic Credit	32	123.9	149.7	222.5	238.5	239.3	233.5	354.7	382.9	625.1	995.2	1,110.5	1,737.9	2,508.0	3,116.2	3,893.9
Claims on Central Govt. (Net)	32an	−42.2	−20.2	27.2	37.5	30.3	23.6	43.6	26.4	79.7	400.9	363.9	580.7	1,155.8	1,608.1	2,172.3
Claims on Private Sector	32d	166.1	169.9	195.3	201.0	209.0	209.9	311.1	356.5	545.4	594.3	746.6	1,157.2	1,352.2	1,508.1	1,721.6
Money	34	188.7	219.9	223.5	191.4	217.5	229.6	261.6	376.3	466.6	783.7	993.2	1,098.6	1,219.2	1,449.2	1,426.2
Quasi-Money	35	57.1	57.5	71.2	102.0	126.5	171.1	203.2	259.3	375.9	755.5	892.8	964.5	1,124.9	1,410.0	1,687.4
Money Market Instruments	36aa	....	....	....	....	....	....	....	....	....	....	....	....	....	....	....
Other Items (Net)	37r	21.4	19.3	39.6	36.5	39.4	53.1	87.9	108.0	141.6	179.2	300.0	274.0	446.1	361.7	480.7
Money plus Quasi-Money	35l	245.8	277.4	294.7	293.4	344.0	400.7	464.8	635.6	842.5	1,539.2	1,886.0	2,063.1	2,344.1	2,859.2	3,113.6
Other Banking Institutions																*Millions of Rupees:*
Deposits	45	34.8	33.9	29.3	27.0	26.7	27.7	30.4	35.3	40.8	48.6	62.1	78.9	93.6	106.9	104.7
Liquid Liabilities	55l	280.6	311.3	324.0	320.4	370.7	428.4	495.2	670.9	883.3	1,587.8	1,948.1	2,142.0	2,437.7	2,966.1	3,218.3
Interest Rates																*Percent Per Annum*
Discount Rate (End of Period)	60	....	....	7.5	7.5	7.5	6.0	6.0	6.0	6.0	6.0	6.0	6.0	7.0	9.0	10.5
Money Market Rate	60b	....	....	....	....	....	....	....	....	....	....	....	....	....	....	....
Deposit Rate	60l	....	....	....	....	....	....	....	....	....	....	....	....	....	7.9	10.0
Lending Rate	60p	....	....	....	....	....	....	....	....	....	....	....	....	....	....	....
Prices																*Index Numbers (1990=100):*
Share Prices	62	....	....	....	....	....	....	....	....	....	....	....	....	....	....	....
Consumer Prices	64	10.1	10.4	10.6	11.3	11.6	11.8	11.8	12.4	14.1	18.2	↕20.9	23.6	25.8	28.0	32.0

Mauritius

	1980	1981	1982	1983	1984	1985	1986	1987	1988	1989	1990	1991	1992	1993	1994		
	End of Period															**Exchange Rates**	
	10.000	12.000	12.000	13.321	15.295	15.718	16.069	17.272	18.616	19.707	20.375	21.162	23.372	25.625	26.077	Official Rate	aa
	End of Period (ae)	*Period Average (rf)*															
	7.835	10.329	10.861	12.723	15.603	14.310	13.137	12.175	13.834	14.996	14.322	14.794	16.998	18.656	17.863	Official Rate	ae
	7.684[e]	8.937[e]	10.873[e]	11.706	13.800	15.442	13.466	12.878	13.438	15.250	14.863	15.652	15.563	17.648	17.960	Official Rate	rf
	End of Period															**Fund Position**	
	40.5	40.5	40.5	53.6	53.6	53.6	53.6	53.6	53.6	53.6	53.6	53.6	53.6	73.3	73.3	73.3	Quota	2f. s
	—	5.6	1.7	.1	.1	—	.5	4.1	3.7	5.0	10.3	18.0	17.6	21.0	21.3	SDRs	1b. s
	—	—	—	—	—	—	—	—	—	—	.1	1.3	6.2	7.3	7.3	Reserve Position in the Fund	1c. s
	79.9	136.9	159.4	172.8	164.2	150.1	132.1	106.9	76.5	47.6	15.5	—	—	—	—	Total Fund Cred.&Loans Outstg.	2tl
	End of Period															**International Liquidity**	
	90.7	35.1	38.0	17.9	23.6	29.9	136.0	343.5	442.0	517.8	737.6	893.2	820.1	757.0	747.6	Total Reserves minus Gold	1l. d
	—	6.5	1.9	.1	.1	—	.6	5.9	5.0	6.6	14.6	25.7	24.3	28.9	31.2	SDRs	1b. d
	—	—	—	—	—	—	—	.1	.1	.1	.1	1.8	8.6	10.1	10.7	Reserve Position in the Fund	1c. d
	90.7	28.6	36.1	17.8	23.5	29.9	135.4	337.5	437.0	511.2	722.9	865.8	787.3	718.1	705.7	Foreign Exchange	1d. d
	.038	.038	.038	.038	.038	.038	.038	.038	.052	.061	.061	.061	.061	.062	.062	Gold (Million Fine Troy Ounces)	1ad
	4.7	4.3	4.1	3.5	2.8	3.1	3.3	3.6	4.4	4.8	5.0	4.9	4.2	3.9	4.0	Gold (National Valuation)	1an d
	.9	.1	.1	—	—	—	.1	.3	.3	.3	—	.1	.1	.1	.1	Government Assets	3ba d
	.5	.4	.4	.4	.3	.5	.5	.7	—	—	—	....	....	....	....	Other Official Inst. Assets	3bb d
	13.3	12.5	13.5	15.3	18.1	41.1	49.2	80.0	89.0	101.7	121.9	135.8	124.2	160.4	178.3	Deposit Money Banks: Assets	7a. d
	7.3	7.2	7.1	7.6	8.9	26.3	35.5	54.8	62.6	78.5	79.2	84.1	89.0	81.3	90.6	of which: Claims on Nonbanks	7ad d
	19.7	16.4	2.6	6.3	8.4	6.0	2.7	5.4	8.3	9.0	12.8	9.9	3.3	28.2	39.8	Deposit Money Banks: Liabilities	7b. d
	17.3	14.0	1.5	4.3	6.8	4.5	—	—	—	—	—	—	—	—	—	of which: Liab. to Nonbanks	7bd d
	End of Period															**Monetary Authorities**	
	747.0	406.1	456.3	271.5	411.9	472.5	1,830.9	4,225.8	6,174.7	7,837.0	10,635.6	13,286.3	14,011.5	14,194.9	13,425.7	Foreign Assets	11
	1,577.3	2,943.5	3,311.1	4,059.6	4,496.4	3,868.6	2,732.0	1,085.6	272.5	289.5	301.8	3,108.2	1,351.4	1,021.4	1,741.8	Claims on Central Government	12a
	55.0	64.5	20.1	15.0	54.2	48.1	31.9	76.5	120.5	173.5	172.2	301.8	411.2	523.5	291.0	Claims on Deposit Money Banks	12e
	1,155.0	1,203.1	1,334.5	1,417.8	1,512.5	1,787.1	2,152.6	2,729.0	3,387.4	4,054.3	4,816.3	11,260.0	10,207.5	9,510.3	8,837.1	Reserve Money	14
	735.0	791.3	875.2	922.4	958.2	1,095.7	1,304.9	1,663.4	2,008.7	2,403.6	2,848.7	3,407.5	3,820.1	4,230.9	4,412.2	of which: Currency Outside DMBs	14a
	—	—	—	—	—	—	—	—	—	—	—	1,057.0	448.6	61.3	—	Money Market Instruments	16aa
	798.0	1,645.5	1,909.1	2,454.8	2,621.0	2,488.1	2,161.7	1,890.3	1,427.5	944.6	322.7	76.0	74.7	11.1	33.2	Foreign Liabilities	16c
	3.4	.1	1.0	2.3	.6	2.2	6.0	3.0	571.1	1,553.8	2,886.9	21.3	17.5	12.0	6.2	Central Government Deposits	16d
	162.8	222.2	221.6	242.7	273.7	280.4	285.9	304.9	326.0	343.2	353.7	366.1	400.9	436.3	443.4	Capital Accounts	17a
	260.1	341.6	321.4	228.6	554.7	-169.2	-11.5	460.7	855.7	1,404.1	2,730.0	3,916.0	4,624.9	5,708.8	6,143.0	Other Items (Net)	17r
	End of Period															**Deposit Money Banks**	
	388.0	400.9	454.9	458.3	536.2	648.5	839.9	1,056.9	1,366.4	1,639.5	1,954.8	7,846.3	6,381.7	5,275.5	4,416.4	Reserves	20
	104.4	129.6	146.9	194.8	282.6	588.1	645.9	974.0	1,230.9	1,525.1	1,745.8	2,008.3	2,110.8	2,991.6	3,185.7	Foreign Assets	21
	989.9	717.8	1,161.2	1,225.1	1,412.0	1,616.7	2,795.0	3,611.5	5,149.5	5,858.5	7,361.6	3,956.7	6,451.2	8,329.5	10,344.5	Claims on Central Government	22a
	1,881.1	2,259.1	2,460.9	2,796.9	3,407.3	4,615.5	5,441.8	7,033.0	8,940.3	10,850.7	13,043.4	15,234.2	18,684.9	23,923.9	28,714.4	Claims on Private Sector	22d
	953.3	731.2	861.5	844.3	1,074.0	900.2	1,119.5	1,631.6	1,799.2	2,096.1	2,716.4	3,262.8	3,383.4	3,188.3	4,443.3	Demand Deposits	24
	2,116.9	2,458.8	3,185.4	3,622.3	4,145.0	6,109.1	8,084.6	10,350.5	13,748.6	15,764.8	18,990.0	23,278.1	27,501.1	33,198.5	36,754.5	Time and Savings Deposits	25
	154.3	169.9	28.5	79.6	130.4	85.3	35.1	65.5	114.4	135.6	183.9	147.1	56.7	525.7	710.7	Foreign Liabilities	26c
	45.3	56.8	10.0	9.3	34.5	25.0	15.0	66.4	116.2	108.6	87.7	157.0	267.5	329.0	156.2	Credit from Monetary Authorities	26g
	198.4	217.0	235.3	289.9	307.4	411.9	469.0	658.7	885.0	1,576.9	1,859.1	2,356.6	3,439.0	4,758.6	5,144.4	Capital Accounts	27a
	-104.8	-126.3	-96.8	-170.3	-53.2	-62.7	-.6	-97.3	23.9	191.8	268.6	-156.1	-1,019.1	-1,479.6	-548.1	Other Items (Net)	27r
	End of Period															**Monetary Survey**	
	-100.9	-1,279.6	-1,334.4	-2,068.0	-2,056.9	-1,513.4	280.0	3,244.0	5,863.7	8,282.0	11,874.7	15,071.5	15,990.9	16,649.7	15,867.5	Foreign Assets (Net)	31n
	4,435.3	5,902.2	6,897.3	8,051.3	9,269.5	10,081.9	10,947.4	11,619.6	13,620.4	15,278.8	17,708.9	22,224.5	26,550.1	33,222.9	40,856.8	Domestic Credit	32
	2,554.2	3,643.1	4,436.4	5,254.4	5,862.6	5,466.4	5,505.6	4,586.6	4,680.1	4,428.1	4,587.1	6,843.1	7,560.3	9,061.0	11,995.9	Claims on Central Govt. (Net)	32an
	1,881.1	2,259.1	2,460.9	2,796.9	3,407.3	4,615.5	5,441.8	7,033.0	8,940.3	10,850.7	13,043.4	15,234.2	18,684.9	23,923.9	28,714.4	Claims on Private Sector	32d
	1,720.3	1,533.4	1,741.6	1,803.8	2,050.3	2,038.6	2,432.2	3,303.7	3,820.4	4,510.9	5,577.8	6,676.5	7,209.2	7,423.2	8,864.0	Money	34
	2,116.9	2,458.8	3,185.4	3,622.3	4,145.0	6,109.1	8,084.6	10,350.5	13,748.6	15,764.8	18,990.0	23,278.1	27,501.1	33,198.5	36,754.5	Quasi-Money	35
	—	—	—	—	—	—	—	—	—	—	—	1,057.0	448.6	61.3	—	Money Market Instruments	36aa
	497.2	630.4	636.5	557.2	1,017.8	420.6	710.6	1,209.4	1,915.5	3,285.0	5,015.9	6,284.5	7,382.1	9,189.6	11,110.3	Other Items (Net)	37r
	3,837.2	3,992.2	4,926.5	5,426.1	6,195.3	8,147.9	10,516.8	13,654.2	17,568.6	20,275.7	24,567.8	29,954.6	34,710.3	40,621.7	45,618.5	Money plus Quasi-Money	35l
	End of Period															**Other Banking Institutions**	
	101.5	101.0	121.4	129.8	146.5	167.4	188.8	196.9	228.4	266.2	295.5	311.7	346.3	373.8	397.0	Deposits	45
	3,938.7	4,093.2	5,047.9	5,555.9	6,341.8	8,315.3	10,705.6	13,851.1	17,797.0	20,541.9	24,863.3	30,266.3	35,056.6	40,995.5	46,015.5	Liquid Liabilities	55l
	Percent Per Annum															**Interest Rates**	
	10.5	12.0	12.0	11.0	11.0	11.0	11.0	10.0	10.0	12.0	12.0	11.3	8.3	8.3	13.8	Discount Rate (End of Period)	60
	9.9	9.9	9.9	10.8	11.0	11.2	11.1	10.3	....	....	13.3	12.2	9.1	7.7	10.2	Money Market Rate	60b
	....	9.25	11.15	12.06	10.29	9.46	9.50	9.38	10.00	11.06	12.56	12.31	10.07	8.40	11.04	Deposit Rate	60l
	....	12.19	13.38	15.08	13.25	13.83	14.33	14.13	14.96	16.13	18.00	17.75	17.13	16.58	18.92	Lending Rate	60p
	Period Averages															**Prices**	
	....	....	....	....	....	....	....	....	76.5	100.0	101.8	107.0	170.0	....	....	Share Prices	62
	45.4	I 52.0	58.0	61.2	65.7	I 70.1	71.3	71.6	78.2	88.1	100.0	I 107.0	112.0	123.7	132.8	Consumer Prices	64

Mauritius
684

		1965	1966	1967	1968	1969	1970	1971	1972	1973	1974	1975	1976	1977	1978	1979
International Transactions																*Millions of Rupees*
Exports	70	313	338	307	354	365	383	361	574	748	1,788	1,839	1,770	2,042	1,987	2,433
Imports, cif	71	367	333	371	421	376	420	462	636	916	1,760	1,995	2,409	2,951	3,076	3,634
Imports, fob	71.v	319	292	321	362	323	360	392	536	787	1,533	1,688	2,046	2,459	2,572	3,004
																1990=100
Unit Value of Exports	74	⊺5.6	5.8	6.1	6.0	6.1	6.5	7.0	⊺8.3	9.7	24.2	31.8	26.1	25.6	25.1	28.3
Unit Value of Imports	75	⊺7.2	7.4	7.5	8.8	8.6	8.5	9.3	⊺9.9	12.8	20.9	23.7	26.5	28.9	30.6	36.8
Balance of Payments																*Millions of US Dollars:*
Goods: Exports f.o.b.	78aa d	....	....	....	....	....	....	....	....	....	....	....	264.0	309.8	324.6	360.4
Goods: Imports f.o.b.	78ab d	....	....	....	....	....	....	....	....	....	....	....	−306.8	−369.9	−422.3	−457.8
Trade Balance	78ac d	....	....	....	....	....	....	....	....	....	....	....	−42.7	−60.2	−97.7	−97.3
Services: Credit	78ad d	....	....	....	....	....	....	....	....	....	....	....	60.9	93.2	119.2	122.9
Services: Debit	78ae d	....	....	....	....	....	....	....	....	....	....	....	−66.5	−121.3	−145.0	−163.9
Balance on Goods and Services	78af d	....	....	....	....	....	....	....	....	....	....	....	−48.3	−88.2	−123.5	−138.3
Income: Credit	78ag d	....	....	....	....	....	....	....	....	....	....	....	14.7	5.0	5.7	3.7
Income: Debit	78ah d	....	....	....	....	....	....	....	....	....	....	....	−8.7	−7.8	−13.7	−19.3
Balance on Goods, Serv., & Inc.	78ai d	....	....	....	....	....	....	....	....	....	....	....	−42.2	−91.0	−131.5	−153.9
Current Transfers, n.i.e.: Credit	78aj d	....	....	....	....	....	....	....	....	....	....	....	10.2	16.7	18.9	18.6
Current Transfers: Debit	78ak d	....	....	....	....	....	....	....	....	....	....	....	−3.0	−3.2	−3.3	−6.0
Current Account, n.i.e.	78al d	....	....	....	....	....	....	....	....	....	....	....	−35.0	−77.5	−115.9	−141.3
Capital Account, n.i.e.: Credit	78ba d	....	....	....	....	....	....	....	....	....	....	....				
Capital Account: Debit	78bb d	....	....	....	....	....	....	....	....	....	....	....	−.9	−.9	−1.6	−1.1
Capital Account, n.i.e.	78bc d	....	....	....	....	....	....	....	....	....	....	....	−.9	−.9	−1.6	−1.1
Direct Investment Abroad	78bd d	....	....	....	....	....	....	....	....	....	....	....	.4	.8	.2	2.3
Dir. Invest. in Rep. Econ., n.i.e.	78be d	....	....	....	....	....	....	....	....	....	....	....	3.1	2.3	4.5	1.8
Portfolio Investment Assets	78bf d	....	....	....	....	....	....	....	....	....	....	....				
Portfolio Investment Liab., n.i.e.	78bg d	....	....	....	....	....	....	....	....	....	....	....	—	—	—	—
Other Investment Assets	78bh d	....	....	....	....	....	....	....	....	....	....	....	−30.1	−5.5	10.2	7.0
Other Investment Liab., n.i.e.	78bi d	....	....	....	....	....	....	....	....	....	....	....	−18.1	32.2	21.1	40.2
Financial Account, n.i.e.	78bj d	....	....	....	....	....	....	....	....	....	....	....	−44.7	29.7	35.9	51.3
Net Errors and Omissions	78ca d	....	....	....	....	....	....	....	....	....	....	....	5.2	11.1	11.5	−1.9
Overall Balance	78cb d	....	....	....	....	....	....	....	....	....	....	....	−75.4	−37.7	−70.1	−93.0
Reserves and Related Items	79da d	....	....	....	....	....	....	....	....	....	....	....	75.4	37.7	70.1	93.0
Reserve Assets	79db d	....	....	....	....	....	....	....	....	....	....	....	75.4	24.8	21.1	9.9
Use of Fund Credit and Loans	79dc d	....	....	....	....	....	....	....	....	....	....	....	—	12.9	11.5	36.7
Liabs.Constit.For.Auth.Reserves	79dd d	....	....	....	....	....	....	....	....	....	....	....	—	—	—	—
Exceptional Financing	79de d	....	....	....	....	....	....	....	....	....	....	....	—	—	37.5	46.3
Government Finance																*Millions of Rupees:*
Deficit (−) or Surplus	80	....	−20.2	−57.9	−33.8	5.0	−6.6	−20.2	−45.1	⊺−27.1	−201.7	−186.0	−208.9	−456.8	−727.2	−882.2
Revenue	81	....	221.6	199.7	239.6	234.2	235.4	259.9	284.7	⊺341.6	456.1	715.6	1,062.3	1,168.2	1,232.2	1,417.0
Grants Received	81z	....	....	....	....	....	....	....	....	⊺13.8	4.1	7.4	3.0	5.0	1.9	1.0
Expenditure	82	....	227.7	248.8	265.1	226.3	240.7	287.9	320.6	⊺355.8	588.9	840.1	1,181.0	1,525.5	1,784.6	2,135.4
Lending Minus Repayments	83	....	14.1	8.8	8.3	2.9	1.3	−7.8	9.2	⊺26.7	73.0	68.9	93.2	104.5	176.7	164.8
Financing																
Net Borrowing: Domestic	84a	....	4.6	5.5	−3.3	20.8	6.9	37.8	76.2	⊺95.3	200.4	249.5	164.4	427.5	397.4	543.8
Foreign	85a	....	16.2	21.9	43.0	−44.3	−6.8	−22.6	3.2	⊺10.7	30.4	44.0	16.6	69.4	284.2	316.2
Use of Cash Balances	87	....	−.5	30.6	−5.8	18.5	6.4	5.0	−34.3	⊺−78.9	−29.1	−107.5	27.9	−40.1	45.6	22.2
Unallocated Financing	87c	....	....	....	....	....	....	....	....	⊺—	—	—	—	—	—	—
Debt: Domestic	88a	....	....	....	....	....	....	....	317.1	⊺415.6	537.6	794.3	966.2	1,322.2	1,724.9	2,246.1
Foreign	89a	....	....	....	....	....	....	....	168.1	⊺139.4	208.0	247.1	262.9	323.0	630.3	910.6
National Accounts																*Millions of Rupees*
Exports of Goods & Services	90c	429	372	419	440	504	518	599	777	1,052	2,324	2,184	2,388	2,656	2,705	3,260
Government Consumption	91f	138	152	163	154	156	166	182	219	235	360	443	586	798	933	1,009
Gross Fixed Capital Formation	93e	155	133	145	141	144	145	184	229	480	750	1,138	1,450	1,510	1,770	1,965
Increase/Decrease(−) in Stocks	93i	—	—	—	—	—	—	—	—	—	—	—	213	120	153	420
Private Consumption	96f	634	654	688	711	681	734	783	929	1,122	1,684	1,878	2,178	3,593	4,174	5,144
Imports of Goods & Services	98c	−434	−399	−446	−480	−449	−515	−587	−722	−1,037	−1,902	−2,227	−2,712	−3,235	−3,477	−4,158
Gross Domestic Product	99b	922	912	969	966	1,036	1,048	1,161	1,432	1,852	3,216	3,416	4,103	5,442	6,258	7,640
Net Factor Inc/Pmts(−) Abroad	98.n	−6	−1	−5	−3	1	7	7	2	16	10	17	47	−17	−48	−106
Gross Nat'l Expenditure = GNP	99a	916	911	964	963	1,037	1,055	1,168	1,434	1,868	3,226	3,433	4,150	5,425	6,210	7,534
Gross Dom. Prod. 1990 Prices	99b.p	12,924	12,478	12,972	12,117	12,731	12,623	13,189	14,249	15,935	17,212	17,428	⊺20,331	21,667	22,497	23,288
GDP Deflator (1990=100)	99bi p	7.1	7.3	7.5	8.0	8.1	8.3	8.8	10.1	11.6	18.7	19.6	20.2	25.1	27.8	32.8
																Millions
Population	99z	.74	.76	.77	.79	.80	.81	.82	.83	.84	.85	.86	.87	.88	.90	.91

Government Finance: ⊺ Beginning in 1973, data are as published in the *Government Finance Statistics Yearbook (GFSY)* and cover budgetary central government. Prior to 1973, data are as reported by the Bank of Mauritius for publication in *IFS*. Data relate to a fiscal year different from calendar year. ⊺ Changes in the coverage of the consolidated central government in 1988, 1989, 1992, and 1993 are as specified in the *GFSY*.

Mauritius

International Transactions (Millions of Rupees)

	1980	1981	1982	1983	1984	1985	1986	1987	1988	1989	1990	1991	1992	1993	1994		Code
	3,341	2,999	3,989	4,311	5,180	6,729	9,062	11,336	13,455	15,049	17,677	18,700	20,244	22,992	24,097	Exports	70
	4,721	4,977	5,048	5,175	6,494	8,119	9,199	13,037	17,242	20,217	24,019	24,383	25,280	30,319	34,473	Imports, cif	71
	3,902	4,260	4,319	4,473	5,662	6,988	8,294	11,701	15,628	18,295	21,921	22,212	22,931	27,507	....	Imports, fob	71.v

1990=100

	1980	1981	1982	1983	1984	1985	1986	1987	1988	1989	1990	1991	1992	1993	1994		Code
	ɪ39.1	42.2	46.8	50.1	55.7	63.6	67.3	75.3	ɪ80.0	95.4	100.0	106.4	113.8	123.5	129.2	Unit Value of Exports	74
	ɪ53.7	57.4	71.1	69.7	78.2	86.0	69.7	72.1	ɪ78.7	93.7	100.0	104.7	106.9	118.0	126.5	Unit Value of Imports	75

Balance of Payments

Minus Sign Indicates Debit

	1980	1981	1982	1983	1984	1985	1986	1987	1988	1989	1990	1991	1992	1993	1994		Code
	430.1	309.6	363.8	361.2	365.4	440.9	677.8	902.3	1,000.5	986.5	1,205.2	1,215.1	1,302.6	1,304.4	....	Goods: Exports f.o.b.	78aa d
	-511.8	-456.5	-394.2	-378.5	-406.4	-466.7	-620.0	-918.7	-1,166.1	-1,196.0	-1,474.8	-1,419.1	-1,473.4	-1,558.6	....	Goods: Imports f.o.b.	78ab d
	-81.7	-146.8	-30.4	-17.3	-41.0	-25.9	57.7	-16.3	-165.6	-209.5	-269.6	-204.0	-170.9	-254.2	....	Trade Balance	78ac d
	138.8	166.5	139.8	134.9	126.9	148.4	212.8	322.2	378.2	400.4	516.7	566.6	609.6	596.3	....	Services: Credit	78ad d
	-172.6	-143.3	-140.1	-124.4	-123.8	-141.8	-171.7	-266.8	-322.6	-349.7	-440.9	-467.9	-543.3	-539.1	....	Services: Debit	78ae d
	-115.5	-123.7	-30.6	-6.9	-37.9	-19.2	98.8	39.1	-110.0	-158.8	-193.8	-105.2	-104.5	-197.1	....	Balance on Goods and Services	78af d
	5.0	7.1	3.9	2.4	2.8	2.0	5.7	14.1	26.6	50.6	55.9	82.5	91.0	70.0	....	Income: Credit	78ag d
	-28.0	-50.4	-49.4	-43.1	-46.9	-48.1	-60.1	-56.0	-70.7	-70.3	-78.7	-76.9	-80.1	-66.4	....	Income: Debit	78ah d
	-138.5	-167.0	-76.1	-47.5	-82.0	-65.4	44.4	-2.8	-154.1	-178.5	-216.6	-99.5	-93.6	-193.5	....	Balance on Goods, Serv., & Inc.	78ai d
	28.5	22.0	37.8	30.4	32.0	40.7	55.8	75.8	103.6	84.3	108.5	98.6	109.9	115.9	....	Current Transfers, n.i.e.: Credit	78aj d
	-6.3	-5.5	-3.9	-5.6	-4.6	-4.2	-5.2	-7.5	-9.7	-8.6	-11.2	-15.7	-16.4	-14.4	....	Current Transfers: Debit	78ak d
	-116.3	-150.5	-42.2	-22.8	-54.6	-28.8	95.0	65.6	-60.2	-102.8	-119.3	-16.6	-.1	-92.0	....	Current Account, n.i.e.	78al d
	—	—	—	—	—	—	—	—	—	—	—	—	—	—	....	Capital Account, n.i.e.: Credit	78ba d
	-1.5	-1.3	-.9	-1.1	-.8	-.8	-1.1	-1.8	-1.1	-.8	-.6	-1.6	-1.4	-1.5	....	Capital Account: Debit	78bb d
	-1.5	-1.3	-.9	-1.1	-.8	-.8	-1.1	-1.8	-1.1	-.8	-.6	-1.6	-1.4	-1.5	....	Capital Account, n.i.e.	78bc d
	—	—	—	—	—	—	—	—	—	-.1	-.6	-.6	-10.9	-43.3	-33.2	Direct Investment Abroad	78bd d
	1.2	.7	1.7	1.6	4.8	8.2	7.5	17.3	23.8	35.5	41.0	19.0	14.7	14.7	....	Dir. Invest. in Rep. Econ., n.i.e.	78be d
	—	—	—	—	—	—	—	—	—	—	—	-2.2	-.4	—	-2.2	Portfolio Investment Assets	78bf d
	—	—	—	—	—	—	—	—	—	—	—	—	—	—	....	Portfolio Investment Liab., n.i.e.	78bg d
	24.8	-17.5	-8.1	-12.0	-4.9	-25.2	-15.3	-23.9	-33.8	-49.0	-7.1	-36.2	14.3	-26.7	....	Other Investment Assets	78bh d
	39.9	25.0	-3.9	-5.5	-6.9	-7.2	3.8	66.5	135.3	63.9	107.4	70.4	-.5	66.6	....	Other Investment Liab., n.i.e.	78bi d
	65.8	8.2	-10.3	-15.8	-7.0	-24.2	-3.9	60.0	125.1	49.8	138.6	41.8	-14.8	19.3	....	Financial Account, n.i.e.	78bj d
	24.0	12.3	-6.9	9.1	23.7	51.7	32.7	97.1	121.5	198.5	213.2	167.2	59.6	81.2	....	Net Errors and Omissions	78ca d
	-28.1	-131.3	-60.3	-30.6	-38.8	-2.2	122.6	220.8	185.3	144.7	231.9	190.8	43.3	7.0	....	Overall Balance	78cb d
	28.1	131.3	60.3	30.6	38.8	2.2	-122.6	-220.8	-185.3	-144.7	-231.9	-190.8	-43.3	-7.0	....	Reserves and Related Items	79da d
	-58.8	47.1	-4.6	15.2	-12.2	-3.9	-102.0	-188.3	-144.5	-107.6	-188.3	-168.9	-43.3	-7.0	....	Reserve Assets	79db d
	41.4	68.5	24.6	14.5	-8.4	-14.6	-21.2	-32.8	-41.0	-37.1	-43.6	-21.9	—	—	....	Use of Fund Credit and Loans	79dc d
	—	—	—	—	—	—	—	—	—	—	—	—	—	—	....	Liabs.Constit.For.Auth.Reserves	79dd d
	45.5	15.8	40.3	1.0	59.4	20.7	.5	.2	.2	—	—	—	—	—	....	Exceptional Financing	79de d

Government Finance

Year Ending June 30

	1980	1981	1982	1983	1984	1985	1986	1987	1988	1989	1990	1991	1992	1993	1994		Code
	-896.6	-1,293.3	-1,388.4	ɪ-977.6	-648.7	-580.4	-346.5	54.1	ɪ87.3	ɪ-468.1	-157.5	1.9	ɪ-358.4	ɪ18.7	39.3 f	Deficit (-) or Surplus	80
	1,810.7	2,059.1	2,220.9	ɪ2,962.3	3,241.9	3,592.5	4,128.3	5,202.6	ɪ6,466.8	ɪ7,630.5	8,884.8	10,114.9	ɪ11378.0	ɪ12363.2	13,798.7 f	Revenue	81
	2.0	13.9	67.8	ɪ22.6	53.2	165.9	233.0	187.7	ɪ214.4	ɪ67.6	116.4	61.4	ɪ25.2	ɪ78.0	173.0 f	Grants Received	81z
	2,369.9	2,953.7	3,336.2	ɪ3,560.2	3,707.1	4,229.2	4,444.9	5,125.0	ɪ6,376.7	ɪ7,482.8	8,879.9	9,943.5	ɪ11517.6	ɪ12147.8	14,315.4 f	Expenditure	82
	339.4	412.6	340.9	ɪ402.3	236.7	109.6	262.9	211.2	ɪ217.2	ɪ683.4	278.8	230.9	ɪ244.0	ɪ274.7	-383.0 f	Lending Minus Repayments	83

Financing

	1980	1981	1982	1983	1984	1985	1986	1987	1988	1989	1990	1991	1992	1993	1994		Code
	656.7	588.7	730.8	ɪ1,132.3	721.6	-117.8	524.7	-1.8	ɪ71.4	ɪ2,317.7	1,606.6	2,151.8	ɪ-2738.8	ɪ1724.9	....	Net Borrowing: Domestic	84a
	218.5	701.0	794.1	ɪ-176.0	-140.0	720.8	-116.5	147.7	ɪ602.2	ɪ-461.1	-165.8	-284.2	ɪ-330.6	ɪ-312.8	....	Foreign	85a
	21.4	3.6	-136.5	ɪ17.4	68.2	-28.1	-61.7	-200.0	ɪ-760.9	ɪ-1388.5	-1,283.3	-1,869.5	ɪ3,427.8	ɪ-430.8	....	Use of Cash Balances	87
	—	—	—	ɪ3.9	—	-1.1	5.5	—	ɪ—	ɪ—	—	—	ɪ—	ɪ—	....	Unallocated Financing	87c
	2,932.5	3,593.8	4,452.7	ɪ5,208.0	5,848.6	5,964.0	6,250.9	6,100.3	ɪ5,998.6	ɪ8,375.6	9,770.0	11,889.2	ɪ10559.9	ɪ11695.5	....	Debt: Domestic	88a
	1,431.7	2,218.4	3,540.0	ɪ3,462.7	3,944.7	5,207.3	4,632.5	4,843.8	ɪ5,801.1	ɪ5,735.5	5,868.1	5,964.0	ɪ5,475.6	ɪ5,712.1	....	Foreign	89a

National Accounts (Millions of Rupees)

	1980	1981	1982	1983	1984	1985	1986	1987	1988	1989	1990	1991	1992	1993	1994		Code
	4,450	4,566	5,529	5,955	6,989	8,895	11,919	15,639	18,565	21,363	25,619	27,861	29,759	33,515	36,260	Exports of Goods & Services	90c
	1,224	1,422	1,624	1,720	1,835	1,915	2,076	2,722	3,509	3,936	4,456	5,005	5,500	6,620	7,935	Government Consumption	91f
	2,028	2,240	2,100	2,300	2,595	3,100	3,890	5,090	7,990	8,565	11,865	12,385	13,630	15,835	19,260	Gross Fixed Capital Formation	93e
	-225	338	30	-50	570	800	422	871	512	1,352	-287	-404	87	954	343	Increase/Decrease(-) in Stocks	93i
	6,562	7,277	8,326	8,835	9,841	11,118	12,000	14,395	17,215	20,850	24,840	27,542	30,336	34,973	39,496	Private Consumption	96f
	-5,342	-5,634	-5,859	-5,985	-7,470	-9,210	-10,607	-15,141	-19,988	-23,801	-28,458	-29,535	-31,386	-37,020	-43,080	Imports of Goods & Services	98c
	8,697	10,209	11,725	12,763	14,360	16,618	19,700	23,576	27,803	32,265	38,035	42,854	47,926	54,877	61,544	Gross Domestic Product	99b
	-178	-408	-498	-485	-626	-700	-729	-538	-593	-303	-339	89	171	63	-400	Net Factor Inc/Pmts(-) Abroad	98.n
	8,519	9,801	11,227	12,278	13,734	15,918	18,971	23,038	27,210	31,962	37,696	42,943	48,097	54,940	61,144	Gross Nat'l Expenditure = GNP	99a
	20,945	22,177	ɪ23,396	23,486	24,607	26,300	28,862	ɪ31,795	33,949	35,497	38,035	39,605	ɪ42,063	44,327	....	Gross Dom. Prod. 1990 Prices	99b.p
	41.5	46.0	50.1	54.3	58.4	63.2	68.3	74.2	81.9	90.9	100.0	108.2	113.9	123.8	....	GDP Deflator (1990=100)	99bi p

Midyear Estimates

	1980	1981	1982	1983	1984	1985	1986	1987	1988	1989	1990	1991	1992	1993	1994		Code
	.94	.95	.96	.97	.98	.99	.99	1.00	1.02	1.03	1.07	1.07	1.08	1.09	....	**Population**	99z

Mexico

273

		1965	1966	1967	1968	1969	1970	1971	1972	1973	1974	1975	1976	1977	1978	1979
Exchange Rates																
New Pesos per Thousand SDRs through 1985																
Market Rate..........aa=..........	**wa**	12.500	12.500	12.500	12.500	12.500	12.500	13.571	13.571	15.079	15.304	14.633	23.179	27.618	29.605	30.038
New Pesos per Thousand US Dollars through 1985																
Market Rate..........ae=..........	**we**	12.500	12.500	12.500	12.500	12.500	12.500	12.500	12.500	12.500	12.500	12.500	19.950	22.736	22.724	22.803
Market Rate..........rf=..........	**wf**	12.500	12.500	12.500	12.500	12.500	12.500	12.500	12.500	12.500	12.500	12.500	15.426	22.573	22.767	22.805
Fund Position																
Millions of SDRs:																
Quota	**2f. *s***	180	270	270	270	270	370	370	370	370	370	370	370	370	535	535
SDRs	**1b. *s***	—	—	—	—	—	48	88	128	128	129	86	1	47	43	152
Reserve Position in the Fund	**1c. *s***	55	86	95	133	112	135	98	98	98	98	98	—	—	—	—
Total Fund Cred.&Loans Outstg.	**2tl**	—	—	—	—	—	—	—	—	—	—	—	319	419	229	103
International Liquidity																
Millions of US Dollars Unless Otherwise Indicated:																
Total Reserves minus Gold	**1l. *d***	379	455	420	492	493	568	752	976	1,160	1,238	1,383	1,188	1,649	1,842	2,072
SDRs	**1b. *d***	—	—	—	—	—	48	96	139	154	158	101	1	57	56	201
Reserve Position in the Fund	**1c. *d***	54	86	95	133	112	135	106	106	118	120	114	—	—	—	—
Foreign Exchange	**1d. *d***	325	369	325	359	381	385	550	731	888	960	1,168	1,187	1,592	1,786	1,871
Gold (Million Fine Troy Ounces)	**1ad**	4.514	3.114	4.743	4.714	4.829	5.029	5.257	4.943	4.629	3.663	3.660	1.602	1.755	1.893	1.984
Gold (National Valuation)	**1an *d***	158	109	166	165	169	176	184	188	195	155	155	210	279	404	955
Deposit Money Banks: Assets	**7a. *d***	....	....	....	....	....	....	....	....	....	....	....	....	299	414	710
Liabilities	**7b. *d***	....	....	....	....	....	....	....	....	....	....	....	....	1,817	2,663	3,872
Other Banking Insts.: Assets	**7e. *d***	....	....	....	....	....	....	....	....	....	....	....	....	31	31	31
Liabilities	**7f. *d***	....	....	....	....	....	....	....	....	....	....	....	....	10,950	11,259	12,810
Monetary Authorities																
Thousands of New Pesos through 1976;																
Foreign Assets	**11**	6,720	7,230	7,980	8,550	8,980	10,330	12,860	16,800	17,980	18,180	20,150	28,160	I 45	52	70
Claims on Central Government	**12a**	8,040	9,100	3,450	3,720	17,170	17,760	14,620	38,430	60,950	95,790	127,470	133,990	I 286	351	459
Claims on Private Sector	**12d**	....	....	....	....	....	....	....	....	....	....	....	....	I 1	3	3
Claims on Deposit Money Banks	**12e**	310	1,610	5,210	7,290	210	110	950	180	440	320	1,150	18,940	I 15	9	9
Claims on Other Banking Insts.	**12f**	2,400	2,580	4,340	3,230	1,910	2,270	2,840	1,720	2,690	3,850	4,680	11,970	I 5	9	12
Reserve Money	**14**	16,920	18,820	21,200	24,490	27,350	29,300	33,440	57,580	75,210	105,320	140,840	130,950	I 296	381	513
of which: Currency Outside DMBs	**14a**	12,580	13,700	14,820	16,750	18,630	20,210	21,890	26,880	34,310	42,900	52,510	80,230	I 89	115	150
Time & Foreign Currency Deposits	**15**	970	730	670	590	770	820	760	680	1,770	1,380	1,750	11,740	I 13	12	16
Foreign Liabilities	**16c**	—	—	—	—	—	—	—	—	—	—	—	7,400	I 11	6	3
Central Govt. Lending Funds(Net)	**16f**	....	....	....	....	....	....	....	....	....	....	....	....	....	....	....
Capital Accounts	**17a**	....	....	....	....	....	....	....	....	....	....	....	....	I 4	4	6
Other Items (Net)	**17r**	–420	970	–890	–2,290	150	350	–2,930	–1,130	5,080	11,440	10,860	42,970	I 28	21	16
Deposit Money Banks																
Thousands of New Pesos through 1976;																
Reserves	**20**	4,080	4,660	5,050	6,320	7,040	7,830	7,580	17,830	26,240	32,910	40,700	37,480	I 202	261	355
Foreign Assets	**21**	....	....	....	....	....	....	....	....	....	....	....	....	I 7	9	16
Claims on Central Government	**22a**	5,600	6,270	7,410	8,270	7,680	7,530	9,420	1,950	2,290	5,500	4,480	25,780	I 8	8	18
Claims on Local Government	**22b**	—	—	—	—	—	—	—	—	—	—	—	—	I 2	4	5
Claims on Nonfin.Pub.Enterprises	**22c**	....	....	....	....	....	....	....	....	....	....	....	....	I 15	21	24
Claims on Private Sector	**22d**	14,410	16,030	17,720	20,650	23,880	28,310	30,610	33,930	36,650	42,680	52,600	63,040	I 247	353	487
Claims on Other Banking Insts.	**22f**	2,740	3,220	2,950	3,030	4,520	4,450	4,680	5,450	7,660	7,690	9,700	13,510	I 15	15	22
Demand Deposits	**24**	16,560	18,640	19,990	23,650	27,260	30,380	32,650	37,900	45,720	56,300	68,560	76,900	I 106	143	197
Time, Savings,& Fgn.Currency Dep.	**25**	9,420	10,700	12,010	13,790	15,340	16,940	18,270	21,310	28,640	31,630	35,680	51,360	I 305	418	574
Money Market Instruments	**26aa**	....	....	....	....	....	....	....	....	....	....	....	....	....	....	....
Foreign Liabilities	**26c**	....	....	....	....	....	....	....	....	....	....	....	....	....	....	....
Long-Term Foreign Liabilities	**26cl**	....	....	....	....	....	....	....	....	....	....	....	....	I 41	61	88
Central Government Deposits	**26d**	....	....	....	....	....	....	....	....	....	....	....	....	....	....	....
Central Govt. Lending Funds(Net)	**26f**	....	....	....	....	....	....	....	....	....	....	....	....	....	....	....
Credit from Monetary Authorities	**26g**	....	....	....	....	....	....	....	....	....	....	....	....	I 14	8	7
Capital Accounts	**27a**	....	....	....	....	....	....	....	....	....	....	....	....	I 16	19	27
Other Items (Net)	**27r**	850	840	1,130	830	520	800	1,370	–50	–1,520	850	3,240	11,550	I 14	23	33
Monetary Survey																
Thousands of New Pesos through 1976;																
Foreign Assets (Net)	**31n**	7,370	7,640	9,000	9,770	9,870	11,440	13,930	17,470	18,330	18,790	20,830	22,060	I 41	55	83
Domestic Credit	**32**	33,850	37,430	36,160	38,760	54,770	60,030	62,220	80,990	108,830	155,160	197,150	239,300	I 577	762	1,028
Claims on Central Govt. (Net)	**32an**	13,550	14,920	10,790	11,740	24,380	24,680	23,520	39,530	61,490	100,060	129,780	150,360	I 292	357	475
Claims on Local Government	**32b**	—	—	—	—	—	—	—	—	—	—	—	—	I 2	4	5
Claims on Nonfin.Pub.Enterprises	**32c**	....	....	....	....	....	....	....	....	....	....	....	....	I 15	21	24
Claims on Private Sector	**32d**	15,160	16,710	18,080	20,760	23,960	28,630	31,180	34,290	36,990	43,560	52,990	63,460	I 248	356	490
Claims on Other Banking Insts.	**32f**	5,140	5,800	7,290	6,260	6,430	6,720	7,520	7,170	10,350	11,540	14,380	25,480	I 20	24	34
Money	**34**	30,210	33,890	37,020	42,260	48,590	53,800	57,890	68,240	83,520	100,770	122,360	157,970	I 212	270	363
Quasi-Money	**35**	10,390	11,810	13,120	14,790	16,850	18,200	19,640	22,910	31,570	38,390	41,740	85,020	I 317	429	588
Money Market Instruments	**36aa**	....	....	....	....	....	....	....	....	....	....	....	....	....	....	....
Long-Term Foreign Liabilities	**36cl**	....	....	....	....	....	....	....	....	....	....	....	....	I 41	61	88
Central Govt. Lending Funds(Net)	**36f**	....	....	....	....	....	....	....	....	....	....	....	....	....	....	....
Other Items (Net)	**37r**	620	–630	–4,980	–8,520	–800	–530	–1,380	7,310	12,070	34,790	53,880	18,370	I 48	57	72
Money plus Quasi-Money	**35l**	40,600	45,700	50,140	57,050	65,440	72,000	77,530	91,150	115,090	139,160	164,100	242,990	I 525	699	949
Other Banking Institutions																
Thousands of New Pesos through 1976;																
Cash	**40**	1,290	1,950	2,110	2,810	3,840	4,000	6,920	14,950	18,800	34,500	54,280	23,790	I 16	9	15
Foreign Assets	**41**	....	....	....	....	....	....	....	....	....	....	....	....	I 1	1	1
Claims on Central Government	**42a**	7,890	12,160	19,340	23,250	17,730	21,960	27,870	24,940	22,160	17,400	28,450	66,490	I 83	70	88
Claims on Local Government	**42b**	—	—	—	—	—	—	—	—	—	—	—	—	I 4	4	9
Claims on Nonfin.Pub.Enterprises	**42c**	....	....	....	....	....	....	....	....	....	....	....	....	I 168	186	226
Claims on Private Sector	**42d**	50,900	59,770	72,380	82,330	99,930	117,900	136,700	156,380	181,010	215,620	267,810	379,070	I 76	98	123
Claims on Deposit Money Banks	**42e**	....	....	....	....	....	....	....	....	....	....	....	....	I 6	12	15
Demand Deposits	**44**	....	....	....	....	....	....	....	....	....	....	....	....	I 3	5	7
Time, Savings,& Fgn.Currency Dep.	**45**	31,720	33,920	39,470	43,070	53,820	66,890	79,210	91,930	112,960	140,240	185,810	310,790	I 38	55	73
Money Market Instruments	**46aa**	....	....	....	....	....	....	....	....	....	....	....	....	....	....	....
Bonds	**46ab**	18,420	27,010	37,660	46,970	54,360	62,000	73,660	82,390	85,700	100,390	131,200	136,830	I 17	16	15
Foreign Liabilities	**46c**	....	....	....	....	....	....	....	....	....	....	....	....	....	....	....
Long-Term Foreign Liabilities	**46cl**	—	—	—	—	—	—	—	—	—	—	—	—	I 249	256	292
Central Government Deposits	**46d**	....	....	....	....	....	....	....	....	....	....	....	....	....	....	....
Central Govt. Lending Funds(Net)	**46f**	....	....	....	....	....	....	....	....	....	....	....	....	....	....	....
Credit from Monetary Authorities	**46g**	1,120	1,800	3,190	2,150	1,250	1,570	2,180	1,560	2,370	3,630	4,020	11,780	I 5	9	12
Credit from Deposit Money Banks	**46h**	3,550	4,970	8,260	11,900	7,220	7,960	9,540	13,200	18,610	24,910	32,340	37,420	I 15	15	22
Capital Accounts	**47a**	7,770	7,780	8,160	8,580	10,100	10,840	14,220	17,000	19,730	22,060	19,740	22,000	I 13	16	18
Other Items (Net)	**47r**	–2,500	–1,600	–2,910	–4,280	–5,250	–5,400	–7,320	–9,810	–17,400	–23,710	–22,570	–49,470	I 13	8	38

Mexico
273

1980	1981	1982	1983	1984	1985	1986	1987	1988	1989	1990	1991	1992	1993	1994		
															Exchange Rates	
and per SDR thereafter: End of Period																
29.661	30.529	106.428	150.688	188.749	408.283	I 1.130	3.135	3.070	3.471	4.190	4.393	4.284	4.266	7.774	Market Rate ....aa=	wa
and per US Dollar thereafter: End of Period (we) Period Average (wf)																
23.256	26.229	96.480	143.930	192.560	371.700	I .924	2.210	2.281	2.641	2.945	3.071	3.115	3.106	5.325	Market Rate ....ae=	we
22.951	24.515	56.402	120.094	167.828	256.872	I .612	1.378	2.273	2.461	2.813	3.018	3.095	3.116	3.375	Market Rate ....rf=	wf
															Fund Position	
End of Period																
803	803	803	1,166	1,166	1,166	1,166	1,166	1,166	1,166	1,166	1,166	1,753	1,753	1,753	Quota	2f.s
113	153	5	22	3	—	7	498	293	292	293	409	399	163	121	SDRs	1b.s
100	161	—	91	—	—	—	—	—	—	—	—	—	—	—	Reserve Position in the Fund	1c.s
—	—	201	1,204	2,408	2,703	3,319	3,639	3,570	3,874	4,605	4,730	4,327	3,485	2,644	Total Fund Cred.&Loans Outstg.	2tl
															International Liquidity	
End of Period																
2,960	4,074	834	3,913	7,272	4,906	5,670	12,464	5,279	6,329	9,863	17,726	18,942	25,110	6,278	Total Reserves minus Gold	1l.d
144	178	6	23	3	—	9	706	394	383	417	586	548	223	177	SDRs	1b.d
128	187	—	95	—	—	—	—	—	—	—	—	—	—	—	Reserve Position in the Fund	1c.d
2,688	3,709	828	3,795	7,269	4,906	5,661	11,758	4,885	5,946	9,446	17,140	18,394	24,886	6,101	Foreign Exchange	1d.d
2.062	2.256	2.065	2.308	2.422	2.362	2.568	2.536	2.555	1.025	.919	.923	.688	.484	.426	Gold (Million Fine Troy Ounces)	1ad
852	852	826	831	709	....	....	....	....	....	....	....	....	....	....	Gold (National Valuation)	1and
1,320	984	1,433	2,179	1,912	2,121	2,003	2,824	2,574	2,573	3,532	4,434	4,858	5,945	5,752	Deposit Money Banks: Assets	7a.d
7,174	10,156	9,221	10,751	10,284	9,446	8,672	7,020	8,378	9,492	13,921	18,722	19,205	22,871	24,054	Liabilities	7b.d
47	38	152	338	386	383	484	377	463	412	336	628	1,164	961	2,394	Other Banking Insts.: Assets	7e.d
13,755	21,231	22,991	23,137	23,715	25,342	27,310	29,635	28,214	26,881	20,926	22,987	25,795	31,170	37,029	Liabilities	7f.d
															Monetary Authorities	
Millions of New Pesos Beginning 1977: End of Period																
93	132	176	708	1,561	2,168	6,214	30,306	15,027	18,116	30,260	55,570	59,992	78,704	32,739	Foreign Assets	11
611	900	2,038	3,177	4,120	6,300	10,235	11,215	32,657	38,733	40,958	21,867	16,064	-8,708	-69,270	Claims on Central Government	12a
3	5	2	4	6	10	16	37	71	95	137	297	379	450	—	Claims on Private Sector	12d
16	12	235	53	54	45	51	52	171	42	37	46	13	810	97,732	Claims on Deposit Money Banks	12e
29	35	73	73	130	79	93	126	853	142	558	1,224	2,405	2,831	4,368	Claims on Other Banking Insts.	12f
722	1,045	2,068	3,225	4,879	5,706	8,444	14,402	20,874	23,012	31,135	39,797	45,535	50,274	60,923	Reserve Money	14
195	283	505	681	1,122	1,738	3,067	7,339	13,201	18,030	24,689	32,513	38,116	43,351	52,035	*of which: Currency Outside DMBs*	14a
15	23	48	198	376	565	373	1,350	1,193	643	834	383	528	592	10	Time & Foreign Currency Deposits	15
—	—	25	181	453	1,094	3,716	11,411	10,966	14,115	19,307	21,019	18,826	15,101	20,906	Foreign Liabilities	16c
....	....	-85	13	77	426	1,542	4,338	5,494	4,682	2,965	-4,247	-11,139	-15,426	-29,159	Central Govt. Lending Funds(Net)	16f
7	9	31	44	55	165	373	957	938	1,055	1,263	1,322	1,313	1,309	2,327	Capital Accounts	17a
8	8	437	354	31	645	2,161	9,277	9,314	13,621	16,446	20,730	23,790	22,236	10,562	Other Items (Net)	17r
															Deposit Money Banks	
Millions of New Pesos Beginning 1977: End of Period																
515	746	1,480	2,514	3,801	3,927	5,310	7,075	7,390	5,710	6,637	7,436	7,824	6,293	9,277	Reserves	20
31	26	138	313	367	781	1,833	6,241	5,871	6,794	10,402	13,617	15,133	18,466	30,631	Foreign Assets	21
22	57	I 483	707	974	3,460	10,888	26,452	31,436	34,028	44,909	62,184	25,016	4,998	9,583	Claims on Central Government	22a
4	5	24	20	73	76	92	251	322	1,506	2,695	3,902	4,913	9,027	14,912	Claims on Local Government	22b
37	76	228	578	1,011	1,355	2,838	5,789	6,737	9,484	6,835	3,321	3,170	2,076	2,005	Claims on Nonfin.Pub.Enterprises	22c
696	1,015	I 1,269	1,822	3,376	5,167	8,742	22,571	41,275	81,598	141,596	228,627	337,800	419,941	589,810	Claims on Private Sector	22d
27	40	71	162	213	340	974	2,759	2,155	2,590	703	1,928	2,828	7,275	14,792	Claims on Other Banking Insts.	22f
260	315	I 455	676	1,075	1,610	2,468	4,928	7,130	10,279	21,847	72,772	82,604	98,725	91,106	Demand Deposits	24
806	1,282	I 1,976	3,300	5,641	7,909	15,136	38,679	21,064	64,088	116,679	139,725	179,845	201,974	276,310	Time, Savings,& Fgn.Currency Dep.	25
....	....	8	21	149	386	2,245	4,762	35,469	22,800	6,503	5,481	5,094	5,447	7,732	Money Market Instruments	26aa
....	....	71	104	140	209	477	1,748	3,439	3,407	11,487	24,210	25,049	33,221	53,417	Foreign Liabilities	26c
167	266	817	1,440	1,834	3,269	7,459	13,764	15,672	21,662	29,516	33,286	34,774	37,815	74,671	Long-Term Foreign Liabilities	26cl
....	....	8	15	24	20	63	82	178	210	441	706	957	1,194	2,028	Central Government Deposits	26d
....	....	199	320	508	890	1,799	4,248	7,476	9,705	10,915	13,603	19,091	23,930	36,458	Central Govt. Lending Funds(Net)	26f
15	8	22	38	83	128	159	385	606	681	246	1,118	1,141	4,323	41,100	Credit from Monetary Authorities	26g
39	52	68	96	169	281	633	2,105	4,084	6,040	8,931	12,452	19,113	25,234	31,091	Capital Accounts	27a
43	41	69	106	192	404	238	437	68	2,838	7,212	17,662	29,016	36,213	57,097	Other Items (Net)	27r
															Monetary Survey	
Millions of New Pesos Beginning 1977: End of Period																
124	158	I 218	736	1,335	1,646	3,854	23,388	6,493	7,388	9,868	23,958	31,250	48,848	-10,953	Foreign Assets (Net)	31n
1,429	2,126	I 4,180	6,528	9,879	16,767	33,815	69,118	115,328	167,930	237,896	322,574	391,532	436,590	564,172	Domestic Credit	32
633	950	I 2,513	3,869	5,070	9,740	21,060	37,585	63,915	72,515	85,372	83,275	40,037	-5,010	-61,715	Claims on Central Govt. (Net)	32an
4	5	24	20	73	76	92	251	322	1,506	2,695	3,902	4,913	9,027	14,912	Claims on Local Government	32b
37	76	228	578	1,011	1,355	2,838	5,789	6,737	9,484	6,835	3,321	3,170	2,076	2,005	Claims on Nonfin.Pub.Enterprises	32c
699	1,020	I 1,271	1,826	3,382	5,177	8,758	22,608	41,346	81,693	141,733	228,924	338,179	420,391	589,810	Claims on Private Sector	32d
56	75	144	235	343	419	1,067	2,885	3,008	2,732	1,261	3,152	5,233	10,106	19,160	Claims on Other Banking Insts.	32f
481	643	I 1,031	1,447	2,315	3,462	5,790	12,627	21,191	29,087	47,439	106,227	122,220	143,902	145,429	Money	34
820	1,298	I 2,024	3,498	6,017	8,474	15,509	40,029	22,257	64,731	117,513	140,108	180,373	202,566	276,320	Quasi-Money	35
....	....	8	21	149	386	2,245	4,762	35,469	22,800	6,503	5,481	5,094	5,447	7,732	Money Market Instruments	36aa
167	266	817	1,440	1,834	3,269	7,459	13,764	15,672	21,662	29,516	33,286	34,774	37,815	74,671	Long-Term Foreign Liabilities	36cl
....	....	114	333	585	1,316	3,341	8,586	12,970	14,387	13,880	9,356	7,952	8,504	7,299	Central Govt. Lending Funds(Net)	36f
85	77	404	525	314	1,506	3,325	12,738	14,262	22,651	32,913	52,074	72,369	87,204	41,768	Other Items (Net)	37r
1,297	1,933	I 3,055	4,945	8,332	11,936	21,299	52,656	43,448	93,818	164,952	246,335	302,593	346,468	421,749	Money plus Quasi-Money	35l
															Other Banking Institutions	
Millions of New Pesos Beginning 1977: End of Period																
21	40	77	92	111	142	264	632	783	875	628	670	787	1,386	1,611	Cash	40
1	1	15	49	74	141	443	834	1,057	1,089	989	1,930	3,626	2,985	12,750	Foreign Assets	41
108	307	I 1,055	1,595	2,248	4,823	13,354	40,304	45,395	50,898	47,524	49,551	52,568	54,014	99,942	Claims on Central Government	42a
14	25	128	133	240	280	155	239	493	531	1,178	2,592	4,816	5,593	8,861	Claims on Local Government	42b
295	424	1,016	1,394	1,922	3,226	7,208	13,282	11,251	8,969	7,241	3,540	3,341	3,125	6,266	Claims on Nonfin.Pub.Enterprises	42c
167	178	I 248	448	839	1,577	2,939	7,192	12,725	14,813	16,082	21,107	33,982	50,076	75,044	Claims on Private Sector	42d
17	43	41	96	130	183	418	1,017	2,277	3,630	11,581	19,906	25,334	42,268	69,769	Claims on Deposit Money Banks	42e
8	16	I 21	28	61	78	87	167	255	348	437	1,088	1,360	1,824	1,974	Demand Deposits	44
121	192	I 254	470	793	1,241	2,226	5,732	9,014	4,455	8,274	11,132	12,485	18,975	26,757	Time, Savings,& Fgn.Currency Dep.	45
....	....	6	8	47	165	432	113	263	4,235	2,645	3,097	10,632	19,578	23,638	Money Market Instruments	46aa
12	20	18	28	33	32	50	53	56	174	210	210	174	188	323	Bonds	46ab
....	....	5	1	5	5	46	18	112	1	—	1	—	6	7	Foreign Liabilities	46c
320	557	2,209	3,322	4,547	9,326	24,945	65,466	64,245	70,991	61,636	70,593	80,351	96,805	197,173	Long-Term Foreign Liabilities	46cl
....	....	180	266	384	674	430	1,932	7,521	4,127	3,330	1,434	1,445	1,712	2,299	Central Government Deposits	46d
....	....	-38	-30	-88	-225	-544	-2,070	-2,029	-1,757	-1,207	-387	1,386	1,559	-330	Central Govt. Lending Funds(Net)	46f
29	35	106	102	154	228	483	1,429	816	355	119	247	1,537	1,665	6,526	Credit from Monetary Authorities	46g
26	40	181	163	247	367	626	1,046	1,557	2,377	903	949	814	894	1,510	Credit from Deposit Money Banks	46h
19	38	86	127	234	329	541	932	3,664	7,930	8,259	8,000	11,426	11,404	12,439	Capital Accounts	47a
88	119	I -448	-678	-853	-1,848	-4,541	-11,318	-11,493	-12,431	617	2,932	2,844	4,837	1,927	Other Items (Net)	47r

Mexico

273

		1965	1966	1967	1968	1969	1970	1971	1972	1973	1974	1975	1976	1977	1978	1979
Banking Survey														*Thousands of New Pesos through 1976;*		
Foreign Assets (Net)	51n	7,370	7,640	9,000	9,770	9,870	11,440	13,930	17,470	18,330	18,790	20,830	22,060	I41	55	83
Domestic Credit	52	87,500	103,560	120,590	138,080	166,000	193,170	219,270	255,140	301,650	376,640	479,030	659,380	I886	1,092	1,435
Claims on Central Govt. (Net)	52an	21,440	27,080	30,130	34,990	42,110	46,640	51,390	64,470	83,650	117,460	158,230	216,850	I375	427	563
Claims on Local Government	52b	—	—	—	—	—	—	—	—	—	—	—	—	I6	8	13
Claims on Nonfin.Pub.Enterprises	52c	....	....	....	....	....	....	....	....	....	....	....	....	I183	207	250
Claims on Private Sector	52d	66,060	76,480	90,460	103,090	123,890	146,530	167,880	190,670	218,000	259,180	320,800	442,530	I328	458	622
Liquid Liabilities	55l	72,320	79,620	89,610	100,120	119,260	138,890	156,740	183,080	228,050	279,400	349,910	553,780	I566	759	1,029
Money Market Instruments	56aa	....	....	....	....	....	....	....	....	....	....	....	....	....	....	....
Bonds	56ab	18,420	27,010	37,660	46,970	54,360	62,000	73,660	82,390	85,700	100,390	131,200	136,830	I17	16	15
Long-Term Foreign Liabilities	56cl	—	—	—	—	—	—	—	—	—	—	—	—	I290	316	380
Central Govt. Lending Funds(Net)	56f	....	....	....	....	....	....	....	....	....	....	....	....	....	....	....
Capital Accounts	57a	7,770	7,780	8,160	8,580	10,100	10,840	14,220	17,000	19,730	22,060	19,740	22,000	I33	39	51
Other Items (Net)	57r	−3,640	−3,210	−5,840	−7,820	−7,850	−7,120	−11,420	−9,860	−13,500	−6,420	−990	−31,170	I21	17	43
Interest Rates														*Percent Per Annum*		
Money Market Rate	60b															
Treasury Bill Rate	60c														10.53	15.02
Deposit Rate	60l														11.17	13.23
Average Cost of Funds	60n												11.92	11.83		
Lending Rate	60p													12.88	15.13	16.35
															18.20	19.90
Prices and Production														*Index Numbers (1990=100):*		
Share Prices	62	....	....	....	....	....	....	....	....	....	....	....	....	....	....	....
Wholesale Prices	63	.1	.1	.1	.1	.1	.1	.2	.2	.2	.2	.2	.3	.4	I.5	.6
Consumer Prices	64	.1	.1	.1	I.1	.1	.1	.2	.2	.2	.2	.3	.3	.4	.4	.5
Wages, Monthly	65	....	....	....	.2	.2	.2	.2	.2	.2	.2	.3	.4	.5	.6	.7
Industrial Production	66	29.2	31.9	I34.4	36.6	39.8	42.5	43.4	47.8	52.6	56.4	I59.1	60.7	62.8	69.1	76.2
Manufacturing Production	66ey	30.0	32.8	I34.9	37.7	41.7	44.1	45.4	49.7	54.3	58.0	I60.4	62.1	64.3	70.1	76.6
Mining Production	66zx	40.6	42.0	I43.2	45.6	47.8	49.1	47.5	49.7	52.9	58.5	I55.4	58.6	59.1	60.3	63.2
Crude Petroleum	66aa															54.5
International Transactions														*Thousands of New Pesos through 1976;*		
Exports	70	14,005	14,986	14,195	15,674	17,874	17,540	18,844	21,243	28,267	37,343	36,300	53,517	I102	136	205
Imports, cif	71	19,497	20,065	21,853	24,502	26,005	30,760	30,090	33,981	47,669	75,707	82,252	90,902	I124	185	276
Imports, fob	71.v	18,569	19,110	20,812	23,335	24,767	29,295	28,657	32,363	45,399	72,102	78,335	86,409	I118	176	263
Balance of Payments														*Millions of US Dollars:*		
Goods: Exports f.o.b.	78aa d															9,939
Goods: Imports f.o.b.	78ab d															−12,131
Trade Balance	78ac d															−2,192
Services: Credit	78ad d															5,192
Services: Debit	78ae d															−4,901
Balance on Goods and Services	78af d															−1,901
Income: Credit	78ag d															872
Income: Debit	78ah d															−4,655
Balance on Goods, Serv., & Inc.	78ai d															−5,684
Current Transfers, n.i.e.: Credit	78aj d															257
Current Transfers: Debit	78ak d															−32
Current Account, n.i.e.	78al d															−5,459
Capital Account, n.i.e.: Credit	78ba d															—
Capital Account: Debit	78bb d															—
Capital Account, n.i.e.	78bc d															—
Direct Investment Abroad	78bd d															—
Dir. Invest. in Rep. Econ., n.i.e.	78be d															1,332
Portfolio Investment Assets	78bf d															−51
Portfolio Investment Liab., n.i.e.	78bg d															−342
Other Investment Assets	78bh d															−1,751
Other Investment Liab., n.i.e.	78bi d															5,932
Financial Account, n.i.e.	78bj d															5,120
Net Errors and Omissions	78ca d															654
Overall Balance	78cb d															315
Reserves and Related Items	79da d															−315
Reserve Assets	79db d															−155
Use of Fund Credit and Loans	79dc d															−160
Liabs.Constit.For.Auth.Reserves	79dd d															—
Exceptional Financing	79de d															—
Government Finance														*Thousands of New Pesos through 1976;*		
Deficit (−) or Surplus	80	....	−4,860	−5,010	−5,030	−9,080	−6,080	−4,160	I−16,930	−27,390	−34,250	−53,620	−64,020	I−61	−63	−102
Revenue	81	....	27,010	28,860	34,320	37,850	42,480	47,490	I58,240	69,540	95,310	133,400	168,580	I241	323	439
Grants Received	81z	....	....	....	....	....	....	I200	320	240	380	410	I—	....	....	
Expenditure	82	....	31,870	33,870	39,350	46,930	48,560	51,650	I67,200	88,050	123,920	161,610	211,610	I286	367	505
Lending Minus Repayments	83	....	....	....	....	....	....	....	I8,170	9,200	5,880	25,790	21,400	I17	18	36
Financing																
Net Borrowing: Domestic	84a	....	4,140	4,220	5,540	7,480	5,040	5,020	I13,600	25,000	27,850	40,200	50,480	I55	65	103
Foreign	85a	....	670	1,480	1,800	1,490	2,040	340	I2,500	3,400	11,700	15,600	25,200	I10	7	−7
Use of Cash Balances	87	....	40	−700	−2,300	110	−1,000	−1,190	I900	−920	−5,300	−2,170	−11,680	I−4	−9	6
Total Debt	88	32,220	37,020	42,730	50,070	59,040	71,120	71,480	88,510	116,690	156,940	217,680	372,650	....	....	....
Debt: Domestic	88a	27,420	31,560	35,780	41,320	48,800	58,840	58,860	74,580	99,000	127,300	177,260	282,380	....	....	....
Foreign	89a	4,800	5,460	6,950	8,750	10,240	12,280	12,620	13,930	17,690	29,640	40,420	90,270	....	....	....
National Accounts														*Thousands of New Pesos through 1976;*		
Exports of Goods & Services	90c	25,000	26,600	26,800	29,000	34,400	34,500	37,400	45,500	58,100	75,700	75,800	116,400	I191	245	343
Government Consumption	91f	18,000	20,400	22,500	25,900	28,800	32,200	37,300	48,700	63,400	82,300	113,500	150,900	I199	255	334
Gross Fixed Capital Formation	93e	44,000	50,200	59,600	65,700	72,800	88,700	88,100	107,100	133,300	178,900	235,600	288,400	I363	492	719
Increase/Decrease(−) in Stocks	93i	—	3,000	....	4,900	6,400	12,300	11,100	7,600	14,400	29,700	25,000	17,200	I59	59	78
Private Consumption	96f	191,000	209,100	226,200	247,800	270,000	319,500	358,800	405,600	487,000	628,300	755,900	933,400	I1,226	1,544	1,976
Imports of Goods & Services	98c	−25,000	−26,500	−28,800	−34,200	−37,500	−42,900	−42,700	−49,800	−65,400	−95,200	−105,800	−135,300	I−189	−258	−382
Gross Domestic Product	99b	252,000	282,800	306,300	339,100	374,900	444,300	490,100	564,700	690,900	899,700	1,100,100	1,371,000	I1,849	2,337	3,068
Net Factor Inc/Pmts(−) Abroad	98.n	−1,000	−2,000	−2,000	−3,000	−3,000	−5,600	−6,500	−7,400	−10,000	−15,000	−17,900	−29,000	I−43	−53	−77
Gross Nat'l Expenditure = GNP	99a	251,000	281,000	304,100	336,000	371,600	438,700	483,500	557,300	680,900	884,700	1,082,100	1,342,000	I1,806	2,285	2,990
GDP 1990 Prices *(Millions)*	99b.p	221,376	236,704	251,615	272,053	289,258	I309,279	322,157	349,514	378,890	402,070	424,624	442,583	457,828	495,626	541,012
GDP Deflator (1990=100)	99bi p	—	—	—	—	—	—	—	—	—	—	—	—	—	—	1
																Millions:
Population	99z	42.69	44.14	45.67	47.27	48.93	50.69	52.45	54.27	56.16	58.12	60.15	61.98	63.81	65.66	67.52

Mexico

273

1980	1981	1982	1983	1984	1985	1986	1987	1988	1989	1990	1991	1992	1993	1994		
Millions of New Pesos Beginning 1977: End of Period															**Banking Survey**	
124	158	I 227	784	1,404	1,782	4,251	24,204	7,438	8,476	10,857	25,887	34,876	51,827	1,790	Foreign Assets (Net)	**51n**
1,953	2,980	I 6,303	9,597	14,401	25,580	55,974	125,318	174,663	236,282	305,330	394,778	479,561	537,580	732,826	Domestic Credit	**52**
741	1,257	I 3,388	5,198	6,934	13,889	33,984	75,957	101,789	119,286	129,566	131,392	91,160	47,292	35,928	Claims on Central Govt. (Net)	**52an**
18	30	152	153	313	356	247	490	815	2,037	3,873	6,494	9,729	14,620	23,773	Claims on Local Government	**52b**
332	500	1,244	1,972	2,933	4,581	10,046	19,071	17,988	18,453	14,076	6,861	6,511	5,201	8,271	Claims on Nonfin.Pub.Enterprises	**52c**
880	1,223	I 1,519	2,274	4,221	6,754	11,697	29,800	54,071	96,506	157,815	250,031	372,161	470,467	664,854	Claims on Private Sector	**52d**
1,426	2,141	I 3,330	5,443	9,186	13,255	23,612	58,555	52,717	98,621	173,663	258,555	316,438	367,267	450,480	Liquid Liabilities	**55l**
....	....	14	29	196	551	2,677	4,875	35,732	27,035	9,148	8,578	15,726	25,025	31,370	Money Market Instruments	**56aa**
12	20	18	28	33	32	50	53	56	174	210	210	174	188	323	Bonds	**56ab**
487	823	3,026	4,762	6,381	12,595	32,404	79,230	79,917	92,653	91,152	103,879	115,125	134,620	271,844	Long-Term Foreign Liabilities	**56cl**
....	....	76	303	497	1,091	2,797	6,516	10,941	12,630	12,673	8,969	9,338	10,063	6,969	Central Govt. Lending Funds(Net)	**56f**
65	99	185	267	458	775	1,547	3,994	8,686	15,025	18,453	21,774	31,852	37,947	45,857	Capital Accounts	**57a**
87	54	I -118	-451	-946	-938	-2,862	-3,702	-5,948	-1,380	10,888	18,700	25,784	14,296	-72,227	Other Items (Net)	**57r**
Percent Per Annum															**Interest Rates**	
....	....	45.86	57.51	49.94	62.44	88.01	95.59	69.01	I 47.43	37.36	23.58	18.87	17.39	16.47	Money Market Rate	**60b**
22.46	30.77	45.75	59.07	49.32	63.20	....	103.07	I 69.15	44.99	34.76	19.28	15.62	15.03	14.10	Treasury Bill Rate	**60c**
20.63	29.57	43.62	54.70	48.36	59.48	84.68	97.24	I 63.65	36.29	31.24	17.10	15.68	15.46	13.26	Deposit Rate	**60l**
20.71	28.62	40.40	56.65	51.08	56.07	80.88	94.64	67.64	44.61	37.07	22.56	18.78	18.56	15.50	Average Cost of Funds	**60n**
28.10	36.60	45.77	63.03	54.73	....	....	....	....	....	....	....	....	....	....	Lending Rate	**60p**
Period Averages															**Prices and Production**	
....	.2	.1	.4	.6	1.1	4.1	28.4	33.1	57.7	100.0	190.1	291.3	324.2	446.3	Share Prices	**62**
.7	.9	1.4	2.9	4.9	7.6	14.3	33.6	69.8	81.1	100.0	120.5	136.7	148.8	158.9	Wholesale Prices	**63**
.7	.8	1.4	2.7	4.5	7.1	13.3	30.7	65.8	79.0	100.0	122.7	I 141.7	154.0	164.7	Consumer Prices	**64**
.8	1.1	1.7	2.7	4.1	6.6	11.5	27.0	I 57.3	76.6	100.0	129.1	151.7	164.7	174.6	Wages, Monthly	**65**
83.6	91.0	89.3	81.9	85.0	89.4	I 84.6	88.1	90.1	94.8	100.0	104.1	107.3	106.9	111.9	Industrial Production	**66**
82.5	88.6	85.1	78.8	82.7	88.2	I 84.0	87.2	89.4	95.1	100.0	103.9	106.7	104.5	109.5	Manufacturing Production	**66ey**
77.2	89.1	98.6	94.5	95.8	96.6	I 92.6	96.1	96.6	96.1	100.0	100.6	101.5	102.6	104.2	Mining Production	**66zx**
72.3	85.9	100.4	97.0	97.6	96.5	I 92.3	96.4	96.4	97.2	100.0	104.0	103.7	103.7	104.6	Crude Petroleum	**66aa**
Millions of New Pesos Beginning 1977															**International Transactions**	
358	481	1,232	2,632	4,082	5,705	10,150	28,939	47,202	56,769	76,611	82,508	85,830	94,062	116,742	Exports	**70**
447	590	775	972	2,014	3,598	7,230	17,951	44,574	60,342	88,058	115,436	149,038	154,618	206,162	Imports, cif	**71**
426	564	743	923	1,920	3,456	6,905	17,145	42,573	57,633	84,105	110,254	142,348	147,677	196,908	Imports, fob	**71.v**
Minus Sign Indicates Debit															Balance of Payments	
18,031	23,307	24,056	25,953	29,101	26,758	21,803	27,599	30,692	35,171	40,711	42,687	46,196	51,885	60,882	Goods: Exports f.o.b.	**78aa*d***
-21,087	-27,184	-17,009	-11,848	-15,915	-18,359	-16,784	-18,813	-28,081	-34,766	-41,592	-49,966	-62,130	-65,366	-79,347	Goods: Imports f.o.b.	**78ab*d***
-3,056	-3,877	7,047	14,105	13,186	8,399	5,019	8,786	2,611	405	-881	-7,279	-15,934	-13,481	-18,465	Trade Balance	**78ac*d***
4,591	4,983	4,136	4,087	4,839	4,808	4,591	5,437	6,084	7,208	8,094	8,869	9,275	9,517	9,843	Services: Credit	**78ad*d***
-6,514	-8,489	-6,066	-4,477	-5,235	-5,524	-5,194	-5,310	-6,281	-7,880	-10,323	-10,959	-11,959	-12,046	-12,432	Services: Debit	**78ae*d***
-4,979	-7,383	5,117	13,715	12,790	7,683	4,416	8,913	2,414	-267	-3,110	-9,369	-18,618	-16,010	-21,054	Balance on Goods and Services	**78af*d***
1,365	1,746	1,709	1,686	2,507	2,281	1,943	2,397	3,049	3,160	3,273	3,523	2,789	2,694	3,348	Income: Credit	**78ag*d***
-7,642	-11,621	-13,758	-10,710	-12,474	-11,148	-9,310	-8,982	-10,092	-11,261	-11,589	-11,788	-11,998	-13,724	-15,093	Income: Debit	**78ah*d***
-11,256	-17,258	-6,932	4,691	2,823	-1,184	-2,951	2,328	-4,629	-8,368	-11,426	-17,634	-27,827	-27,040	-32,799	Balance on Goods, Serv., & Inc.	**78ai*d***
877	1,076	1,072	1,206	1,384	2,012	1,589	1,937	2,270	2,559	3,990	2,765	3,404	3,656	4,031	Current Transfers, n.i.e.: Credit	**78aj*d***
-43	-58	-29	-31	-24	-28	-15	-18	-15	-16	-15	-19	-19	-16	-16	Current Transfers: Debit	**78ak*d***
-10,422	-16,240	-5,889	5,866	4,183	800	-1,377	4,247	-2,374	-5,825	-7,451	-14,888	-24,442	-23,400	-28,784	Current Account, n.i.e.	**78al*d***
—	—	—	—	—	—	—	—	—	—	—	—	—	—	—	Capital Account, n.i.e.: Credit	**78ba*d***
—	—	—	—	—	—	—	—	—	—	—	—	—	—	—	Capital Account: Debit	**78bb*d***
—	—	—	—	—	—	—	—	—	—	—	—	—	—	—	Capital Account, n.i.e.	**78bc*d***
—	—	—	—	—	—	—	—	—	—	—	—	—	—	—	Direct Investment Abroad	**78bd*d***
2,090	3,078	1,901	2,192	1,542	1,984	2,036	1,184	2,011	2,785	2,549	4,742	4,393	4,389	7,978	Dir. Invest. in Rep. Econ., n.i.e.	**78be*d***
-17	165	275	-134	-320	-389	-709	-397	-880	-56	-7,354	-603	1,165	-564	-615	Portfolio Investment Assets	**78bf*d***
60	996	645	-519	-435	-595	-517	-1,002	1,001	354	3,369	12,741	18,041	28,919	8,189	Portfolio Investment Liab., n.i.e.	**78bg*d***
-1,229	-4,425	-1,101	-3,551	-1,580	-989	874	-4,401	-874	-1,114	-1,345	-395	4,387	-3,038	-4,857	Other Investment Assets	**78bh*d***
10,604	26,787	-14	-46	874	-623	-50	1,549	-5,753	-859	11,222	8,654	-947	4,054	2,059	Other Investment Liab., n.i.e.	**78bi*d***
11,508	26,601	1,706	-2,058	81	-612	1,634	-3,067	-4,495	1,110	8,441	25,139	27,039	33,760	12,754	Financial Account, n.i.e.	**78bj*d***
-269	-9,087	-7,454	-3,116	-2,115	-2,917	-738	2,954	-3,193	4,504	1,228	-2,278	-852	-3,128	-1,636	Net Errors and Omissions	**78ca*d***
817	1,274	-11,637	692	2,149	-2,729	-481	4,134	-10,062	-211	2,218	7,973	1,745	7,232	-17,666	Overall Balance	**78cb*d***
-817	-1,274	11,637	-692	-2,149	2,729	481	-4,134	10,062	211	-2,218	-7,973	-1,745	-7,232	17,666	Reserves and Related Items	**79da*d***
-684	-1,274	3,354	-3,102	-3,390	2,434	-595	-5,986	6,721	-542	-3,261	-8,154	-1,173	-6,057	18,864	Reserve Assets	**79db*d***
-133	—	219	1,069	1,241	295	712	401	-84	364	958	161	-572	-1,175	-1,199	Use of Fund Credit and Loans	**79dc*d***
—	—	1,217	-1,217	—	—	—	—	—	—	—	—	—	—	—	Liabs.Constit.For.Auth.Reserves	**79dd*d***
—	—	6,846	2,558	—	—	364	1,450	3,424	389	85	20	—	—	—	Exceptional Financing	**79de*d***
Millions of New Pesos Beginning 1977: Year Ending December 31															**Government Finance**	
-134	-392	-1,454	-1,363	-2,095	-3,978	-10,407	-26,224	-40,343	-26,494	5,104 p	....	....	....	....	Deficit (-) or Surplus	**80**
675	894	1,520	3,222	4,773	7,820	12,643	33,683	67,476	92,841	96,407 p	....	....	....	....	Revenue	**81**
—	—	—	—	—	—	—	—	—	—	— p	....	....	....	....	Grants Received	**81z**
750	1,182	2,829	4,468	6,747	11,784	22,799	59,702	107,273	118,619	119,252 p	....	....	....	....	Expenditure	**82**
59	105	144	117	121	15	251	205	546	716	-27,949 p	....	....	....	....	Lending Minus Repayments	**83**
															Financing	
147	268	1,228	807	1,527	3,692	9,391	22,151	40,271	25,688	....	....	....	....	....	Net Borrowing: Domestic	**84a**
-3	124	228	561	586	309	1,024	4,117	908	1,458	....	....	....	....	....	Foreign	**85a**
-11	1	-2	-5	-18	-23	-8	-44	-836	-652	....	....	....	....	....	Use of Cash Balances	**87**
....	....	....	....	....	....	....	....	....	....	....	....	....	....	....	Total Debt	**88**
....	....	....	....	....	....	....	....	....	....	....	....	....	....	....	Debt: Domestic	**88a**
....	....	....	....	....	....	....	....	....	....	....	....	....	....	....	Foreign	**89a**
Millions of New Pesos Beginning 1977															**National Accounts**	
479	638	1,502	3,397	5,122	7,305	13,732	37,692	65,568	81,148	108,299	119,535	128,325	139,948	....	Exports of Goods & Services	**90c**
449	660	1,026	1,574	2,722	4,374	7,208	16,995	33,741	42,915	57,798	77,971	102,751	121,952	....	Government Consumption	**91f**
1,214	1,678	2,244	3,710	5,853	9,048	15,415	35,667	75,199	92,220	127,728	168,487	211,934	229,541	....	Gross Fixed Capital Formation	**93e**
107	61	-4	573	566	987	-734	1,566	4,501	16,480	22,544	25,327	25,254	18,289	....	Increase/Decrease(-) in Stocks	**93i**
2,909	3,945	6,036	10,882	18,590	30,575	54,209	127,268	270,998	356,900	486,354	621,208	735,865	805,684	....	Private Consumption	**96f**
-580	-793	-1,011	-1,684	-2,815	-4,897	-10,639	-25,877	-59,555	-82,045	-116,318	-147,363	-184,972	-187,831	....	Imports of Goods & Services	**98c**
4,470	6,128	9,798	17,879	29,472	47,392	79,191	193,312	390,451	507,618	686,406	865,166	1,019,156	1,127,584	....	Gross Domestic Product	**99b**
-129	-217	-558	-1,055	-1,618	-2,122	-4,255	-8,849	-14,588	-17,511	-20,369	-18,164	-26,302	-30,656	....	Net Factor Inc/Pmts(-) Abroad	**98.n**
4,341	5,911	9,240	16,824	27,854	45,270	74,936	184,462	375,864	490,107	666,037	847,002	992,854	1,096,928	....	Gross Nat'l Expenditure = GNP	**99a**
586,050	632,620	I 629,139	602,733	624,504	640,689	616,639	628,085	635,910	657,200	686,406	711,302	731,258	735,648	....	GDP 1990 Prices *(Millions)*	**99b.*p***
1	1	2	3	5	7	13	31	61	77	100	122	139	153	....	GDP Deflator (1990=100)	**99bi*p***
Midyear Estimates																
69.66	71.35	73.02	74.67	76.31	77.94	79.57	81.20	82.84	84.49	86.15	87.84	89.54	91.21	93.01	**Population**	**99z**

(Notes in the back of the book)

Moldova

921

		1965	1966	1967	1968	1969	1970	1971	1972	1973	1974	1975	1976	1977	1978	1979
Exchange Rates															*Lei per SDR:*	
Official Rate	aa	....	....	....	....	....	....	....	....	....	....	....	....	....	....	....
															Lei per US Dollar:	
Official Rate	ae	....	....	....	....	....	....	....	....	....	....	....	....	....	....	....
Official Rate	rf	....	....	....	....	....	....	....	....	....	....	....	....	....	....	....
Fund Position															*Millions of SDRs:*	
Quota	2f. s	....	....	....	....	....	....	....	....	....	....	....	....	....	....	....
SDRs	1b. s	....	....	....	....	....	....	....	....	....	....	....	....	....	....	....
Reserve Position in the Fund	1c. s	....	....	....	....	....	....	....	....	....	....	....	....	....	....	....
Total Fund Cred.&Loans Outstg.	2tl	....	....	....	....	....	....	....	....	....	....	....	....	....	....	....
International Liquidity												*Millions of US Dollars Unless Otherwise Indicated:*				
Total Reserves minus Gold	1l. d	....	....	....	....	....	....	....	....	....	....	....	....	....	....	....
SDRs	1b. d	....	....	....	....	....	....	....	....	....	....	....	....	....	....	....
Reserve Position in the Fund	1c. d	....	....	....	....	....	....	....	....	....	....	....	....	....	....	....
Foreign Exchange	1d. d	....	....	....	....	....	....	....	....	....	....	....	....	....	....	....
Gold (Million Fine Troy Ounces)	1ad	....	....	....	....	....	....	....	....	....	....	....	....	....	....	....
Gold (National Valuation)	1and	....	....	....	....	....	....	....	....	....	....	....	....	....	....	....
Monetary Authorities: Other Liab.	4..d	....	....	....	....	....	....	....	....	....	....	....	....	....	....	....
Dep.Money Banks: Assets Conv.	7ax d	....	....	....	....	....	....	....	....	....	....	....	....	....	....	....
Assets Nonconv.	7ay d	....	....	....	....	....	....	....	....	....	....	....	....	....	....	....
Dep.Money Banks: Liab. Conv.	7bx d	....	....	....	....	....	....	....	....	....	....	....	....	....	....	....
Liab. Nonconv.	7by d	....	....	....	....	....	....	....	....	....	....	....	....	....	....	....
Monetary Authorities															*Thousands of Lei:*	
Foreign Assets	11	....	....	....	....	....	....	....	....	....	....	....	....	....	....	....
Claims on Central Government	12a	....	....	....	....	....	....	....	....	....	....	....	....	....	....	....
Claims on Nonfin.Pub.Enterprises	12c	....	....	....	....	....	....	....	....	....	....	....	....	....	....	....
Claims on Deposit Money Banks	12e	....	....	....	....	....	....	....	....	....	....	....	....	....	....	....
Reserve Money	14	....	....	....	....	....	....	....	....	....	....	....	....	....	....	....
of which: Currency Outside Banks	14a	....	....	....	....	....	....	....	....	....	....	....	....	....	....	....
Foreign Liabilities	16c	....	....	....	....	....	....	....	....	....	....	....	....	....	....	....
Long-Term Foreign Liabilities	16cl	....	....	....	....	....	....	....	....	....	....	....	....	....	....	....
Central Government Deposits	16d	....	....	....	....	....	....	....	....	....	....	....	....	....	....	....
Capital Accounts	17a	....	....	....	....	....	....	....	....	....	....	....	....	....	....	....
Other Items (Net)	17r	....	....	....	....	....	....	....	....	....	....	....	....	....	....	....
Deposit Money Banks															*Thousands of Lei:*	
Reserves	20	....	....	....	....	....	....	....	....	....	....	....	....	....	....	....
Foreign Assets	21	....	....	....	....	....	....	....	....	....	....	....	....	....	....	....
Claims on Central Government	22a	....	....	....	....	....	....	....	....	....	....	....	....	....	....	....
Claims on Local Government	22b	....	....	....	....	....	....	....	....	....	....	....	....	....	....	....
Claims on Nonfin.Pub.Enterprises	22c	....	....	....	....	....	....	....	....	....	....	....	....	....	....	....
Claims on Private Sector	22d	....	....	....	....	....	....	....	....	....	....	....	....	....	....	....
Claims on Nonbk.Financial Insts	22g	....	....	....	....	....	....	....	....	....	....	....	....	....	....	....
Demand Deposits	24	....	....	....	....	....	....	....	....	....	....	....	....	....	....	....
Time,Savings,& Fgn.Currency Dep.	25	....	....	....	....	....	....	....	....	....	....	....	....	....	....	....
Foreign Liabilities	26c	....	....	....	....	....	....	....	....	....	....	....	....	....	....	....
Long-Term Foreign Liabilities	26cl	....	....	....	....	....	....	....	....	....	....	....	....	....	....	....
Central Government Deposits	26d	....	....	....	....	....	....	....	....	....	....	....	....	....	....	....
Credit from Monetary Authorities	26g	....	....	....	....	....	....	....	....	....	....	....	....	....	....	....
Capital Accounts	27a	....	....	....	....	....	....	....	....	....	....	....	....	....	....	....
Other Items (Net)	27r	....	....	....	....	....	....	....	....	....	....	....	....	....	....	....
Monetary Survey															*Thousands of Lei:*	
Foreign Assets (Net)	31n	....	....	....	....	....	....	....	....	....	....	....	....	....	....	....
Domestic Credit	32	....	....	....	....	....	....	....	....	....	....	....	....	....	....	....
Claims on Central Govt. (Net)	32an	....	....	....	....	....	....	....	....	....	....	....	....	....	....	....
Claims on Local Government	32b	....	....	....	....	....	....	....	....	....	....	....	....	....	....	....
Claims on Nonfin.Pub.Enterprises	32c	....	....	....	....	....	....	....	....	....	....	....	....	....	....	....
Claims on Private Sector	32d	....	....	....	....	....	....	....	....	....	....	....	....	....	....	....
Claims on Nonbk.Financial Insts	32g	....	....	....	....	....	....	....	....	....	....	....	....	....	....	....
Money	34	....	....	....	....	....	....	....	....	....	....	....	....	....	....	....
Quasi-Money	35	....	....	....	....	....	....	....	....	....	....	....	....	....	....	....
Capital Accounts	37a	....	....	....	....	....	....	....	....	....	....	....	....	....	....	....
Other Items (Net)	37r	....	....	....	....	....	....	....	....	....	....	....	....	....	....	....
Money plus Quasi-Money	35l	....	....	....	....	....	....	....	....	....	....	....	....	....	....	....
															Millions:	
Population	99z	....	....	....	....	....	....	....	....	....	....	....	....	....	....	....

Exchange Rates: Up to July 1993, the Russian ruble (supplemented by ruble-denominated coupons) was the legal tender in Moldova. On August 9, 1993 the Moldovan ruble was introduced. On November 29, 1993 the Moldovan leu, equal to 1,000 Moldovan rubles, was introduced.

Moldova

	1991	1992	1993	1994		
					Exchange Rates	
End of Period	.0024	.5699	4.9998	6.2336	Official Rate	aa
End of Period (ae) Period Average (rf)	.0017	.4145	3.6400	4.2700	Official Rate	ae
	....	....	....	....	Official Rate	rf
					Fund Position	
End of Period	....	90.00	90.00	90.00	Quota	2f. s
	—	—	25.05	14.62	SDRs	1b. s
	—	.01	.01	.01	Reserve Position in the Fund	1c. s
	....	—	63.00	112.45	Total Fund Cred.&Loans Outstg.	2tl
					International Liquidity	
End of Period	—	2.45	76.34	179.92	Total Reserves minus Gold	1l. d
	....	—	34.41	21.34	SDRs	1b. d
	—	.01	.01	.01	Reserve Position in the Fund	1c. d
	—	2.44	41.92	158.57	Foreign Exchange	1d. d
	....	....	....	—	Gold (Million Fine Troy Ounces)	1ad
	—	—	—	—	Gold (National Valuation)	1and d
	—	35.27	1.01	.81	Monetary Authorities: Other Liab.	4.. d
	2.02	2.19	14.92	18.86	Dep.Money Banks: Assets Conv.	7ax d
	—	.20	2.14	7.79	Assets Nonconv.	7ay d
	—	—	—	—	Dep.Money Banks: Liab. Conv.	7bx d
	—	—	1.51	.41	Liab. Nonconv.	7by d
					Monetary Authorities	
End of Period	—	6,684	305,350	785,486	Foreign Assets	11
	485	120,795	742,589	1,729,436	Claims on Central Government	12a
	92	787	—	—	Claims on Nonfin.Pub.Enterprises	12c
	1,141	3,371	98,685	274,672	Claims on Deposit Money Banks	12e
	7,739	49,448	242,378	552,410	Reserve Money	14
	1,827	9,754	119,448	345,550	of which: Currency Outside Banks	14a
	—	14,618	318,660	704,436	Foreign Liabilities	16c
	—	—	—	—	Long-Term Foreign Liabilities	16cl
	6	68,748	596,500	1,462,868	Central Government Deposits	16d
	84	60	1,721	24,720	Capital Accounts	17a
	−6,110	−1,238	−12,636	45,160	Other Items (Net)	17r
					Deposit Money Banks	
End of Period	1,481	10,598	48,870	52,443	Reserves	20
	3	991	62,107	113,755	Foreign Assets	21
	9,461	73,357	382,155	551,019	Claims on Central Government	22a
	3	4,025	10,207	22,823	Claims on Local Government	22b
	6,789	32,811	243,284	493,907	Claims on Nonfin.Pub.Enterprises	22c
	1,519	11,232	91,062	174,786	Claims on Private Sector	22d
	—	—	—	—	Claims on Nonbk.Financial Insts	22g
	7,959	52,968	115,810	136,325	Demand Deposits	24
	9,169	23,607	123,420	274,961	Time,Savings,& Fgn.Currency Dep.	25
	—	—	5,512	1,736	Foreign Liabilities	26c
	—	—	—	—	Long-Term Foreign Liabilities	26cl
	2,070	66,870	409,675	576,004	Central Government Deposits	26d
	2,776	6,469	104,701	292,233	Credit from Monetary Authorities	26g
	1,208	9,568	136,649	333,049	Capital Accounts	27a
	−3,927	−26,468	−58,082	−205,573	Other Items (Net)	27r
					Monetary Survey	
End of Period	3	−6,942	43,285	193,070	Foreign Assets (Net)	31n
	16,273	107,389	463,122	933,099	Domestic Credit	32
	7,870	58,534	118,569	241,584	Claims on Central Govt. (Net)	32an
	3	4,025	10,207	22,823	Claims on Local Government	32b
	6,881	33,598	243,284	493,907	Claims on Nonfin.Pub.Enterprises	32c
	1,519	11,232	91,062	174,786	Claims on Private Sector	32d
	—	—	—	—	Claims on Nonbk.Financial Insts	32g
	9,794	63,219	236,734	486,971	Money	34
	9,169	23,607	124,568	275,288	Quasi-Money	35
	1,292	9,628	138,370	357,769	Capital Accounts	37a
	−3,979	3,991	6,735	6,141	Other Items (Net)	37r
	18,963	86,827	361,301	762,260	Money plus Quasi-Money	35l
Midyear Estimates	4.36	4.35	4.36	4.35	Population	99z

Mongolia
948

	1965	1966	1967	1968	1969	1970	1971	1972	1973	1974	1975	1976	1977	1978	1979

Exchange Rates
Tugriks per SDR:
Market Rate .... aa

Tugriks per US Dollar:
Market Rate .... ae
Market Rate .... rf

Fund Position
Millions of SDRs:
Quota .... 2f. s
SDRs .... 1b. s
Reserve Position in the Fund .... 1c. s
Total Fund Cred.&Loans Outstg. 2tl

International Liquidity
Millions of US Dollars Unless Otherwise Indicated:
Total Reserves Minus Gold .... 1l. d
  SDRs .... 1b. d
  Reserve Position in the Fund .... 1c. d
  Foreign Exchange .... 1d. d
Gold (Million Fine Troy Ounces) 1ad
Gold (National Valuation) .... 1an d
Deposit Money Banks: Assets .... 7a. d
                                Liabilities .... 7b. d
  of which: Liab. to Nonbanks .... 7bd d

Monetary Authorities
Millions of Tugriks:
Foreign Assets 11
Claims on Central Government 12a
Claims on Deposit Money Banks 12e
Reserve Money 14
Foreign Liabilities 16c
Central Government Deposits 16d
Capital Accounts 17a
Other Items (Net) 17r

Deposit Money Banks
Millions of Tugriks:
Reserves 20
Foreign Assets 21
Claims on Central Government 22a
Claims on Nonfin.Pub.Enterprises 22c
Claims on Private Sector 22d
Demand Deposits 24
Time, Savings,& Fgn.Currency Dep. 25
Foreign Liabilities 26c
Central Government Deposits 26d
Credit from Central Bank 26g
Capital Accounts 27a
Other Items (Net) 27r

Monetary Survey
Millions of Tugriks:
Foreign Assets (Net) 31n
Domestic Credit 32
  Claims on Central Govt. (Net) 32an
  Claims on Nonfin.Pub.Enterprises 32c
  Claims on Private Sector 32d
Money 34
Quasi-Money 35
Other Items (Net) 37r
Money plus Quasi-Money 35l

Interest Rates
Percent per Annum
Bank Rate *(End of Period)* 60
Deposit Rate *(End of Period)* 60l
Lending Rate *(End of Period)* 60p

Prices, Production, Employment
Index Numbers (1990=100):
Consumer Prices (Jan.'91=100) 64
Wages: Average Earnings 65
Industrial Production 66
Industrial Employment 67

Mongolia

948

	1980	1981	1982	1983	1984	1985	1986	1987	1988	1989	1990	1991	1992	1993	1994		
Exchange Rates																	
End of Period																	
Market Rate	...	...	...	...	...	...	...	...	...	...	19.92	56.36	144.47	ℐ544.63	604.51		aa
End of Period (ae) Period Average (rf)																	
Market Rate	...	...	...	...	...	...	...	...	...	...	14.00	39.40	105.07	ℐ396.51	414.09		ae
Market Rate	...	...	...	...	...	...	...	...	...	...	...	9.52	42.56	...	ℐ412.72		rf
Fund Position																	
End of Period																	
Quota	...	...	...	...	...	...	...	...	...	...	...	25.00	37.10	37.10	37.10		2f. s
SDRs	...	...	...	...	...	...	...	...	...	...	...	.03	.01	.02	1.98		1b. s
Reserve Position in the Fund	...	...	...	...	...	...	...	...	...	...	...	—	.01	.01	—		1c. s
Total Fund Cred.&Loans Outstg.	...	...	...	...	...	...	...	...	...	...	...	11.25	13.75	23.03	37.87		2tl
International Liquidity																	
End of Period																	
Total Reserves Minus Gold	...	...	...	...	...	...	...	...	...	...	...	...	16.35	59.74	81.39		1l. d
SDRs	...	...	...	...	...	...	...	...	...	...	...	.04	.01	.03	2.89		1b. d
Reserve Position in the Fund	...	...	...	...	...	...	...	...	...	...	...	—	.01	.01	.01		1c. d
Foreign Exchange	...	...	...	...	...	...	...	...	...	...	...	...	16.33	59.70	78.49		1d. d
Gold (Million Fine Troy Ounces)	.04	.05	.04	.04	.04	.05	.03	.03	.03	.03	.04	.14	.02	.02	.03		1ad
Gold (National Valuation)	11.00	12.60	13.10	13.50	12.90	18.00	18.00	18.50	19.70	19.00	22.90	49.70	24.20	5.31	11.00		1an d
Deposit Money Banks: Assets	...	...	...	...	...	...	...	...	...	...	...	81.59	19.90	41.17	41.71		7a. d
Liabilities	...	...	...	...	...	...	...	...	...	...	...	169.52	62.02	11.67	11.90		7b. d
of which: Liab. to Nonbanks	...	...	...	...	...	...	...	...	...	...	...	32.01	23.36	6.43	8.12		7bd d
Monetary Authorities																	
End of Period																	
Foreign Assets	...	...	...	...	...	...	...	...	...	...	...	1,989	1,030	25,616	42,589		11
Claims on Central Government	...	...	...	...	...	...	...	...	...	...	...	716	1,986	7,489	14,858		12a
Claims on Deposit Money Banks	...	...	...	...	...	...	...	...	...	...	...	1,529	6,153	6,637	10,375		12e
Reserve Money	...	...	...	...	...	...	...	...	...	...	...	2,068	5,317	14,277	29,318		14
Foreign Liabilities	...	...	...	...	...	...	...	...	...	...	...	645	2,000	22,899	34,804		16c
Central Government Deposits	...	...	...	...	...	...	...	...	...	...	...	784	1,202	580	2,465		16d
Capital Accounts	...	...	...	...	...	...	...	...	...	...	...	3,285	3,700	2,980	3,347		17a
Other Items (Net)	...	...	...	...	...	...	...	...	...	...	...	−2,549	−3,050	−995	−2,112		17r
Deposit Money Banks																	
End of Period																	
Reserves	...	...	...	...	...	...	...	...	...	...	...	345	3,023	5,690	10,319		20
Foreign Assets	...	...	...	...	...	...	...	...	...	...	...	3,215	2,091	16,325	17,272		21
Claims on Central Government	...	...	...	...	...	...	...	...	...	...	...	1,358	2,793	513	737		22a
Claims on Nonfin.Pub.Enterprises	...	...	...	...	...	...	...	...	...	...	...	9,501	11,789	16,938	12,193		22c
Claims on Private Sector	...	...	...	...	...	...	...	...	...	...	...	3,351	7,340	14,675	40,763		22d
Demand Deposits	...	...	...	...	...	...	...	...	...	...	...	5,592	5,790	9,756	14,104		24
Time, Savings,& Fgn.Currency Dep.	...	...	...	...	...	...	...	...	...	...	...	2,601	5,412	24,216	43,906		25
Foreign Liabilities	...	...	...	...	...	...	...	...	...	...	...	6,679	6,517	4,629	4,926		26c
Central Government Deposits	...	...	...	...	...	...	...	...	...	...	...	1,186	1,950	7,498	8,451		26d
Credit from Central Bank	...	...	...	...	...	...	...	...	...	...	...	1,523	6,288	5,391	10,152		26g
Capital Accounts	...	...	...	...	...	...	...	...	...	...	...	2,139	3,782	11,460	15,892		27a
Other Items (Net)	...	...	...	...	...	...	...	...	...	...	...	−1,950	−2,702	−8,807	−16,146		27r
Monetary Survey																	
End of Period																	
Foreign Assets (Net)	...	...	...	...	...	...	...	...	...	...	...	−2,120	−5,397	14,413	20,130		31n
Domestic Credit	...	...	...	...	...	...	...	...	...	...	...	12,958	20,758	31,547	57,643		32
Claims on Central Govt. (Net)	...	...	...	...	...	...	...	...	...	...	...	103	1,628	−76	4,679		32an
Claims on Nonfin.Pub.Enterprises	...	...	...	...	...	...	...	...	...	...	...	9,501	11,789	16,938	12,193		32c
Claims on Private Sector	...	...	...	...	...	...	...	...	...	...	...	3,354	7,341	14,684	40,770		32d
Money	...	...	...	...	...	...	...	...	...	...	...	7,660	11,106	24,033	43,422		34
Quasi-Money	...	...	...	...	...	...	...	...	...	...	...	2,601	5,412	24,216	43,906		35
Other Items (Net)	...	...	...	...	...	...	...	...	...	...	...	577	−1,157	−2,289	−9,555		37r
Money plus Quasi-Money	...	...	...	...	...	...	...	...	...	...	...	10,261	16,518	48,249	87,328		35l
Interest Rates																	
Percent per Annum																	
Bank Rate *(End of Period)*	...	...	...	...	...	...	...	...	...	...	...	...	...	628.8	435.0		60
Deposit Rate *(End of Period)*	...	...	...	...	...	...	300.0	300.0	300.0	300.0	300.0	400.0	500.0	125.2	92.3		60l
Lending Rate *(End of Period)*	...	...	...	...	...	...	...	...	...	...	...	...	...	300.0	233.6		60p
Prices, Production, Employment																	
Period Averages																	
Consumer Prices (Jan.'91=100)	...	...	...	...	...	...	...	...	...	...	...	...	363.7	1,339.8	2,513.2		64
Wages: Average Earnings	...	...	...	...	...	93.9	94.2	94.2	95.3	99.4	100.0	228.9	348.7	...	...		65
Industrial Production	...	...	...	...	...	88.8	95.8	99.8	103.3	106.0	100.0	84.9	72.4	63.0	65.3		66
Industrial Employment	...	...	...	...	...	85.9	90.2	95.1	101.3	101.3	100.0	98.4	97.9	...	...		67

Mongolia

948

	1965	1966	1967	1968	1969	1970	1971	1972	1973	1974	1975	1976	1977	1978	1979
International Transactions															*Millions of US Dollars*
Exports .... 70.. *d*	...	...	...	...	...	...	...	...	...	...	...	...	...	...	...
Imports, cif .... 71.. *d*	...	...	...	...	...	...	...	...	...	...	...	...	...	...	...
Balance of Payments															*Millions of US Dollars:*
Goods: Exports f.o.b. .... 78aa *d*	...	...	...	...	...	...	...	...	...	...	...	...	...	...	...
Goods: Imports f.o.b. .... 78ab *d*	...	...	...	...	...	...	...	...	...	...	...	...	...	...	...
Trade Balance .... 78ac *d*	...	...	...	...	...	...	...	...	...	...	...	...	...	...	...
Services: Credit .... 78ad *d*	...	...	...	...	...	...	...	...	...	...	...	...	...	...	...
Services: Debit .... 78ae *d*	...	...	...	...	...	...	...	...	...	...	...	...	...	...	...
Balance on Goods and Services .... 78af *d*	...	...	...	...	...	...	...	...	...	...	...	...	...	...	...
Income: Credit .... 78ag *d*	...	...	...	...	...	...	...	...	...	...	...	...	...	...	...
Income: Debit .... 78ah *d*	...	...	...	...	...	...	...	...	...	...	...	...	...	...	...
Balance on Goods, Serv., & Inc. .... 78ai *d*	...	...	...	...	...	...	...	...	...	...	...	...	...	...	...
Current Transfers, n.i.e.: Credit .... 78aj *d*	...	...	...	...	...	...	...	...	...	...	...	...	...	...	...
Current Transfers: Debit .... 78ak *d*	...	...	...	...	...	...	...	...	...	...	...	...	...	...	...
Current Account, n.i.e. .... 78al *d*	...	...	...	...	...	...	...	...	...	...	...	...	...	...	...
Capital Account, n.i.e.: Credit .... 78ba *d*	...	...	...	...	...	...	...	...	...	...	...	...	...	...	...
Capital Account: Debit .... 78bb *d*	...	...	...	...	...	...	...	...	...	...	...	...	...	...	...
Capital Account, n.i.e. .... 78bc *d*	...	...	...	...	...	...	...	...	...	...	...	...	...	...	...
Direct Investment Abroad .... 78bd *d*	...	...	...	...	...	...	...	...	...	...	...	...	...	...	...
Dir. Invest. in Rep. Econ., n.i.e. .... 78be *d*	...	...	...	...	...	...	...	...	...	...	...	...	...	...	...
Portfolio Investment Assets .... 78bf *d*	...	...	...	...	...	...	...	...	...	...	...	...	...	...	...
Portfolio Investment Liab., n.i.e. .... 78bg *d*	...	...	...	...	...	...	...	...	...	...	...	...	...	...	...
Other Investment Assets .... 78bh *d*	...	...	...	...	...	...	...	...	...	...	...	...	...	...	...
Other Investment Liab., n.i.e. .... 78bi *d*	...	...	...	...	...	...	...	...	...	...	...	...	...	...	...
Financial Account, n.i.e. .... 78bj *d*	...	...	...	...	...	...	...	...	...	...	...	...	...	...	...
Net Errors and Omissions .... 78ca *d*	...	...	...	...	...	...	...	...	...	...	...	...	...	...	...
Overall Balance .... 78cb *d*	...	...	...	...	...	...	...	...	...	...	...	...	...	...	...
Reserves and Related Items .... 79da *d*	...	...	...	...	...	...	...	...	...	...	...	...	...	...	...
Reserve Assets .... 79db *d*	...	...	...	...	...	...	...	...	...	...	...	...	...	...	...
Use of Fund Credit and Loans .... 79dc *d*	...	...	...	...	...	...	...	...	...	...	...	...	...	...	...
Liabs.Constit.For.Auth.Reserves .... 79dd *d*	...	...	...	...	...	...	...	...	...	...	...	...	...	...	...
Exceptional Financing .... 79de *d*	...	...	...	...	...	...	...	...	...	...	...	...	...	...	...
Government Finance															*Millions of Tugriks:*
Deficit(-) or Surplus 80	...	...	...	...	...	...	...	...	...	...	...	...	...	...	...
Revenue 81	...	...	...	...	...	...	...	...	...	...	...	...	...	...	...
Grants Received 81z	...	...	...	...	...	...	...	...	...	...	...	...	...	...	...
Expenditure 82	...	...	...	...	...	...	...	...	...	...	...	...	...	...	...
Lending Minus Repayment 83	...	...	...	...	...	...	...	...	...	...	...	...	...	...	...
Financing															
Domestic 84a	...	...	...	...	...	...	...	...	...	...	...	...	...	...	...
Foreign 85a	...	...	...	...	...	...	...	...	...	...	...	...	...	...	...
Debt: Domestic 88a	...	...	...	...	...	...	...	...	...	...	...	...	...	...	...
Foreign 89a	...	...	...	...	...	...	...	...	...	...	...	...	...	...	...
National Accounts															*Millions of Tugriks*
Gross Domestic Product 99b	...	...	...	...	...	...	...	...	...	...	...	...	...	...	...
Gross Dom. Prod. 1990 Prices .... 99b. *p*	...	...	...	...	...	...	...	...	...	...	...	...	...	...	...
GDP Deflator (1990=100) .... 99bi *p*	...	...	...	...	...	...	...	...	...	...	...	...	...	...	...
															Millions:
Population 99z	1.09	1.12	1.15	1.18	1.21	1.25	1.28	1.32	1.36	1.40	1.44	1.47	1.51	1.55	1.60

Exchange Rates: ℓ From May 27, 1993, the midpoint of the average buying and selling rates that are freely determined on the basis of market transactions between commercial banks and the nonbank public. Also beginning on May 27, 1993, all exchange rates were unified in the context of the floating exchange rate system.

Government Finance: ℓ Beginning in 1992, annual data are as reported in the *Government Finance Statistics Yearbook (GFSY)* and cover consolidated central government.

Mongolia
948

1980	1981	1982	1983	1984	1985	1986	1987	1988	1989	1990	1991	1992	1993	1994		
Millions of US Dollars															**International Transactions**	
....	....	....	....	....	689.1	716.1	717.9	739.1	721.5	660.7	348.0	388.5	380.9	324.2	Exports......................	70..d
....	....	....	....	....	1,095.5	1,139.7	1,104.6	1,113.6	963.0	924.0	360.9	418.3	361.5	222.7	Imports, cif...............	71..d
Minus Sign Indicates Debit															Balance of Payments	
....	438.1	518.6	556.8	596.2	566.9	740.9	817.1	829.1	795.8	468.1	....	....	....	....	Goods: Exports f.o.b....................	78aa d
....	−1,240.7	−1,352.5	−1,362.3	−1,308.8	−1,365.7	−1,839.1	−1,827.6	−1,849.9	−1,913.6	−1,051.0	....	....	....	....	Goods: Imports f.o.b.	78ab d
....	−802.6	−833.9	−805.5	−712.6	−798.8	−1,098.2	−1,010.5	−1,020.8	−1,117.8	−582.9	....	....	....	....	Trade Balance...............	78ac d
....	38.4	49.2	56.3	53.7	71.7	84.2	89.0	94.3	36.4	48.1	....	....	....	....	Services: Credit.............	78ad d
....	−32.9	−41.3	−44.4	−42.0	−41.1	−44.7	−57.5	−72.3	−104.1	−72.6	....	....	....	....	Services: Debit..............	78ae d
....	−797.1	−826.0	−793.6	−700.9	−768.2	−1,058.7	−979.0	−998.8	−1,185.5	−607.4	....	....	....	....	Balance on Goods and Services........	78af d
....	.2	.2	—	.1	.1	.1	.2	.2	7.5	5.1	....	....	....	....	Income: Credit.................	78ag d
....	−11.1	−20.6	−31.1	−39.1	−45.1	−1.8	−11.5	−34.4	−56.4	−48.7	....	....	....	....	Income: Debit..................	78ah d
....	−808.0	−846.4	−824.7	−739.9	−813.2	−1,060.4	−990.3	−1,033.0	−1,234.4	−651.0	....	....	....	....	Balance on Goods, Serv., & Inc........	78ai d
....	—	—	—	—	—	—	—	—	—	3.9	....	....	....	....	Current Transfers, n.i.e.: Credit........	78aj d
....	−.1	−.1	−.1	−.4	−.1	−.2	−.3	−.3	—	7.4	....	....	....	....	Current Transfers: Debit..................	78ak d
....	−808.1	−846.5	−824.8	−740.3	−813.3	−1,060.6	−990.6	−1,033.3	−1,230.5	−643.6	....	....	....	....	Current Account, n.i.e.	78al d
....	—	—	—	—	—	—	—	—	—	—	....	....	....	....	Capital Account, n.i.e.: Credit.........	78ba d
....	—	—	—	—	—	—	—	—	—	—	....	....	....	....	Capital Account: Debit...................	78bb d
....	—	—	—	—	—	—	—	—	—	—	....	....	....	....	Capital Account, n.i.e.....................	78bc d
....	—	—	—	—	—	—	—	—	—	—	....	....	....	....	Direct Investment Abroad................	78bd d
....	—	—	—	—	—	—	—	—	—	—	....	....	....	....	Dir. Invest. in Rep. Econ., n.i.e.........	78be d
....	—	—	—	—	—	—	—	—	—	—	....	....	....	....	Portfolio Investment Assets.............	78bf d
....	—	—	—	—	—	—	—	—	—	—	....	....	....	....	Portfolio Investment Liab., n.i.e........	78bg d
....	—	—	—	—	—	—	—	—	—	−2.0	....	....	....	....	Other Investment Assets.................	78bh d
....	807.5	867.3	739.3	742.9	754.5	1,086.6	1,143.4	1,019.4	1,318.7	548.8	....	....	....	....	Other Investment Liab., n.i.e...........	78bi d
....	807.5	867.3	739.3	742.9	754.5	1,086.6	1,143.4	1,019.4	1,318.7	546.8	....	....	....	....	Financial Account, n.i.e.................	78bj d
....	−.6	−18.9	81.1	11.0	83.4	−11.3	−76.5	14.6	41.5	−4.8	....	....	....	....	Net Errors and Omissions...............	78ca d
....	−1.2	1.9	−4.4	13.6	24.6	14.7	76.3	.7	129.7	−101.6	....	....	....	....	Overall Balance................................	78cb d
....	1.2	−1.9	4.4	−13.6	−24.6	−14.7	−76.3	−.7	−129.7	101.6	....	....	....	....	Reserves and Related Items............	79da d
....	1.2	−1.9	4.4	−13.6	−24.6	−14.7	−76.3	−.7	−129.7	101.6	....	....	....	....	Reserve Assets..............................	79db d
....	—	—	—	—	—	—	—	—	—	—	....	....	....	....	Use of Fund Credit and Loans........	79dc d
....	—	—	—	—	—	—	—	—	—	—	....	....	....	....	Liabs.Constit.For.Auth.Reserves.....	79dd d
....	—	—	—	—	—	—	—	—	—	—	....	....	....	....	Exceptional Financing....................	79de d
Year Ending December 31															**Government Finance**	
....	....	....	....	....	−783	−1,696	−1,868	−2,061	−1,807	−1,449	−1,774	⅋−2,840	−3,522 P	....	Deficit(-) or Surplus.....................	80
....	....	....	....	....	4,918	4,360	4,540	4,681	5,243	5,329	6,065	⅋8,672	45,397 P	....	Revenue..	81
....	....	....	....	....	—	—	—	—	12	34	1,090	⅋1,224	3,027 P	....	Grants Received..............................	81z
....	....	....	....	....	5,701	6,056	6,408	6,742	7,062	6,812	8,929	⅋10,187	44,680 P	....	Expenditure.....................................	82
....	....	....	....	....	—	—	—	—	—	—	—	⅋2,549	7,266 P	....	Lending Minus Repayment.............	83
															Financing	
....	....	....	....	....	−40	−292	−46	223	159	858	−647	⅋−470	....	....	Domestic..	84a
....	....	....	....	....	823	1,988	1,914	1,838	1,648	591	2,421	⅋3,310	....	....	Foreign..	85a
....	....	....	....	....	....	....	....	....	....	....	....	⅋1,063	....	....	Debt: Domestic...............................	88a
....	....	....	....	....	....	....	....	....	....	....	....	⅋6,733	....	....	Foreign..	89a
Millions of Tugriks															**National Accounts**	
6,755	7,426	8,205	8,762	8,996	9,372	9,310	9,710	10,301	10,731	10,465	18,910	47,298	....	....	Gross Domestic Product..................	99b
6,227	6,747	7,310	7,730	8,195	8,664	9,380	9,804	10,304	10,735	10,465	9,497	8,392	....	....	Gross Dom. Prod. 1990 Prices...........	99b.p
108.5	110.1	112.2	113.3	109.8	108.2	99.2	99.0	100.0	100.0	100.0	199.1	563.6	....	....	GDP Deflator (1990=100)................	99bi p
Midyear																
1.66	1.70	1.75	1.79	1.83	1.88	1.93	1.97	2.02	2.07	2.18	2.23	2.27	2.32	....	**Population**.......................................	99z

Morocco
686

		1965	1966	1967	1968	1969	1970	1971	1972	1973	1974	1975	1976	1977	1978	1979
Exchange Rates															*Dirhams per SDR:*	
Official Rate	aa	5.027	5.074	5.035	5.074	5.064	5.029	5.168	5.066	5.175	5.087	4.898	5.210	5.256	5.063	4.925
															Dirhams per US Dollar:	
Official Rate	ae	5.027	5.074	5.035	5.074	5.064	5.029	4.760	4.666	4.290	4.155	4.184	4.484	4.327	3.886	3.739
Official Rate	rf	5.060	5.060	5.060	5.060	5.060	5.060	5.050	4.592	4.107	4.370	4.052	4.419	4.503	4.167	3.899
															Index Numbers (1990=100):	
Official Rate	ahx	163.9	163.5	163.3	162.2	162.5	163.5	164.0	179.3	200.9	188.5	203.3	186.4	182.8	197.9	211.2
Nominal Effective Exchange Rate	nec	....	....	....	....	....	....	....	....	....	....	....	....	....	....	120.8
Real Effective Exchange Rate	rec	....	....	....	....	....	....	....	....	....	....	....	....	....	....	178.8
Fund Position															*Millions of SDRs:*	
Quota	2f.s	72	76	79	83	90	113	113	113	113	113	113	113	113	150	150
SDRs	1b.s	—	—	—	—	—	—	2	17	16	16	15	10	9	13	15
Reserve Position in the Fund	1c.s	11	12	13	—	—	—	—	28	28	28	28	—	—	—	—
Total Fund Cred.&Loans Outstg.	2tl	—	—	—	34	37	28	—	—	—	—	—	115	128	220	232
International Liquidity												*Millions of US Dollars Unless Otherwise Indicated:*				
Total Reserves minus Gold	1l.d	78	66	55	64	93	119	151	214	241	391	352	467	505	618	557
SDRs	1b.d	—	—	—	—	—	—	3	18	20	19	17	12	10	16	20
Reserve Position in the Fund	1c.d	11	12	13	—	—	—	31	34	35	33	—	—	—	—	—
Foreign Exchange	1d.d	67	54	42	64	93	119	148	165	187	337	302	455	495	602	537
Gold (Million Fine Troy Ounces)	1ad	.600	.600	.600	.600	.600	.600	.600	.600	.600	.608	.608	.608	.632	.680	.704
Gold (National Valuation)	1and	21	21	21	21	21	21	....	....	26	26	26	24	26	31	33
Monetary Authorities: Other Assets	3..d	22	25	13	20	18	15	22	13	27	16	25	17	9	15	5
Other Liab.	4..d	13	15	12	9	11	16	12	5	1	10	13	29	23	−7	−56
Deposit Money Banks: Assets	7a.d	26	24	25	28	33	39	43	59	75	91	86	88	97	127	215
of which: Claims on Nonbanks	7add	....	....	13	14	15	22	25	32	43	47	50	47	59	74	128
Deposit Money Banks: Liabilities	7b.d	13	13	14	18	16	17	15	21	18	23	23	27	39	41	83
of which: Liab. to Nonbanks	7bdd	....	....	3	7	7	7	4	10	4	4	6	6	8	14	22
Other Banking Insts.: Liabilities	7f.d	....	....	....	....	33	39	54	63	79	94	166	263	466	647	680
Monetary Authorities															*Millions of Dirhams:*	
Foreign Assets	11	610	567	449	532	719	796	919	1,162	1,241	1,795	1,714	2,276	2,340	2,584	2,226
Claims on Central Government	12a	615	615	920	1,191	1,393	1,563	1,474	1,724	1,919	2,184	3,019	3,727	5,209	6,389	7,266
Claims on Private Sector	12d	332	364	338	450	496	480	493	546	670	536	655	824	627	827	1,237
Claims on Deposit Money Banks	12e	162	172	148	228	213	207	280	284	411	769	592	1,153	1,200	1,160	1,931
Reserve Money	14	1,605	1,592	1,798	2,050	2,339	2,527	2,801	3,326	3,815	4,607	5,298	6,450	7,450	8,595	10,013
of which: Currency Outside DMBs	14a	1,386	1,429	1,614	1,859	2,121	2,261	2,461	2,944	3,411	4,063	4,650	5,732	6,650	7,676	9,020
Private Sector Deposits	14d	151	89	102	80	72	81	106	123	128	206	191	207	219	265	262
Foreign Liabilities	16c	65	74	60	266	384	308	81	31	26	94	75	735	850	1,335	1,382
Central Government Deposits	16d	46	25	29	30	29	36	42	47	48	63	72	68	137	95	113
Other Items (Net)	17r	2	26	−32	55	68	176	242	313	351	520	535	727	939	934	1,152
Deposit Money Banks															*Millions of Dirhams:*	
Reserves	20	56	65	76	108	143	185	234	246	272	334	434	511	571	674	733
Foreign Assets	21	133	122	125	140	167	195	199	276	315	380	358	394	421	492	803
Claims on Central Government	22a	557	569	556	647	859	896	1,011	1,181	1,406	1,986	2,496	2,761	3,335	5,410	6,040
Claims on Private Sector	22d	1,648	1,681	1,782	2,188	2,094	2,119	2,441	2,798	3,406	4,537	5,668	6,869	8,116	8,785	9,753
Claims on Other Financial Insts.	22f	....	....	....	....	....	....	....	....	....	....	....	....	....	....	....
Demand Deposits	24	1,854	1,862	1,968	2,204	2,309	2,634	3,042	3,544	4,313	5,346	6,881	7,772	9,362	10,750	11,741
Time Deposits	25	232	212	245	347	417	393	476	547	620	1,017	1,437	1,756	2,179	2,959	3,681
Foreign Liabilities	26c	67	67	68	90	81	86	69	100	77	96	96	120	170	160	309
Credit from Monetary Authorities	26g	163	172	148	228	213	207	280	284	411	769	592	1,153	1,200	1,160	1,931
Other Items (Net)	27r	78	124	109	214	241	76	17	26	−23	9	−51	−266	−467	332	−334
Post Office: Checking Deposits	24..i	244	202	221	232	274	288	324	362	361	547	636	687	853	912	1,118
Treasury: Checking Deposits	24..r	176	217	231	216	282	251	260	363	359	708	479	705	918	1,182	1,211
Monetary Survey															*Millions of Dirhams:*	
Foreign Assets (Net)	31n	611	548	446	316	421	598	969	1,307	1,452	1,985	1,901	1,815	1,741	1,580	1,337
Domestic Credit	32	3,526	3,623	4,019	4,894	5,368	5,561	5,960	6,927	8,072	10,434	12,881	15,505	18,921	23,409	26,512
Claims on Central Govt. (Net)	32an	1,546	1,578	1,899	2,255	2,778	2,962	3,026	3,583	3,997	5,361	6,558	7,812	10,178	13,798	15,522
Claims on Private Sector	32d	1,980	2,045	2,120	2,639	2,590	2,599	2,934	3,344	4,076	5,073	6,323	7,693	8,743	9,612	10,990
Claims on Other Financial Insts.	32f	....	....	....	....	....	....	....	....	....	....	....	....	....	....	....
Money	34	3,811	3,799	4,136	4,591	5,058	5,514	6,193	7,336	8,572	10,869	12,838	15,102	18,002	20,785	23,352
Quasi-Money	35	232	212	245	347	417	393	476	547	620	1,017	1,437	1,756	2,179	2,959	3,681
Other Items (Net)	37r	93	161	84	272	313	252	260	352	333	534	507	461	481	1,245	816
Money plus Quasi-Money	35l	4,043	4,011	4,381	4,938	5,476	5,908	6,669	7,883	9,192	11,886	14,274	16,858	20,181	23,744	27,033
Other Banking Institutions															*Millions of Dirhams:*	
Reserves	40	....	....	....	....	123	81	79	88	200	201	303	293	488	663	405
Claims on Central Government	42a	....	....	....	....	211	200	213	257	292	260	322	385	515	600	844
Claims on Official Entities	42bx	....	....	....	....	72	80	85	101	105	163	215	243	292	280	326
Claims on Private Sector	42d	....	....	....	....	1,030	1,185	1,392	1,699	1,809	2,236	2,966	3,815	4,853	5,981	6,769
Time Deposits	45	....	....	....	....	593	683	757	882	1,006	1,190	1,450	1,588	2,039	2,589	3,049
Bonds	46ab	....	....	....	....	62	84	117	138	206	320	436	421	480	651	822
Long-Term Foreign Liabilities	46cl	....	....	....	....	169	198	252	293	333	389	696	1,180	2,015	2,516	2,542
Central Govt. Lending Funds	46f	....	....	....	....	143	148	157	160	139	173	270	390	358	347	375
Credit from Monetary Authorities	46g	....	....	....	....	332	300	294	351	375	396	469	563	632	543	719
Credit from Deposit Money Banks	46h	....	....	....	....	—	—	—	86	76	52	71	124	151	134	110
Capital Accounts	47a	....	....	....	....	154	183	195	240	310	364	439	502	591	700	751
Other Items (Net)	47r	....	....	....	....	−17	−50	−3	−5	−39	−24	−25	−32	−118	44	−24
Liquid Liabilities	55l	....	....	....	....	5,946	6,510	7,347	8,677	9,998	12,875	15,421	18,153	21,732	25,670	29,677

Morocco

686

	1980	1981	1982	1983	1984	1985	1986	1987	1988	1989	1990	1991	1992	1993	1994	
End of Period																**Exchange Rates**
	5.528	6.208	6.914	8.439	9.362	10.568	10.656	11.066	11.049	10.673	11.442	11.658	12.442	13.257	13.080	Official Rate **aa**
End of Period (ae) Period Average (rf)																
	4.334	5.333	6.268	8.061	9.551	9.621	8.712	7.800	8.211	8.122	8.043	8.150	9.049	9.651	8.960	Official Rate **ae**
	3.937	5.172	6.023	7.111	8.811	10.062	9.104	8.359	8.209	8.488	8.242	8.707	8.538	9.299	9.203	Official Rate **rf**
Period Averages																
	209.5	160.0	137.0	116.7	93.8	81.9	90.5	98.5	100.4	97.0	100.0	94.8	96.5	88.6	89.6	Official Rate **ahx**
	122.4	113.2	113.1	109.6	101.3	95.9	88.9	88.2	91.0	98.1	100.0	100.3	104.0	109.5	117.4	Nominal Effective Exchange Rate **nec**
	156.4	143.1	141.0	131.7	124.1	115.9	110.8	107.1	104.9	105.2	100.0	100.8	102.3	104.0	106.8	Real Effective Exchange Rate **rec**
End of Period																**Fund Position**
	225	225	225	307	307	307	307	307	307	307	307	307	428	428	428	Quota **2f.s**
	—	1	1	1	1	—	16	3	—	—	1	103	56	25	18	SDRs **1b.s**
	—	—	—	—	—	—	—	—	—	—	—	—	30	30	30	Reserve Position in the Fund **1c.s**
	358	497	898	985	1,107	1,161	894	789	711	647	527	402	319	207	101	Total Fund Cred.&Loans Outstg. **2tl**
End of Period																**International Liquidity**
	399	230	218	107	49	115	211	411	547	488	2,066	3,100	3,584	3,655	4,352	Total Reserves minus Gold **1l.d**
	1	2	1	1	1	—	19	4	—	—	1	147	77	34	26	SDRs **1b.d**
	—	—	—	—	—	—	—	—	—	—	—	—	42	42	44	Reserve Position in the Fund **1c.d**
	398	228	217	106	48	115	192	407	547	488	2,065	2,953	3,465	3,579	4,281	Foreign Exchange **1d.d**
	.704	.704	.704	.704	.704	.704	.704	.704	.704	.704	.704	.704	.704	.704	.704	Gold (Million Fine Troy Ounces) **1ad**
	29	23	20	15	13	13	14	16	15	15	16	15	14	202	218	Gold (National Valuation) **1and**
	4	3	3	2	2	-13	....	....	....	....	....	....	....	....	....	Monetary Authorities: Other Assets **3..d**
	-84	-52	-85	-33	-79	-44	-15	23	44	38	44	144	139	53	47	Other Liab. **4..d**
	246	326	282	266	255	322	388	439	495	569	781	690	598	518	755	Deposit Money Banks: Assets **7a.d**
	155	243	240	225	214	....	....	....	....	....	....	....	....	....	....	*of which:* Claims on Nonbanks **7add**
	69	68	35	38	34	49	85	70	103	127	226	267	354	386	672	Deposit Money Banks: Liabilities **7b.d**
	30	36	20	25	23	....	....	....	....	....	....	....	....	....	....	*of which:* Liab. to Nonbanks **7bdd**
	623	586	477	457	439	594	891	1,170	1,171	1,187	1,448	1,585	1,523	1,450	....	Other Banking Insts.: Liabilities **7f.d**
End of Period																**Monetary Authorities**
	1,871	1,366	1,507	1,001	612	1,247	1,987	3,351	4,639	4,111	I 16,760	25,410	32,570	37,243	41,001	Foreign Assets **11**
	I 9,516	12,062	13,676	17,211	18,548	18,766	15,584	13,224	13,881	13,693	I 13,435	16,994	9,861	8,752	8,305	Claims on Central Government **12a**
	I 601	542	809	1,189	1,380	3,383	7,663	8,606	8,901	8,814	I 7,661	7,535	7,611	8,803	8,416	Claims on Private Sector **12d**
	1,631	2,662	2,870	3,041	4,123	3,753	5,315	5,577	5,969	10,948	I 2,118	2,699	1,828	599	512	Claims on Deposit Money Banks **12e**
	10,532	11,952	12,777	14,472	16,137	17,351	21,471	22,636	26,200	30,839	I 38,341	47,847	44,023	47,796	50,709	Reserve Money **14**
	9,807	11,133	12,022	13,636	14,770	16,192	18,694	20,003	21,914	24,814	I 29,543	34,298	35,745	37,202	41,071	*of which: Currency Outside DMBs* **14a**
	324	323	275	356	559	449	479	534	861	1,017	I 1,108	1,184	1,140	1,692	1,295	*Private Sector Deposits* **14d**
	2,399	3,688	6,443	8,967	10,519	12,664	9,994	9,284	8,388	7,248	I 6,381	5,853	5,227	3,256	1,745	Foreign Liabilities **16c**
	125	151	171	184	220	482	560	424	481	407	I 482	517	498	523	642	Central Government Deposits **16d**
	562	841	-529	-1,181	-2,214	-3,348	-1,476	-1,586	-1,679	-928	I -5,230	-1,579	2,122	3,822	5,139	Other Items (Net) **17r**
End of Period																**Deposit Money Banks**
	389	474	417	434	816	695	2,269	2,050	3,497	5,007	I 8,086	12,633	7,439	8,956	8,582	Reserves **20**
	1,066	1,737	I 1,769	2,148	2,432	3,100	3,378	3,428	4,068	4,618	I 6,281	5,621	5,408	5,002	6,765	Foreign Assets **21**
	7,165	8,077	8,577	12,144	12,496	16,977	24,646	28,810	30,428	34,453	I 29,766	28,293	39,545	44,652	50,746	Claims on Central Government **22a**
	11,038	13,066	I 16,264	18,654	21,385	22,920	....	....	....	....	I 34,095	48,500	56,581	62,351	70,408	Claims on Private Sector **22d**
	....	....	689	392	142	242	....	....	....	....	I 1,101	1,011	994	355	1,409	Claims on Other Financial Insts. **22f**
	12,970	15,062	I 15,021	18,064	19,366	21,378	25,978	28,390	32,128	34,732	I 54,171	61,757	66,636	70,033	79,099	Demand Deposits **24**
	4,649	5,872	I 8,691	11,412	13,491	16,592	18,819	21,056	24,627	28,458	I 24,143	30,383	36,425	42,687	45,958	Time Deposits **25**
	300	360	I 217	303	323	472	740	549	842	1,028	I 1,819	2,179	3,205	3,729	6,020	Foreign Liabilities **26c**
	1,661	2,674	2,870	3,041	3,734	3,753	7,490	7,682	8,244	12,492	I 5,862	8,398	2,566	965	1,108	Credit from Monetary Authorities **26g**
	78	-614	916	955	357	1,739	....	....	....	....	I -6,666	-6,659	1,135	3,902	5,725	Other Items (Net) **27r**
	1,169	1,371	1,468	959	1,010	951	1,001	1,129	1,207	1,406	1,420	1,777	1,520	1,625	1,833	Post Office: Checking Deposits **24..i**
	1,042	1,127	1,278	1,182	1,075	1,319	1,523	1,979	3,468	4,077	4,417	4,693	5,041	6,531	4,793	Treasury: Checking Deposits **24..r**
End of Period																**Monetary Survey**
	239	-946	I -3,385	-6,121	-7,798	-8,789	-5,369	-3,054	-523	453	I 14,841	22,999	29,546	35,260	40,002	Foreign Assets (Net) **31n**
	I 31,215	36,939	43,719	52,321	56,759	64,938	72,114	77,243	84,026	92,644	I 91,413	108,782	120,655	132,546	145,268	Domestic Credit **32**
	I 18,766	22,486	24,827	31,312	32,909	37,531	42,194	44,718	48,503	53,222	I 48,556	51,240	55,469	61,037	65,035	Claims on Central Govt. (Net) **32an**
	12,449	14,453	I 17,073	19,843	22,765	26,303	....	....	....	....	I 41,756	56,035	64,192	71,154	78,824	Claims on Private Sector **32d**
	....	....	1,818	1,166	1,086	1,104	....	....	....	....	I 1,101	1,507	994	355	1,409	Claims on Other Financial Insts. **32f**
	25,312	29,016	I 30,064	34,197	36,779	40,289	47,675	52,035	59,578	66,046	I 90,659	103,709	110,082	117,083	128,091	Money **34**
	4,649	5,872	I 8,691	11,412	13,491	16,592	18,819	21,056	24,627	28,458	I 24,143	30,383	36,425	42,687	45,958	Quasi-Money **35**
	1,493	1,106	1,579	593	-1,309	-724	259	1,098	-702	-1,407	I -8,548	-2,311	3,694	8,036	11,221	Other Items (Net) **37r**
	29,961	34,888	I 38,755	45,608	50,270	56,881	66,494	73,091	84,205	94,504	I 114,802	134,092	146,507	159,770	174,049	Money plus Quasi-Money **35l**
End of Period																**Other Banking Institutions**
	378	369	359	622	576	397	781	464	709	474	594	899	1,428	1,938	....	Reserves **40**
	1,062	1,138	1,726	1,827	1,683	2,081	2,516	2,662	3,545	5,421	5,881	6,567	7,191	7,980	....	Claims on Central Government **42a**
	392	408	387	418	462	552	800	204	262	162	42	1	—	—	....	Claims on Official Entities **42bx**
	7,578	8,782	10,024	11,418	13,267	15,702	18,096	21,281	23,786	26,408	30,674	34,525	37,601	39,365	....	Claims on Private Sector **42d**
	3,625	3,967	4,609	5,659	6,508	7,342	8,597	9,294	10,890	12,978	15,014	17,410	19,670	21,836	....	Time Deposits **45**
	1,038	1,617	2,251	3,179	3,556	4,219	5,138	5,281	6,302	7,476	8,432	8,164	9,663	10,134	....	Bonds **46ab**
	2,702	3,128	2,990	3,684	4,196	5,712	7,763	9,124	9,613	9,641	11,643	12,917	13,779	13,997	....	Long-Term Foreign Liabilities **46cl**
	373	404	399	424	608	606	589	594	610	274	143	216	617	547	....	Central Govt. Lending Funds **46f**
	780	834	1,123	796	944	936	—	—	—	145	53	554	14	5	....	Credit from Monetary Authorities **46g**
	123	337	690	392	142	242	303	436	484	377	269	988	515	508	....	Credit from Deposit Money Banks **46h**
	855	882	1,104	1,087	1,366	1,539	2,066	2,715	2,903	3,978	4,713	5,271	5,958	6,911	....	Capital Accounts **47a**
	-86	-472	-670	-936	-1,332	-1,864	-2,263	-2,833	-2,500	-2,404	-3,076	-3,528	-3,996	-4,655	....	Other Items (Net) **47r**
	33,208	38,486	I 43,364	51,267	56,778	64,223	75,091	82,385	95,095	107,482	I 129,816	151,502	166,177	181,606	....	Liquid Liabilities **55l**

Morocco
686

		1965	1966	1967	1968	1969	1970	1971	1972	1973	1974	1975	1976	1977	1978	1979
Interest Rates																*Percent Per Annum*
Discount Rate *(End of Period)*	60	3.50	3.50	3.50	3.50	3.50	3.50	3.50	3.50	3.50	4.50	4.50	4.50	4.50	4.50	4.50
Money Market Rate	60b	....	....	....	....	....	....	....	....	....	....	....	....	....	....	....
Treasury Bill Rate	60c	....	....	....	....	....	....	....	....	....	....	....	....	....	....	....
Deposit Rate	60l	....	....	....	....	....	....	....	....	....	....	....	....	....	6.0	6.0
Lending Rate	60p	....	....	....	....	....	....	....	....	....	....	....	....	....	4.5	4.5
															7.0	7.0
Prices and Production															*Index Numbers (1990=100):*	
Wholesale Prices	63	18.0	18.4	18.9	17.3	17.5	18.9	19.7	20.1	23.6	29.1	30.1	31.5	ɪ36.0	....	42.5
Consumer Prices	64	21.3	21.0	20.9	21.0	21.6	21.9	22.8	23.6	ɪ24.6	28.9	31.2	33.9	38.1	41.8	45.3
Manufacturing Production	66ey	31.4	33.0	34.6	35.5	39.7	41.6	44.3	46.1	51.2	52.6	55.4	59.3	63.4	ɪ68.0	71.2
Mining Production	66zx	50.6	50.9	51.3	51.3	ɪ51.4	55.3	....	63.2	71.4	80.7	66.8	64.6	73.5	ɪ79.6	83.6
Energy Production	66ze	....	....	....	....	....	....	....	....	....	....	....	....	....	....	....
International Transactions															*Millions of Dirhams*	
Exports	70	2,177	2,168	2,146	2,279	2,455	2,471	2,533	2,953	3,746	7,440	6,238	5,579	5,858	6,261	7,622
Imports, cif	71	2,291	2,418	2,620	2,793	2,844	3,463	3,537	3,577	4,683	8,292	10,398	11,555	14,400	12,361	14,328
Imports, fob	71.v	2,019	2,243	2,428	2,586	2,609	3,158	3,216	3,256	4,261	7,297	9,148	10,168	12,671	10,878	12,609
															1990=100	
Volume of Exports	72	32	31	31	34	37	37	39	ɪ45	54	52	40	ɪ45	51	42	52
Volume of Imports	73	13	16	18	19	19	23	22	ɪ20	24	29	36	40	64	66	ɪ70
Unit Value of Imports	75	20	17	16	16	17	17	18	ɪ19	21	31	31	ɪ31	24	27	36
Balance of Payments															*Millions of US Dollars:*	
Goods: Exports f.o.b.	78aa d											1,539	1,262	1,301	1,503	1,955
Goods: Imports f.o.b.	78ab d											−2,252	−2,287	−2,800	−2,614	−3,244
Trade Balance	78ac d											−712	−1,025	−1,498	−1,112	−1,289
Services: Credit	78ad d											459	434	539	636	717
Services: Debit	78ae d											−710	−1,192	−1,276	−1,322	−1,473
Balance on Goods and Services	78af d											−963	−1,783	−2,236	−1,799	−2,044
Income: Credit	78ag d											28	24	31	26	39
Income: Debit	78ah d											−94	−123	−189	−310	−448
Balance on Goods, Serv., & Inc.	78ai d											−1,030	−1,882	−2,394	−2,082	−2,453
Current Transfers, n.i.e.: Credit	78aj d											607	618	677	881	1,081
Current Transfers: Debit	78ak d											−81	−105	−108	−110	−130
Current Account, n.i.e.	78al d											−504	−1,368	−1,825	−1,311	−1,502
Capital Account, n.i.e.: Credit	78ba d											—	—	1	1	1
Capital Account: Debit	78bb d											−10	−10	−9	−12	−13
Capital Account, n.i.e.	78bc d											−10	−10	−9	−11	−13
Direct Investment Abroad	78bd d											—	—	—	—	—
Dir. Invest. in Rep. Econ., n.i.e.	78be d											−1	38	8	12	7
Portfolio Investment Assets	78bf d											—	—	—	—	—
Portfolio Investment Liab., n.i.e.	78bg d											—	—	—	—	—
Other Investment Assets	78bh d											81	26	−44	−64	−141
Other Investment Liab., n.i.e.	78bi d											743	2,309	3,101	2,246	1,577
Financial Account, n.i.e.	78bj d											823	2,373	3,066	2,194	1,444
Net Errors and Omissions	78ca d											−337	−1,013	−1,248	−943	40
Overall Balance	78cb d											−28	−18	−16	−72	−111
Reserves and Related Items	79da d											28	18	16	72	111
Reserve Assets	79db d											27	−131	−9	−55	101
Use of Fund Credit and Loans	79dc d											—	133	14	116	15
Liabs.Constit.For.Auth.Reserves	79dd d											1	16	10	10	−6
Exceptional Financing	79de d											—	—	—	—	—
Government Finance															*Millions of Dirhams:*	
Deficit (-) or Surplus	80	−767	−422	−709	−567	−834	ɪ−619	−658	−897	−526	−1,348	−3,341	−7,217	−7,647	−5,773	−6,039
Revenue	81	1,909	2,088	2,466	2,842	3,102	ɪ3,862	3,890	4,335	5,164	8,468	9,529	9,601	12,333	13,346	15,803
Expenditure	82	2,676	2,510	3,175	3,409	3,936	ɪ4,490	4,544	5,265	5,630	9,879	12,399	16,495	19,904	18,986	21,673
Lending Minus Repayments	83	....	....	....	....	....	ɪ−9	4	−33	60	−63	471	323	76	133	169
Financing																
Net Borrowing: Domestic	84a	240	232	474	459	672	ɪ342	91	521	475	779	1,474	2,197	2,210	2,528	1,759
Foreign	85a	473	169	238	109	161	ɪ277	321	296	−2	185	1,350	4,474	5,195	3,365	4,014
Use of Cash Balances	87	54	21	−3	−1	1	ɪ—	246	80	53	384	517	546	242	−120	266
Debt: Domestic	88a	1,000	1,064	1,156	1,369	1,690	ɪ1,878	2,056	2,349	2,641	3,172	3,770	5,245	5,908	7,360	8,611
Foreign	89a	2,354	2,676	2,930	3,151	3,181	ɪ3,622	4,026	4,338	4,177	4,341	5,168	7,881	11,438	13,722	16,071
National Accounts															*Billions of Dirhams*	
Exports of Goods & Services	90c	2.71	2.76	2.76	3.06	3.40	3.54	3.76	4.37	5.41	9.42	8.43	7.89	8.83	9.36	10.83
Government Consumption	91f	1.80	1.88	1.93	2.13	2.24	2.44	2.71	2.96	2.99	4.04	5.92	9.21	10.25	11.47	13.23
Gross Fixed Capital Formation	93e	1.44	1.53	1.89	1.97	2.43	2.99	3.27	3.18	3.47	4.93	9.04	12.18	15.90	13.73	14.88
Increase/Decrease(-) in Stocks	93i	−.02	−.15	.03	.72	−.32	.09	.06	−.33	.13	1.99	.13	−.64	1.13	.46	.32
Private Consumption	96f	9.55	9.46	9.89	10.50	13.73	14.53	15.81	16.88	18.40	22.45	24.81	27.66	31.81	36.28	40.81
Imports of Goods & Services	98c	−2.33	−2.61	−2.89	−3.06	−3.48	−4.15	−4.22	−4.36	−5.50	−9.23	−11.93	−15.28	−18.16	−16.14	−18.02
Gross Domestic Product	99b	13.16	12.84	13.60	15.31	17.99	19.43	21.38	22.68	24.92	33.60	36.39	41.01	49.76	55.15	62.04
Net Factor Inc/Pmts(-) Abroad	98.n	.09	.04	.11	.05	.02	.04	.18	.24	.63	1.08	1.45	1.74	1.39	1.38	1.41
Gross Nat'l Expenditure = GNP	99a	13.25	12.88	13.71	15.36	18.01	19.47	21.57	22.93	25.54	34.68	37.86	42.75	51.15	56.53	63.46
Nat'l Income, Market Prices	99e	12.85	12.47	13.29	14.94	17.61	18.97	20.96	22.43	24.70	33.50	36.22	42.10	49.00	54.00	60.60
Gross Dom. Prod. 1990 Prices	99b.p	69.10	68.14	72.56	81.57	ɪ82.27	86.39	91.42	93.34	96.91	110.76	115.34	123.43	131.43	135.87	142.04
GDP Deflator (1990=100)	99bi p	19.0	18.8	18.7	18.8	21.9	22.5	23.4	24.3	25.7	30.3	31.6	33.2	37.9	40.6	43.7
															Millions	
Population	99z	13.02	13.37	13.70	14.20	14.80	15.31	15.38	15.70	16.31	16.80	17.31	17.83	18.36	18.91	19.47

Monetary Authorities: ɪ Beginning in December 1980, *Claims on Central Government* (line 12a) include the Fund drawings that have been transferred to the Treasury, and *Claims on Private Sector* (line 12d) exclude *Claims on Other Financial Institutions* (line 12f). ɪ Beginning in 1990, data are based on a more detailed classification of accounts.
Deposit Money Banks: ɪ Beginning in 1982, data are based on improved classification. ɪ About data beginning in 1990, see note to section 10.
Monetary Survey: ɪ See notes to sections 10 and 20.

Government Finance: ɪ Beginning in 1970, data are as reported in the *Government Finance Statistics Yearbook* and cover budgetary central government, the Moroccan Pension Fund, and the National Social Security Fund. Prior to 1970, data are as reported for publication in *IFS*.

Morocco
686

	1980	1981	1982	1983	1984	1985	1986	1987	1988	1989	1990	1991	1992	1993	1994		
Percent Per Annum																**Interest Rates**	
	6.00	6.00	7.00	7.00	7.00	8.50	8.50	8.50	8.50	....	....	....	....	....	7.00	Discount Rate (End of Period)	60
	9.00	9.00	10.92	....	....	9.41	9.44	....	....	....	....	....	....	....	....	Money Market Rate	60b
	6.4	7.5	8.3	8.5	8.5	10.0	10.5	10.5	10.5	10.5	10.5	9.5	9.5	....	....	Treasury Bill Rate	60c
	4.9	6.0	6.4	6.5	6.5	8.0	8.5	8.5	8.5	8.5	8.5	8.5	8.5	....	....	Deposit Rate	60l
	7.0	7.0	7.0	7.0	7.0	7.8	8.8	9.0	9.0	9.0	9.0	9.0	9.0	....	10.0	Lending Rate	60p
Period Averages																**Prices and Production**	
	46.1	54.2	60.7	65.2	74.1	81.2	87.5	88.4	92.1	95.6	100.0	106.4	109.4	114.3	117.0	Wholesale Prices	63
	49.6	55.8	61.7	65.5	73.6	79.3	86.3	88.6	90.7	93.5	100.0	I108.0	114.2	120.1	126.3	Consumer Prices	64
	72.7	72.5	74.6	77.8	77.6	I78.1	81.3	I83.3	90.4	92.3	100.0	102.4	104.2	102.5	....	Manufacturing Production	66ey
	79.2	77.0	80.4	87.4	91.0	91.0	89.2	I99.4	113.9	85.6	100.0	87.8	89.2	90.8	....	Mining Production	66zx
	....	....	....	....	....	....	....	81.5	88.3	94.1	100.0	96.3	105.3	107.3	....	Energy Production	66ze
Millions of Dirhams																**International Transactions**	
	9,645	12,354	12,461	14,324	19,110	21,740	22,103	23,390	29,751	28,271	35,135	37,283	33,954	31,839	36,815	Exports	70
	16,793	22,692	25,983	25,542	34,397	38,675	34,604	35,271	39,133	46,594	57,021	59,720	62,804	66,576	66,119	Imports, cif	71
	14,781	19,760	22,866	22,497	31,300	35,194	31,493	32,097	35,604	42,401	51,890	50,859	57,146	60,579	60,168	Imports, fob	71.v
1990=100																	
	53	55	55	61	64	65	67	72	83	I82	100	108	102	105	....	Volume of Exports	72
	66	69	77	66	73	71	70	77	83	I89	100	112	128	120	....	Volume of Imports	73
	45	57	59	68	82	92	82	80	82	I91	100	96	92	101	....	Unit Value of Imports	75
Minus Sign Indicates Debit																**Balance of Payments**	
	2,450	2,321	2,070	2,075	2,170	2,162	2,428	2,798	3,624	3,331	4,229	4,282	5,010	4,936	....	Goods: Exports f.o.b.	78aa d
	−3,771	−3,840	−3,816	−3,302	−3,571	−3,515	−3,481	−3,864	−4,384	−5,027	−6,338	−6,264	−6,809	−6,401	....	Goods: Imports f.o.b.	78ab d
	−1,321	−1,520	−1,746	−1,227	−1,401	−1,353	−1,053	−1,066	−760	−1,697	−2,108	−1,981	−1,799	−1,466	....	Trade Balance	78ac d
	783	727	849	845	830	983	1,133	1,379	1,764	1,650	2,009	1,771	2,131	2,051	....	Services: Credit	78ad d
	−1,436	−1,435	−1,333	−876	−781	−829	−1,156	−1,141	−1,106	−1,204	−1,445	−1,363	−1,588	−1,594	....	Services: Debit	78ae d
	−1,975	−2,228	−2,230	−1,257	−1,352	−1,199	−1,076	−828	−102	−1,251	−1,544	−1,574	−1,256	−1,009	....	Balance on Goods and Services	78af d
	38	36	25	11	16	15	15	16	18	32	83	199	292	224	....	Income: Credit	78ag d
	−600	−738	−675	−631	−592	−781	−704	−782	−1,055	−1,191	−1,071	−1,315	−1,357	−1,473	....	Income: Debit	78ah d
	−2,537	−2,930	−2,880	−1,878	−1,927	−1,965	−1,765	−1,595	−1,139	−2,411	−2,532	−2,689	−2,320	−2,258	....	Balance on Goods, Serv., & Inc.	78ai d
	1,235	1,189	1,088	1,067	1,005	1,119	1,602	1,822	1,663	1,669	2,383	2,356	2,614	2,361	....	Current Transfers, n.i.e.: Credit	78aj d
	−106	−91	−78	−77	−64	−47	−45	−46	−51	−46	−47	−58	−81	−66	....	Current Transfers: Debit	78ak d
	−1,408	−1,833	−1,864	−888	−986	−893	−209	182	473	−787	−196	−392	213	36	....	Current Account, n.i.e.	78al d
	—	—	—	1	2	5	1	2	1	—	—	—	—	—	....	Capital Account, n.i.e.: Credit	78ba d
	−12	−12	−9	−4	−4	−4	−3	−8	−7	−3	−5	−5	−6	−3	....	Capital Account: Debit	78bb d
	−12	−12	−8	−3	−2	2	−2	−6	−6	−3	−5	−5	−6	−3	....	Capital Account, n.i.e.	78bc d
	—	—	—	—	—	—	—	—	—	—	—	—	−32	−53	....	Direct Investment Abroad	78bd d
	89	59	80	46	47	20	1	60	85	167	165	320	422	481	....	Dir. Invest. in Rep. Econ., n.i.e.	78be d
	—	—	—	—	—	—	—	—	—	—	—	—	—	—	....	Portfolio Investment Assets	78bf d
	—	—	—	—	—	—	—	—	—	—	—	—	1	24	....	Portfolio Investment Liab., n.i.e.	78bg d
	−14	−146	−99	−163	−173	−16	−212	−105	−376	−94	−267	−235	199	669	....	Other Investment Assets	78bh d
	1,041	1,554	1,469	756	908	811	790	129	65	749	1,991	1,390	879	−240	....	Other Investment Liab., n.i.e.	78bi d
	1,116	1,466	1,449	639	783	815	579	84	−226	822	1,889	1,475	1,469	881	....	Financial Account, n.i.e.	78bj d
	15	60	32	26	96	42	−38	38	22	−11	9	88	−1,130	−682	....	Net Errors and Omissions	78ca d
	−289	−319	−391	−226	−109	−34	331	298	264	21	1,697	1,167	546	231	....	Overall Balance	78cb d
	289	319	391	226	109	34	−331	−298	−264	−21	−1,697	−1,167	−546	−231	....	Reserves and Related Items	79da d
	110	116	−24	71	35	−17	−19	−165	−158	63	−1,537	−996	−675	−280	....	Reserve Assets	79db d
	163	168	441	95	128	49	−311	−133	−105	−83	−161	−171	−116	−156	....	Use of Fund Credit and Loans	79dc d
	15	30	−29	58	−56	—	—	—	—	—	—	—	−3	−7	....	Liabs.Constit.For.Auth.Reserves	79dd d
	1	5	3	2	2	2	−1	—	—	—	—	—	248	212	....	Exceptional Financing	79de d
Year Ending December 31																**Government Finance**	
	−7,184	−10,557	−10,630	−7,680	−6,762	−9,424	−11,872	−7,025	−5,841	−9,951	−4,760	−5,083	−3,368	....	....	Deficit (-) or Surplus	80
	17,502	20,418	24,388	24,516	26,684	30,213	32,884	37,089	45,454	49,238	56,635	62,437	69,907	....	....	Revenue	81
	24,520	30,903	34,822	32,043	33,399	39,336	44,752	44,163	51,300	59,121	61,342	67,400	73,008	....	....	Expenditure	82
	166	72	196	153	47	301	4	−49	−5	68	53	120	267	....	....	Lending Minus Repayments	83
																Financing	
	3,426	4,131	3,230	7,129	3,063	6,686	7,787	3,813	....	5,719	−2,725	427	5,816	....	....	Net Borrowing: Domestic	84a
	3,910	7,116	6,471	3,290	5,319	4,506	−225	1,001	3,588	3,650	8,258	4,588	−445	....	....	Foreign	85a
	−152	−690	929	−2,739	−1,620	−1,768	4,310	2,211	....	582	−773	68	−2,003	....	....	Use of Cash Balances	87
	10,197	11,632	13,519	17,166	19,003	26,009	....	....	51,571	58,987	57,501	58,920	67,225	....	....	Debt: Domestic	88a
	20,697	30,557	40,704	55,387	75,368	84,835	....	....	156,786	161,608	159,404	115,549	136,952	....	....	Foreign	89a
Billions of Dirhams																**National Accounts**	
	11.13	14.02	15.44	17.64	22.47	25.81	26.03	27.46	44.88	42.75	52.26	53.60	55.87	....	....	Exports of Goods & Services	90c
	13.59	15.08	17.00	16.63	17.48	20.52	23.75	24.71	28.04	30.41	32.98	36.80	39.74	....	....	Government Consumption	91f
	16.48	20.51	25.38	24.23	25.95	29.93	32.99	31.63	37.24	44.17	51.00	53.79	57.37	....	....	Gross Fixed Capital Formation	93e
	1.45	.13	.84	−.45	2.45	5.20	2.18	1.41	1.03	1.76	2.58	1.27	1.00	....	....	Increase/Decrease(-) in Stocks	93i
	50.93	55.32	63.57	69.30	81.15	89.83	110.61	111.83	115.99	127.20	138.70	160.74	159.67	....	....	Private Consumption	96f
	−19.49	−26.02	−29.33	−28.21	−37.15	−41.77	−40.84	−40.27	−44.93	−52.36	−63.55	−65.45	−68.07	....	....	Imports of Goods & Services	98c
	74.09	79.03	92.90	99.14	112.34	129.51	154.73	156.69	182.30	193.93	213.99	240.76	245.57	....	....	Gross Domestic Product	99b
	1.63	1.23	.89	1.77	2.64	2.56	7.60	8.04	4.38	3.52	10.45	9.27	9.92	....	....	Net Factor Inc/Pmts(-) Abroad	98.n
	75.72	80.26	93.79	100.91	114.98	132.07	162.33	164.73	186.61	197.46	224.44	250.03	255.50	....	....	Gross Nat'l Expenditure = GNP	99a
	67.40	72.61	85.24	89.59	....	....	....	....	....	....	....	....	....	....	....	Nat'l Income, Market Prices	99e
	I146.94	142.87	156.62	155.74	162.51	172.78	187.26	182.34	201.36	206.31	213.99	225.02	218.41	217.87	....	Gross Dom. Prod. 1990 Prices	99b.p
	50.4	55.3	59.3	63.7	69.1	75.0	82.6	85.9	90.5	94.0	100.0	107.0	112.4	....	....	GDP Deflator (1990=100)	99bi p
Midyear Estimates																	
	20.05	20.65	I20.31	20.91	21.33	21.84	22.35	22.88	23.41	23.95	24.49	25.02	25.55	26.07	26.59	Population	99z

Mozambique

688

		1965	1966	1967	1968	1969	1970	1971	1972	1973	1974	1975	1976	1977	1978	1979
Exchange Rates															*Meticais per SDR:*	
Market Rate	aa	28.83	28.98	28.86	28.77	28.65	28.75	29.92	29.31	31.18	30.11	32.16	36.65	39.54	42.24	42.50
											Meticais per US Dollar: End of Period (ae)					
Market Rate	ae	28.83	28.98	28.86	28.77	28.65	28.75	27.56	27.00	25.84	24.60	27.47	31.55	32.55	32.42	32.26
Market Rate	rf	28.75	28.75	28.75	28.75	28.75	28.75	29.60	27.05	24.52	25.41	25.55	30.23	33.02	33.00	32.56
Fund Position															*Millions of SDRs:*	
Quota	2f.s	....	....	....	....	....	....	....	....	....	....	....	....	....	....	....
SDRs	1b.s	....	....	....	....	....	....	....	....	....	....	....	....	....	....	....
Reserve Position in the Fund	1c.s	....	....	....	....	....	....	....	....	....	....	....	....	....	....	....
Total Fund Cred.&Loans Outstg.	2tl	....	....	....	....	....	....	....	....	....	....	....	....	....	....	....
International Liquidity															*Millions of US Dollars Unless Otherwise Indicated:*	
Total Reserves minus Gold	1l.d	....	....	....	....	....	....	....	....	....	....	....	....	....	....	....
SDRs	1b.d	....	....	....	....	....	....	....	....	....	....	....	....	....	....	....
Reserve Position in the Fund	1c.d	....	....	....	....	....	....	....	....	....	....	....	....	....	....	....
Foreign Exchange	1d.d	....	....	....	....	....	....	....	....	....	....	....	....	....	....	....
Monetary Authorities: Other Liab.	4..d	....	....	....	....	....	....	....	....	....	....	....	....	....	....	....
Deposit Money Banks: Assets	7a.d	....	....	....	....	....	....	....	....	....	....	....	....	....	....	....
Liabilities	7b.d	....	....	....	....	....	....	....	....	....	....	....	....	....	....	....
Monetary Authorities															*Billions of Meticais:*	
Foreign Assets	11	....	....	....	....	....	....	....	....	....	....	....	....	....	....	....
Claims on Central Government	12a	....	....	....	....	....	....	....	....	....	....	....	....	....	....	....
Claims on Local Government	12b	....	....	....	....	....	....	....	....	....	....	....	....	....	....	....
Claims on Nonfin.Pub.Enterprises	12c	....	....	....	....	....	....	....	....	....	....	....	....	....	....	....
Claims on Private Sector	12d	....	....	....	....	....	....	....	....	....	....	....	....	....	....	....
Reserve Money	14	....	....	....	....	....	....	....	....	....	....	....	....	....	....	....
of which: Currency Outside DMBs	14a	....	....	....	....	....	....	....	....	....	....	....	....	....	....	....
Time & Fgn. Currency Deposits	15	....	....	....	....	....	....	....	....	....	....	....	....	....	....	....
Foreign Liabilities	16c	....	....	....	....	....	....	....	....	....	....	....	....	....	....	....
Long-Term Foreign Liabilities	16cl	....	....	....	....	....	....	....	....	....	....	....	....	....	....	....
Government Deposits	16d	....	....	....	....	....	....	....	....	....	....	....	....	....	....	....
Central Govt. Lending Funds	16f	....	....	....	....	....	....	....	....	....	....	....	....	....	....	....
Other Items (Net)	17r	....	....	....	....	....	....	....	....	....	....	....	....	....	....	....
of which: Valuation Adjustment	17rv	....	....	....	....	....	....	....	....	....	....	....	....	....	....	....
Deposit Money Banks															*Billions of Meticais:*	
Reserves	20	....	....	....	....	....	....	....	....	....	....	....	....	....	....	....
Foreign Assets	21	....	....	....	....	....	....	....	....	....	....	....	....	....	....	....
Claims on Central Government	22a	....	....	....	....	....	....	....	....	....	....	....	....	....	....	....
Claims on Local Government	22b	....	....	....	....	....	....	....	....	....	....	....	....	....	....	....
Claims on Nonfin.Pub.Enterprises	22c	....	....	....	....	....	....	....	....	....	....	....	....	....	....	....
Claims on Private Sector	22d	....	....	....	....	....	....	....	....	....	....	....	....	....	....	....
Demand Deposits	24	....	....	....	....	....	....	....	....	....	....	....	....	....	....	....
Time Deposits	25	....	....	....	....	....	....	....	....	....	....	....	....	....	....	....
Foreign Liabilities	26c	....	....	....	....	....	....	....	....	....	....	....	....	....	....	....
Long-Term Foreign Liabilities	26cl	....	....	....	....	....	....	....	....	....	....	....	....	....	....	....
Government Deposits	26d	....	....	....	....	....	....	....	....	....	....	....	....	....	....	....
Central Govt. Lending Funds	26f	....	....	....	....	....	....	....	....	....	....	....	....	....	....	....
Other Items (Net)	27r	....	....	....	....	....	....	....	....	....	....	....	....	....	....	....
Other Banking Institutions															*Billions of Meticais:*	
Claims on Nonfin.Pub.Enterprises	42c	....	....	....	....	....	....	....	....	....	....	....	....	....	....	....
Claims on Private Sector	42d	....	....	....	....	....	....	....	....	....	....	....	....	....	....	....
Claims on Deposit Money Banks	42e	....	....	....	....	....	....	....	....	....	....	....	....	....	....	....
Central Govt. Lending Funds	46f	....	....	....	....	....	....	....	....	....	....	....	....	....	....	....
Credit from Deposit Money Banks	46h	....	....	....	....	....	....	....	....	....	....	....	....	....	....	....
Other Items (Net)	47r	....	....	....	....	....	....	....	....	....	....	....	....	....	....	....
Banking Survey															*Billions of Meticais:*	
Foreign Assets (Net)	51n	....	....	....	....	....	....	....	....	....	....	....	....	....	....	....
Domestic Credit	52	....	....	....	....	....	....	....	....	....	....	....	....	....	....	....
Claims on Government (Net)	52an	....	....	....	....	....	....	....	....	....	....	....	....	....	....	....
Claims on Nonfin.Pub.Enterprises	52c	....	....	....	....	....	....	....	....	....	....	....	....	....	....	....
Claims on Private Sector	52d	....	....	....	....	....	....	....	....	....	....	....	....	....	....	....
Liquid Liabilities	55l	....	....	....	....	....	....	....	....	....	....	....	....	....	....	....
Central Govt. Lending Funds	56f	....	....	....	....	....	....	....	....	....	....	....	....	....	....	....
Other Items (Net)	57r	....	....	....	....	....	....	....	....	....	....	....	....	....	....	....
Prices															*Index Numbers (1990=100):*	
Consumer Prices	64	....	....	....	....	....	....	....	....	....	....	....	....	....	....	....

Mozambique
688

	1980	1981	1982	1983	1984	1985	1986	1987	1988	1989	1990	1991	1992	1993	1994		
End of Period																**Exchange Rates**	
	41.77	41.61	42.12	43.09	42.69	45.22	48.12	573.13	842.67	1,077.22	1,476.91	2,639.68	ℐ4058.18	7,339.15	9,709.46	Market Rate	aa
Period Average (rf)																	
	32.75	35.75	38.18	41.16	43.55	41.17	39.34	403.99	626.19	819.70	1,038.14	1,845.37	ℐ2951.40	5,343.16	6,651.00	Market Rate	ae
	32.40	35.35	37.77	40.18	42.44	43.18	40.43	290.73	524.64	744.92	929.09	1,434.47	2,516.55	3,874.24	6,038.59	Market Rate	rf
End of Period																**Fund Position**	
	....	....	....	....	61.00	61.00	61.00	61.00	61.00	61.00	61.00	61.00	84.00	84.00	84.00	Quota	2f. s
	....	....	....	....	—	—	—	.02	.02	.02	.02	.03	.03	.03	.03	SDRs	1b. s
	....	....	....	....	—	—	.01	.01	.01	.01	.01	.01	.01	.01	.01	Reserve Position in the Fund	1c. s
	....	....	....	....	—	—	—	12.20	30.50	42.70	51.85	82.35	126.88	137.86	145.24	Total Fund Cred.&Loans Outstg.	2tl
End of Period																**International Liquidity**	
	....	....	....	....	55.29	45.89	56.75	118.02	173.60	203.50	231.75	239.70	....	....	....	Total Reserves minus Gold	1l. d
	....	....	....	....	—	—	—	.03	.03	.03	.03	.04	.04	.04	.05	SDRs	1b. d
	....	....	....	....	—	—	.01	.01	.01	.01	.01	.01	.01	.01	.01	Reserve Position in the Fund	1c. d
	....	....	....	....	55.29	45.89	56.74	117.98	173.56	203.46	231.70	239.64	....	....	....	Foreign Exchange	1d. d
	....	....	....	....	694.78	886.92	1,057.17	1,116.49	1,070.74	1,066.41	1,072.74	867.20	....	....	....	Monetary Authorities: Other Liab.	4.. d
	....	....	....	....	1.26	1.43	1.50	.21	.21	.66	5.94	14.09	....	....	....	Deposit Money Banks: Assets	7a. d
	....	....	....	....	—	.02	.03	.01	.01	.38	5.26	15.47	....	....	....	Liabilities	7b. d
End of Period																**Monetary Authorities**	
	....	....	....	....	4.0	2.8	3.3	61.0	126.1	189.3	267.9	486.7	....	....	....	Foreign Assets	11
	....	....	....	....	72.1	74.4	82.4	89.6	129.9	173.9	190.5	244.1	....	....	....	Claims on Central Government	12a
	....	....	....	....	—	—	—	—	—	2.5	9.7	9.8	....	....	....	Claims on Local Government	12b
	....	....	....	....	—	—	—	—	—	—	1.6	5.0	....	....	....	Claims on Nonfin.Pub.Enterprises	12c
	....	....	....	....	78.7	91.9	104.7	136.4	183.5	242.2	315.2	443.1	....	....	....	Claims on Private Sector	12d
	....	....	....	....	62.9	73.8	88.1	140.1	216.5	ℐ312.6	383.5	517.0	....	....	....	Reserve Money	14
	....	....	....	....	28.8	31.2	35.0	38.6	64.6	94.1	147.1	189.6	....	....	....	of which: Currency Outside DMBs	14a
	....	....	....	....	—	—	—	—	4.4	3.5	5.1	10.3	27.9	....	....	Time & Fgn. Currency Deposits	15
	....	....	....	....	3.0	2.3	3.0	45.1	84.9	ℐ118.7	173.1	299.7	....	....	....	Foreign Liabilities	16c
	....	....	....	....	27.2	34.2	38.6	412.9	611.0	801.3	1,017.6	1,516.6	....	....	....	Long-Term Foreign Liabilities	16cl
	....	....	....	....	49.5	47.8	47.9	38.1	—	62.6	ℐ116.0	135.2	210.7	....	....	Government Deposits	16d
	....	....	....	....	—	—	—	—	41.0	90.2	127.1	191.1	....	....	....	Central Govt. Lending Funds	16f
	....	....	....	....	12.1	11.0	12.7	−353.7	−580.0	−836.0	−1,061.8	−1,574.3	....	....	....	Other Items (Net)	17r
	....	....	....	....	....	....	....	....	−563.0	−760.8	−1,051.0	−1,675.0	....	....	....	of which: Valuation Adjustment	17rv
End of Period																**Deposit Money Banks**	
	....	....	....	....	7.7	13.6	15.8	29.2	44.7	80.1	102.5	101.5	....	....	....	Reserves	20
	....	....	....	....	.1	.1	.1	.1	.1	.5	6.2	26.0	....	....	....	Foreign Assets	21
	....	....	....	....	7.9	8.4	8.4	9.0	12.1	12.2	10.2	12.7	....	....	....	Claims on Central Government	22a
	....	....	....	....	—	—	—	—	—	—	.1	—	....	....	....	Claims on Local Government	22b
	....	....	....	....	16.3	18.2	19.9	23.8	29.6	32.2	37.6	41.6	....	....	....	Claims on Nonfin.Pub.Enterprises	22c
	....	....	....	....	6.9	7.1	8.9	10.0	22.4	56.1	79.4	132.1	....	....	....	Claims on Private Sector	22d
	....	....	....	....	25.8	32.8	38.9	40.2	71.8	129.3	178.2	224.1	....	....	....	Demand Deposits	24
	....	....	....	....	2.8	3.9	4.1	5.4	7.1	10.8	16.2	20.8	....	....	....	Time Deposits	25
	....	....	....	....	—	—	—	—	—	.3	5.3	28.4	....	....	....	Foreign Liabilities	26c
	....	....	....	....	—	—	—	—	—	—	.2	.2	....	....	....	Long-Term Foreign Liabilities	26cl
	....	....	....	....	8.2	8.0	8.0	21.0	26.9	39.1	40.4	60.8	....	....	....	Government Deposits	26d
	....	....	....	....	—	—	—	.7	.7	.7	.7	.7	....	....	....	Central Govt. Lending Funds	26f
	....	....	....	....	2.2	2.6	2.1	4.7	2.5	.9	−4.9	−21.1	....	....	....	Other Items (Net)	27r
End of Period																**Other Banking Institutions**	
	....	....	....	....	....	....	....	....	4.0	18.7	17.4	17.1	....	....	....	Claims on Nonfin.Pub.Enterprises	42c
	....	....	....	....	....	....	....	....	2.9	13.1	15.9	15.8	....	....	....	Claims on Private Sector	42d
	....	....	....	....	....	....	....	....	—	5.1	−2.1	−.8	....	....	....	Claims on Deposit Money Banks	42e
	....	....	....	....	....	....	....	....	6.5	22.1	22.9	23.1	....	....	....	Central Govt. Lending Funds	46f
	....	....	....	....	....	....	....	....	6.6	10.0	8.5	—	....	....	....	Credit from Deposit Money Banks	46h
	....	....	....	....	....	....	....	....	−1.1	−.3	−.2	9.1	....	....	....	Other Items (Net)	47r
End of Period																**Banking Survey**	
	....	....	....	....	−26.2	−33.6	−38.2	−397.0	−569.7	ℐ−730.5	−922.0	−1,332.2	....	....	....	Foreign Assets (Net)	51n
	....	....	....	....	124.2	144.2	168.4	209.7	295.0	ℐ395.8	502.2	649.9	....	....	....	Domestic Credit	52
	....	....	....	....	22.3	27.0	34.9	39.5	52.5	ℐ33.5	35.1	−4.8	....	....	....	Claims on Government (Net)	52an
	....	....	....	....	16.3	18.2	19.9	23.8	33.6	50.9	56.6	63.7	....	....	....	Claims on Nonfin.Pub.Enterprises	52c
	....	....	....	....	85.7	99.0	113.6	146.4	208.9	311.4	410.5	591.0	....	....	....	Claims on Private Sector	52d
	....	....	....	....	83.6	96.5	113.7	162.6	255.0	381.0	522.3	709.0	....	....	....	Liquid Liabilities	55l
	....	....	....	....	—	—	—	.7	48.2	113.0	150.8	214.9	....	....	....	Central Govt. Lending Funds	56f
	....	....	....	....	14.4	14.0	16.5	−350.6	−577.9	−828.8	−1,092.9	−1,606.1	....	....	....	Other Items (Net)	57r
Period Averages																**Prices**	
	....	....	....	....	....	8.9	....	32.3	48.5	68.0	ℐ100.0	132.9	193.4	275.0	....	Consumer Prices	64

Mozambique
688

		1965	1966	1967	1968	1969	1970	1971	1972	1973	1974	1975	1976	1977	1978	1979
International Transactions															*Millions of US Dollars*	
Exports	70..d	108	112	122	154	142	156	163	176	225	298	198	150	149	162	255
Imports, cif	71..d	174	208	206	238	261	326	341	330	460	467	411	300	328	521	571
Imports, fob	71.vd	155	185	184	212	233	291	305	294	411	417	367	268	293	465	509
Balance of Payments															*Millions of US Dollars*	
Goods: Exports f.o.b.	78aa d	....	....	....	....	....	....	....	....	....	....	....	....	....	....	....
Goods: Imports f.o.b.	78ab d	....	....	....	....	....	....	....	....	....	....	....	....	....	....	....
Trade Balance	78ac d	....	....	....	....	....	....	....	....	....	....	....	....	....	....	....
Services: Credit	78ad d	....	....	....	....	....	....	....	....	....	....	....	....	....	....	....
Services: Debit	78ae d	....	....	....	....	....	....	....	....	....	....	....	....	....	....	....
Balance on Goods and Services	78af d	....	....	....	....	....	....	....	....	....	....	....	....	....	....	....
Income: Credit	78ag d	....	....	....	....	....	....	....	....	....	....	....	....	....	....	....
Income: Debit	78ah d	....	....	....	....	....	....	....	....	....	....	....	....	....	....	....
Balance on Goods, Serv., & Inc.	78ai d	....	....	....	....	....	....	....	....	....	....	....	....	....	....	....
Current Transfers, n.i.e.: Credit	78aj d	....	....	....	....	....	....	....	....	....	....	....	....	....	....	....
Current Transfers: Debit	78ak d	....	....	....	....	....	....	....	....	....	....	....	....	....	....	....
Current Account, n.i.e.	78al d	....	....	....	....	....	....	....	....	....	....	....	....	....	....	....
Capital Account, n.i.e.: Credit	78ba d	....	....	....	....	....	....	....	....	....	....	....	....	....	....	....
Capital Account: Debit	78bb d	....	....	....	....	....	....	....	....	....	....	....	....	....	....	....
Capital Account, n.i.e.	78bc d	....	....	....	....	....	....	....	....	....	....	....	....	....	....	....
Direct Investment Abroad	78bd d	....	....	....	....	....	....	....	....	....	....	....	....	....	....	....
Dir. Invest. in Rep. Econ., n.i.e.	78be d	....	....	....	....	....	....	....	....	....	....	....	....	....	....	....
Portfolio Investment Assets	78bf d	....	....	....	....	....	....	....	....	....	....	....	....	....	....	....
Portfolio Investment Liab., n.i.e.	78bg d	....	....	....	....	....	....	....	....	....	....	....	....	....	....	....
Other Investment Assets	78bh d	....	....	....	....	....	....	....	....	....	....	....	....	....	....	....
Other Investment Liab., n.i.e.	78bi d	....	....	....	....	....	....	....	....	....	....	....	....	....	....	....
Financial Account, n.i.e.	78bj d	....	....	....	....	....	....	....	....	....	....	....	....	....	....	....
Net Errors and Omissions	78ca d	....	....	....	....	....	....	....	....	....	....	....	....	....	....	....
Overall Balance	78cb d	....	....	....	....	....	....	....	....	....	....	....	....	....	....	....
Reserves and Related Items	79da d	....	....	....	....	....	....	....	....	....	....	....	....	....	....	....
Reserve Assets	79db d	....	....	....	....	....	....	....	....	....	....	....	....	....	....	....
Use of Fund Credit and Loans	79dc d	....	....	....	....	....	....	....	....	....	....	....	....	....	....	....
Liabs.Constit.For.Auth.Reserves	79dd d	....	....	....	....	....	....	....	....	....	....	....	....	....	....	....
Exceptional Financing	79de d	....	....	....	....	....	....	....	....	....	....	....	....	....	....	....
National Accounts															*Billions of Meticais*	
Exports of Goods & Services	90c	....	....	....	....	....	....	....	....	....	....	....	....	....	....	....
Government Consumption	91f	....	....	....	....	....	....	....	....	....	....	....	....	....	....	....
Gross Fixed Capital Formation	93e	....	....	....	....	....	....	....	....	....	....	....	....	....	....	....
Net Increase/Decrease(-) in Stocks	93i	....	....	....	....	....	....	....	....	....	....	....	....	....	....	....
Private Consumption	96f	....	....	....	....	....	....	....	....	....	....	....	....	....	....	....
Imports of Goods & Services	98c	....	....	....	....	....	....	....	....	....	....	....	....	....	....	....
Gross Domestic Product	99b	....	....	....	....	....	....	....	....	....	....	....	....	....	....	....
Gross Nat'l Expenditure = GNP	99a	....	....	....	....	....	....	....	....	....	....	....	....	....	....	....
Gross Dom. Prod. 1990 Prices	99b.p	....	....	....	....	....	....	....	....	....	....	....	....	....	....	....
GDP Deflator (1990=100)	99bi p	....	....	....	....	....	....	....	....	....	....	....	....	....	....	....
																Millions
Population	99z	7.37	7.53	7.68	7.86	7.95	8.14	8.36	8.52	....	....	9.72	10.16	10.66	11.17	11.66

Mozambique

688

1980	1981	1982	1983	1984	1985	1986	1987	1988	1989	1990	1991	1992	1993	1994		
Millions of US Dollars															**International Transactions**	
281	281	229	132	96	77	79	97	103	105	126	162	139	132	....	Exports	70..d
800	801	836	636	540	424	543	642	736	808	878	899	855	955	....	Imports, cif	71..d
714	715	746	568	482	378	485	573	657	721	784	803	763	853	....	Imports, fob	71.v d
Minus Sign Indicates Debit															**Balance of Payments**	
280.8	280.8	229.2	131.6	95.7	76.6	79.1	97.0	103.0	104.8	126.4	162.3	139.3	....	....	Goods: Exports f.o.b.	78aa d
−720.1	−721.0	−752.3	−572.8	−485.7	−381.4	−488.4	−577.8	−662.0	−726.9	−789.7	−808.8	−798.5	....	....	Goods: Imports f.o.b.	78ab d
−439.3	−440.2	−523.1	−441.2	−390.0	−304.8	−409.3	−480.8	−559.0	−622.1	−663.3	−646.5	−659.2	....	....	Trade Balance	78ac d
117.9	114.0	107.8	90.6	61.0	66.3	62.9	79.0	85.0	95.4	103.0	147.2	164.6	....	....	Services: Credit	78ad d
−123.5	−137.5	−140.2	−121.4	−97.6	−100.1	−154.3	−175.8	−190.9	−195.5	−206.0	−236.8	−246.4	....	....	Services: Debit	78ae d
−444.9	−463.7	−555.5	−472.0	−426.6	−338.6	−500.7	−577.6	−664.9	−722.2	−766.3	−736.1	−741.0	....	....	Balance on Goods and Services	78af d
53.4	64.5	63.5	75.2	57.0	40.8	50.0	58.0	71.6	71.3	70.4	55.6	58.0	....	....	Income: Credit	78ag d
−31.4	−65.3	−83.9	−108.1	−106.6	−142.3	−177.7	−173.4	−142.0	−196.8	−167.8	−165.5	−197.7	....	....	Income: Debit	78ah d
−422.9	−464.5	−575.9	−504.9	−476.2	−440.1	−628.4	−693.0	−735.3	−847.7	−863.7	−846.0	−880.7	....	....	Balance on Goods, Serv., & Inc.	78ai d
55.9	57.4	79.4	89.6	167.8	139.0	219.1	304.2	376.8	387.5	448.4	501.7	499.4	....	....	Current Transfers, n.i.e.: Credit	78aj d
—	—	—	—	—	—	—	—	—	—	—	—	—	....	....	Current Transfers: Debit	78ak d
−367.0	−407.1	−496.5	−415.3	−308.4	−301.1	−409.3	−388.8	−358.5	−460.2	−415.3	−344.3	−381.3	....	....	Current Account, n.i.e.	78al d
—	—	—	—	—	—	—	—	—	—	—	—	—	....	....	Capital Account, n.i.e.: Credit	78ba d
—	—	—	—	—	—	—	—	—	—	—	—	—	....	....	Capital Account: Debit	78bb d
—	—	—	—	—	—	—	—	—	—	—	—	—	....	....	Capital Account, n.i.e.	78bc d
—	—	—	—	—	—	—	—	—	—	—	—	—	....	....	Direct Investment Abroad	78bd d
—	—	—	—	—	—	1.5	6.2	4.5	3.4	9.2	22.5	25.3	....	....	Dir. Invest. in Rep. Econ., n.i.e.	78be d
—	—	—	—	—	—	—	—	—	—	—	—	—	....	....	Portfolio Investment Assets	78bf d
—	—	—	—	—	—	—	—	—	—	—	—	—	....	....	Portfolio Investment Liab., n.i.e.	78bg d
—	−2.2	−5.8	−3.3	−9.1	1.9	4.5	—	—	—	—	—	—	....	....	Other Investment Assets	78bh d
364.2	412.7	404.0	108.9	−104.0	−54.3	−26.7	−98.4	−130.7	−58.4	−92.7	−210.0	−148.2	....	....	Other Investment Liab., n.i.e.	78bi d
364.2	410.5	398.2	105.6	−113.1	−52.4	−20.7	−92.2	−126.2	−55.0	−83.5	−187.5	−122.9	....	....	Financial Account, n.i.e.	78bj d
−29.6	−70.1	−42.3	9.0	25.8	−12.8	−28.7	40.0	84.7	56.7	66.3	−3.9	32.5	....	....	Net Errors and Omissions	78ca d
−32.4	−66.7	−140.6	−300.7	−395.7	−366.3	−458.7	−441.0	−400.0	−458.5	−432.5	−535.7	−471.7	....	....	Overall Balance	78cb d
32.4	66.7	140.6	300.7	395.7	366.3	458.7	441.0	400.0	458.5	432.5	535.7	471.7	....	....	Reserves and Related Items	79da d
32.4	66.7	140.6	15.4	−23.0	20.5	−23.5	−58.2	−25.2	2.9	−5.9	−12.7	−37.2	....	....	Reserve Assets	79db d
—	—	—	—	—	—	—	15.7	25.3	15.9	12.0	41.2	62.5	....	....	Use of Fund Credit and Loans	79dc d
—	—	—	—	—	—	—	—	—	—	—	—	—	....	....	Liabs.Constit.For.Auth.Reserves	79dd d
—	—	—	285.3	418.7	345.8	482.2	483.5	399.9	439.7	426.4	507.2	446.4	....	....	Exceptional Financing	79de d
Billions of Meticais															**National Accounts**	
....	....	18	9	7	6	6	51	99	149	213	444	739	1,162	....	Exports of Goods & Services	90c
14	17	19	22	21	23	27	68	115	195	271	378	598	925	....	Government Consumption	91f
15	16	18	15	18	19	23	179	362	557	791	1,250	2,016	3,759	....	Gross Fixed Capital Formation	93e
....	....	....	....	....	....	....	....	....	....	....	....	....	....	....	Net Increase/Decrease(−) in Stocks	93i
64	65	62	57	61	83	90	298	482	742	946	1,420	2,131	3,829	....	Private Consumption	96f
....	....	−34	−28	−25	−21	−24	−202	−427	−652	−881	−1,436	−2,360	−4,031	....	Imports of Goods & Services	98c
78	82	79	75	82	111	122	393	631	991	1,341	2,056	3,126	5,463	....	Gross Domestic Product	99b
79	81	91	77	87	113	123	432	810	1,214	1,713	2,699	4,164	7,155	....	Gross Nat'l Expenditure = GNP	99a
....	....	....	....	1,018	1,031	1,006	1,155	1,254	1,329	1,341	1,416	1,403	1,527	....	Gross Dom. Prod. 1990 Prices	99b.p
....	....	....	....	8.1	10.8	12.1	34.0	50.3	74.6	100.0	145.2	222.8	357.7	....	GDP Deflator (1990=100)	99bi p
Midyear Estimates																
12.13	12.45	12.78	13.11	13.51	13.87	14.16	14.12	13.95	13.96	ɪ14.15	14.42	14.79	15.58	16.61	**Population**	99z

Myanmar

518

		1965	1966	1967	1968	1969	1970	1971	1972	1973	1974	1975	1976	1977	1978	1979
Exchange Rates															*Kyats per SDR*	
Official Rate	aa	4.7820	4.8050	4.8000	4.8100	4.7920	4.8020	5.9377	5.8650	5.8653	5.8891	7.7429	7.7429	8.5085	8.5085	8.5085
															Kyats per US Dollar	
Official Rate	ae	4.7820	4.8050	4.8000	4.8100	4.7920	4.8020	5.4690	5.4020	4.8620	4.8100	6.6777	6.7324	7.0873	6.6028	6.5186
Official Rate	rf	4.7619	4.7619	4.7619	4.7619	4.7619	4.7619	4.7648	5.4565	4.9283	4.8598	6.3676	6.7673	7.1194	6.8844	6.6538
Fund Position															*Millions of SDRs*	
Quota	2f.s	30.0	30.0	30.0	48.0	48.0	60.0	60.0	60.0	60.0	60.0	60.0	60.0	60.0	73.0	73.0
SDRs	1b.s	—	—	—	—	—	—	—	5.6	9.7	9.5	8.0	7.6	7.5	2.9	4.7
Reserve Position in the Fund	1c.s	7.5	7.5	—	—	—	—	—	—	—	—	—	—	—	—	—
Total Fund Cred.&Loans Outstg.	2tl	—	—	7.5	7.5	7.5	16.5	18.0	8.0	15.0	36.5	40.5	34.5	58.1	85.3	97.0
International Liquidity											*Millions of US Dollars Unless Otherwise Indicated*					
Total Reserves minus Gold	1l.d	96.9	100.3	71.4	68.9	45.6	ɪ31.4	48.8	40.2	91.9	182.4	132.8	118.3	103.3	96.4	203.3
SDRs	1b.d	—	—	—	—	—	—	—	6.1	11.7	11.7	9.4	8.8	9.1	3.8	6.2
Reserve Position in the Fund	1c.d	7.5	7.5	—	—	—	—	—	—	—	—	—	—	—	—	—
Foreign Exchange	1d.d	89.4	92.8	71.4	68.9	45.6	ɪ31.4	48.8	34.1	80.2	170.7	123.4	109.5	94.2	92.6	197.1
Gold (Million Fine Troy Ounces)	1ad	2.389	2.389	2.389	2.389	2.389	1.791	.617	.320	.200	.200	.200	.200	.226	.238	.251
Gold (National Valuation)	1and	83.6	83.6	83.6	83.6	83.6	62.7	23.4	12.2	8.4	8.5	8.2	8.1	9.6	10.9	11.6
Monetary Authorities: Other Assets	3..d	....	....	....	....	....	....	....	....	....	....	....	10.5	25.5	21.4	47.9
Other Liab.	4..d	....	....	....	....	....	5.3	2.3	6.7	7.0	10.1	9.3	9.6	17.0	57.1	50.6
Deposit Money Banks: Assets	7a.d	14.3	14.7	35.3	28.6	11.6	—	—	—	—	—	—	.1	.1	.3	.3
of which: Claims on Nonbanks	7ad d	....	....	....	....	....	—	—	—	—	—	—	.1	.1	.3	.3
Deposit Money Banks: Liabilities	7b.d	....	....	3.6	31.5	35.9	68.7	62.8	91.5	138.8	157.7	135.2	151.8	167.3	158.6	309.6
of which: Liab. to Nonbanks	7bd d	....	....	....	....	....	....	....	....	....	....	....	116.7	155.2	158.6	309.3
Monetary Authorities															*Millions of Kyats*	
Foreign Assets	11	853	873	734	720	610	ɪ477	442	366	541	1,066	1,132	841	858	908	1,705
Claims on Central Govt. (Net)	12an	1,401	1,331	1,534	1,644	1,760	ɪ2,240	2,634	3,390	3,537	4,603	5,720	5,501	5,044	3,885	2,846
Claims on Nonfin.Pub.Ents.(Net)	12cn	....	....	....	....	....	....	....	....	....	....	....	....	....	....	....
Claims on Deposit Money Banks	12e	....	....	....	....	....	242	117	162	309	106	191	181	621	3,165	4,933
Reserve Money	14	1,819	1,759	1,813	1,902	1,988	ɪ1,631	1,672	3,078	4,162	4,865	5,394	6,007	5,736	6,402	7,672
of which: Currency Outside DMBs	14a	1,700	1,645	1,719	1,742	1,844	ɪ1,742	1,786	2,222	2,840	3,647	4,448	4,945	5,146	5,783	6,448
Foreign Liabilities	16c	....	....	....	....	....	104	117	82	121	263	379	334	620	863	921
Long-Term Foreign Liabilities	16cl	....	....	....	....	....	—	—	—	—	—	—	—	—	248	242
Other Items (Net)	17r	435	445	455	462	382	ɪ1,284	1,569	794	−120	563	1,116	ɪ191	172	449	650
Deposit Money Banks															*Millions of Kyats*	
Reserves	20	....	....	....	....	....	−139	−162	817	1,272	1,173	923	1,466	1,029	1,097	2,334
Claims on Central Govt. (Net)	22an	547	544	463	589	654	ɪ491	402	482	360	582	979	608	2,602	3,570	2,576
Claims on Nonfin.Pub.Enterprises	22c	....	....	....	....	....	2	21	440	618	1,033	1,151	2,518	1,089	2,758	7,025
Claims on Private Sector	22d	145	172	155	179	217	ɪ482	488	685	773	580	790	1,336	1,743	2,363	2,009
Demand Deposits	24	364	576	591	588	513	ɪ167	196	233	253	305	388	442	439	515	555
Time, Savings,& Fgn.Currency Dep.	25	53	63	45	45	40	ɪ567	590	631	626	609	607	642	708	990	1,500
Long-Term Foreign Liabilities	26cl	....	....	....	....	....	53	78	152	336	305	450	561	962	878	1,734
Credit from Monetary Authorities	26g	....	....	....	....	....	242	117	162	309	106	191	181	621	3,165	4,933
Nonfin.Pub.Enterprises' Deposits	26k	....	....	....	....	....	194	117	583	651	1,260	1,792	2,484	2,409	3,006	2,994
Other Items (Net)	27r	....	....	....	....	....	47	8	159	221	20	132	1,259	924	798	1,741
Monetary Survey															*Millions of Kyats*	
Foreign Assets (Net)	31n	921	943	849	670	665	ɪ100	67	−54	89	349	301	47	15	−122	502
Domestic Credit	32	1,997	ɪ1,934	2,035	2,332	2,617	ɪ3,322	3,710	4,611	4,721	5,560	6,883	7,489	8,076	9,575	11,464
Claims on Central Govt. (Net)	32an	1,852	ɪ1,762	1,880	2,153	2,400	ɪ2,731	3,036	3,872	3,897	5,185	6,699	6,109	7,646	7,455	5,422
Claims on Nonfin.Pub.Ents(Net)	32cn	....	....	....	....	....	109	186	54	51	−204	−606	44	−1,313	−243	4,033
Claims on Private Sector	32d	145	172	155	179	217	ɪ482	488	685	773	580	790	1,336	1,743	2,363	2,009
Money	34	2,064	2,221	2,310	2,330	2,357	ɪ1,937	2,030	2,494	3,143	3,997	4,859	5,425	5,619	6,305	7,004
Quasi-Money	35	53	63	45	45	40	ɪ567	590	631	626	609	607	642	708	990	1,500
Long-Term Foreign Liabilities	36cl	....	....	....	....	....	53	78	152	336	305	450	561	962	1,126	1,976
Other Items (Net)	37r	800	591	529	627	741	ɪ864	1,079	1,281	704	998	1,268	557	409	604	1,007
Money plus Quasi-Money	35l	2,117	2,284	2,355	2,375	2,397	ɪ2,504	2,620	3,125	3,769	4,606	5,466	6,067	6,327	7,295	8,504
Interest Rates															*Percent Per Annum*	
Deposit Rate	60l	....	....	.75	.75	.75	.75	.75	.75	.75	.75	.75	.75	.88	1.50	1.50
Lending Rate	60p	....	....	....	....	....	....	....	....	....	....	....	6.00	6.33	8.00	8.00
Prices															*Index Numbers (1990=100)*	
Consumer Prices	64	10.4	13.0	13.1	13.4	12.8	12.3	12.6	13.5	17.0	21.2	28.0	34.2	33.8	31.8	33.6

Myanmar

	1980	1981	1982	1983	1984	1985	1986	1987	1988	1989	1990	1991	1992	1993	1994		
Exchange Rates																	
End of Period																	
Official Rate	8.5085	8.5085	8.5085	8.5085	8.5085	8.5085	8.5085	8.5085	8.5085	8.5085	8.5085	8.5085	8.5085	8.5085	8.5085	aa
End of Period (ae) Period Average (rf)																	
Official Rate	6.7572	7.3970	7.7775	8.2231	8.7512	7.8420	7.0395	6.1097	6.4104	6.4942	6.0804	6.0137	6.2411	6.2456	5.9030	ae
Official Rate	6.5983	7.2807	7.7903	8.0355	8.3855	8.4749	7.3304	6.6535	6.3945	6.7049	6.3386	6.2837	6.1045	6.1570	5.9749	rf
Fund Position																	
End of Period																	
Quota	109.5	109.5	109.5	137.0	137.0	137.0	137.0	137.0	137.0	137.0	137.0	137.0	184.9	184.9	184.9	2f. s
SDRs	5.4	2.4	1.1	.2	.1	—	—	.1	.1	.4	.6	.1	—	—	.2	.1	1b. s
Reserve Position in the Fund	—	9.0	13.0	6.9	6.9	—	—	—	—	—	—	—	—	—	—	1c. s
Total Fund Cred.&Loans Outstg.	87.7	107.6	130.3	141.5	129.7	106.4	68.0	28.9	8.0	2.0	.2	—	—	—	—	2tl
International Liquidity																	
End of Period																	
Total Reserves minus Gold	260.6	229.0	104.3	89.4	62.1	33.9	33.1	27.2	77.4	263.4	312.8	258.4	280.1	302.9	422.0	1l. d
SDRs	6.9	2.7	1.2	.2	.1	—	—	.1	.1	.6	.8	.2	—	.3	.1	1b. d
Reserve Position in the Fund	—	10.5	14.3	7.2	6.7	—	—	—	—	—	—	—	—	—	—	1c. d
Foreign Exchange	253.7	215.8	88.8	82.0	55.3	33.9	33.1	27.1	77.3	262.8	312.0	258.2	280.1	302.6	421.9	1d. d
Gold (Million Fine Troy Ounces)	.251	.251	.251	.251	.251	.251	.251	.251	.251	.251	.251	.251	.251	.251	.251	1ad
Gold (National Valuation)	11.2	10.2	9.7	9.2	8.6	9.7	10.8	12.5	11.8	11.6	12.5	12.6	12.1	12.1	12.8	1an d
Monetary Authorities: Other Assets	75.2	47.9	45.7	19.1	26.4	30.0	13.0	. . .	. . .	. . .	. . .	. . .	. . .	. . .	. . .	3..d
Other Liab.	53.2	48.4	43.8	46.1	42.7	68.4	84.6	114.3	120.8	349.4	337.1	338.1	. . .	. . .	. . .	4..d
Deposit Money Banks: Assets	.7	1.9	1.4	1.6	1.4	1.5	2.6	2.5	2.0	3.4	26.8	. . .	. . .	. . .	. . .	7a. d
of which: Claims on Nonbanks	.7	1.9	1.4	1.6	1.4	1.5	2.6	2.5	2.0	3.4	26.8	. . .	. . .	. . .	. . .	7ad d
Deposit Money Banks: Liabilities	393.8	515.6	514.7	605.0	604.9	796.0	1,155.5	1,469.3	1,610.0	59.0	45.9	. . .	. . .	. . .	. . .	7b. d
of which: Liab. to Nonbanks	393.8	515.6	514.7	605.0	604.9	740.2	1,133.0	1,455.6	1,602.6	53.4	44.9	. . .	. . .	. . .	. . .	7bd d
Monetary Authorities																	
End of Period																	
Foreign Assets	2,201	2,124	1,242	968	850	577	400	363	659	1,537	1,796	. . .	. . .	. . .	. . .	11
Claims on Central Govt. (Net)	1,122	−1,529	−3,547	−5,451	−7,879	−9,605	−5,950	−10,365	−10,650	⌶42,740	51,813	. . .	. . .	. . .	. . .	12an
Claims on Nonfin.Pub.Ents.(Net)																	12cn
Claims on Deposit Money Banks	7,012	12,273	13,554	17,887	21,846	28,533	29,481	31,227	37,564	11,208	10,607	. . .	. . .	. . .	. . .	12e
Reserve Money	8,560	10,278	9,752	10,823	12,360	11,034	15,627	8,710	15,318	42,263	51,387	. . .	. . .	. . .	. . .	14
of which: Currency Outside DMBs	7,289	8,410	9,045	10,165	11,768	10,504	15,218	8,299	14,659	19,926	29,211	. . .	. . .	. . .	. . .	14a
Foreign Liabilities	838	992	1,189	1,288	1,173	1,104	787	540	509	⌶11,898	1,671	. . .	. . .	. . .	. . .	16c
Long-Term Foreign Liabilities	277	292	269	309	313	348	394	409	334	⌶388	381	. . .	. . .	. . .	. . .	16cl
Other Items (Net)	660	1,308	41	983	970	7,020	7,123	11,565	11,411	10,938	10,777	. . .	. . .	. . .	. . .	17r
Deposit Money Banks																	
End of Period																	
Reserves	2,419	2,740	1,290	1,196	1,055	879	645	659	1,148	23,340	22,955	. . .	. . .	. . .	. . .	20
Claims on Central Govt. (Net)	2,948	4,491	4,085	5,680	5,728	6,378	7,315	7,488	9,011	⌶−8,373	−10,240	. . .	. . .	. . .	. . .	22an
Claims on Nonfin.Pub.Enterprises	10,158	15,202	21,020	25,734	31,678	35,926	41,939	46,056	51,113	⌶619	918	. . .	. . .	. . .	. . .	22c
Claims on Private Sector	2,131	2,540	2,470	2,628	2,396	2,762	3,009	2,998	2,801	3,262	7,208	. . .	. . .	. . .	. . .	22d
Demand Deposits	611	696	751	894	1,002	1,040	1,112	1,175	1,009	1,391	1,376	. . .	. . .	. . .	. . .	24
Time, Savings,& Fgn.Currency Dep.	2,047	2,866	3,752	4,603	5,659	6,558	7,447	8,446	7,615	9,467	11,789	. . .	. . .	. . .	. . .	25
Long-Term Foreign Liabilities	2,331	3,056	3,623	4,656	4,980	5,440	7,685	8,659	10,089	. . .	. . .	. . .	. . .	. . .	. . .	26cl
Credit from Monetary Authorities	7,012	12,273	13,554	17,887	21,846	28,533	29,481	31,227	37,564	11,208	10,607	. . .	. . .	. . .	. . .	26g
Nonfin.Pub.Enterprises' Deposits	3,402	4,154	4,292	4,606	4,597	4,320	4,829	4,358	5,446	555	—	. . .	. . .	. . .	. . .	26k
Other Items (Net)	1,688	1,314	2,231	1,886	1,937	−920	1,203	1,991	713	⌶2,858	4,805	. . .	. . .	. . .	. . .	27r
Monetary Survey																	
End of Period																	
Foreign Assets (Net)	1,038	388	−316	−627	−625	−1,317	−818	−480	−69	−723	9	. . .	. . .	. . .	. . .	31n
Domestic Credit	12,958	16,551	19,737	23,986	27,326	31,141	41,484	41,819	46,829	⌶37,693	49,699	. . .	. . .	. . .	. . .	32
Claims on Central Govt. (Net)	4,070	2,962	538	229	−2,151	−3,227	1,365	−2,877	−1,639	⌶34,367	41,573	. . .	. . .	. . .	. . .	32an
Claims on Nonfin.Pub.Ents(Net)	6,757	11,049	16,729	21,129	27,081	31,606	37,110	41,698	45,667	⌶64	918	. . .	. . .	. . .	. . .	32cn
Claims on Private Sector	2,131	2,540	2,470	2,628	2,396	2,762	3,009	2,998	2,801	3,262	7,208	. . .	. . .	. . .	. . .	32d
Money	7,900	9,112	9,803	11,067	12,777	11,551	16,337	9,474	15,668	21,317	30,587	. . .	. . .	. . .	. . .	34
Quasi-Money	2,047	2,866	3,752	4,603	5,659	6,558	7,447	8,446	7,615	9,467	11,789	. . .	. . .	. . .	. . .	35
Long-Term Foreign Liabilities	2,608	3,348	3,892	4,965	5,293	5,788	8,079	9,068	10,423	⌶388	381	. . .	. . .	. . .	. . .	36cl
Other Items (Net)	884	1,000	1,313	2,017	2,135	4,954	7,652	13,005	11,416	12,432	14,687	. . .	. . .	. . .	. . .	37r
Money plus Quasi-Money	9,947	11,978	13,555	15,670	18,436	18,109	23,784	17,920	23,283	30,784	42,376	51,006	77,773	. . .	. . .	35l
Interest Rates																	
Percent Per Annum																	
Deposit Rate	1.50	1.50	1.50	1.50	1.50	1.50	1.50	1.50	1.50	1.50	5.88	. . .	. . .	. . .	. . .	60l
Lending Rate	8.00	8.00	8.00	8.00	8.00	8.00	8.00	8.00	8.00	8.00	8.00	. . .	. . .	. . .	. . .	60p
Prices																	
Period Averages																	
Consumer Prices	33.8	⌶33.9	35.7ᵉ	37.7	⌶39.5	42.2	46.2	57.6	66.8	85.0	100.0	132.3	161.3	212.6	263.8	64

Myanmar
518

		1965	1966	1967	1968	1969	1970	1971	1972	1973	1974	1975	1976	1977	1978	1979
International Transactions															*Millions of Kyats*	
Exports	70	1,072.2	925.8	589.5	530.6	627.1	513.0	594.6	653.5	640.4	911.8	1,102.0	1,394.9	1,516.7	1,665.9	2,547.7
Imports, cif	71	1,178.1	754.0	588.4	540.7	784.7	738.0	805.1	723.1	522.2	855.4	1,245.0	1,198.3	1,704.6	2,114.0	2,116.1
Imports, fob	71.v	1,071.0	685.5	534.9	491.5	713.4	670.9	731.9	657.4	474.7	777.6	1,131.8	1,089.4	1,549.6	1,921.8	1,923.7
																1990=100
Volume of Exports	72	145	122	71	54	72	77	94	80	58	53	51	73	75	67	97
Unit Value of Exports	74	25	27	30	35	29	23	22	25	47	93	98	99	113	114	114
Balance of Payments															*Millions of US Dollars:*	
Goods: Exports f.o.b.	78aa d	...	...	...	...	...	...	...	...	...	...	...	173	206	272	363
Goods: Imports f.o.b.	78ab d	...	...	...	...	...	...	...	...	...	...	...	–213	–307	–495	–732
Trade Balance	78ac d	...	...	...	...	...	...	...	...	...	...	...	–40	–101	–223	–369
Services: Credit	78ad d	...	...	...	...	...	...	...	...	...	...	...	27	36	26	40
Services: Debit	78ae d	...	...	...	...	...	...	...	...	...	...	...	–23	–31	–27	–59
Balance on Goods and Services	78af d	...	...	...	...	...	...	...	...	...	...	...	–36	–97	–224	–388
Income: Credit	78ag d	...	...	...	...	...	...	...	...	...	...	...	3	4	5	9
Income: Debit	78ah d	...	...	...	...	...	...	...	...	...	...	...	–18	–19	–23	–38
Balance on Goods, Serv., & Inc.	78ai d	...	...	...	...	...	...	...	...	...	...	...	–50	–111	–243	–416
Current Transfers, n.i.e.: Credit	78aj d	...	...	...	...	...	...	...	...	...	...	...	18	12	28	60
Current Transfers: Debit	78ak d	...	...	...	...	...	...	...	...	...	...	...	–1	–1	–1	–2
Current Account, n.i.e.	78al d	...	...	...	...	...	...	...	...	...	...	...	–34	–100	–215	–359
Capital Account, n.i.e.: Credit	78ba d	...	...	...	...	...	...	...	...	...	...	...	—	—	—	—
Capital Account: Debit	78bb d	...	...	...	...	...	...	...	...	...	...	...				
Capital Account, n.i.e.	78bc d	...	...	...	...	...	...	...	...	...	...	...	—	—	—	—
Direct Investment Abroad	78bd d	...	...	...	...	...	...	...	...	...	...	...				
Dir. Invest. in Rep. Econ., n.i.e.	78be d	...	...	...	...	...	...	...	...	...	...	...				
Portfolio Investment Assets	78bf d	...	...	...	...	...	...	...	...	...	...	...				
Portfolio Investment Liab., n.i.e.	78bg d	...	...	...	...	...	...	...	...	...	...	...	—	—	—	—
Other Investment Assets	78bh d	...	...	...	...	...	...	...	...	...	...	...	2	—	—	—
Other Investment Liab., n.i.e.	78bi d	...	...	...	...	...	...	...	...	...	...	...	14	56	184	429
Financial Account, n.i.e.	78bj d	...	...	...	...	...	...	...	...	...	...	...	16	56	184	429
Net Errors and Omissions	78ca d	...	...	...	...	...	...	...	...	...	...	...	3	–6	–32	–13
Overall Balance	78cb d	...	...	...	...	...	...	...	...	...	...	...	–15	–51	–64	57
Reserves and Related Items	79da d	...	...	...	...	...	...	...	...	...	...	...	15	51	64	–57
Reserve Assets	79db d	...	...	...	...	...	...	...	...	...	...	...	22	15	7	–96
Use of Fund Credit and Loans	79cc d	...	...	...	...	...	...	...	...	...	...	...	–7	28	34	15
Liabs.Constit.For.Auth.Reserves	79dd d	...	...	...	...	...	...	...	...	...	...	...	—	—	—	—
Exceptional Financing	79de d	...	...	...	...	...	...	...	...	...	...	...	—	8	23	24
Government Finance															*Millions of Kyats:*	
Deficit (-) or Surplus	80	502	426	...	...	...	...	...	...	I–855	I–572	–678	–129	196	196	851
Revenue	81	2,109	1,965	...	...	...	...	...	...	I1,453	I1,934	2,172	3,277	4,266	4,755	5,690
Grants Received	81z	...	...	...	...	...	...	...	...	73	I110	149	141	86	248	326
Expenditure	82	1,607	1,539	...	...	...	...	...	...	I2,349	I2,601	2,990	3,533	4,147	4,787	5,194
Lending Minus Repayments	83	...	...	...	...	...	...	...	...	32	I15	9	14	9	20	–29
Financing																
Domestic	84a	...	...	...	...	...	...	...	...	941	I626	669	123	–769	–467	–1,200
Foreign	85a	...	...	...	...	...	...	...	...	–86	I–54	9	6	573	271	349
National Accounts															*Millions of Kyats:*	
Exports of Goods & Services	90c	1,082	926	669	552	535	585	664	680	953	912	1,192	1,414	1,729	1,842	2,679
Gross Fixed Capital Formation	93e	807	856	990	1,077	1,160	1,056	1,184	1,111	1,146	1,525	1,681	2,320	3,753	5,364	7,389
Increase/Decrease(-) in Stocks	93i	615	–530	7	I194	293	175	133	156	352	475	659	515	92	414	486
Private Consumption	96f	6,651	7,178	7,348	8,846	9,168	9,474	9,712	10,493	12,824	I17,452	21,389	24,805	26,132	27,404	28,980
Imports of Goods & Services	98c	–1,413	–803	–817	I–753	–897	–852	–921	–704	–575	–1,016	–1,443	–1,628	–2,087	–3,224	–4,201
Gross Domestic Product	99b	7,742	7,627	8,198	9,916	10,259	10,438	10,772	11,736	14,700	19,348	23,478	27,426	29,619	31,800	35,333
Gross Dom. Prod. 1990 Prices	99b.p	...	...	66,137	I72,826	78,619	79,608	81,547	80,765	82,865	85,072	88,597	94,000	99,594	I106,085	111,595
GDP Deflator (1990=100)	99bi p	...	...	12.4	13.6	13.0	13.1	13.2	14.5	17.7	22.7	26.5	29.2	29.7	30.0	31.7
																Millions:
Population	99z	24.73	25.25	25.44	25.87	26.44	27.03	27.64	28.26	28.89	29.52	30.17	30.83	31.51	32.21	32.91

International Liquidity: I In February 1970 the Union of Myanmar Bank assumed the foreign assets of all banks and the small holdings of the insurance board. Data for other banks were formerly reported separately in *line 7a.d*.

Deposit Money Banks: I Beginning in 1989, claims on government and on nonfinancial public enterprises have been settled through budgetary operations. At the same time, long-term foreign liabilities have been incurred by the government.

Monetary Survey: I The 1970 consolidation of all financial institutions into a Union of Myanmar Bank resulted in substantial changes in the structure of banking statistics. Postal deposits, which were reported in *line 34* since 1966, are now included in *line 35*. Line *31n* is net of foreign liabilities, which were not identified before 1970. In addition, accounts of public enterprises now reported in *line 32cn* were previously reported partly in *line 32an* and partly in *line 32d*.

Government Finance: Data relate to a fiscal year different from calendar year (fiscal year ends September 30 through 1973; ends March 31 thereafter).

National Accounts: I Data for 1974 relate to the new fiscal year, beginning in April 1974 and ending in March 1975. For the year ending September 1974, i.e., based on the old fiscal year, GDP at current market prices was estimated to be 14,852 million kyats. I Data prior to 1968 refer to fiscal years ending September 30.

Myanmar

518

	1980	1981	1982	1983	1984	1985	1986	1987	1988	1989	1990	1991	1992	1993	1994		
International Transactions																	
Millions of Kyats																	
Exports	3,122.7	3,352.7	3,040.0	3,039.4	2,512.0	2,575.9	2,116.5	1,449.8	1,051.4	1,410.4	2,037.0	2,633.0	3,241.1	3,609.4	4,609.6		70
Imports, cif	2,337.3	2,702.5	3,178.1	2,150.8	2,016.2	2,401.5	2,245.2	1,785.6	1,538.0	1,280.5	1,709.4	4,058.8	3,971.0	5,007.0	5,285.9		71
Imports, fob	2,124.8	2,456.8	2,889.2	1,955.3	1,832.9	2,183.2	2,041.1	1,623.3	1,398.2	1,164.1	1,554.0	3,689.8	3,610.0	4,551.8	4,805.4		71.v
1990=100																	
Volume of Exports	98	99	114	124	118	100	113	82	53	72	100	96	108	149	137		72
Unit Value of Exports	136	151	126	123	130	133	112	94	92	111	100	101	88	81	85		74
Balance of Payments																	
Minus Sign Indicates Debit																	
Goods: Exports f.o.b.	429	533	423	375	364	311	331	220	166	223	223	....	....	....	....		78aa d
Goods: Imports f.o.b.	−788	−863	−913	−728	−565	−513	−621	−453	−370	−304	−524	....	....	....	....		78ab d
Trade Balance	−360	−330	−490	−353	−200	−202	−290	−233	−205	−82	−302	....	....	....	....		78ac d
Services: Credit	52	73	82	64	62	67	66	69	47	57	93	....	....	....	....		78ad d
Services: Debit	−73	−92	−106	−75	−71	−82	−57	−47	−34	−44	−72	....	....	....	....		78ae d
Balance on Goods and Services	−381	−348	−514	−364	−209	−217	−281	−211	−192	−69	−281	....	....	....	....		78af d
Income: Credit	14	20	13	4	5	2	4	6	3	3	2	....	....	....	....		78ag d
Income: Debit	−61	−70	−64	−72	−81	−71	−111	−83	−79	−57	−192	....	....	....	....		78ah d
Balance on Goods, Serv., & Inc.	−428	−398	−565	−432	−286	−286	−387	−287	−268	−124	−470	....	....	....	....		78ai d
Current Transfers, n.i.e.: Credit	81	85	67	82	68	82	97	107	93	56	39	....	....	....	....		78aj d
Current Transfers: Debit	−1	−1	—	—	—	−1	−3	—	−1	—	—	....	....	....	....		78ak d
Current Account, n.i.e.	−347	−314	−499	−350	−218	−205	−294	−180	−176	−68	−431	....	....	....	....		78al d
Capital Account, n.i.e.: Credit	—	—	—	—	—	—	—	—	—	—	—	....	....	....	....		78ba d
Capital Account: Debit	—	—	—	—	—	—	—	—	—	—	—	....	....	....	....		78bb d
Capital Account, n.i.e.	—	—	—	—	—	—	—	—	—	—	—	....	....	....	....		78bc d
Direct Investment Abroad	—	—	—	—	—	—	—	—	—	—	—	....	....	....	....		78bd d
Dir. Invest. in Rep. Econ., n.i.e.	—	—	—	—	—	—	—	—	—	8	161	....	....	....	....		78be d
Portfolio Investment Assets	—	—	—	—	—	—	—	—	—	—	—	....	....	....	....		78bf d
Portfolio Investment Liab., n.i.e.	—	—	—	—	—	—	—	—	—	84	233	....	....	....	....		78bg d
Other Investment Assets	—	—	—	—	—	—	—	—	—	—	—	....	....	....	....		78bh d
Other Investment Liab., n.i.e.	371	318	340	246	194	149	274	203	140	74	25	....	....	....	....		78bi d
Financial Account, n.i.e.	371	318	340	246	194	149	274	203	140	166	419	....	....	....	....		78bj d
Net Errors and Omissions	8	−33	30	80	15	42	69	15	117	53	21	....	....	....	....		78ca d
Overall Balance	31	−29	−128	−24	−9	−15	49	38	80	151	9	....	....	....	....		78cb d
Reserves and Related Items	−31	29	128	24	9	15	−49	−38	−80	−151	−9	....	....	....	....		79da d
Reserve Assets	−40	6	103	13	21	39	−4	13	−52	−143	−6	....	....	....	....		79db d
Use of Fund Credit and Loans	−12	23	25	11	−12	−24	−45	−50	−28	−8	−2	....	....	....	....		79cd d
Liabs.Constit.For.Auth.Reserves												....	....	....	....		79dd d
Exceptional Financing	20	—	—	—	—	—	—	—	—	—	—	....	....	....	....		79de d
Government Finance																	
Year Beginning April 1																	
Deficit (-) or Surplus	473	709	338	307	−93	−443	−1,482	−1,515	−2,300	−5,189	−7,789	−8,993	−7,054	....	....		80
Revenue	6,176	7,303	7,445	7,640	7,741	7,620	7,320	7,201	6,463	11,842	16,048	18,039	20,313	....	....		81
Grants Received	415	269	658	405	404	587	564	566	347	152	140	300	358	....	....		81z
Expenditure	6,119	7,046	7,898	7,936	8,509	9,015	9,790	9,621	9,443	17,566	24,349	27,621	27,931	....	....		82
Lending Minus Repayments	−1	−183	−133	−198	−271	−365	−424	−339	−333	−383	−372	−289	−206	....	....		83
Financing																	
Domestic	−941	−1,136	−886	−779	−485	−214	690	960	2,125	5,200	7,763	9,001	7,038	....	....		84a
Foreign	468	427	548	472	578	657	792	555	175	−11	26	−8	16	....	....		85a
National Accounts																	
Year Beginning April 1																	
Exports of Goods & Services	3,177	3,432	3,003	3,373	3,133	2,566	2,418	1,655	2,169	2,834	2,953	2,926	3,590	4,071	....		90c
Gross Fixed Capital Formation	7,228	8,635	10,044	9,057	8,476	8,649	8,618	8,683	7,296	11,827	22,318	27,571	31,028	35,670	....		93e
Increase/Decrease(-) in Stocks	1,065	1,205	331	−95	−367	44	−1,139	−742	2,467	−325	−1,995	1,032	2,601	5,226	....		93i
Private Consumption	31,774	35,218	39,747	42,685	47,396	49,532	53,067	63,168	67,754	113,726	134,188	160,610	216,062	301,335	....		96f
Imports of Goods & Services	−4,635	−5,611	−6,314	−5,197	−5,041	−4,802	−3,936	−4,066	−3,443	−3,395	−5,523	−5,337	−5,365	−7,218	....		98c
Gross Domestic Product	38,609	42,879	46,811	49,823	53,597	55,989	59,028	68,698	76,243	124,666	151,941	186,802	247,917	339,084	....		99b
Gross Dom. Prod. 1990 Prices	136,614	142,560	150,290	156,832	164,568	169,260	167,471	160,762	142,512	147,778	151,941	148,232	164,977	174,811	....		99b. p
GDP Deflator (1990=100)	28.3	30.1	31.1	31.8	32.6	33.1	35.2	42.7	53.5	84.4	100.0	126.0	150.3	194.0	....		99bi p
Midyear Estimates																	
Population	33.64	35.09	35.91	36.75	37.61	38.54	39.41	39.19	40.04	40.92	41.81	42.72	43.65	44.60	....		99z

Namibia

728

		1965	1966	1967	1968	1969	1970	1971	1972	1973	1974	1975	1976	1977	1978	1979
Exchange Rates																*Namibia Dollars per SDR:*
Market Rate	aa	.7144	.7177	.7134	.7196	.7149	.7172	.8308	.8500	.8097	.8444	1.0180	1.0103	1.0563	1.1329	1.0892
																Namibia Dollars per US Dollar:
Market Rate	ae	.7144	.7177	.7134	.7196	.7149	.7172	.7653	.7829	.6712	.6896	.8696	.8696	.8696	.8696	.8269
Market Rate	rf	.7163	.7170	.7170	.7170	.7181	.7164	.7130	.7728	.6941	.6795	.7395	.8696	.8696	.8696	.8420
Fund Position																*Millions of SDRs:*
Quota	2f.s	....	....	....	....	....	....	....	....	....	....	....	....	....	....	....
SDRs	1b.s	....	....	....	....	....	....	....	....	....	....	....	....	....	....	....
Reserve Position in the Fund	1c.s	....	....	....	....	....	....	....	....	....	....	....	....	....	....	....
Total Fund Cred.&Loans Outstg.	2tl	....	....	....	....	....	....	....	....	....	....	....	....	....	....	....
International Liquidity															*Millions of US Dollars Unless Otherwise Indicated:*	
Total Reserves minus Gold	1l.d	....	....	....	....	....	....	....	....	....	....	....	....	....	....	....
SDRs	1b.d	....	....	....	....	....	....	....	....	....	....	....	....	....	....	....
Reserve Position in the Fund	1c.d	....	....	....	....	....	....	....	....	....	....	....	....	....	....	....
Foreign Exchange	1d.d	....	....	....	....	....	....	....	....	....	....	....	....	....	....	....
Gold (Million Fine Troy Ounces)	1ad	....	....	....	....	....	....	....	....	....	....	....	....	....	....	....
Gold (National Valuation)	1and	....	....	....	....	....	....	....	....	....	....	....	....	....	....	....
Monetary Authorities																*Millions of Namibia Dollars:*
Foreign Assets	11	....	....	....	....	....	....	....	....	....	....	....	....	....	....	....
Claims on Central Government	12a	....	....	....	....	....	....	....	....	....	....	....	....	....	....	....
Reserve Money	14	....	....	....	....	....	....	....	....	....	....	....	....	....	....	....
Foreign Liabilities	16c	....	....	....	....	....	....	....	....	....	....	....	....	....	....	....
Central Government Deposits	16d	....	....	....	....	....	....	....	....	....	....	....	....	....	....	....
Other Items (Net)	17r	....	....	....	....	....	....	....	....	....	....	....	....	....	....	....
Deposit Money Banks																*Millions of Namibia Dollars:*
Reserves	20	....	....	....	....	....	....	....	....	....	....	....	....	....	....	....
Foreign Assets	21	....	....	....	....	....	....	....	....	....	....	....	....	....	....	....
Claims on Central Government	22a	....	....	....	....	....	....	....	....	....	....	....	....	....	....	....
Claims on Private Sector	22d	....	....	....	....	....	....	....	....	....	....	....	....	....	....	....
Demand Deposits	24	....	....	....	....	....	....	....	....	....	....	....	....	....	....	....
Time,Savings,& Fgn.Currency Dep.	25	....	....	....	....	....	....	....	....	....	....	....	....	....	....	....
Foreign Liabilities	26c	....	....	....	....	....	....	....	....	....	....	....	....	....	....	....
Central Government Deposits	26d	....	....	....	....	....	....	....	....	....	....	....	....	....	....	....
Capital Accounts	27a	....	....	....	....	....	....	....	....	....	....	....	....	....	....	....
Other Items (Net)	27r	....	....	....	....	....	....	....	....	....	....	....	....	....	....	....
Monetary Survey																*Millions of Namibia Dollars:*
Foreign Assets (Net)	31n	....	....	....	....	....	....	....	....	....	....	....	....	....	....	....
Domestic Credit	32	....	....	....	....	....	....	....	....	....	....	....	....	....	....	....
Claims on Central Govt. (Net)	32an	....	....	....	....	....	....	....	....	....	....	....	....	....	....	....
Claims on Local Government	32b	....	....	....	....	....	....	....	....	....	....	....	....	....	....	....
Claims on Nonfin.Pub.Enterprises	32c	....	....	....	....	....	....	....	....	....	....	....	....	....	....	....
Claims on Private Sector	32d	....	....	....	....	....	....	....	....	....	....	....	....	....	....	....
Claims on Other Banking Insts	32f	....	....	....	....	....	....	....	....	....	....	....	....	....	....	....
Money	34	....	....	....	....	....	....	....	....	....	....	....	....	....	....	....
Quasi-Money	35	....	....	....	....	....	....	....	....	....	....	....	....	....	....	....
Other Items (Net)	37r	....	....	....	....	....	....	....	....	....	....	....	....	....	....	....
Money plus Quasi-Money	35l	....	....	....	....	....	....	....	....	....	....	....	....	....	....	....
Other Banking Institutions																*Millions of Namibia Dollars:*
Reserves	40	....	....	....	....	....	....	....	....	....	....	....	....	....	....	....
Claims on Private Sector	42d	....	....	....	....	....	....	....	....	....	....	....	....	....	....	....
Time,Savings,& Fgn.Currency Dep.	45	....	....	....	....	....	....	....	....	....	....	....	....	....	....	....
Money Market Instruments	46aa	....	....	....	....	....	....	....	....	....	....	....	....	....	....	....
Central Government Deposits	46d	....	....	....	....	....	....	....	....	....	....	....	....	....	....	....
Capital Accounts	47a	....	....	....	....	....	....	....	....	....	....	....	....	....	....	....
Other Items (Net)	47r	....	....	....	....	....	....	....	....	....	....	....	....	....	....	....
Banking Survey																*Millions of Namibia Dollars:*
Foreign Assets (Net)	51n	....	....	....	....	....	....	....	....	....	....	....	....	....	....	....
Domestic Credit	52	....	....	....	....	....	....	....	....	....	....	....	....	....	....	....
Claims on Central Govt. (Net)	52an	....	....	....	....	....	....	....	....	....	....	....	....	....	....	....
Claims on Local Government	52b	....	....	....	....	....	....	....	....	....	....	....	....	....	....	....
Claims on Nonfin.Pub.Enterprises	52c	....	....	....	....	....	....	....	....	....	....	....	....	....	....	....
Claims on Private Sector	52d	....	....	....	....	....	....	....	....	....	....	....	....	....	....	....
Money	54	....	....	....	....	....	....	....	....	....	....	....	....	....	....	....
Quasi-Money	55	....	....	....	....	....	....	....	....	....	....	....	....	....	....	....
Other Items (Net)	57r	....	....	....	....	....	....	....	....	....	....	....	....	....	....	....
Interest Rates																*Percent Per Annum*
BoN Overdraft Rate	60	....	....	....	....	....	....	....	....	....	....	....	....	....	....	....
Treasury Bill Rate	60c	....	....	....	....	....	....	....	....	....	....	....	....	....	....	....
Deposit Rate	60l	....	....	....	....	....	....	....	....	....	....	....	....	....	....	....
Lending Rate	60p	....	....	....	....	....	....	....	....	....	....	....	....	....	....	....
Government Bond Yield	61	....	....	....	....	....	....	....	....	....	....	....	....	....	....	....
Prices																*Index Numbers (1990=100):*
Consumer Prices	64	....	....	....	....	....	....	....	....	....	....	....	....	....	....	....

Namibia

728

	1980	1981	1982	1983	1984	1985	1986	1987	1988	1989	1990	1991	1992	1993	1994		
End of Period																**Exchange Rates**	
	.9507	1.1134	1.1873	1.2793	1.9456	2.8093	2.6707	2.7379	3.1997	3.3327	3.6456	3.9237	4.1979	4.6667	5.1730	Market Rate	aa
End of Period (ae)	**Period Average (rf)**																
	.7454	.9566	1.0763	1.2219	1.9849	2.5575	2.1834	1.9299	2.3777	2.5360	2.5625	2.7430	3.0530	3.3975	3.5435	Market Rate	ae
	.7788	.8776	1.0858	1.1141	1.4753	2.2287	2.2850	2.0360	2.2735	2.6227	2.5873	2.7613	2.8520	3.2677	3.5508	Market Rate	rf
End of Period																**Fund Position**	
	....	....	....	....	....	....	....	....	....	....	70	70	100	100	100	Quota	2f. s
	....	....	....	....	....	....	....	....	....	....	—	—	—	—	—	SDRs	1b. s
	....	....	....	....	....	....	....	....	....	....	—	—	—	—	—	Reserve Position in the Fund	1c. s
	....	....	....	....	....	....	....	....	....	....	—	—	—	—	—	Total Fund Cred.&Loans Outstg.	2tl
End of Period																**International Liquidity**	
	....	....	....	....	....	....	....	....	....	....	....	....	49.72	133.70	202.62	Total Reserves minus Gold	1l. d
	....	....	....	....	....	....	....	....	....	....	—	.01	.01	.02	.02	SDRs	1b. d
	....	....	....	....	....	....	....	....	....	....	—	.01	.01	.01	.01	Reserve Position in the Fund	1c. d
	....	....	....	....	....	....	....	....	....	....	....	....	49.69	133.67	202.59	Foreign Exchange	1d. d
	....	....	....	....	....	....	....	....	....	....	—	—	—	—	—	Gold (Million Fine Troy Ounces)	1ad
	....	....	....	....	....	....	....	....	....	—	—	—	—	—	—	Gold (National Valuation)	1and
End of Period																**Monetary Authorities**	
	....	....	....	....	....	....	....	....	....	....	243.0	226.0	346.8	465.9	725.8	Foreign Assets	11
	....	....	....	....	....	....	....	....	....	....	—	—	510.3	619.6	720.0	Claims on Central Government	12a
	....	....	....	....	....	....	....	....	....	....	90.0	97.1	221.8	233.3	373.6	Reserve Money	14
	....	....	....	....	....	....	....	....	....	....	.1	.1	508.8	611.3	711.8	Foreign Liabilities	16c
	....	....	....	....	....	....	....	....	....	....	150.4	123.1	143.5	221.7	291.2	Central Government Deposits	16d
	....	....	....	....	....	....	....	....	....	....	2.5	5.7	−17.0	19.2	69.2	Other Items (Net)	17r
End of Period																**Deposit Money Banks**	
	....	....	....	....	....	....	....	....	....	....	81.3	84.7	83.4	99.5	156.2	Reserves	20
	....	....	....	....	....	....	....	....	....	....	374.1	585.5	375.7	195.0	194.4	Foreign Assets	21
	....	....	....	....	....	....	....	....	....	....	40.0	40.8	171.6	279.2	238.8	Claims on Central Government	22a
	....	....	....	....	....	....	....	....	....	....	1,372.6	1,599.9	2,079.2	2,705.5	3,542.6	Claims on Private Sector	22d
	....	....	....	....	....	....	....	....	....	....	605.6	809.5	1,002.4	1,333.1	1,465.3	Demand Deposits	24
	....	....	....	....	....	....	....	....	....	....	863.1	1,103.1	1,420.1	1,529.5	2,086.1	Time,Savings,& Fgn.Currency Dep.	25
	....	....	....	....	....	....	....	....	....	....	275.6	126.4	99.3	160.9	391.5	Foreign Liabilities	26c
	....	....	....	....	....	....	....	....	....	....	82.3	232.6	109.9	113.3	83.1	Central Government Deposits	26d
	....	....	....	....	....	....	....	....	....	....	87.9	162.8	204.5	273.2	293.8	Capital Accounts	27a
	....	....	....	....	....	....	....	....	....	....	−46.5	−123.5	−126.5	−130.7	−187.8	Other Items (Net)	27r
																Monetary Survey	
	....	....	....	....	....	....	....	....	....	....	341.4	685.0	114.3	−111.3	−183.0	Foreign Assets (Net)	31n
	....	....	....	....	....	....	....	....	....	....	1,233.6	1,357.5	2,586.3	3,336.9	4,282.1	Domestic Credit	32
	....	....	....	....	....	....	....	....	....	....	−192.7	−314.9	428.5	563.8	584.5	Claims on Central Govt. (Net)	32an
	....	....	....	....	....	....	....	....	....	....	2.2	9.3	15.2	15.0	17.2	Claims on Local Government	32b
	....	....	....	....	....	....	....	....	....	....	4.0	50.1	42.1	42.2	42.1	Claims on Nonfin.Pub.Enterprises	32c
	....	....	....	....	....	....	....	....	....	....	1,372.6	1,599.9	2,079.2	2,705.5	3,542.6	Claims on Private Sector	32d
	....	....	....	....	....	....	....	....	....	....	47.6	13.1	21.3	10.5	95.6	Claims on Other Banking Insts	32f
	....	....	....	....	....	....	....	....	....	....	614.3	821.9	1,002.4	1,466.8	1,682.8	Money	34
	....	....	....	....	....	....	....	....	....	....	863.1	1,103.1	1,420.1	1,529.5	2,086.1	Quasi-Money	35
	....	....	....	....	....	....	....	....	....	....	97.6	117.4	278.1	229.3	330.2	Other Items (Net)	37r
	....	....	....	....	....	....	....	....	....	....	1,477.4	1,925.0	2,422.6	2,996.4	3,768.9	Money plus Quasi-Money	35l
End of Period																**Other Banking Institutions**	
	....	....	....	....	....	....	....	....	....	....	....	....	138.4	43.1	.6	Reserves	40
	....	....	....	....	....	....	....	....	....	....	....	....	1,003.8	1,148.7	1,374.3	Claims on Private Sector	42d
	....	....	....	....	....	....	....	....	....	....	....	....	479.8	499.4	701.7	Time,Savings,& Fgn.Currency Dep.	45
	....	....	....	....	....	....	....	....	....	....	....	....	153.1	223.8	190.9	Money Market Instruments	46aa
	....	....	....	....	....	....	....	....	....	....	....	....	10.9	21.8	16.4	Central Government Deposits	46d
	....	....	....	....	....	....	....	....	....	....	....	....	563.2	634.2	763.1	Capital Accounts	47a
	....	....	....	....	....	....	....	....	....	....	....	....	−64.8	−187.5	−297.1	Other Items (Net)	47r
End of Period																**Banking Survey**	
	....	....	....	....	....	....	....	....	....	....	....	....	106.4	−120.8	−200.7	Foreign Assets (Net)	51n
	....	....	....	....	....	....	....	....	....	....	....	....	3,569.0	4,473.1	5,597.5	Domestic Credit	52
	....	....	....	....	....	....	....	....	....	....	....	....	420.6	548.0	599.1	Claims on Central Govt. (Net)	52an
	....	....	....	....	....	....	....	....	....	....	....	....	20.9	21.1	22.7	Claims on Local Government	52b
	....	....	....	....	....	....	....	....	....	....	....	....	44.5	49.8	58.8	Claims on Nonfin.Pub.Enterprises	52c
	....	....	....	....	....	....	....	....	....	....	....	....	3,082.9	3,854.2	4,917.0	Claims on Private Sector	52d
	....	....	....	....	....	....	....	....	....	....	614.3	821.9	1,002.4	1,466.8	1,682.8	Money	54
	....	....	....	....	....	....	....	....	....	....	....	....	1,854.9	2,021.3	2,782.7	Quasi-Money	55
	....	....	....	....	....	....	....	....	....	....	....	....	818.1	864.0	931.3	Other Items (Net)	57r
Percent Per Annum																**Interest Rates**	
	....	....	....	....	....	....	....	....	....	....	....	20.50	16.50	14.50	15.50	BoN Overdraft Rate	60
	....	....	....	....	....	....	....	....	....	....	....	....	13.88	12.16	11.35	Treasury Bill Rate	60c
	....	....	....	....	....	....	....	....	....	....	....	12.77	11.36	9.61	9.18	Deposit Rate	60l
	....	....	....	....	....	....	....	....	....	....	....	23.36	20.21	18.02	17.05	Lending Rate	60p
	....	....	....	....	....	....	....	....	....	....	....	....	15.44	13.94	14.63	Government Bond Yield	61
Period Averages																**Prices**	
	29.7	34.1	39.3	44.1	48.1	53.8	61.0	68.7	77.5	89.3	100.0	111.9	131.7	143.0	158.4	Consumer Prices	64

Namibia

728   1965 1966 1967 1968 1969 1970 1971 1972 1973 1974 1975 1976 1977 1978 1979

International Transactions
Millions of Namibia Dollars

		1965	1966	1967	1968	1969	1970	1971	1972	1973	1974	1975	1976	1977	1978	1979
Exports	70	....	....	....	....	....	....	....	....	....	....	....	....	....	....	....
Imports, cif	71	....	....	....	....	....	....	....	....	....	....	....	....	....	....	....
Imports, fob	71.v	....	....	....	....	....	....	....	....	....	....	....	....	....	....	....

Balance of Payments
Millions of US Dollars:

		1965	1966	1967	1968	1969	1970	1971	1972	1973	1974	1975	1976	1977	1978	1979
Goods: Exports f.o.b.	78aa *d*	....	....	....	....	....	....	....	....	....	....	....	....	....	....	....
Goods: Imports f.o.b.	78ab *d*	....	....	....	....	....	....	....	....	....	....	....	....	....	....	....
Trade Balance	78ac *d*	....	....	....	....	....	....	....	....	....	....	....	....	....	....	....
Services: Credit	78ad *d*	....	....	....	....	....	....	....	....	....	....	....	....	....	....	....
Services: Debit	78ae *d*	....	....	....	....	....	....	....	....	....	....	....	....	....	....	....
Balance on Goods and Services	78af *d*	....	....	....	....	....	....	....	....	....	....	....	....	....	....	....
Income: Credit	78ag *d*	....	....	....	....	....	....	....	....	....	....	....	....	....	....	....
Income: Debit	78ah *d*	....	....	....	....	....	....	....	....	....	....	....	....	....	....	....
Balance on Goods, Serv., & Inc.	78ai *d*	....	....	....	....	....	....	....	....	....	....	....	....	....	....	....
Current Transfers, n.i.e.: Credit	78aj *d*	....	....	....	....	....	....	....	....	....	....	....	....	....	....	....
Current Transfers: Debit	78ak *d*	....	....	....	....	....	....	....	....	....	....	....	....	....	....	....
Current Account, n.i.e.	78al *d*	....	....	....	....	....	....	....	....	....	....	....	....	....	....	....
Capital Account, n.i.e.: Credit	78ba *d*	....	....	....	....	....	....	....	....	....	....	....	....	....	....	....
Capital Account: Debit	78bb *d*	....	....	....	....	....	....	....	....	....	....	....	....	....	....	....
Capital Account, n.i.e.	78bc *d*	....	....	....	....	....	....	....	....	....	....	....	....	....	....	....
Direct Investment Abroad	78bd *d*	....	....	....	....	....	....	....	....	....	....	....	....	....	....	....
Dir. Invest. in Rep. Econ., n.i.e.	78be *d*	....	....	....	....	....	....	....	....	....	....	....	....	....	....	....
Portfolio Investment Assets	78bf *d*	....	....	....	....	....	....	....	....	....	....	....	....	....	....	....
Portfolio Investment Liab., n.i.e.	78bg *d*	....	....	....	....	....	....	....	....	....	....	....	....	....	....	....
Other Investment Assets	78bh *d*	....	....	....	....	....	....	....	....	....	....	....	....	....	....	....
Other Investment Liab., n.i.e.	78bi *d*	....	....	....	....	....	....	....	....	....	....	....	....	....	....	....
Financial Account, n.i.e.	78bj *d*	....	....	....	....	....	....	....	....	....	....	....	....	....	....	....
Net Errors and Omissions	78ca *d*	....	....	....	....	....	....	....	....	....	....	....	....	....	....	....
Overall Balance	78cb *d*	....	....	....	....	....	....	....	....	....	....	....	....	....	....	....
Reserves and Related Items	79da *d*	....	....	....	....	....	....	....	....	....	....	....	....	....	....	....
Reserve Assets	79db *d*	....	....	....	....	....	....	....	....	....	....	....	....	....	....	....
Use of Fund Credit and Loans	79dc *d*	....	....	....	....	....	....	....	....	....	....	....	....	....	....	....
Liabs.Constit.For.Auth.Reserves	79dd *d*	....	....	....	....	....	....	....	....	....	....	....	....	....	....	....
Exceptional Financing	79de *d*	....	....	....	....	....	....	....	....	....	....	....	....	....	....	....

Government Finance
Millions of Namibia Dollars:

		1965	1966	1967	1968	1969	1970	1971	1972	1973	1974	1975	1976	1977	1978	1979
Deficit (-) or Surplus	80	....	....	....	....	....	....	....	....	....	....	....	....	....	....	....
Revenue	81	....	....	....	....	....	....	....	....	....	....	....	....	....	....	....
Grants Received	81z	....	....	....	....	....	....	....	....	....	....	....	....	....	....	....
Expenditure	82	....	....	....	....	....	....	....	....	....	....	....	....	....	....	....
Lending Minus Repayments	83	....	....	....	....	....	....	....	....	....	....	....	....	....	....	....
Financing																
Domestic	84a	....	....	....	....	....	....	....	....	....	....	....	....	....	....	....
Foreign	85a	....	....	....	....	....	....	....	....	....	....	....	....	....	....	....

National Accounts
Millions of Namibia Dollars

		1965	1966	1967	1968	1969	1970	1971	1972	1973	1974	1975	1976	1977	1978	1979
Exports of Goods & Services	90c	....	....	....	....	....	....	....	....	....	....	....	....	....	....	....
Government Consumption	91f	....	....	....	....	....	....	....	....	....	....	....	....	....	....	....
Gross Fixed Capital Formation	93e	....	....	....	....	....	....	....	....	....	....	....	....	....	....	....
Increase/Decrease(-) in Stocks	93i	....	....	....	....	....	....	....	....	....	....	....	....	....	....	....
Private Consumption	96f	....	....	....	....	....	....	....	....	....	....	....	....	....	....	....
Imports of Goods & Services	98c	....	....	....	....	....	....	....	....	....	....	....	....	....	....	....
Gross Domestic Product	99b	....	....	....	....	....	....	....	....	....	....	....	....	....	....	....
Net Factor Inc/Pmts(-) Abroad	98.n	....	....	....	....	....	....	....	....	....	....	....	....	....	....	....
Gross Nat'l Expenditure = GNP	99a	....	....	....	....	....	....	....	....	....	....	....	....	....	....	....
Gross Dom. Prod. 1990 Prices	99b. *p*	....	....	....	....	....	....	....	....	....	....	....	....	....	....	....
GDP Deflator (1990=100)	99bi *p*	....	....	....	....	....	....	....	....	....	....	....	....	....	....	....

Millions:

		1965	1966	1967	1968	1969	1970	1971	1972	1973	1974	1975	1976	1977	1978	1979
Population	99z	....	....	....	....	....	....	....	....	....	....	....	....	....	....	....

Government Finance: ℓ Data are as reported in the *Government Finance Statistics Yearbook* and cover, prior to 1990, budgetary central government and one extrabudgetary fund (the University of Namibia). Beginning in 1990, data cover budgetary central government only. Data relate to a fiscal year different from calendar year.

Namibia

728

1980	1981	1982	1983	1984	1985	1986	1987	1988	1989	1990	1991	1992	1993	1994		
Millions of Namibia Dollars															**International Transactions**	
....	....	....	....	....	....	....	....	2,400	2,943	2,804	3,401	3,826	4,263	....	Exports	70
....	....	....	....	....	....	....	....	....	....	3,008	3,173	3,553	3,804	....	Imports, cif	71
....	....	....	....	....	....	....	....	1,937	2,447	2,897	3,094	3,551	3,694	....	Imports, fob	71.v
Minus Sign Indicates Debit															Balance of Payments	
....	....	....	....	....	....	....	....	....	....	1,090	1,222	1,342	1,290	1,274	Goods: Exports f.o.b.	78aa d
....	....	....	....	....	....	....	....	....	....	−1,118	−1,120	−1,263	−1,167	−1,156	Goods: Imports f.o.b.	78ab d
....	....	....	....	....	....	....	....	....	....	−28	102	79	122	118	Trade Balance	78ac d
....	....	....	....	....	....	....	....	....	....	115	131	146	192	219	Services: Credit	78ad d
....	....	....	....	....	....	....	....	....	....	−365	−482	−519	−465	−469	Services: Debit	78ae d
....	....	....	....	....	....	....	....	....	....	−278	−248	−294	−151	−133	Balance on Goods and Services	78af d
....	....	....	....	....	....	....	....	....	....	188	244	204	216	219	Income: Credit	78ag d
....	....	....	....	....	....	....	....	....	....	−150	−150	−178	−157	−175	Income: Debit	78ah d
....	....	....	....	....	....	....	....	....	....	−241	−154	−268	−92	−89	Balance on Goods, Serv., & Inc.	78ai d
....	....	....	....	....	....	....	....	....	....	376	392	463	364	369	Current Transfers, n.i.e.: Credit	78aj d
....	....	....	....	....	....	....	....	....	....	−126	−124	−138	−128	−130	Current Transfers: Debit	78ak d
....	....	....	....	....	....	....	....	....	....	10	114	58	144	150	Current Account, n.i.e.	78al d
....	....	....	....	....	....	....	....	....	....	46	39	47	34	21	Capital Account, n.i.e.: Credit	78ba d
....	....	....	....	....	....	....	....	....	....	−4	−4	—	—	—	Capital Account: Debit	78bb d
....	....	....	....	....	....	....	....	....	....	42	35	47	34	21	Capital Account, n.i.e.	78bc d
....	....	....	....	....	....	....	....	....	....	−1	−7	2	−9	−5	Direct Investment Abroad	78bd d
....	....	....	....	....	....	....	....	....	....	29	121	79	32	30	Dir. Invest. in Rep. Econ., n.i.e.	78be d
....	....	....	....	....	....	....	....	....	....	−5	−11	1	18	−17	Portfolio Investment Assets	78bf d
....	....	....	....	....	....	....	....	....	....	15	−15	15	60	37	Portfolio Investment Liab., n.i.e.	78bg d
....	....	....	....	....	....	....	....	....	....	−331	−268	−205	−194	−265	Other Investment Assets	78bh d
....	....	....	....	....	....	....	....	....	....	87	−6	11	38	97	Other Investment Liab., n.i.e.	78bi d
....	....	....	....	....	....	....	....	....	....	−206	−186	−97	−54	−124	Financial Account, n.i.e.	78bj d
....	....	....	....	....	....	....	....	....	....	191	25	−13	−34	28	Net Errors and Omissions	78ca d
....	....	....	....	....	....	....	....	....	....	37	−12	−7	91	75	Overall Balance	78cb d
....	....	....	....	....	....	....	....	....	....	−37	12	7	−91	−75	Reserves and Related Items	79da d
....	....	....	....	....	....	....	....	....	....	−37	12	7	−91	−75	Reserve Assets	79db d
....	....	....	....	....	....	....	....	....	....	—	—	—	—	—	Use of Fund Credit and Loans	79dc d
....	....	....	....	....	....	....	....	....	....	—	—	—	—	—	Liabs.Constit.For.Auth.Reserves	79dd d
....	....	....	....	....	....	....	....	....	....	—	—	—	—	—	Exceptional Financing	79de d
Year Beginning April 1															**Government Finance**	
....	....	....	....	....	....	200.8	−141.9	2.1	324.7	I−71.7	−189.0	−435.0 P	−402.7 f	....	Deficit (-) or Surplus	80
....	....	....	....	....	....	1,107.8	1,219.8	1,478.0	2,011.8	I1,905.9	2,534.6	2,833.7 P	2,958.5 f	....	Revenue	81
....	....	....	....	....	....	499.6	308.0	317.2	280.9	I101.1	67.8	73.5 P	70.0 f	....	Grants Received	81z
....	....	....	....	....	....	1,408.4	1,666.4	1,800.2	1,970.8	I2,027.4	2,778.9	3,311.9 P	3,407.5 f	....	Expenditure	82
....	....	....	....	....	....	−1.8	3.3	−7.1	−2.8	I51.3	12.5	30.3 P	23.7 f	....	Lending Minus Repayments	83
															Financing	
....	....	....	....	....	....	−162.2	131.8	43.9	−248.1	I−38.8	−.9	297.8 P	391.9 f	....	Domestic	84a
....	....	....	....	....	....	−38.6	10.1	−46.0	−76.6	I110.5	189.9	137.2 P	10.8 f	....	Foreign	85a
Millions of Namibia Dollars															**National Accounts**	
....	....	....	....	....	1,881.7	2,368.3	2,194.3	2,635.8	3,244.3	3,164.1	3,766.6	4,223.0	4,803.0	....	Exports of Goods & Services	90c
....	....	....	....	....	795.1	959.1	1,164.2	1,330.2	1,441.5	1,698.0	2,148.5	2,617.7	2,708.4	....	Government Consumption	91f
....	....	....	....	....	380.1	425.6	504.2	658.5	828.6	930.6	653.1	907.4	868.2	....	Gross Fixed Capital Formation	93e
....	....	....	....	....	5.4	−6.8	15.3	198.4	4.6	149.6	−3.5	−73.0	−80.4	....	Increase/Decrease(-) in Stocks	93i
....	....	....	....	....	1,328.4	1,632.0	2,203.0	2,357.0	3,008.7	3,473.8	4,073.8	4,588.8	5,181.5	....	Private Consumption	96f
....	....	....	....	....	−1,536.5	−2,038.0	−2,565.7	−2,701.6	−3,286.0	−3,907.6	−4,386.3	−4,995.4	−5,286.3	....	Imports of Goods & Services	98c
....	....	....	....	....	2,854.2	3,340.2	3,515.3	4,478.3	5,241.7	5,508.5	6,252.2	7,268.5	8,194.4	....	Gross Domestic Product	99b
....	....	....	....	....	−628.7	−562.2	−217.9	−594.7	−341.6	99.0	278.0	120.0	178.0	....	Net Factor Inc/Pmts(-) Abroad	98.n
....	....	....	....	....	2,225.5	2,778.0	3,297.4	3,883.6	4,900.1	5,607.5	6,530.2	7,388.5	8,372.4	....	Gross Nat'l Expenditure = GNP	99a
....	....	....	....	....	4,691.3	4,863.4	4,973.5	5,413.8	5,453.1	5,508.5	5,820.3	6,190.9	6,056.5	....	Gross Dom. Prod. 1990 Prices	99b.p
....	....	....	....	....	60.8	68.7	70.7	82.7	96.1	100.0	107.4	117.4	135.3	....	GDP Deflator (1990=100)	99bi p
Midyear Estimates																
....	....	....	1.16	1.15	1.18	1.21	1.24	1.28	1.31	1.35	1.38	1.42	1.46	....	Population	99z

Nepal

		1965	1966	1967	1968	1969	1970	1971	1972	1973	1974	1975	1976	1977	1978	1979
Exchange Rates																*Rupees per SDR:*
Market Rate	aa	7.619	7.616	10.125	10.125	10.125	10.125	10.993	10.993	12.739	12.929	14.633	14.523	15.184	15.633	15.808
																Rupees per US Dollar:
Market Rate	ae	7.619	7.616	10.125	10.125	10.125	10.125	10.125	10.125	10.560	10.560	12.500	12.500	12.500	12.000	12.000
Market Rate	rf	7.619	7.617	8.034	10.125	10.125	10.125	10.125	10.125	10.472	10.560	11.003	12.500	12.500	12.111	12.000
Fund Position																*Millions of SDRs:*
Quota	2f. s	7.5	10.0	10.0	10.0	10.0	10.0	10.8	11.6	12.4	12.4	12.4	12.4	12.4	19.0	19.0
SDRs	1b. s	—	—	—	—	—	—	1.1	2.2	2.2	2.2	2.2	2.1	1.9	1.2	1.7
Reserve Position in the Fund	1c. s	.3	.9	.9	.9	2.4	2.5	2.7	2.9	3.1	3.1	3.1	—	—	2.4	2.3
Total Fund Cred.&Loans Outstg.	2tl												4.5	6.0	15.3	18.6
International Liquidity												*Millions of US Dollars Unless Otherwise Indicated:*				
Total Reserves minus Gold	1l. d	56.5	41.7	43.1	54.2	75.5	88.7	96.1	98.4	117.5	121.3	95.7	‡127.5	139.5	145.1	159.2
SDRs	1b. d	—	—	—	—	—	—	1.2	2.4	2.7	2.7	2.6	2.5	2.3	1.6	2.3
Reserve Position in the Fund	1c. d	.3	.9	.9	.9	2.4	2.5	2.9	3.2	3.8	3.8	3.6	—	—	3.1	3.1
Foreign Exchange	1d. d	56.2	40.8	42.2	53.3	73.1	86.2	92.0	92.8	111.1	114.8	89.5	‡125.1	137.2	140.4	153.8
Gold (Million Fine Troy Ounces)	1ad	.087	.094	.094	.265	.233	.147	.142	.136	.130	.130	.130	.130	.133	.146	.149
Gold (National Valuation)	1and	3.0	3.3	3.3	9.3	8.2	5.2	5.0	5.2	5.5	5.5	5.5	5.5	5.6	6.2	6.3
Monetary Authorities: Other Assets	3.. d	....	....	....	....	....	....	....	....	....	....	....	1.8	2.7	2.3	4.9
Other Liab.	4.. d	....	....	....	....	....	7.5	4.4	4.7	6.1	14.4	12.6	4.0	6.0	5.6	10.4
Deposit Money Banks: Assets	7a. d	2.7	2.1	3.1	6.8	10.1	9.1	8.9	17.6	17.2	18.8	26.6	34.1	45.3	52.2	55.5
of which: Claims on Nonbanks	7ad d	....	....	....	2.1	1.5	1.5	1.3	2.4	2.8	2.6	3.0	5.7	6.8	11.1	17.7
Deposit Money Banks: Liabilities	7b. d	....	....	....	.8	.9	1.6	1.4	1.7	1.7	6.3	5.1	16.3	22.5	16.4	11.8
of which: Liab. to Nonbanks	7bd d	....	....	....	....	.9	1.6	1.4	1.7	1.7	6.3	4.7	15.8	21.9	15.4	11.8
Monetary Authorities																*Millions of Rupees:*
Foreign Assets	11	464	345	467	627	825	940	1,000	1,014	1,250	1,269	1,240	1,678	1,839	1,827	2,027
Claims on Central Government	12a	102	141	115	89	66	110	143	173	389	529	724	892	1,105	1,454	1,708
Claims on Private Sector	12d	3	12	6	5	11	11	11	8	19	21	21	17	18	20	34
Claims on Deposit Money Banks	12e	—	3	—	1	—	4	1	3	3	61	164	3	2	134	87
Claims on Other Financial Insts.	12f	18	24	21	27	33	13	27	37	49	56	134	123	211	314	353
Reserve Money	14	419	440	468	556	679	‡645	697	792	1,020	1,063	1,162	1,497	1,627	1,913	2,156
of which: Currency Outside DMBs	14a	310	337	350	420	487	526	549	596	747	882	882	996	1,212	1,379	1,627
Private Sector Deposits	14d	84	76	83	89	129	‡42	69	44	77	82	98	127	142	164	184
Foreign Liabilities	16c	....	....	....	....	....	76	45	47	64	153	157	115	166	306	418
Central Government Deposits	16d	147	148	121	180	146	181	230	194	409	479	514	571	744	735	858
Capital Accounts	17a	29	38	46	53	64	82	107	189	230	250	405	411	497	572	681
Other Items (Net)	17r	44	−58	14	−1	22	70	116	95	75	83	138	220	243	301	191
Deposit Money Banks																*Millions of Rupees:*
Reserves	20	24	21	29	41	65	75	131	135	207	120	163	353	348	325	406
Foreign Assets	21	20	16	31	69	103	93	90	179	181	199	332	426	567	626	666
Claims on Central Government	22a	7	14	23	10	10	17	36	70	100	100	101	320	640	418	347
Claims on Nonfin.Pub.Enterprises	22c	—	9	10	7	11	21	10	23	41	222	380	307	270	604	715
Claims on Private Sector	22d	103	112	117	154	182	240	332	356	459	605	710	614	810	1,106	1,393
Claims on Other Financial Insts.	22f	....	....	....	....	....	....	....	....	....	....	....	....	....	....	....
Demand Deposits	24	87	93	99	‡87	123	131	167	202	267	326	353	513	579	657	723
Time and Savings Deposits	25	44	50	70	122	183	232	324	451	573	658	847	1,175	1,468	1,870	2,178
Foreign Liabilities	26c	....	....	....	8	9	16	14	17	18	66	63	204	281	197	142
Credit from Monetary Authorities	26g	—	3	—	1	—	4	1	3	3	61	164	3	2	134	87
Other Items (Net)	27r	22	26	42	64	55	63	94	88	127	134	258	126	304	221	397
Monetary Survey																*Millions of Rupees:*
Foreign Assets (Net)	31n	484	362	498	688	923	‡941	1,032	1,128	1,349	1,249	1,352	1,785	1,958	1,949	2,132
Domestic Credit	32	84	161	169	‡80	70	123	227	460	620	1,036	1,514	1,648	2,183	3,024	3,692
Claims on Central Govt. (Net)	32an	−23	28	36	‡−104	−80	−79	−93	36	52	133	269	587	875	981	1,198
Claims on Nonfin.Pub.Enterprises	32c	—	9	10	7	11	21	10	23	41	222	380	307	270	604	715
Claims on Private Sector	32d	106	124	123	159	193	252	343	365	478	626	731	631	827	1,126	1,426
Claims on Other Financial Insts.	32f	....	....	....	....	....	....	....	....	....	....	....	....	....	....	....
Money	34	481	506	532	‡596	739	‡699	784	842	1,090	1,290	1,334	1,636	1,933	2,200	2,534
Quasi-Money	35	44	50	70	122	183	232	324	451	573	658	847	1,175	1,468	1,870	2,178
Other Items (Net)	37r	96	11	107	98	127	192	223	376	394	429	777	723	843	982	1,209
Money plus Quasi-Money	35l	525	556	602	718	922	931	1,108	1,293	1,663	1,948	2,180	2,811	3,401	4,070	4,712
Interest Rates																*Percent Per Annum*
Discount Rate (End of Period)	60	....	....	....	....	....	....	....	....	....	....	....	12.00	12.00	12.00	12.00
Treasury Bill Rate	60c	....	....	....	....	....	....	....	....	....	....	....	....	....	....	....
Deposit Rate	60l	....	....	....	....	....	....	....	....	....	....	4.00	4.00	4.00	4.00	4.00
Lending Rate	60p	....	....	....	....	....	....	....	....	....	....	12.00	13.00	14.00	14.00	14.00
Government Bond Yield	61	....	....	....	....	....	....	....	....	....	....	....	....	....	....	....
Prices																*Index Numbers (1990=100):*
Consumer Prices	64	13.6	15.6	15.2	15.3	16.0	18.4	18.0	19.5	21.8	‡26.1	28.1	27.2	29.9	32.1	33.2

Nepal

1980	1981	1982	1983	1984	1985	1986	1987	1988	1989	1990	1991	1992	1993	1994		
End of Period															**Exchange Rates**	
15.305	15.364	15.774	15.914	17.644	22.737	26.910	30.643	33.912	37.585	43.249	61.079	59.400	67.634	72.817	Market Rate	aa
End of Period (ae) Period Average (rf)																
12.000	13.200	14.300	15.200	18.000	20.700	22.000	21.600	25.200	28.600	30.400	42.700	43.200	49.240	49.880	Market Rate	ae
12.000	12.336	13.244	14.545	16.459	18.246	21.230	21.819	23.289	27.189	29.369	37.255	42.718	48.607	49.398	Market Rate	rf
End of Period															**Fund Position**	
28.5	28.5	28.5	37.3	37.3	37.3	37.3	37.3	37.3	37.3	37.3	37.3	52.0	52.0	52.0	Quota	2f. s
.1	—	.8	.2	.1	—	.1	.1	.1	.1	.1	.1	.1	—	.1	SDRs	1b. s
5.2	5.7	5.7	5.7	5.7	5.7	5.7	5.7	5.7	5.7	5.7	5.7	5.7	5.7	5.7	Reserve Position in the Fund	1c. s
32.6	32.5	27.7	22.4	15.8	19.8	19.2	30.3	39.2	39.9	30.9	26.9	31.7	35.8	37.7	Total Fund Cred.&Loans Outstg.	2tl
Data as of Middle of Month															**International Liquidity**	
182.8	201.9	199.2	133.3	82.0	56.0	86.7	178.2	220.3	211.6	295.3	397.0	467.4	640.2	693.6	Total Reserves minus Gold	1l. d
.1	—	.9	.2	.1	—	.1	.1	.1	.2	.2	.1	.2	—	.1	SDRs	1b. d
6.6	6.6	6.3	6.0	5.6	6.3	7.0	8.1	7.7	7.5	8.1	8.2	7.9	7.9	8.4	Reserve Position in the Fund	1c. d
176.0	195.3	192.1	127.2	76.3	49.7	79.7	170.0	212.5	203.9	287.0	388.7	459.4	632.3	685.1	Foreign Exchange	1d. d
.151	.151	.151	.151	.151	.151	.151	.151	.151	.152	.153	.153	.153	.153	.153	Gold (Million Fine Troy Ounces)	1ad
6.4	6.4	6.4	6.4	6.4	6.4	6.4	6.4	6.4	6.4	6.5	6.5	6.5	6.5	6.5	Gold (National Valuation)	1an d
6.4	4.3	2.3	1.4	.4	...	...	...	...	...	...	...	...	...	...	Monetary Authorities: Other Assets	3..d
11.5	15.8	15.1	3.1	3.7	10.8	8.7	31.4	18.0	38.3	39.7	32.2	51.6	55.3	...	Other Liab.	4..d
59.3	71.8	57.9	81.5	71.8	83.5	65.3	90.1	96.8	97.1	128.9	123.1	151.0	129.9	...	Deposit Money Banks: Assets	7a. d
16.2	20.6	11.5	12.6	17.1	24.9	19.7	19.7	20.2	21.0	27.6	30.6	39.7	37.1	...	*of which:* Claims on Nonbanks	7ad d
6.3	8.7	7.4	12.6	16.1	24.4	24.8	26.0	29.4	30.7	32.8	35.8	57.8	68.6	...	Deposit Money Banks: Liabilities	7b. d
6.3	8.6	7.4	12.6	16.1	24.4	24.8	26.0	29.4	29.5	31.3	35.6	57.2	68.6	...	*of which:* Liab. to Nonbanks	7bd d
Data as of Middle of December															**Monetary Authorities**	
2,364	2,773	2,743	2,113	2,224	1,299	1,839	3,830	5,816	7,492	10,329	17,894	21,320	32,721	...	Foreign Assets	11
1,896	2,611	3,312	4,626	5,696	7,040	8,468	8,835	9,956	12,871	14,097	15,276	17,907	19,032	...	Claims on Central Government	12a
41	53	55	64	113	254	185	194	167	205	349	494	501	544	...	Claims on Private Sector	12d
131	264	113	10	226	364	497	341	155	—	42	34	49	39	...	Claims on Deposit Money Banks	12e
373	398	428	501	557	706	749	876	916	818	761	837	690	499	...	Claims on Other Financial Insts.	12f
2,379	2,722	3,394	3,927	4,555	5,152	6,549	7,745	8,917	10,917	13,372	17,138	19,817	25,783	...	Reserve Money	14
1,814	2,147	2,408	2,783	3,302	3,797	4,787	5,827	6,671	7,905	9,818	12,465	14,201	17,390	...	*of which:* Currency Outside DMBs	14a
229	154	270	306	351	332	391	547	580	572	540	864	897	1,307	...	Private Sector Deposits	14d
637	707	653	403	345	675	708	1,607	1,782	2,593	2,543	3,018	3,780	4,389	...	Foreign Liabilities	16c
926	1,471	1,491	1,663	1,898	2,250	2,685	3,302	3,863	4,777	4,661	7,073	7,845	7,870	...	Central Government Deposits	16d
738	890	919	1,154	2,308	2,489	2,925	3,207	3,998	4,383	5,774	8,344	8,259	10,633	...	Capital Accounts	17a
210	367	195	166	−290	−904	−1,129	−1,786	−1,549	−1,285	−777	−1,036	766	4,160	...	Other Items (Net)	17r
Data as of Middle of December															**Deposit Money Banks**	
369	518	611	614	650	914	1,047	1,364	1,364	2,451	2,943	2,999	3,943	5,837	...	Reserves	20
712	948	827	1,239	1,293	1,728	1,437	1,946	2,440	2,778	3,918	5,256	6,525	6,397	...	Foreign Assets	21
387	355	796	1,422	1,654	2,073	2,001	3,024	3,819	4,046	4,395	8,238	9,677	10,734	...	Claims on Central Government	22a
780	946	874	1,075	940	1,296	1,662	1,859	1,921	1,644	2,005	1,310	1,144	1,954	...	Claims on Nonfin.Pub.Enterprises	22c
1,961	2,456	2,620	2,670	3,230	4,336	5,712	6,481	8,897	11,443	12,897	16,038	19,991	25,059	...	Claims on Private Sector	22d
...	...	86	130	157	155	116	105	29	28	28	29	29	29	...	Claims on Other Financial Insts.	22f
821	904	1,027	1,278	1,289	1,487	1,773	2,309	2,575	3,243	3,847	4,286	5,331	6,622	...	Demand Deposits	24
2,661	3,375	4,283	5,228	5,899	7,398	8,592	10,343	13,394	16,386	19,098	23,240	28,888	36,218	...	Time and Savings Deposits	25
76	115	106	191	290	505	546	561	742	878	997	1,529	2,498	3,380	...	Foreign Liabilities	26c
131	264	113	10	226	364	497	341	155	—	42	34	49	39	...	Credit from Monetary Authorities	26g
520	564	286	442	220	746	567	1,228	1,604	1,883	2,202	4,781	5,330	3,749	...	Other Items (Net)	27r
Data as of Middle of December															**Monetary Survey**	
2,362	2,898	2,812	2,758	2,883	1,847	2,023	3,609	5,733	6,799	10,707	18,603	21,566	31,349	...	Foreign Assets (Net)	31n
4,513	5,348	6,685	8,828	10,453	13,613	16,212	18,077	21,849	26,286	29,879	35,157	42,101	49,986	...	Domestic Credit	32
1,357	1,495	2,617	4,385	5,452	6,863	7,785	8,557	9,912	12,139	13,831	16,442	19,739	21,895	...	Claims on Central Govt. (Net)	32an
780	946	879	1,080	945	1,301	1,667	1,864	1,928	1,652	2,012	1,317	1,152	1,961	...	Claims on Nonfin.Pub.Enterprises	32c
2,002	2,510	2,675	2,733	3,343	4,590	5,897	6,675	9,064	11,648	13,246	16,532	20,492	25,602	...	Claims on Private Sector	32d
...	...	514	631	713	860	864	981	945	846	789	866	719	527	...	Claims on Other Financial Insts.	32f
2,864	3,205	3,705	4,366	4,942	5,616	6,951	8,682	9,826	11,720	14,205	17,614	20,428	25,320	...	Money	34
2,661	3,375	4,283	5,228	5,899	7,398	8,592	10,343	13,394	16,386	19,098	23,240	28,888	36,218	...	Quasi-Money	35
1,434	1,725	1,510	1,992	2,495	2,446	2,691	2,662	4,362	4,978	7,278	12,907	15,138	19,797	...	Other Items (Net)	37r
5,526	6,580	7,987	9,594	10,841	13,014	15,543	19,024	23,219	28,106	33,304	40,855	49,316	61,537	...	Money plus Quasi-Money	35l
Percent Per Annum															**Interest Rates**	
12.00	12.00	15.00	15.00	15.00	15.00	11.00	11.00	11.00	11.00	11.00	13.00	13.00	11.00	11.00	Discount Rate (End of Period)	60
...	5.00	5.00	5.00	5.00	5.00	5.00	5.00	5.00	5.62	7.93	8.80	9.00	...	6.50	Treasury Bill Rate	60c
4.00	4.00	4.29	4.50	4.50	4.50	7.17	8.50	8.50	8.50	...	...	...	...	...	Deposit Rate	60l
14.00	14.00	15.50	17.00	17.00	17.00	15.67	15.00	15.00	15.00	14.42	...	...	...	...	Lending Rate	60p
...	10.50	10.50	10.50	10.50	10.50	10.50	10.50	10.50	10.50	10.50	10.00	10.50	...	3.00	Government Bond Yield	61
Period Averages															**Prices**	
38.1	42.4	47.3	53.2	54.7	59.1	70.3	77.9	84.9	92.4	100.0	115.6	135.4	145.5	...	Consumer Prices	64

Nepal

558

		1965	1966	1967	1968	1969	1970	1971	1972	1973	1974	1975	1976	1977	1978	1979
International Transactions															*Millions of Rupees*	
Exports, fob	70	435	390	398	491	550	430	483	587	659	698	1,097	1,229	1,007	1,100	1,306
Imports, cif	71	819	574	483	565	857	764	856	862	1,086	1,419	1,885	2,035	2,104	2,677	3,053
Imports, fob	71.v	780	547	460	538	816	728	816	821	1,034	1,351	1,795	1,938	2,004	2,549	2,908
Balance of Payments															*Millions of US Dollars:*	
Goods: Exports f.o.b.	78aa d	....	....	....	....	....	....	....	....	....	....	....	102.1	81.2	89.4	110.3
Goods: Imports f.o.b.	78ab d	....	....	....	....	....	....	....	....	....	....	....	−154.1	−165.7	−220.5	−251.4
Trade Balance	78ac d	....	....	....	....	....	....	....	....	....	....	....	−52.0	−84.5	−131.1	−141.1
Services: Credit	78ad d	....	....	....	....	....	....	....	....	....	....	....	61.4	72.2	99.1	111.5
Services: Debit	78ae d	....	....	....	....	....	....	....	....	....	....	....	−42.8	−46.0	−57.1	−74.3
Balance on Goods and Services	78af d	....	....	....	....	....	....	....	....	....	....	....	−33.5	−58.3	−89.1	−103.8
Income: Credit	78ag d	....	....	....	....	....	....	....	....	....	....	....	6.7	8.9	6.8	14.2
Income: Debit	78ah d	....	....	....	....	....	....	....	....	....	....	....	−1.6	−.8	−1.2	−2.9
Balance on Goods, Serv., & Inc.	78ai d	....	....	....	....	....	....	....	....	....	....	....	−28.4	−50.3	−83.6	−92.6
Current Transfers, n.i.e.: Credit	78aj d	....	....	....	....	....	....	....	....	....	....	....	48.3	50.4	59.0	82.4
Current Transfers: Debit	78ak d	....	....	....	....	....	....	....	....	....	....	....	−1.4	−1.7	−1.2	−1.2
Current Account, n.i.e.	78al d	....	....	....	....	....	....	....	....	....	....	....	18.5	−1.6	−25.7	−11.4
Capital Account, n.i.e.: Credit	78ba d	....	....	....	....	....	....	....	....	....	....	....	—	—	—	—
Capital Account: Debit	78bb d	....	....	....	....	....	....	....	....	....	....	....				
Capital Account, n.i.e.	78bc d	....	....	....	....	....	....	....	....	....	....	....	—	—	—	—
Direct Investment Abroad	78bd d	....	....	....	....	....	....	....	....	....	....	....				
Dir. Invest. in Rep. Econ., n.i.e.	78be d	....	....	....	....	....	....	....	....	....	....	....				
Portfolio Investment Assets	78bf d	....	....	....	....	....	....	....	....	....	....	....				
Portfolio Investment Liab., n.i.e.	78bg d	....	....	....	....	....	....	....	....	....	....	....				
Other Investment Assets	78bh d	....	....	....	....	....	....	....	....	....	....	....	1.5	−15.3	−20.4	3.3
Other Investment Liab., n.i.e.	78bi d	....	....	....	....	....	....	....	....	....	....	....	12.6	35.5	13.9	30.8
Financial Account, n.i.e.	78bj d	....	....	....	....	....	....	....	....	....	....	....	14.2	20.1	−6.5	34.1
Net Errors and Omissions	78ca d	....	....	....	....	....	....	....	....	....	....	....	−4.1	−.7	10.5	4.8
Overall Balance	78cb d	....	....	....	....	....	....	....	....	....	....	....	28.6	17.8	−21.7	27.5
Reserves and Related Items	79da d	....	....	....	....	....	....	....	....	....	....	....	−28.6	−17.8	21.7	−27.5
Reserve Assets	79db d	....	....	....	....	....	....	....	....	....	....	....	−33.7	−22.1	12.5	−31.7
Use of Fund Credit and Loans	79dc d	....	....	....	....	....	....	....	....	....	....	....	5.2	1.7	11.7	4.2
Liabs.Constit.For.Auth.Reserves	79dd d	....	....	....	....	....	....	....	....	....	....	....	—	2.6	−2.5	—
Exceptional Financing	79de d	....	....	....	....	....	....	....	....	....	....	....	—	—	—	—
Government Finance															*Millions of Rupees:*	
Deficit (-) or Surplus	80	25	−36	−40	22	62	24	−39	ꭍ−126	−223	−248	−236	−422	−576	−582	ꭍ−588
Revenue	81	192	217	257	326	413	464	460	ꭍ541	602	752	995	1,088	1,291	1,522	ꭍ1,758
Grants Received	81z	183	175	142	158	186	244	271	ꭍ242	180	223	283	360	393	467	ꭍ564
Expenditure	82	350	428	439	462	537	684	770	ꭍ880	966	1,191	1,488	1,884	2,269	2,586	ꭍ2,928
Lending Minus Repayments	83	....	....	....	....	....	....	....	ꭍ29	39	31	25	−14	−10	−15	ꭍ−17
Financing																
Net Borrowing: Domestic	84a	10	10	2	11	8	14	32	ꭍ87	127	162	112	212	417	230	ꭍ241
Foreign	85a	6	3	4	—	—	8	33	ꭍ39	47	86	95	137	153	364	ꭍ352
Use of Cash Balances	87	−41	23	34	−33	−70	−45	−25	ꭍ—	48	−1	29	73	6	−12	ꭍ−5
Debt: Domestic	88a	....	....	....	....	....	ꭍ190	272	359		476	605	743	1,014	1,225	ꭍ1,395
Foreign	89a	....	....	....	....	....	....	....	....	....	310	378	513	665	1,029	....
National Accounts															*Millions of Rupees:*	
Exports of Goods & Services	90c	....	....	....	....	....	....	....	....	....	....	1,475	1,874	2,037	2,086	2,618
Government Consumption	91f	....	....	....	....	....	....	....	....	....	....	1,257	1,294	1,260	1,471	1,889
Gross Fixed Capital Formation	93e	....	....	....	....	....	....	....	....	....	....	2,223	2,443	2,580	3,294	3,263
Increase/Decrease(-) in Stocks	93i	....	....	....	....	....	....	....	....	....	....	179	189	188	213	251
Private Consumption	96f	....	....	....	....	....	....	....	....	....	....	13,652	14,060	13,689	15,721	17,741
Imports of Goods & Services	98c	....	....	....	....	....	....	....	....	....	....	−2,215	−2,466	−2,474	−3,053	−3,547
Gross Domestic Product	99b	5,602	6,907	6,415	7,173	7,985	8,768	8,938	10,369	9,969	12,808	ꭍ16,571	17,394	17,280	19,732	22,215
Gross Dom. Prod. 1990 Prices	99b.p	46,657	49,938	49,155	49,489	51,696	53,028	52,395	54,028	53,770	57,176	ꭍ58,009	60,561	62,388	65,136	66,680
GDP Deflator (1990=100)	99bi p	12	14	13	14	15	17	17	19	19	22	29	29	28	30	33
															Millions:	
Population	99z	10.10	10.31	10.53	10.76	10.99	ꭍ11.42	11.56	11.81	12.06	12.32	12.59	12.86	13.14	13.42	13.71

Monetary Authorities: ꭍ Prior to 1970, *line 14d* includes foreign liabilities. Hence, *lines 14, 31n,* and *34* are overstated before this date. **Deposit Money Banks:** ꭍ Beginning in 1968, *line 24* excludes government deposits. **Monetary Survey:** ꭍ See note to section 20. **Government Finance:** ꭍ Beginning in 1972 (1971 for debt data), data are as reported in the *Government Finance Statistics Yearbook* and cover consolidated central government. Prior to 1972 (1971 for debt data), data are as reported by Nepal Rastra Bank for publication in *IFS*.

Prior to 1972, foreign grants received for budgetary support are reported as deficit finance. *Use of Cash Balances* includes the residual, which reflects mainly unspent balances of foreign grants and timing differences. ꭍ Beginning in 1979, data for foreign grants and borrowing have been adjusted to eliminate receivable items. Data relate to a fiscal year different from calendar year.

Nepal

558

	1980	1981	1982	1983	1984	1985	1986	1987	1988	1989	1990	1991	1992	1993	1994	International Transactions	
Millions of Rupees																	
	964	1,731	1,161	1,361	2,109	2,915	3,005	3,290	4,433	4,303	6,160	9,831	15,977	18,935	....	Exports, fob	70
	4,107	4,549	5,237	6,746	6,847	8,267	9,751	12,444	15,850	15,780	20,157	28,235	33,843	42,752	....	Imports, cif	71
	3,912	4,332	4,988	6,425	6,521	7,874	9,286	11,851	15,095	15,029	19,197	26,890	32,232	40,716	....	Imports, fob	71.v
Minus Sign Indicates Debit																Balance of Payments	
	102.1	144.2	87.6	101.5	130.1	161.3	142.6	162.2	193.8	161.2	217.9	274.5	376.3	397.0	....	Goods: Exports f.o.b.	78aa d
	−328.0	−362.4	−406.3	−468.3	−402.9	−444.0	−436.5	−512.4	−664.9	−568.1	−666.6	−756.9	−752.1	−858.6	....	Goods: Imports f.o.b.	78ab d
	−225.9	−218.2	−318.7	−366.8	−272.8	−282.8	−293.9	−350.2	−471.1	−407.0	−448.7	−482.4	−375.8	−461.6	....	Trade Balance	78ac d
	155.0	155.5	160.2	171.0	159.2	157.4	176.6	217.7	223.8	203.1	204.4	239.8	273.8	333.2	....	Services: Credit	78ad d
	−87.7	−94.0	−85.1	−88.0	−99.5	−115.7	−113.7	−131.2	−150.8	−147.7	−167.3	−183.9	−225.0	−251.8	....	Services: Debit	78ae d
	−158.6	−156.6	−243.7	−283.8	−213.2	−241.1	−231.0	−263.7	−398.1	−351.6	−411.7	−426.4	−327.0	−380.2	....	Balance on Goods and Services	78af d
	14.5	14.2	18.0	8.1	5.2	4.7	4.4	6.8	16.2	21.2	25.1	27.0	33.5	28.9	....	Income: Credit	78ag d
	−2.9	−3.2	−2.3	−2.4	−4.9	−3.9	−3.7	−6.7	−14.4	−10.5	−11.2	−16.2	−16.8	−23.7	....	Income: Debit	78ah d
	−147.0	−145.7	−228.0	−278.1	−212.9	−240.3	−230.3	−263.6	−396.3	−340.9	−397.8	−415.6	−310.3	−375.0	....	Balance on Goods, Serv., & Inc.	78ai d
	109.5	127.6	144.9	135.3	119.7	122.2	115.7	143.6	130.5	109.2	115.7	121.3	133.6	155.5	....	Current Transfers, n.i.e.: Credit	78aj d
	−1.4	−1.0	−2.4	−2.8	−2.0	−3.4	−4.6	−3.3	−5.6	−11.6	−7.1	−10.1	−4.6	−3.0	....	Current Transfers: Debit	78ak d
	−38.9	−19.1	−85.4	−145.6	−95.2	−121.6	−119.2	−123.3	−271.5	−243.3	−289.2	−304.4	−181.3	−222.5	....	Current Account, n.i.e.	78al d
	—	—	—	—	—	—	—	—	—	—	—	—	—	—	....	Capital Account, n.i.e.: Credit	78ba d
	—	—	—	—	—	—	—	—	—	—	—	—	—	—	....	Capital Account: Debit	78bb d
	—	—	—	—	—	—	—	—	—	—	—	—	—	—	....	Capital Account, n.i.e.	78bc d
	—	—	—	—	—	—	—	—	—	—	—	—	—	—	....	Direct Investment Abroad	78bd d
	—	—	—	—	—	—	—	—	—	—	—	—	—	—	....	Dir. Invest. in Rep. Econ., n.i.e.	78be d
	—	—	—	—	—	—	—	—	—	—	—	—	—	—	....	Portfolio Investment Assets	78bf d
	—	—	—	—	—	—	—	—	—	—	—	—	—	—	....	Portfolio Investment Liab., n.i.e.	78bg d
	−18.7	−8.1	10.1	42.3	−11.8	−96.0	.8	59.8	38.5	−19.0	116.2	220.0	182.3	149.6	....	Other Investment Assets	78bh d
	40.8	69.0	52.6	65.5	73.3	121.8	86.7	130.9	214.2	215.1	188.3	237.1	153.7	133.9	....	Other Investment Liab., n.i.e.	78bi d
	22.2	60.9	62.7	107.8	61.5	25.8	87.4	190.7	252.7	196.1	304.5	457.1	335.9	283.5	....	Financial Account, n.i.e.	78bj d
	3.5	9.2	24.4	30.1	12.8	2.3	−.8	−3.6	12.5	5.2	4.9	10.7	.8	4.6	....	Net Errors and Omissions	78ca d
	−13.1	51.0	1.6	−7.6	−20.9	−93.5	−32.5	63.8	−6.3	−42.1	20.2	163.4	155.4	65.6	....	Overall Balance	78cb d
	13.1	−51.0	−1.6	7.6	20.9	93.5	32.5	−63.8	6.3	42.1	−20.2	−163.4	−155.4	−65.6	....	Reserves and Related Items	79da d
	−5.3	−50.9	3.0	13.3	27.6	88.5	33.1	−78.1	−5.7	41.2	−8.1	−157.9	−162.3	−71.4	....	Reserve Assets	79db d
	18.5	−.2	−5.3	−5.6	−6.8	4.9	−.6	14.3	12.0	.9	−12.2	−5.4	6.9	5.8	....	Use of Fund Credit and Loans	79dc d
	—	—	—	—	—	—	—	—	—	—	—	—	—	—	....	Liabs.Constit.For.Auth.Reserves	79dd d
	—	—	.8	—	—	—	—	—	—	—	—	—	—	—	....	Exceptional Financing	79de d
Year Ending July 15																Government Finance	
	−705	−728	−1,591	−2,954	−2,985	−3,380	−3,637	−3,902	−4,280	−8,014	−7,013ᵖ	−6,428ᶠ	....	....	....	Deficit (-) or Surplus	80
	1,829	2,375	2,639	2,778	3,310	3,855	4,508	5,780	7,140	7,540	8,767ᵖ	9,847ᶠ	....	....	....	Revenue	81
	791	859	988	1,089	877	917	1,173	1,285	2,077	1,681	1,829ᵖ	2,509ᶠ	....	....	....	Grants Received	81z
	3,340	3,967	5,221	6,852	7,238	8,209	9,445	11,110	13,644	17,405	17,811ᵖ	18,989ᶠ	....	....	....	Expenditure	82
	−15	−5	−4	−31	−67	−56	−128	−142	−148	−170	−202ᵖ	−205ᶠ	....	....	....	Lending Minus Repayments	83
																Financing	
	252	161	1,180	2,006	1,370	....	....	1,545	1,030	2,731	1,433ᵖ	1,492ᶠ	....	....	....	Net Borrowing: Domestic	84a
	432	472	339	948	1,615	....	....	2,455	3,518	5,282	5,580ᵖ	4,935ᶠ	....	....	....	Foreign	85a
	21	95	72	—	—	....	....	−98	−268	—	—ᵖ	—ᶠ	....	....	....	Use of Cash Balances	87
	1,503	1,444	1,900	2,878	4,337	6,032	....	10,017	11,047	13,778	15,428ᵖ	16,920ᶠ	....	....	....	Debt: Domestic	88a
	....	....	....	....	....	8,516	....	15,172	20,826	29,217	38,990ᵖ	43,926ᶠ	....	....	....	Foreign	89a
Year Ending July 15																National Accounts	
	2,695	3,523	3,592	3,455	4,196	5,372	6,506	7,555	8,717	9,897	10,887	14,226	23,909	30,948	....	Exports of Goods & Services	90c
	1,565	1,922	2,638	3,416	3,644	4,371	5,065	5,797	6,895	8,947	9,598	11,085	11,908	14,900	....	Government Consumption	91f
	3,681	4,299	5,465	6,576	6,907	9,386	9,431	11,825	13,414	16,392	17,002	22,780	29,277	33,928	....	Gross Fixed Capital Formation	93e
	589	509	−151	52	444	798	1,168	1,073	1,823	3,023	2,074	2,294	2,342	2,375	....	Increase/Decrease(-) in Stocks	93i
	19,195	22,411	25,272	27,458	31,860	35,977	44,782	50,746	62,407	70,172	86,314	97,901	121,370	135,279	....	Private Consumption	96f
	−4,374	−5,357	−5,828	−7,196	−7,661	−9,317	−11,218	−13,132	−16,350	−19,162	−21,820	−27,785	−39,321	−47,429	....	Imports of Goods & Services	98c
	23,351	27,307	30,988	33,761	39,390	46,587	55,734	63,864	76,906	89,269	103,416	120,371	149,485	170,001	196,969	Gross Domestic Product	99b
	65,133	70,566	73,233	71,052	77,931	82,720	86,496	87,963	94,733	98,833	103,416	110,002	114,519	118,027	127,007	Gross Dom. Prod. 1990 Prices	99b.p
	36	39	42	48	51	56	64	73	81	90	100	109	131	144	155	GDP Deflator (1990=100)	99bi p
Midyear Estimates																	
	14.01	15.02	15.42	15.83	16.25	16.69	17.13	17.56	17.99	18.44	18.92	19.60	20.28	20.81	....	Population	99z

Netherlands

		1965	1966	1967	1968	1969	1970	1971	1972	1973	1974	1975	1976	1977	1978	1979
Exchange Rates																
														Guilders per SDR:		
Market Rate	aa	3.6110	3.6140	3.5960	3.6060	3.6240	3.5970	3.5374	3.5030	3.4073	3.0688	3.1473	2.8546	2.7695	2.5652	2.5102
														Guilders per US Dollar:		
Market Rate	ae	3.6110	3.6140	3.5960	3.6060	3.6240	3.5970	3.2581	3.2265	2.8245	2.5065	2.6885	2.4570	2.2800	1.9690	1.9055
Market Rate	rf	3.6200	3.6200	3.6200	3.6200	3.6200	3.6200	3.5171	3.2095	2.7956	2.6884	2.5290	2.6439	2.4543	2.1636	2.0060
														Guilders per ECU:		
ECU Rate	ea	....	....	....	....	....	....	....	....	....	....	....	....	....	....	2.7460
ECU Rate	eb	....	....	....	....	....	....	....	....	....	....	....	2.9570	2.7998	2.7535	2.7481
														Index Numbers (1990=100):		
Market Rate	ah x	50.5	50.2	50.4	50.2	50.1	50.2	93.9	56.6	65.3	67.7	72.0	68.8	74.0	84.1	90.6
Nominal Effective Exchange Rate	ne u	65.1	65.1	65.3	67.0	67.0	66.0	66.5	67.6	70.1	73.9	75.9	78.4	82.5	84.5	86.4
Real Effective Exchange Rate	re u	....	....	....	....	....	....	....	....	....	....	131.3	133.1	133.9	132.7	128.6
Fund Position														*Millions of SDRs:*		
Quota	2f. s	413	520	520	520	520	700	700	700	700	700	700	700	700	948	948
SDRs	1b. s	—	—	—	—	—	144	570	650	475	486	520	531	564	244	394
Reserve Position in the Fund	1c. s	358	413	352	497	439	539	644	554	309	442	747	900	954	632	458
of which: Outstg.Fund Borrowing	2c	78	78	38	105	123	130	—	—	—	87	325	350	416	294	126
International Liquidity											*Millions of US Dollars Unless Otherwise Indicated:*					
Total Reserves minus Gold	1l. d	657	718	908	766	809	1,454	1,724	2,726	4,253	4,630	4,884	5,178	5,742	5,088	7,591
SDRs	1b. d	—	—	—	—	—	144	619	705	573	595	609	617	685	318	519
Reserve Position in the Fund	1c. d	358	413	352	497	439	539	699	601	373	541	874	1,045	1,158	823	603
Foreign Exchange	1d. d	299	305	556	269	370	771	406	1,420	3,306	3,495	3,401	3,515	3,899	3,947	6,469
Gold (Million Fine Troy Ounces)	1ad	50.19	49.45	48.91	48.51	49.16	51.06	54.53	54.17	54.33	54.33	54.33	54.33	54.63	54.78	43.97
Gold (National Valuation)	1an d	1,752	1,725	1,715	1,696	1,710	1,790	2,110	2,117	2,425	2,732	2,548	2,788	3,021	6,490	5,383
Monetary Authorities: Other Liab.	4.. d	14	10	11	12	12	14	39	104	705	63	69	47	270	511	114
Deposit Money Banks: Assets	7a. d	1,558	1,845	1,809	2,337	3,746	5,279	6,928	8,389	12,344	15,903	20,145	25,503	33,377	46,684	57,250
of which: Claims on Nonbanks	7ad d	....	....	....	....	....	....	....	....	....	....	....	4,161	5,627	7,044	10,561	13,302
Deposit Money Banks: Liabilities	7b. d	1,232	1,633	1,699	2,122	3,373	5,058	6,087	7,353	11,078	14,379	17,504	22,625	31,075	44,688	56,305
of which: Liab. to Nonbanks	7bd d	....	....	....	....	....	....	....	....	....	....	2,514	3,430	4,424	6,041	8,959
Monetary Authorities														*Billions of Guilders:*		
Foreign Assets	11	8.75	8.89	9.50	8.91	9.14	11.70	12.46	15.61	18.85	18.92	20.45	20.07	20.47	23.04	24.99
Claims on Central Government	12a	1.34	1.87	1.73	2.49	2.32	2.31	2.53	1.17	1.03	.89	1.19	.94	1.09	1.38	1.68
Claims on Deposit Money Banks	12e	.11	.18	.14	.38	.71	.05	.19	.53	1.15	1.26	1.84	1.65	2.20	5.21	5.17
Reserve Money	14	8.26	8.83	9.11	9.29	9.97	10.52	11.03	12.04	12.61	13.60	15.35	16.74	18.26	19.70	21.25
of which: Currency Outside DMBs	14a	7.87	8.46	8.72	8.84	9.43	9.95	10.49	11.41	11.92	12.85	14.49	15.89	17.41	18.71	19.98
Central Government Deposits	16d	1.73	1.86	2.09	2.23	1.93	2.84	3.32	3.87	5.14	6.78	5.69	5.37	5.22	4.64	2.38
Other Items (Net)	17r	.22	.25	.18	.26	.28	.71	.82	1.41	3.28	.68	2.45	.55	.29	5.29	8.21
of which: Valuation Adjustment	17rv	—	—	—	—	—	—	—	—	—	—	—	—	—	2.81	6.44
Deposit Money Banks														*Billions of Guilders:*		
Reserves	20	.35	.34	.33	.38	.39	.67	.48	.58	.67	.71	.74	.81	.77	.91	1.05
Foreign Assets	21	5.64	6.68	6.55	8.46	13.56	19.11	22.48	27.22	34.33	39.86	54.16	62.66	76.10	91.92	109.09
Claims on Central Government	22a	7.80	8.00	8.95	9.62	10.12	10.23	10.49	10.71	9.97	10.45	12.44	14.74	16.25	17.69	20.88
Claims on Local Government	22b	6.78	7.32	8.05	9.04	9.43	10.36	11.57	13.39	13.91	15.00	15.62	15.63	15.35	17.05	18.61
Claims on Private Sector	22d	19.92	22.53	26.61	31.29	36.50	42.19	48.34	57.19	71.96	85.75	97.02	117.06	147.34	178.58	204.79
Demand Deposits	24	9.09	9.67	10.52	12.60	13.75	15.96	19.32	23.68	23.19	26.54	32.67	35.09	40.30	41.40	41.65
Time, Savings,& Fgn.Currency Dep.	25	24.72	26.94	31.29	35.76	40.59	45.35	51.23	57.30	70.99	82.11	90.30	108.64	122.70	141.28	161.73
Bonds	26ab	.28	.44	.51	.41	.60	.87	.93	.97	1.46	1.67	2.63	2.93	12.11	19.43	25.70
Foreign Liabilities	26c	4.46	5.91	6.15	7.68	12.21	18.31	19.75	23.86	30.81	36.04	47.06	55.59	70.85	87.99	107.29
Credit from Monetary Authorities	26g	.10	.17	.11	.46	.57	.05	.25	.41	1.10	1.24	1.79	1.75	2.31	5.13	5.27
Other Items (Net)	27r	1.84	1.76	1.91	1.88	2.28	2.02	1.88	2.87	3.29	4.17	5.53	6.90	7.54	10.92	12.78
Monetary Survey														*Billions of Guilders:*		
Foreign Assets (Net)	31n	9.88	9.62	9.87	9.65	10.44	12.45	15.07	18.63	20.41	22.58	27.36	27.03	25.11	25.96	26.58
Domestic Credit	32	34.20	37.95	43.44	50.36	56.66	62.43	69.81	78.88	92.10	105.72	121.03	143.49	175.32	210.70	244.53
Claims on Central Govt. (Net)	32an	7.41	8.01	8.60	9.88	10.51	9.70	9.69	8.01	5.86	4.56	7.95	10.32	12.12	14.44	20.18
Claims on Local Government	32b	6.83	7.37	8.10	9.12	9.54	10.46	11.69	13.53	14.06	15.19	15.81	15.84	15.62	17.39	18.98
Claims on Private Sector	32d	19.96	22.57	26.74	31.36	36.60	42.27	48.43	57.33	72.17	85.98	97.28	117.34	147.58	178.87	205.38
Money	34	16.99	18.16	19.29	21.49	23.23	25.95	29.85	35.13	35.14	39.43	47.20	51.05	57.77	60.19	61.88
Quasi-Money	35	24.73	26.95	31.30	35.77	40.60	45.35	51.23	57.30	70.99	82.11	90.30	108.64	122.70	141.28	161.73
Bonds	36ab	.28	.44	.51	.41	.60	.87	.93	.97	1.46	1.67	2.63	2.93	12.11	19.43	25.70
Other Items (Net)	37r	2.08	2.02	2.21	2.35	2.68	2.70	2.87	4.11	4.91	5.09	8.26	7.90	7.85	15.76	21.80
Money plus Quasi-Money	35l	41.72	45.11	50.59	57.25	63.82	71.31	81.08	92.43	106.13	121.54	137.50	159.69	180.47	201.47	223.61
Money (National Definitions)																
M3H	38n	23.32	24.70	27.39	31.45	34.64	38.46	41.91	46.90	57.19	68.66	72.58	90.74	92.29	95.71	102.88
M3H, Seasonally Adjusted	38n. c	23.57	25.11	27.82	31.95	35.37	38.91	42.20	49.83	57.34	66.28	72.64	88.76	94.11	98.86	105.45
Nonbank Financial Institutions														*Billions of Guilders:*		
Cash	40.. l	.26	.24	.30	.25	.23	.34	.37	.33	.61	.94	1.33	2.40	2.09	1.18	1.50
Foreign Assets	41.. l	1.11	1.14	1.24	1.49	1.79	1.93	2.46	2.98	3.29	3.80	4.07	4.50	4.48	4.53	4.97
Claims on Central Government	42a. l	7.00	8.05	9.31	10.35	11.66	12.84	14.28	16.29	18.25	20.79	24.18	28.62	33.36	38.38	43.11
Claims on Local Government	42b. l	6.26	6.46	6.89	7.07	7.40	8.37	9.22	9.58	10.83	13.55	15.24	17.72	20.18	22.17	25.55
Claims on Private Sector	42d. l	13.47	15.29	17.28	19.71	22.30	24.83	27.88	32.77	37.53	44.93	51.79	58.64	66.34	78.58	87.33
Real Estate	42h. l	2.42	2.97	3.58	4.42	5.10	5.74	6.59	7.74	8.81	10.41	12.36	14.07	15.72	17.89	19.88
Capital Accounts	47a. l	30.42	34.00	38.38	43.35	48.53	54.24	60.86	69.78	79.82	94.53	109.96	126.86	143.73	164.58	185.92
Other Items (Net)	47r. l	.09	.13	.21	−.07	−.05	−.19	−.06	−.11	−.50	−.12	−1.00	−.90	−1.57	−1.85	−3.58
Interest Rates														*Percent Per Annum*		
Discount Rate (End of Period)	60	4.50	5.00	4.50	5.00	6.00	6.00	5.00	4.00	8.00	7.00	4.50	6.00	4.50	6.50	9.50
Rate on Advances	60a	....	....	....	....	....	....	....	....	....	....	....	....	....	....	....
Money Market Rate	60b	4.73	6.42	5.67	5.19	7.76	7.96	l4.85	1.93	6.44	9.20	4.17	7.28	3.80	6.24	9.03
Deposit Rate	60l	....	....	....	....	....	....	....	....	....	....	....	....	....	....	....
Lending Rate	60p	....	....	....	....	....	....	....	....	....	....	....	....	....	5.04	5.54
Government Bond Yield	61	5.50	6.59	6.18	6.49	7.51	8.22	7.35	6.88	l7.92	9.83	8.79	8.95	8.10	13.25	16.50
															7.74	8.78

Netherlands

	1980	1981	1982	1983	1984	1985	1986	1987	1988	1989	1990	1991	1992	1993	1994		
Exchange Rates																	
End of Period	2.7160	2.8732	2.8951	3.2084	3.4793	3.0448	2.6812	2.5217	2.6907	2.5173	2.4043	2.4466	2.4944	2.6659	2.5330	Market Rate	aa
End of Period (ae) Period Average (rf)																	
	2.1295	2.4685	2.6245	3.0645	3.5495	2.7720	2.1920	1.7775	1.9995	1.9155	1.6900	1.7104	1.8141	1.9409	1.7351	Market Rate	ae
	1.9881	2.4952	2.6702	2.8541	3.2087	3.3214	2.4500	2.0257	1.9766	2.1207	1.8209	1.8697	1.7585	1.8573	1.8200	Market Rate	rf
End of Period (ea) Period Average (eb)																	
	2.7901	2.6831	2.5421	2.5371	2.5185	2.4585	2.3440	2.3160	2.3440	2.2730	2.3125	2.2885	2.1925	2.1670	2.1280	ECU Rate	ea
	2.7606	2.7758	2.6153	2.5372	2.5233	2.5111	2.4015	2.3340	2.3343	2.3335	2.3162	2.3127	2.2725	2.1723	2.1528	ECU Rate	eb
Period Averages																	
	91.5	73.1	68.1	63.8	56.8	55.2	74.5	89.8	92.1	85.8	100.0	97.5	103.5	97.9	100.0	Market Rate	ahx
	85.5	82.0	86.3	88.3	87.2	87.3	93.6	98.0	97.5	96.6	100.0	99.3	101.5	104.7	105.1	Nominal Effective Exchange Rate	neu
	118.4	107.0	109.1	108.2	101.2	98.5	104.2	107.6	104.2	98.8	100.0	98.9	103.0	105.7	....	Real Effective Exchange Rate	reu
End of Period																**Fund Position**	
	1,422	1,422	1,422	2,265	2,265	2,265	2,265	2,265	2,265	2,265	2,265	2,265	2,265	3,444	3,444	Quota	2f.s
	439	592	772	502	525	569	598	637	576	590	504	530	403	424	442	SDRs	1b.s
	510	498	561	901	963	898	717	652	563	537	519	559	834	795	802	Reserve Position in the Fund	1c.s
	101	77	74	99	93	79	59	36	15	5	—	—	—	—	—	of which: Outstg.Fund Borrowing	2c
End of Period																**International Liquidity**	
	11,645	9,339	10,132	10,171	9,237	10,782	11,191	16,003	16,075	16,508	17,484	17,798	21,937	31,344	34,532	Total Reserves minus Gold	1l.d
	561	689	851	525	515	625	731	903	776	776	718	758	554	583	645	SDRs	1b.d
	651	579	619	943	944	987	877	926	757	706	738	800	1,147	1,092	1,171	Reserve Position in the Fund	1c.d
	10,434	8,071	8,662	8,702	7,778	9,170	9,583	14,174	14,542	15,027	16,028	16,240	20,237	29,669	32,716	Foreign Exchange	1d.d
	43.94	43.94	43.94	43.94	43.94	43.94	43.94	43.94	43.94	43.94	43.94	43.94	43.94	35.05	34.77	Gold (Million Fine Troy Ounces)	1ad
	4,814	5,204	4,895	4,192	8,702	11,143	14,091	15,532	13,807	14,413	14,719	14,543	13,712	7,639	8,477	Gold (National Valuation)	1and
	182	111	109	133	76	110	235	94	26	87	85	245	38	152	263	Monetary Authorities: Other Liab.	4..d
	62,625	66,352	63,922	58,862	57,520	72,876	91,099	115,975	120,572	146,271	185,921	189,048	190,591	195,752	200,374	Deposit Money Banks: Assets	7a.d
	14,448	16,073	17,790	16,838	15,210	19,061	27,877	32,869	35,590	41,571	46,668	49,014	53,429	56,057	61,018	of which: Claims on Nonbanks	7ad d
	64,353	65,181	62,733	56,217	53,052	65,677	83,456	108,672	109,884	121,329	153,434	157,364	165,530	169,204	186,507	Deposit Money Banks: Liabilities	7b.d
	12,430	14,182	15,205	14,349	15,437	19,444	25,828	32,448	35,483	45,559	59,664	63,186	60,409	63,042	72,596	of which: Liab. to Nonbanks	7bd d
End of Period																**Monetary Authorities**	
	35.30	36.25	39.78	44.34	64.57	61.66	56.41	56.90	60.66	60.10	55.27	56.20	65.61	76.24	75.69	Foreign Assets	11
	2.20	1.92	2.18	2.97	3.97	4.20	3.13	2.97	4.52	6.86	5.96	6.29	6.07	4.17	4.14	Claims on Central Government	12a
	5.80	8.08	4.70	7.54	5.80	6.75	10.91	6.84	6.45	6.39	9.18	3.06	5.35	4.46	8.26	Claims on Deposit Money Banks	12e
	23.00	23.40	25.18	28.17	29.82	30.98	32.10	35.29	39.26	45.33	46.80	40.32	52.46	56.35	59.74	Reserve Money	14
	22.00	22.34	I 23.39	26.35	27.80	28.60	29.77	32.85	34.61	36.00	36.47	36.99	36.99	37.59	38.11	of which: Currency Outside DMBs	14a
	3.85	3.38	3.42	3.36	1.73	3.39	5.80	3.40	3.09	.03	1.36	3.27	3.13	7.99	9.61	Central Government Deposits	16d
	16.45	19.48	18.06	23.31	42.79	38.24	32.55	28.01	29.14	27.98	22.25	21.95	21.44	20.53	18.73	Other Items (Net)	17r
	13.95	16.85	15.45	20.40	40.35	35.01	30.47	25.60	26.69	25.26	20.22	20.44	19.38	17.39	15.54	of which: Valuation Adjustment	17rv
End of Period																**Deposit Money Banks**	
	1.03	.95	I 1.57	1.64	1.91	2.10	2.09	2.06	2.23	2.62	2.87	2.87	2.88	2.81	2.80	Reserves	20
	133.36	163.79	I 167.76	180.38	204.17	202.01	199.69	206.15	241.08	280.18	314.21	323.35	345.75	379.94	347.67	Foreign Assets	21
	24.19	29.05	I 37.84	44.97	51.97	57.73	61.48	55.28	64.88	59.61	62.35	60.70	60.09	62.89	65.28	Claims on Central Government	22a
	21.21	21.02	I 22.27	21.32	18.79	20.60	27.36	32.01	60.11	60.38	59.90	58.67	59.27	62.04	63.92	Claims on Local Government	22b
	224.76	236.84	I 242.42	250.45	259.46	270.93	290.74	306.38	375.09	399.91	427.18	460.32	485.59	518.79	559.34	Claims on Private Sector	22d
	43.54	41.56	I 48.71	53.16	57.11	62.00	67.25	70.56	76.10	82.42	86.63	92.00	98.00	111.92	114.04	Demand Deposits	24
	170.65	190.48	I 195.83	201.65	214.70	229.33	239.98	239.76	257.45	287.29	310.49	325.65	342.32	355.15	353.92	Time, Savings,& Fgn.Currency Dep.	25
	31.47	31.01	31.16	33.08	33.90	35.55	43.84	50.54	128.39	143.91	149.18	150.93	150.11	154.41	169.53	Bonds	26ab
	137.04	160.90	I 164.64	172.28	188.31	182.06	182.94	193.17	219.71	232.41	259.30	269.16	300.29	328.41	323.61	Foreign Liabilities	26c
	5.95	8.69	I 5.26	7.03	5.85	5.67	10.70	7.36	6.14	4.89	9.33	3.08	6.65	4.06	7.92	Credit from Monetary Authorities	26g
	15.90	19.01	I 26.32	31.57	36.65	38.78	36.65	40.49	45.70	51.77	51.58	65.10	56.22	72.52	69.99	Other Items (Net)	27r
																Monetary Survey	
	31.23	38.87	I 42.62	52.04	80.16	81.31	72.65	69.71	81.97	107.71	110.03	109.97	111.01	127.48	99.29	Foreign Assets (Net)	31n
	269.29	286.58	I 301.83	316.80	333.72	350.57	378.03	393.64	501.77	527.52	555.05	583.07	608.15	639.18	682.64	Domestic Credit	32
	22.54	27.59	I 35.82	43.94	53.62	57.87	57.86	53.53	64.82	65.32	66.08	61.80	61.89	57.74	59.02	Claims on Central Govt. (Net)	32an
	21.57	21.46	I 22.67	21.63	19.46	20.92	27.89	32.28	60.36	60.55	60.05	58.91	59.42	62.04	63.92	Claims on Local Government	32b
	225.18	237.52	I 243.34	251.24	260.65	271.78	292.28	307.83	376.59	401.64	428.93	462.45	486.84	519.40	559.69	Claims on Private Sector	32d
	65.58	64.03	I 72.30	79.66	85.00	90.77	97.21	103.71	111.31	119.02	123.93	129.33	135.07	149.64	152.24	Money	34
	170.65	190.48	I 195.83	201.65	214.71	229.34	239.99	239.77	257.46	287.30	310.50	325.66	342.32	355.15	353.92	Quasi-Money	35
	31.47	31.01	31.16	33.08	33.90	35.55	43.84	50.54	138.21	143.91	149.18	150.93	150.11	154.41	169.53	Bonds	36ab
	32.81	39.92	I 45.22	54.45	80.49	76.22	69.63	69.33	76.54	84.99	81.47	87.12	91.66	107.45	106.23	Other Items (Net)	37r
	236.24	254.51	268.13	281.31	299.71	320.11	337.20	343.48	368.77	406.32	434.43	454.99	477.39	504.79	506.16	Money plus Quasi-Money	35l
																Money (National Definitions)	
	106.82	112.46	I 217.95	228.96	242.23	264.13	282.73	294.21	319.81	359.72	386.02	407.19	432.15	465.08	466.91	M3H	38n
	109.45	116.90	I 221.45	233.07	247.57	267.88	283.90	291.96	325.80	369.59	387.24	408.98	434.02	474.64	470.63	M3H, Seasonally Adjusted	38n.c
End of Period																**Nonbank Financial Institutions**	
	1.37	2.07	1.78	2.03	1.82	4.23	3.39	2.85	4.13	6.38	8.87	9.58	9.86	13.56	10.43	Cash	40..l
	5.81	6.64	9.02	12.76	15.77	I 28.52	37.78	41.06	49.05	55.38	57.16	69.33	83.26	106.67	116.01	Foreign Assets	41..l
	50.22	58.42	65.32	76.24	88.96	I 107.31	114.71	118.01	124.01	131.04	138.87	147.12	151.57	153.05	161.63	Claims on Central Government	42a.l
	30.11	36.61	43.88	48.86	54.17	I 62.15	69.10	76.88	25.03	25.18	26.04	27.28	28.49	30.89	31.80	Claims on Local Government	42b.l
	95.53	100.79	108.58	116.41	123.12	I 147.59	158.43	165.06	234.57	254.36	261.61	275.75	289.97	323.76	343.75	Claims on Private Sector	42d.l
	23.34	26.28	30.23	31.93	34.51	I 38.41	40.33	42.22	45.50	47.79	50.64	54.86	58.34	59.68	59.77	Real Estate	42h.l
	210.34	233.97	262.43	293.15	323.80	I 376.77	408.04	433.48	468.80	506.47	526.49	565.73	604.01	668.13	696.73	Capital Accounts	47a.l
	-3.96	-3.16	-3.63	-4.91	-5.45	11.82	14.70	13.49	12.70	13.66	16.69	18.18	17.47	19.47	26.66	Other Items (Net)	47r.l
Percent Per Annum																**Interest Rates**	
	8.00	9.00	5.00	5.00	5.00	5.00	4.50	3.75	4.50	7.00	7.25	8.50	7.75	5.00	....	Discount Rate (End of Period)	60
	....	....	....	....	....	5.50	5.00	4.27	5.01	7.75	8.00	8.94	8.33	5.52	....	Rate on Advances	60a
	10.13	11.01	8.06	5.28	5.78	6.30	5.83	5.16	4.48	6.99	8.29	9.01	9.27	7.10	5.14	Money Market Rate	60b
	5.96	6.06	5.88	4.03	4.10	4.10	3.93	3.55	3.48	3.49	3.31	3.18	3.20	3.11	2.95	Deposit Rate	60l
	13.50	14.25	11.17	8.46	8.88	9.25	8.63	8.15	7.77	10.75	11.75	12.40	12.75	10.40	8.29	Lending Rate	60p
	10.21	11.55	10.10	8.61	8.33	7.34	6.32	6.40	6.42	7.22	8.92	8.74	8.10	6.51	7.20	Government Bond Yield	61

Netherlands

		1965	1966	1967	1968	1969	1970	1971	1972	1973	1974	1975	1976	1977	1978	1979
Prices, Production, Employment																*Index Numbers (1990=100):*
Share Prices: General	62	31.0	25.3	I26.6	34.3	38.1	I35.0	33.0	38.0	40.5	31.1	31.6	33.1	31.6	31.8	31.4
Manufacturing	62a	61.8	52.4	I58.7	68.7	75.6	I77.2	73.1	87.9	97.0	75.0	74.5	71.2	64.3	64.1	57.9
Prices: Final Products	63	42.9	45.1	45.5	46.4	45.2	47.3	I49.4	51.8	55.0	60.0	63.6	68.0	71.7	72.7	74.6
Consumer Prices	64	30.7	32.4	33.6	34.8	37.4	38.8	41.7	44.9	48.5	53.2	58.6	63.9	68.0	70.8	73.8
Wages: Hourly Rates	65	19.6	21.6	23.0	24.7	27.1	30.0	33.6	I37.8	42.8	50.1	56.9	62.0	66.3	70.2	73.3
Industrial Production	66..c	47.5	49.2	51.0	55.3	57.9	63.0	67.4	70.0	76.0	79.5	78.6	83.8	83.8	83.8	87.2
Industrial Employment	67	138.2	137.6	133.0	130.6	131.5	131.5	130.0	126.2	122.7	121.2	117.4	113.6	109.8	106.5	I104.8
International Transactions																*Millions of Guilders*
Exports	70	26,583	28,131	30,267	34,518	41,206	48,345	55,366	61,490	76,039	100,322	100,761	121,662	122,914	124,292	147,395
Imports, cif	71	32,309	34,533	35,748	39,686	46,999	56,791	62,763	66,343	79,774	104,386	103,258	123,209	129,777	132,304	154,964
Imports, fob	71.v	30,480	32,578	33,725	37,440	44,352	53,309	59,030	62,711	74,874	98,137	97,514	116,827	122,983	125,194	146,572
																1990=100
Volume of Exports	72	21	23	24	28	33	36	39	43	48	55	52	59	58	60	66
Volume of Imports	73	28	30	32	36	41	46	47	49	54	59	56	63	64	68	72
Unit Value of Exports	74	45	45	45	45	I45	I47	48	49	52	67	I70	74	76	I75	81
Unit Value of Imports	75	42	42	42	40	I42	I45	46	46	50	67	I70	74	76	I75	84
Balance of Payments																*Millions of US Dollars:*
Goods: Exports f.o.b.	78aa *d*	....	....	7,364	8,339	9,906	11,637	13,450	16,687	23,497	32,965	34,724	39,279	42,994	49,189	63,721
Goods: Imports f.o.b.	78ab *d*	....	....	−7,931	−8,622	−10,333	−12,541	−14,070	−16,187	−22,362	−31,959	−33,398	−37,406	−42,645	−50,173	−64,390
Trade Balance	78ac *d*	....	....	−567	−283	−427	−904	−621	500	1,134	1,006	1,326	1,873	349	−984	−669
Services: Credit	78ad *d*	....	....	1,620	1,796	2,043	2,585	3,568	4,288	5,787	7,333	8,549	8,919	9,927	12,005	13,417
Services: Debit	78ae *d*	....	....	−1,284	−1,546	−1,749	−2,293	−3,152	−3,561	−4,902	−6,411	−7,150	−7,868	−9,118	−11,345	−13,965
Balance on Goods and Services	78af *d*	....	....	−231	−32	−133	−611	−205	1,227	2,019	1,928	2,725	2,924	1,157	−324	−1,217
Income: Credit	78ag *d*	....	....	760	799	962	1,209	1,424	1,584	2,463	4,453	3,886	4,371	4,870	5,566	10,239
Income: Debit	78ah *d*	....	....	−522	−616	−723	−1,041	−1,299	−1,319	−1,948	−3,009	−3,549	−3,381	−3,962	−5,329	−7,960
Balance on Goods, Serv., & Inc.	78ai *d*	....	....	7	150	106	−442	−79	1,492	2,534	3,372	3,062	3,913	2,065	−87	1,061
Current Transfers, n.i.e.: Credit	78aj *d*	....	....	99	132	170	256	516	592	1,048	945	1,045	1,436	1,816	2,292	2,927
Current Transfers: Debit	78ak *d*	....	....	−178	−199	−223	−293	−597	−735	−1,157	−1,302	−1,746	−1,877	−2,631	−3,405	−3,870
Current Account, n.i.e.	78al *d*	....	....	−72	83	53	−479	−159	1,349	2,426	3,015	2,362	3,472	1,250	−1,199	119
Capital Account, n.i.e.: Credit	78ba *d*	....	....	12	14	15	17	41	39	39	32	39	42	57	63	102
Capital Account: Debit	78bb *d*	....	....	−10	−10	−15	−23	−20	−26	−22	−33	−41	−73	−78	−110	−129
Capital Account, n.i.e.	78bc *d*	....	....	2	4	—	−6	21	13	17	−1	−2	−31	−21	−47	−27
Direct Investment Abroad	78bd *d*	....	....	−315	−350	−544	−562	−509	−759	−1,033	−2,788	−2,519	−2,352	−3,039	−3,385	−6,282
Dir. Invest. in Rep. Econ., n.i.e.	78be *d*	....	....	265	327	416	546	599	642	916	1,103	1,233	580	606	1,081	1,715
Portfolio Investment Assets	78bf *d*	....	....	−50	−260	−239	−246	−403	−681	−877	−402	−578	8	−52	−290	482
Portfolio Investment Liab., n.i.e.	78bg *d*	....	....	40	300	380	668	717	280	−100	128	1,002	125	1,802	1,413	2,075
Other Investment Assets	78bh *d*	....	....	−167	−688	−1,677	−1,861	−1,296	−1,711	−3,211	−2,956	−5,838	−5,885	−5,500	−8,943	−11,137
Other Investment Liab., n.i.e.	78bi *d*	....	....	312	425	1,522	2,232	1,050	1,500	2,708	2,898	4,288	4,785	5,509	10,799	12,706
Financial Account, n.i.e.	78bj *d*	....	....	85	−246	−143	778	158	−729	−1,596	−2,017	−2,412	−2,739	−674	675	−440
Net Errors and Omissions	78ca *d*	....	....	155	−9	152	327	142	231	−125	−15	368	−373	−257	−346	−241
Overall Balance	78cb *d*	....	....	170	−168	63	620	161	865	723	983	315	328	299	−917	−588
Reserves and Related Items	79da *d*	....	....	−170	168	−63	−620	−161	−865	−723	−983	−315	−328	−299	917	588
Reserve Assets	79db *d*	....	....	−172	158	−67	−622	−185	−929	−735	−306	−323	−295	−507	770	980
Use of Fund Credit and Loans	79dc *d*	....	....	—	—	—	—	—	—	—	—	—	—	—	—	—
Liabs.Constit.For.Auth.Reserves	79dd *d*	....	....	2	9	4	1	24	65	12	−678	8	−34	208	148	−392
Exceptional Financing	79de *d*	....	....	....	....	....	....	....	....	....	....	....	....	....	....	....
Government Finance																*Millions of Guilders:*
Deficit (-) or Surplus	80	−1,117	−1,678	−2,124	−2,161	−2,311	−1,319	−1,651	−92	I−40	−40	−6,350	−6,120	−8,370	−9,200	−14,530
Revenue	81	17,332	19,104	21,780	24,216	27,573	31,657	37,551	43,896	I76,960	89,530	103,580	119,380	132,730	143,340	154,100
Grants Received	81z	....	....	....	....	....	....	....	....	I310	390	350	340	500	520	660
Expenditure	82	16,876	18,906	21,762	24,417	27,776	31,100	37,095	41,024	I72,690	86,730	106,460	121,440	134,840	149,230	164,510
Lending Minus Repayments	83	1,573	1,876	2,142	1,960	2,108	1,876	2,107	2,964	I4,620	3,270	3,230	3,570	3,500	3,240	3,100
Overall Adj.Cash Basis &Stat.Adj.	80x	....	....	....	....	....	....	....	....	I—	40	−590	−830	−3,260	−590	−1,680
Financing																
Net Borrowing: Domestic	84a	963	1,657	2,615	1,970	2,338	1,819	1,884	1,083	I1,340	2,530	5,640	7,390	8,020	8,970	10,660
Long-Term	84x	....	....	....	....	....	....	....	....	....	....	....	....	....	....	....
Short-Term	84y	....	....	....	....	....	....	....	....	....	....	....	....	....	....	....
Foreign	85a	−52	−22	—	−237	—	−10	−24	−14	I−10	−420	−10	−10	—	—	—
Use of Cash Balances	87	207	43	−491	428	−27	−488	−211	−977	I−1,290	−2,070	720	−1,260	350	230	3,870
Debt: Domestic	88a	....	....	....	....	....	....	....	....	I37,040	39,980	46,170	53,770	61,740	70,670	81,240
Foreign	89a	....	....	....	....	....	....	....	....	....	....	....	....	....	....	....
Guilders	88b	21,573	23,182	25,697	28,420	30,616	32,850	35,045	36,488	....	....	....	....	....	....	....
Foreign Currency	89b	367	345	345	108	108	98	74	60	....	....	....	....	....	....	....
National Accounts																*Billions of Guilders*
Exports of Goods & Services	90c. *c*	30.8	32.6	34.8	39.0	45.9	54.3	62.0	69.4	83.4	107.8	109.7	128.5	130.7	133.3	155.1
Government Consumption	91f. *c*	10.5	11.7	13.2	14.3	16.2	18.7	21.9	24.4	27.4	32.5	38.3	43.5	47.9	52.6	57.2
Gross Fixed Capital Formation	93e. *c*	17.0	19.3	21.3	24.0	26.5	31.4	34.6	36.4	40.7	43.9	46.3	49.0	57.9	63.3	66.5
Increase/Decrease(-) in Stocks	93i. *c*	1.3	1.0	.7	.6	2.3	2.5	1.5	.7	2.5	4.6	−.9	3.0	1.5	1.8	1.5
Private Consumption	96f. *c*	39.5	43.0	46.6	51.0	63.2	70.8	78.9	88.5	99.8	113.4	129.0	148.0	164.3	179.2	192.4
Imports of Goods & Services	98c. *c*	−31.3	−33.7	−35.5	−39.0	−46.1	−56.4	−62.4	−65.2	−77.8	−102.3	−102.3	−119.9	−127.4	−133.2	−156.7
Gross Domestic Product = GDP	99b. *c*	67.8	73.8	81.0	89.8	101.7	121.2	136.5	154.3	176.0	199.8	220.0	251.9	274.9	297.0	316.0
Net Factor Inc/Pmts(-) Abroad	98.n	.8	.6	.8	.6	.8	.6	.4	.7	1.3	1.7	—	.1	.5	−.7	−.7
Gross National Product = GNP	99a	68.6	74.4	81.8	90.4	102.5	121.7	136.9	155.0	177.3	201.5	219.9	252.1	275.4	296.3	315.2
Nat'l Income, Market Prices	99e	62.5	67.8	74.7	82.7	99.9	111.5	125.1	141.7	162.6	184.2	199.9	229.6	251.2	269.7	285.9
Gross Dom. Prod. 1990 Prices	99b. *r*	228.6	235.2	248.0	264.1	296.8	313.7	327.0	337.8	353.5	367.6	367.3	386.1	395.0	404.9	414.7
GDP Deflator (1990=100)	99bi *r*	29.7	31.4	32.7	34.0	34.3	38.6	41.7	45.7	49.8	54.3	59.9	65.2	69.6	73.3	76.2
																Millions:
Population	99z	12.29	12.45	12.60	12.72	12.87	13.03	13.19	13.33	13.44	13.54	13.65	13.77	13.85	13.94	14.03

Deposit Money Banks: I Beginning in 1982, the data reflect improved classifications on the report forms used to collect these data from the banks.

Money (National Definitions): I Prior to December 1982, the concept of domestic liquidity (also referred to as M2, *line 38n*) comprised certain liquid liabilities of the central and local governments. From December 1982, new monetary aggregates, which are denoted as *M3H* and *M3H seasonally adjusted*, have been introduced. Contrary to M2, the broader M3H includes savings with an original maturity of less than two years but excludes liquid liabilities of the central and local governments.

Nonbank Financial Institutions: I Beginning in 1985, the data for insurance companies are based on a new and extended survey of the largest seven insurance companies, covering about 85 to 90 percent of the balance sheet total of all insurance companies. Prior to 1985, data for insurance companies relate only to life insurance. The data for pension funds cover the General Public Service Fund and other pension funds: the data for the latter are based on returns from the largest such funds.

Interest Rates: *Money Market Rate:* I Prior to December 1971, data refer to the short-term lending rate to local authorities.

Government Finance: I Beginning in 1973, data are as reported in the *Government Finance Statistics Yearbook* and relate to the consolidated central government. I Break symbols in data for financing and debt indicate that, from 1987 onward, foreign financing and debt include external borrowing in national currency which, in earlier years, was included in domestic financing and debt.

Netherlands

	1980	1981	1982	1983	1984	1985	1986	1987	1988	1989	1990	1991	1992	1993	1994		Prices, Production, Employment	
Period Averages																		
	29.4	31.1	31.6	45.6	57.9	ℐ74.9	86.0	89.5	81.1	102.6	100.0	102.8	107.8	125.0	148.0		Share Prices: General	62
	49.6	52.5	55.0	83.1	102.6	77.2	98.7	88.0	80.3	103.5	100.0	100.1	107.0	125.4	152.1		Manufacturing	62a
	80.1	87.1	92.1	93.3	97.5	99.0	96.3	95.1	95.6	99.0	100.0	102.3	105.0	ℐ105.8	106.4		Prices: Final Products	63
	ℐ78.6	83.9	88.8	91.3	94.3	96.4	96.5	95.8	96.6	97.6	ℐ100.0	103.1	106.4	109.2	112.2		Consumer Prices	64
	76.5	79.1	84.4	86.6	87.6	91.9	93.4	94.7	95.9	97.2	100.0	ℐ103.7	108.2	111.7	113.8		Wages: Hourly Rates	65
	ℐ86.4	84.5	80.9	83.9	87.3	90.9	90.9	91.8	94.5	98.2	100.0	102.7	102.7	ℐ101.8	105.6		Industrial Production	66..c
	ℐ103.7	100.7	86.2	93.5	92.4	93.5	95.3	96.3	96.3	97.9	100.0	100.2	100.7	ℐ96.5	....		Industrial Employment	67
Millions of Guilders																	**International Transactions**	
	168,850	195,259	201,921	209,954	240,081	257,267	197,285	188,016	203,730	228,544	239,181	249,105	246,541	258,343	....		Exports	70
	175,732	188,916	193,088	194,733	221,657	241,587	185,053	184,844	196,347	220,987	229,708	236,924	236,597	231,043	....		Imports, cif	71
	166,250	178,267	182,665	185,211	209,759	ℐ228,697	175,240	175,042	185,935	209,268	217,527	224,360	224,050	218,791	....		Imports, fob	71.v
1990=100																		
	ℐ66	67	66	69	ℐ74	77	79	83	91	95	100	105	108	ℐ115	....		Volume of Exports	72
	ℐ70	65	66	67	ℐ72	77	80	85	91	95	100	104	106	ℐ110	....		Volume of Imports	73
	ℐ92	107	111	111	119	122	103	94	94	101	100	98	95	ℐ93	....		Unit Value of Exports	74
	ℐ96	111	113	114	120	122	100	94	94	103	100	100	97	ℐ93	....		Unit Value of Imports	75
Minus Sign Indicates Debit																	**Balance of Payments**	
	73,626	68,431	66,004	64,350	65,222	67,571	78,456	91,894	103,099	107,730	129,988	131,482	138,427	127,936	137,587		Goods: Exports f.o.b.	78aa d
	−73,720	−63,396	−60,375	−58,809	−58,691	−61,298	−70,641	−85,460	−93,357	−98,582	−118,334	−119,065	−125,344	−113,525	−123,171		Goods: Imports f.o.b.	78ab d
	−94	5,035	5,630	5,541	6,531	6,273	7,815	6,434	9,741	9,148	11,654	12,417	13,083	14,411	14,416		Trade Balance	78ac d
	15,937	14,746	15,139	12,997	13,372	13,845	16,327	20,078	21,611	24,141	29,238	30,944	34,731	35,108	38,778		Services: Credit	78ad d
	−17,067	−14,933	−14,829	−13,612	−13,792	−14,591	−18,017	−21,595	−23,486	−24,213	−28,139	−32,056	−35,993	−35,404	−38,416		Services: Debit	78ae d
	−1,224	4,848	5,941	4,926	6,112	5,527	6,126	4,917	7,866	9,076	12,753	11,305	11,821	14,114	14,778		Balance on Goods and Services	78af d
	12,763	12,673	12,366	11,190	11,807	9,466	12,708	15,835	18,360	23,525	26,296	27,831	27,820	27,606	25,955		Income: Credit	78ag d
	−11,227	−12,303	−11,984	−10,077	−10,457	−9,690	−12,906	−14,512	−17,243	−20,564	−26,876	−27,196	−28,281	−26,961	−24,084		Income: Debit	78ah d
	312	5,218	6,323	6,039	7,462	5,304	5,927	6,241	8,983	12,038	12,173	11,940	11,360	14,759	16,649		Balance on Goods, Serv., & Inc.	78ai d
	2,790	1,947	1,980	2,066	2,071	2,147	3,055	4,200	5,677	5,198	4,550	4,714	4,715	4,514	4,280		Current Transfers, n.i.e.: Credit	78aj d
	−4,081	−3,543	−3,533	−3,168	−3,173	−3,256	−4,916	−6,233	−7,670	−7,348	−7,565	−8,889	−9,189	−9,072	−9,681		Current Transfers: Debit	78ak d
	−979	3,623	4,769	4,937	6,360	4,195	4,066	4,208	6,990	9,889	9,158	7,764	6,885	10,201	11,249		Current Account, n.i.e.	78al d
	86	106	152	115	97	107	140	164	210	243	243	233	295	422	470		Capital Account, n.i.e.: Credit	78ba d
	−193	−178	−213	−140	−128	−116	−162	−416	−285	−347	−471	−468	−803	−1,078	−1,271		Capital Account: Debit	78bb d
	−107	−72	−61	−25	−31	−8	−22	−252	−75	−104	−228	−235	−507	−656	−801		Capital Account, n.i.e.	78bc d
	−5,917	−4,527	−3,263	−3,835	−4,844	−2,705	−4,093	−8,654	−7,112	−14,826	−15,422	−13,594	−14,588	−10,256	−11,407		Direct Investment Abroad	78bd d
	2,278	1,799	1,227	1,358	1,717	1,493	3,135	3,028	4,779	8,346	12,319	6,282	7,814	5,775	3,403		Dir. Invest. in Rep. Econ., n.i.e.	78be d
	176	−92	−1,202	−1,197	−1,033	−2,438	−7,257	−3,999	−6,921	−593	−3,566	−4,971	−13,028	−11,303	−11,824		Portfolio Investment Assets	78bf d
	3,026	1,186	1,069	1,391	999	2,710	2,132	5,864	10,294	7,846	−1,607	4,113	3,878	12,978	−2,335		Portfolio Investment Liab., n.i.e.	78bg d
	−9,648	−8,225	−2,015	−622	−4,519	−5,502	−7,382	−12,402	−14,081	−27,976	−24,234	−5,609	−7,779	−10,634	10,752		Other Investment Assets	78bh d
	12,468	5,691	1,377	−2,031	148	4,061	11,385	15,046	12,458	19,179	27,858	7,448	16,424	2,874	3,876		Other Investment Liab., n.i.e.	78bi d
	2,382	−4,168	−2,807	−4,937	−7,532	−2,382	−2,080	−1,118	−585	−8,023	−4,652	−6,331	−7,278	−10,566	−7,535		Financial Account, n.i.e.	78bj d
	−115	−210	−120	−203	1,241	−1,054	−2,349	23	−4,704	−1,312	−4,001	−1,121	7,327	7,563	−2,503		Net Errors and Omissions	78ca d
	1,180	−827	1,781	−228	38	751	−386	2,861	1,626	450	277	77	6,427	6,542	410		Overall Balance	78cb d
	−1,180	827	−1,781	228	−38	−751	386	−2,861	−1,626	−450	−277	−77	−6,427	−6,542	−410		Reserves and Related Items	79da d
	−1,263	891	−1,795	158	11	−772	330	−2,694	−1,567	−506	−268	−507	−6,118	−6,641	−501		Reserve Assets	79db d
	—	—	—	—	—	—	—	—	—	—	—	—	—	—	—		Use of Fund Credit and Loans	79dc d
	83	−64	13	70	−50	21	55	−167	−59	57	−9	430	−309	99	91		Liabs.Constit.For.Auth.Reserves	79dd d
	....	....	....	....	....	....	....	....	....	....	....	....	....	....	....		Exceptional Financing	79de d
Year Ending December 31																	**Government Finance**	
	−15,560	−22,970	−28,050	−29,550	−29,920	−23,370	−8,210	−13,770	−19,250	−20,990	−24,700	−14,940	−19,140	−5,450	....		Deficit (-) or Surplus	80
	168,880	179,070	189,320	200,100	206,190	217,120	223,220	224,260	230,120	229,840	243,000	270,860	279,070	291,160	....		Revenue	81
	710	670	820	1,060	960	930	1,080	1,680	850	1,250	200	240	240	180	....		Grants Received	81z
	180,590	195,670	212,910	223,680	232,100	236,030	243,630	251,580	250,940	256,550	266,630	283,650	298,340	309,390	....		Expenditure	82
	4,100	6,210	5,620	4,950	4,440	1,750	−11,760	−10,280	−1,750	−1,930	−390	730	680	−11,110	....		Lending Minus Repayments	83
	−460	−830	340	−2,080	−530	−3,640	−640	1,590	−1,030	2,540	−1,660	−1,660	570	1,490	....		Overall Adj.Cash Basis &Stat.Adj.	80x
																	Financing	
	17,130	22,150	28,500	30,300	29,770	26,200	11,690	ℐ4,040	12,300	14,450	23,230	3,550	−3,120	−4,940	....		Net Borrowing: Domestic	84a
	....	....	....	....	....	....	....	....	....	....	....	....	....	....	....		Long-Term	84x
	....	....	....	....	....	....	....	....	....	....	....	....	....	....	....		Short-Term	84y
	....	....	....	....	....	....	—	ℐ8,600	11,100	5,700	−1,000	17,300	22,600	18,200	....		Foreign	85a
	−1,570	820	−450	−750	150	−2,830	−3,480	ℐ1,130	−4,150	840	2,470	−5,910	−340	−7,810	....		Use of Cash Balances	87
	98,050	118,340	144,760	175,250	204,090	229,020	238,810	ℐ208,370	218,550	232,430	256,580	259,640	256,510	25,151	....		Debt: Domestic	88a
	....	....	....	....	....	....	—	ℐ43,400	55,700	61,400	60,400	78,900	101,500	119,700	....		Foreign	89a
	....	....	....	....	....	....	....	....	....	....	....	....	....	....	....		Guilders	88b
	....	....	....	....	....	....	....	....	....	....	....	....	....	....	....		Foreign Currency	89b
Billions of Guilders																	**National Accounts**	
	176.8	204.6	212.6	219.8	248.6	258.7	222.0	219.3	240.3	267.7	279.7	294.4	294.4	290.7	309.5		Exports of Goods & Services	90c. c
	60.3	62.8	65.1	66.6	66.4	66.9	67.7	69.8	70.2	71.8	74.8	77.9	81.5	83.6	85.7		Government Consumption	91f. c
	70.8	67.6	67.2	69.5	74.3	83.7	89.4	91.6	97.4	104.1	107.9	110.8	114.2	113.0	118.0		Gross Fixed Capital Formation	93e. c
	1.7	−3.1	−1.0	.6	2.0	1.4	3.8	−.4	.3	5.4	6.5	5.2	1.2	−1.4	1.5		Increase/Decrease(-) in Stocks	93i. c
	205.8	213.2	221.8	229.9	236.8	252.9	260.2	267.9	271.6	284.5	303.1	322.5	340.7	350.3	363.4		Private Consumption	96f. c
	−178.6	−192.2	−196.8	−205.2	−227.8	−238.3	−205.4	−207.6	−222.4	−248.8	−255.8	−267.4	−269.0	−261.9	−277.7		Imports of Goods & Services	98c. c
	336.7	352.9	368.9	381.0	400.3	425.4	437.7	440.6	457.4	484.7	516.3	542.2	563.1	574.3	600.3		Gross Domestic Product = GDP	99b. c
	−.6	−1.0	−.4	.6	−.5	—	−.7	−1.2	−3.5	−.2	−.9	−.9	−2.2	−.5	2.5		Net Factor Inc/Pmts(-) Abroad	98.n
	336.1	351.9	368.5	381.6	399.8	425.3	437.0	439.4	453.9	484.5	515.4	541.3	560.9	573.8	602.7		Gross National Product = GNP	99a
	303.6	316.3	330.6	342.4	358.6	379.1	389.8	390.9	402.7	429.6	457.1	479.7	496.3	507.2	532.9		Nat'l Income, Market Prices	99e
	418.4	415.5	409.3	415.1	428.1	439.3	448.1	462.8	474.9	497.0	516.3	528.2	537.5	539.8	553.1		Gross Dom. Prod. 1990 Prices	99b. r
	80.5	84.9	90.1	91.8	93.5	96.8	97.7	95.2	96.3	97.5	100.0	102.6	104.8	106.4	108.5		GDP Deflator (1990=100)	99bi r
Midyear Estimates																		
	14.14	14.25	14.31	14.36	14.42	14.48	14.56	14.66	14.76	14.85	14.95	15.07	15.18	15.29	15.38		Population	99z

Netherlands Antilles
353

		1965	1966	1967	1968	1969	1970	1971	1972	1973	1974	1975	1976	1977	1978	1979
Exchange Rates														*Guilders per SDR: End of Period (aa)*		
Official Rate	aa	1.881	1.883	1.873	1.879	1.888	1.874	1.954	1.954	2.171	2.204	2.107	2.091	2.186	2.345	2.371
Official Rate	ae	1.881	1.883	1.873	1.879	1.888	1.874	1.800	1.800	1.800	1.800	1.800	1.800	1.800	1.800	1.800
													Index Numbers (1990=100):			
Official Rate	ah x	95.4ᵉ	94.9ᵉ	95.3ᵉ	95.5	95.5	95.5	95.4	99.4	99.4	99.4	99.4	99.4	99.4	99.4	99.4
Nominal Effective Exchange Rate	ne c	....	....	....	....	....	....	....	....	....	....	....	....	....	....	70.8
Real Effective Exchange Rate	re c	....	....	....	....	....	....	....	....	....	....	....	....	....	....	93.9
International Liquidity												*Millions of US Dollars Unless Otherwise Indicated:*				
Total Reserves minus Gold	1l. d	....	....	....	20	28	25	36	50	50	62	71	93	101	67	73
Foreign Exchange	1d. d	....	....	....	20	28	25	36	50	50	62	71	93	101	67	73
Gold (Million Fine Troy Ounces)	1ad	.558	.558	.558	.558	.558	.558	.548	.548	.548	.548	.548	.548	.548	.548	.548
Gold (National Valuation)	1an d	19	19	19	19	19	19	19	21ᵉ	23ᵉ	23	23	23	23	23	23
Deposit Money Banks: Assets	7a. d	....	....	....	94	107	118	143	148	125	118	125	318	584	887	1,529
of which: Claims on Nonbanks	7ad d	....	....	....	23	10	11	13	12	42	13	9	122	264	535	998
Deposit Money Banks: Liabilities	7b. d	....	....	....	75	105	115	137	152	122	115	113	289	570	881	1,526
of which: Liab. to Nonbanks	7bd d	....	....	....	73	96	106	120	134	98	98	100	137	371	656	684
OBU: Assets	7k. d	....	....	....	....	....	....	....	....	....	....	....	1,228	1,799	2,283	3,588
of which: Claims on Nonbanks	7kd d	....	....	....	....	....	....	....	....	....	....	....	1,033	1,438	1,732	2,733
OBU: Liabilities	7m. d	....	....	....	....	....	....	....	....	....	....	....	1,154	1,706	2,099	3,360
of which: Liab. to Nonbanks	7md d	....	....	....	....	....	....	....	....	....	....	....	331	470	609	789
Monetary Authorities													*Millions of Guilders*			
Foreign Assets	11	....	....	....	66.6	77.4	78.3	105.0	125.7	127.8	149.2	168.1	206.9	217.3	161.1	172.5
Claims on Central Government	12a	....	....	....	-1.6	-5.1	3.7	6.3	14.3	26.1	56.5	94.7	96.9	93.2	134.4	131.4
Reserve Money	14	....	....	....	56.7	63.5	69.8	95.5	109.9	118.0	127.6	162.7	175.2	201.2	199.8	228.1
of which: Currency Outside DMBs	14a	....	....	....	38.6	48.2	52.6	56.1	60.4	62.8	76.8	88.0	94.7	104.9	125.8	137.7
Time Deposits	15	....	....	....	—	—	—	—	—	—	23.0	44.0	55.0	38.0	12.0	—
Central Government Deposits	16d	....	....	....	—	—	—	.7	8.0	8.6	15.0	13.7	26.2	29.1	25.0	28.7
Capital Accounts	17a	....	....	....	8.8	8.7	9.7	12.6	15.0	23.1	27.1	35.2	35.4	37.2	39.9	42.3
Other Items (Net)	17r	....	....	....	1.3	1.7	4.0	5.1	8.6	2.6	11.0	5.7	10.7	4.3	18.8	4.6
Deposit Money Banks													*Millions of Guilders:*			
Reserves	20	....	....	....	18.5	15.7	17.6	38.7	37.4	55.0	39.2	70.0	77.2	81.4	51.7	76.8
Foreign Assets	21	....	....	....	176.5	201.6	221.8	256.2	264.6	223.9	211.7	224.9	572.9	1,052.0	1,596.5	2,752.6
Claims on Local Government	22b	....	....	....	9.1	7.2	5.7	3.0	2.5	9.1	4.9	2.6	2.7	6.1	15.3	18.4
Claims on Private Sector	22d	....	....	....	146.7	183.5	226.5	244.3	305.5	327.8	379.1	374.5	409.4	492.6	624.1	658.5
Demand Deposits	24	....	....	....	42.8	47.1	59.1	72.8	91.7	98.5	98.9	115.7	135.3	159.6	197.7	192.2
Time and Savings Deposits	25a	....	....	....	95.0	100.3	124.3	154.1	180.1	205.4	250.3	275.6	310.1	340.4	397.7	427.5
Foreign Currency Deposits	25b	....	....	....	32.2	25.6	32.0	31.0	34.0	37.7	44.7	45.5	50.4	65.2	62.2	77.1
Foreign Liabilities	26c	....	....	....	139.0	192.0	211.2	226.6	249.9	198.7	187.1	192.2	516.9	1,007.6	1,577.0	2,731.2
Long-Term Foreign Liabilities	26cl	....	....	....	2.6	5.3	5.3	18.0	21.6	19.8	20.7	10.3	2.8	18.7	9.1	15.7
Central Government Deposits	26d	....	....	....	5.1	4.5	4.3	6.4	4.2	5.4	4.2	4.2	4.8	5.2	5.1	4.8
Capital Accounts	27a	....	....	....	27.0	27.0	29.0	29.8	31.9	33.2	29.1	34.8	44.4	47.7	53.9	70.1
Other Items (Net)	27r	....	....	....	7.4	6.2	6.4	3.5	-3.4	17.1	-.1	-6.1	-3.2	-12.3	-15.1	-12.7
Girosystem Curacao																
Private Sector Deposits	24.. i	....	....	....	6.5	5.2	5.0	6.3	11.1	11.3	11.1	15.5	14.6	30.4	28.0	25.5
Central Government Deposits	26d. i	....	....	....	3.6	2.0	2.0	2.0	6.0	2.8	6.4	5.8	3.7	3.6	8.0	41.6
Monetary Survey													*Millions of Guilders*			
Foreign Assets (Net)	31n	....	....	....	104.1	87.0	87.7	134.6	137.3	152.9	170.8	197.5	259.2	261.7	167.7	193.8
Domestic Credit	32	....	....	....	157.7	187.9	238.1	255.4	323.0	366.2	436.7	473.8	496.3	608.1	804.4	840.5
Claims on Central Govt. (Net)	32an	....	....	....	-10.3	-11.6	-2.6	-2.8	-3.7	9.6	31.0	71.2	62.6	71.6	125.3	93.6
Claims on Local Government	32b	....	....	....	19.2	14.4	12.7	11.3	19.6	23.6	22.6	24.2	21.0	40.6	51.8	86.0
Claims on Private Sector	32d	....	....	....	148.8	185.1	228.0	246.9	307.1	333.0	383.1	378.4	412.7	495.9	627.3	660.9
Money	34	....	....	....	88.3	100.9	117.2	135.8	173.7	173.9	198.3	223.6	247.9	309.8	373.8	369.4
Quasi-Money	35	....	....	....	127.2	125.9	156.3	185.1	214.1	243.1	318.0	365.1	415.5	443.6	471.9	504.6
Long-Term Foreign Liabilities	36cl	....	....	....	2.6	5.3	5.3	18.0	21.6	23.2	23.7	13.0	5.1	20.7	10.7	17.0
Other Items (Net)	37r	....	....	....	43.7	42.8	47.0	51.1	50.8	75.5	64.5	67.1	84.0	93.7	114.1	142.0
Money plus Quasi-Money	35l	....	....	....	215.5	226.8	273.5	320.9	387.8	417.0	516.3	588.7	663.4	753.4	845.7	874.0
Interest Rates													*Percent Per Annum*			
Discount Rate *(End of Period)*	60	....	....	....	....	....	....	....	....	....	....	....	....	....	....	....
Treasury Bill Rate	60c	....	....	....	....	....	....	....	....	....	....	....	....	....	....	....
Deposit Rate	60l	....	....	....	....	....	....	....	....	....	....	....	....	....	....	....
Lending Rate	60p	....	....	....	....	....	....	....	....	....	....	9.25	9.13	9.75	9.75	11.40
Government Bond Yield	61	....	....	....	....	....	....	....	....	....	....	....	....	....	....	....
Prices													*Index Numbers (1990=100):*			
Consumer Prices	64	25.9	26.2	26.5	26.8	27.2	I28.2	28.8	30.0	32.4	38.7	I44.7	47.1	49.6	53.7	59.8
International Transactions													*Millions of Guilders*			
Exports	70	1,137	1,116	1,146	1,130	1,178	1,275	1,366	1,364	2,465	5,815	4,315	4,544	4,764	5,357	7,139
Imports, cif	71	1,359	1,362	1,475	1,482	1,529	1,504	1,661	1,565	2,868	6,536	5,088	6,601	5,631	6,284	7,911
Crude Petroleum	71aa	....	....	905	865	877	948	1,079	988	1,977	5,409	3,490	5,207	4,129	....	....
Imports, fob	71.v	1,189	1,192	1,292	1,300	1,343	1,327	1,411	1,338	2,452	5,588	4,350	5,894	5,029	5,612	7,065

Netherlands Antilles

1980	1981	1982	1983	1984	1985	1986	1987	1988	1989	1990	1991	1992	1993	1994		
Guilders per US Dollar: End of Period (ae)															**Exchange Rates**	
2.296	2.095	1.986	1.885	1.764	1.977	2.202	2.554	2.422	2.352	2.547	2.560	2.461	2.459	2.613	Official Rate	aa
1.800	1.800	1.800	1.800	1.800	1.800	1.800	1.800	1.800	1.790	1.790	1.790	1.790	1.790	1.790	Official Rate	ae
Period Averages																
99.4	99.4	99.4	99.4	99.4	99.4	99.4	99.4	99.4	99.4	99.8	100.0	100.0	100.0	100.0	Official Rate	ah x
70.7	73.9	75.6	78.7	84.1	86.6	83.3	85.8	86.2	97.5	100.0	103.2	104.8	110.3	117.2	Nominal Effective Exchange Rate	ne c
94.6	100.4	102.0	105.1	109.0	107.8	101.9	102.7	99.0	103.1	100.0	98.8	95.1	....	....	Real Effective Exchange Rate	re c
End of Period															**International Liquidity**	
95	135	187	164	118	176	239	217	263	207	215	177	220	234	179	Total Reserves minus Gold	1l. d
95	135	187	164	118	176	239	217	263	207	215	177	220	234	179	Foreign Exchange	1d. d
.548	.548	.548	.548	.548	.548	.548	.548	.548	.548	.548	.548	.548	.548	.548	Gold (Million Fine Troy Ounces)	1ad
23	23	23	23	23	23	23	38	38	38	38	38	38	38	38	Gold (National Valuation)	1an d
2,634	3,055	3,341	2,459	1,331	1,197	361	399	571	880	555	681	748	825	747	Deposit Money Banks: Assets	7a. d
991	875	572	608	431	409	77	91	316	497	182	335	383	496	460	of which: Claims on Nonbanks	7ad d
2,631	3,043	3,322	2,443	1,303	1,155	294	354	532	840	548	660	722	780	719	Deposit Money Banks: Liabilities	7b. d
778	1,188	1,085	774	777	650	197	291	261	529	449	471	581	669	567	of which: Liab. to Nonbanks	7bd d
4,759	7,513	8,512	7,788	6,377	5,417	5,610	6,548	8,011	13,047	15,881	20,327	24,237	29,155	28,623	OBU: Assets	7k. d
3,742	6,549	6,443	5,405	3,826	3,277	3,543	3,596	4,295	6,599	8,391	10,597	12,217	14,750	11,282	of which: Claims on Nonbanks	7kd d
4,503	7,207	8,097	7,435	5,886	4,922	4,990	5,907	7,280	12,418	15,199	19,401	22,935	27,619	27,862	OBU: Liabilities	7m. d
835	1,060	1,577	1,513	1,856	2,426	2,604	3,239	5,176	6,261	7,516	8,731	12,000	15,457	10,138	of which: Liab. to Nonbanks	7md d
End of Period															**Monetary Authorities**	
211.2	285.9	375.5	337.3	253.4	367.6	501.4	459.3	538.2	445.2	454.0	385.1	461.9	490.1	435.1	Foreign Assets	11
111.1	101.5	100.4	111.0	119.7	188.9	130.0	124.0	131.0	91.5	75.4	75.3	71.0	65.1	57.8	Claims on Central Government	12a
247.5	251.6	269.8	247.1	220.6	385.2	469.0	426.1	434.5	302.0	355.6	294.3	380.2	400.3	372.9	Reserve Money	14
139.2	161.6	167.0	162.6	167.8	137.5	122.2	124.4	128.0	144.6	160.8	168.2	178.6	183.4	196.1	of which: Currency Outside DMBs	14a
—	26.5	86.4	81.4	32.4	2.0	2.1	2.3	59.2	17.5	17.6	26.8	2.9	11.0	13.2	Time Deposits	15
26.7	39.7	31.4	44.2	43.2	78.1	77.8	62.1	77.5	91.0	47.4	44.7	40.0	71.2	13.0	Central Government Deposits	16d
45.9	52.1	63.8	63.8	63.8	63.8	44.6	54.7	63.5	63.5	66.4	66.4	65.8	65.8	65.8	Capital Accounts	17a
3.3	18.3	25.2	12.4	13.7	28.0	38.2	38.7	34.6	63.2	42.9	28.7	44.4	7.6	28.4	Other Items (Net)	17r
End of Period															**Deposit Money Banks**	
84.8	73.8	91.7	63.8	41.7	155.9	265.8	216.7	234.1	127.7	138.4	74.9	122.2	176.9	128.5	Reserves	20
4,741.4	5,499.1	6,014.2	4,425.8	2,396.5	2,155.0	649.2	718.5	1,027.7	1,575.5	993.0	1,219.3	1,339.6	1,477.0	1,336.8	Foreign Assets	21
13.3	10.9	5.2	4.3	12.7	9.5	3.0	4.1	5.2	1.5	9.8	72.1	94.7	125.1	126.5	Claims on Local Government	22b
746.8	895.5	979.4	1,112.1	1,112.5	1,041.1	777.8	982.6	1,126.5	1,371.4	1,549.5	1,679.6	1,716.6	1,796.9	2,035.8	Claims on Private Sector	22d
197.6	221.0	269.1	280.7	251.1	260.8	271.4	317.1	333.7	354.6	384.0	413.6	424.8	501.9	561.0	Demand Deposits	24
504.1	595.9	699.6	744.2	754.0	741.8	663.5	697.5	784.6	789.9	869.1	912.8	1,018.6	1,136.5	1,202.3	Time and Savings Deposits	25a
90.0	110.5	98.2	117.3	133.9	149.0	154.1	183.3	220.4	263.1	275.8	330.8	350.8	375.5	399.9	Foreign Currency Deposits	25b
4,706.3	5,442.7	5,956.5	4,376.7	2,333.7	2,076.3	527.1	609.6	937.4	1,471.6	950.9	1,162.2	1,274.8	1,358.9	1,257.1	Foreign Liabilities	26c
29.5	34.2	23.4	21.3	11.8	3.2	2.1	27.8	20.7	31.5	30.9	18.9	18.1	37.9	30.5	Long-Term Foreign Liabilities	26cl
7.5	5.7	7.2	7.0	6.8	9.0	14.1	21.9	11.1	19.6	36.9	50.9	47.5	39.0	36.0	Central Government Deposits	26d
81.1	95.2	105.8	116.9	135.0	147.3	137.0	135.4	140.0	168.8	227.6	242.8	236.6	252.3	277.8	Capital Accounts	27a
−29.8	−26.1	−69.3	−58.2	−62.9	−25.8	−73.3	−70.6	−54.3	−23.2	−84.2	−86.1	−98.0	−124.8	−137.0	Other Items (Net)	27r
															Girosystem Curacao	
26.2	24.2	27.6	28.8	36.7	39.0	38.9	42.6	44.3	40.5	42.0	45.7	55.5	60.1	87.1	Private Sector Deposits	24.. i
37.0	32.8	31.9	32.1	32.3	34.4	32.9	39.4	34.0	35.1	33.6	34.2	34.5	34.3	34.9	Central Government Deposits	26d. i
End of Period															**Monetary Survey**	
245.9	342.2	433.1	385.8	315.8	445.0	621.2	567.7	627.9	548.7	495.3	441.0	526.0	605.1	467.8	Foreign Assets (Net)	31n
914.9	1,050.6	1,180.8	1,302.8	1,324.6	1,243.5	939.4	1,147.8	1,296.1	1,462.9	1,676.7	1,845.2	1,962.3	2,054.8	2,376.8	Domestic Credit	32
90.2	86.0	135.6	124.5	129.5	118.6	86.1	78.4	85.8	13.8	25.6	7.6	59.0	37.9	84.0	Claims on Central Govt. (Net)	32an
76.9	68.3	65.1	65.5	82.0	83.2	75.0	86.3	83.6	77.2	101.1	157.5	186.2	219.5	256.5	Claims on Local Government	32b
747.8	896.3	980.1	1,112.8	1,113.1	1,041.7	778.3	983.1	1,126.7	1,371.9	1,550.1	1,680.1	1,717.1	1,797.4	2,036.3	Claims on Private Sector	32d
386.5	423.0	474.8	493.0	466.7	527.7	513.5	569.1	578.4	569.4	643.2	678.7	738.3	785.0	892.5	Money	34
594.1	732.9	884.2	942.9	920.3	892.8	819.7	883.1	1,064.2	1,070.5	1,162.5	1,270.4	1,372.5	1,523.0	1,615.4	Quasi-Money	35
29.5	34.2	23.4	21.3	11.8	3.2	2.1	27.8	20.7	31.5	30.9	18.9	18.1	37.9	30.5	Long-Term Foreign Liabilities	36cl
150.8	202.5	231.5	231.3	241.6	264.9	225.3	235.7	260.7	340.0	335.7	318.2	359.6	315.5	306.1	Other Items (Net)	37r
980.6	1,155.9	1,359.0	1,435.9	1,387.0	1,420.5	1,333.2	1,452.2	1,642.6	1,639.9	1,805.7	1,949.1	2,110.6	2,308.0	2,507.9	Money plus Quasi-Money	35l
Percent Per Annum															**Interest Rates**	
9.00	9.00	9.00	8.00	8.00	8.00	8.00	6.00	6.00	6.00	6.00	6.00	6.00	6.00	5.00	Discount Rate *(End of Period)*	60
....	....	7.50	7.25	7.35	7.21	7.34	6.36	5.79	5.96	6.10	....	....	4.83	4.48	Treasury Bill Rate	60c
....	....	5.10	5.10	5.20	5.20	5.19	4.82	4.63	4.71	4.97	....	....	4.33	4.05	Deposit Rate	60l
11.88	11.88	11.40	11.00	11.20	11.46	11.59	11.37	11.24	11.23	9.25	....	....	12.59	12.73	Lending Rate	60p
....	....	....	10.65	10.63	9.46	9.29	10.36	10.74	10.63	10.74	....	....	8.14	7.48	Government Bond Yield	61
Period Averages															**Prices**	
68.6	76.9	81.6	I 83.9	85.6	86.1	87.2	90.5	92.8	96.4	I 100.0	104.0	105.5	107.6	109.5	Consumer Prices	64
Millions of Guilders															**International Transactions**	
9,292	9,750	8,803	7,937	6,719	1,856	1,664	2,354	2,041	2,608	3,204	2,862	2,790	2,297	....	Exports	70
10,216	10,551	9,157	8,148	7,258	2,498	2,002	2,703	2,526	2,888	3,833	3,828	3,344	3,485	....	Imports, cif	71
....	....	....	....	....	....	....	....	....	....	....	....	....	....	....	Crude Petroleum	71aa
9,123	9,422	8,178	7,276	6,480	2,230	1,788	2,413	2,255	2,579	3,422	3,418	2,986	3,112	....	Imports, fob	71.v

Netherlands Antilles
353

		1965	1966	1967	1968	1969	1970	1971	1972	1973	1974	1975	1976	1977	1978	1979
Balance of Payments														*Millions of US Dollars:*		
Goods: Exports f.o.b.	78aa d	...	...	...	...	...	...	...	...	...	...	...	2,905.9	3,209.7	3,165.8	4,602.2
Goods: Imports f.o.b.	78ab d	...	...	...	...	...	...	...	...	...	...	...	–3,058.3	–3,312.7	–3,330.6	–4,459.4
Trade Balance	78ac d	...	...	...	...	...	...	...	...	...	...	...	–152.4	–102.9	–164.7	142.8
Services: Credit	78ad d	...	...	...	...	...	...	...	...	...	...	...	405.2	516.7	565.3	690.0
Services: Debit	78ae d	...	...	...	...	...	...	...	...	...	...	...	–289.7	–316.6	–330.0	–413.3
Balance on Goods and Services	78af d	...	...	...	...	...	...	...	...	...	...	...	–36.9	97.1	70.6	419.5
Income: Credit	78ag d	...	...	...	...	...	...	...	...	...	...	...	20.2	39.4	44.8	63.9
Income: Debit	78ah d	...	...	...	...	...	...	...	...	...	...	...	–104.5	–109.9	–192.8	–507.9
Balance on Goods, Serv., & Inc.	78ai d	...	...	...	...	...	...	...	...	...	...	...	–121.3	26.6	–77.4	–24.6
Current Transfers, n.i.e.: Credit	78aj d	...	...	...	...	...	...	...	...	...	...	...	51.7	48.9	72.8	71.7
Current Transfers: Debit	78ak d	...	...	...	...	...	...	...	...	...	...	...	–13.4	–18.9	–20.2	–23.3
Current Account, n.i.e.	78al d	...	...	...	...	...	...	...	...	...	...	...	–83.0	56.6	–24.8	23.8
Capital Account, n.i.e.: Credit	78ba d	...	...	...	...	...	...	...	...	...	...	...	.6	.6	1.7	1.1
Capital Account: Debit	78bb d	...	...	...	...	...	...	...	...	...	...	...	–2.8	–4.1	–4.4	–6.1
Capital Account, n.i.e.	78bc d	...	...	...	...	...	...	...	...	...	...	...	–2.3	–3.5	–2.7	–5.0
Direct Investment Abroad	78bd d	...	...	...	...	...	...	...	...	...	...	...	–1.1	–1.1	–2.8	–3.9
Dir. Invest. in Rep. Econ., n.i.e.	78be d	...	...	...	...	...	...	...	...	...	...	...	1.1	4.4	13.3	278.3
Portfolio Investment Assets	78bf d	...	...	...	...	...	...	...	...	...	...	...	–2.2	–3.9	–15.0	–14.4
Portfolio Investment Liab., n.i.e.	78bg d	...	...	...	...	...	...	...	...	...	...	...	.6	—	—	1.7
Other Investment Assets	78bh d	...	...	...	...	...	...	...	...	...	...	...	–110.6	–337.2	–196.1	–842.2
Other Investment Liab., n.i.e.	78bi d	...	...	...	...	...	...	...	...	...	...	...	227.2	285.6	176.7	557.2
Financial Account, n.i.e.	78bj d	...	...	...	...	...	...	...	...	...	...	...	115.0	–52.2	–23.9	–23.3
Net Errors and Omissions	78ca d	...	...	...	...	...	...	...	...	...	...	...	4.9	–1.9	7.3	11.6
Overall Balance	78cb d	...	...	...	...	...	...	...	...	...	...	...	34.7	–1.1	–44.2	7.1
Reserves and Related Items	79da d	...	...	...	...	...	...	...	...	...	...	...	–34.7	1.1	44.2	–7.1
Reserve Assets	79db d	...	...	...	...	...	...	...	...	...	...	...	–34.7	1.1	44.2	–7.1
Use of Fund Credit and Loans	79dc d	...	...	...	...	...	...	...	...	...	...	...				
Liabs.Constit.For.Auth.Reserves	79dd d	...	...	...	...	...	...	...	...	...	...	...	—	—	—	—
Exceptional Financing	79de d	...	...	...	...	...	...	...	...	...	...	...				
Government Finance														*Millions of Guilders:*		
Deficit (–) or Surplus	80	...	...	...	...	...	...	...	...	–28.6	–35.5	–55.2	–21.4	–27.6	–71.3	–71.4
Revenue	81	...	...	...	...	...	...	...	...	119.1	112.9	85.1	125.8	138.4	177.6	213.3
Grants Received	81z	...	...	...	...	...	...	...	...	19.6	16.9	27.2	27.0	21.5	26.7	33.4
Expenditure	82	...	...	...	...	...	...	...	...	167.3	163.9	159.5	140.7	171.5	245.6	255.8
Lending Minus Repayments	83	...	...	...	...	...	...	...	...	—	1.4	8.0	33.5	16.0	30.0	62.3
Financing																
Domestic	84a	...	...	...	...	...	...	...	...	8.3	20.0	41.4	–4.2	11.0	58.3	50.0
Foreign	85a	...	...	...	...	...	...	...	...	20.3	15.5	13.8	25.6	16.6	13.0	21.4
Debt: Domestic	88a	...	...	...	...	...	...	...	...	3.7	3.4	3.1	2.8	24.6	65.8	105.2
Foreign	89a	...	...	...	...	...	...	...	...	282.3	335.6	326.4	385.9	446.3	495.0	538.0
																Millions:
Population	99z	.21	.21	.21	.22	.22	.22	.23	.23	.23	.24	.24	I .24	.24	.23	.23

Government Finance: I Beginning in 1980, data also cover social security operations. I Beginning in 1986, the island government of Aruba became independent of the Netherlands Antilles.

Netherlands Antilles

	1980	1981	1982	1983	1984	1985	1986	1987	1988	1989	1990	1991	1992	1993	1994			
Minus Sign Indicates Debit																	**Balance of Payments**	
	6,380.6	6,173.1	5,265.1	4,794.9	3,949.1	1,810.8	155.0	157.2	225.8	313.4	302.7	301.8	332.3	302.1	....		Goods: Exports f.o.b.	78aa*d*
	−6,503.9	−6,360.2	−5,481.3	−4,966.1	−4,248.8	−2,132.3	−675.6	−771.7	−879.4	−1,017.8	−1,112.3	−1,118.9	−1,168.5	−1,130.3	....		Goods: Imports f.o.b.	78ab*d*
	−123.3	−187.1	−216.2	−171.1	−299.8	−321.5	−520.6	−614.4	−653.6	−704.4	−809.7	−817.2	−836.2	−828.2	....		Trade Balance	78ac*d*
	878.3	1,010.9	964.8	733.6	697.7	674.2	646.3	671.1	892.6	960.8	1,161.4	1,227.9	1,339.6	1,330.8	....		Services: Credit	78ad*d*
	−529.1	−564.0	−557.6	−520.2	−454.7	−452.3	−284.4	−299.4	−378.2	−407.5	−518.2	−544.2	−606.9	−616.1	....		Services: Debit	78ae*d*
	225.9	259.8	191.0	42.3	−56.8	−99.6	−158.7	−242.8	−139.1	−151.1	−166.5	−133.5	−103.5	−113.5	....		Balance on Goods and Services	78af*d*
	13.9	25.5	24.1	18.5	72.8	49.3	76.7	77.2	80.9	108.9	126.1	126.8	160.3	122.6	....		Income: Credit	78ag*d*
	−343.1	−286.8	−118.8	−103.8	4.9	−19.5	−56.1	−41.1	−41.3	−73.0	−109.6	−109.6	−146.6	−131.2	....		Income: Debit	78ah*d*
	−103.3	−1.5	96.3	−43.0	20.9	−69.7	−138.2	−206.7	−99.5	−115.2	−149.9	−116.3	−89.8	−122.1	....		Balance on Goods, Serv., & Inc.	78ai*d*
	129.4	121.1	152.2	213.3	253.9	565.6	277.2	241.1	268.7	260.9	213.1	228.7	217.4	250.7	....		Current Transfers, n.i.e.: Credit	78aj*d*
	−25.6	−66.7	−70.6	−82.8	−99.4	−92.8	−88.3	−83.9	−94.1	−107.6	−107.3	−118.6	−115.5	−143.7	....		Current Transfers: Debit	78ak*d*
	.6	52.9	178.0	87.6	175.4	403.1	50.7	−49.4	75.2	38.1	−44.0	−6.2	12.2	−15.1	....		Current Account, n.i.e.	78al*d*
	.6	1.2	1.3	.8	1.1	.5	.6	.6	.4	.1	.5	.9	1.7	.8	....		Capital Account, n.i.e.: Credit	78ba*d*
	−6.7	−4.7	−6.9	−7.1	−9.1	−12.3	−6.7	−3.3	−3.3	−3.3	−2.2	−1.7	−2.3	−1.7	....		Capital Account: Debit	78bb*d*
	−6.1	−3.6	−5.6	−6.3	−8.0	−11.8	−6.1	−2.8	−2.9	−3.2	−1.7	−.7	−.6	−.8	....		Capital Account, n.i.e.	78bc*d*
	−.6	−.7	−.6	−.9	−1.7	3.3	−.8	−.1	−2.8	−4.8	−2.4	−1.1	−1.5	2.2	....		Direct Investment Abroad	78bd*d*
	35.0	15.1	−153.9	−95.6	3.4	−281.7	115.8	2.5	6.7	17.4	8.1	33.4	40.1	11.0	....		Dir. Invest. in Rep. Econ., n.i.e.	78be*d*
	−10.0	−28.7	−19.5	−31.3	−37.3	−48.6	−47.2	16.7	−55.1	−76.9	−50.3	−29.2	−21.6	−13.9	....		Portfolio Investment Assets	78bf*d*
	.6	−3.3	−2.4	−1.6	1.0	6.1	−2.2	−2.8	−2.1	1.1	1.2	−1.5	2.8	1.5	....		Portfolio Investment Liab., n.i.e.	78bg*d*
	−1,106.7	−411.8	62.6	−42.9	−117.6	76.0	−87.1	−73.6	−194.2	−335.5	−249.4	−165.8	−68.5	−40.0	....		Other Investment Assets	78bh*d*
	1,101.7	422.8	−15.5	43.2	−40.9	−79.2	108.2	45.3	189.1	305.0	302.1	122.7	90.6	61.5	....		Other Investment Liab., n.i.e.	78bi*d*
	20.0	−6.6	−129.3	−129.1	−193.2	−324.1	86.7	−12.1	−58.3	−93.7	9.4	−41.5	41.8	22.2	....		Financial Account, n.i.e.	78bj*d*
	.3	10.3	7.8	21.6	−13.1	4.8	−33.4	34.7	19.5	14.6	6.5	6.2	5.8	37.8	....		Net Errors and Omissions	78ca*d*
	14.8	53.2	50.8	−26.3	−38.9	71.9	97.9	−29.6	33.4	−44.2	−29.8	−42.2	59.2	44.0	....		Overall Balance	78cb*d*
	−14.8	−53.2	−50.8	26.3	38.9	−71.9	−97.9	29.6	−33.4	44.2	29.8	42.2	−59.2	−44.0	....		Reserves and Related Items	79da*d*
	−14.8	−53.2	−50.8	26.3	38.9	−71.9	−97.9	29.6	−33.4	44.2	29.8	42.2	−59.2	−44.0	....		Reserve Assets	79db*d*
	—	—	—	—	—	—	—	—	—	—	—	—	—	—	....		Use of Fund Credit and Loans	79dc*d*
	—	—	—	—	—	—	—	—	—	—	—	—	—	—	....		Liabs.Constit.For.Auth.Reserves	79dd*d*
	....	....	....	....	....	....	....	....	....	....	....	....	....	....	....		Exceptional Financing	79de*d*
Year Ending December 31																	**Government Finance**	
	Ɨ−76.2	−100.8	−106.6	−87.9	−75.0	−20.8	Ɨ−57.5	−55.6	−11.1	−60.1	−51.3	−45.3	−49.2ᴾ	....	....		Deficit (−) or Surplus	80
	Ɨ253.4	275.4	343.3	345.5	355.5	356.4	Ɨ320.2	334.1	365.2	337.7	438.0	463.1	507.5ᴾ	....	....		Revenue	81
	Ɨ137.7	89.0	93.9	149.8	151.6	200.5	Ɨ112.0	149.0	145.9	77.3	56.2	78.3	66.5ᴾ	....	....		Grants Received	81z
	Ɨ465.2	459.6	540.8	556.9	570.4	552.6	Ɨ488.5	536.9	521.4	475.1	536.0	586.7	611.1ᴾ	....	....		Expenditure	82
	Ɨ2.1	5.6	3.0	26.3	11.7	25.1	Ɨ1.2	1.8	.8	—	9.5	—	12.1ᴾ	....	....		Lending Minus Repayments	83
																	Financing	
	Ɨ75.5	100.7	77.4	68.5	31.3	21.7	Ɨ11.1	6.0	−24.5	75.1	−19.0	106.8	49.2ᴾ	....	....		Domestic	84a
	Ɨ.7	.1	29.2	19.4	43.7	−.9	Ɨ46.4	49.6	35.5	−15.0	70.3	−61.5	—ᴾ	....	....		Foreign	85a
	Ɨ238.8	296.3	282.6	311.3	416.5	217.7	Ɨ417.3	432.0	451.7	447.6	424.0	431.7	458.4ᴾ	....	....		Debt: Domestic	88a
	Ɨ525.8	499.6	449.9	542.4	403.0	541.1	Ɨ215.5	260.0	248.9	235.4	307.0	208.5	187.8ᴾ	....	....		Foreign	89a
Midyear Estimates																		
	.19	.19	.18	.17	.18	.18	.18	.19	.19	.19	.19	.19	.19	.19	....		**Population**	99z

New Zealand

196

		1965	1966	1967	1968	1969	1970	1971	1972	1973	1974	1975	1976	1977	1978	1979
Exchange Rates															*SDRs per New Zealand Dollar:*	
Market Rate	ac	1.3912	1.3850	1.1227	1.1121	1.1198	1.1161	1.1008	1.1008	1.1841	1.0744	.8915	.8177	.8395	.8187	.7486
													US Dollars per New Zealand Dollar:			
Market Rate	ag	1.3912	1.3850	1.1227	1.1121	1.1198	1.1161	1.1952	1.1952	1.4284	1.3155	1.0437	.9500	1.0197	1.0666	.9862
Market Rate	rh	1.3904	1.3904	1.3679	1.1200	1.1200	1.1200	1.1361	1.1952	1.3615	1.4004	1.2157	.9963	.9708	1.0378	1.0229
													Index Numbers (1990=100):			
Market Rate	ahx	232.6	231.9	227.1	187.1	186.8	187.5	191.2	200.2	228.1	234.6	203.6	166.9	162.6	173.8	171.4
Nominal Effective Exchange Rate	nec	....	....	....	....	....	....	....	....	....	....	....	....	....	....	159.9
Real Effective Exchange Rate	rec	....	....	....	....	....	....	....	....	....	....	....	....	....	....	92.2
Fund Position															*Millions of SDRs:*	
Quota	2f.s	125	157	157	157	157	202	202	202	202	202	202	202	202	232	232
SDRs	1b.s	—	—	—	—	—	—	28	58	58	1	1	8	34	46	9
Reserve Position in the Fund	1c.s	—	—	—	—	—	51	51	51	51	—	—	—	—	23	—
Total Fund Cred.&Loans Outstg.	2tl	31	31	120	21	—	—	—	—	—	86	242	390	388	361	270
International Liquidity												*Millions of US Dollars Unless Otherwise Indicated:*				
Total Reserves minus Gold	1l.d	173	179	218	161	209	257	492	832	1,045	639	427	491	443	451	451
SDRs	1b.d	—	—	—	—	—	—	30	63	70	1	1	10	42	60	12
Reserve Position in the Fund	1c.d	—	—	—	—	—	51	55	55	61	—	—	—	—	30	—
Foreign Exchange	1d.d	173	179	218	161	209	206	407	714	914	638	426	481	401	361	439
Monetary Authorities	1da.d	97	95	134	75	112	74	229	459	619	331	193	212	121	172	134
Government	1db.d	76	84	84	86	97	132	178	255	295	307	233	269	280	189	305
Gold (Million Fine Troy Ounces)	1a.d	.008	.005	.016	.017	.024	.023	.023	.023	.023	.023	.023	.023	.044	.066	.045
Gold (National Valuation)	1an.d	....	....	....	1	1	1	1	1	1	1	1	1	2	3	2
Monetary Authorities: Other Liab.	4..d	1	34	84	43	12	10	4	1	—	51	199	278	345	373	381
Deposit Money Banks: Assets	7a.d	61	44	41	63	81	83	85	117	118	163	183	185	263	321	349
Liabilities	7b.d	18	16	15	15	23	18	26	74	80	140	142	106	137	140	152
Monetary Authorities													*Millions of New Zealand Dollars:*			
Foreign Assets	11	125	129	195	144	187	229	405	685	740	488	426	555	431	378	573
Claims on Central Government	12a	241	255	290	188	146	164	85	48	141	511	621	897	1,102	1,041	1,091
Claims on Deposit Money Banks	12e	23	3	—	10	17	30	8	—	—	15	—	3	5	186	22
Reserve Money	14	334	308	308	295	270	308	309	509	749	785	637	669	729	880	956
of which: Currency Outside DMBs	14a	161	160	153	157	168	195	212	242	290	336	352	418	460	536	590
Bonds	16aa	....	....	....	....	....	....	....	....	....	....	....	....	....	....	....
Foreign Liabilities	16c	23	47	182	57	11	9	3	—	—	118	462	770	801	791	1747
Central Government Deposits	16d	107	125	122	120	205	216	269	398	377	349	308	343	359	366	484
Other Items (Net)	17r	-74	-93	-127	-130	-136	-109	-82	-174	-245	-238	-360	-326	-351	-431	-500
Deposit Money Banks													*Millions of New Zealand Dollars:*			
Reserves	20	163	138	145	124	88	96	81	228	335	286	112	131	118	128	118
Reserve Bank Bills	20r	....	....	....	....	....	....	....	....	....	....	....	....	....	....	....
Foreign Assets	21	44	32	37	56	72	74	70	96	87	124	175	195	258	301	354
Claims on Central Government	22a	59	69	78	83	220	176	307	540	509	213	601	646	757	1,209	1,354
Claims on Private Sector	22d	460	479	455	528	582	688	726	789	1,227	1,555	1,679	2,073	2,458	3,001	3,635
Demand Deposits	24	617	643	621	613	622	654	724	956	1,151	1,115	1,245	1,385	1,370	1,637	1,741
Time and Savings Deposits	25	126	140	144	172	269	307	410	630	930	1,022	1,155	1,526	1,995	2,537	3,369
Foreign Currency Deposits	25.a	....	....	....	....	....	....	....	....	....	....	....	....	....	....	....
Foreign Liabilities	26c	10	9	10	11	16	11	13	37	29	62	86	84	116	109	129
Capital Accounts	27a	....	....	....	....	....	....	....	....	....	....	....	....	....	....	....
Other Items (Net)	27r	-29	-75	-61	-4	54	63	37	30	48	-21	81	49	111	357	221
Monetary Survey													*Millions of New Zealand Dollars:*			
Foreign Assets (Net)	31n	135	105	39	133	232	284	458	743	798	432	53	-104	-227	-220	150
Domestic Credit	32	644	665	693	663	727	800	838	967	1,488	1,908	2,555	3,249	3,938	4,859	5,563
Claims on Central Govt. (Net)	32an	184	186	237	135	145	113	112	178	261	353	876	1,176	1,480	1,858	1,929
Claims on Local Government	32b	....	....	....	....	....	....	....	....	....	....	....	....	....	....	....
Claims on Private Sector	32d	460	479	455	528	582	688	726	789	1,227	1,555	1,679	2,073	2,458	3,001	3,635
Money	34	784	810	781	780	801	861	949	1,219	1,545	1,601	1,749	1,910	1,946	2,378	2,458
Quasi-Money	35	126	140	144	172	269	307	410	630	930	1,022	1,155	1,526	1,995	2,537	3,369
Other Items (Net)	37r	-130	-181	-194	-156	-111	-83	-62	-139	-188	-283	-296	-291	-230	-276	-214
Money plus Quasi-Money	35l	910	951	925	952	1,070	1,167	1,359	1,850	2,474	2,623	2,905	3,436	3,941	4,915	5,827
Money (National Definitions)													*Millions of New Zealand Dollars:*			
M3	38n	....	....	....	....	....	....	....	....	....	....	....	....	....	....	....
Unused Overdrafts	39b	333	362	331	302	314	326	380	529	638	556	740	931	933	1,286	1,228
Other Banking Institutions													*Millions of New Zealand Dollars:*			
Claims on Central Government	42a.g	.6	2.8	.2	.2	2.6	11.4	16.5	17.2	19.6	16.1	24.5	36.2	54.8	62.1	90.3
Claims on Private Sector	42d.g	55.4	71.7	76.5	84.1	105.3	144.8	192.0	249.8	334.5	317.4	378.8	546.9	826.7	954.5	1,187.5
Time Dep. Debentures & Notes	45..g	35.4	52.4	53.9	61.7	82.9	122.0	169.9	204.9	240.2	203.8	270.2	466.8	693.5	812.6	1,048.9
Foreign Liabilities	46c.g	2.9	2.8	3.0	3.1	4.8	4.9	8.4	23.6	30.4	44.3	49.8	27.5	18.1	22.9	25.3
Cred.from Deposit Money Banks	46h.g	3.5	4.2	3.5	4.5	4.4	8.8	7.8	10.6	33.5	26.4	25.8	26.5	28.4	27.7	34.8
Capital Accounts	47a.g	13.6	16.6	18.6	19.6	21.8	27.0	37.5	47.8	65.0	67.1	70.7	88.2	131.2	150.5	158.2
Other Items (Net)	47r.g	.6	-1.5	-2.4	-4.6	-5.7	-6.6	-15.1	-19.9	-15.0	-8.2	-13.1	-25.9	10.3	2.9	10.6
Post Office: Savings Deposits	45..i	853.3	865.4	866.2	876.3	898.0	936.8	947.3	1,015.4	1,118.3	1,170.8	1,242.3	1,308.7	1,417.0	1,567.9	1,686.0
Trustee Savings Banks: Deposits	45..k	302.6	333.2	368.4	404.4	439.4	476.1	510.2	590.2	707.5	758.3	850.0	944.9	1,075.7	1,357.1	1,567.6
Private Savings Banks: Deposits	45..r	117.6	179.8	231.1	284.0	328.2	364.0	365.1	399.8	470.4	480.3	565.8	636.4	680.3	853.3	977.6
Nonbank Financial Institutions													*Millions of New Zealand Dollars:*			
Claims on Central Government	42a.s	171.9	192.3	216.2	242.6	259.0	287.0	312.9	349.8	391.8	406.1	445.7	485.2	504.2	549.9	616.8
Claims on Local Government	42b.s	77.3	75.3	74.1	83.8	91.5	100.8	113.5	124.8	142.9	160.0	184.7	215.9	255.7	284.6	316.0
Claims on Private Sector	42d.s	513.6	565.8	630.6	682.6	743.8	800.7	850.9	918.9	989.0	1,080.7	1,153.1	1,251.2	1,359.5	1,462.3	1,584.9
Real Estate	42h.s	62.0	69.5	80.7	91.3	111.9	147.9	186.0	219.4	263.1	324.1	371.1	422.2	479.0	545.4	608.1
Incr.in Total Assets(Within Per.)	49z.s	77.7	78.1	99.1	98.9	105.7	134.1	126.2	154.4	174.5	188.2	185.0	218.6	233.5	258.5	295.6
Liquid Liabilities	55l	2,218.8	2,381.5	2,444.6	2,578.5	2,818.7	3,066.3	3,351.1	4,059.8	5,010.8	5,235.9	5,832.8	6,792.5	7,807.2	9,506.0	11,107.6
Interest Rates															*Percent Per Annum*	
Discount Rate (End of Period)	60	7.00	7.00	7.00	7.00	7.00	7.00	7.00	6.00	6.00	7.00	7.00	8.50	10.00	10.50	13.00
Treasury Bill Rate	60c	....	....	....	....	....	....	....	....	....	....	....	....	....	8.25	10.75
Deposit Rate	60l	....	....	....	....	....	....	....	....	....	....	....	....	....	....	....
Lending Rate	60p	....	....	....	....	....	....	....	....	....	....	....	....	8.16	9.65	10.26
Government Bond Yield	61	5.10	5.28	5.51	5.53	5.54	5.51	5.52	5.52	5.80	6.09	6.33	8.34	9.23	9.97	12.04

New Zealand

	1980	1981	1982	1983	1984	1985	1986	1987	1988	1989	1990	1991	1992	1993	1994		
End of Period																**Exchange Rates**	
	.7545	.7083	.6640	.6252	.4872	.4538	.4280	.4635	.4669	.4544	.4132	.3783	.3740	.4068	.4401	Market Rate	**ac**
End of Period (ag) Period Average (rh)																	
	.9623	.8244	.7325	.6546	.4776	.4985	.5235	.6575	.6283	.5972	.5878	.5411	.5143	.5588	.6425	Market Rate	**ne c**
	.9742	.8700	.7519	.6688	.5785	.4984	.5239	.5922	.6560	.5985	.5970	.5792	.5381	.5407	.5937	Market Rate	**rh**
Period Averages																	
	163.2	145.7	125.9	112.0	96.9	83.5	87.8	99.2	109.9	100.3	100.0	97.0	90.1	90.6	99.5	Market Rate	**ah x**
	151.0	145.5	139.0	131.5	120.1	110.5	102.1	105.3	109.8	103.7	100.0	96.8	89.0	93.1	99.6	Nominal Effective Exchange Rate	**ne c**
	91.4	92.7	95.5	92.1	85.6	87.1	88.1	101.8	108.5	103.0	100.0	95.3	86.2	89.0ᵉ	94.4ᵉ	Real Effective Exchange Rate	**re c**
End of Period																**Fund Position**	
	348	348	348	462	462	462	462	462	462	462	462	462	650	650	650	Quota	**2f. s**
	—	20	2	3	7	6	9	1	1	1	—	—	—	—	—	SDRs	**1b. s**
	28	28	—	28	—	—	—	—	8	40	40	54	109	104	101	Reserve Position in the Fund	**1c. s**
	132	34	3	—	—	—	—	—	—	—	—	—	—	—	—	Total Fund Cred.&Loans Outstg.	**2tl**
End of Period																**International Liquidity**	
	352	674	636	778	1,787	1,596	3,771	3,260	2,836	3,027	4,129	2,950	3,079	3,337	3,709	Total Reserves minus Gold	**1l. d**
	—	23	2	3	7	7	11	1	1	1	—	—	—	—	—	SDRs	**1b. d**
	35	32	—	30	—	—	—	—	11	52	57	77	150	142	147	Reserve Position in the Fund	**1c. d**
	317	619	634	745	1,780	1,589	3,760	3,258	2,824	2,974	4,071	2,872	2,929	3,195	3,561	Foreign Exchange	**1d. d**
	68	367	178	128	1,304	984	2,834	1,369	908	2,422	2,473	2,522	2,366	2,378	2,351	Monetary Authorities	**1da d**
	249	252	456	617	476	605	926	1,889	1,916	552	1,598	350	563	817	1,210	Government	**1db d**
	.022	.022	.022	.022	.022	.022	.022	.022	.022	.022	.001	.001	.001	.001	—	Gold (Million Fine Troy Ounces)	**1ad**
	1	1	1	1	1	1	1	1	1	1	—	—	—	—	—	Gold (National Valuation)	**1an d**
	573	1,012	1,071	866	776	614	2,738	1,159	I 82	60	6	20	100	96	—	Monetary Authorities: Other Liab.	**4.. d**
	435	414	402	457	338	474	579	915	I 1,306	803	1,863	1,276	1,163	2,253	1,316	Deposit Money Banks: Assets	**7a. d**
	182	159	208	346	318	447	833	1,294	I 3,164	2,837	6,495	6,537	8,959	9,550	12,348	Liabilities	**7b. d**
																Monetary Authorities	
	381	817	873	1,240	3,762	2,936	7,375	4,999	I 4,545	5,083	6,979	5,454	5,967	5,974	5,772	Foreign Assets	**11**
	1,057	1,413	1,454	1,369	2,435	1,066	1,648	2,216	I 3,258	3,640	2,931	2,840	2,147	2,273	2,921	Claims on Central Government	**12a**
	31	34	54	51	12	5	4	7	I 26	28	313	236	789	796	301	Claims on Deposit Money Banks	**12e**
	852	972	1,048	1,172	1,263	1,409	1,227	1,488	I 1,716	1,655	1,646	1,613	1,648	1,695	1,891	Reserve Money	**14**
	577	683	714	739	867	940	1,006	1,059	I 1,128	1,152	1,007	1,118	1,173	1,199	1,325	of which: Currency Outside DMBs	**14a**
	....	....	....	....	....	....	....	....	1,278	1,166	1,226	1,208	1,056	1,149	1,185	Bonds	**16aa**
	771	1,275	1,466	1,323	1,626	1,232	5,231	1,763	I 131	100	11	37	194	172	—	Foreign Liabilities	**16c**
	419	638	1,081	1,372	4,994	2,181	2,922	3,416	I 4,373	5,156	6,649	4,896	5,297	5,342	5,219	Central Government Deposits	**16d**
	−573	−621	−1,214	−1,208	−1,673	−814	−353	549	I 330	674	692	777	708	685	699	Other Items (Net)	**17r**
End of Period																**Deposit Money Banks**	
	93	109	116	140	87	182	97	316	I 280	437	1,746	1,679	1,562	1,639	1,694	Reserves	**20**
										1,278	1,167	1,226	1,208	1,064	1,149	1,185	Reserve Bank Bills	**20r**
	452	503	549	699	707	950	1,107	1,392	I 2,078	1,345	3,169	2,358	2,261	4,032	2,049	Foreign Assets	**21**
	1,385	1,203	1,701	2,012	2,849	4,496	4,565	4,941	I 4,768	5,313	7,113	7,636	8,588	7,205	6,049	Claims on Central Government	**22a**
	4,230	5,305	6,002	6,569	7,843	10,020	14,230	18,315	I 19,293	29,321	50,300	52,399	61,528	65,420	71,069	Claims on Private Sector	**22d**
	1,876	2,129	2,259	2,629	2,855	3,135	3,634	5,579	I 13,247	20,193	23,170	23,039	24,616	24,919	27,577	Demand Deposits	**24**
	3,829	4,481	5,419	5,581	7,079	10,267	13,286	14,448	I 2,564	4,347	20,025	28,413	29,886	34,695	35,064	Time and Savings Deposits	**25**
	....	....	....	....	....	....	....	....	1,158	1,673	3,440	2,839	1,967	2,925	1,845	Foreign Currency Deposits	**25.a**
	157	164	249	488	597	773	1,120	1,555	I 5,035	4,750	11,050	12,081	17,420	17,091	19,219	Foreign Liabilities	**26c**
	....	....	....	....	....	....	....	....	3,355	3,795	4,699	4,846	5,883	5,435	4,905	Capital Accounts	**27a**
	297	344	441	722	955	1,474	1,959	3,380	I 2,338	2,825	1,169	−5,938	−4,751	−5,621	−6,564	Other Items (Net)	**27r**
End of Period																**Monetary Survey**	
	−96	−119	−293	128	2,246	1,882	2,131	3,072	I 1,457	1,578	−913	−4,306	−9,386	−7,257	−11,398	Foreign Assets (Net)	**31n**
	6,154	7,227	8,035	8,522	8,080	13,349	17,457	21,996	I 22,902	32,629	53,648	57,952	66,952	69,553	74,810	Domestic Credit	**32**
	1,924	1,922	2,033	1,953	238	3,329	3,228	3,681	I 3,609	3,303	3,348	5,553	5,424	4,133	3,741	Claims on Central Govt. (Net)	**32an**
										5						Claims on Local Government	**32b**
	4,230	5,305	6,002	6,569	7,843	10,020	14,230	18,315	I 19,293	29,321	50,300	52,399	61,528	65,420	71,069	Claims on Private Sector	**32d**
	2,555	2,926	3,030	3,426	3,761	4,104	4,668	6,667	I 14,673	21,382	24,217	24,197	25,848	26,182	28,974	Money	**34**
	3,829	4,481	5,419	5,581	7,079	10,267	13,286	14,448	I 3,722	6,020	23,465	31,252	31,835	37,620	36,909	Quasi-Money	**35**
	−306	−300	−706	−357	−514	859	1,635	3,953	I 5,964	6,805	5,053	−1,801	−117	−1,507	−2,472	Other Items (Net)	**37r**
	6,364	7,407	8,448	9,007	10,840	14,371	17,953	21,115	I 18,394	27,402	47,682	55,449	57,683	63,802	65,883	Money plus Quasi-Money	**35l**
End of Period																**Money (National Definitions)**	
	....	16,009	18,066	20,669	25,020	31,397	37,807	42,932	44,418	46,137	52,832	56,489	64,239	65,873	68,151	M3	**38n**
	1,743	2,165	2,395	3,111	3,628	4,121	4,269	....	....	....	....	....	....	....	....	Unused Overdrafts	**39b**
End of Period																**Other Banking Institutions**	
	130.0	145.6	168.1	318.1	591.9	458.8ᵉ	432.4	....	....	....	....	....	....	....	....	Claims on Central Government	**42a. g**
	1,497.7	1,974.7	2,591.2	3,135.7	3,995.4	5,389.9	5,978.9	....	....	....	....	....	....	....	....	Claims on Private Sector	**42d. g**
	1,332.0	1,762.4	2,326.0	2,974.9	3,974.4	5,088.3	5,289.3	....	....	....	....	....	....	....	....	Time Dep. Debentures & Notes	**45.. g**
	31.9	28.4	34.6	40.5	68.9	123.7	470.8	....	....	....	....	....	....	....	....	Foreign Liabilities	**46c. g**
	27.2	34.0	40.1	30.5	38.8	48.1	61.5	....	....	....	....	....	....	....	....	Cred.from Deposit Money Banks	**46h. g**
	206.9	241.5	292.3	352.4	425.5	492.0	640.3	....	....	....	....	....	....	....	....	Capital Accounts	**47a. g**
	29.7	54.0	66.3	55.5	79.3	96.6	−50.6	....	....	....	....	....	....	....	....	Other Items (Net)	**47r. g**
	1,792.4	1,948.9	2,050.4	2,347.9	2,592.7	2,827.3	3,084.6	....	....	....	....	....	....	....	....	Post Office: Savings Deposits	**45.. i**
	1,872.5	2,242.1	2,493.3	2,989.5	3,399.4	3,750.3	4,202.6	....	....	....	....	....	....	....	....	Trustee Savings Banks: Deposits	**45.. k**
	1,039.3	1,095.4	935.8	828.2	671.0	564.2	488.6	....	....	....	....	....	....	....	....	Private Savings Banks: Deposits	**45.. r**
End of Period																**Nonbank Financial Institutions**	
	687.4	776.2	860.6	988.9	1,303.2	1,626.4	1,923.1	2,116.9	2,172.0	1,659.5	1,398.1	1,954.3	2,349.7	2,328.6	2,435.4	Claims on Central Government	**42a. s**
	344.8	378.1	467.2	511.4	575.6	562.3	471.5	452.7	607.8	706.9	906.9	864.1	738.6	782.3	546.4	Claims on Local Government	**42b. s**
	1,776.9	1,997.6	2,240.5	2,517.1	2,789.6	3,007.6	4,566.1	3,602.8	3,301.1	4,412.7	3,427.8	3,848.1	4,545.8	5,369.7	4,507.9	Claims on Private Sector	**42d. s**
	674.2	727.8	797.3	880.4	958.1	1,113.0	1,745.6	2,725.3	2,746.4	3,091.8	2,580.0	2,061.4	1,740.6	1,488.7	1,590.5	Real Estate	**42h. s**
	343.7	419.3	477.8	585.0	770.1	921.6	3,528.4	833.6	391.3	1,432.7	−1,559.2	522.9	765.3	2,178.4	−618.4	Incr.in Total Assets(Within Per.)	**49z. s**
	12,400.1	14,456.3	16,253.8	18,147.4	21,477.7	26,601.3	31,018.5	....	....	....	....	....	....	....	....	Liquid Liabilities	**55l**
Percent Per Annum																**Interest Rates**	
	14.00	13.00	13.00	7.50	13.50	19.80	24.60	18.55	15.10	15.00	13.25	8.30	9.15	5.70	9.75	Discount Rate (End of Period)	**60**
	11.25	11.25	11.25	10.13	9.23	....	19.97	20.50	....	13.51	13.78	9.74	6.72	6.21	6.69	Treasury Bill Rate	**60c**
	....	11.00	10.79	9.75	10.46	14.71	16.32	....	I 13.41	10.92	I 11.65	8.93	6.58	6.24	6.38	Deposit Rate	**60l**
	12.63	13.50	13.73	13.83	12.53	....	....	I 20.84	17.17	15.78	16.01	14.01	11.39	10.34	9.69	Lending Rate	**60p**
	13.29	12.83	12.91	12.18	12.57	17.71	16.52	I 16.35	13.45	12.78	12.46	10.00	7.87	6.69	7.48	Government Bond Yield	**61**

New Zealand

		1965	1966	1967	1968	1969	1970	1971	1972	1973	1974	1975	1976	1977	1978	1979
Prices, Production, Employment														*Index Numbers (1990=100):*		
Share Prices	62	18	17	⸸15	18	22	23	20	21	25	21	20	21	19	19	21
Input Prices: All Industry	63	9.4	9.5	9.8	10.4	11.0	11.6	12.5	13.4	15.1	16.3	18.4	22.6	⸸26.3	29.3	34.5
Consumer Prices	64	8.8	9.1	9.6	10.0	10.5	⸸11.2	12.4	13.2	14.3	15.9	18.2	21.3	24.4	27.2	31.0
Wages: Weekly Rates	65	8.7	9.0	9.5	9.9	10.4	12.1	14.5	15.8	17.7	19.8	22.5	25.5	⸸28.8	32.2	37.2
Labor Cost Index (Q492=100)	65a															
Manufacturing Production	66ey c													88.3	86.1	92.1
Manufacturing Employment	67ey						97.2	96.8	101.1	105.5	103.9	105.5	106.8	102.4	105.7e	
International Transactions													*Millions of New Zealand Dollars*			
Exports	70	723.9	774.1	725.4	901.6	1,080.9	1,091.6	1,199.8	1,499.5	1,913.2	1,733.9	1,796.3	2,815.5	3,294.9	⸸3,603.5	4,606.7
Butter	70fl	113.6	102.6	116.4	111.3	120.6	101.8	132.7	163.8	137.3	119.4	166.8	227.5	254.6	257.0	318.6
Imports, cif	71	756.7	787.5	695.6	799.0	895.5	1,112.0	1,186.1	1,274.0	1,591.5	2,615.0	2,613.5	3,270.8	3,464.0	⸸3,359.4	4,466.1
Imports, fob	71.v	701.3	723.8	644.1	743.3	839.3	1,038.3	1,102.3	1,189.5	1,480.5	2,396.9	2,386.8	3,028.5	3,189.7	3,110.6	4,052.7
														1990=100		
Volume of Exports	72	39	41	42	49	54	52	54	56	55	51	52	62	63	64	69
Butter	72fl	92	92	107	99	107	89	88	87	94	85	89	103	96	88	105
Volume of Imports	73	45	47	41	40	43	49	50	52	61	80	60	62	59	54	64
Export Prices	74	13	13	12	13	14	14	15	18	23	22	22	29	34	36	43
Butter (Unit Value)	74fl	18	16	16	17	17	17	22	28	21	21	27	32	38	42	45
Butter (Wholesale Price)	76fl	12	11	11	12	12	12	17	18	13	15	24	31	35	43	52
Unit Value of Imports	75	11	11	11	13	14	14	15	16	17	21	28	35	38	39	44
Balance of Payments													*Millions of US Dollars:*			
Goods: Exports f.o.b.	78aa d								1,955	2,511	2,277	2,449	3,009	3,225	4,020	4,988
Goods: Imports f.o.b.	78ab d								−1,457	−2,148	−3,595	−3,095	−3,129	−3,116	−3,418	−4,698
Trade Balance	78ac d								498	362	−1,318	−646	−119	110	602	290
Services: Credit	78ad d								327	491	653	729	698	787	852	1,036
Services: Debit	78ae d								−549	−837	−1,060	−1,008	−962	−1,144	−1,339	−1,677
Balance on Goods and Services	78af d								277	16	−1,725	−925	−384	−247	116	−351
Income: Credit	78ag d								75	122	122	105	103	119	116	132
Income: Debit	78ah d								−225	−307	−239	−401	−523	−554	−701	−649
Balance on Goods, Serv., & Inc.	78ai d								128	−168	−1,842	−1,222	−804	−682	−469	−868
Current Transfers, n.i.e.: Credit	78aj d								76	90	95	109	105	126	139	181
Current Transfers: Debit	78ak d								−51	−69	−99	−109	−96	−105	−108	−115
Current Account, n.i.e.	78al d								153	−148	−1,847	−1,222	−794	−661	−438	−802
Capital Account, n.i.e.: Credit	78ba d								42	77	77	62	37	32	33	48
Capital Account: Debit	78bb d								−31	−50	−73	−60	−61	−60	−84	−89
Capital Account, n.i.e.	78bc d								11	27	4	2	−24	−28	−51	−41
Direct Investment Abroad	78bd d								−4	−19	−21	−22	−36	−32	−56	−75
Dir. Invest. in Rep. Econ., n.i.e.	78be d								127	208	252	138	278	154	274	351
Portfolio Investment Assets	78bf d								—	—	—	—	—	—	—	—
Portfolio Investment Liab., n.i.e.	78bg d								—	—	—	—	—	—	—	—
Other Investment Assets	78bh d								8	—	−42	−65	−26	−46	−40	3
Other Investment Liab., n.i.e.	78bi d								12	26	315	103	−156	−276	−307	−291
Financial Account, n.i.e.	78bj d								143	214	503	155	60	−199	−130	−12
Net Errors and Omissions	78ca d								145	−67	244	66	30	216	−265	−111
Overall Balance	78cb d								452	27	−1,095	−999	−728	−672	−883	−966
Reserves and Related Items	79da d								−452	−27	1,095	999	728	672	883	966
Reserve Assets	79db d								−488	−30	390	−34	15	−201	235	245
Use of Fund Credit and Loans	79dc d								—	—	103	188	171	−2	−34	−118
Liabs.Constit.For.Auth.Reserves	79dd d								—	—	—	—	—	—	—	—
Exceptional Financing	79de d								36	3	602	845	542	875	682	839
Government Finance													*Millions of New Zealand Dollars:*			
Deficit (-) or Surplus	80	−114	−137	−118	−123	−95	⸸−108	−93	−298	−225	−416	−1,194	−614	−789	−1,502	−1,127
Revenue	81	1,019	1,095	1,123	1,173	1,309	⸸1,620	1,908	2,146	2,632	3,124	3,503	4,283	5,153	5,651	6,827
Expenditure	82	1,075	1,172	1,187	1,238	1,329	⸸1,571	1,821	2,231	2,614	3,107	3,873	4,276	5,232	6,404	7,338
Lending Minus Repayments	83	58	59	53	57	75	⸸157	180	213	243	433	824	621	710	749	616
Financing																
Domestic	84a						⸸71	100	409	341	68	755	382	576	837	919
Foreign	85a						⸸51	72	−49	−58	301	422	226	483	340	399
Use of Cash Balances	87a						⸸−14	−79	−62	−58	47	17	6	−270	325	−191
Debt: Domestic	88a						⸸2,445	2,546	2,956	3,295	3,365	4,121	4,478	5,061	5,917	6,806
Foreign	89a						⸸576	654	564	465	863	1,463	1,827	2,447	2,920	3,568
Financing (by Currency)																
Use of Cash Balances	87	4	2	−41	−26	−13										
Debt: New Zealand Dollars	88b		2,007	2,102	2,247	2,351										
National Accounts													*Millions of New Zealand Dollars;*			
Exports of Goods & Services	90c. c	839	893	867	1,123	1,263	1,296	1,560	1,946	2,241	2,117	2,666	3,765	4,125	4,687	5,996
Government Consumption	91f. c	516	565	598	650	643	770	886	1,023	1,176	1,443	1,732	1,937	2,363	2,882	3,314
Gross Fixed Capital Formation	93e. c	915	960	869	964	1,007	1,214	1,420	1,778	2,091	2,695	3,246	3,538	3,545	3,880	4,067
Increase/Decrease(-) in Stocks	93i. c	147	139	139	81	140	204	306	154	452	1,036	459	810	133	−246	470
Private Consumption	96f. c	2,403	2,447	2,587	2,598	3,344	3,742	4,210	4,764	5,488	6,206	7,098	8,162	9,181	10,353	12,105
Imports of Goods & Services	98c. c	−943	−965	−877	−980	−1,142	−1,456	−1,505	−1,710	−2,233	−3,344	−3,430	−4,057	−4,378	−4,647	−6,256
Gross Domestic Product	99b. c	3,877	4,039	4,183	4,436	5,134	5,832	6,874	7,901	9,199	10,095	11,668	14,101	14,879	16,856	19,688
Net Factor Inc/Pmts(-) Abroad	98.n c	54	66	55	81	−41	−41	−46	−54	−37	−82	−165	−265	−336	−409	−460
Gross Nat'l Expenditure = GNP	99a. c	3,823	3,973	4,128	4,355	5,092	5,791	6,828	7,847	9,162	10,013	11,503	13,836	14,543	16,447	19,228
Nat'l Income, Market Prices	99e. c	3,550	3,673	3,809	4,022	4,626	5,268	6,276	7,234	8,470	9,216	10,563	12,758	13,379	15,117	17,774
Gross Dom. Prod. 1990 Prices	99b. r	42,432	44,041	43,658	44,599	46,843	48,583	49,820	52,020	55,752	58,007	58,981	59,068	57,448	57,296	58,757
GDP Deflator (1990=100)	99bi r	9.1	9.2	9.6	9.9	11.0	12.0	13.8	15.2	16.5	17.4	19.8	23.9	25.9	29.4	33.5
														Millions:		
Population	99z	2.63	2.68	2.72	2.75	2.77	2.81	2.85	2.90	2.96	3.01	3.07	3.09	3.11	3.11	3.10

Exchange Rates: On July 10, 1967 the New Zealand dollar, equal to one half the New Zealand pound, was introduced.

Deposit Money Banks: ⸸ Prior to August 1988, data refer to the four trading banks. From that date, data refer to registered banks and 'other M3 institutions' (certain corporations and savings institutions).

Monetary Survey: ⸸ See note to section 20.

Interest Rates: *Deposit Rate:* ⸸ Data refer to the weighted average interest rate for New Zealand's four largest banks for six-month deposits of NZ$10,000 or more, each bank's rate being weighted according to its total New Zealand dollar deposits. ⸸ Prior to 1990, data refer to the quarterly weighted averages for registered banks' total N.Z. dollar deposits. ⸸ Prior to 1988, data refer to upper rates offered by trading banks for three-month deposits.

Lending Rate: ⸸ Data refer to the weighted average base business lending rate for New Zealand's four largest banks, each bank's rate being weighted according to its New Zealand dollar claims on the private sector. ⸸ Prior to 1987, data refer to the quarterly averages for registered banks' total N.Z. dollar claims.

Government Bond Yield: Unweighted average yield to maturity of ten issues with five years or more to maturity. ⸸ Prior to 1987, unweighted average yield to maturity of ten issues with ten years or more to maturity.

International Transactions: ⸸ Prior to September 1978, data exclude veal.

1980	1981	1982	1983	1984	1985	1986	1987	1988	1989	1990	1991	1992	1993	1994		196
Period Averages															**Prices, Production, Employment**	
27	39	38	50	71	84	143	I 167	104	114	100	88	101	132	167	Share Prices	62
42.4	49.5	I 57.0	60.1	64.4	74.3	78.6	84.8	89.3	95.6	100.0	100.9	103.0	105.5	106.9	Input Prices: All Industry	63
36.3	41.8	48.6	52.2	55.4	I 64.0	72.4	83.8	89.2	94.3	100.0	102.6	103.6	105.0	106.8	Consumer Prices	64
44.1	52.6	58.8	59.0	60.4	I 65.1	75.7	85.7	92.2	95.8	100.0	102.6	103.5	....	....	Wages: Weekly Rates	65
....	....	....	....	....	....	....	....	....	....	....	....	....	101	102	Labor Cost Index (Q492=100)	65a
91.1	96.0	100.2	98.3	111.9	110.7	108.9	106.9	103.0	104.0	100.0	95.0	101.0	107.7	112.2	Manufacturing Production	66ey c
106.1	104.0	106.2	100.8	104.0	105.1	125.9	119.3	108.9	102.5	100.0	98.8	95.1	100.9	112.0	Manufacturing Employment	67ey
Millions of New Zealand Dollars															**International Transactions**	
5,568.5	6,471.2	7,414.4	8,110.0	9,584.1	11,603.2	11,225.1	12,149.7	13,488.2	14,819.5	15,760.0	16,671.0	18,208.0	19,492.0	20,517.0	Exports	70
354.1	489.4	683.9	545.3	567.8	670.6	498.8	517.7	554.9	560.4	654.2	733.7	677.5	828.5	790.4	Butter	70fl
5,615.9	6,635.5	7,699.0	7,991.9	10,939.0	12,075.5	11,622.1	12,242.5	11,216.9	14,710.1	15,895.5	14,526.8	17,132.0	17,781.0	19,981.0	Imports, cif	71
5,171.2	5,587.3	7,044.8	6,928.2	8,197.9	10,966.8	10,646.5	11,221.8	10,273.2	13,438.9	14,566.2	13,280.5	15,804.0	16,372.0	18,491.0	Imports, fob	71.v
1990=100																
73	74	76	80	84	I 93	91	93	97	95	100	110	113	118	130	Volume of Exports	72
105	98	118	89	94	123	103	107	117	82	100	121	89	123	124	Butter	72fl
63	65	69	64	77	I 76	75	83	77	93	100	90	100	104	121	Volume of Imports	73
50	57	63	66	75	I 82	80	84	90	102	100	96	104	106	102	Export Prices	74
51	75	89	94	92	I 89	79	73	75	97	100	98	114	111	101	Butter (Unit Value)	74fl
63	65	69	67	67	83	89	78	87	100	100	98	113	105	96	Butter (Wholesale Price)	76fl
58	66	73	79	90	I 100	97	93	92	99	100	101	108	107	104	Unit Value of Imports	75
Minus Sign Indicates Debit															Balance of Payments	
5,394	5,603	5,323	5,328	5,385	5,595	5,836	7,245	8,831	8,846	9,191	9,555	9,781	10,463	....	Goods: Exports f.o.b.	78aa *d*
-5,091	-5,346	-5,603	-4,991	-5,857	-5,654	-5,741	-6,663	-6,667	-7,873	-8,294	-7,483	-8,108	-8,749	....	Goods: Imports f.o.b.	78ab *d*
303	257	-280	337	-472	-59	95	582	2,164	973	897	2,072	1,674	1,714	....	Trade Balance	78ac *d*
1,009	1,249	1,270	1,383	1,487	1,457	1,714	2,191	2,549	2,395	2,492	2,532	2,557	2,749	....	Services: Credit	78ad *d*
-1,843	-2,001	-2,034	-1,867	-1,860	-1,814	-2,184	-2,658	-3,153	-3,167	-3,324	-3,413	-3,568	-3,474	....	Services: Debit	78ae *d*
-531	-495	-1,043	-146	-845	-416	-374	115	1,560	201	65	1,191	662	989	....	Balance on Goods and Services	78af *d*
159	216	224	228	208	272	378	627	542	490	687	32	-95	143	....	Income: Credit	78ag *d*
-697	-860	-965	-1,125	-1,338	-1,604	-1,844	-2,655	-2,689	-2,432	-2,339	-2,566	-2,121	-2,592	....	Income: Debit	78ah *d*
-1,069	-1,139	-1,785	-1,043	-1,975	-1,748	-1,840	-1,913	-587	-1,741	-1,587	-1,343	-1,554	-1,460	....	Balance on Goods, Serv., & Inc.	78ai *d*
226	220	226	222	288	335	376	464	546	575	638	647	635	630	....	Current Transfers, n.i.e.: Credit	78aj *d*
-130	-126	-136	-139	-156	-229	-249	-313	-326	-336	-438	-444	-425	-421	....	Current Transfers: Debit	78ak *d*
-973	-1,045	-1,694	-960	-1,842	-1,642	-1,713	-1,761	-367	-1,501	-1,387	-1,140	-1,343	-1,251	....	Current Account, n.i.e.	78al *d*
55	63	75	80	62	55	69	113	211	368	533	605	589	432	....	Capital Account, n.i.e.: Credit	78ba *d*
-93	-133	-79	-79	-76	-78	-96	-127	-164	-143	-129	-124	-115	-113	....	Capital Account: Debit	78bb *d*
-38	-71	-3	2	-14	-23	-27	-14	47	225	404	481	474	319	....	Capital Account, n.i.e.	78bc *d*
-107	-104	-69	-75	-163	-105	-394	-245	-152	-1,791	-588	—	—	—	....	Direct Investment Abroad	78bd *d*
178	275	328	175	270	424	283	293	441	1,365	419	—	—	—	....	Dir. Invest. in Rep. Econ., n.i.e.	78be *d*
—	—	—	—	—	—	—	—	—	-40	-13	—	—	—	....	Portfolio Investment Assets	78bf *d*
—	—	—	—	—	—	—	—	—	70	24	—	—	—	....	Portfolio Investment Liab., n.i.e.	78bg *d*
-114	-34	-77	-100	26	31	-47	-85	628	-230	67	—	—	—	....	Other Investment Assets	78bh *d*
-601	-846	161	48	-571	-1,237	-574	-754	-3,762	-303	-383	-1,239	-2,352	-2,774	....	Other Investment Liab., n.i.e.	78bi *d*
-644	-710	343	48	-437	-886	-731	-791	-2,845	-931	-474	-1,239	-2,352	-2,774	....	Financial Account, n.i.e.	78bj *d*
230	-277	-859	-204	748	418	-140	317	244	981	1,636	386	1,743	1,933	....	Net Errors and Omissions	78ca *d*
-1,424	-2,102	-2,214	-1,114	-1,546	-2,134	-2,612	-2,248	-2,921	-1,226	178	-1,511	-1,477	-1,773	....	Overall Balance	78cb *d*
1,424	2,102	2,214	1,114	1,546	2,134	2,612	2,248	2,921	1,226	-178	1,511	1,477	1,773	....	Reserves and Related Items	79da *d*
314	-344	31	-209	-1,027	389	-2,044	389	735	-240	-1,013	1,319	-131	74	....	Reserve Assets	79db *d*
-179	-116	-34	-3	—	—	—	—	—	—	—	—	—	—	....	Use of Fund Credit and Loans	79dc *d*
—	—	—	—	—	—	—	—	—	—	—	—	—	—	....	Liabs.Constit.For.Auth.Reserves	79dd *d*
1,289	2,562	2,217	1,325	2,574	1,745	4,656	1,860	2,186	1,466	835	192	1,608	1,699	....	Exceptional Financing	79de *d*
Fiscal Year (see note)															**Government Finance**	
-1,541	-2,111	-2,389	-3,209	-3,234	-2,082	-1,990	642	1,354	....	I 2,894	1,419	-1,677	84	....	Deficit (-) or Surplus	80
7,877	9,753	11,207	11,724	13,705	16,933	20,843	26,668	27,160	....	I 30,866	28,457	26,616	26,742	....	Revenue	81
8,802	11,075	12,880	14,108	16,155	18,330	22,711	27,815	28,492	....	I 31,758	30,084	28,598	28,440	....	Expenditure	82
616	789	716	825	784	685	122	-1,789	-2,686	....	I -3,786	-3,046	-305	-1,782	....	Lending Minus Repayments	83
															Financing	
523	1,451	2,085	2,612	1,653	1,167	I 2,357	....	....	....	....	....	....	....	....	Domestic	84a
816	799	1,322	823	1,839	946	I -367	....	....	....	....	....	....	....	....	Foreign	85a
202	-139	-1,018	-226	-258	-31	....	....	....	....	....	....	....	....	....	Use of Cash Balances	87a
7,399	8,858	11,004	13,701	15,875	17,276	20,744	21,855	23,008	....	I 20,452	20,981	....	....	....	Debt: Domestic	88a
4,236	5,549	7,765	8,227	12,409	14,726	21,735	17,257	16,593	....	I 23,897	22,952	....	....	....	Foreign	89a
															Financing (by Currency)	
....	....	....	....	....	....	....	....	....	....	....	....	....	....	....	Use of Cash Balances	87
....	....	....	....	....	....	....	....	....	....	....	....	....	....	....	Debt: New Zealand Dollars	88b
Year Beginning April 1															**National Accounts**	
7,003	8,249	9,266	10,507	13,229	13,947	15,122	16,663	18,064	19,154	19,935	21,519	23,764	25,030	....	Exports of Goods & Services	90c. *c*
4,134	4,989	5,566	5,858	6,334	7,345	8,930	10,128	11,023	11,728	12,529	12,464	12,572	12,530	....	Government Consumption	91f. *c*
4,754	6,597	7,774	8,612	9,994	11,978	12,363	13,382	12,892	14,303	13,837	11,643	12,564	14,856	....	Gross Fixed Capital Formation	93e. *c*
43	290	400	586	1,442	340	887	503	767	2,083	709	372	1,753	2,176	....	Increase/Decrease(-) in Stocks	93i. *c*
14,181	16,639	19,018	20,718	23,582	27,869	32,962	37,432	40,523	43,455	45,642	45,782	46,725	48,467	....	Private Consumption	96f. *c*
-7,272	-9,168	-10,318	-11,063	-14,539	-15,311	-15,240	-15,635	-15,616	-18,972	-19,527	-19,201	-21,775	-22,642	....	Imports of Goods & Services	98c. *c*
23,089	27,991	31,561	35,049	39,677	45,777	55,024	62,536	67,228	71,410	73,126	72,909	76,111	80,864	....	Gross Domestic Product	99b. *c*
-511	-615	-858	-1,275	-2,002	-2,520	-2,767	-3,270	-3,319	-4,769	-4,243	-4,425	-3,042	-3,220	....	Net Factor Inc/Pmts(-) Abroad	98.n *c*
22,578	27,276	30,703	33,774	37,675	43,257	52,257	59,267	63,909	66,641	68,882	68,484	73,069	77,644	....	Gross Nat'l Expenditure = GNP	99a. *c*
20,934	25,486	28,567	31,210	34,692	39,655	48,014	54,326	58,485	60,863	62,693	61,931	66,236	70,506	....	Nat'l Income, Market Prices	99e. *c*
59,388	62,270	63,727	67,448	70,975	70,819	73,152	73,606	74,720	73,757	73,126	71,279	72,640	76,442	....	Gross Dom. Prod. 1990 Prices	99b. *r*
38.9	45.0	49.5	52.0	55.9	64.6	75.2	85.0	90.0	96.8	100.0	102.3	104.8	105.8	....	GDP Deflator (1990=100)	99bi *r*
Midyear Estimates																
3.11	3.12	3.16	3.20	3.23	3.25	3.25	3.28	3.29	3.31	3.35	3.38	3.41	3.46	3.49	**Population**	99z

Balance of Payments: Annual balance of payments data for years prior to 1980 are compiled on the basis of fiscal years commencing April 1. From 1980 onwards, the data are on a calendar year basis.

Government Finance: I Beginning in 1970, data are as reported in the *Government Finance Statistics Yearbook*. Prior to that date, the data are as reported by the Department of Statistics for publication in *IFS*. The data cover budgetary central government only. I Beginning in 1986, data for *lines 84a* and *85a* cover domestic and foreign financing respectively. I Fiscal year ends June 30 beginning in 1990; begins April 1 through 1988.

Nicaragua
278

		1965	1966	1967	1968	1969	1970	1971	1972	1973	1974	1975	1976	1977	1978	1979
Exchange Rates															Gold Córdobas per Bill. SDRs through 1987, per Million SDRs in 1988, per	
Principal Rate	aa	1.41	1.41	1.41	1.41	1.41	1.41	1.53	1.53	1.70	1.72	1.65	1.63	1.71	1.83	2.65
													Gold Córd.per Bill.US$ through 1987, per Mill.US$ in 1988,per Thous.US$			
Principal Rate	ae	1.41	1.41	1.41	1.41	1.41	1.41	1.41	1.41	1.41	1.41	1.41	1.41	1.41	1.41	2.01
Principal Rate	rf	2.06	2.06	2.06	2.06	2.06	2.06	2.06	2.06	2.06	2.06	2.06	2.06	2.06	2.06	2.79
															Index Numbers (1990=100):	
Principal Rate	ahx	....	....	....	....	....	....	....	....	....	....	....	....	....	....	....
Nominal Effective Exchange Rate	nec	....	....	....	....	....	....	....	....	....	....	....	....	....	....	....
Real Effective Exchange Rate	rec	....	....	....	....	....	....	....	....	....	....	....	....	....	....	22.74
Fund Position																Millions of SDRs:
Quota	2f.s	11.25	19.00	19.00	19.00	19.00	27.00	27.00	27.00	27.00	27.00	27.00	27.00	27.00	34.00	34.00
SDRs	1b.s	—	—	—	—	—	.96	3.68	6.22	5.71	5.80	4.57	3.47	3.77	4.34	.02
Reserve Position in the Fund	1c.s	—	—	4.75	—	—	—	—	—	—	—	—	—	—	—	—
Total Fund Cred.&Loans Outstg.	2tl	8.43	6.49	—	14.25	13.25	8.00	10.99	8.25	12.24	10.06	15.50	8.74	2.00	2.01	43.51
International Liquidity												Millions of US Dollars Unless Otherwise Indicated:				
Total Reserves minus Gold	1l.d	56.94	57.23	31.28	47.65	43.72	48.59	58.11	80.11	116.26	104.49	121.59	146.05	148.33	50.77	146.62
SDRs	1b.d	—	—	—	—	—	.96	4.00	6.75	6.89	7.10	5.35	4.03	4.58	5.65	.03
Reserve Position in the Fund	1c.d	—	—	4.75	—	—	—	—	—	—	—	—	—	—	—	—
Foreign Exchange	1d.d	56.94	57.23	26.53	47.65	43.72	47.63	54.11	73.36	109.37	97.39	116.24	142.02	143.75	45.12	146.59
Gold (Million Fine Troy Ounces)	1ad	.011	.025	.023	.023	.014	.017	.018	.009	.015	.019	.018	.017	.026	.027	.018
Gold (National Valuation)	1and	.39	.88	.81	.81	.49	.60	.63	.34	.63	.80	.76	.72	1.10	1.14	.76
Monetary Authorities: Other Liab.	4..d	6.20	5.98	4.87	.76	.95	.26	−.30	.74	6.35	23.56	47.24	49.42	57.99	139.05	215.29
Deposit Money Banks: Assets	7a.d	5.34	6.99	4.10	5.96	4.44	5.67	8.19	11.04	16.61	10.28	14.32	17.80	16.71	31.01	24.06
Liabilities	7b.d	34.26	54.61	59.57	75.03	77.29	76.80	82.27	74.14	85.03	94.25	113.97	95.87	150.19	198.68	166.00
Monetary Authorities										Thousandths (.000) of Gold Córdobas through 1985; Gold Córd. 1986-87:						
Foreign Assets	11	88	89	52	68	62	69	82	111	164	147	172	205	209	72	244
Claims on Central Government	12a	16	16	15	33	39	38	39	40	74	63	75	79	85	244	364
Claims on Nonfin.Pub.Enterprises	12c	....	....	....	....	....	....	....	....	....	....	....	....	....	....	....
Claims on Deposit Money Banks	12e	2	8	23	20	19	19	19	17	38	122	100	81	79	137	268
Claims on Nonbank Financial Insts.	12g	....	....	....	....	....	....	....	....	....	....	....	....	....	....	....
Reserve Money	14	64	71	69	78	79	88	91	106	150	166	171	217	230	207	472
of which: Currency Outside DMBs	14a	40	45	44	42	44	50	50	66	82	90	89	127	138	177	314
Time, Savings,& Fgn.Currency Dep.	15	1	2	2	1	1	1	1	3	2	4	5	7	5	16	5
Foreign Liabilities	16c	20	17	7	21	20	11	16	14	27	48	67	46	44	145	305
Long-Term Foreign Liabilities	16cl	—	—	—	—	—	—	—	—	3	3	25	38	41	54	243
Central Government Deposits	16d	18	14	5	10	7	7	7	16	53	68	40	31	29	20	152
Liab. to Nonbank Financial Insts.	16j	....	....	....	....	....	....	....	....	....	....	....	....	....	....	....
Capital Accounts	17a	5	5	5	5	5	10	14	19	21	21	21	20	21	21	38
Other Items (Net)	17r	−2	4	2	6	8	9	11	10	20	22	18	6	3	−10	−339
of which: Valuation Adjustment	17rv	....	....	....	....	....	....	....	....	....	....	....	....	....	....	....
Deposit Money Banks										Thousandths (.000) of Gold Córdobas through 1985; Gold Córd. 1986-87;						
Reserves	20	25	36	39	36	35	39	42	41	68	78	84	90	95	77	82
Foreign Assets	21	7	10	6	8	6	8	11	15	23	14	20	25	23	44	46
Claims on Local Government	22b	....	....	....	....	....	....	....	....	....	....	....	....	....	....	....
Claims on Nonfin.Pub.Enterprises	22c	....	....	....	....	....	....	....	....	....	....	....	....	....	....	....
Claims on Private Sector	22d	143	177	201	220	234	249	273	293	398	531	532	594	708	775	1,393
Demand Deposits	24	68	68	64	55	59	65	73	83	147	172	162	195	200	183	305
Time, Savings,& Fgn.Currency Dep.	25	26	35	42	38	41	49	65	93	115	137	150	210	226	198	262
Foreign Liabilities	26c	48	76	83	52	52	49	42	24	30	43	75	59	147	227	335
Long-Term Foreign Liabilities	26cl	—	—	—	54	56	59	73	79	89	89	85	75	64	52	77
Central Government Deposits	26d	—	—	—	9	9	8	7	14	33	58	32	30	33	30	80
Credit from Monetary Authorities	26g	2	8	23	20	18	18	18	16	37	121	98	75	73	134	436
Liab. to Nonbank Financial Insts.	26j	....	....	....	....	....	....	....	....	....	....	....	....	....	....	....
Capital Accounts	27a	43	49	51	53	53	60	66	70	76	80	92	99	102	112	142
Other Items (Net)	27r	−11	−12	−17	−15	−12	−13	−19	−29	−38	−77	−58	−34	−18	−40	−116
Monetary Survey										Thousandths (.000) of Gold Córdobas through 1985; Gold Córd. 1986-87;						
Foreign Assets (Net)	31n	27	5	−33	4	−3	16	35	88	130	71	50	125	41	−256	−349
Domestic Credit	32	140	179	212	235	258	272	298	310	391	486	541	618	748	977	1,590
Claims on Central Govt. (Net)	32an	−2	1	10	14	24	22	25	17	−6	−45	9	24	40	202	197
Claims on Local Government	32b	....	....	....	....	....	....	....	....	....	....	....	....	....	....	....
Claims on Nonfin.Pub.Enterprises	32c	....	....	....	....	....	....	....	....	....	....	....	....	....	....	....
Claims on Private Sector	32d	143	177	201	220	234	249	273	293	398	531	532	594	708	775	1,393
Claims on Nonbank Fin. Insts.	32g	....	....	....	....	....	....	....	....	....	....	....	....	....	....	....
Money	34	107	113	108	97	103	116	124	150	229	263	251	323	340	316	620
Quasi-Money	35	27	37	44	39	42	50	66	95	118	141	155	217	231	215	267
Liab. to Nonbank Financial Insts.	36j	....	....	....	....	....	....	....	....	....	....	....	....	....	....	....
Capital Accounts	37a	48	54	56	58	58	70	80	89	97	101	113	119	122	133	180
Other Items (Net)	37r	−15	−20	−29	45	52	52	63	64	77	52	72	84	96	57	174
Money plus Quasi-Money	35l	135	150	152	136	144	166	190	245	347	403	406	540	571	530	886
Nonbank Financial Institutions												Thousands of Gold Córdobas through 1989;				
Reserves	40	....	....	....	....	....	....	....	....	....	....	....	....	....	....	....
Foreign Assets	41	....	....	....	....	....	....	....	....	....	....	....	....	....	....	....
Claims on Private Sector	42d	....	....	....	....	....	....	....	....	....	....	....	....	....	....	....
Claims on Deposit Money Banks	42e	....	....	....	....	....	....	....	....	....	....	....	....	....	....	....
Credit from Monetary Authorities	46g	....	....	....	....	....	....	....	....	....	....	....	....	....	....	....
Capital Accounts	47a	....	....	....	....	....	....	....	....	....	....	....	....	....	....	....
Other Items (Net)	47r	....	....	....	....	....	....	....	....	....	....	....	....	....	....	....
Financial Survey												Thousands of Gold Córdobas through 1989;				
Foreign Assets (Net)	51n	....	....	....	....	....	....	....	....	....	....	....	....	....	....	....
Domestic Credit	52	....	....	....	....	....	....	....	....	....	....	....	....	....	....	....
Claims on Central Govt. (Net)	52an	....	....	....	....	....	....	....	....	....	....	....	....	....	....	....
Claims on Local Government	52b	....	....	....	....	....	....	....	....	....	....	....	....	....	....	....
Claims on Nonfin.Pub.Enterprises	52c	....	....	....	....	....	....	....	....	....	....	....	....	....	....	....
Claims on Private Sector	52d	....	....	....	....	....	....	....	....	....	....	....	....	....	....	....
Liquid Liabilities	55l	....	....	....	....	....	....	....	....	....	....	....	....	....	....	....
Capital Accounts	57a	....	....	....	....	....	....	....	....	....	....	....	....	....	....	....
Other Items (Net)	57r	....	....	....	....	....	....	....	....	....	....	....	....	....	....	....

Nicaragua

1980	1981	1982	1983	1984	1985	1986	1987	1988	1989	1990	1991	1992	1993	1994		
Thousand SDRs in 1989-1990, per SDR Thereafter: End of Period															**Exchange Rates**	
2.56	2.34	2.22	2.10	1.97	6.15	17.12	19.86	ℐ247.61	ℐ10.03	853.60	ℐ7.15	6.88	8.72	10.38	Principal Rate	**aa**
in 1989-1990,per US$ thereafter; End of Period (ae) Period Average (rf)																
2.01	2.01	2.01	2.01	2.01	5.60	14.00	14.00	ℐ184.00	ℐ7.63	600.00	ℐ5.00	5.00	6.35	7.11	Principal Rate	**ae**
2.95	2.95	2.95	2.95	2.95	7.77	19.50	20.53	ℐ53.95	ℐ3.13	140.92	....	....	5.62	6.72	Principal Rate	**rf**
Period Averages																
....	....	....	....	....	....	....	....	....	1,469.95	100.00	.81	.43	.40	.32	Principal Rate	**ah x**
										100.00	1.06	.65	.65	.71	Nominal Effective Exchange Rate	**ne c**
25.19	31.41	31.87	38.77	44.53	63.06	74.90	109.15	109.24	66.87	100.00	95.70	93.21	90.43	84.74	Real Effective Exchange Rate	**re c**
End of Period															**Fund Position**	
51.00	51.00	51.00	51.00	68.20	68.20	68.20	68.20	68.20	68.20	68.20	68.20	96.10	96.10	96.10	Quota	**2f. s**
—	.06	.88	—	—	—	—	—	.01	—	—	.02	.02	.06	.01	SDRs	**1b. s**
—	—	—	—	—	—	—	—	—	—	—	—	—	—	—	Reserve Position in the Fund	**1c. s**
38.67	21.19	17.54	13.29	9.04	.01	—	—	—	—	—	17.03	17.03	17.03	34.92	Total Fund Cred.&Loans Outstg.	**2tl**
End of Period															**International Liquidity**	
64.52	111.43	171.17	174.70	....	....	....	17.41	38.10	115.80	106.63	134.13	130.48	55.04	141.01	Total Reserves minus Gold	**1l. d**
—	.07	.97	—	—	—	—	.01	—	—	.03	.03	.08	.04	.01	SDRs	**1b. d**
—	—	—	—	—	—	—	—	—	—	—	—	—	—	—	Reserve Position in the Fund	**1c. d**
64.52	111.36	170.20	174.70	—	—	—	17.40	38.10	115.80	106.60	134.10	130.40	55.00	141.00	Foreign Exchange	**1d. d**
.018	.018	.018	.120	—	—	—	.198	.312	.120	.153	.100	.475	.010	.013	Gold (Million Fine Troy Ounces)	**1ad**
.76	.76	.76	5.07	....	....	....	9.60	12.80	4.80	5.90	3.60	17.10	.42	.55	Gold (National Valuation)	**1an d**
399.74	789.78	1,099.85	1,721.93	2,351.35	2,720.96	2,819.85	3,237.13	3,637.93	3,560.99	3,809.93	4,120.70	4,340.22	3,586.04	3,499.77	Monetary Authorities: Other Liab.	**4..d**
23.76	46.87	58.45	38.03	13.32	11.56	2.77	8.81	2.28	2.98	5.45	32.80	43.30	47.35	53.54	Deposit Money Banks: Assets	**7a. d**
270.54	109.00	104.28	132.92	98.25	98.39	20.97	30.94	1.09	.97	2.20	20.54	24.38	18.74	31.62	Liabilities	**7b. d**
Thousands 1988-89; Millions Beginning 1990: End of Period															**Monetary Authorities**	
92	254	266	ℐ369	915	2,602	ℐ4	4	ℐ11	893	ℐ45	840	896	558	1,227	Foreign Assets	**11**
772	991	1,594	ℐ3,852	5,625	11,704	ℐ26	119	ℐ15	77	ℐ52	1,080	20,498	21,646	23,257	Claims on Central Government	**12a**
....	....	....	70	108	206	ℐ—	1	ℐ—	17	ℐ6	135	170	169	381	Claims on Nonfin.Pub.Enterprises	**12c**
663	1,076	1,247	ℐ761	840	1,271	ℐ4	70	ℐ23	328	ℐ61	1,101	767	798	824	Claims on Deposit Money Banks	**12e**
....	....	....	84	316	1,962	ℐ6	27	ℐ3	51	ℐ51	834	1,107	1,705	1,206	Claims on Nonbank Financial Insts.	**12g**
440	691	910	ℐ1,611	3,021	8,564	ℐ29	201	ℐ23	604	ℐ63	883	933	1,006	1,533	Reserve Money	**14**
393	475	617	ℐ1,085	2,268	5,712	ℐ20	146	ℐ13	324	ℐ29	401	468	509	688	*of which: Currency Outside DMBs*	**14a**
3	2	14	ℐ297	453	779	ℐ2	3	ℐ—	—	ℐ—	—	50	18	18	Time, Savings,& Fgn.Currency Dep.	**15**
532	883	1,128	ℐ1,042	1,548	6,548	ℐ13	16	ℐ234	11,522	ℐ1,023	10,514	10,625	9,704	14,019	Foreign Liabilities	**16c**
371	754	1,121	ℐ2,447	3,196	8,690	ℐ26	30	ℐ435	15,648	ℐ1,263	10,212	11,193	13,216	11,026	Long-Term Foreign Liabilities	**16cl**
216	45	130	ℐ34	167	470	ℐ2	21	ℐ3	37	ℐ13	207	1,253	397	330	Central Government Deposits	**16d**
....	....	....	50	87	573	ℐ1	2	ℐ1	4	ℐ1	29	29	44	184	Liab. to Nonbank Financial Insts.	**16j**
48	57	56	ℐ54	52	126	ℐ—	—	ℐ3	123	ℐ13	187	183	188	213	Capital Accounts	**17a**
−83	−111	−252	ℐ−400	−722	−8,004	ℐ−33	−53	ℐ−646	−26,571	ℐ−2,162	−18,043	−828	302	−428	Other Items (Net)	**17r**
....	....	....	....	....	−7,324	ℐ−27	−26	ℐ−576	−23,413	ℐ−1,923	−12,718	—	—	—	*of which: Valuation Adjustment*	**17rv**
Thousands 1988-89; Millions Beginning 1990: End of Period															**Deposit Money Banks**	
86	200	293	ℐ571	961	2,740	ℐ7	53	ℐ16	249	ℐ33	496	463	491	774	Reserves	**20**
48	94	117	ℐ76	27	65	ℐ—	—	ℐ—	23	ℐ3	164	217	301	381	Foreign Assets	**21**
....	....	....	59	82	77	ℐ—	—	ℐ—	—	ℐ—	—	2	8	5	Claims on Local Government	**22b**
....	....	....	1,825	2,609	4,684	ℐ12	116	ℐ27	1,035	ℐ104	728	17	12	41	Claims on Nonfin.Pub.Enterprises	**22c**
2,010	2,573	3,132	ℐ1,844	1,581	3,737	ℐ14	71	ℐ10	345	ℐ57	1,119	2,035	3,050	4,076	Claims on Private Sector	**22d**
427	531	664	ℐ1,170	1,873	5,151	ℐ18	138	ℐ19	451	ℐ21	324	373	295	408	Demand Deposits	**24**
326	542	656	ℐ1,063	1,673	3,387	ℐ10	38	ℐ8	325	ℐ37	691	846	1,356	2,501	Time, Savings,& Fgn.Currency Dep.	**25**
443	115	124	ℐ125	59	162	ℐ—	—	ℐ—	7	ℐ1	101	114	89	201	Foreign Liabilities	**26c**
101	104	86	ℐ142	139	389	ℐ—	—	ℐ—	—	ℐ—	1	8	30	24	Long-Term Foreign Liabilities	**26cl**
129	503	580	ℐ400	229	1,102	ℐ3	17	ℐ2	56	ℐ2	35	268	421	540	Central Government Deposits	**26d**
737	1,073	1,243	ℐ754	853	1,215	ℐ4	70	ℐ29	885	ℐ75	1,054	698	759	779	Credit from Monetary Authorities	**26g**
....	....	....	234	272	314	ℐ1	5	ℐ—	7	ℐ1	116	267	714	1,091	Liab. to Nonbank Financial Insts.	**26j**
171	112	495	ℐ665	781	788	ℐ1	—	ℐ7	69	ℐ48	55	187	503	649	Capital Accounts	**27a**
−190	−114	−304	ℐ−178	−619	−1,206	ℐ−4	−28	ℐ−12	−149	ℐ12	183	160	−307	−916	Other Items (Net)	**27r**
Thousands 1988-89; Millions Beginning 1990: End of Period															**Monetary Survey**	
−834	−650	−869	ℐ−3,311	−4,000	−13,121	ℐ−36	−42	ℐ−658	−26,262	ℐ−2,239	−19,824	−20,828	−22,180	−23,663	Foreign Assets (Net)	**31n**
3,058	3,133	4,080	ℐ7,340	9,997	21,044	ℐ54	298	ℐ50	1,432	ℐ255	3,653	22,312	25,770	28,096	Domestic Credit	**32**
1,048	560	948	ℐ3,445	5,289	10,378	ℐ21	82	ℐ10	−16	ℐ37	838	18,980	20,828	22,387	Claims on Central Govt. (Net)	**32an**
....	....	....	59	82	77	ℐ—	—	ℐ—	—	ℐ—	—	2	8	5	Claims on Local Government	**32b**
....	....	....	1,895	2,717	4,890	ℐ12	117	ℐ27	1,052	ℐ110	862	188	180	422	Claims on Nonfin.Pub.Enterprises	**32c**
2,010	2,573	3,132	ℐ1,844	1,581	3,737	ℐ14	71	ℐ10	345	ℐ57	1,119	2,035	3,050	4,076	Claims on Private Sector	**32d**
....	....	....	97	329	1,962	ℐ6	27	ℐ3	51	ℐ51	834	1,107	1,705	1,206	Claims on Nonbank Fin. Insts.	**32g**
820	1,041	1,309	ℐ2,271	4,169	10,955	ℐ39	284	ℐ33	826	ℐ53	758	845	806	1,097	Money	**34**
329	544	670	ℐ1,360	2,126	4,166	ℐ12	41	ℐ8	325	ℐ37	691	896	1,374	2,519	Quasi-Money	**35**
....	....	....	284	359	887	ℐ2	7	ℐ1	11	ℐ2	146	295	759	1,276	Liab. to Nonbank Financial Insts.	**36j**
219	169	551	ℐ718	834	914	ℐ1	—	ℐ10	192	ℐ61	187	183	691	862	Capital Accounts	**37a**
855	679	682	ℐ−604	−1,491	−8,999	ℐ−36	−78	ℐ−659	−26,184	ℐ−2,137	−17,954	−735	−39	−1,320	Other Items (Net)	**37r**
1,149	1,585	1,979	ℐ3,632	6,295	15,121	ℐ51	326	ℐ41	1,151	ℐ90	1,450	1,741	2,179	3,616	Money plus Quasi-Money	**35l**
Millions of Gold Córdobas beginning 1990: End of Period															**Nonbank Financial Institutions**	
....	....	....	....	....	....	....	....	ℐ—	5	ℐ1	21	24	39	....	Reserves	**40**
....	....	....	....	....	....	....	....	ℐ—	4	ℐ—	3	13	20	....	Foreign Assets	**41**
....	....	....	....	....	....	....	....	ℐ3	55	ℐ119	1,011	1,014	1,140	....	Claims on Private Sector	**42d**
....	....	....	....	....	....	....	....	ℐ—	4	ℐ1	113	354	742	....	Claims on Deposit Money Banks	**42e**
....	....	....	....	....	....	....	....	ℐ3	60	ℐ87	1,064	1,086	1,705	....	Credit from Monetary Authorities	**46g**
....	....	....	....	....	....	....	....	ℐ—	−53	ℐ30	−122	117	23	....	Capital Accounts	**47a**
....	....	....	....	....	....	....	....	ℐ1	62	ℐ3	206	201	214	....	Other Items (Net)	**47r**
Millions of Gold Córdobas beginning 1990: End of Period															**Financial Survey**	
....	....	....	....	....	....	....	....	ℐ−658	−26,257	ℐ−2,239	−19,821	−20,816	−22,161	....	Foreign Assets (Net)	**51n**
....	....	....	....	....	....	....	....	ℐ51	1,436	ℐ323	3,830	22,219	25,206	....	Domestic Credit	**52**
....	....	....	....	....	....	....	....	ℐ10	−16	ℐ37	838	18,980	20,820	....	Claims on Central Govt. (Net)	**52an**
....	....	....	....	....	....	....	....	ℐ—	—	ℐ—	—	2	8	....	Claims on Local Government	**52b**
....	....	....	....	....	....	....	....	ℐ27	1,052	ℐ110	862	188	180	....	Claims on Nonfin.Pub.Enterprises	**52c**
....	....	....	....	....	....	....	....	ℐ13	400	ℐ176	2,130	3,049	4,190	....	Claims on Private Sector	**52d**
....	....	....	....	....	....	....	....	ℐ41	1,146	ℐ89	1,428	1,717	2,140	....	Liquid Liabilities	**55l**
....	....	....	....	....	....	....	....	ℐ10	139	ℐ92	66	300	714	....	Capital Accounts	**57a**
....	....	....	....	....	....	....	....	ℐ−658	−26,106	ℐ−2,096	−17,485	−613	191	....	Other Items (Net)	**57r**

Nicaragua
278

		1965	1966	1967	1968	1969	1970	1971	1972	1973	1974	1975	1976	1977	1978	1979
Interest Rates														*Percent Per Annum*		
Discount Rate (End of period)	60	...	...	...	...	...	...	...	...	...	...	...	...	...	...	...
Savings Rate	60k	...	...	...	...	...	...	...	...	...	...	...	...	...	...	...
Deposit Rate	60l	...	...	...	...	...	...	...	...	...	...	...	...	...	...	...
Lending Rate	60p	...	...	...	...	...	...	...	...	...	...	...	...	...	...	...
Prices														*Index Numbers (1990=100):*		
Consumer Prices	64.a	...	...	...	...	...	...	...	...	...	...	...	...	—	—	—
Cons. Prices (1990=1 million)	64.b	...	...	...	...	...	...	...	...	...	...	...	...	—	—	—
Consumer Prices	64.c	...	...	...	...	...	...	...	...	...	...	...	...	...	...	...
International Transactions														*Millions of US Dollars*		
Exports	70..d	148.9	142.2	151.7	162.3	158.8	178.6	187.2	249.4	277.9	380.9	375.2	541.9	636.8	646.0	566.6
Imports, cif	71..d	160.3	181.9	203.9	184.7	177.0	198.8	210.4	218.5	327.0	561.7	516.9	532.1	762.0	596.0	360.2
Imports, fob	71.v d	146.8	166.1	186.2	169.1	161.5	178.7	190.4	197.2	299.4	504.7	466.1	481.9	659.4	540.4	335.5
Balance of Payments														*Millions of US Dollars:*		
Goods: Exports f.o.b.	78aa d													636.2	646.0	615.9
Goods: Imports f.o.b.	78ab d													−704.2	−553.3	−388.9
Trade Balance	78ac d													−68.0	92.7	227.0
Services: Credit	78ad d													83.1	74.2	56.3
Services: Debit	78ae d													−139.2	−106.6	−123.6
Balance on Goods and Services	78af d													−124.1	60.3	159.7
Income: Credit	78ag d													13.6	11.7	11.0
Income: Debit	78ah d													−82.6	−106.4	−82.1
Balance on Goods, Serv., & Inc.	78ai d													−193.1	−34.4	88.6
Current Transfers, n.i.e.: Credit	78aj d													12.7	10.8	92.1
Current Transfers: Debit	78ak d													−1.5	−1.3	−.5
Current Account, n.i.e.	78al d													−181.9	−24.9	180.2
Capital Account, n.i.e.: Credit	78ba d													—	—	—
Capital Account: Debit	78bb d													—	—	—
Capital Account, n.i.e.	78bc d													—	—	—
Direct Investment Abroad	78bd d													—	—	—
Dir. Invest. in Rep. Econ., n.i.e.	78be d													10.0	7.0	2.8
Portfolio Investment Assets	78bf d													—	—	—
Portfolio Investment Liab., n.i.e.	78bg d													—	—	—
Other Investment Assets	78bh d													−115.7	−296.0	—
Other Investment Liab., n.i.e.	78bi d													292.2	195.8	−147.2
Financial Account, n.i.e.	78bj d													186.5	−93.2	−144.4
Net Errors and Omissions	78ca d													−3.9	−10.5	−38.5
Overall Balance	78cb d													.7	−128.6	−2.7
Reserves and Related Items	79da d													−.7	128.6	2.7
Reserve Assets	79db d													−1.0	84.4	−50.6
Use of Fund Credit and Loans	79dc d													−7.9	—	53.3
Liabs.Constit.For.Auth.Reserves	79dd d													5.6	−10.9	—
Exceptional Financing	79de d													2.6	55.1	—
Government Finance											*Thousandths (.000) of Gold Córdobas through 1985; Gold Córd. in 1986;*					
Deficit (-) or Surplus	80	2.8	−8.3	−19.6	−11.9	−16.5	I−10.6	−27.4	−46.8	−26.8	−123.4	−124.6	−98.6	−199.0	−167.4	−187.6
Revenue	81	88.8	96.0	96.6	94.0	99.8	I 133.4	147.2	152.0	208.6	295.8	306.0	351.2	413.0	378.6	420.8
Grants Received	81z	...	...	...	...	...	I —	—	—	4.2	.4	—	1.4	—	—	8.2
Exp. & Lending Minus Repay.	82z	86.0	104.2	116.2	105.8	116.4	I 144.0	174.6	198.8	239.6	419.6	430.6	451.2	612.0	546.0	616.6
Expenditure	82	86.3	104.0	116.7	105.9	116.2	I 143.6	174.2	183.6	194.4	326.2	383.2	408.0	587.2	505.2	599.8
Lending Minus Repayments	83	−.3	.3	−.4	—	.1	I .4	.4	15.2	45.2	93.4	47.4	43.2	24.8	40.8	16.8
Financing																
Domestic	84a	...	...	...	...	...	I −1.8	3.6	2.4	−13.0	−22.2	53.8	50.0	3.2	154.4	160.0
Foreign	85a	...	...	...	...	...	I 12.4	23.8	44.4	39.8	145.6	70.8	48.6	195.8	13.0	27.6
Debt: Domestic	88a	...	...	...	...	...	I 16.4	29.4	30.8	60.2	56.8	53.4		114.0	175.4	...
Foreign	89a	...	...	...	...	...	I 66.0	89.8	99.0	210.6	336.4	439.6		607.4	688.6	...
Financing (by Currency)																
Net Borrowing: Cordobas	84b	−1.0	−.2	3.8	8.1	9.9										
Foreign Currency	85b	1.8	5.8	10.5	7.5	5.7										
Financing from Foreign Aid	86a	—	.8	.5	—	—										
Use of Cash Balances	87	−3.9	4.7	3.7	−3.7	9.6										
Debt: Cordobas	88b	30.8	27.8	29.3	29.9	31.2										
Foreign Currency	89b	16.2	23.0	33.4	53.0	56.7										
National Accounts										*Thousandths (.000) of Gold Córdobas through 1985; Gold Córd. 1986-87;*						
Exports of Goods & Services	90c	232.4	230.4	243.4	260.0	255.4	290.6	304.6	435.2	432.0	619.0	624.4	853.6	1,006.4	1,032.6	1,220.0
Government Consumption	91f	63.2	73.2	85.6	87.6	91.2	103.9	112.3	115.5	124.3	164.0	200.9	241.0	278.5	351.5	516.8
Gross Fixed Capital Formation	93e	...	...	...	...	...	...	...	...	...	...	...	...	...	...	...
Increase/Decrease(-) in Stocks	93i	...	...	...	...	...	...	...	...	...	...	...	...	...	...	...
Private Consumption	96f	589.7	641.4	721.3	751.2	787.9	809.1	867.2	869.0	1,173.6	1,584.9	1,725.0	1,778.5	2,051.4	2,030.2	2,151.8
Imports of Goods & Services	98c	−257.1	−289.9	−322.5	−296.3	−284.7	−317.5	−330.3	−365.8	−579.0	−907.6	−822.7	−824.1	−1,174.1	−937.6	−816.9
Gross Domestic Product	99b	792.1	848.2	918.7	972.8	1,045.7	1,085.7	1,155.6	1,210.3	1,513.5	2,126.0	2,187.7	2,515.3	2,944.7	2,849.2	2,898.7
Net Factor Inc/Pmts(-) Abroad	98..n	...	...	...	...	...	...	...	...	...	...	...	...	...	...	...
Gross Nat'l Expenditure = GNP	99a	...	...	...	...	...	...	...	...	...	...	...	...	...	...	...
Nat'l Income, Market Prices	99e	...	...	...	...	...	...	...	...	...	...	...	...	...	...	...
GDP 1990 Prices (Millions)	99b.p	276.4	285.5	305.4	309.5	328.8	333.2	349.7	I 360.8	387.8	442.9	442.2	465.2	504.3	464.8	342.0
GDP Deflator (1990=100)	99bi p	—	—	—	—	—	—	—	—	—	—	—	—	—	—	—
																Millions:
Population	99z	1.62	1.66	1.70	1.74	1.79	1.83	1.89	1.95	2.01	2.08	2.15	2.24	2.32	2.41	2.64

Exchange Rates: On February 15, 1988 the new cordoba, equal to 1000 old cordobas, was introduced. A new currency unit called cordoba oro, equivalent to one U.S. dollar, was introduced as a unit of account on May 1, 1990 and began to be circulated in August 1990. On March 4, 1991, the gold cordoba was devalued to US$0.2 per gold cordoba, equal to five million old cordobas. On April 30, 1991 the gold cordoba completely replaced the old cordoba as the sole legal tender. *IFS* money and banking accounts are now expressed in gold cordobas.

Monetary Authorities: I Beginning in 1983, data are based on a new reporting system.
Deposit Money Banks: I See note to section 10.
Monetary Survey: I See note to section 10.
Government Finance: I Beginning in 1970, data are as reported in the *Government Finance Statistics Yearbook* and relate to the consolidated central government.

Nicaragua

1980	1981	1982	1983	1984	1985	1986	1987	1988	1989	1990	1991	1992	1993	1994		
Percent Per Annum															**Interest Rates**	
....	....	....	....	....	....	....	....	12,874.6	311.0	10.0	15.0	15.0	11.8	10.5	Discount Rate *(End of period)*	60
....	....	....	....	....	....	....	....	2,229.8	125.2	7.0	7.8	8.1	8.5	8.8	Savings Rate	60k
....	....	....	....	....	....	....	....	107,379.1	1,585.9	9.5	11.6	12.0	11.6	11.7	Deposit Rate	60l
....	....	....	....	....	....	....	....	121,906.0	558.0	22.0	17.9	19.3	18.7	20.1	Lending Rate	60p
Period Averages															**Prices**	
—	—	1	1	1	3	26	263	....	....	....	....	....	....	....	Consumer Prices	64.a
							3	271	13,184	1,000,000	....	....	....	....	Cons. Prices (1990=1 million)	64.b
										100	2,842	3,418	....	....	Consumer Prices	64.c
Millions of US Dollars															**International Transactions**	
450.6	508.2	405.6	428.8	385.7	301.5	247.2	272.8	232.7	310.7	330.6	274.9	217.5	267.0	....	Exports	70..d
887.2	999.4	775.6	825.6	848.4	964.3	856.8	826.8	805.2	614.9	637.5	751.4	892.4	746.0	....	Imports, cif	71.d
822.3	932.5	723.6	778.1	799.6	878.2	782.0	734.4	716.6	547.3	567.4	694.0	793.7	678.5	....	Imports, fob	71.vd
Minus Sign Indicates Debit															Balance of Payments	
450.4	508.2	406.0	451.9	412.4	305.1	257.8	295.1	235.7	318.7	332.4	268.1	223.1	267.0	351.2	Goods: Exports f.o.b.	78aad
-802.9	-922.4	-723.5	-742.3	-735.3	-794.1	-677.4	-734.4	-718.3	-547.3	-569.7	-688.0	-770.8	-659.4	-784.7	Goods: Imports f.o.b.	78abd
-352.5	-414.2	-317.5	-290.4	-322.9	-489.0	-419.6	-439.3	-482.6	-228.6	-237.3	-419.9	-547.7	-392.4	-433.5	Trade Balance	78acd
44.4	45.1	40.8	46.1	48.4	39.3	29.5	29.5	37.4	22.0	59.8	70.2	86.2	100.2	101.4	Services: Credit	78add
-103.7	-110.2	-103.5	-128.2	-149.0	-129.6	-159.1	-160.5	-138.1	-119.2	-112.3	-136.2	-148.3	-156.6	-172.2	Services: Debit	78aed
-411.8	-479.3	-380.2	-372.5	-423.5	-579.3	-549.2	-570.3	-583.3	-325.8	-289.8	-485.9	-609.8	-448.8	-504.3	Balance on Goods and Services	78afd
19.2	28.3	8.7	6.5	4.6	1.5	.7	1.4	2.1	6.8	11.8	9.7	7.5	5.4	6.7	Income: Credit	78agd
-142.7	-210.9	-193.9	-220.7	-268.0	-274.9	-254.3	-245.3	-264.2	-211.6	-228.8	-373.0	-502.3	-434.5	-472.2	Income: Debit	78ahd
-535.3	-661.9	-565.4	-586.7	-686.9	-852.6	-802.8	-814.2	-845.4	-530.6	-506.8	-849.2	-1,104.6	-877.9	-969.8	Balance on Goods, Serv., & Inc.	78aid
124.0	70.4	51.6	79.3	89.8	126.9	115.1	135.4	130.0	168.9	201.6	844.4	270.6	233.6	240.9	Current Transfers, n.i.e.: Credit	78ajd
-.1	-.1	-.1												—	Current Transfers: Debit	78akd
-411.4	-591.6	-513.9	-507.4	-597.1	-725.7	-687.7	-678.8	-715.4	-361.7	-305.2	-4.8	-834.0	-644.3	-728.9	Current Account, n.i.e.	78ald
—	—	—	—	—	—	—	—	—	—	—	—	—	—	—	Capital Account, n.i.e.: Credit	78bad
—	—	—	—	—	—	—	—	—	—	—	—	—	—	—	Capital Account: Debit	78bbd
—	—	—	—	—	—	—	—	—	—	—	—	—	—	—	Capital Account, n.i.e.	78bcd
—	—	—	—	—	—	—	—	—	—	—	—	—	—	—	Direct Investment Abroad	78bdd
—	—	—	—	—	—	—	—	—	—	—	—	15.0	38.8	40.0	Dir. Invest. in Rep. Econ., n.i.e.	78bed
—	—	—	—	—	—	—	—	—	—	—	—	—	—	—	Portfolio Investment Assets	78bfd
—	—	—	—	—	—	—	—	—	—	—	—	—	—	—	Portfolio Investment Liab., n.i.e.	78bgd
42.7	307.3	284.9	31.7	240.8	353.9	-127.6	125.9	303.5	-89.3	-161.1	-21.1	-5.9	-10.1	-8.8	Other Investment Assets	78bhd
42.7	307.3	284.9	31.7	240.8	353.9	-127.6	125.9	303.5	-89.3	-161.1	-522.5	-547.4	-531.5	-240.3	Other Investment Liab., n.i.e.	78bid
											-543.6	-538.3	-502.8	-209.1	Financial Account, n.i.e.	78bjd
-74.7	15.8	10.8	-106.0	-38.7	-186.8	-183.6	-78.9	51.9	-69.2	-181.2	84.7	60.2	128.1	154.3	Net Errors and Omissions	78cad
-443.4	-268.5	-218.2	-581.6	-395.1	-558.6	-998.9	-631.8	-360.0	-520.2	-647.5	-463.7	-1,312.0	-1,019.0	-783.7	Overall Balance	
443.4	268.5	218.2	581.6	395.1	558.6	998.9	631.8	360.0	520.2	647.5	463.7	1,312.0	1,019.0	783.7	Reserves and Related Items	79dad
207.7	-64.8	-31.3	-13.7	-244.4	-7.8	211.3	-6.2	-43.9	-64.1	39.3	-109.2	-.5	79.4	-80.8	Reserve Assets	79dbd
-6.2	-21.4	-4.1	-4.4	-4.4	-8.9						23.1			26.1	Use of Fund Credit and Loans	79dcd
—	119.4	76.0	-124.7	-57.2	7.8	-66.6	-13.7	-60.5	—	—	—	—	—	—	Liabs.Constit.For.Auth.Reserves.	79ddd
241.9	235.4	177.6	724.5	701.0	567.5	854.2	651.7	464.4	584.3	608.2	549.8	1,312.5	939.6	838.4	Exceptional Financing	79ded
Thousands 1988-89; Millions beg. 1990: Year Ending December 31															**Government Finance**	
-284.4	-525.0	-1,148.6	-2,060.6	-2,121.8	-5,064.8	‡-12.8	....	‡-15.7	-60.8	‡-55.6	410.4	-194.0	41.2	....	Deficit (-) or Surplus	80
968.0	1,339.8	1,589.6	2,313.6	3,564.0	8,549.2	‡32.2	....	‡15.1	813.2	‡52.4	1,631.9	2,195.9	2,556.7	....	Revenue	81
26.8	63.6	61.8	80.6	69.2	135.8	‡.6	....	‡.2	101.0	‡4.7	867.7	403.4	836.2	....	Grants Received	81z
1,279.2	1,928.4	2,800.0	4,454.8	5,755.0	13,749.8	‡45.6	....	‡31.0	975.0	‡112.7	2,089.2	2,793.3	3,351.7	....	Exp. & Lending Minus Repay.	82z
1,266.4	1,924.0	2,798.6	4,454.8	5,755.0	13,749.8	‡45.6	....	‡31.0	973.8	‡112.7	2,055.4	2,767.6	3,317.1	....	Expenditure	82
12.8	4.4	1.4	—	—	—	‡—	....	‡—	1.2	‡.1	33.8	25.7	34.6	....	Lending Minus Repayments	83
															Financing	
134.2	304.2	840.2	1,638.8	1,753.0	3,128.0	‡6.7	....	‡14.7	62.2	‡35.8	-447.9	-676.3	-47.4	....	Domestic	84a
150.2	220.8	308.4	421.8	368.8	1,936.8	‡6.1	....	‡.9	-1.4	‡19.8	37.5	870.3	6.2	....	Foreign	85a
			3,670.8	....	....	....	....	....	....	....	....	....	....	....	Debt: Domestic	88a
2,350.6	2,987.0	3,473.6	3,594.8	....	....	....	....	....	....	....	....	....	....	....	Foreign	89a
															Financing (by Currency)	
															Net Borrowing: Cordobas	84b
															Foreign Currency	85b
															Financing from Foreign Aid	86a
															Use of Cash Balances	87
															Debt: Cordobas	88b
															Foreign Currency	89b
Thousands 1988-89; Millions Beginning 1990															**National Accounts**	
1,007.8	1,094.0	906.0	1,277.4	1,480.7	3,408.1	‡11.1	65.0	‡11.9	1,020.4	‡78.1	1,575.9	1,546.5	2,178.7	3,042.1	Exports of Goods & Services	90c
818.4	1,071.3	1,325.6	2,064.6	3,174.0	8,224.9	‡30.7	189.2	‡21.2	837.2	‡101.7	1,483.9	1,763.4	1,890.7	1,969.7	Government Consumption	91f
....	....	....	....	1,740.2	4,780.6	‡12.1	72.8	‡18.6	881.1	‡60.3	1,358.8	1,799.8	2,293.2	2,751.2	Gross Fixed Capital Formation	93e
....	....	....	249.1	536.6	‡2.5	14.5	‡-.9	-16.8	‡—	139.9	-22.2	-202.3	41.6	Increase/Decrease(-) in Stocks	93i
3,439.6	3,625.5	3,854.6	3,738.0	5,002.3	11,143.9	‡48.7	287.1	‡54.0	2,498.3	‡207.7	6,662.4	8,734.2	9,964.5	11,036.0	Private Consumption	96f
-1,800.6	-2,046.7	-1,477.8	-1,975.6	-2,653.5	-5,039.7	‡-18.2	-76.0	‡-38.7	-2,044.5	‡-135.6	-3,791.7	-4,596.0	-5,053.3	-6,430.4	Imports of Goods & Services	98c
4,154.0	4,889.8	5,662.1	6,574.8	8,993.4	23,048.6	‡87.0	552.6	‡66.3	3,175.7	‡312.0	7,429.2	9,225.7	11,064.7	12,392.8	Gross Domestic Product	99b
....	....	....	....	....	....	....	‡-.5	-11.7	‡-42.7	-1,668.6	-2,399.5	-2,558.5	-3,024.5	Net Factor Inc/Pmts(-) Abroad	98.n
....	....	....	....	....	....	....	‡60.8	3,553.0	‡269.4	5,760.6	6,826.2	8,505.9	9,368.3	Gross Nat'l Expenditure = GNP	99a
....	....	....	....	....	....	....	‡58.4	3,409.7	....	....	....	....	....	Nat'l Income, Market Prices	99e
357.4	376.5	373.5	390.7	384.6	368.9	365.1	362.5	317.4	311.9	312.0	311.5	312.8	311.5	321.4	GDP 1990 Prices *(Millions)*	99b.p
—	—	—	—	—	—	—	—	—	1.0	100.0	2,385.3	2,949.8	3,551.8	3,855.6	GDP Deflator (1990=100)	99bip
Midyear Estimates																
2.73	2.86	2.96	3.06	3.16	3.27	3.38	3.50	3.62	3.74	3.87	4.00	4.13	4.26	4.40	**Population**	99z

Niger

		1965	1966	1967	1968	1969	1970	1971	1972	1973	1974	1975	1976	1977	1978	1979
Exchange Rates																*Francs per SDR:*
Official Rate	aa	245.07	247.59	245.42	247.40	277.91	276.02	283.61	278.00	284.00	272.08	262.55	288.70	285.76	272.28	264.78
																Francs per US Dollar:
Official Rate	ae	245.08	247.59	245.43	247.41	277.92	276.03	261.23	256.05	235.43	222.22	224.27	248.49	235.25	209.00	201.00
Official Rate	rf	245.06	245.68	246.00	247.56	259.96	276.40	275.59	252.03	222.89	240.70	214.31	238.95	245.68	225.66	212.72
Fund Position																*Millions of SDRs:*
Quota	2f. s	7.5	8.0	8.5	9.0	10.0	13.0	13.0	13.0	13.0	13.0	13.0	13.0	13.0	16.0	16.0
SDRs	1b. s	—	—	—	—	—	1.7	3.1	4.4	4.4	4.4	4.4	4.4	4.4	4.4	6.0
Reserve Position in the Fund	1c. s	.8	.9	1.0	1.1	1.4	2.1	2.1	2.1	2.1	2.1	2.1	2.1	3.1	5.0	5.0
Total Fund Cred.&Loans Outstg.	2tl	—	—	—	—	—	—	—	—	—	—	—	—	—	5.4	5.4
International Liquidity														*Millions of US Dollars Unless Otherwise Indicated:*		
Total Reserves minus Gold	1l. d	3.1	3.8	1.1	2.7	6.7	18.7	33.6	41.3	50.8	45.5	50.3	82.5	101.1	128.3	131.7
SDRs	1b. d	—	—	—	—	—	1.7	3.3	4.8	5.3	5.4	5.1	5.1	5.7	5.7	8.0
Reserve Position in the Fund	1c. d	.8	.9	1.0	1.1	1.4	2.1	2.3	2.3	2.5	2.6	2.5	2.5	3.8	6.6	6.6
Foreign Exchange	1d. d	2.3	2.9	.1	1.6	5.3	15.0	28.0	34.3	42.9	37.5	42.6	74.9	92.0	116.1	117.1
Gold (Million Fine Troy Ounces)	1ad	....	....	....	....	....	....	....	....	....	....	....	—	.006	.008	.011
Gold (National Valuation)	1and	....	....	....	....	....	....	....	....	....	....	....	—	.2	.4	.5
Monetary Authorities: Other Liab.	4.. d	—	—	.4	.3	.1	.4	—	.1	.4	.6	1.1	6.1	3.9	3.7	5.0
Deposit Money Banks: Assets	7a. d	1.5	1.0	1.8	2.0	2.1	1.0	4.4	5.7	7.0	9.6	6.8	11.5	23.2	17.3	36.2
Liabilities	7b. d	6.9	6.7	3.7	7.4	6.5	7.9	9.9	9.4	11.1	11.8	12.0	16.7	24.5	45.5	79.9
of which: Liab. to Nonbanks	7bdd	....	....	....	....	....	....	....	....	....	....	....	5.5	7.8	8.5	30.5
Monetary Authorities																*Billions of Francs:*
Foreign Assets	11	.73	.95	.26	.65	1.87	5.20	8.59	10.58	11.68	10.11	11.27	20.50	23.79	26.82	26.47
Claims on Central Government	12a	.02	2.55	6.79	7.40	8.18	.01	—	—	—	—	—	—	.59	4.40	4.56
Claims on Deposit Money Banks	12e	4.21	4.31	4.15	3.33	2.52	1.39	—	.07	.16	4.35	6.22	1.21	1.00	6.42	13.63
Claims on Other Financial Insts.	12f	....	....	....	....	....	....	....	....	....	....	....	.23	.24	.25	.32
Reserve Money	14	4.40	4.88	4.61	4.36	4.93	5.03	6.33	6.45	7.45	10.54	10.07	14.16	17.20	26.47	29.96
of which: Currency Outside DMBs	14a	4.13	4.56	4.33	4.25	4.78	4.87	5.96	6.18	6.66	9.39	9.43	13.42	14.85	19.74	27.28
Foreign Liabilities	16c	.01	.01	.11	.07	.03	.12	.01	.02	.10	.14	.24	1.52	.92	3.73	3.92
Central Government Deposits	16d	.54	.58	.37	.28	.25	.98	1.41	2.83	2.95	2.51	6.05	4.87	6.22	7.41	10.85
Other Items (Net)	17r	.02	2.35	6.11	6.66	7.36	.47	.85	1.24	1.23	1.28	1.14	1.39	1.28	.28	.25
Deposit Money Banks																*Billions of Francs:*
Reserves	20	.27	.31	.26	.10	.14	.17	.36	.25	.48	.94	.64	.70	2.23	6.77	2.52
Foreign Assets	21	.38	.24	.44	.51	.57	.28	1.12	1.47	1.61	2.12	1.52	2.86	5.47	3.61	7.28
Claims on Central Government	22a	.16	.12	.09	.06	.03	.45	.39	.78	.99	1.22	3.23	4.39	4.80	5.16	5.00
Claims on Private Sector	22d	8.36	9.52	8.83	10.22	9.74	9.64	9.35	10.32	12.21	20.69	28.08	27.49	31.35	52.50	74.23
Claims on Other Financial Insts.	22f	....	....	....	....	....	....	....	....	....	....	....	....	....	....	.56
Demand Deposits	24	2.20	2.03	2.69	2.59	3.35	3.55	4.11	4.72	6.42	7.59	10.07	10.67	16.61	25.91	29.00
Time Deposits	25	—	.38	.54	.73	.67	.77	1.56	1.52	1.88	2.68	2.17	4.46	5.30	7.81	7.24
Foreign Liabilities	26c	1.48	1.31	.47	1.19	.68	.89	1.08	1.03	1.29	1.43	1.54	3.09	4.89	8.14	12.57
Long-Term Foreign Liabilities	26cl	.22	.34	.44	.64	1.14	1.31	1.46	1.37	1.27	1.19	1.17	1.05	.88	1.38	3.50
Central Government Deposits	26d	.78	.93	.83	1.05	1.07	1.13	1.42	1.42	1.61	6.25	8.84	11.69	15.36	13.28	17.20
Credit from Monetary Authorities	26g	4.21	4.31	4.17	3.33	2.52	1.39	—	.07	.16	4.35	6.25	1.21	1.00	6.42	13.63
Other Items (Net)	27r	.27	.90	.49	1.37	1.05	1.49	1.58	2.69	2.67	1.49	3.42	3.27	−.20	5.12	6.77
Treasury Claims: Private Sector	22d. i	.28	.32	.30	.28	.33	.41	.39	.35	.26	.28	.47	.84	1.08	1.49	1.17
Post Office: Checking Deposits	24.. i	.39	.36	.35	.41	.41	.41	.50	.48	.54	.66	.63	.69	.87	.74	.98
Monetary Survey																*Billions of Francs:*
Foreign Assets (Net)	31n	−.38	−.13	.12	−.10	1.73	4.47	8.62	10.99	11.91	10.67	11.02	18.75	23.45	18.57	17.27
Domestic Credit	32	7.61	11.04	14.86	16.76	17.03	8.40	7.41	7.33	9.17	13.82	17.06	16.24	16.26	42.36	57.91
Claims on Central Govt. (Net)	32an	−1.03	1.20	5.73	6.26	6.97	−1.64	−2.32	−3.35	−3.29	−7.15	−11.49	−12.33	−16.41	−11.88	−18.36
Claims on Private Sector	32d	8.64	9.84	9.13	10.50	10.06	10.05	9.74	10.68	12.46	20.97	28.55	28.33	32.43	53.99	75.40
Claims on Other Financial Insts.	32f	....	....	....	....	....	....	....	....	....	....	....	.23	.24	.25	.87
Money	34	6.72	6.95	7.36	7.24	8.54	8.83	10.57	11.38	13.62	17.64	20.13	24.78	32.33	46.39	57.27
Quasi-Money	35	—	.38	.54	.73	.67	.77	1.56	1.52	1.88	2.68	2.17	4.46	5.30	7.81	7.24
Long-Term Foreign Liabilities	36cl	.22	.34	.44	.64	1.14	1.31	1.46	1.37	1.27	1.19	1.17	1.05	.88	1.38	3.50
Other Items (Net)	37r	.30	3.24	6.66	8.04	8.42	1.96	2.44	3.95	4.20	2.98	4.59	4.64	1.19	6.78	7.18
Money plus Quasi-Money	35l	6.72	7.33	7.90	7.97	9.21	9.60	12.14	12.90	15.50	20.32	22.31	29.24	37.64	54.20	64.51
Other Banking Institutions																*Billions of Francs:*
Savings Deposits	45	.07	.06	.06	.08	.09	.10	.11	.11	.12	.14	.17	.19	.23	.28	.38
Liquid Liabilities	55l	6.79	7.39	7.96	8.05	9.30	9.69	12.25	13.01	15.62	20.45	22.47	29.43	37.87	54.48	64.89
Interest Rates																*Percent Per Annum*
Discount Rate (End of Period)	60	3.50	3.50	3.50	3.50	3.50	3.50	3.50	3.50	5.50	5.50	8.00	8.00	8.00	8.00	8.00
Money Market Rate	60b	....	....	....	....	....	....	....	....	....	....	....	7.28	7.40	7.38	7.72
Deposit Rate	60l	....	....	....	....	....	3.00	3.00	3.00	5.75	5.75	5.88	6.00	6.00	6.00	6.00
Lending Rate	60p	....	....	....	....	....	....	....	....	....	....	....	....	12.00	12.00	12.00
Prices																*Index Numbers (1990=100):*
Consumer Prices	64	23.5	26.0	26.1	25.3	28.0	28.4	29.5	32.4	36.2	37.5	40.9	50.5	62.3	68.5	73.5
International Transactions																*Millions of Francs:*
Exports	70	6,250	8,574	8,600	7,125	6,250	8,795	10,670	13,712	13,817	12,621	19,556	31,979	39,335	63,706	95,241
Imports, cif	71	9,300	11,115	11,353	10,237	12,570	16,214	14,975	16,576	19,098	23,144	21,889	30,383	48,221	68,896	98,058
Imports, fob	71.v	7,323	8,752	8,939	8,061	9,925	12,819	11,691	13,114	15,036	16,724	15,671	22,250	38,666	57,028	83,016

Niger

	1980	1981	1982	1983	1984	1985	1986	1987	1988	1989	1990	1991	1992	1993	1994		
End of Period																**Exchange Rates**	
	287.99	334.52	370.92	436.97	470.11	415.26	394.78	378.78	407.68	380.32	364.84	370.48	378.57	404.89	ⅰ780.44	Official Rate	aa
End of Period (ae) Period Average (rf)																	
	225.80	287.40	336.25	417.37	479.60	378.05	322.75	267.00	302.95	289.40	256.45	259.00	275.33	294.78	ⅰ534.60	Official Rate	ae
	211.28	271.73	328.61	381.06	436.96	449.26	346.30	300.54	297.85	319.01	272.26	282.11	264.69	283.16	ⅰ555.20	Official Rate	rf
End of Period																**Fund Position**	
	24.0	24.0	24.0	33.7	33.7	33.7	33.7	33.7	33.7	33.7	33.7	33.7	33.7	48.3	48.3	Quota	2f. s
	5.8	7.5	7.5	4.6	2.2	—	1.0	.2	.1	.9	—	.3	—	.4	.3	SDRs	1b. s
	6.0	6.0	6.1	8.6	8.6	8.6	8.6	8.6	8.6	8.6	8.6	8.6	8.6	8.6	8.6	Reserve Position in the Fund	1c. s
	12.7	12.7	12.7	43.5	56.8	71.3	86.8	86.3	70.3	64.4	59.7	51.3	44.6	37.8	42.5	Total Fund Cred.&Loans Outstg.	2tl
End of Period																**International Liquidity**	
	125.9	105.3	29.6	53.2	88.7	136.4	189.2	248.5	232.1	212.3	222.2	202.8	225.0	192.0	110.3	Total Reserves minus Gold	1l. d
	7.4	8.8	8.2	4.8	2.2	—	1.2	.2	.2	1.2	.1	.4	—	.6	.4	SDRs	1b. d
	7.7	7.0	6.8	9.0	8.4	9.4	10.5	12.1	11.5	11.2	12.2	12.2	11.8	11.8	12.5	Reserve Position in the Fund	1c. d
	110.8	89.6	14.6	39.4	78.1	127.0	177.6	236.1	220.4	199.8	210.0	190.1	213.2	179.7	97.3	Foreign Exchange	1d. d
	.011	.011	.011	.011	.011	.011	.011	.011	.011	.011	.011	.011	.011	.011	.011	Gold (Million Fine Troy Ounces)	1ad
	.5	4.7	4.7	4.3	3.7	3.6	4.5	5.2	4.6	4.3	4.2	3.9	3.8	4.1	4.1	Gold (National Valuation)	1and
	4.7	1.1	3.5	12.9	7.8	10.9	14.7	15.6	14.2	16.8	14.7	13.1	45.7	49.8	2.9	Monetary Authorities: Other Liab.	4.. d
	17.9	15.4	8.8	16.4	9.9	6.5	11.9	11.2	19.7	18.7	20.5	25.0	26.7	23.8	40.6	Deposit Money Banks: Assets	7a. d
	126.9	99.3	155.5	130.7	103.6	114.7	124.4	143.8	121.5	125.9	120.3	134.9	130.0	55.5	49.9	Liabilities	7b. d
	49.0	65.0	68.2	79.5	69.7	80.2	91.8	103.2	87.3	85.1	90.1	108.1	105.6	38.5	32.7	of which: Liab. to Nonbanks	7bd d
End of Period																**Monetary Authorities**	
	28.42	30.28	9.96	22.19	42.54	51.57	61.08	66.34	70.31	61.44	56.98	52.51	61.94	56.61	58.95	Foreign Assets	11
	10.93	12.24	15.94	27.86	31.07	38.86	47.73	41.95	37.28	37.88	33.54	32.64	30.97	32.98	47.26	Claims on Central Government	12a
	13.52	22.33	30.68	33.28	20.81	20.31	26.30	30.44	29.09	25.79	27.13	27.10	27.04	26.98	1.10	Claims on Deposit Money Banks	12e
	.36	.42	.43	.22	.09	.02	—	—	—	—	—	—	—	—	—	Claims on Other Financial Insts.	12f
	34.80	41.11	41.70	38.28	48.69	58.31	63.70	65.13	79.41	80.36	82.78	81.33	83.36	79.64	61.03	Reserve Money	14
	31.05	34.84	35.27	31.53	30.72	33.37	40.46	35.59	42.29	41.81	37.64	40.97	39.66	48.35	49.18	of which: Currency Outside DMBs	14a
	8.18	8.04	9.37	27.87	33.63	36.59	42.29	39.00	34.14	29.96	25.55	22.39	29.45	29.96	34.18	Foreign Liabilities	16c
	10.72	16.60	6.80	19.78	16.71	16.50	28.36	31.74	21.08	11.67	3.79	3.23	2.90	3.32	15.06	Central Government Deposits	16d
	−.46	−.49	−.86	−2.38	−4.51	−.65	.76	2.86	2.05	3.12	5.54	5.31	4.23	3.64	−2.96	Other Items (Net)	17r
End of Period																**Deposit Money Banks**	
	3.83	6.31	4.65	6.82	17.66	24.91	27.13	29.18	38.06	38.20	44.82	40.65	43.48	29.89	9.66	Reserves	20
	4.04	4.44	2.95	6.83	4.76	2.44	3.95	3.00	5.96	5.41	5.27	6.47	7.35	7.02	21.73	Foreign Assets	21
	10.40	19.01	23.71	23.86	23.38	21.66	20.71	19.49	18.59	17.12	16.12	16.44	15.99	2.89	13.36	Claims on Central Government	22a
	89.11	102.58	111.30	118.29	108.29	101.18	113.97	108.25	107.01	90.08	83.04	75.34	72.38	64.87	71.41	Claims on Private Sector	22d
	.62	.64	.69	.53	.33	.07	.10	—	—	—	—	—	—	—	.01	Claims on Other Financial Insts.	22f
	32.28	38.78	34.54	33.78	45.92	45.57	41.07	35.86	38.32	44.61	38.38	34.71	30.51	28.83	40.25	Demand Deposits	24
	13.34	19.32	12.05	16.14	22.62	27.51	38.06	41.30	49.68	51.26	55.94	42.03	49.22	41.36	37.22	Time Deposits	25
	19.21	11.99	32.26	26.42	21.69	16.61	13.89	13.81	12.84	13.43	10.59	10.79	12.20	9.99	23.32	Foreign Liabilities	26c
	9.45	16.55	20.03	28.12	28.01	26.74	26.27	24.58	23.96	23.00	20.26	24.15	23.60	6.36	3.34	Long-Term Foreign Liabilities	26cl
	17.79	17.14	15.33	15.27	17.42	19.07	21.81	20.02	23.36	20.81	21.52	27.42	24.06	21.47	21.01	Central Government Deposits	26d
	13.52	22.41	30.68	33.28	20.92	20.60	26.40	30.60	29.38	27.56	26.35	27.13	27.04	26.98	27.81	Credit from Monetary Authorities	26g
	2.41	6.80	−1.57	3.32	−2.16	−5.83	−5.72	−6.23	−7.93	−29.87	−23.80	−27.31	−27.43	−30.32	−36.78	Other Items (Net)	27r
	1.56	1.63	2.29	.04	.09	.11	.62	—	—	.02	—	—	.03	.07	—	Treasury Claims: Private Sector	22d. i
	1.26	1.13	1.11	1.23	1.77	1.67	1.46	1.68	1.51	1.78	1.85	4.25	1.51	1.92	2.10	Post Office: Checking Deposits	24.. i
End of Period																**Monetary Survey**	
	5.08	14.68	−28.71	−25.26	−8.02	.81	8.75	16.54	29.30	23.46	26.11	25.80	27.64	23.68	23.18	Foreign Assets (Net)	31n
	84.16	102.29	131.05	136.93	130.80	127.89	133.80	119.61	119.94	114.37	109.24	98.03	93.89	77.86	98.08	Domestic Credit	32
	−7.49	−2.98	16.34	17.86	22.01	26.52	19.11	11.35	12.93	24.28	26.20	22.69	21.48	12.92	26.65	Claims on Central Govt. (Net)	32an
	90.67	104.21	113.60	118.33	108.37	101.29	114.60	108.25	107.01	90.10	83.04	75.34	72.41	64.93	71.41	Claims on Private Sector	32d
	.99	1.06	1.12	.75	.42	.09	.10	—	—	—	—	—	—	—	.01	Claims on Other Financial Insts.	32f
	64.59	74.75	70.93	66.55	78.41	80.62	82.99	73.15	82.13	88.20	77.87	79.93	71.70	79.52	92.29	Money	34
	13.34	19.32	12.05	16.14	22.62	27.51	38.06	41.30	49.68	51.26	55.94	42.03	49.22	41.36	37.22	Quasi-Money	35
	9.45	16.55	20.03	28.12	28.01	26.74	26.27	24.58	23.96	23.00	20.26	24.15	23.60	6.36	3.34	Long-Term Foreign Liabilities	36cl
	1.86	6.35	−.66	.86	−6.26	−6.17	−4.77	−2.87	−6.53	−24.63	−18.73	−22.27	−22.98	−25.69	−11.60	Other Items (Net)	37r
	77.93	94.07	82.98	82.69	101.02	108.13	121.05	114.44	131.81	139.47	133.81	121.95	120.91	120.87	129.51	Money plus Quasi-Money	35l
End of Period																**Other Banking Institutions**	
	.55	.67	.76	.89	1.00	1.25	1.61	2.15	2.65	3.10	....	....	....	....	....	Savings Deposits	45
	78.48	94.74	83.74	83.58	102.03	109.38	122.66	116.59	134.46	142.56	....	....	....	....	....	Liquid Liabilities	55l
Percent Per Annum																**Interest Rates**	
	10.50	10.50	12.50	10.50	10.50	10.50	8.50	8.50	8.50	11.00	11.00	11.00	12.50	10.50	10.00	Discount Rate (End of Period)	60
	10.13	13.35	14.66	12.23	11.84	10.66	.58	8.37	8.72	10.07	10.98	10.94	11.44	....	....	Money Market Rate	60b
	6.19	6.25	7.75	7.50	7.25	7.25	6.08	5.25	5.25	6.42	7.00	7.00	7.75	....	....	Deposit Rate	60l
	14.50	14.50	16.00	14.50	14.50	14.50	13.50	13.50	13.58	15.13	16.00	16.00	16.75	....	....	Lending Rate	60p
Period Averages																**Prices**	
	81.1	99.7	111.3	108.5	117.6	116.5	112.8	105.2	103.7	100.8	100.0	ⅰ92.2	88.1	87.0	118.4	Consumer Prices	64
Millions of Francs																**International Transactions**	
	119,523	123,589	109,124	113,896	113,030	116,538	109,645	93,863	85,941	77,710	76,939	87,900	....	....	....	Exports	70
	125,426	138,512	153,214	123,287	126,034	165,935	127,559	93,387	115,193	115,822	105,851	100,200	....	....	....	Imports, cif	71
	100,663	121,502	139,285	112,079	114,576	141,462	108,746	79,614	98,204	98,740	90,240	85,422	....	....	....	Imports, fob	71.v

Niger
692

		1965	1966	1967	1968	1969	1970	1971	1972	1973	1974	1975	1976	1977	1978	1979
Balance of Payments																*Millions of US Dollars*
Goods: Exports f.o.b.	78aa d	....	....	....	....	....	....	....	....	....	81.5	138.5	171.6	196.6	287.7	485.0
Goods: Imports f.o.b.	78ab d	....	....	....	....	....	....	....	....	....	−144.9	−148.0	−198.4	−241.3	−410.6	−527.0
Trade Balance	78ac d	....	....	....	....	....	....	....	....	....	−63.4	−9.4	−26.7	−44.7	−123.0	−42.1
Services: Credit	78ad d	....	....	....	....	....	....	....	....	....	17.9	23.9	23.4	26.0	31.5	35.7
Services: Debit	78ae d	....	....	....	....	....	....	....	....	....	−77.1	−87.0	−103.7	−129.3	−163.4	−242.3
Balance on Goods and Services	78af d	....	....	....	....	....	....	....	....	....	−122.6	−72.5	−107.0	−148.0	−254.8	−248.7
Income: Credit	78ag d	....	....	....	....	....	....	....	....	....	8.2	9.7	8.1	9.0	9.3	12.4
Income: Debit	78ah d	....	....	....	....	....	....	....	....	....	8.2	11.1	−11.8	−9.1	−39.1	7.4
Balance on Goods, Serv., & Inc.	78ai d	....	....	....	....	....	....	....	....	....	−106.2	−51.7	−110.8	−148.1	−284.6	−228.9
Current Transfers, n.i.e.: Credit	78aj d	....	....	....	....	....	....	....	....	....	88.7	40.3	99.4	74.6	112.7	148.2
Current Transfers: Debit	78ak d	....	....	....	....	....	....	....	....	....	−22.6	−27.9	−28.2	−29.9	−46.8	−62.8
Current Account, n.i.e.	78al d	....	....	....	....	....	....	....	....	....	−40.0	−39.4	−39.6	−103.5	−218.7	−143.5
Capital Account, n.i.e.: Credit	78ba d															
Capital Account: Debit	78bb d										—	—	—	—	—	—
Capital Account, n.i.e.	78bc d															
Direct Investment Abroad	78bd d	....	....	....	....	....	....	....	....	....	−.3	−6.3	1.4	3.7	6.8	−11.2
Dir. Invest. in Rep. Econ., n.i.e.	78be d	....	....	....	....	....	....	....	....	....	6.9	22.6	9.9	12.9	42.7	46.8
Portfolio Investment Assets	78bf d												—	−1.4	−3.9	—
Portfolio Investment Liab., n.i.e.	78bg d															
Other Investment Assets	78bh d	....	....	....	....	....	....	....	....	....	.7	−4.0	−32.8	−3.6	−10.5	−29.0
Other Investment Liab., n.i.e.	78bi d	....	....	....	....	....	....	....	....	....	16.1	26.4	71.3	102.8	187.4	203.3
Financial Account, n.i.e.	78bj d	....	....	....	....	....	....	....	....	....	23.4	38.7	49.8	114.4	222.5	209.9
Net Errors and Omissions	78ca d	....	....	....	....	....	....	....	....	....	−2.0	−45.0	7.9	−5.3	−14.5	−75.8
Overall Balance	78cb d	....	....	....	....	....	....	....	....	....	−18.6	−45.7	18.1	5.5	−10.7	−9.5
Reserves and Related Items	79da d	....	....	....	....	....	....	....	....	....	18.6	45.7	−18.1	−5.5	10.7	9.5
Reserve Assets	79db d	....	....	....	....	....	....	....	....	....	6.4	−5.7	−37.8	−13.4	−13.8	3.5
Use of Fund Credit and Loans	79dc d										—	—	—	—	6.7	—
Liabs.Constit.For.Auth.Reserves	79dd d															
Exceptional Financing	79de d	....	....	....	....	....	....	....	....	....	12.2	51.4	19.6	7.9	17.7	5.9
Government Finance																*Millions of Francs*
Deficit (−) or Surplus	80	....	....	....	....	....	....	....	....	....	....	....	−5,468	−5,261	−12,622	−12,105
Revenue	81	....	....	....	....	....	....	....	....	....	....	....	29,276	36,957	48,794	62,190
Grants Received	81z	....	....	....	....	....	....	....	....	....	....	....	1,213	698	1,595	369
Expenditure	82	....	....	....	....	....	....	....	....	....	....	....	35,388	42,511	58,552	70,819
Lending Minus Repayments	83	....	....	....	....	....	....	....	....	....	....	....	569	405	4,459	3,845
Financing																
Net Borrowing: Domestic	84a	....	....	....	....	....	....	....	....	....	....	....	4,420	2,941	4,271	1,008
Foreign	85a	....	....	....	....	....	....	....	....	....	....	....	5,813	6,307	9,925	14,278
Use of Cash Balances	87	....	....	....	....	....	....	....	....	....	....	....	−4,765	−3,987	−1,574	−3,181
National Accounts																*Billions of Francs*
Exports of Goods & Services	90c	11.0	13.0	12.6	11.3	10.6	13.2	20.4	23.0	28.2	26.2	34.6	47.1	53.7	71.2	109.7
Government Consumption	91f	8.6	10.8	11.6	11.9	12.6	13.5	13.6	15.0	15.7	17.4	23.6	28.1	31.0	34.0	41.0
Gross Fixed Capital Formation	93e	7.9	8.4	8.6	9.1	6.0	7.5	8.4	8.8	15.0	18.0	36.7	43.6	65.9	90.7	112.8
Increase/Decrease(−) in Stocks	93i	.3	.1	.2	.5	.3	3.0	.4	3.5	3.8	4.1	6.3	19.1	17.7	22.9	28.2
Private Consumption	96f	57.8	79.1	80.1	79.1	85.5	94.9	98.3	114.9	103.5	147.6	138.6	170.7	206.6	264.6	311.1
Imports of Goods & Services	98c	−11.4	−15.4	−15.6	−16.4	−17.2	−24.7	−22.6	−29.2	−38.0	−54.3	−59.5	−70.7	−86.1	−124.2	−159.0
Gross Domestic Product	99b	74.1	96.0	97.5	95.5	97.8	111.1	118.5	136.0	128.2	159.0	180.4	237.9	288.8	359.2	443.2
Gross Dom. Prod. 1980 Prices	99b.p	328.0	404.6	390.7	360.3	354.5	387.4	374.2	345.9	308.2	327.4	388.9	448.3	467.6	513.3	524.9
GDP Deflator (1980=100)	99bi p	22.6	23.7	25.0	26.5	27.6	28.7	31.7	39.3	41.6	48.6	46.4	53.1	61.8	70.0	84.4
																Millions
Population	99z	3.51	3.61	3.71	3.81	3.91	4.02	4.13	4.21	4.30	4.48	4.60	4.73	4.86	4.99	5.17

Niger

692

	1980	1981	1982	1983	1984	1985	1986	1987	1988	1989	1990	1991	1992	1993	1994		
Minus Sign Indicates Debit																	**Balance of Payments**
	576.1	484.6	381.3	335.2	303.3	259.4	331.5	411.9	369.0	311.0	303.4	283.9	265.6	238.4	....	Goods: Exports f.o.b.	78aa *d*
	−677.4	−591.8	−515.3	−331.6	−269.9	−345.6	−309.8	−409.6	−392.5	−368.6	−337.5	−273.3	−266.3	−244.0	....	Goods: Imports f.o.b.	78ab *d*
	−101.3	−107.2	−134.0	3.7	33.4	−86.2	21.7	2.3	−23.5	−57.7	−34.2	10.6	−.8	−5.7	....	Trade Balance	78ac *d*
	40.6	39.8	41.8	40.3	31.4	38.6	—	52.6	48.3	50.8	69.1	57.1	52.1	49.8	....	Services: Credit	78ad *d*
	−279.0	−194.1	−213.0	−153.7	−124.2	−127.5	−84.2	−152.7	−145.4	−139.2	−207.2	−157.0	−148.1	−139.5	....	Services: Debit	78ae *d*
	−339.7	−261.4	−305.1	−109.8	−59.5	−175.1	−62.5	−97.8	−120.5	−146.1	−172.3	−89.3	−96.7	−95.4	....	Balance on Goods and Services	78af *d*
	27.0	18.2	17.6	11.9	13.5	18.4	—	8.0	1.7	6.9	2.2	1.4	—	—	....	Income: Credit	78ag *d*
	−59.9	−46.9	−42.1	−50.6	−55.2	−60.7	−17.5	−92.5	−73.2	−63.3	−49.2	−38.6	−37.4	−36.0	....	Income: Debit	78ah *d*
	−372.6	−290.2	−329.7	−148.4	−101.2	−217.4	−80.0	−182.3	−192.0	−202.5	−219.3	−126.5	−134.1	−131.4	....	Balance on Goods, Serv., & Inc.	78ai *d*
	165.0	161.2	158.4	140.5	144.2	213.1	148.4	142.1	153.8	141.7	171.2	151.0	142.1	148.7	....	Current Transfers, n.i.e.: Credit	78aj *d*
	−69.7	−63.7	−61.8	−55.7	−49.7	−64.3	−43.3	−49.9	−45.0	−50.2	−60.6	−49.6	−52.5	−46.3	....	Current Transfers: Debit	78ak *d*
	−277.3	−192.7	−233.2	−63.6	−6.8	−68.5	25.1	−90.2	−83.3	−111.0	−108.7	−25.2	−44.6	−29.0	....	Current Account, n.i.e.	78al *d*
	—	—	—	—	—	—	—	—	—	—	—	—	—	—	....	Capital Account, n.i.e.: Credit	78ba *d*
	—	—	—	—	—	—	—	—	—	—	—	—	—	—	....	Capital Account: Debit	78bb *d*
	—	—	—	—	—	—	—	—	—	—	—	—	—	—	....	Capital Account, n.i.e.	78bc *d*
	4.2	.6	−3.3	−1.8	−.3	−1.9	—	—	—	—	—	—	—	—	....	Direct Investment Abroad	78bd *d*
	49.1	−6.1	28.2	1.2	1.4	−9.4	—	—	—	—	—	—	—	—	....	Dir. Invest. in Rep. Econ., n.i.e.	78be *d*
	−.3	−.4	—	—	—	—	—	—	—	—	—	—	—	—	....	Portfolio Investment Assets	78bf *d*
	—	—	—	—	—	—	—	—	—	—	—	—	—	—	....	Portfolio Investment Liab., n.i.e.	78bg *d*
	−.5	−13.0	12.8	−15.4	−1.1	5.6	4.2	1.0	−14.8	—	−12.1	2.5	−21.5	−5.5	....	Other Investment Assets	78bh *d*
	254.4	227.2	139.1	73.9	−38.9	−2.4	−12.1	70.7	40.9	35.7	34.9	−24.8	33.9	−19.5	....	Other Investment Liab., n.i.e.	78bi *d*
	307.0	208.2	176.8	57.9	−38.7	−8.2	−7.9	71.7	26.1	35.7	22.8	−22.3	12.5	−25.0	....	Financial Account, n.i.e.	78bj *d*
	−35.1	−24.0	−7.3	−7.9	14.2	26.6	−65.6	−15.4	43.4	−4.1	−25.2	−40.4	15.6	−9.4	....	Net Errors and Omissions	78ca *d*
	−5.4	−8.4	−63.7	−13.6	−31.3	−50.2	−48.4	−33.9	−13.7	−79.3	−111.2	−87.9	−16.5	−63.4	....	Overall Balance	78cb *d*
	5.4	8.4	63.7	13.6	31.3	50.2	48.4	33.9	13.7	79.3	111.2	87.9	16.5	63.4	....	Reserves and Related Items	79da *d*
	−5.8	−2.8	63.3	−29.8	−45.7	−19.1	−27.9	−18.0	−12.5	27.0	15.9	16.0	−35.4	19.6	....	Reserve Assets	79db *d*
	9.6	.1	—	32.7	13.3	15.0	18.6	.6	−21.5	−7.8	−6.1	−11.4	−9.4	−9.6	....	Use of Fund Credit and Loans	79dc *d*
	—	—	—	—	—	—	—	—	—	—	—	—	—	—	....	Liabs.Constit.For.Auth.Reserves	79dd *d*
	1.6	11.2	.3	10.7	63.7	54.3	57.8	51.2	47.7	60.2	101.4	83.3	61.3	53.3	....	Exceptional Financing	79de *d*
Year Ending September 30																	**Government Finance**
	−25,241	....	....	....	....	....	....	....	....	....	....	....	....	....	....	Deficit (-) or Surplus	80
	77,436	....	....	....	....	....	....	....	....	....	....	....	....	....	....	Revenue	81
	—	....	....	....	....	....	....	....	....	....	....	....	....	....	....	Grants Received	81z
	98,727	....	....	....	....	....	....	....	....	....	....	....	....	....	....	Expenditure	82
	3,950	....	....	....	....	....	....	....	....	....	....	....	....	....	....	Lending Minus Repayments	83
																	Financing
	8,256	....	....	....	....	....	....	....	....	....	....	....	....	....	....	Net Borrowing: Domestic	84a
	21,616	....	....	....	....	....	....	....	....	....	....	....	....	....	....	Foreign	85a
	−4,631	....	....	....	....	....	....	....	....	....	....	....	....	....	....	Use of Cash Balances	87
Billions of Francs																	**National Accounts**
	128.8	141.9	139.8	143.7	147.3	135.7	130.9	139.1	140.5	129.1	101.4	96.2	....	....	....	Exports of Goods & Services	90c
	54.0	70.2	81.0	87.5	89.7	97.2	102.3	103.6	105.0	124.4	101.6	101.6	....	....	....	Government Consumption	91f
	136.7	163.9	155.2	119.4	55.0	92.4	84.1	94.1	81.0	85.4	76.7	51.4	....	....	....	Gross Fixed Capital Formation	93e
	32.4	4.5	26.0	−12.4	−21.7	6.6	3.4	−23.3	53.6	−.5	7.3	....	....	....	....	Increase/Decrease(-) in Stocks	93i
	381.7	410.7	483.2	522.8	524.6	510.2	505.3	514.0	446.7	505.3	528.7	539.7	....	....	....	Private Consumption	96f
	−197.4	−189.5	−222.2	−173.9	−156.5	−195.0	−166.5	−156.4	−148.6	−151.1	−145.9	−123.0	....	....	....	Imports of Goods & Services	98c
	536.2	601.5	663.0	687.1	638.4	647.1	659.6	671.2	678.2	692.6	669.8	665.9	....	....	....	Gross Domestic Product	99b
	536.2	502.2	....	....	....	....	....	....	....	....	....	....	....	....	....	Gross Dom. Prod. 1980 Prices	99b. *p*
	100.0	119.8	....	....	....	....	....	....	....	....	....	....	....	....	....	GDP Deflator (1980=100)	99bi *p*
Midyear Estimates																	
	5.31	5.78	5.98	6.18	6.40	6.61	6.82	7.04	7.26	7.49	7.73	7.99	8.26	8.36	....	**Population**	99z

Nigeria

		1965	1966	1967	1968	1969	1970	1971	1972	1973	1974	1975	1976	1977	1978	1979
Exchange Rates																*Naira per SDR:*
Principal Rate	aa	.714	.714	.714	.714	.714	.714	.714	.714	.794	.754	.734	.733	.791	.844	.738
																Naira per US Dollar:
Principal Rate	ae	.714	.714	.714	.714	.714	.714	.658	.658	.658	.616	.627	.631	.651	.648	.561
Principal Rate	rf	.714	.714	.714	.714	.714	.714	.713	.658	.658	.630	.616	.627	.645	.635	.604
																Index Numbers (1990=100):
Principal Rate	ahx	1,124.5	1,124.5	1,124.5	1,124.5	1,124.5	1,124.5	1,126.9	1,220.9	1,220.9	1,277.4	1,305.1	1,281.9	1,246.1	1,264.6	1,332.6
Nominal Effective Exchange Rate	nec	....	....	....	....	....	....	....	....	....	....	....	....	....	....	869.4
Real Effective Exchange Rate	rec	....	....	....	....	....	....	....	....	....	....	....	....	....	....	391.6
Fund Position																*Millions of SDRs:*
Quota	2f.s	50	63	63	100	100	135	135	135	135	135	135	135	135	360	360
SDRs	1b.s	—	—	—	—	—	17	31	46	46	48	57	61	66	67	108
Reserve Position in the Fund	1c.s	5	8	8	8	11	11	11	13	33	34	212	334	340	366	295
of which: Outstg.Fund Borrowing	2c	—	—	—	—	—	—	—	—	—	—	178	300	296	272	203
International Liquidity												*Millions of US Dollars Unless Otherwise Indicated:*				
Total Reserves minus Gold	1l.d	219	195	92	97	112	202	408	355	559	5,602	5,586	5,180	4,232	1,887	5,548
SDRs	1b.d	—	—	—	—	—	17	34	49	55	58	67	71	80	87	142
Reserve Position in the Fund	1c.d	5	8	8	8	11	11	12	14	40	41	248	388	413	477	389
Foreign Exchange	1d.d	214	187	84	89	101	174	362	292	464	5,503	5,270	4,721	3,739	1,323	5,017
Gold (Million Fine Troy Ounces)	1ad	.571	.571	.571	.571	.571	.571	.543	.543	.571	.571	.571	.571	.629	.629	.687
Gold (National Valuation)	1and	20	20	20	20	20	20	....	....	24	26	25	25	25	28	34
Other Official Insts.: Assets	3b.d	30	29	22	11	14	28	32	38	39	44	34	35	20e	....	....
Monetary Authorities: Other Liab.	4..d	—	—	—	1	—	1	2	2	—	2	19	2	6	3	11
Deposit Money Banks: Assets	7a.d	59	69	42	4	8	9	24	19	59	104	170	253	346	275	422
Liabilities	7b.d	74	91	77	10	8	14	24	23	14	26	20	74	39	99	119
Other Banking Insts.: Assets	7e.d	—	—	—	—	—	—	—	—	—	—	7	2	12	18	37
Monetary Authorities																*Millions of Naira:*
Foreign Assets	11	171	154	81	85	96	160	283	249	389	3,454	3,586	3,284	2,766	1,308	3,065
Claims on Central Government	12a	57	93	151	128	168	177	250	157	175	20	314	512	1,683	3,197	2,521
Claims on Private Sector	12d	1	1	13	68	81	95	61	76	10	15	89	118	243	102	96
Claims on Deposit Money Banks	12e	—	—	—	—	—	—	—	—	—	—	—	—	—	—	—
Claims on Other Financial Insts.	12f	1	1	14	5	5	34	32	65	98	180	169	172	244	439	638
Reserve Money	14	224	245	232	214	287	400	423	454	561	1,409	2,203	2,773	3,430	3,312	3,847
of which: Currency Outside DMBs	14a	201	217	207	183	253	342	355	385	436	570	1,031	1,351	1,941	2,157	2,351
Restricted Deposits	16b	—	—	—	—	—	—	—	—	—	—	30	10	191	114	187
Foreign Liabilities	16c	—	—	—	1	—	—	1	1	—	1	12	1	4	2	6
Central Government Deposits	16d	7	13	10	18	11	17	17	24	19	2,098	1,732	1,088	649	820	1,442
Capital Accounts	17a	5	5	6	6	6	19	30	41	45	49	53	60	72	82	115
Other Items (Net)	17r	10	14	18	64	56	39	164	36	48	113	260	374	829	953	723
Deposit Money Banks																*Millions of Naira:*
Reserves	20	20	23	19	23	25	47	38	44	66	331	862	1,237	1,438	1,114	923
Foreign Assets	21	42	49	30	3	6	6	16	12	39	64	107	160	225	178	236
Claims on Central Government	22a	26	41	41	209	336	506	300	385	388	768	787	1,197	1,418	1,118	2,439
Claims on Private Sector	22d	275	312	283	225	234	346	498	601	731	907	1,475	2,063	2,934	3,861	4,362
Claims on Other Financial Insts.	22f	....	....	....	....	....	....	....	6	2	8	27	55	78	50	109
Demand Deposits	24	124	135	110	147	186	289	285	337	‡293	583	1,124	2,050	2,842	2,530	3,061
Time and Savings Deposits	25	141	163	131	184	215	337	372	457	‡582	973	1,572	3,879	2,255	2,420	3,702
Foreign Liabilities	26c	53	65	55	7	6	10	16	15	10	16	13	47	25	64	67
Central Government Deposits	26d	....	....	....	....	—	—	—	—	138	138	143	135	138	352	205
Credit from Monetary Authorities	26g	12	22	25	4	—	—	—	4	—	—	—	—	—	—	—
Capital Accounts	27a	30	34	21	27	54	58	69	77	80	92	124	157	202	267	328
Other Items (Net)	27r	4	7	29	91	144	211	112	167	130	275	281	342	631	688	706
Monetary Survey																*Millions of Naira:*
Foreign Assets (Net)	31n	160	138	56	81	95	156	282	245	418	3,500	3,668	3,396	2,962	1,420	3,228
Domestic Credit	32	353	436	479	613	‡813	1,141	1,124	1,266	1,247	−339	986	2,893	5,813	7,596	8,518
Claims on Central Govt. (Net)	32an	76	121	182	319	‡493	666	532	518	407	−1,448	−774	486	2,314	3,143	3,313
Claims on Private Sector	32d	276	314	296	292	315	441	559	678	741	921	1,564	2,180	3,176	3,963	4,458
Claims on Other Financial Insts.	32f	1	1	1	1	5	34	33	71	100	188	196	226	322	490	747
Money	34	328	357	323	338	447	643	670	747	‡788	1,619	2,463	3,728	5,420	5,101	6,147
Quasi-Money	35	141	163	131	184	215	337	372	457	‡582	973	1,572	3,879	2,255	2,420	3,702
Other Items (Net)	37r	60	82	100	191	257	315	365	313	305	570	750	802	1,339	1,731	1,897
Money plus Quasi-Money	35l	469	520	454	522	663	979	1,042	1,204	‡1,370	2,592	4,035	7,608	7,675	7,521	9,849
Other Banking Institutions																*Millions of Naira:*
Cash	40.m	.1	.1	.1	.1	.2	.1	—	.5	2.0	5.4	16.1	20.3	53.0	59.4	61.4
Foreign Assets	41.m	—	—	—	—	—	—	.1	.1	.3	.3	4.1	1.0	7.5	11.6	20.9
Claims on Central Government	42a.m	—	—	.1	.9	1.1	4.3	2.9	6.4	7.9	12.0	13.4	14.4	31.7	14.1	60.4
Claims on Private Sector	42d.m	2.4	3.3	3.0	2.0	2.0	2.1	8.2	14.1	14.0	26.0	83.7	81.3	109.8	163.7	199.0
Demand Deposits	44.m	.3	.3	1.5	2.0	1.4	1.2	1.4	2.2	5.7	2.9	8.7	2.8	3.5	12.3	53.7
Time and Savings Deposits	45.m	—	—	—	—	—	3.2	5.8	8.5	8.7	19.2	54.8	58.9	82.4	110.7	117.3
Cred.from Deposit Money Banks	46a.m	.7	1.6	−.1	.5	1.3	—	.8	4.8	5.1	14.9	37.7	37.0	58.3	38.0	50.1
Capital Accounts	47a.m	1.5	1.5	1.5	1.5	1.5	1.5	1.6	1.6	2.3	7.0	11.2	9.8	10.9	14.1	19.0
Other Items (Net)	47r.m	....	....	.2	−1.0	−.9	.5	1.8	3.9	2.4	−.3	5.0	8.3	53.4	73.6	101.6
Liquid Liabilities	55l	474	525	460	529	669	989	1,054	1,219	‡1,387	2,614	4,089	7,656	7,716	‡7,593	9,967
Interest Rates																*Percent Per Annum*
Discount Rate (End of Period)	60	5.00	5.00	5.00	4.50	4.50	4.50	4.50	4.50	4.50	4.50	3.50	3.50	4.00	5.00	5.00
Deposit Rate	60l	....	....	....	....	....	3.00	3.00	3.04	3.00	3.00	3.00	2.67	2.83	4.15	4.47
Lending Rate	60p	....	....	....	....	....	7.00	7.00	7.00	7.00	7.00	6.25	6.50	6.00	6.75	7.79
Prices and Production																*Index Numbers (1990=100):*
Consumer Prices	64	2.7	2.9	2.8	2.8	3.1	3.5	4.1	4.2	4.4	5.0	‡6.7	8.3	‡9.5	11.5	12.9
Industrial Production	66	....	13.9	12.3	9.6	17.7	‡26.9	35.8	40.5	47.0	49.6	46.7	55.6	57.9	58.2	78.2
Crude Petroleum Production	66aa	15.0	23.1	17.7	7.9	29.9	59.9	84.6	100.7	113.6	124.7	98.5	114.7	115.8	105.5	127.5
Manufacturing Production	66ey	9.2	10.2	10.5	10.5	13.6	‡15.3	17.4	18.5	22.7	22.2	27.6	33.8	35.9	39.2	60.8

Nigeria
694

	1980	1981	1982	1983	1984	1985	1986	1987	1988	1989	1990	1991	1992	1993	1994		
End of Period																**Exchange Rates**	
	.694	.741	.739	.784	.792	1.098	4.057	5.874	7.204	10.055	12.805	14.107	27.014	30.056	32.113	Principal Rate	aa
End of Period (ae) Period Average (rf)																	
	.544	.637	.670	.749	.808	1.000	3.317	4.141	5.353	7.651	9.001	9.862	19.646	21.882	21.997	Principal Rate	ae
	.547	.618	.673	.724	.767	.894	1.755	4.016	4.537	7.365	8.038	9.909	17.298	22.065	21.996	Principal Rate	rf
Period Averages																	
	1,469.7	1,308.6	1,193.1	1,110.3	1,051.0	900.1	596.4	200.5	179.2	109.2	100.0	81.4	49.2	36.4	36.5	Principal Rate	ahx
	965.8	998.4	1,044.6	1,085.0	1,162.7	1,065.9	594.6	179.2	146.9	98.4	100.0	82.5	53.3	41.4	55.0	Nominal Effective Exchange Rate	nec
	417.2	462.5	474.7	560.8	772.4	692.5	378.4	120.8	121.0	108.0	100.0	84.3	69.8	76.1	139.6	Real Effective Exchange Rate	rec
End of Period																**Fund Position**	
	540	540	540	850	850	850	850	850	850	850	850	850	850	1,282	1,282	1,282 Quota	2f.s
	133	239	40	26	11	1	—	—	—	—	—	1	—	—	—	— SDRs	1b.s
	371	446	—	—	—	—	—	—	—	—	—	—	—	—	—	— Reserve Position in the Fund	1c.s
	179	133	—	—	—	—	—	—	—	—	—	—	—	—	—	— of which: Outstg.Fund Borrowing	2c
End of Period																**International Liquidity**	
	10,235	3,895	1,613	990	1,462	1,667	1,081	1,165	651	1,766	3,864	4,435	967	1,372	1,386	Total Reserves minus Gold	1l.d
	169	278	45	27	10	1	—	—	—	—	—	1	—	—	—	SDRs	1b.d
	473	519	—	—	—	—	—	—	—	—	—	—	—	—	—	Reserve Position in the Fund	1c.d
	9,593	3,098	1,568	963	1,452	1,666	1,081	1,165	651	1,765	3,863	4,435	967	1,372	1,386	Foreign Exchange	1d.d
	.687	.687	.687	.687	.687	.687	.687	.687	.687	.687	.687	.687	.687	.687	.687	Gold (Million Fine Troy Ounces)	1ad
	35	30	28	25	24	19	6	5	4	2	2	2	1	1	1	Gold (National Valuation)	1and
	....	....	3	2	....	....	....	....	....	....	....	....	....	....	....	Other Official Insts.: Assets	3b.d
	60	46	24	40	14	15	19	10	9	6	5	4	....	....	....	Monetary Authorities: Other Liab.	4..d
	458	407	368	459	510	415	525	755	948	979	737	1,081	1,009	....	....	Deposit Money Banks: Assets	7a.d
	162	206	345	351	115	260	247	213	64	112	28	84	64	....	....	Liabilities	7b.d
	54	83	149	123	130	136	342	311	517	495	423	532	437	....	....	Other Banking Insts.: Assets	7e.d
End of Period																**Monetary Authorities**	
	5,479	2,457	1,058	757	1,115	1,676	3,606	4,661	3,290	11,705	34,972	44,267	....	....	....	Foreign Assets	11
	2,861	6,053	8,148	11,871	11,068	11,522	17,722	19,197	28,087	35,378	48,720	83,102	....	....	....	Claims on Central Government	12a
	100	106	112	91	91	91	92	97	176	198	72	1,468	....	....	....	Claims on Private Sector	12d
	—	—	—	—	—	—	—	54	467	313	399		....	....	....	Claims on Deposit Money Banks	12e
	656	804	807	972	1,213	1,332	1,534	1,767	1,775	792	796	862	....	....	....	Claims on Other Financial Insts.	12f
	6,495	6,278	6,803	7,055	7,267	7,785	8,292	9,853	13,982	19,195	24,570	34,892	....	....	....	Reserve Money	14
	3,186	3,862	4,223	4,843	4,884	4,910	5,178	6,299	9,414	12,124	14,951	23,121	....	....	....	of which: Currency Outside DMBs	14a
	96	83	117	1,280	664	371	49	54	51	196	236	935	....	....	....	Restricted Deposits	16b
	33	29	16	30	11	15	64	41	47	45	42	43	....	....	....	Foreign Liabilities	16c
	1,885	1,459	576	1,343	1,659	2,680	2,903	4,904	6,319	18,311	25,885	55,794	....	....	....	Central Government Deposits	16d
	151	208	225	252	289	372	873	1,196	1,466	1,914	2,658	4,210	....	....	....	Capital Accounts	17a
	437	1,363	2,387	3,731	3,598	3,399	10,774	9,727	11,929	8,725	31,541	33,824	....	....	....	Other Items (Net)	17r
End of Period																**Deposit Money Banks**	
	1,552	1,396	2,023	1,285	1,051	824	1,506	2,202	2,355	2,741	4,777	13,736	27,143	....	....	Reserves	20
	249	259	246	344	413	415	1,740	3,128	5,077	7,489	6,634	10,663	19,826	....	....	Foreign Assets	21
	2,987	2,186	3,193	5,514	9,060	10,730	5,009	8,253	7,945	3,777	9,107	7,030	5,881	....	....	Claims on Central Government	22a
	6,046	7,977	9,503	9,765	10,302	11,253	14,916	16,059	18,969	20,920	24,475	29,458	40,099	....	....	Claims on Private Sector	22d
	216	302	279	779	476	456	566	629	1,727	3,055	3,861	5,276	6,315	....	....	Claims on Other Financial Insts.	22f
	4,422	4,702	4,938	5,620	6,051	6,396	6,194	7,708	9,882	9,738	15,000	20,180	31,070	....	....	Demand Deposits	24
	5,163	5,494	6,645	7,752	9,039	9,926	10,942	13,989	16,960	16,707	23,014	30,360	41,425	....	....	Time and Savings Deposits	25
	88	131	231	263	93	260	820	882	345	853	248	832	1,252	....	....	Foreign Liabilities	26c
	424	481	437	567	646	1,275	1,001	1,389	2,223	737	762	1,870	3,578	....	....	Central Government Deposits	26d
	—	—	—	—	—	—	4	7	83	1,263	96	79	102	....	....	Credit from Monetary Authorities	26g
	378	490	659	780	898	1,064	1,231	1,473	1,845	2,628	3,613	4,106	7,985	....	....	Capital Accounts	27a
	574	822	2,336	2,705	4,575	4,757	3,544	4,822	4,734	6,056	6,122	8,739	13,851	....	....	Other Items (Net)	27r
End of Period																**Monetary Survey**	
	5,607	2,556	1,057	808	1,423	1,816	4,463	6,865	7,974	18,296	41,316	54,055	....	....	....	Foreign Assets (Net)	31n
	10,558	15,488	21,028	27,083	29,905	31,430	35,935	39,709	50,135	45,072	60,358	69,533	....	....	....	Domestic Credit	32
	3,539	6,299	10,328	15,475	17,823	18,297	18,827	21,157	27,488	20,107	31,180	32,469	....	....	....	Claims on Central Govt. (Net)	32an
	6,147	8,083	9,615	9,856	10,393	11,345	15,008	16,156	19,145	21,118	24,522	30,926	....	....	....	Claims on Private Sector	32d
	872	1,106	1,085	1,751	1,689	1,788	2,100	2,396	3,502	3,847	4,656	6,139	....	....	....	Claims on Other Financial Insts.	32f
	9,227	9,745	10,049	11,283	12,204	13,227	12,663	14,906	21,446	26,664	34,540	48,708	....	....	....	Money	34
	5,163	5,494	6,645	7,752	9,039	9,926	10,942	13,989	16,960	16,707	23,014	30,360	....	....	....	Quasi-Money	35
	1,775	2,805	5,392	8,856	10,085	10,092	16,793	17,678	19,703	19,997	44,121	44,520	....	....	....	Other Items (Net)	37r
	14,390	15,239	16,694	19,034	21,243	23,153	23,605	28,895	38,406	43,371	57,554	79,067	....	....	....	Money plus Quasi-Money	35l
End of Period																**Other Banking Institutions**	
	94.4	151.7	305.8	325.0	152.1	133.1	177.8	697.1	2,643.5	1,153.5	1,248.1	2,479.2	3,697.1	....	....	Cash	40.m
	29.6	52.6	99.9	92.1	104.8	136.3	1,134.5	1,288.8	2,766.4	3,788.7	3,810.8	5,249.8	8,581.7	....	....	Foreign Assets	41.m
	58.6	69.4	174.7	385.5	894.0	1,132.1	148.2	285.4	167.9	187.1	517.5	808.5	1,189.4	....	....	Claims on Central Government	42a.m
	361.7	585.6	888.4	1,065.9	1,276.0	1,459.6	2,320.3	3,403.1	4,520.4	6,402.0	9,608.7	10,021.8	11,761.0	....	....	Claims on Private Sector	42d.m
	66.5	122.4	272.3	484.7	511.0	530.5	601.9	560.2	834.8	1,294.4	989.2	2,022.2	3,302.9	....	....	Demand Deposits	44.m
	219.6	328.0	691.3	793.7	970.6	1,318.2	1,739.7	2,822.8	3,982.8	2,514.9	4,104.0	5,046.2	8,361.8	....	....	Time and Savings Deposits	45.m
	110.2	177.3	75.7	−50.3	23.5	27.1	132.0	−157.2	1,672.0	4,058.3	4,858.6	6,369.0	6,550.6	....	....	Cred.from Deposit Money Banks	46h.m
	26.0	37.2	63.1	85.4	131.5	163.7	191.8	252.6	471.2	852.7	1,483.6	2,185.9	3,533.9	....	....	Capital Accounts	47a.m
	122.0	194.4	366.5	555.0	790.3	821.6	1,115.4	2,196.0	3,137.4	2,810.9	3,749.8	2,936.0	3,480.0	....	....	Other Items (Net)	47r.m
	14,589	15,545	17,351	19,988	22,572	24,869	25,769	31,581	40,580	46,027	61,399	83,657	135,899	....	....	Liquid Liabilities	55l
Percent Per Annum																**Interest Rates**	
	6.00	6.00	8.00	8.00	10.00	10.00	10.00	12.75	12.75	18.50	18.50	15.50	17.50	26.00	13.50	Discount Rate (End of Period)	60
	5.27	5.72	7.60	7.41	8.25	9.12	9.24	13.09	12.95	14.68	19.78	14.92	18.04	23.24	13.09	Deposit Rate	60l
	8.43	8.92	9.54	9.98	10.24	9.43	9.96	13.96	16.62	20.44	25.30	20.04	24.76	31.65	20.48	Lending Rate	60p
Period Averages																**Prices and Production**	
	14.2	17.1	18.4	22.7	‡31.7	34.1	36.0	40.1	61.9	93.1	100.0	113.0	163.4	256.8	403.3	Consumer Prices	64
	77.4	75.2	79.9	67.4	59.7	68.3	67.9	‡79.5	83.3	95.7	100.0	107.6	107.2	103.3	....	Industrial Production	66
	114.2	79.6	71.0	68.2	76.5	82.8	80.9	73.1	80.2	94.8	100.0	104.5	106.7	106.4	102.9	Crude Petroleum Production	66aa
	64.0	73.4	82.8	84.5	69.9	62.2	60.1	‡80.3	83.0	94.7	100.0	109.3	111.0	99.7	....	Manufacturing Production	66ey

Nigeria

694

		1965	1966	1967	1968	1969	1970	1971	1972	1973	1974	1975	1976	1977	1978	1979
International Transactions																*Millions of Naira*
Exports	70	535	568	484	422	637	886	1,293	1,434	2,278	5,795	4,829	6,623	7,631	6,328	10,398
Crude Petroleum	70aa	136	184	145	74	262	510	953	1,176	1,894	5,366	4,630	6,196	7,083	5,654	9,706
Imports, cif	71	550	513	447	385	497	757	1,079	990	1,225	1,737	3,722	5,148	7,160	8,137	6,161
Imports, fob	71.v	504	470	410	353	456	691	983	903	1,115	1,586	3,358	4,644	6,467	7,350	5,566
Imports, cif, from DOTS	71y	....	....	....	....	....	....	....	....	....	....	....	....	....	....	....
Volume of Exports																*1985=100*
Crude Petroleum	72aa	22	31	24	11	44	84	116	143	160	177	139	161	167	150	180
Export Prices																*1980=100:*
Crude Petrol.(1980=100)	76aa d	5.3	5.3	5.3	5.3	5.3	5.3	7.2	7.8	11.2	31.7	33.5	36.3	40.9	39.5	58.5
Balance of Payments																*Millions of US Dollars:*
Goods: Exports f.o.b.	78aa d	....	....	....	....	....	....	....	....	....	....	....	....	12,366	10,414	16,811
Goods: Imports f.o.b.	78ab d	....	....	....	....	....	....	....	....	....	....	....	....	−9,670	−11,583	−11,887
Trade Balance	78ac d	....	....	....	....	....	....	....	....	....	....	....	....	2,696	−1,169	4,924
Services: Credit	78ad d	....	....	....	....	....	....	....	....	....	....	....	....	563	876	1,028
Services: Debit	78ae d	....	....	....	....	....	....	....	....	....	....	....	....	−3,552	−2,965	−3,441
Balance on Goods and Services	78af d	....	....	....	....	....	....	....	....	....	....	....	....	−293	−3,257	2,510
Income: Credit	78ag d	....	....	....	....	....	....	....	....	....	....	....	....	350	290	269
Income: Debit	78ah d	....	....	....	....	....	....	....	....	....	....	....	....	−886	−520	−722
Balance on Goods, Serv., & Inc.	78ai d	....	....	....	....	....	....	....	....	....	....	....	....	−829	−3,487	2,058
Current Transfers, n.i.e.: Credit	78aj d	....	....	....	....	....	....	....	....	....	....	....	....	42	11	23
Current Transfers: Debit	78ak d	....	....	....	....	....	....	....	....	....	....	....	....	−225	−281	−412
Current Account, n.i.e.	78al d	....	....	....	....	....	....	....	....	....	....	....	....	−1,012	−3,757	1,669
Capital Account, n.i.e.: Credit	78ba d	....	....	....	....	....	....	....	....	....	....	....	....	—	—	—
Capital Account: Debit	78bb d	....	....	....	....	....	....	....	....	....	....	....	....	—	—	—
Capital Account, n.i.e.	78bc d	....	....	....	....	....	....	....	....	....	....	....	....	—	—	—
Direct Investment Abroad	78bd d	....	....	....	....	....	....	....	....	....	....	....	....	—	—	−5
Dir. Invest. in Rep. Econ., n.i.e.	78be d	....	....	....	....	....	....	....	....	....	....	....	....	439	212	310
Portfolio Investment Assets	78bf d	....	....	....	....	....	....	....	....	....	....	....	....	—	—	—
Portfolio Investment Liab., n.i.e.	78bg d	....	....	....	....	....	....	....	....	....	....	....	....	—	—	—
Other Investment Assets	78bh d	....	....	....	....	....	....	....	....	....	....	....	....	−150	−207	−62
Other Investment Liab., n.i.e.	78bi d	....	....	....	....	....	....	....	....	....	....	....	....	−50	1,485	988
Financial Account, n.i.e.	78bj d	....	....	....	....	....	....	....	....	....	....	....	....	239	1,490	1,231
Net Errors and Omissions	78ca d	....	....	....	....	....	....	....	....	....	....	....	....	−50	158	305
Overall Balance	78cb d	....	....	....	....	....	....	....	....	....	....	....	....	−823	−2,109	3,204
Reserves and Related Items	79da d	....	....	....	....	....	....	....	....	....	....	....	....	823	2,109	−3,204
Reserve Assets	79db d	....	....	....	....	....	....	....	....	....	....	....	....	823	2,109	−3,204
Use of Fund Credit and Loans	79dc d	....	....	....	....	....	....	....	....	....	....	....	....	—	—	—
Liabs.Constit.For.Auth.Reserves	79dd d	....	....	....	....	....	....	....	....	....	....	....	....	—	—	—
Exceptional Financing	79de d	....	....	....	....	....	....	....	....	....	....	....	....	—	—	—
Government Finance																*Millions of Naira*
Deficit (−) or Surplus	80	−78	−47	−124	−178	−302	−119	36	37	404	1,487	....	−1,130	1,135	2,122	2,871
Revenue	81	190	182	168	186	246	463	969	1,023	1,769	4,190	4,712	5,523	6,263	5,645	8,609
Grants Received	81z	1	2	2	2	1	—	—	—	—	—	—	—	—	—	—
Expenditure	82	245	217	289	350	541	573	834	898	1,207	2,684	....	6,580	5,255	3,769	5,448
Lending Minus Repayments	83	24	14	6	16	7	8	98	88	158	19	459	72	−127	−246	290
Financing																
Net Borrowing: Domestic	84a	29	76	115	170	303	195	204	−107	−114	....	....	....	....	....	....
Foreign	85a	36	1	18	−2	2	−7	66	−11	5	....	....	....	....	....	....
Use of Cash Balances	87	14	−30	−9	9	−3	−70	−306	81	−295	....	....	−222	−687	....	....
Debt: Domestic	88a	....	....	....	514	762	1,003	822	987	1,057	1,262	1,674	2,630	3,408	5,980	7,217
Central Bank	88aa	....	....	....	....	185	232	343	194	175	20	314	512	457	3,197	2,484
Commercial Banks	88ab	....	....	....	315	459	328	387	388	766	801	1,197	1,683	1,196	2,542	
Other	88ac	....	....	....	....	262	312	152	406	494	477	559	922	1,269	1,587	2,192
Debt: Foreign	89a	....	....	....	179	176	175	179	263	277	322	350	376	364	1,252	1,614
National Accounts																*Millions of Naira*
Exports of Goods & Services	90c	578	599	521	467	683	954	1,422	1,522	2,467	6,244	5,318	6,593	8,370	6,882	10,990
Government Consumption	91f	222	225	215	252	420	578	631	798	976	1,312	2,237	2,585	3,827	4,999	4,882
Gross Capital Formation	93	615	602	484	438	550	883	1,283	1,401	2,615	3,167	5,513	8,577	9,922	9,886	9,594
Private Consumption	96f	2,590	2,828	2,352	2,283	2,901	4,143	5,090	5,267	6,903	10,962	13,689	16,297	19,061	24,341	25,928
Imports of Goods & Services	98c	−645	−639	−621	−561	−702	−937	−1,328	−1,286	−1,762	−2,874	−4,978	−6,480	−8,433	−10,024	−8,243
Gross Domestic Product	99b	3,361	3,614	2,951	2,878	3,851	5,621	7,098	7,703	11,199	18,811	21,779	27,572	32,747	36,084	43,151
Net Factor Inc/Pmts(−) Abroad	98.n	−59	−82	−82	−76	−169	−496	−245	−570	−621	−435	−220	−274	−475	−474	−616
Gross Nat'l Expenditure=GNP	99a	3,302	3,532	2,869	2,802	3,682	5,125	6,853	7,133	10,578	18,376	21,559	27,298	32,272	35,610	42,535
Gross Dom. Prod. 1990 Prices	99b.p	....	....	....	....	....	....	....	....	169,844	190,441	184,699	204,826	221,501	205,282	210,454
GDP Deflator (1990=100)	99bi p	....	....	....	....	....	....	....	....	6.6	9.9	11.8	13.5	14.8	17.6	20.5
																Millions:
Population	99z	58.49	59.96	61.47	63.01	64.58	66.18	67.84	69.56	71.33	73.11	74.88	76.55	78.33	80.27	82.39

Exchange Rates: On January 1, 1973 the naira, equal to one half the Nigerian pound, was introduced.

Deposit Money Banks: ℓ Prior to 1973, central government deposits with commercial banks were included in *Demand Deposits* and *Time and Savings Deposits*.

Monetary Survey: ℓ See note to section 20.

Nigeria

	1980	1981	1982	1983	1984	1985	1986	1987	1988	1989	1990	1991	1992	1993	1994	International Transactions	
Millions of Naira																	
	14,199	11,023	8,206	7,503	9,088	11,215	9,044	29,578	31,193	57,971	109,886	121,534	205,613	218,765	....	Exports	70
	13,632	10,681	8,003	7,201	8,843	10,891	8,368	28,209	28,436	55,017	106,627	116,857	201,384	....	....	Crude Petroleum	70aa
	9,096	12,920	10,771	8,904	7,178	7,933	5,971	15,694	21,446	30,860	45,718	89,488	143,151	165,629	....	Imports, cif	71
	8,216	11,671	9,730	8,043	6,484	7,166	5,394	14,177	19,373	27,877	41,299	80,838	129,315	149,620	....	Imports, fob	71.v
	....	11,498	8,966	7,525	4,446	5,537	5,971	15,712	17,646	25,179	34,704	53,214	158,787	166,398	....	Imports, cif, from DOTS	71y
																Volume of Exports	
1985=100																	
	153		99	81	75	88	100	62	86	96	....	....	....	....	....	Crude Petroleum	72aa
																Export Prices	
Index of Prices in US Dollars																	
	100.0	108.4	99.4	84.6	83.3	....	....	....	....	....	....	....	....	....	....	Crude Petrol.(1980=100)	76aa d
Minus Sign Indicates Debit																Balance of Payments	
	25,929	18,115	12,163	10,344	11,859	13,115	6,015	7,545	6,897	7,870	13,585	12,254	11,791	....	....	Goods: Exports f.o.b.	78aa d
	-14,753	-18,946	-14,894	-11,433	-8,867	-7,499	-3,702	-4,097	-4,271	-3,692	-4,932	-7,813	-7,181	....	....	Goods: Imports f.o.b.	78ab d
	11,176	-831	-2,731	-1,089	2,992	5,616	2,313	3,448	2,626	4,178	8,653	4,441	4,611	....	....	Trade Balance	78ac d
	1,128	924	508	404	433	316	230	225	364	552	965	886	1,053	....	....	Services: Credit	78ad d
	-5,293	-5,017	-3,445	-2,392	-1,793	-1,644	-1,196	-871	-840	-1,374	-1,976	-2,448	-1,810	....	....	Services: Debit	78ae d
	7,012	-4,924	-5,668	-3,077	1,632	4,288	1,347	2,802	2,150	3,355	7,642	2,879	3,853	....	....	Balance on Goods and Services	78af d
	692	698	226	107	57	80	68	46	41	152	211	211	156	....	....	Income: Credit	78ag d
	-1,999	-1,379	-1,414	-989	-1,249	-1,546	-936	-2,892	-2,373	-2,543	-2,949	-2,631	-2,494	....	....	Income: Debit	78ah d
	5,705	-5,605	-6,856	-3,959	441	2,821	479	-44	-182	964	4,904	458	1,515	....	....	Balance on Goods, Serv., & Inc.	78ai d
	33	34	28	18	16	31	13	4	26	157	167	877	817	....	....	Current Transfers, n.i.e.: Credit	78aj d
	-611	-592	-457	-412	-342	-286	-126	-29	-38	-31	-82	-132	-64	....	....	Current Transfers: Debit	78ak d
	5,127	-6,164	-7,285	-4,354	115	2,566	366	-69	-194	1,090	4,988	1,203	2,268	....	....	Current Account, n.i.e.	78al d
	—	—	—	—	—	—	—	—	—	—	—	—	—	....	....	Capital Account, n.i.e.: Credit	78ba d
	—	—	—	—	—	—	—	—	—	—	—	—	—	....	....	Capital Account: Debit	78bb d
	—	—	—	—	—	—	—	—	—	—	—	—	—	....	....	Capital Account, n.i.e.	78bc d
	—	—	—	—	—	—	—	—	—	—	—	—	—	....	....	Direct Investment Abroad	78bd d
	-740	546	433	344	200	478	167	603	377	1,882	588	712	897	....	....	Dir. Invest. in Rep. Econ., n.i.e.	78be d
	—	—	—	—	—	—	—	—	-535	-65	-220	-197	-61	1,884	....	Portfolio Investment Assets	78bf d
	—	—	—	—	—	—	—	—	—	—	—	—	—	....	....	Portfolio Investment Liab., n.i.e.	78bg d
	-26	128	-9	-427	-691	-2,606	-343	-1,795	-1,115	-2,530	-2,886	-2,487	-5,840	....	....	Other Investment Assets	78bh d
	713	852	1,240	1,361	-863	-1,536	-1,015	-2,393	-3,743	-2,777	-1,687	-797	-4,725	....	....	Other Investment Liab., n.i.e.	78bi d
	-53	1,527	1,664	1,278	-1,354	-3,664	-1,191	-4,121	-4,545	-3,644	-4,182	-2,633	-7,784	....	....	Financial Account, n.i.e.	78bj d
	-702	-85	8	87	272	-135	-161	-305	-214	-109	235	-93	-122	....	....	Net Errors and Omissions	78ca d
	4,372	-4,722	-5,613	-2,988	-968	-1,233	-986	-4,495	-4,953	-2,663	1,041	-1,523	-5,638	....	....	Overall Balance	78cb d
	-4,372	4,722	5,613	2,988	968	1,233	986	4,495	4,953	2,663	-1,041	1,523	5,638	....	....	Reserves and Related Items	79aa d
	-4,372	4,666	2,110	441	-482	-488	478	-48	436	-1,185	-2,478	-640	3,727	....	....	Reserve Assets	79ab d
	—	—	—	—	—	—	—	—	—	—	—	—	—	....	....	Use of Fund Credit and Loans	79ac d
	—	—	—	—	—	—	—	—	—	—	—	—	—	....	....	Liabs.Constit.For.Auth.Reserves	79ad d
	—	56	3,503	2,547	1,450	1,721	508	4,542	4,517	3,849	1,437	2,163	1,911	....	....	Exceptional Financing	79ae d
Year Ending December 31																Government Finance	
	9,184	2,055	-6,559	-5,392	-2,614	-3,040	-8,254	-5,889	-12,224	-15,135	-22,116	-35,756	-55,949	-101,126	-70,819	Deficit (-) or Surplus	80
	11,628	7,050	5,819	6,272	6,939	9,640	7,969	16,129	15,525	25,893	39,033	31,774	51,774	73,398	70,796	Revenue	81
	—	—	—	—	—	—	—	—	—	—	—	—	—	—	—	Grants Received	81z
	2,351	4,134	12,378	11,664	9,553	12,680	16,223	22,018	27,749	41,028	61,149	67,530	107,723	174,524	141,615	Expenditure	82
	93	861	—	—	—	—	—	—	—	—	—	—	—	—	—	Lending Minus Repayments	83
																Financing	
	....	....	3,402	7,376	3,450	2,277	499	8,339	10,240	10,020	27,042	32,107	58,119	101,126	62,232	Net Borrowing: Domestic	84a
	....	....	263	1,107	1,184	1,046	708	832	1,919	5,719	1,564	278	—	—	8,587	Foreign	85a
	....	....	2,894	-3,091	-2,019	-283	7,047	-3,283	65	-604	-6,490	3,371	-2,170	—	—	Use of Cash Balances	87
	7,919	11,446	14,848	22,224	25,674	27,982	28,451	36,791	47,031	57,031	84,093	118,200	160,485	252,878	296,381	Debt: Domestic	88a
	2,859	6,047	8,023	11,347	10,701	11,522	17,722	19,197	27,682	38,371	56,564	89,413	134,407	199,993	251,552	Central Bank	88aa
	2,979	2,155	3,169	5,460	8,998	10,699	4,968	8,110	7,715	3,671	8,917	9,526	5,535	29,684	36,184	Commercial Banks	88ab
	2,080	3,244	3,657	5,417	5,975	5,761	5,761	9,484	11,634	14,989	18,612	19,261	20,543	23,201	8,645	Other	88ac
	1,867	3,024	2,595	10,577	14,537	17,290	41,452	100,787	133,956	240,033	298,614	328,051	544,264	633,144	648,813	Debt: Foreign	89a
Millions of Naira																National Accounts	
	14,308	11,478	9,561	7,963	9,548	12,083	9,427	30,013	31,955	94,959	129,910	129,691	196,904	191,982	190,062	Exports of Goods & Services	90c
	5,051	6,619	6,816	7,489	6,925	7,342	7,488	7,395	9,253	10,076	11,469	12,690	20,432	27,583	31,720	Government Consumption	91f
	11,431	11,594	9,734	7,479	4,257	5,126	7,734	9,605	9,392	18,424	31,127	35,620	58,940	81,398	84,442	Gross Capital Formation	93
	31,695	34,563	36,284	41,457	47,962	54,066	56,204	78,329	113,073	138,828	146,420	222,270	404,182	569,793	766,671	Private Consumption	96f
	-11,636	-13,505	-10,686	-7,246	-5,084	-6,262	-7,791	-16,457	-18,430	-37,490	-58,289	-76,260	-130,650	-173,661	-175,397	Imports of Goods & Services	98c
	50,849	50,749	51,709	57,142	63,608	72,355	73,062	108,885	145,243	224,797	260,637	324,011	549,808	697,095	897,498	Gross Domestic Product	99b
	-1,090	-910	-1,162	-974	-1,599	-1,623	-4,380	-11,660	-12,740	-17,619	-22,013	-24,500	-64,400	-73,210	-84,600	Net Factor Inc/Pmts(-) Abroad	98.n
	49,759	49,839	50,547	56,168	62,009	70,732	68,682	97,225	132,503	207,173	238,624	299,511	485,408	623,885	812,898	Gross Nat'l Expenditure=GNP	99a
	221,691	203,090	202,403	191,533	181,773	198,823	205,055	204,088	224,315	240,883	260,637	272,962	281,089	287,488	291,333	Gross Dom. Prod. 1990 Prices	99b.p
	22.9	25.0	25.5	29.8	35.0	36.4	35.6	53.4	64.7	93.3	100.0	118.7	195.6	242.5	308.1	GDP Deflator (1990=100)	99bi p
Midyear Estimates																	
	84.73	87.31	83.62	86.29	I 93.33	95.69	98.17	101.41	104.96	I 93.34	96.15	99.09	102.13	105.26	....	**Population**	99z

Norway
142

		1965	1966	1967	1968	1969	1970	1971	1972	1973	1974	1975	1976	1977	1978	1979
Exchange Rates																*Kroner per SDR:*
Official Rate	aa	7.1500	7.1550	7.1500	7.1500	7.1500	7.1400	7.2851	ɪ7.2091	6.9094	6.3727	6.5381	6.0241	6.2430	6.5433	6.4892
																Kroner per US Dollar:
Official Rate	ae	7.1500	7.1550	7.1500	7.1500	7.1500	7.1400	6.7100	ɪ6.6400	5.7275	5.2050	5.5850	5.1850	5.1395	5.0225	4.9260
Official Rate	rf	7.1429	7.1429	7.1429	7.1429	7.1429	7.1429	7.0559	6.5882	5.7658	5.5397	5.5269	5.4565	5.3235	5.2423	5.0641
																Kroner per ECU:
ECU Rate	ea	....	....	....	....	....	....	....	....	....	....	....	....	....	....	....
ECU Rate	eb	....	....	....	....	....	....	....	....	....	....	....	....	....	....	....
																Index Numbers (1990=100):
Official Rate	ahx	87.4	87.4	87.4	87.5	87.4	87.4	121.2	94.8	108.7	113.1	119.8	114.5	117.4	119.3	123.4
Nominal Effective Exchange Rate	neu	101.5	101.5	102.0	105.5	105.5	104.4	103.8	103.9	108.5	114.4	117.4	120.8	122.7	115.3	114.3
Real Effective Exchange Rate	reu	....	....	....	....	....	....	....	....	....	....	94.7	101.8	106.0	100.7	94.4
Fund Position																*Millions of SDRs:*
Quota	2f. s	100.0	150.0	150.0	150.0	150.0	240.0	240.0	240.0	240.0	240.0	240.0	240.0	240.0	295.0	295.0
SDRs	1b. s	—	—	—	—	—	27.2	54.9	87.9	88.0	88.2	89.0	89.5	92.8	96.3	139.7
Reserve Position in the Fund	1c. s	25.1	42.6	51.3	71.5	87.0	118.8	61.6	69.0	—	63.4	68.9	111.8	247.4	234.7	205.7	188.1
of which: Outstg.Fund Borrowing	2c	—	—	—	—	—	—	—	—	—	—	29.1	100.0	97.4	82.9	66.0
International Liquidity												*Millions of US Dollars Unless Otherwise Indicated:*				
Total Reserves minus Gold	1l. d	445.1	509.4	658.8	678.7	685.0	787.9	1,118.4	1,287.5	1,533.5	1,886.6	2,196.5	2,189.4	2,195.6	2,860.7	4,215.2
SDRs	1b. d	—	—	—	—	—	27.2	59.6	95.4	106.1	108.0	104.2	103.9	112.8	125.4	184.1
Reserve Position in the Fund	1c. d	25.0	42.6	51.3	71.5	87.0	118.8	66.9	74.9	76.5	84.4	130.9	287.4	285.0	268.0	247.8
Foreign Exchange	1d. d	420.1	466.8	607.5	607.2	598.0	641.9	991.9	1,117.5	1,350.8	1,694.2	1,961.4	1,798.1	1,797.8	2,467.2	3,783.4
Gold (Million Fine Troy Ounces)	1ad	.879	.522	.522	.679	.723	.670	.947	.978	.979	.979	.979	.979	1.081	1.133	1.184
Gold (National Valuation)	1and	19.5	11.8	11.8	17.4	25.3	23.4	36.0ᵉ	37.2ᵉ	41.3	45.1	42.1	45.3	50.6	54.2	57.9
Deposit Money Banks: Assets	7a. d	278.6	236.6	259.0	385.0	417.2	396.2	293.4	308.5	410.8	507.2	422.6	520.7	823.8	664.4	634.4
of which: Claims on Nonbanks	7add	....	....	....	....	....	....	....	....	....	....	....	141.8	133.5	171.8	204.4
Deposit Money Banks: Liabilities	7b. d	268.8	274.4	268.8	280.0	372.4	295.4	359.6	365.7	437.1	605.2	472.7	685.4	585.1	752.8	1,279.5
of which: Liab. to Nonbanks	7bdd	....	....	....	....	....	....	....	....	....	....	....	166.4	170.8	224.8	272.6
Other Banking Insts.: Liabilities	7f. d	....	....	....	....	....	....	....	....	....	....	....	1,135.5	2,049.6	3,286.6	
Monetary Authorities																*Billions of Kroner:*
Foreign Assets	11	3.32	3.72	4.79	4.97	5.08	5.81	7.69	8.82	8.99	9.98	12.49	ɪ11.63	11.58	14.63	21.02
Claims on Central Government	12a	5.34	5.22	5.13	4.98	5.65	6.44	6.08	6.22	6.52	6.45	7.72	9.44	12.83	13.04	14.77
Claims on Deposit Money Banks	12e	.01	.07	.15	.03	.48	.06	.30	1.01	1.32	1.92	1.22	1.39	5.53	2.31	1.49
Reserve Money	14	6.28	6.74	6.98	7.45	7.98	8.22	9.17	9.60	10.23	11.64	13.66	ɪ15.37	17.20	19.44	21.19
of which: Currency Outside DMBs	14a	5.05	5.42	5.83	6.14	6.52	7.28	7.99	8.75	9.44	10.77	12.39	14.26	16.08	17.06	17.73
Central Government Deposits	16d	1.93	1.74	2.47	1.75	1.96	2.17	2.86	4.25	5.50	5.48	6.09	5.54	7.03	6.07	8.34
Other Items (Net)	17r	.45	.53	.62	.78	1.27	1.91	2.04	2.21	1.09	1.23	1.68	ɪ1.55	5.71	4.46	7.76
Deposit Money Banks																
Commercial and Savings Banks																*Billions of Kroner:*
Reserves	20	1.28	1.39	1.30	1.42	1.33	1.27	1.42	1.33	1.40	1.44	1.30	ɪ1.01	1.02	1.61	4.21
Foreign Assets	21	1.99	1.69	1.85	2.75	2.98	2.83	1.95	2.05	2.34	2.64	2.36	2.69	4.22	3.32	3.11
Claims on Central Government	22a	1.81	1.96	2.26	2.41	3.08	4.43	5.96	7.26	8.31	7.98	7.49	7.40	9.50	11.40	18.03
Claims on Local Government	22b	....	....	....	....	....	....	....	....	....	....	....	4.36	5.00	5.56	6.22
Claims on Nonfin.Pub.Enterprises	22c	....	....	....	....	....	....	....	....	....	....	....	1.33	1.53	1.51	1.46
Claims on Private Sector	22d	17.90	19.88	21.62	23.53	26.79	29.65	33.74	38.18	43.23	49.10	57.05	ɪ58.90	68.48	74.12	82.38
Claims on Other Financial Insts.	22f	....	....	....	....	....	....	....	....	....	....	....	10.91	14.44	15.41	16.08
Demand Deposits	24	4.52	4.85	5.19	6.30	6.96	7.99	9.12	10.59	12.09	13.70	15.26	ɪ14.70	16.22	17.34	19.46
Time, Savings,& Fgn.Currency Dep.	25	15.37	16.64	18.50	20.46	22.67	26.09	29.58	32.90	37.41	41.62	48.06	ɪ55.94	66.78	75.82	88.67
Foreign Liabilities	26c	1.92	1.96	1.92	2.00	2.66	2.11	2.39	2.43	2.49	3.15	2.64	ɪ3.54	3.00	3.77	6.30
Central Government Deposits	26d	....	....	....	....	....	....	....	....	....	....	....	1.48	1.62	1.94	1.98
Credit from Bank of Norway	26g	....	....	....	....	....	....	....	....	....	....	....	1.34	5.49	2.16	1.32
Other Items (Net)	27r	1.17	1.46	1.41	1.36	1.88	1.99	1.97	2.89	3.33	2.73	2.25	ɪ7.68	8.91	9.04	10.72
P.O. Savings Bank and Postal Giro																*Billions of Kroner:*
Claims on Central Government	22a. i	2.49	2.87	3.36	4.02	4.15	5.08	6.28	7.66	9.44	10.72	12.17	ɪ12.60	13.51	16.86	19.59
Demand Deposits	24.. c	1.03	1.12	1.20	1.58	1.69	1.88	2.05	3.01	4.21	4.30	5.83	ɪ3.26	4.51	4.76	5.21
Time Deposits	25.. i	1.27	1.45	1.61	1.78	1.91	2.37	2.75	3.12	3.45	3.90	4.53	5.16	5.99	6.97	7.66
Central Government Deposits	26d.. i	.72	.81	1.05	1.25	1.40	1.75	2.34	2.36	2.77	3.73	3.29	ɪ6.39	5.57	7.63	8.69
Other Items (Net)	27r.. i	−.53	−.51	−.50	−.59	−.85	−.92	−.86	−.83	−.99	−1.21	−1.48	ɪ−2.22	−2.57	−2.50	−1.97
Monetary Survey																*Billions of Kroner:*
Foreign Assets (Net)	31n	3.33	3.40	4.57	5.59	5.21	6.38	7.12	8.29	8.67	9.21	12.01	ɪ10.59	9.91	13.99	17.54
Domestic Credit	32	26.36	29.09	30.81	34.09	38.62	44.28	49.94	56.31	63.50	70.33	81.22	ɪ94.18	114.31	125.84	143.37
Claims on Central Govt. (Net)	32an	6.99	7.50	7.23	8.41	9.52	12.03	13.12	14.53	16.00	15.94	18.00	ɪ16.03	21.61	25.65	33.38
Claims on Local Government	32b	.89	1.05	1.19	1.33	1.51	1.71	2.17	2.70	3.29	4.08	4.52	ɪ5.24	5.92	6.49	7.12
Claims on Nonfin.Pub.Enterprises	32c	....	....	....	....	....	....	....	....	....	....	....	1.40	1.62	1.58	1.55
Claims on Private Sector	32d	18.48	20.54	22.39	24.35	27.59	30.54	34.65	39.08	44.21	50.31	58.70	ɪ60.18	70.19	76.23	84.81
Claims on Other Financial Insts.	32f	....	....	....	....	....	....	....	....	....	....	....	11.32	14.97	15.89	16.52
Money	34	10.61	11.42	12.26	14.12	15.28	17.20	19.21	22.39	25.81	28.88	33.65	ɪ32.42	37.00	40.19	43.25
Quasi-Money	35	16.92	18.43	20.52	22.64	25.32	29.50	33.72	37.18	41.81	46.22	52.95	ɪ61.29	72.91	82.85	96.42
Other Items (Net)	37r	2.15	2.64	2.60	2.91	3.22	3.97	4.13	5.02	4.59	4.48	6.62	ɪ9.13	12.15	13.92	18.20
Money plus Quasi-Money	35l	27.53	29.85	32.78	36.77	40.60	46.70	52.93	59.56	67.62	75.10	86.60	ɪ93.71	109.91	123.04	139.67
Money (National Definitions)																*Billions of Kroner:*
Broad Money	38n	30.1	32.7	35.4	39.7	43.5	49.6	55.7	62.2	69.2	76.9	88.6	103.9	120.5	133.6	152.2
Broad Money, Seasonally Adj.	38n. c	29.3	31.9	34.6	38.8	42.6	48.6	54.7	61.2	68.1	75.7	87.2	102.2	118.5	131.3	149.5

Norway
142

1980	1981	1982	1983	1984	1985	1986	1987	1988	1989	1990	1991	1992	1993	1994		
															Exchange Rates	
End of Period																
6.6066	6.7597	7.7813	8.0847	8.9072	8.3288	9.0516	8.8418	8.8412	8.6932	8.4044	8.5440	9.5212	10.3264	9.8715	Official Rate	**aa**
End of Period (ae)		*Period Average (rf)*														
5.1800	5.8075	7.0540	7.7222	9.0870	7.5825	7.4000	6.2325	6.5700	6.6150	5.9075	5.9730	6.9245	7.5180	6.7620	Official Rate	**ae**
4.9392	5.7395	6.4540	7.2964	8.1615	8.5972	7.3947	6.7375	6.5170	6.9045	6.2597	6.4829	6.2145	7.0941	7.0576	Official Rate	**rf**
End of Period (ea)		*Period Average (eb)*														
....	....	....	....	....	....	....	....	....	....	8.0230	8.0164	8.3848	8.3878	8.3175	ECU Rate	**ea**
....	....	....	....	....	....	....	....	....	....	....	8.0186	8.0398	8.3505	8.3760	ECU Rate	**eb**
Period Averages																
126.5	109.1	97.4	85.7	76.8	73.0	84.5	92.8	96.0	90.5	100.0	96.7	100.8	87.9	88.6	Official Rate	**ah** *x*
114.6	117.0	118.4	115.9	114.2	112.0	104.9	100.7	100.6	100.7	100.0	98.4	99.4	98.0	96.7	Nominal Effective Exchange Rate	**ne** *u*
93.1	95.8	98.6	99.5	100.2	100.1	97.2	101.2	102.8	100.9	100.0	97.5	97.3	94.6	....	Real Effective Exchange Rate	**re** *u*
End of Period															**Fund Position**	
442.5	442.5	442.5	699.0	699.0	699.0	699.0	699.0	699.0	699.0	699.0	699.0	1,104.6	1,104.6	1,104.6	Quota	**2f.** *s*
157.6	195.3	284.3	257.3	262.2	258.0	318.2	311.2	362.3	345.2	315.5	315.9	139.1	288.4	266.7	SDRs	**1b.** *s*
201.4	213.8	246.4	411.0	470.4	463.7	481.8	498.1	451.3	441.9	407.8	399.0	471.4	425.5	440.9	Reserve Position in the Fund	**1c.** *s*
51.3	31.7	8.1	—	—	—	—	—	—	—	—	—	—	—	—	*of which:* Outstg.Fund Borrowing	**2c**
End of Period															**International Liquidity**	
6,048.0	6,252.9	6,873.5	6,629.2	9,365.0	13,916.7	12,524.6	14,276.5	13,267.7	13,784.8	15,332.3	13,232.0	11,940.4	19,622.4	19,025.5	Total Reserves minus Gold	**1l.** *d*
201.1	227.3	313.7	269.3	257.0	283.4	389.2	441.5	487.5	453.7	448.9	451.9	191.5	396.2	389.4	SDRs	**1b.** *d*
256.8	248.8	271.9	430.3	461.1	509.3	589.4	706.6	607.4	580.7	580.2	570.8	648.1	584.4	643.7	Reserve Position in the Fund	**1c.** *d*
5,590.1	5,776.8	6,288.0	5,929.5	8,647.0	13,124.0	11,546.0	13,128.4	12,172.9	12,750.5	14,303.2	12,209.4	11,101.0	18,641.8	17,992.4	Foreign Exchange	**1d.** *d*
1.184	1.184	1.184	1.184	1.184	1.184	1.184	1.184	1.184	1.184	1.184	1.184	1.184	1.184	1.184	Gold (Million Fine Troy Ounces)	**1ad**
55.0	49.1	40.4	36.9	31.4	37.6	38.5	45.7	43.4	43.1	48.2	47.7	41.2	37.9	42.1	Gold (National Valuation)	**1an** *d*
626.8	1,882.0	2,346.5	2,539.7	2,996.5	3,643.9	6,799.7	8,507.3	6,326.0	6,428.1	7,816.8	8,954.1	11,398.8	6,597.1	7,433.0	Deposit Money Banks: Assets	**7a.** *d*
280.1	494.4	713.1	1,307.1	1,748.1	2,151.5	3,480.8	5,380.5	3,816.3	4,539.8	5,546.4	4,977.2	6,074.1	4,205.2	4,373.0	*of which:* Claims on Nonbanks	**7ad** *d*
2,738.4	3,438.8	3,979.4	4,335.6	5,540.1	9,163.5	13,324.2	19,971.6	19,047.0	20,514.0	22,173.5	16,383.4	11,049.5	9,637.4	8,862.0	Deposit Money Banks· Liabilities	**7b.** *d*
395.0	677.6	762.4	1,101.4	1,515.7	2,761.6	5,626.1	7,323.2	8,602.4	9,548.8	10,424.4	8,467.3	6,802.1	5,173.5	4,770.0	*of which:* Liab. to Nonbanks	**7bd** *d*
3,219.5	2,870.8	2,610.4	2,327.2	1,901.7	2,079.4	2,248.2	2,438.7	2,010.8	1,675.9	1,392.6	1,073.2	760.5	490.7	267.2	Other Banking Insts.: Liabilities	**7f.** *d*
End of Period															**Monetary Authorities**	
31.45	36.72	48.89	51.40	85.53	107.47	93.05	89.62	87.52	91.83	90.92	78.75	82.50	151.43	143.58	Foreign Assets	**11**
9.83	11.12	5.66	11.76	7.67	19.21	47.74	23.93	18.24	24.05	12.56	7.98	12.58	29.25	13.69	Claims on Central Government	**12a**
.97	2.96	2.80	4.62	2.19	8.27	71.46	77.27	79.83	70.77	69.04	66.25	55.40	17.48	5.86	Claims on Deposit Money Banks	**12e**
23.01	22.86	24.36	25.36	29.36	31.44	31.07	33.39	32.56	34.45	34.12	36.73	38.52	42.66	44.09	Reserve Money	**14**
18.82	20.16	20.93	21.75	22.78	25.05	26.58	28.16	28.52	29.20	29.88	31.79	32.45	35.74	37.96	*of which:* Currency Outside DMBs	**14a**
10.18	11.96	8.02	19.45	35.42	81.38	144.65	119.27	116.75	121.09	109.01	85.00	67.62	106.76	87.24	Central Government Deposits	**16d**
9.06	15.98	24.96	22.98	30.61	22.13	36.53	38.17	36.30	31.11	29.74	31.96	45.10	48.75	31.80	Other Items (Net)	**17r**
															Deposit Money Banks	
End of Period															*Commercial and Savings Banks*	
1.49	1.36	1.47	3.43	2.22	2.69	3.30	3.92	2.73	2.69	2.77	3.32	4.57	2.83	3.86	Reserves	**20**
3.23	10.91	16.54	19.60	27.22	27.62	50.27	52.99	41.53	42.33	46.01	53.03	78.66	49.37	47.60	Foreign Assets	**21**
29.05	27.85	27.34	28.08	37.99	38.58	43.37	34.64	33.47	26.90	25.61	13.98	12.52	24.40	22.42	Claims on Central Government	**22a**
7.42	8.71	8.19	8.23	9.88	10.30	9.97	14.02	16.59	16.63	14.69	10.81	9.60	9.53	9.15	Claims on Local Government	**22b**
1.67	2.21	7.42	9.19	11.12	12.58	10.47	12.58	10.20	9.99	8.12	7.11	5.97	4.38	3.98	Claims on Nonfin.Pub.Enterprises	**22c**
94.36	109.47	123.99	141.94	180.11	236.63	303.80	372.59	399.15	432.99	451.57	428.35	431.78	440.06	461.00	Claims on Private Sector	**22d**
18.90	22.35	25.24	30.86	31.87	39.25	45.39	71.59	58.32	51.57	43.48	41.75	44.36	31.65	29.01	Claims on Other Financial Insts.	**22f**
22.53	25.84	29.71	35.81	48.05	63.37	64.69	112.89	145.96	173.10	192.85	206.72	234.94	245.89	258.10	Demand Deposits	**24**
100.79	113.85	126.15	138.66	161.90	182.11	183.58	188.29	168.11	166.22	166.12	153.74	159.72	139.57	149.20	Time, Savings,& Fgn.Currency Dep.	**25**
14.17	19.96	28.05	33.47	50.33	69.46	98.58	124.44	125.11	135.65	130.95	97.78	76.33	72.16	61.31	Foreign Liabilities	**26c**
2.00	2.15	2.48	2.95	3.41	3.66	4.30	4.74	5.18	5.60	6.35	6.77	5.80	6.20	6.44	Central Government Deposits	**26d**
.78	2.77	2.52	4.23	2.03	7.25	69.42	75.64	77.19	60.82	57.62	60.57	55.29	16.98	5.22	Credit from Bank of Norway	**26g**
12.16	13.67	15.58	19.25	23.59	31.64	34.93	56.34	40.44	41.71	38.35	32.77	55.39	81.43	96.76	Other Items (Net)	**27r**
End of Period															*P.O. Savings Bank and Postal Giro*	
19.37	20.19	20.47	21.73	29.75	35.64	41.29	43.51	49.66	56.82	59.85	60.68	64.46	62.92	....	Claims on Central Government	**22a.** *i*
2.96	5.28	6.98	7.03	9.66	8.47	9.10	10.06	11.32	13.57	13.52	15.44	‡53.85	54.55	....	Demand Deposits	**24..** *c*
8.28	8.96	9.56	10.37	11.77	13.20	14.97	17.38	21.20	24.48	28.37	35.44	‡.23	.37	....	Time Deposits	**25..** *i*
10.75	9.60	8.63	8.74	11.77	17.13	17.95	21.83	25.26	26.18	24.20	20.98	25.86	30.35	....	Central Government Deposits	**26d.** *i*
-2.62	-3.64	-4.70	-4.42	-3.44	-3.16	-.73	-5.75	-8.11	-7.41	-6.23	-11.17	-15.48	-22.35	....	Other Items (Net)	**27r.** *i*
End of Period															**Monetary Survey**	
20.25	27.44	36.91	36.78	62.04	65.26	44.24	17.74	3.12	-1.78	5.89	34.11	80.32	123.14	....	Foreign Assets (Net)	**31n**
161.72	182.48	204.01	225.76	263.29	295.87	341.53	433.82	446.30	475.59	487.34	473.64	499.07	486.63	....	Domestic Credit	**32**
35.33	35.46	34.34	30.43	24.81	-8.74	-34.49	-43.75	-45.81	-45.10	-41.54	-30.09	-9.72	-26.74	....	Claims on Central Govt. (Net)	**32an**
8.31	9.52	8.91	8.87	10.31	10.59	10.19	14.20	16.75	16.85	14.77	10.87	9.84	11.62	....	Claims on Local Government	**32b**
1.80	2.43	7.54	9.30	11.30	12.85	10.69	12.79	10.32	10.08	8.18	7.19	6.31	9.05	....	Claims on Nonfin.Pub.Enterprises	**32c**
96.99	112.37	127.66	145.97	184.71	241.66	309.37	378.80	406.56	442.00	462.33	442.02	448.01	457.77	....	Claims on Private Sector	**32d**
19.29	22.71	25.57	31.20	32.17	39.51	45.78	71.79	58.49	51.76	43.60	43.66	44.63	34.92	....	Claims on Other Financial Insts	**32f**
45.56	52.38	58.81	65.92	82.00	98.65	101.76	152.63	187.15	218.30	237.63	255.80	‡323.33	340.12	....	Money	**34**
109.17	122.88	135.79	149.72	174.99	196.82	200.12	207.11	190.30	191.50	195.07	189.48	‡160.02	139.99	....	Quasi-Money	**35**
23.56	29.94	40.63	39.94	57.22	55.49	72.82	91.82	71.96	64.02	60.87	63.17	96.80	129.66	....	Other Items (Net)	**37r**
154.73	175.26	194.60	215.63	256.99	295.47	301.88	359.74	377.45	409.79	432.70	445.28	‡483.35	480.11	....	Money plus Quasi-Money	**35l**
End of Period															**Money (National Definitions)**	
171.0	190.8	210.9	230.7	276.2	317.9	332.4	382.5	404.5	435.0	460.4	509.8	546.9	550.0	586.0	*Broad Money*	**38n**
167.8	187.0	206.4	225.6	270.5	312.2	327.7	378.5	400.9	431.8	457.4	505.7	535.9	538.0	580.0	*Broad Money, Seasonally Adj*	**38n.** *c*

Norway

		1965	1966	1967	1968	1969	1970	1971	1972	1973	1974	1975	1976	1977	1978	1979
Other Banking Institutions																
State Banks															*Billions of Kroner:*	
Claims on State and Local Govt	42b	....	....	....	....	....	....	....	....	....	....	....	....	10.22	13.51	19.21
Claims on Private Sector	42d	10.22	10.96	12.02	13.36	15.74	18.10	21.08	24.77	28.51	32.25	37.97	45.43	↕42.14	50.32	57.08
Bonds (Net)	46ab	.66	.62	.57	.62	.76	1.00	1.44	2.21	2.72	3.15	5.41	7.45	↕6.11	7.42	7.97
Foreign Liabilities	46c													5.84	10.29	16.19
Central Govt. Lending Funds	46f	9.01	9.84	10.95	12.30	14.24	16.27	18.85	21.91	25.11	28.52	32.12	37.11	↕43.21	49.02	55.50
Capital Accounts	47a	.83	.87	.92	.96	1.32	1.37	1.54	1.73	1.80	2.11	2.31	2.65	↕3.65	4.56	4.97
Other Items (Net)	47r	−.29	−.36	−.42	−.52	−.59	−.55	−.77	−1.10	−1.12	−1.53	−1.85	−1.77	↕−6.45	−7.46	−8.33
Credit Associations															*Billions of Kroner:*	
Foreign Assets	41..l	....	....	....	....	....	....	....	....	....	....	....	....	....	....	....
Claims on Central Government	42a.l	....	....	....	....	....	....	....	....	....	....	....	....	....	....	....
Claims on State and Local Govt.	42b.l	....	....	....	....	....	....	....	....	....	....	....	....	....	....	....
Claims on Nonfin.Pub.Enterprises	42c.l	....	....	....	....	....	....	....	....	....	....	....	....	....	....	....
Claims on Private Sector	42d.l	3.05	3.43	3.74	4.09	4.58	5.44	6.40	7.18	8.29	9.48	81.49	81.40	81.29	81.18	81.03
Credit Market Instruments	46aa.l	....	....	....	....	....	....	....	....	....	....	....	....	....	....	....
Bonds (net)	46ab.l	2.83	3.16	3.46	3.82	4.34	5.13	6.04	6.93	8.10	9.37	69.94	69.94	69.95	69.95	69.95
Foreign Liabilities	46c.l	....	....	....	....	....	....	....	....	....	....	....	....	....	....	....
Capital Accounts	47a.l	....	....	....	....	....	....	....	....	....	....	....	....	....	....	....
Other Items (Net)	47r.l	....	....	....	....	....	....	....	....	....	....	....	....	....	....	....
Nonbank Financial Institutions															*Billions of Kroner:*	
Claims on Central Government	42a.s	1.82	1.79	1.74	1.72	1.71	1.72	1.73	1.74	1.78	1.79	1.76	1.75	1.53	2.69	4.30
Claims on Local Government	42b.s	.62	.66	.70	1.19	1.31	1.42	1.51	1.72	1.88	2.17	2.47	2.82	3.06	3.24	3.34
Claims on Private Sector	42d.s	4.47	4.97	5.37	5.33	5.87	6.38	6.89	7.39	8.02	8.76	9.62	10.66	11.56	12.03	12.58
Claims on Other Financial Insts.	42f.s	.73	.86	.99	1.11	1.23	1.40	1.61	1.89	2.23	2.56	3.05	3.80	5.27	5.81	6.37
Incr.in Total Assets(Within Per.)	49z.s	.65	.63	.53	.58	.77	.83	.85	1.01	1.19	1.41	1.64	2.22	2.39	2.89	3.00
Interest Rates															*Percent Per Annum*	
Discount Rate *(End of Period)*	60	3.50	3.50	3.50	3.50	4.50	4.50	4.50	4.50	4.50	5.50	5.00	6.00	6.00	7.00	9.00
Avg.Cost for Centr.Bank Funding	60.a	....	....	....	....	....	....	....	....	....	....	....	....	....	....	....
Deposit Rate	60l	....	....	....	....	....	....	....	....	....	....	....	....	....	....	5.10
Lending Rate	60p	....	....	....	....	....	....	....	....	....	....	....	....	....	....	12.23
Three Month Interbank Rate	60zb	....	....	....	....	....	....	....	....	....	....	....	....	....	....	....
Government Bond Yield	61	4.99	5.00	5.00	4.94	5.12	6.29	6.40	6.27	6.19	7.10	7.29	7.25	7.39	8.45	8.59
Prices, Production, Employment															*Index Numbers (1990=100):*	
Industrial Share Prices	62	13	11	10	10	13	15	15	14	22	20	14	13	12	10	14
Prices: Home & Import Goods	63	21.8	22.1	22.5	22.8	23.5	25.1	26.4	27.2	29.3	34.7	38.0	41.0	43.6	45.7	49.6
Consumer Prices	64	16.9	17.4	18.2	18.8	19.4	21.4	22.8	24.4	26.2	28.7	32.1	35.0	38.2	41.3	43.2
Wages: Hourly Earnings	65	9.5	10.2	↕11.0	11.9	13.0	14.6	16.4	17.9	19.7	23.1	↕27.7	32.0	35.6	38.4	39.6
Industrial Production	66..c	29.7	31.0	32.0	33.4	35.5	36.9	↕38.4	41.3	43.7	45.6	48.0	50.9	50.4	55.7	60.0
Crude Petroleum Production	66aa	....	....	....	....	....	—	.4	2.0	1.9	2.1	11.3	16.7	16.7	20.9	23.0
Manufacturing Employment	67ey	120.2	↕122.4	122.8	122.1	123.1	125.2	126.2	126.9	127.1	130.1	128.4	128.9	128.2	125.7	123.0
Freight Rates: Tramps Voyage	68a	50.4	43.8	46.9	46.0	42.5	59.9	40.4	37.1	80.5	108.6	70.8	66.9	66.2	69.8	89.4
International Transactions															*Millions of Kroner*	
Exports	70	10,309	11,168	12,411	13,841	15,741	17,549	18,003	21,625	27,085	34,732	37,922	43,330	47,263	57,084	68,527
Imports, cif	71	15,787	17,169	19,627	19,331	21,011	26,443	28,714	28,808	36,041	46,556	50,545	60,533	68,579	60,169	69,339
Imports, fob	71.v	15,357	16,701	19,098	18,759	20,418	25,743	28,030	28,035	34,997	45,565	49,043	59,037	66,890	58,675	67,711
															1990=100	
Volume of Exports	72	21.8	23.7	25.3	28.4	31.5	↕33.0	34.0	38.0	41.9	41.6	43.3	49.9	48.2	59.4	62.7
Volume of Imports	73	30.0	33.7	36.5	39.0	44.5	↕50.2	50.7	50.7	57.2	62.2	62.2	69.2	74.7	66.2	69.7
Unit Value of Exports	74	26.3	26.5	26.1	25.4	25.9	↕28.3	29.4	29.1	31.9	41.8	45.5	46.6	49.7	52.6	61.6
Unit Value of Imports	75	28.8	28.8	28.6	28.0	28.5	↕30.7	32.2	32.5	34.7	43.6	46.3	49.4	53.4	56.1	62.0
Balance of Payments															*Millions of US Dollars:*	
Goods: Exports f.o.b.	78aa d	....	....	....	....	....	....	....	....	....	....	7,270	8,047	9,152	11,033	13,747
Goods: Imports f.o.b.	78ab d	....	....	....	....	....	....	....	....	....	....	−10,141	−11,608	−13,205	−11,545	−13,601
Trade Balance	78ac d	....	....	....	....	....	....	....	....	....	....	−2,871	−3,561	−4,053	−512	146
Services: Credit	78ad d	....	....	....	....	....	....	....	....	....	....	4,542	4,779	5,109	5,582	7,054
Services: Debit	78ae d	....	....	....	....	....	....	....	....	....	....	−3,641	−4,228	−4,918	−5,437	−5,977
Balance on Goods and Services	78af d	....	....	....	....	....	....	....	....	....	....	−1,969	−3,010	−3,862	−367	1,223
Income: Credit	78ag d	....	....	....	....	....	....	....	....	....	....	313	288	304	407	597
Income: Debit	78ah d	....	....	....	....	....	....	....	....	....	....	−662	−826	−1,181	−1,775	−2,427
Balance on Goods, Serv., & Inc.	78ai d	....	....	....	....	....	....	....	....	....	....	−2,319	−3,548	−4,740	−1,734	−607
Current Transfers, n.i.e.: Credit	78aj d	....	....	....	....	....	....	....	....	....	....	101	97	50	55	63
Current Transfers: Debit	78ak d	....	....	....	....	....	....	....	....	....	....	−260	−295	−363	−438	−504
Current Account, n.i.e.	78al d	....	....	....	....	....	....	....	....	....	....	−2,478	−3,746	−5,053	−2,118	−1,047
Capital Account, n.i.e.: Credit	78ba d	....	....	....	....	....	....	....	....	....	....	—	—	52	51	54
Capital Account: Debit	78bb d	....	....	....	....	....	....	....	....	....	....	—	—	−33	−36	−50
Capital Account, n.i.e.	78bc d	....	....	....	....	....	....	....	....	....	....	—	—	19	15	3
Direct Investment Abroad	78bd d	....	....	....	....	....	....	....	....	....	....	−172	−193	−125	−66	−44
Dir. Invest. in Rep. Econ., n.i.e.	78be d	....	....	....	....	....	....	....	....	....	....	220	371	768	490	401
Portfolio Investment Assets	78bf d	....	....	....	....	....	....	....	....	....	....	2	−17	5	—	−14
Portfolio Investment Liab., n.i.e.	78bg d	....	....	....	....	....	....	....	....	....	....	610	1,346	2,062	2,458	2,066
Other Investment Assets	78bh d	....	....	....	....	....	....	....	....	....	....	−328	−93	−572	−890	−1,590
Other Investment Liab., n.i.e.	78bi d	....	....	....	....	....	....	....	....	....	....	2,285	2,084	2,383	221	908
Financial Account, n.i.e.	78bj d	....	....	....	....	....	....	....	....	....	....	2,618	3,499	4,521	2,213	1,727
Net Errors and Omissions	78ca d	....	....	....	....	....	....	....	....	....	....	201	219	391	527	601
Overall Balance	78cb d	....	....	....	....	....	....	....	....	....	....	340	−28	−121	637	1,285
Reserves and Related Items	79da d	....	....	....	....	....	....	....	....	....	....	−340	28	121	−637	−1,285
Reserve Assets	79db d	....	....	....	....	....	....	....	....	....	....	−340	28	121	−637	−1,285
Use of Fund Credit and Loans	79dc d	....	....	....	....	....	....	....	....	....	....	—	—	—	—	—
Liabs.Constit.For.Auth.Reserves	79dd d	....	....	....	....	....	....	....	....	....	....	—	—	—	—	—
Exceptional Financing	79de d	....	....	....	....	....	....	....	....	....	....	—	—	—	—	—

Norway 142

1980	1981	1982	1983	1984	1985	1986	1987	1988	1989	1990	1991	1992	1993	1994		
															Other Banking Institutions	
															State Banks	
End of Period																
22.05	23.77	16.69	18.01	19.14	20.18	21.61	23.21	24.90	26.71	27.82	30.79	33.41	34.53	35.40	Claims on State and Local Govt	42b
63.97	70.60	77.05	82.01	89.26	94.13	100.11	107.43	115.53	123.46	131.54	140.95	149.31	145.34	140.71	Claims on Private Sector	42d
8.89	10.48	12.03	11.96	12.71	13.05	12.61	12.82	13.44	14.71	18.72	18.32	20.81	21.39	16.68	Bonds (Net)	46ab
16.68	16.67	18.41	17.97	17.28	15.77	16.64	15.20	13.21	11.09	8.23	6.41	5.27	3.69	1.81	Foreign Liabilities	46c
62.66	67.73	73.77	79.72	87.52	93.87	101.28	112.21	122.54	133.06	140.88	152.07	162.13	160.22	156.44	Central Govt. Lending Funds	46f
5.97	6.58	7.07	7.29	8.06	8.26	8.15	8.04	7.74	8.27	7.87	8.10	9.00	12.23	10.35	Capital Accounts	47a
−8.17	−7.09	−17.54	−16.92	−17.18	−16.64	−16.97	−17.64	−16.48	−16.94	−16.33	−13.15	−14.50	−17.66	−9.11	Other Items (Net)	47r
															Credit Associations	
End of Period																
....	....	....	....	....	....	....	....	I21.49	19.88	20.44	21.92	23.61	19.67	23.95	Foreign Assets	41.. l
....	....	....	....	....	....	....	....	I2.00	1.01	.85	1.05	1.37	2.85	1.48	Claims on Central Government	42a. l
....	....	....	....	....	....	....	....	I3.12	4.56	4.32	3.18	1.82	2.00	1.91	Claims on State and Local Govt	42b. l
....	....	....	....	....	....	....	....	I3.57	3.77	4.00	3.38	2.11	1.65	1.32	Claims on Nonfin.Pub.Enterprises	42c. l
81.11	80.94	80.83	80.62	80.89	81.31	85.61	123.65	I121.50	136.96	138.74	117.00	80.73	72.15	62.34	Claims on Private Sector	42d. l
								I9.24	6.08	5.74	6.67	3.77	5.45	6.97	Credit Market Instruments	46aa l
69.95	69.82	69.94	69.98	69.98	69.98	69.98	87.29	I94.01	115.24	114.40	100.25	55.87	42.16	35.01	Bonds (net)	46ab l
....	....	....	....	....	....	....	....	I23.13	28.23	37.41	37.02	35.91	39.40	39.04	Foreign Liabilities	46c. l
....	....	....	....	....	....	....	....	I4.60	5.39	5.62	4.03	6.38	8.00	7.76	Capital Accounts	47a. l
....	....	....	....	....	....	....	....	I20.69	11.24	5.16	−1.46	7.72	3.30	2.23	Other Items (Net)	47r. l
															Nonbank Financial Institutions	
End of Period																
5.34	4.74	5.01	6.46	7.62	9.37	10.92	7.15	3.86	6.38	5.55	12.53	18.16	32.36	40.47	Claims on Central Government	42a. s
4.04	5.37	6.89	8.73	9.74	11.15	12.99	14.79	18.85	23.00	29.23	28.97	30.54	31.29	32.27	Claims on Local Government	42b. s
13.61	15.32	17.13	19.79	23.16	28.04	35.86	43.57	45.88	45.81	48.10	63.10	73.54	75.78	65.71	Claims on Private Sector	42d. s
7.27	9.10	11.08	12.79	14.59	16.83	21.24	28.33	38.01	44.73	44.43	32.75	28.44	24.30	28.05	Claims on Other Financial Insts.	42f. s
3.93	5.04	6.10	7.14	8.89	11.85	13.64	12.78	12.80	14.56	8.87	9.08	12.61	14.67	7.94	*Incr.in Total Assets(Within Per.)*	49z. s
															Interest Rates	
Percent Per Annum																
9.00	9.00	I9.20	10.00	10.20	10.70	14.80	13.80	12.00	11.00	10.50	10.00	11.00	7.00	6.75	Discount Rate *(End of Period)*	60
								14.28	11.50	11.85	10.93	7.65	5.70	6.46	Avg.Cost for Centr.Bank Funding	60.a
5.00	5.10	5.10	5.30	5.30	10.06	10.97	12.03	11.49	9.63	9.68	9.60	10.69	5.51	5.21	Deposit Rate	60l
12.63	13.90	14.33	14.35	13.69	13.46	14.37	16.31	16.44	14.39	14.15	14.19	14.27	9.17		Lending Rate	60p
....	....	15.37	13.30	13.02	12.53	14.39	14.70	13.51	11.39	11.54	10.56	11.83	7.27	5.85	Three Month Interbank Rate	60zb
10.27	12.31	13.20	12.86	12.16	12.58	13.47	13.56	12.97	10.84	10.72	9.87	9.78	6.52	7.13	Government Bond Yield	61
															Prices, Production, Employment	
Period Averages																
17	16	I15	24	34	45	47	58	50	81	100	93	87	111	143	Industrial Share Prices	62
57.0	I63.4	67.4	71.5	75.9	79.7	81.9	86.8	91.4	96.5	100.0	102.6	102.5	102.5	104.0	Prices: Home & Import Goods	63
47.9	54.5	60.7	65.8	69.9	73.9	79.2	86.1	91.9	96.0	100.0	103.4	105.8	108.2	109.8	Consumer Prices	64
43.3	47.8	52.5	57.0	61.8	66.9	73.7	85.6	90.1	94.5	100.0	105.1	108.5	....	....	Wages: Hourly Earnings	65
I63.9	65.4	64.8	71.0	76.7	79.1	81.9	87.3	89.5	98.4	100.0	102.0	108.5	112.7	121.3	Industrial Production	66.. c
29.8	28.8	30.0	37.4	42.8	46.9	51.8	60.8	69.2	91.5	100.0	114.0	130.4	139.8	158.0	Crude Petroleum Production	66aa
121.6	119.2	115.2	108.2	107.2	113.9	119.0	113.5	108.8	102.5	100.0	95.0	95.3	....	....	Manufacturing Employment	67ey
106.3	97.5	79.2	84.9	86.0	83.4	78.6	86.6	96.9	101.9	100.0	102.2	96.5	97.6	....	Freight Rates: Tramps Voyage	68a
															International Transactions	
Millions of Kroner																
91,672	104,265	113,236	131,397	154,035	170,733	133,847	144,543	146,166	187,146	211,579	220,316	218,474	225,714	243,809	Exports	70
83,602	89,688	99,747	98,408	113,102	132,563	150,052	152,041	151,101	163,380	169,998	165,181	160,821	170,069	192,073	Imports, cif	71
81,846	87,757	97,750	95,828	110,271	129,235	146,250	148,188	146,860	158,700	162,885	157,417	156,746	165,759	187,206	Imports, fob	71.v
1990=100																
I66.4	I65.0	65.9	70.7	77.2	79.7	76.4	82.9	81.3	93.5	100.0	106.5	115.4	121.3	....	Volume of Exports	72
I77.3	74.2	77.3	74.2	84.2	94.2	108.2	I106.2	95.7	90.9	100.0	102.4	106.2	106.7	....	Volume of Imports	73
I80.2	93.1	99.5	102.9	113.1	117.6	88.3	I85.3	85.5	95.7	100.0	95.7	88.0	88.5	....	Unit Value of Exports	74
I69.6	74.5	78.0	81.6	83.2	88.6	88.4	I90.9	93.7	99.3	100.0	98.4	96.5	97.2	....	Unit Value of Imports	75
															Balance of Payments	
Minus Sign Indicates Debit																
18,649	18,494	17,664	18,055	19,115	20,059	18,143	21,191	23,075	27,171	34,313	34,212	35,162	31,989	34,922	Goods: Exports f.o.b.	78aa d
−16,753	−15,459	−15,278	−13,704	−13,957	−15,331	−20,257	−21,951	−23,284	−23,401	−26,552	−25,516	−25,860	−23,995	−26,601	Goods: Imports f.o.b.	78ab d
1,896	3,035	2,386	4,351	5,158	4,728	−2,115	−759	−209	3,770	7,761	8,696	9,303	7,995	8,321	Trade Balance	78ac d
8,615	8,753	7,927	7,109	7,097	7,456	8,142	8,545	9,729	10,770	12,765	13,330	13,642	12,744	13,105	Services: Credit	78ad d
−6,996	−7,283	−7,132	−7,148	−7,253	−7,515	−8,608	−9,623	−10,270	−10,623	−12,358	−12,701	−14,789	−13,848	−14,392	Services: Debit	78ae d
3,516	4,505	3,181	4,312	5,002	4,670	−2,581	−1,837	−750	3,916	8,168	9,326	8,156	6,890	7,034	Balance on Goods and Services	78af d
988	1,443	1,629	1,378	1,616	2,099	2,723	3,039	3,265	3,425	3,896	3,540	3,040	2,448	2,810	Income: Credit	78ag d
−2,909	−3,286	−3,587	−3,125	−3,193	−3,152	−3,883	−4,325	−5,274	−5,995	−6,596	−6,293	−6,457	−5,785	−4,579	Income: Debit	78ah d
1,594	2,662	1,223	2,565	3,425	3,617	−3,741	−3,122	−2,759	1,346	5,468	6,573	4,739	3,553	5,265	Balance on Goods, Serv., & Inc.	78ai d
78	75	98	97	87	85	95	123	168	164	217	239	287	319	266	Current Transfers, n.i.e.: Credit	78aj d
−593	−606	−682	−699	−626	−664	−906	−1,103	−1,305	−1,299	−1,693	−1,780	−2,044	−1,720	−1,886	Current Transfers: Debit	78ak d
1,079	2,131	640	1,962	2,886	3,038	−4,551	−4,102	−3,896	212	3,992	5,032	2,982	2,152	3,645	Current Account, n.i.e.	78al d
76	102	80	79	78	81	81	104	107	101	109	118	143	180	76	Capital Account, n.i.e.: Credit	78ba d
−56	−56	−58	−55	−45	−67	−76	−106	−99	−99	−78	−101	−164	−165	−94	Capital Account: Debit	78bb d
19	45	23	24	33	14	6	−2	8	2	31	17	−21	14	−19	Capital Account, n.i.e.	78bc d
−253	−173	−306	−355	−601	−1,304	−1,600	−873	−978	−1,358	−1,470	−1,782	−411	−877	−1,628	Direct Investment Abroad	78bd d
60	672	442	328	−180	−426	1,017	187	279	1,519	1,003	−398	716	2,003	623	Dir. Invest. in Rep. Econ., n.i.e.	78be d
−88	15	11	−33	143	126	−373	−1,009	−392	−563	−987	−2,523	−192	853	750	Portfolio Investment Assets	78bf d
−54	−714	−679	−867	667	1,650	4,656	3,292	4,618	3,606	1,548	−585	1,054	−1,188	−599	Portfolio Investment Liab., n.i.e.	78bg d
−1,777	−1,707	−1,942	−1,279	−949	−790	−2,341	−1,171	643	−274	−1,502	−326	−1,068	2,146	1,501	Other Investment Assets	78bh d
1,980	176	2,620	−249	1,408	2,204	1,602	4,808	730	−874	648	−1,968	−474	344	−1,968	Other Investment Liab., n.i.e.	78bi d
−133	−1,732	148	−2,455	488	1,459	2,961	5,233	4,900	2,056	−761	−7,581	−375	3,280	−1,321	Financial Account, n.i.e.	78bj d
917	−14	−102	370	−340	−1,059	−1,626	−1,349	−1,149	−1,305	−2,848	−219	−3,442	−1,309	−854	Net Errors and Omissions	78ca d
1,882	431	708	−98	3,068	3,452	−3,211	−220	−138	965	414	2,751	−855	4,138	1,451	Overall Balance	78cb d
−1,882	−431	−708	98	−3,068	−3,452	3,211	220	138	−965	−414	−2,751	855	−4,138	−1,451	Reserves and Related Items	79da d
−1,882	−431	−708	98	−3,068	−3,452	3,211	220	138	−965	−414	−2,751	855	−4,138	−1,451	Reserve Assets	79db d
—	—	—	—	—	—	—	—	—	—	—	—	—	—	—	Use of Fund Credit and Loans	79dc d
—	—	—	—	—	—	—	—	—	—	—	—	—	—	—	Liabs.Constit.For.Auth.Reserves	79dd d
—	—	—	—	—	—	—	—	—	—	—	—	—	—	—	Exceptional Financing	79de d

Norway

142

		1965	1966	1967	1968	1969	1970	1971	1972	1973	1974	1975	1976	1977	1978	1979
Government Finance																*Millions of Kroner:*
Deficit (–) or Surplus	80	–859	–432	–715	–1,295	–1,727	–2,491	–2,331	ℐ–1,438	–1,026	–1,761	–4,716	–10,005	–13,133	–14,472	–14,994
Revenue	81	9,852	10,893	12,164	13,064	14,854	17,203	20,597	ℐ35,992	41,305	47,165	53,648	63,842	73,155	81,596	91,919
Grants Received	81z	....	....	....	....	....	....	....	ℐ1,333	1,605	1,861	2,086	2,281	700	1,092	965
Expenditure	82	9,650	10,400	11,712	12,929	14,718	17,549	20,385	ℐ34,086	38,392	44,554	52,113	63,936	73,354	84,824	93,364
Lending Minus Repayments	83	1,061	925	1,167	1,430	1,863	2,145	2,543	ℐ4,677	5,544	6,233	8,337	12,192	13,634	12,336	14,514
Financing																
Net Borrowing: Domestic	84a	....	....	....	....	....	....	....	ℐ1,499	1,358	1,876	324	5,865	6,178	3,232	10,259
Foreign	85a	....	....	....	....	....	....	....	ℐ–61	–332	–115	4,392	4,140	6,955	11,240	4,735
Unallocable Financing	87c	....	....	....	....	....	....	....	ℐ—	—	—	—	—	—	—	—
Debt: Domestic	88a	....	....	....	....	....	....	ℐ23,007	26,038	28,658	31,004	32,581	37,763	46,681	53,992	68,407
Foreign	89a	....	....	....	....	....	....	ℐ1,684	1,621	1,290	1,179	5,587	9,708	16,666	27,923	32,125
Financing (by Currency)																
Net Borrowing: Kroner	84b	469	615	1,740	1,032	1,847	3,346	3,269	....	....	....	....	....	....	....	....
Foreign Currency	85b	104	152	–59	–102	–672	–149	–161	....	....	....	....	....	....	....	....
Use of Cash Balances	87	286	–335	–966	365	552	–706	–777	....	....	....	....	....	....	....	....
Debt: Kroner	88b	8,631	9,174	11,421	11,923	13,687	16,892	....	....	....	....	....	....	....	....	....
Foreign Currency	89b	2,817	2,969	2,900	2,798	2,137	1,987	....	....	....	....	....	....	....	....	....
National Accounts																*Billions of Kroner*
Exports of Goods & Services	90c	20.57	22.26	25.02	27.49	29.37	33.40	35.81	40.05	48.73	60.01	62.19	70.17	76.26	87.22	105.41
Government Consumption	91f	7.61	8.44	9.62	10.56	11.67	13.53	15.98	17.86	20.39	23.76	28.70	34.09	38.62	43.54	46.59
Gross Fixed Capital Formation	93e	14.27	15.63	17.70	17.12	16.87	21.19	26.45	27.30	32.75	39.60	50.79	62.00	71.07	67.71	66.19
Increase/Decrease(–) in Stocks	93i	.84	1.00	.57	–.40	.15	3.13	1.71	–.08	.97	4.02	1.54	1.38	–1.58	–6.94	–.46
Private Consumption	96f	28.30	30.33	32.92	35.18	39.22	43.05	47.90	52.56	58.29	66.11	77.62	89.49	103.92	110.67	120.10
Imports of Goods & Services	98c	–21.02	–23.08	–26.12	–26.21	–27.86	–34.43	–38.74	–39.29	–49.27	–63.78	–72.14	–86.41	–96.77	–89.12	–99.15
Gross Domestic Product	99b	50.56	54.57	59.70	63.75	69.42	79.88	89.11	98.41	111.85	129.73	148.70	170.71	191.53	213.08	238.67
Net Factor Inc/Pmts(–) Abroad	98.n	–.56	–.63	–.70	–.68	–.57	–.62	–.75	–1.03	–1.19	–1.85	–1.92	–3.05	–4.73	–7.18	–9.33
Gross Nat'l Expenditure = GNP	99a	55.83	60.84	66.54	71.93	77.84	89.70	88.36	97.38	110.67	127.88	146.79	167.66	186.80	205.90	229.34
Nat'l Income, Market Prices	99e	43.90	47.27	51.29	55.03	59.90	68.85	76.72	84.92	95.40	109.18	125.70	141.38	155.74	171.30	129.26
Gross Dom. Prod. 1990 Prices	99b.p	271.04	ℐ281.30	298.91	305.66	319.43	325.81	340.73	358.34	373.08	392.44	408.80	436.65	452.27	473.34	497.32
GDP Deflator (1990=100)	99bi p	18.7	19.4	20.0	20.9	21.7	24.5	26.2	27.5	30.0	33.1	36.4	39.1	42.3	45.0	48.0
																Millions:
Population	99z	3.72	3.75	3.79	3.82	3.85	3.88	3.90	3.93	3.96	3.99	4.01	4.03	4.04	4.06	4.07

Deposit Money Banks: ℐ Prior to December 1992, the Post Office Savings Bank and the Postal Giro reported only aggregate deposits to the authorities who split them into demand and time deposits on the basis of estimated shares. Beginning in December 1992, separate data on demand and time deposits are reported to the authorities. This change affects the composition of money supply in the Monetary Survey.

Monetary Survey: ℐ Beginning in 1976, data for the Bank of Norway, deposit money banks, and state banks are based upon improved sectorization in national source data.

Other Banking Institutions: ℐ Beginning in 1988, data for credit associations are based on a more detailed reporting of accounts.

Government Finance: ℐ Data differ from source A in which government long-term borrowing transactions are included in the measure of the deficit or surplus as revenue and expenditure elements, while, in *IFS* data, total net domestic borrowing and total net foreign borrowing are reported separately as financing transactions. ℐ Beginning in 1972 (except for debt data beginning in 1971), data are as reported in the *Government Finance Statistics Yearbook* and relate to the consolidated central government.

Norway

142

	1980	1981	1982	1983	1984	1985	1986	1987	1988	1989	1990	1991	1992	1993	1994		
Government Finance																	
Year Ending December 31																	
Deficit (-) or Surplus	−5,400	6,817	3,894	9,443	8,963	18,279	17,317	318	−924	−7,625	4,633	....	....	....	....	80
Revenue	116,849	140,094	153,404	176,023	193,630	222,953	245,009	255,607	267,702	278,000	307,083	....	....	....	....	81
Grants Received	998	1,186	1,376	1,529	1,559	1,531	899	1,622	4,781	6,347	5,674	....	....	....	....	81z
Expenditure	108,111	123,585	139,064	154,340	168,126	184,112	205,178	230,000	252,101	273,663	298,647	....	....	....	....	82
Lending Minus Repayments	15,136	10,878	11,822	13,769	18,100	22,093	23,413	26,911	21,306	18,309	9,477	....	....	....	....	83
Financing																	
Net Borrowing: Domestic	7,623	−3,171	711	2,744	−4,191	−20,110	−23,710	1,525	−10,011	5,871	−4,234	....	....	....	....	84a
Foreign	−2,223	−3,646	−4,605	−12,187	−4,535	1,831	6,393	−1,843	10,935	1,754	−399	....	....	....	....	85a
Unallocable Financing	—	—	—	—	−237	—	—	—	—	—	—	....	....	....	....	87c
Debt: Domestic	75,490	78,931	74,729	86,386	105,252	129,625	173,281	142,732	131,287	135,689	123,454	....	....	....	....	88a
Foreign	29,886	26,233	21,629	9,440	4,853	6,650	12,949	11,148	22,113	23,881	23,383	....	....	....	....	89a
Financing (by Currency)																	
Net Borrowing: Kroner	....	....	....	....	....	....	....	....	....	....	....	....	....	....	....	84b
Foreign Currency	....	....	....	....	....	....	....	....	....	....	....	....	....	....	....	85b
Use of Cash Balances	....	....	....	....	....	....	....	....	....	....	....	....	....	....	....	87
Debt: Kroner	....	....	....	....	....	....	....	....	....	....	....	....	....	....	....	88b
Foreign Currency	....	....	....	....	....	....	....	....	....	....	....	....	....	....	....	89b
National Accounts																	
Billions of Kroner																	
Exports of Goods & Services	134.80	156.29	165.02	183.92	214.08	235.56	194.66	200.22	213.67	261.86	293.01	307.53	303.16	316.82	335.67	90c
Government Consumption	53.48	62.62	70.41	78.21	84.10	92.65	101.58	116.04	122.24	131.00	139.12	147.48	157.22	161.78	169.53	91f
Gross Fixed Capital Formation	70.80	91.79	92.26	103.45	117.57	110.04	145.54	157.36	170.34	169.49	124.15	127.05	135.25	161.15	141.80	93e
Increase/Decrease(-) in Stocks	8.10	−7.76	3.81	−4.33	−1.30	11.10	6.07	1.22	−12.52	−18.33	11.06	2.02	−5.78	−18.24	11.17	93i
Private Consumption	135.24	155.21	175.31	192.98	210.92	245.44	278.91	298.05	307.50	311.95	336.06	349.70	365.15	380.46	402.66	96f
Imports of Goods & Services	−117.37	−130.47	−144.54	−152.03	−172.85	−194.60	−213.04	−211.43	−217.96	−234.59	−242.85	−247.10	−252.04	−267.49	−286.58	98c
Gross Domestic Product	285.04	327.67	362.27	402.20	452.51	500.20	513.72	561.48	583.28	621.38	660.55	686.68	702.95	734.49	774.24	99b
Net Factor Inc/Pmts(-) Abroad	−9.52	−10.58	−12.70	−13.00	−13.14	−9.51	−9.09	−9.55	−13.54	−17.84	−17.18	−17.52	−22.04	−24.35	−12.08	98.n
Gross Nat'l Expenditure = GNP	275.53	317.10	349.56	389.20	439.37	490.69	504.63	551.93	569.74	603.54	643.37	669.16	680.91	710.14	762.16	99a
Nat'l Income, Market Prices	234.17	269.04	294.56	329.58	376.86	424.18	432.07	468.63	478.54	506.86	544.55	566.70	576.72	601.11	650.53	99e
Gross Dom. Prod. 1990 Prices	518.24	522.79	524.53	548.84	580.36	610.97	636.51	649.19	645.90	649.73	660.55	670.98	693.60	710.38	746.89	99b.p
GDP Deflator (1990=100)	55.0	62.7	69.1	73.3	78.0	81.9	80.7	86.5	90.3	95.6	100.0	102.3	101.3	103.4	103.7	99bi p
Midyear Estimates																	
Population	4.09	4.10	4.11	4.13	4.14	4.15	4.17	4.19	4.21	4.23	4.24	4.24	4.29	4.31	....	99z

Oman

449

		1965	1966	1967	1968	1969	1970	1971	1972	1973	1974	1975	1976	1977	1978	1979
Exchange Rates															*Rials Omani per SDR: End of Period (aa)*		
Official Rate	aa	.3571	.3571	.4167	.4167	.4167	.4167	.4167	.4167	.4167	.4229	.4043	.4013	.4196	.4500	.4550
Official Rate	ae	.3571	.3571	.4167	.4167	.4167	.4167	.3838	.3838	.3454	.3454	.3454	.3454	.3454	.3454	.3454
														Index Numbers (1990=100):		
Official Rate	ah x	107.7	107.7	105.9	92.3	92.3	92.3	83.1	100.2	109.8	111.3	111.3	111.3	111.3	111.3	111.3
Nominal Effective Exchange Rate	ne c	....	....	....	....	....	....	....	....	....	....	....	....	....	....	114.9
Fund Position														*Millions of SDRs:*		
Quota	2f. s	....	....	....	....	....	....	7.0	7.0	7.0	7.0	7.0	7.0	7.0	20.0	20.0
SDRs	1b. s	....	....	....	....	....	....	—	.7	.7	.7	.7	.7	.7	.7	2.8
Reserve Position in the Fund	1c. s	....	....	....	....	....	....	1.8	1.8	1.8	15.3	24.4	25.0	19.4	13.9	12.8
of which: Outstg.Fund Borrowing	2c	....	....	....	....	....	....	—	—	—	11.6	19.7	20.2	16.4	11.0	8.3
International Liquidity												*Millions of US Dollars Unless Otherwise Indicated:*				
Total Reserves minus Gold	1l. d	....	....	....	....	....	10.3	24.4	36.4	47.1	92.9	161.3	219.6	289.6	254.1	415.6
SDRs	1b. d	....	....	....	....	....	....	—	.8	.9	.9	.9	.9	.9	1.0	3.7
Reserve Position in the Fund	1c. d	....	....	....	....	....	....	1.9	1.9	2.1	18.8	28.6	29.1	23.6	18.2	16.8
Foreign Exchange	1d. d	....	....	....	....	....	10.3	22.5	33.7	44.1	73.3	131.9	189.7	265.1	234.9	395.1
Gold (Million Fine Troy Ounces)	1ad	....	....	....	....	....	.064	.014	.014	.014	.030	.030	.046	.101	.186	.187
Gold (National Valuation)	1and	....	....	....	....	—	.5	.5	.5	.6	3.3	2.9	4.5	12.5	27.6	27.7
Monetary Authorities: Other Assets	3.. d	....	....	....	....	....	....	—	—	—	—	....	....	....	....	....
Other Liab.	4.. d	....	....	....	....	....	....	—	—	—	—	2.8	22.5	24.4	105.3	30.8
Deposit Money Banks: Assets	7a. d	....	....	....	....	....	....	....	58.1	42.8	65.4	66.6	44.3	96.4	106.5	196.4
of which: Claims on Nonbanks	7add	....	....	....	....	....	....	....	....	....	....	24.4	14.8	25.9	27.8	40.3
Deposit Money Banks: Liabilities	7b. d	....	....	....	....	....	....	....	13.8	9.3	163.0	208.5	260.6	195.7	200.9	230.2
of which: Liab. to Nonbanks	7bd d	....	....	....	....	....	....	....	....	....	....	60.7	46.4	55.9	49.0	22.6
Monetary Authorities													*Millions of Rials Omani:*			
Foreign Assets	11	....	....	....	....	....	....	4.5	9.5	14.2	17.0	34.6	56.7	76.8	105.5	97.3	153.3
Claims on Central Government	12a	....	....	....	....	....	....	—	—	—	—	—	7.1	18.4	8.4	49.3	.2
Reserve Money	14	....	....	....	....	....	....	5.1	9.4	13.9	16.3	31.9	49.0	64.3	80.0	88.5	109.7
of which: Currency Outside DMBs	14a	....	....	....	....	....	....	....	....	12.3	15.2	28.9	38.5	47.8	55.1	64.4	74.3
Foreign Liabilities	16c	....	....	....	....	....	....	....	....	—	—	—	1.0	7.8	8.4	36.4	10.7
Central Government Deposits	16d	....	....	....	....	....	....	....	....	—	—	—	8.6	11.3	12.1	2.8	5.3
Capital Accounts	17a	....	....	....	....	....	....	.1	.3	.5	1.3	1.2	7.6	7.9	14.8	19.5	28.5
Other Items (Net)	17r	....	....	....	....	....	....	-.6	-.3	-.2	-.6	1.5	-2.4	3.8	-1.5	-.6	-.6
Deposit Money Banks													*Millions of Rials Omani:*			
Reserves	20	....	....	....	....	....	....	....	....	1.6	1.1	3.0	10.6	16.7	25.6	24.2	32.3
Foreign Assets	21	....	....	....	....	....	....	....	....	22.3	14.8	22.6	23.0	15.3	33.3	36.8	167.8
Claims on Central Government	22a	....	....	....	....	....	....	....	....	7.2	6.6	55.6	62.1	89.5	56.0	20.6	4.0
Claims on Private Sector	22d	....	....	....	....	....	....	....	....	6.6	18.9	65.8	86.0	120.2	167.1	198.4	222.6
Demand Deposits	24	....	....	....	....	....	....	....	....	6.7	9.8	19.5	33.1	54.4	56.2	49.9	48.9
Quasi-Monetary Deposits	25	....	....	....	....	....	....	....	....	25.8	21.7	36.8	46.3	62.5	95.3	116.3	123.1
Foreign Liabilities	26c	....	....	....	....	....	....	....	....	5.3	3.2	56.3	72.0	90.0	67.6	69.4	179.5
Central Government Deposits	26d	....	....	....	....	....	....	....	....	.4	3.1	15.6	24.9	28.0	59.4	39.7	62.8
Capital Accounts	27a	....	....	....	....	....	....	....	....	....	....	....	4.2	6.3	8.9	10.8	13.7
Other Items (Net)	27r	....	....	....	....	....	....	....	....	-.3	3.7	19.7	1.1	.6	-5.5	-6.2	-1.3
Monetary Survey													*Millions of Rials Omani:*			
Foreign Assets (Net)	31n	....	....	....	....	....	....	....	....	31.2	28.6	.9	6.8	-5.7	62.8	28.3	131.0
Domestic Credit	32	....	....	....	....	....	....	....	....	13.5	22.3	106.7	121.6	188.7	159.9	225.8	158.7
Claims on Central Govt. (Net)	32an	....	....	....	....	....	....	....	....	6.8	3.5	40.9	35.6	68.5	-7.2	27.4	-63.9
Claims on Private Sector	32d	....	....	....	....	....	....	....	....	6.6	18.9	65.8	86.0	120.2	167.1	198.4	222.6
Money	34	....	....	....	....	....	....	....	....	19.0	24.9	48.4	71.6	102.1	111.2	114.3	123.1
Quasi-Money	35	....	....	....	....	....	....	....	....	25.8	21.7	36.8	46.3	62.5	95.3	116.3	123.1
Other Items (Net)	37r	....	....	....	....	....	....	....	....	—	4.4	22.4	10.5	18.4	16.1	23.5	43.4
Money plus Quasi-Money	35l	....	....	....	....	....	....	....	....	44.8	46.6	85.2	118.0	164.6	206.6	230.6	246.2
Interest Rates													*Percent Per Annum*			
Deposit Rate	60l	....	....	....	....	....	....	....	....	....	....	....	....	....	....	....
Lending Rate	60p	....	....	....	....	....	....	....	....	....	....	....	....	....	....	....
Production													*Index Numbers (1990=100):*			
Crude Petroleum	66aa	....	....	8.5	35.8	48.5	49.4	43.2	42.0	43.5	43.1	50.5	54.4	50.5	46.6	40.2
International Transactions													*Millions of Rials Omani*			
Exports	70	.8	.6	9.5	43.6	58.8	59.5	63.8	64.2	83.7	284.2	360.6	391.6	393.4	378.7	542.3
Crude Petroleum	70aa	....	....	8.8	42.9	58.1	59.1	63.4	63.8	83.0	283.8	359.5	390.1	391.8	375.4	537.5
Imports, cif	71	3.2	3.4	3.6	4.0	5.6	7.6	13.8	18.7	40.7	135.6	264.3	250.5	302.1	327.2	430.5
Refined Petroleum	71ab	....	....	....	....	....	....	....	....	....	....	....	38.6	40.3	29.5	33.2	52.5
Imports, fob	71.v	2.7	2.9	3.0	3.4	4.7	6.4	11.6	15.7	34.2	114.4	224.6	212.1	263.0	283.4	381.2
Volume of Exports															*1990=100*		
Crude Petroleum	72aa	—	—	9.1	38.4	52.0	52.9	46.3	45.0	46.6	46.3	55.8	58.5	53.2	50.4	46.9
Export Prices															*1985=100:*		
Crude Petroleum	76aa d	....	....	6.0	6.0	6.0	6.0	7.3	8.2	11.3	39.6	41.6	43.1	47.6	48.2	74.0

Oman

	1980	1981	1982	1983	1984	1985	1986	1987	1988	1989	1990	1991	1992	1993	1994		
Rials Omani per US Dollar: End of Period (ae)																**Exchange Rates**	
	.4405	.4020	.3810	.3616	.3386	.3794	.4703	.5455	.5174	.5053	.5470	.5500	.5287	.5281	.5613	Official Rate	aa
	.3454	.3454	.3454	.3454	.3454	.3454	.3845	.3845	.3845	.3845	.3845	.3845	.3845	.3845	.3845	Official Rate	ae
Period Averages																	
	111.3	111.3	111.3	111.3	111.3	111.3	100.7	100.0	100.0	100.0	100.0	100.0	100.0	100.0	100.0	Official Rate	ah x
	113.8	124.5	138.2	144.8	154.8	159.2	118.1	104.5	98.2	104.0	100.0	99.3	97.0	99.8	97.0	Nominal Effective Exchange Rate	ne c
																Fund Position	
End of Period																	
	20.0	30.0	30.0	63.1	63.1	63.1	63.1	63.1	63.1	63.1	63.1	63.1	63.1	119.4	119.4	Quota	2f. s
	5.1	5.2	7.9	11.1	9.4	10.9	11.4	7.2	8.7	10.9	13.4	15.5	3.4	5.0	6.2	SDRs	1b. s
	14.9	16.5	20.8	30.5	33.2	32.1	32.1	32.1	28.7	27.7	25.2	22.7	39.4	37.8	36.0	Reserve Position in the Fund	1c. s
	4.8	1.2	.1	—	—	—	—	—	—	—	—	—	—	—	—	of which: Outstg.Fund Borrowing	2c
																International Liquidity	
End of Period																	
	581.4	744.3	872.4	762.6	900.2	1,090.2	967.9	1,402.2	1,054.2	1,354.3	1,672.4	1,663.3	1,983.5	908.1	979.4	Total Reserves minus Gold	1l. d
	6.5	6.0	8.7	11.6	9.2	12.0	13.9	10.2	11.7	14.3	19.0	22.2	4.7	6.8	9.0	SDRs	1b. d
	19.0	19.2	22.9	31.9	32.5	35.2	39.2	45.5	38.6	36.4	35.8	32.5	54.1	52.0	52.5	Reserve Position in the Fund	1c. d
	555.9	719.1	840.8	719.1	858.4	1,043.0	914.8	1,346.5	1,003.8	1,303.6	1,617.6	1,608.6	1,924.7	849.3	917.9	Foreign Exchange	1d. d
	.209	.274	.279	.288	.289	.289	.289	.289	.289	.289	.289	.289	.289	.289	.289	Gold (Million Fine Troy Ounces)	1ad
	40.0	70.2	71.9	75.6	76.0	76.0	68.3	68.3	68.3	68.3	68.3	68.3	68.3	68.3	68.3	Gold (National Valuation)	1an d
	120.2	237.3	332.4	550.1	620.6	532.3	337.2	312.9	321.0	323.6	484.5	872.5	662.3	162.2	38.4	Monetary Authorities: Other Assets	3. d
	12.4	9.2	14.9	10.6	7.0	10.9	4.3	4.7	3.9	.9	1.0	1.0	1.0	1.0	1.2	Other Liab.	4. d
	402.6	466.8	556.9	826.5	902.8	680.9	596.6	609.9	726.4	755.2	758.7	699.7	532.4	780.1	863.5	Deposit Money Banks: Assets	7a. d
	82.0	68.4	62.8	67.7	65.0	60.6	48.1	37.8	35.6	43.6	54.9	152.9	175.6	97.2	40.4	of which: Claims on Nonbanks	7ad d
	320.1	246.7	268.9	271.1	263.1	249.2	337.7	278.6	313.2	267.8	203.0	104.3	105.8	167.1	239.5	Deposit Money Banks: Liabilities	7b. d
	20.4	21.1	34.4	45.0	36.8	28.5	36.2	24.9	63.6	77.4	53.6	17.8	13.6	15.9	18.2	of which: Liab. to Nonbanks	7bd d
																Monetary Authorities	
End of Period																	
	256.2	363.3	441.0	479.5	551.6	586.6	528.8	687.6	555.8	672.3	856.7	1,002.6	920.5	720.1	635.0	Foreign Assets	11
	—	—	33.6	14.2	5.9	—	116.9	—	121.6	51.0	—	32.3	38.9	49.3	97.0	Claims on Central Government	12a
	144.9	221.8	276.8	210.5	254.4	264.0	280.8	239.7	242.0	295.2	300.6	309.8	299.1	284.7	296.3	Reserve Money	14
	94.8	116.2	129.8	140.4	150.0	178.5	168.8	180.4	176.3	183.6	214.1	215.9	226.7	232.9	245.5	of which: Currency Outside DMBs	14a
	4.3	3.2	5.2	3.7	2.4	3.8	1.7	1.8	1.5	.4	.4	.4	.4	.4	.5	Foreign Liabilities	16c
	66.1	83.6	116.3	190.4	214.4	184.4	129.9	122.4	123.8	124.6	187.6	336.2	255.0	62.4	14.8	Central Government Deposits	16d
	46.8	67.2	74.5	83.3	92.0	104.3	121.8	135.2	144.2	156.9	188.0	202.0	213.7	219.9	235.2	Capital Accounts	17a
	-5.9	-12.5	1.8	5.9	-5.7	30.0	111.6	188.4	165.8	146.3	180.1	186.5	191.2	201.9	185.3	Other Items (Net)	17r
																Deposit Money Banks	
End of Period																	
	50.0	107.6	144.6	67.1	104.6	86.1	111.4	57.8	70.1	110.7	88.2	85.0	72.3	49.4	51.6	Reserves	20
	139.1	161.2	192.3	285.5	311.8	235.2	229.4	234.5	279.3	290.4	291.7	269.0	204.7	299.9	332.0	Foreign Assets	21
	3.2	.6	.3	5.3	16.8	52.8	41.0	84.5	32.8	23.6	48.7	124.8	190.7	154.1	97.9	Claims on Central Government	22a
	283.2	334.8	377.2	468.9	566.5	675.2	674.5	688.5	764.8	823.9	926.1	935.0	1,029.9	1,088.0	1,227.3	Claims on Private Sector	22d
	59.9	96.5	119.0	158.7	134.0	150.1	144.0	154.8	139.0	161.9	176.6	189.8	206.3	218.7	227.4	Demand Deposits	24
	170.3	238.0	322.1	405.5	490.1	608.4	560.6	584.3	658.8	720.3	781.3	830.2	841.1	863.9	931.1	Quasi-Monetary Deposits	25
	110.6	85.2	92.9	93.6	90.9	86.1	129.6	107.1	120.4	103.0	78.0	40.1	40.7	64.2	92.1	Foreign Liabilities	26c
	84.2	111.9	107.2	87.9	155.5	84.9	88.0	82.4	84.6	99.0	130.0	147.8	138.6	153.4	148.9	Central Government Deposits	26d
	23.5	46.0	71.1	90.6	110.6	125.4	138.8	104.6	107.2	104.0	116.5	121.7	129.0	165.8	167.6	Capital Accounts	27a
	27.1	26.6	2.1	-9.4	18.6	-5.7	-4.9	32.1	37.0	60.3	72.2	84.2	141.9	125.5	141.7	Other Items (Net)	27r
																Monetary Survey	
End of Period																	
	280.5	436.2	535.3	667.7	770.1	731.9	626.7	813.2	713.1	859.4	1,070.0	1,231.1	1,084.1	955.4	874.5	Foreign Assets (Net)	31n
	136.1	139.8	187.6	210.1	219.3	458.6	614.6	568.2	710.9	674.9	657.2	608.1	866.0	1,075.6	1,258.5	Domestic Credit	32
	-147.1	-194.9	-189.6	-258.8	-347.2	-216.6	-60.0	-120.3	-54.0	-149.0	-268.9	-327.0	-164.0	-12.5	31.2	Claims on Central Govt. (Net)	32an
	283.2	334.8	377.2	468.9	566.5	675.2	674.5	688.5	764.8	823.9	926.1	935.0	1,029.9	1,088.0	1,227.3	Claims on Private Sector	32d
	154.7	212.7	248.8	299.1	283.9	328.6	312.8	335.2	315.3	345.4	390.8	405.7	433.0	451.5	472.9	Money	34
	170.3	238.0	322.1	405.5	490.1	608.4	560.6	584.3	658.8	720.3	781.3	830.2	841.1	863.9	931.1	Quasi-Money	35
	91.6	125.3	152.0	173.2	215.4	253.5	367.8	461.9	449.9	468.5	555.2	603.2	676.0	715.5	728.9	Other Items (Net)	37r
	325.0	450.7	570.9	704.6	774.0	937.0	873.4	919.5	974.1	1,065.8	1,172.0	1,235.9	1,274.1	1,315.5	1,404.1	Money plus Quasi-Money	35l
																Interest Rates	
Percent Per Annum																	
	....	....	....	....	9.03	9.04	8.33	7.48	7.57	8.66	8.32	7.06	6.29	4.17	4.34	Deposit Rate	60l
	....	....	....	....	10.35	10.24	9.65	9.10	9.40	10.01	9.68	9.50	9.24	8.49	8.57	Lending Rate	60p
																Production	
Period Averages																	
	42.0	48.7	49.8	57.6	63.6	75.0	83.0	86.4	92.2	93.8	100.0	105.2	110.1	115.7	....	Crude Petroleum	66aa
																International Transactions	
Millions of Rials Omani																	
	824.5	1,109.3	1,035.6	1,061.9	1,059.6	1,360.2	698.0	957.9	951.9	1,564.0	2,118.0	1,873.0	....	....	....	Exports	70
	819.5	1,099.7	1,023.9	1,049.8	1,046.9	1,348.2	686.8	945.5	796.9	....	....	....	....	....	....	Crude Petroleum	70aa
	598.2	790.3	926.5	860.9	949.2	1,088.9	916.7	700.7	846.5	867.9	1,031.0	1,228.0	1,449.3	1,581.8	....	Imports, cif	71
	81.7	101.2	94.0	12.2	13.5	....	....	....	....	....	....	....	....	....	....	Refined Petroleum	71ab
	532.3	702.2	827.5	770.3	847.9	972.2	818.5	625.6	755.8	774.9	920.5	1,096.4	1,294.0	1,412.3	....	Imports, fob	71.v
																Volume of Exports	
1990=100																	
	44.4	52.6	51.8	60.2	58.8	72.3	81.8	85.9	92.4	94.2	100.0	102.4	110.1	116.6	....	Crude Petroleum	72aa
																Export Prices	
Index of Prices in US Dollars																	
	119.3	135.5	127.8	112.3	105.9	100.0	49.8	63.9	50.1	....	....	....	....	....	....	Crude Petroleum	76aa d

Oman

449

		1965	1966	1967	1968	1969	1970	1971	1972	1973	1974	1975	1976	1977	1978	1979
Balance of Payments															*Millions of US Dollars:*	
Goods: Exports f.o.b.	78aa d	....	....	....	....	....	....	....	....	....	1,212	1,416	1,596	1,620	1,598	2,280
Goods: Imports f.o.b.	78ab d	....	....	....	....	....	....	....	....	....	−552	−908	−1,000	−1,044	−1,157	−1,285
Trade Balance	78ac d	....	....	....	....	....	....	....	....	....	661	508	596	576	441	994
Services: Credit	78ad d	....	....	....	....	....	....	....	....	....	—	—	—	—	8	8
Services: Debit	78ae d	....	....	....	....	....	....	....	....	....	−104	−155	−177	−186	−193	−235
Balance on Goods and Services	78af d	....	....	....	....	....	....	....	....	....	557	354	419	390	256	767
Income: Credit	78ag d	....	....	....	....	....	....	....	....	....	19	17	6	—	5	—
Income: Debit	78ah d	....	....	....	....	....	....	....	....	....	−310	−312	−220	−160	−118	−149
Balance on Goods, Serv., & Inc.	78ai d	....	....	....	....	....	....	....	....	....	266	58	204	230	142	618
Current Transfers, n.i.e: Credit	78aj d	....	....	....	....	....	....	....	....	....	24	207	52	268	49	212
Current Transfers: Debit	78ak d	....	....	....	....	....	....	....	....	....	−111	−208	−220	−222	−241	−281
Current Account, n.i.e.	78al d	....	....	....	....	....	....	....	....	....	179	57	36	277	−50	549
Capital Account, n.i.e.: Credit	78ba d	....	....	....	....	....	....	....	....	....	—	—	—	—	—	—
Capital Account: Debit	78bb d	....	....	....	....	....	....	....	....	....	—	—	—	—	—	—
Capital Account, n.i.e.	78bc d	....	....	....	....	....	....	....	....	....	—	—	—	—	—	—
Direct Investment Abroad	78bd d	....	....	....	....	....	....	....	....	....	—	—	—	—	—	—
Dir. Invest. in Rep. Econ., n.i.e.	78be d	....	....	....	....	....	....	....	....	....	−61	106	81	48	86	118
Portfolio Investment Assets	78bf d	....	....	....	....	....	....	....	....	....	—	—	—	—	—	—
Portfolio Investment Liab., n.i.e.	78bg d	....	....	....	....	....	....	....	....	....	—	—	—	—	—	—
Other Investment Assets	78bh d	....	....	....	....	....	....	....	....	....	−27	−91	91	−33	6	−110
Other Investment Liab., n.i.e.	78bi d	....	....	....	....	....	....	....	....	....	78	139	217	20	60	−144
Financial Account, n.i.e.	78bj d	....	....	....	....	....	....	....	....	....	−10	155	389	35	151	−136
Net Errors and Omissions	78ca d	....	....	....	....	....	....	....	....	....	−118	−146	−369	−240	−150	−257
Overall Balance	78cb d	....	....	....	....	....	....	....	....	....	50	66	57	72	−49	155
Reserves and Related Items	79da d	....	....	....	....	....	....	....	....	....	−50	−66	−57	−72	49	−155
Reserve Assets	79db d	....	....	....	....	....	....	....	....	....	−50	−66	−57	−72	49	−155
Use of Fund Credit and Loans	79dc d	....	....	....	....	....	....	....	....	....	—	—	—	—	—	—
Liabs.Constit.For.Auth.Reserves	79dd d	....	....	....	....	....	....	....	....	....	—	—	—	—	—	—
Exceptional Financing	79de d	....	....	....	....	....	....	....	....	....	....	....	....	....	....	....
Government Finance															*Millions of Rials Omani:*	
Deficit (−) or Surplus	80	....	....	....	....	....	....	4.1	−17.1	−23.5	−56.4	−37.7	−84.7	58.1	−75.3	85.0
Revenue	81	....	....	....	....	....	....	50.1	53.0	65.0	303.2	358.7	457.3	483.4	440.9	590.6
Grants Received	81z	....	....	....	....	....	....	—	—	3.5	8.3	71.6	18.0	92.7	6.7	61.9
Expenditure	82	....	....	....	....	....	....	46.0	69.4	91.7	329.3	466.5	551.0	497.7	498.7	548.8
Lending Minus Repayments	83	....	....	....	....	....	....	—	.7	.3	38.6	1.5	9.0	20.3	24.2	18.7
Financing																
Net Borrowing: Domestic	84a	....	....	....	....	....	....	−3.3	17.1	−12.5	28.6	−18.1	32.7	−88.8	83.4	−72.8
Foreign	85a	....	....	....	....	....	....	—	—	36.0	27.8	55.8	52.0	30.7	−8.1	−12.2
Debt: Domestic	88a	....	....	....	....	....	....	.7	15.0	12.2	49.7	41.9	69.7	16.1	43.7	4.2
Foreign	89a	....	....	....	....	....	....	—	—	10.9	46.2	102.0	154.0	184.7	176.6	164.4
National Accounts															*Millions of Rials Omani*	
Exports of Goods & Services	90c	....	....	13.1	55.2	74.6	78.7	82.3	83.6	114.9	419.1	489.2	551.2	559.4	552.0	787.4
Government Consumption	91f	....	....	1.7	3.8	5.1	13.7	26.0	41.7	63.0	197.2	229.0	240.9	268.5	272.3	354.7
Gross Capital Formation	93	....	....	12.1	9.9	9.3	14.7	35.6	42.0	44.4	174.1	258.0	317.1	289.9	273.5	335.4
Private Consumption	96f	....	....	20.6	21.4	22.9	20.7	21.4	35.1	40.6	49.6	115.1	181.6	246.2	310.3	337.4
Imports of Goods & Services	98c	....	....	−8.7	−11.6	−11.9	−21.0	−40.2	−61.6	−93.5	−271.5	−367.1	−406.5	−417.0	−461.2	−525.0
Gross Domestic Product = GDP	99b	22.6	24.2	38.8	78.7	100.0	106.8	125.1	140.8	169.4	568.5	724.2	884.3	946.8	946.9	1,289.9
Net Factor Inc/Pmts(−) Abroad	98.n	....	....	−3.6	−19.2	−23.3	−18.2	−20.0	−29.0	−62.7	−152.0	−134.9	−147.9	−130.2	−111.0	−137.3
Gross Nat'l Expenditure = GNP	99a	22.6	24.2	35.2	59.5	76.7	88.6	105.1	111.8	106.7	416.5	589.3	736.4	816.6	835.9	1,152.9
Gross Dom. Prod. 1990 Prices	99b.p	150.7	158.0	262.5	477.9	600.4	620.4	626.7	684.5	588.8	755.0	970.9	I1,126.0	1,324.7e	1,558.6	1,630.3e
GDP Deflator (1990=100)	99bi p	15.0	15.3	14.8	16.5	16.7	17.2	20.0	20.6	28.8	75.3	74.6	78.5	71.5	60.8	79.1
															Millions	
Population	99z	.57	.58	.60	.62	.64	.65	.67	.70	.72	.74	.77	.79	.84	.88	.93

Exchange Rates: On May 7, 1970 the rial saidi replaced the Gulf rupee. On November 11, 1972 the rial saidi was renamed rial Omani.
Deposit Money Banks: I Prior to September 1979, some components of foreign assets and foreign liabilities were reported on a net basis.
Monetary Survey: I See note to section 20.

Oman

	1980	1981	1982	1983	1984	1985	1986	1987	1988	1989	1990	1991	1992	1993	1994			
	Minus Sign Indicates Debit																**Balance of Payments**	
	3,748	4,696	4,423	4,256	4,421	4,971	2,861	3,805	3,342	4,068	5,508	4,871	5,555	5,365	....		Goods: Exports f.o.b.	78aa *d*
	−1,780	−2,296	−2,583	−2,360	−2,640	−3,028	−2,309	−1,769	−2,107	−2,225	−2,623	−3,112	−3,627	−4,030	....		Goods: Imports f.o.b.	78ab *d*
	1,968	2,400	1,840	1,895	1,781	1,943	552	2,036	1,235	1,842	2,885	1,759	1,928	1,336	....		Trade Balance	78ac *d*
	9	9	12	14	14	14	13	13	13	59	68	61	13	13	....		Services: Credit	78ad *d*
	−518	−620	−701	−688	−673	−713	−689	−481	−523	−570	−719	−961	−932	−896	....		Services: Debit	78ae *d*
	1,459	1,788	1,151	1,222	1,123	1,245	−123	1,568	726	1,331	2,235	860	1,009	453	....		Balance on Goods and Services	78af *d*
	96	177	318	307	345	362	597	520	257	338	375	356	328	421	....		Income: Credit	78ag *d*
	−352	−415	−471	−490	−560	−688	−668	−610	−572	−588	−629	−586	−636	−632	....		Income: Debit	78ah *d*
	1,202	1,549	998	1,039	908	919	−194	1,479	411	1,080	1,980	630	701	242	....		Balance on Goods, Serv., & Inc.	78ai *d*
	137	185	87	191	255	43	39	47	81	55	39	39	39	57	....		Current Transfers, n.i.e.: Credit	78aj *d*
	−397	−498	−596	−735	−860	−973	−885	−741	−801	−830	−913	−913	−1,235	−1,368	....		Current Transfers: Debit	78ak *d*
	942	1,237	489	494	303	−10	−1,040	784	−309	305	1,106	−244	−496	−1,069	....		Current Account, n.i.e.	78al *d*
	—	—	—	—	—	—	—	—	—	—	—	—	—	—	....		Capital Account, n.i.e.: Credit	78ba *d*
	—	−3	−3	−3	−3	−3	—	—	—	—	—	—	—	—	....		Capital Account: Debit	78bb *d*
	—	−3	−3	−3	−3	−3	—	—	—	—	—	—	—	—	....		Capital Account, n.i.e.	78bc *d*
	—	—	—	—	—	—	—	—	—	—	—	—	—	—	....		Direct Investment Abroad	78bd *d*
	98	63	182	155	158	161	140	35	92	112	141	149	87	99	....		Dir. Invest. in Rep. Econ., n.i.e.	78be *d*
	—	—	—	—	—	—	—	—	—	—	—	—	—	—	....		Portfolio Investment Assets	78bf *d*
	—	—	—	—	—	—	—	—	—	—	—	—	—	—	....		Portfolio Investment Liab., n.i.e.	78bg *d*
	−257	−96	−139	−299	−146	97	198	−31	−88	−179	−270	146	120	−156	....		Other Investment Assets	78bh *d*
	74	71	149	470	427	199	676	−194	217	52	−369	226	107	107	....		Other Investment Liab., n.i.e.	78bi *d*
	−85	37	192	325	439	458	1,015	−190	221	−15	−499	521	314	49	....		Financial Account, n.i.e.	78bj *d*
	−62	−24	67	−466	−421	−323	−588	−486	−379	33	−472	253	462	−39	....		Net Errors and Omissions	78ca *d*
	796	1,247	744	351	319	122	−613	108	−467	324	135	530	280	−1,058	....		Overall Balance	78cb *d*
	−796	−1,247	−744	−351	−319	−122	613	−108	467	−324	−135	−530	−280	1,058	....		Reserves and Related Items	79da *d*
	−796	−1,247	−744	−351	−319	−122	613	−108	467	−324	−135	−530	−280	1,058	....		Reserve Assets	79db *d*
	—	—	—	—	—	—	—	—	—	—	—	—	—	—	....		Use of Fund Credit and Loans	79dc *d*
	—	—	—	—	—	—	—	—	—	—	—	—	—	—	....		Liabs.Constit.For.Auth.Reserves	79dd *d*
	....	....	....	....	....	....	....	....	....	....	....	....	....	....	....		Exceptional Financing	79de *d*
	Year Ending December 31																**Government Finance**	
	9.1	48.5	−222.8	−242.3	−346.8	−364.2	−700.2	−146.2	−346.7	−289.5	−32.8	−284.3	−584.5	−511.1[p]	....		Deficit (−) or Surplus	80
	793.9	1,075.9	986.5	1,073.7	1,141.6	1,337.8	848.6	1,185.1	998.7	1,125.4	1,580.1	1,261.4	1,338.1	1,357.7[p]	....		Revenue	81
	35.2	50.0	14.7	50.7	72.8	59.8	46.4	14.3	30.5	27.9	6.6	23.0	.9	19.2[p]	....		Grants Received	81z
	794.9	1,028.0	1,176.5	1,308.1	1,501.0	1,731.1	1,587.2	1,330.1	1,363.4	1,425.5	1,601.0	1,575.1	1,900.3	1,871.4[p]	....		Expenditure	82
	25.1	49.4	47.5	58.6	60.2	30.7	8.0	15.5	12.5	17.3	18.5	−6.4	23.2	16.6[p]	....		Lending Minus Repayments	83
																	Financing	
	64.3	−137.7	181.1	−9.3	48.4	−9.5	105.6	54.0	149.5	243.6	191.1	201.6	413.5	337.3[p]	....		Net Borrowing: Domestic	84a
	−73.4	89.2	41.7	251.6	298.4	373.7	594.6	92.2	197.2	45.9	−158.3	82.7	171.0	173.8[p]	....		Foreign	85a
	.8	.4	—	—	—	—	—	—	—	—	32.6	252.9	410.2	329.1[p]	....		Debt: Domestic	88a
	169.1	219.5	261.2	424.0	574.7	648.1	940.2	887.7	959.7	994.4	847.1	932.1	1,036.3	1,019.7[p]	....		Foreign	89a
	Millions of Rials Omani																**National Accounts**	
	1,294.6	1,625.0	1,532.0	1,475.0	1,532.0	1,722.0	1,098.0	1,468.0	1,290.0	1,583.0	2,136.0	1,891.0	2,154.0	....	....		Exports of Goods & Services	90c
	499.2	656.4	715.2	779.8	808.0	938.1	929.0	913.7	956.0	975.6	1,544.9	1,394.7	1,734.9	....	....		Government Consumption	91f
	465.7	583.5	706.7	736.9	913.2	953.1	898.4	564.3	511.1	444.2	529.2	661.4	750.9	....	....		Gross Capital Formation	93
	576.8	590.6	794.7	802.2	938.5	1,125.6	1,020.0	929.6	1,179.8	1,261.8	1,080.6	1,485.3	1,476.6	....	....		Private Consumption	96f
	−789.0	−964.0	−1,134.0	−1,053.0	−1,144.0	−1,285.0	−1,145.0	−873.0	−1,011.0	−1,034.0	−1,240.0	−1,515.0	−1,699.0	....	....		Imports of Goods & Services	98c
	2,047.3	2,491.5	2,614.6	2,740.9	3,047.7	3,453.8	2,800.4	3,002.6	2,925.9	3,230.6	4,050.7	3,917.4	4,417.4	....	....		Gross Domestic Product = GDP	99b
	−212.0	−235.0	−238.0	−297.0	−350.0	−399.0	−336.0	−281.0	−406.0	−406.0	−419.0	−423.0	−574.0	....	....		Net Factor Inc/Pmts(−) Abroad	98.n
	1,835.3	2,256.5	2,376.6	2,443.9	2,697.7	3,054.8	2,464.4	2,721.6	2,519.9	2,824.6	3,631.7	3,494.4	3,843.4	....	....		Gross Nat'l Expenditure = GNP	99a
	1,723.6	2,017.3	2,250.2	2,609.3	3,046.0	3,465.1	3,580.3	3,448.9	3,655.0	3,767.6	4,050.7	4,423.3	4,723.1	....	....		Gross Dom. Prod. 1990 Prices	99b.*p*
	118.8	123.5	116.2	105.0	100.1	99.7	78.2	87.1	80.1	85.7	100.0	88.6	93.5	....	....		GDP Deflator (1990=100)	99bi *p*
	Midyear Estimates																	
	.98	1.03	1.09	1.15	1.21	‡2.00	‡1.46	1.53	1.60	1.67	1.75	1.83	1.91	1.99	....		**Population**	99z

Pakistan

564

		1965	1966	1967	1968	1969	1970	1971	1972	1973	1974	1975	1976	1977	1978	1979
Exchange Rates																*Rupees per SDR:*
Market Rate	aa	4.782	4.805	4.774	4.809	4.791	4.803	5.204	11.976	11.943	12.121	11.590	11.502	12.026	12.898	13.042
																Rupees per US Dollar:
Market Rate	ae	4.782	4.805	4.774	4.809	4.791	4.803	4.793	11.031	9.900	9.900	9.900	9.900	9.900	9.900	9.900
Market Rate	rf	4.762	4.762	4.762	4.762	4.762	4.762	4.762	8.681	9.994	9.900	9.900	9.900	9.900	9.900	9.900
Fund Position																*Millions of SDRs:*
Quota	2f.s	150	188	188	188	188	235	235	235	235	235	235	235	235	285	285
SDRs	1b.s	—	—	—	—	—	10	13	19	27	20	25	32	29	30	34
Reserve Position in the Fund	1c.s	—	—	—	—	—	—	—	—	—	—	—	—	—	—	—
Total Fund Cred.&Loans Outstg.	2tl	37	37	36	61	81	45	43	111	130	239	374	440	463	492	435
International Liquidity													*Millions of US Dollars Unless Otherwise Indicated:*			
Total Reserves minus Gold	1l.d	176	154	111	193	278	136	129	221	412	392	340	466	449	408	213
SDRs	1b.d	—	—	—	—	—	10	14	21	32	24	29	37	35	40	45
Reserve Position in the Fund	1c.d	—	—	—	—	—	—	—	—	—	—	—	—	—	—	—
Foreign Exchange	1d.d	176	154	111	193	278	126	115	200	380	368	311	429	414	368	168
Gold (Million Fine Troy Ounces)	1ad	1.547	1.547	1.548	1.561	1.561	1.561	1.583	1.588	1.588	1.588	1.588	1.618	1.618	1.718	1.818
Gold (National Valuation)	1and	53	53	53	54	54	54	55	....	....	67	67	68	68	332	728
Monetary Authorities: Other Liab.	4..d	5	5	4	4	3	3	3	1	1	4	6	6	7	47	67
Deposit Money Banks: Assets	7a.d	77	86	64	94	92	121	90	71	126	230	222	199	235	350	386
of which: Claims on Nonbanks	7add	57	70	50	73	79	100	76	70	110	201	188	94	94	140	160
Deposit Money Banks: Liabilities	7b.d	191	146	167	162	181	192	202	140	145	122	143	198	212	204	215
Monetary Authorities																*Millions of Rupees:*
Foreign Assets	11	1,535	1,269	1,065	1,458	1,861	1,185	1,159	3,765	5,415	5,191	4,570	5,757	5,544	7,752	9,854
Claims on Central Government	12a	4,611	5,599	5,723	5,671	7,001	7,985	9,661	10,770	9,958	9,094	12,461	13,783	19,764	25,350	32,542
of which: Provincial Government	12ax	229	219	475	438	233	241	503	387	419	415	393	195	443	88	183
Claims on Deposit Money Banks	12e	1,628	1,882	1,856	2,103	1,936	2,182	1,412	1,847	3,102	5,197	5,727	6,688	6,341	6,589	8,646
Reserve Money	14	6,398	7,305	7,322	7,734	8,535	9,512	10,544	12,380	13,861	13,956	15,326	18,358	22,525	26,483	33,564
of which: Currency Outside DMBs	14a	5,498	6,202	5,930	6,505	7,098	8,065	8,156	9,350	10,990	11,427	11,884	13,853	17,349	21,040	26,447
Foreign Liabilities	16c	200	201	187	308	404	230	233	1,337	1,564	2,931	4,399	5,119	5,630	6,813	6,333
Central Government Deposits	16d	155	44	79	45	1,011	485	492	628	597	282	127	315	558	471	409
Counterpart Funds	16e	1,001	954	921	1,004	682	820	926	1,030	1,278	1,502	1,626	1,574	1,894	1,657	2,070
Other Items (Net)	17r	19	248	135	142	166	303	37	1,009	1,177	811	1,279	862	1,042	4,266	8,665
Deposit Money Banks																*Millions of Rupees:*
Reserves	20	834	959	1,053	1,032	1,118	1,156	1,441	1,599	2,062	1,862	2,775	3,738	4,529	5,031	6,742
Foreign Assets	21	365	410	304	448	437	575	427	785	1,247	2,277	2,193	933	1,070	1,733	2,112
Claims on Central Government	22a	2,193	2,616	2,478	3,537	3,829	3,606	4,636	5,361	6,876	6,732	8,861	12,849	12,535	16,997	17,878
of which: Provincial Government	22ax	751	1,041	817	1,541	1,379	1,388	1,479	1,278	1,634	2,249	2,632	4,285	3,983	3,979	4,384
Claims on Private Sector	22d	6,856	7,988	9,000	9,662	10,360	11,948	12,273	14,658	17,074	17,289	20,632	28,435	33,958	38,071	45,853
Demand Deposits	24	3,443	4,271	4,111	4,427	5,303	5,765	7,592	9,427	10,588	10,614	13,107	19,519	21,926	25,887	29,981
Time Deposits	25	3,046	4,008	4,797	5,918	5,960	6,737	7,122	7,796	9,368	8,665	12,177	15,924	18,969	23,436	27,288
Foreign Liabilities	26c	270	286	329	255	294	308	315	405	371	452	623	1,050	1,228	1,144	1,290
Long-Term Foreign Liabilities	26cl	641	408	467	514	566	606	648	1,137	1,062	760	791	906	868	873	834
Central Government Deposits	26d	340	420	460	569	586	722	748	980	1,339	1,410	1,248	2,282	1,669	2,162	2,567
Counterpart Funds	26e	328	337	355	365	383	395	409	420	399	410	428	447	466	487	523
Credit from Monetary Authorities	26g	1,777	1,873	1,832	2,041	1,881	2,098	1,412	1,847	3,102	5,197	5,727	6,688	6,341	6,374	8,431
Other Items (Net)	27r	403	372	484	590	772	655	532	392	1,029	653	361	−860	624	1,468	1,670
Monetary Survey																*Millions of Rupees:*
Foreign Assets (Net)	31n	1,430	1,193	853	1,343	1,599	1,222	1,039	2,808	4,727	4,085	1,741	520	−244	1,527	4,343
Domestic Credit	32	13,415	15,829	16,927	18,402	19,799	22,535	25,553	29,577	32,228	31,683	41,174	53,768	65,994	80,235	96,540
Claims on Central Govt. (Net)	32an	6,308	7,751	7,661	8,595	9,233	10,383	13,057	14,524	14,898	14,134	19,946	24,035	30,072	39,713	47,444
Claims on Private Sector	32d	7,107	8,078	9,266	9,807	10,566	12,152	12,496	15,054	17,329	17,549	21,228	29,733	35,923	40,522	49,097
Money	34	9,012	10,598	10,285	11,042	12,620	14,016	16,488	19,939	22,194	22,517	25,621	34,044	39,966	47,194	56,830
Quasi-Money	35	3,046	4,008	4,797	5,918	5,960	6,737	7,122	7,796	9,368	8,665	12,177	15,924	18,969	23,436	27,288
Long-Term Foreign Liabilities	36cl	641	408	467	514	566	606	648	1,137	1,062	760	791	906	868	873	834
Counterpart Funds	36e	1,329	1,290	1,275	1,368	1,064	1,215	1,335	1,450	1,676	1,912	2,054	2,020	2,360	2,144	2,593
Other Items (Net)	37r	817	719	957	903	1,188	1,184	999	2,065	2,654	1,914	2,272	1,395	3,587	8,116	13,338
Money plus Quasi-Money	35l	12,058	14,605	15,081	16,960	18,580	20,752	23,610	27,734	31,562	31,182	37,798	49,967	58,935	70,629	84,118
Other Banking Institutions																*Millions of Rupees:*
Post Office: Savings Deposits	45..i	574	611	606	618	647	775	974	1,165	1,385	1,418	1,405	1,317	1,360	1,318	1,235
Liquid Liabilities	55l	12,632	15,216	15,687	17,578	19,227	21,527	24,584	28,899	32,947	32,600	39,202	51,285	60,295	71,947	85,352
Interest Rates																*Percent Per Annum*
Bank Rate *(End of Period)*	60	5.00	5.00	5.00	5.00	5.00	5.00	5.00	6.00	8.00	9.00	9.00	9.00	10.00	10.00	10.00
Money Market Rate	60b	5.86	4.70	6.57	6.24	5.40	5.50	6.60	5.34	6.51	10.33	9.87	9.37	10.87	10.41	8.83
Government Bond Yield	61	4.20	4.48	4.47	4.76	5.21	5.50	5.76[e]	5.76	5.76	5.77	5.77	9.04	9.27	9.48	9.75
Prices and Production																*Index Numbers (1990=100):*
Share Prices	62	....	18.7	18.4	21.2	22.7	24.6	20.7	....	19.1	16.4	20.9	21.3	I27.0	30.7	35.4
Wholesale Prices	63	11.2	12.3	13.0	13.0	13.6	13.7	14.5	16.0	20.3	24.9	30.5	32.8	36.0	38.3	41.9
Consumer Prices	64	13.0	13.9	14.9	14.9	15.4	16.2	I17.0	17.8	22.0	27.8	33.6	36.0	I39.7	42.1	45.6
Manufacturing Production	66ey	I19.0	21.1	22.5	24.2	26.8	30.5	30.8	29.8	33.4	I34.6	33.9	33.6	34.3	37.3	40.0

Pakistan

	1980	1981	1982	1983	1984	1985	1986	1987	1988	1989	1990	1991	1992	1993	1994		
End of Period (aa)																**Exchange Rates**	
	12.627	11.523	14.164	14.134	15.056	17.553	21.100	24.756	25.097	28.149	31.156	35.360	35.338	41.372	44.963	Market Rate	aa
End of Period (ae) Period Average (rf)																	
	9.900	9.900	12.840	13.500	15.360	15.980	17.250	17.450	18.650	21.420	21.900	24.720	25.700	30.120	30.800	Market Rate	ae
	9.900	9.900	11.847	13.117	14.046	15.928	16.648	17.399	18.003	20.541	21.707	23.801	25.083	28.107	30.567	Market Rate	rf
End of Period																**Fund Position**	
	428	428	428	546	546	546	546	546	546	546	546	546	546	758	758	758 Quota	2f. s
	23	49	46	1	37	24	11	11	5	1	1	1	5	—	1	— SDRs	1b. s
	—	—	59	89	89	—	—	—	—	—	—	—	—	—	—	— Reserve Position in the Fund	1c. s
	528	880	1,286	1,540	1,469	1,289	973	647	411	710	587	746	820	817	1,097	Total Fund Cred.&Loans Outstg.	2tl
Last Thursday of Period																**International Liquidity**	
	496	721	969	1,973	1,035	807	709	502	395	521	296	527	850	1,197	2,929	Total Reserves minus Gold	1l. d
	29	56	51	1	37	26	13	16	7	1	1	7	—	1	—	SDRs	1b. d
	—	—	65	93	87	—	—	—	—	—	—	—	—	—	—	Reserve Position in the Fund	1c. d
	467	665	853	1,879	912	781	696	486	388	519	295	519	850	1,196	2,929	Foreign Exchange	1d. d
	1.818	1.846	1.848	1.862	1.865	1.902	1.934	1.940	1.945	1.949	1.949	1.961	2.021	2.044	2.052	Gold (Million Fine Troy Ounces)	1ad
	1,188	786	557	756	633	605	654	863	820	716	689	710	681	692	792	Gold (National Valuation)	1and
	347	346	343	340	328	344	303	225	353	417	371	321	690	552	271	Monetary Authorities: Other Liab.	4..d
	309	322	332	462	549	562	687	797	825	934	1,455	1,577	1,384	1,405	1,582	Deposit Money Banks: Assets	7a. d
	169	239	259	331	389	421	504	699	686	782	1,299	1,443	1,246	1,182	1,288	*of which:* Claims on Nonbanks	7ad d
	214	316	290	443	837	1,095	1,460	1,808	1,998	2,349	2,728	3,566	4,431	2,924	2,777	Deposit Money Banks: Liabilities	7b. d
Last Thursday of Period																**Monetary Authorities**	
	17,208	15,414	20,159	37,391	25,930	23,127	24,082	24,296	23,201	27,048	20,406	30,366	39,544	56,923	115,577	Foreign Assets	11
	35,342	39,988	49,774	51,825	66,953	70,119	84,269	93,760	96,674	116,597	137,217	163,007	181,038	210,037	202,251	Claims on Central Government	12a
	134	25	25	25	26	26	26	26	26	26	25	5,451	4,295	8,136	5,524	*of which: Provincial Government*	12ax
	12,553	17,498	17,141	20,682	20,576	24,142	29,368	38,426	43,055	48,826	52,858	62,322	71,593	78,137	89,110	Claims on Deposit Money Banks	12e
	39,157	42,369	49,859	56,719	66,002	71,690	85,893	102,617	113,734	133,146	154,362	196,554	213,817	244,175	282,541	Reserve Money	14
	32,482	34,488	41,153	46,425	52,003	58,678	71,578	81,765	92,168	105,225	125,806	144,530	162,316	177,856	195,827	*of which:* Currency Outside DMBs	14a
	10,108	13,560	26,364	27,164	28,110	25,758	19,940	16,917	28,909	26,429	34,327	46,697	50,415	48,580		Foreign Liabilities	16c
	305	6,719	5,934	13,420	7,772	6,611	17,014	20,930	16,915	18,418	18,343	11,623	15,355	37,304	37,682	Central Government Deposits	16d
	2,077	1,868	1,502	1,729	1,182	918	564	302	350	445	540	542	539	671	614	Counterpart Funds	16e
	13,456	8,384	7,164	11,666	11,339	10,060	8,489	12,693	15,013	11,553	10,807	12,649	15,766	12,533	37,524	Other Items (Net)	17r
Last Thursday of Period																**Deposit Money Banks**	
	6,167	7,451	8,207	10,101	13,809	13,871	15,103	21,994	23,661	29,874	28,931	50,592	51,207	68,030	93,268	Reserves	20
	ꟾ3,060	3,190	4,262	6,243	8,426	8,988	11,848	13,903	15,391	20,008	31,872	38,974	35,563	42,306	48,721	Foreign Assets	21
	23,714	29,527	34,665	47,011	34,240	34,926	44,970	75,978	75,544	78,001	81,079	114,904	191,287	208,114	251,172	Claims on Central Government	22a
	5,836	8,256	10,646	12,598	9,365	3,006	5,057	7,688	5,111	7,336	10,594	7,878	10,395	10,870	11,488	*of which: Provincial Government*	22ax
	51,903	61,313	73,076	88,431	103,071	132,590	155,298	160,908	181,571	195,274	210,491	232,651	290,851	337,082	385,463	Claims on Private Sector	22d
	33,698	37,227	45,641	53,685	53,035	63,668	72,785	90,403	96,563	110,909	127,379	156,588	203,653	191,613	235,265	Demand Deposits	24
	30,650	36,252	44,892	59,316	61,532	68,925	77,592	86,380	89,543	83,028	80,372	92,475	143,406	230,515	278,960	Time Deposits	25
	1,229	2,259	2,493	4,576	10,745	14,931	21,827	26,756	30,346	42,042	50,873	78,115	101,680	74,987	73,295	Foreign Liabilities	26c
	894	868	1,229	1,403	2,106	2,572	3,358	4,801	6,915	8,280	8,870	10,041	12,198	13,074	12,235	Long-Term Foreign Liabilities	26cl
	3,472	3,749	2,799	2,927	948	1,858	1,636	971	966	1,022	1,748	6,613	4,378	19,224	41,168	Central Government Deposits	26d
	566	607	637	701	782	815	837	1,329	131	−12	−24	−238	−20	−196	−181	Counterpart Funds	26e
	12,338	15,424	14,776	18,182	17,948	21,417	26,284	31,359	35,667	40,483	44,313	52,856	61,263	66,564	77,758	Credit from Monetary Authorities	26g
	1,997	5,094	7,743	10,996	12,450	16,188	22,900	30,785	36,036	37,405	38,842	40,673	42,350	59,751	60,123	Other Items (Net)	27r
Last Thursday of Period																**Monetary Survey**	
	8,931	2,785	−689	12,693	−3,554	−10,926	−11,656	−8,497	−8,672	−23,895	−25,024	−43,101	−73,269	−26,173	42,424	Foreign Assets (Net)	31n
	111,499	126,970	157,089	179,914	206,648	242,769	282,908	328,818	357,706	394,776	435,401	520,320	673,944	731,780	797,149	Domestic Credit	32
	55,279	59,046	75,706	82,489	92,474	96,576	110,588	147,838	154,336	175,157	198,204	259,675	352,592	361,623	374,573	Claims on Central Govt. (Net)	32an
	56,220	67,924	81,383	97,426	114,174	146,193	172,321	180,980	203,370	219,619	237,196	260,645	321,352	370,157	422,576	Claims on Private Sector	32d
	66,671	72,285	87,341	100,566	105,780	123,060	145,251	173,016	189,834	217,027	254,620	305,978	371,796	378,111	435,388	Money	34
	30,650	36,252	44,892	59,316	61,532	68,925	77,592	86,380	89,543	83,028	80,372	92,475	143,406	230,515	278,960	Quasi-Money	35
	894	868	1,229	1,403	2,106	2,572	3,358	4,801	6,915	8,870	10,041	12,198	13,074	12,235		Long-Term Foreign Liabilities	36cl
	2,643	2,475	2,139	2,430	1,964	1,733	1,401	1,631	481	433	517	304	520	475	433	Counterpart Funds	36e
	19,572	17,875	20,801	28,894	31,712	35,553	43,651	54,493	62,261	62,115	65,999	68,422	72,755	83,433	112,558	Other Items (Net)	37r
	97,322	108,538	132,233	159,882	167,312	191,985	222,842	259,396	279,378	300,054	334,991	398,453	515,202	608,626	714,348	Money plus Quasi-Money	35l
Last Thursday of Period																**Other Banking Institutions**	
	1,194	1,038	1,347	1,560	1,634	1,838	2,109	3,102	3,814	5,462	5,361	7,028	8,612	8,586	9,891	Post Office: Savings Deposits	45..i
	98,515	109,575	133,580	161,442	168,946	193,823	224,951	262,498	283,191	305,516	340,352	405,481	523,814	617,212	724,239	Liquid Liabilities	55l
Percent Per Annum																**Interest Rates**	
	10.00	10.00	10.00	10.00	10.00	10.00	10.00	10.00	10.00	10.00	10.00	10.00	10.00	....	....	Bank Rate *(End of Period)*	60
	8.63	9.27	9.51	8.15	8.97	8.13	6.59	6.25	6.32	6.30	7.29	7.64	7.51	11.00	8.36	Money Market Rate	60b
	11.20	9.40	9.36	9.31	9.25	9.19	8.77	8.26	8.32	8.18	8.05	7.88	ꟾ13.15	13.31	13.01	Government Bond Yield	61
Period Averages																**Prices and Production**	
	32.7	32.4	ꟾ35.5	45.7	60.1	58.6	60.8	75.6	88.0	94.1	ꟾ100.0	113.9	58.9	58.1	94.4	Share Prices	62
	47.5	52.8	56.4	60.5	66.2	68.1	71.5	77.4	84.9	92.1	100.0	112.0	120.1	131.3	155.9	Wholesale Prices	63
	51.1	57.1	ꟾ60.5	64.4	68.3	72.1	74.6	78.1	85.0	91.7	100.0	111.8	122.4	133.9	150.6	Consumer Prices	64
	ꟾ44.4	ꟾ50.9	58.9	62.8	67.7	73.1	78.3	84.0	91.2	93.4	100.0	106.9	113.8	117.5	....	Manufacturing Production	66ey

Pakistan

564

		1965	1966	1967	1968	1969	1970	1971	1972	1973	1974	1975	1976	1977	1978	1979
International Transactions																*Millions of Rupees*
Exports	70	2,516	2,868	3,071	1,913	1,671	1,892	2,225	ⅼ5,776	9,533	10,970	10,416	11,552	11,766	14,605	20,355
Imports, cif	71	4,987	4,286	5,243	3,204	3,217	3,483	3,229	ⅼ5,938	9,698	17,118	21,361	21,588	24,217	32,523	40,158
Imports, fob	71.v	4,534	3,896	4,775	2,913	2,933	3,175	2,946	ⅼ5,473	8,792	15,576	19,508	19,751	22,116	29,513	36,707
																1990=100
Volume of Exports	72	....	....	....	....	....	14.6ᵉ	20.4	29.2	30.1	27.1	29.7	32.6	ⅼ31.7	35.9	49.5
Volume of Imports	73	....	....	....	....	....	17.9ᵉ	21.0	27.6	36.1	43.1	42.6	49.4	ⅼ55.8	68.5	80.3
Unit Value of Exports	74	....	....	....	....	....	7.0	6.7	12.5	21.9	28.3	25.0	27.2	ⅼ32.6	37.2	43.1
Unit Value of Imports	75	....	....	....	....	....	5.1	5.6	9.6	13.6	23.1	26.2	25.1	ⅼ25.9	27.4	31.0
Balance of Payments																*Millions of US Dollars:*
Goods: Exports f.o.b.	78aa d												1,167	1,121	1,397	1,948
Goods: Imports f.o.b.	78ab d												−2,192	−2,487	−3,221	−4,289
Trade Balance	78ac d												−1,025	−1,366	−1,824	−2,341
Services: Credit	78ad d												276	310	400	544
Services: Debit	78ae d												−440	−492	−617	−788
Balance on Goods and Services	78af d												−1,188	−1,548	−2,040	−2,585
Income: Credit	78ag d												32	34	40	38
Income: Debit	78ah d												−167	−222	−239	−312
Balance on Goods, Serv., & Inc.	78ai d												−1,324	−1,736	−2,240	−2,858
Current Transfers, n.i.e.: Credit	78aj d												562	1,006	1,534	1,749
Current Transfers: Debit	78ak d												−18	−4	−13	−3
Current Account, n.i.e.	78al d												−779	−733	−718	−1,113
Capital Account, n.i.e.: Credit	78ba d												—	—	—	—
Capital Account: Debit	78bb d												—	−1	—	−1
Capital Account, n.i.e.	78bc d												—	−1	—	−1
Direct Investment Abroad	78bd d												—	—	—	—
Dir. Invest. in Rep. Econ., n.i.e.	78be d												8	15	32	58
Portfolio Investment Assets	78bf d												—	—	—	—
Portfolio Investment Liab., n.i.e.	78bg d												—	—	—	—
Other Investment Assets	78bh d												−14	−21	23	−80
Other Investment Liab., n.i.e.	78bi d												511	628	586	608
Financial Account, n.i.e.	78bj d												505	622	640	586
Net Errors and Omissions	78ca d												−76	12	−15	54
Overall Balance	78cb d												−351	−100	−93	−474
Reserves and Related Items	79da d												351	100	93	474
Reserve Assets	79db d												−114	16	28	208
Use of Fund Credit and Loans	79dc d												75	27	34	−74
Liabs.Constit.For.Auth.Reserves	79dd d												—	—	—	—
Exceptional Financing	79de d												390	57	32	340
Government Finance																*Millions of Rupees:*
Deficit (−) or Surplus	80	20	−2,305	−3,857	−2,991	−2,799	−3,945	−3,069	−2,583	ⅼ−4,554	−5,145	−11,466	−12,239	−12,580	−13,247	−17,997
Revenue	81	4,384	ⅼ5,457	5,957	6,048	6,977	8,007	7,342	7,053	ⅼ8,256	11,794	14,259	17,737	20,439	25,171	29,502
Grants Received	81z	527	704	266	334	237	208	327	239	ⅼ486	566	378	1,050	1,092	1,082	848
Expenditure	82	5,003	ⅼ7,560	6,548	6,841	7,304	7,904	7,987	8,784	ⅼ11,128	14,520	19,525	22,390	24,564	30,793	36,241
Lending Minus Repayments	83	−112	906	3,532	2,532	2,709	4,256	2,751	1,091	ⅼ2,168	2,985	6,578	8,636	9,547	8,707	12,106
Financing																
Domestic	84	....	....	....	....	....	....	....	....	....	....	....	....	....	ⅼ7,954	11,513
Foreign	85	....	....	....	....	....	....	....	....	....	....	....	....	....	ⅼ5,293	6,484
Financing																
Net Borrowing: Domestic	84a	−798	1,310	506	452	903	2,328	1,000	1,897	ⅼ1,074	1,884	4,071	5,148	5,201	....	....
Foreign	85a	785	975	3,390	2,475	1,988	1,749	1,719	863	ⅼ3,301	2,976	7,796	6,488	5,153	....	....
Use of Cash Balances	87	−7	19	−39	63	−92	−131	348	−176	ⅼ179	285	−401	603	2,226	....	....
Debt	88	10,762	13,576	15,039	16,882	19,174	22,852	26,096	49,271	50,147	55,475	59,102	74,148	86,279	97,965	117,354
Domestic	88a	....	....	....	....	....	11,426	12,873	16,667	17,818	17,426	21,245	27,420	32,700	38,530	49,371
Foreign	89a	....	....	....	....	....	11,426	13,223	32,604	32,329	38,049	37,857	46,728	53,579	59,435	67,983
Held by: State Bank	88aa	3,474	4,747	4,726	4,819	4,757	6,518	7,492	8,597	8,812	7,875	9,273	12,053	15,529	16,112	24,342
Deposit Money Banks	88ab	1,522	1,519	1,479	1,711	2,188	2,211	2,247	3,627	4,998	4,465	5,415	8,080	9,479	12,678	14,450
Other Financial Inst.	88ac	210	239	238	284	308	330	340	325	395	480	489	744	1,015	1,166	1,449
International Inst.	88ca	603	821	1,183	1,601	1,826	1,996	2,130	5,535	5,624	5,968	6,250	6,977	7,956	10,324	11,503
Foreign Govts. & Bks.	88cb	3,162	4,305	5,496	6,382	7,864	9,430	11,093	27,069	26,705	32,081	31,607	39,751	45,623	49,111	56,480
Others	88d	1,791	1,945	1,917	2,085	2,231	2,367	2,794	4,118	3,613	4,606	6,068	6,543	6,677	8,574	9,130
Intragovernmental Debt	88s	547	587	644	709	753	796	721	631	923	1,024	1,062	1,362	1,538	1,686	1,848
National Accounts																*Billions of Rupees:*
Exports of Goods & Services	90c	2.93	3.11	3.51	3.48	3.64	3.64	3.92	3.92	9.96	11.96	12.99	13.88	13.99	16.63	21.53
Government Consumption	91f	4.10	3.62	3.70	4.12	4.85	4.85	5.27	6.48	7.72	8.54	11.95	15.17	16.71	19.12	20.34
Gross Fixed Capital Formation	93e	5.09	5.60	6.08	6.17	6.84	6.84	7.05	6.81	7.65	10.61	16.22	24.06	27.86	30.51	33.13
Increase/Decrease(−) in Stocks	93i	.07	.94	.37	.95	.71	.71	.85	.85	1.00	1.00	1.00	2.00		1.00	1.75
Private Consumption	96f	25.06	29.34	31.05	34.28	36.67	36.67	38.73	40.72	50.14	69.94	91.04	101.12	116.93	141.68	160.70
Imports of Goods & Services	98c	−4.00	−4.95	−4.48	−4.84	−4.94	−4.94	−5.32	−4.73	−9.60	−15.20	−23.02	−23.85	−26.74	−32.60	−42.53
Gross Domestic Product	99b	33.25	37.66	40.12	44.16	47.75	47.75	50.49	54.06	66.87	86.85	111.18	130.36	149.75	176.33	194.92
Net Factor Inc/Pmts(−) Abroad	98.n	.82	1.11	.10	.01	−.06	—	.08	.10	.46	.62	1.15	2.99	5.48	12.14	14.53
Gross Nat'l Expenditure = GNP	99a	29.92	32.66	37.77	40.23	43.98	47.75	50.41	54.16	67.34	87.47	112.33	133.36	155.23	188.47	209.45
Nat'l Income, Market Prices	99e	45.43	49.73	57.42	61.06	66.67	44.66	47.22	50.78	63.19	82.00	106.04	126.03	146.85	178.65	198.60
Gross Dom. Prod. 1990 Prices	99b.p	265.36	285.82	273.09	286.75	301.83	294.58	296.66	297.86	318.48	336.15	351.60	367.79	381.77	412.32	432.13
GDP Deflator (1990=100)	99bi p	12.5	13.2	14.7	15.4	15.8	16.2	17.0	18.1	21.0	25.8	31.6	35.4	39.2	42.8	45.1
																Millions:
Population	99z	102.87	105.05	107.25	109.52	111.83	114.18	116.62	ⅼ64.30	66.84	68.84	70.90	ⅼ73.21	75.44	77.75	80.13

Interest Rates: *Government Bond Yield:* ⅼ Beginning in 1992, data refer to the three-year federal investment bond yield.

International Transactions: ⅼ Beginning in 1972, data for *lines 70, 71,* and *71.v* exclude trade of former East Pakistan and include trade with Bangladesh.

Government Finance: ⅼ Beginning in 1966, minor modifications to the revenue and expenditure data have been made; comparable data for earlier periods are not available. ⅼ Beginning in 1973, data are as reported in the *Government Finance Statistics Yearbook* and are not comparable with previous years, which included the former East Pakistan. Prior to 1973, data are as reported by the State Bank of Pakistan for publication in *IFS*. ⅼ Beginning in 1978, data on uses of cash balances are not available.

Pakistan

1980	1981	1982	1983	1984	1985	1986	1987	1988	1989	1990	1991	1992	1993	1994		
Millions of Rupees															**International Transactions**	
25,923	28,538	28,275	40,320	35,994	43,645	56,336	72,583	81,348	96,646	121,345	155,398	183,599	187,787	225,200	Exports	70
52,968	55,749	64,712	69,855	82,038	93,793	89,297	101,310	118,681	146,444	160,134	201,409	235,296	265,142	271,744	Imports, cif	71
48,373	50,912	59,098	63,795	74,921	85,656	81,550	92,521	108,384	133,739	146,241	183,935	214,882	242,139	....	Imports, fob	71.v
1990=100																
48.1	57.5	I46.0	64.6	53.1	66.6	116.4	94.7	94.9	100.1	100.0	113.2	123.7	112.3	138.7	Volume of Exports	72
80.2	85.1	I79.3	79.5	82.7	94.2	94.6	95.0	100.0	104.5	100.0	104.6	122.4	123.7	119.5	Volume of Imports	73
46.0	47.7	I52.3	56.2	62.6	62.4	75.8	83.2	84.5	91.3	100.0	103.6	106.4	115.9	135.8	Unit Value of Exports	74
38.6	44.4	I50.1	50.4	55.3	57.6	54.9	66.6	74.1	87.0	100.0	107.3	110.0	117.6	137.7	Unit Value of Imports	75
Minus Sign Indicates Debit															**Balance of Payments**	
2,569	2,730	2,341	2,877	2,480	2,648	3,191	3,938	4,405	4,796	5,380	6,381	6,881	6,760	....	Goods: Exports f.o.b.	78aa d
−5,445	−5,656	−5,744	−5,592	−6,234	−5,878	−5,971	−6,254	−7,097	−7,366	−8,094	−8,642	−9,671	−9,312	....	Goods: Imports f.o.b.	78ab d
−2,876	−2,926	−3,403	−2,715	−3,753	−3,230	−2,780	−2,316	−2,693	−2,571	−2,714	−2,262	−2,790	−2,552	....	Trade Balance	78ac d
649	643	799	769	791	845	826	967	853	1,182	1,423	1,524	1,552	1,516	....	Services: Credit	78ad d
−873	−915	−947	−985	−1,087	−1,179	−1,196	−1,282	−1,486	−1,704	−2,063	−2,303	−2,671	−2,642	....	Services: Debit	78ae d
−3,100	−3,197	−3,550	−2,931	−4,050	−3,564	−3,149	−2,630	−3,326	−3,093	−3,355	−3,041	−3,909	−3,678	....	Balance on Goods and Services	78af d
86	111	127	160	191	112	107	116	94	141	96	73	73	61	....	Income: Credit	78ag d
−357	−377	−532	−578	−662	−692	−754	−905	−907	−1,104	−1,175	−1,256	−1,478	−1,595	....	Income: Debit	78ah d
−3,372	−3,463	−3,955	−3,349	−4,521	−4,144	−3,796	−3,420	−4,140	−4,055	−4,434	−4,224	−5,313	−5,212	....	Balance on Goods, Serv., & Inc.	78ai d
2,456	2,552	3,160	3,381	3,333	3,081	3,170	2,885	2,747	2,757	2,820	2,877	3,485	2,308	....	Current Transfers, n.i.e.: Credit	78aj d
−4	−3	−6	−5	−7	−15	−18	−25	−30	−36	−40	−49	−40	−31	....	Current Transfers: Debit	78ak d
−920	−913	−801	27	−1,195	−1,078	−645	−560	−1,423	−1,334	−1,654	−1,396	−1,868	−2,935	....	Current Account, n.i.e.	78al d
—	—	—	—	—	—	—	—	—	—	—	—	—	—	....	Capital Account, n.i.e.: Credit	78ba d
−1	−1	−1	−2	—	−2	−1	−1	−1	−1	−1	−1	−1	−1	....	Capital Account: Debit	78bb d
−1	−1	−1	−2	—	−2	−1	−1	−1	−1	−1	−1	−1	−1	....	Capital Account, n.i.e.	78bc d
—	—	—	—	5	8	1	−19	−13	−43	−2	4	12	2	....	Direct Investment Abroad	78bd d
63	108	64	29	55	131	105	129	186	210	244	257	335	346	....	Dir. Invest. in Rep. Econ., n.i.e.	78be d
—	—	—	—	9	110	83	132	126	15	87	92	370	292	....	Portfolio Investment Assets	78bf d
—	—	—	—	—	—	—	—	—	—	—	—	—	—	....	Portfolio Investment Liab., n.i.e.	78bg d
−17	12	−13	−10	−103	−78	−198	−166	−188	−199	−363	−309	−565	−285	....	Other Investment Assets	78bh d
592	546	479	513	367	461	540	293	1,436	1,156	1,206	847	2,405	2,594	....	Other Investment Liab., n.i.e.	78bi d
639	665	530	533	333	631	531	368	1,548	1,139	1,173	891	2,556	2,949	....	Financial Account, n.i.e.	78bj d
71	−8	33	−16	−96	33	−42	17	23	−242	−103	−78	120	−91	....	Net Errors and Omissions	78ca d
−211	−257	−240	542	−958	−417	−157	−177	147	−439	−585	−584	808	−78	....	Overall Balance	78cb d
211	257	240	−542	958	417	157	177	−147	439	585	584	−808	78	....	Reserves and Related Items	79aa d
−311	−232	−279	−1,102	870	308	157	325	40	−214	469	−216	−494	−399	....	Reserve Assets	79db d
120	414	452	276	−72	−187	−371	−422	−317	398	−165	227	100	−4	....	Use of Fund Credit and Loans	79dc d
5	−5	—	—	—	—	—	—	—	—	—	—	—	—	....	Liabs.Constit.For.Auth.Reserves	79dd d
398	80	66	284	160	296	371	275	130	254	282	573	−414	481	....	Exceptional Financing	79de d
Year Ending June 30															**Government Finance**	
−13,344	−16,138	−15,351	−24,784	−25,928	−33,783	−46,917	−48,783	−42,426	−56,982	−46,232	−77,105	−95,418	−100,571	−94,453 f	Deficit (-) or Surplus	80
38,102	45,359	50,370	57,750	71,042	76,351	89,716	98,976	119,844	143,370	163,825	170,642	216,586	250,004	288,693 f	Revenue	81
1,826	2,598	2,560	2,189	1,957	2,717	4,510	3,350	5,372	7,831	7,159	10,544	7,511	4,120	2,561 f	Grants Received	81z
41,084	53,392	55,355	70,560	82,627	93,613	120,114	127,822	158,122	191,463	192,079	237,388	294,370	325,499	357,646 f	Expenditure	82
12,188	10,703	12,926	14,163	16,300	19,238	21,029	23,287	9,520	16,720	25,137	20,903	25,145	29,196	28,061 f	Lending Minus Repayments	83
															Financing	
8,022	9,814	11,318	20,617	22,610	31,851	43,108	40,805	30,515	38,352	26,475	61,297	73,110	71,254	62,155 f	Domestic	84
5,322	6,324	4,033	4,167	3,318	1,932	3,809	7,978	11,911	18,630	19,757	15,808	22,308	29,317	32,298 f	Foreign	85
															Financing	
....	....	....	....	....	....	....	....	....	....	....	....	....	....	....	Net Borrowing: Domestic	84a
....	....	....	....	....	....	....	....	....	....	....	....	....	....	....	Foreign	85a
....	....	....	....	....	....	....	....	....	....	....	....	....	....	....	Use of Cash Balances	87
127,492	134,012	177,828	198,582	227,794	284,085	360,388	412,276	492,236	581,192	....	....	....	....	....	Debt	88
56,754	60,088	76,656	87,856	106,554	143,930	193,385	225,246	284,492	327,534	....	....	....	....	....	Domestic	88a
70,738	73,924	101,172	110,726	121,240	140,155	167,003	187,030	207,744	253,658	....	....	....	....	....	Foreign	89a
25,269	25,740	34,756	27,127	35,598	54,704	59,827	55,694	81,957	90,038	110,774	132,845	....	....	....	Held by: State Bank	88aa
19,000	19,457	20,812	25,928	23,152	30,292	38,979	45,597	63,281	61,037	51,177	83,354	....	....	....	Deposit Money Banks	88ab
1,666	2,514	3,162	4,007	4,327	4,103	5,055	8,630	9,194	10,527	10,593	14,810	....	....	....	Other Financial Inst.	88ac
12,477	13,800	19,407	28,100	33,529	41,555	49,649	57,326	69,786	92,533	108,635	137,985	....	....	....	International Inst.	88ca
58,261	60,124	81,765	82,626	87,711	98,600	117,354	129,704	137,958	161,125	189,017	197,018	....	....	....	Foreign Govts. & Bks.	88cb
10,819	12,377	17,926	30,794	43,475	54,831	89,524	115,325	130,060	165,932	204,052	223,571	....	....	....	Others	88d
2,277	2,456	2,662	2,921	2,935	3,897	4,125	5,298	3,130	3,647	4,243	4,989	....	....	....	Intragovernmental Debt	88s
Year Ending June 30															**National Accounts**	
29.49	35.71	33.03	44.40	47.84	49.89	63.27	79.06	93.60	108.32	126.58	172.81	209.22	217.42	245.86	Exports of Goods & Services	90c
23.54	28.28	33.52	41.61	50.74	57.13	65.66	77.48	104.75	129.20	129.56	145.58	155.57	174.66	192.09	Government Consumption	91f
41.35	47.71	54.59	61.76	69.21	77.93	87.55	100.04	111.27	133.17	148.08	177.65	225.36	256.64	287.26	Gross Fixed Capital Formation	93e
2.00	4.50	7.86	6.70	7.49	8.60	9.00	9.50	10.40	14.00	14.00	15.80	18.70	21.10	24.60	Increase/Decrease(-) in Stocks	93i
192.39	224.14	263.66	291.94	336.75	385.35	392.53	415.67	486.57	543.30	611.02	697.45	849.95	968.16	1,128.46	Private Consumption	96f
−54.58	−62.13	−68.50	−82.02	−92.22	−106.73	−103.48	−109.27	−131.20	−156.64	−173.29	−188.68	−247.41	−296.05	−313.30	Imports of Goods & Services	98c
234.18	278.20	324.16	364.39	419.80	472.16	514.53	572.48	675.39	769.75	855.94	1,020.60	1,211.38	1,341.95	1,564.97	Gross Domestic Product	99b
18.28	22.69	25.35	39.40	39.60	38.31	41.36	36.38	29.10	28.01	36.90	23.91	12.54	14.94	14.80	Net Factor Inc/Pmts(-) Abroad	98.n
252.46	300.89	349.51	403.78	459.40	510.47	555.89	608.86	704.48	797.75	892.84	1,044.51	1,223.92	1,356.89	1,579.77	Gross Nat'l Expenditure = GNP	99a
239.41	284.76	330.59	381.89	433.83	481.75	524.37	574.12	665.24	753.98	842.97	983.87	1,148.86	1,272.83	1,480.23	Nat'l Income, Market Prices	99e
469.73	I502.26	535.09	571.36	600.30	645.88	681.41	725.38	780.69	819.41	855.94	902.70	973.35	992.03	1,032.13	Gross Dom. Prod. 1990 Prices	99b.p
49.9	55.4	60.6	63.8	69.9	73.1	75.5	78.9	86.5	93.9	100.0	113.1	124.5	135.3	151.6	GDP Deflator (1990=100)	99bi p
Midyear Estimates																
82.58	85.12	87.76	90.48	93.29	96.18	99.16	102.24	105.41	108.68	112.03	115.52	119.11	122.80	126.61	**Population**	99z

Panama

283

		1965	1966	1967	1968	1969	1970	1971	1972	1973	1974	1975	1976	1977	1978	1979
Exchange Rates															*Balboas per SDR:*	
Official Rate	aa	1.0000	1.0000	1.0000	1.0000	1.0000	1.0000	1.0857	1.0857	1.2064	1.2244	1.1707	1.1618	1.2147	1.3028	1.3173
														Balboas per US Dollar:		
Official Rate	ae	1.0000	1.0000	1.0000	1.0000	1.0000	1.0000	1.0000	1.0000	1.0000	1.0000	1.0000	1.0000	1.0000	1.0000	1.0000
Fund Position														*Millions of SDRs:*		
Quota	2f. s	11.3	11.3	11.3	11.3	28.0	36.0	36.0	36.0	36.0	36.0	36.0	36.0	36.0	45.0	45.0
SDRs	1b. s	—	—	—	—	—	3.2	2.6	2.7	2.6	2.3	6.4	5.2	4.5	4.0	3.9
Reserve Position in the Fund	1c. s	.1	.1	.1	—	—	1.0	4.4	8.0	8.0					3.7	2.5
Total Fund Cred.&Loans Outstg.	2tl	—	—	—	2.3	2.7	—	—	—	—	7.4	17.5	42.6	42.2	40.3	31.5
International Liquidity											*Millions of US Dollars Unless Otherwise Indicated:*					
Total Reserves minus Gold	1l. d	5.7	5.9	6.7	11.1	14.1	15.8	21.0	43.1	41.7	39.3	34.4	78.9	70.9	150.4	118.7
SDRs	1b. d	—	—	—	—	—	3.2	2.9	3.0	3.1	2.8	7.4	6.0	5.5	5.2	5.2
Reserve Position in the Fund	1c. d	.1	.1	.1	—	—	1.0	4.8	8.7	9.6					4.9	3.2
Foreign Exchange	1d. d	5.6	5.8	6.6	11.1	14.1	11.5	13.4	31.5	29.0	36.5	27.0	72.9	65.4	140.4	110.3
Gold (National Valuation)	1and	. . .	. . .	. . .	. . .	. . .	. . .	. . .	. . .	. . .	. . .	. . .	. . .	. . .	. . .	3.7
Monetary Authorities: Other Liab.	4..d	6	6	8	10	37	18	28	30	32	69	93	120	105	107	138
Deposit Money Banks: Assets	7a. d	38	75	61	77	167	287	454	898	2,260	4,795	6,483	7,697	9,970	13,382	19,446
of which: Claims on Nonbanks	7ad d	. . .	. . .	. . .	. . .	. . .	. . .	. . .	. . .	. . .	3,188	4,626	4,944	6,701	8,918	11,701
Deposit Money Banks: Liabilities	7b. d	62	103	96	115	218	364	588	1,097	2,588	5,340	7,116	8,372	10,634	13,846	20,315
of which: Liab. to Nonbanks	7bd d	. . .	. . .	. . .	. . .	. . .	. . .	. . .	. . .	. . .	750	1,278	1,889	1,777	1,865	2,837
ILB: Assets	7k. d	. . .	. . .	. . .	. . .	. . .	35e	38e	59e	57e	1,108	1,670	2,682	4,073	6,039	12,317
of which: Claims on Nonbanks	7kd d	. . .	. . .	. . .	. . .	. . .	. . .	. . .	. . .	. . .	511	918	1,392	2,066	3,416	6,296
ILB: Liabilities	7m. d	. . .	. . .	. . .	. . .	. . .	72e	60e	72e	88e	1,088	1,712	2,719	4,016	5,940	12,198
of which: Liab. to Nonbanks	7md d	. . .	. . .	. . .	. . .	. . .	. . .	. . .	. . .	. . .	. . .	. . .	. . .	. . .	. . .	. . .
Monetary Authorities														*Millions of Balboas:*		
Foreign Assets	11	5.7	5.9	6.7	11.1	I 14.1	15.7	21.0	43.1	41.7	39.3	34.4	78.9	70.9	150.4	122.4
Claims on Central Government	12a	. . .	. . .	. . .	. . .	36.9	26.6	26.7	39.2	35.8	60.1	89.8	168.5	155.4	129.7	170.4
Claims on Official Entities	12bx	. . .	. . .	. . .	. . .	. . .	. . .	. . .	. . .	2.5	2.1	8.2	25.6	12.3	33.7	78.5
Claims on Private Sector	12d	66.6	70.2	77.1	75.9	I 47.7	53.4	67.6	86.6	114.5	130.4	140.7	124.4	121.8	175.5	216.3
Bankers Deposits	14c	. . .	. . .	. . .	. . .	12.6	17.6	19.3	32.9	31.3	32.7	52.0	79.5	88.0	61.5	146.4
Demand Deposits	14d	17.8	18.8	18.9	17.8	I 14.5	15.4	17.1	34.3	29.9	23.5	23.9	26.2	28.2	32.0	38.7
Time, Savings,& Fgn.Currency Dep.	15	31.3	34.5	40.8	35.6	I 12.1	15.1	17.3	22.5	22.3	23.4	25.4	30.5	37.8	45.8	49.3
Foreign Liabilities	16c	6.4	5.5	8.3	12.6	I 22.0	14.6	19.0	10.4	17.3	71.7	103.4	157.6	144.0	147.5	165.8
Long-Term Foreign Liabilities	16cl	. . .	. . .	. . .	. . .	17.6	3.4	8.7	20.0	14.8	6.6	9.1	11.6	12.6	12.3	13.8
Central Government Deposits	16d	11.4	12.3	13.4	10.4	I 18.0	25.3	29.7	48.3	59.2	63.4	68.9	103.0	109.5	205.2	147.5
Capital Accounts	17a	. . .	. . .	. . .	. . .	13.9	18.2	23.7	28.8	32.5	30.9	32.5	32.8	36.5	45.6	52.1
Other Items (Net)	17r	5.3	5.0	2.4	10.6	I -12.0	-13.9	-19.5	-28.3	-12.8	-20.4	-42.9	-43.7	-96.3	-60.6	-26.0
Deposit Money Banks														*Millions of Balboas:*		
Foreign Assets	21	38.0	75.4	61.3	77.3	166.9	287.1	454.2	898.3	2,259.9	4,795.4	6,482.5	7,696.7	9,969.9	13,382.2	19,445.6
Claims on Central Government	22a	. . .	. . .	. . .	. . .	. . .	. . .	9.1	9.9	11.5	19.9	53.9	195.3	224.5	262.5	215.4	165.9
Claims on Private Sector	22d	104.9	126.3	157.8	187.7	233.9	329.4	441.5	596.0	758.2	1,052.6	1,060.6	1,092.0	1,148.7	1,250.0	1,496.3
Demand Deposits	24	37.7	43.1	51.4	63.1	70.3	85.1	88.3	119.3	131.2	172.8	149.2	163.8	185.0	214.0	262.6
Time and Savings Deposits	25	37.9	52.5	69.6	90.0	99.6	140.7	179.5	216.8	261.1	310.5	349.3	357.5	421.5	540.9	692.9
Foreign Liabilities	26c	62.0	103.0	96.0	115.0	218.0	364.0	588.0	1,097.0	2,588.0	5,340.0	7,116.1	8,372.3	10,633.8	13,845.7	20,315.0
Capital Accounts	27a	. . .	. . .	. . .	. . .	11.1	15.8	45.5	53.7	105.9	132.8	181.2	158.9	249.6	287.3	385.9
Other Items (Net)	27r	5.3	3.1	2.1	-3.1	8.6	20.0	4.3	19.0	-48.2	-54.2	-57.4	-39.0	-108.8	-40.3	-549.0
Monetary Survey														*Millions of Balboas:*		
Foreign Assets (Net)	31n	-24.8	-26.7	-36.4	-38.7	-59.0	-75.8	-131.8	-166.0	-303.7	-577.0	-703.5	-754.3	-737.0	-460.6	-913.2
Domestic Credit	32	160.1	184.2	221.5	253.2	307.3	393.2	516.2	685.0	871.7	1,235.7	1,425.7	1,532.3	1,591.2	1,599.1	1,979.9
Claims on Central Govt. (Net)	32an	-11.4	-12.3	-13.4	-10.4	25.7	10.4	6.9	2.4	-3.5	50.6	216.2	290.3	308.4	139.9	188.8
Claims on Private Sector	32d	171.5	196.5	234.9	263.6	281.6	382.8	509.1	682.6	872.7	1,183.0	1,201.3	1,216.4	1,270.5	1,425.5	1,712.6
Deposit Money	34	55.5	61.9	70.3	80.9	84.8	100.5	105.4	153.6	161.1	196.3	173.1	190.0	213.2	246.0	301.3
Quasi-Money	35	69.2	87.0	110.4	125.6	I 111.7	155.8	196.8	239.3	283.4	333.9	374.7	388.0	459.3	586.7	742.2
Other Items (Net)	37r	10.6	8.6	4.4	8.0	51.8	61.2	82.0	126.1	123.5	128.5	174.4	200.0	181.7	305.8	23.2
Money plus Quasi-Money	35l	124.7	148.9	180.7	206.5	I 196.5	256.3	302.2	392.9	444.5	530.2	547.8	578.0	672.5	832.7	1,043.5
Other Banking Institutions														*Millions of Balboas:*		
Claims on Private Sector	42d	. . .	. . .	. . .	. . .	. . .	. . .	. . .	. . .	. . .	. . .	85.7	88.9	98.2	111.2	126.2
Claims on Deposit Money Banks	42e	. . .	. . .	. . .	. . .	. . .	. . .	. . .	. . .	. . .	. . .	—	—	—	—	—
Time and Savings Deposits	45	. . .	. . .	. . .	. . .	. . .	. . .	. . .	. . .	. . .	. . .	87.8	105.5	122.3	115.7	124.3
Capital Accounts	47a	. . .	. . .	. . .	. . .	. . .	. . .	. . .	. . .	. . .	. . .	6.9	7.0	7.0	7.3	7.5
Other Items (Net)	47r	. . .	. . .	. . .	. . .	. . .	. . .	. . .	. . .	. . .	. . .	-9.0	-23.6	-31.1	-11.8	-5.6
Liquid Liabilities	55l	. . .	. . .	. . .	. . .	. . .	. . .	. . .	. . .	. . .	. . .	634.6	682.4	793.7	946.8	1,166.3
Interest Rates														*Percent Per Annum*		
Deposit Rate	60l	. . .	. . .	. . .	. . .	. . .	. . .	. . .	. . .	. . .	. . .	. . .	. . .	. . .	. . .	. . .
Lending Rate	60p	. . .	. . .	. . .	. . .	. . .	. . .	. . .	. . .	. . .	. . .	. . .	. . .	. . .	. . .	. . .
Prices														*Index Numbers (1990=100):*		
Wholesale Prices	63	. . .	31.7	32.0	32.6	33.1	34.1	35.9	39.0	43.1	56.1	64.0	69.0	74.0	77.9	88.9
Consumer Prices	64	39.2	39.2	39.8	40.4	41.2	42.4	43.2	45.6	48.7	56.6	I 60.0	62.3	65.2	67.9	73.4

Panama

	1980	1981	1982	1983	1984	1985	1986	1987	1988	1989	1990	1991	1992	1993	1994		
End of Period																**Exchange Rates**	
	1.2754	1.1640	1.1031	1.0470	.9802	1.0984	1.2232	1.4187	1.3457	1.3142	1.4227	1.4304	1.3750	1.3736	1.4599	Official Rate	aa
End of Period																	
	1.0000	1.0000	1.0000	1.0000	1.0000	1.0000	1.0000	1.0000	1.0000	1.0000	1.0000	1.0000	1.0000	1.0000	1.0000	Official Rate	ae
End of Period																**Fund Position**	
	67.5	67.5	67.5	102.2	102.2	102.2	102.2	102.2	102.2	102.2	102.2	102.2	149.6	149.6	149.6	Quota	2f. s
	1.1	2.8	3.8	.4	—	11.7	1.4	—	—	—	—	19.4	8.1	3.3	.1	SDRs	1b. s
	8.1	—	—	8.7	—	—	—	—	—	—	—	—	—	11.9	11.9	Reserve Position in the Fund	1c. s
	18.1	80.5	76.1	184.1	276.6	283.4	288.6	243.9	243.8	243.2	191.3	150.7	79.8	82.3	91.3	Total Fund Cred.&Loans Outstg.	2tl
End of Period																**International Liquidity**	
	117.4	119.9	101.0	206.7	215.6	98.0	170.2	77.8	72.2	119.4	343.5	499.1	504.4	597.4	704.3	Total Reserves minus Gold	1l. d
	1.4	3.2	4.2	.4	—	12.9	1.8	—	—	—	—	27.6	11.6	4.6	.1	SDRs	1b. d
	10.3	—	—	9.1	—	—	—	—	—	—	—	—	16.3	16.3	17.3	Reserve Position in the Fund	1c. d
	105.7	116.7	96.8	197.2	215.6	85.1	168.4	77.8	72.2	119.4	315.9	487.4	483.5	581.0	686.9	Foreign Exchange	1d. d
	3.7														—	Gold (National Valuation)	1and
	186	221	281	338	352	358	333	351	345	356	345	337	352	334	292	Monetary Authorities: Other Liab.	4..d
	18,970	24,675	27,102	24,649	22,229	22,555	24,459	16,137	6,595	6,287	6,857	8,668	9,714	12,735	16,617	Deposit Money Banks: Assets	7a. d
	14,042	19,349	20,297	17,070	15,661	15,415	16,165	10,412	4,751	4,788	5,131	5,733	6,703	9,425	12,047	of which: Claims on Nonbanks	7ad d
	19,508	25,234	26,965	24,791	22,380	22,385	24,204	16,185	6,923	6,509	6,533	7,860	8,522	11,336	14,846	Deposit Money Banks: Liabilities	7b. d
	3,413	4,939	5,647	6,434	6,655	7,008	7,967	6,629	4,468	4,056	3,319	4,136	3,998	4,686	6,295	of which: Liab. to Nonbanks	7bd d
	15,243	16,424	16,374	12,637	10,107	10,536	9,182	....	3,275	....	....	....	....	....	....	ILB: Assets	7k. d
	9,036	11,585	12,484	8,847	7,572	7,602	6,420	....	2,486	....	....	....	....	....	....	of which: Claims on Nonbanks	7kd d
	15,095	16,061	15,900	12,160	9,566	10,134	8,900	....	3,130	....	....	....	....	....	....	ILB: Liabilities	7m. d
	....	3,542	3,257	2,299	2,133	2,267	4,027	....	1,171	....	....	....	....	....	....	of which: Liab. to Nonbanks	7md d
End of Period																**Monetary Authorities**	
	121.1	119.9	101.0	206.7	215.6	98.0	170.2	77.8	72.2	119.4	343.5	499.1	504.4	597.4	704.3	Foreign Assets	11
	172.3	343.1	346.4	480.0	638.0	737.3	713.8	795.6	988.1	1,150.0	1,115.7	1,033.7	1,019.4	1,050.1	1,014.0	Claims on Central Government	12a
	32.8	59.4	96.5	96.1	93.7	92.3	102.0	105.6	106.8	106.8	106.8	106.8	106.8	—	—	Claims on Official Entities	12bx
	268.0	283.5	339.9	335.9	336.0	322.6	324.3	301.0	300.5	298.8	247.6	234.0	288.0	322.8	300.6	Claims on Private Sector	12d
	155.9	221.5	207.5	207.5	210.2	198.0	223.3	135.5	116.7	104.1	164.6	225.0	237.5	175.6	184.4	167.4	Bankers Deposits	14c
	42.0	40.7	48.8	45.7	46.7	50.0	55.7	46.2	28.6	37.9	52.8	57.9	62.1	63.0	75.4	Demand Deposits	14d
	63.2	83.8	99.7	128.8	157.3	154.4	201.9	179.3	141.2	137.3	148.2	164.7	172.9	187.3	192.5	Time, Savings,& Fgn.Currency Dep.	15
	144.7	196.5	149.6	271.7	348.2	406.1	425.8	479.4	456.1	451.4	390.4	327.0	254.8	244.7	225.5	Foreign Liabilities	16c
	63.9	117.8	215.1	259.4	275.3	263.5	259.8	217.7	216.7	224.0	226.8	225.2	207.1	202.3	199.5	Long-Term Foreign Liabilities	16cl
	144.0	210.3	218.6	243.4	223.7	266.6	305.9	323.1	516.0	686.0	1,060.6	1,262.7	1,358.8	1,550.6	1,716.2	Central Government Deposits	16d
	71.9	82.4	94.0	102.7	101.2	108.6	113.6	120.6	124.1	127.0	76.5	49.2	157.7	196.0	228.3	Capital Accounts	17a
	-91.4	-147.0	-149.5	-140.4	-79.3	-197.1	-275.8	-221.8	-131.8	-92.7	-306.5	-450.5	-470.4	-657.9	-786.0	Other Items (Net)	17r
End of Period																**Deposit Money Banks**	
	18,970.3	24,674.5	27,102.1	24,649.2	22,228.6	22,555.2	24,458.6	16,136.6	6,594.5	6,287.4	6,857.4	8,668.2	9,713.6	12,735.2	16,616.7	Foreign Assets	21
	213.8	207.0	297.6	348.5	377.2	351.4	365.7	201.4	169.4	157.5	157.5	165.8	167.2	144.1	Claims on Central Government	22a
	1,803.2	2,185.8	2,195.2	2,177.4	2,200.5	2,277.1	2,655.9	2,732.1	2,171.9	2,169.0	2,233.5	2,782.5	3,458.9	4,270.0	5,048.8	Claims on Private Sector	22d
	293.3	319.0	330.5	326.9	334.0	359.3	393.8	395.9	275.2	269.0	380.0	499.0	577.1	645.2	728.6	Demand Deposits	24
	917.2	1,117.4	1,270.1	1,246.8	1,324.6	1,388.6	1,708.5	1,657.1	1,203.5	1,156.0	1,604.0	2,141.0	2,765.4	3,296.0	3,845.4	Time and Savings Deposits	25
	19,508.4	25,233.6	26,965.3	24,791.1	22,380.0	22,385.2	24,204.1	16,184.7	6,922.9	6,509.0	6,533.1	7,860.0	8,521.8	11,336.5	14,846.1	Foreign Liabilities	26c
	597.3	682.4	1,202.0	988.0	979.7	1,050.2	1,193.6	1,034.2	671.0	636.0	656.0	736.0	898.0	1,008.0	1,321.3	Capital Accounts	27a
	-328.9	-285.1	-173.0	-177.7	-211.6	.7	-19.8	-201.7	-136.8	45.9	75.3	372.2	576.0	886.8	1,068.2	Other Items (Net)	27r
End of Period																**Monetary Survey**	
	-561.7	-635.7	88.2	-206.9	-284.0	-138.2	-1.2	-449.7	-712.3	-553.6	277.4	980.3	1,441.4	1,751.4	2,249.3	Foreign Assets (Net)	31n
	2,346.1	2,868.5	3,057.0	3,194.5	3,421.5	3,514.1	3,855.8	3,812.6	3,220.7	3,198.1	2,800.5	3,051.9	3,680.1	4,259.6	4,791.3	Domestic Credit	32
	242.1	339.8	425.4	585.1	791.5	822.1	773.6	673.9	641.5	623.5	212.6	-71.4	-173.6	-333.3	-558.1	Claims on Central Govt. (Net)	32an
	2,071.2	2,469.3	2,535.1	2,513.3	2,536.5	2,599.7	2,980.2	3,033.1	2,472.4	2,467.8	2,481.1	3,016.5	3,746.9	4,592.8	5,349.4	Claims on Private Sector	32d
	335.3	359.7	379.3	372.6	380.7	409.3	449.5	442.1	303.8	306.9	413.8	432.8	556.9	639.2	708.2	804.0	Deposit Money	34
	980.4	1,201.1	1,369.8	1,375.6	1,481.9	1,543.0	1,910.4	1,836.4	1,344.7	1,293.3	1,752.4	2,305.7	2,938.3	3,483.5	4,037.9	Quasi-Money	35
	468.7	672.0	1,396.1	1,239.4	1,275.5	1,423.9	1,494.7	1,084.5	859.9	1,044.3	892.7	1,169.6	1,544.0	1,819.6	2,198.6	Other Items (Net)	37r
	1,315.7	1,560.8	1,749.1	1,748.2	1,862.6	1,952.3	2,359.9	2,278.5	1,648.5	1,600.2	2,185.2	2,862.5	3,577.5	4,191.5	4,842.0	Money plus Quasi-Money	35l
End of Period																**Other Banking Institutions**	
	143.1	154.8	164.4	186.2	207.4	230.6	....	....	....	....	....	....	....	....	....	Claims on Private Sector	42d
	.5	.5	3.2	5.2	6.6	5.1	....	....	....	....	....	....	....	....	....	Claims on Deposit Money Banks	42e
	144.2	165.1	202.3	225.9	249.1	250.0	....	....	....	....	....	....	....	....	....	Time and Savings Deposits	45
	7.7	7.9	8.2	8.6	8.8	9.1	....	....	....	....	....	....	....	....	....	Capital Accounts	47a
	-8.3	-17.7	-42.9	-43.1	-43.9	-23.4	....	....	....	....	....	....	....	....	....	Other Items (Net)	47r
	1,458.3	1,723.8	1,949.1	1,970.8	2,108.6	2,194.7	....	....	....	....	....	....	....	....	....	Liquid Liabilities	55l
Percent Per Annum																**Interest Rates**	
	....	....	....	....	....	....	6.50	6.59	7.54	8.49	8.40	7.73	I5.67	5.90	6.11	Deposit Rate	60l
							12.36	12.60	12.47	12.92	11.98	11.79	10.61	10.06	10.15	Lending Rate	60p
Period Averages																**Prices**	
	102.5	112.8	I122.1	117.4	118.7	118.2	99.3	100.8	93.9	I96.2	100.0	100.5	102.3	102.1	104.1	Wholesale Prices	63
	83.5	89.6	93.4	95.4	96.9	97.9	97.8	98.8	I99.1	99.2	100.0	101.3	103.1	103.6	104.9	Consumer Prices	64

Panama
283

		1965	1966	1967	1968	1969	1970	1971	1972	1973	1974	1975	1976	1977	1978	1979
International Transactions																*Millions of Balboas*
Exports	70	70.2	79.7	86.4	95.3	110.5	109.5	116.5	122.6	137.8	210.5	286.4	238.2	251.0	256.4	302.9
Imports, cif	71	208.5	234.8	250.7	266.3	293.6	357.0	395.8	440.5	502.2	822.4	892.0	848.3	861.2	942.4	1,183.8
Imports, fob	71.v	189.6	214.5	229.3	243.3	278.7	326.4	359.0	401.1	454.0	755.7	815.6	779.7	777.8	844.9	1,062.9
																1990=100
Volume of Exports	72	158	170	159	136	164	148	156	133	118	150	202	132	138	138	127
Unit Value of Exports	74	70	71	72	73	69	68	67	71	75	88	102	100	90	89	99
Balance of Payments																*Millions of US Dollars:*
Goods: Exports f.o.b.	78aa d	…	…	…	…	…	…	…	…	…	…	…	…	401.0	385.7	453.2
Goods: Imports f.o.b.	78ab d	…	…	…	…	…	…	…	…	…	…	…	…	−790.4	−862.1	−1,085.7
Trade Balance	78ac d	…	…	…	…	…	…	…	…	…	…	…	…	−389.4	−476.4	−632.5
Services: Credit	78ad d	…	…	…	…	…	…	…	…	…	…	…	…	401.2	442.5	559.5
Services: Debit	78ae d	…	…	…	…	…	…	…	…	…	…	…	…	−205.0	−238.8	−287.7
Balance on Goods and Services	78af d	…	…	…	…	…	…	…	…	…	…	…	…	−193.2	−272.7	−360.7
Income: Credit	78ag d	…	…	…	…	…	…	…	…	…	…	…	…	585.9	915.4	1,570.7
Income: Debit	78ah d	…	…	…	…	…	…	…	…	…	…	…	…	−545.7	−848.3	−1,533.3
Balance on Goods, Serv., & Inc.	78ai d	…	…	…	…	…	…	…	…	…	…	…	…	−153.0	−205.6	−323.3
Current Transfers, n.i.e.: Credit	78aj d	…	…	…	…	…	…	…	…	…	…	…	…	32.4	36.6	57.0
Current Transfers: Debit	78ak d	…	…	…	…	…	…	…	…	…	…	…	…	−34.8	−38.7	−44.7
Current Account, n.i.e.	78al d	…	…	…	…	…	…	…	…	…	…	…	…	−155.4	−207.7	−311.0
Capital Account, n.i.e.: Credit	78ba d	…	…	…	…	…	…	…	…	…	…	…	…	—	—	—
Capital Account: Debit	78bb d	…	…	…	…	…	…	…	…	…	…	…	…	—	—	—
Capital Account, n.i.e.	78bc d	…	…	…	…	…	…	…	…	…	…	…	…	—	—	—
Direct Investment Abroad	78bd d	…	…	…	…	…	…	…	…	…	…	…	…			
Dir. Invest. in Rep. Econ., n.i.e.	78be d	…	…	…	…	…	…	…	…	…	…	…	…	10.9	−2.5	49.8
Portfolio Investment Assets	78bf d	…	…	…	…	…	…	…	…	…	…	…	…	—	—	—
Portfolio Investment Liab., n.i.e.	78bg d	…	…	…	…	…	…	…	…	…	…	…	…	12.6	70.4	203.9
Other Investment Assets	78bh d	…	…	…	…	…	…	…	…	…	…	…	…	−2,328.9	−3,408.0	−6,092.3
Other Investment Liab., n.i.e.	78bi d	…	…	…	…	…	…	…	…	…	…	…	…	2,523.6	3,635.6	6,543.9
Financial Account, n.i.e.	78bj d	…	…	…	…	…	…	…	…	…	…	…	…	218.2	295.5	705.3
Net Errors and Omissions	78ca d	…	…	…	…	…	…	…	…	…	…	…	…	−70.1	−1.6	−421.4
Overall Balance	78cb d	…	…	…	…	…	…	…	…	…	…	…	…	−7.3	86.2	−27.1
Reserves and Related Items	79da d	…	…	…	…	…	…	…	…	…	…	…	…	7.3	−86.2	27.1
Reserve Assets	79db d	…	…	…	…	…	…	…	…	…	…	…	…	7.8	−84.0	38.7
Use of Fund Credit and Loans	79dc d	…	…	…	…	…	…	…	…	…	…	…	…	−.6	−2.3	−11.5
Liabs.Constit.For.Auth.Reserves	79dd d	…	…	…	…	…	…	…	…	…	…	…	…	—	—	—
Exceptional Financing	79de d	…	…	…	…	…	…	…	…	…	…	…	…			
Government Finance																*Millions of Balboas:*
Deficit (−) or Surplus	80	Ɪ−3.4	−6.8	−12.9	−8.3	−62.1	−49.1	−32.3	−105.7	Ɪ−91.0	−119.4	−149.5	−202.7	−119.0	−159.6	−371.8
Revenue	81	Ɪ86.5	100.3	112.7	119.4	133.0	160.1	181.2	197.9	Ɪ306.1	385.5	437.4	425.4	536.8	591.6	690.1
Grants Received	81z	…	…	…	…	…	…	…	…	Ɪ—	6.0	14.3	14.8	9.6	6.0	6.5
Expenditure	82	Ɪ89.9	107.2	125.7	127.7	195.2	209.3	213.5	303.5	Ɪ387.0	503.7	581.7	626.5	649.8	736.7	1,066.0
Lending Minus Repayments	83	…	…	…	…	…	…	…	…	Ɪ10.1	7.2	19.5	16.4	15.6	20.5	2.4
Financing																
Net Borrowing	84	3.0	6.1	11.3	6.6	61.3	49.1	32.3	105.7	Ɪ91.0	119.4	149.5	202.7	119.0	159.6	371.8
Domestic	84a	…	…	…	…	…	…	…	…	Ɪ19.1	54.6	46.3	89.9	40.3	37.2	59.4
Foreign	85a	…	…	…	…	…	…	…	…	Ɪ71.9	64.8	103.2	112.8	78.7	122.4	312.4
Use of Cash Balances	87	Ɪ.3	.7	1.7	1.6	.8	—	—	—	…	…	…	…	…	…	…
Debt: Domestic	88a	71.8	71.5	83.6	97.7	133.9	144.9	155.0	190.4	180.0	231.5	294.6	332.7	330.5	374.8	404.8
Foreign	89a	…	68.3	71.3	70.8	104.8	140.6	173.4	214.9	296.9	358.9	427.4	510.2	614.0	1,025.6	1,344.0
National Accounts																*Millions of Balboas*
Exports of Goods & Services	90c	240.2	268.2	301.7	330.0	362.9	388.0	426.4	460.7	528.1	761.8	865.4	837.8	921.1	986.4	1,124.8
Government Consumption	91f	72.4	86.7	102.6	109.7	118.2	152.0	180.2	226.5	250.1	299.3	353.3	386.1	412.1	482.9	567.2
Gross Fixed Capital Formation	93e	100.1	142.1	152.7	173.5	200.7	261.9	306.3	372.2	434.8	465.0	535.5	608.6	445.9	606.3	661.2
Increase/Decrease(−) in Stocks	93i	15.7	15.1	15.7	18.4	22.0	22.0	43.6	30.3	50.9	91.1	31.9	10.2	45.0	45.4	124.5
Private Consumption	96f	484.9	492.9	536.2	551.8	614.9	619.0	665.2	698.3	767.6	954.0	1,054.1	1,088.6	1,242.6	1,431.7	1,693.8
Imports of Goods & Services	98c	−253.4	−286.0	−308.2	−322.0	−373.3	−422.0	−469.8	−523.1	−584.9	−917.1	−999.4	−975.2	−996.9	−1,100.2	−1,371.3
Gross Domestic Product	99b	659.9	719.0	800.7	861.4	945.4	1,021.0	1,151.9	1,264.9	1,446.6	1,654.1	1,840.8	1,956.3	2,069.8	2,452.5	2,800.2
Net Factor Inc/Pmts(−) Abroad	98.n	−15.9	−16.3	−22.7	−25.3	−25.3	−26.5	−29.6	−31.9	−39.1	−54.4	−19.5	−55.5	−63.1	−57.4	−102.8
Gross Nat'l Expenditure = GNP	99a	644.1	702.7	778.0	836.1	920.1	995.0	1,122.3	1,233.0	1,407.5	1,599.7	1,821.3	1,900.8	2,006.7	2,395.1	2,697.4
Nat'l Income, Market Prices	99e	588.3	642.6	709.5	757.4	833.9	942.0	1,062.4	1,165.5	1,334.3	1,519.2	1,729.5	1,800.4	1,895.1	2,260.2	2,540.1
Gross Dom. Prod. 1990 Prices	99b.p	1,896.4	2,040.2	2,214.6	2,369.2	2,569.2	Ɪ2,748.0	3,012.2	3,150.2	3,319.2	3,400.5	3,459.7	3,517.3	3,555.8	3,904.0	4,080.2
GDP Deflator (1990=100)	99bi p	34.8	35.2	36.2	36.4	36.8	37.2	38.2	40.2	43.6	48.6	53.2	55.6	58.2	62.8	68.6
																Millions:
Population	99z	1.24	1.27	1.31	1.35	1.39	1.43	1.48	1.52	1.57	1.62	1.68	1.72	1.77	1.81	1.85

Monetary Authorities: Ɪ Beginning in October 1969, data are based on improved sectorization.
Deposit Money Banks: Ɪ See note to section 10.
Monetary Survey: Ɪ See note to section 10.
Interest Rates: *Deposit Rate:* Ɪ Beginning in December 1992, weighted average rate offered by domestic deposit money banks on six-month time deposits.

Government Finance: Ɪ Beginning in 1965, data for floating debt have been excluded from *Expenditure* (line 82) and *Net Borrowing* (line 84). Ɪ Beginning in 1973, data are as reported in the *Government Finance Statistics Yearbook* and relate to the consolidated central government.

Panama

	1980	1981	1982	1983	1984	1985	1986	1987	1988	1989	1990	1991	1992	1993	1994		
Millions of Balboas																**International Transactions**	
	360.5	328.1	375.0	320.5	276.0	336.2	348.6	357.7	306.9	317.9	340.1	358.4	501.5	553.2	583.5	Exports	70
	1,449.2	1,540.1	1,570.2	1,411.9	1,423.1	1,391.8	1,229.2	1,306.2	751.0	985.9	1,538.6	1,695.0	2,023.6	2,187.8	2,404.1	Imports, cif	71
	1,288.9	1,393.0	1,406.7	1,267.2	1,276.3	1,238.8	1,103.8	1,165.2	673.4	867.5	1,339.2	1,523.5	1,830.6	1,979.6	2,177.5	Imports, fob	71.v
1990=100																	
	117	103	116	102	81	97	95	94	79	94	100	95	97	116	....	Volume of Exports	72
	110	110	99	110	111	106	93	103	93	95	100	101	....	....	....	Unit Value of Exports	74
Minus Sign Indicates Debit																**Balance of Payments**	
	2,469.3	2,706.7	2,507.4	1,735.9	1,767.9	2,030.7	2,405.0	2,631.1	2,489.7	2,728.5	3,378.8	4,200.1	5,103.8	5,386.3	5,922.2	Goods: Exports f.o.b.	78aa d
	−2,994.5	−3,315.5	−3,044.5	−2,320.8	−2,509.1	−2,731.0	−2,907.1	−3,058.3	−2,531.4	−3,084.2	−3,804.5	−4,960.5	−5,891.5	−6,152.2	−6,824.2	Goods: Imports f.o.b.	78ab d
	−525.2	−608.8	−537.1	−584.9	−741.2	−700.3	−502.1	−427.2	−41.7	−355.7	−425.7	−760.4	−787.7	−765.9	−902.0	Trade Balance	78ac d
	841.2	924.0	1,000.2	1,140.0	1,103.7	1,191.3	1,188.2	1,126.2	1,051.9	978.4	1,066.2	1,174.0	1,203.9	1,228.5	1,083.0	Services: Credit	78ad d
	−648.5	−711.9	−670.1	−385.8	−403.3	−437.8	−480.7	−415.3	−291.7	−311.8	−373.0	−420.5	−455.2	−487.3	−462.0	Services: Debit	78ae d
	−332.5	−396.7	−207.0	169.3	−40.8	53.2	205.4	283.7	718.5	310.9	267.5	−6.9	−39.0	−24.7	−281.0	Balance on Goods and Services	78af d
	4,425.9	6,290.6	5,899.4	4,402.6	3,666.0	3,085.5	2,541.7	2,071.2	969.6	1,075.0	1,074.8	1,018.9	1,117.8	1,031.9	97.0	Income: Credit	78ag d
	−4,418.7	−5,869.3	−5,789.0	−4,200.6	−3,519.2	−2,961.1	−2,487.3	−2,099.4	−1,148.6	−1,301.2	−1,391.6	−1,278.8	−1,281.2	−1,116.7	−263.8	Income: Debit	78ah d
	−325.3	24.6	−96.6	371.3	106.0	177.6	259.8	255.5	539.5	84.7	−49.3	−266.8	−202.4	−109.5	−447.8	Balance on Goods, Serv., & Inc.	78ai d
	72.5	85.9	109.5	114.7	150.9	147.9	128.8	122.5	116.8	114.3	125.7	136.3	155.1	147.8	151.9	Current Transfers, n.i.e.: Credit	78aj d
	−58.0	−54.8	−63.9	−70.4	−38.7	−39.0	−33.7	−59.6	−45.3	−44.2	−29.4	−27.4	−36.6	−36.5	−35.4	Current Transfers: Debit	78ak d
	−310.8	55.7	−51.0	415.6	218.2	286.3	354.9	318.4	611.0	154.8	47.0	−157.9	−83.9	1.8	−331.3	Current Account, n.i.e.	78al d
	—	—	—	—	—	—	—	—	—	—	—	—	—	—	—	Capital Account, n.i.e.: Credit	78ba d
	—	—	—	—	—	—	—	—	—	—	—	—	—	—	—	Capital Account: Debit	78bb d
	—	—	—	—	—	—	—	—	—	—	—	—	—	—	....	Capital Account, n.i.e.	78bc d
	−46.6	5.7	2.8	71.6	9.5	59.2	−62.2	56.8	−51.7	36.6	−17.6	−30.3	1.8	−41.2	....	Direct Investment Abroad	78bd d
	−901.6	176.8	361.2	98.0	76.9	−160.0	96.7	−61.0	276.5	−58.9	−26.2	8.2	−78.0	−504.1	....	Dir. Invest. in Rep. Econ., n.i.e.	78be d
	16.2	26.2	−9.5	−23.4	−17.7	−23.4	−30.3	−10.4	−64.1	−29.9	−35.8	−24.0	−71.2	−54.9	....	Portfolio Investment Assets	78bf d
	−1,656.1	−7,100.3	−2,751.9	6,047.5	4,879.9	−604.6	−635.4	8,458.3	15,050.0	−600.6	−1,947.3	−1,495.4	−1,471.3	−1,316.8	....	Portfolio Investment Liab., n.i.e.	78bg d
	2,247.4	7,002.3	2,473.3	−6,090.7	−4,908.5	567.4	644.3	−8,617.0	−15,455.8	86.3	1,241.9	712.2	945.3	1,312.2	....	Other Investment Assets	78bh d
	−340.7	110.7	75.9	91.0	40.1	−161.4	13.1	−173.8	−245.1	−566.5	−785.0	−829.3	−673.4	−604.8	....	Other Investment Liab., n.i.e.	78bi d
																Financial Account, n.i.e.	78bj d
	662.8	−239.7	−40.4	−563.7	−373.7	−253.5	−373.9	−646.2	−1,369.9	−420.6	377.1	564.9	443.7	196.3	....	Net Errors and Omissions	78ca d
	11.3	−73.3	−15.5	−57.1	−115.4	−128.6	−5.9	−501.2	−1,003.9	−832.3	−360.9	−422.3	−313.6	−406.7	....	Overall Balance	78cb d
	−11.3	73.3	15.5	57.1	115.4	128.6	5.9	501.2	1,003.9	832.3	360.9	422.3	313.6	406.7	25.7	Reserves and Related Items	79da d
	6.1	2.5	20.3	−103.7	−11.1	110.0	−66.3	95.5	5.5	−47.9	−226.9	−143.1	−17.8	−93.0	.1	Reserve Assets	79db d
	−17.3	70.9	−4.8	114.7	94.7	8.0	6.7	−57.9	−.1	−.8	−70.7	−55.7	−98.6	3.4	12.5	Use of Fund Credit and Loans	79dc d
																Liabs.Constit.For.Auth.Reserves	79dd d
	—	—	—	46.1	31.8	10.6	65.5	463.5	998.6	881.0	658.5	621.2	430.0	496.3	13.0	Exceptional Financing	79de d
Year Ending December 31																**Government Finance**	
	−197.6	−334.6	−482.6	−272.5	−340.0	−155.0	−220.7	−227.9	−108.1	−133.7	160.2	315.7	257.9	....	....	Deficit (−) or Surplus	80
	965.0	1,029.8	1,203.8	1,324.3	1,344.1	1,382.8	1,530.8	1,586.0	1,249.4	1,131.5	1,400.9	1,707.0	1,917.0	....	....	Revenue	81
	1.1	—	—	30.0	20.1	8.2	7.1	2.4	—	—	4.9	71.7	26.1	....	....	Grants Received	81z
	1,163.4	1,322.1	1,612.0	1,512.4	1,653.3	1,504.0	1,667.0	1,751.4	1,281.0	1,229.9	1,300.1	1,544.5	1,878.0	....	....	Expenditure	82
	.3	42.3	74.4	84.4	60.8	53.9	92.7	69.6	78.9	35.3	−54.5	−81.5	−192.8	....	....	Lending Minus Repayments	83
																Financing	
	197.6	334.6	482.6	272.5	340.0	155.0	220.7	227.9	108.1	199.6	−160.1	−315.7	−257.8	....	....	Net Borrowing	84
	−8.9	133.2	95.1	49.4	158.6	152.3	37.5	247.7	281.1	....	−266.7	−230.2	−214.2	....	....	Domestic	84a
	206.5	201.4	387.5	223.1	181.4	2.7	183.2	−19.8	−173.0	....	106.6	−85.5	−43.6	....	....	Foreign	85a
																Use of Cash Balances	87
	484.4	691.6	728.4	897.1	957.5	1,055.2	1,191.6	1,143.4	1,088.3	1,208.1	937.4	851.5	999.5	1,810.1	1,805.6	Debt: Domestic	88a
	1,578.6	1,689.8	2,049.8	2,175.1	2,263.9	2,265.5	2,372.5	2,399.1	2,443.5	2,457.7	2,450.4	2,432.9	2,624.9	2,600.2	2,812.9	Foreign	89a
Millions of Balboas																**National Accounts**	
	1,626.2	1,711.3	1,772.9	1,804.7	1,707.3	1,822.1	1,869.7	1,851.8	1,731.4	1,724.2	1,936.0	2,134.4	2,340.5	2,429.9	....	Exports of Goods & Services	90c
	680.5	812.9	962.6	941.5	1,001.3	1,043.6	1,127.8	1,226.9	1,011.6	986.7	939.1	958.1	1,021.6	1,095.8	....	Government Consumption	91f
	866.4	1,079.6	1,185.4	917.8	779.9	773.1	896.7	937.0	407.7	320.0	473.4	923.9	1,270.4	1,603.6	....	Gross Fixed Capital Formation	93e
	120.5	87.6	−.8	16.3	−18.9	−20.1	−37.5	−9.0	−94.0	−161.3	385.7	68.7	102.9	35.3	....	Increase/Decrease(−) in Stocks	93i
	1,975.4	2,060.7	2,261.0	2,423.8	2,819.3	3,020.0	2,910.0	2,966.1	2,606.8	3,005.8	3,003.9	3,377.3	3,593.0	3,897.5	....	Private Consumption	96f
	−1,676.4	−1,830.7	−1,856.1	−1,676.1	−1,679.0	−1,690.4	−1,575.8	−1,609.5	−1,059.0	−1,236.1	−1,728.7	−1,966.0	−2,313.0	−2,497.2	....	Imports of Goods & Services	98c
	3,592.6	3,921.4	4,324.6	4,428.0	4,609.9	4,948.3	5,190.9	5,363.3	4,604.5	4,639.3	5,009.4	5,496.4	6,015.4	6,564.9	....	Gross Domestic Product	99b
	−110.0	−78.6	−138.9	−2.2	−123.9	−46.4	−43.7	−41.1	−234.4	−273.0	−253.6	−244.8	−172.7	−53.0	....	Net Factor Inc/Pmts(−) Abroad	98.n
	3,482.6	3,842.8	4,185.7	4,425.8	4,486.0	4,901.9	5,147.2	5,322.2	4,370.1	4,366.3	4,755.8	5,251.6	5,842.7	6,511.9	....	Gross Nat'l Expenditure = GNP	99a
	3,230.5	3,563.1	3,864.8	4,090.3	4,111.4	4,503.1	4,722.8	4,887.3	3,958.2	3,963.2	4,333.7	4,797.5	5,357.1	6,006.4	....	Nat'l Income, Market Prices	99e
	4,672.5	4,861.7	5,131.6	5,162.5	5,140.2	5,382.9	5,562.1	5,696.7	4,807.9	4,787.5	5,009.4	5,487.8	5,954.7	6,276.0	6,570.9	Gross Dom. Prod. 1990 Prices	99b.p
	76.9	80.7	84.3	85.8	89.7	91.9	93.3	94.1	95.8	96.9	100.0	100.2	101.0	104.6	....	GDP Deflator (1990=100)	99bi p
Midyear Estimates																	
	1.96	2.00	2.04	2.09	2.13	2.17	2.21	2.26	2.30	2.35	2.40	2.44	2.49	2.53	2.56	Population	99z

Papua New Guinea
853

		1965	1966	1967	1968	1969	1970	1971	1972	1973	1974	1975	1976	1977	1978	1979
Exchange Rates																*SDRs per Kina:*
Official Rate	ac	1.1185	1.1140	1.1210	1.1100	1.1180	1.1150	1.0970	1.1743	1.2335	1.0838	1.0738	1.0599	1.0867	1.1153	1.0998
																US Dollars per Kina:
Official Rate	ag	1.1185	1.1140	1.1210	1.1100	1.1180	1.1150	1.1910	1.2750	1.4880	1.3270	1.2571	1.2314	1.3200	1.4530	1.4488
Official Rate	rh	1.1200	1.1200	1.1200	1.1200	1.1200	1.1200	1.1331	1.1923	1.4227	1.4394	1.3102	1.2621	1.2640	1.4117	1.4053
																Index Numbers (1990=100):
Official Rate	ahx	106.4	106.3	106.3	106.3	106.1	106.4	113.5	113.9	135.6	137.4	125.2	120.6	120.8	134.9	134.3
Nominal Effective Exchange Rate	nec	....	....	....	....	....	....	....	....	....	....	....	....	....	....	83.8
Real Effective Exchange Rate	rec	....	....	....	....	....	....	....	....	....	....	....	....	....	....	115.0
Fund Position																*Millions of SDRs:*
Quota	2f.s											20.00	20.00	20.00	30.00	30.00
SDRs	1b.s											—	1.68	.19	.42	.81
Reserve Position in the Fund	1c.s											—	—	—	.01	2.37
Total Fund Cred.&Loans Outstg.	2tl											—	24.80	24.80	23.09	18.10
International Liquidity												*Millions of US Dollars Unless Otherwise Indicated:*				
Total Reserves minus Gold	1l.d									31.26	32.45	179.67	257.20	426.63	404.72	503.55
SDRs	1b.d									....	....	—	1.95	.23	.55	1.07
Reserve Position in the Fund	1c.d									....	....	—	—	—	.01	3.12
Foreign Exchange	1d.d									31.26	32.45	179.67	255.25	426.40	404.16	499.36
Gold (Million Fine Troy Ounces)	1ad									....	....	....	....	.029	.044	.053
Gold (National Valuation)	1and									—	—	—	—	3.55	7.93	11.09
Government Assets	3bad									5.38	16.56	19.09	15.39	21.89	28.20	24.27
Deposit Money Banks: Assets	7a.d									72.06	162.74	.27	10.14	80.18	35.93	21.13
of which: Claims on Nonbanks	7add									....	....	.27	.68	6.45	4.44	13.59
Deposit Money Banks: Liabilities	7b.d									.05	1.59	20.54	22.86	46.00	52.33	22.93
of which: Liab. to Nonbanks	7bdd									.05	.04	.09	10.57	38.16	46.05	17.09
Monetary Authorities																*Millions of Kina:*
Foreign Assets	11									99.37	114.48	194.32	208.77	327.51	297.22	372.94
Claims on Central Government	12a									3.24	3.24	7.57	22.21	11.55	12.75	30.14
Reserve Money	14									64.13	81.62	142.19	168.13	203.51	194.10	235.72
of which: Currency Outside DMBs	14a									57.37	76.61	85.21	47.51	56.66	61.55	67.89
Time Deposits	15									—	—	—	—	49.73	68.37	95.38
Foreign Liabilities	16c									—	—	—	23.40	40.21	20.70	16.55
Central Government Deposits	16d									32.50	27.71	53.74	24.73	34.70	18.36	24.06
Capital Accounts	17a									5.01	5.53	6.26	9.93	12.60	14.86	17.69
Other Items (Net)	17r									.98	2.86	-.30	4.79	-1.68	-6.43	13.67
Deposit Money Banks																*Millions of Kina:*
Reserves	20									6.25	5.09	54.95	116.81	141.57	126.99	160.26
Foreign Assets	21									48.44	122.64	.22	8.24	60.74	24.73	14.59
Claims on Central Government	22a									22.70	35.25	28.27	32.54	44.78	37.75	58.47
Claims on Private Sector	22d									137.16	152.15	164.23	164.08	182.75	180.62	224.45
Demand Deposits	24									41.53	63.22	63.55	83.87	107.44	111.87	119.94
Time and Savings Deposits	25									96.24	179.61	94.66	142.80	209.35	201.67	280.92
Foreign Liabilities	26c									.03	1.20	16.34	18.56	34.85	36.02	15.83
Central Government Deposits	26d									15.02	5.92	12.86	12.00	18.33	18.62	30.30
Capital Accounts	27a									49.53	69.30	71.14	76.14	77.41	29.93	30.07
Other Items (Net)	27r									12.22	-4.11	-10.90	-11.72	-17.53	-28.03	-19.30
Monetary Survey																*Millions of Kina:*
Foreign Assets (Net)	31n									147.78	235.92	178.20	175.05	313.20	265.23	355.15
Domestic Credit	32									115.58	157.65	134.01	185.07	192.30	208.00	263.90
Claims on Central Govt. (Net)	32an									-21.58	4.86	-30.76	18.01	3.31	13.52	34.25
Claims on Private Sector	32d									137.16	152.15	164.23	164.08	182.75	180.62	224.45
Claims on Other Financial Insts.	32f									—	.39	.15	2.27	5.27	13.14	3.20
Money	34									99.40	140.43	150.80	135.02	169.38	178.99	195.41
Quasi-Money	35									96.24	179.61	94.66	142.80	259.08	270.05	376.30
Other Items (Net)	37r									67.74	73.53	66.74	82.30	77.05	24.19	47.34
Money plus Quasi-Money	35l									195.64	320.04	245.46	277.82	428.46	449.03	571.71
Interest Rates																*Percent Per Annum*
Discount Rate (End of Period)	60									....	....	8.18	8.27	7.73	6.38	5.78	6.03
Treasury Bill Rate	60c									....	....	....	....	....	....	....
Deposit Rate	60l									....	....	....	....	....	....	....
Lending Rate	60p									....	....	....	....	....	....	....
Prices and Employment																*Index Numbers (1990=100):*
Consumer Prices	64							25.7	27.3	29.6	36.4	40.3	43.3	45.3	47.9	50.7
Total Employment	67									....	....	....	....	....	83.6	86.8

Papua New Guinea

	1980	1981	1982	1983	1984	1985	1986	1987	1988	1989	1990	1991	1992	1993	1994		
End of Period																**Exchange Rates**	
	1.2177	1.2625	1.2121	1.0910	1.0837	.8992	.8506	.8024	.8992	.8852	.7376	.7339	.7365	.7419	.5812	Official Rate	ac
End of Period (ag) Period Average (rh)																	
	1.5531	1.4695	1.3371	1.1422	1.0623	.9877	1.0404	1.1384	1.2100	1.1633	1.0493	1.0498	1.0127	1.0190	.8485	Official Rate	ag
	1.4916	1.4871	1.3559	1.1989	1.1183	1.0000	1.0296	1.1012	1.1538	1.1685	1.0467	1.0504	1.0367	1.0221	.9950	Official Rate	rh
Period Averages																	
	142.5	142.1	129.5	114.5	106.8	95.5	98.4	105.2	110.2	111.6	100.0	100.4	99.1	97.7	95.1	Official Rate	ah x
	90.6	95.2	96.6	93.3	95.0	94.8	90.1	91.9	94.0	103.4	100.0	104.4	107.7	114.3	117.1	Nominal Effective Exchange Rate	ne c
	123.4	126.3	124.3	120.2	121.2	116.1	109.8	108.5	107.3	110.8	100.0	102.6	102.0	103.4	....	Real Effective Exchange Rate	re c
End of Period																**Fund Position**	
	45.00	45.00	45.00	65.90	65.90	65.90	65.90	65.90	65.90	65.90	65.90	65.90	95.30	95.30	95.30	Quota	2f. s
	—	33.07	31.00	16.95	4.99	5.89	2.61	3.31	3.04	2.67	—	.02	.10	.03	.07	SDRs	1b. s
	3.78	.04	.07	5.31	5.35	5.38	5.42	6.94	6.95	6.98	—	—	.04	.05	.05	Reserve Position in the Fund	1c. s
	24.28	64.55	64.55	64.55	34.59	26.33	12.34	8.44	4.55	2.31	42.91	42.83	42.83	32.12	10.70	Total Fund Cred.&Loans Outstg.	2tl
Approximately End of Period																**International Liquidity**	
	423.43	396.71	452.88	440.07	435.23	442.57	425.46	436.83	393.49	384.38	403.04	323.05	238.58	141.45	96.06	Total Reserves minus Gold	1l. d
	—	38.49	34.20	17.75	4.89	6.47	3.19	4.70	4.09	3.51	—	.03	.14	.05	.11	SDRs	1b. d
	4.82	.05	.08	5.56	5.24	5.91	6.63	9.85	9.35	9.17	—	—	.06	.07	.08	Reserve Position in the Fund	1c. d
	418.61	357.63	418.61	416.76	425.09	430.19	415.64	422.29	380.05	371.70	403.04	323.02	238.39	141.34	95.88	Foreign Exchange	1d. d
	.058	.062	.062	.063	.063	.063	.063	.063	.063	.063	.063	.063	.063	.063	.063	Gold (Million Fine Troy Ounces)	1ad
	14.74	15.91	14.54	12.53	11.71	10.93	11.08	11.08	11.09	11.09	11.09	11.09	11.09	11.09	11.09	Gold (National Valuation)	1an d
	....	....	....	....	....	....	2.83	4.00	....	....	....	....	....	....	....	Government Assets	3ba d
	16.02	18.28	7.15	10.59	14.28	16.21	10.06	24.27	29.92	22.32	20.65	39.72	61.61	160.59	175.61	Deposit Money Banks: Assets	7a. d
	6.56	6.19	6.41	2.58	2.94	3.82	3.28	3.78	8.29	4.53	2.76	2.66	3.75	6.82	24.33	of which: Claims on Nonbanks	7ad d
	9.88	38.30	26.76	33.63	54.61	56.23	43.55	68.21	109.35	143.31	113.17	150.27	118.34	88.07	120.46	Deposit Money Banks: Liabilities	7b. d
	3.48	29.69	19.21	26.22	47.29	50.58	40.04	61.53	94.21	126.45	100.47	140.68	115.59	88.05	100.55	of which: Liab. to Nonbanks	7bd d
Last Wednesday of Period																**Monetary Authorities**	
	293.56	290.19	269.84	395.45	416.78	460.51	455.06	446.14	396.23	342.42	376.53	306.44	242.31	138.61	112.51	Foreign Assets	11
	39.39	52.76	72.88	27.51	12.52	60.99	53.22	78.53	107.24	174.14	227.01	251.35	284.20	421.02	776.65	Claims on Central Government	12a
	99.46	88.82	90.46	138.04	128.25	130.53	125.56	134.16	141.91	152.24	176.04	164.64	168.93	199.20	221.65	Reserve Money	14
	70.49	73.39	72.41	79.95	88.90	94.26	95.74	106.35	115.20	122.03	134.77	137.36	141.17	160.70	179.00	of which: Currency Outside DMBs	14a
	102.27	90.60	90.73	83.30	80.15	80.55	89.15	64.97	12.69	2.64	1.39	1.15	.50	.50	.50	Time Deposits	15
	20.02	51.41	53.42	59.36	32.27	29.76	14.97	10.83	5.31	4.25	59.78	56.06	61.38	46.89	40.60	Foreign Liabilities	16c
	91.79	80.09	55.99	71.50	103.83	96.37	120.71	172.96	172.98	196.02	171.18	171.79	221.02	366.60	663.21	Central Government Deposits	16d
	37.62	24.34	37.69	61.72	90.12	112.28	143.51	154.81	174.32	198.46	225.66	223.88	209.35	208.82	140.62	Capital Accounts	17a
	−18.21	7.69	14.44	9.05	−5.32	72.01	14.38	−13.05	−3.75	−37.05	−30.53	−59.72	−134.67	−262.38	−177.43	Other Items (Net)	17r
Last Wednesday of Period																**Deposit Money Banks**	
	26.09	18.35	16.07	56.02	35.67	22.57	29.02	24.76	23.78	23.21	35.33	22.52	24.61	36.68	40.67	Reserves	20
	10.32	12.44	5.34	9.27	13.44	16.41	9.67	21.32	24.73	19.19	19.68	37.84	60.84	157.59	206.97	Foreign Assets	21
	88.13	92.29	78.74	91.92	108.72	80.79	130.42	105.59	140.10	110.36	121.92	232.60	364.57	502.65	446.27	Claims on Central Government	22a
	301.31	348.79	378.42	446.34	502.98	563.78	668.22	738.58	823.53	937.72	951.15	1,081.33	1,124.08	1,114.97	1,272.69	Claims on Private Sector	22d
	128.18	120.71	114.25	124.42	156.12	146.22	160.16	172.24	200.32	215.48	203.12	275.03	293.10	431.77	433.46	Demand Deposits	24
	249.32	269.77	288.49	360.78	418.88	495.42	583.13	597.00	649.99	690.36	736.38	854.16	993.78	1,091.68	1,049.85	Time and Savings Deposits	25
	6.36	26.06	20.02	29.44	51.41	56.93	41.86	59.92	90.37	123.19	107.85	143.14	116.85	86.43	141.97	Foreign Liabilities	26c
	22.71	26.05	27.21	45.93	24.25	20.20	18.55	17.72	18.71	18.75	33.22	39.78	43.46	51.45	73.13	Central Government Deposits	26d
	41.54	48.68	45.36	56.46	47.00	49.35	66.46	79.70	93.27	66.56	68.88	64.45	65.21	60.63	78.36	Capital Accounts	27a
	−22.27	−19.40	−16.75	−13.49	−36.85	−84.02	−32.07	−36.32	−40.53	−23.84	−21.38	−2.27	61.68	89.92	189.83	Other Items (Net)	27r
Last Wednesday of Period																**Monetary Survey**	
	277.50	225.15	201.75	315.92	346.54	390.24	407.90	396.71	325.28	234.17	228.56	145.08	124.91	162.88	136.91	Foreign Assets (Net)	31n
	318.87	390.77	449.74	456.43	499.76	594.65	718.63	740.48	884.81	1,012.70	1,101.72	1,357.22	1,521.59	1,633.63	1,765.21	Domestic Credit	32
	13.01	38.92	68.42	2.00	−6.85	25.21	44.38	−6.55	55.64	69.73	144.53	272.38	384.29	505.61	486.57	Claims on Central Govt. (Net)	32an
	301.31	348.79	378.42	446.34	502.98	563.78	668.22	738.58	823.53	937.72	951.15	1,081.33	1,124.08	1,114.97	1,272.69	Claims on Private Sector	32d
	2.54	.99	1.01	5.74	2.20	2.00	1.95	4.63	3.20	4.17	2.25	2.35	8.91	6.84	—	Claims on Other Financial Insts.	32f
	201.56	194.36	188.64	205.97	248.99	244.15	256.68	281.33	322.17	344.50	343.84	417.16	437.42	594.29	614.48	Money	34
	351.59	360.37	379.22	444.08	499.03	575.97	672.28	661.96	662.68	693.00	737.77	855.31	994.28	1,092.18	1,050.35	Quasi-Money	35
	43.22	61.18	83.64	122.30	98.29	165.31	198.32	193.90	225.24	209.38	248.68	229.84	214.44	110.05	237.29	Other Items (Net)	37r
	553.15	554.74	567.85	650.04	748.02	820.12	928.96	943.29	984.85	1,037.50	1,081.61	1,272.46	1,431.70	1,686.46	1,664.83	Money plus Quasi-Money	35l
Percent Per Annum																**Interest Rates**	
	....	....	....	8.75	8.75	9.75	11.40	8.80	10.80	9.55	9.30	9.30	7.12	16.39	....	Discount Rate (End of Period)	60
	7.16	11.56	13.80	10.92	9.28	10.40	12.32	10.44	10.12	10.50	11.40	10.33	8.88	6.25	....	Treasury Bill Rate	60c
	6.90	10.00	8.00	9.54	8.13	9.49	11.49	9.60	9.28	8.23	8.67	9.06	7.85	5.03	....	Deposit Rate	60l
	11.15	14.40	12.25	11.58	10.64	11.54	12.33	11.94	12.68	14.62	15.52	14.17	14.53	11.29	....	Lending Rate	60p
Period Averages																**Prices and Employment**	
	56.8	61.4	64.8	69.9	75.1	77.9	82.1	84.9	89.5	93.5	100.0	107.0	111.6	117.1	....	Consumer Prices	64
	94.6	97.4	87.8	85.6	87.0	89.9	92.1	94.2	97.6	105.0	100.0	96.3	99.4	96.7	....	Total Employment	67

Papua New Guinea

853

		1965	1966	1967	1968	1969	1970	1971	1972	1973	1974	1975	1976	1977	1978	1979
International Transactions																Millions of Kina
Exports	70	52.8	50.8	58.8	74.5	89.0	92.8	106.3	184.4	359.7	451.3	335.9	435.5	539.8	504.0	686.9
Imports, cif	71	109.9	133.5	160.0	158.3	197.0	270.0	313.7	280.7	250.1	352.4	424.1	397.9	507.4	545.3	643.0
Imports, fob	71.v	97.1	118.5	142.9	140.6	174.1	238.5	274.4	244.7	214.4	301.4	368.5	351.5	448.3	478.3	561.6
																1990=100
Unit Value of Exports	74	....	....	....	....	....	....	....	....	38.8	ᵢ59.5	44.0	54.0	71.6	63.3	85.8
Balance of Payments																Millions of US Dollars:
Goods: Exports f.o.b.	78aa d	....	....	....	....	....	....	....	....	....	....	....	550.4	683.1	713.4	1,010.3
Goods: Imports f.o.b.	78ab d	....	....	....	....	....	....	....	....	....	....	....	-434.2	-559.9	-688.4	-783.3
Trade Balance	78ac d	....	....	....	....	....	....	....	....	....	....	....	116.2	123.3	25.1	226.9
Services: Credit	78ad d	....	....	....	....	....	....	....	....	....	....	....	68.9	38.0	35.7	41.8
Services: Debit	78ae d	....	....	....	....	....	....	....	....	....	....	....	-175.6	-183.7	-217.2	-237.8
Balance on Goods and Services	78af d	....	....	....	....	....	....	....	....	....	....	....	9.5	-22.4	-156.4	31.0
Income: Credit	78ag d	....	....	....	....	....	....	....	....	....	....	....	19.8	30.3	38.3	49.4
Income: Debit	78ah d	....	....	....	....	....	....	....	....	....	....	....	-75.2	-81.3	-103.4	-158.1
Balance on Goods, Serv., & Inc.	78ai d	....	....	....	....	....	....	....	....	....	....	....	-45.9	-73.4	-221.5	-77.8
Current Transfers, n.i.e.: Credit	78aj d	....	....	....	....	....	....	....	....	....	....	....	159.5	245.5	270.5	268.3
Current Transfers: Debit	78ak d	....	....	....	....	....	....	....	....	....	....	....	-62.8	-57.8	-81.2	-83.5
Current Account, n.i.e.	78al d	....	....	....	....	....	....	....	....	....	....	....	50.8	114.3	-32.2	107.0
Capital Account, n.i.e.: Credit	78ba d	....	....	....	....	....	....	....	....	....	....	....	14.0	8.7	9.2	9.1
Capital Account: Debit	78bb d	....	....	....	....	....	....	....	....	....	....	....	-24.5	-24.4	-32.4	-37.5
Capital Account, n.i.e.	78bc d	....	....	....	....	....	....	....	....	....	....	....	-10.5	-15.7	-23.2	-28.3
Direct Investment Abroad	78bd d	....	....	....	....	....	....	....	....	....	....	....	1.9	-1.8	-4.9	-3.2
Dir. Invest. in Rep. Econ., n.i.e.	78be d	....	....	....	....	....	....	....	....	....	....	....	20.8	19.8	38.9	44.2
Portfolio Investment Assets	78bf d	....	....	....	....	....	....	....	....	....	....	....	-3.1	-.9	-5.1	-2.9
Portfolio Investment Liab., n.i.e.	78bg d	....	....	....	....	....	....	....	....	....	....	....	-3.3	-3.5	-8.4	—
Other Investment Assets	78bh d	....	....	....	....	....	....	....	....	....	....	....	-10.8	-67.0	48.2	14.5
Other Investment Liab., n.i.e.	78bi d	....	....	....	....	....	....	....	....	....	....	....	25.5	66.8	-55.1	-17.2
Financial Account, n.i.e.	78bj d	....	....	....	....	....	....	....	....	....	....	....	31.0	13.5	13.7	35.4
Net Errors and Omissions	78ca d	....	....	....	....	....	....	....	....	....	....	....	-28.5	25.9	37.8	-5.1
Overall Balance	78cb d	....	....	....	....	....	....	....	....	....	....	....	42.8	138.0	-3.9	108.9
Reserves and Related Items	79da d	....	....	....	....	....	....	....	....	....	....	....	-42.8	-138.0	3.9	-108.9
Reserve Assets	79db d	....	....	....	....	....	....	....	....	....	....	....	-70.3	-159.8	29.6	-105.8
Use of Fund Credit and Loans	79dc d	....	....	....	....	....	....	....	....	....	....	....	28.6	—	-2.0	-6.4
Liabs.Constit.For.Auth.Reserves	79dd d	....	....	....	....	....	....	....	....	....	....	....	-1.0	21.8	-23.8	—
Exceptional Financing	79de d	....	....	....	....	....	....	....	....	....	....	....	—	—	—	3.2
Government Finance																Millions of Kina:
Deficit (-) or Surplus	80	....	....	....	....	....	....	....	....	....	....	-56.96	-26.80	-19.36	ᵢ-21.48	-62.80
Revenue	81	....	....	....	....	....	....	....	....	....	....	173.98	234.20	214.09	ᵢ259.41	283.99
Grants Received	81z	....	....	....	....	....	....	....	....	....	....	156.28	119.39	174.93	ᵢ171.96	174.83
Expenditure	82	....	....	....	....	....	....	....	....	....	....	365.73	368.57	400.80	ᵢ448.95	511.48
Lending Minus Repayments	83	....	....	....	....	....	....	....	....	....	....	21.49	11.82	7.58	ᵢ3.90	10.14
Financing																
Domestic	84a	....	....	....	....	....	....	....	....	....	....	25.97	15.85	9.39	ᵢ19.30	39.76
Foreign	85a	....	....	....	....	....	....	....	....	....	....	30.99	10.95	9.97	ᵢ2.18	23.04
Debt: Domestic	88a	....	....	....	....	....	....	....	....	....	....	58.39	81.74	78.01	ᵢ75.06	139.34
Foreign	89a	....	....	....	....	....	....	....	....	....	....	211.43	232.14	237.91	ᵢ250.97	291.25
National Accounts																Millions of Kina
Exports of Goods & Services	90c	54	57	61	77	87	99	114	157	290	531	428	400	591	586	752
Government Consumption	91f	96	114	135	140	151	164	183	207	228	270	328	367	358	374	393
Gross Fixed Capital Formation	93e	51	66	79	83	91	182	276	242	128	130	187	164	241	270	329
Increase/Decrease(-) in Stocks	93i	9	8	4	7	7	6	16	9	19	4	35	30	41	28	57
Private Consumption	96f	186	208	247	270	303	347	387	407	428	446	521	591	770	876	990
Imports of Goods & Services	98c	-103	-131	-150	-163	-184	-268	-354	-384	-308	-329	-486	-471	-609	-636	-755
Gross Domestic Product	99b	292	323	376	413	453	531	622	645	786	1,040	1,004	1,069	1,410	1,535	1,773
Net Factor Inc/Pmts(-) Abroad	98.n	3	3	1	3	4	9	27	35	37	79	72	39	27	19	40
Gross Nat'l Expenditure = GNP	99a	292	323	376	413	453	531	622	645	789	1,041	1,004	1,107	1,437	1,554	1,813
Nat'l Income, Market Prices	99e	282	310	363	396	433	500	566	574	695	895	862	952	1,187	1,290	1,486
Gross Dom. Prod. 1990 Prices	99b.p	....	....	....	....	....	....	....	....	2,499	2,595	2,618	2,575	2,464	2,675	2,724
GDP Deflator (1990=100)	99bi p	....	....	....	....	....	....	....	....	31.5	40.1	38.4	41.5	57.2	57.4	65.1
																Millions:
Population	99z	2.15	2.19	2.25	2.31	2.36	2.42	2.52	2.58	2.59	2.64	2.69	2.75	2.81	2.87	2.93

Interest Rates: *Discount Rate (line 60):* ᵢ Period average data beginning in 1993; end-of-period data prior to 1993.
Government Finance: ᵢ Prior to 1978, data relate to a fiscal year different from calendar year. ᵢ Through 1984 and beginning in 1993, data cover budgetary central government. For the period 1985-92, data also cover extrabudgetary accounts.
National Accounts: ᵢ Prior to 1977, data relate to fiscal years ending June 30. Since this date, data refer to calendar years.

Papua New Guinea

1980	1981	1982	1983	1984	1985	1986	1987	1988	1989	1990	1991	1992	1993	1994		International Transactions	
Millions of Kina																	
691.7	564.4	570.9	687.5	822.1	926.2	1,000.8	1,123.2	1,256.3	1,111.6	1,122.4	1,390.5	1,730.6	2,429.3	....		Exports	70
786.8	848.9	887.4	944.9	971.4	1,006.0	1,037.4	1,144.9	1,378.9	1,324.8	1,215.0	1,537.0	1,466.3	1,277.0	....		Imports, cif	71
684.2	738.2	771.7	821.7	844.7	874.8	902.1	995.6	1,199.0	1,152.0	1,056.5	1,336.5	1,275.0	1,110.4	....		Imports, fob	71.v
1990=100																	
‡89.1	69.6	68.8	80.2	88.7	91.4	90.1	98.4	114.2	95.7	100.0	99.1	100.9	112.8	....		Unit Value of Exports	74
Minus Sign Indicates Debit																Balance of Payments	
985.5	840.1	768.8	820.3	915.3	926.3	1,030.7	1,243.9	1,475.3	1,318.5	1,173.8	1,482.6	1,950.9	2,504.7	....		Goods: Exports f.o.b.	78aa *d*
−1,020.5	−1,096.4	−1,017.6	−974.8	−962.8	−874.8	−928.8	−1,129.6	−1,384.5	−1,341.3	−1,106.8	−1,403.8	−1,321.7	−1,134.8	....		Goods: Imports f.o.b.	78ab *d*
−35.0	−256.3	−248.8	−154.5	−47.5	51.5	101.8	114.3	90.8	−22.8	67.0	78.8	629.2	1,369.9	....		Trade Balance	78ac *d*
43.3	84.7	95.4	75.7	64.4	64.0	72.5	97.3	122.3	167.9	205.4	303.5	349.9	315.0	....		Services: Credit	78ad *d*
−301.6	−342.1	−347.8	−333.4	−356.1	−288.5	−302.7	−377.6	−435.1	−408.8	−402.6	−542.5	−687.8	−800.5	....		Services: Debit	78ae *d*
−293.3	−513.7	−501.2	−412.2	−339.2	−173.0	−128.5	−166.0	−222.0	−263.7	−130.2	−160.2	291.3	884.4	....		Balance on Goods and Services	78af *d*
59.8	47.4	59.6	58.3	50.6	55.5	91.5	57.9	118.6	87.0	106.5	70.6	39.2	23.4	....		Income: Credit	78ag *d*
−239.0	−209.2	−180.9	−180.3	−199.2	−161.8	−202.5	−206.3	−326.2	−265.2	−209.8	−320.5	−425.8	−396.3	....		Income: Debit	78ah *d*
−472.5	−675.4	−622.4	−534.2	−487.7	−279.2	−239.3	−314.4	−429.6	−441.9	−233.5	−410.1	−95.4	511.5	....		Balance on Goods, Serv., & Inc.	78ai *d*
283.9	300.8	293.6	293.8	291.1	247.3	248.8	238.4	249.4	256.3	273.8	365.7	303.6	220.8	....		Current Transfers, n.i.e.: Credit	78aj *d*
−100.2	−109.8	−115.9	−97.1	−92.9	−89.8	−82.9	−108.8	−116.2	−127.2	−118.1	−106.1	−111.2	−178.0	....		Current Transfers: Debit	78ak *d*
−288.7	−484.3	−444.8	−337.4	−289.5	−121.8	−73.4	−184.8	−296.4	−312.7	−77.8	−150.6	97.0	554.3	....		Current Account, n.i.e.	78al *d*
5.4	4.7	6.1	4.3	5.4	5.6	7.0	13.4	10.0	7.2	5.4	21.0	20.7	20.4	....		Capital Account, n.i.e.: Credit	78ba *d*
−28.2	−41.4	−45.7	−41.8	−36.7	−33.5	−38.9	−43.3	−50.1	−49.8	−42.8	−21.0	−20.7	−20.4	....		Capital Account: Debit	78bb *d*
−22.8	−36.7	−39.6	−37.4	−31.3	−27.9	−31.9	−29.8	−40.1	−42.6	−37.4	—	—	—	....		Capital Account, n.i.e.	78bc *d*
−15.7	−.6	−1.8	−1.1	−2.3	−.9	8.7	22.2	−33.8	17.9	—	—	—	—	....		Direct Investment Abroad	78bd *d*
75.5	86.2	85.9	138.9	115.7	83.3	90.8	93.2	153.5	203.4	62.8	116.8	100.4	62.0	....		Dir. Invest. in Rep. Econ., n.i.e.	78be *d*
—	−1.6	—	—	—	—	—	—	—	—	—	—	—	—	....		Portfolio Investment Assets	78bf *d*
—	—	—	—	—	—	—	—	—	—	93.5	86.0	190.4	−61.3	....		Portfolio Investment Liab., n.i.e.	78bg *d*
7.1	—	—	—	—	—	—	—	—	—	—	—	—	—	....		Other Investment Assets	78bh *d*
29.1	333.4	395.6	214.2	144.6	41.6	35.0	61.7	125.4	43.7	60.4	−140.0	−442.6	−661.1	....		Other Investment Liab., n.i.e.	78bi *d*
96.0	417.4	479.7	352.0	258.1	124.0	134.5	177.1	245.1	265.0	216.8	62.8	−151.8	−660.5	....		Financial Account, n.i.e.	78bj *d*
131.8	52.5	−31.2	120.0	111.6	24.3	−26.0	39.5	37.9	31.6	−78.6	2.2	−17.5	24.2	....		Net Errors and Omissions	78ca *d*
−83.7	−51.1	−35.9	97.2	48.8	−1.4	3.3	2.0	−53.5	−58.7	22.9	−85.5	−72.2	−82.0	....		Overall Balance	78cb *d*
83.7	51.1	35.9	−97.2	−48.8	1.4	−3.3	−2.0	53.5	58.7	−22.9	85.5	72.2	82.0	....		Reserves and Related Items	79da *d*
75.4	4.2	35.9	−97.2	−18.1	9.3	13.2	3.0	58.7	61.6	−76.4	85.6	72.2	97.0	....		Reserve Assets	79db *d*
8.3	46.9	—	—	−30.7	−8.0	−16.5	−4.9	−5.2	−2.9	53.5	−.1	—	−15.0	....		Use of Fund Credit and Loans	79dc *d*
—	—	—	—	—	—	—	—	—	—	—	—	—	—	....		Liabs.Constit.For.Auth.Reserves	79dd *d*
—	.1	−.1	—	—	—	—	—	—	—	—	—	—	—	....		Exceptional Financing	79de *d*
Year Ending December 31																Government Finance	
−33.02	−107.72	−97.18	−94.57	−21.13	−55.54	−80.07	−38.79	−32.60	−35.07	−106.65	−68.01	−220.38	‡−283.55	−228.78[f]		Deficit (-) or Surplus	80
392.34	371.85	369.79	404.09	496.37	‡490.77	550.84	637.59	711.11	809.65	777.58	901.47	921.32	‡1128.95	1,220.53[f]		Revenue	81
174.60	184.33	186.70	213.09	231.96	‡216.35	204.68	184.25	189.87	189.72	222.09	311.71	196.32	‡181.70	176.97[f]		Grants Received	81z
587.56	649.52	633.91	679.26	733.56	‡752.88	795.65	828.90	890.00	987.84	1,066.52	1,273.56	1,348.69	‡1588.71	1,630.23[f]		Expenditure	82
12.40	14.38	19.76	32.49	15.90	‡9.78	39.94	31.73	43.58	46.60	39.80	7.63	−10.67	‡5.49	−3.95[f]		Lending Minus Repayments	83
																Financing	
−8.87	33.85	20.62	−22.28	−27.45	‡40.00	20.32	30.03	42.90	30.41	93.15	125.17	181.52	‡237.83	238.08[f]		Domestic	84a
41.89	73.87	76.56	116.85	48.58	‡15.54	59.75	8.76	−10.30	4.66	13.50	−57.16	38.86	‡45.72	−9.30[f]		Foreign	85a
174.32	151.96	158.44	143.80	179.48	‡192.44	201.50	259.54	286.80	374.02	412.38	564.39	676.41	‡1036.60	....		Debt: Domestic	88a
328.18	389.85	481.57	668.78	740.14	‡852.78	951.94	1,034.78	881.75	875.35	1,093.52	1,116.21	1,218.21	‡1120.80	....		Foreign	89a
Millions of Kina																National Accounts	
747	651	652	776	905	1,021	1,121	1,232	1,371	1,238	1,250	1,524	1,870	2,419	....		Exports of Goods & Services	90c
436	481	496	499	532	572	591	640	663	745	764	808	930	1,022	....		Government Consumption	91f
397	454	581	637	548	447	539	551	737	791	773	1,010	984	935	....		Gross Fixed Capital Formation	93e
36	7	−14	−6	72	34	−32	34	126	−83	−21	−22	—	—	....		Increase/Decrease(-) in Stocks	93i
1,168	1,227	1,242	1,386	1,446	1,600	1,674	1,815	1,919	1,962	1,816	2,166	2,396	2,574	....		Private Consumption	96f
−923	−1,001	−1,073	−1,145	−1,219	−1,271	−1,321	−1,418	−1,646	−1,607	−1,506	−1,881	−2,040	−1,972	....		Imports of Goods & Services	98c
1,855	1,826	1,900	2,146	2,282	2,403	2,572	2,854	3,170	3,046	3,076	3,606	4,140	4,979	....		Gross Domestic Product	99b
59	60	73	119	73	89	72	131	122	115	118	118	110	....			Net Factor Inc/Pmts(-) Abroad	98.n
1,914	1,886	1,972	2,265	2,355	2,491	2,645	2,985	3,292	3,161	3,194	3,723	4,250	....			Gross Nat'l Expenditure = GNP	99a
1,525	1,483	1,527	1,973	2,064	2,179	2,259	2,462	2,769	2,615	2,619	3,071	3,152	....			Nat'l Income, Market Prices	99e
2,661	2,692	2,714	‡2,807	2,780	2,879	3,042	3,126	3,217	3,171	3,076	3,369	3,767	4,311	....		Gross Dom. Prod. 1990 Prices	99b.*p*
69.7	67.8	70.0	76.4	82.1	83.4	84.6	91.3	98.5	96.0	100.0	107.0	109.9	115.5	....		GDP Deflator (1990=100)	99bi *p*
Midyear Estimates																	
2.98	3.04	3.11	3.19	3.26	3.34	3.41	3.48	3.56	3.63	3.70	3.77	3.85	3.92	4.00		Population	99z

Paraguay

288

		1965	1966	1967	1968	1969	1970	1971	1972	1973	1974	1975	1976	1977	1978	1979
Exchange Rates														*Guaranies per SDR:*		
Market Rate......aa=	wa	126.0	126.0	126.0	126.0	126.0	126.0	136.8	136.8	152.0	154.3	147.5	146.4	153.1	164.2	166.0
														Guaranies per US Dollar:		
Market Rate......ae=	we	126.0	126.0	126.0	126.0	126.0	126.0	126.0	126.0	126.0	126.0	126.0	126.0	126.0	126.0	126.0
Market Rate......rf=	wf	126.0	126.0	126.0	126.0	126.0	126.0	126.0	126.0	126.0	126.0	126.0	126.0	126.0	126.0	126.0
Secondary Rate	xf	....	....	....	....	....	....	....	....	....	136.4	138.3	138.6	134.0	138.6	139.3
Tertiary Rate	yf	....	....	....	....	....	....	....	....	....	....	....	....	....	....	....
													Index Numbers (1990=100):			
Market Rate	ahx	975.8	975.8	975.8	975.8	975.8	975.8	975.8	975.8	975.8	975.8	975.8	975.8	975.8	975.8	975.8
Nominal Effective Exchange Rate	nec	....	....	....	....	....	....	....	....	....	....	....	....	....	....	.5
Real Effective Exchange Rate	rec	....	....	....	....	....	....	....	....	....	....	....	....	....	....	200.0
Fund Position															*Millions of SDRs:*	
Quota	2f.s	11.25	15.00	15.00	15.00	15.00	19.00	19.00	19.00	19.00	19.00	19.00	19.00	19.00	23.00	23.00
SDRs	1b.s	—	—	—	—	—	2.52	4.55	6.57	6.57	6.57	6.57	6.57	6.58	6.64	9.41
Reserve Position in the Fund	1c.s	2.81	3.76	3.77	3.77	3.77	4.77	4.77	4.77	4.77	4.77	4.77	5.77	6.62	6.48	8.19
International Liquidity											*Millions of US Dollars Unless Otherwise Indicated:*					
Total Reserves minus Gold	11.d	10.19	11.46	12.18	12.14	10.25	17.52	21.04	31.39	57.01	87.13	115.02	157.51	267.84	448.73	609.09
SDRs	1b.d	....	....	....	....	....	2.52	4.94	7.13	7.93	8.04	7.69	7.63	7.99	8.65	12.40
Reserve Position in the Fund	1c.d	2.81	3.76	3.77	3.77	3.77	4.77	5.18	5.18	5.75	5.84	5.58	6.70	8.04	8.44	10.79
Foreign Exchange	1d.d	7.38	7.70	8.41	8.37	6.48	10.23	10.92	19.08	43.33	73.25	101.74	143.17	251.81	431.64	585.90
of which: US Dollars	1dx d	5.84	6.11	7.30	5.26	3.47	7.55	2.73	13.86	16.14	47.53	93.99	116.26	111.67	226.32	288.89
Gold (Million Fine Troy Ounces)	1ad	.002	.002	.002	.002	.002	.002	.002	.002	.002	.002	.002	.002	.006	.011	.035
Gold (National Valuation)	1and	.08	.08	.08	.08	.08	.08	.08	.09	.10	.10	.10	.10	.26	.45	4.36
Monetary Authorities: Other Liab.	4..d	.70	1.18	1.29	2.40	1.45	1.01	.96	.89	3.98	3.57	3.37	6.21	7.74	9.16	17.42
Deposit Money Banks: Assets	7a.d	1.16	4.56	1.29	1.26	2.81	2.15	2.49	3.09	4.30	12.06	12.47	16.49	18.96	17.09	35.32
of which: Claims on Nonbanks	7add	....	....	....	....	....	....	....	....	....	....	....	....	....	....	....
Deposit Money Banks: Liabilities	7b.d	5.12	9.17	11.02	13.25	16.26	19.78	19.52	20.86	20.57	18.68	14.26	7.10	14.22	21.21	30.02
of which: Liab. to Nonbanks	7bdd	....	....	....	....	....	....	....	....	....	....	....	....	....	....	....
Other Banking Insts.: Liabilities	7f.d	....	....	20.49	27.13	34.96	40.98	45.19	52.50	59.96	69.91	81.89	84.46	93.19	103.22	116.98
of which: Liab. to Nonbanks	7fdd	....	....	20.41	27.01	34.92	40.76	44.75	52.50	59.68	69.81	81.86	84.09	93.09	102.32	116.27
Monetary Authorities															*Billions of Guaranies:*	
Foreign Assets	11	1.38	1.45	I 1.54	1.56	1.31	2.33	2.78	4.00	7.20	10.99	14.51	19.85	33.78	56.60	77.29
Claims on Central Government	12a	1.93	2.05	I 2.72	2.81	2.73	2.75	3.17	4.21	4.43	3.18	2.97	2.67	2.92	4.29	4.38
Claims on Local Government	12b	....	....	....	....	....	....	....	....	....	....	....	....	....	....	....
Claims on Nonfin.Pub.Enterprises	12c	1.34	1.45	I 3.17	2.13	2.73	2.79	2.60	2.89	2.58	3.02	3.64	3.17	2.69	2.79	2.97
Claims on Private Sector	12d	1.31	1.26	1.75	1.78	1.78	1.81	1.85	1.84	1.85	1.91	1.87	1.99	2.02	2.02	2.01
Claims on Deposit Money Banks	12e	.80	.89	I .10	.11	.16	.34	.35	.26	.52	.84	.64	.53	.76	2.27	3.74
Claims on Other Banking Insts.	12f	.08	.07	.10	.04	.31	.49	1.28	1.54	1.98	2.78	3.26	4.03	3.68	3.09	3.37
Reserve Money	14	5.05	5.24	I 7.18	6.58	7.33	8.61	9.71	11.84	15.04	17.69	21.74	26.24	34.47	45.89	56.16
of which: Currency Outside DMBs	14a	2.93	2.90	I 3.05	3.27	3.45	4.02	4.41	5.14	6.49	7.55	8.90	10.29	13.34	18.69	24.31
Quasi-Monetary Deposits	15	.13	.13	I .06	.07	.10	.13	.13	.15	.17	.20	.68	.69	.64	1.08	3.92
Restricted Deposits	16b	.04	.05	.41	.49	.48	.40	.31	.27	.45	.53	.46	.65	1.07	1.72	2.19
Foreign Liabilities	16c	—	.01	I .15	.23	.19	.14	.18	.16	.56	.56	.55	.72	1.00	1.42	2.54
Long-Term Foreign Liabilities	16cl	....	....	....	....	....	....	....	....	....	....	....	....	....	....	....
Central Government Deposits	16d	.58	.75	I .69	.67	.69	.81	.92	1.00	1.24	1.89	2.12	2.18	5.37	12.15	19.04
Capital Accounts	17a	.06	.08	I .04	.05	.05	.38	.64	.98	1.11	1.25	1.69	2.04	2.54	3.37	5.01
Other Items (Net)	17r	−.07	.07	I .84	.34	.16	.06	.14	.33	−.02	.62	−.37	−.30	.76	5.43	4.90
Deposit Money Banks															*Billions of Guaranies:*	
Reserves	20	2.16	2.34	I 2.72	3.21	3.25	4.23	5.12	6.45	8.17	9.86	12.50	15.75	20.77	26.64	30.47
Foreign Assets	21	−.42	−.43	I .16	.16	.35	.27	.31	.39	.54	1.52	1.57	2.08	2.39	2.15	4.45
Claims on Central Government	22a	—	—	I —	—	—	—	—	—	—	—	—	—	.55	.97	.84
Claims on Local Government	22b	....	....	....	....	....	....	....	....	....	....	....	....	....	....	....
Claims on Nonfin.Pub.Enterprises	22c	....	....	....	....	....	....	....	....	....	....	....	....	....	....	....
Claims on Private Sector	22d	5.07	6.61	I 5.35	6.03	6.98	7.99	9.11	9.85	12.45	14.56	17.78	21.72	28.05	40.66	53.88
Claims on Other Banking Insts.	22f	....	....	....	....	....	....	....	....	....	....	....	....	....	....	....
Demand Deposits	24	1.99	2.13	I 2.25	2.42	2.48	2.93	3.21	4.04	5.60	7.28	8.55	11.03	14.69	20.30	23.29
Quasi-Monetary Liabilities	25	2.23	2.69	I 3.59	4.26	5.20	6.08	7.27	9.27	11.64	14.06	18.58	23.47	30.94	37.60	44.04
Bonds	26ab	....	....	....	....	....	....	....	....	....	....	....	....	....	....	....
Foreign Liabilities	26c	.56	1.01	1.39	1.67	1.98	2.30	1.83	1.54	1.92	1.89	1.54	.71	1.24	2.27	3.26
Long-Term Foreign Liabilities	26cl	.08	.15	—	—	.06	.19	.63	1.09	.67	.46	.25	.19	.55	.40	.52
Central Government Deposits	26d	—	—	I .01	.01	.01	.01	.01	.03	.05	.04	.05	.07	.09	.11	.16
Credit from Monetary Authorities	26g	.50	.73	I .16	.11	.13	.42	.47	.29	.57	.90	.67	.54	.75	2.24	3.71
Liab. to Other Banking Insts.	26i	....	....	....	....	....	....	....	....	....	....	....	....	....	....	....
Capital Accounts	27a	1.94	2.41	I 1.57	1.85	1.98	2.10	2.55	2.56	2.78	3.90	4.92	5.68	7.19	9.91	16.13
Other Items (Net)	27r	.16	.56	I −.73	−.91	−1.26	−1.53	−1.42	−2.13	−2.06	−2.60	−2.71	−2.13	−3.70	−2.40	−1.47
Monetary Survey															*Billions of Guaranies:*	
Foreign Assets (Net)	31n	.96	1.01	I .16	−.18	−.51	.16	1.08	2.69	5.26	10.06	13.99	20.49	33.93	55.07	75.94
Domestic Credit	32	9.07	10.62	I 12.39	12.10	13.83	15.01	17.08	19.31	22.00	23.52	27.33	31.33	34.45	41.55	48.24
Claims on Central Govt. (Net)	32an	1.35	1.30	I 2.02	2.13	2.03	1.93	2.24	3.19	3.14	1.25	.79	.42	−1.99	−7.00	−13.98
Claims on Local Government	32b	....	....	....	....	....	....	....	....	....	....	....	....	....	....	....
Claims on Nonfin.Pub.Enterprises	32c	1.34	1.45	I 3.17	2.13	2.73	2.79	2.60	2.89	2.58	3.02	3.64	3.17	2.69	2.79	2.97
Claims on Private Sector	32d	6.38	7.87	I 7.10	7.81	8.76	9.80	10.96	11.68	14.30	16.47	19.64	23.71	30.07	42.67	55.88
Claims on Other Banking Insts.	32f	.08	.07	.10	.04	.31	.49	1.28	1.54	1.98	2.78	3.26	4.03	3.68	3.09	3.37
Money	34	4.91	5.03	I 6.69	5.79	6.56	7.31	7.85	9.42	12.49	15.12	17.83	21.59	28.57	39.81	49.54
Quasi-Money	35	2.37	2.82	I 3.65	4.32	5.30	6.20	7.39	9.42	11.81	14.26	19.26	24.16	31.58	38.68	47.95
Bonds	36ab	....	....	....	....	....	....	....	....	....	....	....	....	....	....	....
Restricted Deposits	36b	.04	.05	.41	.49	.48	.40	.31	.27	.45	.53	.46	.65	1.07	1.72	2.19
Long-Term Foreign Liabilities	36cl	.08	.15	—	—	.06	.19	.63	1.09	.67	.46	.25	.19	.55	.40	.52
Liab. to Other Banking Insts.	36i	....	....	....	....	....	....	....	....	....	....	....	....	....	....	....
Capital Accounts	37a	2.00	2.48	I 1.61	1.90	2.03	2.48	3.19	3.54	3.90	5.15	6.61	7.72	9.73	13.28	21.14
Other Items (Net)	37r	1.49	2.64	I −.66	−1.21	−1.67	−1.91	−1.71	−2.34	−2.14	−1.94	−3.10	−2.49	−3.12	2.72	2.84
Money plus Quasi-Money	35l	7.28	7.86	I 10.34	10.11	11.86	13.51	15.24	18.84	24.30	29.38	37.09	45.75	60.15	78.49	97.49

Paraguay

288

1980	1981	1982	1983	1984	1985	1986	1987	1988	1989	1990	1991	1992	1993	1994		
End of Period															**Exchange Rates**	
160.7	146.7	139.0	131.9	235.3	351.5	672.8	780.3	740.1	1,600.6	1,789.7	1,934.4	2,200.3	2,582.3	2,832.1	Market Rate……aa= ……	**wa**
End of Period (we) Period Average (wf)																
126.0	126.0	126.0	126.0	240.0	320.0	550.0	550.0	550.0	1,218.0	1,258.0	1,352.3	1,600.2	1,880.0	1,940.0	Market Rate……ae= ……	**we**
126.0	126.0	126.0	126.0	201.0	306.7	339.2	550.0	550.0	1,056.2	1,229.8	1,325.2	1,500.3	1,744.3	1,911.5	Market Rate……rf= ……	**wf**
136.1	148.4	160.5	160.0	321.8	602.8	700.3	....	....	....	....	....	....	....	....	Secondary Rate	**xf**
....	....	....	315.2	224.3	226.7	253.3	400.0	400.0	....	....	....	....	....	....	Tertiary Rate	**yf**
Period Averages																
975.8	975.8	975.8	975.8	653.5	405.5	370.8	223.5	223.5	126.3	100.0	92.7	79.8	70.6	64.3	Market Rate	**ah*x***
.7	1.0	1.2	1.7	2.7	3.7	4.5	5.0	10.7	23.5	100.0	201.5	427.6	1,119.8	3,421.2	Nominal Effective Exchange Rate	**ne*c***
222.2	239.2	211.0	196.8	185.3	159.9	161.1	129.6	133.9	102.4	100.0	116.4	113.9	110.1	109.5	Real Effective Exchange Rate	**re*c***
End of Period															**Fund Position**	
34.50	34.50	34.50	48.40	48.40	48.40	48.40	48.40	48.40	48.40	48.40	48.40	72.10	72.10	72.10	Quota	**2f.*s***
11.05	15.09	23.67	30.41	35.03	38.80	42.08	44.78	47.38	50.83	54.93	58.76	62.12	65.08	67.63	SDRs	**1b.*s***
14.88	25.16	27.64	32.25	32.25	31.58	24.86	19.57	14.97	12.48	11.02	11.02	16.94	16.48	14.53	Reserve Position in the Fund	**1c.*s***
End of Period															**International Liquidity**	
761.85	805.70	739.00	680.19	666.27	533.62	446.67	497.02	323.66	432.55	661.42	962.12	561.53	631.18	1,016.43	Total Reserves minus Gold	**1l.*d***
14.09	17.56	26.11	31.84	34.34	42.62	51.47	63.53	63.76	66.80	78.15	84.05	85.42	89.39	98.73	SDRs	**1b.*d***
18.98	29.29	30.49	33.76	31.61	34.69	30.41	27.76	20.15	16.40	15.68	15.76	23.29	22.63	21.20	Reserve Position in the Fund	**1c.*d***
728.78	758.85	682.40	614.59	600.32	456.31	364.79	405.73	239.76	349.35	567.60	862.30	452.82	519.16	896.50	Foreign Exchange	**1d.*d***
404.33	456.22	453.02	334.72	482.86	336.89	268.20	106.23	81.13	50.27	382.15	462.70	329.34	416.00	569.20	*of which: US Dollars*	**1dx*d***
.035	.035	.035	.035	.035	.035	.035	.035	.035	.035	.035	.035	.035	.035	.035	Gold (Million Fine Troy Ounces)	**1ad**
4.62	4.30	4.05	3.88	2.96	11.68	13.82	17.01	14.31	13.98	13.97	12.79	11.60	13.70	13.40	Gold (National Valuation)	**1an*d***
17.83	29.65	36.62	58.71	152.23	98.81	77.98	89.22	34.26	21.99	24.10	1.22	....	....	....	Monetary Authorities: Other Liab.	**4..*d***
53.75	94.20	80.68	111.43	71.86	43.12	31.49	31.37	59.12	134.84	158.15	152.70	240.30	300.39	298.21	Deposit Money Banks: Assets	**7a.*d***
—	—	—	—	—	—	—	—	1.91	4.16	9.51	13.38	19.56	32.45	56.95	*of which:* Claims on Nonbanks	**7ad*d***
34.13	67.48	52.69	98.14	60.20	44.18	18.39	9.02	34.56	20.91	23.29	48.47	89.18	147.37	124.57	Deposit Money Banks: Liabilities	**7b.*d***
....	....	....	....	....	....	....	....	15.14	11.60	8.11	29.31	47.73	65.62	14.75	*of which:* Liab. to Nonbanks	**7bd*d***
131.34	136.20	164.48	173.98	107.86	94.78	62.35	70.60	64.44	41.65	46.38	52.18	41.51	36.40	....	Other Banking Insts.: Liabilities	**7f.*d***
130.13	136.05	164.44	173.98	107.86	94.78	62.35	70.60	64.44	40.47	45.24	48.81	38.14	33.10	....	*of which:* Liab. to Nonbanks	**7fd*d***
End of Period															**Monetary Authorities**	
96.58	102.06	86.54	85.98	109.41	100.01	167.05	168.56	I 135.19	537.60	853.59	1,292.09	993.43	1,289.15	2,016.58	Foreign Assets	**11**
3.85	3.96	3.54	20.33	28.89	32.52	39.03	49.25	I 27.38	103.34	230.46	76.98	794.81	916.73	1,047.15	Claims on Central Government	**12a**
....	....	....	....	....	....	....	....	1.11	1.08	.94	.89	.83	.82	.82	Claims on Local Government	**12b**
7.65	8.25	9.19	9.31	12.87	25.51	35.25	65.51	I 106.49	176.53	142.32	185.73	242.74	266.79	222.35	Claims on Nonfin.Pub.Enterprises	**12c**
2.08	2.19	2.24	2.78	2.74	2.63	4.14	4.39	I 1.58	2.79	5.39	6.55	6.30	6.29	6.58	Claims on Private Sector	**12d**
6.76	9.62	7.81	11.84	22.19	20.52	51.60	45.91	I 93.26	111.10	117.11	112.10	170.29	102.77	98.07	Claims on Deposit Money Banks	**12e**
3.03	3.75	10.06	11.09	13.34	11.55	22.34	22.67	I 10.58	17.40	18.70	21.53	16.53	16.21	15.65	Claims on Other Banking Insts.	**12f**
71.59	84.24	84.75	111.03	130.02	154.65	209.17	293.37	I 379.06	506.43	644.79	863.55	1,185.63	1,422.54	1,803.48	Reserve Money	**14**
31.18	31.15	33.17	38.47	48.60	62.61	84.48	119.57	I 149.10	216.19	300.52	379.92	531.26	635.77	800.46	*of which: Currency Outside DMBs*	**14a**
6.62	11.62	17.03	18.43	20.05	31.85	38.09	34.47	I —	—	32.74	80.60	50.75	75.70	66.43	Quasi-Monetary Deposits	**15**
2.14	1.90	.87	.19	.25	.17	.15	.37	I 3.92	3.96	5.51	8.13	10.12	17.11	26.47	Restricted Deposits	**16b**
2.66	4.08	5.00	8.79	31.90	15.55	17.97	26.29	I 19.42	26.35	26.95	2.76	7.49	17.36	16.21	Foreign Liabilities	**16c**
....	....	....	....	....	....	....	....	1.17	3.01	3.02	75.58	92.09	98.31	96.99	Long-Term Foreign Liabilities	**16cl**
21.18	9.23	5.47	5.08	5.78	8.96	13.54	23.43	I 51.82	224.25	382.06	288.49	228.31	134.37	414.23	Central Government Deposits	**16d**
9.64	16.13	18.86	18.27	19.68	22.22	28.35	35.91	I 40.02	59.82	100.88	169.11	286.93	304.13	331.91	Capital Accounts	**17a**
6.11	2.63	-12.60	-20.46	-18.24	-40.66	12.15	-57.55	I -119.83	126.02	172.59	207.63	363.63	529.23	651.47	Other Items (Net)	**17r**
End of Period															**Deposit Money Banks**	
38.66	52.83	50.75	69.74	78.27	84.28	117.09	174.02	I 209.06	264.24	301.07	411.01	588.19	752.52	948.78	Reserves	**20**
6.77	11.87	10.17	14.04	17.25	13.80	17.32	17.25	I 23.65	164.50	198.01	208.44	388.08	549.71	573.75	Foreign Assets	**21**
1.02	1.54	2.16	1.81	1.35	.81	.64	1.32	I .07	1.58	.33	.18	—	.18	—	Claims on Central Government	**22a**
....	....	....	....	....	....	....	....	—	—	.02	.02	.30	.55	.01	Claims on Local Government	**22b**
....	....	....	....	....	....	....	....	.38	.34	1.71	1.88	1.79	1.45	1.46	Claims on Nonfin.Pub.Enterprises	**22c**
77.34	89.50	94.41	99.68	116.59	128.66	170.19	215.12	I 350.06	492.99	768.44	1,226.37	1,705.83	2,315.36	3,164.92	Claims on Private Sector	**22d**
....	....	....	....	....	....	....	....	1.71	2.30	2.96	4.73	4.93	11.08	11.58	Claims on Other Banking Insts.	**22f**
28.57	29.28	25.70	34.92	44.76	56.25	67.44	113.73	I 163.52	188.97	215.27	288.88	306.57	367.48	499.43	Demand Deposits	**24**
62.27	82.73	88.46	99.41	108.08	115.88	150.89	191.20	I 192.80	405.69	690.94	1,077.61	1,628.79	2,170.28	2,663.58	Quasi-Monetary Liabilities	**25**
....	....	....	....	....	....	....	....	2.76	1.53	3.10	7.00	2.21	4.00	3.76	Bonds	**26ab**
3.82	7.76	5.39	11.76	13.88	13.70	9.55	4.34	I 8.38	11.97	19.61	26.74	71.07	149.61	211.29	Foreign Liabilities	**26c**
.48	.74	1.25	.61	.57	.44	.56	.62	I 5.44	13.55	9.56	39.42	72.96	120.08	28.39	Long-Term Foreign Liabilities	**26cl**
.20	.18	.13	.13	.15	.35	.64	.98	I 19.27	35.79	50.91	63.99	97.40	209.98	432.74	Central Government Deposits	**26d**
6.75	9.25	7.41	13.51	24.94	20.87	51.94	46.01	I 92.14	114.08	116.51	111.34	169.18	102.45	94.01	Credit from Monetary Authorities	**26g**
....	....	....	....	....	....	....	....	6.32	11.94	2.63	5.39	2.85	.86	.01	Liab. to Other Banking Insts.	**26i**
21.29	26.77	30.36	30.54	32.79	35.88	39.13	47.36	I 86.50	131.12	188.84	256.33	342.21	483.01	719.50	Capital Accounts	**27a**
.42	-.96	-1.23	-5.61	-11.70	-15.80	-14.92	3.48	I 7.80	11.32	-24.82	-24.07	-4.12	23.11	47.82	Other Items (Net)	**27r**
End of Period															**Monetary Survey**	
96.87	102.09	86.31	79.47	80.87	84.55	156.84	155.18	I 131.03	663.79	1,005.04	1,471.02	1,302.95	1,671.89	2,362.84	Foreign Assets (Net)	**31n**
73.59	99.80	116.00	139.77	169.86	192.38	257.42	333.85	I 428.28	538.31	738.31	1,172.38	2,448.35	3,191.11	3,623.54	Domestic Credit	**32**
-16.51	-3.89	.10	16.92	24.31	24.03	25.49	26.16	I -43.64	-155.12	-202.18	-275.31	469.10	572.56	200.17	Claims on Central Govt. (Net)	**32an**
....	....	....	....	....	....	....	....	1.11	1.08	.96	.91	1.13	1.37	.83	Claims on Local Government	**32b**
7.65	8.25	9.19	9.31	12.87	25.51	35.25	65.51	I 106.87	176.88	144.03	187.61	244.53	268.23	223.81	Claims on Nonfin.Pub.Enterprises	**32c**
79.42	91.69	96.65	102.45	119.33	131.30	174.33	219.51	I 351.64	495.78	773.83	1,232.92	1,712.14	2,321.65	3,171.50	Claims on Private Sector	**32d**
3.03	3.75	10.06	11.09	13.34	11.55	22.34	22.67	I 12.29	19.69	21.66	26.26	21.46	27.29	27.23	Claims on Other Banking Insts.	**32f**
62.36	62.43	60.20	75.59	97.81	125.20	158.67	243.67	I 330.16	434.89	558.06	738.91	905.03	1,054.01	1,370.31	Money	**34**
68.89	94.35	105.49	117.84	128.13	147.73	188.98	225.67	I 192.80	405.69	723.67	1,158.21	1,679.54	2,245.98	2,730.01	Quasi-Money	**35**
....	....	....	....	....	....	....	....	2.76	1.53	3.10	7.00	2.21	4.00	3.76	Bonds	**36ab**
2.14	1.90	.87	.19	.25	.17	.15	.37	I 3.92	3.96	5.51	8.13	10.12	17.11	26.47	Restricted Deposits	**36b**
.48	.74	1.25	.61	.57	.44	.56	.62	I 6.61	16.56	12.57	115.00	165.05	218.39	125.38	Long-Term Foreign Liabilities	**36cl**
....	....	....	....	....	....	....	....	6.32	11.94	2.63	5.39	2.85	.86	.01	Liab. to Other Banking Insts.	**36i**
30.93	42.90	49.22	48.81	52.46	58.09	67.48	83.26	I 126.52	190.93	289.71	425.44	629.13	787.14	1,051.41	Capital Accounts	**37a**
5.65	-.44	-14.72	-23.78	-28.48	-54.70	-1.58	-64.56	I -109.78	136.59	148.09	185.32	357.37	535.53	679.04	Other Items (Net)	**37r**
131.26	156.79	165.69	193.43	225.94	272.94	347.65	469.34	I 522.96	840.58	1,281.73	1,897.12	2,584.57	3,299.99	4,100.32	Money plus Quasi-Money	**35l**

Paraguay

288

		1965	1966	1967	1968	1969	1970	1971	1972	1973	1974	1975	1976	1977	1978	1979
Other Banking Institutions																*Billions of Guaranies:*
Reserves	40	....	....	—	—	—	—	—	—	—	—	—	—	—	-.01	—
Claims on Local Government	42b	....	....	....	....	....	....	....	....	....	....	....	....	....	....	....
Claims on Nonfin.Pub.Enterprises	42c	....	....	....	....	....	....	....	....	....	....	....	....	....	....	....
Claims on Private Sector	42d	....	....	3.41	4.46	6.13	7.33	8.03	9.51	11.22	13.40	14.78	16.65	19.88	19.96	24.34
Claims on Deposit Money Banks	42e	....	....	—	—	.01	.01	.01	.01	.01	—	.03	.01	.01	.01	.01
Time, Savings,& Fgn.Currency Dep.	45	....	....	—	—	—	—	—	—	—	—	—	—	—	—	—
Bonds	46ab	....	....	....	....	....	....	....	....	....	....	....	....	....	....	....
Foreign Liabilities	46c	....	....	.17	.09	.16	.14	.05	.19	.12	.01	.10	—	—	—	—
Long-Term Foreign Liabilities	46cl	....	....	2.41	3.33	4.24	5.02	5.65	6.43	7.44	8.80	10.22	10.64	11.74	13.01	14.74
Credit from Monetary Authorities	46g	....	....	—	—	.26	.45	1.09	1.50	1.83	2.48	2.95	3.64	3.66	3.09	3.32
Credit from Deposit Money Banks	46h	....	....	—	—	—	—	—	.01	—	—	—	.01	.02	.02	.03
Capital Accounts	47a	....	....	1.16	1.31	1.50	1.70	2.06	2.20	2.43	2.49	2.48	3.18	4.23	5.24	5.98
Other Items (Net)	47r	....	....	-.33	-.27	-.02	.02	-.81	-.80	-.60	-.37	-.93	-.81	.25	-1.39	.28
Banking Survey																*Billions of Guaranies:*
Foreign Assets (Net)	51n	....	....	-.02	-.27	-.67	.02	1.03	2.50	5.13	10.01	13.85	20.45	33.90	55.06	75.91
Domestic Credit	52	....	....	15.60	16.42	19.55	21.70	23.62	27.07	31.04	33.92	38.62	43.35	50.65	58.42	69.20
Claims on Central Govt. (Net)	52an	....	....	1.91	2.03	1.93	1.78	2.04	2.98	2.94	1.02	.56	-.17	-1.99	-7.00	-13.98
Claims on Local Government	52b	....	....	....	....	....	....	....	....	....	....	....	....	....	....	....
Claims on Nonfin.Pub.Enterprises	52c	....	....	3.17	2.13	2.73	2.79	2.60	2.89	2.58	3.02	3.64	3.17	2.69	2.79	2.97
Claims on Private Sector	52d	....	....	10.51	12.27	14.90	17.13	18.99	21.20	25.52	29.87	34.42	40.35	49.95	62.63	80.22
Liquid Liabilities	55l	....	....	10.34	10.11	11.86	13.51	15.25	18.84	24.30	29.38	37.09	45.75	60.15	78.50	97.49
Bonds	56ab	....	....	....	....	....	....	....	....	....	....	....	....	....	....	....
Restricted Deposits	56b	....	....	.41	.49	.48	.40	.31	.27	.45	.53	.46	.65	1.07	1.72	2.19
Long-Term Foreign Liabilities	56cl	....	....	2.41	3.33	4.31	5.21	6.28	7.52	8.11	9.27	10.47	10.83	12.29	13.41	15.26
Capital Accounts	57a	....	....	2.77	3.21	3.52	4.18	5.26	5.74	6.33	7.63	9.09	10.90	13.96	18.53	27.12
Other Items (Net)	57r	....	....	-.35	-.99	-1.29	-1.58	-2.44	-2.80	-3.03	-2.88	-4.63	-4.33	-2.92	1.31	3.06
Interest Rates																*Percent Per Annum*
Discount Rate (End of Period)	60	....	....	....	....	....	....	....	....	....	....	....	....	....	....	....
Savings Rate	60k	....	....	....	....	....	....	....	....	....	....	....	....	....	....	....
Deposit Rate	60l	....	....	....	....	....	....	....	....	....	....	....	....	....	....	....
Lending Rate	60p	....	....	....	....	....	....	....	....	....	....	....	....	....	....	....
Prices																*Index Numbers (1990=100):*
Wholesale Prices	63	2.5	2.6	2.6	2.5	2.6	2.5	2.8	I3.3	4.4	5.8	6.8	6.9	7.4	8.4	10.6
Consumer Prices	64	3.8	3.9	4.0	4.0	4.1	4.1	4.3	4.7	5.3	6.6	7.1	7.4	8.1	8.9	11.4
International Transactions																*Millions of U.S. Dollars:*
Exports	70..d	56.2	48.5	47.4	45.9	50.0	63.0	64.0	84.6	124.2	166.5	176.3	181.2	278.9	257.0	305.2
Imports, cif	71..d	55.4	58.8	70.8	72.8	82.3	76.2	83.2	82.6	122.3	198.3	205.6	220.2	308.3	383.0	521.1
Imports, fob	71.vd	47.4	50.2	60.7	61.5	70.4	63.8	70.3	69.9	104.8	171.4	178.4	180.2	255.4	317.7	437.7
																1990=100
Volume of Exports	72	59.4	49.6	53.0	48.0	53.2	60.7	58.1	67.0	11.0	14.0	13.5	16.8	23.4	26.0	32.2
																1985=100:
Unit Value of Exports	74	36.3	37.1	33.7	36.3	37.2	39.9	40.6	44.9	56.3	28.3	25.5	31.9	43.6	39.1	40.7
Balance of Payments																*Millions of US Dollars:*
Goods: Exports f.o.b.	78aa d	....	....	....	....	....	....	....	....	....	....	188.0	202.1	327.1	356.1	384.5
Goods: Imports f.o.b.	78ab d	....	....	....	....	....	....	....	....	....	....	-227.3	-236.4	-360.0	-432.0	-577.1
Trade Balance	78ac d	....	....	....	....	....	....	....	....	....	....	-39.3	-34.3	-32.9	-75.9	-192.6
Services: Credit	78ad d	....	....	....	....	....	....	....	....	....	....	34.1	39.9	62.9	78.2	129.1
Services: Debit	78ae d	....	....	....	....	....	....	....	....	....	....	-55.1	-57.8	-72.1	-95.6	-154.2
Balance on Goods and Services	78af d	....	....	....	....	....	....	....	....	....	....	-60.3	-52.2	-42.1	-93.3	-217.7
Income: Credit	78ag d	....	....	....	....	....	....	....	....	....	....	11.7	15.8	29.6	54.8	80.1
Income: Debit	78ah d	....	....	....	....	....	....	....	....	....	....	-37.6	-36.3	-47.3	-80.2	-75.7
Balance on Goods, Serv., & Inc.	78ai d	....	....	....	....	....	....	....	....	....	....	-86.2	-72.7	-59.8	-118.7	-213.3
Current Transfers, n.i.e.: Credit	78aj d	....	....	....	....	....	....	....	....	....	....	16.0	7.1	3.8	8.5	10.0
Current Transfers: Debit	78ak d	....	....	....	....	....	....	....	....	....	....	-2.0	-2.9	-2.6	-2.7	-2.6
Current Account, n.i.e.	78al d	....	....	....	....	....	....	....	....	....	....	-72.2	-68.5	-58.6	-112.9	-205.9
Capital Account, n.i.e.: Credit	78ba d	....	....	....	....	....	....	....	....	....	....	—	—	—	—	—
Capital Account: Debit	78bb d	....	....	....	....	....	....	....	....	....	....	—	—	—	—	—
Capital Account, n.i.e.	78bc d	....	....	....	....	....	....	....	....	....	....	—	—	—	—	—
Direct Investment Abroad	78bd d	....	....	....	....	....	....	....	....	....	....	—	-25.0	—	-5.0	—
Dir. Invest. in Rep. Econ., n.i.e.	78be d	....	....	....	....	....	....	....	....	....	....	24.4	22.0	21.7	24.6	50.2
Portfolio Investment Assets	78bf d	....	....	....	....	....	....	....	....	....	....	—	—	—	—	—
Portfolio Investment Liab., n.i.e.	78bg d	....	....	....	....	....	....	....	....	....	....	—	—	—	—	—
Other Investment Assets	78bh d	....	....	....	....	....	....	....	....	....	....	22.2	9.4	74.0	106.4	130.7
Other Investment Liab., n.i.e.	78bi d	....	....	....	....	....	....	....	....	....	....	51.3	103.1	93.1	146.7	175.8
Financial Account, n.i.e.	78bj d	....	....	....	....	....	....	....	....	....	....	97.9	109.5	188.8	272.7	356.7
Net Errors and Omissions	78ca d	....	....	....	....	....	....	....	....	....	....	3.9	-.4	-20.6	17.1	8.9
Overall Balance	78cb d	....	....	....	....	....	....	....	....	....	....	29.6	40.6	109.6	176.9	159.7
Reserves and Related Items	79da d	....	....	....	....	....	....	....	....	....	....	-29.6	-40.6	-109.6	-176.9	-159.7
Reserve Assets	79db d	....	....	....	....	....	....	....	....	....	....	-28.6	-42.4	-111.8	-178.4	-161.7
Use of Fund Credit and Loans	79dc d	....	....	....	....	....	....	....	....	....	....	—	—	—	—	—
Liabs.Constit.For.Auth.Reserves	79dd d	....	....	....	....	....	....	....	....	....	....	-1.0	1.8	2.2	1.5	2.0
Exceptional Financing	79de d	....	....	....	....	....	....	....	....	....	....	—	—	—	—	—

Paraguay
288

1980	1981	1982	1983	1984	1985	1986	1987	1988	1989	1990	1991	1992	1993	1994		
End of Period															**Other Banking Institutions**	
—	.01	—	—	—	—	—	—	‡16.58	21.25	12.13	13.57	26.85	30.25	....	Reserves	40
....	....	....	....	....	....	....	....		.29	1.99	—	—	—	—	Claims on Local Government	42b
....	....	....	....	....	....	....	....		.01	—	—	—	—	—	Claims on Nonfin.Pub.Enterprises	42c
26.54	33.19	40.23	41.81	50.27	55.39	73.34	84.58	‡133.44	172.92	249.42	335.32	432.03	600.11	....	Claims on Private Sector	42d
.01	—	.01	—	.02	.02	—	—	‡8.25	15.16	27.70	76.48	59.07	68.59	....	Claims on Deposit Money Banks	42e
—	—	—	—	—	—	—	—	‡63.30	79.15	117.44	174.25	179.67	201.09	....	Time, Savings,& Fgn.Currency Dep.	45
—	—	—	—	—	—	—	—		15.50	21.13	10.74	14.04	58.71	119.50	Bonds	46ab
—	—	—	—	—	—	—	—	‡	—	—	—	—	—	—	Foreign Liabilities	46c
16.55	17.16	20.72	21.92	25.89	30.33	34.29	38.83	‡25.78	50.81	58.07	71.22	67.03	66.62	....	Long-Term Foreign Liabilities	46cI
3.01	2.22	10.04	10.90	12.43	11.50	18.74	22.57	‡10.38	16.31	15.67	12.57	11.57	11.57	....	Credit from Monetary Authorities	46g
.03	.03	.01	—	—	.02	—	—	‡.43	.49	1.74	4.08	1.41	2.31	....	Credit from Deposit Money Banks	46h
6.87	8.81	9.99	12.04	13.80	14.38	19.59	29.42	‡47.92	50.70	93.32	165.24	234.45	273.00	....	Capital Accounts	47a
.09	4.98	–.51	–3.06	–1.83	–.81	.72	–6.24	‡–4.74	–7.25	–7.72	–16.03	–34.89	24.87	....	Other Items (Net)	47r
End of Period															**Banking Survey**	
96.85	102.05	86.29	79.44	80.87	84.55	156.84	155.18	‡131.03	663.79	1,005.04	1,471.02	1,302.95	1,671.89	....	Foreign Assets (Net)	51n
97.10	129.24	146.17	170.49	206.79	236.23	308.42	395.76	‡549.72	693.53	966.06	1,481.44	2,858.92	3,763.93	....	Domestic Credit	52
–16.51	–3.89	.10	16.92	24.31	24.03	25.49	26.16	‡–43.64	–155.12	–202.18	–275.31	469.10	572.56	....	Claims on Central Govt. (Net)	52an
....	....	....	....	....	....	....	....		1.40	3.07	.96	.91	1.13	1.37	Claims on Local Government	52b
7.65	8.25	9.19	9.31	12.87	25.51	35.25	65.51	‡106.88	176.88	144.03	187.61	244.53	268.23	....	Claims on Nonfin.Pub.Enterprises	52c
105.96	124.88	136.89	144.26	169.60	186.69	247.67	304.09	‡485.08	668.70	1,023.25	1,568.24	2,144.16	2,921.76	....	Claims on Private Sector	52d
131.25	156.78	165.69	193.42	225.94	272.94	347.65	469.34	‡569.68	898.48	1,387.03	2,057.80	2,737.39	3,470.82	....	Liquid Liabilities	55l
....	....	....	....	....	....	....	....		18.25	22.66	13.84	21.04	60.92	123.49	Bonds	56ab
2.14	1.90	.87	.19	.25	.17	.15	.37	‡3.92	3.96	5.51	8.13	10.12	17.11	....	Restricted Deposits	56b
17.03	17.90	21.97	22.53	26.45	30.77	34.86	39.45	‡32.39	67.37	70.64	186.22	232.08	285.01	....	Long-Term Foreign Liabilities	56cl
37.80	51.71	59.21	60.86	66.27	72.47	87.07	112.68	‡174.43	241.63	383.03	590.68	863.58	1,060.14	....	Capital Accounts	57a
5.72	3.00	–15.29	–27.06	–31.25	–55.56	–4.46	–70.89	‡–117.92	123.22	111.05	88.59	257.78	479.25	....	Other Items (Net)	57r
Percent Per Annum															**Interest Rates**	
....	....	....	....	....	....	....	....		10.00	21.00	30.00	18.00	18.00	18.00	18.00	Discount Rate *(End of Period)*	60
....	....	....	....	....	....	....	....	....	....		10.50	12.04	10.37	10.60	11.35	Savings Rate	60k
....	....	....	....	....	....	....	....	....	....		22.92	22.53	20.15	22.10	23.12	Deposit Rate	60l
....	....	....	....	....	....	....	....	....	....		31.00	34.94	27.96	30.78	32.46	Lending Rate	60p
Period Averages															**Prices**	
11.4	12.8	13.3	16.2	20.8	25.6	37.2	41.6	52.9	64.5	100.0	131.7	....	....	....	Wholesale Prices	63
14.0	15.9	17.0	19.3	23.3	29.1	38.3	46.7	57.2	72.4	100.0	124.3	143.1	169.2	....	Consumer Prices	64
Millions of U.S. Dollars															**International Transactions**	
310.2	295.6	329.8	269.2	334.5	303.9	232.5	353.4	509.8	1,009.4	958.7	737.1	656.6	725.2	....	Exports	70..d
614.7	599.6	672.0	545.9	586.0	501.5	578.1	595.3	573.9	759.7	1,352.0	1,460.3	1,421.6	1,688.8	....	Imports, cif	71..d
517.1	506.1	581.5	478.3	513.1	442.3	509.4	517.5	494.8	660.8	1,193.4	1,275.4	1,237.1	1,477.5	....	Imports, fob	71.vd
1990=100																
30.7	28.6	38.2	32.6	34.0	50.0	47.5	54.7	69.2	98.3	100.0	80.6	....	....	....	Volume of Exports	72
Indexes of Unit Values in Guaranies																
42.4	44.9	41.8	45.6	84.1	74.4	60.9	146.1	204.6	401.3	....	....	....	....	....	Unit Value of Exports	74
Minus Sign Indicates Debit															Balance of Payments	
400.3	398.5	396.2	326.0	361.3	465.6	575.8	597.4	871.0	1,180.0	1,382.3	1,120.8	1,081.5	1,653.0	....	Goods: Exports f.o.b.	78aa d
–675.3	–772.4	–711.3	–551.1	–649.1	–659.3	–864.2	–918.7	–1,030.1	–1,015.9	–1,635.8	–1,867.6	–1,950.6	–2,671.6	....	Goods: Imports f.o.b.	78ab d
–275.0	–373.9	–315.1	–225.4	–287.8	–193.7	–288.4	–321.3	–159.1	164.1	–253.5	–746.8	–869.1	–1,018.6	....	Trade Balance	78ac d
164.0	156.2	120.4	138.0	210.8	152.7	183.8	172.1	295.9	394.9	497.5	903.6	825.6	1,018.7	....	Services: Credit	78ad d
–165.1	–203.9	–250.3	–157.4	–211.9	–180.3	–224.9	–256.3	–300.8	–303.5	–457.6	–546.9	–541.9	–608.8	....	Services: Debit	78ae d
–276.1	–421.6	–445.0	–244.8	–288.9	–221.3	–329.5	–405.5	–164.0	255.5	–213.6	–390.1	–585.4	–608.7	....	Balance on Goods and Services	78af d
126.8	163.8	129.7	96.0	93.9	68.5	70.5	50.3	56.7	88.7	106.8	108.6	129.6	90.5	....	Income: Credit	78ag d
–132.3	–121.5	–97.5	–105.3	–131.7	–106.8	–117.0	–161.5	–138.0	–112.1	–121.1	–114.9	–178.2	–126.8	....	Income: Debit	78ah d
–281.6	–379.3	–379.8	–254.1	–326.7	–259.6	–376.0	–516.7	–245.3	232.1	–227.9	–396.2	–634.0	–645.0	....	Balance on Goods, Serv., & Inc.	78ai d
8.7	8.5	5.9	6.8	9.8	9.2	11.9	28.6	37.7	24.3	55.9	73.7	34.2	42.4	....	Current Transfers, n.i.e.: Credit	78aj d
–4.1	–2.7	–.9	–.6	–.5	–1.3	–.8	–1.7	–2.6	–.8	–.3	–1.4	–.3	–.4	....	Current Transfers: Debit	78ak d
–277.0	–373.5	–374.8	–247.9	–317.4	–251.7	–364.9	–489.8	–210.2	255.6	–172.3	–324.1	–600.1	–603.0	....	Current Account, n.i.e.	78al d
—	—	—	—	—	.1	—	.1	.2	.4	—	—	—	—	....	Capital Account, n.i.e.: Credit	78ba d
—	—	—	—	—	–.5	—	—	–.1	—	—	—	—	—	....	Capital Account: Debit	78bb d
—	—	—	—	—	–.4	—	.1	.1	.4	—	—	—	—	....	Capital Account, n.i.e.	78bc d
—	—	—	—	—	—	—	—	—	—	—	—	—	—	....	Direct Investment Abroad	78bd d
31.7	31.9	36.6	4.9	5.2	.7	.6	5.3	8.4	12.8	76.3	83.5	136.6	111.0	....	Dir. Invest. in Rep. Econ., n.i.e.	78be d
—	5.9	–7.5	3.3	—	—	—	—	—	—	—	—	—	—	....	Portfolio Investment Assets	78bf d
—	—	—	—	—	—	—	—	—	—	—	—	—	—	....	Portfolio Investment Liab., n.i.e.	78bg d
191.2	182.6	175.5	131.6	97.0	69.5	2.5	68.4	–49.0	–63.5	–70.3	–38.5	–16.6	51.0	....	Other Investment Assets	78bh d
225.1	205.5	139.6	150.2	182.0	–37.8	92.3	18.3	–158.7	–123.2	–81.8	169.9	72.0	147.2	....	Other Investment Liab., n.i.e.	78bi d
448.0	425.9	344.2	290.0	284.2	32.4	95.4	92.0	–199.3	–173.9	–75.8	215.0	192.0	309.2	....	Financial Account, n.i.e.	78bj d
–20.1	–13.1	–25.7	–92.3	17.6	73.7	43.8	338.3	198.3	–90.6	362.4	472.0	457.7	483.2	....	Net Errors and Omissions	78ca d
150.9	39.3	–56.5	–50.2	–15.6	–146.0	–225.7	–59.4	–211.1	–8.5	114.3	362.9	49.6	189.4	....	Overall Balance	78cb d
–150.9	–39.3	56.5	50.2	15.6	146.0	225.7	59.4	211.1	8.5	–114.3	–362.9	–49.6	–189.4	....	Reserves and Related Items	79a d
–150.5	–43.5	62.3	52.9	13.8	97.8	139.8	–37.8	168.2	–145.2	–219.3	–298.9	346.9	–86.3	....	Reserve Assets	79db d
—	—	—	—	—	—	—	—	—	—	—	—	—	—	....	Use of Fund Credit and Loans	79dc d
–.4	4.2	–6.0	–2.7	1.8	6.2	19.3	–13.9	–17.2	—	—	—	—	—	....	Liabs.Constit.For.Auth.Reserves	79dd d
—	—	—	—	—	42.0	66.6	111.1	60.1	153.7	105.0	–64.0	–396.5	–103.1	....	Exceptional Financing	79de d

Paraguay

288

		1965	1966	1967	1968	1969	1970	1971	1972	1973	1974	1975	1976	1977	1978	1979
Government Finance																*Millions of Guaranies:*
Deficit (-) or Surplus	80	−37	163	−278	−267	195	161	−310	∫−1,608	−39	1,736	−558	−2,223	1,628	3,060	4,335
Revenue	81	5,710	6,241	6,632	7,284	8,567	8,819	8,970	∫10,995	13,466	18,417	21,177	23,905	31,350	40,520	51,195
Grants Received	81z	....	....	....	....	....	....	....	∫44	28	25	18	17	19	333	46
Expenditure	82	5,747	∫6,078	6,910	7,551	8,372	8,658	9,280	∫12,398	13,301	16,332	21,166	25,267	29,200	37,719	45,467
Lending Minus Repayments	83	....	....	....	....	....	....	....	∫249	232	374	587	878	541	74	1,439
Exch.Rate Adj.to Overall Def./Sur	80x	....	....	....	....	....	....	....	∫—	—	—	—	—	—	—	—
Financing																
Net Borrowing	84	158	∫16	160	160	−96	−48	402	....	....	....	....	....	....	....	....
Net Borrowing: Domestic	84a	....	....	....	....	....	....	....	∫1,074	269	−1,337	−51	−327	425	1,126	1,567
Foreign	85a	....	....	....	....	....	....	....	∫656	66	546	1,967	4,712	3,178	5,717	2,863
Use of Cash Balances	87	−120	−179	118	107	−99	−112	−92	∫−122	−296	−945	−1,358	−2,162	−5,231	−9,903	−8,765
Debt: Domestic	88a	....	....	....	....	....	....	....	....	4,228	2,849	2,505	2,504	3,003	4,369	5,944
Foreign	89a	....	....	....	....	....	....	....	....	7,312	7,548	9,221	13,537	16,251	22,048	24,916
National Accounts																*Billions of Guaranies*
Exports of Goods & Services	90c	8.4	7.8	7.6	8.1	9.5	11.2	11.2	13.3	18.8	26.1	29.3	31.4	51.3	59.4	69.1
Government Consumption	91f	3.8	4.6	4.8	5.4	6.3	6.8	7.1	7.8	8.2	9.2	12.0	13.4	16.4	21.5	24.7
Gross Fixed Capital Formation	93e	8.0	9.1	10.1	10.0	10.8	10.9	11.8	13.3	20.4	30.9	39.5	48.8	62.9	81.3	116.1
Increase/Decrease(-) in Stocks	93i	.4	.2	.2	.3	.4	.2	.4	1.3	3.5	4.4	6.4	4.0	2.2	6.5	6.8
Private Consumption	96f	44.1	46.5	49.1	52.3	55.8	58.0	66.6	74.6	92.5	126.3	141.1	155.2	190.1	225.2	306.5
Imports of Goods & Services	98c	−8.8	−9.5	−9.7	−10.9	−12.8	−12.1	−13.4	−13.4	−17.9	−28.8	−37.5	−38.6	−59.2	−71.3	−92.8
Gross Domestic Product = GDP	99b	55.9	58.7	62.1	65.2	70.1	74.9	83.7	96.9	125.4	168.0	190.4	214.1	263.6	322.5	430.5
Net Factor Inc/Pmts(-) Abroad	98.n	−.6	−.6	−1.0	−1.1	−1.5	−1.8	−1.6	−2.0	−2.1	−2.0	−1.5	−1.1	.4	1.8	1.3
Gross National Product = GNP	99a	55.3	58.1	61.1	64.2	68.6	73.1	82.1	95.0	123.3	166.0	188.9	213.0	264.0	324.3	431.8
Nat'l Income, Market Prices	99e	51.9	54.0	56.7	59.7	64.2	69.1	77.9	89.9	116.8	158.4	179.1	199.0	239.4	292.1	382.6
Gross Dom. Prod. 1990 Prices	99b.p	1,751.6	1,771.4	1,883.8	1,951.1	2,026.9	2,152.4	2,246.8	∫2,362.3	2,532.2	2,740.9	2,914.0	∫3,118.6	3,459.5	3,852.2	4,289.7
GDP Deflator (1990=100)	99bi p	3.2	3.3	3.3	3.3	3.5	3.5	3.7	4.1	5.0	6.1	6.5	6.9	7.6	8.4	10.0
																Millions:
Population	99z	2.03	2.07	2.13	2.18	2.24	2.30	2.36	2.43	2.50	2.57	2.69	2.78	2.87	2.95	3.05

Monetary Authorities: ∫ Beginning in 1967, data have been improved regarding coverage and sectoring. Also, the commercial bank data exclude the noncommercial banking operations of the National Development Bank, subsequently shown separately in section 40. ∫ Beginning in December 1988, data are based on improved sectorization.

Deposit Money Banks: ∫ Beginning in December 1988, consolidates commercial banks and the National Development Bank. See note to section 10.

Monetary Survey: ∫ See notes to sections 10 and 20.

Other Banking Institutions: ∫ Beginning in December 1988, consolidates savings and loans associations for housing, National Housing Bank, Cattle Fund, Credit Agency for Farm Equipment, Bank Employees Retirement and Pension Fund, finance companies, and Paraguayan Institute for Housing and Urbanization, which was abolished in March 1992.

Banking Survey: ∫ See notes to sections 10, 20, and 40.

Government Finance: ∫ Beginning in 1966, debt amortization has been excluded from *Expenditure* and included as a financing item. ∫ Beginning in 1972, data are as reported in the *Government Finance Statistics Yearbook* and relate to the consolidated central government. ∫ Beginning in 1989, data cover budgetary central government only. However, data on outstanding debt relate to the budgetary central government for all years.

Paraguay

	1980	1981	1982	1983	1984	1985	1986	1987	1988	1989	1990	1991	1992	1993	1994		
Year Ending December 31																**Government Finance**	
	1,809	−10,590	2,985	−7,727	−20,381	−6,906	517	−961	21,674	Ɪ112,526	189,590	−12,916	77,687	138,669	....	Deficit (−) or Surplus	80
	61,989	72,743	85,773	84,033	102,170	135,312	178,637	252,978	323,101	Ɪ524,352	796,297	979,661	1,391,563	1,688,014	....	Revenue	81
	202	97	139	1	342	201	121	317	601	Ɪ1,724	1,066	1,568	2,976	4,020	....	Grants Received	81z
	56,847	75,619	86,715	87,315	115,385	126,661	148,307	224,660	295,389	Ɪ412,187	608,819	991,471	1,307,449	1,559,382	....	Expenditure	82
	3,535	7,811	−3,788	4,446	5,563	6,119	5,204	7,798	6,639	Ɪ1,363	−1,046	2,674	9,403	−6,017	....	Lending Minus Repayments	83
	—	—	—	—	−1,945	−9,639	−24,730	−21,798	—	Ɪ—	—	—	—	—	....	Exch.Rate Adj.to Overall Def./Sur	80x
																Financing	
	−359	−1,755	−864	−6,147	1,976	−7,971	−5,742	−3,181	−16,094	Ɪ−2,120	1,982	−151,227	−2,082	−2,004	....	Net Borrowing	84
	12,819	4,880	564	13,874	18,405	14,877	5,225	4,142	−5,580	Ɪ−6,246	−55,094	10,543	20,277	−96,185	....	Net Borrowing: Domestic	84a
	−14,269	7,465	−2,685	....	....	....	....	....	....	Ɪ−104160	−136,478	153,600	−95,882	−40,480	....	Foreign	85a
	4,279	4,378	4,042	....	....	18,365	23,616	21,098	32,896	....	....	....	....	....	....	Use of Cash Balances	87
	37,798	42,828	43,452	....	....	111,798	....	....	341,992	....	....	....	....	....	....	Debt: Domestic	88a
																Foreign	89a
Billions of Guaranies																**National Accounts**	
	77.6	79.1	89.5	70.1	170.0	355.0	399.0	704.7	1,137.4	1,645.2	2,138.0	2,045.8	2,092.5	2,792.7	....	Exports of Goods & Services	90c
	34.7	48.6	52.3	58.0	69.3	90.2	121.8	176.6	209.1	306.7	401.9	546.5	629.1	801.9	....	Government Consumption	91f
	152.7	194.2	176.9	164.5	231.2	288.0	431.8	591.4	768.2	1,045.6	1,425.4	1,961.8	2,117.4	2,642.1	....	Gross Fixed Capital Formation	93e
	8.6	10.1	12.1	10.7	14.3	18.5	27.1	34.4	40.6	53.2	55.0	93.9	97.6	109.6	....	Increase/Decrease(−) in Stocks	93i
	399.4	504.1	552.0	642.2	822.0	1,066.9	1,434.8	1,882.6	2,281.3	3,035.3	5,014.9	6,483.2	7,611.7	9,119.3	....	Private Consumption	96f
	−112.4	−127.4	−145.6	−127.4	−236.3	−424.7	−580.7	−896.1	−1,117.5	−1,477.6	−2,560.7	−2,850.6	−2,877.5	−3,473.7	....	Imports of Goods & Services	98c
	560.5	708.7	737.0	818.1	1,070.4	1,393.9	1,833.8	2,493.6	3,319.1	4,608.4	6,474.4	8,280.8	9,670.8	11,991.7	....	Gross Domestic Product = GDP	99b
	5.3	8.8	8.3	5.0	−2.4	−13.0	−21.1	−68.2	−8.8	92.5	143.6	114.8	22.1	43.0	....	Net Factor Inc/Pmts(−) Abroad	98.n
	565.7	717.5	745.3	823.1	1,068.0	1,380.9	1,812.7	2,425.4	3,310.3	4,700.9	6,618.0	8,395.6	9,692.9	12,034.7	....	Gross National Product = GNP	99a
	507.1	639.8	671.0	750.9	960.1	1,235.7	1,628.0	2,136.3	2,954.7	4,241.7	5,924.1	7,705.3	8,923.8	11,104.0	....	Nat'l Income, Market Prices	99e
	4,780.5	5,197.1	5,146.0	4,991.6	5,145.1	5,349.3	5,349.7	5,581.3	5,936.1	6,280.3	6,474.4	6,634.3	6,753.7	7,033.7	....	Gross Dom. Prod. 1990 Prices	99b.p
	11.7	13.6	14.3	16.4	20.8	26.1	34.3	44.7	55.9	73.4	100.0	124.8	143.2	170.5	....	GDP Deflator (1990=100)	99bi p
Midyear Estimates																	
	3.15	3.25	3.36	3.47	3.58	3.61	3.72	3.84	3.96	4.09	4.22	4.33	4.45	4.57	4.70	**Population**	99z

Peru

		1965	1966	1967	1968	1969	1970	1971	1972	1973	1974	1975	1976	1977	1978	1979
Exchange Rates														*New Soles per Billion SDRs through 1987; per Million SDRs 1988-89;*		
Market Rate	aa	26.8	26.8	38.7	38.7	38.7	38.7	42.0	42.0	46.7	47.4	52.7	80.6	158.4	255.6	329.5
														New Soles per Billion US$ through 1987; per Million US$ 1988-89;		
Market Rate	ae	26.8	26.8	38.7	38.7	38.7	38.7	38.7	38.7	38.7	38.7	45.0	69.4	130.4	196.2	250.1
Market Rate	rf	26.8	26.8	30.2	38.7	38.7	38.7	38.7	38.7	38.7	38.7	40.4	55.8	84.2	156.3	224.7
Fund Position															*Millions of SDRs:*	
Quota	2f.s	37.5	47.0	85.0	85.0	85.0	123.0	123.0	123.0	123.0	123.0	123.0	123.0	123.0	164.0	164.0
SDRs	1b.s	—	—	—	—	—	14.3	28.4	41.0	37.3	37.2	37.1	3.3	2.7	4.8	81.3
Reserve Position in the Fund	1c.s	9.4	11.8	.1	—	—	—	—	—	30.8	30.8	30.8	—	—	—	—
Total Fund Cred.&Loans Outstg.	2tl	—	—	—	3.8	28.3	9.9	3.3	30.8	13.6	—	—	158.8	168.8	256.1	373.1
International Liquidity													*Millions of US Dollars Unless Otherwise Indicated:*			
Total Reserves minus Gold	1l.d	107.5	90.2	105.6	91.4	142.2	↕296.3	380.9	442.5	526.1	925.2	425.5	289.3	356.8	389.7	1,520.7
SDRs	1b.d	—	—	—	—	—	14.3	30.9	44.5	45.0	45.6	43.4	3.8	3.3	6.3	107.1
Reserve Position in the Fund	1c.d	9.4	11.8	—	—	—	—	—	—	37.1	37.6	36.0	—	—	—	—
Foreign Exchange	1d.d	98.1	78.4	105.5	91.4	142.2	↕282.0	350.0	398.0	444.0	842.0	346.1	285.5	353.5	383.4	1,413.6
Gold (Million Fine Troy Ounces)	1ad	1.920	1.849	.577	.566	.709	1.134	1.131	1.089	1.003	1.003	1.003	1.003	1.003	1.004	1.158
Gold (National Valuation)	1an.d	67.2	64.7	20.2	19.8	24.8	39.7	39.6	41.4	42.3	42.3	42.3	42.3	42.3	42.4	106.4
Monetary Authorities: Other Liab.	4..d	10.5	23.4	44.6	33.7	18.6	.8	1.9	13.4	17.2	—	20.0	263.7	651.8	688.1	346.0
Deposit Money Banks: Assets	7a.d	6.8	10.5	7.5	8.4	6.3	126.6	118.9	2.6	2.6	165.4	48.9	61.5	48.2	138.4	582.8
Liabilities	7b.d	11.9	5.3	20.3	22.5	15.3	25.8	77.5	69.8	219.6	410.9	537.8	810.8	786.4	644.7	505.0
Other Banking Insts.: Liabilities	7f.d	....	....	....	....	....	46.5	49.1	38.8	69.8	98.2	111.1	133.8	146.4	164.2	152.0
Monetary Authorities										*Thousandths(.000) New Soles through 1976; New Soles from 1977 to 1987;*						
Foreign Assets	11	5,452	5,016	6,502	6,100	8,300	15,500	14,100	22,600	25,836	35,557	24,120	24,500	↕50	104	342
Claims on Central Government	12a	4,600	6,700	7,600	9,500	9,500	9,500	9,600	9,900	9,800	9,700	9,700	10,000	↕10	23	33
Claims on Official Entities	12bx													↕—		
Claims on Deposit Money Banks	12e	100	200	100	200	500	1,200	3,900	3,800	2,700	3,200	15,900	52,300	↕74	106	140
Claims on Other Banking Insts.	12f	2,000	1,300	1,700	1,400	1,400	2,200	2,800	4,900	6,900	10,400	14,400	28,900	↕44	72	86
Reserve Money	14	11,400	12,100	13,700	14,700	16,300	24,200	25,500	33,500	35,700	50,400	53,300	79,100	↕98	153	347
of which: Currency Outside DMBs	14a	7,000	7,900	9,000	10,000	11,800	16,300	18,900	21,900	27,200	33,500	42,600	49,500	↕61	91	162
Time, Savings,& Fgn.Currency Dep.	15															1
Restricted Deposits	16b	—	—	100	—	—	100	100	100	—	—	100	—	↕—	—	5
Foreign Liabilities	16c	—	100	179	279	1,079	412	210	1,810	1,303	—	900	29,127	↕94	194	208
Long-Term Foreign Liabilities	16cl	800	1,000	1,800	1,800	1,900	2,700	2,900	4,400	4,500	5,000	5,900	8,900	↕11	27	43
Central Government Deposits	16d	—	—	100	100	100	100	100	—	—	600	400	100	↕—	—	—
Capital Accounts	17a	200	200	200	300	600	1,453	2,053	2,601	2,990	3,518	3,832	4,463	↕11	21	39
Other Items (Net)	17r	−248	−184	−177	21	−279	−565	−463	−1,211	742	−661	−313	−5,990	↕−36	−91	−42
Deposit Money Banks										*Thousandths(.000) New Soles through 1976; New Soles from 1977 to 1987;*						
Reserves	20	4,100	4,200	4,300	4,000	4,000	7,400	6,200	10,500	7,700	15,700	9,500	26,900	↕36	58	158
Foreign Assets	21	1,200	1,900	1,800	1,900	1,500	4,900	4,600	100	100	6,400	2,200	4,000	↕5	26	145
Claims on Central Government	22a	4,600	4,300	7,300	7,100	11,500	13,300	14,900	20,500	28,200	29,700	47,700	87,700	↕126	189	215
Claims on Local Government	22b	100	200	200	200	100	200	600	1,000	1,400	1,300	1,400	1,100	↕1	1	1
Claims on Official Entities	22bx	900	1,000	1,200	1,000	2,000	3,700	4,100	4,500	10,000	25,700	40,200	59,200	↕83	139	118
Claims on Private Sector	22d	15,500	16,900	18,400	19,800	21,700	24,700	30,200	36,700	44,900	49,300	63,700	76,400	↕87	119	220
Claims on Other Banking Insts.	22f	500	800	600	1,500	2,400	2,100	1,800	2,200	4,200	4,600	5,200	3,200	↕4	6	7
Demand Deposits	24	8,600	10,300	11,600	12,500	15,400	26,600	27,400	37,600	47,900	71,300	80,100	103,500	↕122	177	268
Time, Savings,& Fgn.Currency Dep.	25	12,200	13,700	14,000	14,300	14,500	14,100	15,500	16,700	19,100	21,200	23,400	26,900	↕40	92	233
Bonds	26ab	—	—	100	300	400	1,100	1,600	2,400	3,200	3,800	4,700	5,300	↕4	4	6
Foreign Liabilities	26c	400	700	2,200	1,700	1,300	900	2,200	1,700	4,800	10,600	14,900	41,100	↕72	105	105
Long-Term Foreign Liabilities	26cl	1,100	—	200	300	100	100	800	1,000	3,700	5,300	9,300	11,600	↕14	18	21
Central Government Deposits	26d	3,100	2,400	4,000	3,700	8,400	11,800	8,800	9,600	10,900	14,200	19,100	16,300	↕16	25	75
Credit from Monetary Authorities	26g	100	200	200	200	500	1,700	3,900	3,900	2,700	3,300	16,000	52,300	↕74	106	141
Capital Accounts	27a	1,800	3,500	4,000	4,800	5,400	6,900	7,600	8,700	10,400	13,100	16,000	20,500	↕27	43	84
Other Items (Net)	27r	−400	−1,500	−2,500	−2,300	−2,800	−6,900	−5,400	−6,100	−6,200	−10,100	−13,600	−19,000	↕−27	−29	−69
Monetary Survey										*Thousandths(.000) New Soles through 1976; New Soles from 1977 to 1987;*						
Foreign Assets (Net)	31n	6,252	6,116	5,923	6,021	7,421	19,088	16,290	19,190	19,832	31,357	10,520	−41,727	↕−111	−169	174
Domestic Credit	32	25,100	28,800	32,900	36,700	40,100	43,800	55,100	70,100	94,500	115,900	162,800	250,100	↕340	523	604
Claims on Central Govt. (Net)	32an	6,100	8,600	10,800	12,800	12,500	10,900	15,600	20,800	27,100	24,600	37,900	81,300	↕120	186	173
Claims on Local Government	32b	100	200	200	200	100	200	600	1,000	1,400	1,300	1,400	1,100	↕1	1	1
Claims on Official Entities	32bx	900	1,000	1,200	1,000	2,000	3,700	4,100	4,500	10,000	25,700	40,200	59,200	↕83	139	118
Claims on Private Sector	32d	15,500	16,900	18,400	19,800	21,700	24,700	30,200	36,700	44,900	49,300	63,700	76,400	↕87	119	220
Claims on Other Banking Insts.	32f	2,500	2,100	2,300	2,900	3,800	4,300	4,600	7,100	11,100	15,000	19,600	32,100	↕49	78	93
Money	34	15,800	18,200	20,700	22,800	27,500	43,300	46,600	60,300	75,700	105,500	123,300	155,000	↕185	270	461
Quasi-Money	35	12,200	13,700	14,000	14,300	14,500	14,100	15,500	16,700	19,100	21,200	23,400	26,900	↕40	92	235
Bonds	36ab	—	—	100	300	400	1,100	1,600	2,400	3,200	3,800	4,700	5,300	↕4	4	6
Restricted Deposits	36b	—	—	100	—	—	100	100	100	—	—	100	—	↕—	—	5
Long-Term Foreign Liabilities	36cl	1,900	1,000	2,000	2,100	2,000	2,800	3,700	5,400	8,200	10,300	15,200	20,500	↕25	44	63
Other Items (Net)	37r	1,452	2,016	1,923	3,221	3,121	1,488	3,890	4,390	8,132	6,457	6,620	673	↕−25	−56	9
Money plus Quasi-Money	35l	28,000	31,900	34,700	37,100	42,000	57,400	62,100	77,000	94,800	126,700	146,700	181,900	↕225	362	695
Other Banking Institutions										*Thousandths(.000) New Soles through 1976; New Soles from 1977 to 1987;*						
Cash	40	400	200	300	300	600	600	600	900	800	1,200	1,100	1,900	↕2	4	32
Foreign Assets	41	100	100	200	200	100	200	100	200	100	—	100	600	↕1	1	6
Claims on Central Government	42a	200	400	600	600	400	1,400	4,000	4,900	5,900	7,700	10,000	10,800	↕18	39	34
Claims on Official Entities	42bx	300	500	600	100	—	—	200	500	3,600	4,400	4,600	7,000	↕10	11	11
Claims on Private Sector	42d	6,000	8,000	10,400	12,800	14,200	15,400	18,200	23,200	29,800	36,600	46,800	60,300	↕82	118	171
Claims on Deposit Money Banks	42e	1,100	700	800	900	1,500	3,900	2,500	3,400	3,200	3,800	3,900	4,100	↕4	7	11
Demand Deposits	44	400	700	900	900	900	1,300	1,400	2,300	2,100	2,400	2,700	6,000	↕7	11	23
Time, Savings,& Fgn.Currency Dep.	45	—	—	100	100	300	700	900	1,100	1,200	1,500	1,900	1,500	↕4	12	18
Bonds	46ab	1,100	1,700	2,000	2,500	3,100	6,900	9,100	11,800	15,100	18,000	22,000	22,700	↕27	34	61
Foreign Liabilities	46c	400	400	900	800	700	400	400	—	—	—	—	—	↕—	1	2
Long-Term Foreign Liabilities	46cl	800	1,500	2,200	1,900	1,600	1,400	1,500	1,500	2,700	3,800	5,000	8,700	↕16	30	36
Central Government Deposits	46d	400	200	300	300	300	100	200	100	100	300	100	100	↕—	—	—
Credit from Monetary Authorities	46g	2,000	1,100	1,700	1,400	1,400	2,200	2,800	4,900	6,900	10,300	14,400	25,700	↕39	64	76
Credit from Deposit Money Banks	46h	600	700	600	1,700	2,700	1,900	2,000	2,200	4,200	4,800	5,300	3,400	↕4	6	11
Capital Accounts	47a	2,300	2,900	3,600	4,300	5,000	5,600	6,600	6,900	8,200	9,400	11,900	16,700	↕22	33	62
Other Items (Net)	47r	100	600	600	700	800	1,000	700	2,300	2,900	3,200	3,200	−100	↕−4	−11	−23

Peru

1980	1981	1982	1983	1984	1985	1986	1987	1988	1989	1990	1991	1992	1993	1994		
per Thousand SDRs thereafter: End of Period															**Exchange Rates**	
435.8	590.1	1,091.7	2,377.8	5,583.3	15,317.5	17,063.5	46,815.8	‡672.9	6,914.3	‡735.4	1,373.2	2,241.3	2,966.9	3,182.5	Market Rate	aa
per Thousand US$ thereafter: End of Period(ae) Period Avg.(rf)																
341.7	507.0	989.7	2,271.2	5,696.0	13,945.0	13,950.0	33,000.0	‡500.0	5,261.4	‡516.9	960.0	1,630.0	2,160.0	2,180.0	Market Rate	ae
288.9	422.3	697.6	1,628.6	3,466.9	10,974.9	13,947.5	16,835.8	‡128.8	2,666.2	‡187.9	772.5	1,245.8	1,988.3	2,195.0	Market Rate	rf
End of Period															**Fund Position**	
246.0	246.0	246.0	246.0	330.9	330.9	330.9	330.9	330.9	330.9	330.9	330.9	330.9	466.1	466.1	Quota	2f. s
9.7	9.8	29.9	.6	22.9	—	—	—	—	—	—	—	—	.7	.3	SDRs	1b. s
—	—	—	—	—	—	—	—	—	—	—	—	—	—	—	Reserve Position in the Fund	1c. s
371.6	332.9	588.8	666.3	688.3	639.0	595.5	595.4	595.4	577.0	530.5	493.4	458.7	642.7	642.7	Total Fund Cred.&Loans Outstg.	2tl
End of Period															**International Liquidity**	
1,979.8	1,199.5	1,349.6	1,365.7	1,630.5	1,842.0	1,407.2	645.8	511.0	808.4	1,039.8	2,443.0	2,849.0	3,407.9	6,992.4	Total Reserves minus Gold	1l. d
12.3	11.4	32.9	.6	22.4	—	—	—	—	—	—	—	—	.9	.4	SDRs	1b. d
—	—	—	—	—	—	—	—	—	—	—	—	—	—	—	Reserve Position in the Fund	1c. d
1,967.5	1,188.1	1,316.7	1,365.1	1,608.1	1,842.0	1,407.2	645.8	511.0	808.4	1,039.8	2,443.0	2,849.0	3,407.0	6,992.0	Foreign Exchange	1d. d
1.398	1.398	1.398	1.398	1.398	1.954	2.137	1.497	1.712	1.967	2.210	1.831	1.822	1.305	1.116	Gold (Million Fine Troy Ounces)	1ad
281.0	400.3	400.3	400.3	400.3	419.6	458.9	513.4	587.1	671.6	728.9	556.5	515.6	434.0	362.9	Gold (National Valuation)	1an d
196.9	32.7	39.7	107.0	116.7	22.6	136.8	260.4	752.0	543.4	664.3	777.8	666.2	95.3	124.8	Monetary Authorities: Other Liab.	4..d
387.3	568.1	388.4	312.8	330.7	241.1	320.1	365.1	399.7	589.7	527.9	1,052.6	991.2	871.8	1,134.5	Deposit Money Banks: Assets	7a. d
624.2	763.2	446.9	433.2	362.0	298.2	268.0	262.8	282.0	308.4	250.2	275.9	396.9	415.3	583.8	Liabilities	7b. d
190.0	217.6	345.7	299.4	212.5	136.9	140.6	100.1	91.1	79.7	108.0	108.5	108.7	107.3	120.4	Other Banking Insts.: Liabilities	7f. d
Thousands from 1988 to 1989;Millions Beginning 1990: End of Period															**Monetary Authorities**	
764	657	1,653	4,060	10,746	33,009	28,953	34,118	‡527	7,649	‡920	2,681	5,461	9,335	16,001	Foreign Assets	11
186	351	518	2,867	3,220	2,986	5,003	32,514	‡55	404	‡5	117	90	55	614	Claims on Central Government	12a
—	—	—	—	—	—	1	10	—	—	‡—	—	—	—	—	Claims on Official Entities	12bx
45	174	35	281	1,753	3,507	5,694	13,274	‡151	3,079	‡109	152	197	149	-196	Claims on Deposit Money Banks	12e
122	209	378	966	2,039	3,754	8,964	23,039	‡121	3,446	‡104	108	173	209	—	Claims on Other Banking Insts.	12f
734	1,139	1,787	3,845	9,328	29,372	40,979	86,262	‡576	8,896	‡699	1,831	3,627	5,721	7,227	Reserve Money	14
273	437	622	1,116	2,502	8,145	16,435	41,945	‡261	5,372	‡273	643	1,101	1,591	2,381	of which: Currency Outside DMBs	14a
1	2	5	28	87	128	47	161	‡6	18	‡23	101	152	189	202	Time, Savings,& Fgn.Currency Dep.	15
9	1	14	25	124	188	179	962	‡71	701	‡21	5	7	1	1	Restricted Deposits	16b
226	209	654	1,800	4,115	10,102	12,061	30,998	‡777	6,460	‡733	1,424	2,114	2,103	2,317	Foreign Liabilities	16c
76	104	200	851	1,375	4,421	5,507	6,599	‡35	828	‡27	330	505	1,104	1,179	Long-Term Foreign Liabilities	16cl
2	11	12	41	58	619	551	602	‡6	26	‡1	3	55	96	3,684	Central Government Deposits	16d
38	57	105	269	743	1,441	1,628	4,492	‡64	680	‡91	137	224	254	377	Capital Accounts	17a
30	-132	-192	1,315	1,929	-3,014	-12,338	-27,121	‡-681	-3,030	‡-458	-773	-765	280	1,433	Other Items (Net)	17r
Thousands from 1988 to 1989;Millions Beginning 1990: End of Period															**Deposit Money Banks**	
360	560	1,088	2,469	6,314	19,081	22,548	37,298	‡260	3,391	‡267	852	2,040	3,519	5,330	Reserves	20
131	283	369	700	1,720	3,362	4,462	10,240	‡200	2,927	‡273	1,011	1,616	1,874	2,473	Foreign Assets	21
189	320	551	1,259	4,132	9,120	16,483	35,377	‡217	4,697	‡497	854	1,422	1,913	1,660	Claims on Central Government	22a
1	22	25	6	1	27	25	77	‡2	13	‡1	5	19	35	83	Claims on Local Government	22b
129	237	229	380	1,257	2,774	3,989	8,277	‡153	1,321	‡95	343	331	369	263	Claims on Official Entities	22bx
469	1,063	1,756	3,779	7,324	16,096	25,682	46,300	‡340	7,451	‡437	1,857	4,076	7,694	13,217	Claims on Private Sector	22d
8	5	31	99	496	1,621	2,726	4,482	‡53	676	‡9	19	7	7	3	Claims on Other Banking Insts.	22f
367	519	822	1,639	3,211	13,063	24,940	48,967	‡285	4,738	‡275	656	1,298	2,142	3,102	Demand Deposits	24
545	1,076	2,186	4,532	10,952	20,657	24,070	42,930	‡407	9,865	‡584	2,641	5,148	9,528	13,915	Time, Savings,& Fgn.Currency Dep.	25
10	28	34	42	78	177	404	943	‡4	124	‡3	11	12	55	102	Bonds	26ab
172	310	263	616	1,537	3,417	3,573	7,101	‡130	1,482	‡127	232	590	796	1,060	Foreign Liabilities	26c
38	70	161	353	345	741	163	269	‡11	49	‡2	33	57	97	212	Long-Term Foreign Liabilities	26cl
81	197	189	608	1,598	4,923	7,768	14,874	‡79	983	‡159	764	1,041	1,248	2,382	Central Government Deposits	26d
49	174	62	281	1,762	3,511	5,694	13,692	‡156	3,150	‡119	153	207	149	64	Credit from Monetary Authorities	26g
144	254	450	975	3,579	9,908	12,694	31,457	‡459	7,492	‡565	1,269	2,096	3,181	4,800	Capital Accounts	27a
-120	-139	-117	-355	-1,818	-4,297	-3,392	-18,184	‡-305	-7,406	‡-257	-816	-939	-1,785	-2,611	Other Items (Net)	27r
Thousands from 1988 to 1989;Millions Beginning 1990: End of Period															**Monetary Survey**	
496	421	1,105	2,344	6,813	22,852	17,780	6,258	‡-180	2,634	‡333	2,035	4,372	8,311	15,097	Foreign Assets (Net)	31n
1,020	1,998	3,291	8,717	16,845	30,973	54,721	134,821	‡859	17,040	‡988	2,544	5,029	8,947	9,774	Domestic Credit	32
291	462	869	3,477	5,696	6,565	13,167	52,415	‡188	4,092	‡342	204	416	625	-3,792	Claims on Central Govt. (Net)	32an
1	22	25	6	1	27	25	77	‡2	13	‡1	5	19	35	83	Claims on Local Government	32b
129	237	229	380	1,257	2,774	3,990	8,287	‡153	1,321	‡95	343	331	369	263	Claims on Official Entities	32bx
469	1,064	1,759	3,790	7,355	16,232	25,849	46,522	‡342	7,491	‡438	1,864	4,083	7,702	13,217	Claims on Private Sector	32d
130	214	409	1,064	2,536	5,375	11,690	27,521	‡174	4,122	‡112	127	179	216	3	Claims on Other Banking Insts.	32f
730	1,075	1,509	2,965	6,060	23,098	43,424	96,390	‡593	10,403	‡708	1,608	2,884	4,343	5,495	Money	34
546	1,077	2,191	4,560	11,038	20,765	24,117	43,091	‡413	9,883	‡607	2,741	5,300	9,717	14,117	Quasi-Money	35
10	28	34	42	78	177	404	943	‡4	124	‡3	11	12	55	102	Bonds	36ab
9	1	14	25	124	188	179	962	‡71	701	‡21	5	7	1	1	Restricted Deposits	36b
114	174	361	1,204	1,720	5,162	5,670	6,868	‡46	877	‡29	362	562	1,201	1,391	Long-Term Foreign Liabilities	36cl
108	65	287	2,265	4,639	4,435	-1,293	-7,174	‡-447	-2,313	‡-49	-147	637	1,940	3,764	Other Items (Net)	37r
1,276	2,152	3,701	7,525	17,098	43,864	67,541	139,481	‡1,006	20,286	‡1,316	4,349	8,184	14,060	19,612	Money plus Quasi-Money	35l
Thousands from 1988 to 1989;Millions Beginning 1990: End of Period															**Other Banking Institutions**	
86	124	62	175	241	1,245	897	3,151	‡33	273	‡11	33	5	4	—	Cash	40
7	12	58	160	171	397	257	1,239	‡23	280	‡30	18	27	24	24	Foreign Assets	41
28	132	155	72	53	811	666	957	‡35	361	‡17	35	49	54	55	Claims on Central Government	42a
14	13	31	81	139	373	958	3,047	‡18	198	‡4	40	45	20	20	Claims on Official Entities	42bx
301	570	1,265	2,639	6,483	12,195	21,127	47,500	‡242	3,744	‡204	607	769	743	761	Claims on Private Sector	42d
24	42	110	229	138	330	964	2,283	‡7	76	‡6	23	11	1	5	Claims on Deposit Money Banks	42e
36	62	83	145	307	987	1,151	3,820	‡19	349	‡13	37	32	9	9	Demand Deposits	44
26	58	124	369	1,143	2,135	2,202	3,696	‡23	622	‡34	102	78	44	44	Time, Savings,& Fgn.Currency Dep.	45
106	229	310	403	521	1,182	2,724	4,768	‡15	487	‡8	28	17	11	11	Bonds	46ab
11	18	104	216	118	338	301	1,389	‡29	239	‡39	74	125	162	193	Foreign Liabilities	46c
54	91	224	454	988	1,571	1,659	1,420	‡16	156	‡17	31	52	69	70	Long-Term Foreign Liabilities	46cl
—	1	10	17	55	130	77	312	‡1	5	‡1	5	5	5	5	Central Government Deposits	46d
108	189	348	880	1,889	3,495	8,563	22,764	‡122	3,499	‡106	108	168	209	—	Credit from Monetary Authorities	46g
9	11	37	51	529	1,653	2,710	4,687	‡54	656	‡13	18	14	13	3	Credit from Deposit Money Banks	46h
112	187	313	450	1,256	2,838	2,838	10,580	‡105	1,249	‡190	388	506	709	715	Capital Accounts	47a
-1	48	129	371	419	1,023	2,645	4,740	‡-26	-2,330	‡-148	-35	-91	-385	-184	Other Items (Net)	47r

Peru

293		1965	1966	1967	1968	1969	1970	1971	1972	1973	1974	1975	1976	1977	1978	1979
Banking Survey																*Thousandths(.000) New Soles through 1976; New Soles from 1977 to 1987;*
Foreign Assets (Net)	**51n**	5,952	5,716	5,223	5,421	6,821	18,888	15,990	19,390	19,932	31,357	10,620	–41,127	I –111	–169	179
Domestic Credit	**52**	28,700	35,400	41,900	46,700	50,600	56,200	72,700	91,500	122,600	149,300	204,500	296,000	I 401	614	727
Claims on Central Govt. (Net)	**52an**	5,900	8,800	11,100	12,800	12,600	12,200	19,400	25,600	32,900	32,000	47,800	92,000	I 138	226	207
Claims on Local Government	**52b**	100	200	200	200	100	200	600	1,000	1,400	1,300	1,400	1,100	I 1	1	1
Claims on Official Entities	**52bx**	1,200	1,500	1,800	1,100	2,000	3,700	4,300	5,000	13,600	30,100	44,800	66,200	I 93	151	128
Claims on Private Sector	**52d**	21,500	24,900	28,800	32,600	35,900	40,100	48,400	59,900	74,700	85,900	110,500	136,700	I 170	237	391
Liquid Liabilities	**55l**	28,000	32,400	35,400	37,800	42,600	58,800	63,800	79,500	97,300	129,400	150,200	187,500	I 234	382	705
Bonds	**56ab**	1,100	1,700	2,100	2,800	3,500	8,000	10,700	14,200	18,300	21,800	26,700	28,000	I 31	38	66
Restricted Deposits	**56b**	—	—	100	—	—	100	100	100	—	—	100	—	I —	—	5
Long-Term Foreign Liabilities	**56cl**	2,700	2,500	4,200	4,000	3,600	4,200	5,200	6,900	10,900	14,100	20,200	29,200	I 41	75	99
Capital Accounts	**57a**	4,300	6,600	7,800	9,400	11,000	13,953	16,253	18,201	21,590	26,018	31,732	41,663	I 60	96	185
Other Items (Net)	**57r**	–1,448	–2,084	–2,477	–1,879	–3,279	–9,965	–7,363	–8,011	–5,558	–10,661	–13,813	–31,490	I –76	–145	–154
Interest Rates																*Percent Per Annum*
Discount Rate *(End of Period)*	**60**	9.5	9.5	9.5	9.5	9.5	9.5	9.5	9.5	9.5	9.5	9.5	12.5	14.5	28.5	29.5
Deposit Rate	**60l**	....	....	....	....	....	....	....	....	....	....	....	....	....	....	....
Lending Rate	**60p**	....	....	....	....	....	....	....	....	....	....	....	....	....	....	....
Prices, Production, Employment																*Index Numbers (1990=100):*
Share Prices	**62**	....	....	....	....	....	....	....	....	....	....	....	....	....	....	....
Cons. Prices(1990=100,000)	**64.b**	....	....	....	....	....	....	....	....	....	....	....	....	....	....	....
Consumer Prices	**64.c**	....	....	....	....	....	....	....	....	....	....	....	....	....	....	....
Manufacturing Production	**66ey**	....	....	....	....	....	....	....	....	....	....	....	....	....	....	114.9
Industrial Employment	**67**	....	....	....	....	....	....	....	....	....	....	....	....	....	....	....
International Transactions																*Millions of US Dollars*
Exports	***70..d***	667.3	764.4	753.8	866.0	865.5	1,047.9	892.9	944.4	1,111.8	1,503.3	I 1,290.9	1,359.6	1,725.6	1,940.7	3,490.9
Imports, cif	***71..d***	729.7	828.7	825.2	645.5	612.7	622.9	763.0	796.5	1,018.6	1,530.5	2,550.0	2,037.3	1,910.9	1,174.7	1,820.1
Imports, fob	***71.vd***	583.7	663.0	660.2	516.4	490.8	499.0	611.2	638.0	815.3	1,275.7	2,124.8	1,697.7	1,592.4	978.9	1,516.7
																1990=100
Volume of Exports	**72**	1,211.1	1,242.8	1,289.0	1,430.0	1,313.3	1,417.9	1,306.0	1,374.1	1,087.9	1,103.1	78.6	87.4	93.9	115.1	139.3
																1990=100:
Unit Value of Exports	***74..d***	25	31	30	32	35	36	30	31	50	90	55	62	68	68	106
Balance of Payments																*Millions of US Dollars:*
Goods: Exports f.o.b.	***78aad***	....	....	....	....	....	....	....	....	....	....	....	....	1,726	1,941	3,491
Goods: Imports f.o.b.	***78abd***	....	....	....	....	....	....	....	....	....	....	....	....	–2,164	–1,601	–1,951
Trade Balance	***78acd***	....	....	....	....	....	....	....	....	....	....	....	....	–438	340	1,540
Services: Credit	***78add***	....	....	....	....	....	....	....	....	....	....	....	....	406	459	594
Services: Debit	***78aed***	....	....	....	....	....	....	....	....	....	....	....	....	–523	–470	–560
Balance on Goods and Services	***78afd***	....	....	....	....	....	....	....	....	....	....	....	....	–556	330	1,573
Income: Credit	***78agd***	....	....	....	....	....	....	....	....	....	....	....	....	13	16	58
Income: Debit	***78ahd***	....	....	....	....	....	....	....	....	....	....	....	....	–436	–594	–1,025
Balance on Goods, Serv., & Inc.	***78aid***	....	....	....	....	....	....	....	....	....	....	....	....	–979	–248	607
Current Transfers, n.i.e.: Credit	***78ajd***	....	....	....	....	....	....	....	....	....	....	....	....	60	59	126
Current Transfers: Debit	***78akd***	....	....	....	....	....	....	....	....	....	....	....	....	–3	–4	–4
Current Account, n.i.e.	***78ald***	....	....	....	....	....	....	....	....	....	....	....	....	–923	–193	730
Capital Account, n.i.e.: Credit	***78bad***	....	....	....	....	....	....	....	....	....	....	....	....	—	—	—
Capital Account: Debit	***78bbd***	....	....	....	....	....	....	....	....	....	....	....	....	—	—	—
Capital Account, n.i.e.	***78bcd***	....	....	....	....	....	....	....	....	....	....	....	....	—	—	—
Direct Investment Abroad	***78bdd***	....	....	....	....	....	....	....	....	....	....	....	....	—	—	—
Dir. Invest. in Rep. Econ., n.i.e.	***78bed***	....	....	....	....	....	....	....	....	....	....	....	....	54	25	71
Portfolio Investment Assets	***78bfd***	....	....	....	....	....	....	....	....	....	....	....	....	—	—	—
Portfolio Investment Liab., n.i.e.	***78bgd***	....	....	....	....	....	....	....	....	....	....	....	....	—	—	—
Other Investment Assets	***78bhd***	....	....	....	....	....	....	....	....	....	....	....	....	—	—	—
Other Investment Liab., n.i.e.	***78bid***	....	....	....	....	....	....	....	....	....	....	....	....	593	–208	–304
Financial Account, n.i.e.	***78bjd***	....	....	....	....	....	....	....	....	....	....	....	....	647	–183	–233
Net Errors and Omissions	***78cad***	....	....	....	....	....	....	....	....	....	....	....	....	–111	53	112
Overall Balance	***78cbd***	....	....	....	....	....	....	....	....	....	....	....	....	–387	–322	609
Reserves and Related Items	***79dad***	....	....	....	....	....	....	....	....	....	....	....	....	387	322	–609
Reserve Assets	***79dbd***	....	....	....	....	....	....	....	....	....	....	....	....	–80	–134	–1,236
Use of Fund Credit and Loans	***79dcd***	....	....	....	....	....	....	....	....	....	....	....	....	12	111	151
Liabs.Constit.For.Auth.Reserves	***79ddd***	....	....	....	....	....	....	....	....	....	....	....	....	22	7	–63
Exceptional Financing	***79ded***	....	....	....	....	....	....	....	....	....	....	....	....	433	338	539
Government Finance																*Thousandths(.000) New Soles through 1976; New Soles from 1977 to 1987;*
Deficit (-) or Surplus	**80**	–3,900	–5,700	–6,500	I –5,600	–2,000	–3,300	–8,100	–10,800	–14,100	–14,100	–30,600	–48,400	I –79	–80	–18
Revenue	**81**	17,400	20,300	23,700	I 28,500	32,300	38,800	41,400	45,600	53,300	68,600	87,900	111,400	I 154	264	552
Grants Received	**81z**	....	....	....	—	—	—	—	—	—	—	—	—	I —	—	—
Expenditure	**82**	21,500	25,400	29,900	I 34,100	34,300	42,100	49,500	56,400	67,400	82,700	118,500	159,800	I 233	344	570
Lending Minus Repayments	**83**	....	....	....	—	—	—	—	—	—	—	—	—	I —	—	—
Financing																
Net Borrowing: Domestic	**84a**	2,800	3,300	1,200	I 3,800	800	1,800	9,100	8,900	7,100	3,100	13,800	32,600	I 45	72	49
Foreign	**85a**	1,400	1,900	3,200	I 1,900	1,300	1,500	–1,000	1,900	7,000	11,000	16,800	15,800	I 35	8	–31
National Accounts																*Thousandths(.000) New Soles through 1976; New Soles from 1977 to 1987;*
Exports of Goods & Services	**90c**	20,600	24,300	27,500	38,200	41,200	47,500	42,100	45,500	53,100	72,100	71,700	95,700	I 176	375	957
Government Consumption	**91f**	12,500	14,800	16,700	24,100	25,400	29,000	33,000	38,400	45,400	54,700	75,500	101,000	I 157	209	301
Gross Fixed Capital Formation	**93e**	19,200	22,600	23,400	24,100	25,900	29,900	33,300	37,800	45,400	68,000	96,800	127,800	I 154	230	720
Increase/Decrease(-) in Stocks	**93i**	2,200	4,900	7,600	1,700	2,000	1,200	6,400	4,000	10,800	16,500	12,400	9,200	I 5	9	33
Private Consumption	**96f**	82,600	96,700	113,500	130,000	154,200	I 170,000	190,000	210,000	260,000	330,000	420,000	570,000	I 780	1,170	2,031
Imports of Goods & Services	**98c**	–22,200	–26,400	–31,800	–35,300	–35,200	–37,700	–39,900	–43,200	–54,900	–96,400	–126,100	–139,100	I –214	–320	–559
Gross Domestic Product = GDP	**99b**	114,900	136,800	156,900	185,800	209,000	240,700	264,400	294,700	359,200	447,500	550,200	764,500	I 1,058	1,678	I 3,490
Net Factor Inc/Pmts(-) Abroad	**98.n**	–1,900	—	—	—	—	—	—	—	—	—	–10,000	–10,000	I –20	–70	–140
Gross National Product = GNP	**99a**	113,000	134,000	152,800	181,200	204,100	237,300	262,500	292,200	355,200	444,100	545,200	752,800	I 1,035	1,609	2,977
Nat'l Income, Market Prices	**99e**	....	....	....	....	....	....	....	....	....	....	....	....	....	....	....
GDP 1990 Prices *(Millions)*	***99b.p***	3,884	4,210	4,370	4,385	4,550	4,816	5,018	5,162	5,439	5,942	6,144	6,265	6,290	6,308	6,674
GDP Deflator (1990=100)	***99bip***	—	—	—	—	—	—	—	—	—	—	—	—	—	—	—
																Millions:
Population	**99z**	11.65	12.01	12.31	12.67	13.05	13.45	13.59	13.95	14.35	14.75	15.16	15.57	15.99	16.41	16.85

Exchange Rates: On February 1, 1985, the inti, equal to 1,000 soles, was introduced. On July 1, 1991, the new sol, equal to one million intis, replaced the inti as the currency unit of Peru.

International Liquidity: I In 1970 essentially all foreign exchange reserves of banks were transferred to the Central Reserve Bank.

International Transactions: I Prior to 1975, data on exports and imports in U.S. dollars were derived by conversion of national currency data into U.S. dollars. Annual figures include grants and other adjustments.

Peru

1980	1981	1982	1983	1984	1985	1986	1987	1988	1989	1990	1991	1992	1993	1994		
Thousands from 1988 to 1989;Millions Beginning 1990: End of Period															**Banking Survey**	
492	416	1,059	2,287	6,867	22,911	17,737	6,108	ℐ−186	2,675	ℐ323	1,979	4,273	8,173	14,928	Foreign Assets (Net)	51n
1,233	2,499	4,324	10,428	20,929	38,847	65,705	158,492	ℐ980	17,216	ℐ1,100	3,094	5,708	9,543	10,602	Domestic Credit	52
320	593	1,014	3,532	5,694	7,246	13,757	53,060	ℐ222	4,448	ℐ358	235	459	674	−3,742	Claims on Central Govt. (Net)	52an
1	22	25	7	1	27	25	77	ℐ2	13	ℐ1	5	19	35	83	Claims on Local Government	52b
143	250	261	460	1,396	3,147	4,947	11,333	ℐ171	1,519	ℐ99	383	377	389	283	Claims on Official Entities	52bx
769	1,634	3,024	6,429	13,838	28,427	46,976	94,022	ℐ585	11,236	ℐ642	2,471	4,852	8,445	13,978	Claims on Private Sector	52d
1,251	2,148	3,845	7,865	18,308	45,741	69,997	143,847	ℐ1,015	20,983	ℐ1,351	4,455	8,289	14,108	19,665	Liquid Liabilities	55l
116	257	343	444	599	1,359	3,128	5,711	ℐ18	610	ℐ11	38	29	66	113	Bonds	56ab
9	1	14	25	124	188	179	962	ℐ71	701	ℐ21	5	7	1	1	Restricted Deposits	56b
168	265	585	1,658	2,708	6,732	7,329	8,288	ℐ62	1,033	ℐ46	393	614	1,270	1,461	Long-Term Foreign Liabilities	56cl
294	498	868	1,693	5,578	14,187	17,160	46,529	ℐ628	9,420	ℐ845	1,794	2,826	4,144	5,892	Capital Accounts	57a
−112	−254	−272	1,030	480	−6,449	−14,351	−40,736	ℐ−1,001	−12,857	ℐ−852	−1,612	−1,784	−1,875	−1,602	Other Items (Net)	57r
Percent Per Annum															**Interest Rates**	
29.5	44.5	44.5	60.0	60.0	42.6	36.1	29.8	748.0	865.6	289.6	67.7	48.5	28.6	16.1	Discount Rate *(End of Period)*	60
....	....	....	....	....	....	....	....	....	161.8	1,135.6	2,439.6	170.5	59.7	44.1	22.3	Deposit Rate	60l
....	....	....	....	....	....	40.5	35.7	174.3	1,515.9	4,774.5	751.5	173.8	97.4	53.6	Lending Rate	60p
Period Averages															**Prices, Production, Employment**	
....	....	....	....	....	....	....	....	....	....	1.0	100.0	462.7	1,537.9	6,064.2	11,111.5	Share Prices	62
....	....	....	....	....	....	....	....	38	1,319	100,000	....	....	....	....	Cons. Prices(1990=100,000)	64.b
....	....	....	....	....	....	....	....	....	....	100	510	884	1,314	1,626	Consumer Prices	64.c
124.8	125.8	119.6	97.5	104.8	111.3	131.3	149.6	130.4	105.2	100.0	104.2	100.1	106.7	124.8	Manufacturing Production	66ey
123.0	124.3	122.6	116.1	103.9	102.6	108.8	117.9	115.4	ℐ102.7	100.0	95.0	85.3	78.3	77.4	Industrial Employment	67
Millions of US Dollars															**International Transactions**	
3,898.3	3,255.0	3,258.9	3,015.2	3,147.1	2,978.5	2,530.6	2,660.8	2,701.0	3,488.0	3,230.9	3,329.1	3,484.4	3,463.0	4,506.7	Exports	70..d
2,499.5	3,481.6	3,600.7	2,547.9	2,212.0	1,835.0	2,908.8	3,562.3	3,348.0	2,749.2	3,469.8	4,194.7	4,860.4	4,901.3	6,751.6	Imports, cif	71..d
2,082.9	2,901.3	3,000.6	2,123.3	1,843.3	1,529.2	2,424.0	2,968.6	2,790.0	2,291.0	2,891.5	3,495.6	4,050.0	4,084.4	5,626.3	Imports, fob	71.vd
1990=100																
125.6	123.5	132.3	112.3	113.8	117.7	106.4	97.0	85.2	100.1	100.0	102.9	....	....	....	Volume of Exports	72
Indexes of Unit Values in US Dollars																
139	117	100	104	95	85	69	85	95	104	100	88	87	74	84	Unit Value of Exports	74..d
Minus Sign Indicates Debit															Balance of Payments	
3,916	3,249	3,293	3,015	3,147	2,978	2,531	2,661	2,691	3,488	3,231	3,330	3,485	3,463	....	Goods: Exports f.o.b.	78aa d
−3,090	−3,802	−3,721	−2,722	−2,140	−1,806	−2,596	−3,182	−2,790	−2,291	−2,892	−3,495	−4,050	−4,043	....	Goods: Imports f.o.b.	78ab d
826	−553	−428	293	1,007	1,172	−65	−521	−99	1,197	339	−165	−565	−580	....	Trade Balance	78ac d
715	770	784	711	670	814	836	931	995	891	845	877	846	892	....	Services: Credit	78ad d
−880	−1,087	−1,098	−965	−891	−984	−1,179	−1,353	−1,371	−1,305	−1,259	−1,329	−1,514	−1,548	....	Services: Debit	78ae d
661	−870	−742	39	786	1,002	−408	−943	−475	783	−75	−617	−1,233	−1,236	....	Balance on Goods and Services	78af d
202	204	109	116	157	133	93	67	43	80	72	117	137	153	....	Income: Credit	78ag d
−1,111	−1,223	−1,143	−1,246	−1,334	−1,177	−1,007	−944	−1,025	−1,023	−1,173	−1,149	−1,047	−1,134	....	Income: Debit	78ah d
−248	−1,889	−1,776	−1,091	−391	−42	−1,322	−1,820	−1,457	−160	−1,176	−1,649	−2,143	−2,217	....	Balance on Goods, Serv., & Inc.	78ai d
147	156	164	216	156	132	149	180	211	235	275	318	433	417	....	Current Transfers, n.i.e.: Credit	78aj d
—	—	—	—	—	—	—	—	—	—	—	—	—	—	....	Current Transfers: Debit	78ak d
−101	−1,733	−1,612	−875	−235	90	−1,173	−1,640	−1,246	75	−901	−1,331	−1,710	−1,800	....	Current Account, n.i.e.	78al d
—	—	—	—	—	—	—	—	—	—	—	—	—	—	....	Capital Account, n.i.e.: Credit	78ba d
—	—	—	—	—	—	—	—	—	—	—	—	—	—	....	Capital Account: Debit	78bb d
—	—	—	—	—	—	—	—	—	—	—	—	—	—	....	Capital Account, n.i.e.	78bc d
—	—	—	—	—	—	—	—	—	—	—	—	—	—	....	Direct Investment Abroad	78bd d
27	125	48	38	−89	1	22	32	26	59	41	−7	127	349	....	Dir. Invest. in Rep. Econ., n.i.e.	78be d
—	—	—	—	—	—	—	—	—	—	—	—	—	—	....	Portfolio Investment Assets	78bf d
—	—	—	—	—	—	—	—	—	—	—	—	—	222	....	Portfolio Investment Liab., n.i.e.	78bg d
—	—	—	—	—	—	—	—	—	—	—	−476	83	151	....	Other Investment Assets	78bh d
−75	252	1,770	−344	−681	−1,165	−1,162	−1,180	−909	−1,193	−923	−483	−274	−747	....	Other Investment Liab., n.i.e.	78bi d
−48	377	1,818	−306	−770	−1,164	−1,140	−1,148	−883	−1,134	−882	−966	−64	−25	....	Financial Account, n.i.e.	78bj d
414	582	−402	120	−566	−297	46	−34	−187	−195	312	1,618	1,348	1,278	....	Net Errors and Omissions	78ca d
264	−774	−196	−1,061	−1,571	−1,371	−2,267	−2,822	−2,316	−1,254	−1,471	−679	−426	−547	....	Overall Balance	78cb d
−264	774	196	1,061	1,571	1,371	2,267	2,822	2,316	1,254	1,471	679	426	547	....	Reserves and Related Items	79da d
−650	735	−198	−50	−274	−137	346	648	−11	−570	−222	−836	−519	−699	....	Reserve Assets	79db d
−1	−46	281	84	24	−49	−51	—	—	−24	−63	−51	−49	254	....	Use of Fund Credit and Loans	79dc d
15	—	—	—	—	—	—	—	—	—	—	—	—	—	....	Liabs.Constit.For.Auth.Reserves	79dd d
372	85	112	1,027	1,821	1,557	1,972	2,174	2,327	1,848	1,757	1,566	994	992	....	Exceptional Financing	79de d
Thousands from 1988 to 1989;Millions Beginning 1990: Yr. Ending Dec. 31															**Government Finance**	
−140	−416	−557	−2,351	ℐ−3,064	−4,563	−14,734	−44,988	ℐ−155	−5,956	ℐ−234	−471	−927	ℐ−657	....	Deficit (-) or Surplus	80
1,019	1,523	2,493	3,732	ℐ9,646	28,235	45,331	66,424	ℐ403	7,499	ℐ597	3,025	5,838	ℐ10,937	....	Revenue	81
								ℐ—		ℐ—			ℐ149	....	Grants Received	81z
1,159	1,938	3,050	6,083	ℐ12,710	32,798	60,065	111,412	ℐ558	13,455	ℐ831	3,496	6,765	ℐ11,187	....	Expenditure	82
—	—	—	—	—	—	—	—	ℐ—	—	ℐ—	—	—	ℐ556	....	Lending Minus Repayments	83
															Financing	
125	283	133	1,177	ℐ708	−931	8,453	35,971	ℐ64	4,131	ℐ115	−181	442	....	....	Net Borrowing: Domestic	84a
15	133	424	1,174	ℐ2,356	5,494	6,281	9,017	ℐ91	1,825	ℐ119	652	485	....	....	Foreign	85a
Thousands from 1988 to 1989; Millions Beginning 1990															**National Accounts**	
1,337	1,697	2,861	6,140	13,310	43,267	50,131	78,661	ℐ583	15,450	ℐ827	3,424	5,478	8,734	12,423	Exports of Goods & Services	90c
628	1,096	1,908	3,486	6,682	17,920	34,653	71,515	ℐ320	7,300	ℐ378	1,858	3,492	5,363	8,052	Government Consumption	91f
1,497	3,041	5,150	7,389	14,424	34,292	73,640	142,700	ℐ967	18,000	ℐ945	4,719	8,055	13,699	22,433	Gross Fixed Capital Formation	93e
239	575	664	172	−220	410	3,230	16,280	ℐ73	1,000	ℐ52	739	609	1,420	1,124	Increase/Decrease(-) in Stocks	93i
3,470	6,230	10,120	20,030	45,210	123,490	252,990	504,120	ℐ3,062	78,000	ℐ4,906	25,926	42,125	63,420	81,706	Private Consumption	96f
−1,159	−2,077	−3,383	−6,074	−10,601	−31,002	−55,100	−91,210	ℐ−699	−12,000	ℐ−741	−3,728	−6,959	−11,137	−16,059	Imports of Goods & Services	98c
6,010	10,540	17,310	31,160	68,800	188,380	359,550	722,030	ℐ4,306	106,000	ℐ6,367	32,756	52,800	81,498	109,678	Gross Domestic Product = GDP	99b
−140	−420	−680	−1,770	−3,980	−10,010	−10,460	−9,850	ℐ−107	−1,616	ℐ−160	−773	−1,083	−1,930	....	Net Factor Inc/Pmts(-) Abroad	98.n
4,830	10,125	16,632	29,387	64,823	178,374	349,088	712,178	ℐ4,199	113,499	ℐ6,630	32,164	50,977	78,598	....	Gross National Product = GNP	99a
....	....	....	....	....	....	....	....	....	....	....	....	....	....	....	Nat'l Income, Market Prices	99e
7,002	7,362	7,345	6,419	6,790	6,933	7,575	8,206	7,532	6,701	6,416	6,598	6,443	6,858	....	GDP 1990 Prices *(Millions)*	99b.p
—	—	—	—	—	—	—	—	—	2	100	498	813	1,190	....	GDP Deflator (1990=100)	99bi p
Midyear Estimates																
17.30	17.75	18.14	18.57	18.99	19.42	19.84	20.26	20.68	21.11	21.55	22.00	22.45	22.64	23.09	**Population**	99z

Government Finance: ℐ Beginning in 1968, the coverage of government agencies has been expanded, and transactions carried out after the close of the year for which they were budgeted are included in the year in which they are effected rather than in the year to which their budget relates. ℐ Beginning in 1984, data are as reported in the *Government Finance Statistics Yearbook* and relate to the budgetary central government only; expenditure data include interest arrears.

Philippines

566

		1965	1966	1967	1968	1969	1970	1971	1972	1973	1974	1975	1976	1977	1978	1979
Exchange Rates																*Pesos per SDR:*
Market Rate	aa	3.910	3.900	3.930	3.930	3.930	‖6.435	6.987	7.362	8.119	8.650	8.778	8.630	8.952	9.608	9.768
																Pesos per US Dollar:
Market Rate	ae	3.910	3.900	3.930	3.930	3.930	‖6.435	6.435	6.781	6.730	7.065	7.498	7.428	7.370	7.375	7.415
Market Rate	rf	3.909	3.900	3.900	3.900	3.900	5.904	6.432	6.675	6.756	6.788	7.248	7.440	7.403	7.366	7.378
															Index Numbers (1990=100):	
Market Rate	ah x	618.0ᵉ	618.9ᵉ	615.8ᵉ	614.9ᵉ	614.5ᵉ	420.0	375.7	362.2	357.6	356.1	333.7	324.5	326.2	327.3	327.1
Nominal Effective Exchange Rate	ne c	....	....	....	....	....	....	....	....	....	....	....	....	....	....	346.8
Real Effective Exchange Rate	re c	....	....	....	....	....	....	....	....	....	....	....	....	....	....	133.4
Fund Position																*Millions of SDRs:*
Quota	2f. s	75	110	110	110	110	155	155	155	155	155	155	155	155	210	210
SDRs	1b. s	—	—	—	—	—	—	—	22	24	28	23	14	19	13	26
Reserve Position in the Fund	1c. s	4	28	—	—	—	—	—	—	—	—	—	—	—	—	—
Total Fund Cred.&Loans Outstg.	2tl	—	—	—	55	55	69	90	95	76	68	165	348	435	506	618
International Liquidity												*Millions of US Dollars Unless Otherwise Indicated:*				
Total Reserves minus Gold	1l. d	155	149	120	99	76	195	309	480	993	1,459	1,314	1,597	1,479	1,763	2,250
SDRs	1b. d	—	—	—	—	—	—	—	24	29	34	27	16	23	17	34
Reserve Position in the Fund	1c. d	4	27	—	—	—	—	—	—	—	—	—	—	—	—	—
Foreign Exchange	1d. d	151	122	120	99	76	195	309	456	964	1,425	1,287	1,581	1,456	1,746	2,216
Gold (Million Fine Troy Ounces)	1ad	1.086	1.257	1.714	1.771	1.286	1.600	1.914	1.857	1.057	1.056	1.056	1.056	1.056	1.513	1.702
Gold (National Valuation)	1an d	38	44	60	62	45	56	67	71	45	45	45	45	45	118	166
Monetary Authorities: Other Liab.	4.. d	110	128	236	206	273	212	233	157	187	282	577	595	49	881	1,562
Deposit Money Banks: Assets	7a. d	124	169	173	197	171	162	187	355	675	1,004	1,121	716	639	1,033	1,436
of which: Claims on Nonbanks	7ad d	....	....	....	....	....	....	....	....	....	....	....	173	149	183	238
Deposit Money Banks: Liabilities	7b. d	113	100	93	131	127	155	260	484	716	1,087	1,176	1,209	1,480	2,606	3,721
of which: Liab. to Nonbanks	7bd d	....	....	....	....	....	....	....	....	....	....	....	980	1,109	1,862	2,822
Other Banking Insts.: Liabilities	7f. d	....	....	....	....	....	....	....	....	....	....	163	160	271	516	582	731
of which: Liab. to Nonbanks	7fd d	....	....	....	....	....	....	....	....	....	....	163	160	271	516	582	731
OBU: Foreign Assets	7k. d	....	....	....	....	....	....	....	....	....	....	....	....	366	719	819
of which: Claims on Nonbanks	7kd d	....	....	....	....	....	....	....	....	....	....	....	....	17	27	82
OBU: Foreign Liabilities	7m.. d	....	....	....	....	....	....	....	....	....	....	....	....	359	1,248	1,998
of which: Liab. to Nonbanks	7md d	....	....	....	....	....	....	....	....	....	....	....	....	5	2	57
Monetary Authorities																*Billions of Pesos:*
Foreign Assets	11	.75	.75	.70	.63	.47	1.18	1.78	2.77	7.05	10.63	10.20	12.54	11.86	14.57	18.68
Claims on Central Government	12a	.81	.89	1.05	1.18	1.70	2.03	2.14	2.91	3.36	4.47	3.32	3.84	4.46	5.98	6.91
Claims on Local Government	12b	.42	.42	.42	.50	.52	.50	.44	.46	.26	.27	.35	.72	.81	.74	.68
Claims on Nonfin.Publ.Enterprises	12c	....	....	....	....	....	....	....	....	....	....	....	....	....	....	....
Claims on Deposit Money Banks	12e	.51	.63	1.15	1.35	1.44	1.15	1.03	1.24	1.04	2.23	6.27	4.28	2.90	5.86	9.74
Claims on Other Financial Insts.	12f	.33	.45	.63	.59	.66	.71	.84	.96	.57	.84	1.52	2.27	2.66	3.83	5.11
Reserve Money	14	1.73	1.87	2.42	2.59	2.95	3.24	3.57	4.47	5.03	6.27	7.12	8.01	9.90	12.30	15.08
of which: Currency Outside DMBs	14a	1.48	1.54	1.76	1.78	2.12	2.41	2.65	3.43	3.45	4.31	4.75	5.65	6.73	8.14	9.18
Restricted Deposits	16b	....	....	....	....	....	....	....	....	....	....	....	....	....	....	....
Foreign Liabilities	16c	.43	.50	.92	1.02	1.28	1.81	2.12	1.76	1.88	2.58	5.77	7.43	4.25	11.32	17.57
o/w: Med.&Long-Term Fgn Liabs	16cl	....	....	....	....	....	....	....	....	....	....	....	....	....	....	....
Central Government Deposits	16d	.08	.19	.19	.17	.13	.22	.29	.74	1.91	3.40	1.26	.97	1.49	2.63	2.30
Capital Accounts	17a	.22	.23	.29	.29	.27	.27	.29	.34	.31	.33	.34	.37	.42	.41	.68
Other Items (Net)	17r	.37	.35	.12	.19	.16	.02	−.05	1.02	3.15	5.87	7.17	6.86	6.63	4.33	5.49
Deposit Money Banks																*Billions of Pesos:*
Reserves	20	.25	.33	.67	.81	.83	.83	.92	1.03	1.58	1.96	2.26	2.30	3.09	3.96	5.45
Nonreserve Claims on Mon. Auths.	20r	—	—	—	—	—	—	.29	.45	1.80	2.25	3.51	3.92	5.23	6.91	7.11
Foreign Assets	21	.48	.66	.68	.77	.67	1.04	1.21	2.41	4.54	7.10	8.40	‖5.32	4.71	7.62	10.65
Claims on Central Government	22a	.45	.54	.64	.78	1.04	.90	.91	.83	1.53	1.38	1.25	1.68	3.27	3.93	4.45
Claims on Local Government	22b	.65	.59	1.01	1.10	1.46	1.58	1.47	1.36	1.09	1.70	4.58	5.87	6.05	6.43	7.38
Claims on Nonfin.Publ.Enterprises	22c	....	....	....	....	....	....	....	....	....	....	....	....	....	....	....
Claims on Private Sector	22d	4.35	4.89	5.83	6.41	6.79	8.06	9.52	11.65	15.63	23.34	26.98	‖32.36	38.61	49.23	63.32
Claims on Other Financial Insts.	22f	....	....	....	....	....	....	....	....	....	....	....	....	....	....	....
Demand Deposits	24	1.11	1.20	1.43	1.50	1.90	1.90	2.36	3.03	3.81	4.70	5.57	6.42	8.21	8.81	9.66
Time,Savings,&Fgn.Currency Deps.	25	2.45	3.08	3.88	4.53	4.68	5.48	6.32	6.45	8.69	9.55	10.80	12.95	17.59	23.40	26.57
Money Market Instruments	26a	....	....	....	....	....	—	.99	1.29	4.04	7.47	9.63	10.87	11.40	11.49	11.95
Foreign Liabilities	26c	.44	.39	.36	.51	.49	1.00	1.67	3.28	4.82	7.68	8.82	8.98	10.90	19.22	27.59
Central Government Deposits	26d	.67	.49	.64	.63	.64	.73	.69	.92	1.89	2.46	2.39	2.23	2.11	2.55	4.17
Credit from Monetary Authorities	26g	.51	.63	1.15	1.35	1.44	1.15	1.03	1.24	1.04	2.23	6.12	4.41	3.13	4.02	7.00
Capital Accounts	27a	.86	.98	1.09	1.19	1.35	1.52	1.72	2.06	2.77	3.64	5.05	5.67	6.73	7.76	8.90
Other Items (Net)	27r	.14	.25	.29	.17	.29	.63	−.46	−.55	−.88	—	−1.40	−.07	.88	.82	2.52
Monetary Survey																*Billions of Pesos:*
Foreign Assets (Net)	31n	.36	.52	.09	−.13	−.64	−.58	−.81	.13	4.90	7.46	4.02	‖1.45	1.42	−8.35	−15.84
Domestic Credit	32	6.27	7.11	8.76	9.77	11.39	12.81	14.34	16.50	18.65	26.15	34.34	‖43.55	52.26	64.96	81.38
Claims on Central Govt. (Net)	32an	.51	.76	.86	1.16	1.97	1.97	2.07	2.08	1.09	−.01	.91	2.32	4.13	4.74	4.89
Claims on Local Government	32b	....	....	....	....	....	....	....	....	....	....	....	....	....	....	....
Claims on Nonfin.Pub.Enterprises	32c	....	....	....	....	....	....	....	....	....	....	....	....	....	....	....
Claims on Private Sector	32d	4.35	4.89	5.83	6.41	6.79	8.06	9.52	11.65	15.63	23.34	26.98	‖32.36	38.61	49.23	63.32
Claims on Other Financial Insts.	32f	.33	.45	.63	.59	.66	.71	.84	.96	.57	.84	1.52	2.27	2.66	3.83	5.11
Money	34	2.60	2.74	3.19	3.28	4.02	4.31	5.01	6.47	7.27	9.01	10.31	12.07	14.94	16.95	18.84
Quasi-Money	35	2.45	3.08	3.88	4.53	4.68	5.48	6.32	6.45	8.69	9.55	10.80	12.95	17.59	23.40	26.57
Money Market Instruments	36a	....	....	....	....	....	....	....	....	....	....	....	....	....	....	....
Other Items (Net)	37r	1.59	1.81	1.79	1.83	2.06	2.44	2.20	3.71	7.59	15.06	17.24	19.98	21.14	16.27	20.13
Money plus Quasi-Money	35l	6.44	7.44	9.02	9.97	11.11	12.50	14.47	16.49	20.37	23.69	26.96	31.96	41.54	51.52	57.99
Other Banking Institutions																*Billions of Pesos:*
Claims on Central Government	42a	.13	.12	.11	.12	.12	.11	.22	.59	.41	.74	1.39	2.00	2.10	2.62	2.62
Claims on Private Sector	42d	1.30	1.43	1.83	2.22	2.69	3.26	4.03	4.49	5.26	5.55	7.12	10.19	13.35	15.76	20.11
Time and Savings Deposits	45	.27	.40	.58	.67	.80	.94	1.15	1.24	1.63	2.21	4.73	5.56	6.18	7.91	9.93
Bonds	46ab	.38	.41	.69	.86	1.15	1.13	1.12	1.11	.54	.64	.55	.46	.30	1.81	2.25
Foreign Liabilities	46c	....	....	....	....	....	....	....	....	....	1.15	1.20	2.01	3.80	4.29	5.42
Capital Accounts	47a	.42	.64	.67	.73	.75	.78	.82	.87	2.21	2.31	2.54	3.11	3.61	4.00	4.65
Other Items (Net)	47r	.36	.10	−.01	.08	.11	.52	1.16	1.86	1.28	−.02	−.51	1.05	1.56	.25	.49
Liquid Liabilities	55l	5.3	6.2	7.6	8.5	9.5	10.7	12.5	14.2	17.6	20.8	25.8	30.6	38.7	48.3	55.3

Philippines

566

	1980	1981	1982	1983	1984	1985	1986	1987	1988	1989	1990	1991	1992	1993	1994		
End of Period																**Exchange Rates**	
	9.693	9.544	10.117	14.659	19.369	20.905	25.112	29.508	28.711	29.490	39.834	38.121	34.507	38.046	35.647	Market Rate	**aa**
End of Period (ae) Period Average (rf)																	
	7.600	8.200	9.171	14.002	19.760	19.032	20.530	20.800	21.335	22.440	28.000	26.650	25.096	27.699	24.418	Market Rate	**ae**
	7.511	7.900	8.540	11.113	16.699	18.607	20.386	20.568	21.095	21.737	24.311	27.479	25.512	27.120	26.417	Market Rate	**rf**
Period Averages																	
	321.3	305.6	282.8	222.0	147.9	129.9	118.6	117.4	114.6	111.2	100.0	88.0	94.8	89.3	91.7	Market Rate	**ahx**
	344.6	343.4	342.2	273.3	187.9	169.9	133.9	121.5	112.0	111.8	100.0	86.5	90.9	84.8	85.2	Nominal Effective Exchange Rate	**nec**
	140.5	145.0	150.5	126.6	125.4	137.2	107.1	98.5	95.8	102.8	100.0	98.8	109.6	106.9	114.1	Real Effective Exchange Rate	**rec**
End of Period																**Fund Position**	
	315	315	315	440	440	440	440	440	440	440	440	440	633	633	633	Quota	**2f.s**
	—	2	3	1	20	35	5	—	—	1	1	3	—	7	17	SDRs	**1b.s**
	—	—	—	—	9	24	39	39	39	39	39	39	87	87	87	Reserve Position in the Fund	**1c.s**
	820	975	906	1,046	903	1,049	1,035	888	813	895	641	759	800	881	729	Total Fund Cred.&Loans Outstg.	**2tl**
End of Period																**International Liquidity**	
	2,846	2,066	888	747	602	615	1,728	968	1,003	1,417	924	3,246	4,403	4,676	6,017	Total Reserves minus Gold	**1l.d**
	—	2	3	1	19	39	6	—	—	1	1	4	1	10	24	SDRs	**1b.d**
	—	—	—	—	9	26	47	55	52	51	55	56	120	120	127	Reserve Position in the Fund	**1c.d**
	2,846	2,064	885	746	574	550	1,675	913	951	1,365	868	3,186	4,283	4,546	5,866	Foreign Exchange	**1d.d**
	1.920	1.659	1.866	.289	.786	1.478	2.259	2.776	2.841	2.447	2.888	3.366	2.798	3.221	2.892	Gold (Million Fine Troy Ounces)	**1ad**
	294	508	823	117	288	501	799	1,046	1,108	959	1,124	1,280	935	1,245	1,104	Gold (National Valuation)	**1and**
	2,500	2,802	4,308	4,288	4,575	6,252	7,824	7,178	6,744	6,026	6,166	6,080	4,527	2,663	2,294	Monetary Authorities: Other Liab.	**4..d**
	2,170	2,322	2,629	1,873	2,171	2,158	2,158	2,640	3,259	3,539	3,910	3,947	4,691	4,778	6,036	Deposit Money Banks: Assets	**7a.d**
	285	285	304	396	528	574	447	591	561	803	1,077	1,549	1,787	2,105	2,470	*of which:* Claims on Nonbanks	**7ad d**
	4,846	4,609	4,843	3,157	3,044	2,500	1,827	1,940	2,099	2,024	2,378	2,059	2,995	2,913	4,640	Deposit Money Banks: Liabilities	**7b.d**
	3,785	3,350	3,701	2,214	2,131	1,650	1,045	1,023	1,120	1,316	1,640	1,377	1,773	1,821	3,460	*of which:* Liab. to Nonbanks	**7bd d**
	986	1,253	1,643	1,646	1,701	1,203	5	5	6	16	67	213	480	911	963	Other Banking Insts.: Liabilities	**7f.d**
	986	1,253	1,643	1,646	1,701	1,203	5	5	6	16	67	213	480	911	963	*of which:* Liab. to Nonbanks	**7fd d**
	995	1,035	1,253	887	676	643	441	505	549	518	508	357	483	508	485	OBU: Foreign Assets	**7k.d**
	61	131	232	400	286	269	145	142	165	108	98	55	52	106	190	*of which:* Claims on Nonbanks	**7kd d**
	2,916	3,798	4,321	4,164	3,809	3,751	3,473	2,946	2,513	2,265	1,950	1,524	1,418	1,055	1,674	OBU: Foreign Liabilities	**7m.d**
	111	147	65	39	12	23	8	11	25	43	105	82	67	15	18	*of which:* Liab. to Nonbanks	**7md d**
End of Period																**Monetary Authorities**	
	24.73	22.43	24.49	I 12.11	17.69	20.66	51.42	41.88	45.04	53.23	57.61	122.43	133.45	I 164.04	173.77	Foreign Assets	**11**
	7.79	12.47	19.07	I 28.65	33.95	33.34	58.67	45.72	40.92	40.03	39.80	32.14	76.24	I 293.48	233.87	Claims on Central Government	**12a**
	.56	—	—	I —	—	—	—	—	—	—	—	—	—	I —	—	Claims on Local Government	**12b**
	....	.01	.08	I .81	.42	4.49	4.09	4.38	5.05	5.97	6.29	5.99	3.45	I 2.31	1.97	Claims on Nonfin.Publ.Enterprises	**12c**
	14.09	16.88	18.50	I 18.06	19.86	27.78	16.00	19.01	20.54	22.49	28.00	29.14	15.38	I 7.27	6.17	Claims on Deposit Money Banks	**12e**
	6.88	10.17	12.53	I 19.83	27.52	27.79	9.29	8.72	8.18	8.01	7.62	6.80	6.45	I 5.91	4.60	Claims on Other Financial Insts.	**12f**
	16.95	18.64	19.67	I 28.85	34.62	39.48	52.13	59.42	69.10	96.00	112.98	135.68	153.36	I 182.27	191.56	Reserve Money	**14**
	10.18	11.63	12.71	I 19.59	21.76	24.03	29.26	35.37	40.64	52.94	61.92	69.39	74.30	I 84.08	95.68	*of which: Currency Outside DMBs*	**14a**
	....	....	....	21.60	46.98	58.17	48.98	30.40	31.09	29.56	34.26	80.61	94.72	I 60.97	45.43	Restricted Deposits	**16b**
	26.91	32.18	48.67	I 73.22	105.35	138.69	184.71	174.13	166.62	161.46	198.16	190.98	141.22	I 107.27	81.99	Foreign Liabilities	**16c**
	....	3.68	4.27	I 36.95	53.79	85.16	116.96	120.00	113.58	111.81	142.41	127.26	53.38	I 42.84	37.47	*o/w:* Med.&Long-Term Fgn Liabs	**16cl**
	2.33	I 2.69	2.44	6.17	13.00	8.70	17.13	47.55	64.38	79.23	81.78	96.73	168.23	I 120.22	108.67	Central Government Deposits	**16d**
	.50	.81	.96	I 1.99	2.63	3.08	3.60	4.15	4.13	4.31	6.58	6.60	6.59	I 21.10	26.46	Capital Accounts	**17a**
	7.34	7.65	2.99	–52.37	–103.15	–134.05	–167.09	–195.94	–215.60	–240.84	–294.43	–314.10	–329.14	I –18.83	–33.72	Other Items (Net)	**17r**
End of Period																**Deposit Money Banks**	
	6.02	6.17	5.94	I 8.37	11.87	14.42	21.77	22.37	26.65	40.05	46.80	59.97	70.54	87.66	86.74	Reserves	**20**
	6.17	5.58	4.37	I 18.77	31.43	37.19	32.84	29.95	32.29	30.52	37.76	57.21	35.39	29.20	37.50	Nonreserve Claims on Mon. Auths.	**20r**
	16.49	19.04	24.11	21.11	26.22	41.08	44.31	54.92	69.54	79.42	109.49	105.18	117.73	132.35	147.38	Foreign Assets	**21**
	4.98	6.13	9.62	I 13.03	15.44	13.65	21.44	24.21	38.69	54.84	59.70	61.33	84.34	98.89	147.56	Claims on Central Government	**22a**
	8.68	7.39	.03	I .22	.21	.26	.25	.20	.17	.17	.16	.16	.36	.80	2.37	Claims on Local Government	**22b**
	....	....	10.61	I 15.37	21.19	20.97	13.63	13.29	13.15	14.83	19.27	19.87	21.50	22.84	17.07	Claims on Nonfin.Publ.Enterprises	**22c**
	76.64	92.50	103.40	136.23	128.35	115.03	90.45	109.08	128.85	159.87	206.56	221.64	276.30	388.87	491.98	Claims on Private Sector	**22d**
	....	....	....	2.38	4.45	3.51	2.74	3.52	3.62	3.23	5.45	7.91	10.17	11.50	24.61	Claims on Other Financial Insts.	**22f**
	12.36	11.90	10.82	I 13.07	11.69	11.70	12.81	16.75	18.74	25.21	26.76	31.98	34.72	49.10	55.08	Demand Deposits	**24**
	32.89	42.11	56.00	I 90.87	111.49	123.27	119.68	130.77	168.86	218.09	273.91	322.67	371.44	477.63	613.16	Time,Savings,&Fgn.Currency Deps.	**25**
	12.37	16.45	18.82	I 20.00	14.59	11.03	7.83	6.76	5.38	6.88	14.56	7.35	7.39	8.86	8.03	Money Market Instruments	**26a**
	36.83	37.79	53.28	I 44.20	60.16	47.58	37.52	40.34	44.77	45.42	66.59	54.87	75.17	80.70	113.29	Foreign Liabilities	**26c**
	4.13	4.50	4.29	I 11.53	12.29	15.25	17.29	13.26	16.70	17.09	13.78	16.23	26.55	41.76	26.62	Central Government Deposits	**26d**
	10.09	12.98	13.67	I 16.33	20.36	29.20	16.17	20.31	25.46	25.27	32.58	35.77	22.58	23.82	17.41	Credit from Monetary Authorities	**26g**
	10.47	13.79	I 16.16	22.43	27.41	24.77	31.85	35.51	42.28	47.34	61.65	76.32	91.07	107.10	132.36	Capital Accounts	**27a**
	–.18	–2.72	–14.95	2.16	–2.14	–16.68	–15.71	–6.19	–9.24	–2.35	–4.65	–11.94	–12.57	–16.86	–10.75	Other Items (Net)	**27r**
End of Period																**Monetary Survey**	
	–22.52	–28.50	–53.36	I –79.10	–104.92	–124.54	–126.49	–117.67	–96.81	–74.23	–97.65	–18.25	34.80	108.42	125.87	Foreign Assets (Net)	**31n**
	99.05	122.14	150.98	I 198.83	206.25	195.11	166.15	148.32	157.55	191.41	250.27	243.86	286.82	663.21	789.29	Domestic Credit	**32**
	6.30	11.63	22.00	I 23.98	24.11	23.05	45.69	9.13	–1.48	–1.45	3.94	–19.50	–34.20	230.39	246.14	Claims on Central Govt. (Net)	**32an**
	....	....	....	.22	.21	.26	.25	.20	.17	.17	.16	.16	.36	.80	2.37	Claims on Local Government	**32b**
	....	....	....	16.19	21.61	25.46	17.73	17.67	18.19	20.80	25.55	25.86	24.96	25.14	19.04	Claims on Nonfin.Pub.Enterprises	**32c**
	76.64	92.50	103.40	136.23	128.35	115.03	90.46	109.08	128.85	160.65	207.54	222.63	279.08	389.47	492.53	Claims on Private Sector	**32d**
	6.88	10.17	12.53	I 22.21	31.97	31.31	12.03	12.24	11.81	11.24	13.07	14.71	16.62	17.41	29.21	Claims on Other Financial Insts.	**32f**
	22.54	23.52	23.52	I 33.55	34.44	36.76	43.17	53.80	61.20	81.28	92.94	107.69	117.54	143.71	159.90	Money	**34**
	32.89	42.11	56.00	I 90.87	111.49	123.27	119.68	130.77	168.86	218.09	273.91	322.67	371.44	477.63	613.16	Quasi-Money	**35**
	....	....	....	20.00	14.59	11.03	7.83	6.76	5.38	6.88	14.56	7.35	7.39	8.86	8.03	Money Market Instruments	**36a**
	21.10	28.01	18.09	–24.69	–59.19	–100.48	–131.02	–160.70	–174.70	–189.06	–228.79	–212.10	–174.75	141.43	134.07	Other Items (Net)	**37r**
	70.79	83.82	101.55	I 124.42	145.93	160.02	162.85	184.58	230.05	299.37	366.85	430.36	488.97	621.34	773.06	Money plus Quasi-Money	**35l**
End of Period																**Other Banking Institutions**	
	2.69	3.19	2.99	2.54	2.93	6.85	2.78	5.06	5.28	3.65	5.95	7.92	11.41	10.82	12.93	Claims on Central Government	**42a**
	26.23	36.03	42.29	54.17	56.31	39.36	15.63	17.69	21.36	29.05	33.07	45.95	61.24	82.32	115.93	Claims on Private Sector	**42d**
	12.36	14.44	16.04	14.49	9.78	13.52	13.32	15.49	20.14	24.84	29.60	40.72	51.30	63.19	69.09	Time and Savings Deposits	**45**
	2.65	3.23	4.78	6.03	6.53	5.96	1.45	1.09	.48	.33	.19	—	—	.15	2.28	Bonds	**46ab**
	7.49	10.27	15.07	23.05	33.61	22.90	.09	.10	.14	.36	1.87	5.69	12.04	25.23	23.51	Foreign Liabilities	**46c**
	5.82	6.57	7.72	8.37	7.46	7.88	6.50	7.23	8.88	11.08	12.17	13.13	16.11	18.97	27.08	Capital Accounts	**47a**
	.60	4.71	1.67	4.77	1.87	–4.05	–2.96	–1.16	–2.99	–3.91	–4.81	–5.67	–6.79	–14.39	6.90	Other Items (Net)	**47r**
	67.8	80.1	95.6	138.9	155.7	173.5	176.2	200.1	250.2	324.2	396.5	471.1	540.3	684.5	842.2	Liquid Liabilities	**55l**

Philippines

566

	1965	1966	1967	1968	1969	1970	1971	1972	1973	1974	1975	1976	1977	1978	1979
Interest Rates															*Percent Per Annum*
Discount Rate *(End of Period)* ... 60	6.00	4.75	6.00	7.50	10.00	10.00	10.00	10.00	10.00	6.00	6.00	6.00	6.00	4.00	11.00
Treasury Bill Rate ... 60c	....	....	....	....	....	....	....	....	....	....	....	10.186	10.885	10.880	12.255
Deposit Rate ... 60l	....	....	....	....	....	....	....	....	....	....	....	8.500	8.500	8.500	8.667
Lending Rate ... 60p	....	....	....	....	....	....	....	....	....	....	....	12.000	12.000	12.000	14.000
Prices and Employment															*Index Numbers (1990=100):*
Share Prices: Commercial ... 62	15.9	19.4	21.7	31.2	57.1	40.8	24.8	19.1	26.8	22.8	16.5	16.8	13.4	17.0	16.7
Mining(1980=100) ... 62a	164.6	220.9	228.5	349.5	770.3	548.4	307.4	191.2	297.0	218.0	138.6	130.7	91.5	109.2	147.6
Sugar(1980=100) ... 62b	185.9	135.1	205.6	245.7	179.0	142.6	110.6	88.1	90.9	112.1	135.1	175.7	129.4	108.7	101.9
Wholesale Prices ... 63	3.8	4.1	4.2	4.2	5.2	5.2	6.1	6.7	8.2	12.2	12.8	14.6	15.7	16.5	19.6
Consumer Prices ... 64	5.2	5.5	5.8	5.9	6.0	6.9	8.4	9.1	10.6	14.2	15.1	16.5	18.1	19.5	22.9
Manufacturing Employment ... 67ey	....	....	....	....	....	....	....	....	....	....	....	....	....	....	....
International Transactions															*Millions of Pesos*
Exports ... 70	2,728	3,220	3,199	3,345	3,332	6,183	7,064	7,351	12,735	18,505	16,607	19,005	23,148	25,051	33,696
Sugar ... 70i	....	....	....	....	....	....	....	....	....	....	....	....	....	....	....
Coconut Oil ... 70ai	266	291	231	302	197	564	665	562	1,015	2,483	1,669	2,222	2,950	4,293	5,462
Imports, cif ... 71	3,493	3,739	4,601	5,031	4,933	7,299	8,523	9,474	12,156	23,556	27,226	29,328	31,606	37,885	48,786
Imports, fob ... 71.v	3,148	3,338	4,146	4,533	4,452	6,570	7,594	8,504	10,846	21,346	24,937	26,954	28,983	34,856	45,310
															1990=100
Volume of Exports ... 72	21	23	22	23	24	27	30	31	33	30	31	40	49	47	51
Sugar ... 72i	415	400	398	394	400	501	549	494	602	629	397	598	997	474	511
Coconut Oil ... 72ai	20	26	20	22	17	29	34	40	37	36	53	74	64	84	68
Volume of Imports ... 73	32	34	41	41	40	37	40	40	38	44	47	49	48	57	62
Unit Value of Exports ... 74	8	8	8	8	8	13	13	13	19	32	28	25	25	28	34
Sugar (Wholesale Price) ... 76i	4	5	5	5	6	7	9	10	11	22	22	19	14	14	14
Coconut Oil (W'sale price) ... 76ai	14	12	14	17	15	22	19	15	40	85	34	37	53	63	83
Unit Value of Imports ... 75	4	4	4	4	4	7	7	8	10	17	19	19	21	22	26
Balance of Payments															*Millions of US Dollars:*
Goods: Exports f.o.b. ... 78aa *d*	....	....	....	....	....	....	....	....	....	....	....	3,151	3,425	4,601	
Goods: Imports f.o.b. ... 78ab *d*	....	....	....	....	....	....	....	....	....	....	....	−3,915	−4,732	−6,142	
Trade Balance ... 78ac *d*	....	....	....	....	....	....	....	....	....	....	....	−764	−1,307	−1,541	
Services: Credit ... 78ad *d*	....	....	....	....	....	....	....	....	....	....	....	733	1,013	1,076	
Services: Debit ... 78ae *d*	....	....	....	....	....	....	....	....	....	....	....	−856	−1,000	−1,180	
Balance on Goods and Services ... 78af *d*	....	....	....	....	....	....	....	....	....	....	....	−887	−1,294	−1,645	
Income: Credit ... 78ag *d*	....	....	....	....	....	....	....	....	....	....	....	352	472	578	
Income: Debit ... 78ah *d*	....	....	....	....	....	....	....	....	....	....	....	−477	−591	−784	
Balance on Goods, Serv., & Inc. ... 78ai *d*	....	....	....	....	....	....	....	....	....	....	....	−1,012	−1,413	−1,851	
Current Transfers, n.i.e.: Credit ... 78aj *d*	....	....	....	....	....	....	....	....	....	....	....	272	328	369	
Current Transfers: Debit ... 78ak *d*	....	....	....	....	....	....	....	....	....	....	....	−14	−10	−14	
Current Account, n.i.e. ... 78al *d*	....	....	....	....	....	....	....	....	....	....	....	−754	−1,095	−1,496	
Capital Account, n.i.e.: Credit ... 78ba *d*	....	....	....	....	....	....	....	....	....	....	....	1	1	—	
Capital Account: Debit ... 78bb *d*	....	....	....	....	....	....	....	....	....	....	....	—	—	—	
Capital Account, n.i.e. ... 78bc *d*	....	....	....	....	....	....	....	....	....	....	....	1	1	—	
Direct Investment Abroad ... 78bd *d*	....	....	....	....	....	....	....	....	....	....	....	....	....	....	
Dir. Invest. in Rep. Econ., n.i.e. ... 78be *d*	....	....	....	....	....	....	....	....	....	....	....	210	101	7	
Portfolio Investment Assets ... 78bf *d*	....	....	....	....	....	....	....	....	....	....	....	−3	−5	−1	
Portfolio Investment Liab., n.i.e. ... 78bg *d*	....	....	....	....	....	....	....	....	....	....	....	9	4	14	
Other Investment Assets ... 78bh *d*	....	....	....	....	....	....	....	....	....	....	....	−337	−343	−889	
Other Investment Liab., n.i.e. ... 78bi *d*	....	....	....	....	....	....	....	....	....	....	....	618	1,984	2,432	
Financial Account, n.i.e. ... 78bj *d*	....	....	....	....	....	....	....	....	....	....	....	497	1,741	1,563	
Net Errors and Omissions ... 78ca *d*	....	....	....	....	....	....	....	....	....	....	....	210	113	249	
Overall Balance ... 78cb *d*	....	....	....	....	....	....	....	....	....	....	....	−46	760	316	
Reserves and Related Items ... 79da *d*	....	....	....	....	....	....	....	....	....	....	....	46	−760	−316	
Reserve Assets ... 79db *d*	....	....	....	....	....	....	....	....	....	....	....	−56	−898	−462	
Use of Fund Credit and Loans ... 79dc *d*	....	....	....	....	....	....	....	....	....	....	....	102	90	146	
Liabs.Constit.For.Auth.Reserves ... 79dd *d*	....	....	....	....	....	....	....	....	....	....	....	—	—	—	
Exceptional Financing ... 79de *d*	....	....	....	....	....	....	....	....	....	....	....	—	47	—	
Government Finance															*Millions of Pesos:*
Deficit (−) or Surplus ... 80	−302	−153	−236	−262	−996	59	−183	ⅉ−1,101	−843	445	−1,360	ⅉ−2,352	−2,807	−2,171	−349
Revenue ... 81	2,533	3,038	3,576	4,056	4,510	4,849	5,869	ⅉ6,950	9,430	11,919	16,657	ⅉ17,895	19,782	23,826	29,095
Grants Received ... 81z	....	....	....	....	....	....	....	ⅉ22	69	238	181	ⅉ405	177	181	224
Expenditure ... 82	2,835	3,191	3,812	4,318	5,506	4,790	6,052	ⅉ7,507	10,060	9,968	17,276	ⅉ18,706	20,542	23,502	25,417
Lending Minus Repayments ... 83	....	....	....	....	....	....	....	ⅉ566	282	1,744	922	ⅉ1,946	2,224	2,676	4,251
Financing															
Net Borrowing ... 84	434	112	348	215	897	316	216	ⅉ1,101	843	−445	1,360	ⅉ2,352	2,807	2,171	349
Domestic ... 84a	....	....	....	....	....	....	....	ⅉ695	594	−631	1,106	ⅉ2,302	2,561	362	−2,762
Foreign ... 85a	....	....	....	....	....	....	....	ⅉ406	249	186	254	ⅉ50	246	1,809	3,111
Use of Cash Balances ... 87	−132	41	−112	46	99	−385	−38	....	....	....	....	....	....	....	....
Debt: Domestic ... 88a	1,987	2,234	2,669	2,825	3,700	4,019	4,287	ⅉ4,627	6,356	9,379	11,414	ⅉ13,171	15,301	15,571	16,191
Foreign ... 89a	519	682	757	850	948	1,105	1,388	ⅉ1,536	1,272	3,071	4,937	ⅉ6,210	8,517	12,266	20,829
National Accounts															*Billions of Pesos:*
Exports of Goods & Services ... 90c	4.0	4.7	4.9	4.7	4.6	8.1	9.3	9.9	8.1	22.3	21.3	23.2	28.9	32.4	41.5
Government Consumption ... 91f	2.1	2.3	2.6	2.8	3.1	3.5	4.3	5.3	6.2	8.9	11.1	13.2	14.3	16.1	18.3
Gross Fixed Capital Formation ... 93e	4.1	4.3	5.3	5.5	5.7	6.7	8.2	8.8	11.4	18.4	27.1	33.7	36.4	42.3	56.3
Increase/Decrease(−) in Stocks ... 93i	.7	.8	.8	1.3	1.5	2.3	2.3	2.7	3.2	6.6	6.7	8.3	7.9	9.0	11.4
Private Consumption ... 96f	17.9	19.7	21.8	23.9	25.9	29.6	35.6	39.9	48.2	67.2	76.2	87.1	102.6	118.8	146.6
Imports of Goods & Services ... 98c	−4.0	−4.3	−5.4	−5.8	−5.8	−8.2	−9.6	−10.3	−8.2	−25.4	−29.1	−31.8	−34.8	−41.3	−53.6
Gross Domestic Product ... 99b	23.5	25.9	29.0	32.1	35.3	42.4	50.1	56.1	72.3	99.5	114.7	135.3	154.2	177.7	217.5
Net Factor Inc/Pmts(−) Abroad ... 98.n	−.1	−.1	−.3	−.3	−.3	−.7	−.5	−.5	−.1	.4	−.3	−1.1	−1.0	−.6	.5
Gross Nat'l Expenditure = GNP ... 99a	23.4	25.7	28.7	31.8	35.0	41.8	49.6	55.5	72.2	99.9	114.4	134.2	153.3	177.0	218.0
Nat'l Income, Market Prices ... 99e	21.6	23.8	26.5	29.4	32.3	38.0	44.9	50.2	65.2	91.4	103.1	121.3	138.7	160.3	197.5
Gross Dom. Prod. 1990 Prices ... 99b.p	394.0	411.5	436.6	460.8	483.0	505.1	530.0	555.2	606.4	636.8	677.6	731.9	776.9	819.6	870.9
GDP Deflator (1990=100) ... 99bi p	5.96	6.29	6.65	6.97	7.31	8.40	9.46	10.10	11.93	15.63	16.93	18.48	19.85	21.68	24.98
															Millions:
Population ... 99z	31.77	32.73	33.71	34.73	35.77	36.85	37.90	38.99	40.12	41.30	42.07	43.41	44.58	45.79	47.04

Philippines

1980	1981	1982	1983	1984	1985	1986	1987	1988	1989	1990	1991	1992	1993	1994		
Percent Per Annum															**Interest Rates**	
4.54	6.69	6.30	8.05	12.11	12.75	10.00	10.00	10.00	12.00	14.00	14.00	14.30	9.40	8.30	Discount Rate (End of Period)	60
12.136	12.547	13.780	14.231	28.529	26.725	16.081	11.509	14.667	18.646	23.672	21.478	16.018	12.448	12.714	Treasury Bill Rate	60c
12.250	13.717	13.742	13.581	21.172	18.914	11.253	8.202	11.315	14.126	19.538	18.802	14.275	9.606	10.542	Deposit Rate	60l
14.000	15.335	18.120	19.238	28.195	28.612	17.534	13.338	15.921	19.270	24.118	23.074	19.479	14.683	15.057	Lending Rate	60p
Period Averages															**Prices and Employment**	
12.6	11.0	9.0	8.9	7.9	7.0	33.1	76.4	79.8	114.1	100.0	104.8	123.0	145.9	....	Share Prices: Commercial	62
100.0	77.2	....	....	....	....	....	....	....	....	....	....	....	....	....	Mining(1980=100)	62a
100.0	110.2	....	....	....	....	....	....	....	....	....	....	....	....	....	Sugar(1980=100)	62b
23.2	26.6	29.4	34.1	57.0	67.4	66.3	72.3	82.0	90.8	100.0	113.4	118.6	117.3	....	Wholesale Prices	63
27.0	30.6	33.7	37.1	55.8	68.7	69.2	71.8	78.1	87.6	100.0	118.7	129.3	139.1	151.7	Consumer Prices	64
....	111.6	103.6	101.5	95.8	88.4	82.8	88.5	97.6	102.3	100.0	91.5	88.3	87.0	85.8	Manufacturing Employment	67ey
Millions of Pesos															**International Transactions**	
43,142	44,620	42,411	54,641	88,339	85,283	97,375	116,237	148,151	168,928	211,052	241,612	248,393	302,998	....	Exports	70
....	....	....	....	....	....	....	....	....	....	....	2,555	3,169	2,225	2,740	Sugar	70i
4,258	4,214	3,422	5,666	9,677	6,460	6,727	7,827	8,608	8,190	8,770	8,203	12,030	9,697	....	Coconut Oil	70ai
62,308	66,984	70,569	88,657	107,670	101,518	107,324	147,875	184,246	243,013	317,977	353,191	393,723	511,311	....	Imports, cif	71
57,698	62,773	65,322	83,207	99,246	93,396	102,897	138,605	172,174	226,643	297,657	331,079	369,635	479,296	....	Imports, fob	71.v
1990=100																
62	63	66	I63	62	60	70	75	83	93	100	103	....	....	....	Volume of Exports	72
708	499	509	399	390	233	91	67	58	86	100	112	85	132	....	Sugar	72i
78	89	79	82	50	56	106	88	68	65	100	72	74	71	....	Coconut Oil	72ai
63	58	66	I63	45	41	49	64	78	93	100	102	....	....	....	Volume of Imports	73
36	37	34	46	76	75	73	80	91	92	100	115	....	....	....	Unit Value of Exports	74
18	20	25	28	50	66	62	69	91	98	100	103	102	....	....	Sugar (Wholesale Price)	76i
54	51	45	81	196	108	64	113	155	145	100	154	192	196	....	Coconut Oil (W'sale price)	76ai
32	38	35	46	78	81	73	74	76	83	100	108	....	....	....	Unit Value of Imports	75
Minus Sign Indicates Debit															**Balance of Payments**	
5,788	5,722	5,021	5,005	5,391	4,629	4,842	5,720	7,074	7,821	8,186	8,840	9,824	11,375	....	Goods: Exports f.o.b.	78aad
−7,727	−7,946	−7,667	−7,487	−6,070	−5,111	−5,044	−6,737	−8,159	−10,419	−12,206	−12,051	−14,519	−17,597	....	Goods: Imports f.o.b.	78abd
−1,939	−2,224	−2,646	−2,482	−679	−482	−202	−1,017	−1,085	−2,598	−4,020	−3,211	−4,695	−6,222	....	Trade Balance	78acd
1,447	1,791	1,804	1,808	1,642	2,235	2,860	2,345	2,413	3,225	3,244	3,654	4,742	4,673	....	Services: Credit	78add
−1,439	−1,632	−1,823	−1,733	−1,194	−867	−844	−1,155	−1,308	−1,564	−1,761	−1,804	−2,308	−3,090	....	Services: Debit	78aed
−1,931	−2,065	−2,665	−2,407	−231	886	1,814	173	20	−937	−2,537	−1,361	−2,261	−4,639	....	Balance on Goods and Services	78afd
762	1,070	1,179	1,319	984	1,053	931	1,109	1,179	1,361	1,598	1,969	2,755	2,855	....	Income: Credit	78agd
−1,182	−1,573	−2,200	−2,155	−2,433	−2,353	−2,232	−2,299	−2,364	−2,710	−2,470	−2,469	−2,310	−2,204	....	Income: Debit	78ahd
−2,351	−2,568	−3,686	−3,243	−1,680	−414	513	−1,017	−1,165	−2,286	−3,409	−1,861	−1,816	−3,988	....	Balance on Goods, Serv., & Inc.	78aid
451	485	486	483	387	387	443	575	778	832	717	828	825	746	....	Current Transfers, n.i.e.: Credit	78ajd
−17	−13	−12	−11	−1	−9	−4	−2	−3	−2	−3	−1	−9	−47	....	Current Transfers: Debit	78akd
−1,917	−2,096	−3,212	−2,771	−1,294	−36	952	−444	−390	−1,456	−2,695	−1,034	−1,000	−3,289	....	Current Account, n.i.e.	78ald
—	—	—	—	—	1	2	—	—	—	—	—	—	1	—	Capital Account, n.i.e.: Credit	78bad
—	—	—	—	—	—	—	—	—	—	—	—	—	—	—	Capital Account: Debit	78bbd
—	—	—	—	—	1	2	—	—	—	—	—	—	1	—	Capital Account, n.i.e.	78bcd
—	—	—	—	—	—	—	—	—	—	—	—	—	—	—	Direct Investment Abroad	78bdd
−106	172	16	105	9	12	127	307	936	563	530	544	228	763	....	Dir. Invest. in Rep. Econ., n.i.e.	78bed
−1	−2	—	—	−3	−12	—	−2	−1	−14	—	−15	−115	−1,061	....	Portfolio Investment Assets	78bfd
5	5	1	7	—	17	13	21	51	294	−50	125	155	897	....	Portfolio Investment Liab., n.i.e.	78bgd
−389	−713	−355	108	100	—	—	—	—	—	—	—	—	—	....	Other Investment Assets	78bhd
3,175	2,556	3,185	−609	675	311	6	−8	−415	511	1,577	2,273	2,940	2,687	....	Other Investment Liab., n.i.e.	78bid
2,684	2,018	2,847	−389	781	328	146	318	571	1,354	2,057	2,927	3,208	3,286	....	Financial Account, n.i.e.	78bjd
124	−487	−364	635	65	545	34	68	493	402	593	−138	−520	292	....	Net Errors and Omissions	78cad
891	−565	−729	−3,496	−448	838	1,134	−58	674	300	−45	1,755	1,689	289	....	Overall Balance	78cbd
−891	565	729	3,496	448	−838	−1,134	58	−674	−300	45	−1,755	−1,689	−289	....	Reserves and Related Items	79dad
−1,163	151	792	1,886	−49	98	−1,124	249	−570	−408	388	−1,937	−1,746	−400	....	Reserve Assets	79dbd
259	182	−75	155	−149	164	−10	−190	−104	108	−343	182	58	111	....	Use of Fund Credit and Loans	79dcd
—	—	—	—	—	—	—	—	—	—	—	—	—	—	—	Liabs.Constit.For.Auth.Reserves	79ddd
13	232	12	1,455	647	−1,100	—	—	—	—	—	—	—	—	—	Exceptional Financing	79ded
Year Ending December 31															**Government Finance**	
−3,385	−12,154	−14,414	−7,468	−9,957	−11,158	−30,648	−16,728	−23,244	−19,568	−37,194	−26,349	−15,966	−21,891	18,114	Deficit (−) or Surplus	80
34,151	35,478	37,710	45,290	56,467	68,577	78,714	101,495	111,086	150,709	178,346	217,598	240,570	258,855	334,488	Revenue	81
222	258	283	101	359	380	531	1,719	1,775	1,701	2,556	3,189	2,144	1,550	739	Grants Received	81z
32,561	38,880	40,821	44,942	52,753	64,084	82,409	108,451	128,867	166,205	211,184	239,470	265,629	272,391	309,942	Expenditure	82
5,197	9,010	11,586	8,132	14,030	16,031	27,484	11,491	7,238	5,773	6,912	7,666	−6,949	9,905	7,171	Lending Minus Repayments	83
															Financing	
3,385	12,154	14,414	7,468	9,957	11,158	30,648	16,728	23,244	19,568	37,194	26,349	15,966	21,891	−18,114	Net Borrowing	84
1,152	6,180	9,735	2,048	8,123	11,308	27,068	9,947	19,002	11,358	33,068	19,469	1,576	8,979	−4,408	Domestic	84a
2,233	5,974	4,679	5,420	1,834	−150	3,580	6,781	4,242	8,210	4,126	6,880	14,390	12,912	−13,706	Foreign	85a
—	—	—	—	—	—	—	—	—	—	—	—	—	—	—	Use of Cash Balances	87
18,534	23,227	31,772	42,639	61,350	79,940	116,236	224,697	260,359	284,073	293,821	330,380	435,110	640,867	....	Debt: Domestic	88a
22,569	29,992	40,118	41,784	97,996	107,992	123,540	155,308	165,539	176,037	258,820	289,858	278,150	348,955	....	Foreign	89a
Billions of Pesos															**National Accounts**	
57.5	67.1	64.5	78.8	126.0	137.3	160.3	181.9	226.9	260.2	296.4	369.4	393.7	462.4	583.3	Exports of Goods & Services	90c
22.1	24.7	28.9	30.6	36.9	43.5	48.4	57.3	72.2	88.2	108.8	123.9	130.5	149.1	168.3	Government Consumption	91f
66.4	78.1	87.3	110.2	121.0	94.2	97.7	112.7	142.2	192.7	249.0	250.1	282.8	358.4	418.2	Gross Fixed Capital Formation	93e
4.5	−.8	1.1	−.9	−14.3	−12.1	−4.9	6.8	7.0	7.2	11.2	2.2	5.6	3.1	8.3	Increase/Decrease(−) in Stocks	93i
156.8	181.5	208.1	237.5	362.3	420.8	444.5	482.3	558.8	649.3	767.1	916.4	1,019.2	1,122.5	1,258.8	Private Consumption	96f
−69.4	−76.5	−82.9	−103.6	−131.5	−125.2	−136.2	−179.0	−215.3	−280.1	−358.5	−406.7	−459.9	−592.6	−715.6	Imports of Goods & Services	98c
243.7	281.6	317.2	369.1	524.5	571.9	608.9	682.8	799.2	925.4	1,077.2	1,248.6	1,351.6	1,475.0	1,687.6	Gross Domestic Product	99b
.5	−1.1	−3.6	−5.8	−16.0	−15.8	−12.6	−11.9	−7.2	−13.4	5.3	18.1	34.0	44.8	63.9	Net Factor Inc/Pmts(−) Abroad	98.n
243.2	280.5	313.5	363.3	508.5	556.1	596.3	670.8	792.0	912.0	1,082.6	1,266.1	1,385.6	1,519.8	1,751.5	Gross Nat'l Expenditure = GNP	99a
240.0	273.0	300.8	340.4	472.5	530.5	543.0	625.7	743.2	841.8	994.0	1,246.4	1,262.2	1,369.8	1,553.3	Nat'l Income, Market Prices	99e
I916.5	942.6	976.8	995.1	922.2	854.8	884.0	922.1	984.4	1,045.5	1,077.2	1,071.0	1,074.6	1,097.6	1,144.6	Gross Dom. Prod. 1990 Prices	99b.p
26.60	29.87	32.47	37.09	56.87	66.90	68.88	74.04	81.18	88.52	100.00	116.53	125.77	134.39	147.44	GDP Deflator (1990=100)	99bip
Midyear Estimates																
48.32	49.54	50.78	52.06	53.35	54.67	56.00	57.36	58.72	60.10	61.48	62.87	64.26	65.65	67.04	Population	99z

(Notes in the back of the book)

Poland

964

		1965	1966	1967	1968	1969	1970	1971	1972	1973	1974	1975	1976	1977	1978	1979
Exchange Rates																
											Zlotys per MILlion sdrs through 1977, per Thousand SDRs 1978-89					
Market Rate	aa	400.00	400.00	400.00	400.00	400.00	400.00	399.54	399.54	400.51	406.48	388.66	385.73	403.28	I 4.33	5.14
											Zlotys per Million US$ through 1977, per Thousand US$ 1978-89					
Market Rate	ae	400.00	400.00	400.00	400.00	400.00	400.00	368.00	368.00	332.00	332.00	332.00	332.00	332.00	I 3.32	3.90
Market Rate	rf	400.00	400.00	400.00	400.00	400.00	400.00	389.33	368.00	335.00	332.00	332.00	332.00	332.00	332.00	4.02
															Index Numbers (1990=100):	
Market Rate	ah x	237,500.0	237,500.0	237,500.0	237,500.0	237,500.0	237,500.0	244,384.1	258,152.2	283,811.9	286,144.6	286,144.6	286,144.6	286,144.6	....	23,655.4
Nominal Effective Exchange Rate	ne c	....	....	....	....	....	....	....	....	....	....	....	....	....	....	13,667.4
Real Effective Exchange Rate	re c	....	....	....	....	....	....	....	....	....	....	....	....	....	....	
Fund Position																*Millions of SDRs:*
Quota	2f. s															....
SDRs	1b. s															....
Reserve Position in the Fund	1c. s															....
Total Fund Cred.&Loans Outstg.	2tl															....
International Liquidity															*Millions of US Dollars Unless Otherwise Indicated:*	
Total Reserves minus Gold	1l. d															565.1
SDRs	1b. d															....
Reserve Position in the Fund	1c. d															....
Foreign Exchange	1d. d															565.1
Gold (Million Fine Troy Ounces)	1ad															1.285
Gold (National Valuation)	1an d															267.3
Monetary Authorities: Other Liab.	4..d															510.1
Deposit Money Banks: Assets	7a. d															1,576.5
Liabilities	7b. d															23,476.0
Monetary Authorities																*Millions of Zlotys:*
Foreign Assets	11															3
Claims on General Government	12a															—
Claims on Nonfin.Pub.Enterprises	12c															
Claims on Private Sector	12d															
Claims on Deposit Money Banks	12e															180
Reserve Money	14															109
of which: Currency Outside DMBs	14a															24
Nonreserve Liabilities to Banks	16b															
Foreign Liabilities	16c															2
General Government Deposits	16d															68
Capital Accounts	17a															
Other Items (Net)	17r															4
Deposit Money Banks																*Millions of Zlotys:*
Reserves	20															85
Nonreserve Claims on Mon.Auth.	20c															—
Foreign Assets	21															6
Claims on General Government	22a															8
Claims on Nonfin.Pub.Enterprises	22c															283
Claims on Private Sector	22d															15
Demand Deposits	24															55
Time, Savings,& Fgn.Currency Dep.	25															56
Foreign Liabilities	26c															17
General Government Deposits	26d															7
of which: Local Govt. Dep.	26db															4
Credit from Monetary Authorities	26g															180
Capital Accounts	27a															3
Other Items (Net)	27r															80
Monetary Survey																*Millions of Zlotys:*
Foreign Assets (Net)	31n															−10
Domestic Credit	32															232
Claims on General Govt. (Net)	32an															−66
Claims on Nonfin.Pub.Enterprises	32c															283
Claims on Private Sector	32d															15
Money	34															78
Quasi-Money	35															56
Capital Accounts	37a															7
Other Items (Net)	37r															81
Money plus Quasi-Money	35l															134
Interest Rates																*Percent Per Annum*
Refinancing Rate (End of Period)	60															
Money Market Rate	60b															
Treasury Bill Rate	60c															
Demand Deposit Rate	60j															
Deposit Rate	60l															
Lending Rate	60p															8.0
Prices, Production, Employment																*Index Numbers (1990=100):*
Producer Prices: Industry	63														.4	.5	.5
Consumer Prices	64						.3	.3	.3	.3	.3	.3	.4	I .4	.4	.4
Wages: Average Earnings	65														.5	.5	.5
Industrial Production	66														118.0	122.2	124.5
Industrial Employment	67											127.9	128.4	131.0	130.9	130.6

Poland

	1980	1981	1982	1983	1984	1985	1986	1987	1988	1989	1990	1991	1992	1993	1994		
End of Period																**Exchange Rates**	
	5.87	6.50	9.54	10.30	12.37	16.24	24.17	44.76	67.63	854.20	ꞁ1.35	1.57	2.17	2.93	3.56	Market Rate	aa
and per US$ thereafter: End of Period (ae) Period Average (rf)																	
	4.61	5.58	8.65	9.84	12.62	14.79	19.76	31.55	50.26	650.00	ꞁ.95	1.10	1.58	2.13	2.44	Market Rate	ae
	4.42	5.12	8.48	9.16	11.32	14.71	17.53	26.51	43.05	143.92	ꞁ.95	1.06	1.36	1.81	2.27	Market Rate	rf
Period Averages																	
	21,490.1	18,687.4	11,207.2	10,410.5	8,449.5	6,473.8	5,475.0	3,644.6	2,242.7	1,086.6	100.0	90.4	70.2	52.9	41.9	Market Rate	ahx
	13,612.9	13,977.7	9,510.9	9,776.8	8,961.2	7,443.8	5,274.3	3,180.4	1,978.2	1,066.4	100.0	96.3	77.8	67.8	58.6	Nominal Effective Exchange Rate	ne c
	146.2	162.1	201.6	242.3	236.6	203.2	159.4	116.0	105.1	118.6	100.0	154.0	152.3	162.9	165.5	Real Effective Exchange Rate	re c
End of Period																**Fund Position**	
	....	....	....	....	....	....	680	680	680	680	680	680	989	989	989	Quota	2f. s
	....	....	....	....	....	....	—	—	—	—	1	5	1	1	1	SDRs	1b. s
	....	....	....	....	....	....	—	—	—	—	—	—	77	77	77	Reserve Position in the Fund	1c. s
	....	....	....	....	....	....	—	—	—	—	358	597	597	498	919	Total Fund Cred.&Loans Outstg.	2tl
End of Period																**International Liquidity**	
	127.6	277.8	646.8	765.2	1,106.0	870.4	697.8	1,494.7	2,055.3	2,314.3	4,492.1	3,632.6	4,099.1	4,091.9	5,841.8	Total Reserves minus Gold	1l. d
	....	....	....	....	....	....	.1	.1	.1	.1	.8	7.7	1.1	.7	1.5	SDRs	1b. d
	....	....	....	....	....	....	—	—	—	—	—	—	106.1	105.9	112.6	Reserve Position in the Fund	1c. d
	127.6	277.8	646.8	765.2	1,106.0	870.4	697.7	1,494.6	2,055.2	2,314.2	4,491.3	3,624.9	3,992.0	3,985.3	5,727.7	Foreign Exchange	1d. d
	.758	.470	.471	.472	.472	.472	.472	.472	.472	.472	.472	.473	.473	.473	.473	Gold (Million Fine Troy Ounces)	1ad
	303.0	188.0	188.5	188.8	188.8	188.8	188.9	189.0	189.0	189.0	189.0	189.1	189.0	189.0	189.0	Gold (National Valuation)	1an d
	427.8	428.0	387.5	668.9	640.1	771.6	700.3	680.4	503.0	664.3	939.9	1,199.1	1,224.5	1,108.7	1,686.7	Monetary Authorities: Other Liab.	4..d
	1,476.7	2,034.4	1,713.1	1,639.7	1,895.6	2,295.1	2,373.2	2,782.5	2,794.7	2,773.1	6,091.2	5,306.4	6,648.3	5,925.5	7,742.2	Deposit Money Banks: Assets	7a. d
	25,318.1	27,593.1	25,544.2	24,039.8	23,394.3	26,681.1	30,876.9	35,014.6	33,198.1	32,811.4	1,923.0	1,580.9	1,921.0	1,469.8	1,543.2	Liabilities	7b. d
End of Period																**Monetary Authorities**	
	2	ꞁ3	7	10	17	17	24	60	127	1,719	4,717	ꞁ5,080	7,912	10,113	15,475	Foreign Assets	11
	3	ꞁ20	23	39	52	68	72	84	137	595	601	ꞁ4,365	12,170	15,729	19,530	Claims on General Government	12a
													15	8	6	3	Claims on Nonfin.Pub.Enterprises	12c
	....	....	....	....	....	....	....	....	....	....	....	5	15	21	20	Claims on Private Sector	12d
	200	ꞁ189	197	207	202	216	227	208	483	2,691	7,613	ꞁ7,512	4,848	6,362	7,450	Claims on Deposit Money Banks	12e
	142	ꞁ168	190	207	219	233	244	246	570	3,275	8,535	ꞁ10,943	14,860	15,993	19,615	Reserve Money	14
	29	ꞁ40	61	72	82	101	117	131	252	988	3,934	ꞁ5,618	7,798	9,982	12,274	of which: Currency Outside DMBs	14a
	—	—	—	—	—	—	—	—	—	—	55	ꞁ841	757	1,406	3,462	Nonreserve Liabilities to Banks	16b
	2	ꞁ2	3	7	8	11	14	21	25	432	1,376	ꞁ2,249	3,224	3,825	7,379	Foreign Liabilities	16c
	56	ꞁ37	25	32	47	64	72	78	116	146	1,369	ꞁ1,109	1,285	2,272	2,773	General Government Deposits	16d
	4	ꞁ4	4	4	4	4	4	5	7	15	82	ꞁ100	150	210	300	Capital Accounts	17a
	1	ꞁ1	5	6	-7	-11	-11	1	29	1,137	1,515	ꞁ1,736	4,676	8,525	8,949	Other Items (Net)	17r
End of Period																**Deposit Money Banks**	
	113	ꞁ128	130	135	136	131	127	115	318	1,889	3,909	ꞁ4,749	5,816	6,045	7,343	Reserves	20
	—	—	—	—	—	—	—	—	—	—	9	ꞁ860	757	1,406	2,877	Nonreserve Claims on Mon.Auth.	20c
	7	ꞁ11	15	16	24	34	47	88	140	1,803	5,787	ꞁ5,814	10,482	12,647	18,869	Foreign Assets	21
	11	ꞁ13	18	15	16	28	25	44	108	403	1,321	ꞁ7,445	12,037	19,278	27,402	Claims on General Government	22a
	308	ꞁ331	379	415	454	529	629	721	1,002	3,061	10,105	ꞁ10,379	11,770	14,252	16,751	Claims on Nonfin.Pub.Enterprises	22c
	16	ꞁ16	23	29	36	46	58	74	110	199	1,719	ꞁ8,979	13,111	19,022	25,165	Claims on Private Sector	22d
	59	ꞁ67	90	93	108	128	163	220	280	864	5,411	ꞁ5,113	7,096	9,654	15,175	Demand Deposits	24
	64	ꞁ80	107	129	158	192	253	363	636	5,078	9,022	ꞁ14,609	25,041	36,268	49,844	Time, Savings,& Fgn.Currency Dep.	25
	25	ꞁ27	36	40	58	70	82	111	174	2,053	1,679	ꞁ1,732	3,029	3,137	3,761	Foreign Liabilities	26c
	5	ꞁ4	14	10	10	17	21	31	49	264	1,472	ꞁ1,870	3,921	2,706	3,688	General Government Deposits	26d
	3	ꞁ4	9	10	10	16	21	27	43	54	490	ꞁ857	860	1,149	1,503	of which: Local Govt. Dep.	26db
	200	ꞁ189	197	207	202	216	227	208	483	2,691	7,613	ꞁ7,512	4,848	6,338	7,020	Credit from Monetary Authorities	26g
	3	ꞁ3	3	5	6	6	7	9	14	107	1,503	ꞁ3,374	4,323	7,129	9,990	Capital Accounts	27a
	98	ꞁ129	118	126	124	141	133	100	42	-3,703	-3,852	ꞁ4,015	5,715	7,419	8,928	Other Items (Net)	27r
End of Period																**Monetary Survey**	
	-18	ꞁ-15	-17	-20	-25	-31	-25	15	68	1,037	7,448	ꞁ6,913	12,142	15,798	23,204	Foreign Assets (Net)	31n
	276	ꞁ339	404	455	501	591	691	814	1,192	3,847	10,905	ꞁ28,210	43,904	63,330	82,410	Domestic Credit	32
	-48	ꞁ-8	2	11	10	16	4	19	80	587	-919	ꞁ8,832	19,001	30,029	40,471	Claims on General Govt. (Net)	32an
	308	ꞁ331	379	415	454	529	629	721	1,002	3,061	10,105	ꞁ10,394	11,778	14,258	16,754	Claims on Nonfin.Pub.Enterprises	32c
	16	ꞁ16	23	29	36	46	58	74	110	199	1,719	ꞁ8,984	13,125	19,043	25,185	Claims on Private Sector	32d
	88	ꞁ107	150	165	190	229	279	352	532	1,881	9,426	ꞁ10,783	14,963	19,646	27,450	Money	34
	64	ꞁ80	107	129	158	192	253	363	636	5,446	9,633	ꞁ15,319	26,145	36,278	49,852	Quasi-Money	35
	7	ꞁ7	7	9	10	10	11	14	21	122	1,585	ꞁ3,474	4,473	7,339	10,290	Capital Accounts	37a
	99	ꞁ130	122	132	118	129	122	100	71	-2,566	-2,291	ꞁ5,546	10,464	15,864	18,022	Other Items (Net)	37r
	152	ꞁ187	257	294	348	421	533	715	1,168	7,327	19,060	ꞁ26,102	41,108	55,924	77,302	Money plus Quasi-Money	35l
Percent Per Annum																**Interest Rates**	
	....	....	....	3.0	4.0	4.0	4.0	4.0	6.0	140.0	55.0	40.0	38.0	35.0	33.0	Refinancing Rate (End of Period)	60
	....	....	....	....	....	....	....	....	....	....	....	49.9	ꞁ29.5	24.5	23.3	Money Market Rate	60b
	....	....	....	....	....	....	....	....	....	....	....	....	44.0	33.2	28.8	Treasury Bill Rate	60c
	3.0	4.0	6.0	6.0	6.0	6.0	6.0	6.0	21.0	21.0	34.3	14.3	6.1	5.0	5.0	Demand Deposit Rate	60j
	....	....	....	....	....	....	....	....	....	....	100.0	41.7	ꞁ53.5	37.8	30.6	Deposit Rate	60l
	8.0	8.0	9.0	9.0	9.0	12.0	12.0	12.0	16.7	64.0	504.2	54.6	39.0	35.3	32.8	Lending Rate	60p
Period Averages																**Prices, Production, Employment**	
	.5	.5	1.2	1.4	1.6	1.9	2.2	2.8	4.4	13.8	100.0	ꞁ148.1	189.6	250.7	326.2	Producer Prices: Industry	63
	.5	.6	1.2	1.5	1.7	1.9	2.2	2.8	4.4	15.3	100.0	ꞁ176.7	256.8	351.5	468.4	Consumer Prices	64
	.6	.8	1.1	1.5	1.7	2.0	2.5	3.0	5.6	21.5	ꞁ100.0	167.1	228.5	320.0	421.4	Wages: Average Earnings	65
	123.3	106.5	103.3	112.1	117.7	121.9	127.5	131.8	138.1	134.1	100.0	84.0	87.3	....	....	Industrial Production	66
	130.2	129.6	122.9	121.7	121.0	120.3	120.6	119.9	118.0	114.5	ꞁ100.0	91.1	87.7	83.1	81.7	Industrial Employment	67

Poland

964

		1965	1966	1967	1968	1969	1970	1971	1972	1973	1974	1975	1976	1977	1978	1979
International Transactions															*Millions of Zlotys*	
Exports	70	1	1	1	1	1	1	2	2	3	3	42	41	46	50	57
Imports, cif	71	....	....	....	....	....	....	....	....	....	....	56	56	58	61	65
Imports, fob	71.v											54	54	56	58	62
															1990=100	
Volume of Exports	72											57.5	61.0	66.0	69.8	74.5
Volume of Imports	73											119.2	131.5	129.9	132.0	130.3
Export Prices	76											.6	.5	.5	.6	.6
Import Prices	76.x											.6	.5	.6	.6	.6
Balance of Payments															*Millions of US Dollars:*	
Goods: Exports f.o.b.	78aa d											....	9,506	10,506	11,967	13,276
Goods: Imports f.o.b.	78ab d												−12,263	−12,724	−14,259	−15,660
Trade Balance	78ac d												−2,757	−2,218	−2,292	−2,384
Services: Credit	78ad d												1,180	1,385	1,586	1,874
Services: Debit	78ae d												−1,144	−1,309	−1,521	−1,863
Balance on Goods and Services	78af d												−2,721	−2,142	−2,227	−2,373
Income: Credit	78ag d												37	36	40	71
Income: Debit	78ah d												−688	−924	−1,244	−1,738
Balance on Goods, Serv., & Inc.	78ai d												−3,372	−3,030	−3,431	−4,040
Current Transfers, n.i.e.: Credit	78aj d												597	660	909	953
Current Transfers: Debit	78ak d												−18	−22	−23	−278
Current Account, n.i.e.	78al d												−2,793	−2,392	−2,545	−3,365
Capital Account, n.i.e.: Credit	78ba d												—	—	—	—
Capital Account: Debit	78bb d															
Capital Account, n.i.e.	78bc d												—	—	—	—
Direct Investment Abroad	78bd d												−12	−17	−16	−13
Dir. Invest. in Rep. Econ., n.i.e.	78be d												6	5	25	30
Portfolio Investment Assets	78bf d												—	—	—	—
Portfolio Investment Liab., n.i.e.	78bg d															
Other Investment Assets	78bh d												−338	−378	−195	−252
Other Investment Liab., n.i.e.	78bi d												3,489	2,672	3,113	3,714
Financial Account, n.i.e.	78bj d												3,145	2,282	2,927	3,479
Net Errors and Omissions	78ca d												−167	−261	−253	161
Overall Balance	78cb d												185	−371	129	275
Reserves and Related Items	79da d												−185	371	−129	−275
Reserve Assets	79db d												−185	371	−129	−275
Use of Fund Credit and Loans	79dc d												—	—	—	—
Liabs.Constit.For.Auth.Reserves	79dd d												—	—	—	—
Exceptional Financing	79de d												—	—	—	—
Government Finance															*Millions of Zlotys:*	
Deficit (−) or Surplus	80														....	....
Revenue	81															
Grants Received	81z															
Expenditure	82															
Lending Minus Repayments	83															
Financing																
Domestic	84a															
Foreign	85a															
National Accounts															*Millions of Zlotys*	
Exports of Goods & Services	90c														....	....
Government Consumption	91f	....	....	6	7	7	8	9	10	11	13	15	18	21	23	....
Gross Fixed Capital Formation	93e	....	....	12	13	14	14	18	24	30	35	39	46	49	51	....
Increase/Decrease(−) in Stocks	93i	....	....	4	5	3	4	6	7	9	11	10	13	9	10	....
Private Consumption	96f	....	....	39	42	44	47	50	55	61	70	81	92	104	113	....
Imports of Goods & Services	98c															
Gross Domestic Product	99b	53	57	61	67	70	75	86	95	107	121	135	159	174	190	200
Net Material Product	99m															
															Millions:	
Population	99z	31.34	31.54	31.75	32.08	32.30	32.53	32.80	33.07	33.36	33.69	34.02	34.36	34.70	35.01	35.26

Exchange Rates: The post-January 1, 1995 zloty is equal to 10,000 of the pre-January 1, 1995 zlotys.

Monetary Authorities: ▮ Beginning in December 1981, data are based on an improved reporting system. ▮ Beginning in December 1991, data are based on a new system of accounts and an improved reporting system.

Deposit Money Banks: ▮ See note to section 10.

Monetary Survey: ▮ See note to section 10.

Interest Rates: *Money Market Rate:* ▮ Beginning in January 1992, weighted average rate on outstanding deposits of one month or less in the interbank market.

Deposit Rate: ▮ Beginning in January 1991, lowest rate offered on 12-month deposits in zlotys by main commercial banks.

Poland

964

	1980	1981	1982	1983	1984	1985	1986	1987	1988	1989	1990	1991	1992	1993	1994		
	\multicolumn{16}{l	}{}	**International Transactions**	
Millions of Zlotys																	
	63	55	95	106	134	169	212	324	601	1,948	13,606	15,772	17,969	25,757	38,767	Exports	70
	74	65	90	100	125	165	202	297	547	1,542	9,292	16,426	21,995	34,018	48,630	Imports, cif	71
	71	62	87	97	121	159	196	288	527	1,486	7,752	16,426	19,126	29,581	42,287	Imports, fob	71.v
1990=100																	
	71.4	57.8	62.5	69.3	75.9	76.9	80.7	84.5	92.2	92.4	100.0	102.6	....	96.4	114.0	Volume of Exports	72
	127.9	106.3	91.7	96.4	104.7	113.0	118.5	123.9	135.5	137.6	100.0	155.6	....	210.3	238.1	Volume of Imports	73
	.7	.7	1.2	1.2	1.4	1.7	2.0	2.9	5.0	16.2	100.0	118.0	....	190.6	245.7	Export Prices	76
	.7	.8	1.3	1.3	1.5	1.9	2.2	3.1	5.2	14.2	100.0	135.9	....	182.3	230.8	Import Prices	76.x
	\multicolumn{16}{l	}{}	**Balance of Payments**	
Minus Sign Indicates Debit																	
	14,043	10,542	11,547	11,615	11,654	10,945	11,926	12,026	13,846	12,869	15,837	14,393	13,929	13,582	....	Goods: Exports f.o.b.	78aa *d*
	−15,819	−12,723	−11,631	−11,312	−10,995	−10,598	−11,459	−11,236	−12,757	−12,822	−12,248	−15,104	−14,060	−17,087	....	Goods: Imports f.o.b.	78ab *d*
	−1,776	−2,181	−84	303	659	347	467	790	1,089	47	3,589	−711	−131	−3,505	....	Trade Balance	78ac *d*
	2,018	1,913	1,842	1,990	2,017	2,104	2,015	2,216	2,472	3,201	3,200	3,687	4,773	4,201	....	Services: Credit	78ad *d*
	−2,023	−1,727	−1,467	−1,783	−1,853	−1,846	−2,012	−2,028	−2,404	−3,053	−2,847	−2,994	−4,045	−3,631	....	Services: Debit	78ae *d*
	−1,781	−1,995	291	510	823	605	470	978	1,157	195	3,942	−18	597	−2,935	....	Balance on Goods and Services	78af *d*
	139	171	93	184	195	173	188	217	271	410	603	573	728	579	....	Income: Credit	78ag *d*
	−2,496	−3,395	−3,156	−2,978	−2,833	−2,730	−2,861	−3,132	−3,226	−3,623	−3,989	−3,469	−4,895	−4,192	....	Income: Debit	78ah *d*
	−4,138	−5,219	−2,772	−2,284	−1,815	−1,952	−2,203	−1,937	−1,798	−3,018	556	−2,914	−3,570	−6,548	....	Balance on Goods, Serv., & Inc.	78ai *d*
	1,234	1,878	926	942	1,106	1,351	1,483	2,154	2,777	4,246	6,865	6,707	6,214	5,840	....	Current Transfers, n.i.e.: Credit	78aj *d*
	−513	−645	−95	−239	−374	−381	−386	−596	−1,086	−2,637	−4,354	−5,939	−5,748	−5,080	....	Current Transfers: Debit	78ak *d*
	−3,417	−3,986	−1,941	−1,581	−1,083	−982	−1,106	−379	−107	−1,409	3,067	−2,146	−3,104	−5,788	....	Current Account, n.i.e.	78al *d*
	—	—	—	—	—	—	—	—	—	—	—	—	—	—	....	Capital Account, n.i.e.: Credit	78ba *d*
	—	—	—	—	—	—	—	—	—	—	—	—	—	—	....	Capital Account: Debit	78bb *d*
	—	—	—	—	—	—	—	—	—	—	—	—	—	—	....	Capital Account, n.i.e.	78bc *d*
	−21	−3	−4	−1	−12	−1	−22	−8	−22	−18	—	7	−13	−18	....	Direct Investment Abroad	78bd *d*
	10	18	14	16	28	15	16	12	15	11	89	291	678	1,715	....	Dir. Invest. in Rep. Econ., n.i.e.	78be *d*
	—	—	—	—	—	—	—	—	—	—	—	—	—	—	....	Portfolio Investment Assets	78bf *d*
	—	—	—	—	—	—	—	—	—	—	—	—	—	—	....	Portfolio Investment Liab., n.i.e.	78bg *d*
	−182	−711	−543	−336	−767	−39	−1,128	−1,415	−1,226	−155	−4,504	−1,497	−958	848	....	Other Investment Assets	78bh *d*
	3,063	−790	−4,473	−3,360	−2,769	−1,451	−3,692	−1,907	−9,428	−1,634	−4,316	−2,984	−752	−204	....	Other Investment Liab., n.i.e.	78bi *d*
	2,870	−1,486	−5,006	−3,681	−3,520	−1,476	−4,826	−3,318	−10,661	−1,796	−8,731	−4,183	−1,045	2,341	....	Financial Account, n.i.e.	78bj *d*
	−90	−206	−217	344	333	118	731	91	−267	−110	162	−745	−181	−104	....	Net Errors and Omissions	78ca *d*
	−637	−5,678	−7,164	−4,918	−4,270	−2,340	−5,201	−3,606	−11,035	−3,315	−5,502	−7,074	−4,330	−3,551	....	Overall Balance	78cb *d*
	637	5,678	7,164	4,918	4,270	2,340	5,201	3,606	11,035	3,315	5,502	7,074	4,330	3,551	....	Reserves and Related Items	79da *d*
	637	−35	−370	−118	−341	236	173	−797	−561	−259	−2,418	830	−616	223	....	Reserve Assets	79db *d*
	—	—	—	—	—	—	—	—	—	—	479	323	—	−138	....	Use of Fund Credit and Loans	79dc *d*
	—	—	—	—	—	—	—	—	—	—	—	—	—	—	....	Liabs.Constit.For.Auth.Reserves	79dd *d*
	—	5,713	7,534	5,036	4,611	2,104	5,028	4,403	11,596	3,574	7,440	5,921	4,946	3,466	....	Exceptional Financing	79de *d*
	\multicolumn{16}{l	}{}	**Government Finance**	
Year Ending December 31																	
	....	....	....	....	−3.99	−18.04	−4.13	−24.16	−67.30	....	....	....	....	....	....	Deficit (-) or Surplus	80
	....	....	....	....	374.63	453.81	532.34	657.09	1,096.61	....	....	....	....	....	....	Revenue	81
	....	....	....	....	.45	—	9.41	2.85	4.72	....	....	....	....	....	....	Grants Received	81z
	....	....	....	....	379.52	471.90	541.71	675.13	1,145.78	....	....	....	....	....	....	Expenditure	82
	....	....	....	....	−.45	−.05	4.17	8.97	22.85	....	....	....	....	....	....	Lending Minus Repayments	83
	\multicolumn{16}{l	}{}	Financing	
	....	....	....	....	−.25	13.25	−7.82	18.88	74.03	....	....	....	....	....	....	Domestic	84a
	....	....	....	....	4.24	4.79	11.95	5.28	−6.73	....	....	....	....	....	....	Foreign	85a
	\multicolumn{16}{l	}{}	**National Accounts**	
Millions of Zlotys																	
	71	64	108	119	152	190	236	363	674	2,257	16,051	16,773	22,732	....	....	Exports of Goods & Services	90c
	23	26	45	61	80	189	230	294	474	707	10,890	7,631	10,752	....	....	Government Consumption	91f
	62	51	112	139	178	221	284	382	666	1,935	11,607	15,503	....	....	....	Gross Fixed Capital Formation	93e
	4	−1	43	34	48	68	90	106	299	2,618	4,682	2,226	....	....	....	Increase/Decrease(-) in Stocks	93i
	168	204	348	449	543	551	679	874	1,460	6,076	26,972	56,827	77,472	....	....	Private Consumption	96f
	−78	−70	−96	−107	−135	−176	−217	−322	−593	−1,761	−11,050	−16,433	−23,430	....	....	Imports of Goods & Services	98c
	251	275	555	692	858	1,045	1,295	1,694	2,963	11,832	59,152	82,527	114,944	155,605	....	Gross Domestic Product	99b
	199	216	475	592	718	859	1,070	1,401	2,499	10,495	50,625	....	....	....	....	Net Material Product	99m
Midyear Estimates																	
	35.58	35.90	36.23	36.57	36.91	37.20	37.46	37.66	37.86	37.96	38.12	38.24	38.36	38.46	38.54	Population	99z

Portugal

		1965	1966	1967	1968	1969	1970	1971	1972	1973	1974	1975	1976	1977	1978	1979
Exchange Rates																*Escudos per SDR:*
Market Rate	aa	28.83	28.98	28.86	28.77	28.65	28.75	29.92	29.31	31.18	30.11	32.16	36.65	48.41	59.94	65.58
																Escudos per US Dollar:
Market Rate	ae	28.83	28.98	28.86	28.77	28.65	28.75	27.56	27.00	25.85	24.60	27.47	31.55	39.86	46.01	49.78
Market Rate	rf	28.75	28.75	28.75	28.75	28.75	28.75	28.36	27.05	24.52	25.41	25.55	30.23	38.28	43.94	48.92
																Escudos per ECU:
ECU Rate	ea	....	....	....	....	....	....	....	....	....	....	....	....	....	....	....
ECU Rate	eb	....	....	....	....	....	....	....	....	....	....	....	....	....	....	....
															Index Numbers (1990=100):	
Market Rate	ahx	494.1	493.4	493.1	495.0	497.9	496.8	602.6	525.7	581.8	560.0	557.9	471.6	373.7	324.7	290.8
Nominal Effective Exchange Rate	nec	....	....	....	....	....	....	....	....	....	....	....	....	....	....	270.1
Real Effective Exchange Rate	rec	....	....	....	....	....	....	....	....	....	....	....	....	....	....	89.6
Fund Position																*Millions of SDRs:*
Quota	2f.s	60	75	75	75	75	75	117	117	117	117	117	117	117	172	172
SDRs	1b.s	—	—	—	—	—	—	—	—	—	—	7	8	4	—	1
Reserve Position in the Fund	1c.s	15	19	19	19	19	19	29	29	29	29	—	—	—	—	—
Total Fund Cred.&Loans Outstg.	2tl	—	—	—	—	—	—	—	—	—	—	—	173	245	203	172
International Liquidity												*Millions of US Dollars Unless Otherwise Indicated:*				
Total Reserves minus Gold	1l.d	362	434	535	507	570	602	945	1,291	1,676	1,161	398	176	366	871	931
SDRs	1b.d	—	—	—	—	—	—	—	—	—	—	8	10	5	—	1
Reserve Position in the Fund	1c.d	15	19	19	19	19	19	32	32	35	36	—	—	—	—	—
Foreign Exchange	1d.d	347	415	516	488	551	583	913	1,259	1,641	1,125	390	166	361	871	930
Bank of Portugal	1da.d	324	379	474	456	516	553	894	1,242	1,622	1,104	355	156	326	762	698
Treasury	1db.d	23	36	42	32	35	30	19	17	19	21	35	10	35	109	232
Gold (Million Fine Troy Ounces)	1ad	16.46	18.37	19.97	24.46	25.00	25.77	26.31	26.88	27.54	27.84	27.72	27.67	24.11	22.13	22.13
Gold (National Valuation)	1an.d	576	643	699	856	875	902	1,000	1,021	1,163	1,193	1,136	1,125	1,025	1,009	1,020
Monetary Authorities: Other Liab.	4..d	8	10	10	10	10	4	4	4	4	4	4	34	878		
Deposit Money Banks: Assets	7a.d	152	178	200	215	274	299	281	298	304	412	347	702	881	996	1,508
Liabilities	7b.d	40	65	48	65	34	41	61	69	85	114	94	600	2,146	2,999	3,628
of which: Liab. to Nonbanks	7bd.d	....	....	....	....	....	....	....	....	....	....	....	2	37	56	32
Monetary Authorities														*Billions of Escudos:*		
Foreign Assets	11	‡29.0	32.2	36.2	39.9	41.9	43.5	52.5	62.4	70.4	54.7	40.1	‡40.6	54.1	81.6	85.7
Claims on Central Government	12a	‡2.3	2.1	2.2	1.9	2.5	2.7	2.7	3.2	3.5	10.7	34.9	‡71.7	134.4	169.4	265.6
Claims on State and Local Govts.	12b	....	....	....	....	....	....	....	....	....	....	....	....	....	....	....
Claims on Deposit Money Banks	12e	1.8	1.7	1.6	1.7	1.9	2.2	1.9	2.0	2.2	3.7	2.3	‡99.7	92.4	73.8	24.4
Claims on Other Financial Insts.	12f	....	....	....	....	....	....	....	....	....	....	....	7.1	10.7	13.2	18.3
of which: Claims on Nonbk.Fin.Ins	12g	....	....	....	....	....	....	....	....	....	....	....	....	....	....	....
Reserve Money	14	‡30.8	32.1	35.2	38.8	41.5	45.9	52.5	62.5	70.6	94.9	130.7	‡139.6	147.3	169.5	223.1
of which: Currency Outside DMBs	14a	‡19.7	19.9	20.3	19.8	26.7	29.7	31.9	36.1	38.3	69.7	109.8	‡109.2	113.3	121.4	142.1
Restricted Deposits	16b	....	....	....	....	....	....	....	....	....	....	....	....	....	....	....
Foreign Liabilities	16c	....	....	....	....	....	....	....	....	....	....	....	1.9	6.2	5.1	10.0
Central Government Deposits	16d	‡4.0	5.2	5.5	5.0	5.4	4.7	5.8	4.1	6.0	3.8	1.0	36.9	58.4	52.6	40.4
Capital Accounts	17a	....	....	....	....	....	....	....	....	....	....	....	‡12.2	22.2	10.9	22.7
Other Items (Net)	17r	‡-.6	.1	.3	.7	6.3	7.1	8.2	10.6	11.1	14.7	33.7	‡-1.2	20.9	56.0	63.6
Deposit Money Banks														*Billions of Escudos:*		
Reserves	20	‡10.7	11.9	14.3	19.0	14.4	15.8	20.0	25.8	31.7	23.8	18.9	‡29.2	33.7	47.5	78.2
Nonreserve Claims on Mon.Auths	20n	....	....	....	....	....	....	....	....	....	....	....	1.9	6.2	7.1	10.0
Foreign Assets	21	4.4	5.1	5.8	6.2	7.9	8.6	7.7	8.1	7.7	10.1	9.5	‡22.2	35.1	45.8	75.7
Claims on Central Government	22a	‡14.3	15.1	15.9	15.3	12.5	13.7	14.6	20.8	21.6	26.1	32.0	‡47.9	48.6	54.1	65.4
Claims on State and Local Govts.	22b	....	....	....	....	....	....	....	....	....	....	....	3.0	3.0	2.7	2.7
Claims on Nonfin.Pub.Enterprises	22c	....	....	....	....	....	....	....	....	....	....	....	2.8	152.6	201.8	233.5
Claims on Private Sector	22d	‡62.4	69.8	76.8	88.9	98.3	116.6	144.2	178.1	238.3	250.1	312.9	‡391.6	346.6	387.7	491.5
Claims on Other Financial Insts.	22f	....	....	....	....	....	....	....	....	....	....	....	12.0	16.2	19.6	16.8
of which: Claims on Nonbk.Fin.Ins	22g	....	....	....	....	....	....	....	....	....	....	....	....	....	....	....
Demand Deposits	24	‡48.7	52.8	57.0	63.9	64.3	62.5	72.4	85.6	126.7	111.4	115.5	‡141.5	168.4	199.1	262.4
Time and Savings Deposits	25	‡20.1	23.6	30.7	38.3	46.2	63.1	84.1	112.5	135.7	159.8	158.2	‡209.9	258.7	331.5	463.9
Money Market Instruments	26aa	....	....	....	....	....	....	....	....	....	....	....	....	....	....	....
Foreign Liabilities	26c	‡1.1	1.9	1.4	1.9	1.0	1.2	1.7	1.9	2.2	2.8	2.6	‡16.3	78.6	128.9	162.2
Long-Term Foreign Liabilities	26cl	....	....	....	....	....	....	....	....	....	....	....	2.7	6.9	9.1	18.4
Central Government Deposits	26d	7.9	7.9	8.0	9.2	10.2	14.3	16.2	17.9	20.2	24.0	32.5	‡29.2	33.4	39.4	50.6
Credit from Monetary Authorities	26g	....	....	....	....	....	....	....	....	....	....	....	99.7	92.4	73.8	24.4
Capital Accounts	27a	‡7.3	8.2	9.8	10.2	10.9	12.2	14.1	18.8	22.4	23.7	24.2	‡35.2	34.8	42.3	48.9
Other Items (Net)	27r	‡6.8	7.5	6.0	6.0	.5	1.4	-2.1	-3.7	-7.9	-11.6	40.4	‡-24.0	-31.1	-57.8	-57.0
Monetary Survey														*Billions of Escudos:*		
Foreign Assets (Net)	31n	32.5	36.3	41.0	44.1	47.9	49.8	58.4	68.6	75.9	62.0	38.8	‡9.5	-47.8	-54.1	-41.2
Domestic Credit	32	76.3	83.2	90.5	102.2	104.6	123.3	148.8	189.9	248.8	303.4	434.5	‡495.2	656.8	798.4	1,020.5
Claims on Central Govt. (Net)	32an	12.6	12.0	12.5	12.2	12.4	15.0	-4.7	2.0	-1.2	9.0	33.4	‡78.2	127.4	173.2	257.8
Claims on State and Local Govts.	32b	....	....	....	....	....	....	....	....	....	....	....	3.0	3.0	2.7	2.7
Claims on Nonfin.Pub.Enterprises	32c	....	....	....	....	....	....	....	....	....	....	....	3.1	152.8	202.0	233.5
Claims on Private Sector	32d	63.7	71.2	77.9	89.9	107.6	126.4	153.5	187.9	250.0	294.4	401.1	‡391.8	346.7	387.7	491.5
Claims on Other Financial Insts.	32f	....	....	....	....	....	....	....	....	....	....	....	19.1	27.0	32.8	35.0
o/w: Claims on Nonbk.Fin.Inst.	32g	....	....	....	....	....	....	....	....	....	....	....	....	....	....	....
Money	34	68.8	73.1	77.9	84.5	93.9	100.5	104.9	122.3	165.6	182.5	227.3	‡251.9	281.9	321.1	407.3
Quasi-Money	35	20.1	23.6	30.7	38.3	51.0	66.1	84.1	112.5	135.7	159.8	158.2	‡209.9	258.7	331.5	463.9
Money Market Instruments	36aa	....	....	....	....	....	....	....	....	....	....	....	....	....	....	....
Long-Term Foreign Liabilities	36cl	....	....	....	....	....	....	....	....	....	....	....	3.1	15.9	42.9	55.9
Other Items (Net)	37r	19.9	22.8	23.0	23.5	22.9	24.7	18.3	23.7	23.4	23.0	87.8	‡39.7	52.5	48.8	52.1
Money plus Quasi-Money	35l	88.9	96.7	108.5	122.8	144.9	166.5	189.0	234.8	301.3	342.3	385.5	‡461.8	540.6	652.6	871.2
Interest Rates														*Percent Per Annum*		
Discount Rate *(End of Period)*	60	2.17	2.50	2.50	2.52	2.75	3.31	3.73	3.77	4.08	5.83	7.42	6.50	9.83	16.33	17.33
Money Market Rate	60b	....	....	....	....	....	....	....	....	....	....	....	....	....	18.42	14.87
Treasury Bill Rate	60c	....	....	....	....	....	....	....	....	....	....	....	....	....	....	....
Deposit Rate	60l	....	....	....	....	....	....	....	....	....	....	....	9.50	12.54	17.67	19.00
Lending Rate	60p	....	....	....	....	....	....	....	....	....	....	....	8.75	12.50	17.58	18.75
Government Bond Yield	61	3.87	3.96	5.00	5.11	5.15	5.28	5.69	6.01	5.50	....	....	9.74	10.80	16.17	16.68

	1980	1981	1982	1983	1984	1985	1986	1987	1988	1989	1990	1991	1992	1993	1994		
End of Period																**Exchange Rates**	
	67.65	75.95	98.25	137.62	165.93	172.99	178.73	184.23	196.97	196.92	190.07	191.94	201.79	242.86	232.25	Market Rate	aa
End of Period (ae) Period Average (rf)																	
	53.04	65.25	89.06	131.45	169.28	157.49	146.12	129.87	146.37	149.84	133.60	134.18	146.76	176.81	159.09	Market Rate	ae
	50.06	61.55	79.47	110.78	146.39	170.39	149.59	140.88	143.95	157.46	142.55	144.48	135.00	160.80	165.99	Market Rate	rf
End of Period (ea) Period Average (eb)																	
	....	....	....	....	....	140.28	156.39	169.39	171.69	177.90	183.20	179.31	177.35	197.20	195.17	ECU Rate	ea
	....	....	....	....	....	....	148.84	162.49	169.19	173.32	181.43	178.83	174.44	187.80	196.37	ECU Rate	eb
Period Averages																	
	284.2	232.1	181.4	130.9	97.8	83.6	95.1	101.0	99.0	90.4	100.0	98.7	105.6	88.8	85.9	Market Rate	ahx
	262.4	255.7	225.4	178.8	148.2	131.3	119.3	110.4	104.5	101.2	100.0	100.3	104.0	96.4	91.8	Nominal Effective Exchange Rate	nec
	91.1	96.3	95.7	88.9	90.3	91.3	90.5	89.2	89.8	93.8	100.0	106.8	116.6	111.7	109.3	Real Effective Exchange Rate	rec
End of Period																**Fund Position**	
	258	258	258	377	377	377	377	377	377	377	377	377	558	558	558	Quota	2f.s
	—	9	2	1	13	16	54	56	3	1	40	68	34	42	48	SDRs	1b.s
	35	49	49	30	30	30	30	30	30	95	124	189	228	219	231	Reserve Position in the Fund	1c.s
	94	47	10	355	572	572	572	373	—	—	—	—	—	—	—	Total Fund Cred.&Loans Outstg.	2tl
End of Period																**International Liquidity**	
	795	534	447	385	516	1,395	1,456	3,327	5,127	9,952	14,485	20,629	19,129	15,840	15,513	Total Reserves minus Gold	1l.d
	—	10	2	1	12	17	66	80	4	2	57	98	46	58	71	SDRs	1b.d
	44	57	54	31	29	33	36	42	40	125	176	270	314	301	337	Reserve Position in the Fund	1c.d
	751	467	391	353	475	1,345	1,354	3,205	5,083	9,826	14,252	20,261	18,769	15,481	15,106	Foreign Exchange	1d.d
	602	399	371	290	390	1,277	1,287	3,192	5,075	9,823	14,230	20,221	18,744	15,442	15,095	Bank of Portugal	1dad
	149	68	20	63	85	68	67	13	8	3	22	40	25	39	11	Treasury	1dbd
	22.17	22.14	22.09	20.43	20.30	20.23	20.16	20.06	16.07	16.05	15.83	15.87	16.06	16.06	16.07	Gold (Million Fine Troy Ounces)	1ad
	5,652	5,644	5,631	5,209	5,174	5,159[e]	5,139	5,114	5,190	5,184	5,113	5,125	5,188	5,189	5,185	Gold (National Valuation)	1and
	222	251	277	378	201	6	5	6	I10	21	24	12	20	18	91	Monetary Authorities: Other Liab.	4..d
	1,739	1,553	1,537	1,704	1,843	1,925	1,929	2,738	4,181	4,660	5,495	6,961	9,627	14,887	21,023	Deposit Money Banks: Assets	7a.d
	5,163	6,332	6,906	6,689	7,057	8,781	10,057	11,734	I11,750	13,685	17,815	21,218	23,203	23,577	31,620	Liabilities	7b.d
	41	40	40	30	39	46	78	139	I170	228	395	380	I1,113	1,038	1,173	*of which:* Liab. to Nonbanks	7bdd
End of Period																**Monetary Authorities**	
	334.5	399.4	540.6	730.5	952.5	1,023.1	956.3	1,098.7	I1,517.5	2,283.0	2,622.3	3,449.3	3,568.2	3,706.7	3,294.8	Foreign Assets	11
	190.6	293.7	422.7	562.3	782.7	1,047.0	1,177.7	1,159.0	I1,073.4	1,071.9	962.2	259.3	290.6	266.5	242.4	Claims on Central Government	12a
	—	—	—	—	5.0	10.0	24.7	27.5	I27.5	27.5	30.9	44.9	44.7	46.6	46.1	Claims on State and Local Govts.	12b
	13.6	28.1	18.5	42.7	31.9	56.0	72.8	52.0	I17.7	112.0	9.5	150.6	9.5	266.1	542.1	Claims on Deposit Money Banks	12e
	19.7	20.7	26.9	35.8	41.1	38.8	33.9	15.1	I12.2	9.3	5.8	9.5	8.9	8.6	17.4	Claims on Other Financial Insts.	12f
	....	....	....	....	....	....	....	....	12.2	9.3	5.8	8.0	8.2	8.1	8.9	*of which: Claims on Nonbk.Fin.Ins*	12g
	272.1	370.5	478.8	540.3	557.9	595.7	667.4	815.0	I943.5	1,856.4	1,997.9	2,475.6	2,740.5	3,001.3	1,249.4	Reserve Money	14
	165.2	188.4	219.5	240.1	267.4	319.0	399.3	457.7	I509.5	577.3	623.9	683.1	708.2	752.9	796.3	*of which: Currency Outside DMBs*	14a
	62.3	76.0	98.2	85.8	375.1	772.8	1,008.9	979.6	I919.6	775.3	818.2	245.1	346.7	23.3	1,732.9	Restricted Deposits	16b
	18.1	20.0	25.6	98.5	128.9	99.9	102.9	69.5	I1.5	3.2	3.3	1.6	2.9	3.1	14.4	Foreign Liabilities	16c
	33.2	48.9	36.5	70.7	60.4	101.1	12.5	91.6	I145.8	252.9	356.1	848.4	573.9	539.8	510.6	Central Government Deposits	16d
	101.0	106.1	110.0	144.6	107.2	263.7	398.0	395.4	I482.0	474.9	385.6	267.3	184.0	493.9	395.7	Capital Accounts	17a
	71.8	120.5	259.6	431.4	583.7	341.8	75.7	1.2	I155.9	141.0	69.8	75.7	74.8	233.0	240.8	Other Items (Net)	17r
End of Period																**Deposit Money Banks**	
	106.1	180.4	255.5	297.4	287.0	273.7	256.4	352.4	I424.1	1,272.1	1,354.1	1,734.3	1,938.0	2,135.5	415.6	Reserves	20
	62.3	76.0	98.2	85.8	375.1	772.8	1,008.9	979.6	I920.6	775.3	818.2	109.5	346.7	23.3	1,741.7	Nonreserve Claims on Mon.Auths	20n
	92.5	101.6	137.4	224.3	312.5	357.3	339.3	403.4	I612.0	698.2	734.1	934.0	1,412.8	2,632.1	3,344.7	Foreign Assets	21
	79.3	136.6	175.7	218.5	254.5	447.1	560.1	907.1	I1,322.5	1,401.9	1,717.9	3,209.8	3,156.1	3,159.1	3,851.3	Claims on Central Government	22a
	5.0	15.3	30.2	42.6	43.9	47.3	51.9	55.0	I69.4	70.3	104.0	111.8	134.5	170.5	176.7	Claims on State and Local Govts.	22b
	263.5	298.2	350.2	488.4	614.6	607.4	667.4	619.9	I645.3	614.9	678.6	772.0	687.9	657.1	624.1	Claims on Nonfin.Pub.Enterprises	22c
	672.7	892.0	1,116.7	1,288.6	1,500.5	1,689.4	1,892.6	2,024.3	I2,764.7	2,944.8	4,002.0	5,014.8	6,164.7	7,176.8	7,888.6	Claims on Private Sector	22d
	17.9	15.5	16.9	20.3	21.8	25.9	39.3	76.1	I103.5	135.4	285.1	485.7	700.1	801.8	965.2	Claims on Other Financial Insts.	22f
	....	....	....	....	....	....	....	....	103.3	134.9	280.6	479.6	688.3	792.9	957.4	*of which: Claims on Nonbk.Fin.Ins*	22g
	331.4	350.3	404.8	436.4	513.1	678.3	948.5	1,074.3	I1,284.5	1,319.2	1,810.8	2,130.6	2,613.8	2,908.7	3,115.3	Demand Deposits	24
	628.4	850.2	1,086.1	1,316.4	1,705.5	2,083.9	2,330.8	2,677.8	I2,947.3	3,362.6	3,801.1	4,928.4	6,136.5	6,937.5	7,684.2	Time and Savings Deposits	25
	....	....	....	....	....	....	....	....	182.3	141.2	124.7	356.8	167.4	76.0	163.3	Money Market Instruments	26aa
	246.6	366.7	508.3	675.8	916.3	1,157.1	1,283.8	1,371.1	I1,585.5	1,928.9	2,266.1	2,719.2	3,235.6	3,947.0	4,747.3	Foreign Liabilities	26c
	27.3	46.4	106.7	203.5	278.3	225.7	185.7	152.7	I134.4	121.6	113.9	128.0	169.7	221.6	283.2	Long-Term Foreign Liabilities	26cl
	58.7	69.1	90.3	102.5	136.0	209.9	280.6	251.7	I259.8	331.8	397.7	481.9	411.8	434.4	511.9	Central Government Deposits	26d
	13.6	28.1	18.5	42.7	31.9	56.0	72.8	52.0	I17.7	112.0	9.5	150.6	9.5	266.1	542.7	Credit from Monetary Authorities	26g
	65.3	84.8	117.4	117.4	157.1	198.1	291.6	436.0	I667.5	852.4	1,196.1	1,610.9	1,970.2	2,296.2	2,426.7	Capital Accounts	27a
	-72.1	-80.0	-151.5	-228.8	-328.2	-388.0	-577.8	-597.9	I-217.0	-257.7	-25.9	-134.3	-173.7	-331.2	-466.4	Other Items (Net)	27r
End of Period																**Monetary Survey**	
	162.3	114.3	144.1	180.5	219.9	123.4	-91.1	61.5	I542.5	1,049.2	1,087.0	1,662.6	1,742.5	2,388.7	1,877.8	Foreign Assets (Net)	31n
	1,156.7	1,554.1	2,012.4	2,483.4	3,067.8	3,602.1	4,154.5	4,540.6	I5,612.9	5,691.3	7,047.4	8,592.1	10,227.9	11,340.5	12,818.6	Domestic Credit	32
	178.0	312.4	471.5	607.6	840.9	1,183.2	1,444.7	1,722.9	I1,990.2	1,889.1	1,926.4	2,138.8	2,460.9	2,451.4	3,071.2	Claims on Central Govt. (Net)	32an
	5.0	15.3	30.2	42.6	48.9	57.3	76.6	82.5	I97.0	97.9	134.9	156.7	179.1	217.0	222.9	Claims on State and Local Govts.	32b
	263.5	298.2	350.2	488.4	614.6	607.4	667.4	619.9	I645.3	614.9	693.2	786.6	702.4	671.6	639.2	Claims on Nonfin.Pub.Enterprises	32c
	672.7	892.0	1,116.7	1,288.6	1,500.5	1,689.4	1,892.6	2,024.3	I2,764.7	2,944.8	4,002.0	5,014.8	6,176.3	7,190.0	7,902.8	Claims on Private Sector	32d
	37.6	36.2	43.8	56.1	62.8	64.7	73.2	91.1	I115.7	144.7	291.0	495.1	709.1	810.5	982.6	Claims on Other Financial Insts.	32f
	....	....	....	....	....	....	....	....	115.5	144.1	286.4	487.7	696.5	801.0	966.3	*o/w: Claims on Nonbk.Fin.Inst.*	32g
	497.3	540.4	628.1	679.3	784.0	1,000.3	1,359.4	1,537.0	I1,803.9	1,903.4	2,454.6	2,871.8	3,416.4	3,774.5	3,949.1	Money	34
	628.4	850.2	1,086.1	1,316.4	1,705.5	2,083.9	2,330.8	2,677.8	I2,947.3	3,362.6	3,801.1	4,928.4	6,136.5	6,937.5	7,684.2	Quasi-Money	35
	....	....	....	....	....	....	....	....	182.3	141.2	124.7	356.8	167.4	76.0	163.3	Money Market Instruments	36aa
	66.8	88.2	154.7	258.6	327.5	261.6	207.4	161.4	I134.4	121.6	113.9	128.0	169.7	221.6	283.2	Long-Term Foreign Liabilities	36cl
	126.5	189.5	287.5	409.5	470.5	379.7	165.8	226.1	I1,087.5	1,210.6	1,640.0	1,969.7	2,081.5	2,719.7	2,617.8	Other Items (Net)	37r
	1,125.8	1,390.6	1,714.2	1,995.7	2,489.5	3,084.1	3,690.2	4,214.7	I4,751.2	5,266.0	6,255.7	7,800.2	9,552.9	10,712.0	11,633.2	Money plus Quasi-Money	35l
Percent Per Annum																**Interest Rates**	
	18.00	18.00	18.75	23.17	25.00	23.50	17.00	14.96	13.71	14.33	14.50	14.50	14.50	13.71	11.63	Discount Rate *(End of Period)*	60
	9.95	9.24	12.42	18.24	21.27	20.17	I14.52	13.69	12.34	12.84	13.73	15.81	I17.48	13.25	10.62	Money Market Rate	60b
	12.37	13.48	14.37	18.14	21.15	20.90	I15.56	13.89	12.97	....	13.52	14.19	12.88	....	....	Treasury Bill Rate	60c
	19.00	19.25	21.00	26.08	28.00	25.08	17.13	14.46	13.21	13.00	13.58	14.63	14.59	11.06	8.37	Deposit Rate	60l
	18.75	20.13	23.00	27.88	29.42	27.29	19.63	I18.92	I17.53	19.59	21.71	I25.02	20.43	16.48	15.01	Lending Rate	60p
	16.68	16.71	16.79	19.22	21.50	20.75	15.54	15.02	13.87	14.74	15.17	17.77	15.38	12.45	10.83	Government Bond Yield	61

Portugal

		1965	1966	1967	1968	1969	1970	1971	1972	1973	1974	1975	1976	1977	1978	1979
Prices and Production																*Index Numbers (1990=100):*
Share Prices	62	...	...	...	...	...	...	...	...	...	...	...	...	...	...	...
Prices: Home & Import Goods ('85=100)	63	6.1	6.4	6.6	6.9	7.1	7.4	7.5	7.9	8.8	11.4	12.9	15.3	19.7	25.9	33.6
Home Goods ('85=100)	63a	6.0	6.3	6.7	7.0	7.4	7.9	8.0	8.7	9.7	12.2	13.1	15.8	20.4	28.7	37.9
Consumer Prices	64	2.9	3.1	3.3	I3.5	3.7	3.9	4.2	4.6	5.0	6.4	7.7	9.1	11.6	14.3	17.6
Wages: Daily Earnings (Mfg.)	65ey	...	...	...	...	...	...	...	...	...	...	...	...	...	...	15.5
Industrial Production	66	...	...	...	...	...	...	...	...	...	...	...	...	...	...	...
International Transactions																*Billions of Escudos*
Exports	70	16.8	18.0	20.0	21.1	23.7	27.2	29.7	35.1	44.8	57.5	49.3	54.7	75.7	106.5	170.5
Imports, cif	71	25.8	29.1	29.2	30.0	35.4	44.7	50.9	59.6	73.2	113.3	97.5	127.8	182.7	230.1	320.1
Imports, fob	71.v	23.0	26.0	26.1	26.8	31.6	39.9	45.5	53.2	65.7	102.6	88.4	115.1	165.6	208.6	290.2
																1990=100
Volume of Exports	72	...	...	...	...	...	...	...	...	...	...	...	...	...	...	...
Volume of Imports	73	...	...	...	...	...	...	...	...	...	...	...	...	...	...	...
Export Prices	76	...	...	...	...	...	...	...	...	...	...	...	...	...	...	...
Import Prices	76.x	6.3	6.5	6.7	6.9	6.9	6.9	7.0	7.2	8.2	10.7	12.0	14.3	19.8	23.7	28.8
Balance of Payments																*Millions of US Dollars:*
Goods: Exports f.o.b.	78aa d											1,942	1,825	2,564	2,782	3,608
Goods: Imports f.o.b.	78ab d											-3,544	-3,960	-4,528	-4,783	-6,183
Trade Balance	78ac d											-1,603	-2,136	-1,964	-2,001	-2,575
Services: Credit	78ad d											941	756	840	1,076	1,592
Services: Debit	78ae d											-1,110	-730	-785	-849	-1,128
Balance on Goods and Services	78af d											-1,772	-2,110	-1,909	-1,774	-2,110
Income: Credit	78ag d											115	47	67	87	133
Income: Debit	78ah d											-139	-184	-249	-410	-553
Balance on Goods, Serv., & Inc.	78ai d											-1,796	-2,247	-2,090	-2,098	-2,531
Current Transfers, n.i.e.: Credit	78aj d											1,103	1,007	1,222	1,718	2,536
Current Transfers: Debit	78ak d											-62	-42	-89	-83	-59
Current Account, n.i.e.	78al d											-755	-1,282	-957	-463	-54
Capital Account, n.i.e.: Credit	78ba d											—	—	—	—	—
Capital Account: Debit	78bb d											—	—	—	—	—
Capital Account, n.i.e.	78bc d											—	—	—	—	—
Direct Investment Abroad	78bd d											-8	-5	-3	-6	8
Dir. Invest. in Rep. Econ., n.i.e.	78be d											115	63	58	66	78
Portfolio Investment Assets	78bf d											-1	1	1	1	1
Portfolio Investment Liab., n.i.e.	78bg d											-5	7	1	-4	-4
Other Investment Assets	78bh d											-15	-157	-231	-218	-503
Other Investment Liab., n.i.e.	78bi d											-227	246	866	1,220	152
Financial Account, n.i.e.	78bj d											-140	155	692	1,059	-267
Net Errors and Omissions	78ca d											-150	58	-70	-293	597
Overall Balance	78cb d											-1,045	-1,069	-334	304	276
Reserves and Related Items	79da d											1,045	1,069	334	-304	-276
Reserve Assets	79db d											725	168	-171	-474	-25
Use of Fund Credit and Loans	79dc d											—	201	84	-54	-40
Liabs.Constit.For.Auth.Reserves	79dd d											320	665	422	197	-210
Exceptional Financing	79de d												35	—	28	—
Government Finance																*Billions of Escudos:*
Deficit (-) or Surplus	80						-3.1	-2.2	-5.6	-3.6	-8.9	I-31.8	-54.0	-40.9	-92.8	-100.5
Revenue	81						27.8	30.0	33.8	39.9	47.2	I96.0	127.4	176.7	217.4	272.1
Grants Received	81z						...	...	...	...	...	I—	.1	1.5	.6	1.0
Expenditure	82						27.4	30.6	33.8	41.3	55.4	I123.5	172.8	210.0	283.8	352.8
Lending Minus Repayments	83						1.4	1.6	1.5	1.3	1.4	I4.3	8.7	9.1	27.0	20.8
Unclass. Transactions (Net)	83x						2.0	-.1	4.1	.9	-.7	...	...	...	...	...
Financing																
Domestic	84a						2.5	1.2	3.5	3.9	6.2	I32.3	52.9	41.3	73.1	95.1
Foreign	85a						.6	.8	-.3	.2	-.2	I-.6	1.2	-.4	19.7	5.4
Use of Cash Balances	87						-.1	.1	2.5	-.5	2.9	...	...	...	...	...
Debt: Escudos	88b	11.02	12.12	11.87	11.92	12.34	13.10	12.42	15.32	39.62	48.91	90.09	147.18	...	...	...
Held By: Bk of Portugal	88ba	1.35	1.42	1.45	1.41	1.55	1.69	1.63	1.54	1.74	8.73	44.08	68.79			
Commercial Banks	88bb	3.93	3.91	3.90	3.85	3.86	4.10	3.87	4.84	8.82	8.49	7.88	14.23			
Savings Banks	88bc	2.13	2.20	2.30	2.27	2.44	2.62	2.59	3.53	6.36	6.10	5.40	8.20			
Others	88bd	3.61	4.59	4.22	4.39	4.49	4.69	4.33	5.41	22.70	25.59	32.73	55.96			
Intragovernmental Debt	88s	9.26	8.94	10.08	10.86	11.56	12.16	13.64	13.48	13.22	13.14	9.58	3.48			
Held by: Social Insur. System	88sz	7.99	7.71	8.90	9.73	10.52	11.23	12.81	12.80	12.62	12.62	9.12	3.12			
National Accounts																*Billions of Escudos*
Exports of Goods & Services	90c	25.9	29.9	32.4	32.8	35.3	41.2	47.7	56.9	75.4	91.2	76.9	81.7	104.7	138.8	232.2
Government Consumption	91f	13.2	14.6	17.7	19.6	21.2	25.2	27.7	31.8	36.1	47.9	56.5	64.4	89.7	111.9	143.9
Gross Fixed Capital Formation	93e	22.5	26.7	32.4	33.4	38.0	43.5	52.0	66.5	75.6	88.2	97.8	117.5	165.8	219.8	264.0
Increase/Decrease(-) in Stocks	93i	5.0	1.6	1.0	1.9	.8	4.0	4.0	2.4	7.3	8.6	-21.3	-1.8	15.9	23.2	51.9
Private Consumption	96f	75.1	82.8	88.0	97.9	108.5	119.2	131.7	148.4	183.0	246.5	290.9	351.7	452.3	540.1	665.2
Imports of Goods & Services	98c	-31.8	-35.2	-36.9	-39.2	-43.3	-52.9	-61.2	-71.0	-95.2	-143.1	-123.6	-144.6	-202.7	-246.6	-361.6
Gross Domestic Product	99b	109.9	120.4	134.6	146.4	160.5	180.2	201.9	235.0	282.2	339.3	377.2	468.9	625.8	787.3	995.5
Net Factor Inc/Pmts(-) Abroad	98.n	.7	.3	.6	.6	.9	.9	.4	.6	2.4	3.8	-.4	-4.6	-7.9	15.6	-22.3
Gross Nat'l Expenditure = GNP	99a	110.6	120.7	135.2	147.0	161.4	181.1	202.3	235.6	284.6	343.1	376.8	464.2	617.9	771.6	971.9
Nat'l Income, Market Prices	99e	104.9	114.5	128.4	139.3	152.9	171.7	191.8	223.3	271.3	328.0	359.4	448.8	591.8	735.8	927.7
Gross Dom. Prod. 1990 Prices	99b.p	...	3,135.8	3,383.0	3,680.8	3,752.2	4,100.7	4,371.7	4,723.1	I5,250.2	5,310.6	5,079.7	5,429.7	I5,733.9	5,928.2	6,292.6
GDP Deflator (1990=100)	99bi p	...	3.8	4.0	4.0	4.3	4.4	4.6	5.0	5.4	6.4	7.4	8.6	10.9	13.3	15.8
																Millions:
Population	99z	8.78	8.75	8.72	8.69	9.10	9.04	8.99	8.97	8.98	8.99	9.43	9.67	9.74	9.80	I9.66

Monetary Authorities: ℐ Beginning in 1976, data are based on fully sectored and consolidated accounts, not available before that date. ℐ Annual data beginning in 1965, quarterly data beginning in 1968, and monthly data beginning in December 1976 are based upon improved sectorization in national source data for the Bank of Portugal and commercial and savings banks. ℐ From December 1988, data reflect major changes in statistical reporting arrangements in Portugal.

Deposit Money Banks: ℐ See note to section 10.

Interest Rates: *Money Market Rate:* ℐ Beginning in August 1985, data relate to deposits for up to five days. Prior to that date, they relate to deposits of up to three days. ℐ Beginning in July 1991, weighted average interbank rate for overnight transactions.

Lending Rate: ℐ Beginning in March 20, 1987, maximum interest rate legally authorized on all loans. ℐ Beginning in November 7, 1988, rate that the banks intend to apply during the reporting week to 90-day operations with their average clients. ℐ Beginning in October 1990, rate charged by deposit money banks on 91- to 180-day loans and advances to nonfinancial private enterprises.

Government Finance: ℐ Beginning in 1975, data are as reported in the *Government Finance Statistics Yearbook* and relate to the consolidated central government. However, data on outstanding debt are derived from the *Annual Report* of the Finance Ministry.

Portugal
182

	1980	1981	1982	1983	1984	1985	1986	1987	1988	1989	1990	1991	1992	1993	1994		
Period Averages																**Prices and Production**	
	....	....	....	....	....	....	....	....	99.6	103.7	100.0	85.0	75.0	88.4	116.1	Share Prices	62
	35.8	43.5	55.5	64.7	82.5	100.0	109.2	....	....	....	....	....	....	....	....	Prices: Home & Import Goods('85=100).	63
	36.4	45.0	53.5	65.2	83.3	100.0	109.1	....	....	....	....	....	....	....	....	Home Goods ('85=100)	63a
	20.6	24.7	30.3	I37.9	49.0	58.5	65.3	71.5	78.3	88.2	100.0	I111.4	121.3	129.6	136.0	Consumer Prices	64
	19.5	23.4	32.7	38.0	45.8	54.2	63.6	72.4	76.0	86.2	100.0	113.5	....	....	....	Wages: Daily Earnings (Mfg.)	65ey
	....	64.3	69.3	71.5	73.6	I74.4	79.3	82.9	86.0	91.3	100.0	100.0	97.3	90.7	....	Industrial Production	66
Billions of Escudos																**International Transactions**	
	232.2	254.9	331.7	508.6	760.6	967.4	1,082.3	1,311.0	1,582.0	2,015.7	2,335.8	2,352.5	2,473.9	2,474.0	2,900.0	Exports	70
	465.8	599.7	754.0	899.4	1,160.6	1,302.8	1,442.5	1,965.3	2,581.0	3,024.0	3,603.0	3,811.0	4,093.0	3,889.0	4,404.0	Imports, cif	71
	422.2	543.6	683.4	817.3	1,052.3	1,181.1	1,307.8	1,781.8	2,340.0	2,741.6	3,266.5	3,455.1	3,710.8	3,525.8	3,992.7	Imports, fob	71.v
1990=100																	
	....	....	....	44.4	50.9	56.3	60.7	67.8	74.1	89.1	I100.0	100.6	107.0	....	....	Volume of Exports	72
	....	....	....	43.2	40.7	43.4	51.7	66.2	80.8	87.7	I100.0	106.0	118.6	....	....	Volume of Imports	73
	....	....	....	49.1	64.1	74.1	76.6	83.0	91.6	97.1	I100.0	100.2	98.1	....	....	Export Prices	76
	33.7	38.9	45.7	I59.7	80.6	86.3	78.9	83.8	89.7	96.6	I100.0	100.2	95.2	....	....	Import Prices	76.x
Minus Sign Indicates Debit																Balance of Payments	
	4,668	4,185	4,194	4,646	5,246	5,749	7,265	9,335	11,015	12,843	16,458	16,391	18,348	15,695	....	Goods: Exports f.o.b.	78aa d
	−8,611	−11,132	−8,953	−7,631	−7,297	−7,179	−8,876	−12,847	−16,392	−17,585	−23,141	−24,079	−27,735	−22,330	....	Goods: Imports f.o.b.	78ab d
	−3,943	−6,948	−4,759	−2,985	−2,051	−1,430	−1,611	−3,513	−5,377	−4,742	−6,684	−7,688	−9,387	−6,636	....	Trade Balance	78ac d
	2,006	1,946	1,536	1,478	1,656	1,931	2,425	3,165	3,418	3,789	5,096	5,231	5,497	6,449	....	Services: Credit	78ad d
	−1,525	−1,639	−1,462	−1,254	−1,244	−1,269	−1,585	−2,157	−2,668	−2,830	−4,005	−4,420	−4,732	−5,665	....	Services: Debit	78ae d
	−3,462	−6,640	−4,685	−2,761	−1,638	−768	−772	−2,505	−4,627	−3,784	−5,592	−6,877	−8,621	−5,851	....	Balance on Goods and Services	78af d
	173	206	153	167	195	277	300	414	477	719	1,360	1,550	2,067	2,442	....	Income: Credit	78ag d
	−781	−1,141	−1,405	−1,212	−1,355	−1,373	−1,276	−1,245	−1,238	−1,322	−1,457	−1,364	−1,456	−2,359	....	Income: Debit	78ah d
	−4,070	−7,575	−5,937	−3,806	−2,798	−1,864	−1,748	−3,336	−5,388	−4,387	−5,689	−6,691	−8,010	−5,768	....	Balance on Goods, Serv., & Inc.	78ai d
	3,047	2,918	2,718	2,245	2,257	2,329	3,306	4,365	4,946	5,227	6,433	7,237	9,344	8,425	....	Current Transfers, n.i.e.: Credit	78aj d
	−41	−29	−40	−71	−82	−85	−392	−594	−624	−687	−926	−1,263	−1,518	−1,710	....	Current Transfers: Debit	78ak d
	−1,064	−4,686	−3,258	−1,632	−623	380	1,166	435	−1,066	153	−181	−716	−184	947	....	Current Account, n.i.e.	78al d
	—	—	—	—	—	—	—	—	—	—	—	—	—	—	....	Capital Account, n.i.e.: Credit	78ba d
	—	—	—	—	—	—	—	—	—	—	—	—	—	—	....	Capital Account: Debit	78bb d
	—	—	—	—	—	—	—	—	—	—	—	—	—	—	....	Capital Account, n.i.e.	78bc d
	−14	−16	−8	−17	−7	−22	—	10	−80	−84	−163	−463	−687	−165	....	Direct Investment Abroad	78bd d
	157	174	144	146	195	274	238	466	922	1,737	2,610	2,448	1,873	1,301	....	Dir. Invest. in Rep. Econ., n.i.e.	78be d
	2	8	1	1	—	1	—	—	—	−27	—	—	−379	−2,169	....	Portfolio Investment Assets	78bf d
	−9	−3	153	132	149	123	404	816	1,841	1,050	961	1,895	−2,685	1,638	....	Portfolio Investment Liab., n.i.e.	78bg d
	−259	1,017	671	−946	−572	−385	−1,095	−87	−1,145	−7	−2,442	−1,511	−1,923	−530	....	Other Investment Assets	78bh d
	327	1,657	2,315	1,065	895	791	−979	−517	−1,218	1,310	1,598	2,168	2,851	−3,699	....	Other Investment Liab., n.i.e.	78bi d
	203	2,837	3,276	381	660	781	−1,432	689	293	4,005	2,563	4,537	−950	−3,624	....	Financial Account, n.i.e.	78bj d
	1,218	1,707	100	−11	−31	−253	156	653	1,640	497	1,160	1,893	978	−171	....	Net Errors and Omissions	78ca d
	357	−142	118	−1,262	6	908	−111	1,777	867	4,654	3,542	5,713	−156	−2,847	....	Overall Balance	78cb d
	−357	142	−118	1,262	−6	−908	111	−1,777	−867	−4,654	−3,542	−5,713	156	2,847	....	Reserves and Related Items	79da d
	107	167	56	687	−127	−707	111	−1,521	−365	−4,654	−3,542	−5,713	156	2,847	....	Reserve Assets	79db d
	−102	−55	−42	366	221	—	—	−256	−502	—	—	—	—	—	....	Use of Fund Credit and Loans	79dc d
	−362	29	−132	210	−100	−201	—	—	—	—	—	—	—	—	....	Liabs.Constit.For.Auth.Reserves	79dd d
	....	....	....	....	....	....	....	....	....	....	....	....	....	....	....	Exceptional Financing	79de d
Year Ending December 31																**Government Finance**	
	−121.5	−179.6	−195.0	−219.7	−272.4	−522.0	−543.2	−538.8	−523.0	−287.1	−449.6	−666.8	−289.9	....	....	Deficit (−) or Surplus	80
	377.2	480.9	603.5	809.8	951.4	1,182.3	1,553.9	1,768.5	2,030.5	2,726.4	3,215.9	3,869.5	4,594.5	....	....	Revenue	81
	2.9	1.5	1.2	1.9	3.9	5.1	56.6	94.3	105.9	140.7	153.4	259.1	429.9	....	....	Grants Received	81z
	475.9	620.2	751.0	974.1	1,141.7	1,626.6	2,033.5	2,245.0	2,492.9	3,146.2	3,828.9	4,722.6	5,527.0	....	....	Expenditure	82
	25.7	41.8	48.7	57.3	86.0	82.8	120.2	156.6	166.5	8.0	−10.0	72.8	−212.7	....	....	Lending Minus Repayments	83
	....	....	....	....	....	....	....	....	....	....	....	....	....	....	....	Unclass. Transactions (Net)	83x
																Financing	
	93.8	141.8	141.9	143.2	174.8	465.5	589.2	466.3	546.4	457.7	582.0	806.3	296.4	....	....	Domestic	84a
	27.7	37.8	53.1	76.5	97.6	56.5	−46.0	72.5	−23.4	−170.6	−132.4	−139.5	−6.7	....	....	Foreign	85a
	....	....	....	....	....	....	....	....	....	....	....	....	....	....	....	Use of Cash Balances	87
																Debt: Escudos	88b
	....	....	....	....	....	....	....	....	....	....	....	....	....	....	....	Held By: Bk of Portugal	88ba
	....	....	....	....	....	....	....	....	....	....	....	....	....	....	....	Commercial Banks	88bb
	....	....	....	....	....	....	....	....	....	....	....	....	....	....	....	Savings Banks	88bc
	....	....	....	....	....	....	....	....	....	....	....	....	....	....	....	Others	88bd
	....	....	....	....	....	....	....	....	....	....	....	....	....	....	....	Intragovernmental Debt	88s
	....	....	....	....	....	....	....	....	....	....	....	....	....	....	....	Held by: Social Insur. System	88sz
Billions of Escudos																**National Accounts**	
	298.5	338.6	431.7	644.5	933.9	1,158.5	1,279.9	1,525.1	1,841.4	2,320.6	2,684.2	2,704.8	2,821.1	....	....	Exports of Goods & Services	90c
	187.4	231.2	282.3	360.0	433.0	558.8	693.2	803.5	970.5	1,168.5	1,448.5	1,797.8	2,114.2	....	....	Government Consumption	91f
	358.8	463.0	574.8	671.5	663.7	767.9	977.0	1,250.9	1,611.2	1,885.0	2,243.3	2,574.9	2,981.2	....	....	Gross Fixed Capital Formation	93e
	72.7	116.5	112.5	−.8	−37.7	−40.8	13.6	167.8	179.8	239.2	284.3	254.9	209.9	....	....	Increase/Decrease(−) in Stocks	93i
	848.9	1,011.6	1,257.6	1,610.4	2,055.5	2,491.4	2,989.4	3,501.1	4,088.5	4,747.0	5,614.3	6,548.2	7,454.8	....	....	Private Consumption	96f
	−510.3	−659.7	−808.5	−983.9	−1,232.6	−1,411.9	−1,532.6	−2,073.8	−2,688.9	−3,183.1	−3,714.1	−3,945.1	−4,238.2	....	....	Imports of Goods & Services	98c
	1,256.0	1,501.1	1,850.4	2,301.7	2,815.7	3,523.9	4,420.4	5,174.7	6,002.8	7,177.2	8,560.6	9,935.5	11,343.0	....	....	Gross Domestic Product	99b
	−32.6	−61.0	−103.0	−119.5	−177.3	−196.4	−151.6	−130.8	−125.8	−113.1	−34.1	10.8	81.7	....	....	Net Factor Inc/Pmts(−) Abroad	98.n
	1,225.4	1,440.1	1,747.4	2,182.2	2,638.4	3,327.5	4,268.8	5,043.9	5,876.9	7,064.0	8,526.5	9,948.0	11,424.7	....	....	Gross Nat'l Expenditure = GNP	99a
	1,169.5	1,376.9	1,665.4	2,061.0	2,506.7	3,176.7								....	....	Nat'l Income, Market Prices	
	6,595.1	6,678.2	6,817.3	6,803.8	6,680.2	6,880.9	7,165.9	7,534.8	7,837.1	8,220.1	8,560.6	8,744.2	8,839.8	....	....	Gross Dom. Prod. 1990 Prices	99b.p
	19.0	22.5	27.1	33.8	42.2	51.2	61.7	68.7	76.6	87.3	100.0	113.6	128.3	....	....	GDP Deflator (1990=100)	99bi p
Midyear Estimates																	
	9.77	9.86	9.86	9.88	9.90	9.91	9.91	9.91	9.90	9.89	9.88	9.86	9.86	9.86	....	Population	99z

Qatar
453

		1965	1966	1967	1968	1969	1970	1971	1972	1973	1974	1975	1976	1977	1978	1979
Exchange Rates															*Riyals per SDR:*	
Official Rate	aa	4.7619e	4.7619	4.7619	4.7619	4.7619	4.7619	4.7619	4.7619	4.7619	4.8330	4.6679	4.5989	4.8100	5.0008	4.8807
															Riyals per US Dollar:	
Official Rate	ae	4.7619e	4.7619	4.7619	4.7619	4.7619	4.7619	4.3860	4.3860	3.9474	3.9474	3.9874	3.9583	3.9598	3.8385	3.7050
Official Rate	rf	....	4.7619	4.7619	4.7619	4.7619	4.7619	4.7480	4.3860	3.9963	3.9474	3.9307e	3.9634	3.9590	3.8769	3.7733
															Index Numbers (1990=100):	
Official Rate	ah x	....	76.4	76.4	76.4	76.4	76.4	76.7	83.0	91.1	92.2	92.6e	91.8	91.9	93.9	96.5
Nominal Effective Exchange Rate	ne c	....	....	....	....	....	....	....	....	....	....	....	....	....	....	97.2
Fund Position															*Millions of SDRs:*	
Quota	2f. s	....	....	....	....	....	....	....	20.0	20.0	20.0	20.0	20.0	20.0	40.0	40.0
SDRs	1b. s								—	—	—	—	—	—	—	4.2
Reserve Position in the Fund	1c. s	....	....	....	....	....	....	....	5.0	5.0	6.1	13.1	16.2	14.5	14.7	13.6
International Liquidity											*Millions of US Dollars Unless Otherwise Indicated:*					
Total Reserves minus Gold	1l. d	....	18.0	22.6	25.7	28.6	30.5	38.4	53.4	67.7	63.7	96.7	129.3	161.7	210.7	288.0
SDRs	1b. d								—	—	—	—	—	—	—	5.5
Reserve Position in the Fund	1c. d								5.4	6.0	6.1	15.3	18.8	17.6	19.2	17.9
Foreign Exchange	1d. d	....	18.0	22.6	25.7	28.6	30.5	38.4	48.0	61.7	57.6	81.4	110.5	144.1	191.5	264.6
Gold (Million Fine Troy Ounces)	1ad		—	.139	.185	.185	.185	.186	.186	.186	.186	.189	.192	.183	.252	.269
Gold (National Valuation)	1an d		—	4.9	6.5	6.5	6.5	7.0	7.0	7.8	7.8	7.7	7.8	7.8	11.5	12.4
Deposit Money Banks: Assets	7a. d	....	44.2	29.6	32.1	39.5	44.9	64.0	72.9	82.5	143.1	278.0	381.8	456.7	576.5	681.3
of which: Claims on Nonbanks	7ad d		.5	1.1	1.3	1.0	1.4	3.1	4.6	5.0	3.3	1.5	11.2	35.0	25.0	21.4
Deposit Money Banks: Liabilities	7b. d	....	3.1	3.6	1.9	3.3	8.3	5.9	.6	7.9	26.2	56.4	87.4	120.8	166.0	270.0
Monetary Authorities															*Millions of Riyals:*	
Foreign Assets	11	....	34	52	65	76	85	94	126	164	282	416	542	671	853	1,113
Claims on Deposit Money Banks	12e	....	—	—	—	—	—	—	4	—	—	—	16	51	88	96
Reserve Money	14	....	34	52	59	61	61	70	93	129	188	298	428	582	774	988
of which: Currency Outside DMBs	14a	....	25	47	51	52	54	60	77	111	158	240	376	505	573	715
Central Government Deposits	16d	....	1	—	—	—	11	9	24	30	49	109	147	101	125	180
Capital Accounts	17a	....	—	1	8	15	15	17	16	16	26	30	30	30	30	50
Other Items (Net)	17r	....	–1	–1	–1	–1	–2	–2	–3	–11	20	–21	–47	9	12	–9
Deposit Money Banks																
Reserves	20	....	10	6	8	10	7	9	16	18	30	58	52	77	213	276
Foreign Assets	21	....	210	141	153	188	214	281	320	326	565	1,109	1,511	1,809	2,213	2,524
Claims on Private Sector	22d	....	103	113	154	183	215	262	333	503	752	1,126	1,559	2,464	2,889	3,278
Demand Deposits	24	....	92	106	123	128	143	177	269	302	406	765	1,200	1,582	1,733	1,776
Time and Savings Deposits	25	....	112	125	123	188	187	226	319	364	485	744	1,129	1,480	1,809	2,020
Foreign Liabilities	26c	....	15	17	9	16	40	26	3	31	104	225	346	478	637	1,000
Central Government Deposits	26d	....	106	22	23	9	12	56	20	39	127	229	120	252	448	434
Credit from Monetary Authorities	26g		—	—	—	—	—	—	—	—	—	—	—	63	82	39
Capital Accounts	27a	....	20	18	26	32	53	67	67	95	169	252	210	232	284	386
Other Items (Net)	27r	....	–22	–29	10	8	—	2	–9	15	57	77	118	263	322	423
Monetary Survey															*Millions of Riyals:*	
Foreign Assets (Net)	31n	....	230	176	209	248	259	349	443	458	744	1,300	1,708	2,002	2,429	2,637
Claims on Private Sector	32d	....	103	113	154	183	215	262	333	503	752	1,126	1,559	2,464	2,889	3,278
Money	34	....	117	153	174	180	198	237	345	413	564	1,005	1,576	2,087	2,307	2,492
Quasi-Money	35	....	112	125	123	188	187	226	319	364	485	744	1,129	1,480	1,809	2,020
Central Government Deposits	36d	....	107	22	23	9	23	65	44	69	175	338	266	353	573	614
Other Items (Net)	37r	....	–4	–11	43	54	66	84	68	115	272	338	296	545	629	790
Money plus Quasi-Money	35l	....	229	278	297	368	385	463	664	777	1,049	1,749	2,705	3,567	4,116	4,511
Interest Rates															*Percent Per Annum*	
Deposit Rate	60l	....	....	....	....	....	....	....	....	....	....	....	....	....	....	6.0
Lending Rate	60p	....	....	....	....	....	....	....	....	....	....	....	....	....	....	
Prices and Production															*Index Numbers (1990=100):*	
Consumer Prices	64															66.4
Crude Petroleum	66aa	55.3	71.9	80.4	84.1	90.3	94.0	111.6	123.4	143.3	132.1	113.8	126.9	113.3	125.2	131.5
International Transactions															*Millions of Riyals*	
Exports	70	....	....	....	....	....	1,142	1,496	1,740	2,511	7,954	7,094	8,757	8,205	9,268	14,120
Crude Petroleum	70aa	....	855	963	1,007	1,056	1,099	1,441	1,673	2,444	7,811	6,893	8,470	8,134	8,955	13,398
Imports, cif	71	....	....	....	....	252	306	516	616	778	1,070	1,622	3,237	4,850	4,590	5,378
Imports, fob	71.v	....	....	....	....	225	273	461	550	695	955	1,448	2,890	4,330	4,098	4,802
Volume of Exports															*1985=100*	
Crude Petroleum	72aa	71.4	90.0	101.3	105.9	111.2	115.6	136.4	154.1	181.9	162.9	137.1	158.9	132.1	152.9	159.7
Export Prices															*1985=100:*	
Crude Petroleum	76aa d	6.0	6.0	6.0	6.0	6.0	6.0	6.7	7.4	10.1	36.4	38.4	40.3	44.9	44.9	67.2
Government Finance															*Millions of Riyals:*	
Deficit (–) or Surplus	80						75	255	272	178	3,565	1,832	3,118	837	1,752	3,820
Revenue	81	....	....	....	....	....	579	945	1,230	1,720	5,497	7,135	8,927	8,155	8,225	12,090
Expenditure	82	....	....	....	....	....	505	690	959	1,542	1,931	5,302	5,809	7,318	6,473	8,270
Financing																
Use of Cash Balances	87	....	....	....	....	....	–75	–255	–272	–178	–3,565	–1,832	–3,118	–837	–1,752	–3,820
National Accounts															*Millions of Riyals*	
Gross Domestic Product	99b	....	848	974	1,082	1,220	1,313	1,850	2,172	2,615	7,895	9,877	13,017	14,322	15,709	21,783
															Millions:	
Population	99z	.07	.07	.08	.08	.10	.11	.12	.13	.15	.16	.17	.18	.19	.20	.22

Exchange Rates: On May 19, 1973 the Qatar riyal replaced at par the Qatar-Dubai riyal, which replaced the rupee in 1966.

Qatar

	1980	1981	1982	1983	1984	1985	1986	1987	1988	1989	1990	1991	1992	1993	1994		
																Exchange Rates	
End of Period																	
	4.6425	4.2368	4.0153	3.8109	3.5680	3.9982	4.4524	5.1639	4.8983	4.7835	5.1785	5.2068	5.0050	4.9998	5.3139	Official Rate	aa
End of Period (ae) Period Average (rf)																	
	3.6400	3.6400	3.6400	3.6400	3.6400	3.6400	3.6400	3.6400	3.6400	3.6400	3.6400	3.6400	3.6400	3.6400	3.6400	Official Rate	ae
	3.6570	3.6400	3.6400	3.6400	3.6400	3.6400	3.6400	3.6400	3.6400	3.6400	3.6400	3.6400	3.6400	3.6400	3.6400	Official Rate	rf
Period Averages																	
	99.5	100.0	100.0	100.0	100.0	100.0	100.0	100.0	100.0	100.0	100.0	100.0	100.0	100.0	100.0	Official Rate	ah x
	99.4	111.0	123.3	130.0	139.9	143.8	117.4	104.8	99.4	105.6	100.0	100.0	97.6	101.2	98.2	Nominal Effective Exchange Rate	ne c
End of Period																**Fund Position**	
	66.2	66.2	66.2	114.9	114.9	114.9	114.9	114.9	114.9	114.9	114.9	114.9	190.5	190.5	190.5	Quota	2f. s
	2.7	8.6	14.0	8.7	16.2	18.9	21.1	24.7	26.4	28.7	31.3	33.8	17.1	18.7	19.9	SDRs	1b. s
	18.1	18.1	19.4	37.2	38.4	35.8	30.7	27.8	21.1	19.5	17.3	18.7	36.4	33.8	30.7	Reserve Position in the Fund	1c. s
End of Period																**International Liquidity**	
	343.4	365.8	386.6	384.1	380.0	446.1	571.9	618.4	474.5	533.4	631.1	667.7	683.3	693.7	657.7	Total Reserves minus Gold	1l. d
	3.5	10.0	15.4	9.1	15.9	20.7	25.8	35.0	35.6	37.7	44.6	48.3	23.6	25.6	29.0	SDRs	1b. d
	23.1	21.1	21.4	38.9	37.6	39.3	37.6	39.5	28.4	25.7	24.6	26.8	50.1	46.4	44.7	Reserve Position in the Fund	1c. d
	316.8	334.7	349.8	336.1	326.5	386.2	508.5	543.9	410.5	470.0	561.9	592.6	609.8	621.7	584.0	Foreign Exchange	1d. d
	.474	.713	.897	1.066	1.205	1.075	.966	.833	.880	.901	.833	.828	.861	.862	.814	Gold (Million Fine Troy Ounces)	1ad
	21.2	29.0	34.6	39.0	41.3	41.3	41.3	41.3	41.5	41.5	41.5	41.5	41.5	41.5	41.6	Gold (National Valuation)	1an d
	732.7	1,204.5	1,271.0	1,059.1	1,726.2	1,918.7	1,982.8	2,499.2	2,701.7	2,081.4	2,273.6	2,537.6	2,195.0	2,259.3	2,000.4	Deposit Money Banks: Assets	7a. d
	36.2	25.5	30.3	26.1	126.6	208.7	263.9	369.5	378.1	443.0	308.8	453.6	107.8	63.2	99.3	of which: Claims on Nonbanks	7ad d
	174.4	200.0	245.0	311.5	234.2	246.6	430.6	734.1	977.5	409.7	578.7	1,192.7	58.2	49.2	39.8	Deposit Money Banks: Liabilities	7b. d
End of Period																**Monetary Authorities**	
	1,327	1,437	1,533	1,540	1,534	1,774	2,232	2,401	2,064	2,278	2,633	2,767	2,824	2,861	2,731	Foreign Assets	11
	8	—	25	6	18	5	4	5	24	106	155	150	151	150	260	Claims on Deposit Money Banks	12e
	1,159	1,193	1,325	1,335	1,350	1,307	1,699	1,692	1,542	1,761	1,917	1,934	2,086	2,181	2,030	Reserve Money	14
	808	992	1,151	1,068	1,186	1,120	1,288	1,249	1,178	1,245	1,350	1,275	1,321	1,350	1,350	of which: Currency Outside DMBs	14a
	187	311	316	367	445	560	422	308	241	178	265	346	320	218	201	Central Government Deposits	16d
	69	84	81	79	76	81	87	96	93	91	96	97	94	220	252	Capital Accounts	17a
	−80	−152	−165	−235	−319	−169	29	311	212	354	510	539	473	393	509	Other Items (Net)	17r
End of Period																**Deposit Money Banks**	
	335	196	185	278	170	192	421	449	374	519	581	662	768	830	680	Reserves	20
	2,667	4,384	4,626	3,855	6,283	6,984	7,217	9,097	9,834	7,576	8,276	9,237	7,990	8,224	7,282	Foreign Assets	21
	3,693	4,507	5,576	6,056	5,440	6,445	8,031	8,743	9,265	10,553	9,906	13,344	18,113	18,724	20,663	Claims on Private Sector	22d
	1,466	2,412	2,644	2,556	2,948	2,897	3,199	3,530	2,221	2,158	2,705	2,353	2,669	2,805	2,561	Demand Deposits	24
	3,003	4,072	4,772	4,863	6,220	7,289	8,082	8,872	9,109	10,847	9,544	10,290	11,036	11,748	14,508	Time and Savings Deposits	25
	635	728	892	1,134	853	898	1,567	2,672	3,558	1,491	2,107	4,342	212	179	145	Foreign Liabilities	26c
	592	549	437	456	419	486	312	331	1,003	282	817	2,425	5,020	4,317	1,903	Central Government Deposits	26d
	—	—	25	5	—	—	—	—	23	2	—	—	43	18	73	Credit from Monetary Authorities	26g
	563	572	700	859	1,040	1,129	1,416	1,522	1,750	1,990	2,271	2,525	2,762	2,997	3,236	Capital Accounts	27a
	437	755	918	317	413	923	1,093	1,363	1,808	1,878	1,319	1,308	5,129	5,714	6,199	Other Items (Net)	27r
End of Period																**Monetary Survey**	
	3,359	5,093	5,268	4,261	6,964	7,861	7,882	8,826	8,340	8,363	8,803	7,662	10,601	10,906	9,868	Foreign Assets (Net)	31n
	3,693	4,507	5,576	6,056	5,440	6,445	8,031	8,743	9,265	10,553	9,906	13,344	18,113	18,724	20,663	Claims on Private Sector	32d
	2,274	3,403	3,795	3,625	4,135	4,017	4,487	4,778	3,399	3,403	4,055	3,629	3,990	4,156	3,910	Money	34
	3,003	4,072	4,772	4,863	6,220	7,289	8,082	8,872	9,109	10,847	9,544	10,290	11,036	11,748	14,508	Quasi-Money	35
	779	860	753	822	864	1,047	734	639	1,244	460	1,082	2,771	5,341	4,535	2,104	Central Government Deposits	36d
	996	1,266	1,524	1,008	1,186	1,954	2,610	3,281	3,853	4,206	4,028	4,316	8,348	9,192	10,008	Other Items (Net)	37r
	5,277	7,475	8,567	8,488	10,354	11,305	12,569	13,650	12,507	14,250	13,599	13,918	15,026	15,904	18,419	Money plus Quasi-Money	35l
Percent Per Annum																**Interest Rates**	
	6.0	6.0	6.0	6.0	6.0	6.0	6.0	6.0	6.0	6.0	6.0	6.0	4.8	4.1	....	Deposit Rate	60l
	9.5	9.5	9.5	9.5	9.5	9.5	9.5	9.5	9.5	9.5	9.5	9.5	8.1	7.2	....	Lending Rate	60p
Period Averages																**Prices and Production**	
	70.9	77.0	81.3	83.6	84.5	86.1	87.5	89.8	94.0	97.1	100.0	104.4	....	....	....	Consumer Prices	64
	122.8	105.2	85.2	76.4	111.3	85.6	93.0	79.9	81.8	101.6	100.0	98.6	103.1	107.4	105.5	Crude Petroleum	66aa
Millions of Riyals																**International Transactions**	
	20,768	20,696	15,802	12,221	....	....	....	....	....	....	....	....	....	....	....	Exports	70
	19,728	19,331	14,840	11,132	15,943	12,147	....	....	....	....	....	....	....	....	....	Crude Petroleum	70aa
	5,203	5,525e	7,088	4,230	4,147	4,000	4,128	4,613	4,827	6,169	6,261	7,336	....	....	....	Imports, cif	71
	4,646	4,933	6,328	4,731	3,776	3,702	3,571	3,686	4,119	4,310	5,508	5,590	6,550	....	....	Imports, fob	71.v
1985=100																Volume of Exports	
	148.8	125.2	102.9	89.3	130.1	100.0	108.7	....	....	....	....	....	....	....	....	Crude Petroleum	72aa
Index of Prices in US Dollars																Export Prices	
	108.6	127.1	118.7	102.6	100.9	100.0	....	....	....	....	....	....	....	....	....	Crude Petroleum	76aa d
Lunar Years																**Government Finance**	
	8,066	4,500	815	....	....	....	....	....	....	....	....	....	....	....	....	Deficit (-) or Surplus	80
	19,003	19,243	13,434	....	....	....	....	....	....	....	....	....	....	....	....	Revenue	81
	10,937	14,743	12,619	....	....	....	....	....	....	....	....	....	....	....	....	Expenditure	82
																Financing	
	−8,066	−4,500	−815	....	....	....	....	....	....	....	....	....	....	....	....	Use of Cash Balances	87
Millions of Riyals																**National Accounts**	
	28,663	31,568	27,705	23,605	25,008	22,398	18,393	19,825	21,979	23,616	26,792	25,056	27,202	....	....	Gross Domestic Product	99b
Midyear Estimates																	
	.23	.24	.26	.31	.33	.36	.39	.41	.43	.46	.49	.50	.52	.56	....	Population	99z

Romania

968

		1965	1966	1967	1968	1969	1970	1971	1972	1973	1974	1975	1976	1977	1978	1979
Exchange Rates															*Lei per SDR:*	
Market Rate	aa	6.00	6.00	6.00	6.00	6.00	6.00	6.00	6.00	24.13	24.49	23.41	23.24	24.29	23.45	23.71
															Lei per US Dollar:	
Market Rate	ae	6.00	6.00	6.00	6.00	6.00	6.00	5.53	5.53	20.00	20.00	20.00	20.00	20.00	18.00	18.00
Market Rate	rf	6.00	6.00	6.00	6.00	6.00	6.00	6.00	5.53	20.25	20.00	20.00	20.00	20.00	18.36	18.00
Fund Position															*Millions of SDRs:*	
Quota	2f. s	....	....	....	....	....	....	....	190	190	190	190	190	190	245	245
SDRs	1b. s	....	....	....	....	....	....	....	—	6	5	8	13	7	—	1
Reserve Position in the Fund	1c. s	....	....	....	....	....	....	....	48	—	—	—	—	—	—	—
Total Fund Cred.&Loans Outstg.	2tl	....	....	....	....	....	....	....	—	48	48	88	238	270	256	247
International Liquidity											*Millions of US Dollars Unless Otherwise Indicated:*					
Total Reserves minus Gold	1l. d	....	....	....	....	....	....	....	....	215	241	539	562	256	376	525
SDRs	1b..d	....	....	....	....	....	....	....	....	7	7	9	15	8	—	1
Reserve Position in the Fund	1c. d	....	....	....	....	....	....	....	52	—	—	—	—	—	—	—
Foreign Exchange	1d. d	....	....	....	....	....	....	....	....	208	234	530	547	248	376	524
o/w: Held by Dep.Money Banks	1e. d	....	....	....	....	....	....	....	....	....	....	....	....	....	....	....
Gold (Million Fine Troy Ounces)	1ad	....	....	....	....	....	....	....	....	2.275	2.447	2.597	2.749	3.057	3.347	3.535
Gold (National Valuation)	1and	....	....	....	....	....	....	....	....	96	105	106	112	130	153	141
Monetary Authorities: Other Liab.	4..d	....	....	....	....	....	....	....	....	51	86	35	83	101	124	159
Deposit Money Banks: Assets	7a. d	....	....	....	....	....	....	....	....	105	220	248	98	161	264	123
Liabilities	7b..d	....	....	....	....	....	....	....	....	290	460	610	2,320	2,984	4,143	6,534
Monetary Authorities															*Billions of Lei:*	
Foreign Assets	11	....	....	....	....	....	....	....	....	.6	.6	.7	.8	.8	1.8	4.0
Claims on Government	12a	....	....	....	....	....	....	....	....	....	....	....	....	....	....	....
Claims on Private Sector	12d	....	....	....	....	....	....	....	....	75.1	98.9	111.3	122.7	111.1	119.4	133.3
Claims on Deposit Money Banks	12e	....	....	....	....	....	....	....	....	28.2	23.3	28.4	32.7	45.0	65.1	73.6
Reserve Money	14	....	....	....	....	....	....	....	....	38.3	57.4	74.4	77.8	77.2	95.9	121.3
of which: Currency Outside DMBs	14a	....	....	....	....	....	....	....	....	17.6	18.2	21.1	23.6	27.0	28.2	34.1
Transit Accounts	14x	....	....	....	....	....	....	....	....	....	....	....	....	....	....	....
Deposits of Savings Bank	15a	....	....	....	....	....	....	....	....	10.1	12.9	17.2	22.3	45.6	62.1	70.9
Foreign Currency Deposits	15b	....	....	....	....	....	....	....	....	—	—	—	—	—	.1	.1
Foreign Liabilities	16c	....	....	....	....	....	....	....	....	.3	.4	.2	1.7	2.0	2.2	2.9
Central Government Deposits	16d	....	....	....	....	....	....	....	....	37.7	30.2	19.9	21.6	17.1	16.4	6.7
Other Items (Net)	17r	....	....	....	....	....	....	....	....	17.5	21.8	28.8	32.8	15.0	9.6	9.1
Deposit Money Banks															*Billions of Lei:*	
Reserves	20	....	....	....	....	....	....	....	....	5.5	11.0	24.2	21.5	14.2	34.0	52.7
Foreign Assets	21	....	....	....	....	....	....	....	....	1.9	2.7	4.1	12.8	8.1	10.5	8.5
Claims on Central Government	22a	....	....	....	....	....	....	....	....	....	....	....	....	....	....	....
Claims on Private Sector	22d	....	....	....	....	....	....	....	....	128.0	153.3	165.3	200.9	231.3	275.9	286.2
Demand Deposits	24	....	....	....	....	....	....	....	....	11.9	14.2	15.4	19.6	21.2	32.7	33.3
Transit Accounts	24x	....	....	....	....	....	....	....	....	....	....	....	....	....	....	....
Savings Deposits	25	....	....	....	....	....	....	....	....	35.5	40.8	47.4	55.0	64.3	80.1	89.6
Other Term Deposits	25a	....	....	....	....	....	....	....	....	....	....	....	....	....	....	....
Foreign Currency Deposits	25b	....	....	....	....	....	....	....	....	.2	.2	.2	1.0	1.4	1.1	2.1
Foreign Liabilities	26c	....	....	....	....	....	....	....	....	5.8	9.2	12.2	46.4	59.7	74.6	117.6
Government Deposits	26d	....	....	....	....	....	....	....	....	....	....	....	....	....	....	....
Investment Funds	26h	....	....	....	....	....	....	....	....	46.0	67.0	59.0	65.6	68.6	75.7	73.6
Credit from Monetary Authorities	26g	....	....	....	....	....	....	....	....	28.2	23.3	28.4	32.7	45.0	65.1	73.6
Capital Accounts	27a	....	....	....	....	....	....	....	....	....	....	....	....	....	....	....
Other Items (Net)	27r	....	....	....	....	....	....	....	....	17.4	25.2	30.1	17.6	21.8	29.1	28.4
Monetary Survey															*Billions of Lei:*	
Foreign Assets (Net)	31n	....	....	....	....	....	....	....	....	−3.6	−6.3	−7.6	−34.4	−53.5	−64.5	−108.0
Domestic Credit	32	....	....	....	....	....	....	....	....	203.2	252.2	276.7	323.6	343.2	395.3	419.5
Money	34	....	....	....	....	....	....	....	....	44.7	60.6	65.7	75.9	84.2	94.5	101.8
Transit Accounts	34x	....	....	....	....	....	....	....	....	....	....	....	....	....	....	....
Quasi-Money	35	....	....	....	....	....	....	....	....	35.7	41.0	47.6	56.0	65.7	81.2	91.8
Central Government Deposits	36d	....	....	....	....	....	....	....	....	37.7	30.2	19.9	21.6	17.1	16.4	6.7
Investment Funds	36h	....	....	....	....	....	....	....	....	.5	—	18.0	19.6	17.2	24.2	12.6
Other Liquid Liabilities	36x	....	....	....	....	....	....	....	....	9.1	10.5	12.1	13.8	15.9	18.3	20.8
Other Items (Net)	37r	....	....	....	....	....	....	....	....	71.9	103.5	105.9	102.2	89.4	96.0	77.8
Money plus Quasi-Money	35l	....	....	....	....	....	....	....	....	80.4	101.6	113.3	131.9	150.0	175.7	193.6
Prices, Production, Employment															*Index Numbers (1990=100):*	
Consumer Prices(Oct.'90=100)	64	....	....	....	....	....	....	....	....	....	....	....	....	....	....	....
Consumer Prices	64a	....	....	....	....	....	64.8	65.2	65.2	65.6	66.4	66.5	66.8	67.2	68.5	69.8
Wages: Average Earnings	65	....	....	....	....	....	....	....	....	40.6	43.1	47.1	49.8	....	....	....
Industrial Production	66	....	....	....	....	....	....	....	....	45.1	51.7	57.9	64.6	72.7	....	....
Industrial Employment	67	....	....	....	....	....	....	....	....	64.4	68.9	72.6	75.3	78.4	80.5	83.7
International Transactions															*Millions of US Dollars*	
Exports	70..d	1,101.5	1,186.2	1,395.3	1,468.5	1,633.2	1,850.8	2,107.3	2,601.0	3,691.0	4,874.5	5,341.5	6,137.7	7,021.0	8,086.4	9,724.2
Imports, cif	71..d	1,163.3	1,310.2	1,669.9	1,737.7	1,879.7	2,117.0	2,277.7	2,827.0	3,737.7	5,554.9	5,769.0	6,583.0	7,579.3	9,638.1	11,788.7
Imports, fob	71.v d	....	....	....	....	....	....	....	....	....	....	....	....	....	....	....

Romania

968

	1980	1981	1982	1983	1984	1985	1986	1987	1988	1989	1990	1991	1992	1993	1994		
																Exchange Rates	
End of Period	22.96	17.46	16.55	19.19	17.44	17.28	18.69	19.49	19.34	18.98	49.38	ɪ270.35	632.50	1,752.66	2,579.55	Market Rate	aa
End of Period (ae) Period Average (rf)																	
	18.00	15.00	15.00	18.33	17.79	15.73	15.28	13.74	14.37	14.44	34.71	ɪ189.00	460.00	1,276.00	1,767.00	Market Rate	ae
	18.00	15.00	15.00	17.18	21.28	17.14	16.15	14.56	14.28	14.92	22.43	76.39	ɪ307.95	760.05	1,655.09	Market Rate	rf
																Fund Position	
End of Period	368	368	368	523	523	523	523	523	523	523	523	523	754	754	754	Quota	2f. s
	—	—	12	—	—	—	—	—	—	76	—	40	8	1	38	SDRs	1b. s
	—	—	—	—	—	—	—	—	—	—	—	—	—	—	—	Reserve Position in the Fund	1c. s
	257	507	782	905	956	783	584	358	107	—	—	566	751	751	906	Total Fund Cred.&Loans Outstg.	2tl
																International Liquidity	
End of Period	323	404	450	525	709	199	582	1,402	780	1,859	524	695	826	995	2,086	Total Reserves minus Gold	1l. d
	—	1	13	—	—	—	—	—	—	100	—	58	11	2	56	SDRs	1b. d
	—	—	—	—	—	—	—	—	—	—	—	—	—	—	—	Reserve Position in the Fund	1c. d
	323	403	437	525	709	199	582	1,402	780	1,759	524	637	815	994	2,031	Foreign Exchange	1d. d
	....	....	....	....	....	....	....	....	....	....	....	480	730	....	....	o/w: Held by Dep.Money Banks	1e. d
	3.712	3.591	3.553	3.620	3.731	3.818	3.247	1.364	1.449	2.174	2.208	2.247	2.307	2.370	2.625	Gold (Million Fine Troy Ounces)	1ad
	43	50	49	41	44	50	44	21	1,236	1,845	780	666	780	924	965	Gold (National Valuation)	1an d
	470	968	1,199	1,300	1,247	1,272	972	....	....	....	—	241	—	....	....	Monetary Authorities: Other Liab.	4.. d
	260	187	254	353	317	1,000	507	570	1,021	799	682	261	132	222	129	Deposit Money Banks: Assets	7a. d
	8,381	9,056	8,034	7,603	6,460	6,046	5,948	5,896	1,972	512	1,723	724	461	560	687	Liabilities	7b. d
																Monetary Authorities	
End of Period	2.9	ɪ9.2	10.6	13.4	13.3	ɪ2.8	3.9	.7	18.1	27.8	ɪ28.2	171.3	404.8	1,234.2	2,795.6	Foreign Assets	11
	151.7	168.1	187.8	194.3	208.7	ɪ226.8	227.2	260.7	266.5	331.5	....	3.8	41.1	263.0	336.3	Claims on Government	12a
															1,771.4	Claims on Private Sector	12d
	149.3	157.1	170.0	189.9	222.4	ɪ284.3	321.8	356.7	444.3	409.1	ɪ361.5	390.2	352.7	1,568.6	2,334.3	Claims on Deposit Money Banks	12e
	166.8	182.8	187.7	177.9	158.3	ɪ128.1	146.2	155.4	180.9	251.8	ɪ324.3	397.1	859.1	2,503.9	4,619.6	Reserve Money	14
	39.3	41.3	44.7	44.9	49.1	ɪ54.8	60.0	60.6	65.0	74.7	ɪ92.4	176.5	411.7	1,048.1	2,200.6	of which: Currency Outside DMBs	14a
												49.4	95.4	-35.8	26.8	20.6	Transit Accounts	14x
	104.6	119.3	128.3	143.5	159.8	ɪ180.9	203.5	221.9	239.7	266.7	....	....	....	....	....	Deposits of Savings Bank	15a
	.1	.1	.1	.1	.4	ɪ.1	.1	.1	.1	.1	....	....	....	....	....	Foreign Currency Deposits	15b
	8.5	14.5	18.0	23.8	22.2	ɪ14.5	3.9	2.2	1.6	.2	ɪ—	198.4	474.9	1,316.1	2,444.2	Foreign Liabilities	16c
	14.3	12.9	31.3	51.9	101.5	ɪ145.0	173.3	226.5	281.5	228.0	.3	42.3	163.1	485.3	1,351.8	Central Government Deposits	16d
	9.7	4.8	3.1	.3	2.3	ɪ55.4	25.9	12.3	25.1	21.7	ɪ19.6	-130.6	-440.7	-1,193.0	-1,534.9	Other Items (Net)	17r
																Deposit Money Banks	
End of Period	81.3	86.1	78.3	67.9	43.6	ɪ35.9	8.3	.4	.4	.4	ɪ8.7	ɪ177.1	443.4	989.7	1,606.8	Reserves	20
	9.1	8.5	9.9	15.7	17.6	ɪ19.8	24.8	27.5	25.8	38.4	ɪ41.1	104.7	297.6	1,324.2	2,746.0	Foreign Assets	21
	....	....	....	....	....	....	....	....	....	....	—	124.1	198.2	398.0	584.2	Claims on Central Government	22a
	309.4	ɪ292.9	315.9	349.8	380.6	ɪ439.1	469.8	513.0	546.6	478.9	ɪ684.0	1,375.2	1,911.6	4,891.5	9,484.5	Claims on Private Sector	22d
	61.7	ɪ38.8	57.6	46.2	47.4	ɪ37.6	33.0	34.3	37.3	48.6	ɪ140.6	554.8	599.8	1,138.2	2,691.8	Demand Deposits	24
	....	....	....	....	....	....	....	....	....	....	2.8	225.0	152.1	208.0	173.9	Transit Accounts	24x
	101.4	114.6	118.2	127.8	138.9	ɪ153.2	167.3	176.5	185.6	201.7	ɪ193.7	188.3	375.6	785.4	3,252.6	Savings Deposits	25
	....	....	....	....	....	....	....	....	....	....	71.5	71.0	121.4	218.6	144.4	Other Term Deposits	25a
	2.3	3.0	3.6	2.7	3.2	ɪ3.7	4.1	5.4	4.5	3.9	ɪ15.1	40.4	281.3	1,324.6	2,358.1	Foreign Currency Deposits	25b
	150.9	135.8	120.5	139.4	114.9	ɪ95.1	90.9	81.0	28.3	7.4	ɪ59.8	136.8	212.2	714.9	1,213.1	Foreign Liabilities	26c
	....	....	....	....	....	....	....	....	....	....	72.3	125.2	357.6	856.4	1,302.9	Government Deposits	26d
	.8	15.6	12.6	14.4	15.0	ɪ14.3	13.9	13.0	21.6	15.7	....	....	....	....	....	Investment Funds	26h
	149.3	157.1	170.0	189.9	218.2	ɪ273.5	310.9	346.5	434.0	409.1	ɪ361.5	390.1	343.3	1,567.8	2,316.2	Credit from Monetary Authorities	26g
	....	....	....	....	....	....	....	....	....	....	26.6	69.5	253.5	493.0	1,337.9	Capital Accounts	27a
	35.4	41.8	49.9	56.5	63.9	ɪ98.2	86.2	105.7	101.2	98.0	ɪ275.8	81.9	-131.0	656.7	-239.5	Other Items (Net)	27r
																Monetary Survey	
End of Period	-147.3	-132.1	-118.1	-134.1	-106.2	ɪ-77.0	-66.2	-55.0	14.0	58.7	ɪ9.4	-59.2	15.3	527.4	1,884.3	Foreign Assets (Net)	31n
	ɪ427.6	459.3	503.7	544.1	589.3	ɪ665.9	697.0	773.6	813.1	810.4	ɪ684.0	1,375.2	1,911.6	4,891.5	9,484.5	Domestic Credit	32
	ɪ114.5	135.5	167.0	156.3	162.3	ɪ165.8	169.5	171.3	199.4	204.5	ɪ233.0	731.3	1,011.5	2,186.3	4,892.4	Money	34
	....	....	....	....	....	....	....	....	....	....	52.2	320.4	116.3	234.8	194.5	Transit Accounts	34x
	103.8	117.7	121.9	130.6	142.5	ɪ157.0	171.5	182.0	190.1	205.7	ɪ280.3	299.7	778.2	2,328.5	5,755.1	Quasi-Money	35
	14.3	13.4	31.3	51.9	101.5	ɪ152.1	174.8	245.8	283.0	234.4	ɪ68.7	2.3	59.5	607.4	299.2	Central Government Deposits	36d
	2.6	15.2	12.6	14.4	15.0	ɪ14.3	13.9	13.0	21.6	15.7	....	....	....	....	....	Investment Funds	36h
	23.6	26.7	29.8	32.8	36.0	ɪ39.3	43.4	48.3	52.9	58.2	....	....	....	....	....	Other Liquid Liabilities	36x
	ɪ21.5	18.1	23.2	24.0	25.8	ɪ60.5	57.6	58.2	80.2	150.6	ɪ59.1	64.2	-323.6	422.1	357.5	Other Items (Net)	37r
	ɪ218.3	253.2	288.8	286.8	304.8	ɪ322.8	341.0	353.2	389.5	410.2	ɪ513.3	1,031.0	1,789.7	4,514.9	10,647.5	Money plus Quasi-Money	35l
																Prices, Production, Employment	
Period Averages												274.4	854.0	3,033.1	7,181.2	Consumer Prices(Oct.'90=100)	64
	ɪ70.9	72.4	84.7	89.1	90.1	89.7	91.7	92.7	95.3	96.0	100.0	....	....	....	....	Consumer Prices	64a
	67.5	69.3	74.7	76.9	82.7	83.2	84.4	84.9	87.0	90.5	100.0	221.3	597.4	1,804.8	....	Wages: Average Earnings	65
	91.1	92.6	94.6	99.1	105.7	112.1	117.5	120.4	124.5	121.7	100.0	80.4	62.7	ɪ63.0	....	Industrial Production	66
	86.1	87.8	89.8	94.4	91.2	97.4	94.2	95.7	95.7	98.3	100.0	88.3	78.2	....	....	Industrial Employment	67
																International Transactions	
Millions of US Dollars																	
	11,209.0	12,610.0	11,559.0	11,512.0	12,646.0	12,167.0	9,763.1	10,491.8	11,392.4	10,487.3	5,775.4	4,265.7	4,363.4	4,892.2	6,151.3	Exports	70..d
	13,843.4	13,453.6	10,524.6	10,414.4	11,160.7	11,266.6	11,437.2	8,977.7	8,254.0	9,122.4	9,843.4	5,793.4	6,259.6	6,521.7	7,109.0	Imports, cif	71..d
	12,818.0	12,457.0	9,745.0	9,643.0	10,334.0	10,432.0	10,590.0	8,312.7	7,642.6	8,437.7	9,202.5	5,372.0	5,784.1	6,020.1	6,562.4	Imports, fob	71.v d

Romania

968

		1965	1966	1967	1968	1969	1970	1971	1972	1973	1974	1975	1976	1977	1978	1979
Balance of Payments																*Millions of US Dollars:*
Goods: Exports f.o.b.	78aa d	....	....	....	....	....	....	2,102	2,599	3,667	4,858	5,341	6,134	6,859	8,022	9,303
Goods: Imports f.o.b.	78ab d	....	....	....	....	....	....	−2,102	−2,616	−3,425	−5,049	−5,342	−6,087	−7,002	−8,628	−10,519
Trade Balance	78ac d							—	−17	242	−191	−1	47	−143	−606	−1,216
Services: Credit	78ad d	....	....	....	....	....	....	280	265	338	419	471	508	498	706	830
Services: Debit	78ae d	....	....	....	....	....	....	−303	−295	−373	−518	−516	−453	−527	−691	−909
Balance on Goods and Services	78af d							−23	−47	207	−290	−46	102	−172	−591	−1,295
Income: Credit	78ag d	....	....	....	....	....	....	—	—	16	18	25	37	50	56	77
Income: Debit	78ah d	....	....	....	....	....	....	—	—	−74	−87	−114	−155	−182	−224	−435
Balance on Goods, Serv., & Inc.	78ai d							−23	−47	149	−359	−135	−16	−304	−759	−1,653
Current Transfers, n.i.e.: Credit	78aj d	....	....	....	....	....	....	—	—	—	—	—	—	—	—	—
Current Transfers: Debit	78ak d	....	....	....	....	....	....	—	—	—	—	—	—	—	—	—
Current Account, n.i.e.	78al d							−23	−47	149	−359	−135	−16	−304	−759	−1,653
Capital Account, n.i.e.: Credit	78ba d	....	....	....	....	....	....	—	—	—	—	—	—	—	—	—
Capital Account: Debit	78bb d	....	....	....	....	....	....	—	—	—	—	—	—	—	—	—
Capital Account, n.i.e.	78bc d							—	—	—	—	—	—	—	—	—
Direct Investment Abroad	78bd d	....	....	....	....	....	....	—	—	—	—	—	—	—	—	—
Dir. Invest. in Rep. Econ., n.i.e.	78be d	....	....	....	....	....	....	—	—	—	—	—	—	—	—	—
Portfolio Investment Assets	78bf d	....	....	....	....	....	....	—	—	—	—	—	—	—	—	—
Portfolio Investment Liab., n.i.e.	78bg d	....	....	....	....	....	....	—	—	—	—	—	—	—	—	—
Other Investment Assets	78bh d	....	....	....	....	....	....	—	—	−43	−141	−198	−296	−151	−302	−418
Other Investment Liab., n.i.e.	78bi d	....	....	....	....	....	....	−15	38	−223	507	288	183	120	1,227	2,282
Financial Account, n.i.e.	78bj d							−15	38	−266	366	90	−113	−31	925	1,864
Net Errors and Omissions	78ca d	....	....	....	....	....	....	—	10	−9	—	13	9	1	−16	−73
Overall Balance	78cb d							−38	1	−126	7	−32	−120	−334	150	138
Reserves and Related Items	79da d	....	....	....	....	....	....	38	−1	126	−7	32	120	334	−150	−138
Reserve Assets	79db d							38	−5	69	−7	−15	−52	297	−132	−126
Use of Fund Credit and Loans	79dc d							—	—	57	—	47	173	37	−19	−12
Liabs.Constit.For.Auth.Reserves	79dd d							—	4	—	—	—	—	—	—	—
Exceptional Financing	79de d							—	—	—	—	—	—	—	—	—
Government Finance																*Billions of Lei:*
Deficit(−) or Surplus	80	....	....	....	....	....	1.2	3.2	6.6	6.9	1.7	1.1	2.8	.9	.9	1.2
Revenue	81	....	....	....	....	....	116.0	119.1	130.3	152.0	186.2	216.9	230.3	260.2	277.8	317.5
Expenditure	82	....	....	....	....	....	114.8	115.9	123.7	145.1	184.5	215.8	227.5	259.4	276.9	316.3
Lending Minus Repayments	83						—	—	—	—	—	—	—	—	—	—
Financing																
Domestic	84a	....	....	....	....	....	....	....	....	....	....	....	....	....	....	....
Foreign	85a	....	....	....	....	....	....	....	....	....	....	....	....	....	....	....
National Accounts																*Billions of Lei*
Exports of Goods & Services	90c	....	....	....	....	....	....	....	....	....	....	....	....	....	....	....
Government Consumption	91f	....	....	....	....	....	....	....	....	....	....	....	....	....	....	....
Gross Fixed Capital Formation	93e	....	....	....	....	....	....	....	....	....	....	....	....	....	....	....
Increase/Decrease(−) in Stocks	93i	....	....	....	....	....	....	....	....	....	....	....	....	....	....	....
Private Consumption	96f	....	....	....	....	....	....	....	....	....	....	....	....	....	....	....
Imports of Goods & Services	98c	....	....	....	....	....	....	....	....	....	....	....	....	....	....	....
Gross Domestic Product	99b	....	....	....	....	....	....	....	....	....	....	....	....	....	....	....
Gross Dom. Prod. 1990 Prices	99b.p	....	....	....	....	....	....	....	....	....	....	....	....	....	....	....
GDP Deflator (1990=100)	99bi p	....	....	....	....	....	....	....	....	....	....	....	....	....	....	....
																Millions:
Population	99z	19.03	19.14	19.28	19.72	20.01	20.25	20.47	20.66	20.83	21.03	21.24	21.45	21.66	21.85	22.05

Monetary Authorities: I Beginning in 1981, data are based on improved classification.

Romania

968

1980	1981	1982	1983	1984	1985	1986	1987	1988	1989	1990	1991	1992	1993	1994		
Minus Sign Indicates Debit															**Balance of Payments**	
11,024	12,367	11,559	11,512	12,646	10,174	9,763	10,491	11,392	10,487	5,770	4,266	4,364	4,892	5,998	Goods: Exports f.o.b.	78aa *d*
−12,685	−12,264	−9,745	−9,643	−10,334	−8,402	−8,083	−8,313	−7,642	−8,437	−9,114	−5,372	−5,558	−6,020	−6,328	Goods: Imports f.o.b.	78ab *d*
−1,661	103	1,814	1,869	2,312	1,772	1,680	2,178	3,750	2,050	−3,344	−1,106	−1,194	−1,128	−330	Trade Balance	78ac *d*
1,063	1,095	825	727	840	746	681	770	850	834	610	680	659	799	1,044	Services: Credit	78ad *d*
−1,045	−1,014	−748	−726	−774	−524	−424	−515	−480	−450	−787	−819	−946	−910	−1,131	Services: Debit	78ae *d*
−1,643	184	1,891	1,870	2,378	1,994	1,937	2,433	4,120	2,434	−3,521	−1,245	−1,481	−1,239	−417	Balance on Goods and Services	78af *d*
73	113	119	97	117	116	120	138	173	181	175	104	54	63	116	Income: Credit	78ag *d*
−850	−1,130	−970	−807	−776	−729	−662	−528	−371	−101	−14	−89	−144	−208	−245	Income: Debit	78ah *d*
−2,420	−833	1,040	1,160	1,719	1,381	1,395	2,043	3,922	2,514	−3,360	−1,230	−1,571	−1,384	−546	Balance on Goods, Serv., & Inc.	78ai *d*
—	—	—	—	—	—	—	—	—	—	138	277	136	239	348	Current Transfers, n.i.e.: Credit	78aj *d*
—	—	—	—	—	—	—	—	—	—	−32	−59	−71	−17	−61	Current Transfers: Debit	78ak *d*
−2,420	−833	1,040	1,160	1,719	1,381	1,395	2,043	3,922	2,514	−3,254	−1,012	−1,506	−1,162	−259	Current Account, n.i.e.	78al *d*
—	—	—	—	—	—	—	—	—	—	—	—	—	—	—	Capital Account, n.i.e.: Credit	78ba *d*
—	—	—	—	—	—	—	—	—	—	—	—	—	—	—	Capital Account: Debit	78bb *d*
—	—	—	—	—	—	—	—	—	—	—	—	—	—	—	Capital Account, n.i.e.	78bc *d*
—	—	—	—	—	—	—	—	—	—	−18	−3	−4	−7	−1	Direct Investment Abroad	78bd *d*
—	—	—	—	—	—	—	—	—	—	—	40	77	94	340	Dir. Invest. in Rep. Econ., n.i.e.	78be *d*
—	—	—	—	—	—	—	—	—	—	—	—	—	—	75	Portfolio Investment Assets	78bf *d*
—	—	—	—	—	—	—	—	—	—	—	—	—	−73	—	Portfolio Investment Liab., n.i.e.	78bg *d*
−137	−153	−625	−659	−701	−578	−1	191	−765	98	562	−86	94	−180	−662	Other Investment Assets	78bh *d*
2,312	−402	392	−489	−990	−1,002	−790	−1,274	−3,458	−1,474	1,069	369	1,213	1,135	1,159	Other Investment Liab., n.i.e.	78bi *d*
2,175	−555	−233	−1,148	−1,691	−1,580	−791	−1,083	−4,223	−1,376	1,613	320	1,380	969	911	Financial Account, n.i.e.	78bj *d*
−1	7	—	−2	100	−118	8	81	16	114	147	15	−12	139	−254	Net Errors and Omissions	78ca *d*
−246	−1,381	807	10	128	−317	612	1,041	−285	1,252	−1,494	−677	−138	−54	399	Overall Balance	78cb *d*
246	1,381	−807	−10	−128	317	−612	−1,041	285	−1,252	1,494	677	138	54	−399	Reserves and Related Items	79da *d*
232	−46	−353	245	−184	492	−376	−749	622	−1,111	1,494	−93	−124	54	−616	Reserve Assets	79db *d*
15	284	301	133	56	−175	−236	−292	−337	−141	—	770	262	—	217	Use of Fund Credit and Loans	79dc *d*
—	—	—	—	—	—	—	—	—	—	—	—	—	—	—	Liabs.Constit.For.Auth.Reserves	79dd *d*
—	1,143	−755	−388	—	—	—	—	—	—	—	—	—	—	—	Exceptional Financing	79de *d*
Year Ending December 31															**Government Finance**	
3.0	10.4	21.9	24.7	52.9	20.9	36.0	60.1	50.0	65.8	8.0	42.8	−282.3	....	....	Deficit(−) or Surplus	80
279.3	260.4	255.5	236.8	288.8	360.9	392.3	403.9	364.1	386.3	297.9	822.8	2,200.5	....	....	Revenue	81
276.3	250.0	233.6	212.0	235.9	340.0	356.3	343.8	314.1	320.6	289.9	780.0	2,406.0	....	....	Expenditure	82
—	—	—	—	—	—	—	—	—	—	—	—	76.7	....	....	Lending Minus Repayments	83
															Financing	
....	....	....	....	....	....	....	....	....	....	−8.0	−42.8	282.3	....	....	Domestic	84a
										—	—	—	....	....	Foreign	85a
Billions of Lei															**National Accounts**	
138.8	174.1	172.7	204.2	227.4	235.8	227.0	224.6	218.9	167.0	143.5	388.0	1,623.3	4,282.0	....	Exports of Goods & Services	90c
31.1	32.0	30.0	30.9	30.6	32.0	30.3	27.8	31.0	44.0	47.2	128.1	362.4	....	....	Government Consumption	91f
212.8	209.4	216.4	230.7	244.7	246.3	249.0	245.5	240.2	238.9	169.8	317.0	888.6	2,521.4	....	Gross Fixed Capital Formation	93e
32.9	17.1	28.9	30.9	34.1	23.6	39.4	23.5	13.1	−24.6	89.7	301.1	968.7	2,647.3	....	Increase/Decrease(−) in Stocks	93i
357.3	379.7	438.4	432.7	463.2	459.9	466.9	489.1	501.3	520.0	632.3	1,544.4	4,221.5	14,756.0	....	Private Consumption	96f
137.2	156.8	134.3	143.3	163.9	163.3	151.7	150.1	134.7	145.2	224.6	474.6	2,082.1	5,371.5	....	Imports of Goods & Services	98c
616.9	623.7	727.4	768.7	816.1	817.3	838.6	845.2	857.0	800.0	857.9	2,203.9	5,982.3	18,835.2	....	Gross Domestic Product	99b
820.2	821.2	853.7	905.9	959.3	958.3	980.3	988.1	983.2	925.9	857.9	747.2	646.0	....	....	Gross Dom. Prod. 1990 Prices	99b.*p*
75.2	76.0	85.2	84.9	85.1	85.3	85.5	85.5	87.2	86.4	100.0	295.0	926.1	....	....	GDP Deflator (1990=100)	99bi *p*
Midyear Estimates																
22.20	22.35	22.48	22.55	22.62	22.72	22.82	22.94	23.05	23.15	23.21	23.19	22.79	22.76	22.73	Population	99z

Rwanda
714

		1965	1966	1967	1968	1969	1970	1971	1972	1973	1974	1975	1976	1977	1978	1979
Exchange Rates																*Francs per SDR:*
Official Rate	aa	50.00	100.00	100.00	100.00	100.00	100.00	100.00	100.00	100.00	113.67	108.68	107.86	112.77	120.95	122.30
																Francs per US Dollar:
Official Rate	ae	50.00	100.00	100.00	100.00	100.00	100.00	92.11	92.11	82.90	92.84	92.84	92.84	92.84	92.84	92.84
Official Rate	rf	50.00	87.50	100.00	100.00	100.00	100.00	99.74	92.11	84.05	92.84	92.84	92.84	92.84	92.84	92.84
Fund Position																*Millions of SDRs:*
Quota	2f.s	11.25	12.00	12.75	15.00	15.00	19.00	19.00	19.00	19.00	19.00	19.00	19.00	19.00	23.00	23.00
SDRs	1b.s	—	—	—	—	—	.50	1.43	.39	2.43	2.48	2.39	2.39	2.35	2.39	4.58
Reserve Position in the Fund	1c.s	.13	—	—	—	—	—	.07	—	—	—	—	2.07	2.07	2.93	5.47
Total Fund Cred.&Loans Outstg.	2tl	—	4.68	5.50	5.93	4.94	2.93	—	—	—	—	—	—	—	—	5.76
International Liquidity											*Millions of US Dollars Unless Otherwise Indicated:*					
Total Reserves minus Gold	1l.d	3.69	5.13	6.69	5.78	3.01	7.70	5.78	6.37	15.18	12.96	25.59	64.29	82.87	87.60	152.31
SDRs	1b.d	—	—	—	—	—	.50	1.55	.42	2.93	3.04	2.80	2.78	2.85	3.11	6.03
Reserve Position in the Fund	1c.d	.13	—	—	—	—	—	.08	—	—	—	—	2.40	2.51	3.82	7.21
Foreign Exchange	1d.d	3.56	5.13	6.69	5.78	3.01	7.20	4.15	5.95	12.25	9.92	22.79	59.10	77.51	80.67	139.07
Monetary Authorities: Other Liab.	4..d	3.28	8.14	7.88	7.72	6.72	5.07	1.89	2.87	4.63	5.53	5.65	15.52	18.85	19.25	17.06
Deposit Money Banks: Assets	7a.d	1.56	.32	.42	1.05	.54	.89	1.97	.31	1.18	1.36	2.89	3.34	13.92	12.41	25.28
of which: Claims on Nonbanks	7ad d	....	....	....	....	....	....	....	....	....	....	....	....	....	....	....
Deposit Money Banks: Liabilities	7b.d	.16	.25	.40	.46	.18	.31	2.93	.48	.86	.01	2.03	3.17	6.67	4.75	7.27
of which: Liab. to Nonbanks	7bd d	....	....	....	....	....	....	....	....	....	.52	1.32	2.61	6.42	3.88	5.69
Other Banking Insts.: Liabilities	7f.d	....	....	....	....	....	....	....	....	....	1.11	1.19	1.85	3.67	5.99	
Monetary Authorities																*Millions of Francs:*
Foreign Assets	11	225	554	708	578	302	770	532	586	1,259	1,203	2,376	5,968	7,710	8,133	14,141
Claims on Central Government	12a	545	797	918	1,165	1,305	985	1,146	1,623	2,105	2,199	1,604	1,583	1,211	1,399	1,205
Claims on Official Entities	12bx	—	—	—	17	34	21	81	68	147	116	194	166	100	78	51
Claims on Private Sector	12d	—	—	—	—	—	—	10	10	39	59	18	334	295	301	456
Claims on Deposit Money Banks	12e	—	45	9	36	41	58	204	31	73	721	531	51	562	671	249
Claims on Other Financial Insts.	12f	—	—	—	—	69	123	162	130	121	160	87	67	40	38	
Reserve Money	14	939	1,079	1,266	1,411	1,655	2,073	2,021	2,258	2,921	3,842	3,905	5,109	5,803	5,930	8,532
of which: Currency Outside DMBs	14a	845	899	1,032	987	1,092	1,238	1,409	1,446	2,003	2,553	2,722	3,070	3,948	4,443	5,242
Time Deposits	15										110	153	224	131	88	94
Foreign Liabilities	16c	164	814	788	772	672	507	174	265	384	513	525	1,441	1,750	1,787	2,287
Central Government Deposits	16d	100	114	118	107	94	87	130	218	490	386	600	783	1,364	1,786	1,850
Counterpart Funds	16e	—	70	203	186	81	86	64	41	39	22	8	117	108	73	46
Capital Accounts	17a	39	39	58	67	62	299	506	710	799	806	951	1,309	1,409	1,708	3,030
Other Items (Net)	17r	–472	–720	–798	–643	–710	–689	–646	–586	–509	–528	–513	–793	–620	–750	302
Deposit Money Banks																*Millions of Francs:*
Reserves	20	100	162	221	264	340	275	345	245	483	328	200	1,345	1,087	673	2,328
Foreign Assets	21	78	32	42	105	54	89	182	29	98	127	269	310	1,292	1,152	2,347
Claims on Central Government	22a	201	205	263	268	322	437	576	775	779	1,123	1,430	784	600	504	596
Claims on Official Entities	22bx	—	—	—	—	—	—	10	10	—	—	194	237	121	148	183
Claims on Private Sector	22d	82	216	234	234	313	529	636	453	855	1,717	1,640	1,782	3,662	4,478	3,793
Demand Deposits	24	326	319	444	519	678	828	949	936	1,449	1,518	1,869	2,702	3,429	4,016	4,745
Time and Savings Deposits	25	153	202	242	250	295	404	449	453	464	953	994	1,306	1,973	2,132	2,738
Foreign Liabilities	26c	8	25	40	46	18	31	270	44	72	49	188	294	619	441	675
Central Government Deposits	26d	—	—	—	5	10	—	6	15	53	5	5	28	137	143	1,423
Credit from Monetary Authorities	26g	—	44	10	13	12	16	5	3	9	578	494	56	529	350	137
Capital Accounts	27a	30	33	94	99	106	115	134	148	164	190	170	230	314	369	447
Other Items (Net)	27r	–56	–8	–70	–61	–90	–64	–65	–86	5	—	12	–159	–239	–495	–920
Monetary Survey																*Millions of Francs:*
Foreign Assets (Net)	31n	131	–253	–78	–135	–335	321	270	306	902	768	1,932	4,544	6,633	7,057	13,526
Domestic Credit	32	728	1,104	1,296	1,591	1,888	1,977	2,465	2,888	3,555	5,001	4,729	4,334	4,677	5,134	3,114
Claims on Central Govt. (Net)	32an	646	888	1,062	1,331	1,531	1,348	1,595	2,176	2,359	2,958	2,464	1,605	327	—	–1,449
Claims on Official Entities	32bx	—	—	—	17	34	21	91	78	147	116	387	403	221	225	234
Claims on Private Sector	32d	82	216	234	234	313	529	646	462	893	1,775	1,658	2,115	3,957	4,779	4,249
Claims on Other Financial Insts.	32f	—	—	—	10	10	79	133	172	156	151	220	212	173	130	81
Money	34	1,171	1,230	1,478	1,564	1,825	2,165	2,472	2,520	3,565	4,288	4,850	6,516	8,035	8,961	11,255
Quasi-Money	35	153	202	242	250	295	404	449	453	464	1,063	1,147	1,530	2,104	2,220	2,831
Other Items (Net)	37r	–465	–581	–501	–358	–567	–272	–187	221	427	417	662	831	1,171	1,010	2,555
Money plus Quasi-Money	35l	1,324	1,432	1,720	1,814	2,120	2,568	2,921	2,973	4,029	5,350	5,997	8,047	10,138	11,181	14,086
Other Banking Institutions																*Millions of Francs:*
Cash	40..k	....	....	....	—	23	10	2	59	36	109	92	53	45	45	73
Claims on Official Entities	42bx k	....	....	....	—	55	55	55	—	—	—	—	77	28	26	125
Claims on Private Sector	42d.k	....	....	....	—	6	27	90	159	216	239	449	455	545	670	955
Long Term Foreign Liabilities	46cl k	....	....	....	....	....	....	....	....	....	....	103	110	172	340	556
Cred.from Monetary Authorities	46g.k	....	....	....	—	60	69	121	162	130	117	157	85	63	40	38
Cred.from Deposit Money Banks	46h.k	....	....	....	....	....	....	....	....	....	....	....	20	85	60	20	80
Capital Accounts	47a.k	....	....	....	50	50	50	51	63	169	215	221	286	318	450	469
Other Items (Net)	47r.k	....	....	....	–50	–26	–25	–26	–7	–47	16	40	34	20	–109	10

Rwanda
714

1980	1981	1982	1983	1984	1985	1986	1987	1988	1989	1990	1991	1992	1993	1994			
End of Period																**Exchange Rates**	
118.41	108.06	102.41	102.71	102.71	102.71	102.71	102.71	102.71	102.71	102.71	171.18	171.18	201.39	201.39	....	Official Rate	aa
End of Period (ae)	*Period Average (rf)*																
92.84	92.84	92.84	98.54	104.36	93.49	84.18	73.02	76.71	77.62	121.12	119.79	146.27	146.37	....		Official Rate	ae
92.84	92.84	92.84	94.34	100.17	101.26	87.64	79.67	76.45	79.98	82.60	125.14	133.35	144.25	....		Official Rate	rf
End of Period																**Fund Position**	
34.50	34.50	34.50	43.80	43.80	43.80	43.80	43.80	43.80	43.80	43.80	43.80	43.80	59.50	59.50	59.50	Quota	2f. s
7.72	9.83	10.83	8.40	8.29	8.19	8.10	8.01	7.85	7.54	7.15	6.73	2.43	2.11	1.75	SDRs	1b. s
8.36	7.28	7.30	9.64	9.66	9.32	9.32	9.33	7.08	7.10	6.44	6.46	10.40	9.79	9.79	Reserve Position in the Fund	1c. s
10.62	10.69	10.69	10.69	10.69	9.15	7.02	4.90	2.77	.65	.07	8.76	8.76	8.76	8.76	Total Fund Cred.&Loans Outstg.	2tl
End of Period																**International Liquidity**	
186.57	173.10	128.40	110.89	106.86	113.33	162.30	164.19	118.33	70.37	44.35	110.12	78.72	47.46	....		Total Reserves minus Gold	1l. d
9.85	11.44	11.95	8.79	8.13	9.00	9.91	11.36	10.56	9.91	10.17	9.63	3.34	2.90	2.55	SDRs	1b. d
10.66	8.47	8.05	10.09	9.47	10.24	11.40	13.24	9.53	9.33	9.16	9.24	14.30	13.45	14.29	Reserve Position in the Fund	1c. d
166.06	153.18	108.40	92.00	89.26	94.09	141.00	139.59	98.24	51.13	25.01	91.25	61.08	31.11	....	Foreign Exchange	1d. d
23.81	20.63	11.55	17.36	14.93	9.28	11.48	17.19	20.52	14.38	46.41	32.77	29.14	28.50	....	Monetary Authorities: Other Liab.	4.. d
21.29	26.11	28.00	20.90	31.57	28.90	21.12	28.99	35.03	29.80	32.44	45.27	41.66	31.68	....	Deposit Money Banks: Assets	7a. d
...	5.60	4.94	7.44	12.47	5.72	—	.26	.24	1.10	.70	1.68	—	.03	....	*of which:* Claims on Nonbanks	7ad d
8.41	13.63	25.10	17.90	15.78	24.79	9.89	9.23	12.88	6.77	7.45	8.60	8.76	6.07	....	Deposit Money Banks: Liabilities	7b. d
6.55	6.26	24.30	17.31	15.10	22.26	7.81	8.06	10.54	6.03	6.60	7.27	8.12	4.46	....	*of which:* Liab. to Nonbanks	7bd d
5.10	6.42	6.20	8.81	7.66	9.36	8.78	18.70	22.30	25.99	17.56	17.92	15.59	14.73	....	Other Banking Insts.: Liabilities	7f. d
																Monetary Authorities	
17,321	16,071	11,921	10,927	11,151	10,595	13,663	11,989	9,077	5,462	5,372	13,191	11,514	6,946	....		Foreign Assets	11
1,232	1,219	2,483	3,887	3,937	3,519	4,375	7,151	6,348	9,667	18,608	20,611	29,127	34,915	....	Claims on Central Government	12a
25	7	14	2	2	2	2	—	—	—	—	—	—	—	....	Claims on Official Entities	12bx
517	635	285	264	248	267	240	223	191	178	144	128	115	123	....	Claims on Private Sector	12d
504	417	730	1,027	1,643	2,830	928	872	3,095	3,050	1,327	655	917	1,321	....	Claims on Deposit Money Banks	12e
36	93	356	601	532	598	548	321	631	816	555	378	32	....	....	Claims on Other Financial Insts.	12f
7,978	6,964	7,237	8,065	8,559	9,584	10,877	12,051	10,822	9,261	10,129	14,588	14,097	18,024	....	Reserve Money	14
5,689	6,086	6,260	6,662	7,030	7,161	7,686	8,203	8,439	7,744	8,593	8,822	10,321	11,522	....	*of which:* Currency Outside DMBs	14a
135	972	623	453	395	547	633	663	688	544	1,216	601	913	346	....	Time Deposits	15
3,469	3,203	2,360	3,078	3,006	1,807	1,688	1,758	1,859	1,183	5,634	5,426	6,024	5,932	....	Foreign Liabilities	16c
4,542	3,973	3,488	2,825	2,872	3,082	3,048	3,076	2,320	1,243	2,452	5,911	7,527	4,492	....	Central Government Deposits	16d
21	99	61	118	86	62	50	42	33	766	732	1,083	4,098	4,157	....	Counterpart Funds	16e
3,357	3,917	4,494	4,659	4,727	4,923	4,965	4,965	5,139	5,486	6,526	8,024	8,631	....	....	Capital Accounts	17a
131	−687	−2,475	−2,489	−2,133	−2,194	−1,505	−1,998	−1,518	692	−683	−671	416	....	....	Other Items (Net)	17r
End of Period																**Deposit Money Banks**	
999	433	585	874	966	1,391	1,870	2,277	966	701	1,040	5,097	3,117	5,778	....		Reserves	20
1,976	‡2,424	2,600	2,060	3,294	2,702	1,778	2,117	2,687	2,313	3,929	5,423	6,093	4,637	....	Foreign Assets	21
426	648	1,220	1,982	2,757	3,068	3,698	4,851	7,100	6,348	5,421	5,448	6,667	4,495	....	Claims on Central Government	22a
194	269	400	852	701	677	641	688	853	1,533	2,533	810	298	679	....	Claims on Official Entities	22bx
5,689	7,090	7,742	8,085	10,021	13,140	13,198	13,356	16,302	17,597	14,629	12,122	15,308	17,875	....	Claims on Private Sector	22d
5,020	‡5,191	4,777	5,056	5,743	6,306	8,234	7,922	8,228	7,305	7,346	8,587	11,571	12,876	....	Demand Deposits	24
3,065	‡3,237	4,090	5,306	6,154	8,184	8,641	10,885	12,471	13,588	13,804	14,879	14,249	13,356	....	Time and Savings Deposits	25
781	‡1,265	2,330	1,764	1,647	2,317	832	674	988	525	903	1,030	1,281	889	....	Foreign Liabilities	26c
166	‡714	837	917	1,824	1,711	2,256	2,103	2,621	3,457	3,220	2,800	2,953	2,854	....	Central Government Deposits	26d
572	512	742	1,113	1,810	2,729	1,634	610	2,829	2,820	1,399	600	469	719	....	Credit from Monetary Authorities	26g
500	788	1,015	1,330	2,096	2,458	2,595	2,681	3,001	3,348	3,469	2,876	3,535	3,778	....	Capital Accounts	27a
−818	−843	−1,244	−1,635	−1,533	−2,728	−3,007	−1,586	−2,230	−2,552	−2,589	−1,873	−2,575	−1,614	....	Other Items (Net)	27r
End of Period																**Monetary Survey**	
15,047	‡14,026	9,830	8,145	9,793	9,173	12,921	11,674	8,918	6,068	2,764	12,157	10,303	4,763	....		Foreign Assets (Net)	31n
3,481	‡5,373	8,247	12,038	13,597	16,683	17,611	21,626	26,698	31,653	36,569	31,210	41,471	....	....	Domestic Credit	32
−3,034	‡−2,775	−604	2,151	2,009	1,915	2,890	6,945	8,630	11,437	18,480	17,469	25,436	32,186	....	Claims on Central Govt. (Net)	32an
219	276	414	853	703	678	643	688	853	1,533	2,533	810	298	679	....	Claims on Official Entities	32bx
6,207	7,724	8,027	8,348	10,269	13,407	13,438	13,580	16,493	17,776	14,773	12,250	15,423	17,998	....	Claims on Private Sector	32d
90	147	410	685	616	682	640	413	723	908	783	682	314	....	....	Claims on Other Financial Insts.	32f
12,026	‡11,774	11,460	12,317	13,343	14,699	17,334	17,791	18,332	16,053	16,846	18,145	22,631	25,041	....	Money	34
3,200	‡4,209	4,712	5,759	6,549	8,731	9,274	11,549	13,159	14,132	15,020	15,480	15,162	13,701	....	Quasi-Money	35
3,302	3,416	1,904	2,106	3,498	2,426	3,924	3,960	4,125	7,536	7,467	9,743	13,981	....	....	Other Items (Net)	37r
15,226	‡15,983	16,172	18,077	19,892	23,430	26,608	29,339	31,491	30,184	31,866	33,625	37,793	38,743	....	Money plus Quasi-Money	35l
End of Period																**Other Banking Institutions**	
80	263	187	396	183	292	200	292	191	127	134	584	887	1,332	....		Cash	40..k
191	188	214	195	154	106	98	70	45	119	143	131	108	83	....	Claims on Official Entities	42bx k
1,019	1,166	1,436	1,863	2,088	2,258	2,456	2,961	4,184	4,264	4,362	3,162	3,038	2,732	....	Claims on Private Sector	42d. k
474	596	575	868	800	875	740	1,366	1,711	2,017	2,127	2,147	2,281	2,155	....	Long Term Foreign Liabilities	46cl k
36	93	356	601	532	598	548	321	631	816	555	354	10	9	....	Cred.from Monetary Authorities	46g. k
—	—	—	—	—	—	—	—	—	—	—	—	—	—	....	Cred.from Deposit Money Banks	46h. k
1,080	956	1,001	1,240	1,444	1,572	1,970	2,133	2,221	2,168	2,567	2,009	2,272	2,395	....	Capital Accounts	47a. k
−300	−29	−95	−256	−350	−390	−503	−496	−144	−491	−609	−634	−531	−411	....	Other Items (Net)	47r. k

Rwanda

714

	1965	1966	1967	1968	1969	1970	1971	1972	1973	1974	1975	1976	1977	1978	1979
Interest Rates														*Percent Per Annum*	
Discount Rate *(End of Period)* 60	5.00	5.00	5.00	5.00	5.00	5.00	5.00	5.00	5.00	5.00	5.00	5.00	5.00	5.00	9.00
Deposit Rate 60l	....	....	....	....	....	....	....	....	....	....	....	....	....	2.00	2.71
Lending Rate 60p	....	....	....	....	....	....	....	....	....	....	....	....	....	12.50	13.04
Prices														*Index Numbers (1990=100):*	
Consumer Prices 64	....	18.7	19.0	19.6	19.7	19.8	19.9	20.5	22.4	29.4	I 38.2	41.0	46.6	52.7	61.0
International Transactions														*Millions of Francs*	
Exports 70	1,406	1,174	1,404	1,487	1,424	2,481	2,233	1,795	2,787	3,372	3,872	7,471	8,511	6,655	10,961
Imports, cif 71	2,094	2,047	2,022	2,246	2,362	2,910	3,305	3,183	2,819	5,416	9,167	9,858	11,406	17,447	17,856
Imports, fob 71.v	1,675	1,638	1,618	1,797	1,890	2,328	2,644	2,546	2,253	4,261	7,174	8,010	9,212	11,864	11,951
														1990=100	
Volume of Exports 72	33	29	32	35	32	42	44	36	42	32	57	56	47	41	79
Export Prices 74	21	67	66	65	62	79	67	68	77	89	79	134	212	147	134
Balance of Payments														*Millions of US Dollars:*	
Goods: Exports f.o.b. .... 78aa d	....	....	....	....	....	....	....	....	....	....	....	114.2	126.5	111.7	203.0
Goods: Imports f.o.b. .... 78ab d	....	....	....	....	....	....	....	....	....	....	....	-104.5	-102.3	-144.9	-159.5
Trade Balance .... 78ac d	....	....	....	....	....	....	....	....	....	....	....	9.7	24.2	-33.3	43.5
Services: Credit .... 78ad d	....	....	....	....	....	....	....	....	....	....	....	8.0	11.0	14.2	23.7
Services: Debit .... 78ae d	....	....	....	....	....	....	....	....	....	....	....	-49.5	-74.7	-116.4	-147.6
Balance on Goods and Services .... 78af d	....	....	....	....	....	....	....	....	....	....	....	-31.8	-39.5	-135.6	-80.4
Income: Credit .... 78ag d	....	....	....	....	....	....	....	....	....	....	....	1.2	3.4	4.5	8.4
Income: Debit .... 78ah d	....	....	....	....	....	....	....	....	....	....	....	-5.1	-7.9	-9.5	-11.9
Balance on Goods, Serv., & Inc. .... 78ai d	....	....	....	....	....	....	....	....	....	....	....	-35.7	-44.0	-140.6	-83.9
Current Transfers, n.i.e.: Credit .... 78aj d	....	....	....	....	....	....	....	....	....	....	....	68.8	85.0	113.7	150.8
Current Transfers: Debit .... 78ak d	....	....	....	....	....	....	....	....	....	....	....	-14.3	-18.9	-19.1	-21.1
Current Account, n.i.e. .... 78al d	....	....	....	....	....	....	....	....	....	....	....	18.8	22.1	-46.0	45.8
Capital Account, n.i.e.: Credit .... 78ba d	....	....	....	....	....	....	....	....	....	....	....	—	—	—	1.7
Capital Account: Debit .... 78bb d	....	....	....	....	....	....	....	....	....	....	....	-.7	-1.3	-.6	-1.4
Capital Account, n.i.e. .... 78bc d	....	....	....	....	....	....	....	....	....	....	....	-.7	-1.3	-.6	.3
Direct Investment Abroad .... 78bd d	....	....	....	....	....	....	....	....	....	....	....	—	—	—	—
Dir. Invest. in Rep. Econ., n.i.e. .... 78be d	....	....	....	....	....	....	....	....	....	....	....	5.9	5.0	4.7	12.6
Portfolio Investment Assets .... 78bf d	....	....	....	....	....	....	....	....	....	....	....	—	—	—	—
Portfolio Investment Liab., n.i.e. .... 78bg d	....	....	....	....	....	....	....	....	....	....	....	—	.1	—	—
Other Investment Assets .... 78bh d	....	....	....	....	....	....	....	....	....	....	....	-2.8	-17.5	11.3	-12.3
Other Investment Liab., n.i.e. .... 78bi d	....	....	....	....	....	....	....	....	....	....	....	13.5	31.3	31.2	14.9
Financial Account, n.i.e. .... 78bj d	....	....	....	....	....	....	....	....	....	....	....	16.6	18.8	47.1	15.1
Net Errors and Omissions .... 78ca d	....	....	....	....	....	....	....	....	....	....	....	-2.0	-5.2	.1	.5
Overall Balance .... 78cb d	....	....	....	....	....	....	....	....	....	....	....	32.6	34.5	.7	61.7
Reserves and Related Items .... 79da d	....	....	....	....	....	....	....	....	....	....	....	-32.6	-34.5	-.7	-61.7
Reserve Assets .... 79db d	....	....	....	....	....	....	....	....	....	....	....	-32.6	-34.5	-.7	-70.0
Use of Fund Credit and Loans .... 79dc d	....	....	....	....	....	....	....	....	....	....	....	—	—	—	7.5
Liabs.Constit.For.Auth.Reserves .... 79dd d	....	....	....	....	....	....	....	....	....	....	....	—	—	—	—
Exceptional Financing .... 79de d	....	....	....	....	....	....	....	....	....	....	....	—	—	—	.8
Government Finance														*Millions of Francs:*	
Deficit (-) or Surplus 80	....	....	....	-201	-403	57	-466	-818	-653	-728	-727	-1,225	-1,026	-1,291	-1,618
Revenue 81	....	....	....	1,334	1,320	1,946	1,856	1,880	2,419	3,369	4,539	6,749	8,703	9,180	12,478
Grants Received 81z	....	....	....	—	—	—	—	—	—	—	471	1	—	—	—
Expenditure 82	....	....	....	1,540	1,720	1,888	2,319	2,696	3,069	4,060	5,651	7,881	9,610	10,370	13,790
Lending Minus Repayments 83	....	....	....	-5	3	1	3	2	3	37	86	94	119	101	306
Financing															
Net Borrowing: Domestic 84a	....	....	....	278	223	-12	403	802	521	246	140	-687	-426	-766	-487
Foreign 85a	....	....	....	-5	23	-18	-3	32	235	377	1,321	2,117	2,213	1,567	2,664
Use of Cash Balances 87	....	....	....	-71	157	-27	66	-16	-103	105	-734	-205	-761	490	-559
Debt: Domestic 88a	....	....	....	....	....	....	....	....	374	392	470	506	853	824	832
Foreign 89a	....	....	....	....	....	....	....	....	....	....	....	....	5,246	8,964	10,715
National Accounts														*Billions of Francs*	
Exports of Goods & Services 90c	....	....	....	1.5	1.5	2.5	2.3	1.9	2.8	3.5	4.8	9.0	10.2	12.0	20.2
Government Consumption 91f	....	....	....	1.5	1.7	1.9	2.2	2.4	2.8	3.4	8.8	10.2	12.1	12.8	13.0
Gross Fixed Capital Formation 93e	....	....	....	1.2	1.2	1.6	2.0	2.2	2.3	3.0	7.0	8.0	9.1	11.3	14.3
Increase/Decrease(-) in Stocks 93i	....	....	....	10.4	13.7	15.7	15.7	16.2	17.4	20.5	.3	.6	1.7	2.1	-2.7
Private Consumption 96f	....	....	....	15.4	17.2	19.3	19.5	19.9	19.8	24.9	41.2	46.1	51.2	62.1	74.5
Imports of Goods & Services 98c	....	....	....	-2.6	-2.7	-3.4	-3.8	-3.7	-3.3	-6.1	-9.3	-12.0	-12.7	-19.3	-21.9
Gross Domestic Product 99b	19.4	20.5	23.6	27.4	32.4	37.7	38.1	38.9	41.7	49.2	52.8	61.9	71.6	81.1	97.4
Gross Dom. Prod. 1990 Prices 99b.p	76.9	77.2	84.5	92.4	102.5	113.8	115.2	115.5	119.4	120.3	122.7	124.9	131.4	144.2	157.7
GDP Deflator (1990=100) .... 99bi p	25.3	26.6	27.9	29.7	31.6	33.1	33.0	33.7	34.9	40.9	43.0	49.6	54.5	56.2	61.7
														Millions:	
Population 99z	3.13	3.26	3.37	3.46	3.57	3.68	3.79	3.90	4.01	4.12	4.20	4.29	4.36	4.80	4.98

Deposit Money Banks: I Beginning in December 1981, the classification of external and government accounts has been improved.
Monetary Survey: I See note to section 20.

Rwanda

714

	1980	1981	1982	1983	1984	1985	1986	1987	1988	1989	1990	1991	1992	1993	1994		
Percent Per Annum																**Interest Rates**	
	9.00	9.00	9.00	9.00	9.00	9.00	9.00	9.00	9.00	9.00	14.00	14.00	11.00	11.00	....	Discount Rate (End of Period)	60
	6.25	6.25	6.25	6.25	6.25	6.25	6.25	6.25	6.25	6.31	6.88	8.75	7.73	5.00	....	Deposit Rate	60l
	13.50	13.50	13.50	13.50	13.50	13.88	14.00	13.00	12.00	12.00	13.17	19.00	16.67	15.00	....	Lending Rate	60p
Period Averages																**Prices**	
	65.4	69.7	78.4	83.6	88.1	89.6	88.6	92.3	95.0	96.0	100.0	119.6	131.1	147.3	....	Consumer Prices	64
Millions of Francs																**International Transactions**	
	10,354	10,199	9,550	11,405	14,496	13,221	16,466	8,949	8,291	7,635	9,224	11,598	8,917	....	....	Exports	70
	22,568	23,775	25,666	25,453	27,872	30,244	30,624	28,018	28,280	26,642	23,059	38,454	38,263	....	....	Imports, cif	71
	14,904	17,230	17,961	17,947	19,408	21,061	21,326	19,511	19,694	18,553	16,058	26,779	26,646	....	....	Imports, fob	71.v
1990=100																	
	44	69	61	63	71	67	76	94	72	72	100	87	78	....	....	Volume of Exports	72
	118	150	159	188	191	196	209	112	....	115	100	131	105	....	....	Export Prices	74
Minus Sign Indicates Debit																**Balance of Payments**	
	133.6	113.3	108.5	124.1	142.6	126.1	184.1	121.4	117.9	104.7	102.6	95.6	68.5			Goods: Exports f.o.b.	78aa d
	−195.8	−207.1	−214.7	−197.6	−197.5	−219.3	−259.2	−267.0	−278.6	−254.1	−227.7	−228.1	−240.4			Goods: Imports f.o.b.	78ab d
	−62.2	−93.8	−106.2	−73.6	−54.9	−93.2	−75.1	−145.5	−160.7	−149.4	−125.0	−132.5	−171.9			Trade Balance	78ac d
	31.8	37.3	33.3	27.9	31.9	34.9	43.3	46.2	48.2	43.0	42.2	43.0	31.4			Services: Credit	78ad d
	−123.4	−121.7	−120.9	−113.0	−113.2	−114.2	−148.4	−147.0	−134.3	−118.6	−131.1	−111.6	−114.6			Services: Debit	78ae d
	−153.9	−178.2	−193.8	−158.7	−136.2	−172.6	−180.2	−246.4	−246.8	−225.0	−213.9	−201.1	−255.1			Balance on Goods and Services	78af d
	17.1	25.2	16.1	8.6	8.2	9.2	9.3	10.3	8.7	9.3	4.4	3.5	4.7			Income: Credit	78ag d
	−15.4	−16.7	−18.8	−16.5	−14.6	−17.0	−22.4	−24.2	−30.7	−23.4	−20.9	−17.2	−17.4			Income: Debit	78ah d
	−152.2	−169.6	−196.5	−166.5	−142.7	−180.5	−193.2	−260.4	−268.9	−239.1	−230.4	−214.8	−267.8			Balance on Goods, Serv., & Inc.	78ai d
	126.9	119.2	129.7	141.3	122.5	136.7	151.6	155.0	153.0	141.6	147.4	209.3	213.6			Current Transfers, n.i.e.: Credit	78aj d
	−23.1	−23.5	−23.7	−23.4	−21.4	−20.0	−27.6	−29.4	−29.0	−25.5	−25.1	−28.3	−30.4			Current Transfers: Debit	78ak d
	−48.3	−74.0	−90.5	−48.6	−41.5	−63.7	−69.2	−134.8	−144.9	−123.0	−108.1	−33.8	−84.6			Current Account, n.i.e.	78al d
	1.8	1.8	5.5	1.7	1.6	1.3	2.0	2.3	2.4	2.7	1.7	2.6	—			Capital Account, n.i.e.: Credit	78ba d
	−1.4	−1.4	−1.6	−1.7	−1.7	−1.7	−2.0	−1.9	−2.0	−2.2	−2.4	−2.9	—			Capital Account: Debit	78bb d
	.4	.4	3.9	—	−.1	−.3	—	.4	.4	.5	−.6	−.3	—			Capital Account, n.i.e.	78bc d
																Direct Investment Abroad	78bd d
	16.4	18.0	20.7	11.1	15.1	14.6	17.6	17.5	21.0	15.5	7.7	4.6	2.2			Dir. Invest. in Rep. Econ., n.i.e.	78be d
	—	—	—	—	—	—	—	—	—	—	−.3	−.1	—			Portfolio Investment Assets	78bf d
	.6	.6	—	—	.1	—	—	—	—	—	—	—	—			Portfolio Investment Liab., n.i.e.	78bg d
	16.2	9.9	15.4	2.9	.4	−6.7	−1.6	12.8	17.7	8.8	8.3	23.8	19.2			Other Investment Assets	78bh d
	39.6	23.4	16.4	17.3	37.5	61.4	87.9	91.9	55.0	29.6	40.0	70.8	41.0			Other Investment Liab., n.i.e.	78bi d
	72.8	51.9	52.5	31.4	53.0	69.3	103.9	122.3	93.7	53.9	55.7	99.1	62.4			Financial Account, n.i.e.	78bj d
	−1.9	14.9	−2.5	−1.1	−3.6	−3.6	−4.5	1.5	.4	1.9	30.3	.2	18.2			Net Errors and Omissions	78ca d
	23.0	−6.7	−36.6	−18.4	7.8	1.7	30.2	−10.6	−50.4	−66.7	−22.9	65.2	−4.0			Overall Balance	78cb d
	−23.0	6.7	36.6	18.4	−7.8	−1.7	−30.2	10.6	50.4	66.7	22.9	−65.2	4.0			Reserves and Related Items	79da d
	−29.3	.1	36.6	18.4	−7.8	−.1	−27.7	13.3	27.8	48.9	1.2	−77.0	4.0			Reserve Assets	79db d
	6.3	.1	—	—	—	−1.6	−2.5	−2.8	−2.9	−2.7	−.8	11.7	—			Use of Fund Credit and Loans	79dc d
	—	6.6	—	—	—	—	—	—	25.5	20.5	22.4	—	—			Liabs.Constit.For.Auth.Reserves	79dd d
																Exceptional Financing	79de d
Year Ending December 31																**Government Finance**	
	−1,875	....	....	....	....	....	....	....	−6,317ᵖ	−11,280ᵖ	−7,551ᵖ	−15,034ᵖ				Deficit (−) or Surplus	80
	13,805								25,987ᵖ	23,144ᵖ	26,056ᵖ	28,723ᵖ				Revenue	81
									5,291ᵖ	5,871ᵖ	13,682ᵖ	10,796ᵖ				Grants Received	81z
	15,458								37,706ᵖ	40,436ᵖ	47,658ᵖ	54,868ᵖ				Expenditure	82
	222								−111ᵖ	−141ᵖ	−369ᵖ	−315ᵖ				Lending Minus Repayments	83
																Financing	
	1,139								1,975ᵖ	7,048ᵖ	3,806ᵖ	7,951ᵖ				Net Borrowing: Domestic	84a
	2,858								4,101ᵖ	5,370ᵖ	6,784ᵖ	8,852ᵖ				Foreign	85a
	−2,122								241ᵖ	−1,138ᵖ	−3,039ᵖ	−1,769ᵖ				Use of Cash Balances	87
	940								17,179ᵖ	23,773ᵖ	25,500ᵖ	35,796ᵖ				Debt: Domestic	88a
	15,979								49,416ᵖ	82,524ᵖ	89,012ᵖ	95,817ᵖ				Foreign	89a
Billions of Francs																**National Accounts**	
	15.6	12.1	15.1	16.1	20.0	18.7	21.4	16.9	16.1	16.4	13.4	18.0	16.1	....		Exports of Goods & Services	90c
	13.5	24.6	16.9	16.7	16.2	19.5	20.1	23.2	24.7	24.4	29.1	44.3	54.5	....		Government Consumption	91f
	13.2	16.0	18.7	20.7	24.6	27.0	26.8	26.9	25.5	25.7	25.7	29.1	32.3	....		Gross Fixed Capital Formation	93e
	4.2	.3	4.5	−1.5	.5	3.0	.2	—	1.0	.1	−1.1	−2.9	−.1	....		Increase/Decrease(−) in Stocks	93i
	90.0	96.4	107.2	119.2	128.9	139.8	134.7	137.9	149.4	159.5	156.2	172.4	166.9	....		Private Consumption	96f
	−28.5	−26.7	−31.6	−29.5	−31.2	−34.5	−34.3	−36.1	−34.5	−34.9	−32.4	−48.0	−52.5	....		Imports of Goods & Services	98c
	108.0	122.6	130.9	142.1	159.1	173.7	170.3	174.4	183.9	193.3	193.9	212.8	217.3	....		Gross Domestic Product	99b
	152.1	155.9	162.2	171.9	164.6	171.8	181.3	180.2	189.2	190.1	193.9	195.4	196.4	....		Gross Dom. Prod. 1990 Prices	99b.p
	71.0	78.6	80.7	82.7	96.6	101.1	93.9	96.8	97.2	101.7	100.0	108.9	110.7	....		GDP Deflator (1990=100)	99bi p
Midyear Estimates																	
	5.16	5.35	5.55	5.76	5.87	6.06	6.24	6.42	6.61	6.80	7.18	7.17	7.36	7.55	....	Population	99z

St. Kitts and Nevis

361

		1965	1966	1967	1968	1969	1970	1971	1972	1973	1974	1975	1976	1977	1978	1979
Exchange Rates																
													E. Caribbean Dollars per SDR:			
Official Rate	aa	1.7126	1.7203	1.9948	2.0131	1.9994	2.0053	2.0417	2.2194	2.4925	2.5024	2.7770	3.1369	3.2797	3.5175	3.5568
													E. Caribbean Dollars per US Dollar			
Official Rate	ae	1.7126	1.7203	1.9948	2.0131	1.9994	2.0053	1.8805	2.0442	2.0661	2.0439	2.3721	2.7000	2.7000	2.7000	2.7000
													Index Numbers (1990=100):			
Nominal Effective Exchange Rate	ne c	....	....	....	....	....	....	....	....	....	....	....	....	....	....	86.22
Real Effective Exchange Rate	re c	....	....	....	....	....	....	....	....	....	....	....	....	....	....	111.74
Fund Position													*Millions of SDRs:*			
Quota	2f. s	....	....	....	....	....	....	....	....	....	....	....	....	....	....	....
SDRs	1b. s	....	....	....	....	....	....	....	....	....	....	....	....	....	....	....
Reserve Position in the Fund	1c. s	....	....	....	....	....	....	....	....	....	....	....	....	....	....	....
International Liquidity												*Millions of US Dollars Unless Otherwise Indicated:*				
Total Reserves minus Gold	1l. d	....	....	....	....	....	....	....	....	....	....	....	....	....	....	....
SDRs	1b. d	....	....	....	....	....	....	....	....	....	....	....	....	....	....	....
Reserve Position in the Fund	1c. d	....	....	....	....	....	....	....	....	....	....	....	....	....	....	....
Foreign Exchange	1d. d	....	....	....	....	....	....	....	....	....	....	....	....	....	....	....
Deposit Money Banks: Assets	7a. d	....	....	....	....	....	....	....	....	....	....	....	....	....	....	22.18
of which: Claims on Nonbanks	7ad d	....	....	....	....	....	....	....	....	....	....	....	....	....	....	14.02
Deposit Money Banks: Liabilities	7b. d	....	....	....	....	....	....	....	....	....	....	....	....	....	....	11.25
of which: Liab. to Nonbanks	7bd d	....	....	....	....	....	....	....	....	....	....	....	....	....	....	4.79
Monetary Authorities													*Millions of E. Caribbean Dollars:*			
Foreign Assets	11	....	....	....	....	....	....	....	....	....	....	....	....	....	....	3.65
Claims on Central Government	12a	....	....	....	....	....	....	....	....	....	1.96	1.96	3.35	3.36	3.36	3.36
Claims on Deposit Money Banks	12e	....	....	....	....	....	....	....	....	....	....	....	....	....	....	....
Reserve Money	14	....	....	....	....	....	....	....	....	....	....	....	....	....	....	7.01
of which: Currency Outside DMBs	14a	....	....	....	....	....	....	....	....	....	....	....	....	....	....	....
Foreign Liabilities	16c	....	....	....	....	....	....	....	....	....	....	....	....	....	....	—
Central Government Deposits	16d	....	....	....	....	....	....	....	....	....	....	....	....	....	....	—
Other Items (Net)	17r	....	....	....	....	....	....	....	....	....	....	....	....	....	....	—
Deposit Money Banks													*Millions of E. Caribbean Dollars:*			
Reserves	20	....	....	....	....	....	....	....	....	....	....	....	....	....	....	8.56
Foreign Assets	21	....	....	....	....	....	....	....	....	....	....	....	....	....	....	59.89
Claims on Central Government	22a	....	....	....	....	....	....	....	....	....	....	....	....	....	....	6.94
Claims on Local Government	22b	....	....	....	....	....	....	....	....	....	....	....	....	....	....	—
Claims on Nonfin.Pub.Enterprises	22c	....	....	....	....	....	....	....	....	....	....	....	....	....	....	8.19
Claims on Private Sector	22d	....	....	....	....	....	....	....	....	....	....	....	....	....	....	43.24
Claims on Nonbank Financial Insts	22f	....	....	....	....	....	....	....	....	....	....	....	....	....	....	3.36
Demand Deposits	24	....	....	....	....	....	....	....	....	....	....	....	....	....	....	10.81
Time, Savings,& Fgn.Currency Dep.	25	....	....	....	....	....	....	....	....	....	....	....	....	....	....	74.73
Foreign Liabilities	26c	....	....	....	....	....	....	....	....	....	....	....	....	....	....	30.37
Central Government Deposits	26d	....	....	....	....	....	....	....	....	....	....	....	....	....	....	15.62
Credit from Monetary Authorities	26g	....	....	....	....	....	....	....	....	....	....	....	....	....	....	5.70
Capital Accounts	27a	....	....	....	....	....	....	....	....	....	....	....	....	....	....	7.29
Other Items (Net)	27r	....	....	....	....	....	....	....	....	....	....	....	....	....	....	−14.32
Monetary Survey													*Millions of E. Caribbean Dollars*			
Foreign Assets (Net)	31n	....	....	....	....	....	....	....	....	....	....	....	....	....	....	33.17
Domestic Credit	32	....	....	....	....	....	....	....	....	....	....	....	....	....	....	49.48
Claims on Central Govt.(Net)	32an	....	....	....	....	....	....	....	....	....	....	....	....	....	....	−5.32
Claims on Local Government	32b	....	....	....	....	....	....	....	....	....	....	....	....	....	....	—
Claims on Nonfin.Pub.Enterprises	32c	....	....	....	....	....	....	....	....	....	....	....	....	....	....	8.19
Claims on Private Sector	32d	....	....	....	....	....	....	....	....	....	....	....	....	....	....	43.24
Claims on Nonbank Financial Inst	32f	....	....	....	....	....	....	....	....	....	....	....	....	....	....	3.36
Money	34	....	....	....	....	....	....	....	....	....	....	....	....	....	....	9.25
Quasi-Money	35	....	....	....	....	....	....	....	....	....	....	....	....	....	....	74.73
Other Items (Net)	37r	....	....	....	....	....	....	....	....	....	....	....	....	....	....	−1.34
Money plus Quasi-Money	35l	....	....	....	....	....	....	....	....	....	....	....	....	....	....	83.98
Interest Rates													*Percent Per Annum*			
Treasury Bill Rate	60c	....	....	....	....	....	....	....	....	....	....	....	....	....	....	....
Deposit Rate	60l	....	....	....	....	....	....	....	....	....	....	....	....	....	....	....
Lending Rate	60p	....	....	....	....	....	....	....	....	....	....	....	....	....	....	....
Prices													*Index Numbers (1990=100)*			
Consumer Prices	64	....	....	....	....	....	....	....	....	....	....	....	....	....	....	60.7

St. Kitts and Nevis

	1980	1981	1982	1983	1984	1985	1986	1987	1988	1989	1990	1991	1992	1993	1994		
End of Period																**Exchange Rates**	
	3.4436	3.1427	2.9784	2.8268	2.6466	2.9657	3.3026	3.8304	3.6334	3.5482	3.8412	3.8622	3.7125	3.7086	3.9416	Official Rate	aa
End of Period (ae)																	
	2.7000	2.7000	2.7000	2.7000	2.7000	2.7000	2.7000	2.7000	2.7000	2.7000	2.7000	2.7000	2.7000	2.7000	2.7000	Official Rate	ae
Period Averages																	
	84.04	87.59	91.68	95.68	100.76	102.89	102.80	100.15	97.98	101.91	100.00	100.84	102.45	110.73	112.82	Nominal Effective Exchange Rate	ne c
	111.21	114.88	117.99	119.28	121.57	121.11	116.90	109.70	102.60	105.02	100.00	99.54	99.28	105.22	106.16	Real Effective Exchange Rate	re c
End of Period																**Fund Position**	
	....	....	....	....	4.50	4.50	4.50	4.50	4.50	4.50	4.50	4.50	4.50	6.50	6.50	Quota	2f. s
	....	....	....	....	—	—	—	—	—	—	—	—	—	—	—	SDRs	1b. s
	....	....	....	....	—	—	.01	.01	.01	.01	.01	.01	.01	.02	.01	Reserve Position in the Fund	1c. s
End of Period																**International Liquidity**	
	....	4.02	3.33	3.15	5.65	7.41	10.23	10.57	10.32	16.39	16.28	16.63	26.24	29.42	31.82	Total Reserves minus Gold	1l. d
	....	....	....	....	—	—	—	—	—	—	—	—	—	—	—	SDRs	1b. d
	....	....	....	....	—	—	.01	.01	.01	.01	.01	.01	.01	.02	.02	Reserve Position in the Fund	1c. d
	....	4.02	3.33	3.15	5.65	7.41	10.22	10.56	10.31	16.38	16.27	16.62	26.23	29.40	31.80	Foreign Exchange	1d. d
	33.13	15.48	12.37	24.81	21.86	27.92	27.22	46.98	43.06	31.40	32.62	33.68	45.57	59.65	70.62	Deposit Money Banks: Assets	7a. d
	20.04	8.37	5.76	7.63	11.54	8.24	11.97	20.67	1.25	1.62	1.78	2.34	5.36	16.75	19.50	of which: Claims on Nonbanks	7ad d
	13.71	14.91	10.65	24.34	17.47	24.21	20.99	33.53	29.20	22.35	22.52	27.24	45.10	58.96	73.35	Deposit Money Banks: Liabilities	7b. d
	6.75	6.32	6.44	7.08	6.52	9.78	10.33	10.84	11.07	12.32	15.22	15.35	13.92	15.98	20.77	of which: Liab. to Nonbanks	7bd d
End of Period																**Monetary Authorities**	
	−.48	20.27	11.01	14.44	15.26	20.02	27.63	28.56	27.86	44.27	43.97	44.96	70.93	79.54	85.80	Foreign Assets	11
	3.36	3.36	5.91	6.40	14.10	16.07	16.04	16.03	14.91	10.71	14.63	14.15	7.80	8.34	4.95	Claims on Central Government	12a
	—	—	—	—	1.03	.21	.10	1.68	1.61	.06	.05	.05	.03	.01	3.52	Claims on Deposit Money Banks	12e
	2.88	23.63	16.92	20.84	30.39	36.30	43.77	46.27	44.39	55.04	58.65	59.10	78.70	87.89	94.27	Reserve Money	14
	....	10.33	11.10	11.59	12.61	9.39	12.22	13.00	16.08	22.65	21.43	23.86	23.04	28.08	28.28	of which: Currency Outside DMBs	14a
	—	—	—	—	—	—	—	—	—	—	—	—	—	—	—	Foreign Liabilities	16c
	—	—	—	—	—	—	—	—	—	—	—	—	.06	.06	—	Central Government Deposits	16d
	—	—	—	—	—	—	—	—	—	—	—	—	—	—	—	Other Items (Net)	17r
End of Period																**Deposit Money Banks**	
	4.20	13.29	5.82	9.25	17.33	26.81	30.54	33.22	30.10	32.62	34.68	38.69	57.09	63.95	65.79	Reserves	20
	89.45	41.78	33.40	66.99	59.01	75.39	73.49	126.85	116.25	84.79	88.07	90.93	123.05	161.06	190.68	Foreign Assets	21
	5.00	6.68	15.26	21.97	26.76	35.65	41.21	39.37	48.48	53.56	65.95	71.31	70.63	57.69	63.70	Claims on Central Government	22a
	—	—	—	—	—	—	—	—	5.49	6.33	6.88	6.57	7.52	6.97	Claims on Local Government	22b
	21.48	32.57	35.78	43.60	45.51	56.20	58.20	2.31	8.52	19.75	34.55	31.64	30.17	32.46	41.50	Claims on Nonfin.Pub.Enterprises	22c
	52.77	67.40	75.71	84.80	96.58	104.76	102.64	122.81	170.08	223.98	231.91	262.49	334.56	375.78	416.36	Claims on Private Sector	22d
	.36	.31	.31	.30	.29	.25	.25	.25	.25	.25	.25	1.00	1.00	1.18	.03	Claims on Nonbank Financial Insts	22f
	9.34	16.09	14.39	15.99	16.64	23.51	37.59	42.25	32.40	38.58	38.56	36.49	42.07	47.83	44.54	Demand Deposits	24
	87.31	90.41	105.43	123.11	141.64	171.31	182.75	156.98	182.42	218.54	241.44	258.69	302.55	332.09	339.43	Time, Savings,& Fgn.Currency Dep.	25
	37.02	40.26	28.74	65.71	47.18	65.36	56.68	90.52	78.85	60.36	60.81	73.55	121.76	159.18	198.05	Foreign Liabilities	26c
	21.87	18.10	22.56	24.29	33.87	28.88	11.92	12.14	45.43	61.47	70.68	81.52	100.42	112.65	141.51	Central Government Deposits	26d
	5.44	3.65	2.81	3.16	.58	1.02	2.90	.65	—	1.88	—	.03	—	3.50	3.50	Credit from Monetary Authorities	26g
	10.02	13.35	12.30	13.80	13.70	14.25	16.88	22.00	24.22	33.96	42.13	51.90	55.82	58.70	63.12	Capital Accounts	27a
	2.25	−19.82	−19.94	−19.15	−8.12	−5.28	−2.39	.27	15.85	5.85	8.10	.75	.46	−14.32	−5.12	Other Items (Net)	27r
End of Period																**Monetary Survey**	
	51.95	21.79	15.66	15.71	27.10	30.05	44.45	64.88	65.26	68.70	71.22	62.34	72.22	81.42	78.44	Foreign Assets (Net)	31n
	61.08	92.22	110.42	132.78	149.38	184.04	206.41	168.64	202.31	252.47	282.93	305.88	350.24	370.31	391.99	Domestic Credit	32
	−13.52	−8.06	−1.39	4.08	7.00	22.84	45.32	43.26	17.97	2.80	9.90	3.88	−22.06	−46.62	−72.86	Claims on Central Govt.(Net)	32an
	—	—	—	—	—	—	—	—	5.49	5.69	6.33	6.88	6.57	7.52	6.97	Claims on Local Government	32b
	21.48	32.57	35.78	43.60	45.51	56.20	58.20	2.31	8.52	19.75	34.55	31.64	30.17	32.46	41.50	Claims on Nonfin.Pub.Enterprises	32c
	52.77	67.40	75.71	84.80	96.58	104.76	102.64	122.81	170.08	223.98	231.91	262.49	334.56	375.78	416.36	Claims on Private Sector	32d
	.36	.31	.31	.30	.29	.25	.25	.25	.25	.25	.25	1.00	1.00	1.18	.03	Claims on Nonbank Financial Inst	32f
	8.02	26.42	25.49	27.58	29.26	32.90	49.81	55.26	48.48	61.23	59.99	60.35	65.12	75.92	72.84	Money	34
	87.31	90.41	105.43	123.11	141.64	171.31	182.75	156.98	182.42	218.54	241.44	258.69	302.55	332.09	339.43	Quasi-Money	35
	17.71	−2.83	−4.84	−2.19	5.57	9.89	18.30	21.28	36.66	41.39	52.72	49.18	54.80	43.72	58.17	Other Items (Net)	37r
	95.32	116.84	130.92	150.69	170.90	204.21	232.56	212.24	230.90	279.78	301.44	319.04	367.66	408.01	412.26	Money plus Quasi-Money	35l
Percent Per Annum																**Interest Rates**	
	6.5	6.5	6.5	6.5	6.5	6.5	6.5	6.5	6.5	6.5	6.5	6.5	6.5	6.5	6.5	Treasury Bill Rate	60c
	6.0	6.0	6.0	6.0	6.0	6.3	6.0	5.3	7.0	7.0	7.0	7.0	7.0	5.5	5.5	Deposit Rate	60l
	....	9.0	9.0	9.0	10.0	10.2	10.2	12.0	12.0	12.0	12.0	12.0	12.0	12.7	13.0	13.0	Lending Rate	60p
Period Averages																**Prices**	
	71.5	79.0	83.7	85.6	87.9	90.2	90.2	91.1	91.3	95.9	100.0	104.2	107.2	109.1	112.0	Consumer Prices	64

St. Kitts and Nevis

361

		1965	1966	1967	1968	1969	1970	1971	1972	1973	1974	1975	1976	1977	1978	1979
Balance of Payments															*Millions of US Dollars:*	
Goods: Exports f.o.b.	78aa *d*	...	...	...	...	...	...	...	...	...	...	...	...	...	...	...
Goods: Imports f.o.b.	78ab *d*	...	...	...	...	...	...	...	...	...	...	...	...	...	...	...
Trade Balance	78ac *d*	...	...	...	...	...	...	...	...	...	...	...	...	...	...	...
Services: Credit	78ad *d*	...	...	...	...	...	...	...	...	...	...	...	...	...	...	...
Services: Debit	78ae *d*	...	...	...	...	...	...	...	...	...	...	...	...	...	...	...
Balance on Goods and Services	78af *d*	...	...	...	...	...	...	...	...	...	...	...	...	...	...	...
Income: Credit	78ag *d*	...	...	...	...	...	...	...	...	...	...	...	...	...	...	...
Income: Debit	78ah *d*	...	...	...	...	...	...	...	...	...	...	...	...	...	...	...
Balance on Goods, Serv., & Inc.	78ai *d*	...	...	...	...	...	...	...	...	...	...	...	...	...	...	...
Current Transfers, n.i.e.: Credit	78aj *d*	...	...	...	...	...	...	...	...	...	...	...	...	...	...	...
Current Transfers: Debit	78ak *d*	...	...	...	...	...	...	...	...	...	...	...	...	...	...	...
Current Account, n.i.e.	78al *d*	...	...	...	...	...	...	...	...	...	...	...	...	...	...	...
Capital Account, n.i.e.: Credit	78ba *d*	...	...	...	...	...	...	...	...	...	...	...	...	...	...	...
Capital Account: Debit	78bb *d*	...	...	...	...	...	...	...	...	...	...	...	...	...	...	...
Capital Account, n.i.e.	78bc *d*	...	...	...	...	...	...	...	...	...	...	...	...	...	...	...
Direct Investment Abroad	78bd *d*	...	...	...	...	...	...	...	...	...	...	...	...	...	...	...
Dir. Invest. in Rep. Econ., n.i.e.	78be *d*	...	...	...	...	...	...	...	...	...	...	...	...	...	...	...
Portfolio Investment Assets	78bf *d*	...	...	...	...	...	...	...	...	...	...	...	...	...	...	...
Portfolio Investment Liab., n.i.e.	78bg *d*	...	...	...	...	...	...	...	...	...	...	...	...	...	...	...
Other Investment Assets	78bh *d*	...	...	...	...	...	...	...	...	...	...	...	...	...	...	...
Other Investment Liab., n.i.e.	78bi *d*	...	...	...	...	...	...	...	...	...	...	...	...	...	...	...
Financial Account, n.i.e.	78bj *d*	...	...	...	...	...	...	...	...	...	...	...	...	...	...	...
Net Errors and Omissions	78ca *d*	...	...	...	...	...	...	...	...	...	...	...	...	...	...	...
Overall Balance	78cb *d*	...	...	...	...	...	...	...	...	...	...	...	...	...	...	...
Reserves and Related Items	79da *d*	...	...	...	...	...	...	...	...	...	...	...	...	...	...	...
Reserve Assets	79db *d*	...	...	...	...	...	...	...	...	...	...	...	...	...	...	...
Use of Fund Credit and Loans	79dc *d*	...	...	...	...	...	...	...	...	...	...	...	...	...	...	...
Liabs.Constit.For.Auth.Reserves	79dd *d*	...	...	...	...	...	...	...	...	...	...	...	...	...	...	...
Exceptional Financing	79de *d*	...	...	...	...	...	...	...	...	...	...	...	...	...	...	...
Government Finance															*Millions of E. Caribbean Dollars:*	
Deficit (-) or Surplus	80	...	...	...	...	...	...	...	...	...	...	...	...	...	...	...
Revenue	81	...	...	...	...	...	...	...	...	...	...	...	...	...	...	...
Grants Received	81z	...	...	...	...	...	...	...	...	...	...	...	...	...	...	...
Expenditure	82	...	...	...	...	...	...	...	...	...	...	...	...	...	...	...
Lending Minus Repayments	83	...	...	...	...	...	...	...	...	...	...	...	...	...	...	...
Financing																	
Domestic	84a	...	...	...	...	...	...	...	...	...	...	...	...	...	...	...
Foreign	85a	...	...	...	...	...	...	...	...	...	...	...	...	...	...	...
National Accounts															*Millions of E. Caribbean Dollars*	
Exports of Goods & Services	90c	...	...	...	...	...	...	...	...	16.6	...	46.8	...	51.5	58.6	64.3
Government Consumption	91f	...	...	...	...	...	...	...	...	10.5	...	12.1	...	16.1	20.6	22.9
Gross Fixed Capital Formation	93e	...	...	...	...	...	...	...	...	7.1	...	7.7	...	30.8	25.1	37.3
Private Consumption	96f	...	...	...	...	...	...	...	...	47.4	...	57.1	...	47.2	57.3	73.5
Imports of Goods & Services	98c	...	...	...	...	...	...	...	...	−35.6	...	−51.4	...	−64.8	−69.1	−90.2
Gross Domestic Product	99b	...	...	...	...	...	...	...	...	48.6	...	74.1	75.5	80.7	92.6	107.7
GDP at Factor Cost, 1990 Prices	99b.*p*	...	...	...	...	...	...	...	...	...	...	...	...	...	...	...
GDP Deflator (1990=100)	99bi *p*	...	...	...	...	...	...	...	...	...	...	...	...	...	...	...
																Millions:
Population	99z	...	...	...	...	...	.04	.04	.04	.04	.04	.04	.04	.04	.04	.04

Government Finance: 1 Data prior to 1988 cover operations of the budgetary central government and the Social Security Fund. Beginning in 1988, data also cover operations of the trust funds.

St. Kitts and Nevis

	1980	1981	1982	1983	1984	1985	1986	1987	1988	1989	1990	1991	1992	1993	1994	
Minus Sign Indicates Debit																**Balance of Payments**
	24.12	24.26	18.84	18.43	20.15	20.37	25.15	27.99	27.44	28.61	27.65	27.89	32.33	31.31	....	Goods: Exports f.o.b. .... 78aa *d*
	−40.80	−43.42	−39.82	−46.74	−47.23	−46.70	−55.35	−69.96	−81.96	−90.19	−97.44	−97.05	−84.15	−88.36	....	Goods: Imports f.o.b. .... 78ab *d*
	−16.68	−19.16	−20.99	−28.32	−27.09	−26.33	−30.20	−41.96	−54.52	−61.58	−69.79	−69.16	−51.83	−57.05	....	Trade Balance .... 78ac *d*
	8.10	10.00	13.20	13.00	20.32	22.80	32.70	41.14	47.71	50.60	54.73	69.11	79.78	83.03	....	Services: Credit .... 78ad *d*
	−5.84	−7.19	−12.64	−10.82	−9.17	−10.32	−18.20	−22.37	−26.26	−30.49	−37.13	−37.68	−43.34	−47.78	....	Services: Debit .... 78ae *d*
	−14.42	−16.35	−20.42	−26.14	−15.94	−13.84	−15.71	−23.20	−33.06	−41.47	−52.19	−37.73	−15.39	−21.80	....	Balance on Goods and Services .... 78af *d*
	.70	1.20	1.30	1.80	.90	.30	2.27	3.22	4.51	3.54	3.31	2.65	2.51	2.14	....	Income: Credit .... 78ag *d*
	−1.94	−2.24	−.70	−.70	−.80	−1.60	−3.96	−5.05	−8.63	−12.71	−7.77	−9.87	−12.99	−14.81	....	Income: Debit .... 78ah *d*
	−15.66	−17.40	−19.82	−25.04	−15.84	−15.14	−17.40	−25.03	−37.18	−50.64	−56.65	−44.95	−25.86	−34.47	....	Balance on Goods, Serv., & Inc. ..... 78ai *d*
	13.00	12.70	13.10	13.20	14.80	12.62	14.93	17.63	19.50	22.76	20.22	17.77	17.58	17.69	....	Current Transfers, n.i.e.: Credit .... 78aj *d*
	—	—	−2.00	−2.90	−3.30	−4.15	−2.37	−2.98	−3.77	−6.41	−7.90	−4.51	−4.17	−4.13	....	Current Transfers: Debit .... 78ak *d*
	−2.66	−4.70	−8.72	−14.74	−4.34	−6.68	−4.84	−10.37	−21.46	−34.29	−44.33	−31.69	−12.45	−20.91	....	Current Account, n.i.e. .... 78al *d*
	—	—	—	—	—	—	—	—	—	—	—	—	—	—	....	Capital Account, n.i.e.: Credit ..... 78ba *d*
	—	—	—	—	—	—	—	—	—	—	—	—	—	—	....	Capital Account: Debit .... 78bb *d*
	—	—	—	—	—	—	—	—	—	—	—	—	—	—	....	Capital Account, n.i.e. .... 78bc *d*
	—	—	—	—	—	—	—	—	—	—	—	—	—	—	....	Direct Investment Abroad .... 78bd *d*
	1.00	.90	2.20	13.50	6.00	8.00	9.20	16.65	13.13	40.80	48.79	21.44	12.51	9.27	....	Dir. Invest. in Rep. Econ., n.i.e. ... 78be *d*
	—	—	—	—	—	—	—	—	—	—	—	−.07	—	—	....	Portfolio Investment Assets .... 78bf *d*
	—	—	—	—	—	—	—	—	—	—	—	—	—	2.22	....	Portfolio Investment Liab., n.i.e. .. 78bg *d*
	—	—	3.10	−12.44	2.95	−5.90	—	—	—	4.80	—	3.66	5.95	—	....	Other Investment Assets .... 78bh *d*
	3.94	4.80	−3.57	14.49	−1.60	7.05	−3.16	−2.78	5.89	5.99	2.68	.89	5.67	9.59	....	Other Investment Liab., n.i.e. ...... 78bi *d*
	4.94	5.70	1.74	15.55	7.35	9.15	6.04	13.87	19.02	51.59	51.47	25.92	24.13	21.08	....	Financial Account, n.i.e. .... 78bj *d*
	−3.88	−.90	3.19	.39	−1.21	−.53	1.81	−2.95	2.35	−10.97	−7.05	6.42	−1.87	3.20	....	Net Errors and Omissions .... 78ca *d*
	−1.60	.10	−3.80	1.20	1.80	1.94	3.01	.54	−.08	6.33	.09	.65	9.81	3.37	....	Overall Balance .... 78cb *d*
	1.60	−.10	3.80	−1.20	−1.80	−1.94	−3.01	−.54	.08	−6.33	−.09	−.65	−9.81	−3.37	....	Reserves and Related Items .... 79da *d*
	1.60	−.10	3.80	−1.20	−1.80	−1.94	−3.01	−.54	.08	−6.33	−.09	−.65	−9.81	−3.37	....	Reserve Assets .... 79db *d*
	—	—	—	—	—	—	—	—	—	—	—	—	—	—	....	Use of Fund Credit and Loans......... 79dc *d*
	—	—	—	—	—	—	—	—	—	—	—	—	—	—	....	Liabs.Constit.For.Auth.Reserves........ 79dd *d*
	....	....	....	....	....	....	....	....	....	....	....	....	....	....	....	Exceptional Financing .... 79de *d*
Year Ending December 31																**Government Finance**
	....	....	....	....	....	−13.12	2.85	−47.46	‡−23.95	−3.77	−.05	−1.28	6.61^P	9.90^P	....	Deficit (-) or Surplus 80
	....	....	....	....	....	59.95	71.71	82.26	‡93.57	111.60	122.87	121.43	137.42^P	165.33^P	....	Revenue 81
	....	....	....	....	....	4.07	5.45	7.99	11.81	7.52	3.45	4.97	2.79^P	.59^P	....	Grants Received 81z
	....	....	....	....	....	74.57	71.75	80.90	‡124.79	122.13	123.69	126.51	134.97^P	155.98^P	....	Expenditure 82
	....	....	....	....	....	2.57	2.56	56.81	4.54	.76	2.68	1.17	−1.37^P	.04^P	....	Lending Minus Repayments 83
																Financing
	....	....	....	....	....	....	....	....	‡3.83	−9.06	−1.58	−.39	−5.37^P	−14.20^P	....	Domestic 84a
	....	....	....	....	....	....	....	....	‡20.12	12.83	1.63	1.67	−1.24^P	4.30^P	....	Foreign 85a
Millions of E. Caribbean Dollars																**National Accounts**
	86.7	92.2	80.6	78.8	104.1	116.6	156.2	186.7	202.9	215.8	224.3	263.9	287.9	....	....	Exports of Goods & Services 90c
	27.1	39.7	36.5	36.8	45.4	47.4	50.3	56.7	60.2	68.7	79.2	79.9	82.9	....	....	Government Consumption............... 91f
	49.4	46.1	55.0	59.9	57.1	63.9	69.4	98.0	191.3	224.8	238.1	190.8	191.6	....	....	Gross Fixed Capital Formation 93e
	92.3	108.9	120.0	133.1	139.6	146.7	177.0	199.9	179.7	204.9	254.6	263.7	264.1	....	....	Private Consumption 96f
	−125.9	−136.6	−130.4	−150.4	−157.1	−164.0	−198.6	−249.3	−292.0	−327.8	−365.5	−351.7	−348.8	....	....	Imports of Goods & Services 98c
	129.6	150.3	161.9	158.3	189.2	210.6	254.2	292.0	342.0	386.5	430.8	446.5	477.8	....	....	Gross Domestic Product 99b
	206.4	217.0	230.6	228.1	248.7	262.5	278.7	299.4	328.7	350.8	361.3	375.2	388.5	403.9	....	GDP at Factor Cost, 1990 Prices .... 99b. *p*
	52.65	58.10	58.86	58.19	63.80	67.27	76.49	81.80	87.26	92.41	100.00	99.79	103.14	....	....	GDP Deflator (1990=100) .... 99bi *p*
Midyear Estimates																
	.04	.04	.04	.05	.04	.04	.04	.04	.04	.04	.04	.04	.04	.04	....	**Population** 99z

St. Lucia

		1965	1966	1967	1968	1969	1970	1971	1972	1973	1974	1975	1976	1977	1978	1979
Exchange Rates																*E.Caribbean Dollars per SDR: End of Period (aa)*
Official Rate	aa	1.7126	1.7203	1.9948	2.0131	1.9994	2.0053	2.0417	2.2194	2.4925	2.5024	2.7770	3.1369	3.2797	3.5175	3.5568
Official Rate	ae	1.7126	1.7203	1.9948	2.0131	1.9994	2.0053	1.8805	2.0442	2.0661	2.0439	2.3721	2.7000	2.7000	2.7000	2.7000
														Index Numbers (1990=100):		
Official Rate	ah x	157.3	157.1	154.5	134.6	134.5	134.8	137.3	140.7	137.9	131.6	125.0	103.5	100.0	100.0	100.0
Nominal Effective Exchange Rate	ne c	....	....	....	....	....	....	....	....	....	....	....	....	....	....	87.3
Real Effective Exchange Rate	re c	....	....	....	....	....	....	....	....	....	....	....	....	....	....	100.5
Fund Position																*Millions of SDRs:*
Quota	2f. s	....	....	....	....	....	....	....	....	....	....	....	....	....	....	3.60
SDRs	1b. s	....	....	....	....	....	....	....	....	....	....	....	....	....	....	—
Reserve Position in the Fund	1c. s	....	....	....	....	....	....	....	....	....	....	....	....	....	....	—
Total Fund Cred.&Loans Outstg.	2tl	....	....	....	....	....	....	....	....	....	....	....	....	....	....	
International Liquidity												*Millions of US Dollars Unless Otherwise Indicated:*				
Total Reserves minus Gold	1l. d	....	....	....	....	....	....	....	....	....	....	3.24	5.19	5.65	6.76	8.12
SDRs	1b. d	....	....	....	....	....	....	....	....	....	....	....	—	—	....	—
Reserve Position in the Fund	1c. d	....	....	....	....	....	....	....	....	....	....	....	—	—	....	—
Foreign Exchange	1d. d	....	....	....	....	....	....	....	....	....	....	3.24	5.19	5.65	6.76	8.12
Deposit Money Banks: Assets	7a. d	....	....	....	....	....	....	....	....	....	....	5.06	5.32	4.70	5.60	7.44
of which: Claims on Nonbanks	7ad d	....	....	....	....	....	....	....	....	....	....	.51	.56	.56	.85	2.16
Deposit Money Banks: Liabilities	7b. d	....	....	....	....	....	....	....	....	....	....	8.94	9.12	7.82	9.82	15.05
of which: Liab. to Nonbanks	7bd d	....	....	....	....	....	....	....	....	....	....	5.44	3.81	4.00	5.22	7.92
Monetary Authorities												*Millions of E. Caribbean Dollars:*				
Foreign Assets	11	....	....	....	....	....	....	....	....	....	....	7.69	14.02	15.26	18.24	21.94
Claims on Central Government	12a	....	....	....	....	....	....	....	....	....	....	3.87	3.87	3.87	5.87	9.13
Claims on Deposit Money Banks	12e	....	....	....	....	....	....	....	....	....	....	—	—	—	—	—
Reserve Money	14	....	....	....	....	....	....	....	....	....	....	11.56	17.89	19.14	24.12	31.06
of which: Currency Outside DMBs	14a	....	....	....	....	....	....	....	....	....	....	9.56	12.07	15.04	17.67	22.05
Foreign Liabilities	16c	....	....	....	....	....	....	....	....	....	....	—	—	—	—	—
Central Government Deposits	16d	....	....	....	....	....	....	....	....	....	....	—	—	—	—	—
Other Items (Net)	17r	....	....	....	....	....	....	....	....	....	....					
Deposit Money Banks												*Millions of E. Caribbean Dollars:*				
Reserves	20	....	....	....	....	....	....	....	....	....	....	2.00	5.82	4.10	6.45	9.01
Foreign Assets	21	....	....	....	....	....	....	....	....	....	....	12.01	14.35	12.68	15.12	20.10
Claims on Central Government	22a	....	....	....	....	....	....	....	....	....	....	19.66	16.23	15.86	10.86	19.30
Claims on Local Government	22b	....	....	....	....	....	....	....	....	....	....					
Claims on Nonfin.Pub.Enterprises	22c	....	....	....	....	....	....	....	....	....	....	2.60	3.00	3.90	4.70	5.21
Claims on Private Sector	22d	....	....	....	....	....	....	....	....	....	....	61.14	70.01	90.53	110.75	128.40
Claims on Nonbank Financial Insts	22f	....	....	....	....	....	....	....	....	....	....					.80
Demand Deposits	24	....	....	....	....	....	....	....	....	....	....	11.07	16.98	17.97	20.72	23.16
Time, Savings,& Fgn.Currency Dep.	25	....	....	....	....	....	....	....	....	....	....	61.46	71.46	73.47	88.99	104.41
Foreign Liabilities	26c	....	....	....	....	....	....	....	....	....	....	21.20	24.64	21.11	26.52	40.62
Central Government Deposits	26d	....	....	....	....	....	....	....	....	....	....	—	—	—	1.70	3.13
Credit from Monetary Authorities	26g	....	....	....	....	....	....	....	....	....	....	.30	.90	.50	1.20	.61
Capital Accounts	27a	....	....	....	....	....	....	....	....	....	....	2.00	2.00	2.00	2.00	2.22
Other Items (Net)	27r	....	....	....	....	....	....	....	....	....	....	1.39	−6.56	12.02	6.75	8.68
Monetary Survey												*Millions of E. Caribbean Dollars:*				
Foreign Assets (Net)	31n	....	....	....	....	....	....	....	....	....	....	−1.50	3.74	6.83	6.84	1.41
Domestic Credit	32	....	....	....	....	....	....	....	....	....	....	87.27	93.11	114.17	130.48	159.72
Claims on Central Govt. (Net)	32an	....	....	....	....	....	....	....	....	....	....	23.53	20.10	19.73	15.03	25.31
Claims on Local Government	32b	....	....	....	....	....	....	....	....	....	....					
Claims on Nonfin.Pub.Enterprises	32c	....	....	....	....	....	....	....	....	....	....	2.60	3.00	3.90	4.70	5.21
Claims on Private Sector	32d	....	....	....	....	....	....	....	....	....	....	61.14	70.01	90.53	110.75	128.40
Claims on Nonbank Financial Inst	32f	....	....	....	....	....	....	....	....	....	....	—	—	—	—	.80
Money	34	....	....	....	....	....	....	....	....	....	....	20.63	29.05	33.01	38.39	45.22
Quasi-Money	35	....	....	....	....	....	....	....	....	....	....	61.46	71.46	73.47	88.99	104.41
Other Items (Net)	37r	....	....	....	....	....	....	....	....	....	....	3.69	−3.66	14.52	9.95	11.51
Money plus Quasi-Money	35l	....	....	....	....	....	....	....	....	....	....	82.09	100.50	106.48	127.37	149.63
Interest Rates															*Percent Per Annum*	
Treasury Bill Rate	60c	....	....	....	....	....	....	....	....	....	....	....	....	....	....	....
Deposit Rate	60l	....	....	....	....	....	....	....	....	....	....	....	....	....	....	....
Lending Rate	60p	....	....	....	....	....	....	....	....	....	....	....	....	....	7.5	7.5
Prices															*Index Numbers (1990=100):*	
Consumer Prices	64	14.3	14.7	15.1	15.7	16.1	18.2	19.8	21.3	24.2	32.5	38.2	41.9	45.6	50.6	55.4
International Transactions															*Millions of E. Caribbean Dollars*	
Exports	70	11.17	12.11	11.66	12.55	16.54	18.73	12.23	15.11	19.23	32.91	36.81	54.19	66.29	77.68	96.63
Imports, cif	71	22.01	28.39	29.55	29.54	41.50	54.59	69.00	68.69	74.17	91.12	100.43	125.71	160.23	223.50	273.20
Imports, fob	71.v	20.01	25.81	26.86	26.86	37.73	49.62	62.73	62.45	67.43	82.83	91.30	114.28	145.65	203.17	248.34
																1980=100
Unit Value of Exports	74	....	....	....	....	....	....	....	....	....	....	62.7	60.3	I71.7	74.7	87.0

St. Lucia

1980	1981	1982	1983	1984	1985	1986	1987	1988	1989	1990	1991	1992	1993	1994		
\multicolumn{15}{l}{E.Caribbean Dollars per US Dollar: End of Period (ae)}	**Exchange Rates**	
3.4436	3.1427	2.9784	2.8268	2.6466	2.9657	3.3026	3.8304	3.6334	3.5482	3.8412	3.8622	3.7125	3.7086	3.9416	Official Rate	aa
2.7000	2.7000	2.7000	2.7000	2.7000	2.7000	2.7000	2.7000	2.7000	2.7000	2.7000	2.7000	2.7000	2.7000	2.7000	Official Rate	ae
\multicolumn{15}{l}{Period Averages}		
100.0	100.0	100.0	100.0	100.0	100.0	100.0	100.0	100.0	100.0	100.0	100.0	100.0	100.0	100.0	Official Rate	ah x
85.2	90.3	95.3	100.4	108.4	112.1	106.6	101.7	98.6	102.3	100.0	102.3	105.4	112.5	114.3	Nominal Effective Exchange Rate	ne c
102.2	112.1	115.0	116.8	121.7	120.0	112.8	110.7	103.6	105.6	100.0	101.9	104.5	108.4	108.8	Real Effective Exchange Rate	re c
\multicolumn{15}{l}{End of Period}	**Fund Position**	
5.40	5.40	5.40	7.50	7.50	7.50	7.50	7.50	7.50	7.50	7.50	7.50	7.50	11.00	11.00	Quota	2f. s
.07	.23	.01	.01	—	—	—	—	—	—	—	1.23	1.27	1.31	1.34	SDRs	1b. s
—	—	—	—	—	—	—	—	—	—	—	—	—	—	—	Reserve Position in the Fund	1c. s
1.35	4.05	2.55	2.55	2.02	.30	—	—	—	—	—	—	—	—	—	Total Fund Cred.&Loans Outstg.	2tl
\multicolumn{15}{l}{End of Period}	**International Liquidity**	
8.29	7.61	8.21	8.87	12.38	12.65	25.11	30.80	32.65	38.21	44.59	48.75	55.46	59.94	57.59	Total Reserves minus Gold	1l. d
.09	.27	.01	.01	—	—	—	—	—	—	—	1.75	1.82	1.80	1.84	SDRs	1b. d
—	—	—	—	—	—	—	—	—	—	—	—	—	—	1.99	Reserve Position in the Fund	1c. d
8.20	7.34	8.20	8.86	12.38	12.65	25.11	30.80	32.65	38.21	42.84	46.93	53.66	58.10	55.60	Foreign Exchange	1d. d
10.07	7.09	8.71	15.00	12.37	19.45	30.42	41.77	53.12	39.67	43.66	46.84	48.60	35.08	25.23	Deposit Money Banks: Assets	7a. d
1.50	1.26	1.45	2.76	1.80	1.88	2.55	3.66	1.89	4.08	9.12	8.97	8.86	10.53	9.04	of which: Claims on Nonbanks	7ad d
18.62	14.79	15.48	14.94	15.25	15.78	15.02	18.74	19.44	24.14	30.12	32.81	36.37	39.84	55.33	Deposit Money Banks: Liabilities	7b. d
8.79	8.84	9.40	9.60	9.49	9.93	9.39	11.97	14.34	16.17	19.08	21.44	26.07	30.03	31.96	of which: Liab. to Nonbanks	7bd d
\multicolumn{15}{l}{End of Period}	**Monetary Authorities**	
22.38	20.55	22.44	23.94	25.97	39.17	67.81	83.12	88.16	105.62	128.65	141.52	149.75	162.21	156.86	Foreign Assets	11
15.81	24.40	20.03	20.06	37.45	35.00	36.08	34.26	30.70	31.60	29.91	30.43	13.82	11.85	9.71	Claims on Central Government	12a
—	—	—	.34	—	—	1.45	1.68	1.10	.48	.04	.81	.02	.02	.02	Claims on Deposit Money Banks	12e
33.54	32.22	34.87	36.80	58.41	73.20	103.87	118.84	120.52	135.87	150.78	162.31	160.48	168.11	160.52	Reserve Money	14
24.61	27.69	28.04	30.26	30.08	33.01	39.05	52.06	56.28	67.28	64.23	68.09	64.26	67.88	66.85	of which: Currency Outside DMBs	14a
4.65	12.73	7.59	7.21	5.35	.97	.02	—	—	—	—	—	—	—	—	Foreign Liabilities	16c
—	—	—	—	—	—	—	—	.01	2.45	8.25	9.68	3.90	5.97	6.06	Central Government Deposits	16d
—	—	—	—	—	—	—	—	—	—	—	—	—	—	—	Other Items (Net)	17r
\multicolumn{15}{l}{End of Period}	**Deposit Money Banks**	
8.93	4.53	6.82	6.54	29.08	36.01	63.19	65.96	61.67	69.15	84.98	93.01	97.73	102.30	103.66	Reserves	20
27.18	19.14	23.53	40.49	33.41	52.52	82.13	112.77	143.42	107.11	117.88	126.46	131.23	94.72	68.12	Foreign Assets	21
14.97	12.68	17.41	19.22	20.96	31.01	41.91	43.53	38.42	36.92	34.80	32.63	47.91	52.12	47.49	Claims on Central Government	22a
—	—	—	—	—	—	—	—	.24	.24	.64	3.91	6.44	1.84	2.09	Claims on Local Government	22b
2.17	5.88	4.81	2.47	3.44	2.84	1.99	2.75	2.96	10.61	14.61	11.44	31.27	49.25	57.48	Claims on Nonfin.Pub.Enterprises	22c
163.53	184.98	196.95	208.06	237.22	251.61	275.15	310.21	401.52	519.42	578.48	623.78	683.36	751.43	860.16	Claims on Private Sector	22d
.32	.65	.93	1.27	1.56	1.62	1.66	4.72	10.18	7.88	11.12	10.64	9.59	2.84	8.69	Claims on Nonbank Financial Insts	22f
28.06	25.84	29.52	28.13	32.98	38.04	58.58	70.53	84.00	90.27	103.26	99.84	147.62	157.78	166.37	Demand Deposits	24
114.56	142.91	157.06	187.39	210.97	257.59	314.58	356.75	375.16	444.02	509.31	561.49	546.91	547.77	618.95	Time, Savings,& Fgn.Currency Dep.	25
50.28	39.92	41.79	40.33	41.18	42.59	40.56	50.59	52.50	65.17	81.32	88.60	98.20	107.57	143.99	Foreign Liabilities	26c
5.81	6.31	7.70	3.37	.62	1.63	6.20	8.30	88.53	97.49	117.86	123.47	158.49	174.24	170.92	Central Government Deposits	26d
.80	—	.40	—	—	—	—	—	.16	—	—	2.20	.70	9.03	9.60	Credit from Monetary Authorities	26g
3.46	6.23	7.12	8.01	9.16	9.40	9.79	11.06	17.73	26.97	26.36	47.44	64.46	65.08	71.81	Capital Accounts	27a
14.11	6.66	6.86	10.82	30.75	26.36	36.33	42.71	40.33	27.41	4.40	−21.18	−8.85	−6.97	−33.95	Other Items (Net)	27r
\multicolumn{15}{l}{End of Period}	**Monetary Survey**	
−5.38	−12.96	−3.42	16.89	12.85	48.13	109.36	145.30	179.08	147.56	165.21	179.39	182.78	149.35	80.99	Foreign Assets (Net)	31n
190.99	222.28	232.42	247.72	300.01	320.45	350.60	387.17	395.49	506.72	543.45	579.67	630.00	689.13	808.63	Domestic Credit	32
24.97	30.77	29.73	35.92	57.79	64.38	71.79	69.50	−19.41	−31.42	−61.41	−70.09	−100.66	−116.24	−119.78	Claims on Central Govt. (Net)	32an
—	—	—	—	—	—	—	—	.24	.24	.64	3.91	6.44	1.84	2.09	Claims on Local Government	32b
2.17	5.88	4.81	2.47	3.44	2.84	1.99	2.75	2.96	10.61	14.61	11.44	31.27	49.25	57.48	Claims on Nonfin.Pub.Enterprises	32c
163.53	184.98	196.95	208.06	237.22	251.61	275.15	310.21	401.52	519.42	578.48	623.78	683.36	751.43	860.16	Claims on Private Sector	32d
.32	.65	.93	1.27	1.56	1.62	1.66	4.72	10.18	7.88	11.12	10.64	9.59	2.84	8.69	Claims on Nonbank Financial Inst	32f
52.67	53.53	57.57	58.39	63.06	71.05	97.62	122.58	140.28	157.54	167.50	168.13	212.47	226.02	233.85	Money	34
114.56	142.91	157.06	187.39	210.97	257.59	314.58	356.75	375.16	444.02	509.31	561.49	546.91	547.77	618.95	Quasi-Money	35
18.37	12.88	14.37	18.84	38.83	39.94	47.75	53.13	59.13	52.72	31.86	29.43	53.39	64.69	36.83	Other Items (Net)	37r
167.24	196.44	214.62	245.78	274.03	328.64	412.21	479.34	515.44	601.56	676.80	729.63	759.39	773.79	852.80	Money plus Quasi-Money	35l
\multicolumn{15}{l}{Percent Per Annum}	**Interest Rates**	
6.5	6.5	6.5	6.5	6.5	7.0	7.0	7.0	7.0	7.0	7.0	7.0	7.0	7.0	7.0	Treasury Bill Rate	60c
5.5	8.0	8.0	8.0	8.6	9.1	7.5	5.0	5.0	5.0	5.6	6.1	5.5	5.0	4.5	Deposit Rate	60l
11.0	13.0	13.0	13.0	13.3	14.0	14.0	11.6	10.6	10.0	10.5	10.5	10.5	10.2	10.1	Lending Rate	60p
\multicolumn{15}{l}{Period Averages}	**Prices**	
66.2	76.2	79.7	80.8	81.8	83.0	84.7	91.1	91.8	95.5	100.0	105.7	111.1	112.0	....	Consumer Prices	64
\multicolumn{15}{l}{Millions of E. Caribbean Dollars}	**International Transactions**	
157.41	124.36	122.83	149.63	132.40	152.73	234.59	214.80	312.00	294.70	343.70	297.80	331.50	....	....	Exports	70
334.20	348.90	318.70	388.40	320.00	337.50	417.90	483.90	595.00	739.10	731.60	797.00	845.00	....	....	Imports, cif	71
303.83	317.16	289.71	353.06	290.91	306.82	379.91	439.91	540.91	671.91	665.09	724.55	768.18	....	....	Imports, fob	71.v
\multicolumn{15}{l}{1980=100}		
100.0	107.4	116.6	123.3	....	....	....	....	....	....	....	....	....	....	....	Unit Value of Exports	74

St. Lucia
362

		1965	1966	1967	1968	1969	1970	1971	1972	1973	1974	1975	1976	1977	1978	1979
Balance of Payments													*Millions of US Dollars:*			
Goods: Exports f.o.b.	78aa d	....	....	....	....	....	....	....	....	....	....	....	19.10	22.60	26.80	31.90
Goods: Imports f.o.b.	78ab d	....	....	....	....	....	....	....	....	....	....	....	-43.63	-53.90	-75.27	-91.99
Trade Balance	78ac d	....	....	....	....	....	....	....	....	....	....	....	-24.53	-31.30	-48.47	-60.09
Services: Credit	78ad d	....	....	....	....	....	....	....	....	....	....	....	12.50	17.80	27.70	33.80
Services: Debit	78ae d	....	....	....	....	....	....	....	....	....	....	....	-6.46	-8.40	-12.83	-13.41
Balance on Goods and Services	78af d	....	....	....	....	....	....	....	....	....	....	....	-18.50	-21.90	-33.60	-39.70
Income: Credit	78ag d	....	....	....	....	....	....	....	....	....	....	....	.50	.90	1.30	1.00
Income: Debit	78ah d	....	....	....	....	....	....	....	....	....	....	....	-.30	—	-.50	-.60
Balance on Goods, Serv., & Inc.	78ai d	....	....	....	....	....	....	....	....	....	....	....	-18.30	-21.00	-32.80	-39.30
Current Transfers, n.i.e.: Credit	78aj d	....	....	....	....	....	....	....	....	....	....	....	12.90	10.10	9.80	11.20
Current Transfers: Debit	78ak d	....	....	....	....	....	....	....	....	....	....	....	—	—	—	—
Current Account, n.i.e.	78al d	....	....	....	....	....	....	....	....	....	....	....	-5.40	-10.90	-23.00	-28.10
Capital Account, n.i.e.: Credit	78ba d	....	....	....	....	....	....	....	....	....	....	....	—	—	—	—
Capital Account: Debit	78bb d	....	....	....	....	....	....	....	....	....	....	....	—	—	—	—
Capital Account, n.i.e.	78bc d	....	....	....	....	....	....	....	....	....	....	....	—	—	—	—
Direct Investment Abroad	78bd d	....	....	....	....	....	....	....	....	....	....	....	—	—	—	—
Dir. Invest. in Rep. Econ., n.i.e.	78be d	....	....	....	....	....	....	....	....	....	....	....	3.00	13.00	20.60	26.00
Portfolio Investment Assets	78bf d	....	....	....	....	....	....	....	....	....	....	....	—	—	—	—
Portfolio Investment Liab., n.i.e.	78bg d	....	....	....	....	....	....	....	....	....	....	....	-.13	—	—	.08
Other Investment Assets	78bh d	....	....	....	....	....	....	....	....	....	....	....	-7.65	.80	-.24	-1.69
Other Investment Liab., n.i.e.	78bi d	....	....	....	....	....	....	....	....	....	....	....	7.91	.59	4.70	7.54
Financial Account, n.i.e.	78bj d	....	....	....	....	....	....	....	....	....	....	....	3.13	14.40	25.07	31.93
Net Errors and Omissions	78ca d	....	....	....	....	....	....	....	....	....	....	....	4.79	-2.93	-1.06	-2.27
Overall Balance	78cb d	....	....	....	....	....	....	....	....	....	....	....	2.52	.56	1.00	1.57
Reserves and Related Items	79da d	....	....	....	....	....	....	....	....	....	....	....	-2.52	-.56	-1.00	-1.57
Reserve Assets	79db d	....	....	....	....	....	....	....	....	....	....	....	-2.52	-.56	-1.00	-1.57
Use of Fund Credit and Loans	79dc d	....	....	....	....	....	....	....	....	....	....	....	—	—	—	—
Liabs.Constit.For.Auth.Reserves	79dd d	....	....	....	....	....	....	....	....	....	....	....	—	—	—	—
Exceptional Financing	79de d	....	....	....	....	....	....	....	....	....	....	....	—	—	—	—
Government Finance													*Millions of E. Caribbean Dollars:*			
Deficit (-) or Surplus	80	....	....	....	....	....	....	....	....	....	....	....			-1.48	4.73
Revenue	81	....	....	....	....	....	....	....	....	....	....	....			60.03	83.14
Grants Received	81z	....	....	....	....	....	....	....	....	....	....	....			5.71	13.12
Expenditure	82	....	....	....	....	....	....	....	....	....	....	....			66.58	90.73
Lending Minus Repayments	83	....	....	....	....	....	....	....	....	....	....	....			.64	.80
Domestic	84a	....	....	....	....	....	....	....	....	....	....	....			-2.72	-8.35
Foreign	85a	....	....	....	....	....	....	....	....	....	....	....			4.20	3.62
National Accounts													*Millions of E. Caribbean Dollars*			
Exports of Goods & Services	90c	....	....	....	....	....	....	....	....	....	....	51.5	82.8	107.1	147.2	176.3
Government Consumption	91f	....	....	....	....	....	....	....	....	....	....	23.2	26.5	37.0	44.7	44.8
Gross Capital Formation	93	....	....	....	....	....	....	....	....	....	....	56.8	65.6	87.7	124.8	155.8
Private Consumption	96f	....	....	....	....	....	....	....	....	....	....	96.5	108.9	110.5	145.2	194.3
Imports of Goods & Services	98c	....	....	....	....	....	....	....	....	....	....	-104.8	-131.3	-166.2	-237.9	-284.6
Gross Domestic Product	99b	....	....	....	....	....	....	....	....	....	....	123.2	152.5	176.1	191.0	229.1
Gross Dom. Prod. 1990 Prices	99b.p	....	....	....	....	....	....	....	....	....	....	....	....	....	522.6	541.7
GDP Deflator (1990=100)	99bi p	....	....	....	....	....	....	....	....	....	....	....	....	....	36.6	42.3
																Millions:
Population	99z	....	....	....	....	....	.10	....	....	.11	.12	.11	.11	.11	.11	.12

Government Finance: ℓ Beginning in 1984, data cover budgetary operations only. For earlier years, data refer to the consolidated central government.

St. Lucia

	1980	1981	1982	1983	1984	1985	1986	1987	1988	1989	1990	1991	1992	1993	1994		
Minus Sign Indicates Debit																**Balance of Payments**	
	46.00	41.60	41.60	47.50	47.80	52.00	82.93	79.48	119.11	111.96	127.30	110.30	122.78	119.74	....	Goods: Exports f.o.b.	78aa d
	−112.55	−117.17	−107.35	−97.08	−107.71	−113.63	−136.22	−156.70	−194.48	−240.89	−238.71	−261.39	−269.54	−264.00	....	Goods: Imports f.o.b.	78ab d
	−66.55	−75.57	−65.75	−49.58	−59.91	−61.63	−53.30	−77.22	−75.37	−128.93	−111.41	−151.10	−146.76	−144.26	....	Trade Balance	78ac d
	40.50	38.50	44.70	54.20	64.00	69.50	83.56	100.67	120.33	140.51	154.26	181.34	204.12	213.26	....	Services: Credit	78ad d
	−22.15	−23.63	−27.75	−30.02	−38.29	−37.97	−48.65	−51.52	−66.15	−76.35	−88.90	−90.13	−101.50	−105.15	....	Services: Debit	78ae d
	−48.20	−60.70	−48.80	−25.40	−34.20	−30.10	−18.39	−28.07	−21.19	−64.77	−46.06	−59.89	−44.14	−36.15	....	Balance on Goods and Services	78af d
	1.00	1.50	—	.69	—	—	3.30	4.11	6.41	5.85	5.94	4.63	5.46	4.36	....	Income: Credit	78ag d
	−.70	−.90	−1.20	−1.50	−3.20	−3.30	−8.11	−9.15	−17.22	−16.44	−32.13	−34.28	−34.23	−29.28	....	Income: Debit	78ah d
	−47.90	−60.10	−50.00	−26.21	−37.40	−33.40	−23.20	−33.11	−32.00	−75.36	−72.25	−89.53	−72.91	−61.07	....	Balance on Goods, Serv., & Inc.	78ai d
	14.60	20.30	24.00	27.50	30.40	27.60	26.37	29.93	20.59	20.78	17.52	22.14	25.26	25.21	....	Current Transfers, n.i.e.: Credit	78aj d
	—	—	−4.80	−6.20	−6.40	−6.70	−.89	−1.07	−1.00	−1.85	−2.19	−1.68	−3.07	−5.81	....	Current Transfers: Debit	78ak d
	−33.30	−39.80	−30.80	−4.91	−13.40	−12.50	2.28	−4.26	−12.41	−56.43	−56.92	−69.07	−50.72	−41.67	....	Current Account, n.i.e.	78al d
	—	—	—	—	—	—	—	—	—	—	—	—	—	—	....	Capital Account, n.i.e.: Credit	78ba d
	—	—	—	—	—	—	—	—	—	—	—	—	—	—	....	Capital Account: Debit	78bb d
	—	—	—	—	—	—	—	—	—	—	—	—	—	—	....	Capital Account, n.i.e.	78bc d
	—	—	—	—	—	—	—	—	—	—	—	—	—	—	....	Direct Investment Abroad	78bd d
	30.90	38.20	26.50	10.00	12.00	17.00	14.52	15.00	16.44	26.63	44.79	57.74	40.89	34.09	....	Dir. Invest. in Rep. Econ., n.i.e.	78be d
	—	—	—	—	—	—	—	—	—	—	—	−.14	—	—	....	Portfolio Investment Assets	78bf d
	—	.37	—	—	—	—	—	—	—	—	.18	—	−.51	—	....	Portfolio Investment Liab., n.i.e.	78bg d
	−3.27	2.75	−1.42	−5.00	1.29	−7.15	−11.63	−7.15	−11.52	18.15	4.51	.21	2.23	19.84	....	Other Investment Assets	78bh d
	5.76	−1.03	6.19	1.66	.89	2.34	4.69	6.25	5.04	9.07	5.59	3.86	21.43	6.31	....	Other Investment Liab., n.i.e.	78bi d
	33.39	40.29	31.27	6.66	14.17	12.18	7.58	14.10	9.96	53.85	54.93	61.81	64.03	60.24	....	Financial Account, n.i.e.	78bj d
	−2.03	−5.26	1.89	−2.19	−.57	1.47	1.42	−.73	4.30	8.17	8.29	15.00	−6.53	−14.08	....	Net Errors and Omissions	78ca d
	−1.95	−4.77	2.36	−.44	.20	1.16	11.28	9.11	1.85	5.59	6.30	7.74	6.78	4.49	....	Overall Balance	78cb d
	1.95	4.77	−2.36	.44	−.20	−1.16	−11.28	−9.11	−1.85	−5.59	−6.30	−7.74	−6.78	−4.49	....	Reserves and Related Items	79da d
	.21	1.50	−.75	−.80	−1.19	−3.00	−11.11	−9.11	−1.85	−5.59	−6.30	−7.74	−6.78	−4.49	....	Reserve Assets	79db d
	1.74	3.27	−1.60	—	−.54	−1.75	−.34	—	—	—	—	—	—	—	....	Use of Fund Credit and Loans	79dc d
	—	—	—	.74	—	—	—	—	—	—	—	—	—	—	....	Liabs.Constit.For.Auth.Reserves	79dd d
	—	—	—	.50	1.53	3.59	.17	—	—	—	—	—	—	—	....	Exceptional Financing	79de d
Year Beginning April 1																**Government Finance**	
	−12.85	−7.84	−15.81	14.30	....	−11.10	−11.40	8.10	19.10	10.90	−1.10	....	....	....	....	Deficit (-) or Surplus	80
	91.79	103.45	116.19	122.28	I 119.26	145.80	169.50	193.90	229.90	268.00	265.00	299.80 p	....	....	....	Revenue	81
	8.95	16.57	21.09	31.81	....	16.30	16.60	27.90	16.70	11.80	3.90	3.30 p	....	....	....	Grants Received	81z
	112.71	126.95	152.19	138.67	....	173.20	197.50	211.60	224.20	267.70	257.70	280.20 p	....	....	....	Expenditure	82
	.88	.91	.90	1.12	I —	—	—	2.10	3.30	1.20	12.30	....	....	....	....	Lending Minus Repayments	83
	1.32	−5.25	....	....	....	....	....	....	....	....	....	....	....	....	....	Domestic	84a
	11.53	13.09	....	....	....	....	....	....	....	....	....	....	....	....	....	Foreign	85a
Millions of E. Caribbean Dollars																**National Accounts**	
	233.6	216.3	224.1	248.4	261.4 e	....	....	....	....	....	....	....	....	....	....	Exports of Goods & Services	90c
	63.7	71.1	92.1	90.8	102.7 e	....	....	....	....	....	....	....	....	....	....	Government Consumption	91f
	181.2	198.8	144.7	116.5	126.0	....	....	....	....	....	....	....	....	....	....	Gross Capital Formation	93
	176.6	221.8	244.4	238.2	266.7 e	....	....	....	....	....	....	....	....	....	....	Private Consumption	96f
	−351.5	−369.1	−344.3	−316.4	−348.4 e	....	....	....	....	....	....	....	....	....	....	Imports of Goods & Services	98c
	264.2	299.4	312.5	323.4	353.0	504.9	601.9	646.9	728.7	820.6	898.9	967.7	1,060.3	....	....	Gross Domestic Product	99b
	537.6	544.1	560.6	583.4	612.6	I 649.2	726.5	737.3	826.5	864.6	I 898.9	913.3	973.2	....	....	Gross Dom. Prod. 1990 Prices	99b. p
	49.1	55.0	55.7	55.4	57.6	77.8	82.9	87.7	88.2	94.9	100.0	105.9	109.0	....	....	GDP Deflator (1990=100)	99bi p
Midyear Estimates																	
	.12	.13	.13	.13	.13	.14	.14	.14	.15	.15	I .13	.13	.14	.14	....	Population	99z

1995 INTERNATIONAL FINANCIAL STATISTICS YEARBOOK

St. Vincent & Grens.
364

		1965	1966	1967	1968	1969	1970	1971	1972	1973	1974	1975	1976	1977	1978	1979
Exchange Rates													E. Caribbean Dollars per SDR: End of Period (aa)			
Official Rate	aa	1.7126	1.7203	1.9948	2.0131	1.9994	2.0053	2.0417	2.2194	2.4925	2.5024	2.7770	3.1369	3.2797	3.5175	3.5568
Official Rate	ae	1.7126	1.7203	1.9948	2.0131	1.9994	2.0053	1.8805	2.0442	2.0661	2.0439	2.3721	2.7000	2.7000	2.7000	2.7000
														Index Numbers (1990=100):		
Official Rate	ah x	157.3	157.1	154.5	134.6	134.5	134.8	137.3	140.7	137.9	131.6	125.0	103.5	100.0	100.0	100.0
Nominal Effective Exchange Rate	ne c	...	...	...	...	...	...	...	...	...	...	...	...	...	...	84.7
Real Effective Exchange Rate	re c	...	...	...	...	...	...	...	...	...	...	...	...	...	...	102.7
Fund Position																Millions of SDRs:
Quota	2f. s	...	...	...	...	...	...	...	...	...	...	...	...	...	...	1.70
SDRs	1b. s	...	...	...	...	...	...	...	...	...	...	...	...	...	...	—
Reserve Position in the Fund	1c. s	...	...	...	...	...	...	...	...	...	...	...	...	...	...	—
Total Fund Cred.&Loans Outstg.	2tl	...	...	...	...	...	...	...	...	...	...	...	...	...	...	
International Liquidity												Millions of US Dollars Unless Otherwise Indicated:				
Total Reserves minus Gold	1l. d	...	...	...	...	...	...	...	...	...	...	...	4.66	4.81	5.26	8.90
SDRs	1b. d	...	...	...	...	...	...	...	...	...	...	...	...	...	...	...
Reserve Position in the Fund	1c. d	...	...	...	...	...	...	...	...	...	...	...	...	...	...	...
Foreign Exchange	1d. d	...	...	...	...	...	...	...	...	...	...	...	4.66	4.81	5.26	8.90
Deposit Money Banks: Assets	7a. d	...	...	...	...	...	...	...	...	...	...	6.02	7.91	7.90	9.03	7.08
of which: Claims on Nonbanks	7ad d	...	...	...	...	...	...	...	...	...	...	3.31	4.76	4.46	5.33	2.13
Deposit Money Banks: Liabilities	7b. d	...	...	...	...	...	...	...	...	...	...	5.67	6.34	8.87	9.21	10.29
of which: Liab. to Nonbanks	7bd d	...	...	...	...	...	...	...	...	...	...	4.77	5.15	5.95	6.31	7.53
Monetary Authorities													Millions of E. Caribbean Dollars:			
Foreign Assets	11	...	...	...	...	...	...	...	...	...	...	...	12.58	12.99	14.19	24.04
Claims on Central Government	12a	...	...	...	...	...	...	...	...	...	...	...	2.94	4.09	4.09	4.09
Claims on Deposit Money Banks	12e	...	...	...	...	...	...	...	...	...	...	—	—	—	—	—
Reserve Money	14	...	...	...	...	...	...	...	...	...	...	8.90	15.52	17.07	18.28	28.12
of which: Currency Outside DMBs	14a	...	...	...	...	...	...	...	...	...	...	8.00	9.52	9.50	11.07	12.94
Foreign Liabilities	16c	...	...	...	...	...	...	...	...	...	...	—	—	—	—	—
Central Government Deposits	16d	...	...	...	...	...	...	...	...	...	...	—	—	—	—	—
Other Items (Net)	17r	...	...	...	...	...	...	...	...	...	...	—	—	—	—	—
Deposit Money Banks																
Reserves	20	...	...	...	...	...	...	...	...	...	...	.90	6.00	7.57	7.21	15.18
Foreign Assets	21	...	...	...	...	...	...	...	...	...	...	14.29	21.35	21.32	24.37	19.11
Claims on Central Government	22a	...	...	...	...	...	...	...	...	...	...	4.80	3.40	6.10	7.00	9.58
Claims on Local Government	22b	...	...	...	...	...	...	...	...	...	...	—	—	—	—	—
Claims on Nonfin.Pub.Enterprises	22c	...	...	...	...	...	...	...	...	...	...	2.70	2.50	3.30	4.70	9.52
Claims on Private Sector	22d	...	...	...	...	...	...	...	...	...	...	26.34	26.55	35.88	48.00	54.35
Claims on Nonbank Financial Insts	22f	...	...	...	...	...	...	...	...	...	...	.06	.06	.06	.06	.34
Demand Deposits	24	...	...	...	...	...	...	...	...	...	...	5.34	6.55	7.10	11.55	14.78
Time, Savings,& Fgn.Currency Dep.	25	...	...	...	...	...	...	...	...	...	...	33.76	39.72	44.71	55.58	68.71
Foreign Liabilities	26c	...	...	...	...	...	...	...	...	...	...	13.46	17.13	23.94	24.88	27.77
Central Government Deposits	26d	...	...	...	...	...	...	...	...	...	...	—	1.50	1.50	1.70	.28
Credit from Monetary Authorities	26g	...	...	...	...	...	...	...	...	...	...	—	.70	.80	1.00	—
Capital Accounts	27a	...	...	...	...	...	...	...	...	...	...	.40	.40	.40	.40	.45
Other Items (Net)	27r	...	...	...	...	...	...	...	...	...	...	-3.87	-6.14	-4.22	-3.77	-3.90
Monetary Survey													Millions of E. Caribbean Dollars:			
Foreign Assets (Net)	31n	...	...	...	...	...	...	...	...	...	...	...	16.80	10.37	13.68	15.38
Domestic Credit	32	...	...	...	...	...	...	...	...	...	...	...	33.96	47.92	62.15	77.60
Claims on Central Govt. (Net)	32an	...	...	...	...	...	...	...	...	...	...	...	4.84	8.69	9.39	13.39
Claims on Local Government	32b	...	...	...	...	...	...	...	...	...	...	—	—	—	—	—
Claims on Nonfin.Pub.Enterprises	32c	...	...	...	...	...	...	...	...	...	...	2.70	2.50	3.30	4.70	9.52
Claims on Private Sector	32d	...	...	...	...	...	...	...	...	...	...	26.34	26.55	35.88	48.00	54.35
Claims on Nonbank Financial Inst	32f	...	...	...	...	...	...	...	...	...	...	.06	.06	.06	.06	.34
Money	34	...	...	...	...	...	...	...	...	...	...	13.35	16.08	16.61	22.62	27.72
Quasi-Money	35	...	...	...	...	...	...	...	...	...	...	33.76	39.72	44.71	55.58	68.71
Other Items (Net)	37r	...	...	...	...	...	...	...	...	...	...	-3.47	-5.04	-3.02	-2.37	-3.45
Money plus Quasi-Money	35l	...	...	...	...	...	...	...	...	...	...	47.11	55.79	61.31	78.20	96.43
Interest Rates															Percent Per Annum	
Treasury Bill Rate	60c	...	...	...	...	...	...	...	...	...	...	...	...	...	...	...
Deposit Rate	60l	...	...	...	...	...	...	...	...	...	...	...	...	...	...	...
Lending Rate	60p	...	...	...	...	...	...	...	...	...	...	...	...	8.5	8.5	8.5
Prices													Index Numbers (1990=100):			
Consumer Prices	64	...	...	...	...	...	...	...	...	...	33.6	35.9	39.9	44.0	47.7	55.1
International Transactions													Millions of E. Caribbean Dollars			
Exports	70	6.4	6.7	6.3	7.5	7.6	7.1	5.9	6.6	10.1	14.6	16.4	24.5	26.8	44.0	39.3
Imports, cif	71	14.8	16.1	15.8	20.0	24.4	30.5	36.0	35.2	38.1	52.3	53.9	62.0	81.9	97.7	125.8
Imports, fob	71.v	13.5	14.6	14.4	18.2	22.2	27.7	32.7	32.0	34.6	47.5	49.0	56.4	74.5	88.8	114.4

St. Vincent & Grens.

1980	1981	1982	1983	1984	1985	1986	1987	1988	1989	1990	1991	1992	1993	1994		
E.Caribbean Dollars per US Dollar: End of Period (ae)															**Exchange Rates**	
3.4436	3.1427	2.9784	2.8268	2.6466	2.9657	3.3026	3.8304	3.6334	3.5482	3.8412	3.8622	3.7125	3.7086	3.9416	Official Rate	**aa**
2.7000	2.7000	2.7000	2.7000	2.7000	2.7000	2.7000	2.7000	2.7000	2.7000	2.7000	2.7000	2.7000	2.7000	2.7000	Official Rate	**ae**
Period Averages																
100.0	100.0	100.0	100.0	100.0	100.0	100.0	100.0	100.0	100.0	100.0	100.0	100.0	100.0	100.0	Official Rate	**ah** *x*
82.6	86.5	90.7	94.7	99.7	101.8	102.6	99.9	98.0	102.5	100.0	100.7	101.9	111.3	114.0	Nominal Effective Exchange Rate	**ne** *c*
101.8	107.7	111.5	115.6	117.4	116.3	114.4	109.1	102.4	102.6	100.0	101.2	101.4	111.2	110.3	Real Effective Exchange Rate	**re** *c*
End of Period															**Fund Position**	
2.60	2.60	2.60	4.00	4.00	4.00	4.00	4.00	4.00	4.00	4.00	4.00	6.00	6.00	6.00	Quota	**2f.** *s*
.05	.15	.03	.01	—	—	.01	—	—	—	—	.01	.09	.09	.09	SDRs	**1b.** *s*
—	—	—	.35	—	—	—	—	—	—	—	—	.50	.50	.50	Reserve Position in the Fund	**1c.** *s*
.20	1.50	1.50	1.50	1.01	.33	—	—	—	—	—	—	—	—	—	Total Fund Cred.&Loans Outstg.	**2tl**
End of Period															**International Liquidity**	
7.27	9.00	4.78	5.70	12.82	13.80	25.83	20.22	21.82	22.77	26.49	22.68	33.38	31.31	30.45	Total Reserves minus Gold	**1l.** *d*
.06	.17	.03	.01	—	—	.01	—	—	—	—	.01	.12	.12	.12	SDRs	**1b.** *d*
—	—	—	.37	—	—	—	—	—	—	—	—	.69	.69	.73	Reserve Position in the Fund	**1c.** *d*
7.21	8.83	4.75	5.32	12.82	13.80	25.82	20.22	21.82	22.77	26.49	22.67	32.57	30.50	29.60	Foreign Exchange	**1d.** *d*
8.84	11.21	10.70	9.81	8.49	12.69	19.66	25.23	34.31	37.29	48.65	43.82	41.84	47.01	49.54	Deposit Money Banks: Assets	**7a.** *d*
1.28	1.68	1.80	3.55	2.47	5.69	8.17	2.56	2.93	3.40	8.56	6.98	14.04	18.64	14.25	of which: Claims on Nonbanks	**7ad** *d*
12.15	12.02	14.26	12.19	13.25	14.18	16.14	17.46	14.49	19.40	19.99	21.76	28.80	29.45	26.77	Deposit Money Banks: Liabilities	**7b.** *d*
9.28	8.87	10.89	9.32	10.58	12.51	12.10	13.72	11.91	14.95	16.55	19.57	26.37	26.68	24.81	of which: Liab. to Nonbanks	**7bd** *d*
End of Period															**Monetary Authorities**	
19.63	24.31	18.58	17.31	25.45	41.93	69.76	54.99	60.05	63.90	75.35	65.85	96.75	84.64	82.33	Foreign Assets	**11**
5.10	8.93	11.48	11.03	19.71	16.37	15.45	17.46	10.57	12.79	11.93	15.02	9.04	9.94	9.25	Claims on Central Government	**12a**
—	—	—	—	2.45	.95	—	—	—	—	—	1.32	.01	.01	.01	Claims on Deposit Money Banks	**12e**
24.04	28.53	25.59	24.10	44.93	58.28	85.21	72.06	69.49	74.27	84.79	76.27	99.19	94.58	91.52	Reserve Money	**14**
12.85	15.36	17.61	20.14	22.53	32.03	41.42	23.27	25.15	32.12	23.96	19.09	30.30	28.22	32.02	of which: Currency Outside DMBs	**14a**
.69	4.71	4.47	4.24	2.67	.98	—	—	—	—	—	—	—	—	—	Foreign Liabilities	**16c**
—	—	—	—	—	—	—	.39	1.13	2.43	3.81	4.61	6.62	—	.07	Central Government Deposits	**16d**
—	—	—	—	—	—	—	—	—	—	—	—	—	—	—	Other Items (Net)	**17r**
End of Period															**Deposit Money Banks**	
11.18	13.17	7.98	3.95	27.05	26.81	41.81	45.10	40.92	40.11	60.56	55.40	65.36	73.06	60.14	Reserves	**20**
23.87	30.25	28.89	26.48	22.93	34.27	53.07	68.12	92.64	100.69	131.35	118.31	112.97	126.94	133.75	Foreign Assets	**21**
4.77	6.16	12.36	12.68	10.67	9.59	31.96	37.92	35.94	44.38	31.27	29.34	39.80	42.34	44.25	Claims on Central Government	**22a**
—	—	—	—	—	—	—	—	2.39	—	—	3.29	3.29	—	.26	Claims on Local Government	**22b**
11.65	4.57	30.45	35.37	43.96	45.03	21.86	22.58	25.37	23.67	24.88	25.14	32.16	38.39	47.55	Claims on Nonfin.Pub.Enterprises	**22c**
68.03	87.88	83.97	97.54	104.56	107.35	108.18	130.05	159.41	189.83	204.33	238.67	258.45	265.98	285.12	Claims on Private Sector	**22d**
.39	.62	.86	.67	.78	.47	1.23	1.33	.72	1.14	3.10	2.91	1.11	2.65	5.85	Claims on Nonbank Financial Insts	**22f**
15.21	17.93	17.27	20.42	25.27	20.52	21.74	29.89	37.50	37.73	49.37	41.41	61.10	62.86	76.54	Demand Deposits	**24**
73.03	86.70	100.24	111.49	123.58	143.68	163.97	190.87	184.16	209.67	245.33	254.37	249.83	279.28	282.14	Time, Savings,& Fgn.Currency Dep.	**25**
32.81	32.44	38.49	32.93	35.79	38.29	43.58	47.15	39.13	52.37	53.96	58.76	77.76	79.51	72.28	Foreign Liabilities	**26c**
.14	.19	.23	5.84	3.78	3.18	10.42	18.18	76.90	75.67	80.55	95.03	95.88	101.95	110.64	Central Government Deposits	**26d**
—	1.34	5.66	1.92	2.07	—	—	—	—	.94	—	—	—	—	—	Credit from Monetary Authorities	**26g**
1.57	3.47	5.73	8.41	10.51	10.97	13.91	15.18	24.18	20.72	24.26	36.65	31.99	35.65	47.87	Capital Accounts	**27a**
-2.88	.60	-3.11	-4.31	8.94	6.88	4.50	3.82	-4.48	2.71	5.31	-13.15	-6.71	-9.89	-12.57	Other Items (Net)	**27r**
End of Period															**Monetary Survey**	
10.00	17.41	4.51	6.62	9.92	36.93	79.25	75.96	113.55	112.22	152.73	125.40	131.96	132.07	143.79	Foreign Assets (Net)	**31n**
89.79	107.97	138.89	151.45	175.88	175.64	168.27	190.77	156.36	193.70	194.44	214.74	238.06	257.36	281.56	Domestic Credit	**32**
9.72	14.89	23.61	17.87	26.59	22.79	36.99	36.80	-31.53	-20.93	-41.16	-55.28	-53.66	-49.66	-57.21	Claims on Central Govt. (Net)	**32an**
—	—	—	—	—	—	—	—	2.39	—	—	3.29	3.29	—	.26	Claims on Local Government	**32b**
11.65	4.57	30.45	35.37	43.96	45.03	21.86	22.58	25.37	23.67	24.88	25.14	32.16	38.39	47.55	Claims on Nonfin.Pub.Enterprises	**32c**
68.03	87.88	83.97	97.54	104.56	107.35	108.18	130.05	159.41	189.83	204.33	238.67	258.45	265.98	285.12	Claims on Private Sector	**32d**
.39	.62	.86	.67	.78	.47	1.23	1.33	.72	1.14	3.10	2.91	1.11	2.65	5.85	Claims on Nonbank Financial Inst	**32f**
28.06	33.28	34.88	40.56	47.79	52.55	63.16	53.16	62.64	69.85	73.33	60.51	91.40	91.10	108.57	Money	**34**
73.03	86.70	100.24	111.49	123.58	143.68	163.97	190.87	184.16	209.67	245.33	254.37	249.83	279.28	282.14	Quasi-Money	**35**
-1.30	5.40	8.28	6.02	14.43	16.33	20.39	22.70	23.11	26.40	28.52	25.27	28.80	19.05	34.64	Other Items (Net)	**37r**
101.10	119.98	135.12	152.05	171.37	196.23	227.13	244.03	246.80	279.52	318.66	314.87	341.23	370.37	390.71	Money plus Quasi-Money	**35l**
Percent Per Annum															**Interest Rates**	
6.5	6.5	6.5	6.5	6.5	6.5	6.5	6.5	6.5	6.5	6.5	6.5	6.5	6.5	6.5	Treasury Bill Rate	**60c**
4.5	4.5	5.5	5.5	5.8	5.9	6.0	5.3	4.8	4.3	4.3	4.4	5.0	4.3	4.0	Deposit Rate	**60l**
10.0	10.0	10.0	10.7	12.0	12.1	12.5	12.5	12.1	12.4	12.5	13.5	11.4	11.2	11.0	Lending Rate	**60p**
Period Averages															**Prices**	
64.6	72.8	78.1	82.4	84.6	86.4	87.3	90.2	90.4	92.9	100.0	105.5	109.1	113.8	115.0	Consumer Prices	**64**
Millions of E. Caribbean Dollars															**International Transactions**	
41.7	64.9	87.0	110.8	144.6	170.8	172.3	141.3	230.2	201.4	223.4	181.6	210.9	156.1	....	Exports	**70**
154.2	157.1	175.8	190.0	206.8	213.9	235.7	266.4	330.1	344.2	367.4	377.1	356.6	362.7	....	Imports, cif	**71**
140.2	142.8	159.8	172.7	188.0	194.5	214.3	242.2	300.1	312.9	334.0	342.8	324.2	329.7	....	Imports, fob	**71.v**

St. Vincent & Grens.

364

		1965	1966	1967	1968	1969	1970	1971	1972	1973	1974	1975	1976	1977	1978	1979
Balance of Payments															*Millions of US Dollars:*	
Goods: Exports f.o.b.	78aa d	....	....	....	....	....	....	....	....	....	....	....	....	....	18.10	19.10
Goods: Imports f.o.b.	78ab d	....	....	....	....	....	....	....	....	....	....	....	....	....	−32.91	−42.09
Trade Balance	78ac d	....	....	....	....	....	....	....	....	....	....	....	....	....	−14.81	−22.99
Services: Credit	78ad d	....	....	....	....	....	....	....	....	....	....	....	....	....	11.10	13.70
Services: Debit	78ae d	....	....	....	....	....	....	....	....	....	....	....	....	....	−5.59	−9.81
Balance on Goods and Services	78af d	....	....	....	....	....	....	....	....	....	....	....	....	....	−9.30	−19.10
Income: Credit	78ag d	....	....	....	....	....	....	....	....	....	....	....	....	....	.20	.60
Income: Debit	78ah d	....	....	....	....	....	....	....	....	....	....	....	....	....	−.20	−1.20
Balance on Goods, Serv., & Inc.	78ai d	....	....	....	....	....	....	....	....	....	....	....	....	....	−9.30	−19.70
Current Transfers, n.i.e.: Credit	78aj d	....	....	....	....	....	....	....	....	....	....	....	....	....	12.00	21.40
Current Transfers: Debit	78ak d	....	....	....	....	....	....	....	....	....	....	....	....	....	—	−5.30
Current Account, n.i.e.	78al d	....	....	....	....	....	....	....	....	....	....	....	....	....	2.70	−3.60
Capital Account, n.i.e.: Credit	78ba d	....	....	....	....	....	....	....	....	....	....	....	....	....	—	—
Capital Account: Debit	78bb d	....	....	....	....	....	....	....	....	....	....	....	....	....	—	—
Capital Account, n.i.e.	78bc d	....	....	....	....	....	....	....	....	....	....	....	....	....	—	—
Direct Investment Abroad	78bd d	....	....	....	....	....	....	....	....	....	....	....	....	....	—	—
Dir. Invest. in Rep. Econ., n.i.e.	78be d	....	....	....	....	....	....	....	....	....	....	....	....	....	−.50	.60
Portfolio Investment Assets	78bf d	....	....	....	....	....	....	....	....	....	....	....	....	....	—	—
Portfolio Investment Liab., n.i.e.	78bg d	....	....	....	....	....	....	....	....	....	....	....	....	....	—	—
Other Investment Assets	78bh d	....	....	....	....	....	....	....	....	....	....	....	....	....	−1.13	1.95
Other Investment Liab., n.i.e.	78bi d	....	....	....	....	....	....	....	....	....	....	....	....	....	1.45	3.27
Financial Account, n.i.e.	78bj d	....	....	....	....	....	....	....	....	....	....	....	....	....	−.18	5.82
Net Errors and Omissions	78ca d	....	....	....	....	....	....	....	....	....	....	....	....	....	−2.37	1.63
Overall Balance	78cb d	....	....	....	....	....	....	....	....	....	....	....	....	....	.15	3.84
Reserves and Related Items	79da d	....	....	....	....	....	....	....	....	....	....	....	....	....	−.15	−3.84
Reserve Assets	79db d	....	....	....	....	....	....	....	....	....	....	....	....	....	−.15	−3.84
Use of Fund Credit and Loans	79dc d	....	....	....	....	....	....	....	....	....	....	....	....	....	—	—
Liabs.Constit.For.Auth.Reserves	79dd d	....	....	....	....	....	....	....	....	....	....	....	....	....	—	—
Exceptional Financing	79de d	....	....	....	....	....	....	....	....	....	....	....	....	....	....	....
Government Finance															*Millions of E. Caribbean Dollars:*	
Deficit (−) or Surplus	80	....	....	....	....	....	....	....	....	....	....	....	....	....	....	....
Revenue	81	....	....	....	....	....	....	....	....	....	....	....	....	....	24.5	31.8
Grants Received	81z	....	....	....	....	....	....	....	....	....	....	....	....	....	6.4	7.4
Expenditure	82	....	....	....	....	....	....	....	....	....	....	....	....	....	30.3	41.1
Lending Minus Repayments	83	....	....	....	....	....	....	....	....	....	....	....	....	....	....	....
Debt: Domestic	88a	....	....	....	....	....	....	....	....	....	....	....	....	....	....	....
Foreign	89a	....	....	....	....	....	....	....	....	....	....	....	....	....	....	....
National Accounts															*Millions of E. Caribbean Dollars*	
Exports of Goods & Services	90c	....	....	....	....	....	....	....	....	....	....	....	....	....	74.0	76.3
Government Consumption	91f	....	....	....	....	....	....	....	....	....	....	17.0	17.9	21.9	27.6	34.0
Gross Fixed Capital Formation	93e	....	....	....	....	....	....	....	....	....	....	18.4	17.1	33.9	34.4	48.6
Increase/Decrease(−) in Stocks	93i	....	....	....	....	....	....	....	....	....	....	.3	.7	2.6	—	—
Private Consumption	96f	....	....	....	....	....	....	....	....	....	....	56.0	66.1	84.4	90.6	123.8
Imports of Goods & Services	98c	....	....	....	....	....	....	....	....	....	....	—	—	−86.0	−103.9	−140.2
Gross Domestic Product	99b	....	....	....	....	....	....	....	....	....	....	70.4	83.7	97.3	122.6	142.6
Gross Dom. Prod. 1990 Prices	99b.p	....	....	....	....	....	....	....	....	....	....	234.2	258.4	265.7	257.6	269.7
GDP Deflator (1990=100)	99bi p	....	....	....	....	....	....	....	....	....	....	30.0	32.4	36.6	47.6	52.9
															Millions:	
Population	99z	....	....	....	....	....	....	....	....	....	....	....	.11	.11	.12	.12

St. Vincent & Grens.

	1980	1981	1982	1983	1984	1985	1986	1987	1988	1989	1990	1991	1992	1993	1994		
Minus Sign Indicates Debit																	**Balance of Payments**
	21.10	29.80	32.19	41.10	53.60	63.20	63.89	51.67	85.30	74.70	82.74	67.25	78.87	57.05	….	….	Goods: Exports f.o.b. .... 78aa *d*
	−51.91	−52.91	−58.59	−63.36	−68.94	−71.28	−76.81	−85.96	−107.59	−112.19	−119.78	−119.71	−116.23	−117.35	….	….	Goods: Imports f.o.b. .... 78ab *d*
	−30.81	−23.11	−26.40	−22.26	−15.34	−8.08	−12.93	−34.30	−22.30	−37.48	−37.04	−52.47	−37.36	−60.30	….	….	Trade Balance .... 78ac *d*
	17.70	18.90	15.70	17.80	19.10	19.20	29.00	39.43	39.21	40.81	47.43	45.43	47.48	48.66	….	….	Services: Credit .... 78ad *d*
	−11.39	−13.29	−15.01	−15.24	−17.26	−17.92	−27.95	−30.48	−30.59	−36.32	−34.00	−36.60	−39.71	−38.81	….	….	Services: Debit .... 78ae *d*
	−24.50	−17.50	−25.71	−19.70	−13.50	−6.80	−11.87	−25.35	−13.68	−33.00	−23.61	−43.63	−29.59	−50.45	….	….	Balance on Goods and Services .... 78af *d*
	.80	1.40	.20	.20	—	.20	2.26	3.96	4.48	4.63	4.62	5.10	4.83	2.89	….	….	Income: Credit .... 78ag *d*
	−1.70	−2.10	−2.90	−2.50	−3.00	−3.10	−10.70	−8.22	−15.74	−11.48	−15.67	−16.30	−11.77	−11.11	….	….	Income: Debit .... 78ah *d*
	−25.40	−18.20	−28.41	−22.00	−16.50	−9.70	−20.32	−29.61	−24.94	−39.85	−34.66	−54.83	−36.53	−58.67	….	….	Balance on Goods, Serv., & Inc. .... 78ai *d*
	23.90	26.50	26.20	27.10	22.80	22.10	20.67	19.52	22.48	25.15	33.33	35.45	28.87	21.75	….	….	Current Transfers, n.i.e.: Credit .... 78aj *d*
	−7.80	−9.10	−8.60	−7.70	−7.30	−8.70	−2.81	−4.05	−5.07	−3.70	−4.15	−4.39	−4.90	−4.76	….	….	Current Transfers: Debit .... 78ak *d*
	−9.30	−.80	−10.81	−2.60	−1.00	3.70	−2.47	−14.14	−7.53	−18.40	−5.47	−23.78	−12.56	−41.68	….	….	Current Account, n.i.e. .... 78al *d*
	—	—	—	—	—	—	—	—	—	—	—	—	—	—	….	….	Capital Account, n.i.e.: Credit .... 78ba *d*
	—	—	—	—	—	—	—	—	—	—	—	—	—	—	….	….	Capital Account: Debit .... 78bb *d*
	—	—	—	—	—	—	—	—	—	—	—	—	—	—	….	….	Capital Account, n.i.e. .... 78bc *d*
	—	—	—	—	—	—	—	—	—	—	—	—	—	—	….	….	Direct Investment Abroad .... 78bd *d*
	1.10	.50	1.50	2.10	1.40	1.80	7.37	4.96	9.11	10.59	7.67	8.83	18.85	31.36	….	….	Dir. Invest. in Rep. Econ., n.i.e. .... 78be *d*
	—	—	—	—	—	—	—	—	—	—	—	—	—	—	….	….	Portfolio Investment Assets .... 78bf *d*
	—	—	—	—	—	—	—	—	—	—	—	—	—	.03	….	….	Portfolio Investment Liab., n.i.e. .... 78bg *d*
	−1.72	−2.20	.50	.89	1.31	−4.20	—	—	—	1.96	—	5.68	2.96	—	….	….	Other Investment Assets .... 78bh *d*
	6.27	2.56	4.64	.54	2.76	3.23	.29	12.89	−4.96	5.67	−5.11	7.28	4.94	3.03	….	….	Other Investment Liab., n.i.e. .... 78bi *d*
	5.65	.87	6.64	3.53	5.47	.83	7.66	17.85	4.15	18.22	2.56	21.79	26.75	34.42	….	….	Financial Account, n.i.e. .... 78bj *d*
	1.73	.08	.46	−.64	.04	1.86	6.30	−9.10	5.31	1.63	6.95	−1.82	−2.85	5.77	….	….	Net Errors and Omissions .... 78ca *d*
	−1.92	.14	−3.70	.30	4.52	6.38	11.49	−5.39	1.93	1.44	4.04	−3.81	11.34	−1.49	….	….	Overall Balance .... 78cb *d*
	1.92	−.14	3.70	−.30	−4.52	−6.38	−11.49	5.39	−1.93	−1.44	−4.04	3.81	−11.34	1.49	….	….	Reserves and Related Items .... 79da *d*
	1.66	−1.74	3.70	−.30	−4.02	−5.70	−11.12	5.39	−1.93	−1.44	−4.04	3.81	−11.34	1.49	….	….	Reserve Assets .... 79db *d*
	.26	1.60	—	—	−.49	−.68	−.37	—	—	—	—	—	—	—	….	….	Use of Fund Credit and Loans .... 79dc *d*
	….	….	….	….	….	….	….	….	….	….	….	….	….	….	….	….	Liabs.Constit.For.Auth.Reserves .... 79dd *d*
	….	….	….	….	….	….	….	….	….	….	….	….	….	….	….	….	Exceptional Financing .... 79de *d*
Year Ending June 30																	**Government Finance**
	−.3	1.6	−7.1	−.4	−8.3	6.1	4.4	5.2	−5.7	….	126.9	137.2	….	….	….	….	Deficit (-) or Surplus 80
	43.2	45.9	62.9	74.9	78.6	90.8	100.8	107.5	116.4	….	126.9	137.2	….	….	….	….	Revenue 81
	3.8	12.9	5.3	4.7	4.7	6.1	5.0	5.9	3.9	….	….	….	….	….	….	….	Grants Received 81z
	47.3	57.2	75.3	80.0	91.6	90.8	101.4	108.2	126.0	139.8	155.4	….	….	….	….	….	Expenditure 82
	….	….	—	….	….	….	….	—	—	—	—	….	….	….	….	….	Lending Minus Repayments 83
	….	….	….	….	….	….	59.0	68.4	68.3	57.2	59.3	….	….	….	….	….	Debt: Domestic 88a
	….	….	….	….	….	….	74.7	84.4	100.2	118.0	145.3	….	….	….	….	….	Foreign 89a
Millions of E. Caribbean Dollars																	**National Accounts**
	89.5	116.0	135.9	155.7	193.0	222.5	257.2	245.2	334.6	299.5	370.5	308.9	337.5	….	….	….	Exports of Goods & Services 90c
	37.4	46.8	54.0	58.3	62.9	60.2	67.8	76.6	80.3	92.0	93.6	117.6	149.8	….	….	….	Government Consumption 91f
	62.8	64.2	64.7	62.9	70.5	76.2	98.9	115.0	121.1	125.5	159.1	168.9	152.8	….	….	….	Gross Fixed Capital Formation 93e
	—	—	—	—	6.9	9.9	2.8	9.9	13.6	12.5	7.1	7.7	13.9	….	….	….	Increase/Decrease(-) in Stocks 93i
	140.9	147.9	177.4	195.4	175.6	175.7	197.5	250.3	252.8	349.3	351.3	432.0	397.4	….	….	….	Private Consumption 96f
	−170.9	−178.8	−204.7	−217.5	−231.6	−239.9	−280.7	−313.3	−368.6	−409.5	−458.2	−470.4	−428.4	….	….	….	Imports of Goods & Services 98c
	159.7	196.1	227.4	254.9	277.2	304.6	343.5	383.7	433.7	469.3	523.3	564.7	622.9	….	….	….	Gross Domestic Product 99b
	279.8	298.4	315.6	332.0	349.4	368.3	395.1	420.2	456.2	488.9	523.3	539.6	574.9	582.8	….	….	Gross Dom. Prod. 1990 Prices 99b.*p*
	57.1	65.7	72.0	76.8	79.3	82.7	86.9	91.3	95.1	96.0	100.0	104.6	108.4	….	….	….	GDP Deflator (1990=100) .... 99bi *p*
Midyear Estimates																	
	.10	.10	.11	.11	.11	.11	.11	.11	.11	.11	.11	.11	.11	.11	….	….	Population 99z

Saudi Arabia
456

		1965	1966	1967	1968	1969	1970	1971	1972	1973	1974	1975	1976	1977	1978	1979
Exchange Rates																*Riyals per SDR:*
Official Rate	aa	4.5000	4.5000	4.5000	4.5000	4.5000	4.5000	4.5057	4.5057	4.2825	4.3464	4.1324	4.1013	4.2576	4.3187	4.4328
																Riyals per US Dollar:
Official Rate	ae	4.5000	4.5000	4.5000	4.5000	4.5000	4.5000	4.1500	4.1500	3.5500	3.5500	3.5300	3.5300	3.5050	3.3150	3.3650
Official Rate	rf	4.5000	4.5000	4.5000	4.5000	4.5000	4.5000	4.4868	4.1448	3.7066	3.5500	3.5176	3.5300	3.5251	3.3996	3.3608
																Index Numbers (1990=100):
Official Rate	ah x	83.2	83.2	83.2	83.2	83.2	83.2	80.7	90.2	101.0	105.5	106.5	106.1	106.2	110.2	111.4
Nominal Effective Exchange Rate	ne c	....	....	....	....	....	....	....	....	....	....	....	....	....	....	115.8
Real Effective Exchange Rate	re c	....	....	....	....	....	....	....	....	....	....	....	....	....	....	....
Fund Position																*Millions of SDRs:*
Quota	2f. s	72	90	90	90	90	90	134	134	134	134	134	134	134	600	600
SDRs	1b. s	—	—	—	—	—	—	—	—	—	—	—	—	—	—	149
Reserve Position in the Fund	1c. s	18	23	23	23	23	23	34	34	34	595	1,570	2,206	2,215	1,896	1,290
of which: Outstg. Fund Borrowing	2c	—	—	—	—	—	—	—	—	—	562	1,515	2,150	2,124	1,658	970
International Liquidity											*Millions of US Dollars Unless Otherwise Indicated:*					
Total Reserves minus Gold	1l. d	653	678	692	542	487	542	1,327	2,383	3,747	14,153	23,193	26,900	29,903	ꭵ19,200	19,273
SDRs	1b. d	—	—	—	—	—	—	—	—	—	—	—	—	—	—	196
Reserve Position in the Fund	1c. d	18	22	22	22	22	22	36	36	40	729	1,838	2,563	2,691	2,470	1,699
Foreign Exchange	1d. d	635	656	670	520	465	520	1,291	2,347	3,707	13,424	21,355	24,337	27,212	ꭵ16,730	17,378
Gold (Million Fine Troy Ounces)	1ad	2.086	1.971	1.971	3.400	3.400	3.400	3.086	3.086	3.086	3.081	3.081	3.081	3.081	4.539	4.567
Gold (National Valuation)	1an d	73	69	69	119	119	119	117	117	130	130	126	125	131	207	211
Monetary Authorities: Other Assets	3.. d	....	....	....	....	....	....	....	....	....	....	15,385	22,564	....	....	....
Deposit Money Banks: Assets	7a. d	42	39	52	61	80	99	155	320	386	458	1,025	2,348	3,218	3,484	5,390
of which: Claims on Nonbanks	7ad d	....	....	....	1	1	1	1	5	6	26	127	224	257	543	449
Deposit Money Banks: Liabilities	7b. d	40	53	38	40	42	36	68	55	91	245	506	1,323	1,238	1,830	2,219
of which: Liab. to Nonbanks	7bd d	....	....	....	—	—	—	—	—	—	—	—	35	—	2	4
Other Banking Insts.: Assets	7e. d	....	....	....	....	....	....	....	....	....	....	....	168	249	286	294
of which: Claims on Nonbanks	7ed d	....	....	....	....	....	....	....	....	....	....	....	168	249	286	294
Monetary Authorities																*Billions of Riyals:*
Foreign Assets	11	3.40	3.66	4.25	3.92	3.53	4.02	6.95	11.99	16.99	78.19	136.54	180.84	208.27	198.95	207.95
Reserve Money	14	1.14	1.26	1.44	1.66	1.79	1.82	2.19	2.87	4.34	5.85	11.84	19.13	31.13	43.40	38.72
of which: Currency Outside DMBs	14a	.94	1.06	1.20	1.45	1.56	1.63	1.67	2.42	3.05	4.14	6.68	10.59	16.25	19.18	23.71
Central Government Deposits	16d	1.96	1.95	2.44	1.83	1.08	1.38	3.64	8.26	11.88	44.92	89.53	125.14	133.74	112.97	110.85
Other Items (Net)	17r	.30	.45	.37	.42	.67	.82	1.12	.87	.78	27.42	35.17	36.57	43.40	42.57	58.38
Deposit Money Banks																*Billions of Riyals:*
Reserves	20	.19	.21	.23	.22	.23	.22	.53	.46	1.23	1.61	4.85	7.11	13.03	22.12	13.59
Foreign Assets	21	.19	.18	.23	.27	.36	.45	.64	1.32	1.37	1.63	3.62	8.29	11.28	11.55	18.14
Claims on Central Government	22a	—	—	.10	.16	—	—	—	—	—	—	—	—	.01	.10	.23
Claims on Public Enterprises	22c	....	....	....	....	....	....	....	....	....	....	....	....	....	.08	....
Claims on Private Sector	22d	1.03	1.24	1.23	1.39	1.61	1.71	1.82	1.82	2.36	4.43	6.72	9.88	10.68	14.40	26.73
Demand Deposits	24	.55	.66	.72	.75	.77	.77	.98	1.36	2.23	3.19	7.50	13.68	22.16	30.03	31.00
Quasi-Monetary Deposits	25a	.25	.36	.43	.55	.59	.70	.90	1.21	1.42	1.94	3.13	4.31	5.85	7.63	9.38
Foreign Currency Deposits	25b	.05	.04	.07	.04	.05	.04	.03	.06	.10	.50	.47	1.03	1.30	1.20	1.90
Foreign Liabilities	26c	.18	.24	.17	.18	.19	.16	.28	.23	.32	.87	1.79	4.67	4.34	6.07	7.47
Credit from Monetary Authorities	26g	....	....	....	—	—	—	—	—	—	—	—	—	—	1.32	.03
Capital Accounts	27a	.14	.14	.14	.15	.17	.17	.19	.20	.24	.33	.68	.94	1.25	1.85	2.54
Other Items (Net)	27r	.24	.18	.26	.37	.43	.53	.60	.55	.64	.83	1.62	.66	.20	.06	6.38
Monetary Survey																*Billions of Riyals:*
Foreign Assets (Net)	31n	3.40	3.60	4.31	4.01	3.71	4.31	7.30	13.09	18.04	78.94	138.37	184.46	215.21	204.43	218.62
Domestic Credit	32	−.98	−.75	−1.15	−.34	.46	.24	−1.94	−6.56	−9.63	−40.65	−83.08	−115.66	−123.34	−99.24	−84.73
Claims on Central Govt. (Net)	32an	−2.01	−1.99	−2.38	−1.73	−1.16	−1.47	−3.76	−8.38	−11.99	−45.09	−89.81	−125.55	−134.02	−113.64	−111.46
Claims on Public Enterprises	32c	....	....	....	....	....	....	....	....	....	....	....	....	....	....	....
Claims on Private Sector	32d	1.03	1.24	1.23	1.39	1.61	1.71	1.82	1.82	2.36	4.43	6.72	9.88	10.68	14.40	26.73
Money	34	1.50	1.72	1.92	2.20	2.32	2.40	2.65	3.78	5.29	7.33	14.18	24.27	38.41	49.21	54.70
Quasi-Money	35	.29	.40	.50	.60	.64	.74	.94	1.26	1.52	2.44	3.60	5.34	7.14	8.82	11.28
Other Items (Net)	37r	.64	.73	.74	.87	1.20	1.40	1.78	1.49	1.60	28.51	37.51	39.19	46.31	47.15	67.91
Money plus Quasi-Money	35l	1.79	2.12	2.42	2.80	2.97	3.14	3.59	5.04	6.81	9.78	17.78	29.61	45.56	58.03	65.98
Other Banking Institutions																*Millions of Riyals:*
Cash	40	....	2	2	7	14	13	11	19	17	18	8	ꭵ3,729	2,058	3,971	3,573
Foreign Assets	41	....	....	....	....	....	....	....	....	....	....	....	....	592	873	948	990
Claims on Private Sector	42d	....	14	25	31	38	42	43	45	47	52	132	ꭵ12,135	33,309	47,121	63,594
Capital Accounts	47a	....	16	24	37	50	53	53	63	63	72	173	ꭵ15,097	32,689	42,827	69,519
Other Items (Net)	47r	....	—	3	1	2	22	3	1	1	−2	−33	ꭵ1,361	3,553	9,212	−1,360
Prices																*Index Numbers (1990=100):*
Wholesale Prices	63	....	....	....	....	....	....	....	....	....	....	....	....	....	....	....
Consumer Prices	64	29.4	29.8	30.5	31.0	32.0	ꭵ32.1	33.5	35.0	40.8	49.5	66.6	87.6	97.6	ꭵ96.1	ꭵ97.8
International Transactions																*Billions of Riyals*
Exports	70	6.28	7.43	8.03	8.75	9.24	10.67	17.27	19.78	28.92	126.22	104.41	135.15	153.21	138.24	213.18
Petroleum	70a	4.83	5.84	6.23	9.09	9.48	10.88	16.66	22.71	28.92	126.46	104.05	135.91	153.47	127.11	197.02
Crude Petroleum	70aa	4.78	5.84	6.25	6.83	7.54	8.27	13.09	16.90	26.55	118.93	97.26	127.73	146.00	120.16	186.03
Refined Petroleum	70ab	....	....	....	....	....	1.81	1.93	2.09	2.47	7.53	6.79	8.18	7.47	6.95	10.99
Imports, cif	71	2.28	2.66	2.58	2.49	3.31	3.12	3.63	4.71	7.31	10.15	14.82	30.69	51.66	69.18	82.22
Imports, fob	71.v	2.07	2.42	2.32	2.15	2.95	2.76	3.25	4.18	6.54	8.70	12.86	25.60	44.54	59.13	70.28
Volume of Exports																*1990=100*
Petroleum	72a	43.4	52.8	56.5	61.9	68.3	75.4	246.2	125.8	161.2	181.7	151.4	184.6	196.8	176.3	201.6
Crude Petroleum	72aa	44.3	54.2	57.9	63.3	69.9	76.7	99.8	129.8	167.0	188.7	157.1	191.7	204.9	183.4	210.0
Refined Petroleum	72ab	26.6	27.2	29.4	36.5	38.0	50.0	46.6	49.8	51.1	50.6	42.1	49.5	45.3	42.8	42.9
Export Prices																*1990=100:*
Crude Petroleum	76aa d	....	....	....	....	....	....	....	....	....	....	....	....	....	....	85.3

Saudi Arabia

	1980	1981	1982	1983	1984	1985	1986	1987	1988	1989	1990	1991	1992	1993	1994		
																Exchange Rates	
End of Period	4.2407	3.9749	3.7892	3.6591	3.5043	4.0037	4.5808	5.3129	5.0396	4.9215	5.3279	5.3570	5.1494	5.1440	5.4671	Official Rate	aa
End of Period (ae) Period Average (rf)	3.3250	3.4150	3.4350	3.4950	3.5750	3.6450	3.7450	3.7450	3.7450	3.7450	3.7450	3.7450	3.7450	3.7450	3.7450	Official Rate	ae
	3.3267	3.3825	3.4282	3.4548	3.5238	3.6221	3.7033	3.7450	3.7450	3.7450	3.7450	3.7450	3.7450	3.7450	3.7450	Official Rate	rf
Period Averages	112.6	110.7	109.3	108.4	106.3	103.4	101.1	100.0	100.0	100.0	100.0	100.0	100.0	100.0	100.0	Official Rate	ah x
	118.3	128.3	138.6	143.1	148.6	148.2	119.4	105.5	100.4	104.8	100.0	99.6	96.8	99.4	97.1	Nominal Effective Exchange Rate	ne c
	187.6	189.9	193.8	191.9	188.1	175.3	134.1	114.1	106.4	107.7	100.0	100.1	94.1	95.1	91.2	Real Effective Exchange Rate	re c
End of Period																**Fund Position**	
	1,040	2,100	2,100	3,202	3,202	3,202	3,202	3,202	3,202	3,202	3,202	3,202	3,202	3,202	5,131	Quota	2f. s
	213	213	579	487	586	529	336	371	396	467	70	62	202	403	416	SDRs	1b. s
	1,896	3,428	4,621	8,903	10,188	9,707	8,838	8,016	6,540	3,688	2,099	1,292	797	869	604	Reserve Position in the Fund	1c. s
	1,352	2,439	3,212	6,913	8,104	7,837	7,748	7,352	6,051	3,224	1,712	950	525	175	—	*of which:* Outstg.Fund Borrowing	2c
Approximately End of Period																**International Liquidity**	
	23,437	32,236	29,549	27,287	24,748	25,004	18,324	22,684	20,553	16,748	11,668	11,673	5,935	7,428	7,378	Total Reserves minus Gold	1l. d
	271	248	638	510	574	581	411	526	532	614	99	89	278	553	607	SDRs	1b. d
	2,418	3,990	5,098	9,321	9,986	10,662	10,811	11,372	8,801	4,847	2,986	1,848	1,096	1,193	882	Reserve Position in the Fund	1c. d
	20,747	27,998	23,813	17,457	14,188	13,761	7,102	10,786	11,219	11,287	8,582	9,737	4,561	5,682	5,888	Foreign Exchange	1d. d
	4.567	4.567	4.596	4.596	4.596	4.596	4.596	4.596	4.596	4.596	4.596	4.596	4.596	4.596	4.596	Gold (Million Fine Troy Ounces)	1ad
	204	186	177	168	158	177	197	228	216	211	229	230	221	221	235	Gold (National Valuation)	1an d
	....	....	....	....	....	....	....	....	....	....	....	....	....	....	....	Monetary Authorities: Other Assets	3..d
	9,692	15,625	17,757	17,848	18,808	19,384	23,143	27,289	30,639	31,734	32,967	31,761	27,147	29,796	26,208	Deposit Money Banks: Assets	7a. d
	634	671	718	1,580	1,581	1,499	2,989	3,317	3,588	3,523	3,631	6,303	11,954	14,405	13,956	*of which:* Claims on Nonbanks	7ad d
	2,752	2,656	1,737	1,945	2,231	2,848	3,815	6,538	7,671	9,240	8,057	7,453	7,660	9,958	10,454	Deposit Money Banks: Liabilities	7b. d
	1	45	16	27	41	51	37	38	30	30	84	65	405	885	1,827	*of which:* Liab. to Nonbanks	7bd d
	303	379	389	419	406	402	423	1,107	1,122	1,124	1,196	1,138	1,148	1,153	1,150	Other Banking Insts.: Assets	7e. d
	303	379	389	419	406	402	423	1,107	1,122	1,124	1,196	1,138	1,148	1,153	1,150	*of which:* Claims on Nonbanks	7ed d
Approximately End of Period																**Monetary Authorities**	
	293.06	444.04	472.93	470.49	427.84	358.33	316.59	299.06	265.70	244.73	223.33	215.80	....	....	....	Foreign Assets	11
	34.46	39.20	44.65	43.73	43.00	42.12	45.83	46.34	43.44	41.83	52.48	54.53	....	....	....	Reserve Money	14
	25.68	29.49	34.44	35.42	35.11	35.77	38.81	38.84	35.95	33.88	44.78	44.62	43.77	42.62	44.97	*of which:* Currency Outside DMBs	14a
	187.41	333.20	332.73	335.86	294.45	271.14	158.93	97.53	77.53	44.91	33.44	31.36	....	....	....	Central Government Deposits	16d
	71.19	71.64	95.55	90.90	90.40	45.06	111.83	155.19	144.72	157.99	137.42	129.90	....	....	....	Other Items (Net)	17r
Approximately End of Period																**Deposit Money Banks**	
	8.19	8.27	10.81	I 8.26	11.04	12.56	13.92	18.59	10.69	11.75	11.64	12.68	10.65	11.53	11.65	Reserves	20
	32.23	53.36	61.00	I 62.38	67.24	70.65	86.67	102.20	114.74	118.84	123.46	118.95	I 101.67	111.59	98.15	Foreign Assets	21
	.21	.24	1.97	I —	—	—	.08	.12	7.76	10.29	13.33	31.71	I 37.92	43.46	50.03	Claims on Central Government	22a
	....	....	....	....	....	....	....	....	....	....	....	....	24.67	22.60	26.93	Claims on Public Enterprises	22c
	37.25	43.25	50.16	I 58.54	62.18	63.49	62.64	62.14	74.01	78.23	70.99	82.65	I 86.04	101.93	113.19	Claims on Private Sector	22d
	33.28	43.49	49.34	I 49.51	47.86	46.06	47.47	51.70	57.48	57.51	57.17	75.38	I 79.67	78.88	80.68	Demand Deposits	24
	13.83	21.93	29.68	I 34.13	41.79	44.09	44.92	45.25	44.23	48.30	42.82	48.69	I 53.72	56.89	60.47	Quasi-Monetary Deposits	25a
	4.65	8.08	10.33	I 18.02	20.58	21.09	29.36	31.37	40.23	39.76	42.90	46.29	I 42.21	48.41	47.13	Foreign Currency Deposits	25b
	9.15	9.07	5.97	I 6.80	7.97	10.38	14.29	24.49	28.73	34.60	30.17	27.91	I 28.69	37.29	39.15	Foreign Liabilities	26c
	—	.02	.05	I 2.06	1.63	5.78	7.43	8.81	10.95	14.11	15.91	16.02	13.37	19.80	21.42	Credit from Monetary Authorities	26g
	4.15	5.56	7.82	I 14.47	18.16	19.09	20.92	22.96	26.76	29.82	31.94	34.50	I 28.17	34.48	36.96	Capital Accounts	27a
	12.82	16.97	20.75	I 4.19	2.47	.22	-1.07	-1.53	-1.18	-4.99	-1.50	-2.80	I 15.11	15.36	14.14	Other Items (Net)	27r
Approximately End of Period																**Monetary Survey**	
	316.13	488.33	527.96	I 526.07	487.11	418.60	388.97	376.78	351.72	328.97	316.62	306.84	....	....	....	Foreign Assets (Net)	31n
	-153.51	-296.51	-288.81	I -280.50	-236.52	-212.70	-100.14	-40.06	-.11	37.57	43.90	72.48	....	....	....	Domestic Credit	32
	-190.76	-339.76	-338.97	I -337.34	-296.16	-272.51	-159.40	-98.86	-70.63	-35.71	-21.40	-1.16	....	....	....	Claims on Central Govt. (Net)	32an
	....	....	....	....	....	....	....	....	....	....	....	....	24.67	22.60	26.93	Claims on Public Enterprises	32c
	37.25	43.25	50.16	56.84	59.63	59.81	59.26	58.80	70.52	73.28	65.30	73.64	I 86.04	101.93	113.19	Claims on Private Sector	32d
	58.96	72.98	83.78	84.93	82.98	81.83	86.28	90.54	93.43	91.38	101.94	120.00	123.45	121.50	125.64	Money	34
	18.48	30.01	40.01	52.16	62.37	65.18	74.28	76.62	84.46	88.06	85.72	94.97	I 95.94	105.30	107.60	Quasi-Money	35
	85.19	88.83	115.36	I 108.48	105.24	58.89	128.28	169.55	173.71	187.09	172.85	164.29	....	....	....	Other Items (Net)	37r
	77.44	102.99	123.79	137.09	145.35	147.01	160.56	167.16	177.89	179.44	187.67	214.98	219.38	226.80	233.25	Money plus Quasi-Money	35l
Approximately End of Period																**Other Banking Institutions**	
	8,044	7,348	6,326	4,291	3,906	5,282	6,964	11,767	14,666	14,890	12,656	12,775	18,601	21,876	17,206	Cash	40
	1,007	1,293	1,337	1,463	1,450	1,465	1,584	4,144	4,201	4,208	4,479	4,261	4,299	4,317	4,307	Foreign Assets	41
	81,201	103,462	132,656	152,833	168,452	173,014	176,493	176,849	175,078	175,779	173,986	172,173	171,364	168,811	172,896	Claims on Private Sector	42d
	91,443	113,750	142,242	160,261	176,728	182,371	185,009	190,586	190,658	188,160	190,908	191,415	190,658	190,658	190,458	Capital Accounts	47a
	-1,189	-1,647	-1,923	-1,674	-2,921	-2,612	32	2,174	3,287	6,717	213	-2,206	3,606	4,346	3,951	Other Items (Net)	47r
Period Averages																**Prices**	
	....	....	....	....	....	77.1	80.0	85.7	97.2	98.3	100.0	103.0	104.3	105.0	106.9	Wholesale Prices	63
	I 101.6	100.4	105.5	105.7	104.0	100.8	97.6	96.1	97.0	98.0	100.0	104.9	104.8	105.9	106.5	Consumer Prices	64
Billions of Riyals																**International Transactions**	
	362.89	405.48	271.09	158.44	132.30	99.54	74.75	86.88	91.29	106.29	166.34	179.00	134.28	113.11	....	Exports	70
	337.40	377.30	251.16	147.89	120.73	....	66.88	76.50	75.67	90.24	150.28	163.49	....	....	....	Petroleum	70a
	320.45	359.56	235.21	142.15	114.57	....	54.26	55.17	55.05	70.62	123.28	139.83	....	....	....	Crude Petroleum	70aa
	16.95	17.75	15.95	5.74	6.16	....	12.62	21.33	20.62	19.61	27.00	23.66	....	....	....	Refined Petroleum	70ab
	100.35	119.30	139.34	135.42	118.74	85.56	70.78	75.31	81.58	79.22	90.14	108.90	124.50	105.70	87.42	Imports, cif	71
	85.77	101.96	119.09	115.74	102.21	79.35	66.15	70.39	76.24	74.04	84.24	101.78	116.36	98.79	81.70	Imports, fob	71.v
1990=100																Volume of Exports	
	211.4	206.5	130.1	90.6	74.4	49.6	77.2	55.5	73.8	76.3	100.0	145.9	....	....	....	Petroleum	72a
	220.4	215.0	134.5	94.9	76.2	49.5	77.9	53.7	72.4	75.3	100.0	148.3	....	....	....	Crude Petroleum	72aa
	43.5	46.8	47.1	35.7	40.4	52.0	64.3	89.6	100.4	95.2	100.0	100.1	....	....	....	Refined Petroleum	72ab
Index of Prices in US Dollars																Export Prices	
	142.2	160.4	163.9	142.2	138.7	135.9	97.0	85.2	68.8	79.0	100.0	81.1	84.9	73.8	74.1	Crude Petroleum	76aa d

Saudi Arabia

456

		1965	1966	1967	1968	1969	1970	1971	1972	1973	1974	1975	1976	1977	1978	1979
Balance of Payments															*Millions of US Dollars:*	
Goods: Exports f.o.b.	78aa d	....	....	....	....	....	....	2,706	4,058	7,702	30,870	27,888	36,314	41,052	37,534	58,771
Goods: Imports f.o.b.	78ab d	....	....	....	....	....	....	−805	−1,197	−1,853	−3,569	−6,004	−10,385	−14,698	−20,020	−20,911
Trade Balance	78ac d	....	....	....	....	....	....	1,901	2,861	5,849	27,301	21,884	25,929	26,354	17,514	37,860
Services: Credit	78ad d	....	....	....	....	....	....	154	217	356	645	841	1,074	1,407	1,627	4,079
Services: Debit	78ae d	....	....	....	....	....	....	−374	−509	−955	−2,163	−4,375	−7,935	−10,272	−14,396	−27,318
Balance on Goods and Services	78af d	....	....	....	....	....	....	1,680	2,570	5,250	25,783	18,351	19,068	17,489	4,745	14,621
Income: Credit	78ag d	....	....	....	....	....	....	67	106	205	1,220	1,839	2,884	3,989	4,301	4,915
Income: Debit	78ah d	....	....	....	....	....	....	−421	−162	−2,048	−2,445	−2,124	−3,280	−4,079	−4,512	−2,065
Balance on Goods, Serv., & Inc.	78ai d	....	....	....	....	....	....	1,326	2,514	3,407	24,558	18,066	18,671	17,398	4,533	17,472
Current Transfers, n.i.e.: Credit	78aj d	....	....	....	....	....	....	—	—	—	—	—	—	—	—	—
Current Transfers: Debit	78ak d	....	....	....	....	....	....	−354	−425	−888	−1,532	−3,681	−4,312	−5,407	−6,745	−7,266
Current Account, n.i.e.	78al d	....	....	....	....	....	....	972	2,089	2,520	23,025	14,385	14,360	11,991	−2,212	10,206
Capital Account, n.i.e.: Credit	78ba d	....	....	....	....	....	....	—	—	—	—	—	—	—	—	—
Capital Account: Debit	78bb d	....	....	....	....	....	....	—	—	—	—	—	—	—	—	—
Capital Account, n.i.e.	78bc d	....	....	....	....	....	....	—	—	—	—	—	—	—	—	—
Direct Investment Abroad	78bd d	....	....	....	....	....	....	—	—	—	—	—	—	—	—	—
Dir. Invest. in Rep. Econ., n.i.e.	78be d	....	....	....	....	....	....	−111	34	−626	−3,732	1,865	−397	783	556	−1,271
Portfolio Investment Assets	78bf d	....	....	....	....	....	....	−7	−31	−283	−5,101	−9,922	−9,456	−8,258	2,256	−1,021
Portfolio Investment Liab., n.i.e.	78bg d	....	....	....	....	....	....	—	—	—	—	—	—	—	—	—
Other Investment Assets	78bh d	....	....	....	....	....	....	−198	−1,047	−715	−3,918	3,551	−293	−1,698	−7,810	−8,096
Other Investment Liab., n.i.e.	78bi d	....	....	....	....	....	....	18	12	22	115	−819	−487	−122	509	417
Financial Account, n.i.e.	78bj d	....	....	....	....	....	....	−299	−1,033	−1,603	−12,637	−5,325	−10,633	−9,295	−4,489	−9,971
Net Errors and Omissions	78ca d	....	....	....	....	....	....	—	—	—	—	—	—	—	—	—
Overall Balance	78cb d	....	....	....	....	....	....	673	1,057	917	10,388	9,059	3,727	2,697	−6,700	234
Reserves and Related Items	79da d	....	....	....	....	....	....	−673	−1,057	−917	−10,388	−9,059	−3,727	−2,697	6,700	−234
Reserve Assets	79db d	....	....	....	....	....	....	−673	−1,057	−917	−10,388	−9,059	−3,727	−2,697	6,700	−234
Use of Fund Credit and Loans	79dc d	....	....	....	....	....	....	—	—	—	—	—	—	—	—	—
Liabs.Constit.For.Auth.Reserves	79dd d	....	....	....	....	....	....	—	—	—	—	—	—	—	—	—
Exceptional Financing	79de d	....	....	....	....	....	....	....	....	....	....	....	....	....	....	....
National Accounts															*Billions of Riyals*	
Exports of Goods & Services	90c	6.29	7.27	7.65	8.59	9.09	10.30	19.86	30.01	85.68	114.46	120.28	140.32	140.76	147.24	258.49
Government Consumption	91f	1.65	1.92	2.67	2.75	3.03	3.42	4.29	5.34	9.86	15.91	28.88	41.03	47.03	71.90	77.56
Gross Fixed Capital Formation	93e	1.71	2.33	2.16	2.39	2.63	2.60	3.40	5.69	8.40	17.70	33.54	51.19	66.89	76.65	97.07
Increase/Decrease(-) in Stocks	93i	−.21	—	.20	.74	.72	.21	.10	−.11	.84	.75	.78	.84	7.61	−7.38	−17.35
Private Consumption	96f	2.91	3.03	4.00	4.59	5.36	5.86	6.92	7.90	9.83	18.04	23.90	34.37	54.61	68.61	102.39
Imports of Goods & Services	98c	−1.95	−2.26	−3.54	−4.39	−4.85	−4.99	−6.30	−8.27	−15.29	−27.26	−42.86	−62.70	−91.51	−107.48	−132.35
Gross Domestic Product	99b	10.40	11.94	13.14	14.66	15.98	17.40	28.26	40.55	99.32	139.60	164.53	205.06	225.40	249.54	385.81
Net Factor Inc/Pmts(-) Abroad	98.n	....	2.96	−2.96	−3.20	−3.25	−3.83	−7.67	−10.46	−16.97	−14.20	.87	2.67	−1.78	−6.64	−4.75
Gross Nat'l Expenditure = GNP	99a	8.17	10.00	10.43	11.45	12.73	13.57	20.59	30.15	82.35	125.40	165.39	207.72	223.62	242.90	381.06
Gross Dom. Prod. 1990 Prices	99b.p	....	....	....	98.50	105.19	121.26	160.04	191.63	220.53	221.11	240.19	276.48	292.92	312.51	344.10
GDP Deflator (1990=100)	99bi p	....	....	....	14.88	15.19	14.35	17.66	21.16	45.03	63.14	68.50	74.17	76.95	79.85	112.12
																Millions:
Population	99z	5.41	5.55	5.70	5.86	6.03	6.20	6.38	6.57	6.76	6.97	7.25	7.62	8.06	8.49	8.93

International Liquidity: ⅃ Beginning in April 1978, *line 1d.d* excludes the foreign exchange cover against the note issue, which together with *line 3..d* is included in *line 11*. As of March 1978, this foreign exchange cover amounted to about US$5.3 billion.

Deposit Money Banks: ⅃ Beginning in October 1983, data are based on an improved classification. ⅃ Beginning in December 1992, claims on public enterprises *(line 22c)* include claims on financial and nonfinancial public enterprises, and may include a small amount of loans and advances to central government. Demand deposits *(line 24)*, quasi-monetary deposits *(line 25a)*, and foreign currency deposits *(line 25b)* may include some central government deposits.

Monetary Survey: ⅃ See note to section 20.

Other Banking Institutions: ⅃ Beginning in 1976, consolidates the Saudi Agricultural Bank, the Saudi Industrial Development Fund, the Public Investment Fund, the Real Estate Development Fund, and the Saudi Credit Bank. Prior to 1976, data refer only to the Saudi Agricultural Bank.

Prices: ⅃ Prior to 1979, the index is based on 1970 weights and covers Riyadh only. Thereafter, the index covers middle-income population of ten cities, base 1988.

Saudi Arabia

1980	1981	1982	1983	1984	1985	1986	1987	1988	1989	1990	1991	1992	1993	1994		
Minus Sign Indicates Debit																**Balance of Payments**
101,574	112,422	74,203	45,864	37,545	27,478	20,185	23,199	24,377	28,385	44,414	47,744	47,180	45,048	....	Goods: Exports f.o.b.	78aa *d*
−25,563	−29,889	−34,444	−33,218	−28,557	−20,364	−17,066	−18,283	−19,805	−19,231	−21,490	−25,968	−30,248	−25,897	....	Goods: Imports f.o.b.	78ab *d*
76,011	82,533	39,759	12,646	8,987	7,115	3,119	4,916	4,571	9,154	22,924	21,776	16,932	19,150	....	Trade Balance	78ac *d*
5,191	7,021	4,565	4,151	4,112	3,561	2,606	2,515	2,294	2,510	3,031	2,908	3,346	3,396	....	Services: Credit	78ad *d*
−30,231	−40,236	−34,852	−37,259	−32,856	−25,822	−20,336	−18,830	−14,935	−19,874	−22,414	−38,804	−31,782	−24,311	....	Services: Debit	78ae *d*
50,972	49,318	9,472	−20,462	−19,757	−15,146	−14,611	−11,399	−8,069	−8,211	3,541	−14,120	−11,504	−1,764	....	Balance on Goods and Services	78af *d*
7,443	10,956	14,060	15,868	13,366	12,418	11,279	10,537	10,454	10,433	9,199	8,700	7,378	6,154	....	Income: Credit	78ag *d*
−6,917	−9,599	−6,210	−3,022	−3,127	−1,756	−659	−676	−716	−1,017	−1,220	−1,933	−1,944	−1,951	....	Income: Debit	78ah *d*
51,498	50,675	17,321	−7,616	−9,518	−4,484	−3,991	−1,538	1,669	1,204	11,519	−7,354	−6,069	2,439	....	Balance on Goods, Serv., & Inc.	78ai *d*
—	—	—	—	—	—	—	—	—	—	—	—	—	—	....	Current Transfers, n.i.e.: Credit	78aj *d*
−9,995	−11,048	−9,746	−9,237	−8,882	−8,448	−7,804	−8,235	−9,009	−10,742	−15,637	−20,235	−14,898	−16,657	....	Current Transfers: Debit	78ak *d*
41,503	39,627	7,575	−16,852	−18,401	−12,932	−11,795	−9,773	−7,340	−9,538	−4,117	−27,589	−20,967	−14,218	....	Current Account, n.i.e.	78al *d*
—	—	—	—	—	—	—	—	—	—	—	—	—	—	....	Capital Account, n.i.e.: Credit	78ba *d*
—	—	—	—	—	—	—	—	—	—	—	—	—	—	....	Capital Account: Debit	78bb *d*
—	—	—	—	—	—	—	—	—	—	—	—	—	—	....	Capital Account, n.i.e.	78bc *d*
—	—	—	—	—	—	—	—	—	—	—	—	—	—	....	Direct Investment Abroad	78bd *d*
−3,192	6,498	11,128	4,944	4,850	491	967	−1,175	−328	−654	1,864	160	−79	−79	....	Dir. Invest. in Rep. Econ., n.i.e.	78be *d*
−22,010	−32,804	−11,490	7,529	13,406	8,412	3,451	6,150	3,057	−1,786	−3,340	470	−3,646	8,448	....	Portfolio Investment Assets	78bf *d*
—	—	—	—	—	—	—	—	—	—	—	—	—	—	....	Portfolio Investment Liab., n.i.e.	78bg *d*
−12,868	−3,729	−8,618	2,632	−1,669	2,658	−1,298	4,714	1,960	6,903	1,400	27,605	17,808	5,519	....	Other Investment Assets	78bh *d*
505	−24	−904	240	332	663	1,056	2,724	1,132	1,567	−1,183	−598	1,220	1,826	....	Other Investment Liab., n.i.e.	78bi *d*
−37,565	−30,059	−9,884	15,345	16,919	12,224	4,176	12,413	5,821	6,030	−1,259	27,637	15,303	15,714	....	Financial Account, n.i.e.	78bj *d*
—	—	—	—	—	—	—	—	—	—	—	—	—	—	....	Net Errors and Omissions	78ca *d*
3,937	9,568	−2,308	−1,508	−1,480	−709	−7,619	2,640	−1,519	−3,508	−5,376	49	−5,664	1,496	....	Overall Balance	78cb *d*
−3,937	−9,568	2,308	1,508	1,480	709	7,619	−2,640	1,519	3,508	5,376	−49	5,664	−1,496	....	Reserves and Related Items	79da *d*
−3,937	−9,568	2,308	1,508	1,480	709	7,619	−2,640	1,519	3,508	5,376	−49	5,664	−1,496	....	Reserve Assets	79db *d*
—	—	—	—	—	—	—	—	—	—	—	—	—	—	....	Use of Fund Credit and Loans	79dc *d*
—	—	—	—	—	—	—	—	—	—	—	—	—	—	....	Liabs.Constit.For.Auth.Reserves	79dd *d*
....	....	....	....	....	....	....	....	....	....	....	....	....	....	....	Exceptional Financing	79de *d*
Billions of Riyals																**National Accounts**
368.43	354.92	219.45	167.18	145.53	113.16	85.99	99.05	103.08	118.21	181.13	197.28	196.10	....	....	Exports of Goods & Services	90c
81.92	128.53	126.85	121.33	121.06	114.39	106.37	107.71	97.42	96.56	120.13	165.00	148.97	....	....	Government Consumption	91f
106.38	122.31	115.45	103.23	96.49	76.31	66.14	65.20	56.92	60.41	73.80	86.51	98.98	....	....	Gross Fixed Capital Formation	93e
6.43	−19.80	−2.56	9.33	19.60	−10.62	−12.32	−12.87	2.73	6.76	2.75	7.34	8.95	....	....	Increase/Decrease(-) in Stocks	93i
114.91	126.51	151.29	157.37	159.35	158.59	140.15	135.54	139.40	145.03	155.87	168.75	183.92	....	....	Private Consumption	96f
−157.46	−187.76	−195.26	−186.41	−190.64	−137.89	−115.24	−119.17	−114.40	−116.15	−141.69	−182.84	−181.77	....	....	Imports of Goods & Services	98c
520.59	524.72	415.23	372.02	351.40	313.94	271.09	275.45	285.15	310.82	391.99	442.04	455.13	....	....	Gross Domestic Product	99b
−12.16	−1.82	18.16	20.44	20.94	13.59	18.58	17.38	19.51	20.14	6.43	−2.36	....	....	....	Net Factor Inc/Pmts(-) Abroad	98.n
508.42	522.90	433.39	392.46	372.34	327.53	289.67	292.84	304.65	330.96	398.42	439.68	....	....	....	Gross Nat'l Expenditure = GNP	99a
371.36	377.50	336.93	336.54	329.09	315.75	333.32	328.72	353.59	354.23	391.99	430.03	434.43	....	....	Gross Dom. Prod. 1990 Prices	99b.*p*
140.19	139.00	123.24	110.54	106.78	99.43	81.33	83.79	80.64	87.75	100.00	102.79	104.76	....	....	GDP Deflator (1990=100)	99bi *p*
Midyear Estimates																
9.37	9.81	10.25	11.17	11.98	12.65	13.36	13.61	14.02	14.43	14.87	Ⅰ16.49	16.82	17.12	....	**Population**	99z

Senegal
722

		1965	1966	1967	1968	1969	1970	1971	1972	1973	1974	1975	1976	1977	1978	1979
Exchange Rates															*Francs per SDR:*	
Official Rate	aa	245.07	247.59	245.42	247.40	277.91	276.02	283.61	278.00	284.00	272.08	262.55	288.70	285.76	272.28	264.78
															Francs per US Dollar:	
Official Rate	ae	245.08	247.59	245.43	247.41	277.92	276.03	261.23	256.05	235.43	222.22	224.27	248.49	235.25	209.00	201.00
Official Rate	rf	245.06	245.68	246.00	247.56	259.96	276.40	275.59	252.03	222.89	240.70	214.31	238.95	245.68	225.66	212.72
Fund Position															*Millions of SDRs:*	
Quota	2f. s	25.0	25.0	25.0	25.0	25.0	34.0	34.0	34.0	34.0	34.0	34.0	34.0	34.0	42.0	42.0
SDRs	1b. s	—	—	—	—	—	1.2	2.5	5.7	5.3	4.6	3.3	1.2	1.7	9.7	11.5
Reserve Position in the Fund	1c. s	2.5	2.5	2.5	2.5	2.5	3.3	3.6	3.9	4.2	—	—	—	—	2.1	—
Total Fund Cred.&Loans Outstg.	2tl	—	—	—	—	—	—	—	—	—	—	25.4	25.4	25.4	57.0	70.5
International Liquidity											*Millions of US Dollars Unless Otherwise Indicated:*					
Total Reserves minus Gold	1l. d	38.0	46.2	37.2	16.0	6.2	22.1	24.6	38.5	12.1	6.3	31.1	25.2	33.7	18.8	19.1
SDRs	1b. d	—	—	—	—	—	1.2	2.7	6.2	6.4	5.7	3.9	1.3	2.1	12.7	15.1
Reserve Position in the Fund	1c. d	2.5	2.5	2.5	2.5	2.5	3.3	3.9	4.2	5.0	—	—	—	—	2.8	—
Foreign Exchange	1d. d	35.5	43.7	34.7	13.5	3.7	17.6	18.1	28.1	.6	.6	27.3	23.9	31.6	3.4	4.0
Gold (Million Fine Troy Ounces)	1ad	....	....	....	....	....	....	....	....	....	....	....	—	.015	.022	.029
Gold (National Valuation)	1and	....	....	....	....	....	....	....	....	....	....	....	—	.6	1.0	1.3
Monetary Authorities: Other Liab.	4.. d	4.5	.6	3.0	1.3	.2	.4	1.1	1.0	11.6	11.9	.5	14.4	19.3	36.0	117.6
Deposit Money Banks: Assets	7a. d	9.2	8.0	7.9	5.9	7.4	8.9	8.4	10.9	15.5	19.0	22.8	37.2	46.0	46.6	53.2
Deposit Money Banks: Liabilities	7b. d	19.4	21.1	17.9	17.2	27.5	23.6	30.8	41.3	47.2	57.7	85.8	77.5	101.0	144.2	228.6
of which: Liab. to Nonbanks	7bdd	....	....	....	....	....	....	....	....	....	....	....	18.7	20.1	34.9	73.0
Monetary Authorities															*Billions of Francs:*	
Foreign Assets	11	9.37	11.41	9.19	3.95	1.71	6.10	7.50	9.85	2.78	1.40	6.98	6.27	7.92	3.93	3.85
Claims on Central Government	12a	—	.01	.02	.01	—	.01	—	.01	—	—	.45	3.41	8.14	8.21	16.53
Claims on Deposit Money Banks	12e	14.02	11.63	8.29	12.89	13.01	13.50	13.57	12.94	25.24	38.55	39.49	42.81	44.34	71.17	79.16
Claims on Other Financial Insts.	12f	....	....	....	....	....	....	....	....	....	....	....	1.05	1.45	1.21	1.18
Reserve Money	14	15.41	13.25	10.92	12.84	12.73	16.07	16.92	17.73	21.46	32.15	34.57	38.74	44.63	55.81	51.09
of which: Currency Outside DMBs	14a	14.72	12.56	10.21	11.92	11.58	15.24	15.94	16.49	19.45	28.96	29.46	33.74	39.47	46.23	42.94
Foreign Liabilities	16c	1.12	.14	.75	.31	.05	.10	.28	.26	2.66	2.64	6.79	10.92	11.80	27.00	49.15
Central Government Deposits	16d	6.86	9.66	5.83	3.62	1.90	2.20	1.68	1.57	.72	1.98	2.58	.98	1.43	1.87	1.41
Other Items (Net)	17r	—	—	—	.07	.04	1.23	2.19	3.23	3.18	3.19	2.99	2.91	3.99	−.16	−.94
Deposit Money Banks															*Billions of Francs:*	
Reserves	20	.90	.52	.63	1.30	1.25	.76	1.46	1.31	2.16	2.33	4.75	5.17	5.43	9.15	6.57
Foreign Assets	21	2.28	1.97	1.95	1.45	2.06	2.48	2.14	2.80	3.56	4.22	5.11	9.23	10.83	9.73	10.69
Claims on Central Government	22a	2.20	2.20	1.97	1.90	3.30	3.37	3.57	5.34	6.27	8.00	10.61	14.40	12.59	12.26	I 14.10
Claims on Private Sector	22d	33.41	29.85	26.00	31.63	33.87	36.56	38.59	45.97	62.75	88.84	106.18	121.08	143.31	194.33	I 230.60
Claims on Other Financial Insts.	22f	....	....	....	....	....	....	....	....	....	....	....	....	....	....	6.72
Demand Deposits	24	11.99	12.76	13.04	14.48	14.66	17.26	17.35	20.99	23.00	36.89	42.85	58.63	66.70	76.54	I 74.28
Time Deposits	25	1.04	.70	.74	1.28	1.76	2.77	2.84	3.72	8.17	9.49	10.92	18.76	21.85	32.31	I 39.91
Foreign Liabilities	26c	3.44	3.73	2.44	2.16	3.94	3.27	4.95	6.56	7.07	8.90	15.43	15.27	19.87	26.31	35.16
Long-Term Foreign Liabilities	26cl	1.35	1.47	1.99	2.09	3.70	3.28	2.93	4.01	3.80	3.92	3.82	3.99	3.89	3.82	10.79
Central Government Deposits	26d	3.11	2.14	1.66	1.65	2.09	2.21	2.52	4.15	4.31	6.06	8.17	4.44	4.22	4.45	I 12.26
Credit from Monetary Authorities	26g	14.02	11.79	8.39	12.89	13.01	13.50	13.57	12.94	25.24	38.55	39.49	42.81	44.34	71.17	78.17
Other Items (Net)	27r	3.84	1.96	2.29	1.73	1.32	.89	1.59	3.04	3.16	−.42	5.96	5.99	11.29	10.87	18.12
Treasury Claims: Private Sector	22d. i	1.13	.96	1.08	1.00	.86	1.00	1.23	1.30	.74	.81	.76	.84	1.31	1.82	1.78
Post Office: Checking Deposits	24.. i	2.25	1.79	2.06	1.97	1.73	2.00	1.91	1.64	1.69	1.88	2.31	2.46	2.89	3.66	3.59
Monetary Survey															*Billions of Francs:*	
Foreign Assets (Net)	31n	7.09	9.51	7.95	2.93	−.23	5.21	4.40	5.83	−3.39	−5.91	−10.13	−10.69	−12.92	−39.65	−69.76
Domestic Credit	32	27.89	22.05	22.56	30.24	34.91	37.52	39.87	47.22	65.68	90.69	108.81	136.99	162.73	213.35	I 259.05
Claims on Central Govt. (Net)	32an	−6.65	−8.76	−4.52	−2.39	.17	−.03	.05	−.04	2.19	1.04	1.87	14.02	16.66	16.00	I 18.76
Claims on Private Sector	32d	34.54	30.81	27.08	32.63	34.73	37.56	39.82	47.26	63.49	89.65	106.94	121.92	144.62	196.14	I 232.38
Claims on Other Financial Insts.	32f	....	....	....	....	....	....	....	....	....	....	....	1.05	1.45	1.21	I 7.90
Money	34	28.96	27.11	25.31	28.36	27.97	34.50	35.20	39.12	44.20	67.77	75.18	94.89	109.12	126.53	I 121.21
Quasi-Money	35	1.04	.70	.74	1.28	1.76	2.77	2.84	3.72	8.17	9.49	10.92	18.76	21.85	32.31	I 39.91
Long-Term Foreign Liabilities	36cl	1.35	1.47	1.99	2.09	3.70	3.28	2.93	4.01	3.80	3.92	3.82	3.99	3.89	3.82	10.79
Other Items (Net)	37r	3.63	2.28	2.48	1.42	1.26	2.19	3.29	6.20	6.12	3.60	8.76	8.66	14.95	11.05	17.37
Money plus Quasi-Money	35l	30.00	27.81	26.05	29.64	29.73	37.27	38.05	42.83	52.37	77.26	86.10	113.65	130.97	158.83	I 161.12
Other Banking Institutions															*Billions of Francs:*	
Savings Deposits	45	.35	.38	.40	.45	.46	.51	.56	.66	.72	.86	....	....	....	....	1.62
Liquid Liabilities	55l	30.35	28.19	26.45	30.09	30.19	37.78	38.61	43.49	53.09	78.12	....	....	....	....	I 162.75
Interest Rates															*Percent Per Annum*	
Discount Rate (End of Period)	60	3.50	3.50	3.50	3.50	3.50	3.50	3.50	3.50	5.50	5.50	8.00	8.00	8.00	8.00	8.00
Money Market Rate	60b	....	....	....	....	....	....	....	....	....	....	....	7.28	7.40	7.40	7.80
Deposit Rate	60l	....	....	....	....	3.00	3.00	3.00	3.00	5.75	5.75	5.88	6.00	6.00	6.00	6.00
Lending Rate	60p	....	....	....	....	....	....	....	....	....	....	....	....	12.00	12.00	12.00
Prices and Production															*Index Numbers (1990=100):*	
Consumer Prices	64	....	....	20.3	20.3	21.1	21.7	22.5	23.9	26.6	31.0	40.8	41.3	45.9	47.5	52.1
Industrial Production	66	....	....	....	62.7	I 61.6	65.4	64.6	80.7	73.5	78.1	90.9	93.4	I 98.6	88.5	99.4

Senegal

1980	1981	1982	1983	1984	1985	1986	1987	1988	1989	1990	1991	1992	1993	1994		
End of Period															**Exchange Rates**	
287.99	334.52	370.92	436.97	470.11	415.26	394.78	378.78	407.68	380.32	364.84	370.48	378.57	404.89	I 780.44	Official Rate	aa
End of Period (ae) Period Average (rf)																
225.80	287.40	336.25	417.37	479.60	378.05	322.75	267.00	302.95	289.40	256.45	259.00	275.33	294.78	I 534.60	Official Rate	ae
211.28	271.73	328.61	381.06	436.96	449.26	346.30	300.54	297.85	319.01	272.26	282.11	264.69	283.16	I 555.20	Official Rate	rf
															Fund Position	
End of Period																
63.0	63.0	63.0	85.1	85.1	85.1	85.1	85.1	85.1	85.1	85.1	85.1	85.1	118.9	118.9	Quota	2f. s
—	3.7	4.9	3.8	.1	.1	2.5	—	—	3.6	.2	.3	—	.3	.7	SDRs	1b. s
—	—	.9	.9	1.0	1.0	1.0	1.0	1.0	1.0	1.0	1.0	1.1	1.1	1.1	Reserve Position in the Fund	1c. s
109.9	160.2	200.0	220.5	234.7	243.7	236.3	241.6	236.5	240.4	221.0	228.9	197.4	177.8	205.4	Total Fund Cred.&Loans Outstg.	2tl
															International Liquidity	
End of Period																
8.1	8.7	11.4	12.2	3.7	5.1	9.4	9.2	10.5	19.0	11.0	13.2	12.4	3.4	179.6	Total Reserves minus Gold	1l. d
—	4.4	5.4	3.9	.1	.1	3.0	—	—	4.7	.2	.4	—	.4	1.1	SDRs	1b. d
—	—	1.0	1.0	.9	1.1	1.2	1.4	1.3	1.3	1.4	1.5	1.4	1.5	1.7	Reserve Position in the Fund	1c. d
8.1	4.3	5.0	7.3	2.6	3.9	5.2	7.8	9.1	13.0	9.3	11.3	10.9	1.5	176.9	Foreign Exchange	1d. d
.029	.029	.029	.029	.029	.029	.029	.029	.029	.029	.029	.029	.029	.029	.029	Gold (Million Fine Troy Ounces)	1ad
1.3	12.2	12.4	11.2	9.6	9.4	11.7	13.7	12.0	11.3	11.0	10.3	10.1	10.8	10.8	Gold (National Valuation)	1and
158.9	210.8	255.5	241.0	196.2	334.8	289.8	317.8	407.1	303.7	330.0	282.2	298.2	408.2	144.4	Monetary Authorities: Other Liab.	4..d
57.7	43.1	55.4	45.1	40.4	41.9	40.0	39.7	58.3	84.8	51.2	66.7	72.8	68.6	131.4	Deposit Money Banks: Assets	7a. d
211.4	173.9	159.5	112.5	133.2	167.1	150.9	204.3	226.9	259.7	183.1	192.2	171.8	154.7	134.0	Deposit Money Banks: Liabilities	7b. d
78.1	64.4	54.3	46.6	40.9	42.0	60.5	63.9	70.5	141.4	83.9	70.7	79.5	54.2	45.0	of which: Liab. to Nonbanks	7bd d
															Monetary Authorities	
End of Period																
1.82	2.49	3.84	5.09	1.77	1.91	3.03	2.46	3.17	5.50	2.81	3.42	3.41	1.01	96.02	Foreign Assets	11
36.80	59.61	116.17	132.27	145.30	158.15	164.53	170.11	172.87	173.96	163.94	165.46	163.60	158.39	265.55	Claims on Central Government	12a
108.06	146.67	168.55	173.82	157.90	179.71	160.64	156.35	194.52	190.00	183.86	179.83	188.98	172.27	11.50	Claims on Deposit Money Banks	12e
.48	1.36	1.66	2.36	2.61	3.14	3.65	3.64	3.65	.49	.49	.63	.63	.63	.62	Claims on Other Financial Insts.	12f
62.02	85.80	106.65	103.14	102.15	108.16	125.75	132.59	131.82	164.42	158.46	169.61	181.74	126.62	189.80	Reserve Money	14
51.36	73.61	84.49	78.28	77.32	86.22	104.30	100.70	92.78	102.68	95.24	97.53	107.18	93.03	146.58	of which: Currency Outside DMBs	14a
76.71	123.41	169.32	205.99	212.67	234.51	194.01	180.66	221.72	179.82	165.28	157.88	156.82	192.31	237.54	Foreign Liabilities	16c
12.87	6.22	20.47	15.95	13.51	6.05	5.98	9.27	9.90	7.58	5.81	6.02	4.03	5.72	12.85	Central Government Deposits	16d
-4.42	-5.30	-6.22	-11.53	-20.74	-5.81	6.09	10.04	10.76	18.13	21.54	15.83	14.02	7.64	-66.51	Other Items (Net)	17r
															Deposit Money Banks	
End of Period																
10.14	11.70	21.92	21.22	24.19	22.36	28.35	32.12	39.65	67.64	62.34	71.32	74.14	34.07	31.84	Reserves	20
13.02	12.40	18.64	18.81	19.39	15.84	12.90	10.61	17.68	24.55	13.12	17.27	20.06	20.22	70.23	Foreign Assets	21
15.60	14.53	13.53	13.45	14.92	14.50	15.35	15.69	24.81	21.66	15.49	32.75	22.85	28.64	57.85	Claims on Central Government	22a
268.25	322.79	353.76	366.67	372.16	394.55	389.67	401.46	431.40	441.49	410.27	396.08	417.47	424.31	349.89	Claims on Private Sector	22d
2.89	2.43	2.14	2.32	2.54	3.57	4.16	4.20	5.34	2.68	2.03	1.87	2.09	1.58	1.28	Claims on Other Financial Insts.	22f
81.97	85.12	98.73	106.06	109.58	103.44	117.15	109.67	117.03	124.48	104.68	112.28	106.63	101.43	155.35	Demand Deposits	24
39.75	53.69	73.34	83.85	95.47	106.62	106.68	118.41	119.59	138.11	146.98	158.39	167.56	138.78	161.38	Time Deposits	25
34.79	35.80	38.32	30.93	47.68	52.05	37.08	43.12	57.05	63.68	38.61	41.86	38.26	36.36	58.26	Foreign Liabilities	26c
12.95	14.18	15.30	16.01	16.19	11.11	11.60	11.42	11.70	11.47	8.35	7.92	9.04	9.23	13.38	Long-Term Foreign Liabilities	26cl
13.60	18.99	15.14	16.37	18.83	17.49	23.85	32.08	38.05	61.39	66.69	83.13	100.76	118.05	136.36	Central Government Deposits	26d
107.64	146.87	169.61	175.32	156.04	182.09	167.46	158.99	196.79	194.75	184.26	181.42	190.18	176.83	11.50	Credit from Monetary Authorities	26g
19.21	9.20	-.45	-6.06	-10.59	-21.98	-13.38	-9.61	-21.33	-35.86	-46.32	-65.71	-75.83	-71.86	-25.13	Other Items (Net)	27r
1.40	1.33	1.12	1.90	1.49	2.25	2.07	2.20	2.76	2.97	3.22	2.22	2.44	2.30	....	Treasury Claims: Private Sector	22d. i
4.15	4.04	5.29	4.81	4.74	3.83	5.54	3.76	4.90	3.47	3.95	3.01	3.40	2.96	....	Post Office: Checking Deposits	24.. i
															Monetary Survey	
End of Period																
-96.65	-144.32	-185.17	-213.01	-239.20	-268.81	-215.18	-210.71	-257.92	-213.44	-187.97	-179.05	-171.62	-207.45	-129.55	Foreign Assets (Net)	31n
301.70	379.55	456.93	489.56	509.94	554.20	553.07	557.51	595.00	574.78	523.66	510.65	505.24	492.74	525.98	Domestic Credit	32
28.67	51.64	98.26	116.31	131.13	150.70	153.53	146.01	151.87	127.16	107.66	109.85	82.62	63.92	174.19	Claims on Central Govt. (Net)	32an
269.65	324.12	354.88	368.58	373.65	396.79	391.74	403.66	434.16	444.46	413.49	398.30	419.90	426.61	349.89	Claims on Private Sector	32d
3.38	3.79	3.79	4.67	5.15	6.70	7.80	7.85	8.98	3.17	2.52	2.50	2.72	2.20	1.90	Claims on Other Financial Insts.	32f
137.94	163.23	189.00	189.15	191.65	193.49	226.99	214.42	214.91	230.83	204.20	213.22	217.39	197.75	302.34	Money	34
39.75	53.69	73.34	83.85	95.47	106.62	106.68	118.41	119.59	138.11	146.98	158.39	167.56	138.78	161.38	Quasi-Money	35
12.95	14.18	15.30	16.01	16.19	11.11	11.60	11.42	11.70	11.47	8.35	7.92	9.04	9.23	13.38	Long-Term Foreign Liabilities	36cl
14.41	4.13	-5.86	-12.46	-32.57	-25.84	-7.37	2.55	-9.11	-19.08	-23.83	-47.53	-60.37	-60.47	-80.66	Other Items (Net)	37r
177.69	216.92	262.34	273.00	287.12	300.11	333.67	332.83	334.49	368.94	351.18	371.61	384.95	336.52	463.72	Money plus Quasi-Money	35l
															Other Banking Institutions	
End of Period																
1.68	1.74	1.86	1.87	1.88	1.94	2.36	2.38	3.47	3.79	4.17	....	....	....	....	Savings Deposits	45
179.37	218.66	264.19	274.86	288.99	302.05	336.02	335.21	337.96	372.73	355.35	....	....	....	....	Liquid Liabilities	55l
															Interest Rates	
Percent Per Annum																
10.50	10.50	12.50	10.50	10.50	10.50	8.50	8.50	9.50	11.00	11.00	11.00	12.50	10.50	10.00	Discount Rate (End of Period)	60
10.00	13.67	14.66	12.23	11.84	10.66	8.58	8.37	8.72	10.07	10.98	10.94	11.44	....	....	Money Market Rate	60b
6.19	6.25	7.75	7.50	7.25	7.25	6.08	5.25	5.25	6.42	7.00	7.00	7.75	....	....	Deposit Rate	60l
14.50	14.50	16.00	14.50	14.50	14.50	13.50	13.50	13.58	15.13	16.00	16.00	16.75	....	....	Lending Rate	60p
															Prices and Production	
Period Averages																
56.7	60.0	70.4	78.6	87.9	99.3	105.4	101.1	99.2	99.7	100.0	98.2	98.1	97.6	129.1	Consumer Prices	64
81.9	89.7	93.1	96.5	94.6	96.9	103.7	104.4	88.9	84.7	100.0	....	....	....	....	Industrial Production	66

Senegal

		1965	1966	1967	1968	1969	1970	1971	1972	1973	1974	1975	1976	1977	1978	1979
International Transactions																*Billions of Francs*
Exports	70	32.05	37.11	34.27	37.85	31.91	42.18	34.71	54.41	43.24	93.98	99.10	115.93	152.92	101.40	113.86
Exports, from DOTS	70y	....	....	....	....	....	....	....	....	....	....	....	....	....	....	....
Imports, cif	71	40.20	39.48	40.83	45.80	50.41	53.86	60.60	70.55	80.17	119.38	124.62	153.89	187.55	170.31	197.98
Imports, fob	71.v	35.58	34.94	36.13	40.38	44.75	47.55	53.76	62.61	70.91	103.04	110.06	136.38	167.13	151.01	177.84
Imports, cif, from DOTS	71y	....	....	....	....	....	....	....	....	....	....	....	....	....	....	....
																1985=100
Unit Value of Exports	74	....	17.8	20.4	20.2	17.4	19.4	21.6	21.1	25.0	47.5	ɪ40.2	39.2	47.1	50.8	54.4
Unit Value of Imports	75	....	24.1	25.4	19.5	19.2	19.5	22.8	23.6	26.9	38.5	ɪ40.8	42.9	46.7	46.1	51.8
Balance of Payments																*Millions of US Dollars:*
Goods: Exports f.o.b.	78aa d	....	....	....	....	....	....	....	....	....	472.6	542.6	536.5	685.3	434.7	517.6
Goods: Imports f.o.b.	78ab d	....	....	....	....	....	....	....	....	....	−552.5	−611.5	−659.6	−772.5	−744.2	−813.3
Trade Balance	78ac d	....	....	....	....	....	....	....	....	....	−79.9	−69.0	−123.1	−87.2	−309.5	−295.7
Services: Credit	78ad d	....	....	....	....	....	....	....	....	....	127.3	145.6	159.5	169.9	240.4	298.6
Services: Debit	78ae d	....	....	....	....	....	....	....	....	....	−126.6	−170.4	−174.6	−202.7	−210.8	−287.9
Balance on Goods and Services	78af d	....	....	....	....	....	....	....	....	....	−79.2	−93.7	−138.2	−120.0	−279.9	−285.1
Income: Credit	78ag d	....	....	....	....	....	....	....	....	....	8.8		7.7	9.7	11.7	16.5
Income: Debit	78ah d	....	....	....	....	....	....	....	....	....	−58.6	−83.8	−68.6	−63.9	−87.6	−95.6
Balance on Goods, Serv., & Inc.	78ai d	....	....	....	....	....	....	....	....	....	−129.0	−169.6	−199.2	−174.3	−355.8	−364.2
Current Transfers, n.i.e.: Credit	78aj d	....	....	....	....	....	....	....	....	....	102.0	134.2	152.5	158.1	208.2	223.4
Current Transfers: Debit	78ak d	....	....	....	....	....	....	....	....	....	−38.6	−50.2	−46.1	−51.3	−88.2	−123.4
Current Account	78al d	....	....	....	....	....	....	....	....	....	−65.6	−85.6	−92.8	−67.5	−235.8	−264.2
Capital Account, n.i.e.: Credit	78ba d	....	....	....	....	....	....	....	....	....	—	—	—	—	—	—
Capital Account: Debit	78bb d	....	....	....	....	....	....	....	....	....						
Capital Account, n.i.e.	78bc d	....	....	....	....	....	....	....	....	....						
Direct Investment Abroad	78bd d	....	....	....	....	....	....	....	....	....	−3.2	6.9	.4	−2.9	−.5	−3.9
Dir. Invest. in Rep. Econ., n.i.e.	78be d	....	....	....	....	....	....	....	....	....	10.3	22.5	35.9	28.0	−5.0	8.9
Portfolio Investment Assets	78bf d	....	....	....	....	....	....	....	....	....	.2	—	—	—	.7	—
Portfolio Investment Liab., n.i.e.	78bg d	....	....	....	....	....	....	....	....	....	2.9	2.9	.6	.6	8.3	−2.6
Other Investment Assets	78bh d	....	....	....	....	....	....	....	....	....	−42.7	2.3	−22.4	−14.2	−4.0	−57.8
Other Investment Liab., n.i.e.	78bi d	....	....	....	....	....	....	....	....	....	78.0	57.6	44.4	58.4	191.6	333.2
Financial Account, n.i.e.	78bj d	....	....	....	....	....	....	....	....	....	45.4	92.2	67.4	69.9	191.0	277.8
Net Errors and Omissions	78ca d	....	....	....	....	....	....	....	....	....	14.3	−11.2	6.2	.5	−14.7	−40.6
Overall Balance	78cb d	....	....	....	....	....	....	....	....	....	−5.9	−4.5	−19.1	2.9	−59.4	−27.0
Reserves and Related Items	79da d	....	....	....	....	....	....	....	....	....	5.9	4.5	19.1	−2.9	59.4	27.0
Reserve Assets	79db d	....	....	....	....	....	....	....	....	....	5.9	−26.3	6.2	−3.7	20.1	8.9
Use of Fund Credit and Loans	79dc d	....	....	....	....	....	....	....	....	....	—	30.8	—	—	39.9	17.7
Liabs.Constit.For.Auth.Reserves	79dd d	....	....	....	....	....	....	....	....	....	—	—	12.6	.4	−1.2	−.1
Exceptional Financing	79de d	....	....	....	....	....	....	....	....	....	—	—	.3	.5	.5	.5
Government Finance																*Billions of Francs:*
Deficit (-) or Surplus	80	....	....	....	....	....	1.24	−1.20	....	−7.51	....	−2.15	....	−15.09	1.49	−4.26
Revenue	81	....	....	....	....	....	39.98	41.43	....	47.70	....	77.03	....	86.22	98.14	107.55
Grants Received	81z	....	....	....	....	....	.01	.01	....	—	....	.02	.17	.05	.04	.26
Expenditure	82	....	....	....	....	....	38.20	42.31	....	51.00	....	75.64	90.80	96.96	96.80	111.50
Lending Minus Repayments	83	....	....	....	....	....	.55	.33	....	4.21	....	3.56	.62	4.40	−.11	.57
Financing																
Net Borrowing: Domestic	84a	....	....	....	....	....	....	....	....	....	....	2.31	....	....	....	....
Foreign	85a	....	....	....	....	....	....	....	....	....	....	−.16	....	....	....	....
Use of Cash Balances	87	....	....	....	....	....	....	....	....	....	....	....	....	....	....	....
Debt: Domestic	88a	....	....	....	....	....	....	....	....	....	....	....	....	....	....	....
Foreign	89a	....	....	....	....	....	....	....	....	....	....	....	....	....	....	....
National Accounts																*Billions of Francs*
Exports of Goods & Services	90c	....	....	....	49.7	53.8	65.3	66.0	83.8	79.2	144.6	147.9	166.7	209.2	142.6	186.6
Government Consumption	91f	34.5	35.7	36.1	34.9	33.6	35.7	38.8	40.8	43.8	50.0	61.8	71.7	77.9	91.1	111.0
Gross Fixed Capital Formation	93e	....	....	....	21.0	22.7	30.0	31.2	37.5	39.6	51.8	56.6	61.4	62.2	67.2	82.6
Increase/Decrease(-) in Stocks	93i	....	....	....	4.0	6.4	7.7	9.0	9.0	13.0	23.3	15.7	14.3	22.4	5.2	26.7
Private Consumption	96f	148.7	151.6	152.9	172.7	171.5	177.3	185.6	198.1	210.2	235.1	294.5	348.8	363.6	419.2	460.1
Imports of Goods & Services	98c	....	....	....	−65.1	−71.4	−75.9	−83.4	−95.6	−107.5	−166.0	−170.1	−203.6	−251.7	−230.6	−285.9
Gross Domestic Product	99b	198.8	205.3	205.5	217.2	216.6	240.1	247.2	273.6	278.3	338.8	406.4	459.3	487.5	494.1	581.1
Gross Dom. Prod. 1985 Prices	99b.p	....	....	....	....	....	....	....	....	....	....	....	1,004.1	976.8	938.3	1,033.2
GDP Deflator (1985=100)	99bi p	....	....	....	....	....	....	....	....	....	....	....	45.7	49.9	52.7	56.2
																Millions:
Population	99z	3.37	3.42	3.50	4.00	4.13	4.27	4.40	4.55	4.70	4.84	4.98	5.12	5.25	5.40	5.55

Deposit Money Banks: ɪ Beginning in October 1979, *Central Government Deposits* include the deposits of public establishments of an administrative or social nature (EPAS) and exclude those of the savings bank; *Demand* and *Time Deposits* include deposits of the savings bank and exclude deposits of EPAS; and *Claims on Private Sector* exclude claims on other financial institutions.

Monetary Survey: ɪ Beginning in October 1979, line 32f includes claims of deposit money banks on other financial institutions; see deposit money bank notes for explanation of other break symbols.

Government Finance: ɪ Beginning in 1980, data include social security operations. ɪ Beginning in 1982, data also cover extrabudgetary foreign grants and loans for capital expenditure not recorded in the treasury accounts.

Senegal

722

	1980	1981	1982	1983	1984	1985	1986	1987	1988	1989	1990	1991	1992	1993	1994	International Transactions	
Billions of Francs																	
	100.77	135.88	180.04	235.48	277.02	252.49	216.58	182.25	176.08	221.10	207.38	183.77	180.41	....	....	Exports	70
	....	135.88	180.03	235.48	294.55	311.92	267.83	235.84	176.08	253.14	234.42	183.77	180.41	....	....	Exports, from DOTS	70y
	222.26	292.34	325.94	390.72	428.60	370.97	332.93	307.60	321.57	389.54	357.67	309.35	309.68	....	....	Imports, cif	71
	194.24	255.54	284.91	341.54	374.65	324.27	291.02	268.88	281.09	340.51	312.65	270.41	270.70	....	....	Imports, fob	71.v
	....	292.34	325.92	424.45	469.36	418.26	381.19	356.66	321.57	421.68	377.56	309.42	309.68	....	....	Imports, cif, from DOTS	71y
1985=100																	
	53.2	73.0	ℐ70.7	78.7	100.3	100.0	70.0	66.6	....	....	....	....	....	....	....	Unit Value of Exports	74
	67.4	75.6	ℐ85.3	93.3	102.4	100.0	72.4	68.9	....	....	....	....	....	....	....	Unit Value of Imports	75
																Balance of Payments	
Minus Sign Indicates Debit																	
	470.2	603.4	564.5	642.1	632.5	548.1	694.5	707.5	713.2	758.6	911.6	824.2	831.9	722.6	....	Goods: Exports f.o.b.	78aa d
	−875.1	−1,020.3	−815.1	−917.2	−818.9	−795.8	−883.3	−955.8	−956.0	−998.4	−1,176.1	−1,114.1	−1,200.3	−1,105.4	....	Goods: Imports f.o.b.	78ab d
	−404.9	−416.8	−250.5	−275.1	−186.4	−247.7	−188.7	−248.3	−242.8	−239.8	−264.4	−290.0	−368.4	−382.8	....	Trade Balance	78ac d
	336.7	379.6	319.7	306.0	268.4	297.4	369.7	405.3	442.3	472.9	563.1	560.4	592.4	563.6	....	Services: Credit	78ad d
	−339.9	−494.7	−414.6	−391.9	−370.0	−366.7	−484.7	−503.8	−528.9	−500.5	−573.0	−573.2	−606.6	−574.6	....	Services: Debit	78ae d
	−408.1	−531.9	−345.4	−361.0	−288.0	−317.1	−303.8	−346.7	−329.5	−267.4	−274.4	−302.7	−382.6	−393.8	....	Balance on Goods and Services	78af d
	23.6	19.1	19.3	24.5	14.9	9.8	12.5	11.3	14.5	25.1	22.8	24.1	26.1	24.7	....	Income: Credit	78ag d
	−122.0	−115.9	−117.0	−123.9	−138.3	−133.9	−173.7	−205.1	−223.0	−221.9	−258.6	−220.1	−228.3	−215.8	....	Income: Debit	78ah d
	−506.5	−628.6	−443.2	−460.5	−411.4	−441.2	−465.0	−540.5	−538.0	−464.3	−510.2	−498.7	−584.8	−584.8	....	Balance on Goods, Serv., & Inc.	78ai d
	245.4	275.5	274.4	238.9	212.4	248.5	290.6	344.8	386.3	367.9	387.1	382.8	414.1	371.2	....	Current Transfers, n.i.e.: Credit	78aj d
	−125.4	−109.1	−97.8	−84.6	−75.2	−80.4	−93.9	−110.8	−109.6	−101.9	−92.6	−89.3	−97.5	−91.1	....	Current Transfers: Debit	78ak d
	−386.6	−462.3	−266.6	−306.1	−274.1	−273.0	−268.2	−306.5	−261.4	−198.3	−215.6	−205.2	−268.2	−304.8	....	Current Account, n.i.e.	78al d
	—	—	—	—	—	—	—	—	—	—	—	—	—	—	....	Capital Account, n.i.e.: Credit	78ba d
	—	—	—	—	—	—	—	—	—	—	—	—	—	—	....	Capital Account: Debit	78bb d
	—	—	—	—	—	—	—	—	—	—	—	—	—	—	....	Capital Account, n.i.e.	78bc d
	−1.6	−14.8	−18.0	1.6	−1.9	−3.1	4.7	1.9	−13.7	—	—	—	—	—	....	Direct Investment Abroad	78bd d
	14.5	34.4	28.1	−34.7	29.1	−15.8	−8.4	−3.9	14.4	—	—	—	—	—	....	Dir. Invest. in Rep. Econ., n.i.e.	78be d
	−.4	−1.8	−.3	−1.0	−.1	—	—	—	−.1	—	—	—	—	—	....	Portfolio Investment Assets	78bf d
	3.2	1.1	.9	−.8	1.7	.6	2.1	.7	1.2	—	—	—	—	—	....	Portfolio Investment Liab., n.i.e.	78bg d
	—	—	—	—	—	—	—	−.6	7.9	−41.9	−15.5	—	−14.7	−10.5	−.6	Other Investment Assets	78bh d
	−25.8	−59.3	−63.1	−22.4	20.3	6.3	—	205.4	202.7	189.9	48.8	4.2	65.8	89.5	42.7	Other Investment Liab., n.i.e.	78bi d
	375.2	356.4	89.6	246.8	140.8	180.6	205.4	202.7	189.9	48.8	4.2	4.2	51.0	79.0	42.2	Financial Account, n.i.e.	78bj d
	365.1	316.0	37.2	189.4	190.0	168.6	203.1	209.3	149.9	33.4	4.2	−16.7	−26.2	82.6	114.8	Net Errors and Omissions	78ca d
	−36.6	13.6	−4.7	6.6	−14.2	13.5	30.0	−.2	−3.3	1.6	−16.7	9.8	−2.1	.1	−147.8	Overall Balance	78cb d
	−58.1	−132.6	−234.1	−110.1	−98.2	−90.9	−35.1	−97.4	−114.8	−163.3	−228.1	−180.4	−106.7	147.8	....	Reserves and Related Items	79da d
	58.1	132.6	234.1	110.1	98.2	90.9	35.1	97.4	114.8	163.3	228.1	180.4	106.7	147.8	....	Reserve Assets	79db d
	15.8	2.9	−3.5	−2.2	7.8	−.2	−3.3	1.9	−2.3	−7.8	9.8	−2.1	.1	8.5	....	Use of Fund Credit and Loans	79dc d
	50.9	57.4	43.8	21.1	15.7	8.5	−8.4	6.8	−6.5	6.2	−27.7	10.6	−44.2	−27.4	....	Liabs.Constit.For.Auth.Reserves	79dd d
	−9.1	−.3	97.7	.2	−.2	−.3	.1	1.3	9.3	−9.8	—	—	—	—	....	Exceptional Financing	79de d
	.5	72.6	96.1	91.0	74.9	83.0	46.7	87.5	114.3	174.8	246.1	171.9	150.7	166.7			
																Government Finance	
Year Ending June 30																	
	ℐ5.44	−22.63	ℐ−52.30	−55.47	−82.44	....	....	....	....	....	....	....	....	....	....	Deficit (-) or Surplus	80
	ℐ153.67	150.89	ℐ170.63	182.71	192.46	....	....	....	....	....	....	....	....	....	....	Revenue	81
	ℐ.36	1.18	ℐ9.89	13.59	24.77	....	....	....	....	....	....	....	....	....	....	Grants Received	81z
	ℐ147.18	171.89	ℐ231.01	250.04	298.46	....	....	....	....	....	....	....	....	....	....	Expenditure	82
	ℐ1.41	2.81	ℐ1.81	1.73	1.21	....	....	....	....	....	....	....	....	....	....	Lending Minus Repayments	83
																Financing	
	ℐ10.60	23.51	ℐ49.64	15.91	23.86	....	....	....	....	....	....	....	....	....	....	Net Borrowing: Domestic	84a
	ℐ−16.90	6.47	ℐ26.08	41.78	40.60	....	....	....	....	....	....	....	....	....	....	Foreign	85a
	ℐ.86	−7.35	ℐ−23.42	−2.22	17.98	....	....	....	....	....	....	....	....	....	....	Use of Cash Balances	87
	....	....	ℐ123.59	147.28	172.58	....	....	....	....	....	....	....	....	....	....	Debt: Domestic	88a
	....	....	ℐ313.96	423.84	520.68	....	....	....	....	....	....	....	....	....	....	Foreign	89a
																National Accounts	
Billions of Francs																	
	161.6	178.3	293.2	334.7	367.4	351.8	349.3	345.3	344.3	393.6	406.4	418.9	....	....	....	Exports of Goods & Services	90c
	140.3	150.7	173.8	177.8	206.8	213.0	224.7	215.6	218.1	229.8	215.3	215.1	....	....	....	Government Consumption	91f
	100.2	102.4	129.1	173.1	152.8	161.5	151.9	172.1	188.6	195.8	197.1	210.4	....	....	....	Gross Fixed Capital Formation	93e
	−2.9	7.7	12.9	36.6	20.6	45.3	36.2	.3	—	−20.9	1.8	28.4	....	....	....	Increase/Decrease(-) in Stocks	93i
	504.1	551.9	662.4	746.7	731.5	849.5	929.7	1,072.1	1,163.8	1,151.9	1,170.4	1,171.3	....	....	....	Private Consumption	96f
	−275.7	−321.2	−410.7	−477.3	−478.8	−494.6	−462.6	−423.1	−431.5	−474.0	−474.9	−492.7	....	....	....	Imports of Goods & Services	98c
	627.6	669.8	860.7	991.6	1,000.3	1,126.5	1,229.2	1,382.3	1,483.3	1,476.2	1,516.1	1,551.5	....	....	....	Gross Domestic Product	99b
	ℐ971.0	959.5	1,106.7	1,130.8	1,085.5	1,126.5	1,177.8	1,224.9	1,287.0	1,267.2	....	....	....	....	....	Gross Dom. Prod. 1985 Prices	99b.p
	64.6	69.8	77.8	87.7	92.2	100.0	104.4	112.9	115.3	116.5	....	....	....	....	....	GDP Deflator (1985=100)	99bi p
Midyear Estimates																	
	5.70	5.86	6.03	6.40	6.37	6.55	6.73	6.92	7.11	7.13	7.33	7.52	7.71	7.90	....	Population	99z

Seychelles
718

		1965	1966	1967	1968	1969	1970	1971	1972	1973	1974	1975	1976	1977	1978	1979
Exchange Rates																
Official Rate	aa	4.7571	4.7786	5.5410	5.5919	5.5539	5.5702	5.6713	I6.1650	6.9235	6.9511	7.7137	9.0995	8.4974	8.5380	8.3197
														\multicolumn{3}{r}{Rupees per US Dollar:}
Official Rate	ae	4.7571	4.7786	5.5410	5.5919	5.5539	5.5702	5.2236	I5.6783	5.7392	5.6774	6.5892	7.8321	6.9954	6.5536	6.3156
Official Rate	rf	4.7619	4.7619	4.8280	5.5555	5.5555	5.5555	5.4858	5.3385	5.4423	5.7031	6.0268	7.4189	7.6434	6.9525	6.3327
Fund Position																Millions of SDRs:
Quota	2f. s	...	...	...	...	...	...	...	...	...	...	...	...	1.00	1.30	1.30
SDRs	1b. s	...	...	...	...	...	...	...	...	...	...	...	...	—	—	.09
Reserve Position in the Fund	1c. s	...	...	...	...	...	...	...	...	...	...	...	...	.10	.10	.25
International Liquidity														Millions of US Dollars Unless Otherwise Indicated:		
Total Reserves minus Gold	11. d	...	...	...	...	...	...	...	...	4.27	5.04	6.34	6.49	11.51	9.26	12.15
SDRs	1b. d	...	...	...	...	...	...	...	...	...	...	...	...	—	—	.12
Reserve Position in the Fund	1c. d	...	...	...	...	...	...	...	...	...	...	...	...	.12	.13	.33
Foreign Exchange	1d. d	...	...	...	...	...	...	...	...	4.27	5.04	6.34	6.49	11.39	9.13	11.70
Deposit Money Banks: Assets	7a. d	...	...	...	...	...	...	2.27	2.79	.10	—	1.81	4.09	3.40	6.32	5.57
Liabilities	7b. d	...	...	...	...	...	...	—	—	—	—	—	—	—	1.24	1.08
Monetary Authorities																Millions of Rupees:
Foreign Assets	11	...	...	...	...	...	...	13.4	17.1	17.8	18.9	26.7	31.8	48.0	45.5	70.7
Claims on Central Government	12a	...	...	...	...	...	...	1.8	1.8	1.5	1.5	1.5	1.5	1.5	9.3	4.4
Claims on Deposit Money Banks	12e	...	...	...	...	...	...	...	...	...	...	...	...	...	...	...
Reserve Money	14	...	...	...	...	...	...	13.0	17.8	20.1	21.1	24.9	33.2	42.3	48.7	64.3
of which: Currency Outside DMBs	14a	...	...	...	...	...	...	12.4	17.0	18.9	20.1	22.7	31.1	40.1	43.9	52.9
Central Government Deposits	16d	...	...	...	...	...	...	—	—	—	—	—	—	—	—	—
Capital Accounts	17a	...	...	...	...	...	...	...	...	...	...	...	...	...	4.0	9.6
Other Items (Net)	17r	...	...	...	...	...	...	2.2	1.1	-.8	-.7	3.3	.1	7.1	2.1	1.2
Deposit Money Banks																Millions of Rupees:
Reserves	20	...	...	...	...	...	...	.6	.8	1.2	1.0	2.2	2.1	2.2	4.8	5.8
Foreign Assets	21	...	...	...	...	...	...	11.6	14.3	.6	-4.0	11.9	32.0	23.8	41.4	35.2
Claims on Central Government	22a	...	...	...	...	...	...	2.0	1.4	5.2	5.9	7.0	10.2	8.4	6.8	17.7
Claims on Official Entities	22bx	...	...	...	...	...	...	...	...	...	...	...	...	—	1.0	1.0
Claims on Private Sector	22d	...	...	...	...	...	...	19.0	33.7	48.1	50.7	54.8	83.5	117.0	137.1	155.4
Demand Deposits	24	...	...	...	...	...	...	13.0	20.7	21.4	21.8	25.1	36.5	43.7	51.1	56.2
Time and Savings Deposits	25	...	...	...	...	...	...	19.9	27.1	31.7	32.6	48.6	70.7	78.3	91.9	118.6
Foreign Liabilities	26c	...	...	...	...	...	...	...	...	2.8	1.8	2.9	8.8	14.6	14.1	9.6
Central Government Deposits	26d	...	...	...	...	...	...	...	...	...	...	...	...	...	8.1	6.8
Capital Accounts	27a	...	...	...	...	...	...	—	—	—	—	—	16.0	16.0	28.8	24.0
Other Items (Net)	27r	...	...	...	...	...	...	.3	2.4	-.8	-2.6	-.9	-4.2	-1.2	-2.9	-.1
Monetary Survey																Millions of Rupees:
Foreign Assets (Net)	31n	...	...	...	...	...	...	25.0	31.4	18.4	14.9	38.6	63.8	71.8	78.8	99.1
Domestic Credit	32	...	...	...	...	...	...	22.8	36.9	52.0	56.3	60.4	86.4	112.3	140.1	168.9
Claims on Central Govt. (Net)	32an	...	...	...	...	...	...	3.8	3.2	3.9	5.6	5.6	2.9	-4.7	2.0	12.5
Claims on Official Entities	32bx	...	...	...	...	...	...	...	...	...	...	...	...	—	1.0	1.0
Claims on Private Sector	32d	...	...	...	...	...	...	19.0	33.7	48.1	50.7	54.8	83.5	117.0	137.1	155.4
Money	34	...	...	...	...	...	...	25.4	37.7	40.3	41.9	47.8	67.6	83.8	95.0	114.7
Quasi-Money	35	...	...	...	...	...	...	19.9	27.1	31.7	32.6	48.6	70.7	78.3	91.9	118.6
Other Items (Net)	37r	...	...	...	...	...	...	2.5	3.5	-1.6	-3.3	2.4	11.9	21.9	32.0	34.7
Money plus Quasi-Money	35l	...	...	...	...	...	...	45.3	64.8	72.0	74.5	96.4	138.3	162.1	186.9	233.3
Interest Rates																Percent Per Annum
Treasury Bill Rate	60c	...	...	...	...	...	...	...	...	...	...	...	...	...	...	...
Concessionary Refinance Rate	60e	...	...	...	...	...	...	...	...	...	...	...	...	...	...	...
Deposit Rate	60l	...	...	...	...	...	...	...	...	...	...	...	...	...	...	...
Lending Rate	60p	...	...	...	...	...	...	...	...	...	...	...	...	...	...	...
Prices																Index Numbers (1990=100):
Consumer Prices	64	...	...	...	...	...	16.2	18.6	22.5	26.7	33.2	39.3	45.2	I52.0	58.1	65.3
International Transactions																Millions of Rupees
Exports	70	7.33	8.60	10.04	17.39	13.91	11.90	10.16	13.99	19.68	41.56	38.27	64.34	84.76	105.43	138.63
Imports, cif	71	11.40	19.96	24.60	33.88	40.00	55.92	84.00	111.67	135.12	160.46	191.35	290.62	349.74	402.05	534.78
Imports, fob	71.v	10.18	17.82	21.96	30.25	35.71	49.93	75.00	97.10	117.50	139.53	166.39	252.71	304.12	349.61	465.03

Seychelles

	1980	1981	1982	1983	1984	1985	1986	1987	1988	1989	1990	1991	1992	1993	1994		
																Exchange Rates	
End of Period	8.3197	7.2345	7.2345	7.2345	7.2345	7.2345	7.2345	7.2345	7.2345	7.2345	7.2345	7.2345	7.2345	7.2345	7.2345	Official Rate	aa
End of Period (ae) Period Average (rf)																	
	6.5184	6.2273	6.5475	6.9227	7.3578	6.6018	5.9290	5.1435	5.3966	5.4672	5.1188	5.0627	5.2545	5.2579	4.9695	Official Rate	ae
	6.3920	6.3149	6.5525	6.7676	7.0589	7.1343	6.1768	5.6000	5.3836	5.6457	5.3369	5.2893	5.1220	5.1815	5.0559	Official Rate	rf
																Fund Position	
End of Period																	
	2.00	2.00	2.00	3.00	3.00	3.00	3.00	3.00	3.00	3.00	3.00	3.00	6.00	6.00	6.00	Quota	2f. s
	.04	.17	.16	.05	.02	.01	.02	—	.01	.01	.01	.04	.01	.01	.02	SDRs	1b. s
	.43	.44	.44	—	—	—	.02	.03	.04	.05	.05	.05	.80	.80	.80	Reserve Position in the Fund	1c. s
																International Liquidity	
End of Period																	
	18.44	13.80	13.07	9.97	5.40	8.50	7.75	13.71	8.71	12.11	16.64	27.65	31.26	35.65	30.15	Total Reserves minus Gold	1l. d
	.05	.20	.18	.05	.02	.01	.02	—	.01	.01	.01	.06	.01	.02	.02	SDRs	1b. d
	.55	.51	.49	—	—	—	.02	.04	.05	.07	.07	.07	1.10	1.10	1.17	Reserve Position in the Fund	1c. d
	17.84	13.09	12.41	9.92	5.38	8.49	7.70	13.67	8.64	12.04	16.55	27.52	30.14	34.53	28.96	Foreign Exchange	1d. d
	7.49	7.19	2.93	3.08	3.67	4.85	5.48	5.99	6.58	4.99	11.23	17.88	9.44	7.66	5.03	Deposit Money Banks: Assets	7a. d
	1.20	3.65	3.88	3.58	2.43	3.57	3.41	4.94	4.65	7.85	11.55	13.95	6.76	7.32	6.42	Liabilities	7b. d
																Monetary Authorities	
End of Period																	
	122.5	88.3	87.7	71.5	62.4	59.9	49.6	72.7	46.5	65.6	84.4	138.4	157.6	180.5	142.8	Foreign Assets	11
	1.5	18.6	33.3	58.0	69.7	106.3	101.5	139.3	165.7	103.3	105.4	110.9	241.4	302.0	529.2	Claims on Central Government	12a
	—	10.5	13.8	13.7	9.6	6.5	20.7	13.7	21.4	30.7	18.5	13.0	4.0	21.5	7.0	Claims on Deposit Money Banks	12e
	108.7	98.3	93.2	99.6	96.1	107.7	106.1	105.6	134.0	140.0	164.0	206.3	311.8	383.8	566.7	Reserve Money	14
	61.7	65.3	62.6	64.3	69.9	75.8	78.1	82.4	95.6	99.5	104.5	113.6	122.5	134.5	141.6	*of which:* Currency Outside DMBs	14a
	—	1.0	1.0	2.0	13.7	24.4	28.6	93.8	91.3	26.8	21.4	30.3	64.3	58.8	30.9	Central Government Deposits	16d
	13.2	13.9	13.9	13.9	13.9	13.9	13.9	13.9	13.9	13.9	13.9	15.8	13.9	13.9	13.9	Capital Accounts	17a
	2.1	4.2	26.7	27.7	17.9	26.7	23.2	12.4	−5.6	18.9	7.1	11.8	13.0	47.5	67.4	Other Items (Net)	17r
																Deposit Money Banks	
End of Period																	
	27.3	18.6	15.4	21.9	16.5	31.2	27.3	22.5	38.0	39.8	58.8	91.9	188.5	248.7	424.5	Reserves	20
	48.8	44.8	19.2	21.3	27.0	32.0	32.5	30.8	35.5	27.3	57.5	90.5	49.6	40.3	25.0	Foreign Assets	21
	26.2	39.2	36.2	48.3	69.6	184.2	270.0	335.8	411.8	526.1	547.2	633.6	632.9	779.0	692.3	Claims on Central Government	22a
	10.4	32.8	69.1	63.9	87.1	24.9	21.9	23.3	35.7	40.3	41.4	58.4	54.1	80.9	118.9	Claims on Official Entities	22bx
	160.1	155.3	143.7	137.4	120.4	104.6	90.8	88.6	96.2	127.0	137.2	150.2	157.8	172.8	209.0	Claims on Private Sector	22d
	77.3	78.2	65.5	53.6	55.1	78.8	76.2	72.1	91.8	119.4	111.6	151.8	170.0	200.7	184.4	Demand Deposits	24
	155.1	149.3	139.9	158.2	187.9	208.1	250.3	285.9	351.7	412.9	507.3	541.4	620.3	768.5	768.7	Time and Savings Deposits	25
	7.8	22.7	25.4	24.8	17.9	23.6	20.2	25.4	25.1	42.9	59.1	70.6	35.5	38.5	31.9	Foreign Liabilities	26c
	8.7	11.4	14.8	17.2	19.6	21.2	34.0	48.3	60.1	84.3	46.0	80.1	83.9	107.7	118.8	Central Government Deposits	26d
	24.0	24.0	24.0	24.0	24.0	24.7	24.8	24.8	25.8	26.3	27.7	75.5	71.8	74.7	76.0	Capital Accounts	27a
	−.1	5.1	14.0	15.0	16.1	20.5	37.0	44.5	62.7	74.7	90.4	105.2	101.4	131.6	289.8	Other Items (Net)	27r
																Monetary Survey	
End of Period																	
	163.5	110.4	81.5	68.0	71.5	68.3	61.9	78.1	56.9	50.0	82.8	158.3	171.7	182.3	135.9	Foreign Assets (Net)	31n
	189.5	233.5	266.5	288.4	313.5	374.4	421.6	444.9	558.0	685.9	763.8	842.7	938.0	1,168.2	1,399.7	Domestic Credit	32
	19.0	45.4	53.7	87.1	106.0	244.9	308.9	333.0	426.1	518.3	585.2	634.1	726.1	914.5	1,071.8	Claims on Central Govt. (Net)	32an
	10.4	32.8	69.1	63.9	87.1	24.9	21.9	23.3	35.7	40.3	41.4	58.4	54.1	80.9	118.9	Claims on Official Entities	32bx
	160.1	155.3	143.7	137.4	120.4	104.6	90.8	88.6	96.2	127.0	137.2	150.2	157.8	172.8	209.0	Claims on Private Sector	32d
	158.7	157.9	143.3	131.3	134.7	155.3	155.0	155.2	187.8	219.6	216.8	266.2	293.3	335.8	326.6	Money	34
	155.1	149.3	139.9	158.2	187.9	208.1	250.3	285.9	351.7	412.9	507.3	541.4	620.3	768.5	768.7	Quasi-Money	35
	39.2	36.7	64.8	66.9	62.3	79.3	78.2	81.9	75.4	103.1	122.5	193.4	196.1	246.2	440.1	Other Items (Net)	37r
	313.8	307.2	283.2	289.5	322.6	363.4	405.3	441.1	539.5	632.5	724.1	807.6	913.6	1,104.3	1,095.3	Money plus Quasi-Money	35l
																Interest Rates	
Percent Per Annum																	
	9.57	9.15	10.10	12.07	12.61	12.44	12.91	15.15	13.90	13.41	13.17	13.30	13.28	13.18	12.51	Treasury Bill Rate	60c
	....	6.0	6.0	6.0	6.0	6.0	6.0	6.0	6.0	6.0	6.0	1.0	1.0	1.0	1.0	Concessionary Refinance Rate	60e
	....	9.0	9.0	9.1	9.5	9.6	10.0	10.0	10.0	9.6	9.5	9.6	9.6	9.5	....	Deposit Rate	60l
	....	....	....	....	....	....	....	....	....	15.52	15.65	15.57	15.58	15.66	15.62	Lending Rate	60p
																Prices	
Period Averages																	
	74.2	82.0	81.3	86.2	89.7	90.5	90.7	93.0	94.8	96.3	100.0	102.0	105.3	106.7	108.7	Consumer Prices	64
																International Transactions	
Millions of Rupees																	
	135.21	108.34	100.09	137.25	181.47	199.69	113.66	124.07	171.33	193.52	301.50	258.27	245.66	265.02	....	Exports	70
	631.44	589.01	641.32	594.08	618.73	704.72	651.96	633.90	856.63	930.15	993.78	910.42	984.28	980.90	1,234.90	Imports, cif	71
	549.08	512.18	557.67	516.59	538.03	612.80	566.92	551.22	744.90	808.83	864.16	791.67	855.90	852.96	....	Imports, fob	71.v

Seychelles

718

	1965	1966	1967	1968	1969	1970	1971	1972	1973	1974	1975	1976	1977	1978	1979
Balance of Payments												\multicolumn{4}{r}{*Millions of US Dollars:*}			
Goods: Exports f.o.b. .... 78aa d	....	....	....	....	....	....	....	....	....	....	....	3.05	4.83	6.63	6.22
Goods: Imports f.o.b. .... 78ab d	....	....	....	....	....	....	....	....	....	....	....	–33.19	–38.63	–51.82	–71.58
Trade Balance .... 78ac d	....	....	....	....	....	....	....	....	....	....	....	–30.14	–33.81	–45.19	–65.35
Services: Credit .... 78ad d	....	....	....	....	....	....	....	....	....	....	....	33.89	48.24	63.80	83.62
Services: Debit .... 78ae d	....	....	....	....	....	....	....	....	....	....	....	–10.80	–21.72	–27.87	–35.74
Balance on Goods and Services ... 78af d	....	....	....	....	....	....	....	....	....	....	....	–7.05	–7.29	–9.26	–17.47
Income: Credit .... 78ag d	....	....	....	....	....	....	....	....	....	....	....	.80	1.58	2.29	4.91
Income: Debit .... 78ah d	....	....	....	....	....	....	....	....	....	....	....	–2.87	–4.97	–6.04	–7.64
Balance on Goods, Serv., & Inc. . 78ai d	....	....	....	....	....	....	....	....	....	....	....	–9.13	–10.68	–13.02	–20.19
Current Transfers, n.i.e.: Credit .. 78aj d	....	....	....	....	....	....	....	....	....	....	....	6.17	10.24	11.26	10.45
Current Transfers: Debit .... 78ak d	....	....	....	....	....	....	....	....	....	....	....	–.94	–1.44	–2.23	–2.52
Current Account, n.i.e. .... 78al d	....	....	....	....	....	....	....	....	....	....	....	–3.90	–1.87	–3.98	–12.26
Capital Account, n.i.e.: Credit .... 78ba d	....	....	....	....	....	....	....	....	....	....	....				
Capital Account: Debit .... 78bb d	....	....	....	....	....	....	....	....	....	....	....				
Capital Account, n.i.e. .... 78bc d	....	....	....	....	....	....	....	....	....	....	....	—	—	—	—
Direct Investment Abroad .... 78bd d	....	....	....	....	....	....	....	....	....	....	....				
Dir. Invest. in Rep. Econ., n.i.e. ... 78be d	....	....	....	....	....	....	....	....	....	....	....	–2.02	–2.26	–2.68	–3.13
Portfolio Investment Assets .... 78bf d	....	....	....	....	....	....	....	....	....	....	....	6.34	7.06	6.33	7.51
Portfolio Investment Liab., n.i.e. . 78bg d	....	....	....	....	....	....	....	....	....	....	....				
Other Investment Assets .... 78bh d	....	....	....	....	....	....	....	....	....	....	....				
Other Investment Liab., n.i.e. .... 78bi d	....	....	....	....	....	....	....	....	....	....	....	–3.48	–1.27	.60	4.56
Financial Account, n.i.e. .... 78bj d	....	....	....	....	....	....	....	....	....	....	....	2.12	.46	4.11	7.71
Net Errors and Omissions .... 78ca d	....	....	....	....	....	....	....	....	....	....	....	2.95	3.99	8.37	16.65
Overall Balance .... 78cb d	....	....	....	....	....	....	....	....	....	....	....	1.63	.12	–5.26	–.76
Reserves and Related Items .... 79da d	....	....	....	....	....	....	....	....	....	....	....	.69	2.24	–.88	3.63
Reserve Assets .... 79db d	....	....	....	....	....	....	....	....	....	....	....	–.69	–2.24	.88	–3.63
Use of Fund Credit and Loans ... 79dc d	....	....	....	....	....	....	....	....	....	....	....	–.69	–2.24	.88	–3.63
Liabs.Constit.For.Auth.Reserves .. 79dd d	....	....	....	....	....	....	....	....	....	....	....				
Exceptional Financing .... 79de d	....	....	....	....	....	....	....	....	....	....	....	—	—	—	—
Government Finance												\multicolumn{4}{r}{*Millions of Rupees:*}			
Deficit (–) or Surplus 80	....	....	....	....	....	....	....	5.5	–11.0	–.8	–.7	–3.1	20.1	–28.8	....
Revenue 81	....	....	....	....	....	....	....	35.7	44.6	52.3	58.7	90.3	133.9	165.5	....
Grants Received 81z	....	....	....	....	....	....	....	44.5	23.1	38.6	37.9	36.1	50.6	31.0	....
Expenditure 82	....	....	....	....	....	....	....	74.1	76.0	81.8	94.2	126.4	156.0	218.2	....
Lending Minus Repayments 83	....	....	....	....	....	....	....	.6	2.7	9.9	3.1	3.1	8.4	7.1	....
Financing															
Domestic 84a	....	....	....	....	....	....	....	–4.8	11.0	3.1	3.2	5.7	–20.0	12.0	....
Foreign 85a	....	....	....	....	....	....	....	–.7	—	–2.3	–2.5	–2.6	–.1	16.8	....
Debt: Domestic 88a	....	....	....	....	....	....	....	4.1	4.3	6.3	11.5	11.5	15.8	....	....
Foreign 89a	....	....	....	....	....	....	....	6.5	6.1	5.8	5.5	4.9	8.6	....	....
National Accounts												\multicolumn{4}{r}{*Millions of Rupees*}			
Exports of Goods & Services 90c	....	....	....	....	....	....	....	....	....	....	....	271.9	386.3	488.4	582.6
Government Consumption 91f	....	....	....	....	....	....	....	....	....	....	....	81.5	117.1	149.5	211.4
Gross Fixed Capital Formation 93e	....	....	....	....	....	....	....	....	....	....	....	134.5	190.5	253.5	256.6
Increase/Decrease(–) in Stocks 93i	....	....	....	....	....	....	....	....	....	....	....	8	7	4	9
Private Consumption 96f	....	....	....	....	....	....	....	....	....	....	....	200.3	198.5	195.3	377.6
Imports of Goods & Services 98c	....	....	....	....	....	....	....	....	....	....	....	–330.4	–406.2	–495.8	–630.8
Gross Domestic Product 99b	....	....	....	....	....	....	....	138.0	168.0	194.0	235.0	365.6	493.0	595.0	806.3
Net Factor Inc/Pmts(–) Abroad ... 98.n	....	....	....	....	....	....	....	....	....	....	....	–15.8	–29.6	–38.3	–56.3
Gross Nat'l Expenditure = GNP .. 99a	....	....	....	....	....	....	....	....	....	....	....	349.8	463.4	556.7	750.0
Gross Dom. Prod. 1990 Prices ... 99b.p	....	....	....	....	....	....	....	....	....	....	....	1,079.9	1,165.0 ⅼ	1,243.6	1,429.5
GDP Deflator (1990=100) .... 99bi p	....	....	....	....	....	....	....	11.5	13.9	16.1	19.5	33.9	42.3	47.8	56.4
												\multicolumn{4}{r}{*Millions:*}			
Population 99z	.05	.05	.05	.05	.05	.05	.05	.06	.06	.06	.06	.06	.06	.06	.06

Government Finance: Data cover budgetary central government operations. From 1972–78, data are as reported by the Ministry of Finance for the *Government Finance Statistics Yearbook*. ⅼ Beginning in 1985, data are as reported by the Central Bank of Seychelles.

Seychelles 718

	1980	1981	1982	1983	1984	1985	1986	1987	1988	1989	1990	1991	1992	1993	1994		
	Minus Sign Indicates Debit															**Balance of Payments**	
	5.65	4.64	3.84	4.99	4.98	4.64	4.41	8.09	17.26	14.48	28.11	18.76	19.58	....	....	Goods: Exports f.o.b.	78aa d
	−83.66	−79.19	−83.00	−74.50	−73.94	−84.14	−89.34	−96.25	−134.96	−139.61	−158.44	−146.25	−162.90			Goods: Imports f.o.b.	78ab d
	−78.01	−74.55	−79.16	−69.51	−68.97	−79.50	−84.93	−88.16	−117.70	−125.13	−130.33	−127.49	−143.32			Trade Balance	78ac d
	91.22	88.69	77.76	76.80	95.07	111.99	123.27	144.85	164.42	186.37	229.18	235.03	247.04			Services: Credit	78ad d
	−40.10	−40.50	−41.83	−40.08	−46.36	−59.27	−74.53	−85.06	−81.61	−95.62	−106.45	−111.46	−113.03			Services: Debit	78ae d
	−26.89	−26.35	−43.23	−32.78	−20.26	−26.79	−36.19	−28.37	−34.89	−34.39	−7.60	−3.92	−9.31			Balance on Goods and Services	78af d
	5.90	4.29	2.79	2.37	2.09	2.16	2.06	2.70	3.09	3.51	4.07	4.65	4.80			Income: Credit	78ag d
	−7.68	−6.88	−6.72	−7.12	−7.82	−8.09	−10.55	−16.67	−20.53	−18.43	−23.62	−19.86	−18.18			Income: Debit	78ah d
	−28.67	−28.95	−47.17	−37.54	−25.98	−32.71	−44.68	−42.35	−52.33	−49.31	−27.16	−19.13	−22.69			Balance on Goods, Serv., & Inc.	78ai d
	16.18	14.78	12.80	17.63	18.30	17.02	19.85	27.62	34.00	36.17	37.08	32.81	34.62			Current Transfers, n.i.e.: Credit	78aj d
	−3.13	−4.62	−6.28	−6.15	−5.60	−3.51	−8.46	−6.39	−10.08	−9.70	−10.34	−9.94	−13.61			Current Transfers: Debit	78ak d
	−15.62	−18.79	−40.64	−26.05	−13.29	−19.20	−33.29	−21.11	−28.41	−22.83	−.42	3.74	−1.67			Current Account, n.i.e.	78al d
	—	—	—	—	—	—	—	—	—	—	—	—	—			Capital Account, n.i.e.: Credit	78ba d
	—	—	—	—	—	—	—	—	—	—	—	—	—			Capital Account: Debit	78bb d
	—	—	—	—	—	—	—	—	—	—	—	—	—			Capital Account, n.i.e.	78bc d
	−3.81	−7.23	−4.94	−3.24	−3.92	−10.56	−5.78	−5.39	−4.29	−6.31	−5.73	−2.91	−2.52			Direct Investment Abroad	78bd d
	9.52	10.07	10.01	9.12	9.77	11.65	14.20	19.40	23.20	22.90	27.14	21.79	21.13			Dir. Invest. in Rep. Econ., n.i.e.	78be d
																Portfolio Investment Assets	78bf d
																Portfolio Investment Liab., n.i.e.	78bg d
	.81	3.21	4.73	−.42	−1.78	.03	−.61	1.13	−.93	4.58	−2.67	−4.15	1.26			Other Investment Assets	78bh d
	11.84	7.79	24.21	10.38	11.92	15.33	25.76	3.73	3.35	13.36	−4.31	13.46	−7.42			Other Investment Liab., n.i.e.	78bi d
	18.35	13.85	34.02	15.85	16.00	16.45	33.57	18.88	21.33	34.52	14.43	28.20	12.45			Financial Account, n.i.e.	78bj d
	5.23	−.38	6.41	7.71	−4.25	2.70	−1.64	6.19	2.82	−8.18	−9.97	−21.46	−6.92			Net Errors and Omissions	78ca d
	7.96	−5.33	−.21	−2.50	−1.54	−.06	−1.36	−3.96	−4.26	3.51	4.04	10.47	3.86			Overall Balance	78cb d
	−7.96	5.33	.21	2.50	1.54	.06	1.36	−3.96	4.26	−3.51	−4.04	−10.47	−3.86			Reserves and Related Items	79da d
	−7.96	5.33	.21	2.50	1.54	.06	1.36	−3.96	4.26	−3.51	−4.04	−10.47	−3.86			Reserve Assets	79db d
	—	—	—	—	—	—	—	—	—	—	—	—	—			Use of Fund Credit and Loans	79dc d
	—	—	—	—	—	—	—	—	—	—	—	—	—			Liabs.Constit.For.Auth.Reserves	79dd d
	—	—	—	—	—	—	—	—	—	—	—	—	—			Exceptional Financing	79de d
	Year Ending December 31															**Government Finance**	
	....	....	....	....	....	I−179.8	−251.8	−53.0	−61.1	−152.4	−.9	−105.7	−111.0	−181.9	18.2	Deficit (−) or Surplus	80
	....	....	....	....	....	I 476.4	515.6	639.3	763.4	898.7	989.1	961.4	1,097.6	1,209.6	1,319.5	Revenue	81
	....	....	....	....	....	I 31.1	31.7	42.6	24.0	33.9	46.8	40.2	39.2	38.1	18.6	Grants Received	81z
	....	....	....	....	....	I 685.8	767.3	701.9	768.8	971.5	958.7	1,078.9	1,216.2	1,393.6	1,297.4	Expenditure	82
	....	....	....	....	....	I 1.5	31.8	33.0	79.7	113.5	78.1	28.4	31.6	36.0	22.5	Lending Minus Repayments	83
																Financing	
	....	....	....	....	....	I 134.0	106.4	73.5	105.2	119.9	36.2	44.7	144.0	161.8	16.3	Domestic	84a
	....	....	....	....	....	I 45.7	145.4	−20.5	−44.1	32.5	−35.3	61.0	−33.0	20.2	−34.6	Foreign	85a
	....	....	....	....	....	....	....	....	....	....	....	....	....	....	....	Debt: Domestic	88a
	....	....	....	....	....	....	....	....	....	....	....	....	....	....	....	Foreign	89a
	Millions of Rupees															**National Accounts**	
	640.1	467.0	404.4	415.0	539.7	596.5	496.9	541.7	737.3	833.8	1,056.2	952.7	1,016.9	....	....	Exports of Goods & Services	90c
	270.0	308.5	338.0	326.0	327.7	417.4	497.6	406.6	415.6	474.7	544.4	558.4	674.6			Government Consumption	91f
	344.2	329.7	302.9	219.9	226.9	273.5	309.6	260.1	357.3	418.0	451.9	422.1	465.2			Gross Fixed Capital Formation	93e
	17	−13	10	−10	5	—	6	16	33	55	32	20	6			Increase/Decrease(−) in Stocks	93i
	416.3	515.5	598.6	673.3	653.0	700.7	700.3	870.5	909.9	968.4	981.3	1,003.1	1,124.7			Private Consumption	96f
	−745.4	−636.2	−686.0	−635.3	−684.0	−783.2	−720.0	−698.8	−925.2	−1,028.5	−1,098.2	−975.9	−1,066.2			Imports of Goods & Services	98c
	941.9	971.9	968.2	989.4	1,067.9	1,204.9	1,290.0	1,395.9	1,527.9	1,721.0	1,967.1	1,980.4	2,221.1			Gross Domestic Product	99b
	−34.1	−16.3	−26.2	−32.6	−41.2	−42.2	−52.4	−78.2	−93.6	−84.2	−103.5	−80.2	−68.4			Net Factor Inc/Pmts(−) Abroad	98.n
	907.8	955.6	942.0	956.8	1,026.7	1,162.7	1,237.6	1,317.7	1,434.3	1,636.8	1,863.6	1,899.8	2,152.7			Gross Nat'l Expenditure = GNP	99a
	1,385.1	1,293.1	1,273.6	1,251.9	1,352.2	1,491.3	1,509.8	1,576.0	1,659.9	1,830.6	1,967.1	2,010.5	....	....	....	Gross Dom. Prod. 1990 Prices	99b.p
	68.0	75.2	76.0	79.0	79.0	80.8	85.4	88.6	92.0	94.0	100.0	98.5	....	....	....	GDP Deflator (1990=100)	99bi p
	Midyear Estimates																
	.06	.06	.06	.06	.06	.07	.07	.07	.07	.07	.07	.07	.07	.07	.07	Population	99z

Sierra Leone

724

		1965	1966	1967	1968	1969	1970	1971	1972	1973	1974	1975	1976	1977	1978	1979
Exchange Rates																*Leones per SDR:*
Market Rate	aa	.71	.72	.83	.84	.83	.84	.85	.92	1.04	1.04	1.16	1.36	1.27	1.37	1.37
																Leones per US Dollar:
Market Rate	ae	.71	.72	.83	.84	.83	.84	.78	.85	.86	.85	.99	1.17	1.05	1.05	1.04
Market Rate	rf	.71	.71	.72	.83	.83	.83	.83	.80	.82	.86	.90	1.11	1.15	1.05[e]	1.06
																Index Numbers (1990=100):
Market Rate	ah x	20,189.3	20,167.9	19,831.4	17,283.0	17,258.7	17,299.5	577.2	18,063.8	17,705.2	16,888.4	16,042.0	13,041.2	12,603.1	13,807.2[e]	13,663.8
Nominal Effective Exchange Rate	nec	....	....	....	....	....	....	....	....	....	....	....	....	....	....	9,274.4
Real Effective Exchange Rate	rec	....	....	....	....	....	....	....	....	....	....	....	....	....	....	123.6
Fund Position																*Millions of SDRs:*
Quota	2f. s	11.3	15.0	15.0	15.0	15.0	25.0	25.0	25.0	25.0	25.0	25.0	25.0	25.0	31.0	31.0
SDRs	1b. s	—	—	—	—	—	.5	3.1	5.7	5.7	4.4	3.9	2.9	1.4	.2	—
Reserve Position in the Fund	1c. s	1.3	.8	—	—	—	4.9	4.9	4.9	4.9	—	—	—	—	—	—
Total Fund Cred.&Loans Outstg.	2tl	—	—	4.6	4.5	3.0	—	—	—	—	4.3	4.9	22.4	32.1	35.6	43.8
International Liquidity												*Millions of US Dollars Unless Otherwise Indicated:*				
Total Reserves minus Gold	1l.d	22.6	20.0	15.9	27.5	35.4	39.4	38.4	46.5	51.8	54.6	28.4	25.2	33.4	34.8	46.7
SDRs	1b.d	—	—	—	—	—	.5	3.4	6.2	6.9	5.4	4.6	3.4	1.7	.3	—
Reserve Position in the Fund	1c.d	1.3	.8	—	—	—	4.9	5.3	5.3	5.9	—	—	—	—	—	—
Foreign Exchange	1d.d	21.3	19.2	15.9	27.5	35.4	34.0	29.7	34.9	39.0	49.2	23.8	21.8	31.7	34.5	46.7
Monetary Authorities: Other Liab.	4..d	—	—	—	—	—	—	—	—	1.4	5.2	8.3	6.3	—	13.4	25.5
Deposit Money Banks: Assets	7a.d	.3	.3	.3	1.2	.5	.1	1.0	.5	2.7	4.2	2.4	3.5	7.7	11.6	11.0
Liabilities	7b.d	8.0	8.3	6.2	5.2	2.9	1.9	5.8	.1	3.0	5.6	2.5	.5	.9	.3	.2
Monetary Authorities																*Millions of Leones:*
Foreign Assets	11	15	14	13	23	29	29	29	36	43	47	28	29	36	37	48
Claims on Central Government	12a	5	8	7	3	1	6	8	7	14	16	42	60	69	117	214
Reserve Money	14	18	19	18	21	25	23	25	28	35	39	43	50	58	94	144
of which: Currency Outside DMBs	14a	14	14	14	18	20	19	21	25	30	31	37	41	52	63	72
Private Sector Deposits	14d	1	—	—	—	1	—	—	1	1	2	2	1	1	1	—
Foreign Liabilities	16c	—	—	4	4	3	—	—	—	1	9	14	38	41	63	86
Central Government Deposits	16d	—	—	1	3	4	5	2	2	6	5	—	5	6	7	36
Other Items (Net)	17r	1	1	-3	-3	-1	8	11	13	15	6	10	-34	-37	-42	-38
of which: Valuation Adjustment	17rv	....	....	-4	-4	-2	4	4	4	5	4	4	—	—	-3	-1
Deposit Money Banks																*Millions of Leones:*
Reserves	20	3	5	3	3	4	3	3	3	4	6	4	8	5	29	71
Foreign Assets	21	—	—	—	1	—	—	1	—	2	4	2	4	8	12	11
Claims on Central Government	22a	—	2	3	6	5	5	7	8	13	16	19	31	38	51	54
Claims on Official Entities	22bx	—	1	1	2	1	—	—	—	—	—	3	1	3	6	4
Claims on Private Sector	22d	15	15	15	14	16	19	20	22	28	35	40	43	46	63	68
Demand Deposits	24	7	7	8	9	11	10	11	13	17	22	22	30	32	43	55
Time and Savings Deposits	25	8	9	9	12	14	14	16	18	23	30	31	40	52	72	87
Foreign Liabilities	26c	6	6	5	4	2	2	4	—	2	5	3	1	1	—	—
Capital Accounts	27a	—	1	1	3	2	4	3	3	4	4	5	5	7	8	10
Other Items (Net)	27r	-2	-1	-1	-2	-3	-1	-3	-1	1	4	5	11	9	37	57
Monetary Survey																*Millions of Leones:*
Foreign Assets (Net)	31n	10	8	4	16	25	27	26	36	42	37	14	-5	2	-14	-27
Domestic Credit	32	20	24	23	21	19	26	32	35	49	70	102	130	151	231	307
Claims on Central Govt. (Net)	32an	5	8	8	5	2	7	12	14	20	27	61	86	101	160	232
Claims on Official Entities	32bx	—	1	1	2	1	—	—	—	—	3	1	1	3	6	4
Claims on Private Sector	32d	15	15	15	14	16	19	20	22	28	40	41	44	47	65	71
Money	34	22	22	22	27	32	29	32	39	48	55	60	72	84	107	128
Quasi-Money	35	8	9	9	12	14	14	16	18	23	30	31	40	52	72	87
Other Items (Net)	37r	-1	1	-8	-6	-4	14	14	19	24	19	22	-17	-20	5	31
Money plus Quasi-Money	35l	30	31	32	39	46	43	48	57	71	85	92	112	136	179	215
Interest Rates																*Percent Per Annum*
Treasury Bill Rate	60c	....	5.50	5.58	6.00	5.50	5.50	5.50	5.50	5.50	5.50	5.50	5.50	5.50	5.50	6.25
Deposit Rate	60l	....	....	....	....	....	....	....	....	....	....	....	....	7.00	7.00	7.25
Lending Rate	60p	8.00	8.00	8.00	8.00	8.00	8.00	8.00	8.00	8.00	8.00	8.50	9.00	11.00	11.00	11.00
Prices																*Index Numbers (1990=100):*
Consumer Prices	64	.2	.2	.2	.2	.2	.2	.2	.2	.2	.2	.2	.3	.3	.4	.4	.5

Sierra Leone

724

1980	1981	1982	1983	1984	1985	1986	1987	1988	1989	1990	1991	1992	1993	1994		
End of Period															**Exchange Rates**	
1.37	1.37	1.36	2.63	2.46	5.74	43.53	32.69	52.57	85.89	268.43	621.93	723.68	793.41	894.90	Market Rate	aa
End of Period (ae) Period Average (rf)																
1.06	1.17	1.23	2.51	5.21	35.59	23.04	39.06	65.36	188.68	434.78	526.32	577.63	613.01		Market Rate	ae
1.05	1.16	1.24	1.89	2.51	5.09	16.09	34.04	32.51	59.81	151.45	295.34	499.44	567.46	586.74	Market Rate	rf
Period Averages																
13,759.0	12,475.1	11,665.0	8,604.2	5,753.1	3,053.2	1,720.0	468.7	462.6	248.3	100.0	52.6	29.1	25.5	24.6	Market Rate	ahx
9,284.3	9,724.7	10,319.5	8,367.8	6,366.8	3,605.9	1,742.1	424.4	414.1	247.5	100.0	54.5	31.2	31.3	32.2	Nominal Effective Exchange Rate	nec
122.8	141.8	175.6	213.7	264.7	234.5	172.2	133.3	157.5	137.3	100.0	100.4	91.8	103.7	119.2	Real Effective Exchange Rate	rec
End of Period															**Fund Position**	
46.5	46.5	46.5	57.9	57.9	57.9	57.9	57.9	57.9	57.9	57.9	57.9	57.9	57.9	77.2	Quota	2f.s
—	.1	.5	.1	—	—	.3	—	—	—	—	—	—	1.2	2.8	SDRs	1b.s
—	1.1	—	—	—	—	—	—	—	—	—	—	—	—	—	Reserve Position in the Fund	1c.s
46.6	72.2	70.9	88.9	97.5	92.0	82.9	81.5	80.8	79.5	76.2	70.7	67.0	61.0	100.2	Total Fund Cred.&Loans Outstg.	2tl
End of Period															**International Liquidity**	
30.6	16.0	8.4	16.2	7.7	10.8	13.7	6.3	7.4	3.7	5.4	9.6	20.6	32.8	49.7	Total Reserves minus Gold	1l.d
—	.1	.5	.1	—	—	.3	—	—	—	—	—	1.7	3.8	9.0	SDRs	1b.d
—	1.2	—	—	—	—	—	—	—	—	—	—	—	—	—	Reserve Position in the Fund	1c.d
30.6	14.6	7.9	16.1	7.7	10.8	13.3	6.3	7.4	3.7	5.4	9.6	18.9	28.9	40.6	Foreign Exchange	1d.d
102.4	152.0	157.4	208.5	216.9	247.8	176.4	276.7	263.9	254.5	243.6	248.4	302.4	322.1	470.2	Monetary Authorities: Other Liab.	4..d
14.0	5.3	7.4	7.6	16.0	10.0	13.8	12.5	11.4	12.7	8.7	7.5	16.1	22.5	16.9	Deposit Money Banks: Assets	7a.d
—	—	.1	.3	3.9	2.1	4.7	1.4	1.0	.1	—	—	—	2.7	2.9	Liabilities	7b.d
End of Period															**Monetary Authorities**	
32	19	7	33	9	7	232	1	791	2,067	1,016	4,169	11,143	18,943	30,443	Foreign Assets	11
296	425	583	719	924	1,202	1,976	3,560	4,684	7,531	11,251	14,594	9,338	4,657	6,135	Claims on Central Government	12a
133	134	253	317	450	691	1,423	2,916	4,274	7,449	12,395	20,258	24,095	24,995	31,352	Reserve Money	14
86	86	121	197	260	442	1,006	1,364	2,255	4,058	8,337	15,650	18,270	21,882	23,604	of which: Currency Outside DMBs	14a
2	3	4	6	4	4	13	30	51	104	96	104	112	418	219	Private Sector Deposits	14d
172	277	290	728	760	1,727	9,358	8,697	13,987	22,546	63,955	146,330	201,044	227,256	316,556	Foreign Liabilities	16c
26	28	20	52	5	13	299	−27	297	713	828	1,974	6,598	5,936		Central Government Deposits	16d
−4	5	27	−344	−309	−1,214	−8,586	−8,352	−12,752	−20,661	−64,798	−148,654	−206,632	−235,248	−317,267	Other Items (Net)	17r
4	−1	—	−293	−176	−409	−6,609	−3,731	−4,842	−6,586	−19,102	−60,400	−40,542	−83,035	−47,334	of which: Valuation Adjustment	17rv
End of Period															**Deposit Money Banks**	
121	158	261	297	365	418	570	1,515	1,968	3,287	3,963	4,498	5,707	2,855	7,523	Reserves	20
15	6	9	19	40	52	493	288	445	830	1,644	3,255	8,462	12,986	10,378	Foreign Assets	21
51	53	62	121	169	406	556	811	988	1,193	1,379	1,819	2,795	8,589	9,921	Claims on Central Government	22a
4	4	4	4	6	15	21	—	51	53	67	50	50	26	81	Claims on Official Entities	22bx
83	96	110	129	108	133	370	605	1,105	2,592	3,092	8,008	10,257	14,847	16,576	Claims on Private Sector	22d
65	63	128	156	222	454	833	1,494	2,332	4,513	5,820	9,338	13,005	12,753	14,719	Demand Deposits	24
108	116	166	193	223	313	433	859	1,241	1,565	3,565	6,306	10,446	15,951	16,955	Time and Savings Deposits	25
—	—	—	1	10	11	169	33	40	5	3	13	11	1,551	1,761	Foreign Liabilities	26c
11	12	17	18	21	24	28	82	118	155	627	850	1,025	1,292	5,483	Capital Accounts	27a
90	126	134	203	213	223	546	752	799	1,716	129	1,123	2,784	7,755	5,559	Other Items (Net)	27r
End of Period															**Monetary Survey**	
−124	−252	−274	−676	−721	−1,679	−8,802	−8,441	−12,791	−19,653	−61,299	−138,919	−181,449	−196,878	−277,496	Foreign Assets (Net)	31n
413	551	738	919	1,172	1,748	2,957	4,446	6,852	10,923	15,011	23,510	19,944	20,290	25,021	Domestic Credit	32
318	448	621	783	1,055	1,598	2,509	3,829	5,602	8,176	11,749	15,345	9,525	5,292	8,203	Claims on Central Govt. (Net)	32an
4	4	4	4	6	15	21	—	51	53	67	50	50	26	81	Claims on Official Entities	32bx
91	99	114	132	111	135	427	617	1,199	2,694	3,195	8,115	10,369	14,973	16,736	Claims on Private Sector	32d
153	152	253	359	486	900	1,852	2,889	4,637	8,675	14,253	25,092	31,387	35,053	38,542	Money	34
108	116	166	193	223	313	433	859	1,241	1,565	3,565	6,306	10,446	15,951	16,955	Quasi-Money	35
27	32	44	−310	−258	−1,143	−8,129	−7,743	−11,837	−18,937	−64,106	−146,806	−203,339	−227,592	−307,974	Other Items (Net)	37r
261	268	420	552	709	1,213	2,285	3,747	5,879	10,240	17,818	31,397	41,834	51,004	55,497	Money plus Quasi-Money	35l
Percent Per Annum															**Interest Rates**	
9.38	10.00	10.00	11.00	12.00	12.00	14.50	16.50	18.00	22.00	47.50	50.67	78.63	28.64	12.19	Treasury Bill Rate	60c
9.17	10.00	10.00	11.00	12.00	11.33	14.17	12.67	16.33	20.00	40.50	47.80	54.67	27.00	11.63	Deposit Rate	60l
11.00	15.00	15.00	17.25	18.00	17.00	17.19	28.54	28.00	29.67	52.50	56.25	62.83	50.46	27.33	Lending Rate	60p
Period Averages															**Prices**	
.6	.7	.9	1.5	2.5	4.4	7.9	22.2	29.1	47.4	100.0	202.7	335.4	409.9	509.1	Consumer Prices	64

Sierra Leone
724

		1965	1966	1967	1968	1969	1970	1971	1972	1973	1974	1975	1976	1977	1978	1979
International Transactions																*Millions of Leones*
Exports	70	63.2	59.2	50.0	79.2	91.1	83.0	81.4	93.5	106.0	123.0	112.5	112.5	140.3	175.1	204.6
Imports, cif	71	77.4	71.4	65.3	76.4	93.0	96.8	93.1	94.2	127.2	188.4	167.9	171.3	206.2	290.8	334.4
Imports, fob	71.v	70.4	64.9	59.4	69.6	84.7	88.1	84.7	85.7	115.7	171.5	152.8	155.8	187.6	264.6	304.3
Balance of Payments																*Millions of US Dollars:*
Goods: Exports f.o.b.	78aa d	....	....	....	....	....	....	....	....	....	....	....	....	150.3	193.6	211.6
Goods: Imports f.o.b.	78ab d	....	....	....	....	....	....	....	....	....	....	....	....	−165.0	−253.0	−336.3
Trade Balance	78ac d	....	....	....	....	....	....	....	....	....	....	....	....	−14.7	−59.4	−124.7
Services: Credit	78ad d	....	....	....	....	....	....	....	....	....	....	....	....	10.7	17.7	31.2
Services: Debit	78ae d	....	....	....	....	....	....	....	....	....	....	....	....	−50.7	−56.2	−72.6
Balance on Goods and Services	78af d	....	....	....	....	....	....	....	....	....	....	....	....	−54.7	−97.9	−166.0
Income: Credit	78ag d	....	....	....	....	....	....	....	....	....	....	....	....	1.8	.4	.3
Income: Debit	78ah d	....	....	....	....	....	....	....	....	....	....	....	....	−16.7	−33.9	−42.3
Balance on Goods, Serv., & Inc.	78ai d	....	....	....	....	....	....	....	....	....	....	....	....	−69.6	−131.4	−208.0
Current Transfers, n.i.e.: Credit	78aj d	....	....	....	....	....	....	....	....	....	....	....	....	22.1	21.8	31.7
Current Transfers: Debit	78ak d	....	....	....	....	....	....	....	....	....	....	....	....	−2.1	−2.4	−2.7
Current Account, n.i.e.	78al d	....	....	....	....	....	....	....	....	....	....	....	....	−49.6	−112.0	−179.1
Capital Account, n.i.e.: Credit	78ba d	....	....	....	....	....	....	....	....	....	....	....	....	—	—	—
Capital Account: Debit	78bb d	....	....	....	....	....	....	....	....	....	....	....	....	—	—	—
Capital Account, n.i.e.	78bc d	....	....	....	....	....	....	....	....	....	....	....	....	—	—	—
Direct Investment Abroad	78bd d	....	....	....	....	....	....	....	....	....	....	....	....			
Dir. Invest. in Rep. Econ., n.i.e.	78be d	....	....	....	....	....	....	....	....	....	....	....	....	5.1	24.3	16.1
Portfolio Investment Assets	78bf d	....	....	....	....	....	....	....	....	....	....	....	....	—	2.4	2.4
Portfolio Investment Liab., n.i.e.	78bg d	....	....	....	....	....	....	....	....	....	....	....	....			
Other Investment Assets	78bh d	....	....	....	....	....	....	....	....	....	....	....	....	−3.1	2.0	4.9
Other Investment Liab., n.i.e.	78bi d	....	....	....	....	....	....	....	....	....	....	....	....	15.4	47.5	82.7
Financial Account, n.i.e.	78bj d	....	....	....	....	....	....	....	....	....	....	....	....	17.3	76.1	106.1
Net Errors and Omissions	78ca d	....	....	....	....	....	....	....	....	....	....	....	....	11.9	27.0	17.9
Overall Balance	78cb d	....	....	....	....	....	....	....	....	....	....	....	....	−20.4	−8.9	−55.2
Reserves and Related Items	79da d	....	....	....	....	....	....	....	....	....	....	....	....	20.4	8.9	55.2
Reserve Assets	79db d	....	....	....	....	....	....	....	....	....	....	....	....	−5.0	−1.6	−3.9
Use of Fund Credit and Loans	79cc d	....	....	....	....	....	....	....	....	....	....	....	....	11.3	4.3	10.6
Liabs.Constit.For.Auth.Reserves	79dd d	....	....	....	....	....	....	....	....	....	....	....	....			
Exceptional Financing	79de d	....	....	....	....	....	....	....	....	....	....	....	....	14.1	6.2	48.5
Government Finance																*Millions of Leones:*
Deficit (-) or Surplus	80	−7	−7	−3	−2	6	....	I−4	−8	−12	I−21	−60	−48	−51	−79	−119
Revenue	81	35	34	37	39	51	....	I 54	60	64	I 92	97	95	119	157	174
Grants Received	81z	....	....	....	....	....	....	....	....	....	I —	—	—	—	12	19
Expenditure	82	34	40	39	41	43	....	I 58	68	76	I 113	157	144	170	249	311
Lending Minus Repayments	83	8	2	2	—	1	....	....	....	....	I —	—	—	—	—	1
Financing																
Domestic	84a	....	....	....	....	....	....	5	—	11	I 8	27	30	36	39	81
Foreign	85a	....	....	....	....	....	....	−1	8	1	I 13	33	19	15	41	38
Debt: Domestic	88a	....	....	....	....	....	....	....	....	....	I 45	69	109	143	196	292
Foreign	89a	....	....	....	....	....	....	....	....	....	I 71	118	136	153	229	290
National Accounts																*Millions of Leones:*
Exports of Goods & Services	90c	74.1	74.5	68.4	65.1	94.1	112.3	109.0	103.5	115.7	133.7	154.2	142.6	156.4	199.4	233.4
Government Consumption	91f	19.8	19.8	19.7	21.3	22.5	24.7	31.5	31.8	41.7	49.3	63.5	59.0	71.2	76.8	95.5
Gross Fixed Capital Formation	93e	31.8	38.9	32.8	31.7	36.8	53.4	47.4	42.7	44.2	56.6	76.0	71.5	80.6	99.7	128.0
Increase/Decrease(-) in Stocks	93i	−2.7	1.1	.9	1.1	3.7	2.3	5.9	−1.2	2.0	19.1	14.1	−2.3	17.2	−3.6	10.1
Private Consumption	96f	205.0	212.4	219.3	229.8	243.6	268.6	267.7	287.2	299.6	364.1	476.6	534.2	630.8	719.3	879.8
Imports of Goods & Services	98c	−80.3	−84.8	−79.1	−73.8	−85.8	−106.0	−112.9	−108.2	−109.9	−145.0	−211.7	−191.5	−212.0	−241.5	−317.6
Gross Domestic Product	99b	247.7	261.9	262.0	275.2	314.9	355.3	348.6	355.8	393.3	477.8	572.7	613.5	744.2	850.1	1,029.2
Net Factor Inc/Pmts(-) Abroad	98.n	−6.5	−8.5	−5.4	−8.2	−8.1	−6.6	−3.4	−7.6	−5.8	−6.6	−6.8	−9.8	−11.2	−17.0	−40.7
Gross Nat'l Expenditure = GNP	99a	241.2	253.4	256.6	267.0	306.8	348.7	345.2	348.2	387.5	471.2	565.9	603.7	733.0	833.1	988.5
Nat'l Income, Market Prices	99e	222.9	239.2	241.9	238.1	275.9	314.6	314.0	317.3	355.2	433.2	521.4	554.4	674.5	764.0	907.0
Gross Dom. Prod. 1990 Prices	99b.p	....	....	....	....	....	....	63,724.1	63,046.7	64,979.7	67,590.1	69,622.3	67,507.5	68,482.3	68,697.1	73,802.3
GDP Deflator (1990=100)	99bi p	....	....	....	....	....	....	.5	.6	.6	.7	.8	.9	1.1	1.2	1.4
																Millions:
Population	99z	2.37	2.40	2.44	2.48	2.63	2.69	2.76	2.83	2.90	2.97	3.05	3.09	3.14	3.19	3.19

Government Finance: I Prior to 1974, data are a consolidation of central government current, capital, and extrabudgetary accounts, given separately in Sierra Leone *Government Financial Reports*. In 1968 and 1969, expenditure is larger than total expenditure given in the *Reports*, because capital expenditure financed by certain long-term foreign loans is included here but not in the *Reports*. From 1974, data are as reported in the *Government Finance Statistics Yearbook*. Data cover transactions of the recurrent and development budgets of the central government.

Sierra Leone

724

1980	1981	1982	1983	1984	1985	1986	1987	1988	1989	1990	1991	1992	1993	1994		
Millions of Leones															**International Transactions**	
217.3	157.6	137.0	201.9	328.9	667.3	1,951.7	4,656.0	3,329.0	8,270.0	21,093.0	44,079.0	75,034.0	67,077.0	67,930.0	Exports	70
447.5	360.4	368.5	286.9	394.3	781.6	2,022.3	4,423.7	5,215.0	10,901.8	23,606.8	45,487.9	77,671.0	83,460.0	87,973.0	Imports, cif	71
407.2	322.4	324.3	252.5	347.0	688.0	1,780.2	3,894.1	4,590.6	9,596.7	20,780.6	40,042.2	68,372.4	73,468.3	77,441.0	Imports, fob	71.v
Minus Sign Indicates Debit															Balance of Payments	
226.6	165.9	122.6	115.1	139.2	135.8	131.7	142.0	107.9	142.0	148.5	155.1	....	....	....	Goods: Exports f.o.b.	78aa *d*
−385.9	−282.0	−260.3	−133.0	−149.7	−141.2	−111.4	−114.8	−138.2	−160.4	−140.4	−138.3	....	....	....	Goods: Imports f.o.b.	78ab *d*
−159.3	−116.1	−137.7	−17.9	−10.5	−5.4	20.3	27.1	−30.3	−18.3	8.1	16.8	....	....	....	Trade Balance	78ac *d*
48.9	37.2	25.3	26.7	34.5	24.0	20.8	40.9	48.6	35.8	61.1	61.9	....	....	....	Services: Credit	78ad *d*
−85.3	−59.6	−72.7	−42.1	−47.6	−42.9	−33.9	−42.0	−34.6	−44.8	−74.4	−63.8	....	....	....	Services: Debit	78ae *d*
−195.8	−138.6	−185.1	−33.3	−23.6	−24.2	7.2	26.0	−16.3	−27.3	−5.2	15.0	....	....	....	Balance on Goods and Services	78af *d*
.6	.5	.2	.3	.2	.2	.1	.2	.2	.2	.7	.9	....	....	....	Income: Credit	78ag *d*
−22.5	−37.4	−35.2	−21.2	−32.6	7.6	127.3	−63.2	4.6	−39.9	−71.8	−14.9	....	....	....	Income: Debit	78ah *d*
−217.6	−175.5	−220.2	−54.2	−56.0	−16.4	134.6	−37.0	−11.5	−67.0	−76.3	.9	....	....	....	Balance on Goods, Serv., & Inc.	78ai *d*
56.7	44.4	54.3	39.0	34.6	21.2	6.5	7.3	9.3	7.9	7.1	10.0	....	....	....	Current Transfers, n.i.e.: Credit	78aj *d*
−4.2	−1.0	−4.0	−2.4	−1.6	−2.0	−.3	−.6	−.6	−.7	−.2	−.2	....	....	....	Current Transfers: Debit	78ak *d*
−165.2	−132.1	−169.9	−17.6	−23.0	2.8	140.7	−30.3	−2.8	−59.7	−69.4	10.7	....	....	....	Current Account, n.i.e.	78al *d*
.1	—	.1	.1	.1	—	—	.1	.1	.1	—	—	....	....	....	Capital Account, n.i.e.: Credit	78ba *d*
—	—	—	—	—	—	—	—	—	—	—	—	....	....	....	Capital Account: Debit	78bb *d*
.1	—	.1	.1	.1	—	—	.1	.1	.1	—	—	....	....	....	Capital Account, n.i.e.	78bc *d*
—	—	—	—	—	—	—	—	—	—	—	—	....	....	....	Direct Investment Abroad	78bd *d*
−18.7	7.5	4.7	1.7	5.9	−31.0	−140.3	39.4	−23.1	22.4	32.4	7.5	....	....	....	Dir. Invest. in Rep. Econ., n.i.e.	78be *d*
—	—	—	—	—	—	—	—	—	—	—	—	....	....	....	Portfolio Investment Assets	78bf *d*
−1.4	—	—	—	—	—	—	—	—	—	—	—	....	....	....	Portfolio Investment Liab., n.i.e.	78bg *d*
2.0	9.6	16.1	−38.6	−16.2	−10.5	−48.4	7.3	32.0	23.4	−20.1	−9.5	....	....	....	Other Investment Assets	78bh *d*
129.6	54.3	1.0	−41.2	−50.4	−26.2	−90.7	−47.9	−15.6	−63.7	−13.1	−.3	....	....	....	Other Investment Liab., n.i.e.	78bi *d*
111.5	71.4	21.8	−78.1	−60.8	−67.6	−279.4	−1.2	−6.7	−17.9	−.8	−2.3	....	....	....	Financial Account, n.i.e.	78bj *d*
−22.3	−46.2	68.3	2.9	−12.4	−9.3	42.0	−21.9	−62.5	29.2	49.2	11.1	....	....	....	Net Errors and Omissions	78ca *d*
−75.9	−107.0	−79.7	−92.8	−96.1	−74.1	−96.6	−53.4	−71.9	−48.4	−20.9	19.4	....	....	....	Overall Balance	78cb *d*
75.9	107.0	79.7	92.8	96.1	74.1	96.6	53.4	71.9	48.4	20.9	−19.4	....	....	....	Reserves and Related Items	79da *d*
19.3	15.4	9.8	−13.6	9.6	.6	−13.6	−.7	−6.7	9.3	−5.1	−10.7	....	....	....	Reserve Assets	79db *d*
3.8	30.7	−1.4	19.7	9.4	−5.4	−11.2	−1.7	−1.0	−1.6	−4.5	−7.5	....	....	....	Use of Fund Credit and Loans	79dc *d*
—	—	—	—	—	—	—	—	—	—	—	—	....	....	....	Liabs.Constit.For.Auth.Reserves	79dd *d*
52.7	60.9	71.3	86.7	77.2	78.8	121.4	55.8	79.6	40.7	30.6	−1.3	....	....	....	Exceptional Financing	79de *d*
Year Ending June 30															**Government Finance**	
−148	−121	−167	−271	−206	−376	−184	−3,337	−2,157	−2,865	−2,413	−10,477	−16,502	−17,099	....	Deficit (−) or Surplus	80
190	221	182	156	229	286	490	1,264	2,333	3,693	5,499	17,902	35,384	54,294	....	Revenue	81
7	16	10	15	37	41	105	838	305	532	322	2,522	5,107	7,302	....	Grants Received	81z
334	358	353	416	451	578	778	5,412	4,656	7,090	8,191	30,901	56,993	78,695	....	Expenditure	82
12	—	6	26	21	124	—	27	139	—	—	43	—	—	....	Lending Minus Repayments	83
															Financing	
105	105	134	229	206	322	147	2,406	1,290	2,952	1,929	5,127	356	−3,798	....	Domestic	84a
44	16	34	43	—	54	37	931	867	−87	484	5,350	16,146	20,897	....	Foreign	85a
391	487	648	878	1,078	1,402	2,124	4,353	5,986	7,304	10,642	16,140	16,508	....	....	Debt: Domestic	88a
366	396	485	518	870	1,995	4,961	17,138	17,431	32,821	87,566	156,136	367,739	....	....	Foreign	89a
Year Ending June 30															**National Accounts**	
264.2	297.4	252.8	207.7	290.0	647.0	940.0	5,509.0	3,580.0	6,158.0	18,118.0	39,127.0	77,527.0	93,558.0	84,118.0	Exports of Goods & Services	90c
97.3	90.1	137.6	166.6	189.2	345.4	497.6	1,208.8	1,389.3	3,311.1	5,492.0	15,591.0	32,101.0	48,608.0	....	Government Consumption	91f
171.6	236.2	205.1	235.3	331.8	424.2	729.7	1,853.9	2,274.9	5,574.9	10,510.0	15,855.0	27,206.0	27,081.0	....	Gross Fixed Capital Formation	93e
15.7	10.5	9.6	32.6	15.0	52.6	109.3	204.0	22.3	335.7	414.7	5,015.0	12,950.0	3,628.0	....	Increase/Decrease(−) in Stocks	93i
1,048.3	1,171.5	1,415.5	1,647.3	2,242.1	4,002.2	6,238.2	16,267.0	25,295.4	38,117.1	70,851.0	141,064.0	179,310.0	274,151.0	....	Private Consumption	96f
−441.6	−513.5	−416.1	−413.4	−338.6	−725.0	−1,184.0	−5,514.0	−4,937.0	−9,860.0	−25,741.0	−47,047.0	−86,963.0	111,377.0	111,559.0	Imports of Goods & Services	98c
1,155.5	1,292.2	1,604.5	1,876.1	2,729.5	4,365.0	7,888.0	21,100.0	32,321.0	51,317.0	90,016.0	181,624.0	272,533.0	396,073.0	474,845.0	Gross Domestic Product	99b
−44.5	−22.9	−42.7	−43.4	−39.5	−12.0	954.0	−100.0	−848.1	−243.0	−5,032.0	−5,561.0	−3,520.0	....	....	Net Factor Inc/Pmts(−) Abroad	98.n
1,111.0	1,269.3	1,561.8	1,832.7	2,690.0	4,703.9	7,541.8	21,562.8	27,101.2	44,341.0	83,517.8	169,684.0	255,688.0	....	....	Gross Nat'l Expenditure = GNP	99a
1,008.1	1,145.0	1,409.6	1,650.0	2,410.0	4,048.0	8,356.0	19,815.0	29,606.0	47,636.0	79,429.0	168,034.0	259,507.0	....	....	Nat'l Income, Market Prices	99e
76,016.2	80,724.9	‡82046.6	80,860.2	81,984.2	‡79736.3	77,791.7	82,029.2	84,238.8	86,126.7	90,016.0	92,115.6	90,415.9	88,216.3	....	Gross Dom. Prod. 1990 Prices	99b.*p*
1.5	1.6	2.0	2.3	3.3	5.5	10.1	25.7	38.4	59.6	100.0	197.2	301.4	449.0	....	GDP Deflator (1990=100)	99bi *p*
Midyear Estimates																
3.26	3.34	3.41	3.49	3.51	3.58	3.66	3.74	3.82	4.91	4.00	4.09	4.19	4.30	....	Population	99z

Singapore

576

		1965	1966	1967	1968	1969	1970	1971	1972	1973	1974	1975	1976	1977	1978	1979
Exchange Rates																*Singapore Dollars per SDR:*
Market Rate	aa	3.0600	3.0800	3.0700	3.0800	3.0900	3.0800	3.1486	3.0617	I2.9991	2.8307	2.9144	2.8529	2.8406	2.8186	2.8441
																Singapore Dollars per US Dollar:
Market Rate	ae	3.0600	3.0800	3.0700	3.0800	3.0900	3.0800	2.9000	2.8200	I2.4861	2.3120	2.4895	2.4555	2.3385	2.1635	2.1590
Market Rate	rf	3.0612	3.0612	3.0612	3.0612	3.0612	3.0612	3.0507^e	2.8125^e	2.4574	2.4369	2.3713	2.4708	2.4394	2.2740	2.1746
																Index Numbers (1990=100):
Market Rate	ahx	59.0^e	59.0^e	58.8^e	58.8^e	58.8^e	58.5^e	59.7^e	64.4^e	73.9	74.3	76.5	73.3	74.2	79.7	83.3
Nominal Effective Exchange Rate	nec	....	....	....	....	....	....	....	....	....	....	....	....	....	....	83.3
Fund Position																*Millions of SDRs:*
Quota	2f. s	....	30.0	30.0	30.0	30.0	30.0	37.0	37.0	37.0	37.0	37.0	37.0	37.0	49.0	49.0
SDRs	1b. s	....	—	—	—	—	—	—	—	—	—	—	—	—	—	12.2
Reserve Position in the Fund	1c. s	....	7.5	7.5	7.5	7.5	7.5	9.3	9.3	9.3	9.3	9.3	9.4	9.4	13.1	21.5
International Liquidity													*Millions of US Dollars Unless Otherwise Indicated:*				
Total Reserves (see notes)	1l. d	430	394	496	712	827	1,012	1,452	1,748	2,286	2,812	3,007	3,364	3,858	5,303	5,818
SDRs	1b. d	....	—	—	—	—	—	—	—	—	—	—	—	—	—	16
Reserve Position in the Fund	1c. d	....	7	7	8	8	8	10	10	11	11	11	11	11	17	28
Foreign Exchange	1d. d	430	387	488	705	819	1,005	1,442	1,738	2,275	2,801	2,996	3,353	3,846	5,286	5,774
Deposit Money Banks: Assets	7a. d	232	238	167	170	210	214	307	383	603	828	956	1,317	1,681	2,190	3,233
of which: Claims on Nonbanks	7ad d	141	143	80	77	109	107	145	182	252	300	327	438	634	936	1,537
Deposit Money Banks: Liabilities	7b. d	207	204	109	150	132	171	400	604	1,083	1,173	1,191	1,696	2,186	3,053	3,866
of which: Liab. to Nonbanks	7bd d	6	12	14	16	21	26	123	158	239	306	315	450	572	786	995
Other Banking Insts.: Assets	7e. d	....	....	....	27	14	10	12	15	11	10	8	9	8	6	7
Liabilities	7f. d	....	....	....	2	4	4	4	3	4	4	2	4	4	3	4
ACU: Foreign Assets	7k. d	....	....	....	30	121	315	888	2,229	4,202	7,721	9,590	13,292	16,381	21,621	29,478
of which: Claims on Nonbanks	7kd d	....	....	....	1	1	14	188	601	1,214	2,629	3,303	4,048	4,782	6,377	8,484
ACU: Foreign Liabilities	7m. d	....	....	....	31	122	323	880	2,201	4,056	7,325	9,406	13,273	16,142	20,425	27,315
of which: Liab. to Nonbanks	7md d	....	....	....	18	98	244	238	399	913	1,614	2,068	1,960	2,255	3,599	5,771
Monetary Authorities																*Millions of Singapore Dollars:*
Foreign Assets	11	1,317	1,456	1,684	2,205	2,533	3,102	4,095	4,930	5,800	6,503	7,486	8,262	9,023	11,474	12,562
Reserve Money	14	555	624	560	647	765	891	996	1,296	1,779	1,850	2,197	2,563	2,904	3,369	3,838
of which: Currency Outside DMBs	14a	469	508	423	501	617	727	806	1,005	1,114	1,306	1,638	1,947	2,243	2,583	2,941
Central Government Deposits	16d	695	758	1,077	1,545	1,786	2,201	2,897	3,444	3,816	4,191	4,676	4,755	5,423	6,123	7,019
Other Items (Net)	17r	67	74	47	13	–18	10	202	190	205	462	613	944	696	1,982	1,705
Deposit Money Banks																*Millions of Singapore Dollars:*
Reserves	20	86	116	137	146	150	168	190	291	664	541	560	616	661	787	898
Foreign Assets	21	709	730	512	521	642	656	I866	1,079	1,529	1,915	2,379	3,234	3,932	4,739	6,979
Claims on Central Government	22a	77	104	356	714	609	686	971	1,202	967	1,021	1,179	1,477	1,640	1,761	1,833
Claims on Private Sector	22d	1,112	1,258	1,356	1,671	2,124	2,664	3,110	4,172	6,141	6,840	7,688	8,601	9,511	11,035	13,652
Demand Deposits	24	413	498	562	695	800	904	I954	1,380	1,518	1,552	1,834	2,053	2,169	2,343	2,765
Time and Savings Deposits	25	767	886	1,227	1,562	1,915	2,217	I2,445	2,897	3,470	4,066	4,692	5,202	5,394	5,936	7,193
Foreign Liabilities	26c	634	623	335	459	405	523	I1,129	1,704	2,747	2,712	2,964	4,164	5,111	6,606	8,347
Central Government Deposits	26d	34	35	48	75	56	82	107	293	715	1,052	1,144	1,119	1,092	1,209	1,488
Other Items (Net)	27r	136	166	189	261	349	448	502	470	851	935	1,171	1,390	1,978	2,228	3,539
Monetary Survey																*Millions of Singapore Dollars:*
Foreign Assets (Net)	31n	1,392	1,563	1,861	2,267	2,770	3,235	I3,829	4,303	4,578	5,702	6,896	7,326	7,837	9,597	11,179
Domestic Credit	32	494	612	628	834	968	1,163	1,090	1,637	2,578	2,619	3,048	4,206	4,638	5,467	6,951
Claims on Central Govt. (Net)	32an	–618	–646	–728	–831	–1,156	–1,501	–2,020	–2,535	–3,564	–4,222	–4,641	–4,397	–4,875	–5,571	–6,704
Claims on Private Sector	32d	1,112	1,258	1,356	1,665	2,124	2,664	3,110	4,172	6,142	6,841	7,689	8,603	9,513	11,038	13,655
Money	34	882	1,006	985	1,196	1,417	1,631	I1,760	2,385	2,632	2,858	3,472	4,000	4,412	4,926	5,706
Quasi-Money	35	767	886	1,227	1,562	1,915	2,217	I2,445	2,897	3,470	4,066	4,692	5,202	5,394	5,936	7,193
Other Items (Net)	37r	237	283	277	343	407	550	714	658	1,054	1,397	1,780	2,330	2,669	4,202	5,231
Money plus Quasi-Money	35l	1,649	1,892	2,212	2,758	3,332	3,848	I4,205	5,282	6,102	6,924	8,164	9,202	9,806	10,862	12,899
Other Banking Institutions																
Finance Companies																*Millions of Singapore Dollars:*
Cash	40	....	....	....	108	118	184	240	279	318	395	366	398	384	380	393
Foreign Assets	41	....	....	....	82	41	31	33	42	28	24	21	22	20	13	15
Claims on Private Sector	42d	....	....	....	217	218	278	372	479	738	888	947	1,082	1,229	1,486	1,936
Time and Savings Deposits	45	....	....	....	274	295	389	542	675	843	1,021	1,043	1,183	1,295	1,503	1,806
Foreign Liabilities	46c	....	....	....	5	11	12	11	9	11	10	5	9	10	7	9
Capital Accounts	47a	....	....	....	111	74	89	102	119	181	227	242	268	286	308	363
Other Items (Net)	47r	....	....	....	16	–1	3	–11	–2	49	48	43	43	42	61	166
Post Office: Savings Deposits	45.. i	39	37	38	43	58	73	91	125	171	269	548	957	1,589	2,029	2,525
Nonbank Financial Institutions																*Millions of Singapore Dollars:*
Cash	40.. s	....	....	....	13	14	18	21	32	17	25	45	52	56	67	74
Foreign Assets	41.. s	....	....	....	21	22	23	25	23	22	20	78	78	78	78	78
Claims on Central Government	42a. s	....	....	....	29	39	42	46	55	62	70	79	97	127	135	156
Claims on Private Sector	42d. s	....	....	....	54	55	59	69	80	119	129	732	732	732	732	732
Fixed Assets	42h. s	....	....	....	13	13	14	16	19	19	27	30	31	32	34	35
Incr.in Total Assets(Within Per.)	49z. s	....	....	....	16	15	15	21	37	28	33	51	50	57	68	74
Liquid Liabilities	55l	....	....	....	2,967	3,566	4,125	I4,599	5,803	6,797	7,819	9,390	10,944	12,306	14,014	16,837
Interest Rates																*Percent Per Annum*
Money Market Rate	60b	....	....	....	....	....	....	....	3.57	11.69	8.90	4.39	4.15	4.76	5.93	7.76
Eurodollar Rate in Singapore	60d	....	....	....	....	....	....	....	....	....	....	6.44	5.12	7.31	11.88	15.06
Deposit Rate	60l	....	....	....	....	....	....	....	....	....	....	....	....	4.06	4.75	6.20
Lending Rate	60p	....	....	....	....	....	....	....	....	....	....	....	....	....	7.17	8.50

Singapore

1980	1981	1982	1983	1984	1985	1986	1987	1988	1989	1990	1991	1992	1993	1994		
End of Period															**Exchange Rates**	
2.6701	2.3836	2.3259	2.2269	2.1349	2.3122	2.6604	2.8352	2.6190	2.4895	2.4818	2.3323	2.2617	2.2087	2.1324	Market Rate	**aa**
End of Period (ae)	*Period Average (rf)*															
2.0935	2.0478	2.1085	2.1270	2.1780	2.1050	2.1750	1.9985	1.9462	1.8944	1.7445	1.6305	1.6449	1.6080	1.4607	Market Rate	**ae**
2.1412	2.1127	2.1400	2.1131	2.1331	2.2002	2.1774	2.1060	2.0124	1.9503	1.8125	1.7276	1.6290	1.6158	1.5274	Market Rate	**rf**
Period Averages																
84.6	85.8	84.7	85.7	84.9	82.3	83.2	86.0	90.0	92.8	100.0	104.8	111.1	112.1	118.6	Market Rate	**ah x**
85.4	91.1	97.1	100.8	103.7	103.8	91.3	87.4	87.0	92.8	100.0	103.8	106.9	106.8	111.5	Nominal Effective Exchange Rate	**ne c**
End of Period															**Fund Position**	
92.4	92.4	92.4	92.4	92.4	92.4	92.4	92.4	92.4	92.4	92.4	92.4	357.6	357.6	357.6	Quota	**2f. s**
15.1	27.5	49.4	59.7	58.0	66.0	73.8	81.2	79.0	79.4	81.4	81.3	49.4	56.9	24.1	SDRs	**1b. s**
44.3	63.4	67.7	68.5	69.1	80.6	79.9	79.1	77.9	80.1	68.9	60.1	113.4	157.4	172.8	Reserve Position in the Fund	**1c. s**
End of Period															**International Liquidity**	
6,567	7,549	8,480	9,264	10,416	12,847	12,939	15,227	17,073	20,345	27,748	34,133	39,885	48,361	58,177	Total Reserves (see notes)	**1l. d**
19	32	54	62	57	72	90	115	106	104	116	116	68	78	35	SDRs	**1b. d**
57	74	75	72	68	89	98	112	105	105	98	86	156	216	252	Reserve Position in the Fund	**1c. d**
6,491	7,443	8,351	9,130	10,291	12,686	12,751	15,000	16,861	20,136	27,535	33,931	39,661	48,066	57,890	Foreign Exchange	**1d. d**
3,706	5,630	5,073	5,824	7,869	9,595	12,052	14,761	17,763	25,744	25,142	25,814	31,396	31,345	38,992	Deposit Money Banks: Assets	**7a. d**
1,736	1,906	2,182	1,885	1,797	2,171	2,175	2,361	2,579	3,369	3,864	3,760	3,355	3,080	4,068	*of which:* Claims on Nonbanks	**7ad d**
4,513	6,942	6,686	8,751	11,463	12,829	13,441	15,367	17,360	23,947	24,937	24,569	29,450	32,085	40,976	Deposit Money Banks: Liabilities	**7b. d**
1,144	1,509	1,713	1,718	1,739	1,637	1,585	1,796	2,010	2,282	3,307	3,648	3,813	4,181	5,859	*of which:* Liab. to Nonbanks	**7bd d**
8	9	38	58	103	115	101	113	89	97	139	120	129	124	163	Other Banking Insts.: Assets	**7e. d**
7	3	4	10	7	5	2	5	11	6	3	3	6	10	27	Liabilities	**7f. d**
40,914	64,608	76,218	82,350	93,400	110,763	149,821	194,968	230,252	280,224	321,451	296,259	292,475	306,703	326,698	ACU: Foreign Assets	**7k. d**
12,402	19,452	27,606	30,385	33,766	37,440	38,742	55,011	66,551	86,394	125,516	134,078	134,184	136,857	145,823	*of which:* Claims on Nonbanks	**7kd d**
38,942	62,685	76,130	83,878	96,901	116,881	157,710	201,466	235,012	284,414	329,919	304,431	298,497	321,390	340,295	ACU: Foreign Liabilities	**7m. d**
9,322	13,659	17,630	20,620	21,524	28,019	33,805	41,576	47,453	55,019	66,886	63,500	63,612	62,669	65,788	*of which:* Liab. to Nonbanks	**7md d**
End of Period															**Monetary Authorities**	
13,758	15,491	17,918	19,755	22,748	27,080	28,158	30,442	33,277	38,607	48,521	55,803	65,788	77,867	85,166	Foreign Assets	**11**
4,340	4,809	5,690	6,220	6,656	6,944	7,319	7,910	8,932	10,316	11,056	12,232	13,531	14,669	15,577	Reserve Money	**14**
3,137	3,382	3,996	4,335	4,619	4,739	5,034	5,440	5,997	6,610	7,109	7,497	8,279	8,942	9,420	*of which:* Currency Outside DMBs	**14a**
7,026	2,442	6,771	3,943	2,806	6,159	5,491	6,247	7,676	13,465	17,678	20,177	25,077	30,080	35,669	Central Government Deposits	**16d**
2,392	8,240	5,457	9,592	13,286	13,977	15,348	16,285	16,669	14,826	19,787	23,394	27,180	33,118	33,920	Other Items (Net)	**17r**
End of Period															**Deposit Money Banks**	
1,192	1,428	1,720	1,900	2,060	2,219	2,318	2,476	2,932	3,709	3,951	4,750	5,301	5,770	6,150	Reserves	**20**
7,758	11,530	10,697	12,387	17,139	20,197	26,214	29,499	34,570	48,769	43,860	42,089	51,644	50,402	56,956	Foreign Assets	**21**
2,214	2,587	2,946	3,505	3,753	4,020	3,976	5,287	5,412	6,826	7,923	9,765	11,587	12,758	13,568	Claims on Central Government	**22a**
17,823	22,867	27,222	32,578	35,602	35,790	34,484	36,693	40,789	48,757	55,798	62,725	68,851	79,282	91,375	Claims on Private Sector	**22d**
2,998	3,860	4,161	4,272	4,247	4,046	4,788	5,591	5,961	7,135	8,152	8,933	10,236	13,940	13,991	Demand Deposits	**24**
9,930	12,429	14,647	16,918	18,254	19,363	21,134	26,059	30,130	37,801	46,584	53,112	57,213	59,248	70,569	Time and Savings Deposits	**25**
9,448	14,216	14,098	18,614	24,966	27,006	29,235	30,710	33,786	45,366	43,502	40,060	48,443	51,592	59,854	Foreign Liabilities	**26c**
2,360	2,818	3,212	3,354	3,526	3,525	2,507	2,212	3,560	5,344	4,733	5,268	5,744	6,385	6,584	Central Government Deposits	**26d**
4,251	5,089	6,466	7,212	7,560	8,286	9,329	9,383	10,266	12,415	8,560	11,955	15,746	17,047	17,050	Other Items (Net)	**27r**
End of Period															**Monetary Survey**	
11,901	12,691	14,429	13,439	14,833	19,930	25,002	29,137	33,979	41,933	48,780	57,718	68,397	76,196	81,833	Foreign Assets (Net)	**31n**
10,654	20,195	20,189	28,789	33,029	30,134	30,471	33,530	34,973	36,782	41,317	47,053	49,624	55,583	62,699	Domestic Credit	**32**
–7,172	–2,673	–7,037	–3,792	–2,579	–5,664	–4,022	–3,172	–5,824	–11,983	–14,488	–15,680	–19,234	–23,707	–28,685	Claims on Central Govt. (Net)	**32an**
17,826	22,868	27,226	32,581	35,608	35,798	34,493	36,702	40,797	48,765	55,805	62,733	68,858	79,290	91,384	Claims on Private Sector	**32d**
6,135	7,242	8,157	8,607	8,866	8,785	9,822	11,031	11,958	13,745	15,261	16,430	18,515	22,882	23,411	Money	**34**
9,930	12,429	14,647	16,918	18,254	19,363	21,134	26,059	30,130	37,801	46,584	53,112	57,213	59,248	70,569	Quasi-Money	**35**
6,490	13,215	11,814	16,703	20,742	21,917	24,518	25,577	26,864	27,169	28,251	35,228	42,292	49,649	50,551	Other Items (Net)	**37r**
16,065	19,671	22,804	25,525	27,120	28,148	30,956	37,090	42,088	51,546	61,845	69,542	75,728	82,130	93,980	Money plus Quasi-Money	**35l**
															Other Banking Institutions	
															Finance Companies	
End of Period																
441	677	662	608	724	875	1,085	1,136	1,010	1,117	1,557	1,996	1,953	1,788	2,574	Cash	**40**
18	19	81	122	225	242	221	225	173	183	243	196	212	200	238	Foreign Assets	**41**
2,509	3,422	4,421	5,593	6,027	5,549	5,338	5,759	6,684	8,196	8,958	9,555	10,251	12,047	15,110	Claims on Private Sector	**42d**
2,108	2,937	3,707	4,544	5,265	5,004	4,886	5,372	5,821	7,422	8,520	9,097	9,552	10,558	13,753	Time and Savings Deposits	**45**
15	6	9	22	15	11	4	10	22	12	6	6	10	17	39	Foreign Liabilities	**46c**
476	672	816	1,043	1,117	1,132	1,148	1,177	1,250	1,333	1,416	1,510	1,679	1,850	2,203	Capital Accounts	**47a**
368	502	632	714	580	519	607	562	774	728	815	1,133	1,176	1,611	1,927	Other Items (Net)	**47r**
2,757	3,266	5,058	5,917	7,287	9,129	559	11,165	12,140	13,050	13,240	15,531	18,007	20,085	20,127	Post Office: Savings Deposits	**45.. i**
End of Period															**Nonbank Financial Institutions**	
106	146	180	235	298	420	353	384	478	697	974	954	761	1,160	1,090	Cash	**40.. s**
78	78	78	78	78	78	171	250	175	200	205	246	830	1,160	1,060	Foreign Assets	**41.. s**
152	171	211	241	238	232	217	232	300	422	440	567	1,337	1,190	918	Claims on Central Government	**42a. s**
732	732	732	732	732	732	980	1,215	1,524	1,766	2,198	2,854	2,919	4,270	5,488	Claims on Private Sector	**42d. s**
37	41	58	63	70	66	71	85	95	105	116	131	237	313	335	Fixed Assets	**42h. s**
126	142	154	193	189	198	269	391	422	644	785	830	1,375	1,944	1,682	Incr.in Total Assets(Within Per.)	**49z. s**
20,489	25,198	30,908	35,378	38,948	41,407	35,315	52,492	59,040	70,901	82,048	92,174	101,333	110,985	125,286	Liquid Liabilities	**55l**
Percent Per Annum															**Interest Rates**	
10.98	11.54	7.92	7.11	7.67	5.38	4.27	3.89	4.30	5.34	6.61	4.76	2.74	2.50	3.68	Money Market Rate	**60b**
18.25	14.38	9.56	9.94	8.75	8.13	6.75	8.00	9.31	8.38	7.75	4.38	3.50	3.38	6.50	Eurodollar Rate in Singapore	**60d**
9.37	10.71	7.22	6.31	6.98	4.99	3.91	2.89	2.74	3.21	4.67	4.63	2.86	2.30	3.00	Deposit Rate	**60l**
11.72	13.65	10.23	9.05	9.72	7.93	6.82	6.10	5.96	6.21	7.36	7.58	5.95	5.39	5.88	Lending Rate	**60p**

Singapore

		1965	1966	1967	1968	1969	1970	1971	1972	1973	1974	1975	1976	1977	1978	1979
Prices and Production														*Index Numbers (1990=100):*		
Wholesale Prices	63	....	....	....	....	....	....	....	....	....	75.2	74.1	79.1	82.6	83.9	96.0
Consumer Prices	64	38.2	39.0	40.2	40.5	40.4	40.6	41.3	42.2	I 53.2	65.1	66.8	65.6	67.7	70.9	73.8
Manufacturing Production	66ey	....	9.4	10.4	I 12.2	14.5	17.0	20.3	24.1	28.1	29.3	29.0	32.5	35.5	39.6	45.6
International Transactions														*Millions of Singapore Dollars*		
Exports	70	3,004	3,374	3,491	3,891	4,741	4,756	5,371	6,149	8,907	14,155	12,758	16,266	20,091	22,986	30,940
Imports, cif	71	3,806	4,065	4,406	5,083	6,243	7,535	8,658	9,539	12,513	20,406	19,269	22,406	25,522	29,630	38,352
Imports, fob	71.v	3,577	3,820	4,141	4,777	5,867	7,070	8,117	8,909	11,709	19,086	18,005	21,040	23,990	27,982	36,211
																1990=100
Volume of Exports	72	....	....	....	....	....	....	....	14	17	19	17	20	24	26	I 32
Volume of Imports	73	....	....	....	....	....	....	....	19	22	I 25	24	26	28	31	35
Exports (Direct Prices)	76	....	....	....	....	....	....	....	....	....	....	....	....	....	....	102.5
Imports (Direct Prices)	76.x	....	....	....	....	....	....	....	....	....	74.6	73.3	80.0	84.0	87.2	98.5
Balance of Payments														*Millions of US Dollars:*		
Goods: Exports f.o.b.	78aa d								2,170	3,599	5,906	5,481	6,654	8,245	10,123	14,248
Goods: Imports f.o.b.	78ab d								-3,127	-4,735	-7,764	-7,511	-8,442	-9,729	-12,090	-16,450
Trade Balance	78ac d								-958	-1,137	-1,859	-2,030	-1,788	-1,484	-1,967	-2,202
Services: Credit	78ad d								961	1,377	1,931	2,416	2,364	2,594	3,127	3,595
Services: Debit	78ae d								-484	-655	-900	-966	-1,054	-1,277	-1,547	-2,050
Balance on Goods and Services	78af d								-481	-414	-828	-580	-478	-167	-388	-657
Income: Credit	78ag d								113	167	225	380	370	391	528	806
Income: Debit	78ah d								-129	-268	-380	-345	-410	-475	-554	-849
Balance on Goods, Serv., & Inc.	78ai d								-497	-515	-982	-545	-518	-251	-414	-701
Current Transfers, n.i.e.: Credit	78aj d								79	103	70	65	49	48	64	86
Current Transfers: Debit	78ak d								-76	-107	-109	-104	-98	-93	-102	-121
Current Account, n.i.e.	78al d								-495	-519	-1,021	-584	-567	-295	-453	-736
Capital Account, n.i.e.: Credit	78ba d								—	—	—	—	—	—	—	—
Capital Account: Debit	78bb d								—	—	—	—	—	—	—	—
Capital Account, n.i.e.	78bc d								—	—	—	—	—	—	—	—
Direct Investment Abroad	78bd d								-20	-26	-30	-38	-45	-85	-113	-167
Dir. Invest. in Rep. Econ., n.i.e.	78be d								161	353	340	292	231	291	300	836
Portfolio Investment Assets	78bf d								-13	-17	-20	-29	-32	-40	-139	-108
Portfolio Investment Liab., n.i.e.	78bg d								77	50	35	27	82	136	12	30
Other Investment Assets	78bh d								-98	-212	-195	-235	-399	-347	-545	-1,112
Other Investment Liab., n.i.e.	78bi d								289	575	370	563	1,012	651	1,499	1,519
Financial Account, n.i.e.	78bj d								395	722	500	580	849	607	1,013	998
Net Errors and Omissions	78ca d								435	210	816	412	17	1	104	254
Overall Balance	78cb d								335	413	295	407	298	313	665	516
Reserves and Related Items	79da d								-335	-413	-295	-407	-298	-313	-665	-516
Reserve Assets	79db d								-335	-413	-295	-407	-298	-313	-665	-516
Use of Fund Credit and Loans	79dc d								—	—	—	—	—	—	—	—
Liabs.Constit.For.Auth.Reserves	79dd d								—	—	—	—	—	—	—	—
Exceptional Financing	79de d								....	....	....	....	....	....	....	....
Government Finance														*Millions of Singapore Dollars:*		
Deficit (-) or Surplus	80	-80	-56	-20	70	76	I 90	40	108	-12	197	121	31	164	146	468
Revenue	81	538	623	710	857	950	I 1,301	1,505	1,820	2,284	2,729	3,391	3,497	3,990	4,247	5,181
Expenditure	82	510	594	676	720	785	I 1,038	1,247	1,369	1,588	1,916	2,401	2,893	3,290	3,491	4,026
Lending Minus Repayments	83	108	85	54	67	89	I 173	218	343	708	616	869	573	536	610	687
Financing																
Net Borrowing	84	27	133	477	622	185	I 275	793	531	716	972	1,131	1,884	1,736	1,776	1,874
Domestic	84a	....	....	....	....	....	I 107	722	315	683	924	1,097	1,718	1,446	1,768	1,917
Foreign	85a	....	....	....	....	....	I 168	71	216	33	48	34	166	290	8	-43
Use of Foreign Exchange	86b	56	-75	-415	-614	-231	....	....	....	....	....	....	....	....	....	....
Use of Cash Balances	87	-2	-2	-42	-78	-30	I -365	-833	-639	-704	-1,169	-1,252	-1,915	-1,900	-1,922	-2,342
Debt: Domestic	88a	....	....	....	....	....	I 2,140	2,814	3,238	3,827	4,725	5,804	7,527	8,966	10,726	12,650
Foreign	89a	....	....	....	....	....	I 199	264	453	482	524	549	717	1,007	1,019	975
Singapore Dollars	88b	514	700	1,024	1,637	1,753	....	....	....	....	....	....	....	....	....	....
National Accounts														*Millions of Singapore Dollars*		
Exports (Net)	90n	-356	-274	-316	-284	-532	-1,179	-1,484	-1,378	-1,041	-2,133	-1,508	-1,199	-424	-898	-1,445
Government Consumption	91f	308	351	383	449	560	693	861	990	1,118	1,298	1,423	1,542	1,716	1,965	2,034
Gross Fixed Capital Formation	93e	625	655	738	997	1,326	1,889	2,473	3,054	3,561	4,695	4,698	5,288	5,458	6,365	7,520
Increase/Decrease(-) in Stocks	93i	23	74	93	78	112	356	271	300	439	897	336	694	341	592	1,380
Private Consumption	96f	2,341	2,556	2,852	3,180	3,440	3,920	4,532	5,071	6,340	7,658	8,121	8,606	9,269	10,149	11,245
Gross Domestic Product	99b	2,956	3,331	3,746	4,315	5,020	5,805	6,823	8,156	10,205	12,543	13,373	14,651	16,039	17,830	20,523
Net Factor Inc/Pmts(-) Abroad	98.n	....	....	....	87	85	56	-10	-21	-224	-288	-28	-81	-187	-43	-79
Gross Nat'l Expenditure = GNP	99a	....	....	....	4,402	5,105	5,861	6,813	8,135	9,981	12,255	13,345	14,570	15,852	17,787	20,444
Gross Dom. Prod. 1990 Prices	99b.p	7,663	8,515	9,523	10,845	12,330	14,022	15,776	17,895	19,958	21,225	22,092	I 23,743	25,585	27,784	30,371
GDP Deflator (1990=100)	99bi p	38.6	39.1	39.3	39.8	40.7	41.4	43.2	45.6	51.1	59.1	60.5	61.7	62.7	64.2	67.6
																Millions:
Population	99z	1.89	1.93	1.98	2.01	2.04	2.07	2.11	2.15	2.19	2.23	2.26	2.29	2.33	2.35	2.38

Deposit Money Banks: I Beginning in April 1971, data are not comparable with earlier data, owing to improved sector classification in regard to resident and nonresident accounts.

Monetary Survey: I See note to section 20.

Government Finance: I Beginning in 1970, data are as reported in the *Government Finance Statistics Yearbook* and cover budgetary and some extrabudgetary accounts. Also beginning in 1970, data relate to a fiscal year different from calendar year.

Singapore

	1980	1981	1982	1983	1984	1985	1986	1987	1988	1989	1990	1991	1992	1993	1994		
Period Averages																**Prices and Production**	
	114.8	119.3	114.3	110.1	109.4	107.0	90.8	97.6	95.8	I98.3	100.0	95.9	91.7	87.7	87.3	Wholesale Prices	63
	80.0	86.6	90.0	I91.0	93.4	93.8	92.6	93.0	94.4	I96.7	I100.0	103.4	105.8	108.2	111.6	Consumer Prices	64
	51.2	56.2	I53.1	54.2	59.1	I54.8	59.5	69.9	82.6	91.0	100.0	105.4	108.0	119.0	134.3	Manufacturing Production	66ey
Millions of Singapore Dollars																**International Transactions**	
	41,452	44,291	44,473	46,155	51,340	50,179	48,986	60,266	79,051	87,117	95,206	101,880	103,351	119,475	147,328	Exports	70
	51,355	58,249	60,244	59,504	61,134	57,819	55,543	68,416	88,228	96,864	109,806	114,195	117,530	137,602	156,397	Imports, cif	71
	48,493	55,095	56,639	56,117	57,660	54,525	52,399	64,543	83,234	91,381	103,591	107,731	110,877	129,813	147,544	Imports, fob	71.v
1990=100																	
	34	35	37	40	46	46	52	62	83	92	100	113	123	145	187	Volume of Exports	72
	41	45	49	50	52	50	54	62	80	87	100	107	114	137	157	Volume of Imports	73
	126.4	131.1	127.0	121.0	116.3	114.1	98.0	101.4	100.0	I99.5	100.0	94.6	88.4	86.4	82.9	Exports (Direct Prices)	76
	115.0	116.8	111.7	108.8	108.1	105.2	92.9	100.6	101.0	I100.9	100.0	96.8	93.5	91.6	90.7	Imports (Direct Prices)	76.x
Minus Sign Indicates Debit																**Balance of Payments**	
	19,430	21,090	21,016	21,894	24,091	22,854	22,383	28,657	39,122	44,829	52,714	58,995	63,527	73,608	....	Goods: Exports f.o.b.	78aa*d*
	−22,400	−25,785	−26,196	−26,252	−26,734	−24,362	−23,402	−29,910	−40,338	−45,687	−55,812	−60,948	−67,850	−80,025	....	Goods: Imports f.o.b.	78ab*d*
	−2,971	−4,695	−5,181	−4,358	−2,643	−1,508	−1,019	−1,253	−1,216	−858	−3,099	−1,952	−4,323	−6,417	....	Trade Balance	78ac*d*
	4,856	7,184	8,128	7,834	6,153	5,062	5,173	6,254	8,243	10,500	13,820	14,982	17,335	19,230	....	Services: Credit	78ad*d*
	−2,912	−3,254	−3,613	−3,782	−4,024	−3,976	−4,165	−5,015	−6,227	−7,306	−9,297	−9,863	−10,231	−11,635	....	Services: Debit	78ae*d*
	−1,027	−765	−665	−306	−513	−421	−11	−14	800	2,337	1,423	3,166	2,781	1,178	....	Balance on Goods and Services	78af*d*
	953	1,092	1,243	1,300	1,603	1,814	2,219	2,900	3,790	4,657	6,469	7,464	8,407	9,091	....	Income: Credit	78ag*d*
	−1,382	−1,644	−1,668	−1,390	−1,252	−1,183	−1,707	−2,810	−3,402	−3,843	−5,355	−6,140	−6,844	−7,534	....	Income: Debit	78ah*d*
	−1,456	−1,317	−1,091	−396	−162	210	502	76	1,188	3,151	2,537	4,491	4,343	2,736	....	Balance on Goods, Serv., & Inc.	78ai*d*
	87	130	98	121	121	111	119	127	132	156	187	186	197	176	....	Current Transfers, n.i.e.: Credit	78aj*d*
	−194	−283	−303	−336	−344	−325	−302	−361	−431	−523	−630	−684	−792	−873	....	Current Transfers: Debit	78ak*d*
	−1,563	−1,470	−1,296	−610	−385	−4	319	−157	889	2,785	2,094	3,992	3,748	2,039	....	Current Account, n.i.e.	78al*d*
	—	—	—	—	—	—	—	—	—	—	—	—	—	—	....	Capital Account, n.i.e.: Credit	78ba*d*
	—	—	—	—	—	—	—	—	—	—	—	—	—	—	....	Capital Account: Debit	78bb*d*
	—	—	—	—	—	—	—	—	—	—	—	—	—	—	....	Capital Account, n.i.e.	78bc*d*
	−98	15	−304	−49	−92	−238	−181	−206	−118	−882	−1,570	−444	−748	−767	....	Direct Investment Abroad	78bd*d*
	1,236	1,660	1,602	1,134	1,302	1,047	1,710	2,836	3,655	2,887	5,575	4,888	6,730	6,829	....	Dir. Invest. in Rep. Econ., n.i.e.	78be*d*
	−121	−193	−106	−160	−161	−347	−287	−67	−329	−451	−1,713	−592	−834	−959	....	Portfolio Investment Assets	78bf*d*
	134	145	78	111	10	521	−261	320	36	375	573	−210	15	14	....	Portfolio Investment Liab., n.i.e.	78bg*d*
	−741	−2,645	184	−824	−3,071	−2,250	−3,370	−2,233	−2,625	−7,864	1,673	199	−5,255	343	....	Other Investment Assets	78bh*d*
	1,173	3,186	856	2,251	3,593	1,965	1,945	−179	369	6,391	121	−2,906	5,651	3,991	....	Other Investment Liab., n.i.e.	78bi*d*
	1,582	2,167	2,309	2,463	1,580	699	−445	470	987	456	4,658	934	5,559	9,452	....	Financial Account, n.i.e.	78bj*d*
	643	212	165	−793	329	642	664	782	−217	−503	−1,322	−728	−3,208	−3,913	....	Net Errors and Omissions	78ca*d*
	663	909	1,177	1,059	1,524	1,337	538	1,095	1,659	2,738	5,431	4,198	6,100	7,578	....	Overall Balance	78cb*d*
	−663	−909	−1,177	−1,059	−1,524	−1,337	−538	−1,095	−1,659	−2,738	−5,431	−4,198	−6,100	−7,578	....	Reserves and Related Items	79da*d*
	−663	−909	−1,177	−1,059	−1,524	−1,337	−538	−1,095	−1,659	−2,738	−5,431	−4,198	−6,100	−7,578	....	Reserve Assets	79db*d*
	—	—	—	—	—	—	—	—	—	—	—	—	—	—	....	Use of Fund Credit and Loans	79dc*d*
	—	—	—	—	—	—	—	—	—	—	—	—	—	—	....	Liabs.Constit.For.Auth.Reserves	79dd*d*
	....	....	....	....	....	....	....	....	....	....	....	....	....	....	....	Exceptional Financing	79de*d*
Year Beginning April 1																**Government Finance**	
	538	213	1,098	661	1,643	816	561	−1,165	3,485	5,889	7,192	6,455	10,170	....	....	Deficit (-) or Surplus	80
	6,620	8,696	10,086	11,717	11,697	14,764	14,971	13,805	14,459	17,267	21,636	23,234	26,617	....	....	Revenue	81
	5,027	6,833	6,961	8,273	10,474	10,580	11,437	15,271	11,742	13,115	14,223	15,966	15,858	....	....	Expenditure	82
	1,055	1,650	2,027	2,783	−420	3,368	2,973	−301	−768	−1,737	221	813	589	....	....	Lending Minus Repayments	83
Financing																	
	2,595	3,515	3,788	4,499	3,384	3,222	1,523	5,495	2,627	4,838	8,591	7,199	7,103	....	....	Net Borrowing	84
	2,639	3,552	3,825	4,677	3,422	3,266	1,711	5,547	2,726	4,881	8,679	7,224	7,118	....	....	Domestic	84a
	−44	−37	−37	−178	−38	−44	−188	−52	−99	−43	−88	−25	−15	....	....	Foreign	85a
	....	....	....	....	....	....	....	....	....	....	....	....	....	....	....	Use of Foreign Exchange	86b
	−3,133	−3,728	−4,886	−5,160	−5,027	−4,038	−2,084	−4,330	−6,112	−10,727	−15,783	−13,654	−17,273	....	....	Use of Cash Balances	87
	15,307	17,161	20,752	25,482	29,718	32,984	34,175	40,086	42,476	47,313	54,821	61,993	69,513	....	....	Debt: Domestic	88a
	928	890	869	673	635	591	336	291	178	130	61	38	22	....	....	Foreign	89a
	....	....	....	....	....	....	....	....	....	....	....	....	....	....	....	Singapore Dollars	88b
Millions of Singapore Dollars																**National Accounts**	
	−2,216	−1,634	−1,441	−664	−1,113	−946	143	589	2,527	5,701	4,075	6,852	5,702	3,194	....	Exports (Net)	90n
	2,447	2,789	3,570	3,995	4,333	5,549	5,270	5,315	5,337	5,899	6,694	7,346	7,434	8,341	....	Government Consumption	91f
	10,203	12,785	15,506	17,464	19,122	16,425	14,310	15,165	17,344	20,356	23,412	27,557	30,886	36,056	....	Gross Fixed Capital Formation	93e
	1,425	802	153	132	295	126	585	1,472	1,091	18	2,731	189	1,098	2,925	....	Increase/Decrease(-) in Stocks	93i
	12,911	14,329	15,283	16,202	17,570	17,553	18,192	20,249	23,415	26,040	29,024	31,601	33,974	38,042	....	Private Consumption	96f
	25,091	29,339	32,670	36,732	40,048	38,924	38,664	42,636	49,998	57,462	66,174	73,038	79,083	89,007	....	Gross Domestic Product	99b
	−902	−1,148	−894	−172	767	1,407	949	−429	−136	445	524	906	1,373	1,226	....	Net Factor Inc/Pmts(-) Abroad	98.n
	24,189	28,191	31,776	36,560	40,815	40,331	39,613	42,207	49,862	57,907	66,698	73,944	80,456	90,233	....	Gross Nat'l Expenditure = GNP	99a
	33,315	36,515	39,021	42,216	45,724	44,974	45,803	50,114	55,695	60,842	66,174	70,575	74,839	82,281	....	Gross Dom. Prod. 1990 Prices	99b.*p*
	75.3	80.3	83.7	87.0	87.6	86.5	84.4	85.1	89.8	94.4	100.0	103.5	105.7	108.2	....	GDP Deflator (1990=100)	99bi *p*
Midyear Estimates																	
	2.41	2.44	2.47	2.41	2.44	2.48	2.52	2.55	2.60	2.65	2.71	2.76	2.82	2.87	2.93	Population	99z

Slovak Republic
936

		1965	1966	1967	1968	1969	1970	1971	1972	1973	1974	1975	1976	1977	1978	1979
Exchange Rates																*Koruny per SDR:*
Official Rate	aa	...	...	...	...	...	...	...	...	...	...	...	...	...	...	...
																Koruny per US Dollar:
Official Rate	ae	...	...	...	...	...	...	...	...	...	...	...	...	...	...	...
Official Rate	rf	...	...	...	...	...	...	...	...	...	...	...	...	...	...	...
Fund Position																*Millions of SDRs:*
Quota	2f.s	...	...	...	...	...	...	...	...	...	...	...	...	...	...	...
SDRs	1b.s	...	...	...	...	...	...	...	...	...	...	...	...	...	...	...
Reserve Position in the Fund	1c.s	...	...	...	...	...	...	...	...	...	...	...	...	...	...	...
Total Fund Cred.&Loans Outstg.	2tl	...	...	...	...	...	...	...	...	...	...	...	...	...	...	...
International Liquidity													*Millions of US Dollars Unless Otherwise Indicated:*			
Total Reserves minus Gold	1l.d	...	...	...	...	...	...	...	...	...	...	...	...	...	...	...
SDRs	1b.d	...	...	...	...	...	...	...	...	...	...	...	...	...	...	...
Reserve Position in the Fund	1c.d	...	...	...	...	...	—	...	...	...	...	...	...	...	...	...
Foreign Exchange	1d.d	...	...	...	...	...	...	...	...	...	...	...	...	...	...	...
Gold (Million Fine Troy Ounces)	1ad	...	...	...	...	...	...	...	...	...	...	...	...	...	...	...
Gold (National Valuation)	1and	...	...	...	...	...	...	...	...	...	...	...	...	...	...	...
Mon. Auth.: Other Assets Conv.	3a.d	...	...	...	...	...	...	...	...	...	...	...	...	...	...	...
Other Assets Nonconv.	3b.d	...	...	...	...	...	...	...	...	...	...	...	...	...	...	...
Monetary Authorities: Other Liab.	4..d	...	...	...	...	...	...	...	...	...	...	...	...	...	...	...
Dep.Money Banks: Assets Conv.	7ax d	...	...	...	...	...	...	...	...	...	...	...	...	...	...	...
Assets Nonconv.	7ay d	...	...	...	...	...	...	...	...	...	...	...	...	...	...	...
Dep.Money Banks: Liab. Conv.	7bx d	...	...	...	...	...	...	...	...	...	...	...	...	...	...	...
Liab. Nonconv.	7by d	...	...	...	...	...	...	...	...	...	...	...	...	...	...	...
Monetary Authorities																*Millions of Koruny:*
Foreign Assets	11	...	...	...	...	...	...	...	...	...	...	...	...	...	...	...
of which: Nonconv. Fgn. Assets	11..y	...	...	...	...	...	...	...	...	...	...	...	...	...	...	...
Claims on Central Government	12a	...	...	...	...	...	...	...	...	...	...	...	...	...	...	...
Claims on Nonfin.Pub.Enterprises	12c	...	...	...	...	...	...	...	...	...	...	...	...	...	...	...
Claims on Deposit Money Banks	12e	...	...	...	...	...	...	...	...	...	...	...	...	...	...	...
Reserve Money	14	...	...	...	...	...	...	...	...	...	...	...	...	...	...	...
of which: Currency Outside DMBs	14a	...	...	...	...	...	...	...	...	...	...	...	...	...	...	...
Time & Fgn. Currency Deposits	15	...	...	...	...	...	...	...	...	...	...	...	...	...	...	...
Foreign Liabilities	16c	...	...	...	...	...	...	...	...	...	...	...	...	...	...	...
of which: Nonconv. Fgn. Liab.	16c.y	...	...	...	...	...	...	...	...	...	...	...	...	...	...	...
Long-Term Foreign Liabilities	16cl	...	...	...	...	...	...	...	...	...	...	...	...	...	...	...
Central Government Deposits	16d	...	...	...	...	...	...	...	...	...	...	...	...	...	...	...
Capital Accounts	17a	...	...	...	...	...	...	...	...	...	...	...	...	...	...	...
Other Items (Net)	17r	...	...	...	...	...	...	...	...	...	...	...	...	...	...	...
Deposit Money Banks																*Millions of Koruny:*
Reserves	20	...	...	...	...	...	...	...	...	...	...	...	...	...	...	...
Foreign Assets	21	...	...	...	...	...	...	...	...	...	...	...	...	...	...	...
of which: Nonconv. Fgn. Assets	21..y	...	...	...	...	...	...	...	...	...	...	...	...	...	...	...
Claims on Central Government	22a	...	...	...	...	...	...	...	...	...	...	...	...	...	...	...
Claims on National Property Fund	22ae	...	...	...	...	...	...	...	...	...	...	...	...	...	...	...
Claims on Local Government	22b	...	...	...	...	...	...	...	...	...	...	...	...	...	...	...
Claims on Nonfin.Pub.Enterprises	22c	...	...	...	...	...	...	...	...	...	...	...	...	...	...	...
Claims on Private Sector	22d	...	...	...	...	...	...	...	...	...	...	...	...	...	...	...
Claims on Other Financial Insts.	22f	...	...	...	...	...	...	...	...	...	...	...	...	...	...	...
Demand Deposits	24	...	...	...	...	...	...	...	...	...	...	...	...	...	...	...
Time & Fgn. Currency Deposits	25	...	...	...	...	...	...	...	...	...	...	...	...	...	...	...
of which: Fgn. Currency Deposits	25b	...	...	...	...	...	...	...	...	...	...	...	...	...	...	...
Bonds	26ab	...	...	...	...	...	...	...	...	...	...	...	...	...	...	...
Foreign Liabilities	26c	...	...	...	...	...	...	...	...	...	...	...	...	...	...	...
of which: Nonconv. Fgn. Liab.	26c.y	...	...	...	...	...	...	...	...	...	...	...	...	...	...	...
Long-Term Foreign Liabilities	26cl	...	...	...	...	...	...	...	...	...	...	...	...	...	...	...
o/w: L-T Nonconv. Fgn. Liab.	26cly	...	...	...	...	...	...	...	...	...	...	...	...	...	...	...
Central Government Deposits	26d	...	...	...	...	...	...	...	...	...	...	...	...	...	...	...
National Property Fund Deposits	26de	...	...	...	...	...	...	...	...	...	...	...	...	...	...	...
Local Government Deposits	26db	...	...	...	...	...	...	...	...	...	...	...	...	...	...	...
Credit from Monetary Authorities	26g	...	...	...	...	...	...	...	...	...	...	...	...	...	...	...
Liabilities to Other Fin. Insts.	26i	...	...	...	...	...	...	...	...	...	...	...	...	...	...	...
Capital Accounts	27a	...	...	...	...	...	...	...	...	...	...	...	...	...	...	...
Other Items (Net)	27r	...	...	...	...	...	...	...	...	...	...	...	...	...	...	...
Monetary Survey																*Millions of Koruny:*
Foreign Assets (Net)	31n	...	...	...	...	...	...	...	...	...	...	...	...	...	...	...
Domestic Credit	32	...	...	...	...	...	...	...	...	...	...	...	...	...	...	...
Claims on General Govt. (Net)	32an	...	...	...	...	...	...	...	...	...	...	...	...	...	...	...
Claims on Nonfin.Pub.Enterprises	32c	...	...	...	...	...	...	...	...	...	...	...	...	...	...	...
Claims on Private Sector	32d	...	...	...	...	...	...	...	...	...	...	...	...	...	...	...
Claims on Other Financial Insts.	32f	...	...	...	...	...	...	...	...	...	...	...	...	...	...	...
Money	34	...	...	...	...	...	...	...	...	...	...	...	...	...	...	...
Quasi-Money	35	...	...	...	...	...	...	...	...	...	...	...	...	...	...	...
Bonds	36ab	...	...	...	...	...	...	...	...	...	...	...	...	...	...	...
Long-Term Foreign Liabilities	36cl	...	...	...	...	...	...	...	...	...	...	...	...	...	...	...
Capital Accounts	37a	...	...	...	...	...	...	...	...	...	...	...	...	...	...	...
Other Items (Net)	37r	...	...	...	...	...	...	...	...	...	...	...	...	...	...	...
Money plus Quasi-Money	35l	...	...	...	...	...	...	...	...	...	...	...	...	...	...	...

Slovak Republic
936

	1980	1981	1982	1983	1984	1985	1986	1987	1988	1989	1990	1991	1992	1993	1994		
End of Period																**Exchange Rates**	
	....	....	....	....	....	....	....	....	....	....	....	....	....	45.605	45.660	Official Rate	aa
End of Period (ae) Period Averages (rf)																	
	....	....	....	....	....	....	....	....	....	....	....	....	....	33.202	31.277	Official Rate	ae
	....	....	....	....	....	....	....	....	....	....	....	....	....	30.770	32.045	Official Rate	rf
End of Period																**Fund Position**	
	....	....	....	....	....	....	....	....	....	....	....	....	....	257.4	257.4	Quota	2f. s
	....	....	....	....	....	....	....	....	....	....	....	....	....	.3	58.9	SDRs	1b. s
	....	....	....	....	....	....	....	....	....	....	....	....	....	—	—	Reserve Position in the Fund	1c. s
	....	....	....	....	....	....	....	....	....	....	....	....	....	405.2	439.8	Total Fund Cred.&Loans Outstg.	2tl
End of Period																**International Liquidity**	
	....	....	....	....	....	....	....	....	....	....	....	....	....	416	1,691	Total Reserves minus Gold	1l. d
	....	....	....	....	....	....	....	....	....	....	....	....	....	—	86	SDRs	1b. d
	....	....	....	....	....	....	....	....	....	....	....	....	....	—	—	Reserve Position in the Fund	1c. d
	....	....	....	....	....	....	....	....	....	....	....	....	....	415	1,605	Foreign Exchange	1d. d
	....	....	....	....	....	....	....	....	....	....	....	....	....	1.290	1.290	Gold (Million Fine Troy Ounces)	1ad
	....	....	....	....	....	....	....	....	....	....	....	....	....	76	80	Gold (National Valuation)	1an d
	....	....	....	....	....	....	....	....	....	....	....	....	....	114	322	Mon. Auth.: Other Assets Conv.	3a. d
	....	....	....	....	....	....	....	....	....	....	....	....	....	—	—	Other Assets Nonconv.	3b. d
	....	....	....	....	....	....	....	....	....	....	....	....	....	1,040	1,355	Monetary Authorities: Other Liab.	4..d
	....	....	....	....	....	....	....	....	....	....	....	....	....	952	1,350	Dep.Money Banks: Assets Conv.	7ax d
	....	....	....	....	....	....	....	....	....	....	....	....	....	35	78	Assets Nonconv.	7ay d
	....	....	....	....	....	....	....	....	....	....	....	....	....	294	405	Dep.Money Banks: Liab. Conv.	7bx d
	....	....	....	....	....	....	....	....	....	....	....	....	....	131	94	Liab. Nonconv.	7by d
																Monetary Authorities	
	....	....	....	....	....	....	....	....	....	....	....	....	....	19,557	60,184	Foreign Assets	11
	....	....	....	....	....	....	....	....	....	....	....	....	....	7	—	of which: Nonconv. Fgn. Assets	11..y
	....	....	....	....	....	....	....	....	....	....	....	....	....	46,476	46,456	Claims on Central Government	12a
	....	....	....	....	....	....	....	....	....	....	....	....	....	352	294	Claims on Nonfin.Pub.Enterprises	12c
	....	....	....	....	....	....	....	....	....	....	....	....	....	40,654	36,143	Claims on Deposit Money Banks	12e
	....	....	....	....	....	....	....	....	....	....	....	....	....	39,494	48,544	Reserve Money	14
	....	....	....	....	....	....	....	....	....	....	....	....	....	25,122	28,101	of which: Currency Outside DMBs	14a
	....	....	....	....	....	....	....	....	....	....	....	....	....	9	25	Time & Fgn. Currency Deposits	15
	....	....	....	....	....	....	....	....	....	....	....	....	....	43,064	46,342	Foreign Liabilities	16c
	....	....	....	....	....	....	....	....	....	....	....	....	....	24,573	24,573	of which: Nonconv. Fgn. Liab.	16c.y
	....	....	....	....	....	....	....	....	....	....	....	....	....	9,933	16,112	Long-Term Foreign Liabilities	16cl
	....	....	....	....	....	....	....	....	....	....	....	....	....	6,458	11,726	Central Government Deposits	16d
	....	....	....	....	....	....	....	....	....	....	....	....	....	4,151	7,977	Capital Accounts	17a
	....	....	....	....	....	....	....	....	....	....	....	....	....	3,930	12,351	Other Items (Net)	17r
End of Period																**Deposit Money Banks**	
	....	....	....	....	....	....	....	....	....	....	....	....	....	13,961	19,656	Reserves	20
	....	....	....	....	....	....	....	....	....	....	....	....	....	32,773	44,634	Foreign Assets	21
	....	....	....	....	....	....	....	....	....	....	....	....	....	1,171	2,425	of which: Nonconv. Fgn. Assets	21..y
	....	....	....	....	....	....	....	....	....	....	....	....	....	16,715	42,471	Claims on Central Government	22a
	....	....	....	....	....	....	....	....	....	....	....	....	....	12,083	7,803	Claims on National Property Fund	22ae
	....	....	....	....	....	....	....	....	....	....	....	....	....	—	419	Claims on Local Government	22b
	....	....	....	....	....	....	....	....	....	....	....	....	....	114,419	93,158	Claims on Nonfin.Pub.Enterprises	22c
	....	....	....	....	....	....	....	....	....	....	....	....	....	118,563	107,195	Claims on Private Sector	22d
	....	....	....	....	....	....	....	....	....	....	....	....	....	1,310	1,290	Claims on Other Financial Insts.	22f
	....	....	....	....	....	....	....	....	....	....	....	....	....	90,742	94,931	Demand Deposits	24
	....	....	....	....	....	....	....	....	....	....	....	....	....	137,344	174,427	Time & Fgn. Currency Deposits	25
	....	....	....	....	....	....	....	....	....	....	....	....	....	28,509	38,395	of which: Fgn. Currency Deposits	25b
	....	....	....	....	....	....	....	....	....	....	....	....	....	564	952	Bonds	26ab
	....	....	....	....	....	....	....	....	....	....	....	....	....	13,762	14,909	Foreign Liabilities	26c
	....	....	....	....	....	....	....	....	....	....	....	....	....	4,347	2,933	of which: Nonconv. Fgn. Liab.	26c.y
	....	....	....	....	....	....	....	....	....	....	....	....	....	341	686	Long-Term Foreign Liabilities	26cl
	....	....	....	....	....	....	....	....	....	....	....	....	....	—	—	o/w: L-T Nonconv. Fgn. Liab.	26cl y
	....	....	....	....	....	....	....	....	....	....	....	....	....	2,015	8,743	Central Government Deposits	26d
	....	....	....	....	....	....	....	....	....	....	....	....	....	5,151	1,506	National Property Fund Deposits	26de
	....	....	....	....	....	....	....	....	....	....	....	....	....	2,292	1,902	Local Government Deposits	26db
	....	....	....	....	....	....	....	....	....	....	....	....	....	41,204	37,705	Credit from Monetary Authorities	26g
	....	....	....	....	....	....	....	....	....	....	....	....	....	—	—	Liabilities to Other Fin. Insts.	26i
	....	....	....	....	....	....	....	....	....	....	....	....	....	48,722	63,813	Capital Accounts	27a
	....	....	....	....	....	....	....	....	....	....	....	....	....	-32,313	-82,948	Other Items (Net)	27r
End of Period																**Monetary Survey**	
	....	....	....	....	....	....	....	....	....	....	....	....	....	-4,496	43,567	Foreign Assets (Net)	31n
	....	....	....	....	....	....	....	....	....	....	....	....	....	294,005	275,220	Domestic Credit	32
	....	....	....	....	....	....	....	....	....	....	....	....	....	59,358	73,272	Claims on General Govt. (Net)	32an
	....	....	....	....	....	....	....	....	....	....	....	....	....	114,771	93,452	Claims on Nonfin.Pub.Enterprises	32c
	....	....	....	....	....	....	....	....	....	....	....	....	....	118,566	107,206	Claims on Private Sector	32d
	....	....	....	....	....	....	....	....	....	....	....	....	....	1,310	1,290	Claims on Other Financial Insts.	32f
	....	....	....	....	....	....	....	....	....	....	....	....	....	116,615	123,820	Money	34
	....	....	....	....	....	....	....	....	....	....	....	....	....	137,353	174,452	Quasi-Money	35
	....	....	....	....	....	....	....	....	....	....	....	....	....	564	952	Bonds	36ab
	....	....	....	....	....	....	....	....	....	....	....	....	....	10,274	16,798	Long-Term Foreign Liabilities	36cl
	....	....	....	....	....	....	....	....	....	....	....	....	....	52,873	71,790	Capital Accounts	37a
	....	....	....	....	....	....	....	....	....	....	....	....	....	-28,170	-69,025	Other Items (Net)	37r
	....	....	....	....	....	....	....	....	....	....	....	....	....	253,968	298,272	Money plus Quasi-Money	35l

Slovak Republic

936		1965	1966	1967	1968	1969	1970	1971	1972	1973	1974	1975	1976	1977	1978	1979

Interest Rates
Percent Per Annum

Discount Rate *(End of Period)*	60	…	…	…	…	…	…	…	…	…	…	…	…	…	…	…
Refinancing Rate	60a	…	…	…	…	…	…	…	…	…	…	…	…	…	…	…
Deposit Rate	60l	…	…	…	…	…	…	…	…	…	…	…	…	…	…	…
Lending Rate	60p	…	…	…	…	…	…	…	…	…	…	…	…	…	…	…

Prices, Production, Employment
Index Numbers (1990=100):

Producer Prices	63	…	…	…	…	…	…	…	…	…	…	…	…	…	…	…
Consumer Prices	64	…	…	…	…	…	…	…	…	…	…	…	…	…	…	…
Wages	65	…	…	…	…	…	…	…	…	…	…	…	…	…	…	…
Industrial Production	66	…	…	…	…	…	…	…	…	…	…	…	…	…	…	…
Industrial Employment	67	…	…	…	…	…	…	…	…	…	…	…	…	…	…	…

International Transactions
Millions of Koruny

Exports	70	…	…	…	…	…	…	…	…	…	…	…	…	…	…	…
Imports, fob	71.v	…	…	…	…	…	…	…	…	…	…	…	…	…	…	…

Balance of Payments
Millions of US Dollars:

Goods: Exports f.o.b.	78aa*d*	…	…	…	…	…	…	…	…	…	…	…	…	…	…	…
Goods: Imports f.o.b.	78ab*d*	…	…	…	…	…	…	…	…	…	…	…	…	…	…	…
Trade Balance	78ac*d*	…	…	…	…	…	…	…	…	…	…	…	…	…	…	…
Services: Credit	78ad*d*	…	…	…	…	…	…	…	…	…	…	…	…	…	…	…
Services: Debit	78ae*d*	…	…	…	…	…	…	…	…	…	…	…	…	…	…	…
Balance on Goods and Services	78af*d*	…	…	…	…	…	…	…	…	…	…	…	…	…	…	…
Income: Credit	78ag*d*	…	…	…	…	…	…	…	…	…	…	…	…	…	…	…
Income: Debit	78ah*d*	…	…	…	…	…	…	…	…	…	…	…	…	…	…	…
Balance on Goods, Serv., & Inc.	78ai*d*	…	…	…	…	…	…	…	…	…	…	…	…	…	…	…
Current Transfers, n.i.e.: Credit	78aj*d*	…	…	…	…	…	…	…	…	…	…	…	…	…	…	…
Current Transfers: Debit	78ak*d*	…	…	…	…	…	…	…	…	…	…	…	…	…	…	…
Current Account, n.i.e.	78al*d*	…	…	…	…	…	…	…	…	…	…	…	…	…	…	…
Capital Account, n.i.e.: Credit	78ba*d*	…	…	…	…	…	…	…	…	…	…	…	…	…	…	…
Capital Account: Debit	78bb*d*	…	…	…	…	…	…	…	…	…	…	…	…	…	…	…
Capital Account, n.i.e.	78bc*d*	…	…	…	…	…	…	…	…	…	…	…	…	…	…	…
Direct Investment Abroad	78bd*d*	…	…	…	…	…	…	…	…	…	…	…	…	…	…	…
Dir. Invest. in Rep. Econ., n.i.e.	78be*d*	…	…	…	…	…	…	…	…	…	…	…	…	…	…	…
Portfolio Investment Assets	78bf*d*	…	…	…	…	…	…	…	…	…	…	…	…	…	…	…
Portfolio Investment Liab., n.i.e.	78bg*d*	…	…	…	…	…	…	…	…	…	…	…	…	…	…	…
Other Investment Assets	78bh*d*	…	…	…	…	…	…	…	…	…	…	…	…	…	…	…
Other Investment Liab., n.i.e.	78bi*d*	…	…	…	…	…	…	…	…	…	…	…	…	…	…	…
Financial Account, n.i.e.	78bj*d*	…	…	…	…	…	…	…	…	…	…	…	…	…	…	…
Net Errors and Omissions	78ca*d*	…	…	…	…	…	…	…	…	…	…	…	…	…	…	…
Overall Balance	78cb*d*	…	…	…	…	…	…	…	…	…	…	…	…	…	…	…
Reserves and Related Items	79da*d*	…	…	…	…	…	…	…	…	…	…	…	…	…	…	…
Reserve Assets	79db*d*	…	…	…	…	…	…	…	…	…	…	…	…	…	…	…
Use of Fund Credit and Loans	79dc*d*	…	…	…	…	…	…	…	…	…	…	…	…	…	…	…
Liabs.Constit.For.Auth.Reserves	79dd*d*	…	…	…	…	…	…	…	…	…	…	…	…	…	…	…
Exceptional Financing	79de*d*	…	…	…	…	…	…	…	…	…	…	…	…	…	…	…

National Accounts
Millions of Koruny

Exports of Goods & Services	90c	…	…	…	…	…	…	…	…	…	…	…	…	…	…	…
Government Consumption	91f	…	…	…	…	…	…	…	…	…	…	…	…	…	…	…
Gross Fixed Capital Formation	93e	…	…	…	…	…	…	…	…	…	…	…	…	…	…	…
Increase/Decrease(-) in Stocks	93i	…	…	…	…	…	…	…	…	…	…	…	…	…	…	…
Private Consumption	96f	…	…	…	…	…	…	…	…	…	…	…	…	…	…	…
Imports of Goods & Services	98c	…	…	…	…	…	…	…	…	…	…	…	…	…	…	…
Gross Domestic Product	99b	…	…	…	…	…	…	…	…	…	…	…	…	…	…	…
Gross Dom. Prod. 1990 Prices	99b.*p*	…	…	…	…	…	…	…	…	…	…	…	…	…	…	…
GDP Deflator (1990=100)	99bi*p*	…	…	…	…	…	…	…	…	…	…	…	…	…	…	…

Millions:

Population	99z	…	…	…	…	…	…	…	…	…	…	…	…	…	…	…

Slovak Republic

936

	1980	1981	1982	1983	1984	1985	1986	1987	1988	1989	1990	1991	1992	1993	1994		
Percent Per Annum																**Interest Rates**	
	....	....	....	....	....	....	....	....	....	....	....	....	....	12.00	12.00	Discount Rate *(End of Period)*	60
	....	....	....	....	....	....	....	....	....	....	....	....	....	16.30	12.00	Refinancing Rate	60a
	....	....	....	....	....	....	....	....	....	....	....	....	....	8.02	9.32	Deposit Rate	60l
	....	....	....	....	....	....	....	....	....	....	....	....	....	14.41	14.56	Lending Rate	60p
Period Averages																**Prices, Production, Employment**	
	....	....	....	....	....	....	....	....	....	....	....	....	....	208.5	229.3	Producer Prices	63
	....	....	....	....	....	....	....	....	....	....	....	....	....	218.5	247.7	Consumer Prices	64
	....	....	....	....	....	....	....	....	....	....	....	....	....	161.1	190.8	Wages	65
	....	....	....	....	....	....	....	....	....	....	....	....	....	62.2	69.3	Industrial Production	66
	....	....	....	....	....	....	....	....	....	....	....	....	....	77.7	79.0	Industrial Employment	67
Millions of Koruny																**International Transactions**	
	....	....	....	....	....	....	....	....	....	....	....	....	....	167,724	211,085	Exports	70
	....	....	....	....	....	....	....	....	....	....	....	....	....	195,034	208,227	Imports, fob	71.v
Minus Sign Indicates Debit																Balance of Payments	
	....	....	....	....	....	....	....	....	....	....	....	....	....	5,452	....	Goods: Exports f.o.b.	78aa *d*
	....	....	....	....	....	....	....	....	....	....	....	....	....	−6,365	....	Goods: Imports f.o.b.	78ab *d*
	....	....	....	....	....	....	....	....	....	....	....	....	....	−912	....	Trade Balance	78ac *d*
	....	....	....	....	....	....	....	....	....	....	....	....	....	1,939	....	Services: Credit	78ad *d*
	....	....	....	....	....	....	....	....	....	....	....	....	....	−1,666	....	Services: Debit	78ae *d*
	....	....	....	....	....	....	....	....	....	....	....	....	....	−640	....	Balance on Goods and Services	78af *d*
	....	....	....	....	....	....	....	....	....	....	....	....	....	185	....	Income: Credit	78ag *d*
	....	....	....	....	....	....	....	....	....	....	....	....	....	−224	....	Income: Debit	78ah *d*
	....	....	....	....	....	....	....	....	....	....	....	....	....	−678	....	Balance on Goods, Serv., & Inc.	78ai *d*
	....	....	....	....	....	....	....	....	....	....	....	....	....	215	....	Current Transfers, n.i.e.: Credit	78aj *d*
	....	....	....	....	....	....	....	....	....	....	....	....	....	−118	....	Current Transfers: Debit	78ak *d*
	....	....	....	....	....	....	....	....	....	....	....	....	....	−580	....	Current Account, n.i.e.	78al *d*
	....	....	....	....	....	....	....	....	....	....	....	....	....	771	....	Capital Account, n.i.e.: Credit	78ba *d*
	....	....	....	....	....	....	....	....	....	....	....	....	....	−207	....	Capital Account: Debit	78bb *d*
	....	....	....	....	....	....	....	....	....	....	....	....	....	564	....	Capital Account, n.i.e.	78bc *d*
	....	....	....	....	....	....	....	....	....	....	....	....	....	−61	....	Direct Investment Abroad	78bd *d*
	....	....	....	....	....	....	....	....	....	....	....	....	....	199	....	Dir. Invest. in Rep. Econ., n.i.e.	78be *d*
	....	....	....	....	....	....	....	....	....	....	....	....	....	−773	....	Portfolio Investment Assets	78bf *d*
	....	....	....	....	....	....	....	....	....	....	....	....	....	464	....	Portfolio Investment Liab., n.i.e.	78bg *d*
	....	....	....	....	....	....	....	....	....	....	....	....	....	−412	....	Other Investment Assets	78bh *d*
	....	....	....	....	....	....	....	....	....	....	....	....	....	430	....	Other Investment Liab., n.i.e.	78bi *d*
	....	....	....	....	....	....	....	....	....	....	....	....	....	−153	....	Financial Account, n.i.e.	78bj *d*
	....	....	....	....	....	....	....	....	....	....	....	....	....	180	....	Net Errors and Omissions	78ca *d*
	....	....	....	....	....	....	....	....	....	....	....	....	....	11	....	Overall Balance	78cb *d*
	....	....	....	....	....	....	....	....	....	....	....	....	....	−11	....	Reserves and Related Items	79da *d*
	....	....	....	....	....	....	....	....	....	....	....	....	....	−104	....	Reserve Assets	79db *d*
	....	....	....	....	....	....	....	....	....	....	....	....	....	92	....	Use of Fund Credit and Loans	79dc *d*
	....	....	....	....	....	....	....	....	....	....	....	....	....	—	....	Liabs.Constit.For.Auth.Reserves	79dd *d*
	....	....	....	....	....	....	....	....	....	....	....	....	....	—	....	Exceptional Financing	79de *d*
Millions of Koruny																**National Accounts**	
	....	....	....	....	....	....	....	....	....	....	....	....	....	227,800	287,800	Exports of Goods & Services	90c
	....	....	....	....	....	....	....	....	....	....	....	....	....	87,800	....	Government Consumption	91f
	....	....	....	....	....	....	....	....	....	....	....	....	....	93,500	101,800	Gross Fixed Capital Formation	93e
	....	....	....	....	....	....	....	....	....	....	....	....	....	−19,000	....	Increase/Decrease(−) in Stocks	93i
	....	....	....	....	....	....	....	....	....	....	....	....	....	199,000	225,600	Private Consumption	96f
	....	....	....	....	....	....	....	....	....	....	....	....	....	−248,200	−263,500	Imports of Goods & Services	98c
	....	....	....	....	....	....	....	....	....	....	....	....	....	340,200	398,300	Gross Domestic Product	99b
	....	....	....	....	....	....	....	....	....	....	....	....	....	196,539	206,038	Gross Dom. Prod. 1990 Prices	99b.*p*
	....	....	....	....	....	....	....	....	....	....	....	....	....	173.1	193.3	GDP Deflator (1990=100)	99bi *p*
Midyear Estimates																	
	....	....	....	....	....	....	....	....	....	....	....	....	....	5.32	5.35	**Population**	99z

Slovenia
961

		1965	1966	1967	1968	1969	1970	1971	1972	1973	1974	1975	1976	1977	1978	1979
Exchange Rates															*Tolars per SDR:*	
Official Rate	aa	....	....	....	....	....	....	....	....	....	....	....	....	....	....	....
															Tolars per US Dollar:	
Official Rate	ae	....	....	....	....	....	....	....	....	....	....	....	....	....	....	....
Official Rate	rf	....	....	....	....	....	....	....	....	....	....	....	....	....	....	....
Fund Position															*Millions of SDRs:*	
Quota	2f.s	....	....	....	....	....	....	....	....	....	....	....	....	....	....	....
SDRs	1b.s	....	....	....	....	....	....	....	....	....	....	....	....	....	....	....
Reserve Position in the Fund	1c.s	....	....	....	....	....	....	....	....	....	....	....	....	....	....	....
Total Fund Cred.&Loans Outstg.	2tl	....	....	....	....	....	....	....	....	....	....	....	....	....	....	....
International Liquidity													*Millions of US Dollars Unless Otherwise Indicated:*			
Total Reserves minus Gold	1l.d	....	....	....	....	....	....	....	....	....	....	....	....	....	....	....
SDRs	1b.d	....	....	....	....	....	....	....	....	....	....	....	....	....	....	....
Reserve Position in the Fund	1c.d	....	....	....	....	....	....	....	....	....	....	....	....	....	....	....
Foreign Exchange	1d.d	....	....	....	....	....	....	....	....	....	....	....	....	....	....	....
Gold (Million Fine Troy Ounces)	1ad	....	....	....	....	....	....	....	....	....	....	....	....	....	....	....
Gold (National Valuation)	1and	....	....	....	....	....	....	....	....	....	....	....	....	....	....	....
Monetary Authorities: Other Assets	3..d	....	....	....	....	....	....	....	....	....	....	....	....	....	....	....
Other Liab.	4..d	....	....	....	....	....	....	....	....	....	....	....	....	....	....	....
Deposit Money Banks: Assets	7a.d	....	....	....	....	....	....	....	....	....	....	....	....	....	....	....
of which: Claims on Nonbanks	7ad d	....	....	....	....	....	....	....	....	....	....	....	....	....	....	....
Deposit Money Banks: Liabilities	7b.d	....	....	....	....	....	....	....	....	....	....	....	....	....	....	....
of which: Liab. to Nonbanks	7bd d	....	....	....	....	....	....	....	....	....	....	....	....	....	....	....
Monetary Authorities															*Billions of Tolars:*	
Foreign Assets	11	....	....	....	....	....	....	....	....	....	....	....	....	....	....	....
Claims on Central Government	12a	....	....	....	....	....	....	....	....	....	....	....	....	....	....	....
Claims on Private Sector	12d	....	....	....	....	....	....	....	....	....	....	....	....	....	....	....
Claims on Deposit Money Banks	12e	....	....	....	....	....	....	....	....	....	....	....	....	....	....	....
Reserve Money	14	....	....	....	....	....	....	....	....	....	....	....	....	....	....	....
of which: Currency Outside DMBs	14a	....	....	....	....	....	....	....	....	....	....	....	....	....	....	....
Bonds	16ab	....	....	....	....	....	....	....	....	....	....	....	....	....	....	....
Restricted Deposits	16b	....	....	....	....	....	....	....	....	....	....	....	....	....	....	....
Foreign Liabilities	16c	....	....	....	....	....	....	....	....	....	....	....	....	....	....	....
Central Government Deposits	16d	....	....	....	....	....	....	....	....	....	....	....	....	....	....	....
Capital Accounts	17a	....	....	....	....	....	....	....	....	....	....	....	....	....	....	....
Other Items (Net)	17r	....	....	....	....	....	....	....	....	....	....	....	....	....	....	....
Deposit Money Banks															*Billions of Tolars:*	
Reserves	20	....	....	....	....	....	....	....	....	....	....	....	....	....	....	....
Foreign Assets	21	....	....	....	....	....	....	....	....	....	....	....	....	....	....	....
Claims on Central Government	22a	....	....	....	....	....	....	....	....	....	....	....	....	....	....	....
Claims on Local Government	22b	....	....	....	....	....	....	....	....	....	....	....	....	....	....	....
Claims on Private Sector	22d	....	....	....	....	....	....	....	....	....	....	....	....	....	....	....
Claims on Other Financial Insts.	22f	....	....	....	....	....	....	....	....	....	....	....	....	....	....	....
Demand Deposits	24	....	....	....	....	....	....	....	....	....	....	....	....	....	....	....
Time, Savings,& Fgn.Currency Dep.	25	....	....	....	....	....	....	....	....	....	....	....	....	....	....	....
Money Market Instruments	26aa	....	....	....	....	....	....	....	....	....	....	....	....	....	....	....
Bonds	26ab	....	....	....	....	....	....	....	....	....	....	....	....	....	....	....
Restricted Deposits	26b	....	....	....	....	....	....	....	....	....	....	....	....	....	....	....
Foreign Liabilities	26c	....	....	....	....	....	....	....	....	....	....	....	....	....	....	....
Central Government Deposits	26d	....	....	....	....	....	....	....	....	....	....	....	....	....	....	....
Central Govt. Lending Funds	26f	....	....	....	....	....	....	....	....	....	....	....	....	....	....	....
Credit from Monetary Authorities	26g	....	....	....	....	....	....	....	....	....	....	....	....	....	....	....
Liabs. to Other Financial Insts.	26i	....	....	....	....	....	....	....	....	....	....	....	....	....	....	....
Capital Accounts	27a	....	....	....	....	....	....	....	....	....	....	....	....	....	....	....
Other Items (Net)	27r	....	....	....	....	....	....	....	....	....	....	....	....	....	....	....
Monetary Survey															*Billions of Tolars:*	
Foreign Assets (Net)	31n	....	....	....	....	....	....	....	....	....	....	....	....	....	....	....
Domestic Credit	32	....	....	....	....	....	....	....	....	....	....	....	....	....	....	....
Claims on Central Govt. (Net)	32an	....	....	....	....	....	....	....	....	....	....	....	....	....	....	....
Claims on Local Government	32b	....	....	....	....	....	....	....	....	....	....	....	....	....	....	....
Claims on Private Sector	32d	....	....	....	....	....	....	....	....	....	....	....	....	....	....	....
Claims on Other Financial Insts.	32f	....	....	....	....	....	....	....	....	....	....	....	....	....	....	....
Money	34	....	....	....	....	....	....	....	....	....	....	....	....	....	....	....
Quasi-Money	35	....	....	....	....	....	....	....	....	....	....	....	....	....	....	....
Money Market Instruments	36aa	....	....	....	....	....	....	....	....	....	....	....	....	....	....	....
Bonds	36ab	....	....	....	....	....	....	....	....	....	....	....	....	....	....	....
Restricted Deposits	36b	....	....	....	....	....	....	....	....	....	....	....	....	....	....	....
Central Govt. Lending Funds	36f	....	....	....	....	....	....	....	....	....	....	....	....	....	....	....
Liabs. to Other Financial Insts.	36i	....	....	....	....	....	....	....	....	....	....	....	....	....	....	....
Capital Accounts	37a	....	....	....	....	....	....	....	....	....	....	....	....	....	....	....
Other Items (Net)	37r	....	....	....	....	....	....	....	....	....	....	....	....	....	....	....
Interest Rates															*Percent Per Annum*	
Discount Rate *(End of Period)*	60	....	....	....	....	....	....	....	....	....	....	....	....	....	....	....
Interbank Market Rate	60bs	....	....	....	....	....	....	....	....	....	....	....	....	....	....	....
Deposit Rate	60l	....	....	....	....	....	....	....	....	....	....	....	....	....	....	....
Lending Rate	60p	....	....	....	....	....	....	....	....	....	....	....	....	....	....	....

Slovenia

	1980	1981	1982	1983	1984	1985	1986	1987	1988	1989	1990	1991	1992	1993	1994		
																Exchange Rates	
End of Period	....	....	....	....	....	....	....	....	....	....	....	81.09	135.71	181.09	184.61	Official Rate	aa
End of Period (ae) Period Average (rf)																	
	....	....	....	....	....	....	....	....	....	....	....	56.69	98.70	131.84	126.46	Official Rate	ae
	....	....	....	....	....	....	....	....	....	....	....	27.57	81.29	113.24	128.81	Official Rate	rf
																Fund Position	
End of Period	....	....	....	....	....	....	....	....	....	....	....	....	....	150.50	150.50	Quota	2f. s
	....	....	....	....	....	....	....	....	....	....	....	....	....	.03	.04	SDRs	1b. s
	....	....	....	....	....	....	....	....	....	....	....	....	....	12.88	12.87	Reserve Position in the Fund	1c. s
	....	....	....	....	....	....	....	....	....	....	....	....	....	8.53	4.94	Total Fund Cred.&Loans Outstg.	2tl
																International Liquidity	
End of Period	....	....	....	....	....	....	....	....	....	....	....	112.10	715.50	805.43	1,513.76	Total Reserves minus Gold	1l. d
	....	....	....	....	....	....	....	....	....	....	....	....	....	.05	.06	SDRs	1b. d
	....	....	....	....	....	....	....	....	....	....	....	....	....	17.68	18.80	Reserve Position in the Fund	1c. d
	....	....	....	....	....	....	....	....	....	....	....	112.10	715.50	787.70	1,494.90	Foreign Exchange	1d. d
	....	....	....	....	....	....	....	....	....	....	....	.0003	.0003	.0003	.0003	Gold (Million Fine Troy Ounces)	1ad
	....	....	....	....	....	....	....	....	....	....	....	.11	.11	.13	.12	Gold (National Valuation)	1an d
	....	....	....	....	....	....	....	....	....	....	....	2.40	1.30	1.10	102.10	Monetary Authorities: Other Assets	3.. d
	....	....	....	....	....	....	....	....	....	....	....	—	—	.1	.1	Other Liab.	4.. d
	....	....	....	....	....	....	....	....	....	....	....	1,989.8	2,065.9	1,432.0	2,389.4	Deposit Money Banks: Assets	7a. d
	....	....	....	....	....	....	....	....	....	....	....	163.6	165.9	43.5	289.3	of which: Claims on Nonbanks	7ad d
	....	....	....	....	....	....	....	....	....	....	....	1,282.2	1,183.5	1,059.0	1,182.2	Deposit Money Banks: Liabilities	7b. d
	....	....	....	....	....	....	....	....	....	....	....	93.5	166.0	189.2	241.5	of which: Liab. to Nonbanks	7bd d
																Monetary Authorities	
End of Period	....	....	....	....	....	....	....	....	....	....	....	6.50	70.77	104.02	189.91	Foreign Assets	11
	....	....	....	....	....	....	....	....	....	....	....	8.65	8.88	18.78	15.65	Claims on Central Government	12a
	....	....	....	....	....	....	....	....	....	....	....	.02	.05	.08	.10	Claims on Private Sector	12d
	....	....	....	....	....	....	....	....	....	....	....	3.82	16.29	16.00	29.90	Claims on Deposit Money Banks	12e
	....	....	....	....	....	....	....	....	....	....	....	15.92	37.11	51.29	80.49	Reserve Money	14
	....	....	....	....	....	....	....	....	....	....	....	9.18	24.18	32.72	47.28	of which: Currency Outside DMBs	14a
	....	....	....	....	....	....	....	....	....	....	....	—	40.76	50.39	99.77	Bonds	16ab
	....	....	....	....	....	....	....	....	....	....	....	.05	.04	.37	1.82	Restricted Deposits	16b
	....	....	....	....	....	....	....	....	....	....	....	—	—	1.55	.92	Foreign Liabilities	16c
	....	....	....	....	....	....	....	....	....	....	....	1.64	5.78	5.99	27.41	Central Government Deposits	16d
	....	....	....	....	....	....	....	....	....	....	....	1.50	12.40	29.33	29.05	Capital Accounts	17a
	....	....	....	....	....	....	....	....	....	....	....	-.13	-.10	-.03	-3.92	Other Items (Net)	17r
																Deposit Money Banks	
End of Period	....	....	....	....	....	....	....	....	....	....	....	6.77	43.94	55.40	114.53	Reserves	20
	....	....	....	....	....	....	....	....	....	....	....	112.81	203.90	188.79	302.15	Foreign Assets	21
	....	....	....	....	....	....	....	....	....	....	....	13.25	24.86	208.60	231.95	Claims on Central Government	22a
	....	....	....	....	....	....	....	....	....	....	....	.01	—	.02	.04	Claims on Local Government	22b
	....	....	....	....	....	....	....	....	....	....	....	120.08	236.17	315.91	417.66	Claims on Private Sector	22d
	....	....	....	....	....	....	....	....	....	....	....	.50	.91	2.03	5.00	Claims on Other Financial Insts.	22f
	....	....	....	....	....	....	....	....	....	....	....	20.21	44.48	64.36	92.19	Demand Deposits	24
	....	....	....	....	....	....	....	....	....	....	....	90.06	197.72	334.95	482.62	Time, Savings,& Fgn.Currency Dep.	25
	....	....	....	....	....	....	....	....	....	....	....	2.55	10.00	16.44	12.51	Money Market Instruments	26aa
	....	....	....	....	....	....	....	....	....	....	....	.13	.66	2.57	8.27	Bonds	26ab
	....	....	....	....	....	....	....	....	....	....	....	3.48	6.04	9.51	10.28	Restricted Deposits	26b
	....	....	....	....	....	....	....	....	....	....	....	72.69	116.81	139.62	149.50	Foreign Liabilities	26c
	....	....	....	....	....	....	....	....	....	....	....	12.20	33.55	57.93	78.92	Central Government Deposits	26d
	....	....	....	....	....	....	....	....	....	....	....	.74	.91	2.43	4.88	Central Govt. Lending Funds	26f
	....	....	....	....	....	....	....	....	....	....	....	1.40	15.61	15.48	29.64	Credit from Monetary Authorities	26g
	....	....	....	....	....	....	....	....	....	....	....	3.01	6.00	9.92	14.71	Liabs. to Other Financial Insts.	26i
	....	....	....	....	....	....	....	....	....	....	....	65.04	104.77	151.07	231.05	Capital Accounts	27a
	....	....	....	....	....	....	....	....	....	....	....	-18.09	-26.76	-33.53	-43.24	Other Items (Net)	27r
																Monetary Survey	
End of Period	....	....	....	....	....	....	....	....	....	....	....	46.61	157.86	151.65	341.64	Foreign Assets (Net)	31n
	....	....	....	....	....	....	....	....	....	....	....	128.66	231.54	481.50	564.06	Domestic Credit	32
	....	....	....	....	....	....	....	....	....	....	....	8.05	-5.59	163.46	141.26	Claims on Central Govt. (Net)	32an
	....	....	....	....	....	....	....	....	....	....	....	.01	—	.02	.04	Claims on Local Government	32b
	....	....	....	....	....	....	....	....	....	....	....	120.10	236.22	315.99	417.76	Claims on Private Sector	32d
	....	....	....	....	....	....	....	....	....	....	....	.50	.91	2.03	5.00	Claims on Other Financial Insts.	32f
	....	....	....	....	....	....	....	....	....	....	....	29.45	69.53	97.99	140.58	Money	34
	....	....	....	....	....	....	....	....	....	....	....	90.06	197.72	334.95	482.62	Quasi-Money	35
	....	....	....	....	....	....	....	....	....	....	....	2.55	10.00	16.44	12.51	Money Market Instruments	36aa
	....	....	....	....	....	....	....	....	....	....	....	.13	41.42	52.96	108.04	Bonds	36ab
	....	....	....	....	....	....	....	....	....	....	....	3.53	6.08	9.88	12.10	Restricted Deposits	36b
	....	....	....	....	....	....	....	....	....	....	....	.74	.91	2.43	4.88	Central Govt. Lending Funds	36f
	....	....	....	....	....	....	....	....	....	....	....	3.01	6.00	9.92	14.71	Liabs. to Other Financial Insts.	36i
	....	....	....	....	....	....	....	....	....	....	....	66.54	117.17	180.40	260.10	Capital Accounts	37a
	....	....	....	....	....	....	....	....	....	....	....	-20.74	-59.43	-71.83	-129.84	Other Items (Net)	37r
																Interest Rates	
Percent Per Annum	....	....	....	....	....	....	....	....	....	....	....	....	25.00	18.00	16.00	Discount Rate (End of Period)	60
	....	....	....	....	....	....	....	....	....	....	....	....	60.40	39.15	29.07	Interbank Market Rate	60bs
	....	....	....	....	....	....	....	....	....	....	....	673.60	151.42	32.67	27.89	Deposit Rate	60l
	....	....	....	....	....	....	....	....	....	....	....	853.50	203.68	49.62	39.41	Lending Rate	60p

Slovenia

961		1965	1966	1967	1968	1969	1970	1971	1972	1973	1974	1975	1976	1977	1978	1979
Prices, Production, Employment																*Index Numbers (1990=100):*
Producer Prices	63	....	....	....	....	....	....	....	....	....	....	....	....	....	....	....
Consumer Prices	64	....	....	....	....	....	....	....	....	....	....	....	....	....	....	....
Wages	65	....	....	....	....	....	....	....	....	....	....	....	....	....	....	....
Industrial Production	66	....	....	....	....	....	....	....	....	....	....	....	....	....	....	....
Employment	67	....	....	....	....	....	....	....	....	....	....	....	....	....	....	....
International Transactions																*Millions of US Dollars*
Exports	70..*d*	....	....	....	....	....	....	....	....	....	....	....	....	....	....	....
Imports, cif	71..*d*	....	....	....	....	....	....	....	....	....	....	....	....	....	....	....
Balance of Payments																*Millions of US Dollars:*
Goods: Exports f.o.b.	78aa *d*	....	....	....	....	....	....	....	....	....	....	....	....	....	....	....
Goods: Imports f.o.b.	78ab *d*	....	....	....	....	....	....	....	....	....	....	....	....	....	....	....
Trade Balance	78ac *d*	....	....	....	....	....	....	....	....	....	....	....	....	....	....	....
Services: Credit	78ad *d*	....	....	....	....	....	....	....	....	....	....	....	....	....	....	....
Services: Debit	78ae *d*	....	....	....	....	....	....	....	....	....	....	....	....	....	....	....
Balance on Goods and Services	78af *d*	....	....	....	....	....	....	....	....	....	....	....	....	....	....	....
Income: Credit	78ag *d*	....	....	....	....	....	....	....	....	....	....	....	....	....	....	....
Income: Debit	78ah *d*	....	....	....	....	....	....	....	....	....	....	....	....	....	....	....
Balance on Goods, Serv., & Inc.	78ai *d*	....	....	....	....	....	....	....	....	....	....	....	....	....	....	....
Current Transfers, n.i.e.: Credit	78aj *d*	....	....	....	....	....	....	....	....	....	....	....	....	....	....	....
Current Transfers: Debit	78ak *d*	....	....	....	....	....	....	....	....	....	....	....	....	....	....	....
Current Account, n.i.e.	78al *d*	....	....	....	....	....	....	....	....	....	....	....	....	....	....	....
Capital Account, n.i.e.: Credit	78ba *d*	....	....	....	....	....	....	....	....	....	....	....	....	....	....	....
Capital Account: Debit	78bb *d*	....	....	....	....	....	....	....	....	....	....	....	....	....	....	....
Capital Account, n.i.e.	78bc *d*	....	....	....	....	....	....	....	....	....	....	....	....	....	....	....
Direct Investment Abroad	78bd *d*	....	....	....	....	....	....	....	....	....	....	....	....	....	....	....
Dir. Invest. in Rep. Econ., n.i.e.	78be *d*	....	....	....	....	....	....	....	....	....	....	....	....	....	....	....
Portfolio Investment Assets	78bf *d*	....	....	....	....	....	....	....	....	....	....	....	....	....	....	....
Portfolio Investment Liab., n.i.e.	78bg *d*	....	....	....	....	....	....	....	....	....	....	....	....	....	....	....
Other Investment Assets	78bh *d*	....	....	....	....	....	....	....	....	....	....	....	....	....	....	....
Other Investment Liab., n.i.e.	78bi *d*	....	....	....	....	....	....	....	....	....	....	....	....	....	....	....
Financial Account, n.i.e.	78bj *d*	....	....	....	....	....	....	....	....	....	....	....	....	....	....	....
Net Errors and Omissions	78ca *d*	....	....	....	....	....	....	....	....	....	....	....	....	....	....	....
Overall Balance	78cb *d*	....	....	....	....	....	....	....	....	....	....	....	....	....	....	....
Reserves and Related Items	79da *d*	....	....	....	....	....	....	....	....	....	....	....	....	....	....	....
Reserve Assets	79db *d*	....	....	....	....	....	....	....	....	....	....	....	....	....	....	....
Use of Fund Credit and Loans	79dc *d*	....	....	....	....	....	....	....	....	....	....	....	....	....	....	....
Liabs.Constit.For.Auth.Reserves	79dd *d*	....	....	....	....	....	....	....	....	....	....	....	....	....	....	....
Exceptional Financing	79de *d*	....	....	....	....	....	....	....	....	....	....	....	....	....	....	....
Government Finance																*Billions of Tolars:*
Deficit (-) or Surplus	80	....	....	....	....	....	....	....	....	....	....	....	....	....	....	....
Revenue	81	....	....	....	....	....	....	....	....	....	....	....	....	....	....	....
Grants Received	81z	....	....	....	....	....	....	....	....	....	....	....	....	....	....	....
Expenditure	82	....	....	....	....	....	....	....	....	....	....	....	....	....	....	....
Lending Minus Repayments	83	....	....	....	....	....	....	....	....	....	....	....	....	....	....	....
Financing																
Domestic	84a	....	....	....	....	....	....	....	....	....	....	....	....	....	....	....
Foreign	85a	....	....	....	....	....	....	....	....	....	....	....	....	....	....	....
Use of Cash Balances	87	....	....	....	....	....	....	....	....	....	....	....	....	....	....	....
National Accounts																*Billions of Tolars*
Exports of Goods & Services	90c	....	....	....	....	....	....	....	....	....	....	....	....	....	....	....
Government Consumption	91f	....	....	....	....	....	....	....	....	....	....	....	....	....	....	....
Gross Fixed Capital Formation	93e	....	....	....	....	....	....	....	....	....	....	....	....	....	....	....
Increase/Decrease(-) in Stocks	93i	....	....	....	....	....	....	....	....	....	....	....	....	....	....	....
Private Consumption	96f	....	....	....	....	....	....	....	....	....	....	....	....	....	....	....
Imports of Goods & Services	98c	....	....	....	....	....	....	....	....	....	....	....	....	....	....	....
Gross Domestic Product	99b	....	....	....	....	....	....	....	....	....	....	....	....	....	....	....
Gross Dom. Prod. 1990 Prices	99b. *p*	....	....	....	....	....	....	....	....	....	....	....	....	....	....	....
GDP Deflator (1990=100)	99bi *p*	....	....	....	....	....	....	....	....	....	....	....	....	....	....	....
																Millions:
Population	99z	....	....	....	....	....	....	....	....	....	....	....	....	....	....	....

Slovenia

961

	1980	1981	1982	1983	1984	1985	1986	1987	1988	1989	1990	1991	1992	1993	1994	
Period Averages																**Prices, Production, Employment**
	....	....	....	....	....	....	....	....	....	....	....	....	707.4	860.1	1,012.5	Producer Prices 63
	....	....	....	....	....	....	....	....	....	....	....	....	658.5	868.6	1,040.4	Consumer Prices 64
	....	....	....	....	....	....	....	....	....	....	....	....	545.5	825.7	1,058.5	Wages 65
	....	....	....	....	....	....	....	....	....	....	....	....	76.0	73.9	....	Industrial Production 66
	....	....	....	....	....	....	....	....	....	....	....	....	86.1	83.6	82.0	Employment 67
Millions of US Dollars																**International Transactions**
	....	....	....	....	....	....	....	....	....	....	....	....	....	6,088	6,825	Exports .... 70..*d*
	....	....	....	....	....	....	....	....	....	....	....	....	....	6,498	7,334	Imports, cif .... 71..*d*
Minus Sign Indicates Debit																Balance of Payments
	....	....	....	....	....	....	....	....	....	....	....	....	6,683.0	6,082.9	6,806.3	Goods: Exports f.o.b. 78aa*d*
	....	....	....	....	....	....	....	....	....	....	....	....	-5,891.9	-6,237.1	-6,952.5	Goods: Imports f.o.b. 78ab*d*
	....	....	....	....	....	....	....	....	....	....	....	....	791.1	-154.2	-146.2	Trade Balance 78ac*d*
	....	....	....	....	....	....	....	....	....	....	....	....	1,219.4	1,402.9	1,693.2	Services: Credit 78ad*d*
	....	....	....	....	....	....	....	....	....	....	....	....	-1,038.8	-1,049.5	-1,065.4	Services: Debit 78ae*d*
	....	....	....	....	....	....	....	....	....	....	....	....	971.7	199.2	481.6	Balance on Goods and Services 78af*d*
	....	....	....	....	....	....	....	....	....	....	....	....	69.9	114.8	128.0	Income: Credit 78ag*d*
	....	....	....	....	....	....	....	....	....	....	....	....	-161.3	-166.6	-167.2	Income: Debit 78ah*d*
	....	....	....	....	....	....	....	....	....	....	....	....	880.3	147.4	442.4	Balance on Goods, Serv., & Inc. 78ai*d*
	....	....	....	....	....	....	....	....	....	....	....	....	92.9	163.1	188.5	Current Transfers, n.i.e.: Credit 78aj*d*
	....	....	....	....	....	....	....	....	....	....	....	....	-47.1	-122.2	-138.5	Current Transfers: Debit 78ak*d*
	....	....	....	....	....	....	....	....	....	....	....	....	926.1	188.3	492.4	Current Account, n.i.e. 78al*d*
	....	....	....	....	....	....	....	....	....	....	....	....	—	6.7	3.4	Capital Account, n.i.e.: Credit 78ba*d*
	....	....	....	....	....	....	....	....	....	....	....	....	—	-2.6	-4.2	Capital Account: Debit 78bb*d*
	....	....	....	....	....	....	....	....	....	....	....	....	—	4.1	-.8	Capital Account, n.i.e. 78bc*d*
	....	....	....	....	....	....	....	....	....	....	....	....	2.0	1.3	15.8	Direct Investment Abroad 78bd*d*
	....	....	....	....	....	....	....	....	....	....	....	....	111.0	110.8	72.4	Dir. Invest. in Rep. Econ., n.i.e. 78be*d*
	....	....	....	....	....	....	....	....	....	....	....	....	-8.9	-1.4	-84.1	Portfolio Investment Assets 78bf*d*
	....	....	....	....	....	....	....	....	....	....	....	....	—	4.5	51.6	Portfolio Investment Liab., n.i.e. 78bg*d*
	....	....	....	....	....	....	....	....	....	....	....	....	-157.6	-297.7	-248.0	Other Investment Assets 78bh*d*
	....	....	....	....	....	....	....	....	....	....	....	....	40.4	118.3	284.0	Other Investment Liab., n.i.e. 78bi*d*
	....	....	....	....	....	....	....	....	....	....	....	....	-13.1	-64.2	91.7	Financial Account, n.i.e. 78bj*d*
	....	....	....	....	....	....	....	....	....	....	....	....	-280.5	-3.4	64.2	Net Errors and Omissions 78ca*d*
	....	....	....	....	....	....	....	....	....	....	....	....	632.5	124.8	647.5	Overall Balance 78cb*d*
	....	....	....	....	....	....	....	....	....	....	....	....	-632.5	-124.8	-647.5	Reserves and Related Items 79da*d*
	....	....	....	....	....	....	....	....	....	....	....	....	-632.5	-111.0	-642.3	Reserve Assets 79db*d*
	....	....	....	....	....	....	....	....	....	....	....	....	—	-13.8	-5.2	Use of Fund Credit and Loans 79dc*d*
	....	....	....	....	....	....	....	....	....	....	....	....	—	—	—	Liabs.Constit.For.Auth.Reserves 79dd*d*
	....	....	....	....	....	....	....	....	....	....	....	....	—	—	—	Exceptional Financing 79de*d*
Year Ending December 31																**Government Finance**
	....	....	....	....	....	....	....	....	....	....	....	....	....	5.3	-5.1	Deficit (-) or Surplus 80
	....	....	....	....	....	....	....	....	....	....	....	....	....	611.3	768.5	Revenue 81
	....	....	....	....	....	....	....	....	....	....	....	....	....	—	—	Grants Received 81z
	....	....	....	....	....	....	....	....	....	....	....	....	....	606.0	773.6	Expenditure 82
	....	....	....	....	....	....	....	....	....	....	....	....	....	—	—	Lending Minus Repayments 83
																Financing
	....	....	....	....	....	....	....	....	....	....	....	....	....	-3.3	-5.4	Domestic 84a
	....	....	....	....	....	....	....	....	....	....	....	....	....	6.8	3.8	Foreign 85a
	....	....	....	....	....	....	....	....	....	....	....	....	....	-8.9	6.7	Use of Cash Balances 87
Billions of Tolars																**National Accounts**
	....	....	....	....	....	....	....	....	....	....	....	....	....	846.8	....	Exports of Goods & Services 90c
	....	....	....	....	....	....	....	....	....	....	....	....	....	306.3	....	Government Consumption 91f
	....	....	....	....	....	....	....	....	....	....	....	....	....	254.4	....	Gross Fixed Capital Formation 93e
	....	....	....	....	....	....	....	....	....	....	....	....	....	14.9	....	Increase/Decrease(-) in Stocks 93i
	....	....	....	....	....	....	....	....	....	....	....	....	....	767.2	....	Private Consumption 96f
	....	....	....	....	....	....	....	....	....	....	....	....	....	-796.6	....	Imports of Goods & Services 98c
	....	....	....	....	....	....	....	....	....	....	....	....	....	1,414.7	....	Gross Domestic Product 99b
	....	....	....	....	....	....	....	....	....	....	....	....	....	691.2	....	Gross Dom. Prod. 1990 Prices 99b.*p*
	....	....	....	....	....	....	....	....	....	....	....	....	....	204.7	....	GDP Deflator (1990=100) 99bi*p*
Midyear Estimates																
	....	....	....	....	....	....	....	....	....	....	....	2.00	1.99	1.99	....	Population 99z

Solomon Islands
813

		1965	1966	1967	1968	1969	1970	1971	1972	1973	1974	1975	1976	1977	1978	1979
Exchange Rates													*Solomon Islands Dollars per SDR:*			
Official Rate	aa	.8941	1.8977	.8921	.9009	.8945	.8969	.9116	.8515	.8107	.9226	.9312	1.0694	1.0642	1.1324	1.1306
													Solomon Islands Dollars per US Dollar:			
Official Rate	ae	.8941	1.8977	.8921	.9009	.8945	.8969	.8396	.7843	.6720	.7536	.7955	.9205	.8761	.8692	.8582
Official Rate	rf	.8929	.8929	.8929	.8929	.8929	.8929	.8816	.8373^e	.7041	.6981^e	.7639	.8183	.9018	.8737	.8660
													Index Numbers (1990=100):			
Official Rate	ahx	282.0^e	281.8^e	281.8^e	281.6^e	281.3^e	282.1^e	168.6	301.9^e	358.9^e	363.2^e	331.1	309.6	280.3	289.3	291.9
Nominal Effective Exchange Rate	nec	....	....	....	....	....	....	....	....	....	....	....	....	....	....	266.6
Real Effective Exchange Rate	rec	....	....	....	....	....	....	....	....	....	....	....	....	....	....	144.8
Fund Position															*Millions of SDRs:*	
Quota	2f.s														2.10	2.10
SDRs	1b.s														—	.04
Reserve Position in the Fund	1c.s														—	.43
Total Fund Cred.&Loans Outstg.	2tl															
International Liquidity												*Millions of US Dollars Unless Otherwise Indicated:*				
Total Reserves minus Gold	1l.d													2.87	29.19	36.96
SDRs	1b.d													—	—	.05
Reserve Position in the Fund	1c.d													—	—	.57
Foreign Exchange	1d.d													2.87	29.19	36.34
Deposit Money Banks: Assets	7a.d										6.2	7.3	7.8	12.5	.7	1.1
Liabilities	7b.d								1.8	1.9	2.2	2.3	1.8	1.9	1.9	1.2
Monetary Authorities													*Millions of Solomon Islands Dollars:*			
Foreign Assets	11														25.37	31.72
Claims on Central Government	12a															
Claims on Nonfin.Pub.Enterprises	12c															
Claims on Deposit Money Banks	12e															
Reserve Money	14														24.20	26.91
of which: Currency Outside DMBs	14a														3.85	4.84
Foreign Liabilities	16c														.16	.16
Central Government Deposits	16d														.65	1.81
Capital Accounts	17a														.75	3.03
Other Items (Net)	17r														−.18	−.45
Deposit Money Banks													*Millions of Solomon Islands Dollars:*			
Reserves	20														19.18	24.24
Foreign Assets	21														.64	.97
Claims on Central Government	22a														.09	.53
Claims on Nonfin.Pub.Enterprises	22c															
Claims on Private Sector	22d														5.70	13.14
Demand Deposits	24														3.97	6.15
Time and Savings Deposits	25														19.48	28.57
Foreign Liabilities	26c														1.61	1.03
Central Government Deposits	26d														1.29	3.03
Credit from Monetary Authorities	26g														.20	.16
Capital Accounts	27a															
Other Items (Net)	27r														−.94	−.05
Monetary Survey													*Millions of Solomon Islands Dollars:*			
Foreign Assets (Net)	31n														24.24	31.50
Domestic Credit	32														3.85	8.83
Claims on Central Govt. (Net)	32an														−1.85	−4.31
Claims on Nonfin.Pub.Enterprises	32c														....	....
Claims on Private Sector	32d														5.70	13.14
Claims on Other Financial Insts.	32f															
Money	34														7.82	10.99
Quasi-Money	35														19.48	28.57
Money Market Instruments	36aa															
Restricted Deposits	36b														....	....
Other Items (Net)	37r														.79	.77
Money plus Quasi-Money	35l														27.29	39.56
Other Banking Institutions													*Millions of Solomon Islands Dollars:*			
Reserves	40													.90	.81	3.61
Claims on Private Sector	42d													1.22	4.76	7.79
Quasi-Monetary Liabilities	45															
Central Govt. Lending Funds	46f													1.48	5.27	7.19
Credit from Monetary Section	46h													—	—	2.84
Credit from Nonbank Fin. Insts.	46i													—	—	.50
Other Items (Net)	47r													.64	.30	.88
Banking Survey													*Millions of Solomon Islands Dollars:*			
Foreign Assets (Net)	51n														24.24	31.50
Domestic Credit	52														8.61	16.63
Claims on Central Govt. (Net)	52an														−1.85	−4.31
Claims on Nonfin.Pub.Enterprises	52c															
Claims on Private Sector	52d														10.46	20.93
Liquid Liabilities	55l														26.59	38.88
Money Market Instruments	56aa														....	....
Restricted Deposits	56b															
Central Govt. Lending Funds	56f													1.48	5.27	7.19
Other Items (Net)	57r														.99	2.06
Nonbank Financial Institutions													*Millions of Solomon Islands Dollars:*			
Claims on Banking System	40.m															
Claims on Central Government	42a.m															
Claims on Nonfin.Pub.Enterprises	42c.m															
Claims on Private Sector	42d.m															
Capital Accounts	47a.m															
Other Items (Net)	47r.m															

Solomon Islands

	1980	1981	1982	1983	1984	1985	1986	1987	1988	1989	1990	1991	1992	1993	1994		
	End of Period															**Exchange Rates**	
	1.0172	1.0346	1.1527	1.2788	1.3170	1.7714	2.4299	2.8009	2.8505	3.1500	3.7184	3.9978	4.2622	4.4611	4.8597	Official Rate	aa
	End of Period (ae) Period Average (rf)																
	.7975	.8889	1.0449	1.2214	1.3435	1.6126	1.9865	1.9743	2.1182	2.3969	2.6137	2.7949	3.0998	3.2478	3.3289	Official Rate	ae
	.8298	.8702	.9711	1.1486	1.2737	1.4808	1.7415	2.0033	2.0825	2.2932	2.5288	2.7148	2.9281	3.1877	3.2914	Official Rate	rf
	Period Averages																
	304.8	290.9	261.6	220.4	198.6	170.5	145.8	126.1	121.4	110.4	100.0	93.2	86.2	79.3	76.8	Official Rate	ah x
	278.6	280.3	273.8	243.7	233.0	213.5	163.8	131.8	120.1	112.6	100.0	92.6	84.0	78.5	73.5	Nominal Effective Exchange Rate	ne c
	153.3	163.5	168.3	152.6	154.1	140.6	118.9	102.9	105.7	108.9	100.0	101.9	99.3	98.7	....	Real Effective Exchange Rate	re c
	End of Period															**Fund Position**	
	3.20	3.20	3.20	5.00	5.00	5.00	5.00	5.00	5.00	5.00	5.00	5.00	7.50	7.50	7.50	Quota	2f. s
	.97	1.22	1.24	1.65	1.34	.77	1.29	.17	—	.05	.25	.07	.04	.03	.01	SDRs	1b. s
	.72	.01	.02	.47	.48	.51	.51	.52	.52	.53	.53	.54	.54	.54	.54	Reserve Position in the Fund	1c. s
	—	.80	2.40	3.36	3.16	2.76	2.83	1.55	1.25	1.09	.47	—	—	—	—	Total Fund Cred.&Loans Outstg.	2tl
	End of Period															**International Liquidity**	
	29.60	21.59	37.23	47.33	44.70	35.61	29.57	36.75	39.62	26.16	17.60	8.54	23.50	20.07	....	Total Reserves minus Gold	1l. d
	1.24	1.42	1.37	1.73	1.31	.85	1.58	.24	—	.07	.36	.10	.06	.04	.01	SDRs	1b. d
	.92	.01	.02	.49	.47	.56	.62	.74	.70	.70	.75	.77	.74	.74	.79	Reserve Position in the Fund	1c. d
	27.45	20.16	35.84	45.11	42.92	34.20	27.37	35.77	38.92	25.40	16.49	7.67	22.70	19.29	....	Foreign Exchange	1d. d
	1.0	1.0	.8	1.7	1.6	2.5	1.9	3.4	2.5	.5	1.2	2.3	2.1	2.1	3.6	Deposit Money Banks: Assets	7a. d
	2.1	3.1	2.5	2.7	1.4	2.1	1.7	2.8	1.2	1.3	3.8	2.9	1.7	1.7	4.8	Liabilities	7b. d
	Approximately End of Period															**Monetary Authorities**	
	23.61	I 19.19	38.91	55.57	59.04	46.07	58.79	71.07	82.95	62.47	44.85	23.59	73.45	65.07	57.78	Foreign Assets	11
	.13	.42	3.23	3.27	I 3.35	10.00	5.90	10.14	13.94	21.00	31.70	58.01	37.92	45.39	64.47	Claims on Central Government	12a
	....	....	....	....	.50	.50	.50	.58	1.25	6.25	6.65	5.59	4.05	4.05	2.89	Claims on Nonfin.Pub.Enterprises	12c
	....	.20	.70	—	—	7.80	6.55	.10	.15	6.76	.06	.03	—	—	4.20	Claims on Deposit Money Banks	12e
	17.36	9.69	15.58	20.73	28.79	22.39	22.98	23.83	32.21	27.01	31.02	42.11	42.06	46.97	61.48	Reserve Money	14
	5.66	6.42	7.15	9.30	13.75	13.89	13.58	16.84	20.21	22.65	25.22	27.80	30.83	42.11	50.23	*of which: Currency Outside DMBs*	14a
	.24	I 5.64	19.09	28.97	18.32	22.29	18.44	8.92	5.90	10.40	3.56	1.16	1.67	5.70	1.39	Foreign Liabilities	16c
	I 3.13	.43	2.19	6.38	3.57	4.82	5.88	25.82	32.85	23.24	8.56	1.80	4.85	5.98	10.67	Central Government Deposits	16d
	2.88	5.48	8.54	12.11	18.16	19.62	29.12	35.70	42.51	46.94	49.13	52.16	50.99	52.31	57.39	Capital Accounts	17a
	-.06	-1.43	-2.56	-9.35	I -5.94	-4.74	-4.60	-11.72	-10.18	-10.72	-10.08	-11.55	15.84	2.38	-4.49	Other Items (Net)	17r
	Approximately End of Period															**Deposit Money Banks**	
	11.59	2.20	7.41	9.42	16.01	7.70	9.40	7.16	12.28	4.41	5.78	14.06	6.64	4.86	12.50	Reserves	20
	.82	.85	.85	2.04	2.12	3.96	3.81	6.70	5.20	1.25	3.13	6.50	6.2	6.91	11.88	Foreign Assets	21
	1.24	1.68	3.05	5.83	4.62	8.10	11.60	25.79	32.64	31.97	39.36	69.94	105.47	130.86	152.14	Claims on Central Government	22a
	5.15	5.78	5.26	5.13	5.90	1.05	.23	.06	.86	1.58	6.89	6.13	1.46	2.71	.91	Claims on Nonfin.Pub.Enterprises	22c
	17.34	21.39	22.45	20.56	29.88	47.10	51.62	55.02	69.52	92.23	82.31	75.64	72.22	84.22	107.06	Claims on Private Sector	22d
	I 9.48	7.81	8.63	9.13	15.57	14.45	16.80	20.39	28.82	28.25	39.23	51.74	74.08	81.82	112.65	Demand Deposits	24
	I 23.87	17.92	23.90	29.16	35.91	37.59	41.65	59.76	79.04	76.68	75.65	94.02	111.12	125.88	149.70	Time and Savings Deposits	25
	I 1.69	2.73	2.59	3.34	1.93	3.38	3.33	5.51	2.54	3.14	9.97	8.05	5.32	5.67	16.05	Foreign Liabilities	26c
	I 2.54	3.08	1.76	1.05	1.53	.33	2.03	2.03	4.08	6.01	2.21	7.94	4.31	5.17	5.24	Central Government Deposits	26d
	I —	.20	.70	—	—	6.40	6.55	.10	.15	5.76	.06	.03	—	—	—	Credit from Monetary Authorities	26g
	—	—	2.97	—	5.68	8.83	9.26	10.04	10.29	13.62	16.57	18.39	22.72	32.30	30.87	Capital Accounts	27a
	-1.45	.15	-1.54	.30	-2.09	I -3.07	-2.95	-3.09	-4.42	-2.03	-6.23	-7.90	-25.16	-21.28	-30.02	Other Items (Net)	27r
	Approximately End of Period															**Monetary Survey**	
	22.49	11.67	18.07	25.29	40.91	24.36	40.83	63.34	79.72	50.18	34.45	20.88	73.08	60.61	52.21	Foreign Assets (Net)	31n
	18.19	25.75	30.04	27.36	39.15	62.59	63.37	71.29	91.99	129.95	162.28	210.32	220.60	256.67	314.12	Domestic Credit	32
	I -4.30	-1.42	2.33	1.67	2.87	12.95	9.59	8.08	9.65	23.71	60.29	118.21	134.20	165.10	200.70	Claims on Central Govt. (Net)	32an
	5.15	5.78	5.26	5.13	6.40	1.55	.81	1.31	7.11	8.23	12.47	10.18	5.52	5.60	5.11	Claims on Nonfin.Pub.Enterprises	32c
	17.34	21.39	22.45	20.56	29.88	47.10	51.62	55.02	69.52	92.23	82.31	75.64	72.22	84.22	107.06	Claims on Private Sector	32d
	....	....	....	....	....	.64	1.22	6.89	5.71	5.73	6.57	6.01	8.18	1.34	....	Claims on Other Financial Insts.	32f
	15.14	14.23	15.78	18.43	28.32	28.33	30.38	37.23	49.03	50.90	64.46	79.54	104.91	123.93	162.88	Money	34
	23.87	17.92	23.90	29.16	35.91	37.59	41.65	59.76	79.04	76.68	75.65	94.02	111.12	125.88	149.70	Quasi-Money	35
	.03	.04	.10	.31	.41	.43	.64	.61	.49	.56	.26	.16	.13	.49	.54	Money Market Instruments	36aa
	....	....	....	—	5.44	.07	.09	.10	.86	.03	2.70	.34	.14	1.02	.83	Restricted Deposits	36b
	1.64	5.23	8.34	4.75	9.99	20.53	31.45	36.93	42.29	51.96	53.65	57.14	77.36	65.95	52.38	Other Items (Net)	37r
	39.01	32.15	39.68	47.59	64.23	65.92	72.03	96.98	128.07	127.58	140.11	173.56	216.03	249.81	312.58	Money plus Quasi-Money	35l
	End of Period															**Other Banking Institutions**	
	4.00	3.47	5.78	8.22	8.36	7.59	8.17	I 12.62	....	....	I 9.77	14.57	17.05	11.35	....	Reserves	40
	12.32	17.00	18.06	24.35	26.17	31.28	33.12	I 40.81	....	....	18.17	20.42	54.50	65.65	....	Claims on Private Sector	42d
	....	....	....	....	....	....	....	.36	.97	2.57	2.94	3.34	5.96	9.12	10.00	Quasi-Monetary Liabilities	45
	11.92	15.26	20.73	24.68	25.75	25.79	26.11	I 28.65	....	....	6.71	6.50	6.47	12.22	....	Central Govt. Lending Funds	46f
	2.93	2.87	3.51	5.44	.57	.64	1.12	7.16	....	....	6.75	9.98	9.38	6.85	....	Credit from Monetary Section	46h
	.50	1.52	1.51	1.95	5.70	9.91	13.61	13.15	....	....	10.38	10.13	9.22	8.31	....	Credit from Nonbank Fin. Insts.	46i
	.98	.82	-1.91	.50	2.50	2.53	.45	I 4.11	....	....	1.06	5.10	39.31	40.51	....	Other Items (Net)	47r
	Approximately End of Period															**Banking Survey**	
	22.49	11.67	18.07	25.29	40.91	24.36	40.83	63.34	79.72	50.18	34.45	20.88	73.08	60.61	52.21	Foreign Assets (Net)	51n
	30.51	42.75	48.10	51.71	65.32	93.23	95.28	105.21	99.55	141.18	173.87	224.73	266.92	320.98	....	Domestic Credit	52
	-4.30	-1.42	2.33	1.67	2.87	12.95	9.59	8.08	9.65	23.71	60.29	118.21	134.20	165.10	200.70	Claims on Central Govt. (Net)	52an
	5.15	5.78	5.26	5.13	6.40	1.55	.81	1.31	7.11	8.23	12.47	10.18	5.52	5.60	5.11	Claims on Nonfin.Pub.Enterprises	52c
	29.66	38.39	40.51	44.90	56.05	78.38	84.74	I 95.83	82.79	109.18	100.47	96.06	126.72	149.88	....	Claims on Private Sector	52d
	38.24	32.07	39.51	47.36	63.67	65.63	70.95	I 95.13	....	....	140.87	173.52	217.46	255.14	....	Liquid Liabilities	55l
	.03	.04	.10	.31	.41	.43	.64	.61	.49	.56	.26	.16	.13	.49	.54	Money Market Instruments	56aa
	....	—	—	—	5.44	.07	.09	.10	.86	.03	2.70	.34	.14	1.02	.83	Restricted Deposits	56b
	11.92	15.26	20.73	24.68	25.75	25.79	26.11	28.65	5.00	4.74	6.71	6.50	6.47	12.22	....	Central Govt. Lending Funds	56f
	2.81	7.05	5.83	4.70	10.97	25.67	38.32	I 44.06	....	....	57.67	65.15	114.57	112.73	....	Other Items (Net)	57r
	End of Period															**Nonbank Financial Institutions**	
	5.75	6.12	9.52	11.34	13.45	13.85	18.98	23.28	24.49	25.22	26.23	35.31	30.87	30.04	34.35	Claims on Banking System	40.m
	1.25	2.68	4.88	7.41	12.66	18.24	21.47	25.04	28.66	31.81	29.51	38.61	49.14	68.00	73.98	Claims on Central Government	42a m
	1.00	1.25	.99	.97	1.96	2.76	2.43	5.46	5.74	8.40	12.20	11.14	17.75	23.72	39.95	Claims on Nonfin.Pub.Enterprises	42c m
	.69	.67	.73	.31	.42	.20	.27	.41	2.98	4.23	12.25	16.72	15.24	24.69	31.83	Claims on Private Sector	42d m
	8.88	11.54	16.73	22.37	30.79	39.28	50.12	62.42	74.05	90.20	105.71	129.45	153.64	187.03	223.57	Capital Accounts	47a m
	-.19	-.82	-.61	-2.34	-2.29	-4.23	-6.98	-8.23	-12.17	-20.55	-25.53	-27.66	-40.65	-40.58	-43.46	Other Items (Net)	47r m

Solomon Islands

813

		1965	1966	1967	1968	1969	1970	1971	1972	1973	1974	1975	1976	1977	1978	1979
Interest Rates																*Percent Per Annum*
Treasury Bill Rate	60c	…	…	…	…	…	…	…	…	…	…	…	…	…	…	…
Deposit Rate	60l	…	…	…	…	…	…	…	…	…	…	…	…	…	…	…
Lending Rate	60p	…	…	…	…	…	…	…	…	…	…	…	…	…	…	…
Government Bond Yield	61	…	…	…	…	…	…	…	…	…	…	…	…	…	…	…
Prices and Production																*Index Numbers (1990=100):*
Consumer Prices	64	…	…	…	…	…	…	15.1	16.1	16.6	19.8	ɪ21.8	22.7	24.6	26.2	28.3
Copra Production	66ag	79.1	75.2	75.8	66.2	79.7	78.1	82.7	67.2	51.1	90.6	84.0	75.6	92.7	87.4	106.7
Fish Catch	66al	…	…	…	…	…	…	14.5	28.0	22.7	32.1	24.9	55.0	42.0	60.8	83.1
International Transactions													*Millions of Solomon Islands Dollars*			
Exports	70	4.84	3.75	5.09	5.54	6.46	7.13	9.08	9.14	9.55	18.25	11.82	19.95	29.61	32.95	59.26
Imports, cif	71	7.56	9.80	9.43	10.58	9.83	11.52	13.25	13.86	12.94	18.82	25.04	24.25	29.62	37.05	60.96
Imports, fob	71.v	6.58	8.52	8.20	9.20	8.54	10.02	11.52	12.05	11.26	16.37	21.77	21.09	25.75	30.88	50.80
																1990=100
Volume of Exports (1985=100)	72	…	…	…	…	…	40.9	48.1	50.3	41.9	46.1	44.6	50.0	51.2	60.1	76.6
Unit Value of Exports	74	…	…	…	…	…	18.3	19.8	ɪ16.3	19.8	36.9	24.0	37.5	54.9	52.0	74.6
Balance of Payments														*Millions of US Dollars:*		
Goods: Exports f.o.b.	78aa d	…	…	…	…	…	…	…	…	…	…	15.45	24.32	32.82	35.03	68.48
Goods: Imports f.o.b.	78ab d	…	…	…	…	…	…	…	…	…	…	−28.54	−25.79	−28.61	−35.37	−58.43
Trade Balance	78ac d	…	…	…	…	…	…	…	…	…	…	−13.09	−1.47	4.21	−.34	10.05
Services: Credit	78ad d	…	…	…	…	…	…	…	…	…	…	2.49	3.06	3.33	5.27	5.77
Services: Debit	78ae d	…	…	…	…	…	…	…	…	…	…	−9.82	−9.04	−10.65	−17.40	−20.79
Balance on Goods and Services	78af d	…	…	…	…	…	…	…	…	…	…	−20.42	−7.45	−3.10	−12.48	−4.97
Income: Credit	78ag d	…	…	…	…	…	…	…	…	…	…	…	…	…	…	…
Income: Debit	78ah d	…	…	…	…	…	…	…	…	…	…	−1.96	−3.91	−4.10	−3.43	−4.62
Balance on Goods, Serv., & Inc.	78ai d	…	…	…	…	…	…	…	…	…	…	−22.39	−11.37	−7.21	−15.91	−9.58
Current Transfers, n.i.e.: Credit	78aj d	…	…	…	…	…	…	…	…	…	…	9.82	13.08	12.97	19.23	19.86
Current Transfers: Debit	78ak d	…	…	…	…	…	…	…	…	…	…	…	…	…	…	…
Current Account, n.i.e.	78al d	…	…	…	…	…	…	…	…	…	…	−12.57	1.71	5.77	3.32	10.28
Capital Account, n.i.e.: Credit	78ba d	…	…	…	…	…	…	…	…	…	…	—	—	—	—	—
Capital Account: Debit	78bb d	…	…	…	…	…	…	…	…	…	…	—	—	—	—	—
Capital Account, n.i.e.	78bc d	…	…	…	…	…	…	…	…	…	…	—	—	—	—	—
Direct Investment Abroad	78bd d	…	…	…	…	…	…	…	…	…	…	—	—	—	—	—
Dir. Invest. in Rep. Econ., n.i.e.	78be d	…	…	…	…	…	…	…	…	…	…	7.85	4.89	4.44	4.58	3.46
Portfolio Investment Assets	78bf d	…	…	…	…	…	…	…	…	…	…	—	—	—	—	—
Portfolio Investment Liab., n.i.e.	78bg d	…	…	…	…	…	…	…	…	…	…	—	—	—	—	—
Other Investment Assets	78bh d	…	…	…	…	…	…	…	…	…	…	—	—	—	—	.58
Other Investment Liab., n.i.e.	78bi d	…	…	…	…	…	…	…	…	…	…	—	—	2.88	1.60	2.31
Financial Account, n.i.e.	78bj d	…	…	…	…	…	…	…	…	…	…	7.85	4.89	7.32	6.18	6.35
Net Errors and Omissions	78ca d	…	…	…	…	…	…	…	…	…	…	6.02	−4.77	−6.21	5.72	−9.05
Overall Balance	78cb d	…	…	…	…	…	…	…	…	…	…	1.31	1.83	6.88	15.22	7.57
Reserves and Related Items	79da d	…	…	…	…	…	…	…	…	…	…	−1.31	−1.83	−6.88	−15.22	−7.57
Reserve Assets	79db d	…	…	…	…	…	…	…	…	…	…	−1.31	−1.83	−6.88	−15.22	−7.54
Use of Fund Credit and Loans	79dc d	…	…	…	…	…	…	…	…	…	…	—	—	—	—	−.04
Liabs.Constit.For.Auth.Reserves	79dd d	…	…	…	…	…	…	…	…	…	…	—	—	—	—	—
Exceptional Financing	79de d	…	…	…	…	…	…	…	…	…	…	—	—	—	—	—
Government Finance													*Millions of Solomon Islands Dollars:*			
Deficit (-) or Surplus	80	…	…	…	…	…	…	…	…	…	…	.04	.03	−.63	.72	−2.94
Revenue	81	…	…	…	…	…	…	…	…	…	…	6.82	8.28	11.05	13.45	20.93
Grants Received	81z	…	…	…	…	…	…	…	…	…	…	6.23	8.51	8.90	14.68	11.39
Expenditure	82	…	…	…	…	…	…	…	…	…	…	12.87	16.29	19.48	27.61	31.91
Lending Minus Repayments	83	…	…	…	…	…	…	…	…	…	…	.14	.47	1.10	−.20	3.35
Financing																
Net Borrowing: Domestic	84a	…	…	…	…	…	…	…	…	…	…	.01	−.04	−.01	−.01	2.11
Foreign	85a	…	…	…	…	…	…	…	…	…	…	.13	.06	.17	.69	2.03
Use of Cash Balances	87	…	…	…	…	…	…	…	…	…	…	−.18	−.05	.47	−1.40	−1.20
Debt: Domestic	88a	…	…	…	…	…	…	…	…	…	…	.09	.08	.07	.06	…
Foreign	89a	…	…	…	…	…	…	…	…	…	…	.59	.64	.79	1.51	…
National Accounts													*Millions of Solomon Islands Dollars*			
Exports of Goods & Services	90c	…	…	…	…	…	7.1	9.1	9.1	9.6	18.3	11.8	20.0	29.6	30.6	60.2
Government Consumption	91f	…	…	…	…	…	5.5	5.1	5.5	…	…	…	…	…	…	…
Gross Fixed Capital Formation	93e	…	…	…	…	…	4.2	7.2	7.4	…	…	…	…	…	…	…
Increase/Decrease(-) in Stocks	93i	…	…	…	…	…	…	…	…	…	…	…	…	…	…	…
Private Consumption	96f	…	…	…	…	…	23.3	24.5	23.6	…	…	…	…	…	85.0	103.0
Imports of Goods & Services	98c	…	…	…	…	…	−10.0	−11.5	−12.1	−11.3	−16.4	−21.8	−21.1	−25.8	−30.9	−50.5
Gross Domestic Product	99b	…	…	…	…	25.7	28.6	30.5	31.7	35.6	50.9	49.5	59.0	73.5	85.8	112.7
Gross Dom. Prod. 1985 Prices	99b.p	…	…	…	…	…	…	…	…	…	…	…	…	…	…	…
GDP Deflator (1985=100)	99bi p	…	…	…	…	…	…	…	…	…	…	…	…	…	…	…
																Millions:
Population	99z	.14	.15	.15	.16	.16	.16	.17	.18	.18	.19	.19	.20	.20	.21	.22

Other Banking Institutions: ɪ Beginning in December 1989, includes data for the credit unions.
Banking Survey: ɪ See note to section 40.

Solomon Islands

	1980	1981	1982	1983	1984	1985	1986	1987	1988	1989	1990	1991	1992	1993	1994		
Percent Per Annum																**Interest Rates**	
	....	5.83	7.50	8.92	9.00	9.58	12.00	11.33	11.00	11.00	11.00	13.71	13.50	12.15	11.25	Treasury Bill Rate	60c
	....	6.23	6.92	8.38	8.00	8.73	10.50	10.67	10.23	10.46	10.50	10.50	12.00	9.77	9.00	Deposit Rate	60l
	....	9.00	10.58	11.50	12.00	12.83	15.13	17.33	18.00	18.00	18.00	19.46	19.75	17.80	15.72	Lending Rate	60p
	....	10.00	11.00	11.00	11.00	12.00	13.00	12.33	12.00	12.44	12.75	12.92	13.00	13.00	13.00	Government Bond Yield	61
Period Averages																**Prices and Production**	
	32.0	37.2	42.1	44.7	49.6	54.4	61.8	68.5	80.0	92.0	I100.0	115.1	118.3	138.7	157.6	Consumer Prices	64
	92.6	106.9	102.1	90.2	135.2	133.0	100.5	86.2	92.9	110.7	100.0	68.5	72.3	....	....	Copra Production	66ag
	79.8	88.8	71.8	120.9	125.1	108.3	154.0	112.9	146.0	128.7	100.0	132.3	149.0	....	....	Fish Catch	66al
Millions of Solomon Islands Dollars																**International Transactions**	
	61.28	57.56	56.56	71.20	118.56	103.81	114.90	128.30	170.57	171.45	178.11	225.90	297.40	301.10	....	Exports	70
	73.77	79.30	68.92	84.76	100.57	123.20	125.19	162.08	203.30	262.50	238.97	299.60	285.90	321.10	....	Imports, cif	71
	61.48	66.08	57.43	70.63	83.81	102.67	104.33	135.07	169.41	218.75	199.14	249.67	238.25	267.58	....	Imports, fob	71.v
1990=100																	
	79.0	86.2	82.2	99.1	109.5	100.0	122.9	90.1	99.7	....	....	....	....	....	....	Volume of Exports (1985=100)	72
	80.3	64.4	65.7	67.2	100.6	95.2	67.0	79.5	96.3	122.2	100.0	54.3	....	....	....	Unit Value of Exports	74
Minus Sign Indicates Debit																**Balance of Payments**	
	73.27	66.19	58.28	61.99	93.11	70.98	63.85	63.20	81.92	74.70	70.11	83.43	101.74	....	....	Goods: Exports f.o.b.	78aa d
	−74.11	−75.85	−59.11	−61.47	−67.60	−71.85	−67.41	−69.49	−104.63	−94.28	−77.35	−91.98	−87.43	....	....	Goods: Imports f.o.b.	78ab d
	−.84	−9.65	−.82	.52	25.52	−.88	−3.56	−6.29	−22.71	−19.58	−7.24	−8.55	14.31	....	....	Trade Balance	78ac d
	11.69	12.99	13.70	15.15	9.50	9.39	16.65	21.03	21.99	26.51	25.35	31.61	36.03	....	....	Services: Credit	78ad d
	−27.96	−37.69	−36.97	−34.13	−38.63	−43.15	−49.90	−49.77	−66.22	−75.26	−78.69	−88.26	−78.04	....	....	Services: Debit	78ae d
	−17.11	−34.36	−24.10	−18.46	−3.61	−34.64	−36.81	−35.03	−66.94	−68.33	−60.58	−65.20	−27.70	....	....	Balance on Goods and Services	78af d
			2.37	1.83	5.02	3.58	3.33	3.29	3.55	3.88	2.33	1.36	.99	....	....	Income: Credit	78ag d
	−14.94	−3.91	−11.22	−10.19	−13.82	−8.64	−9.24	−11.03	−12.10	−11.77	−7.59	−10.39	−10.89	....	....	Income: Debit	78ah d
	−32.05	−38.27	−32.95	−26.82	−12.40	−39.71	−42.72	−42.77	−75.49	−76.22	−65.84	−74.22	−37.60	....	....	Balance on Goods, Serv., & Inc.	78ai d
	19.88	17.47	15.34	17.24	17.12	16.01	34.34	29.45	42.93	47.14	43.66	46.82	43.78	....	....	Current Transfers, n.i.e.: Credit	78aj d
		−5.75	−7.41	−5.05	−4.55	−4.12	−3.56	−3.49	−5.09	−4.14	−5.58	−8.44	−7.62	....	....	Current Transfers: Debit	78ak d
	−12.17	−26.55	−25.02	−14.63	.16	−27.82	−11.94	−16.81	−37.65	−33.23	−27.76	−35.84	−1.43	....	....	Current Account, n.i.e.	78al d
	—	—	—	—	—	—	—	—	—	—	—	—	—	....	....	Capital Account, n.i.e.: Credit	78ba d
	—	—	−1.03	−.96	−.86	−.95	−.52	−.35	−.38	−.17	−.16	−.26	−.44	....	....	Capital Account: Debit	78bb d
	—	—	−1.03	−.96	−.86	−.95	−.52	−.35	−.38	−.17	−.16	−.26	−.44	....	....	Capital Account, n.i.e.	78bc d
	—	—	—	—	—	—	—	—	—	—	—	—	—	....	....	Direct Investment Abroad	78bd d
	2.41	.23	1.03	.44	1.96	.68	3.10	10.48	1.68	11.60	10.44	14.51	14.17	....	....	Dir. Invest. in Rep. Econ., n.i.e.	78be d
	—	—	—	—	—	—	—	—	—	—	—	—	—	....	....	Portfolio Investment Assets	78bf d
	—	—	—	—	—	—	—	—	—	—	—	—	—	....	....	Portfolio Investment Liab., n.i.e.	78bg d
	−3.25	2.64	—	−1.04	−.16	−.27	−5.05	−11.28	18.82	−.74	−.75	−1.25	−.07	....	....	Other Investment Assets	78bh d
	3.98	3.91	13.39	13.84	−12.95	13.98	4.59	8.54	23.29	14.26	13.17	1.84	8.33	....	....	Other Investment Liab., n.i.e.	78bi d
	3.13	6.78	14.42	13.23	−11.15	14.38	2.64	7.74	43.79	25.12	22.86	15.10	22.44	....	....	Financial Account, n.i.e.	78bj d
	—	13.13	16.86	5.99	1.31	−.41	−8.47	2.82	−10.87	−5.21	−8.60	8.36	−6.16	....	....	Net Errors and Omissions	78ca d
	−9.04	−6.64	5.22	3.64	−10.54	−14.80	−18.29	−6.61	−5.10	−13.49	−13.67	−12.64	14.40	....	....	Overall Balance	78cb d
	9.04	6.64	−5.22	−3.64	10.54	14.80	18.29	6.61	5.10	13.49	13.67	12.64	−14.40	....	....	Reserves and Related Items	79da d
	9.04	5.71	−16.41	−10.58	−.72	9.74	8.57	−4.28	−4.28	11.61	8.58	8.34	−17.14	....	....	Reserve Assets	79db d
	—	.93	1.71	1.02	−.20	−.41	.13	−1.64	−.41	−.21	−.84	−.64	—	....	....	Use of Fund Credit and Loans	79dc d
	—	—	—	—	—	—	—	—	—	—	—	—	—	....	....	Liabs.Constit.For.Auth.Reserves	79dd d
	—	—	9.47	5.92	11.46	5.47	9.59	12.53	9.80	2.09	5.93	4.94	2.73	....	....	Exceptional Financing	79de d
Year Ending December 31																**Government Finance**	
	−3.60	−9.21	−13.04	−13.38	−6.53	−19.33ᴾ	−15.06ᴾ	−34.05ᴾ	−32.96ᴾ	....	114.31ᴾ	122.80ᴾ	132.38ᶠ	....	....	Deficit (−) or Surplus	80
	23.38	29.92	33.25	34.36	47.71	53.19ᴾ	57.10ᴾ	69.45ᴾ	82.44ᴾ	....	114.31ᴾ	122.80ᴾ	132.38ᶠ	....	....	Revenue	81
	13.47	7.33	5.51	6.04	4.70	2.05ᴾ	25.39ᴾ	30.20ᴾ	37.56ᴾ	....	....	....	....	....	....	Grants Received	81z
	36.17	41.83	46.38	49.94	56.24	73.29ᴾ	96.22ᴾ	125.73ᴾ	138.26ᴾ	....	145.05ᴾ	167.57ᴾ	231.67ᶠ	....	....	Expenditure	82
	4.28	4.63	5.42	3.84	2.70	1.28ᴾ	1.33ᴾ	7.97ᴾ	14.70ᴾ	....	2.35ᴾ	4.89ᴾ	6.46ᶠ	....	....	Lending Minus Repayments	83
																Financing	
	3.13	2.97	4.69	6.44	....	....	....	14.01ᴾ	15.03ᴾ	....	....	....	....	....	....	Net Borrowing: Domestic	84a
	3.42	3.24	5.01	7.64	....	....	....	35.14ᴾ	20.36ᴾ	....	....	....	....	....	....	Foreign	85a
	−2.95	3.00	3.34	−.70	....	....	....	−15.10ᴾ	−2.43ᴾ	....	....	....	....	....	....	Use of Cash Balances	87
	9.44	12.05	17.37	21.24	25.32	....	....	....	....	....	....	....	....	....	....	Debt: Domestic	88a
	6.36	9.90	11.94	24.20	29.60	....	....	....	....	....	....	....	....	....	....	Foreign	89a
Millions of Solomon Islands Dollars																**National Accounts**	
	60.8	....	....	....	135.2	121.1	132.9	163.6	227.0	249.0	....	....	....	....	....	Exports of Goods & Services	90c
	....	....	....	....	52.1	66.6	84.1	106.3	123.8	133.4	....	....	....	....	....	Government Consumption	91f
	....	....	....	....	43.0	49.9	63.6	59.6	122.1	....	....	....	....	....	....	Gross Fixed Capital Formation	93e
	....	....	....	....	7.9	12.2	2.5	7.9	10.0	....	....	....	....	....	....	Increase/Decrease(−) in Stocks	93i
	118.1	....	....	....	122.0	152.0	159.3	184.9	253.6	300.0	....	....	....	....	....	Private Consumption	96f
	−61.5	....	....	....	−138.5	−164.9	−189.8	−229.6	−380.1	−405.9	....	....	....	....	....	Imports of Goods & Services	98c
	119.1	140.6	158.5	141.4	221.7	236.9	252.5	292.7	356.4	384.4	....	....	....	....	....	Gross Domestic Product	99b
	194.6	207.6	205.3	213.4	231.0	236.9	231.7	219.8	....	....	....	....	....	....	....	Gross Dom. Prod. 1985 Prices	99b.p
	61.2	67.7	77.2	66.3	96.0	100.0	109.0	133.2	....	....	....	....	....	....	....	GDP Deflator (1985=100)	99bi p
Midyear Estimates																	
	.23	.23	.24	.25	.26	.27	.28	.29	.30	.31	.32	.33	.34	.35	....	Population	99z

Somalia

726

	1965	1966	1967	1968	1969	1970	1971	1972	1973	1974	1975	1976	1977	1978	1979
Exchange Rates														*Shillings per SDR:*	
Principal Rate........aa=........wa	7.1	7.1	7.1	7.1	7.1	7.1	7.6	7.6	7.6	7.7	7.4	7.3	7.6	8.2	8.3
													Shillings per US Dollar:		
Principal Rate........ae=........we	7.1	7.1	7.1	7.1	7.1	7.1	7.0	7.0	6.3	6.3	6.3	6.3	6.3	6.3	6.3
Principal Rate........rf=........wf	7.1	7.1	7.1	7.1	7.1	7.1	7.1	7.0	6.3	6.3	6.3	6.3	6.3	6.3	6.3
Secondary Rate........xe	....	....	....	....	....	....	....	....	....	....	....	....	....	....	....
Secondary Rate........xf	....	....	....	....	....	....	....	....	....	....	....	....	....	....	....
Fund Position														*Millions of SDRs:*	
Quota........2f.s	11.3	15.0	15.0	15.0	15.0	19.0	19.0	19.0	19.0	19.0	19.0	19.0	19.0	23.0	23.0
SDRs........1b.s	—	—	—	—	—	.6	2.6	4.6	4.5	4.4	4.4	4.3	4.2	4.1	6.4
Reserve Position in the Fund........1c.s	—	—	—	.1	1.0	3.7	3.8	3.9	3.9	3.9	4.2	4.2	—	—	—
Total Fund Cred.&Loans Outstg........2tl	8.4	8.4	7.7	—	—	—	—	—	—	—	—	—	—	.1	.1
International Liquidity											*Millions of US Dollars Unless Otherwise Indicated:*				
Total Reserves minus Gold........1l.d	8.6	12.3	10.0	6.8	13.4	21.1	26.7	31.3	35.0	42.3	68.4	84.9	120.0	126.3	43.8
SDRs........1b.d	—	—	—	—	—	.6	2.8	5.0	5.4	5.4	5.1	5.0	5.1	5.3	8.4
Reserve Position in the Fund........1c.d	—	—	—	—	1.0	3.7	4.1	4.2	4.7	4.8	5.0	4.9	—	—	—
Foreign Exchange........1d.d	8.6	12.3	10.0	6.7	12.4	16.8	19.7	22.2	24.9	32.1	58.3	75.0	114.9	121.0	35.4
Gold (Million Fine Troy Ounces)........1ad	—	—	—	—	.023	.003	.003	.003	.003	.003	.003	.003	.011	.015	.015
Gold (National Valuation)........1and	.1	.1	.1	.1	.8	.1	.1e	....	....	.1	.1	.1	.5	3.0	7.0
Monetary Authorities: Other Assets........3..d	5.3	4.9	4.3	4.0	4.8	4.9	6.4	4.8	5.7	2.1	1.7	3.4	1.0	1.0	.4
Monetary Authorities: Other Liab........4..d	6	6	7	6	12	10	9	7	6	30	27	25	31	33	39
Deposit Money Banks: Assets........7a.d	.4	.6	1.0	1.0	1.0	.1	7.0	13.2	6.3	18.0	36.7	22.3	39.6	59.8	38.2
Liabilities........7b.d	—	1	1	1	1	—	1	1	1	3	1	1	1	8	—
Monetary Authorities														*Billions of Shillings:*	
Foreign Assets........11	.10	.12	.11	.08	.14	.19	.19	.26	.25	.28	.44	.54	.76	.82	.32
Claims on Central Government........12a	.04	.06	.09	.06	.06	.07	.06	.04	.08	.16	.03	.26	.38	.88	1.66
Claims on Official Entities........12bx	—	—	.01	—	—	.04	.04	.04	.05	.05	.11	.11	.16	.18	.17
Claims on Deposit Money Banks........12e	—	—	—	—	—	—	.06	.11	.22	.47	.55	.21	.41	.37	.30
Reserve Money........14	.13	.15	.17	.18	.22	.31	.21	.29	.34	.41	.53	.63	.84	1.18	1.47
of which: Currency Outside DMBs........14a	.09	.11	.12	.13	.14	.15	.15	.22	.25	.31	.39	.41	.62	.88	1.15
Private Sector Deposits........14d	.03	.03	.03	.04	.07	.16	.03	.01	.02	.03	.06	.12	.10	.12	.08
Time and Savings Deposits........15	—	.01	.01	.01	.02	.06	—	—	—	—	—	—	—	—	—
Foreign Liabilities........16c	.10	.10	.11	.04	.09	.07	.06	.05	.04	.19	.17	.16	.20	.21	.24
Central Government Deposits........16d	—	.01	.01	—	.01	.01	.03	.07	.13	.21	.27	.14	.48	.57	.43
Capital Accounts........17a	.01	.01	.01	.01	.02	.04	.05	.07	.07	.07	.09	.10	.11	.13	.15
Other Items (Net)........17r	−.09	−.09	−.09	−.11	−.15	−.19	—	−.01	.03	.08	.08	.09	.08	.16	.16
Deposit Money Banks														*Billions of Shillings:*	
Reserves........20	.01	.01	.01	.01	.01	.02	.03	.06	.07	.08	.08	.10	.12	.18	.23
Foreign Assets........21	—	—	.01	.01	.01	—	.05	.09	.04	.11	.23	.14	.25	.38	.24
Claims on Official Entities........22bx	—	—	—	—	—	—	—	—	—	....	.42	.54	.74	.82	1.10
Claims on Private Sector........22d	.08	.09	.09	.11	.09	.09	.25	.32	.62	.92	.52	.35	.38	.40	.45
Demand Deposits........24	.07	.06	.08	.09	.07	.07	.15	.21	.24	.29	.38	.46	.60	.72	1.10
Time and Savings Deposits........25	.02	.02	.03	.03	.03	.03	.06	.08	.10	.15	.18	.20	.22	.32	.47
Foreign Liabilities........26c	—	.01	.01	.01	.01	—	.01	.01	.01	.02	—	.01	.01	.05	—
Credit from Monetary Authorities........26g	—	—	—	—	—	—	.05	.06	.22	.48	.50	.23	.42	.38	.37
Capital Accounts........27a	.01	.01	.01	.01	—	—	.01	.01	.01	.01	.01	.01	.01	.01	.01
Other Items (Net)........27r	—	—	−.01	−.01	—	.01	.05	.09	.15	.15	.17	.20	.23	.29	.06
Monetary Survey														*Billions of Shillings:*	
Foreign Assets (Net)........31n	.01	.02	.01	.04	.05	.12	.17	.30	.25	.18	.50	.52	.80	.94	.32
Domestic Credit........32	.21	.23	.27	.27	.30	.40	.33	.33	.63	.92	.80	1.11	1.18	1.72	2.96
Claims on Central Govt. (Net)........32an	.04	.05	.08	.06	.06	.06	.03	−.02	−.05	−.05	−.24	.12	−.10	.31	1.23
Claims on Official Entities........32bx	—	—	.01	—	—	.04	.04	.04	.05	.05	.53	.64	.91	1.00	1.28
Claims on Private Sector........32d	.17	.18	.19	.21	.23	.30	.25	.32	.62	.92	.52	.35	.38	.40	.45
Money........34	.19	.20	.23	.26	.28	.38	.33	.44	.51	.63	.83	.99	1.33	1.73	2.34
Quasi-Money........35	.03	.03	.04	.05	.05	.09	.06	.08	.10	.15	.18	.21	.22	.32	.48
Other Items (Net)........37r	—	.01	.01	.01	.02	.05	.10	.11	.27	.32	.30	.43	.44	.61	.46
Money plus Quasi-Money........35l	.22	.23	.27	.30	.33	.47	.39	.52	.61	.78	1.01	1.20	1.54	2.05	2.81
Interest Rates														*Percent Per Annum*	
Discount Rate (End of Period)........60	....	....	....	....	3.0	3.0	3.0	3.0	3.5	3.5	3.5	3.5	3.5	3.5	4.0
Deposit Rate........60l	....	....	....	....	2.00	2.00	2.00	2.00	2.46	2.50	4.00	4.00	4.00	4.00	4.04
Lending Rate........60p	....	....	....	....	....	....	....	....	....	....	7.0	7.0	7.0	7.0	7.5
Prices													*Index Numbers (1985=100):*		
Consumer Prices........64	3.7	‡3.6	3.6	3.7	3.9	3.9	3.9	3.8	4.0	4.8	5.7	6.5	‡7.2	7.9	9.8

Somalia

	1980	1981	1982	1983	1984	1985	1986	1987	1988	1989	1990	1991	1992	1993	1994		
Exchange Rates																	
End of Period	8.0	7.3	16.5	18.4	25.5	46.7	110.7	141.9	363.3	1,221.5	....	....	....	....	....	Principal Rate....aa=	wa
End of Period (we) Period Average (wf)																	
	6.3	6.3	15.2	17.6	26.0	42.5	90.5	100.0	270.0	929.5	...	...	...	...	...	Principal Rate....ae=	we
	6.3	6.3	10.8	15.8	20.0	39.5	72.0	105.2	170.5	490.7	...	...	...	...	...	Principal Rate....rf=	wf
	....	12.6	....	....	....	84.4	....	....	....	....	....	....	....	....	....	Secondary Rate	xe
	....	....	....	....	....	....	....	....	....	....	....	....	....	....	....	Secondary Rate	xf
Fund Position																	
End of Period																	
	34.5	34.5	34.5	44.2	44.2	44.2	44.2	44.2	44.2	44.2	44.2	44.2	44.2	44.2	44.2	Quota	2f. s
	5.5	4.2	.7	.4	.1	—	—	—	—	—	—	—	—	—	—	SDRs	1b. s
	—	—	—	—	—	—	—	—	—	—	—	—	—	—	—	Reserve Position in the Fund	1c. s
	14.0	40.0	72.2	117.2	114.3	140.1	127.3	123.7	123.0	114.1	112.0	112.0	112.0	112.0	112.0	Total Fund Cred.&Loans Outstg.	2tl
International Liquidity																	
End of Period																	
	14.6	30.7	6.5	9.2	1.0	2.5	12.8	7.3	15.3	15.4	....	....	....	....	....	Total Reserves minus Gold	1l. d
	7.0	4.9	.8	.4	—	—	—	—	—	—	—	—	—	—	—	SDRs	1b. d
	—	—	—	—	—	—	—	—	—	—	—	—	—	—	—	Reserve Position in the Fund	1c. d
	7.6	25.8	5.7	8.8	1.0	2.5	12.8	7.3	15.3	15.4	....	....	....	....	....	Foreign Exchange	1d. d
	.019	.019	.019	.019	.019	.019	.019	.019	.019	.019	....	....	....	....	....	Gold (Million Fine Troy Ounces)	1ad
	10.0	6.8	7.7	6.6	5.3	5.6	6.7	8.3	7.0	6.9	....	....	....	....	....	Gold (National Valuation)	1an d
	.5	—	—	.2	—	—	.1	....	....	....	....	....	....	....	....	Monetary Authorities: Other Assets	3.. d
	52	72	74	83	97	99	127	128	130	134	....	....	....	....	....	Monetary Authorities: Other Liab.	4.. d
	53.9	73.9	93.9	51.7	23.1	104.4	57.7	76.7	56.5	22.4	....	....	....	....	....	Deposit Money Banks: Assets	7a. d
	—	—	—	—	—	—	—	—	—	—	....	....	....	....	....	Liabilities	7b. d
Monetary Authorities																	
End of Period																	
	.16	.26	.22	.28	.17	.35	1.79	1.56	6.02	20.61	....	....	....	....	....	Foreign Assets	11
	2.44	2.96	4.00	6.06	6.33	7.32	8.53	18.80	27.74	28.49	....	....	....	....	....	Claims on Central Government	12a
	.24	.22	.19	.20	.65	1.45	3.01	4.02	6.18	11.18	....	....	....	....	....	Claims on Official Entities	12bx
	.41	.83	1.42	1.90	2.42	2.52	4.39	3.73	6.25	47.15	....	....	....	....	....	Claims on Deposit Money Banks	12e
	1.93	2.45	2.09	2.14	3.46	5.34	8.85	16.19	27.23	79.69	....	....	....	....	....	Reserve Money	14
	1.51	1.89	1.46	1.36	1.90	3.79	5.21	12.33	21.03	70.79	....	....	....	....	....	of which: Currency Outside DMBs	14a
	.09	.09	.16	.16	.54	.49	.94	1.77	1.56	5.07	....	....	....	....	....	Private Sector Deposits	14d
	—	—	.01	.01	.01	.01	.11	.20	.66	.29	....	....	....	....	....	Time and Savings Deposits	15
	.35	.67	2.16	3.41	5.16	10.26	24.65	29.44	77.31	255.74	....	....	....	....	....	Foreign Liabilities	16c
	.54	.71	1.90	4.25	1.96	1.89	2.45	4.54	7.62	14.43	....	....	....	....	....	Central Government Deposits	16d
	.21	.25	.17	.38	.48	.75	1.62	1.90	5.12	16.19	....	....	....	....	....	Capital Accounts	17a
	.22	.19	-.50	-1.75	-1.48	-6.62	-19.97	-24.16	-71.76	-258.91	....	....	....	....	....	Other Items (Net)	17r
Deposit Money Banks																	
End of Period																	
	.33	.47	.46	.66	1.05	1.16	2.56	2.48	5.39	35.06	....	....	....	....	....	Reserves	20
	.34	.47	1.43	.91	.60	4.44	5.22	7.67	15.25	20.81	....	....	....	....	....	Foreign Assets	21
	1.31	1.50	1.11	.96	.86	.63	.72	-2.39	-4.87	-16.11	....	....	....	....	....	Claims on Official Entities	22bx
	.43	.57	1.62	2.29	3.73	4.03	4.10	18.61	29.64	89.79	....	....	....	....	....	Claims on Private Sector	22d
	1.18	1.69	2.42	2.79	2.90	5.50	6.00	15.95	22.85	63.97	....	....	....	....	....	Demand Deposits	24
	.59	.74	1.08	1.19	1.60	2.78	4.58	7.99	14.01	17.87	....	....	....	....	....	Time and Savings Deposits	25
	—	—	—	—	—	—	—	—	—	—	....	....	....	....	....	Foreign Liabilities	26c
	.44	.81	1.47	1.83	2.36	2.59	3.59	3.45	4.94	46.26	....	....	....	....	....	Credit from Monetary Authorities	26g
	.01	.01	.01	.02	.02	.02	.02	.02	.02	.02	....	....	....	....	....	Capital Accounts	27a
	.18	-.25	-.36	-1.00	-.63	-.63	-1.58	-1.04	3.59	1.44	....	....	....	....	....	Other Items (Net)	27r
Monetary Survey																	
End of Period																	
	.14	.06	-.52	-2.23	-4.39	-5.48	-17.64	-20.21	-56.05	-214.31	....	....	....	....	....	Foreign Assets (Net)	31n
	3.88	4.55	5.02	5.26	9.62	11.52	13.90	34.49	51.07	98.93	....	....	....	....	....	Domestic Credit	32
	1.90	2.25	2.10	1.81	4.38	5.42	6.08	14.26	20.12	14.07	....	....	....	....	....	Claims on Central Govt. (Net)	32an
	1.55	1.72	1.30	1.16	1.51	2.07	3.73	1.62	1.31	-4.93	....	....	....	....	....	Claims on Official Entities	32bx
	.43	.57	1.62	2.29	3.73	4.03	4.10	18.61	29.64	89.79	....	....	....	....	....	Claims on Private Sector	32d
	2.78	3.67	4.03	4.31	5.33	9.77	12.14	30.05	45.44	139.83	....	....	....	....	....	Money	34
	.60	.75	1.08	1.19	1.60	2.79	4.69	8.19	14.68	18.16	....	....	....	....	....	Quasi-Money	35
	.64	.19	-.61	-2.47	-1.71	-6.52	-20.57	-23.95	-65.10	-273.37	....	....	....	....	....	Other Items (Net)	37r
	3.38	4.42	5.12	5.50	6.93	12.56	16.83	38.23	60.11	157.99	....	....	....	....	....	Money plus Quasi-Money	35l
Interest Rates																	
Percent Per Annum																	
	4.0	6.0	8.0	8.0	8.0	12.0	12.0	12.0	45.0	45.0	....	....	....	....	....	Discount Rate (End of Period)	60
	4.50	5.50	7.50	8.50	8.50	14.00	15.31	16.25	20.63	25.00	....	....	....	....	....	Deposit Rate	60l
	7.5	10.0	11.5	12.0	12.0	19.0	20.6	22.0	33.7	....	....	....	....	....	....	Lending Rate	60p
Prices																	
Period Averages																	
	15.6	22.6	27.9	38.0	72.6	100.0	135.8	174.0	316.6	....	....	....	....	....	....	Consumer Prices	64

Somalia

726

		1965	1966	1967	1968	1969	1970	1971	1972	1973	1974	1975	1976	1977	1978	1979
International Transactions														*Millions of Shillings*		
Exports	70	237	233	199	212	232	224	246	300	340	391	558	595	397	671	704
Imports, cif	71	354	300	286	340	370	322	448	524	638	815	974	980	1,433	1,539	1,546
Imports, fob	71.v	316	268	256	303	326	285	397	456	555	709	847	853	1,246	1,339	1,345
Balance of Payments														*Millions of US Dollars:*		
Goods: Exports f.o.b.	78aa d	....	....	....	....	....	....	....	....	....	....	....	....	71.3	109.5	106.0
Goods: Imports f.o.b.	78ab d	....	....	....	....	....	....	....	....	....	....	....	....	-179.0	-239.4	-342.9
Trade Balance	78ac d	....	....	....	....	....	....	....	....	....	....	....	....	-107.7	-130.0	-236.8
Services: Credit	78ad d	....	....	....	....	....	....	....	....	....	....	....	....	29.7	36.5	37.7
Services: Debit	78ae d	....	....	....	....	....	....	....	....	....	....	....	....	-65.1	-80.6	-103.1
Balance on Goods and Services	78af d	....	....	....	....	....	....	....	....	....	....	....	....	-143.1	-174.1	-302.2
Income: Credit	78ag d	....	....	....	....	....	....	....	....	....	....	....	....	3.0	5.9	9.5
Income: Debit	78ah d	....	....	....	....	....	....	....	....	....	....	....	....	-.8	-2.4	-7.0
Balance on Goods, Serv., & Inc.	78ai d	....	....	....	....	....	....	....	....	....	....	....	....	-140.8	-170.5	-299.7
Current Transfers, n.i.e.: Credit	78aj d	....	....	....	....	....	....	....	....	....	....	....	....	109.2	106.1	95.0
Current Transfers: Debit	78ak d	....	....	....	....	....	....	....	....	....	....	....	....	-1.1	-.2	-1.0
Current Account, n.i.e.	78al d	....	....	....	....	....	....	....	....	....	....	....	....	-32.8	-64.7	-205.7
Capital Account, n.i.e.: Credit	78ba d	....	....	....	....	....	....	....	....	....	....	....	....	—	—	—
Capital Account: Debit	78bb d	....	....	....	....	....	....	....	....	....	....	....	....	—	—	—
Capital Account, n.i.e.	78bc d	....	....	....	....	....	....	....	....	....	....	....	....	—	—	—
Direct Investment Abroad	78bd d	....	....	....	....	....	....	....	....	....	....	....	....	—	—	—
Dir. Invest. in Rep. Econ., n.i.e.	78be d	....	....	....	....	....	....	....	....	....	....	....	....	7.8	.3	—
Portfolio Investment Assets	78bf d	....	....	....	....	....	....	....	....	....	....	....	....			
Portfolio Investment Liab., n.i.e.	78bg d	....	....	....	....	....	....	....	....	....	....	....	....	—	—	—
Other Investment Assets	78bh d	....	....	....	....	....	....	....	....	....	....	....	....	-1.2	-1.2	1.3
Other Investment Liab., n.i.e.	78bi d	....	....	....	....	....	....	....	....	....	....	....	....	73.8	88.6	85.8
Financial Account, n.i.e.	78bj d	....	....	....	....	....	....	....	....	....	....	....	....	80.4	87.6	87.1
Net Errors and Omissions	78ca d	....	....	....	....	....	....	....	....	....	....	....	....	6.6	4.6	11.3
Overall Balance	78cb d	....	....	....	....	....	....	....	....	....	....	....	....	54.2	27.5	-107.3
Reserves and Related Items	79da d	....	....	....	....	....	....	....	....	....	....	....	....	-54.2	-27.5	107.3
Reserve Assets	79db d	....	....	....	....	....	....	....	....	....	....	....	....	-54.2	-27.7	107.3
Use of Fund Credit and Loans	79dc d	....	....	....	....	....	....	....	....	....	....	....	....	—	.2	—
Liabs.Constit.For.Auth.Reserves	79dd d	....	....	....	....	....	....	....	....	....	....	....	....	—	—	—
Exceptional Financing	79de d	....	....	....	....	....	....	....	....	....	....	....	....			
Government Finance														*Millions of Shillings:*		
Deficit (-) or Surplus	80	....	....	....	....	....	....	....	18.5	-33.4	-59.6	-73.1	-120.3	-367.4	-700.1	....
Revenue	81	....	....	....	....	....	....	....	398.9	438.0	565.7	623.8	669.6	828.8	1,347.6	....
Grants Received	81z	....	....	....	....	....	....	....	13.9	—	19.4	3.1	34.4	35.9	4.9	....
Expenditure	82	....	....	....	....	....	....	....	394.3	471.4	644.7	700.0	824.3	1,228.5	2,050.3	....
Lending Minus Repayments	83	....	....	....	....	....	....	....	—	—	—	—	—	3.6	2.3	....
Financing																
Domestic	84a	....	....	....	....	....	....	....	....	....	....	....	....	-238.6	238.5	....
Foreign	85a	....	....	....	....	....	....	....	....	....	....	....	....	606.0	461.6	....
														Millions:		
Population	99z	2.50	2.56	2.61	2.67	2.73	2.79	2.86	2.94	3.01	3.09	3.13	3.36	3.56	3.72	I 5.11

Somalia

726

	1980	1981	1982	1983	1984	1985	1986	1987	1988	1989	1990	1991	1992	1993	1994		
Millions of Shillings																**International Transactions**	
	835	960	1,993	1,717	1,096	3,577	6,373	10,900	20,400	37,000	97,000	....	....	....	....	Exports	70
	2,191	3,222	2,377	5,509	2,172	4,425	20,474	13,914	18,800	35,400	96,700	....	....	....	....	Imports, cif	71
	1,906	2,803	2,068	4,793	1,890	3,852	17,819	12,109	16,362	30,809	84,160	....	....	....	....	Imports, fob	71.v
Minus Sign Indicates Debit																Balance of Payments	
	133.3	175.4	170.8	98.4	54.8	90.6	94.7	94.0	58.4	67.7	....	....	....	....	....	Goods: Exports f.o.b.	78aa *d*
	−401.5	−370.5	−471.4	−362.1	−465.7	−330.7	−342.1	−358.5	−216.0	−346.3	....	....	....	....	....	Goods: Imports f.o.b.	78ab *d*
	−268.2	−195.2	−300.5	−263.6	−410.9	−240.2	−247.4	−264.5	−157.6	−278.6	....	....	....	....	....	Trade Balance	78ac *d*
	66.2	74.2	83.4	77.0	51.0	35.9	—	—	—	—	....	....	....	....	....	Services: Credit	78ad *d*
	−133.2	−135.0	−131.0	−117.6	−123.5	−96.8	−128.2	−127.7	−104.0	−122.0	....	....	....	....	....	Services: Debit	78ae *d*
	−335.2	−255.9	−348.1	−304.2	−483.4	−301.0	−375.6	−392.2	−261.6	−400.6	....	....	....	....	....	Balance on Goods and Services	78af *d*
	5.0	5.8	1.9	1.7	1.0	1.1	—	—	—	—	....	....	....	....	....	Income: Credit	78ag *d*
	−5.8	−13.9	−8.0	−6.4	−13.7	−26.6	−60.3	−52.0	−60.6	−84.4	....	....	....	....	....	Income: Debit	78ah *d*
	−336.1	−264.0	−354.1	−308.9	−496.1	−326.5	−435.9	−444.2	−322.2	−485.0	....	....	....	....	....	Balance on Goods, Serv., & Inc.	78ai *d*
	199.9	183.3	183.3	169.9	363.5	242.5	310.2	343.3	223.7	331.2	....	....	....	....	....	Current Transfers, n.i.e.: Credit	78aj *d*
		−2.7	−6.6	−2.6	−6.5	−18.7	—	−13.1	—	−2.9	....	....	....	....	....	Current Transfers: Debit	78ak *d*
	−136.2	−83.4	−177.4	−141.6	−139.1	−102.8	−125.7	−114.0	−98.5	−156.7	....	....	....	....	....	Current Account, n.i.e.	78al *d*
	—	—	—	—	—	—	—	—	—	—	....	....	....	....	....	Capital Account, n.i.e.: Credit	78ba *d*
	—	—	—	—	—	—	—	—	—	—	....	....	....	....	....	Capital Account: Debit	78bb *d*
	—	—	—	—	—	—	—	—	—	—	....	....	....	....	....	Capital Account, n.i.e.	78bc *d*
	—	—	—	—	—	—	—	—	—	—	....	....	....	....	....	Direct Investment Abroad	78bd *d*
	—	—	−.8	−8.2	−14.9	−.7	—	—	—	—	....	....	....	....	....	Dir. Invest. in Rep. Econ., n.i.e.	78be *d*
	—	—	—	—	—	—	—	—	—	—	....	....	....	....	....	Portfolio Investment Assets	78bf *d*
	—	—	—	—	—	—	—	—	—	—	....	....	....	....	....	Portfolio Investment Liab., n.i.e.	78bg *d*
	—	—	−1.1	−1.1	−.7	−.7	—	—	—	—	....	....	....	....	....	Other Investment Assets	78bh *d*
	103.6	69.0	140.1	77.6	103.1	77.0	9.8	−22.8	−105.5	−32.6	....	....	....	....	....	Other Investment Liab., n.i.e.	78bi *d*
	103.6	69.0	138.2	68.2	87.5	75.6	9.8	−22.8	−105.5	−32.6	....	....	....	....	....	Financial Account, n.i.e.	78bj *d*
	1.6	18.6	75.2	−4.4	24.5	15.3	19.3	39.0	22.4	−.8	....	....	....	....	....	Net Errors and Omissions	78ca *d*
	−31.0	4.2	36.0	−77.7	−27.1	−11.9	−96.5	−97.9	−181.7	−190.0	....	....	....	....	....	Overall Balance	78cb *d*
	31.0	−4.2	−36.0	77.7	27.1	11.9	96.5	97.9	181.7	190.0	....	....	....	....	....	Reserves and Related Items	79da *d*
	13.3	−34.0	−71.7	29.3	20.9	−31.8	−12.0	−10.7	3.8	32.0	....	....	....	....	....	Reserve Assets	79db *d*
	17.7	29.8	35.7	48.4	−2.9	24.5	−14.9	−4.9	−.9	−11.6	....	....	....	....	....	Use of Fund Credit and Loans	79dc *d*
	—	—	—	—	—	—	—	—	—	—	....	....	....	....	....	Liabs.Constit.For.Auth.Reserves	79dd *d*
	—	—	—	—	9.1	19.2	123.4	113.4	178.8	169.7	....	....	....	....	....	Exceptional Financing	79de *d*
Year Ending December 31																**Government Finance**	
	....	....	....	....	....	....	....	....	....	....	....	....	....	....	....	Deficit (−) or Surplus	80
	....	....	....	....	....	....	....	....	....	....	....	....	....	....	....	Revenue	81
	....	....	....	....	....	....	....	....	....	....	....	....	....	....	....	Grants Received	81z
	....	....	....	....	....	....	....	....	....	....	....	....	....	....	....	Expenditure	82
	....	....	....	....	....	....	....	....	....	....	....	....	....	....	....	Lending Minus Repayments	83
																Financing	
	....	....	....	....	....	....	....	....	....	....	....	....	....	....	....	Domestic	84a
	....	....	....	....	....	....	....	....	....	....	....	....	....	....	....	Foreign	85a
Midyear Estimates																	
	5.35	5.57	5.77	7.46	7.67	7.87	8.07	8.25	8.41	8.55	8.68	8.78	8.86	8.95	....	Population	99z

South Africa

199		1965	1966	1967	1968	1969	1970	1971	1972	1973	1974	1975	1976	1977	1978	1979
Exchange Rates																*SDRs per Rand:*
Principal Rate......ac= ......wc		1.3998	1.3933	1.4018	1.3898	1.3988	1.3943	1.2036	1.1765	1.2351	1.1843	.9824	.9898	.9467	.8827	.9181
																US Dollars per Rand:
Principal Rate......ag= ......wg		1.3998	1.3933	1.4018	1.3898	1.3988	1.3943	1.3068	1.2773	1.4900	1.4501	1.1500	1.1500	1.1500	1.1500	1.2094
Principal Rate......rh= ......wh		1.3960	1.3947	1.3946	1.3947	1.3927	1.3959	1.3982	1.2950	1.4438	1.4722	1.3663	1.1500	1.1500	1.1500	1.1879
Secondary Rate ......xg		....	....	....	....	....	....	....	....	....	....	....	....	....	....	.88880
																Index Numbers (1990=100):
Principal Rate......ah x		361.1	360.7	360.7	360.7	360.2	361.0	306.4	334.9	373.4	380.7	353.4	297.4	297.4	297.4	307.2
Nominal Effective Exchange Rate ......ne c		....	....	....	....	....	....	....	....	....	....	....	....	....	....	315.5
Real Effective Exchange Rate ......re c		....	....	....	....	....	....	....	....	....	....	....	....	....	....	122.2
Fund Position																*Millions of SDRs:*
Quota......2f. s		150	200	200	200	200	200	320	320	320	320	320	320	320	424	424
SDRs......1b. s		—	—	—	—	—	39	—	38	1	40	43	42	40	39	25
Reserve Position in the Fund......1c. s		38	50	60	60	153	50	81	81	81	81	—	—	—	—	—
Total Fund Cred.&Loans Outstg......2tl		—	—	—	—	—	—	—	—	—	—	—	315	392	314	77
International Liquidity												*Millions of US Dollars Unless Otherwise Indicated:*
Total Reserves minus Gold......1l. d		175	194	196	228	283	346	266	609	449	377	489	425	416	423	434
SDRs......1b. d		—	—	—	—	—	39	1	41	2	48	51	48	48	51	33
Reserve Position in the Fund......1c. d		38	50	60	60	153	50	87	87	97	100	—	—	—	—	—
Foreign Exchange......1d. d		137	144	136	168	130	256	178	480	350	229	438	377	368	372	401
Gold (Million Fine Troy Ounces)......1ad		12.14	18.20	16.64	35.51	31.86	19.03	11.72	17.93	18.99	18.25	17.75	12.67	9.72	9.79	10.03
Gold (National Valuation)......1and		421	629	579	1,224	1,105	658	433	677	836	782	603	431	330	1,931	4,451
Monetary Authorities: Other Assets......3..d		5	14	17	19	19	52	70	93	109	181	208	274	270	388	490
Other Liab.......4..d		48	70	36	85	56	94	162	66	3	45	699	805	599	186	16
Deposit Money Banks: Assets......7a. d		80	46	60	114	106	121	163	106	161	162	181	165	158	224	316
Liabilities......7b. d		114	126	120	158	179	164	215	261	347	513	495	823	753	791	815
Monetary Authorities																*Millions of Rand:*
Foreign Assets......11		430	600	564	1,057	1,005	784	585	1,112	939	959	1,168	1,017	917	2,429	4,472
Claims on Central Government......12a		190	236	292	352	459	633	615	620	1,086	1,122	1,598	1,232	962	954	1,163
Claims on Deposit Money Banks......12e		38	78	82	64	39	226	264	44	135	108	286	299	551	230	195
Reserve Money......14		522	580	617	702	766	833	874	943	1,124	1,309	1,503	1,588	1,703	1,906	2,188
of which: Currency Outside DMBs......14a		326	357	384	406	458	513	570	627	747	880	1,026	1,106	1,149	1,285	1,460
Foreign Liabilities......16c		35	50	26	61	40	67	122	52	2	31	608	1,018	935	518	92
Central Government Deposits......16d		43	228	218	619	594	477	294	545	867	745	1,065	1,113	1,218	1,416	1,409
Other Items (Net)......17r		58	55	78	92	103	266	175	237	167	104	-125	-1,173	-1,427	-226	2,136
Deposit Money Banks																*Millions of Rand:*
Reserves......20		185	219	225	289	298	311	293	309	368	416	451	460	529	600	695
Foreign Assets......21		57	33	43	82	76	86	122	83	114	112	158	144	138	195	261
Claims on Central Government......22a		577	802	779	947	915	814	874	1,212	1,233	1,441	2,070	2,576	3,237	3,380	3,721
Claims on Private Sector......22d		2,114	2,218	2,479	2,744	3,231	3,571	3,844	4,302	5,830	6,934	8,335	8,882	9,419	10,759	12,274
Demand Deposits......24		1,124	1,235	1,313	1,637	1,754	1,735	1,863	2,170	2,622	3,114	3,229	3,305	3,470	3,819	4,701
Time and Savings Deposits......25		1,458	1,646	1,796	2,029	2,299	2,477	2,617	3,216	4,123	4,944	6,550	7,172	8,014	9,632	10,737
Short & Medium-Term Deposits......25x		1,009	1,025	1,126	1,371	1,551	1,722	1,828	2,052	2,597	3,298	4,302	4,931	5,350	6,143	6,576
Long-Term Deposits......25y		449	621	670	658	749	754	790	1,164	1,527	1,646	2,248	2,242	2,665	3,489	4,162
Foreign Liabilities......26c		81	90	86	113	128	117	161	204	244	354	431	716	655	688	674
Credit from Monetary Authorities......26g		43	91	84	67	39	229	265	47	275	108	463	449	554	433	417
Other Items (Net)......27r		227	209	249	217	300	224	226	270	280	384	341	419	629	361	423
Monetary Survey																*Millions of Rand:*
Foreign Assets (Net)......31n		371	492	496	965	913	686	424	940	806	686	287	-574	-536	1,419	3,963
Domestic Credit......32		2,826	3,014	3,272	3,423	4,011	4,521	5,023	5,562	7,219	8,723	10,909	11,529	12,118	13,341	15,772
Claims on Central Govt. (Net)......32an		705	789	788	658	758	943	1,165	1,256	1,376	1,779	2,556	2,619	2,683	2,540	3,287
Claims on Private Sector......32d		2,121	2,225	2,484	2,765	3,253	3,577	3,858	4,307	5,842	6,944	8,354	8,909	9,435	10,801	12,485
Money......34		1,460	1,596	1,705	2,050	2,223	2,259	2,446	2,808	3,382	4,011	4,286	4,437	4,648	5,133	6,198
Quasi-Money......35		1,458	1,646	1,796	2,029	2,299	2,477	2,617	3,216	4,123	4,944	6,550	7,172	8,014	9,632	10,737
Other Items (Net)......37r		229	200	265	309	402	471	384	478	520	454	361	-654	-1,080	-5	2,800
Money plus Quasi-Money......35l		2,919	3,242	3,501	4,079	4,522	4,736	5,063	6,024	7,505	8,955	10,835	11,609	12,662	14,765	16,935
Other Banking Institutions																
Building Societies																*Millions of Rand:*
Claims on Private Sector......42d		1,774	1,856	2,000	2,170	2,434	2,872	3,277	3,681	4,356	4,985	5,634	6,410	7,063	7,821	9,077
Time and Savings Deposits......45a		769	858	992	1,067	1,193	1,414	1,505	1,627	1,905	2,217	2,764	2,997	3,301	3,866	4,727
Building Societies Shares......45c		1,001	1,009	988	1,088	1,261	1,488	1,723	2,153	2,580	2,830	3,065	3,403	3,714	4,112	4,901
Bonds......46ab		94	119	144	154	184	184	206	274	348	356	446	439	484	627	772
Other Items (Net)......47r		-89	-130	-124	-140	-203	-214	-157	-374	-477	-418	-642	-428	-436	-785	-1,323
Post Office: Savings Deposits......45.. i		132	138	148	153	157	165	168	171	177	212	303	463	664	854	998
Nonbank Financial Institutions																*Millions of Rand:*
Cash......40.. s		91	100	98	125	158	190	175	183	234	413	410	506	431	493	1,037
Claims on Central Government......42a. s		94	154	222	309	374	424	529	778	923	1,059	1,303	1,730	2,168	2,634	2,987
Claims on Local Government......42b. s		542	498	546	581	517	569	634	708	758	840	1,050	1,274	1,514	1,605	1,682
Claims on Private Sector......42d. s		1,522	1,670	1,841	2,059	2,331	2,665	3,003	3,191	3,574	3,919	4,277	5,703	5,409	6,345	7,796
Real Estate......42h. s		32	180	195	225	260	304	351	395	547	685	943	1,223	1,429	1,627	1,801
Incr.in Total Assets(Within Per.)......49z. s		136	321	300	397	341	512	540	563	781	880	1,067	2,453	515	1,753	2,599
Financial Survey																*Millions of Rand:*
Foreign Assets (Net)......51n		371	492	496	965	913	686	424	940	806	686	287	-574	-536	1,419	3,963
Domestic Credit......52		6,984	7,499	8,199	8,880	9,999	11,408	12,829	14,326	17,230	19,885	23,709	27,270	29,276	33,103	39,072
Claims on Central Govt. (Net)......52an		1,005	1,177	1,255	1,232	1,394	1,643	1,974	2,356	2,605	3,117	4,233	4,877	5,753	6,415	7,868
Claims on Private Sector......52d		6,034	6,321	6,945	7,648	8,605	9,765	10,855	11,970	14,625	16,768	19,476	22,393	23,523	26,687	31,204
Liquid Liabilities......55l		4,807	5,230	5,601	6,372	7,124	7,801	8,459	9,975	12,167	14,214	16,968	18,471	20,341	23,597	27,570
Bonds......56ab		94	119	144	154	184	184	206	274	348	356	446	439	484	627	772
Other Items (Net)......57r		2,440	2,625	2,923	3,304	3,596	4,107	4,588	5,017	5,522	6,000	6,583	7,787	7,915	10,297	14,702
Interest Rates																*Percent Per Annum*
Discount Rate *(End of Period)*......60		5.00	6.00	6.00	5.50	5.50	5.50	6.50	6.00	3.78	6.48	7.42	8.28	8.41	7.87	4.70
Money Market Rate......60b		3.94	4.15	4.89	4.83	4.51	4.55	5.61	5.37	4.12	6.13	6.24	8.50	8.29	7.99	5.39
Treasury Bill Rate......60c		4.04	4.20	4.87	4.90	4.61	4.39	5.38	5.30	3.18	5.43	6.12	7.44	7.87	7.81	5.26
Deposit Rate......60l		....	....	....	....	....	....	....	....	....	....	....	....	....	7.67	6.00
Lending Rate......60p		6.92	7.50	8.25	8.33	8.00	8.17	8.83	8.79	8.00	10.17	11.79	12.25	12.50	12.13	10.00
Government Bond Yield......61		5.60	6.25	6.50	6.50	6.50	7.15	8.38	8.35	7.83	8.96	9.71	10.44	11.01	10.40	9.26

South Africa

1980	1981	1982	1983	1984	1985	1986	1987	1988	1989	1990	1991	1992	1993	1994		
															Exchange Rates	
End of Period																
1.0519	.8981	.8423	.7817	.5140	.3560	.3744	.3652	.3125	.3001	.2743	.2549	.2382	.2143	.1933	Principal Rate............ac=	wc
End of Period (wg)	*Period Average (wh)*															
1.3416	1.0454	.9291	.8184	.5038	.3910	.4580	.5182	.4206	.3943	.3902	.3646	.3275	.2943	.2822	Principal Rate............ag=	wg
1.2854	1.1491	.9245	.8991	.6954	.4564	.4408	.4914	.4423	.3822	.3866	.3628	.3509	.3064	.2818	Principal Rate............rh=	wh
.93560	.80000	.75750	....	....	.27250	.21500	....	....	....	....	....	....	....	....	Secondary Rate..........................	xg
Period Averages																
332.5	297.2	239.1	232.5	179.8	118.0	114.0	127.1	114.4	98.8	100.0	93.8	90.8	79.2	72.9	Principal Rate..........................	ahx
337.7	337.7	298.4	305.6	252.8	172.1	135.8	134.7	116.1	105.9	100.0	93.8	88.2	80.3	72.3	Nominal Effective Exchange Rate	nec
133.7	140.6	133.3	146.8	129.6	98.3	90.8	102.4	96.8	97.1	100.0	103.9	107.8	104.9	100.6	Real Effective Exchange Rate	rec
End of Period															**Fund Position**	
636	636	636	916	916	916	916	916	916	916	916	916	1,365	1,365	1,365	Quota	2f. s
37	115	99	27	2	1	—	1	1	1	2	1	—	9	1	SDRs	1b. s
128	107	—	70	70	—	—	—	—	—	—	—	—	—	—	Reserve Position in the Fund	1c. s
—	—	795	745	745	745	398	—	—	—	—	—	—	614	614	Total Fund Cred.&Loans Outstg.	2tl
End of Period															**International Liquidity**	
726	666	485	823	242	315	370	641	780	960	1,008	899	992	1,020	1,685	Total Reserves minus Gold........	1l. d
47	134	109	29	2	1	—	2	1	2	2	2	—	12	1	SDRs	1b. d
164	125	—	73	69	—	—	—	—	—	—	—	—	—	—	Reserve Position in the Fund	1c. d
515	407	376	721	171	314	370	639	779	958	1,006	897	991	1,008	1,684	Foreign Exchange	1d. d
12.15	9.29	7.57	7.79	7.36	4.84	4.82	5.83	3.47	3.08	4.09	6.47	6.65	4.76	4.20	Gold (Million Fine Troy Ounces)	1ad
6,512	3,339	3,075	2,660	2,039	1,420	1,698	2,541	1,295	1,137	1,415	2,074	1,992	1,658	1,445	Gold (National Valuation)	1and d
506	515	488	427	281	251	335	374	271	271	365	....	....	....	....	Monetary Authorities: Other Assets	3..d
—	1,204	539	1,187	1,228	1,201	511	499	545	570	324	126	385	1,812	....	Other Liab.	4..d
542	465	482	613	473	734	835	1,089	757	679	465	....	....	....	....	Deposit Money Banks: Assets ...	7a. d
804	1,476	1,481	1,623	1,275	1,750	2,141	2,262	2,060	2,372	2,613	....	....	....	....	Liabilities......	7b. d
End of Period															**Monetary Authorities**	
5,811	4,453	4,472	4,812	5,089	5,093	5,247	6,865	5,579	6,008	I7,144	8,847	10,570	10,627	12,481	Foreign Assets	11
2,679	3,508	2,917	2,246	499	774	1,255	494	1,304	1,519	I6,739	7,547	4,935	8,844	....	Claims on Central Government .	12a
127	105	434	1,393	1,902	857	658	988	1,633	2,513	I3,620	3,774	4,901	6,219	5,995	Claims on Deposit Money Banks	12e
3,560	4,159	3,687	4,204	4,860	5,426	5,800	6,819	9,398	12,077	I14,588	17,912	17,952	16,428	20,625	Reserve Money	14
1,861	2,273	2,491	2,763	3,190	3,552	4,181	5,025	6,128	7,314	I8,064	8,836	9,536	10,490	13,495	of which: Currency Outside DMBs	14a
—	1,152	1,523	2,404	3,887	5,165	2,177	963	1,296	1,445	I832	347	1,176	9,023	....	Foreign Liabilities	16c
2,391	1,649	3,708	3,369	1,277	197	2,368	2,474	5,239	9,863	I10,701	13,737	9,419	12,180	10,962	Central Government Deposits ...	16d
2,667	1,105	−1,095	−1,526	−2,533	−4,064	−3,185	−1,908	−7,417	−13,345	I−8,617	−11,827	−8,142	−10,911	....	Other Items (Net)	17r
End of Period															**Deposit Money Banks**	
1,660	1,826	1,158	1,394	1,621	1,860	1,580	1,748	3,006	4,468	....	....	....	....	....	Reserves	20
404	445	518	750	938	1,876	1,822	2,101	1,801	1,721	....	....	....	....	....	Foreign Assets	21
3,310	2,657	3,085	2,896	1,987	2,486	3,569	4,808	6,590	10,322	....	....	....	....	....	Claims on Central Government .	22a
15,712	21,419	25,873	30,298	39,529	46,273	49,413	56,765	76,660	103,299	....	....	....	....	....	Claims on Private Sector	22d
6,472	8,892	10,553	13,721	20,110	17,689	18,898	26,893	33,375	35,559	....	....	....	....	....	Demand Deposits	24
12,490	13,838	15,649	15,611	17,229	24,757	24,268	26,807	39,881	65,551	....	....	....	....	....	Time and Savings Deposits	25
7,861	9,075	10,796	11,251	12,640	19,244	18,424	19,978	32,997	51,869	....	....	....	....	....	Short & Medium-Term Deposits	25x
4,629	4,763	4,853	4,360	4,589	5,513	5,844	6,829	6,884	13,683	....	....	....	....	....	Long-Term Deposits	25y
600	1,412	1,594	1,983	2,531	4,476	4,675	4,365	4,898	6,016	....	....	....	....	....	Foreign Liabilities	26c
965	284	660	1,513	2,213	1,007	1,156	1,048	1,707	2,568	....	....	....	....	....	Credit from Monetary Authorities	26g
559	1,922	2,179	2,510	1,993	4,566	7,388	6,308	8,196	10,116	....	....	....	....	....	Other Items (Net)	27r
End of Period															**Monetary Survey**	
5,615	2,333	1,873	1,175	−390	−2,671	218	3,638	1,186	268	....	....	....	....	....	Foreign Assets (Net)	31n
19,433	25,933	28,161	32,390	40,942	49,639	51,850	60,000	79,872	106,051	....	....	....	....	....	Domestic Credit	32
3,319	4,187	1,798	1,179	594	2,422	1,893	2,064	1,432	512	....	....	....	....	....	Claims on Central Govt. (Net) .	32an
16,115	21,746	26,363	31,211	40,348	47,217	49,957	57,936	78,441	105,539	....	....	....	....	....	Claims on Private Sector	32d
8,398	11,273	13,124	16,586	23,413	21,332	23,207	32,026	39,934	43,343	....	....	....	....	....	Money	34
12,490	13,838	15,649	15,611	17,229	24,757	24,268	26,807	39,881	65,551	....	....	....	....	....	Quasi-Money	35
4,160	3,155	1,261	1,367	−89	878	4,593	4,806	1,243	−2,576	....	....	....	....	....	Other Items (Net)	37r
20,888	25,112	28,773	32,197	40,642	46,090	47,474	58,833	79,815	108,895	....	....	....	....	....	Money plus Quasi-Money	35l
End of Period															**Other Banking Institutions**	
															Building Societies	
11,137	13,009	14,348	17,752	20,284	22,846	26,020	29,977	33,923	29,021	33,224	....	....	....	....	Claims on Private Sector	42d
5,857	7,378	9,087	10,622	12,400	14,409	16,446	20,891	25,911	24,117	29,245	....	....	....	....	Time and Savings Deposits	45a
5,975	6,087	6,090	7,056	6,768	7,568	9,220	8,615	7,414	4,353	3,347	....	....	....	....	Building Societies Shares	45c
877	977	2,155	2,195	1,794	1,972	2,579	2,429	2,526	1,942	2,506	3,070	2,847	....	....	Bonds	46ab
−1,572	−1,433	−2,984	−2,120	−678	−1,103	−2,225	−1,959	−1,927	−1,391	−1,874	....	....	....	....	Other Items (Net)	47r
1,122	1,085	1,059	1,346	1,534	2,226	3,326	3,045	2,891	2,604	1,937	1,572	1,324	1,189	1,092	Post Office: Savings Deposits ...	45.. i
End of Period															**Nonbank Financial Institutions**	
1,969	2,913	2,552	2,618	4,477	4,790	7,980	14,825	22,613	25,438	24,580	24,444	27,794	30,938	....	Cash	40.. s
3,450	4,792	6,844	8,205	9,861	11,334	12,886	14,261	16,651	17,969	22,988	28,767	36,243	55,216	....	Claims on Central Government .	42a. s
1,740	1,850	2,002	2,070	2,144	2,474	2,885	3,243	3,684	3,778	4,119	4,303	5,034	6,268	....	Claims on Local Government ...	42b. s
9,753	12,214	15,110	19,399	23,026	30,361	46,053	48,309	54,472	72,109	87,642	153,699	170,906	225,784	....	Claims on Private Sector	42d. s
2,282	2,760	3,911	4,821	6,273	7,750	9,459	10,246	11,659	15,189	17,565	28,117	32,258	35,175	....	Real Estate	42h. s
3,891	5,335	5,890	6,694	8,668	10,928	22,554	11,621	18,195	25,404	22,411	82,436	32,905	81,146	....	Incr.in Total Assets(Within Per.)	49z. s
End of Period															**Financial Survey**	
5,615	2,333	1,873	1,175	−390	−2,671	218	3,638	1,186	268	....	....	....	....	....	Foreign Assets (Net)	51n
47,262	59,267	68,159	81,765	98,456	119,849	143,997	160,198	193,516	233,411	....	....	....	....	....	Domestic Credit	52
8,367	10,318	10,227	11,231	12,566	16,878	19,054	20,709	22,955	22,919	....	....	....	....	....	Claims on Central Govt. (Net) .	52an
38,895	48,949	57,932	70,534	85,890	102,971	124,943	139,490	170,561	210,492	....	....	....	....	....	Claims on Private Sector	52d
33,842	39,661	45,010	51,220	61,343	70,293	76,466	91,384	116,031	139,976	....	....	....	....	....	Liquid Liabilities	55l
877	977	2,155	2,195	1,794	1,972	2,579	2,429	2,526	1,942	2,506	3,070	2,847	....	....	Bonds	56ab
18,157	20,962	22,867	29,525	34,929	44,913	65,170	70,023	76,145	91,768	....	....	....	....	....	Other Items (Net)	57r
Percent Per Annum															**Interest Rates**	
6.54	14.54	14.35	17.75	20.75	13.00	9.50	9.50	14.50	18.00	18.00	17.00	14.00	12.00	13.00	Discount Rate (End of Period)...	60
4.40	10.25	16.90	13.98	20.31	18.21	10.92	9.50	13.90	18.77	19.46	17.02	14.11	10.83	10.24	Money Market Rate	60b
4.65	9.80	15.59	13.45	19.33	17.56	10.43	8.71	12.03	16.84	17.80	16.68	13.77	11.31	10.93	Treasury Bill Rate	60c
5.54	8.19	13.00	13.71	18.29	17.02	10.98	8.70	13.54	18.13	18.86	17.30	13.78	11.50	11.11	Deposit Rate	60l
9.50	14.00	19.33	16.67	22.33	21.50	14.33	12.50	15.33	19.83	21.00	20.31	18.91	16.16	15.58	Lending Rate	60p
10.09	12.99	13.51	12.67	15.23	16.79	16.37	15.30	16.37	16.90	16.15	16.34	15.44	13.97	14.83	Government Bond Yield	61

South Africa

199		1965	1966	1967	1968	1969	1970	1971	1972	1973	1974	1975	1976	1977	1978	1979
Prices, Production, Employment																*Index Numbers (1990=100):*
Share Prices: Industry & Comm.	62a	37	37	41	57	69	48	41	49	59	48	47	47	44	51	68
Gold Mining	62b	13	13	11	13	12	10	11	15	25	54	41	26	25	33	48
Prices: Home & Import Goods	63	7.2	7.4	7.6	7.7	7.9	8.1	8.5	9.2	10.5	12.3	14.4	16.7	18.9	20.7	23.9
Home Goods	63a	7.5	7.8	8.1	8.1	8.3	8.6	9.1	9.7	11.0	12.8	14.6	16.9	19.3	21.2	24.1
Consumer Prices	64	7.9	8.2	8.5	8.7	8.9	9.3	9.8	10.5	11.5	12.8	I 14.5	16.2	18.0	19.8	22.4
Manufacturing Production	66ey c	35.2	37.7	40.6	42.7	47.1	50.3	53.6	55.7	60.7	64.5	67.1	68.7	66.1	74.3	79.5
Mining Production	66zx c	111.7	106.4	106.0	109.8	111.8	117.0	114.1	107.5	110.5	103.1	98.8	99.8	101.4	102.4	105.8
Volume of Gold Produced	66kr	158.1	159.8	156.9	160.8	161.3	166.7	162.4	151.1	142.3	126.3	118.7	118.3	116.3	117.5	117.3
Manufacturing Employment	67ey c	58.5	61.4	63.8	65.4	69.5	I 73.9	76.3	78.2	82.3	86.9	90.2	92.4	90.7	90.9	93.1
Mining Employment	67zx c	80.8	81.4	79.2	80.8	80.8	I 84.5	83.3	80.6	86.6	85.5	80.2	84.2	89.4	90.7	94.6
International Transactions																*Millions of Rand*
Exports	70	1,819	1,958	2,151	2,289	2,398	2,389	2,491	3,160	I 4,187	5,908	6,448	6,826	8,612	11,106	15,345
Gold Output (Net)	70kr	775	769	775	769	847	837	922	1,161	1,769	2,565	2,540	2,346	2,795	3,907	6,003
Imports, cif	71	1,831	1,711	1,986	1,992	2,278	2,745	3,121	3,031	I 3,564	5,344	6,084	6,335	5,452	6,622	7,562
Imports, fob	71.v	1,756	1,646	1,919	1,880	2,135	2,547	2,887	2,813	I 3,275	4,909	5,545	5,859	5,118	6,263	7,027
																1990=100
Volume of Exports	72	29	33	39	44	42	43	44	I 53	54	56	55	60	71	77	88
Volume of Imports	73	68	61	70	71	79	93	101	I 85	97	121	113	96	75	84	83
Unit Value of Exports	74	9	9	9	9	9	9	9	I 10	12	15	17	20	21	23	26
Unit Value of Imports	75	6	6	6	6	6	6	6	I 7	8	10	13	16	18	20	25
Import Prices (1985=100)	76.x	12.1	12.4	12.6	12.8	13.0	13.3	13.9	15.6	17.4	21.3	26.1	30.8	33.8	37.2	44.5
Balance of Payments																*Millions of US Dollars:*
Goods: Exports f.o.b.	78aa d	....	....	....	....	....	....	....	....	....	....	....	8,296	10,443	13,041	17,696
Goods: Imports f.o.b.	78ab d	....	....	....	....	....	....	....	....	....	....	....	-8,559	-7,913	-9,222	-11,589
Trade Balance	78ac d	....	....	....	....	....	....	....	....	....	....	....	-263	2,530	3,819	6,107
Services: Credit	78ad d	....	....	....	....	....	....	....	....	....	....	....	1,400	1,598	1,863	2,226
Services: Debit	78ae d	....	....	....	....	....	....	....	....	....	....	....	-1,662	-1,919	-2,290	-2,700
Balance on Goods and Services	78af d	....	....	....	....	....	....	....	....	....	....	....	-526	2,209	3,392	5,633
Income: Credit	78ag d	....	....	....	....	....	....	....	....	....	....	....	329	247	378	550
Income: Debit	78ah d	....	....	....	....	....	....	....	....	....	....	....	-1,815	-1,976	-2,318	-2,880
Balance on Goods, Serv., & Inc.	78ai d	....	....	....	....	....	....	....	....	....	....	....	-2,011	481	1,452	3,302
Current Transfers, n.i.e.: Credit	78aj d	....	....	....	....	....	....	....	....	....	....	....	210	220	251	336
Current Transfers: Debit	78ak d	....	....	....	....	....	....	....	....	....	....	....	-107	-91	-121	-194
Current Account, n.i.e.	78al d	....	....	....	....	....	....	....	....	....	....	....	-1,908	609	1,582	3,445
Capital Account, n.i.e.: Credit	78ba d	....	....	....	....	....	....	....	....	....	....	....	92	38	43	46
Capital Account: Debit	78bb d	....	....	....	....	....	....	....	....	....	....	....	-61	-114	-92	-74
Capital Account, n.i.e.	78bc d	....	....	....	....	....	....	....	....	....	....	....	31	-76	-49	-27
Direct Investment Abroad	78bd d	....	....	....	....	....	....	....	....	....	....	....	-32	-68	-238	-11
Dir. Invest. in Rep. Econ., n.i.e.	78be d	....	....	....	....	....	....	....	....	....	....	....	18	-122	-109	-488
Portfolio Investment Assets	78bf d	....	....	....	....	....	....	....	....	....	....	....	-2	7	3	-238
Portfolio Investment Liab., n.i.e.	78bg d	....	....	....	....	....	....	....	....	....	....	....	-29	1	125	-244
Other Investment Assets	78bh d	....	....	....	....	....	....	....	....	....	....	....	-250	-215	-213	-601
Other Investment Liab., n.i.e.	78bi d	....	....	....	....	....	....	....	....	....	....	....	1,672	198	-2	-678
Financial Account, n.i.e.	78bj d	....	....	....	....	....	....	....	....	....	....	....	1,378	-199	-434	-2,259
Net Errors and Omissions	78ca d	....	....	....	....	....	....	....	....	....	....	....	-201	-661	-520	-685
Overall Balance	78cb d	....	....	....	....	....	....	....	....	....	....	....	-700	-326	580	474
Reserves and Related Items	79da d	....	....	....	....	....	....	....	....	....	....	....	700	326	-580	-474
Reserve Assets	79db d	....	....	....	....	....	....	....	....	....	....	....	311	415	-40	3
Use of Fund Credit and Loans	79dc d	....	....	....	....	....	....	....	....	....	....	....	365	89	-97	-308
Liabs.Constit.For.Auth.Reserves	79dd d	....	....	....	....	....	....	....	....	....	....	....	3	2	-93	-8
Exceptional Financing	79de d	....	....	....	....	....	....	....	....	....	....	....	21	-181	-350	-161
Government Finance																*Millions of Rand:*
Deficit (-) or Surplus	80	-275	-332	-323	-322	-326	-447	-811	-587	-391	-810	-1,300	-2,045	-1,807	-2,032	-1,959
Revenue	81	1,302	1,436	1,655	1,685	2,143	2,318	2,730	3,182	4,202	4,986	5,685	6,516	7,274	8,515	10,217
Expenditure	82	1,577	1,768	1,978	2,007	2,469	2,765	3,541	3,769	4,593	5,796	6,985	8,561	9,081	10,547	12,176
Total Financing	84	278	335	321	324	331	445	811	589	393	815	1,298	2,044	1,803	2,029	1,959
Net Domestic Borrowing	84a	196	394	495	655	287	87	557	906	731	604	1,319	1,492	2,236	2,457	1,966
Monetary Sector	84aa	114	61	115	122	-64	-83	178	350	377	205	849	410	471	-322	227
Public Investment Commission	84ab	17	166	121	232	291	124	24	126	255	259	38	183	575	1,290	742
Private Sector	84ac	65	167	259	301	60	46	355	430	99	140	432	899	1,190	1,489	997
Net Foreign Borrowing	85a	-10	-15	-47	20	53	123	113	83	-84	93	347	356	-157	-347	-34
Adj: Extraord. Recpts and Trans.	86a	....	....	....	....	....	....	....	....	....	....	....	....	....	....	....
Minus: Disc.on New Iss.Govt Stock	86b	....	....	....	....	....	....	....	....	....	....	....	....	....	....	....
Use of Cash Balances	87	92	-44	-127	-351	-9	235	141	-400	-254	118	-368	196	-276	-81	27
Total Debt	88	3,414	3,779	4,229	4,893	5,239	5,484	6,205	7,173	7,799	8,505	10,291	12,110	14,270	16,324	18,182
Domestic Debt	88a	3,238	3,651	4,123	4,781	5,086	5,204	5,755	6,640	7,364	7,948	9,259	10,753	13,006	15,484	17,420
Held By: Reserve Bank	88aa	80	98	114	96	129	177	201	146	516	421	860	643	526	481	316
Deposit Money Bks.	88ab	696	741	897	1,002	973	820	986	1,387	1,924	2,197	2,653	3,257	3,847	3,052	3,371
Other Finan. Inst.	88ac	220	310	373	469	515	551	711	1,011	1,128	1,253	1,590	1,914	2,634	3,317	3,825
Public Invest.Comm.	88ad	2,080	2,242	2,362	2,608	2,902	3,027	3,053	3,178	3,432	3,692	3,731	3,916	4,492	5,783	6,525
Other	88ae	191	301	468	662	677	677	867	1,006	979	972	1,064	1,639	2,123	2,935	3,392
Gold and Foreign Exchange Contingency Reserve Account	88b	....	....	....	....	....	....	....	....	....	....	....	....	....	....	....
Foreign Debt	89a	176	128	106	112	153	280	450	533	435	557	1,032	1,357	1,264	840	762
TBVC Ctries & Self-Gov.St.Debt	89c	....	....	....	....	....	....	....	....	....	....	....	....	....	....	....
National Accounts																*Millions of Rand*
Exports of Goods & Services	90c. c	2,071	2,220	2,397	2,652	2,718	2,747	3,054	3,987	4,953	6,716	7,480	8,504	10,339	12,681	16,470
Government Consumption	91f. c	851	958	1,022	1,121	1,283	1,516	1,828	1,937	2,219	2,802	3,687	4,465	5,034	5,526	6,329
Gross Fixed Capital Formation	93e. c	1,901	1,974	2,094	2,230	2,559	3,085	3,605	4,176	4,885	5,945	7,846	9,046	9,312	10,087	12,015
Increase/Decrease(-) in Stocks	93i. c	164	30	420	281	359	403	575	-184	110	1,066	681	-490	-370	-434	238
Private Consumption	96f. c	4,619	5,031	5,465	6,037	6,769	7,613	8,536	9,503	11,134	13,106	15,167	17,116	18,914	21,086	24,427
Imports of Goods & Services	98c. c	-2,136	-2,007	-2,345	-2,324	-2,644	-3,189	-3,629	-3,568	-4,406	-6,838	-8,128	-8,795	-8,491	-9,931	-11,969
Gross Domestic Product	99b. c	7,682	8,364	9,355	10,125	11,395	12,473	13,767	15,535	19,218	23,690	26,646	30,020	33,263	38,247	45,772
Net Factor Inc/Pmts(-) Abroad	98.n	-322	-345	-358	-410	-474	-523	-524	-605	-724	-938	-1,249	-1,443	-1,659	-1,877	-2,144
Gross Nat'l Expenditure = GNP	99a	6,561	7,116	8,005	8,641	9,749	10,621	11,710	13,122	16,382	20,183	22,087	24,433	26,811	30,697	36,884
Nat'l Income, Market Prices	99e	6,855	7,477	8,336	8,964	10,099	10,974	12,148	13,513	17,042	20,931	22,862	25,403	27,825	31,637	37,683
Gross Dom. Prod. 1990 Prices	99b. r	132,744	138,635	148,612	154,785	162,084	170,592	177,891	180,834	189,103	200,659	204,061	208,652	208,456	214,740	I 222,879
GDP Deflator (1990=100)	99bi r	5.8	6.0	6.3	6.5	7.0	7.3	7.7	8.6	10.2	11.8	13.1	14.4	16.0	17.8	20.5
																Millions:
Population	99z	19.61	20.16	20.73	21.29	21.88	22.47	23.03	23.67	24.30	24.92	25.47	26.13	26.68	27.30	27.67

South Africa
199

1980	1981	1982	1983	1984	1985	1986	1987	1988	1989	1990	1991	1992	1993	1994		
Period Averages															**Prices, Production, Employment**	
100	99	86	109	I107	114	59	87	68	95	100	133	149	162	224	Share Prices: Industry & Comm.	62a
100	79	64	99	I112	119	94	130	80	96	100	69	58	90	129	Gold Mining	62b
27.7	31.5	35.9	39.7	43.0	50.3	60.1	68.5	77.5	89.3	100.0	111.4	120.6	128.5	139.1	Prices: Home & Import Goods	63
27.8	31.8	36.1	40.0	43.3	49.8	59.1	68.1	77.5	88.9	100.0	112.1	122.3	130.9	142.5	Home Goods	63a
I25.5	29.4	33.7	I37.8	42.2	49.0	58.2	67.5	76.2	I87.4	100.0	115.3	131.3	144.0	157.1	Consumer Prices	64
88.3	95.9	92.1	89.3	93.7	94.0	92.4	94.7	101.2	102.4	100.0	95.5	92.4	92.2	94.7	Manufacturing Production	66ey c
104.4	104.3	103.5	103.9	108.6	109.4	106.1	101.5	103.3	101.9	100.0	99.1	99.5	102.5	99.8	Mining Production	66zx c
112.3	109.1	110.5	113.0	113.6	110.6	105.2	100.1	101.9	100.1	100.0	99.3	102.1	....	....	Volume of Gold Produced	66kr
97.0	I99.3	100.5	96.7	96.8	94.2	I93.3	94.1	100.4	100.4	100.0	97.4	94.3	92.2	....	Manufacturing Employment	67ey c
97.6	98.3	94.6	92.7	I96.2	100.0	I103.7	103.7	101.4	100.0	100.0	92.7	85.3	79.6	....	Mining Employment	67zx c
Millions of Rand															**International Transactions**	
19,880	18,129	19,189	20,620	25,320	36,312	42,011	43,202	49,724	58,199	60,929	64,355	66,774	79,279	88,724	Exports	70
10,140	8,338	8,641	9,929	11,684	15,461	16,727	17,768	19,280	19,095	18,070	19,648	18,195	22,229	22,661	Gold Output (Net)	70kr
I15,264	20,118	19,987	17,617	23,538	25,226	29,688	31,105	42,566	48,515	47,605	52,006	56,358	65,411	83,042	Imports, cif	71
I14,363	18,439	18,374	16,204	21,636	22,691	26,864	28,673	39,484	44,741	44,212	48,209	52,857	58,779	76,379	Imports, fob	71.v
1990=100																
I85	77	77	69	76	90	93	91	I98	106	100	100	88	107	....	Volume of Exports	72
I108	123	103	86	103	88	85	89	I109	109	100	100	103	107	....	Volume of Imports	73
30	I33	36	40	46	58	66	69	I79	95	100	106	112	122	....	Unit Value of Exports	74
30	I34	41	44	48	62	72	75	I83	93	100	110	117	127	....	Unit Value of Imports	75
53.4	59.1	68.0	74.8	80.9	100.0	122.6	134.5	....	....	....	....	....	....	....	Import Prices (1985=100)	76.x
Minus Sign Indicates Debit															Balance of Payments	
25,698	20,632	17,328	18,241	16,948	16,244	18,330	21,088	22,432	22,399	23,560	23,289	23,645	24,068	....	Goods: Exports f.o.b.	78aa d
–18,268	–20,622	–16,683	–14,202	–14,774	–10,402	–11,130	–13,925	–17,210	–16,810	–16,778	–17,156	–18,216	–18,287	....	Goods: Imports f.o.b.	78ab d
7,430	10	645	4,039	2,174	5,842	7,200	7,163	5,222	5,589	6,783	6,134	5,429	5,781	....	Trade Balance	78ac d
2,929	3,005	2,790	2,676	2,484	1,995	2,048	2,469	2,585	2,729	3,559	3,474	3,611	3,571	....	Services: Credit	78ad d
–3,805	–4,202	–3,689	–3,407	–3,209	–2,488	–2,899	–3,367	–3,484	–3,655	–4,239	–4,238	–4,833	–5,101	....	Services: Debit	78ae d
6,554	–1,187	–254	3,308	1,449	5,349	6,348	6,265	4,323	4,664	6,102	5,370	4,207	4,251	....	Balance on Goods and Services	78af d
631	525	446	524	565	610	678	641	659	815	833	1,012	1,058	872	....	Income: Credit	78ag d
–3,916	–4,168	–3,627	–4,018	–3,701	–3,410	–3,962	–4,183	–3,940	–4,101	–4,929	–4,195	–3,983	–3,449	....	Income: Debit	78ah d
3,269	–4,831	–3,435	–186	–1,687	2,549	3,064	2,723	1,043	1,378	2,006	2,187	1,282	1,675	....	Balance on Goods, Serv., & Inc.	78ai d
526	582	448	459	369	299	324	367	309	325	298	242	215	262	....	Current Transfers, n.i.e.: Credit	78aj d
–287	–240	–190	–264	–272	–226	–226	–157	–148	–139	–238	–186	–121	–132	....	Current Transfers: Debit	78ak d
3,508	–4,489	–3,178	9	–1,589	2,622	3,163	2,934	1,204	1,564	2,065	2,243	1,376	1,804	....	Current Account, n.i.e.	78al d
64	45	42	45	37	27	19	21	29	23	23	27	25	24	....	Capital Account, n.i.e.: Credit	78ba d
–64	–67	–48	–44	–36	–26	–30	–19	–15	–8	–12	–12	–14	–23	....	Capital Account: Debit	78bb d
—	–23	–6	1	2	—	–11	2	14	15	12	16	11	1	....	Capital Account, n.i.e.	78bc d
–746	–700	43	–157	–184	–47	–63	–88	–18	2	—	—	—	—	....	Direct Investment Abroad	78bd d
–19	121	338	69	435	–449	–53	–75	116	8	–5	–8	–5	–8	....	Dir. Invest. in Rep. Econ., n.i.e.	78be d
–18	6	6	66	—	12	–3	—	—	—	—	—	—	—	....	Portfolio Investment Assets	78bf d
–372	–294	–196	–600	1,115	297	–708	–181	–54	–138	–50	78	1,496	225	....	Portfolio Investment Liab., n.i.e.	78bg d
–250	–528	–144	–387	–360	–802	–905	–38	–175	–742	–97	–492	–704	–583	....	Other Investment Assets	78bh d
142	3,318	3,168	1,690	1,150	–996	–793	–973	–1,507	–248	495	898	–601	–1,298	....	Other Investment Liab., n.i.e.	78bi d
–1,262	1,924	3,215	681	2,156	–1,985	–2,525	–1,355	–1,640	–1,117	344	476	187	–1,664	....	Financial Account, n.i.e.	78bj d
–1,451	388	–276	–403	–1,149	–1,145	–134	–220	–965	–575	–1,016	–1,228	–1,443	–2,936	....	Net Errors and Omissions	78ca d
795	–2,200	–245	287	–581	–507	493	1,361	–1,386	–113	1,405	1,506	131	–2,795	....	Overall Balance	78cb d
–795	2,200	245	–287	581	507	–493	–1,361	1,386	113	–1,405	–1,506	–131	2,795	....	Reserves and Related Items	79da d
–690	1,046	49	–942	525	526	570	–906	766	–527	–356	–1,111	–402	575	....	Reserve Assets	79db d
–101	—	848	–52	—	—	–409	–515	—	—	—	—	—	850	....	Use of Fund Credit and Loans	79dc d
20	8	–2	13	—	–7	16	–14	8	27	11	–7	–10	51	....	Liabs.Constit.For.Auth.Reserves	79dd d
–24	1,145	–650	694	56	–12	–669	75	612	613	–1,060	–389	282	1,319	....	Exceptional Financing	79de d
Year Beginning April 1															**Government Finance**	
–551	–2,341	–2,370	–4,586	–4,350	–4,479	–6,903	–10,557	–9,162	–8,400	–16,581	–13,094	–27,254	–25,346	....	Deficit (-) or Surplus	80
13,388	14,526	17,196	19,103	23,533	29,765	34,557	38,384	49,684	66,081	68,168	77,105	81,875	96,226	....	Revenue	81
13,939	16,867	19,566	23,689	27,883	34,244	41,460	48,941	58,846	74,481	84,749	90,199	109,129	121,572	....	Expenditure	82
558	2,344	2,371	4,589	4,353	4,477	6,904	10,552	9,164	8,400	16,577	13,096	27,252	25,342	....	Total Financing	84
1,613	1,773	3,579	3,888	4,098	4,802	7,479	10,659	11,453	13,061	I13,681	17,283	31,945	41,559	....	Net Domestic Borrowing	84a
–34	–148	198	1,391	–1,126	1,476	903	3,051	288	3,291	I1,457	–2,560	258	13,976	....	Monetary Sector	84aa
1,049	330	894	815	2,123	2,920	5,621	3,706	6,629	4,111	4,201	4,554	13,994	14,527	....	Public Investment Commission	84ab
598	1,591	2,487	1,682	3,101	406	955	3,902	4,536	5,659	I8,023	15,289	17,693	13,056	....	Private Sector	84ac
–94	425	26	184	254	–135	–86	–92	–96	58	–80	899	807	–319	....	Net Foreign Borrowing	85a
....	....	....	....	....	....	....	....	....	....	I319	–991	–4,633	–13,430	....	Adj: Extraord. Recpts and Trans.	86a
....	....	....	....	....	....	....	....	....	....	I357	4,299	4,080	2,630	....	Minus: Disc.on New Iss.Govt Stock	86b
–961	146	–1,234	517	1	–190	–489	–15	–2,193	–4,719	3,014	204	3,213	162	....	Use of Cash Balances	87
19,883	22,091	26,484	30,506	36,449	41,086	47,619	57,503	68,737	81,905	105,658	126,615	154,668	192,159	....	Total Debt	88
19,223	20,821	24,300	28,077	32,837	37,190	44,399	55,061	66,510	79,815	93,536	111,167	143,386	184,768	....	Domestic Debt	88a
904	684	755	926	522	1,278	486	447	373	535	1,723	490	2,214	7,894	....	Held By: Reserve Bank	88aa
3,733	3,721	3,343	4,144	3,587	4,184	5,841	8,915	9,495	13,219	15,120	13,743	12,183	20,623	....	Deposit Money Bks.	88ab
3,831	5,522	7,613	8,925	10,959	12,516	12,520	13,882	18,794	22,715	24,035	22,322	30,606	40,076	....	Other Finan. Inst.	88ac
7,573	7,903	8,797	9,489	11,611	14,530	20,151	23,860	30,489	34,599	38,798	43,303	57,329	71,872	....	Public Invest.Comm.	88ad
3,901	3,788	4,214	4,606	5,700	4,541	5,423	7,963	7,550	9,595	13,860	31,309	41,054	44,303	....	Other	88ae
															Gold and Foreign Exchange	
....	....	....	....	....	....	....	....	....	....	10,351	12,508	8,934	2,190	....	Contingency Reserve Account	88b
660	1,270	2,184	2,429	3,612	3,896	3,220	2,442	2,227	2,090	1,771	2,940	2,348	5,201	....	Foreign Debt	89a
....	....	....	....	....	....	....	....	....	....	—	—	—	—	....	TBVC Ctries & Self-Gov.St.Debt	89c
Millions of Rand															**National Accounts**	
22,022	20,661	21,778	23,079	28,015	I39,698	45,508	48,627	57,890	66,021	70,714	74,220	78,070	91,013	102,682	Exports of Goods & Services	90c. c
8,158	9,877	12,361	14,115	17,927	I21,297	25,672	30,516	35,865	44,713	52,702	61,169	70,196	79,047	91,349	Government Consumption	91f. c
16,040	19,238	22,459	24,498	26,209	I28,715	28,992	30,850	39,717	49,585	54,113	55,285	56,711	58,837	68,101	Gross Fixed Capital Formation	93e. c
2,569	3,807	–2,167	–893	485	I–3,734	–1,609	28	2,311	1,249	–5,479	–2,937	–2,608	2,407	10,209	Increase/Decrease(-) in Stocks	93i. c
30,797	38,086	44,564	51,596	59,705	I65,890	78,211	93,277	113,151	133,955	159,530	183,005	207,769	230,630	256,320	Private Consumption	96f. c
–17,034	–21,749	–21,897	–19,512	–25,931	I–28,546	–32,239	–35,187	–47,027	–53,449	–54,046	–58,726	–65,285	–76,155	–94,415	Imports of Goods & Services	98c. c
60,328	71,080	80,531	91,457	107,221	I123,126	143,255	167,098	200,448	240,639	276,060	310,074	340,963	383,071	432,753	Gross Domestic Product	99b. c
–2,739	–3,314	–3,703	–4,164	–4,655	I–5,986	–7,010	–6,693	–7,572	–9,310	–11,529	–9,509	–9,145	–9,458	–10,561	Net Factor Inc/Pmts(-) Abroad	98.n
49,570	67,664	76,828	87,293	102,566	I117,140	136,245	160,405	192,876	231,329	264,531	300,565	331,818	373,613	422,192	Gross Nat'l Expenditure = GNP	99a
52,307	57,976	64,829	73,077	86,445	I97,495	111,548	132,407	160,492	192,955	221,594	253,845	281,546	319,492	362,655	Nat'l Income, Market Prices	99e
237,635	250,375	249,415	244,809	257,292	I254,175	254,221	259,561	270,463	276,940	276,060	273,249	267,257	270,181	276,464	Gross Dom. Prod. 1990 Prices	99b. r
25.4	28.4	32.3	37.4	41.7	I48.4	56.4	64.4	74.1	86.9	100.0	113.5	127.6	141.8	156.5	GDP Deflator (1990=100)	99bi r
Midyear Estimates																
28.28	28.90	29.54	31.93	32.25	33.04	33.83	34.63	35.42	36.24	37.07	37.91	38.78	39.66	40.44	**Population**	99z

(Notes in the back of the book)

Spain
184

		1965	1966	1967	1968	1969	1970	1971	1972	1973	1974	1975	1976	1977	1978	1979
Exchange Rates															*Pesetas per SDR:*	
Market Rate	aa	59.99	60.00	69.70	69.82	70.06	69.72	71.68	69.02	68.70	ɪ68.70	69.98	79.34	98.28	91.34	87.14
															Pesetas per US Dollar:	
Market Rate	ae	59.99	60.00	69.70	69.82	70.06	69.72	66.02	63.57	56.95	ɪ56.11	59.77	68.29	80.91	70.11	66.15
Market Rate	rf	60.00	60.00	61.67	70.00	70.00	70.00	69.47	64.27	58.26	57.69	57.41	66.90	75.96	76.67	67.13
														Index Numbers (1990=100):		
Market Rate	ahx	169.7	169.6	166.7	145.8	145.5	145.8	146.8	158.1	174.6	176.2	176.8	152.1	135.1	133.0	151.5
Nominal Effective Exchange Rate	neu	190.5	190.5	186.1	166.5	167.7	167.2	165.3	165.9	166.4	173.2	167.2	158.0	139.6	125.1	139.6
Real Effective Exchange Rate	reu	....	....	....	....	....	....	....	....	....	....	78.9	84.9	89.9	90.1	104.7
Fund Position															*Millions of SDRs:*	
Quota	2f. s	150	250	250	250	250	395	395	395	395	395	395	395	395	557	557
SDRs	1b. s	—	—	—	—	—	43	87	129	129	134	121	91	48	103	206
Reserve Position in the Fund	1c. s	141	166	—	—	—	45	104	104	104	121	—	—	—	136	133
Total Fund Cred.&Loans Outstg.	2tl	—	—	—	—	—	—	—	—	—	—	—	496	572	615	205
International Liquidity											*Millions of US Dollars Unless Otherwise Indicated:*					
Total Reserves minus Gold	1l. d	612	468	315	364	497	1,319	2,727	4,473	6,170	5,874	5,506	4,704	5,977	10,112	13,224
SDRs	1b. d	—	—	—	—	—	43	94	140	155	164	142	105	59	134	272
Reserve Position in the Fund	1c. d	141	166	—	—	—	45	113	113	125	148	—	—	—	178	176
Foreign Exchange	1d. d	471	302	315	364	497	1,231	2,520	4,221	5,889	5,562	5,364	4,599	5,918	9,801	12,777
Gold (Million Fine Troy Ounces)	1ad	23.15	22.44	22.42	22.42	22.41	14.23	14.23	14.23	14.27	14.27	14.27	14.27	14.44	14.52	14.61
Gold (National Valuation)	1and	810	785	785	785	784	498	498	541	602	602	602	602	609	613	617
Deposit Money Banks: Assets	7a. d	232	245	301	333	546	1,004	1,569	2,514	3,774	3,033	3,242	3,644	4,583	7,228	10,535
of which: Claims on Nonbanks	7add	17	17	15	24	28	37	44	67	109	107	125	127	163	226	326
Deposit Money Banks: Liabilities	7b. d	353	353	459	450	612	1,216	2,035	3,104	4,658	5,016	6,060	7,909	10,275	13,949	19,179
of which: Liabs. to Nonbanks	7bdd	212	236	263	286	364	549	873	1,292	1,761	2,138	2,356	3,275	4,181	5,751	7,338
Other Banking Insts.: Assets	7e. d	—	—	—	—	—	—	—	—	—	1	1	1	....	....	....
Liabilities	7f. d	—	—	—	20	46	68	89	92	109	336	306	391	566	864	1,389
Monetary Authorities															*Billions of Pesetas:*	
Foreign Assets	11	84	74	79	83	92	127	227	320	399	359	354	329	486	777	939
Claims on Central Government	12a	59	80	103	116	136	134	117	97	120	202	296	321	458	570	833
Claims on Deposit Money Banks	12e	44	65	76	81	116	104	61	72	73	154	180	367	360	230	325
Reserve Money	14	181	205	228	250	279	314	391	455	542	664	780	897	1,092	1,365	1,832
of which: Currency Outside DMBs	14a	151	175	199	218	243	263	294	328	387	447	524	614	777	946	1,039
Central Government Deposits	16d	10	10	13	15	19	26	34	34	44	52	45	45	90	74	109
Capital Accounts	17a	....	....	....	....	....	....	....	....	....	....	....	....	....	....	....
Other Items (Net)	17r	–3	4	17	15	45	24	–21	–1	7	–2	4	75	122	139	156
Deposit Money Banks															*Billions of Pesetas:*	
Reserves	20	27	27	25	29	32	45	89	119	143	208	241	269	291	392	762
Foreign Assets	21	14	15	21	23	38	70	101	162	219	170	194	249	371	507	697
Claims on Central Government	22a	176	208	243	290	336	363	435	491	523	542	605	752	774	1,018	1,255
Claims on Local Government	22b	....	....	....	....	....	....	....	....	....	....	....	....	....	....	....
Claims on Private Sector	22d	635	742	873	1,065	1,310	1,524	1,833	2,329	3,019	3,810	4,674	5,746	6,979	7,891	9,072
Claims on Other Financial Insts.	22f	3	3	4	3	3	3	5	4	10	7	9	13	18	23	32
Demand Deposits	24	273	299	341	389	452	473	614	802	1,011	1,199	1,424	1,759	2,038	2,353	2,546
Time and Savings Deposits	25	484	563	658	818	997	1,211	1,505	1,843	2,300	2,764	3,294	3,877	4,605	5,628	6,942
Bonds	26ab	10	13	16	20	27	34	38	59	114	166	221	260	281	290	281
Foreign Liabilities	26c	21	21	32	31	43	85	131	200	270	281	362	540	831	978	1,269
Central Government Deposits	26d	9	10	17	18	27	27	35	36	45	53	69	75	95	92	121
Credit from Monetary Authorities	26g	44	65	75	80	116	104	61	72	73	148	180	368	359	236	301
Capital Accounts	27a	50	66	95	125	145	166	193	236	305	392	490	589	669	800	1,085
Other Items (Net)	27r	–36	–43	–70	–70	–87	–94	–114	–144	–203	–266	–317	–439	–446	–545	–726
Monetary Survey															*Billions of Pesetas:*	
Foreign Assets (Net)	31n	77	66	64	71	56	106	196	282	348	247	150	–10	–32	249	349
Domestic Credit	32	857	1,016	1,194	1,443	1,741	1,974	2,323	2,851	3,583	4,457	5,470	6,713	8,048	9,341	10,967
Claims on Central Govt. (Net)	32an	215	268	315	373	426	444	483	518	554	639	787	953	1,048	1,422	1,858
Claims on Local Government	32b	....	....	....	....	....	....	....	....	....	....	....	....	....	....	....
Claims on Private Sector	32d	638	745	875	1,067	1,312	1,526	1,835	2,329	3,019	3,811	4,675	5,748	6,982	7,895	9,077
Money	34	429	480	545	612	701	743	920	1,142	1,410	1,654	1,963	2,392	2,836	3,325	3,610
Quasi-Money	35	484	563	658	818	997	1,211	1,505	1,843	2,300	2,764	3,294	3,877	4,605	5,628	6,942
Other Items (Net)	37r	21	38	55	85	98	125	94	148	221	286	363	433	575	636	765
Money plus Quasi-Money	35l	913	1,043	1,204	1,430	1,698	1,955	2,424	2,985	3,710	4,419	5,257	6,270	7,441	8,953	10,551
Other Banking Institutions															*Billions of Pesetas:*	
Cash	40	2	2	2	2	3	5	8	10	10	8	10	18	37	30	31
Foreign Assets	41	....	....	....	....	....	....	....	....	....	....	....	....	....	....	....
Claims on Central Government	42a	20	23	28	34	39	43	50	58	82	96	115	145	194	233	305
Claims on Local Government	42b	....	....	....	....	....	....	....	....	....	....	....	....	....	....	....
Claims on Private Sector	42d	112	140	166	193	221	232	243	238	241	290	372	481	612	768	950
Claims on Deposit Money Banks	42e	....	....	....	....	....	....	....	....	....	....	....	....	....	....	....
Time Deposits	45	....	....	....	....	....	1	3	4	4	6	7	12	15	13	12
Bonds	46ab	25	24	24	23	23	23	22	22	22	21	21	25	35	39	55
Foreign Liabilities	46c	—	—	—	1	3	5	6	6	6	19	18	27	46	61	92
Central Government Deposits	46d	....	....	....	....	....	....	....	....	....	....	....	....	....	....	....
Credit from Deposit Money Banks	46h	4	4	5	6	6	6	6	4	4	4	4	4	4	4	20
Other Items (Net)	47r	11	20	30	22	20	20	19	7	9	22	25	54	ɪ51	70	101
Banking Survey															*Billions of Pesetas:*	
Foreign Assets (Net)	51n	....	....	....	....	....	....	....	....	....	....	....	....	....	....	....
Domestic Credit	52	....	....	....	....	....	....	....	....	....	....	....	....	....	....	....
Claims on Central Govt. (Net)	52an	....	....	....	....	....	....	....	....	....	....	....	....	....	....	....
Claims on Local Government	52b	....	....	....	....	....	....	....	....	....	....	....	....	....	....	....
Claims on Private Sector	52d	....	....	....	....	....	....	....	....	....	....	....	....	....	....	....
Liquid Liabilities	55l	911	1,041	1,202	1,428	1,696	1,950	2,416	2,975	3,700	4,411	5,247	6,252	7,403	8,923	10,520
Bonds	56ab	....	....	....	....	....	....	....	....	....	....	....	....	....	....	....
Central Govt. Lending Funds	56f	....	....	....	....	....	....	....	....	....	....	....	....	....	....	....
Capital Accounts	57a	....	....	....	....	....	....	....	....	....	....	....	....	....	....	....
Other Items (Net)	57r	....	....	....	....	....	....	....	....	....	....	....	....	....	....	....

Spain

1980	1981	1982	1983	1984	1985	1986	1987	1988	1989	1990	1991	1992	1993	1994		
End of Period															**Exchange Rates**	
101.08	113.43	138.55	164.06	169.97	169.32	161.94	154.63	152.67	144.19	137.87	138.31	157.61	195.34	192.32	Market Rate	aa
End of Period (ae) Period Average (rf)																
79.25	97.45	125.60	156.70	173.40	154.15	132.40	109.00	113.45	109.72	96.91	96.69	114.62	142.21	131.74	Market Rate	ae
71.70	92.32	109.86	143.43	160.76	170.04	140.05	123.48	116.49	118.38	101.93	103.91	102.38	127.26	133.96	Market Rate	rf
Period Averages																
142.1	110.5	93.0	71.2	63.4	59.9	72.7	82.5	87.4	86.0	100.0	98.1	99.6	80.3	76.0	Market Rate	ah x
125.9	119.1	114.0	96.3	96.3	94.6	90.9	89.6	92.7	97.2	100.0	100.2	97.9	86.9	81.1	Nominal Effective Exchange Rate	ne u
97.0	94.6	94.0	81.2	83.9	83.5	81.7	83.2	87.0	94.1	100.0	101.8	102.5	94.0	....	Real Effective Exchange Rate	re u
End of Period															**Fund Position**	
836	836	836	1,286	1,286	1,286	1,286	1,286	1,286	1,286	1,286	1,286	1,935	1,935	1,935	Quota	2f. s
231	319	186	65	155	254	353	420	457	523	489	319	134	157	174	SDRs	1b. s
206	206	206	322	363	369	423	554	786	930	797	749	832	751	760	Reserve Position in the Fund	1c. s
205	142	5	—	—	—	—	—	—	—	—	—	—	—	—	Total Fund Cred.&Loans Outstg.	2tl
End of Period															**International Liquidity**	
11,863	10,805	7,655	7,402	11,955	11,175	14,755	30,669	37,074	41,467	51,228	65,822	45,504	41,045	41,569	Total Reserves minus Gold	1l. d
294	371	205	68	151	280	432	596	615	687	696	456	184	216	255	SDRs	1b. d
262	239	227	337	356	405	518	785	1,058	1,222	1,134	1,071	1,144	1,031	1,109	Reserve Position in the Fund	1c. d
11,307	10,195	7,223	6,997	11,448	10,490	13,805	29,287	35,401	39,558	49,398	64,295	44,176	39,798	40,205	Foreign Exchange	1d. d
14.61	14.61	14.61	14.61	14.63	14.65	14.82	11.92	14.04	15.72	15.61	15.62	15.62	15.62	15.62	Gold (Million Fine Troy Ounces)	1ad
617	4,353	3,666	3,827	3,832	3,722	3,785	3,767	4,766	5,419	4,777	4,498	4,217	4,217	4,217	Gold (National Valuation)	1an d
12,790	14,824	I 17,362	15,712	17,524	20,039	23,817	25,728	24,571	27,511	39,107	46,642	68,542	117,311	110,693	Deposit Money Banks: Assets	7a. d
387	410	I 5,734	5,739	6,177	7,108	8,358	9,253	8,688	10,409	13,602	17,275	18,000	27,287	27,666	*of which:* Claims on Nonbanks	7ad d
22,856	26,175	I 21,534	19,417	21,209	20,939	25,409	33,186	36,998	43,627	63,986	73,724	81,501	87,093	100,658	Deposit Money Banks: Liabilities	7b. d
8,850	10,290	I 9,670	9,377	10,410	11,781	13,459	15,915	18,115	21,439	26,500	28,194	30,855	29,379	37,301	*of which:* Liabs. to Nonbanks	7bd d
....	....	....	418	476	579	690	863	1,212	1,193	1,521	2,290	2,695	3,736	4,082	4,714	Other Banking Insts.: Assets	7e. d
1,643	1,696	1,974	1,977	1,778	1,515	I —	—	—	—	—	1	5	845	510	471	Liabilities	7f. d
End of Period															**Monetary Authorities**	
906	1,182	930	I 1,245	2,096	1,696	I 1,996	3,643	4,609	4,938	5,348	6,731	5,604	6,152	5,796	Foreign Assets	11
1,227	1,821	2,687	I 3,616	2,723	3,295	I 2,498	2,865	2,917	2,740	2,459	3,011	1,881	−219	2,981	Claims on Central Government	12a
315	384	531	I 752	1,053	975	I 1,426	1,384	958	2,128	1,595	1,545	4,296	6,525	5,949	Claims on Deposit Money Banks	12e
2,107	2,366	2,866	I 5,413	5,627	5,859	I 6,221	6,974	7,580	9,354	6,346	7,746	7,767	7,800	8,603	Reserve Money	14
1,185	1,333	1,531	I 1,688	1,867	2,083	I 2,402	2,736	3,241	3,836	4,534	5,608	6,025	6,509	7,165	*of which:* Currency Outside DMBs	14a
98	118	203	I 273	338	216	I 86	131	168	167	128	110	81	184	2,049	Central Government Deposits	16d
....	....	....	441	527	469	I 334	478	452	417	392	690	1,506	2,207	1,166	Capital Accounts	17a
242	903	1,079	I −515	−621	−579	I −720	309	285	−133	2,535	2,740	2,427	2,267	2,908	Other Items (Net)	17r
End of Period															**Deposit Money Banks**	
884	988	1,292	I 3,601	3,649	3,678	I 3,798	5,045	5,165	5,945	5,057	5,798	4,999	4,314	4,300	Reserves	20
1,014	1,445	2,103	I 2,462	3,039	3,089	I 3,152	2,804	2,800	3,019	3,800	4,517	7,861	16,683	14,561	Foreign Assets	21
1,507	2,104	2,778	I 2,067	5,478	7,083	I 8,588	9,343	9,336	10,202	11,839	10,027	10,783	12,035	16,286	Claims on Central Government	22a
....	....	....	141	159	183	I 1,154	1,297	1,432	1,710	2,257	3,004	3,713	4,017	4,506	Claims on Local Government	22b
10,714	12,519	14,724	I 15,680	15,832	16,887	I 20,624	23,251	27,785	32,248	35,042	39,287	41,821	43,052	44,906	Claims on Private Sector	22d
36	67	149	I 309	520	732	I 406	757	1,075	1,820	2,314	2,725	2,807	2,742	2,219	Claims on Other Financial Insts.	22f
2,882	3,263	3,583	I 3,428	3,718	4,262	I 5,574	6,509	7,897	9,684	11,059	11,486	10,944	10,878	11,411	Demand Deposits	24
8,221	9,639	11,409	I 10,806	11,137	12,279	I 16,030	16,785	17,886	19,521	21,870	25,171	28,208	32,053	34,395	Time and Savings Deposits	25
319	363	444	I 3,552	5,631	6,519	I 1,796	1,547	1,511	1,223	1,113	1,422	1,449	1,906	2,214	Bonds	26ab
1,811	2,551	3,577	I 3,043	3,678	3,228	I 3,378	3,634	4,258	4,904	6,468	7,419	9,400	12,386	13,241	Foreign Liabilities	26c
166	209	344	I 764	983	1,139	I 596	624	720	906	1,079	1,533	1,509	1,627	1,437	Central Government Deposits	26d
306	392	554	I 758	1,058	984	I 1,426	1,384	957	2,112	1,590	1,572	4,282	6,525	6,063	Credit from Monetary Authorities	26g
1,230	1,531	1,628	I 2,140	2,623	3,161	I 3,959	4,789	6,020	6,963	7,851	9,472	9,424	10,234	10,709	Capital Accounts	27a
−782	−824	−493	I −231	−151	81	I 4,966	7,225	8,345	9,630	9,276	7,284	6,770	7,231	7,308	Other Items (Net)	27r
End of Period															**Monetary Survey**	
87	58	−546	I 664	1,456	1,554	I 1,715	2,764	3,059	2,965	2,629	3,783	4,013	10,383	7,048	Foreign Assets (Net)	31n
13,224	16,189	19,797	I 20,851	23,455	26,878	I 32,899	37,146	42,012	47,720	52,757	56,457	59,450	59,837	67,433	Domestic Credit	32
2,469	3,598	4,918	I 4,645	6,880	9,023	I 10,405	11,454	11,366	11,868	13,090	11,395	11,074	10,004	15,781	Claims on Central Govt. (Net)	32an
....	....	....	141	159	183	I 1,155	1,297	1,432	1,710	2,257	3,004	3,713	4,017	4,506	Claims on Local Government	32b
10,719	12,524	14,730	I 15,686	15,838	16,893	I 20,933	23,573	28,128	32,322	35,097	39,334	41,857	43,052	44,927	Claims on Private Sector	32d
4,098	4,630	5,158	I 5,277	5,746	6,589	I 7,996	9,271	11,165	13,546	15,682	17,179	17,003	17,409	18,593	Money	34
8,221	9,639	11,409	I 10,806	11,137	12,279	I 16,030	16,785	17,886	19,521	21,870	25,171	28,208	32,053	34,395	Quasi-Money	35
992	1,978	2,684	I 5,432	8,027	9,565	I 10,588	13,854	16,020	17,618	17,833	17,890	18,252	20,756	21,493	Other Items (Net)	37r
12,319	14,269	16,259	I 16,082	16,883	18,867	I 24,026	26,056	29,051	33,068	37,553	42,350	45,212	49,462	52,988	Money plus Quasi-Money	35l
End of Period															**Other Banking Institutions**	
43	52	I 54	98	204	238	I 46	199	129	103	106	114	44	35	28	Cash	40
....	....	53	75	100	106	I —	—	—	—	—	—	7	6	4	Foreign Assets	41
347	388	I 33	27	71	81	I 116	97	101	67	64	31	89	63	61	Claims on Central Government	42a
....	....	352	367	376	450	....	....	....	....	....	....	....	....	....	Claims on Local Government	42b
1,141	1,393	I 1,248	1,492	1,768	1,949	I 997	1,845	2,802	3,628	4,128	4,368	4,124	3,563	3,013	Claims on Private Sector	42d
....	....	507	645	729	822	I 217	235	201	144	165	188	308	244	207	Claims on Deposit Money Banks	42e
13	12	16	39	85	129	I 436	482	689	930	1,129	1,049	208	156	97	Time Deposits	45
71	90	I 52	49	107	157	I —	—	—	—	—	—	—	—	—	Bonds	46ab
130	165	I 248	309	308	259	I —	—	—	—	—	1	97	73	62	Foreign Liabilities	46c
....	....	....	....	....	....	....	....	....	....	....	....	21	17	17	Central Government Deposits	46d
28	59	I 192	287	459	609	I 581	1,282	1,846	2,331	2,568	2,815	2,616	2,650	2,293	Credit from Deposit Money Banks	46h
109	96	59	58	63	101	I 359	611	698	681	764	836	1,630	1,016	844	Other Items (Net)	47r
End of Period															**Banking Survey**	
....	....	....	430	1,248	1,401	I 1,715	2,764	3,059	2,965	2,628	3,782	3,923	10,317	6,990	Foreign Assets (Net)	51n
....	....	....	22,419	25,141	28,626	33,605	38,266	43,828	49,595	54,635	58,131	60,835	60,704	68,270	Domestic Credit	52
....	....	....	4,673	6,950	9,104	I 10,520	11,551	11,467	11,935	13,153	11,425	11,142	10,050	15,824	Claims on Central Govt. (Net)	52an
....	....	....	I 508	535	633	I 1,155	1,297	1,432	1,710	2,257	3,004	3,713	4,017	4,506	Claims on Local Government	52b
....	....	....	17,178	17,606	18,842	I 21,930	25,417	30,930	35,950	39,225	43,702	45,981	46,637	47,940	Claims on Private Sector	52d
12,276	14,217	16,221	I 16,023	16,764	18,758	I 24,201	26,263	29,559	33,804	38,395	43,128	45,097	49,150	52,582	Liquid Liabilities	55l
....	....	....	3,601	5,738	6,675	I 1,796	1,547	1,511	1,223	1,113	1,422	1,449	1,906	2,214	Bonds	56ab
....	....	1,680	1,963	2,226	2,392	....	....	....	....	....	....	....	....	....	Central Govt. Lending Funds	56f
....	....	....	2,711	3,333	3,864	I 4,434	5,467	6,760	7,721	8,654	10,652	11,474	12,979	12,382	Capital Accounts	57a
....	....	....	−1,450	−1,673	−1,661	I 4,891	7,752	9,056	9,814	9,102	6,710	6,738	6,984	8,082	Other Items (Net)	57r

Spain

184

		1965	1966	1967	1968	1969	1970	1971	1972	1973	1974	1975	1976	1977	1978	1979
Money (National Definitions)																*Billions of Pesetas:*
M1	59ma	....	....	....	....	....	....	....	....	....	....	....	....	....	....	....
M2	59mb	....	....	....	....	....	....	....	....	....	....	....	....	....	....	....
M3	59mc	....	....	....	....	....	....	....	....	....	....	....	....	....	....	....
ALP	59md	....	....	....	....	....	....	....	....	....	....	....	....	....	....	....
Interest Rates																*Percent Per Annum*
Bank of Spain Rate(End of Period)	60	4.60	4.60	5.10	5.10	5.50	6.50	5.00	5.00	6.00	7.00	7.00	7.00	‡8.03	9.02	7.98
Money Market Rate	60b	....	....	....	....	....	....	....	....	....	....	9.61	6.70	9.96	13.12	20.77	13.13
Treasury Bill Rate	60c	....	....	....	....	....	....	....	....	....	....	....	....	....	14.41	15.70
Deposit Rate	60l	....	....	....	....	....	....	....	....	....	....	....	....	....	....	9.61
Lending Rate	60p	....	....	....	....	....	....	....	....	....	....	....	....	....	14.96	15.77
Government Bond Yield	61	....	....	....	....	....	....	....	....	....	....	....	....	....	....	13.31
Prices, Production, Employment																*Index Numbers (1990=100):*
Share Prices	62	14.7	15.3	15.9	18.7	27.0	28.8	‡29.2	38.2	48.3	48.9	42.0	36.3	24.9	20.1	17.3
Industrial Prices	63	13.3	13.6	13.7	14.0	14.4	14.6	15.4	16.5	18.2	‡21.5	‡23.4	26.5	31.9	37.1	42.5
Consumer Prices	64	7.6	8.2	8.7	9.2	9.4	9.9	10.7	11.6	12.9	14.9	17.5	20.6	25.6	30.7	35.5
Wages	65	2.5	2.9	3.3	3.6	3.9	‡4.6	5.2	6.0	7.2	9.1	11.7	15.2	19.8	25.0	‡30.9
Industrial Production	66..c	‡32.0	36.7	37.9	40.8	47.4	50.8	54.2	62.8	69.9	75.1	71.7	76.0	79.9	82.0	82.9
Total Employment	67	94.9	95.5	96.3	97.0	97.8	98.5	99.2	100.4	99.5	100.9	99.5	99.8	98.8	96.8	94.6
International Transactions																*Billions of Pesetas*
Exports	70	56.1	75.2	84.7	111.3	133.0	167.2	205.7	245.3	302.5	408.6	441.5	583.5	775.3	1,001.4	1,221.2
Imports, cif	71	182.4	215.5	211.8	245.4	296.3	332.3	347.9	438.8	561.6	889.0	932.2	1,170.4	1,350.6	1,431.5	1,704.1
Imports, fob	71.v	164.3	194.1	190.8	221.0	268.2	300.7	316.6	397.1	508.3	812.9	861.7	1,082.2	1,257.1	1,332.7	1,596.3
																1990=100
Volume of Exports	72	15.1	18.3	20.4	24.6	30.0	37.3	44.9	50.9	58.7	62.8	64.8	‡74.4	83.8	93.7	104.2
Volume of Imports	73	22.2	27.0	26.7	28.5	32.9	34.0	33.9	42.2	47.6	49.1	48.7	‡53.8	50.3	48.5	54.2
Unit Value of Exports	74	16.7	17.4	18.5	20.1	19.7	‡20.0	19.7	20.3	23.1	28.4	29.8	31.5	37.0	41.6	45.5
Unit Value of Imports	75	15.3	14.9	14.9	‡16.1	16.5	‡17.4	18.3	18.2	20.9	29.7	31.8	35.2	41.7	45.7	46.9
Export Prices (1975=100)	76	55.3	56.6	54.8	57.9	60.7	57.9	60.2	66.6	78.3	85.9	100.0	116.5	135.9	156.1	179.6
Balance of Payments																*Millions of US Dollars:*
Goods: Exports f.o.b.	78aa d	....	....	....	....	....	....	....	....	....	....	7,821	9,015	10,601	13,491	18,357
Goods: Imports f.o.b.	78ab d	....	....	....	....	....	....	....	....	....	....	−15,207	−16,299	−16,736	−17,555	−24,041
Trade Balance	78ac d	....	....	....	....	....	....	....	....	....	....	−7,386	−7,284	−6,135	−4,064	−5,684
Services: Credit	78ad d	....	....	....	....	....	....	....	....	....	....	5,434	5,105	6,152	8,195	10,285
Services: Debit	78ae d	....	....	....	....	....	....	....	....	....	....	−2,539	−2,807	−2,895	−3,184	−4,284
Balance on Goods and Services	78af d	....	....	....	....	....	....	....	....	....	....	−4,491	−4,986	−2,879	947	317
Income: Credit	78ag d	....	....	....	....	....	....	....	....	....	....	597	425	449	758	1,348
Income: Debit	78ah d	....	....	....	....	....	....	....	....	....	....	−769	−875	−1,111	−1,730	−2,324
Balance on Goods, Serv., & Inc.	78ai d	....	....	....	....	....	....	....	....	....	....	−4,662	−5,437	−3,541	−25	−658
Current Transfers, n.i.e.: Credit	78aj d	....	....	....	....	....	....	....	....	....	....	1,068	1,145	1,228	1,487	1,745
Current Transfers: Debit	78ak d	....	....	....	....	....	....	....	....	....	....	−299	−330	−142	−211	−330
Current Account, n.i.e.	78al d	....	....	....	....	....	....	....	....	....	....	−3,893	−4,622	−2,455	1,251	757
Capital Account, n.i.e.: Credit	78ba d	....	....	....	....	....	....	....	....	....	....	379	331	323	383	373
Capital Account: Debit	78bb d	....	....	....	....	....	....	....	....	....	....	—	—	—	—	−1
Capital Account, n.i.e.	78bc d	....	....	....	....	....	....	....	....	....	....	379	331	323	383	371
Direct Investment Abroad	78bd d	....	....	....	....	....	....	....	....	....	....	−170	−193	−115	−102	−133
Dir. Invest. in Rep. Econ., n.i.e.	78be d	....	....	....	....	....	....	....	....	....	....	683	478	608	1,178	1,397
Portfolio Investment Assets	78bf d	....	....	....	....	....	....	....	....	....	....	−17	−13	−1	−4	−16
Portfolio Investment Liab., n.i.e.	78bg d	....	....	....	....	....	....	....	....	....	....	−70	−85	9	77	102
Other Investment Assets	78bh d	....	....	....	....	....	....	....	....	....	....	−341	−553	−363	−1,046	−832
Other Investment Liab., n.i.e.	78bi d	....	....	....	....	....	....	....	....	....	....	2,554	3,099	4,295	2,041	4,154
Financial Account, n.i.e.	78bj d	....	....	....	....	....	....	....	....	....	....	2,638	2,732	4,432	2,144	4,672
Net Errors and Omissions	78ca d	....	....	....	....	....	....	....	....	....	....	47	469	−1,154	−19	−2,350
Overall Balance	78cb d	....	....	....	....	....	....	....	....	....	....	−829	−1,090	1,146	3,759	3,450
Reserves and Related Items	79da d	....	....	....	....	....	....	....	....	....	....	829	1,090	−1,146	−3,759	−3,450
Reserve Assets	79db d	....	....	....	....	....	....	....	....	....	....	223	1,001	−1,146	−3,809	−2,925
Use of Fund Credit and Loans	79dc d	....	....	....	....	....	....	....	....	....	....	606	89	—	50	−525
Liabs.Constit.For.Auth.Reserves	79dd d	....	....	....	....	....	....	....	....	....	....	—	—	—	—	—
Exceptional Financing	79de d	....	....	....	....	....	....	....	....	....	....	—	—	—	—	—
Government Finance																*Billions of Pesetas:*
Deficit (−) or Surplus	80	−26.7	−36.0	−31.2	−42.4	−36.7	−19.7	−63.5	−36.1	−23.4	−82.3	−111.2	−128.3	−248.6	−254.4	−400.9
Revenue	81	155.5	193.9	221.8	244.9	287.8	327.3	377.3	443.7	531.2	629.8	758.4	899.7	1,159.2	1,479.4	1,762.4
Expenditure	82	157.4	197.6	220.7	255.0	289.2	326.5	414.6	456.8	526.2	659.2	766.2	905.7	1,249.4	1,571.8	1,994.5
Lending Minus Repayments	83	24.8	32.3	32.3	32.3	35.4	20.5	26.2	23.0	28.4	52.9	103.4	122.3	158.4	162.0	168.8
Financing																	
Net Borrowing: Domestic	84a	22.6	24.6	23.5	40.3	29.8	17.9	61.9	58.8	8.7	22.3	52.0	148.0	103.5	151.3	237.1
Foreign	85a	.6	1.4	1.2	6.3	1.7	.6	−.7	−.5	.4	5.6	1.8	33.7	87.1	−37.9	5.2
Other Net Liabilities	86	....	....	....	....	....	....	....	....	....	....	....	....	....	....	....
Use of Cash Balances	87	3.5	9.9	6.1	−4.3	5.2	1.0	2.2	−22.2	14.4	54.3	57.4	−53.6	57.9	140.8	158.5
Debt: Domestic	88a	195.8	229.9	257.4	292.0	326.0	344.1	421.3	458.2	481.6	558.0	666.2	757.9	934.7	1,220.4	1,619.4
Foreign	89a	14.0	15.8	18.6	20.8	21.3	21.6	22.3	24.9	24.1	30.2	33.4	64.7	178.1	137.8	129.4
National Accounts																*Billions of Pesetas*
Exports of Goods & Services	90c. c	80	101	109	153	282	348	422	507	611	740	816	997	1,334	1,710	1,975
Government Consumption	91f. c	104	125	153	167	192	249	286	331	399	509	631	820	1,059	1,344	1,639
Gross Fixed Capital Formation	93e. c	304	356	405	465	539	684	706	868	1,108	1,436	1,593	1,808	2,201	2,551	2,843
Increase/Decrease(−) in Stocks	93i. c	42	47	25	15	57	21	26	32	31	113	127	145	97	28	99
Private Consumption	96f. c	1,058	1,216	1,350	1,506	1,578	1,701	1,926	2,245	2,694	3,333	3,920	4,817	6,050	7,272	8,582
Imports of Goods & Services	98c. c	−189	−226	−224	−269	−331	−373	−397	−500	−644	−988	−1,047	−1,320	−1,522	−1,621	−1,936
Gross Domestic Product	99b. c	1,399	1,618	1,818	2,037	2,317	2,630	2,968	3,483	4,199	5,143	6,039	7,267	9,220	11,285	13,201
Net Factor Inc/Pmts(−) Abroad	98.n	....	....	....	....	....	−17	−16	−16	−12	−1	−19	−40	−62	−87	−78
Gross Nat'l Expenditure = GNP	99a	1,287	1,477	1,632	1,805	2,011	2,559	2,904	3,416	4,128	5,101	6,000	7,194	9,116	11,143	13,052
Nat'l Income, Market Prices	99e	1,208	1,384	1,524	1,683	1,869	2,324	2,641	3,124	3,786	4,667	5,470	6,558	8,312	10,166	11,858
Gross Dom. Prod. 1990 Prices	99b. r	19,497	20,872	21,774	23,249	25,328	26,362	27,587	29,836	32,159	33,966	34,150	35,278	36,279	36,810	36,826
GDP Deflator (1990=100)	99bi r	7	8	8	9	9	10	11	12	13	15	18	21	25	31	36
																Millions:
Population	99z	32.06	32.39	32.73	33.08	33.43	33.78	34.13	34.49	34.86	35.22	35.60	35.97	36.35	36.67	36.99

1980	1981	1982	1983	1984	1985	1986	1987	1988	1989	1990	1991	1992	1993	1994		
End of Period															**Money (National Definitions)**	
....	....	....	....	....	....	7,450.2	8,650.8	10,319.7	11,859.6	14,163.1	15,898.8	15,631.3	16,180.5	17,337.6	*M1*	**59ma**
....	....	....	....	....	....	13,425.5	15,078.3	17,563.4	19,611.5	23,037.3	25,797.5	25,690.3	26,966.7	28,753.3	*M2*	**59mb**
....	....	....	....	....	....	28,251.2	31,724.0	35,777.6	40,896.6	46,309.3	51,301.2	53,700.3	59,263.2	63,684.3	*M3*	**59mc**
....	....	....	....	....	....	30,345.2	34,794.1	39,443.6	45,278.4	50,685.6	56,439.2	59,374.9	65,373.9	69,990.3	*ALP*	**59md**
Percent Per Annum															**Interest Rates**	
10.90	10.51	18.40	21.40	12.50	10.50	11.84	13.50	12.40	14.52	14.71	12.50	13.25	9.00	7.38	Bank of Spain Rate *(End of Period)*	**60**
15.46	16.56	17.21	19.40	12.60	11.60	11.50	16.07	11.30	14.39	14.76	13.20	13.01	....	....	Money Market Rate	**60b**
15.70	15.80	15.70	19.80	13.43	10.90	8.63	8.03	I 10.79	13.57	14.17	12.45	12.44	10.53	8.11	Treasury Bill Rate	**60c**
13.05	11.41	12.26	12.31	12.30	10.53	9.05	8.97	9.06	9.55	10.65	10.47	10.43	9.33	6.70	Deposit Rate	**60l**
16.85	15.26	14.98	15.00	16.58	13.52	12.19	16.36	12.43	15.84	16.01	14.38	14.23	12.78	8.95	Lending Rate	**60p**
15.96	15.81	15.99	16.91	16.52	13.37	11.36	12.81	11.74	13.70	14.68	12.43	12.17	10.16	9.69	Government Bond Yield	**61**
Period Averages															**Prices, Production, Employment**	
16.2	20.6	18.9	19.1	26.1	33.0	I 67.2	96.6	107.1	116.3	100.0	102.6	89.1	104.6	121.6	Share Prices	**62**
49.9	57.7	64.9	74.0	83.0	89.7	90.5	91.2	94.0	97.9	100.0	101.5	102.9	105.5	110.0	Industrial Prices	**63**
41.1	47.0	53.8	60.4	67.2	73.1	79.5	83.7	87.7	93.7	100.0	105.9	112.2	117.3	122.9	Consumer Prices	**64**
36.6	41.2	47.7	54.9	61.3	67.5	74.9	80.5	85.7	92.0	100.0	108.2	116.5	124.4	....	Wages	**65**
82.8	I 82.3	81.4	83.8	84.4	86.1	88.6	92.6	95.6	100.1	100.0	99.3	96.1	....	....	Industrial Production	**66..c**
90.7	87.6	86.5	85.7	84.8	84.0	88.3	91.0	93.7	97.4	100.0	100.2	98.3	94.1	93.3	Total Employment	**67**
Billions of Pesetas															**International Transactions**	
1,493.2	1,888.4	2,258.0	2,838.6	3,778.1	4,099.2	3,801.8	4,195.6	4,686.4	5,134.5	5,642.8	6,225.7	6,605.7	7,982.3	9,795.2	Exports	**70**
2,450.7	2,970.4	3,465.6	4,176.5	4,629.0	5,073.2	4,890.8	6,029.9	7,039.5	8,396.4	8,914.7	9,672.1	10,205.0	10,402.4	12,348.0	Imports, cif	**71**
2,313.4	2,808.5	3,289.7	3,944.1	4,366.4	4,786.1	4,613.9	5,688.6	6,641.1	7,921.1	8,410.1	9,124.7	9,627.4	9,813.6	11,649.1	Imports, fob	**71.v**
1990=100																
109.9	I 52.8	57.2	62.3	74.1	76.0	74.0	79.5	85.0	89.0	100.0	111.5	117.0	135.4	160.4	Volume of Exports	**72**
58.2	I 41.5	41.8	41.6	40.9	44.1	52.5	65.8	78.1	91.0	100.0	111.7	121.5	117.8	130.5	Volume of Imports	**73**
54.1	62.8	69.2	80.2	90.8	96.4	92.2	94.3	98.7	103.5	100.0	99.4	99.9	104.5	109.8	Unit Value of Exports	**74**
63.9	82.5	92.9	112.8	126.6	128.3	106.3	102.6	101.1	103.4	100.0	97.1	92.7	99.4	106.0	Unit Value of Imports	**75**
....	....	....	....	....	....	....	....	....	....	....	....	....	....	....	Export Prices (1975=100)	**76**
Minus Sign Indicates Debit															Balance of Payments	
20,547	20,974	21,288	20,794	23,737	24,851	27,755	34,753	40,692	44,945	55,812	59,173	65,210	61,006	73,363	Goods: Exports f.o.b.	**78aa*d***
-32,272	-31,086	-30,542	-28,601	-28,380	-29,611	-34,953	-48,495	-59,396	-70,351	-86,764	-89,709	-95,782	-76,026	-88,035	Goods: Imports f.o.b.	**78ab*d***
-11,725	-10,113	-9,254	-7,806	-4,643	-4,759	-7,197	-13,742	-18,703	-25,406	-30,952	-30,536	-30,572	-15,020	-14,672	Trade Balance	**78ac*d***
11,593	11,331	11,542	11,365	12,325	12,723	17,836	21,705	24,457	24,618	29,832	32,418	38,461	30,764	34,032	Services: Credit	**78ad*d***
-5,732	-5,714	-5,953	-5,136	-4,502	-4,551	-5,983	-8,255	-10,732	-11,983	-16,544	-20,397	-26,210	-19,657	-19,665	Services: Debit	**78ae*d***
-5,864	-4,496	-3,665	-1,577	3,180	3,412	4,655	-291	-4,979	-12,772	-17,664	-18,515	-18,322	-3,912	-305	Balance on Goods and Services	**78af*d***
1,723	2,027	1,936	1,325	1,489	1,817	1,666	1,862	2,690	3,775	7,793	10,954	14,092	11,905	8,892	Income: Credit	**78ag*d***
-3,085	-4,210	-4,095	-3,658	-3,746	-3,505	-3,488	-4,438	-5,999	-6,544	-11,580	-15,474	-20,161	-15,694	-17,133	Income: Debit	**78ah*d***
-7,226	-6,680	-5,825	-3,910	923	1,724	2,833	-2,868	-8,287	-15,540	-21,451	-23,035	-24,391	-7,700	-8,546	Balance on Goods, Serv., & Inc.	**78ai*d***
1,956	1,596	1,503	1,324	1,281	1,722	2,783	4,584	7,478	8,496	7,849	9,767	11,410	8,902	9,104	Current Transfers, n.i.e.: Credit	**78aj*d***
-310	-279	-226	-427	-426	-660	-1,702	-1,979	-2,986	-3,880	-5,050	-6,870	-9,015	-7,250	-7,390	Current Transfers: Debit	**78ak*d***
-5,580	-5,363	-4,548	-3,013	1,778	2,785	3,914	-263	-3,795	-10,924	-18,653	-20,137	-21,996	-6,048	-6,832	Current Account, n.i.e.	**78al*d***
411	382	312	278	253	78	71	50	48	50	1,753	3,535	3,978	3,366	3,134	Capital Account, n.i.e.: Credit	**78ba*d***
-4	-8	-9	-10	-13	-13	-20	-19	-37	-59	-302	-370	-493	-449	-501	Capital Account: Debit	**78bb*d***
407	374	303	268	240	65	51	31	11	-9	1,451	3,166	3,484	2,918	2,632	Capital Account, n.i.e.	**78bc*d***
-311	-271	-511	-243	-248	-250	-378	-745	-1,235	-1,473	-3,522	-4,442	-2,192	-2,652	-4,170	Direct Investment Abroad	**78bd*d***
1,493	1,707	1,783	1,622	1,772	1,968	3,451	4,571	7,021	8,428	13,984	12,493	13,276	8,144	9,700	Dir. Invest. in Rep. Econ., n.i.e.	**78be*d***
-14	-12	-81	-6	-175	-259	-469	29	-136	-166	-1,367	-2,410	-2,811	-6,772	-1,228	Portfolio Investment Assets	**78bf*d***
14	115	13	48	229	491	1,697	3,770	2,427	8,155	9,328	21,700	1,394	29,589	1,089	Portfolio Investment Liab., n.i.e.	**78bg*d***
-765	-787	-2,151	-388	-616	-1,391	-322	793	-596	-108	-12,683	-7,700	-40,525	-75,218	11,178	Other Investment Assets	**78bh*d***
4,830	5,244	3,281	2,972	3,961	-3,776	-5,620	5,812	7,134	3,506	10,474	12,726	21,143	2,478	12,127	Other Investment Liab., n.i.e.	**78bi*d***
5,247	5,996	2,334	4,005	4,922	-3,217	-1,641	14,229	14,615	18,342	16,214	32,367	-9,715	-44,430	28,695	Financial Account, n.i.e.	**78bj*d***
-869	-1,734	-1,194	-1,525	-2,123	-1,908	20	-1,291	-2,414	-2,693	7,949	-1,254	10,755	42,720	-24,446	Net Errors and Omissions	**78ca*d***
-795	-727	-3,104	-265	4,817	-2,275	2,344	12,706	8,416	4,716	6,962	14,141	-17,472	-4,840	49	Overall Balance	**78cb*d***
795	727	3,104	265	-4,817	2,275	-2,344	-12,706	-8,416	-4,716	-6,962	-14,141	17,472	4,840	-49	Reserves and Related Items	**79da*d***
795	802	3,256	270	-4,817	2,275	-2,344	-12,706	-8,416	-4,716	-6,962	-14,141	17,472	4,840	-49	Reserve Assets	**79db*d***
—	-75	-151	-5	—	—	—	—	—	—	—	—	—	—	—	Use of Fund Credit and Loans	**79dc*d***
—	—	—	—	—	—	—	—	—	—	—	—	—	—	—	Liabs.Constit.For.Auth.Reserves	**79dd*d***
—	—	—	—	—	—	—	—	—	—	—	—	—	—	—	Exceptional Financing	**79de*d***
Year Ending December 31															**Government Finance**	
I -555.8	-780.2	-1,450.2	-1,714.9	-2,502.1	-2,199.7	-1,940.6	-1,608.8	-166.1	-1,500.1	-1,677.6	-1,758.0	-2,523.5	-4,221.4	-4,943.9	Deficit (-) or Surplus	**80**
I 2,179.1	2,574.7	3,002.8	3,631.4	4,218.5	4,780.0	6,039.9	7,129.5	8,178.1	9,847.0	10,435.3	11,478.1	12,826.2	13,499.7	12,992.9	Revenue	**81**
I 2,552.7	3,097.2	4,058.5	4,809.9	5,909.3	6,615.8	7,709.7	8,705.4	9,517.0	10,951.3	11,815.3	13,102.1	14,835.5	17,503.0	17,034.0	Expenditure	**82**
I 182.2	257.8	394.5	536.4	811.3	363.9	270.9	32.9	-1,172.9	395.8	297.6	133.9	514.1	218.1	902.9	Lending Minus Repayments	**83**
															Financing	
I 579.2	742.2	1,345.9	1,661.8	2,421.1	2,332.0	2,118.1	1,727.4	-96.8	1,395.0	2,731.8	-82.5	2,402.5	4,236.4	3,486.5	Net Borrowing: Domestic	**84a**
I —	43.0	77.2	124.0	120.7	32.9	-174.4	58.0	163.6	305.0	359.2	1,775.0	124.2	2,712.9	-462.4	Foreign	**85a**
I -23.4	2.0	78.9	-50.0	1.1	-158.0	-7.5	-184.1	128.7	-101.4	-38.4	371.0	48.0	-240.4	138.9	Other Net Liabilities	**86**
I —	-6.9	-51.7	-21.0	-40.7	-7.2	4.5	7.5	-29.5	-98.5	-1,374.9	-305.6	-51.3	-2,487.5	1,781.0	Use of Cash Balances	**87**
I 2,183.1	2,930.8	4,428.8	6,198.1	8,657.9	11,023.1	13,131.6	14,819.4	14,695.3	15,920.1	17,430.5	17,868.5	20,292.8	22,344.3	28,555.0	Debt: Domestic	**88a**
I 133.6	204.7	352.9	565.3	738.0	708.5	470.8	535.1	655.1	865.9	1,201.5	2,968.8	3,259.9	6,364.6	5,893.0	Foreign	**89a**
Billions of Pesetas															**National Accounts**	
2,387	3,042	3,631	4,667	5,865	6,407	6,417	6,996	7,575	8,150	8,555	9,409	10,410	11,784	14,419	Exports of Goods & Services	**90c.*c***
2,008	2,370	2,784	3,280	3,647	4,152	4,740	5,452	5,924	6,831	7,815	8,882	10,027	10,669	10,992	Government Consumption	**91f.*c***
3,368	3,729	4,264	4,686	4,779	5,409	6,297	7,518	9,083	10,868	12,261	13,041	12,859	12,040	12,709	Gross Fixed Capital Formation	**93e.*c***
157	-1	116	155	254	14	162	258	419	449	464	461	529	69	43	Increase/Decrease(-) in Stocks	**93i.*c***
9,992	11,301	12,939	14,604	16,305	18,080	20,438	22,856	25,180	28,367	31,303	34,244	37,220	38,511	40,854	Private Consumption	**96f.*c***
-2,743	-3,397	-4,011	-4,860	-5,329	-5,860	-5,730	-6,935	-8,023	-9,621	-10,251	-11,137	-12,053	-12,183	-14,363	Imports of Goods & Services	**98c.*c***
15,168	17,045	19,723	22,532	25,520	28,201	32,324	36,144	40,159	45,044	50,145	54,901	59,002	60,904	64,673	Gross Domestic Product	**99b.*c***
-130	-238	-285	-358	-397	-331	-296	-304	-411	-384	-451	-554	-708	-650	....	Net Factor Inc/Pmts(-) Abroad	**98.n**
15,079	16,751	19,283	21,877	24,715	27,870	32,028	35,840	39,748	44,660	49,693	54,347	58,294	60,255	....	Gross Nat'l Expenditure = GNP	**99a**
13,464	14,820	17,029	19,239	21,685	24,521	28,170	31,662	35,148	39,627	44,148	48,321	51,853	53,305	....	Nat'l Income, Market Prices	**99e**
37,305	37,239	37,823	38,662	39,229	40,254	41,542	43,885	46,151	48,337	50,145	51,269	51,625	51,054	52,064	Gross Dom. Prod. 1990 Prices	**99b.*r***
41	46	52	58	65	70	78	82	87	93	100	107	114	119	124	GDP Deflator (1990=100)	**99bi*r***
Midyear Estimates																
37.54	37.75	37.97	38.16	38.33	38.41	38.52	38.61	38.69	38.77	38.84	38.92	39.01	39.08	39.14	**Population**	**99z**

(Notes in the back of the book)

Sri Lanka
524

		1965	1966	1967	1968	1969	1970	1971	1972	1973	1974	1975	1976	1977	1978	1979
Exchange Rates															*Rupees per SDR:*	
Market Rate	aa	4.775	4.775	5.928	5.928	5.958	5.958	6.469	7.272	8.140	8.195	9.029	10.257	18.901	20.200	20.346
															Rupees per US Dollar:	
Market Rate	ae	4.775	4.775	5.928	5.928	5.958	5.958	5.958	6.698	6.748	6.693	7.713	8.828	15.560	15.505	15.445
Market Rate	rf	4.762	4.762	4.861	5.952	5.952	5.952	5.935	5.970^e	6.403^e	6.651^e	7.007^e	8.412^e	8.873^e	15.611^e	15.572^e
Fund Position															*Millions of SDRs:*	
Quota	2f.s	62	78	78	78	78	98	98	98	98	98	98	98	98	119	119
SDRs	1b.s	—	—	—	—	—	—	—	13	13	14	11	12	20	26	22
Reserve Position in the Fund	1c.s	—	—	—	—	—	—	—	—	—	—	—	—	—	—	—
Total Fund Cred.&Loans Outstg.	2tl	24	39	62	92	93	79	72	75	74	102	125	134	170	227	305
International Liquidity												*Millions of US Dollars Unless Otherwise Indicated:*				
Total Reserves minus Gold	1l.d	73	43	55	52	40	43	50	59	87	78	57	92	293	398	517
SDRs	1b.d	—	—	—	—	—	—	—	14	16	18	13	14	24	34	29
Reserve Position in the Fund	1c.d	—	—	—	—	—	—	—	—	—	—	—	—	—	—	—
Foreign Exchange	1d.d	73	43	55	52	40	43	50	46	70	60	45	78	269	363	488
Gold (Million Fine Troy Ounces)	1ad	....	....	....	....	....	....	....	....	....	....	....	....	....	.042	.063
Gold (National Valuation)	1and	....	....	....	....	....	....	....	....	....	....	....	....	—	9	18
Monetary Authorities: Other Liab.	4..d	1	8	28	19	53	75	59	55	40	48	45	63	44	20	39
Deposit Money Banks: Assets	7a.d	19	24	20	26	23	25	34	48	44	59	51	65	80	85	109
of which: Claims on Nonbanks	7ad d	10	11	9	13	14	18	21	29	30	45	41	54	61	68	78
Deposit Money Banks: Liabilities	7b.d	7	9	9	12	11	10	12	22	11	11	11	12	9	14	22
of which: Liab. to Nonbanks	7bd d	6	9	8	10	9	9	10	9	9	9	9	8	5	6	7
FCBU: Assets	7k.d	....	....	....	....	....	....	....	....	....	....	....	....	....	....	29
of which: Claims on Nonbanks	7kd d	....	....	....	....	....	....	....	....	....	....	....	....	....	....	—
FCBU: Liabilities	7m.d	....	....	....	....	....	....	....	....	....	....	....	....	....	....	14
of which: Liab. to Nonbanks	7md d	....	....	....	....	....	....	....	....	....	....	....	....	....	....	8
Monetary Authorities															*Millions of Rupees:*	
Foreign Assets	11	282	143	260	236	165	194	238	302	510	453	442	829	4,534	6,170	7,972
Claims on Central Government	12a	1,271	1,435	1,631	1,938	2,043	2,197	2,286	2,368	2,353	2,447	2,537	3,760	4,978	5,868	7,768
Claims on Deposit Money Banks	12e	6	45	107	99	190	204	229	125	239	679	594	401	894	1,091	693
Reserve Money	14	1,206	1,145	1,289	1,401	1,431	1,381	1,575	1,856	2,179	2,357	2,202	2,769	4,028	4,535	5,538
of which: Currency Outside DMBs	14a	902	883	980	1,066	1,084	935	1,115	1,202	1,437	1,539	1,610	2,081	2,792	3,016	3,774
Foreign Liabilities	16c	118	225	538	659	868	916	749	912	872	1,156	1,472	1,932	3,897	4,892	6,810
Central Government Deposits	16d	75	161	126	176	109	145	104	91	94	120	15	31	....	1,049	740
Capital Accounts	17a	....	....	....	....	....	....	....	....	....	....	....	....	....	....	....
Other Items (Net)	17r	295	316	243	292	184	365	511	113	73	168	–42	359	2,669	3,976	4,324
Deposit Money Banks															*Millions of Rupees:*	
Reserves	20	277	242	272	288	289	406	404	606	802	789	562	652	1,145	1,342	1,742
Foreign Assets	21	92	113	120	157	138	151	185	320	297	394	395	573	1,243	1,316	1,681
Claims on Central Government	22a	545	482	556	441	446	639	692	745	499	386	1,415	782	914	801	864
Claims on Nonfin.Pub.Enterprises	22ca	....	....	....	....	....	....	....	....	....	....	....	....	....	....	3,347
Claims on Cooperatives	22cb	....	....	....	....	....	....	....	....	....	....	....	....	....	....	....
Claims on Private Sector	22d	742	815	935	1,211	1,445	1,599	1,736	2,117	2,134	3,188	3,363	3,919	5,714	8,666	11,853
Demand Deposits	24	791	757	805	823	781	1,005	1,009	1,241	1,312	1,377	1,443	2,038	2,526	2,863	3,857
Time and Savings Deposits	25	549	557	656	767	934	1,112	1,251	1,456	1,337	1,582	1,648	2,117	3,303	5,425	8,668
Foreign Liabilities	26c	35	45	52	73	64	60	68	145	75	75	86	103	135	224	337
Central Government Deposits	26d	172	144	126	152	147	221	199	514	446	530	452	714	871	990	1,073
Credit from Monetary Authorities	26g	....	....	....	....	....	....	....	....	....	....	....	....	....	....	609
Capital Accounts	27a	68	84	91	97	112	130	154	162	171	214	239	281	374	520	906
Other Items (Net)	27r	–10	–29	9	57	100	83	143	60	85	310	206	132	685	2,534	2,271
Monetary Survey															*Millions of Rupees:*	
Foreign Assets (Net)	31n	221	–14	–210	–340	–629	–630	–394	–435	–140	–384	–721	–633	1,744	2,371	2,506
Domestic Credit	32	2,378	2,489	2,935	3,333	3,750	4,126	4,473	4,696	4,519	5,435	5,823	7,644	10,547	13,184	18,556
Claims on Central Govt. (Net)	32an	1,636	1,674	2,000	2,122	2,305	2,527	2,737	2,579	2,386	2,247	2,460	3,725	4,834	4,518	6,703
Claims on Nonfin.Pub.Enterprise	32ca	....	....	....	....	....	....	....	....	....	....	....	....	....	....	3,347
Claims on Cooperatives	32cb	....	....	....	....	....	....	....	....	....	....	....	....	....	....	....
Claims on Private Sector	32d	742	815	935	1,211	1,445	1,599	1,736	2,117	2,134	3,188	3,363	3,919	5,714	8,666	11,853
Money	34	1,703	1,645	1,790	1,896	1,868	1,949	2,128	2,461	2,755	2,923	3,064	4,133	5,332	5,895	7,643
Quasi-Money	35	608	620	727	846	1,019	1,179	1,333	1,541	1,361	1,685	1,706	2,186	3,492	5,698	8,908
Other Items (Net)	37r	347	274	280	332	320	435	701	345	286	546	390	761	3,655	4,752	6,106
Money plus Quasi-Money	35l	2,311	2,265	2,517	2,742	2,886	3,128	3,461	4,002	4,116	4,608	4,770	6,319	8,824	11,593	16,551
Liquid Liabilities	55l	2,312	2,265	2,518	2,742	2,887	3,129	3,462	4,969	5,263	5,950	6,351	8,207	11,204	14,619	20,701
Interest Rates															*Percent Per Annum*	
Bank Rate (End of Period)	60	5.00	5.00	5.00	5.50	5.50	6.50	6.50	6.50	6.50	6.50	6.50	6.50	10.00	10.00	10.00
Money Market Rate	60b	....	....	....	....	....	....	....	....	....	....	....	....	....	9.50	11.00
Treasury Bill Rate	60c	....	....	....	....	....	....	....	....	....	....	....	....	....	....	....
Deposit Rate	60l	....	....	....	....	....	....	....	....	....	....	....	....	....	8.50	8.50
Lending Rate	60p	....	....	....	....	....	....	....	....	....	....	....	....	....	18.00	18.00
Government Bond Yield	61	....	....	....	....	....	....	....	....	....	....	....	....	....	....	....
Prices															*Index Numbers (1990=100):*	
Wholesale Prices	63	....	....	....	....	....	....	....	....	....	15.4	15.9	17.2	20.8	24.1	26.4
Consumer Prices	64	11.2	11.1	11.4	12.0	12.9	13.7	14.1	15.0	16.4	18.4	19.6	19.9	20.1	22.6	25.0
Domestic Goods (1985=100)	64a	21.8	21.8	21.9	23.0	25.1	26.7	27.8	30.2	31.3	32.9	35.4	36.6	37.5	42.8	46.6
Import Goods (1985=100)	64b	16.0	15.9	16.8	17.7	18.6	19.5	19.5	20.5	24.5	29.5	32.2	31.5	29.5	36.7	42.7
Wages: Agr. Minimum Rates	65	5.0	5.0	5.2	6.0	6.0	6.0	6.1	6.4	7.1	9.0	10.3	10.6	13.3	19.3	23.8

Sri Lanka

	1980	1981	1982	1983	1984	1985	1986	1987	1988	1989	1990	1991	1992	1993	1994		
End of Period																**Exchange Rates**	
	22.957	23.919	23.518	26.174	25.760	30.105	34.885	43.642	44.453	52.566	57.248	60.908	63.250	68.076	72.963	Market Rate	aa
End of Period (ae) Period Average (rf)																	
	18.000	20.550	21.320	25.000	26.280	27.408	28.520	30.763	33.033	40.000	40.240	42.580	46.000	49.562	49.980	Market Rate	ae
	16.534	19.246	20.812	23.529	25.438	27.163	28.017	29.445	31.807	36.047	40.063	41.372	43.830	48.322	49.415	Market Rate	rf
End of Period																**Fund Position**	
	179	179	179	223	223	223	223	223	223	223	223	223	304	304	304	Quota	2f. s
	—	20	6	1	—	—	—	—	—	10	—	—	—	—	—	SDRs	1b. s
	—	1	6	17	6	6	—	—	—	—	—	—	20	20	20	Reserve Position in the Fund	1c. s
	307	443	437	425	413	361	284	195	267	278	288	280	338	376	423	Total Fund Cred.&Loans Outstg.	2tl
End of Period																**International Liquidity**	
	246	327	351	297	511	451	353	279	222	244	423	685	927	1,629	2,046	Total Reserves minus Gold	1l. d
	—	23	7	1	—	—	—	—	—	13	—	—	—	—	—	SDRs	1b. d
	—	1	6	18	6	7	—	—	—	—	—	—	28	28	30	Reserve Position in the Fund	1c. d
	246	304	338	278	505	445	353	279	222	231	422	685	899	1,601	2,016	Foreign Exchange	1d. d
	.063	.063	.063	.063	.063	.063	.063	.063	.063	.063	.063	.111	.160	.145	....	Gold (Million Fine Troy Ounces)	1ad
	16	14	13	11	11	10	10	10	10	10	10	10	37	....	....	Gold (National Valuation)	1an d
	42	8	89	76	1	10	8	67	11	꞊207	291	363	420	625	713	Monetary Authorities: Other Liab.	4..d
	130	114	168	205	199	209	239	301	298	294	422	438	504	516	639	Deposit Money Banks: Assets	7a. d
	83	77	73	84	77	78	79	94	66	103	119	112	109	101	102	of which: Claims on Nonbanks	7ad d
	26	30	75	114	120	149	185	251	229	249	303	394	464	547	615	Deposit Money Banks: Liabilities	7b. d
	8	8	56	78	89	109	131	163	188	213	265	354	456	538	607	of which: Liab. to Nonbanks	7bd d
	114	205	379	545	463	458	430	382	422	492	524	432	539	456	540	FCBU: Assets	7k. d
	7	22	131	182	203	143	138	139	143	132	124	121	183	84	78	of which: Claims on Nonbanks	7kd d
	131	231	428	640	498	489	447	408	371	400	448	428	635	601	665	FCBU: Liabilities	7m. d
	31	45	22	29	21	41	47	42	41	65	53	53	42	62	103	of which: Liab. to Nonbanks	7md d
End of Period																**Monetary Authorities**	
	꞊4,706	6,929	7,494	7,760	13,725	12,650	10,341	8,871	7,620	꞊10,056	17,304	30,581	41,868	78,290	96,807	Foreign Assets	11
	꞊16,081	19,334	23,142	25,331	20,732	29,524	32,386	34,178	46,570	꞊51,466	55,023	61,318	50,072	35,515	38,275	Claims on Central Government	12a
	꞊1,070	1,278	1,159	2,662	2,041	1,824	2,811	3,136	3,480	꞊4,312	5,570	5,344	5,506	4,900	3,376	Claims on Deposit Money Banks	12e
	6,629	7,822	9,679	12,240	14,296	18,084	18,695	20,626	25,941	꞊27,482	33,141	42,374	45,972	57,539	68,518	Reserve Money	14
	4,181	4,823	5,988	7,200	8,561	9,816	11,570	13,495	18,484	꞊19,644	22,120	24,852	27,280	32,133	38,906	of which: Currency Outside DMBs	14a
	꞊7,790	10,760	12,183	13,025	10,678	11,157	10,124	10,571	12,241	꞊22,912	28,215	29,121	30,077	41,297	46,076	Foreign Liabilities	16c
	1,364	1,450	1,286	1,772	2,337	3,161	2,514	1,587	3,528	꞊2,776	3,604	9,027	2,666	1,801	2,813	Central Government Deposits	16d
	5,763	7,140	8,256	8,475	8,450	10,612	11,654	13,334	14,675	꞊14,853	13,324	14,550	18,156	17,251	19,873	Capital Accounts	17a
	꞊310	368	391	241	737	983	2,552	67	1,285	꞊-2,189	-387	2,172	575	817	1,178	Other Items (Net)	17r
End of Period																**Deposit Money Banks**	
	2,049	2,730	3,069	4,678	5,670	8,228	8,040	5,728	6,802	꞊7,611	9,406	15,421	16,289	20,562	25,389	Reserves	20
	2,347	2,342	3,585	5,126	5,233	5,726	6,803	9,265	9,875	꞊11,753	16,967	18,634	23,162	25,567	31,918	Foreign Assets	21
	939	1,563	1,719	1,579	2,878	2,897	2,753	5,362	7,862	꞊8,382	14,701	13,861	13,886	18,782	21,039	Claims on Central Government	22a
	4,123	4,488	4,677	4,385	4,148	4,438	4,739	7,366	10,787	꞊13,862	15,636	14,077	15,032	7,775	5,163	Claims on Nonfin.Pub.Enterprises	22ca
	1,368	1,294	1,188	1,823	1,568	1,304	1,425	1,123	1,319	꞊1,178	1,139	1,238	1,739	1,903	2,541	Claims on Cooperatives	22cb
	꞊11,344	15,396	19,379	25,552	29,656	32,793	35,400	39,653	48,322	꞊50,781	63,122	76,734	93,826	113,544	140,820	Claims on Private Sector	22d
	5,139	5,111	5,665	7,334	8,002	8,761	9,358	11,243	13,511	꞊15,375	17,256	21,641	22,741	27,169	31,415	Demand Deposits	24
	11,624	15,269	19,779	23,523	27,674	30,803	31,085	34,697	37,469	꞊40,078	50,668	63,519	79,741	100,780	121,210	Time and Savings Deposits	25
	472	613	1,606	2,857	3,141	4,078	5,290	7,714	9,122	꞊9,962	12,191	16,793	21,356	27,119	30,746	Foreign Liabilities	26c
	1,642	1,503	1,568	1,763	2,299	3,687	3,863	3,357	5,011	꞊5,851	9,723	8,639	9,075	6,304	9,290	Central Government Deposits	26d
	1,180	1,436	1,413	2,875	2,401	2,165	3,140	3,479	3,906	꞊4,046	6,625	5,614	5,603	5,843	4,054	Credit from Monetary Authorities	26g
	1,272	2,268	2,602	2,705	2,932	3,164	3,410	3,954	4,774	꞊5,395	6,690	8,960	9,868	21,851	28,278	Capital Accounts	27a
	꞊841	1,612	984	2,085	2,703	2,729	3,013	4,053	11,172	꞊12,860	18,625	14,799	15,552	-932	1,877	Other Items (Net)	27r
End of Period																**Monetary Survey**	
	꞊-1,210	-2,102	-2,709	-2,996	5,138	3,140	1,730	-149	-3,868	꞊-11,065	-6,135	3,301	13,598	35,442	51,902	Foreign Assets (Net)	31n
	꞊31,088	39,383	47,695	55,604	54,748	65,707	72,280	83,743	107,368	꞊117,313	138,426	150,156	163,657	170,050	197,073	Domestic Credit	32
	꞊14,014	17,944	22,008	23,375	18,974	25,573	28,763	34,596	45,893	꞊51,220	56,397	57,514	52,218	46,192	47,211	Claims on Central Govt. (Net)	32an
	4,123	4,488	4,677	4,385	4,148	4,438	4,739	7,366	10,787	꞊13,862	15,636	14,077	15,032	7,775	5,163	Claims on Nonfin.Pub.Enterprise	32ca
	1,368	1,294	1,188	1,823	1,568	1,304	1,425	1,123	1,319	꞊1,178	1,139	1,238	1,739	1,903	2,541	Claims on Cooperatives	32cb
	꞊11,420	15,417	19,475	25,629	29,677	33,585	36,533	39,722	48,391	꞊50,833	63,122	76,819	93,872	113,616	141,597	Claims on Private Sector	32d
	9,333	9,949	11,672	14,589	16,647	18,662	21,051	24,901	32,155	꞊35,088	39,596	46,600	50,057	59,355	70,462	Money	34
	11,970	15,587	20,342	24,123	28,265	31,994	31,750	36,052	37,857	꞊40,780	52,241	65,847	80,867	101,852	121,674	Quasi-Money	35
	꞊8,576	11,745	12,972	13,896	14,974	18,192	21,209	22,641	33,488	꞊30,380	41,332	41,009	46,330	44,285	56,839	Other Items (Net)	37r
	21,303	25,536	32,014	38,712	44,912	50,656	52,801	60,953	70,012	75,867	91,838	112,447	130,923	161,206	192,136	Money plus Quasi-Money	35l
	26,256	30,975	39,668	48,221	56,145	63,884	67,002	77,332	88,077	95,818	113,332	138,892	163,746	203,364	245,462	Liquid Liabilities	55l
Percent Per Annum																**Interest Rates**	
	12.00	14.00	14.00	13.00	13.00	11.00	11.00	10.00	10.00	14.00	15.00	17.00	17.00	17.00	17.00	Bank Rate (End of Period)	60
	21.06	19.00	16.88	23.88	21.42	14.56	12.95	13.14	18.65	22.19	21.56	25.42	21.63	25.65	18.54	Money Market Rate	60b
	....	15.60	12.28	12.38	13.08	13.39	10.48	7.30	13.59	14.81	14.08	13.75	16.19	16.52	12.68	Treasury Bill Rate	60c
	14.50	17.88	17.50	18.25	19.79	17.33	12.21	11.50	13.23	16.43	19.42	18.54	18.33	18.42	15.33	Deposit Rate	60l
	19.00	19.00	17.75	13.25	13.15	13.40	11.57	9.80	12.42	13.17	13.00	13.83	13.00	16.43	12.96	Lending Rate	60p
	....	....	....	....	14.67	15.33	12.00	12.00	11.49	11.71	12.20	15.68	16.00	16.25	....	Government Bond Yield	61
Period Averages																**Prices**	
	35.3	41.2	43.5	54.4	68.3	57.9	56.2	63.7	75.1	81.9	100.0	109.2	118.7	127.7	134.1	Wholesale Prices	63
	31.6	37.2	41.2	47.0	54.8	55.6	60.1	64.7	73.8	82.3	100.0	112.2	125.0	139.6	151.4	Consumer Prices	64
	54.0	63.8	71.8	81.0	93.7	100.0	112.2	119.5	....	....	....	....	....	....	....	Domestic Goods (1985=100)	64a
	62.9	74.3	80.3	87.8	96.9	100.0	106.8	110.4	....	....	....	....	....	....	....	Import Goods (1985=100)	64b
	29.7	29.8	35.0	38.4	48.4	52.9	55.7	58.5	73.2	81.3	100.0	111.7	128.4	155.4	158.8	Wages: Agr. Minimum Rates	65

Sri Lanka
524

		1965	1966	1967	1968	1969	1970	1971	1972	1973	1974	1975	1976	1977	1978	1979
International Transactions																*Millions of Rupees*
Exports	70	1,949	1,700	1,690	2,035	1,916	2,033	2,039	2,016	2,630	3,503	3,969	4,840	6,570	13,193	15,282
Tea	70s	1,210	1,024	1,061	1,161	1,061	1,119	1,144	1,162	1,261	1,360	1,932	2,100	3,503	6,401	5,722
Imports, cif	71	1,474	1,907	1,773	2,139	2,499	2,295	2,100	2,199	2,763	4,770	5,196	4,902	6,061	15,100	22,603
Imports, fob	71.v	1,328	1,718	1,597	1,927	2,251	2,066	1,890	1,979	2,487	4,293	4,677	4,412	5,455	13,590	20,342
																1990=100
Volume of Exports	72	65.2	59.3	61.7	63.4	60.5	62.9	61.1	59.9	60.5	52.3	62.9	59.9	55.2	58.7	I59.3
Tea	72s	105.1	93.8	101.4	96.6	93.3	96.5	96.1	88.1	95.3	81.2	98.5	92.6	86.0	89.2	86.8
Volume of Imports	73	41.6	56.9	48.6	49.3	52.5	49.3	43.5	42.9	38.4	26.9	33.3	36.5	46.7	64.0	I78.7
Unit Value of Exports	74	4.9	4.6	4.3	5.2	5.2	5.2	5.2	5.2	6.2	9.6	9.0	10.5	17.0	30.9	I33.6
Tea	74s	5.8	5.5	5.3	6.1	5.7	5.8	6.0	6.7	6.7	8.4	9.9	11.4	20.5	36.2	33.2
Unit Value of Imports	75	2.0	2.0	2.0	2.6	2.8	2.9	3.1	3.3	4.4	7.7	9.0	8.1	9.9	18.4	I28.0
Balance of Payments																*Millions of US Dollars*
Goods: Exports f.o.b.	78aa d	....	....	....	....	....	....	....	....	....	....	558.4	559.6	761.6	845.7	981.1
Goods: Imports f.o.b.	78ab d	....	....	....	....	....	....	....	....	....	....	-686.2	-579.5	-655.1	-898.7	-1,304.3
Trade Balance	78ac d	....	....	....	....	....	....	....	....	....	....	-127.7	-20.0	106.5	-52.9	-323.2
Services: Credit	78ad d	....	....	....	....	....	....	....	....	....	....	73.5	72.5	93.5	104.4	152.9
Services: Debit	78ae d	....	....	....	....	....	....	....	....	....	....	-117.5	-103.4	-113.7	-181.5	-232.8
Balance on Goods and Services	78af d	....	....	....	....	....	....	....	....	....	....	-171.7	-50.9	86.3	-130.1	-403.1
Income: Credit	78ag d	....	....	....	....	....	....	....	....	....	....	7.1	3.9	11.8	20.2	39.5
Income: Debit	78ah d	....	....	....	....	....	....	....	....	....	....	-25.5	-24.1	-27.5	-35.2	-54.8
Balance on Goods, Serv., & Inc.	78ai d	....	....	....	....	....	....	....	....	....	....	-190.1	-71.1	70.5	-145.1	-418.4
Current Transfers, n.i.e.: Credit	78aj d	....	....	....	....	....	....	....	....	....	....	85.9	70.9	77.6	94.6	201.6
Current Transfers: Debit	78ak d	....	....	....	....	....	....	....	....	....	....	-5.9	-6.3	-7.8	-17.1	-11.7
Current Account, n.i.e.	78al d	....	....	....	....	....	....	....	....	....	....	-110.0	-6.5	140.3	-67.7	-228.5
Capital Account, n.i.e.: Credit	78ba d	....	....	....	....	....	....	....	....	....	....					
Capital Account: Debit	78bb d	....	....	....	....	....	....	....	....	....	....	—	—	—	—	—
Capital Account, n.i.e.	78bc d	....	....	....	....	....	....	....	....	....	....					
Direct Investment Abroad	78bd d	....	....	....	....	....	....	....	....	....	....					
Dir. Invest. in Rep. Econ., n.i.e.	78be d	....	....	....	....	....	....	....	....	....	....	.1	—	-1.2	1.5	46.9
Portfolio Investment Assets	78bf d	....	....	....	....	....	....	....	....	....	....	10.6	—	—	—	—
Portfolio Investment Liab., n.i.e.	78bg d	....	....	....	....	....	....	....	....	....	....	—	.5	—	.5	—
Other Investment Assets	78bh d	....	....	....	....	....	....	....	....	....	....	-2.1	-18.8	-62.6	-6.4	-22.3
Other Investment Liab., n.i.e.	78bi d	....	....	....	....	....	....	....	....	....	....	77.9	61.1	53.4	90.8	160.6
Financial Account, n.i.e.	78bj d	....	....	....	....	....	....	....	....	....	....	86.5	42.8	-10.4	86.4	185.2
Net Errors and Omissions	78ca d	....	....	....	....	....	....	....	....	....	....	-2.4	.1	20.7	-17.7	49.4
Overall Balance	78cb d	....	....	....	....	....	....	....	....	....	....	-25.9	36.3	150.6	1.1	6.1
Reserves and Related Items	79da d	....	....	....	....	....	....	....	....	....	....	25.9	-36.3	-150.6	-1.1	-6.1
Reserve Assets	79db d	....	....	....	....	....	....	....	....	....	....	-1.1	-50.4	-198.6	-80.5	-102.7
Use of Fund Credit and Loans	79dc d	....	....	....	....	....	....	....	....	....	....	27.0	11.0	43.5	71.7	101.8
Liabs.Constit.For.Auth.Reserves	79dd d	....	....	....	....	....	....	....	....	....	....	—	2.5	2.6	5.6	-7.3
Exceptional Financing	79de d	....	....	....	....	....	....	....	....	....	....	—	.6	1.9	2.1	2.2
Government Finance																*Millions of Rupees*
Deficit (-) or Surplus	80	-492	-518	-616	-702	-825	-898	-1,153	-1,168	I-960	-767	-1,704	-2,518	-1,671	-5,290	-6,300
Revenue	81	1,826	1,903	1,942	2,290	2,555	2,698	2,997	3,322	I3,670	4,360	4,668	5,340	6,277	11,245	12,158
Grants Received	81z	....	....	....	....	....	....	....	....	I49	253	405	381	500	661	1,390
Expenditure	82	2,311	2,411	2,547	3,026	3,355	3,594	4,146	4,493	I4,637	5,332	6,715	8,072	8,364	16,626	19,426
Lending Minus Repayments	83	7	10	12	-34	24	3	3	-3	I42	48	62	167	84	570	422
Financing (by Residence of Lender)																
Domestic	84a	....	....	....	....	....	....	....	....	I828	641	1,395	1,927	917	1,998	3,953
Foreign	85a	....	....	....	....	....	....	....	....	I132	126	309	591	754	3,292	2,347
Debt: Domestic	88a	....	....	....	....	....	....	....	....	I8,585	9,444	10,859	12,692	14,392	16,368	19,634
Foreign	89a	....	....	....	....	....	....	....	....	I2,989	3,302	4,288	5,406	10,593	14,582	15,841
Financing (by Currency)																
Net Borrowing: Rupees	84b	246	422	304	563	223	696	727	701	....	....	....	....	....	....	....
Foreign Currency	85b	51	126	177	160	357	168	278	248	....	....	....	....	....	....	....
Finance from Foreign Aid	86a	24	42	19	29	24	53	—	—	....	....	....	....	....	....	....
Treasury Depository Functions	86c	172	10	84	-27	90	156	-10	231	....	....	....	....	....	....	....
Use of Cash Balances	87	-2	-82	32	-22	131	-175	157	-12	....	....	....	....	....	....	....
Debt: Rupees	88b	3,408	3,839	4,120	4,709	4,922	5,808	6,444	7,096	....	....	....	....	....	....	....
Intragovernmental Debt	88s	413	495	552	609	661	528	718	870	....	....	....	....	....	....	....
Debt: Foreign Currency	89b	447	576	876	1,116	1,399	1,567	1,887	2,352	....	....	....	....	....	....	....
National Accounts																*Millions of Rupees*
Exports of Goods & Services	90c	2,095	1,865	1,849	2,210	2,152	3,478	3,458	3,404	4,481	6,283	7,306	8,773	12,311	14,835	17,660
Government Consumption	91f	1,157	1,158	1,240	1,408	1,471	1,623	1,764	1,897	2,016	2,743	2,480	3,021	3,118	4,043	4,798
Gross Fixed Capital Formation	93e	1,043	1,187	1,366	1,568	2,276	2,359	2,140	2,206	2,493	2,972	3,699	4,595	5,035	8,521	13,246
Increase/Decrease(-) in Stocks	93i	-30	8	11	132	-23	230	258	432	35	763	441	301	224	33	281
Private Consumption	96f	5,881	6,274	6,677	7,928	8,698	9,882	10,169	10,952	14,083	19,068	21,942	22,991	26,698	32,105	40,371
Imports of Goods & Services	98c	-2,061	-2,155	-2,106	-2,528	-2,879	-3,908	-3,739	-3,644	-4,704	-8,058	-9,291	-9,478	-10,979	-16,872	-23,969
Gross Domestic Product	99b	8,084	8,337	9,037	10,718	11,695	13,664	14,050	15,247	18,404	23,771	26,577	30,203	36,407	42,665	52,387
Net Factor Inc/Pmts(-) Abroad	98.n	-15	-37	-54	-54	-109	-220	-188	-178	-183	-213	-282	-252	-237	-240	
Gross Nat'l Expenditure = GNP	99a	8,013	8,334	9,018	10,540	11,624	12,746	12,798	14,042	16,784	21,482	23,619	25,704	31,256	42,428	52,147
Nat'l Income, Market Prices	99e	7,735	8,033	8,645	9,964	10,836	12,237	12,426	13,576	15,869	20,489	22,439	24,212	29,707	37,110	49,700
Gross Dom. Prod. 1990 Prices	99b.p	119,781	125,938	133,567	139,383	150,785	174,637	174,531	I179,795	186,132	193,489	202,568	211,557	219,640	235,911	250,249
GDP Deflator (1990=100)	99bi p	6.7	6.6	6.8	7.7	7.8	7.8	8.1	8.5	9.9	12.3	13.1	14.3	16.6	18.1	20.9
																Millions
Population	99z	11.16	11.44	11.70	11.99	12.25	12.52	12.61	12.86	13.09	13.28	13.50	13.72	13.94	14.19	14.47

Monetary Authorities: I Beginning in 1989, data are compiled from a new report form.
Deposit Money Banks: I See note to section 10.
Monetary Survey: I See note to section 10.

Government Finance: I Beginning in 1973, data are as reported in the *Government Finance Statistics Yearbook* and relate to the consolidated central government.

Sri Lanka

524

	1980	1981	1982	1983	1984	1985	1986	1987	1988	1989	1990	1991	1992	1993	1994		
Millions of Rupees																**International Transactions**	
	17,595	21,043	21,454	25,096	37,347	36,207	34,072	41,133	46,928	56,175	76,624	82,225	107,855	138,175	158,554	Exports	**70**
	6,170	6,444	6,342	8,295	15,764	12,003	9,253	10,654	12,299	13,664	19,823	17,867	14,893	19,911	20,964	Tea	**70s**
	33,942	36,583	41,946	45,558	47,541	54,049	54,559	60,528	71,200	80,225	107,729	126,643	153,555	193,550	236,030	Imports, cif	**71**
	30,548	32,924	37,750	41,000	42,787	48,645	49,108	54,481	64,086	72,210	96,966	113,990	138,213	174,212^p	212,448	Imports, fob	**71.v**
1990=100																	
	63.3	66.7	70.0	66.0	77.3	80.0	85.3	I86.7	84.2	85.8	100.0	104.2	120.0	136.7	153.3	Volume of Exports	**72**
	85.5	84.9	83.8	73.1	94.5	91.7	96.2	93.1	101.8	94.5	100.0	98.3	84.1	101.1	106.3	Tea	**72s**
	92.9	83.7	83.7	92.1	95.4	91.2	103.8	I106.3	101.1	94.7	100.0	113.7	125.3	144.2	162.1	Volume of Imports	**73**
	37.6	40.8	39.9	51.1	65.2	57.8	51.6	I59.8	69.8	82.3	100.0	101.9	115.4	127.5	127.9	Unit Value of Exports	**74**
	36.4	38.3	38.2	57.2	84.1	66.1	48.5	57.7	61.0	72.9	100.0	91.7	89.3	99.3	99.5	Tea	**74s**
	35.5	41.2	42.9	44.7	46.9	50.8	47.0	I53.0	65.7	78.7	100.0	103.9	113.2	122.6	129.1	Unit Value of Imports	**75**
Minus Sign Indicates Debit																**Balance of Payments**	
	1,061.6	1,062.5	1,013.9	1,061.2	1,461.6	1,315.8	1,208.5	1,393.9	1,477.1	1,505.1	1,853.0	2,003.3	2,301.4	2,785.7	3,201.8	Goods: Exports f.o.b.	**78aa** *d*
	-1,845.1	-1,694.5	-1,794.3	-1,725.6	-1,698.7	-1,838.5	-1,764.3	-1,866.0	-2,017.5	-2,055.1	-2,325.6	-2,808.0	-3,016.5	-3,527.8	-4,072.5	Goods: Imports f.o.b.	**78ab** *d*
	-783.5	-632.0	-780.4	-664.4	-237.1	-522.6	-555.7	-472.1	-540.5	-550.1	-472.5	-804.7	-715.1	-742.1	-870.7	Trade Balance	**78ac** *d*
	231.1	279.4	290.6	297.9	276.2	245.4	305.3	328.2	339.2	345.6	439.6	546.6	621.4	634.4	753.9	Services: Credit	**78ad** *d*
	-351.4	-359.2	-390.6	-407.3	-383.5	-457.1	-499.7	-533.2	-547.1	-565.8	-639.2	-762.5	-823.2	-874.3	-1,053.2	Services: Debit	**78ae** *d*
	-903.8	-711.8	-880.5	-773.7	-344.4	-734.4	-750.2	-677.2	-748.4	-770.3	-672.0	-1,020.6	-916.9	-982.1	-1,170.0	Balance on Goods and Services	**78af** *d*
	47.2	33.0	43.8	44.7	58.1	83.3	68.0	69.3	68.7	58.6	93.0	54.5	68.1	111.4	143.2	Income: Credit	**78ag** *d*
	-72.8	-128.8	-137.8	-181.8	-191.9	-210.1	-206.0	-210.8	-240.8	-221.3	-259.8	-232.5	-246.2	-234.3	-310.3	Income: Debit	**78ah** *d*
	-929.4	-807.6	-974.4	-910.8	-478.3	-861.2	-888.1	-818.7	-920.5	-933.0	-838.8	-1,198.5	-1,094.9	-1,105.0	-1,337.0	Balance on Goods, Serv., & Inc.	**78ai** *d*
	287.8	388.7	451.0	464.6	503.6	468.9	502.9	530.0	563.7	546.6	578.8	644.5	730.4	795.4	878.5	Current Transfers, n.i.e.: Credit	**78aj** *d*
	-15.5	-26.6	-25.5	-20.0	-24.4	-26.1	-31.8	-37.3	-37.7	-27.3	-38.3	-40.8	-86.1	-72.6	-88.1	Current Transfers: Debit	**78ak** *d*
	-657.2	-445.6	-548.9	-466.2	.9	-418.5	-417.1	-326.1	-394.5	-413.7	-298.3	-594.8	-450.7	-382.2	-546.7	Current Account, n.i.e.	**78al** *d*
	—	—	—	—	—	—	—	—	—	—	—	—	—	—	—	Capital Account, n.i.e.: Credit	**78ba** *d*
	—	—	—	—	—	—	—	—	—	—	—	—	—	—	—	Capital Account: Debit	**78bb** *d*
	—	—	—	—	—	—	—	—	—	—	—	—	—	—	—	Capital Account, n.i.e.	**78bc** *d*
	—	—	—	—	—	-1.4	-.5	-1.3	-2.1	-2.0	-.8	-4.5	-1.6	-6.9	-8.3	Direct Investment Abroad	**78bd** *d*
	43.0	49.3	63.6	37.8	32.6	26.2	29.7	59.5	45.7	19.7	43.4	48.4	122.6	194.5	164.4	Dir. Invest. in Rep. Econ., n.i.e.	**78be** *d*
	—	—	—	—	—	—	—	—	—	—	—	—	32.1	25.7	27.0	Portfolio Investment Assets	**78bf** *d*
	—	—	—	—	—	—	—	—	—	—	—	—	—	—	—	Portfolio Investment Liab., n.i.e.	**78bg** *d*
	-40.0	-7.2	-72.8	-57.3	-35.2	-20.9	-30.0	-56.9	-15.8	-11.3	-115.8	-51.6	-100.3	16.4	-134.0	Other Investment Assets	**78bh** *d*
	321.9	340.2	509.6	465.9	361.7	359.1	362.6	393.6	228.2	570.6	551.4	664.8	454.9	725.0	860.5	Other Investment Liab., n.i.e.	**78bi** *d*
	324.9	382.2	500.4	446.4	359.1	363.0	361.8	394.9	256.0	577.0	478.1	689.0	501.3	994.2	911.7	Financial Account, n.i.e.	**78bj** *d*
	16.2	24.0	.6	14.8	-39.7	-43.0	-34.4	-122.5	37.4	-115.0	-115.1	225.6	173.3	130.1	-66.9	Net Errors and Omissions	**78ca** *d*
	-316.0	-39.4	-47.9	-4.9	320.3	-98.5	-89.6	-53.6	-101.2	48.3	64.8	319.9	223.9	742.0	298.1	Overall Balance	**78cb** *d*
	316.0	39.4	47.9	4.9	-320.3	98.5	89.6	53.6	101.2	-48.3	-64.8	-319.9	-223.9	-742.0	-298.1	Reserves and Related Items	**79da** *d*
	290.4	-108.0	-25.7	16.9	-235.1	141.4	182.7	167.9	3.2	-65.1	-132.3	-312.5	-284.6	-820.7	-373.5	Reserve Assets	**79db** *d*
	3.3	156.6	-6.3	-14.1	-11.9	-53.2	-90.7	-114.6	100.7	13.6	16.5	-11.2	82.9	52.8	65.9	Use of Fund Credit and Loans	**79dc** *d*
	20.5	-10.3	79.3	2.0	-73.3	10.3	-2.4	.4	-2.7	3.3	51.0	3.8	-22.2	25.9	9.6	Liabs.Constit.For.Auth.Reserves	**79dd** *d*
	1.9	1.2	.6	.2	—	—	—	—	—	—	—	—	—	—	—	Exceptional Financing	**79de** *d*
Year Ending December 31																**Government Finance**	
	-12,157	-10,518	-13,927	-12,846	-10,482	-15,678	-18,202	-17,073	-28,195	-21,778	-25,153	-35,197	-22,912	-32,084	....	Deficit (-) or Surplus	**80**
	13,444	14,775	16,209	23,318	34,062	36,248	37,238	42,144	41,749	53,979	67,964	76,460	85,780	98,495	....	Revenue	**81**
	2,620	2,721	3,376	3,473	3,293	3,307	3,753	4,677	6,588	6,407	6,697	7,870	8,280	8,025	....	Grants Received	**81z**
	27,515	25,901	33,768	37,865	44,546	54,174	57,202	62,376	69,010	77,634	91,300	109,060	114,586	134,728	....	Expenditure	**82**
	706	2,113	-256	1,772	3,291	1,059	1,991	1,518	7,522	4,530	8,514	10,467	2,386	3,876	....	Lending Minus Repayments	**83**
																Financing (by Residence of Lender)	
	9,162	5,638	9,183	6,534	3,989	8,569	9,141	11,357	21,067	15,852	13,509	15,868	15,551	22,229	....	Domestic	**84a**
	2,995	4,880	4,744	6,312	6,493	7,109	9,061	5,716	7,128	5,926	11,644	19,329	7,361	9,855	....	Foreign	**85a**
	29,070	35,828	45,575	52,355	52,237	63,197	70,085	80,133	98,595	117,562	133,897	152,118	....	....	....	Debt: Domestic	**88a**
	22,277	30,050	35,376	46,729	54,192	68,196	86,723	92,857	125,997	156,631	176,990	214,579	....	....	....	Foreign	**89a**
																Financing (by Currency)	
	....	....	....	....	....	....	....	....	....	....	....	....	....	....	....	Net Borrowing: Rupees	**84b**
	....	....	....	....	....	....	....	....	....	....	....	....	....	....	....	Foreign Currency	**85b**
	....	....	....	....	....	....	....	....	....	....	....	....	....	....	....	Finance from Foreign Aid	**86a**
	....	....	....	....	....	....	....	....	....	....	....	....	....	....	....	Treasury Depository Functions	**86c**
	....	....	....	....	....	....	....	....	....	....	....	....	....	....	....	Use of Cash Balances	**87**
	....	....	....	....	....	....	....	....	....	....	....	....	....	....	....	Debt: Rupees	**88b**
	....	....	....	....	....	....	....	....	....	....	....	....	....	....	....	Intragovernmental Debt	**88s**
	....	....	....	....	....	....	....	....	....	....	....	....	....	....	....	Debt: Foreign Currency	**89b**
Millions of Rupees																**National Accounts**	
	21,434	25,892	27,148	32,016	44,285	42,237	42,568	49,559	57,885	68,666	97,117	107,016	135,114	168,858	195,808	Exports of Goods & Services	**90c**
	5,685	6,310	8,242	9,889	11,935	16,599	18,480	19,538	21,849	26,410	31,405	36,633	40,972	45,791	56,099	Government Consumption	**91f**
	20,845	23,279	30,279	35,342	39,558	38,457	42,326	45,752	49,961	54,249	70,417	84,206	100,039	126,070	154,310	Gross Fixed Capital Formation	**93e**
	1,620	331	248	-210	150	225	137	148	601	473	1,038	950	3,200	1,800	2,250	Increase/Decrease(-) in Stocks	**93i**
	53,399	68,751	79,226	94,945	111,235	126,503	139,370	151,949	173,457	194,680	244,288	288,214	320,466	373,785	434,933	Private Consumption	**96f**
	-36,456	-39,558	-45,905	-50,381	-53,417	-61,646	-63,407	-70,223	-81,771	-92,587	-122,481	-144,674	-174,508	-216,544	-264,602	Imports of Goods & Services	**98c**
	66,527	85,005	99,238	121,601	153,746	162,375	179,474	196,723	221,982	251,891	321,784	372,345	425,283	499,760	578,795	Gross Domestic Product	**99b**
	-432	-1,868	-1,959	-3,214	-3,401	-3,400	-3,861	-4,336	-5,266	-5,739	-6,685	-7,367	-7,821	-5,979	-8,028	Net Factor Inc/Pmts(-) Abroad	**98.n**
	67,906	82,659	97,279	118,387	149,293	158,975	175,613	192,387	216,716	246,152	315,099	364,978	417,462	493,781	570,767	Gross Nat'l Expenditure = GNP	**99a**
	63,457	77,868	89,983	109,671	137,091	146,788	160,870	175,333	203,938	232,298	298,256	345,111	....	....	....	Nat'l Income, Market Prices	**99e**
	264,497	279,165	235,214	I246,878	259,467	272,438	284,155	288,419	296,184	302,998	321,784	337,231	....	....	....	Gross Dom. Prod. 1990 Prices	**99b.***p*
	25.2	30.4	42.2	49.3	59.3	59.6	63.2	68.2	74.9	83.1	100.0	110.4	....	....	....	GDP Deflator (1990=100)	**99bi** *p*
Midyear Estimates																	
	14.75	15.01	15.19	15.42	15.60	15.84	16.13	16.37	16.60	16.83	16.99	17.25	17.40	17.62	17.86	**Population**	**99z**

Sudan
732

		1965	1966	1967	1968	1969	1970	1971	1972	1973	1974	1975	1976	1977	1978	1979
Exchange Rates															*Pounds per SDR:*	
Market Rate	aa	.3482	.3482	.3482	.3482	.3482	.3482	.3781	.3781	.4201	.4264	.4077	.4046	.4230	.5211	.6587
															Pounds per US Dollar:	
Market Rate	ae	.3482	.3482	.3482	.3482	.3482	.3482	.3482	.3482	.3482	.3482	.3482	.3482	.3482	.4000	.5000
Market Rate	rf	.3482	.3482	.3482	.3482	.3482	.3482	.3482	.3482	.3482	.3482	.3482	.3482	.3482	.3775	.4292
Fund Position															*Millions of SDRs:*	
Quota	2f.s	45.0	57.0	57.0	57.0	57.0	72.0	72.0	72.0	72.0	72.0	72.0	72.0	72.0	88.0	88.0
SDRs	1b.s	—	—	—	—	—	.1	—	4.9	13.6	21.5	7.3	—	—	6.0	10.0
Reserve Position in the Fund	1c.s															
Total Fund Cred.&Loans Outstg.	2tl	15.0	27.0	39.2	40.5	39.9	30.9	15.2	28.1	29.0	71.7	113.4	119.1	99.5	150.6	222.4
International Liquidity													*Millions of US Dollars Unless Otherwise Indicated:*				
Total Reserves minus Gold	1l.d	59.7	57.2	54.7	47.7	36.4	21.7	27.9	35.6	61.3	124.3	36.4	23.6	23.1	28.4	67.4
SDRs	1b.d	—	—	—	—	—	.1	—	5.3	16.4	26.4	8.6	—	—	7.9	13.2
Reserve Position in the Fund	1c.d															
Foreign Exchange	1d.d	59.7	57.2	54.7	47.7	36.4	21.6	27.9	30.3	44.9	97.9	27.8	23.6	23.1	20.5	54.2
Monetary Authorities: Other Liab.	4..d	1.6	12.5	5.5	19.4	15.6	34.1	106.6	127.5	136.5	144.0	362.1	483.6	536.1	501.8	559.8
Deposit Money Banks: Assets	7a.d	1.2	1.1	2.9	2.2	1.6	1.4	1.2	2.7	13.4	17.4	18.1	67.8	172.6	168.1	193.7
Liabilities	7b.d	14.6	16.1	15.8	28.7	15.4	14.0	14.0	21.9	45.4	34.9	57.2	72.1	145.3	106.9	73.2
Monetary Authorities														*Millions of Pounds through 1991;*			
Foreign Assets	11	26	27	24	21	16	9	10	13	23	39	12	8	9	13	34
Claims on Central Govt. (Net)	12an															
Claims on Nonfin.Pub.Enterprises	12c	4	2	—	—	5	25	38	50	49	84	160	182	181	227	284
Claims on Deposit Money Banks	12e	4	7	12	19	17	15	8	7	9	9	11	5	13	32	43
Claims on Other Banking Insts.	12f	3	3	4	7	8	8	14	14	15	19	21	23	23	23	23
Reserve Money	14	46	51	55	57	71	78	85	93	119	163	193	235	380	502	667
of which: Currency Outside DMBs	14a	35	41	42	47	59	67	70	75	93	119	129	153	199	279	380
Quasi-Monetary Deposits	15															
Foreign Liabilities	16c	6	14	16	21	19	23	39	51	50	81	172	217	229	264	392
Capital Accounts	17a	4	4	4	4	4	8	11	14	14	14	14	17	24	28	128
Rescheduling Adjustment	17rr															
Valuation Adjustment	17rv															
Other Items (Net)	17r	−20	−30	−35	−36	−49	−52	−65	−74	−86	−107	−175	−251	−407	−500	−704
Deposit Money Banks														*Millions of Pounds through 1991;*			
Reserves	20	8	5	4	7	4	5	5	11	19	24	34	44	115	176	240
Foreign Assets	21	—	—	1	1	1	1	—	1	4	6	6	24	60	67	97
Claims on Central Government	22a	11	14	17	18	20	21	23	29	37	54	60	76	106	133	159
Claims on Private Sector	22d	46	49	62	71	66	71	70	85	99	123	186	228	265	343	461
Demand Deposits	24	27	29	33	31	36	43	45	62	74	99	121	155	226	292	392
Time and Savings Deposits	25	11	14	17	18	20	21	23	29	37	54	60	66	108	126	159
Foreign Liabilities	26c	5	6	6	10	5	5	4	7	13	12	20	25	51	43	37
Central Government Deposits	26d	—	—	—	1	1	1	1	3	2	2	3	8	15	19	15
Credit from Monetary Authorities	26g	4	7	12	19	17	15	8	6	9	9	13	9	14	33	40
Capital Accounts	27a	6	6	6	6	6	6	6	6	6	6	6	10	16	19	21
Valuation Adjustment	27rv															
Other Items (Net)	27r	11	7	11	12	6	6	10	11	16	25	64	99	117	187	293
Monetary Survey														*Millions of Pounds through 1991;*			
Foreign Assets (Net)	31n	16	8	4	−9	−8	−18	−33	−44	−36	−48	−174	−210	−210	−227	−298
Domestic Credit	32	76	93	109	126	143	176	206	246	275	357	567	726	956	1,186	1,455
Claims on Central Govt. (Net)	32an	23	38	42	48	62	72	84	98	112	132	200	294	488	593	687
Claims on Nonfin.Pub.Enterprises	32c	4	2	—	—	7	25	38	50	49	84	160	182	181	227	284
Claims on Private Sector	32d	46	49	62	71	66	71	70	85	99	123	186	228	265	343	461
Claims on Other Banking Insts.	32f															
Money	34	66	74	82	81	101	116	124	144	176	237	281	350	497	634	837
Quasi-Money	35	8	9	12	17	14	14	16	22	30	41	49	62	92	117	141
Rescheduling Adjustment	37rr															
Valuation Adjustment	37rv															
Other Items (Net)	37r	18	18	19	19	20	28	32	36	34	32	63	104	157	208	180
Money plus Quasi-Money	35l	74	83	93	98	115	130	140	166	205	278	330	412	589	751	977
Other Banking Institutions															*Millions of Pounds:*	
Savings Deposits	45	4	5	5	6	6	7	7	7	7	14	12	14	14	16	19
Liquid Liabilities	55l	78	88	99	104	122	137	147	173	213	292	342	426	603	766	996
Interest Rates															*Percent Per Annum*	
Deposit Rate	60l														6.0	6.0
Prices															*Index Numbers (1990=100):*	
Consumer Prices	64	.6	.7	.7	.6	.7	1.8	.8	.9	1.0	1.3	1.6	1.6	1.9	2.2	2.9

Sudan
732

1980	1981	1982	1983	1984	1985	1986	1987	1988	1989	1990	1991	1992	1993	1994		
End of Period															**Exchange Rates**	
.6377	1.0486	1.4341	1.3611	1.2743	2.7461	3.0580	6.3846	6.0563	5.9143	6.4026	21.4457	185.8108	298.6000	583.9400	Market Rate	aa
End of Period (ae) Period Average (rf)																
.5000	.9009	1.3001	1.3001	1.3001	2.5000	2.5000	4.5005	4.5005	4.5005	4.5005	14.9925	135.1351	217.3913	400.0000	Market Rate	ae
.5000	.5589	.9523	1.3000	1.3000	2.3040	2.5000	3.0000	4.5000	4.5000	4.5000	6.9556	97.4317	159.3139	289.6089	Market Rate	rf
End of Period															**Fund Position**	
132.0	132.0	132.0	169.7	169.7	169.7	169.7	169.7	169.7	169.7	169.7	169.7	169.7	169.7	169.7	Quota	2f. s
—	.5	—	.1	—	—	—	—	—	—	—	—	—	—	—	SDRs	1b. s
—	—	—	—	—	—	—	—	—	—	—	—	—	—	—	Reserve Position in the Fund	1c. s
338.0	484.8	524.6	666.7	677.6	672.7	672.7	672.7	672.7	672.7	671.6	671.6	671.6	671.6	671.6	Total Fund Cred.&Loans Outstg.	2tl
End of Period															**International Liquidity**	
48.7	17.0	20.5	16.6	17.2	12.2	58.5	11.7	12.1	15.9	11.4	7.6	27.5	37.4	78.2	Total Reserves minus Gold	1l. d
—	.6	—	.1	—	—	—	—	—	—	—	—	—	—	—	SDRs	1b. d
—	—	—	—	—	—	—	—	—	—	—	—	—	—	—	Reserve Position in the Fund	1c. d
48.7	16.4	20.5	16.5	17.2	12.2	58.5	11.7	12.1	15.9	11.4	7.6	27.5	37.4	78.1	Foreign Exchange	1d. d
682.6	898.3	873.9	1,520.2	1,614.7	1,180.0	1,308.7	1,016.3	1,703.6	1,809.5	2,400.6	1,340.4	2,165.8	2,288.0	2,471.8	Monetary Authorities: Other Liab.	4..d
435.0	309.5	289.2	409.4	512.7	618.1	493.9	354.5	500.2	539.8	616.9	599.5	322.0	447.7	270.1	Deposit Money Banks: Assets	7a. d
144.1	146.8	122.0	117.2	136.7	215.5	165.9	137.5	136.2	134.4	154.6	106.6	70.1	68.8	37.8	Liabilities	7b. d
Billions of Pounds Beginning 1992: End of Period															**Monetary Authorities**	
20	15	27	⌶22	22	34	156	67	89	80	446	720	⌶4	8	31	Foreign Assets	11
....	....	....	1,631	1,985	2,894	4,285	6,174	8,726	15,907	22,314	35,932	⌶108	165	220	Claims on Central Govt. (Net)	12an
377	534	796	⌶473	582	1,147	1,656	2,283	2,724	3,568	3,888	2,698	⌶2	2	2	Claims on Nonfin.Pub.Enterprises	12c
50	67	91	⌶23	146	150	139	164	210	216	272	179	⌶1	5	3	Claims on Deposit Money Banks	12e
23	30	31	⌶45	57	72	84	84	84	139	169	169	⌶—	—	—	Claims on Other Banking Insts.	12f
751	1,211	1,582	⌶1,740	2,444	3,950	5,615	7,160	9,447	17,515	23,338	34,608	⌶88	144	202	Reserve Money	14
508	630	820	⌶1,022	1,247	1,930	2,760	3,625	5,601	9,240	13,113	21,663	⌶44	95	148	of which: Currency Outside DMBs	14a
....	....	....	13	103	102	89	175	190	224	268	389	⌶6	6	21	Quasi-Monetary Deposits	15
512	1,244	1,788	⌶2,788	2,877	4,612	5,123	8,438	11,333	11,723	14,673	33,055	⌶405	678	1,342	Foreign Liabilities	16c
28	18	19	45	42	42	59	128	212	348	374	394	⌶—	1	2	Capital Accounts	17a
....	....	....	—576	—576	—743	—743	—743	—759	—199	—743	—743	⌶—1	—1	—1	Rescheduling Adjustment	17rr
....	....	....	—1,532	—1,532	—3,209	—3,418	—5,925	—8,364	—8,949	—10,606	—29,464	⌶—392	—631	—1,249	Valuation Adjustment	17rv
—822	—1,827	—2,444	⌶—284	—566	—457	—404	—462	—226	—752	—217	1,458	⌶8	—18	—60	Other Items (Net)	17r
Billions of Pounds Beginning 1992: End of Period															**Deposit Money Banks**	
196	391	408	826	937	⌶2,009	2,695	3,283	3,203	7,258	8,315	10,085	⌶37	46	56	Reserves	20
217	279	376	532	667	⌶1,545	1,235	1,595	2,251	2,429	2,776	8,988	⌶44	97	108	Foreign Assets	21
186	285	466	94	96	100	112	60	60	243	10	—	⌶—	5	2	Claims on Central Government	22a
593	778	1,143	1,377	1,609	⌶1,882	2,638	3,793	4,509	4,941	7,667	14,049	⌶27	45	88	Claims on Private Sector	22d
540	653	884	1,165	1,326	⌶1,925	2,636	3,633	4,744	8,470	11,443	18,714	⌶46	62	95	Demand Deposits	24
182	288	465	761	852	⌶1,862	1,875	2,720	2,756	2,593	4,375	9,428	⌶34	101	137	Time and Savings Deposits	25
72	132	159	152	178	⌶539	415	619	613	605	696	1,599	⌶9	15	15	Foreign Liabilities	26c
13	25	12	46	57	265	664	1,121	1,079	1,109	1,216	1,717	⌶2	3	2	Central Government Deposits	26d
53	71	93	148	127	31	12	10	12	14	15	84	⌶—	1	1	Credit from Monetary Authorities	26g
29	45	94	247	326	⌶652	773	764	1,157	1,414	1,607	2,422	⌶6	17	39	Capital Accounts	27a
....	....	....	....	....	300	300	300	300	300	496	3,000	⌶12	11	7	Valuation Adjustment	27rv
304	517	685	311	443	⌶—36	6	—434	—638	367	—1,080	—3,841	⌶—2	—17	—42	Other Items (Net)	27r
Billions of Pounds Beginning 1992: End of Period															**Monetary Survey**	
—347	—1,082	—1,543	⌶—2,386	—2,366	⌶—3,572	—4,146	—7,395	—9,606	—9,819	—12,147	—24,946	⌶—367	—587	—1,217	Foreign Assets (Net)	31n
1,770	2,378	2,761	3,574	4,272	⌶5,830	8,111	11,274	15,024	23,689	32,831	51,131	⌶129	214	315	Domestic Credit	32
777	1,037	791	⌶1,679	2,025	2,729	3,733	5,114	7,707	15,041	21,108	34,216	⌶94	158	211	Claims on Central Govt. (Net)	32an
377	534	796	⌶473	582	1,147	1,656	2,283	2,724	3,568	3,888	2,698	⌶8	9	14	Claims on Nonfin.Pub.Enterprises	32c
593	778	1,143	1,377	1,609	⌶1,882	2,638	3,793	4,509	4,941	7,667	14,049	⌶27	45	88	Claims on Private Sector	32d
....	....	....	45	57	72	84	84	84	139	169	169	⌶1	1	1	Claims on Other Banking Insts.	32f
1,097	1,531	2,091	2,336	2,764	⌶4,145	5,849	7,768	11,218	18,899	27,659	44,305	⌶89	157	243	Money	34
167	264	443	774	955	⌶1,964	1,964	2,895	2,946	2,817	4,643	9,817	⌶41	108	158	Quasi-Money	35
....	....	....	—576	—576	—743	—743	—743	—759	—199	—743	—743	⌶—1	—1	—1	Rescheduling Adjustment	37rr
....	....	....	—1,532	—1,532	—2,909	—3,118	—5,625	—8,064	—8,649	—10,110	—26,464	⌶—380	—620	—1,243	Valuation Adjustment	37rv
159	—499	—1,317	⌶185	296	⌶—198	13	—416	77	1,002	—765	—730	⌶13	—17	—59	Other Items (Net)	37r
1,264	1,795	2,534	3,110	3,719	⌶6,108	7,813	10,664	14,164	21,716	32,302	54,122	⌶130	265	400	Money plus Quasi-Money	35l
End of Period															**Other Banking Institutions**	
20	21	23	25	27	30	....	....	....	....	....	....	....	....	....	Savings Deposits	45
1,284	1,816	2,557	3,135	3,746	5,713	....	....	....	....	....	....	....	....	....	Liquid Liabilities	55l
Percent Per Annum															**Interest Rates**	
6.0	8.6	10.5	13.5	13.5	....	....	....	....	....	....	....	....	....	....	Deposit Rate	60l
Period Averages															**Prices**	
3.7	4.6	5.8	7.5	10.1	⌶14.7	18.3	....	⌶36.3	60.5	100.0	223.6	486.6	979.9	....	Consumer Prices	64

Sudan
732

		1965	1966	1967	1968	1969	1970	1971	1972	1973	1974	1975	1976	1977	1978	1979
International Transactions																*Millions of Pounds*
Exports	70	68.0	70.8	74.2	81.2	86.3	103.9	114.4	124.4	151.2	122.0	152.5	193.0	230.2	195.6	232.7
Cotton	70f	31.4	34.9	40.9	51.3	51.8	63.7	69.9	72.8	84.3	43.3	70.2	97.8	133.2	122.9	151.3
Imports, cif	71	72.3	77.5	74.3	89.7	89.3	100.1	115.4	117.9	151.9	247.5	359.9	341.4	376.5	449.5	477.3
Imports, fob	71.v	64.5	69.2	66.4	80.1	79.8	89.4	103.1	107.4	138.4	225.5	327.4	310.7	342.7	409.0	430.1
Balance of Payments																*Millions of US Dollars:*
Goods: Exports f.o.b.	78aa d	....	....	....	....	....	....	....	....	....	....	....	....	658.2	563.0	514.1
Goods: Imports f.o.b.	78ab d	....	....	....	....	....	....	....	....	....	....	....	....	−644.2	−623.9	−735.8
Trade Balance	78ac d	....	....	....	....	....	....	....	....	....	....	....	....	14.1	−60.9	−221.7
Services: Credit	78ad d	....	....	....	....	....	....	....	....	....	....	....	....	120.9	162.4	202.9
Services: Debit	78ae d	....	....	....	....	....	....	....	....	....	....	....	....	−199.3	−229.9	−269.4
Balance on Goods and Services	78af d	....	....	....	....	....	....	....	....	....	....	....	....	−64.3	−128.5	−288.3
Income: Credit	78ag d	....	....	....	....	....	....	....	....	....	....	....	....	5.2	14.5	3.8
Income: Debit	78ah d	....	....	....	....	....	....	....	....	....	....	....	....	−87.6	−74.9	−78.9
Balance on Goods, Serv., & Inc.	78ai d	....	....	....	....	....	....	....	....	....	....	....	....	−146.7	−188.8	−363.4
Current Transfers, n.i.e.: Credit	78aj d	....	....	....	....	....	....	....	....	....	....	....	....	60.0	81.7	118.0
Current Transfers: Debit	78ak d	....	....	....	....	....	....	....	....	....	....	....	....	−2.9	−2.9	−12.2
Current Account, n.i.e.	78al d	....	....	....	....	....	....	....	....	....	....	....	....	−89.6	−110.0	−257.6
Capital Account, n.i.e.: Credit	78ba d	....	....	....	....	....	....	....	....	....	....	....	....	.3	1.3	9.9
Capital Account: Debit	78bb d	....	....	....	....	....	....	....	....	....	....	....	....	−.6	—	—
Capital Account, n.i.e.	78bc d	....	....	....	....	....	....	....	....	....	....	....	....	−.3	1.3	9.9
Direct Investment Abroad	78bd d	....	....	....	....	....	....	....	....	....	....	....	....	—	—	—
Dir. Invest. in Rep. Econ., n.i.e.	78be d	....	....	....	....	....	....	....	....	....	....	....	....			
Portfolio Investment Assets	78bf d	....	....	....	....	....	....	....	....	....	....	....	....	—	—	—
Portfolio Investment Liab., n.i.e.	78bg d	....	....	....	....	....	....	....	....	....	....	....	....	—	—	—
Other Investment Assets	78bh d	....	....	....	....	....	....	....	....	....	....	....	....	−104.8	−13.2	−26.1
Other Investment Liab., n.i.e.	78bi d	....	....	....	....	....	....	....	....	....	....	....	....	41.6	5.5	201.5
Financial Account, n.i.e.	78bj d	....	....	....	....	....	....	....	....	....	....	....	....	−63.2	−7.7	175.4
Net Errors and Omissions	78ca d	....	....	....	....	....	....	....	....	....	....	....	....	−15.1	14.5	−35.0
Overall Balance	78cb d	....	....	....	....	....	....	....	....	....	....	....	....	−168.2	−101.9	−107.3
Reserves and Related Items	79da d	....	....	....	....	....	....	....	....	....	....	....	....	168.2	101.9	107.3
Reserve Assets	79db d	....	....	....	....	....	....	....	....	....	....	....	....	−3.2	−7.8	−55.4
Use of Fund Credit and Loans	79dc d	....	....	....	....	....	....	....	....	....	....	....	....	−22.9	64.5	93.1
Liabs.Constit.For.Auth.Reserves	79dd d	....	....	....	....	....	....	....	....	....	....	....	....			
Exceptional Financing	79de d	....	....	....	....	....	....	....	....	....	....	....	....	194.3	45.2	69.6
Government Finance																*Millions of Pounds:*
Deficit (-) or Surplus	80	....	....	−34.0	−8.0	−20.6	−15.8	2.7	I−6.3	−16.2	−9.7	−74.8	−58.9	−168.4	−151.7	−135.9
Revenue	81	....	....	75.8	92.0	104.4	122.6	149.6	I149.5	153.7	189.4	253.6	298.3	326.7	403.5	547.2
Grants Received	81z	....	....	2.8	1.1	1.4	1.4	1.6	I6.3	3.0	3.6	5.2	.5	24.0	—	—
Expenditure	82	....	....	100.9	99.4	122.5	140.0	156.4	I158.9	171.7	197.1	333.5	357.7	516.6	554.3	682.6
Lending Minus Repayments	83	....	....	11.7	1.7	3.9	−.2	−7.9	I3.2	1.2	5.6	.1	—	2.5	.9	.5
Financing																
Domestic	84a	....	2.9	25.2	2.9	11.4	12.5	−5.4	I−3.1	3.2	−14.2	34.0	−46.8	127.2	172.1	126.6
Foreign	85a	....	....	8.2	7.4	9.6	2.8	1.0	I9.4	13.0	23.9	40.8	105.7	41.2	−20.4	9.3
Use of Cash Balances	87	....	....	.7	−2.3	−.5	.5	1.7	....	....	....	....	....	....	....	....
Debt: Domestic	88a	....	....	....	....	....	....	58.1	I88.7	91.4	125.7	....	....	....	....	....
Foreign	89a	....	....	....	....	....	....	91.7	I101.1	114.1	138.0	....	....	....	....	....
National Accounts																*Millions of Pounds:*
Exports of Goods & Services	90c	86	82	I89	93	103	113	126	126	145	167	184	193	218	257	395
Government Consumption	91f	56	63	I94	105	112	148	141	141	166	181	208	278	331	407	501
Gross Fixed Capital Formation	93e	69	52	I72	70	71	76	73	73	95	140	214	400	414	431	379
Increase/Decrease(-) in Stocks	93i	2	11	I4	3	10	−6	3	3	10	89	51	87	90	92	−160
Private Consumption	96f	371	382	I343	372	409	479	543	543	611	846	1,171	1,827	2,380	2,606	3,481
Imports of Goods & Services	98c	−107	−94	I−103	−107	−122	−108	−134	−134	−136	−177	−316	−341	−459	−447	−784
Gross Domestic Product	99b	477	497	I498	536	583	761	832	897	1,246	1,511	1,848	2,340	2,883	3,254	3,972
Net Factor Inc/Pmts(-) Abroad	98.n	−5	−5	I6	5	6	−3	−4	−8	−10	−16	−20	−17	−14	−24	....
Gross Nat'l Expenditure = GNP	99a	472	492	I504	541	589	758	829	889	1,236	1,495	1,828	2,323	2,868	3,230	....
Nat'l Income, Market Prices	99e	458	460	I472	507	555	649	712	779	831	1,131	1,375	1,665	2,108	2,595	....
																Millions:
Population	99z	13.30	13.48	13.60	13.69	13.75	14.09	14.44	14.81	14.96	15.34	15.73	16.13	16.95	17.56	18.11

Monetary Authorities: I Beginning in 1983 and again in 1992, data reflect improvements in classification.
Deposit Money Banks: I Beginning in June 1985, data are based on a new bank reporting system. I Beginning in 1992, data reflect improvements in classification.
Monetary Survey: I See notes to sections 10 and 20.

Government Finance: I Data for 1972 onwards are as reported in the *Government Finance Statistics Yearbook* and relate to the budgetary central government.

Sudan
732

	1980	1981	1982	1983	1984	1985	1986	1987	1988	1989	1990	1991	1992	1993	1994		
	\multicolumn{15}{l}{}	**International Transactions**	
Millions of Pounds																	
	271.3	357.0	483.1	810.6	817.3	844.7	833.3	1,497.1	2,290.9	3,023.2	....	....	....	....	....	Exports	70
	121.9	66.5	122.0	395.9	405.0	374.3	366.7	455.2	978.4		....	....	....	....	....	Cotton	70f
	788.2	839.8	1,213.8	1,760.8	1,490.8	1,739.1	2,402.2	2,612.9	4,772.2		....	....	....	....	....	Imports, cif	71
	717.3	764.3	1,104.4	1,602.2	1,367.9	1,631.2	2,253.5	2,451.2	4,476.7		....	....	....	....	....	Imports, fob	71.v
Minus Sign Indicates Debit																**Balance of Payments**	
	689.4	792.7	400.9	514.2	519.0	444.2	326.8	265.0	427.0	544.4	326.5	302.5	213.4	....	....	Goods: Exports f.o.b.	78aa d
	−1,127.4	−1,633.6	−750.3	−703.2	−599.8	−579.0	−633.7	−694.8	−948.5	−1,051.0	−648.8	−1,138.2	−810.2	....	....	Goods: Imports f.o.b.	78ab d
	−438.0	−840.9	−349.4	−188.9	−80.8	−134.8	−306.9	−429.7	−521.5	−506.6	−322.3	−835.7	−596.8	....	....	Trade Balance	78ac d
	292.4	425.5	471.7	269.2	258.5	374.2	220.5	184.7	161.7	272.6	172.5	77.0	155.5	....	....	Services: Credit	78ad d
	−353.0	−466.1	−328.7	−343.7	−284.6	−346.4	−188.0	−228.6	−244.6	−378.2	−228.0	−197.3	−204.1	....	....	Services: Debit	78ae d
	−498.6	−881.4	−206.4	−263.4	−107.0	−107.0	−274.4	−473.7	−604.4	−612.2	−377.8	−956.0	−645.4	....	....	Balance on Goods and Services	78af d
	48.8	44.0	44.1	25.8	9.8	12.1	8.3	7.5	9.9	7.0	12.4	2.7	—	....	....	Income: Credit	78ag d
	−96.0	−146.5	−193.3	−227.8	−163.4	−113.5	−93.6	−94.4	−96.7	−117.5	−148.0	−129.1	−93.5	....	....	Income: Debit	78ah d
	−545.8	−983.9	−355.6	−465.3	−260.6	−208.3	−359.8	−560.6	−691.2	−722.6	−513.4	−1,082.4	−738.9	....	....	Balance on Goods, Serv., & Inc.	78ai d
	272.2	403.7	131.9	274.5	306.5	369.5	357.6	332.4	334.4	576.7	143.3	127.9	232.7	....	....	Current Transfers, n.i.e.: Credit	78aj d
	−43.4	−68.1	−25.4	−28.3	−9.5	−12.2	−24.1	−4.1	−1.1	−4.4	−2.1	−.2	—	....	....	Current Transfers: Debit	78ak d
	−317.0	−648.3	−249.1	−219.2	36.5	148.9	−26.3	−232.4	−358.0	−150.3	−372.2	−954.7	−506.2	....	....	Current Account, n.i.e.	78al d
	6.6	14.7	1.2	—	—	—	—	—	—	—	—	—	—	....	....	Capital Account, n.i.e.: Credit	78ba d
	−9.8	−6.3	−.6	−.3	—	—	—	—	—	—	—	—	—	....	....	Capital Account: Debit	78bb d
	−3.2	8.3	.6	−.3	—	—	—	—	—	—	—	—	—	....	....	Capital Account, n.i.e.	78bc d
	—	—	—	—	—	—	—	—	—	—	—	—	—	....	....	Direct Investment Abroad	78bd d
	—	—	—	—	9.1	−3.0	—	—	—	3.5	—	—	—	....	....	Dir. Invest. in Rep. Econ., n.i.e.	78be d
	—	—	—	—	—	—	—	—	—	—	—	—	—	....	....	Portfolio Investment Assets	78bf d
	—	—	—	—	—	—	—	—	—	—	—	—	—	....	....	Portfolio Investment Liab., n.i.e.	78bg d
	−241.0	105.2	20.3	−120.2	−41.9	−497.4	90.6	116.6	−65.3	−39.6	−28.5	−74.0	−82.8	....	....	Other Investment Assets	78bh d
	−22.7	123.6	13.7	−28.6	−120.2	56.5	−176.8	−30.8	132.8	153.9	145.4	658.1	399.2	....	....	Other Investment Liab., n.i.e.	78bi d
	−263.7	228.8	34.0	−148.8	−153.0	−443.9	−86.2	85.8	67.5	117.8	116.9	584.1	316.4	....	....	Financial Account, n.i.e.	78bj d
	58.0	14.7	12.6	145.5	−1.4	−126.0	−88.5	−196.5	3.1	−160.3	10.9	97.9	31.0	....	....	Net Errors and Omissions	78ca d
	−525.9	−396.4	−201.9	−222.8	−118.0	−420.9	−201.0	−343.0	−287.4	−192.8	−244.4	−272.8	−158.8	....	....	Overall Balance	78cb d
	525.9	396.4	201.9	222.8	118.0	420.9	201.0	343.0	287.4	192.8	244.4	272.8	158.8	....	....	Reserves and Related Items	79da d
	35.4	−199.2	−136.5	34.4	−.6	5.0	−46.3	46.8	−.4	−3.8	4.5	3.8	29.3	....	....	Reserve Assets	79db d
	147.5	172.3	45.6	152.7	11.4	−4.9	—	—	—	—	−1.4	—	—	....	....	Use of Fund Credit and Loans	79dc d
	—	—	—	—	—	—	—	—	—	—	—	—	—	....	....	Liabs.Constit.For.Auth.Reserves.	79dd d
	342.9	423.2	292.8	35.7	107.1	420.8	247.3	296.2	287.8	196.6	241.3	269.0	129.5	....	....	Exceptional Financing	79de d
Year Ending June 30																**Government Finance**	
	−129.9	....	−326.4	....	....	....	....	....	....	....	....	....	....	....	....	Deficit (-) or Surplus	80
	558.6	....	839.8	....	....	....	....	....	....	....	....	....	....	....	....	Revenue	81
	107.2	....	194.0	....	....	....	....	....	....	....	....	....	....	....	....	Grants Received	81z
	779.7	....	1,198.2	....	....	....	....	....	....	....	....	....	....	....	....	Expenditure	82
	16.0	....	161.7	....	....	....	....	....	....	....	....	....	....	....	....	Lending Minus Repayments	83
																Financing	
	18.0	....	197.9	....	....	....	....	....	....	....	....	....	....	....	....	Domestic	84a
	111.9	....	128.5	....	....	....	....	....	....	....	....	....	....	....	....	Foreign	85a
	....	....	....	....	....	....	....	....	....	....	....	....	....	....	....	Use of Cash Balances	87
	....	....	....	....	....	....	....	....	....	....	....	....	....	....	....	Debt: Domestic	88a
	....	....	....	....	....	....	....	....	....	....	....	....	....	....	....	Foreign	89a
Year Ending June 30																**National Accounts**	
	554	647	483	811	817	845	1,172	1,493	2,433	3,423	4,657	2,548	....	....	....	Exports of Goods & Services	90c
	648	726	....	....	....	....	1,808	2,035	3,574	5,428	7,783	9,471	....	....	....	Government Consumption	91f
	241	304	....	....	....	....	2,058	3,338	5,395	6,546	9,008	22,632	....	....	....	Gross Fixed Capital Formation	93e
	−421	−449	....	....	....	....	−345	−1,390	−1,767	−4,454	−1,260	−3,257	....	....	....	Increase/Decrease(-) in Stocks	93i
	4,505	5,943	....	....	....	....	17,477	30,508	37,915	68,789	93,450	164,698	....	....	....	Private Consumption	96f
	−998	−1,222	−1,214	−1,761	−1,491	−1,737	−2,720	−2,294	−4,294	−6,078	−6,046	−9,946	....	....	....	Imports of Goods & Services	98c
	4,951	6,398	6,720	9,178	11,311	13,913	20,141	36,471	46,791	82,562	110,111	192,660	....	....	....	Gross Domestic Product	99b
	....	....	....	....	....	....	....	....	....	....	....	....	....	....	....	Net Factor Inc/Pmts(-) Abroad	98.n
	....	....	....	....	....	....	17,726	33,168	42,466	76,615	101,721	178,337	....	....	....	Gross Nat'l Expenditure = GNP	99a
	....	....	....	....	....	....	....	....	....	....	....	....	....	....	....	Nat'l Income, Market Prices	99e
Midyear Estimates																	
	18.68	19.28	19.90	20.53	21.43	22.11	22.80	23.52	24.24	24.99	25.75	26.53	27.32	28.13	....	**Population**	99z

Suriname
366

		1965	1966	1967	1968	1969	1970	1971	1972	1973	1974	1975	1976	1977	1978	1979
Exchange Rates																*Guilders per SDR:*
Market Rate	aa	1.89	1.89	1.89	1.89	1.89	1.89	1.84	1.94ᵉ	....	2.19	2.09	2.07	2.17	2.33	2.35
																Guilders per US Dollar:
Market Rate	ae	1.89	1.89	1.89	1.89	1.89	1.89	1.69	1.79ᵉ	....	1.79	1.79	1.79	1.79	1.79	1.79
Market Rate	rf	1.89	1.89	1.89	1.89	1.89	1.89	1.88	1.79ᵉ	1.79	1.79	1.79	1.79	1.79	1.79	1.79
Fund Position																*Millions of SDRs:*
Quota	2f.s	....	....	....	....	....	....	....	....	....	....	....	....	....	25.00	25.00
SDRs	1b.s	....	....	....	....	....	....	....	....	....	....	....	....	....	—	2.60
Reserve Position in the Fund	1c.s	....	....	....	....	....	....	....	....	....	....	....	....	....	4.75	4.75
International Liquidity													*Millions of US Dollars Unless Otherwise Indicated:*			
Total Reserves minus Gold	1l.d	17.40	17.25	8.36	9.10	23.76	27.83	33.09	37.59	56.44	67.55	91.41	110.22	94.03	132.42	169.53
SDRs	1b.d	....	....	....	....	....	....	....	....	....	....	....	....	....	—	3.43
Reserve Position in the Fund	1c.d	....	....	....	....	....	....	....	....	....	....	....	....	....	6.19	6.26
Foreign Exchange	1d.d	17.40	17.25	8.36	9.10	23.76	27.83	33.09	37.59	56.44	67.55	91.41	110.22	94.03	126.24	159.84
Gold (Million Fine Troy Ounces)	1ad	.207	.279	.534	.534	.248	.248	.248	.248	.148	.148	.148	.148	.148	.054	.054
Gold (National Valuation)	1and	....	....	18.55	18.48	8.57	8.57	9.83	9.29ᵉ	6.16	6.16	6.16	6.16	6.16	2.26	2.26
Deposit Money Banks: Assets	7a.d	....	....	6.81	9.79	9.67	12.69	10.10	13.50	15.54	10.04	22.08	28.55	28.90	41.65	37.36
Liabilities	7b.d	....	....	3.03	3.25	4.39	5.58	7.54	6.32	6.80	6.83	7.99	13.15	13.47	16.07	18.89
Monetary Authorities																*Millions of Guilders:*
Foreign Assets	11	....	....	50.6	51.9	61.0	69.3	75.1	79.5	110.7	130.6	172.8	206.1	177.4	237.3	304.2
Claims on Central Government	12a	....	....	6.2	6.8	7.9	6.3	6.0	8.4	12.6	22.8	53.0	124.1	186.5	62.5	55.3
Claims on Private Sector	12d	....	....	1.5	1.4	1.3	1.2	—	1.1	1.0	.9	.8	.7	.6	.6	.5
Claims on Deposit Money Banks	12e	....	....	.3	.2	.2	.2	.4	.3	.3	.2	.3	.3	.2	.3	.3
Reserve Money	14	....	....	48.4	49.2	57.9	60.6	67.1	69.7	99.3	98.8	124.4	159.5	197.0	198.7	241.4
of which: Currency Outside DMBs	14a	....	....	37.9	39.9	45.4	48.6	53.2	58.2	73.5	78.8	88.6	109.6	125.3	145.1	156.3
Time Deposits	15	....	....	—	—	—	—	—	—	—	—	—	—	—	—	—
Foreign Liabilities	16c	....	....	.2	—	—	.2	—	—	.1	.1	.1	.2	.1	7.6	10.0
Central Government Deposits	16d	....	....	.6	2.7	4.3	5.3	5.9	9.5	.5	18.7	52.4	116.9	116.3	18.6	24.8
Capital Accounts	17a	....	....	6.6	7.0	7.0	7.5	8.0	7.0	7.0	7.0	14.5	22.0	22.0	22.0	28.1
Other Items (Net)	17r	....	....	2.8	1.4	1.1	3.4	.5	3.0	17.7	29.8	35.5	32.6	29.4	53.7	56.0
Deposit Money Banks																*Millions of Guilders:*
Reserves	20	....	....	10.1	9.0	12.0	11.4	13.0	10.6	24.4	18.5	33.4	49.1	70.0	52.2	79.9
Foreign Assets	21	....	....	12.9	18.5	18.2	23.9	17.1	24.1	27.8	17.9	39.4	51.0	51.6	74.4	66.7
Claims on Central Government	22a	....	....	3.0	3.6	2.9	1.7	5.8	5.5	13.1	15.5	15.3	23.7	18.5	17.8	18.5
Claims on Private Sector	22d	....	....	52.5	62.2	76.3	91.0	105.5	117.5	121.3	148.9	156.6	229.6	283.9	360.4	420.6
Demand Deposits	24	....	....	27.1	29.9	34.5	36.8	44.1	44.2	58.2	59.8	77.7	87.9	92.3	99.5	111.9
Quasi-Monetary Liabilities	25	....	....	33.0	42.2	51.0	59.3	66.9	83.3	95.6	105.0	122.3	199.0	252.3	301.9	338.6
Bonds	26ab	....	....	—	.8	.8	2.4	2.4	2.5	2.1	2.2	2.2	2.2	2.2	6.9	6.9
Foreign Liabilities	26c	....	....	2.6	3.0	4.6	5.9	6.6	4.4	5.7	4.8	6.9	14.6	17.7	22.2	27.1
Long-Term Foreign Liabilities	26cl	....	....	3.1	3.1	3.7	4.7	6.1	7.0	6.5	7.4	7.4	8.9	6.3	6.5	6.6
Central Government Deposits	26d	....	....	.3	—	1.3	2.2	.2	3.1	.4	.9	1.7	12.6	7.1	1.2	8.7
Credit from Monetary Authorities	26g	....	....	.3	.2	.2	.2	.4	.3	.3	.2	.3	.3	.2	.3	.3
Capital Accounts	27a	....	....	9.4	10.9	11.2	12.6	13.3	13.7	15.6	18.0	23.5	29.5	44.1	55.8	66.4
Other Items (Net)	27r	....	....	2.6	3.1	2.2	4.0	1.4	–.6	2.3	2.6	2.7	–1.5	1.5	10.5	19.2
Monetary Survey																*Millions of Guilders:*
Foreign Assets (Net)	31n	....	....	60.7	67.3	74.6	87.2	85.5	99.2	132.7	143.6	205.2	242.3	211.2	281.8	333.8
Domestic Credit	32	....	....	62.2	71.3	82.9	92.7	111.2	119.8	147.1	168.4	171.5	248.7	366.0	421.5	461.4
Claims on Central Govt. (Net)	32an	....	....	8.2	7.7	5.3	.5	5.7	1.3	24.8	18.6	14.1	18.3	81.6	60.5	40.3
Claims on Private Sector	32d	....	....	54.0	63.6	77.6	92.2	105.5	118.6	122.3	149.8	157.4	230.4	284.5	360.9	421.1
Money	34	....	....	65.4	70.0	80.4	86.1	98.2	103.3	133.1	140.0	168.7	198.2	219.6	246.1	273.5
Quasi-Money	35	....	....	33.0	42.2	51.0	59.3	66.9	83.3	95.6	105.0	122.3	199.0	252.3	301.9	338.6
Bonds	36ab	....	....	—	.8	.8	2.4	2.4	2.5	2.1	2.2	2.2	2.2	2.2	6.9	6.9
Long-Term Foreign Liabilities	36cl	....	....	3.1	3.1	3.7	4.7	6.1	7.0	6.5	7.4	7.4	8.9	6.3	6.5	6.6
Other Items (Net)	37r	....	....	21.5	22.4	21.5	27.5	23.1	23.1	42.5	57.4	76.2	82.6	96.7	142.0	169.7
Money plus Quasi-Money	35l	....	....	98.4	112.3	131.4	145.3	165.0	186.5	228.7	245.0	290.9	397.3	472.0	548.0	612.1
Prices															*Index Numbers (1990=100):*	
Consumer Prices	64	8.8	9.2	10.2	10.2	11.4	11.7	11.7	12.1	13.6	15.9	17.3	19.0	20.9	22.7	26.1
International Transactions																*Millions of Guilders:*
Exports	70	110.5	164.7	201.0	218.5	246.5	272.1	296.2	305.7	319.8	481.1	495.3	492.3	552.8	658.3	792.7
Imports, cif	71	179.5	168.9	193.8	188.9	207.6	217.7	237.8	258.2	280.1	410.5	449.8	525.1	709.9	724.5	733.5
Imports, fob	71.v	164.7	154.9	177.8	173.3	190.4	199.7	218.2	236.8	257.0	376.5	412.5	481.2	639.0	652.1	660.2
																1985=100
Volume of Exports	72	65.4	96.0	106.7	113.1	124.9	123.6	139.2	146.4	145.8	142.6	106.8	110.4	117.5	121.0	120.9
Unit Value of Exports	74	41.3	41.3	41.3	42.3	43.7	46.8	47.7	46.0	46.2	62.2	83.4	91.4	101.3	109.9	120.3

Suriname

	1980	1981	1982	1983	1984	1985	1986	1987	1988	1989	1990	1991	1992	1993	1994		
																Exchange Rates	
End of Period	2.28	2.08	1.97	1.87	1.75	1.96	2.18	2.53	2.40	2.35	2.54	2.55	2.45	2.45	597.81	Market Rate	**aa**
End of Period (ae) Period Average (rf)																	
	1.79	1.79	1.79	1.79	1.79	1.79	1.79	1.79	1.79	1.79	1.79	1.79	1.79	1.79	409.50	Market Rate	**ae**
	1.79	1.79	1.79	1.79	1.79	1.79	1.79	1.79	1.79	1.79	1.79	1.79	1.79	1.79	134.12	Market Rate	**rf**
End of Period																**Fund Position**	
	37.50	37.50	37.50	49.30	49.30	49.30	49.30	49.30	49.30	49.30	49.30	49.30	49.30	67.60	67.60	Quota	**2f. s**
	2.07	5.40	8.48	1.74	1.28	.76	.28	—	—	—	—	—	—	—	—	SDRs	**1b. s**
	7.87	7.87	7.88	2.95	—	—	—	—	—	—	—	—	—	—	—	Reserve Position in the Fund	**1c. s**
End of Period																**International Liquidity**	
	189.25	207.09	175.76	59.15	24.87	23.42	20.89	15.10	12.56	9.25	21.07	—	—	—	21.70	Total Reserves minus Gold	**1l. d**
	2.64	6.29	9.35	1.82	1.25	.83	.34	—	—	—	—	—	—	—	—	SDRs	**1b. d**
	10.04	9.16	8.69	3.09	—	—	—	—	—	—	—	—	—	—	—	Reserve Position in the Fund	**1c. d**
	176.57	191.64	157.71	54.24	23.62	22.59	20.55	15.10	12.56	9.25	21.07	—	—	—	21.70	Foreign Exchange	**1d. d**
	.054	.054	.054	.054	.054	.054	.054	.054	.054	.054	.054	.054	.054	.054	.054	Gold (Million Fine Troy Ounces)	**1ad**
	2.26	2.26	2.26	19.60	14.89	15.83	18.75	23.84	20.44	19.79	18.66	17.71	16.21	841.65	14.32	Gold (National Valuation)	**1and**
	51.94	52.25	49.11	31.03	16.81	11.52	5.20	11.59	9.89	17.55	21.98	21.63	20.20	1,093.52	….	Deposit Money Banks: Assets	**7a. d**
	22.78	25.67	27.96	21.85	28.04	31.70	49.41	57.28	61.50	69.19	82.39	90.01	93.38	379.48	….	Liabilities	**7b. d**
End of Period																**Monetary Authorities**	
	339.2	370.8	315.4	139.7	70.6	70.0	72.2	69.0	58.7	51.7	70.6	45.3	64.9	3,276.6	23,545.9	Foreign Assets	**11**
	36.9	81.4	181.7	460.6	716.9	1,062.1	1,494.1	1,997.5	2,478.9	2,853.4	2,627.3	3,260.6	3,511.9	5,224.4	5,306.7	Claims on Central Government	**12a**
	.4	.3	.2	.2	.1	—	—	—	15.0	15.2	15.3	15.4	1.1	1.5	8.7	Claims on Private Sector	**12d**
	.2	.2	.2	.2	.2	.5	19.4	2.5	3.1	2.4	.3	.4	1.6	3.5	12.6	Claims on Deposit Money Banks	**12e**
	241.9	297.7	327.3	422.7	627.0	956.8	1,302.5	1,564.4	1,903.0	2,195.0	2,321.9	2,946.4	3,317.1	5,640.3	17,361.4	Reserve Money	**14**
	177.8	197.0	268.1	265.0	305.2	405.4	451.3	638.0	788.3	874.2	958.2	1,143.0	1,347.2	2,638.2	….	of which: Currency Outside DMBs	**14a**
	—	—	—	—	—	—	29.7	248.5	362.5	431.8	120.0	63.5	2.4	—	—	Time Deposits	**15**
	.4	.4	.4	.4	.6	.7	23.3	26.0	59.0	71.0	64.5	99.0	83.5	2,349.5	7,403.0	Foreign Liabilities	**16c**
	28.6	24.2	31.9	24.8	16.1	22.2	14.1	14.5	11.5	11.5	13.4	12.7	14.9	29.4	843.5	Central Government Deposits	**16d**
	39.0	49.4	50.5	49.4	49.1	48.5	49.6	54.0	54.0	54.0	52.7	52.7	52.7	52.7	52.7	Capital Accounts	**17a**
	66.8	81.0	87.5	103.3	94.9	104.4	166.6	161.7	165.8	159.4	140.9	147.6	108.8	434.4	3,213.4	Other Items (Net)	**17r**
End of Period																**Deposit Money Banks**	
	53.3	79.1	53.9	152.6	316.3	543.7	827.9	912.4	1,098.1	1,299.4	1,339.5	1,767.8	1,914.4	2,873.3	….	Reserves	**20**
	92.7	93.3	87.7	55.4	30.0	20.6	9.3	20.7	17.7	31.3	39.2	38.6	36.1	1,951.9	….	Foreign Assets	**21**
	17.4	27.6	29.8	72.6	110.0	123.8	142.3	123.2	128.7	140.4	206.9	225.5	224.9	266.2	….	Claims on Central Government	**22a**
	460.5	546.1	615.1	620.0	627.4	689.8	727.6	773.0	923.8	1,145.5	1,453.8	1,809.4	2,464.1	3,133.2	….	Claims on Private Sector	**22d**
	105.6	139.4	147.8	184.9	266.6	467.1	754.1	910.0	1,140.4	1,269.0	1,268.3	1,707.6	1,818.4	3,275.8	….	Demand Deposits	**24**
	365.4	430.4	454.5	516.3	591.2	663.6	675.8	664.6	752.6	1,021.2	1,400.9	1,712.2	2,343.7	3,179.5	….	Quasi-Monetary Liabilities	**25**
	6.9	6.9	6.9	6.9	6.9	6.9	5.0	5.0	5.0	5.0	5.0	5.8	22.8	104.2	….	Bonds	**26ab**
	33.9	39.2	43.0	32.1	43.1	49.6	81.3	95.3	102.8	116.6	139.8	153.2	158.9	668.9	….	Foreign Liabilities	**26c**
	6.8	6.6	7.0	7.0	7.0	7.0	7.0	7.0	7.0	7.0	7.0	7.3	7.4	7.8	8.5	Long-Term Foreign Liabilities	**26cl**
	6.1	5.4	3.4	7.4	6.9	13.3	14.6	10.9	9.3	22.8	23.5	39.5	25.5	103.0	….	Central Government Deposits	**26d**
	.2	.2	.2	.2	.2	.5	19.4	2.5	3.1	2.4	.3	.4	1.6	3.5	….	Credit from Monetary Authorities	**26g**
	75.0	84.2	96.3	103.2	108.2	124.6	133.8	136.5	155.5	176.4	245.4	295.9	369.1	602.4	….	Capital Accounts	**27a**
	24.2	33.8	27.4	42.6	53.7	45.2	16.2	−2.5	−7.6	−3.8	−51.1	−80.7	−108.2	279.0	….	Other Items (Net)	**27r**
End of Period																**Monetary Survey**	
	397.6	424.4	359.7	162.7	56.9	40.2	−23.1	−31.6	−85.5	−104.6	−94.5	−168.3	−141.5	2,210.3	….	Foreign Assets (Net)	**31n**
	480.5	625.7	791.5	1,121.0	1,431.3	1,840.2	2,335.4	2,868.3	3,525.6	4,120.1	4,266.4	5,258.7	6,161.7	8,493.0	….	Domestic Credit	**32**
	19.6	79.4	176.2	500.9	803.9	1,150.4	1,607.8	2,095.3	2,586.8	2,959.4	2,797.3	3,433.9	3,696.5	5,358.3	….	Claims on Central Govt. (Net)	**32an**
	460.9	546.4	615.3	620.1	627.4	689.8	727.6	773.0	938.8	1,160.6	1,469.1	1,824.8	2,465.2	3,134.7	….	Claims on Private Sector	**32d**
	294.2	358.0	421.2	455.0	577.3	880.2	1,228.8	1,561.9	1,945.4	2,164.6	2,250.8	2,886.1	3,221.1	6,042.8	….	Money	**34**
	365.4	430.4	454.5	516.3	591.2	663.6	705.5	913.1	1,115.1	1,453.0	1,520.9	1,775.7	2,346.1	3,179.5	….	Quasi-Money	**35**
	6.9	6.9	6.9	6.9	6.9	6.9	5.0	5.0	5.0	5.0	5.0	5.8	22.8	104.2	….	Bonds	**36ab**
	6.8	6.6	7.0	7.0	7.0	7.0	7.0	7.0	7.0	7.0	7.0	7.3	7.4	7.8	8.5	Long-Term Foreign Liabilities	**36cl**
	204.9	248.3	261.6	298.5	305.9	322.7	366.1	349.7	367.7	386.0	387.9	415.4	422.3	1,368.4	….	Other Items (Net)	**37r**
	659.5	788.4	875.8	971.3	1,168.5	1,543.8	1,934.3	2,475.0	3,060.5	3,617.6	3,771.7	4,661.7	5,567.2	9,222.2	….	Money plus Quasi-Money	**35l**
Period Averages																**Prices**	
	29.8	32.4	34.8	36.3	37.6	41.7	49.5	76.0	81.5	82.1	100.0	126.0	181.0	440.7	….	Consumer Prices	**64**
Millions of Guilders																**International Transactions**	
	918.2	845.7	765.1	654.7	635.0	587.0	597.8	546.3	730.6	966.5	843.3	….	….	….	….	Exports	**70**
	900.3	1,013.6	912.8	808.5	617.3	532.9	584.4	525.9	626.4	790.6	842.5	….	….	….	….	Imports, cif	**71**
	810.5	904.0	814.2	721.2	550.5	474.7	520.4	467.8	557.8	704.0	750.2	….	….	….	….	Imports, fob	**71.v**
1985=100																	
	121.7	99.0	94.9	84.9	90.2	100.0	102.8	83.2	97.0	….	….	….	….	….	….	Volume of Exports	**72**
	148.4	160.6	155.0	138.2	130.4	100.0	97.1	102.9	134.3	….	….	….	….	….	….	Unit Value of Exports	**74**

Suriname

366

		1965	1966	1967	1968	1969	1970	1971	1972	1973	1974	1975	1976	1977	1978	1979
Balance of Payments														*Millions of US Dollars:*		
Goods: Exports f.o.b.	78aa d	....	....	....	....	....	....	....	....	....	....	....	....	346.2	411.1	444.1
Goods: Imports f.o.b.	78ab d	....	....	....	....	....	....	....	....	....	....	....	....	−324.1	−343.5	−369.9
Trade Balance	78ac d	....	....	....	....	....	....	....	....	....	....	....	....	22.1	67.6	74.2
Services: Credit	78ad d	....	....	....	....	....	....	....	....	....	....	....	....	50.2	62.3	69.5
Services: Debit	78ae d	....	....	....	....	....	....	....	....	....	....	....	....	−115.2	−124.6	−142.7
Balance on Goods and Services	78af d	....	....	....	....	....	....	....	....	....	....	....	....	−42.9	5.3	1.0
Income: Credit	78ag d	....	....	....	....	....	....	....	....	....	....	....	....	7.2	8.3	14.1
Income: Debit	78ah d	....	....	....	....	....	....	....	....	....	....	....	....	−47.4	−45.5	−59.1
Balance on Goods, Serv., & Inc.	78ai d	....	....	....	....	....	....	....	....	....	....	....	....	−83.1	−31.9	−44.0
Current Transfers, n.i.e.: Credit	78aj d	....	....	....	....	....	....	....	....	....	....	....	....	87.2	66.4	94.6
Current Transfers: Debit	78ak d	....	....	....	....	....	....	....	....	....	....	....	....	−5.6	−5.5	−6.6
Current Account, n.i.e.	78al d	....	....	....	....	....	....	....	....	....	....	....	....	−1.5	29.0	44.0
Capital Account, n.i.e.: Credit	78ba d	....	....	....	....	....	....	....	....	....	....	....	....	1.1	1.9	2.0
Capital Account: Debit	78bb d	....	....	....	....	....	....	....	....	....	....	....	....	−3.0	−3.4	−2.3
Capital Account, n.i.e.	78bc d	....	....	....	....	....	....	....	....	....	....	....	....	−1.9	−1.5	−.3
Direct Investment Abroad	78bd d	....	....	....	....	....	....	....	....	....	....	....	....	—	—	—
Dir. Invest. in Rep. Econ., n.i.e.	78be d	....	....	....	....	....	....	....	....	....	....	....	....	−12.7	−7.6	−15.4
Portfolio Investment Assets	78bf d	....	....	....	....	....	....	....	....	....	....	....	....	—	—	—
Portfolio Investment Liab., n.i.e.	78bg d	....	....	....	....	....	....	....	....	....	....	....	....	−.1	−.3	—
Other Investment Assets	78bh d	....	....	....	....	....	....	....	....	....	....	....	....	−.8	−4.8	—
Other Investment Liab., n.i.e.	78bi d	....	....	....	....	....	....	....	....	....	....	....	....	−1.1	26.3	−1.5
Financial Account, n.i.e.	78bj d	....	....	....	....	....	....	....	....	....	....	....	....	−14.6	13.7	−16.8
Net Errors and Omissions	78ca d	....	....	....	....	....	....	....	....	....	....	....	....	.2	.5	−.2
Overall Balance	78cb d	....	....	....	....	....	....	....	....	....	....	....	....	−17.8	41.7	26.7
Reserves and Related Items	79da d	....	....	....	....	....	....	....	....	....	....	....	....	17.8	−41.7	−26.7
Reserve Assets	79db d	....	....	....	....	....	....	....	....	....	....	....	....	17.8	−41.7	−26.7
Use of Fund Credit and Loans	79dc d	....	....	....	....	....	....	....	....	....	....	....	....	—	—	—
Liabs.Constit.For.Auth.Reserves	79dd d	....	....	....	....	....	....	....	....	....	....	....	....	—	—	—
Exceptional Financing	79de d	....	....	....	....	....	....	....	....	....	....	....	....			
Government Finance														*Millions of Guilders:*		
Deficit (−) or Surplus	80	....	....	....	....	....	....	−2.05	−1.76	−19.12	−8.80	−2.15	−21.85	−63.10	−22.72	20.01
Revenue	81	....	....	....	....	....	....	146.72	158.10	166.14	186.59	297.37	286.38	335.46	413.02	418.24
Grants Received	81z	....	....	....	....	....	....	18.34	37.83	33.78	41.86	20.76	116.72	138.45	99.03	144.08
Expenditure	82	....	....	....	....	....	....	166.61	196.26	217.53	237.27	318.48	424.21	540.54	536.78	542.32
Lending Minus Repayments	83	....	....	....	....	....	....	.50	1.43	1.51	−.02	1.80	.74	−3.53	−2.01	−.01
Financing																
Domestic	84a	....	....	....	....	....	....	5.91	1.76	9.12	8.80	2.15	21.85	66.35	−15.86	−22.81
Foreign	85a	....	....	....	....	....	....	−3.86	—	10.00	—	—	—	−3.25	38.58	2.80
Debt: Domestic	88a	....	....	....	....	....	....	17.60	21.30	31.20	43.11	41.52	58.93	43.22	....	....
Foreign	89a	....	....	....	....	....	....	156.90	187.50	197.30	194.71	10.99	8.77	7.83	....	....
National Accounts														*Millions of Guilders*		
Exports of Goods & Services	90c	....	....	....	....	....	....	....	350.6	369.1	543.4	577.7	617.9	707.2	813.6	916.7
Government Consumption	91f	60.3	86.0	91.3	104.5	105.8	128.1	138.4	135.5	116.0	133.3	137.3	123.4	282.0	335.1	342.7
Gross Capital Formation	93	130.4	125.0	94.9	100.7	93.4	100.6	105.4	134.5	156.4	245.3	353.0	303.8	478.8	477.3	357.3
Private Consumption	96f	184.0	171.6	250.2	259.7	284.0	293.2	308.8	315.6	385.7	433.5	503.0	604.2	609.3	692.5	870.3
Imports of Goods & Services	98c	....	....	....	....	....	....	....	−316.8	−348.5	−536.3	−634.4	−619.7	−794.5	−847.5	−921.6
Gross Domestic Product	99b	308.3	380.7	441.4	490.7	519.3	549.6	599.6	619.3	679.7	819.7	930.0	1,029.6	1,282.7	1,471.0	1,565.3
Net Factor Inc/Pmts(−) Abroad	98.n	−30.3	−32.0	−39.2	−71.6	−79.4	−74.7	−85.2	−84.3	−70.5	−45.3	−25.3	−66.7	−61.3	−55.2	−73.7
Gross Nat'l Expenditure = GNP	99a	278.0	348.7	402.2	419.1	439.9	474.9	514.4	535.0	609.2	774.4	904.7	962.9	1,221.4	1,415.8	1,491.6
Nat'l Income, Market Prices	99e	248.6	....	....	....	....	....	....	475.6	530.2	673.6	796.5	861.9	1,091.3	1,262.1	1,323.3
Gross Dom. Prod. 1990 Prices	99b. p	....	....	....	....	....	....	....	....	726.9	674.7	742.7	865.5	962.8	944.1	3,219.9
GDP Deflators (1990=100)	99bi p	....	....	....	....	....	....	....	....	93.5	121.5	125.2	119.0	133.2	155.8	48.6
																Millions:
Population	99z	.33	.34	.35	.36	.37	.37	.37	I.38	.38	.38	.36	.35	.36	.37	.37

International Transactions: I Trade data, which are compiled by the Central Bureau of Statistics, have been updated with the Bank of Suriname balance of payments data on a cash basis for current periods.

Suriname

	1980	1981	1982	1983	1984	1985	1986	1987	1988	1989	1990	1991	1992	1993	1994		
Minus Sign Indicates Debit																**Balance of Payments**	
	514.4	473.8	428.6	366.8	374.1	336.1	337.1	338.8	358.4	549.2	465.9	345.9	341.0	298.3	293.6	Goods: Exports f.o.b.	78aa *d*
	−454.0	−506.4	−460.3	−401.6	−391.6	−309.5	−304.1	−274.3	−239.4	−330.9	−374.4	−347.1	−272.5	−213.9	−194.3	Goods: Imports f.o.b.	78ab *d*
	60.4	−32.7	−31.7	−34.8	−17.5	26.6	33.0	64.5	118.9	218.3	91.5	−1.1	68.4	84.4	99.3	Trade Balance	78ac *d*
	98.6	91.9	80.9	67.7	55.2	44.3	25.7	80.9	22.7	23.7	20.7	22.3	22.6	46.5	72.6	Services: Credit	78ad *d*
	−204.0	−197.1	−206.8	−177.0	−113.1	−79.2	−77.0	−68.0	−76.3	−90.7	−96.0	−97.7	−98.7	−101.6	−113.5	Services: Debit	78ae *d*
	−45.0	−137.8	−157.6	−144.2	−75.3	−8.4	−18.3	77.4	65.3	151.3	16.2	−76.5	−7.6	29.3	58.4	Balance on Goods and Services	78af *d*
	25.6	36.2	35.8	16.5	5.0	2.7	1.6	1.2	1.3	1.0	2.2	1.4	.7	.2	.9	Income: Credit	78ag *d*
	−45.4	−24.6	−29.0	−27.7	−3.6	−3.2	−4.6	−5.8	−9.8	−7.3	−10.8	−12.6	−8.2	−6.4	−4.7	Income: Debit	78ah *d*
	−64.8	−126.2	−150.8	−155.4	−73.9	−8.9	−21.3	72.8	56.9	145.0	7.7	−87.7	−15.1	23.1	54.6	Balance on Goods, Serv., & Inc.	78ai *d*
	91.0	107.6	106.6	9.7	5.9	4.1	5.2	6.7	11.3	24.1	35.5	20.4	37.9	26.7	6.2	Current Transfers, n.i.e.: Credit	78aj *d*
	−8.6	−8.6	−10.4	−12.5	−9.1	−5.5	−4.5	−3.5	−4.1	−4.6	−5.8	−7.5	−8.6	−5.8	−2.2	Current Transfers: Debit	78ak *d*
	17.6	−27.2	−54.7	−158.2	−77.1	−10.3	−20.7	76.0	64.0	164.4	37.4	−74.7	14.2	44.0	58.6	Current Account, n.i.e.	78al *d*
	1.9	2.1	1.8	2.6	3.2	2.0	.9	1.1	1.5	1.1	.3	2.3	2.6	3.5	.2	Capital Account, n.i.e.: Credit	78ba *d*
	−4.1	−2.7	−3.8	−5.3	−4.8	−3.3	−2.6	−2.3	−3.0	−2.7	−3.1	−3.4	−5.8	−3.0	−.4	Capital Account: Debit	78bb *d*
	−2.2	−.6	−1.9	−2.7	−1.6	−1.3	−1.7	−1.2	−1.5	−1.6	−2.8	−1.1	−3.2	.5	−.2	Capital Account, n.i.e.	78bc *d*
	—	—	—	—	—	—	—	—	—	—	—	—	—	—	—	Direct Investment Abroad	78bd *d*
	10.1	34.6	−6.2	45.7	−39.7	11.9	−33.8	−72.6	−95.8	−167.9	−43.0	10.4	−30.4	−46.6	−30.2	Dir. Invest. in Rep. Econ., n.i.e.	78be *d*
	—	−.6	−.8	—	—	—	—	—	—	—	—	—	—	—	—	Portfolio Investment Assets	78bf *d*
	—	−.3	−.4	—	—	−.2	−.2	−.1	—	−.5	.5	−2.3	1.5	—	—	Portfolio Investment Liab., n.i.e.	78bg *d*
	−9.5	−14.8	−7.4	18.8	−.5	1.9	1.8	.7	−.5	−13.3	15.6	2.7	−.1	−4.4	−19.1	Other Investment Assets	78bh *d*
	9.1	9.7	27.3	−14.7	29.8	.9	33.3	21.3	30.4	8.3	12.0	21.6	−19.5	−22.1	−34.8	Other Investment Liab., n.i.e.	78bi *d*
	9.7	28.5	12.5	49.7	−10.4	14.5	1.1	−50.6	−65.9	−172.9	−15.0	32.4	−48.5	−73.1	−84.1	Financial Account, n.i.e.	78bj *d*
	.7	12.4	1.2	2.0	36.6	−11.4	−18.7	−33.6	−1.8	9.9	−9.4	−.5	25.4	41.3	60.0	Net Errors and Omissions	78ca *d*
	25.9	13.1	−42.8	−109.1	−52.5	−8.5	−40.0	−9.4	−5.2	−.1	10.3	−43.9	−12.0	12.7	34.3	Overall Balance	78cb *d*
	−25.9	−13.1	42.8	109.1	52.5	8.5	40.0	9.4	5.2	.1	−10.3	43.9	12.0	−12.7	−34.3	Reserves and Related Items	79da *d*
	−25.9	−13.1	42.8	109.1	52.5	8.5	40.0	9.4	5.2	.1	−10.3	43.9	12.0	−12.7	−34.3	Reserve Assets	79db *d*
	—	—	—	—	—	—	—	—	—	—	—	—	—	—	—	Use of Fund Credit and Loans	79dc *d*
	—	—	—	—	—	—	—	—	—	—	—	—	—	—	—	Liabs.Constit.For.Auth.Reserves	79dd *d*
	....	....	....	....	....	....	....	....	....	....	....	....	....	....	—	Exceptional Financing	79de *d*
Year Ending December 31																**Government Finance**	
	24.40	−56.53	−98.85	−309.59	−263.19	−349.18	−445.74	....	....	....	....	....	....	....	....	Deficit (-) or Surplus	80
	477.82	488.26	516.64	486.78	515.38	490.38	494.88	....	....	....	....	....	....	....	....	Revenue	81
	131.56	168.89	172.96	4.46	3.60	1.40	2.78	....	....	....	....	....	....	....	....	Grants Received	81z
	580.81	713.56	788.15	801.26	768.12	803.35	925.69	....	....	....	....	....	....	....	....	Expenditure	82
	4.17	.12	.30	−.43	14.05	37.61	17.71	....	....	....	....	....	....	....	....	Lending Minus Repayments	83
																Financing	
	−20.30	56.29	98.33	310.10	263.31	349.18	421.59	....	....	....	....	....	....	....	....	Domestic	84a
	−4.10	.24	.52	−.51	−.12	—	24.15	....	....	....	....	....	....	....	....	Foreign	85a
	....	....	....	....	782.40	1,137.08	1,582.01	....	....	....	....	....	....	....	....	Debt: Domestic	88a
	....	....	....	....	55.50	38.37	124.24	....	....	....	....	....	....	....	....	Foreign	89a
Millions of Guilders																**National Accounts**	
	1,094.2	1,009.4	909.5	775.5	749.4	641.7	581.0	608.8	680.6	1,022.6	868.6	657.3	649.1	544.0	....	Exports of Goods & Services	90c
	338.5	430.7	520.1	437.2	498.8	588.5	655.8	736.5	848.3	814.7	777.0	1,085.0	1,239.3	1,827.1	....	Government Consumption	91f
	420.6	555.0	507.3	275.6	203.9	252.2	391.2	508.8	387.3	565.2	660.3	828.7	1,163.0	2,435.1	....	Gross Capital Formation	93
	915.6	1,040.7	1,084.3	1,314.0	1,119.3	961.0	757.8	622.1	971.3	1,064.7	1,623.9	1,940.5	2,719.4	6,379.4	....	Private Consumption	96f
	−1,179.2	−1,258.1	−1,190.8	−1,035.1	−843.1	−696.9	−582.9	−502.1	−566.2	−754.7	−844.4	−793.9	−667.2	−613.4	....	Imports of Goods & Services	98c
	1,589.7	1,778.1	1,830.4	1,767.2	1,728.3	1,746.5	1,802.8	1,974.1	2,321.3	2,712.6	3,085.4	3,717.5	5,103.3	10,572.2	....	Gross Domestic Product	99b
	−30.4	23.0	12.8	−19.9	−2.5	−.9	−5.4	−8.2	−15.3	−11.1	−15.2	−20.0	−13.3	−12.6	....	Net Factor Inc/Pmts(-) Abroad	98.n
	1,559.3	1,801.1	1,843.2	1,747.3	1,725.8	1,745.6	1,797.4	1,965.9	2,306.0	2,701.5	3,070.2	3,697.5	5,090.0	10,559.6	....	Gross Nat'l Expenditure = GNP	99a
	1,387.7	1,614.7	1,660.9	1,564.8	1,557.8	1,583.7	1,640.5	1,778.0	2,120.3	2,404.2	2,717.2	3,217.0	4,441.0	9,087.7	....	Nat'l Income, Market Prices	99e
	2,943.9	3,152.7	3,020.5	2,901.8	2,847.2	2,904.7	2,926.8	2,746.7	2,971.1	3,084.3	3,085.4	3,193.5	3,378.5	3,226.0	....	Gross Dom. Prod. 1990 Prices	99b.*p*
	54.0	56.4	60.6	60.9	60.7	60.1	61.6	71.9	78.1	87.9	100.0	116.4	151.1	327.7	....	GDP Deflators (1990=100)	99bi *p*
Midyear Estimates																	
	.35	.36	.36	.37	.37	.38	.38	.39	.39	.40	.40	.40	.40	.41	.41	**Population**	99z

Swaziland

734

		1965	1966	1967	1968	1969	1970	1971	1972	1973	1974	1975	1976	1977	1978	1979
Exchange Rates															*SDRs per Lilangeni:*	
Official Rate	ac	1.39975	1.39325	1.40175	1.38975	1.39875	1.39425	1.20359	1.17647	1.23509	1.18434	.98235	.98982	.94673	.88272	.91807
														US Dollars per Lilangeni:		
Official Rate	ag	1.39975	1.39325	1.40175	1.38975	1.39875	1.39425	1.30675	1.27731	1.48995	1.45005	1.15000	1.15000	1.15000	1.15000	1.20940
Official Rate	rh	1.40000	1.40000	1.40000	1.40000	1.40000	1.40000	1.39820	1.30181	1.44408	1.47216	1.36629	1.15000	1.15000	1.15000	1.18785
Fund Position															*Millions of SDRs*	
Quota	2f. s	....	....	....	....	6.00	8.00	8.00	8.00	8.00	8.00	8.00	8.00	8.00	12.00	12.00
SDRs	1b. s	....	....	....	....	—	.01	.01	.75	.82	.87	1.01	.94	.87	.96	2.16
Reserve Position in the Fund	1c. s	....	....	....	.18	.11	.20	.29	.20	.39	1.05	2.00	2.00	2.80	2.74	
Total Fund Cred.&Loans Outstg.	2tl	....	....	....	....	—	—	—	—	—	—	—	—	—	—	2.43
International Liquidity											*Millions of US Dollars Unless Otherwise Indicated:*					
Total Reserves minus Gold	1l. d	....	....	....	....	....	....	....	....	....	13.47	45.61	73.39	94.71	113.61	113.70
SDRs	1b. d	....	....	....	....	—	.01	.01	.81	.99	1.07	1.18	1.09	1.06	1.25	2.85
Reserve Position in the Fund	1c. d	....	....	....	....	.18	.11	.22	.31	.24	.48	1.23	2.32	2.43	3.65	3.61
Foreign Exchange	1d. d	....	....	....	....	....	....	....	....	....	11.93	43.20	69.97	91.22	108.71	107.25
Monetary Authorities: Other Liab.	4.. d	....	....	....	....	....	....	....	....	....	.18	.19	.04	.40	3.80	3.81
Deposit Money Banks: Assets	7a. d	....	....	....	....	....	8.74	.17	14.66	7.18	17.36	22.25	9.63	13.70	8.22	5.73
Liabilities	7b. d	....	....	....	....	....	8.10	16.77	2.06	.01	—	.03	.07	.03	.24	1.11
Monetary Authorities															*Millions of Emalangeni:*	
Foreign Assets	11	....	....	....	....	....	....	....	....	....	10.19	39.97	64.48	83.45	98.16	92.44
Claims on Central Government	12a	....	....	....	....	....	....	....	....	....	.67	.75	.88	.66	10.51	3.52
Claims on Deposit Money Banks	12e	....	....	....	....	....	....	....	....	....	.02	4.20	—	—	—	2.70
Reserve Money	14	....	....	....	....	....	....	....	....	....	6.34	13.51	33.60	46.53	44.40	46.20
of which: Currency Outside DMBs	14a	....	....	....	....	....	....	....	....	....	3.33	5.11	6.52	7.31	8.90	9.59
Time Deposits	15	....	....	....	....	....	....	....	....	....	....	....	....	....	....	....
Foreign Liabilities	16c	....	....	....	....	....	....	....	....	....	.13	.17	.04	.35	3.30	5.79
Central Government Deposits	16d	....	....	....	....	....	....	....	....	....	3.14	29.20	27.51	31.44	54.84	42.28
Capital Accounts	17a	....	....	....	....	....	....	....	....	....	.50	1.01	1.33	1.74	5.39	7.34
Other Items (Net)	17r	....	....	....	....	....	....	....	....	....	.91	1.03	2.89	4.06	.89	-2.32
Deposit Money Banks															*Millions of Emalangeni:*	
Reserves	20	....	....	....	....	....	1.02	1.26	1.36	1.57	2.58	8.51	25.97	32.72	34.48	34.30
Foreign Assets	21	....	....	....	....	....	6.24	.12	11.48	5.06	11.97	19.34	8.37	11.91	7.15	4.74
Claims on Central Government	22a	....	....	....	....	....	1.41	2.13	2.49	9.07	8.05	13.09	2.68	2.00	9.54	7.00
Claims on Private Sector	22d	....	....	....	....	....	16.49	24.20	17.40	22.60	29.25	43.43	46.32	48.38	74.78	84.69
Demand Deposits	24	....	....	....	....	....	6.43	10.06	13.01	11.70	13.59	18.23	22.17	20.67	27.72	30.58
Time and Savings Deposits	25	....	....	....	....	....	10.78	14.13	13.96	22.32	23.72	38.08	48.31	55.33	77.37	76.69
Foreign Liabilities	26c	....	....	....	....	....	5.79	12.58	1.61	.01	.03	.06	.03	.21	.92	
Central Government Deposits	26d	....	....	....	....	....	2.49	2.68	4.48	.29	10.78	16.96	5.69	6.74	9.56	16.77
Capital Accounts	27a	....	....	....	....	....	—	—	—	3.19	4.63	4.63	7.15	8.27	14.12	14.34
Other Items (Net)	27r	....	....	....	....	....	-.33	-11.73	-.34	.80	-.87	6.44	-.03	3.97	-3.02	-8.58
Monetary Survey															*Millions of Emalangeni:*	
Foreign Assets (Net)	31n	....	....	....	....	....	....	....	....	....	22.04	59.12	72.76	94.99	101.80	90.47
Domestic Credit	32	....	....	....	....	....	....	....	....	....	24.07	11.27	16.93	13.27	31.03	37.03
Claims on Central Govt. (Net)	32an	....	....	....	....	....	....	....	....	....	-5.20	-32.33	-29.63	-35.53	-44.36	-48.54
Claims on Private Sector	32d	....	....	....	....	....	....	....	....	22.60	29.26	43.59	46.56	48.80	75.39	85.57
Money	34	....	....	....	....	....	....	....	....	....	16.93	23.42	28.79	34.16	37.21	40.91
Quasi-Money	35	....	....	....	....	....	10.78	14.13	13.96	22.32	23.72	38.08	48.31	55.33	77.37	76.69
Other Items (Net)	37r	....	....	....	....	....	....	....	....	....	5.59	8.89	12.60	18.79	18.41	10.53
Money plus Quasi-Money	35l	....	....	....	....	....	....	....	....	....	40.65	61.50	77.11	89.48	114.58	117.60
Interest Rates															*Percent Per Annum*	
Discount Rate (End of Period)	60	....	....	....	....	....	....	....	....	....	....	....	....	9.00	9.00	8.50	7.00
Money Market Rate	60b	....	....	....	....	....	....	....	....	....	....	....	....	....	....	....
Treasury Bill Rate	60c	....	....	....	....	....	....	....	....	....	....	....	6.00	6.00	6.00	7.71	7.71
Deposit Rate	60l	....	....	....	....	....	....	....	....	5.50	8.25	7.75	7.75	7.75	7.25	4.50
Lending Rate	60p	....	....	....	....	....	....	9.00	8.50	8.00	11.00	10.50	10.50	10.50	10.25	9.50
Prices															*Index Numbers (1990=100):*	
Consumer Prices	64	8.3	8.5	8.7	9.0	9.3	9.4	9.7	9.9	11.0	13.1	14.7	15.7	19.0	20.6	124.0
International Transactions															*Millions of Emalangeni*	
Exports	70	30.76	38.35	40.23	39.35	44.52	50.89	55.72	62.98	74.22	121.50	145.72	159.05	143.11	170.62	194.83
Imports, cif	71	26.11	24.23	35.03	34.10	35.50	42.75	47.82	53.31	66.62	93.44	131.59	174.08	158.32	270.82	365.74
Imports, fob	71.v	25.62	23.78	34.38	33.46	34.84	41.95	46.93	52.32	65.38	91.74	128.99	170.08	155.64	264.62	361.74

Swaziland

734

	1980	1981	1982	1983	1984	1985	1986	1987	1988	1989	1990	1991	1992	1993	1994		
	End of Period															**Exchange Rates**	
	1.05190	.89814	.84226	.78170	.51397	.35597	.37443	.36524	.31253	.30005	.27430	.25486	.23821	.21429	.19331	Official Rate	ac
	End of Period (ag)	*Period Average (rh)*															
	1.34160	1.04540	.92910	.81840	.50380	.39100	.45800	.51815	.42057	.39432	.39024	.36456	.32754	.29433	.28221	Official Rate	ag
	1.28543	1.14914	.92451	.89909	.69536	.45783	.44082	.49141	.44227	.38218	.38665	.36280	.35092	.30641	.28177	Official Rate	rh
																Fund Position	
	18.00	18.00	18.00	24.70	24.70	24.70	24.70	24.70	24.70	24.70	24.70	24.70	36.50	36.50	36.50	Quota	2f. s
	1.82	5.92	4.98	1.47	2.29	.26	2.24	2.79	1.23	.80	8.49	8.65	5.84	5.88	5.89	SDRs	1b. s
	4.26	4.28	.01	1.70	1.73	1.76	.03	.03	.01	.01	.02	.02	3.00	3.00	3.00	Reserve Position in the Fund	1c. s
	4.47	4.50	4.50	14.48	14.48	12.85	8.57	4.30	1.16	.26	—	—	—	—	—	Total Fund Cred.&Loans Outstg.	2tl
	End of Period															**International Liquidity**	
	158.74	96.36	76.12	92.50	80.10	83.42	96.45	127.16	140.01	180.61	216.47	171.93	309.06	264.29	296.97	Total Reserves minus Gold	1l. d
	2.32	6.89	5.49	1.54	2.24	.29	2.74	3.96	1.66	1.05	12.08	12.37	8.03	8.08	8.60	SDRs	1b. d
	5.43	4.98	.01	1.78	1.70	1.93	.04	.04	.01	.01	.03	.03	4.13	4.12	4.38	Reserve Position in the Fund	1c. d
	150.99	84.49	70.62	89.18	76.16	81.20	93.67	123.16	138.34	179.55	204.36	159.53	296.90	252.09	283.99	Foreign Exchange	1d. d
	1.15	1.43	1.11	.95	3.89	1.05	1.60	2.39	3.98	2.59	2.65	2.81	1.55	1.48	32.02	Monetary Authorities: Other Liab.	4..d
	4.18	7.17	9.03	11.50	4.93	7.31	6.33	17.82	64.40	63.90	58.16	41.13	52.01	52.43	43.59	Deposit Money Banks: Assets	7a. d
	4.66	5.52	6.71	10.97	4.38	3.31	6.58	6.21	16.40	14.43	12.33	10.68	20.82	19.69	17.83	Liabilities	7b. d
	End of Period															**Monetary Authorities**	
	114.60	88.25	84.21	117.89	163.31	213.40	214.25	244.39	328.23	467.10	537.75	↕806.91	929.80	875.03	872.21	Foreign Assets	11
	5.12	5.96	7.29	6.63	19.82	25.97	31.70	11.51	3.71	.87	.02	—	—	—	40.00	Claims on Central Government	12a
	—	4.00	—	1.17	1.17	—	1.10	.10	.60	2.93	11.41	12.81	9.60	6.82	5.65	Claims on Deposit Money Banks	12e
	57.24	49.20	54.97	79.52	106.10	118.35	188.97	189.47	157.29	204.60	200.79	181.98	287.97	255.34	300.24	Reserve Money	14
	11.90	14.41	15.03	15.23	16.77	17.45	25.21	27.19	32.20	37.20	50.89	52.99	56.09	75.19	69.59	of which: Currency Outside DMBs	14a
	1.88	2.54	3.60	3.77	9.71	49.50	8.21	5.88	48.00	36.56	21.98	23.72	25.11	43.92	36.90	Time Deposits	15
	5.11	6.38	6.54	19.68	35.89	38.78	26.39	16.38	13.18	7.43	6.79	7.70	4.74	5.02	113.47	Foreign Liabilities	16c
	52.64	33.26	17.51	13.20	18.13	10.94	12.09	33.73	87.07	192.08	211.47	↕515.06	500.36	508.31	385.92	Central Government Deposits	16d
	8.91	11.11	12.12	12.73	15.63	22.57	21.81	21.95	25.05	26.69	30.10	31.88	33.48	36.53	40.09	Capital Accounts	17a
	-6.31	-4.53	-3.49	-3.47	-1.41	-1.01	-10.41	-11.41	1.95	3.29	78.11	59.37	87.74	32.73	41.24	Other Items (Net)	17r
	End of Period															**Deposit Money Banks**	
	45.23	32.51	42.09	59.34	86.47	93.38	159.65	163.60	138.62	165.74	129.83	125.94	217.80	185.65	227.46	Reserves	20
	3.12	6.86	9.72	14.05	9.79	18.68	13.82	34.39	153.13	162.05	149.04	112.82	158.78	178.14	154.45	Foreign Assets	21
	4.00	5.92	8.44	14.26	7.12	11.67	25.08	5.50	11.25	9.75	—	—	—	30.00	38.00	Claims on Central Government	22a
	97.11	130.04	138.13	143.26	152.54	151.94	161.24	202.62	260.87	335.83	465.99	654.58	673.59	739.14	902.68	Claims on Private Sector	22d
	37.93	36.59	42.11	44.21	48.74	56.55	86.80	94.94	110.42	131.67	146.90	158.41	197.76	215.06	241.75	Demand Deposits	24
	81.97	87.70	99.70	133.53	161.15	166.84	202.55	240.46	319.26	435.43	430.19	539.03	659.16	731.45	833.28	Time and Savings Deposits	25
	3.47	5.28	7.22	13.40	8.70	8.46	14.37	11.99	39.01	36.60	31.60	29.29	63.58	66.89	63.17	Foreign Liabilities	26c
	17.93	25.71	23.85	18.36	13.60	17.83	14.02	6.23	15.37	35.72	87.43	92.96	89.16	73.71	90.88	Central Government Deposits	26d
	17.53	19.53	22.13	26.40	26.65	26.83	31.28	44.78	67.08	46.99	61.85	67.69	74.36	96.20	92.33	Capital Accounts	27a
	-9.37	.51	3.37	-4.99	-2.93	-.83	10.76	7.72	13.34	-12.96	-10.40	5.96	-33.83	-50.37	1.17	Other Items (Net)	27r
	End of Period															**Monetary Survey**	
	109.14	83.45	80.17	98.86	128.51	184.85	187.29	250.39	429.14	585.08	648.30	↕882.74	1,020.26	981.26	850.02	Foreign Assets (Net)	31n
	36.85	85.33	114.86	135.82	151.22	168.03	196.02	183.89	178.09	124.15	174.22	↕55.80	93.71	195.99	514.51	Domestic Credit	32
	-61.45	-47.09	-25.62	-10.67	-4.79	8.87	30.69	-22.93	-87.44	-217.16	-298.77	↕-608.02	-589.52	-552.02	-398.80	Claims on Central Govt. (Net)	32an
	98.30	132.42	140.48	146.49	156.01	159.15	165.33	206.82	265.53	341.30	472.99	663.83	683.22	748.00	913.30	Claims on Private Sector	32d
	49.86	51.08	58.09	60.84	67.81	76.92	115.14	125.42	142.77	169.01	197.97	211.54	254.29	290.50	311.59	Money	34
	83.85	90.23	103.30	137.30	170.86	216.34	210.76	246.33	367.26	471.98	452.17	562.75	684.27	775.37	870.18	Quasi-Money	35
	12.04	27.21	33.39	36.28	40.81	59.36	57.41	62.53	97.81	68.06	175.13	164.23	175.41	111.39	182.76	Other Items (Net)	37r
	133.70	141.32	161.38	198.14	238.67	293.26	325.90	371.75	510.02	641.00	650.14	774.29	938.56	1,065.87	1,181.76	Money plus Quasi-Money	35l
	Percent Per Annum															**Interest Rates**	
	7.00	10.50	16.00	13.50	19.00	12.50	9.50	9.00	11.00	12.00	12.00	13.00	12.00	11.00	12.00	Discount Rate (End of Period)	60
	....	....	....	....	....	....	....	....	....	8.39	10.50	10.61	10.25	9.73	7.01	Money Market Rate	60b
	7.71	12.00	14.60	13.04	17.74	16.47	9.76	5.96	7.28	10.16	11.14	12.67	12.34	8.25	8.35	Treasury Bill Rate	60c
	4.50	9.00	12.00	12.50	16.50	10.19	5.75	4.81	9.23	8.92	8.85	10.85	9.00	7.38	8.00	Deposit Rate	60l
	9.50	13.50	18.00	18.00	22.00	17.00	12.50	11.88	15.00	14.50	14.50	16.25	15.00	14.00	15.00	Lending Rate	60p
	Period Averages															**Prices**	
	28.4	34.1	37.8	↕42.2	↕47.7	57.4	65.3	74.0	83.2	90.1	100.0	110.8	119.9	140.3	160.4	Consumer Prices	64
	Millions of Emalangeni															**International Transactions**	
	286.86	340.30	351.84	338.50	345.62	392.86	635.54	862.36	1,059.86	1,313.92	1,422.09	1,647.30	1,818.60	2,123.50	....	Exports	70
	484.73	516.76	569.29	612.77	642.74	707.12	798.87	885.77	1,167.63	1,524.50	1,714.13	1,979.04	2,468.03	....	....	Imports, cif	71
	481.83	508.70	560.29	603.72	634.06	697.35	787.84	873.54	1,151.51	1,503.45	1,690.46	1,951.72	2,433.96	....	....	Imports, fob	71.v

Swaziland

734

	1965	1966	1967	1968	1969	1970	1971	1972	1973	1974	1975	1976	1977	1978	1979
Balance of Payments													*Millions of US Dollars:*		
Goods: Exports f.o.b. .... 78aa d	....	....	....	....	....	....	....	....	....	178.8	197.0	193.4	183.9	198.7	241.6
Goods: Imports f.o.b. .... 78ab d	....	....	....	....	....	....	....	....	....	−111.9	−139.7	−155.9	−171.2	−247.7	−363.3
Trade Balance .... 78ac d	....	....	....	....	....	....	....	....	....	67.0	57.3	37.5	12.6	−49.0	−121.6
Services: Credit .... 78ad d	....	....	....	....	....	....	....	....	....	23.0	25.0	25.8	29.2	20.1	31.4
Services: Debit .... 78ae d	....	....	....	....	....	....	....	....	....	−28.8	−39.5	−42.1	−46.0	−63.7	−83.3
Balance on Goods and Services .... 78af d	....	....	....	....	....	....	....	....	....	61.1	42.9	21.2	−4.1	−92.6	−173.6
Income: Credit .... 78ag d	....	....	....	....	....	....	....	....	....	4.4	13.3	15.8	20.7	25.4	27.4
Income: Debit .... 78ah d	....	....	....	....	....	....	....	....	....	−38.3	−23.1	−15.2	−17.8	−29.9	−20.0
Balance on Goods, Serv., & Inc. .... 78ai d	....	....	....	....	....	....	....	....	....	27.2	33.0	21.7	−1.3	−97.1	−166.1
Current Transfers, n.i.e.: Credit .... 78aj d	....	....	....	....	....	....	....	....	....	28.6	37.2	44.0	50.4	70.5	95.0
Current Transfers: Debit .... 78ak d	....	....	....	....	....	....	....	....	....	−13.2	−18.7	−35.4	−37.5	−44.2	−48.2
Current Account, n.i.e. .... 78al d	....	....	....	....	....	....	....	....	....	42.5	51.5	30.4	11.6	−70.7	−119.3
Capital Account, n.i.e.: Credit .... 78ba d	....	....	....	....	....	....	....	....	....	—	—	—	—	—	—
Capital Account: Debit .... 78bb d	....	....	....	....	....	....	....	....	....	—	—	—	—	−1.5	−1.4
Capital Account, n.i.e. .... 78bc d	....	....	....	....	....	....	....	....	....	—	—	—	—	−1.5	−1.4
Direct Investment Abroad .... 78bd d	....	....	....	....	....	....	....	....	....	—	—	—	—	—	—
Dir. Invest. in Rep. Econ., n.i.e. .... 78be d	....	....	....	....	....	....	....	....	....	3.5	14.5	7.4	20.0	21.7	55.5
Portfolio Investment Assets .... 78bf d	....	....	....	....	....	....	....	....	....						
Portfolio Investment Liab., n.i.e. .... 78bg d	....	....	....	....	....	....	....	....	....						
Other Investment Assets .... 78bh d	....	....	....	....	....	....	....	....	....	−25.0	−9.1	−.7	−3.3	11.2	9.9
Other Investment Liab., n.i.e. .... 78bi d	....	....	....	....	....	....	....	....	....	6.6	6.5	13.8	7.9	47.5	34.8
Financial Account, n.i.e. .... 78bj d	....	....	....	....	....	....	....	....	....	−14.9	11.9	20.5	24.6	80.4	100.1
Net Errors and Omissions .... 78ca d	....	....	....	....	....	....	....	....	....	−17.7	−24.2	−23.1	−14.5	7.7	12.0
Overall Balance .... 78cb d	....	....	....	....	....	....	....	....	....	10.0	39.2	27.7	21.8	15.9	−8.5
Reserves and Related Items .... 79da d	....	....	....	....	....	....	....	....	....	−10.0	−39.2	−27.7	−21.8	−15.9	8.5
Reserve Assets .... 79db d	....	....	....	....	....	....	....	....	....	−10.2	−39.2	−27.8	−21.8	−15.9	5.3
Use of Fund Credit and Loans .... 79dc d	....	....	....	....	....	....	....	....	....	—	—	—	—	—	3.2
Liabs.Constit.For.Auth.Reserves ...... 79dd d	....	....	....	....	....	....	....	....	....	.1	—	.1	—	—	.1
Exceptional Financing .... 79de d	....	....	....	....	....	....	....	....	....	—	—	—	—	—	—
Government Finance													*Millions of Emalangeni:*		
Deficit(−) or Surplus 80	....	....	....	....	....	....	−2.02	−4.62	−10.77	1.66	17.39	−8.48	−8.56	−39.97	3.87
Revenue 81	....	....	....	....	....	....	17.40	21.22	28.47	45.64	69.93	54.61	80.82	98.65	126.04
Grants Received 81z	....	....	....	....	....	....	.07	.14	.10	.67	.09	.05	.35	6.63	8.01
Expenditure 82	....	....	....	....	....	....	19.14	23.31	38.31	39.52	46.83	57.61	75.20	119.04	97.50
Lending Minus Repayments 83	....	....	....	....	....	....	.35	2.67	1.03	5.13	5.80	5.53	14.53	26.21	32.68
Statistical Adjustment 80x	....	....	....	....	....	....	—	—	—	—	—	—	—	—	—
Financing															
Net Borrowing: Domestic 84a	....	....	....	....	....	....	1.14	−.82	3.68	−10.99	−20.85	8.98	2.93	−5.66	−10.46
Foreign 85a	....	....	....	....	....	....	.88	5.44	7.09	9.33	3.46	−.50	5.63	45.63	6.59
Use of Cash Balances 87	....	....	....	....	....	....	—	—	—	—	—	—	—	—	—
Debt: Domestic 88a	....	....	....	....	....	1.99	3.21	4.13	10.79	12.01	12.76	9.17	10.25	15.28	15.04
Foreign 89a	....	....	....	....	....	....	....	....	....	....	4.07	....	....	94.40	116.40
National Accounts													*Millions of Emalangeni:*		
Exports of Goods & Services 90c	....	....	34.0	41.1	43.1	48.9	56.0	65.3	72.9	94.9	155.4	179.4	172.4	186.4	221.1
Government Consumption 91f	....	6.4	6.7	7.0	8.6	10.4	10.9	13.6	13.0	17.7	36.8	43.3	54.1	70.2	74.9
Gross Fixed Capital Formation 93e	....	....	10.5	11.2	10.7	9.5	16.1	20.0	19.9	21.6	41.6	50.5	68.1	144.8	142.1
Increase/Decrease(−) in Stocks 93i	....	....	2.6	−.9	.5	2.8	2.4	2.7	4.7	6.1	−2.0	2.0	3.0	−3.0	6.0
Private Consumption 96f	....	....	30.1	29.8	35.2	45.3	44.0	59.2	78.1	105.6	102.7	120.1	146.8	153.5	249.2
Imports of Goods & Services 98c	....	....	−29.0	−34.8	−41.1	−40.8	−48.4	−63.2	−75.7	−93.4	−121.2	−160.2	−181.4	−256.7	−344.6
Gross Domestic Product 99b	....	50.2	54.9	53.4	57.0	76.1	81.0	97.6	116.6	136.4	161.2	186.3	263.0	295.2	348.7
Net Factor Inc/Pmts(−) Abroad 98.n	....	−7.5	−6.6	−7.4	−6.6	−9.6	−9.4	−13.5	−19.3	−3.7	50.4	46.1	−2.3	−14.6	−22.2
Gross Nat'l Expenditure = GNP 99a	....	42.7	48.3	46.0	50.4	66.5	71.6	84.1	97.3	132.7	211.6	232.4	260.7	280.6	326.5
Nat'l Income, Market Prices 99e	....	38.5	43.9	40.7	44.5	59.7	63.9	75.6	87.5	121.3	211.7	232.4	260.7	280.6	277.1
Gross Dom. Prod. 1990 Prices 99b.p	....	....	....	....	....	....	....	....	....	....	....	....	717.5	788.4	902.7
GDP Deflator (1990=100) .... 99bi p	....	....	....	....	....	....	....	....	....	....	....	....	36.7	37.4	38.6
															Millions:
Population 99z	.36	.37	.39	.40	.41	.42	.44	.45	.46	.48	.49	.50	.51	.53	.53

Exchange Rates: On September 6, 1974 the lilangeni, equal to the South African rand, was introduced.
Monetary Authorities: I Beginning in April 1991, the Capital Investment Fund of the central government is included in *line 11*, with a contra-entry in *line 16d*.
Monetary Survey: I See note to section 10.

Government Finance: I Beginning in 1990, data are as reported by the Bank of Swaziland and cover budgetary central government. Prior to 1990, data are as reported in the *Government Finance Statistics Yearbook* and cover budgetary central government.

Swaziland

1980	1981	1982	1983	1984	1985	1986	1987	1988	1989	1990	1991	1992	1993	1994		
Minus Sign Indicates Debit															**Balance of Payments**	
368.3	388.3	324.0	303.8	230.8	176.7	278.1	423.6	466.2	493.8	556.6	596.6	637.7	649.8	....	Goods: Exports f.o.b.	78aa *d*
−538.1	−504.0	−439.0	−464.8	−372.1	−272.7	−296.7	−370.0	−441.5	−515.8	−587.6	−632.9	−765.3	−775.0	....	Goods: Imports f.o.b.	78ab *d*
−169.9	−115.7	−115.0	−160.9	−141.3	−95.9	−18.6	53.6	24.7	−22.1	−31.0	−36.3	−127.7	−125.1	....	Trade Balance	78ac *d*
36.1	41.4	32.9	41.2	43.7	27.8	30.5	51.1	61.1	88.6	107.9	96.4	105.3	99.6	....	Services: Credit	78ad *d*
−80.0	−100.9	−107.4	−93.0	−86.5	−62.5	−61.7	−86.7	−119.8	−98.5	−143.6	−152.5	−118.5	−124.2	....	Services: Debit	78ae *d*
−213.8	−175.1	−189.5	−212.7	−184.2	−130.6	−49.7	17.9	−34.0	−32.0	−66.7	−92.5	−140.9	−149.7	....	Balance on Goods and Services	78af *d*
46.4	68.6	54.6	66.9	70.9	71.8	73.0	97.1	123.5	128.2	165.1	170.5	163.2	125.3	....	Income: Credit	78ag *d*
−41.1	−48.4	−40.2	−27.5	−31.4	−32.8	−57.4	−101.8	−97.0	−179.8	−148.0	−142.4	−140.9	−127.5	....	Income: Debit	78ah *d*
−208.5	−154.9	−175.1	−173.3	−144.7	−91.6	−34.1	13.2	−7.5	−83.6	−49.6	−64.3	−118.6	−151.9	....	Balance on Goods, Serv., & Inc.	78ai *d*
143.7	131.7	123.6	128.1	113.0	88.4	86.7	108.8	129.2	142.0	169.7	169.5	216.8	205.2	....	Current Transfers, n.i.e.: Credit	78aj *d*
−64.8	−58.1	−62.3	−61.8	−45.8	−35.3	−40.8	−59.5	−56.5	−54.7	−73.6	−80.1	−93.3	−90.9	....	Current Transfers: Debit	78ak *d*
−129.7	−81.4	−113.8	−107.0	−77.5	−38.4	11.8	62.6	65.3	3.7	46.5	25.1	4.9	−37.5	....	Current Account, n.i.e.	78al *d*
—	—	—	—	—	—	—	.3	.3	.7	2.3	.3	.4	.3	....	Capital Account, n.i.e.: Credit	78ba *d*
−2.1	−1.9	−.6	−1.7	−1.9	−.9	−.8	−.7	−.2	−.1	—	−.3	−.1	—	....	Capital Account: Debit	78bb *d*
−2.1	−1.9	−.6	−1.7	−1.9	−.9	−.8	−.4	.1	.6	2.2	.1	.2	.3	....	Capital Account, n.i.e.	78bc *d*
−9.0	−5.4	2.9	.1	−4.9	−2.7	−2.4	−6.7	−12.3	−14.7	−7.8	−30.8	−8.9	−11.2	....	Direct Investment Abroad	78bd *d*
26.5	37.1	−13.6	−5.7	5.0	11.7	25.6	60.9	50.6	72.0	39.0	77.3	56.0	40.2	....	Dir. Invest. in Rep. Econ., n.i.e.	78be *d*
—	—	—	−.1	−.7	.1	−.1	−.1	−1.2	−.2	−.5	−.4	−.5	−1.1	−.1	....	Portfolio Investment Assets	78bf *d*
—	—	−.2	.4	−.1	2.0	−.4	2.4	6.3	7.4	−8.4	.1	1.1	−1.0	....	Portfolio Investment Liab., n.i.e.	78bg *d*
—	−24.8	−19.9	7.6	−4.2	−16.5	−7.0	−55.9	−110.3	−81.7	−38.7	−40.2	−39.7	−110.1	....	Other Investment Assets	78bh *d*
19.0	14.4	63.5	64.8	32.9	27.0	−13.4	−8.9	7.6	4.8	−21.7	2.3	27.1	45.4	....	Other Investment Liab., n.i.e.	78bi *d*
36.5	21.3	32.5	66.5	28.7	21.4	2.2	−9.5	−58.3	−12.7	−38.1	8.2	34.7	−36.8	....	Financial Account, n.i.e.	78bj *d*
129.4	13.3	73.1	53.8	41.7	13.7	−5.7	−31.2	7.6	59.6	.4	−20.0	51.8	26.3	....	Net Errors and Omissions	78ca *d*
34.1	−48.7	−8.7	11.6	−9.0	−4.2	7.5	21.5	14.6	51.3	11.1	13.4	91.7	−47.6	....	Overall Balance	78cb *d*
−34.1	48.7	8.7	−11.6	9.0	4.2	−7.5	−21.5	−14.6	−51.3	−11.1	−13.4	−91.7	47.6	....	Reserves and Related Items	79da *d*
−36.8	48.3	9.1	−22.3	8.3	6.1	−2.5	−15.7	−10.6	−50.0	−10.7	−13.4	−91.7	47.6	....	Reserve Assets	79db *d*
2.6	—	—	10.7	—	−1.6	−5.0	−5.6	−4.2	−1.2	−.3	—	—	—	....	Use of Fund Credit and Loans	79dc *d*
—	.3	−.4	—	—	.7	−.3	.1	−.2	.3	−.2	—	—	—	....	Liabs.Constit.For.Auth.Reserves	79dd *d*
—	—	—	—	—	—	—	—	—	—	—	—	—	—	....	Exceptional Financing	79de *d*
Year Beginning April 1															**Government Finance**	
27.55	−48.90	−31.85	−19.55	−3.63	−27.57	−48.85	21.58	59.20	95.46	ⅈ165.55	121.18	−42.22	−171.47	−282.28	Deficit(−) or Surplus	80
148.80	131.11	178.60	179.63	210.75	232.33	243.91	330.70	422.64	570.06	ⅈ745.57	795.46	925.58	953.00	1,200.49	Revenue	81
7.65	5.00	5.40	5.94	10.71	10.17	11.77	6.62	5.55	14.24	ⅈ10.80	20.65	46.33	28.70	39.20	Grants Received	81z
117.28	166.06	183.19	190.53	209.67	257.85	290.99	301.34	354.83	427.28	ⅈ581.94	698.12	1,025.44	1,139.43	1,487.90	Expenditure	82
11.62	18.95	17.70	14.59	15.42	12.22	13.54	14.40	14.16	61.56	ⅈ8.88	−3.19	−11.31	13.74	34.07	Lending Minus Repayments	83
—	—	−14.96	—	—	—	—	—	—	—	ⅈ—	—	—	—	—	Statistical Adjustment	80x
															Financing	
−27.67	42.54	14.90	18.11	9.21	24.82	7.41	2.29	15.78	−5.97	ⅈ−160.00	−105.38	50.40	196.78	241.85	Net Borrowing: Domestic	84a
.12	6.36	16.95	1.44	−5.58	2.75	27.75	5.52	−7.18	−3.10	ⅈ−5.56	−15.79	−8.18	−25.31	40.43	Foreign	85a
—	—	—	—	—	—	13.69	−29.39	−67.80	−86.39	ⅈ—	—	—	—	—	Use of Cash Balances	87
12.02	17.02	22.02	26.62	27.34	40.87	50.00	53.87	51.61	37.23	ⅈ25.96	25.65	25.45	53.75	....	Debt: Domestic	88a
116.50	127.00	166.40	198.60	371.54	471.70	509.62	532.50	565.70	555.40	ⅈ570.20	583.90	630.20	671.40	....	Foreign	89a
Year Ending June 30															**National Accounts**	
325.7	388.0	416.8	400.6	432.8	474.6	705.3	959.4	1,182.4	1,512.3	1,767.0	1,917.1	....	....	....	Exports of Goods & Services	90c
103.9	133.8	141.0	135.8	182.1	177.6	198.6	208.3	262.9	296.5	412.3	474.4	....	....	....	Government Consumption	91f
147.8	140.2	152.8	208.5	208.5	225.4	163.6	196.2	350.7	419.6	467.8	441.0	....	....	....	Gross Fixed Capital Formation	93e
23.8	15.3	23.4	−5.7	.9	12.2	41.2	−19.5	20.0	21.4	16.3	22.5	....	....	....	Increase/Decrease(−) in Stocks	93i
286.9	360.2	394.9	450.4	510.8	591.5	654.3	675.9	853.8	1,054.5	1,215.3	1,448.2	....	....	....	Private Consumption	96f
−465.9	−536.6	−582.2	−610.0	−672.8	−738.0	−736.7	−814.1	−1,096.5	−1,478.9	−1,539.1	−1,890.2	....	....	....	Imports of Goods & Services	98c
422.1	500.9	546.7	579.6	662.3	743.3	1,026.3	1,206.1	1,573.3	1,825.4	2,339.6	2,413.3	....	....	....	Gross Domestic Product	99b
−5.7	5.7	15.5	30.6	53.1	76.5	34.1	−19.3	46.2	−148.5	20.2	50.6	....	....	....	Net Factor Inc/Pmts(−) Abroad	98.n
416.4	506.6	562.2	610.2	715.4	819.8	1,060.4	1,186.8	1,619.5	1,676.9	2,359.0	2,463.9	....	....	....	Gross Nat'l Expenditure = GNP	99a
390.3	476.5	524.9	563.6	668.2	764.5	986.1	1,131.9	....	....	....	....	....	....	....	Nat'l Income, Market Prices	99e
862.8	ⅈ922.1	932.7	943.5	1,002.3	1,040.0	1,138.5	1,347.3	1,748.3	2,008.9	2,339.6	....	....	....	....	Gross Dom. Prod. 1990 Prices	99b.*p*
48.9	54.3	58.6	61.4	66.1	71.5	90.2	89.5	90.0	90.9	100.0	....	....	....	....	GDP Deflator (1990=100)	99bi *p*
Midyear Estimates																
.55	.57	.59	.60	.63	.65	.68	.69	.71	.72	.77	.77	.82	.81	....	Population	99z

Sweden
144

		1965	1966	1967	1968	1969	1970	1971	1972	1973	1974	1975	1976	1977	1978	1979
Exchange Rates																*Kronor per SDR:*
Official Rate	aa	5.1800	5.1800	5.1650	5.1800	5.1700	5.1700	5.2820	15.1495	5.5341	4.9960	5.1339	4.7943	5.6721	5.5961	5.4623
																Kronor per US Dollar:
Official Rate	ae	5.1800	5.1800	5.1650	5.1800	5.1700	5.1700	4.8650	14.7430	4.5875	4.0805	4.3855	4.1265	4.6695	4.2955	4.1465
Official Rate	rf	5.1732	5.1732	5.1732	5.1732	5.1732	5.1732	5.1259	4.7624	4.3673	4.4394	4.1522	4.3559	4.4816	4.5185	4.2871
																Kronor per ECU:
ECU Rate	ea	....	....	....	....	....	....	....	....	....	....	....	....	....	....	5.9729
ECU Rate	eb	....	....	....	....	....	....	....	....	....	....	....	....	....	....	5.8729
																Index Numbers (1990=100):
Official Rate	ahx	114.6	114.4	114.5	114.4	114.3	114.0	167.4	124.1	135.6	133.3	142.7	135.7	132.2	130.9	137.9
Nominal Effective Exchange Rate	neu	140.0	140.0	141.0	146.8	146.6	144.9	143.4	144.6	143.4	142.3	147.9	151.3	145.2	131.6	133.3
Real Effective Exchange Rate	reu	....	....	....	....	....	....	....	....	....	....	116.9	122.9	117.0	107.0	105.6
Fund Position																*Millions of SDRs:*
Quota	2f.s	150	225	225	225	225	325	325	325	325	325	325	325	325	450	450
SDRs	1b.s	—	—	—	—	—	38	73	107	107	107	107	107	107	112	173
Reserve Position in the Fund	1c.s	143	165	139	164	101	126	84	90	88	89	95	232	225	191	181
of which: Outstg.Fund Borrowing	2c	33	33	18	56	45	45	—	—	—	—	—	50	64	55	43
International Liquidity													*Millions of US Dollars Unless Otherwise Indicated:*			
Total Reserves minus Gold	1l.d	770	824	638	590	470	561	893	1,358	2,284	1,487	2,839	2,255	3,415	4,124	3,514
SDRs	1b.d	—	—	—	—	—	38	79	116	129	131	125	124	130	146	228
Reserve Position in the Fund	1c.d	143	165	139	164	101	126	91	98	106	109	111	269	274	249	238
Foreign Exchange	1d.d	627	659	499	426	369	397	723	1,144	2,049	1,247	2,602	1,862	3,011	3,729	3,048
Gold (Million Fine Troy Ounces)	1ad	5.771	5.800	5.804	6.426	6.449	5.715	5.778	5.782	5.790	5.790	5.790	5.790	5.929	5.999	6.069
Gold (National Valuation)	1and	202	203	203	225	226	200	220	220	244	248	237	235	252	274	280
Deposit Money Banks: Assets	7a.d	556	674	802	849	846	985	1,187	1,418	2,214	3,177	3,629	4,145	4,609	4,902	5,948
of which: Claims on Nonbanks	7add	87	94	98	114	140	137	186	192	346	503	665	693	698	972	1,015
Deposit Money Banks: Liabilities	7b.d	422	506	470	541	720	769	940	1,019	1,393	1,782	2,478	3,236	4,414	5,811	9,070
of which: Liab. to Nonbanks	7bdd	100	122	120	156	151	150	171	170	224	266	285	275	278	367	766
Other Banking Insts.: Assets	7e.d	—	—	—	—	—	—	—	—	—	—	—	—	—	—	—
of which: Claims on Nonbanks	7edd	....	....	....	....	....	....	....	....	....	....	....	....	....	....	....
Other Banking Insts.: Liabilities	7f.d															
Monetary Authorities																*Billions of Kronor:*
Foreign Assets	11	4.96	5.13	4.20	4.12	3.41	3.62	5.07	7.33	11.24	7.62	12.82	11.37	17.66	19.79	16.27
Claims on Central Government	12a	5.25	6.24	6.57	7.75	8.92	10.17	11.33	10.85	8.89	16.67	16.40	17.88	15.65	20.96	34.68
Claims on Deposit Money Banks	12e	—	—	—	.85	1.56	1.11	.01	—	—	2.96	.25	2.75	3.61	—	6.01
Reserve Money	14	9.40	9.97	10.65	11.35	12.15	12.56	14.07	15.44	16.92	22.83	22.68	25.10	27.62	31.41	43.13
of which: Currency Outside DMBs	14a	8.69	9.24	10.00	10.46	10.94	11.40	12.81	14.14	15.38	17.32	20.13	22.16	24.41	27.57	30.94
Restricted Deposits	16b	1.14	1.28	.99	.88	1.07	1.25	1.05	1.05	1.24	2.28	4.47	3.32	2.86	2.39	5.57
Foreign Liabilities	16c	—	—	—	—	—	—	—	—	—	—	—	.91	1.98	1.87	1.80
Central Government Deposits	16d	.07	.07	.11	.10	.09	.04	.05	.39	.34	.26	.22	.19	.04	.15	.18
Other Items (Net)	17r	–.43	.06	–.96	.40	.58	1.05	1.25	1.31	1.63	1.88	2.10	2.48	4.42	4.93	6.27
Deposit Money Banks																*Billions of Kronor:*
Reserves	20	.71	.74	.76	.92	1.26	1.30	1.33	1.42	1.55	5.73	2.74	3.13	3.33	3.96	12.30
Foreign Assets	21	2.87	3.49	4.15	4.39	4.38	5.10	5.72	6.83	10.10	12.96	15.91	17.10	21.52	21.06	24.66
Claims on Central Government	22a	4.32	4.20	4.90	5.38	6.81	6.41	7.56	11.50	15.11	13.83	20.38	15.62	17.88	34.41	36.10
Claims on Private Sector	22d	47.74	52.24	58.08	66.32	69.49	72.45	78.40	87.49	97.72	108.14	120.72	136.27	154.87	171.81	197.84
Claims on Other Financial Insts.	22f	7.58	9.16	11.24	13.13	15.61	19.36	20.08	22.54	23.50	25.15	28.47	30.60	34.89	39.95	47.02
Demand,Time,Sav.& Fgn Cur.Deps.	25l	55.59	61.14	69.36	78.10	82.40	87.47	96.12	108.87	124.55	136.17	151.24	157.85	171.97	202.96	239.04
Foreign Liabilities	26c	2.18	2.62	2.43	2.80	3.72	3.98	4.53	4.91	6.35	7.27	10.87	13.36	20.61	24.96	37.61
Central Government Deposits	26d	—	—	—	—	—	—	.01	—	.01	.01	.01	.02	.05	.08	.12
Credit from Monetary Authorities	26g	—	—	—	.85	1.56	1.11	.01	—	—	2.96	.25	2.75	3.77	.09	6.32
Credit from Other Financial Insts.	26i	—	—	—	.53	1.00	1.37	2.21	2.27	4.22	4.22	4.52	6.15	7.63	9.18	10.25
Other Items (Net)	27r	5.46	6.06	7.30	7.86	8.86	10.69	10.21	13.72	12.84	15.18	21.36	22.62	28.51	34.01	24.70
Monetary Survey																*Billions of Kronor:*
Foreign Assets (Net)	31n	5.65	6.00	5.92	5.71	4.06	4.74	6.26	9.25	14.99	13.31	17.86	14.21	16.59	14.02	1.53
Domestic Credit	32	65.75	72.38	82.49	93.15	101.35	108.87	117.85	132.53	145.47	164.11	186.38	200.90	223.97	267.71	316.30
Claims on Central Govt. (Net)	32an	9.50	10.37	11.36	13.03	15.64	16.54	18.84	21.96	23.65	30.23	36.54	33.29	33.44	55.13	70.47
Claims on Private Sector	32d	48.20	52.37	59.43	66.49	69.66	72.65	78.55	87.64	97.90	108.38	121.03	136.67	155.30	172.25	198.46
Claims on Other Financial Insts.	32f	8.06	9.64	11.70	13.63	16.05	19.68	20.46	22.93	23.92	25.50	28.81	30.94	35.23	40.32	47.37
Restricted Deposits	36b	1.14	1.28	.99	.88	1.07	1.25	1.05	1.05	1.24	2.28	4.47	3.32	2.86	2.39	5.57
Other Items (Net)	37r	5.97	6.71	8.04	9.43	10.99	13.49	14.12	17.71	19.26	21.65	28.39	31.76	41.30	48.79	42.25
Money plus Quasi-Money	35l	64.28	70.39	79.36	88.56	93.35	98.88	108.94	123.02	139.94	153.50	171.39	180.03	196.40	230.54	270.00
Unused Bank Credits	39b	4.34	4.88	5.83	6.91	7.27	6.29	8.61	9.69	10.40	11.89	14.78	15.70	16.09	19.89	18.94
Money (National Definitions)																*Billions of Kronor:*
Broad Money	38n	68.57	74.11	83.89	93.40	97.89	103.32	113.58	126.95	143.24	155.99	175.76	184.70	202.04	238.45	277.53
Other Banking Institutions																*Billions of Kronor:*
Cash	40	.26	.44	.50	1.30	.22	.74	.59	.74	1.19	.81	1.18	.93	1.15	2.46	2.31
Foreign Assets	41															
Claims on Private Sector	42d	21.50	26.33	31.71	37.67	46.24	53.81	63.01	71.61	81.08	93.09	108.05	121.96	137.45	155.48	174.09
Bonds	46ab	3.11	3.20	3.28	3.48	3.19	46.91	1.85	2.59	4.80	6.71	10.14	14.27	15.81	18.17	21.43
Foreign Liabilities	46c															
Central Govt. Lending Funds	46f	5.25	8.01	10.43	14.10	17.79	22.22	27.81	31.83	37.16	43.04	48.18	54.05	60.52	67.30	73.18
Cred.from Deposit Money Banks	46h	7.58	9.16	11.24	13.13	15.61	19.36	20.08	22.54	23.50	25.15	28.47	30.60	34.89	39.95	47.02
Capital Accounts	47a	....	....	....	....	....	....	....	....	....	....	....	....	....	....	....
Other Items (Net)	47r	–12.22	–16.51	–20.78	–26.36	–32.36	–39.32	–45.12	–51.72	–58.04	–65.36	–73.06	–81.37	–91.68	–102.17	–116.27

Sweden

144

	1980	1981	1982	1983	1984	1985	1986	1987	1988	1989	1990	1991	1992	1993	1994		
End of Period																**Exchange Rates**	
	5.5771	6.4844	8.0466	8.3766	8.8116	8.3650	8.3409	8.2963	8.2855	8.1833	8.1063	7.9096	9.6841	11.4054	10.8927	Official Rate	aa
End of Period (ae)		*Period Average (rf)*															
	4.3728	5.5710	7.2945	8.0010	8.9895	7.6155	6.8190	5.8480	6.1570	6.2270	5.6980	5.5295	7.0430	8.3035	7.4615	Official Rate	ae
	4.2296	5.0634	6.2826	7.6671	8.2718	8.6039	7.1236	6.3404	6.1272	6.4469	5.9188	6.0475	5.8238	7.7834	7.7160	Official Rate	rf
End of Period (ea)		*Period Average (eb)*															
	5.7329	6.0037	7.0809	6.6260	6.3699	6.7172	7.2518	7.5529	7.1762	7.4106	7.6754	7.4502	8.5490	9.2963	9.1779	ECU Rate	ea
	5.8797	5.6327	6.1417	6.8243	6.5113	6.5198	6.9944	7.3096	7.2439	7.1013	7.5200	7.4798	7.5299	9.1146	9.1579	ECU Rate	eb
Period Averages																	
	139.8	117.4	95.0	77.2	71.6	69.0	83.0	93.3	96.6	91.7	100.0	98.0	102.0	76.1	76.7	Official Rate	ah x
	131.9	130.6	117.5	104.2	106.6	106.0	103.2	101.5	101.6	102.3	100.0	99.8	101.2	82.6	81.5	Nominal Effective Exchange Rate	ne u
	104.7	103.6	91.8	82.4	87.9	89.0	90.3	90.2	93.4	99.7	100.0	99.1	98.5	74.2	....	Real Effective Exchange Rate	re u
End of Period																**Fund Position**	
	675	675	675	1,064	1,064	1,064	1,064	1,064	1,064	1,064	1,064	1,064	1,614	1,614	1,614	Quota	2f. s
	174	225	233	123	181	224	261	208	299	260	204	290	33	42	46	SDRs	1b. s
	194	166	149	241	258	250	253	277	251	254	234	308	451	451	451	Reserve Position in the Fund	1c. s
	31	18	6	—	—	—	—	—	—	—	—	—	—	—	—	*of which:* Outstg.Fund Borrowing	2c
End of Period																**International Liquidity**	
	3,418	3,601	3,513	4,034	3,845	5,793	6,551	8,174	8,492	9,559	17,988	18,331	22,624	19,050	23,254	Total Reserves minus Gold	1l. d
	222	261	257	129	178	246	320	296	402	341	290	414	45	58	68	SDRs	1b. d
	247	193	164	252	253	274	310	394	337	333	333	441	621	620	659	Reserve Position in the Fund	1c. d
	2,949	3,147	3,091	3,653	3,414	5,273	5,921	7,485	7,752	8,885	17,365	17,476	21,959	18,372	22,527	Foreign Exchange	1d. d
	6.069	6.069	6.069	6.069	6.069	6.069	6.069	6.069	6.069	6.069	6.069	6.069	6.069	6.069	6.069	Gold (Million Fine Troy Ounces)	1ad
	271	247	234	222	208	233	260	301	286	279	302	304	292	292	310	Gold (National Valuation)	1an d
	8,036	7,515	6,725	7,122	6,741	8,943	10,787	15,023	14,905	30,505	I 34,919	34,247	32,056	26,261	24,727	Deposit Money Banks: Assets	7a. d
	1,146	1,403	1,507	1,781	1,846	2,011	2,336	3,136	4,398	12,777	I 14,748	15,279	14,534	11,364	10,445	*of which:* Claims on Nonbanks	7ad d
	12,518	14,100	13,157	13,980	13,098	17,199	23,621	35,051	43,924	72,015	I 99,361	93,185	62,745	50,253	50,925	Deposit Money Banks: Liabilities	7b. d
	1,286	1,908	676	1,306	1,302	2,398	2,093	5,208	7,023	11,339	I 12,126	13,954	9,215	9,452	7,412	*of which:* Liab. to Nonbanks	7bd d
	947	1,215	1,542	1,964	1,944	2,394	3,465	4,519	5,107	7,629	I 6,027	5,513	4,395	3,743	4,661	Other Banking Insts.: Assets	7e. d
	643	772	408	1,362	1,339	1,745	2,941	3,209	2,942	3,936	I 4,017	3,581	3,448	3,009	3,764	*of which:* Claims on Nonbanks	7ed d
	1,045	1,609	2,337	3,189	3,855	4,343	5,556	7,430	9,401	10,829	I 5,269	6,623	22,534	20,605	22,196	Other Banking Insts.: Liabilities	7f. d
End of Period																**Monetary Authorities**	
	15.73	20.87	25.99	32.64	33.91	44.41	45.74	50.29	53.74	60.69	103.77	99.85	163.29	175.69	177.95	Foreign Assets	11
	33.19	43.16	50.46	37.73	67.20	68.14	88.93	96.14	93.35	89.50	53.24	132.31	145.98	98.99	87.52	Claims on Central Government	12a
	6.23	1.23	—	13.06	.55	5.86	4.15	2.40	17.40	27.87	19.68	23.55	61.02	1.26	.01	Claims on Deposit Money Banks	12e
	38.98	43.55	46.46	47.44	50.54	52.04	65.28	68.37	80.91	89.56	96.86	89.36	110.95	163.84	200.59	Reserve Money	14
	33.58	36.06	38.06	41.93	45.11	46.12	50.38	52.22	55.14	60.66	62.00	64.80	64.30	67.05	68.81	*of which:* Currency Outside DMBs	14a
	5.72	4.17	3.89	14.92	12.95	28.20	36.22	28.01	23.51	26.53	12.96	6.07	2.39	1.46	.92	Restricted Deposits	16b
	1.47	1.57	1.90	1.15	.44	.29	1.40	.04	—	.09	.05	—	12.47	.08	.22	Foreign Liabilities	16c
	.07	.06	.08	.02	.14	.09	.03	.01	.01	—	—	88.89	159.57	21.79	—	Central Government Deposits	16d
	8.91	15.92	24.12	19.91	37.59	37.77	35.90	52.48	60.06	61.88	66.82	71.40	84.92	88.78	63.75	Other Items (Net)	17r
End of Period																**Deposit Money Banks**	
	5.65	8.49	8.41	I 4.77	5.26	7.71	13.85	15.38	18.81	19.88	24.91	15.50	35.40	21.25	8.75	Reserves	20
	35.14	41.87	51.31	I 59.59	63.82	67.80	71.09	97.46	131.34	186.70	242.68	272.46	328.95	329.24	281.57	Foreign Assets	21
	54.27	79.56	77.70	I 99.71	99.66	87.29	85.96	104.81	110.62	134.54	86.39	89.11	65.32	149.50	162.35	Claims on Central Government	22a
	219.18	241.08	273.39	I 289.03	323.52	340.62	398.71	453.89	581.82	705.26	791.16	785.40	784.30	631.41	605.08	Claims on Private Sector	22d
	51.39	61.15	71.44	I 86.30	102.64	120.94	135.27	131.61	137.07	164.33	225.84	235.30	169.86	182.54	247.87	Claims on Other Financial Insts.	22f
	269.34	307.13	332.30	I 342.32	379.60	392.57	451.60	473.10	513.10	567.10	567.10	592.33	611.20	636.85	639.32	Demand,Time,Sav.& Fgn Cur.Deps.	25l
	54.74	78.55	102.74	I 120.44	139.57	144.66	160.50	214.66	311.77	420.48	616.56	615.87	545.64	532.70	504.20	Foreign Liabilities	26c
	.13	.15	.17	I .95	1.41	1.22	1.72	1.99	.37	1.10	.89	.53	.38	.34	.43	Central Government Deposits	26d
	6.51	1.82	.19	I 13.07	.62	6.74	5.76	3.02	19.50	27.51	20.25	31.14	82.15	.74	.02	Credit from Monetary Authorities	26g
	9.39	16.77	16.82	I 16.30	23.05	22.42	21.31	38.44	45.57	47.23	38.69	38.80	49.57	40.96	40.16	Credit from Other Financial Insts.	26i
	25.64	27.87	30.13	I 46.55	51.17	56.96	64.78	71.93	89.70	147.25	127.48	119.09	94.89	102.35	121.49	Other Items (Net)	27r
																Monetary Survey	
	−5.34	−17.38	−27.34	I −29.36	−42.27	−32.75	−45.07	−66.95	−126.70	−173.18	−270.16	−243.56	−65.87	−27.85	−44.90	Foreign Assets (Net)	31n
	358.81	425.52	473.38	I 523.44	603.99	626.43	717.62	796.90	934.12	1,107.09	1,177.11	1,176.29	1,025.20	1,054.89	1,119.92	Domestic Credit	32
	87.26	122.51	127.90	I 136.46	165.31	154.11	173.14	198.95	203.60	222.93	138.73	132.00	51.35	226.37	249.43	Claims on Central Govt. (Net)	32an
	219.83	241.52	273.72	I 289.66	324.33	341.38	399.35	454.23	581.96	705.30	791.16	785.40	784.30	631.41	605.08	Claims on Private Sector	32d
	51.72	61.49	71.76	I 86.61	102.91	120.94	135.27	131.61	137.07	164.33	225.84	235.30	169.86	182.54	247.87	Claims on Other Financial Insts.	32f
	5.72	4.17	3.89	14.92	12.95	28.20	36.22	28.01	23.51	26.53	12.96	6.07	2.39	1.46	.92	Restricted Deposits	36b
	44.79	60.74	71.31	I 94.24	123.93	126.05	133.81	174.11	212.38	274.21	255.91	259.62	270.19	308.72	350.89	Other Items (Net)	37r
	302.95	343.24	370.76	I 385.15	425.35	439.64	503.31	527.91	571.88	633.14	638.08	667.04	686.75	716.86	723.21	Money plus Quasi-Money	35l
	29.16	25.64	28.12	I 44.30	45.78	46.65	63.28	87.93	120.22	134.76	152.30	154.42	166.20	173.66	184.13	*Unused Bank Credits*	39b
End of Period																**Money (National Definitions)**	
	307.44	349.22	376.21	402.52	431.52	428.82	474.26	494.05	519.65	571.68	636.46	661.79	682.85	710.06	712.33	*Broad Money*	38n
End of Period																**Other Banking Institutions**	
	2.52	I 4.87	6.86	4.90	8.33	9.99	2.65	4.94	7.56	7.37	I 4.30	.34	.08	.03	.64	Cash	40
	4.14	I 6.77	11.25	15.72	17.48	18.54	26.19	26.43	36.87	43.90	I 48.90	43.70	46.54	37.45	46.15	Foreign Assets	41
	194.19	I 248.70	282.39	331.48	379.14	436.34	555.81	437.97	524.09	604.80	I 1020.15	1,113.06	1,133.15	1,124.98	1,133.60	Claims on Private Sector	42d
	28.66	I 176.20	186.36	208.35	233.07	280.12	363.92	430.60	515.71	616.43	I 786.09	863.74	946.30	1,026.65	1,007.87	Bonds	46ab
	4.57	I 8.96	21.19	25.52	34.66	33.60	38.58	34.59	46.86	57.03	I 37.78	43.07	42.10	26.57	41.49	Foreign Liabilities	46c
	79.70	86.87	93.31	99.65	110.99	127.30	155.06	168.26	194.40	225.27	239.54	262.71	279.97	278.12	247.18	Central Govt. Lending Funds	46f
	51.39	I 61.15	71.44[c]	86.30	102.64	120.94	135.27	131.61	137.07	164.33	I 116.31	150.85	93.48	51.38	66.74	Cred.from Deposit Money Banks	46h
	....	7.36	8.19	9.21	10.11	11.36	12.73	14.46	17.74	19.38	21.34	23.12	47.15	66.72	73.35	Capital Accounts	47a
	−126.65	I −80.20	−80.00	−76.93	−86.52	−108.44	−120.91	−309.48	−343.20	−426.39	I −127.72	−186.39	−228.96	−286.99	−256.27	Other Items (Net)	47r

Sweden

144

		1965	1966	1967	1968	1969	1970	1971	1972	1973	1974	1975	1976	1977	1978	1979
Banking Survey															*Billions of Kronor:*	
Foreign Assets (Net)	51n	5.65	6.00	5.92	5.71	4.06	4.74	6.26	9.25	14.99	13.31	17.86	14.21	16.59	14.02	1.53
Domestic Credit	52	....	....	....	....	....	....	....	....	....	....	....	....	....	....	....
Claims on Central Govt. (Net)	52an	9.50	10.37	11.36	13.03	15.64	16.56	18.84	21.96	24.15	30.58	36.84	33.45	33.47	55.21	70.55
Claims on Private Sector	52d	69.70	78.71	91.14	104.16	115.89	126.46	141.56	159.25	178.97	201.47	229.08	258.63	292.75	327.74	372.55
Liquid Liabilities	55l	64.02	69.95	78.86	87.26	93.13	98.14	108.36	122.29	138.75	152.69	170.21	179.11	195.24	228.08	267.70
Bonds	56ab	....	....	....	....	....	....	....	....	....	....	....	....	....	....	....
Central Govt. Lending Funds	56f	5.82	8.96	11.57	15.51	19.79	24.66	30.55	34.90	40.63	47.30	53.00	59.61	67.28	75.40	82.53
Other Items (Net)	57r	....	....	....	....	....	....	....	....	....	....	....	....	....	....	....
Nonbank Financial Institutions															*Billions of Kronor:*	
Cash	40..l	.35	.36	.42	.53	.62	.78	1.02	1.10	1.20	1.49	1.22	1.28	1.70	1.81	2.70
Foreign Assets	41..l	....	....	....	....	....	....	....	....	....	....	....	....	....	....	....
Claims on Central Government	42a.l	2.95	2.97	2.93	3.14	2.80	3.20	3.01	3.57	4.27	5.49	6.13	7.49	9.04	12.24	15.82
Claims on Private Sector	42d.l	12.52	13.20	13.97	14.48	15.11	15.98	17.00	18.01	19.42	21.66	24.14	27.31	30.93	34.81	39.29
Claims on Other Banking Insts.	42f.l	4.73	5.25	5.92	6.91	8.40	8.99	10.69	12.35	13.76	15.81	18.51	20.34	23.30	27.08	30.49
Interest Rates															*Percent Per Annum*	
Discount Rate (End of Period)	60	5.50	6.00	6.00	5.00	7.00	7.00	5.00	5.00	5.00	7.00	6.00	8.00	8.00	6.50	9.00
Repurchase Rate (End of Period)	60a	....	....	....	....	....	....	....	....	3.34	3.83	9.00	7.83	7.93	9.96	7.16	8.19
Money Market Rate	60b	....	7.31	5.56	6.67	9.00	9.83	5.79	3.06	3.27	7.33	7.83	7.93	9.96	7.16	8.19
Treasury Bill Rate	60c	5.98	6.18	4.80	5.90	7.04	8.44	5.85	3.75	2.79	6.85	7.29	6.50	9.42	6.63	6.79
Deposit Rate (End of Period)	60l	6.25	6.75	6.50	5.50	7.50	7.50	5.50	5.50	5.50	7.50	6.50	8.50	8.50	7.00	9.50
Lending Rate (End of Period)	60p	....	....	....	....	....	9.39	9.39	8.93	8.93	11.19	10.25	12.91	12.79	11.16	13.67
Government Bond Yield	61	6.18	6.57	6.06	6.31	6.98	7.39	7.23	7.29	7.39	7.79	8.79	9.28	9.74	10.09	10.47
Prices, Production, Employment															*Index Numbers (1990=100):*	
Share Prices	62	6	6	5	6	7	6	6	7	8	8	9	10	9	9	9
Forest Industries	62a	6	5	4	4	5	5	4	5	7	8	9	13	10	9	9
Engineering Industries	62b	7	7	7	8	10	8	9	10	11	10	11	12	10	10	9
Prices: Domestic Supply	63	....	....	....	18.5	19.2	20.5	21.0	21.9	24.4	30.4	32.4	35.3	38.7	41.8	46.7
Consumer Prices	64	16	17	18	18	19	20	21	23	24	27	29	32	36	39	42
Wages: Hourly Earnings	65	12	13	14	15	16	18	18	20	22	25	29	33	35	38	41
Industrial Production	66..c	61	63	65	68	73	78	I79	80	86	90	88	86	81	80	86
Industrial Employment	67	117	114	109	106	108	111	110	109	111	117	119	114	110	106	107
International Transactions															*Millions of Kronor:*	
Exports	70	20,542	22,071	23,422	25,403	29,459	35,150	38,224	41,749	53,153	70,514	72,012	80,195	I85,677	98,206	118,210
Wood Pulp	70sl	2,232	2,337	2,274	2,243	2,441	2,964	2,806	2,841	4,003	5,825	5,528	5,498	I4,869	5,190	5,706
Imports, cif	71	1,887	1,975	2,027	2,210	2,548	3,021	3,016	3,218	3,958	6,154	6,033	7,108	I7,518	7,729	10,247
Imports, fob	71.v	1,762	1,844	1,892	2,062	2,371	2,809	2,805	2,993	3,681	5,723	5,610	6,612	I6,992	7,187	10,064
															1990=100	
Volume of Exports	72	I28	30	32	35	40	45	47	51	59	63	I57	59	60	65	70
Volume of Imports	73	I30	31	33	36	41	46	44	46	50	58	I59	62	61	57	66
Export Prices	76	20	20	19	19	I20	22	22	22	26	34	36	38	40	43	48
Imports (Direct Prices)	76.x	17	18	17	17	I19	20	20	21	24	33	34	37	42	45	53
Balance of Payments															*Millions of US Dollars:*	
Goods: Exports f.o.b.	78aa d	....	....	....	....	....	6,750	7,402	8,697	12,097	15,797	17,259	18,287	18,930	21,598	27,377
Goods: Imports f.o.b.	78ab d	....	....	....	....	....	−6,447	−6,508	−7,479	−10,066	−15,405	−16,181	−18,124	−18,654	−19,023	−28,072
Trade Balance	78ac d	....	....	....	....	....	303	894	1,218	2,031	392	1,078	162	275	2,574	−695
Services: Credit	78ad d	....	....	....	....	....	1,353	1,615	1,917	2,482	3,041	3,431	3,624	3,909	4,654	6,619
Services: Debit	78ae d	....	....	....	....	....	−1,776	−1,957	−2,285	−2,775	−3,555	−4,144	−4,517	−5,037	−5,610	−6,471
Balance on Goods and Services	78af d	....	....	....	....	....	−120	552	850	1,738	−122	365	−730	−852	1,619	−546
Income: Credit	78ag d	....	....	....	....	....	153	133	153	261	306	351	492	511	831	1,008
Income: Debit	78ah d	....	....	....	....	....	−145	−156	−183	−259	−318	−404	−665	−962	−1,490	−1,755
Balance on Goods, Serv., & Inc.	78ai d	....	....	....	....	....	−112	529	821	1,740	−133	312	−902	−1,303	959	−1,293
Current Transfers, n.i.e.: Credit	78aj d	....	....	....	....	....	15	14	17	16	29	26	44	40	49	148
Current Transfers: Debit	78ak d	....	....	....	....	....	−157	−178	−252	−305	−426	−647	−744	−857	−1,199	−1,204
Current Account, n.i.e.	78al d	....	....	....	....	....	−253	365	586	1,452	−529	−308	−1,602	−2,120	−191	−2,349
Capital Account, n.i.e.: Credit	78ba d	....	....	....	....	....	....	....	....	....	....	....	....	....	....	....
Capital Account: Debit	78bb d	....	....	....	....	....	−12	−14	−19	−23	−23	−34	−46	−60	−60	−65
Capital Account, n.i.e.	78bc d	....	....	....	....	....	−12	−14	−19	−23	−23	−34	−46	−60	−60	−65
Direct Investment Abroad	78bd d	....	....	....	....	....	−213	−176	−265	−293	−430	−434	−596	−737	−415	−618
Dir. Invest. in Rep. Econ., n.i.e.	78be d	....	....	....	....	....	108	84	65	84	77	80	5	81	70	112
Portfolio Investment Assets	78bf d	....	....	....	....	....	−6	12	—	−23	−11	−4	5	9	17	−23
Portfolio Investment Liab., n.i.e.	78bg d	....	....	....	....	....	54	62	176	103	47	599	712	573	129	−265
Other Investment Assets	78bh d	....	....	....	....	....	−178	−84	−254	−607	−795	−733	−1,049	−1,253	221	−366
Other Investment Liab., n.i.e.	78bi d	....	....	....	....	....	377	226	443	442	1,212	2,153	1,894	2,132	59	839
Financial Account, n.i.e.	78bj d	....	....	....	....	....	143	125	166	−294	99	1,660	971	805	80	−320
Net Errors and Omissions	78ca d	....	....	....	....	....	151	−228	−382	−265	−301	−122	153	300	−523	−133
Overall Balance	78cb d	....	....	....	....	....	29	248	351	870	−753	−1,196	−524	−1,075	−693	−2,868
Reserves and Related Items	79da d	....	....	....	....	....	−29	−248	−351	−870	753	1,196	524	1,075	693	2,868
Reserve Assets	79db d	....	....	....	....	....	−29	−248	−351	−870	753	−1,404	513	−1,101	−654	676
Use of Fund Credit and Loans	79dc d	....	....	....	....	....	—	—	—	—	—	—	—	—	—	—
Liabs.Constit.For.Auth.Reserves	79dd d	....	....	....	....	....	—	—	—	—	—	—	—	—	—	—
Exceptional Financing	79de d	....	....	....	....	....	—	—	—	—	—	208	12	2,176	1,347	2,191

Sweden

1980	1981	1982	1983	1984	1985	1986	1987	1988	1989	1990	1991	1992	1993	1994		
End of Period															**Banking Survey**	
−5.77	−19.57	−37.29	−39.16	−59.45	−47.81	−57.46	−75.10	−136.69	−186.32	−259.04	−242.93	−61.44	−16.98	−40.24	Foreign Assets (Net)	51n
....	....	....	771.41	885.11	949.89	1,146.09	1,113.63	1,333.40	1,557.78	I 1978.41	2,071.73	2,006.50	2,014.73	2,034.50	Domestic Credit	52
87.34	122.94	129.59	I 139.56	170.19	162.17	181.07	208.63	215.79	233.16	I 145.71	149.49	69.36	243.76	278.27	Claims on Central Govt. (Net)	52an
414.02	490.22	556.11	621.14	703.47	777.72	955.16	892.20	1,106.05	1,310.09	I 1811.31	1,898.46	1,917.45	1,756.39	1,738.68	Claims on Private Sector	52d
300.43	338.36	363.90	380.25	417.02	429.65	500.65	522.97	564.32	625.77	I 633.79	666.70	686.67	716.83	722.57	Liquid Liabilities	55l
....	....	....	222.89	241.10	288.27	372.12	446.45	534.89	641.54	I 819.14	894.55	982.56	1,060.59	1,039.71	Bonds	56ab
90.54	98.46	106.07	112.16	121.59	135.75	159.35	170.61	195.72	226.08	239.54	262.71	279.70	278.12	247.18	Central Govt. Lending Funds	56f
....	....	....	16.95	45.95	48.62	57.29	−100.73	−97.80	−121.97	26.91	4.84	−3.86	−57.80	−15.21	Other Items (Net)	57r
End of Period															**Nonbank Financial Institutions**	
2.59	3.91	3.21	3.11	6.17	5.83	7.57	4.54	9.32	7.53	6.94	7.74	9.67	9.08	8.63	Cash	40.. l
....	1.38	2.19	2.88	2.96	3.49	3.71	4.98	6.70	18.98	55.96	74.17	77.98	100.48	102.79	Foreign Assets	41.. l
19.59	24.35	34.57	46.20	57.50	59.67	56.93	48.58	47.51	52.82	50.52	73.97	77.43	130.95	161.20	Claims on Central Government	42a. l
44.92	35.72	37.91	41.60	43.99	51.15	53.83	122.25	150.81	176.69	153.11	155.86	160.00	201.46	215.18	Claims on Private Sector	42d. l
33.55	52.28	55.97	63.71	73.49	88.59	113.52	125.84	159.04	183.06	175.10	204.02	231.03	242.55	188.15	Claims on Other Banking Insts.	42f. l
Percent Per Annum															**Interest Rates**	
10.00	11.00	10.00	8.50	9.50	10.50	7.50	7.50	8.50	10.50	11.50	8.00	I 10.00	5.00	7.00	Discount Rate (End of Period)	60
12.17	14.35	13.29	10.85	11.77	13.94	10.02	9.04	9.70	11.09	12.60	11.28	16.62	8.83	I 7.51	Repurchase Rate (End of Period)	60a
12.17	14.35	13.29	10.85	11.77	13.85	10.15	9.16	10.08	11.52	13.45	11.81	18.42	9.08	7.36	Money Market Rate	60b
11.58	12.54	13.22	12.34	11.93	14.17	9.83	9.39	10.08	11.50	13.66	11.59	12.85	8.35	7.40	Treasury Bill Rate	60c
11.25	11.75	11.25	9.75	10.75	12.00	9.00	8.75	9.50	I 9.16	9.93	7.96	I 7.80	5.10	4.91	Deposit Rate (End of Period)	60l
15.18	16.73	16.52	14.91	16.00	16.89	I 12.57	12.65	13.29	14.81	16.69	16.05	I 15.20	11.40	10.64	Lending Rate (End of Period)	60p
11.74	13.49	13.04	12.30	12.28	13.09	10.26	I 11.68	11.35	11.18	13.08	10.69	10.02	8.54	I 9.41	Government Bond Yield	61
Period Averages															**Prices, Production, Employment**	
10	15	18	35	39	36	59	70	78	108	100	94	80	106	133	Share Prices	62
10	15	18	41	48	43	75	97	113	132	100	108	93	115	139	Forest Industries	62a
9	14	18	40	42	39	63	62	66	101	100	96	91	132	174	Engineering Industries	62b
53.3	59.3	66.9	74.4	80.1	84.3	81.9	84.2	88.7	95.5	100.0	101.7	101.0	108.1	I 112.3	Prices: Domestic Supply	63
I 48	54	59	64	69	74	77	80	85	91	100	109	112	117	120	Consumer Prices	64
44	50	53	56	62	67	71	77	83	91	100	105	110	113	118	Wages: Hourly Earnings	65
85	84	83	86	92	95	95	98	99	103	I 100	95	93	94	104	Industrial Production	66.. c
107	103	99	99	100	102	103	101	102	102	100	92	84	77	76	Industrial Employment	67
Millions of Kronor															**International Transactions**	
130,747	144,876	168,134	210,516	242,809	260,500	265,104	281,333	305,040	332,570	339,860	332,800	326,010	97,075	77,120	Exports	70
6,075	6,807	6,444	8,441	11,328	9,627	8,795	10,450	12,105	13,336	11,557	9,341	....	....	....	Wood Pulp	70sl
11,777	12,170	14,494	16,697	18,214	20,384	19,373	21,449	23,272	26,302	26,698	25,105	24,209	27,708	33,118	Imports, cif	71
11,600	11,962	14,098	16,304	17,801	19,924	18,938	20,967	22,749	25,710	26,098	24,541	23,665	27,085	32,373	Imports, fob	71.v
1990=100																
68	69	71	I 80	86	89	91	95	97	100	100	98	99	I 107	114	Volume of Exports	72
67	63	67	I 69	72	79	82	88	92	99	100	93	95	I 97	108	Volume of Imports	73
54	59	66	73	79	82	83	86	90	97	100	101	98	108	113	Export Prices	76
62	69	78	89	93	96	86	88	91	97	100	101	99	112	117	Imports (Direct Prices)	76.x
Minus Sign Indicates Debit															**Balance of Payments**	
30,662	28,389	26,575	27,204	29,123	30,173	36,845	44,013	49,367	51,071	56,835	54,543	55,366	49,347	60,146	Goods: Exports f.o.b.	78aa d
−32,860	−28,226	−26,797	−25,303	−25,701	−27,788	−31,811	−39,528	−44,487	−47,056	−53,433	−48,184	−48,643	−41,679	−50,563	Goods: Imports f.o.b.	78ab d
−2,198	163	−222	1,901	3,422	2,385	5,035	4,485	4,880	4,015	3,402	6,359	6,723	7,669	9,583	Trade Balance	78ac d
7,489	7,035	6,521	6,292	6,293	6,121	6,664	8,946	10,420	11,361	13,720	14,731	16,207	12,587	13,645	Services: Credit	78ad d
−7,018	−6,863	−6,909	−6,224	−6,334	−6,681	−8,463	−10,634	−12,662	−14,393	−17,077	−17,368	−19,097	−13,371	−14,472	Services: Debit	78ae d
−1,727	336	−610	1,968	3,381	1,825	3,236	2,798	2,637	982	45	3,722	3,833	6,885	8,757	Balance on Goods and Services	78af d
1,238	1,682	2,431	2,125	2,312	2,584	3,142	4,372	5,277	6,970	9,694	9,440	8,150	7,134	10,112	Income: Credit	78ag d
−2,617	−3,790	−4,159	−3,962	−4,201	−4,561	−5,187	−5,935	−7,070	−9,306	−14,141	−15,808	−18,162	−16,290	−16,203	Income: Debit	78ah d
−3,107	−1,773	−2,338	131	1,492	−152	1,191	1,234	844	−1,353	−4,403	−2,646	−6,179	−2,271	2,665	Balance on Goods, Serv., & Inc.	78ai d
92	92	81	124	100	117	111	267	382	297	387	395	404	456	542	Current Transfers, n.i.e.: Credit	78aj d
−1,317	−1,097	−1,028	−980	−856	−975	−1,269	−1,523	−1,760	−2,048	−2,323	−2,380	−3,015	−2,264	−2,380	Current Transfers: Debit	78ak d
−4,331	−2,778	−3,285	−725	736	−1,010	32	−21	−534	−3,104	−6,338	−4,632	−8,790	−4,078	826	Current Account, n.i.e.	78al d
—	—	—	1	—	—	—	38	29	39	39	38	38	37	37	Capital Account, n.i.e.: Credit	78ba d
−73	−69	−80	−82	−171	−221	−182	−177	−263	−335	−393	−101	−33	−16	−14	Capital Account: Debit	78bb d
−73	−69	−80	−81	−171	−221	−182	−139	−234	−296	−354	−63	5	21	22	Capital Account, n.i.e.	78bc d
−625	−825	−1,212	−1,458	−1,497	−1,805	−3,963	−4,780	−7,471	−10,198	−14,573	−7,254	−251	−1,417	−6,302	Direct Investment Abroad	78bd d
251	181	355	226	290	393	1,083	639	1,673	1,811	1,979	6,345	−94	3,773	6,699	Dir. Invest. in Rep. Econ., n.i.e.	78be d
−35	14	−34	−60	3	−47	−153	−327	−686	−4,477	−3,645	−2,313	−1,580	−93	−1,921	Portfolio Investment Assets	78bf d
−231	473	180	749	219	609	—	−738	−673	3,227	6,112	8,859	2,561	1,383	−203	Portfolio Investment Liab., n.i.e.	78bg d
−183	−1,130	−1,744	−1,903	−939	−219	−875	−2,274	−2,133	−4,831	−9,620	−943	1,725	1,162	−2,390	Other Investment Assets	78bh d
1,277	1,940	1,123	−2,276	−3,888	−1,823	4,168	8,251	12,187	24,394	39,064	−6,026	8,109	6,733	10,167	Other Investment Liab., n.i.e.	78bi d
454	652	−1,333	−4,722	−5,812	−2,893	259	770	2,897	9,927	19,318	−1,332	10,469	11,541	6,049	Financial Account, n.i.e.	78bj d
−1,447	−596	408	47	−586	−527	68	153	−1,190	−5,303	−5,130	6,159	5,269	−4,955	−4,566	Net Errors and Omissions	78ca d
−5,398	−2,790	−4,291	−5,481	−5,834	−4,651	177	762	938	1,223	7,495	133	6,952	2,530	2,331	Overall Balance	78cb d
5,398	2,790	4,291	5,481	5,834	4,651	−177	−762	−938	−1,223	−7,495	−133	−6,952	−2,530	−2,331	Reserves and Related Items	79da d
105	−203	41	−686	43	−1,551	−177	−762	−938	−1,223	−7,495	−133	−6,952	−2,530	−2,331	Reserve Assets	79db d
—	—	—	—	—	—	—	—	—	—	—	—	—	—	—	Use of Fund Credit and Loans	79dc d
—	—	—	—	—	—	—	—	—	—	—	—	—	—	—	Liabs.Constit.For.Auth.Reserves	79dd d
5,292	2,994	4,249	6,167	5,790	6,201	—	—	—	—	—	—	—	—	—	Exceptional Financing	79de d

Sweden

144

		1965	1966	1967	1968	1969	1970	1971	1972	1973	1974	1975	1976	1977	1978	1979
Government Finance																*Billions of Kronor:*
Deficit (-) or Surplus	80	.02	ℐ1.74	1.01	2.25	.88	ℐ–3.10	–2.44	–2.47	–3.21	–7.98	–7.55	–1.17	–6.06	–20.45	–33.22
Revenue	81	26.58	ℐ37.59	41.27	46.12	51.25	ℐ51.05	58.37	66.10	70.08	78.77	93.35	122.49	140.24	153.85	165.53
Grants Received	81z	....	....	....	....	....	ℐ.24	.27	.37	.42	.38	.37	.39	.53	.80	1.04
Expenditure	82	24.33	ℐ32.55	37.70	40.99	45.72	ℐ43.86	49.10	56.93	63.39	74.78	88.57	108.79	131.66	156.38	182.76
Lending Minus Repayments	83	2.23	ℐ3.30	2.56	2.88	4.65	ℐ10.53	11.98	12.01	10.32	12.35	12.70	15.26	15.17	18.72	17.03
Financing																
Domestic	84a	....	....	....	....	....	ℐ3.17	2.44	2.47	3.21	7.95	7.47	1.09	1.19	14.31	29.55
Foreign	85a	....	....	....	....	....	ℐ–.07	—	—	—	.03	.08	.08	4.87	6.14	3.67
Financing																
Net Borrowing	84	....	ℐ1.77	2.20	3.10	2.53	....	....	....	....	....	....	....	....	....	....
Other Financing	86c	.24	ℐ–2.98	–3.42	–4.94	–3.44	....	....	....	....	....	....	....	....	....	....
Use of Cash Balances	87	—	ℐ–.53	.21	–.41	.02	....	....	....	....	....	....	....	....	....	....
Total Debt	88	19.73	21.36	23.90	27.31	30.88	ℐ27.85	29.92	32.39	36.00	44.09	52.50	54.58	65.00	83.31	112.20
Debt: Domestic	88a	....	....	....	....	....	ℐ27.85	29.92	32.39	36.00	44.05	52.39	54.39	59.93	72.11	97.32
Other Levels of Government	88aa	....	....	....	....	....	....	....	....	....	....	2.48	3.17	3.80	3.73	4.51
Monetary Authorities	88ab	....	....	....	....	....	....	....	....	....	....	18.46	11.55	13.15	12.69	15.16
Deposit Money Banks	88ac	....	....	....	....	....	....	....	....	....	....	13.71	17.91	16.49	24.44	37.28
Other Domestic	88ad	....	....	....	....	....	....	....	....	....	....	17.74	21.76	26.49	31.25	40.37
Debt: Foreign	89a	....	....	....	....	....	ℐ—	—	—	—	.04	.11	.19	5.07	11.20	14.88
Intragovernmental Debt	88s	1.77	1.84	1.88	2.10	2.05	ℐ3.11	3.49	4.83	7.20	8.59	11.18	14.17	17.35	21.92	26.89
Total Debt	88	19.73	21.36	23.90	27.31	30.88	ℐ27.85	29.92	32.39	36.00	44.09	52.50	54.58	65.00	83.31	112.20
Debt: Kronor	88b	19.60	21.23	23.77	27.18	30.88	....	....	....	....	....	....	....	....	....	....
Held By: Bank of Sweden	88ba	5.52	6.40	6.73	7.76	9.27	....	....	....	....	....	....	....	....	....	....
Commercial Banks	88bb	3.59	3.94	4.81	5.34	6.58	....	....	....	....	....	....	....	....	....	....
Other Financial Inst.	88bc	6.19	6.30	7.31	8.41	8.88	....	....	....	....	....	....	....	....	....	....
Local Governments	88bd	.31	.31	.23	.23	.21	....	....	....	....	....	....	....	....	....	....
Bus. & Individuals	88be	3.88	4.17	4.63	5.36	5.85	....	....	....	....	....	....	....	....	....	....
Nonresidents	88bf	.11	.11	.06	.08	.09	....	....	....	....	....	....	....	....	....	....
Intragovernmental Debt	88s	1.77	1.84	1.88	2.10	2.05	ℐ3.11	3.49	4.83	7.20	8.59	11.18	14.17	17.35	21.92	26.89
Debt: Foreign Currency	89b	.13	.13	.13	.13	—	....	....	....	....	....	....	....	....	....	....
National Accounts																*Billions of Kronor*
Exports of Goods & Services	90c	24.62	26.24	28.07	30.43	35.01	41.52	45.32	49.28	62.13	82.49	84.68	94.07	101.33	116.40	140.57
Government Consumption	91f	20.00	23.20	26.07	28.99	31.73	36.47	41.21	45.50	50.98	59.01	70.69	83.19	101.14	116.89	132.72
Gross Fixed Capital Formation	93e	27.40	29.80	32.48	33.17	34.90	38.11	39.72	44.44	48.22	55.24	59.99	67.22	76.78	78.52	89.76
Increase/Decrease(-) in Stocks	93i	2.76	1.38	.25	.44	2.00	5.27	1.98	–.18	–1.19	6.07	10.01	7.87	–2.40	–7.42	.96
Private Consumption	96f	62.62	68.01	73.31	77.64	83.78	91.99	98.96	108.82	119.92	136.86	156.07	180.49	197.75	219.26	242.31
Imports of Goods & Services	98c	–25.59	–27.09	–28.14	–30.70	–35.59	–42.48	–43.17	–46.21	–55.88	–84.45	–85.26	–99.77	–107.51	–112.17	–145.20
Gross Domestic Product	99b	111.66	121.62	132.07	140.02	152.13	172.23	186.22	203.76	226.74	256.13	300.79	340.20	370.02	412.45	462.31
Net Factor Inc/Pmts(-) Abroad	98.n	.16	.12	.03	–.04	–.11	–.06	.18	.36	.77	.71	.81	.46	–.69	–1.38	–1.27
Gross Nat'l Expenditure = GNP	99a	111.82	121.74	132.10	139.99	152.02	172.17	186.40	204.12	227.51	256.84	301.59	340.66	369.33	413.55	463.82
Nat'l Income, Market Prices	99e	101.96	110.74	119.85	127.31	138.98	154.76	165.17	178.86	204.80	230.40	271.10	305.50	328.80	367.60	412.04
Gross Dom. Prod. 1990 Prices	99b.p	745.65	762.06	788.10	816.11	857.18	ℐ913.49	922.12	943.22	980.65	1,012.01	1,037.85	1,048.83	1,032.09	1,050.17	1,090.49
GDP Deflator (1990=100)	99bi p	15.0	16.0	16.8	17.2	17.7	18.9	20.2	21.6	23.1	25.3	29.0	32.4	35.9	39.3	42.4
																Millions:
Population	99z	7.73	7.81	7.87	7.91	7.97	8.04	8.10	8.12	8.14	8.16	8.19	8.22	8.25	8.28	8.29

International Liquidity: ℐ *Lines 7a.d, 7b.d, 7e.d,* and *7f.d:* The banks' positions with their branches abroad are included from 1990.
Deposit Money Banks: ℐ Beginning in 1983, data reflect improved classification of accounts.
Monetary Survey: ℐ See note to section 20.
Interest Rates: ℐ *Discount Rate (End of Period):* ℐ Before March 1992, rate charged by the Riksbank to commercial banks on short-term loans. Beginning in March 1992, the official discount rate is calculated on a quarterly basis as a rounded value of the average of long-term bond rates minus 2.5 percent.
Deposit Rate: ℐ Before December 1992, average quarterly rate on savings deposits with the deposit money banks. Beginning in December 1992, average deposit rate of the six largest banks, at quarter end.
Lending Rate: ℐ Before December 1992, deposit money banks' average lending rate to households at quarter end. Beginning in December 1992, average rate of the six largest banks' loans to households, at quarter end.
International Transactions: ℐ Beginning in January 1977, data refer to actual imports and exports of the period. Prior to January 1977, data refer to exports and imports for which customs documents were processed by the Customs Office during the period.
Government Finance: ℐ Beginning in 1966, coverage has been expanded to include social security funds. ℐ Beginning in 1970, data are as reported in the *Government Finance Statistics Yearbook* and cover consolidated central government. However, data on outstanding debt relate to the budgetary central government. Beginning in 1970, data relate to a fiscal year different from calendar year.

Sweden

144

1980	1981	1982	1983	1984	1985	1986	1987	1988	1989	1990	1991	1992	1993	1994	Government Finance	
Year Ending June 30																
-43.03	-51.52	-52.59	-68.68	-62.88	-61.51	-57.17	4.08	8.10	6.69	8.25	-14.92	-33.01	-169.27	....	Deficit (-) or Surplus	80
185.75	212.65	240.08	272.38	309.76	351.83	377.72	440.30	476.09	532.20	601.67	624.91	625.74	561.36	....	Revenue	81
1.00	1.11	1.33	—	—	—	—	—	—	—	—	—	—	—	....	Grants Received	81z
208.79	245.39	273.44	320.73	348.76	388.32	406.96	423.32	445.98	484.45	554.83	615.52	665.96	747.22	....	Expenditure	82
20.99	19.89	20.56	20.33	23.88	25.02	27.93	12.90	22.01	41.06	38.59	24.31	-7.21	-16.59	....	Lending Minus Repayments	83
															Financing	
25.81	36.90	36.77	49.79	41.36	25.39	75.75	-11.85	10.04	-.17	-7.81	5.45	29.79	-76.65	....	Domestic	84a
17.22	14.62	15.82	18.88	21.52	36.12	-18.58	7.77	-18.14	-6.52	-.44	9.47	3.22	245.92	....	Foreign	85a
															Financing	
....	....	....	....	....	....	....	....	....	....	....	....	....	....	....	Net Borrowing	84
....	....	....	....	....	....	....	....	....	....	....	....	....	....	....	Other Financing	86c
....	....	....	....	....	....	....	....	....	....	....	....	....	....	....	Use of Cash Balances	87
159.57	213.21	272.80	352.52	414.48	480.48	529.89	532.53	510.33	516.75	506.15	532.91	607.32	890.66	1,007.60	Total Debt	88
127.47	166.49	210.26	271.09	311.53	341.41	409.40	404.27	400.21	413.15	402.99	411.35	471.33	441.02	494.13	Debt: Domestic	88a
4.51	5.63	7.10	17.79	15.03	14.38	10.99	8.41	8.90	13.32	28.35	29.75	15.39	8.38	—	Other Levels of Government	88aa
26.05	36.64	58.00	39.52	45.78	45.52	90.29	86.45	68.65	81.95	79.13	53.71	32.98	—	78.12	Monetary Authorities	88ab
44.54	61.39	72.79	96.69	92.37	88.74	60.65	58.49	45.45	41.02	46.86	48.80	52.23	61.27	77.56	Deposit Money Banks	88ac
52.37	62.83	72.37	117.09	158.35	192.77	247.47	250.92	277.21	276.86	248.65	279.09	370.73	371.37	338.45	Other Domestic	88ad
32.10	46.72	62.54	81.43	102.95	139.07	120.49	128.26	110.12	103.60	103.16	121.56	135.99	449.64	513.47	Debt: Foreign	89a
32.52	39.76	46.89	54.80	68.16	71.98	66.11	76.72	87.29	72.96	76.30	93.79	103.66	135.97	171.05	Intragovernmental Debt	88s
159.57	213.21	272.80	352.52	414.48	480.48	529.89	532.53	510.33	516.75	506.15	532.91	607.32	890.66	1,007.60	Total Debt	88
															Debt: Kronor	88b
....	....	....	....	....	....	....	....	....	....	....	....	....	....	....	Held By: Bank of Sweden	88ba
....	....	....	....	....	....	....	....	....	....	....	....	....	....	....	Commercial Banks	88bb
....	....	....	....	....	....	....	....	....	....	....	....	....	....	....	Other Financial Inst.	88bc
....	....	....	....	....	....	....	....	....	....	....	....	....	....	....	Local Governments	88bd
....	....	....	....	....	....	....	....	....	....	....	....	....	....	....	Bus. & Individuals	88be
....	....	....	....	....	....	....	....	....	....	....	....	....	....	....	Nonresidents	88bf
32.52	39.76	46.89	54.80	68.16	71.98	66.11	76.72	87.29	72.96	76.30	93.79	103.66	135.97	171.05	Intragovernmental Debt	88s
....	....	....	....	....	....	....	....	....	....	....	....	....	....	....	Debt: Foreign Currency	89b
															National Accounts	
Billions of Kronor																
156.47	174.11	204.76	253.26	289.82	305.87	311.13	332.48	359.69	394.47	406.83	404.18	401.59	473.09	556.75	Exports of Goods & Services	90c
153.76	170.16	185.67	203.51	221.06	239.16	257.25	269.88	286.81	322.63	372.13	394.39	400.28	401.70	413.51	Government Consumption	91f
106.43	109.40	118.09	132.30	148.79	166.98	175.50	197.95	225.11	271.00	292.53	280.37	244.60	205.63	208.24	Gross Fixed Capital Formation	93e
5.92	-4.07	-6.29	-10.26	-7.76	-.48	-5.84	-4.76	-3.56	-.49	-2.48	-21.17	-6.66	-11.63	10.53	Increase/Decrease(-) in Stocks	93i
273.33	305.55	340.04	369.44	403.78	443.67	487.33	537.87	584.35	632.74	692.67	771.31	777.32	792.08	820.94	Private Consumption	96f
-166.55	-175.30	-208.23	-238.14	-260.70	-291.19	-281.03	-313.31	-341.35	-387.75	-401.80	-381.76	-377.64	-420.49	-492.30	Imports of Goods & Services	98c
528.26	578.91	633.68	709.85	794.30	866.60	947.26	1,023.60	1,114.50	1,232.60	1,359.88	1,447.33	1,441.72	1,442.18	1,516.95	Gross Domestic Product	99b
-4.02	-8.65	-13.29	-16.59	-19.81	-21.09	-20.02	-16.47	-21.08	-28.86	-40.62	-41.44	-53.04	-57.01	....	Net Factor Inc/Pmts(-) Abroad	98.n
524.23	570.26	620.40	693.26	774.49	844.70	925.57	1,003.08	1,089.39	1,198.49	1,310.55	1,393.64	1,391.30	1,400.49	....	Gross Nat'l Expenditure = GNP	99a
464.81	503.79	545.72	608.93	682.74	745.23	818.35	886.61	961.56	1,203.75	1,319.26	1,405.89	1,388.69	1,385.17	....	Nat'l Income, Market Prices	99e
Ƚ1108.69	1,109.06	1,121.37	1,141.69	1,187.15	1,213.52	1,240.44	1,275.77	1,310.45	1,341.60	1,359.88	Ƚ1337.25	1,318.23	1,284.40	1,312.28	Gross Dom. Prod. 1990 Prices	99b.*p*
47.6	52.2	56.5	62.2	66.9	71.4	76.4	80.2	85.0	91.9	100.0	108.2	109.4	112.3	115.6	GDP Deflator (1990=100)	99bi *p*
Midyear Estimates																
8.31	8.32	8.33	8.33	8.34	8.36	8.38	8.41	8.46	8.53	8.59	8.64	8.69	8.75	....	Population	99z

Switzerland

146		1965	1966	1967	1968	1969	1970	1971	1972	1973	1974	1975	1976	1977	1978	1979
Exchange Rates																*Francs per SDR:*
Market Rate	aa	4.3180	4.3270	4.3250	4.3020	4.3180	4.3160	4.2506	4.0975	3.9134	3.1098	3.0671	2.8459	2.4294	2.1105	2.0814
																Francs per US Dollar:
Market Rate	ae	4.3180	4.3270	4.3250	4.3020	4.3180	4.3160	3.9150	3.7740	3.2440	2.5400	2.6200	2.4495	2.0000	1.6200	1.5800
Market Rate	rf	4.3730	4.3730	4.3730	4.3730	4.3730	4.3730	4.1339	3.8193	3.1648	2.9793	2.5813	2.4996	2.4035	1.7880	1.6627
																Index Numbers (1990=100):
Market Rate	ahx	31.9	32.0	31.9	32.0	32.1	32.1	33.7	36.2	43.9	46.6	53.6	55.3	57.7	77.9	83.2
Nominal Effective Exchange Rate	neu	41.7	41.7	41.8	42.5	42.6	41.9	43.3	43.5	47.4	51.3	57.2	63.8	65.0	79.1	80.8
Real Effective Exchange Rate	reu	....	....	....	....	....	....	....	....	....	....	97.0	99.1	93.1	106.7	101.2
Fund Position																*Millions of SDRs:*
Quota	2f.s	....	....	....	....	....	....	....	....	....	....	....	....	....	....	....
SDRs	1b.s	....	....	....	....	....	....	....	....	....	....	—	—	—	—	—
Reserve Position in the Fund	1c.s	....	....	....	....	....	....	....	....	....	....	81	250	391	308	207
of which: Outstg.Fund Borrowing	2c	....	....	....	....	....	....	....	....	....	....	81	250	391	308	207
International Liquidity													*Millions of US Dollars Unless Otherwise Indicated:*				
Total Reserves minus Gold	1l.d	402	704	607	1,669	1,783	2,401	3,808	4,399	5,007	5,446	7,019	9,606	10,289	17,763	16,435
SDRs	1b.d	....	....	....	....	....	....	....	....	....	....	—	—	—	—	—
Reserve Position in the Fund	1c.d	....	....	....	....	....	....	....	....	....	....	95	290	475	402	273
Foreign Exchange	1d.d	402	704	607	1,669	1,783	2,401	3,808	4,399	5,007	5,446	6,924	9,316	9,814	17,361	16,162
Gold (Million Fine Troy Ounces)	1ad	86.91	81.17	88.26	74.97	75.49	78.03	83.11	83.11	83.20	83.20	83.20	83.28	83.28	83.28	83.28
Gold (National Valuation)	1and	3,010	2,812	3,057	2,597	2,615	2,703	3,093	3,094	3,666	4,682	4,539	4,860	5,952	7,348	7,534
Monetary Authorities: Other Liab.	4..d	15	13	19	25	21	14	34	91	115	78	62	111	90	240	1,409
Deposit Money Banks: Assets	7a.d	4,242	4,974	6,469	8,736	12,667	16,199	23,924	25,521	29,992	I23,778	27,533	32,072	40,986	54,407	64,946
of which: Claims on Nonbanks	7add	1,864	2,198	2,802	3,582	4,842	5,682	8,655	8,914	11,581	I10,213	9,836	13,014	16,990	23,509	32,987
Deposit Money Banks: Liabilities	7b.d	4,315	4,630	6,058	7,703	11,224	13,890	20,189	20,987	24,958	I19,954	19,513	23,396	28,249	38,779	44,009
of which: Liab. to Nonbanks	7bdd	3,055	3,266	3,774	4,819	6,907	8,372	11,586	10,369	11,882	I8,416	8,418	9,416	11,689	14,871	15,648
Trustee Accounts: Assets	7k.d	....	....	....	....	....	....	9,375	8,203	12,238	18,156	20,107	23,404	29,749	37,120	53,326
Liabilities	7m.d	....	....	....	....	....	....	8,516	7,422	9,988	14,600	17,103	20,330	25,952	32,014	44,226
Monetary Authorities																*Billions of Francs:*
Foreign Assets	11	14.90	15.33	16.00	18.53	19.10	22.14	26.50	28.51	29.03	28.87	32.00	37.55	36.37	42.92	38.29
Claims on Central Government	12a	.77	.92	.95	1.17	1.60	1.67	1.30	1.34	.98	1.48	1.23	1.49	1.91	1.49	2.21
Claims on Deposit Money Banks	12e	.24	.33	.30	.54	.98	.63	.18	1.35	1.74	3.08	2.05	1.24	1.62	.47	2.75
Reserve Money	14	15.50	15.91	16.57	19.19	20.50	23.02	27.24	29.42	30.57	31.64	32.32	34.69	35.99	42.29	38.97
of which: Currency Outside DMBs	14a	10.71	11.37	12.09	13.03	13.83	14.54	15.60	17.82	19.08	20.33	20.12	20.78	21.49	23.64	24.99
Central Government Deposits	16d	.14	.39	.25	.51	.49	.57	.99	1.33	.39	.63	1.61	3.69	2.48	4.04	2.24
Other Items (Net)	17r	.38	.40	.52	.67	.84	.95	−.17	.55	.90	1.34	1.49	1.93	1.50	−1.33	2.12
Deposit Money Banks																*Billions of Francs:*
Reserves	20	6.17	6.12	7.12	9.10	9.80	10.70	13.61	11.92	10.94	I11.26	12.98	14.34	15.53	17.04	15.80
Foreign Assets	21	18.55	21.75	28.29	38.20	55.39	70.84	91.87	98.00	97.29	I60.40	72.14	78.56	81.97	88.14	102.61
Claims on Central Government	22a	5.50	6.01	6.58	7.19	7.92	8.20	10.86	12.60	13.32	I6.94	7.44	7.70	7.85	7.68	8.05
Claims on Private Sector	22d	64.70	69.05	74.27	81.14	89.38	98.72	106.93	116.48	126.30	I118.05	126.25	137.41	148.41	164.12	175.47
Demand Deposits	24	12.12	11.94	12.53	14.33	13.47	15.84	20.48	21.19	20.28	I17.81	19.63	22.97	24.19	33.30	27.93
Time and Savings Deposits	25	37.66	41.53	44.98	50.19	58.28	64.05	68.08	78.02	85.43	I71.69	78.61	84.56	93.37	97.30	114.15
Bonds	26ab	18.46	19.83	22.70	25.58	27.89	30.00	34.32	36.01	36.23	I21.87	28.07	31.23	33.62	35.23	34.05
Foreign Liabilities	26c	18.87	20.25	26.49	33.68	49.08	60.74	77.53	80.59	80.96	I50.68	51.12	57.31	56.50	62.82	69.54
Other Items (Net)	27r	7.81	9.39	9.55	11.84	13.78	17.83	22.87	23.21	24.97	I34.60	41.38	41.95	46.08	48.33	56.27
Post Office: Checking Deposits	24..i	3.81	4.07	4.43	4.89	5.09	5.51	6.31	7.36	8.57	7.59	7.96	9.52	8.04	9.40	12.19
Monetary Survey																*Billions of Francs:*
Foreign Assets (Net)	31n	14.52	16.78	17.71	22.94	25.32	32.17	40.71	45.57	44.98	I38.38	52.85	58.53	61.66	67.84	69.15
Domestic Credit	32	74.65	79.67	85.97	93.89	103.50	113.69	124.68	136.40	148.71	I133.42	141.26	152.44	163.73	178.65	195.68
Claims on Central Govt. (Net)	32an	9.95	10.62	11.71	12.75	14.12	14.97	17.75	19.92	22.41	I15.37	15.01	15.02	15.33	14.53	20.21
Claims on Private Sector	32d	64.70	69.05	74.27	81.14	89.38	98.72	106.93	116.48	126.30	I118.05	126.25	137.41	148.41	164.12	175.47
Money	34	26.01	26.99	28.99	32.59	36.39	40.38	47.51	50.09	49.68	I48.03	50.11	55.76	56.43	69.69	68.40
Quasi-Money	35	37.66	41.53	44.98	50.19	58.28	64.05	68.08	78.02	85.43	I71.69	78.61	84.56	93.37	97.30	114.15
Bonds	36ab	18.46	19.83	22.70	25.58	27.89	30.00	34.32	36.01	36.23	I21.87	28.07	31.23	33.62	35.23	34.05
Other Items (Net)	37r	7.03	8.10	7.01	8.46	6.27	11.43	15.49	17.87	22.36	I30.21	37.33	39.22	41.98	44.28	48.24
Money plus Quasi-Money	35l	63.67	68.52	73.97	82.78	94.67	104.43	115.59	128.11	135.11	I117.64	128.72	140.52	149.80	166.99	182.55
Other Banking Institutions																*Billions of Francs:*
Foreign Assets	41.x	5.56	8.37	9.89	12.93	25.04	35.94	36.00	31.50	39.70	46.12	52.68	57.33	59.50	60.13	84.26
Domestic Liabilities	45.x	.58	.84	.97	1.27	2.48	10.31	3.30	3.00	7.30	9.03	7.87	7.53	7.59	8.27	14.38
Foreign Liabilities	46c.x	4.98	7.53	8.92	11.66	22.56	25.63	32.70	28.50	32.40	37.09	44.81	49.80	51.90	51.86	69.88
Nonbank Financial Institutions																*Billions of Francs:*
Claims on Central Government	42a.s	.50	.47	.45	.45	.44	.43	.40	.40	.38	.41	.46	.66	.67	.68	.67
Claims on Priv.Sec.& Local Govt.	42d.s	8.33	9.02	9.76	10.73	11.73	12.86	13.98	15.39	16.73	17.79	19.74	22.06	24.23	26.60	29.73
Real Estate	42h.s	2.04	2.26	2.51	2.81	3.17	3.56	4.04	4.52	5.03	5.38	5.69	5.94	6.28	6.88	7.60
Incr.in Total Assets(Within Per.)	49z.s	.89	.96	1.03	1.24	1.42	1.53	1.75	1.97	1.93	1.63	2.42	2.84	2.58	3.21	4.13
Liquid Liabilities	55l	57.65	63.25	68.70	77.94	93.27	106.11	115.87	125.11	132.08	I126.67	134.36	145.42	154.80	172.08	193.78
Interest Rates																*Percent Per Annum*
Discount Rate *(End of Period)*	60	2.50	3.50	3.00	3.00	3.75	3.75	3.75	3.75	4.50	5.50	3.00	2.00	1.50	1.00	2.00
Money Market Rate	60b	....	....	....	....	6.25	6.75	1.15	2.69	3.64	5.97	2.75	1.51	2.47	.66	I1.00
Treasury Bill Rate	60c	....	....	....	....	....	....	....	....	....	....	....	....	....	....	....
Deposit Rate	60l	....	....	....	....	....	....	....	....	....	....	....	....	....	....	....
Lending Rate	60p	....	....	....	....	....	....	....	....	....	....	....	....	....	....	....
Government Bond Yield	61	3.95	4.16	4.61	4.37	4.90	5.82	5.27	4.97	5.60	7.15	6.44	4.99	4.05	3.33	3.45

Switzerland

146

1980	1981	1982	1983	1984	1985	1986	1987	1988	1989	1990	1991	1992	1993	1994		
															Exchange Rates	
End of Period																
2.2492	2.0934	2.2002	2.2818	2.5338	2.2809	1.9858	1.8130	2.0239	2.0323	1.8431	1.9389	2.0020	2.0322	1.9146	Market Rate	aa
End of Period (ae)			*Period Average (rf)*													
1.7635	1.7985	1.9945	2.1795	2.5850	2.0765	1.6235	1.2780	1.5040	1.5465	1.2955	1.3555	1.4560	1.4795	1.3115	Market Rate	ae
1.6757	1.9642	2.0303	2.0991	2.3497	2.4571	1.7989	1.4912	1.4633	1.6359	1.3892	1.4340	1.4062	1.4776	1.3677	Market Rate	rf
Period Averages																
82.6	70.7	68.3	65.9	59.0	56.8	77.3	92.9	94.8	84.6	100.0	96.8	98.7	93.6	101.4	Market Rate	ahx
79.0	81.1	87.7	91.8	90.9	90.2	96.9	101.1	100.2	95.0	100.0	98.5	96.6	99.8	106.3	Nominal Effective Exchange Rate	neu
109.9	108.9	112.1	114.4	108.5	103.2	108.2	109.5	106.4	98.0	100.0	97.6	93.7	92.1	....	Real Effective Exchange Rate	reu
End of Period															**Fund Position**	
....	....	....	....	....	....	....	....	....	....	....	....	2,470	2,470	2,470	Quota	2f.s
5	—	4	13	9	3	....	10	15	4	1	2	12	113	162	SDRs	1b.s
252	397	467	636	593	501	370	212	102	32	—	—	581	605	643	Reserve Position in the Fund	1c.s
252	397	467	636	593	501	370	212	102	32	—	—	—	—	—	*of which*: Outstg.Fund Borrowing	2c
End of Period															**International Liquidity**	
15,656	13,979	15,460	15,034	15,296	18,016	21,786	27,476	24,203	25,276	29,223	29,004	33,255	32,635	34,729	Total Reserves minus Gold	1l.d
6	....	4	13	9	3	....	14	20	5	2	2	16	155	236	SDRs	1b.d
322	462	515	666	581	550	452	300	137	42	—	—	799	830	939	Reserve Position in the Fund	1c.d
15,328	13,517	14,941	14,355	14,706	17,463	21,334	27,162	24,045	25,230	29,221	29,002	32,440	31,650	33,554	Foreign Exchange	1d.d
83.28	83.28	83.28	83.28	83.28	83.28	83.28	83.28	83.28	83.28	83.28	83.28	83.28	83.28	83.28	Gold (Million Fine Troy Ounces)	1ad
6,750	6,619	5,968	5,462	4,605	5,733	7,332	9,315	7,915	7,697	9,189	8,782	8,176	8,046	9,077	Gold (National Valuation)	1and
1,298	915	456	84	49	54	79	101	123	123	—	—	—	—	—	Monetary Authorities: Other Liab.	4..d
66,452	70,672	I69,446	68,374	I62,091	85,244	116,102	158,534	140,737	132,779	153,254	147,565	143,589	154,224	187,875	Deposit Money Banks: Assets	7a.d
34,938	35,471	I34,192	49,264	I28,190	37,382	48,671	66,013	59,197	62,554	73,518	72,005	67,468	75,869	86,093	*of which*: Claims on Nonbanks	7add
47,949	58,606	I56,124	54,517	I49,078	63,396	82,400	109,973	102,794	110,325	133,572	131,765	125,791	129,333	171,093	Deposit Money Banks: Liabilities	7b.d
13,869	21,266	I24,538	24,942	I20,417	23,908	30,360	40,097	32,457	30,679	33,176	30,624	29,093	33,895	40,829	*of which*: Liab. to Nonbanks	7bdd
73,238	92,778	92,950	94,011	I99,738	120,219	137,338	173,415	178,320	222,824	290,797	281,023	268,344	235,558	271,584	Trustee Accounts: Assets	7k.d
60,635	76,195	85,074	82,968	I85,513	100,398	111,322	137,912	140,664	170,156	219,395	213,727	204,428	182,470	213,280	Liabilities	7m.d
End of Period															**Monetary Authorities**	
39.27	37.40	43.79	44.61	50.80	50.04	48.17	49.38	47.91	51.74	49.23	52.35	59.22	60.94	59.98	Foreign Assets	11
2.70	2.67	2.88	3.26	3.46	3.74	3.90	3.83	4.08	4.31	4.62	4.95	4.99	5.02	5.13	Claims on Central Government	12a
3.54	5.67	3.95	5.28	5.63	5.97	6.18	5.83	3.35	1.71	1.44	1.18	1.34	1.36	1.30	Claims on Deposit Money Banks	12e
39.49	37.75	40.27	40.60	42.19	41.51	43.54	46.06	37.42	35.94	36.92	35.96	39.60	39.10	39.33	Reserve Money	14
25.44	24.74	25.98	26.31	27.88	27.31	28.54	28.92	30.64	30.90	31.45	31.28	31.37	31.38	32.64	*of which*: Currency Outside DMBs	14a
.37	.80	.76	.76	1.11	2.57	.98	1.38	2.51	2.50	.69	.22	.42	.49	.75	Central Government Deposits	16d
5.72	7.19	9.58	11.80	16.61	15.67	13.72	11.60	15.41	19.32	17.69	22.31	25.53	27.73	26.33	Other Items (Net)	17r
End of Period															**Deposit Money Banks**	
16.50	15.35	I17.89	18.62	I15.75	15.78	17.15	18.74	9.29	8.59	8.27	7.90	7.82	8.01	7.64	Reserves	20
117.19	127.10	I138.51	149.02	I160.51	177.01	188.49	202.61	211.67	205.34	198.54	200.02	209.07	228.17	246.40	Foreign Assets	21
7.92	8.72	I11.23	11.81	I14.72	15.43	14.11	14.49	12.85	15.24	17.09	20.72	22.15	33.53	35.13	Claims on Central Government	22a
195.78	213.66	I262.06	281.61	I305.10	335.25	355.19	388.23	431.83	490.01	532.78	552.02	563.92	574.31	594.37	Claims on Private Sector	22d
27.19	27.47	I34.09	36.82	I32.84	34.49	35.41	43.20	43.98	40.30	38.59	38.83	40.84	45.98	47.79	Demand Deposits	24
115.10	130.44	I160.54	177.49	I197.99	211.30	219.20	239.91	255.57	279.51	283.91	293.89	300.34	329.73	343.60	Time and Savings Deposits	25
39.63	44.93	I60.22	61.44	I103.97	116.63	125.64	135.43	145.67	157.12	172.43	181.45	183.49	173.22	164.72	Bonds	26ab
84.56	105.40	I111.94	118.82	I126.87	131.64	133.78	140.55	154.60	171.02	173.04	178.61	183.15	191.35	224.39	Foreign Liabilities	26c
70.91	56.60	I62.90	66.50	I34.06	49.24	60.76	64.90	65.81	71.64	88.72	87.89	95.13	103.74	103.04	Other Items (Net)	27r
12.42	12.68	11.02[e]	12.63	15.02	12.03	11.50	13.77	13.29	14.36	14.17	12.79	14.02	13.87	14.43	Post Office: Checking Deposits	24..i
End of Period															**Monetary Survey**	
69.61	57.46	I69.45	74.63	I84.32	95.30	102.75	111.31	104.79	86.28	74.73	73.77	85.13	97.76	81.99	Foreign Assets (Net)	31n
218.45	236.94	I286.42	308.56	I337.20	363.88	383.71	418.94	459.54	521.42	567.97	590.26	604.67	626.24	648.31	Domestic Credit	32
22.67	23.27	I24.36	26.95	I32.10	28.63	28.52	30.71	27.71	31.41	35.19	38.23	40.75	51.93	53.94	Claims on Central Govt. (Net)	32an
195.78	213.66	I262.06	281.61	I305.10	335.25	355.19	388.23	431.83	490.01	532.78	552.02	563.92	574.31	594.37	Claims on Private Sector	32d
68.33	64.79	I71.14	75.82	I75.82	73.93	75.54	85.98	88.00	85.65	84.30	82.89	86.23	91.74	94.86	Money	34
115.10	130.44	I160.54	177.49	I197.99	211.30	219.20	239.91	255.57	279.51	283.91	293.89	300.34	329.73	343.60	Quasi-Money	35
39.63	44.93	I60.22	61.44	I103.97	116.63	125.64	135.43	145.67	157.12	172.43	181.45	183.49	173.22	164.72	Bonds	36ab
65.41	55.76	I63.98	68.45	I43.38	57.16	65.93	68.85	75.09	85.42	102.07	105.79	119.74	129.82	127.11	Other Items (Net)	37r
183.43	195.23	I231.67	253.31	I273.81	285.23	294.74	325.89	343.57	365.16	368.20	376.79	386.57	420.97	438.46	Money plus Quasi-Money	35l
End of Period															**Other Banking Institutions**	
129.16	166.86	185.39	204.90	257.82	249.63	222.97	221.63	268.19	344.60	376.73	380.93	390.71	348.51	356.18	Foreign Assets	41..x
22.23	29.83	15.71	24.07	36.77	41.16	42.24	45.37	56.64	81.45	92.50	91.22	93.06	78.54	76.47	Domestic Liabilities	45..x
106.93	137.04	169.68	180.83	221.05	208.48	180.73	176.25	211.56	263.15	284.23	289.71	297.65	269.96	279.72	Foreign Liabilities	46c.x
End of Period															**Nonbank Financial Institutions**	
.63	....	.73	.74	....	....	....	....	....	....	....	....	....	....	....	Claims on Central Government	42a.s
33.03	....	39.56	43.61	52.71	59.09	66.26	73.75	84.75	96.37	102.44	114.79	127.21	139.24	....	Claims on Priv.Sec.& Local Govt.	42d.s
8.32	....	9.87	10.68	11.62	12.46	13.49	14.41	15.45	16.77	17.64	18.65	19.75	20.82	....	Real Estate	42h.s
4.17	....	....	4.95	6.42	7.23	8.19	8.41	12.04	12.95	6.93	13.35	13.54	13.09	....	Incr.in Total Assets(Within Per.)	49z.s
202.49	225.19	I247.38	277.38	I310.58	326.40	337.35	371.26	400.20	446.61	460.71	468.01	479.63	499.51	514.93	Liquid Liabilities	55l
Percent Per Annum															**Interest Rates**	
3.00	6.00	4.50	4.00	4.00	4.00	4.00	2.50	3.50	6.00	6.00	7.00	6.00	4.00	3.50	Discount Rate (End of Period)	60
2.29	2.93	1.32	1.84	3.34	3.75	3.17	2.51	2.22	6.50	8.33	7.73	7.47	4.94	3.85	Money Market Rate	60b
5.15	7.82	3.87	3.04	3.58	4.15	3.54	3.18	3.01	6.60	8.32	7.74	7.76	4.75	3.97	Treasury Bill Rate	60c
....	7.75	4.40	3.31	3.77	4.36	3.51	3.08	4.50	8.08	8.28	7.63	5.50	3.50	3.63	Deposit Rate	60l
....	5.56	5.98	5.49	5.49	5.43	5.46	5.24	5.07	5.85	7.42	7.83	7.80	6.40	5.51	Lending Rate	60p
4.77	5.57	4.83	4.52	4.70	4.78	4.29	4.12	4.15	5.20	I6.68	6.35	5.48	4.05	5.23	Government Bond Yield	61

Switzerland
146

		1965	1966	1967	1968	1969	1970	1971	1972	1973	1974	1975	1976	1977	1978	1979
Prices, Production, Employment														*Index Numbers (1990=100):*		
Industrial Share Prices	62	39.2	ɪ33.6	34.2	48.9	58.4	51.7	52.0	57.4	53.1	40.2	36.1	39.9	41.9	40.4	44.7
Prices: Home & Imported Goods	63	55.7	56.7	56.9	56.9	58.6	61.0	62.4	64.6	71.5	83.1	81.2	80.7	80.9	78.1	81.1
Home Goods	63a	53.8	54.8	55.1	54.9	55.8	57.9	60.2	62.6	67.9	77.4	78.4	77.5	77.5	76.5	77.9
Total Supply (May 93=100)	63s	….	….	….	….	….	….	….	….	….	….	….	….	….	….	….
Producer Pr. (May 93=100)	63b	….	….	….	….	….	….	….	….	….	….	….	….	….	….	….
Consumer Prices	64	37.2	39.0	ɪ40.5	41.5	42.5	44.1	47.0	50.1	54.5	59.8	63.6	64.9	65.7	ɪ66.4	68.9
Wages: Hourly Earnings	65	ɪ27.6	ɪ29.3	ɪ30.9	32.1	ɪ33.5	ɪ35.6	ɪ39.0	ɪ42.5	46.3	ɪ51.1	54.8	55.5	ɪ58.2	59.7	61.8
Industrial Production	66	56	57	60	62	68	74	75	77	81	82	72	72	76	76	78
Manufacturing Employment	67ey	ɪ131.7	128.8	127.4	126.6	126.4	125.7	124.0	120.8	119.7	119.4	108.5	ɪ101.0	100.6	101.1	101.0
International Transactions														*Millions of Francs*		
Exports	70	12,861	14,204	15,165	17,349	20,009	22,140	23,631	26,114	29,943	35,353	33,418	37,015	42,011	41,779	ɪ44,080
Imports, cif	71	15,929	17,004	17,786	19,425	22,734	27,874	29,649	32,332	36,574	42,929	34,271	36,874	42,932	42,300	ɪ48,739
Imports, fob	71.v	15,709	16,769	17,540	19,157	22,423	27,529	29,244	31,839	35,864	41,997	33,412	36,034	41,867	41,105	47,376
														1990=100		
Volume of Exports (1985=100)	72	33.6	36.4	ɪ38.0	43.2	49.0	52.1	53.6	56.8	63.0	65.6	60.4	67.7	75.5	79.2	80.7
Volume of Exports	72.a	….	….	….	….	….	….	….	….	….	….	….	….	….	….	….
Volume of Imports (1985=100)	73	….	….	….	….	….	….	….	….	….	….	….	….	70.3	76.7	82.1
Volume of Imports	73.a	….	….	….	….	….	….	….	….	….	….	….	….	….	….	….
Unit Value of Exp. (1985=100)	74	54.0	56.4	ɪ57.9	58.6	59.2	61.6	64.1	67.2	69.0	78.3	80.1	79.5	81.4	78.3	80.7
Unit Value of Exports	74.a	….	….	….	….	….	….	….	….	….	….	….	….	….	….	….
Unit Value of Imp. (1985=100)	75	58.8	60.1	ɪ60.8	60.8	62.1	66.1	66.8	68.1	72.7	87.3	83.3	79.3	84.0	74.7	79.3
Unit Value of Imports	75.a	….	….	….	….	….	….	….	….	….	….	….	….	….	….	….
Import Prices	76.x	61.4	62.1	62.1	62.6	66.3	69.9	68.8	70.3	81.5	98.8	89.1	89.4	90.4	82.6	89.9
Import Prices (May 1993=100)	76.w	….	….	….	….	….	….	….	….	….	….	….	….	….	….	….
Balance of Payments														*Millions of US Dollars:*		
Goods: Exports f.o.b.	78aa d	….	….	….	….	….	….	….	….	….	….	….	….	20,992	28,837	33,827
Goods: Imports f.o.b.	78ab d	….	….	….	….	….	….	….	….	….	….	….	….	–22,710	–31,014	–38,727
Trade Balance	78ac d	….	….	….	….	….	….	….	….	….	….	….	….	–1,718	–2,178	–4,900
Services: Credit	78ad d	….	….	….	….	….	….	….	….	….	….	….	….	4,289	5,436	5,957
Services: Debit	78ae d	….	….	….	….	….	….	….	….	….	….	….	….	–2,524	–3,516	–4,237
Balance on Goods and Services	78af d	….	….	….	….	….	….	….	….	….	….	….	….	47	–257	–3,180
Income: Credit	78ag d	….	….	….	….	….	….	….	….	….	….	….	….	4,953	7,075	8,805
Income: Debit	78ah d	….	….	….	….	….	….	….	….	….	….	….	….	–2,411	–3,820	–4,808
Balance on Goods, Serv., & Inc.	78ai d	….	….	….	….	….	….	….	….	….	….	….	….	2,590	2,998	816
Current Transfers, n.i.e.: Credit	78aj d	….	….	….	….	….	….	….	….	….	….	….	….	304	425	490
Current Transfers: Debit	78ak d	….	….	….	….	….	….	….	….	….	….	….	….	–969	–1,348	–1,552
Current Account, n.i.e.	78al d	….	….	….	….	….	….	….	….	….	….	….	….	1,924	2,075	–245
Capital Account, n.i.e.: Credit	78ba d	….	….	….	….	….	….	….	….	….	….	….	….	—	—	—
Capital Account: Debit	78bb d	….	….	….	….	….	….	….	….	….	….	….	….	—	—	—
Capital Account, n.i.e.	78bc d	….	….	….	….	….	….	….	….	….	….	….	….	—	—	—
Direct Investment Abroad	78bd d	….	….	….	….	….	….	….	….	….	….	….	….	—	—	—
Dir. Invest. in Rep. Econ., n.i.e.	78be d	….	….	….	….	….	….	….	….	….	….	….	….	—	—	—
Portfolio Investment Assets	78bf d	….	….	….	….	….	….	….	….	….	….	….	….	–4,761	–6,210	–7,113
Portfolio Investment Liab., n.i.e.	78bg d	….	….	….	….	….	….	….	….	….	….	….	….	—	—	—
Other Investment Assets	78bh d	….	….	….	….	….	….	….	….	….	….	….	….	–1,440	–3,807	–12,383
Other Investment Liab., n.i.e.	78bi d	….	….	….	….	….	….	….	….	….	….	….	….	–337	3,538	4,036
Financial Account, n.i.e.	78bj d	….	….	….	….	….	….	….	….	….	….	….	….	–6,537	–6,479	–15,460
Net Errors and Omissions	78ca d	….	….	….	….	….	….	….	….	….	….	….	….	4,763	3,497	11,772
Overall Balance	78cb d	….	….	….	….	….	….	….	….	….	….	….	….	150	–906	–3,934
Reserves and Related Items	79da d	….	….	….	….	….	….	….	….	….	….	….	….	–150	906	3,934
Reserve Assets	79db d	….	….	….	….	….	….	….	….	….	….	….	….	–164	368	3,175
Use of Fund Credit and Loans	79dc d	….	….	….	….	….	….	….	….	….	….	….	….	—	—	—
Liabs.Constit.For.Auth.Reserves	79dd d	….	….	….	….	….	….	….	….	….	….	….	….	14	539	759
Exceptional Financing	79de d	….	….	….	….	….	….	….	….	….	….	….	….	—	—	—
Government Finance														*Millions of Francs:*		
Deficit (–) or Surplus	80	–244	–127	–268	32	–387	295	–869	–54	–1,425	–884	–1,766	–1,377	–1,291	–64	–2,352
Revenue	81	4,831	5,590	5,493	6,336	6,666	7,661	8,003	10,060	10,111	11,835	11,599	13,781	12,959	15,079	13,655
Expenditure	82	4,973	5,351	5,475	6,018	6,698	7,169	8,374	9,426	10,786	11,905	12,662	15,185	14,211	15,428	15,951
Lending Minus Repayments	83	102	366	286	286	355	197	498	688	750	814	703	–27	39	–285	56
Financing																
Net Domestic Borrowing	84a	–334	–94	131	155	135	–320	1,085	601	88	1,472	1,880	4,623	888	751	1,070
Other Financing	86c	343	489	–75	198	376	–103	426	–105	91	242	94	–901	133	509	392
Use of Cash Balances	87	235	–268	211	–386	–125	128	–642	–442	1,246	–830	–208	–2,345	270	–1,196	890
Total Debt	88	4,894	4,836	4,918	5,079	5,305	7,496	8,606	9,572	10,014	11,760	14,405	18,390	19,372	20,549	22,405
National Accounts														*Billions of Francs*		
Exports of Goods & Services	90c.c	17.5	19.2	20.5	23.2	26.6	29.7	32.1	35.8	40.2	45.9	44.0	47.7	53.4	53.2	56.0
Government Consumption	91f.c	6.5	6.9	7.3	7.9	8.7	9.6	11.4	12.9	14.8	16.6	17.9	18.9	19.2	19.8	20.8
Gross Fixed Capital Formation	93e.c	17.5	17.9	18.3	19.2	21.0	25.0	30.1	34.6	38.2	38.9	33.7	29.2	30.2	32.5	34.6
Increase/Decrease(–) in Stocks	93i.c	1.1	1.3	2.2	1.9	2.0	4.3	3.3	2.5	2.5	5.2	–1.5	.2	—	.4	3.3
Private Consumption	96f.c	36.4	39.2	42.2	44.9	48.7	53.3	59.7	67.8	75.9	83.1	86.0	88.9	92.6	95.3	100.7
Imports of Goods & Services	98c.c	–18.0	–19.2	–20.1	–22.0	–25.6	–31.3	–33.6	–36.8	–41.7	–48.7	–40.0	–43.0	–49.7	–49.5	–56.8
Gross Domestic Product	99b.c	60.9	65.4	70.4	75.1	81.4	90.7	103.0	116.7	130.1	141.1	140.2	142.0	145.8	151.7	158.5
Net Factor Inc/Pmts (–) Abroad	98.n	1.3	1.6	1.8	2.3	2.6	3.3	3.5	3.8	4.5	5.4	4.5	5.2	6.1	5.8	6.6
Gross Nat'l Expenditure = GNP	99a	62.2	67.0	72.1	77.4	84.0	93.9	106.5	120.5	134.5	146.5	144.6	147.2	151.9	157.5	165.2
Nat'l Income, Market Prices	99e	55.6	59.7	64.3	68.9	74.7	83.2	94.2	106.4	119.3	130.3	129.4	132.3	135.9	141.1	148.5
Gross Dom. Prod. 1990 Prices	99b.r	181.3	185.6	191.2	198.3	209.4	222.7	232.2	240.3	247.9	250.8	234.0	232.0	237.5	238.9	244.7
GDP Deflator (1990=100)	99bi r	33.6	35.2	36.8	37.9	38.9	40.7	44.3	48.6	52.5	56.3	59.9	61.2	61.4	63.5	64.8
														Millions:		
Population	99z	5.86	5.92	5.99	6.07	6.14	6.19	6.23	6.39	6.43	6.44	6.41	6.35	6.33	6.34	6.36

International Liquidity: ɪ Beginning in September 1971, *line 7a.d* includes all foreign investments on behalf of trustee accounts (*line 7k.d*), and *line 7b.d* includes all funds deposited in trustee accounts by nonresidents (*line 7m.d*). Prior to that date, practices with regard to trustee accounts varied from bank to bank and from time to time, and some accounts that were not recorded in the balance sheets of individual banks are excluded. Banks were required to separate all trustee accounts from their balance sheets by the end of 1974. As a result, the proportion of trustee accounts included in banks' balance sheets declined from about 50 percent at the end of 1971 to 40 percent at the end of 1972 and to 17 percent at the end of 1973. ɪ See note to section 20.

Deposit Money Banks: ɪ Before 1974, data relate to all banks in Switzerland, with nonresident branches of Swiss banks being consolidated. Beginning in December 1974, data relate to resident banks which are subject to minimum reserves on external liabilities. ɪ From August 1982, data relate to all banks. Before that date, data relate to a similar sample of banks as shown in present data. ɪ Beginning in December 1984, data relate to those banks that are subject to minimum reserves on foreign liabilities only.

Monetary Survey: ɪ See note to section 20.

Switzerland

146

	1980	1981	1982	1983	1984	1985	1986	1987	1988	1989	1990	1991	1992	1993	1994		
Period Averages																**Prices, Production, Employment**	
	42.3	38.5	38.0	49.1	55.9	72.7	88.6	91.7	I 86.5	105.8	100.0	101.0	107.8	137.4	159.2	Industrial Share Prices	62
	85.3	90.2	92.5	92.9	96.0	98.2	94.3	92.4	94.5	98.5	100.0	100.4	100.5	....	....	Prices: Home & Imported Goods	63
	81.4	86.0	89.1	90.1	92.8	94.6	93.4	92.8	94.8	97.7	100.0	101.3	102.1	....	....	Home Goods	63a
	....	....	....	....	....	....	....	....	....	....	....	99.6	99.7	99.9	99.6	Total Supply (May 93=100)	63s
	....	....	....	....	....	....	....	....	....	....	....	98.8	99.5	99.9	99.5	Producer Pr. (May 93=100)	63b
	71.6	76.3	I 80.6	83.0	85.4	88.3	89.0	90.3	92.0	94.9	100.0	105.8	I 110.1	113.8	114.7	Consumer Prices	64
	65.1	69.2	74.2	77.1	79.1	82.1	85.4	87.5	90.7	94.3	100.0	107.5	113.4	116.2	....	Wages: Hourly Earnings	65
	82	81	78	78	80	85	88	89	96	97	100	101	100	100	108	Industrial Production	66
	102.7	102.8	99.6	96.1	95.6	96.4	I 97.7	97.6	97.6	98.5	100.0	98.3	93.2	89.0	85.3	Manufacturing Employment	67ey
Millions of Francs																**International Transactions**	
	49,645	52,857	52,687	53,764	60,630	66,624	67,004	67,477	74,064	84,268	88,257	87,947	I 86,148	86,659	90,213	Exports	70
	60,883	60,093	58,115	61,276	69,150	74,750	73,513	75,171	82,399	95,209	96,611	95,032	I 86,739	83,767	87,279	Imports, cif	71
	58,802	58,285	57,270	60,635	68,482	74,010	72,785	74,427	81,583	94,266	95,654	94,091	85,880	82,938	86,415	Imports, fob	71.v
1990=100																	
	82.3	85.9	82.8	82.8	88.5	100.0	102.1	102.6	....	....	....	....	....	....	....	Volume of Exports(1985=100)	72
	....	....	....	....	....	....	....	....	I 91.0	95.7	100.0	98.6	103.4	104.0	109.1	Volume of Exports	72.a
	88.0	86.6	84.8	89.0	89.6	100.0	108.3	115.3	....	....	....	....	....	....	....	Volume of Imports(1985=100)	73
	....	....	....	....	....	....	....	....	I 92.5	97.4	100.0	98.6	94.3	93.2	101.9	Volume of Imports	73.a
	89.4	91.8	94.9	96.8	101.7	100.0	98.0	101.7	....	....	....	....	....	....	....	Unit Value of Exp.(1985=100)	74
	....	....	....	....	....	....	....	....	I 93.0	99.0	100.0	102.8	103.1	103.0	102.3	Unit Value of Exports	74.a
	95.9	93.2	91.9	92.6	96.5	100.0	89.9	86.6	....	....	....	....	....	....	....	Unit Value of Imp.(1985=100)	75
	....	....	....	....	....	....	....	....	I 92.9	100.7	100.0	100.1	102.3	100.1	95.3	Unit Value of Imports	75.a
	96.1	102.0	102.0	100.9	105.0	108.0	96.6	91.4	93.9	100.9	100.0	97.9	96.3	....	....	Import Prices	76.x
	....	....	....	....	....	....	....	....	....	....	....	....	....	....	99.8	Import Prices (May 1993=100)	76.w
Minus Sign Indicates Debit																Balance of Payments	
	41,708	40,104	36,073	33,907	36,658	37,057	48,453	55,219	62,725	65,366	77,488	73,745	79,353	74,932	....	Goods: Exports f.o.b.	78aa *d*
	–46,958	–42,488	–39,292	–39,298	–37,747	–38,618	–53,412	–60,647	–67,301	–69,690	–83,878	–77,550	–78,863	–72,695	....	Goods: Imports f.o.b.	78ab *d*
	–5,250	–2,384	–3,219	–5,391	–1,089	–1,561	–4,960	–5,427	–4,576	–4,323	–6,391	–3,806	490	2,237	....	Trade Balance	78ac *d*
	6,888	6,816	6,979	7,422	7,301	7,928	10,809	13,716	14,366	14,015	16,809	17,635	18,681	18,787	....	Services: Credit	78ad *d*
	–4,885	–4,696	–4,733	–4,710	–4,697	–4,977	–6,539	–8,145	–9,168	–9,021	–10,935	–10,868	–11,534	–10,998	....	Services: Debit	78ae *d*
	–3,248	–264	–973	–2,678	1,516	1,390	–690	144	622	671	–516	2,961	7,637	10,026	....	Balance on Goods and Services	78af *d*
	10,867	12,330	11,959	11,167	11,788	11,627	15,007	18,768	21,521	24,189	30,416	29,345	28,293	26,201	....	Income: Credit	78ag *d*
	–6,681	–7,637	–7,432	–6,363	–6,327	–6,171	–8,572	–11,121	–11,586	–15,135	–20,628	–19,361	–18,743	–16,671	....	Income: Debit	78ah *d*
	939	4,430	3,554	2,126	6,977	6,846	5,745	7,790	10,556	9,725	9,272	12,946	17,187	19,556	....	Balance on Goods, Serv., & Inc.	78ai *d*
	522	733	823	946	929	1,017	1,548	1,911	2,054	1,919	2,357	2,367	2,531	2,499	....	Current Transfers, n.i.e.: Credit	78aj *d*
	–1,662	–1,736	–1,842	–1,860	–1,763	–1,823	–2,638	–3,415	–3,768	–3,602	–4,686	–4,987	–5,528	–5,359	....	Current Transfers: Debit	78ak *d*
	–201	3,427	2,534	1,211	6,143	6,040	4,654	6,286	8,843	8,042	6,942	10,325	14,190	16,696	....	Current Account, n.i.e.	78al *d*
	—	—	—	—	—	—	—	—	—	—	—	—	—	—	....	Capital Account, n.i.e.: Credit	78ba *d*
	—	—	—	—	—	—	—	—	—	—	—	—	—	—	....	Capital Account: Debit	78bb *d*
	—	—	—	—	—	—	—	—	—	—	—	—	—	—	....	Capital Account, n.i.e.	78bc *d*
	—	—	—	–492	–1,139	–4,573	–1,460	–1,273	–8,695	–7,850	–6,370	–6,541	–5,671	–6,538	....	Direct Investment Abroad	78bd *d*
	—	—	—	643	777	1,267	2,122	2,320	405	2,827	4,961	3,178	1,249	808	....	Dir. Invest. in Rep. Econ., n.i.e.	78be *d*
	–7,068	–8,488	–12,480	–5,754	–4,660	–6,535	–7,538	–6,371	–13,837	–9,394	–577	–17,549	–9,698	–29,809	....	Portfolio Investment Assets	78bf *d*
	—	—	—	1,766	1,784	5,431	8,940	4,639	6,421	6,371	–551	5,570	3,571	12,501	....	Portfolio Investment Liab., n.i.e.	78bg *d*
	–13,145	–9,502	–2,689	–1,605	–3,965	–10,158	–13,459	–24,089	–7,641	–14,202	–28,846	2,828	–8,495	8,039	....	Other Investment Assets	78bh *d*
	8,871	10,614	3,090	–332	1,376	7,292	8,236	16,712	8,604	14,631	19,924	836	3,675	–2,444	....	Other Investment Liab., n.i.e.	78bi *d*
	–11,342	–7,376	–12,079	–5,774	–5,827	–7,276	–3,160	–8,063	–14,742	–7,618	–11,458	–11,677	–15,369	–17,443	....	Financial Account, n.i.e.	78bj *d*
	11,880	3,429	13,044	4,947	1,164	2,460	–402	4,984	3,473	995	5,688	2,322	5,599	1,150	....	Net Errors and Omissions	78ca *d*
	337	–520	3,499	384	1,480	1,224	1,093	3,206	–2,426	1,419	1,172	970	4,420	404	....	Overall Balance	78cb *d*
	–337	520	–3,499	–384	–1,480	–1,224	–1,093	–3,206	2,426	–1,419	–1,172	–970	–4,420	–404	....	Reserves and Related Items	79da *d*
	–337	951	–3,366	110	–1,491	–1,228	–1,091	–3,213	2,382	–1,369	–1,169	–992	–4,397	–486	....	Reserve Assets	79db *d*
	—	—	—	—	—	—	—	—	—	—	—	—	—	—	....	Use of Fund Credit and Loans	79dc *d*
	1	–431	–133	–494	11	4	–2	7	44	–51	–3	22	–23	82	....	Liabs.Constit.For.Auth.Reserves	79dd *d*
	—	—	—	—	—	—	—	—	—	—	—	—	—	—	....	Exceptional Financing	79de *d*
Year Ending December 31																**Government Finance**	
	–76	–1,491	901	–1,446	I –241	–1,183	2,372	670	1,980	157	1,276	–3,297	–2,437	–8,351	–4,443	Deficit (-) or Surplus	80
	16,456	15,939	18,857	17,752	I 20,282	20,702	24,347	23,296	27,066	26,427	30,385	30,247	32,355	29,559	33,752	Revenue	81
	16,474	17,140	18,001	18,897	I 20,160	21,534	21,671	22,219	24,099	25,964	28,764	32,422	34,354	35,443	36,759	Expenditure	82
	58	290	–45	301	I 363	351	304	407	987	306	345	1,122	438	2,467	1,436	Lending Minus Repayments	83
																Financing	
	1,217	465	–369	547	I 1,870	3,509	–1,603	1,145	–1,676	1,321	–203	5,408	8,801	14,923	7,399	Net Domestic Borrowing	84a
	116	92	98	62	I –417	–1,124	59	–1,329	299	–2,884	–26	–1,812	–1,810	–1,131	–1,598	Other Financing	86c
	–1,257	934	–630	837	I –1,212	–1,202	–828	–486	–603	1,406	–1,047	–299	–4,554	–5,441	–1,359	Use of Cash Balances	87
	I 31,680	31,612	33,111	33,340	36,610	39,161	38,782	38,597	39,289	38,287	40,569	45,487	55,296	69,427	77,774	Total Debt	88
Billions of Francs																**National Accounts**	
	62.6	69.1	69.6	71.8	80.6	89.0	89.1	90.5	98.0	110.5	115.1	116.7	122.2	125.0	127.8	Exports of Goods & Services	90c. *c*
	22.0	23.9	25.9	27.8	28.9	30.9	32.3	33.0	35.4	38.5	42.9	46.6	49.3	49.7	50.9	Government Consumption	91f. *c*
	40.5	44.6	45.3	47.5	49.8	54.2	59.0	64.4	71.5	79.9	84.5	84.8	80.4	77.0	80.8	Gross Fixed Capital Formation	93e. *c*
	5.8	2.5	1.8	1.3	1.5	1.4	4.4	5.0	3.4	6.4	7.3	4.5	–1.0	–3.2	.8	Increase/Decrease(-) in Stocks	93i. *c*
	108.0	115.7	122.1	127.3	133.6	140.6	144.9	150.2	157.0	166.2	177.7	190.5	198.1	202.3	206.5	Private Consumption	96f. *c*
	–68.6	–70.9	–68.7	–71.9	–81.2	–88.1	–86.4	–88.4	–96.8	–111.1	–113.4	–112.1	–110.2	–107.8	–110.7	Imports of Goods & Services	98c. *c*
	170.3	184.8	196.0	203.9	213.2	228.0	243.4	254.7	268.4	290.4	314.0	331.1	338.8	343.0	356.2	Gross Domestic Product	99b. *c*
	7.0	9.2	9.2	10.1	12.8	13.4	11.6	11.4	14.5	14.8	13.6	14.3	13.4	14.1	....	Net Factor Inc/Pmts(-) Abroad	98.n
	177.3	194.0	205.2	214.0	226.1	241.4	254.9	266.1	283.0	305.2	327.6	345.4	352.2	357.1	....	Gross Nat'l Expenditure = GNP	99a
	159.4	174.4	184.8	193.1	204.4	218.0	230.5	240.5	255.2	274.7	294.8	311.1	316.7	320.9	....	Nat'l Income, Market Prices	99e
	255.4	259.1	256.7	259.3	263.9	273.6	281.5	287.2	295.5	306.9	314.0	313.9	312.9	310.3	316.9	Gross Dom. Prod. 1990 Prices	99b. *r*
	66.7	71.3	76.4	78.6	80.8	83.3	86.5	88.7	90.8	94.6	100.0	105.5	108.2	110.6	112.4	GDP Deflator (1990=100)	99bi *r*
Midyear Estimates																	
	6.32	6.35	6.39	6.42	6.44	6.47	6.50	6.55	6.59	6.65	6.71	6.79	6.90	6.94	6.99	**Population**	99z

Nonbank Financial Institutions: Comprises life insurance companies.

International Transactions: I Since 1979, the data for the volume and unit value of imports include trade of gems, semi-precious stones, and antiques. I Since 1992, the data for exports and imports exclude diamonds and precious metals.

Government Finance: I Beginning in 1980, debt data were redefined. I Beginning in 1984, federal accounts are harmonized with the cantonal accounting model.

Syrian Arab Republic
463

		1965	1966	1967	1968	1969	1970	1971	1972	1973	1974	1975	1976	1977	1978	1979
Exchange Rates															*Pounds per SDR: End of Period (aa)*		
Principal Rate	aa	3.820	3.820	3.820	3.820	3.820	3.820	4.147	4.147	4.584	4.530	4.331	4.560	4.768	5.113	5.171
Principal Rate	ae	3.820	3.820	3.820	3.820	3.820	3.820	3.820	3.820	3.800	3.700	3.700	3.925	3.925	3.925	3.925
Fund Position															*Millions of SDRs:*		
Quota	2f.s	25	38	38	38	38	50	50	50	50	50	50	50	50	63	63
SDRs	1b.s	—	—	—	—	—	—	—	4	8	8	7	7	6	6	12
Reserve Position in the Fund	1c.s	—	—	—	—	—	—	—	—	—	—	7	13	—	—	—
Total Fund Cred.&Loans Outstg.	2tl	18	12	17	10	10	10	5	23	18	5	—	—	—	—	1
International Liquidity												*Millions of US Dollars Unless Otherwise Indicated:*					
Total Reserves minus Gold	1l.d	26	34	55	39	31	27	58	105	379	466	702	293	484	382	581
SDRs	1b.d	—	—	—	—	—	—	—	4	10	10	9	8	8	8	16
Reserve Position in the Fund	1c.d	—	—	—	—	—	—	—	—	—	—	8	15	—	—	—
Foreign Exchange	1d.d	26	34	55	39	31	27	58	101	369	456	685	271	476	374	565
Gold (Million Fine Troy Ounces)	1ad	.543	.543	.543	.800	.800	.800	.800	.800	.800	.789	.789	.789	.811	.811	.833
Gold (National Valuation)	1and	19	19	19	27	27	27	27	27	28	28	28	27	28	27	29e
Monetary Authorities: Other Assets	3..d	11	12	12	15	22	15	10	16	16	34	28	32	74	41	19
Other Liab.	4..d	51	50	23	53	58	85	104	134	101	56	287	347	296	352	409
Deposit Money Banks: Assets	7a.d	16	14	18	41	16	12	10	22	33	62	88	125	65	73	188
Liabilities	7b.d	18	19	13	11	12	16	39	49	61	88	42	155	210	126	139
Monetary Authorities															*Millions of Pounds:*		
Foreign Assets	11	212	246	327	312	307	264	362	571	1,605	1,956	2,808	1,382	2,297	1,766	2,485
Claims on Central Government	12a	960	1,023	1,295	1,569	1,848	2,275	2,711	3,208	2,588	3,486	4,445	7,175	7,932	11,934	12,447
Claims on Official Entities	12bx	83	113	97	93	129	132	115	81	78	40	28	23	13	12	9
Claims on Deposit Money Banks	12e	357	353	327	436	292	330	234	346	432	629	756	1,306	1,191	842	1,532
Reserve Money	14	1,086	1,162	1,399	1,656	1,807	2,093	2,264	2,684	3,301	4,300	5,142	6,431	8,026	10,463	11,905
of which: Currency Outside DMBs	14a	959	1,031	1,304	1,491	1,577	1,795	1,846	2,245	2,757	3,413	3,945	5,259	6,797	8,459	9,903
Foreign Liabilities	16c	261	238	150	239	258	359	418	606	464	230	1,061	1,363	1,163	1,382	1,609
Central Government Deposits	16d	128	229	383	438	419	419	536	586	715	995	1,611	1,745	1,782	2,008	2,459
Capital Accounts	17a	30	31	31	31	28	47	68	93	100	100	96	100	100	110	141
Other Items (Net)	17r	106	75	85	47	64	83	136	237	121	485	128	247	361	590	359
Deposit Money Banks															*Millions of Pounds:*		
Reserves	20	83	77	58	86	121	194	291	296	390	468	603	817	736	1,411	938
Foreign Assets	21	59	54	68	156	60	48	40	83	126	229	327	490	255	287	737
Claims on Central Government	22a	27	38	43	52	62	84	101	136	173	230	295	405	485	612	782
Claims on Official Entities	22bx	50	50	514	578	722	840	965	1,347	1,744	3,027	4,647	6,746	8,148	8,089	9,819
Claims on Private Sector	22d	934	1,046	581	584	596	551	570	578	653	694	861	1,146	1,339	1,651	2,437
Demand Deposits	24	238	248	249	294	404	441	566	786	957	1,784	2,640	3,091	3,676	4,883	5,552
Time and Savings Deposits	25	84	92	85	112	126	180	213	277	317	456	619	826	1,111	1,427	1,785
Restricted Deposits	26b	156	174	159	94	140	152	272	267	436	537	444	1,090	1,258	1,106	1,586
Foreign Liabilities	26c	69	71	50	42	46	60	147	186	231	327	155	610	824	495	545
Central Government Deposits	26d	89	113	122	109	129	133	154	169	181	259	1,128	1,485	1,569	1,669	1,839
Credit from Monetary Authorities	26g	351	359	324	436	292	326	234	345	421	629	756	1,298	1,190	842	1,232
Capital Accounts	27a	130	139	154	161	174	174	181	186	190	227	248	338	384	445	532
Other Items (Net)	27r	36	71	120	207	253	249	202	224	354	428	743	866	952	1,184	1,643
Monetary Survey															*Millions of Pounds:*		
Foreign Assets (Net)	31n	−59	−9	194	187	64	−108	−163	−138	1,036	1,627	1,919	−102	565	175	1,068
Domestic Credit	32	1,837	1,927	2,026	2,329	2,809	3,330	3,773	4,595	4,339	6,222	7,538	12,264	14,566	18,621	21,196
Claims on Central Govt. (Net)	32an	770	719	833	1,073	1,362	1,807	2,122	2,589	1,864	2,462	2,001	4,350	5,065	8,869	8,931
Claims on Official Entities	32bx	133	163	611	672	850	972	1,080	1,428	1,822	3,066	4,675	6,768	8,162	8,101	9,828
Claims on Private Sector	32d	934	1,046	581	584	596	551	570	578	653	694	861	1,146	1,339	1,651	2,437
Money	34	1,240	1,350	1,619	1,867	2,088	2,341	2,502	3,151	3,797	5,540	6,966	8,561	10,924	13,866	16,119
Quasi-Money	35	84	92	85	112	126	180	213	277	317	456	619	826	1,111	1,427	1,785
Restricted Deposits	36b	156	174	159	94	140	152	272	267	436	537	444	1,090	1,258	1,106	1,586
Other Items (Net)	37r	299	302	358	442	520	549	622	762	825	1,316	1,428	1,686	1,839	2,398	2,774
Money plus Quasi-Money	35l	1,324	1,442	1,704	1,980	2,214	2,521	2,716	3,428	4,114	5,996	7,585	9,387	12,035	15,293	17,904
Interest Rates															*Percent Per Annum*		
Discount Rate (End of Period)	60	5.00	5.00	5.00	5.00	5.00	5.00	5.00	5.00	5.00	5.00	5.00	5.00	5.00	5.00	5.00
Prices and Production															*Index Numbers (1990=100):*		
Wholesale Prices	63	4.1	4.4	4.9	4.7	4.6	5.0	5.5	5.2	6.9	7.9	8.5	9.5	10.3	11.7	12.7
Consumer Prices	64	4.4	4.6	4.9	5.0	4.9	5.1	5.4	5.5	6.7	I7.7	8.6	9.6	10.7	11.2	11.7
Industrial Production	66	17.6	18.3	17.7	19.0	22.8	I25.5	27.5	30.3	32.3	37.9	I44.0	48.0	46.9	50.9	50.9

Syrian Arab Republic

1980	1981	1982	1983	1984	1985	1986	1987	1988	1989	1990	1991	1992	1993	1994		
Pounds per US Dollar: End of Period (ae)															**Exchange Rates**	
5.006	4.569	4.330	4.109	3.847	4.311	4.801	5.568	15.105	14.751	15.969	16.057	15.434	15.418	16.387	Principal Rate	aa
3.925	3.925	3.925	3.925	3.925	3.925	3.925	3.925	3.925	11.225	11.225	11.225	11.225	11.225	11.225	Principal Rate	ae
End of Period															**Fund Position**	
95	95	95	95	139	139	139	139	139	139	139	139	139	210	210	Quota	2f. s
10	15	12	9	5	3	—	—	—	—	—	—	—	—	—	SDRs	1b. s
7	7	—	—	—	—	—	—	—	—	—	—	—	—	—	Reserve Position in the Fund	1c. s
—	—	—	—	—	—	—	—	—	—	—	—	—	—	—	Total Fund Cred.&Loans Outstg.	2tl
End of Period															**International Liquidity**	
337	291	198	52^e	268	83	144	223	193	....	....	....	....	....	....	Total Reserves minus Gold	1l. d
12	17	13	9	5	3	—	—	—	—	—	—	—	—	—	SDRs	1b. d
9	8	—	—	—	—	—	—	—	—	—	—	—	—	—	Reserve Position in the Fund	1c. d
315	266	185	43^e	263	80	144	223	193	....	....	....	....	....	....	Foreign Exchange	1d. d
.833	.833	.833	.833	.833	.833	.833	.833	.833	.833	.833	.833	.833	.833	.833	Gold (Million Fine Troy Ounces)	1ad
29	29	29	29	29	29	29	29	29	29	29	29	29	29	29	Gold (National Valuation)	1an d
15	124	92	149	195	194	430	942	1,140	....	....	....	....	....	....	Monetary Authorities: Other Assets	3.. d
530	672	929	904	1,641	2,362	2,858	3,629	3,578	3,680	4,019	3,863	3,873	....	....	Other Liab.	4.. d
109	69	292	244	141	152	223	241	302	500	992	1,730	2,326	2,667	....	Deposit Money Banks: Assets	7a. d
377	637	722	990	928	1,166	1,263	1,311	1,126	1,062	919	742	587	493	....	Liabilities	7b. d
End of Period															**Monetary Authorities**	
1,499	1,749	1,253	902	1,916	1,193	2,352	4,653	15,265	25,868	37,540	42,955	43,720	....	....	Foreign Assets	11
18,228	22,560	35,248	41,519	55,165	74,003	79,407	83,159	83,334	88,713	104,776	114,228	136,065	....	....	Claims on Central Government	12a
62	59	57	56	56	56	56	106	106	106	106	106	106	....	....	Claims on Official Entities	12bx
1,493	1,496	1,429	2,246	1,179	1,825	1,197	915	3,126	8,356	18,697	32,730	51,827	....	....	Claims on Deposit Money Banks	12e
15,896	17,250	25,700	32,548	43,095	58,516	62,753	68,590	64,983	78,421	100,745	118,986	150,370	....	....	Reserve Money	14
13,422	14,046	17,348	20,500	25,155	29,562	36,262	41,852	52,171	59,962	76,202	92,450	107,557	....	....	of which: Currency Outside DMBs	14a
2,080	2,637	3,645	3,546	6,441	9,273	11,218	14,244	40,160	41,304	45,112	43,357	43,470	....	....	Foreign Liabilities	16c
3,011	4,986	7,351	7,391	7,255	8,305	9,098	8,839	17,593	24,711	35,276	46,362	57,640	....	....	Central Government Deposits	16d
176	195	185	185	185	185	185	185	185	185	185	558	399	399	....	Capital Accounts	17a
119	796	1,105	1,054	1,340	797	−242	−3,024	−21,090	−21,578	−20,571	−19,086	−20,161	....	....	Other Items (Net)	17r
End of Period															**Deposit Money Banks**	
1,622	1,994	6,466	9,816	14,935	25,334	23,729	23,309	9,467	11,939	17,503	20,149	23,773	24,814	....	Reserves	20
426	272	1,144	957	555	597	876	947	3,389	5,610	11,132	19,423	26,105	29,932	....	Foreign Assets	21
918	1,383	1,700	2,136	2,849	3,532	3,772	5,004	5,566	5,873	6,915	16,502	20,179	21,827	....	Claims on Central Government	22a
14,176	21,672	20,802	22,468	19,556	16,279	18,918	22,035	47,162	52,579	59,134	72,383	89,540	120,043	....	Claims on Official Entities	22bx
2,944	3,489	4,472	5,938	6,580	6,825	7,601	8,971	12,068	16,073	20,009	26,787	35,556	44,067	....	Claims on Private Sector	22d
7,611	9,917	10,895	15,174	17,872	22,222	22,962	23,438	24,595	28,987	35,888	41,973	53,341	63,918	....	Demand Deposits	24
2,176	3,009	3,993	5,204	7,167	8,517	9,907	11,529	17,044	21,341	28,054	45,303	54,929	64,386	....	Time and Savings Deposits	25
2,505	5,162	7,783	7,887	7,616	9,841	11,587	17,535	11,262	10,156	11,039	13,022	15,121	16,051	....	Restricted Deposits	26b
1,479	2,500	2,833	3,884	3,644	4,575	4,959	5,147	12,642	11,918	10,316	8,327	6,593	5,538	....	Foreign Liabilities	26c
2,211	3,226	4,132	3,826	4,008	3,561	3,555	3,912	3,880	4,114	3,919	4,781	5,973	6,668	....	Central Government Deposits	26d
1,493	1,495	1,421	2,246	1,179	1,825	1,199	924	3,138	8,724	18,770	27,890	51,671	71,340	....	Credit from Monetary Authorities	26g
607	914	1,032	1,139	1,301	1,423	1,505	1,831	2,228	2,647	3,148	7,318	10,344	13,234	....	Capital Accounts	27a
2,005	2,585	2,495	1,954	1,688	604	−779	−4,051	2,864	4,187	3,558	6,631	−2,818	−453	....	Other Items (Net)	27r
End of Period															**Monetary Survey**	
−1,634	−3,117	−4,081	−5,572	−7,614	−12,057	−12,948	−13,791	−34,148	−21,744	−6,756	10,694	19,762	....	....	Foreign Assets (Net)	31n
31,105	40,950	50,795	60,900	72,942	88,828	97,101	106,523	126,763	134,518	151,744	178,864	217,834	....	....	Domestic Credit	32
13,924	15,730	25,465	32,438	46,751	65,669	70,527	75,412	67,427	65,761	72,495	79,587	92,632	....	....	Claims on Central Govt. (Net)	32an
14,238	21,731	20,858	22,524	19,612	16,335	18,974	22,141	47,268	52,685	59,240	72,489	89,646	....	....	Claims on Official Entities	32bx
2,944	3,489	4,472	5,938	6,580	6,825	7,601	8,971	12,068	16,073	20,009	26,787	35,556	44,067	....	Claims on Private Sector	32d
21,854	24,832	29,518	36,978	45,607	54,976	61,214	67,821	79,814	95,030	118,717	146,263	181,979	....	....	Money	34
2,176	3,009	3,993	5,204	7,167	8,517	9,907	11,529	17,044	21,341	28,054	45,303	54,929	64,386	....	Quasi-Money	35
2,505	5,162	7,783	7,887	7,616	9,841	11,587	17,535	11,262	10,156	11,039	13,022	15,121	16,051	....	Restricted Deposits	36b
2,936	4,829	5,420	5,259	4,939	3,437	1,444	−4,151	−15,504	−13,752	−12,823	−15,031	−14,433	....	....	Other Items (Net)	37r
24,030	27,841	33,511	42,182	52,774	63,493	71,121	79,349	96,857	116,370	146,772	191,566	236,908	....	....	Money plus Quasi-Money	35l
Percent Per Annum															**Interest Rates**	
5.00	5.00	5.00	5.00	5.00	5.00	5.00	5.00	5.00	5.00	5.00	5.00	5.00	5.00	5.00	Discount Rate *(End of Period)*	60
Period Averages															**Prices and Production**	
ℐ14.6	17.4	19.3	19.8	21.6	23.8	33.4	ℐ49.0	72.0	82.0	100.0	114.0	123.0	117.0	126.0	Wholesale Prices	63
14.0	16.6	18.9	20.1	22.0	25.7	35.0	55.9	75.2	83.8	100.0	107.7	117.9	131.8	....	Consumer Prices	64
57.2	64.6	68.0	79.5	ℐ79.5	75.7	78.7	ℐ81.0	79.0	91.0	100.0	107.0	114.0	116.0	....	Industrial Production	66

Syrian Arab Republic

463

		1965	1966	1967	1968	1969	1970	1971	1972	1973	1974	1975	1976	1977	1978	1979
International Transactions																*Millions of Pounds*
Exports	70	644	662	591	643	790	775	743	1,098	1,341	2,914	3,441	4,141	4,199	4,160	6,453
Imports, cif	71	815	1,105	1,011	1,194	1,412	1,377	1,677	2,061	2,341	4,572	6,236	9,203	10,605	9,650	13,067
Imports, fob	71.v	755	1,024	937	1,107	1,309	1,273	1,554	1,907	2,168	4,234	5,774	8,520	9,525	8,642	11,991
																1990=100
Volume of Exports	72	59	52	43	47	59	58	47	58	54	I 52	63	67	65	69	63
Volume of Imports	73	29	36	31	34	47	42	44	I 44	52	65	102	104	129	116	130
Unit Value of Exports	74	14.8	12.0	14.5	15.4	15.4	15.0	18.0	I 21.0	26.2	49.2	41.9	53.4	57.6	61.8	80.7
Unit Value of Imports	75	10.9	12.0	12.1	11.6	11.3	11.6	13.5	I 16.2	19.9	28.0	31.1	39.2	36.1	38.6	47.9
Balance of Payments																*Millions of US Dollars:*
Goods: Exports f.o.b.	78aa d	....	....	....	....	....	....	....	....	....	....	....	....	1,070	1,061	1,648
Goods: Imports f.o.b.	78ab d	....	....	....	....	....	....	....	....	....	....	....	....	-2,402	-2,204	-3,055
Trade Balance	78ac d	....	....	....	....	....	....	....	....	....	....	....	....	-1,332	-1,142	-1,407
Services: Credit	78ad d	....	....	....	....	....	....	....	....	....	....	....	....	330	259	376
Services: Debit	78ae d	....	....	....	....	....	....	....	....	....	....	....	....	-418	-579	-590
Balance on Goods and Services	78af d	....	....	....	....	....	....	....	....	....	....	....	....	-1,421	-1,463	-1,621
Income: Credit	78ag d	....	....	....	....	....	....	....	....	....	....	....	....	54	51	54
Income: Debit	78ah d	....	....	....	....	....	....	....	....	....	....	....	....	-35	-22	-15
Balance on Goods, Serv., & Inc.	78ai d	....	....	....	....	....	....	....	....	....	....	....	....	-1,402	-1,434	-1,583
Current Transfers, n.i.e.: Credit	78aj d	....	....	....	....	....	....	....	....	....	....	....	....	1,236	1,418	2,530
Current Transfers: Debit	78ak d	....	....	....	....	....	....	....	....	....	....	....	....	—	—	-2
Current Account, n.i.e.	78al d	....	....	....	....	....	....	....	....	....	....	....	....	-167	-15	946
Capital Account, n.i.e.: Credit	78ba d	....	....	....	....	....	....	....	....	....	....	....	....	—	—	—
Capital Account: Debit	78bb d	....	....	....	....	....	....	....	....	....	....	....	....	—	—	—
Capital Account, n.i.e.	78bc d	....	....	....	....	....	....	....	....	....	....	....	....	—	—	—
Direct Investment Abroad	78bd d	....	....	....	....	....	....	....	....	....	....	....	....	—	—	—
Dir. Invest. in Rep. Econ., n.i.e.	78be d	....	....	....	....	....	....	....	....	....	....	....	....	—	—	—
Portfolio Investment Assets	78bf d	....	....	....	....	....	....	....	....	....	....	....	....	—	—	—
Portfolio Investment Liab., n.i.e.	78bg d	....	....	....	....	....	....	....	....	....	....	....	....	—	—	—
Other Investment Assets	78bh d	....	....	....	....	....	....	....	....	....	....	....	....	18	25	-148
Other Investment Liab., n.i.e.	78bi d	....	....	....	....	....	....	....	....	....	....	....	....	318	360	272
Financial Account, n.i.e.	78bj d	....	....	....	....	....	....	....	....	....	....	....	....	337	385	124
Net Errors and Omissions	78ca d	....	....	....	....	....	....	....	....	....	....	....	....	22	-473	-875
Overall Balance	78cb d	....	....	....	....	....	....	....	....	....	....	....	....	192	-103	195
Reserves and Related Items	79da d	....	....	....	....	....	....	....	....	....	....	....	....	-192	103	-195
Reserve Assets	79db d	....	....	....	....	....	....	....	....	....	....	....	....	-192	103	-196
Use of Fund Credit and Loans	79dc d	....	....	....	....	....	....	....	....	....	....	....	....	—	—	1
Liabs.Constit.For.Auth.Reserves	79dd d	....	....	....	....	....	....	....	....	....	....	....	....	—	—	....
Exceptional Financing	79de d	....	....	....	....	....	....	....	....	....	....	....	....	....	....	....
Government Finance																*Millions of Pounds:*
Deficit (-) or Surplus	80	....	....	....	....	....	....	....	-327	-574	-740	-992	-2,332	-2,928	-2,935	303
Revenue	81	....	....	....	....	....	....	....	2,346	2,766	4,285	8,698	9,058	10,320	7,341	9,201
Grants Received	81z	....	....	....	....	....	....	....	—	—	—	550	665	100	3,070	6,384
Expenditure	82	....	....	....	....	....	....	....	2,673	3,340	5,575	9,690	12,055	13,348	13,346	15,282
Financing																
Total Financing	84	....	....	....	....	....	....	....	....	....	....	....	2,332	2,928	2,935	-303
Domestic	84a	....	....	....	....	....	....	....	....	....	....	....	1,564	2,034	....	....
Foreign	85a	....	....	....	....	....	....	....	....	....	....	....	768	894	....	....
Unallocable Financing	87c	....	....	....	....	....	....	....	....	....	....	....	—	—	....	....
National Accounts																*Millions of Pounds*
Exports of Goods & Services	90c	872	929	851	1,014	1,149	1,190	1,390	1,674	2,175	3,816	4,409	4,828	4,908	4,808	7,458
Government Consumption	91f	716	738	834	1,065	1,116	1,187	1,427	1,637	2,122	2,815	4,343	4,960	5,293	6,470	8,424
Gross Capital Formation	93	484	583	625	773	1,021	937	1,194	1,868	1,229	3,963	5,916	7,759	9,597	8,887	10,194
Private Consumption	96f	3,435	3,647	4,200	4,296	5,018	4,966	5,823	6,294	6,960	10,704	13,685	15,657	18,199	22,338	26,931
Imports of Goods & Services	98c	-893	-1,199	-1,073	-1,201	-1,460	-1,432	-1,790	-2,187	-2,541	-5,347	-6,996	-8,479	-10,984	-10,114	-14,033
Gross Domestic Product	99b	4,614	4,698	5,437	5,947	6,844	6,848	8,044	9,286	9,945	15,951	20,597	24,725	27,013	32,389	38,974
Gross Dom. Prod. 1990 Prices	99b.p	71,527	69,470	73,151	I 76,333	91,567	86,155	I 94,344	114,701	111,284	132,707	160,767	175,123	172,674	I 186,239	193,004
GDP Deflator (1990=100)	99bi p	6.45	6.76	7.43	7.79	7.47	7.95	8.53	8.10	8.94	12.02	12.81	14.12	15.64	17.39	20.19
																Millions:
Population	99z	5.33	5.50	5.68	5.87	6.06	6.26	6.48	6.71	6.94	7.19	7.44	7.72	8.02	I 8.15	8.42

Syrian Arab Republic

1980	1981	1982	1983	1984	1985	1986	1987	1988	1989	1990	1991	1992	1993	1994		
Millions of Pounds															**International Transactions**	
8,273	8,254	7,954	7,548	7,275	6,427	5,199	15,192	15,093	33,740	45,591	35,280	34,720	35,319	39,810	Exports	70
16,187	20,302	15,808	17,829	16,155	15,570	10,709	27,915	25,040	23,544	28,353	35,365	39,178	46,468	60,270	Imports, cif	71
15,737	19,511	14,567	16,318	14,827	14,284	9,825	25,610	22,972	21,600	26,012	32,445	35,943	42,631	55,294	Imports, fob	71.v
1990=100																
55	50	53	52	49	45	‡44	‡46	51	78	100	104	105	158	....	Volume of Exports	72
133	174	150	164	153	161	‡152	‡114	98	92	100	163	143	225	....	Volume of Imports	73
104.8	116.3	101.6	95.3	97.4	95.3	‡70.2	‡65.0	62.0	77.0	100.0	98.0	68.0	67.0	....	Unit Value of Exports	74
62.3	80.9	75.9	87.8	82.2	69.1	‡82.2	‡83.0	102.0	99.0	100.0	101.0	98.0	93.0	....	Unit Value of Imports	75
Minus Sign Indicates Debit															Balance of Payments	
2,112	2,212	2,002	1,918	1,834	1,856	1,037	1,357	1,348	3,013	4,156	3,438	3,100	3,153	....	Goods: Exports f.o.b.	78aa *d*
−4,010	−4,404	−3,636	−4,024	−3,687	−3,946	−2,363	−2,226	−1,986	−1,821	−2,062	−2,354	−2,941	−3,475	....	Goods: Imports f.o.b.	78ab *d*
−1,898	−2,193	−1,633	−2,106	−1,853	−2,090	−1,326	−869	−639	1,192	2,094	1,084	159	−322	....	Trade Balance	78ac *d*
365	431	483	560	512	656	566	600	667	893	874	1,065	1,281	1,498	....	Services: Credit	78ad *d*
−521	−814	−757	−854	−906	−975	−699	−690	−636	−792	−892	−1,002	−1,102	−1,228	....	Services: Debit	78ae *d*
−2,054	−2,575	−1,907	−2,400	−2,247	−2,409	−1,459	−958	−608	1,293	2,075	1,146	338	−52	....	Balance on Goods and Services	78af *d*
91	94	26	16	30	29	10	25	22	22	45	65	69	80	....	Income: Credit	78ag *d*
−79	−111	−177	−148	−128	−139	−137	−459	−461	−745	−831	−1,096	−1,214	−1,276	....	Income: Debit	78ah *d*
−2,043	−2,592	−2,059	−2,532	−2,344	−2,519	−1,586	−1,392	−1,047	570	1,289	115	−808	−1,247	....	Balance on Goods, Serv., & Inc.	78ai *d*
2,296	2,287	1,811	1,691	1,553	1,564	1,082	1,095	897	657	476	588	871	649	....	Current Transfers, n.i.e.: Credit	78aj *d*
−2	−3	−2	−3	−3	−2	—	−1	−1	−5	−3	−4	−8	−8	....	Current Transfers: Debit	78ak *d*
251	−308	−250	−844	−794	−958	−504	−298	−151	1,222	1,762	699	55	−607	....	Current Account, n.i.e.	78al *d*
—	—	—	—	—	—	—	—	—	—	—	—	—	—	....	Capital Account, n.i.e.: Credit	78ba *d*
—	—	—	—	—	—	—	—	—	—	—	—	—	—	....	Capital Account: Debit	78bb *d*
—	—	—	—	—	—	—	—	—	—	—	—	—	—	....	Capital Account, n.i.e.	78bc *d*
—	—	—	—	—	—	—	—	—	—	—	—	—	—	....	Direct Investment Abroad	78bd *d*
—	—	—	—	—	—	—	—	—	—	—	—	—	—	....	Dir. Invest. in Rep. Econ., n.i.e.	78be *d*
—	—	—	—	—	—	—	—	—	—	—	—	—	—	....	Portfolio Investment Assets	78bf *d*
—	—	—	—	—	—	—	—	—	—	—	—	—	—	....	Portfolio Investment Liab., n.i.e.	78bg *d*
47	−64	−172	−3	83	−50	−307	−530	−256	−1,580	−2,008	−1,294	−1,175	−1,130	....	Other Investment Assets	78bh *d*
149	351	346	716	952	839	898	929	341	−128	172	779	1,126	1,701	....	Other Investment Liab., n.i.e.	78bi *d*
196	287	175	714	1,035	789	591	399	85	−1,708	−1,836	−515	−50	571	....	Financial Account, n.i.e.	78bj *d*
−701	−30	−17	−15	−25	−17	−26	−23	34	420	110	−112	70	100	....	Net Errors and Omissions	78ca *d*
−254	−51	−92	−145	216	−186	61	79	−32	−66	36	72	76	64	....	Overall Balance	78cb *d*
254	51	92	145	−216	186	−61	−79	32	66	−36	−72	−76	−64	....	Reserves and Related Items	79ca *d*
255	51	92	145	−216	186	−61	−79	32	66	−36	−72	−76	−64	....	Reserve Assets	79db *d*
−1	—	—	—	—	—	—	—	—	—	—	—	—	—	....	Use of Fund Credit and Loans	79dc *d*
—	—	—	—	—	—	—	—	—	—	—	—	—	—	....	Liabs.Constit.For.Auth.Reserves	79dd *d*
....	....	....	....	....	....	....	....	....	....	....	....	....	....	....	Exceptional Financing	79de *d*
Year Ending December 31															**Government Finance**	
−4,976	−4,157	....	....	....	....	−8,267	−3,355	2,319	−1,267	921	4,184	6,273	....	....	Deficit (-) or Surplus	80
13,759	14,844	....	....	....	....	24,128	28,276	38,181	48,374	58,639	70,965	85,788	....	....	Revenue	81
5,967	6,359	....	....	....	....	2,061	3,812	6,156	3,426	763	9,995	6,250	....	....	Grants Received	81z
24,702	25,360	....	....	....	....	34,456	35,443	42,018	53,067	58,481	76,776	85,765	....	....	Expenditure	82
															Financing	
4,976	4,157	....	....	....	....	....	....	....	....	....	....	....	....	....	Total Financing	84
5,032	1,765	....	....	....	....	....	....	....	....	....	....	....	....	....	Domestic	84a
−99	1,598	....	....	....	....	....	....	....	....	....	....	....	....	....	Foreign	85a
43	794	....	....	....	....	....	....	....	....	....	....	....	....	....	Unallocable Financing	87c
Millions of Pounds															**National Accounts**	
9,345	10,290	9,572	9,714	9,360	9,949	11,256	20,003	31,212	62,811	76,042	76,038	97,577	113,985	....	Exports of Goods & Services	90c
11,870	13,656	15,103	16,154	18,448	19,785	21,440	22,945	24,529	33,433	38,502	47,582	53,588	57,459	....	Government Consumption	91f
14,116	15,262	16,270	17,508	18,082	20,016	22,443	23,223	25,992	33,808	44,395	55,992	86,120	102,633	....	Gross Capital Formation	93
34,107	48,256	44,992	49,464	47,535	54,650	67,026	98,496	152,683	141,717	184,389	231,883	273,196	294,417	....	Private Consumption	96f
−18,168	−21,687	−17,149	−19,549	−18,083	−21,175	−22,232	−36,955	−48,369	−62,877	−75,000	−99,931	−139,850	−169,979	....	Imports of Goods & Services	98c
51,270	65,777	68,788	73,291	75,342	83,225	99,933	127,712	186,047	208,892	268,328	311,564	370,631	398,515	....	Gross Domestic Product	99b
216,132	236,681	241,704	245,158	235,176	249,557	237,215	241,740	273,809	249,281	268,328	287,513	317,841	330,297	....	Gross Dom. Prod. 1990 Prices	99b.*p*
23.72	27.79	28.46	29.90	32.04	33.35	42.13	52.83	67.95	83.80	100.00	108.37	116.61	120.65	....	GDP Deflator (1990=100)	99bi *p*
Midyear Estimates																
8.70	9.00	9.30	9.61	9.93	10.27	10.61	10.97	11.34	11.72	12.12	12.53	12.96	13.31	13.88	**Population**	99z

Tanzania
738

		1965	1966	1967	1968	1969	1970	1971	1972	1973	1974	1975	1976	1977	1978	1979
Exchange Rates															*Shillings per SDR:*	
Official Rate	aa	7.14	7.14	7.14	7.14	7.14	7.14	7.76	7.76	8.32	8.75	9.66	9.66	9.66	9.66	10.83
															Shillings per US Dollar:	
Official Rate	ae	7.14	7.14	7.14	7.14	7.14	7.14	7.14	7.14	6.90	7.14	8.26	8.32	7.96	7.41	8.22
Official Rate	rf	7.14	7.14	7.14	7.14	7.14	7.14	7.14	7.14	7.02	7.13	7.37e	8.38e	8.29e	7.71e	8.22e
Fund Position															*Millions of SDRs:*	
Quota	2f.s	25.0	32.0	32.0	32.0	32.0	42.0	42.0	42.0	42.0	42.0	42.0	42.0	42.0	55.0	55.0
SDRs	1b.s	—	—	—	—	—	1.9	6.3	6.7	6.6	1.7	1.2	5.1	5.6	6.1	2.8
Reserve Position in the Fund	1c.s	2.2	4.0	4.0	4.2	4.4	6.9	6.9	6.9	10.5	—	—	—	—	—	—
Total Fund Cred.&Loans Outstg.	2tl	—	—	—	—	—	—	—	—	—	38.9	62.6	83.6	91.2	81.5	115.5
International Liquidity											*Millions of US Dollars Unless Otherwise Indicated:*					
Total Reserves minus Gold	1l.d	....	61.3	61.7	77.5	80.3	65.0	60.3	119.6	144.6	50.2	65.4	112.3	281.8	99.9	68.0
SDRs	1b.d	—	—	—	—	—	1.9	6.9	7.3	8.0	2.0	1.3	5.9	6.8	7.9	3.7
Reserve Position in the Fund	1c.d	2.2	4.0	4.0	4.2	4.4	6.9	7.5	7.5	12.7	—	—	—	—	—	—
Foreign Exchange	1d.d	....	57.3	57.7	73.3	75.9	56.2	45.9	104.8	124.0	48.2	64.1	106.4	275.0	91.9	64.3
Monetary Authorities: Other Liab.	4..d	....	2.0	.7	.6	1.2	1.2	1.4	6.2	3.7	21.6	26.4	2.4	42.3	57.3	34.4
Deposit Money Banks: Assets	7a.d	22.4	16.8	27.1	26.9	41.3	53.6	85.6	97.1	100.1	113.1	91.9	82.9	91.8	84.5	122.5
Deposit Money Banks: Liabilities	7b.d	21.1	6.3	6.2	5.9	5.8	9.8	18.0	14.2	14.3	18.1	15.0	28.4	37.0	92.9	45.3
of which: Liab. to Nonbanks	7bd d	....	....	....	....	4.9	3.8	6.1	8.9	9.6	11.2	10.1	20.2	30.9	84.5	36.7
Monetary Authorities															*Billions of Shillings:*	
Foreign Assets	11	....	.53	.45	.56	.57	.46	.43	.83	1.04	.40	.55	.94	2.30	.76	.72
Claims on Central Government	12a	....	.08	.06	.03	.15	.42	.64	.55	.51	1.06	1.37	1.60	1.31	2.87	5.04
Claims on Deposit Money Banks	12c	....	.09	.05	.08	.03	.07	.16	.14	—	.90	1.01	.73	.38	.84	.23
Reserve Money	14	....	.56	.54	.62	.65	.86	1.05	1.28	1.29	1.62	1.88	2.23	2.60	3.16	4.39
of which: Currency Outside DMBs	14a	....	.50	.51	.53	.61	.82	.99	1.20	1.20	1.52	1.76	2.07	2.38	2.92	4.06
Foreign Liabilities	16c	....	.01	.01	—	.01	.01	.01	.04	.03	.49	.82	.83	1.22	1.21	1.53
Other Items (Net)	17r	....	.13	.02	.05	.09	.08	.17	.20	.23	.24	.22	.21	.17	.11	.08
Deposit Money Banks															*Billions of Shillings:*	
Reserves	20	.04	.06	.03	.09	.08	.05	.06	.08	.09	.11	.13	.16	.21	.29	.30
Foreign Assets	21	.16	.12	.19	.19	.30	.38	.61	.69	.69	.81	.76	.69	.73	.63	1.01
Claims on Central Government	22a	.21	.02	.05	.14	.18	.15	.29	.46	.61	.90	1.51	2.16	1.87	2.13	3.39
Claims on Official Entities	22bx	.10	.01	.07	.14	.30	.68	.91	.85	1.24	2.21	2.63	3.08	3.65	5.01	5.60
Claims on Private Sector	22d	.60	.79	.76	.75	.77	.63	.52	.63	.50	.61	.64	.54	.68	.98	1.03
Claims on Other Financial Insts.	22f	....	....	....	.01	.02	.03	.07	.07	.08	.08	.08	.05	.07	.07	.10
Demand Deposits	24	.47	.63	.68	.77	1.05	.86	1.07	1.13	1.58	1.94	2.53	3.26	4.00	3.91	6.38
Time and Savings Deposits	25	.24	.24	.35	.52	.33	.54	.57	.76	.88	1.01	1.27	1.62	1.96	2.57	3.37
Foreign Liabilities	26c	.15	.05	.04	.04	.04	.07	.13	.10	.10	.13	.12	.24	.29	.69	.37
Central Government Deposits	26d	.25	.06	.14	.10	.19	.38	.52	.54	.53	.49	.65	.52	.29	.40	.47
Credit from Monetary Authorities	26g	.01	.09	.05	.08	.06	.07	.16	.14	—	.90	1.02	.74	.38	.90	.26
Capital Accounts	27a	.02	.03	.05	.05	.05	.08	.12	.14	.17	.21	.27	.34	.41	.52	.81
Other Items (Net)	27r	−.04	−.09	−.08	−.23	−.07	−.08	−.10	−.02	−.03	.03	−.12	−.04	−.13	.12	−.22
Monetary Survey															*Billions of Shillings:*	
Foreign Assets (Net)	31n	....	.60	.59	.70	.82	.77	.90	1.38	1.61	.58	.36	.56	1.51	−.51	−.17
Domestic Credit	32	....	.67	.75	.84	1.16	1.53	1.91	2.02	2.40	4.33	5.57	6.90	7.28	10.66	14.70
Claims on Central Govt. (Net)	32an	....	−.13	−.07	−.06	.07	.18	.41	.47	.58	1.44	2.22	3.22	2.89	4.60	7.96
Claims on Official Entities	32bx	.10	.01	.07	.14	.30	.68	.91	.85	1.24	2.21	2.63	3.08	3.65	5.01	5.60
Claims on Private Sector	32d	.60	.79	.76	.75	.77	.63	.52	.63	.50	.61	.64	.54	.68	.98	1.03
Claims on Other Financial Insts.	32f	....	....	....	.01	.02	.03	.07	.07	.08	.08	.08	.05	.07	.07	.10
Money	34	....	1.12	1.19	1.30	1.66	1.68	2.06	2.33	2.77	3.46	4.28	5.33	6.38	6.83	10.44
Quasi-Money	35	.24	.24	.35	.52	.33	.54	.57	.76	.88	1.01	1.27	1.62	1.96	2.57	3.37
Other Items (Net)	37r	....	−.10	−.19	−.19	−.17	.06	.22	.32	.40	.47	.39	.51	.39	.74	.71
Money plus Quasi-Money	35l	....	1.36	1.54	1.81	1.98	2.22	2.62	3.09	3.65	4.46	5.55	6.95	8.35	9.40	13.81
Other Banking Institutions															*Billions of Shillings:*	
Deposits	45	.03	.04	.04	.04	.05	.05	.05	.05	.06	.08	.09	.09	.11	.16	.18
Liquid Liabilities	55l	....	1.40	1.58	1.86	2.03	2.27	2.67	3.14	3.72	4.54	5.64	7.04	8.46	9.56	13.99
Interest Rates															*Percent Per Annum*	
Discount Rate (End of Period)	60	....	....	....	....	....	....	....	4.27	4.27	I4.77	4.77	4.77	4.77	4.77	4.77
Deposit Rate	60l	....	....	....	....	....	....	....	....	....	4.00	4.00	4.00	4.00	4.00	4.00
Lending Rate	60p	....	....	....	....	....	....	....	....	....	....	....	....	....	6.54	11.50
Prices and Production															*Index Numbers (1990=100):*	
Consumer Prices	64	1.3	1.4	1.6	1.9	2.2	2.2	2.3	2.5	2.8	3.3	4.2	4.5	I5.0	5.4	6.0
Manufacturing Production	66ey	....	....	....	....	....	....	....	....	....	....	....	....	....	....	....

Tanzania

738

	1980	1981	1982	1983	1984	1985	1986	1987	1988	1989	1990	1991	1992	1993	1994		
Exchange Rates																	
End of Period																	
Official Rate	10.44	9.69	10.55	13.04	17.75	18.12	63.26	118.77	168.21	252.71	279.69	334.58	460.63	659.13	764.16		aa
End of Period (ae) Period Average (rf)																	
Official Rate	8.18	8.32	9.57	12.46	18.11	16.50	51.72	83.72	125.00	192.30	196.60	233.90	335.00	479.87	523.45		ae
Official Rate	8.20ᵉ	8.28ᵉ	9.28ᵉ	11.14ᵉ	15.29	17.47	32.70	64.26	99.29	143.38	195.06	219.16	297.71	405.27	509.63		rf
Fund Position																	
End of Period																	
Quota	82.5	82.5	82.5	107.0	107.0	107.0	107.0	107.0	107.0	107.0	107.0	107.0	146.9	146.9	146.9		2f. s
SDRs	—	.3	—	.1	.1	—	4.6	.1	—	—	—	—	—	—	—		1b. s
Reserve Position in the Fund	—	1.7	—	—	—	—	—	—	—	—	—	—	10.0	10.0	10.0		1c. s
Total Fund Cred.&Loans Outstg.	134.3	125.7	114.4	88.1	60.2	52.6	58.2	80.0	105.1	97.8	98.4	100.2	160.5	156.2	145.5		2tl
International Liquidity																	
End of Period																	
Total Reserves minus Gold	20.3	18.8	4.8	19.4	26.9	16.0	61.1	31.8	77.7	54.2	192.8	203.9	327.3	203.3	332.1		1l. d
SDRs	—	.4	—	.1	.1	—	5.6	.1	—	—	—	—	—	—	—		1b. d
Reserve Position in the Fund	—	1.9	—	—	—	—	—	—	—	—	—	—	13.7	13.7	14.6		1c. d
Foreign Exchange	20.3	16.5	4.8	19.3	26.8	16.0	55.5	31.7	77.7	54.2	192.8	203.9	313.6	189.6	317.5		1d. d
Monetary Authorities: Other Liab.	19.6	-5.2	6.8	18.9	36.5	181.4	148.1	336.4	537.8	497.8	759.7	796.5	991.9	957.8	....		4.. d
Deposit Money Banks: Assets	172.1	127.5	170.0	206.0	86.8	52.4	39.7	18.8	17.8	....	....	....	31.1	40.7	131.1		7a. d
Deposit Money Banks: Liabilities	23.0	23.0	65.0	26.0	376.2	710.6	745.9	553.2	639.8	....	....	....	81.3	119.4	....		7b. d
of which: Liab. to Nonbanks	14.0	14.2	49.4	....	366.8	495.9	141.4	545.3	620.7	....	....	....	78.6	110.0	....		7bd d
Monetary Authorities																	
End of Period																	
Foreign Assets	.38	.35	.27	.34	.51	.26	2.54	2.66	9.71	10.43	37.90	47.70	139.86	97.56	....		11
Claims on Central Government	6.55	7.99	9.48	10.02	13.26	25.17	32.53	35.26	33.78	44.47	129.35	130.37	179.07	262.38	....		12a
Claims on Deposit Money Banks	.29	.47	.50	.34	.47	.01	1.73	19.78	43.98	55.56	60.09	58.32	2.30	2.07	....		12e
Reserve Money	5.56	7.14	8.63	8.89	11.57	14.03	19.72	27.88	36.18	43.76	62.28	70.35	112.75	152.32	....		14
of which: Currency Outside DMBs	5.25	6.61	7.99	8.19	10.47	12.67	18.31	24.55	31.23	....	57.92	63.60	95.45	122.47	....		14a
Foreign Liabilities	1.56	1.17	1.27	1.38	1.73	3.95	11.34	37.66	84.90	120.44	176.87	212.67	366.80	506.18	....		16c
Other Items (Net)	.10	.50	.35	.42	.94	7.47	5.73	-7.85	-33.61	-53.75	-11.82	-46.63	-158.31	-296.50	....		17r
Deposit Money Banks																	
End of Period																	
Reserves	.32	.53	.62	.81	1.30	1.62	1.22	3.09	4.95	....	....	....	18.05	35.04	....		20
Foreign Assets	1.41	1.06	1.63	2.57	1.57	.87	2.05	1.57	2.23	....	....	....	10.43	19.53	....		21
Claims on Central Government	4.87	6.65	9.49	11.43	12.74	8.50	3.76	3.64	17.30	....	....	....	33.14	32.48	....		22a
Claims on Official Entities	6.14	7.19	7.77	8.68	12.01	16.20	19.73	46.62	62.34	....	....	....	98.18	157.40	....		22bx
Claims on Private Sector	1.14	1.22	1.71	1.89	1.39	2.40	2.94	5.85	8.02	....	....	....	79.97	103.47	....		22d
Claims on Other Financial Insts.	.07	.07	.06	—	.01	—	.05	.03	.02	....	....	....	.06	1.48	....		22f
Demand Deposits	8.10	8.79	10.33	12.37	10.14	12.80	17.50	22.58	32.90	....	....	....	90.42	115.41	....		24
Time and Savings Deposits	4.17	5.29	6.41	8.56	9.59	13.88	14.50	19.31	23.65	....	....	....	99.09	116.36	....		25
Foreign Liabilities	.19	.19	.62	.32	6.81	11.72	38.58	46.32	79.97	....	....	....	27.23	57.29	....		26c
Central Government Deposits	.52	.79	1.44	.81	.85	.79	.73	1.65	1.23	....	....	....	5.44	5.19	....		26d
Credit from Monetary Authorities	.32	.28	.41	.40	.43	.50	1.24	18.09	43.98	....	....	....	75.00	8.86	....		26g
Capital Accounts	1.05	1.15	1.41	1.58	1.70	1.99	2.57	3.84	3.81	....	....	....	12.42	63.42	....		27a
Other Items (Net)	-.40	.23	.65	1.33	-.50	-12.10	-45.38	-50.98	-90.68	....	....	....	-69.79	-17.14	....		27r
Monetary Survey																	
End of Period																	
Foreign Assets (Net)	.04	.05	—	1.20	-6.46	-14.54	-45.33	-79.75	-152.93	....	....	....	-243.74	-446.37	....		31n
Domestic Credit	18.25	22.33	27.07	31.13	38.51	51.40	56.66	87.51	119.94	....	....	....	401.16	526.66	....		32
Claims on Central Govt. (Net)	10.90	13.84	17.54	20.57	25.11	32.80	33.95	35.02	49.56	....	....	....	222.96	264.31	....		32an
Claims on Official Entities	6.14	7.19	7.77	8.68	12.01	16.20	19.73	46.62	62.34	....	....	....	98.18	157.40	....		32bx
Claims on Private Sector	1.14	1.22	1.71	1.89	1.39	2.40	2.94	5.85	8.02	....	....	....	79.97	103.47	....		32d
Claims on Other Financial Insts.	.07	.07	.06	—	.01	—	.05	.03	.02	....	....	....	.06	1.48	....		32f
Money	13.35	15.40	18.32	20.56	20.61	25.47	35.81	47.13	64.13	....	....	....	185.88	237.88	....		34
Quasi-Money	4.17	5.29	6.41	8.56	9.59	13.88	14.50	19.31	23.65	....	....	....	99.09	116.36	....		35
Other Items (Net)	.82	1.67	2.32	3.32	1.85	-2.49	-38.98	-58.68	-120.78	....	....	....	-127.54	-273.96	....		37r
Money plus Quasi-Money	17.52	20.69	24.73	29.13	30.20	39.34	50.31	66.44	87.78	....	....	....	284.97	354.25	....		35l
Other Banking Institutions																	
End of Period																	
Deposits	.21	.25	.29	.36	.44	.55	.68	.87	.11	....	....	....	.80	1.12	....		45
Liquid Liabilities	17.73	20.94	25.02	29.48	30.64	39.89	50.99	67.31	87.89	....	....	....	285.77	355.36	....		55l
Interest Rates																	
Percent Per Annum																	
Discount Rate (End of Period)	4.77	4.00	4.00	4.00	4.00	4.25	6.50	11.31	12.67	15.17	....	....	....	14.50	34.63		60
Deposit Rate	4.00	4.00	4.00	4.00	4.00	4.50	8.50	15.75	17.46	17.00	....	....	....	....	....		60l
Lending Rate	11.50	12.00	12.00	13.00	13.00	12.29	18.50	27.50	29.63	31.00	....	....	....	31.00	39.00		60p
Prices and Production																	
Period Averages																	
Consumer Prices	7.9	9.9	12.8	16.2	22.1	29.4	38.9	50.6	66.4	83.5	100.0	122.3	149.3	184.3	....		64
Manufacturing Production	....	....	....	....	....	88	85	94	101	103	100	103	96	....	....		66ey

Tanzania
738

		1965	1966	1967	1968	1969	1970	1971	1972	1973	1974	1975	1976	1977	1978	1979
International Transactions															*Millions of Shillings*	
Exports	70	1,476	1,890	1,797	1,719	1,757	1,797	1,913	2,313	2,581	2,878	2,764	3,683	4,198	3,669	4,096
Imports, cif	71	1,410	1,695	1,638	1,834	1,710	2,274	2,726	2,883	3,479	5,377	5,710	5,350	6,161	8,798	9,073
Imports, fob	71.v	1,216	1,461	1,409	1,589	1,477	1,971	2,358	2,498	3,020	4,672	4,967	4,655	5,360	7,654	7,894
Balance of Payments															*Millions of US Dollars:*	
Goods: Exports f.o.b.	78aa d	....	....	....	....	....	....	....	....	....	....	....	490.4	538.5	476.0	545.7
Goods: Imports f.o.b.	78ab d	....	....	....	....	....	....	....	....	....	....	....	−555.7	−646.7	−992.5	−960.7
Trade Balance	78ac d	....	....	....	....	....	....	....	....	....	....	....	−65.3	−108.2	−516.5	−415.0
Services: Credit	78ad d	....	....	....	....	....	....	....	....	....	....	....	135.4	106.8	130.2	140.0
Services: Debit	78ae d	....	....	....	....	....	....	....	....	....	....	....	−141.0	−163.9	−245.3	−237.6
Balance on Goods and Services	78af d	....	....	....	....	....	....	....	....	....	....	....	−70.9	−165.4	−631.6	−512.6
Income: Credit	78ag d	....	....	....	....	....	....	....	....	....	....	....	7.4	11.1	19.1	11.6
Income: Debit	78ah d	....	....	....	....	....	....	....	....	....	....	....	−25.7	−31.8	−24.8	−20.2
Balance on Goods, Serv., & Inc.	78ai d	....	....	....	....	....	....	....	....	....	....	....	−89.2	−186.1	−637.3	−521.3
Current Transfers, n.i.e.: Credit	78aj d	....	....	....	....	....	....	....	....	....	....	....	105.5	144.9	194.8	200.3
Current Transfers: Debit	78ak d	....	....	....	....	....	....	....	....	....	....	....	−44.2	−24.9	−24.8	−25.6
Current Account, n.i.e.	78al d	....	....	....	....	....	....	....	....	....	....	....	−27.8	−66.1	−467.3	−346.5
Capital Account, n.i.e.: Credit	78ba d	....	....	....	....	....	....	....	....	....	....	....	—	—	.1	
Capital Account: Debit	78bb d	....	....	....	....	....	....	....	....	....	....	....	−6.8	−5.3	−6.1	
Capital Account, n.i.e.	78bc d	....	....	....	....	....	....	....	....	....	....	....	−6.8	−5.3	−6.0	
Direct Investment Abroad	78bd d	....	....	....	....	....	....	....	....	....	....	....	—	—	—	—
Dir. Invest. in Rep. Econ., n.i.e.	78be d	....	....	....	....	....	....	....	....	....	....	....	—	—	—	—
Portfolio Investment Assets	78bf d	....	....	....	....	....	....	....	....	....	....	....	—	—	—	—
Portfolio Investment Liab., n.i.e.	78bg d	....	....	....	....	....	....	....	....	....	....	....	—	—	—	—
Other Investment Assets	78bh d	....	....	....	....	....	....	....	....	....	....	....	8.2	−4.9	14.1	−47.2
Other Investment Liab., n.i.e.	78bi d	....	....	....	....	....	....	....	....	....	....	....	52.2	116.0	200.1	197.5
Financial Account, n.i.e.	78bj d	....	....	....	....	....	....	....	....	....	....	....	60.4	111.0	214.2	150.3
Net Errors and Omissions	78ca d	....	....	....	....	....	....	....	....	....	....	....	−4.3	69.1	8.4	23.8
Overall Balance	78cb d	....	....	....	....	....	....	....	....	....	....	....	21.5	108.7	−250.7	−172.4
Reserves and Related Items	78da d	....	....	....	....	....	....	....	....	....	....	....	−21.5	−108.7	250.7	172.4
Reserve Assets	79db d	....	....	....	....	....	....	....	....	....	....	....	−46.5	−163.7	199.2	30.2
Use of Fund Credit and Loans	79dc d	....	....	....	....	....	....	....	....	....	....	....	24.2	8.8	−12.0	43.4
Liabs.Constit.For.Auth.Reserves	79dd d	....	....	....	....	....	....	....	....	....	....	....	—	—	—	—
Exceptional Financing	79de d	....	....	....	....	....	....	....	....	....	....	....	.8	46.2	63.5	98.9
Government Finance															*Millions of Shillings:*	
Deficit (−) or Surplus	80	....	....	....	−305	−412	−369	−688	−555	−360	−851	−1,865	−1,805	−855	−1,936	−4,134
Revenue	81	....	....	....	1,129	1,263	1,595	1,683	1,855	2,295	3,000	3,944	4,062	4,896	7,096	6,833
Grants Received	81z	....	....	....	9	1	12	12	38	284	399	377	469	626	709	1,114
Expenditure	82	....	....	....	1,417	1,642	1,918	2,405	2,376	2,995	4,230	6,163	6,326	6,270	9,622	11,921
Lending Minus Repayments	83	....	....	....	26	33	58	−23	72	−57	20	24	11	108	119	160
Financing																
Domestic	84a	....	....	....	271	244	253	441	312	155	634	1,267	1,354	124	1,140	3,411
Foreign	85a	....	....	....	58	80	105	236	243	209	222	597	448	739	783	727
Use of Cash Balances	87	....	....	....	−24	88	11	11	—	−4	−4	2	3	−8	13	−4
National Accounts															*Millions of Shillings*	
Exports of Goods & Services	90c	1,600	2,013	1,948	1,906	2,041	2,200	2,366	2,745	2,939	3,400	3,462	5,297	5,627	4,692	5,131
Government Consumption	91f	642	725	803	884	995	1,208	1,365	1,494	1,968	2,604	3,259	3,989	4,308	5,585	5,956
Gross Fixed Capital Formation	93e	789	982	1,232	1,302	1,213	1,878	2,372	2,364	2,600	3,032	3,540	5,159	6,663	7,330	8,592
Increase/Decrease(−) in Stocks	93i	107	110	80	94	72	189	219	75	160	484	464	438	861	764	866
Private Consumption	96f	4,458	5,288	5,225	5,674	5,829	6,396	6,726	7,822	9,277	12,044	14,171	15,377	17,979	23,363	25,497
Imports of Goods & Services	98c	−1,544	−1,903	−1,927	−2,102	−2,016	−2,607	−3,234	−3,328	−3,840	−5,570	−5,885	−5,841	−6,570	−9,565	−9,759
Gross Domestic Product	99b	6,140	7,042	7,343	7,874	8,271	9,174	9,814	11,172	13,103	15,994	19,011	24,419	28,868	32,169	36,283
Net Factor Inc/Pmts(−) Abroad	98.n	−74	−136	−92	−33	−39	−24	−47	−42	−51	−37	−53	−100	−88	−45	−71
Gross Nat'l Expenditure = GNP	99a	6,066	6,906	7,251	7,841	8,232	9,148	9,767	11,130	13,052	15,957	18,958	24,319	28,780	32,124	36,212
Nat'l Income, Market Prices	99e	5,744	6,540	6,837	7,388	7,763	8,637	9,211	10,518	12,179	15,123	18,051	23,406	27,766	30,985	34,942
Gross Dom. Prod. 1990 Prices	99b.p	207,670	234,326	243,786	256,413	261,125	276,270	287,817	307,170	316,559	324,473	342,927	365,590	367,059	374,876	383,943
GDP Deflator (1990=100)	99bi p	3.0	3.0	3.0	3.1	3.2	3.3	3.4	3.6	4.1	4.9	5.5	6.7	7.9	8.6	9.5
															Millions:	
Population	99z	11.67	11.96	12.26	12.59	12.93	13.27	13.63	14.00	14.37	14.76	15.31	16.41	16.92	17.44	17.98

Exchange Rates: On June 14, 1966 the Tanzania shilling, equal to the East African shilling, was introduced.
International Transactions: Before 1968, data exclude trade of Zanzibar.
Government Finance: Data relate to a fiscal year different from calendar year.

Tanzania

738

	1980	1981	1982	1983	1984	1985	1986	1987	1988	1989	1990	1991	1992	1993	1994		
Millions of Shillings																**International Transactions**	
	4,192	4,706	4,144	4,138	4,388	4,265	11,285	18,512	27,041	52,777	64,512	74,709	123,966	180,034	....	Exports	70
	10,308	9,739	10,499	8,877	9,653	14,959	30,577	59,340	80,828	146,705	136,091	335,994	449,480	605,459	....	Imports, cif	71
	8,760	8,279	8,928	7,548	8,208	12,720	26,001	50,459	68,731	124,749	115,724	285,709	382,211	514,846	....	Imports, fob	71.v
Minus Sign Indicates Debit																**Balance of Payments**	
	582.7	613.0	412.9	383.2	398.5	328.5	335.9	287.9	386.5	415.1	407.8	362.2	400.7	462.0	....	Goods: Exports f.o.b.	78aa *d*
	−1,089.1	−1,061.3	−952.0	−708.4	−760.3	−869.2	−913.3	−1,000.5	−1,033.0	−1,070.1	−1,186.4	−1,284.7	−1,313.6	−1,299.9	....	Goods: Imports f.o.b.	78ab *d*
	−506.4	−448.2	−539.1	−325.2	−361.8	−540.7	−577.5	−712.6	−646.5	−655.0	−778.6	−922.5	−912.9	−837.9	....	Trade Balance	78ac *d*
	165.1	184.8	114.5	106.3	105.8	105.6	100.7	105.3	117.4	117.3	134.9	142.1	147.4	270.9	....	Services: Credit	78ad *d*
	−295.0	−252.1	−193.0	−161.5	−174.8	−208.7	−219.0	−224.4	−263.4	−272.5	−281.8	−308.1	−336.1	−413.0	....	Services: Debit	78ae *d*
	−636.4	−515.5	−617.6	−380.4	−430.7	−643.8	−695.7	−831.7	−792.5	−810.2	−925.5	−1,088.5	−1,101.6	−980.1	....	Balance on Goods and Services	78af *d*
	14.0	10.9	2.8	1.7	1.6	2.5	9.5	5.9	3.2	5.4	6.2	7.9	8.2	19.3	....	Income: Credit	78ag *d*
	−27.6	−32.2	−27.7	−29.2	−89.4	−100.4	−108.9	−203.2	−207.7	−214.7	−199.3	−194.1	−233.5	−167.4	....	Income: Debit	78ah *d*
	−649.9	−536.8	−642.5	−407.9	−518.5	−741.7	−795.1	−1,029.0	−997.1	−1,019.6	−1,118.6	−1,274.7	−1,326.9	−1,128.2	....	Balance on Goods, Serv., & Inc.	78ai *d*
	153.2	152.5	136.5	127.6	180.4	394.2	501.2	609.9	642.9	682.0	723.5	856.0	940.0	749.7	....	Current Transfers, n.i.e.: Credit	78aj *d*
	−25.5	−23.2	−18.1	−24.9	−21.4	−27.6	−28.0	−27.0	−21.7	−29.8	−30.0	−32.6	−35.0	−30.0	....	Current Transfers: Debit	78ak *d*
	−522.2	−407.6	−524.1	−305.2	−359.5	−375.1	−322.0	−446.0	−375.9	−367.3	−425.1	−451.3	−421.9	−408.5	....	Current Account, n.i.e.	78al *d*
	—	—	—	—	—	—	—	—	—	—	—	—	—	—	....	Capital Account, n.i.e.: Credit	78ba *d*
	—	—	—	—	—	—	—	—	—	—	—	—	—	—	....	Capital Account: Debit	78bb *d*
	—	—	—	—	—	—	—	—	—	—	—	—	—	—	....	Capital Account, n.i.e.	78bc *d*
	—	—	—	—	—	—	—	—	—	—	—	—	—	—	....	Direct Investment Abroad	78bd *d*
	—	—	—	—	—	—	—	—	—	—	—	—	12.0	20.0	....	Dir. Invest. in Rep. Econ., n.i.e.	78be *d*
	—	—	—	—	—	—	—	—	—	—	—	—	—	—	....	Portfolio Investment Assets	78bf *d*
	—	—	—	—	—	—	—	—	—	—	—	—	—	—	....	Portfolio Investment Liab., n.i.e.	78bg *d*
	—	—	—	—	—	—	—	—	—	—	—	—	—	—	....	Other Investment Assets	78bh *d*
	218.7	242.5	193.4	278.5	11.3	−72.3	9.5	60.4	33.9	21.8	126.5	108.1	76.9	55.0	....	Other Investment Liab., n.i.e.	78bi *d*
	218.7	242.5	193.4	278.5	11.3	−72.3	9.5	60.4	33.9	21.8	126.5	108.1	88.9	75.0	....	Financial Account, n.i.e.	78bj *d*
	−46.6	78.7	58.2	−61.7	126.9	−39.6	−40.1	94.1	−42.0	18.8	216.9	−20.1	44.6	−18.6	....	Net Errors and Omissions	78ca *d*
	−350.1	−86.3	−272.5	−88.4	−221.2	−487.0	−352.5	−291.5	−383.9	−326.8	−81.6	−363.3	−288.4	−352.1	....	Overall Balance	78cb *d*
	350.1	86.3	272.5	88.4	221.2	487.0	352.5	291.5	383.9	326.8	81.6	363.3	288.4	352.1	....	Reserves and Related Items	79da *d*
	54.9	8.4	13.9	−14.6	−7.5	10.9	−45.0	30.7	−45.9	23.5	−140.8	−12.6	−92.8	57.2	....	Reserve Assets	79db *d*
	25.0	−11.3	−12.4	−28.1	−28.4	−7.5	7.3	28.4	34.2	−9.3	—	2.1	83.7	−6.0	....	Use of Fund Credit and Loans	79dc *d*
	—	—	—	—	—	—	—	—	—	—	—	—	—	—	....	Liabs.Constit.For.Auth.Reserves	79dd *d*
	270.1	89.1	271.0	131.1	257.1	483.7	390.3	232.4	395.6	312.6	222.5	373.9	297.5	301.0	....	Exceptional Financing	79de *d*
Year Ending June 30																**Government Finance**	
	−4,046	−5,026	−7,024	−5,383	−5,669	−8,409	−8,643	−15,406	−11,908	−14,698	−15,340	−47,324	−54,688	−113,592	−135,982	Deficit (−) or Surplus	80
	8,963	8,571	9,406	12,581	13,506	18,638	22,032	29,321	47,480	70,415	97,867	137,093	173,566	164,110	242,444	Revenue	81
	1,000	1,158	957	1,029	1,234	1,462	1,035	3,144	15,909	20,985	27,664	22,875	32,798	58,313	106,790	Grants Received	81z
	13,943	14,755	17,387	18,993	20,409	28,509	31,710	47,871	75,297	106,098	140,871	207,292	261,051	336,015	485,216	Expenditure	82
	65															Lending Minus Repayments	83
																Financing	
	3,545	....	6,226	4,735	5,630	7,989	8,638	12,315	−2,728	21,188	12,361	29,608	9,335	84,156	112,581	Domestic	84a
	755	612	797	648	39	420	5	3,091	14,636	−6,490	2,979	17,716	45,353	29,436	23,401	Foreign	85a
	−255	....	—	—	—	—	—	—	—	—	—	—	—	—	—	Use of Cash Balances	87
Millions of Shillings																**National Accounts**	
	5,540	5,994	4,546	5,111	6,321	7,453	14,580	26,452	45,541	77,677	103,457	112,466	170,170	189,914	....	Exports of Goods & Services	90c
	5,494	6,105	8,046	9,443	13,844	18,555	23,621	25,433	35,855	45,380	52,637	71,027	85,531	95,110	....	Government Consumption	91f
	8,630	10,624	10,825	7,752	11,973	16,872	28,679	65,075	97,296	129,022	217,404	231,430	305,076	487,195	....	Gross Fixed Capital Formation	93e
	1,055	1,498	1,410	1,836	1,645	2,091	2,487	3,685	4,122	11,075	18,022	36,996	37,402	50,100	....	Increase/Decrease(−) in Stocks	93i
	32,486	35,043	42,261	55,128	68,652	93,490	127,307	175,049	311,330	350,614	394,530	596,099	684,359	77,135	....	Private Consumption	96f
	−11,087	−10,162	−8,862	−8,761	−13,543	−17,480	−37,026	−69,250	−162,928	−206,683	−280,840	−350,330	−475,202	−56,553	....	Imports of Goods & Services	98c
	42,118	49,102	58,226	70,509	88,892	120,621	159,721	226,444	331,217	407,085	505,210	697,688	807,336	845,485	....	Gross Domestic Product	99b
	−112	−176	−231	−211	−173	−704	−3,281	−11,038	−18,542	−29,377	−40,981	−42,180	−54,808	−75,502	....	Net Factor Inc/Pmts(−) Abroad	98.n
	42,006	48,926	57,995	70,298	88,719	119,917	156,367	215,406	312,675	377,708	464,229	655,508	752,528	769,983	....	Gross Nat'l Expenditure = GNP	99a
	40,466	47,384	56,427	68,679	86,840	117,435	152,606	210,066	305,779	363,751	449,865	640,771	736,907	753,532	....	Nat'l Income, Market Prices	99e
	395,425	393,433	395,763	386,358	399,427	409,929	423,302	444,830	463,657	482,196	505,210	524,847	543,741	....	....	Gross Dom. Prod. 1990 Prices	99b.*p*
	10.7	12.5	14.7	18.2	22.3	29.4	37.7	50.9	71.4	84.4	100.0	132.9	148.5	....	....	GDP Deflator (1990=100)	99bi *p*
Midyear Estimates																	
	18.58	19.17	19.78	20.41	21.06	21.73	22.46	23.22	24.00	24.80	25.63	26.40	27.20	28.02	....	**Population**	99z

Thailand

578

		1965	1966	1967	1968	1969	1970	1971	1972	1973	1974	1975	1976	1977	1978	1979
Exchange Rates																*Baht per SDR:*
Official Rate	aa	20.830	20.750	20.800	20.850	20.927	20.927	Ι22.721	22.721	24.579	24.946	23.881	23.701	24.780	26.564	26.906
																Baht per US Dollar:
Official Rate	ae	20.830	20.750	20.800	20.850	20.928	20.928	Ι20.928	20.928	20.375	20.375	20.400	20.400	20.400	20.390	20.425
Official Rate	rf	20.800	20.800	20.800	20.800	20.800	20.800	20.800	20.800	20.620	20.375	20.379	20.400	20.400	20.336	20.419
Fund Position																*Millions of SDRs:*
Quota	2f.s	76	95	95	95	95	134	134	134	134	134	134	134	134	181	181
SDRs	1b.s	—	—	—	—	—	—	14	29	29	30	30	29	30	27	37
Reserve Position in the Fund	1c.s	19	24	24	24	24	34	34	34	34	34	34	34	34	—	—
Total Fund Cred.&Loans Outstg.	2tl	—	—	—	—	—	—	—	—	—	—	—	67	81	191	278
International Liquidity												*Millions of US Dollars Unless Otherwise Indicated:*				
Total Reserves minus Gold	11.d	643	832	917	929	893	824	788	963	1,207	1,758	1,679	1,798	1,813	2,009	1,843
SDRs	1b.d							16	31	34	36	35	34	37	35	49
Reserve Position in the Fund	1c.d	19	24	24	24	24	34	36	36	40	41	39	39	41	—	—
Foreign Exchange	1d.d	624	808	893	905	869	790	736	896	1,132	1,681	1,605	1,725	1,735	1,974	1,794
Gold (Million Fine Troy Ounces)	1ad	2.756	2.620	2.620	2.620	2.620	2.342	2.340	2.340	2.340	2.340	2.340	2.340	2.397	2.426	2.455
Gold (National Valuation)	1and	96	92	92	92	92	82	82	89	99	100	96	95	102	548	1,286
Monetary Authorities: Other Liab.	4.d	....	....	....	—	—	—	—	—	—	—	—	—	—	—	—
Deposit Money Banks: Assets	7a.d	83	94	76	95	130	128	178	226	298	299	290	384	446	565	771
of which: Claims on Nonbanks	7add	83	94	76	46	52	57	78	94	138	155	163	229	240	346	424
Deposit Money Banks: Liabilities	7b.d	117	154	169	132	152	176	184	198	366	421	466	528	868	1,453	1,846
of which: Liab. to Nonbanks	7bdd	117	154	169	9	8	19	20	22	25	40	40	43	63	47	44
Other Banking Insts.: Liabilities	7f.d	1	2	3	4	7	8	11	11	10	14	28	181	235	289	378
of which: Liab. to Nonbanks	7fdd	—	—	—	—	—	—	—	—	—	—	1	39	49	60	84
Monetary Authorities																*Billions of Baht:*
Foreign Assets	11	15.8	19.7	21.5	21.7	21.0	19.5	19.2	23.3	27.6	39.4	37.7	37.9	38.3	51.8	63.9
Claims on Central Government	12a	2.7	2.8	2.3	4.6	8.5	11.7	13.4	15.6	17.0	14.1	13.8	19.6	26.1	35.3	44.0
Claims on Deposit Money Banks	12e	.4	.5	.4	.4	.3	.8	1.3	1.3	2.9	3.9	7.2	5.4	5.9	8.0	16.5
Claims on Other Financial Insts.	12f	....	....	....	.1	.2	.2	.1	.3	.4	.7	.9	1.3	1.1	2.1	3.0
Reserve Money	14	9.9	11.2	12.2	13.2	14.0	15.4	17.0	20.1	23.7	26.8	29.7	33.5	36.6	42.9	50.3
of which: Currency Outside DMBs	14a	8.1	9.4	9.8	10.7	11.0	11.9	13.1	15.3	18.7	20.5	22.3	25.8	28.7	33.2	40.8
Foreign Liabilities	16c	....	....	....	—	—	—	—	—	—	—	—	1.6	2.0	5.1	7.5
Central Government Deposits	16d	4.5	6.8	6.9	5.6	7.2	6.4	4.9	6.5	8.0	10.5	7.2	5.4	4.6	5.9	5.8
Capital Accounts	17a	4.0	4.4	4.8	8.0	8.9	10.3	11.9	14.0	16.4	20.8	22.5	23.0	27.6	43.6	63.7
Other Items (Net)	17r	.4	.4	.4	—	-.1	.1	.1	-.2	-.1	.1	.7	.5	.7	-.3	.4
Deposit Money Banks																*Billions of Baht:*
Reserves	20	1.3	1.5	1.7	Ι2.0	2.3	2.4	3.0	3.4	3.6	5.2	6.5	6.3	6.8	8.4	7.6
Foreign Assets	21	1.7	2.0	1.6	2.0	2.7	2.7	3.7	4.7	6.1	6.1	5.9	Ι7.8	9.1	11.5	15.7
Claims on Central Government	22a	2.6	4.1	4.9	5.6	5.5	5.9	8.3	13.9	15.0	15.9	17.7	Ι21.0	22.5	24.5	26.1
Claims on Nonfin.Pub.Enterprises	22c				.3	.3	.3	.5	.5	.9	1.2	1.4	Ι1.8	2.5	3.8	4.5
Claims on Private Sector	22d	12.0	14.4	16.8	18.8	21.9	26.6	29.3	33.0	47.1	63.6	77.3	Ι89.4	114.3	146.8	179.3
Claims on Other Financial Insts.	22f	....	....	....	1.3	1.5	1.9	1.9	1.6	2.0	3.7	6.6	Ι5.4	8.3	11.0	12.1
Demand Deposits	24	4.5	5.0	5.4	6.1	6.4	6.7	7.5	8.7	10.5	11.7	12.0	Ι15.1	16.4	21.1	22.2
Time and Savings Deposits	25	7.9	10.8	13.1	15.7	18.8	22.3	27.3	35.4	43.7	55.9	68.5	Ι84.3	105.4	125.7	142.1
Foreign Liabilities	26c	2.4	3.2	3.5	2.8	3.2	3.7	3.8	4.1	7.5	8.6	9.5	Ι10.8	17.7	29.6	37.7
Central Government Deposits	26d	1.1	1.2	1.5	1.8	1.8	2.0	2.0	2.6	3.0	3.4	3.3	Ι4.7	5.0	5.6	7.5
Credit from Monetary Authorities	26g				.4	.3	.8	1.3	1.3	2.9	4.0	7.3	5.5	6.0	8.1	16.7
Capital Accounts	27a	....	....	....	2.5	2.9	3.4	4.0	4.4	5.7	8.0	9.8	Ι10.2	12.1	15.0	18.2
Other Items (Net)	27r	1.7	1.8	1.3	.8	.8	.9	.8	.6	1.4	3.9	4.9	Ι1.1	.9	.7	.9
Monetary Survey																*Billions of Baht:*
Foreign Assets (Net)	31n	15.1	18.5	19.5	20.9	20.5	18.5	19.1	23.9	26.2	36.9	34.1	Ι33.4	27.7	28.6	34.4
Domestic Credit	32	11.6	13.3	15.6	23.2	28.8	38.0	46.6	55.8	71.5	85.2	107.1	Ι128.6	165.4	212.3	256.0
Claims on Central Govt. (Net)	32an	-.4	-1.1	-1.2	2.8	5.0	9.0	14.7	20.3	20.9	16.0	20.9	Ι30.5	39.0	48.2	56.8
Claims on Nonfin.Pub.Enterprises	32c				.3	.3	.3	.5	.5	.9	1.2	1.4	Ι1.9	2.6	3.8	4.6
Claims on Private Sector	32d	12.0	14.4	16.8	18.8	21.9	26.6	29.3	33.1	47.2	63.6	77.4	Ι89.6	114.5	147.0	179.6
Claims on Other Financial Insts.	32f	—	—	—	1.4	1.6	2.1	2.0	1.9	2.4	4.4	7.4	Ι6.7	9.3	13.1	15.1
Money	34	12.9	14.6	15.6	17.2	17.9	19.4	21.3	24.8	30.0	32.7	34.7	Ι41.4	45.4	54.5	63.5
Quasi-Money	35	7.9	10.8	13.1	15.7	18.8	22.3	27.3	35.4	43.7	55.9	68.5	Ι84.3	105.4	125.7	142.1
Other Items (Net)	37r	5.9	6.4	6.4	11.3	12.6	14.9	17.0	19.5	24.1	33.4	38.1	Ι36.3	42.2	60.6	84.8
Money plus Quasi-Money	35l	20.8	25.4	28.8	32.9	36.7	41.7	48.6	60.2	73.6	88.7	103.2	Ι125.7	150.8	180.3	205.7
Other Banking Institutions																
Development Institutions																*Billions of Baht:*
Cash	40	.1	.3	.1	.1	.1	.1	.2	.2	.3	Ι.5	.8	1.9	2.7	4.4	4.6
Claims on Private Sector	42d	.3	.4	.6	.9	1.3	1.6	1.9	2.3	2.6	Ι3.7	6.2	9.0	11.5	14.0	18.2
Time and Savings Deposits	45	—	—	.1	.1	.1	.2	.2	.3	.4	Ι.8	1.4	1.7	2.2	2.6	2.8
Bonds	46ab	—	—	—	—	—	.2	.2	.2	.2	.2	.2	.4	.2	.2	.2
Long-Term Foreign Liabilities	46cl	—	—	.1	.1	.1	.2	.2	.2	.2	Ι.3	.6	.9	1.4	2.7	4.8
Central Govt. Lending Funds	46f	.1	.2	.2	.1	.1	.1	.1	.1	.1	Ι.5	.5	.6	.6	.8	.6
Credit from Monetary Authorities	46g	—	—	—	.1	.2	.2	.1	.3	.4	Ι.7	.8	1.3	1.2	2.1	2.6
Credit from Deposit Money Banks	46h	—	—	—	.1	.1	.1	—	—	—	Ι.2	2.0	4.4	6.3	7.8	9.3
Capital Accounts	47a	.1	.2	.4	.5	.6	.9	1.3	1.3	1.5	Ι1.6	1.7	1.9	2.3	2.8	3.2
Other Items (Net)	47r	—	—	—	—	—	—	—	—	—	Ι-.1	-.2	-.2	—	-.5	-.7

Thailand

1980	1981	1982	1983	1984	1985	1986	1987	1988	1989	1990	1991	1992	1993	1994		
End of Period															**Exchange Rates**	
26.312	26.771	25.372	24.080	26.613	29.273	31.962	35.566	33.965	33.761	35.979	36.161	35.090	35.081	36.628	Official Rate	**aa**
End of Period (ac)				*Period Average (rf)*												
20.630	23.000	23.000	23.000	27.150	26.650	26.130	25.070	25.240	25.690	25.290	25.280	25.520	25.540	25.090	Official Rate	**ae**
20.476	21.820	23.000	23.000	23.639	27.159	26.299	25.723	25.294	25.702	25.585	25.517	25.400	25.319	25.150	Official Rate	**rf**
End of Period															**Fund Position**	
272	272	272	387	387	387	387	387	387	387	387	387	387	574	574	574 Quota	**2f. s**
6	52	22	15	2	1	27	42	45	13	9	6	9	16	22	SDRs	**1b. s**
—	—	—	29	29	29	29	29	29	29	29	32	155	243	272	285 Reserve Position in the Fund	**1c. s**
273	737	767	994	922	1,021	874	686	492	207	1	—	—	—	—	Total Fund Cred.&Loans Outstg.	**2tl**
End of Period															**International Liquidity**	
1,560	1,732	1,538	1,607	1,921	2,190	2,804	4,007	6,097	9,515	13,305	17,517	20,359	24,473	29,332	Total Reserves minus Gold	**1l. d**
8	61	25	16	2	1	33	60	61	16	13	8	12	22	32	SDRs	**1b. d**
—	—	—	30	28	32	35	41	39	38	45	222	335	373	416	Reserve Position in the Fund	**1c. d**
1,552	1,671	1,513	1,561	1,890	2,157	2,736	3,906	5,997	9,461	13,247	17,287	20,012	24,078	28,884	Foreign Exchange	**1d. d**
2.487	2.487	2.487	2.487	2.487	2.487	2.487	2.476	2.476	2.476	2.476	2.476	2.474	2.474	2.474	Gold (Million Fine Troy Ounces)	**1ad**
1,466	995	1,114	949	768	813	972	1,204	1,015	993	968	899	823	967	947	Gold (National Valuation)	**1and**
—	—	—	—	—	—	—	1	—	4	3	4	5	6	6	Monetary Authorities: Other Liab.	**4..d**
919	1,118	1,318	1,069	1,134	1,263	1,606	1,538	1,782	2,733	2,229	2,872	3,046	6,167	6,740	Deposit Money Banks: Assets	**7a. d**
493	391	511	355	414	410	475	606	780	981	1,064	1,276	1,568	1,783	2,463	of which: Claims on Nonbanks	**7add d**
1,379	1,462	1,276	1,865	1,875	1,722	1,215	1,482	2,444	3,319	4,340	4,902	6,567	13,799	31,151	Deposit Money Banks: Liabilities	**7b. d**
86	111	89	150	119	177	182	243	265	430	378	555	620	901	969	of which: Liab. to Nonbanks	**7bd d**
394	473	458	571	803	776	860	857	869	1,021	1,557	1,894	5,194	5,611	6,839	Other Banking Insts.: Liabilities	**7f. d**
85	117	137	175	206	290	306	398	402	518	554	573	2,685	2,890	3,573	of which: Liab. to Nonbanks	**7fd d**
End of Period															**Monetary Authorities**	
62.4	62.7	61.0	58.8	72.9	80.0	98.6	130.5	179.3	269.7	360.6	465.1	539.1	649.1	759.0	Foreign Assets	**11**
59.9	71.3	87.7	100.7	96.0	106.9	98.9	92.5	47.2	36.2	57.9	54.9	60.6	50.7	32.5	Claims on Central Government	**12a**
16.5	19.8	20.7	22.9	23.8	25.5	34.8	42.0	57.8	41.6	42.5	37.5	34.8	18.9	12.4	Claims on Deposit Money Banks	**12e**
5.4	4.8	5.3	5.0	8.3	12.8	14.1	13.6	15.0	16.1	17.6	19.1	24.7	27.5	35.8	Claims on Other Financial Insts.	**12f**
57.3	61.1	68.4	75.6	79.8	86.5	95.3	116.7	134.0	156.7	185.8	210.5	248.0	288.1	329.9	Reserve Money	**14**
45.9	47.8	54.0	59.6	63.5	64.0	71.1	86.7	99.0	119.0	137.5	149.3	180.2	208.6	242.0	of which: Currency Outside DMBs	**14a**
7.2	19.7	19.5	23.9	24.5	29.9	27.9	24.4	16.7	7.1	.1	.1	.1	.7	.1	Foreign Liabilities	**16c**
6.7	5.9	6.5	5.8	5.7	8.0	10.3	9.0	15.0	58.2	115.5	173.9	201.6	213.7	235.8	Central Government Deposits	**16d**
72.5	75.0	79.6	81.6	93.4	103.3	117.3	136.0	138.4	148.6	172.0	202.2	231.8	263.1	290.3	Capital Accounts	**17a**
.7	-3.1	.7	.4	-2.3	-2.6	-4.6	-7.4	-4.8	-7.0	5.3	-10.1	-22.5	-18.9	-16.5	Other Items (Net)	**17r**
End of Period															**Deposit Money Banks**	
10.4	11.8	12.8	15.0	14.6	21.2	22.1	25.7	32.4	33.8	51.6	60.4	60.9	73.4	79.4	Reserves	**20**
19.0	25.7	30.3	24.6	30.8	33.7	42.0	38.6	45.0	70.2	56.4	72.6	77.7	157.5	169.1	Foreign Assets	**21**
29.1	38.7	53.7	53.1	80.6	77.7	104.8	115.6	124.3	123.3	110.7	82.9	69.7	50.3	36.0	Claims on Central Government	**22a**
5.4	6.4	6.2	12.0	13.0	13.6	14.6	14.9	14.5	15.9	18.1	47.7	53.2	76.5	94.2	Claims on Nonfin.Pub.Enterprises	**22c**
201.3	237.3	281.6	371.7	433.5	481.2	501.5	614.8	796.1	1,045.4	1,408.8	1,696.9	2,045.1	2,532.6	3,304.0	Claims on Private Sector	**22d**
15.4	14.9	15.7	25.1	34.0	32.5	36.3	51.7	52.8	60.4	69.0	91.2	113.1	126.6	158.0	Claims on Other Financial Insts.	**22f**
25.1	25.0	23.5	21.3	24.5	21.1	30.5	44.5	48.1	53.9	55.0	70.0	66.1	82.4	96.4	Demand Deposits	**24**
180.3	219.1	284.6	365.6	449.1	507.6	569.3	676.2	807.6	1,032.4	1,333.7	1,610.6	1,868.1	2,210.9	2,482.9	Time and Savings Deposits	**25**
28.4	33.6	29.3	42.9	50.9	45.9	31.8	37.2	61.7	85.3	109.8	123.9	167.6	352.4	781.6	Foreign Liabilities	**26c**
7.7	11.8	11.6	15.8	16.5	19.7	20.9	23.6	28.4	32.7	35.6	50.5	76.5	92.7	122.5	Central Government Deposits	**26d**
16.7	20.2	20.9	23.4	24.3	26.1	33.6	42.0	57.6	41.2	42.3	37.6	36.3	21.2	13.7	Credit from Monetary Authorities	**26g**
19.5	21.5	24.6	28.1	36.3	42.4	44.1	57.5	68.3	83.1	111.3	143.5	170.2	222.4	280.9	Capital Accounts	**27a**
2.7	3.6	5.7	4.4	4.8	-3.0	-9.0	-19.7	-6.6	20.5	26.9	16.1	34.8	33.3	62.7	Other Items (Net)	**27r**
End of Period															**Monetary Survey**	
45.7	35.1	42.5	16.5	28.3	37.8	80.8	107.5	145.9	247.5	307.1	413.7	449.1	454.0	146.3	Foreign Assets (Net)	**31n**
302.5	356.1	432.7	546.6	643.9	697.9	739.7	871.2	1,007.4	1,207.3	1,531.1	1,768.1	2,088.2	2,557.6	3,302.2	Domestic Credit	**32**
74.6	92.3	123.3	132.2	154.4	156.9	172.4	175.5	128.1	68.6	17.5	-86.7	-147.8	-205.5	-289.8	Claims on Central Govt. (Net)	**32an**
5.4	6.4	6.2	12.0	13.0	13.6	14.6	14.9	14.5	15.9	18.1	47.7	53.2	76.5	94.2	Claims on Nonfin.Pub.Enterprises	**32c**
201.7	237.8	282.5	372.3	434.2	482.0	502.3	615.6	796.9	1,046.2	1,408.8	1,696.9	2,045.1	2,532.6	3,304.0	Claims on Private Sector	**32d**
20.8	19.7	21.0	30.1	42.3	45.4	50.4	65.3	67.9	76.6	86.6	110.3	137.8	154.0	193.8	Claims on Other Financial Insts.	**32f**
71.4	73.3	78.3	81.8	88.8	85.8	102.4	132.4	148.5	174.7	195.4	222.4	249.7	296.2	346.4	Money	**34**
180.3	219.1	284.6	365.6	449.1	507.6	569.3	676.2	807.6	1,032.4	1,333.7	1,610.6	1,868.1	2,210.9	2,482.9	Quasi-Money	**35**
96.5	98.7	112.5	115.7	134.2	142.2	148.8	170.2	197.2	247.7	309.1	349.6	419.5	503.1	619.2	Other Items (Net)	**37r**
251.8	292.4	362.9	447.4	537.9	593.5	671.8	808.6	956.1	1,207.1	1,529.1	1,832.4	2,117.8	2,507.1	2,829.4	Money plus Quasi-Money	**35l**
															Other Banking Institutions	
															Development Institutions	
End of Period																
4.1	5.6	3.4	2.9	4.3	4.9	4.2	5.0	6.1	13.9	15.7	16.0	8.1	13.0	21.1	Cash	**40**
24.0	28.1	30.4	32.4	38.3	43.3	45.5	49.0	55.3	69.7	94.0	121.2	159.3	207.5	264.6	Claims on Private Sector	**42d**
3.6	4.4	4.8	6.0	9.5	11.7	14.0	15.1	20.6	32.3	43.3	58.2	71.5	91.0	....	Time and Savings Deposits	**45**
.9	2.0	2.1	2.6	2.9	2.5	1.7	3.0	5.5	10.3	15.0	25.7	37.0	67.3	....	Bonds	**46ab**
5.9	7.6	8.3	9.3	13.5	16.3	18.2	19.1	19.3	19.9	21.7	20.2	23.1	26.0	29.9	Long-Term Foreign Liabilities	**46cl**
.7	.8	.6	.5	.8	.7	.7	.7	.4	.5	1.4	1.4	1.4	4.4	2.7	Central Govt. Lending Funds	**46f**
4.6	4.2	4.7	4.2	4.1	4.6	3.6	4.0	4.1	4.8	6.0	6.9	8.6	9.7	9.0	Credit from Monetary Authorities	**46g**
9.5	9.7	10.0	9.3	9.8	10.7	11.1	12.3	14.1	14.5	15.3	17.1	12.5	7.6	11.6	Credit from Deposit Money Banks	**46h**
3.2	3.7	4.7	5.1	6.2	7.0	6.7	7.3	7.7	11.8	12.3	15.4	17.0	21.6	30.0	Capital Accounts	**47a**
-.4	1.1	-1.3	-1.7	-4.4	-5.3	-6.3	-7.6	-10.1	-10.4	-5.2	-7.7	-3.8	-7.1	....	Other Items (Net)	**47r**

Thailand

578

		1965	1966	1967	1968	1969	1970	1971	1972	1973	1974	1975	1976	1977	1978	1979
Finance and Securities Companies																*Billions of Baht:*
Reserves	40..f	....	....	....	....	....	....	....	....	....	....	....	1.2	1.2	1.4	2.0
Claims on Central Government	42a.f	....	....	....	....	....	....	....	....	....	....	....	—	—	—	—
Claims on Nonfin.Pub.Enterprises	42c.f	....	....	....	....	....	....	....	....	....	....	....	.9	1.5	2.3	2.6
Claims on Private Sector	42d.f	....	....	....	....	....	....	....	....	....	....	....	22.5	30.7	44.0	45.0
Bonds	46ab f	....	....	....	....	....	....	....	....	....	....	....	15.3	21.3	32.1	33.8
Foreign Liabilities	46c.f	....	....	....	....	....	....	....	....	....	....	....	2.8	3.4	3.2	2.9
Credit from Monetary Authorities	46g.f	....	....	....	....	....	....	....	....	....	....	....	—	—	—	.3
Cred. from Deposit Money Banks	46h.f	....	....	....	....	....	....	....	....	....	....	....	3.1	4.1	5.0	5.3
Capital Accounts	47a.f	....	....	....	....	....	....	....	....	....	....	....	2.8	4.2	6.3	8.2
Other Items (Net)	47r.f	....	....	....	....	....	....	....	....	....	....	....	.6	.5	1.0	−.8
Government Savings Bank																*Billions of Baht:*
Cash	40..g	.1	.1	.1	.3	.1	.2	.1	.1	.2	.7	.7	.3	.3	.4	.8
Claims on Central Government	42a.g	2.4	3.5	4.3	4.9	5.5	5.9	6.8	8.4	10.8	11.9	12.7	14.1	16.3	17.5	20.3
Claims on Nonfin.Pub.Enterprise	42c.g	.4	.2	.1	.1	.1	.2	.1	.1	.1	.1	.1	.4	.6	.5	.6
Claims on Private Sector	42d.g	.1	.1	.2	.2	.3	.2	.3	.3	.3	.3	.3	.3	.3	.3	.3
Demand Deposits	44..g	.2	.2	.2	.2	.2	.2	.2	.1	.1	.3	.2	.2	.1	.1	.1
Time and Savings Deposits	45..g	2.1	2.6	3.2	3.6	4.1	4.4	5.0	6.4	8.3	9.5	10.2	11.4	13.9	15.2	19.0
Bonds	46ab g	.7	.9	1.0	1.1	1.2	1.3	1.3	1.4	1.6	1.6	1.6	1.5	1.6	1.7	1.8
Central Government Deposits	46d.g	—	—	—	—	—	—	—	—	—	—	.1	.1	.2	.1	.2
Capital Accounts	47a.g	.2	.2	.3	.3	.4	.5	.6	.7	.9	1.1	1.2	1.4	1.4	1.8	2.0
Other Items (Net)	47r.g	−.2	—	—	.2	.1	.2	.1	.2	.4	.5	.5	.5	.4	−.3	−.9
Banking Survey																*Billions of Baht:*
Foreign Assets (Net)	51n	15.1	18.5	19.5	20.9	20.5	18.5	19.1	23.9	26.2	36.9	34.1	I30.6	24.3	25.4	31.5
Domestic Credit	52	....	....	....	28.0	34.4	43.9	53.7	65.0	82.7	I96.6	118.7	I169.1	216.7	277.5	328.5
Claims on Central Govt. (Net)	52an	2.0	2.3	3.1	7.6	10.4	14.9	21.5	28.7	31.7	27.8	33.5	I44.4	55.1	65.6	77.6
Claims on Nonfin.Pub.Enterprises	52c	....	....	....	.4	.4	.5	.7	.6	.9	1.3	1.4	I3.2	4.7	6.6	7.8
Claims on Private Sector	52d	12.5	14.9	17.5	19.9	23.5	28.4	31.5	35.7	50.0	67.5	83.8	I121.4	156.9	205.3	243.1
Liquid Liabilities	55l	23.1	28.2	32.2	36.8	41.1	46.5	54.0	67.0	82.4	I99.1	114.7	I135.7	162.9	192.0	220.3
Bonds	56ab	.7	.9	1.0	1.1	1.2	1.3	1.5	1.6	1.8	1.7	1.7	I17.2	23.1	34.0	35.7
Other Items (Net)	57r	....	....	....	11.0	12.6	14.6	17.2	20.3	24.7	32.6	36.4	I46.8	55.1	77.0	104.1
Interest Rates																*Percent Per Annum*
Discount Rate (End of Period)	60	....	....	....	....	....	....	....	....	....	....	....	7.70	9.00	12.50	12.50
Money Market Rate	60b													8.27	10.40	13.28
Treasury Bill Rate	60c													6.32	7.04	7.40
Deposit Rate	60l													8.00	8.00	8.25
Lending Rate	60p													15.00	15.00	15.00
Government Bond Yield	61												8.50	8.90	9.25	13.25
Prices																*Index Numbers (1990=100):*
Wholesale Prices	63	21.5	24.6	26.4	25.2	26.1	25.9	26.0	28.0	34.5	44.4	46.1	47.9	51.6	55.5	61.7
Consumer Prices	64	22.7	23.6	24.6	25.1	25.7	25.7	25.8	27.0	31.2	38.8	I40.9	42.6	45.8	49.4	54.3
International Transactions																*Millions of Baht*
Exports	70	12,941	14,099	14,166	13,679	14,709	14,772	17,275	22,491	32,226	49,799	45,007	60,797	71,198	83,065	108,179
Rice	70n	4,344	4,001	4,653	3,775	2,945	2,517	2,909	4,437	3,593	9,778	5,852	8,603	13,383	10,425	15,592
Rubber	70l	1,999	1,861	1,574	1,816	2,664	2,232	1,905	1,862	4,573	5,035	3,474	5,297	6,163	8,030	12,351
Maize	70j	1,004	1,577	1,431	1,647	1,767	1,969	2,286	2,085	2,969	6,078	5,705	5,677	3,345	3,975	5,644
Tin	70q	1,166	1,316	1,822	1,510	1,631	1,618	1,570	1,664	2,035	3,097	2,247	2,973	4,542	7,229	9,252
Imports, cif	71	15,433	18,504	22,188	24,103	25,966	27,009	26,794	30,875	42,184	64,044	66,835	72,877	94,177	108,899	146,161
Imports, fob	71.v	13,904	16,670	19,989	21,753	23,430	24,366	24,144	27,803	37,980	57,649	60,383	65,732	84,572	97,815	130,772
																1990=100
Volume of Exports	72	8.1	I8.6	8.7	8.4	8.8	9.3	12.1	14.3	13.4	15.0	14.4	20.0	22.8	24.7	I26.9
Rice	72n	47.2	37.5	36.9	26.6	25.5	26.5	39.2	52.6	21.1	25.6	23.7	49.1	73.3	40.0	69.6
Rubber	72l	18.1	17.4	18.1	21.7	23.7	23.7	26.5	27.3	33.6	31.2	28.5	32.1	34.5	38.0	44.8
Maize	72j	67.3	102.1	92.8	126.1	125.0	117.2	151.7	149.2	112.2	180.7	170.4	195.8	124.8	159.7	163.0
Tin	72q	172.6	159.1	228.2	202.1	197.2	187.2	184.1	183.8	190.8	174.8	140.2	168.7	180.4	243.6	263.5
Volume of Imports	73	10.5	I12.9	15.5	17.7	19.4	19.9	16.8	19.4	24.0	22.2	21.9	23.0	27.2	29.1	I33.8
Unit Value of Exports	74	25.9	26.7	26.5	26.4	27.4	25.9	25.0	26.0	40.8	60.3	I53.2	51.8	52.9	57.2	I68.3
Rice (Unit Value)	74n	33.2	38.4	45.4	51.1	41.6	34.2	26.7	30.4	61.2	137.4	89.0	63.1	65.7	93.9	80.6
Rice (Wholesale Price)	76n	38.6	46.9	62.6	57.9	52.4	40.5	36.9	42.4	83.2	150.2	100.7	70.5	75.6	102.0	92.9
Rubber (Unit Value)	74l	46.8	45.4	36.8	35.6	47.6	40.0	30.6	29.0	57.9	68.6	51.7	70.1	75.8	89.7	117.1
Rubber (Wholesale Price)	76l	47.5	44.3	36.7	35.9	47.2	38.3	31.3	31.2	63.2	69.2	51.7	71.3	75.1	90.6	116.5
Maize (Unit Value)	74j	36.0	37.3	37.2	31.5	34.1	40.5	36.4	33.7	63.8	81.2	80.8	70.0	64.7	60.1	83.5
Tin (Unit Value)	74q	35.9	44.0	42.5	39.7	44.0	46.0	45.4	48.2	56.7	94.2	85.2	93.7	133.9	157.8	186.7
Unit Value of Imports	75	15.8	15.5	15.4	14.6	14.3	15.5	16.3	17.2	20.1	32.4	I36.2	38.2	41.0	44.3	I51.2

Thailand

578

	1980	1981	1982	1983	1984	1985	1986	1987	1988	1989	1990	1991	1992	1993	1994		
	End of Period															**Finance and Securities Companies**	
	2.0	3.9	5.8	4.1	3.6	4.8	3.8	4.9	6.1	9.7	9.2	12.3	29.6	31.2	33.7	Reserves	40..f
	—	3.5	5.5	5.3	9.5	14.7	16.7	20.2	20.3	23.0	26.2	30.8	18.6	23.9	59.2	Claims on Central Government	42a.f
	3.0	.2	.5	.7	.5	.9	1.1	.9	1.3	1.4	3.8	6.9	19.1	27.0	39.6	Claims on Nonfin.Pub.Enterprises	42c.f
	50.3	59.1	71.5	83.3	88.0	90.1	95.5	107.5	145.7	217.1	311.3	408.2	572.2	648.1	501.8	Claims on Private Sector	42d.f
	41.3	53.2	66.6	70.1	66.3	76.9	80.0	85.0	116.9	173.2	230.3	301.2	340.7	340.7	340.7	Bonds	46ab f
	2.3	3.3	2.3	3.8	8.3	4.4	4.3	2.3	2.6	6.4	17.6	27.7	109.5	117.3	141.7	Foreign Liabilities	46c.f
	1.1	.2	.2	.7	3.9	7.8	10.4	9.4	10.3	9.6	9.0	8.5	8.3	8.3	8.3	Credit from Monetary Authorities	46g.f
	5.2	4.1	6.0	10.0	15.1	15.2	17.2	31.2	25.1	28.4	27.7	39.2	3.3	3.5	1.6	Cred. from Deposit Money Banks	46h.f
	7.9	8.0	8.8	10.3	9.0	9.0	9.7	10.9	15.6	21.0	31.6	44.8	64.8	90.0	....	Capital Accounts	47a.f
	-2.3	-2.1	-.6	-1.6	-1.1	-2.7	-4.4	-5.3	2.7	12.6	34.3	36.9	123.8	170.4	....	Other Items (Net)	47r.f
	End of Period															**Government Savings Bank**	
	.8	.8	.8	1.6	4.6	3.4	7.6	15.2	13.2	7.6	8.7	20.2	25.0	28.7	51.1	Cash	40..g
	24.7	26.2	31.1	38.8	46.6	57.7	81.1	85.7	95.9	100.0	93.0	80.7	69.0	64.7	50.1	Claims on Central Government	42a.g
	.4	.9	.8	.2	.1	.1	.4	2.1	3.7	5.4	9.7	12.5	18.9	27.3	28.5	Claims on Nonfin.Pub.Enterprise	42c.g
	.4	.3	.4	.6	.8	1.0	1.2	1.6	2.1	2.9	6.3	7.0	14.7	14.5	18.4	Claims on Private Sector	42d.g
	.1	.1	.1	.1	—	.1	—	.1	—	-.1	.1	-.2	-.7	-.4	-.6	Demand Deposits	44..g
	22.3	24.9	29.5	36.0	42.4	52.3	60.4	69.5	76.5	89.7	97.3	101.5	111.6	122.0	132.4	Time and Savings Deposits	45..g
	1.7	1.8	2.2	2.8	3.2	3.5	20.4	26.8	28.8	16.7	13.7	16.6	16.4	16.9	19.1	Bonds	46ab g
	.1	.1	.2	.2	1.1	.4	2.5	2.2	2.8	.4	.6	.7	.8	1.0	1.2	Central Government Deposits	46d.g
	2.1	2.3	2.3	2.9	2.9	4.3	5.7	5.6	6.1	9.2	8.9	9.9	11.1	13.1	15.9	Capital Accounts	47a.g
	-.2	-1.2	-1.2	-.8	2.5	1.7	1.4	.5	.7	.1	-3.0	-8.1	-11.5	-17.4	-19.7	Other Items (Net)	47r.g
	End of Period															**Banking Survey**	
	43.5	31.8	40.2	12.7	20.0	33.4	76.6	105.2	143.3	241.2	289.5	386.0	339.6	335.2	....	Foreign Assets (Net)	51n
	385.7	454.6	551.9	677.8	784.2	860.3	928.5	1,070.8	1,260.9	1,550.6	1,988.2	2,324.5	2,821.5	3,415.5	3,752.3	Domestic Credit	52
	100.7	121.8	159.8	176.4	209.3	229.2	267.8	279.2	241.5	192.0	136.1	24.1	-60.9	-117.9	-181.7	Claims on Central Govt. (Net)	52an
	8.8	7.5	7.5	12.8	13.7	14.6	16.2	18.0	19.4	22.7	31.7	67.1	91.2	130.7	162.4	Claims on Nonfin.Pub.Enterprises	52c
	276.3	325.3	384.7	488.6	561.3	616.4	644.5	773.6	1,000.0	1,335.9	1,820.4	2,233.3	2,791.3	3,402.6	3,771.7	Claims on Private Sector	52d
	271.0	311.6	387.3	480.9	577.4	644.5	730.5	868.2	1,027.8	1,297.9	1,636.2	1,943.7	2,237.7	2,647.1	....	Liquid Liabilities	55l
	44.0	57.0	71.0	75.6	72.3	82.8	102.0	114.9	151.2	200.2	259.0	343.5	394.1	424.9	....	Bonds	56ab
	114.3	117.8	133.9	134.0	154.5	166.4	172.5	192.9	225.2	293.7	382.4	423.4	529.4	678.8	....	Other Items (Net)	57r
	Percent Per Annum															**Interest Rates**	
	13.50	14.50	12.50	13.00	12.00	11.00	8.00	8.00	8.00	8.00	12.00	11.00	11.00	9.00	9.50	Discount Rate *(End of Period)*	60
	14.66	17.25	14.95	12.15	13.58	13.48	8.07	5.91	8.66	9.82	12.73	10.58	7.06	....	....	Money Market Rate	60b
	9.16	11.57	11.64	9.35	10.00	11.02	6.76	3.63	5.08	....	....	....	....	....	....	Treasury Bill Rate	60c
	12.00	12.50	13.00	13.00	13.00	13.00	9.75	9.50	9.50	9.50	12.25	13.67	8.88	8.63	8.46	Deposit Rate	60l
	18.00	19.00	19.00	17.63	18.75	19.00	17.00	15.00	15.00	15.00	16.54	19.00	17.54	15.60	14.38	Lending Rate	60p
	13.00	13.06	13.85	11.13	12.41	12.11	9.11	7.48	7.50	8.09	10.60	10.75	10.75	10.75	10.75	Government Bond Yield	61
	Period Averages															**Prices**	
	74.1	81.2	81.9	‡83.6	81.0	81.0	80.6	85.4	92.4	96.7	100.0	106.8	107.0	106.6	110.7	Wholesale Prices	63
	65.1	73.3	77.1	80.0	80.7	82.7	‡84.2	86.3	89.6	94.4	100.0	105.7	110.1	114.0	120.1	Consumer Prices	64
	Millions of Baht															**International Transactions**	
	133,197	153,001	159,728	146,472	175,237	193,366	233,383	301,453	403,570	516,315	589,813	725,630	824,644	940,862	....	Exports	70
	19,508	26,366	22,510	20,157	25,932	22,524	20,315	22,703	34,676	45,462	27,770	30,516	36,214	32,637	....	Rice	70n
	12,351	10,841	9,490	11,786	13,004	13,567	15,116	20,539	27,189	26,423	23,557	24,953	28,925	30,384	....	Rubber	70l
	7,300	8,349	8,330	8,485	10,147	7,700	5,233	3,928	3,828	4,093	4,144	3,925	537	673	....	Maize	70j
	11,347	9,091	7,773	5,265	5,280	5,646	3,097	2,344	2,229	2,497	1,880	877	1,076	455	....	Tin	70q
	188,686	216,746	196,616	236,609	245,155	251,169	241,358	334,209	513,114	662,679	844,448	958,832	1,033,244	1,166,130	....	Imports, cif	71
	169,685	195,143	177,279	213,178	220,923	226,651	217,832	301,633	463,099	598,086	762,137	865,372	932,531	1,052,464	....	Imports, fob	71.v
	1990=100																
	28.0	31.2	35.1	31.7	38.3	‡41.1	48.2	58.2	71.9	89.4	100.0	119.1	133.8	149.5	....	Volume of Exports	72
	69.7	75.5	94.2	86.5	114.9	101.1	112.6	110.6	126.7	152.9	100.0	103.7	122.0	124.8	....	Rice	72n
	39.1	40.6	46.8	47.7	50.8	59.3	65.4	76.1	80.6	95.6	100.0	108.3	125.8	133.4	....	Rubber	72l
	178.3	208.4	229.1	215.2	254.5	225.2	324.9	133.5	98.3	95.7	100.0	99.9	11.8	16.0	....	Maize	72j
	285.8	253.1	209.5	149.2	155.3	151.2	158.8	115.5	110.1	97.3	100.0	52.6	61.9	29.5	....	Tin	72q
	35.2	34.2	30.3	38.6	39.7	‡37.1	38.4	49.2	68.4	82.5	100.0	108.7	116.7	130.8	....	Volume of Imports	73
	80.8	83.2	77.3	78.4	77.7	‡79.8	82.1	87.8	95.2	98.0	100.0	103.3	104.5	105.5	....	Unit Value of Exports	74
	100.8	125.8	86.0	83.9	81.3	80.2	65.0	73.9	98.6	107.1	100.0	106.0	106.9	94.2	....	Rice (Unit Value)	74n
	120.9	143.4	91.8	86.7	81.2	80.4	75.2	80.4	103.8	112.1	100.0	108.6	99.4	92.3	122.6	Rice (Wholesale Price)	76n
	134.1	113.4	86.1	104.9	108.6	97.1	98.1	114.5	143.2	117.3	100.0	97.8	97.6	96.7	....	Rubber (Unit Value)	74l
	131.8	110.7	89.2	110.6	102.3	93.1	95.9	114.5	135.5	112.7	100.0	95.2	98.9	95.1	128.0	Rubber (Wholesale Price)	76l
	98.8	96.7	87.7	95.1	96.2	82.5	68.8	71.0	94.0	103.2	100.0	94.8	109.7	101.3	....	Maize (Unit Value)	74j
	211.2	191.0	197.4	187.7	180.8	198.6	103.7	108.0	107.7	136.5	100.0	88.6	92.5	82.0	....	Tin (Unit Value)	74q
	63.5	75.1	77.0	72.7	73.2	‡80.2	74.4	80.5	88.8	95.1	100.0	104.4	104.9	105.2	....	Unit Value of Imports	75

Thailand

578

		1965	1966	1967	1968	1969	1970	1971	1972	1973	1974	1975	1976	1977	1978	1979
Balance of Payments																*Millions of US Dollars:*
Goods: Exports f.o.b.	78aa d	....	....	....	....	....	....	....	....	....	....	2,177	2,959	3,454	4,045	5,234
Goods: Imports f.o.b.	78ab d	....	....	....	....	....	....	....	....	....	....	−2,850	−3,152	−4,238	−4,904	−6,785
Trade Balance	78ac d	....	....	....	....	....	....	....	....	....	....	−673	−193	−784	−858	−1,550
Services: Credit	78ad d	....	....	....	....	....	....	....	....	....	....	603	508	531	819	1,034
Services: Debit	78ae d	....	....	....	....	....	....	....	....	....	....	−628	−748	−845	−1,005	−1,352
Balance on Goods and Services	78af d	....	....	....	....	....	....	....	....	....	....	−698	−433	−1,099	−1,045	−1,868
Income: Credit	78ag d	....	....	....	....	....	....	....	....	....	....	209	154	194	269	394
Income: Debit	78ah d	....	....	....	....	....	....	....	....	....	....	−198	−208	−232	−418	−672
Balance on Goods, Serv., & Inc.	78ai d	....	....	....	....	....	....	....	....	....	....	−687	−487	−1,137	−1,193	−2,146
Current Transfers, n.i.e.: Credit	78aj d	....	....	....	....	....	....	....	....	....	....	91	59	52	52	71
Current Transfers: Debit	78ak d	....	....	....	....	....	....	....	....	....	....	−10	−12	−13	−12	−12
Current Account, n.i.e.	78al d	....	....	....	....	....	....	....	....	....	....	−606	−440	−1,097	−1,153	−2,087
Capital Account, n.i.e.: Credit	78ba d	....	....	....	....	....	....	....	....	....	....	—	—	—	—	1
Capital Account: Debit	78bb d	....	....	....	....	....	....	....	....	....	....	−1	−1	−1	−1	—
Capital Account, n.i.e.	78bc d	....	....	....	....	....	....	....	....	....	....	−1	—	—	—	1
Direct Investment Abroad	78bd d	....	....	....	....	....	....	....	....	....	....	—	—	—	−6	−4
Dir. Invest. in Rep. Econ., n.i.e.	78be d	....	....	....	....	....	....	....	....	....	....	86	79	106	56	55
Portfolio Investment Assets	78bf d	....	....	....	....	....	....	....	....	....	....					
Portfolio Investment Liab., n.i.e.	78bg d	....	....	....	....	....	....	....	....	....	....	1	−1	—	76	180
Other Investment Assets	78bh d	....	....	....	....	....	....	....	....	....	....	−1	10	4	−12	−43
Other Investment Liab., n.i.e.	78bi d	....	....	....	....	....	....	....	....	....	....	383	451	936	1,246	1,789
Financial Account, n.i.e.	78bj d	....	....	....	....	....	....	....	....	....	....	469	539	1,046	1,360	1,977
Net Errors and Omissions	78ca d	....	....	....	....	....	....	....	....	....	....	86	−19	44	−231	20
Overall Balance	78cb d	....	....	....	....	....	....	....	....	....	....	−51	81	−8	−25	−88
Reserves and Related Items	79da d	....	....	....	....	....	....	....	....	....	....	51	−81	8	25	88
Reserve Assets	79db d	....	....	....	....	....	....	....	....	....	....	51	−158	−9	−112	−24
Use of Fund Credit and Loans	79dc d	....	....	....	....	....	....	....	....	....	....	—	77	17	137	112
Liabs.Constit.For.Auth.Reserves	79dd d	....	....	....	....	....	....	....	....	....	....	—	—	—	—	—
Exceptional Financing	79de d	....	....	....	....	....	....	....	....	....	....					
Government Finance																*Millions of Baht:*
Deficit (−) or Surplus	80	−521	−1,086	−1,625	−2,371	−2,742	−5,400	−7,176	ℐ−7,092	−7,041	2,489	−6,236	−13,823	−13,082	−17,700	−20,400
Revenue	81	11,954	13,210	14,886	16,954	18,429	18,886	19,992	ℐ21,151	25,428	36,970	38,074	42,184	51,560	62,210	75,391
Grants Received	81z	....	....	....	....	....	....	....	ℐ952	971	823	802	781	634	1,100	1,427
Expenditure	82	12,475	14,296	16,511	19,325	21,171	24,286	27,168	ℐ28,316	32,676	34,958	44,253	55,254	64,163	80,137	95,856
Lending Minus Repayments	83	....	....	....	....	....	....	....	ℐ879	764	346	859	1,534	1,113	873	1,362
Financing																
Net Borrowing	84	1,496	2,973	1,264	1,356	4,115	4,206	6,221	ℐ6,773	8,651	3,005	5,749	13,187	14,606	18,983	20,724
Domestic	84a	....	....	....	....	....	....	....	ℐ6,749	8,411	2,895	5,801	11,728	13,630	14,125	14,347
Foreign	85a	....	....	....	....	....	....	....	ℐ24	240	110	−52	1,459	976	4,858	6,377
Use of Cash Balances	87	−975	−1,887	361	1,015	−1,373	1,199	955	ℐ319	−1,610	−5,494	487	636	−1,524	−1,283	−324
Debt: Domestic	88a	....	....	....	....	....	....	....	ℐ39,275	48,075	50,783	56,535	67,897	80,645	94,338	106,768
Foreign	89a	....	....	....	....	....	....	....	ℐ3,611	3,848	3,855	3,804	6,030	6,580	13,261	20,166
Debt: Baht	88b	10,009	12,683	13,497	15,028	19,494	23,644	29,012	....	....	....	....	....	....	....	....
Held By: Bank of Thailand	88ba	3,637	3,466	2,897	2,969	6,842	9,997	12,144								
Deposit Money Banks	88bb	4,945	7,576	9,148	10,413	10,920	11,825	15,022								
Others	88bc	1,427	1,641	1,452	1,646	1,732	1,822	1,846								
Debt: Foreign Currency	89b	2,471	2,577	2,770	3,128	3,265	3,671	3,978	....	....	....	....	....	....	....	....
National Accounts																*Billions of Baht*
Exports of Goods & Services	90c	15.4	19.3	21.3	21.4	22.4	22.1	24.5	30.9	41.3	60.3	55.7	70.1	80.5	97.1	126.2
Government Consumption	91f	8.3	9.3	10.4	12.7	14.1	16.6	17.7	18.6	21.6	26.1	31.3	38.0	42.9	54.6	66.8
Gross Fixed Capital Formation	93e	16.0	20.4	24.9	27.5	30.8	35.0	35.8	38.6	49.9	65.0	69.4	79.4	104.6	123.3	142.9
Increase/Decrease (−) in Stocks	93i	1.0	3.6	.8	2.0	3.1	2.7	1.4	−1.8	10.0	9.3	11.8	3.7	3.9	14.3	9.2
Private Consumption	96f	58.6	66.7	75.2	80.9	86.5	103.2	104.8	117.6	149.0	190.1	211.3	237.7	271.9	315.0	364.0
Imports of Goods & Services	98c	−16.5	−19.7	−23.7	−26.2	−27.9	−28.6	−28.9	−32.6	−44.5	−66.9	−69.7	−78.7	−102.4	−117.7	−163.7
Gross Domestic Product	99b	84.3	101.4	108.3	116.8	128.6	147.4	153.4	170.1	222.1	279.2	303.3	346.5	403.5	488.2	558.9
Net Factor Inc/Pmts (−) Abroad	98.n	—	—	.2	.3	.2	.2	−1.1	−.6	−.9	−.1	—	−1.3	−3.6	−6.2
Gross Nat'l Expenditure = GNP	99a	84.3	101.4	108.5	117.0	128.8	147.6	153.3	169.5	221.2	279.1	303.3	345.6	402.3	484.6	552.6
Nat'l Income, Market Prices	99e	80.1	96.2	102.2	109.5	119.9	137.4	141.7	156.5	206.5	261.9	283.1	322.2	375.2	453.0	515.4
Gross Dom. Prod. 1990 Prices	99b.p	340.7	382.3	412.0	447.0	482.4	ℐ532.8	559.3	582.1	639.5	667.3	699.7	765.2	841.0	928.8	978.1
GDP Deflator (1990=100)	99bi p	24.7	26.5	26.3	26.1	26.7	27.7	27.4	29.2	34.7	41.8	43.4	45.3	48.0	52.6	57.1
																Millions:
Population	99z	31.03	32.00	33.00	34.04	35.11	36.37	37.49	38.59	39.69	40.78	41.87	42.96	44.04	45.10	46.14

Deposit Money Banks: ℐ Beginning in 1976, a new system of bank returns was introduced that led to changes in the coverage of commercial bank data.
Monetary Survey: ℐ See note to section 20.
Other Banking Institutions: ℐ Beginning in 1974, revised data are based on a new reporting system, providing an improved sectoral classification.
Banking Survey: ℐ About 1974 data, see note to section 40. ℐ Beginning in 1976, revised data include the Government Housing Bank and the finance and securities companies, for which earlier data are not available. See note to section 20.
Government Finance: ℐ Beginning in 1972, data are as reported in the *Government Finance Statistics Yearbook* and cover consolidated central government. Beginning in 1972, data relate to a fiscal year different from calendar year.

Thailand

	1980	1981	1982	1983	1984	1985	1986	1987	1988	1989	1990	1991	1992	1993	1994		
Minus Sign Indicates Debit																**Balance of Payments**	
	6,449	6,902	6,835	6,308	7,338	7,059	8,803	11,595	15,781	19,834	22,811	28,232	32,100	36,410	....	Goods: Exports f.o.b.	78aa d
	-8,352	-8,931	-7,565	-9,169	-9,236	-8,391	-8,415	-12,019	-17,856	-22,750	-29,561	-34,222	-36,261	-40,556	....	Goods: Imports f.o.b.	78ab d
	-1,902	-2,029	-731	-2,861	-1,898	-1,332	388	-424	-2,074	-2,916	-6,751	-5,989	-4,161	-4,146	....	Trade Balance	78ac d
	1,490	1,612	1,717	1,846	1,964	2,041	2,302	3,070	4,648	5,457	6,419	7,272	8,567	10,103	....	Services: Credit	78ad d
	-1,644	-1,819	-1,658	-1,909	-1,910	-1,815	-1,852	-2,406	-3,569	-4,505	-6,309	-8,040	-9,942	-11,959	....	Services: Debit	78ae d
	-2,057	-2,236	-672	-2,924	-1,843	-1,105	839	239	-996	-1,964	-6,641	-6,757	-5,537	-6,002	....	Balance on Goods and Services	78af d
	636	740	864	1,073	1,113	1,122	1,031	1,098	1,297	1,589	2,059	2,254	2,202	2,252	....	Income: Credit	78ag d
	-865	-1,243	-1,378	-1,300	-1,554	-1,719	-1,848	-1,928	-2,191	-2,369	-2,913	-3,329	-3,397	-3,490	....	Income: Debit	78ah d
	-2,286	-2,739	-1,186	-3,151	-2,284	-1,703	22	-590	-1,891	-2,744	-7,494	-7,832	-6,731	-7,240	....	Balance on Goods, Serv., & Inc.	78ai d
	229	181	198	296	194	190	250	247	268	281	278	411	578	511	....	Current Transfers, n.i.e.: Credit	78aj d
	-19	-14	-15	-19	-19	-25	-25	-23	-31	-34	-65	-150	-202	-199	....	Current Transfers: Debit	78ak d
	-2,076	-2,571	-1,003	-2,873	-2,109	-1,537	247	-366	-1,654	-2,498	-7,281	-7,571	-6,355	-6,928	....	Current Account, n.i.e.	78al d
	7	2	—	—	—	1	1	2	—	—	—	—	—	—	....	Capital Account, n.i.e.: Credit	78ba d
	-1	-1	—	-1	-1	-1	—	—	—	—	-1	—	—	—	....	Capital Account: Debit	78bb d
	6	2	—	-1	-1	—	—	2	—	—	-1	—	—	—	....	Capital Account, n.i.e.	78bc d
	-3	-2	-2	-1	-1	-1	-1	-1	-170	-24	-50	-140	-167	-147	-221	Direct Investment Abroad	78bd d
	190	291	191	350	401	163	263	352	1,105	1,775	2,444	2,014	2,116	1,715	....	Dir. Invest. in Rep. Econ., n.i.e.	78be d
	—	—	—	—	—	—	—	—	—	—	—	—	—	—	....	Portfolio Investment Assets	78bf d
	96	44	68	108	155	895	-29	346	530	1,486	-38	-81	927	5,455	....	Portfolio Investment Liab., n.i.e.	78bg d
	-21	-42	-84	-108	-79	-242	-150	141	269	-313	-164	352	-125	-447	....	Other Investment Assets	78bh d
	1,782	2,189	1,120	1,618	2,091	722	-213	393	1,960	3,700	6,996	9,642	7,025	7,942	....	Other Investment Liab., n.i.e.	78bi d
	2,044	2,480	1,293	1,966	2,567	1,538	-131	1,062	3,840	6,599	9,098	11,759	9,797	14,443	....	Financial Account, n.i.e.	78bj d
	-180	133	-521	587	71	103	598	248	411	928	1,419	431	-517	-347	....	Net Errors and Omissions	78ca d
	-206	43	-231	-320	529	105	714	945	2,596	5,029	3,235	4,618	2,925	7,169	....	Overall Balance	78cb d
	206	-43	231	320	-529	-105	-714	-945	-2,596	-5,029	-3,235	-4,618	-2,925	-7,169	....	Reserves and Related Items	79da d
	212	-574	50	-84	-457	-205	-545	-700	-2,336	-4,667	-2,961	-4,618	-2,925	-7,169	....	Reserve Assets	79db d
	-6	532	31	240	-72	100	-168	-245	-260	-363	-274	-1	—	—	....	Use of Fund Credit and Loans	79dc d
	—	-1	—	—	—	—	—	—	—	—	—	—	—	—	....	Liabs.Constit.For.Auth.Reserves	79dd d
	—	—	150	164	—	—	—	—	—	—	—	—	—	—	....	Exceptional Financing	79de d
Year Ending September 30																**Government Finance**	
	-32,150	-25,505	-53,537	-36,408	-33,728	-55,403	-47,914	-28,983	10,643	54,732	99,360	118,414	80,163 P	66,290 P	....	Deficit (-) or Surplus	80
	94,945	113,848	118,310	143,199	153,516	163,071	172,346	197,018	251,468	317,128	404,556	480,123	508,056 P	569,313 P	....	Revenue	81
	1,949	3,705	2,615	2,977	3,917	3,778	5,464	6,870	5,817	6,353	6,605	5,006	3,472 P	3,608 P	....	Grants Received	81z
	124,551	144,693	169,785	180,249	191,203	216,969	220,979	227,248	236,195	266,337	307,426	364,019	425,422 P	504,703 P	....	Expenditure	82
	4,493	-1,635	4,677	2,335	-42	5,283	4,745	5,623	10,447	2,412	4,375	2,696	5,943 P	1,928 P	....	Lending Minus Repayments	83
																Financing	
	24,659	28,533	53,031	41,148	35,175	54,941	50,901	28,190	-894	-19,426	-26,527	-64,107	-27,697 P	-44,010 P	....	Net Borrowing	84
	17,105	22,908	38,851	32,934	30,428	36,769	39,518	23,198	-10,767	-20,875	5,737	-67,744	-16,936 P	-47,560 P	....	Domestic	84a
	7,554	5,625	14,180	8,214	4,747	18,172	11,383	4,992	9,873	1,449	-32,264	3,637	-10,761 P	3,550 P	....	Foreign	85a
	7,491	-3,028	506	-4,740	-1,447	462	-2,987	793	-9,749	-35,306	-72,833	-54,307	-52,466 P	-22,280 P	....	Use of Cash Balances	87
	107,914	122,349	147,310	183,518	209,515	248,760	288,866	317,661	319,677	302,862	307,675	235,373	210,565 P	163,968 P	....	Debt: Domestic	88a
	27,895	36,630	49,583	58,505	62,873	93,223	112,470	119,677	132,513	129,679	95,140	99,653	97,410 P	103,184 P	....	Foreign	89a
	....	....	....	....	....	....	....	....	....	....	....	....	....	....	....	Debt: Baht	88b
	....	....	....	....	....	....	....	....	....	....	....	....	....	....	....	Held By: Bank of Thailand	88ba
	....	....	....	....	....	....	....	....	....	....	....	....	....	....	....	Deposit Money Banks	88bb
	....	....	....	....	....	....	....	....	....	....	....	....	....	....	....	Others	88bc
	....	....	....	....	....	....	....	....	....	....	....	....	....	....	....	Debt: Foreign Currency	89b
Billions of Baht																**National Accounts**	
	159.7	181.3	192.9	185.2	216.4	245.3	290.2	375.6	514.9	648.5	745.3	887.2	1,019.6	....	....	Exports of Goods & Services	90c
	81.4	97.0	110.2	118.6	130.1	142.9	144.6	147.2	156.7	176.8	206.8	233.3	283.2	....	....	Government Consumption	91f
	184.0	212.8	226.7	262.1	282.6	287.0	292.2	359.3	478.5	642.9	881.8	1,033.2	1,113.7	....	....	Gross Fixed Capital Formation	93e
	9.1	12.8	-3.6	13.9	8.6	11.4	1.0	3.1	29.8	8.3	18.2	19.8	11.7	....	....	Increase/Decrease(-) in Stocks	93i
	433.6	496.4	535.0	599.6	628.9	657.4	695.8	781.1	885.0	1,030.6	1,223.9	1,390.2	1,544.9	....	....	Private Consumption	96f
	-201.2	-229.0	-207.3	-251.2	-258.6	-274.1	-267.1	-368.3	-536.9	-696.1	-909.6	-1,064.3	-1,146.5	....	....	Imports of Goods & Services	98c
	662.5	760.4	841.6	921.0	988.1	1,056.5	1,133.4	1,299.9	1,559.8	1,857.0	2,191.1	2,505.6	2,804.9	....	....	Gross Domestic Product	99b
	-5.4	-12.0	-12.9	-6.7	-11.5	-17.6	-22.4	-22.4	-24.8	-23.7	-27.3	-38.9	-47.0	....	....	Net Factor Inc/Pmts(-) Abroad	98.n
	657.1	748.3	828.6	914.3	976.6	1,038.9	1,111.0	1,277.5	1,535.0	1,833.3	2,163.8	2,466.7	2,758.0	....	....	Gross Nat'l Expenditure = GNP	99a
	609.7	698.2	750.1	838.7	889.0	915.4	979.5	1,127.6	1,363.7	1,608.8	1,869.1	....	....	....	....	Nat'l Income, Market Prices	99e
	I 1,024.9	1,085.5	1,143.6	1,207.4	1,276.9	1,336.2	1,410.2	1,544.4	1,749.6	1,962.9	2,191.1	2,367.9	2,546.8	....	....	Gross Dom. Prod. 1990 Prices	99b.p
	64.6	70.0	73.6	76.3	77.4	79.1	80.4	84.2	89.2	94.6	100.0	105.8	110.1	....	....	GDP Deflator (1990=100)	99bi p
Midyear Estimates																	
	46.72	47.74	48.71	49.68	50.64	51.58	52.51	53.43	54.33	55.21	56.08	56.92	57.76	58.58	59.40	Population	99z

Togo
742

		1965	1966	1967	1968	1969	1970	1971	1972	1973	1974	1975	1976	1977	1978	1979
Exchange Rates																*Francs per SDR:*
Official Rate	aa	245.07	247.59	245.42	247.40	277.91	276.02	283.61	278.00	284.00	272.08	262.55	288.70	285.76	272.28	264.78
																Francs per US Dollar:
Official Rate	ae	245.08	247.59	245.43	247.41	277.92	276.03	261.23	256.05	235.43	222.22	224.27	248.49	235.25	209.00	201.00
Official Rate	rf	245.06	245.68	246.00	247.56	259.96	276.40	275.59	252.03	222.89	240.70	214.31	238.95	245.68	225.66	212.72
																Index Numbers (1990=100):
Official Rate	ahx	110.8	110.5	110.4	109.7	104.8	98.2	98.6	107.8	122.3	112.8	126.9	113.8	110.5	120.6	127.7
Nominal Effective Exchange Rate	nec	....	....	....	....	....	....	....	....	....	....	....	....	....	....	69.4
Real Effective Exchange Rate	rec	....	....	....	....	....	....	....	....	....	....	....	....	....	....	127.6
Fund Position																*Millions of SDRs:*
Quota	2f.s	11.3	11.3	11.3	11.3	11.3	15.0	15.0	15.0	15.0	15.0	15.0	15.0	15.0	19.0	19.0
SDRs	1b.s	—	—	—	—	—	1.9	3.5	5.1	5.1	5.1	5.1	5.0	4.8	4.4	6.3
Reserve Position in the Fund	1c.s	1.1	1.1	1.1	1.1	1.1	2.1	2.1	2.1	2.1	2.1	2.1	2.1	2.1	2.0	3.3
Total Fund Cred.&Loans Outstg.	2tl	—	—	—	—	—	—	—	—	—	—	—	7.5	7.5	6.2	10.8
International Liquidity													*Millions of US Dollars Unless Otherwise Indicated:*			
Total Reserves minus Gold	1l.d	17.5	18.6	22.3	25.5	26.3	35.4	40.5	36.5	37.9	54.5	41.2	66.6	46.1	70.0	65.5
SDRs	1b.d	—	—	—	—	—	1.9	3.8	5.5	6.1	6.2	5.9	5.8	5.8	5.7	8.3
Reserve Position in the Fund	1c.d	1.1	1.1	1.1	1.1	1.1	2.1	2.2	2.2	2.5	2.5	2.4	2.4	2.5	2.6	4.4
Foreign Exchange	1d.d	16.4	17.5	21.2	24.4	25.2	31.4	34.5	28.7	29.3	45.7	32.8	58.4	37.9	61.7	52.8
Gold (Million Fine Troy Ounces)	1ad	....	....	....	....	....	....	....	....	....	....	....	—	.006	.010	.013
Gold (National Valuation)	1and	....	....	....	....	....	....	....	....	....	....	....	—	.3	.4	.6
Monetary Authorities: Other Liab.	4..d	—	—	.2	.3	.3	.3	.8	1.4	.1	1.4	3.9	2.2	1.4	4.3	20.7
Deposit Money Banks: Assets	7a.d	4.5	6.5	6.0	6.4	17.2	10.9	10.8	8.1	7.2	63.0	13.9	21.5	27.3	63.7	69.0
Deposit Money Banks: Liabilities	7b.d	4.8	5.9	4.5	6.3	6.9	8.9	11.0	12.0	18.4	22.7	32.7	32.8	51.5	81.5	61.0
of which: Liab. to Nonbanks	7bdd	....	....	....	....	....	....	....	....	....	....	....	7.7	16.1	33.8	24.3
Monetary Authorities																*Billions of Francs:*
Foreign Assets	11	4.32	4.58	5.51	6.30	7.32	9.83	10.36	9.33	8.73	12.10	9.24	16.56	10.85	14.63	13.16
Claims on Central Government	12a	—	—	.08	.01	—	—	—	—	—	—	.01	2.40	2.46	10.35	13.10
Claims on Deposit Money Banks	12e	.07	.08	.07	—	—	—	.08	.18	.68	.64	4.25	4.19	6.82	5.09	9.83
Claims on Other Financial Insts.	12f	....	....	....	....	....	....	....	....	....	....	—	.18	.36	.56	.57
Reserve Money	14	2.91	3.01	3.26	3.90	4.83	4.82	5.91	5.74	6.47	9.09	11.75	18.93	19.89	25.84	26.95
of which: Currency Outside DMBs	14a	2.80	2.88	3.17	3.77	4.52	4.56	5.58	5.45	6.03	8.37	9.99	14.20	15.97	20.80	21.53
Foreign Liabilities	16c	.01	.01	.04	.09	.09	.09	.21	.35	.02	.31	.89	2.72	2.48	4.35	10.05
Central Government Deposits	16d	1.48	1.64	2.28	2.32	2.40	4.38	3.35	2.01	1.46	1.96	.29	.28	.45	.76	.67
Other Items (Net)	17r	—	—	.07	.01	—	.54	.97	1.41	1.39	1.41	1.45	1.47	–.32	–1.01	
Deposit Money Banks																*Billions of Francs:*
Reserves	20	.13	.09	.08	.11	.28	.17	.38	.25	.39	.56	1.63	4.23	3.86	4.93	4.94
Foreign Assets	21	1.11	1.61	1.48	1.58	4.79	3.04	2.77	2.07	1.67	14.00	3.11	5.34	6.41	13.32	13.87
Claims on Central Government	22a	.01	.01	.02	.01	.01	.01	.01	—	.02	.01	.03	.03	.62	1.27	I4.06
Claims on Private Sector	22d	2.70	3.17	3.86	5.61	5.89	7.79	8.90	9.75	13.12	15.99	24.29	31.71	43.11	49.20	I56.17
Claims on Other Financial Insts.	22f	....	....	....	....	....	....	....	....	....	....	....	....	....	....	.74
Demand Deposits	24	2.26	2.69	3.29	3.64	4.96	5.31	5.95	6.05	5.19	16.30	11.08	18.19	19.89	26.57	I30.42
Time Deposits	25	.23	.15	.30	1.01	1.80	2.53	2.23	2.08	4.35	5.38	6.72	8.27	11.63	16.85	I13.88
Foreign Liabilities	26c	.60	.78	.35	.73	1.12	1.77	2.09	1.95	2.87	3.40	5.66	6.45	10.47	15.36	10.34
Long-Term Foreign Liabilities	26cl	.59	.68	.76	.82	.81	.70	.74	1.12	1.36	1.65	1.68	1.70	1.64	1.67	1.91
Central Government Deposits	26d	.01	.02	.02	.12	.05	.06	.12	.15	.53	.69	.88	1.26	4.04	3.59	I11.21
Credit from Monetary Authorities	26g	.07	.08	.07	—	—	—	.08	.19	.68	.64	2.59	4.19	6.82	5.09	9.83
Other Items (Net)	27r	.24	.47	.63	.99	2.24	.63	.85	.53	.21	2.49	.45	1.24	–.48	–.42	2.20
Treasury Claims: Private Sector	22d.i	.44	.52	.46	.36	.48	.58	.54	.45	.21	.27	.35	.35	1.12	1.81	2.04
Post Office: Checking Deposits	24..i	.16	.17	.21	.15	.22	.28	.35	.33	.33	.41	.49	.56	.57	.72	.71
Monetary Survey																*Billions of Francs:*
Foreign Assets (Net)	31n	4.82	5.40	6.60	7.06	10.90	11.01	10.83	9.10	7.51	22.38	5.81	12.72	4.32	8.24	6.64
Domestic Credit	32	1.38	1.69	1.87	3.33	3.68	3.63	5.79	7.92	11.48	13.77	26.04	33.39	46.44	57.75	I63.47
Claims on Central Govt. (Net)	32an	–1.76	–2.00	–2.45	–2.63	–2.69	–4.74	–3.65	–2.27	–1.85	–2.48	–1.40	1.16	1.85	6.18	I3.96
Claims on Private Sector	32d	3.14	3.69	4.32	5.97	6.37	8.38	9.44	10.19	13.34	16.26	24.64	32.05	44.23	51.01	I58.21
Claims on Other Financial Insts.	32f	....	....	....	....	....	....	....	....	....	....	....	.18	.36	.56	1.31
Money	34	5.22	5.74	6.67	7.55	9.69	10.15	11.88	11.82	11.56	25.08	21.56	32.94	36.45	48.10	I52.66
Quasi-Money	35	.23	.15	.30	1.01	1.80	2.53	2.23	2.08	4.35	5.38	6.72	8.27	11.63	16.85	I13.88
Long-Term Foreign Liabilities	36cl	.59	.68	.76	.82	.81	.70	.74	1.12	1.36	1.65	1.68	1.70	1.64	1.67	1.91
Other Items (Net)	37r	.16	.52	.73	1.04	2.28	1.27	1.76	2.00	1.72	4.03	1.89	3.17	1.04	1.06	1.66
Money plus Quasi-Money	35l	5.45	5.89	6.97	8.56	11.49	12.68	14.11	13.90	15.91	30.47	28.28	41.21	48.08	64.94	I66.54
Other Banking Institutions																*Billions of Francs:*
Savings Deposits	45	.35	.42	.45	.53	.65	.74	.89	1.00	1.10	1.27	1.56	1.90	2.17	2.37	2.57
Liquid Liabilities	55l	5.80	6.31	7.42	9.09	12.14	13.42	15.00	14.90	17.01	31.74	29.84	43.11	50.25	67.31	76.24
Interest Rates																*Percent Per Annum*
Discount Rate (End of Period)	60	3.50	3.50	3.50	3.50	3.50	3.50	3.50	3.50	5.50	5.50	8.00	8.00	8.00	8.00	8.00
Money Market Rate	60b	....	....	....	....	....	....	....	....	....	....	....	7.28	7.38	7.42	7.72
Deposit Rate	60l	....	....	....	....	....	3.00	3.00	3.00	5.75	5.75	5.88	6.00	6.00	6.00	6.00
Lending Rate	60p	....	....	....	....	....	....	....	....	....	....	....	....	12.00	12.00	12.00
Prices																*Index Numbers (1990=100):*
Consumer Prices	64	....	24.4	23.9	24.0	25.4	26.5	28.3	30.4	I31.5	35.6	42.0	46.9	57.4	57.7	62.0

Togo

742

1980	1981	1982	1983	1984	1985	1986	1987	1988	1989	1990	1991	1992	1993	1994		
End of Period															**Exchange Rates**	
287.99	334.52	370.92	436.97	470.11	415.26	394.78	378.78	407.68	380.32	364.84	370.48	378.57	404.89	‡780.44	Official Rate	aa
End of Period (ae)	*Period Average (rf)*															
225.80	287.40	336.25	417.37	479.60	378.05	322.75	267.00	302.95	289.40	256.45	259.00	275.33	294.78	‡534.60	Official Rate	ae
211.28	271.73	328.61	381.06	436.96	449.26	346.30	300.54	297.85	319.01	272.26	282.11	264.69	283.16	‡555.20	Official Rate	rf
Period Averages																
128.7	100.5	83.1	71.6	62.3	60.9	78.6	90.5	91.4	85.2	100.0	96.6	102.8	96.0	49.0	Official Rate	ah x
71.0	66.8	63.7	63.6	64.4	67.9	74.4	78.4	80.8	84.9	100.0	103.8	113.8	122.6	70.0	Nominal Effective Exchange Rate	ne c
128.1	126.7	121.6	121.0	108.0	103.4	111.4	110.7	104.3	97.1	100.0	95.4	98.0	92.3	65.1	Real Effective Exchange Rate	re c
End of Period															**Fund Position**	
28.5	28.5	28.5	38.4	38.4	38.4	38.4	38.4	38.4	38.4	38.4	38.4	38.4	54.3	54.3	54.3 Quota	2f. s
5.8	6.5	3.9	1.2	2.1	.1	.5	.1	.1	1.3	.1	.3	.2	.1	—	SDRs	1b. s
—	—	.2	.2	.2	.2	.2	.2	.2	.2	.2	.3	.3	.2	.3	Reserve Position in the Fund	1c. s
25.5	32.8	32.8	51.9	63.5	67.6	73.8	60.1	57.9	57.4	61.1	55.3	55.8	49.9	56.0	Total Fund Cred.&Loans Outstg.	2tl
End of Period															**International Liquidity**	
77.6	151.5	167.7	172.8	203.3	296.6	342.0	354.9	232.1	285.3	353.2	364.9	272.5	156.3	94.4	Total Reserves minus Gold	1l. d
7.4	7.6	4.3	1.3	2.0	.1	.6	.1	.1	1.7	.2	.4	.3	.1	.1	SDRs	1b. d
—	—	.2	.2	.2	.2	.2	.3	.3	.3	.3	.4	.3	.3	.4	Reserve Position in the Fund	1c. d
70.2	143.9	163.2	171.4	201.1	296.3	341.1	354.5	231.7	283.3	352.7	364.1	271.9	155.9	94.0	Foreign Exchange	1d. d
.013	.013	.013	.013	.013	.013	.013	.013	.013	.013	.013	.013	.013	.013	.013	Gold (Million Fine Troy Ounces)	1ad
.6	5.3	5.3	4.8	4.2	4.1	5.0	5.9	5.2	4.9	4.7	4.4	4.3	4.7	4.7	Gold (National Valuation)	1an d
6.6	1.7	2.2	3.7	2.3	3.8	16.5	-3.2	10.4	6.1	4.6	12.1	-.1	10.3	5.5	Monetary Authorities: Other Liab.	4..d
49.4	69.7	64.8	46.5	46.7	50.1	43.3	64.3	78.4	117.9	84.4	93.6	87.9	58.4	109.7	Deposit Money Banks: Assets	7a. d
77.6	79.4	64.2	46.2	52.9	67.7	88.2	104.7	88.0	93.0	83.0	92.0	95.1	64.8	40.6	Deposit Money Banks: Liabilities	7b. d
27.0	19.8	17.1	14.6	12.9	14.1	29.2	38.0	28.2	31.8	38.9	38.2	37.8	26.3	10.2	*of which:* Liab. to Nonbanks	7bd d
End of Period															**Monetary Authorities**	
17.51	43.54	56.37	72.14	97.49	112.14	110.37	94.76	70.32	82.56	90.58	94.50	75.02	46.08	50.47	Foreign Assets	11
12.80	21.89	22.63	32.01	33.71	40.72	42.83	42.71	42.47	39.64	41.90	39.49	40.00	40.40	49.82	Claims on Central Government	12a
13.17	7.11	7.24	6.35	6.64	3.95	5.97	5.19	3.85	4.80	4.50	6.40	6.40	6.40	7.18	Claims on Deposit Money Banks	12e
.46	.45	.44	.51	.58	.80	1.13	1.56	1.54	1.63	.50	1.60	1.58	1.50	1.31	Claims on Other Financial Insts.	12f
31.74	57.93	70.97	78.40	99.07	116.27	118.77	115.22	86.08	93.90	104.36	110.08	90.62	61.72	63.17	Reserve Money	14
27.76	50.74	54.29	45.50	36.99	39.21	46.02	48.27	23.20	21.33	32.09	36.29	22.34	10.72	45.19	*of which:* Currency Outside DMBs	14a
12.89	15.55	16.99	28.24	34.62	32.49	37.67	23.82	27.61	23.80	23.50	23.61	21.10	23.24	46.65	Foreign Liabilities	16c
.67	1.13	.74	7.56	10.62	10.83	2.51	.50	1.26	6.60	3.78	2.56	6.21	6.17	9.26	Central Government Deposits	16d
-1.35	-1.61	-2.02	-3.19	-5.88	-1.98	1.35	4.67	3.23	4.32	5.84	5.75	5.08	3.26	-10.30	Other Items (Net)	17r
End of Period															**Deposit Money Banks**	
4.37	7.56	16.51	33.02	63.11	77.59	72.94	67.18	62.68	70.47	72.63	73.70	68.98	54.15	15.13	Reserves	20
11.17	20.03	21.80	19.40	22.40	18.93	13.98	17.17	23.76	34.12	21.66	24.25	24.21	17.22	58.62	Foreign Assets	21
4.62	3.82	3.41	3.17	2.30	.75	.95	.82	1.16	1.71	1.56	1.36	2.09	1.91	12.35	Claims on Central Government	22a
64.13	61.98	69.17	67.28	70.84	69.72	89.28	96.41	99.69	95.29	99.09	111.97	110.62	101.89	101.84	Claims on Private Sector	22d
.60	.46	.68	.64	.45	.58	.63	.66	.66	.93	.88	.75	.55	.58	.48	Claims on Other Financial Insts.	22f
26.82	28.51	34.87	36.59	52.70	42.22	42.81	41.77	40.27	40.82	42.15	41.19	34.14	35.13	49.35	Demand Deposits	24
17.23	20.60	27.10	34.69	45.39	60.46	75.82	72.77	79.93	82.77	84.58	86.37	78.06	66.72	68.18	Time Deposits	25
15.30	20.83	19.31	17.44	23.47	23.83	26.05	24.76	23.69	24.96	18.94	21.56	24.32	17.24	19.94	Foreign Liabilities	26c
2.23	1.99	2.26	1.86	1.91	1.78	2.42	3.19	2.98	1.96	2.35	2.27	1.87	1.87	1.75	Long-Term Foreign Liabilities	26cl
11.18	9.47	11.39	16.62	24.15	35.20	32.12	40.81	38.34	50.55	46.58	49.84	53.25	43.14	39.08	Central Government Deposits	26d
12.85	6.68	7.26	6.36	6.66	4.09	8.00	5.35	3.92	2.82	3.42	6.40	6.40	7.11	7.40	Credit from Monetary Authorities	26g
-.72	5.79	9.39	9.94	4.83	-.01	-9.44	-6.41	-1.18	-1.37	-2.22	4.40	8.41	4.55	2.74	Other Items (Net)	27r
1.80	1.50	2.03	1.98	1.47	1.63	2.12	1.58	2.09	2.22	1.99	1.40	....	....	....	Treasury Claims: Private Sector	22d. i
.76	.72	.87	.97	.97	1.26	.82	1.00	.89	1.00	1.00	1.00	....	....	....	Post Office: Checking Deposits	24.. i
End of Period															**Monetary Survey**	
.49	27.20	41.88	45.86	61.82	74.75	60.63	63.35	42.77	67.92	69.80	73.59	53.82	22.82	42.50	Foreign Assets (Net)	31n
71.51	78.73	85.08	80.38	74.08	67.79	101.01	101.84	106.81	83.05	94.56	103.77	95.38	96.98	117.48	Domestic Credit	32
4.53	14.33	12.76	9.98	.75	-4.93	7.85	1.64	2.83	-17.02	-7.89	-11.95	-17.36	-6.99	13.84	Claims on Central Govt. (Net)	32an
65.93	63.49	71.20	69.26	72.31	71.35	91.40	97.99	101.78	97.51	101.08	113.37	110.62	101.89	101.84	Claims on Private Sector	32d
1.06	.91	1.12	1.14	1.03	1.38	1.76	2.22	2.20	2.56	1.38	2.35	2.12	2.08	1.79	Claims on Other Financial Insts.	32f
55.34	79.97	90.07	83.07	90.69	82.74	89.67	91.04	64.38	63.16	75.25	78.48	56.48	45.96	94.64	Money	34
17.23	20.60	27.10	34.69	45.39	60.46	75.82	72.77	79.93	82.77	84.58	86.37	78.06	66.72	68.18	Quasi-Money	35
2.23	1.99	2.26	1.86	1.91	1.78	2.42	3.19	2.98	1.96	2.35	2.27	1.87	1.87	1.75	Long-Term Foreign Liabilities	36cl
-2.79	3.38	7.52	6.62	-2.09	-2.43	-6.27	-1.81	2.30	3.08	2.18	10.23	12.78	5.25	-4.59	Other Items (Net)	37r
72.57	100.57	117.17	117.76	136.08	143.20	165.49	163.82	144.31	145.92	159.83	164.86	134.54	112.68	162.82	Money plus Quasi-Money	35l
End of Period															**Other Banking Institutions**	
2.62	3.52	3.79	3.87	4.20	5.51	6.19	6.42	6.19	9.89	....	....	....	....	....	Savings Deposits	45
75.19	104.09	120.96	121.63	140.28	148.71	171.68	170.23	150.50	155.82	....	....	....	....	....	Liquid Liabilities	55l
Percent Per Annum															**Interest Rates**	
10.50	10.50	12.50	10.50	10.50	10.50	8.50	8.50	9.50	11.00	11.00	11.00	12.50	10.50	10.00	Discount Rate (*End of Period*)	60
10.13	13.35	14.66	12.23	11.84	10.66	8.58	8.37	8.72	10.07	10.98	10.94	11.44	....	....	Money Market Rate	60b
6.19	6.25	7.75	7.50	7.25	7.25	6.08	5.25	5.25	6.42	7.00	7.00	7.75	....	....	Deposit Rate	60l
14.50	14.50	16.00	14.50	14.50	14.50	13.50	13.50	14.50	16.00	16.00	16.00	17.50	....	....	Lending Rate	60p
Period Averages															**Prices**	
69.6	83.4	92.7	101.3	97.7	96.0	99.9	100.0	99.8	99.0	100.0	100.4	101.8	100.8	....	Consumer Prices	64

Togo
742

		1965	1966	1967	1968	1969	1970	1971	1972	1973	1974	1975	1976	1977	1978	1979
International Transactions																*Millions of Francs*
Exports	70	6,679	8,872	7,894	9,549	11,477	15,176	13,626	12,659	13,755	45,174	26,962	24,914	39,115	54,238	46,432
Imports, cif	71	11,100	11,668	11,133	11,623	14,572	17,928	19,455	21,381	22,388	28,612	37,270	44,420	69,834	100,898	110,208
Imports, fob	71.v	9,737	10,235	9,766	10,196	12,832	15,847	17,148	18,589	19,838	24,100	29,307	36,774	57,965	83,375	91,668
															1985=100	
Volume of Exports	72	71	80	70	78	88	117	117	115	110	118	73	89	118	169	119
															1985=100	
Export Prices	74	....	15	14	15	17	17	16	15	17	43	I44	33	45	47	52
Unit Value of Imports	75	....	21	21	20	22	24	24	26	28	36	I40	47	53	59	66
Balance of Payments																*Millions of US Dollars:*
Goods: Exports f.o.b.	78aa d										215.1	141.0	158.9	199.3	262.0	290.6
Goods: Imports f.o.b.	78ab d										-98.0	-211.5	-180.6	-252.7	-410.9	-464.3
Trade Balance	78ac d										117.0	-70.6	-21.8	-53.4	-148.9	-173.8
Services: Credit	78ad d										14.5	27.9	23.8	27.6	36.0	45.2
Services: Debit	78ae d										-38.2	-69.1	-60.0	-90.3	-134.2	-145.4
Balance on Goods and Services	78af d										93.3	-111.7	-58.0	-116.1	-247.1	-273.9
Income: Credit	78ag d										6.4	6.5	6.5	7.0	7.3	10.2
Income: Debit	78ah d										-6.0	-11.3	-10.4	-20.2	-27.7	-32.0
Balance on Goods, Serv., & Inc.	78ai d										93.7	-116.6	-61.9	-129.3	-267.6	-295.8
Current Transfers, n.i.e.: Credit	78aj d										44.6	49.9	43.2	53.9	66.0	99.9
Current Transfers: Debit	78ak d										-6.5	-8.8	-8.8	-11.8	-15.8	-16.9
Current Account, n.i.e.	78al d										131.8	-75.5	-27.6	-87.3	-217.4	-212.7
Capital Account, n.i.e.: Credit	78ba d										—	—	—	—	—	—
Capital Account: Debit	78bb d										—	—	—	—	—	—
Capital Account, n.i.e.	78bc d										—	—	—	—	—	—
Direct Investment Abroad	78bd d															
Dir. Invest. in Rep. Econ., n.i.e.	78be d										-44.3	5.2	5.6	11.3	92.9	52.6
Portfolio Investment Assets	78bf d										—					
Portfolio Investment Liab., n.i.e.	78bg d										.8	.6	21.0	1.5	—	2.5
Other Investment Assets	78bh d										-65.6	51.2	-26.0	-12.9	-42.3	5.4
Other Investment Liab., n.i.e.	78bi d										27.7	35.4	23.5	70.6	186.1	147.1
Financial Account, n.i.e.	78bj d										-81.5	92.5	24.1	70.4	236.6	207.5
Net Errors and Omissions	78ca d										-16.0	-6.1	.2	-15.4	.5	-10.3
Overall Balance	78cb d										34.3	10.9	-3.3	-32.2	19.7	-15.6
Reserves and Related Items	79da d										-34.3	-10.9	3.3	32.2	-19.7	15.6
Reserve Assets	79db d										-34.3	-10.9	-8.3	32.2	-18.2	9.7
Use of Fund Credit and Loans	79dc d										—	—	8.6	—	-1.5	5.9
Liabs.Constit.For.Auth.Reserves	79dd d										—	—	—	—	—	—
Exceptional Financing	79de d										—	—	3.0	—	—	—
Government Finance																*Millions of Francs:*
Deficit (-) or Surplus	80													-39,222	-58,836	-17,942
Revenue	81													47,002	56,549	69,674
Grants Received	81z													20	97	334
Expenditure	82													72,677	84,667	68,297
Lending Minus Repayments	83													13,567	30,815	19,653
Financing																
Total Financing	84													39,222	58,836	17,942
Net Borrowing: Domestic	84a													8,869	5,746	-1,312
Foreign	85a													31,438	55,411	23,196
Use of Cash Balances	87													-1,085	-2,321	-3,942
Debt: Domestic	88a													....	....	....
Debt: Foreign	89a													....	....	....
National Accounts																*Billions of Francs:*
Exports of Goods & Services	90c	9.1	12.8	13.4	15.7	19.8	21.5	22.8	20.2	18.3	55.2	35.6	43.4	45.0	66.8	71.6
Government Consumption	91f	3.5	3.9	3.9	4.1	4.4	5.2	6.4	7.3	8.2	10.8	19.2	22.2	28.6	29.2	32.3
Gross Fixed Capital Formation	93e	8.2	7.3	10.2	7.0	8.7	9.2	13.3	16.2	18.9	20.0	29.2	33.7	58.7	88.5	101.4
Increase/Decrease(-) in Stocks	93i	2.1	1.4	-2.9	-.4	.5	1.4	1.6	1.4	2.4	2.1	7.4	3.1	6.9	4.6	6.4
Private Consumption	96f	32.4	41.4	45.5	48.0	54.8	59.6	63.4	69.5	70.0	72.8	95.6	90.8	106.1	123.1	131.0
Imports of Goods & Services	98c	-11.8	-13.7	-13.0	-14.4	-18.6	-23.5	-27.6	-27.9	-26.0	-32.2	-58.7	-56.9	-76.6	-123.2	-129.9
Gross Domestic Product	99b	43.5	53.1	57.0	59.9	69.6	73.7	81.8	87.6	90.4	130.6	128.3	136.3	168.8	189.0	212.8
Nat'l Income, Market Prices	99e	38.7	48.2	51.2	53.7	62.9	67.8	76.8	80.7	82.9	121.8	121.7	129.2	159.1	173.3	194.0
Gross Dom. Prod. 1985 Prices	99b.p	....	....	....	....	....	255.3	270.8	281.0	269.3	280.7	279.0	277.7	293.1	I322.7	340.1
GDP Deflator (1985=100)	99bi p	....	....	....	....	....	28.9	30.2	31.2	33.6	46.5	46.0	49.1	57.6	58.6	62.6
																Millions:
Population	99z	1.70	1.75	1.80	1.85	1.90	1.96	2.01	2.07	2.12	2.17	2.23	2.29	2.35	2.41	2.47

Deposit Money Banks: I Beginning in October 1979, *Central Government Deposits* include the deposits of public establishments of an administrative or social nature (EPAS) and exclude those of the savings bank; *Demand* and *Time Deposits* include deposits of the savings bank and exclude deposits of EPAS; and *Claims on Private Sector* exclude claims on other financial institutions.

Monetary Survey: I Beginning in October 1979, *line 32f* includes claims of deposit money banks on other financial institutions; see deposit money bank notes for explanation of other break symbols.

Togo

	1980	1981	1982	1983	1984	1985	1986	1987	1988	1989	1990	1991	1992	1993	1994		
Millions of Francs																**International Transactions**	
	71,285	57,469	58,173	61,921	83,588	85,380	70,551	73,212	72,209	78,188	72,942	71,433	....	....	....	Exports	70
	116,357	117,769	128,354	108,141	118,460	129,406	107,983	127,308	145,170	150,533	158,287	125,222	....	....	....	Imports, cif	71
	95,624	96,803	105,416	89,313	101,760	111,174	92,769	109,371	124,716	129,324	135,985	107,579	....	....	....	Imports, fob	71.v
1985=100																	
	163	110	93	83	118	100	100	121	131	....	....	....	....	....	....	Volume of Exports	72
1985=100																	
	49	51	54	61	84	100	....	....	....	....	....	....	....	....	....	Export Prices	74
	71	80	83	100	100	100	....	....	....	....	....	....	....	....	....	Unit Value of Imports	75
Minus Sign Indicates Debit																**Balance of Payments**	
	475.8	377.1	344.8	273.5	291.0	282.0	362.4	397.5	435.3	411.7	395.2	393.1	322.3	214.7	....	Goods: Exports f.o.b.	78aa d
	−524.1	−413.9	−408.2	−291.8	−263.2	−303.7	−418.6	−437.1	−504.5	−470.1	−513.1	−452.3	−417.8	−248.6	....	Goods: Imports f.o.b.	78ab d
	−48.3	−36.2	−63.3	−18.3	27.8	−21.7	−56.2	−39.6	−69.1	−58.4	−117.9	−59.2	−95.6	−33.9	....	Trade Balance	78ac d
	73.9	97.1	88.3	70.6	76.8	87.0	103.7	118.8	105.1	128.0	150.2	142.9	129.2	68.6	....	Services: Credit	78ad d
	−166.8	−146.0	−136.0	−117.7	−112.6	−131.8	−172.3	−196.6	−200.2	−195.8	−227.0	−213.0	−203.3	−135.6	....	Services: Debit	78ae d
	−141.2	−85.1	−111.1	−65.4	−8.1	−66.6	−124.8	−117.4	−164.1	−126.2	−194.7	−129.4	−169.6	−100.9	....	Balance on Goods and Services	78af d
	20.7	15.6	16.7	16.1	17.2	23.5	27.5	18.9	20.8	24.0	30.5	29.4	31.4	19.5	....	Income: Credit	78ag d
	−60.6	−43.4	−59.0	−59.2	−56.0	−61.5	−69.5	−66.1	−70.5	−63.8	−61.0	−60.3	−58.6	−57.6	....	Income: Debit	78ah d
	−181.2	−112.9	−153.4	−108.5	−46.9	−104.6	−166.8	−164.6	−213.8	−166.0	−225.1	−160.2	−196.8	−139.0	....	Balance on Goods, Serv., & Inc.	78ai d
	101.4	83.3	80.1	73.6	75.5	90.5	120.4	125.2	148.4	134.0	145.8	126.9	112.6	61.8	....	Current Transfers, n.i.e.: Credit	78aj d
	−15.2	−14.5	−13.6	−13.0	−12.3	−19.4	−19.1	−21.2	−21.8	−18.8	−22.0	−21.3	−22.7	−21.2	....	Current Transfers: Debit	78ak d
	−95.0	−44.2	−86.8	−47.9	16.3	−33.5	−65.6	−60.5	−87.2	−50.8	−101.4	−54.6	−106.9	−98.4	....	Current Account, n.i.e.	78al d
	—	—	—	—	—	—	—	—	—	—	—	—	—	—	....	Capital Account, n.i.e.: Credit	78ba d
	—	—	—	—	—	—	—	—	—	—	—	—	—	—	....	Capital Account: Debit	78bb d
	—	—	—	—	—	—	—	—	—	—	—	—	—	—	....	Capital Account, n.i.e.	78bc d
	—	—	—	—	—	—	—	—	—	—	—	—	—	—	....	Direct Investment Abroad	78bd d
	42.7	10.2	16.1	1.4	−9.9	16.3	6.1	7.2	13.0	7.4	—	—	—	—	....	Dir. Invest. in Rep. Econ., n.i.e.	78be d
	−.3	−.2	−.2	−.9	−.3	−.3	−4.0	.7	−.3	−1.3	—	—	—	—	....	Portfolio Investment Assets	78bf d
	2.2	—	—	.7	.1	.7	1.4	.7	1.0	1.3	—	—	—	—	....	Portfolio Investment Liab., n.i.e.	78bg d
	4.9	−60.3	−31.5	16.9	−15.4	−16.1	−4.5	−39.9	−12.9	−52.7	43.1	−10.1	.2	24.7	....	Other Investment Assets	78bh d
	13.3	50.8	27.4	−15.9	−11.5	30.5	24.5	−22.8	32.0	66.8	19.1	56.4	10.4	−71.6	....	Other Investment Liab., n.i.e.	78bi d
	62.8	.4	11.8	2.3	−37.0	31.1	23.5	−54.2	32.7	21.5	62.2	46.4	10.6	−46.9	....	Financial Account, n.i.e.	78bj d
	−.6	−2.6	−3.2	7.5	−.1	−.7	−1.0	−15.7	6.6	1.8	10.8	−33.7	−62.1	−42.2	....	Net Errors and Omissions	78ca d
	−32.8	−46.3	−78.2	−38.1	−20.8	−3.1	−43.1	−130.4	−47.9	−27.6	−28.4	−42.0	−158.5	−187.5	....	Overall Balance	78cb d
	32.8	46.3	78.2	38.1	20.8	3.1	43.1	130.4	47.9	27.6	28.4	42.0	158.5	187.5	....	Reserves and Related Items	79da d
	−12.6	−92.5	−38.4	−40.9	−57.6	−32.6	10.9	52.0	3.5	−38.6	−29.5	−13.9	73.6	102.2	....	Reserve Assets	79db d
	19.3	9.0	—	20.1	11.7	4.5	7.4	−17.7	−2.8	−.7	5.3	−7.9	.6	−8.3	....	Use of Fund Credit and Loans	79dc d
	—	—	—	—	—	—	—	—	—	—	—	—	—	—	....	Liabs.Constit.For.Auth.Reserves	79dd d
	26.1	129.9	116.6	58.8	66.9	31.2	24.8	96.2	47.1	66.9	52.5	63.8	84.2	93.6	....	Exceptional Financing	79de d
Year Ending December 31																**Government Finance**	
	−4,689	−14,821	−4,794	−5,607	−7,862	−6,104	−16,644	−9,380	....	....	....	....	....	....	....	Deficit (-) or Surplus	80
	72,833	66,660	76,771	79,406	91,987	107,212	104,880	99,492	....	....	....	....	....	....	....	Revenue	81
	63	4,231	4,878	6,515	10,717	9,386	15,600	8,382	....	....	....	....	....	....	....	Grants Received	81z
	73,943	85,137	86,410	91,863	110,567	122,702	137,121	117,144	....	....	....	....	....	....	....	Expenditure	82
	3,642	575	33	−335	−1	—	3	110	....	....	....	....	....	....	....	Lending Minus Repayments	83
																Financing	
	4,689	14,821	4,794	5,607	7,862	6,104	16,644	....	....	....	....	....	....	....	....	Total Financing	84
	−53	7,362	5,351	17,266	....	3,264	13	....	....	....	....	....	....	....	....	Net Borrowing: Domestic	84a
	4,247	6,597	3,103	5,562	....	2,840	11,691	....	....	....	....	....	....	....	....	Foreign	85a
	495	862	−3,660	−17,221	....	....	4,940	....	....	....	....	....	....	....	....	Use of Cash Balances	87
	....	....	....	16,282	4,277	6,412	4,213	....	....	....	....	....	....	....	....	Debt: Domestic	88a
	....	209,964	231,683	292,270	320,487	293,683	283,430	280,615	308,066	....	....	....	....	....	....	Debt: Foreign	89a
Billions of Francs																**National Accounts**	
	114.9	103.4	110.7	131.1	160.7	165.8	133.2	128.6	....	....	....	....	....	....	....	Exports of Goods & Services	90c
	35.4	38.7	41.8	48.3	49.4	44.5	44.6	53.4	....	....	....	....	....	....	....	Government Consumption	91f
	82.3	67.7	63.6	66.6	55.7	91.8	101.7	92.8	....	....	....	....	....	....	....	Gross Fixed Capital Formation	93e
	.6	11.4	7.3	−1.6	−8.5	−5.7	4.5	1.2	....	....	....	....	....	....	....	Increase/Decrease(-) in Stocks	93i
	151.6	180.6	194.9	208.6	219.6	235.4	258.8	262.5	....	....	....	....	....	....	....	Private Consumption	96f
	−146.4	−143.8	−148.6	−155.0	−163.1	−193.8	−177.5	−166.6	....	....	....	....	....	....	....	Imports of Goods & Services	98c
	238.4	258.0	269.7	298.0	313.8	338.2	365.3	371.9	....	....	....	....	....	....	....	Gross Domestic Product	99b
	212.2	224.3	230.0	247.4	266.3	287.7	313.5	320.4	....	....	....	....	....	....	....	Nat'l Income, Market Prices	99e
	346.4	334.3	321.5	323.9	328.1	338.2	349.8	355.1	....	....	....	....	....	....	....	Gross Dom. Prod. 1985 Prices	99b.p
	68.8	77.2	83.9	92.0	95.6	100.0	104.4	104.7	....	....	....	....	....	....	....	GDP Deflator (1985=100)	99bi p
Midyear Estimates																	
	2.55	2.69	2.70	2.85	2.94	3.03	3.12	3.22	3.32	3.42	3.53	3.64	3.76	3.88	....	Population	99z

Tonga
866

		1965	1966	1967	1968	1969	1970	1971	1972	1973	1974	1975	1976	1977	1978	1979
Exchange Rates															*Pa'anga per SDR:*	
Official Rate	aa	.8941	1.8977	.8921	.9009	.8945	.8969	.9116	.8515	.8107	.9226	.9312	1.0694	1.0642	1.1324	1.1916
															Pa'anga per US Dollar:	
Official Rate	ae	.8941	1.8977	.8921	.9009	.8945	.8969	.8396	.7843	.6720	.7536	.7955	.9205	.8761	.8692	.9046
Official Rate	rf	.8929	.8929	.8929	.8929	.8929	.8929	.8806	.8192	.7041	.6958	.7639	.8183	.9018	.8737	.8946
Fund Position															*Millions of SDRs:*	
Quota	2f.s	…	…	…	…	…	…	…	…	…	…	…	…	…	…	…
SDRs	1b.s	…	…	…	…	…	…	…	…	…	…	…	…	…	…	…
Reserve Position in the Fund	1c.s	…	…	…	…	…	…	…	…	…	…	…	…	…	…	…
International Liquidity												*Millions of US Dollars Unless Otherwise Indicated:*				
Total Reserves minus Gold	1l.d	…	…	…	…	…	…	…	…	…	…	…	…	9.00	10.12	12.56
SDRs	1b.d	…	…	…	…	…	…	…	…	…	…	…	…	…	…	…
Reserve Position in the Fund	1c.d	…	…	…	…	…	…	…	…	…	…	…	…	…	…	…
Foreign Exchange	1d.d	…	…	…	…	…	…	…	…	…	…	…	…	9.00	10.12	12.56
Monetary Authorities															*Thousands of Pa'anga:*	
Foreign Assets (Net)	11n	…	…	…	…	…	…	…	…	…	…	…	…	…	…	…
Claims on Central Government	12a	…	…	…	…	…	…	…	…	…	…	…	…	…	…	…
Claims on Nonmonetary Fin. Insts.	12g	…	…	…	…	…	…	…	…	…	…	…	…	…	…	…
Reserve Money	14	…	…	…	…	…	…	…	…	…	…	…	…	…	…	…
of which: Currency Outside DMBs	14a	…	…	…	…	…	…	…	…	…	…	…	…	…	…	…
Bonds	16ab	…	…	…	…	…	…	…	…	…	…	…	…	…	…	…
Central Government Deposits	16d	…	…	…	…	…	…	…	…	…	…	…	…	…	…	…
Capital Accounts	17a	…	…	…	…	…	…	…	…	…	…	…	…	…	…	…
Other Items (Net)	17r	…	…	…	…	…	…	…	…	…	…	…	…	…	…	…
Deposit Money Banks															*Thousands of Pa'anga:*	
Reserves	20	…	…	…	…	…	…	…	…	…	5,710	5,276	5,645	8,373	9,536	11,939
Claims on Central Government	22a	…	…	…	…	…	…	…	…	…	—	518	—	—	—	200
Claims on Nonfin.Pub.Enterprises	22c	…	…	…	…	…	…	…	…	…	—	—	—	—	—	—
Claims on Private Sector	22d	…	…	…	…	…	…	…	…	…	40	668	2,088	3,012	3,088	4,090
Claims on Nonmonetary Fin. Insts.	22g	…	…	…	…	…	…	…	…	…	—	—	—	50	50	100
Demand Deposits	24	…	…	…	…	…	…	…	…	…	1,190	1,382	1,445	2,224	2,651	2,705
Time and Savings Deposits	25	…	…	…	…	…	…	…	…	…	2,324	2,381	3,497	5,860	6,038	7,084
Central Government Deposits	26d	…	…	…	…	…	…	…	…	…	1,500	1,573	1,142	1,482	1,309	2,237
Capital Accounts	27a	…	…	…	…	…	…	…	…	…	794	1,313	1,861	2,223	3,065	4,457
Other Items (Net)	27r	…	…	…	…	…	…	…	…	…	−57	−187	−212	−355	−386	−152
Monetary Survey															*Thousands of Pa'anga:*	
Foreign Assets (Net)	31n	…	…	…	…	…	…	…	…	…	…	…	…	…	…	…
Domestic Credit	32	…	…	…	…	…	…	…	…	…	…	…	…	…	…	…
Claims on Central Govt. (Net)	32an	…	…	…	…	…	…	…	…	…	…	…	…	…	…	…
Claims on Nonfin.Pub.Enterprises	32c	…	…	…	…	…	…	…	…	…	…	…	…	…	…	…
Claims on Private Sector	32d	…	…	…	…	…	…	…	…	…	…	…	…	…	…	…
Claims on Nonmonetary Fin. Insts.	32g	…	…	…	…	…	…	…	…	…	…	…	…	…	…	…
Money	34	…	…	…	…	…	…	…	…	…	…	…	…	…	…	…
Quasi-Money	35	…	…	…	…	…	…	…	…	…	…	…	…	…	…	…
Other Items (Net)	37r	…	…	…	…	…	…	…	…	…	…	…	…	…	…	…
Money plus Quasi-Money	35l	…	…	…	…	…	…	…	…	…	…	…	…	…	…	…
Other Banking Institutions															*Thousands of Pa'anga:*	
Reserves	40	…	…	…	…	…	…	…	…	…	…	…	…	175	121	1,147
Claims on Central Government	42a	…	…	…	…	…	…	…	…	…	…	…	…	—	—	—
Claims on Private Sector	42d	…	…	…	…	…	…	…	…	…	…	…	…	196	706	1,398
Long-Term Foreign Liabilities	46cl	…	…	…	…	…	…	…	…	…	…	…	…	—	—	—
Central Government Deposits	46d	…	…	…	…	…	…	…	…	…	…	…	…	—	—	—
Central Govt. Lending Funds	46f	…	…	…	…	…	…	…	…	…	…	…	…	—	—	1,054
Credit from Monetary Authorities	46g	…	…	…	…	…	…	…	…	…	…	…	…	33	—	—
Capital Accounts	47a	…	…	…	…	…	…	…	…	…	…	…	…	332	796	1,490
Other Items (Net)	47r	…	…	…	…	…	…	…	…	…	…	…	…	7	31	2
Banking Survey															*Thousands of Pa'anga:*	
Foreign Assets (Net)	51n	…	…	…	…	…	…	…	…	…	…	…	…	…	…	…
Domestic Credit	52	…	…	…	…	…	…	…	…	…	…	…	…	…	…	…
Claims on Government (Net)	52an	…	…	…	…	…	…	…	…	…	…	…	…	…	…	…
Claims on Nonfin.Pub.Enterprises	52c	…	…	…	…	…	…	…	…	…	…	…	…	…	…	…
Claims on Private Sector	52d	…	…	…	…	…	…	…	…	…	…	…	…	…	…	…
Liquid Liabilities	55l	…	…	…	…	…	…	…	…	…	…	…	…	…	…	…
Long-Term Foreign Liabilities	56cl	…	…	…	…	…	…	…	…	…	…	…	…	…	…	…
Other Items (Net)	57r	…	…	…	…	…	…	…	…	…	…	…	…	…	…	…
Interest Rates															*Percent Per Annum*	
Deposit Rate	60l	…	…	…	…	…	…	…	…	…	…	…	…	…	…	…
Lending Rate	60p	…	…	…	…	…	…	…	…	…	…	…	…	…	…	…
Prices															*Index Numbers (1990=100):*	
Consumer Prices	64	…	…	…	…	…	…	…	…	…	…	21.5	23.0	27.1	29.6	31.3

Tonga

866

	1980	1981	1982	1983	1984	1985	1986	1987	1988	1989	1990	1991	1992	1993	1994		
																Exchange Rates	
End of Period	1.0802	1.0320	1.1249	1.1607	1.1841	1.6132	1.8399	1.9635	1.5748	1.6539	1.8435	1.9050	1.9116	1.8946	1.8371	Official Rate	aa
End of Period (ae) Period Average (rf)	.8470	.8866	1.0198	1.1086	1.2080	1.4686	1.5042	1.3841	1.1703	1.2585	1.2958	1.3317	1.3902	1.3793	1.2584	Official Rate	ae
	.8782	.8702	.9859	1.1100	1.1395	1.4319	1.4960	1.4282	1.2750	1.2612	1.2800	1.2961	1.3471	1.3841	1.3202	Official Rate	rf
																Fund Position	
End of Period	....	....	....	....	....	3.25	3.25	3.25	3.25	3.25	3.25	3.25	3.25	5.00	5.00	5.00 Quota	2f. s
	....	....	....	....	....	—	.03	.05	.08	.12	.17	.74	.38	.44	.49	SDRs	1b. s
	....	....	....	....	....	.74	.74	.74	.74	.74	.74	.74	1.18	1.19	1.20	Reserve Position in the Fund	1c. s
																International Liquidity	
End of Period	13.75	13.98	15.56	20.95	26.02	27.51	22.48	28.88	30.51	24.85	31.34	32.28	31.77	37.06	35.54	Total Reserves minus Gold	1l. d
						—	.04	.07	.11	.16	.24	1.06	.52	.60	.71	SDRs	1b. d
	....	....	....	....	....	.81	.91	1.05	1.00	.97	1.05	1.06	1.62	1.64	1.76	Reserve Position in the Fund	1c. d
	13.75	13.98	15.56	20.95	26.02	26.70	21.54	27.76	29.41	23.72	30.04	30.17	29.62	34.82	33.07	Foreign Exchange	1d. d
																Monetary Authorities	
End of Period			15,554	20,874	25,928	27,772	34,726	40,491	35,775	44,089	39,886	42,316	44,438	51,316	43,671	Foreign Assets (Net)	11n
	....	....	2,734	3,379	3,095	2,730	3,374	3,760	4,184	5,336	13,121	10,407	10,432	11,236	9,516	Claims on Central Government	12a
	....	....	—	—	—	—	—	—	—	—	—	—	650	—	—	Claims on Nonmonetary Fin. Insts.	12g
	....	....	17,860	23,715	28,421	29,986	37,127	42,879	38,532	45,606	49,261	48,975	52,155	21,351	20,682	Reserve Money	14
	....	....	2,505	3,168	3,404	3,569	4,474	4,892	5,503	5,971	6,767	7,165	7,127	7,894	7,346	of which: Currency Outside DMBs	14a
	....	....	....	....	....	....	....	....	....	....	....	....	....	42,590	39,200	Bonds	16ab
	....	....	409	469	513	400	771	873	1,002	1,432	488	488	1,091	3,432	2,142	Central Government Deposits	16d
	....	....	—	—	—	—	—	—	—	1,001	2,786	3,659	2,725	2,789	2,922	Capital Accounts	17a
	....	....	19	69	89	117	202	499	425	1,386	473	253	-1,102	-7,611	-11,760	Other Items (Net)	17r
																Deposit Money Banks	
End of Period	13,342	13,697	15,355	20,547	25,017	26,417	32,653	37,987	33,029	39,635	42,494	41,810	42,457	50,707	49,002	Reserves	20
	200	431	431	431	431	431	200	200	2,213	2,305	2,203	5,974	6,898	6,816	6,262	Claims on Central Government	22a
									832	—	1,437	1,188	413	55	152	Claims on Nonfin.Pub.Enterprises	22c
	5,170	6,921	9,555	9,600	9,849	15,330	16,783	23,957	28,756	33,555	33,271	32,730	31,051	31,351	47,174	Claims on Private Sector	22d
	150	150	233	274	311	311	350	350	350	350	350	350	350	350	3,850	Claims on Nonmonetary Fin. Insts.	22g
	....	3,505	4,912	6,451	6,650	7,360	8,817	10,306	10,182	11,200	15,529	18,509	15,285	19,713	18,612	Demand Deposits	24
	....	8,226	8,928	10,035	11,870	16,632	19,489	23,959	22,523	23,725	27,017	29,557	30,173	33,971	42,730	Time and Savings Deposits	25
	....	2,795	4,054	5,930	7,375	6,427	7,339	11,543	13,584	12,415	16,413	10,931	10,382	12,324	15,335	Central Government Deposits	26d
	....	6,526	7,964	8,993	10,333	12,200	15,342	19,515	21,290	22,843	26,731	27,627	32,559	30,758	36,561	Capital Accounts	27a
	....	148	-284	-558	-621	-132	-1,001	-2,829	-2,399	7,754	-5,935	-4,572	-7,230	-7,485	-6,798	Other Items (Net)	27r
																Monetary Survey	
End of Period	....	....	15,083	20,611	25,668	26,863	33,608	39,871	35,143	43,639	39,258	41,823	43,784	50,437	42,490	Foreign Assets (Net)	31n
	....	....	8,490	7,285	5,798	11,975	12,597	15,851	21,749	29,791	33,481	39,880	37,671	34,052	49,477	Domestic Credit	32
	....	....	-1,298	-2,589	-4,362	-3,666	-4,536	-8,456	-8,189	-6,206	-1,577	4,962	5,857	2,296	-1,699	Claims on Central Govt. (Net)	32an
	....	....	—	—	—	—	—	—	832	2,092	1,437	1,188	413	55	152	Claims on Nonfin.Pub.Enterprises	32c
	....	....	9,555	9,600	9,849	15,330	16,783	23,957	28,756	33,555	33,271	32,730	31,051	31,351	47,174	Claims on Private Sector	32d
	....	....	233	274	311	311	350	350	350	350	350	1,000	350	350	3,850	Claims on Nonmonetary Fin. Insts.	32g
	....	....	7,417	9,619	10,054	10,929	13,291	15,198	15,685	17,171	22,296	25,674	22,412	27,760	27,510	Money	34
	....	....	8,928	10,035	11,870	16,632	19,489	23,959	22,523	23,725	27,017	29,557	30,173	33,971	42,730	Quasi-Money	35
	....	....	7,228	8,241	9,541	11,276	13,425	16,565	18,684	32,534	23,427	26,474	28,869	22,759	21,726	Other Items (Net)	37r
	....	....	16,345	19,654	21,924	27,561	32,780	39,157	38,208	40,896	49,313	55,231	52,585	61,731	70,240	Money plus Quasi-Money	35l
																Other Banking Institutions	
End of Period	1,230	725	926	947	841	1,288	1,150	2,392	657	300	2,941	4,752	3,097	4,277	9,895	Reserves	40
	—	—	—	—	—	—	—	—	—	100	100	400	900	900	2,000	Claims on Central Government	42a
	2,135	3,043	4,031	4,391	5,880	6,551	8,441	10,370	16,474	18,749	22,187	23,042	25,222	30,131	31,176	Claims on Private Sector	42d
	36	133	419	419	668	977	1,235	2,144	3,125	3,169	3,052	3,516	3,973	5,040	5,444	Long-Term Foreign Liabilities	46cl
	—	—	—	—	—	6	—	—	—	—	—	—	—	—	—	Central Government Deposits	46d
	1,593	1,917	2,065	2,041	2,640	3,272	4,124	4,703	7,259	7,825	11,219	12,485	14,029	14,597	15,761	Central Govt. Lending Funds	46f
	—	41	—	284	350	200	178	347	307	328	226	169	—	—	—	Credit from Monetary Authorities	46g
	1,736	1,811	2,874	3,162	3,653	4,149	4,825	6,218	7,235	8,936	10,681	12,980	15,514	16,643	17,703	Capital Accounts	47a
	-2	-134	-402	-570	-591	-766	-768	-651	-797	-1,107	50	-956	-4,297	-972	7,810	Other Items (Net)	47r
																Banking Survey	
End of Period	....	....	15,083	20,611	25,668	26,863	33,608	39,871	35,143	43,639	39,258	41,823	43,784	50,437	42,490	Foreign Assets (Net)	51n
	....	....	12,288	11,402	11,367	18,209	20,688	25,871	37,873	48,290	55,418	62,322	63,443	64,733	82,450	Domestic Credit	52
	....	....	-1,298	-2,589	-4,362	-3,672	-4,536	-8,456	-8,189	-6,106	-1,477	5,362	6,757	3,196	301	Claims on Government (Net)	52an
	....	....	—	—	—	—	—	—	832	2,092	1,437	1,188	413	55	3,799	Claims on Nonfin.Pub.Enterprises	52c
	....	....	13,586	13,991	15,729	21,881	25,224	34,327	45,230	52,304	55,458	55,772	56,273	61,482	78,350	Claims on Private Sector	52d
	....	....	15,419	18,707	21,083	26,273	31,630	36,765	37,551	40,596	46,372	50,479	49,488	57,454	60,345	Liquid Liabilities	55l
	....	....	419	419	668	977	1,235	2,144	3,125	3,169	3,052	3,516	3,973	5,040	5,444	Long-Term Foreign Liabilities	56cl
	....	....	11,532	12,884	15,282	17,820	21,434	26,832	32,338	48,166	45,253	50,152	53,765	52,677	59,150	Other Items (Net)	57r
																Interest Rates	
Percent Per Annum	6.25	6.25	6.25	6.25	6.25	6.25	6.25	6.25	6.25	7.25	7.25	7.25	4.25	4.25	4.67	Deposit Rate	60l
	....	....	....	....	....	....	....	....	....	....	....	....	....	9.94	....	Lending Rate	60p
																Prices	
Period Averages	38.3	44.0	48.7	53.5	53.6	62.6	76.1	79.7	87.6	91.1	100.0	110.6	119.4	120.5	121.8	Consumer Prices	64

Tonga
866

		1965	1966	1967	1968	1969	1970	1971	1972	1973	1974	1975	1976	1977	1978	1979
International Transactions																*Thousands of Pa'anga*
Exports	70	2,506	3,618	3,566	3,846	3,398	2,673	2,200	2,050	3,200	4,600	4,433	3,220	6,352	4,750	6,134
Imports, cif	71	3,404	4,141	5,730	5,150	5,087	5,539	6,305	7,456	7,997	11,819	12,972	11,655	17,698	22,317	26,210
Balance of Payments																*Millions of US Dollars:*
Goods: Exports f.o.b.	78aa d	....	....	....	....	....	....	2.66	2.87	3.24	4.99	7.76	4.52	4.26	7.56	5.85
Goods: Imports f.o.b.	78ab d	....	....	....	....	....	....	-5.15	-6.61	-7.54	-11.08	-19.08	-16.19	-15.35	-18.49	-22.72
Trade Balance	78ac d	....	....	....	....	....	....	-2.49	-3.74	-4.30	-6.09	-11.32	-11.67	-11.09	-10.93	-16.87
Services: Credit	78ad d	....	....	....	....	....	....	1.01	1.40	1.80	3.55	7.94	4.81	5.55	5.83	6.22
Services: Debit	78ae d	....	....	....	....	....	....	-.91	-1.36	-1.37	-1.97	-4.13	-3.02	-3.79	-4.89	-3.87
Balance on Goods and Services	78af d	....	....	....	....	....	....	-2.39	-3.70	-3.86	-4.52	-7.51	-9.88	-9.32	-9.98	-14.53
Income: Credit	78ag d	....	....	....	....	....	....	.26	.44	.24	.34	.37	.68	.70	.97	1.90
Income: Debit	78ah d	....	....	....	....	....	....	-.02	-.03	-.07	-.15	-.06	-.23	-.35	-.21	-.38
Balance on Goods, Serv., & Inc.	78ai d	....	....	....	....	....	....	-2.15	-3.29	-3.69	-4.32	-7.20	-9.43	-8.98	-9.23	-13.00
Current Transfers, n.i.e.: Credit	78aj d	....	....	....	....	....	....	1.83	2.06	2.86	5.54	7.95	8.35	8.42	9.39	11.49
Current Transfers: Debit	78ak d	....	....	....	....	....	....	-.29	-.25	-.41	-.41	-.50	-1.01	-1.49	-.87	-.89
Current Account, n.i.e.	78al d	....	....	....	....	....	....	-.61	-1.48	-1.24	.80	.24	-2.09	-2.05	-.72	-2.40
Capital Account, n.i.e.: Credit	78ba d	....	....	....	....	....	....	.10	.12	.59	.21	.16	.14	.14	—	—
Capital Account: Debit	78bb d	....	....	....	....	....	....	-.02	-.02	-.07	-.06	-.05	-.06	-.08	—	—
Capital Account, n.i.e.	78bc d	....	....	....	....	....	....	.08	.09	.52	.15	.10	.08	.06	—	—
Direct Investment Abroad	78bd d	....	....	....	....	....	....	—	—	—	—	—	—	—	—	—
Dir. Invest. in Rep. Econ., n.i.e.	78be d	....	....	....	....	....	....	—	—	—	—	—	—	—	—	—
Portfolio Investment Assets	78bf d	....	....	....	....	....	....	—	—	—	—	—	—	—	—	—
Portfolio Investment Liab., n.i.e.	78bg d	....	....	....	....	....	....	—	—	—	—	—	—	—	—	—
Other Investment Assets	78bh d	....	....	....	....	....	....	—	—	—	—	—	—	—	—	—
Other Investment Liab., n.i.e.	78bi d	....	....	....	....	....	....	1.28	.78	1.09	.26	2.36	2.10	1.52	3.92	3.13
Financial Account, n.i.e.	78bj d	....	....	....	....	....	....	1.28	.78	1.09	.26	2.36	2.10	1.52	3.92	3.13
Net Errors and Omissions	78ca d	....	....	....	....	....	....	-.72	.36	-.41	.56	-.64	-2.48	2.89	-.23	.02
Overall Balance	78cb d	....	....	....	....	....	....	.03	-.25	-.03	1.78	2.07	-2.40	2.42	2.97	.74
Reserves and Related Items	79da d	....	....	....	....	....	....	-.03	.25	.03	-1.78	-2.07	2.40	-2.42	-2.97	-.74
Reserve Assets	79db d	....	....	....	....	....	....	-.03	.25	.03	-1.78	-2.07	2.40	-2.42	-2.97	-.74
Use of Fund Credit and Loans	79dc d	....	....	....	....	....	....	—	—	—	—	—	—	—	—	—
Liabs.Constit.For.Auth.Reserves	79dd d	....	....	....	....	....	....	—	—	—	—	—	—	—	—	—
Exceptional Financing	79de d	....	....	....	....	....	....	—	—	—	—	—	—	—	—	—
Government Finance																*Thousands of Pa'anga:*
Deficit (-) or Surplus	80	....	....	....	....	....	....	....	....	....	....	....	....	....	....	....
Revenue	81	....	....	....	....	....	....	....	....	....	....	....	....	....	....	....
Grants Received	81z	....	....	....	....	....	....	....	....	....	....	....	....	....	....	....
Expenditure	82	....	....	....	....	....	....	....	....	....	....	....	....	....	....	....
Lending Minus Repayments	83	....	....	....	....	....	....	....	....	....	....	....	....	....	....	....
Financing																
Domestic	84a	....	....	....	....	....	....	....	....	....	....	....	....	....	....	....
Foreign	85a	....	....	....	....	....	....	....	....	....	....	....	....	....	....	....
National Accounts																*Millions of Pa'anga:*
Gross Domestic Product	99b	....	....	....	....	....	....	....	....	....	....	24.83	24.58	30.79	36.32	39.94
Gross Dom. Prod. 1990 Prices	99b.p	....	....	....	....	....	....	....	....	....	....	52.39	52.82	55.35	56.41	57.46
GDP Deflator (1990=100)	99bi p	....	....	....	....	....	....	....	....	....	....	47.39	46.53	55.62	64.38	69.51
																Millions:
Population	99z	.08	.08	.08	.08	.08	.08	.08	.08	.09	.09	.09	.09	.09	.09	.09

Government Finance: Data relate to a fiscal year different from calendar year.

Tonga 866

	1980	1981	1982	1983	1984	1985	1986	1987	1988	1989	1990	1991	1992	1993	1994		
	\multicolumn{15}{l}{}	**International Transactions**	
	Thousands of Pa'anga																
	6,351	6,549	3,661	5,842	9,996	7,171	8,711	8,804	9,502	11,633	14,463	17,454	16,617	23,430	18,367	Exports	70
	33,134	35,002	41,198	41,664	46,315	58,928	60,823	68,459	70,689	68,336	78,991	76,817	84,294	84,933	91,210	Imports, cif	71
	Minus Sign Indicates Debit															Balance of Payments	
	7.25	7.62	7.97	3.51	7.18	7.86	5.87	7.04	6.42	9.91	9.00	10.57	14.28	11.90	....	Goods: Exports f.o.b.	78aa *d*
	−27.08	−37.12	−38.64	−37.49	−33.40	−31.76	−32.28	−35.10	−44.06	−48.02	−49.45	−51.42	−50.72	−49.50	....	Goods: Imports f.o.b.	78ab *d*
	−19.83	−29.50	−30.66	−33.97	−26.22	−23.90	−26.41	−28.06	−37.64	−38.11	−40.45	−40.85	−36.44	−37.60	....	Trade Balance	78ac *d*
	7.12	8.34	10.81	9.99	12.00	15.06	14.77	18.01	18.37	21.73	29.76	21.77	17.47	16.20	....	Services: Credit	78ad *d*
	−4.95	−5.18	−5.31	−9.45	−10.88	−14.65	−16.33	−16.49	−23.89	−22.70	−21.96	−23.74	−22.84	−19.09	....	Services: Debit	78ae *d*
	−17.66	−26.34	−25.17	−33.44	−25.10	−23.49	−27.97	−26.54	−43.16	−39.08	−32.64	−42.83	−41.81	−40.49	....	Balance on Goods and Services	78af *d*
	2.96	4.48	4.23	3.16	3.23	2.94	3.00	4.07	6.31	3.60	5.20	4.59	3.78	5.10	....	Income: Credit	78ag *d*
	−.48	−.57	−.96	−.10	−.16	−.11	−.41	−.50	−1.47	−1.29	−1.09	−1.07	−.98	−2.32	....	Income: Debit	78ah *d*
	−15.18	−22.44	−21.90	−30.38	−22.03	−20.66	−25.38	−22.96	−38.33	−36.77	−28.54	−39.31	−39.02	−37.70	....	Balance on Goods, Serv., & Inc.	78ai *d*
	13.08	17.31	28.49	36.18	26.37	20.60	28.93	30.86	33.07	39.94	46.53	43.99	43.93	52.04	....	Current Transfers, n.i.e.: Credit	78aj *d*
	−1.12	−2.34	−3.20	−5.00	−4.59	−2.04	−3.01	−3.01	−5.99	−5.05	−5.21	−6.58	−6.68	−11.07	....	Current Transfers: Debit	78ak *d*
	−3.22	−7.47	3.39	.80	−.26	−2.09	.54	4.88	−11.24	−1.88	12.78	−1.90	−1.77	3.27	....	Current Account, n.i.e.	78al *d*
	—	—	—	.38	1.54	.97	.80	1.43	.33	.08	.25	.27	.59	1.18	....	Capital Account, n.i.e.: Credit	78ba *d*
	—	—	—	−.99	−.99	−.21	−.47	−.56	−.46	−.09	−.53	−.37	−.24	−.35	....	Capital Account: Debit	78bb *d*
	—	—	—	−.61	.55	.75	.33	.87	−.13	−.01	−.28	−.11	.35	.83	....	Capital Account, n.i.e.	78bc *d*
	—	—	—	—	—	—	—	—	—	—	—	—	—	—	....	Direct Investment Abroad	78bd *d*
	—	—	—	—	—	.02	.11	.19	.06	.11	.10	.20	1.24	.35	....	Dir. Invest. in Rep. Econ., n.i.e.	78be *d*
	—	—	—	—	—	—	—	—	—	—	—	.03	—	.13	....	Portfolio Investment Assets	78bf *d*
	—	—	—	—	—	.02	—	—	—	—	−2.17	−13.64	−3.73	−.57	−.10	Portfolio Investment Liab., n.i.e.	78bg *d*
	—	—	—	—	—	—	.03	−.55	.27	.75	1.84	4.69	4.57	—	....	Other Investment Assets	78bh *d*
	6.89	8.19	2.18	1.18	4.29	4.73	−.80	.61	4.55	2.46	−1.87	.75	.85	3.02	....	Other Investment Liab., n.i.e.	78bi *d*
	6.89	8.19	2.18	1.18	4.29	4.77	−.65	.25	4.88	1.15	−13.55	1.92	6.21	3.27	....	Financial Account, n.i.e.	78bj *d*
	−.36	−.34	−4.07	−1.45	1.47	.37	.27	−4.88	7.24	−1.29	1.93	−.91	−1.18	.29	....	Net Errors and Omissions	78ca *d*
	3.31	.38	1.51	−.08	6.05	3.80	.48	1.12	.74	−2.03	.88	−1.00	3.62	7.65	....	Overall Balance	78cb *d*
	−3.31	−.38	−1.51	.08	−6.05	−3.80	−.48	−1.12	−.74	2.03	−.88	1.00	−3.62	−7.65	....	Reserves and Related Items	79da *d*
	−3.31	−.38	−1.51	.08	−6.05	−3.80	−.48	−1.12	−.74	2.03	−.88	1.00	−3.62	−7.65	....	Reserve Assets	79db *d*
	—	—	—	—	—	—	—	—	—	—	—	—	—	—	....	Use of Fund Credit and Loans	79dc *d*
	—	—	—	—	—	—	—	—	—	—	—	—	—	—	....	Liabs.Constit.For.Auth.Reserves	79dd *d*
	—	—	—	—	—	—	—	—	—	—	—	—	—	—	....	Exceptional Financing	79de *d*
	Year Ending June 30															**Government Finance**	
	....	....	—	−1,524	1,061	324	−2,104	−4,781	−6,693	622	−64	−1,893^P	−10,051^f	....	....	Deficit (-) or Surplus	80
	....	....	—	15,529	18,054	17,786	22,204	26,218	29,210	33,750	32,740	39,806^P	51,686^f	....	....	Revenue	81
	....	....	—	10,658	7,422	9,616	18,668	8,431	15,585	16,278	23,778	29,384^P	51,530^f	....	....	Grants Received	81z
	....	....	—	26,178	23,698	26,239	37,983	37,923	42,425	43,985	54,150	68,862^P	99,175^f	....	....	Expenditure	82
	....	....	—	1,533	717	839	4,993	1,507	9,063	5,421	2,432	2,221^P	14,092^f	....	....	Lending Minus Repayments	83
																Financing	
	....	....	1,026	−1,824	−757	979	3,301	−805	−622	64	293^P	2,717^f	....	....	....	Domestic	84a
	....	....	498	763	433	1,125	1,480	7,498	—	—	1,600^P	7,334^f	....	....	....	Foreign	85a
	Year Ending June 30															**National Accounts**	
	52.88	66.39	79.69	86.28	74.48	80.01	100.03	114.84	141.30	146.00	158.40	193.20	198.20	201.00	214.80	Gross Domestic Product	99b
	66.55	75.84	87.04	92.11	132.76	I 140.20	152.49	155.06	I 149.61	151.31	158.40	167.82	161.36	161.26	168.99	Gross Dom. Prod. 1990 Prices	99b. *p*
	79.45	87.54	91.55	93.66	56.10	57.07	65.59	74.07	94.44	96.49	100.00	115.12	122.83	124.64	127.11	GDP Deflator (1990=100)	99bi *p*
	Midyear Estimates																
	.09	.09	.09	.10	.10	.10	.09	.09	.09	.10	.10	.10	.10	.10	....	Population	99z

Trinidad and Tobago
369

		1965	1966	1967	1968	1969	1970	1971	1972	1973	1974	1975	1976	1977	1978	1979
Exchange Rates														*TT Dollars per SDR:*		
Market Rate	aa	1.7126	1.7203	1.9948	2.0131	1.9994	2.0053	2.0417	2.2194	2.4924	2.5024	2.7769	2.7884	2.9153	3.1267	3.1616
														TT Dollars per US Dollar:		
Market Rate	ae	1.7126	1.7203	1.9948	2.0131	1.9994	2.0053	1.8805	2.0442	2.0661	2.0439	2.3721	2.4000	2.4000	2.4000	2.4000
Market Rate	rf	1.7143	1.7143	1.7381	2.0000	2.0000	2.0000	1.9749	1.9213	1.9592	2.0532	2.1698	2.4358	2.4000	2.4000	2.4000
														Index Numbers (1990=100):		
Nominal Effective Exchange Rate	ne c	....	....	....	....	....	....	....	....	....	....	....	....	....	....	172.16
Real Effective Exchange Rate	re c	....	....	....	....	....	....	....	....	....	....	....	....	....	....	95.82
Fund Position														*Millions of SDRs:*		
Quota	2f. s	20.0	25.0	25.0	44.0	44.0	63.0	63.0	63.0	63.0	63.0	63.0	63.0	63.0	82.0	82.0
SDRs	1b. s	—	—	—	—	—	.5	7.2	7.3	7.1	7.9	7.6	7.6	12.2	16.9	31.2
Reserve Position in the Fund	1c. s	.5	1.8	1.8	1.8	2.8	6.6	6.6	6.6	—	—	4.8	18.7	27.8	27.6	29.8	37.8
of which: Outstg.Fund Borrowing	2c												2.9	10.0	10.0	10.0	7.9
Total Fund Cred.&Loans Outstg.	2tl																
International Liquidity													*Millions of US Dollars Unless Otherwise Indicated:*				
Total Reserves minus Gold	1l. d	28.5	29.7	30.3	49.4	44.7	43.0	69.4	58.3	47.0	390.3	751.0	1,013.5	1,481.7	1,804.8	2,140.0
SDRs	1b. d						.5	7.8	7.9	8.6	9.6	8.9	8.8	14.8	22.0	41.1
Reserve Position in the Fund	1c. d	.5	1.8	1.8	1.8	2.8	6.6	7.1	7.1	—	5.8	21.9	32.2	33.5	38.8	49.7
Foreign Exchange	1d. d	28.0	27.9	28.5	47.6	41.9	35.9	54.4	43.2	38.4	374.9	720.2	972.5	1,433.4	1,744.0	2,049.2
Gold (Million Fine Troy Ounces)	1ad	....	....	....	....	....	....	....	....	....	....	....	....	.027	.040	.054
Gold (National Valuation)	1and	....	....	....	....	....	....	....	....	....	....	....	....	1.1	1.7	2.3
Monetary Authorities: Other Liab.	4..d	—	—	—	—	—	—	—	—	—	—	—	—	—	—	—
Deposit Money Banks: Assets	7a. d	15.7	8.1	6.0	-3.3	4.7	3.9	11.9	3.4	3.8	3.4	3.6	5.9	12.9	19.1	41.1
of which: Claims on Nonbanks	7add	15.0	7.6	5.0	-4.3	3.5	2.6	9.7	.9	.5	.5	.1	1.0	1.8	.6	3.0
Deposit Money Banks: Liabilities	7b. d	3.3	3.8	3.4	4.6	12.2	7.7	13.6	15.3	25.0	19.3	23.2	21.3	34.6	57.5	47.9
of which: Liab. to Nonbanks	7bdd	3.2	3.5	3.1	3.9	4.1	5.1	11.7	11.8	4.9	5.9	6.0	9.0	11.4	12.5	15.3
Other Banking Insts.: Assets	7e. d	....	....	....	....	....	.7	.8	.8	.8	1.0	3.3	2.3	2.8	2.4	2.5
Liabilities	7f. d											4.8	5.1	5.5	4.7	10.2
Monetary Authorities													*Millions of TT Dollars:*				
Foreign Assets	11	48.9	51.0	60.6	98.7	89.3	85.8	136.5	106.7	97.5	796.2	1,778.8	2,461.8	3,586.7	4,363.5	5,163.5
Claims on Central Government	12a	7.5	22.7	2.6	27.2	46.3	43.5	23.2	52.3	77.2	20.6	11.6	11.2	24.6	33.5	17.6
Claims on Deposit Money Banks	12e	—	—	—	—	—	—	—	1.7	3.0	.1	—	—	—	—	—
Claims on Other Banking Insts	12f	—	—	.3	—	—	—	—	—	—	—	—	—	—	—	—
Reserve Money	14	51.3	63.1	63.7	87.0	82.4	91.6	119.7	131.4	151.8	303.2	478.8	639.2	664.4	695.6	1,225.6
of which: Currency Outside DMBs	14a	36.1	40.8	42.3	48.5	50.5	56.5	68.4	81.2	79.7	98.5	138.2	177.2	230.9	295.5	412.1
Foreign Liabilities	16c															
Central Government Deposits	16d	1.3	.4	9.4	36.9	50.8	24.8	16.4	-3.4	-15.2	460.1	1,202.7	1,694.8	2,891.1	3,436.6	3,609.7
Capital Accounts	17a	4.3	6.6	9.5	13.4	15.4	29.8	43.7	55.0	64.7	88.3	283.1	263.9	257.7	433.5	747.6
Other Items (Net)	17r	-.5	3.6	-19.1	-11.4	-13.0	-16.8	-20.1	-22.3	-23.6	-34.6	-174.1	-124.9	-201.9	-168.7	-401.7
Deposit Money Banks													*Millions of TT Dollars:*				
Reserves	20	15.2	22.7	21.7	38.5	31.9	35.1	51.3	50.2	72.1	204.7	340.6	462.0	433.6	400.1	813.7
Foreign Assets	21	27.0	13.9	12.0	-6.6	9.4	7.8	21.9	6.3	7.9	7.0	8.5	14.1	31.0	45.8	98.7
Claims on Central Government	22a	36.5	40.6	53.5	70.3	52.7	61.9	119.6	115.0	147.0	168.8	158.7	157.3	172.9	213.8	276.3
Claims on Local Government	22b	—	—	.1	—	.1	.1	.1	—	—	1.3	.6	1.4	5.1	7.2	12.0	8.0
Claims on Nonfin.Pub.Enterprises	22c	—	—	—	—	—	—	—	10.5	9.0	8.4	5.0	1.7	—	—	—
Claims on Private Sector	22d	143.7	158.8	184.4	202.9	271.8	330.4	361.5	502.7	585.5	665.7	888.1	1,247.6	1,761.7	2,341.0	2,745.5
Demand Deposits	24	79.8	84.9	87.3	90.4	89.1	94.9	108.4	129.9	132.9	171.4	254.2	394.6	494.4	640.8	734.6
Time and Savings Deposits	25	147.7	169.1	185.7	223.4	275.5	337.2	429.1	511.8	610.2	802.7	995.9	1,291.5	1,634.5	2,004.9	2,669.0
Foreign Liabilities	26c	5.6	6.5	6.8	9.1	24.4	15.4	25.1	28.2	51.7	39.5	55.1	51.1	83.0	138.0	114.9
Central Government Deposits	26d	17.3	6.8	13.4	6.7	6.6	12.1	13.5	19.1	19.0	35.5	58.8	66.2	79.1	86.3	194.8
Credit from Monetary Authorities	26g	—	—	.3	—	—	—	—	1.7	3.0	—	—	—	—	—	—
Capital Accounts	27a	.4	1.0	.5	.3	—	5.1	6.4	30.0	41.8	51.5	74.2	110.0	139.3	192.0	262.0
Other Items (Net)	27r	-28.4	-32.3	-22.3	-24.4	-29.7	-29.4	-28.1	-36.0	-35.8	-45.4	-35.9	-25.6	-23.9	-49.3	-33.1
Monetary Survey													*Millions of TT Dollars:*				
Foreign Assets (Net)	31n	70.3	58.4	65.8	83.0	74.3	78.2	133.3	84.8	53.7	763.7	1,732.2	2,424.8	3,534.7	4,271.3	5,147.3
Domestic Credit	32	169.1	214.9	217.8	256.8	313.5	399.0	474.5	664.8	816.2	368.5	-196.7	-338.1	-1,003.8	-922.6	-757.1
Claims on Central Govt. (Net)	32an	25.4	56.1	33.3	53.9	41.6	68.5	112.9	151.6	220.4	-306.2	-1,091.2	-1,592.5	-2,772.7	-3,275.6	-3,510.6
Claims on Local Government	32b	—	—	.1	—	.1	.1	.1	—	—	1.3	.6	1.4	5.1	7.2	12.0	8.0
Claims on Nonfin.Pub.Enterprises	32c	—	—	—	—	—	—	—	10.5	9.0	8.4	5.0	1.7	—	—	—
Claims on Private Sector	32d	143.7	158.8	184.4	202.9	271.8	330.4	361.5	502.7	585.5	665.7	888.1	1,247.6	1,761.7	2,341.0	2,745.5
Claims on Other Banking Insts	32f															
Money	34	115.9	125.7	129.6	138.5	139.6	151.4	176.8	211.1	212.6	269.9	392.4	571.8	725.3	936.3	1,146.7
Quasi-Money	35	147.7	169.1	185.7	223.4	275.5	337.2	429.1	511.8	610.2	802.7	995.9	1,291.5	1,634.5	2,004.9	2,669.0
Capital Accounts	37a	4.7	7.6	10.0	13.7	15.4	34.9	50.1	85.0	106.5	139.8	357.3	373.9	397.0	625.5	1,009.6
Other Items (Net)	37r	-28.9	-29.1	-41.7	-35.8	-42.7	-46.2	-48.2	-58.3	-59.4	-80.1	-210.0	-150.5	-225.9	-218.0	-435.0
Money plus Quasi-Money	35l	263.6	294.8	315.3	361.9	415.1	488.6	605.9	722.9	822.8	1,072.6	1,388.3	1,863.3	2,359.8	2,941.2	3,815.7
Other Banking Institutions																
Other Banklike Institutions													*Millions of TT Dollars:*				
Reserves	40	....	....	....	....	....	.4	.8	.4	.8	1.2	1.0	1.8	2.6	3.9	4.4
Foreign Assets	41	....	....	....	....	....	1.3	1.4	1.6	1.7	2.1	7.8	5.6	6.8	5.9	5.9
Claims on Central Government	42a	9.5	9.4	8.7	8.4	8.7	8.3	7.8	8.2	8.3	7.8	16.4	3.8	5.0	4.1	6.2
Claims on Nonfin.Pub.Enterprises	42c	....	....	....	....	....	....	....	....	....	....	....	.1	....	.1	—
Claims on Private Sector	42d	....	....	....	....	....	25.5	26.6	37.5	39.5	33.5	134.7	192.6	276.1	447.7	521.3
Claims on Deposit Money Banks	42e												24.9	16.4	11.8	41.0	14.6
Time and Savings Deposits	45	9.5	9.4	8.7	8.4	8.7	16.0	15.2	19.5	21.6	29.0	133.0	175.8	238.7	376.9	431.3
Credit from Deposit Money Banks	46h						10.3	10.5	15.5	14.0	1.7	3.0	8.7	18.4	46.1	52.3
Capital Accounts	47a											14.6	15.7	17.7	23.1	30.4
Other Items (Net)	47r						9.2	10.9	12.8	14.6	13.9	34.3	20.1	27.4	56.6	38.4
Development Banks													*Millions of TT Dollars:*				
Reserves	40..n											.1	.3	.2	.2	.4
Claims on Private Sector	42d. n											58.0	65.2	97.1	129.8	197.6
Claims on Deposit Money Banks	42e. n											15.4	18.5	20.5	26.6	12.4
Foreign Liabilities	46c. n											11.1	12.0	12.7	10.8	24.4
Central Government Deposits	46d. n											35.4	50.0	76.0	124.4	156.9
Credit from Dep. Money Banks	46h. n											—	—	—	—	—
Capital Accounts	47a. n											22.3	19.6	21.8	27.3	38.7
Other Items (Net)	47r. n											4.6	2.5	7.3	-6.0	-9.6

Trinidad and Tobago
369

1980	1981	1982	1983	1984	1985	1986	1987	1988	1989	1990	1991	1992	1993	1994	Item	Code
															Exchange Rates	
End of Period																
3.0610	2.7935	2.6475	2.5127	2.3525	3.9543	4.4035	5.1072	5.7192	5.5852	6.0463	6.0793	5.8438	7.9860	8.6616	Market Rate	aa
End of Period (ae) Period Average (rf)																
2.4000	2.4000	2.4000	2.4000	2.4000	3.6000	3.6000	3.6000	4.2500	4.2500	4.2500	4.2500	4.2500	5.8141	5.9332	Market Rate	ae
2.4000	2.4000	2.4000	2.4000	2.4000	2.4500	3.6000	3.6000	3.8438	4.2500	4.2500	4.2500	4.2500	5.3511	5.9249	Market Rate	rf
Period Averages																
170.26	180.57	191.84	199.09	211.73	215.24	141.71	122.27	110.43	102.52	100.00	100.89	101.72	85.74	75.03	Nominal Effective Exchange Rate	ne c
98.28	108.12	119.82	137.26	157.62	164.78	113.99	105.65	99.09	97.76	100.00	99.28	101.80	91.88	84.96	Real Effective Exchange Rate	re c
															Fund Position	
End of Period																
123.0	123.0	123.0	170.1	170.1	170.1	170.1	170.1	170.1	170.1	170.1	170.1	246.8	246.8	246.8	Quota	2f. s
35.8	51.3	73.5	94.4	103.1	107.8	112.0	—	—	6.9	.8	1.5	.2	.2	.1	SDRs	1b. s
63.0	78.3	96.7	118.6	126.8	124.4	77.2	53.0	—	—	—	—	—	—	—	Reserve Position in the Fund	1c. s
5.4	2.9	.4	—	—	—	—	—	—	—	—	—	—	—	—	*of which:* Outstg.Fund Borrowing	2c
—	—	—	—	—	—	—	—	85.1	155.8	231.6	269.1	205.3	112.8	62.4	Total Fund Cred.&Loans Outstg.	2tl
															International Liquidity	
End of Period																
2,780.8	3,347.5	3,080.5	2,104.5	1,356.7	1,128.5	474.1	187.8	127.1	246.5	492.0	338.6	172.2	206.3	352.4	Total Reserves minus Gold	1l. d
45.7	59.7	81.0	98.9	101.1	118.4	136.9	—	—	9.0	1.1	2.1	.3	.3	.1	SDRs	1b. d
80.3	91.1	106.7	124.2	124.3	136.6	94.4	75.2	—	—	—	—	—	—	—	Reserve Position in the Fund	1c. d
2,654.8	3,196.7	2,892.8	1,881.5	1,131.3	873.5	242.8	112.6	127.1	237.5	490.9	336.5	171.9	206.0	352.3	Foreign Exchange	1d. d
.054	.054	.054	.054	.054	.054	.054	.054	.054	.054	.054	.054	.054	.056	.054	Gold (Million Fine Troy Ounces)	1ad
2.3	2.3	2.3	2.3	2.3	1.5	1.5	2.3	2.0	2.0	2.0	2.0	2.0	1.4	1.4	Gold (National Valuation)	1and
—	—	—	—	—	—	67.6	50.9	50.7	74.0	116.2	113.9	86.9	99.8	55.0	Monetary Authorities: Other Liab.	4.. d
48.0	49.6	63.8	50.3	56.3	56.3	81.8	77.2	112.1	131.4	114.8	97.9	99.3	208.4	294.1	Deposit Money Banks: Assets	7a. d
7.1	9.8	8.1	7.0	5.0	4.4	9.9	1.2	1.4	3.9	5.8	5.1	30.4	36.9	115.4	*of which:* Claims on Nonbanks	7ad d
76.1	86.9	104.5	119.1	141.1	85.7	70.8	91.4	56.4	48.2	49.7	39.9	60.8	66.5	50.5	Deposit Money Banks: Liabilities	7b. d
30.6	41.9	49.9	67.0	71.2	41.8	31.4	30.2	26.8	25.1	27.0	22.9	20.4	10.2	12.5	*of which:* Liab. to Nonbanks	7bd d
2.4	2.4	2.4	2.2	3.8	2.4	3.8	2.5	3.9	4.0	24.1	4.6	5.2	3.0	. . . .	Other Banking Insts.: Assets	7e. d
10.6	14.3	15.9	17.8	28.4	14.1	16.9	16.8	15.6	23.6	23.7	35.5	53.5	53.2	. . . .	Liabilities	7f. d
															Monetary Authorities	
End of Period																
6,694.7	8,064.1	7,410.4	5,087.1	3,322.5	4,096.4	1,748.2	1,481.0	1,509.2	2,274.6	3,321.6	2,825.1	2,180.4	3,610.2	4,602.3	Foreign Assets	11
85.7	45.4	38.8	77.0	173.6	220.0	1,356.3	1,579.4	2,128.6	2,440.8	2,480.2	2,806.2	3,249.6	2,150.8	1,542.5	Claims on Central Government	12a
—	—	—	—	53.8	125.4	360.7	535.0	542.1	258.2	109.5	644.1	260.1	250.0	507.2	Claims on Deposit Money Banks	12e
—	—	—	—	—	—	—	1.5	15.9	15.9	15.9	23.5	23.5	21.7	18.7	Claims on Other Banking Insts	12f
1,335.8	1,637.4	2,631.9	2,488.1	2,291.2	2,452.6	2,069.8	1,619.0	1,650.2	1,869.4	2,068.1	2,421.0	2,185.9	2,083.4	3,269.7	Reserve Money	14
467.2	532.2	725.9	758.1	709.7	684.7	723.1	702.6	671.8	693.3	735.3	747.8	698.2	707.4	744.6	*of which: Currency Outside DMBs*	14a
—	—	—	—	—	—	243.3	183.4	702.0	1,184.5	1,893.8	2,119.7	1,568.9	1,480.8	867.3	Foreign Liabilities	16c
5,020.6	5,748.5	3,786.3	2,137.7	1,101.1	995.5	750.6	747.2	876.9	782.3	760.5	872.4	927.1	526.8	780.1	Central Government Deposits	16d
884.3	1,320.9	1,629.9	1,708.5	824.0	1,070.6	1,126.9	1,329.3	1,389.5	1,483.1	1,699.3	1,721.3	1,564.3	2,513.8	2,651.5	Capital Accounts	17a
-460.3	-597.3	-598.8	-1,170.2	-666.3	-76.9	-725.3	-282.0	-422.9	-329.8	-494.6	-835.6	-532.6	-572.1	-897.8	Other Items (Net)	17r
															Deposit Money Banks	
End of Period																
868.6	1,070.0	1,856.8	1,629.2	1,497.2	1,673.2	1,241.9	805.4	857.0	1,065.1	1,195.8	1,540.1	1,348.8	1,221.2	2,320.3	Reserves	20
115.2	119.0	153.1	120.8	135.2	202.6	294.3	278.0	476.5	558.5	487.8	416.0	421.9	1,211.6	1,745.0	Foreign Assets	21
399.9	491.0	707.2	1,072.4	570.6	569.5	575.6	1,221.3	978.2	834.1	913.5	559.3	568.6	774.9	899.4	Claims on Central Government	22a
5.7	5.1	33.5	3.5	32.2	37.9	12.7	11.5	9.2	—	—	—	—	.7	1.9	Claims on Local Government	22b
44.9	235.7	340.6	520.8	596.7	752.5	861.1	1,050.0	1,376.0	1,240.3	1,002.2	969.6	689.8	747.7	377.9	Claims on Nonfin.Pub.Enterprises	22c
3,310.3	4,058.4	4,893.8	5,671.5	6,075.2	5,843.6	5,917.4	6,130.8	5,900.5	6,181.9	6,428.3	7,608.5	7,710.0	7,995.1	7,625.6	Claims on Private Sector	22d
869.8	1,287.4	1,772.2	1,575.6	1,500.3	1,483.0	1,260.3	1,357.0	1,082.3	1,327.6	1,703.6	2,040.7	1,858.9	2,274.3	2,798.8	Demand Deposits	24
2,960.9	3,637.4	4,847.7	5,499.3	6,048.1	6,183.3	6,124.7	6,327.2	6,673.6	6,960.6	7,085.7	6,984.4	6,525.9	7,492.1	8,651.1	Time and Savings Deposits	25
182.7	208.5	250.9	285.9	338.7	308.4	254.7	329.0	239.9	204.8	211.1	169.5	258.4	386.6	299.8	Foreign Liabilities	26c
281.5	374.3	452.2	507.2	233.3	208.8	134.1	147.3	111.6	131.0	201.8	162.4	135.2	143.2	102.1	Central Government Deposits	26d
—	—	—	—	19.0	47.5	355.3	476.4	542.1	258.2	109.5	641.7	260.1	288.7	507.1	Credit from Monetary Authorities	26g
361.4	411.7	531.2	636.6	781.4	890.9	668.1	1,163.5	1,284.4	1,443.9	1,358.4	1,450.1	1,525.6	1,669.4	1,748.2	Capital Accounts	27a
88.3	59.9	130.8	513.6	-13.7	-42.6	105.8	-303.4	-336.5	-446.2	-642.5	-355.3	175.0	-303.1	-1,137.0	Other Items (Net)	27r
															Monetary Survey	
End of Period																
6,627.2	7,974.6	7,312.6	4,922.0	3,119.0	3,990.6	1,544.5	1,246.6	1,043.7	1,443.8	1,704.5	951.9	774.9	2,954.4	5,180.3	Foreign Assets (Net)	31n
-1,455.6	-1,287.2	1,775.4	4,700.3	6,113.9	6,219.2	7,838.4	9,100.0	9,419.9	9,799.7	9,877.8	10,932.3	11,179.2	11,020.9	9,583.8	Domestic Credit	32
-4,816.5	-5,586.4	-3,492.5	-1,495.5	-590.2	-414.8	1,047.2	1,906.2	2,118.3	2,361.6	2,431.4	2,330.7	2,755.9	2,255.7	1,559.7	Claims on Central Govt. (Net)	32an
5.7	5.1	33.5	3.5	32.2	37.9	12.7	11.5	9.2	—	—	—	—	.7	1.9	Claims on Local Government	32b
44.9	235.7	340.6	520.8	596.7	752.5	861.1	1,050.0	1,376.0	1,240.3	1,002.2	969.6	689.8	747.7	377.9	Claims on Nonfin.Pub.Enterprises	32c
3,310.3	4,058.4	4,893.8	5,671.5	6,075.2	5,843.6	5,917.4	6,130.8	5,900.5	6,181.9	6,428.3	7,608.5	7,710.0	7,995.1	7,625.6	Claims on Private Sector	32d
—	—	—	—	—	—	—	1.5	15.9	15.9	15.9	23.5	23.5	21.7	18.7	Claims on Other Banking Insts	32f
1,337.0	1,854.7	2,547.2	2,434.5	2,294.0	2,260.5	2,088.2	2,170.3	1,875.5	2,133.1	2,575.9	2,921.6	2,696.0	3,136.5	3,748.2	Money	34
2,960.9	3,637.4	4,847.7	5,499.3	6,048.1	6,183.3	6,124.7	6,327.2	6,673.6	6,960.6	7,085.7	6,984.4	6,525.9	7,492.1	8,651.1	Quasi-Money	35
1,245.7	1,732.6	2,161.1	2,345.1	1,605.4	1,961.5	1,795.0	2,492.8	2,673.9	2,927.0	3,057.7	3,171.4	3,089.9	4,183.2	4,399.7	Capital Accounts	37a
-372.0	-537.3	-467.9	-656.6	-714.5	-195.5	-624.9	-643.7	-759.4	-777.2	-1,137.1	-1,193.3	-357.6	-836.5	-2,034.9	Other Items (Net)	37r
4,297.9	5,492.1	7,394.9	7,933.8	8,342.1	8,443.8	8,212.9	8,497.5	8,549.1	9,093.7	9,661.6	9,906.0	9,221.9	10,628.6	12,399.3	Money plus Quasi-Money	35l
															Other Banking Institutions	
															Other Banklike Institutions	
End of Period																
5.9	19.1	28.3	51.1	49.0	35.6	22.0	111.9	117.8	104.9	114.8	118.4	128.7	143.7	148.0	Reserves	40
5.8	5.7	5.7	5.2	9.1	8.7	13.6	9.1	16.6	17.0	102.5	19.6	22.3	17.5	50.3	Foreign Assets	41
3.7	4.1	.7	22.3	13.7	15.1	10.6	.8	.3	87.8	151.2	165.0	181.3	505.7	588.7	Claims on Central Government	42a
—	—	3.4	—	—	.9	—	—	—	—	9.6	85.6	12.4	9.2	65.5	Claims on Nonfin.Pub.Enterprises	42c
723.4	970.5	1,390.2	1,721.5	2,333.9	2,594.9	2,053.1	2,197.6	2,234.4	1,965.4	2,184.2	2,436.0	2,749.3	2,852.1	3,341.6	Claims on Private Sector	42d
33.2	45.8	98.6	81.8	185.2	153.8	102.3	161.6	199.8	301.2	222.7	216.5	356.7	381.8	325.2	Claims on Deposit Money Banks	42e
608.0	883.1	1,335.0	1,685.1	2,228.2	2,399.9	1,964.1	2,071.2	2,189.2	2,096.1	2,221.2	2,272.5	2,471.7	2,805.5	2,894.1	Time and Savings Deposits	45
39.5	49.2	30.7	59.2	125.2	200.3	76.3	209.8	251.4	96.2	213.1	165.5	147.0	138.9	30.3	Credit from Deposit Money Banks	46h
51.8	71.1	191.5	210.3	297.3	245.6	261.2	302.3	300.8	322.2	341.6	428.0	464.4	470.6	512.2	Capital Accounts	47a
72.9	41.8	-30.4	-72.9	-59.8	-36.9	-100.0	-102.3	-172.3	-38.2	9.1	175.1	367.6	495.0	1,082.7	Other Items (Net)	47r
															Development Banks	
End of Period																
.4	-.3	3.0	9.5	5.0	4.4	3.3	—	—	4.8	.9	.5	—	—	. . . .	Reserves	40.. n
265.1	368.1	638.7	763.7	836.8	883.5	922.7	965.3	919.4	940.6	1,007.9	987.2	1,126.5	1,165.7	. . . .	Claims on Private Sector	42d. n
14.0	19.4	66.2	52.5	50.6	37.5	35.9	2.5	3.9	1.5	.9	32.9	72.5	99.4	. . . .	Claims on Deposit Money Banks	42e. n
24.8	33.7	32.7	34.2	37.3	32.7	50.6	60.6	66.5	100.1	99.0	150.5	226.9	309.1	. . . .	Foreign Liabilities	46c. n
220.4	308.1	363.3	582.4	604.3	591.3	610.0	720.4	598.1	416.3	614.8	427.3	419.2	401.6	. . . .	Central Government Deposits	46d. n
—	—	—	—	—	—	—	17.0	19.6	26.2	26.4	21.7	33.6	27.3	. . . .	Credit from Dep. Money Banks	46h. n
48.0	60.3	315.9	102.2	127.7	153.6	160.8	150.9	193.4	345.5	194.9	346.2	389.9	389.2	. . . .	Capital Accounts	47a. n
-13.7	-14.9	-4.0	106.9	123.2	147.7	140.6	19.0	45.9	58.7	74.5	75.0	129.4	137.9	. . . .	Other Items (Net)	47r. n

Trinidad and Tobago
369

		1965	1966	1967	1968	1969	1970	1971	1972	1973	1974	1975	1976	1977	1978	1979
Nonbank Financial Institutions														*Millions of TT Dollars:*		
Reserves	40..s	...	...	...	...	...	...	...	...	...	16.8	34.9	48.4	54.3	74.7	85.7
Foreign Assets	41..s	...	...	...	...	...	...	...	...	...	65.6	63.7	55.8	75.2	58.9	75.0
Claims on Central Government	42a.s	...	...	...	...	...	...	...	...	...	88.9	82.1	90.6	93.3	139.7	130.2
Claims on Private Sector	42d.s	...	...	...	...	...	...	...	...	...	164.2	162.3	229.1	263.3	310.7	339.9
Fixed Assets	42h.s	...	...	...	...	...	...	...	...	...	11.2	19.1	20.5	25.2	45.0	35.1
Incr.in Total Assets(Within Per.)	49z.s	...	...	...	...	...	...	...	...	...	...	15.4	82.2	67.0	117.7	36.8
Liquid Liabilities	55l	272.9	304.2	323.8	370.1	424.0	504.3	620.1	742.1	843.7	1,100.4	1,520.2	2,037.0	2,595.7	3,314.1	4,242.2
Interest Rates														*Percent Per Annum*		
Bank Rate (End of Period)	60	...	6.00	6.50	6.00	6.00	6.00	5.00	5.00	6.00	6.00	6.00	6.00	6.00	6.00	6.00
Treasury Bill Rate	60c	4.82	4.94	5.13	5.82	5.15	5.32	5.11	3.74	4.37	5.57	3.99	3.98	3.94	3.60	3.16
Deposit Rate	60l															
Lending Rate	60p															
Government Bond Yield	61	...	...	8.00	7.96	8.00	8.16	8.27	7.83	7.99	8.31	8.25	8.18	8.07	8.07	8.12
Prices, Production, Employment														*Index Numbers (1990=100):*		
Producer Prices	63															39.2
Consumer Prices	64	8.5	8.9	9.0	9.8	10.0	10.3	10.6	11.6	13.4	16.3	ǀ19.1	21.1	23.6	26.0	29.8
Wages: Average Weekly Earnings	65												23.7	27.6	34.1
Industrial Production	66														74.8	76.5
Crude Petroleum Production	66aa	88.9	101.2	118.3	121.8	104.5	92.9	85.8	93.2	110.3	124.0	143.1	141.4	152.2	152.5	142.4
Total Employment	67	165.1	...	...	...	...	...	131.0	...	147.8	144.2	146.1	153.4	ǀ154.8	157.9	157.7
International Transactions														*Millions of TT Dollars*		
Exports	70	690.5	735.1	763.4	943.3	947.7	963.1	1,040.2	1,068.4	1,371.4	4,162.8	3,875.2	5,391.8	5,231.5	4,895.1	6,265.0
Imports, cif	71	808.2	777.7	723.9	840.1	965.4	1,087.0	1,314.2	1,467.6	1,560.1	3,774.9	3,239.2	4,904.3	4,365.2	4,721.0	5,051.0
Imports, fob	71.v	748.8	722.8	664.1	714.2	826.6	936.7	1,139.4	1,409.5	1,489.7	3,680.6	3,045.7	4,651.7	4,082.9	4,380.5	4,615.6
																1990=100
Volume of Exports	72	...	103.5	105.8	116.0	118.4	118.9	114.8	117.6	116.9	ǀ125.6	108.2	126.5	118.5	107.5	104.7
Volume of Imports	73	...	69.8	56.0	62.1	66.2	72.7	82.6	81.1	89.3	ǀ111.2	81.2	111.9	92.2	95.6	107.2
Unit Value of Exports	74	...	4.9	5.1	5.5	5.5	5.6	6.3	6.4	8.3	ǀ22.3	25.8	29.8	32.5	32.5	42.9
Unit Value of Imports	75	...	3.9	3.9	4.6	4.8	4.9	5.4	5.9	6.9	ǀ15.7	18.1	21.3	21.9	22.9	26.0
Balance of Payments														*Millions of US Dollars:*		
Goods: Exports f.o.b.	78aa d										1,072.5	1,153.3	1,284.7	1,301.0	1,759.1
Goods: Imports f.o.b.	78ab d										-658.1	-766.0	-867.8	-1,057.5	-1,334.1
Trade Balance	78ac d										414.4	387.3	416.8	243.5	425.0
Services: Credit	78ad d										217.3	237.4	263.8	263.8	308.5
Services: Debit	78ae d										-197.3	-235.8	-289.2	-355.3	-474.2
Balance on Goods and Services	78af d										434.5	388.9	391.5	151.9	259.4
Income: Credit	78ag d										43.3	60.3	77.0	125.0	159.9
Income: Debit	78ah d										-124.8	-163.7	-263.2	-196.3	-407.5
Balance on Goods, Serv., & Inc.	78ai d										352.9	285.5	205.3	80.6	11.7
Current Transfers, n.i.e.: Credit	78aj d										2.8	1.9	1.7	1.8	1.8
Current Transfers: Debit	78ak d										-15.4	-26.4	-24.1	-28.0	-32.6
Current Account, n.i.e.	78al d										340.3	260.9	182.8	54.4	-19.2
Capital Account, n.i.e.: Credit	78ba d														
Capital Account: Debit	78bb d										-8.5	-5.5	-8.7	-11.8	-14.8
Capital Account, n.i.e.	78bc d										-8.5	-5.5	-8.7	-11.8	-14.8
Direct Investment Abroad	78bd d														
Dir. Invest. in Rep. Econ., n.i.e.	78be d										93.0	132.2	83.5	128.8	93.8
Portfolio Investment Assets	78bf d										—	—	—	-7.9	-2.7
Portfolio Investment Liab., n.i.e.	78bg d										-1.1	-9.4	-1.1	107.5	-1.1
Other Investment Assets	78bh d										-35.6	-100.5	-1.0	-27.3	-87.6
Other Investment Liab., n.i.e.	78bi d										-19.0	-38.3	201.0	86.5	370.0
Financial Account, n.i.e.	78bj d										37.2	-16.1	282.4	287.5	372.3
Net Errors and Omissions	78ca d										89.1	-38.9	-12.6	7.3	5.4
Overall Balance	78cb d										458.1	200.5	443.9	337.5	343.8
Reserves and Related Items	79da d										-458.1	-200.5	-443.9	-337.5	-343.8
Reserve Assets	79db d										-458.1	-200.5	-443.9	-337.5	-343.8
Use of Fund Credit and Loans	79dc d										—	—	—	—	—
Liabs.Constit.For.Auth.Reserves	79dd d										—	—	—	—	—
Exceptional Financing	79de d										—	—	—	—	—
Government Finance														*Millions of TT Dollars:*		
Deficit (-) or Surplus	80	-8.9	-32.3	-21.7	-6.2	-.8	32.8	-57.7	-39.2		...	ǀ499.9	799.7	301.6	-61.0
Revenue	81	233.3	228.3	239.4	284.1	308.4	313.2	346.6	528.9		...	ǀ2,340.1	3,043.9	3,155.5	4,118.8
Grants Received	81z											ǀ—			
Expenditure	82	242.2	260.6	261.1	290.3	309.2	280.4	404.3	568.1		...	ǀ1,599.7	1,913.4	2,680.5	3,654.7
Lending Minus Repayments	83											ǀ241.2	330.8	173.4	525.1
Financing (by Residence of Lender)																
Net Borrowing: Domestic	84a											ǀ49.7	62.8	42.1	40.9
Foreign	85a											-80.2	360.2	259.3	132.3
Use of Cash Balances	87	-5.9	1.5	-3.7	-35.5	-23.2	3.1	15.8f	-57.0f	3.5	-417.8	-465.3	ǀ-469.4	-1,222.7	-603.0	-112.2
Financing (by Currency)																
Net Borrowing: TT Dollars	84b	12.8	24.1	7.3	25.2	20.4	-22.8	39.8	56.6	36.6	16.6	24.3			
Foreign Currency	85b	2.0	6.7	18.1	16.5	3.7	-13.1	2.1	39.6	49.2	-17.9	-22.7			
Use of Cash Balances	87	-5.9	1.5	-3.7	-35.5	-23.2	3.1	15.8f	-57.0f	3.5	-417.8	-465.3	ǀ-469.4	-1,222.7	-603.0	-112.2
Debt: TT Dollars	88b	108.0	129.8	154.8	181.6	202.6	234.4	275.9	333.9	370.2	387.3	411.7			
Foreign Currency	89b	124.5	136.3	143.4	157.2	167.9	158.2	163.7	199.2	255.7	241.4	215.7			
National Accounts														*Millions of TT Dollars*		
Exports of Goods & Services	90c	815	517	551	649	677	703	757	824	1,132	2,378	2,808	3,401	3,733	3,766	4,979
Government Consumption	91f	153	154	161	175	187	215	280	334	366	475	652	743	967	1,148	1,536
Gross Fixed Capital Formation	93e	326	258	223	292	272	344	581	615	579	651	1,085	1,398	1,735	2,323	2,952
Increase/Decrease(-) in Stocks	93i	2	28	10	8	-5	81	21	37	86	264	364	98	272	261	261
Private Consumption	96f	842	731	818	900	1,038	986	980	1,234	1,385	1,774	2,257	2,896	3,605	4,443	5,663
Imports of Goods & Services	98c	-876	-447	-438	-506	-611	-685	-848	-963	-984	-1,350	-1,866	-2,445	-2,779	-3,391	-4,345
Gross Domestic Product	99b	1,263	1,241	1,324	1,518	1,558	1,644	1,771	2,082	2,564	4,193	5,300	6,091	7,533	8,550	11,046
Net Factor Inc/Pmts(-) Abroad	98.n	-96	-117	-119	-137	-143	-130	-132	-136	-180	-586	-551	-836	-1,193	-611	-756
Gross Nat'l Expenditure = GNP	99a	1,166	1,123	1,205	1,381	1,415	1,514	1,639	1,946	2,384	3,607	4,749	5,255	6,340	7,938	10,290
Nat'l Income, Market Prices	99e	1,064	1,006	1,082	1,278	1,274	1,367	1,472	1,705	2,166	3,316	4,795	5,328	6,414	7,314	9,592
Gross Dom. Prod. 1990 Prices	99b.p	...	14,229	14,519	15,277	15,694	16,248	16,417	17,366	17,654	18,326	18,597	19,788	21,593	23,756	24,611
GDP Deflator (1990=100)	99bi p	...	8.7	9.1	9.9	9.9	10.1	10.8	12.0	14.5	22.9	28.5	30.8	34.9	36.0	44.9
														Millions:		
Population	99z	.97	.99	1.01	1.02	1.03	1.03	1.03	1.05	1.06	1.07	ǀ1.01	1.02	1.04	1.06	1.06

Trinidad and Tobago

369

Series	Code	1980	1981	1982	1983	1984	1985	1986	1987	1988	1989	1990	1991	1992	1993	1994
Nonbank Financial Institutions		*End of Period*														
Reserves	40..s	23.8	63.8	44.3	98.0	132.4	62.0	24.5	75.0	135.7	20.0	23.6	....	....	....	....
Foreign Assets	41..s	52.0	25.6	43.1	83.5	126.8	163.0	171.2	550.0	432.9	235.3	347.5	....	....	....	....
Claims on Central Government	42a.s	121.6	132.5	133.8	140.7	106.3	200.3	295.8	322.6	447.0	452.3	619.3	....	....	....	....
Claims on Private Sector	42d.s	566.7	751.9	818.4	913.5	1,138.5	1,438.6	1,679.2	1,245.8	1,653.9	1,625.6	2,406.2	....	....	....	....
Fixed Assets	42h.s	41.0	53.1	87.9	131.0	157.4	169.8	205.5	209.7	204.9	243.2	289.2	....	....	....	....
Incr.in Total Assets(Within Per.)	49z.s	140.3	220.4	101.0	239.3	294.6	372.2	342.7	26.9	471.2	–297.9	1,109.4	....	....	....	....
Liquid Liabilities	55l	4,899.5	6,356.4	8,698.6	9,558.4	10,516.3	10,803.8	10,151.7	10,456.8	10,620.4	11,080.1	11,767.1	12,059.6	11,564.9	13,290.4	15,145.4
Interest Rates		*Percent Per Annum*														
Bank Rate *(End of Period)*	60	6.00	6.00	6.00	7.50	7.50	7.50	5.97	7.50	9.50	9.50	9.50	11.50	13.00	13.00	13.00
Treasury Bill Rate	60c	3.07	3.06	3.05	3.08	3.39	3.47	3.99	4.63	....	7.13	7.50	7.67	9.26	9.45	....
Deposit Rate	60l	....	6.57	6.25	6.40	6.76	5.31	6.04	6.03	....	6.28	5.96	5.79	6.99	7.06	6.91
Lending Rate	60p	10.00	11.38	11.50	11.71	12.75	12.69	12.00	11.50	12.58	13.31	12.87	13.17	15.33	15.50	15.98
Government Bond Yield	61	8.61	8.84	9.84	9.88	9.89	9.89	9.62	9.54	....	10.77	10.73	10.85	13.30	....	....
Prices, Production, Employment		*Period Averages*														
Producer Prices	63	46.8	54.7	62.2	70.0	73.6	77.1	82.0	85.4	90.5	98.6	100.0	100.2	101.0	106.4	....
Consumer Prices	64	35.1	40.1	I44.8	51.5	58.4	62.9	67.7	75.0	80.8	I90.0	100.0	103.8	110.6	122.4	133.2
Wages: Average Weekly Earnings	65	41.9	50.5	59.2	70.6	80.8	86.8	88.4	92.2	93.7	94.5	100.0	100.1	103.0	....	....
Industrial Production	66	81.1	72.0	74.9	68.4	83.7	80.5	97.9	101.6	I97.5	97.7	100.0	111.6	122.3	114.6	....
Crude Petroleum Production	66aa	141.3	125.8	117.6	106.2	113.0	117.0	112.2	103.7	100.5	99.2	100.0	95.7	90.2	82.3	87.1
Total Employment	67	158.9	155.7	150.5	152.9	145.0	127.8	120.4	114.4	107.7	107.7	100.0	100.9	99.6	....	....
International Transactions		*Millions of TT Dollars*														
Exports	70	9,784.8	9,026.0	7,372.4	5,646.3	5,216.2	5,247.1	4,988.6	5,264.6	5,424.2	6,706.9	8,842.0	8,436.4	7,943.0	8,800.9	....
Imports, cif	71	7,626.4	7,498.9	8,873.1	6,196.7	4,605.9	3,739.0	4,860.2	4,387.5	4,310.3	5,190.4	5,361.8	7,084.8	6,101.2	7,495.3	....
Imports, fob	71.v	7,055.5	6,922.6	8,065.9	5,569.4	4,137.0	3,365.1	4,374.6	3,949.1	3,879.7	4,671.8	4,826.1	6,377.0	5,491.6	6,746.4	....
		1990=100														
Volume of Exports	72	101.0	90.0	92.1	90.2	103.4	I95.0	93.7	92.1	95.0	93.1	100.0	....	....	....	....
Volume of Imports	73	121.9	113.7	111.6	126.0	I142.4	125.6	128.4	101.5	85.4	104.1	100.0	....	....	....	....
Unit Value of Exports	74	68.6	75.6	72.4	71.9	I71.4	68.2	66.4	69.6	66.1	83.6	100.0	....	....	....	....
Unit Value of Imports	75	39.0	44.0	49.8	50.2	I50.3	49.8	67.6	77.4	85.7	98.6	100.0	....	....	....	....
Balance of Payments		*Minus Sign Indicates Debit*														
Goods: Exports f.o.b.	78aa*d*	2,728.3	2,725.6	2,317.3	2,102.7	2,173.4	2,141.7	1,378.4	1,414.3	1,469.5	1,550.8	1,960.1	1,774.5	1,691.4	1,500.1	....
Goods: Imports f.o.b.	78ab*d*	–1,789.1	–1,763.5	–2,486.8	–2,233.3	–1,704.9	–1,354.6	–1,209.4	–1,057.6	–1,064.2	–1,045.2	–947.6	–1,210.3	–995.6	–952.9	....
Trade Balance	78ac*d*	939.2	962.1	–169.4	–130.6	468.5	787.1	168.9	356.7	405.3	505.5	1,012.5	564.2	695.7	547.2	....
Services: Credit	78ad*d*	410.6	418.0	471.9	242.9	266.3	264.1	271.7	209.3	271.3	280.8	328.5	405.3	452.7	353.4	....
Services: Debit	78ae*d*	–645.3	–714.8	–882.4	–897.4	–849.4	–725.5	–613.6	–493.5	–453.9	–439.8	–479.2	–534.4	–561.9	–466.4	....
Balance on Goods and Services	78af*d*	704.5	665.3	–580.0	–785.1	–114.5	325.7	–172.9	72.5	222.6	346.6	861.9	435.1	586.6	434.2	....
Income: Credit	78ag*d*	232.3	344.7	357.0	230.3	141.5	195.8	96.8	16.8	20.3	32.4	39.6	48.6	29.8	40.2	....
Income: Debit	78ah*d*	–537.9	–543.1	–281.9	–367.5	–466.2	–545.2	–307.4	–291.7	–322.3	–410.1	–436.4	–490.7	–477.9	–366.0	....
Balance on Goods, Serv., & Inc.	78ai*d*	398.9	466.9	–504.8	–922.3	–439.3	–23.7	–383.5	–202.4	–79.4	–31.1	465.2	–7.0	138.5	108.4	....
Current Transfers, n.i.e.: Credit	78aj*d*	1.8	1.9	2.0	5.9	13.2	10.1	.8	6.3	3.5	5.2	7.8	15.6	11.1	23.7	....
Current Transfers: Debit	78ak*d*	–43.8	–54.2	–96.6	–30.2	–40.6	–34.3	–29.2	–28.9	–12.7	–12.7	–13.9	–13.3	–10.7	–19.0	....
Current Account, n.i.e.	78al*d*	357.0	414.6	–599.5	–946.6	–466.7	–47.9	–411.9	–225.0	–88.6	–38.5	459.0	–4.7	138.9	113.1	....
Capital Account, n.i.e.: Credit	78ba*d*	4.6	2.8	3.5	3.5	3.4	3.1	—	1.8	—	.4	.4	.4	.4	1.3	....
Capital Account: Debit	78bb*d*	–26.8	–42.9	–49.0	–59.8	–59.2	–38.3	–21.5	–16.0	–20.4	–17.5	–19.6	–16.5	–16.9	–12.8	....
Capital Account, n.i.e.	78bc*d*	–22.3	–40.1	–45.4	–56.3	–55.8	–35.2	–21.5	–14.2	–20.4	–17.2	–19.2	–16.1	–16.5	–11.5	....
Direct Investment Abroad	78bd*d*	—	—	—	–3.6	–3.5	–8.2	–7.3	1.9	—	—	—	—	—	—	....
Dir. Invest. in Rep. Econ., n.i.e.	78be*d*	184.5	258.1	203.5	117.7	113.2	1.2	–14.5	33.1	62.9	148.9	109.4	169.3	177.9	379.2	....
Portfolio Investment Assets	78bf*d*	–12.7	1.8	.3	.1	—	—	—	—	—	—	—	—	—	—	....
Portfolio Investment Liab., n.i.e.	78bg*d*	–6.5	–.5	—	—	—	—	—	—	—	—	—	—	—	—	....
Other Investment Assets	78bh*d*	–87.4	–100.4	–49.5	–79.6	–166.0	–73.2	–12.2	58.8	60.9	44.5	63.0	4.4	–31.3	–76.2	....
Other Investment Liab., n.i.e.	78bi*d*	148.8	144.1	284.8	346.2	–66.5	100.6	–162.3	–15.5	–265.4	–359.8	–678.8	–400.5	–300.8	–204.2	....
Financial Account, n.i.e.	78bj*d*	226.8	303.1	439.0	380.8	–122.8	20.4	–196.4	78.4	–141.5	–166.5	–506.3	–226.8	–154.2	98.8	....
Net Errors and Omissions	78ca*d*	86.8	–109.0	–1.1	–250.7	–47.6	–238.6	–91.8	–94.8	21.1	45.4	–112.0	–29.0	–72.6	–41.8	....
Overall Balance	78cb*d*	648.3	568.6	–206.9	–872.8	–692.9	–301.3	–721.6	–255.6	–229.4	–176.8	–178.5	–276.5	–104.4	158.6	....
Reserves and Related Items	79da*d*	–648.3	–568.6	206.9	872.8	692.9	301.3	721.6	255.6	229.4	176.8	178.5	276.5	104.4	–158.6	....
Reserve Assets	79db*d*	–648.3	–568.6	206.9	872.8	692.9	301.3	721.6	255.6	27.4	–158.5	–197.7	102.7	124.4	–29.4	....
Use of Fund Credit and Loans	79dc*d*	—	—	—	—	—	—	—	—	115.4	91.4	100.9	50.7	–89.8	–129.2	....
Liabs.Constit.For.Auth.Reserves	79dd*d*	—	—	—	—	—	—	—	—	—	—	—	—	—	—	....
Exceptional Financing	79de*d*	—	—	—	—	—	—	—	—	86.6	243.8	275.3	123.1	69.8	—	....
Government Finance		*Year Ending December 31*														
Deficit (-) or Surplus	80	1,105.6	545.8	I-2346.7	–2,216.0	–1,655.7	–917.4	–1,012.3	–1,012.0	–983.7	–709.6	....	....	....	....	....
Revenue	81	6,487.8	7,232.8	I7,066.9	6,552.0	6,612.8	6,664.0	5,455.8	5,300.0	4,947.6	4,965.2	....	....	....	....	....
Grants Received	81z	—	—	I—	—	—	.8	—	—	—	12.3	....	....	....	....	....
Expenditure	82	4,621.7	5,061.5	I9,464.4	8,779.6	8,276.0	7,684.1	6,569.7	6,386.8	6,060.6	5,854.9	....	....	....	....	....
Lending Minus Repayments	83	760.5	1,625.5	I-50.8	–11.6	–7.5	–101.9	–101.6	–74.8	–129.3	–167.8	....	....	....	....	....
Financing (by Residence of Lender)																
Net Borrowing: Domestic	84a	14.3	–12.4	....	....	....	....	....	....	....	....	....	....	....	....	....
Foreign	85a	162.1	25.9	....	....	....	....	....	....	....	....	....	....	....	....	....
Use of Cash Balances	87	–1,282.0	–559.3	....	....	....	....	....	....	....	....	....	....	....	....	....
Financing (by Currency)																
Net Borrowing: TT Dollars	84b	....	....	....	....	....	....	....	....	....	....	....	....	....	....	....
Foreign Currency	85b	....	....	....	....	....	....	....	....	....	....	....	....	....	....	....
Use of Cash Balances	87	–1,282.0	–559.3	....	....	....	....	....	....	....	....	....	....	....	....	....
Debt: TT Dollars	88b	....	....	....	....	....	....	....	....	....	....	....	....	....	....	....
Foreign Currency	89b	....	....	....	....	....	....	....	....	....	....	....	....	....	....	....
National Accounts		*Millions of TT Dollars*														
Exports of Goods & Services	90c	7,550	7,542	6,694	5,756	5,981	5,883	5,740	5,854	6,727	7,834	9,771	9,264	9,112	9,752	....
Government Consumption	91f	1,805	2,110	4,032	3,907	4,179	4,109	4,042	3,730	3,424	3,099	3,487	3,824	4,117	4,121	....
Gross Fixed Capital Formation	93e	4,204	4,342	5,189	4,770	3,954	3,656	3,593	3,200	2,185	2,714	2,756	3,044	2,756	3,168	....
Increase/Decrease(-) in Stocks	93i	376	199	228	199	165	–265	135	139	70	331	–43	–20	93	108	....
Private Consumption	96f	6,865	8,197	11,103	11,594	10,224	9,824	10,717	9,959	10,768	10,773	11,694	13,835	13,629	15,230	....
Imports of Goods & Services	98c	–5,834	–5,952	–8,070	–7,606	–6,283	–5,136	–6,967	–5,610	–5,889	–6,378	–6,126	–7,388	–6,589	–7,392	....
Gross Domestic Product	99b	14,966	16,438	19,176	18,719	18,615	18,071	17,260	17,272	17,285	18,373	21,539	22,559	23,118	24,987	....
Net Factor Inc/Pmts(-) Abroad	98.n	–481	–154	–295	–339	–765	–859	–911	–1,003	–1,176	–1,635	–1,710	–1,906	....	....	....
Gross Nat'l Expenditure = GNP	99a	14,485	16,284	18,881	18,381	17,850	16,942	16,349	16,269	16,109	16,738	19,830	20,474	....	....	....
Nat'l Income, Market Prices	99e	13,637	15,354	17,739	16,923	16,231	15,309	14,552	14,398	14,165	14,708	17,697	18,128	....	....	....
Gross Dom. Prod. 1990 Prices	99b.*p*	27,168	28,412	29,559	I26,838	25,165	24,125	23,333	22,269	21,396	21,220	21,539	22,117	21,744	21,381	....
GDP Deflator (1990=100)	99bi*p*	55.1	57.9	64.9	69.7	74.0	74.9	74.0	77.6	80.8	86.6	100.0	102.0	106.3	116.9	....
		Midyear Estimates														
Population	99z	1.08	1.09	1.12	1.14	1.17	1.18	1.20	1.21	1.21	1.21	1.23	1.25	1.25	1.26	....

(Notes in the back of the book)

Tunisia

744		1965	1966	1967	1968	1969	1970	1971	1972	1973	1974	1975	1976	1977	1978	1979
Exchange Rates															*Dinars per SDR:*	
Market Rate	aa	.5200	.5200	.5200	.5200	.5200	.5200	.5211	1.5255	.5369	.4978	.4979	.5007	.5005	.5255	.5215
															Dinars per US Dollar:	
Market Rate	ae	.5200	.5200	.5200	.5200	.5200	.5200	.4800	1.4840	.4451	.4066	.4253	.4310	.4121	.4034	.3959
Market Rate	rf	.5250	.5250	.5250	.5250	.5250	.5250	.5229e	.4771e	.4216e	.4365	.4023	.4288	.4290	.4162	.4065
Fund Position															*Millions of SDRs*	
Quota	2f. s	22.5	35.0	35.0	35.0	35.0	35.0	48.0	48.0	48.0	48.0	48.0	48.0	48.0	63.0	63.0
SDRs	1b. s	—	—	—	—	—	—	2.0	7.9	7.6	8.5	8.2	10.0	9.6	8.5	14.6
Reserve Position in the Fund	1c. s	—	—	—	—	—	—	—	5.9	12.0	12.0	12.0	12.0	12.0	11.7	11.3
Total Fund Cred.&Loans Outstg.	2tl	14.0	19.2	20.3	17.3	13.1	13.3	2.6	—	—	—	—	—	24.0	24.0	24.0
International Liquidity												*Millions of US Dollars Unless Otherwise Indicated:*				
Total Reserves minus Gold	1l. d	32.2	24.1	36.0	31.2	32.6	55.2	142.9	217.8	301.8	412.8	379.9	365.8	351.2	443.0	579.3
SDRs	1b. d	—	—	—	—	—	—	2.2	8.6	9.2	10.4	9.6	11.6	11.6	11.1	19.3
Reserve Position in the Fund	1c. d	—	—	—	—	—	—	—	6.4	14.5	14.7	14.1	14.0	14.6	15.2	14.9
Foreign Exchange	1d. d	32.2	24.1	36.0	31.2	32.6	55.2	140.7	202.8	278.1	387.7	356.2	340.3	325.0	416.7	545.1
Gold (Million Fine Troy Ounces)	1ad	.109	.109	.117	.120	.123	.126	.129	.129	.129	.129	.129	.129	.150	.160	.170
Gold (National Valuation)	1and	3.8	3.9	4.1	4.2	4.3	4.4	....	....	....	5.8	5.6	5.5	6.7	7.3	7.9
Deposit Money Banks: Assets	7a. d	4.5	8.2	10.3	7.0	8.3	9.8	15.4	19.1	25.5	47.8	45.1	36.7	44.9	61.7	104.7
of which: Claims on Nonbanks	7ad d	3.6	7.1	8.6	5.8	5.0	7.2	10.1	13.6	18.8	39.2	28.8	22.8	25.7	40.7	60.5
Deposit Money Banks: Liabilities	7b. d	36.8	46.0	68.7	61.4	54.4	62.8	88.6	105.4	140.2	198.6	212.1	233.3	254.4	316.4	352.8
of which: Liab. to Nonbanks	7bd d	24.6	32.4	37.7	45.0	52.3	60.8	84.4	96.2	124.6	174.9	189.9	210.2	231.1	280.9	319.6
Other Banking Insts.: Liabilities	7f. d	1.0	.2	1.3	4.9	9.2	14.1	18.8	26.0	30.3	56.7	58.4	121.3	152.5	197.5	257.0
Monetary Authorities															*Millions of Dinars*	
Foreign Assets	11	21	16	21	21	22	32	74	110	144	176	169	159	144	166	200
Claims on Central Government	12a	47	50	46	45	50	50	50	50	49	48	47	48	46	52	46
Claims on Deposit Money Banks	12e	19	24	23	28	29	31	12	24	36	55	106	111	151	167	153
Reserve Money	14	52	63	65	73	77	80	104	119	140	182	209	223	234	274	301
of which: Currency Outside DMBs	14a	47	55	57	62	65	67	80	94	112	140	163	185	214	250	265
Foreign Liabilities	16c	18	20	21	16	14	14	9	4	2	3	1	2	15	22	18
Central Government Deposits	16d	7	4	1	1	1	5	11	39	53	44	42	17	28	35	29
Capital Accounts	17a	3	3	3	3	4	7	10	13	17	31	42	48	53	59	63
Other Items (Net)	17r	6	1	—	—	5	7	3	9	16	18	28	27	11	-6	-13
Deposit Money Banks															*Millions of Dinars:*	
Reserves	20	4	7	6	9	11	11	20	24	26	41	46	36	25	32	48
Foreign Assets	21	2	4	5	4	4	5	7	9	11	19	19	16	18	25	41
Claims on Central Government	22a	28	27	27	27	30	32	30	41	49	49	49	71	102	136	173
Claims on Private Sector	22d	149	179	199	223	234	255	285	332	396	518	673	757	872	987	1,088
Demand Deposits	24	77	80	88	99	109	118	153	175	202	251	296	305	337	412	493
Quasi-Monetary Liabilities	25	29	38	40	45	48	58	63	76	103	142	192	258	300	362	434
Foreign Liabilities	26c	12	15	26	21	14	15	18	24	26	35	41	43	46	55	58
Long-Term Foreign Liabilities	26cl	8	9	10	11	15	18	25	27	35	46	50	57	58	73	81
Counterpart Funds	26e	9	10	10	10	10	10	10	10	10	10	9	9	9	9	9
Central Govt. Lending Funds	26f	10	12	12	15	16	17	19	28	30	38	41	43	50	60	72
Credit from Monetary Authorities	26g	19	26	28	28	29	30	9	24	35	56	106	114	169	153	125
Capital Accounts	27a	12	14	17	22	26	29	32	34	39	44	50	60	69	77	86
Other Items (Net)	27r	8	12	5	10	12	8	14	9	3	7	2	-9	-21	-20	-8
Post Office: Checking Deposits	24.. i	6	6	7	9	8	7	7	9	10	13	15	23	25	26	26
Monetary Survey															*Millions of Dinars:*	
Foreign Assets (Net)	31n	-7	-14	-21	-12	-2	8	55	91	126	157	146	130	101	114	165
Domestic Credit	32	223	258	277	304	321	340	362	394	452	585	744	888	1,033	1,184	1,321
Claims on Central Govt. (Net)	32an	74	79	78	80	86	85	77	61	55	66	70	125	145	178	214
Claims on Private Sector	32d	149	179	199	223	235	256	286	333	397	520	675	763	888	1,005	1,107
Money	34	130	142	152	171	181	193	241	278	323	404	475	514	576	688	786
Quasi-Money	35	29	38	40	45	48	58	63	76	103	142	192	258	300	362	434
Long-Term Foreign Liabilities	36cl	8	9	10	11	15	18	25	27	35	46	50	57	58	73	81
Counterpart Funds	36e	15	12	10	12	14	17	12	13	15	15	17	13	12	11	11
Central Govt. Lending Funds	36f	10	12	12	15	16	17	19	28	30	38	41	43	50	60	72
Other Items (Net)	37r	25	31	32	37	44	46	58	63	72	97	114	133	137	104	102
Money plus Quasi-Money	35l	160	181	192	217	230	251	304	355	426	546	668	772	876	1,050	1,219
Other Banking Institutions															*Millions of Dinars:*	
Claims on Central Govt. (Net)	42an	....	....	....	....	....	....	....	12	17	21	28	33	37	45	54
Claims on Private Sector	42d	3	3	5	8	11	15	20	127	37	59	81	124	157	205	255
Monetary Deposits	44	....	....	....	....	....	....	....	4	6	10	9	9	10	15	15
Time and Savings Deposits	45	6	7	7	8	9	9	11	115	20	34	64	80	92	113	138
Long-Term Foreign Liabilities	46cl	1		1	3	5	7	9	13	13	23	25	52	63	80	102
Central Govt. Lending Funds	46f	—	1	1	1	1	3	3	15	5	6	6	6	6	6	10
Capital Accounts	47a	2	2	3	3	3	6	9	9	13	13	18	20	23	29	31
Other Items (Net)	47r	-6	-7	-7	-7	-7	-11	-12	1-6	-3	-7	-12	-10	-1	7	13
Liquid Liabilities	55l	166	187	199	225	238	260	315	1373	453	591	740	860	978	1,178	1,373
Interest Rates															*Percent Per Annum*	
Discount Rate (End of Period)	60	4.00	5.00	5.00	5.00	5.00	5.00	5.00	5.00	5.00	5.00	5.00	5.00	5.75	5.75	5.75
Money Market Rate	60b	....	....	....	....	....	....	....	....	....	....	....	....	....	....	....
Deposit Rate	60l	....	....	....	....	....	....	....	....	....	....	....	....	2.50	2.50	2.50
Lending Rate	60p	....	....	....	....	....	....	....	....	....	....	....	....	....	7.25	7.25

Tunisia
744

1980	1981	1982	1983	1984	1985	1986	1987	1988	1989	1990	1991	1992	1993	1994		
End of Period															**Exchange Rates**	
.5340	.6002	.6792	.7612	.8494	.8314	1.0277	1.1035	1.2090	1.1888	1.1904	1.2366	1.3071	1.4376	1.4470	Market Rate	**aa**
End of Period (ae) Period Average (rf)																
.4187	.5157	.6158	.7271	.8666	.7570	.8402	.7779	.8985	.9046	.8368	.8645	.9507	1.0466	.9912	Market Rate	**ae**
.4050	.4938	.5907	.6788	.7768	.8345	.7940	.8287	.8578	.9493	.8783	.9246	.8844	1.0037	1.0116	Market Rate	**rf**
End of Period															**Fund Position**	
94.5	94.5	94.5	138.2	138.2	138.2	138.2	138.2	138.2	138.2	138.2	138.2	206.0	206.0	206.0	Quota	**2f. s**
11.8	17.4	16.0	3.6	1.9	.5	22.6	38.1	21.0	6.4	1.7	23.0	8.8	1.3	1.8	SDRs	**1b. s**
19.2	19.2	19.2	30.1	29.4	26.4	—	—	—	—	—	—	—	—	—	Reserve Position in the Fund	**1c. s**
—	—	—	—	—	—	149.7	190.7	205.7	205.7	123.7	180.1	211.1	207.3	207.3	Total Fund Cred.&Loans Outstg.	**2tl**
End of Period															**International Liquidity**	
590.1	536.1	606.5	567.3	406.3	232.7	305.3	525.5	899.3	961.9	794.8	789.9	852.0	853.8	1,461.5	Total Reserves minus Gold	**1l. d**
15.1	20.3	17.7	3.7	1.9	.5	27.6	54.1	28.3	8.5	2.5	32.9	12.1	1.8	2.7	SDRs	**1b. d**
24.5	22.3	21.2	31.5	28.8	29.0	—	—	—	—	—	—	—	—	.1	Reserve Position in the Fund	**1c. d**
550.6	493.5	567.6	532.0	375.6	203.2	277.7	471.4	871.0	953.4	792.3	757.0	839.9	852.0	1,458.8	Foreign Exchange	**1d. d**
.187	.187	.187	.187	.187	.187	.187	.187	.187	.187	.187	.215	.215	.215	.216	Gold (Million Fine Troy Ounces)	**1ad**
8.2	6.6	5.6	4.7	4.0	4.5	4.5	4.8	4.2	4.2	5.2	5.0	4.6	4.2	4.4	Gold (National Valuation)	**1an d**
125.4	162.0	195.7	233.6	225.5	223.7	218.3	365.5	392.2	453.9	610.0	603.7	570.6	545.2	536.9	Deposit Money Banks: Assets	**7a. d**
64.8	95.0	108.1	131.1	120.9	115.3	147.4	221.7	238.2	288.0	372.1	407.9	381.0	379.8	340.5	*of which:* Claims on Nonbanks	**7ad d**
410.1	402.9	391.2	397.9	410.0	471.6	425.0	....	578.3	584.9	753.9	1,342.7	1,461.9	1,374.3	1,729.3	Deposit Money Banks: Liabilities	**7b. d**
376.6	364.7	350.3	352.3	377.3	439.1	398.3	....	515.8	527.7	655.0	1,249.8	1,231.7	1,230.2	1,466.4	*of which:* Liab. to Nonbanks	**7bd d**
266.6	252.4	259.5	292.3	....	....	....	....	....	....	....	....	....	....	....	Other Banking Insts.: Liabilities	**7f. d**
End of Period															**Monetary Authorities**	
220	260	265	381	331	210	187	386	762	843	629	671	868	930	1,462	Foreign Assets	**11**
47	48	73	59	56	50	62	71	49	54	64	95	117	122	93	Claims on Central Government	**12a**
199	304	446	549	697	819	980	840	557	603	911	1,134	1,079	1,177	835	Claims on Deposit Money Banks	**12e**
338	426	525	617	680	740	747	806	858	991	1,129	1,264	1,355	1,420	1,521	Reserve Money	**14**
300	343	440	533	573	633	651	705	801	875	1,005	1,104	1,156	1,179	1,194	*of which:* Currency Outside DMBs	**14a**
5	8	10	—	44	1	155	226	251	246	165	234	296	324	326	Foreign Liabilities	**16c**
63	80	103	108	92	81	87	72	119	139	119	164	71	128	200	Central Government Deposits	**16d**
77	90	128	150	204	232	266	264	58	60	68	92	99	108	119	Capital Accounts	**17a**
–17	7	19	113	63	25	–25	–71	83	64	122	146	243	248	224	Other Items (Net)	**17r**
End of Period															**Deposit Money Banks**	
40	52	36	51	68	67	47	55	86	89	118	130	129	181	294	Reserves	**20**
53	84	120	170	195	169	183	284	352	411	510	522	542	571	532	Foreign Assets	**21**
204	245	284	335	405	501	575	631	652	715	762	793	535	536	544	Claims on Central Government	**22a**
1,334	1,756	2,207	2,675	3,024	3,481	3,736	4,017	4,449	5,648	5,957	6,466	7,402	7,907	8,510	Claims on Private Sector	**22d**
619	729	886	1,050	1,107	1,261	1,322	1,253	1,595	1,561	1,565	1,437	1,555	1,676	1,957	Demand Deposits	**24**
495	609	672	776	950	1,103	1,206	1,687	1,986	2,650	2,892	3,196	3,490	3,777	4,003	Quasi-Monetary Liabilities	**25**
77	98	120	159	191	178	167	253	314	328	378	424	605	614	780	Foreign Liabilities	**26c**
95	110	121	130	164	179	190	....	206	201	253	736	785	824	934	Long-Term Foreign Liabilities	**26cl**
9	9	10	10	10	10	10	....	16	3	3	—	—	—	—	Counterpart Funds	**26e**
80	96	111	136	159	194	214	....	236	367	412	—	—	—	—	Central Govt. Lending Funds	**26f**
180	366	563	743	929	1,059	1,239	1,152	840	1,308	1,356	1,536	1,485	1,494	1,175	Credit from Monetary Authorities	**26g**
96	134	158	192	228	270	321	368	419	530	592	710	885	1,053	1,246	Capital Accounts	**27a**
–21	–14	8	36	–45	–36	–128	....	–72	–86	–104	–128	–196	–244	–214	Other Items (Net)	**27r**
31	42	52	67	82	84	77	91	95	....	100	128	157	110	122	Post Office: Checking Deposits	**24.. i**
End of Period															**Monetary Survey**	
191	237	255	391	290	201	49	192	550	679	596	535	509	562	888	Foreign Assets (Net)	**31n**
1,573	2,040	2,561	3,101	3,592	4,175	4,521	4,917	5,131	6,367	6,765	7,319	8,141	8,546	9,070	Domestic Credit	**32**
219	255	307	354	451	554	627	721	677	715	808	853	739	639	560	Claims on Central Govt. (Net)	**32an**
1,354	1,784	2,255	2,747	3,142	3,621	3,894	4,196	4,454	5,653	5,957	6,466	7,402	7,907	8,510	Claims on Private Sector	**32d**
951	1,165	1,455	1,699	1,814	2,059	2,112	2,126	2,494	2,524	2,678	2,697	2,894	2,998	3,317	Money	**34**
495	609	672	776	950	1,103	1,206	1,687	1,986	2,650	2,892	3,196	3,490	3,777	4,003	Quasi-Money	**35**
95	110	121	130	164	179	190	....	206	201	253	736	785	824	934	Long-Term Foreign Liabilities	**36cl**
11	14	29	27	28	32	57	....	95	97	69	70	64	78	49	Counterpart Funds	**36e**
80	96	111	136	159	194	214	....	236	367	412	—	—	—	—	Central Govt. Lending Funds	**36f**
132	284	429	725	767	808	792	....	663	1,208	1,058	1,155	1,417	1,430	1,655	Other Items (Net)	**37r**
1,445	1,774	2,127	2,475	2,764	3,162	3,318	3,813	4,481	5,174	5,570	5,893	6,384	6,775	7,320	Money plus Quasi-Money	**35l**
End of Period															**Other Banking Institutions**	
62	80	97	116	121	131	148	....	....	....	....	....	....	....	....	Claims on Central Govt. (Net)	**42an**
291	351	450	662	867	1,068	1,203	....	....	....	....	....	....	....	....	Claims on Private Sector	**42d**
16	21	22	37	55	43	62	....	....	....	....	....	....	....	....	Monetary Deposits	**44**
149	184	230	274	303	336	402	....	....	....	....	....	....	....	....	Time and Savings Deposits	**45**
112	130	160	213	—	—	—	....	....	....	....	....	....	....	....	Long-Term Foreign Liabilities	**46cl**
19	35	46	78	347	460	457	....	....	....	....	....	....	....	....	Central Govt. Lending Funds	**46f**
33	85	154	211	302	397	462	....	....	....	....	....	....	....	....	Capital Accounts	**47a**
25	–24	–65	–33	–18	–38	–32	....	....	....	....	....	....	....	....	Other Items (Net)	**47r**
1,610	1,979	2,379	2,786	3,122	3,542	3,781	....	....	....	....	....	....	....	....	Liquid Liabilities	**55l**
Percent Per Annum															**Interest Rates**	
5.75	7.00	7.00	7.00	7.00	9.25	9.25	9.25	9.25	....	....	....	....	....	....	Discount Rate *(End of Period)*	**60**
....	8.50	8.25	8.38	8.89	10.28	9.95	10.00	9.15	9.40	11.53	11.79	11.73	10.48	8.81	Money Market Rate	**60b**
2.50	4.00	4.50	4.50	4.50	5.35	6.75	7.22	7.37	....	....	....	....	....	....	Deposit Rate	**60l**
7.25	8.10	8.50	8.50	8.50	9.63	9.17	11.08	9.87	....	....	....	....	....	....	Lending Rate	**60p**

Tunisia
744

		1965	1966	1967	1968	1969	1970	1971	1972	1973	1974	1975	1976	1977	1978	1979
Prices and Production																*Index Numbers (1990=100):*
Producer Prices	63	18.0	18.6	19.3	20.0	20.2	I21.0	22.5	22.9	24.1	29.2	32.0	32.4	33.9	35.0	37.5
Home Goods (1985=100)	63a	25.5	26.4	28.1	29.5	29.8	I31.0	33.9	34.4	36.1	41.3	45.0	46.4	49.4	51.2	54.9
Consumer Prices	64	....	....	....	....	....	....	....	....	....	....	....	....	....	....	....
Industrial Production	66	....	34.3	35.5	38.8	38.8	I42.0	45.2	48.6	50.7	54.8	56.3	57.7	I63.2	70.0	78.0
Mining Production	66zx	....	52.9	45.5	59.2	53.0	I58.5	58.8	58.9	59.9	64.2	66.8	58.1	I64.3	72.6	75.2
Crude Petroleum Production	66aa	....	17.1	49.8	70.9	82.3	92.2	91.0	88.3	86.1	91.9	102.4	82.4	94.7	108.8	123.6
International Transactions																*Millions of Dinars*
Exports	70	62.9	73.7	78.4	82.8	87.0	95.8	113.3	150.3	178.8	397.7	345.6	338.3	398.3	468.4	726.7
Imports, cif	71	129.1	131.2	137.1	114.5	139.8	160.4	180.0	222.2	286.1	488.7	572.8	656.7	782.5	889.7	1,156.8
Imports, fob	71.v	120.5	122.5	128.0	106.9	130.5	153.6	172.3	210.4	268.7	455.6	537.3	619.7	739.5	833.3	1,088.6
																1990=100
Volume of Exports	72	50	58	I60	67	70	75	81	105	92	95	87	92	88	102	108
Volume of Imports	73	29	I30	29	23	29	27	33	38	38	50	49	56	73	77	96
Unit Value of Exports	74	8	8	I9	9	9	9	10	10	13	27	27	24	25	27	37
Balance of Payments																*Millions of US Dollars:*
Goods: Exports f.o.b.	78aa d												788	788	942	1,557
Goods: Imports f.o.b.	78ab d												-1,434	-1,613	-1,788	-2,487
Trade Balance	78ac d												-646	-825	-846	-930
Services: Credit	78ad d												515	539	711	999
Services: Debit	78ae d												-296	-315	-365	-445
Balance on Goods and Services	78af d												-427	-601	-500	-376
Income: Credit	78ag d												26	16	19	52
Income: Debit	78ah d												-191	-196	-231	-312
Balance on Goods, Serv., & Inc.	78ai d												-592	-781	-711	-637
Current Transfers, n.i.e.: Credit	78aj d												208	231	274	359
Current Transfers: Debit	78ak d												-12	-16	-22	-22
Current Account, n.i.e.	78al d												-396	-566	-459	-300
Capital Account, n.i.e.: Credit	78ba d															
Capital Account: Debit	78bb d												-12	-12	-14	-7
Capital Account, n.i.e.	78bc d												-12	-12	-14	-7
Direct Investment Abroad	78bd d												—	—	2	—
Dir. Invest. in Rep. Econ., n.i.e.	78be d												110	93	91	49
Portfolio Investment Assets	78bf d															
Portfolio Investment Liab., n.i.e.	78bg d												-5	2	-2	-2
Other Investment Assets	78bh d												-9	-7	-144	-209
Other Investment Liab., n.i.e.	78bi d												352	450	569	485
Financial Account, n.i.e.	78bj d												448	539	517	322
Net Errors and Omissions	78ca d												-49	-19	39	92
Overall Balance	78cb d												-10	-59	82	107
Reserves and Related Items	79da d												10	59	-82	-107
Reserve Assets	79db d												10	31	-82	-117
Use of Fund Credit and Loans	79dc d												—	28	—	—
Liabs.Constit.For.Auth.Reserves	79dd d												—	—	—	10
Exceptional Financing	79de d															
Government Finance																*Millions of Dinars:*
Deficit (-) or Surplus	80							-9.5	-17.1	-15.4	-25.2	-62.4	-132.2	-101.2	-139.6
Revenue	81							246.3	279.1	388.1	486.8	526.9	626.4	779.8	941.2
Grants Received	81z							16.5	14.9	18.4	18.9	15.4	13.4	7.7	10.8
Expenditure	82							241.1	291.1	396.1	506.0	577.2	729.8	845.5	993.6
Lending Minus Repayments	83							31.2	20.0	25.8	24.9	27.5	42.2	43.2	98.0
Financing																
Domestic	84a							7.4	1.8	9.0	7.6	42.2	36.4	25.7	2.8
Foreign	85a							2.1	15.3	6.4	17.6	20.2	95.8	75.5	136.8
Debt: Domestic	88a						110.7	123.2	146.9	140.5	147.1	175.5	230.8	293.1	267.8
Foreign	89a						251.0	276.9	287.4	318.3	353.0	441.9	550.1	676.9	804.5
National Accounts																*Millions of Dinars*
Exports of Goods & Services	90c	99	115	121	134	150	166	212	271	300	547	546	562	649	769	1,139
Government Consumption	91f	79	92	101	110	118	127	134	151	169	199	250	293	355	405	444
Gross Fixed Capital Formation	93e	145	131	134	137	148	151	168	214	248	315	461	558	665	765	894
Increase/Decrease(-) in Stocks	93i	—	7	9	9	8	-1	10	19	-5	36	85	20	-5	-7	-27
Private Consumption	96f	372	377	387	397	443	517	596	707	790	971	1,032	1,205	1,409	1,563	1,775
Imports of Goods & Services	98c	-168	-168	-176	-152	-180	-200	-230	-283	-328	-542	-630	-716	-873	-1,008	-1,285
Gross Domestic Product	99b	527	554	576	634	686	759	891	1,078	1,174	1,527	1,744	1,922	2,199	2,487	2,940
Net Primary Inc/Pmts(-) Abroad	98.n b															
Gross National Income	99i															
Net Current Transfers from Abroad	98.n a															
Gross Nat'l Disposable Income	99a	519	545	563	615	667	744	888	1,070	1,162	1,508	1,746	1,897	2,217	2,491	2,934
National Disposable Income	99e	510	528	539	586	634	707	842	1,018	1,106	1,442	1,647	1,752	2,040	2,276	2,674
Gross Dom. Prod. 1990 Prices	99b.p	....	....	....	3,037	3,178	3,418	3,815	4,470	4,492	4,943	5,343	5,781	6,062	6,436	6,896
GDP Deflator (1990=100)	99bi p	....	....	....	20.9	21.6	22.2	23.4	24.1	26.1	30.9	32.6	33.2	36.3	38.6	42.6
																Millions:
Population	99z	4.62	4.72	4.82	4.92	5.03	5.13	5.20	5.28	I5.33	5.46	5.61	5.77	5.93	6.08	6.22

Government Finance: I Beginning in 1985, data for budgetary central government are based on a revised budgetary nomenclature.

Tunisia 744

	1980	1981	1982	1983	1984	1985	1986	1987	1988	1989	1990	1991	1992	1993	1994		
Period Averages																**Prices and Production**	
	41.6	46.8	54.7	⌐58.3	63.3	70.5	77.5	84.6	92.0	97.3	100.0	102.6	104.3	106.4	108.2	Producer Prices	63
	60.2	65.7	80.6	86.9	93.1	100.0	106.4	109.5	....	....	....	....	....	....	....	Home Goods (1985=100)	63a
	....	....	....	60.6	65.9	70.7	75.1	81.3	⌐87.1	93.9	100.0	108.2	114.5	119.0	124.7	Consumer Prices	64
	83.7	86.7	85.8	⌐93.2	93.5	94.6	94.8	95.0	98.4	100.4	100.0	103.1	104.7	101.5	102.0	Industrial Production	66
	83.7	82.7	79.7	⌐95.3	86.3	74.4	91.1	97.8	99.0	107.9	100.0	100.3	95.6	80.9	88.9	Mining Production	66zx
	124.1	119.9	113.3	122.8	121.7	120.1	116.6	110.8	109.0	109.4	100.0	115.4	115.5	103.2	97.2	Crude Petroleum Production	66aa
Millions of Dinars																**International Transactions**	
	904.8	1,233.0	1,164.7	1,263.9	1,399.1	1,443.0	1,403.7	1,770.7	2,055.4	2,782.0	3,087.4	3,417.1	3,549.7	3,818.1	4,696.6	Exports	70
	1,427.4	1,866.0	2,008.5	2,109.8	2,508.9	2,287.0	2,295.1	2,509.2	3,167.0	4,163.6	4,826.4	4,789.0	5,688.8	6,237.2	6,647.3	Imports, cif	71
	1,348.6	1,765.5	1,900.1	1,968.1	2,340.4	2,133.4	2,141.0	2,340.6	2,954.3	3,884.0	4,502.2	4,467.4	5,306.7	5,818.3	6,200.8	Imports, fob	71.v
1990=100																	
	102	⌐100	100	92	91	82	92	95	96	116	⌐100	110	111	121	....	Volume of Exports	72
	91	⌐92	96	91	99	76	76	67	83	99	⌐100	94	104	116	....	Volume of Imports	73
	48	⌐61	66	69	75	76	68	77	83	94	⌐100	98	95	96	....	Unit Value of Exports	74
Minus Sign Indicates Debit																Balance of Payments	
	2,195	2,490	2,004	1,862	1,782	1,708	1,768	2,107	2,401	2,934	3,516	3,702	4,023	3,806	....	Goods: Exports f.o.b.	78aa d
	-3,166	-3,457	-3,167	-2,947	-2,948	-2,593	-2,715	-2,838	-3,503	-4,146	-5,201	-4,901	-6,086	-5,879	....	Goods: Imports f.o.b.	78ab d
	-970	-967	-1,163	-1,084	-1,166	-886	-947	-731	-1,102	-1,212	-1,685	-1,199	-2,063	-2,073	....	Trade Balance	78ac d
	1,067	1,043	997	1,003	915	965	950	1,236	1,849	1,538	1,676	1,397	1,952	2,009	....	Services: Credit	78ad d
	-600	-553	-611	-616	-611	-612	-599	-597	-696	-669	-787	-756	-890	-914	....	Services: Debit	78ae d
	-504	-476	-777	-697	-862	-533	-597	-93	51	-343	-796	-558	-1,002	-977	....	Balance on Goods and Services	78af d
	94	98	105	88	99	40	29	25	54	77	105	69	122	127	....	Income: Credit	78ag d
	-353	-392	-400	-357	-353	-400	-450	-512	-553	-554	-601	-686	-744	-767	....	Income: Debit	78ah d
	-763	-770	-1,072	-965	-1,116	-894	-1,018	-579	-448	-821	-1,292	-1,175	-1,624	-1,618	....	Balance on Goods, Serv., & Inc.	78ai d
	430	409	430	414	368	328	417	538	680	718	847	728	681	728	....	Current Transfers, n.i.e.: Credit	78aj d
	-20	-20	-20	-19	-17	-16	-14	-13	-13	-14	-24	-17	-18	-15	....	Current Transfers: Debit	78ak d
	-353	-381	-662	-570	-765	-581	-615	-54	219	-116	-469	-464	-961	-905	....	Current Account, n.i.e.	78al d
	—	—	—	—	—	—	—	—	—	—	—	—	—	—	....	Capital Account, n.i.e.: Credit	78ba d
	-7	-10	-5	-7	-5	-6	-4	-6	-3	-7	-7	-5	-5	-7	....	Capital Account: Debit	78bb d
	-7	-10	-5	-7	-5	-6	-4	-6	-3	-7	-7	-5	-5	-7	....	Capital Account, n.i.e.	78bc d
	—	-2	-2	1	1	6	-1	-1	2	-5	1	-3	-5	—	....	Direct Investment Abroad	78bd d
	235	293	340	184	113	108	63	92	61	79	76	125	369	239	....	Dir. Invest. in Rep. Econ., n.i.e.	78be d
	—	—	-7	-22	-8	-5	-5	-7	-5	-1	-1	-2	-3	-11	....	Portfolio Investment Assets	78bf d
	15	-2	69	60	99	35	38	16	9	-5	3	23	50	24	....	Portfolio Investment Liab., n.i.e.	78bg d
	-119	-305	-125	-301	-49	2	-63	-169	-131	-9	-232	-267	-53	-179	....	Other Investment Assets	78bh d
	237	453[e]													....	Other Investment Liab., n.i.e.	78bi d
	368	436	718	385	622	381	441	138	198	194	381	337	1,058	903	....	Financial Account, n.i.e.	78bj d
	69	18	112	228	48	-19	94	48	27	-5	-28	77	5	16	....	Net Errors and Omissions	78ca d
	76	63	163	35	-100	-225	-84	126	441	65	-123	-55	97	7	....	Overall Balance	78cb d
	-76	-63	-163	-35	100	225	84	-126	-441	-65	123	55	-97	-7	....	Reserves and Related Items	79da d
	-35	-67	-159	-35	100	225	-96	-181	-462	-65	235	-19	-143	-2	....	Reserve Assets	79db d
	-32	—	—	—	—	—	179	53	21	—	-112	74	45	—	....	Use of Fund Credit and Loans	79dc d
	-10	4	-3	—	—	—	—	2	—	—	—	—	—	-5	....	Liabs.Constit.For.Auth.Reserves	79dd d
															....	Exceptional Financing	79de d
Year Ending December 31																**Government Finance**	
	-98.9	-105.5	-277.4	-458.8	-307.3	⌐-354.2	-510.9	-372.1	-326.9	-411.6	-585.5	-497.0[P]	-349.0[f]	....	....	Deficit (-) or Surplus	80
	1,109.2	1,328.7	1,649.3	1,848.0	2,276.1	⌐2,328.3	2,400.2	2,497.2	2,728.4	2,927.9	3,325.8	3,491.6[P]	3,956.4[f]	....	....	Revenue	81
	22.0	5.4	8.4	6.5	9.3	⌐3.4	4.1	23.6	30.3	143.2	70.5	32.5[P]	72.0[f]	....	....	Grants Received	81z
	1,117.4	1,353.4	1,814.5	2,142.0	2,438.0	⌐2,559.0	2,697.4	2,800.1	3,004.0	3,424.6	3,742.6	4,017.2[P]	4,391.7[f]	....	....	Expenditure	82
	112.7	86.2	120.6	171.3	154.7	⌐126.9	217.8	92.8	81.4	58.1	239.2	3.9[P]	-14.3[f]	....	....	Lending Minus Repayments	83
																Financing	
	18.5	-3.2	81.2	174.7	160.5	⌐155.6	273.8	285.5	157.5	294.1	393.8	404.8[P]	....	....	....	Domestic	84a
	80.4	108.7	196.2	284.1	146.8	⌐198.6	237.1	86.6	169.4	117.5	191.7	92.2[P]	....	....	....	Foreign	85a
	313.3	358.4	405.8	485.0	601.8	⌐750.6	867.1	949.1	1,062.3	1,275.7	1,614.4	1,965.0[P]	....	....	....	Debt: Domestic	88a
	897.1	1,102.6	1,430.5	1,867.2	2,108.7	⌐2,441.8	3,178.4	3,190.9	3,750.5	3,847.5	4,309.4	4,435.0[P]	....	....	....	Foreign	89a
Millions of Dinars																**National Accounts**	
	1,425	1,722	1,773	1,948	2,114	2,253	2,161	2,799	3,639	4,315	4,662	4,802	5,357	5,994	6,896	Exports of Goods & Services	90c
	510	616	794	927	1,030	1,142	1,217	1,305	1,387	1,656	1,769	1,974	2,168	2,380	2,641	Government Consumption	91f
	982	1,290	1,635	1,750	1,920	1,850	1,685	1,620	1,680	2,157	2,635	2,912	3,634	4,168	4,658	Gross Fixed Capital Formation	93e
	37	56	-116	-140	75	-15	-36	27	5	103	242	231	497	160	102	Increase/Decrease(-) in Stocks	93i
	2,171	2,553	2,997	3,434	3,944	4,356	4,665	5,124	5,582	6,022	6,866	7,459	8,354	8,975	9,840	Private Consumption	96f
	-1,615	-2,074	-2,279	-2,421	-2,843	-2,676	-2,671	-2,878	-3,608	-4,722	-5,376	-5,382	-6,256	-6,989	-8,003	Imports of Goods & Services	98c
	3,510	4,162	4,804	5,497	6,240	6,910	7,021	7,997	8,685	9,531	10,798	11,997	13,754	14,688	16,134	Gross Domestic Product	99b
	....	....	....	....	....	....	....	....	....	⌐-390	-359	-500	-519	-763	-687	Net Primary Inc/Pmts(-) Abroad	98.n b
	....	....	....	....	....	....	....	....	....	9,142	10,438	11,498	13,236	13,926	15,447	Gross National Income	99i
	....	....	....	....	....	....	....	....	....	⌐450	504	515	501	574	656	Net Current Transfers from Abroad	98.n a
	3,488	4,194	4,857	5,562	6,289	6,842	6,971	7,995	8,737	9,591	10,943	12,013	13,736	14,500	16,102	Gross Nat'l Disposable Income	99a
	3,163	3,814	4,393	4,994	5,617	6,058	6,093	7,024	7,691	8,541	10,109	11,054	12,621	....	....	National Disposable Income	99e
	7,547	⌐8,040	8,002	8,376	8,856	9,358	⌐9,222	9,840	9,847	10,019	10,798	11,217	12,110	12,365	12,906	Gross Dom. Prod. 1990 Prices	99b.p
	46.5	51.8	60.0	65.6	70.5	73.8	76.1	81.3	88.2	95.1	100.0	107.0	113.6	118.8	125.0	GDP Deflator (1990=100)	99bi p
Midyear Estimates																	
	6.39	6.57	6.70	6.84	7.03	7.26	7.46	7.64	7.77	7.91	8.07	8.24	8.41	8.57	....	Population	99z

Turkey
186

		1965	1966	1967	1968	1969	1970	1971	1972	1973	1974	1975	1976	1977	1978	1979
Exchange Rates															*Liras per SDR:*	
Market Rate	aa	9.0	9.0	9.0	9.0	9.0	14.9	15.4	15.4	17.1	17.1	17.7	19.4	23.6	32.9	46.6
														Liras per US Dollar:		
Market Rate	ae	9.0	9.0	9.0	9.0	9.0	14.9	14.2	14.2	14.2	14.0	15.2	16.7	19.4	25.3	35.4
Market Rate	rf	9.0	9.0	9.0	9.0	9.0	11.5	15.0	14.2	14.2	13.9	14.4	16.1	18.0	24.3	31.1
Fund Position														*Millions of SDRs:*		
Quota	2f. s	86	86	108	108	108	151	151	151	151	151	151	151	151	200	200
SDRs	1b. s	—	—	—	—	—	—	5	38	28	35	27	18	—	—	—
Reserve Position in the Fund	1c. s	—	—	—	—	—	—	—	28	38	38	—	—	—	—	—
Total Fund Cred.&Loans Outstg.	2tl	19	19	21	48	37	74	62	—	—	—	208	337	337	478	480
International Liquidity												*Millions of US Dollars Unless Otherwise Indicated:*				
Total Reserves minus Gold	1l. d	25	29	22	26	128	304	631	1,262	1,986	1,562	944	990	638	801	658
SDRs	1b. d	—	—	—	—	—	—	5	42	34	42	32	21	—	—	—
Reserve Position in the Fund	1c. d	—	—	—	—	—	—	—	31	46	46	—	—	—	—	—
Foreign Exchange	1d. d	25	29	22	26	128	304	626	1,190	1,906	1,473	912	969	638	801	658
Gold (Million Fine Troy Ounces)	1ad	3.314	2.914	2.771	2.771	3.343	3.629	3.429	3.571	3.571	3.569	3.570	3.570	3.634	3.667	3.765
Gold (National Valuation)	1and	116	102	97	97	117	127	130	136	151	151	151	151	153	155	155
Monetary Authorities: Other Liab.	4..d	132	199	201	121	63	461	440	989	1,249	1,445	2,233	4,258	4,188	5,166	5,544
Deposit Money Banks: Assets	7a. d	—	—	—	—	—	25	38	50	74	58	309	191	137	215	258
Liabilities	7b. d	—	—	—	—	—	34	50	101	104	100	73	135	58	58	80
Other Banking Insts.: Assets	7e. d	....	....	....	....	....	....	....	....	....	....	....	....	....	....	....
Liabilities	7f. d	....	....	....	....	....	115	135	147	201	238	288	526	580	656	853
Monetary Authorities													*Millions of Liras through 1977;*			
Foreign Assets	11	1,930	1,930	1,980	2,482	3,151	⁑8,162	12,895	21,680	31,893	25,306	17,968	23,591	16,252	⁑42	59
Claims on Central Government	12a	7,660	8,350	8,860	9,322	10,724	⁑10,532	12,987	13,985	14,331	18,857	41,966	51,767	90,297	⁑144	262
of which: Revaluation Account	12ag e	....	....	....	....	....	....	....	....	....	....	....	....	....	....	....
Claims on Official Entities	12bx	810	1,240	1,620	1,497	1,684	⁑3,584	5,459	5,809	5,688	9,946	9,551	25,528	46,510	⁑68	124
Claims on Nonfin.Pub.Enterprises	12c	....	....	....	....	....	....	....	....	....	....	....	....	....	....	....
Claims on Deposit Money Banks	12e	1,600	2,590	3,790	4,887	6,357	⁑8,969	7,624	13,702	18,319	26,192	41,770	71,843	100,138	⁑151	214
Claims on Other Banking Insts.	12f	....	....	....	....	....	⁑—	—	14	78	6,245	13,514	22,281	35,840	⁑42	47
Claims on Nonbank Financial Insts.	12g	....	....	....	....	....	....	....	....	....	....	....	....	....	....	....
Reserve Money	14	9,040	10,840	12,780	14,250	16,302	⁑19,790	26,312	35,877	45,364	58,413	76,906	93,045	136,680	⁑199	309
of which: Currency Outside DMBs	14a	6,310	7,190	8,740	8,237	9,081	⁑11,851	13,918	15,980	20,703	26,154	32,909	42,471	62,961	⁑94	144
Time and Savings Deposits	15	....	....	....	....	....	37	75	211	787	859	680	909	769	⁑2	1
Foreign Currency Deposits	15.a	....	....	....	....	....	....	....	....	....	....	....	....	....	....	....
Restricted Deposits	16b	....	....	....	....	....	2,189	1,819	1,558	1,922	1,958	3,000	13,249	50,385	⁑96	150
Foreign Liabilities	16c	1,360	1,960	2,000	1,527	895	⁑8,025	7,098	13,847	17,481	20,210	37,504	77,487	89,390	⁑146	218
Central Government Deposits	16d	360	380	370	282	443	⁑675	789	1,150	1,279	972	1,460	2,072	2,571	⁑2	5
Central Govt. Lending Funds	16f	....	....	....	....	....	104	990	696	578	1,180	1,068	1,858	3,050	⁑4	9
Capital Accounts	17a	260	180	190	430	533	⁑854	1,345	1,691	1,905	2,380	3,122	3,970	5,101	⁑7	9
Other Items (Net)	17r	980	750	910	1,699	3,743	⁑–427	536	160	994	574	1,028	2,419	1,091	⁑–9	3
Deposit Money Banks													*Millions of Liras through 1977;*			
Reserves	20	1,590	1,920	1,960	⁑7,450	8,832	⁑7,710	12,087	19,095	23,539	30,303	42,688	49,355	72,040	⁑100	151
Nonreserve Claims on Monet.Auth.	20n	....	....	....	....	....	....	....	....	....	....	....	....	....	....	....
Central Bank Bonds	20r	....	....	....	....	....	2,189	1,819	1,558	1,922	1,958	3,000	13,249	50,385	⁑96	150
Foreign Assets	21	....	....	....	....	376	529	700	1,038	815	4,677	3,175	2,668	⁑5	9	
Claims on Central Government	22a	4,550	5,370	5,870	⁑2,868	1,677	⁑3,735	6,189	7,551	7,242	7,450	9,878	16,056	23,756	⁑32	42
Claims on Local Government	22b	....	....	....	....	....	....	....	....	....	....	....	....	....	....	....
Claims on Official Entities	22bx	....	....	....	1,225	2,154	⁑6,069	7,669	9,881	14,641	19,131	25,699	33,568	36,194	⁑40	78
Claims on Nonfin.Pub.Enterprises	22c	....	....	....	....	....	....	....	....	....	....	....	....	....	....	....
Claims on Private Sector	22d	17,460	21,580	24,880	⁑28,070	33,182	⁑32,536	37,196	49,420	64,989	84,172	121,233	161,596	205,772	⁑261	381
Claims on Other Banking Insts.	22f	....	....	....	....	....	2,062	2,125	2,255	2,330	2,427	2,481	2,795	1,843	⁑2	2
Claims on Nonbank Financial Insts.	22g	....	....	....	....	....	....	....	....	....	....	....	....	....	....	....
Demand Deposits	24	10,088	12,590	13,950	17,726	21,032	⁑23,542	29,766	36,943	49,239	62,559	84,725	108,073	145,642	⁑190	298
Time and Savings Deposits	25	2,652	3,660	4,420	18,230	4,741	⁑8,894	13,020	18,008	20,542	24,577	29,002	30,776	34,403	⁑44	84
Foreign Currency Deposits	25.a	....	....	....	....	....	....	....	....	....	....	....	....	....	....	....
Money Market Instruments	26aa	....	....	....	....	....	....	....	....	....	....	....	....	....	....	....
Bonds	26ab	550	540	500	474	443	418	402	360	375	386	767	833	1,302	⁑1	2
Restricted Deposits	26b	330	540	580	914	1,698	⁑21	21	20	20	404	2,993	7,634	27,859	⁑28	25
Foreign Liabilities	26c	....	....	....	....	....	504	701	1,419	1,454	1,398	1,103	2,248	1,130	⁑1	3
Central Government Deposits	26d	2,050	2,230	2,640	2,959	3,288	⁑3,933	5,780	7,908	10,493	11,607	17,100	20,032	26,048	⁑35	51
Central Govt. Lending Funds	26f	3,820	4,300	4,720	5,449	6,261	⁑440	439	369	374	551	1,145	2,084	3,135	⁑5	2
Credit from Monetary Authorities	26g	1,600	2,590	3,790	⁑4,427	5,766	6,300	4,434	5,993	14,119	23,178	22,226	34,927	55,796	⁑151	214
Credit from Other Financial Insts.	26i	....	....	....	....	....	2,502	2,535	2,894	3,814	4,919	6,159	9,440	12,852	⁑9	10
Capital Accounts	27a	4,970	5,400	5,940	6,501	7,143	⁑7,494	9,410	11,418	12,507	13,972	17,057	19,658	22,498	⁑27	52
Other Items (Net)	27r	–2,460	–2,980	–3,830	⁑–17,100	–4,527	636	1,109	5,121	2,778	2,779	27,398	44,110	62,046	⁑44	72
Monetary Survey													*Millions of Liras through 1977;*			
Foreign Assets (Net)	31n	1,930	1,930	1,980	2,200	3,420	⁑9	5,625	7,114	13,996	4,513	–15,962	–52,969	–71,600	⁑–100	–153
Domestic Credit	32	28,080	33,930	38,220	⁑40,179	48,068	⁑53,910	65,056	79,857	97,527	135,649	205,762	291,487	411,593	⁑551	880
Claims on Central Govt. (Net)	32an	9,810	11,110	11,720	⁑8,949	10,245	⁑9,659	12,607	12,478	9,801	13,728	33,284	45,719	85,434	⁑139	248
Claims on Local Government	32b	....	....	....	....	....	....	....	....	....	....	....	....	....	....	....
Claims on Official Entities	32bx	810	1,240	1,620	1,500	1,680	⁑9,653	13,128	15,690	20,329	29,077	35,250	59,096	82,704	⁑108	202
Claims on Nonfin.Pub.Enterprises	32c	....	....	....	....	....	....	....	....	....	....	....	....	....	....	....
Claims on Private Sector	32d	17,460	21,580	24,880	⁑28,070	33,838	⁑32,536	37,196	49,420	64,989	84,172	121,233	161,596	205,772	⁑261	381
Claims on Other Banking Insts.	32f	—	—	—	—	—	⁑2,062	2,125	2,269	2,408	8,672	15,995	25,076	37,683	⁑44	50
Claims on Nonbank Fin. Insts.	32g	....	....	....	....	....	....	....	....	....	....	....	....	....	....	....
Money	34	16,398	19,780	22,690	25,800	30,110	⁑35,622	43,991	53,725	71,063	90,668	118,943	151,763	210,282	⁑289	456
Quasi-Money	35	2,652	3,660	4,420	5,430	6,440	⁑8,931	13,095	18,219	21,329	25,436	29,682	31,685	35,172	⁑46	85
Money Market Instruments	36aa	....	....	....	....	....	....	....	....	....	....	....	....	....	....	....
Bonds	36ab	....	....	....	....	....	....	....	....	....	....	....	....	....	....	....
Restricted Deposits	36b	....	....	....	....	....	....	....	....	....	....	....	....	....	....	....
Central Govt. Lending Funds	36f	3,820	4,300	4,720	5,449	6,261	⁑544	1,429	1,065	952	1,731	2,213	3,942	6,185	⁑9	11
Other Items (Net)	37r	7,140	8,120	8,370	9,980	13,340	⁑8,829	12,168	13,955	18,194	22,401	38,980	51,148	88,407	⁑107	173
Money plus Quasi-Money	35l	19,050	23,440	27,110	31,230	36,550	⁑44,553	57,086	71,944	92,392	116,104	148,625	183,448	245,454	⁑335	542

Turkey

1980	1981	1982	1983	1984	1985	1986	1987	1988	1989	1990	1991	1992	1993	1994		
End of Period															**Exchange Rates**	
115.0	155.5	206.0	296.1	435.9	633.6	926.9	1,448.3	2,442.2	3,040.6	4,168.5	7,266.5	11,776.1	19,878.9	56,534.2	Market Rate	aa
End of Period (ae) Period Average (rf)																
90.1	133.6	186.8	282.8	444.7	576.9	757.8	1,020.9	1,814.8	2,313.7	2,930.1	5,079.9	8,564.4	14,472.5	38,726.0	Market Rate	ae
76.0	111.2	162.6	225.5	366.7	522.0	674.5	857.2	1,422.3	2,121.7	2,608.6	4,171.8	6,872.4	10,984.6	29,608.7	Market Rate	rf
End of Period															**Fund Position**	
300	300	300	429	429	429	429	429	429	429	429	429	429	642	642	642 Quota	2f. s
—	—	—	1	—	—	—	—	—	—	—	—	—	—	—	1 SDRs	1b. s
—	—	—	32	32	32	32	32	32	32	32	32	32	32	32	32 Reserve Position in the Fund	1c. s
827	1,136	1,319	1,497	1,455	1,208	887	543	222	36	—	—	—	—	236	Total Fund Cred.&Loans Outstg.	2tl
End of Period															**International Liquidity**	
1,077	928	1,080	1,288	1,271	1,056	1,412	1,776	2,344	4,780	6,050	5,144	6,159	6,272	7,169	Total Reserves minus Gold	1l. d
—	—	—	1	—	—	—	—	—	—	1	—	—	—	1	SDRs	1b. d
—	—	—	34	32	35	39	46	43	42	46	46	44	44	47	Reserve Position in the Fund	1c. d
1,077	928	1,080	1,253	1,239	1,020	1,372	1,730	2,301	4,738	6,003	5,098	6,115	6,227	7,121	Foreign Exchange	1d. d
3.768	3.768	3.769	3.775	3.800	3.858	3.840	3.831	3.822	3.785	4.095	4.163	4.047	4.031	3.820	Gold (Million Fine Troy Ounces)	1ad
155	155	155	155	823	1,069	1,237	1,535	1,368	1,354	1,512	1,536	1,494	1,488	1,410	Gold (National Valuation)	1and
7,086	6,160	6,047	7,084	7,440	9,507	ɪ8,118	10,583	9,911	8,993	8,725	7,399	6,985	7,490	9,939	Monetary Authorities: Other Liab.	4..d
547	794	950	992	2,076	1,994	ɪ2,728	3,075	4,892	4,222	4,973	5,486	8,540	10,708	8,655	Deposit Money Banks: Assets	7a. d
82	46	343	446	1,693	2,507	ɪ1,563	1,885	1,712	1,957	3,796	3,688	6,379	9,369	3,245	Liabilities	7b. d
....	....	....	....	....	....	13	786	148	467	540	620	555	612	478	Other Banking Insts.: Assets	7e. d
619	529	504	439	492	551	ɪ210	334	382	451	594	998	928	937	799	Liabilities	7f. d
Billions of Liras Beginning 1978: End of Period															**Monetary Authorities**	
270	496	808	1,404	1,662	2,241	ɪ2,681	3,738	9,643	16,939	24,249	37,875	73,521	124,914	372,848	Foreign Assets	11
631	993	1,349	1,803	4,441	6,668	ɪ9,500	14,352	22,672	26,947	31,654	50,033	87,974	141,746	349,901	Claims on Central Government	12a
....	....	....	....	....	....	4,339	8,249	15,852	21,100	26,394	32,426	34,745	31,932	133,417	of which: Revaluation Account	12ag e
180	236	261	256	41	122	....	....	....	....	....	....	....	....	....	Claims on Official Entities	12bx
....	....	....	....	....	....	57	91	466	553	902	4,728	11,601	12,515	25,930	Claims on Nonfin.Pub.Enterprises	12c
317	420	377	629	307	369	ɪ711	1,646	3,165	3,140	4,511	4,477	8,655	16,866	20,503	Claims on Deposit Money Banks	12e
49	54	67	76	37	50	ɪ78	835	628	1,137	1,519	1,332	1,517	1,996	71	Claims on Other Banking Insts.	12f
....	....	....	....	....	....	27	30	25	21	—	—	—	—	—	Claims on Nonbank Financial Insts.	12g
458	717	1,011	1,397	2,101	2,900	ɪ4,588	6,759	12,084	20,780	28,746	43,077	76,773	128,902	282,973	Reserve Money	14
218	280	412	548	736	1,011	ɪ1,300	2,208	3,424	6,833	11,343	16,834	30,244	51,364	101,401	of which: Currency Outside DMBs	14a
1	64	3	4	2	5	ɪ373	110	190	207	365	667	1,982	2,942	6,773	Time and Savings Deposits	15
....	....	....	....	....	....	151	115	531	611	743	1,052	1,843	3,827	3,130	Foreign Currency Deposits	15.a
142	94	73	61	90	72	ɪ148	213	341	221	39	15	14	11	12	Restricted Deposits	16b
734	1,000	1,401	2,447	3,943	6,249	ɪ6,974	11,590	18,529	20,916	25,564	37,587	59,826	108,401	398,227	Foreign Liabilities	16c
49	269	301	191	37	120	ɪ1,012	1,842	3,850	4,578	5,057	6,366	14,309	16,541	22,482	Central Government Deposits	16d
26	38	11	16	10	30	....	....	....	....	....	....	....	....	....	Central Govt. Lending Funds	16f
17	26	39	55	75	103	ɪ135	209	348	486	1,246	1,327	3,468	8,784	13,753	Capital Accounts	17a
20	-10	23	-3	230	-30	ɪ-328	-145	726	938	1,075	8,355	25,054	28,630	41,901	Other Items (Net)	17r
Billions of Liras Beginning 1978: End of Period															**Deposit Money Banks**	
220	429	592	827	1,299	1,834	ɪ3,400	5,103	9,134	13,603	16,967	25,834	44,839	74,625	172,477	Reserves	20
....	....	....	....	....	....	-169	514	-138	28	6	3,660	14,213	14,396	8,449	Nonreserve Claims on Monet.Auth.	20n
....	....	....	....	....	....	....	....	....	....	....	....	....	....	....	Central Bank Bonds	20r
142	94	73	61	90	72	....	....	....	....	....	....	....	....	....		
49	106	177	281	923	1,150	ɪ2,067	3,139	8,878	9,769	14,571	27,867	73,144	154,976	335,160	Foreign Assets	21
68	159	384	376	915	2,030	ɪ2,644	4,512	7,413	14,702	20,064	35,090	56,219	100,523	224,793	Claims on Central Government	22a
....	....	....	....	....	....	149	383	545	563	753	—	—	—	2,756	Claims on Local Government	22b
159	161	156	199	174	439	....	....	....	....	....	....	....	....	....	Claims on Official Entities	22bx
....	....	....	....	....	....	1,371	2,249	3,401	3,221	6,814	9,095	7,120	24,052	65,820	Claims on Nonfin.Pub.Enterprises	22c
660	1,231	1,814	2,708	3,625	5,725	ɪ9,454	14,484	20,617	34,828	61,060	98,780	182,233	336,615	550,331	Claims on Private Sector	22d
2	3	12	17	26	32	ɪ29	40	49	579	568	1,030	2,489	4,856	17,848	Claims on Other Banking Insts.	22f
....	....	....	....	....	....	22	79	233	284	397	660	992	1,893	2,192	Claims on Nonbank Financial Insts.	22g
ɪ520	736	994	1,520	1,686	2,402	ɪ3,710	6,175	7,480	12,082	18,671	27,114	45,590	73,402	125,850	Demand Deposits	24
ɪ186	690	1,272	1,393	3,045	5,120	ɪ6,698	8,023	15,516	27,779	41,408	75,477	124,654	183,910	434,518	Time and Savings Deposits	25
....	....	....	....	....	....	2,285	5,241	8,981	13,524	21,051	49,889	101,391	186,790	561,875	Foreign Currency Deposits	25.a
....	....	....	....	....	....	787	1,367	1,251	1,979	2,382	3,397	3,709	3,064	4,633	Money Market Instruments	26aa
2	2	7	12	9	7	ɪ7	7	54	389	413	704	6,192	24,524	15,757	Bonds	26ab
38	101	181	379	512	550	....	....	....	....	....	....	....	....	....	Restricted Deposits	26b
7	6	64	126	753	1,446	ɪ1,184	1,924	3,107	4,528	11,122	18,736	54,629	135,596	125,647	Foreign Liabilities	26c
ɪ42	85	94	173	255	491	ɪ2,747	5,115	8,124	12,542	20,329	26,333	38,069	65,803	91,715	Central Government Deposits	26d
7	67	218	268	376	576	....	....	....	....	....	....	....	....	....	Central Govt. Lending Funds	26f
317	420	377	629	307	369	ɪ806	2,226	2,813	3,205	3,516	4,450	8,652	17,903	12,661	Credit from Monetary Authorities	26g
7	—	2	1	2	4	....	....	....	....	....	....	....	....	....	Credit from Other Financial Insts.	26i
81	80	174	291	455	676	ɪ1,624	3,039	6,816	9,341	16,680	28,044	50,209	99,670	182,053	Capital Accounts	27a
93	-5	-175	-323	-347	-359	ɪ-880	-2,613	-4,013	-7,793	-14,371	-32,126	-51,846	-78,726	-174,883	Other Items (Net)	27r
Billions of Liras Beginning 1978: End of Period															**Monetary Survey**	
-422	-404	-480	-889	-2,111	-4,304	ɪ-3,410	-6,637	-3,116	1,264	2,134	9,419	32,211	35,893	184,134	Foreign Assets (Net)	31n
1,659	2,482	3,648	5,071	8,965	14,456	ɪ19,572	30,100	44,074	65,713	98,346	168,049	297,767	541,851	1,125,444	Domestic Credit	32
609	798	1,339	1,815	5,062	8,088	ɪ8,385	11,908	18,111	24,529	26,332	52,424	91,815	159,925	460,497	Claims on Central Govt. (Net)	32an
....	....	....	....	....	....	149	383	545	563	753	—	—	—	2,756	Claims on Local Government	32b
339	397	417	456	215	561	....	....	....	....	....	....	....	....	....	Claims on Official Entities	32bx
....	....	....	....	....	....	1,428	2,340	3,866	3,774	7,716	13,823	18,721	36,567	91,749	Claims on Nonfin.Pub.Enterprises	32c
660	1,231	1,814	2,708	3,625	5,725	ɪ9,454	14,484	20,617	34,828	61,060	98,780	182,233	336,615	550,331	Claims on Private Sector	32d
51	56	79	93	62	82	ɪ107	875	677	1,716	2,087	2,362	4,007	6,852	17,918	Claims on Other Banking Insts.	32f
....	....	....	....	....	....	49	109	258	305	397	660	992	1,893	2,192	Claims on Nonbank Fin. Insts.	32g
758	1,024	1,413	2,090	2,487	3,468	ɪ5,062	8,438	11,020	19,092	30,237	44,279	76,373	125,868	228,413	Money	34
187	755	1,275	1,397	3,047	5,125	ɪ9,507	13,489	25,219	42,121	63,566	127,085	229,870	377,469	1,006,296	Quasi-Money	35
....	....	....	....	....	....	787	1,367	1,251	1,979	2,382	3,397	3,709	3,064	4,633	Money Market Instruments	36aa
....	....	....	....	....	....	7	7	54	389	413	704	6,192	24,524	15,757	Bonds	36ab
....	....	....	....	....	....	148	213	341	221	39	15	14	11	12	Restricted Deposits	36b
33	105	229	284	386	606	....	....	....	....	....	....	....	....	....	Central Govt. Lending Funds	36f
259	195	251	412	935	953	ɪ651	-51	3,073	3,176	3,843	1,990	13,821	46,809	54,467	Other Items (Net)	37r
945	1,779	2,688	3,487	5,534	8,593	ɪ14,568	21,926	36,239	61,213	93,803	171,363	306,242	503,336	1,234,709	Money plus Quasi-Money	35l

Turkey

		1965	1966	1967	1968	1969	1970	1971	1972	1973	1974	1975	1976	1977	1978	1979
Other Banking Institutions													*Millions of Liras through 1977;*			
Reserves	40	...	...	...	...	...	211	218	264	333	360	513	608	383	⌡1	1
Foreign Assets	41	...	...	...	...	...	—	—	—	—	—	74	299	3	⌡—	—
Claims on Central Government	42a	...	...	...	...	...	102	102	335	185	343	305	764	1,842	⌡2	2
Claims on Local Government	42b															
Claims on Official Entities	42bx	...	...	...	...	...	10,398	10,636	10,421	12,688	22,312	33,437	55,401	77,766	⌡95	115
Claims on Nonfin.Pub.Enterprises	42c															
Claims on Private Sector	42d	...	...	...	...	...	2,861	2,737	3,092	4,066	4,751	5,931	7,709	9,692	⌡15	27
Claims on Deposit Money Banks	42e	...	...	...	...	...	2,502	2,535	2,894	3,814	4,919	6,159	9,440	12,852	⌡9	10
Claims on Nonbank Fin. Insts.	42g															
Time and Savings Deposits	45															
Bonds	46ab	...	...	...	...	...	7,973	7,927	8,563	11,583	14,930	19,312	30,410	38,526	⌡45	50
Foreign Liabilities	46c															
Long-Term Foreign Liabilities	46cl	...	...	...	...	...	1,729	1,897	2,061	2,815	3,326	4,358	8,759	11,275	⌡17	30
Central Government Deposits	46d	...	...	...	...	...					2,275	2,110	4,466	4,557	⌡6	5
Central Govt. Lending Funds	46f	...	...	...	...	...	2,974	2,602	1,949	1,631						
Credit from Monetary Authorities	46g	...	...	...	...	...	—	—	14	78	6,245	13,514	22,281	35,840	⌡42	47
Credit from Deposit Money Banks	46h	...	...	...	...	...	1,869	1,932	2,028	2,103	2,200	2,157	2,471	1,452	⌡2	2
Capital Accounts	47a	...	...	...	...	...	1,588	1,647	2,075	2,388	2,664	3,060	3,787	6,405	⌡7	11
Other Items (Net)	47r	...	...	...	...	...	−59	223	316	488	1,045	1,908	2,047	4,483	⌡4	9
Banking Survey													*Millions of Liras through 1977;*			
Foreign Assets (Net)	51n	...	...	...	...	...	9	5,625	7,114	13,996	4,513	−15,888	−52,670	−71,597	⌡−100	−153
Domestic Credit	52	...	...	...	...	...	65,209	76,406	91,436	112,058	154,383	229,440	330,285	463,210	⌡620	974
Claims on Central Govt. (Net)	52an	...	...	...	...	...	9,761	12,709	12,813	9,986	14,071	33,589	46,483	87,276	⌡141	250
Claims on Local Government	52b															
Claims on Official Entities	52bx	...	...	...	...	...	20,051	23,764	26,111	33,017	51,389	68,687	114,497	160,470	⌡203	316
Claims on Nonfin.Pub.Enterprises	52c															
Claims on Private Sector	52d	...	...	...	...	...	35,397	39,933	52,512	69,055	88,923	127,164	169,305	215,464	⌡276	408
Claims on Nonbank Fin. Insts.	52g															
Liquid Liabilities	55l	...	...	...	...	...	44,342	56,868	71,680	92,059	115,744	148,112	182,840	245,071	⌡334	541
Bonds	56ab	...	...	...	...	...	8,391	8,329	8,923	11,958	15,316	20,079	31,243	39,828	⌡46	51
Long-Term Foreign Liabilities	56cl	...	...	...	...	...	1,729	1,897	2,061	2,815	3,326	4,358	8,759	11,275	⌡17	30
Central Govt. Lending Funds	56f	...	...	...	...	...	3,518	4,031	3,014	2,583	4,006	4,323	8,408	10,742	⌡15	17
Other Items (Net)	57r	...	...	...	...	...	7,245	10,908	12,865	16,654	20,578	36,698	46,385	84,750	⌡108	181
Interest Rates													*Percent Per Annum*			
Discount Rate (End of Period)	60	7.50	7.50	7.50	7.50	7.50	9.00	9.00	9.00	8.75	9.00	9.00	9.00	9.00	10.00	10.75
Interbank Money Market Rate	60b															
Treasury Bill Rate	60c															
Deposit Rate	60l	...	...	...	...	...	...	...	...	4.00	6.00	6.00	6.00	6.00	6.00	7.33
Prices and Production													*Index Numbers (1990=100):*			
Wholesale Prices	63															
Consumer Prices	64	.1	.1	.1	.1	.1	.2	.2	.2	.2	.3	.3	.4	.5	.7	1.1
Industrial Production	66															
International Transactions													*Millions of Liras through 1977;*			
Exports	70	4,174	4,415	4,701	4,468	4,832	6,408	9,090	11,876	18,038	21,197	20,075	30,775	31,339	⌡55	76
Imports, cif	71	5,193	6,222	6,217	6,934	6,786	10,348	17,726	22,346	29,976	53,362	68,987	82,941	105,000	⌡115	179
Imports, fob	71.v	4,637	5,555	5,536	6,172	6,040	9,213	15,778	19,892	26,676	50,692	65,537	78,785	99,746	⌡109	170
													Millions of US Dollars			
Exports	70..d	464	491	522	496	537	588	677	885	1,317	1,532	1,401	1,960	1,753	2,288	2,261
Imports, cif	71..d	572	718	685	764	801	948	1,171	1,563	2,086	3,778	4,739	5,129	5,796	4,599	5,070
Imports, fob	71.v d	511	641	610	680	713	844	1,042	1,391	1,857	3,589	4,502	4,872	5,506	4,369	4,816
													1990=100			
Volume of Exports	72															
Volume of Imports	73															
Unit Value of Exports	74															
Unit Value of Imports	75															
Balance of Payments													*Millions of US Dollars:*			
Goods: Exports f.o.b.	78aa d										1,532	1,401	1,960	1,753	2,288	2,261
Goods: Imports f.o.b.	78ab d										−3,589	−4,502	−4,872	−5,506	−4,369	−4,815
Trade Balance	78ac d										−2,057	−3,101	−2,912	−3,753	−2,081	−2,554
Services: Credit	78ad d										549	616	580	534	467	674
Services: Debit	78ae d										−366	−436	−517	−687	−310	−367
Balance on Goods and Services	78af d										−1,874	−2,921	−2,849	−3,906	−1,924	−2,247
Income: Credit	78ag d										1	1	1	6	66	34
Income: Debit	78ah d										−178	−165	−301	−347	−506	−1,010
Balance on Goods, Serv., & Inc.	78ai d										−2,051	−3,085	−3,149	−4,247	−2,364	−3,223
Current Transfers, n.i.e.: Credit	78aj d										1,508	1,449	1,134	1,123	1,116	1,829
Current Transfers: Debit	78ak d										−18	−12	−14	−16	−17	−19
Current Account, n.i.e.	78al d										−561	−1,648	−2,029	−3,140	−1,265	−1,413
Capital Account, n.i.e.: Credit	78ba d										—	—	—	—	—	—
Capital Account: Debit	78bb d															
Capital Account, n.i.e.	78bc d										—	—	—	—	—	—
Direct Investment Abroad	78bd d															
Dir. Invest. in Rep. Econ., n.i.e.	78be d										64	114	10	27	34	75
Portfolio Investment Assets	78bf d										—	—	—	—	—	—
Portfolio Investment Liab., n.i.e.	78bg d															
Other Investment Assets	78bh d										—	—	—	149	−17	−109
Other Investment Liab. n.i.e.	78bi d										114	213	1,122	1,469	785	−362
Financial Account, n.i.e.	78bj d										178	327	1,132	1,645	802	−396
Net Errors and Omissions	78ca d										−170	−351	−831	−634	−874	651
Overall Balance	78cb d										−553	−1,672	−1,728	−2,129	−1,337	−1,158
Reserves and Related Items	79da d										553	1,672	1,728	2,129	1,337	1,158
Reserve Assets	79db d										551	383	79	366	−153	148
Use of Fund Credit and Loans	79dc d										—	254	149	—	175	4
Liabs.Constit.For.Auth.Reserves	79dd d										—	—	—	—	—	—
Exceptional Financing	79de d										2	1,035	1,500	1,763	1,315	1,006

Turkey

186

1980	1981	1982	1983	1984	1985	1986	1987	1988	1989	1990	1991	1992	1993	1994		
Billions of Liras Beginning 1978: End of Period															**Other Banking Institutions**	
2	3	3	4	10	14	I 88	294	663	1,746	2,400	5,938	10,381	19,738	52,327	Reserves	**40**
—	1	2	3	4	9	I 10	802	269	1,081	1,582	3,152	4,757	8,859	18,513	Foreign Assets	**41**
2	5	4	4	35	32	I 42	44	119	323	330	449	461	2,623	4,579	Claims on Central Government	**42a**
....	....	....	....	....	....	—	—	—	—	—	1,158	2,292	5,717	5,942	Claims on Local Government	**42b**
127	173	251	304	333	418	....	....	....	....	....	....	....	....	....	Claims on Official Entities	**42bx**
....	....	....	....	....	....	512	613	1,206	1,108	1,614	1,453	1,320	1,713	1,272	Claims on Nonfin.Pub.Enterprises	**42c**
50	84	126	179	301	390	I 585	895	1,778	2,989	4,480	9,406	13,931	22,562	45,137	Claims on Private Sector	**42d**
7	—	2	1	2	4	....	....	....	....	....	....	....	....	....	Claims on Deposit Money Banks	**42e**
....	....	....	....	....	....	—	—	—	18	21	10	119	710	230	Claims on Nonbank Fin. Insts.	**42g**
....	....	....	....	....	....	97	140	321	387	718	793	1,255	1,664	1,827	Time and Savings Deposits	**45**
57	70	71	121	103	147	I 226	510	1,228	2,205	3,102	5,075	8,856	16,545	39,255	Bonds	**46ab**
....	....	....	....	....	....	159	341	693	1,044	1,741	5,071	7,946	13,558	30,961	Foreign Liabilities	**46c**
56	71	94	124	219	318	....	....	....	....	....	....	....	....	....	Long-Term Foreign Liabilities	**46cl**
....	....	....	....	....	....	185	240	311	263	794	4,643	5,309	13,202	23,550	Central Government Deposits	**46d**
9	46	75	70	99	127	....	....	....	....	....	....	....	....	....	Central Govt. Lending Funds	**46f**
49	54	67	76	37	50	I 84	891	711	1,435	1,514	1,121	775	1,364	71	Credit from Monetary Authorities	**46g**
1	1	7	9	18	16	I 281	309	1,166	1,121	1,760	3,348	5,900	11,252	42,689	Credit from Deposit Money Banks	**46h**
14	17	64	79	189	227	I 333	461	603	1,148	2,457	4,825	7,495	12,058	13,174	Capital Accounts	**47a**
3	7	10	16	22	–18	I –128	–243	–997	–337	–1,657	–3,311	–4,278	–7,720	–23,527	Other Items (Net)	**47r**
Billions of Liras Beginning 1978: End of Period															**Banking Survey**	
–421	–403	–478	–885	–2,106	–4,295	I –3,559	–6,175	–3,540	1,301	1,976	7,500	29,021	31,194	171,686	Foreign Assets (Net)	**51n**
1,787	2,688	3,950	5,466	9,571	15,215	I 20,418	30,537	46,189	68,172	101,911	173,519	306,573	555,122	1,141,136	Domestic Credit	**52**
610	803	1,343	1,819	5,098	8,120	I 8,241	11,712	17,919	24,589	25,869	48,230	86,966	149,346	441,527	Claims on Central Govt. (Net)	**52an**
....	....	....	....	....	....	149	383	545	563	753	1,158	2,292	5,717	8,698	Claims on Local Government	**52b**
466	570	668	760	548	980	....	....	....	....	....	....	....	....	....	Claims on Official Entities	**52bx**
....	....	....	....	....	....	1,940	2,954	5,072	4,881	9,330	15,276	20,041	38,279	93,022	Claims on Nonfin.Pub.Enterprises	**52c**
711	1,315	1,939	2,887	3,926	6,116	I 10,039	15,379	22,395	37,817	65,540	108,186	196,164	359,178	595,467	Claims on Private Sector	**52d**
....	....	....	....	....	....	49	109	258	323	419	670	1,110	2,602	2,422	Claims on Nonbank Fin. Insts.	**52g**
943	1,776	2,685	3,483	5,524	8,579	I 15,420	23,325	37,595	62,168	94,611	169,760	300,968	488,455	1,189,694	Liquid Liabilities	**55l**
60	73	78	133	112	154	I 233	517	1,283	2,594	3,515	5,779	15,048	41,069	55,012	Bonds	**56ab**
56	71	94	124	219	318	....	....	....	....	....	....	....	....	....	Long-Term Foreign Liabilities	**56cl**
42	151	304	354	484	734	....	....	....	....	....	....	....	....	....	Central Govt. Lending Funds	**56f**
265	214	311	486	1,127	1,135	I 1,206	520	3,772	4,711	5,761	5,481	19,579	56,791	68,116	Other Items (Net)	**57r**
Percent Per Annum															**Interest Rates**	
26.00	31.50	31.50	48.50	52.00	52.00	48.00	45.00	54.00	54.00	45.00	45.00	....	....	....	Discount Rate *(End of Period)*	**60**
....	....	....	....	....	....	....	39.82	60.62	40.66	51.91	72.75	65.35	62.83	136.47	Interbank Money Market Rate	**60b**
....	....	....	....	....	....	....	41.92	54.56	48.01	43.46	67.01	72.17	....	....	Treasury Bill Rate	**60c**
8.00	26.50	45.00	45.33	51.42	49.25	40.58	35.00	49.08	53.45	47.60	62.93	68.74	64.58	87.79	Deposit Rate	**60l**
Period Averages															**Prices and Production**	
....	3.8	4.9	6.4	9.6	13.7	17.8	I 23.5	40.0	65.7	100.0	155.3	251.8	397.8	880.1	Wholesale Prices	**63**
2.3	3.2	I 4.2	5.5	8.1	11.8	15.8	I 22.0	38.2	62.4	100.0	166.0	282.3	468.8	967.0	Consumer Prices	**64**
....	....	....	....	....	....	78.5	86.8	88.2	91.4	100.0	105.6	111.1	118.6	....	Industrial Production	**66**
Billions of Liras Beginning 1978															**International Transactions**	
221	531	937	1,299	2,608	4,153	5,012	8,844	16,810	24,826	34,034	57,388	101,901	170,699	529,527	Exports	**70**
586	1,006	1,463	2,125	4,023	5,994	7,562	12,357	20,477	33,759	58,819	88,920	159,628	329,022	665,207	Imports, cif	**71**
557	965	1,391	2,016	3,791	5,671	7,154	11,691	19,373	31,939	55,647	84,125	151,020	311,279	629,335	Imports, fob	**71.v**
Millions of US Dollars																
2,910	4,703	5,746	5,728	7,134	7,958	7,457	10,190	11,662	11,625	12,959	13,594	14,716	15,343	....	Exports	**70..*d***
7,910	8,933	8,843	9,235	10,757	11,343	11,105	14,158	14,335	15,792	22,302	21,047	22,872	29,174	....	Imports, cif	**71..*d***
7,514	8,567	8,406	8,761	10,137	10,732	10,506	13,394	13,562	14,940	21,100	19,912	21,638	27,601	....	Imports, fob	**71.v*d***
1990=100																
....	....	....	....	....	....	....	....	....	94.7	100.0	106.7	109.9	117.0	134.3	Volume of Exports	**72**
....	....	....	....	....	....	....	....	....	87.0	100.0	96.1	97.7	133.8	105.0	Volume of Imports	**73**
....	....	....	....	....	....	....	....	....	90.7	100.0	99.0	100.4	97.6	95.0	Unit Value of Exports	**74**
....	....	....	....	....	....	....	....	....	95.0	100.0	97.0	95.1	89.1	90.1	Unit Value of Imports	**75**
Minus Sign Indicates Debit															Balance of Payments	
2,910	4,703	5,890	5,905	7,389	8,255	7,583	10,322	11,929	11,780	13,026	13,672	14,892	15,610	....	Goods: Exports f.o.b.	**78aa*d***
–7,513	–8,567	–8,518	–8,895	–10,331	–11,230	–10,664	–13,551	–13,706	–15,999	–22,581	–20,998	–23,082	–29,772	....	Goods: Imports f.o.b.	**78ab*d***
–4,603	–3,864	–2,628	–2,990	–2,942	–2,975	–3,081	–3,229	–1,777	–4,219	–9,555	–7,326	–8,190	–14,162	....	Trade Balance	**78ac*d***
711	1,264	1,918	1,939	2,157	2,618	2,696	3,520	5,176	5,832	7,275	7,659	8,452	9,511	....	Services: Credit	**78ad*d***
–569	–468	–1,031	–1,166	–1,296	–1,333	–1,428	–1,695	–1,925	–2,465	–3,071	–3,218	–3,625	–3,949	....	Services: Debit	**78ae*d***
–4,461	–3,068	–1,741	–2,217	–2,081	–1,690	–1,813	–1,404	1,474	–852	–5,351	–2,885	–3,363	–8,600	....	Balance on Goods and Services	**78af*d***
51	52	120	102	209	544	642	675	850	1,266	1,658	1,656	1,999	2,332	....	Income: Credit	**78ag*d***
–1,169	–1,478	–1,608	–1,568	–1,649	–1,851	–2,218	–2,467	–2,887	–3,011	–3,425	–3,598	–3,637	–3,880	....	Income: Debit	**78ah*d***
–5,579	–4,494	–3,229	–3,683	–3,521	–2,997	–3,389	–3,196	–563	–2,597	–7,118	–4,827	–5,001	–10,148	....	Balance on Goods, Serv., & Inc.	**78ai*d***
2,184	2,575	2,295	1,806	2,131	2,022	2,030	2,456	2,220	3,574	4,525	5,131	4,075	3,800	....	Current Transfers, n.i.e.: Credit	**78aj*d***
–13	–17	–18	–46	–17	–38	–106	–66	–61	–39	–32	–32	–16	–32	....	Current Transfers: Debit	**78ak*d***
–3,408	–1,936	–952	–1,923	–1,407	–1,013	–1,465	–806	1,596	938	–2,625	272	–942	–6,380	....	Current Account, n.i.e.	**78al*d***
—	—	—	—	—	—	—	—	—	23	—	—	—	—	....	Capital Account, n.i.e.: Credit	**78ba*d***
—	—	—	—	—	—	—	—	—	—	—	—	—	—	....	Capital Account: Debit	**78bb*d***
—	—	—	—	—	—	—	—	—	23	—	—	—	—	....	Capital Account, n.i.e.	**78bc*d***
—	—	—	—	—	—	—	–9	—	—	16	–27	–65	–14	....	Direct Investment Abroad	**78bd*d***
18	95	55	46	113	99	125	115	354	663	684	810	844	636	....	Dir. Invest. in Rep. Econ., n.i.e.	**78be*d***
—	—	—	—	—	—	—	–25	–6	–59	–134	–91	–754	–563	....	Portfolio Investment Assets	**78bf*d***
—	—	—	—	—	—	146	307	1,184	1,445	681	714	3,165	4,480	....	Portfolio Investment Liab., n.i.e.	**78bg*d***
85	360	–181	177	–1,654	127	–313	–945	–1,428	371	–409	–2,563	–2,438	–3,291	....	Other Investment Assets	**78bh*d***
542	444	406	660	1,734	839	2,166	2,448	–1,062	–1,640	3,199	–1,240	2,896	7,715	....	Other Investment Liab., n.i.e.	**78bi*d***
645	899	280	883	193	1,065	2,124	1,891	–958	780	4,037	–2,397	3,648	8,963	....	Financial Account, n.i.e.	**78bj*d***
1,435	650	–76	408	317	–836	–119	–505	515	969	–469	926	–1,222	–2,275	....	Net Errors and Omissions	**78ca*d***
–1,328	–387	–748	–632	–897	–784	540	580	1,153	2,710	943	–1,199	1,484	308	....	Overall Balance	**78cb*d***
1,328	387	748	632	897	784	–540	–580	–1,153	–2,710	–943	1,199	–1,484	–308	....	Reserves and Related Items	**79da*d***
–529	–293	–358	–186	–63	360	–162	–137	–721	–2,471	–895	1,199	–1,484	–308	....	Reserve Assets	**79db*d***
456	365	204	196	–43	–251	–378	–443	–432	–239	–48	—	—	—	....	Use of Fund Credit and Loans	**79dc*d***
—	—	—	—	—	—	—	—	—	—	—	—	—	—	....	Liabs.Constit.For.Auth.Reserves	**79dd*d***
1,400	315	902	622	1,002	676	—	—	—	—	—	—	—	—	....	Exceptional Financing	**79de*d***

Turkey
186

		1965	1966	1967	1968	1969	1970	1971	1972	1973	1974	1975	1976	1977	1978	1979
Government Finance															*Millions of Liras through 1977; Billions of Liras Beginning 1978:*	
Deficit (-) or Surplus	80	....	....	–1,917	–2,636	–3,719	ℐ–3,620	–6,457	–5,105	–5,499	–7,451	–6,998	–13,235	–52,839	ℐ–55	–137
Revenue	81	....	....	16,804	18,743	21,605	ℐ28,820	38,481	47,500	59,384	71,710	109,003	143,732	186,900	ℐ291	497
Grants Received	81z	....	....	—	—	—	ℐ—	—	—	—	—	10	—	—	ℐ—	—
Expenditure	82	....	....	18,721	21,379	25,324	ℐ31,640	44,330	52,393	64,403	77,098	112,931	154,209	229,414	ℐ328	610
Lending Minus Repayments	83	....	....	....	....	....	ℐ800	608	212	480	2,073	3,070	2,758	10,325	ℐ18	23
Financing																
Domestic	84a	....	....	1,099	1,654	3,238	ℐ3,200	5,900	4,360	4,940	7,240	6,920	13,300	52,180	ℐ53	133
Foreign	85a	....	....	818	982	481	ℐ370	484	742	560	206	82	25	567	ℐ2	3
Total Debt	88	....	....	....	....	....	ℐ45,040	58,030	64,490	68,000	78,050	101,100	135,220	207,170	ℐ325	508
Domestic	88a	....	....	....	....	....	ℐ24,330	32,890	36,990	41,560	46,960	70,080	100,280	164,480	ℐ244	405
Foreign	89a	....	....	....	....	....	ℐ20,710	25,140	27,500	26,440	31,090	30,960	34,940	42,690	ℐ80	103
National Accounts															*Billions of Liras*	
Exports of Goods & Services	90c	....	....	....	....	....	....	....	....	....	....	....	....	....	....	....
Government Consumption	91f	....	....	....	....	....	....	....	....	....	....	....	....	....	....	....
Gross Fixed Capital Formation	93e	....	....	....	....	....	....	....	....	....	....	....	....	....	....	....
Increase/Decrease(-) in Stocks	93i	....	....	....	....	....	....	....	....	....	....	....	....	....	....	....
Private Consumption	96f	....	....	....	....	....	....	....	....	....	....	....	....	....	....	....
Imports of Goods & Services	98c	....	....	....	....	....	....	....	....	....	....	....	....	....	....	....
Gross Domestic Product	99b	....	....	....	....	....	....	....	....	....	....	....	....	....	....	....
GDP 1990 Prices *(Billions)*	99b.p	....	....	....	....	....	....	....	....	....	....	....	....	....	....	....
GDP Deflator (1990=100)	99bi p	74,408	79,103	84,375	87,686	92,361	102,924	121,384	141,280	172,247	220,101	256,097	302,020	376,482	540,093	919,999
																Millions:
Population	99z	31.37	32.02	32.66	33.59	34.44	35.32	36.22	37.13	38.07	39.04	40.09	40.92	41.77	42.64	43.53

Monetary Authorities: ℐ Beginning in 1970, data are based on a more detailed classification of accounts and therefore are not strictly comparable with data for earlier periods.
Deposit Money Banks: ℐ Prior to 1968, bankers' required deposits with the State Investment Bank are included in *line 22a* rather than in *line 20*, and claims on government enterprises are included in *line 22d*. ℐ See note to section 10.
Monetary Survey: ℐ See note to section 10.

Government Finance: ℐ Beginning in 1970, data are as reported in the *Government Finance Statistics Yearbook* and cover budgetary central government and some extrabudgetary accounts. ℐ Prior to 1982, data relate to a fiscal year different from calendar year.

Turkey

Government Finance

	1980	1981	1982	1983	1984	1985	1986	1987	1988	1989	1990	1991	1992	1993	1994		Code
	\multicolumn{6}{l}{*Year Ending February 28/29 through 1981, December 31 Thereafter*}												
Deficit (-) or Surplus	−161	−117	....	‡483	−1,815	−2,050	−1,259	−2,346	−3,858	−7,502	−11,781	−33,317	−47,328	−133,011 P	....		80
Revenue	957	1,446	....	‡2,309	2,721	4,836	7,052	10,430	17,547	31,254	54,937	90,650	176,370	355,736 P	....		81
Grants Received	—	—	—	‡—	—	—	—	15	41	115	1,636	8,434	1,700	1,597 P	....		81z
Expenditure	1,117	1,526	....	‡2,791	4,535	6,884	8,294	12,773	21,424	38,840	68,316	132,350	225,256	490,129 P	....		82
Lending Minus Repayments	1	37	....	‡2	2	1	18	18	22	32	38	51	142	215 P	....		83
Financing																	
Domestic	137	29	....	....	....	....	1,158	....	3,683	7,907	11,913	31,596	43,395	112,701 P	....		84a
Foreign	24	88	....	....	....	....	101	....	176	−404	−131	1,721	3,933	20,310 P	....		85a
Total Debt	968	2,052	....	....	5,033	7,101	10,801	....	57,937	86,925	118,883	202,456	371,934	667,854 P	....		88
Domestic	621	1,131	....	....	....	3,671	6,417	....	28,458	41,934	57,180	97,647	194,237	356,555 P	....		88a
Foreign	347	922	....	‡2,567	....	3,431	4,384	....	29,479	44,991	61,703	104,809	177,697	311,299 P	....		89a

National Accounts

Billions of Liras

	1980	1981	1982	1983	1984	1985	1986	1987	1988	1989	1990	1991	1992	1993	1994		Code
Exports of Goods & Services	....	....	....	....	....	....	....	11,642	24,106	36,833	52,214	87,216	157,360	270,995	....		90c
Government Consumption	....	....	....	....	....	....	....	5,845	9,836	21,239	43,082	78,255	141,317	254,889	....		91f
Gross Fixed Capital Formation	....	....	....	....	....	....	....	18,491	33,738	51,836	89,892	149,272	251,435	484,587	....		93e
Increase/Decrease(-) in Stocks	....	....	....	....	....	....	....	688	−1,245	1,523	6,602	−6,159	4,000	21,620	....		93i
Private Consumption	....	....	....	....	....	....	....	51,017	82,050	149,140	269,564	434,365	734,305	1,289,008	....		96f
Imports of Goods & Services	....	....	....	....	....	....	....	−13,268	−22,682	−40,420	−69,043	−104,820	−189,645	−383,357	....		98c
Gross Domestic Product	....	....	....	....	....	....	....	74,416	125,801	220,151	392,312	638,129	1,098,772	1,937,742	....		99b
GDP 1990 Prices *(Billions)*	....	....	....	....	....	....	....	350,177	358,299	359,344	392,312	395,465	415,384	439,628	....		99b.p
GDP Deflator (1990=100)	1,861,226	2,642,770	3,389,625	4,364,155	6,518,130	9,382,138		21	35	61	100	161	265	441	....		99bi p

Midyear Estimates

	1980	1981	1982	1983	1984	1985	1986	1987	1988	1989	1990	1991	1992	1993	1994		Code
Population	44.47	45.47	46.69	47.86	49.07	50.31	51.43	52.56	53.71	54.89	56.10	57.33	58.58	59.87	61.18		99z

Uganda

		1965	1966	1967	1968	1969	1970	1971	1972	1973	1974	1975	1976	1977	1978	1979
Exchange Rates														*Shillings per thousand SDRs through 1984*		
Principal Rate	aa	71.4	71.4	71.4	71.4	71.4	71.4	77.6	77.6	83.2	87.5	96.6	96.6	96.6	96.6	96.6
												Shillings per Thousand US Dollars through 1984				
Principal Rate	ae	71.4	71.4	71.4	71.4	71.4	71.4	71.4	71.4	69.0	71.4	82.6	83.1	79.5	74.2	73.3
Principal Rate	rf	71.4	71.4	71.4	71.4	71.4	71.4	71.4	71.4	70.2	71.4	74.2	82.7	82.6	77.4	74.8
														Index Numbers (1990=100):		
Principal Rate	ah x	....	....	....	....	....	....	....	....	....	....	....	....	....	....	....
Nominal Effective Exchange Rate	ne c	....	....	....	....	....	....	....	....	....	....	....	....	....	....	....
Real Effective Exchange Rate	re c	....	....	....	....	....	....	....	....	....	....	....	....	....	....	524.24
Fund Position															*Millions of SDRs:*	
Quota	2f.s	25.0	32.0	32.0	32.0	32.0	40.0	40.0	40.0	40.0	40.0	40.0	40.0	40.0	50.0	50.0
SDRs	1b.s	—	—	—	—	—	5.4	9.6	13.7	13.4	5.0	3.2	.9	4.5	8.1	8.4
Reserve Position in the Fund	1c.s	2.3	4.0	4.0	4.0	4.5	6.5	—	—	—	—	—	—	—	5.9	—
Total Fund Cred.&Loans Outstg.	2tl	—	—	—	—	—	—	10.0	10.0	10.0	15.0	24.1	32.7	32.7	29.2	26.2
International Liquidity												*Millions of US Dollars Unless Otherwise Indicated:*				
Total Reserves minus Gold	1l.d	....	40.9	34.9	49.0	52.3	56.6	26.9	36.0	29.1	16.8	31.0	44.5	47.2	52.7	22.8
SDRs	1b.d	—	—	—	—	—	5.4	10.4	14.9	16.2	6.2	3.7	1.0	5.4	10.5	11.0
Reserve Position in the Fund	1c.d	2.3	4.0	4.0	4.0	4.5	6.5	—	—	—	—	—	—	—	7.7	—
Foreign Exchange	1d.d	....	36.9	30.9	45.0	47.8	44.8	16.5	21.1	12.9	10.6	27.3	43.5	41.8	34.5	11.8
Deposit Money Banks: Assets	7a.d	16.2	7.7	12.5	6.9	11.0	9.9	8.7	9.0	5.5	9.9	12.2	17.7	32.2	31.5	33.3
Liabilities	7b.d	32.1	16.2	10.1	7.2	3.4	2.2	5.6	8.4	3.3	7.1	2.7	7.4	12.0	5.6	18.8
Monetary Authorities												*Thousands of Shillings through 1978;*				
Foreign Assets	11	....	4,200	I 2,495	3,511	3,734	4,079	1,923	2,568	2,009	1,197	2,561	3,703	3,755	3,909	I 2
Claims on Central Government	12a	....	1,460	1,720	1,437	1,812	3,369	6,951	7,952	12,383	16,702	23,547	31,912	38,662	54,424	I 73
Claims on Official Entities	12bx	....	450	600	600	600	600	600	600	600	600	600	693	1,062	1,466	I 1
Claims on Private Sector	12d	....	....	....	....	....	....	....	....	....	....	....	....	....	....	....
Claims on Deposit Money Banks	12e	....	—	100	211	637	277	30	—	—	—	—	—	—	—	I —
Reserve Money	14	....	4,290	4,840	5,411	5,989	6,971	7,019	7,956	10,120	13,353	21,004	30,077	34,374	51,109	I 85
of which: Currency Outside DMBs	14a	....	3,470	3,670	4,284	5,177	5,901	5,934	6,157	7,959	10,920	13,672	22,052	28,891	35,312	I 58
Foreign Liabilities	16c	....	1,430	10	—	—	—	775	1,147	1,232	1,724	2,610	3,461	3,662	3,222	I 4
Central Government Deposits	16d	....	470	360	3	133	7	13	12	16	8	3	6	6	1	I —
Capital Accounts	17a	....	50	150	173	400	938	1,214	1,563	1,675	1,721	1,876	1,897	2,440	2,446	I 2
Other Items (Net)	17r	....	−130	−450	151	214	457	427	413	1,913	1,728	1,256	901	3,035	2,979	I −16
of which: Valuation Adjustment	17rv	....	....	....	−320	−340	−519	−427	−429	−514	−458	−671	−673	−631	−26	I —
Deposit Money Banks												*Thousands of Shillings through 1978;*				
Reserves	20	470	680	789	868	710	988	1,083	1,550	2,058	2,995	8,754	8,599	5,233	14,844	I 31
Foreign Assets	21	I 1,160	550	896	490	788	706	620	640	380	710	1,010	1,468	2,565	2,336	I 2
Claims on Central Government	22a	2,400	470	297	1,186	1,848	2,642	2,760	6,800	10,880	14,500	12,510	16,881	17,345	19,731	I 23
Claims on Official Entities	22bx												1,000	4,000	5,000	I 6
Claims on Private Sector	22d	5,050	5,830	6,004	6,691	8,270	8,493	8,740	9,390	11,470	14,840	16,290	17,312	23,155	24,978	I 26
Demand Deposits	24	2,660	3,270	3,310	4,229	4,423	5,090	5,283	9,081	13,070	19,013	18,672	22,372	28,826	34,453	I 47
Time and Savings Deposits	25	2,120	3,360	3,446	3,998	4,417	5,617	5,283	6,025	7,700	8,533	14,256	17,428	16,126	22,937	I 31
Foreign Liabilities	26c	2,290	1,160	724	517	242	159	400	600	230	510	220	613	953	418	I 1
Central Government Deposits	26d	2,220	100	791	211	225	217	321	304	344	171	421	176	327	708	I 1
Credit from Monetary Authorities	26g	30	—	85	215	708	229	30	—	—	—	—	—	—	—	I —
Capital Accounts	27a	40	310	344	414	1,608	1,459	1,480	1,310	1,520	1,770	1,800	4,635	5,878	7,293	I 9
Other Items (Net)	27r	−260	−660	−716	−350	139	232	−71	573	851	1,612	1,046	38	188	1,079	I —
Monetary Survey												*Thousands of Shillings through 1978;*				
Foreign Assets (Net)	31n	....	2,160	I 2,657	3,484	4,279	4,625	1,368	1,461	927	−327	741	1,097	1,705	2,605	I −1
Domestic Credit	32	....	7,640	7,980	9,700	12,174	14,875	18,795	24,426	34,991	46,723	52,584	67,689	84,087	105,094	I 129
Claims on Central Govt. (Net)	32an	....	1,360	1,390	2,413	3,304	5,785	9,377	14,436	22,903	31,023	35,633	48,611	55,674	73,446	I 95
Claims on Official Entities	32bx	....	450	600	600	600	600	600	600	600	600	600	1,693	5,062	6,466	I 7
Claims on Private Sector	32d	5,050	5,830	5,990	6,690	8,270	8,490	8,740	9,390	11,470	14,840	16,290	17,312	23,155	24,978	I 26
Money	34	....	6,740	7,280	8,819	9,685	11,001	11,240	15,325	21,140	29,975	32,391	44,472	57,724	69,780	I 106
Quasi-Money	35	2,120	3,360	3,446	3,998	4,417	5,617	5,283	6,025	7,700	8,533	14,256	17,428	16,126	22,937	I 31
Other Items (Net)	37r	....	−290	−600	65	2,407	2,549	3,107	4,021	5,969	6,487	4,570	6,922	11,980	14,939	I −10
Money plus Quasi-Money	35l	....	10,100	10,726	12,817	14,102	16,618	16,523	21,350	28,840	38,508	46,647	61,900	73,850	92,717	I 137
Interest Rates															*Percent Per Annum*	
Bank Rate (End of Period)	60	....	....	....	....	....	....	....	....	....	....	....	....	....	....	....
Treasury Bill Rate	60c	....	....	....	....	....	....	....	....	....	....	....	....	....	....	....
Deposit Rate	60l	....	....	....	....	....	....	....	....	....	....	....	....	....	....	....
Lending Rate	60p	....	....	....	....	....	....	....	....	....	....	....	....	....	....	....
Government Bond Yield	61	....	....	....	....	....	....	....	....	....	....	....	....	....	....	....
Prices															*Index Numbers (1990=100):*	
Consumer Prices	64	....	....	....	....	....	....	....	....	....	....	....	....	....	....	....

Uganda

	1980	1981	1982	1983	1984	1985	1986	1987	1988	1989	1990	1991	1992	1993	1994		
Exchange Rates																	
and per SDR thereafter: End of Period																	
Principal Rate	96.6	991.1	1,167.3	2,512.7	5,097.1	‡15.4	17.1	85.1	222.0	486.2	768.2	1,308.8	1,673.6	1,552.3	1,352.9	aa	
and per US Dollar thereafter: End of Period (ae) Period Average (rf)																	
Principal Rate	75.7	851.5	1,058.2	2,400.0	5,200.0	‡14.0	14.0	60.0	165.0	370.0	540.0	915.0	1,217.2	1,130.2	926.8	ae	
Principal Rate	74.2	500.5	940.5	1,538.6	3,597.0	‡6.7	14.0	42.8	106.1	223.1	428.9	734.0	1,133.8	1,195.0	979.4	rf	
Period Averages																	
Principal Rate	....	....	45,262.09	29,221.64	12,647.52	6,667.06	3,023.64	1,512.03	491.90	201.58	100.00	59.31	37.57	35.44	43.64	ah x	
Nominal Effective Exchange Rate	....	59,066.61	12,441.42	9,104.99	5,321.70	3,433.91	1,507.53	753.69	284.46	155.91	100.00	71.97	55.50	74.32	120.24	ne c	
Real Effective Exchange Rate	931.24	659.16	228.67	179.76	121.40	158.52	166.88	213.95	193.06	163.75	100.00	76.67	69.94	72.71	91.24	re c	
Fund Position																	
End of Period																	
Quota	75.0	75.0	75.0	99.6	99.6	99.6	99.6	99.6	99.6	99.6	99.6	99.6	133.9	133.9	133.9	2f. s	
SDRs	—	2.6	10.1	.9	.2	—	—	—	—	—	4.8	7.2	6.6	—	2.1	1b. s	
Reserve Position in the Fund	—	—	3.5	3.5	3.5	3.5	3.5	—	—	—	—	—	—	—	—	1c. s	
Total Fund Cred.&Loans Outstg.	70.1	182.5	265.9	360.6	343.8	277.6	203.4	192.8	187.6	171.2	198.2	230.9	250.1	243.0	262.6	2tl	
International Liquidity																	
End of Period																	
Total Reserves minus Gold	3.0	30.0	78.3	106.5	‡67.9	27.3	29.2	54.6	49.3	14.1	44.0	58.9	94.4	146.4	321.2	1l. d	
SDRs	—	3.0	11.1	.9	.2	—	—	—	—	—	6.8	10.3	9.0	.1	3.1	1b. d	
Reserve Position in the Fund	—	—	3.9	3.7	3.5	3.9	4.3	—	—	—	—	—	—	—	—	1c. d	
Foreign Exchange	3.0	27.0	63.3	101.9	‡64.3	23.4	24.9	54.6	49.3	14.1	37.2	48.6	85.4	146.3	318.1	1d. d	
Deposit Money Banks: Assets	18.5	11.7	25.1	29.6	26.8	11.5	21.4	29.5	15.5	15.7	27.3	43.0	72.2	91.3	....	7a. d	
Liabilities	4.2	1.0	6.3	9.8	7.2	3.4	7.3	5.2	6.4	6.6	14.5	13.2	21.6	78.6	....	7b. d	
Monetary Authorities																	
Millions of Shillings Beginning 1979: End of Period																	
Foreign Assets	—	36	83	256	353	382	409	....	....	....	....	....	‡117,077	172,280	299,209	11	
Claims on Central Government	127	232	328	‡866	1,334	2,814	4,735	....	....	....	....	....	‡792,168	791,086	963,068	12a	
Claims on Official Entities	1	2	3	62	22	108	39	....	....	....	....	....	‡24,257	20,753	23,188	12bx	
Claims on Private Sector	....	....	....	....	....	—	—	....	....	....	....	....	‡4,768	4,357	4,244	12d	
Claims on Deposit Money Banks	—	2	20	45	89	—	22	....	....	....	....	....	‡10,126	6,272	1,085	12e	
Reserve Money	116	152	180	293	649	1,816	4,717	....	....	....	....	....	‡147,046	181,523	262,675	14	
of which: Currency Outside DMBs	73	114	128	189	487	1,050	3,509	....	....	....	....	....	‡98,335	132,638	....	14a	
Foreign Liabilities	8	217	351	915	1,802	4,314	3,591	....	....	....	....	....	‡421,733	379,308	362,371	16c	
Central Government Deposits	—	7	11	‡445	576	1,106	2,452	....	....	....	....	....	‡464,830	550,278	829,914	16d	
Capital Accounts	2	32	33	76	176	204	217	....	....	....	....	....	‡80,792	61,501	20,493	17a	
Other Items (Net)	2	-135	-141	-501	-1,405	-4,137	-5,772	....	....	....	....	....	‡-166006	-177,863	-184,660	17r	
of which: Valuation Adjustment	-1	131	90	451	1,369	4,271	7,155	....	....	....	....	....	....	....	....	17rv	
Deposit Money Banks																	
Millions of Shillings Beginning 1979: End of Period																	
Reserves	46	41	26	60	246	715	968	2,481	2,750	4,829	11,989	27,386	34,640	37,059	....	20	
Foreign Assets	1	10	27	71	140	161	299	1,773	2,550	5,802	14,742	39,334	87,883	103,218	....	21	
Claims on Central Government	26	92	51	41	26	30	46	38	338	126	2,740	986	5,846	14,273	....	22a	
Claims on Official Entities	9	5	82	66	123	424	1,699	3,423	4,370	6,343	12,120	23,713	27,909	35,456	....	22bx	
Claims on Private Sector	49	107	129	214	222	608	1,236	3,496	10,866	29,633	49,364	64,572	105,081	142,761	....	22d	
Demand Deposits	66	166	165	235	460	1,140	2,449	7,465	15,948	32,871	47,660	78,626	107,676	126,757	....	24	
Time and Savings Deposits	45	62	87	109	176	366	1,056	2,014	3,227	8,480	19,400	30,837	57,880	99,742	....	25	
Foreign Liabilities	—	1	7	24	37	48	102	314	1,052	2,427	7,834	12,115	26,272	88,873	....	26c	
Central Government Deposits	1	1	1	1	1	2	5	154	485	1,174	1,762	2,153	8,152	11,194	....	26d	
Credit from Monetary Authorities	—	3	3	—	—	—	—	—	492	1,303	4,809	9,617	7,582	10,474	....	26g	
Capital Accounts	10	14	58	247	221	415	533	1,723	4,848	8,942	39,704	48,947	51,137	37,701	....	27a	
Other Items (Net)	9	9	-6	-164	-140	-32	102	-460	-5,178	-8,463	-30,214	-26,305	2,660	-41,973	....	27r	
Monetary Survey																	
Millions of Shillings Beginning 1979: End of Period																	
Foreign Assets (Net)	-6	-171	-248	-612	-1,347	-3,819	-2,985	....	....	....	....	....	‡-243046	-192,683	....	31n	
Domestic Credit	211	430	582	803	1,152	2,876	5,299	....	....	....	....	....	‡487,348	448,155	....	32	
Claims on Central Govt. (Net)	151	316	367	461	783	1,736	2,324	....	....	....	....	....	‡325,033	243,887	....	32an	
Claims on Official Entities	10	7	85	128	145	532	1,738	....	....	....	....	....	‡52,166	56,209	....	32bx	
Claims on Private Sector	49	107	129	214	222	608	1,236	....	....	....	....	....	‡109,849	147,118	....	32d	
Money	140	283	298	435	987	2,256	6,062	....	....	....	....	....	‡214,463	269,945	....	34	
Quasi-Money	45	62	87	109	176	366	1,056	2,014	3,227	8,480	19,400	30,837	57,880	99,742	....	35	
Other Items (Net)	20	-87	-51	-353	-1,358	-3,565	-4,804	....	....	....	....	....	‡-28,041	-114,215	....	37r	
Money plus Quasi-Money	185	346	385	544	1,163	2,622	7,118	....	....	....	....	....	‡272,342	369,687	....	35l	
Interest Rates																	
Percent Per Annum																	
Bank Rate (End of Period)	8.00	10.00	11.00	15.50	24.00	24.00	36.00	31.00	45.00	55.00	50.00	46.00	41.00	24.00	15.00	60	
Treasury Bill Rate	5.08	6.08	9.50	11.17	18.00	22.00	30.67	30.50	33.00	42.17	41.00	34.17	....	‡21.30	12.52	60c	
Deposit Rate	6.80	7.23	9.00	10.67	16.00	‡20.00	23.33	20.00	21.50	32.17	31.25	31.17	35.83	16.26	9.99	60l	
Lending Rate	10.80	12.50	14.50	16.17	21.92	24.00	33.33	34.67	35.00	40.00	38.67	34.42	....	....	....	60p	
Government Bond Yield	....	10.00	12.00	12.63	18.00	24.00	38.33	40.00	38.50	45.33	44.50	42.00	43.50	....	....	61	
Prices																	
Period Averages																	
Consumer Prices	....	—	—	1	‡1	2	5	16	47	75	100	128	195	207	227	64	

Uganda
746

		1965	1966	1967	1968	1969	1970	1971	1972	1973	1974	1975	1976	1977	1978	1979
International Transactions													*Thousands of Shillings through 1978;*			
Exports	70	1,474	1,551	1,563	1,541	1,661	2,013	1,857	2,019	2,043	2,250	1,902	3,006	4,859	2,682	ℐ32
Imports, cif (Cash Basis)	71	11,510	11,880	11,380	11,760	12,470	12,290	17,830	11,570	11,380	15,220	15,270	14,240	19,920	19,630	ℐ15
Imports, fob (Cash Basis)	71.v	10,369	10,703	10,252	10,595	11,234	11,072	16,063	10,423	10,252	13,712	13,757	12,829	17,946	17,685	ℐ13
Balance of Payments													*Millions of US Dollars:*			
Goods: Exports f.o.b.	78aa d	....	....	....	....	....	....	....	....	....	....	....	....	....	....	....
Goods: Imports f.o.b.	78ab d	....	....	....	....	....	....	....	....	....	....	....	....	....	....	....
Trade Balance	78ac d	....	....	....	....	....	....	....	....	....	....	....	....	....	....	....
Services: Credit	78ad d	....	....	....	....	....	....	....	....	....	....	....	....	....	....	....
Services: Debit	78ae d	....	....	....	....	....	....	....	....	....	....	....	....	....	....	....
Balance on Goods and Services	78af d	....	....	....	....	....	....	....	....	....	....	....	....	....	....	....
Income: Credit	78ag d	....	....	....	....	....	....	....	....	....	....	....	....	....	....	....
Income: Debit	78ah d	....	....	....	....	....	....	....	....	....	....	....	....	....	....	....
Balance on Goods, Serv., & Inc.	78ai d	....	....	....	....	....	....	....	....	....	....	....	....	....	....	....
Current Transfers, n.i.e.: Credit	78aj d	....	....	....	....	....	....	....	....	....	....	....	....	....	....	....
Current Transfers: Debit	78ak d	....	....	....	....	....	....	....	....	....	....	....	....	....	....	....
Current Account, n.i.e.	78al d	....	....	....	....	....	....	....	....	....	....	....	....	....	....	....
Capital Account, n.i.e.: Credit	78ba d	....	....	....	....	....	....	....	....	....	....	....	....	....	....	....
Capital Account: Debit	78bb d	....	....	....	....	....	....	....	....	....	....	....	....	....	....	....
Capital Account, n.i.e.	78bc d	....	....	....	....	....	....	....	....	....	....	....	....	....	....	....
Direct Investment Abroad	78bd d	....	....	....	....	....	....	....	....	....	....	....	....	....	....	....
Dir. Invest. in Rep. Econ., n.i.e.	78be d	....	....	....	....	....	....	....	....	....	....	....	....	....	....	....
Portfolio Investment Assets	78bf d	....	....	....	....	....	....	....	....	....	....	....	....	....	....	....
Portfolio Investment Liab., n.i.e.	78bg d	....	....	....	....	....	....	....	....	....	....	....	....	....	....	....
Other Investment Assets	78bh d	....	....	....	....	....	....	....	....	....	....	....	....	....	....	....
Other Investment Liab., n.i.e.	78bi d	....	....	....	....	....	....	....	....	....	....	....	....	....	....	....
Financial Account, n.i.e.	78bj d	....	....	....	....	....	....	....	....	....	....	....	....	....	....	....
Net Errors and Omissions	78ca d	....	....	....	....	....	....	....	....	....	....	....	....	....	....	....
Overall Balance	78cb d	....	....	....	....	....	....	....	....	....	....	....	....	....	....	....
Reserves and Related Items	79da d	....	....	....	....	....	....	....	....	....	....	....	....	....	....	....
Reserve Assets	79db d	....	....	....	....	....	....	....	....	....	....	....	....	....	....	....
Use of Fund Credit and Loans	79dc d	....	....	....	....	....	....	....	....	....	....	....	....	....	....	....
Liabs.Constit.For.Auth.Reserves	79dd d	....	....	....	....	....	....	....	....	....	....	....	....	....	....	....
Exceptional Financing	79de d	....	....	....	....	....	....	....	....	....	....	....	....	....	....	....
Government Finance													*Thousands of Shillings through 1978;*			
Deficit (-) or Surplus	80	....	....	....	....	....	−4,134	−7,519	ℐ−8,990	−8,610	−15,260	−12,370	−13,180	−12,780	−1,600	ℐ−35
Revenue	81	....	....	....	....	....	10,838	12,880	ℐ15,320	12,400	11,400	20,890	23,510	34,200	57,930	ℐ26
Grants Received	81z	....	....	....	....	....	....	....	ℐ60	30	390	20	1,060	190	—	ℐ—
Expenditure	82	....	....	....	....	....	14,972	20,399	ℐ24,370	21,040	27,050	33,280	37,750	47,170	59,530	ℐ61
Lending Minus Repayments	83	....	....	....	....	....	....	....	ℐ—	....	....	....	....	....	....	ℐ—
Financing																
Total Financing	84	....	....	....	....	....	....	....	....	....	....	....	....	....	....	....
Net Borrowing: Domestic	84a	....	....	....	....	....	2,770	3,819	....	....	....	....	....	....	....	....
Foreign	85a	....	....	....	....	....	1,663	3,642	....	....	....	ℐ4,430	3,120	2,620	1,100	ℐ5
Use of Cash Balances	87	....	....	....	....	....	−299	58	....	....	....	....	....	....	....	....
Adj. to Total Financing	84x	....	....	....	....	....	....	....	....	....	....	....	....	....	....	....
Debt: Domestic	88a	....	....	....	....	....	....	....	....	....	....	....	....	....	....	ℐ84
National Accounts													*Thousands of Shillings through 1978;*			
Exports of Goods & Services	90c	....	....	....	ℐ17,000	18,000	21,000	20,000	21,000	20,000	22,000	18,000	28,000	46,000	26,000	....
Government Consumption	91f	....	....	....	....	....	....	....	....	....	....	....	....	....	....	....
Gross Fixed Capital Formation	93e	....	....	....	ℐ11,000	12,000	12,000	17,000	13,000	10,000	16,000	15,000	12,000	18,000	19,000	....
Increase/Decrease(-) in Stocks	93i	....	....	....	ℐ—	2,000	1,000	—	−1,000	1,000	1,000	2,000	3,000	5,000	6,000	....
Private Consumption	96f	....	....	....	ℐ62,000	68,000	79,000	91,000	98,000	115,000	144,000	213,000	245,000	456,000	628,000	....
Imports of Goods & Services	98c	....	....	....	ℐ−16,000	−17,000	−18,000	−24,000	−18,000	−16,000	−22,000	−23,000	−24,000	−39,000	−35,000	....
Gross Domestic Product	99b	44,700	46,700	49,600	ℐ74,000	83,400	94,500	103,700	113,900	129,500	160,300	225,000	264,500	485,700	643,000	ℐ996
GDP 1990 Prices *(Millions)*	99b.p	....	....	....	....	....	1,188,122	1,222,889	1,231,050	1,223,542	1,225,664	1,200,854	1,209,668	1,228,602	1,161,353	1,033,220
GDP Deflator *(1990=100)*	99bi p	....	....	....	....	....	—	—	—	—	—	—	—	—	.1	.1
																Millions:
Population	99z	8.58	8.81	9.05	9.30	9.55	9.81	10.13	10.46	10.81	11.17	11.55	11.94	12.35	12.78	13.22

Exchange Rates: On August 15, 1966 the Uganda shilling, equal to the East African shilling, was introduced.
International Liquidity: ℐ Beginning in October 1984, data for *Foreign Exchange (line 1d.d)* are based on the U.S. dollar values of the Bank of Uganda's foreign exchange holdings, as reported by the Foreign Exchange Operations Department of the Bank of Uganda. Previous data were obtained by converting the shilling values of these assets, as maintained by the Accounts Department of the Bank of Uganda, using the prevailing exchange rate given in *line ae.*
Monetary Authorities: ℐ Beginning in June 1983, *Claims on Central Government (line 12a)* and *Central Government Deposits (line 16d)* are presented on a gross basis. Prior to that date, the main government accounts were shown on a net basis in *line 12a.* ℐ Data for 1987 onwards are not comparable with prior periods, owing to a reclassification of accounts. For 1987 through 1991, data are available only as of June each year, which is the end of the financial year for the Bank of Uganda. *Other Items (Net) (line 17r):* A large component of this aggregate represents valuation adjustments related to Fund accounts.
Deposit Money Banks: ℐ Before 1965, data for *line 21* are net of foreign liabilities and exclude intraterritorial claims.
Interest Rates: *Treasury Bill Rate:* ℐ Through April 1992, rates were determined by the Bank of Uganda. From May 1992, rates are determined at auctions held every two weeks.
Government Finance: ℐ Beginning in 1972, data are as reported in the *Government Finance Statistics Yearbook* and cover budgetary central government. ℐ Beginning in 1986, data are as reported by the Bank of Uganda for inclusion in *IFS* and cover budgetary central government. Data relate to a fiscal year different from calendar year.

Uganda

	1980	1981	1982	1983	1984	1985	1986	1987	1988	1989	1990	1991	1992	1993	1994		
Millions of Shillings Beginning 1979																**International Transactions**	
	26	122	328	593	1,388	2,600	6,100	13,684	29,070	55,674	64,653	146,661	159,387	213,846	393,960	Exports	70
	22	....	....	....	....	....	4,300	36,336	94,112	87,851	125,059	137,250	580,685	....	850,411	Imports, cif (Cash Basis)	71
	20	....	....	....	....	....	3,874	32,735	84,786	79,145	112,666	123,649	523,140	....	766,136	Imports, fob (Cash Basis)	71.v
Minus Sign Indicates Debit																**Balance of Payments**	
	319.4	228.8	347.1	367.7	407.3	347.8	406.8	333.6	266.3	277.7	177.8	173.2	151.2	196.7	....	Goods: Exports f.o.b.	78aa *d*
	−317.6	−284.3	−337.6	−342.5	−286.8	−238.3	−360.9	−475.6	−523.5	−588.3	−491.0	−377.1	−421.9	−474.7	....	Goods: Imports f.o.b.	78ab *d*
	1.8	−55.5	9.5	25.2	120.5	109.5	45.9	−142.0	−257.2	−310.6	−313.2	−203.9	−270.7	−278.0	....	Trade Balance	78ac *d*
	9.9	44.3	—	—	16.8	23.1	11.8	—	—	—	—	20.8	34.5	93.6	....	Services: Credit	78ad *d*
	−123.4	−100.4	−160.4	−150.0	−82.3	−129.9	−130.5	−218.2	−235.2	−237.2	−195.3	−241.8	−247.7	−283.1	....	Services: Debit	78ae *d*
	−111.7	−111.6	−150.9	−124.8	55.0	2.7	−72.8	−360.2	−492.4	−547.8	−508.5	−424.9	−483.9	−467.5	....	Balance on Goods and Services	78af *d*
	1.4	.8	—	—	—	1.5	2.9	—	—	—	—	2.8	4.1	6.4	....	Income: Credit	78ag *d*
	−8.8	−13.2	−26.3	−50.9	−36.9	−21.0	−38.9	−18.0	−25.2	−23.3	−47.8	−76.7	−88.3	−71.2	....	Income: Debit	78ah *d*
	−119.1	−124.0	−177.2	−175.7	18.1	−16.8	−108.8	−378.2	−517.6	−571.1	−556.3	−498.8	−568.1	−532.3	....	Balance on Goods, Serv., & Inc.	78ai *d*
	40.0	125.7	107.3	103.5	85.4	21.7	66.6	266.2	322.4	311.6	293.0	329.0	468.5	425.0	....	Current Transfers, n.i.e.: Credit	78aj *d*
	−3.6	−.5	—	—	—	−.3	−1.1	—	—	—	—	—	—	—	....	Current Transfers: Debit	78ak *d*
	−82.7	1.2	−69.9	−72.2	103.5	4.6	−43.3	−112.0	−195.2	−259.5	−263.3	−169.8	−99.6	−107.3	....	Current Account, n.i.e.	78al *d*
	—	—	—	—	—	—	—	—	—	—	—	—	—	—	....	Capital Account, n.i.e.: Credit	78ba *d*
	−.5	—	—	—	—	—	—	—	—	—	—	—	—	—	....	Capital Account: Debit	78bb *d*
	−.5	—	—	—	—	—	—	—	—	—	—	—	—	—	....	Capital Account, n.i.e.	78bc *d*
	—	—	—	—	—	—	—	—	—	—	—	—	—	—	....	Direct Investment Abroad	78bd *d*
	—	—	—	—	—	—	—	—	—	—	—	1.0	3.0	3.4	....	Dir. Invest. in Rep. Econ., n.i.e.	78be *d*
	—	—	—	—	—	—	—	—	—	—	—	—	—	—	....	Portfolio Investment Assets	78bf *d*
	—	—	—	—	—	—	—	—	—	—	—	—	—	—	....	Portfolio Investment Liab., n.i.e.	78bg *d*
	14.7	6.8	−13.4	−4.5	30.1	69.3	131.8	—	—	—	—	.4	1.8	37.4	....	Other Investment Assets	78bh *d*
	−81.2	−103.1	28.2	32.2	−88.3	11.5	−114.7	31.2	3.6	213.0	211.8	136.2	110.0	119.2	....	Other Investment Liab., n.i.e.	78bi *d*
	−66.5	−96.3	14.8	27.7	−58.2	80.8	17.1	31.2	3.6	213.0	211.8	137.6	114.8	160.0	....	Financial Account, n.i.e.	78bj *d*
	−64.6	−31.7	−24.7	−36.6	21.6	−52.2	−.6	26.4	154.9	−38.0	9.5	.6	9.0	5.5	....	Net Errors and Omissions	78ca *d*
	−214.3	−126.8	−79.8	−81.1	66.9	33.2	−26.8	−54.4	−36.7	−84.5	−41.9	−31.7	24.2	58.1	....	Overall Balance	78cb *d*
	214.3	126.8	79.8	81.1	−66.9	−33.2	26.8	54.4	36.7	84.5	41.9	31.7	−24.2	−58.1	....	Reserves and Related Items	79da *d*
	26.1	−34.6	−34.5	−28.6	26.5	17.3	36.2	−20.3	2.4	1.8	5.2	−12.7	−50.6	−48.3	....	Reserve Assets	79db *d*
	58.4	129.5	92.0	101.4	−16.1	−67.8	−87.2	−15.1	−7.8	−20.7	36.5	44.4	26.4	−9.8	....	Use of Fund Credit and Loans	79dc *d*
															....	Liabs.Constit.For.Auth.Reserves	79dd *d*
	129.8	31.9	22.4	8.3	−77.3	17.3	77.8	89.8	42.1	103.4	.3	—	—	—	....	Exceptional Financing	79de *d*
Millions of Shillings Beginning 1979: Year Ending June 30																**Government Finance**	
	−39	−100	−146	−134	−221	−640	I−1,639	−5,557	−5,499	−14,436	−57,914	−78,295	−196,103	−159,597 P	....	Deficit (-) or Surplus	80
	39	28	247	527	903	1,621	I2,844	5,005	22,262	46,719	86,459	136,808	187,901	287,112 P	....	Revenue	81
	1	3	30	10	35	48	I384	853	5,640	11,408	24,891	143,189	185,909	281,386 P	....	Grants Received	81z
	77	128	417	664	1,151	2,300	I4,867	11,415	33,401	72,563	166,977	353,792	561,413	720,595 P	....	Expenditure	82
	2	4	6	6	8	9	I—	—	—	—	—	2,287	4,500	8,500	7,500 P	....	Lending Minus Repayments	83
																Financing	
	39	100	146	134	221	640	I1,639	5,557	5,499	14,436	57,914	78,295	196,103	159,597 P	....	Total Financing	84
	I39	100	148	120	229	496	I1,164	4,195	4,943	1,524	−16,384	8,171	38,799	−45,097 P	....	Net Borrowing: Domestic	84a
	—	1	−1	15	−8	135	I474	1,362	556	12,912	74,299	70,124	159,824	204,695 P	....	Foreign	85a
	I—	—	—	—	—	—	I—	—	—	—	—	—	—	— P	....	Use of Cash Balances	87
	—	—	−1	−1	—	9	I1	—	—	—	−1	—	−2,520	−1 P	....	Adj. to Total Financing	84x
	123	223	371	491	720	1,251	I2,016	4,775	5,233	11,612	12,280	19,082	75,580	47,265 P	....	Debt: Domestic	88a
Millions of Shillings Beginning 1979																**National Accounts**	
	....	....	....	....	1,451	2,784	6,764	15,969	39,619	74,317	91,932	154,548	198,904	233,296	....	Exports of Goods & Services	90c
	....	....	....	....	1,538	3,325	5,771	16,541	52,101	91,462	140,825	237,145	407,032	498,057	....	Government Consumption	91f
	....	....	....	....	866	2,030	5,643	25,347	65,755	122,122	218,460	350,654	521,401	603,302	....	Gross Fixed Capital Formation	93e
	....	....	....	....	44	−48	44	−217	−49	−1,886	2,046	−1,486	7,792	12,647	....	Increase/Decrease(-) in Stocks	93i
	....	....	....	....	8,676	24,128	60,295	210,316	614,588	1,132,741	1,150,407	2,009,043	3,369,562	3,733,693	....	Private Consumption	96f
	....	....	....	....	−1,393	−3,256	−10,898	−42,226	−99,747	−183,057	−303,054	−499,513	−737,924	−776,217	....	Imports of Goods & Services	98c
	1,352	2,665	3,953	5,980	10,645	27,645	65,368	223,525	632,055	1,174,452	1,601,398	2,227,955	3,707,842	4,305,085	....	Gross Domestic Product	99b
	998,127	I1036648	1,098,395	I1184154	1,232,103	1,230,287	1,235,854	1,322,025	1,418,385	1,520,199	1,601,398	1,678,061	1,752,429	1,890,509	....	GDP 1990 Prices (Millions)	99b.*p*
	.1	.3	.4	.5	.9	2.2	5.3	16.9	44.6	77.3	100.0	132.8	211.6	227.7	....	GDP Deflator (1990=100)	99bi *p*
Midyear Estimates																	
	13.12	13.58	14.01	14.23	14.66	15.11	15.61	16.15	16.72	17.32	17.95	18.59	19.26	19.94	....	Population	99z

United Arab Emirates

		1965	1966	1967	1968	1969	1970	1971	1972	1973	1974	1975	1976	1977	1978	1979
Exchange Rates															*Dirhams*	*per SDR:*
Official Rate	aa	....	4.7619	4.7619	4.7619	4.7619	4.7619	4.7619	4.7619	4.8344	4.8735	4.6791	4.6206	4.7349	5.0001	4.9611
															Dirhams per	*US Dollar:*
Official Rate	ae	....	4.7619	4.7619	4.7619	4.7619	4.7619	4.3860	4.3860	4.0075	3.9805	3.9970	3.9770	3.8980	3.8380	3.7660
Official Rate	rf	....	4.7619	4.7619	4.7619	4.7619	4.7619	4.7480	4.3860	3.9963	3.9590	3.9613	3.9531	3.9032	3.8712	3.8157
														Index Numbers	*(1990=100):*	
Official Rate	ahx	....	77.1	77.1	77.1	77.1	77.1	77.3	83.7	91.7	92.5	92.7	92.9	93.8	94.8	96.2
Nominal Effective Exchange Rate	nec	....	....	....	....	....	....	....	....	....	....	....	....	....	....	97.8
Fund Position															*Millions*	*of SDRs:*
Quota	2f.s	....	....	....	....	....	....	....	15.0	15.0	15.0	15.0	15.0	15.0	120.0	120.0
SDRs	1b.s	....	....	....	....	....	....	....	....	—	—	—	—	—	—	15.4
Reserve Position in the Fund	1c.s	....	....	....	....	....	....	....	3.8	3.8	69.6	114.8	114.1	96.5	71.7	62.1
of which: Outstg.Fund Borrowing	2c	....	....	....	....	....	....	....	—	—	63.8	100.0	100.0	84.0	57.9	46.5
International Liquidity											*Millions of US Dollars Unless Otherwise Indicated:*					
Total Reserves minus Gold	1l.d	....	....	....	....	....	....	....	....	91.7	452.9	987.9	1,906.5	800.3	811.8	1,432.3
SDRs	1b.d	....	....	....	....	....	....	....	....	....	....	....	....	....	....	20.2
Reserve Position in the Fund	1c.d	....	....	....	....	....	....	....	4.1	4.5	85.2	134.4	132.6	117.2	93.4	81.7
Foreign Exchange	1d.d	....	....	....	....	....	....	....	....	87.2	367.7	853.5	1,773.9	683.1	718.4	1,330.3
Gold (Million Fine Troy Ounces)	1ad	....	....	....	....	....	....	....	....	—	—	—	.545	.569	.576	.577
Gold (National Valuation)	1and	....	....	....	....	....	....	....	....	....	....	....	67.8	72.7	75.3	76.8
Monetary Authorities: Other Assets	3..d	....	....	....	....	....	....	....	....	....	....	....	....	....	....	....
Deposit Money Banks: Assets	7a.d	....	....	....	....	....	....	....	....	402.2	1,106.4	1,794.3	2,574.7	2,077.4	2,584.2	3,556.7
of which: Claims on Nonbanks	7ad d	....	....	....	....	....	....	....	....	11.6	17.5	112.2	242.3	540.5	700.5	870.7
Deposit Money Banks: Liabilities	7b.d	....	....	....	....	....	....	....	....	108.6	225.7	436.5	892.7	2,262.8	2,761.1	4,028.3
of which: Liab. to Nonbanks	7bd d	....	....	....	....	....	....	....	....	21.8	70.1	133.4	163.6	170.7	182.6	210.9
RLB: Foreign Assets	7k.d	....	....	....	....	....	....	....	....	....	....	....	....	85.8	268.0	313.3
Foreign Liabilities	7m.d	....	....	....	....	....	....	....	....	....	....	....	....	115.3	316.1	376.2
Monetary Authorities															*Millions of*	*Dirhams:*
Foreign Assets	11	....	....	....	....	....	....	....	....	365	1,976	4,189	9,001	3,419	3,405	5,721
Claims on Central Government	12a	....	....	....	....	....	....	....	....	45	120	459	1,307	1,712	1,540	1,538
Claims on Official Entities	12bx	....	....	....	....	....	....	....	....	—	—	—	100	12	12	11
Claims on Deposit Money Banks	12e	....	....	....	....	....	....	....	....	16	172	527	1,013	1,199	1,391	1,042
Claims on Other Financial Insts.	12f	....	....	....	....	....	....	....	....	—	2	18	31	16	22	18
Reserve Money	14	....	....	....	....	....	....	....	....	411	1,051	1,526	2,776	3,796	4,259	5,475
of which: Currency Outside DMBs	14a	....	....	....	....	....	....	....	....	265	429	628	1,077	1,392	1,704	1,965
Quasi-Monetary Deposits	15	....	....	....	....	....	....	....	....	—	293	60	52	34	10	—
Foreign Liabilities	16c	....	....	....	....	....	....	....	....	—	—	1	824	616	487	513
Central Government Deposits	16d	....	....	....	....	....	....	....	....	18	919	3,578	7,631	2,041	1,776	2,173
Capital Accounts	17a	....	....	....	....	....	....	....	....	9	10	20	30	30	30	237
Other Items (Net)	17r	....	....	....	....	....	....	....	....	-12	-4	9	140	-161	-194	-70
Deposit Money Banks															*Millions of*	*Dirhams:*
Reserves	20	....	....	....	....	....	....	....	....	146	594	898	1,699	2,404	2,553	3,507
Foreign Assets	21	....	....	....	....	....	....	....	....	1,588	4,404	7,172	10,240	8,098	9,918	13,395
Claims on Central Government	22a	....	....	....	....	....	....	....	....	137	273	358	737	1,498	1,907	2,958
Claims on Official Entities	22bx	....	....	....	....	....	....	....	....	—	9	91	299	713	584	892
Claims on Private Sector	22d	....	....	....	....	....	....	....	....	1,627	3,362	5,691	10,472	15,819	19,357	21,212
Claims on Other Financial Insts.	22f	....	....	....	....	....	....	....	....	14	37	125	186	170	210	283
Demand Deposits	24	....	....	....	....	....	....	....	....	705	1,107	1,975	3,648	3,822	4,072	4,303
Time and Savings Deposits	25	....	....	....	....	....	....	....	....	1,287	4,207	6,157	11,977	10,291	11,790	11,954
Foreign Liabilities	26c	....	....	....	....	....	....	....	....	429	898	1,745	3,550	8,821	10,597	15,171
Central Government Deposits	26d	....	....	....	....	....	....	....	....	979	2,159	3,578	2,949	2,324	2,503	4,358
Central Govt. Lending Funds	26f	....	....	....	....	....	....	....	....	7	6	5	5	290	658	925
Credit from Monetary Authorities	26g	....	....	....	....	....	....	....	....	16	172	527	1,013	1,192	1,391	1,039
Capital Accounts	27a	....	....	....	....	....	....	....	....	125	175	392	609	1,867	3,548	4,553
Other Items (Net)	27r	....	....	....	....	....	....	....	....	-34	-46	-45	-119	95	-31	-56
Monetary Survey															*Millions of*	*Dirhams:*
Foreign Assets (Net)	31n	....	....	....	....	....	....	....	....	1,524	5,481	9,615	14,866	2,080	2,239	3,432
Domestic Credit	32	....	....	....	....	....	....	....	....	826	724	-412	2,555	15,582	19,359	20,385
Claims on Central Govt. (Net)	32an	....	....	....	....	....	....	....	....	-815	-2,685	-6,339	-8,536	-1,155	-832	-2,035
Claims on Official Entities	32bx	....	....	....	....	....	....	....	....	—	9	91	399	725	596	903
Claims on Private Sector	32d	....	....	....	....	....	....	....	....	1,627	3,362	5,693	10,475	15,826	19,363	21,218
Claims on Other Financial Insts.	32f	....	....	....	....	....	....	....	....	14	39	142	217	186	232	300
Money	34	....	....	....	....	....	....	....	....	970	1,536	2,603	4,725	5,215	5,776	6,269
Quasi-Money	35	....	....	....	....	....	....	....	....	1,287	4,499	6,217	12,029	10,325	11,800	11,954
Other Items (Net)	37r	....	....	....	....	....	....	....	....	94	170	383	667	2,122	4,022	5,595
Money plus Quasi-Money	35l	....	....	....	....	....	....	....	....	2,257	6,036	8,820	16,754	15,540	17,576	18,222
Production														*Index Numbers*	*(1990=100):*	
Crude Petroleum	66aa	13.6	17.4	18.5	24.2	29.5	37.6	51.2	58.3	73.6	81.0	82.0	94.0	96.6	88.5	88.5

United Arab Emirates

	1980	1981	1982	1983	1984	1985	1986	1987	1988	1989	1990	1991	1992	1993	1994		
End of Period																**Exchange Rates**	
	4.6820	4.2729	4.0495	3.8434	3.5984	4.0323	4.4903	5.2079	4.9401	4.8243	5.2226	5.2511	5.0476	5.0423	5.3591	Official Rate	aa
End of Period (ae) Period Average (rf)																	
	3.6710	3.6710	3.6710	3.6710	3.6710	3.6710	3.6710	3.6710	3.6710	3.6710	3.6710	3.6710	3.6710	3.6710	3.6710	Official Rate	ae
	3.7074	3.6710	3.6710	3.6710	3.6710	3.6710	3.6710	3.6710	3.6710	3.6710	3.6710	3.6710	3.6710	3.6710	3.6710	Official Rate	rf
Period Averages																	
	99.0	100.0	100.0	100.0	100.0	100.0	100.0	100.0	100.0	100.0	100.0	100.0	100.0	100.0	100.0	Official Rate	ahx
	100.6	112.6	124.7	130.6	139.7	143.8	118.0	105.3	99.6	104.7	100.0	99.5	96.6	99.7	97.6	Nominal Effective Exchange Rate	nec
End of Period																**Fund Position**	
	202.6	202.6	202.6	202.6	202.6	202.6	202.6	202.6	202.6	202.6	202.6	202.6	392.1	392.1	392.1	Quota	2f.s
	8.0	29.5	50.3	61.5	66.0	68.3	76.5	79.8	82.3	85.9	90.8	95.5	52.4	54.1	55.0	SDRs	1b.s
	93.1	147.9	201.4	214.6	222.3	201.7	181.0	159.1	135.3	138.4	126.3	126.1	158.3	162.8	149.1	Reserve Position in the Fund	1c.s
	44.7	75.4	105.0	102.9	93.9	72.6	46.4	22.5	3.2	.1	—	—	—	—	—	of which: Outstg.Fund Borrowing	2c
End of Period																**International Liquidity**	
	2,014.7	3,202.2	‡2,215.5	2,072.4	2,286.9	3,204.3	3,369.9	4,725.3	4,433.5	4,456.6	4,583.9	5,365.4	5,711.8	6,103.7	6,658.8	Total Reserves minus Gold	1l.d
	10.2	34.4	55.5	64.7	75.0	93.5	113.2	110.8	112.9	129.1	136.6	72.1	74.4	80.3		SDRs	1b.d
	118.8	172.1	222.2	224.7	217.9	221.5	221.4	225.6	182.0	181.9	179.7	180.4	217.6	223.6	217.7	Reserve Position in the Fund	1c.d
	1,885.8	2,995.7	‡1,937.8	1,783.3	2,004.3	2,907.8	3,054.9	4,386.5	4,140.7	4,161.8	4,275.1	5,048.4	5,422.1	5,805.7	6,360.8	Foreign Exchange	1d.d
	.577	.678	.817	.817	.817	.817	.817	.817	.817	.817	.797	.797	.796	.798	.795	Gold (Million Fine Troy Ounces)	1ad
	78.8	184.6	184.6	184.6	184.6	184.6	184.6	184.6	184.6	184.6	182.0	181.7	181.7	182.0	182.5	Gold (National Valuation)	1and
	....	....	1,132.7	....	....	....	....	....	....	....	....	....	....	....	181.6	Monetary Authorities: Other Assets	3..d
	5,286.4	7,914.3	9,548.5	9,538.0	12,100.6	12,070.1	13,475.9	13,188.7	15,505.7	16,378.1	17,134.0	18,931.9	18,496.6	17,997.8	....	Deposit Money Banks: Assets	7a.d
	1,092.0	1,660.4	1,743.1	2,084.1	2,254.8	3,194.5	3,453.4	3,552.2	4,059.6	4,414.6	4,033.8	4,248.3	4,352.8	5,022.9	....	of which: Claims on Nonbanks	7add
	4,571.2	6,142.9	7,229.5	6,719.6	5,666.5	5,422.6	4,594.9	4,789.9	6,153.1	5,603.4	6,779.1	7,042.0	7,157.7	7,221.7	....	Deposit Money Banks: Liabilities	7b.d
	251.5	271.5	253.9	326.5	339.4	708.8	472.0	633.9	797.3	856.4	751.6	720.0	1,074.1	1,097.5	....	of which: Liab. to Nonbanks	7bdd
	378.8	332.9	490.5	601.1	459.5	540.6	498.4	448.1	475.4	433.4	386.0	210.3	162.9	118.8	....	RLB: Foreign Assets	7k.d
	424.9	419.9	343.4	515.9	332.7	308.7	239.4	259.2	300.5	186.6	94.5	113.6	79.0	60.2	....	Foreign Liabilities	7m.d
End of Period																**Monetary Authorities**	
	7,726	12,629	13,271	10,204	11,029	14,543	13,805	18,322	17,225	17,211	17,734	20,654	21,804	23,357	....	Foreign Assets	11
	1,544	1,484	1,486	1,488	1,491	1,493	2,226	—	—	13	364	—	425	—	....	Claims on Central Government	12a
	5	—	12	12	5	5	5	—	—	—	—	—	—	—	....	Claims on Official Entities	12bx
	689	335	239	1,469	1,081	190	1,076	1,080	1,076	555	50	50	50	50	....	Claims on Deposit Money Banks	12e
	14	7	4	—	—	—	—	—	—	—	—	—	—	—	....	Claims on Other Financial Insts.	12f
	4,451	5,321	6,044	5,992	6,529	7,562	7,756	11,864	10,902	9,600	9,663	11,192	13,576	13,124	....	Reserve Money	14
	2,143	2,771	2,990	2,879	2,929	3,161	3,246	3,511	3,600	3,612	4,392	4,676	5,108	5,667	....	of which: Currency Outside DMBs	14a
	—	—	—	—	—	—	—	—	—	—	—	—	—	—	....	Quasi-Monetary Deposits	15
	390	233	8	6	5	6	5	5	7	10	202	252	336	313	....	Foreign Liabilities	16c
	4,508	6,938	6,078	3,527	3,340	3,308	1,985	4,815	4,615	4,621	5,069	7,057	6,166	6,788	....	Central Government Deposits	16d
	711	2,074	3,084	3,758	3,816	5,405	7,367	2,628	2,631	2,649	2,664	1,738	1,696	1,695	....	Capital Accounts	17a
	−83	−111	−203	−112	−85	−49	−2	88	146	899	549	464	505	1,486	....	Other Items (Net)	17r
End of Period																**Deposit Money Banks**	
	2,295	2,543	3,043	3,099	3,590	4,394	4,514	8,286	7,264	5,963	5,247	6,525	8,466	7,452	....	Reserves	20
	19,406	29,054	35,052	35,014	44,421	44,309	49,470	48,416	56,922	60,124	62,899	69,499	67,901	66,070	....	Foreign Assets	21
	2,305	2,418	3,641	4,177	4,330	9,491	5,892	7,491	6,856	7,250	8,251	10,040	10,806	12,334	....	Claims on Central Government	22a
	840	1,015	916	798	659	636	612	704	1,058	785	1,187	1,323	1,421	2,791	....	Claims on Official Entities	22bx
	25,173	29,902	31,713	33,467	33,385	33,628	36,232	38,975	42,493	46,086	46,897	50,618	53,713	57,691	....	Claims on Private Sector	22d
	606	537	924	1,236	2,349	2,064	1,961	1,634	1,721	1,637	2,482	1,477	2,193	3,014	....	Claims on Other Financial Insts.	22f
	5,212	6,198	6,749	6,245	5,963	6,344	5,956	6,585	7,154	7,444	6,370	8,336	9,873	12,507	....	Demand Deposits	24
	16,172	20,125	23,907	27,217	37,978	40,381	42,875	44,844	47,403	52,132	47,246	53,432	54,530	50,240	....	Time and Savings Deposits	25
	16,781	22,551	26,540	24,668	20,802	19,906	16,868	17,584	22,588	20,570	24,886	25,851	26,276	26,511	....	Foreign Liabilities	26c
	3,675	3,737	3,791	3,326	4,108	3,882	4,335	5,158	5,907	6,292	10,662	10,619	11,008	14,830	....	Central Government Deposits	26d
	1,569	2,054	907	736	526	559	482	434	385	353	332	307	282	243	....	Central Govt. Lending Funds	26f
	689	335	239	1,469	1,031	190	1,076	1,080	1,076	555	605	911	51	50	....	Credit from Monetary Authorities	26g
	5,523	8,397	10,756	11,583	12,027	14,286	12,659	13,138	13,378	14,395	15,254	16,063	16,838	17,516	....	Capital Accounts	27a
	1,005	2,071	2,399	2,547	6,301	8,973	14,431	16,684	18,422	20,104	21,607	23,963	25,642	27,455	....	Other Items (Net)	27r
End of Period																**Monetary Survey**	
	9,962	18,898	21,776	20,544	34,643	38,940	46,401	49,148	51,552	56,755	55,545	64,050	63,093	62,603	....	Foreign Assets (Net)	31n
	22,310	24,692	28,831	34,330	34,777	40,134	40,614	38,839	41,617	44,872	43,466	45,800	51,400	54,229	....	Domestic Credit	32
	−4,335	−6,773	−4,742	−1,188	−1,627	3,795	1,797	−2,482	−3,666	−3,650	−7,116	−7,636	−5,943	−9,284	....	Claims on Central Govt. (Net)	32an
	846	1,015	928	810	664	641	617	704	1,058	785	1,187	1,323	1,421	2,791	....	Claims on Official Entities	32bx
	25,179	29,907	31,718	33,471	33,390	33,635	36,238	38,983	42,504	46,100	46,913	50,636	53,729	57,708	....	Claims on Private Sector	32d
	620	543	928	1,236	2,349	2,064	1,961	1,634	1,721	1,637	2,482	1,477	2,193	3,014	....	Claims on Other Financial Insts.	32f
	7,355	8,969	9,739	9,124	8,892	9,505	9,201	10,096	10,753	11,056	10,762	13,012	14,981	18,174	....	Money	34
	16,172	20,125	23,907	27,218	37,978	40,382	42,875	44,844	47,403	52,132	47,246	53,432	54,530	50,240	....	Quasi-Money	35
	8,745	14,496	16,961	18,531	22,550	29,188	34,939	33,047	35,013	38,439	41,001	43,405	44,982	48,417	....	Other Items (Net)	37r
	23,527	29,094	33,646	36,342	46,870	49,887	52,076	54,940	58,156	63,188	58,008	66,444	69,511	68,414	....	Money plus Quasi-Money	35l
Period Averages																**Production**	
	82.9	72.6	61.3	57.1	54.3	54.0	67.4	69.4	72.7	90.7	100.0	115.8	110.3	105.9	105.4	Crude Petroleum	66aa

United Arab Emirates

		1965	1966	1967	1968	1969	1970	1971	1972	1973	1974	1975	1976	1977	1978	1979
International Transactions																*Millions of Dirhams*
Exports	70	....	1,149	1,246	1,593	2,016	2,613	4,294	5,076	7,198	25,389	27,565	34,344	37,891	35,434	52,023
Crude Petroleum	70aa	....	1,149	1,246	1,593	1,940	2,492	4,133	4,872	6,953	25,050	26,962	33,140	36,138	33,529	49,078
Imports, cif	71	....	....	....	....	1,462	1,272	1,469	2,113	3,279	6,750	10,635	13,192	19,733	20,791	26,581
Imports, fob	71.v	....	....	....	....	1,329	1,156	1,335	1,921	2,981	6,136	9,668	11,993	17,939	18,901	24,165
Volume of Exports																*1985=100*
Crude Petroleum	72aa	25.0	32.5	33.7	44.5	54.5	69.7	94.2	107.8	135.4	149.9	151.7	173.9	178.8	163.7	163.7
Export Prices																*1985=100:*
Crude Petroleum (Murban)	76aa d	5.8	5.8	5.8	5.8	5.8	5.8	6.9	7.8	10.9	38.7	39.4	42.2	45.6	46.9	70.1
Government Finance																*Millions of Dirhams:*
Deficit (-) or Surplus	80	....	....	....	....	....	....	....	37	30	62	590	596	-211	-503	202
Revenue	81	....	....	....	....	....	....	....	5	17	21	51	96	259	204	252
Grants Received	81z	....	....	....	....	....	....	....	196	403	780	1,722	3,006	5,736	6,780	8,610
Expenditure	82	....	....	....	....	....	....	....	164	390	734	1,157	2,144	5,068	6,815	8,132
Lending Minus Repayment	83	....	....	....	....	....	....	....	—	—	4	26	361	1,138	672	528
Financing																
Domestic	84a	....	....	....	....	....	....	....	-37	-30	-62	-590	-596	211	503	-202
Foreign	85a	....	....	....	....	....	....	....	—	—	—	—	—	—	—	—
National Accounts																*Billions of Dirhams*
Exports of Goods & Services	90c	....	....	....	....	....	....	....	5.5	9.4	29.4	29.5	36.6	41.8	40.2	57.2
Government Consumption	91f	....	....	....	....	....	....	....	.9	1.3	2.7	3.3	4.6	7.4	8.2	9.6
Gross Fixed Capital Formation	93e	....	....	....	....	....	....	....	1.8	2.1	4.1	12.1	16.6	22.7	25.8	28.4
Increase/Decrease(-) in Stocks	93i	....	....	....	....	....	....	....	—	.8	.7	—	.4	2.1	-2.3	-.8
Private Consumption	96f	....	....	....	....	....	....	....	.9	1.5	2.2	6.2	7.7	11.6	12.5	15.2
Imports of Goods & Services	98c	....	....	....	....	....	....	....	-2.5	-3.7	-8.0	-11.6	-14.8	-22.3	-23.9	-29.7
Gross Domestic Product	99b	....	....	....	....	....	....	....	6.6	11.4	31.1	39.5	51.0	63.4	60.7	79.9
Gross Dom. Prod. 1990 Prices	99b.p	....	....	....	....	....	....	....	....	47.3	54.1	57.5	66.1	77.6	75.8	94.7
GDP Deflator (1990=100)	99bi p	....	....	....	....	....	....	....	....	24.1	57.5	68.7	77.1	81.7	80.1	84.4
																Millions:
Population	99z	.16	.16	.17	.18	.19	.23	.28	.34	.42	.49	.51	.59	.69	.79	.92

Exchange Rates: On May 19, 1973 the dirham replaced the Bahrain dinar and the Qatar / Dubai riyal.

International Liquidity: ℓ Beginning in June 1982, *Foreign Exchange (line 1d.d)* excludes foreign assets of the Central Bank and the accrued interest attributable to the Emirate Governments.

United Arab Emirates

466

	1980	1981	1982	1983	1984	1985	1986	1987	1988	1989	1990	1991	1992	1993	1994		
Millions of Dirhams																**International Transactions**	
	76,627	74,302	63,614	55,378	50,759	48,180	58,139	....	....	....	....	....	....	....	....	Exports	70
	71,886	68,870	58,573	47,783	44,189	42,661	....	....	....	....	....	....	....	....	....	Crude Petroleum	70aa
	32,425	35,410	34,654	30,447	25,464	24,040	23,575	26,526	31,283	36,746	41,111	50,462	63,912	71,659	....	Imports, cif	71
	29,478	32,191	31,504	27,679	23,149	21,855	21,432	24,115	28,439	33,406	37,374	45,874	58,102	65,144	....	Imports, fob	71.v
1985=100																Volume of Exports	
	153.4	134.4	113.3	105.6	100.4	100.0	124.8	128.4	134.5	....	....	....	....	....	....	Crude Petroleum	72aa
Index of Prices in US Dollars																Export Prices	
	111.7	128.9	123.1	107.6	104.6	100.0	49.3	62.7	48.7	....	....	....	....	....	....	Crude Petroleum (Murban)	76aa d
Year Ending December 31																**Government Finance**	
								−624	−314	−780	456	−625	1,050	−260 P	....	Deficit (−) or Surplus	80
	2,302	2,355	....	....	....	....	....	2,769	1,921	1,355	1,971	1,626	4,110	2,503 P	....	Revenue	81
	269	201	....	....	....	....	....	9,865	10,950	11,332	12,927	12,997	12,511	12,659 P	....	Grants Received	81z
	17,339	22,259	....	....	....	....	....	13,258	13,185	13,467	14,442	15,248	15,571	15,422 P	....	Expenditure	82
	13,332	18,666	19,980	16,310	15,669	....	....	—	—	—	—	—	—	— P	....	Lending Minus Repayment	83
	1,974	1,439	....	....	....	....	....									Financing	
	−2,302	−2,355	....	....	....	....	....	624	314	780	−456	625	−1,050	260 P	....	Domestic	84a
	—	—	....	....	....	....	....	—	—	—	—	—	—	— P	....	Foreign	85a
Billions of Dirhams																**National Accounts**	
	85.6	83.7	71.6	60.9	59.8	57.7	37.9	48.5	46.8	59.4	82.0	84.2	88.7	....	....	Exports of Goods & Services	90c
	12.0	21.5	22.0	19.0	17.7	19.5	17.5	17.8	18.5	20.1	20.1	21.1	22.8	....	....	Government Consumption	91f
	30.1	30.6	31.7	31.7	29.1	24.5	23.4	20.3	20.8	22.4	24.1	25.8	29.8	....	....	Gross Fixed Capital Formation	93e
	1.0	1.2	.5	.5	.3	.5	.5	.6	.9	1.2	1.3	1.4	1.6	....	....	Increase/Decrease(−) in Stocks	93i
	19.0	24.9	26.8	27.5	27.5	28.3	31.6	33.8	38.7	41.9	46.7	51.5	58.4	....	....	Private Consumption	96f
	−37.9	−40.8	−40.2	−36.7	−32.7	−31.3	−31.7	−34.0	−38.8	−44.9	−50.6	−59.4	−72.9	....	....	Imports of Goods & Services	98c
	109.8	121.1	112.4	102.9	101.8	99.4	79.5	87.3	87.1	101.0	123.6	124.5	128.4	....	....	Gross Domestic Product	99b
	119.7	123.2	112.9	110.0	114.9	112.0	88.3	91.4	91.2	105.2	123.6	124.6	128.0	....	....	Gross Dom. Prod. 1990 Prices	99b.p
	91.7	98.3	99.5	93.6	88.6	88.7	90.0	95.5	95.5	96.0	100.0	99.9	100.3	....	....	GDP Deflator (1990=100)	99bi p
Midyear Estimates																	
	1.01	1.10	1.17	1.21	I 1.31	1.38	1.44	1.50	1.56	1.62	1.67	1.72	1.77	I 1.21	....	Population	99z

United Kingdom

		1965	1966	1967	1968	1969	1970	1971	1972	1973	1974	1975	1976	1977	1978	1979
Exchange Rates																*SDRs per Pound:*
Market Rate	ac	2.8028	2.7902	2.4063	2.3844	2.4007	2.3937	2.3510	ℐ2.1627	1.9258	1.9182	1.7285	1.4653	1.5691	1.5616	1.6883
																US Dollars per Pound:
Market Rate	ag	2.8028	2.7902	2.4063	2.3844	2.4007	2.3937	2.5525	ℐ2.3481	2.3232	2.3485	2.0235	1.7024	1.9060	2.0345	2.2240
Market Rate	rh	2.8000	2.8000	2.7667	2.4000	2.4000	2.4000	2.4344	2.5018	2.4522	2.3390	2.2218	1.8062	1.7455	1.9195	2.1216
																ECUs per Pound:
ECU Rate	ec	....	....	....	....	....	....	....	....	....	....	....	....	....	....	....
ECU Rate	ed	....	....	....	....	....	....	....	....	....	....	....	....	....	....	1.5445
															Index Numbers (1990=100):	
Market Rate	ah x	156.7	156.5	153.9	134.1	133.9	134.3	136.9	140.2	137.4	131.1	124.5	101.2	97.8	107.6	118.9
Nominal Effective Exchange Rate	ne u	201.3	201.3	199.1	175.3	175.8	174.4	173.4	165.8	147.1	142.2	129.9	112.5	106.8	107.3	114.9
Real Effective Exchange Rate	re u	....	....	....	....	....	....	....	....	....	....	84.5	77.7	76.4	82.9	95.3
Fund Position																*Millions of SDRs:*
Quota	2f. s	1,950	2,440	2,440	2,440	2,440	2,800	2,800	2,800	2,800	2,800	2,800	2,800	2,800	2,925	2,925
SDRs	1b. s	—	—	—	—	—	266	591	604	600	688	696	603	501	415	965
Reserve Position in the Fund	1c. s	—	—	—	—	—	—	—	116	117	206	304	—	—	—	—
Total Fund Cred.&Loans Outstg.	2tl	1,907	1,865	1,013	2,275	2,241	1,829	497	—	—	—	—	1,700	3,340	1,805	813
International Liquidity												*Billions of US Dollars Unless Otherwise Indicated:*				
Total Reserves minus Gold	1l. d	.74	1.16	1.40	.95	1.06	1.48	7.99	4.85	5.59	6.04	4.60	3.37	20.11	16.03	19.74
SDRs	1b. d	—	—	—	—	—	.27	.64	.66	.72	.84	.82	.70	.61	.54	1.27
Reserve Position in the Fund	1c. d	—	—	—	—	—	—	—	.13	.14	.25	.36	—	—	—	—
Foreign Exchange	1d. d	.74	1.16	1.40	.95	1.06	1.21	7.35	4.06	4.72	4.94	3.43	2.67	19.50	15.49	18.47
Gold (Million Fine Troy Ounces)	1ad	64.70	55.47	36.86	42.09	42.06	38.52	22.18	21.08	21.01	21.03	21.03	21.03	22.23	22.83	18.25
Gold (National Valuation)	1an d	2.27	1.94	1.29	1.47	1.47	1.35	.84	.80	.89	.89	.89	.89	.94	.96	3.26
Deposit Money Banks: Assets	7a. d	7.57	10.21	12.20	18.93	30.78	37.03	45.49	60.14	88.59	108.55	125.74	145.61	ℐ171.53	217.69	285.49
Claims on Nonbanks	7ad d	3.09	3.38	....	....	....	....	....	....	....	33.99ᵉ	36.21ᵉ	40.18ᵉ	ℐ54.19	67.72	81.49
Deposit Money Banks: Liabilities	7b. d	10.85	12.75	14.29	20.43	31.94	39.95	51.07	64.81	96.23	119.03	135.62	154.52	ℐ183.66	226.89	304.43
Liabilities to Nonbanks	7bd d	....	....	....	....	....	....	....	....	....	21.50ᵉ	20.66ᵉ	23.73ᵉ	ℐ36.38	49.17	75.40
Monetary Authorities																*Billions of Pounds:*
Foreign Assets	11	1.07	1.11	1.12	1.01	1.08	1.37	3.82	2.66	2.64	2.51	1.95	ℐ2.43	10.72	7.69	10.13
Claims on Central Govt. (Net)	12an	7.51	7.84	8.74	10.44	9.92	8.97	5.60	7.98	9.18	11.03	11.41	ℐ9.33	2.05	6.52	5.41
Claims on Deposit Money Banks	12e	.03	.08	.12	—	—	—	.08	—	—	—	—	.45	.47	—	.05
Reserve Money	14	3.59	3.81	3.98	4.14	4.22	4.71	4.47	5.42	7.13	7.41	8.16	9.78	10.30	11.30	12.41
of which: Currency Outside DMBs	14a	2.64	2.70	2.82	2.86	3.01	3.32	3.59	4.08	4.38	5.09	5.81	6.58	7.56	8.73	9.51
Foreign Liabilities	16c	4.94	5.12	5.91	7.19	6.67	5.33	4.51	4.59	4.21	5.39	4.73	ℐ1.92	2.15	2.19	2.40
Other Items (Net)	17r	.09	.11	.09	.13	.11	.29	.51	.63	.48	.74	.47	.50	.79	.71	.78
Deposit Money Banks																*Billions of Pounds:*
Reserves	20	1.10	1.25	1.32	1.44	1.38	1.57	1.08	1.56	3.00	2.61	2.68	3.56	3.15	3.04	3.44
Foreign Assets	21	2.70	3.66	5.07	7.94	12.82	15.47	17.82	25.61	38.13	46.22	ℐ62.14	85.53	88.13	105.93	128.68
Claims on Central Govt. (Net)	22an	3.61	3.60	3.84	3.41	2.89	2.98	4.39	2.65	2.52	3.35	5.91	5.60	7.42	6.36	6.17
Claims on Official Entities	22bx	1.00	1.10	1.61	1.82	2.12	2.75	3.55	3.74	4.52	4.62	5.82	6.41	6.74	6.73	7.45
Claims on Private Sector	22d	7.50	7.56	8.12	8.85	ℐ9.39	10.79	12.63	19.43	26.38	31.04	ℐ30.94	35.42	39.34	44.84	53.61
Demand Deposits	24	5.21	5.15	5.63	5.93	5.81	6.32	7.50	8.58	8.93	9.65	ℐ11.58	12.75	15.96	18.63	20.35
Time, Savings,& Fgn.Currency Dep.	25	5.09	5.55	6.40	7.12	7.59	8.31	9.23	13.33	19.84	22.69	ℐ22.62	25.27	25.46	28.76	33.27
Foreign Liabilities	26c	3.87	4.57	5.94	8.57	13.30	16.69	20.01	27.60	41.42	50.69	67.02	90.77	95.17	110.52	135.82ᵉ
Other Items (Net)	27r	1.73	1.90	1.99	1.84	1.90	2.24	2.73	3.48	4.36	4.82	ℐ6.27	7.72	8.18	9.01	9.90
Banking Survey																*Billions of Pounds:*
Foreign Assets (Net)	31n	−5.04	−4.92	−5.66	−6.81	−6.11	−5.18	−2.88	−3.92	−4.86	−7.34	ℐ−7.65	ℐ−4.73	1.52	.91	.59
Domestic Credit	32	19.62	20.10	22.31	24.52	24.33	25.48	26.16	33.79	42.60	50.04	ℐ54.07	56.76	55.56	64.45	72.63
Claims on Central Govt. (Net)	32an	11.12	11.44	12.58	13.85	12.81	11.95	9.99	10.62	11.71	14.38	17.31	14.93	9.48	12.88	11.58
Claims on Official Entities	32bx	1.00	1.10	1.61	1.82	2.14	2.75	3.55	3.74	4.52	4.62	5.82	6.41	6.74	6.73	7.45
Claims on Private Sector	32d	7.50	7.56	8.12	8.85	9.39	10.79	12.63	19.43	26.38	31.04	ℐ30.94	35.42	39.34	44.84	53.61
Money	34	7.85	7.84	8.44	8.78	8.81	9.64	11.09	12.66	13.30	14.74	ℐ17.48	19.47	23.52	27.36	29.86
Quasi-Money	35	5.09	5.55	6.40	7.12	7.59	8.31	9.23	13.33	19.84	22.69	ℐ22.62	25.27	25.46	28.76	33.27
Other Items (Net)	37r	1.64	1.78	1.81	1.81	1.82	2.36	2.96	3.89	4.59	5.28	ℐ6.32	7.28	8.09	9.25	10.09
Money plus Quasi-Money	35l	12.93	13.40	14.84	15.91	16.40	17.95	20.18	25.67	32.84	37.11	40.10	44.74	48.99	56.12	63.13
Money (National Definitions)																*Billions of Pounds:*
M0	59mc	....	....	....	....	3.99	4.21	4.43	5.05	5.59	6.45	7.19	7.99	9.12	10.36	11.62
M4	59md	....	....	....	....	....	....	....	....	....	....	....	....	....	....	....
																Millions of Pounds:
M0, Seasonally Adjusted	59mc c	....	....	....	....	....	180	191	555	494	819	689	762	1,017	1,190	1,188
M4, Seasonally Adjusted	59md c	....	....	....	....	....	....	....	....	....	....	....	....	....	....	....
Interest Rates																*Percent Per Annum*
Money Market Rate	60b	....	....	....	....	3.95	2.00	1.42	3.45	1.92	4.63	6.08	5.54	2.13	4.29	6.01
Treasury Bill Rate	60c	5.91	6.10	5.82	7.09	7.64	7.02	5.58	5.52	9.34	11.37	10.17	11.12	7.68	7.84	12.97
Treas. Bill Rate(Bond Equivalent)	60cs	....	....	....	....	....	....	....	....	....	....	....	10.56	11.62	8.06	8.74	12.52
Eurodollar Rate in London	60d	4.81	6.12	5.46	6.36	9.76	8.51	6.08	4.97	9.16	11.01	6.99	5.58	6.05	8.78	12.01
Deposit Rate	60l	4.42	4.50	4.21	5.42	5.92	5.21	3.83	4.15	8.02	9.50	7.08	7.54	4.90	6.08	11.71
Lending Rate	60p	....	....	5.50	6.13	6.63	7.25	7.50	7.50	8.00	9.00	9.00	9.00	9.75	9.25	13.92
Govt. Bond Yield: Short-Term	61a	6.57	6.77	6.66	7.59	8.81	7.26	6.69	7.55	10.41	12.51	11.48	12.06	10.08	11.32	12.64
Long-Term	61	6.56	6.94	6.80	7.55	9.04	9.22	8.90	8.90	10.71	14.77	14.39	14.43	12.73	12.47	12.99
Prices, Production, Employment																*Index Numbers (1990=100):*
Industrial Share Prices	62	8.9	9.0	9.6	13.5	13.4	11.9	14.0	17.8	15.4	9.1	11.3	15.6	17.4	19.6	22.3
Prices: Manufacturing Output	63	13.2	13.5	13.7	14.2	14.8	15.8	17.2	18.1	19.5	23.8	29.3	34.2	40.6	44.3	49.5
Consumer Prices	64	11.8	12.2	12.5	13.1	13.8	14.7	16.1	17.2	18.8	ℐ21.8	27.1	31.6	36.6	39.6	44.9
Wages: Avg. Monthly Earnings	65.. c	8.4	9.0	9.3	10.0	10.8	12.1	13.5	15.2	17.3	20.3	25.7	ℐ29.7	32.7	37.5	43.3
Industrial Production	66.. c	64.2	65.2	65.7	70.7	73.1	73.5	73.1	74.4	81.0	79.4	75.1	77.6	81.6	83.9	87.2
Employment	67.. c	99.6	100.3	98.4	97.7	97.5	96.8	97.3	97.3	99.8	100.3	100.0	99.2	97.3	100.2	101.9

United Kingdom

	1980	1981	1982	1983	1984	1985	1986	1987	1988	1989	1990	1991	1992	1993	1994		
	End of Period															**Exchange Rates**	
	1.8700	1.6392	1.4636	1.3855	1.1798	1.3151	1.2055	1.3192	1.3447	1.2217	1.3552	1.3078	1.0996	1.0784	1.0703	Market Rate	ac
	End of Period (ag) Period Average (rh)																
	2.3850	1.9080	1.6145	1.4506	1.1565	1.4445	1.4745	1.8715	1.8095	1.6055	1.9280	1.8707	1.5120	1.4812	1.5625	Market Rate	ag
	2.3263	2.0279	1.7505	1.5170	1.3363	1.2963	1.4670	1.6389	1.7814	1.6397	1.7847	1.7694	1.7655	1.5020	1.5316	Market Rate	rh
	End of Period (ec) Period Average (ed)																
	1.8062	1.7652	1.6659	1.7525	1.6398	1.6251	1.3794	1.4351	1.5419	1.3463	1.4126	1.3964	1.2528	1.3225	1.2705	ECU Rate	ec
	....	1.8136	1.7846	1.7072	1.6932	1.6989	1.4948	1.4138	1.5057	1.4872	1.4011	1.4265	1.3607	1.2822	1.2897	ECU Rate	ed
	Period Averages																
	130.3	113.6	98.1	85.0	74.9	72.6	82.2	91.8	99.8	91.9	100.0	99.1	98.9	84.2	85.8	Market Rate	ahx
	124.5	128.0	123.3	115.7	111.5	111.4	101.5	99.4	105.4	102.4	100.0	100.8	97.0	89.0	89.3	Nominal Effective Exchange Rate	neu
	114.2	121.7	116.1	107.4	102.8	103.8	96.2	98.6	106.0	106.2	100.0	103.9	103.6	96.7	....	Real Effective Exchange Rate	reu
	End of Period															**Fund Position**	
	4,388	4,388	4,388	6,194	6,194	6,194	6,194	6,194	6,194	6,194	6,194	6,194	6,194	7,415	7,415	7,415	Quota	2f.s
	447	852	1,061	494	507	1,030	1,270	974	981	870	878	919	393	210	335	SDRs	1b.s
	1,045	1,236	1,408	2,010	2,012	1,810	1,621	1,253	1,239	1,246	1,179	1,293	1,464	1,354	1,366	Reserve Position in the Fund	1c.s
	563	313	52	—	—	—	—	—	—	—	—	—	—	—	—	Total Fund Cred.&Loans Outstg.	2tl
	End of Period															**International Liquidity**	
	20.65	15.24	12.40	11.34	9.44	12.86	18.42	41.72	44.10	34.77	35.85	41.89	36.64	36.78	41.01	Total Reserves minus Gold	1l.d
	.57	.99	1.17	.52	.50	1.13	1.55	1.38	1.32	1.14	1.25	1.31	.54	.29	.49	SDRs	1b.d
	1.33	1.44	1.55	2.10	1.97	1.99	1.98	1.78	1.67	1.64	1.68	1.85	2.01	1.86	1.99	Reserve Position in the Fund	1c.d
	18.75	12.81	9.67	8.72	6.97	9.74	14.89	38.56	41.12	31.99	32.93	38.73	34.09	34.63	38.53	Foreign Exchange	1d.d
	18.84	19.03	19.01	19.01	19.03	19.03	19.01	19.01	19.00	18.99	18.94	18.89	18.61	18.45	18.44	Gold (Million Fine Troy Ounces)	1ad
	6.99	7.33	4.56	5.91	5.48	4.31	4.90	5.79	6.47	5.46	5.24	5.04	4.77	4.56	5.31	Gold (National Valuation)	1and
	356.32	432.71	462.82	485.21	489.71	I 590.07	715.54	875.31	883.08	922.94	1,068.97	I 982.81	1,018.98	1,051.27	1,200.17	Deposit Money Banks: Assets	7a.d
	103.50	130.80	142.78	148.65	144.55	I 173.08	188.95	212.67	209.79	219.22	259.92	I 269.23	291.94	322.58	334.21	Claims on Nonbanks	7add
	377.71	I 451.40	489.64	519.63	538.22	625.74	758.98	926.53	960.09	1,024.56	1,201.03	I 1113.16	1,114.77	1,133.51	1,278.85	Deposit Money Banks: Liabilities	7b.d
	95.46	123.40	151.61	150.53	146.10	157.87	198.82	247.79	248.26	265.74	334.76	I 314.24	296.00	279.71	294.47	Liabilities to Nonbanks	7bdd
	End of Period															**Monetary Authorities**	
	11.49	12.22	10.51	12.27	13.55	10.75	I 16.74	24.36	29.26	24.27	20.43	24.35	30.08	31.05	....	Foreign Assets	11
	4.66	4.40	7.23	6.35	3.98	9.16	I 8.67	4.00	1.79	10.22	15.60	14.22	14.60	14.04	....	Claims on Central Govt. (Net)	12an
	—	—	.10	.05	.10	.20	I —	.05	.04	.11	.04	—	—	.18	—	Claims on Deposit Money Banks	12e
	12.05	12.51	13.05	13.41	11.95	12.72	I 17.03	18.26	20.04	21.74	22.01	22.24	23.58	25.19	26.53	Reserve Money	14
	10.24	I 10.77	11.22	I 11.01	9.16	9.84	13.39	14.18	15.34	16.20	16.35	16.71	17.76	18.87	19.94	of which: Currency Outside DMBs	14a
	3.28	3.25	3.77	4.04	4.31	5.98	I 7.92	9.41	10.39	12.13	13.10	15.46	20.16	25.89	....	Foreign Liabilities	16c
	.82	.85	1.02	1.22	1.37	1.41	I .46	.74	.65	.73	.96	.86	.94	−5.80	−1.52	Other Items (Net)	17r
	End of Period															**Deposit Money Banks**	
	2.39	2.38	2.56	2.41	2.79	2.88	I 3.76	4.26	5.01	5.83	5.97	5.88	6.28	6.78	7.04	Reserves	20
	150.86	225.02	285.59	339.91	435.15	403.28	I 479.92	460.81	484.11	566.13	545.18	516.71	646.94	682.18	736.37	Foreign Assets	21
	7.19	I 8.05	7.15	7.15	7.27	7.89	I 17.20	16.16	15.28	12.07	11.37	11.14	14.98	25.18	....	Claims on Central Govt. (Net)	22an
	8.83	I 13.13	11.81	9.94	10.84	8.40	I 7.73	6.09	4.58	3.20	3.26	3.14	4.46	5.87	6.24	Claims on Official Entities	22bx
	63.73	I 83.04	100.38	119.74	146.54	167.39	I 318.45	377.41	468.57	583.11	645.26	663.09	685.18	708.31	....	Claims on Private Sector	22d
	20.81	I 25.77	29.44	I 31.46	38.89	46.84	58.85	I 140.13	155.64	179.39	198.90	212.83	221.37	233.64	....	Demand Deposits	24
	43.74	59.02	65.74	74.85	82.77	88.85	109.09	I 183.57	223.31	277.98	308.14	302.57	326.66	349.60	....	Time, Savings,& Fgn.Currency Dep.	25
	157.16	232.32	295.38	350.71	453.62	416.01	493.40	I 473.34	510.86	608.30	590.45	563.99	680.89	706.38	....	Foreign Liabilities	26c
	11.27	I 14.52	16.91	22.13	27.32	38.15	41.42	I 60.22	75.20	92.26	99.02	105.24	115.56	128.53	....	Other Items (Net)	27r
	End of Period															**Banking Survey**	
	1.91	1.67	−3.06	−2.56	−9.23	−7.97	−4.91	I 2.42	−7.88	−30.04	−37.94	−38.39	−24.03	−19.03	....	Foreign Assets (Net)	31n
	84.40	I 108.62	126.55	143.18	168.63	192.84	I 352.05	403.65	490.22	608.60	675.49	691.59	719.22	753.40	....	Domestic Credit	32
	11.85	I 12.45	14.37	13.50	11.25	17.05	I 25.87	20.16	17.07	22.29	26.97	25.36	29.58	39.22	....	Claims on Central Govt. (Net)	32an
	I 8.83	I 13.13	11.81	9.94	10.84	8.40	I 7.73	6.09	4.58	3.20	3.26	3.14	4.46	5.87	6.24	Claims on Official Entities	32bx
	63.73	I 83.04	100.38	119.74	146.54	167.39	I 318.45	377.41	468.57	583.11	645.26	663.09	685.18	708.31	....	Claims on Private Sector	32d
	31.04	I 34.59	40.66	42.46	48.05	56.67	69.27	I 154.12	170.67	195.31	214.94	229.20	238.67	252.05	....	Money	34
	43.74	I 59.02	65.74	I 74.85	82.77	88.85	109.09	I 183.57	223.31	277.98	308.14	302.57	326.66	349.60	....	Quasi-Money	35
	11.52	I 14.73	17.10	23.30	28.59	39.35	41.96	I 60.91	75.82	92.88	99.93	106.11	116.50	122.54	....	Other Items (Net)	37r
	74.79	I 95.55	106.41	I 120.02	134.91	150.46	183.79	I 337.69	393.99	473.28	523.08	531.77	565.32	601.65	....	Money plus Quasi-Money	35l
	End of Period															**Money (National Definitions)**	
	12.24	12.56	12.95	13.85	14.62	15.16	15.95	16.63	18.04	19.01	19.49	20.09	20.58	21.73	23.32	M0	59mc
	....	....	154.91	175.30	198.93	224.79	257.89	304.37	358.37	426.19	478.10	504.72	520.24	546.69	569.60	M4	59md
	Period Change																
	650	589	376	755	708	531	749	638	1,203	1,005	476	557	527	1,162	1,376	M0, Seasonally Adjusted	59mc c
	....	....	....	20,146	23,072	26,291	35,131	43,135	53,042	64,830	51,768	28,292	18,947	25,053	24,816	M4, Seasonally Adjusted	59md c
	Percent Per Annum															**Interest Rates**	
	15.62	13.12	11.36	9.09	7.62	10.78	10.68	9.66	10.31	13.88	14.68	11.75	9.55	5.46	4.76	Money Market Rate	60b
	15.16	13.03	11.47	9.59	9.30	11.56	10.37	9.25	9.78	13.05	14.08	10.96	8.94	5.18	5.21	Treasury Bill Rate	60c
	16.10	12.41	12.02	9.90	9.61	12.00	10.77	9.54	10.05	13.74	14.63	11.23	9.21	5.35	5.18	Treas. Bill Rate(Bond Equivalent)	60cs
	14.06	16.82	13.16	9.60	10.78	8.34	6.77	7.11	7.91	9.10	8.21	5.89	3.77	3.25	4.67	Eurodollar Rate in London	60d
	14.13	10.67	12.42	11.19	I 7.14	11.79	9.85	8.57	8.54	11.43	12.22	10.06	7.30	3.76	3.44	Deposit Rate	60l
	16.17	13.25	11.84	9.85	9.75	12.33	10.83	9.64	10.29	13.92	14.75	11.54	9.41	5.92	5.48	Lending Rate	60p
	13.84	14.65	12.79	11.19	11.29	11.13	10.01	9.36	9.66	10.73	12.08	10.18	8.96	6.65	7.83	Govt. Bond Yield: Short-Term	61a
	13.79	14.74	12.88	10.81	10.69	10.62	9.87	9.48	9.36	9.58	11.08	9.92	9.15	7.87	8.05	Long-Term	61
	Period Averages															**Prices, Production, Employment**	
	23.8	26.9	31.1	39.3	46.7	57.7	71.6	94.5	85.0	101.9	100.0	109.8	114.7	131.7	141.5	Industrial Share Prices	62
	57.4	63.6	69.0	73.5	77.9	82.7	83.8	86.7	89.8	94.1	100.0	105.4	108.7	113.0	115.8	Prices: Manufacturing Output	63
	53.0	59.3	64.4	67.4	70.7	75.0	77.6	80.8	84.7	91.3	100.0	105.9	109.8	111.5	114.3	Consumer Prices	64
	I 51.4	58.0	63.4	68.8	73.0	79.0	85.3	92.0	83.5	91.1	100.0	108.0	114.6	118.5	123.3	Wages: Avg. Monthly Earnings	65..c
	81.5	78.9	80.4	83.3	83.4	88.0	90.1	93.7	98.2	100.3	100.0	96.1	95.9	98.1	103.2	Industrial Production	66..c
	101.1	96.3	94.2	92.7	93.4	94.3	94.1	95.0	98.0	99.8	100.0	96.9	94.8	95.2	95.6	Employment	67..c

United Kingdom

		1965	1966	1967	1968	1969	1970	1971	1972	1973	1974	1975	1976	1977	1978	1979
International Transactions																*Millions of Pounds*
Exports	**70**	4,932	5,275	5,244	6,442	7,352	8,096	9,070	9,602	12,087	16,309	19,607	25,277	31,990	35,380	40,637
Imports, cif	**71**	5,760	5,951	6,439	7,900	8,317	9,113	9,799	11,073	15,723	23,139	24,046	31,084	36,219	39,533	46,925
Imports, fob(on a b.o.p. basis)	**71.v**	5,173	5,384	5,840	7,145	7,478	8,142	8,820	10,154	14,448	21,513	22,440	29,041	34,006	36,573	43,814
																1990=100
Volume of Exports	**72**	31.4	32.6	32.4	36.6	40.6	I 41.6	44.4	45.1	50.3	52.5	51.5	56.1	61.6	63.2	65.7
Volume of Imports	**73**	37.1	37.8	40.7	44.9	45.6	I 47.8	49.4	52.1	57.9	57.3	52.0	54.9	54.8	57.0	61.6
Unit Value of Exports	**74**	14.3	14.8	15.1	16.3	16.8	I 17.9	18.9	19.9	22.4	28.5	35.0	42.0	49.7	54.4	60.3
Unit Value of Imports	**75**	14.1	14.3	14.4	16.1	16.6	I 17.4	18.2	19.0	24.1	34.9	39.6	48.5	55.8	57.4	61.1
Balance of Payments																*Millions of US Dollars:*
Goods: Exports f.o.b.	**78aa *d***	....	....	14,474	15,439	17,446	19,507	21,994	23,510	29,106	38,105	42,475	45,033	55,319	67,121	86,018
Goods: Imports f.o.b.	**78ab *d***	....	....	–16,128	–17,148	–17,947	–19,541	–21,474	–25,353	–35,361	–50,347	–49,747	–52,103	–59,323	–70,185	–92,991
Trade Balance	**78ac *d***	....	....	–1,654	–1,709	–502	–34	520	–1,844	–6,256	–12,242	–7,272	–7,070	–4,004	–3,064	–6,973
Services: Credit	**78ad *d***	....	....	5,929	6,113	6,763	8,117	9,468	10,506	12,714	15,441	16,965	17,934	20,282	23,999	30,737
Services: Debit	**78ae *d***	....	....	–5,565	–5,364	–5,885	–7,106	–8,133	–8,947	–11,034	–13,190	–14,063	–13,605	–14,624	–16,872	–22,433
Balance on Goods and Services	**78af *d***	....	....	–1,290	–960	377	977	1,855	–285	–4,575	–9,991	–4,371	–2,741	1,653	4,063	1,331
Income: Credit	**78ag *d***	....	....	2,767	2,724	3,300	3,586	3,739	8,513	12,068	14,523	14,562	15,086	15,397	21,473	37,250
Income: Debit	**78ah *d***	....	....	–1,657	–1,862	–2,026	–2,155	–2,400	–7,015	–8,814	–10,993	–12,603	–12,294	–14,938	–19,929	–34,687
Balance on Goods, Serv., & Inc.	**78ai *d***	....	....	–180	–98	1,651	2,407	3,195	1,212	–1,322	–6,461	–2,412	51	2,112	5,607	3,893
Current Transfers, n.i.e.: Credit	**78aj *d***	....	....	445	444	494	552	599	660	947	1,143	1,684	1,420	1,594	2,330	2,976
Current Transfers: Debit	**78ak *d***	....	....	–1,331	–1,582	–989	–989	–1,077	–1,339	–2,037	–2,130	–2,738	–2,852	–3,560	–5,774	–7,652
Current Account, n.i.e.	**78al *d***	....	....	–1,066	–1,236	1,157	1,970	2,717	533	–2,412	–7,448	–3,465	–1,380	145	2,163	–783
Capital Account, n.i.e.: Credit	**78ba *d***	....	....	—	—	—	—	—	—	—	—	—	—	—	—	—
Capital Account: Debit	**78bb *d***	....	....	—	—	—	—	—	—	—	—	—	—	—	—	—
Capital Account, n.i.e.	**78bc *d***	....	....	—	—	—	—	—	—	—	—	—	—	—	—	—
Direct Investment Abroad	**78bd *d***	....	....	–1,102	–1,181	–1,558	–1,678	–1,988	–2,017	–4,981	–4,376	–3,001	–4,338	–4,173	–6,815	–12,539
Dir. Invest. in Rep. Econ., n.i.e.	**78be *d***	....	....	978	1,200	1,070	1,488	1,771	1,208	2,723	4,374	3,319	3,006	4,427	3,787	6,469
Portfolio Investment Assets	**78bf *d***	....	....	–180	–574	–115	–317	–112	–1,510	681	1,698	–122	134	17	–2,065	–1,899
Portfolio Investment Liab., n.i.e.	**78bg *d***	....	....	91	120	146	194	694	724	941	751	28	718	2,489	–369	2,302
Other Investment Assets	**78bh *d***	....	....	–1,130	–1,716	–1,632	–1,157	–3,477	–634	–2,490	–3,680	–1,986	–4,622	–3,265	–4,069	–69,841
Other Investment Liab., n.i.e.	**78bi *d***	....	....	425	826	895	2,290	3,587	1,872	3,102	1,373	3,161	1,408	5,846	1,543	55,774
Financial Account, n.i.e.	**78bj *d***	....	....	–917	–1,325	–1,193	821	474	–357	–24	138	1,399	–3,693	5,340	–7,987	–19,734
Net Errors and Omissions	**78ca *d***	....	....	520	–434	893	–65	652	–2,464	309	332	–4	738	6,645	3,432	1,888
Overall Balance	**78cb *d***	....	....	–1,463	–2,994	857	2,726	3,843	–2,288	–2,127	–6,978	–2,070	–4,335	12,130	–2,392	–18,628
Reserves and Related Items	**79da *d***	....	....	1,463	2,994	–857	–2,726	–3,843	2,288	2,127	6,978	2,070	4,335	–12,130	2,392	18,628
Reserve Assets	**79db *d***	....	....	928	271	–105	19	–3,471	1,975	–577	–256	1,419	1,413	–16,706	4,319	–1,759
Use of Fund Credit and Loans	**79dc *d***	....	....	–851	1,262	–34	–412	–1,332	–540	—	—	—	1,975	1,902	–1,962	–1,271
Liabs.Constit.For.Auth.Reserves	**79dd *d***	....	....	1,386	1,462	–852	–2,333	764	853	225	3,122	–1,294	–2,455	674	–198	20,770
Exceptional Financing	**79de *d***	....	....	—	—	134	—	197	—	2,479	4,113	1,946	3,402	1,999	233	888
Government Finance																*Millions of Pounds*
Deficit (-) or Surplus	**80**	–591	–535	–1,150	–734	906	I 923	–384	–1,742	–2,524	–3,828	–7,796	–7,251	–4,934	–8,808	–11,164
Revenue	**81**	10,528	11,610	12,750	14,812	16,884	I 19,088	20,170	21,311	23,158	29,442	37,683	44,145	50,125	55,042	64,369
Grants Received	**81z**	....	....	....	....	....	I —	—	—	7	23	27	46	117	110	179
Expenditure	**82**	10,357	10,649	12,247	13,779	14,435	I 16,301	18,231	20,781	23,503	30,335	41,190	48,634	53,513	61,884	72,188
Lending Minus Repayments	**83**	762	1,496	1,653	1,767	1,543	I 1,864	2,323	2,272	2,186	2,958	4,316	2,808	1,663	2,076	3,524
Financing																
Domestic Borrowing	**84a**	499	85	663	–407	–208	I 389	2,725	96	3,263	2,917	8,426	7,468	11,556	6,451	10,376
Bank of England, Banking Dept	**84aa**	152	44	–19	128	–128	....	....	....	....	....	....	....	....	....	....
Notes and Coin	**84ab**	204	148	152	186	197	....	....	....	....	....	....	....	....	....	....
Dep Money Bks: Bills & Bonds	**84ac**	158	–77	233	–394	–592	....	....	....	....	....	....	....	....	....	....
National Savings	**84ad**	–28	–202	–43	–93	–224	....	....	....	....	....	....	....	....	....	....
Tax Certificates	**84ae**	–106	79	36	21	–27	....	....	....	....	....	....	....	....	....	....
Other Dom. Hold. Bills & Bonds	**84af**	117	84	283	–257	347	....	....	....	....	....	....	....	....	....	....
Other Transactions (Net)	**84ag**	2	9	21	2	219	....	....	....	....	....	....	....	....	....	....
Foreign Borrowing	**85a**	111	458	492	1,164	–689	I –965	51	213	–319	1,084	–465	–527	1,345	130	1,389
EEA External Currency Flow	**85aa**	353	591	671	1,410	–743	....	....	....	....	....	....	....	....	....	....
of which: Treasury IMF Acct.	**85ab**	489	15	–339	506	–30	....	....	....	....	....	....	....	....	....	....
Fgn Hold.of Treas.Bills &Bonds	**85ac**	–274	–67	–112	–79	42	....	....	....	....	....	....	....	....	....	....
Other Fgn. Hold. of Govt. Debt	**85ad**	32	–66	–67	–167	12	....	....	....	....	....	....	....	....	....	....
Use of Cash Balances	**87**	–19	–8	–5	–23	–9	I –318	–2,416	1,438	–329	–359	263	–169	–8,544	2,058	–1,477
Adj. to Total Financing	**84x**	....	....	....	....	....	I –29	24	–5	–91	186	–428	479	577	169	876
																Millions of Pounds
Debt: Domestic	**88a**	....	....	....	....	....	I 25,921	28,168	29,017	31,988	36,045	46,699	57,219	66,817	75,327	80,496
Foreign	**89a**	....	....	....	....	....	I 5,158	5,289	5,613	5,528	6,825	6,675	6,414	6,873	6,505	8,632
National Accounts																*Billions of Pounds*
Exports of Goods & Services	**90c. *c***	6.61	7.17	7.39	8.98	10.09	11.51	12.92	13.62	17.07	22.88	26.86	35.09	43.30	47.48	54.90
Government Consumption	**91f. *c***	6.12	6.67	7.37	7.84	8.19	9.25	10.55	12.06	13.77	17.15	23.65	27.70	30.18	34.13	39.61
Gross Fixed Capital Formation	**93e. *c***	6.63	7.06	7.71	8.51	8.83	9.74	10.89	11.94	14.73	17.50	21.04	24.50	27.04	31.06	36.93
Increase/Decrease(-) in Stocks	**93i. *c***	.46	.29	.29	.45	.54	.38	.11	.03	1.53	1.05	–1.35	.90	1.82	1.80	2.16
Private Consumption	**96f. *c***	23.04	24.37	25.62	27.59	29.29	31.91	35.76	40.44	46.21	53.26	65.59	76.23	87.17	100.52	119.21
Imports of Goods & Services	**98c. *c***	–6.97	–7.26	–7.85	–9.38	–9.93	–11.10	–12.16	–13.74	–18.95	–27.15	–28.80	–36.64	–42.38	–45.37	–54.35
Gross Domestic Product	**99b. *c***	36.04	38.37	40.40	43.81	47.15	51.77	57.75	64.66	74.26	83.86	105.85	125.25	145.98	168.53	198.22
Net Factor Inc/Pmts(-) Abroad	**98.n *c***	.45	.40	.40	.36	.53	.60	.55	.59	1.33	1.51	.89	1.56	.27	.81	1.21
Gross Nat'l Expenditure = GNP	**99a. *c***	36.49	38.77	40.80	44.17	47.68	52.37	58.30	65.26	75.58	85.37	106.74	126.81	146.25	169.33	199.43
Gross Dom. Prod. 1990 Prices	**99b. *r***	308.91	314.75	321.96	335.08	341.99	349.79	356.74	369.24	396.41	389.67	386.87	397.61	407.00	421.07	432.85
GDP Deflator (1990=100)	**99bi *r***	11.7	12.2	12.5	13.1	13.8	14.8	16.2	17.5	18.7	21.5	27.4	31.5	35.9	40.0	45.8
																Millions:
Population	**99z**	54.18	54.50	54.80	55.05	55.27	55.42	55.61	55.78	55.91	55.92	55.90	55.89	55.85	55.84	55.88

International Liquidity: I Banks began to report foreign accounts according to a new system in 1975. I From 1985 onwards, deposit money banks' assets *(line 7a.d)* and their claims on nonbanks *(line 7add)* include holdings of bonds issued by nonresidents.

Monetary Authorities: I The breaks in series in 1981 and 1983 reflect the redefinition of the banking sector referred to in the notes for deposit money banks.

Deposit Money Banks: I A new system of bank returns was introduced in mid-May 1975, as described in the June 1975 issue of source B. As a result of this change, (1) money at call and money placed overnight are now reported in *line 24* rather than in *line 25,* a shift of approximately 700 million pounds sterling in the second quarter of 1975, and (2) *line 21* is estimated to have increased by about 1,300 million pounds sterling. I Beginning November 1981, they comprise the U.K. monetary sector as described in the December 1981 issue of source B, subject to the same exclusions as the banking sector. I Forty-three new banks were included in the quarterly survey of banking statistics at the end of March 1983. I Comprise U.K. banks authorized under the Banking Act of 1987, the Banking Department of the Bank of England, certain institutions in the Channel Islands and the Isle of Man, and, beginning 1987, building societies as defined by the Building Societies Act of 1986. Prior to January 1987, building societies are treated as part of the private sector.

Banking Survey: I Breaks in series occur as a result of changes in coverage referred to in the notes for deposit money banks.

Government Finance: I Beginning in 1970, data are as reported in the *Government Finance Statistics Yearbook* and cover consolidated central government.

United Kingdom

	1980	1981	1982	1983	1984	1985	1986	1987	1988	1989	1990	1991	1992	1993	1994		
Millions of Pounds																**International Transactions**	
	47,357	50,998	55,558	60,684	70,488	78,392	72,988	79,849	81,655	93,771	103,692	104,877	108,508	120,936	133,030	Exports	70
	49,773	51,169	56,978	66,101	78,967	85,027	86,176	94,026	106,571	121,699	126,086	118,786	125,867	137,404	147,564	Imports, cif	71
	45,792	47,416	53,421	62,237	75,601	81,336	82,186	90,735	101,826	116,837	120,527	113,697	120,447	134,787	145,059	Imports, fob(on a b.o.p. basis)	71.v
1990=100																	
	66.5	65.6	67.8	69.0	74.9	79.2	82.4	87.0	89.1	93.9	100.0	100.6	102.7	103.0	115.1	Volume of Exports	72
	57.9	55.1	57.9	61.6	68.2	70.8	75.8	81.2	92.3	99.6	100.0	94.7	100.8	101.2	107.8	Volume of Imports	73
	68.7	74.8	80.0	86.5	93.3	98.2	88.6	92.1	92.5	96.6	100.0	101.1	102.9	115.4	117.9	Unit Value of Exports	74
	66.9	72.3	78.0	85.1	92.4	96.7	92.2	94.5	93.8	97.6	100.0	101.0	101.9	111.5	115.2	Unit Value of Imports	75
Minus Sign Indicates Debit																**Balance of Payments**	
	109,620	102,158	96,660	91,963	93,487	100,862	106,429	129,847	143,078	150,696	181,729	182,579	188,451	181,914	207,283	Goods: Exports f.o.b.	78aa *d*
	−106,267	−95,198	−93,492	−94,340	−100,601	−104,817	−120,488	−148,866	−181,237	−191,239	−214,471	−200,853	−211,879	−202,060	−223,291	Goods: Imports f.o.b.	78ab *d*
	3,353	6,960	3,167	−2,377	−7,114	−3,955	−14,058	−19,019	−38,160	−40,544	−32,742	−18,274	−23,428	−20,146	−16,009	Trade Balance	78ac *d*
	36,452	34,010	30,861	29,070	28,429	31,306	37,092	44,599	47,822	47,930	56,234	54,223	58,602	55,562	59,277	Services: Credit	78ad *d*
	−27,933	−26,306	−25,553	−23,270	−22,828	−22,957	−27,992	−34,417	−40,759	−42,403	−49,671	−47,635	−51,481	−47,779	−51,980	Services: Debit	78ae *d*
	11,872	14,663	8,475	3,423	−1,513	4,394	−4,958	−8,837	−31,097	−35,017	−26,179	−11,686	−16,307	−12,363	−8,712	Balance on Goods and Services	78af *d*
	55,065	74,883	77,586	64,364	68,522	66,812	69,401	78,615	100,592	120,999	141,293	136,051	121,586	109,453	120,708	Income: Credit	78ag *d*
	−55,483	−72,344	−75,060	−60,073	−62,794	−63,932	−62,605	−72,537	−92,731	−115,388	−139,410	−136,545	−114,023	−107,014	−103,457	Income: Debit	78ah *d*
	11,454	17,203	11,000	7,714	4,216	7,274	1,838	−2,759	−23,237	−29,406	−24,296	−12,181	−8,743	−9,923	8,540	Balance on Goods, Serv., & Inc.	78ai *d*
	4,414	5,751	5,996	5,699	5,337	4,573	5,676	6,410	6,817	6,423	7,215	12,056	8,557	8,068	8,241	Current Transfers, n.i.e.: Credit	78aj *d*
	−9,005	−8,827	−9,011	−8,121	−7,718	−8,538	−8,848	−11,955	−13,154	−13,879	−15,956	−14,518	−17,663	−15,920	−16,793	Current Transfers: Debit	78ak *d*
	6,862	14,127	7,985	5,292	1,835	3,309	−1,334	−8,304	−29,574	−36,862	−33,037	−14,643	−17,850	−17,776	−12	Current Account, n.i.e.	78al *d*
	—	—	—	—	—	—	—	—	—	—	—	—	—	—	—	Capital Account, n.i.e.: Credit	78ba *d*
	—	—	—	—	—	—	—	—	—	—	—	—	—	—	—	Capital Account: Debit	78bb *d*
	—	—	—	—	—	—	—	—	—	—	—	—	—	—	—	Capital Account, n.i.e.	78bc *d*
	−11,229	−12,153	−7,163	−8,184	−7,969	−10,606	−17,018	−31,335	−37,287	−35,484	−19,327	−16,403	−19,347	−25,638	−29,951	Direct Investment Abroad	78bd *d*
	10,123	5,879	5,413	5,179	−347	5,480	8,570	15,696	21,414	30,553	32,430	16,059	16,491	14,559	10,942	Dir. Invest. in Rep. Econ., n.i.e.	78be *d*
	−7,787	−9,197	−13,209	−11,165	−12,926	−21,251	−32,821	9,739	−20,146	−59,265	−31,825	−51,768	−46,380	−126,915	28,211	Portfolio Investment Assets	78bf *d*
	878	−57	426	2,238	1,641	10,573	16,740	34,398	30,136	29,600	23,974	26,408	35,116	60,319	37,916	Portfolio Investment Liab., n.i.e.	78bg *d*
	−81,221	−86,313	−37,571	−27,363	−24,273	−32,872	−83,948	−92,727	−39,212	−63,224	−95,859	36,039	−84,168	−80,473	−44,997	Other Investment Assets	78bh *d*
	79,754	86,335	53,059	30,362	20,355	40,317	108,584	68,199	63,195	115,375	120,590	19,057	96,617	163,738	−29,843	Other Investment Liab., n.i.e.	78bi *d*
	−9,482	−15,507	956	−8,934	−23,519	−8,358	106	3,970	18,101	17,556	29,983	29,393	−1,671	5,590	−27,723	Financial Account, n.i.e.	78bj *d*
	1,931	1,787	−3,788	1,525	9,348	915	5,814	−2,700	10,009	3,781	521	−1,142	12,008	5,760	9,044	Net Errors and Omissions	78ca *d*
	−689	407	5,153	−2,117	−12,336	−4,134	4,586	−7,035	−1,464	−15,525	−2,533	13,608	−7,513	−6,426	−18,691	Overall Balance	78cb *d*
	689	−407	−5,153	2,117	12,336	4,134	−4,586	7,035	1,464	15,525	2,533	−13,608	7,513	6,426	18,691	Reserves and Related Items	79aa *d*
	−224	5,028	2,419	910	1,302	−551	−1,430	−20,187	−4,885	8,805	−121	−4,996	2,609	−1,084	−1,597	Reserve Assets	79db *d*
	−326	−298	−290	−57	—	—	—	—	—	—	—	—	—	—	—	Use of Fund Credit and Loans	79dc *d*
	1,989	−4,002	−7,803	353	9,429	3,676	−4,813	26,136	6,427	7,769	2,565	−8,567	4,937	7,323	20,262	Liabs.Constit.For.Auth.Reserves	79dd *d*
	−749	−1,135	521	910	1,605	1,009	1,657	1,086	−78	−1,048	89	−45	−33	187	26	Exceptional Financing	79de *d*
Year Ending December 31																**Government Finance**	
	−10,733	−12,141	−9,514	−13,372	−10,282	−10,268	−9,112	−2,880	7,284	7,971	4,000	−5,689	−29,995	....	....	Deficit (−) or Surplus	80
	81,640	91,806	106,449	112,590	120,665	133,839	139,836	151,367	169,355	182,897	203,022	212,683	215,076	....	....	Revenue	81
	408	992	1,363	1,153	1,039	667	753	937	736	828	735	3,138	1,078	....	....	Grants Received	81z
	88,475	103,089	113,762	122,347	130,718	141,102	147,419	155,882	162,909	174,578	207,442	229,150	257,887	....	....	Expenditure	82
	4,306	1,850	3,564	4,768	1,268	3,672	2,282	−698	−102	1,176	−7,685	−7,640	−11,738	....	....	Lending Minus Repayments	83
																Financing	
	9,419	8,040	6,083	14,189	10,044	8,615	7,831	11,525	−4,245	−11,940	−716	3,924	22,918	....	....	Domestic Borrowing	84a
	....	....	....	....	....	....	....	....	....	....	....	....	....	....	....	Bank of England, Banking Dept	84aa
	....	....	....	....	....	....	....	....	....	....	....	....	....	....	....	Notes and Coin	84ab
	....	....	....	....	....	....	....	....	....	....	....	....	....	....	....	Dep Money Bks: Bills & Bonds	84ac
	....	....	....	....	....	....	....	....	....	....	....	....	....	....	....	National Savings	84ad
	....	....	....	....	....	....	....	....	....	....	....	....	....	....	....	Tax Certificates	84ae
	....	....	....	....	....	....	....	....	....	....	....	....	....	....	....	Other Dom. Hold. Bills & Bonds	84af
	....	....	....	....	....	....	....	....	....	....	....	....	....	....	....	Other Transactions (Net)	84ag
	1,425	154	286	873	665	3,490	3,413	4,530	2,243	1,556	−3,717	5,496	4,713	....	....	Foreign Borrowing	85a
	....	....	....	....	....	....	....	....	....	....	....	....	....	....	....	EEA External Currency Flow	85aa
	....	....	....	....	....	....	....	....	....	....	....	....	....	....	....	of which: Treasury IMF Acct.	85ab
	....	....	....	....	....	....	....	....	....	....	....	....	....	....	....	Fgn Hold.of Treas.Bills &Bonds	85ac
	....	....	....	....	....	....	....	....	....	....	....	....	....	....	....	Other Fgn. Hold. of Govt. Debt	85ad
	−286	2,862	1,546	−616	−427	−166	−2,780	−12,360	−2,801	5,415	−57	−2,515	1,489	....	....	Use of Cash Balances	87
	175	1,085	1,599	−1,072	−3	−1,671	648	−815	−2,481	−3,002	490	−1,216	875	....	....	Adj. to Total Financing	84x
Year Beginning April 1																	
	96,606	100,629	112,609	126,680	139,899	151,448	161,726	169,590	178,613	164,853	158,508	161,195	168,613	....	....	Debt: Domestic	88a
	10,142	10,462	10,799	12,354	12,990	15,113	18,452	22,008	24,164	27,514	27,068	28,451	34,892	....	....	Foreign	89a
Billions of Pounds																**National Accounts**	
	62.62	67.43	72.69	79.88	91.63	102.04	97.89	106.40	107.27	121.49	133.17	134.23	141.82	159.39	173.93	Exports of Goods & Services	90c.*c*
	49.98	56.51	61.64	67.20	71.20	75.27	80.91	87.05	93.64	101.80	112.93	124.11	131.88	137.97	144.08	Government Consumption	91f.*c*
	41.56	41.30	44.82	48.62	55.18	60.72	65.03	75.16	91.53	105.44	107.58	97.75	93.64	94.64	100.08	Gross Fixed Capital Formation	93e.*c*
	−2.57	−2.77	−1.19	1.47	1.30	.82	.68	1.23	4.33	2.68	−1.80	−4.93	−1.94	.33	3.30	Increase/Decrease(−) in Stocks	93i.*c*
	138.56	154.27	169.37	185.61	198.82	217.49	241.55	265.29	299.45	327.36	347.53	364.97	381.72	405.46	428.08	Private Consumption	96f.*c*
	−57.61	−60.39	−67.76	−77.59	−92.76	−98.99	−101.22	−111.74	−124.80	−142.81	−148.29	−140.81	−149.87	−167.08	−180.73	Imports of Goods & Services	98c.*c*
	231.77	254.93	279.04	304.46	325.85	357.34	384.84	423.38	471.43	515.96	551.12	575.32	597.24	630.71	668.87	Gross Domestic Product	99b.*c*
	−.18	1.25	1.46	2.83	4.34	2.30	4.63	3.93	4.57	3.50	.72	−.57	3.69	1.89	10.52	Net Factor Inc/Pmts(−) Abroad	98.n *c*
	231.59	256.18	280.50	307.29	330.20	359.64	389.47	427.31	476.00	519.46	551.84	574.75	600.94	632.60	679.39	Gross Nat'l Expenditure = GNP	99a.*c*
	423.49	418.03	425.25	440.89	451.13	468.07	488.12	511.62	537.22	548.94	551.12	540.31	537.45	549.59	570.72	Gross Dom. Prod. 1990 Prices	99b.*r*
	54.7	61.0	65.6	69.1	72.2	76.3	78.8	82.8	87.8	94.0	100.0	106.5	111.1	114.8	117.2	GDP Deflator (1990=100)	99bi *r*
Midyear Estimates																	
	56.33	56.35	56.31	56.35	56.51	56.68	56.85	57.01	57.16	57.35	57.56	57.80	58.00	I 57.92	....	Population	99z

United States

111

		1965	1966	1967	1968	1969	1970	1971	1972	1973	1974	1975	1976	1977	1978	1979
Exchange Rates														*End of Period (sa and sc)*	*Period Averages (sb and sd)*	
US Dollar/SDR Rate.........aa=	sa	1.0000	1.0000	1.0000	1.0000	1.0000	1.0000	1.0857	1.0857	1.2064	1.2244	1.1707	1.1618	1.2147	1.3028	1.3173
US Dollar/SDR Rate	sb	1.0000	1.0000	1.0000	1.0000	1.0000	1.0000	1.0030	1.0857	1.1921	1.2026	1.2142	1.1545	1.1675	1.2520	1.2920
SDR/US Dollar Rate.........ac=	sc	1.0000	1.0000	1.0000	1.0000	1.0000	1.0000	.9211	.9211	.8290	.8168	.8542	.8607	.8232	.7676	.7591
SDR/US Dollar Rate	sd	1.0000	1.0000	1.0000	1.0000	1.0000	1.0000	.9970	.9211	.8388	.8315	.8236	.8662	.8565	.7987	.7740
															Dollars per ECU:	
ECU Rate	ea	....	....	....	....	....	....	....	....	....	....	....	....	....	....	1.4419
ECU Rate	eb	....	....	....	....	....	....	....	....	....	....	....	....	....	1.2740	1.3706
															Index Numbers (1990=100):	
Nominal Effective Exchange Rate	ne u	136.7	136.7	137.0	139.4	139.6	137.9	134.2	123.8	115.0	117.8	117.9	122.6	120.8	109.2	108.7
Real Effective Exchange Rate	re u	....	....	....	....	....	....	....	....	....	....	117.6	120.6	118.6	108.8	109.9
Fund Position															*Billions of SDRs:*	
Quota	2f. s	4.13	5.16	5.16	5.16	5.16	6.70	6.70	6.70	6.70	6.70	6.70	6.70	6.70	8.41	8.41
SDRs	1b. s	—	—	—	—	—	.85	1.10	1.80	1.80	1.94	1.99	2.06	2.16	1.20	2.07
Reserve Position in the Fund	1c. s	.60	.33	.42	1.29	2.32	1.94	.58	.43	.46	1.51	1.89	3.82	4.07	.80	.95
of which: Outstg.Fund Borrowing	2c	—	—	—	—	—	—	—	—	—	—	—	—	.58	—	—
International Liquidity												*Billions of US Dollars Unless Otherwise Indicated:*				
Total Reserves minus Gold	1l. d	1.39	1.65	2.77	4.82	5.10	3.41	2.11	2.66	2.73	4.23	4.63	7.15	7.59	6.98	7.78
SDRs	1b. d	—	—	—	—	—	.85	1.19	1.96	2.17	2.37	2.33	2.39	2.63	1.56	2.72
Reserve Position in the Fund	1c. d	.60	.33	.42	1.29	2.32	1.94	.63	.46	.55	1.85	2.21	4.43	4.95	1.05	1.25
Foreign Exchange	1d. d	.78	1.32	2.35	3.53	2.78	.63	.28	.24	.01	.01	.08	.32	.02	4.37	3.81
Gold (Million Fine Troy Ounces)	1ad	401.86	378.14	344.71	311.20	338.83	316.34	291.60	275.97	275.97	275.97	274.71	274.68	277.55	276.41	264.60
Gold (National Valuation)	1an d	14.07	13.24	12.07	10.89	11.86	11.07	10.21	10.49	11.65	11.65	11.60	11.60	11.72	11.67	11.17
Deposit Money Banks: Assets	7a. d	9.83	10.00	9.80	9.80	10.99	11.80	13.61	17.99	23.89	42.47	54.70	72.68	88.05	I 118.58	136.03
of which: Claims on Nonbanks	7ad d	6.72	6.67	6.71	6.45	6.48	6.74	7.82	9.38	11.48	19.64	20.87	24.17	27.00	I 33.39	45.63
Deposit Money Banks: Liabilities	7b. d	17.27	20.96	23.32	26.45	37.66	31.27	26.91	34.43	40.02	64.05	62.72	71.15	87.33	I 101.08	141.00
of which: Liabilities to Nonbanks	7bd d	12.45	13.18	14.82	15.61	18.41	17.78	17.64	22.57	28.64	45.60	44.21	48.01	55.13	I 18.15	20.43
Monetary Authorities															*Billions of US Dollars:*	
Foreign Assets	11	13.1	12.5	12.3	14.8	15.1	13.9	11.8	13.0	14.2	15.9	16.2	18.7	19.3	18.7	18.9
Claims on Central Government	12a	45.4	49.6	55.3	58.4	61.7	66.8	76.4	78.1	86.7	87.5	95.2	100.9	108.6	121.6	129.8
Federal Reserve Float	13a	2.2	2.5	2.6	3.4	3.4	4.3	4.3	4.0	3.1	2.0	10.1	2.5	3.6	6.5	6.8
Reserve Money	14	60.5	64.4	68.2	72.8	76.0	81.2	88.8	92.2	99.6	105.6	112.6	118.8	130.5	145.3	155.0
of which: Currency Outside Banks	14a	37.2	39.2	41.3	43.8	46.6	50.0	53.5	57.8	61.9	69.1	74.2	79.7	88.0	97.4	107.6
Foreign Liabilities	16c	.2	.2	.1	.2	.1	.1	.3	.3	.3	.4	.4	.4	.4	.4	.4
Central Government Deposits	16d	.8	.9	1.9	2.2	2.1	1.5	1.7	1.4	1.9	2.7	6.9	10.3	7.0	5.5	3.9
Other Items (Net)	17r	−.7	−.9	—	1.6	2.0	2.0	1.9	1.1	2.2	−3.3	1.7	−7.3	−6.3	−4.5	−3.9
Banking Institutions																
Commercial Banks															*Billions of US Dollars:*	
Reserves	20	23.4	25.3	27.0	29.1	29.4	31.3	35.3	34.4	37.8	37.4	38.4	37.3	40.8	46.7	48.3
Foreign Assets	21	8.5	8.4	9.2	8.8	9.6	10.9	12.7	15.2	21.9	38.8	52.2	66.7	78.9	93.2	114.5
Claims on Central Government	22a	60.2	56.8	63.3	65.3	55.6	62.5	65.6	68.1	59.2	55.1	85.0	103.8	102.0	95.3	95.6
Claims on State and Local Govts.	22b	38.8	41.2	50.3	58.9	59.5	70.2	82.8	90.0	95.7	101.2	102.9	106.0	115.2	126.2	135.6
Claims on Private Sector	22d	207.9	227.7	249.7	280.1	307.7	327.9	362.7	426.3	510.9	574.9	572.7	618.0	702.5	812.9	921.1
Demand Deposits	24	138.7	140.9	152.4	165.4	169.6	175.5	186.7	203.8	214.6	216.9	226.5	236.9	254.6	273.6	295.2
Time and Savings Deposits	25	116.7	127.8	145.8	159.8	165.9	180.1	208.7	233.2	264.2	264.2	304.3	358.9	387.2	401.1	431.1
Money Market Instruments	26aa	28.3	30.5	35.9	43.0	31.4	56.2	68.9	83.3	122.7	167.3	156.1	145.7	175.7	228.3	252.7
Bonds	26ab	1.6	1.7	2.0	2.2	2.0	3.2	5.2	8.3	9.2	10.4	14.5	18.0	21.1	22.1	21.9
Foreign Liabilities	26c	15.3	18.7	21.1	23.6	33.8	27.0	22.8	30.4	35.7	53.1	55.0	60.8	72.8	84.5	121.2
Central Government Deposits	26d	5.5	5.0	5.2	5.0	5.1	7.9	10.2	10.9	9.9	4.8	3.1	3.0	7.3	14.1	14.5
Credit from Monetary Authorities	26g	4.6	5.2	5.1	7.2	7.0	8.9	8.7	10.0	7.5	4.3	7.6	5.2	7.9	14.2	15.0
Other Items (Net)	27r	28.1	29.6	32.0	36.0	47.0	44.0	47.9	54.1	79.9	86.4	84.1	103.3	112.8	136.4	163.5
Thrift Institutions															*Billions of US Dollars:*	
Reserves	20.. t	6.7	6.1	6.1	5.5	4.9	5.9	8.5	10.8	10.0	11.5	16.9	15.5	16.5	17.0	16.1
Claims on Central Government	22a. t	12.0	11.8	13.0	13.2	11.3	10.2	9.8	9.2	7.8	6.8	11.4	15.3	16.8	14.0	12.3
Claims on State and Local Govts.	22b. t	.3	.3	.2	.3	.3	.3	.5	1.0	1.1	1.4	3.1	3.6	4.0	4.6	4.1
Claims on Private Sector	22d. t	171.8	181.0	194.4	209.7	226.2	244.7	282.6	328.8	367.0	392.0	437.4	502.5	579.8	654.4	710.7
Demand Deposits	24.. t	.3	.3	.3	.4	.4	.4	.5	.6	.8	.9	1.3	2.1	3.1	4.2	5.4
Time and Savings Deposits	25.. t	171.8	178.8	195.4	208.1	216.0	232.4	272.0	317.1	343.6	363.1	421.1	488.1	554.5	606.1	636.3
Money Market Instruments	26aa t	—	—	—	—	—	.7	1.5	2.7	3.8	7.2	8.2	9.5	13.8	22.8	40.0
Bonds	26ab t	—	—	—	—	—	—	—	—	—	—	.1	.1	1.3	2.0	3.4
Other Items (Net)	27r. t	18.7	20.1	18.0	20.2	26.3	27.6	27.4	29.4	37.7	40.5	38.1	37.1	44.4	54.9	58.1
Money Market Funds															*Billions of US Dollars:*	
Foreign Assets	21. m	—	—	—	—	—	—	—	—	—	—	—	—	—	.5	5.1
Claims on Central Government	22a m	—	—	—	—	—	—	—	—	—	.1	.9	1.2	.9	.9	1.6
Claims on Local Government	22b m	—	—	—	—	—	—	—	—	—	—	—	—	—	—	—
Claims on Private Sector	22d m	—	—	—	—	—	—	—	—	—	.7	.5	.9	1.1	4.3	23.3
Claims on Banks	22e m	—	—	—	—	—	—	—	—	—	1.6	2.1	1.5	1.8	4.6	12.1
Time Deposits	25. m	—	—	—	—	—	—	—	—	—	2.4	3.7	3.7	3.9	10.8	45.2
Other Items (Net)	27r m	—	—	—	—	—	—	—	—	—	—	−.2	−.1	−.1	−.5	−3.1
Banking Survey															*Billions of US Dollars:*	
Foreign Assets (Net)	31n	6.1	2.0	.3	−.2	−9.2	−2.4	1.4	−2.6	.1	1.2	13.1	24.3	25.0	27.5	16.8
Domestic Credit	32	530.1	562.6	619.2	678.8	715.1	773.1	869.0	990.5	1,118.5	1,216.9	1,305.2	1,445.7	1,624.6	1,822.4	2,023.9
Claims on Central Govt. (Net)	32an	111.3	112.4	124.6	129.8	121.4	130.0	139.9	143.1	141.8	142.0	182.5	207.9	214.0	212.1	220.9
Claims on State and Local Govts.	32b	39.1	41.5	50.5	59.2	59.8	70.5	83.3	91.0	96.8	102.6	106.0	109.6	119.2	130.8	139.7
Claims on Private Sector	32d	379.7	408.7	444.1	489.8	533.9	572.6	645.8	756.4	879.8	972.3	1,016.7	1,128.2	1,291.4	1,479.5	1,663.3
Money	34	176.2	180.4	194.0	209.6	216.6	225.9	240.7	262.2	277.3	286.9	302.0	318.7	345.7	375.2	408.2
Quasi-Money	35	288.5	306.6	341.2	367.9	381.9	412.5	480.7	550.3	589.6	629.7	729.1	850.7	945.6	1,018.0	1,112.6
Money Market Instruments	36aa	28.3	30.5	35.9	43.0	31.4	56.9	70.4	86.0	126.5	174.5	164.3	155.2	189.5	251.1	292.7
Bonds	36ab	1.6	1.7	2.0	2.2	2.0	3.2	5.2	8.3	9.2	10.4	14.6	18.1	22.4	24.1	25.3
Other Items (Net)	37r	41.7	45.4	46.3	55.9	74.0	72.3	73.5	81.1	116.0	116.5	108.2	127.3	146.5	181.5	201.9
Money plus Quasi-Money	35l	464.7	487.0	535.2	577.5	598.5	638.4	721.4	812.5	866.9	916.6	1,031.1	1,169.4	1,291.3	1,393.2	1,520.8

1980	1981	1982	1983	1984	1985	1986	1987	1988	1989	1990	1991	1992	1993	1994		
End of Period (sa and sc) Period Averages (sb and sd)															**Exchange Rates**	
1.2754	1.1640	1.1031	1.0470	.9802	1.0984	1.2232	1.4187	1.3457	1.3142	1.4227	1.4304	1.3750	1.3736	1.4599	US Dollar/SDR Rate ... aa=	sa
1.3015	1.1792	1.1040	1.0690	1.0250	1.0153	1.1732	1.2931	1.3439	1.2818	1.3568	1.3682	1.4084	1.3963	1.4317	US Dollar/SDR Rate	sb
.7841	.8591	.9065	.9552	1.0202	.9104	.8175	.7049	.7431	.7609	.7029	.6991	.7273	.7280	.6850	SDR/US Dollar Rate ... ac=	sc
.7683	.8481	.9058	.9355	.9756	.9849	.8524	.7734	.7441	.7802	.7371	.7309	.7100	.7162	.6985	SDR/US Dollar Rate	sd
End of Period (ea) Period Average (eb)																
1.3096	1.0852	.9677	.8274	.7089	.8879	1.0704	1.3034	1.1726	1.1970	1.3633	1.3409	1.2109	1.1200	1.2300	ECU Rate	ea
1.3910	1.1176	.9812	.8913	.7890	.7622	.9812	1.1543	1.1839	1.1024	1.2730	1.2405	1.2968	1.1723	1.1886	ECU Rate	eb
Period Averages																
108.0	118.2	130.9	135.7	145.0	149.9	122.0	107.8	100.4	104.8	100.0	98.4	96.5	99.4	97.6	Nominal Effective Exchange Rate	ne*u*
112.3	123.4	139.4	141.8	149.9	154.3	124.6	108.2	101.5	104.9	100.0	98.5	96.5	100.4	....	Real Effective Exchange Rate	re*u*
End of Period															**Fund Position**	
12.61	12.61	12.61	17.92	17.92	17.92	17.92	17.92	17.92	17.92	17.92	17.92	26.53	26.53	26.53	Quota	2f.*s*
2.05	3.52	4.76	4.80	5.75	6.64	6.86	7.25	7.16	7.57	7.72	7.86	6.18	6.57	6.88	SDRs	1b.*s*
2.24	4.34	6.66	10.81	11.77	10.88	9.59	8.00	7.24	6.88	6.38	6.63	8.55	8.59	8.24	Reserve Position in the Fund	1c.*s*
.30	.75	1.14	1.43	1.32	1.10	.77	.42	.19	.04	—	—	—	—	—	*of which:* Outstg.Fund Borrowing	2c
End of Period															**International Liquidity**	
15.60	18.92	22.81	22.63	23.84	32.10	37.45	34.72	36.74	63.55	72.26	66.66	60.27	62.35	63.28	Total Reserves minus Gold	1l.*d*
2.61	4.10	5.25	5.03	5.64	7.29	8.39	10.28	9.64	9.95	10.99	11.24	8.50	9.02	10.04	SDRs	1b.*d*
2.85	5.05	7.35	11.31	11.54	11.95	11.73	11.35	9.75	9.05	9.08	9.49	11.76	11.80	12.03	Reserve Position in the Fund	1c.*d*
10.13	9.77	10.21	6.29	6.66	12.86	17.33	13.09	17.36	44.55	52.19	45.93	40.01	41.53	41.22	Foreign Exchange	1d.*d*
264.32	264.11	264.03	263.39	262.79	262.65	262.04	262.38	261.87	261.93	261.91	261.91	261.84	261.79	261.73	Gold (Million Fine Troy Ounces)	1ad
11.16	11.15	11.15	11.12	11.10	11.09	11.06	11.08	11.06	11.06	11.06	11.06	11.06	11.05	11.05	Gold (National Valuation)	1an*d*
176.91	254.62	360.54	397.17	409.88	417.32	470.29	511.25	560.15	599.62	578.34	587.53	562.24	545.23	532.66	Deposit Money Banks: Assets	7a.*d*
57.35	80.21	107.04	121.08	119.01	110.69	110.27	107.54	104.30	103.60	89.96	78.94	86.10	99.56	86.06	*of which:* Claims on Nonbanks	7ad*d*
151.45	189.92	254.55	305.78	338.12	381.26	477.22	572.95	645.26	713.61	733.32	720.46	755.41	823.18	942.65	Deposit Money Banks: Liabilities	7b.*d*
21.53	27.47	45.55	58.83	67.45	73.84	80.59	81.16	86.84	103.37	92.82	92.14	91.42	96.88	109.80	*of which:* Liabilities to Nonbanks	7bd*d*
End of Period															**Monetary Authorities**	
26.8	30.1	33.9	33.7	34.9	43.2	48.4	45.8	47.8	75.5	85.2	75.9	72.0	73.4	74.3	Foreign Assets	11
132.4	139.7	146.7	157.7	168.7	187.6	208.5	230.8	247.7	245.7	256.0	288.4	312.4	350.3	383.5	Claims on Central Government	12a
4.5	1.8	2.7	1.6	.8	1.0	1.3	.8	1.3	1.0	2.2	.7	3.3	.9	–.7	Federal Reserve Float	13a
164.3	170.0	181.4	191.5	205.6	226.1	260.1	272.0	287.0	298.8	325.6	337.2	366.8	400.2	434.6	Reserve Money	14
116.8	122.8	131.9	146.6	160.5	175.3	186.3	201.8	217.3	228.9	254.8	277.0	298.5	327.5	363.5	*of which:* Currency Outside Banks	14a
.4	.5	.3	.2	.3	.5	.3	.2	.3	.6	.4	1.0	.2	.4	.3	Foreign Liabilities	16c
5.5	7.3	9.3	6.2	9.2	17.1	17.8	14.0	19.9	23.7	34.0	38.8	28.0	36.3	29.2	Central Government Deposits	16d
–6.6	–6.3	–7.7	–4.8	–10.6	–11.9	–20.0	–8.8	–10.5	–.9	–16.6	–11.9	–7.4	–12.3	–7.0	Other Items (Net)	17r
															Banking Institutions	
End of Period															Commercial Banks	
47.2	43.7	45.6	41.1	43.8	50.2	68.2	61.8	61.7	59.8	67.9	60.1	60.9	64.2	66.3	Reserves	20
160.8	196.7	202.4	208.7	204.7	197.9	192.5	174.6	180.7	157.0	169.4	190.5	245.6	228.8	221.3	Foreign Assets	21
111.5	113.8	134.0	179.5	181.5	189.4	197.7	194.4	185.7	166.1	172.1	232.5	294.4	322.2	290.4	Claims on Central Government	22a
148.8	154.0	158.3	162.1	174.6	231.8	203.4	174.3	151.6	133.8	117.4	103.2	97.5	99.2	97.6	Claims on State and Local Govts.	22b
989.4	1,081.3	1,159.9	1,252.2	1,419.7	1,563.9	1,783.7	1,945.8	2,137.5	2,360.1	2,494.4	2,546.0	2,625.4	2,757.0	2,943.9	Claims on Private Sector	22d
307.1	320.8	337.3	357.2	380.1	422.3	511.9	499.4	509.4	508.7	583.6	621.3	714.3	788.4	756.3	Demand Deposits	24
476.7	517.6	615.6	745.5	820.6	902.1	975.9	1,003.9	1,077.5	1,177.7	1,307.6	1,386.5	1,389.3	1,377.4	1,375.8	Time and Savings Deposits	25
311.5	378.6	390.1	350.8	393.8	393.6	388.2	435.7	471.3	501.7	463.2	419.7	348.3	326.5	350.0	Money Market Instruments	26aa
23.2	26.1	32.4	42.0	55.5	74.4	90.5	104.0	109.1	113.7	108.9	113.2	127.7	134.9	140.8	Bonds	26ab
131.1	113.4	108.1	124.5	132.0	153.6	168.7	194.2	213.8	187.1	209.8	219.2	248.1	241.3	296.1	Foreign Liabilities	26c
11.9	10.8	16.9	11.5	15.6	25.8	27.5	21.6	29.0	25.6	30.9	36.4	30.6	42.6	23.8	Central Government Deposits	26d
10.8	5.2	6.2	4.1	5.3	5.1	4.1	5.4	4.8	2.7	5.3	2.3	7.2	1.9	–1.2	Credit from Monetary Authorities	26g
185.4	217.0	193.6	208.0	221.4	256.3	278.7	286.7	302.3	359.6	311.7	333.7	458.4	558.2	678.0	Other Items (Net)	27r
End of Period															Thrift Institutions	
22.6	24.4	42.3	47.3	40.6	51.1	65.0	53.9	52.9	47.2	46.1	52.9	52.7	54.0	43.4	Reserves	20.. *t*
14.1	14.3	17.9	34.6	43.4	40.7	46.0	58.8	49.3	38.9	34.4	39.0	53.9	50.8	48.1	Claims on Central Government	22a. *t*
3.6	3.6	3.3	3.1	2.8	3.4	3.1	3.1	2.8	2.6	3.0	2.4	2.1	2.1	2.0	Claims on State and Local Govts.	22b. *t*
762.2	789.0	796.2	915.7	1,061.7	1,157.1	1,262.9	1,386.9	1,514.5	1,444.9	1,291.8	1,161.4	1,089.7	1,092.4	1,128.6	Claims on Private Sector	22d. *t*
8.3	16.7	25.0	36.5	44.4	57.4	77.9	85.0	93.4	93.3	86.3	105.9	109.0	115.1	111.6	Demand Deposits	24.. *t*
674.1	681.9	722.9	808.6	884.8	945.6	993.9	1,035.6	1,100.0	1,099.7	1,041.6	964.2	904.2	845.8	807.6	Time and Savings Deposits	25.. *t*
54.7	69.7	79.4	127.9	193.7	196.9	215.8	252.5	282.3	222.5	165.7	108.4	101.3	106.1	124.1	Money Market Instruments	26aa *t*
3.7	3.2	3.7	4.0	5.9	10.5	15.4	19.8	21.7	18.3	12.7	8.6	5.5	3.9	3.1	Bonds	26ab *t*
61.7	59.8	28.7	23.7	19.7	41.9	74.0	109.8	122.1	99.8	69.0	68.7	78.3	128.4	175.7	Other Items (Net)	27r. *t*
End of Period															Money Market Funds	
6.8	18.9	23.8	21.9	21.2	19.0	22.2	21.6	29.7	26.4	27.1	21.6	20.5	10.1	16.0	Foreign Assets	21.*m*
3.5	21.5	42.7	22.8	25.4	24.6	28.0	14.3	11.6	14.8	45.5	79.6	79.7	80.8	67.4	Claims on Central Government	22a*m*
1.9	4.3	13.2	16.8	23.8	36.3	63.8	61.4	65.7	69.4	83.6	89.9	94.8	103.2	110.7	Claims on Local Government	22b*m*
36.4	80.8	81.1	79.6	115.0	117.2	120.4	138.3	147.5	207.6	243.6	233.2	229.5	234.8	271.2	Claims on Private Sector	22d*m*
21.2	43.3	41.1	23.7	22.3	17.0	19.1	33.3	33.5	41.3	32.4	32.8	28.2	23.8	20.0	Claims on Banks	22e*m*
76.4	186.2	219.8	179.4	233.6	243.8	292.1	316.1	337.9	428.1	498.4	539.6	543.6	558.9	605.3	Time Deposits	25.*m*
–6.6	–17.4	–17.9	–14.6	–25.9	–29.7	–38.6	–47.2	–49.9	–68.6	–66.3	–82.4	–90.8	–106.2	–120.0	Other Items (Net)	27r*m*
End of Period															**Banking Survey**	
62.8	131.8	151.7	139.7	128.6	106.0	94.2	47.6	44.1	71.2	71.4	67.8	89.8	70.6	15.4	Foreign Assets (Net)	31n
2,195.1	2,393.3	2,536.0	2,815.0	3,200.2	3,517.3	3,880.1	4,180.0	4,472.0	4,641.1	4,683.3	4,706.5	4,826.3	5,018.4	5,294.0	Domestic Credit	32
244.0	271.1	315.1	376.9	394.2	399.4	434.9	462.7	445.4	416.2	443.1	564.4	681.8	725.1	736.4	Claims on Central Govt. (Net)	32an
154.3	161.9	174.8	182.0	201.2	271.5	270.3	238.8	220.1	205.8	201.1	195.5	194.4	204.4	210.3	Claims on State and Local Govts.	32b
1,796.7	1,960.2	2,046.1	2,256.1	2,604.8	2,846.4	3,174.8	3,478.6	3,806.5	4,019.1	4,036.1	3,946.6	3,950.0	4,088.8	4,347.3	Claims on Private Sector	32d
432.2	460.3	494.2	540.3	585.0	655.0	776.1	786.2	820.1	830.9	924.7	1,004.1	1,121.9	1,231.0	1,231.4	Money	34
1,227.2	1,385.7	1,558.3	1,733.5	1,939.0	2,091.5	2,261.9	2,355.6	2,515.4	2,705.5	2,847.6	2,890.3	2,837.0	2,782.1	2,788.7	Quasi-Money	35
366.2	448.3	469.5	478.7	587.5	590.5	604.0	688.2	753.6	724.2	628.9	528.1	449.7	432.6	474.1	Money Market Instruments	36aa
26.9	29.3	36.1	46.0	61.4	84.9	105.9	123.8	130.8	132.0	121.6	121.8	133.1	138.8	143.9	Bonds	36ab
205.4	201.5	129.6	156.2	155.9	201.5	226.3	273.8	296.1	319.7	231.9	230.1	374.3	504.4	671.3	Other Items (Net)	37r
1,659.4	1,846.0	2,052.5	2,273.8	2,524.0	2,746.5	3,038.0	3,141.8	3,335.5	3,536.4	3,772.3	3,894.4	3,958.9	4,013.1	4,020.1	Money plus Quasi-Money	35l

United States

111

		1965	1966	1967	1968	1969	1970	1971	1972	1973	1974	1975	1976	1977	1978	1979
Other Financial Institutions														*Billions of US Dollars*		
Claims on Central Government	42a	2.4	3.7	2.4	3.4	6.8	9.1	7.0	7.4	8.2	9.5	9.9	15.7	11.7	10.0	5.7
Claims on State and Local Govts.	42b	.5	.4	.5	.5	10.3	11.9	14.2	15.3	16.4	14.9	16.5	21.8	26.0	27.8	30.7
Claims on Private Sector	42d	85.5	86.9	98.2	111.7	213.1	214.7	252.9	292.1	286.7	252.7	278.8	312.4	319.3	349.1	396.6
Claims on Banks	42e	3.3	3.3	3.7	4.7	6.9	7.1	8.1	9.1	9.3	9.6	9.7	11.2	12.1	12.3	13.6
Claims on Other Financial Insts.	42f	—	.1	—	.1	4.1	4.0	4.9	5.8	5.0	3.6	4.3	5.2	4.8	5.4	6.3
Credit Market Instruments	46aa	37.7	39.9	54.0	62.8	61.3	59.8	71.5	76.0	59.2	41.5	54.0	62.5	65.4	61.4	71.4
Bonds	46ab	15.1	16.6	17.3	17.7	18.9	20.2	23.0	27.3	31.8	37.6	42.5	45.9	53.9	58.8	61.2
Liabilities to Banks	46h	11.7	11.1	10.7	12.3	129.8	134.5	158.7	187.6	182.2	156.1	163.4	190.1	188.1	198.0	219.0
Other Items (Net)	47r	27.2	26.8	22.8	27.6	31.2	32.3	33.9	38.8	52.4	55.1	59.3	67.8	66.5	86.4	101.3
Insurance Companies & Pension Funds														*Billions of US Dollars:*		
Claims on Central Government	42a. s	20.3	19.3	17.2	16.7	15.2	14.6	13.0	13.7	14.1	16.5	24.3	34.9	43.2	48.0	56.3
Claims on State and Local Govts	42b. s	17.5	17.8	19.1	20.0	21.0	22.3	26.1	30.2	33.6	35.4	39.7	47.7	59.0	73.3	83.1
Claims on Private Sector	42d. s	248.1	262.6	293.6	323.4	337.7	364.1	411.7	469.0	474.2	469.8	555.5	622.6	668.1	762.3	862.6
Claims on Banks	42e. s	6.9	7.5	8.4	9.4	9.8	11.2	12.7	14.8	17.5	20.8	24.0	26.6	30.5	36.7	42.7
Claims on Other Financial Insts.	42f. s	.5	.5	.7	.8	1.3	1.7	1.8	1.8	2.2	2.5	3.4	4.1	4.7	5.1	8.2
Insurance and Pension Reserves	47a. s	240.5	254.3	280.8	307.3	323.0	348.5	391.3	450.5	464.1	476.5	579.2	650.3	707.8	812.2	922.1
Other Items (Net)	47r. s	52.8	53.4	58.2	63.0	62.0	65.4	74.0	79.0	77.5	68.5	67.7	85.6	97.7	113.2	130.8
Financial Survey														*Billions of US Dollars:*		
Foreign Assets (Net)	51n	6.1	2.0	.3	−.2	−9.2	−2.4	1.4	−2.6	.1	1.2	13.1	24.3	25.0	27.5	16.8
Domestic Credit	52	618.5	653.6	720.3	794.4	945.3	1,008.8	1,143.1	1,305.3	1,429.8	1,494.0	1,610.4	1,795.6	1,981.6	2,209.3	2,456.9
Claims on Central Govt. (Net)	52an	113.7	116.1	127.0	133.2	128.2	139.1	146.9	150.5	150.0	151.5	192.4	223.6	225.7	222.1	226.6
Claims on State and Local Govts.	52b	39.6	41.9	51.0	59.7	70.1	82.4	97.5	106.3	113.2	117.5	122.5	131.4	145.2	158.6	170.4
Claims on Private Sector	52d	465.2	495.6	542.3	601.5	747.0	787.3	898.7	1,048.5	1,166.5	1,225.0	1,295.5	1,440.6	1,610.7	1,828.6	2,059.9
Liquid Liabilities	55l	464.7	487.0	535.2	577.5	598.5	638.4	721.4	812.5	866.9	916.6	1,031.1	1,169.4	1,291.3	1,393.2	1,520.8
Credit Market Instruments	56aa	66.0	70.4	89.9	105.8	92.7	116.7	141.9	162.0	185.7	216.0	218.3	217.7	254.9	312.5	364.1
Bonds	56ab	16.7	18.3	19.3	19.9	20.9	23.4	28.2	35.6	41.0	48.0	57.1	64.0	76.3	82.9	86.5
Other Items (Net)	57r	77.3	79.9	76.1	91.0	224.0	228.0	253.1	292.6	336.3	314.5	316.9	368.8	384.2	448.2	502.3
Money Stock, Liquid Assets, and																
Debt Measures (National Definitions)														*Billions of US Dollars:*		
M1	59ma	172.7	176.9	188.4	202.8	209.4	220.1	234.5	256.2	270.2	281.9	295.4	314.5	340.0	368.0	393.1
M1, Seasonally Adjusted	59ma c	167.9	172.0	183.3	197.4	203.9	214.4	228.3	249.2	262.8	274.3	287.5	306.3	331.1	358.2	382.5
M2	59mb	463.1	483.7	528.0	569.7	592.4	629.2	713.5	806.0	861.9	909.6	1,024.2	1,164.8	1,288.8	1,392.5	1,501.8
M2, Seasonally Adjusted	59mb c	459.3	480.0	524.3	566.3	589.5	628.0	712.6	805.1	860.9	908.4	1,023.1	1,163.5	1,286.4	1,388.5	1,496.4
M3	59mc	485.5	508.6	560.8	610.1	618.2	678.2	776.6	886.2	985.2	1,071.1	1,173.7	1,314.1	1,476.7	1,652.7	1,810.4
M3, Seasonally Adjusted	59mc c	482.2	505.1	557.1	606.2	615.0	677.3	776.1	886.0	984.9	1,070.4	1,172.1	1,311.6	1,472.3	1,646.2	1,802.6
L	59md	587.0	617.4	669.5	731.9	765.9	816.9	903.5	1,023.6	1,143.5	1,251.6	1,369.3	1,519.5	1,709.7	1,916.4	2,122.8
L, Seasonally Adjusted	59md c	584.4	614.7	666.5	728.9	763.5	816.2	902.9	1,022.9	1,142.5	1,250.2	1,369.3	1,516.4	1,705.0	1,910.3	2,115.6
Debt	59me	1,002.9	1,069.9	1,144.0	1,235.3	1,326.3	1,416.4	1,548.7	1,704.7	1,892.1	2,064.8	2,249.1	2,494.8	2,812.1	3,189.4	3,564.2
Debt, Seasonally Adjusted	59me c	1,005.1	1,072.3	1,146.6	1,238.2	1,329.3	1,419.6	1,552.0	1,707.5	1,894.1	2,067.0	2,251.4	2,496.3	2,813.7	3,192.2	3,568.2
Treasury Securities by Holders														*Billions of US Dollars:*		
Total	59t	257.0	259.3	268.2	277.6	276.8	289.9	315.9	330.1	336.7	348.8	434.9	503.7	561.0	614.9	652.1
Nonresidents	59ta	13.1	11.2	13.3	12.7	10.3	19.8	46.3	54.8	55.2	60.1	68.0	80.8	108.7	132.9	116.0
Residents	59tb	244.0	248.2	254.9	264.9	266.6	270.2	269.6	275.4	281.5	288.8	366.9	422.9	452.3	482.0	536.1
Monetary Authorities	59tb a	40.5	43.7	49.0	52.9	57.2	62.1	69.0	69.8	78.5	80.1	86.7	93.3	100.9	109.5	116.3
Commercial Banks	59tb b	60.2	56.8	63.3	65.3	55.6	62.5	65.6	68.1	59.2	55.1	85.0	103.8	102.0	95.3	95.6
Govt. Sponsored Enterprises	59tb c	1.8	2.7	2.7	2.6	2.0	3.1	2.5	1.3	1.2	1.4	2.9	4.4	1.0	1.4	1.2
Other Financial Institutions	59tb d	34.7	34.8	32.6	33.3	33.3	33.9	29.8	30.3	30.1	32.9	46.5	67.1	72.6	72.9	75.9
Nonfinancial Sectors	59tb e	106.8	110.2	107.4	110.8	118.5	108.5	102.7	105.9	112.7	119.2	145.8	154.3	175.8	202.8	247.1
Interest Rates														*Percent Per Annum*		
Discount Rate (End of Period)	60	4.50	4.50	4.50	5.50	6.00	5.50	4.50	4.50	7.50	7.75	6.00	5.25	6.00	9.50	12.00
Federal Funds Rate	60b	4.07	5.12	4.22	5.67	8.21	7.18	4.66	4.43	8.73	10.50	5.82	5.05	5.54	7.93	11.20
Commercial Paper Rate	60bc	....	....	....	....	....	....	....	....	....	....	....	5.24	5.54	7.94	10.97
Treasury Bill Rate	60c	3.95	4.88	4.33	5.35	6.69	6.44	4.34	4.07	7.03	7.87	5.82	4.99	5.27	7.22	10.04
Treas. Bill Rate(Bond Equivalent)	60cs	....	....	....	....	....	....	....	....	....	....	5.78	4.99	5.29	7.19	10.07
Certificates of Deposit Rate	60lc	....	....	....	....	....	....	....	....	....	....	....	5.26	5.58	8.20	11.22
Lending Rate (Prime Rate)	60p	4.54	5.63	5.63	6.31	7.95	7.91	5.72	5.25	8.02	10.80	7.86	6.84	6.82	9.06	12.67
Govt. Bond Yield: Med.-Term	61a	4.22	5.23	5.03	5.69	7.02	7.29	5.66	5.72	6.95	7.82	7.49	6.77	6.69	8.29	9.71
Long-Term	61	4.28	4.92	5.07	5.65	6.67	7.35	6.16	6.21	6.84	7.56	7.99	7.61	7.42	8.41	9.44
Prices, Production, Employment														*Index Numbers (1990=100):*		
Industrial Share Prices	62	23.9	23.3	25.4	27.5	27.2	23.4	27.7	31.2	30.8	23.8	24.7	29.3	27.7	27.2	29.4
Producer Prices	63	27.8	28.7	28.7	29.5	30.6	31.7	32.8	34.2	38.7	46.0	50.3	52.6	55.8	60.2	67.7
Industrial Goods	63a	26.7	27.3	27.7	28.4	29.3	30.4	31.6	32.6	34.8	42.6	47.5	50.5	54.0	57.9	65.4
Finished Goods	63b	28.6	29.6	29.9	30.8	31.9	33.0	34.0	35.1	38.3	44.1	48.9	51.0	54.4	58.6	65.1
Consumer Goods	63ba	28.9	29.9	30.1	30.9	32.1	33.1	34.0	35.1	38.9	45.0	49.3	51.1	54.4	58.7	65.6
Capital Equipment	63bb	27.5	28.2	29.1	30.2	31.2	32.6	34.0	34.8	36.0	41.1	47.4	50.5	53.8	58.0	63.1
Consumer Prices	64	24.1	24.9	25.5	26.6	28.1	29.7	31.0	32.0	34.0	37.8	41.2	43.6	46.4	49.9	55.6
Wages: Hourly Earnings(Mfg)	65ey	24.1	25.1	26.1	27.8	29.4	31.0	33.0	35.3	37.7	40.9	44.6	48.2	52.4	57.0	61.8
Industrial Production	66.. c	46.6	50.8	51.9	54.7	57.3	55.4	56.1	61.6	66.6	65.6	59.9	65.3	70.5	75.1	78.1
Crude Petroleum Production	66aa	108.7	114.0	120.7	124.9	126.3	131.9	129.6	129.6	126.1	120.1	114.7	111.7	112.9	119.2	117.1
Nonagr.Employment	67.. c	55.5	58.4	60.1	62.1	64.3	64.8	65.1	67.3	70.2	71.5	70.3	72.5	75.4	79.2	82.1
International Transactions														*Billions of US Dollars*		
Exports	70	26.70	29.38	30.93	34.06	37.33	42.66	43.55	49.20	70.82	99.44	108.86	116.79	123.18	145.85	186.36
Imports, cif	71	23.23	27.79	28.82	35.44	38.50	42.39	48.34	58.86	73.20	110.88	105.88	132.50	160.41	186.05	222.23
Imports, fob	71.v	21.37	25.54	26.81	33.23	36.04	39.95	45.56	55.58	69.48	I 103.32	I 99.31	124.61	151.53	176.05	210.29
														1990=100		
Volume of Exports	72	26.3	28.1	29.0	31.5	33.5	36.3	35.9	39.3	48.6	53.4	52.3	54.3	55.2	61.2	68.7
Volume of Imports	73	23.0	26.8	27.6	33.5	35.4	36.5	39.5	44.9	47.0	48.1	42.1	51.1	57.2	61.4	61.5
Export Prices	74	25.8	26.5	27.1	27.4	I 28.3	29.9	30.8	31.8	37.1	47.3	52.9	54.7	56.7	60.6	68.9
Import Prices	75	19.5	20.1	20.2	20.4	I 21.1	22.5	23.7	25.4	30.1	44.6	48.6	50.2	54.3	58.6	69.9

1980	1981	1982	1983	1984	1985	1986	1987	1988	1989	1990	1991	1992	1993	1994		
End of Period															**Other Financial Institutions**	
10.0	22.1	33.5	28.1	51.1	85.7	142.3	141.1	115.9	215.2	154.1	199.5	224.6	208.4	131.9	Claims on Central Government	**42a**
29.4	29.9	41.7	53.0	68.0	102.9	142.9	145.6	161.0	187.9	211.7	263.4	321.3	388.1	393.3	Claims on State and Local Govts.	**42b**
442.0	457.1	504.0	585.1	665.3	822.3	1,030.4	1,136.5	1,278.2	1,489.2	1,641.1	1,938.4	2,175.1	2,608.4	2,772.2	Claims on Private Sector	**42d**
15.1	15.8	18.2	18.7	20.3	26.0	34.5	36.4	42.4	45.8	49.6	49.8	49.7	57.0	57.6	Claims on Banks	**42e**
8.3	11.5	14.5	15.2	20.0	33.5	65.6	66.8	64.0	77.8	125.8	177.2	236.3	310.0	328.7	Claims on Other Financial Insts.	**42f**
73.5	69.2	85.5	140.3	163.5	292.8	487.6	541.0	597.2	727.4	821.0	1,060.5	1,308.6	1,684.3	1,751.5	Credit Market Instruments	**46aa**
66.9	69.6	77.6	84.6	113.2	143.1	211.2	269.7	311.7	377.1	450.7	518.2	591.6	705.2	801.1	Bonds	**46ab**
244.7	245.0	276.8	305.4	323.3	381.4	444.1	439.8	465.4	544.9	582.1	677.8	701.2	719.0	697.0	Liabilities to Banks	**46h**
119.7	152.6	172.0	169.8	224.7	253.1	272.8	275.9	287.2	366.5	328.5	371.9	405.8	463.4	434.1	Other Items (Net)	**47r**
End of Period															**Insurance Companies & Pension Funds**	
71.2	86.5	127.3	171.0	223.0	278.7	334.2	375.4	411.0	460.9	501.4	586.5	624.3	692.1	719.4	Claims on Central Government	**42a. s**
91.3	95.0	99.8	99.2	95.8	100.6	118.0	137.4	144.8	145.7	151.0	138.8	147.8	163.3	171.6	Claims on State and Local Govts	**42b. s**
1,004.9	1,075.5	1,239.2	1,417.9	1,522.8	1,813.4	2,093.9	2,241.4	2,540.1	2,984.5	3,028.1	3,560.0	3,819.7	4,150.9	4,189.7	Claims on Private Sector	**42d. s**
46.6	51.6	66.3	80.4	93.0	119.1	143.9	158.5	186.1	224.6	204.9	257.3	265.2	274.4	245.2	Claims on Banks	**42e. s**
12.8	17.8	20.0	20.3	24.8	32.6	49.5	60.8	71.5	84.7	111.9	154.9	207.6	303.9	349.6	Claims on Other Financial Insts.	**42f. s**
1,080.4	1,169.1	1,386.5	1,618.6	1,775.8	2,129.3	2,491.0	2,701.9	2,954.7	3,470.0	3,601.8	4,256.1	4,634.5	5,100.8	5,180.0	Insurance and Pension Reserves	**47a. s**
146.4	157.3	166.1	170.2	183.6	215.1	248.5	271.6	398.8	430.4	395.6	441.4	430.2	483.8	495.3	Other Items (Net)	**47r. s**
End of Period															**Financial Survey**	
62.8	131.8	151.7	139.7	128.6	106.0	94.2	47.6	44.1	71.2	71.4	67.8	89.8	70.6	15.4	Foreign Assets (Net)	**51n**
2,676.5	2,902.4	3,115.2	3,481.2	3,984.6	4,528.2	5,195.7	5,603.2	6,027.1	6,533.4	6,690.2	7,107.8	7,547.3	8,223.2	8,591.4	Domestic Credit	**52**
254.0	293.2	348.6	405.0	445.3	485.1	577.2	603.8	561.3	631.4	597.2	763.9	906.4	933.6	868.2	Claims on Central Govt. (Net)	**52an**
183.7	191.8	216.5	235.0	269.2	374.4	413.2	384.4	381.1	393.7	415.8	458.9	515.8	592.5	603.7	Claims on State and Local Govts.	**52b**
2,238.7	2,417.3	2,550.1	2,841.2	3,270.1	3,668.7	4,205.2	4,615.1	5,084.7	5,508.3	5,677.2	5,885.0	6,125.2	6,697.2	7,119.5	Claims on Private Sector	**52d**
1,659.4	1,846.0	2,052.5	2,273.8	2,524.0	2,746.5	3,038.0	3,141.8	3,335.5	3,536.4	3,772.3	3,894.4	3,958.9	4,013.1	4,020.1	Liquid Liabilities	**55l**
439.7	517.5	555.0	619.0	751.0	883.3	1,091.6	1,229.2	1,350.8	1,451.6	1,449.9	1,588.6	1,758.2	2,116.8	2,225.7	Credit Market Instruments	**56aa**
93.8	98.9	113.7	130.6	174.6	228.0	317.1	393.5	442.5	509.1	572.4	640.0	724.8	844.1	944.9	Bonds	**56ab**
546.4	571.8	545.7	597.5	663.6	776.5	843.1	886.3	942.3	1,107.5	967.1	1,052.6	1,195.2	1,319.8	1,416.0	Other Items (Net)	**57r**
End of Period															**Money Stock, Liquid Assets, and Debt Measures (National Definitions)**	
419.5	447.0	485.8	533.2	564.6	633.5	740.1	765.9	803.8	811.5	843.7	916.4	1,046.7	1,153.8	1,173.5	*M1*	**59ma**
408.5	436.3	474.4	521.2	552.4	620.1	724.5	750.0	787.1	794.6	827.2	899.3	1,024.8	1,128.4	1,147.8	*M1, Seasonally Adjusted*	**59ma c**
1,635.1	1,798.5	1,959.8	2,194.9	2,384.9	2,582.6	2,828.3	2,929.3	3,090.3	3,245.1	3,357.0	3,457.9	3,527.6	3,590.5	3,638.0	*M2*	**59mb**
1,629.2	1,792.6	1,952.7	2,186.5	2,376.0	2,572.4	2,816.0	2,917.2	3,078.3	3,233.3	3,345.5	3,445.8	3,509.0	3,567.9	3,614.5	*M2, Seasonally Adjusted*	**59mb c**
1,994.8	2,241.4	2,449.8	2,703.3	2,999.0	3,215.2	3,504.6	3,686.7	3,926.5	4,066.4	4,126.3	4,178.1	4,198.2	4,251.4	4,329.6	*M3*	**59mc**
1,986.8	2,233.4	2,440.6	2,693.1	2,988.2	3,203.6	3,491.6	3,674.8	3,915.5	4,056.1	4,116.7	4,168.1	4,183.0	4,232.0	4,303.6	*M3, Seasonally Adjusted*	**59mc c**
2,330.9	2,603.2	2,858.6	3,164.1	3,540.3	3,843.4	4,146.9	4,349.0	4,686.1	4,906.0	4,986.5	5,004.2	5,087.6	5,169.9	5,324.5	*L*	**59md**
2,323.5	2,596.0	2,850.3	3,154.4	3,529.6	3,830.9	4,131.9	4,333.5	4,669.4	4,886.1	4,965.2	4,982.3	5,057.1	5,135.0	5,287.0	*L, Seasonally Adjusted*	**59md c**
3,892.9	4,274.1	4,684.9	5,247.3	5,997.3	6,893.3	7,769.5	8,539.6	9,301.0	10,026.5	10,667.7	11,141.0	11,708.9	12,327.6	12,956.8	*Debt*	**59me**
3,896.8	4,278.7	4,691.6	5,257.5	6,006.1	6,901.1	7,778.6	8,543.3	9,306.1	10,030.7	10,670.1	11,141.9	11,706.1	12,335.4	12,965.0	*Debt, Seasonally Adjusted*	**59me c**
End of Period															**Treasury Securities by Holders**	
730.0	815.9	978.1	1,163.5	1,360.8	1,586.6	1,802.2	1,944.6	2,082.3	2,227.0	2,465.8	2,757.8	3,061.6	3,309.8	3,465.6	Total	**59t**
127.5	135.5	150.7	163.6	200.3	226.4	269.4	296.3	353.8	383.6	450.3	496.6	547.8	625.0	688.3	Nonresidents	**59ta**
602.6	680.4	827.4	999.9	1,160.5	1,360.2	1,532.9	1,648.3	1,728.5	1,843.4	2,015.5	2,261.2	2,513.8	2,684.8	2,777.3	Residents	**59tb**
119.3	127.7	135.6	150.6	159.2	177.8	197.6	222.6	233.7	226.8	235.1	266.5	295.0	332.0	364.5	Monetary Authorities	**59tb a**
111.5	113.8	134.0	179.5	181.5	189.4	197.7	194.4	185.7	166.1	172.1	232.5	294.4	322.2	290.4	Commercial Banks	**59tb b**
1.7	1.9	3.4	2.6	3.9	7.1	12.3	17.2	22.9	9.6	38.0	43.7	61.9	60.4	64.4	Govt. Sponsored Enterprises	**59tb c**
98.8	144.4	221.4	256.5	342.9	429.7	550.5	589.6	587.8	729.8	735.4	904.7	982.6	1,032.1	966.7	Other Financial Institutions	**59tb d**
271.2	292.6	333.0	410.8	472.9	556.2	574.7	624.6	698.3	711.1	834.9	813.8	879.9	938.1	1,091.3	Nonfinancial Sectors	**59tb e**
Percent Per Annum															**Interest Rates**	
13.00	12.00	8.50	8.50	8.00	7.50	5.50	6.00	6.50	7.00	6.50	3.50	3.00	3.00	4.75	Discount Rate *(End of Period)*	**60**
13.36	16.38	12.26	9.09	10.23	8.10	6.81	6.66	7.61	9.22	8.10	5.70	3.52	3.02	4.20	Federal Funds Rate	**60b**
12.66	15.32	11.89	8.87	10.10	7.95	6.50	6.81	7.66	8.99	8.06	5.87	3.75	3.22	4.66	Commercial Paper Rate	**60bc**
11.62	14.08	10.72	8.62	9.57	7.49	5.97	5.83	6.67	8.11	7.51	5.41	3.46	3.02	4.27	Treasury Bill Rate	**60c**
11.33	14.70	11.07	8.95	9.89	7.73	6.13	6.01	6.89	7.96	7.36	5.52	3.62	3.32	4.98	Treas. Bill Rate(Bond Equivalent)	**60cs**
13.07	15.91	12.35	9.09	10.37	8.05	6.52	6.86	7.73	9.09	8.16	5.84	3.68	3.17	4.63	Certificates of Deposit Rate	**60lc**
15.27	18.87	14.86	10.79	12.04	9.93	8.35	8.21	9.32	10.92	10.01	8.46	6.25	6.00	7.14	Lending Rate (Prime Rate)	**60p**
11.55	14.44	12.92	10.45	11.89	9.64	7.06	7.67	8.24	8.56	8.25	6.81	5.31	4.44	6.26	Govt. Bond Yield: Med.-Term	**61a**
11.46	13.91	13.00	11.11	12.52	10.62	7.68	8.38	8.85	8.50	8.55	7.86	7.01	5.82	7.11	Long-Term	**61**
Period Averages															**Prices, Production, Employment**	
34.4	36.9	34.2	46.2	46.4	53.2	67.1	84.7	78.5	94.7	100.0	114.1	125.5	132.3	138.0	Industrial Share Prices	**62**
77.3	84.3	86.0	87.1	89.2	I 88.7	86.2	88.4	92.0	96.6	100.0	100.2	100.8	102.3	103.6	Producer Prices	**63**
76.0	84.1	I 86.4	87.4	89.3	89.6	86.4	88.6	91.8	96.4	100.0	100.6	101.4	102.9	104.2	Industrial Goods	**63a**
73.9	80.7	I 84.0	85.3	87.1	87.9	86.7	88.5	90.7	95.3	100.0	102.1	103.3	104.7	105.5	Finished Goods	**63b**
75.0	81.7	I 84.6	85.7	87.4	87.9	85.8	87.6	89.9	94.9	100.0	102.0	102.9	104.0	104.3	Consumer Goods	**63ba**
69.9	77.0	I 81.4	83.7	85.7	87.6	89.3	90.9	93.1	96.7	100.0	103.1	105.0	106.9	109.2	Capital Equipment	**63bb**
I 63.1	69.6	73.9	76.2	79.5	82.4	83.9	87.0	90.5	94.9	100.0	104.2	107.4	110.6	113.4	Consumer Prices	**64**
67.2	73.8	78.5	81.5	84.8	88.1	89.9	91.5	94.1	96.8	100.0	103.3	105.8	108.5	111.4	Wages: Hourly Earnings(Mfg)	**65ey**
76.6	78.3	72.7	77.0	85.7	87.4	88.3	I 91.6	96.5	99.0	100.0	98.1	99.6	101.7	107.9	Industrial Production	**66.. c**
118.0	117.4	118.4	119.0	121.9	122.8	118.9	114.3	111.7	104.9	100.0	101.0	98.2	93.6	91.3	Crude Petroleum Production	**66aa**
82.6	83.3	81.8	82.4	86.3	89.0	90.8	93.2	96.2	98.6	100.0	98.9	99.2	100.7	103.7	Nonagr.Employment	**67.. c**
Billions of US Dollars															**International Transactions**	
225.57	238.72	216.44	205.64	223.98	218.82	227.16	254.12	322.43	363.81	393.59	421.73	448.16	464.77	512.52	Exports	**70**
256.98	273.35	254.88	269.88	346.36	352.46	382.30	424.44	459.54	492.92	516.99	508.36	553.92	603.44	689.22	Imports, cif	**71**
245.26	260.98	243.95	258.05	330.68	336.53	365.44	406.24	440.95	473.21	495.31	488.45	532.67	580.51	663.83	Imports, fob	**71.v**
1990=100																
73.2	71.0	63.6	59.8	64.3	63.3	65.1	71.6	84.8	93.3	100.0	106.2	112.7	116.4	125.7	Volume of Exports	**72**
56.7	57.2	54.2	59.9	75.5	78.8	88.5	91.6	94.6	98.4	100.0	98.3	106.3	116.6	130.9	Volume of Imports	**73**
78.3	85.4	86.4	87.3	88.5	87.8	88.7	90.2	I 96.6	99.1	I 100.0	100.9	101.0	101.4	103.6	Export Prices	**74**
87.6	92.4	90.9	87.2	88.8	86.5	83.6	89.7	I 94.0	96.9	I 100.0	100.0	100.8	100.1	101.8	Import Prices	**75**

United States

111

Balance of Payments		1965	1966	1967	1968	1969	1970	1971	1972	1973	1974	1975	1976	1977	1978	1979
Goods: Exports f.o.b.	78aa d	....	....	....	....	....	42.45	43.31	49.38	71.41	98.31	107.09	114.74	120.81	142.05	184.47
Goods: Imports f.o.b.	78ab d	....	....	....	....	....	-39.86	-45.58	-55.80	-70.50	-103.82	-98.18	-124.23	-151.91	-176.00	-212.01
Trade Balance	78ac d	....	....	....	....	....	2.59	-2.27	-6.42	.91	-5.51	8.91	-9.49	-31.10	-33.95	-27.54
Services: Credit	78ad d	....	....	....	....	....	11.45	12.80	13.35	17.04	20.77	23.33	27.58	31.09	35.45	38.83
Services: Debit	78ae d	....	....	....	....	....	-14.65	-15.57	-17.05	-19.09	-21.66	-22.27	-24.91	-27.63	-31.69	-36.23
Balance on Goods and Services	78af d	....	....	....	....	....	-.61	-5.04	-10.12	-1.14	-6.40	9.97	-6.82	-27.64	-30.19	-24.94
Income: Credit	78ag d	....	....	....	....	....	11.75	12.71	14.77	21.78	27.63	25.37	29.29	32.40	42.47	64.37
Income: Debit	78ah d	....	....	....	....	....	-5.07	-4.81	-5.85	-8.95	-12.11	-12.58	-13.32	-14.67	-22.16	-33.43
Balance on Goods, Serv., & Inc.	78ai d	....	....	....	....	....	6.07	2.86	-1.20	11.69	9.12	22.76	9.15	-9.91	-9.88	6.00
Current Transfers, n.i.e.: Credit	78aj d	....	....	....	....	....	.38	.40	.61	.70	.72	.72	.76	.70	.81	1.14
Current Transfers: Debit	78ak d	....	....	....	....	....	-3.83	-4.24	-4.67	-4.81	-8.14	-5.60	-6.07	-5.89	-6.70	-7.27
Current Account, n.i.e.	78al d	....	....	....	....	....	2.62	-.98	-5.26	7.58	1.70	17.88	3.84	-15.10	-15.77	-.13
Capital Account, n.i.e.: Credit	78ba d	....	....	....	....	....	—	—	—	—	—	—	—	.26	.40	.25
Capital Account: Debit	78bb d	....	....	....	....	....	—	—	—	—	—	—	—	-.06	-.10	-.10
Capital Account, n.i.e.	78bc d	....	....	....	....	....	—	—	—	—	—	—	—	.20	.30	.15
Direct Investment Abroad	78bd d	....	....	....	....	....	-6.53	-5.72	-7.41	-9.53	-4.95	-13.98	-11.66	-11.26	-14.72	-25.37
Dir. Invest. in Rep. Econ., n.i.e.	78be d	....	....	....	....	....	1.26	.87	1.35	2.12	3.33	2.56	3.25	2.90	5.85	8.70
Portfolio Investment Assets	78bf d	....	....	....	....	....	-1.08	-1.10	-.62	-.67	-1.82	-6.23	-8.87	-5.45	-3.63	-4.70
Portfolio Investment Liab., n.i.e.	78bg d	....	....	....	....	....	2.28	2.30	4.55	3.84	.44	2.88	4.27	4.95	4.86	6.20
Other Investment Assets	78bh d	....	....	....	....	....	-3.27	-5.89	-6.72	-10.69	-22.60	-18.51	-27.90	-17.64	-43.01	-32.79
Other Investment Liab., n.i.e.	78bi d	....	....	....	....	....	-4.66	-7.31	6.26	6.32	19.04	4.85	14.87	7.82	20.92	33.79
Financial Account, n.i.e.	78bj d	....	....	....	....	....	-12.00	-16.85	-2.59	-8.61	-6.56	-28.43	-26.04	-18.68	-29.73	-14.17
Net Errors and Omissions	78ca d	....	....	....	....	....	-.54	-11.75	-2.67	-4.19	-3.89	5.82	11.68	-1.46	13.32	27.78
Overall Balance	78cb d	....	....	....	....	....	-9.92	-29.58	-10.52	-5.22	-8.75	-4.73	-10.52	-35.04	-31.88	13.63
Reserves and Related Items	79da d	....	....	....	....	....	9.92	29.58	10.52	5.22	8.75	4.73	10.52	35.04	31.88	-13.63
Reserve Assets	79db d	....	....	....	....	....	2.56	2.17	.22	.12	-1.48	-.77	-2.56	-.37	.69	—
Use of Fund Credit and Loans	79dc d	....	....	....	....	....	—	—	—	—	—	—	—	—	—	—
Liabs.Constit.For.Auth.Reserves	79dd d	....	....	....	....	....	7.36	27.41	10.30	5.10	10.23	5.50	13.08	35.41	31.19	-13.63
Exceptional Financing	79de d	....	....	....	....	....	....	....	....	....	....	....	....	....	....	....

Government Finance
Billions of US Dollars

		1965	1966	1967	1968	1969	1970	1971	1972	1973	1974	1975	1976	1977	1978	1979
Deficit (-) or Surplus	80	-1.6	-3.8	-8.7	-15.2	5.4	-11.4	-24.8	‡-18.7	-16.2	-4.5	-53.9	-74.9	‡-52.2	-58.9	-36.0
Revenue	81	116.8	130.9	149.6	169.4	195.7	190.5	194.0	‡214.1	244.4	279.0	292.7	311.3	‡371.5	416.7	488.8
Grants Received	81z	....	....	....	....	....	—	—	‡—	—	—	—	—	‡—	—	—
Exp. & Lending Minus Repay.	82z	118.4	134.7	158.3	184.6	190.3	201.9	218.8	‡232.8	260.6	283.4	346.6	386.2	‡423.8	475.7	524.7
Expenditure	82	117.2	130.8	153.2	180.0	188.5	201.0	216.8	‡231.4	258.8	280.5	333.1	375.1	‡414.3	457.7	506.3
Lending Minus Repayments	83	1.3	3.8	5.1	4.5	1.9	.9	2.0	‡1.4	1.8	2.9	13.5	11.1	‡9.5	17.9	18.5
Financing																
Net Borrowing	84	4.1	3.1	2.8	5.4	-2.6	11.9	24.8	‡20.7	18.0	2.0	53.1	82.8	‡55.8	62.0	39.8
Domestic	84a	....	....	....	....	....	....	....	‡3.1	7.7	5.0	44.6	78.0	‡34.6	38.6	36.9
Foreign	85a	....	....	....	....	....	....	....	‡17.5	10.3	-2.9	8.5	4.8	‡21.2	23.4	2.9
Other Financing	86c	-.1	.3	.9	3.4	-.9	1.1	1.7								
Use of Cash Balances	87	-2.3	.5	4.9	-1.3	-2.0	-1.5	-1.7	‡-2.0	-1.8	2.5	.8	-7.9	‡-3.6	-3.1	-3.9

Billions of US Dollars

		1965	1966	1967	1968	1969	1970	1971	1972	1973	1974	1975	1976	1977	1978	1979
Debt	88	257.6	259.8	268.6	279.6	278.4	291.2	317.3	331.6	339.4	351.5	437.3	506.5	563.8	618.2	658.0
Held by: Monetary Authorities	88aa	40.8	44.3	49.1	52.9	57.2	62.1	70.2	69.9	78.5	80.5	87.9	97.0	102.5	109.6	117.5
Commercial Banks	88ab	60.7	57.4	63.8	66.0	56.8	62.7	65.3	67.7	60.3	55.6	85.1	103.5	98.9	95.0	88.1
Other Financial Inst.	88ac	15.8	14.5	13.1	12.0	10.5	12.0	9.7	10.0	9.3	8.7	14.0	16.2	19.9	20.0	21.4
State & Local Govts	88ad	22.9	24.3	24.1	24.9	27.2	27.8	25.4	28.9	29.2	29.2	34.2	40.9	58.1	76.1	81.7
Corporations	88ae	15.8	14.9	12.2	14.2	10.4	7.3	11.4	9.8	10.9	12.4	21.3	23.5	18.2	17.3	17.0
Individuals	88af	71.9	74.2	73.5	75.1	80.8	81.2	73.2	73.9	77.3	84.2	90.8	101.6	107.8	114.0	118.0
Money Market Funds	88ag	....	....	....	....	....	....	....	....	....	....	....	1.1	.9	1.5	5.6
Foreign & International	88ca	13.0	10.8	12.9	12.5	10.4	19.8	46.1	54.5	54.7	58.8	66.5	78.1	109.6	133.1	119.0
Others	88d	16.7	19.4	19.9	21.9	25.0	19.9	15.6	17.0	19.3	22.1	37.4	44.6	47.9	51.6	89.7
Intragovernmental Debt	88s	65.5	64.8	73.8	79.1	91.9	99.7	108.7	119.2	131.7	143.4	141.4	149.3	156.8	171.7	188.7

National Accounts
Billions of US Dollars

		1965	1966	1967	1968	1969	1970	1971	1972	1973	1974	1975	1976	1977	1978	1979
Exports of Goods & Services	90c. c	35.4	39.0	41.4	45.3	49.3	57.0	59.3	66.2	91.8	124.3	136.3	148.9	158.8	186.2	228.9
Gov't Consumption & Investment	91ff c	136.3	155.9	175.6	191.5	201.8	212.7	224.4	241.5	257.7	288.3	321.4	341.3	368.0	403.6	448.5
of which: Gross Capital Form	93gf c	20.5	21.7	24.5	28.0	29.2	28.6	30.1	34.3	37.0	44.0	48.3	48.7	49.2	54.5	62.8
Priv. Gross Fixed Capital Form	93ee c	108.3	116.6	117.6	130.8	145.5	147.7	167.2	195.3	224.8	230.8	230.7	268.3	333.5	406.1	467.5
Increase/Decrease(-) in Stocks	93i. c	9.7	13.8	10.5	9.1	9.7	2.3	8.1	9.9	17.7	14.3	-5.7	16.7	24.7	27.9	12.8
Private Consumption	96f. c	444.6	481.6	509.3	559.1	603.7	646.5	700.3	767.8	848.2	927.7	1,024.9	1,143.1	1,271.5	1,421.2	1,583.7
Imports of Goods & Services	98c. c	-31.5	-37.1	-39.9	-46.6	-50.5	-55.8	-62.4	-74.2	-91.2	-127.5	-122.7	-151.2	-182.5	-212.3	-252.7
Gross Domestic Product	99b. c	702.7	769.8	814.3	889.3	959.5	1,010.4	1,096.1	1,206.5	1,349.1	1,458.0	1,584.8	1,767.1	1,974.1	2,232.7	2,488.7
Net Factor Inc/Pmts(-) Abroad	98.n c	5.4	5.2	5.5	6.2	6.2	6.4	7.7	8.7	12.7	15.7	13.2	17.0	20.5	21.9	32.2
Gross Nat'l Expenditure = GNP	99a. c	708.1	774.9	819.8	895.5	965.6	1,016.8	1,104.5	1,215.2	1,361.8	1,473.7	1,598.1	1,784.1	1,994.6	2,254.6	2,520.8
Nat'l Income, Market Prices	99e. c	650.7	712.8	752.4	821.5	884.2	928.0	1,006.9	1,105.3	1,241.4	1,333.4	1,432.9	1,601.3	1,789.4	2,019.8	2,248.4
Gross Dom. Prod. 1990 Prices	99b. r	2,800.4	2,968.9	3,045.9	3,171.2	3,257.4	3,256.0	3,357.0	3,517.8	3,700.6	3,677.4	3,647.5	3,827.7	4,000.3	4,193.0	4,298.7
GDP Deflator (1990=100)	99bi r	25.1	25.9	26.7	28.0	29.5	31.0	32.7	34.3	36.5	39.6	43.4	46.2	49.3	53.2	57.9

Millions:

		1965	1966	1967	1968	1969	1970	1971	1972	1973	1974	1975	1976	1977	1978	1979
Population	99z	194.30	196.56	198.71	200.71	202.68	205.05	207.66	209.90	211.91	213.85	215.97	218.04	220.24	222.59	225.06

Prices: ‡ Beginning in January 1983, the cost of shelter to the homeowner is measured by a rental equivalence, and since January 1987 an enhanced housing survey represents optimally both owners and renters in the estimation of shelter costs. Reference base 1982-84=100.
International Transactions: ‡ Beginning in January 1975, data include exports and imports, respectively, of nonmonetary gold, which prior to January 1975 are excluded.

Government Finance: ‡ Beginning in 1972, data are as reported in the *Government Finance Statistics Yearbook* and cover consolidated central government. Also beginning in 1972, data relate to a fiscal year different from calendar year (fiscal year ends June 30 through 1976; ends September 30 thereafter).

United States

1980	1981	1982	1983	1984	1985	1986	1987	1988	1989	1990	1991	1992	1993	1994		
Minus Sign Indicates Debit															**Balance of Payments**	
224.25	237.05	211.17	201.80	219.93	215.91	223.35	250.21	320.23	362.13	389.31	416.92	440.36	456.87	502.73	Goods: Exports f.o.b.	78aa *d*
−249.76	−265.07	−247.65	−268.89	−332.41	−338.09	−368.41	−409.77	−447.19	−477.38	−498.33	−490.98	−536.46	−589.44	−669.09	Goods: Imports f.o.b.	78ab *d*
−25.51	−28.02	−36.48	−67.09	−112.48	−122.18	−145.06	−159.56	−126.96	−115.25	−109.02	−74.06	−96.10	−132.57	−166.36	Trade Balance	78ac *d*
47.55	57.25	63.99	64.11	70.89	72.84	86.07	97.70	109.84	126.73	147.13	163.11	176.42	184.64	195.09	Services: Credit	78ad *d*
−40.97	−44.88	−51.04	−54.18	−66.82	−71.98	−79.04	−89.35	−96.89	−100.91	−115.86	−116.45	−119.66	−126.62	−133.92	Services: Debit	78ae *d*
−18.93	−15.65	−23.53	−57.16	−108.41	−121.32	−138.03	−151.21	−114.01	−89.43	−77.76	−27.41	−39.34	−74.55	−105.19	Balance on Goods and Services	78af *d*
72.67	86.65	86.32	84.85	104.18	92.82	90.97	99.36	127.53	152.63	160.42	137.06	114.61	114.00	135.02	Income: Credit	78ag *d*
−43.09	−54.26	−57.14	−54.45	−74.86	−73.94	−79.95	−92.20	−116.77	−139.90	−140.71	−123.24	−111.09	−111.22	−151.41	Income: Debit	78ah *d*
10.65	16.74	5.65	−26.76	−79.09	−102.44	−127.01	−144.05	−103.26	−76.69	−58.05	−13.59	−35.83	−71.77	−121.58	Balance on Goods, Serv., & Inc.	78ai *d*
1.32	1.23	2.04	2.00	2.16	2.50	2.72	3.01	3.66	4.09	8.79	46.89	6.48	5.38	5.21	Current Transfers, n.i.e.: Credit	78aj *d*
−9.82	−13.13	−19.29	−19.91	−22.91	−25.64	−27.07	−26.27	−28.87	−30.37	−42.72	−40.51	−38.95	−37.97	−39.79	Current Transfers: Debit	78ak *d*
2.15	4.84	−11.60	−44.67	−99.84	−125.58	−151.36	−167.31	−128.47	−102.97	−91.98	−7.21	−68.30	−104.36	−156.16	Current Account, n.i.e.	78ac *d*
.26	.19	.18	.16	.16	.16	.20	.22	.23	.24	.26	.28	.43	.47	.47	Capital Account, n.i.e.: Credit	78ba *d*
−.12	—	—	—	—	—	—	—	—	—	—	—	—	—	—	Capital Account: Debit	78bb *d*
.14	.19	.18	.16	.16	.16	.20	.22	.23	.24	.26	.28	.43	.47	.47	Capital Account, n.i.e.	78bc *d*
−19.23	−9.62	.98	−4.91	−10.94	−13.40	−17.12	−27.18	−15.45	−36.83	−29.95	−31.30	−41.01	−57.87	−58.44	Direct Investment Abroad	78bd *d*
16.93	25.19	12.47	10.47	24.76	20.01	35.64	58.22	57.27	67.73	47.92	26.09	9.89	21.37	60.07	Dir. Invest. in Rep. Econ., n.i.e.	78be *d*
−3.57	−5.70	−7.98	−6.78	−4.77	−7.50	−4.33	−5.25	−7.88	−22.10	−28.80	−44.74	−45.11	−120.00	−60.59	Portfolio Investment Assets	78bf *d*
7.67	8.33	7.07	11.52	33.51	71.91	75.92	36.31	48.18	65.60	−4.20	53.29	61.75	102.45	94.02	Portfolio Investment Liab., n.i.e.	78bg *d*
−57.12	−93.13	−111.85	−46.19	−15.96	−13.37	−83.38	−48.17	−73.28	−83.40	−10.10	19.18	19.22	30.93	−11.97	Other Investment Assets	78bh *d*
19.73	43.66	71.34	56.48	53.20	50.17	80.76	100.73	95.72	75.69	47.09	2.34	38.12	37.28	124.00	Other Investment Liab., n.i.e.	78bi *d*
−35.59	−31.27	−27.96	20.59	79.80	107.82	87.49	114.67	104.56	66.69	21.95	24.86	42.85	14.15	147.19	Financial Account, n.i.e.	78bj *d*
25.41	25.00	41.41	19.86	20.59	23.39	29.89	−4.44	−12.59	52.97	39.96	−39.71	−17.18	21.09	−33.24	Net Errors and Omissions	78ca *d*
−7.89	−1.24	2.03	−4.05	.72	5.80	−33.78	−56.86	−36.27	16.93	−29.81	−21.78	−42.20	−68.65	−41.74	Overall Balance	78cb *d*
7.89	1.24	−2.03	4.05	−.72	−5.80	33.78	56.86	36.27	−16.93	29.81	21.78	42.20	68.65	41.74	Reserves and Related Items	79da *d*
−6.99	−4.06	−4.98	−1.20	−3.13	−3.84	.32	9.14	−3.92	−25.27	−2.23	5.76	3.92	−1.37	5.34	Reserve Assets	79db *d*
—	—	—	—	—	—	—	—	—	—	—	—	—	—	—	Use of Fund Credit and Loans	79dc *d*
14.88	5.30	2.95	5.25	2.41	−1.96	33.46	47.72	40.19	8.34	32.04	16.02	38.27	70.02	36.40	Liabs.Constit.For.Auth.Reserves	79dd *d*
....	....	....	....	....	....	....	....	....	....	....	....	....	....	....	Exceptional Financing	79de *d*
Year Ending September 30															**Government Finance**	
−76.2	−78.7	−125.7	−202.5	−178.3	−212.1	−212.6	−147.5	−155.5	−143.8	−218.1	−272.5	−289.3	−254.1	....	Deficit (-) or Surplus	80
546.1	639.9	659.9	653.4	718.5	791.7	823.2	910.0	962.7	1,046.7	1,085.9	1,116.8	1,151.8	1,238.8	....	Revenue	81
—	—	—	—	—	—	—	—	—	—	—	43.2	4.9	—	....	Grants Received	81z
622.3	718.6	785.6	856.0	896.8	1,003.8	1,035.8	1,057.5	1,118.2	1,190.5	1,304.0	1,432.4	1,446.0	1,492.9	....	Exp. & Lending Minus Repay.	82z
596.6	687.6	764.9	842.6	881.9	977.3	1,032.5	1,054.1	1,118.8	1,194.6	1,304.5	1,429.1	1,445.1	1,492.4	....	Expenditure	82
25.6	31.0	20.7	13.4	14.9	26.5	3.3	3.4	−.6	−4.1	−.5	3.4	.8	.5	....	Lending Minus Repayments	83
															Financing	
76.6	84.8	138.8	215.6	174.1	200.5	233.1	148.6	161.4	139.5	219.7	276.4	309.7	248.0	....	Net Borrowing	84
76.4	75.0	129.3	200.1	158.5	167.9	191.4	119.5	94.8	92.0	209.2	207.6	252.1	156.6	....	Domestic	84a
.2	9.8	9.5	15.5	15.6	32.6	41.6	29.0	66.6	47.5	10.5	68.8	57.6	91.4	....	Foreign	85a
....	....	....	....	....	....	....	....	....	....	....	....	....	....	....	Other Financing	86c
−.4	−6.1	−13.1	−13.1	4.2	11.6	−20.4	−1.0	−5.9	4.3	−1.6	−3.9	−20.5	6.1	....	Use of Cash Balances	87
Year Ending December 31																
737.7	825.4	987.7	1,174.5	1,373.4	1,598.5	1,813.3	1,953.9	2,096.9	2,244.2	2,548.1	2,845.0	3,142.4	3,391.9	....	Debt	88
121.3	130.9	139.3	151.9	160.9	181.3	211.3	222.5	238.4	228.4	259.8	281.8	302.5	344.2	374.1	Held by: Monetary Authorities	88aa
112.1	111.4	134.0	179.5	181.5	189.4	197.7	194.4	185.3	165.3	172.1	232.5	294.4	322.2	....	Commercial Banks	88ab
24.0	29.0	30.6	46.0	64.5	80.5	101.6	108.1	118.6	123.9	138.2	181.8	197.5	234.5	....	Other Financial Inst.	88ac
87.9	96.8	118.6	153.0	188.4	299.0	342.1	403.9	435.4	442.5	462.5	485.1	476.7	508.9	....	State & Local Govts	88ad
19.3	17.9	24.5	39.7	50.1	59.0	68.8	84.6	86.0	93.4	108.9	150.8	192.5	213.0	....	Corporations	88ae
117.1	110.8	116.5	133.4	143.8	154.8	162.7	172.4	190.4	216.4	233.8	263.9	289.2	309.9	....	Individuals	88af
3.5	21.5	42.6	22.8	25.9	25.1	28.6	14.6	11.8	14.9	45.5	80.0	79.7	80.8	....	Money Market Funds	88ag
129.7	136.6	149.5	166.3	205.9	224.8	263.4	299.7	362.2	429.6	458.4	491.7	549.7	622.6	....	Foreign & International	88ca
122.8	170.5	232.0	281.9	352.4	384.6	437.1	453.7	468.8	529.8	668.9	677.4	760.2	755.8	....	Others	88d
194.1	204.9	210.7	237.5	290.8	350.1	404.3	478.6	589.5	708.0	828.5	968.8	1,047.9	1,153.5	1,257.1	Intragovernmental Debt	88s
Billions of US Dollars															**National Accounts**	
279.2	303.0	282.6	276.7	302.4	302.1	319.2	364.0	444.2	508.0	557.0	601.5	638.1	659.1	718.7	Exports of Goods & Services	90c. *c*
507.1	561.1	607.6	652.3	700.8	772.4	833.0	881.5	918.7	975.2	1,043.9	1,099.3	1,125.9	1,148.4	1,175.9	Gov't Consumption & Investment	91ff *c*
72.7	74.6	75.7	79.1	81.5	95.2	109.4	109.9	108.2	122.9	136.1	139.9	150.6	155.1	160.8	*of which:* Gross Capital Form	93gf *c*
477.1	532.6	519.4	552.2	647.8	690.0	709.0	723.0	777.4	798.9	793.2	736.9	788.3	882.0	1,032.9	Priv. Gross Fixed Capital Form	93ee *c*
−9.5	25.5	−16.0	−5.5	71.1	24.6	8.7	26.3	16.3	33.3	6.3	−.1	3.0	15.4	52.2	Increase/Decrease(-) in Stocks	93i. *c*
1,748.1	1,926.3	2,059.2	2,257.6	2,460.3	2,667.4	2,850.6	3,052.2	3,296.1	3,523.1	3,748.4	3,906.4	4,136.9	4,378.2	4,628.4	Private Consumption	96f. *c*
−293.9	−317.7	−303.2	−328.1	−405.1	−417.6	−451.7	−507.1	−552.2	−587.7	−625.9	−621.1	−668.4	−724.3	−816.9	Imports of Goods & Services	98c. *c*
2,708.1	3,030.6	3,149.6	3,405.1	3,777.2	4,038.7	4,268.6	4,539.9	4,900.4	5,250.8	5,522.2	5,722.9	6,020.2	6,343.3	6,738.4	Gross Domestic Product	99b. *c*
34.1	33.2	30.2	29.4	24.3	14.8	9.1	4.6	7.9	4.2	10.7	14.2	5.6	4.5	−11.5	Net Factor Inc/Pmts(-) Abroad	98.n *c*
2,742.1	3,063.8	3,179.8	3,434.5	3,801.5	4,053.6	4,277.8	4,544.5	4,908.2	5,248.2	5,524.6	5,737.1	6,025.8	6,347.8	6,726.9	Gross Nat'l Expenditure = GNP	99a. *c*
2,430.2	2,701.4	2,780.8	3,016.0	3,368.3	3,599.1	3,799.2	4,042.4	4,374.3	4,673.7	4,929.8	5,111.0	5,367.3	5,678.7	6,011.5	Nat'l Income, Market Prices	99e. *c*
4,275.6	4,351.1	4,257.3	4,423.0	4,696.8	4,845.5	4,986.7	5,140.1	5,342.3	5,477.6	5,522.2	5,458.3	5,637.5	5,813.2	6,050.4	Gross Dom. Prod. 1990 Prices	99b. *r*
63.3	69.7	74.0	77.0	80.4	83.4	85.6	88.3	91.7	95.9	100.0	104.8	106.8	109.1	111.4	GDP Deflator (1990=100)	99bi *r*
Midyear Estimates																
227.76	229.94	232.17	234.30	236.37	238.49	240.68	242.84	245.06	247.34	249.91	252.64	255.41	258.12	260.65	**Population**	99z

Uruguay

		1965	1966	1967	1968	1969	1970	1971	1972	1973	1974	1975	1976	1977	1978	1979
Exchange Rates														*Pesos per Thousand SDRs through 1978*		
Market Rate	aa	.0599	.0762	.2000	.2501	.2501	.2501	.4018	.7949	1.1306	2.0280	3.1966	4.6484	6.5730	9.1919	ɪ.0112
												Pesos per Thousand US Dollars through 1978				
Market Rate	ae	.0599	.0762	.2000	.2501	.2501	.2501	.3701	.7322	.9372	1.6564	2.7306	4.0009	5.4112	7.0556	ɪ.0085
Market Rate	rf	.0304	.0647	.1023	.2354	.2500	.2500	.2550	.5361	.8658	1.1962	2.2542^e	3.3358	4.6783	6.0600	ɪ.0079
														Index Numbers (1990=100):		
Market Rate	ah x	....	....	....	483,937.9	451,536.0	451,536.0	444,253.1	235,911.0	130,838.0	96,772.7^e	50,842.7^e	34,290.6^e	24,342.4^e	18,784.9^e	14,404.7^e
Nominal Effective Exchange Rate	ne c	....	....	....	....	....	....	....	....	....	....	....	....	....	....	161.3
Real Effective Exchange Rate	re c	....	....	....	....	....	....	....	....	....	....	....	....	....	....	138.6
Fund Position															*Millions of SDRs:*	
Quota	2f. s	30	30	30	55	55	69	69	69	69	69	69	69	69	84	84
SDRs	1b. s	—	—	—	—	—	—	—	8	11	12	2	4	8	11	26
Reserve Position in the Fund	1c. s	—	—	3	—	—	—	—	—	—	—	—	—	—	17	16
Total Fund Cred.&Loans Outstg.	2tl	8	6	—	21	10	18	17	37	32	64	100	125	98	—	—
International Liquidity											*Millions of US Dollars Unless Otherwise Indicated:*					
Total Reserves minus Gold	1l. d	24	30	22	34	19	14	20	69	101	81	59	176	322	352	ɪ323
SDRs	1b. d								8	13	15	2	4	10	15	34
Reserve Position in the Fund	1c. d			3											22	21
Foreign Exchange	1d. d	24	30	20	34	19	14	20	61	88	66	57	172	312	316	ɪ267
Gold (Million Fine Troy Ounces)	1ad	4.426	4.186	3.986	3.809	4.711	4.614	4.229	3.536	3.536	3.536	3.539	3.544	3.576	3.640	ɪ3.310
Gold (National Valuation)	1and	....	....	....	....	....	....	161	135	149	152	319	319	435	562	ɪ513
Monetary Authorities: Other Assets	3..d	12	21	16	27	13	5	5	61	20	19	8	10	19	74	....
Monetary Authorities: Other Liab.	4..d											182	151	175	141	171
Deposit Money Banks: Assets	7a. d															
of which: Claims on Nonbanks	7ad d															
Deposit Money Banks: Liabilities	7b. d															
Monetary Authorities									*Pesos through 1971; Thousands of Pesos from 1972 to 1985;*							
Foreign Assets	11	3,954	ɪ14,997	34,717	48,138	48,251	43,276	46,051	ɪ190	242	412	ɪ469	1,004	1,815	2,503	4,031
Claims on Central Government	12a	5,543	ɪ7,912	14,833	19,240	31,746	36,637	70,328	ɪ116	172	351	ɪ531	942	1,157	1,382	2,231
Claims on Nonfin.Pub.Enterprises	12c															
Claims on Private Sector	12d	4,464	ɪ8,313	13,628	19,868	21,681	34,043	61,844	ɪ124	207	470	ɪ12	16	22	29	33
Claims on Deposit Money Banks	12e	1,102	ɪ2,426	1,812	2,004	2,166	6,085	17,198	ɪ30	51	100	ɪ552	721	894	1,043	1,504
Claims on Other Financial Insts.	12f	474	ɪ15	345	425	735	1,015	1,481	ɪ3	3	9	ɪ23	24	16	15	39
Reserve Money	14	9,318	ɪ13,671	28,988	42,537	69,372	78,799	121,247	ɪ181	320	517	ɪ613	1,186	1,727	3,180	4,508
of which: Currency Outside DMBs	14a	ɪ6,678	10,332	19,611	31,389	50,573	56,959	84,408	ɪ121	202	316	ɪ469	781	1,114	1,814	3,186
Quasi-Monetary Deposits	15	2,089	ɪ2,936	4,823	6,714	7,135	10,231	19,379	ɪ33	69	107	ɪ70	64	175	211	247
Foreign Liabilities	16c	10,102	ɪ14,932	33,636	37,728	33,800	35,314	43,338	ɪ170	137	407	ɪ807	1,436	1,426	917	1,445
Long-Term Foreign Liabilities	16cl	....	457	1,380	1,837	2,953	3,320	3,541	ɪ10	16	32	ɪ28	86	120	155	232
Central Government Deposits	16d	2,268	ɪ3,693	5,279	13,504	13,223	16,630	26,129	ɪ48	101	189	ɪ35	167	192	171	634
Other Items (Net)	17r	-8,240	ɪ-2,026	-8,771	-12,645	-21,904	-23,238	-16,732	ɪ21	33	90	34	-232	264	338	772
Deposit Money Banks									*Pesos through 1971; Thousands of Pesos from 1972 to 1985;*							
Reserves	20	ɪ2,110	1,838	6,739	8,769	10,649	10,304	22,950	ɪ58	69	134	ɪ370	811	1,650	1,864	1,520
Foreign Assets	21	ɪ1,037	1,205	2,944	3,691	7,862	3,632	3,040	ɪ13	19	40	ɪ209	499	862	1,885	3,094
Claims on Central Government	22a	129	327	2,038	2,975	3,527	2,949	5,467	ɪ12	23	35	ɪ260	379	585	722	533
Claims on Local Government	22b	....	36	1,239	1,047	—	—	38	ɪ—	—	—	ɪ156	149	157	389	683
Claims on Nonfin.Pub.Enterprises	22c															
Claims on Private Sector	22d	ɪ8,030	9,940	15,798	26,252	35,290	49,321	61,590	ɪ128	207	372	ɪ1,531	2,635	4,881	8,659	19,076
Claims on Other Financial Insts.	22f												16	43	54	205	425
Demand Deposits	24	ɪ2,762	3,040	8,820	13,402	16,454	17,399	29,423	ɪ57	106	174	ɪ489	785	1,052	1,718	3,351
Time, Savings,& Fgn.Currency Dep.	25	ɪ3,567	6,261	10,970	17,036	23,988	31,616	42,519	ɪ85	117	225	ɪ733	1,816	3,809	7,540	14,631
Foreign Liabilities	26c	ɪ4,016	4,933	12,846	19,346	24,208	22,098	12,723	ɪ36	38	64	ɪ167	97	483	284	1,271
Long-Term Foreign Liabilities	26cl											27	51	71	85	89
Central Government Deposits	26d											134	199	300	470	799
Credit from Monetary Authorities	26g	1,400	2,000	900	1,100	1,500	6,500	15,000	ɪ34	53	98	534	667	1,064	907	1,343
Other Items (Net)	27r	ɪ-439	-2,888	-4,778	-8,150	-8,822	-11,407	-6,580	ɪ1	4	20	458	901	1,410	2,720	3,847
Monetary Survey									*Pesos through 1971; Thousands of Pesos from 1972 to 1985;*							
Foreign Assets (Net)	31n	ɪ-10,460	ɪ-3,663	-8,821	-5,245	-1,895	-10,504	-6,970	ɪ-3	86	-19	-309	225	768	3,188	4,409
Domestic Credit	32	ɪ21,410	ɪ23,314	43,456	58,784	84,384	112,243	179,851	ɪ349	538	1,082	ɪ2,442	3,902	6,444	10,839	21,619
Claims on Central Govt. (Net)	32an	3,337	ɪ4,546	11,592	8,711	22,054	22,956	49,666	ɪ81	94	197	ɪ622	955	1,250	1,463	1,331
Claims on Local Government	32b	....	500	2,093	3,528	4,624	4,908	5,270	ɪ12	28	35	ɪ185	174	204	478	715
Claims on Nonfin.Pub.Enterprises	32c															
Claims on Private Sector	32d	ɪ18,080	ɪ18,253	29,426	46,120	56,971	83,364	123,434	ɪ253	414	841	ɪ1,596	2,706	4,920	8,678	19,109
Claims on Other Financial Insts.	32f	474	ɪ15	345	425	735	1,015	1,481	ɪ3	3	9	ɪ39	67	70	220	464
Money	34	ɪ10,510	13,372	28,431	44,792	67,027	74,358	113,831	ɪ178	308	490	ɪ834	1,380	1,938	3,588	6,160
Quasi-Money	35	ɪ8,040	ɪ9,197	15,793	23,750	31,123	41,847	61,898	ɪ118	186	332	ɪ803	1,880	3,984	7,751	14,878
Long-Term Foreign Liabilities	36cl	....	457	1,380	1,837	2,953	3,320	3,541	ɪ10	16	32	ɪ55	137	191	240	321
Other Items (Net)	37r	ɪ-7,600	ɪ-3,375	-10,969	-16,840	-18,614	-17,786	-6,389	ɪ40	115	209	441	730	1,099	2,448	4,669
Money plus Quasi-Money	35l	18,550	ɪ22,569	44,224	68,542	98,150	116,205	175,729	ɪ295	493	822	ɪ1,637	3,260	5,922	11,339	21,038
Interest Rates															*Percent Per Annum*	
Discount Rate *(End of Period)*	60															
Deposit Rate	60l												30.2	51.4	42.6	50.6
Lending Rate	60p												62.0	76.6	71.2	68.1
Prices and Production															*Index Numbers (1990=100):*	
Wholesale Prices	63	—	—	ɪ—	—	—	—	—	—	—	.1	.1	.1	.2	.3	.6
Consumer Prices	64	—	—	ɪ—	—	—	—	—	—	ɪ—	.1	.1	.1	.2	.3	.5
Manufacturing Production	66ey	73	74	71	74	77	ɪ81	81	83	82	84	89	91	96	102	109

Uruguay

1980	1981	1982	1983	1984	1985	1986	1987	1988	1989	1990	1991	1992	1993	1994		
															Exchange Rates	
.0128	.0135	.0372	.0453	.0728	.1373	.2214	.3987	.6070	1.0581	2.2682	3.5611	4.7861	6.0684	8.1971	Market Rate	aa
and per SDR thereafter: End of Period																
and per US Dollar thereafter: End of Period (ae) Period Average (rf)																
.0100	.0116	.0338	.0433	.0743	.1250	.1810	.2811	.4511	.8052	1.5944	2.4896	3.4808	4.4180	5.6150	Market Rate	ae
.0091	.0108	.0139	.0345	.0561	.1014	.1520	.2267	.3594	.6055	1.1710	2.0188	3.0270	3.9484	5.0529	Market Rate	rf
Period Averages																
12,441.5[e]	10,452.4[e]	8,583.3[e]	3,300.2[e]	2,044.6	1,135.6	751.0	505.8	319.9	192.1	100.0	56.8	37.6	28.7	22.5	Market Rate	ah x
163.6	180.9	209.5	123.3	119.8	108.4	79.0	63.0	61.7	78.5	100.0	86.7	85.7	112.4	153.6	Nominal Effective Exchange Rate	ne c
174.5	196.1	205.1	126.1	120.8	116.5	114.9	112.2	105.7	110.6	100.0	114.1	122.1	143.1	150.9	Real Effective Exchange Rate	re c
End of Period															**Fund Position**	
126	126	126	164	164	164	164	164	164	164	164	164	225	225	225	Quota	2f. s
26	37	2	4	5	13	10	48	22	17	8	3	—	—	—	SDRs	1b. s
27	28	—	9	—	—	—	—	—	—	—	—	15	15	15	Reserve Position in the Fund	1c. s
—	—	87	227	227	319	323	277	230	153	71	40	38	28	20	Total Fund Cred.&Loans Outstg.	2tl
End of Period															**International Liquidity**	
384	430	116	207	134	174	482	530	532	501	524	336	509	758	969	Total Reserves minus Gold	1l. d
33	43	2	4	5	15	12	68	30	23	11	5	—	—	—	SDRs	1b. d
34	33	—	10	—	—	—	—	—	—	—	—	21	21	22	Reserve Position in the Fund	1c. d
317	354	114	193	129	160	470	462	502	478	512	331	488	737	946	Foreign Exchange	1d. d
3.422	3.392	2.858	2.602	2.618	2.619	2.605	2.609	2.609	2.609	2.609	2.395	2.263	2.028	1.700	Gold (Million Fine Troy Ounces)	1ad
530	526	443	403	647	648	678	817	970	855	737	640	541	454	497	Gold (National Valuation)	1an d
….	….	….	….	….	….	….	….	….	….	….	….	….	….	….	Monetary Authorities: Other Assets	3.. d
117	119	263	116	96	82	89	94	110	109	190	201	54	46	54	Monetary Authorities: Other Liab.	4.. d
….	….	821	727	681	792	907	1,143	1,455	2,070	2,630	3,334	3,941	3,897	3,655	Deposit Money Banks: Assets	7a. d
….	….	298	274	339	428	463	650	878	907	945	1,116	1,505	1,550	1,374	of which: Claims on Nonbanks	7ad d
….	….	1,406	1,197	1,219	1,066	1,128	1,216	1,713	2,263	2,599	2,828	3,338	3,393	3,335	Deposit Money Banks: Liabilities	7b. d
Millions of Pesos Beginning 1986: End of Period															**Monetary Authorities**	
5,454	6,609	I18,816	31,365	57,899	102,661	I210	421	686	1,111	2,169	2,809	3,969	5,496	8,536	Foreign Assets	11
3,963	4,440	I12,496	31,917	88,011	119,097	I315	681	998	1,161	1,749	1,969	3,972	5,816	7,854	Claims on Central Government	12a
		1,486	12,979	19,803	36,478	I89	144	289	549	1,165	1,806	2,538	2,568	3,227	Claims on Nonfin.Pub.Enterprises	12c
32	30	3,212	17,815	30,322	47,923	I57	77	85	15	145	108	62	145	130	Claims on Private Sector	12d
1,505	1,891	I6,893	10,409	14,726	18,651	I27	46	75	124	244	309	562	918	865	Claims on Deposit Money Banks	12e
132	251	I9,962	21,515	35,407	62,473	I96	172	194	355	804	1,300	1,810	2,354	3,206	Claims on Other Financial Insts.	12f
7,040	8,222	I14,458	25,137	48,033	89,225	I158	273	490	968	2,329	3,828	5,665	8,286	10,989	Reserve Money	14
5,103	6,145	I7,879	8,405	12,106	23,309	I43	76	125	219	420	851	1,426	2,313	3,314	of which: Currency Outside DMBs	14a
655	740	I2,392	1,454	5,188	6,820	I27	52	110	181	425	436	600	716	997	Quasi-Monetary Deposits	15
1,171	1,370	12,025	15,211	23,585	53,830	I88	136	188	250	463	645	370	372	471	Foreign Liabilities	16c
297	354	I9,889	58,894	104,717	180,422	I303	521	842	1,443	2,787	2,851	3,733	4,417	5,396	Long-Term Foreign Liabilities	16cl
2,286	2,467	I2,588	13,767	63,418	88,099	I297	650	927	1,092	1,811	2,627	4,227	5,427	7,890	Central Government Deposits	16d
−363	68	I11,514	11,537	1,227	−31,113	I−78	−91	−229	−619	−1,538	−2,086	−1,874	−1,923	−1,925	Other Items (Net)	17r
Millions of Pesos Beginning 1986: End of Period															**Deposit Money Banks**	
2,374	3,328	I10,896	30,233	39,805	76,370	I172	275	530	1,059	2,534	3,623	4,926	6,622	7,875	Reserves	20
3,762	7,318	I27,505	31,917	50,359	98,804	I164	319	655	1,664	4,192	8,299	13,712	17,207	20,470	Foreign Assets	21
1,141	1,933	I8,400	12,813	40,842	48,338	I60	71	152	306	791	1,161	1,708	2,055	3,918	Claims on Central Government	22a
870	1,040	I917	1,065	1,756	3,109	I5	6	13	21	30	44	58	71	116	Claims on Local Government	22b
….	….	4,183	2,666	5,395	5,348	I8	12	23	30	64	65	97	161	285	Claims on Nonfin.Pub.Enterprises	22c
34,301	48,175	I88,827	83,847	112,894	216,717	I359	538	1,043	1,890	3,382	5,660	9,801	14,556	20,896	Claims on Private Sector	22d
478	525	I316	308	457	875	I1	1	1	1	8	14	21	44	52	Claims on Other Financial Insts.	22f
4,734	4,385	I5,448	6,235	9,895	22,221	I41	58	94	155	348	675	1,148	1,735	2,350	Demand Deposits	24
26,697	43,662	I56,377	65,480	105,527	206,976	I355	514	1,038	2,209	4,789	8,751	13,201	17,364	24,540	Time, Savings,& Fgn.Currency Dep.	25
2,356	3,081	I23,237	25,959	57,373	78,282	I91	148	285	607	1,341	2,514	4,609	6,726	7,864	Foreign Liabilities	26c
89	72	I23,877	25,496	32,812	54,712	I113	191	486	1,212	2,802	4,526	7,004	8,260	10,813	Long-Term Foreign Liabilities	26cl
1,327	1,045	I2,573	3,437	4,014	9,399	I17	55	96	147	382	553	1,014	1,093	1,570	Central Government Deposits	26d
1,524	2,065	I7,887	10,873	16,215	22,049	I37	46	101	123	274	391	660	996	818	Credit from Monetary Authorities	26g
6,199	8,008	I21,645	24,714	25,672	55,922	I114	208	316	519	1,065	1,456	2,688	4,543	5,657	Other Items (Net)	27r
Millions of Pesos Beginning 1986: End of Period															**Monetary Survey**	
5,689	9,475	I11,060	21,456	27,301	69,352	I196	456	867	1,918	4,557	7,948	12,511	15,605	20,671	Foreign Assets (Net)	31n
37,354	53,056	I124,638	167,721	267,455	442,860	I677	996	1,774	3,090	5,946	8,949	14,827	21,249	30,224	Domestic Credit	32
1,491	2,861	I15,735	27,526	61,421	69,937	I62	46	127	229	347	−49	440	1,351	2,312	Claims on Central Govt. (Net)	32an
920	1,214	I917	1,065	1,756	3,109	I5	6	13	21	30	44	58	71	116	Claims on Local Government	32b
….	….	5,669	15,645	25,198	41,826	I97	155	311	579	1,229	1,871	2,634	2,729	3,512	Claims on Nonfin.Pub.Enterprises	32c
34,333	48,205	I92,039	101,662	143,216	264,640	I417	616	1,128	1,904	3,528	5,768	9,863	14,700	21,027	Claims on Private Sector	32d
610	776	I10,278	21,823	35,864	63,348	I97	173	195	356	812	1,314	1,832	2,397	3,258	Claims on Other Financial Insts.	32f
9,082	9,838	I13,696	14,922	22,151	45,985	I86	135	222	383	770	1,528	2,583	4,074	5,678	Money	34
27,352	44,402	I58,769	66,934	110,715	213,796	I382	567	1,147	2,390	5,214	9,187	13,802	18,080	25,537	Quasi-Money	35
386	426	I33,766	84,390	137,529	235,134	I417	712	1,327	2,656	5,589	7,377	10,737	12,677	16,210	Long-Term Foreign Liabilities	36cl
6,223	7,865	I29,467	22,931	24,361	17,297	I−11	38	−55	−421	−1,070	−1,195	216	2,023	3,470	Other Items (Net)	37r
36,434	54,240	I72,465	81,856	132,866	259,781	I468	702	1,369	2,773	5,984	10,715	16,385	22,154	31,215	Money plus Quasi-Money	35l
Percent Per Annum															**Interest Rates**	
….	72.1	83.7	112.7	133.2	145.1	138.4	143.4	154.5	219.6	251.6	219.0	162.4	164.3	182.3	Discount Rate (End of Period)	60
50.3	47.4	50.1	71.4	68.4	81.9	61.7	60.8	67.8	84.7	97.8	75.2	54.5	39.4	37.0	Deposit Rate	60l
66.6	60.4	58.5	93.6	83.2	94.6	94.7	95.8	102.0	127.6	174.5	152.9	117.8	97.3	95.1	Lending Rate	60p
Period Averages															**Prices and Production**	
.9	1.1	1.2	2.1	3.7	6.5	10.8	17.7	27.8	48.2	100.0	187.6	297.0	396.1	….	Wholesale Prices	63
.9	1.2	1.4	2.1	3.2	I5.6	9.8	16.1	26.1	47.1	100.0	202.0	340.2	524.3	758.9	Consumer Prices	64
112	106	88	82	85	83	I93	103	102	101	100	100	….	….	….	Manufacturing Production	66ey

Uruguay

		1965	1966	1967	1968	1969	1970	1971	1972	1973	1974	1975	1976	1977	1978	1979
International Transactions																*Millions of US Dollars*
Exports	70..d	191.2	185.8	158.7	179.2	200.3	232.7	205.7	214.1	321.5	382.2	383.9	546.5	607.5	686.1	788.1
Imports, cif	71..d	150.8	164.2	171.4	157.4	197.3	230.9	228.9	211.6	284.8	486.7	556.5	587.2	729.9	757.3	1,206.3
Imports, fob	71.v d	127.8	139.2	145.3	133.9	166.4	196.8	193.2	176.2	244.5	419.8	491.6	534.3	672.3	693.4	1,103.5
Balance of Payments																*Millions of US Dollars*
Goods: Exports f.o.b.	78aa d	…	…	…	…	…	…	…	…	…	…	…	…	…	686.1	788.1
Goods: Imports f.o.b.	78ab d	…	…	…	…	…	…	…	…	…	…	…	…	…	−709.8	−1,166.2
Trade Balance	78ac d	…	…	…	…	…	…	…	…	…	…	…	…	…	−23.7	−378.1
Services: Credit	78ad d	…	…	…	…	…	…	…	…	…	…	…	…	…	226.8	406.1
Services: Debit	78ae d	…	…	…	…	…	…	…	…	…	…	…	…	…	−260.4	−337.3
Balance on Goods and Services	78af d	…	…	…	…	…	…	…	…	…	…	…	…	…	−57.3	−309.3
Income: Credit	78ag d	…	…	…	…	…	…	…	…	…	…	…	…	…	18.4	54.2
Income: Debit	78ah d	…	…	…	…	…	…	…	…	…	…	…	…	…	−95.2	−109.1
Balance on Goods, Serv., & Inc.	78ai d	…	…	…	…	…	…	…	…	…	…	…	…	…	−134.1	−364.2
Current Transfers, n.i.e.: Credit	78aj d	…	…	…	…	…	…	…	…	…	…	…	…	…	8.8	9.2
Current Transfers: Debit	78ak d	…	…	…	…	…	…	…	…	…	…	…	…	…	−1.7	−2.1
Current Account, n.i.e.	78al d	…	…	…	…	…	…	…	…	…	…	…	…	…	−127.0	−357.1
Capital Account, n.i.e.: Credit	78ba d	…	…	…	…	…	…	…	…	…	…	…	…	…	—	—
Capital Account: Debit	78bb d	…	…	…	…	…	…	…	…	…	…	…	…	…	—	—
Capital Account, n.i.e.	78bc d	…	…	…	…	…	…	…	…	…	…	…	…	…	—	—
Direct Investment Abroad	78bd d	…	…	…	…	…	…	…	…	…	…	…	…	…	—	—
Dir. Invest. in Rep. Econ., n.i.e.	78be d	…	…	…	…	…	…	…	…	…	…	…	…	…	128.8	215.5
Portfolio Investment Assets	78bf d	…	…	…	…	…	…	…	…	…	…	…	…	…	—	—
Portfolio Investment Liab., n.i.e.	78bg d	…	…	…	…	…	…	…	…	…	…	…	…	…	−11.6	−35.7
Other Investment Assets	78bh d	…	…	…	…	…	…	…	…	…	…	…	…	…	−45.8	−99.2
Other Investment Liab., n.i.e.	78bi d	…	…	…	…	…	…	…	…	…	…	…	…	…	33.1	361.1
Financial Account, n.i.e.	78bj d	…	…	…	…	…	…	…	…	…	…	…	…	…	104.5	441.7
Net Errors and Omissions	78ca d	…	…	…	…	…	…	…	…	…	…	…	…	…	160.8	−10.8
Overall Balance	78cb d	…	…	…	…	…	…	…	…	…	…	…	…	…	138.3	73.8
Reserves and Related Items	79da d	…	…	…	…	…	…	…	…	…	…	…	…	…	−138.3	−73.8
Reserve Assets	79db d	…	…	…	…	…	…	…	…	…	…	…	…	…	−5.5	−85.1
Use of Fund Credit and Loans	79dc d	…	…	…	…	…	…	…	…	…	…	…	…	…	−125.5	—
Liabs.Constit.For.Auth.Reserves	79dd d	…	…	…	…	…	…	…	…	…	…	…	…	…	−7.4	11.3
Exceptional Financing	79de d	…	…	…	…	…	…	…	…	…	…	…	…	…		
Government Finance													*Pesos through 1971; Thousands of Pesos from 1972 to 1985;*
Deficit (−) or Surplus	80	−1,900	−300	−4,700	−4,100	−11,800	−8,300	−42,200	I−31	−31	−174	−359	−262	−264	−280	−1
Revenue	81	6,300	13,500	20,100	48,700	61,800	82,900	103,100	I 278	552	914	1,519	2,800	4,539	6,923	12,188
Expenditure	82	8,200	13,800	24,800	52,800	73,600	91,200	145,300	I 306	580	1,084	1,877	3,054	4,677	7,068	11,615
Lending Minus Repayments	83	…	…	…	…	…	…	…	I 3	3	4	1	8	126	135	574
Financing																
Net Borrowing	84	100	−300	400	5,800	12,400	7,600	42,500	I 7	12	201	482	558	329	490	923
Domestic	84a	…	…	…	…	…	…	…	I 4	−5	104	220	349	246	423	512
Foreign	85a	…	…	…	…	…	…	…	I 3	17	97	262	209	83	67	411
Use of Cash Balances	87	…	…	…	…	…	…	…	I 24	19	−27	−123	−296	−65	−210	−922
Debt: Domestic	88a	…	…	…	…	…	…	…	I 112	138	404	429	1,135	1,450	1,790	2,462
Foreign	89a	…	…	…	…	…	…	…	I 129	179	419	968	1,622	2,187	3,514	4,743
National Accounts													*Pesos through 1971; Thousands of Pesos from 1972 to 1985;*
Exports of Goods & Services	90c	10,000	16,600	24,300	55,700	66,100	72,500	70,800	I 178	354	641	1,317	2,350	3,774	5,530	9,400
Government Consumption	91f	7,700	13,000	23,900	49,100	75,400	92,100	118,600	I 153	364	680	1,116	1,755	2,451	3,821	6,789
Gross Fixed Capital Formation	93e	5,700	10,900	22,800	38,300	56,000	68,500	82,800	I 121	229	465	1,090	1,952	3,030	4,943	9,312
Increase/Decrease(−) in Stocks	93i	…	1,100	600	−300	−800	1,000	8,400	I 26	93	60	12	−81	−2	8	663
Private Consumption	96f	35,600	69,300	120,400	277,000	369,900	448,000	522,000	I 938	1,844	3,463	6,244	9,107	15,018	22,919	43,441
Imports of Goods & Services	98c	−6,300	−11,300	−22,200	−45,300	−60,600	−80,900	−80,100	I −174	−323	−763	−1,613	−2,445	−4,356	−6,291	−11,980
Gross Domestic Product = GDP	99b	52,500	99,600	169,800	374,500	506,100	601,000	722,000	I 1,242	2,561	4,546	8,166	12,638	19,915	30,930	57,625
Net Factor Inc/Pmts(−) Abroad	98.n	−1,000	−1,000	−3,000	−6,000	−7,000	−6,000	−6,000	I −15	−22	−54	−168	−244	−317	−465	−454
Gross National Product = GNP	99a	51,900	98,400	167,100	368,600	498,900	595,000	716,000	I 1,227	2,539	4,492	7,998	12,394	19,598	30,465	57,171
Gross Nat'l Inc., Factor Cost	99g	…	…	…	…	…	…	…	…	…	…	…	…	…	…	…
GDP 1990 Prices (Millions)	99b.p	6,268	6,483	6,232	6,303	6,697	7,020	I 6,948	6,840	6,865	7,081	7,496	7,795	7,886	8,301	8,813
GDP Deflator (1990=100)	99bi p	—	—	—	—	—	—	—	—	—	—	—	—	—	—	1
																Millions:
Population	99z	2.71	2.75	2.69	2.70	2.71	2.73	2.74	2.75	2.76	2.77	I 2.83	2.85	2.86	2.88	2.89

Exchange Rates: On July 1, 1975, the new peso, equal to 1,000 old pesos, was introduced. On March 1, 1993, the Uruguayan peso, equal to 1,000 new Uruguayan pesos, was introduced.

Monetary Authorities: ❈ Before 1965, data for *line 14a* and for commercial banks are averages of weekly data of last month of period. Beginning in 1966, data are based on balance sheets in which sectoring of assets and liabilities is improved. ❈ Beginning in December 1975, data include only the Central Bank accounts which have been generated from the end-of-month issue of provisional balance sheets produced every ten days by the Central Bank of Uruguay. ❈ Beginning in 1982, data for *Long-Term Foreign Liabilities* (*line 16cl*) include long-term foreign financing and, beginning in August 1983, include liabilities relating to external debt refinancing. Prior to 1982, gold holdings are valued at the historical price of gold, and the gold component of *line 11* is not comparable with *line 1and* converted into national currency. Beginning in 1982, however, the national currency value of gold holdings is based on the national valuation.

Deposit Money Banks: ❈ See note to section 10. ❈ Beginning in December 1975, data consolidate also the Bank of the Republic accounts. ❈ Beginning in 1982, data are based on improved sectorization, which properly distinguishes between resident and nonresident transactions; in addition, data are based on actual, rather than preliminary, information.

Monetary Survey: ❈ See notes to sections 10 and 20.

Government Finance: ❈ Beginning in 1972, data are as reported in the *Government Finance Statistics Yearbook* and cover consolidated central government, including extrabudgetary and social security accounts. Data show the transactions of nonfinancial public enterprises on a net basis.

Uruguay

1980	1981	1982	1983	1984	1985	1986	1987	1988	1989	1990	1991	1992	1993	1994		
Millions of US Dollars															**International Transactions**	
1,058.6	1,215.4	1,022.9	1,045.1	933.8	909.0	1,087.8	1,189.2	1,404.5	1,598.8	1,692.9	1,604.7	1,702.5	1,645.3	1,913.4	Exports	70..*d*
1,680.3	1,641.1	1,110.0	787.5	776.7	707.7	870.0	1,141.9	1,157.2	1,202.8	1,342.9	1,636.5	2,045.1	2,324.4	2,772.6	Imports, cif	71..*d*
1,541.3	1,499.9	1,038.2	739.7	733.4	675.3	830.2	1,089.6	1,104.2	1,147.7	1,281.4	1,561.5	1,951.4	2,217.9	2,645.6	Imports, fob	71.v*d*
Minus Sign Indicates Debit															Balance of Payments	
1,058.5	1,229.7	1,256.4	1,156.4	924.6	853.6	1,087.8	1,182.3	1,404.5	1,599.0	1,692.9	1,604.7	1,801.4	1,731.6	....	Goods: Exports f.o.b.	78aa*d*
−1,668.2	−1,592.1	−1,038.4	−739.7	−732.2	−675.4	−814.5	−1,079.9	−1,112.2	−1,136.2	−1,266.9	−1,543.7	−1,923.2	−2,118.3	....	Goods: Imports f.o.b.	78ab*d*
−609.7	−362.4	218.0	416.7	192.4	178.2	273.3	102.4	292.3	462.8	426.0	61.0	−121.8	−386.7	....	Trade Balance	78ac*d*
467.5	471.0	280.9	278.2	364.8	403.5	422.1	406.9	348.3	433.3	465.6	596.2	830.3	916.8	....	Services: Credit	78ad*d*
−475.5	−505.9	−547.1	−472.5	−334.7	−339.6	−387.1	−356.3	−315.4	−421.7	−392.5	−422.5	−558.8	−640.6	....	Services: Debit	78ae*d*
−617.7	−397.3	−48.2	222.4	222.5	242.1	308.3	153.0	325.2	474.4	499.1	234.7	149.7	−110.5	....	Balance on Goods and Services	78af*d*
67.7	145.8	147.2	62.5	87.2	77.4	92.7	103.5	114.7	203.2	258.3	234.7	225.0	249.7	....	Income: Credit	78ag*d*
−167.8	−219.6	−344.0	−358.5	−448.8	−428.3	−384.4	−405.3	−439.0	−552.1	−579.6	−467.1	−412.1	−390.8	....	Income: Debit	78ah*d*
−717.8	−471.1	−245.0	−73.6	−139.1	−108.8	16.6	−148.8	.9	125.5	177.8	2.3	−37.4	−251.6	....	Balance on Goods, Serv., & Inc.	78ai*d*
11.2	12.5	13.4	14.1	13.0	15.2	29.6	14.5	26.0	15.0	15.8	50.1	36.0	32.6	....	Current Transfers, n.i.e.: Credit	78aj*d*
−2.5	−2.8	−3.0	−3.1	−3.0	−4.4	−4.3	−6.5	−4.7	−7.0	−7.7	−10.0	−7.4	−7.8	....	Current Transfers: Debit	78ak*d*
−709.1	−461.4	−234.6	−62.6	−129.1	−98.0	41.9	−140.8	22.2	133.5	185.9	42.4	−8.8	−226.8	....	Current Account, n.i.e.	78al*d*
—	—	—	—	—	—	—	—	—	—	—	—	—	—	....	Capital Account, n.i.e.: Credit	78ba*d*
—	—	—	—	—	—	—	—	—	—	—	—	—	—	....	Capital Account: Debit	78bb*d*
—	—	—	—	—	—	—	—	—	—	—	—	—	—	....	Capital Account, n.i.e.	78bc*d*
—	—	−13.7	5.6	3.4	−7.9	−4.5	4.9	−2.3	—	—	—	—	—	....	Direct Investment Abroad	78bd*d*
289.5	48.6	—	—	—	—	37.0	50.1	46.8	—	—	—	—	75.8	....	Dir. Invest. in Rep. Econ., n.i.e.	78be*d*
—	—	—	—	—	—	—	—	−60.1	—	—	—	—	—	....	Portfolio Investment Assets	78bf*d*
−11.8	3.1	77.6	28.3	62.5	221.4	91.9	183.0	224.3	129.8	107.8	47.4	83.4	29.3	....	Portfolio Investment Liab., n.i.e.	78bg*d*
−26.9	−389.1	54.6	98.0	38.1	−126.2	−190.9	−245.7	−390.4	−764.3	−632.0	−399.0	−589.8	−18.6	....	Other Investment Assets	78bh*d*
487.0	994.2	964.6	117.5	61.9	−161.6	85.1	297.0	368.2	628.6	438.3	−77.6	414.9	108.0	....	Other Investment Liab., n.i.e.	78bi*d*
737.8	656.8	1,083.1	249.4	165.9	−74.3	18.6	289.3	186.5	−5.9	−85.9	−429.2	−91.5	194.5	....	Financial Account, n.i.e.	78bj*d*
89.5	−161.5	−1,264.5	−252.5	−121.2	238.7	221.3	−104.6	−247.1	−62.6	35.7	468.8	238.3	220.8	....	Net Errors and Omissions	78ca*d*
118.2	33.9	−416.0	−65.7	−84.4	66.4	281.8	43.9	−38.4	65.0	135.7	82.0	138.0	188.5	....	Overall Balance	78cb*d*
−118.2	−33.9	416.0	65.7	84.4	−66.4	−281.8	−43.9	38.4	−65.0	−135.7	−82.0	−138.0	−188.5	....	Reserves and Related Items	79da*d*
−95.4	−25.5	322.6	−82.7	85.6	−164.0	−287.0	−26.9	46.8	3.2	−40.2	−113.5	−186.2	−178.6	....	Reserve Assets	79db*d*
—	—	94.5	148.2	—	97.9	5.5	−61.1	−63.3	−98.0	−111.5	−41.3	−2.5	−14.4	....	Use of Fund Credit and Loans	79dc*d*
−22.8	−8.4	−1.1	.3	−1.2	−.3	−.2	4.1	14.9	−5.2	−3.8	−2.2	—	4.4	....	Liabs.Constit.For Auth.Reserves	79dd*d*
—	—	—	—	—	—	—	40.0	40.0	35.0	19.8	75.0	50.7	—	....	Exceptional Financing	79de*d*
Millions of Pesos Beginning 1986: Year Ending December 31															**Government Finance**	
30	−1,835	−11,654	−7,273	−15,308	−11,651	I−6	−14	−46	−146	36	184	222	....	....	Deficit (−) or Surplus	80
20,525	29,077	27,454	40,139	55,513	109,323	I220	395	668	1,157	2,598	5,768	10,421	....	....	Revenue	81
20,136	30,487	38,107	46,305	69,373	118,413	I223	406	708	1,292	2,539	5,550	10,165	....	....	Expenditure	82
359	425	1,001	1,107	1,448	2,561	I4	3	5	11	23	34	34	....	....	Lending Minus Repayments	83
															Financing	
1,846	1,305	9,570	5,388	28,063	35,370	I26	375	286	222	220	63	615	....	....	Net Borrowing	84
1,030	289	8,402	5,588	21,767	18,320	I15	334	207	129	69	−53	386	....	....	Domestic	84a
816	1,016	1,168	−200	6,296	17,050	I11	42	79	93	151	116	229	....	....	Foreign	85a
−1,876	530	2,084	1,885	−12,755	−23,720	I−20	−361	−240	−76	−256	−247	−837	....	....	Use of Cash Balances	87
3,964	4,305	16,904	23,860	51,376	75,227	I102	153	245	483	802	1,176	2,058	....	....	Debt: Domestic	88a
4,278	5,897	18,547	34,411	58,344	120,712	I176	330	626	1,231	2,634	4,384	7,137	....	....	Foreign	89a
Millions of Pesos Beginning 1986															**National Accounts**	
13,861	17,987	18,072	45,100	72,065	128,100	I233	360	650	1,232	2,559	4,679	7,908	10,495	....	Exports of Goods & Services	90c
11,482	17,336	20,100	25,500	36,851	69,154	I128	220	359	647	1,362	2,731	4,523	7,299	....	Government Consumption	91f
15,422	19,205	19,382	24,000	29,600	46,100	I88	189	325	560	1,055	2,418	4,634	7,382	....	Gross Fixed Capital Formation	93e
572	−403	−827	1,000	3,200	8,400	I12	48	34	−14	18	318	238	714	....	Increase/Decrease(−) in Stocks	93i
69,890	91,147	94,076	121,300	187,300	327,970	I610	1,164	1,880	3,343	6,758	14,164	25,651	37,115	....	Private Consumption	96f
−19,023	−22,819	−22,107	−41,400	−57,950	−101,050	I−181	−319	−522	−928	−1,968	−4,039	−7,608	−11,108	....	Imports of Goods & Services	98c
92,204	122,453	128,696	175,400	271,000	478,600	I891	1,662	2,726	4,839	9,784	20,271	35,346	51,896	....	Gross Domestic Product = GDP	99b
−912	−797	−2,729	−9,950	−20,310	−35,630	I−44	−68	−113	−212	−377	−478	−578	−572	....	Net Factor Inc/Pmts(−) Abroad	98.n
91,292	121,656	125,967	165,460	250,720	443,010	I846	1,593	2,613	4,628	9,407	19,793	34,767	51,324	....	Gross National Product = GNP	99a
....	105,100	109,300	142,700	211,500	365,900	I691	1,319	2,170	3,895	7,717	15,858	27,715	....	....	Gross Nat'l Inc., Factor Cost	99g
9,342	9,520	8,626	I8,121	8,032	8,150	8,872	9,576	9,575	9,698	9,784	10,098	10,894	11,169	11,737	GDP 1990 Prices *(Millions)*	99b.*p*
1	1	1	2	3	6	10	17	28	50	100	201	325	470	....	GDP Deflator (1990=100)	99bi*p*
Midyear Estimates																
2.91	2.93	2.95	2.97	2.99	3.01	3.03	3.04	3.06	3.08	3.09	3.11	3.13	3.15	3.17	Population	99z

Vanuatu
846

		1965	1966	1967	1968	1969	1970	1971	1972	1973	1974	1975	1976	1977	1978	1979
Exchange Rates													*Vatu per SDR: Unless Otherwise Indicated:*				
Official Rate	aa	89.12	90.03	89.25	89.97	89.83	84.44	91.67	89.86	91.80	87.95	84.86	93.32	92.37	88.01	85.59
															Vatu per US Dollar:	
Official Rate	ae	89.12	90.03	89.25	89.97	89.83	84.44	84.44	82.76	76.10	71.83	72.49	80.32	76.04	67.56	64.97
Official Rate	rf	89.77	89.77	89.77	89.77	94.44	100.99	100.69	81.61	72.04	77.80	69.27	77.24	79.41	72.94	68.76
Fund Position													*Millions of SDRs: Unless Otherwise Indicated:*				
Quota	2f. s	...	...	...	...	...	...	...	...	...	...	...	...	...	...	...
SDRs	1b. s	...	...	...	...	...	...	...	...	...	...	...	...	...	...	...
Reserve Position in the Fund	1c. s	...	...	...	...	...	...	...	...	...	...	...	...	...	...	...
International Liquidity													*Millions of US Dollars Unless Otherwise Indicated:*				
Total Reserves minus Gold	1l. d	...	...	...	...	...	...	...	...	...	...	...	...	...	...	...
SDRs	1b. d	...	...	...	...	...	...	...	...	...	...	...	...	...	...	...
Reserve Position in the Fund	1c. d	...	...	...	...	...	...	...	...	...	...	...	...	...	...	...
Foreign Exchange	1d. d	...	...	...	...	...	...	...	...	...	...	...	...	...	...	...
Monetary Authorities	1da d	...	...	...	...	...	...	...	...	...	...	...	...	...	...	...
Government	1db d	...	...	...	...	...	...	...	...	...	...	...	...	...	...	...
Deposit Money Banks: Assets	7a. d								3.61	7.49	2.75	5.52	29.26	42.49	45.31	52.59
of which: Claims on Nonbanks	7ad d															
Deposit Money Banks: Liabilities	7b. d												6.31	8.02	5.06	7.11
of which: Liab. to Nonbanks	7bd d												—	—	—	—
Monetary Authorities															*Millions of Vatu:*		
Foreign Assets	11												594	682	836	1,079
Claims on Central Government	12a												...	...	...	...
Claims on Deposit Money Banks	12e															
of which: Fgn.Currency Claims	12ex															
Reserve Money	14												567	670	776	965
of which: Currency Outside DMBs	14a												494	564	699	846
Foreign Liabilities	16c															
Central Government Deposits	16d												26	9	62	104
Capital Accounts	17a												...	...	...	...
Valuation Adjustment	17rv												...	...	...	...
Other Items (Net)	17r												1	3	−2	10
Deposit Money Banks																
Reserves	20												26	48	51	83
Foreign Assets	21												2,350	3,231	3,061	3,417
Claims on Central Government	22a												305	272	225	121
Claims on Nonfin.Pub.Enterprises	22c															
Claims on Private Sector	22d												2,123	2,169	2,747	2,480
Claims on Other Financial Insts.	22f															
Demand Deposits	24												1,135	1,206	1,189	1,248
Time, Savings,& Fgn.Currency Dep.	25												3,763	4,046	3,981	3,949
of which: Nonreporting Bks' Deps	25e															
Foreign Liabilities	26c												507	610	342	462
Central Government Deposits	26d												53	286	594	686
Credit from Monetary Authorities	26g															
Capital Accounts	27a												276	342	346	259
Other Items (Net)	27r												−930	−770	−368	−503
Monetary Survey															*Millions of Vatu:*		
Foreign Assets (Net)	31n												2,437	3,303	3,555	4,034
Domestic Credit	32												2,349	2,146	2,316	1,811
Claims on Central Govt. (Net)	32an												226	−23	−431	−669
Claims on Nonfin.Pub.Enterprises	32c												—	—	—	—
Claims on Private Sector	32d												2,123	2,169	2,747	2,480
Claims on Other Financial Insts.	32f															
Money	34												1,629	1,770	1,888	2,094
Quasi-Money	35												3,763	4,046	3,981	3,949
Other Items (Net)	37r												−606	−367	2	−198
Money plus Quasi-Money	35l												5,392	5,816	5,869	6,043
Other Banking Institutions															*Millions of Vatu:*		
Cash	40															
Foreign Assets	41															
Claims on Central Government	42a															
Claims on Private Sector	42d															
Claims on Deposit Money Banks	42e															
Time and Savings Deposits	45															
Foreign Liabilities	46c															
Capital Accounts	47a															
Other Items (Net)	47r															
Banking Survey															*Millions of Vatu:*		
Foreign Assets (Net)	51n															
Domestic Credit	52															
Claims on Central Govt. (Net)	52an															
Claims on Nonfin.Pub.Enterprises	52c															
Claims on Private Sector	52d															
Liquid Liabilities	55l															
Other Items (Net)	57r															

Vanuatu

846

1980	1981	1982	1983	1984	1985	1986	1987	1988	1989	1990	1991	1992	1993	1994		
End of Period															**Exchange Rates**	
93.09	106.19	106.06	106.55	100.55	110.12	142.18	142.00	141.37	145.48	155.43	158.48	163.63	165.93	163.62	Official Rate	aa
End of Period (ae) Period Average (rf)																
72.99	91.23	96.15	101.77	102.58	100.25	116.24	100.56	105.05	110.70	109.25	110.79	119.00	120.80	112.08	Official Rate	ae
68.29	87.83	96.21	99.37	99.23	106.03	106.08	109.85	104.43	116.04	117.06	111.68	113.39	121.58	116.41	Official Rate	rf
End of Period															**Fund Position**	
....	6.90	6.90	9.00	9.00	9.00	9.00	9.00	9.00	9.00	9.00	9.00	9.00	9.00	12.50	12.50	Quota	2f. s
....	—	—	.02	.09	.15	.20	.26	.31	.40	.50	.59	.68	.15	.22	SDRs	1b. s
....	—	1.04	1.57	1.58	1.58	1.59	1.59	1.60	1.61	1.61	1.61	1.61	2.49	2.49	Reserve Position in the Fund	1c. s
End of Period															**International Liquidity**	
....	8.46	5.67	6.59	8.09	10.61	21.42	40.17	40.67	35.08	37.69	39.84	42.46	45.59	43.58	Total Reserves minus Gold	1l. d
....	—	—	.02	.09	.16	.24	.37	.42	.53	.71	.84	.94	.21	.31	SDRs	1b. d
....	—	1.15	1.64	1.55	1.74	1.94	2.26	2.15	2.12	2.29	2.30	2.21	3.42	3.63	Reserve Position in the Fund	1c. d
....	8.46	4.52	4.93	6.45	8.71	19.23	37.55	38.10	32.44	34.69	36.69	39.31	41.96	39.63	Foreign Exchange	1d. d
....	7.13	4.27	4.75	6.20	8.48	18.89	36.93	37.54	31.91	34.25	35.97	39.00	41.95	39.62	Monetary Authorities	1da d
....	1.33	.25	.18	.25	.23	.34^e	.62	.56	.53	.44	.72	.31	.01	.01	Government	1db d
34.98	137.26	195.93	170.31	196.57	288.38	274.75	284.51	139.14	209.94	235.09	183.03	150.93	157.83	158.73	Deposit Money Banks: Assets	7a. d
—	33.27	75.60	68.45	39.19	124.06	122.67	126.65	6.58	5.90	4.52	3.71	.81	1.76	.40	of which: Claims on Nonbanks	7ad d
5.80	117.09	146.14	111.74	114.17	190.45	177.57	190.14	38.75	51.98	64.10	22.54	20.07	29.48	26.54	Deposit Money Banks: Liabilities	7b. d
—	104.56	89.18	64.70	58.36	135.55	123.27	133.14	30.79	45.73	58.23	17.20	18.77	23.38	23.60	of which: Liab. to Nonbanks	7bd d
End of Period															**Monetary Authorities**	
1,158	772	671	674	829	1,063	2,496	4,040	4,272	4,012	4,120	4,413	4,978	5,519	4,919	Foreign Assets	11
....	10	23	39	39	12	—	—	—	—	—	—	—	—	76	Claims on Central Government	12a
....	49	194	183	167	395	363	—	4	2	8	8	—	4	1	Claims on Deposit Money Banks	12e
....	—	180	121	60	395	363	—	4	2	8	8	—	4	1	of which: Fgn.Currency Claims	12ex
849	642	678	796	981	1,228	1,371	1,233	1,380	1,823	1,570	2,008	1,956	3,005	2,801	Reserve Money	14
720	597	634	748	922	963	906	1,000	954	1,037	934	1,148	901	1,224	1,351	of which: Currency Outside DMBs	14a
....	1	46	23	12	24	35	5	25	4	45	42	1	21	25	Foreign Liabilities	16c
309	122	152	21	30	32	795	2,199	2,286	1,737	1,633	2,039	2,594	2,315	2,138	Central Government Deposits	16d
....	106	132	155	182	253	359	508	624	538	814	589	780	748	740	Capital Accounts	17a
....	—	—	—	—	18	436	409	364	295	584	330	319	248	134	Valuation Adjustment	17rv
—	-40	-120	-99	-170	-85	-137	-314	-403	-385	-519	-586	-673	-814	-842	Other Items (Net)	17r
End of Period															**Deposit Money Banks**	
105	42	42	47	58	236	357	276	349	826	546	972	1,070	1,821	1,397	Reserves	20
2,553	12,523	18,838	17,332	20,164	28,910	31,937	28,611	14,617	23,241	25,684	20,278	17,960	19,065	17,790	Foreign Assets	21
102	103	85	67	194	187	210	384	553	591	583	560	833	937	527	Claims on Central Government	22a
....	—	—	68	30	32	90	82	19	27	15	11	20	6	105	Claims on Nonfin.Pub.Enterprises	22c
2,646	3,135	3,252	3,492	3,497	3,287	3,485	4,079	4,365	4,799	5,966	6,226	7,914	7,944	8,540	Claims on Private Sector	22d
....	1,310	714	30	482	324	348	—	2	3	3	4	6	100	38	Claims on Other Financial Insts.	22f
1,162	851	1,110	1,525	2,104	1,679	1,904	3,219	2,441	3,270	2,918	3,209	4,119	4,448	4,339	Demand Deposits	24
3,379	3,874	6,192	6,353	7,926	9,749	12,828	10,386	11,953	18,460	20,203	19,560	18,248	18,778	19,443	Time, Savings,& Fgn.Currency Dep.	25
....	1,562	2,073	813	395	1,260	3,140	1,676	3,469	6,650	6,099	1,683	1,487	80	—	of which: Nonreporting Bks' Deps	25e
423	10,682	14,052	11,372	11,712	19,093	20,641	19,121	4,070	5,754	7,003	2,497	2,388	3,561	2,975	Foreign Liabilities	26c
347	1,314	840	780	1,465	1,544	276	359	322	394	396	629	376	709	296	Central Government Deposits	26d
....	—	246	202	176	398	364	—	4	2	8	1	—	3	1	Credit from Monetary Authorities	26g
370	586	720	1,188	1,476	1,188	1,354	1,130	1,449	2,083	1,034	2,557	3,124	2,297	1,726	Capital Accounts	27a
-275	-193	-227	-383	-434	-676	-939	-784	-335	-475	1,234	-402	-452	76	-381	Other Items (Net)	27r
End of Period															**Monetary Survey**	
3,288	2,611	5,412	6,611	9,270	10,856	13,757	13,525	14,794	21,494	22,755	22,152	20,549	21,003	19,710	Foreign Assets (Net)	31n
2,092	3,123	3,082	2,895	2,746	2,265	3,062	1,986	2,332	3,289	4,537	4,133	5,803	5,963	6,853	Domestic Credit	32
-554	-1,322	-885	-695	-1,263	-1,377	-861	-2,175	-2,055	-1,541	-1,446	-2,108	-2,137	-2,087	-1,831	Claims on Central Govt. (Net)	32an
....	—	—	68	30	32	90	82	19	27	15	11	20	6	105	Claims on Nonfin.Pub.Enterprises	32c
2,646	3,135	3,252	3,492	3,497	3,287	3,485	4,079	4,365	4,799	5,966	6,226	7,914	7,944	8,540	Claims on Private Sector	32d
—	1,310	714	30	482	324	348	—	2	3	3	4	6	100	38	Claims on Other Financial Insts.	32f
1,882	1,451	1,746	2,274	3,027	2,643	2,811	4,219	3,516	4,369	3,894	4,377	5,056	5,679	5,728	Money	34
3,379	3,874	6,192	6,353	7,926	9,749	12,828	10,386	11,953	18,460	20,203	19,560	18,248	18,778	19,443	Quasi-Money	35
119	410	557	880	1,063	729	1,179	905	1,656	1,955	3,196	2,349	3,049	2,509	1,392	Other Items (Net)	37r
5,261	5,325	7,938	8,627	10,953	12,392	15,639	14,606	15,469	22,829	24,097	23,936	23,303	24,457	25,171	Money plus Quasi-Money	35l
End of Period															**Other Banking Institutions**	
....	....	....	....	129	97	187	125	61	69	76	....	30	43	36	Cash	40
....	....	....	....	18	23	24	145	147	—	—	....	41	41	—	Foreign Assets	41
....	....	....	....	—	—	30	210	245	245	250	....	51	50	26	Claims on Central Government	42a
....	....	....	....	530	545	562	510	611	606	612	....	507	681	653	Claims on Private Sector	42d
....	....	....	....	231	278	292	25	9	17	129	....	—	—	—	Claims on Deposit Money Banks	42e
....	....	....	....	228	294	315	341	370	395	403	....	—	—	—	Time and Savings Deposits	45
....	....	....	....	159	230	291	323	188	362	430	....	349	583	631	Foreign Liabilities	46c
....	....	....	....	298	259	390	384	517	356	266	....	373	342	220	Capital Accounts	47a
....	....	....	....	223	161	99	-33	-2	-176	-32	....	-94	-109	-137	Other Items (Net)	47r
End of Period															**Banking Survey**	
....	....	....	....	9,129	10,649	13,490	13,346	14,752	21,133	22,325	....	20,240	20,461	19,079	Foreign Assets (Net)	51n
....	....	....	....	2,794	2,487	3,306	2,706	3,186	4,136	5,397	....	6,355	6,594	7,493	Domestic Credit	52
....	....	....	....	-1,263	-1,377	-831	-1,965	-1,810	-1,296	-1,196	....	-2,086	-2,037	-1,805	Claims on Central Govt. (Net)	52an
....	....	....	....	30	32	90	82	19	27	15	....	20	6	105	Claims on Nonfin.Pub.Enterprises	52c
....	....	....	....	4,027	3,832	4,047	4,589	4,977	5,405	6,578	....	8,421	8,625	9,193	Claims on Private Sector	52d
....	....	....	....	11,053	12,589	15,767	14,822	15,778	23,155	24,424	....	23,274	24,414	25,135	Liquid Liabilities	55l
....	....	....	....	871	546	1,028	1,230	2,160	2,114	3,298	....	3,323	2,642	1,437	Other Items (Net)	57r

Vanuatu

846

		1965	1966	1967	1968	1969	1970	1971	1972	1973	1974	1975	1976	1977	1978	1979
Interest Rates															*Percent Per Annum*	
Money Market Rate	60b	...	...	...	...	...	...	...	...	...	...	...	...	...	...	...
Deposit Rate	60l	...	...	...	...	...	...	...	...	...	...	...	...	...	...	...
Lending Rate	60p	...	...	...	...	...	...	...	...	...	...	...	...	...	...	...
Government Bond Yield	61	...	...	...	...	...	...	...	...	...	...	...	...	...	...	...
Prices													*Index Numbers (1990=100):*			
Consumer Prices	64	...	...	...	...	...	...	...	...	...	...	...	35.0	37.0	39.4	41.1
International Transactions															*Millions of Vatu*	
Exports	70	820	932	1,063	1,043	1,002	1,162	1,285	1,206	1,498	2,380	800	1,309	2,536	2,682	2,851
Imports, cif	71	647	735	865	908	1,057	1,311	1,844	2,373	2,552	3,860	2,754	2,628	3,146	3,739	4,232
Balance of Payments															*Millions of US Dollars:*	
Goods: Exports f.o.b.	78aa d	...	...	...	...	...	...	...	...	...	...	...	...	...	...	...
Goods: Imports f.o.b.	78ab d	...	...	...	...	...	...	...	...	...	...	...	...	...	...	...
Trade Balance	78ac d	...	...	...	...	...	...	...	...	...	...	...	...	...	...	...
Services: Credit	78ad d	...	...	...	...	...	...	...	...	...	...	...	...	...	...	...
Services: Debit	78ae d	...	...	...	...	...	...	...	...	...	...	...	...	...	...	...
Balance on Goods and Services	78af d	...	...	...	...	...	...	...	...	...	...	...	...	...	...	...
Income: Credit	78ag d	...	...	...	...	...	...	...	...	...	...	...	...	...	...	...
Income: Debit	78ah d	...	...	...	...	...	...	...	...	...	...	...	...	...	...	...
Balance on Goods, Serv., & Inc.	78ai d	...	...	...	...	...	...	...	...	...	...	...	...	...	...	...
Current Transfers, n.i.e.: Credit	78aj d	...	...	...	...	...	...	...	...	...	...	...	...	...	...	...
Current Transfers: Debit	78ak d	...	...	...	...	...	...	...	...	...	...	...	...	...	...	...
Current Account, n.i.e.	78al d	...	...	...	...	...	...	...	...	...	...	...	...	...	...	...
Capital Account, n.i.e.: Credit	78ba d	...	...	...	...	...	...	...	...	...	...	...	...	...	...	...
Capital Account: Debit	78bb d	...	...	...	...	...	...	...	...	...	...	...	...	...	...	...
Capital Account, n.i.e.	78bc d	...	...	...	...	...	...	...	...	...	...	...	...	...	...	...
Direct Investment Abroad	78bd d	...	...	...	...	...	...	...	...	...	...	...	...	...	...	...
Dir. Invest. in Rep. Econ., n.i.e.	78be d	...	...	...	...	...	...	...	...	...	...	...	...	...	...	...
Portfolio Investment Assets	78bf d	...	...	...	...	...	...	...	...	...	...	...	...	...	...	...
Portfolio Investment Liab., n.i.e.	78bg d	...	...	...	...	...	...	...	...	...	...	...	...	...	...	...
Other Investment Assets	78bh d	...	...	...	...	...	...	...	...	...	...	...	...	...	...	...
Other Investment Liab., n.i.e.	78bi d	...	...	...	...	...	...	...	...	...	...	...	...	...	...	...
Financial Account, n.i.e.	78bj d	...	...	...	...	...	...	...	...	...	...	...	...	...	...	...
Net Errors and Omissions	78ca d	...	...	...	...	...	...	...	...	...	...	...	...	...	...	...
Overall Balance	78cb d	...	...	...	...	...	...	...	...	...	...	...	...	...	...	...
Reserves and Related Items	79da d	...	...	...	...	...	...	...	...	...	...	...	...	...	...	...
Reserve Assets	79db d	...	...	...	...	...	...	...	...	...	...	...	...	...	...	...
Use of Fund Credit and Loans	79dc d	...	...	...	...	...	...	...	...	...	...	...	...	...	...	...
Liabs.Constit.For.Auth.Reserves	79dd d	...	...	...	...	...	...	...	...	...	...	...	...	...	...	...
Exceptional Financing	79de d	...	...	...	...	...	...	...	...	...	...	...	...	...	...	...
Government Finance															*Millions of Vatu*	
Deficit (-) or Surplus	80	...	...	...	...	...	...	...	...	...	...	...	...	...	...	...
Revenue	81	...	...	...	...	...	...	...	...	...	...	...	...	...	...	...
Grants Received	81z	...	...	...	...	...	...	...	...	...	...	...	...	...	...	...
Expenditure	82	...	...	...	...	...	...	...	...	...	...	...	...	...	...	...
Lending Minus Repayments	83	...	...	...	...	...	...	...	...	...	...	...	...	...	...	...
Financing																
Domestic	84a	...	...	...	...	...	...	...	...	...	...	...	...	...	...	...
Foreign	85a	...	...	...	...	...	...	...	...	...	...	...	...	...	...	...
Debt: Domestic	88a	...	...	...	...	...	...	...	...	...	...	...	...	...	...	...
Foreign	89a	...	...	...	...	...	...	...	...	...	...	...	...	...	...	...
National Accounts															*Millions of Vatu*	
Exports of Goods & Services	90c	...	...	...	...	...	...	...	...	...	...	...	...	...	...	...
Government Consumption	91f	...	...	...	...	...	...	...	...	...	...	...	...	...	...	...
Gross Fixed Capital Formation	93e	...	...	...	...	...	...	...	...	...	...	...	...	...	...	...
Increase/Decrease(-) in Stocks	93i	...	...	...	...	...	...	...	...	...	...	...	...	...	...	...
Private Consumption	96f	...	...	...	...	...	...	...	...	...	...	...	...	...	...	...
Imports of Goods & Services	98c	...	...	...	...	...	...	...	...	...	...	...	...	...	...	...
Gross Domestic Product = GDP	99b	...	...	...	...	...	...	...	...	...	...	...	...	...	...	...
Net Factor Inc/Pmts(-) Abroad	98.n	...	...	...	...	...	...	...	...	...	...	...	...	...	...	...
Gross National Product = GNP	99a	...	...	...	...	...	...	...	...	...	...	...	...	...	...	...
Gross Dom. Prod. 1990 Prices	99b.p	...	...	...	...	...	...	...	...	...	...	...	...	...	...	...
GDP Deflator (1990=100)	99bi p	...	...	...	...	...	...	...	...	...	...	...	...	...	...	...
																Millions:
Population	99z	.07	.08	.08	.08	.08	.08	.08	.09	.09	.09	.10	.10	.10	.10	I.11

Deposit Money Banks: I Beginning on October 31, 1992, includes the National Bank of Vanuatu—a government-owned commercial bank that took over the assets and liabilities of the Vanuatu Cooperative Savings Bank.
Monetary Survey: I See note to section 20.
Other Banking Institutions: I Prior to October 31, 1992, comprised the Development Bank of Vanuatu and the Vanuatu Cooperative Savings Bank. Beginning with October 31, 1992, includes only the Development Bank of Vanuatu.
Interest Rates: *Government Bond Yield:* I Prior to January 1989, data refer to the yield on three-year maturities. Beginning in January 1989, data refer to the yield on ten-year maturities.

Vanuatu

	1980	1981	1982	1983	1984	1985	1986	1987	1988	1989	1990	1991	1992	1993	1994			
Percent Per Annum																	**Interest Rates**	
	....	....	....	....	....	7.00	6.96	6.50	7.50	7.08	7.00	7.00	5.92	6.00	6.00	Money Market Rate	60b
	....	10.75	10.42	9.44	8.75	7.34	6.81	5.48	6.94	6.58	7.00	7.00	4.69	5.00	5.06	Deposit Rate	60l
	....	17.00	17.17	17.50	16.83	15.75	16.00	15.42	17.04	17.00	17.33	18.00	16.25	16.00	16.00	Lending Rate	60p
	....	....	....	....	....	9.50	9.50	9.50	9.50	ℐ8.00	8.00	8.00	8.00	8.00	8.00	Government Bond Yield	61
Period Averages																	**Prices**	
	45.7	57.9	61.8	62.8	66.3	67.0	ℐ70.2	81.5	88.6	95.5	100.0	106.5	108.8	114.7	117.4	Consumer Prices	64
Millions of Vatu																	**International Transactions**	
	2,449	2,833	2,201	2,941	4,395	3,252	1,841	1,943	2,066	2,560	2,202	2,035	2,677	2,758	2,911	Exports	70
	4,993	5,116	5,819	6,356	6,881	7,378	6,105	7,638	7,361	8,250	11,211	9,216	9,276	9,167	....	Imports, cif	71
Minus Sign Indicates Debit																	Balance of Payments	
	....	....	10.67	17.92	32.54	18.67	8.81	13.73	15.39	13.74	13.73	14.86	17.80	17.43	....	Goods: Exports f.o.b.	78aa d
	....	....	-43.27	-45.82	-51.48	-52.29	-46.81	-57.09	-57.89	-57.92	-79.34	-74.01	-66.79	-64.71	....	Goods: Imports f.o.b.	78ab d
	....	....	-32.60	-27.90	-18.94	-33.62	-37.99	-43.36	-42.50	-44.18	-65.61	-59.15	-48.99	-47.28	....	Trade Balance	78ac d
	....	....	36.99	38.11	42.43	38.16	30.58	36.15	39.97	40.29	60.17	66.09	69.40	61.01	....	Services: Credit	78ad d
	....	....	-14.35	-16.82	-20.07	-20.37	-15.80	-15.59	-17.79	-19.11	-23.86	-26.95	-26.79	-26.92	....	Services: Debit	78ae d
	....	....	-9.96	-6.60	3.42	-15.83	-23.21	-22.80	-20.32	-23.01	-29.30	-20.01	-6.39	-13.19	....	Balance on Goods and Services	78af d
	....	....	5.59	6.50	8.78	26.73	40.82	31.14	23.38	23.42	31.92	24.88	17.60	17.62	....	Income: Credit	78ag d
	....	....	-26.70	-23.71	-27.90	-40.22	-48.96	-51.86	-40.99	-29.18	-33.32	-49.18	-47.55	-48.23	....	Income: Debit	78ah d
	....	....	-31.07	-23.81	-15.70	-29.31	-31.35	-43.52	-37.93	-28.76	-30.70	-44.31	-36.34	-43.80	....	Balance on Goods, Serv., & Inc.	78ai d
	....	....	24.78	17.17	20.84	20.97	20.94	24.61	26.28	20.42	25.01	31.10	23.23	23.24	....	Current Transfers, n.i.e.: Credit	78aj d
	....	....	-1.37	-1.65	-2.02	-2.02	-1.28	-5.46	-3.54	-3.90	-.50	-.50	-.55	-.58	....	Current Transfers: Debit	78ak d
	....	....	-7.66	-8.29	3.12	-10.37	-11.70	-24.37	-15.19	-12.25	-6.18	-13.71	-13.66	-21.14	....	Current Account, n.i.e.	78al d
	....	....	19.96	17.11	16.57	12.32	9.30	19.54	17.96	8.91	16.51	19.34	26.59	25.90	....	Capital Account, n.i.e.: Credit	78ba d
	....	....	-.46	-.45	-.47	-.67	-.41	-.50	-.10	-.13	-.04	-.20	-9.37	-5.74	....	Capital Account: Debit	78bb d
	....	....	19.50	16.66	16.10	11.65	8.90	19.04	17.87	8.78	16.47	19.14	17.22	20.16	....	Capital Account, n.i.e.	78bc d
	....	....	—	—	—	—	—	—	—	—	—	—	—	—	....	Direct Investment Abroad	78bd d
	....	....	6.93	5.87	7.44	4.63	2.02	12.89	10.81	9.17	13.11	25.47	26.45	26.65	....	Dir. Invest. in Rep. Econ., n.i.e.	78be d
	....	....	—	—	—	—	—	—	—	—	—	—	—	—	....	Portfolio Investment Assets	78bf d
	....	....	—	—	—	—	—	—	—	—	—	—	—	—	....	Portfolio Investment Liab., n.i.e.	78bg d
	....	....	-60.81	22.19	-35.57	-81.72	-20.11	18.59	145.38	-.79	-.93	15.28	-8.57	-26.60	....	Other Investment Assets	78bh d
	....	....	38.58	-39.24	.62	82.17	31.02	-12.14	-146.25	15.81	1.60	-68.55	5.83	16.05	....	Other Investment Liab., n.i.e.	78bi d
	....	....	-15.29	-11.18	-27.51	5.07	12.92	19.35	9.95	24.19	13.79	-27.79	23.71	16.10	....	Financial Account, n.i.e.	78bj d
	....	....	6.37	3.79	2.13	-6.62	-5.34	-15.12	-17.30	-12.96	-19.38	19.31	-26.52	-11.67	....	Net Errors and Omissions	78ca d
	....	....	2.91	.98	-6.17	-.26	4.78	-1.10	-4.67	7.77	4.69	-3.05	.75	3.45	....	Overall Balance	78cb d
	....	....	-2.91	-.98	6.17	.26	-4.78	1.10	4.67	-7.77	-4.69	3.05	-.75	-3.45	....	Reserves and Related Items	79da d
	....	....	-3.25	-.98	2.55	.26	-4.78	-12.93	-.68	-7.77	-4.69	-.40	-4.16	-6.70	....	Reserve Assets	79db d
	....	....	—	—	—	—	—	—	—	—	—	—	—	—	....	Use of Fund Credit and Loans	79dc d
	....	....	—	—	—	—	—	—	—	—	—	—	—	—	....	Liabs.Constit.For.Auth.Reserves	79dd d
	....	....	.33	—	3.62	—	—	14.04	5.36	—	—	3.45	3.41	3.26	....	Exceptional Financing	79de d
Year Ending December 31																	**Government Finance**	
	....	650.7	-338.3	-57.2	432.5	-62.3	-855.2	511.6	-629.5	....	....	....	....	....	....	Deficit (-) or Surplus	80
	....	1,366.1	1,607.4	1,897.7	2,503.4	2,851.2	2,778.1	3,367.3	3,850.2	....	....	....	....	....	....	Revenue	81
	....	1,756.4	1,204.7	1,007.0	1,376.5	843.4	543.5	2,385.0	1,806.0	....	....	....	....	....	....	Grants Received	81z
	....	2,456.8	2,750.4	2,961.9	3,215.5	3,696.9	4,131.8	5,214.0	6,236.2	....	....	....	....	....	....	Expenditure	82
	....	15.0	400.0	—	231.9	60.0	45.0	26.7	49.5	....	....	....	....	....	....	Lending Minus Repayments	83
																Financing	
	....	-627.7	364.3	78.2	-413.8	19.1	798.7	-816.9	336.7	....	....	....	....	....	....	Domestic	84a
	....	-23.0	-26.0	-21.0	-18.7	43.2	56.5	305.3	292.8	....	....	....	....	....	....	Foreign	85a
	....	....	....	....	252.5	194.5	250.7	702.2	885.5	....	....	....	....	....	....	Debt: Domestic	88a
	....	....	....	....	325.2	600.2	757.1	900.4	1,117.8	....	....	....	....	....	....	Foreign	89a
Millions of Vatu																	**National Accounts**	
	....	....	....	5,934	5,934	5,652	5,001	4,421	4,232	6,099	8,301	9,263	9,677	9,743	....	Exports of Goods & Services	90c
	....	....	....	3,660	3,660	4,237	4,123	3,814	3,817	4,881	5,054	5,868	5,988	6,029	....	Government Consumption	91f
	....	....	....	2,142	2,142	2,619	3,183	3,321	2,847	5,470	7,241	5,258	5,645	6,075	....	Gross Fixed Capital Formation	93e
	....	....	....	463	463	634	559	267	350	606	488	500	520	540	....	Increase/Decrease(-) in Stocks	93i
	....	....	....	5,450	5,450	6,079	6,118	6,051	6,330	10,545	11,267	11,301	11,662	11,701	....	Private Consumption	96f
	....	....	....	-7,326	-7,326	-8,737	-7,754	-7,696	-7,362	-10,670	-13,714	-12,045	-12,270	-13,262	....	Imports of Goods & Services	98c
	....	....	9,442	10,150	10,150	10,966	10,743	10,789	10,850	16,367	17,899	19,212	20,524	21,959	....	Gross Domestic Product = GDP	99b
	....	....	....	-497	-497	378	460	-690	-287	553	1,283	-1,028	-1,707	-1,970	....	Net Factor Inc/Pmts(-) Abroad	98.n
	....	....	....	9,653	9,653	11,344	11,203	10,099	10,563	16,920	19,182	18,184	18,817	19,989	....	Gross National Product = GNP	99a
	....	....	....	15,218	16,262	16,442	16,107	16,176	16,268	17,007	17,899	18,631	18,775	19,494	....	Gross Dom. Prod. 1990 Prices	99b.p
	....	....	....	66.7	62.4	66.7	66.7	66.7	66.7	96.2	100.0	103.1	109.3	112.6	....	GDP Deflator (1990=100)	99bi p
Midyear Estimates																		
	.12	.12	.12	.13	.13	.14	.14	.14	.15	ℐ.14	.14	.15	.15	.16	....	Population	99z

Venezuela

		1965	1966	1967	1968	1969	1970	1971	1972	1973	1974	1975	1976	1977	1978	1979
Exchange Rates																*Bolivares per SDR:*
Official Rate	aa	4.450	4.450	4.450	4.450	4.450	4.450	4.723	4.723	5.169	5.246	5.016	4.987	5.214	5.592	5.655
																Bolivares per US Dollar:
Official Rate	ae	4.450	4.450	4.450	4.450	4.450	4.450	4.350	4.350	4.285	4.285	4.285	4.293	4.293	4.293	4.293
Official Rate	rf	4.450	4.450	4.450	4.450	4.450	4.450	4.447	4.400	4.305	4.285	4.285	4.290	4.293	4.293	4.293
Secondary Rate	xe	....	....	....	....	....	....	....	....	....	....	....	....	....	....	....
Tertiary Rate	ye	....	....	....	....	....	....	....	....	....	....	....	....	....	....	....
Tertiary Rate	yf	....	....	....	....	....	....	....	....	....	....	....	....	....	....	....
																Index Numbers (1990=100):
Market Rate	ahx	1,050.4	1,050.4	1,050.4	1,050.4	1,050.4	1,050.4	1,051.2	1,074.5	1,088.6	1,090.8	1,090.8	1,089.7	1,088.9	1,088.9	1,088.9
Nominal Effective Exchange Rate	nec	....	....	....	....	....	....	....	....	....	....	....	....	....	....	604.8
Real Effective Exchange Rate	rec	....	....	....	....	....	....	....	....	....	....	....	....	....	....	200.9
Fund Position																*Millions of SDRs:*
Quota	2f.s	150	250	250	250	250	330	330	330	330	330	330	330	330	660	660
SDRs	1b.s	—	—	—	—	—	48	83	118	118	120	124	126	136	167	268
Reserve Position in the Fund	1c.s	38	63	73	81	89	117	111	111	111	401	805	926	833	588	408
of which: Outstg.Fund Borrowing	2c	—	—	—	—	—	—	—	—	—	252	602	610	559	361	185
Total Fund Cred.&Loans Outstg.	2tl	—	—	—	—	—	—	—	—	—	—	—	—	—	—	—
International Liquidity												*Millions of US Dollars Unless Otherwise Indicated:*				
Total Reserves minus Gold	1l.d	418	376	471	519	530	637	1,097	1,307	1,940	6,034	8,403	8,124	7,735	6,035	7,320
SDRs	1b.d	—	—	—	—	—	47	90	128	143	147	145	146	166	218	353
Reserve Position in the Fund	1c.d	38	63	73	81	89	117	121	121	134	491	942	1,075	1,011	766	538
Foreign Exchange	1d.d	380	313	398	438	441	472	886	1,058	1,663	5,396	7,316	6,902	6,558	5,051	6,430
Gold (Million Fine Troy Ounces)	1ad	11.46	11.46	11.46	11.51	11.51	10.97	11.17	11.17	11.17	11.18	11.18	11.18	11.32	11.39	11.46
Gold (National Valuation)	1and	401	401	401	403	403	384	425	425	472	472	472	472	478	481	484
Monetary Authorities: Other Liab.	4..d	38	7	5	5	3	5	13	11	9	16	28	39	69	49	38
Deposit Money Banks: Assets	7a.d	33	27	27	23	29	30	43	112	62	130	221	214	329	614	765
of which: Claims on Nonbanks	7add	5	5	5	4	4	2	2	2	2	44	48	33	26	24	21
Deposit Money Banks: Liabilities	7b.d	46	53	44	40	65	79	70	102	168	171	216	370	691	1,002	778
Other Banking Insts.: Assets	7e.d	—	—	—	1	—	6	2	67	70	48	17	47	47	99	161
Liabilities	7f.d	39	56	59	61	98	122	146	249	307	253	59	157	402	729	1,770
Monetary Authorities																*Billions of Bolivares:*
Foreign Assets	11	3.06	2.88	3.30	3.53	3.58	4.00	6.01	6.84	10.22	27.39	37.89	36.76	35.17	27.93	33.45
Claims on Central Government	12a	.27	.35	.34	.41	.52	.53	.36	.38	.43	.54	.93	.93	1.37	1.41	2.65
Claims on Local Government	12b	.01	.01	.02	.01	—	—	—	—	—	—	—	—	—	—	—
Claims on Nonfin.Pub.Enterprises	12c	.05	.05	.06	.07	.06	.05	.04	.02	.01	.01	—	—	—	—	—
Claims on Private Sector	12d	.07	.09	.07	.07	.07	.02	.01	—	—	.01	—	.10	.25	.05	.12
Claims on Deposit Money Banks	12e	.24	.29	.16	.11	.04	.05	.04	.06	.06	.16	.25	.20	1.02	2.21	2.12
Claims on Other Banking Insts.	12f	.02	.04	.08	.07	.14	.15	.01	.01	.11	.22	.09	—	.64	2.45	2.63
Reserve Money	14	2.83	2.94	3.24	3.64	3.85	3.96	4.87	5.46	6.78	9.63	13.55	16.34	20.06	21.88	24.69
of which: Currency Outside DMBs	14a	1.55	1.65	1.79	1.94	2.03	2.16	2.34	2.58	2.87	3.81	4.72	5.82	7.38	9.01	10.01
Time, Savings,& Fgn.Currency Dep.	15	.03	.02	.01	.01	.01	.01	.01	.13	.24	.26	1.03	.17	.47	.18	.19
Bonds	16ab	—	—	—	—	—	—	.13	.05	—	—	—	—	—	—	—
Foreign Liabilities	16c	.17	.03	.02	.02	.01	.02	.06	.05	.04	.07	.09	.14	.24	.20	.16
Long-Term Foreign Liabilities	16cl	—	—	—	—	—	—	—	—	—	—	—	.03	.03	.01	—
Central Government Deposits	16d	.43	.44	.59	.44	.45	.39	.66	.68	1.86	16.07	21.62	18.31	14.09	7.41	10.80
Capital Accounts	17a	.34	.37	.34	.38	.43	.69	.93	1.15	2.24	2.50	2.83	3.15	3.54	4.24	5.46
Other Items (Net)	17r	−.08	−.10	−.17	−.22	−.35	−.29	−.18	−.20	−.32	−.18	.01	−.15	−.01	.12	−.34
Deposit Money Banks																*Billions of Bolivares:*
Reserves	20	1.22	1.24	1.46	1.66	1.80	1.73	2.45	2.90	3.80	4.90	5.87	8.71	10.66	10.97	12.09
Foreign Assets	21	.15	.12	.12	.10	.13	.13	.19	.49	.27	.56	.95	.92	1.41	2.63	3.28
Claims on Central Government	22a	.02	—	—	—	.28	.28	—	.36	.42	.65	.90	.90	1.97	1.63	1.50
Claims on Local Government	22b	—	—	—	—	—	—	—	—	—	—	—	—	—	—	.03
Claims on Nonfin.Pub.Enterprises	22c	.06	.06	.07	.11	.10	.07	.46	.27	.50	.53	.56	.50	.56	.71	.77
Claims on Private Sector	22d	5.85	5.94	6.50	7.27	7.84	8.68	9.58	11.20	14.20	18.97	28.70	39.29	46.46	56.52	59.04
Claims on Other Banking Insts.	22f	—	—	—	—	—	—	—	.03	.06	.07	.03	.07	.13	.12	.33
Demand Deposits	24	3.18	3.30	3.73	4.07	4.52	4.82	5.73	6.92	8.44	12.12	17.85	21.21	27.58	33.25	33.75
Time & Foreign Currency Deposits	25	2.96	2.89	3.43	3.77	4.29	4.71	5.56	6.80	8.20	9.75	14.89	21.48	26.22	29.02	32.01
Foreign Liabilities	26c	.07	.11	.09	.06	.09	.10	.10	.12	.22	.29	.31	.46	1.00	.92	1.33
Long-Term Foreign Liabilities	26cl	.13	.13	.10	.12	.20	.25	.20	.33	.51	.45	.61	1.13	1.97	3.38	2.00
Central Government Deposits	26d	.22	.22	.25	.41	.35	.43	.42	.40	.55	1.46	1.36	2.99	4.40	6.93	5.34
Credit from Monetary Authorities	26g	.17	.22	.11	.09	.04	.03	.02	.02	—	.13	—	.15	.97	2.14	2.65
Liabs. to Other Banking Insts.	26i	.04	.05	.08	.06	.08	.12	.17	.49	.56	.78	.84	1.09	1.09	1.28	1.55
Capital Accounts	27a	1.23	1.29	1.33	1.46	1.55	1.66	1.83	1.95	2.21	2.58	3.17	3.67	4.51	5.12	5.77
Other Items (Net)	27r	−.71	−.84	−.97	−.89	−.98	−1.23	−1.35	−1.76	−1.43	−1.89	−2.04	−1.79	−6.54	−9.46	−7.38
Monetary Survey																*Billions of Bolivares:*
Foreign Assets (Net)	31n	2.97	2.86	3.31	3.55	3.60	4.01	6.04	7.17	10.23	27.60	38.43	37.08	35.34	29.44	35.24
Domestic Credit	32	5.70	5.87	6.30	7.17	8.20	8.96	9.39	11.20	13.33	3.46	8.23	20.50	32.89	48.55	50.91
Claims on Central Govt. (Net)	32an	−.36	−.32	−.50	−.43	—	−.01	−.72	−.34	−1.55	−16.34	−21.15	−19.48	−15.15	−11.30	−12.00
Claims on Local Government	32b	.01	.01	.02	.01	—	—	—	—	—	—	—	—	—	—	.03
Claims on Nonfin.Pub.Enterprises	32c	.11	.11	.13	.18	.16	.12	.50	.29	.51	.53	.56	.51	.56	.71	.77
Claims on Private Sector	32d	5.91	6.03	6.57	7.35	7.91	8.70	9.60	11.21	14.20	18.98	28.70	39.39	46.71	56.57	59.16
Claims on Other Banking Insts.	32f	.02	.04	.08	.07	.14	.15	.01	.04	.16	.29	.12	.07	.77	2.57	2.96
Money	34	4.79	5.02	5.57	6.09	6.64	7.07	8.19	9.65	11.49	16.94	25.60	29.00	37.41	44.05	46.55
Quasi-Money	35	2.99	2.91	3.44	3.78	4.30	4.72	5.57	6.93	8.44	10.00	15.92	21.66	26.69	29.21	32.20
Bonds	36ab	—	—	—	—	—	—	.13	.05	—	—	—	—	—	—	—
Long-Term Foreign Liabilities	36cl	.13	.13	.10	.12	.20	.25	.20	.33	.51	.45	.64	1.16	2.02	3.39	2.01
Liabs. to Other Banking Insts.	36i	.04	.05	.08	.06	.08	.12	.17	.49	.56	.78	.84	1.09	1.09	1.28	1.55
Other Items (Net)	37r	.72	.64	.42	.67	.58	.80	1.16	.92	2.57	2.89	3.65	4.66	1.01	.07	3.84
Money plus Quasi-Money	35l	7.78	7.93	9.01	9.87	10.95	11.79	13.76	16.58	19.92	26.94	41.52	50.66	64.10	73.26	78.75

Venezuela

	1980	1981	1982	1983	1984	1985	1986	1987	1988	1989	1990	1991	1992	1993	1994		
End of Period																**Exchange Rates**	
	5.475	4.996	4.735	4.502	7.352	8.238	17.736	20.571	19.513	56.612	71.673	88.048	109.244	145.102	I248.175	Official Rate	aa
End of Period (ae)	**Period Average (rf)**																
	4.293	4.293	4.293	4.300	7.500	7.500	14.500	14.500	14.500	43.079	50.380	61.554	79.450	105.640	I170.000	Official Rate	ae
	4.293	4.293	4.293	4.297	7.017	7.500	8.083	14.500	14.500	34.681	46.900	56.816	68.376	90.826	148.503	Official Rate	rf
	....	....	....	6.0000	6.0000	6.0000	7.5000	7.5000	39.1820	....	....	....	....	....	....	Secondary Rate	xe
	....	....	....	9.900	12.650	14.400	22.700	30.250	39.182	....	....	....	....	....	....	Tertiary Rate	ye
	....	....	....	....	12.655	13.758	5.783	27.533	33.555	....	....	....	....	....	....	Tertiary Rate	yf
Period Averages																	
	1,088.9	1,088.9	1,088.9	1,087.6	693.1	623.2	598.1	322.4	322.4	154.7	100.0	82.5	68.7	51.8	32.8	Market Rate	ahx
	624.6	682.8	742.7	690.0	572.6	536.2	427.7	257.9	246.4	137.6	100.0	88.4	79.0	67.9	48.1	Nominal Effective Exchange Rate	nec
	219.1	245.0	265.1	241.6	204.0	195.7	163.5	117.2	130.7	111.3	100.0	106.8	111.7	115.5	111.3	Real Effective Exchange Rate	rec
End of Period																**Fund Position**	
	990	990	990	1,372	1,372	1,372	1,372	1,372	1,372	1,372	1,372	1,372	1,951	1,951	1,951	Quota	2f.s
	270	382	399	337	382	451	498	534	534	56	36	7	188	55	354	317	SDRs	1b.s
	490	549	682	877	827	745	656	473	30	3	—	—	145	145	145	Reserve Position in the Fund	1c.s
	206	276	348	361	330	265	176	91	30	3	—	—	—	—	—	of which: Outstg.Fund Borrowing	2c
	—	—	—	—	—	—	—	—	—	759	2,117	2,271	2,143	1,951	1,810	Total Fund Cred.&Loans Outstg.	2tl
End of Period																**International Liquidity**	
	6,604	8,164	6,579	7,643	8,901	10,251	6,437	5,963	3,092	4,106	8,321	10,666	9,562	9,216	8,067	Total Reserves minus Gold	1l.d
	344	445	440	353	375	496	609	757	76	47	10	269	75	486	463	SDRs	1b.d
	625	639	752	918	811	818	802	671	41	4	—	—	199	199	212	Reserve Position in the Fund	1c.d
	5,635	7,081	5,386	6,372	7,716	8,937	5,026	4,535	2,975	4,055	8,311	10,397	9,288	8,531	7,393	Foreign Exchange	1d.d
	11.46	11.46	11.46	11.46	11.46	11.46	11.46	11.46	11.46	11.46	11.46	11.46	11.46	11.46	11.46	Gold (Million Fine Troy Ounces)	1ad
	484	484	3,439	3,439	3,439	3,439	3,439	3,439	3,439	3,439	3,439	3,439	3,439	3,440	3,440	Gold (National Valuation)	1and
	170	151	79	63	41	47	36	306	1,188	1,419	1,280	2,636	2,777	3,361	2,950	Monetary Authorities: Other Liab.	4..d
	770	719	525	1,296	1,118	927	636	1,061	1,321	1,004	1,286	1,400	1,425	1,495	1,093	Deposit Money Banks: Assets	7a.d
	25	21	15	14	7	8	1	112	128	107	106	350	554	407	380	of which: Claims on Nonbanks	7add
	837	1,189	2,035	1,974	1,455	1,956	2,066	3,068	4,421	1,059	839	950	613	634	256	Deposit Money Banks: Liabilities	7b.d
	212	168	130	120	75	73	40	57	51	28	17	11	6	28	16	Other Banking Insts.: Assets	7e.d
	1,862	2,044	2,510	2,460	1,362	1,352	1,042	1,025	988	321	214	—	4	1	1	Liabilities	7f.d
End of Period																**Monetary Authorities**	
	30.38	37.06	41.59	47.90	71.89	80.99	86.22	109.44	95.16	324.04	593.78	867.53	1,033.90	1,341.12	1,953.60	Foreign Assets	11
	2.08	3.82	6.86	5.48	8.70	13.47	14.32	20.06	49.29	115.83	193.51	244.75	281.71	348.25	1,299.38	Claims on Central Government	12a
	.12	.13	.13	.10	.22	.14	—	.06	.05	.02	.04	—	—	—	—	Claims on Local Government	12b
	—	—	—	—	—	—	.37	—	—	—	5.27	10.90	9.77	9.18	9.10	Claims on Nonfin.Pub.Enterprises	12c
	.49	.49	.03	.02	.30	.41	.26	.41	.52	.93	.58	.40	.26	.32	-.06	Claims on Private Sector	12d
	2.28	.92	4.71	1.52	3.07	1.00	3.72	4.03	19.05	16.88	15.93	14.71	14.79	33.05	17.74	Claims on Deposit Money Banks	12e
	4.06	6.43	8.05	9.04	11.04	5.75	5.97	7.33	11.46	7.88	7.31	3.41	2.03	1.11	1.11	Claims on Other Banking Insts.	12f
	26.45	30.89	36.25	46.33	58.31	60.10	49.29	62.80	67.41	109.50	217.57	349.96	391.74	430.14	713.19	Reserve Money	14
	12.34	13.52	13.09	14.73	15.13	16.16	18.70	I24.83	31.20	40.29	56.42	76.46	108.63	136.55	278.53	of which: Currency Outside DMBs	14a
	.14	.12	.16	.23	.19	.22	.23	.28	.42	6.58	8.82	2.77	4.67	3.64	5.65	Time, Savings,& Fgn.Currency Dep.	15
	—	—	—	—	—	—	—	—	—	4.84	100.04	49.65	52.81	70.85	744.71	Bonds	16ab
	.24	.24	.17	.20	.25	.30	.48	4.29	17.13	92.88	197.11	266.84	349.13	512.58	808.98	Foreign Liabilities	16c
	.49	.41	.17	.06	.05	.05	.04	.14	.10	11.27	19.09	95.42	105.59	125.50	141.83	Long-Term Foreign Liabilities	16cl
	5.59	9.08	5.49	3.66	8.08	16.46	15.07	29.57	20.23	59.36	149.14	254.87	177.67	149.04	292.15	Central Government Deposits	16d
	7.01	8.94	6.04	11.99	22.10	15.13	29.75	31.28	71.80	204.05	78.43	96.80	105.35	115.78	179.51	Capital Accounts	17a
	-.51	-.82	13.10	1.59	6.24	9.52	15.99	12.96	-1.55	-17.64	51.84	24.25	154.90	325.42	394.84	Other Items (Net)	17r
End of Period																**Deposit Money Banks**	
	11.61	15.39	13.73	23.24	19.87	22.04	23.62	I25.15	32.62	52.71	171.73	294.74	294.06	305.50	782.42	Reserves	20
	3.30	3.09	2.25	5.57	8.39	6.95	9.22	I15.39	19.15	43.26	64.81	86.19	113.22	157.94	185.81	Foreign Assets	21
	1.38	7.12	4.10	5.95	7.88	13.59	16.55	I22.75	24.27	31.96	46.97	25.76	39.83	139.48	416.03	Claims on Central Government	22a
	.12	.12	.11	.17	.07	.09	.07	.05	.06	.22	.04	.02	.53	—	—	Claims on Local Government	22b
	.78	.86	1.13	1.30	.77	1.07	1.20	1.33	1.06	3.95	2.28	31.73	26.71	79.64	131.23	Claims on Nonfin.Pub.Enterprises	22c
	69.33	75.65	85.15	89.04	103.64	115.39	149.75	I201.25	261.92	300.88	379.38	570.16	769.55	859.84	801.50	Claims on Private Sector	22d
	.60	.52	.51	.47	.50	.48	.60	I1.78	1.78	2.34	2.94	3.18	.99	.80	11.59	Claims on Other Banking Insts.	22f
	39.44	42.58	38.22	52.24	57.45	66.62	83.48	I82.88	105.84	109.37	150.91	241.61	245.24	256.54	664.92	Demand Deposits	24
	37.64	46.21	52.60	63.82	70.65	82.29	101.36	I137.34	152.86	259.87	465.12	679.92	827.16	1,093.93	1,646.25	Time & Foreign Currency Deposits	25
	1.17	1.10	1.87	1.79	2.45	1.86	3.17	5.56	11.44	6.87	8.21	22.54	22.04	32.29	10.40	Foreign Liabilities	26c
	2.42	4.00	6.87	6.70	8.47	12.81	26.79	I38.93	52.66	38.76	34.06	35.97	26.68	34.71	33.16	Long-Term Foreign Liabilities	26cl
	6.45	5.89	3.91	3.42	4.96	7.76	8.09	9.39	6.20	7.62	13.88	23.74	24.68	27.81	47.20	Central Government Deposits	26d
	2.35	.56	5.04	2.50	4.75	1.96	3.75	I4.83	20.49	8.98	14.31	14.70	14.82	33.02	17.73	Credit from Monetary Authorities	26g
	1.57	2.53	2.17	2.62	2.11	2.56	2.83	I3.75	5.98	8.52	16.45	27.80	32.90	37.02	12.69	Liabs. to Other Banking Insts.	26i
	6.55	7.35	8.56	9.09	6.96	4.31	6.76	I8.80	23.71	31.17	44.32	68.14	100.37	146.86	90.55	Capital Accounts	27a
	-10.47	-7.47	-12.25	-16.46	-16.67	-20.57	-35.22	I-23.77	-38.32	-35.83	-79.11	-102.63	-49.02	-119.02	-203.17	Other Items (Net)	27r
End of Period																**Monetary Survey**	
	32.28	38.82	41.80	51.48	77.57	85.78	91.79	I114.99	85.75	267.56	453.28	664.35	775.95	954.19	1,320.02	Foreign Assets (Net)	31n
	66.91	80.17	96.67	104.49	120.08	126.16	165.91	I216.05	323.97	402.30	480.92	610.57	928.43	1,261.68	2,331.73	Domestic Credit	32
	-8.58	-4.03	1.57	4.34	3.54	2.83	7.70	I3.85	47.13	80.81	77.46	-8.10	119.20	310.88	1,376.06	Claims on Central Govt. (Net)	32an
	.23	.25	.24	.27	.29	.22	.07	.10	.11	.24	.08	.02	.53	—	1.20	Claims on Local Government	32b
	.78	.86	1.13	1.30	.77	1.07	1.57	1.33	1.06	9.21	13.18	41.51	35.89	88.74	140.34	Claims on Nonfin.Pub.Enterprises	32c
	69.82	76.14	85.17	89.07	103.94	115.80	150.01	I201.65	262.44	301.81	379.96	570.56	769.80	860.16	801.44	Claims on Private Sector	32d
	4.66	6.95	8.56	9.51	11.54	6.24	6.57	I9.11	13.24	10.23	10.26	6.58	3.01	1.91	12.69	Claims on Other Banking Insts.	32f
	54.54	58.30	60.81	76.25	96.68	105.22	109.85	I122.56	145.45	169.95	269.26	347.59	375.45	416.85	991.38	Money	34
	37.77	46.33	52.76	64.05	70.84	82.51	101.59	I137.62	153.27	266.46	473.94	682.69	831.83	1,097.57	1,651.91	Quasi-Money	35
	—	—	—	—	—	—	—	—	—	4.84	100.04	49.65	52.81	70.85	744.71	Bonds	36ab
	2.91	4.42	7.03	6.76	8.52	12.86	26.83	I39.07	52.76	50.03	53.15	131.39	132.28	160.22	174.99	Long-Term Foreign Liabilities	36cl
	1.57	2.53	2.17	2.62	2.11	2.56	2.83	I3.75	5.98	8.52	16.45	27.80	32.90	37.02	22.73	Liabs. to Other Banking Insts.	36i
	2.38	7.41	15.70	6.28	19.52	8.79	16.60	I28.04	52.25	170.07	21.36	35.80	279.11	433.37	66.03	Other Items (Net)	37r
	92.31	104.63	113.57	140.31	167.51	187.73	211.44	I260.18	298.72	436.41	743.20	1,030.28	1,207.28	1,514.42	2,643.29	Money plus Quasi-Money	35l

Venezuela
299

		1965	1966	1967	1968	1969	1970	1971	1972	1973	1974	1975	1976	1977	1978	1979
Other Banking Institutions														*Billions of Bolivares:*		
Cash	40	.01	.01	.01	.03	.08	.05	.09	.09	.18	.52	.28	.65	1.00	.71	1.35
Foreign Assets	41	—	—	—	.01	—	.03	.01	.29	.30	.20	.07	.20	.20	.43	.69
Claims on Central Government	42a	.24	.32	.45	.52	.58	.81	1.13	1.18	1.07	1.08	.43	.63	.71	1.01	.91
Claims on Local Government	42b	...	...	...	...	...	...	...	...	...	...	...	...	...	...	...
Claims on Nonfin.Pub.Enterprises	42c						—	.01	.02	.02	.01	.02	.02	.46	.01	.01
Claims on Private Sector	42d	4.10	3.25	3.61	4.03	5.17	5.89	7.54	8.79	13.30	16.69	18.39	24.97	34.06	43.59	56.28
Claims on Deposit Money Banks	42e	.01	.02	.03	.05	.13	.13	.22	.58	.74	1.12	1.13	1.43	1.50	2.09	2.22
														Billions of Bolivares:		
Demand Deposits	44	.04	.04	.07	.05	.06	.07	.10	.15	.26	.57	.70	1.01	1.63	2.79	3.19
Time and Savings Deposits	45	.11	1.34	1.56	1.81	2.70	3.32	4.92	6.44	9.56	12.33	15.20	20.30	25.56	29.82	36.40
Bonds	46ab	.65	.22	.36	.59	.55	.48	.56	.52	.65	.79	.83	1.03	1.66	3.21	5.11
Foreign Liabilities	46c	—	—	—	—	—	—	—	—	—	—	—	—	.02	.05	1.01
Long-Term Foreign Liabilities	46cl	.18	.25	.26	.27	.44	.54	.64	1.08	1.32	1.08	.25	.67	1.71	3.08	6.59
Central Government Deposits	46d	.67	.75	.81	.93	.94	.94	1.06	.77	.92	1.26	.63	1.41	1.74	1.49	2.10
Credit from Monetary Authorities	46g	.06	.08	.07	.14	.21	.18	.04	.01	.11	.22	.09		.64	1.97	1.98
Credit from Deposit Money Banks	46h	—	—	—	—	—	.14	.24	.31	1.19	1.48	1.66	2.23	3.21	2.98	3.09
Capital Accounts	47a	2.54	2.88	3.20	3.61	4.43	4.97	4.69	5.04	6.09	7.49	1.87	2.37	3.15	3.90	4.32
Other Items (Net)	47r	.13	−1.96	−2.24	−2.77	−3.36	−3.73	−3.24	−3.38	−4.49	−5.60	−.91	−1.14	−1.38	−1.47	−2.32
Banking Survey														*Billions of Bolivares:*		
Foreign Assets (Net)	51n	2.97	2.87	3.31	3.56	3.60	4.03	6.05	7.46	10.53	27.80	38.50	37.28	35.52	29.82	35.52
Domestic Credit	52	9.35	8.66	9.47	10.72	12.88	14.57	16.98	20.37	26.62	19.69	26.31	44.62	65.60	89.09	103.05
Claims on Central Govt. (Net)	52an	−.79	−.75	−.86	−.84	−.36	−.14	−.65	.07	−1.41	−16.53	−21.36	−20.26	−16.19	−11.78	−13.18
Claims on Local Government	52b	.01	.01	.02	.01	—	—	—	—	—	—	—	—	—	—	.03
Claims on Nonfin.Pub.Enterprises	52c	.11	.11	.13	.18	.16	.12	.51	.30	.52	.54	.58	.52	1.03	.71	.77
Claims on Private Sector	52d	10.01	9.28	10.19	11.37	13.08	14.59	17.13	20.00	27.50	35.67	47.09	64.36	80.76	100.16	115.44
Liquid Liabilities	55l	7.93	9.30	10.62	11.70	13.63	15.14	18.68	23.09	29.56	39.32	57.14	71.33	90.28	105.16	116.99
Bonds	56ab	.65	.22	.36	.59	.55	.48	.69	.57	.65	.79	.83	1.03	1.66	3.21	5.11
Long-Term Foreign Liabilities	56cl	.31	.38	.37	.39	.63	.79	.84	1.41	1.82	1.53	.89	1.84	3.73	6.47	8.59
Capital Accounts	57a	4.11	4.54	4.87	5.46	6.42	7.32	7.45	8.14	10.53	12.58	7.87	9.18	11.21	13.26	15.55
Other Items (Net)	57r	−.68	−2.91	−3.44	−3.86	−4.74	−5.12	−4.62	−5.38	−5.41	−6.73	−1.92	−1.47	−5.75	−9.19	−8.26
Interest Rates														*Percent Per Annum*		
Discount Rate (End of Period)	60	4.50	4.50	4.50	4.50	5.50	5.00	5.00	5.00	5.00	5.00	7.00	7.00	7.00	7.50	11.00
Deposit Rate	60l	...	...	...	...	...	...	...	...	...	...	...	...	...	...	...
Lending Rate	60p	...	...	...	...	...	...	...	...	...	...	...	...	...	...	...
Government Bond Yield	61	...	...	...	...	...	...	...	...	...	...	...	...	...	...	...
Prices and Production														*Index Numbers (1990=100):*		
Industrial Share Prices	62	50.8	49.7	46.2	48.8	53.4	55.8	58.4	64.3	78.2	99.1	112.3	131.2	136.9	95.5	77.2
Prices: Home & Import Goods	63	4.0	4.1	4.2	4.2	4.3	4.4	4.5	4.7	5.0	5.8	6.6	7.1	7.8	8.4	9.2
Home Goods	63a	3.9	3.9	3.9	4.0	4.1	4.1	4.2	4.3	4.6	5.4	6.1	6.6	7.4	8.0	8.8
Consumer Prices	64	5.1	5.2	5.2	5.3	5.4	5.5	5.7	5.9	6.1	6.6	7.3	7.9	8.5	9.1	10.2
Crude Petroleum Production	66aa	160	156	163	167	166	171	164	149	155	137	108	106	103	100	109
International Transactions														*Billions of Bolivares*		
Exports	70	10.9	10.6	11.2	11.2	11.1	11.7	13.5	13.8	21.0	47.4	37.7	39.9	41.0	39.4	61.5
Petroleum	70a	10.1	9.7	10.3	10.4	10.1	10.6	12.8	12.6	18.6	45.2	35.7	37.6	39.1	37.5	58.5
Crude Petroleum	70aa	7.2	6.9	7.4	7.2	7.1	6.9	8.4	8.1	11.6	27.9	24.8	24.0	25.6	23.8	36.6
Imports, cif	71	6.2	6.0	6.4	7.4	7.6	8.3	9.2	10.6	12.1	17.9	25.7	29.2	47.0	50.5	45.8
Imports, fob	71.v	5.6	5.5	5.8	6.7	6.9	7.5	8.3	9.5	10.9	16.2	22.8	25.9	41.9	45.5	41.3
														Millions of US Dollars		
Exports	70..d	2,455	2,373	3,077	2,779	3,083	3,169	3,124	3,166	3,298	11,153	8,800	9,299	9,551	9,187	14,317
Petroleum	70a.d	2,280	2,190	2,307	2,330	2,279	2,371	2,882	2,857	4,328	10,548	8,324	8,763	9,110	8,740	13,633
Imports, c.i.f.	71..d	1,421	1,307	1,445	1,665	1,720	1,869	2,103	2,463	2,812	4,148	6,000	7,663	10,938	11,767	10,670
Imports, f.o.b.	71.vd	1,281	1,178	1,301	1,506	1,544	1,684	1,878	2,207	2,534	3,757	5,324	6,787	9,766	10,601	9,613
Volume of Exports															*1990=100*	
Petroleum	72a	169.3	165.9	174.6	175.0	176.9	181.6	171.6	161.3	162.9	150.6	109.0	114.4	104.0	105.3	111.3
Crude Petroleum	72aa	187.8	182.2	195.6	198.2	199.4	196.0	186.3	172.2	171.0	142.4	118.5	110.6	106.4	100.2	112.9
Refined Petroleum	72ab	144.2	143.7	146.0	143.5	146.3	162.0	151.7	146.4	151.8	161.7	96.1	119.6	100.7	112.3	109.1
Import Prices (Wholesale)	76.x	4.2	4.3	4.5	4.5	4.6	4.8	5.0	5.2	5.5	6.4	7.2	7.8	8.3	8.9	9.6
Balance of Payments														*Millions of US Dollars:*		
Goods: Exports f.o.b.	78aa d	...	...	...	...	...	2,640	3,152	3,202	4,803	11,290	8,982	9,342	9,661	9,174	14,360
Goods: Imports f.o.b.	78ab d	...	...	...	...	...	−1,713	−1,896	−2,222	−2,626	−3,876	−5,462	−7,337	−10,194	−11,234	−10,004
Trade Balance	78ac d						927	1,256	980	2,177	7,414	3,520	2,005	−533	−2,060	4,356
Services: Credit	78ad d						139	148	159	247	325	370	341	504	629	599
Services: Debit	78ae d						−525	−594	−665	−748	−1,143	−1,646	−2,068	−2,955	−3,935	−4,195
Balance on Goods and Services	78af d						541	810	474	1,676	6,596	2,244	278	−2,984	−5,366	760
Income: Credit	78ag d						54	39	57	229	356	740	693	782	1,052	1,346
Income: Debit	78ah d						−607	−777	−537	−917	−993	−640	−485	−694	−1,014	−1,349
Balance on Goods, Serv., & Inc.	78ai d						−12	72	−6	988	5,959	2,344	486	−2,896	−5,328	757
Current Transfers, n.i.e.: Credit	78aj d						2	2	2	2	2	2	2	1	1	1
Current Transfers: Debit	78ak d						−94	−85	−97	−113	−201	−175	−234	−284	−408	−408
Current Account, n.i.e.	78al d						−104	−11	−101	877	5,760	2,171	254	−3,179	−5,735	350
Capital Account, n.i.e.: Credit	78ba d						—	—	—	—	—	—	—	—	—	—
Capital Account: Debit	78bb d						—	—	—	—	—	—	—	—	—	—
Capital Account, n.i.e.	78bc d						—	—	—	—	—	—	—	—	—	—
Direct Investment Abroad	78bd d						—	—	—	—	—	—	—	—	—	—
Dir. Invest. in Rep. Econ., n.i.e.	78be d						−23	211	−376	−84	−430	418	−889	−3	67	88
Portfolio Investment Assets	78bf d						−11	−9	1	−11	−14	−63	−191	−108	−239	6
Portfolio Investment Liab., n.i.e.	78bg d						−1	−1	14	−1	−5	−6	914	67	363	−80
Other Investment Assets	78bh d						−67	80	−108	14	−483	−760	−1,182	−722	−991	−988
Other Investment Liab., n.i.e.	78bi d						183	223	243	290	57	575	1,413	2,468	3,982	4,225
Financial Account, n.i.e.	78bj d						81	504	−226	208	−875	164	65	1,702	3,182	3,251
Net Errors and Omissions	78ca d						69	−75	497	−474	−417	380	2,024	2,276	1,488	497
Overall Balance	78cb d						46	418	170	611	4,468	2,715	2,343	799	−1,065	4,098
Reserves and Related Items	79da d						−46	−418	−170	−611	−4,468	−2,715	−2,343	−799	1,065	−4,098
Reserve Assets	79db d						−46	−418	−170	−611	−4,468	−2,715	−2,343	−799	1,065	−4,098
Use of Fund Credit and Loans	79dc d						—	—	—	—	—	—	—	—	—	—
Liabs.Constit.For.Auth.Reserves	79dd d						—	—	—	—	—	—	—	—	—	—
Exceptional Financing	79de d	...	...	...	...	...	—	—	—	—	—	—	—	—	—	—

Venezuela

299

1980	1981	1982	1983	1984	1985	1986	1987	1988	1989	1990	1991	1992	1993	1994		
End of Period															**Other Banking Institutions**	
1.65	1.68	.98	.78	1.43	1.08	.73	I 1.11	.95	2.46	4.82	4.99	7.99	12.41	22.51	Cash	40
.91	.72	.56	.52	.56	.55	.58	I .82	.74	1.21	.85	.68	.50	2.99	2.73	Foreign Assets	41
.73	4.98	1.52	.92	2.37	2.64	2.88	I 3.01	4.52	5.06	13.60	19.46	40.74	32.00	76.80	Claims on Central Government	42a
....	....	....	....	....	....	....	—	—	—	—	—	—	—	—	Claims on Local Government	42b
.01	.01	.01	.22	—	—	—	I .04	.03	.31	2.15	3.63	1.13	.81	1.71	Claims on Nonfin.Pub.Enterprises	42c
73.86	87.55	101.14	105.46	109.28	116.82	126.02	I 143.56	157.61	172.95	200.02	265.93	341.90	361.62	343.85	Claims on Private Sector	42d
2.40	3.50	2.88	3.53	3.25	4.06	4.20	I 5.63	8.55	11.65	20.99	34.35	44.89	81.30	38.94	Claims on Deposit Money Banks	42e
End of Period																
3.33	3.26	4.20	4.23	5.63	5.13	5.39	I 7.30	7.28	6.91	7.90	6.95	8.11	11.15	13.84	Demand Deposits	44
45.34	56.84	64.28	76.43	82.81	84.19	80.63	I 80.47	83.41	144.98	198.03	288.21	388.50	453.32	435.47	Time and Savings Deposits	45
9.78	11.92	15.53	9.78	7.62	17.79	25.10	I 34.26	45.51	15.24	16.88	11.06	8.86	11.03	8.52	Bonds	46ab
.74	1.15	1.62	.89	.74	.73	.69	I .68	1.16	1.12	.39	—	—	—	—	Foreign Liabilities	46c
7.25	7.62	9.15	9.69	9.48	9.41	14.43	I 14.19	13.17	12.69	10.37	.02	.29	.07	.12	Long-Term Foreign Liabilities	46cl
4.60	4.69	3.53	7.91	8.64	12.05	18.11	I 17.45	13.30	14.95	10.36	20.82	19.76	5.27	1.00	Central Government Deposits	46d
3.41	6.18	8.34	7.80	9.19	4.21	5.78	I 9.44	14.60	8.64	3.55	3.19	1.90	.56	.50	Credit from Monetary Authorities	46g
3.03	3.01	2.22	2.74	3.11	3.29	3.45	I 4.96	6.56	5.36	4.10	6.85	6.08	8.40	8.17	Credit from Deposit Money Banks	46h
5.15	6.01	6.47	6.59	7.90	8.13	7.99	I 9.44	11.18	12.65	19.31	30.01	40.17	60.63	63.36	Capital Accounts	47a
-3.07	-2.23	-8.26	-14.62	-18.22	-19.78	-27.15	I -24.01	-23.77	-28.90	-28.45	-38.06	-36.52	-59.30	-44.44	Other Items (Net)	47r
End of Period															**Banking Survey**	
32.44	38.39	40.74	51.11	77.40	85.60	91.68	I 115.13	85.32	267.64	453.74	665.03	776.45	957.18	1,322.75	Foreign Assets (Net)	51n
132.24	161.07	187.24	193.67	211.56	227.34	270.13	I 336.10	459.61	555.44	676.08	872.18	1,289.42	1,648.93	2,740.39	Domestic Credit	52
-12.46	-3.74	-.44	-2.64	-2.73	-6.58	-7.53	I -10.59	38.35	70.92	80.70	-9.46	140.17	337.61	1,451.86	Claims on Central Govt. (Net)	52an
.23	.25	.24	.27	.29	.22	.07	I .11	.11	.24	.08	.02	.53	—	1.20	Claims on Local Government	52b
.78	.87	1.14	1.52	.77	1.07	1.57	I 1.37	1.10	9.52	15.33	45.13	37.01	89.55	142.05	Claims on Nonfin.Pub.Enterprises	52c
143.68	163.69	186.31	194.52	213.22	232.62	276.03	I 345.21	420.05	474.75	579.98	836.49	1,111.71	1,221.78	1,145.29	Claims on Private Sector	52d
139.33	163.05	181.07	220.18	254.52	275.98	296.72	I 346.84	388.46	585.83	944.31	1,320.44	1,595.90	1,966.47	3,070.10	Liquid Liabilities	55l
9.78	11.92	15.53	9.78	7.62	17.79	25.10	I 34.26	45.51	20.08	116.92	60.70	61.67	81.89	753.23	Bonds	56ab
10.16	12.04	16.19	16.45	18.00	22.27	41.25	I 53.26	65.93	62.72	63.51	131.40	132.57	160.29	175.11	Long-Term Foreign Liabilities	56cl
18.70	22.30	21.07	27.67	36.95	27.57	44.50	I 49.51	106.69	247.87	142.06	194.95	245.88	323.27	333.42	Capital Accounts	57a
-13.28	-9.85	-5.87	-29.30	-28.14	-30.67	-45.76	I -32.64	-61.66	-93.41	-136.98	-170.29	29.85	74.21	-268.71	Other Items (Net)	57r
Percent Per Annum															**Interest Rates**	
13.00	14.00	13.00	11.00	11.00	8.00	8.00	8.00	8.00	45.00	43.00	43.00	52.20	71.25	48.00	Discount Rate *(End of Period)*	60
....	....	....	....	12.29	10.52	8.93	8.94	8.95	29.23	27.78	31.10	35.42	53.75	39.02	Deposit Rate	60l
....	....	....	....	9.57	9.33	8.49	8.48	8.50	22.57	28.23	29.78	33.91	48.88	46.55	Lending Rate	60p
....	....	....	....	13.15	12.55	12.07	13.49	14.86	17.32	20.06	27.14	31.66	41.03	54.73	Government Bond Yield	61
Period Averages															**Prices and Production**	
63.0	54.6	40.9	40.6	53.0	59.0	93.0	206.5	179.4	94.9	I 100.0	230.9	266.9	214.3	384.0	Industrial Share Prices	62
11.0	12.5	13.6	14.5	I 17.0	19.6	23.0	33.4	39.8	78.6	100.0	122.3	151.1	203.9	363.2	Prices: Home & Import Goods	63
10.9	12.5	13.6	14.6	I 17.1	19.8	23.0	31.7	38.2	76.8	100.0	123.5	155.5	211.0	372.3	Home Goods	63a
12.4	14.4	15.8	16.8	18.7	20.8	23.2	29.8	38.5	71.1	100.0	134.2	176.4	243.6	391.8	Consumer Prices	64
100	100	90	83	83	78	82	79	88	90	100	110	110	113	117	Crude Petroleum Production	66aa
Billions of Bolivares															**International Transactions**	
82.5	86.4	70.8	64.7	97.2	94.0	77.8	I 123.4	154.7	470.5	831.2	863.0	975.4	1,272.0	2,352.1	Exports	70
78.3	81.7	67.1	59.5	85.2	77.6	53.8	I 100.9	118.2	347.5	665.4	700.2	770.9	940.1	....	Petroleum	70a
53.2	58.4	44.7	36.6	53.7	44.7	29.9	I 64.5	68.9	201.6	415.1	432.9	492.4	597.7	....	Crude Petroleum	70aa
50.8	56.3	55.6	37.5	52.8	61.8	75.1	I 127.8	236.4	266.4	347.9	637.7	961.9	1,107.1	1,323.9	Imports, cif	71
45.8	50.7	50.1	33.7	47.6	55.6	67.6	115.1	213.0	240.0	313.4	574.5	866.6	997.4	1,192.7	Imports, fob	71.v
Millions of US Dollars																
19,221	20,980	16,590	13,937	15,997	14,438	8,660	10,577	10,244	13,286	17,497	15,155	14,185	14,066	15,480	Exports	70..*d*
17,562	18,609	15,633	13,857	14,824	12,956	7,178	9,054	8,158	10,001	13,953	12,302	11,208	10,565	....	Petroleum	70a.*d*
11,827	13,106	12,944	6,419	7,774	8,106	8,504	I 9,659	12,726	7,803	7,335	11,147	14,066	12,200	8,879	Imports, c.i.f.	71..*d*
10,655	11,808	11,661	5,783	7,004	7,303	7,661	8,702	11,465	7,030	6,608	10,042	12,672	10,991	7,999	Imports, f.o.b.	71.v*d*
1990=100															Volume of Exports	
98.2	91.5	81.9	79.9	80.9	74.5	82.9	80.4	89.5	88.1	100.0	112.9	108.1	113.2	....	Petroleum	72a
103.6	102.0	85.5	79.3	81.4	66.8	76.4	82.7	81.8	79.4	100.0	111.2	115.4	124.0	....	Crude Petroleum	72aa
90.9	77.2	77.0	80.7	80.2	84.9	91.8	77.2	100.0	100.0	100.0	115.3	98.1	98.6	....	Refined Petroleum	72ab
10.9	12.4	13.3	14.1	I 16.6	19.1	22.6	37.6	43.9	83.2	100.0	118.9	140.2	188.6	340.7	Import Prices (Wholesale)	76.x
Minus Sign Indicates Debit															Balance of Payments	
19,275	20,181	16,516	14,759	16,075	14,478	8,664	10,564	10,217	13,059	17,623	15,159	14,202	14,215	....	Goods: Exports f.o.b.	78aa*d*
-10,877	-12,123	-13,584	-6,409	-7,246	-7,501	-7,866	-8,870	-12,080	-7,365	-6,917	-10,259	-12,880	-11,257	....	Goods: Imports f.o.b.	78ab*d*
8,398	8,058	2,932	8,350	8,829	6,977	798	1,694	-1,863	5,694	10,706	4,900	1,322	2,958	....	Trade Balance	78ac*d*
693	757	1,041	1,082	688	797	828	864	835	929	1,183	1,229	1,312	1,370	....	Services: Credit	78ad*d*
-4,253	-4,980	-6,050	-2,681	-2,632	-2,043	-2,148	-2,238	-2,863	-1,911	-2,534	-3,431	-4,263	-4,594	....	Services: Debit	78ae*d*
4,838	3,835	-2,077	6,751	6,885	5,731	-522	320	-3,891	4,712	9,355	2,698	-1,629	-266	....	Balance on Goods and Services	78af*d*
2,264	3,581	2,565	1,500	2,097	1,914	1,761	1,455	1,653	1,582	2,658	2,168	1,607	1,689	....	Income: Credit	78ag*d*
-1,935	-3,007	-4,095	-3,613	-4,159	-4,147	-3,363	-3,074	-3,424	-3,950	-3,432	-2,766	-3,357	-3,299	....	Income: Debit	78ah*d*
5,167	4,409	-3,607	4,638	4,823	3,498	-2,124	-1,299	-5,662	2,344	8,581	2,100	-3,379	-1,876	....	Balance on Goods, Serv., & Inc.	78ai*d*
—	—	—	—	61	68	80	137	87	237	444	370	533	467	....	Current Transfers, n.i.e.: Credit	78aj*d*
-439	-409	-639	-211	-233	-239	-201	-228	-234	-420	-746	-734	-907	-814	....	Current Transfers: Debit	78ak*d*
4,728	4,000	-4,246	4,427	4,651	3,327	-2,245	-1,390	-5,809	2,161	8,279	1,736	-3,753	-2,223	....	Current Account, n.i.e.	78al*d*
—	—	—	—	—	—	—	—	—	—	—	—	—	—	....	Capital Account, n.i.e.: Credit	78ba*d*
—	—	—	—	—	—	—	—	—	—	—	—	—	—	....	Capital Account: Debit	78bb*d*
—	—	—	—	—	—	—	—	—	—	—	—	—	—	....	Capital Account, n.i.e.	78bc*d*
—	—	-4	—	-21	-11	-460	-37	-68	-179	-375	-188	-156	-419	....	Direct Investment Abroad	78bd*d*
55	184	257	86	18	68	16	21	89	213	451	1,916	629	372	....	Dir. Invest. in Rep. Econ., n.i.e.	78be*d*
-264	-118	-10	-7	—	—	—	—	—	-8	1,952	-74	-134	-46	....	Portfolio Investment Assets	78bf*d*
1,574	201	1,592	208	—	—	—	—	—	-526	14,974	39	705	542	....	Portfolio Investment Liab., n.i.e.	78bg*d*
-1,807	-2,963	-5,000	-1,059	-1,469	-314	-16	-789	-1,595	-369	-2,305	-834	-454	-614	....	Other Investment Assets	78bh*d*
606	814	1,637	-2,944	-547	-372	-247	1,494	-469	-4,563	-15,816	882	2,110	1,478	....	Other Investment Liab., n.i.e.	78bi*d*
164	-1,882	-1,528	-3,716	-2,019	-629	-707	689	-2,043	-5,432	-5,023	1,741	2,700	1,313	....	Financial Account, n.i.e.	78bj*d*
-1,129	-2,139	-2,386	-265	-996	-999	-930	-505	3,117	1,603	-1,742	-1,516	-295	407	....	Net Errors and Omissions	78ca*d*
3,763	-21	-8,160	446	1,636	1,699	-3,882	-1,206	-4,735	-1,668	1,514	1,961	-1,348	-503	....	Overall Balance	78cb*d*
-3,763	21	8,160	-446	-1,636	-1,699	3,882	1,206	4,735	1,668	-1,514	-1,961	1,348	503	....	Reserves and Related Items	79da*d*
-3,763	21	8,160	-446	-1,636	-1,699	3,882	935	3,872	-1,077	-4,376	-2,645	845	147	....	Reserve Assets	79db*d*
—	—	—	—	—	—	—	—	—	964	1,900	221	-183	-268	....	Use of Fund Credit and Loans	79dc*d*
—	—	—	—	—	—	—	271	863	-70	-473	-90	298	799	....	Liabs.Constit.For.Auth.Reserves	79dd*d*
—	—	—	—	—	—	—	—	—	1,852	1,435	553	388	-175	....	Exceptional Financing	79de*d*

Venezuela
299

		1965	1966	1967	1968	1969	1970	1971	1972	1973	1974	1975	1976	1977	1978	1979
Government Finance																*Billions of Bolivares:*
Deficit (-) or Surplus	80	.1	.1	—	‡–.3	–1.1	‡–.7	.2	–.2	1.2	5.0	1.9	–4.0	–6.7	–6.9	4.0
Revenue	81	7.3	7.8	8.5	‡8.8	8.7	‡10.1	12.4	13.3	17.0	44.3	42.4	39.9	42.9	42.7	50.9
Grants Received	81z	...	...	...	...	...	‡.2	.1	.2	—	.7	.1	.1	.1	.2	.2
Expenditure	82	7.1	7.7	8.5	‡9.0	9.6	‡9.8	11.1	12.7	14.2	22.8	27.5	32.7	42.2	46.3	44.8
Lending Minus Repayments	83	...	...	.1	‡.1	.1	‡1.2	1.2	1.0	1.7	17.3	13.0	11.3	7.5	3.5	2.3
Financing																
Net Borrowing	84	–.2	–.1	.1	‡.2	.8	‡.8	—	.2	.5	–1.2	–1.3	8.0	6.8	8.6	–2.7
Domestic	84a	–.2	–.1	.1	‡.1	.4	‡.4	.2	.2	.5	–.9	–1.3	–.7	.6	–1.5	–1.6
Foreign	85a	—	—	—	‡.1	.4	‡.4	–.2	—	—	–.3	—	8.7	6.2	10.2	–1.1
Use of Cash Balances	87	—	—	–.1	‡.1	.3	‡–.1	–.2	–.1	–1.7	–3.8	–.6	–4.0	–.1	–1.7	–1.3
Debt	88	2.1	2.3	2.8	1.0	1.8	‡2.3	2.1	2.2	2.2	2.1	3.7	12.8	21.4	32.5	32.0
Domestic	88a	...	...	...	...	...	‡.8	.8	.9	1.1	1.2	1.4	1.7	3.8	4.0	4.1
Foreign	89a	...	...	...	...	...	‡1.5	1.3	1.3	1.1	.9	2.3	11.2	17.5	28.4	27.9
National Accounts																*Billions of Bolivares*
Exports of Goods & Services	90c	11.6	11.3	12.0	12.3	12.8	12.4	14.7	14.5	21.2	48.8	39.3	41.1	43.5	42.0	64.0
Government Consumption	91f	4.7	5.1	5.4	5.6	5.9	6.9	7.8	8.5	9.6	12.8	15.9	19.8	23.0	24.1	27.8
Gross Fixed Capital Formation	93e	7.0	7.4	7.9	10.1	11.1	11.5	13.3	15.8	18.6	21.0	30.6	42.8	60.5	71.8	65.6
Increase/Decrease(-) in Stocks	93i	.9	.5	.5	2.7	1.0	3.9	3.8	3.4	2.8	5.9	5.8	3.7	4.2	.6	.1
Private Consumption	96f	21.7	22.7	23.8	23.2	25.1	27.6	29.0	31.8	35.2	44.9	56.3	66.9	80.1	94.8	110.3
Imports of Goods & Services	98c	–8.0	–7.5	–8.0	–9.1	–9.4	–10.0	–11.1	–12.4	–14.2	–21.1	–29.9	–39.2	–55.5	–64.1	–60.0
Gross Domestic Product	99b	37.9	39.5	41.6	44.8	46.4	52.3	57.4	61.5	73.3	112.2	118.1	135.1	155.7	169.1	207.7
Net Factor Inc/Pmts(-) Abroad	98.n	–3.5	–3.4	–3.3	–3.5	–3.7	–2.4	–3.3	–2.1	–3.0	–2.7	.3	.2	–.4	–.6	–.8
Gross Nat'l Expenditure = GNP	99a	34.4	36.1	38.4	41.3	42.8	49.9	54.2	59.4	70.3	109.5	118.4	135.3	155.3	168.4	207.0
Nat'l Income, Market Prices	99e	31.2	32.6	34.5	37.2	38.7	45.0	48.9	53.9	64.4	103.0	110.9	126.8	144.8	155.9	192.1
Gross Dom. Prod. 1990 Prices	99b.p	1,095.3	1,122.6	1,165.4	1,222.4	1,277.0	1,388.8	1,430.8	1,469.8	1,561.7	1,656.4	1,757.0	1,911.1	2,039.5	2,083.2	2,111.0
GDP Deflator (1990=100)	99bi p	3.5	3.5	3.6	3.7	3.6	3.8	4.0	4.2	4.7	6.8	6.7	7.1	7.6	8.1	9.8
																Millions:
Population	99z	8.71	9.03	9.31	9.62	9.94	10.28	10.61	10.94	11.28	11.63	‡12.67	13.12	13.59	14.07	14.55

Deposit Money Banks: ‡ Beginning in December 1987, data are based on an improved reporting system.
Monetary Survey: ‡ See note to section 20.
Other Banking Institutions: ‡ See note to section 20.
Banking Survey: ‡ See note to section 20.
Prices and Production: *Industrial Share Prices:* ‡ Beginning in January 1990, the index, base January 1, 1971, refers to the average of daily quotations on the Caracas Stock Exchange.
Government Finance: ‡ Beginning in 1968, data include extrabudgetary accounts derived from the Annual Report of the Ministry of Finance. ‡ Beginning in 1970, data are as reported in the *Government Finance Statistics Yearbook* and cover, in addition to budgetary central government, some extrabudgetary and social security accounts. ‡ However, operations of social security funds other than the Venezuelan Social Security Institute are covered only beginning in 1983. ‡ Beginning in 1987, data cover budgetary central government and the Venezuelan Social Security Institute only.
National Accounts: ‡ Data on GDP have been revised backward for a longer period than have the data on the components. Hence, components do not add up to GDP for some years.

Venezuela

Government Finance / National Accounts

	1980	1981	1982	1983	1984	1985	1986	1987	1988	1989	1990	1991	1992	1993	1994		
Year Ending December 31																**Government Finance**	
Deficit (-) or Surplus	.1	-3.9	-12.7	‡-4.4	13.5	23.6	-10.0	‡-39.8	-67.7	-23.9	25.2	134.1	-131.2	-160.5ᵖ	....		80
Revenue	66.5	97.5	83.7	‡77.4	104.5	126.5	108.7	‡135.2	167.9	303.1	535.2	734.0	781.2	953.2ᵖ	....		81
Grants Received	.3	.3	.3	‡.1	.1	.1	—	‡—	—	—	—	—	—	—ᵖ	....		81z
Expenditure	55.8	84.5	84.5	‡73.4	82.6	94.6	105.2	‡174.9	235.6	327.1	510.0	723.0	824.5	1,015.1ᵖ	....		82
Lending Minus Repayments	10.9	17.2	12.2	‡8.4	8.5	8.4	13.4	‡—	—	—	—	-123.1	87.9	98.6ᵖ	....		83
Financing																	
Net Borrowing	3.6	6.8	6.3	....	....	....	....	....	....	....	....	....	....	....	....		84
Domestic	-1.9	8.2	-1.6	....	....	....	....	....	....	....	....	....	....	....	....		84a
Foreign	5.5	-1.4	7.9	....	....	....	....	....	....	....	....	....	....	....	....		85a
Use of Cash Balances	-3.7	-2.9	6.4	....	....	....	....	....	....	....	....	....	....	....	....		87
Debt	35.6	46.5	55.3	‡57.8	85.5	98.4	....	....	....	....	....	....	....	....	....		88
Domestic	3.2	16.3	19.3	‡18.1	23.5	38.7	67.7	....	....	....	....	....	....	....	....		88a
Foreign	32.4	30.3	36.0	‡39.7	62.0	59.7	....	....	....	....	....	....	....	....	....		89a
Billions of Bolivares																**National Accounts**	
Exports of Goods & Services	85.5	89.6	75.2	74.1	108.8	108.3	97.5	145.7	180.1	503.0	899.2	952.4	1,088.8	1,428.8	2,556.8		90c
Government Consumption	35.1	42.6	42.6	41.3	43.3	48.6	54.7	71.1	91.9	144.4	191.8	293.2	379.4	472.6	609.7		91f
Gross Fixed Capital Formation	64.1	69.8	70.2	55.4	67.3	80.6	99.8	147.9	199.3	255.0	322.1	552.0	870.7	1,062.7	1,316.0		93e
Increase/Decrease(-) in Stocks	-1.4	-4.4	5.2	-21.2	6.2	5.4	2.6	23.2	44.8	-63.2	-89.2	15.4	109.3	-41.3	-471.0		93i
Private Consumption	135.4	160.5	182.2	183.4	256.3	287.3	337.1	450.4	597.7	977.3	1,415.4	2,021.2	2,877.6	3,989.1	6,039.1		96f
Imports of Goods & Services	-64.6	-73.0	-84.1	-42.5	-76.2	-81.1	-99.6	-158.8	-238.4	-330.9	-460.1	-796.6	-1,194.4	-1,462.8	-1,739.9		98c
Gross Domestic Product	254.2	285.2	291.3	290.5	405.8	449.0	492.1	679.4	875.5	1,485.5	2,279.3	3,037.5	4,131.5	5,449.1	8,310.7		99b
Net Factor Inc/Pmts(-) Abroad	1.2	2.3	-6.6	-9.9	6.8	-10.6	-3.0	-.2	-2.2	-62.4	-67.7	-57.3	-123.8	-156.3	-239.2		98.n
Gross Nat'l Expenditure = GNP	255.4	287.5	284.7	280.6	412.6	438.4	489.2	679.2	873.4	1,423.1	2,211.6	2,980.2	4,007.7	5,292.8	8,071.5		99a
Nat'l Income, Market Prices	238.3	267.6	263.1	256.6	379.8	401.9	446.0	623.0	801.7	1,315.8	2,057.3	2,759.7	3,698.4	4,857.8	7,411.4		99e
Gross Dom. Prod. 1990 Prices	2,069.0	2,062.7	2,076.6	1,960.2	‡1,933.5	1,961.0	2,085.3	2,179.3	2,313.9	2,132.6	2,279.3	2,501.0	2,652.6	2,641.9	2,555.5		99b.p
GDP Deflator (1990=100)	12.3	13.8	14.0	14.8	21.0	22.9	23.6	31.2	37.8	69.7	100.0	121.4	155.8	206.3	325.2		99bi p
Midyear Estimates																	
Population	15.02	15.48	15.94	16.39	16.85	17.32	17.53	17.97	18.42	18.87	19.33	19.79	20.25	20.71	21.18		99z

Western Samoa

862

		1965	1966	1967	1968	1969	1970	1971	1972	1973	1974	1975	1976	1977	1978	1979
Exchange Rates																
Official Rate	ac	1.3905	1.3905	1.3868	1.3868	1.3868	1.3868	1.3631	1.3674	1.3666	1.3465	1.1133	1.0759	1.0998	1.0743	.8332
															SDRs per Tala:	
														US Dollars per Tala:		
Official Rate	ag	1.3905	1.3905	1.3868	1.3868	1.3868	1.3868	1.4799	1.4847	1.6486	1.6486	1.3033	1.2500	1.3359	1.3996	1.0976
Official Rate	rh	1.3905	1.3905	1.3898	1.3868	1.3868	1.3868	1.3910	1.4806ᵉ	1.6281ᵉ	1.6486ᵉ	1.5920	1.2547	1.2706	1.3586	1.2205
													Index Numbers (1990=100):			
Official Rate	ahx	321.1ᵉ	321.1ᵉ	321.0ᵉ	320.3ᵉ	320.3ᵉ	320.3ᵉ	312.1	341.9ᵉ	376.0ᵉ	380.7ᵉ	367.6	289.8	293.4	313.8	281.9
Nominal Effective Exchange Rate	nec	....	....	....	....	....	....	....	....	....	....	....	....	....	....	238.8
Real Effective Exchange Rate	rec	....	....	....	....	....	....	....	....	....	....	....	....	....	....	123.1
Fund Position															*Millions of SDRs:*	
Quota	2f.s	....	....	....	....	....	....	....	2.00	2.00	2.00	2.00	2.00	2.00	3.00	3.00
SDRs	1b.s	....	....	....	....	....	....	—	.21	.21	.21	.04	—	.03	.04	—
Reserve Position in the Fund	1c.s	....	....	....	....	....	....	.36	.36	.36	.36	—	—	—	—	—
Total Fund Cred.&Loans Outstg.	2tl	....	....	....	....	....	....	—	—	—	—	1.26	1.92	1.84	3.49	4.75
International Liquidity									*Millions of US Dollars Unless Otherwise Indicated:*							
Total Reserves minus Gold	1l.d	3.57	2.73	2.16	3.06	5.15	5.22	6.41	4.53	5.08	5.96	6.39	5.24	9.13	4.78	4.82
SDRs	1b.d	....	....	....	....	....	....	—	.23	.25	.26	.05	—	.04	.05	—
Reserve Position in the Fund	1c.d	....	....	....	....	....	....	.39	.39	.43	.44	—	—	—	—	—
Foreign Exchange	1d.d	3.57	2.73	2.16	3.06	5.15	5.22	6.02	3.91	4.39	5.26	6.34	5.24	9.09	4.73	4.82
Other Official Insts.: Assets	3b.d	....	....	....	....	....	4.42	4.85	4.58	3.09	2.30	.91	.69	.74	1.34	.84
Deposit Money Banks: Assets	7a.d	2	2	2	3	5	4	5	3	4	5	5	5	7	4	4
Liabilities	7b.d	—	—	—	—	—	—	—	—	—	—	—	—	—	—	1
Monetary Authorities															*Millions of Tala:*	
Foreign Assets	11	.73	.56	.26	.34	.56	.69	.91	.71	.60	.77	.74	.42	1.18	.64	.61
Claims on Central Government	12a	−.73	−.56	−.21	−.27	−.48	−.59	−.80	.13	.15	.18	.39	.48	.66	.67	.84
Claims on Deposit Money Banks	12e	—	—	—	—	—	—	—	—	—	—	—	—	—	—	—
Reserve Money	14	—	—	.06	.07	.09	.10	.12	.13	.15	.18	.38	.48	.66	.67	.84
of which: Currency Outside DMBs	14a	—	—	.04	.06	.07	.09	.10	.12	.14	.17	.19	.22	.23	.25	.17
Foreign Liabilities	16c	—	—	—	—	—	—	—	—	—	—	1.13	1.78	1.67	3.25	5.70
Central Government Deposits	16d	—	—	—	—	—	—	—	.56	.44	.61	−.58	−1.56	−.69	−2.81	−5.72
Other Items (Net)	17r	—	—	—	—	—	—	—	.15	.15	.16	.19	.20	.19	.20	.62
Deposit Money Banks															*Millions of Tala:*	
Reserves	20	—	—	.01	.01	.01	.01	.01	.01	.01	.01	.02	.26	.43	.41	.66
Foreign Assets	21	1.50	1.71	1.29	1.88	3.33	3.15	3.35	2.29	2.43	3.27	4.16	3.78	5.50	2.78	3.79
Claims on Central Government	22a	.05	.05	.07	.26	.29	.30	.48	.65	1.03	1.03	1.20	1.35	2.67	3.39	4.59
Claims on Nonfin.Pub.Enterprises	22c	—	—	—	—	—	—	—	—	.41	.34	.36	.58	.55	1.93	4.78
Claims on Private Sector	22d	1.40	1.25	1.18	1.15	1.27	1.58	1.99	3.17	2.85	4.06	3.91	5.91	7.15	9.78	10.73
Demand Deposits	24	1.20	1.15	1.05	1.06	.83	1.19	1.83	2.19	2.62	3.04	3.29	3.83	4.52	4.97	5.60
Time and Savings Deposits	25	.65	.74	.83	1.06	1.52	1.40	1.52	1.57	2.12	2.56	2.80	3.59	4.53	5.11	9.01
Foreign Liabilities	26c	.03	—	.04	.02	.08	—	—	.27	.01	—	—	—	—	.03	.60
Central Government Deposits	26d	.43	.40	.23	.34	1.52	1.07	.94	.59	.28	.42	.67	.55	1.72	1.01	1.18
Other Items (Net)	27r	.66	.70	.44	.76	1.05	1.33	1.44	1.50	1.71	2.70	3.07	3.91	5.52	7.18	8.18
Monetary Survey															*Millions of Tala:*	
Foreign Assets (Net)	31n	2.20	2.27	1.52	2.19	3.81	3.84	4.26	2.74	3.02	⅃4.04	3.77	2.41	5.00	.13	−1.89
Domestic Credit	32	.28	.34	.82	.80	−.44	.21	.73	2.79	3.72	4.58	5.75	9.33	9.99	17.57	25.48
Claims on Central Govt. (Net)	32an	−1.11	−.91	−.36	−.35	−1.71	−1.37	−1.25	−.38	.46	.18	1.49	2.84	2.29	5.86	9.97
Claims on Nonfin.Pub.Enterprises	32c	—	—	—	—	—	—	—	—	.41	.34	.36	.58	.55	1.93	4.78
Claims on Private Sector	32d	1.40	1.25	1.18	1.15	1.27	1.58	1.99	3.17	2.85	4.06	3.91	5.91	7.15	9.78	10.73
Money	34	1.20	1.15	1.09	1.12	.90	1.28	1.94	2.31	2.76	⅃3.21	3.48	4.04	4.76	5.23	5.77
Quasi-Money	35	.65	.74	.83	1.06	1.52	1.40	1.52	1.57	2.12	2.56	2.80	3.59	4.53	5.11	9.01
Other Items (Net)	37r	.66	.70	.44	.76	1.05	1.33	1.44	1.65	1.86	2.85	3.44	4.11	5.70	7.39	8.80
Money plus Quasi-Money	35l	1.85	1.89	1.92	2.18	2.42	2.68	3.46	3.88	4.88	5.77	6.28	7.64	9.28	10.33	14.78
Other Banking Institutions															*Millions of Tala:*	
Deposits	45	.60	.56	.53	.50	.53	.56	.59	.66	.70	.87	.83	.88	.85	.81	.85
Liquid Liabilities	55l	2.45	2.46	2.45	2.68	2.95	3.24	4.05	4.54	5.58	6.64	7.11	8.52	10.13	11.14	15.63
Interest Rates															*Percent Per Annum*	
Deposit Rate	60l	....	....	....	....	....	....	....	....	....	....	....	....	....	....	....
Lending Rate	60p	....	....	....	....	....	....	....	....	....	....	....	....	....	....	6.5
Government Bond Yield	61	....	....	....	....	....	....	....	....	....	....	....	....	....	....	8.0
Prices															*Index Numbers (1990=100):*	
Consumer Prices	64	9.7	10.0	9.9	10.1	10.5	10.8	11.3	⅃12.2	13.6	17.0	18.5	19.4	22.2	22.7	25.2

Western Samoa

	1980	1981	1982	1983	1984	1985	1986	1987	1988	1989	1990	1991	1992	1993	1994		
Exchange Rates																	
End of Period																	
Official Rate	.8438	.7816	.7328	.5895	.4673	.3947	.3720	.3505	.3459	.3323	.3013	.2855	.2844	.2792	.2794		ac
End of Period (ag) Period Average (rh)																	
Official Rate	1.0762	.9098	.8083	.6172	.4581	.4336	.4550	.4973	.4655	.4367	.4286	.4084	.3910	.3835	.4079		ag
Official Rate	1.0876	.9649	.8297	.6496	.5441	.4457	.4474	.4716	.4810	.4408	.4330	.4171	.4056	.3894	.3945		rh
Period Averages																	
Official Rate	251.2	222.8	191.6	150.0	125.6	102.9	103.3	108.9	111.1	101.8	100.0	96.3	93.7	89.9	91.1		ah x
Nominal Effective Exchange Rate	214.2	203.4	191.5	159.1	143.1	127.2	117.0	113.6	109.1	104.1	100.0	96.6	94.0	92.0	89.7		ne c
Real Effective Exchange Rate	130.8	135.2	138.5	127.1	121.7	110.6	102.8	98.5	98.4	95.1	100.0	91.3	94.5	91.9	103.2		re c
Fund Position																	
End of Period																	
Quota	4.50	4.50	4.50	6.00	6.00	6.00	6.00	6.00	6.00	6.00	6.00	6.00	8.50	8.50	8.50		2f. s
SDRs	—	.01	.01	.41	.15	.01	—	.79	1.31	2.44	.69	2.94	2.59	1.89	1.99		1b. s
Reserve Position in the Fund	—	—	—	—	—	—	—	—	—	.01	.03	.03	.03	.66	.66		1c. s
Total Fund Cred.&Loans Outstg.	4.51	6.41	5.70	7.56	9.97	9.95	8.28	5.79	2.85	1.23	.59	.16	—	—	—		2tl
International Liquidity																	
End of Period																	
Total Reserves minus Gold	2.77	3.28	3.48	7.23	10.56	14.02	23.75	37.20	49.20	55.07	69.05	67.81	61.16	50.71	50.80		1l. d
SDRs	—	.01	.01	.43	.15	.01	.97	1.86	3.28	.91	4.18	3.70	2.60	2.68	2.91		1b. d
Reserve Position in the Fund	—	—	—	—	—	—	—	—	.01	.04	.04	.04	.91	.91	.97		1c. d
Foreign Exchange	2.77	3.27	3.47	6.80	10.41	14.01	22.78	35.34	45.90	54.12	64.82	64.06	57.65	47.11	46.92		1d. d
Other Official Insts.: Assets	.56	.51	.50	.34	.22	.27	.23	.33	....	....	....	....	....	....	....		3b. d
Deposit Money Banks: Assets	2	3	3	6	7	2	3	5	5	5	5	3	4	3	6		7a. d
Liabilities	3	1	1	—	—	—	1	1	—	1	1	—	—	3		Liabilities	7b. d
Monetary Authorities																	
Foreign Assets	.43	.29	.52	2.01	8.00	27.66	44.68	64.47	86.51	117.15	148.25	159.24	135.99	112.38	109.39		11
Claims on Central Government	2.71	4.79	6.75	6.78	6.66	6.87	1.96	1.88	2.51	2.51	4.23	1.94	1.69	1.69	.07		12a
Claims on Deposit Money Banks	2.73	2.57	1.75	2.03	1.28	4.99	5.05	11.05	5.35	7.81	29.34	16.89	5.85	6.00	6.23		12e
Reserve Money	5.44	7.35	8.41	9.41	10.94	25.09	35.14	40.37	41.81	58.01	88.33	79.77	63.29	58.25	60.11		14
of which: Currency Outside DMBs	3.56	5.28	6.05	6.02	7.08	8.44	9.18	10.53	10.72	12.48	12.94	13.96	12.31	13.95	16.82		14a
Foreign Liabilities	5.34	8.21	7.87	12.84	21.36	25.22	22.26	16.52	8.24	3.70	1.96	.56	—	—	—		16c
Central Government Deposits	-5.91	-9.37	-8.82	-12.75	-18.65	-15.97	-11.90	13.93	33.59	49.97	66.37	79.40	79.89	64.54	49.07		16d
Other Items (Net)	1.00	1.45	1.56	1.32	2.30	5.18	6.19	6.58	10.74	15.78	25.16	18.33	.35	-2.73	6.51		17r
Deposit Money Banks																	
End of Period																	
Reserves	1.89	2.07	2.37	3.39	3.86	16.65	25.96	29.84	31.09	45.53	75.39	65.80	50.98	44.30	43.29		20
Foreign Assets	2.14	3.31	3.88	9.76	15.05	4.68	7.67	10.33	11.60	11.52	12.83	6.84	9.61	8.10	15.34		21
Claims on Central Government	6.08	10.86	15.17	8.30	4.42	1.39	2.40	4.21	4.42	4.29	3.79	3.45	2.99	3.62	3.67		22a
Claims on Nonfin.Pub.Enterprises	6.65	10.51	12.77	10.57	10.11	12.08	12.25	10.48	6.24	4.07	2.57	2.35	2.37	.56	3.16		22c
Claims on Private Sector	11.33	11.99	14.17	15.94	19.04	22.39	26.61	32.63	39.95	42.32	58.81	63.19	70.91	81.29	75.49		22d
Demand Deposits	5.58	8.83	11.37	10.91	12.28	11.52	12.45	18.16	19.47	20.68	34.35	28.97	25.73	29.70	30.38		24
Time and Savings Deposits	10.46	18.67	26.89	21.95	24.15	32.44	41.52	51.96	56.73	68.29	73.69	75.78	81.52	77.63	90.88		25
Foreign Liabilities	2.86	.89	1.39	.37	.52	.67	.04	1.32	1.83	.98	1.34	2.97	.57	1.30	7.00		26c
Central Government Deposits	.60	.98	1.64	1.71	6.16	1.00	6.79	1.95	4.65	5.52	3.01	2.35	1.96	3.01	2.32		26d
Other Items (Net)	8.59	9.38	7.06	13.00	9.37	11.56	14.09	14.10	10.62	12.26	41.00	31.56	27.08	26.23	10.37		27r
Monetary Survey																	
Foreign Assets (Net)	-5.63	-5.49	-4.86	-1.45	1.17	6.45	30.05	56.96	88.04	123.99	157.78	162.55	145.03	119.18	117.73		31n
Domestic Credit	32.08	46.53	56.04	52.63	52.73	57.70	48.33	33.32	14.88	-2.30	.02	-10.82	-3.89	19.61	31.00		32
Claims on Central Govt. (Net)	14.10	24.03	29.10	26.12	23.57	23.23	9.47	-9.79	-31.31	-48.69	-61.36	-76.36	-77.17	-62.24	-47.65		32an
Claims on Nonfin.Pub.Enterprises	6.65	10.51	12.77	10.57	10.11	12.08	12.25	10.48	6.24	4.07	2.57	2.35	2.37	.56	3.16		32c
Claims on Private Sector	11.33	11.99	14.17	15.94	19.04	22.39	26.61	32.63	39.95	42.32	58.81	63.19	70.91	81.29	75.49		32d
Money	9.14	14.11	17.42	16.93	19.36	19.96	21.63	28.69	30.19	33.16	47.29	42.93	38.04	43.65	47.20		34
Quasi-Money	10.46	18.67	26.89	21.95	24.15	32.44	41.52	51.96	56.73	68.29	73.69	75.78	81.52	77.63	90.88		35
Other Items (Net)	6.85	8.26	6.86	12.29	10.39	11.75	15.23	9.63	16.01	20.23	36.82	33.01	21.58	17.50	10.65		37r
Money plus Quasi-Money	19.60	32.77	44.31	38.88	43.51	52.40	63.15	80.65	86.92	101.45	120.98	118.71	119.56	121.28	138.08		35l
Other Banking Institutions																	
End of Period																	
Deposits	.88	.81	1.01	1.15	1.27	1.54	1.59	1.72	1.94	3.50	3.86	8.44	6.60	2.56	2.63		45
Liquid Liabilities	20.48	33.58	45.32	40.03	44.78	53.94	64.74	82.37	88.86	104.95	124.84	127.15	126.16	123.84	140.71		55l
Interest Rates																	
Percent Per Annum																	
Deposit Rate	6.5	6.5	9.0	11.8	12.0	12.0	13.5	12.0	12.0	12.0	8.3	8.3	6.4	5.5	5.5		60l
Lending Rate	....	....	....	20.0	20.0	19.0	18.8	17.5	17.5	17.0	13.3	14.8	12.9	12.0	12.0		60p
Government Bond Yield	8.0	11.5	12.3	14.9	17.5	15.0	14.2	13.5	13.5	13.5	13.5	13.5	13.5	13.5	13.5		61
Prices																	
Period Averages																	
Consumer Prices	33.5	40.4	47.8	55.7	62.3	67.9	71.8	75.1	81.5	86.8	100.0	98.2	107.0	108.9	128.9		64

Western Samoa

862

		1965	1966	1967	1968	1969	1970	1971	1972	1973	1974	1975	1976	1977	1978	1979
International Transactions																*Thousands of Tala*
Exports	70	...	...	...	...	...	...	...	...	...	...	...	5,447	11,584	8,169	14,981
Imports, cif	71	6,581	5,729	5,635	5,498	7,374	9,791	9,614	13,044	14,433	15,909	23,160	23,627	ɪ32,254	38,567	60,946
Imports, fob	71.v	5,929	5,161	5,077	4,948	6,703	8,901	8,740	11,858	13,121	14,262	21,050	21,479	ɪ29,354	35,087	55,476
Balance of Payments																*Millions of US Dollars:*
Goods: Exports f.o.b.	78aa d	....	....	....	....	....	....	....	....	....	....	....	....	14.73	9.74	18.13
Goods: Imports f.o.b.	78ab d	....	....	....	....	....	....	....	....	....	....	....	....	-37.34	-47.66	-67.15
Trade Balance	78ac d	....	....	....	....	....	....	....	....	....	....	....	....	-22.61	-37.92	-49.02
Services: Credit	78ad d	....	....	....	....	....	....	....	....	....	....	....	....	2.42	3.91	3.63
Services: Debit	78ae d	....	....	....	....	....	....	....	....	....	....	....	....	-5.09	-6.76	-9.89
Balance on Goods and Services	78af d	....	....	....	....	....	....	....	....	....	....	....	....	-25.28	-40.77	-55.28
Income: Credit	78ag d	....	....	....	....	....	....	....	....	....	....	....	....	—	—	—
Income: Debit	78ah d	....	....	....	....	....	....	....	....	....	....	....	....	-.11	-1.49	-1.62
Balance on Goods, Serv., & Inc.	78ai d	....	....	....	....	....	....	....	....	....	....	....	....	-25.39	-42.26	-56.90
Current Transfers, n.i.e.: Credit	78aj d	....	....	....	....	....	....	....	....	....	....	....	....	14.20	24.16	34.86
Current Transfers: Debit	78ak d	....	....	....	....	....	....	....	....	....	....	....	....	—	—	—
Current Account, n.i.e.	78al d	....	....	....	....	....	....	....	....	....	....	....	....	-11.19	-18.10	-22.04
Capital Account, n.i.e.: Credit	78ba d	....	....	....	....	....	....	....	....	....	....	....	....	—	—	—
Capital Account: Debit	78bb d	....	....	....	....	....	....	....	....	....	....	....	....	—	—	—
Capital Account, n.i.e.	78bc d	....	....	....	....	....	....	....	....	....	....	....	....	—	—	—
Direct Investment Abroad	78bd d	....	....	....	....	....	....	....	....	....	....	....	....	—	—	—
Dir. Invest. in Rep. Econ., n.i.e.	78be d	....	....	....	....	....	....	....	....	....	....	....	....	—	—	—
Portfolio Investment Assets	78bf d	....	....	....	....	....	....	....	....	....	....	....	....	—	—	—
Portfolio Investment Liab., n.i.e.	78bg d	....	....	....	....	....	....	....	....	....	....	....	....	—	—	—
Other Investment Assets	78bh d	....	....	....	....	....	....	....	....	....	....	....	....	—	—	—
Other Investment Liab., n.i.e.	78bi d	....	....	....	....	....	....	....	....	....	....	....	....	8.87	7.80	19.47
Financial Account, n.i.e.	78bj d	....	....	....	....	....	....	....	....	....	....	....	....	8.87	7.80	19.47
Net Errors and Omissions	78ca d	....	....	....	....	....	....	....	....	....	....	....	....	4.31	3.56	1.67
Overall Balance	78cb d	....	....	....	....	....	....	....	....	....	....	....	....	1.98	-6.75	-.90
Reserves and Related Items	79da d	....	....	....	....	....	....	....	....	....	....	....	....	-1.98	6.75	.90
Reserve Assets	79db d	....	....	....	....	....	....	....	....	....	....	....	....	-3.35	4.65	-.77
Use of Fund Credit and Loans	79dc d	....	....	....	....	....	....	....	....	....	....	....	....	-.09	2.10	1.63
Liabs.Constit.For.Auth.Reserves	79dd d	....	....	....	....	....	....	....	....	....	....	....	....	—	—	—
Exceptional Financing	79de d	....	....	....	....	....	....	....	....	....	....	....	....	1.46	—	.05
																Millions:
Population	99z	.13	.13	.13	.14	.14	.14	.15	.15	.15	.15	ɪ.15	.15	.15	.15	.15

Exchange Rates: On July 10, 1967 the tala, equal to one half the pound, was introduced.

Monetary Survey: ɪ Beginning in April 1974, *line 31n* includes nonresident deposits, which prior to this date were reported in *line 34*.

International Transactions: ɪ Prior to January 1977, data are based on customs clearances; diplomatic imports are included in total imports. After January 1977, data refer to actual imports landed in Western Samoa.

Western Samoa

862

1980	1981	1982	1983	1984	1985	1986	1987	1988	1989	1990	1991	1992	1993	1994	International Transactions	
Thousands of Tala																
15,828	11,150	16,248	27,410	36,781	36,180	23,495	24,968	31,397	29,206	20,494	15,515	14,349	16,522	9,121	Exports	70
57,438	58,396	60,115	75,100	93,285	115,074	105,375	131,010	157,296	171,220	186,120	225,337	271,325	269,079	206,347	Imports, cif	71
52,268	53,139	54,705	68,340	84,889	104,716	95,883	119,208	143,126	155,796	169,354	205,038	246,884	244,840	187,759	Imports, fob	71.v
															Balance of Payments	
Minus Sign Indicates Debit																
17.22	10.78	13.46	17.69	18.34	16.12	10.51	11.77	15.09	12.87	8.85	6.48	5.82	6.43	....	Goods: Exports f.o.b.	78aa *d*
−56.86	−51.38	−45.31	−44.12	−45.55	−46.60	−42.84	−55.79	−66.57	−66.99	−70.00	−77.62	−89.90	−87.37	....	Goods: Imports f.o.b.	78ab *d*
−39.64	−40.60	−31.86	−26.42	−27.21	−30.48	−32.34	−44.02	−51.47	−54.12	−61.15	−71.15	−84.07	−80.94	....	Trade Balance	78ac *d*
8.43	7.48	8.24	9.13	8.53	10.33	13.34	16.43	26.89	30.90	35.58	30.75	36.65	35.78	....	Services: Credit	78ad *d*
−14.86	−11.59	−12.61	−12.45	−12.18	−11.09	−12.38	−14.94	−18.25	−18.80	−24.72	−34.64	−43.43	−38.22	....	Services: Debit	78ae *d*
−46.07	−44.71	−36.22	−29.73	−30.86	−31.23	−31.38	−42.53	−42.83	−42.02	−50.29	−75.04	−90.85	−83.38	....	Balance on Goods and Services	78af *d*
.02	.13	.08	.14	.34	.68	1.26	2.75	2.89	4.48	6.68	7.21	6.15	4.33	....	Income: Credit	78ag *d*
−2.56	−2.79	−2.24	−2.83	−2.33	−2.58	−2.33	−2.22	−2.12	−2.39	−1.53	−2.39	−2.55	−4.42	....	Income: Debit	78ah *d*
−48.60	−47.37	−38.37	−32.43	−32.85	−33.13	−32.45	−42.00	−42.07	−39.94	−45.14	−70.22	−87.25	−83.47	....	Balance on Goods, Serv., & Inc.	78ai *d*
36.17	32.49	32.29	36.67	33.86	35.48	40.74	50.35	52.95	56.29	56.54	44.66	39.07	49.91	....	Current Transfers, n.i.e.: Credit	78aj *d*
−.48	−.25	−.54	−.72	−.35	−.57	−1.06	−1.07	−2.93	−3.54	−4.15	−3.09	−4.32	−5.11	....	Current Transfers: Debit	78ak *d*
−12.91	−15.12	−6.62	3.51	.66	1.78	7.22	7.29	7.95	12.81	7.26	−28.66	−52.50	−38.68	....	Current Account, n.i.e.	78al *d*
—	—	—	—	—	—	—	—	—	—	—	—	—	—	....	Capital Account, n.i.e.: Credit	78ba *d*
—	—	—	—	—	—	—	—	—	—	—	—	—	—	....	Capital Account: Debit	78bb *d*
—	—	—	—	—	—	—	—	—	—	—	—	—	—	....	Capital Account, n.i.e.	78bc *d*
—	—	—	—	—	—	—	—	—	—	—	—	—	—	....	Direct Investment Abroad	78bd *d*
—	—	—	—	—	—	—	—	—	—	—	—	—	—	....	Dir. Invest. in Rep. Econ., n.i.e.	78be *d*
—	—	—	—	—	—	—	—	—	—	—	—	—	—	....	Portfolio Investment Assets	78bf *d*
—	—	—	—	—	—	—	—	—	—	—	—	—	—	....	Portfolio Investment Liab., n.i.e.	78bg *d*
—	—	−.05	.08	.02	−.05	.04	−.13	−.31	−.08	−.03	−.22	—	—	....	Other Investment Assets	78bh *d*
8.19	2.63	−.03	2.50	4.54	−.42	−.78	3.28	.80	.56	9.43	18.83	19.95	15.55	....	Other Investment Liab., n.i.e.	78bi *d*
8.19	2.63	−.08	2.58	4.56	−.47	−.74	3.15	.49	.48	9.40	18.60	19.95	15.55	....	Financial Account, n.i.e.	78bj *d*
2.27	6.80	3.52	1.10	2.00	3.92	.90	−1.85	1.67	−2.61	−5.66	7.97	19.82	13.82	....	Net Errors and Omissions	78ca *d*
−2.45	−5.70	−3.18	7.20	7.22	5.23	7.38	8.59	10.10	10.68	11.00	−2.08	−12.72	−9.31	....	Overall Balance	78cb *d*
2.45	5.70	3.18	−7.20	−7.22	−5.23	−7.38	−8.59	−10.10	−10.68	−11.00	2.08	12.72	9.31	....	Reserves and Related Items	79da *d*
2.28	−.63	−.65	−4.78	−5.90	−4.09	−9.38	−9.28	−8.42	−10.66	−11.49	−.42	12.95	8.29	....	Reserve Assets	79db *d*
−.31	2.32	−.78	1.97	2.48	−.07	−1.94	−3.22	−3.96	−2.09	−.86	−.59	−.22	—	....	Use of Fund Credit and Loans	79dc *d*
														....	Liabs.Constit.For.Auth.Reserves	79dd *d*
.48	4.01	4.61	−4.39	−3.80	−1.07	3.94	3.91	2.28	2.07	1.34	3.09	—	1.01	....	Exceptional Financing	79de *d*
Midyear Estimates																
.16	.16	.16	.16	.16	.16	.16	.16	.16	.16	.16	.16	.16	....	....	Population	99z

Yemen, Republic of

474

		1965	1966	1967	1968	1969	1970	1971	1972	1973	1974	1975	1976	1977	1978	1979
Exchange Rates																*Rials per SDR:*
Principal Rate	aa	....	....	....	....	....	....	....	....	....	....	....	....	....	....	....
																Rials per US Dollar:
Principal Rate	ae	....	....	....	....	....	....	....	....	....	....	....	....	....	....	....
Principal Rate	rf	....	....	....	....	....	....	....	....	....	....	....	....	....	....	....
Fund Position																*Millions of SDRs:*
Quota	2f.s	....	....	....	....	....	....	....	....	....	....	....	....	....	....	....
SDRs	1b.s	....	....	....	....	....	....	....	....	....	....	....	....	....	....	....
Reserve Position in the Fund	1c.s	....	....	....	....	....	....	....	....	....	....	....	....	....	....	....
Total Fund Cred.&Loans Outstg.	2tl	....	....	....	....	....	....	....	....	....	....	....	....	....	....	....
International Liquidity													*Millions of US Dollars Unless Otherwise Indicated:*			
Total Reserves minus Gold	1l.d	....	....	....	....	....	....	....	....	....	....	....	....	....	....	....
SDRs	1b.d	....	....	....	....	....	....	....	....	....	....	....	....	....	....	....
Reserve Position in the Fund	1c.d	....	....	....	....	....	....	....	....	....	....	....	....	....	....	....
Foreign Exchange	1d.d	....	....	....	....	....	....	....	....	....	....	....	....	....	....	....
Gold (Million Fine Troy Ounces)	1ad	....	....	....	....	....	....	....	....	....	....	....	....	....	....	....
Gold (National Valuation)	1and	....	....	....	....	....	....	....	....	....	....	....	....	....	....	....
Deposit Money Banks: Assets	7a.d	....	....	....	....	....	....	....	....	....	....	....	....	....	....	....
of which: Claims on Nonbanks	7add	....	....	....	....	....	....	....	....	....	....	....	....	....	....	....
Deposit Money Banks: Liabilities	7b.d	....	....	....	....	....	....	....	....	....	....	....	....	....	....	....
of which: Liab. to Nonbanks	7bdd	....	....	....	....	....	....	....	....	....	....	....	....	....	....	....
Monetary Authorities																*Millions of Rials:*
Foreign Assets	11	....	....	....	....	....	....	....	....	....	....	....	....	....	....	....
Claims on Central Government	12a	....	....	....	....	....	....	....	....	....	....	....	....	....	....	....
Claims on Nonfin.Pub.Enterprises	12c	....	....	....	....	....	....	....	....	....	....	....	....	....	....	....
Reserve Money	14	....	....	....	....	....	....	....	....	....	....	....	....	....	....	....
o/w: Currency Outside Banks	14a	....	....	....	....	....	....	....	....	....	....	....	....	....	....	....
Time, Savings,& Fgn.Currency Dep.	15	....	....	....	....	....	....	....	....	....	....	....	....	....	....	....
Foreign Liabilities	16c	....	....	....	....	....	....	....	....	....	....	....	....	....	....	....
Central Government Deposits	16d	....	....	....	....	....	....	....	....	....	....	....	....	....	....	....
Capital Accounts	17a	....	....	....	....	....	....	....	....	....	....	....	....	....	....	....
Other Items (Net)	17r	....	....	....	....	....	....	....	....	....	....	....	....	....	....	....
Deposit Money Banks																*Millions of Rials:*
Reserves	20	....	....	....	....	....	....	....	....	....	....	....	....	....	....	....
Foreign Assets	21	....	....	....	....	....	....	....	....	....	....	....	....	....	....	....
Claims on Central Government	22a	....	....	....	....	....	....	....	....	....	....	....	....	....	....	....
Claims on Nonfin.Pub.Enterprises	22c	....	....	....	....	....	....	....	....	....	....	....	....	....	....	....
Claims on Private Sector	22d	....	....	....	....	....	....	....	....	....	....	....	....	....	....	....
Demand Deposits	24	....	....	....	....	....	....	....	....	....	....	....	....	....	....	....
Time, Savings,& Fgn.Currency Dep.	25	....	....	....	....	....	....	....	....	....	....	....	....	....	....	....
Restricted Deposits	26b	....	....	....	....	....	....	....	....	....	....	....	....	....	....	....
Foreign Liabilities	26c	....	....	....	....	....	....	....	....	....	....	....	....	....	....	....
Central Government Deposits	26d	....	....	....	....	....	....	....	....	....	....	....	....	....	....	....
Capital Accounts	27a	....	....	....	....	....	....	....	....	....	....	....	....	....	....	....
Other Items (Net)	27r	....	....	....	....	....	....	....	....	....	....	....	....	....	....	....
Monetary Survey																*Millions of Rials:*
Foreign Assets (Net)	31n	....	....	....	....	....	....	....	....	....	....	....	....	....	....	....
Domestic Credit	32	....	....	....	....	....	....	....	....	....	....	....	....	....	....	....
Claims on Central Govt. (Net)	32an	....	....	....	....	....	....	....	....	....	....	....	....	....	....	....
Claims on Nonfin.Pub.Enterprises	32c	....	....	....	....	....	....	....	....	....	....	....	....	....	....	....
Claims on Private Sector	32d	....	....	....	....	....	....	....	....	....	....	....	....	....	....	....
Money	34	....	....	....	....	....	....	....	....	....	....	....	....	....	....	....
Quasi-Money	35	....	....	....	....	....	....	....	....	....	....	....	....	....	....	....
Restricted Deposits	36b	....	....	....	....	....	....	....	....	....	....	....	....	....	....	....
Capital Accounts	37a	....	....	....	....	....	....	....	....	....	....	....	....	....	....	....
Other Items (Net)	37r	....	....	....	....	....	....	....	....	....	....	....	....	....	....	....
Money plus Quasi-Money	35l	....	....	....	....	....	....	....	....	....	....	....	....	....	....	....
Government Finance																*Millions of Rials:*
Deficit (-) or Surplus	80	....	....	....	....	....	....	....	....	....	....	....	....	....	....	....
Revenue	81	....	....	....	....	....	....	....	....	....	....	....	....	....	....	....
Grants Received	81z	....	....	....	....	....	....	....	....	....	....	....	....	....	....	....
Expenditure	82	....	....	....	....	....	....	....	....	....	....	....	....	....	....	....
Lending Minus Repayments	83	....	....	....	....	....	....	....	....	....	....	....	....	....	....	....
Financing																
Domestic	84a	....	....	....	....	....	....	....	....	....	....	....	....	....	....	....
Foreign	85a	....	....	....	....	....	....	....	....	....	....	....	....	....	....	....
																Millions:
Population	99z	....	....	....	....	....	....	....	....	....	....	....	....	....	....	....

Yemen, Republic of

474

	1980	1981	1982	1983	1984	1985	1986	1987	1988	1989	1990	1991	1992	1993	1994		
End of Period																**Exchange Rates**	
	....	....	....	....	....	....	....	....	....	....	17.0861	17.1795	16.5138	16.4965	17.5328	Principal Rate	**aa**
End of Period (ae) Period Average (rf)																	
	....	....	....	....	....	....	....	....	....	....	12.0100	12.0100	12.0100	12.0100	12.0100	Principal Rate	**ae**
	....	....	....	....	....	....	....	....	....	....	....	12.0100	12.0100	12.0100	12.0100	Principal Rate	**rf**
End of Period																**Fund Position**	
	....	....	....	....	....	....	....	....	....	....	120.5	120.5	176.5	176.5	176.5	Quota	**2f. s**
	....	....	....	....	....	....	....	....	....	....	9.4	11.7	2.9	.5	33.5	SDRs	**1b. s**
	....	....	....	....	....	....	....	....	....	....	—	—	—	—	—	Reserve Position in the Fund	**1c. s**
	....	....	....	....	....	....	....	....	....	....	.1	—	—	—	—	Total Fund Cred.&Loans Outstg.	**2tl**
End of Period																**International Liquidity**	
	....	....	....	....	....	....	....	....	....	....	422.2	679.3	320.5	145.3	....	Total Reserves minus Gold	**1l. d**
	....	....	....	....	....	....	....	....	....	....	13.4	16.8	4.0	.6	48.9	SDRs	**1b. d**
	....	....	....	....	....	....	....	....	....	....	—	—	—	—	—	Reserve Position in the Fund	**1c. d**
	....	....	....	....	....	....	....	....	....	....	408.8	662.5	316.5	144.6	....	Foreign Exchange	**1d. d**
	....	....	....	....	....	....	....	....	....	....	.050	.050	.050	.050	....	Gold (Million Fine Troy Ounces)	**1ad**
	....	....	....	....	....	....	....	....	....	....	2.2	2.5	2.4	2.4	....	Gold (National Valuation)	**1an d**
	....	....	....	....	....	....	....	....	....	....	520.2	565.6	543.7	547.7	....	Deposit Money Banks: Assets	**7a. d**
	....	....	....	....	....	....	....	....	....	....	17.1	8.5	8.0	9.4	....	*of which:* Claims on Nonbanks	**7ad d**
	....	....	....	....	....	....	....	....	....	....	404.9	564.2	590.4	549.4	....	Deposit Money Banks: Liabilities	**7b. d**
	....	....	....	....	....	....	....	....	....	....	203.8	256.7	305.4	302.4	....	*of which:* Liab. to Nonbanks	**7bd d**
End of Period																**Monetary Authorities**	
	....	....	....	....	....	....	....	....	....	....	5,165	8,442	3,896	1,777	....	Foreign Assets	**11**
	....	....	....	....	....	....	....	....	....	....	74,914	82,253	104,818	135,664	....	Claims on Central Government	**12a**
	....	....	....	....	....	....	....	....	....	....	162	318	92	76	....	Claims on Nonfin.Pub.Enterprises	**12c**
	....	....	....	....	....	....	....	....	....	....	63,315	69,148	83,927	108,933	....	Reserve Money	**14**
	....	....	....	....	....	....	....	....	....	....	39,895	45,161	55,531	79,019	....	*o/w:* Currency Outside Banks	**14a**
	....	....	....	....	....	....	....	....	....	....	423	289	316	2,352	....	Time, Savings,& Fgn.Currency Dep.	**15**
	....	....	....	....	....	....	....	....	....	....	2,041	2,149	2,136	1,913	....	Foreign Liabilities	**16c**
	....	....	....	....	....	....	....	....	....	....	6,880	8,803	14,063	16,326	....	Central Government Deposits	**16d**
	....	....	....	....	....	....	....	....	....	....	716	1,094	1,075	1,077	....	Capital Accounts	**17a**
	....	....	....	....	....	....	....	....	....	....	6,865	9,532	7,289	6,919	....	Other Items (Net)	**17r**
End of Period																**Deposit Money Banks**	
	....	....	....	....	....	....	....	....	....	....	20,533	20,097	24,120	25,987	....	Reserves	**20**
	....	....	....	....	....	....	....	....	....	....	6,248	6,792	6,530	6,578	....	Foreign Assets	**21**
	....	....	....	....	....	....	....	....	....	....	155	239	352	281	....	Claims on Central Government	**22a**
	....	....	....	....	....	....	....	....	....	....	2,813	3,968	3,793	3,395	....	Claims on Nonfin.Pub.Enterprises	**22c**
	....	....	....	....	....	....	....	....	....	....	7,723	8,708	10,040	12,653	....	Claims on Private Sector	**22d**
	....	....	....	....	....	....	....	....	....	....	12,640	14,097	18,237	21,489	....	Demand Deposits	**24**
	....	....	....	....	....	....	....	....	....	....	12,782	14,271	15,096	17,251	....	Time, Savings,& Fgn.Currency Dep.	**25**
	....	....	....	....	....	....	....	....	....	....	2,834	1,786	1,329	1,240	....	Restricted Deposits	**26b**
	....	....	....	....	....	....	....	....	....	....	4,863	6,776	7,091	6,599	....	Foreign Liabilities	**26c**
	....	....	....	....	....	....	....	....	....	....	2,182	1,880	1,272	1,543	....	Central Government Deposits	**26d**
	....	....	....	....	....	....	....	....	....	....	1,237	1,443	1,564	1,997	....	Capital Accounts	**27a**
	....	....	....	....	....	....	....	....	....	....	934	−449	247	−1,224	....	Other Items (Net)	**27r**
End of Period																**Monetary Survey**	
	....	....	....	....	....	....	....	....	....	....	4,508	6,310	1,199	−157	....	Foreign Assets (Net)	**31n**
	....	....	....	....	....	....	....	....	....	....	76,704	84,803	103,762	134,201	....	Domestic Credit	**32**
	....	....	....	....	....	....	....	....	....	....	66,007	71,809	89,836	118,076	....	Claims on Central Govt. (Net)	**32an**
	....	....	....	....	....	....	....	....	....	....	2,974	4,286	3,886	3,472	....	Claims on Nonfin.Pub.Enterprises	**32c**
	....	....	....	....	....	....	....	....	....	....	7,723	8,708	10,040	12,653	....	Claims on Private Sector	**32d**
	....	....	....	....	....	....	....	....	....	....	56,498	62,995	78,314	103,306	....	Money	**34**
	....	....	....	....	....	....	....	....	....	....	13,205	14,560	15,412	19,604	....	Quasi-Money	**35**
	....	....	....	....	....	....	....	....	....	....	2,834	1,786	1,329	1,240	....	Restricted Deposits	**36b**
	....	....	....	....	....	....	....	....	....	....	1,953	2,536	2,640	3,073	....	Capital Accounts	**37a**
	....	....	....	....	....	....	....	....	....	....	6,722	9,236	7,266	6,824	....	Other Items (Net)	**37r**
	....	....	....	....	....	....	....	....	....	....	69,703	77,555	93,726	122,909	....	Money plus Quasi-Money	**35l**
Year Ending December 31																**Government Finance**	
	....	....	....	....	....	....	....	....	....	....	−11,167	−7,120	−23,428	....	....	Deficit (−) or Surplus	**80**
	....	....	....	....	....	....	....	....	....	....	23,941	37,982	32,911	....	....	Revenue	**81**
	....	....	....	....	....	....	....	....	....	....	1,397	300	—	....	....	Grants Received	**81z**
	....	....	....	....	....	....	....	....	....	....	35,193	44,067	54,848	....	....	Expenditure	**82**
	....	....	....	....	....	....	....	....	....	....	1,312	1,335	1,491	....	....	Lending Minus Repayments	**83**
																Financing	
	....	....	....	....	....	....	....	....	....	....	7,145	5,803	23,055	....	....	Domestic	**84a**
	....	....	....	....	....	....	....	....	....	....	4,022	1,317	373	....	....	Foreign	**85a**
Midyear Estimates																	
	....	....	....	9.10	9.42	9.60	9.88	10.16	10.61	10.95	11.23	11.61	11.95	12.30	12.67	Population	**99z**

Zaïre

636	1965	1966	1967	1968	1969	1970	1971	1972	1973	1974	1975	1976	1977	1978	1979
Exchange Rates															
N.Zaires per Bill.SDRs through 1980, per Mill. SDRs 1981-90; per Thous.															
Market Rate ... **aa**	55.00	55.00	166.67	166.67	166.67	166.67	180.95	180.95	201.06	204.06	195.11	333.41	336.43	437.14	889.06
N.Zaires per Bill. US$ through 1980, per Mill. US$ 1981-90, per Thous.															
Market Rate ... **ae**	55.00	55.00	166.67	166.67	166.67	166.67	166.67	166.67	166.67	166.67	166.67	286.97	276.96	335.54	674.89
Market Rate ... **rf**	54.99[e]	54.99[e]	115.46[e]	166.63[e]	166.63[e]	166.63[e]	166.63[e]	166.63[e]	166.63[e]	166.63[e]	166.63[e]	264.01	285.55	278.57	576.06
Index Numbers (1990=100):															
Market Rate ... **ahx**	380,212.1[e]	380,212.1[e]	236,879.8[e]	125,470.0[e]	125,470.0[e]	125,470.0[e]	8,124.9	125,470.0[e]	9,912.8	9,912.8	9,912.8	6,581.5	73,225.2	75,542.4	36,884.2[e]
Nominal Effective Exchange Rate ... **nec**	....	....	....	....	....	....	....	....	....	....	....	....	....	....	13,147.2
Real Effective Exchange Rate ... **rec**	....	....	....	....	....	....	....	....	....	....	....	....	....	....	411.0
Fund Position															
Millions of SDRs:															
Quota ... **2f.s**	45.00	47.40	57.00	57.00	90.00	113.00	113.00	113.00	113.00	113.00	113.00	113.00	113.00	152.00	152.00
SDRs ... **1b.s**	—	—	—	—	—	15.62	15.71	7.36	6.88	6.39	19.96	27.10	.03	4.39	.12
Reserve Position in the Fund ... **1c.s**	3.12	3.72	6.13	14.25	22.51	28.27	28.27	28.27	28.27	28.27	—	—	—	—	—
Total Fund Cred.&Loans Outstg. ... **2tl**	—	—	—	—	—	—	—	28.23	28.23	28.23	73.25	180.64	220.33	247.11	271.57
International Liquidity															
Millions of US Dollars Unless Otherwise Indicated:															
Total Reserves minus Gold ... **1l.d**	18.27	17.06	63.49	125.29	144.21	136.00	90.87	123.18	172.79	118.80	47.91	50.28	133.87	125.75	206.69
SDRs ... **1b.d**	—	—	—	—	—	15.62	17.06	7.99	8.30	7.82	23.37	31.49	.04	5.72	.16
Reserve Position in the Fund ... **1c.d**	3.12	3.72	6.13	14.25	22.51	28.27	30.69	30.69	34.10	34.61	—	—	—	—	—
Foreign Exchange ... **1d.d**	15.15	13.34	57.36	111.04	121.70	92.11	43.12	84.50	130.39	76.36	24.54	18.79	133.83	120.03	206.53
Gold (Million Fine Troy Ounces) ... **1ad**	.089	.099	.117	.358	1.569	1.425	1.439	1.454	1.464	.500	.260	.260	.260	.308	.252
Gold (National Valuation) ... **1and**	3.12	3.47	4.10	12.53	54.92	49.88	50.37	50.89	51.24	17.50	9.10	10.98	10.98	58.52	91.44
Monetary Authorities: Other Liab. ... **4..d**	3.03	3.64	1.20	1.60	—	.10	.19	.74	.39	20.82	28.62	18.63	56.86	48.19	47.73
Deposit Money Banks: Assets ... **7a.d**	23.96	48.48	56.59	35.91	31.25	37.16	35.51	37.56	50.53	72.62	105.20	113.39	149.33	162.29	131.97
Liabilities ... **7b.d**	1.48	1.47	1.22	2.17	2.06	2.14	5.70	11.57	14.87	17.04	149.65	48.73	57.34	41.92	47.79
Monetary Authorities															
Thousandths of New Zaïres through 1979; New Zaïres 1980-87;															
Foreign Assets ... **11**	1,067	1,033	11,267	22,967	33,072	30,880	23,545	29,150	37,145	22,716	9,612	30,088	40,136	61,888	201,692
Claims on Central Government ... **12a**	19,533	22,867	27,000	29,933	37,653	56,278	39,374	48,431	57,322	100,734	139,243	249,291	368,144	620,305	827,651
Claims on Nonfin.Pub.Enterprises ... **12c**	—	—	—	—	—	—	—	—	—	—	—	—	—	—	—
Claims on Private Sector ... **12d**	100	133	133	133	—	—	—	—	—	—	—	9,693	10,680	10,789	1,438
Claims on Deposit Money Banks ... **12e**	—	—	—	—	—	—	—	—	1,600	6,100	4,500	700	6,967	3,633	5,933
Claims on Other Banking Insts. ... **12f**	33	33	33	33	21	66	100	148	148	148	173	173	174	358	358
Reserve Money ... **14**	18,104	20,102	28,255	38,764	41,121	47,583	41,408	52,188	61,248	74,819	105,140	191,862	247,423	386,327	316,048
of which: Currency Outside DMBs ... **14a**	9,100	10,467	13,667	17,033	19,010	24,960	27,766	32,552	40,061	53,029	68,457	95,577	155,203	266,599	136,193
Time & Foreign Currency Deposits ... **15**	—	67	100	3,767	4,396	1,396	6,536	3,305	16,014	16,891	1,003	3,010	4,456	13,954	32,011
Restricted Deposits ... **16b**	—	433	733	467	432	614	1,495	1,457	2,037	11,865	7,071	13,923	77,878	149,118	195,836
Foreign Liabilities ... **16c**	167	200	200	267	—	17	32	5,231	5,741	9,231	19,062	65,573	89,875	124,190	273,653
Central Government Deposits ... **16d**	433	1,833	5,300	6,967	16,402	29,456	3,736	3,891	4,077	6,820	8,110	9,205	11,973	89,841	121,779
Counterpart Funds ... **16e**	1,800	2,000	2,733	2,467	2,654	1,917	2,247	1,635	1,318	748	582	2,044	4,617	8,655	12,691
Capital Accounts ... **17a**	200	200	433	433	2,834	5,835	7,727	9,942	9,632	9,659	9,826	49,897	43,358	82,114	100,599
Other Items (Net) ... **17r**	—	−767	667	−100	2,906	407	−161	81	−3,851	−335	2,735	−45,569	−53,483	−157,226	−15,544
Deposit Money Banks															
Thousandths of New Zaïres through 1979; New Zaïres 1980-87;															
Reserves ... **20**	6,910	6,460	8,997	17,884	18,896	18,648	10,802	15,825	15,692	18,868	26,567	90,321	77,147	116,734	137,408
Foreign Assets ... **21**	1,318	2,667	9,432	5,985	5,208	6,193	5,918	6,261	8,422	12,103	17,533	32,538	41,359	54,456	89,063
Claims on Central Government ... **22a**	4,467	4,467	4,433	5,733	5,740	5,834	8,336	8,114	7,637	12,853	15,613	29,778	30,050	39,320	42,217
Claims on Nonfin.Pub.Enterprises ... **22c**	....	....	....	....	316	414	577	582	2,580	4,275	11,499	8,547	9,489	4,910	4,027
Claims on Private Sector ... **22d**	3,233	4,100	5,900	6,733	8,872	13,717	17,992	28,600	43,041	73,438	94,344	109,035	158,357	199,540	276,831
Claims on Other Banking Insts. ... **22f**	—	—	—	—	—	—	—	—	—	—	17	20	30	30	30
Demand Deposits ... **24**	9,300	11,933	19,633	25,100	26,726	32,852	31,399	40,649	50,146	71,813	73,576	113,691	166,342	257,547	364,600
Time & Foreign Currency Deposits ... **25**	1,133	1,333	1,300	1,433	2,087	5,733	6,100	9,886	12,990	20,080	29,163	29,950	55,953	70,969	96,764
Restricted Deposits ... **26b**	2,216	2,039	4,955	6,205	5,538	2,703	1,723	1,505	2,137	6,305	6,725	20,648	26,640	21,320	18,338
Foreign Liabilities ... **26c**	82	81	203	362	343	357	950	1,928	2,478	2,840	24,941	13,983	15,880	14,067	32,254
Central Government Deposits ... **26d**	....	....	....	....	348	284	523	837	857	944	1,262	2,907	2,883	9,781	15,933
Counterpart Funds ... **26e**	978	433	30	238	935	940	34	1	5	3	—	—	56	59	3
Credit from Monetary Authorities ... **26g**	—	—	—	—	—	—	—	—	1,600	6,100	4,500	700	6,967	3,633	5,933
Capital Accounts ... **27a**	1,033	1,267	1,300	1,513	2,759	3,547	4,331	6,782	7,432	8,633	10,090	15,156	17,355	20,538	34,888
Other Items (Net) ... **27r**	1,167	500	1,341	1,484	297	−1,612	−1,435	−2,208	−272	4,820	15,317	73,205	24,354	17,076	−19,136
Post Office: Checking Deposits ... **24..i**	283	322	409	778	671	617	710	959	1,248	1,658	2,151	2,168	2,116	2,006	2,248
Monetary Survey															
Thousandths of New Zaïres through 1979; New Zaïres 1980-87;															
Foreign Assets (Net) ... **31n**	2,136	3,419	20,296	28,323	37,938	36,700	28,481	28,251	37,349	22,748	−16,858	−16,931	−24,261	−21,913	−15,153
Domestic Credit ... **32**	27,200	30,100	32,600	36,367	36,522	47,185	62,829	82,105	107,043	185,342	253,668	396,594	564,182	777,636	1,017,089
Claims on Central Govt. (Net) ... **32an**	23,833	25,867	26,533	29,467	27,313	32,988	44,160	52,776	61,274	107,481	147,635	269,126	385,453	562,009	734,405
Claims on Nonfin.Pub.Enterprises ... **32c**	....	....	....	....	316	414	577	582	2,580	4,275	11,499	8,547	9,489	4,910	4,027
Claims on Private Sector ... **32d**	3,333	4,233	6,033	6,867	8,872	13,717	17,992	28,600	43,041	73,438	94,344	118,728	169,037	210,329	278,269
Claims on Other Banking Insts. ... **32f**	33	33	33	33	21	66	100	148	148	148	189	193	204	388	388
Money ... **34**	20,649	25,889	37,009	45,412	50,177	62,272	62,146	77,659	96,217	129,474	152,964	219,867	342,183	536,191	523,345
Quasi-Money ... **35**	1,133	1,400	1,400	5,200	6,483	7,129	12,636	13,191	29,004	36,971	30,166	32,959	60,410	84,923	128,774
of which: Foreign Currency Deps. ... **35x**	....	....	....	....	....	....	....	....	....	....	....	....	....	....	....
Restricted Deposits ... **36b**	2,216	2,472	5,689	6,672	5,971	3,318	3,217	2,962	4,174	18,170	13,795	34,571	104,519	170,438	214,173
Counterpart Funds ... **36e**	2,778	2,433	2,763	2,704	3,589	2,856	2,281	1,636	1,323	751	582	2,044	4,674	8,715	12,694
Capital Accounts ... **37a**	1,233	1,467	1,733	1,947	5,593	9,382	12,058	16,725	17,064	18,292	19,916	65,053	60,714	102,652	135,488
Revaluation Accounts ... **37ar**	....	....	....	....	....	....	....	....	....	....	....	....	....	....	....
Other Items (Net) ... **37r**	1,326	−142	4,302	2,755	2,647	−1,072	−1,027	−1,816	−3,391	4,432	19,386	25,169	−32,577	−147,196	−12,538
Money plus Quasi-Money ... **35l**	21,783	27,289	38,409	50,612	56,660	69,401	74,782	90,850	125,221	166,445	183,130	252,827	402,593	621,114	652,120
Other Banking Institutions															
Thousandths of New Zaïres through 1979;															
Claims on Private Sector ... **42d**	....	....	....	....	....	....	....	879	1,264	1,932	2,649	3,578	4,356	5,254	7,038
Sight Deposits ... **44**	....	....	....	....	....	....	....	80	244	707	1,069	1,365	2,591	3,066	5,354
Time and Savings Deposits ... **45**	....	....	....	....	....	....	....	2,138	2,445	3,175	3,804	4,930	5,759	7,356	14,527
Central Govt. Lending Funds ... **46f**	....	....	....	....	....	976	992	1,010	1,028	1,046	556	556	556	556	—
Other Items (Net) ... **47r**	....	....	....	....	....	....	....	−2,348	−2,452	−2,997	−2,780	−3,273	−4,550	−5,723	−12,844
Interest Rates															
Percent Per Annum															
Discount Rate *(End of Period)* ... **60**	....	....	....	....	....	....	....	....	....	....	....	....	....	12.0	12.0
Prices															
Index Numbers (1990=100):															
Consumer Prices ... **64.b**	....	....	....	....	....	....	....	....	....	....	....	....	....	....	....
Consumer Prices (1990=.01) ... **64.c**	....	....	....	....	....	....	....	....	....	....	....	....	....	....	....
Mining Production(1980=100) ... **66zx**	....	....	71.9	78.6	94.2	91.7	95.1	100.3[e]	109.7	113.1	109.9	98.1	103.5	94.6	88.7

Zaïre

636

	1980	1981	1982	1983	1984	1985	1986	1987	1988	1989	1990	1991	1992	1993	1994		
Exchange Rates																	
SDRs 1991-92, per SDR thereafter: End of Period																	
Market Rate	1,268.91	‡2.12	2.11	10.51	13.22	20.43	28.99	62.18	122.91	199.15	948.44	‡30.36	912.08	‡48.07	4,744.51	aa
US$ 1991-92, per US$ thereafter: End of Period (ae) Period Average (rf)																	
Market Rate	994.90	‡1.82	1.92	10.04	13.48	18.60	23.70	43.83	91.33	151.54	666.67	‡21.22	663.33	‡35.00	3,250.00	ae
Market Rate	933.11	‡1.46	1.92	4.30	12.04	16.62	19.87	37.46	62.34	127.12	239.47	‡5.19	215.14	‡2.51	1,194.12	rf
Period Averages																	
Market Rate	22,747.5ᵉ	15,434.9ᵉ	10,916.9ᵉ	7,896.2ᵉ	1,746.0	1,265.7	1,056.7	573.3	348.0	167.6	100.0	11.5	.3	3,665.0	329.9	ahx
Nominal Effective Exchange Rate	8,281.2	6,563.7	5,507.0	4,565.8	1,198.4	996.8	734.2	372.9	241.9	146.6	100.0	13.2	.4	—	—	nec
Real Effective Exchange Rate	333.4	308.5	325.1	378.5	151.5	136.9	136.8	118.4	122.1	121.1	100.0	96.7	93.7	117.2	89.4	rec
Fund Position																	
End of Period																	
Quota	228.00	228.00	228.00	291.00	291.00	291.00	291.00	291.00	291.00	291.00	291.00	291.00	291.00	291.00	291.00	2f.s
SDRs	—	.56	.02	20.97	—	.19	—	.08	—	3.74	—	—	—	—	—	1b.s
Reserve Position in the Fund	—	23.46	—	—	—	—	—	—	—	—	—	—	—	—	—	1c.s
Total Fund Cred.&Loans Outstg.	292.75	407.45	492.93	593.87	688.45	735.11	699.67	681.26	584.07	478.19	366.28	330.31	330.31	330.31	327.27	2tl
International Liquidity																	
End of Period																	
Total Reserves minus Gold	204.11	151.55	38.87	101.56	137.37	189.71	268.62	180.77	186.94	195.08	219.07	182.85	156.73	46.20	120.69	1l.d
SDRs	—	.65	.02	21.95	—	.21	—	.11	—	4.91	—	—	—	—	—	1b.d
Reserve Position in the Fund	—	27.31	—	—	—	—	—	—	—	—	—	—	—	—	—	1c.d
Foreign Exchange	204.11	123.59	38.85	79.61	137.37	189.50	268.62	180.66	186.94	190.17	219.07	182.85	156.73	46.20	120.69	1d.d
Gold (Million Fine Troy Ounces)	.298	.358	.410	.440	.466	.445	.467	.488	.450	.216	.108	.029	.028	.022	.028	1ad
Gold (National Valuation)	153.07	136.12	156.94	154.55	141.13	145.52	182.55	237.41	184.57	86.62	42.23	10.25	9.32	8.59	10.71	1and
Monetary Authorities: Other Liab.	133.13	61.33	168.56	6,572.27	205.64	714.57	418.36	198.13	241.88	193.60	217.38	305.63	290.50	272.40	280.95	4..d
Deposit Money Banks: Assets	171.65	146.62	110.66	109.51	74.65	77.49	104.39	125.48	94.58	174.81	131.61	86.13	68.00	62.37	81.18	7a.d
Liabilities	43.97	39.59	50.28	24.69	12.63	17.97	43.50	48.33	47.34	67.55	53.13	39.62	27.72	27.31	31.29	7b.d
Monetary Authorities																	
Thousands 1988-91; Millions 1992-93; Billions Beg. 1994: End of Period																	
Foreign Assets	‡355	526	542	28,659	2,570	2,844	10,641	16,901	‡26	53	171	4,664	‡122	6,682	‡515	11
Claims on Central Government	‡944	1,554	3,096	23,450	4,547	4,756	8,255	10,805	‡44	115	541	7,928	‡243	4,183	‡168	12a
Claims on Nonfin.Pub.Enterprises	‡—	—	—	—	45	57	81	102	‡1	1	8	431	‡1	2	‡1	12c
Claims on Private Sector	‡1	2	37	—	34	44	402	486	‡1	2	3	20	‡3	80	‡3	12d
Claims on Deposit Money Banks	‡43	17	11	191	383	727	1,243	5,075	‡5	13	16	6	‡—	127	‡16	12e
Claims on Other Banking Insts.	‡—	—	—	1	1	7	55	111	134	‡—	—	1	3	‡—	7	‡1	12f
Reserve Money	‡677	1,078	2,065	33,041	5,220	6,666	10,703	21,497	‡47	84	239	5,817	‡258	6,999	‡235	14
of which: Currency Outside DMBs	‡418	697	1,094	2,047	2,934	4,098	6,329	12,085	‡28	51	142	3,615	‡121	4,693	‡277	14a
Time & Foreign Currency Deposits	‡20	46	97	17	36	98	72	133	‡—	1	11	512	‡3	688	‡71	15
Restricted Deposits	‡146	139	272	60,119	751	299	1,032	1,439	‡4	7	41	1,117	‡20	1,262	‡100	16b
Foreign Liabilities	‡504	976	1,364	72,228	11,872	28,306	30,198	51,048	‡94	125	492	16,515	‡494	25,414	‡2,466	16c
Central Government Deposits	‡107	247	408	17,829	140	168	397	406	‡4	10	24	148	‡3	34	‡30	16d
Counterpart Funds	‡1	3	6	621	36	51	38	35	‡—	—	—	—	‡—	—	‡—	16e
Capital Accounts	‡183	222	196	89,990	1,428	2,930	5,115	8,887	‡27	40	117	2,982	‡107	4,537	‡412	17a
Other Items (Net)	‡−294	−611	−722	−221,545	−11,897	−30,034	−26,821	−49,137	‡−100	−83	−185	−14,037	‡−517	−27,853	‡−2,611	17r
Deposit Money Banks																	
Thousands 1988-91; Millions 1992-93; Billions Beg. 1994: End of Period																	
Reserves	‡237	337	800	1,037	2,015	2,241	4,026	9,077	‡15	29	64	1,759	‡131	2,122	‡26	20
Foreign Assets	‡171	267	212	1,099	1,006	1,441	2,474	5,500	‡9	26	88	1,828	‡45	2,183	‡264	21
Claims on Central Government	‡54	58	58	59	84	95	213	839	‡1	2	4	14	‡—	23	‡18	22a
Claims on Nonfin.Pub.Enterprises	‡2	10	5	5	21	4	26	—	‡—	—	2	21	‡—	8	‡8	22c
Claims on Private Sector	‡367	422	597	939	1,469	1,824	3,190	7,644	‡13	21	38	322	‡14	246	‡70	22d
Claims on Other Banking Insts.	‡—	—	—	—	—	—	—	—	‡—	—	—	—	‡—	—	‡—	22f
Demand Deposits	‡453	637	1,227	2,079	2,739	3,173	5,416	10,319	‡19	33	70	1,961	‡126	1,618	‡92	24
Time & Foreign Currency Deposits	‡138	167	254	297	414	519	851	2,284	‡8	9	36	652	‡23	1,077	‡141	25
Restricted Deposits	‡32	124	28	83	61	429	604	1,209	‡1	6	18	158	‡2	194	‡6	26b
Foreign Liabilities	‡44	72	96	248	170	334	1,031	2,118	‡4	10	35	841	‡18	956	‡102	26c
Central Government Deposits	‡22	27	42	268	133	167	145	435	‡1	2	5	60	‡5	100	‡—	26d
Counterpart Funds	‡—	—	—	—	—	—	—	144	‡—	—	—	—	‡—	—	‡—	26e
Credit from Monetary Authorities	‡43	17	11	191	383	727	1,243	5,075	‡5	13	16	6	‡—	127	‡16	26g
Capital Accounts	‡56	86	128	259	469	728	1,576	1,809	‡4	11	32	213	‡10	114	‡20	27a
Other Items (Net)	‡42	−34	−116	−286	228	−472	−938	−332	‡−4	−6	−17	52	‡5	396	‡9	27r
Post Office: Checking Deposits	‡3	3	3	3	4	5	8	40	‡—	—	—	—	‡—	—	‡—	24..i
Monetary Survey																	
Thousands 1988-91; Millions 1992-93; Billions Beg. 1994: End of Period																	
Foreign Assets (Net)	‡−21	−255	−707	−42,717	−8,466	−24,355	−18,114	−30,765	‡−63	−55	−269	−10,864	‡−345	−17,505	‡−1,789	31n
Domestic Credit	‡1,241	1,776	3,346	6,359	5,939	6,506	11,745	19,208	‡55	129	567	8,531	‡253	4,415	‡238	32
Claims on Central Govt. (Net)	‡871	1,341	2,707	5,414	4,362	4,522	7,935	10,843	‡41	104	516	7,734	‡235	4,072	‡156	32an
Claims on Nonfin.Pub.Enterprises	‡2	10	5	5	67	61	107	102	‡1	1	9	452	‡1	10	‡8	32c
Claims on Private Sector	‡368	424	634	939	1,503	1,868	3,592	8,130	‡13	23	41	342	‡16	326	‡73	32d
Claims on Other Banking Insts.	‡—	—	1	1	7	55	111	134	‡—	—	1	3	‡—	7	‡1	32f
Money	‡903	1,400	2,469	33,903	5,811	7,495	11,966	22,829	‡50	88	242	6,019	‡254	6,495	‡373	34
Quasi-Money	‡158	213	351	314	450	617	924	2,417	‡8	10	47	1,164	‡26	1,765	‡211	35
of which: Foreign Currency Deps.	....	....	77	87	118	268	305	736	‡2	5	34	1,088	‡23	1,627	‡209	35x
Restricted Deposits	‡178	262	300	60,202	813	729	1,636	2,647	‡5	13	59	1,275	‡23	1,456	‡107	36b
Counterpart Funds	‡1	3	6	621	36	51	38	179	‡—	—	—	—	‡—	—	‡—	36e
Capital Accounts	‡239	308	325	90,249	1,897	3,659	6,691	9,890	‡31	51	149	3,195	‡117	4,651	‡432	37a
Revaluation Accounts	....	....	....	....	−7,208	−10,019	169	−5,523	‡−29	121	301	−7,861	‡−287	−11,572	‡−1,506	37ar
Other Items (Net)	‡−260	−665	−813	−221,648	−4,325	−20,379	−27,793	−43,997	‡−74	−211	−500	−6,125	‡−225	−15,885	‡−1,168	37r
Money plus Quasi-Money	‡1,061	1,613	2,821	34,217	6,261	8,112	12,890	25,246	‡58	98	289	7,182	‡280	8,260	‡584	35l
Other Banking Institutions																	
New Zaïres in 1980: End of Period																	
Claims on Private Sector	‡10	....	....	....	....	....	....	....	....	....	....	....	....	....	....	42d
Sight Deposits	‡9	....	....	....	....	....	....	....	....	....	....	....	....	....	....	44
Time and Savings Deposits	‡15	....	....	....	....	....	....	....	....	....	....	....	....	....	....	45
Central Govt. Lending Funds	‡—	....	....	....	....	....	....	....	....	....	....	....	....	....	....	46f
Other Items (Net)	‡−14	....	....	....	....	....	....	....	....	....	....	....	....	....	....	47r
Interest Rates																	
Percent Per Annum																	
Discount Rate (End of Period)	12.0	12.0	15.0	20.0	20.0	26.0	26.0	29.0	37.0	50.0	45.0	55.0	55.0	95.0	145.0	60
Prices																	
Period Averages																	
Consumer Prices	....	....	....	....	....	15	‡27	55	100	2,254	‡95,344	....	....	....	....	64.b
Consumer Prices (1990=.01)	....	....	....	....	....	....	....	....	....	....	....	....	10	199	47,501	64.c
Mining Production (1980=100)	100.0	106.6	102.1	106.0	110.5	....	....	....	....	....	....	....	....	....	....	66zx

Zaïre

636

		1965	1966	1967	1968	1969	1970	1971	1972	1973	1974	1975	1976	1977	1978	1979
International Transactions															*Millions of US Dollars*	
Exports	70..d	102	141	135	190	227	259	229	231	335	432	275	301	329	308	499
Imports, cif	71..d	97	104	78	103	132	179	203	208	251	349	300	224	203	196	199
Imports, fob	71.v d	81	86	66	87	112	151	172	177	218	303	260	194	175	169	172
Balance of Payments															*Millions of US Dollars:*	
Goods: Exports f.o.b.	78aa d	....	....	....	....	....	....	....	....	....	....	....	....	....	....	....
Goods: Imports f.o.b.	78ab d	....	....	....	....	....	....	....	....	....	....	....	....	....	....	....
Trade Balance	78ac d	....	....	....	....	....	....	....	....	....	....	....	....	....	....	....
Services: Credit	78ad d	....	....	....	....	....	....	....	....	....	....	....	....	....	....	....
Services: Debit	78ae d	....	....	....	....	....	....	....	....	....	....	....	....	....	....	....
Balance on Goods and Services	78af d	....	....	....	....	....	....	....	....	....	....	....	....	....	....	....
Income: Credit	78ag d	....	....	....	....	....	....	....	....	....	....	....	....	....	....	....
Income: Debit	78ah d	....	....	....	....	....	....	....	....	....	....	....	....	....	....	....
Balance on Goods, Serv., & Inc.	78ai d	....	....	....	....	....	....	....	....	....	....	....	....	....	....	....
Current Transfers, n.i.e.: Credit	78aj d	....	....	....	....	....	....	....	....	....	....	....	....	....	....	....
Current Transfers: Debit	78ak d	....	....	....	....	....	....	....	....	....	....	....	....	....	....	....
Current Account, n.i.e.	78al d	....	....	....	....	....	....	....	....	....	....	....	....	....	....	....
Capital Account, n.i.e.: Credit	78ba d	....	....	....	....	....	....	....	....	....	....	....	....	....	....	....
Capital Account: Debit	78bb d	....	....	....	....	....	....	....	....	....	....	....	....	....	....	....
Capital Account, n.i.e.	78bc d	....	....	....	....	....	....	....	....	....	....	....	....	....	....	....
Direct Investment Abroad	78bd d	....	....	....	....	....	....	....	....	....	....	....	....	....	....	....
Dir. Invest. in Rep. Econ., n.i.e.	78be d	....	....	....	....	....	....	....	....	....	....	....	....	....	....	....
Portfolio Investment Assets	78bf d	....	....	....	....	....	....	....	....	....	....	....	....	....	....	....
Portfolio Investment Liab., n.i.e.	78bg d	....	....	....	....	....	....	....	....	....	....	....	....	....	....	....
Other Investment Assets	78bh d	....	....	....	....	....	....	....	....	....	....	....	....	....	....	....
Other Investment Liab., n.i.e.	78bi d	....	....	....	....	....	....	....	....	....	....	....	....	....	....	....
Financial Account, n.i.e.	78bj d	....	....	....	....	....	....	....	....	....	....	....	....	....	....	....
Net Errors and Omissions	78ca d	....	....	....	....	....	....	....	....	....	....	....	....	....	....	....
Overall Balance	78cb d	....	....	....	....	....	....	....	....	....	....	....	....	....	....	....
Reserves and Related Items	79da d	....	....	....	....	....	....	....	....	....	....	....	....	....	....	....
Reserve Assets	79db d	....	....	....	....	....	....	....	....	....	....	....	....	....	....	....
Use of Fund Credit and Loans	79dc d	....	....	....	....	....	....	....	....	....	....	....	....	....	....	....
Liabs.Constit.For.Auth.Reserves	79dd d	....	....	....	....	....	....	....	....	....	....	....	....	....	....	....
Exceptional Financing	79de d	....	....	....	....	....	....	....	....	....	....	....	....	....	....	....
Government Finance										*Thousandths of New Zaïres through 1979; New Zaïres 1980-87;*						
Deficit (-) or Surplus	80	....	-3,367	-1,900	-6,067	300	-6,767	ⅼ-25,533	-27,333	-47,000	-108,100	-72,033	-209,000	-149,867	-198,467	-182,867
Revenue	81	....	20,600	32,800	62,067	89,833	107,333	ⅼ98,733	102,100	128,433	178,033	145,033	163,533	229,367	246,333	660,100
Grants Received	81z	....	2,100	4,533	6,333	8,067	9,967	ⅼ10,867	12,667	18,100	18,000	18,467	27,400	47,167	57,033	158,567
Expenditure	82	....	26,267	40,800	75,767	99,600	123,267	ⅼ132,300	141,567	192,733	285,400	235,933	402,033	426,100	502,067	1,000,267
Lending Minus Repayments	83	....	-200	-1,567	-1,300	-2,000	800	ⅼ2,833	533	800	18,733	-400	-2,100	300	-233	1,267
Financing																
Domestic	84a	....	1,500	-733	2,700	-1,900	4,200	ⅼ10,600	9,267	10,633	68,600	37,433	173,700	97,467	175,200	161,633
Foreign	85a	....	1,867	2,633	3,367	1,600	2,567	ⅼ14,933	18,067	36,367	39,500	34,600	35,300	52,400	23,267	21,233
Debt: Domestic	88a	....	....	....	....	....	....	ⅼ47,067	57,233	65,367	114,067	154,100	277,467	381,600	568,900	812,967
Foreign	89a	....	....	....	....	....	....	ⅼ53,400	47,700	88,900	127,233	159,567	304,100	358,167	477,767	951,333
National Accounts										*Thousandths of New Zaïres through 1979; New Zaïres 1980-87:*						
Exports of Goods & Services	90c	....	24,600	....	ⅼ97,400	121,333	138,333	124,567	125,833	187,233	272,400	173,167	308,867	372,267	405,433	914,033
Government Consumption	91f	....	21,000	....	46,700	65,600	88,500	94,967	88,333	104,100	142,600	150,633	185,100	257,400	297,800	619,000
Gross Fixed Capital Formation	93e	....	13,833	....	46,500	72,233	67,500	99,767	123,767	124,000	183,667	182,500	218,600	457,200	316,733	508,633
Increase/Decrease(-) in Stocks	93i	....	....	....	133	—	14,000	15,433	5,133	23,333	—	21,767	28,600	50,633	18,933	217,700
Private Consumption	96f	....	65,000	....	ⅼ100,000	141,100	137,733	170,733	216,600	268,300	313,500	406,767	696,400	949,533	1,270,733	2,228,767
Imports of Goods & Services	98c	....	-23,000	....	ⅼ-52,333	-107,133	-133,533	-155,767	-173,900	-215,167	-312,467	-295,133	-484,167	-768,300	-482,800	-786,467
Gross Domestic Product = GDP	99b	....	101,367	....	ⅼ200,000	293,133	312,533	349,700	385,767	491,800	599,700	639,333	953,333	1,318,667	1,826,667	3,701,667
Net Factor Inc/Pmts(-) Abroad	98.n	1,333	4,233	11,400	10,900	19,567	-18,633	-18,500	-19,167	-25,067	-35,033	-31,367	-38,933	-50,200	-59,833	-128,067
Gross National Product = GNP	99a	....	97,133	....	ⅼ300,000	312,700	262,300	283,867	314,000	421,967	505,533	528,433	777,900	1,050,633	1,420,000	2,827,467
Nat'l Income, Market Prices	99e	....	89,000	....	ⅼ200,000	249,233	275,767	291,733	279,333	378,333	463,367	487,200	719,467	848,133	1,186,767	2,323,033
GDP 1990 Prices (Thousands)	99b.p	....	....	....	....	....	2,520	2,672	2,676	2,893	2,984	2,833	2,685	2,705	2,561	2,567
GDP Deflator (1990=100)	99bi p	—	—	—	ⅼ1	1	—	—	—	—	—	—	—	—	—	—
																Millions:
Population	99z	17.57	18.35	19.15	20.00	20.88	21.64	22.22	22.86	23.51	24.17	ⅼ22.58	23.29	24.02	24.78	ⅼ25.56

Exchange Rates: On June 23, 1967, the zaire, equal to 1,000 Congo francs, was introduced. On October 22, 1993, the new zaire, equal to three million old zaires, was introduced.

Government Finance: ⅼ Beginning in 1971, data are as reported in the *Government Finance Statistics Yearbook* and cover consolidated central government.

Zaïre

	1980	1981	1982	1983	1984	1985	1986	1987	1988	1989	1990	1991	1992	1993	1994	International Transactions	
Millions of US Dollars																	
	544	193	133	377	‡1,005	950	1,100	975	1,120	1,254	999	830	427	369	419	Exports	70..d
	278	223	160	157	‡685	792	875	756	763	850	888	711	420	372	382	Imports, cif	71..d
	240	192	138	135	‡590	682	754	652	658	733	765	613	362	321	329	Imports, fob	71.vd
Minus Sign Indicates Debit																**Balance of Payments**	
	....	....	1,601	1,686	1,918	1,853	1,844	1,732	2,178	2,201	2,138	....	....	....	....	Goods: Exports f.o.b.	78aad
	....	....	−1,297	−1,213	−1,176	−1,247	−1,283	−1,376	−1,645	−1,683	−1,539	....	....	....	....	Goods: Imports f.o.b.	78abd
	....	....	304	473	742	606	561	356	533	518	599	....	....	....	....	Trade Balance	78acd
	....	....	57	100	115	125	155	216	150	137	157	....	....	....	....	Services: Credit	78add
	....	....	−608	−690	−694	−596	−662	−723	−895	−921	−907	....	....	....	....	Services: Debit	78aed
	....	....	−247	−117	163	135	54	−151	−212	−266	−151	....	....	....	....	Balance on Goods and Services	78afd
	....	....	26	15	27	27	33	45	36	28	14	....	....	....	....	Income: Credit	78agd
	....	....	−522	−424	−598	−596	−624	−689	−563	−539	−642	....	....	....	....	Income: Debit	78ahd
	....	....	−743	−526	−408	−434	−537	−795	−739	−777	−779	....	....	....	....	Balance on Goods, Serv., & Inc.	78aid
	....	....	—	176	174	199	184	220	226	276	217	....	....	....	....	Current Transfers, n.i.e.: Credit	78ajd
	....	....	−9	....	−91	−55	−62	−70	−67	−109	−81	....	....	....	....	Current Transfers: Debit	78akd
	....	....	−752	−350	−325	−290	−415	−645	−580	−610	−643	....	....	....	....	Current Account, n.i.e.	78ald
	....	....	....	....	....	....	....	....	....	....	....	....	....	....	....	Capital Account, n.i.e.: Credit	78bad
	....	....	....	....	....	....	....	....	....	....	....	....	....	....	....	Capital Account: Debit	78bbd
	....	....	....	....	....	....	....	....	....	....	....	....	....	....	....	Capital Account, n.i.e.	78bcd
	....	....	....	....	....	....	....	....	....	....	....	....	....	....	....	Direct Investment Abroad	78bdd
	....	....	....	....	....	....	....	....	....	....	....	....	....	....	....	Dir. Invest. in Rep. Econ., n.i.e.	78bed
	....	....	....	....	....	....	....	....	....	....	....	....	....	....	....	Portfolio Investment Assets	78bfd
	....	....	....	....	....	....	....	....	....	....	....	....	....	....	....	Portfolio Investment Liab., n.i.e.	78bgd
	....	....	109	−16	80	175	74	102	−54	86	111	....	....	....	....	Other Investment Assets	78bhd
	....	....	−184	−200	−281	−268	−161	−32	43	−146	−331	....	....	....	....	Other Investment Liab., n.i.e.	78bid
	....	....	−75	−216	−201	−93	−87	70	−11	−60	−220	....	....	....	....	Financial Account, n.i.e.	78bjd
	....	....	131	34	−23	—	−17	14	−133	111	102	....	....	....	....	Net Errors and Omissions	78cad
	....	....	−696	−532	−549	−383	−519	−561	−724	−559	−761	....	....	....	....	Overall Balance	78cbd
	....	....	696	532	549	383	519	561	724	559	761	....	....	....	....	Reserves and Related Items	79dad
	....	....	62	−31	48	−30	36	−90	95	−71	65	....	....	....	....	Reserve Assets	79dbd
	....	....	96	105	97	48	−42	−23	−132	−139	−151	....	....	....	....	Use of Fund Credit and Loans	79dcd
	....	....	....	....	....	....	....	....	....	....	....	....	....	....	....	Liabs.Constit.For.Auth.Reserves	79ddd
	....	....	538	458	403	365	525	674	761	769	847	....	....	....	....	Exceptional Financing	79ded
Thousands 1988-91; Millions beg. 1992: Year Ending December 31																**Government Finance**	
	‡−111	−719	−1,161	....	....	....	....	....	‡−44	—	−146	−6,782	‡−213	−3,585	....	Deficit (-) or Surplus	80
	‡1,266	1,581	2,060	3,823	8,953	14,237	16,683	29,347	‡54	131	226	2,351	‡56	1,104	....	Revenue	81
	‡284	387	335	....	....	....	....	....	‡13	25	48	529	‡—	....	....	Grants Received	81z
	‡1,660	2,688	3,549	....	....	....	....	....	‡111	156	420	9,662	‡269	4,689	....	Expenditure	82
	‡1	—	7	....	....	....	....	....	‡—	—	—	—	‡—	—	....	Lending Minus Repayments	83
																Financing	
	‡69	479	1,069	....	....	520	3,330	2,833	‡44	−3	146	6,782	‡213	3,585	....	Domestic	84a
	‡42	241	92	....	....	....	....	....	‡—	4	—	—	‡—	—	....	Foreign	85a
	‡1,041	1,660	2,731	....	....	4,950	8,313	11,100	‡45	30	176	7,734	‡235	4,072	....	Debt: Domestic	88a
	‡2,532	4,378	2,693	....	58,580	....	....	....	‡642	1,090	6,314	49,057	‡2,038	23,925	....	Foreign	89a
Thousands 1988-91; Millions Beginning 1992																**National Accounts**	
	‡2,333	3,000	3,667	8,667	23,667	32,333	39,667	74,667	‡141	292	621	10,323	‡381	....	....	Exports of Goods & Services	90c
	‡919	2,000	2,467	3,567	6,200	9,200	12,867	28,500	‡70	116	258	6,282	‡384	....	....	Government Consumption	91f
	‡1,145	1,558	2,433	4,767	10,033	13,333	20,633	39,833	‡81	153	288	2,878	‡125	....	....	Gross Fixed Capital Formation	93e
	‡281	431	−267	−367	−100	1,600	600	800	‡−1	11	−85	−245	‡−4	....	....	Increase/Decrease(-) in Stocks	93i
	‡11,000	14,667	21,233	38,567	76,800	90,767	124,767	226,100	‡415	860	1,600	37,688	‡1,214	....	....	Private Consumption	96f
	‡−2,126	−3,000	−3,333	−8,000	−22,000	−27,667	−37,667	−82,667	‡−154	−285	−630	−10,438	‡−336	....	....	Imports of Goods & Services	98c
	‡13,333	18,333	26,167	47,267	94,600	119,600	160,867	287,000	‡552	1,147	2,239	47,208	‡1,765	....	....	Gross Domestic Product = GDP	99b
	‡−247	−667	−633	−1,367	−5,533	9,300	−8,800	−13,400	‡−20	−47	−63	−647	‡−2	....	....	Net Factor Inc/Pmts(-) Abroad	98.n
	‡13,000	18,000	25,733	46,267	89,567	111,100	153,267	276,267	‡536	1,109	2,183	46,699	‡1,766	....	....	Gross National Product = GNP	99a
	‡12,667	17,333	24,933	44,833	86,733	107,500	148,433	267,667	‡519	1,075	2,117	45,298	‡1,702	....	....	Nat'l Income, Market Prices	99e
	‡1,992	2,011	2,002	2,029	2,129	2,153	2,255	2,314	2,328	2,295	2,239	1,964	1,759	....	....	GDP 1990 Prices (Thousands)	99b.p
	1	1	1	2	4	6	7	12	24	50	100	2,403	100,384	....	....	GDP Deflator (1990=100)	99bi p
Midyear Estimates																	
	26.38	27.23	28.12	29.04	29.92	30.98	31.50	32.46	33.46	34.49	35.56	36.67	‡39.94	41.23	....	Population	99z

Zambia
754

		1965	1966	1967	1968	1969	1970	1971	1972	1973	1974	1975	1976	1977	1978	1979
Exchange Rates															*SDRs per Kwacha:*	
Principal Rate	ac	1.4000	1.4000	1.4000	1.4000	1.4000	1.4000	1.2895	1.2883	1.2883	1.2693	1.3275	1.0848	1.0848	I.9763	.9763
															US Dollars per Kwacha:	
Principal Rate	ag	1.4000	1.4000	1.4000	1.4000	1.4000	1.4000	1.4000	1.3987	1.5541	1.5541	1.5541	1.2603	1.3161	1.2704	1.2845
Principal Rate	rh	1.4000	1.4000	1.4000	1.4000	1.4000	1.4000	1.4000	1.3999^e	1.5347	1.5541^e	1.5541^e	1.4144	1.2663^e	1.2502	1.2606
															Index Numbers (1990=100):	
Principal Rate	ah x	4,058.6^e	4,058.6^e	4,058.6^e	4,058.6^e	4,058.6^e	4,058.6^e	379.9	4,058.4^e	4,448.9	4,505.3^e	4,505.3^e	4,100.4	3,671.0^e	3,624.3	3,654.4
Nominal Effective Exchange Rate	ne c	....	....	....	....	....	....	....	....	....	....	....	....	....	....	1,014.3
Real Effective Exchange Rate	re c	....	....	....	....	....	....	....	....	....	....	....	....	....	....	170.4
Fund Position															*Millions of SDRs:*	
Quota	2f. s	50.0	50.0	50.0	50.0	50.0	76.0	76.0	76.0	76.0	76.0	76.0	76.0	76.0	141.0	141.0
SDRs	1b. s	—	—	—	—	—	8.9	18.9	.2	—	—	—	—	—	12.1	4.2
Reserve Position in the Fund	1c. s	3.2	3.2	6.3	6.4	8.9	19.0	19.0	—	—	11.7	15.7	19.2	11.4	12.1	4.2
Total Fund Cred.&Loans Outstg.	2tl	—	—	—	—	—	—	19.0	38.0	57.0	57.0	75.9	95.2	95.2	245.1	343.0
International Liquidity											*Millions of US Dollars Unless Otherwise Indicated:*						
Total Reserves minus Gold	1l. d	196.0	204.8	174.5	193.5	362.9	508.0	277.1	158.4	185.5	164.4	142.0	92.7	66.3	51.1	80.0
SDRs	1b. d	—	—	—	—	—	8.9	20.6	.2	—	14.3	18.4	22.3	13.8	15.8	5.6
Reserve Position in the Fund	1c. d	3.2	3.2	6.2	6.4	8.9	19.0	20.6	—	—	—	—	—	—	—	—
Foreign Exchange	1d. d	192.8	201.6	168.3	187.1	354.0	480.1	235.9	158.2	185.5	150.1	123.6	70.4	52.5	35.3	74.4
Gold (Million Fine Troy Ounces)	1ad	.223	.363	.363	.183	.183	.183	.200	.200	.200	.168	.168	.168	.168	.201	.217
Gold (National Valuation)	1an d	3.6	5.8	5.8	5.8	5.8	5.8	....	....	....	7.1	7.1	6.8	7.1	9.1	10.7
Monetary Authorities: Other Liab.	4.. d	—	—	—	—	—	—	—	—	—	—	122.4	77.5	98.0	666.5	471.3
Deposit Money Banks: Assets	7a. d	14.3	23.6	21.3	7.0	14.3	24.8	13.8	10.7	9.0	18.6	7.6	12.5	10.7	33.4	96.6
Deposit Money Banks: Liabilities	7b. d	5.9	13.0	13.4	9.9	7.9	4.2	14.0	25.1	26.8	36.8	37.3	36.6	55.6	59.5	48.2
of which: Liab. to Nonbanks	7bd d	....	....	....	....	....	....	10.7	20.1	24.7	33.1	29.4	27.7	37.3	46.2	41.7
Monetary Authorities															*Millions of Kwacha:*	
Foreign Assets	11	143	150	129	142	263	367	197	115	124	132	96	79	56	47	71
Claims on Central Government	12a	6	6	8	6	—	−5	18	57	104	62	215	276	256	908	854
Claims on Private Sector	12d	—	—	4	—	2	2	2	—	1	1	48	53	124	115	81
Reserve Money	14	33	42	52	63	73	71	89	106	123	128	175	208	222	235	249
of which: Currency Outside DMBs	14a	19	28	35	40	41	43	58	61	69	80	102	121	118	131	126
Priv.Sect.Demand Dep.	14d	....	....	....	....	....	....	....	....	....	....	....	....	....	....	....
Time, Savings,& Fgn.Currency Dep.	15	....	....	....	....	....	....	....	....	....	....	....	....	....	....	....
Foreign Liabilities	16c	—	—	—	—	—	—	15	30	45	45	61	90	89	726	690
Central Government Deposits	16d	112	109	81	77	164	198	32	5	21	24	18	19	23	9	2
Other Items (Net)	17r	4	6	9	9	14	30	81	33	24	−3	21	9	21	45	33
Deposit Money Banks															*Millions of Kwacha:*	
Reserves	20	15	14	16	22	31	28	34	45	57	56	58	87	100	103	222
Foreign Assets	21	10	17	15	5	10	18	10	8	6	12	5	10	8	26	75
Claims on Central Government	22a	21	22	14	40	54	50	39	82	115	39	134	280	531	142	281
Claims on Private Sector	22d	42	67	93	91	111	135	181	165	176	337	347	348	348	312	405
Demand Deposits	24	58	77	87	120	141	143	I 140	140	174	186	220	256	268	261	387
Time and Savings Deposits	25	31	40	48	58	80	104	I 120	140	152	175	163	223	306	243	316
Foreign Liabilities	26c	4	9	10	7	6	3	I 10	18	17	24	24	29	42	47	37
Central Government Deposits	26d	4	6	10	9	10	16	I 15	13	27	28	29	20	32	27	30
Other Items (Net)	27r	−9	−12	−15	−33	−29	−30	I −21	−12	−16	32	108	206	353	10	213
Monetary Survey															*Millions of Kwacha:*	
Foreign Assets (Net)	31n	149	158	134	140	268	382	I 182	75	67	75	16	−30	−68	−699	−582
Domestic Credit	32	−46	−19	28	53	−6	−27	I 192	287	348	386	697	919	1,204	1,440	1,589
Claims on Central Govt. (Net)	32an	−89	−87	−69	−39	−120	−169	I 9	122	171	49	303	518	732	1,014	1,103
Claims on Private Sector	32d	43	67	96	91	113	137	183	165	177	337	394	401	472	426	485
Money	34	76	105	122	161	181	186	I 199	201	259	266	331	400	393	397	517
Quasi-Money	35	31	40	48	58	100	170	....	....	....	....	....	....	....	....	....
Other Items (Net)	37r	−5	−6	−7	−25	−19	—	56	21	5	21	144	215	379	56	147
Money plus Quasi-Money	35l	108	145	169	219	282	356	I 319	341	411	441	494	623	699	639	832
Interest Rates															*Percent Per Annum*	
Discount Rate (End of Period)	60	4.50	4.50	5.00	5.00	5.00	5.00	5.00	5.00	5.00	5.00	5.00	5.00	6.00	6.00	6.50
Treasury Bill Rate	60c	....	....	....	....	....	....	3.34	4.34	3.94	3.96	4.00	4.15	4.38	4.38	4.44
Deposit Rate	60l	....	....	....	....	....	....	3.50	3.75	4.00	4.00	4.00	5.31	6.25	6.25	6.75
Lending Rate	60p	....	....	....	....	....	....	7.00	7.25	7.50	7.50	7.50	8.13	8.25	8.25	9.08
Prices and Production															*Index Numbers (1990=100):*	
Wholesale Prices	63	....	.6	.6	.7	.8	.7	.7	.7	.9	1.0	.9	1.1	1.4	1.6	2.0
Home & Import Goods	63a	....	.5	.5	.5	.5	.6	.6	.6	.7	.8	.9	1.1	1.3	1.6	1.8
Consumer Prices	64	.6	.7	.7	.8	.8	.8	I.9	.9	1.0	1.1	1.2	1.4	1.7	1.9	2.1
Industrial Production	66	....	....	....	....	105.2	100.7	97.7	108.5	108.6	117.8	109.1	116.0	110.8	110.9	104.1
Mining Production	66zx	136.2	117.1	121.9	132.4	I 150.9	139.4	130.4	143.0	140.2	146.3	132.7	144.5	135.0	135.5	115.7

Zambia

754

	1980	1981	1982	1983	1984	1985	1986	1987	1988	1989	1990	1991	1992	1993	1994		
	End of Period															**Exchange Rates**	
	.9763	.9763	.9763	.7810	.4636	.1597	.0643	.0881	.0743	.0351	.0164	.0079	.0020	.0015	.0007	Principal Rate	ac
	End of Period (ag)	*Period Average (rh)*															
	1.2446	1.1328	1.0756	.6619	.4544	.1754	.0787	.1250	.1000	.0462	.0234	.0112	.0028	.0020	.0010	Principal Rate	ag
	1.2682	1.1516	1.0773	.7996	.5573	.3685	.1369	.1125	.1216	.0775	.0345	.0162	.0064	.0023	.0013	Principal Rate	rh
	Period Averages																
	3,676.4	3,338.5	3,123.2	2,318.1	1,615.6	1,068.2	396.9	326.1	352.4	224.7	100.0	46.9	18.5	6.6	3.7	Principal Rate	ah x
	1,044.5	1,092.2	1,213.4	1,074.1	872.5	697.3	238.1	191.3	228.4	183.6	100.0	57.1	24.3	10.4	7.6	Nominal Effective Exchange Rate	ne c
	135.1	138.1	153.9	142.7	122.7	113.4	54.6	57.7	89.5	116.4	100.0	88.6	94.6	108.8	103.4	Real Effective Exchange Rate	re c
	End of Period															**Fund Position**	
	211.5	211.5	211.5	270.3	270.3	270.3	270.3	270.3	270.3	270.3	270.3	270.3	270.3	270.3	270.3	Quota	2f. s
	—	7.7	14.5	—	—	—	—	—	—	—	—	—	—	—	—	SDRs	1b. s
	—	7.5	—	—	—	—	—	—	—	—	—	—	—	—	—	Reserve Position in the Fund	1c. s
	350.8	670.6	618.3	678.5	753.8	728.9	701.6	698.8	698.8	685.0	666.7	641.6	615.6	565.8	551.2	Total Fund Cred.&Loans Outstg.	2tl
	End of Period															**International Liquidity**	
	78.2	56.2	58.2	54.5	54.2	200.1	70.3	108.8	134.0	116.2	193.1	184.6	....	192.3	....	Total Reserves minus Gold	1l. d
	—	8.9	16.0	—	—	—	—	—	—	—	—	—	—	—	—	SDRs	1b. d
	—	8.7	—	—	—	—	—	—	—	—	—	—	—	—	—	Reserve Position in the Fund	1c. d
	78.2	38.5	42.2	54.5	54.2	200.1	70.3	108.8	134.0	116.2	193.1	184.6	....	192.3	....	Foreign Exchange	1d. d
	.217	.217	.217	.217	.002	.003	.003	.004	.013	.017	.021	.022	....	....	....	Gold (Million Fine Troy Ounces)	1ad
	10.4	9.5	83.5	70.9	.7	.9	1.0	1.8	4.1	....	....	....	....	....	....	Gold (National Valuation)	1an d
	650.6	618.6	938.8	699.5	506.7	478.2	343.6	408.2	471.4	523.6	578.4	483.3	....	....	....	Monetary Authorities: Other Liab.	4.. d
	56.1	93.7	33.1	37.7	29.3	48.2	60.7	118.6	141.4	169.6	165.7	134.9	120.7	205.5	53.6	Deposit Money Banks: Assets	7a. d
	77.7	64.8	108.2	46.4	54.6	90.5	44.0	61.8	50.3	55.0	49.3	34.1	20.0	16.8	7.1	Deposit Money Banks: Liabilities	7b. d
	39.0	40.5	44.7	32.2	20.4	10.8	8.7	13.2	12.0	15.8	8.8	6.4	3.2	4.5	....	*of which:* Liab. to Nonbanks	7bd d
	End of Period															**Monetary Authorities**	
	71	53	130	174	123	1,146	906	675	ⅰ1,394	2,602	9,217	14,071	....	....		Foreign Assets	11
	1,114	1,392	1,664	1,850	1,942	2,149	2,629	2,267	ⅰ1,288	918	1,239	1,268	....	....		Claims on Central Government	12a
	62	62	161	166	166	161	161	161	ⅰ79	82	942	374	....	....		Claims on Private Sector	12d
	278	332	379	432	516	632	1,716	2,415	4,832	6,324	11,269	22,704	....	....		Reserve Money	14
	151	190	210	239	286	343	593	974	1,759	2,250	4,610	9,188	....	....		*of which:* Currency Outside DMBs	14a
	....	....	....	....	....	....	....	1	1	2	7	6	....	....		Priv.Sect.Demand Dep.	14d
	....	....	....	....	....	....	....	....	1	3	5	14	....	....		Time, Savings,& Fgn.Currency Dep.	15
	810	1,175	1,295	1,711	2,358	5,548	12,138	9,586	ⅰ14,123	30,825	65,284	124,654	....	....		Foreign Liabilities	16c
	3	1	1	2	1	8	5	4	ⅰ–1,594	–2,641	–472	–29,341	....	....		Central Government Deposits	16d
	51	–64	60	–382	–1,030	–4,701	–13,712	–11,378	ⅰ–14,602	–30,477	–64,694	–122,259	....	....		Other Items (Net)	17r
	End of Period															**Deposit Money Banks**	
	128	139	160	196	276	370	985	1,192	3,191	4,433	7,918	14,296	20,774	49,801	....	Reserves	20
	45	83	31	57	65	275	771	949	1,414	3,672	7,083	12,003	43,404	102,765	....	Foreign Assets	21
	275	118	353	310	431	787	1,394	2,457	2,591	3,436	4,134	14,195	38,255	71,330	....	Claims on Central Government	22a
	447	711	760	887	1,055	1,191	1,790	2,397	4,450	9,013	13,465	22,501	42,585	98,062	....	Claims on Private Sector	22d
	358	371	473	548	581	886	1,708	2,248	3,484	5,695	7,927	13,166	32,403	55,821	....	Demand Deposits	24
	388	415	620	659	834	870	1,758	3,041	4,881	8,778	11,842	25,984	44,865	102,925	....	Time and Savings Deposits	25
	62	57	101	70	120	516	560	495	504	1,190	2,108	3,031	7,197	8,421	....	Foreign Liabilities	26c
	33	21	25	31	38	56	135	231	383	762	1,193	3,168	5,722	5,786	....	Central Government Deposits	26d
	54	192	84	143	253	294	781	981	2,394	4,129	9,531	17,665	54,835	149,003	....	Other Items (Net)	27r
	End of Period															**Monetary Survey**	
	–756	–1,097	–1,235	–1,550	–2,291	–4,644	–11,020	–8,457	ⅰ–11,819	–25,741	–51,091	–101,610	....	....		Foreign Assets (Net)	31n
	1,863	2,261	2,910	3,180	3,554	4,223	5,834	7,047	ⅰ9,619	15,328	19,059	64,510	....	....		Domestic Credit	32
	1,354	1,487	1,990	2,128	2,334	2,871	3,884	4,490	ⅰ5,090	6,233	4,652	41,636	....	....		Claims on Central Govt. (Net)	32an
	509	773	920	1,052	1,220	1,352	1,951	2,558	ⅰ4,529	9,095	14,407	22,874	....	....		Claims on Private Sector	32d
	519	564	689	795	870	1,231	2,304	3,225	ⅰ5,244	7,947	12,543	22,360	....	....		Money	34
	....	....	....	....	....	....	....	....	ⅰ4,882	8,781	11,847	25,997	....	....		Quasi-Money	35
	103	131	154	–242	–823	–4,487	–12,794	–10,148	ⅰ–12,326	–26,707	–56,422	–105,374	....	....		Other Items (Net)	37r
	907	979	1,309	1,454	1,704	2,102	4,062	6,266	ⅰ10,126	16,728	24,390	48,357	....	....		Money plus Quasi-Money	35l
	Percent Per Annum															**Interest Rates**	
	6.50	7.50	7.50	10.00	14.50	25.00	30.00	15.00	15.00	....	....	....	47.00	72.50	20.48	Discount Rate *(End of Period)*	60
	4.50	5.75	6.00	7.50	7.67	13.21	24.25	16.50	15.17	18.50	25.92	....	....	124.03	74.20	Treasury Bill Rate	60c
	7.00	6.17	6.00	7.00	7.71	15.33	17.74	13.23	11.44	11.44	25.65	....	48.50	....	46.14	Deposit Rate	60l
	9.50	9.50	9.50	13.00	14.54	18.60	27.40	21.20	18.39	18.39	35.10	....	54.57	113.31	70.56	Lending Rate	60p
	Period Averages															**Prices and Production**	
	2.2	2.3	2.4	3.0	3.9	5.7	12.2	22.6	25.2	46.4	100.0	191.7	424.2	....	....	Wholesale Prices	63
	2.2	2.3	2.6	3.2	4.0	5.5	11.4	22.9	24.0	46.1	100.0	193.0	447.2	....	....	Home & Import Goods	63a
	2.4	2.7	3.0	3.6	4.4	ⅰ6.0	9.1	13.0	20.2	46.0	100.0	192.6	572.8	1,655.4	....	Consumer Prices	64
	ⅰ107.3	103.1	100.1	107.8	105.4	106.8	104.3	102.2	106.2	103.6	100.0	99.5	105.0	....	....	Industrial Production	66
	ⅰ125.2	114.1	118.1	116.0	111.8	108.6	107.1	104.6	100.9	102.5	100.0	90.1	100.8	93.7	....	Mining Production	66zx

Zambia

754

		1965	1966	1967	1968	1969	1970	1971	1972	1973	1974	1975	1976	1977	1978	1979
International Transactions															*Millions of Kwacha*	
Exports	70	376.2	493.6	467.3	542.0	766.3	715.0	875.8	541.8	742.1	905.1	521.2	749.1	708.0	686.7	1,090.0
Imports, cif	71	246.6	284.5	368.3	386.1	371.4	399.5	463.1	484.9	421.1	622.6	732.1	564.7	621.6	590.9	717.4
Imports, fob	71.v	213.3	246.1	314.0	326.6	311.8	340.9	396.9	403.8	346.9	506.6	597.6	468.6	530.0	492.8	593.8
Balance of Payments															*Millions of US Dollars:*	
Goods: Exports f.o.b.	78aa d														831	1,408
Goods: Imports f.o.b.	78ab d														−618	−756
Trade Balance	78ac d														213	652
Services: Credit	78ad d														113	116
Services: Debit	78ae d														−408	−456
Balance on Goods and Services	78af d														−82	311
Income: Credit	78ag d														8	11
Income: Debit	78ah d														−162	−181
Balance on Goods, Serv., & Inc.	78ai d														−236	142
Current Transfers, n.i.e.: Credit	78aj d														27	38
Current Transfers: Debit	78ak d														−72	−101
Current Account, n.i.e.	78al d														−281	78
Capital Account, n.i.e.: Credit	78ba d														−17	−41
Capital Account: Debit	78bb d															
Capital Account, n.i.e.	78bc d														−17	−41
Direct Investment Abroad	78bd d															
Dir. Invest. in Rep. Econ., n.i.e.	78be d														39	35
Portfolio Investment Assets	78bf d														—	—
Portfolio Investment Liab., n.i.e.	78bg d														—	—
Other Investment Assets	78bh d														17	−25
Other Investment Liab., n.i.e.	78bi d														−25	109
Financial Account, n.i.e.	78bj d														30	119
Net Errors and Omissions	78ca d														−75	−88
Overall Balance	78cb d														−342	68
Reserves and Related Items	79da d														342	−68
Reserve Assets	79db d														5	13
Use of Fund Credit and Loans	79dc d														185	126
Liabs.Constit.For.Auth.Reserves	79dd d														—	—
Exceptional Financing	79de d														152	−207
Government Finance															*Millions of Kwacha:*	
Deficit (-) or Surplus	80	24	30	−39	−105	35	23	−194	I−176	−266	64	−341	−270	−261	−325	−241
Revenue	81	209	212	270	297	403	457	313	I297	469	649	448	453	498	556	594
Grants Received	81z								I1	1	1	15	9	34	20	26
Expenditure	82	175	175	269	392	334	360	482	I433	469	531	678	685	706	669	810
Lending Minus Repayments	83	10	7	40	11	34	74	24	I41	268	54	125	47	87	231	52
Financing																
Net Borrowing: Domestic	84a				56	11	3	8	I129	119		267	240	243	298	
Foreign	85a				20	21	13	36	I15	147	37	59	30	19	21	138
Use of Cash Balances	87	−42	−35	28	30	−67	−40	150	I32	1		15	—	−1	5	
Debt: Domestic	88a							239	I335	469	345	574	818	1,146	1,456	
Foreign	89a							163							557	634	
National Accounts															*Millions of Kwacha*	
Exports of Goods & Services	90c	373	456	475	545	863	685	501	586	780	944	575	832	782	755	1,208
Government Consumption	91f	83	86	115	127	131	199	273	315	345	358	436	501	525	538	633
Gross Fixed Capital Formation	93e	138	195	246	288	277	372	393	445	423	502	602	445	483	437	450
Increase/Decrease(-) in Stocks	93i	36	50	49	56	−39	−12	47	31	42	185	40	7	7	100	−74
Private Consumption	96f	344	397	489	518	508	494	493	536	530	664	815	847	1,023	1,252	1,413
Imports of Goods & Services	98c	−263	−335	−416	−470	−426	−471	−526	−565	−529	−766	−884	−736	−833	−831	−970
Gross Domestic Product	99b	711	848	957	1,062	1,314	1,219	1,181	1,348	1,591	1,888	1,583	1,896	1,986	2,251	2,660
Net Factor Inc/Pmts(-) Abroad	98.n	46	58	51	52	48	33	44	74	−91	−81	−82	−80	−69	50	−83
Gross National Product = GNP	99a	666	790	907	1,010	1,266	1,186	1,137	1,274	1,682	1,969	1,665	1,976	2,055	2,201	2,744
Nat'l Income, Market Prices	99e	619	739	845	926	1,155	1,099	974	1,069	1,294	1,582	1,269	1,522	1,607	1,809	2,124
Gross Dom. Prod. 1990 Prices	99b.p	82,653	79,306	83,304	85,454	88,163	91,022	90,955	99,286	98,359	104,985	102,419	106,838	101,708	102,291	99,178
GDP Deflator (1990=100)	99bi p	.9	1.1	1.1	1.2	1.5	1.3	1.3	1.4	1.6	1.8	1.5	1.8	2.0	2.2	2.7
															Millions:	
Population	99z	3.70	3.80	3.90	4.05	4.12	4.25	4.39	4.53	4.68	4.83	4.98	5.14	5.30	5.47	5.52

Monetary Authorities: I Beginning in December 1988, data reflect the new accounting system adopted by the Bank of Zambia.

Deposit Money Banks: I Beginning in July 1971, data are based on a new reporting system, which resulted mainly in improved sector classification distinguishing between resident and nonresident accounts and the government and private sectors.

Government Finance: I Beginning in 1972, data are as reported in the *Government Finance Statistics Yearbook* and cover budgetary central government. Prior to 1972, data are as reported by the Bank of Zambia for publication in *IFS*. I Beginning in 1986, data cover extrabudgetary accounts.

Zambia

	1980	1981	1982	1983	1984	1985	1986	1987	1988	1989	1990	1991	1992	1993	1994		
Millions of Kwacha																**International Transactions**	
	1,023.2	976.6	950.5	1,047.5	1,199.4	1,508.2	5,366.5	8,058.7	9,786.2	18,434.0	39,143.3	69,607.4	129,475.4	....	....	Exports	70
	1,057.0	1,093.6	1,116.0	1,071.6	1,329.2	1,933.2	4,828.1	6,686.6	6,810.2	12,817.0	37,627.6	59,988.0	50,724.8	....	....	Imports, cif	71
	859.5	923.0	930.0	693.2	1,085.7	2,133.2	4,447.7	6,627.5	6,898.1	12,600.5	36,553.7	51,772.8	144,108.5	....	....	Imports, fob	71.v
Minus Sign Indicates Debit																**Balance of Payments**	
	1,457	996	942	923	893	797	692	852	1,189	1,340	1,254	1,172	....	....	....	Goods: Exports f.o.b.	78aa d
	−1,114	−1,065	−1,003	−711	−612	−571	−518	−585	−687	−774	−1,511	−752	....	....	....	Goods: Imports f.o.b.	78ab d
	343	−69	−61	212	280	226	175	267	502	566	−257	420	....	....	....	Trade Balance	78ac d
	152	153	122	99	75	68	47	48	58	85	107	83	....	....	....	Services: Credit	78ad d
	−651	−584	−409	−334	−291	−254	−199	−223	−289	−444	−386	−363	....	....	....	Services: Debit	78ae d
	−157	−501	−348	−23	65	39	23	91	271	208	−537	140	....	....	....	Balance on Goods and Services	78af d
	16	20	15	3	5	2	1	1	3	1	2	10	....	....	....	Income: Credit	78ag d
	−221	−130	−203	−241	−187	−413	−354	−329	−604	−509	−439	−696	....	....	....	Income: Debit	78ah d
	−362	−610	−537	−261	−117	−371	−330	−236	−330	−300	−974	−546	....	....	....	Balance on Goods, Serv., & Inc.	78ai d
	35	30	32	44	14	8	23	10	64	114	398	262	....	....	....	Current Transfers, n.i.e.: Credit	78aj d
	−190	−148	−57	−46	−44	−32	−41	−19	−27	−32	−18	−22	....	....	....	Current Transfers: Debit	78ak d
	−516	−729	−562	−263	−147	−395	−348	−245	−293	−219	−594	−306	....	....	....	Current Account, n.i.e.	78al d
	—	—	—	—	—	—	—	—	—	—	—	—	....	....	....	Capital Account, n.i.e.: Credit	78ba d
	−21	−13	−4	−8	−6	−3	−3	−2	−2	−3	−3	−1	....	....	....	Capital Account: Debit	78bb d
	−21	−13	−4	−8	−6	−3	−3	−2	−2	−3	−3	−1	....	....	....	Capital Account, n.i.e.	78bc d
	—	—	—	—	—	—	—	—	—	—	—	—	....	....	....	Direct Investment Abroad	78bd d
	62	−38	39	26	17	52	28	75	93	164	203	34	....	....	....	Dir. Invest. in Rep. Econ., n.i.e.	78be d
	—	—	—	—	—	—	—	—	—	—	—	—	....	....	....	Portfolio Investment Assets	78bf d
	—	—	—	—	—	—	—	—	—	—	—	—	....	....	....	Portfolio Investment Liab.	78bg d
	56	−64	30	−19	−7	−26	−38	−57	−347	26	−275	−125	....	....	....	Other Investment Assets	78bh d
	170	561	184	32	141	337	−90	−165	277	1,637	569	108	....	....	....	Other Investment Liab., n.i.e.	78bi d
	287	459	253	38	151	363	−99	−147	23	1,827	497	18	....	....	....	Financial Account, n.i.e.	78bj d
	26	−181	−77	211	−87	−145	315	153	40	−1,712	322	110	....	....	....	Net Errors and Omissions	78ca d
	−225	−464	−390	−21	−89	−181	−134	−242	−232	−106	222	−179	....	....	....	Overall Balance	78cb d
	225	464	390	21	89	181	134	242	232	106	−222	179	....	....	....	Reserves and Related Items	79da d
	22	39	−6	4	59	−127	121	71	−51	−82	−119	−26	....	....	....	Reserve Assets	79db d
	9	373	−57	65	76	−25	−31	−4	—	−17	−25	−35	....	....	....	Use of Fund Credit and Loans	79dc d
	—	—	—	—	—	—	—	—	—	—	—	—	....	....	....	Liabs.Constit.For.Auth.Reserves	79dd d
	194	52	453	−47	−46	332	44	175	284	205	−77	241	....	....	....	Exceptional Financing	79de d
Year Ending December 31																**Government Finance**	
	−568	−450	−668	−327	−414	−1,073	I−2,804	−2,549	−3,466	−2,757 p	....	....	....	....	....	Deficit (−) or Surplus	80
	765	807	840	1,014	1,091	1,556	3,023	4,267	5,142	6,553 p	....	....	....	....	....	Revenue	81
	26	24	29	54	23	20	173	91	495	1,332 p	....	....	....	....	....	Grants Received	81z
	1,135	1,278	1,409	1,346	1,441	2,484	I 5,407	6,820	8,559	11,985 p	....	....	....	....	....	Expenditure	82
	223	3	128	48	86	164	I 594	87	545	−1,343 p	....	....	....	....	....	Lending Minus Repayments	83
																Financing	
	....	161	532	215	290	457	I 1,625	1,095	2,101	....	....	....	....	....	....	Net Borrowing: Domestic	84a
	270	247	112	120	129	600	I 1,156	1,401	1,125	....	....	....	....	....	....	Foreign	85a
	....	42	25	−8	−5	16	24	53	241	....	....	....	....	....	....	Use of Cash Balances	87
	....	2,011	2,746	2,920	3,229	4,077	5,818	7,053	....	....	....	....	....	....	....	Debt: Domestic	88a
	....	1,285	1,846	2,666	3,545	9,542	33,146	20,459	....	....	....	....	....	....	....	Foreign	89a
Millions of Kwacha																**National Accounts**	
	1,268	998	993	1,281	1,807	2,740	5,910	8,512	10,266	14,792	42,302	74,967	180,291	579,036	....	Exports of Goods & Services	90c
	782	986	996	1,009	1,240	1,687	3,481	4,399	4,582	7,574	21,566	35,758	83,497	130,659	....	Government Consumption	91f
	558	610	618	615	623	725	1,386	1,931	2,381	3,643	15,271	24,973	60,187	93,170	....	Gross Fixed Capital Formation	93e
	155	63	−15	−40	101	329	1,701	911	1,032	2,321	4,312	7,201	19,805	60,846	....	Increase/Decrease(−) in Stocks	93i
	1,692	2,262	2,315	2,646	2,779	4,295	6,552	11,820	19,825	45,517	71,616	114,334	421,998	1,173,588	....	Private Consumption	96f
	−1,391	−1,434	−1,312	−1,329	−1,619	−2,703	−5,916	−8,066	−18,665	−41,726	−37,879	−197,048	−596,636		....	Imports of Goods & Services	98c
	3,064	3,485	3,595	4,181	4,931	7,072	13,115	19,778	30,021	55,181	113,341	219,353	568,730	1,440,663	....	Gross Domestic Product	99b
	−139	−115	−36	−4	−64	−86	−973	−1,669	−1,911	−6,486	−9,772	−41,834	−85,961	−377,249	....	Net Factor Inc/Pmts(−) Abroad	98.n
	3,202	3,600	3,632	4,177	4,867	6,986	12,142	18,110	28,110	48,695	103,569	177,519	482,769	1,063,415	....	Gross National Product = GNP	99a
	2,496	3,004	2,870	3,508	3,926	5,430	8,381	14,445	15,541	43,447	92,534	150,965	415,861	923,807	....	Nat'l Income, Market Prices	99e
	102,189	108,492	105,440	103,372	102,993	104,683	105,440	108,257	115,056	113,884	113,341	111,334	....	....	....	Gross Dom. Prod. 1990 Prices	99b.p
	3.0	3.2	3.4	4.0	4.8	6.8	12.4	18.3	26.1	48.5	100.0	197.0	....	....	....	GDP Deflator (1990=100)	99bi p
Midyear Estimates																	
	5.56	5.87	6.05	6.24	6.44	6.73	7.11	7.37	7.53	7.80	8.07	8.41	8.67	8.94	....	Population	99z

Zimbabwe

698

		1965	1966	1967	1968	1969	1970	1971	1972	1973	1974	1975	1976	1977	1978	1979
Exchange Rates														*SDRs per Zimbabwe Dollar:*		
Official Rate	ac	1.4000	1.4000	1.4000	1.4000	1.4000	1.3963	1.3724	1.4127	1.3678	1.4885	1.3672	1.3904	1.2728	1.1369	1.1259
													US Dollars per Zimbabwe Dollar:			
Official Rate	ag	1.4000	1.4000	1.4000	1.4000	1.4000	1.3963	1.4900	1.5338	1.6500	1.8225	1.6005	1.6154	1.5461	1.4811	1.4832
Official Rate	rh	1.4000	1.4000	1.4000	1.4000	1.4000	1.4000	1.4042	1.5161	1.7070	1.6949	1.7603	1.5984	1.5919	1.4764	1.4709
Fund Position														*Millions of SDRs:*		
Quota	2f.s	....	....	....	....	....	....	....	....	....	....	....	....	....	....	....
SDRs	1b.s	....	....	....	....	....	....	....	....	....	....	....	....	....	....	....
Reserve Position in the Fund	1c.s	....	....	....	....	....	....	....	....	....	....	....	....	....	....	....
Total Fund Cred.&Loans Outstg.	2tl	....	....	....	....	....	....	....	....	....	....	....	....	....	....	....
International Liquidity												*Millions of US Dollars Unless Otherwise Indicated:*				
Total Reserves minus Gold	1l.d	....	64.9	58.6	3.6	27.9	20.3	6.1	61.3	124.7	70.8	80.0	76.6	72.6	148.0	298.9
SDRs	1b.d	....	....	....	....	....	....	....	....	....	....	....	....	....	....	....
Reserve Position in the Fund	1c.d	....	....	....	....	....	....	....	....	....	....	....	....	....	....	....
Foreign Exchange	1d.d	....	....	....	....	....	....	....	....	....	....	....	....	....	....	....
Gold (Million Fine Troy Ounces)	1ad	....	.63	.86	.80	.80	1.05	.82	.55	.75	.50	.35	.27	.15	.16	.26
Gold (National Valuation)	1an d	....	22.1	30.3	27.9	28.0	36.5	30.4	21.2	30.9	22.9	14.0	10.7	5.9	6.0	9.6
Monetary Authorities: Other Liab.	4..d	—	—	—	—	—	—	—	—	—	—	47.9	100.0	110.1	23.8	12.0
Deposit Money Banks: Assets	7a.d	—	—	—	—	—	—	—	—	—	—	9.6	19.5	15.9	18.7	65.9
Liabilities	7b.d	—	—	—	—	—	—	—	—	—	—	—	—	—	—	—
Monetary Authorities												*Millions of Zimbabwe Dollars:*				
Foreign Assets	11	....	....	....	....	....	....	....	....	....	....	58.7	54.1	50.7	104.0	139.0
Claims on Central Government	12a	....	....	....	....	....	....	....	....	....	....	80.6	88.9	104.4	76.5	78.4
Claims on Nonfin.Pub.Enterprises	12c	....	....	....	....	....	....	....	....	....	....	....	....	....	....	.6
Reserve Money	14	....	....	....	....	....	....	....	....	....	....	119.7	147.7	164.8	156.0	181.6
of which: Currency Outside DMBs	14a	....	....	....	....	....	....	....	....	....	....	66.9	79.1	83.9	95.2	107.6
Central Bank Bills Outstanding	16ad	....	....	....	....	....	....	....	....	....	....	....	....	....	....	....
Foreign Liabilities	16c	....	....	....	....	....	....	....	....	....	....	29.9	61.9	71.2	16.1	8.1
Central Government Deposits	16d	....	....	....	....	....	....	....	....	....	....	16.6	8.0	.3	25.7	75.9
Other Items (Net)	17r	—	—	—	—	—	—	—	—	—	—	19.7	8.6	31.6	38.6	14.5
Deposit Money Banks												*Millions of Zimbabwe Dollars:*				
Reserves	20	....	....	....	....	....	....	....	....	....	....	42.4	46.7	56.3	55.0	59.8
Nonreserve Claims on Mon. Auths.	20r	....	....	....	....	....	....	....	....	....	....	—	—	—	—	9.5
Foreign Assets	21	....	....	....	....	....	....	....	....	....	....	....	....	....	....	....
Claims on Central Government	22a	....	....	....	....	....	....	....	....	....	....	....	....	....	....	....
Claims on Nonfin.Pub.Enterprises	22c	....	....	....	....	....	....	....	....	....	....	....	....	....	....	....
Claims on Private Sector	22d	....	....	....	....	....	....	....	....	....	....	....	....	....	....	54.5
Demand Deposits	24	....	....	....	....	....	....	....	....	....	....	250.4	269.2	288.1	316.8	353.6
Time and Savings Deposits	25	....	....	....	....	....	....	....	....	....	....	....	....	....	....	469.4
Money Market Instruments	26aa	....	....	....	....	....	....	....	....	....	....	....	....	....	....	—
Foreign Liabilities	26c	....	....	....	....	....	....	....	....	....	....	....	....	....	....	....
Central Government Deposits	26d	....	....	....	....	....	....	....	....	....	....	....	....	....	....	3.6
Capital Accounts	27a	....	....	....	....	....	....	....	....	....	....	33.1	48.4	68.6	74.6	88.2
Other Items (Net)	27r	....	....	....	....	....	....	....	....	....	....	....	....	....	....	3.3
Monetary Survey												*Millions of Zimbabwe Dollars:*				
Foreign Assets (Net)	31n	—	—	—	—	—	—	—	—	—	—	....	....	....	....	....
Domestic Credit	32	....	....	....	....	....	....	....	....	....	....	....	....	....	....	....
Claims on Central Govt. (Net)	32an	....	....	....	....	....	....	....	....	....	....	....	....	....	....	....
Claims on Nonfin.Pub.Enterprises	32c	....	....	....	....	....	....	....	....	....	....	....	....	....	....	31.9
Claims on Private Sector	32d	....	....	....	....	....	....	....	....	....	....	....	....	....	....	117.2
Money	34	....	....	....	....	....	....	....	....	....	....	324.1	351.9	374.5	415.0	463.2
Quasi-Money	35	....	....	....	....	....	....	....	....	....	....	....	....	....	....	....
Money Market Instruments	36aa	....	....	....	....	....	....	....	....	....	....	....	....	....	....	—
Other Items (Net)	37r	—	—	—	—	—	—	—	—	—	—	53.1	57.3	100.6	169.1	155.9
Money plus Quasi-Money	35l	....	....	....	....	....	....	....	....	....	....	324.1	351.9	374.5	415.0	935.3
Other Banking Institutions												*Millions of Zimbabwe Dollars:*				
Reserves	40	....	....	....	....	....	....	....	....	....	....	....	....	....	....	....
Claims on Central Government	42a	....	....	....	....	....	....	....	....	....	....	15.4	15.9	21.9	23.4	....
Claims on Nonfin.Pub.Enterprises	42c	....	....	....	....	....	....	....	....	....	....	....	....	....	....	....
Claims on Private Sector	42d	....	....	....	....	....	....	....	....	....	....	....	....	....	....	....
Time and Savings Deposits	45	....	....	....	....	....	....	....	....	....	....	63.3	47.0	40.8	29.8	28.0
Money Market Instruments	46aa	....	....	....	....	....	....	....	....	....	....	41.2	44.9	48.9	55.2	64.1
Capital Accounts	47a	....	....	....	....	....	....	....	....	....	....	....	....	....	....	....
Other Items (Net)	47r	....	....	....	....	....	....	....	....	....	....	....	....	....	....	....
Banking Survey												*Millions of Zimbabwe Dollars:*				
Foreign Assets (Net)	51n	—	—	—	—	—	—	—	—	—	—	....	....	....	....	....
Domestic Credit	52	....	....	....	....	....	....	....	....	....	....	....	....	....	....	....
Claims on Central Govt. (Net)	52an	....	....	....	....	....	....	....	....	....	....	....	....	....	....	....
Claims on Nonfin.Pub.Enterprises	52c	....	....	....	....	....	....	....	....	....	....	....	....	....	....	....
Claims on Private Sector	52d	....	....	....	....	....	....	....	....	....	....	386.8	400.3	405.0	486.7	464.5
Liquid Liabilities	55l	....	....	....	....	....	....	....	....	....	....	....	....	....	....	....
Money Market Instruments	56aa	....	....	....	....	....	....	....	....	....	....	....	....	....	....	28.0
Capital Accounts	57a	....	....	....	....	....	....	....	....	....	....	80.2	99.7	124.5	137.5	160.3
Other Items (Net)	57r	—	—	—	—	—	—	—	—	—	—	−7.3	−4.8	−7.4	−13.7	87.8
Interest Rates												*Percent Per Annum*				
Rediscount Rate (End of Period)	60	4.50	4.50	4.50	4.50	4.50	4.50	4.50	4.50	4.50	4.50	4.50	4.50	4.50	4.50	4.50
Money Market Rate	60b	....	....	....	....	....	....	....	....	....	....	4.25	4.25	4.25	4.25	4.25
Treasury Bill Rate	60c	....	....	....	....	....	....	....	....	....	....	....	....	....	3.55	3.54
Deposit Rate	60l	....	....	....	....	....	....	....	....	....	....	4.00	3.75	3.50	3.25	3.25
Lending Rate	60p	....	....	....	....	....	....	....	....	....	....	....	....	....	17.54	17.54
Government Bond Yield	61	....	....	....	6.25	6.33	6.50	6.50	6.50	6.50	6.50	6.50	6.54	7.63	8.75	8.75

Zimbabwe

1980	1981	1982	1983	1984	1985	1986	1987	1988	1989	1990	1991	1992	1993	1994		
End of Period															**Exchange Rates**	
1.2434	1.1980	.9859	.8640	.6790	.5547	.4872	.4239	.3825	.3352	.2666	.1384	.1327	.1050	.0817	Official Rate	ac
End of Period (ag) Period Average (rh)																
1.5858	1.3944	1.0876	.9046	.6656	.6093	.5959	.6013	.5147	.4405	.3793	.1980	.1824	.1442	.1192	Official Rate	ag
1.5561	1.4518	1.3205	.9895	.8037	.6204	.6006	.6020	.5550	.4732	.4085	.2917	.1963	.1545	.1227	Official Rate	rh
End of Period															**Fund Position**	
150.0	150.0	150.0	150.0	191.0	191.0	191.0	191.0	191.0	191.0	191.0	191.0	261.3	261.3	261.3	Quota	2f. *s*
—	8.8	6.3	6.1	2.3	13.2	5.0	16.3	.5	.5	.2	.1	.3	.6	—	SDRs	1b. *s*
—	—	—	—	—	—	—	—	—	—	—	.1	.1	.1	.1	Reserve Position in the Fund	1c. *s*
—	37.5	37.5	191.1	261.3	240.5	191.1	110.3	52.2	22.2	4.8	—	157.2	205.0	257.5	Total Fund Cred.&Loans Outstg.	2tl
End of Period															**International Liquidity**	
213.5	169.5	140.4	75.4	45.4	93.4	106.4	166.1	178.6	94.6	149.2	149.7	222.2	432.0	405.3	Total Reserves minus Gold	1l. *d*
—	10.3	6.9	6.4	2.3	14.5	6.2	23.1	.6	.7	.3	.1	.4	.9	.1	SDRs	1b. *d*
—	—	—	—	—	—	—	.1	.1	.1	.1	.1	.1	.1	.1	Reserve Position in the Fund	1c. *d*
213.5	159.2	133.5	68.9	43.1	78.8	100.2	143.0	178.0	93.8	148.9	149.5	221.7	431.1	405.1	Foreign Exchange	1d. *d*
.35	.47	.39	.59	.70	.77	.54	.42	.40	.45	.38	.41	.55	.50	.47	Gold (Million Fine Troy Ounces)	1ad
112.9	99.1	83.6	111.6	110.5	127.8	110.0	98.5	79.1	82.2	69.6	67.9	88.1	79.1	89.7	Gold (National Valuation)	1an *d*
—	173.5	232.2	334.0	95.2	47.6	52.7	36.6	29.7	28.4	163.1	479.6	510.4	408.0	249.1	Monetary Authorities: Other Liab.	4..*d*
60.7	21.5	32.4	24.0	15.6	13.4	25.4	26.1	28.2	32.8	40.2	49.1	95.5	75.4	321.4	Deposit Money Banks: Assets	7a.*d*
56.6	27.6	26.8	23.9	30.2	43.9	62.2	61.3	62.4	66.0	96.8	186.0	220.6	518.6	579.4	Liabilities	7b. *d*
End of Period															**Monetary Authorities**	
170.4	165.2	206.0	206.7	I421.0	522.4	523.8	459.3	519.1	425.2	611.2	1,511.8	1,655.9	3,545.2	4,151.6	Foreign Assets	11
122.4	201.2	346.9	347.2	303.4	244.3	356.3	566.5	398.6	355.0	829.9	963.3	2,033.8	2,759.5	7,101.9	Claims on Central Government	12a
.4	—	96.2	.7	188.8	157.4	236.8	187.7	157.6	123.6	181.6	305.0	263.2	176.5	99.1	133.9	Claims on Nonfin.Pub.Enterprises	12c
245.0	325.4	388.5	407.3	449.4	541.4	625.9	669.1	843.4	1,026.8	1,290.0	1,705.2	1,932.8	2,938.0	3,631.5	Reserve Money	14
157.2	198.6	237.5	227.4	258.8	321.1	379.7	389.3	503.3	617.9	769.8	888.8	861.3	1,191.4	1,467.1	of which: Currency Outside DMBs	14a
....	....	....	....	64.5	55.0	—	50.0	200.0	—	—	—	—	—	2,050.0	Central Bank Bills Outstanding	16ad
—	155.7	251.5	590.4	527.9	511.7	480.7	321.1	194.2	130.8	448.3	2,422.1	3,570.9	3,971.5	3,791.2	Foreign Liabilities	16c
66.1	94.2	.2	.2	.2	4.1	.6	.7	.4	1.1	11.6	1.2	2.3	1.2	3,310.6	Central Government Deposits	16d
31.0	-82.6	-39.5	-38.5	-160.3	-108.7	-39.5	142.5	-196.6	-196.9	-3.7	-1,390.3	-1,639.8	-508.9	-1,396.0	Other Items (Net)	17r
End of Period															**Deposit Money Banks**	
81.6	115.3	143.2	160.5	168.8	208.1	217.3	238.7	312.6	385.1	471.8	766.0	1,046.3	1,188.1	2,019.0	Reserves	20
—	—	—	—	64.5	55.0	—	50.0	99.0	—	—	.1	.1	—	2,050.0	Nonreserve Claims on Mon. Auths.	20r
38.3	15.4	29.8	26.5	23.4	22.0	42.7	43.4	54.8	74.5	106.1	248.0	523.8	523.2	2,695.4	Foreign Assets	21
314.9	203.3	228.1	219.2	312.7	354.9	333.9	480.8	518.9	698.0	597.1	463.8	489.0	1,455.2	968.3	Claims on Central Government	22a
170.5	292.0	422.6	348.7	476.8	659.0	794.0	659.3	721.4	860.7	637.3	501.7	406.3	1,082.9	668.4	Claims on Nonfin.Pub.Enterprises	22c
57.4	47.0	47.1	46.9	I658.8	672.2	748.8	1,032.9	1,489.1	1,987.8	2,502.6	4,241.3	5,966.7	9,236.5	11,797.6	Claims on Private Sector	22d
472.8	477.7	587.7	511.5	608.1	688.3	727.0	835.3	1,103.5	1,292.0	1,650.9	2,094.4	2,293.8	4,786.1	5,728.4	Demand Deposits	24
I578.1	714.0	915.7	941.9	971.3	1,151.9	1,137.7	1,619.6	1,859.8	2,387.4	2,505.9	2,008.9	2,469.7	3,297.5	5,391.1	Time and Savings Deposits	25
....	....	....	....	I124.1	165.9	204.6	—	91.8	4.4	38.4	95.8	29.7	28.2	13.3	Money Market Instruments	26aa
35.7	19.8	24.6	26.4	45.4	72.1	104.3	101.9	121.2	149.9	255.2	939.6	1,209.4	3,596.7	4,859.4	Foreign Liabilities	26c
I4.2	22.9	24.0	19.7	50.0	44.0	67.5	92.1	119.4	133.5	178.9	587.8	694.8	330.5	332.2	Central Government Deposits	26d
102.4	121.2	142.5	149.7	194.3	205.5	242.8	281.9	342.8	424.5	587.4	790.8	1,016.6	1,435.1	1,919.5	Capital Accounts	27a
97.7	121.3	I51.7	104.0	-288.5	-357.3	-350.4	-431.5	-447.7	-386.7	-903.6	-295.6	718.5	11.8	1,954.5	Other Items (Net)	27r
End of Period															**Monetary Survey**	
173.0	5.1	-40.4	-459.8	-129.0	-39.4	-18.5	79.7	258.5	219.0	13.9	-1,601.9	-2,600.6	-3,499.7	-1,803.7	Foreign Assets (Net)	31n
644.6	853.3	1,080.2	1,481.3	1,866.1	2,123.0	2,358.4	2,830.2	3,160.7	4,038.5	4,839.1	6,129.6	8,840.9	14,508.9	17,209.2	Domestic Credit	32
367.0	287.4	550.8	546.5	565.9	551.1	622.1	954.5	797.7	918.4	1,236.5	838.2	1,825.7	3,883.0	4,427.4	Claims on Central Govt. (Net)	32an
I170.9	388.2	423.3	537.5	634.2	895.8	981.7	816.9	845.0	1,042.3	942.3	764.9	582.8	1,182.0	802.3	Claims on Nonfin.Pub.Enterprises	32c
106.7	177.7	106.1	397.3	666.0	676.1	754.6	1,058.8	1,518.0	2,077.8	2,660.5	4,526.5	6,432.4	9,443.9	11,979.5	Claims on Private Sector	32d
632.8	678.8	826.9	751.4	873.9	1,020.8	1,126.8	1,258.9	1,617.3	1,933.1	2,467.2	3,035.6	3,211.2	6,494.5	7,333.3	Money	34
579.8	720.6	921.2	939.3	971.3	1,151.9	1,137.7	1,619.6	1,859.8	2,387.4	2,505.9	2,008.9	2,469.7	3,297.5	5,391.1	Quasi-Money	35
....	....	....	....	124.1	165.9	204.6	—	192.8	4.4	38.4	95.7	29.6	28.2	13.3	Money Market Instruments	36aa
184.4	171.7	214.3	575.1	-232.5	-255.5	-132.5	25.6	-255.0	-68.5	-160.1	-611.8	530.1	1,186.9	2,667.5	Other Items (Net)	37r
1,212.6	1,399.4	1,748.1	1,690.7	1,837.1	2,157.1	2,240.5	2,844.2	3,462.5	4,292.5	4,923.5	4,913.5	5,477.8	8,670.9	11,903.9	Money plus Quasi-Money	35l
End of Period															**Other Banking Institutions**	
....	....	....	....	107.8	100.8	179.5	170.5	924.9	134.3	231.0	258.5	175.3	678.5	913.5	Reserves	40
360.5	349.3	437.0	450.8	565.5	764.8	907.7	1,120.2	1,256.5	1,652.4	1,745.9	2,158.9	2,186.4	2,348.0	2,794.9	Claims on Central Government	42a
....	28.9	31.1	24.2	38.6	53.8	53.3	53.3	58.9	36.0	52.1	82.7	126.2	182.3	404.1	Claims on Nonfin.Pub.Enterprises	42c
532.6	576.2	579.5	628.4	660.7	704.3	800.5	959.7	499.8	1,598.5	2,291.7	3,224.7	3,462.5	3,413.7	4,036.0	Claims on Private Sector	42d
865.1	934.0	1,018.5	1,082.0	1,266.0	1,551.4	1,856.2	2,169.8	2,627.5	3,297.2	4,248.4	5,283.6	5,358.9	6,704.7	9,347.5	Time and Savings Deposits	45
44.0	67.8	72.7	81.8	65.4	33.0	40.1	58.9	76.2	69.4	133.0	226.4	192.2	207.5	385.6	Money Market Instruments	46aa
76.2	87.7	91.2	99.4	105.9	119.7	138.0	163.1	200.0	268.2	372.5	521.2	591.1	638.6	690.7	Capital Accounts	47a
-4.4	-31.1	9.8	11.6	-63.1	-77.0	-88.4	-76.9	-162.2	-209.3	-431.0	-304.5	-191.7	-926.7	-2,275.1	Other Items (Net)	47r
End of Period															**Banking Survey**	
....	....	-164.6	-473.1	-132.5	-41.5	-19.3	78.9	258.2	222.3	13.8	-1,599.6	-2,598.3	-3,489.8	-1,796.7	Foreign Assets (Net)	51n
1,565.1	1,807.7	2,127.8	2,584.7	3,130.9	3,645.9	4,119.9	4,963.4	4,975.7	7,325.4	8,929.0	11,595.9	14,616.2	20,452.9	24,444.2	Domestic Credit	52
727.5	636.7	987.8	997.3	1,131.4	1,315.9	1,529.8	2,074.7	2,054.0	2,570.8	2,982.4	2,997.1	4,012.3	6,231.0	7,222.3	Claims on Central Govt. (Net)	52an
198.3	417.1	454.4	561.7	672.8	949.6	1,035.0	870.2	903.9	1,078.3	994.4	847.6	709.0	1,364.3	1,206.4	Claims on Nonfin.Pub.Enterprises	52c
I639.3	753.9	685.6	1,025.7	1,326.7	1,380.4	1,555.1	2,018.5	2,017.8	3,676.3	4,952.2	7,751.2	9,894.9	12,857.6	16,015.5	Claims on Private Sector	52d
....	....	....	....	3,003.4	3,623.3	3,941.2	4,877.8	5,179.7	7,483.4	8,990.5	10,069.6	10,864.5	15,818.2	21,158.4	Liquid Liabilities	55l
44.0	67.8	72.7	798.1	189.5	198.9	244.7	58.9	269.0	73.8	171.4	322.1	221.8	235.7	398.9	Money Market Instruments	56aa
186.6	216.9	241.7	257.1	308.2	333.2	388.5	453.0	550.8	700.7	967.9	1,320.6	1,615.2	2,465.7	3,279.8	Capital Accounts	57a
67.0	3.2	63.9	413.5	-501.4	-548.4	472.5	342.0	-768.9	-707.0	-1,186.6	-1,712.8	-683.9	-1,557.0	-2,189.7	Other Items (Net)	57r
Percent Per Annum															**Interest Rates**	
4.50	9.00	9.00	9.00	9.00	9.00	9.00	9.00	9.00	9.00	9.00	10.25	20.00	28.50	29.50	Rediscount Rate *(End of Period)*	60
4.15	6.83	9.50	9.09	8.90	8.80	9.10	9.30	9.08	8.73	8.68	17.36	....	34.18	30.90	Money Market Rate	60b
3.39	5.70	8.50	8.52	8.49	8.48	8.71	8.73	8.38	8.17	8.39	13.34	....	33.04	29.22	Treasury Bill Rate	60c
3.52	7.46	14.46	12.80	10.30	10.04	10.28	9.58	9.68	8.85	8.80	14.10	....	29.45	26.75	Deposit Rate	60l
17.54	20.19	23.00	23.08	23.00	17.17	13.00	13.00	13.00	13.00	13.00	11.71	15.50	36.33	34.86	Lending Rate	60p
8.94	11.54	13.00	13.08	13.29	13.26	13.20	13.87	14.00	14.00	15.24	17.27	....	....	....	Government Bond Yield	61

Zimbabwe

698

		1965	1966	1967	1968	1969	1970	1971	1972	1973	1974	1975	1976	1977	1978	1979
Prices and Production														*Index Numbers (1990=100):*		
Consumer Prices	64	12.0	12.4	12.7	12.9	12.9	13.2	13.6	14.0	14.4	15.4	ⅼ16.9	18.7	20.7	21.8	25.8
Manufacturing Production	66ey	34.0	30.8	33.6	36.7	41.4	46.4	50.0	57.5	62.1	66.5	ⅼ65.9	61.8	58.4	56.9	62.7
International Transactions														*Millions of Zimbabwe Dollars*		
Exports	70	322.8	200.0	194.4	187.8	231.9	264.6	287.7	340.6	402.7	503.1	531.3	557.4	550.8	609.3	715.7
Imports, cif	71	275.5	194.9	215.2	238.2	229.4	270.2	324.9	315.9	354.9	504.0	531.2	440.1	446.3	464.3	631.7
Imports, fob	71.v	239.6	169.5	187.1	207.1	199.5	235.0	282.5	274.7	308.6	438.3	461.9	382.7	388.1	403.7	549.3
																1985=100
Volume of Exports	72	104.5	67.0	69.5	68.5	78.3	85.3	94.1	112.7	115.1	119.9	ⅼ112.2	112.8	107.1	111.4	109.8
Volume of Imports	73	120.2	77.3	85.5	96.0	90.9	102.3	115.5	114.7	123.7	128.9	ⅼ122.9	89.8	82.7	75.6	74.6
Unit Value of Exports	74	19.7	17.9	17.3	17.6	18.8	19.3	19.6	19.7	21.5	28.2	ⅼ30.1	31.5	32.7	34.9	40.1
Unit Value of Imports	75	16.7	18.4	18.3	18.0	18.4	19.2	20.5	20.0	20.9	28.5	ⅼ31.4	35.6	39.3	44.7	61.1
Balance of Payments														*Millions of US Dollars:*		
Goods: Exports f.o.b.	78aa d	….	….	….	….	….	….	….	….	….	….	….	900.8	927.7	1,079.8	
Goods: Imports f.o.b.	78ab d	….	….	….	….	….	….	….	….	….	….	….	−671.1	−657.4	−875.2	
Trade Balance	78ac d	….	….	….	….	….	….	….	….	….	….	….	229.6	270.3	204.6	
Services: Credit	78ad d	….	….	….	….	….	….	….	….	….	….	….	65.3	69.9	88.3	
Services: Debit	78ae d	….	….	….	….	….	….	….	….	….	….	….	−226.8	−231.1	−276.4	
Balance on Goods and Services	78af d	….	….	….	….	….	….	….	….	….	….	….	68.1	109.0	16.5	
Income: Credit	78ag d	….	….	….	….	….	….	….	….	….	….	….	39.0	36.3	62.7	
Income: Debit	78ah d	….	….	….	….	….	….	….	….	….	….	….	−105.8	−90.5	−132.0	
Balance on Goods, Serv., & Inc.	78ai d	….	….	….	….	….	….	….	….	….	….	….	1.3	54.9	−52.8	
Current Transfers, n.i.e.: Credit	78aj d	….	….	….	….	….	….	….	….	….	….	….	28.2	26.1	36.0	
Current Transfers: Debit	78ak d	….	….	….	….	….	….	….	….	….	….	….	−28.3	−27.0	−39.7	
Current Account, n.i.e.	78al d	….	….	….	….	….	….	….	….	….	….	….	1.1	54.0	−56.5	
Capital Account, n.i.e.: Credit	78ba d	….	….	….	….	….	….	….	….	….	….	….	5.3	5.6	7.7	
Capital Account: Debit	78bb d	….	….	….	….	….	….	….	….	….	….	….	−20.4	−22.3	−59.9	
Capital Account, n.i.e.	78bc d	….	….	….	….	….	….	….	….	….	….	….	−15.1	−16.6	−52.2	
Direct Investment Abroad	78bd d	….	….	….	….	….	….	….	….	….	….	….	—	—	—	
Dir. Invest. in Rep. Econ., n.i.e.	78be d	….	….	….	….	….	….	….	….	….	….	….	−3.8	2.5	.1	
Portfolio Investment Assets	78bf d	….	….	….	….	….	….	….	….	….	….	….	.2	—	.6	
Portfolio Investment Liab., n.i.e.	78bg d	….	….	….	….	….	….	….	….	….	….	….	−8.4	−8.3	−9.4	
Other Investment Assets	78bh d	….	….	….	….	….	….	….	….	….	….	….	3.2	−3.1	−30.0	
Other Investment Liab., n.i.e.	78bi d	….	….	….	….	….	….	….	….	….	….	….	−5.7	73.6	147.9	
Financial Account, n.i.e.	78bj d	….	….	….	….	….	….	….	….	….	….	….	−14.6	64.7	109.2	
Net Errors and Omissions	78ca d	….	….	….	….	….	….	….	….	….	….	….	20.5	−26.7	119.5	
Overall Balance	78cb d	….	….	….	….	….	….	….	….	….	….	….	−8.1	75.4	119.9	
Reserves and Related Items	79da d	….	….	….	….	….	….	….	….	….	….	….	8.1	−75.4	−119.9	
Reserve Assets	79db d	….	….	….	….	….	….	….	….	….	….	….	8.1	−75.4	−119.9	
Use of Fund Credit and Loans	79dc d	….	….	….	….	….	….	….	….	….	….	….	—	—	—	
Liabs.Constit.For.Auth.Reserves	79dd d	….	….	….	….	….	….	….	….	….	….	….	—	—	—	
Exceptional Financing	79de d	….	….	….	….	….	….	….	….	….	….	….	—	—	—	
Government Finance														*Millions of Zimbabwe Dollars:*		
Deficit (-) or Surplus	80	….	….	….	….	….	….	….	….	….	….	….	−118	−95	−254	−293
Revenue	81	….	….	….	….	….	….	….	….	….	….	….	492	576	573	611
Grants Received	81z	….	….	….	….	….	….	….	….	….	….	….	—	—	—	—
Expenditure	82	….	….	….	….	….	….	….	….	….	….	….	539	674	802	881
Lending Minus Repayments	83	….	….	….	….	….	….	….	….	….	….	….	72	−2	24	24
Financing																
Net Borrowing: Domestic	84a	….	….	….	….	….	….	….	….	….	….	….	123	98	130	172
Foreign	85a	….	….	….	….	….	….	….	….	….	….	….	−1	−3	124	121
Use of Cash Balances	87	….	….	….	….	….	….	….	….	….	….	….	−4	….	….	….
Total Debt	88	….	….	….	….	….	….	….	….	….	….	….	785	864	1,146	1,479
Debt: Domestic	88a	….	….	….	….	….	….	….	….	….	….	….	693	764	914	1,117
Foreign	89a	….	….	….	….	….	….	….	….	….	….	….	92	100	233	361
National Accounts														*Millions of Zimbabwe Dollars*		
Exports of Goods & Services	90c	243	….	….	….	296	324	355	417	….	577	590	617	610	675	798
Government Consumption	91f	83	86	93	101	112	126	143	157	180	221	256	319	382	451	537
Gross Fixed Capital Formation	93e	100	84	106	138	156	175	221	256	330	421	468	427	379	341	395
Increase/Decrease(-) in Stocks	93i	16	38	77	52	42	47	56	40	51	91	72	−18	40	−60	−37
Private Consumption	96f	495	508	523	594	643	715	849	936	988	1,166	1,254	1,354	1,344	1,546	1,933
Imports of Goods & Services	98c	−278	….	….	….	−271	−315	−379	−376	….	−587	−613	−533	−558	−593	−803
Gross Domestic Product	99b	842	733	794	852	977	1,086	1,262	1,429	1,538	1,832	1,995	2,166	2,198	2,359	2,822
Net Factor Inc/Pmts(-) Abroad	98.n	−25	−16	−11	−14	−17	−21	−30	−35	−39	−40	−45	−58	−48	−42	−53
Gross Nat'l Expenditure = GNP	99a	817	….	….	….	….	1,065	1,232	1,394	1,499	1,792	1,950	2,108	2,150	2,317	2,769
Gross Dom. Prod. 1990 Prices	99b.p	….	….	….	….	….	….	….	7,981	ⅼ8,114	9,518	9,172	9,071	8,605	8,420	8,740
GDP Deflator (1990=100)	99bi p	….	….	….	….	….	….	….	17.9	19.0	19.2	21.8	23.9	25.5	28.0	32.3
																Millions:
Population	99z	4.49	4.63	4.79	4.96	5.13	5.31	5.50	5.69	5.89	6.08	ⅼ6.14	6.33	6.52	6.72	6.93

Deposit Money Banks: ⅼ Prior to December 1984, *line 22d* includes claims on state and local governments and claims on public financial enterprises. Subsequently, these claims have been identified and omitted from the series.
Government Finance: ⅼ Beginning in 1985, data cover extrabudgetary accounts in addition to budgetary central government. Also beginning in 1985, data relate to a fiscal year different from calendar year.

Zimbabwe

	1980	1981	1982	1983	1984	1985	1986	1987	1988	1989	1990	1991	1992	1993	1994	
Period Averages																**Prices and Production**
	27.2	30.8	34.0	41.9	50.4	54.6	62.5	70.3	75.5	85.2	ℐ100.0	123.3	175.2	223.6	273.3	Consumer Prices............................ 64
	71.9	78.6	78.1	76.1	72.4	80.7	83.0	84.9	89.1	94.0	100.0	102.8	93.4	82.2	....	Manufacturing Production 66ey
Millions of Zimbabwe Dollars																**International Transactions**
	909.2	971.7	968.4	1,150.2	1,453.0	1,795.5	2,170.3	2,371.4	2,966.4	3,267.3	4,231.4	5,546.5	7,365.7	....	....	Exports 70
	930.8	1,170.4	1,244.1	1,220.8	1,380.8	1,663.5	1,886.5	2,003.0	2,349.7	3,438.1	4,528.4	7,443.1	11,317.5	....	....	Imports, cif 71
	809.4	1,017.7	1,081.8	1,061.6	1,200.7	1,446.5	1,640.4	1,741.7	2,043.2	2,989.7	3,937.8	6,472.3	9,841.3	....	....	Imports, fob 71.v
1985=100																
	104.6	99.6	102.5	106.2	104.8	100.0	124.9	....	....	....	....	....	....	....	....	Volume of Exports 72
	102.8	126.9	136.7	114.6	114.2	100.0	121.0	....	....	....	....	....	....	....	....	Volume of Imports 73
	53.1	58.7	56.9	64.4	84.0	100.0	101.9	....	....	....	....	....	....	....	....	Unit Value of Exports 74
	65.5	65.2	64.9	76.2	85.9	100.0	104.6	....	....	....	....	....	....	....	....	Unit Value of Imports 75
Minus Sign Indicates Debit																**Balance of Payments**
	1,441.1	1,451.4	1,312.1	1,153.7	1,173.6	1,119.6	1,322.7	1,452.0	1,664.9	1,693.5	1,747.9	1,693.8	1,527.6	1,609.1	....	Goods: Exports f.o.b. .... 78aa d
	-1,335.0	-1,534.0	-1,472.0	-1,069.6	-989.3	-918.9	-1,011.6	-1,071.0	-1,163.6	-1,318.3	-1,505.2	-1,645.7	-1,782.1	-1,487.0	....	Goods: Imports f.o.b. .... 78ab d
	106.1	-82.6	-159.9	84.1	184.3	200.6	311.2	381.0	501.3	375.2	242.7	48.1	-254.5	122.1	....	Trade Balance .... 78ac d
	169.1	134.2	181.5	145.1	139.4	295.5	169.0	164.6	190.3	241.8	264.2	273.5	305.1	372.1	....	Services: Credit .... 78ad d
	-394.5	-535.9	-437.4	-430.9	-357.5	-462.3	-316.0	-349.8	-410.9	-457.0	-495.5	-627.4	-660.9	-563.8	....	Services: Debit .... 78ae d
	-119.3	-484.3	-415.8	-201.7	-33.9	33.8	164.2	195.7	280.7	160.0	11.3	-305.9	-610.3	-69.6	....	Balance on Goods and Services .... 78af d
	103.9	94.0	80.4	69.6	55.2	37.8	36.4	33.0	17.4	26.0	22.9	26.1	26.0	35.0	....	Income: Credit .... 78ag d
	-165.1	-211.9	-290.9	-254.8	-170.9	-166.9	-225.5	-228.4	-234.0	-236.1	-286.3	-278.0	-302.3	-287.1	....	Income: Debit .... 78ah d
	-180.4	-602.2	-626.4	-387.0	-149.7	-95.3	-24.9	.4	64.1	-50.0	-252.0	-557.8	-886.6	-321.6	....	Balance on Goods, Serv., & Inc. .... 78ai d
	105.0	141.9	87.3	95.4	193.3	171.7	169.7	220.8	211.2	211.4	204.0	191.7	347.3	270.6	....	Current Transfers, n.i.e.: Credit .... 78aj d
	-74.0	-85.8	-93.1	-106.3	-86.6	-140.6	-128.0	-163.2	-150.1	-144.3	-91.8	-90.9	-64.4	-64.7	....	Current Transfers: Debit .... 78ak d
	-149.4	-546.1	-632.1	-397.9	-42.9	-64.2	16.8	58.0	125.3	17.0	-139.8	-457.0	-603.7	-115.7	....	Current Account, n.i.e. .... 78al d
	3.7	27.3	30.1	18.9	3.3	.1	.2	.2	.3	.2	.4	.1	.2	.6	....	Capital Account, n.i.e.: Credit .... 78ba d
	-97.4	-117.1	-107.1	-81.2	-60.4	-11.7	-10.2	-10.2	-9.0	-7.9	-7.4	-2.9	-1.6	-1.0	....	Capital Account: Debit .... 78bb d
	-93.7	-89.8	-77.0	-62.3	-57.1	-11.5	-10.0	-10.0	-8.6	-7.6	-7.0	-2.8	-1.4	-.4	....	Capital Account, n.i.e. .... 78bc d
										22.2					....	Direct Investment Abroad .... 78bd d
	1.6	3.6	-.8	-2.1	-2.5	2.9	7.5	-30.5	-18.1	-10.2	-12.2	2.8	15.0	28.0	....	Dir. Invest. in Rep. Econ., n.i.e. .... 78be d
	.5	2.3	.7		39.4	45.9	38.2	56.8				10.4	41.8	27.6	....	Portfolio Investment Assets .... 78bf d
	-27.9	-32.3	-47.5	-42.7	-36.6	-36.8	-37.0	-55.9	-60.9	-36.7	-32.1	-34.6	-37.1	-5.1	....	Portfolio Investment Liab., n.i.e. ...... 78bg d
	6.5	-5.4	62.3	36.7	43.2	24.6	34.4	19.8	4.9			38.0	15.9	99.9	....	Other Investment Assets .... 78bh d
	-10.4	531.9	579.9	259.8	-34.8	84.2	75.0	69.6	99.9	94.7	276.5	488.4	352.0	204.4	....	Other Investment Liab., n.i.e. .... 78bi d
	-29.8	499.4	594.5	251.8	8.7	120.7	118.1	59.8	48.0	47.8	242.6	536.5	373.4	327.2	....	Financial Account, n.i.e. .... 78bj d
	186.6	128.4	92.3	34.5	44.9	37.2	-69.4	16.6	-63.0	-103.8	-9.9	-31.4	37.2	14.9	....	Net Errors and Omissions .... 78ca d
	-86.3	-8.1	-22.4	-174.0	-46.3	82.2	55.5	124.5	101.6	-46.8	85.8	45.2	-194.6	225.9	....	Overall Balance .... 78cb d
	86.3	8.1	22.4	174.0	46.3	-82.2	-55.5	-124.5	-101.6	46.8	-85.8	-45.2	194.6	-225.9	....	Reserves and Related Items .... 79da d
	86.3	-37.3	22.4	7.3	-26.7	-61.2	3.0	-19.5	-23.0	85.5	-62.8	-38.4	-31.1	-293.6	....	Reserve Assets .... 79db d
	—	45.4	—	166.6	73.0	-21.0	-58.5	-104.9	-78.6	-38.8	-23.0	-6.9	225.7	67.7	....	Use of Fund Credit and Loans......... 79dc d
	—	—	—	—	—	—	—	—	—	—	—	—	—	—	....	Liabs.Constit.For.Auth.Reserves ...... 79dd d
	—	—	—	—	—	—	—	—	—	—	—	—	—	—	....	Exceptional Financing .... 79de d
Year Ending June 30																**Government Finance**
	-376	-262	-545	-394	-647	ℐ-513	-638	-977	-1,005	-1,111	-1,138^P	-1,430^f	....	....	....	Deficit (-) or Surplus 80
	830	1,130	1,514	1,866	2,034	ℐ2,132	2,500	2,954	3,526	4,267	5,169^P	6,521^f	....	....	....	Revenue 81
	—	2	18	23	77	ℐ173	108	80	118	90	138^P	250^f	....	....	....	Grants Received 81z
	1,198	1,301	1,882	2,079	2,546	ℐ2,617	3,077	3,783	4,264	4,960	5,872^P	7,419^f	....	....	....	Expenditure 82
	7	91	195	205	212	ℐ200	169	228	385	507	573^P	782^f	....	....	....	Lending Minus Repayments 83
																Financing
	297	114	115	238	325	ℐ295	378	639	708	982	937^P	1,313^f	....	....	....	Net Borrowing: Domestic 84a
	79	146	132	44	322	ℐ488	260	212	175	129	201^P	117^f	....	....	....	Foreign 85a
	....	1	299	113	....	ℐ-270	....	126	122	....	....	....	....	....	....	Use of Cash Balances 87
	1,828	2,081	2,464	2,846	3,744	ℐ4,118	5,197	6,137	7,295	8,633	10,412^P	....	....	....	....	Total Debt 88
	1,393	1,507	1,622	1,860	2,306	ℐ2,422	2,977	3,622	4,470	5,397	6,375^P	....	....	....	....	Debt: Domestic 88a
	435	574	841	987	1,438	ℐ1,696	2,221	2,515	2,825	3,236	4,037^P	....	....	....	....	Foreign............................. 89a
Millions of Zimbabwe Dollars																**National Accounts**
	1,043	1,117	1,141	1,345	1,708	2,101	2,559	2,789	3,434	4,142	....	....	....	....	....	Exports of Goods & Services 90c
	677	763	1,027	1,159	1,364	1,560	1,804	2,334	2,770	3,250	....	....	....	....	....	Government Consumption 91f
	528	830	1,039	1,238	1,185	1,133	1,312	1,673	2,043	2,402	....	....	....	....	....	Gross Fixed Capital Formation 93e
	120	196	62	-235	-28	312	229	44	-185	210	....	....	....	....	....	Increase/Decrease(-) in Stocks 93i
	2,219	2,969	3,378	4,341	3,792	4,206	4,674	4,856	5,712	6,915	....	....	....	....	....	Private Consumption 96f
	-1,146	-1,442	-1,450	-1,542	-1,673	-2,015	-2,202	-2,423	-2,835	-3,731	....	....	....	....	....	Imports of Goods & Services 98c
	3,441	4,433	5,197	6,306	6,404	7,297	8,376	9,273	10,925	13,188	15,174	....	....	....	....	Gross Domestic Product 99b
	-47	-115	-194	-248	-195	-284	-384	-355	-478	-538	....	....	....	....	....	Net Factor Inc/Pmts(-) Abroad 98.n
	3,394	4,318	5,003	6,058	6,209	7,013	7,992	8,918	10,447	12,650	....	....	....	....	....	Gross Nat'l Expenditure = GNP 99a
	9,664	10,874	11,161	11,338	11,121	11,894	12,208	12,082	13,200	13,930	15,174	15,430	....	....	....	Gross Dom. Prod. 1990 Prices .... 99b. p
	35.6	40.8	46.6	55.6	57.6	61.4	68.6	76.8	82.8	94.7	100.0	....	....	....	....	GDP Deflator (1990=100) .... 99bi p
Midyear Estimates																
	7.10	7.36	7.48	7.74	7.98	8.38	8.41	8.64	8.88	9.12	9.37	10.19	10.41	10.78	11.15	Population 99z

Wholesale Prices

Note: There is significant diversity in the methodology used by countries to compile these indices.

Bolivia

Exchange Rates: On January 1, 1987 the boliviano, equal to 1,000,000 pesos, was introduced.
Monetary Authorities: ℐ Beginning in December 1987, data reflect the introduction of improved sectorization and classification of domestic and foreign accounts.
Deposit Money Banks: ℐ See note to section 10.
Monetary Survey: ℐ See note to section 10.
Other Banking Institutions: ℐ See note to section 10.
Banking Survey: ℐ See note to section 10.
Interest Rates: *Deposit Rate:* ℐ Beginning in November 1985, average rate, including surcharges and commissions, paid by commercial banks on time deposits in national currency.
Lending Rate: ℐ Beginning in November 1985, average rate, including surcharges and commissions, charged by commercial banks on loans in national currency.
Government Finance: ℐ Beginning in 1986, annual data are as reported in the *Government Finance Statistics Yearbook* and cover consolidated central government.

Ecuador

Monetary Authorities: ℐ Beginning in 1976, data have been revised to accommodate a wider coverage.
Deposit Money Banks: ℐ Beginning in 1966, private sector securities held by private and development banks are included in *Claims on Private Sector* (*lines 22d, 32d,* and *42d*). Prior to that date, these securities were reported in *lines 27r* and *47r*.
Monetary Survey: ℐ See note to section 20.
Other Banking Institutions: ℐ See note to section 20.
International Transactions: ℐ Trade data, which are derived from customs returns, have been updated with central bank payments data for current periods.
Government Finance: ℐ Beginning in 1973, annual data are identical to data reported in the *Government Finance Statistics Yearbook* and cover budgetary central government. ℐ Beginning in 1986, annual data are derived from monthly data.

Ireland

Monetary Authorities: ℐ Beginning in 1968, *line 11* (and *line 1d.d*) increased and *line 21* decreased as a result of the transfer of foreign assets following the Basle Agreement for the support of sterling. Offsetting items affect *line 14* and *line 20*.
Deposit Money Banks: ℐ See note to section 10. ℐ Prior to December 1982, data were based on call report forms that recorded the associated bank data on a location-of-branch basis. Accordingly, *Foreign Assets (line 21)* and *Foreign Liabilities (line 26c)* reflected the activities of nonresident offices of these banks, while *Claims on Private Sector (line 22d)* and *Demand* and *Time Deposits* (*lines 24* and *25,* respectively) included accounts of nonresidents at resident offices of the banks.
ℐ Beginning in December 1982, data reflect the introduction by the Central Bank of Ireland of an improved call report form, which for the first time records the associated bank data, confined to resident offices only, on a residency-of-customer basis. From that date, the activities of nonresident offices are, therefore, excluded from the data, and accounts of nonresidents at resident offices are (properly) classified under *Foreign Assets (line 21)* and *Foreign Liabilities (line 26c)*.
Monetary Survey: ℐ See note to section 10. ℐ Beginning in 1964, data for *line 32an* are net of government deposits at the Central Bank, for which data were not available before that date. ℐ Prior to December 1982, *line 34* differed from the source B (old) measure of M1, as given in the money supply table, in that *IFS* included and source B excluded private sector deposits at the Central Bank, while source B included government demand deposits at deposit money banks, which *IFS* nets in *line 32an*. A timing difference also existed between the two measures, since *IFS* data were as of bank-return dates whereas the currency component of M1 in source B related to the average of Fridays. ℐ Beginning in December 1982, *line 34* reflects changes affecting the data of the deposit money banks, including improved sectorization, the exclusion on nonresident accounts, and a change in the method of allocating items in transit.
Other Banking Institutions: ℐ Prior to December 1982, data were gross of provision for bad and doubtful debts, offsets, and unearned interest and charges, and sectorization of data was incomplete. Beginning in December 1982, data reflect the introduction of an improved call report form, which facilitates the sectorization of accounts. In the case of deposit money banks, data are recorded net of provisions for bad and doubtful debts and certain offsets and are also net of unearned interest and charges. They differ from source B in that *IFS* does not apply a resident / nonresident distinction to capital account items, and *IFS* adjusts certain balance sheet items from an actual to a cash basis.
Banking Survey: ℐ Beginning in December 1982, data reflect an improvement in the sectorization of accounts. Prior to that date, it is assumed that all of the counterpart to the quasi-money liabilities of state and state-sponsored banking institutions and national installment savings reflects in claims on government.
Interest Rates: *Discount Rate (End of Period):* ℐ Short-term facility rate charged by the Bank of Ireland on funds, up to a specified quota, lent to banks experiencing day-to-day liquidity shortages. Prior to August 1981, data refer to the discount rate.

Mexico

Exchange Rates: On January 1, 1993 the new peso, equal to 1,000 pesos, was introduced.
Monetary Authorities: ℐ Beginning in December 1977, data are based on improved sectorization.
Deposit Money Banks: ℐ See note to section 10. Prior to December 1977, data refer only to commercial banks. ℐ Beginning in 1982, data reflect the introduction of a new plan of accounts, which provides an improved sector classification of domestic and foreign accounts.
Monetary Survey: ℐ See notes to sections 10 and 20.
Other Banking Institutions: ℐ See notes to sections 10 and 20. Prior to December 1977, private credit institutions other than commercial banks were also included, and rediscount operations were not included, since they were classified to contingency or memorandum accounts.
Banking Survey: ℐ See notes to sections 10, 20, and 40.

Interest Rates: *Money Market Rate:* ℐ Beginning in July 1988, average of rates quoted by deposit money banks on three-month bankers' acceptances.
Treasury Bill Rate: ℐ Beginning in January 1988, average yield on one-month treasury bills.
Deposit Rate: ℐ Beginning in January 1988, net return offered by deposit money banks on one-month financial promissory notes.
Production: ℐ From 1975 onwards, annual data have been adjusted to include production of petroleum and gas and petroleum refining. Monthly data have been adjusted from January 1979 onwards.
Government Finance: ℐ Beginning in 1972, data are as reported in the *Government Finance Statistics Yearbook* and relate to the consolidated central government.
National Accounts: ℐ Data on GDP have been revised backward for a longer period than have the data on the components. Hence, components do not add up to GDP for some years.

Philippines

Monetary Authorities: ℐ Beginning in 1983, data reflect improved classification in the report forms. ℐ Beginning in 1993, data reflect the financial restructuring of the Central Bank of the Philippines. The Bangko Sentral ng Pilipinas (BSP) was created to take over the monetary authority functions of the former Central Bank of the Philippines. At the same time, the Central Bank–Board of Liquidators (CB-BOL), an agency of the central government, was created to liquidate the nonperforming assets of the former Central Bank of the Philippines. *Line 12a* includes claims on the CB-BOL. *Line 16c* includes foreign liabilities assumed by the BSP which, prior to 1993, were included in *lines 16b* and *16d*.
Deposit Money Banks: ℐ In 1976 the sectorization of foreign accounts was improved. Previously, *line 21* included, and *line 22d* excluded, certain claims on residents. ℐ For beginning of 1983, see note to section 10.
Monetary Survey: ℐ See notes to sections 10 and 20.
Interest Rates: *Discount Rate (End of Period):* ℐ Beginning in December 1985, the rediscount facility was unified, and data refer to the single rate charged on all rediscount loans. Prior to 1985, data refer to the rediscount rate for loans for traditional exports, which account for a large part of total rediscount credits.
Government Finance: ℐ Beginning in 1972, data are derived from *Cash Operations Statements,* Bureau of Treasury. Annual data are identical to data reported in the *Government Finance Statistics Yearbook* and cover budgetary central government. ℐ During the period 1972-75, data relate to a fiscal year different from calendar year (fiscal year ends June 30).

South Africa

Monetary Authorities: ℐ Beginning in 1990, accounts of the Corporation for Public Deposits–a full subsidiary of the South African Reserve Bank–have been included in the compilation of the monetary authorities' accounts.
International Transactions: Foreign trade of Botswana, Lesotho, Swaziland, and Namibia are included in South African trade data. Intertrade of these five countries is not included. ℐ Beginning in January 1973, export data exclude certain mineral oils. *Imports c.i.f.* and *f.o.b.:* Data are from source S. ℐ Prior to January 1980, petroleum products and defense equipment were excluded. ℐ Beginning in June 1981, strategic materials are included in the calculation of the export and import unit values.
Government Finance: ℐ From January 1991 onwards, data include the definition of banks and of net financing to the government as revised by the authorities in August 1994.

Spain

Monetary Authorities: ℐ Beginning in January 1983, data are based on a new system of accounts with a revised transactor breakdown. ℐ From January 1986, data reflect an introduction of a new reporting system.
Deposit Money Banks: ℐ Through December 1982, the coverage of *line 24* is confined to the commercial and savings banks. Beginning in January 1983, cooperative banks and money market intermediary companies are included. ℐ From January 1983, data are based on the new bank returns introduced in 1982, which are aimed at a uniform reporting system for all financial institutions. ℐ Beginning in January 1986, money market intermediary companies are excluded.
Monetary Survey: ℐ See notes to sections 10 and 20.
Other Banking Institutions: ℐ From December 1982 onward, data are based on new returns introduced in 1982. The revised presentation reflects improvement in the sectorization and classification of domestic and foreign accounts. ℐ Beginning in January 1986, other banking institutions have broader coverage, including money market intermediary companies, mortgage loan companies, financial leasing companies, and finance and factoring companies.
Interest Rates: *Bank of Spain Rate:* ℐ Prior to September 1977, rate at which the Bank of Spain discounted financial paper for commercial and savings banks.
Treasury Bill Rate: ℐ Prior to July 1987, discount rate on three-month treasury bills.
Government Finance: ℐ Beginning in 1980, data reflect separation from central government of the autonomous communities and reflect adoption of altered accounting classifications. Also beginning in 1980, data on *Use of Cash Balances (line 87)* reflect only the variation in the deposits with the Bank of Spain, whereas in previous years, data corresponded to the net position of the State with the Bank of Spain. Data on *Net Foreign Borrowing (line 85a)* are now classified on a pure residence criterion, whereas in previous years, data contained proceeds from domestic borrowing issued in foreign currency.

Trinidad and Tobago

Other Banking Institutions: ℐ Prior to 1970, data relate to post office savings deposits only.
Government Finance: ℐ Beginning in 1976, data are as reported in the *Government Finance Statistics Yearbook* and cover budgetary central government, statutory bodies, and the National Insurance Board. Prior to 1976, data are as reported by the Central Bank for Trinidad and Tobago for publication in *IFS*. ℐ Beginning in 1982, data cover budgetary central government only.